The
Bedford
Introduction
to Drama

The Bedford Introduction to Drama

FIFTH EDITION

Lee A. Jacobus
University of Connecticut

BEDFORD / ST. MARTIN'S   BOSTON ◆ NEW YORK

This book is dedicated to David Krause.

For Bedford/St. Martin's

Senior Developmental Editor: Mikola De Roo
Senior Production Editor: Harold Chester
Production Supervisor: Jennifer Wetzel
Marketing Manager: Jenna Bookin Barry
Art Direction and Cover Design: Lucy Krikorian
Text Design: Claire Seng-Niemoeller
Photo Research: Martha Friedman
Cover Photo: James Blendick as Creon and Len Cariou as Oedipus in he 1972
   Guthrie Theater production of *Oedipus the King.* Photo by Act Two Photography.
Composition: Stratford Publishing Services
Printing and Binding: R. R. Donnelley & Sons Company

President: Joan E. Feinberg
Editorial Director: Denise B. Wydra
Editor in Chief: Nancy Perry
Director of Marketing: Karen Melton Soeltz
Director of Editing, Design, and Production: Marcia Cohen
Managing Editor: Erica T. Appel

Library of Congress Control Number: 2004101200

Manufactured in the United States of America.

0 9 8 7 6 5
f   e   d   c   b

For information, write: Bedford/St. Martin's, 75 Arlington Street, Boston, MA 02116
(617-399-4000)

ISBN: 0–312–44576-8

EAN: 978-0-312-44576-8

Acknowledgments

Preface for Instructors

For four best-selling editions, *The Bedford Introduction to Drama* has been the most comprehensive introductory drama resource available. With an abundance of plays, commentaries, and useful editorial features, the text continues to give students a diverse overview of dramatic literature and instructors a text with enough breadth and flexibility to complement a variety of approaches. In its fifth edition, *The Bedford Introduction to Drama* remains first and foremost the most complete anthology available: a collection of fifty-three important plays that have shaped dramatic literature from the time of the early Greek dramatists to the present. A number of important features distinguish this book from other introductory drama texts. Most notably, it presents three major playwrights in greater than usual depth — three plays by William Shakespeare and two each by Sophocles and Tennessee Williams — offering students a unique opportunity to study and write about significant figures in the development of drama. The book also offers a full array of background material about the plays and playwrights, providing more resources for students than any other drama text. Accompanying all the plays are thorough biographical and critical introductions; brief performance histories; commentaries by playwrights, directors, actors, reviewers, and critics; and photographs of landmark productions. To give students a better overall view of the periods and contexts in which individual plays are written and performed, these play-specific materials are complemented by four cultural casebooks interspersed throughout the book. Each casebook presents background materials — journal entries, letters, newspaper accounts, and essays — about specific plays and dramatic periods, enabling students to think critically about a play or group of plays through a focused study of important cultural and historical contexts.

Even when it appears most timeless, all drama, like all literature, is a product of language, style, its era, and a complex range of political, social, and ethnic influences. *The Bedford Introduction to Drama* offers a succinct but thorough history of Western drama, complemented by an important representation of Asian drama. A general introduction gives an overview of the great ages of drama, the major genres and elements, and the cultural value of drama. Throughout the book, introductions to significant periods of drama, the playwrights, and the plays focus on the cultural contexts of the works and on their stage history. Timelines following the introductions to each dramatic period present important developments in theater history in their appropriate cultural contexts.

The Bedford Introduction to Drama is also a complete resource for the beginning student. In the general introduction, a discussion of the elements of drama defines the important terms and concepts and demonstrates these concepts in action, drawing its examples from Lady Isabella Augusta Gregory's one-act play, *The Rising of the Moon*. Nearly every play is accompanied by one or more striking photographs, and the plays by those playwrights who are treated in depth are illustrated by photo essays that often feature more than one production to help students understand the plays as texts to be interpreted through performance.

"Writing about Drama," the first appendix, offers students possible approaches for commenting on dramatic literature and points the way for developing ideas that can result in probing critical essays. From prewriting to outlining and drafting, the process of writing about drama is illustrated by reference to *The Rising of the Moon*, and a sample essay on the play provides one example of drama criticism. Especially useful for assignments involving attendance at theater productions, the section "How to Write a Review" analyzes professional reviews and offers suggestions for students who are writing reviews.

The second appendix, "Glossary of Dramatic Terms," clearly and concisely defines concepts and terms. When these terms are first introduced and defined in the text, they appear in small capital letters.

"Selected Bibliography," the third appendix, includes a list of reference works for the major periods of drama, the playwrights, and the plays by the three playwrights treated in depth. The cited general references, histories, biographies, critical studies, journal articles, reviews, and collections of plays are especially useful for research in drama.

Although the book presents the plays as texts to be read, the fourth appendix, "Selected List of Film, Video, and Audiocassette Resources," reinforces the element of performance. This list, accompanied by a directory of distributors, can help instructors and students find illuminating treatments of the plays in performance.

New to This Edition
New Plays and Commentaries

Fourteen plays are new to the fifth edition. Most notably, the inclusion of three Asian plays complements the text's unparalleled representation of Western drama and gives a more complete view of the world drama landscape. This edition contains two masterpieces of Japanese theater, Chikamatsu Monzaemon's Nō drama, *The Love Suicides at Sonezaki*, and Zeami Motokiyo's kabuki play, *Lady Han*. In addition, *The Other Shore*, by China's Nobel prize winner, Gao Xingjian, offers a view of shifts in contemporary Chinese drama. Also new are award-winning contemporary plays such as Suzan Lori-Parks's *Topdog/Underdog* and Nilo Cruz's *Anna in the Tropics*, which both won the Pulitzer Prize. Other new plays include Oliver Goldsmith's *She Stoops to Conquer*, Brian Friel's *Translations*, David Mamet's *Glengarry Glen Ross*, and Edward Albee's *The Goat, or Who Is Sylvia?* Fourteen of eighty-two commentaries are also new to this edition and continue to provide a variety of ways for students to think about a play — from the perspective of critic, reviewer, actor, director, and playwright.

The fifth edition continues the tradition of offering a strong representation of multicultural and women playwrights and representing them with their most significant works. The most popular, seminal works from the fourth edition have been retained, including *A Raisin in the Sun* by Lorraine Hansberry, *The Strong Breed* by Wole Soyinka, *Zoot Suit* by Luis Valdez, *Fences* by August Wilson, and *How I Learned to Drive* by Paula Vogel; in addition, seven new plays have been added, including *Top Girls* by Caryl Churchill and *Fires in the Mirror* by Anna Deavere Smith.

New Cultural and Production Casebooks

In addition to the cultural casebooks on "The Issue of Race and *Othello*" and "The 'Woman Question' in Late Nineteenth-Century Drama," the fifth edition includes two new casebooks, which enable students to think critically about a play or group of plays through a focused study of important cultural and historical contexts. The new cultural casebook on "Kabuki, Jōruri, and Bunraku Theater" offers students a solid overview of the history of seventeenth- and eighteenth-century Japanese theater. The new production casebook on Arthur Miller's *Death of a Salesman* focuses on multiple dramatic elements of this oft-produced play: the staging, design, casting, and directing of the original 1949 production; the richness of the role of Willy Loman for several generations of actors; and the cultural and racial issues involved in staging international and black productions of the play.

As in the previous edition, each casebook comprises an introduction to the topic followed by selected documents, including journal entries, letters, newspaper accounts, and essays. The documents are accompanied by visual materials that illuminate the subject of the casebook.

More Performance Photographs

Significantly more theater photographs of important productions and illuminating stage diagrams (sixty are new) help students visualize the plays in performance.

Companion Web Site and Video Library

The revised and updated companion Web site at bedfordstmartins.com /jacobus helps students succeed in the course with study questions, writing suggestions, and Web assignments to accompany each play; annotated research links for the plays and playwrights in the book; brand-new interactive multimedia tutorials of specific plays that draw students step by step through the close reading of the work's elements and the in-depth study of its critical and cultural contexts; and links to online reviews, important repertory theaters around the country, and internship opportunities. Sample syllabi and assignment ideas are offered for instructors.

A selection of videotapes of plays included in the book is available from the Bedford/St. Martin's video library for qualified adopters.

Compact Edition

The Bedford Introduction to Drama, Fifth Edition, is also available in a compact edition containing twenty-nine plays, fifty-two commentaries, and two cultural casebooks on "The Issue of Race and *Othello*" and "Kabuki, Jōruri, and Bunraku Theater." The compact edition retains all of the longer book's editorial features for those instructors who want a smaller, less expensive anthology.

Acknowledgments

First, I would like to thank those who offered their advice on what to include in the first edition of this book: Jeff Glauner, Park College; Susan Smith, University of Pittsburgh; and Jordan Miller, University of Rhode Island. Second, I am grateful to those who read the introductions and commentaries in the first edition and who gave me the advantage of their knowledge and wisdom. G. Jennifer Wilson, University of California, Los Angeles; William Carroll, Boston University; Ronald Bryden, Graduate Centre for the Study of Drama, University of Toronto; Robert Dial, University of Akron; Jonnie Guerra, Mount Vernon College; and John Timpane, Lafayette College, were all unhesitating in offering suggestions and improvements.

For the second edition, experts in specific historical periods examined the introductions for accuracy and comprehensiveness. Each of the introductions was revised with their suggestions in mind. These reviewers were Michael Cadden, Princeton University; Mary Coogan, University of Colorado, Boulder; Anthony Graham-White, University of Illinois, Chicago; C. Fenno Hoffman; Robert D. Hume, Pennsylvania State University; Paul G. Reeve, University of Houston, University Park; Laurence Senelick, Tufts University; and Timothy Wiles, Indiana University, Bloomington.

I am also grateful to Keith Hull of the University of Wyoming for the warmth of his response to the book. Especially helpful in preparing the second edition were Elias Abdou, Community College of Allegheny, Pittsburgh; Robert E. Aldridge, Kirkwood Community College; Katya Amato, Portland State University; Keith Appler, University of Illinois, Urbana; Nora Bicki, University of Illinois, Champaign; Reverend Doctor Nadean Bishop, Eastern Michigan University; François Bonneville, State University of New York, Albany; Michael Boudreau, University of Illinois, Urbana; David Bratt, Winona State University; Marianne Cooley, University of Houston, University Park; Walter Creed, University of Hawaii, Manoa; Mary Beth Culp, Marymount College; Merilee Cunningham, University of Houston; Joan D'Antoni, University of Louisville; Wayne G. Deahl, Eastern Wyoming College; Charlotte Doctor, Los Angeles Pierce College; Janet Dow, Western Connecticut State University; Jerry D. Eisenhour, Eastern Illinois University; Fred M. Fetrow, United States Naval Academy; Jane E. Fisher, Canisius College; Charles Frey, University of Washington; Robert W. Funk, Eastern Illinois University; Stephen R. Grecco, Pennsylvania State University; L. W. Harrison, Santa Rosa Junior College; Dave Hartley, Central Florida Community College; Andrew Jay Hoffman, Central Connecticut State University; Claudia L. Johnson, Marquette University; Ellen Redding Kaler, University of Kansas; Harvey Kassebaum, Cuyahoga Community College; Dorothy Louise, Franklin and Marshall College; Annette McGregor, Purdue University; Jack Mahoney, Vincennes University; James Marlow, Southeastern Massachusetts University; Christy Minadeo, Eastern Michigan University; Carol A. Moore, Louisiana State University; Roark Mulligan, University of Oregon; Eric Pederson, Butler County Community College; M. Bernice Pepke, Manatee Community College; Patrick Quade, Saint Olaf College; Carol Replogle, Loyola University, Chicago; William Reynolds, Hope College; Mark Rocha, California State University, Northridge; Matthew C. Roudane, Georgia State University; Dolores J. Sarafinski, Gannon University; Carol Scklenica, Marquette University; Rodney Simard, California State University, San Bernardino; James Stephens, Marquette University; Jeannie B. Thomas, University of Oregon; Gregory Ulmer, Kearney State College; Susan Vick, Worcester Polytechnic Institute; Linda Wells, Boston University; Keith Welsh, Webster University; Virginia West, Franklin and Marshall College; Paul Wood, Villanova University; and J. S. Wszalek, James Madison University.

For the third edition, Samuel Abel of Dartmouth College reviewed the historical material for accuracy and offered a number of very useful suggestions that I incorporated into the text. I am grateful for his help and for the response of those who offered suggestions and advice for improving the book, especially Cora Agatucci, Central Oregon Community College; Joan D'Antoni, University of Louisville; Harold J. Baxter, Trinity International University; Irene Blakely, Northland College; Cynthia Bowers, Loyola University, Chicago; Jody D. Brown, Ferrum College; Mark Browning, Johnson County Community College; William D. Buckley, Indiana University NW; William J. Campbell, SUNY College of Technology at Delhi; Heather S. Collins, Mott Community College; Ruth Contrell, New Mexico State University; Kenneth Cox, Oklahoma State University; Judith P. Cronk, Oklahoma State University; Marsha Cummins, Bronx Community College; James D. Cunningham, Florida Southern College; Tom DeSpain, Chemeketa Community College; Dexter Roger Dixon, University of Arkansas; Nancy Eddy, Indiana University–Purdue University at Indianapolis; Tom Empy, Casper College; Shawn Paul Evans, University of Tennessee at Chattanooga; Harry Feiner, Queens College; Monika Fischer, University of Oregon; James Fisher, Wabash College; Kay Forston, Phillips University; John E. Hallwas, Western Illinois University; Wilma Hahn Hasse, Mitchell University; David Henry, El Paso Community College; Kirsten F. Herdd, Eastern Michigan University; D. E. Jukes, Community College of Allegheny County; E. Kahn, Lehigh University; Jackson Kesler, Western Kentucky University; Lawrence Kinsman, New Hampshire College; Terry A. Klenk, Santa Fe Community College; Marcia K. Morrison, Genesee Community College; Eva Patton, Fordham University; Richard Pettergill, University of Illinois at Chicago; David Pinner, Colgate University; Joseph Rice, University of Cincinnati; Deborah A. Ring, Case Western Reserve University; Hans H. Rudnick, Southern Illinois University; Samuel Schuman, University of North Carolina; William O. Scott, University of Kansas; Rita Smilkstein, North Seattle Community College; Gerald F. Snelson, Frostburg State University; N. J. Stanley, Agnes Scott College; Catherine Stevenson, University of Hartford; John S. Terhes, Chemeketa Community College; Charles Trainor, Siena College; Anita J. Turpin, Roanoke College; Joy Walsh, Butler County Community College; Gladdy White, Notre Dame College; Celeste Wiggins, Ursuline College; Salaam Yousif, California State University; and Ruth Zielke, Concordia College.

For the fourth edition, I am grateful to those who offered suggestions and advice for improving the book, especially David Adamson, University of North Carolina, Chapel Hill; Joan Angelis, Woodbury University; Karen C. Blansfield, University of North Carolina, Chapel Hill; Stephen F. Bloom, Emmanuel College; Cathy A. Brookshire, James Madison University; Barbara Clayton, University of Wisconsin, Madison; John J. Conlon, University of Massachusetts, Boston; Heath A. Diehl, Bowling Green State University; Richard Donnelly, University of Notre Dame; Joseph Fahey, Ohio State University; John E. R. Friedenberg, Wake Forest University; Stanton B. Garner Jr., University of

Tennessee; Anthony Graham-White, University of Illinois at Chicago; Leigh
Harbin, Angelo State University; Jim Hauser, William Patterson University;
Don Haynes, Robert Morris College; Gregory Kable, University of North Car-
olina, Chapel Hill; Theresa M. Kenosa, Lincoln Land Community College;
Sonya Lancaster, University of Kansas; Charlotte Langford, Pima Community
College; Sandee McGlaun, Ohio State University; Deborah Montuori, Ship-
pensburg University; Joan Navarre, Marquette University; Susan Sanders,
Northern Essex Community College; Helen Scheck, University of Albany; Joel
Shatzky, SUNY College at Cortland; Michelle L. Stie, University of Kansas;
James Symmons, Pennsylvania State University, Media; George Wead, James
Madison University; Janet S. Wolf, SUNY College at Cortland; and Tom Zim-
merman, Washtenaw Community College.

For this fifth edition, I am grateful to the following reviewers for their sug-
gestions and feedback: Alan Ackerman, University of Toronto; Sonya Alvarado,
Michigan University; Dennis Black, University of North Carolina at Charlotte;
Kristin Bovaird-Abbo, University of Kansas; Doug Cummins, Furman Univer-
sity; Merilee Cunningham, University of Houston–Downtown; J. K. Curry,
Wake Forest University; Brook Davis, Wake Forest University; Marcia J. Doug-
las, University of Maine; James Fisher, Wabash College; Deborah Payne Fisk,
American University; Christine Frezza, Southern Utah University; Jean Dobie
Giebel, Hofstra University; Kellie L. Grengs, Loyola University; Mark Harvey,
University of Minnesota, Duluth; Peter Hays, University of California at
Davis; Helen Killoran, Ohio University at Lancaster; David Krasner, Yale
University; Holly E. McDonald, University of Central Florida; Walter Metz,
Montana State University–Bozeman; Kimberly A. Miller, University of Kansas;
John Patton, Troy State University; Susan Proctor, St. Gregory's University;
Stephen Slimp, University of West Alabama; Annette Wannamaker, Eastern
Michigan University; and Craig White, University of Houston at Clear Lake.

I am indebted to many talented people who, were they in a drama, could
constitute a crowd scene, and yet each played an indispensable solo role in
making this book a reality. Martha Friedman did the photo research and, as in
previous editions, secured permissions for wonderful images in an outstanding
fashion. Fred Courtright cleared the text permission for the plays and commentaries in record time. Joanna Imm did a thorough job of checking controversial facts and dates throughout the book, scrutinizing the details in the new
material for accuracy and consistency. Lisa Schlein and Nathan Odell updated
the Selected Bibliography and the list of audiovisual materials.

I am especially grateful to the people who worked behind the scenes at
Bedford/St. Martin's to produce this book. I thank editorial assistants Kristy
Bredin, Lisa Schlein, and Nathan Odell for coordinating reviews and managing
tasks large and small in order to prepare the manuscript for production. Managing editor Erica Appel, senior project editor Harold Chester, and production
supervisor Jennifer Wetzel managed the production of this complex project
with aplomb and kept the book on schedule. Sandy Schechter did a great job
overseeing text permissions with efficiency and care. Art director Lucy Krikorian designed the stunning cover. Thanks also to New Media editors Harriet
Wald and Coleen O'Hanley for their work on *The Bedford Introduction to
Drama* Web site.

As always, I owe an immense debt of gratitude to the imaginative and intelligent guidance of Joan Feinberg, president of Bedford/St. Martin's, and her predecessor, Charles Christensen. They have been friends of this book from the beginning and have helped give it special meaning. They have been a continual inspiration. Nancy Perry, editor in chief, offered many useful suggestions, especially in the earlier stages of development. Karen Henry, my editor for the first three editions of this book, is a passionate fan of theater and the values for which this book stands. She has always remained close to this project. Maura Shea, editor of the fourth edition, provided excellent guidance and set a standard for editorial excellence. In her work on this new edition, Mika De Roo, my editor and friend, has worked to maintain the standards for which Bedford/St. Martin's is known. Working with her has been a constant pleasure, especially because I know I can count on her excellent judgment in all matters editorial and literary.

Lee A. Jacobus
University of Connecticut, Storrs

Contents

Introduction: Thinking about Drama   1

Lady Gregory   21

Appendices

Introduction:
Thinking about
Drama

What Is Drama?

DRAMA is the art of representing for the pleasure of others events that happened or that we imagine happening. The primary ingredients of drama are characters, represented by players; action, described by gestures and movement; thought, implied by dialogue, words, and action; spectacle, represented by scenery, music, and costume; and, finally, audiences, who respond to this complex mixture.

When we are in the theater, we see the actors, hear the lines, are aware of the setting, and sense the theatrical community of which we are a part. Even when reading a play, we should imagine actors speaking lines and visualize a setting in which those lines are spoken. Drama is an experience in which we participate on many levels simultaneously. On one level, we may believe that what we see is really happening; on another level, we know it is only make-believe. On one level we may be amused, but on another level we realize that serious statements about our society are being made. Drama both entertains and instructs.

When Aristotle wrote about drama in the *Poetics*, a work providing one of the earliest and most influential theories of drama, he began by explaining it as the imitation of an action (MIMESIS). Those analyzing his work have interpreted this statement in several ways. One interpretation is that drama imitates life. On the surface, such an observation may seem simple, even obvious. But on reflection we begin to find complex significance in his comment. The drama of the Greeks, for example, with its intense mythic structure, its formidable speeches, and its profound actions, often seems larger than life or other than life. Yet we recognize characters saying words that we ourselves are capable of saying, doing things that we ourselves might do. The great Greek tragedies are certainly lifelike and certainly offer literary mirrors in which we can examine human nature. And the same is true of Greek comedies.

The relationship between drama and life has always been subtle and complex. In some plays, such as Luigi Pirandello's *Six Characters in Search of an Author,* it is one of the central issues. We begin our reading or viewing of most plays knowing that the dramatic experience is not absolutely real in the sense that, for example, the actor playing Hamlet does not truly die or truly see a ghost or truly frighten his mother. The play imitates those imagined actions, but when done properly it is realistic enough to make us fear, if only for a moment, that they could be real.

We see significance in the actions Hamlet imitates; his actions help us live our own lives more deeply, more intensely, because they give us insight into the possibilities of life. We are all restricted to living this life as ourselves; drama is one art form that helps us realize the potential of life, for both the good and the bad. In an important sense, we can share the experience of a character such as Hamlet when he soliloquizes over the question of whether it is better to die than to live in a world filled with sin and crime.

Drama and Ritual

Such imaginative participation is only a part of what we derive from drama. In its origins, drama may have evolved from ancient Egyptian and Greek rituals, ceremonies that were performed the same way again and again and were thought to have a propitious effect on the relationship between the people and their gods.

In ancient Egypt some religious rituals evolved into repeated passion plays, such as those celebrating Isis and Osiris at the festivals of Heb-Seb in Abydos some three thousand years ago. Greek drama was first performed during yearly religious celebrations dedicated to the god Dionysus. The early Greek playwrights, such as Sophocles in *Oedipus Rex* and *Antigone,* emphasized the interaction between the will of the gods and the will of human beings, often pitting the truths of men and women against the truths of the gods.

In the thirteenth and fourteenth centuries drama thrived in Japan, reaching a pinnacle in the Nō drama of Zeami Motokiyo and his father, Kan'ami. Japanese Nō drama combines music and movement in intricate patterns of ritualistic formality. Nō developed in a Buddhist environment and expressed the deep religious values associated with Buddhism. Although it began as a provincial form, the beauty of Nō — its deep meditative pauses and extraordinary dancelike movement — quickly made it the major style of drama in medieval Japan.

The rebirth of Western drama in the Middle Ages — after the fall of Rome and the loss of classical artistic traditions — took place first in monasteries, then later in the cathedrals of Europe. It evolved from medieval religious ceremonies that helped the faithful understand more about their own moral predicament. *Everyman,* a late play in the medieval theater (it was written about 1500), concerns itself with the central issue of reward and punishment after this life because the soul is immortal.

Drama: The Illusion of Reality

From the beginning, drama has had the capacity to hold up an illusion of reality like the reflection in a mirror: we take the reality for granted while recognizing that it is nonetheless illusory. As we have seen, Aristotle described DRAMATIC ILLUSION as an imitation of an action. But unlike the reflection in a mirror, the action of most drama is not drawn from our actual experience of life but from our potential or imagined experience. In the great Greek drama, the illusion includes the narratives of ancient myths that were thought to offer profound illumination. The interpretation of the myths by the Greek playwrights over a two-hundred-year period helped the Greek people participate in the myths, understand them, and apply the values of those myths to their daily lives.

Different ages have had different approaches to representing reality onstage. Greek actors spoke in verse and wore masks. The staging consisted of very little setting and no special costumes except for some comedies and satyr plays. Medieval drama was sometimes acted on pushwagons and carts, but the special machinery developed to suggest hellfire and the presence of devils was said to be so realistic as to be frightening. Elizabethan audiences were accustomed to actors who spoke directly to the crowds at their feet near the apron of the stage. All Elizabethan plays were done in essentially contemporary clothing, often with no more scenery than a suggestion in the spoken descriptions of the players. The actors recited their lines in verse, except when the author had a particular reason to use prose — for example, to imply that the speaker was of low social station. Yet Elizabethans reported that their theater was much like life itself.

In Shakespeare's *A Midsummer Night's Dream,* fairies, enchantments, an ass's head on the shoulders of a man — all these are presented as illusions, and we accept them. They inform the audience — in Shakespeare's day and in modern times — not by showing us ourselves in a mirror but by demonstrating that even fantastic realities have significance for us.

Certainly *A Midsummer Night's Dream* gives us insight into the profound range of human emotions. We learn about the pains of rejection when we see Helena longing for Demetrius, who in turn longs for Hermia. We learn about jealousy and possessiveness when we see Oberon cast a spell on his wife, Titania, over a dispute concerning a changeling. And we learn, too, about the worldly ambitions of the "rude mechanicals" who themselves put on a play whose reality they fear might frighten their audience. They solve the problem by reminding their audience that it is only a play and that they need not fear that reality will spoil their pleasure.

In modern drama the dramatic illusion of reality includes not just the shape of an action, the events, and the characters but also the details of everyday life. When the action changes locale, the setting changes as well. Some contemporary playwrights make an effort to re-create a reality close to the one we live in. Some modern plays, like August Wilson's *Fences,* make a precise representation of reality a primary purpose, shaping the tone of the language to reflect the way modern people speak, re-creating contemporary reality in the setting, language, and other elements of the drama.

But describing a play as an illusion of reality in no way means that it represents the precise reality that we take for granted in our everyday experience. Rather, drama ranges widely and explores multiple realities, some of which may seem very close to our own and some of which may seem improbably removed from our everyday experience.

Seeing a Play Onstage

For an audience, drama is one of the most powerful artistic experiences. When we speak about participating in drama, we mean that as a member of the audience we become a part of the action that unfolds. This is a mysterious phenomenon.

When we see a play today, we are usually seated in a darkened theater looking at a lighted stage. In ages past, this contrast was not the norm. Greek plays took place outdoors during the morning and the afternoon; most Elizabethan plays were staged outdoors in the afternoon; in the Renaissance, some plays began to be staged indoors with ingenious systems of lighting that involved candles and reflectors. In the early nineteenth century most theaters used gaslight onstage; electricity took over in the later part of the century, and its use has grown increasingly complex. In most large theaters today computerized lighting boards have replaced Renaissance candles.

Sitting in the darkness has made the experience of seeing Greek and Elizabethan plays much different for us than it was for the original audiences. We do not worry about being seen by the "right people" or about studying the quality of the audience, as people did during the Restoration in the late seventeenth century. The darkness isolates us from all except those who sit adjacent to us. Yet we instantly respond when others in the audience laugh, when they gasp, when they shift restlessly. We recognize in those moments that we are part of a larger community drawn together by theater and that we are all involved in the dramatic experience.

Theaters and Their Effect

Different kinds of theaters make differing demands on actors and audiences. Despite its huge size, the open ARENA style theater of the early Greeks brought the audience into a special kind of intimacy with the actors. The players came very close to the first rows of seats, and the acoustics permitted even a whisper onstage to be audible in the far seats. The Greek theater also imparted a sense of formality to the occasion of drama. For one thing, its regularity and circularity was accompanied by a relatively rigid seating plan. The officials and nobility sat in special seats. Then each section of the theater was given over to specific families, with the edges of the seating area devoted to travelers and strangers to the town. One knew one's place in the Greek theater. Its regularity gave the community a sense of order.

Medieval theater also gave its audiences a sense of community, both when it used playing areas called *mansions* inside and outside the churches and when it used wagons wheeled about in processions in the streets or outside the city walls. That the medieval theater repeated the same cycles of plays again and again for about two hundred years, to the delight of many European communities, tells us something about the stability of those communities. Their drama was integrated with their religion, and both helped them express their sense of belonging to the church and the community.

In some medieval performances the actors came into the audience, breaking the sense of distance or the illusion of separation. It is difficult for us to know how much participation and involvement in the action the medieval audience felt. Modern audiences have responded very well to productions of medieval plays such as *The Second Shepherds' Pageant, Noah's Flood,* and *Everyman,* and we have every reason to think that medieval audiences enjoyed their dramas immensely. The guilds that performed them took pride in making their plays as exciting and involving as possible.

The Elizabethan playhouse was a wooden structure providing an enclosed space, approximately seventy-two feet in diameter, around a courtyard open to the sky. A covered stage thrust into the courtyard. As in the Greek theater, the audience was arranged somewhat by social station. Around the stage, which was about five feet off the ground, stood the groundlings, those who paid the least for their entrance. Then in covered galleries in the building itself sat patrons who paid extra for a seat. The effect of the enclosed structure was of a small, contained world. Actors were in the habit of speaking directly to members of the audience, and the audience rarely kept a polite silence. It was a busy, humming theater that generated intimacy and involvement between actors and audience.

The proscenium stage of the nineteenth and twentieth centuries distanced the audience from the play, providing a clear frame (the PROSCENIUM) behind which the performers acted out their scenes. This detachment was especially effective for plays that demanded a high degree of realism because the effect of the proscenium is to make the audience feel that it is witnessing the action as a silent observer, looking in as if through an imaginary fourth wall on a living room or other intimate space in which the action takes place. The proscenium arch gives the illusion that the actors are in a world of their own, unaware of the audience's presence.

In the twentieth century some of the virtues of the Greek arena theater, or THEATER IN THE ROUND, were rediscovered. In an effort to close the distance between audience and players, Antonin Artaud, the French actor and director, developed in the 1920s and 1930s a concept called the *theater of cruelty*. Using theater in the round, Artaud robbed the audience of the comfort of watching a distant stage and pressed his actors into the space of the viewers. His purpose was to force theatergoers to deal with the primary issues of the drama by stripping them of the security of darkness and anonymity. Theaters in the Soviet Union and Britain developed similar spaces in the 1930s and 1940s, and since the 1950s the Arena Theater in Washington, D.C., and the Circle in the Square in New York City have continued the tradition.

Twenty-first-century theater is eclectic. It uses thrust, arena, proscenium, and every other kind of stage already described. Some contemporary theater also converts nontheatrical space, such as warehouses or city streets, into space for performance.

Reading a Play

Reading a play is a different experience from seeing it enacted. For one thing, readers do not have the benefit of the interpretations made by a director, actors, and scene designers in presenting a performance. These interpretations are all critical judgments based on a director's ideas of how the play should be presented and on actors' insights into the meaning of the play.

A reading of a play produces an interpretation that remains in our heads and is not translated to the stage. The dramatic effect of the staging is lost to us unless we make a genuine effort to visualize it and to understand its contribution to the dramatic experience. For a fuller experience of the drama when reading plays, one should keep in mind the historical period and the conventions of staging that are appropriate to the period and that are specified by the playwright.

Some plays were prepared by their authors for reading as well as for staging, as evident in plays whose stage directions supply information that would be unavailable to an audience, such as the color of the characters' eyes, characters' secret motives, and other such details. Occasionally, stage directions, such as those of Bernard Shaw and Tennessee Williams, are written in a poetic prose that can be appreciated only by a reader.

It is not a certainty that seeing a play will produce an experience more "true" to the play's meaning than reading it. Every act of reading silently or speaking the lines aloud is an act of interpretation. No one can say which is the best interpretation. Each has its own merits, and the ideal is probably to read and see any play.

The Great Ages of Drama

Certain historical periods have produced great plays and great playwrights, although why some periods generate more dramatic activity than others is still a matter of conjecture for scholars examining the social, historical, and religious conditions of the times. Each of the great ages of drama has affected the way plays are written, acted, and staged in successive ages. In every age, drama borrows important elements from each earlier period.

Greek Drama

The Greeks of the fifth century B.C. are credited with the first masterful dramatic age, which lasted from the birth of Aeschylus (c. 525 B.C.) to the death of Aristophanes (c. 385 B.C.). Their theaters were supported by public funds, and the playwrights competed for prizes during the great festivals of Dionysus. Sometimes as many as ten to fifteen thousand people sat in the theaters and watched with a sense of delight and awe as the actors played out their tales.

Theater was extremely important to the Greeks as a way of interpreting their relationships with their gods and of reinforcing their sense of community. The fifth-century B.C. audience, mostly wealthy citizens, came early in the morning and spent the entire day in the theater. Drama for the Greeks was not mere escapism or entertainment, not a frill or a luxury. Connected as it was with religious festivals, it was a cultural necessity.

Sophocles' plays *Oedipus Rex* and *Antigone* are examples of the powerful tragedies that have transfixed audiences for centuries. Euripides, slightly younger than Sophocles, was also a prize-winning tragedian. His *Trojan Women, Alcestis, Medea, Bacchae,* and *Elektra* [*Electra*] are still performed and still exert an influence on today's drama. The same is true of Aeschylus, who was slightly older than both and whose *Agamemnon, The Libation Bearers, The Eumenides* (known collectively as the *Oresteia*), and *Prometheus Bound* have all been among the most lasting of plays.

In addition to such great tragedians, the Greeks also produced the important comedians Aristophanes and Menander (late fourth century B.C.), whose work has been plundered for plays as diverse as a Shakespeare comedy and a Broadway musical. Aristophanes' *Lysistrata,* in which the Athenian and Spartan women agree to withhold sex from their husbands until the men promise to stop making war, is a powerful social comedy. Menander produced a more subtle type of comedy that made the culture laugh at itself. Both styles of comedy are the staple of popular entertainment even today. Menander's social comedies were the basis of comedy in which society's ways of behavior are criticized. Such social comedy is exemplified in Oliver Goldsmith's eighteenth-century *She Stoops to Conquer* and Molière's *The Misanthrope.*

Roman Drama

The Romans became aware of Greek drama in the third century B.C. and began to import Greek actors and playwrights. Because of many social and cultural differences between the societies, however, drama never took a central role in the life of the average Roman. Seneca, who is now viewed as Rome's most important tragedian, almost certainly wrote his plays to be read rather than to be seen onstage.

Roman comedy produced two great playwrights, Plautus and Terence, who helped develop the STOCK (or type) CHARACTER, such as the skinflint or the prude. Plautus was the great Roman comedian in the tradition of Menander. Plautus's best-known plays are *The Braggart Warrior* and *The Twin Menaechmi;* during the Renaissance, when all European schoolchildren read Latin, his works were favorites.

Terence's work was praised during the Middle Ages and the Renaissance as being smoother, more elegant, and more polished and refined than Plautus's. In his own age Terence was less admired by the general populace but more admired by connoisseurs of drama. His best-known plays — *The Woman of Andros, Phormio,* and *The Brothers* — are rarely performed today.

Drama took its place beside many other forms of entertainment in Roman culture — sports events, gladiator battles to the death, chariot races, the slaughter of wild beasts, and sacrifices of Christians and others to animals. The Roman public, when it did attend plays, enjoyed farces and relatively coarse humor. The audiences for Plautus and Terence, aristocratic in taste, may not have represented the cross-section of the community that was typical of Greek audiences.

Medieval Drama

After the fall of Rome and the spread of the Goths and Visigoths across southern Europe in the fifth century A.D., Europe experienced a total breakdown of the strong central government Rome had provided. When Rome fell, Greek and Roman culture virtually disappeared. The great classical texts went largely unread until the end of the medieval period in the fourteenth and fifteenth centuries; however, expressions of culture, including art forms such as drama, did not entirely disappear. During the medieval period the Church's power and influence grew extensively, and it tried to fill the gap left by the demise of the Roman empire. The Church became a focus of both religious and secular activity for people all over Europe.

After almost five centuries of relative inactivity, European drama was reborn in religious ceremonies in monasteries. It moved inside churches, then out of doors by the twelfth century, perhaps because its own demands outgrew its circumstances. Drama had become more than an adjunct of the religious ceremonies that had spawned it.

One reason that the medieval European communities regarded their drama so highly is that it expressed many of their concerns and values. The age was highly religious; in addition, the people who produced the plays were members of guilds whose personal pride was represented in their work. Their plays came to be called MYSTERY PLAYS because the trade that each guild represented was a special skill — a mystery to the average person. Of course, the pun on religious mystery was understood by most audiences.

Many of these plays told stories drawn from the Bible. The tales of Noah's Ark, Abraham and Isaac, and Samson and Delilah all had dramatic potential, and the mystery plays capitalized on that potential, as did plays on the life and crucifixion of Christ. Among mystery plays, *The Second Shepherds' Pageant* and *Abraham and Isaac* are still performed regularly.

Most mystery plays were gathered into groups of plays called CYCLES dramatizing incidents from the Bible, among other sources. They were usually performed outdoors, at times on movable wagons that doubled as stages. The audience either moved from wagon to wagon to see each play in a cycle, or the wagons moved among the audience.

By the fifteenth and sixteenth centuries, another form of play developed that was not associated with cycles or with the guilds. These were the MORALITY PLAYS, and their purpose was to touch on larger contemporary issues that had a moral overtone. *Everyman,* the best known of the morality plays, was performed in many nations in various languages.

Renaissance Drama

The revival of learning in the Renaissance, beginning in Italy in the fourteenth century, had considerable effect on drama because classical Greek and Roman plays were discovered and studied. In the academies in Italy, some experiments in re-creating Greek and Roman plays introduced music into drama. New theaters, such as Teatro Olympico in Vicenza (1579), were built to produce these plays; they allow us to see how the Renaissance reconceived the classical stage. Some of these experiments developed into modern opera. The late medieval traditions of the Italian theater's COMMEDIA DELL'ARTE, a stylized improvisational slapstick comedy performed by actors' guilds, began to move outside Italy into other European nations. The commedia's stock characters, Harlequins and Pulcinellas, began to appear in many countries in Europe.

Elizabethan and Jacobean (named for King James I, who succeeded Elizabeth and reigned from 1603 to 1625) drama developed most fully during the fifty years from approximately 1590 to 1640. Audiences poured into the playhouses eager for plays about history and for the great tragedies of Christopher Marlowe, such as *Doctor Faustus,* and of Shakespeare, including *Macbeth, Hamlet, Othello, Julius Caesar,* and *King Lear.* But there were others as well: Middleton and Rowley's *The Changeling,* Cyril Tourneur's *Revenger's Tragedy,* and John Webster's *The White Devil* and his sensational *The Duchess of Malfi.*

The great comedies of the age came mostly from the pen of William Shakespeare: *A Midsummer Night's Dream, The Comedy of Errors, As You Like It, Much Ado about Nothing, The Taming of the Shrew,* and *Twelfth Night.* Many of these plays derived from Italian originals, usually novellas or popular poems and sometimes comedies. But Shakespeare, of course, elevated and vastly improved everything he borrowed.

Ben Jonson, a playwright who was significantly influenced by the classical writers, was also well represented on the Elizabethan stage, with *Volpone, The Alchemist, Everyman in His Humour, Bartholomew Fair,* and other durable comedies. Jonson is also important for his contributions to the MASQUE, an aristocratic entertainment that featured music, dance, and fantastic costuming. His *Masque of Blackness* was performed in the royal court with the queen as a performer.

The Elizabethan stage sometimes grew bloody, with playwrights and audiences showing a passion for tragedies that, like *Hamlet,* centered on revenge and often ended with most of the characters meeting a premature death. Elizabethan plays also show considerable variety, with many plays detailing the history of English kings and, therefore, the history of England. It was a theater of powerful effect, and contemporary diaries indicate that the audiences delighted in it. Theaters also flourished in Spain in this period, producing Lope de Vega (1562–1635), who may have written as many as seventeen hundred plays.

Vega's immediate successor, Pedro Calderón de la Barca (1600–1681), is sometimes considered to be more polished in style, but also more stiffly aristocratic in appeal. He wrote fewer plays than Vega, but still produced an amazing body of work. He is said to have written at least 111 dramas and seventy or eighty *auto sacramentales,* the Spanish equivalent of religious morality plays designed for special religious ceremonies. Calderón is best known for *La vida es sueño (Life Is a Dream),* which is still performed today.

Theaters in Shakespeare's day were built outside city limits in seamy neighborhoods near brothels and bear-baiting pits, where chained bears were set upon by large dogs for the crowd's amusement. Happily, the theaters' business was good; the plays were constructed of remarkable language that seems to have fascinated all social classes, since all flocked to the theater by the thousands.

Late Seventeenth- and Eighteenth-Century Drama

After the Puritan reign in England from 1642 (when the theaters were closed) to 1660, during which dramatic productions were almost nonexistent, the theater was suddenly revived. In 1660 Prince Charles, sent to France by his father during the English Civil War, was invited back to be king, thus beginning what was known in England as the Restoration. It was a gay, exciting period in stark contrast to the gray Puritan era. During the period new indoor theaters modeled on those in France were built, and a new generation of actors and actresses (women took part in plays for the first time in England) came forth to participate in the dramatic revival.

Since the mid-1600s, French writers, interpreting Aristotle's description of Greek drama, had leaned toward development of a classical theater, which was supposed to observe the "unities" of time, place, and action: a play had one plot and one setting and covered the action of one day. In 1637 Pierre Corneille wrote *Le Cid,* using relatively modern Spanish history as his theme and following certain classical techniques. Jean-Baptiste Racine was Corneille's successor, and his plays became even more classical by centering on classical topics. His work includes *Andromache, Britannicus,* and, possibly his best play, *Phaedra.* Racine retired from the stage at the end of the seventeenth century, but he left a powerful legacy of classicism that reached well into the eighteenth century.

Molière, an actor and producer, was the best comedian of seventeenth-century France. Among his plays, *The Misanthrope* and several others are still produced regularly in the West. Molière was classical in his way, borrowing ancient comedy's technique of using type, or stock, characters in his social satires.

Among the important playwrights of the new generation were Aphra Behn, the first professional English female writer, whose play *The Rover* was one of the most popular plays of the late seventeenth century, and William Congreve, whose best-known play, *The Way of the World,* is often still produced. The latter is a lively comedy that aimed to chasten as well as entertain Congreve's audiences.

The eighteenth century saw the tradition of social comedy continued in Richard Brinsley Sheridan's *School for Scandal* and Oliver Goldsmith's *She Stoops to Conquer.* The drama of this period focuses on social manners, and much of it is SATIRE — that is, drama that offers mild criticism of society and holds society up to comic ridicule. But underlying that ridicule is the relatively noble motive of reforming society. We can see some of that motive at work in the plays of Molière and Goldsmith.

During much of the eighteenth century, theater in France centered on the court and was controlled by a small coterie of snobbish people. The situation

Claques

in England was not quite the same, although the audiences were snobbish and socially conscious. They went to the theater to be seen, and they often went in claques — groups of like-minded patrons who applauded or booed together to express their views. Theater was important, but attendance at it was like a material possession, something to be displayed for others to admire.

A wide variety of drama was extant in Japan in the late sixteenth and early seventeenth centuries. Kabuki theater, the most remarkable of popular Japanese drama, evolved in this period as a lasting form still seen today in theaters around the world. Kabuki is performed with puppets, and the resulting intensity would have surprised Western playwrights and audiences of that time. The emphasis shifted from the personality of the player to the situations and circumstances portrayed in the drama. Chikamatsu Monzaemon developed the form and was the most inventive of the Kabuki playwrights. His play *The Love Suicides at Sonezaki* was based on a genuine love suicide (shinjū in Japanese) and eventually created a craze for love suicide plays that ultimately resulted in an edict in 1722 that banned them entirely. Some modern writers claim that the quality of his drama was not equaled in Japan for more than two hundred years.

Nineteenth-Century Drama through the Turn of the Twentieth Century

English playwrights alone produced more than thirty thousand plays during the nineteenth century. Most of the plays were sentimental, melodramatic, and dominated by a few very powerful actors, stars who often overwhelmed the works written for them. The audiences were quite different from those of the seventeenth and eighteenth centuries. The upwardly mobile urban middle classes and the moneyed factory and mill owners who had benefited economically from the industrial revolution demanded a drama that would entertain them.

The new audiences were not especially well educated, nor were they interested in plays that were intellectually demanding. Instead, they wanted escapist and sentimental entertainment that was easy to respond to and did not challenge their basic values. Revivals of old plays and adaptations of Shakespeare were also common in the age, with great stars like Edmund Kean, Sir Henry Irving, Edwin Forrest, Edwin Booth, and William Macready using the plays as platforms for overwhelming, and sometimes overbearing, performances. Thrillers were especially popular, as were historical plays and melodramatic plays featuring a helpless heroine.

As an antidote to such a diet, the new Realist movement in literature, marked by the achievements of French novelists Émile Zola and Gustave Flaubert, finally struck the stage in the 1870s and 1880s in plays by August Strindberg and Henrik Ibsen. Revolutionizing Western drama, these Scandinavians forced their audiences to pay attention to important issues and deeper psychological concerns than earlier audiences had done.

Strindberg's *Miss Julie*, a psychological study, challenged social complacency based on class and social differences. Ibsen's *A Doll House* was a blow struck for feminism, but it did not amuse all audiences. Some were horrified at the thought that Nora Helmer was to be taken as seriously as her husband. Such a view was heretical, but it was also thrilling for a newly awakened European conscience. Those intellectuals and writers who responded positively to Ibsen, including Bernard Shaw, acted as the new conscience and began a move that soon transformed drama. Feminism is also a theme, but perhaps less directly, of Ibsen's *Hedda Gabler*, the story of a woman whose frustration at being cast into an inferior role contributes toward a destructive — and ultimately self-destructive — impulse. Both plays are acted in a physical setting that seems to be as ordinary as a nineteenth-century sitting room, with characters as small — and yet as large — as the people who watched them.

The Russian Anton Chekhov's plays *Three Sisters, Uncle Vanya,* and *The Cherry Orchard,* written at the turn of the twentieth century, are realistic as well, but they are also patient examinations of character rather than primarily problem plays — like Ibsen's successful dramas *Ghosts* and *The Master Builder.* Chekhov is aware of social change in Russia, especially the changes that revealed a hitherto repressed class of peasants evolving into landowners and merchants. *The Cherry Orchard* is suffused with an overpowering sense of inevitability through which Chekhov depicts the conflict between the necessity for change and a nostalgia for the past. The comedies of Oscar Wilde, such as *Lady Windermere's Fan* and *The Importance of Being Earnest,* poked fun at the foibles of the upper classes. Amusing as they are, their satirical quality constitutes social criticism.

These plays introduced a modern realism of a kind that was rare in earlier drama. Melodrama of the nineteenth century was especially satisfying to mass audiences because the good characters were very good, the bad characters were very bad, and justice was meted out at the end. But it is difficult in Chekhov to be sure who the heroes and villains are. Nothing is as clear-cut in these plays as it is in popular melodramas. Instead, Chekhov's plays are as complicated as life itself. Such difficulties of distinction have become the norm of the most important drama of contemporary drama.

Drama in the Early and Mid-Twentieth Century

The drama of the early twentieth century nurtured the seeds of nineteenth-century realism into bloom, but sometimes this drama experimented with audience expectations. Eugene O'Neill's *Desire under the Elms* is a tragedy that features the ordinary citizen rather than the noble. This play focuses on New England farmers as tragic characters. Arthur Miller's *Death of a Salesman* invokes a sense of dreadful inevitability within the world of the commercial salesman, the ordinary man. As in many other twentieth-century tragedies, the point is that the life of the ordinary man can be as tragic as Oedipus's life.

Luigi Pirandello experiments with reality in *Six Characters in Search of an Author,* a play that has a distinctly absurd quality, since it expects us to accept the notion that the characters on the stage are waiting for an author to put them into a play. Pirandello plays with our sense of illusion and of expectation and realism to such an extent that he forces us to reexamine our concepts of reality.

Bertolt Brecht's *Mother Courage,* an example of what the playwright called EPIC DRAMA, explores war from a complex series of viewpoints. On the one hand Courage is a powerful figure who has been seen as a model of endurance, but Brecht also wanted his audience to see that Courage brings on much of her own suffering by trying to profit from war. The sole act of self-sacrifice in the play comes at the end, when Kattrin beats her drum to warn villagers of the approach of a destroying army. Brecht produced the play early in World War II as a protest. Playwrights around the world responded to events such as World War I, the Communist revolution, and the Great Depression by writing plays that no longer permitted audiences to sit comfortably and securely in darkened theaters. Brecht and other playwrights instead came out to get their audiences, to make them feel and think, to make them realize their true condition.

Samuel Beckett's dramatic career began with *Waiting for Godot,* which audiences interpreted as an examination of humans' eternal vigilance for the revelation of God or of some transcendent meaning in their lives. In the play, Godot never comes, yet the characters do not give up hope. *Endgame*'s characters seem to be awaiting the end of the world: in the 1950s the shadow of nuclear extinction cast by the cold war dominated most people's imagination.

Tennessee Williams examines a physically and psychically frail young woman's withdrawal from life in *The Glass Menagerie.* The play derives from personal experience: Williams's sister was such a woman. Personal experience may also inform his *Cat on a Hot Tin Roof,* which portrays themes of homosexuality and marital sexual tension — themes that were not openly discussed in contemporary American theater except in veiled mythic terms, in the manner, for example, of O'Neill's *Desire under the Elms.*

Nigerian playwright Wole Soyinka, who won the Nobel Prize for literature in 1986, portrays the complex intersection of a person's past and the present in his play *The Strong Breed,* set in an African village reminiscent of the Greek *polis.* Indeed, he has experimented with Greek tragic forms in *The Bacchae of Euripides,* which is also set in Africa. Soyinka's insights into the nature of culture and drama provide us with a new way of reflecting on drama's power in our lives.

Modern dramatists from the turn of the twentieth century to the Korean War explored in many different directions and developed new approaches to themes of dramatic illusion as well as to questions concerning the relationship of an audience to the stage and the players.

Contemporary Drama

As we begin the twenty-first century, the stage is vibrant. The great commercial theaters of England and the United States are sometimes hampered by high production costs, but regional theaters everywhere are producing fine drama. The National Theatre in London has made inexpensive seats available for most of its plays, and other theaters are doing the same. In Latin America, Germany, Japan, China, France, and elsewhere, the theater is active and exciting. Poland's experiments in drama, led by Jerzy Grotowski's "Poor Theater," inspired experimentation that has spread throughout the world of drama. Russia, too, has produced a number of plays that have been given a worldwide currency.

The hallmark of many of these plays has been experimentalism. Caryl Churchill's *Top Girls* features characters who claim to be Pope Joan, Patient Griselda, and Lady Nijo, as well as being "themselves" — all this in the milieu of a feminist employment agency.

Sam Shepard, well known as an actor, was for many years among the most experimental playwrights living in New York's Greenwich Village. His *True West* begins as a relatively straightforward play about Austin and Lee, two brothers, but quickly reveals the drama that lies beneath the surface. Lee has arrived to steal his mother's television set but ends by stealing something of his brother's personality.

Luis Valdez's *Zoot Suit* explores 1940s Los Angeles when the zoot suit riots brought Chicano youth into clashes with sailors and determined police. The play is intense and filled with dynamic music, powerful language, and action.

Not all modern theater is experimental, however. August Wilson's *Fences* shows us the pain of life at the lower end of the economic ladder in a form that is recognizably realistic and plausible. The play is set in the 1950s and focuses on Troy Maxon, a black man, and his relationship with his son and his wife. Tenement life is one subject of the play, but the most important subject is the courage it takes to keep going after tasting defeat. The entire drama develops within the bounds of conventional nineteenth-century realism.

Suzan-Lori Parks has maintained a career of writing experimental plays, from the Brechtian *The Death of the Last Black Man in the Whole Entire World*, which structures itself in "panels" — brief, intense scenes that connect imaginatively — to *Topdog/Underdog*, which features brothers named Lincoln and Booth. In the latter play, this unlikely pair of brothers connects through the con game of three-card monte while the play explores race and reality in America. Tony Kushner employs similar techniques in *Angels in America*. Its brilliantly staged scenes are filled with emotional intensity, and the audience is carried on waves of imaginative speculation on America's history as well as on America's present. Anna Deavere Smith brings an interesting experimentation to a logical conclusion: she writes and performs her work, assuming the parts of multiple characters of every race and gender. Her *Fires in the Mirror: Crown Heights, Brooklyn, and Other Identities,* is an example of PERFORMANCE ART, a form of drama becoming popular in many parts of the world. Laurie Anderson, Karen Finley, Sarah Jones, John Leguizamo, and Eric Bogosian are a few of the better-known performance artists. Experimentation is probably at the heart of the work of many playwrights, although it still does not please mainstream audiences to the same degree that traditional drama does.

The most celebrated of contemporary playwrights seem to mix experimental and conventional dramatic techniques. Tom Stoppard, whose work is cerebral and witty, as in his pastiche of *Hamlet* called *Rosencrantz and Guildenstern Are Dead,* continues to delve into literature for much of his work. *The Invention of Love* treats the hopeless love of the Oxford classical scholar and poet, A. E. Housman, for a young athlete, Moses Jackson. The play begins with Housman crossing the river Styx into the underworld. Throughout, the older Housman watches the action of himself as a young man and offers his sentiments. *Arcadia*, unlike some of Stoppard's early works, is a deeply emotional play about a thirteen-year-old girl, Lady Thomasina Coverly, gifted mathematically in an age in which such fields of study were reserved for men. The play takes place in one country house in Derbyshire, England, in both 1809 and 1989, contrasting several modes of thought and feeling — classical, romantic, and modern. Paula Vogel's plays frequently interrupt the dramatic action with asides, but they are also imaginatively structured so that time feels fluid and the action moves in emotionally significant sweeps. *The Baltimore Waltz,* derived from Vogel's experience of watching her brother die of AIDS, brings humor to a tragic situation. Similarly, *How I Learned to Drive,* which sensitively treats the subject of sexual molestation in families, also has comic moments. Edward Albee, always interested in pushing limits, introduces an unlikely love relationship between a brilliant architect and a goat in *The Goat, or Who Is Sylvia?* This sharply focused play explores the underpinnings of Greek tragedy in a context that is startling for modern audiences. Nilo Cruz, who studied playwriting with Paula Vogel, has explored unusual material in early plays such as *Night Train to Bolina,* a play centered on the efforts of two children to free themselves from an oppressive existence. His *Anna in the*

Tropics connects classic literature, *Anna Karenina,* with the Cuban cigar makers of the 1920s in Tampa, Florida. The cigar rollers usually employed a *lectore,* or reader, to read to them while they worked. In Cruz's play, the lectore's choice of *Anna Karenina* ultimately results in awakening dormant emotions that change everyone's lives. The theater in our times continues with extraordinary energy to explore issues of social, historical, and psychological importance, with a wide range of techniques to which audiences respond positively.

Genres of Drama
Tragedy

Drama since the great age of the Greeks has taken several different forms. As we have seen, tragedies were one genre that pleased Greek audiences, and comedies pleased the Romans. In later ages, a blend of the comic and the tragic produced a hybrid genre: tragicomedy. In our time, unless a play is modeled on the Greek or Shakespearean tragedies, as is O'Neill's *Desire under the Elms,* it is usually considered tragicomic rather than tragic. Our age still enjoys the kind of comedy that people laugh at, although most plays that are strictly comedy are frothy, temporarily entertaining, and not lasting.

TRAGEDY demands a specific worldview. Aristotle, in his *Poetics,* points out that the tragic hero or heroine should be noble of birth, perhaps a king like Oedipus or a princess like Antigone. This has often been interpreted to mean that the tragic hero or heroine should be more magnanimous, more daring, larger in spirit than the average person.

Modern tragedies have rediscovered tragic principles, and while O'Neill and Miller rely on Aristotle's precepts, they have shown that in a modern society shorn of the distinctions between noble and peasant it is possible for audiences to see the greatness in all classes. This has given us a new way of orienting ourselves to the concept of fate; to HAMARTIA, the wrong act that leads people to a tragic end; and to the hero's or heroine's relationship to the social order.

Aristotle suggested that plot was the heart and soul of tragedy and that character came second. But most older tragedies take the name of the tragic hero or heroine as their title; this signifies the importance that dramatists invested in their tragic characters. Yet they also heeded Aristotle's stipulation that tragic action should have one plot rather than the double or triple plots that often characterize comedies. (Shakespeare was soundly criticized in the eighteenth century for breaking this rule in his tragedies.) And they paid attention to the concept of PERIPETEIA, which specifies that the progress of the tragic characters sometimes leads them to a reversal: they get what they want, but what they want turns out to be destructive. Aristotle especially valued a plot in which the reversal takes place simultaneously with the recognition of the truth, or the shift from ignorance to awareness, as it does in Sophocles' *Oedipus Rex.*

Playwrights in the seventeenth and eighteenth centuries in France were especially interested in following classical precepts. They were certain that Greek tragedy and Roman comedy were the epitome of excellence in drama. They interpreted Aristotle's discussion of dramatic integrity to be a set of rules governing dramatic form. These became known as the dramatic UNITIES specifying one plot, a single action that takes place in one day in a single setting. The neoclassical reinterpretation of the unities was probably much stricter than Aristotle intended.

Comedy

Two kinds of comedy developed among the ancient Greeks: OLD COMEDY, which resembles FARCE (light drama characterized by broad satirical comedy and an improbable plot) and often pokes fun at individuals with social and political power, and NEW COMEDY, which is a more refined commentary on the condition of society.

Old Comedy survives in the masterful works of Aristophanes, such as *Lysistrata,* while New Comedy hearkens back to the lost plays of Menander and resurfaces in plays such as Molière's *The Misanthrope.* Molière uses humor but mixes it with a serious level of social commentary. Modern COMEDY OF MANNERS studies and sometimes ridicules modern society as in Oscar Wilde's *The Importance of Being Earnest.*

Comedy is not always funny. Chekhov thought *The Cherry Orchard* was a comedy, while his producer, the great Konstantin Stanislavsky, who trained actors to interpret his lines and who acted in other Chekhov plays, thought it was a tragedy. The argument may have centered on the ultimate effect of the play on its audiences, but it may also have centered on the question of laughter. There are laughs in *The Cherry Orchard,* but they usually come at the expense of a character or a social group. This is true, as well, of Samuel Beckett's *Waiting for Godot* and *Happy Days.* We may laugh, but we also know that the play is at heart very serious.

Tragicomedy

Since the early seventeenth century, serious plays have been called TRAGICOMEDIES when they do not adhere strictly to the structure of tragedy, which emphasizes the nobility of the hero or heroine, fate, the wrong action of the hero or heroine, and a resolution that includes death, exile, or a similar end. Many serious plays have these qualities, but they also have some of the qualities of comedy: a commentary on society, raucous behavior that draws laughs, and a relatively happy ending. Yet their darkness is such that we can hardly feel comfortable regarding them as comedies.

Plays such as Sam Shepard's *True West* and Lorraine Hansberry's *A Raisin in the Sun* can be considered tragicomedy. Indeed, the modern temperament has especially relied on the mixture of comic and tragic elements for its most serious plays. Eugene O'Neill, Tennessee Williams, Harold Pinter, Marsha Norman, and Caryl Churchill have all been masters of tragicomedy.

In contemporary drama tragicomedy takes several forms. One is the play whose seriousness is relieved by comic moments; another is a play whose comic structure absorbs a tragic moment and continues to express affirmation. Yet another is the dark comedy whose sardonic humor leaves us wondering how we can laugh at something that is ultimately frightening. This is the case with some absurdist comedies, which insist that there is no meaning in events other than the meaning we invent for ourselves. Pinter's *Betrayal* and Beckett's *Happy Days* are such plays. They are funny yet sardonic, and when we laugh we do so uneasily.

Other genres of drama exist, although they are generally versions of tragedy, comedy, and tragicomedy. Improvisational theater, in which actors use no scripts and may switch roles at any moment, defies generic description. Musical comedies and operas are dramatic entertainments that have established their own genres related in some ways to the standard genres of drama.

Genre distinctions are useful primarily because they establish expectations in the minds of audiences with theatrical experience. Tragedies and comedies make different demands on an audience. According to Marsha Norman's explanation of the "rules" of drama, you have to know in a play just what is at stake. Understanding the principles that have developed over the centuries to create the genres of drama helps us know what is at stake.

Elements of Drama

All plays share some basic elements with which playwrights and producers work: plots, characters, settings, dialogue, movement, and themes. In addition, many modern plays pay close attention to lighting, costuming, and props. When we respond to a play, we observe the elements of drama in action together, and the total experience is rich, complex, and subtle. Occasionally, we respond primarily to an individual element — the theme or characterization, for instance — but that is rare. Our awareness of the elements of drama is most useful when we are thinking analytically about a play and the way it affects us.

For the sake of discussion, we will consider the way the basic elements of drama function in Lady Gregory's one-act play *The Rising of the Moon* (which follows this section). It has all the elements we expect from drama, and it is both a brief and a very successful play.

Plot

PLOT is a term for the action of a drama. Plot implies that the ACTION has a shape and form that will ultimately prove satisfying to the audience. Generally, a carefully plotted play begins with EXPOSITION, an explanation of what happened before the play began and of how the characters arrived at their present situation. The play then continues, using SUSPENSE to build tension in the audience and in the characters and to develop further the pattern of RISING ACTION. The audience wonders what is going to happen, sees the characters set in motion, and then watches as certain questions implied by the drama are answered one by one. The action achieves its greatest tension as it moves to a point of CLIMAX, when a revelation is experienced, usually by the chief characters. Once the climax has been reached, the plot continues, sometimes very briefly, in a pattern of FALLING ACTION as the drama reaches its conclusion and the characters understand their circumstances and themselves better than they did at the beginning of the play.

The function of plot is to give action a form that helps us understand elements of the drama in relation to one another. Plays can have several interrelated plots or only one. Lady Gregory's *The Rising of the Moon* has one very simple plot: a police sergeant is sent out with two policemen to make sure a political rebel does not escape from the area. The effect of the single plot is that the entire play focuses intensely on the interaction between the rebel, disguised as a ballad singer, and the sergeant. The sergeant meets the rebel, listens to him sing ballads, and then recognizes in him certain qualities they share. The audience wonders if a reward of one hundred pounds will encourage the sergeant to arrest the ballad singer or if, instead, the ballad singer's sense that his cause is just will convince the sergeant to let him go. The climax of the action occurs when the sergeant's two policemen return, as the ballad singer hides behind a barrel, and ask if the sergeant has seen any signs of the rebel. Not until that moment does the audience know for sure what the sergeant will do. When he gives his answer, the falling action begins.

Plots depend on CONFLICT between characters, and in *The Rising of the Moon* the conflict is very deep. It is built into the characters themselves, but it is also part of the institution of law that the sergeant serves and the ongoing struggle for justice that the ballad singer serves. This conflict, still evident today, was a very significant national issue in Ireland when the play was first produced in Dublin in 1907.

Lady Gregory works subtly with the conflict between the sergeant and the ballad singer, showing that although they are on completely opposite sides of the law — and of the important political issues — they are more alike than they are different. The ballad singer begins to sing the "Granuaile," a revolutionary song about England's unlawful dominance over Ireland through seven centuries; when he leaves out a line, the sergeant supplies it. In that action the sergeant reveals that, although he is paid by the English to keep law and order, his roots lie with the Irish people. By his knowledge of the revolutionary songs he reveals his sympathies.

Characterization

Lady Gregory has effectively joined CHARACTER and conflict in *The Rising of the Moon:* as the conflict is revealed, the characters of the sergeant and the ballad singer are also revealed. At first the sergeant seems eager to get the reward, and he acts bossy with Policeman X and Policeman B. And when he first meets the ballad singer he seems demanding and policemanlike. It is only when he begins to sense who the ballad singer really is that he changes and reveals a deep, sympathetic streak.

Lady Gregory, in a note to the play, said that in Ireland when the play was first produced, those who wanted Ireland to become part of England were incensed to see a policeman portrayed so as to show his sympathies with rebels. Those who wished Ireland to become a separate nation from England were equally shocked to see a policeman portrayed so sympathetically.

The sergeant and the ballad singer are both major characters in the play, but it is not clear that either is the villain or the hero. When the play begins, the sergeant seems to be the hero because he represents the law and the ballad singer appears to be the villain because he has escaped from prison. But as the action develops, those characterizations change. What replaces them is an awareness of the complications that underlie the relationship between the law and the lawbreaker in some circumstances. This is part of the point of Lady Gregory's play.

Lady Gregory has given a very detailed portrait of both main characters, although in a one-act play she does not have enough space to be absolutely thorough in developing them. Yet we get an understanding of the personal ambitions of each character, and we understand both their relationship to Ireland and their particular allegiances as individuals. They speak with each other in enough detail to show that they understand each other, and when the ballad singer hides behind the barrel at the approach of the other two policemen, he indicates that he trusts the sergeant not to reveal him.

Policeman X and Policeman B are only sketched in. Yet their presence is important. It is with them that the sergeant reveals his official personality, and it is their presence at the end that represents the most important threat to the security of the ballad singer. We know, though, little or nothing about them personally. They are characters who are functionaries, a little like Rosencrantz and Guildenstern in *Hamlet,* but without the differentiating characterizations that Shakespeare was able to give minor players in his full-length play.

The plays in this collection have some of the most remarkable characters ever created in literature. Tragedy usually demands complex characters, such as Oedipus, Antigone, Medea, Hamlet, and Willy Loman. We come to know them through their own words, through their interaction with other characters, through their expression of feelings, through their decisions, and through their presence onstage depicted in movement and gesture.

Characters in tragicomedies are individualized and complexly portrayed, such as Madame Ranevskaya in *The Cherry Orchard,* Miss Julie, and Nora Helmer in *A Doll House.* But just as effective in certain kinds of drama are characters drawn as types, such as Alceste, the misanthrope in Molière's play, and Everyman in medieval drama.

In many plays we see that the entire shape of the action derives from the characters, from their strengths and weaknesses. In such plays we do not feel that the action lies outside the characters and that they must live through an arbitrary sequence of events. Instead we feel that they create their own opportunities and problems.

Setting

The SETTING of a play includes many things. First, it refers to the time and place in which the action occurs. Second, it refers to the scenery, the physical elements that appear onstage to vivify the author's stage directions. In Lady Gregory's play, we have a dock with barrels to suggest the locale and darkness to suggest night. These are important details that influence the emotional reaction of the audience.

Some plays make use of very elaborate settings, as does August Wilson's *Fences,* which is produced with a detailed tenement backyard onstage. Others make use of simple settings, such as the empty stage of Pirandello's *Six Characters in Search of an Author.*

Lady Gregory's setting derives from her inspiration for the play. She visited the quays — places where boats dock and leave with goods — as a young girl and imagined how someone might escape from the nearby prison and make his getaway "under a load of kelp" in one of the ships. The quay represents the meeting of the land and water, and it represents the getaway, the possibility of freedom. The barrel is a symbol of trade, and the sergeant and the ballad singer sit on its top and trade the words of a revolutionary song with each other.

The title of the play refers to another element of the setting: the moonlight. The night protects the ballad singer, and it permits the sergeant to bend his sworn principles a bit. The rising of the moon, as a rebel song suggests, signifies a change in society, the time when "the small shall rise up and the big shall fall down." Lady Gregory uses these elements in the play in a very effective way, interrelating them so that their significance becomes increasingly apparent as the play progresses.

Dialogue

Plays depend for their unfolding on dialogue. The DIALOGUE is the verbal exchanges between the characters. Since there is no description or commentary on the action, as there is in most novels, the dialogue must tell the whole story. Fine playwrights have developed ways of revealing character, advancing action, and introducing themes by a highly efficient use of dialogue.

Dialogue is spoken by one character to another, who then responds. But sometimes, as in Shakespeare's *Hamlet,* a character delivers a SOLILOQUY, in which he or she speaks onstage to him- or herself. Ordinarily, such speeches take on importance because they are thought to be especially true. Characters, when they speak to each other, may well wish to deceive, but generally, when they speak to themselves, they have no reason to say anything but the truth.

In *The Rising of the Moon* Lady Gregory has written an unusual form of dialogue that reveals a regional way of speech. Lady Gregory was Anglo-Irish, but she lived in the west of Ireland and was familiar with the speech patterns that the characters in this play would have used. She has been recognized for her ability to re-create the speech of the rural Irish, and passages such as the following are meant to reveal the peculiarities of the rhythms and syntax of English as it was spoken in Ireland at the turn of the century:

SERGEANT: Is he as bad as that?
MAN: He is then.
SERGEANT: Do you tell me so?

Lady Gregory makes a considerable effort to create dialogue that is rich in local color as well as in spirit. John Millington Synge, another Irish playwright, whose dialogue in *Riders to the Sea* is also an effort to re-create the sounds and rhythms of rural Irish speech, once said: "In a good play every speech should be as fully flavored as a nut or apple, and such speeches cannot be written by anyone who works among people who have shut their lips on poetry." Lady Gregory, who produced the plays of Synge at the Abbey Theatre in Dublin, would certainly agree, as her dialogue in *The Rising of the Moon* amply shows.

Music

Lady Gregory introduces another dramatic element: music. In *The Rising of the Moon* the music is integral to the plot because it allows the ballad singer, by omitting a line of a rebel song, gradually to expose the sergeant's sympathies with the rebel cause. The sergeant is at first mindful of his duty and insists that the balladeer stop, but eventually he is captivated by the music. As the ballad singer continues, he sings a song containing the title of the play, and the audience or reader realizes that the title exposes the play's rebel sympathies.

Movement

We as readers or witnesses are energized by the movement of the characters in a play. As we read, stage directions inform us where the characters are, when they move, how they move, and perhaps even what the significance of their movement is. In modern plays the author may give many directions for the action; in earlier plays stage directions are few and often supplemented by those of a modern editor. In performance the movements that you see may well have been invented by the director, although the text of a play often requires certain actions, as in the ghost scene and final dueling scene in *Hamlet*. In some kinds of drama, such as musical comedy and Greek drama, part of the action may be danced.

Lady Gregory moves the ballad singer and the sergeant in telling ways. They move physically closer to one another as they become closer in their thinking. Their movement seems to pivot around the barrel, and in one of the most charming moments of the play, they meet each other's eyes when the ballad singer sits on the barrel and comments on the way the sergeant is pacing back and forth. They then both sit on the barrel, facing in opposite directions, and share a pipe between them, almost as a peace offering.

Theme

The theme of a play is its message, its central concerns — in short, what it is about. It is by no means a simple thing to decide what the theme of a play is, and many plays contain several rather than just a single theme. Often, the search for a theme tempts us to oversimplify and to reduce a complex play to a relatively simple catchphrase.

Sophocles' *Antigone* focuses on the conflict between human law and the law of the gods when following both sets of laws seems to be impossible. Antigone wishes to honor the gods by burying her brother, but the law of Kreon decrees that he shall have no burial, since her brother is technically a traitor to the state. Similar themes are present in other Greek plays. *Hamlet* has many themes. On a very elementary level, the main theme of *Hamlet* is revenge. This is played out in the obligation of a son to avenge the murder of a father, even when the murderer is a kinsman. Another theme centers on corruption in the state of Denmark.

Lady Gregory's play has revolution as one theme. The rising of the moon is a sign for "the rising" or revolution of the people against their English oppressors. The sergeant is an especially English emblem of oppression because the police were established by an Englishman, Robert Peele. At one point the balladeer suggests a song, "The Peeler and the Goat," but rejects it because in slang a peeler is a policeman.

Another important theme in *The Rising of the Moon* is that of unity among the Irish people. The sergeant seems to be at an opposite pole from the ballad singer when the play opens. He is posting signs announcing a reward that he could well use, since he is a family man. But as the play proceeds, the sergeant moves closer in thought to the Irish people, represented by the rebel, the ballad singer.

If concerned that readers and viewers will miss their thematic intentions, playwrights sometimes reveal these in one or two speeches. Usually, a careful reader or viewer has already divined the theme, and the speeches are intrusive. But Lady Gregory is able to introduce thematic material in certain moments of dialogue, as in this comment by the sergeant, revealing that the police are necessary to prevent a revolution:

> SERGEANT: Well, we have to do our duty in the force. Haven't we the whole country depending on us to keep law and order? It's those that are down would be up and those that are up would be down, if it wasn't for us.

But the thematic material in *The Rising of the Moon* is spread evenly throughout, as is the case in most good plays.

In every play, the elements of drama will work differently, sometimes giving us the feeling that character is dominant over theme, or plot over character, or setting over both. Ordinarily, critics feel that character, plot, and theme are the most important elements of drama, while setting, dialogue, music, and movement come next. But in the best of dramas each has its importance and each balances the others. The plays in this collection strive for that harmony; most achieve it memorably.

Lady Gregory

Isabella Augusta Persse (1852–1932) was born in the west of Ireland. Her family was known as "ascendancy stock"— that is, it was educated, wealthy, and Protestant living in a land that was largely uneducated, poverty-ridden, and Roman Catholic. A gulf existed between the rich ascendancy families, who lived in great houses with considerable style, partaking in lavish hunts and balls, and the impoverished Irish, who lived in one-room straw-roofed homes and worked the soil with primitive tools.

Lady Gregory took a strong interest in the Irish language, stimulated in part by a nurse who often spoke the language to her when she was a child. Her nurse was an important source of Irish folklore and a contact with the people who lived in the modest cottages around her family estate. It was extraordinary for any wealthy Protestant to pay attention to the language or the life of the poor laborers of the west of Ireland. Yet these are the very people who figure most importantly in the plays that Lady Gregory wrote in later life.

Isabella Persse met Sir William Gregory when she was on a family trip to Nice and Rome. They were actually neighbors in Ireland, but only slightly acquainted. He was also of Irish ascendancy stock and had been a governor of Ceylon. They were married the following year, when she was twenty-eight and he was sixty-three. Their marriage was apparently quite successful, and in 1881 their son, Robert Gregory, was born. They used the family home, Coole Park, as a retreat for short periods, but most of their time was spent traveling and living in London, where Sir William was a trustee of the National Gallery of Art. W. B. Yeats, Bernard Shaw, and numerous other important literary figures spent time in Coole Park and its beautiful great house in the early part of the twentieth century.

Lady Gregory led a relatively conventional life until Sir William Gregory died in 1892. According to the laws of that time, the estate passed to her son, so she anticipated a life of relatively modest circumstances. In the process of finishing Sir William's memoirs, she found herself to be a gifted writer. She used some of her spare time to learn Irish well enough to talk with the old cottagers in the hills, where she went to gather folklore and old songs. Although W. B. Yeats and others had collected volumes of Irish stories and poems, they did not know Irish well enough to authenticate what they heard. Lady Gregory published her Kiltartan tales (she had dubbed her neighborhood Kiltartan) as a way of preserving the rapidly disappearing myths and stories that were still told around the hearth as a matter of course in rural Ireland.

She was already an accomplished writer when she met W. B. Yeats in 1894. Their meeting was of immense importance for the history of drama, since they decided to forge their complementary talents and abilities to create an Irish theater. Their discussions included certain Irish neighbors, among them Edward Martyn, a Catholic whose early plays were very successful. They also talked with Dr. Douglas Hyde, a mythographer and linguist and the first president of modern Ireland. Another neighbor who took part, the flamboyant George Moore, was a well-established novelist and playwright.

The group's first plays — Yeats's *The Countess Cathleen* and Martyn's *The Heather Field* — were performed on May 8 and 9, 1899, under the auspices of the Irish Literary Theatre in Dublin at the Ancient Concert Rooms. Dedicated to producing plays by Irish playwrights on Irish themes, the Irish Literary Theatre became an immediate success. The greatest problem the founders faced was finding more plays. Lady Gregory tried her own hand and discovered herself, at age fifty, to be a playwright.

Her ear for people's speech was unusually good — good enough that she was able to give the great poet Yeats lessons in dialogue and to help him prepare his own plays for the stage. She collaborated with Yeats on *The Pot of Broth* in 1902, the year she wrote her first plays, *The Jackdaw* and *A Losing Game*. Her first produced play, *Twenty-Five*, was put on in 1903. By 1904 the group had rented the historic Abbey Theatre. Some of her plays were quite popular and were successful even in later revivals: *Spreading the News* (1904); *Kincora* and *The White Cockade* (1905); and *Hyacinth Halvey, The Doctor in Spite of Himself, The Gaol Gate,* and *The Canavans* (all 1906). In the next year, there were troubles at the Abbey over John Millington Synge's *Playboy of the Western World*. The middle-class audience resented the portrait of the Irish peasants as people who would celebrate a self-confessed father-killer, even though he had not actually done the "gallous deed." Lady Gregory faced down a rioting audience who were protesting what she felt was excellent drama.

In 1918 her son, a World War I pilot, was shot down over Italy. The years that followed were to some extent years of struggle. Lady Gregory managed the Abbey Theatre, directed its affairs, and developed new playwrights, among them Sean O'Casey. During the Irish Civil War (1920–1922), she was physically threatened, and eventually her family home, Roxborough, was burned. In 1926, after discovering that she had cancer, she made arrangements to sell Coole Park to the government with the agreement that she could remain there for life. She died in 1932, the writer of a large number of satisfying plays and the prime mover in developing one of the twentieth century's most important literary theaters.

THE RISING OF THE MOON

One of Lady Gregory's shortest but most popular plays, *The Rising of the Moon* is openly political in its themes. Lady Gregory had been writing plays only a short time, and she had been directing the Irish Literary Theatre when it became the Abbey Theatre Company and produced this play in 1907. Her interest in Irish politics developed, she said, when she was going through the papers of a distant relative of her husband. That man had been in the Castle, the offices of the English authorities given the task of ruling Ireland from Dublin. She said that the underhanded dealings revealed in those papers convinced her that Ireland should be a nation apart from England if justice were ever to be done.

In 1907 the question of union with England or separation and nationhood was on everyone's lips. Ireland was calm, and the people in Dublin were relatively prosperous and by no means readying for a fight or a revolution. Yet there had been a tradition of risings against the English dating back to the Elizabethan age and earlier. In 1907 the average Irish person believed that revolution was a thing of the past; actually, it was less than ten years in the future. Certain organizations had been developing, notably the widespread Gaelic League and the less-known Sinn Féin (We Ourselves), to promote Irish lore, language, and culture. English was the dominant language in Ireland, since it was the language of commerce, but it tended to obliterate the Irish culture. Lady Gregory's work with the Abbey Theatre, which was making one of the age's most important contributions to Irish culture, thus coincided with growing interest in the rest of Ireland in rediscovering its literary past.

The title *The Rising of the Moon* comes from a popular old rebel song that pointed to the rising of the moon as the signal for the rising of peoples against oppression. The main characters of the play represent the two opposing forces in Ireland: freedom and independence, personified by the ballad singer ("a Ragged Man"); and law and order, represented by the sergeant. The ballad singer is aligned with those who want to change the social structure of Ireland so that the people now on the bottom will be on top. The sergeant's job is to preserve the status quo and avoid such a turning of the tables.

In an important way, the sergeant and the ballad singer represent the two alternatives that face the modern Irish — now as in the past. One alternative is to accept the power of the English and be in their pay, like the sergeant; one would then be well fed and capable of supporting a family. The other alternative is to follow the revolutionary path of the ballad singer and risk prison, scorn, and impoverishment. The ballad singer is a ragged man because he has been totally reduced in circumstances by his political choices.

For Lady Gregory, this play was a serious political statement. She and W. B. Yeats — both aristocratic Protestant Irish — were sympathetic to the Irish revolutionary causes. They each wrote plays that struck a revolutionary note during this period. Neither truly expected a revolution; when the Easter Uprising of 1916 was put down with considerable loss of life and immense destruction of central Dublin, Yeats lamented that his plays may have sent some young men to their deaths.

It is possible that if either Yeats or Lady Gregory had thought there would be a revolution they would not have written such plays. They opposed violence, but it was clear to some that violence was the only means by which Ireland would be made into a separate nation.

The success of *The Rising of the Moon* lies in Lady Gregory's exceptional ear for dialogue. She captures the way people speak, and she also manages to draw the characters of the sergeant and ballad singer so as to gain our sympathies for both. In a remarkably economic fashion she dramatizes the problem of politics in Ireland, characterizing the two polarities and revealing some of the complexities that face anyone who tries to understand them.

Lady Gregory (1852–1932)
THE RISING OF THE MOON

1907

Persons

SERGEANT   POLICEMAN B
POLICEMAN X   A RAGGED MAN

Scene: *Side of a quay in a seaport town. Some posts and chains. A large barrel. Enter three policemen. Moonlight.*

(*Sergeant, who is older than the others, crosses the stage to right and looks down steps. The others put down a pastepot and unroll a bundle of placards.*)

POLICEMAN B: I think this would be a good place to put up a notice. (*He points to barrel.*)

POLICEMAN X: Better ask him. (*Calls to Sergeant.*) Will this be a good place for a placard?

(*No answer.*)

POLICEMAN B: Will we put up a notice here on the barrel?

(*No answer.*)

SERGEANT: There's a flight of steps here that leads to the water. This is a place that should be minded well. If he got down here, his friends might have a boat to meet him; they might send it in here from outside.

POLICEMAN B: Would the barrel be a good place to put a notice up?

SERGEANT: It might; you can put it there.

(*They paste the notice up.*)

SERGEANT (*reading it*): Dark hair — dark eyes, smooth face, height five feet five — there's not much to take hold of in that — It's a pity I had no chance of seeing him before he broke out of jail. They say he's a wonder, that it's he makes all the plans for the whole organization. There isn't another man in Ireland would have broken jail the way he did. He must have some friends among the jailers.

POLICEMAN B: A hundred pounds is little enough for the Government to offer for him. You may be sure any man in the force that takes him will get promotion.

SERGEANT: I'll mind this place myself. I wouldn't wonder at all if he came this way. He might come slipping along there (*points to side of quay*), and his friends might be waiting for him there (*points down steps*), and once he got away it's little chance we'd have of finding him; it's maybe under a load of kelp he'd be in a fishing boat, and not one to help a married man that wants it to the reward.

POLICEMAN X: And if we get him itself, nothing but abuse on our heads for it from the people, and maybe from our own relations.

SERGEANT: Well, we have to do our duty in the force. Haven't we the whole country depending on us to keep law and order? It's those that are down would be up and those that are up would be down, if it wasn't for us. Well, hurry on, you have plenty of other places to placard yet, and come back here then to me. You can take the lantern. Don't be too long now. It's very lonesome here with nothing but the moon.

POLICEMAN B: It's a pity we can't stop with you. The Government should have brought more police into the town, with *him* in jail, and at assize° time too. Well, good luck to your watch.

(*They go out.*)

SERGEANT (*walks up and down once or twice and looks at placard*): A hundred pounds and promotion sure. There must be a great deal of spending in a hundred pounds. It's a pity some honest man not to be better of that.

(*A Ragged Man appears at left and tries to slip past. Sergeant suddenly turns.*)

SERGEANT: Where are you going?

MAN: I'm a poor ballad-singer, your honor. I thought to sell some of these (*holds out bundle of ballads*) to the sailors.

(*He goes on.*)

SERGEANT: Stop! Didn't I tell you to stop? You can't go on there.

MAN: Oh, very well. It's a hard thing to be poor. All the world's against the poor!

SERGEANT: Who are you?

MAN: You'd be as wise as myself if I told you, but I don't mind. I'm one Jimmy Walsh, a ballad-singer.

SERGEANT: Jimmy Walsh? I don't know that name.

MAN: Ah, sure, they know it well enough in Ennis. Were you ever in Ennis, sergeant?

SERGEANT: What brought you here?

MAN: Sure, it's to the assizes I came, thinking I might make a few shillings here or there. It's in the one train with the judges I came.

SERGEANT: Well, if you came so far, you may as well go farther, for you'll walk out of this.

MAN: I will, I will; I'll just go on where I was going.

(*Goes toward steps.*)

SERGEANT: Come back from those steps; no one has leave to pass down them tonight.

MAN: I'll just sit on the top of the steps till I see will some sailor buy a ballad off me that would give me my supper. They do be late going back to the ship. It's often I saw them in Cork carried down the quay in a handcart.

SERGEANT: Move on, I tell you. I won't have anyone lingering about the quay tonight.

MAN: Well, I'll go. It's the poor have the hard life! Maybe yourself might like one, sergeant. Here's a good sheet now. (*Turns one over.*) "Content and a pipe"—that's not much. "The Peeler and the goat"—you wouldn't like that. "Johnny Hart"—that's a lovely song.

SERGEANT: Move on.

MAN: Ah, wait till you hear it. (*Sings.*)

assize: Judicial inquest.

There was a rich farmer's daughter lived near the town of Ross;
She courted a Highland soldier, his name was Johnny Hart;
Says the mother to her daughter, "I'll go distracted mad
If you marry that Highland soldier dressed up in Highland plaid."

SERGEANT: Stop that noise.

(*Man wraps up his ballads and shuffles toward the steps.*)

SERGEANT: Where are you going?

MAN: Sure you told me to be going, and I am going.

SERGEANT: Don't be a fool. I didn't tell you to go that way; I told you to go back to the town.

MAN: Back to the town, is it?

SERGEANT (*taking him by the shoulder and shoving him before him*): Here, I'll show you the way. Be off with you. What are you stopping for?

MAN (*who has been keeping his eye on the notice, points to it*): I think I know what you're waiting for, sergeant.

SERGEANT: What's that to you?

MAN: And I know well the man you're waiting for — I know him well — I'll be going.

(*He shuffles on.*)

SERGEANT: You know him? Come back here. What sort is he?

MAN: Come back is it, sergeant? Do you want to have me killed?

SERGEANT: Why do you say that?

MAN: Never mind. I'm going. I wouldn't be in your shoes if the reward was ten times as much. (*Goes on off stage to left.*) Not if it was ten times as much.

SERGEANT (*rushing after him*): Come back here, come back. (*Drags him back.*) What sort is he? Where did you see him?

MAN: I saw him in my own place, in the County Clare. I tell you you wouldn't like to be looking at him. You'd be afraid to be in the one place with him. There isn't a weapon he doesn't know the use of, and as to strength, his muscles are as hard as that board (*slaps barrel*).

SERGEANT: Is he as bad as that?

MAN: He is then.

SERGEANT: Do you tell me so?

MAN: There was a poor man in our place, a sergeant from Ballyvaughan. — It was with a lump of stone he did it.

SERGEANT: I never heard of that.

MAN: And you wouldn't, sergeant. It's not everything that happens gets into the papers. And there was a policeman in plain clothes, too. . . . It is in Limerick he was. . . . It was after the time of the attack on the police barrack at Kilmallock. . . . Moonlight . . . just like this . . . waterside. . . . Nothing was known for certain.

SERGEANT: Do you say so? It's a terrible county to belong to.

MAN: That's so, indeed! You might be standing there, looking out that way, thinking you saw him coming up this side of the quay (*points*), and he might be coming up this other side (*points*), and he'd be on you before you knew where you were.

SERGEANT: It's a whole troop of police they ought to put here to stop a man like that.

MAN: But if you'd like me to stop with you, I could be looking down this side. I could be sitting up here on this barrel.

SERGEANT: And you know him well, too?

MAN: I'd know him a mile off, sergeant.

SERGEANT: But you wouldn't want to share the reward?

MAN: Is it a poor man like me, that has to be going the roads and singing in fairs, to have the name on him that he took a reward? But you don't want me. I'll be safer in the town.

SERGEANT: Well, you can stop.

MAN (*getting up on barrel*): All right, sergeant. I wonder, now, you're not tired out, sergeant, walking up and down the way you are.

SERGEANT: If I'm tired I'm used to it.

MAN: You might have hard work before you tonight yet. Take it easy while you can. There's plenty of room up here on the barrel, and you see farther when you're higher up.

SERGEANT: Maybe so. (*Gets up beside him on barrel, facing right. They sit back to back, looking different ways.*) You made me feel a bit queer with the way you talked.

MAN: Give me a match, sergeant (*he gives it and man lights pipe*); take a draw yourself? It'll quiet you. Wait now till I give you a light, but you needn't turn round. Don't take your eye off the quay for the life of you.

SERGEANT: Never fear, I won't. (*Lights pipe. They both smoke.*) Indeed it's a hard thing to be in the force, out at night and no thanks for it, for all the danger we're in. And it's little we get but abuse from the people, and no choice but to obey our orders, and never asked when a man is sent into danger, if you are a married man with a family.

MAN (*sings*): As through the hills I walked to view the hills and shamrock plain,
I stood awhile where nature smiles to view the rocks and streams,
On a matron fair I fixed my eyes beneath a fertile vale,
And she sang her song it was on the wrong of poor old Granuaile.

SERGEANT: Stop that; that's no song to be singing in these times.

MAN: Ah, sergeant, I was only singing to keep my heart up. It sinks when I think of him. To think of us two sitting here, and he creeping up the quay, maybe, to get us.

SERGEANT: Are you keeping a good lookout?

MAN: I am; and for no reward too. Amn't I the foolish man? But when I saw a man in trouble, I never could help trying to get him out of it. What's that? Did something hit me?

(*Rubs his heart.*)

SERGEANT (*patting him on the shoulder*): You will get your reward in heaven.

MAN: I know that, I know that, sergeant, but life is precious.

SERGEANT: Well, you can sing if it gives you more courage.

MAN (*sings*): Her head was bare, her hands and feet with iron bands were bound,
Her pensive strain and plaintive wail mingles with the evening gale,
And the song she sang with mournful air, I am old Granuaile.
Her lips so sweet that monarchs kissed . . .

SERGEANT: That's not it. . . . "Her gown she wore was stained with gore." . . . That's it — you missed that.

MAN: You're right, sergeant, so it is; I missed it. (*Repeats line.*) But to think of a man like you knowing a song like that.

SERGEANT: There's many a thing a man might know and might not have any wish for.

MAN: Now, I daresay, sergeant, in your youth, you used to be sitting up on a wall, the way you are sitting up on this barrel now, and the other lads beside you, and you singing "Granuaile"? . . .

SERGEANT: I did then.

MAN: And the "Shan Van Vocht"? . . .

SERGEANT: I did then.

MAN: And the "Green on the Cape"?

SERGEANT: That was one of them.

MAN: And maybe the man you are watching for tonight used to be sitting on the wall, when he was young, and singing those same songs. . . . It's a queer world. . . .

SERGEANT: Whisht! . . . I think I see something coming. . . . It's only a dog.

MAN: And isn't it a queer world? . . . Maybe it's one of the boys you used to be singing with that time you will be arresting today or tomorrow, and sending into the dock. . . .

SERGEANT: That's true indeed.

MAN: And maybe one night, after you had been singing, if the other boys had told you some plan they had, some plan to free the country, you might have joined with them . . . and maybe it is you might be in trouble now.

SERGEANT: Well, who knows but I might? I had a great spirit in those days.

MAN: It's a queer world, sergeant, and it's little any mother knows when she sees her child creeping on the floor what might happen to it before it has gone through its life, or who will be who in the end.

SERGEANT: That's a queer thought now, and a true thought. Wait now till I think it out. . . . If it wasn't for the sense I have, and for my wife and family, and for me joining the force the time I did, it might be myself now would be after breaking jail and hiding in the dark, and it might be him that's hiding in the dark and that got out of jail would be sitting up here where I am on this barrel. . . . And it might be myself would be creeping up trying to make my escape from himself, and it might be himself would be keeping the law, and myself would be breaking it, and myself would be trying to put a bullet in his head, or to take up a lump of stone the way you said he did . . . no, that myself did. . . . Oh! (*Gasps. After a pause.*) What's that? (*Grasps man's arm.*)

MAN (*jumps off barrel and listens, looking out over water*): It's nothing, sergeant.

SERGEANT: I thought it might be a boat. I had a notion there might be friends of his coming about the quays with a boat.

MAN: Sergeant, I am thinking it was with the people you were, and not with the law you were, when you were a young man.

SERGEANT: Well, if I was foolish then, that time's gone.

MAN: Maybe, sergeant, it comes into your head sometimes, in spite of your belt and your tunic, that it might have been as well for you to have followed Granuaile.

SERGEANT: It's no business of yours what I think.

MAN: Maybe, sergeant, you'll be on the side of the country yet.

SERGEANT (*gets off barrel*): Don't talk to me like that. I have my duties and I know them. (*Looks round.*) That was a boat; I hear the oars.

(*Goes to the steps and looks down.*)

MAN (*sings*): O, then, tell me, Shawn O'Farrell,
    Where the gathering is to be.
  In the old spot by the river
    Right well known to you and me!

SERGEANT: Stop that! Stop that, I tell you!

MAN (*sings louder*): One word more, for signal token,
    Whistle up the marching tune,
  With your pike upon your shoulder,
    At the Rising of the Moon.

SERGEANT: If you don't stop that, I'll arrest you.

(*A whistle from below answers, repeating the air.*)

SERGEANT: That's a signal. (*Stands between him and steps.*) You must not pass this way. . . . Step farther back. . . . Who are you? You are no ballad-singer.

MAN: You needn't ask who I am; that placard will tell you. (*Points to placard.*)

SERGEANT: You are the man I am looking for.

MAN (*takes off hat and wig. Sergeant seizes them*): I am. There's a hundred pounds on my head. There is a friend of mine below in a boat. He knows a safe place to bring me to.

SERGEANT (*looking still at hat and wig*): It's a pity! It's a pity. You deceived me. You deceived me well.

MAN: I am a friend of Granuaile. There is a hundred pounds on my head.

SERGEANT: It's a pity, it's a pity!

MAN: Will you let me pass, or must I make you let me?

SERGEANT: I am in the force. I will not let you pass.

MAN: I thought to do it with my tongue. (*Puts hand in breast.*) What is that?

VOICE OF POLICEMAN X (*outside*): Here, this is where we left him.

SERGEANT: It's my comrades coming.

MAN: You won't betray me . . . the friend of Granuaile. (*Slips behind barrel.*)

VOICE OF POLICEMAN B: That was the last of the placards.

POLICEMAN X (*as they come in*): If he makes his escape it won't be unknown he'll make it.

(*Sergeant puts hat and wig behind his back.*)

POLICEMAN B: Did anyone come this way?

SERGEANT (*after a pause*): No one.

POLICEMAN B: No one at all?

SERGEANT: No one at all.

POLICEMAN B: We had no orders to go back to the station; we can stop along with you.

SERGEANT: I don't want you. There is nothing for you to do here.

POLICEMAN B: You bade us to come back here and keep watch with you.

SERGEANT: I'd sooner be alone. Would any man come this way and you making all that talk? It is better the place to be quiet.

POLICEMAN B: Well, we'll leave you the lantern anyhow.

(*Hands it to him.*)

SERGEANT: I don't want it. Bring it with you.

POLICEMAN B: You might want it. There are clouds coming up and you have the darkness of the night before you yet. I'll leave it over here on the barrel. (*Goes to barrel.*)

SERGEANT: Bring it with you, I tell you. No more talk.

POLICEMAN B: Well, I thought it might be a comfort to you. I often think when I have it in my hand and can be flashing it about into every dark corner (*doing so*) that it's the same as being beside the fire at home, and the bits of bogwood blazing up now and again.

(*Flashes it about, now on the barrel, now on Sergeant.*)

SERGEANT (*furious*): Be off the two of you, yourselves and your lantern!

(*They go out. Man comes from behind barrel. He and Sergeant stand looking at one another.*)

SERGEANT: What are you waiting for?

MAN: For my hat, of course, and my wig. You wouldn't wish me to get my death of cold?

(*Sergeant gives them.*)

MAN (*going toward steps*): Well, good night, comrade, and thank you. You did me a good turn tonight, and I'm obliged to you. Maybe I'll be able to do as much for you when the small rise up and the big fall down . . . when we all change places at the Rising (*waves his hand and disappears*) of the Moon.

SERGEANT (*turning his back to audience and reading placard*): A hundred pounds reward! A hundred pounds! (*Turns toward audience.*) I wonder, now, am I as great a fool as I think I am?

Greek Drama

Origins of Greek Drama

Because our historical knowledge of Greek drama is limited by the available contemporary commentaries and by partial archaeological remains — in the form of ruined theaters — we do not know when Greek theater began or what its original impulses were. Our best information points to 534 B.C. as the beginning of the formal competitions among playwrights for coveted prizes that continued to be awarded for several centuries. Thespis, credited as the first tragedy writer, seems to have changed the nature of the form by stepping out of the chorus and taking a solo part. But the origin of *tragedy*, which translates in Greek as "goat-song" or "song for the sacrificial goat," is obscure. One theory is that tragedy may have developed from the rites of rural cults that sacrificed a she-goat at some Dionysian festivals or from masked animal dances at certain cult celebrations.

One source that may well have influenced the Greeks was the Egyptian civilization of the first millennium B.C. Egyptian culture was fully formed, brilliant, and complex. And while Egyptologists do not credit it with having a formal theater, certain ceremonies, repeated annually at major festivals, seem to have counterparts in later Greek rituals and drama. The most important and most impressive Egyptian ritual, described by some scholars as a passion play, concerned the dramatic story of Isis and Osiris and the treachery of Osiris's brother Set.

The closest Greek counterpart to Osiris was DIONYSUS, who inspired orgiastic celebrations that found their way into early Greek drama. Dionysus was an agricultural deity, the Greek god of wine and the symbol of life-giving power. In several myths he, like Osiris, was ritually killed and dismembered and his parts scattered through the land. These myths paralleled the agricultural cycle of death and disintegration during the winter, followed by cultivation and rebirth in the spring, and reinforced the Greeks' understanding of the meaning of birth, life, and death.

Drama developed in ancient Greece in close connection with the Dionysia, religious celebrations dedicated to Dionysus. Four Dionysiac celebrations were held each winter in Athens beginning at the grape harvest and culminating during the first wine tastings: the Rural Dionysia in December, the Lenaia in January, the Anthesteria in February, and the City Dionysia in March. Except for the Anthesteria, the festivals featured drama contests among playwrights, and some of the works performed in those competitions have endured through the centuries. Theories that connect the origins of drama with religion hypothesize that one function of the religious festivals within which the drama competitions took place was the ritual attempt to guarantee fertility and the growth of the crops, on which the society depended.

The CITY DIONYSIA, the most lavish of the festivals, lasted from five to seven days. It was open to non-Athenians and therefore offered Athenians the opportunity to show off their wealth, their glorious history, and their heroes, who were often honored in parades the day before the plays began. There is some question about what was presented on each day. Two days were probably taken up with dithyrambic contests among the ten tribes of Athens. Generally each tribe presented two choruses — one of men and one of boys — each singing a narrative lyric called a DITHYRAMB. A prize was awarded the best performers. Three days were devoted to contests among tragedians, most of whom worked for half the year on three tragedies and a SATYR PLAY, an erotic piece of comic relief that ended the day's performance. A tragedian's three plays sometimes shared related themes or myths, but often they did not. The tragedians wrote the plays; trained and rehearsed the actors; composed music; and created setting, dances, costumes, and masks. After 486 B.C. the first comedy competition was held, when five and later three comedies were also presented during the festival. The performances were paid for by wealthy Athenians as part of their civic duty. The great Greek plays thus were not commercial enterprises but an important part of civic and religious festivals.

Judges chosen by lottery awarded prizes, usually basing their decisions on the merits of the dramas. First prize went to the tragedian whose four plays were most powerful and most beautifully conceived.

The Greeks and Their Gods

The great achievement of Greek religion was the humanizing of their gods. Apollo, Zeus, Aphrodite, Athena, and Bacchus had recognizable emotions and pleasures. The Greeks built temples to their gods and made offerings at appropriate times to avoid catastrophe and bad luck. But the Greeks had no official religious text, no system of religious belief that they all followed, and few ethical teachings derived from religion. The impression we have today is that Greeks' efforts to define and know the gods were shaped by great artists such as Phidias, who sculpted Zeus at Olympia; Homer, who portrayed the gods in *The Iliad* and *The Odyssey*; and the great Greek playwrights, who sometimes revealed the actions of the gods. Our present knowledge of Greek gods resides in the literary and artistic remains of Greek culture.

Fortunately for us, most Greek drama was associated with important celebrations designed to honor Greek gods. We would not, however, call this drama religious in nature — as we characterize the medieval drama designated to celebrate Christian holidays. What we learn from Greek drama is that the gods can favor individual humans for reasons of their own. And likewise, the gods can choose to punish individual humans. To some extent Greek drama is designed to explain the divine approach to favor and disfavor.

The Greek Stage

At the center of the Greek theater was the ORCHESTRA, where the chorus sang and danced (*orches* is derived from the Greek for "dancing place"). The audience, sometimes numbering fifteen thousand, sat in rising rows on three sides of the orchestra. The steep sides of a hill formed a natural amphitheater for Greek audiences. Eventually, on the rim of the orchestra, an oblong building called the SKENE, or scene house, developed as a space for the actors and a background for the action. The term PROSKENION was sometimes used to refer to a raised stage added in later times in front of the *skene* where the actors performed. The theater at Epidaurus (Figures 1 and 2) was a model for the Greek theater plan.

Greek theaters were widely dispersed from Greece to present-day Turkey, to Sicily, and even to southern France. Wherever the Greeks developed new colonies and city-states, they built theaters. In many of the surviving theaters the acoustics are so fine that a human voice onstage can be heard from any seat in the theater.

Perhaps the most spectacular theatrical device used by the Greek playwrights, the MEKANE ("machine"), was implemented onstage by means of elaborate booms or derricks. Actors were lowered onto the stage to enact the roles of Olympian gods intervening in the affairs of humans. Some commentators, such as Aristotle (384–322 B.C.), felt that the *mekane* should be used only if the intercession of deities was in keeping with the character of the play. The last of the great Greek tragedians, Euripides (c. 485–c. 406 B.C.), used the device in almost half of his tragedies. In *Medea* Euripides uses the *mekane* to lift Medea to the roof of the *skene* and into her dragon chariot as a means of resolving the play's conflict. At the end of the play Medea is beyond her persecutors' reach and is headed for safety in another country. Modern dramatists use a version of this, called *deus ex machina,* literally, "the god from the machine," when they rescue characters at the last moment by improbable accidents or strokes of luck. Usually, these are unsatisfying means of solving dramatic problems.

Genres of Greek Drama
Tragedy

Greek tragedy focused on a person of noble birth who in some cases had risen to a great height and then fell precipitately. Tragedies showed humans at the mercy of MOIRA, their fate, which they only partly understood. One objective of Greek drama was to have the audience experience a CATHARSIS, which Aristotle describes as a purging or purifying of the emotions of pity and fear. According to the Greeks, these are emotions that a person associates with the fall of someone in a high social station, such as a king or queen. A central character, or PROTAGONIST, of noble birth was therefore an essential element for the playwright striving to evoke catharsis in an audience. Twentieth-century experiments with tragic figures who are ordinary people, such as Arthur Miller's *Death of a Salesman,* as masterful as they are, would not have made sense to the Greeks. For the Greeks, tragedy could befall only the great.

The modern critic Kenneth Burke identified a pattern for Greek tragedies. The tragic figure — for whom the play is usually named — experiences three stages of development: purpose, passion, and perception. The play begins with a purpose, such as finding the source of the plague in *Oedipus Rex.* Then, as the path becomes tangled and events unfold, the tragic figure begins an

Figure 1. The theater at Epidaurus, Greece, looking east. This is the best preserved (and now restored) Greek theater. Built in the fourth century B.C. by Polykleitos the Younger and approximately 124 feet in diameter, it seats twelve thousand people and remains in use today with excellent acoustics.

Figure 2. Theater at Epidaurus.

extensive process of soul-searching and suffers an inner agony — the passion. The perception of the truth involves a fate that the tragic figure would rather not face. It might be death or, as in *Oedipus Rex,* exile. It always involves separation from the human community. For the Greeks, that was the greatest punishment.

According to Aristotle, the tragic hero's perception of the truth was the most intense moment in the drama. He called it ANAGNORISIS, or recognition. When it came at the same moment that the tragic figure's fortunes reversed — the PERIPETEIA — Aristotle felt that the tragedy was most fulfilling for the audience. This is the case in *Oedipus Rex*. Aristotle's comments in his *Poetics* on the structure and effect of *Oedipus Rex* remain the most significant critical observations made by a contemporary on Greek theater. (See the excerpt from the *Poetics* on page 94.)

The Structure of Greek Tragedies. The earliest tragedies seem to have developed from the emotional, intense dithyrambs sung by Athenian choruses. The CHORUS in most tragedies numbered twelve or fifteen men. They usually represented the citizenry in the drama. They dressed simply, and their song was sometimes sung in unison, sometimes delivered by the chorus leader. Originally, there were no actors separate from the chorus.

According to legend, Thespis (sixth century B.C.) was the first actor — the first to step from the chorus to act in dialogue with it — thus creating the AGON, or dramatic confrontation. He won the first prize for tragedy in 532 B.C. As the only actor, he took several parts, wearing MASKS to distinguish the different characters. One actor was the norm in tragedies until Aeschylus (525–456 B.C.), the first important Greek tragedian whose work survives, introduced a second actor, and then Sophocles (c. 496–c. 406 B.C.) added a third. (Only comedy used more: four actors.)

Like the actors, the members of the chorus wore masks. At first the masks were simple, but they became more ornate, often trimmed with hair and decorated with details that established the gender, age, or station of each character. The chorus and all the actors were male.

Eventually the structure of the plays became elaborated into a series of alternations between the characters' dialogue and the choral odes, with each speaking part developing the action or responding to it. Often crucial information furthering the action came from the mouth of a messenger, as in *Oedipus Rex*. The tragedies were structured in three parts: the PROLOGUE established the conflict; the episodes or agons developed the dramatic relationships between characters; and the EXODOS concluded the action. Between these sections the chorus performed different songs: PARODOS while moving onto the stage and STASIMA while standing still. In some plays the chorus sang choral ODES called the STROPHE as it moved from right to left. It sang the ANTISTROPHE while moving back to the right. The actors' episodes consisted of dialogue with each other and with the chorus. The scholar Bernhard Zimmerman has plotted the structure of *Oedipus Rex* in this fashion:

Prologue: Dialogue with Oedipus, the Priests, and Kreon establishing that the plague afflicting Thebes will cease when Laios's murderer is found.

Parodos: The opening hymn of the Chorus appealing to the gods.

First Episode: Oedipus seeks the murderer; Teiresias says it is Oedipus.

First Stasimon: The Chorus supports Oedipus, disbelieving Teiresias.

Second Episode: Oedipus accuses Kreon of being in league with Teiresias and the real murderer. Iokaste pleads for Kreon and tells the oracle of Oedipus's birth and of the death of Laios at the fork of a road. Oedipus sends for the eyewitness of the murder.

Second Stasimon: The Chorus, in a song, grows agitated for Oedipus.

Third Episode: The messenger from Oedipus's "hometown" tells him that his adoptive father has died and is not his real father. Iokaste guesses the truth and Oedipus becomes deeply worried.

Third Stasimon: The Chorus delivers a reassuring, hopeful song.

Fourth Episode: Oedipus, the Shepherd, and the Messenger confront the facts and Oedipus experiences the turning point of the play: he realizes he is the murderer he seeks.

Fourth Stasimon: The Chorus sings of the illusion of human happiness.

Exodos: Iokaste kills herself; Oedipus puts out his eyes; the Chorus and Kreon try to decide the best future action.

As this brief structural outline of *Oedipus Rex* demonstrates, the chorus assumed an important part in the tragedies. In Aeschylus's *Agamemnon* it represents the elders of the community. In Sophocles' *Oedipus Rex* it is a group of concerned citizens who give Oedipus advice and make demands on him. In *Antigone* the chorus consists of men loyal to the state. In Euripides' *Medea* the chorus is a group of the important women of Corinth.

Satyr Plays

The drama competitions held regularly from 534 B.C. consisted usually of the work of three playwrights who each produced three tragedies and one satyr play, a form of comic relief. In a satyr play, the chorus dressed as satyrs, comic half-beast, half-man figures who cavorted with a PHALLUS, a mock penis, and engaged in riotous, almost slapstick antics. The characters were not psychologically developed, as they were in tragedy; the situations were not socially instructive, as they were in comedy. Rough-hewn and lighthearted, the satyr plays may have been a necessary antidote to the intensity of the tragedies.

Only one satyr play survives, perhaps an indication that the form was not as highly valued as tragedy. In Euripides' *Cyclops*, based on Odysseus's confrontation with the one-eyed giant who dined on a number of his men, Odysseus outwits the giant with the aid of a well-filled wineskin. The powers of Bacchus (Dionysus) are often alluded to, and drunkenness is a prime ingredient. The play is witty, entertaining, and brief. It might well have been the perfect way to end an otherwise serious drama festival.

Comedy

No coherent Greek theories on comedy have come down to us. (Aristotle is said to have written a lost treatise on comedy.) In the *Poetics*, Aristotle points out that comedy shows people from a lower social order than the nobility, who are the main figures in tragedy.

The two greatest Greek comic writers were Aristophanes (c. 448–c. 385 B.C.), whose *Lysistrata* appears in this collection, and Menander (c. 342–c. 291 B.C.). The first was a master of OLD COMEDY (which lasted from c. 486 to c. 400 B.C.), in which individuals — sometimes well known to the audience — could be attacked personally. The nature of the humor was often ribald, coarse, and brassy, but, according to Aristotle, it was not vicious. Physical devices onstage, such as the erect phalluses beneath the men's garments in *Lysistrata,* accompanied ribald lines, and Athenian audiences were mightily entertained. Comedy appears to have provided release, but for entirely different emotions than those evoked by tragedy.

The Old Comedy of Aristophanes concentrated on buffoonery and farce. Although we know little about it, a form known as MIDDLE COMEDY seems to have flourished from approximately 400 to 320 B.C. Our evidence is from statuettes of players that indicate a more realistic portrayal of character and thus a less broad and grotesque form of comedy than in some of the plays of Aristophanes. The NEW COMEDY of Menander and others whose work is now lost provided a less ribald humor that centered on the shortcomings of the middle classes. Although Menander enjoyed a great reputation in his own time and was highly regarded by Roman playwrights much later, very little of his work has survived. He is said to have written a few more than one hundred plays, but only one, *The Grouch,* survives intact. Twenty-three of his plays existed in a manuscript in Constantinople in the sixteenth century, but nothing of that volume seems to have survived. We know a number of titles, such as *The Lady from Andros, The Flatterer,* and *The Suspicious Man.* And we know that the Romans pilfered liberally from his plays. Beyond that we know little.

Menander's New Comedy concentrated on social manners. Instead of attacking individuals, as Aristophanes frequently did, Menander was more likely to attack a vice, such as vanity, or to portray the foibles of a social class. He aimed at his own middle class and established the pattern of parents or guardians struggling, usually over the issue of marriage, against the wishes of their children. The children ordinarily foil their parents' wishes, frequently with the help of an acerbic slave who provides the comedy with most of its humor. This pattern has proved so durable that it is used virtually every day in modern situation comedies on television.

Both Old and New Comedy have influenced theater from the time of the Greeks to the present. The nineteenth-century comedy of Oscar Wilde (in this collection) is an example of New Comedy, while the Marx Brothers' movies are examples of Old Comedy.

The Great Age of Greek Drama

The fifth century B.C. was not only the great creative age of Athenian theater but also the age of Athenian power in Greek politics. By the beginning of the century, Greece dominated trade in the Mediterranean and therefore in many of the major civilized urban centers of the world. The most important threat to Greek power came from the Persians, living to the east. After the Persians attacked in 490, Greek city-states such as Athens formed the Delian League to defend themselves, pouring their funds into the treasury at Delos. When the Persians threatened again in 483 B.C., Themistocles (525?–460? B.C.), Athenian soldier and statesman, realized he could not win a battle on land. By skillful political moves he managed to create a powerful navy. When the Persians attacked Athens in 480 B.C., Themistocles left a small rear guard to defend the Acropolis, the city's religious fortress. The Persians took the fortress, burned everything, and were lured by a clever ruse to Salamis, where they thought that a puny Athenian navy was making a getaway. Once the Persians set sail for

Salamis, Themistocles turned on them and revealed a powerful fighting force that defeated the Persians once and for all.

In the years immediately following, Athens overstated its role in the Persian defeat and assumed an air of imperial importance. It appropriated the gold in the Delian League treasury, using it to rebuild the Acropolis beginning in 448 B.C. The great Greek general and leader Pericles (495?–429? B.C.) chose his friend Phidias to supervise the construction of the Parthenon and the other main buildings that are on the Acropolis even today. The threat of Athenian domination seems to have triggered the Peloponnesian Wars (432–406 B.C.), which pitted the Spartan alliance against the Athenian alliance. Athens eventually lost the war and its democratic government.

The events of these years — dominated by interminable wars, threats of a return to tyranny, and cultural instability — are coterminous with the great flourishing of Greek art, drama, and philosophy. The geniuses of Greek drama cluster in the period dating from the birth of Aeschylus (c. 525 B.C.) to the death of the philosopher Socrates (399 B.C.). Aeschylus wrote *The Persians* (472 B.C.); *Seven against Thebes* (467 B.C.); and the *Oresteia* (458 B.C.), a trilogy centering on Orestes and consisting of *Agamemnon*, *The Libation Bearers*, and *The Eumenides*. *The Suppliants* and *Prometheus Bound* are of uncertain dates.

Aeschylus's introduction of a second actor made it possible to intensify the dramatic value of each *agon*, the confrontation between ANTAGONISTS. He is also notable for giving minor characters, such as the watchman who opens *Agamemnon*, both dimension and depth. Aeschylus's *Oresteia*, the only surviving trilogy, tells of the death of Agamemnon and the efforts of his son Orestes to avenge that death.

Sophocles (c. 496–c. 406 B.C.) and Euripides (c. 485–406 B.C.) learned from Aeschylus and from each other, because they were all sometimes rivals. In addition to *Oedipus Rex* (c. 429 B.C.), Sophocles is known today for *Ajax* (c. 442 B.C.), *Philoctetes* (c. 409 B.C.), *Oedipus at Colonus* (406 B.C.), and *Electra* (date uncertain).

Euripides, the last of the great tragedians, may have written as many as ninety-two plays. Of the nineteen that survive, the best known are *Alcestis* (438 B.C.), *Medea* (431 B.C.), *Electra* (date uncertain), *The Trojan Women* (415 B.C.), and *The Bacchae* (produced in 405 B.C.). He is especially noteworthy for his portrayal of women and for his experimental approach to theater.

These three tragedians, along with Aristophanes, provide us with insight into the Greek dramatic imagination. They also reveal something of our common humanity, since their achievement — lost though it was for many centuries — shapes our current dramatic practice. The Greeks give us not only the beginnings of drama but the basis of drama. We build on it today whenever a play is written, whenever we witness a play.

Greek Drama Timeline

DATE	THEATER	POLITICAL	SOCIAL/CULTURAL
1000–800 B.C.			Classic paganism is in full bloom in Greece.
			Temple of Hera, oldest surviving temple in Olympia, Greece, is built.
			9th c.: Age of the Homeric epic; *The Iliad, The Odyssey*
800–700		First Messenian War: Sparta gains power in Greece.	Choral and dramatic music develop.
			Hesiod, poet whose *Works and Days* classified the five ages of mankind: Golden (peaceful), Silver (less happy), Bronze (art and warfare), Heroic (Trojan War), and Iron (the present)
			776: First Olympian festival (predecessor of the modern Olympic games). Only one event is featured: a footrace of approximately 200 meters.
700–600		First written laws of Athens are recorded by Draco.	Sappho of Lesbos, Greek poet
			Archilochus, Greek lyricist and author of fables
			Construction of the Acropolis begins in Athens.
600–500	**534:** First contest for best tragedy is held in Athens as part of the annual City Dionysia, a major religious festival. The winning playwright (and actor) is Thespis.	**594:** Solon's law allows for the Council of Four Hundred and various reforms pertaining to land ownership and civil liberties.	The influence of the oracle at Delphi and its priestess is at its height.
	c. 501: Satyr plays are added to the City Dionysia play competition. Each playwright now has to present a trilogy of tragedies and a satyr play.	**c. 525–459:** Themistocles, Athenian statesman and naval commander, builds a Greek navy and fortifications.	The theater of Delphi is built.
		525–405: Persians conquer Egypt.	**c. 582–507:** Pythagoras, philosopher, mathematician, and musical theorist
			Public libraries in Athens
			c. 563–483: Siddartha, founder of Buddhism, begins his religious journey in 534.
			c. 520–438: Pindar, Greek musician and poet
500–400	**487–486:** Comedy is introduced as a dramatic form in the City Dionysia.	**500–449:** Persian Wars	**c. 460–370:** Hippocrates, Greek physician who did much to separate medicine from superstition
	c. 471: Aeschylus introduces the second actor in the performance of tragedy at the City Dionysia.	**494:** King Darius of Persia annexes all of Greece.	**485–424:** Herodotus, a Greek historian, writes the history of the Persian Wars.
		490: Athenians defeat the Persians in the Battle of Marathon.	

37

DATE	THEATER	POLITICAL	SOCIAL/CULTURAL
500–400 B.C. (continued)	c. 468: Sophocles is credited with introducing the third actor in the performance of tragedies at the City Dionysia. 458: First performance of Aeschylus's trilogy the *Oresteia* at the City Dionysia 458: *Skene,* or scene house, is introduced in Greek theater. c. 441: First performance of Sophocles' *Antigone* at the City Dionysia c. 430–425: First performance of Sophocles' *Oedipus Rex* at the City Dionysia 411: First performance of Aristophanes' *Lysistrata*	480: At the Battle of Thermopylae, the Spartans defeat the Persians. 479: Xerxes, son of Darius, returns to Persia; the Persian Wars end. 462–429: Periclean Athens 431: The Peloponnesian War begins; Athens is defeated in 404. Thucydides records the events in his history *The Peloponnesian War.*	460–370: Democritus, Greek philosopher who believed that all living things are composed of atoms 438: The Parthenon is completed.
400–300	400–c. 320: Era of Middle Comedy, which concentrates on more accurately portraying daily life rather than the more fantastic plots of Old Comedy (Aristophanes) 336–300: Era of New Comedy. Menander and others move further away from Aristophanes; stock characters are common. 335–323: Aristotle writes *Poetics.*	395: The Corinthian War begins. Athens joins with Corinth, Thebes, and Argos to attack Sparta. Athens emerges from the ten-year war as a partially restored power. 332: Alexander the Great conquers Egypt. 321: Alexander the Great dies of a fever at age thirty-three. His successors divide the empire into Macedon, Egypt, and the Seleucid empire.	399: Socrates is tried and executed for corrupting the youth of Athens. 373: Plato writes *Republic.* 340–271: Epicurus, Greek philosopher who believed in pleasure, spontaneity, and freedom of will 320–330: Hellenistic period of Greek art 307: The museum and library of Alexandria are begun under Ptolemy Soter.
300–100	277: Artists of Dionysis, a performing artists' guild, is formed.		275–195: Eratosthenes, Greek scientist, suggests that the earth moves around the sun; he makes close estimates of the earth's circumference.
100 B.C.–300 A.D.		100 B.C.–1 A.D.: Alexandria is the Mediterranean center of culture and commerce.	
300–400 A.D.			346–395: The Roman emperor Theodosius forbids the celebration of Olympic games in Greece.

Aeschylus

Very little is known for certain about the life of Aeschylus (c. 525–456 B.C.) despite a first attempt at a biographical sketch in 300 B.C. What is known is that he was born in Eleusis near Athens at a time that marked Athens's beginning as an important power in Greece and as the cradle of Western art and thought. When Aeschylus was born, Athens was under the control of tyrants, a control that ended in 510 to 508 B.C.; when he died, Athens was a democracy and one of the strongest states in the Greek confederation. The great threat to Athens's security came from the Persians, powerful Eastern warriors whose aim was the destruction of Greek economic power. Of the three great playwrights who lived in these times, Aeschylus is the only one who actually went to war against the Persians.

The records reveal that in 490 B.C. Aeschylus fought at the battle of Marathon, in which his brother was killed. The Persians were defeated at Marathon, and their king, Darius, died shortly thereafter. For ten years the Athenians enjoyed an uneasy peace, but in 480 B.C. the Persians returned under King Xerxes with a powerful fleet and army. Aeschylus fought at Salamis and probably also at a later victory in Plataea.

He seems to have been writing tragedies for fifteen years before his first victory in the drama competitions. He began competing in 499 to 496 B.C.; he won his first victory in 484 B.C. Aeschylus went on to win a total of thirteen competitions with thirteen tetralogies: groups of three tragedies and a satyr play. He may have written as many as ninety plays; the titles of eighty-three have come down to us, with seven plays and many fragments surviving. *Agamemnon* is the first play in the *Oresteia,* the only surviving trilogy of Greek tragedies that we know were produced together. Sophocles' Oedipus plays were, by contrast, composed over a long period of time and never performed as a trilogy until recent times.

Many efforts have been made to connect Aeschylus's plays to his life and times, but on the whole such efforts have been unprofitable. Clearly, though, he wrote some plays that spoke to the times, such as *The Persians* (472 B.C.), undoubtedly inspired by Athenian success in the Persian Wars. He also wrote plays associated with specific places, as in *The Women of Aetna,* produced in Sicily near Mount Aetna. *The Persians* won first prize, and its expenses were paid for by Athens's ruler, Pericles, who, after the battle of Salamis, rebuilt the Acropolis with the Parthenon and the other important buildings, such as the Erectheum, that still stand there.

Aeschylus is sometimes credited with a rough and powerful style expressed in a language that sometimes forced him to make up new words. The power of his language is always remarked on by those who know his Greek original, and his translators have often been poets in their own right. By contrast, the younger Sophocles uses a language that is smoother, more lyrical, and more graceful. Some critics have asserted that the younger playwrights profited from Aeschylus's development of tragic style.

Aeschylus died at age sixty-eight in Gela, Sicily, where he spent time at the request of a friendly tyrant, Hieron. The story surrounding Aeschylus's death has been told many times and is probably only legend. It was said that an eagle grasping a tortoise flew high into the air and accidentally dropped the tortoise on Aeschylus's head, killing him. His death came at the height of the development of Greek tragedy.

AGAMEMNON

Agamemnon is the first play in the *Oresteia,* the only extant trilogy of Greek tragedies. The trilogy was performed in 458 B.C., winning first prize in the competition. As its name implies, it concerns the fate of Orestes, son of Agamemnon, even though Orestes is not present during *Agamemnon.* He does not enter until *The Libation Bearers* but becomes the center of the action in the third play, *The Eumenides.* As many commentators have observed, the three plays are in essence three acts of one larger play.

Lying behind the action of the three plays is a memory of the horror that has befallen the House of Atreus, the family to which Agamemnon and Aegisthus and Orestes belong. Centuries before Aeschylus, Homer had told part of the story, which was a myth of significant proportions by the time Aeschylus dramatized it. It is recounted by Aegisthus near the end of *Agamemnon* (lines 1731–1766), although he omits at least one important detail. Pelops, son of Tantalus, had two sons: Atreus and Thyestes. The legend has several forms, but in essence Atreus and Thyestes have a falling out over the throne of their father. In addition Atreus suspects that Thyestes has slept with his wife. With Atreus in control of the kingdom, Thyestes is invited to return for a reconciliation, but Atreus plans a fearful revenge. Pretending to prepare a feast of slaughtered animals, Atreus serves Thyestes his own two children chopped into a stew. Once he has eaten, Thyestes is shown the heads, hands, and feet of his children and vomits. He then flees into exile with his remaining infant son, Aegisthus.

Atreus's sons were Menelaus, who led the Greeks to Troy to regain his errant wife, Helen; and Agamemnon, who returned victorious from Troy. Agamemnon's children were Iphigenia, Electra (who figures in *The Libation Bearers*), and Orestes. The *Oresteia,* then, works out the curse on the house of Atreus.

Agamemnon reveals several forceful characters. Clytemnestra, the wife of Agamemnon, presents herself as a faithful, long-suffering wife waiting patiently for her husband's return from war. However, the Chorus, composed of older men, knows that she has taken a lover, Aegisthus. Clytemnestra faces up to the rumors of her infidelity when Agamemnon returns, daring anyone to contradict her. Secretly, though, she plans (with the help of Aegisthus) to kill Agamemnon. Her discovery that her husband is returning with a female slave, the prophetess Cassandra, as his concubine gives her further motivation. When she confesses to the murder of Agamemnon and Cassandra, she tells the Chorus that she is exacting revenge against Agamemnon for sacrificing their daughter Iphigenia in order to get a favorable wind to sail to Troy. Later, Aegisthus justifies his role in the killing as revenge against the crimes of Agamemnon's father, Atreus.

To ensnare Agamemnon, Clytemnestra has woven an intricate web — the image of the spider is invoked in the play. She is warned of his return by the pillars of fire that are set from Troy to Greece as Agamemnon returns, so she is prepared. She produces a richly woven purple cloth — the equivalent of what we call a red carpet — on which she expects Agamemnon to walk into the palace. Knowing that to do so could offend the gods, he at first refuses. Ultimately he yields to her entreaties and enters the palace, leaving Cassandra outside to prophesy his death — and hers — to the unbelieving Chorus. Inside, Clytemnestra continues the pattern by winding a regal cloak about Agamemnon as he is in the bath, disabling him so that she is able to stab him mortally.

Throughout, *Agamemnon* emphasizes issues of gender. Often the Chorus comments on Clytemnestra's speaking with the authority of a man. The invocation of the god Apollo throughout the trilogy has been taken to imply an important cultural shift that Aeschylus recognizes. Is he referring to a distant past in which female deities were dominant but then were replaced by masculine deities? Such speculation is impossible to verify (see Lois Spatz's commentary on p. 63), but it is clear that the women in the *Oresteia* are powerful in their presence, demanding in their actions, and insistent in their demand for justice. *Agamemnon* ends with Clytemnestra facing down an angry and mistrustful Chorus and with Aegisthus claiming the throne and governing as a tyrant.

Agamemnon in Performance

The first production of Aeschylus's trilogy in 458 B.C. won first prize in the drama competitions. Although tragedies were not usually revived, it seems that this trilogy was played again at Greek festivals some few years after Aeschylus's death in 456 B.C. Unfortunately, after the demise of the Greek festivals, Aeschylus was not performed again until the sixteenth century. Early in the twentieth century the *Oresteia* was produced in Greek in the United States to a limited but enthusiastic audience. Harvard University produced *Agamemnon* in 1906, using all male actors, who spoke the lines in Greek. Max Reinhardt produced the trilogy in Berlin in 1915, but problems with the size of the theater and the nature of the stage resulted in an unsuccessful production. In 1968 the Minnesota Theater Company adapted the trilogy as *The House of Atreus,* directed by Tyrone Guthrie, taking it to Broadway at the Billy Rose Theater. Beginning in 1977 in New York, Andrei Serban experimented with performing *Agamemnon* in a mixture of English and Greek because, as he said, "Greek sounds have the power to catch the real emotional experience of the text." Serban produced the play at the Vivian Beaumont Theatre in Lincoln Center, New York. The high-tech staging, with exposed metal mesh floors and walls, created powerful effects. The Royal Shakespeare Company in 1980 put together an eleven-hour sequence of plays of Aeschylus, Euripides, and Sophocles on the fall of Troy, calling it *The Greeks;* it was successful both in England and abroad. The National Theatre in London produced the *Oresteia* in 1981 to considerable acclaim. Interestingly, the reviews of that production describe *Agamemnon* as having been eclipsed in dramatic importance by *The Libation Bearers,* which "becomes the great dramatic moment of the trilogy." Combining Euripides' *Iphigenia in Aulis* with the trilogy, the French Théâtre du Soleil performed *Les Atrides* in Paris, Montreal, and New York in 1992. Ariane Mnouchkine directed and conceived the production (in French with simultaneous translation), using only five actors. Paul Nadler compared *Les Atrides* with bullfights, which "deal with killers and victims acting out their fates upon fields of honor."

Aeschylus (c. 525–456 B.C.)

AGAMEMNON

458 B.C.

TRANSLATED BY DAVID GREENE AND WENDY DONIGER O'FLAHERTY

Dramatis Personae

SENTRY
CHORUS, *old men of Argos left behind after the Argives went to Troy*
CLYTEMNESTRA, *queen of Argos in the absence of King Agamemnon at Troy*
HERALD *from the Greek army*
KING AGAMEMNON
CASSANDRA, *princess of Troy, daughter of King Priam*
AEGISTHUS

SENTRY: You gods, release me.
    Crouched like a dog, I watch always, all year long,
    on the tower of the sons of Atreus.
    I have come to know the nightly gathering of the
        stars
    and those radiant dynasts of the firmament that lead
5   them.
    They bring winter and summer to men.
    Now I watch for a flaming light,
    the beacon fire, the tell-tale witness that Troy is
        captured.
    Such are my orders, orders from a hopeful queen
10   who thinks with the mind of a man.
    I have a bed here, soaked with dew, always shifting.
    But no dreams. Fear is my visitor, not sleep.
    I cannot close my eyes for fear.
    Sometimes I whistle or hum;
15   the tunes are my drug against my sleepiness.
    But then the sorrow comes.
    This house is in bitter trouble.
    Once it was well governed; not now.
    Still, may the fire of good news light the darkness
20   to be the lucky release from our troubles.

    The beacon! Day out of night!
    The dances everywhere in Argos!
    Thanks, good beacon!

    My lady, Agamemnon's wife, get out of bed!
    Cry aloud a blessing on this beacon,   25
    since Troy is surely captured.
    I will myself begin the dance, for I'll score to myself,
        too,
    the winning dice that the beacon threw for my
        master.
    Oh, that I could touch with this hand of mine
    the hand that I love, my lord's.   30
    As for the rest, I haven't a word;
    a great ox stands on my tongue.
    If the house itself had a voice to speak,
    it would tell the clearest story.
    I choose to speak to those who understand;   35
    for the others, I am all forgetfulness.
CHORUS: This is the tenth year
    since they launched from this land
    the Greek fleet of a thousand ships
    to help right wrongs done.   40
    They launched it, King Menelaus,
    great plaintiff against Priam,
    and Agamemnon his brother;
    twin the yoke joining them in honor and throne,
    twin their shared grace of God.   45

    From their hearts the great war cry;
    they screamed like eagles,
    that wheel and wheel high above their eyries,
    driven by the oarage of their wings,
    in lonely agony for the loss of their nestlings,   50
    and all the watchful care they had spent guarding
        them.

    But One yet higher up, some Apollo or Pan or
        Zeus,°

---

52. **Apollo or Pan or Zeus:** Greek gods with the power to avenge crimes.

hears the shrill-voiced sorrow of these settlers in his
  kingdom
and sends on the evildoers
55 the Fury that brings punishment, however late.
So a Lord greater than the kings, Zeus god of guest-
  friends,
sends the sons of Atreus on Alexander;°
in this quarrel over a woman of many men,
he would lay upon Greeks and Trojans alike
60 many wrestlings where the limbs grow heavy
and the knee is pressed into the dust
and the spear is shattered in the first rites of
  engagement.
Yet it is now as it is.
Fulfillment moves toward what is fated.
And not with burnt offerings nor with pouring on
65   of wine
nor sacrifice to the gods below
will you assuage that stubborn anger.

But we, dishonored for the ancientness of our flesh,
were left behind then when the army went;
we remain, propping on staffs a strength like a
70   child's.
For the child's marrow, too, leaps within his breast
but is only the match of an old man's;
the god of war is not there either.
And the overold, the leafage already withering,
walks his three-footed way,° no stronger than a
75   child;
wanders, a dream in the daylight.

You, daughter of Tyndareus, Queen Clytemnestra,
What's the matter? What's the news? What have
  you heard?
What message do you trust, that you order sacrifices
80 at all the altars?
Of all the gods that hold our city,
of those above and those beneath the earth,
of those at the doorpost and those at the
  marketplace,
the altars blaze with offerings.
85 Here one torch sends its flames to the sky,
and another raises its light,
charmed by the soft, guileless urgings of pure
  streams of oil
drawn from the depth of the royal store.
Tell us what you can and what may be said
90 about all these things.
Cure this care that now broods darkly on our
  minds.
But then hope, shining out of the sacrifice,

turns away the insatiable thoughts that might
  otherwise
eat out the heart in sorrow.

It is mine to declare the omens of victory   95
given to princely men on the journey.
For by God's grace, old age, which grows with life,
  my life,
still breathes on my lips persuasion,
the strength of song.
I tell how the princes of the Achaeans,   100
twin-throned, single-hearted
lords of the youth of Greece,
were sent against the land of Troy
with spear in hand to exact vengeance.
The furious omen-birds° sent them,   105
one black eagle, one white-tail,
the kings of birds to the kings of the ships.
Near the palace they came on the spear-striking
  side,
perched where all could see them
as they fed on the womb's gravid load of leverets,°   110
mother and all, pulled down in the hare's last
  course.
Cry sorrow, sorrow, but let the good prevail.

Yet the honest prophet of the army saw
the two sons of Atreus,
twin in military spirit,   115
and knew the princely leaders and hare-
  devourers —
knew that they were one and the same.
And so he declared in his prophecy,
"In time, this journey will capture Troy, Priam's°
  city;
and all the communal herds that graze before her
  towers   120
shall Fate give violently to plunder.
I only pray that no anger from the God will cast a
  cloud
upon this army forged from before to be
a great iron bit in the mouth of Troy.
For Queen Artemis° is full of pity out of jealousy   125
against those winged hounds of her father
who devour in sacrifice
the unhappy cowering mother with her brood
before they come to birth.
She hates the eagles' feast.   130
Cry sorrow, sorrow, but let the good prevail.

57. **Alexander:** Also known as Paris, Alexander was the son of King Priam and Queen Hecuba of Troy. He carried off Helen, the wife of Greek commander Menelaus (Agamemnon's brother), and this action caused the Trojan War.   75. **three-footed way:** Walking with a cane or staff.

105. **omen-birds:** Eagles, thought to be messengers of the gods. 110. **leverets:** Young hares.   119. **Priam:** King of Troy at the time of the Trojan War.   125. **Artemis:** Greek goddess, who was the daughter of Zeus and sister of Apollo. Artemis was the protector of young animals. Angered at the slaughter of the leverets, she caused contrary winds to prevent the Greeks from sailing for Troy. Agamemnon was forced to sacrifice his daughter Iphigeneia to appease Artemis and secure favorable winds.

Yes, she is kindly, that beautiful one,
to cubs, scarcely crawling, of savage lions,
and she finds her delight in all the breast-loving
    infants
135 of wild things of the field.
Yet she grants fulfillment of what the omens imply:
grant, Lady, favorable fulfillment, and void the
    other.
I call on Apollo the Healer
to keep her from setting against the Greeks
140 those contrary winds, winds that hold ships,
staying winds, winds that stop sailing altogether.
She might do this in eagerness for a different
    sacrifice,
one that is lawless and horrible,
a trueborn craftsman of quarrels,
145 that has no awe of a husband.
For full of terrors it lurks,
house keeping, crafty, long-memoried,
an anger that punishes child-slaughter."

Such were the prophecies of Calchas's° voice,
150 mingled with the good things,
and all predicted for our royal house
from omens on the way.
In harmony with these,
cry sorrow, sorrow, but let the good prevail.

155 Zeus, whoever he is,
if it is dear to him to be so called,
this is how I call him.
I have thrown all into the scale,
but cannot find his likeness —
160 there is only Zeus,
if I must cast my burden of vain care from the heart
in honest truth.

Not he that once was great,
swelling with daring, challenging all comers,
165 shall even be spoken of, for he is of the past.
And he that came after him
has had his three falls wrestling,
and is gone.
But whoever sings to Zeus
170 the victory song from a full heart,
he shall win all that his heart desires.

Zeus it is that has made man's road;
he it is who has laid down the rule
that understanding comes through suffering.
175 Instead of sleep, there drips before the heart
the recollected sorrow of past pain.
It is against our wills that we become wise.
Forced indeed upon us is the grace of our gods
that sit on their solemn thrones.

So on that day, the old leader of the Greek ships,   180
faulting no prophet, caught his breath at his sudden
    calamity,
when the Greek host was burdened
with ships halted and empty holds,
as they held the coast over against Chalcis,°
at Aulis° where the tides roar to and fro.   185

The hurricane that came from Strymon,°
breeding deadly delays, starvation, lost anchorages,
driving crews to aimless wanderings,
sparing neither ships nor cables,
wore down the flower of the Argives,   190
doubling their time with enforced lingering.
So when the prophet's voice rang out,
proclaiming to the princes another cure for the
    bitter storm,
a cure yet heavier to bear,
he backed his prophecies with Artemis's name,   195
and the twin sons of Atreus beat the ground with
    their staves
and could not hold back their tears.
Then the old king spoke and said,
"Heavy indeed my fate if I disobey,
but heavy, too, if I must butcher my child,   200
the glory of my house, polluting a father's hands
with streams of a virgin's blood beside the altar.
Which of these two things is without evil?
How shall I become a deserter of my fleet and fail
    my allies?
There is sacred law on their side, that they
    passionately covet   205
a virgin's blood as sacrifice to quell the winds.
May it turn out well."

When he put on the harness of Necessity,
his spirit veered in a breath of change —
to impiety, to unholiness, to desecration,   210
and from it he drew audacity for his heart
to stop at nothing.
For indeed there is a wretched distraction of the
    wits,
a primal source of ruin,
that puts recklessness in man's mind   215
and counsels ugliness.
So he dared to become his daughter's sacrificer
to aid the war waged for a woman —
first rites of deliverance for the ships.
Her prayers, and her cries of "Father," and her
    maiden life   220
they set at nothing, those military umpires.
Her father ordered his servants to lift her
carefully over the altar

---

149. **Calchas:** A prophet who accompanied the Greek army to
Troy.

184. **Chalcis:** City in Asia Minor across the straits from
Aulis, where the Greeks were detained by contrary winds.
185. **Aulis:** City where the Greek fleet collected before sailing to
Troy.   186. **Strymon:** River in Asia Minor across from Aulis.

225 after the prayer, swooning, her clothes all round her,
like a young goat,
and with a gag on her beautiful lips
to restrain the cry that would curse his house.
Constrained to voicelessness by the violence of the
bit,
she slipped to the ground her saffron robes,
230 and with darting, pitiful eyes struck each of her
sacrificers.
She stood out, like a figure in a picture, struggling
to speak,
for often she had sung in her father's hospitable halls,
and with pure maiden voice lovingly honored
her beloved father's victory hymn,
235 with its triple libation to bring good luck.
What happened after that I neither saw nor tell.
But Calchas's divining art bore fruit;
the scales of justice have come down and brought,
with suffering, understanding.
240 You will learn the future when it happens.
Till then, let it be.
To do otherwise is to have sorrow before you need.
For it will come clear with the dawn's light.

(Enter Clytemnestra.)

But at the end of all this let there be good fortune.
245 Surely that is the wish of this *(turning to the queen)*
our sole and closest bulwark against trouble in
Argos.
I have come, Queen Clytemnestra, to pay you my
respects;
for it is right, in the absence of the prince,
to honor the wife of the man whose throne is empty.
250 I would be glad to know
if you are sure of good tidings or not.
Is it in the hope of happy news
that you are ordering sacrifice?
But I won't resent it if you must be silent.
255 CLYTEMNESTRA: As the proverb goes,
"May dawn be the dawn of good news
as she comes from her mother night"—
you shall learn of a joy greater than you hope.
For the Argives have captured Priam's city.
CHORUS: What? I cannot believe you; I cannot
260 understand.
CLYTEMNESTRA: Troy is the Greeks' city now. Are my
words clear?
CHORUS: Joy steals over me, and calls out tears, too.
CLYTEMNESTRA: Your eyes proclaim you a subject true
and loyal.
CHORUS: What makes you trust the news? Have you
proof of it?
CLYTEMNESTRA: I have, of course — unless the gods
265 deceived me.
CHORUS: Dream visions? Do you believe in them?
CLYTEMNESTRA: No sleeping mind for me, no, nor its
fancies.
CHORUS: Have flying rumors bloated you?
CLYTEMNESTRA: As if I were a child, you taunt me.

CHORUS: But when was it that the city was sacked? 270
CLYTEMNESTRA: In this last night that brought this
dawn to birth.
CHORUS: What messenger can be as quick as that?
CLYTEMNESTRA: The god of fire, sending his brilliant
glow from Mount Ida.
Beacon sent beacon here with courier fires,
Ida to the crag of Hermes in Lemnos;° 275
then from that island a third flame sent on
was welcomed by the heights of Athos that belong
to Zeus;
and high, spanning the sea's back,
the strength of the escorting flame went joyously
onward.
The pine fire sent its golden blaze, almost a sun, 280
to the watchtowers of Macistus.
He didn't hesitate nor carelessly succumb to sleep,
but passed his share of the message,
and from afar, over the streams of Euripus,
he gave to the sentries of Messapion 285
the sign that the beacon's light had traveled to him.
They in their turn lit up and sent the message
farther,
firing a great heap of ancient gorse.
Still strong, the beacon's light never flagged,
but leapt over the plain of Asopus like a radiant
moon, 290
to Mount Cithaeron, and there awakened
another relay of traveling fire.
The guard station did not refuse the far-escorted
flame;
it kindled more than was ordered, and launched its
light
over the Gorgon lake; and coming to 295
the goat-haunted mountain,
urged the watchman not to scant the ordinance of
fire.
They lit a huge beard of flame that burnt
ungrudgingly,
and sent it over the Saronic gulf, now become its
mirror,
beyond the headland, till it struck the heights of
Arachnus, 300
our neighboring sentry post here, and then again
struck right here on this roof of the sons of
Atreus —
this fire that is the grandchild of that fire on Mount
Ida.
Such were the courses of the torchbearers,
one from the other in relays, 305
and victor is he that ran first and last.
Such proof I have and such confirmation,
sent me out of Troy by my man.

273–75. Mount Ida . . . Lemnos: Mountain in Asia Minor
southeast of Troy from which the gods could view the battles.
The place names that follow trace the course of beacon fires set
to bring the news of the Greek victory from Troy to Greece.

CHORUS: My lady, to the gods once again
310   I shall give my prayer of thanks,
        but I would like you to tell me all this again,
        that I might hear the words and marvel at them
        from beginning to end.
CLYTEMNESTRA: Troy is captured; this is the day; the
            Greeks hold it.
315   Within that city there rings out
        a volume of cries that do not mingle.
        This is how I see it.
        Mix oil and vinegar in the same jar
        and you could not call them friends;
320   they will not be at one.
        So in Troy you might hear two sorts of crying:
        the conquered and the conquerors.
        The act is single, the meaning double.
        Here are these:
325   throwing themselves on the dead bodies
        of husbands and brothers,
        children on the bodies of their fathers,
        all sorrowing for the destiny of their dead,
        they cry from throats no longer free.
330   Then there are the others:
        roving all night after the fight
        sets them down hungry to breakfast
        on such foods as the city has;
        they all share, no rank or place assigned,
335   but as each has got the luck of the draw.
        They are already living in Troy's captured houses,
        free of the frost beneath the sky, free of the dews.
        They will sleep all night long without a guard,
        like happy men.
        If they revere the gods of that city in that captured
340   land,
        if they revere the gods' sacred places,
        they who are conquerors will not be reconquered.
        Only let no lust seize the army first,
        let no greed conquer them,
345   to make them ravish what they should not.
        They must still make the home voyage safely,
        travel the other leg of the double track.
        But even if the army came through offenseless
        in the sight of the gods,
350   the wrong done to the dead may yet awaken,
        seeking to contrive some sudden mischief.
        This is what you hear from me, a woman.
        But may the good prevail for all to see, past dispute.
        Of the many good things I might have,
355   this is what I would choose.
CHORUS: My lady, you talk wisely, like a sensible man.
        I have learned from you your convincing proofs,
        and now again I prepare to greet the gods.
        Surely we should thank them for what they have
            done for us.
360   O Zeus the king, and friendly night,
        that has endowed us with great glory,
        you that have cast upon the towers of Troy
        a close-fitting mesh so that no one young or old
        can overleap the great net of slavery,

the all-catching trap of ruin —   365
great Zeus of guest-friends I revere.
He has done all this. He has forever bent his bow
against Alexander, that no bolt should fail,
neither missing the mark nor scaling the stars.
They can say, "It is the stroke of Zeus";   370
the track of it is clear to see.
Zeus has acted as he has determined.
Someone has said,
"The gods do not deign to take heed of mortals
who trample underfoot the grace of holiness."   375
But he that said that had no piety in him.
The recklessness stands revealed
of those who breathe war beyond justice.
It is a recklessness that breeds consequences
when houses are overcrammed   380
beyond the measure of the best.
So I escape harm, let but a sufficiency be mine,
with abundance of good judgment.
For wealth gives no defense
for the man insolent with gorging,   385
who kicks the great altar of justice
to where none can see it.
Wretched persuasion,
intolerable child of forecounseling ruin,
drives him on violently.   390
And all cure is vain. It is not hidden, no —
the mischief shines, a lamp of evil light.
The black grain in Paris° shows through the test,
like base copper rubbed bare with use.
He has been like a child that chases a bird;   395
he has brought on this city an intolerable infection,
and no one of the gods will hear his prayer —
rather, pull down the unjust man
conversant with such things.
Such a one is Paris, who came   400
to the house of the sons of Atreus
and stained with shame the table of his host
by the theft of that host's wife.
She has left to her fellow citizens
the clanging of shields, the arming of sailors,
    ambushes.   405
To Ilium she has brought ruin instead of dowry.
Her daring defying all limits,
she darted quickly through the gates.
And many a groan there was
among those that spoke for the palace: 410
"Ah me, ah me, for the house, the house and the
    princes.
Ah me for the bed and the tracks of the love of men
    on it."
There one can see the silence —
dishonored, unreviling, inexorable —
of him that sits apart.   415
Through yearning for the one gone over the sea,
a ghost will seem to rule the house.

393. Paris: A prince of Troy, Paris abducted Helen of Greece,
thus defying Zeus's law of hospitality.

The grace of beautiful statues is hateful to the man.
Their eyes are empty, and before them
420 all passionate love falls dead.
Fancies haunt him in dreams persuasively;
theirs is a grace without substance.
Unsubstantial it is, when one sees,
and dreaming reaches to the touch,
and the phantom is gone, quickly slipping through
425   his hands,
as it follows the winged paths of sleep.
Such are the sorrows at home at the hearth;
but there are worse than these for all,
for those who joined the fleet and left the land of
     Greece.
430 In the house of every one of these
preeminent there is grief that reaches the heart.
They know whom they have sent forth, but instead
     of men
there come home urns and ashes to each house.
The war god is a money changer;
435 men's bodies are his money.
He holds the scales in the battle of the spear.
From Ilium he sends back to those who loved them
the scrapings of dust made heavy with their tears;
he loads the elegant urns with the dust that was
     once a man.
440 They mourn this man as they praise him —
how skilled he was in the fight — and another —
how gallantly he fell in his blood —
for another man's woman.
That is what they whisper and snarl;
445 and pain creeps about, full of ill will
toward the plaintiffs, the sons of Atreus.
But those others keep to their graves in all their
     beauty,
where they were, around the walls of Troy.
The enemy land that they have taken at last
450 has taken them, hidden them in itself.
The malicious speech of citizens is hard to bear;
it is the equal of a public curse.
And still I am troubled, lest I come to hear
something hidden in dark night.

455 For watchful are the gods' eyes
for those that kill by the thousands.
The black Furies reduce to dim nothingness
the man whose success has no justice in it,
wear him down, reversing his life's fortune.
460 And when he is among those we cannot see,
there is no help for him.
To be too well spoken of is heavy indeed.
For the thunderbolt is hurled from the eyes of Zeus.
May I not be a city-sacker, nor yet look upon my
     own life,
465 captured by others.
Swift is the rumor coursing through the city,
spurred by the fire of good tidings.
But whether it is true, who knows, or whether
somehow the gods deceive us.

Who is there so childish, so maimed of wit,   470
that the messages of fire should kindle his heart
only to sicken later when the news changes?
It is like the mettle of a woman's spirit
to praise the gracious gift before it is certainly there.
The limits of a woman's belief can be   475
as easily and quickly crossed
as cattle graze across a boundary.
But quickly, too, dies the report
a woman utters.
Soon we shall know about the lights from the
     beacons   480
and all the exchange of watch fires:
whether they are true or whether, like dreams,
a light of joy has stolen upon us and cheated our
     minds.
Here I see the herald coming from the shore,
shaded with twigs of olive.   485
The thirsty dust, twin sister of mud across the
     boundary,
is my witness; it witnesses to me that he has a *real*
     voice,
and so his testimony is not one of the smoky fire
of some wood on the hillside.
He will rather speak out and tell us to be glad,   490
or — God forbid it is the contrary message.
There *have* been good things that have shown
     through;
grant that this is their consummation.
Whoever prays anything else for this city,
I would he might reap the fruit of his mistaken
     thoughts.   495

(*Enter a herald.*)

HERALD: O my fathers' earth, Argos, Argos,
     ten long years and I have come to you;
     so many shipwrecked hopes, and one a winner.
     I never dreamed that I would have for my share in
          death
     a piece of dearest Argive land.   500
     Now welcome earth, welcome the light of sun,
     and Zeus supreme lord; and the Pythian King,°
     no longer shooting his arrows against us;
     you were harsh enough along Scamander's banks,
     but now you are different, now you are savior and
          healer,   505
     King Apollo. My greetings to all the gods in
          assembly.
     My greeting to my patron god, Hermes, dear herald,
     whom all heralds worship.
     My greetings to the heroes that sent us out
     and kindly welcome back what's left of us after the
          fight.   510
     Hail, royal halls, roofs I have loved,
     hail, holy seats and you divinities that face the
          sunlight.

502. **Pythian King:** The god Apollo.

Receive now with faces bright in joy —
if ever you did in days gone by —
515   now receive the king in glory after so long.
He comes and brings light after night's darkness,
a light to you and to all these —
King Agamemnon.
Give him true welcome; truly it belongs to him,
the king who dug down Troy with the spade of
520   God's justice,
made plowland of Troy;
and the seed has perished from all their country.
Their altars and the shrines of their gods are gone.
Such a yoking chain has he cast on Troy,
525   the king, Atreus's son, the old and happy man.
And now he comes here, most worthy of all
that now live and die.
Neither Paris nor the city that supports him
can boast that they have done more than they have
      paid for.
530   He was condemned for rape and theft —
lost what he carried off.
He has reaped for harvest
the utter ruin of his father's house.
And doubly have the sons of Priam paid for their
      offenses.
CHORUS: Herald of the Argive army, joy on your
535   homecoming!
HERALD: Joy, indeed. If the gods should end my life
      now,
I'd not deny them.
CHORUS: Has the love of your lost homeland tortured
      you so?
HERALD: Yes; the tears you see are tears of joy.
CHORUS: That disease had its pleasure for you, all the
540   same.
HERALD: What disease? What should I understand by
      that?
CHORUS: Love's stroke. But you got love for the love
      you gave.
HERALD: You mean this land has missed the army as
      we missed you?
CHORUS: We were faint and weak and so have groaned
      for you.
HERALD: Why so uneasy? What horror was in your
545   mind?
CHORUS: I say nothing and am safe — a long, long
      silence.
HERALD: How could that be? Your king was away; did
      you fear others?
CHORUS: As you said just now, I would have welcomed
      death.
HERALD: It *has* been a success. Of course, in the length
      of time,
550   one must say some things have gone well, some ill.
Who except the gods lives the whole span of his life
without trouble?
Yes, if I were to speak of the hard work
and the bad quarters,
555   the narrow gangways and the hard beds,

there's plenty to complain about.
Then there were the troubles on land,
disgusting things, too.
Our beds were under the enemy's walls.
Rain from the sky and dew from the grass soaked us   560
and kept rotting our clothing
and bred lice in our hair.
I could talk about the winter, which killed the birds;
Mount Ida and its snow made that intolerable.
And then there was the heat,   565
when the sea fell on its noontide bed and slept.
Not a breath of wind, not a stir on the waves —
Oh, why should I still feel pain for all this?
It's over, isn't it, all the trouble?
It's over indeed, for them, too, the dead;   570
they'll never have to trouble about getting up again.
Why should I reckon up the numbers of those who
      are gone?
Why should the living grieve because
fortune turned against us?
I'm ready to say a long goodbye to all that's
      happened.   575
For us that are left of the Greek army,
the gain certainly wins out,
and the bad side of things doesn't weigh it down.
So, those of us who have sped over land and sea
can stand facing the sunlight and make our boast: 580
"There was a day when the Argive army took Troy.
They have nailed the spoils of it
on the homes of the gods throughout Greece
to be a glory forever and ever."
When they hear this, men must praise   585
the city and its generals.
We shall also honor the grace of God
who brought it to pass.
That's my whole speech.
CHORUS: What you say wins me over; I admit it.   590
To be ready to learn is what makes a young man
out of an old one.
But it is this house and Clytemnestra
that the news most concerns,
though I, too, am the richer for it.   595
CLYTEMNESTRA: I rejoiced long ago,
and raised the cry of joy over the news,
when first the fire came as my messenger in the
      night,
telling of Troy's capture and destruction.
That was when everyone found fault with me: 600
"Is it beacon fires that convince you
that Troy has now been sacked?
How like a woman's heart to be so lifted up."
In rumors such as these I appeared
to have gone astray in my wits.   605
But yet I made the sacrifices,
and following this "woman's fashion"
they all raised the chant, now here, now there,
throughout the city,
the songs of blessing at the gods' shrines,   610
and there they lulled to sleep

the sweet-smelling sacrificial fires.
Why *now* should I depend on you to tell me more?
I shall learn the whole story from my lord himself.
615 How shall I make best haste to receive him home,
my honored husband?
What sweeter day for a wife's eye to see
than when she opens the doors to her man
coming from the army,
620 when the gods have brought him safely back to her?
Tell my husband this:
bid him come as quick as he can,
the city's darling.
And when he comes may he find his wife
625 true as he left her,
the watchdog of his house,
devoted to him, enemy to his enemies,
the same always and ever.
I never broke the seal
630 in all those years.
I know of no pleasure with another man
nor any talk or evil gossip against me,
anymore than I know how to dip this blade
to temper it.
635 Such is my boast, so full of truth
that even a well-bred wife
need not blush to utter it.

(*Exit Clytemnestra.*)

CHORUS: She has spoken very suitably
for those who understand her.
640 But tell me, Herald,
what of Menelaus?
Was he among the returning army?
Is he safe among you?
And will he come back home again, our dear
prince?
645 HERALD: I don't know how to put a fair face on lies:
my friends would only have good of it
for a short time anyway.
CHORUS: Why can't you tell news that is both good
and true?
When you separate them, you can't get away with
it.
HERALD: Then — the man has vanished from the
650 Greek army,
he and his ship. *That* is not a lie.
CHORUS: Did you see him set forth from Ilium on his
own?
Or did some storm that struck you all together
snatch him away?
655 HERALD: You've hit it exactly;
in a few words you've covered a long, sad story.
CHORUS: What do the rest of his shipmates think?
Do they say he's alive or dead?
HERALD: No one knows how to tell the news clearly —
660 except the sun, there, that gives life to the world.
CHORUS: What do you mean? Was there a storm
that came upon the fleet by the gods' anger
and then ended?
HERALD: A day of good news — one should not infect it

with the tongue of bad news.   665
The honor due to the two kinds of gods
is separate.
When a messenger with a gloomy face bears cursed
news
of an army's downfall,
there is one common injury which is public,   670
and then, besides, many a man is banned from his
home;
this is the double lash that the god of war loves,
a two-speared ruin, a bloody pair.
When, I say, a messenger is loaded with such
calamities,
he must sing his news as his hymn to the Furies.   675
But when the saving messenger of good news
comes to a city that rejoices in well-being
— how should I mingle good with bad
in telling you of this storm
which surely did proceed from the gods' anger   680
against the Greeks?
For fire and sea, those two oldest and deepest of
enemies,
swore a conspiracy and pledged their common
allegiance
to destroy the wretched Greek army.
In the night, waves lashed by the storm   685
arose to plague us.
For the Thracian winds battered ship on ship.
Butting one another savagely
in the hurricane and sheets of hail,
they sank from sight, as our evil shepherd   690
drove us here and there.
When the clear light of the day came back,
we saw the sea blooming,
and its flowers were dead Greeks and wrecks.
For ourselves and our boat, we went unharmed;   695
some god stole us through it or begged us off;
he must have steered us himself,
for no man touched the steering oar.
Luck chose to become our savior, and sat on our
ship,
so that we missed the driving waves when we were
at anchor,   700
nor were driven aground on the rugged land.
Afterward, when we had escaped our watery hell,
in the white light of day, we hardly dared to trust
our luck;
and in our own thoughts we were constantly
shepherds of some new calamity,   705
seeing how the fleet had been pounded and ground
to pieces.
Now, if any of them still breathes,
they speak of us as lost; of course they do.
We have much the same idea about them.
Let it turn out well. For Menelaus,   710
in all likelihood you may expect him back.
For if the beams of the sun discover him living and
seeing,
through the workings of God —

715 for surely God will not yet blot out
     the whole family —
     there is some hope that he'll come home again.
     This is really the truth that you have heard.

                                        (*Exit herald.*)

     CHORUS: Who can have named her so,
         with such truth, utterly?
720 Could it be someone we cannot see,
     with foreknowledge of destiny,
     that used his tongue in harmony with fortune?
     She was called Helen,°
     the bride won by the spear, sought in strife.
725 Helen means death, and death indeed she was,
     death to ships and men and city
     as she sailed out of the delicate fabrics of her
             curtained room,
     fanned by the breeze of giant Zephyr;°
     and the man-swarm of shield-bearing hunters
730 came on the track of her,
     the vanished track of the oar blades
     which beached on the ever-green shores of Simoeis
     on the heels of their bloody quarrel.

     To Ilium it drove her,
735 the wrath that brings fulfillment,
     and again the word proved true, that equates
     marriage and mourning,
     for the wrath exacted vengeance at the last
     for the guest-table dishonored at the hearth shared
             by Zeus.
740 Wrath punished as victims those men,
     the new marriage kinsmen,
     who on that day must celebrate,
     sing out of full throats
     the hymn that honored the bride.
745 Perhaps that ancient city of Priam
     has learned another tune now,
     a tuneful dirge that calls him
     Paris the dismally bedded;
     the city has endured the ruin of its life,
750 the voice of countless lamentations,
     through the wretched bloodletting of its citizens.
     Once on a time there was a man
     who raised a lion cub in his home.
     It was a little thing, starved of milk,
755 still a suckling, still in the first rituals of its life,
     gentle, a friend of children,
     and a delight to the old.
     Many a time it lay in their arms,
     like a young baby;
760 its face was bright as it fawned on the hand
     at the dictates of its belly's needs.
     But time passed, and it showed
     what disposition it had from its breeding;

723. Helen: Daughter of Zeus and Leda, a mortal woman, Helen was the wife of the Greek commander Menelaus before she was abducted by Paris and brought to Troy.   **728. Zephyr:** God of the west wind.

it requited the grace of those that brought it up
by horrid slaughtering of their sheep,   765
an unbidden dinner guest.
And the house was confused and befouled with
        blood;
an evil it was that the servants couldn't fight,
a very murderous mischief.
God reared the lion in the house to become   770
an additional priest of ruin.
But on that first day — as I tell the story —
she came to the city of Ilium
a spirit of windless calm,
the delicate glory of wealth,   775
the soft arrow darting from her eyes,
the flower of love that bites the heart.
Then she changed direction, and brought
a bitter ending to the marriage,
hastening to the daughters of Priam   780
to sit with them and live with them
to their ruin.
Zeus, the god of guests, brought her there,
a Fury to make wives weep.
There is an old saying among men, first spoken long
        ago,   785
that a man's great prosperity, when perfected,
gives birth and doesn't die childless,
but from that good fortune in true descent
there grows an ever-greedy misery.
In this, my mind is different from others'.   790
No, I say, it is the wicked deed
that breeds more wickedness, and like to its own
        kind.
For the house that is straight-dealing and just
is fated always to have good children.
The ancient deed of sacrilege always breeds a young
        one,   795
full of disaster for man, now or then,
when comes the dawn appointed for its birth.
A spirit but a clansman —
one cannot war against him nor fight him —
he is a thing unholy,   800
a daring, a black ruin to the halls,
and very like his parents.
For justice shines in houses grimed with smoke,
and she honors the good man.
And those gilded palaces where hands are dirty   805
she leaves, averting her eyes;
she goes to what is clean,
for she doesn't honor power
whose coinage is misstamped by the praise of the
        rich.
And she guides everything to its due end.   810

(*Enter Agamemnon and Cassandra.*)

     My lord, conqueror of Troy, descendant of Atreus,
     how shall I greet you, how do you reverence,
     neither exceeding nor scanting due measure of
             praise?
     Many men, indeed, who transgress justice,

815 honor appearance over reality.
Everyone is ready to cry over the unfortunate,
but the bite of that sorrow doesn't reach the heart.
So, too, there are those that seem to share joy,
yet the faces that they force have no laughter in
them.
820 When one is a good judge of stock,
one doesn't miss the meaning of the man's eyes,
fawning in watery friendship
when they seem all loyalty.
In the days when you led the expedition from
Greece,
825 for Helen's sake,
I saw you painted in ugly colors —
I will not hide that from you —
as one who had an unskillful hand
on the rudder of his wits
830 when you tried to win back through men's dying
a willing whore.
But now from the depth of my heart, in true
friendship,
I say, May the work be kind to those who did it so
well.
In time you shall know by enquiry
835 which of your citizens that stayed here at home
dealt justly, and which did wrong.
AGAMEMNON: First Argos and my country's gods,
I must address you; you and I are coauthors
of my home return and the justice
840 I exacted from Priam's city.
The causes were not spoken aloud,
but the gods heard them
and cast their votes with no opposing voices
into the bloody urn: for Ilium's destruction
845 and the deaths of men.
To the other urn nothing drew near
but the shadowy hope of a hand;
there was no filling that urn.
You can still see the smoke from the city's capture.
850 The hot blasts of ruin live there yet,
but there is ash, too, dying
as it sends into the air its breaths fattened on rich
things.
For all of this we should pay our gods
much-remembering thanks.
855 We have taken vengeance for insolent robbery.
And for the sake of a woman a city has been leveled
by the biting beast of Argos, the colt,
the shield-bearing host,
that made its leap about the time of the setting
Pleiades.
860 A ravening lion leaped over the wall
and licked its fill of royal blood.
So far my prelude stretches; that's for the gods.
What you've said of your feelings, I've heard and
remember.
I say the same. You have me as your advocate.
865 In very few men is it native
to admire a successful friend without envying him.

For the poison of malice, settling on the heart,
doubles its weight in one who is stricken with envy.
He suffers under the load of his own troubles,
and groans to see the prosperity of the other man. 870
I know of what I speak; I very well understand
the glassy mirror of comradeship, that shadow of a
shade,
which those prove to be who seemed my truest
friends.
Only Odysseus,° who joined the fleet unwillingly,
once he was yoked was for me a ready trace horse. 875
Even as I speak of him, I do not know
if I speak of the dead or the living.
For other matters, we will set up public meetings
and take counsel in full assembly.
What is now well shall remain well; we shall see to
it. 880
But where there is need for healing medicines,
we will try by surgery or cautery°
intelligently to avert the disease.
Now I will go in, into my halls, my hearth, my
home,
and there I will first greet the gods 885
who sent me forth and brought me back again.
Victory has followed us;
let her be ours still, constantly!

(Enter Clytemnestra.)

CLYTEMNESTRA: You citizens, elders of Argos,
I will not be ashamed of speaking to you 890
of how l love my husband.
Modest inhibition is something
that dies away in human dealings.
I will tell of how wretched my life has been
while this man was in Troy — 895
at first hand I will tell it; it has been *my* life.
First, that a woman should sit in her house,
lonely without her male,
is something terrifying.
She hears so many hateful rumors; 900
here's one has come, and then another,
announcing a greater disaster still,
mouthing the ruin of the house.
If this man here had had as many wounds
as streams of rumor would have it, 905
he would have had more holes in him than a net.
If he had died, as his deaths multiplied in stories of
him,
he must have had three bodies, like Geryon;
he would have boasted of taking a triple
shroud of earth to himself. 910
It was because of these hateful reports
that others, not I, have loosened many a cord
as it tightened round my neck.

874. Odysseus: Throughout the *Iliad*, Homer's story of the Trojan war, Odysseus is a brave soldier. He gives wise, even wily advice to the Greeks. **882. cautery:** The process of burning with a hot iron in order to heal.

915 And that is why your son
doesn't stand beside me as he should,
the proof of our trust, mine to you, yours to me,
our Orestes.
Do not wonder at this; a loyal ally keeps him safe,
Strophius the Phocian.°
920 He spoke to me of twin troubles:
your danger at Ilium, and then that here, too,
the anarchy of the people's voices
might overturn good counsel.
Indeed, it is inbred in men
925 to kick the man that's down.
That's the advice of Strophius, and there's no deceit
in it.
For my own part, the gushing springs of my grief
have dried up;
there's not a drop left.
930 My eyes are in pain from late watching,
weeping for the beacons that should tell of you,
but never called for firing.
In my dreams, I have started up,
roused by the light strokes of the gnat's flight;
935 I have seen so much more happen to you
than could be contained within the time
with which I shared my sleep.
But now I have come through all this;
my heart is free of sorrow;
940 and so I can describe this man of mine —
a watchdog of the house,
the saving forestay of the ship,
the rooted pillar of the towering roof,
the single child of a father,
the land seen by sailors when they had given over
945 hope,
the fairest day to see after the storm,
the springwater stream for the thirsty traveler.
It is sweet indeed to escape the harsh stroke of
necessity.
Such terms of address would, I think, belong to him.
950 But let no one be jealous.
Many, indeed, were the evils we endured before.
Now, dear heart,
step from the carriage, but do not place on earth,
my king,
this foot that trod Troy to destruction.
955 Servants, to whom I have commanded the task
of strewing his path to the house with tapestries —
let his way lie straight before him strewn with purple,
that justice may guide him to the home he never
hoped for.
Everything else earned by fate
960 an unsleeping mind, with the help of the gods,
will arrange justly.
AGAMEMNON: Daughter of Leda,° guardian of my house,

919. **Strophius the Phocian:** A family friend with whom Orestes stayed at the time of Agamemnon's murder.   962. **Leda:** Mother of Clytemnestra by her husband, Tyndareus, and of Helen by Zeus, who approached Leda in the form of a swan.

your speech is a good fit for my absence:
both have stretched out long.
965 But to praise me in due fashion
is an honor that others should give.
Besides, do not make much of me in this woman's
fashion,
nor grovel and gape flatteringly, like some foreigner,
nor strew my path with garments that would make it
970 an object of ill will;
it is the gods one should honor with such things.
For one who is mortal, for me certainly,
to walk on subtly woven beauties like these
cannot be without fear.
975 I tell you, honor me as man, not god.
Footmats and embroideries — they sound
differently,
they are different.
Not to be presumptuous
is the greatest gift the gods can give you.
980 It's only when a life has ended, and ended well,
that one dare say, "Well done."
I would be cheerful if my life
were like this in everything.
CLYTEMNESTRA: Then tell me this, and let it be your
own true judgment.
985 AGAMEMNON: Be sure, I will not falsify that judgment.
CLYTEMNESTRA: Was it through fear of the gods
that you made this vow?
AGAMEMNON: I said, if any man ever did, what I knew
would happen.
CLYTEMNESTRA: And what of Priam, if he had
conquered as you have?
990 AGAMEMNON: He would certainly have trodden on the
tapestry.
CLYTEMNESTRA: Don't be ashamed, then, of human
reproach.
AGAMEMNON: Yes, but the ill repute of the people's
voices
has a great power.
CLYTEMNESTRA: He that is not envied is also not
admired.
995 AGAMEMNON: A woman should not long so for a fight.
CLYTEMNESTRA: In those that win, yielding is graceful.
AGAMEMNON: Do you set such store on victory in this
dispute?
CLYTEMNESTRA: Let me have my way. You are the victor
if you yield readily.
1000 AGAMEMNON: Well, if you will — here, someone undo
my sandals,
that are like slaves for the treading of my foot.
And as I walk upon these lovely cloths,
I pray against the envious eye of the gods
lest from afar it strike me.
1005 It's a great shame to spoil a house's wealth,
these weavings so dear in price, with the dirt of
treading feet.
Enough of this.
Bring in this stranger here, and use her kindly.
The god looks from afar with approval

1010   on the merciful conqueror.
        No one chooses to become a slave.
        This woman is the very flower, picked out
        from the spoils of war;
        as a gift from the army to me, she followed me.
1015   Well, since I've been subdued to listen to you,
        I will go into my house, treading on purple.
        CLYTEMNESTRA: There is a sea — and who shall drain
            it dry? —
        nourishing a spring, always new, an abundance of
            purple
        to be bought with silver for the dyeing of garments.
1020   This house, my lord, has store enough of it,
        thanks be to the gods.
        This house does not know poverty.
        I would have vowed the treading of many garments,
        had I been so ordered by the shrines of the oracles,
1025   to win the safe return of your life.
        When the root is there, the leaf comes to the house,
        and stretches its shade against the dog star's heat.
        And when you came to this house and hearth of
            yours,
        it meant what heat means in the winter time.
1030   And when Zeus makes wine from the bitter grape,
        it is still cool within the house,
        when its perfected lord paces through the halls.
        Zeus, Zeus, that brings all to perfection,
        perfect my prayer.
1035   Bring to perfection all you have to do.
        CHORUS: Why this fluttering, insistent terror
        that keeps guard before my heart?
        Is the song prophetic
        that rises unhired and unbidden?
1040   My grounded mind has no confidence to dismiss it
        like an obscure nightmare.
        Time has grown old since the boats,
        their hawsers all thrown out along the sands,
        set out to Ilium.
1045   With my eyes I am my own witness
        to their homecoming.
        But nonetheless, my spirit within me
        drones this tune of the Furies,
        accompanied by no lyre,
1050   a song taught by none but itself.
        It has none of the dear confidence of hope.
        Not for nothing is the boding of my entrails,
        the whirling of my heart, harmonized with
        eddies of my mind that will surely bring fulfillment.
1055   But I pray that what I expect may fall away,
        a lie, into unfulfillment.
        There is no limit in health;
        it is insatiable.
        For disease is its next-door neighbor;
1060   there is but a single wall between them.
        A man's destiny, facing straight ahead,
        often crashes on the hidden reef.
        Yet, if beforehand in prudent fear,
        he casts overboard part of what he owns
1065   with the derrick of good measure,

his whole house does not sink utterly,
though overloaded to overflowing,
nor does the frame of the ship sink.
Many times the generous gifts of Zeus,
and those of the furrows yearly tilled,   1070
banish the disease of hunger.
But the black blood of a man,
when once it has fallen to the earth in his death,
who shall conjure it back again with any
    incantation?
Did not Zeus, for the safety of the world,   1075
stop the wizard who would raise the dead?
If there were no fates appointed by the gods
which checked other fates from having overmuch,
my heart would have outstripped my tongue
and poured this out.   1080
But now in the dark it mutters, in heart-anguish,
with never a hope of spinning out of my burning
    mind
what is right for this moment.
CLYTEMNESTRA: In with you too, now, Cassandra,
since Zeus (you cannot be angry with Zeus)   1085
has made you a sharer in the sacrifices in our
    house,
standing near the altar with many slaves that we
    own.
Get down from that carriage;
none of your high spirit of pride.
They say that Heracles, Alcmene's son,°   1090
was sold and forced to eat the bread of slavery.
If then the necessity of fate's scales
has forced this on you,
you should be very grateful for masters anciently
    rich.
Those who have reaped a harvest they never
    expected   1095
are always excessive in harshness toward their
    slaves.
From us you will have all the usual treatment.
CHORUS: She has finished; it is to you she spoke,
and what she says is clear enough.
You are taken, a quarry in fate's net;   1100
obey her, then —
though I will understand if you don't.
CLYTEMNESTRA: If she has anything besides her
    swallow twitterings,
a barbaric speech that no one knows,
I'll try to persuade her within her understanding.   1105
CHORUS: Follow her. What she says is the best there is
    for you;
leave the carriage; obey her.
CLYTEMNESTRA: I have no time to waste here with her
    outside the palace.
The sheep stand ready for slaughter   1110
in front of the hearth at the center of the house.

1090. Heracles, Alcmene's son: Heracles was a popular Greek
hero. According to legend, he was sold into slavery to
Omphale, Queen of Lydia.

(*To Cassandra.*)

You, if you're going to do anything that I tell you,
do it quickly.
But if you disobey because you don't take in my
words —

(*To Chorus.*)

1115 Here, you!
Don't speak to her any more; use your hands;
that's all these foreigners understand.
CHORUS: I think the woman needs a good interpreter;
she looks like a wild thing newly caught.
CLYTEMNESTRA: She's crazy; she hears only her
1120   distraught mind.
Of course she does, she that has left her newly
captured city,
come here not yet knowing how to wear the curb bit,
till she's frothed out her spirit in blood.
I won't throw any more words at her to be belittled.

(*Exit Clytemnestra.*)

1125 CHORUS: I pity her, and so I won't be angry.
Come, you poor girl, desert your place in the
carriage;
yield to what must be; wear your yoke for the first
time.
CASSANDRA: Oh! Oh! Oh! Oh, the land!
Lord Apollo! Lord Apollo!
1130 CHORUS: Why do you raise such dismal cries to
Apollo?
He is no god for the singer of dirges.
CASSANDRA: Oh! Oh! Oh! Oh, the land!
Lord Apollo! Lord Apollo!
1135 CHORUS: Again she calls with her ill omens
upon the god who has no suitable place
at scenes of mourning.
CASSANDRA: Lord Apollo! Lord Apollo! God of the
streets,
god of destruction! Now again, god of my
destruction,
1140 and so easily.
CHORUS: She seems to me about to prophesy her own
misfortunes.
The gift of prophecy still sticks
even though the mind is now a slave's.
CASSANDRA: Lord Apollo! Lord Apollo!
1145 God of my destruction! God of the streets!
Through what streets have you led me now,
to what house?
CHORUS: To that of the sons of Atreus. If you don't
know that,
that I can tell you. And you won't say it's a lie.
1150 CASSANDRA: Yes, to a house the gods hate;
it has been witness of so many
murders of kin, butcheries,
bowl full of man's blood, ground soaked in shed
blood.
CHORUS: The stranger has a nose as keen as a hound;
1155   she's on the trail of a murder and will find it.

CASSANDRA: What convinces me are the witnesses —
the children, the babies screaming of their cut
throats,
of their flesh roasted and eaten by their father.
CHORUS: We have heard of your fame as a prophet;
but we need no foretellers here.   1160
CASSANDRA: Oh, what does she plan?
What is the great new grief?
It is a great evil against the house
that she is planning.
It is unbearable for its friends, uncurable.   1165
Defense stands aloof and keeps away.
CHORUS: These last foretellings are quite beyond my
understanding;
the others I know — indeed the whole city cries
them aloud.
CASSANDRA: Oh, you wretched woman,
is this what you bring to consummation?   1170
You have cleaned him in the bath
till his skin shined,
the husband to share your bed.
And how shall I tell the consummation?
It would be quick: the line of clutching hands,   1175
stretching out, one hooked to another.
CHORUS: I don't understand that yet;
you spoke riddles before,
but now what baffles me is the dimness
of what comes from the gods in words.   1180
CASSANDRA: Oh! Oh! Oh! What is this that appears?
A net, a net of death. Can it be so?
But the meshes are the bedfellow, the accomplice in
murder.
Let the pack that ravens insatiate against the family
bay for a sacrifice that merits death by stoning.   1185
CHORUS: What Fury is this you bid raise its cries
against the house?
I find no cleaning in your words.
To my heart rush back the blood drops of yellowing
stain,
as when the eyes grow dim at the setting of a life's
day,   1190
a man falling by the point of a spear.
And destruction comes quick.
CASSANDRA: Look at that! Look at that!
Keep away the bull from the cow!
She will take him in the folds of the robe   1195
with the trick of the black horn.
She strikes! He falls! He falls
in the water of the bath.
That is his end, I tell you,
a treacherous murder in a cauldron.
CHORUS: I will not boast of being a keen judge of   1200
prophecy,
but this certainly looks like something evil.
Anyway, what good word ever came to mankind
from the prophets?
It is through evils that the wordy tricks of the
prophets   1205
bring terrors for us to understand.

CASSANDRA: Oh, the ill boding of my own sad fate!
　For it is my own suffering, on top of his,
　that my tongue spills out.

(*To the god.*)

1210　Where is this you have brought me to in my
　　sorrow?
　For nothing but to share his death; what else?
CHORUS: You are someone god-possessed;
　the god carries you along.
　It is for yourself you cry out this tuneless tune.
1215　Like the brown nightingale,° that can never have
　　enough of song,
　as she cries "Itys! Itys!" for her life rich in sorrows,
　and her mind loves pity for herself.
CASSANDRA: Oh! The life of the shrill-voiced
　　nightingale!
1220　The gods covered *her* with a feathered body;
　I tell you, they gave her a *sweet* life,
　and her cries are not cries of sorrow.

1215–22. Like the brown nightingale: The chorus alludes to the story of Philomela, who was raped by her brother-in-law, Tereus. Although her tongue was cut out to prevent her from telling anyone of the crime, Philomela sent her sister a piece of embroidery that revealed all. The sisters took their revenge on Tereus by tricking him into eating his son, Itys. According to some accounts, the gods turned Philomela into a nightingale.

But what remains for me
　is the splitting of the flesh with the two-edged spear.
CHORUS: Where do they come from, these rushes　　1225
　of useless agony carried by the god?
　You make music that is a mixture,
　ugly cries of terror and high-pitched melodies.
　Where did you get the milestones of evil words
　that mark your prophetic journey?　　1230
CASSANDRA: The marriage! The marriage of Paris,
　deadly to those who loved him.
　Scamander, river that my fathers drank of,
　in that time I was raised on your shores;
　but now around the banks of Cocytus and Acheron,°　1235
　the rivers of death, I am likely to prophesy,
　and soon.
CHORUS: What is this word you have spoken all too
　　clearly?
　A newborn child could understand.
　The bite of murder has pierced me　　1240
　as you whimper at your painful fortune.
　It is a heartbreak to hear you.
CASSANDRA: The agony, agony of the city utterly
　　ruined.
　The sacrifices that my father made before the walls,
　the multiplied slaughter of cattle and woolly sheep.

1235. Cocytus and Acheron: Rivers flowing together at the entrance to the kingdom of death.

A scene from the American Repertory Theatre's 1994 production of the *Oresteia,* directed by François Rochaix.

1245 None of it helped; it was no cure.
The city suffered as it was fated to suffer.
And I shall soon be thrown on the ground
in my own warm blood.
CHORUS: What you say now follows what you said
before.
Some malevolent god who falls on you with fearful
1250 weight
makes you a singer of these deadly mournful things.
But as for the end — I am at a loss.
CASSANDRA: Now my prophecy shall no longer peer
from behind veils
like a newly married bride.
1255 No, it will rush on, a wind brightly blowing
into the sun's rising,
to send disaster surging like a wave to meet the
sunbeams,
a disaster yet greater than this.
I will not school you in riddles any longer.
1260 And do you be my witness that my nose is keen
and my tracking by shortcuts
on the path of crimes committed long ago.
Never do they leave the house,
that chorus that sings in ugly harmony.
1265 For their speech is of evil.
The revelers have drunk, to whet their courage more,
man's blood, and so they abide in the house,
and none shall expel them: they are the Furies,
that attend on the murder of kin.
1270 The song they sing as they beleaguer the house
is the song of the primal destruction,
when the mind is blinded.
And each of the Furies has spat in disgust
on the brother's bed that hates its violator.
1275 Hah! Am I an archer that missed,
or have I hit the mark?
Or am I a false prophet
that raps on doors and babbles?
Be my witness, you, but first make your sworn oath
1280 that I know the story of the ancient sins
of this house.
CHORUS: How would such an oath, even plighted in all
honesty,
serve as any kind of cure?
True, I do wonder at you,
that you, reared beyond the sea and speaking a
1285 strange tongue
should talk of these things as if you had been there.
CASSANDRA: It was Apollo the prophet
that charged me with the office of prophecy.
CHORUS: He fell in love with you?
1290 Is that possible for a god?
CASSANDRA: Till now I was ashamed to speak of it.
CHORUS: As long as things go well, one has one's
delicacy.
CASSANDRA: He was a wrestler, that breathed his grace
into me.
CHORUS: Did you come to the breeding of children,
1295 like other couples?

CASSANDRA: I promised the god and cheated him.
CHORUS: Had you already got your gift of prophecy?
CASSANDRA: Oh yes, I used to tell my countrymen
all that would happen.
CHORUS: How did you escape the god's anger?   1300
CASSANDRA: Since my offense against him,
no one believed a word of mine.
CHORUS: Ah, but to us right now, you seem to
prophesy truly.
CASSANDRA: Oh, oh, my agony! There it is again!
The fearful pain of true prophecy   1305
that twists me, that drives me wild;
and it is still only prelude.
Look! Look! You see them! The young ones,
sitting on the house like dream phantoms.
They are the likenesses of those children dead and
gone,   1310
killed by those they loved;
their hands are full of meat, their own flesh.
You can see it clearly; they carry the pitiful load
of their guts, and their father has tasted them.
I tell you, there is punishment for this,   1315
and someone is plotting it,
a lion, but a coward, that wallows, a housekeeper
in the bed of the returning lord —
O mine, *my* lord — for I must bear the yoke of
slavery.
The captain of the ships, the sacker of Ilium,   1320
he knows not what tongue is licking him,
the tongue of the hateful bitch, her ears pricked,
like a secret blind vengeance,
that will work out his evil fate.
So far her daring reaches: 1325
the woman will murder the man.
She is — what shall I call her and be right?
this monstrous, biting creature.
A snake with poison at both ends;
some Scylla° living in the rocks, death to sailors; 1330
some murderous, raging mother of hell;
some truceless god of war;
a war she has declared upon her loved ones!
So let her cry her war cry,
whose daring knows no limit,   1335
as at the moment when the battle turns.
Yet she seems to rejoice that he has come safe home.
It is all one to me, if you do not believe any of this;
what difference?
It is to be and will come.   1340
Soon you will stand here and say of me, in pity,
she was too true a prophet.
CHORUS: The feast of Thyestes, and the flesh of the
children,
I understand and shudder; fear is on me
as I hear the truth, and no mere likenesses.   1345

1330. **Scylla:** A sea monster living in a cave opposite the whirlpool, Charybdis. Ships could not escape the double threat.

But for the rest I heard from you,
   I have fallen off the course and run wide.
CASSANDRA: I tell you, you will live to see
   Agamemnon's death.
CHORUS: Wretched one, hold your tongue in piety.
CASSANDRA: No, no holy god of healing presides over
1350   this story.
CHORUS: True, if what you say is so; but God forbid it
   should be.
CASSANDRA: You are all for God forbidding;
   but their job is killing.
CHORUS: What man is he that furnishes this grief?
CASSANDRA: You have surely fallen astray of my
1355   prophecies.
CHORUS: Yes, for I do not understand how the plotter
   will make his plan work.
CASSANDRA: Yet I know Greek rather too well.
CHORUS: So does the Delphic oracle;° but it's hard to
   understand,
1360   all the same.
CASSANDRA: Oh! It attacks me like fire!
   Oh! Oh! O god! O Lycian Apollo!
   There she is, the lioness, two-footed bedfellow of
     the wolf,
   in the absence of the true-bred lion.
1365   She will kill me. Like one that brews a potion,
   She will put my reward, too, in the drink.
   She cries her glee in triumph, as she whets the knife
   for a man, to pay him in murder for bringing me
     here.

(She starts tearing off her robe and garlands.)

   Why should I have these mockeries about me,
1370   this staff, the prophet's garlands round my neck?
   Before I die myself, I shall at least destroy you.
   Go; you shall be no more. Lie on the ground as you
     fall.
   Thus I requite you.
   Enrich some other girl with blinded madness,
1375   some other girl than me.
   Look, Apollo himself undoes his prophetess
   of her prophetic mantle; he has watched me
   laughed to scorn even in this trumpery,
   laughed at by friends turned foes,
1380   with never a quiver in the scale — what hollowness!
   Ill-treated like a wandering beggar priest,
   in misery half-starved to death, I still endured.
   But now the prophet has unmade the prophet
   and brought me here to meet my chance death.
1385   No father's altar, but a chopping block, waits for me,
   to be warmed with my blood as I am butchered,
   the preliminary victim. Yet, all the same, I shall not
     die
   dishonored by the gods.

But another will come° to take vengeance for me;
he will kill the mother in whom he was seeded,   1390
and will avenge his father.
A wanderer outcast, grown alien to this land,
who will return from exile
to put a coping stone of ruin for those he loved,
for he has sworn a great oath by the gods   1395
that his father's corpse shall bring him home again.
Why do I go on this way, crying, full of self-pity? —
now that I have seen Troy's ruin, as I saw it,
now as Troy's conquerors come off in the god's
   judgment,
as I see them now.   1400
I will go and face it; I will face my death.
These gates before me here, I call you now by name:
the gates of death.
But I pray that the stroke that reaches me
may be a mortal stroke,   1405
that without struggle, as the blood runs freely,
in easy death I may close these eyes of mine.
CHORUS: You are a woman that has suffered much,
   and have understood much; and you have said
     much.
   But if you truly know your fate,   1410
   why do you walk up to the altar steadfastly,
   like an ox?
CASSANDRA: There is no escape, my friends; the time is
   full.
CHORUS: Yet the latest moment has a special value.
CASSANDRA: This day has come; there is little I would
   gain by flight.   1415
CHORUS: How courageous and steadfast!
CASSANDRA: No one who's happy hears these
   compliments.
CHORUS: But death, if fame comes with it,
   comes still with grace to those that must die
     anyway.
CASSANDRA: I weep for you, father, and for your noble
   children.   1420

(She recoils.)

CHORUS: What is it? What is the fear that turns you
   back?

(Cassandra shudders.)

CHORUS: What made you shudder?
   Is it something in your mind that disgusts you?
CASSANDRA: The house! It reeks of murder, of dripping
   blood!
CHORUS: What? It's just the blood of sacrificed
   animals.   1425
CASSANDRA: No, it is just like the smell of a grave.
CHORUS: It is no delicate Syrian incense in the house
   that you speak of.

1359. Delphic oracle: The chief oracle of ancient Greece, presided over by Apollo. The utterings of the oracle were ambiguous and had to be interpreted.

1389. another will come: Reference to Orestes, who avenges his father's murder in the second part of Aeschylus's trilogy.

CASSANDRA: Still — I will go into the house,
  to mourn with cries my own and Agamemnon's
1430   deaths.
  I have enough of life.
  My friends, I'm not scared
  like a bird startled at a bush
  in empty terror.
1435   When I die, you will be my witness to this,
  when a woman dies to match my woman's death,
  when a man falls to match that other man,
  whose wife was his assassin.
  This friendly office I lay on you, as I die now.
1440 CHORUS: Poor girl, I pity you for your death,
  that the god predicted.
CASSANDRA: I have one more speech to make,
  or shall I call it a dirge, just for myself.
  As I face this last sunlight,
1445   I call on those who shall be my avengers
  to make my enemies pay for *my* murder too,
  only a dead slave, such an easy victory.
  Men's fortunes, when they are good,
  one might say of them, "They are like shadows only."
1450   When they're bad, a wet sponge
  with one stroke wipes it all out.
  The first truth has my pity, far more than the second.
            (*Exit Cassandra.*)
CHORUS: To be successful is to be endlessly hungry for
      more;
  all men are so.
  There is no one who banishes good fortune from his
1455   house,
  so long as fingers point at it.
  No man says, "Do not come here again, good
      fortune."
  Here is this king, to whom the blessed gods granted
  the sacking of Priam's city;
  he came home with all the honors that the gods
1460   gave him.
  But now, if he shall pay for the blood of the past
  and dying render the price of others' deaths,
  who that hears this and must die himself
  dare boast that a man may be born
1465   to live a whole life unharmed?
AGAMEMNON (*from within*): I've been hit! I am hurt to
      death.
CHORUS: Hush! Who is it that cries out, hurt to death?
AGAMEMNON: I'm hit again!
CHORUS: It is the king crying out; I think all is over.
1470   But let us plan safety for ourselves — if we can.
  1. My vote is to cry, Help! to the citizens
  to come to the palace.
  2. Yes, and at once, I think,
  to catch them red-handed with dripping sword.
  3. I think you're right; at least we should do
1475   something.
  It certainly isn't the moment for hesitation.
  4. But we can see. This is a kind of first act;
  it looks like the beginning of a tyranny.
  5. Yes, it does — because we're wasting time.
1480   Their hands don't sleep, and they trample underfoot

the good reputation of delay.
  6. I really do not know what would be best.
  Those who do the deed of course find it easy to plan.
  7. Yes, I am with you. Anyhow,
  one cannot by talking bring the dead to life again.   1485
  8. Are we then, in order to stretch our own lives,
  to yield to a government that shames our royal
      house?
  9. No, that is awful. Death is better than that.
  Death is better than subjection to a tyranny.
  10. Is the evidence of the cries good enough?   1490
  Are we right to predict that the man is dead?
  11. Yes, one must know before one gets angry.
  Knowing the truth is very far from guessing.
  12. I have the support of many voices among you:
  that we should be told clearly how it is with
      Agamemnon.   1495

(*Enter Clytemnestra.*)

CLYTEMNESTRA: Till now I have said much to meet the
      occasion,
  but now I will not be ashamed to say the opposite.
  How could one, rendering hate to those who hated
  but looked like loved ones,
  hedge the trap about with sides too high to be leapt
      over?   1500
  This was my day of trial; I have thought of it
  enough and long enough, a trial of an old quarrel
  years and years old.
  Now I stand here where I have struck him.
  He is dead, and the sequence ended.   1505
  This is how I managed — I will not disavow it —
  that he should not escape, nor defend himself from
      death.
  I threw about him an encompassing net,
  as it might be for fish, all-entangling,
  an evil wealth of cloak.   1510
  I struck him twice. He gave two groans,
  and his body went limp;
  as he lay there, I gave him a third,
  in honor of the Zeus that keeps the dead
  securely in the underworld.   1515
  This was my grace and prayer for him.
  So, as he lay there, he gasped out his spirit,
  choking, poured out a sharp stream of his blood
  and struck me with the dark bloody shower.
  I rejoiced as much as the new-sown earth   1520
  rejoices in the glad rain of Zeus,
  when the buds strike in earth's womb.
  So it is, you old men of Argos here;
  be glad, if you can. I triumph in it.
  If it were right to pour libations   1525
  on a dead man's body, I would have done so to him,
  and more than justly done so.
  Here's a bowl of horrors, cursed horrors,
  that he filled within our house,
  and then he came and drank it off himself.   1530
CHORUS: I wonder at your tongue, how boldly it wags,
  that you should boast like this over a dead husband.
CLYTEMNESTRA: You try me out as if I were

a woman that cannot think.
1535 But my heart doesn't tremble,
and I speak to you who know;
whether you wish to praise or blame me is all one
     to me.
Here is Agamemnon, my husband, now a corpse —
his death the work of this right hand of mine,
1540 an efficient craftsman.
That is how *that* is.
CHORUS: Woman, what evil thing have you eaten
     that grows in the earth,
what draught have you tasted that comes from the
     salt sea,
1545 that you have taken upon you so horrible a sacrifice
and the curse of the people's voice?
You have cast away, you have torn apart,
and you shall be cast and torn away from the city,
a monstrous object of hate to the citizens.
CLYTEMNESTRA: Now it's against me that you proclaim
1550   banishment,
that the hatred and curses of the citizens shall be
     mine,
but in the old days you brought nothing against
     that man,
who, with all the indifference of one whose pastures
     are full
of teeming flocks, rich in wool,
1555 had no care for the death of a lamb.
He sacrificed his own daughter,
dearest pain of my womb,
to charm the contrariness of Thracian winds.
For this, should you not have banished him,
1560 payment for his polluting wickedness?
No, you are a careful hearer and harsh judge
only of *my* acts.
Threaten away! I tell you now, if once you
     conquer me
in a fair fight, I'll be your subject;
1565 but if God gives another outcome,
you will get an education in discretion
and learn it thoroughly, though the knowledge
     comes very late.
CHORUS: You think big thoughts, and you scream
     proud defiance,
1570 as though the bloody smear of your success
had maddened your mind.
The smear of blood — I can see it in your eyes.
But still you must pay stroke for stroke,
with no friend to take your part.
CLYTEMNESTRA: You may now hear the solemn
1575   swearing of my oath:
By the justice due to my child, and now perfected,
by the Spirit of Destruction and the Fury,
in whose honor I cut this man's throat,
my hope treads not within the hall of Fear
1580 so long as Aegisthus lights the hearth fire for me,
my loyal friend, as he has always been,
shield for my daring — no small one.
There lies Agamemnon, this girl's seducer —
he was the darling of all the women of Troy —

and there she is, our prophet, prisoner of war,   1585
that shared his bed, a faithful whore
that spoke her auguries for him, and knew as well
the rubbing of the sailors' benches.
Both have suffered as they deserved.
He died as I said, and she has sung her swan song in
     death,   1590
and lies with him, her lover.
But to me she has brought an additional side dish
to *my* pleasure in bed.
CHORUS: What day of doom may I look for soon,
one with not too much pain, not too long
     bedridden,   1595
that shall bring me the sleep that has no ending,
now that my kindest of guardians has been
     overcome,
suffering so much at a woman's hands.
By a woman his life has perished.
Curse on you, crazy Helen, that were the single
     murderess   1600
of all those lives, those many lives,
lost under Troy's walls;
now you have made the fulfillment,
the fine flowering, of whatever it was,
that quarrel within the house   1605
built to bring a man to misery.
You have perfected it,
through bloodshed that cannot be washed out.
CLYTEMNESTRA: Do not pray for your end in death
because of the burden of your grief in this,   1610
nor turn your anger against Helen,
as the man-killer who destroyed
those many lives of the Greeks,
and brought into being an incurable pain.
CHORUS: Spirit that attacks the house of the sons of
     Atreus,   1615
you master me to the breaking of my heart;
your power is wielded by two women of like soul.
And now you stand like an evil raven,
and croak over the dead a lawless hymn of victory.
CLYTEMNESTRA: Now indeed you have made right   1620
the judgment of your mouth,
as you name the thrice-glutted spirit of this race.
It is through him that the love of blood-licking
is nourished in the belly,
and before the old wound has healed,   1625
new pus comes.
CHORUS: Yes, the one you name is indeed great,
the spirit whose anger lies heavy on this house.
And the tale you have to tell is evil;
it has an endless appetite for the events of blind
     madness.   1630
But surely these are through Zeus,
who is cause of all, who brings all to pass.
For what is there that is fulfilled for man,
except through Zeus?
What is there of all this   1635
that is not of God's accomplishment?
O my king, my king,
how shall I sorrow for you?

What shall I say from a heart that loves you?
1640   You lie there in that spider's web,
        gasping out your life in an unholy death.
        Oh, oh! Conquered by deadly treachery,
        to fall to such an ignoble bed
        by a wife's hand and a double-edged blade.
1645   CLYTEMNESTRA: You cry aloud on this as *my* work;
        but do not call me Agamemnon's wife.
        No, it is the old, bitter, Evil Genius
        of Atreus, giver of the cruel feast,
        that has likened himself to the wife of this dead man
1650   and has paid him off, sacrificing a full-grown victim
        in fulfillment for those young children.
        CHORUS: But who will bear you witness
        that you are guiltless of the murder?
        How, how so? It is true, there may be,
1655   on his father's side, the Evil Genius to help you.
        And the black god of war presses on
        through tides of kindred blood
        to the place of his advance,
        where he pays just requital
1660   for the congealed fragments of the eaten children.
        O my king, my king,
        how shall I sorrow for you?
        What shall I say from a heart that loves you?
        You lie there in that spider's web,
1665   gasping out your life in an unholy death.
        Oh, oh! Conquered by deadly treachery,
        to fall to such an ignoble bed
        by a wife's hand and a double-edged blade.
        CLYTEMNESTRA: Did *he* not also lay upon the house
1670   a treacherous destruction?
        The victim, my daughter, raised from his loins,
        Iphigeneia, whom I mourn for.
        What he did is what he suffered for.
        Let him not boast of anything in the house of death,
1675   for he paid for what he had done
        with death by the mischief of the sword.
        CHORUS: I am all bewildered about what road to take
        as the house falls;
        my wits are deserted by their skillful carefulness.
1680   I fear the crash of the bloody torrent of rain
        that will shake the house to its foundation.
        Now it is a shower no longer.
        Fate is whetting its justice on other whetstones
        for another deed of injury.
1685   Earth, Earth, would you had received me
        before I lived to see him in his lowly couch
        in a silver-sided bath.
        Who shall bury him? Who shall keen him?
        Will you dare to do this, to make lament for him,
1690   you who killed him, your husband?
        Will you accomplish for his soul a grace no grace
        as thanks for his great deeds?
        Who shall stand at the grave and chant
        a praise of the hero
1695   with tears in the eye and truthful sorrow at heart?
        CLYTEMNESTRA: The care of that concerns you not at all.
        It is by our hand that he fell, that he died,
        and we shall bury him

with no cries of mourning from this house.
But his daughter Iphigeneia, as is right,   1700
will welcome her father by the swift-flowing passage
over the River of Sorrows
and throw her arms around him and kiss him.
CHORUS: This is but the exchange of insult for insult;
it is hard to judge the issue of such a fight.   1705
The pirate plunders the pirate,
the killer pays for the killing.
Still there remains, as long as Zeus remains on his
    throne,
the rule that he who has acted shall suffer accordingly.
That is the divine law.   1710
Who shall expel from the house the brood of curses?
The whole race is welded to destruction.
CLYTEMNESTRA: In what you say now, the prophecy
    has become truth.
For my part, I am willing to make a sworn compact
with the evil spirit of this house   1715
to be satisfied with things as they are, however bad,
on condition that he, in the days to come,
may go from our house and wear out some other
    breed
with murders of one another in the family.
I will be utterly content with a small part of wealth, 1720
if I can banish from these halls
the madness of mutual bloodletting.

(Enter Aegisthus.)

AEGISTHUS: O happy light, day of justified revenge!
Now I will say that the gods
in watchfulness so high above the earth   1725
still bear an eye on the sorrows of mortals to avenge
    them.
Now I take pleasure to have seen this man
lying here in the robes that were
the nets of the Furies for him,
paying for the plots his father's hand contrived.   1730
For Atreus, ruler of this land, was this man's father,
and his brother Thyestes was my father.
Both were Pelops's sons; this is the plain story.
The two of them were in dispute about the throne,
and Atreus banished my father from city and home.   1735
The unlucky Thyestes later returned,
a suppliant at Atreus's hearth, and found safety
    there —
I mean for his own part, for he did not die
nor stained his fatherland with blood.
But the vile Atreus, father of the dead man here,   1740
with show of eagerness rather than love,
gave my father a banquet of welcome.
He pretended to celebrate a day of feasting
on flesh slaughtered for meat,
in all hospitality,   1745
but the meat he gave my father was his own
    children's.
The feet and the ends of the fingers he put apart and
    hid,
as the guests sat man by man at separate tables.
So Thyestes in ignorance ate the other parts,

1750 a meal that brought a curse, as you see, on all the
      race.
Later, when he discovered what awful act he had
      committed,
he moaned aloud, recoiled, and vomited up the
      bloody mess.
"A doom intolerable will overtake," he said,
"the house of Pelops."
1755 He kicked the dinner over to back the oath,
crying, "So perish every one of all your breed."
That is why you can see this man fallen dead here,
and I am justly the one who stitched together his
      murder.
I was the third son, and while I was still in
      swaddling clothes
1760 he drove me out along with my luckless father.
But when I grew to manhood, justice brought me
      back.
And so I laid my hand on him, though not face to
      face;
mine was the whole contriving of the evil plot.
So glorious the result,
1765 that now I would welcome death itself,
having seen him in the traps of justice.
CHORUS: Aegisthus, I do not respect insolence
at the moment of calamity.
Do you say that with aforethought you killed
      Agamemnon,
1770 that you alone planned this miserable murder?
In that case, I do not think your life will escape
the justice of the public curse, the stoning.
That's what I think.
AEGISTHUS: Do you talk back to me, you who sit at the
      lower oar,
1775 when we are in possession of the upper deck?
You will find out, despite your age,
how uncomfortable such learning is for an old man,
when discretion is the lesson set.
Chains in old age and hunger's pangs
1780 are the very sharpest healing prophets of the mind.
Don't you see this when you see?
Kick not against the pricks, lest your own striking
      hurt you.
CHORUS: Woman, you who were his housekeeper
and at the same time sullied his bed,
did you plot his death when the victors were newly
1785 home
and he had been their general?
AEGISTHUS: These words of yours are true progenitors
of sorrows.
Yours is a tongue the opposite of Orpheus's:
he led all things his captive through the joy of his
      own voice,
but you with silly yappings arouse others to lead
1790 *you* captive.
Once you are mastered, you'll be a tamer animal.
CHORUS: I suppose you'll be the sovereign of the
      Argives,
you, who when you plotted this man's murder
didn't dare to do the deed with your own hand.

AEGISTHUS: Well, no. The treachery was a woman's
      part,   1795
clearly so. I would be suspected as his old enemy.
But his wealth will give me a base to rule the citizens,
and the disobedient man I will yoke in heavy chains;
he will not be, I assure you, like a full-fed young
      trace horse.
No, unwelcome hunger and a dark cell   1800
will see him through into submission.
CHORUS: Why didn't you kill him yourself, with your
      cowardly soul?
No, your partner, the woman, did the killing,
to be the pollution of the land and of the gods of the
      land.
But I tell you, Orestes still sees the light of day, 1805
that he may come home, and with good luck on his
      side
be conquerer and the death of both of you.
AEGISTHUS: Since you're resolved to act and talk like
      this,
you'll soon know —
here, my bodyguards, this is your work, right here. 1810
CHORUS: Here, let each one of you be ready, hand on
      sword hilt.
AEGISTHUS: I, too, hold the hilt of my sword.
I will face my death.
CHORUS: You talk of death; I welcome it. But I will try
      my chances.   1815
CLYTEMNESTRA: No, dearest, no. Let us do no further
      evils.
Those that there are, are many, a bloody harvest;
we have a good store of calamity.
No, no bloodletting.
Good old men, off with you to your houses.   1820
Yield to what must be, before you suffer.
What we did had to be done.
If this should be all of troubles, I would gladly
      welcome it,
though struck with misfortune
by the heavy hoof of the evil spirit.   1825
That is a woman's word, if anyone should think it
worth heeding.
AEGISTHUS: No, but to have them letting their tongues
blossom in insolence, to throw their empty threats
      about —
"That they would try their chances"—   1830
You lack all brains, so to abuse your master.
CHORUS: It does not fit an Argive to fawn on a villain.
AEGISTHUS: I will get even with you in the days to come.
CHORUS: Not if the Spirit brings Orestes home.
AEGISTHUS: I know the diet of exiles is rich in hope. 1835
CHORUS: Yes, do things, grow fat, pollute justice —
      while you can.
AEGISTHUS: You know you will pay me for your
      foolishness.
CHORUS: Boast, do; be bold — a cock beside your hen.
CLYTEMNESTRA: Do not pay heed to their vain
      yappings. I
and you together will make all things well,   1840
for we are masters of this house.

COMMENTARIES

Albrecht Dihle (b. 1923)

Orestes and the Gods   *1991*

TRANSLATED BY CLARE KROJZL

Dihle, in his A History of Greek Literature, *takes up the role of the old and the new gods in the* Oresteia. *In Dihle's view the question of interpretation of the will of the gods and of the law becomes central to the drama.*

The act of vengeance perpetrated by Orestes[1] is by the express orders of the god Apollo, but the deed draws the attention of other deities responsible for the sanctity of the bond between mother and child. These, the Erinyes or Furies (goddesses of curses), hound the matricide mercilessly from one town to the next. He finds only fleeting refuge with Apollo in the temple at Delphi. The third play in the trilogy, *The Eumenides*, resolves this apparently hopeless conflict. A legal battle is fought out at the Areopagus, the time-honored murder court of the city of Athens, which convenes under the aegis of the goddess Athena. Apollo, representing the new order established by the Olympian gods, defends the deed of Orestes by pointing out the necessity of punishing the murder of a husband and king. The Erinyes, on the other hand, invoke the earlier order, calling for the expiation of matricide. The Areopagus dismisses the case against Orestes, at the same time mollifying the Erinyes by introducing their cult into Athens, where they are henceforth to dwell as *The Eumenides*, the gracious bestowers of blessings.

Aeschylus's theological interpretation of myth is based on a firm belief in the essential justice of the divine order of the universe. The idea of this justice making the gods into defenders of law and order among humankind had already been put forward by Hesiod, and later with a heightened sense of political responsibility by Solon. The notion that the actions of gods and heroes related in myth ought to correspond to the moral standards of his own day had moreover been the most important motif in the mythical interpretations of Pindar. What was new about Aeschylus's conception is that the law established by Zeus was more than a body of fixed rules whose observance was watched over by the gods with a system of reward and punishment. Instead, it was seen as a vital force constantly proving itself in ever new manifestations, and even able to resolve conflict which seemed hopeless from the human viewpoint. Apollo's claim is as valid as that of the Erinyes, so that Orestes, who must satisfy both, seems bound to be destroyed by this dilemma, as two divine powers conduct a mutual conflict with each other through his action and suffering, without releasing him from his moral responsibility. The trial instigated by Athena, the motherless daughter of Zeus, allows the dynamic nature of his law to manifest itself clearly, thereby resolving a unique, unforeseeable conflict

---

[1]To avenge the murder of his father, Agamemnon.

through a decision that is specific to the situation, but also creates a new order, while at the same time reconciling two equally valid claims that had seemed to be hopelessly at odds. Nevertheless, it is in human action, carried out with a consciousness of responsibility, that this conflict between divine powers is acted out and resolved. Were it not for human beings, as is demonstrated using the metaphor of the court of Athenian citizens, the law of Zeus would have no scope in which to unfold. Human dignity consists in becoming the necessary partner of the gods, and in the right order of human society matching the divine order as closely as possible.

Lois Spatz (b. 1940)
ORESTEIA: TRILOGY PRESERVED   *1982*

In her examination of Aeschylus, Lois Spatz discusses how he conceived of the three plays of the Oresteia *as a unified whole. She also provides some of the key background information that most of the original Greek audience would have known. Spatz connects the plays to events of the time in Athens, so we can better understand* Agamemnon *in the context of history and the other two plays to which it is linked.*

The *Oresteia* won first prize at the Great Dionysia of 458 B.C., just two years before Aeschylus's death. The three tragedies, *Agamemnon, The Libation Bearers (Choephoroi),* and *The Eumenides,* were presented in a sequence which concluded with a lost satyr play, *Proteus,* about the wanderings of Agamemnon's brother, Menelaus. Modern readers often study *Agamemnon* alone, although it is extremely difficult to follow and does not resolve the dramatic questions it raises, but the ancient spectators would have considered the drama as a first act in a larger whole. The trilogy is composed so that the *Agamemnon* and *The Libation Bearers* define a conflict which can only be resolved by a third and different action. *Agamemnon,* taken alone, seems an obscure play, for the extreme complexity of image, diction, and action is a dramatic device which conveys the moral, emotional, and political confusion of the initial situation. In the second play, where the next generation of characters better understand their positions and motivations, the action is clearer. In *The Eumenides,* Aeschylus illuminates the issues underlying the action and resolves them.

Because one must study the parts together to appreciate the whole, the trilogy will be treated as a single play. Although Aeschylus begins his drama *in medias res,* as Agamemnon is about to return from Troy, the audience was familiar with the stories concerning the crimes of Agamemnon's father, Atreus. Therefore, it would have suspected with increasing dread some relationship between the events of the present generation and the horrors of the past, which the poet does not mention directly until the last third of the play, when the curse on the House of Atreus becomes a central theme of the trilogy. Atreus was head of the house and ruler of Argos when Thyestes, his brother, raped his wife and attempted to steal his property and power. First Atreus exiled his brother, but judging that penalty inadequate, he invited him home and cooked and served Thyestes' children to him at a feast celebrating the reunion. When Thyestes discovered he had eaten his own sons, he cursed Atreus, promising revenge, and left Argos with his one remaining son, Aegisthus.

The curse arising from this horrible act brought misfortune to the next generation. Atreus's sons, Agamemnon and Menelaus, had married sisters, Clytemnestra and Helen, respectively. Helen, the most beautiful woman in Greece, was seduced and stolen away from the hearth of the House of Atreus by their guest, Paris (Alexander), son of King Priam of Troy. Paris's adultery was a violation of the sacred relationship between guest and host protected by Zeus Xenios ("Guest-Friend"). Therefore, the Argives considered it a serious crime demanding revenge, and launched the Trojan War, subject of the *Iliad* and epic cycle.

The Greek warriors who had sworn to support Menelaus met at Aulis under the leadership of Agamemnon, elder brother of the wronged husband and most powerful king in Greece. When rough seas prevented the fleet's passage to Troy, the priest Calchas informed Agamemnon that he must sacrifice his daughter, Iphigenia, to the goddess Artemis in order to calm the winds. Agamemnon, confident of the justice of the war and fearful of his restive troops, decided to slaughter Iphigenia so that the expedition could set sail.

Aeschylus begins his drama just as the Argives receive the news that Agamemnon has defeated Troy. The audience would know, however, from such sources as the *Odyssey*, the return stories of the cycle, and the *Oresteia* by the lyric poet Stesichorus, that, during these ten years of war, Clytemnestra had sent her son Orestes away and taken Aegisthus as a lover, and that the Greek soldiers in Troy had committed crimes which were punished on the return voyages. Aeschylus's gradual and sparing presentation of this background increases the mystery surrounding the events of the play itself.

Act I and Act II are both return and revenge stories. In *Agamemnon* several characters in sequence, the watchman, citizen/chorus, Queen Clytemnestra, and the herald, express hope and anxiety about the general's experiences in the Trojan War and his safe victorious return. Tension builds because the expectation of victory as the just punishment of Troy is constantly undercut by suggestions that the general and his men have themselves committed atrocities to insure victory. In fact, the Greek fleet has already been punished, destroyed by a god-sent storm at sea. At the mid-point in the drama, Agamemnon enters in triumph with his war prize, Cassandra, and is welcomed with Eastern pomp by his queen, Clytemnestra, who entices him to enter the palace on a luxurious tapestry. This greeting initiates the revenge story. After Agamemnon's entrance into the palace, Cassandra, the Trojan priestess of Apollo, predicts his murder and hers and relates it to the bloody history of the House of Atreus. Then Clytemnestra murders Agamemnon and his mistress and justifies her deed to the citizens as divine retribution for his sacrifice of their daughter, Iphigenia. Aegisthus, Clytemnestra's lover, later explains that history more precisely, justifying his part in Agamemnon's death as revenge for his uncle Atreus's slaughter of his brothers. Thus, the cycle of revenge as punishment which demands further revenge is clearly established by the end of the play. It is equally clear that Clytemnestra's act of revenge cannot break the cycle. She and her lover plan to replace Agamemnon as rulers of Argos, but they respond with threats of violence to the chorus's protests against their tyranny. *Agamemnon* ends with the chorus cowed for the moment, but predicting that Orestes, Agamemnon's son, sent away by Clytemnestra, will someday return to avenge the death of his father and assume his rightful place as head of the family and ruler of the state.

Act II, *The Libation Bearers,* also exhibits the return and revenge patterns, in dramatizing the murder of Agamemnon's murderers. First Orestes returns, fulfilling the hopes of his sister, Electra, and the chorus of household slaves, captives from Troy loyal to their conqueror, Agamemnon. Orestes later learns that his return has also fulfilled the nightmares of his mother, Clytemnestra. He enters, not as a conquering hero like his father, to be warmly welcomed and then duped, but as an exile in disguise, announcing his own death in order to deceive his mother and her lover. He has been spurred on by Apollo's demand that he avenge his father's death or suffer dire punishments, but he also acts from private motives as son, disinherited heir, and legitimate ruler of Argos. After praying with his sister and the chorus at the tomb of Agamemnon to invoke the aid of the gods and the powerful dead, he tricks Clytemnestra, kills Aegisthus, and then confronts his mother again. She tries to dissuade him, but he leads her into the house for the slaughter. When Orestes afterwards proclaims the justice of the matricide to the satisfied chorus, he does not gloat, as his mother before him did, for he recognizes that his deed was a crime as well as a necessity. He confesses that his pollution is a danger to himself and his community and prepares to leave Argos to be purified of blood guilt by Apollo. As he announces his plans, however, madness overtakes him; he seems to see the very Furies (Erinyes) from Hell descending on him to avenge his matricide. The chorus is puzzled that this act has not ended the chain of reciprocal revenge in the House of Atreus, but sends him forward to Apollo with prayers for success.

Act III, *The Eumenides,* introduces a new story pattern, "suppliant received"; a new setting, the shrines of the gods in Delphi and Athens; and new characters, the gods themselves — Apollo, the Furies, and Athena. The play begins at the shrine of Apollo in Delphi, where Orestes has arrived as a suppliant begging asylum from the Furies and release from blood guilt. Although Apollo has temporarily drugged the Furies into sleep, he cannot permanently protect Orestes from their vengeance. The god directs the matricide to the shrine of Athena in the Acropolis of Athens, where the goddess will release him from the curse. Once Orestes has fled, the ghost of Clytemnestra angrily arouses the sleeping Furies and sends them to track their prey. Orestes arrives in Athens and clings to the goddess's shrine, but the Furies enter soon after and threaten to destroy him. Athena returns just in time, and after questioning Orestes and the chorus of Furies, she decides the conflict is too important for her to resolve alone. Instead, she establishes a homicide court (modeled on the murder trials of the Court of the Areopagus) where citizen-judges (dicasts) will hear arguments for both sides and decide between them. The two present their cases, with Apollo supporting Orestes' plea. When the jury's vote is equally split, Orestes is set free by Athena's order. Before he returns home, he thanks Apollo, Athena, and the court, promising eternal peace between Argos and Athens and wishing the city prosperity and victory forever. The Furies, incensed by the verdict, call down curses on Athens, but Athena persuades them to become honored participants in the new procedure, ever punishing injustice, but showering blessings on the good as well. When they accept her offer, they exchange their loathsome black garments for the red robes of metics (foreign residents in Athens), a visible sign of their transformation from Furies to Eumenides ("Kindly Ones"). The trilogy ends with a torchlight procession, similar to the Panathenaic Festival, in which the citizens escort the goddesses to their new home, a hallowed cave at the foot of the Acropolis.

It is a long way from the polluted House of Atreus in Argos, whose bloody Furies roost like metics on the roof (*L.B.,* 1023), to the clear bright light of Athens, with its court system, public festivals, rites of Apollo, and the patronage of Zeus's daughter, Athena. Aeschylus has chosen a primitive myth about a blood-vendetta which extends for generations and includes cannibalism and child sacrifice. But he has dramatized the saga in a way which makes it relevant to his fifth-century audience. In none of the earlier versions of the story (i.e., *Odyssey, Cypria, Nostoi,* Stesichorus's *Oresteia*) was Orestes freed by a verdict of the Court of the Areopagus in Athens. Aeschylus originated this resolution so that he could trace the development of human justice — from the blood-vendetta carried out by the family with the support of the Furies who automatically avenge kindred bloodshed, through the purification rituals performed at the shrines of Apollo, to its culmination in the state court system, established by Athena with Zeus's blessing.[1] In dramatizing the progress of justice from vendetta to trial, he is also tracing the evolution of social institutions, from family and clan united by kindred blood, through cult united by ritual and a common patron, up to its perfection in the democratic polis, exemplified by Athens, where the families were ruled by law, the gods supported the new institutions, and the citizens united into a harmonious and effective whole.[2] No Athenian could sit unmoved while Athena voted like a citizen according to the procedures established in mythic time, but still in effect in 458 B.C. Nor could he watch without pride the imitation of his great Panathenaic Festival and the respectful acceptance of the dread Furies as metics in his own state. Thus would the contemporary Athenian recognize the ideals and glory of his city in the resolution of the myth.

But if this resolution represents the culmination of human progress, at least two problems disturbed the polis in 458. The Court of the Areopagus (the aristocratic body of ex-archons which once functioned as supreme overseer of the laws of the land) had recently been a target of the democratic reform. In 462, Ephialtes and Pericles carried through the Assembly an act which removed the court's right to interfere with democratic legislation and reduced its jurisdiction to cases of premeditated murder. The aristocrats were incensed and Ephialtes himself was assassinated. Although Aeschylus's own position on this democratic reform cannot be determined with certainty, in *The Eumenides* the court's function as a tribunal for murder is given a divine validation. Ephialtes and Pericles had also favored challenging Spartan hegemony in Greece by allying with Argos, Sparta's main rival in the Peloponnese. In 461, the leader of the aristocrats, Cimon, was ostracized and the alliance with Argos approved. This change, which also produced fierce debate in the ensuing years, received attention from Aeschylus in the *Oresteia.* Orestes is clearly a political representative of Argos who allies himself with Athens, seemingly with Aeschylus's approval.[3]

---

[1]For a different opinion of Apollo's place, see George Derwent Thomson, *Aeschylus and Athens: A Study in the Social Origins of Drama,* 2nd ed. (London: Lawrence & Wishart, 1967), pp. 259–61, and R. P. Winnington-Ingram, "The Role of Apollo in the Oresteia," *Classical Review* 47 (1933): 97–104. On the relation of purification to the laws on homicide, see D. M. MacDowell, *Athenian Homicide Law in the Age of the Orators* (Manchester: University of Manchester Press, 1963), pp. 4–5, 141–50.

[2]The family remained important, however, even in the legal prosecution for homicide, as MacDowell points out (*Athenian Homicide,* pp. 8–30). For a study of this evolution, see Richard Kuhns, *The House, the City, and the Judge: The Growth of Moral Awareness in the "Oresteia"* (Indianapolis: Bobbs-Merrill, 1962). George Thomson also traces the development from tribe to state and its influence on the form and ideas of drama, and on the *Oresteia* in particular (*Aeschylus,* pp. 229–78).

[3]The debate about Aeschylus's position on the reforms is summarized by Anthony J. Podlecki in *The Political Background of Aeschylean Tragedy* (Ann Arbor: U of Michigan P, 1966), pp. 81–92.

It is not as important to label Aeschylus an aristocrat or radical as it is to recognize in the entire trilogy a paradigm for necessary compromise between disparate elements in the state.[4] If political vendettas are not controlled, there can be no civil order and consequently no peace and prosperity. Traditional groups like the Furies must be reconciled to the new system, treated with honor, and allowed to serve the state so that they can preserve for themselves and the community whichever of their principles remain valuable. Athena, establishing the Court of the Areopagus, defines its functions in words which echo the Furies' defense of their grim penalties:

> Here the reverence
> of citizens, their fear and kindred do-no-wrong
> shall hold by day and in the blessing of night alike
> all while the people do not muddy their own laws
> with foul infusions. But if bright water you stain
> with mud, you nevermore will find it fit to drink.
> No anarchy, no rule of a single master. Thus
> I advise my citizens to govern and to grace,
> and not to cast fear utterly from your city. What
> man who fears nothing at all is ever righteous? Such
> be your just terrors, and you may deserve and have
> salvation for your citadel, your land's defence
> such as is nowhere else found among men . . .
> (*The Eumenides*, 11. 690–702)[5]

Her admonitions provide not only an eternal definition of good government, but also a timely warning to a population recently embroiled in civil strife.

---

[4]A forceful spokesman for this view is E. R. Dodds, "Morals and Politics," from *The Ancient Concept of Progress and Other Essays* (Oxford UP, 1973), pp. 54–62.

[5]I have used the translation of Richmond Lattimore which appears in *The Complete Greek Tragedies: Aeschylus I* (New York, n.d.).

Sophocles

Sophocles (c. 496–c. 406 B.C.) won more prizes than any other tragedian in the Greek drama competitions, and he never came in lower than second place. His first victory was against the grand old master Aeschylus in 468 B.C. Sophocles' last plays, which he wrote in his eighties, were among his greatest. We have fragments of some ninety plays or poems and seven complete tragedies, while records suggest that his output numbered something over a hundred and twenty plays.

Sophocles lived in interesting times. He would have recalled the first defeat of the Persians in 490 B.C., when the news came by a messenger who had run twenty-six miles from Marathon to Athens. In his adolescence, Athens achieved its astonishing and decisive victory over the Persians at Salamis. His popularity as a tragedian and as a statesman coincided with the development of an imperial attitude in Athens. Athenian society honored the greatness of men like Aeschylus, Sophocles, Euripides, the historian Herodotus, and all the politicians and artists that Pericles drew to Athens for its rebuilding. It was a golden age shadowed by war.

Sophocles was both sociable and religious, serving as the priest of several religious cults. He was also a man of action, popular enough to be elected as one of Athens's twelve generals; he participated with Pericles in the Samian War (440–439 B.C.). His plays — especially *Antigone* (441 B.C.), which preceded his election to generalship — often have deep political concerns. One of his primary themes concerns the relation of the individual to the *polis,* the state itself. Since the Greeks valued the individual and at the same time regarded the *polis* as a sacred bulwark against a return to barbarism, conflicts between the individual and the *polis* were immensely painful.

When Sophocles began writing, he broke with an old tradition. From the time of Thespis (mid-sixth century B.C.), each playwright acted in his own plays. Aeschylus probably did so, but it is on record that Sophocles' voice was not strong enough to permit him to take a part in his plays. He played the lyre well enough to appear onstage, and he participated in a game of ball in one of his plays, but he did not appear as an actor. He also introduced innovations in the structure of his plays by changing the size of the chorus to fifteen and by adding painted scenery, more props, and a third actor to the two that Aeschylus and other tragedians had used. Sophocles wrote some of his plays with specific actors in mind, much as Shakespeare, Molière, and many other first-rank playwrights have done.

Sophocles was versed in the epics of Homer. Some of his plays derive from the *Iliad* or the *Odyssey,* although Sophocles always adapted the material of others to his own purposes. His nickname was the Attic Bee because he could investigate wonderful pieces of literature and always return with a useful idea. The approach he took to the structure of the play, measuring the effect of the rising action of complication and then ensuring that the moment of recognition occurred at the same time the falling action began, was recognized as a

Bust of Sophocles. The Capitoline Museum, Rome.

supremely elegant skill. Nowhere is this illustrated with more completeness than in *Oedipus Rex*.

The plays of Aeschylus, powerful though they are, do not have the same delicacy of construction as do Sophocles'. They are forceful but, in terms of structure, somewhat simpler. The structure of the plays of Euripides, Sophocles' successor, was never as fully worked out; and when Aristotle discussed the nature of tragedy in his *Poetics*, it was to Sophocles he turned for a model, not to the other two master playwrights of the genre.

Besides the Oedipus plays, Sophocles' other surviving plays are *Philoctetes, Ajax, Trachiniae,* and *Elektra.*

OEDIPUS REX

Oedipus Rex is one of three plays by Sophocles that treat the fate of Oedipus and his children. The plays were written over a period of thirty years: *Antigone* (first produced in 441 B.C.), *Oedipus Rex* (produced approximately fifteen years later, between 430 and 427 B.C.), and *Oedipus at Colonus* (produced in

401 B.C., after Sophocles' death). When these plays are produced together today, they are usually given in an order that follows the events of Oedipus's and Antigone's lives — *Oedipus Rex, Oedipus at Colonus,* and *Antigone* — almost like the trilogies that Athenian audiences often viewed in the early years of the drama competitions. In fact, they were never a unified trilogy, and one of Sophocles' distinctions is that he did not present as trilogies plays that were thematically related, as poets before him had done.

The original narratives of the Oedipus plays were known to Sophocles' audience — with the possible exception of the story of Antigone — and one of the special pleasures for the audience watching the action of *Oedipus Rex* was that they knew the outcome. They watched for the steps, the choices, that led Oedipus to his fate.

Oedipus Rex is the story of a noble man who seeks knowledge that in the end destroys him. His greatness is measured in part by the fact that the gods have prophesied his fate: the gods do not take interest in insignificant men. Before the action of the play begins, Oedipus has set out to discover whether he is truly the son of Polybos and Merope, the people who have reared him. He learns from the oracle of Apollo at Delphi, the most powerful interpreter of the voice and the will of the gods, that he will kill his father and marry his mother. His response is overwhelmingly human: he has seen his *moira,* his fate, and he cannot accept it. His reaction is to do everything he can, including leaving his homeland as quickly as possible, to avoid the possibility of killing Polybos and marrying Merope.

The Greek audience would have known that Oedipus was a descendant of Kadmos, founder of Thebes, who had sown the dragon teeth that produced the Spartoi (the sown men). Legend determined that the rulership of Thebes would be in dispute, with fraternal rivalry resembling that of the Spartoi, who fought and killed each other. This bloody legacy follows Oedipus, but it also reaches into all the plays of the trilogy. For example, in *Antigone* we learn that Antigone's brothers Polyneices and Eteocles killed each other in the shadow of the city walls. Thus, the fate Oedipus attempts to avoid actually dooms most of the characters in the three plays, including his true father, Laios, and his daughter Antigone.

Sophocles develops the drama in terms of IRONY — the disjunction between what seems to be true and what is true. Knowing the outcome of the action, the audience savors the ironic moments from the beginning of the play to the end. Oedipus flees his homeland to avoid fulfilling the prophecy, only to run headlong into the fate foretold by the oracle. He unwittingly returns to his original home, Thebes, and to his parents, murdering Laios, his true father, at a crossroads on the way and marrying Iokaste, his true mother, and becoming king of Thebes. The blind seer Teiresias warns Oedipus not to pursue the truth, but, in human fashion, Oedipus refuses to heed Teiresias's warnings. When the complete truth becomes clear to Oedipus, he physically blinds himself in horror and expiation. Like the blind Teiresias, Oedipus must now look inward for the truth, without the distractions of surface experiences.

The belief that the moral health of the ruler directly affected the security of the *polis* was widespread in Athenian Greece. Indeed, the Athenians regarded their state as fragile — like a human being whose health, physical and moral, could change suddenly. Because the Greeks were concerned for the well-being of their state, the *polis* often figures in the tragedies. The Sophoclean Oedipus trilogy is usually called the Theban plays, a nomenclature that reminds us that the story of Oedipus can be read as the story of an individual or as the story of a state.

Oedipus Rex examines the tension between and interdependence of the individual and the state. The agricultural and ritual basis of the Dionysian festivals — in which Greek drama developed — underscores the importance the Greeks attached to the individual's dependence on the state that feeds him and on the proper ways of doing things. This could be planting and harvesting or worshiping the gods or living as part of a political entity.

The underlying conflict in the play is political. The political relationship of human beings to the gods, the arbiters of their fate, is dramatized in Oedipus's relationship with the seer Teiresias. If he had his way, Oedipus might disregard Teiresias entirely. But Oedipus cannot command everything, even as ruler. His incomplete knowledge, despite his wisdom, is symptomatic of the limitations of every individual.

The contrast of Oedipus and Kreon, Iokaste's brother, is one of political style. Oedipus is a fully developed character who reveals himself as sympathetic but willful. He acts on his misunderstanding of the prophecy without reconsulting the oracle. He marries Iokaste and blinds himself without reconsulting the oracle. Kreon, who is much less complicated, never acts without consulting the oracle and thoughtfully reflecting on the oracle's message. Oedipus sometimes behaves tyrannically, and he appears eager for power. Kreon takes power only when forced to do so.

The depth of Sophocles' character development was unmatched, except by his contemporary Euripides, for almost two thousand years. Sophocles' drama is one of psychological development. His audiences saw Oedipus as a model for human greatness but also as a model for the human capacity to fall from a great height. The play is about the limits of human knowledge; it is also about the limits and frailty of human happiness.

Oedipus Rex in Performance

Oedipus Rex has enjoyed great popularity since its first performance. The Greeks, who originally restricted their plays to one performance, eventually began to revive plays of the masters. *Oedipus* was one of the most popular. In modern times, performance has been almost constant since the seventeenth century. Great dramatists have produced it in their own adaptations — Corneille (1659), John Dryden (1679), Voltaire (1718), William Butler Yeats (1923), and Jean Cocteau (1931) — proving the durability of the themes and the adaptability of the play. The early American performances (beginning in 1881) were in Greek but soon gave way to English. Modern versions have been both very traditional, such as those developed by the Royal Shakespeare Company in the 1970s, and experimental, such as that of Peter Brook (1968). Brook's production began with a huge golden cube reflecting brilliant light like the sun and ended with the ritual unveiling of a giant phallus. John Gielgud played Oedipus and Irene Worth, all in black, played Iokaste. Currently, Greek companies perform the play regularly in the theater of Dionysus in Athens as well as in Epidaurus and elsewhere.

Sophocles (c. 496–c. 406 B.C.)

OEDIPUS REX

c. 430 B.C.

TRANSLATED BY DUDLEY FITTS AND ROBERT FITZGERALD

Characters

OEDIPUS, *King of Thebes, supposed son of Polybos and Merope, King and Queen of Corinth*
IOKASTE, *wife of Oedipus and widow of the late King Laios*
KREON, *brother of Iokaste, a prince of Thebes*
TEIRESIAS, *a blind seer who serves Apollo*
PRIEST
MESSENGER, *from Corinth*
SHEPHERD, *former servant of Laios*
SECOND MESSENGER, *from the palace*
CHORUS OF THEBAN ELDERS
CHORAGOS, *leader of the Chorus*
ANTIGONE *and* ISMENE, *young daughters of Oedipus and Iokaste. They appear in the Exodos but do not speak.*
SUPPLIANTS, GUARDS, SERVANTS

The Scene: *Before the palace of Oedipus, King of Thebes. A central door and two lateral doors open onto a platform which runs the length of the facade. On the platform, right and left, are altars; and three steps lead down into the orchestra, or chorus-ground. At the beginning of the action these steps are crowded by suppliants who have brought branches and chaplets of olive leaves and who sit in various attitudes of despair. Oedipus enters.*

PROLOGUE°

OEDIPUS: My children, generations of the living
　In the line of Kadmos,° nursed at his ancient hearth:
　Why have you strewn yourselves before these altars
　In supplication, with your boughs and garlands?
5　The breath of incense rises from the city
　With a sound of prayer and lamentation.
　　　　　　　　　　　　　　　　Children,
　I would not have you speak through messengers,
　And therefore I have come myself to hear you —
　I, Oedipus, who bear the famous name.
　(*To a Priest.*) You, there, since you are eldest in the
10　　company,
　Speak for them all, tell me what preys upon you,
　Whether you come in dread, or crave some blessing:

Prologue: Portion of the play explaining the background and current action.　**2. Kadmos:** Founder of Thebes.

Tell me, and never doubt that I will help you
In every way I can; I should be heartless
Were I not moved to find you suppliant here.　　　15
PRIEST: Great Oedipus, O powerful king of Thebes!
You see how all the ages of our people
Cling to your altar steps: here are boys
Who can barely stand alone, and here are priests
By weight of age, as I am a priest of God,　　　20
And young men chosen from those yet unmarried;
As for the others, all that multitude,
They wait with olive chaplets in the squares,
At the two shrines of Pallas,° and where Apollo°
Speaks in the glowing embers.
　　　　　　　　　　　Your own eyes　　　25
Must tell you: Thebes is tossed on a murdering sea
And can not lift her head from the death surge.
A rust consumes the buds and fruits of the earth;
The herds are sick; children die unborn,
And labor is vain. The god of plague and pyre　　　30
Raids like detestable lightning through the city,
And all the house of Kadmos is laid waste,
All emptied, and all darkened: Death alone
Battens upon the misery of Thebes.

You are not one of the immortal gods, we know;　　　35
Yet we have come to you to make our prayer
As to the man surest in mortal ways
And wisest in the ways of God. You saved us
From the Sphinx,° that flinty singer, and the tribute
We paid to her so long; yet you were never　　　40
Better informed than we, nor could we teach you:
A god's touch, it seems, enabled you to help us.

Therefore, O mighty power, we turn to you:
Find us our safety, find us a remedy,
Whether by counsel of the gods or of men.　　　45
A king of wisdom tested in the past
Can act in a time of troubles, and act well.
Noblest of men, restore
Life to your city! Think how all men call you
Liberator for your boldness long ago;　　　50
Ah, when your years of kingship are remembered,

---

24. Pallas: Pallas Athene, daughter of Zeus and goddess of wisdom.　**Apollo:** Son of Zeus and god of the sun, of light and truth.　**39. Sphinx:** A winged monster with the body of a lion and the face of a woman, the Sphinx had tormented Thebes with her riddle, killing those who could not solve it. When Oedipus solved the riddle, the Sphinx killed herself.

Let them not say *We rose, but later fell* —
Keep the State from going down in the storm!
Once, years ago, with happy augury,
55   You brought us fortune; be the same again!
No man questions your power to rule the land:
But rule over men, not over a dead city!
Ships are only hulls, high walls are nothing,
When no life moves in the empty passageways.
60 OEDIPUS: Poor children! You may be sure I know
All that you longed for in your coming here.
I know that you are deathly sick; and yet,
Sick as you are, not one is as sick as I.
Each of you suffers in himself alone
65   His anguish, not another's; but my spirit
Groans for the city, for myself, for you.

I was not sleeping, you are not waking me.
No, I have been in tears for a long while
And in my restless thought walked many ways.
70 In all my search I found one remedy,
And I have adopted it: I have sent Kreon,
Son of Menoikeus, brother of the queen,
To Delphi,° Apollo's place of revelation,
To learn there, if he can,
75   What act or pledge of mine may save the city.
I have counted the days, and now, this very day,
I am troubled, for he has overstayed his time.
What is he doing? He has been gone too long.
Yet whenever he comes back, I should do ill
80   Not to take any action the god orders.
PRIEST: It is a timely promise. At this instant
They tell me Kreon is here.
OEDIPUS: O Lord Apollo!
May his news be fair as his face is radiant!
PRIEST: Good news, I gather! he is crowned with bay,
The chaplet is thick with berries.
85 OEDIPUS: We shall soon know;
He is near enough to hear us now.   (*Enter Kreon.*)
O prince:
Brother: son of Menoikeus:
What answer do you bring us from the god?
KREON: A strong one. I can tell you, great afflictions
90   Will turn out well, if they are taken well.
OEDIPUS: What was the oracle? These vague words
Leave me still hanging between hope and fear.
KREON: Is it your pleasure to hear me with all these
Gathered around us? I am prepared to speak,
But should we not go in?
95 OEDIPUS: Speak to them all,
It is for them I suffer, more than for myself.
KREON: Then I will tell you what I heard at Delphi.
In plain words
The god commands us to expel from the land of
Thebes
100   An old defilement we are sheltering.

73. **Delphi:** Site of the oracle, source of religious authority and prophecy, under the protection of Apollo.

It is a deathly thing, beyond cure;
We must not let it feed upon us longer.
OEDIPUS: What defilement? How shall we rid ourselves
of it?
KREON: By exile or death, blood for blood. It was
Murder that brought the plague-wind on the city.   105
OEDIPUS: Murder of whom? Surely the god has named
him?
KREON: My Lord: Laios once ruled this land,
Before you came to govern us.
OEDIPUS: I know;
I learned of him from others; I never saw him.
KREON: He was murdered; and Apollo commands us
now   110
To take revenge upon whoever killed him.
OEDIPUS: Upon whom? Where are they? Where shall
we find a clue
To solve that crime, after so many years?
KREON: Here in this land, he said. Search reveals
Things that escape an inattentive man.   115
OEDIPUS: Tell me: Was Laios murdered in his house,
Or in the fields, or in some foreign country?
KREON: He said he planned to make a pilgrimage.
He did not come home again.
OEDIPUS: And was there no one,
No witness, no companion, to tell what happened?   120
KREON: They were all killed but one, and he got away
So frightened that he could remember one thing
only.
OEDIPUS: What was that one thing? One may be the
key
To everything, if we resolve to use it.
KREON: He said that a band of highwaymen attacked
them,   125
Outnumbered them, and overwhelmed the king.
OEDIPUS: Strange, that a highwayman should be so
daring —
Unless some faction here bribed him to do it.
KREON: We thought of that. But after Laios' death
New troubles arose and we had no avenger.   130
OEDIPUS: What troubles could prevent your hunting
down the killers?
KREON: The riddling Sphinx's song
Made us deaf to all mysteries but her own.
OEDIPUS: Then once more I must bring what is dark to
light.
It is most fitting that Apollo shows,   135
As you do, this compunction for the dead.
You shall see how I stand by you, as I should,
Avenging this country and the god as well,
And not as though it were for some distant friend,
But for my own sake, to be rid of evil.   140
Whoever killed King Laios might — who knows? —
Lay violent hands even on me — and soon.
I act for the murdered king in my own interest.

Come, then, my children: leave the altar steps,
Lift up your olive boughs!
                        One of you go   145

And summon the people of Kadmos to gather here.
I will do all that I can; you may tell them that.
                                        (*Exit a Page.*)
So, with the help of God,
We shall be saved — or else indeed we are lost.
150 PRIEST: Let us rise, children. It was for this we came,
And now the king has promised it.
Phoibos° has sent us an oracle; may he descend
Himself to save us and drive out the plague.

(*Exeunt*° *Oedipus and Kreon into the palace by the
central door. The Priest and the Suppliants disperse right
and left. After a short pause the Chorus enters the orchestra.*)

PARODOS° • *Strophe°* 1

CHORUS: What is God singing in his profound
Delphi of gold and shadow?
What oracle for Thebes, the Sunwhipped city?
Fear unjoints me, the roots of my heart tremble.
Now I remember, O Healer, your power, and
5   wonder:
Will you send doom like a sudden cloud, or weave it
Like nightfall of the past?
Speak to me, tell me, O
Child of golden Hope, immortal Voice.

Antistrophe° 1

Let me pray to Athene, the immortal daughter of
10   Zeus,
And to Artemis° her sister
Who keeps her famous throne in the market ring,
And to Apollo, archer from distant heaven —
O gods, descend! Like three streams leap against
15 The fires of our grief, the fires of darkness;
Be swift to bring us rest!
As in the old time from the brilliant house
Of air you stepped to save us, come again!

Strophe 2

Now our afflictions have no end,
20 Now all our stricken host lies down
And no man fights off death with his mind;
The noble plowland bears no grain,
And groaning mothers can not bear —
See, how our lives like birds take wing,

Like sparks that fly when a fire soars,   25
To the shore of the god of evening.

Antistrophe 2

The plague burns on, it is pitiless,
Though pallid children laden with death
Lie unwept in the stony ways,
And old gray women by every path   30
Flock to the strand about the altars
There to strike their breasts and cry
Worship of Phoibos in wailing prayers:
Be kind, God's golden child!

Strophe 3

There are no swords in this attack by fire,   35
No shields, but we are ringed with cries.
Send the besieger plunging from our homes
Into the vast sea-room of the Atlantic
Or into the waves that foam eastward of Thrace —
For the day ravages what the night spares —   40
Destroy our enemy, lord of the thunder!
Let him be riven by lightning from heaven!

Antistrophe 3

Phoibos Apollo, stretch the sun's bowstring,
That golden cord, until it sing for us,
Flashing arrows in heaven!
                        Artemis, Huntress,   45
Race with flaring lights upon our mountains!
O scarlet god,° O golden-banded brow,
O Theban Bacchos in a storm of Maenads,°

(*Enter Oedipus, center.*)

Whirl upon Death, that all the Undying hate!
Come with blinding torches, come in joy!   50

SCENE 1

OEDIPUS: Is this your prayer? It may be answered.
    Come,
Listen to me, act as the crisis demands,
And you shall have relief from all these evils.

Until now I was a stranger to this tale,
As I had been a stranger to the crime.   5
Could I track down the murderer without a clue?
But now, friends,
As one who became a citizen after the murder,

I make this proclamation to all Thebans:
If any man knows by whose hand Laios, son of
10   Labdakos,
Met his death, I direct that man to tell me everything,
No matter what he fears for having so long
    withheld it.
Let it stand as promised that no further trouble
Will come to him, but he may leave the land in safety.
Moreover: If anyone knows the murderer to be
15   foreign,
Let him not keep silent: he shall have his reward
    from me.
However, if he does conceal it; if any man
Fearing for his friend or for himself disobeys this
    edict,
Hear what I propose to do:

20   I solemnly forbid the people of this country,
Where power and throne are mine, ever to receive
    that man
Or speak to him, no matter who he is, or let him
Join in sacrifice, lustration, or in prayer.
I decree that he be driven from every house,
25   Being, as he is, corruption itself to us: the Delphic
Voice of Apollo has pronounced this revelation.
Thus I associate myself with the oracle
And take the side of the murdered king.

As for the criminal, I pray to God —
30   Whether it be a lurking thief, or one of a number —
I pray that that man's life be consumed in evil and
    wretchedness.
And as for me, this curse applies no less
If it should turn out that the culprit is my guest here,
Sharing my hearth.
                You have heard the penalty.
35   I lay it on you now to attend to this
For my sake, for Apollo's, for the sick
Sterile city that heaven has abandoned.
Suppose the oracle had given you no command:
Should this defilement go uncleansed for ever?
40   You should have found the murderer: your king,
A noble king, had been destroyed!
                      Now I,
Having the power that he held before me,
Having his bed, begetting children there
Upon his wife, as he would have, had he lived —
45   Their son would have been my children's brother,
If Laios had had luck in fatherhood!
(And now his bad fortune has struck him down) —
I say I take the son's part, just as though
I were his son, to press the fight for him
50   And see it won! I'll find the hand that brought
Death to Labdakos' and Polydoros' child,
Heir of Kadmos' and Agenor's line.°

51–52. Labdakos, Polydoros, Kadmos, and Agenor: Father,
grandfather, great-grandfather, and great-great-grandfather of
Laios.

And as for those who fail me,
May the gods deny them the fruit of the earth,
Fruit of the womb, and may they rot utterly!   55
Let them be wretched as we are wretched, and
    worse!

For you, for loyal Thebans, and for all
Who find my actions right, I pray the favor
Of justice, and of all the immortal gods.
CHORAGOS: Since I am under oath, my lord, I swear   60
    I did not do the murder, I can not name
    The murderer. Phoibos ordained the search;
    Why did he not say who the culprit was?
OEDIPUS: An honest question. But no man in the world
    Can make the gods do more than the gods will.   65
CHORAGOS: There is an alternative, I think —
OEDIPUS: Tell me.
    Any or all, you must not fail to tell me.
CHORAGOS: A lord clairvoyant to the lord Apollo,
    As we all know, is the skilled Teiresias.
    One might learn much about this from him, Oedipus.   70
OEDIPUS: I am not wasting time:
    Kreon spoke of this, and I have sent for him —
    Twice, in fact; it is strange that he is not here.
CHORAGOS: The other matter — that old report —
    seems useless.
OEDIPUS: What was that? I am interested in all reports.   75
CHORAGOS: The king was said to have been killed by
    highwaymen.
OEDIPUS: I know. But we have no witnesses to that.
CHORAGOS: If the killer can feel a particle of dread,
    Your curse will bring him out of hiding!
OEDIPUS: No.
    The man who dared that act will fear no curse.   80

(*Enter the blind seer Teiresias, led by a Page.*)

CHORAGOS: But there is one man who may detect the
    criminal.
    This is Teiresias, this is the holy prophet
    In whom, alone of all men, truth was born.
OEDIPUS: Teiresias: seer: student of mysteries,   *seer*
    Of all that's taught and all that no man tells,   85
    Secrets of Heaven and secrets of the earth:
    Blind though you are, you know the city lies
    Sick with plague; and from this plague, my lord,
    We find that you alone can guard or save us.

    Possibly you did not hear the messengers?   90
    Apollo, when we sent to him,
    Sent us back word that this great pestilence
    Would lift, but only if we established clearly
    The identity of those who murdered Laios.
    They must be killed or exiled.
                         Can you use   95
    Birdflight° or any art of divination
    To purify yourself, and Thebes, and me

96. Birdflight: Prophets used the flight of birds to predict the
future.

OEDIPUS: What a wicked old man you are! You'd try a stone's
    Patience! Out with it! Have you no feeling at all?
TEIRESIAS: You call me unfeeling. If you could only see   120
    The nature of your own feelings . . .
OEDIPUS: Why,
    Who would not feel as I do? Who could endure
    Your arrogance toward the city?
TEIRESIAS: What does it matter?
    Whether I speak or not, it is bound to come.
OEDIPUS: Then, if "it" is bound to come, you are
    bound to tell me.   125
TEIRESIAS: No, I will not go on. Rage as you please.
OEDIPUS: Rage? Why not!
                And I'll tell you what I think:
    You planned it, you had it done, you all but
    Killed him with your own hands: if you had eyes,
    I'd say the crime was yours, and yours alone.   130
TEIRESIAS: So? I charge you, then,
    Abide by the proclamation you have made:
    From this day forth
    Never speak again to these men or to me;
    You yourself are the pollution of this country.   135
OEDIPUS: You dare say that! Can you possibly think you have
    Some way of going free, after such insolence?
TEIRESIAS: I have gone free. It is the truth sustains me.
OEDIPUS: Who taught you shamelessness? It was not your craft.
TEIRESIAS: You did. You made me speak. I did not want to.   140
OEDIPUS: Speak what? Let me hear it again more clearly.
TEIRESIAS: Was it not clear before? Are you tempting me?
OEDIPUS: I did not understand it. Say it again.
TEIRESIAS: I say that you are the murderer whom you seek.
OEDIPUS: Now twice you have spat out infamy. You'll pay for it!   145
TEIRESIAS: Would you care for more? Do you wish to be really angry?
OEDIPUS: Say what you will. Whatever you say is worthless.
TEIRESIAS: I say you live in hideous shame with those
    Most dear to you. You can not see the evil.
OEDIPUS: Can you go on babbling like this for ever?   150
TEIRESIAS: I can, if there is power in truth.
OEDIPUS: There is:
    But not for you, not for you,
    You sightless, witless, senseless, mad old man!
TEIRESIAS: You are the madman. There is no one here
    Who will not curse you soon, as you curse me.   155
OEDIPUS: You child of total night! I would not touch you;
    Neither would any man who sees the sun.
TEIRESIAS: True: it is not from you my fate will come.
    That lies within Apollo's competence,
    As it is his concern.

    From this contagion? We are in your hands.
    There is no fairer duty
100   Than that of helping others in distress.
TEIRESIAS: How dreadful knowledge of the truth can be
    When there's no help in truth! I knew this well,
    But did not act on it; else I should not have come.
OEDIPUS: What is troubling you? Why are your eyes so
    cold?
105 TEIRESIAS: Let me go home. Bear your own fate, and I'll
    Bear mine. It is better so: trust what I say.
OEDIPUS: What you say is ungracious and unhelpful
    To your native country. Do not refuse to speak.
TEIRESIAS: When it comes to speech, your own is
    neither temperate
110   Nor opportune. I wish to be more prudent.
OEDIPUS: In God's name, we all beg you —
TEIRESIAS: You are all ignorant.
    No; I will never tell you what I know.
    Now it is my misery; then, it would be yours.
OEDIPUS: What! You do know something, and will not tell us?
115   You would betray us all and wreck the State?
TEIRESIAS: I do not intend to torture myself, or you.
    Why persist in asking? You will not persuade me.

FAR LEFT: Le Clanche Du Rand as Iokaste in Donald Sutherland and Robert Loper's production of *Oedipus Rex* at the 1975 Oregon Shakespeare Festival in Ashland. RIGHT: Philip L. Jones as the Shepherd. (Photos by Henry S. Kranzler.) BELOW: Franz Mertz's design for a 1952 production of *Oedipus Rex* directed by G. R. Sellner at Darmstadt Landestheater.

160 OEDIPUS: Tell me, who made
      These fine discoveries? Kreon? or someone else?
    TEIRESIAS: Kreon is no threat. You weave your own
      doom.
    OEDIPUS: Wealth, power, craft of statemanship!
      Kingly position, everywhere admired!
165 What savage envy is stored up against these,
      If Kreon, whom I trusted, Kreon my friend,
      For this great office which the city once
      Put in my hands unsought — if for this power
      Kreon desires in secret to destroy me!

170 He has bought this decrepit fortune-teller, this
      Collector of dirty pennies, this prophet fraud —
      Why, he is no more clairvoyant than I am!
                                          Tell us:
      Has your mystic mummery ever approached the
        truth?
      When that hellcat the Sphinx was performing here,
175 What help were you to these people?
      Her magic was not for the first man who came along:
      It demanded a real exorcist. Your birds —
      What good were they? or the gods, for the matter of
        that?
      But I came by,
180 Oedipus, the simple man, who knows nothing —
      I thought it out for myself, no birds helped me!
      And this is the man you think you can destroy,
      That you may be close to Kreon when he's king!
      Well, you and your friend Kreon, it seems to me,
185 Will suffer most. If you were not an old man,
      You would have paid already for your plot.
    CHORAGOS: We can not see that his words or yours
      Have been spoken except in anger, Oedipus,
      And of anger we have no need. How to accomplish
190 The god's will best: that is what most concerns us.
    TEIRESIAS: You are a king. But where argument's
        concerned
      I am your man, as much a king as you.
      I am not your servant, but Apollo's.
      I have no need of Kreon or Kreon's name.

195 Listen to me. You mock my blindness, do you?
      But I say that you, with both your eyes, are blind:
      You can not see the wretchedness of your life,
      Nor in whose house you live, no, nor with whom.
      Who are your father and mother? Can you tell me?
200 You do not even know the blind wrongs
      That you have done them, on earth and in the world
        below.
      But the double lash of your parents' curse will whip
        you
      Out of this land some day, with only night
      Upon your precious eyes.
205 Your cries then — where will they not be heard?
      What fastness of Kithairon° will not echo them?

    206. Kithairon: The mountain where Oedipus was abandoned
    as an infant.

      And that bridal-descant of yours — you'll know it
        then,
      The song they sang when you came here to Thebes
      And found your misguided berthing.
      All this, and more, that you can not guess at now,   210
      Will bring you to yourself among your children.

      Be angry, then. Curse Kreon. Curse my words.
      I tell you, no man that walks upon the earth
      Shall be rooted out more horribly than you.
    OEDIPUS: Am I to bear this from him? — Damnation   215
      Take you! Out of this place! Out of my sight!
    TEIRESIAS: I would not have come at all if you had not
        asked me.
    OEDIPUS: Could I have told that you'd talk nonsense,
        that
      You'd come here to make a fool of yourself, and of
        me?
    TEIRESIAS: A fool? Your parents thought me sane
        enough.   220
    OEDIPUS: My parents again! — Wait: who were my
        parents?
    TEIRESIAS: This day will give you a father, and break
        your heart.
    OEDIPUS: Your infantile riddles! Your damned
        abracadabra!
    TEIRESIAS: You were a great man once at solving riddles.
    OEDIPUS: Mock me with that if you like; you will find
        it true.   225
    TEIRESIAS: It was true enough. It brought about your
        ruin.
    OEDIPUS: But if it saved this town?
    TEIRESIAS (to the Page):   Boy, give me your hand.
    OEDIPUS: Yes, boy; lead him away.
                                      — While you are here
      We can do nothing. Go; leave us in peace.   230
    TEIRESIAS: I will go when I have said what I have to say.
      How can you hurt me? And I tell you again:
      The man you have been looking for all this time,
      The damned man, the murderer of Laios,
      That man is in Thebes. To your mind he is
        foreign-born,   235
      But it will soon be shown that he is a Theban,
      A revelation that will fail to please.
                                          A blind man,
      Who has his eyes now; a penniless man, who is rich
        now;
      And he will go tapping the strange earth with his staff.
      To the children with whom he lives now he will be   240
      Brother and father — the very same; to her
      Who bore him, son and husband — the very same
      Who came to his father's bed, wet with his father's
        blood.
      Enough. Go think that over.
      If later you find error in what I have said,   245
      You may say that I have no skill in prophecy.

      (Exit Teiresias, led by his Page.
      Oedipus goes into the palace.)

ODE° 1 • Strophe 1

CHORUS: The Delphic stone of prophecies
    Remembers ancient regicide
    And a still bloody hand.
    That killer's hour of flight has come.
5   He must be stronger than riderless
    Coursers of untiring wind,
    For the son of Zeus° armed with his father's thunder
    Leaps in lightning after him;
    And the Furies° hold his track, the sad Furies.

Ode: Song sung by the Chorus.   **7. son of Zeus:** Apollo.
9. Furies: Spirits called on to avenge crimes, especially against kin.

Antistrophe 1

Holy Parnassos'° peak of snow   10
Flashes and blinds that secret man,
That all shall hunt him down:
Though he may roam the forest shade
Like a bull gone wild from pasture
To rage through glooms of stone.   15
Doom comes down on him; flight will not avail him;
For the world's heart calls him desolate,
And the immortal voices follow, for ever follow.

10. Parnassos: Mountain sacred to Apollo.

Josef Svoboda's stage design
for M. Machacek's 1963
production of *Oedipus Rex*
in Prague.

Strophe 2

But now a wilder thing is heard
From the old man skilled at hearing Fate in the
20   wing-beat of a bird.
Bewildered as a blown bird, my soul hovers and can
        not find
Foothold in this debate, or any reason or rest of
        mind.
But no man ever brought — none can bring
Proof of strife between Thebes' royal house,
25   Labdakos' line, and the son of Polybos;°
And never until now has any man brought word
Of Laios' dark death staining Oedipus the King.

Antistrophe 2

Divine Zeus and Apollo hold
Perfect intelligence alone of all tales ever told;
And well though this diviner works, he works in his
30   own night;
No man can judge that rough unknown or trust in
        second sight,
For wisdom changes hands among the wise.
Shall I believe my great lord criminal
At a raging word that a blind old man let fall?
I saw him, when the carrion woman° faced him of
35   old,
Prove his heroic mind. These evil words are lies.

SCENE 2

KREON: Men of Thebes:
   I am told that heavy accusations
   Have been brought against me by King Oedipus.

   I am not the kind of man to bear this tamely.

5   If in these present difficulties
   He holds me accountable for any harm to him
   Through anything I have said or done — why, then,
   I do not value life in this dishonor.
   It is not as though this rumor touched upon
10   Some private indiscretion. The matter is grave.
   The fact is that I am being called disloyal
   To the State, to my fellow citizens, to my friends.
CHORAGOS: He may have spoken in anger, not from his
        mind.
KREON: But did you not hear him say I was the one
15   Who seduced the old prophet into lying?
CHORAGOS: The thing was said; I do not know how
        seriously.
KREON: But you were watching him! Were his eyes
        steady?

25. Polybos: King who adopted Oedipus.   **35. woman:** The
Sphinx.

Did he look like a man in his right mind?
CHORAGOS: I do not know.
   I can not judge the behavior of great men.
   But here is the king himself.

(*Enter Oedipus.*)

OEDIPUS: So you dared come back.   20
   Why? How brazen of you to come to my house,
   You murderer!
                    Do you think I do not know
   That you plotted to kill me, plotted to steal my
        throne?
   Tell me, in God's name: am I coward, a fool,
   That you should dream you could accomplish this?   25
   A fool who could not see your slippery game?
   A coward, not to fight back when I saw it?
   You are the fool, Kreon, are you not? hoping
   Without support or friends to get a throne?
   Thrones may be won or bought: you could do
        neither.   30
KREON: Now listen to me. You have talked; let me talk,
        too.
   You can not judge unless you know the facts.
OEDIPUS: You speak well: there is one fact; but I find it
        hard
   To learn from the deadliest enemy I have.
KREON: That above all I must dispute with you.   35
OEDIPUS: That above all I will not hear you deny.
KREON: If you think there is anything good in being
        stubborn
   Against all reason, then I say you are wrong.
OEDIPUS: If you think a man can sin against his own
        kind
   And not be punished for it, I say you are mad.   40
KREON: I agree. But tell me: what have I done to
        you?
OEDIPUS: You advised me to send for that wizard,
        did you not?
KREON: I did. I should do it again.
OEDIPUS: Very well. Now tell me:
   How long has it been since Laios —
KREON: What of Laios?
OEDIPUS: Since he vanished in that onset by the road?   45
KREON: It was long ago, a long time.
OEDIPUS: And this prophet,
   Was he practicing here then?
KREON: He was; and with honor,
        as now.
OEDIPUS: Did he speak of me at that time?
KREON: He never did,
   At least, not when I was present.
OEDIPUS: But . . . the enquiry?
   I suppose you held one?
KREON: We did, but we learned nothing.   50
OEDIPUS: Why did the prophet not speak against me
        then?
KREON: I do not know; and I am the kind of man
   Who holds his tongue when he has no facts to
        go on.

OEDIPUS: There's one fact that you know, and you
    could tell it.
KREON: What fact is that? If I know it, you shall
55   have it.
OEDIPUS: If he were not involved with you, he could
    not say
    That it was I who murdered Laios.
KREON: If he says that, you are the one that knows
    it! —
    But now it is my turn to question you.
60 OEDIPUS: Put your questions. I am no murderer.
KREON: First, then: You married my sister?
OEDIPUS: I married your sister.
KREON: And you rule the kingdom equally with her?
OEDIPUS: Everything that she wants she has from me.
KREON: And I am the third, equal to both of you?
65 OEDIPUS: That is why I call you a bad friend.
KREON: No. Reason it out, as I have done.
    Think of this first: would any sane man prefer
    Power, with all a king's anxieties,
    To that same power and the grace of sleep?
70   Certainly not I.
    I have never longed for the king's power — only his
      rights.
    Would any wise man differ from me in this?
    As matters stand, I have my way in everything
    With your consent, and no responsibilities.
75   If I were king, I should be a slave to policy.
    How could I desire a scepter more
    Than what is now mine — untroubled influence?
    No, I have not gone mad; I need no honors,
    Except those with the perquisites I have now.
80   I am welcome everywhere; every man salutes me,
    And those who want your favor seek my ear,
    Since I know how to manage what they ask.
    Should I exchange this ease for that anxiety?
    Besides, no sober mind is treasonable.
85   I hate anarchy
    And never would deal with any man who likes it.
    Test what I have said. Go to the priestess
    At Delphi, ask if I quoted her correctly.
    And as for this other thing: if I am found
90   Guilty of treason with Teiresias,
    Then sentence me to death. You have my word
    It is a sentence I should cast my vote for —
    But not without evidence!
                     You do wrong
    When you take good men for bad, bad men for
      good.
95   A true friend thrown aside — why, life itself
    Is not more precious!
                  In time you will know this well:
    For time, and time alone, will show the just man,
    Though scoundrels are discovered in a day.
CHORAGOS: This is well said, and a prudent man
    would ponder it.
100   Judgments too quickly formed are dangerous.
OEDIPUS: But is he not quick in his duplicity?
    And shall I not be quick to parry him?

Would you have me stand still, hold my peace,
    and let
This man win everything, through my inaction?
KREON: And you want — what is it, then? To banish
    me?   105
OEDIPUS: No, not exile. It is your death I want,
    So that all the world may see what treason means.
KREON: You will persist, then? You will not believe
    me?
OEDIPUS: How can I believe you?
KREON: Then you are a fool.
OEDIPUS: To save myself?
KREON: In justice, think of me.   110
OEDIPUS: You are evil incarnate.
KREON: But suppose that you are wrong?
OEDIPUS: Still I must rule.
KREON: But not if you rule badly.
OEDIPUS: O city, city!
KREON: It is my city, too!
CHORAGOS: Now, my lords, be still. I see the queen,
    Iokaste, coming from her palace chambers;   115
    And it is time she came, for the sake of you both.
    This dreadful quarrel can be resolved through her.

(*Enter Iokaste.*)

IOKASTE: Poor foolish men, what wicked din is this?
    With Thebes sick to death, is it not shameful
    That you should take some private quarrel up?   120
    (*To Oedipus.*) Come into the house.
                    — And you, Kreon, go now:
    Let us have no more of this tumult over nothing.
KREON: Nothing? No, sister: what your husband plans
    for me
    Is one of two great evils: exile or death.
OEDIPUS: He is right.
               Why, woman I have caught him squarely   125
    Plotting against my life.
KREON: No! Let me die
    Accurst if ever I have wished you harm!
IOKASTE: Ah, believe it, Oedipus!
    In the name of the gods, respect this oath of his
    For my sake, for the sake of these people here!   130

Strophe 1

CHORAGOS: Open your mind to her, my lord. Be ruled
    by her, I beg you!
OEDIPUS: What would you have me do?
CHORAGOS: Respect Kreon's word. He has never
    spoken like a fool,
    And now he has sworn an oath.
OEDIPUS: You know what you ask?
CHORAGOS: I do.
OEDIPUS: Speak on, then.
CHORAGOS: A friend so sworn should not be baited so,   135
    In blind malice, and without final proof.
OEDIPUS: You are aware, I hope, that what you say
    Means death for me, or exile at the least.

Strophe 2

CHORAGOS: No, I swear by Helios, first in heaven!
140   May I die friendless and accurst,
          The worst of deaths, if ever I meant that!
          It is the withering fields
              That hurt my sick heart:
          Must we bear all these ills,
145   And now your bad blood as well?
      OEDIPUS: Then let him go. And let me die, if I must,
          Or be driven by him in shame from the land of
              Thebes.
          It is your unhappiness, and not his talk,
          That touches me.
                        As for him —
150   Wherever he goes, hatred will follow him.
      KREON: Ugly in yielding, as you were ugly in rage!
          Natures like yours chiefly torment themselves.
      OEDIPUS: Can you not go? Can you not leave me?
      KREON: I can.
          You do not know me; but the city knows me,
155   And in its eyes I am just, if not in yours.
                                              (*Exit Kreon.*)

Antistrophe 1

CHORAGOS: Lady Iokaste, did you not ask the King to
          go to his chambers?
      IOKASTE: First tell me what has happened.
      CHORAGOS: There was suspicion without evidence; yet
          it rankled
          As even false charges will.
      IOKASTE: On both sides?
      CHORAGOS: On both.
160   IOKASTE: But what was said?
      CHORAGOS: Oh let it rest, let it be done with!
          Have we not suffered enough?
      OEDIPUS: You see to what your decency has brought
          you:
          You have made difficulties where my heart saw
              none.

Antistrophe 2

CHORAGOS: Oedipus, it is not once only I have told
165   you —
          You must know I should count myself
              unwise
          To the point of madness, should I now forsake
              you —
                      You, under whose hand,
                          In the storm of another time,
170   Our dear land sailed out free.
          But now stand fast at the helm!
      IOKASTE: In God's name, Oedipus, inform your wife as
          well:
          Why are you so set in this hard anger?

OEDIPUS: I will tell you, for none of these men deserves
      My confidence as you do. It is Kreon's work,   175
      His treachery, his plotting against me.
IOKASTE: Go on, if you can make this clear to me.
OEDIPUS: He charges me with the murder of Laios.
IOKASTE: Has he some knowledge? Or does he speak
      from hearsay?
OEDIPUS: He would not commit himself to such a
      charge,   180
      But he has brought in that damnable soothsayer
      To tell his story.
IOKASTE: Set your mind at rest.
      If it is a question of soothsayers, I tell you
      That you will find no man whose craft gives
          knowledge
      Of the unknowable.
                        Here is my proof: 185
      An oracle was reported to Laios once
      (I will not say from Phoibos himself, but from
      His appointed ministers, at any rate)
      That his doom would be death at the hands of his
          own son —
      His son, born of his flesh and of mine!   190

      Now, you remember the story: Laios was killed
      By marauding strangers where three highways meet;
      But his child had not been three days in this world
      Before the king had pierced the baby's ankles
      And left him to die on a lonely mountainside.   195

      Thus, Apollo never caused that child
      To kill his father, and it was not Laios' fate
      To die at the hands of his son, as he had feared.
      This is what prophets and prophecies are worth!
      Have no dread of them.
                            It is God himself   200
      Who can show us what he wills, in his own way.
OEDIPUS: How strange a shadowy memory crossed my
      mind,
      Just now while you were speaking; it chilled my
      heart.
IOKASTE: What do you mean? What memory do you
      speak of?
OEDIPUS: If I understand you, Laios was killed   205
      At a place where three roads meet.
IOKASTE: So it was said;
      We have no later story.
OEDIPUS: Where did it happen?
IOKASTE: Phokis, it is called: at a place where the
      Theban Way
      Divides into the roads toward Delphi and Daulia.
OEDIPUS: When?
IOKASTE: We had the news not long before you came 210
      And proved the right to your succession here.
OEDIPUS: Ah, what net has God been weaving for me?
IOKASTE: Oedipus! Why does this trouble you?
OEDIPUS: Do not ask me yet.
      First, tell me how Laios looked, and tell me
      How old he was.

215 IOKASTE: He was tall, his hair just touched
      With white; his form was not unlike your own.
   OEDIPUS: I think that I myself may be accurst
      By my own ignorant edict.
   IOKASTE: You speak strangely.
      It makes me tremble to look at you, my king.
220 OEDIPUS: I am not sure that the blind man can not see.
      But I should know better if you were to tell me —
   IOKASTE: Anything — though I dread to hear you ask
      it.
   OEDIPUS: Was the king lightly escorted, or did he ride
      With a large company, as a ruler should?
   IOKASTE: There were five men with him in all: one was
225   a herald;
      And a single chariot, which he was driving.
   OEDIPUS: Alas, that makes it plain enough!
                                    But who —
      Who told you how it happened?
   IOKASTE: A household servant,
      The only one to escape.
   OEDIPUS: And is he still
      A servant of ours?
230 IOKASTE: No; for when he came back at last
      And found you enthroned in the place of the dead
         king,
      He came to me, touched my hand with his, and
         begged
      That I would send him away to the frontier district
      Where only the shepherds go —
235   As far away from the city as I could send him.
      I granted his prayer; for although the man was a
         slave,
      He had earned more than this favor at my hands.
   OEDIPUS: Can he be called back quickly?
   IOKASTE: Easily.
      But why?
240 OEDIPUS: I have taken too much upon myself
      Without enquiry; therefore I wish to consult him.
   IOKASTE: Then he shall come.
                        But am I not one also
      To whom you might confide these fears of yours?
   OEDIPUS: That is your right; it will not be denied you,
245   Now least of all; for I have reached a pitch
      Of wild foreboding. Is there anyone
      To whom I should sooner speak?

      Polybos of Corinth is my father.
      My mother is a Dorian: Merope.
250   I grew up chief among the men of Corinth
      Until a strange thing happened —
      Not worth my passion, it may be, but strange.
      At a feast, a drunken man maundering in his cups
      Cries out that I am not my father's son!
255   I contained myself that night, though I felt anger
      And a sinking heart. The next day I visited
      My father and mother, and questioned them. They
         stormed,
      Calling it all the slanderous rant of a fool;
      And this relieved me. Yet the suspicion

      Remained always aching in my mind;   260
      I knew there was talk; I could not rest;
      And finally, saying nothing to my parents,
      I went to the shrine at Delphi.

      The god dismissed my question without reply;
      He spoke of other things.
                        Some were clear,   265
      Full of wretchedness, dreadful, unbearable:
      As, that I should lie with my own mother, breed
      Children from whom all men would turn their
         eyes;
      And that I should be my father's murderer.

      I heard all this, and fled. And from that day   270
      Corinth to me was only in the stars
      Descending in that quarter of the sky,
      As I wandered farther and farther on my way
      To a land where I should never see the evil
      Sung by the oracle. And I came to this country   275
      Where, so you say, King Laios was killed.

      I will tell you all that happened there, my lady.
      There were three highways
      Coming together at a place I passed;
      And there a herald came towards me, and a chariot   280
      Drawn by horses, with a man such as you describe
      Seated in it. The groom leading the horses
      Forced me off the road at his lord's command;
      But as this charioteer lurched over towards me
      I struck him in my rage. The old man saw me   285
      And brought his double goad down upon my head
      As I came abreast.
                        He was paid back, and more!
      Swinging my club in this right hand I knocked him
      Out of his car, and he rolled on the ground.
                                    I killed him.

      I killed them all.   290
      Now if that stranger and Laios were — kin,
      Where is a man more miserable than I?
      More hated by the gods? Citizen and alien alike
      Must never shelter me or speak to me —
      I must be shunned by all.
                              And I myself   295
      Pronounced this malediction upon myself!

      Think of it: I have touched you with these hands,
      These hands that killed your husband. What
         defilement!

      Am I all evil, then? It must be so,
      Since I must flee from Thebes, yet never again   300
      See my own countrymen, my own country,
      For fear of joining my mother in marriage
      And killing Polybos, my father.
                              Ah,
      If I was created so, born to this fate,
      Who could deny the savagery of God?   305

O holy majesty of heavenly powers!
May I never see that day! Never!
Rather let me vanish from the race of men
Than know the abomination destined me!
310 CHORAGOS: We too, my lord, have felt dismay at this.
But there is hope: you have yet to hear the shepherd.
OEDIPUS: Indeed, I fear no other hope is left me.
IOKASTE: What do you hope from him when he comes?
OEDIPUS: This much:
If his account of the murder tallies with yours,
Then I am cleared.
315 IOKASTE: What was it that I said
Of such importance?
OEDIPUS: Why, "marauders," you said,
Killed the king, according to this man's story.
If he maintains that still, if there were several,
Clearly the guilt is not mine: I was alone.
320 But if he says one man, singlehanded, did it,
Then the evidence all points to me.
IOKASTE: You may be sure that he said there were
several;
And can he call back that story now? He can not.
The whole city heard it as plainly as I.
325 But suppose he alters some detail of it:
He can not ever show that Laios' death
Fulfilled the oracle: for Apollo said
My child was doomed to kill him; and my child —
Poor baby! — it was my child that died first.

330 No. From now on, where oracles are concerned,
I would not waste a second thought on any.
OEDIPUS: You may be right.
                              But come: let someone go
For the shepherd at once. This matter must be
settled.
IOKASTE: I will send for him.
335 I would not wish to cross you in anything,
And surely not in this. — Let us go in.
                              (*Exeunt into the palace.*)

ODE 2 • *Strophe 1*

CHORUS: Let me be reverent in the ways of right,
Lowly the paths I journey on;
Let all my words and actions keep
The laws of the pure universe
5 From highest Heaven handed down.
For Heaven is their bright nurse,
Those generations of the realms of light;
Ah, never of mortal kind were they begot,
Nor are they slaves of memory, lost in sleep:
10 Their Father is greater than Time, and ages not.

Antistrophe 1

The tyrant is a child of Pride
Who drinks from his great sickening cup

Recklessness and vanity,
Until from his high crest headlong
He plummets to the dust of hope.   15
That strong man is not strong.
But let no fair ambition be denied;
May God protect the wrestler for the State
In government, in comely policy,
Who will fear God, and on his ordinance wait.   20

Strophe 2

Haughtiness and the high hand of disdain
Tempt and outrage God's holy law;
And any mortal who dares hold
No immortal Power in awe
Will be caught up in a net of pain: 25
The price for which his levity is sold.
Let each man take due earnings, then,
And keep his hands from holy things,
And from blasphemy stand apart —
Else the crackling blast of heaven   30
Blows on his head, and on his desperate heart.
Though fools will honor impious men,
In their cities no tragic poet sings.

Antistrophe 2

Shall we lose faith in Delphi's obscurities,
We who have heard the world's core   35
Discredited, and the sacred wood
Of Zeus at Elis praised no more?
The deeds and the strange prophecies
Must make a pattern yet to be understood.
Zeus, if indeed you are lord of all,   40
Throned in light over night and day,
Mirror this in your endless mind:
Our masters call the oracle
Words on the wind, and the Delphic vision blind!
Their hearts no longer know Apollo,   45
And reverence for the gods has died away.

SCENE 3

(*Enter Iokaste.*)

IOKASTE: Princes of Thebes, it has occurred to me
To visit the altars of the gods, bearing
These branches as a suppliant, and this incense.
Our king is not himself: his noble soul
Is overwrought with fantasies of dread,   5
Else he would consider
The new prophecies in the light of the old.
He will listen to any voice that speaks disaster,
And my advice goes for nothing. (*She approaches
the altar, right.*)
                    To you, then, Apollo,

10   Lycean lord, since you are nearest, I turn in prayer
      Receive these offerings, and grant us deliverance
      From defilement. Our hearts are heavy with fear
      When we see our leader distracted, as helpless
          sailors
      Are terrified by the confusion of their helmsman.

(Enter Messenger.)

15   MESSENGER: Friends, no doubt you can direct me:
      Where shall I find the house of Oedipus,
      Or, better still, where is the king himself?
      CHORAGOS: It is this very place, stranger; he is inside.
      This is his wife and mother of his children.
20   MESSENGER: I wish her happiness in a happy house,
      Blest in all the fulfillment of her marriage.
      IOKASTE: I wish as much for you: your courtesy
      Deserves a like good fortune. But now, tell me:
      Why have you come? What have you to say to us?
      MESSENGER: Good news, my lady, for your house and
25   your husband.
      IOKASTE: What news? Who sent you here?
      MESSENGER: I am from Corinth.
      The news I bring ought to mean joy for you,
      Though it may be you will find some grief in it.
      IOKASTE: What is it? How can it touch us in both
          ways?
      MESSENGER: The word is that the people of the
30   Isthmus
      Intend to call Oedipus to be their king.
      IOKASTE: But old King Polybos — is he not reigning
          still?
      MESSENGER: No. Death holds him in his sepulchre.
      IOKASTE: What are you saying? Polybos is dead?
      MESSENGER: If I am not telling the truth, may I die
35   myself.
      IOKASTE (*to a Maidservant*): Go in, go quickly; tell this
          to your master.
      O riddlers of God's will, where are you now!
      This was the man whom Oedipus, long ago,
      Feared so, fled so, in dread of destroying him —
40   But it was another fate by which he died.

(Enter Oedipus, center.)

      OEDIPUS: Dearest Iokaste, why have you sent for me?
      IOKASTE: Listen to what this man says, and then tell
          me
      What has become of the solemn prophecies.
      OEDIPUS: Who is this man? What is his news for me?
      IOKASTE: He has come from Corinth to announce your
45   father's death!
      OEDIPUS: Is it true, stranger? Tell me in your own
          words.
      MESSENGER: I can not say it more clearly: the king is
          dead.
      OEDIPUS: Was it by treason? Or by an attack of
          illness?
      MESSENGER: A little thing brings old men to their rest.
      OEDIPUS: It was sickness, then?
50   MESSENGER: Yes, and his many years.

OEDIPUS: Ah!
      Why should a man respect the Pythian hearth,° or
      Give heed to the birds that jangle above his head?
      They prophesied that I should kill Polybos,
      Kill my own father; but he is dead and buried,   55
      And I am here — I never touched him, never,
      Unless he died of grief for my departure,
      And thus, in a sense, through me. No. Polybos
      Has packed the oracles off with him underground.
      They are empty words.
IOKASTE: Had I not told you so?   60
OEDIPUS: You had; it was my faint heart that betrayed
          me.
IOKASTE: From now on never think of those things
          again.
OEDIPUS: And yet — must I not fear my mother's bed?
IOKASTE: Why should anyone in this world be afraid
      Since Fate rules us and nothing can be foreseen?   65
      A man should live only for the present day.

      Have no more fear of sleeping with your mother:
      How many men, in dreams, have lain with their
          mothers!
      No reasonable man is troubled by such things.
OEDIPUS: That is true, only —   70
      If only my mother were not still alive!
      But she is alive. I can not help my dread.
IOKASTE: Yet this news of your father's death is
          wonderful.
OEDIPUS: Wonderful. But I fear the living woman.
MESSENGER: Tell me, who is this woman that you fear?   75
OEDIPUS: It is Merope, man; the wife of King Polybos.
MESSENGER: Merope? Why should you be afraid of
          her?
OEDIPUS: An oracle of the gods, a dreadful saying.
MESSENGER: Can you tell me about it or are you sworn
          to silence?
OEDIPUS: I can tell you, and I will.   80
      Apollo said through his prophet that I was the man
      Who should marry his own mother, shed his father's
          blood
      With his own hands. And so, for all these years
      I have kept clear of Corinth, and no harm has
          come —
      Though it would have been sweet to see my parents
          again.   85
MESSENGER: And is this the fear that drove you out of
          Corinth?
OEDIPUS: Would you have me kill my father?
MESSENGER: As for that
      You must be reassured by the news I gave you.
OEDIPUS: If you could reassure me, I would reward
          you.
MESSENGER: I had that in mind, I will confess: I
          thought   90
      I could count on you when you returned to Corinth.
OEDIPUS: No: I will never go near my parents again.

52. Pythian hearth: Delphi.

MESSENGER: Ah, son, you still do not know what you
    are doing —
OEDIPUS: What do you mean? In the name of God tell
    me!
MESSENGER: — If these are your reasons for not going
95   home.
OEDIPUS: I tell you, I fear the oracle may come true.
MESSENGER: And guilt may come upon you through
    your parents?
OEDIPUS: That is the dread that is always in my heart.
MESSENGER: Can you not see that all your fears are
    groundless?
100 OEDIPUS: Groundless? Am I not my parents' son?
MESSENGER: Polybos was not your father.
OEDIPUS: Not my father?
MESSENGER: No more your father than the man
    speaking to you.
OEDIPUS: But you are nothing to me!
MESSENGER: Neither was he.
OEDIPUS: Then why did he call me son?
MESSENGER: I will tell you:
105   Long ago he had you from my hands, as a gift.
OEDIPUS: Then how could he love me so, if I was not
    his?
MESSENGER: He had no children, and his heart turned
    to you.
OEDIPUS: What of you? Did you buy me? Did you find
    me by chance?
MESSENGER: I came upon you in the woody vales of
    Kithairon.
OEDIPUS: And what were you doing there?
110 MESSENGER: Tending my flocks.
OEDIPUS: A wandering shepherd?
MESSENGER: But your savior, son, that day.
OEDIPUS: From what did you save me?
MESSENGER: Your ankles should tell you that.
OEDIPUS: Ah, stranger, why do you speak of that
    childhood pain?
MESSENGER: I pulled the skewer that pinned your feet
    together.
OEDIPUS: I have had the mark as long as I can
115   remember.
MESSENGER: That was why you were given the name°
    you bear.
OEDIPUS: God! Was it my father or my mother who
    did it?
    Tell me!
MESSENGER: I do not know. The man who gave you
    to me
    Can tell you better than I.
120 OEDIPUS: It was not you that found me, but another?
MESSENGER: It was another shepherd gave you to me.
OEDIPUS: Who was he? Can you tell me who he was?
MESSENGER: I think he was said to be one of Laios'
    people.
OEDIPUS: You mean the Laios who was king here years
    ago?

116. name: "Oedipus" literally means swollen foot.

MESSENGER: Yes; King Laios; and the man was one of
    his herdsmen.   125
OEDIPUS: Is he still alive? Can I see him?
MESSENGER: These men here
    Know best about such things.
OEDIPUS: Does anyone here
    Know this shepherd that he is talking about?
    Have you seen him in the fields, or in the town?
    If you have, tell me. It is time things were made
    plain.   130
CHORAGOS: I think the man he means is that same
    shepherd
    You have already asked to see. Iokaste perhaps
    Could tell you something.
OEDIPUS: Do you know anything
    About him, Lady? Is he the man we have
    summoned?
    Is that the man this shepherd means?
IOKASTE: Why think of him? 135
    Forget this herdsman. Forget it all. *possibly sensing*
    This talk is a waste of time. *something wrong?*
OEDIPUS: How can you say that,
    When the clues to my true birth are in my hands?
IOKASTE: For God's love, let us have no more
    questioning!
    Is your life nothing to you?   140
    My own is pain enough for me to bear.
OEDIPUS: You need not worry. Suppose my mother a
    slave,
    And born of slaves: no baseness can touch you.
IOKASTE: Listen to me, I beg you: do not do this thing!
OEDIPUS: I will not listen; the truth must be made
    known.   145
IOKASTE: Everything that I say is for your own good!
OEDIPUS: My own good
    Snaps my patience, then; I want none of it.
IOKASTE: You are fatally wrong! May you never learn
    who you are!
OEDIPUS: Go, one of you, and bring the shepherd here.
    Let us leave this woman to brag of her royal name. 150
IOKASTE: Ah, miserable!
    That is the only word I have for you now.
    That is the only word I can ever have.

                      (Exit into the palace.)
CHORAGOS: Why has she left us, Oedipus? Why has
    she gone
    In such a passion of sorrow? I fear this silence: 155
    Something dreadful may come of it.
OEDIPUS: Let it come!
    However base my birth, I must know about it.
    The Queen, like a woman, is perhaps ashamed
    To think of my low origin. But I
    Am a child of Luck, I can not be dishonored. 160
    Luck is my mother; the passing months, my
    brothers,
    Have seen me rich and poor.
                      If this is so,
    How could I wish that I were someone else?
    How could I not be glad to know my birth?

ODE 3 • *Strophe*

CHORUS: If ever the coming time were known
    To my heart's pondering,
    Kithairon, now by Heaven I see the torches
    At the festival of the next full moon
5   And see the dance, and hear the choir sing
    A grace to your gentle shade:
    Mountain where Oedipus was found,
    O mountain guard of a noble race!
    May the god° who heals us lend his aid,
10   And let that glory come to pass
    For our king's cradling-ground.

Antistrophe

    Of the nymphs that flower beyond the years,
    Who bore you,° royal child,
    To Pan° of the hills or the timberline Apollo,
15   Cold in delight where the upland clears,
    Or Hermes° for whom Kyllene's° heights are piled?
    Or flushed as evening cloud,
    Great Dionysos,° roamer of mountains,
    He — was it he who found you there,
20   And caught you up in his own proud
    Arms from the sweet god-ravisher
    Who laughed by the Muses'° fountains?

SCENE 4

OEDIPUS: Sirs: though I do not know the man,
    I think I see him coming, this shepherd we want:
    He is old, like our friend here, and the men
    Bringing him seem to be servants of my house.
5   But you can tell, if you have ever seen him.

(*Enter Shepherd escorted by Servants.*)

CHORAGOS: I know him, he was Laios' man. You can
    trust him.
OEDIPUS: Tell me first, you from Corinth: is this the
    shepherd
    We were discussing?
MESSENGER: This is the very man.
OEDIPUS (*to Shepherd*): Come here. No, look at me.
    You must answer
10   Everything I ask. — You belonged to Laios?

9. **god:** Apollo. 13. **Who bore you:** The Chorus is asking if Oedipus is the son of an immortal nymph and a god: Pan, Apollo, Hermes, or Dionysus. 14. **Pan:** God of nature, forests, flocks, and shepherds, depicted as half-man and half-goat. 16. **Hermes:** Son of Zeus, messenger of the gods. **Kyllene:** Mountain reputed to be the birthplace of Hermes; also the center of a cult to Hermes. 18. **Dionysos:** (Dionysus) God of wine around whom wild, orgiastic rituals developed; also called Bacchus. 22. **Muses:** Nine sister goddesses who presided over poetry and music, art and sciences.

SHEPHERD: Yes: born his slave, brought up in his
    house.
OEDIPUS: Tell me: what kind of work did you do for
    him?
SHEPHERD: I was a shepherd of his, most of my life.
OEDIPUS: Where mainly did you go for pasturage?
SHEPHERD: Sometimes Kithairon, sometimes the hills
    near-by.   15
OEDIPUS: Do you remember ever seeing this man out
    there?
SHEPHERD: What would he be doing there? This man?
OEDIPUS: This man standing here. Have you ever seen
    him before?
SHEPHERD: No. At least, not to my recollection.
MESSENGER: And that is not strange, my lord. But I'll
    refresh   20
    His memory: he must remember when we two
    Spent three whole seasons together, March to
    September,
    On Kithairon or thereabouts. He had two flocks;
    I had one. Each autumn I'd drive mine home
    And he would go back with his to Laios'
    sheepfold. —   25
    Is this not true, just as I have described it?
SHEPHERD: True, yes; but it was all so long ago.
MESSENGER: Well, then: do you remember, back in
    those days,
    That you gave me a baby boy to bring up as my
    own?
SHEPHERD: What if I did? What are you trying to say?   30
MESSENGER: King Oedipus was once that little child.
SHEPHERD: Damn you, hold your tongue! ← *Why such anger?*
OEDIPUS: No more of that!
    It is your tongue needs watching, not this man's.
SHEPHERD: My king, my master, what is it I have done
    wrong?
OEDIPUS: You have not answered his question about
    the boy.   35
SHEPHERD: He does not know . . . He is only making
    trouble . . .
OEDIPUS: Come, speak plainly, or it will go hard with
    you.
SHEPHERD: In God's name, do not torture an old man!
OEDIPUS: Come here, one of you; bind his arms behind
    him.
SHEPHERD: Unhappy king! What more do you wish to
    learn?   40
OEDIPUS: Did you give this man the child he speaks of?
SHEPHERD: I did.
    And I would to God I had died that very day.
OEDIPUS: You will die now unless you speak the truth.
SHEPHERD: Yet if I speak the truth, I am worse than
    dead.
OEDIPUS (*to Attendant*): He intends to draw it out,
    apparently —   45
SHEPHERD: No! I have told you already that I gave him
    the boy.
OEDIPUS: Where did you get him? From your house?
    From somewhere else?

The Shepherd (Oliver Cliff) tells Oedipus (Kenneth Welsh) the truth about his birth in the Guthrie Theater Company's 1973 production directed by Michael Langham.

SHEPHERD: Not from mine, no. A man gave him
        to me.
OEDIPUS: Is that man here? Whose house did he
        belong to?
SHEPHERD: For God's love, my king, do not ask me any
50   more!
OEDIPUS: You are a dead man if I have to ask you
        again.
SHEPHERD: Then . . . Then the child was from the
        palace of Laios.
OEDIPUS: A slave child? or a child of his own line?
SHEPHERD: Ah, I am on the brink of dreadful speech!
55 OEDIPUS: And I of dreadful hearing. Yet I must hear.
SHEPHERD: If you must be told, then . . .
                        They said it was Laios' child;
        But it is your wife who can tell you about that.
OEDIPUS: My wife — Did she give it to you?
SHEPHERD: My lord, she did.
OEDIPUS: Do you know why?
SHEPHERD: I was told to get rid of it.
OEDIPUS: Oh heartless mother!
60 SHEPHERD: But in dread of prophecies . . .
OEDIPUS: Tell me.
SHEPHERD: It was said that the boy would kill
        his own father.
OEDIPUS: Then why did you give him over to this old
        man?
SHEPHERD: I pitied the baby, my king,
        And I thought that this man would take him far
        away
        To his own country.
65   He saved him — but for what a fate!
        For if you are what this man says you are,
        No man living is more wretched than Oedipus.
OEDIPUS: Ah God!
        It was true!
                All the prophecies!
                                — Now,
70   O Light, may I look on you for the last time!
        I, Oedipus,
        Oedipus, damned in his birth, in his marriage
        damned,
        Damned in the blood he shed with his own hand!
(*He rushes into the palace.*)

ODE 4 • *Strophe 1*

CHORUS: Alas for the seed of men.
        What measure shall I give these generations
        That breathe on the void and are void
        And exist and do not exist?
5   Who bears more weight of joy
        Than mass of sunlight shifting in images,
        Or who shall make his thought stay on
        That down time drifts away?
        Your splendor is all fallen.
10   O naked brow of wrath and tears,

O change of Oedipus!
I who saw your days call no man blest —
Your great days like ghosts gone.

Antistrophe 1

That mind was a strong bow.
Deep, how deep you drew it then, hard archer,   15
At a dim fearful range,
And brought dear glory down!
You overcame the stranger° —
The virgin with her hooking lion claws —
And though death sang, stood like a tower   20
To make pale Thebes take heart.
Fortress against our sorrow!
True king, giver of laws,
Majestic Oedipus!
No prince in Thebes had ever such renown,   25
No prince won such grace of power.

Strophe 2

And now of all men ever known
Most pitiful is this man's story:
His fortunes are most changed; his state
Fallen to a low slave's   30
Ground under bitter fate.
O Oedipus, most royal one!
The great door° that expelled you to the light
Gave at night — ah, gave night to your glory:
As to the father, to the fathering son.   35
All understood too late.
How could that queen whom Laios won,
The garden that he harrowed at his height,
Be silent when that act was done?

Antistrophe 2

But all eyes fail before time's eye,   40
All actions come to justice there.
Though never willed, though far down the deep
        past,
Your bed, your dread sirings,
Are brought to book at last.
Child by Laios doomed to die,   45
Then doomed to lose that fortunate little death,
Would God you never took breath in this air
That with my wailing lips I take to cry:
For I weep the world's outcast.
I was blind, and now I can tell why: 50
Asleep, for you had given ease of breath
To Thebes, while the false years went by.

18. stranger: The Sphinx.   **33. door:** Iokaste's womb.

EXODOS°

(*Enter, from the palace, Second Messenger.*)

SECOND MESSENGER: Elders of Thebes, most honored
    in this land,
    What horrors are yours to see and hear, what
        weight
    Of sorrow to be endured, if, true to your birth,
    You venerate the line of Labdakos!
5   I think neither Istros nor Phasis, those great rivers,
    Could purify this place of all the evil
    It shelters now, or soon must bring to light —
    Evil not done unconsciously, but willed.

    The greatest griefs are those we cause ourselves.
CHORAGOS: Surely, friend, we have grief enough
10   already;
    What new sorrow do you mean?
SECOND MESSENGER: The queen is dead.
CHORAGOS: O miserable queen! But at whose hand?
SECOND MESSENGER: Her own.
    The full horror of what happened you can not
        know,
    For you did not see it; but I, who did, will tell you
15 As clearly as I can how she met her death.

    When she had left us,
    In passionate silence, passing through the court,
    She ran to her apartment in the house,
    Her hair clutched by the fingers of both hands.
20 She closed the doors behind her; then, by that bed
    Where long ago the fatal son was conceived —
    That son who should bring about his father's
        death —
    We heard her call upon Laios, dead so many years,
    And heard her wail for the double fruit of her
        marriage,
25 A husband by her husband, children by her child.

    Exactly how she died I do not know:
    For Oedipus burst in moaning and would not let us
    Keep vigil to the end: it was by him
    As he stormed about the room that our eyes were
        caught.
    From one to another of us he went, begging a
30   sword,
    Hunting the wife who was not his wife, the mother
    Whose womb had carried his own children and
        himself.
    I do not know: it was none of us aided him,
    But surely one of the gods was in control!
35 For with a dreadful cry
    He hurled his weight, as though wrenched out of
        himself,
    At the twin doors: the bolts gave, and he rushed in.
    And there we saw her hanging, her body swaying

Exodos: Final scene.

From the cruel cord she had noosed about her neck.
A great sob broke from him, heartbreaking to hear,   40
As he loosed the rope and lowered her to the
    ground.

I would blot out from my mind what happened
    next!
For the king ripped from her gown the golden
    brooches
That were her ornament, and raised them, and
    plunged them down
Straight into his own eyeballs, crying, "No more,   45
No more shall you look on the misery about me,
The horrors of my own doing! Too long you have
    known
The faces of those whom I should never have seen,
Too long been blind to those for whom I was
    searching!
From this hour, go in darkness!" And as he spoke,   50
He struck at his eyes — not once, but many times;
And the blood spattered his beard,
Bursting from his ruined sockets like red hail.

So from the unhappiness of two this evil has sprung,
A curse on the man and woman alike. The old   55
Happiness of the house of Labdakos
Was happiness enough: where is it today?
It is all wailing and ruin, disgrace, death — all
The misery of mankind that has a name —
And it is wholly and for ever theirs.   60
CHORAGOS: Is he in agony still? Is there no rest for
    him?
SECOND MESSENGER: He is calling for someone to open
    the doors wide
So that all the children of Kadmos may look upon
His father's murderer, his mother's — no,
I can not say it!
                And then he will leave Thebes,   65
Self-exiled, in order that the curse
Which he himself pronounced may depart from the
    house.
He is weak, and there is none to lead him,
So terrible is his suffering.
                But you will see:
Look, the doors are opening; in a moment   70
You will see a thing that would crush a heart of
    stone.

(*The central door is opened; Oedipus, blinded, is led in.*)

CHORAGOS: Dreadful indeed for men to see.
    Never have my own eyes
    Looked on a sight so full of fear.

    Oedipus!   75
    What madness came upon you, what demon
    Leaped on your life with heavier
    Punishment than a mortal man can bear?
    No: I can not even
    Look at you, poor ruined one.   80

And I would speak, question, ponder,
If I were able. No.
You make me shudder.
OEDIPUS: God. God.
85   Is there a sorrow greater?
Where shall I find harbor in this world?
My voice is hurled far on a dark wind.
What has God done to me?
CHORAGOS: Too terrible to think of, or to see.

Strophe 1

90   OEDIPUS: O cloud of night,
Never to be turned away: night coming on,
I can not tell how: night like a shroud!
My fair winds brought me here.
                     O God. Again
The pain of the spikes where I had sight,
95   The flooding pain
Of memory, never to be gouged out.
CHORAGOS: This is not strange.
You suffer it all twice over, remorse in pain,
Pain in remorse.

Antistrophe 1

100   OEDIPUS: Ah dear friend
Are you faithful even yet, you alone?
Are you still standing near me, will you stay here,
Patient, to care for the blind?
                    The blind man!
Yet even blind I know who it is attends me,
105   By the voice's tone —
Though my new darkness hide the comforter.
CHORAGOS: Oh fearful act!
What god was it drove you to rake black
Night across your eyes?

Strophe 2

110   OEDIPUS: Apollo. Apollo. Dear
Children, the god was Apollo.
He brought my sick, sick fate upon me.
But the blinding hand was my own!
How could I bear to see
115   When all my sight was horror everywhere?
CHORAGOS: Everywhere; that is true.
OEDIPUS: And now what is left?
Images? Love? A greeting even,
Sweet to the senses? Is there anything?
120   Ah, no, friends: lead me away.
Lead me away from Thebes.
                Lead the great wreck
And hell of Oedipus, whom the gods hate.
CHORAGOS: Your misery, you are not blind to that.
Would God you had never found it out!

Antistrophe 2

OEDIPUS: Death take the man who unbound			125
My feet on that hillside
And delivered me from death to life! What life?
If only I had died,
This weight of monstrous doom
Could not have dragged me and my darlings down.			130
CHORAGOS: I would have wished the same.
OEDIPUS: Oh never to have come here
With my father's blood upon me! Never
To have been the man they call his mother's husband!
Oh accurst! Oh child of evil,			135
To have entered that wretched bed —
                     the selfsame one!
More primal than sin itself, this fell to me.
CHORAGOS: I do not know what words to offer you.
You were better dead than alive and blind.
OEDIPUS: Do not counsel me any more. This
punishment			140
That I have laid upon myself is just.
If I had eyes,
I do not know how I could bear the sight
Of my father, when I came to the house of Death,
Or my mother: for I have sinned against them both			145
So vilely that I could not make my peace
By strangling my own life.
                  Or do you think my children,
Born as they were born, would be sweet to my eyes?
Ah never, never! Nor this town with its high walls,
Nor the holy images of the gods.
                 For I,			150
Thrice miserable! — Oedipus, noblest of all the line
Of Kadmos, have condemned myself to enjoy
These things no more, by my own malediction
Expelling that man whom the gods declared
To be a defilement in the house of Laios.			155
After exposing the rankness of my own guilt,
How could I look men frankly in the eyes?
No, I swear it,
If I could have stifled my hearing at its source,
I would have done it and made all this body
A tight cell of misery, blank to light and sound:			160
So I should have been safe in my dark mind
Beyond external evil.
              Ah Kithairon!
Why did you shelter me? When I was cast upon you,
Why did I not die? Then I should never			165
Have shown the world my execrable birth.

Ah Polybos! Corinth, city that I believed
The ancient seat of my ancestors: how fair
I seemed, your child! And all the while this evil
Was cancerous within me!
              For I am sick			170
In my own being, sick in my origin.
O three roads, dark ravine, woodland and way
Where three roads met; you, drinking my father's
   blood,

My own blood, spilled by my own hand: can you
        remember
175   The unspeakable things I did there, and the things
        I went on from there to do?
                        O marriage, marriage!
        The act that engendered me, and again the act
        Performed by the son in the same bed —
                                Ah, the net
        Of incest, mingling fathers, brothers, sons,
180   With brides, wives, mothers: the last evil
        That can be known by men: no tongue can say
        How evil!
                No. For the love of God, conceal me
        Somewhere far from Thebes; or kill me; or hurl me
        Into the sea, away from men's eyes for ever.

185   Come, lead me. You need not fear to touch me.
        Of all men, I alone can bear this guilt.

(*Enter Kreon.*)

CHORAGOS: Kreon is here now. As to what you ask,
        He may decide the course to take. He only
        Is left to protect the city in your place.
OEDIPUS: Alas, how can I speak to him? What right
190   have I
        To beg his courtesy whom I have deeply wronged?
KREON: I have not come to mock you, Oedipus,
        Or to reproach you, either.
        (*To Attendants.*)   — You, standing there:
        If you have lost all respect for man's dignity,
195   At least respect the flame of Lord Helios:°
        Do not allow this pollution to show itself
        Openly here, an affront to the earth
        And Heaven's rain and the light of day. No, take
        him
        Into the house as quickly as you can.
200   For it is proper
        That only the close kindred see his grief.
OEDIPUS: I pray you in God's name, since your
        courtesy
        Ignores my dark expectation, visiting
        With mercy this man of all men most execrable:
205   Give me what I ask — for your good, not for mine.
KREON: And what is it that you turn to me begging for?
OEDIPUS: Drive me out of this country as quickly as
        may be
        To a place where no human voice can ever greet
        me.
KREON: I should have done that before now — only,
210   God's will had not been wholly revealed to me.
OEDIPUS: But his command is plain: the parricide
        Must be destroyed. I am that evil man.
KREON: That is the sense of it, yes; but as things are,
        We had best discover clearly what is to be done.
215 OEDIPUS: You would learn more about a man like me?
KREON: You are ready now to listen to the god.

195. Lord Helios: The sun god.

OEDIPUS: I will listen. But it is to you
        That I must turn for help. I beg you, hear me.

        The woman is there —
        Give her whatever funeral you think proper: 220
        She is your sister.
                        — But let me go, Kreon!
        Let me purge my father's Thebes of the pollution
        Of my living here, and go out to the wild hills,
        To Kithairon, that has won such fame with me,
        The tomb my mother and father appointed for me,   225
        And let me die there, as they willed I should.
        And yet I know
        Death will not ever come to me through sickness
        Or in any natural way: I have been preserved
        For some unthinkable fate. But let that be.   230

        As for my sons, you need not care for them.
        They are men, they will find some way to live.
        But my poor daughters, who have shared my table,
        Who never before have been parted from their
        father —
        Take care of them, Kreon; do this for me.   235

        And will you let me touch them with my hands
        A last time, and let us weep together?
        Be kind, my lord,
        Great prince, be kind!
                        Could I but touch them,
        They would be mine again, as when I had my eyes.   240

(*Enter Antigone and Ismene, attended.*)

        Ah, God!
        Is it my dearest children I hear weeping?
        Has Kreon pitied me and sent my daughters?
KREON: Yes, Oedipus: I knew that they were dear to
        you
        In the old days, and know you must love them still.   245
OEDIPUS: May God bless you for this — and be a
        friendlier
        Guardian to you than he has been to me!

        Children, where are you?
        Come quickly to my hands: they are your
        brother's —
        Hands that have brought your father's once clear
        eyes   250
        To this way of seeing —
                        Ah dearest ones,
        I had neither sight nor knowledge then, your father
        By the woman who was the source of his own life!
        And I weep for you — having no strength to see
        you — ,
        I weep for you when I think of the bitterness   255
        That men will visit upon you all your lives.
        What homes, what festivals can you attend
        Without being forced to depart again in tears?
        And when you come to marriageable age,

260 Where is the man, my daughters, who would dare
Risk the bane that lies on all my children?
Is there any evil wanting? Your father killed
His father; sowed the womb of her who bore him;
Engendered you at the fount of his own existence!
That is what they will say of you.

265   Then, whom
Can you ever marry? There are no bridegrooms for
    you,
And your lives must wither away in sterile
    dreaming.

O Kreon, son of Menoikeus!
You are the only father my daughters have,
270 Since we, their parents, are both of us gone for ever.
They are your own blood: you will not let them
Fall into beggary and loneliness;
You will keep them from the miseries that are mine!
Take pity on them; see, they are only children,
275 Friendless except for you. Promise me this,
Great prince, and give me your hand in token of it.

(*Kreon clasps his right hand.*)

Children:
I could say much, if you could understand me,
But as it is, I have only this prayer for you:
280 Live where you can, be as happy as you can —
Happier, please God, than God has made your
    father.
KREON: Enough. You have wept enough. Now go
    within.

OEDIPUS: I must, but it is hard.
KREON: Time eases all things.
OEDIPUS: You know my mind, then?
KREON: Say what you desire.
OEDIPUS: Send me from Thebes!
KREON: God grant that I may!   285
OEDIPUS: But since God hates me . . .
KREON: No, he will grant your wish.
OEDIPUS: You promise?
KREON: I can not speak beyond my knowledge.
OEDIPUS: Then lead me in.
KREON: Come now, and leave your children.   290
OEDIPUS: No! Do not take them from me!
KREON: Think no longer
That you are in command here, but rather think
How, when you were, you served your own
    destruction.

(*Exeunt into the house all but
the Chorus; the Choragos
chants directly to the audience.*)

CHORAGOS: Men of Thebes: look upon Oedipus.

This is the king who solved the famous riddle   295
And towered up, most powerful of men.
No mortal eyes but looked on him with envy,
Yet in the end ruin swept over him.

Let every man in mankind's frailty
Consider his last day; and let none   300
Presume on his good fortune until he find
Life, at his death, a memory without pain.

COMMENTARIES

Critical comment on the plays of Sophocles has been rich and various and has spanned the centuries. We are especially fortunate to have a commentary from the great age of Greek thought a century after Sophocles himself flourished. In *Oedipus Rex* Sophocles gave the philosopher Aristotle a perfect drama on which to build a theory of tragedy, and Aristotle's observations have remained the most influential comments made on drama in the West. In some ways they have established the function, limits, and purposes of drama. In the twentieth century, for instance, when Bertolt Brecht tried to create a new theory of the drama, he specifically described his ideas as an alternative to Aristotelian notions.

Although not a critic, Sigmund Freud saw in the Oedipus myth as interpreted by Sophocles a basic psychological phenomenon experienced by all people in their infancy. This "Oedipus complex" is now well established in psychology and in the popular imagination.

The extraordinary range of commentary on the Oedipus story is demonstrated nowhere more amazingly than in Claude Lévi-Strauss's structural reading of the myth, both in Sophocles' version and in other versions. Lévi-Strauss shows that a pattern emerges when certain actions in the play are placed side by side. If he is correct, his theory offers a way to interpret myths and to see why they were valued so highly by the Greeks in their drama.

Aristotle (384–322 B.C.)
POETICS: COMEDY AND EPIC AND TRAGEDY   *c. 334–323 B.C.*

TRANSLATED BY GERALD F. ELSE

Aristotle was Plato's most brilliant student and the heir of his teaching mantle. He remained with Plato for twenty years and then began his own school, called the Lyceum. His extant work consists mainly of his lectures, which were recorded by his students and carefully preserved. Called his treatises, they greatly influenced later thought and deal with almost every branch of philosophy, science, and the arts. His Poetics *remains, more than two thousand years later, a document of immense importance for literary criticism. Although sometimes ambiguous, difficult, and unfinished, it provides insight into the theoretical basis of Greek tragedy and comedy, and it helps us see that the drama was significant enough in intellectual life to warrant an examination by the best Greek minds.*

Comedy

Comedy is, as we said it was, an imitation of persons who are inferior; not, however, going all the way to full villainy, but imitating the ugly, of which the ludicrous is one part. The ludicrous, that is, is a failing or a piece of ugliness which causes no pain or destruction; thus, to go on farther, the comic mask° is something ugly and distorted but painless.

Now the stages of development of tragedy, and the men who were responsible for them, have not escaped notice but comedy did escape notice in the beginning because it was not taken seriously. (In fact it was late in its history that the presiding magistrate officially "granted a chorus" to the comic poets; until then they were volunteers.) Thus comedy already possessed certain defining characteristics when the first "comic poets," so-called, appear in the record. Who gave it masks, or prologues, or troupes of actors and all that sort of thing is not known. The composing of plots came originally from Sicily; of the Athenian poets, Crates° was the first to abandon the lampooning mode and compose arguments, that is, plots, of a general nature.

---

the comic mask: Actors in Greek drama wore masks behind which they spoke their lines. The masks were made individually for each character.

Crates: Greek actor and playwright (fl. 470 B.C.), credited by Aristotle with developing Greek comedy into a fully plotted, credible form. Aristophanes (c. 448–c. 385 B.C.), another Greek comic playwright, says that Crates was the first to portray a drunkard onstage.

Epic and Tragedy

Well, then, epic poetry followed in the wake of tragedy up to the point of being a (1) good-sized (2) imitation (3) in verse (4) of people who are to be taken seriously; but in its having its verse unmixed with any other and being narrative in character, there they differ. Further, so far as its length is concerned, tragedy tries as hard as it can to exist during a single daylight period, or to vary but little, while the epic is not limited in its time and so differs in that respect. Yet originally they used to do this in tragedies just as much as they did in epic poems.

The constituent elements are partly identical and partly limited to tragedy. Hence anybody who knows about good and bad tragedy knows about epic also; for the elements that the epic possesses appertain to tragedy as well, but those of tragedy are not all found in the epic.

Tragedy and Its Six Constituent Elements

Our discussions of imitative poetry in hexameters,° and of comedy, will come later; at present let us deal with tragedy, recovering from what has been said so far the definition of its essential nature, as it was in development. Tragedy, then, is a process of imitating an action which has serious implications, is complete, and possesses magnitude; by means of language which has been made sensuously attractive, with each of its varieties found separately in the parts; enacted by the persons themselves and not presented through narrative; through a course of pity and fear completing the purification of tragic acts which have those emotional characteristics. By "language made sensuously attractive" I mean language that has rhythm and melody, and by "its varieties found separately" I mean the fact that certain parts of the play are carried on through spoken verses alone and others the other way around, through song.

Now first of all, since they perform the imitation through action (by acting it), the adornment of their visual appearance will perforce constitute some part of the making of tragedy; and song-composition and verbal expression also, for those are the media in which they perform the imitation. By "verbal expression" I mean the actual composition of the verses, and by "song-composition" something whose meaning is entirely clear.

Next, since it is an imitation of an action and is enacted by certain people who are performing the action, and since those people must necessarily have certain traits both of character and thought (for it is thanks to these two factors that we speak of people's actions also as having a defined character, and it is in accordance with their actions that all either succeed or fail); and since the imitation of the action is the plot, for by "plot" I mean here the structuring of the events, and by the "characters" that in accordance with which we say that the persons who are acting have a defined moral character, and by "thought" all the passages in which they attempt to prove some thesis or set forth an opinion — it follows of necessity, then, that tragedy as a whole has just six constituent elements, in relation to the essence that makes it a distinct species; and they are plot, characters, verbal expression, thought, visual adornment, and song-composition. For the elements by which they imitate are two (i.e., verbal expression and song-composition), the manner in

---

hexameters: The first known metrical form for classical verse. Each line had six metrical feet, some of which were prescribed in advance. It is the meter used for epic poetry and for poetry designed to teach a lesson. The form has sometimes been used in comparatively modern poetry but rarely with success except in French.

which they imitate is one (visual adornment), the things they imitate are three (plot, characters, thought), and there is nothing more beyond these. These then are the constituent forms they use.

The Relative Importance of the Six Elements

The greatest of these elements is the structuring of the incidents. For tragedy is an imitation not of men but of a life, an action, and they have moral quality in accordance with their characters but are happy or unhappy in accordance with their actions; hence they are not active in order to imitate their characters, but they include the characters along with the actions for the sake of the latter. Thus the structure of events, the plot, is the goal of tragedy, and the goal is the greatest thing of all.

Again: a tragedy cannot exist without a plot, but it can without characters: thus the tragedies of most of our modern poets are devoid of character, and in general many poets are like that; so also with the relationship between Zeuxis and Polygnotus,° among the painters: Polygnotus is a good portrayer of character, while Zeuxis's painting has no dimension of character at all.

Again: if one strings end to end speeches that are expressive of character and carefully worked in thought and expression, he still will not achieve the result which we said was the aim of tragedy; the job will be done much better by a tragedy that is more deficient in these other respects but has a plot, a structure of events. It is much the same case as with painting: the most beautiful pigments smeared on at random will not give as much pleasure as a black-and-white outline picture. Besides, the most powerful means tragedy has for swaying our feelings, namely the peripeties and recognitions,° are elements of plot.

Again: an indicative sign is that those who are beginning a poetic career manage to hit the mark in verbal expression and character portrayal sooner than they do in plot construction; and the same is true of practically all the earliest poets.

So plot is the basic principle, the heart and soul, as it were, of tragedy, and the characters come second: [. . .] it is the imitation of an action and imitates the persons primarily for the sake of their action.

Third in rank is thought. This is the ability to state the issues and appropriate points pertaining to a given topic, an ability which springs from the arts of politics and rhetoric; in fact the earlier poets made their characters talk "politically," the present-day poets rhetorically. But "character" is that kind of utterance which clearly reveals the bent of a man's moral choice (hence there is no character in that class of utterances in which there is nothing at all that the speaker is choosing or rejecting), while "thought" is the passages in which they try to prove that something is so or not so, or state some general principle.

Fourth is the verbal expression of the speeches. I mean by this the same thing that was said earlier, that the "verbal expression" is the conveyance of thought through language: a statement which has the same meaning whether one says "verses" or "speeches."

Zeuxis and Polygnotus: Zeuxis (fl. 420–390 B.C.) developed a method of painting in which the figures were rounded and apparently three-dimensional. Thus, he was an illusionistic painter, imitating life in a realistic style. Polygnotus (c. 470–440 B.C.) was famous as a painter, and his works were on the Acropolis as well as at Delphi. His draftsmanship was especially praised.

peripeties and recognitions: The turning about of fortune and the recognition on the part of the tragic hero of the truth. This is, for Aristotle, a critical moment in the drama, especially if both events happen simultaneously, as they do in *Oedipus Rex*. It is quite possible for these moments to happen apart from one another.

The song-composition of the remaining parts is the greatest of the sensuous attractions, and the visual adornment of the dramatic persons can have a strong emotional effect but is the least artistic element, the least connected with the poetic art; in fact the force of tragedy can be felt even without benefit of public performance and actors, while for the production of the visual effect the property man's art is even more decisive than that of the poets.

General Principles of the Tragic Plot

With these distinctions out of the way, let us next discuss what the structuring of the events should be like, since this is both the basic and the most important element in the tragic art. We have established, then, that tragedy is an imitation of an action which is complete and whole and has some magnitude (for there is also such a thing as a whole that has no magnitude). "Whole" is that which has beginning, middle, and end. "Beginning" is that which does not necessarily follow on something else, but after it something else naturally is or happens; "end," the other way around, is that which naturally follows on something else, either necessarily or for the most part, but nothing else after it; and "middle" that which naturally follows on something else and something else on it. So, then, well constructed plots should neither begin nor end at any chance point but follow the guidelines just laid down.

Furthermore, since the beautiful, whether a living creature or anything that is composed of parts, should not only have these in a fixed order to one another but also possess a definite size which does not depend on chance — for beauty depends on size and order; hence neither can a very tiny creature turn out to be beautiful (since our perception of it grows blurred as it approaches the period of imperceptibility) nor an excessively huge one (for then it cannot all be perceived at once and so its unity and wholeness are lost), if for example there were a creature a thousand miles long — so, just as in the case of living creatures they must have some size, but one that can be taken in a single view, so with plots: they should have length, but such that they are easy to remember. As to a limit of the length, the one is determined by the tragic competitions and the ordinary span of attention. (If they had to compete with a hundred tragedies they would compete by the water clock, as they say used to be done [?].) But the limit fixed by the very nature of the case is: the longer the plot, up to the point of still being perspicuous as a whole, the finer it is so far as size is concerned; or to put it in general terms, the length in which, with things happening in unbroken sequence, a shift takes place either probably or necessarily from bad to good fortune or from good to bad — that is an acceptable norm of length.

But a plot is not unified, as some people think, simply because it has to do with a single person. A large, indeed an indefinite number of things can happen to a given individual, some of which go to constitute no unified event; and in the same way there can be many acts of a given individual from which no single action emerges. Hence it seems clear that those poets are wrong who have composed *Heracleïds*, *Theseïds*, and the like. They think that since Heracles was a single person it follows that the plot will be single too. But Homer, superior as he is in all other respects, appears to have grasped this point well also, thanks either to art or nature, for in composing an *Odyssey* he did not incorporate into it everything that happened to the hero, for example how he was wounded on Mt. Parnassus° or how he

---

Mt. Parnassus: A mountain in central Greece traditionally sacred to Apollo. In legend, Odysseus was wounded there, but the point Aristotle is making is that the writer of epics need not include every detail of his hero's life in a given work. Homer, in writing the *Odyssey,* was working with a hero, Odysseus, whose story had been legendary long before he began writing.

feigned madness at the muster, neither of which events, by happening, made it at all necessary or probable that the other should happen. Instead, he composed the *Odyssey* — and the *Iliad* similarly — around a unified action of the kind we have been talking about.

A poetic imitation, then, ought to be unified in the same way as a single imitation in any other mimetic field, by having a single object: since the plot is an imitation of an action, the latter ought to be both unified and complete, and the component events ought to be so firmly compacted that if any one of them is shifted to another place, or removed, the whole is loosened up and dislocated; for an element whose addition or subtraction makes no perceptible extra difference is not really a part of the whole.

From what has been said it is also clear that the poet's job is not to report what has happened but what is likely to happen: that is, what is capable of happening according to the rule of probability or necessity. Thus the difference between the historian and the poet is not in their utterances being in verse or prose (it would be quite possible for Herodotus's work to be translated into verse, and it would not be any the less a history with verse than it is without it); the difference lies in the fact that the historian speaks of what has happened, the poet of the kind of thing that *can* happen. Hence also poetry is a more philosophical and serious business than history; for poetry speaks more of universals, history of particulars. "Universal" in this case is what kind of person is likely to do or say certain kinds of things, according to probability or necessity; that is what poetry aims at, although it gives its persons particular names afterward; while the "particular" is what Alcibiades did or what happened to him.

In the field of comedy this point has been grasped: our comic poets construct their plots on the basis of general probabilities and then assign names to the persons quite arbitrarily, instead of dealing with individuals as the old iambic poets° did. But in tragedy they still cling to the historically given names. The reason is that what is possible is persuasive; so what has not happened we are not yet ready to believe is possible, while what has happened is, we feel, obviously possible: for it would not have happened if it were impossible. Nevertheless, it is a fact that even in our tragedies, in some cases only one or two of the names are traditional, the rest being invented, and in some others none at all. It is so, for example, in Agathon's *Antheus* — the names in it are as fictional as the events — and it gives no less pleasure because of that. Hence the poets ought not to cling at all costs to the traditional plots, around which our tragedies are constructed. And in fact it is absurd to go searching for this kind of authentication, since even the familiar names are familiar to only a few in the audience and yet give the same kind of pleasure to all.

So from these considerations it is evident that the poet should be a maker of his plots more than of his verses, insofar as he is a poet by virtue of his imitations and what he imitates is actions. Hence even if it happens that he puts something that has actually taken place into poetry, he is none the less a poet; for there is nothing to prevent some of the things that have happened from being the kind of things that can happen, and that is the sense in which he is their maker.

old iambic poets: Aristotle may be referring to Archilochus (fl. 650 B.C.) and the iambic style he developed. The iamb is a metrical foot of two syllables, a short and a long syllable, and was the most popular metrical style before the time of Aristotle. "Dealing with individuals" implies using figures already known to the audience rather than figures whose names can be arbitrarily assigned because no one knows who they are.

*Simple and Complex
Plots*

Among simple plots and actions the episodic are the worst. By "episodic" plot I mean one in which there is no probability or necessity for the order in which the episodes follow one another. Such structures are composed by the bad poets because they are bad poets, but by the good poets because of the actors: in composing contest pieces for them, and stretching out the plot beyond its capacity, they are forced frequently to dislocate the sequence.

Furthermore, since the tragic imitation is not only of a complete action but also of events that are fearful and pathetic,° and these come about best when they come about contrary to one's expectation yet logically, one following from the other; that way they will be more productive of wonder than if they happen merely at random, by chance — because even among chance occurrences the ones people consider most marvelous are those that seem to have come about as if on purpose: for example the way the statue of Mitys at Argos killed the man who had been the cause of Mitys's death, by falling on him while he was attending the festival; it stands to reason, people think, that such things don't happen by chance — so plots of that sort cannot fail to be artistically superior.

Some plots are simple, others are complex; indeed the actions of which the plots are imitations already fall into these two categories. By "simple" action I mean one the development of which being continuous and unified in the manner stated above, the reversal comes without peripety or recognition, and by "complex" action one in which the reversal is continuous but with recognition or peripety or both. And these developments must grow out of the very structure of the plot itself, in such a way that on the basis of what has happened previously this particular outcome follows either by necessity or in accordance with probability; for there is a great difference in whether these events happen because of those or merely after them.

"Peripety" is a shift of what is being undertaken to the opposite in the way previously stated, and that in accordance with probability or necessity as we have just been saying; as for example in the *Oedipus* the man who has come, thinking that he will reassure Oedipus, that is, relieve him of his fear with respect to his mother, by revealing who he once was, brings about the opposite; and in the *Lynceus*, as he (Lynceus) is being led away with every prospect of being executed, and Danaus pursuing him with every prospect of doing the executing, it comes about as a result of the other things that have happened in the play that *he* is executed and Lynceus is saved. And "recognition" is, as indeed the name indicates, a shift from ignorance to awareness, pointing in the direction either of close blood ties or of hostility, of people who have previously been in a clearly marked state of happiness or unhappiness.

The finest recognition is one that happens at the same time as a peripety, as is the case with the one in the *Oedipus*. Naturally, there are also other kinds of recognition: it is possible for one to take place in the prescribed manner in relation to inanimate objects and chance occurrences, and it is possible to recognize whether a person has acted or not acted. But the form that is most integrally a part of the plot, the action, is the one aforesaid; for that kind of recognition combined with peripety will excite either pity or fear (and these are the kinds of action of which tragedy is

---

fearful and pathetic: Aristotle said that tragedy should evoke two emotions: terror and pity. The terror results from our realizing that what is happening to the hero might just as easily happen to us; the pity results from our human sympathy with a fellow sufferer. Therefore, the fearful and pathetic represent significant emotions appropriate to our witnessing drama.

an imitation according to our definition), because both good and bad fortune will also be most likely to follow that kind of event. Since, further, the recognition is a recognition of persons, some are of one person by the other one only (when it is already known who the "other one" is), but sometimes it is necessary for both persons to go through a recognition, as for example Iphigenia is recognized by her brother° through the sending of the letter, but of him by Iphigenia another recognition is required.

These then are two elements of plot: peripety and recognition; third is the *pathos*. Of these, peripety and recognition have been discussed; a *pathos* is a destructive or painful act, such as deaths on stage, paroxysms of pain, woundings, and all that sort of thing.

Sigmund Freud (1856–1939)
THE OEDIPUS COMPLEX   *1900–1930°*

TRANSLATED BY JAMES STRACHEY

Sigmund Freud was the most celebrated psychiatrist of the twentieth century and the father of psychoanalytic theory. His researches into the unconscious changed the way we think about the human mind, and his explorations into the symbolic meaning of dreams have been widely regarded as a breakthrough in connecting the meaning of world myth to personal life.

In his Interpretation of Dreams *he turned to Sophocles' drama and developed his theories of the Oedipus complex: the desire to kill one parent and marry the other may be rooted in the deepest natural psychological development of the individual. The following passage provides insight not only into a psychological state that all humans may share but also into the way in which a man of Freud's temperament read and interpreted a great piece of literature. Like Sophocles himself, Freud believed that the myth underlying* Oedipus Rex *has a meaning and importance for all human beings.*

In my experience, which is already extensive, the chief part in the mental lives of all children who later become psychoneurotics is played by their parents. Being in love with the one parent and hating the other are among the essential constituents of the stock of psychical impulses which is formed at that time and which is of such importance in determining the symptoms of the later neurosis. It is not my belief, however, that psychoneurotics differ sharply in this respect from other human beings who remain normal — that they are able, that is, to create something absolutely new and peculiar to themselves. It is far more probable — and this is confirmed by occasional observations on normal children — that they are only distinguished by exhibiting on a magnified scale feelings of love and hatred to their parents which occur less obviously and less intensely in the minds of most children.

---

her brother: Orestes is Iphigenia's brother. Aristotle may be referring to a lost play.
1900–1930: *Interpretation of Dreams* was first published in 1900 and updated regularly by Freud through eight editions. This passage is taken from the eighth edition, published in 1930.

This discovery is confirmed by a legend that has come down to us from classical antiquity: a legend whose profound and universal power to move can only be understood if the hypothesis I have put forward in regard to the psychology of children has an equally universal validity. What I have in mind is the legend of King Oedipus and Sophocles' drama which bears his name.

Oedipus, son of Laïus, King of Thebes, and of Jocasta, was exposed [to the elements and left to die] as an infant because an oracle had warned Laïus that the still unborn child would be his father's murderer. The child was rescued and grew up as a prince in an alien court, until, in doubts as to his origin, he too questioned the oracle and was warned to avoid his home since he was destined to murder his father and take his mother in marriage. On the road leading away from what he believed was his home, he met King Laïus and slew him in a sudden quarrel. He came next to Thebes and solved the riddle set him by the Sphinx who barred his way. Out of gratitude the Thebans made him their king and gave him Jocasta's hand in marriage. He reigned long in peace and honor, and she who, unknown to him, was his mother bore him two sons and two daughters. Then at last a plague broke out and the Thebans made inquiry once more of the oracle. It is at this point that Sophocles' tragedy opens. The messengers bring back the reply that the plague will cease when the murderer of Laïus has been driven from the land.

> But he, where is he? Where shall now be read
> The fading record of this ancient guilt?[1]

The action of the play consists in nothing other than the process of revealing, with cunning delays and ever-mounting excitement — a process that can be likened to the work of a psychoanalysis — that Oedipus himself is the murderer of Laïus, but further that he is the son of the murdered man and of Jocasta. Appalled at the abomination which he has unwittingly perpetrated, Oedipus blinds himself and forsakes his home. The oracle has been fulfilled.

Oedipus Rex is what is known as a tragedy of destiny. Its tragic effect is said to lie in the contrast between the supreme will of the gods and the vain attempts of mankind to escape the evil that threatens them. The lesson which, it is said, the deeply moved spectator should learn from the tragedy is submission to the divine will and realization of his own impotence. Modern dramatists have accordingly tried to achieve a similar tragic effect by weaving the same contrast into a plot invented by themselves. But the spectators have looked on unmoved while a curse or an oracle was fulfilled in spite of all the efforts of some innocent man: later tragedies of destiny have failed in their effect.

If *Oedipus Rex* moves a modern audience no less than it did the contemporary Greek one, the explanation can only be that its effect does not lie in the contrast between destiny and human will, but is to be looked for in the particular nature of the material on which that contrast is exemplified. There must be something which makes a voice within us ready to recognize the compelling force of destiny in the *Oedipus,* while we can dismiss as merely arbitrary such dispositions as are laid down in [Grillparzer's] *Die Ahnfrau* or other modern tragedies of destiny. And a factor of this kind is in fact involved in the story of King Oedipus. His destiny

---

[1]Lewis Campbell's translation (1883), lines 108ff [Dudley Fitts and Robert Fitzgerald, *Sophocles: The Oedipus Cycle, an English Version* (Harcourt Brace & Company, 1949), Prologue, lines 112–13].

moves us only because it might have been ours — because the oracle laid the same curse upon us before our birth as upon him. It is the fate of all of us, perhaps, to direct our first sexual impulse toward our mother and our first hatred and our first murderous wish against our father. Our dreams convince us that that is so. King Oedipus, who slew his father Laïus and married his mother Jocasta, merely shows us the fulfillment of our own childhood wishes. But, more fortunate than he, we have meanwhile succeeded, in so far as we have not become psychoneurotics, in detaching our sexual impulses from our mothers and in forgetting our jealousy of our fathers. Here is one in whom these primeval wishes of our childhood have been fulfilled, and we shrink back from him with the whole force of the repression by which those wishes have since that time been held down within us. While the poet, as he unravels the past, brings to light the guilt of Oedipus, he is at the same time compelling us to recognize our own inner minds, in which those same impulses, though suppressed, are still to be found. The contrast with which the closing Chorus leaves us confronted —

> . . . Fix on Oedipus your eyes,
> Who resolved the dark enigma, noblest champion and most wise.
> Like a star his envied fortune mounted beaming far and wide:
> Now he sinks in seas of anguish, whelmed beneath a raging tide . . .[2]

— strikes as a warning at ourselves and our pride, at us who since our childhood have grown so wise and so mighty in our own eyes. Like Oedipus, we live in ignorance of these wishes, repugnant to morality, which have been forced upon us by Nature, and after their revelation we may all of us well seek to close our eyes to the scenes of our childhood.[3]

There is an unmistakable indication in the text of Sophocles' tragedy itself that the legend of Oedipus sprang from some primeval dream material which had as its content the distressing disturbance of a child's relation to his parents owing to the first stirrings of sexuality. At a point when Oedipus, though he is not yet enlightened, has begun to feel troubled by his recollection of the oracle, Jocasta consoles him by referring to a dream which many people dream, though, as she thinks, it has no meaning:

> Many a man ere now in dreams hath lain
> With her who bare him. He hath least annoy
> Who with such omens troubleth not his mind.[4]

Today, just as then, many men dream of having sexual relations with their mothers, and speak of the fact with indignation and astonishment. It is clearly the key to the tragedy and the complement to the dream of the dreamer's father being dead. The story of Oedipus is the reaction of the imagination to these two typical dreams.

---

[2]Lewis Campbell's translation, lines 1524ff [Fitts and Fitzgerald, antistrophe 2, lines 292–96].

[3][*Footnote added by Freud in 1914 edition.*] None of the findings of psychoanalytic research has provoked such embittered denials, such fierce opposition — or such amusing contortions — on the part of critics as this indication of the childhood impulses toward incest which persist in the unconscious. An attempt has even been made recently to make out, in the face of all experience, that the incest should only be taken as "symbolic."— Ferenczi (1912) has proposed an ingenious "overinterpretation" of the Oedipus myth, based on a passage in one of Schopenhauer's letters. [*Added 1919.*] Later studies have shown that the "Oedipus complex," which was touched upon for the first time in the above paragraphs in the *Interpretation of Dreams*, throws a light of undreamt-of importance on the history of the human race and the evolution of religion and morality.

[4]Lewis Campbell's translation, lines 982ff [Fitts and Fitzgerald, scene 3, lines 67–69].

And just as these dreams, when dreamt by adults, are accompanied by feelings of repulsion, so too the legend must include horror and self-punishment. Its further modification originates once again in a misconceived secondary revision of the material, which has sought to exploit it for theological purposes. . . . The attempt to harmonize divine omnipotence with human responsibility must naturally fail in connection with this subject matter just as with any other.

Claude Lévi-Strauss (b. 1908)
FROM *THE STRUCTURAL STUDY OF MYTH*   1955

Claude Lévi-Strauss is one of a handful of modern anthropologists whose interests span the range of thought, culture, and understanding. His work has been of immense influence on French intellectual life and, by extension, on the intellectual life of modern times. His works include Triste Tropiques *(translated as* A World on the Wane*), about his own experiences as an anthropologist;* Structural Anthropology, *about the ways in which the study of anthropology implies a study of the structure of thought; and* Mythologies, *a four-volume summation of his thought. The excerpt that follows is structuralist in scope in that it attempts to understand the myth of Oedipus by examining the patterns of repetition in the original narrative. By setting up a grid, Lévi-Strauss begins to sort out the implications of the myth and to seek a meaning that is not necessarily apparent in the chronological order of the narrative. He examines the myth diachronically — across the lines of time — and thereby sees a new range of implications, which he treats as the structural implications of the myth. His reading is complex, suggesting that the Oedipus myth is a vegetation myth explaining the origins of mankind. Lévi-Strauss gives us a new way to interpret the significance of literary myths.*

The time has come to give a concrete example of the method we propose. We will use the Oedipus myth which has the advantage of being well known to everybody and for which no preliminary explanation is therefore needed. By doing so, I am well aware that the Oedipus myth has only reached us under late forms and through literary transfigurations concerned more with esthetic and moral preoccupations than with religious or ritual ones, whatever these may have been. But as will be shown later, this apparently unsatisfactory situation will strengthen our demonstration rather than weaken it.

The myth will be treated as would be an orchestra score perversely presented as a unilinear series and where our task is to reestablish the correct disposition. As if, for instance, we were confronted with a sequence of the type: 1,2,4,7,8,2,3,4,6,8,1,4,5,7,8,1,2,5,7,3,4,5,6,8 . . . , the assignment being to put all the 1's together, all the 2's, the 3's, etc.; the result is a chart:

```
1 2    4      7 8
  2 3 4    6     8
1       4 5    7 8
1 2       5  7
    3 4 5
              6   8
```

We will attempt to perform the same kind of operation on the Oedipus myth, trying out several dispositions. [. . .] Let us suppose, for the sake of argument, that the best arrangement is the following (although it might certainly be improved by the help of a specialist in Greek mythology):

Kadmos seeks his sister Europa ravished by Zeus.			
		Kadmos kills the dragon.	
	The Spartoi kill each other.		
			Labdacos (Laios's father) = *lame* (?).
		Oedipus kills his father Laios.	Laios (Oedipus's father) = *left-sided* (?).
			Oedipus kills the Sphinx.
Oedipus marries his mother Jocasta.			
	Eteocles kills his brother Polyneices.		Oedipus = *swollen-foot* (?).
Antigone buries her brother Polyneices despite prohibition.			

Thus, we find ourselves confronted with four vertical columns each of which includes several relations belonging to the same bundle. Were we to *tell* the myth, we would disregard the columns and read the rows from left to right and from top to bottom. But if we want to *understand* the myth, then we will have to disregard one half of the diachronic° dimension (top to bottom) and read from left to right, column after column, each one being considered as a unit.

All the relations belonging to the same column exhibit one common feature which it is our task to unravel. For instance, all the events grouped in the first column on the left have something to do with blood relations which are overemphasized, i.e., are subject to a more intimate treatment than they should be. Let us say, then, that the first column has as its common feature the *overrating of blood relations*. It is obvious that the second column expresses the same thing, but inverted: *underrating of blood relations*. The third column refers to monsters being slain. As

---

diachronic: Not ordered linearly in time but through time.

to the fourth, a word of clarification is needed. The remarkable connotation of the surnames in Oedipus's father-line has often been noticed. However, linguists usually disregard it, since to them the only way to define the meaning of a term is to investigate all the contexts in which it appears, and personal names, precisely because they are used as such, are not accompanied by any context. With the method we propose to follow the objection disappears since the myth itself provides its own context. The meaningful fact is no longer to be looked for in the eventual sense of each name, but in the fact that all the names have a common feature: i.e., that they may eventually mean something and that all these hypothetical meanings (which may well remain hypothetical) exhibit a common feature, namely they refer to *difficulties to walk and to behave straight.*

What is then the relationship between the two columns on the right? Column three refers to monsters. The dragon is a chthonian° being which has to be killed in order that mankind be born from the earth; the Sphinx is a monster unwilling to permit men to live. The last unit reproduces the first one which has to do with the *autochthonous°* origin of mankind. Since the monsters are overcome by men, we may thus say that the common feature of the third column is *the denial of the autochthonous origin of man.*

This immediately helps us to understand the meaning of the fourth column. In mythology it is a universal character of men born from the earth that at the moment they emerge from the depth, they either cannot walk or do it clumsily. This is the case of the chthonian beings in the mythology of the Pueblo: Masauwu, who leads the emergence, and the chthonian Shumaikoli are lame ("bleeding-foot," "sore-foot"). The same happens to the Koskimo of the Kwakiutl after they have been swallowed by the chthonian monster, Tsiakish: when they returned to the surface of the earth "they limped forward or tripped sideways." Then the common feature of the fourth column is: *the persistence of the autochthonous origin of man.* It follows that column four is to column three as column one is to column two. The inability to connect two kinds of relationships is overcome (or rather replaced) by the positive statement that contradictory relationships are identical inasmuch as they are both self-contradictory in a similar way. Although this is still a provisional formulation of the structure of mythical thought, it is sufficient at this stage.

Turning back to the Oedipus myth, we may now see what it means. The myth has to do with the inability, for a culture which holds the belief that mankind is autochthonous [. . .] to find a satisfactory transition between this theory and the knowledge that human beings are actually born from the union of man and woman. Although the problem obviously cannot be solved, the Oedipus myth provides a kind of logical tool which, to phrase it coarsely, replaces the original problem: born from one or born from two? born from different or born from same? By a correlation of this type, the overrating of blood relations is to the underrating of blood relations as the attempt to escape autochthony is to the impossibility to succeed in it. Although experience contradicts theory, social life verifies the cosmology by its similarity of structure. Hence cosmology is true.

Two remarks should be made at this stage.

In order to interpret the myth, we were able to leave aside a point which has until now worried the specialists, namely, that in the earlier (Homeric) versions of

---

chthonian: From the underworld.
autochthonous: Native, aboriginal; in this case, born of the earth.

the Oedipus myth, some basic elements are lacking, such as Jocasta killing herself and Oedipus piercing his own eyes. These events do not alter the substance of the myth although they can easily be integrated, the first one as a new case of auto-destruction (column three) while the second is another case of crippledness (column four). At the same time there is something significant in these additions since the shift from foot to head is to be correlated with the shift from: autochthonous origin negated to: self-destruction.

Thus, our method eliminates a problem which has been so far one of the main obstacles to the progress of mythological studies, namely, the quest for the *true* version, or the *earlier* one. On the contrary, we define the myth as consisting of all its versions; to put it otherwise: a myth remains the same as long as it is felt as such. A striking example is offered by the fact that our interpretation may take into account, and is certainly applicable to, the Freudian use of the Oedipus myth. Although the Freudian problem has ceased to be that of autochthony *versus* bisexual reproduction, it is still the problem of understanding how *one* can be born from *two*: how is it that we do not have only one procreator, but a mother plus a father? Therefore, not only Sophocles, but Freud himself, should be included among the recorded versions of the Oedipus myth on a par with earlier or seemingly more "authentic" versions.

ANTIGONE

Antigone was Sophocles' thirty-second play, produced in March 441 B.C., when he was in his mid-fifties. It draws a powerful response from its audience partly because it portrays the conflict between two proud, willful people: Antigone, a daughter of Oedipus and Iokaste, and Kreon, Iokaste's brother and the king of Thebes. Its original success was due in part to its portrayal of the individual's struggle against a tyrannical king. After enjoying thirty years of peace with its archrival Sparta, Athens was moving slowly toward war; and the memory of previous tyrants — both good, like Peisistratus, and bad, like his son Hippias — remained in the minds of Sophocles' audience.

It has never been easy to determine which of the two main characters is correct. Kreon's portrayal as a tyrant content to take up the state as his private property tells us that he is not to be fully trusted. At the same time, Antigone knows that the social mores of Thebes imply that a citizen must obey the ruler. Antigone's great courage makes the audience feel sympathy and admiration for her. She is a martyr to her beliefs, an ancient Joan of Arc.

The main conflict in *Antigone* centers on a distinction between law and justice, the conflict between a human law and a higher law. Kreon, the uncle of Antigone and Ismene, has made a decree: Polyneices, the brother of Antigone and Ismene, was guilty not only of killing his brother Eteocles but also of attacking the state and, like all traitors, will be denied a proper burial. When the action of the play begins, Antigone is determined to give her brother the burial that ancient tradition and her religious beliefs demand.

The opening dialogue with Ismene clarifies the important distinction between human law and the higher law on which Antigone says she must act. Ismene declares simply that she cannot go against the law of the citizens. Kreon has been willful in establishing the law, but it is nonetheless the law. Antigone, knowing full well the consequences of defying Kreon, nonetheless acts on her principles.

The complex conflict between Antigone and Kreon occurs on the level of citizen and ruler and is affected on the personal level by the relationship between Haimon, Kreon's son, and his intended bride, Antigone. The antagonism between Kreon and Haimon begins slowly, as Haimon appears to yield to the will of his father, but culminates in Haimon's ultimate rejection of his father by choosing to join Antigone in death.

When Teiresias reveals a prophecy of death and punishment and begs Kreon, for the sake of the suffering Thebes, to rescind his decree and give Polyneices a proper burial, Kreon willfully continues to heed his own declarations rather than oracular wisdom or the pleas of others.

By the time Kreon accepts Teiresias's prophecy, it is too late: he has lost his son, and his wife has killed herself. Power not only has corrupted Kreon but also has taken from him the people about whom he cared most. He emerges as an unyielding tyrant, guilty of making some of the same mistakes that haunted Oedipus.

Antigone emerges as a heroine who presses forward in the full conviction that she is right. She must honor her dead brother at all costs. Even if she must break the law of the state, she must answer to what she regards as a higher law. As she says early in the play, she has "dared the crime of piety." Yet she has within her the complexity of all humans: she in one sense acts in the knowledge that she is right but in another dares Kreon to punish her. She challenges Kreon so boldly that her every move forces the proud Kreon to harden his position and set in motion the ultimate tragedy — the loss of all he holds dear. This is yet one more tragic irony in the Theban trilogy.

Antigone in Performance

Since the eighteenth century *Antigone* has been produced in Europe and the Western Hemisphere in more or less its original form and in various adaptations and rewritings. Jean Cocteau combined his version with music by Arthur Honegger in 1930. It was rewritten and produced by Walter Hasenclever in 1917 as a protest against the First World War and then in 1944 by Jean Anouilh as a protest against Nazi occupation of Paris during World War II (see the excerpt on p. 127). The Royal Shakespeare Company produced *Antigone* along with all the surviving Greek tragedies in 1980. Bertolt Brecht's production of *Antigone* in 1948 introduced a Gestapo officer and Nazi brutality. Athol Fugard's *The Island* (1973) features a remarkable production of *Antigone* as a play within a play, produced by convicts in a South African island jail as a Christmas entertainment for their jailers and specially invited white guests. Fugard found, as have so many other adapters and producers, that the political power of *Antigone* leaps out for virtually all contemporary audiences. Janusz Glowacki, a Polish playwright, produced *Antigone in New York* at the Arena

Stage in Washington in March 1993. Inspired by both Sophocles and Beckett, it is set in Tompkins Square Park in New York. The action centers on a homeless Puerto Rican woman's efforts to bury a homeless man in the park. The action of the play demonstrates the durability of *Antigone*'s basic concept — that a decent burial is an essential vestige of humanity.

Sophocles (*c. 496–c. 406 B.C.*)

ANTIGONE   *441 B.C.*

TRANSLATED BY DUDLEY FITTS AND ROBERT FITZGERALD

Characters

ANTIGONE, } *daughters of Oedipus*
ISMENE,
EURYDICE, *wife of Kreon*
KREON, *King of Thebes*
HAIMON, *son of Kreon*
TEIRESIAS, *a blind seer*
A SENTRY
A MESSENGER
CHORUS

Scene: *Before the palace of Kreon, King of Thebes. A central double door, and two lateral doors. A platform extends the length of the facade, and from this platform three steps lead down into the orchestra, or chorus-ground.*

Time: *Dawn of the day after the repulse of the Argive army from the assault on Thebes.*

PROLOGUE°

(*Antigone and Ismene enter from the central door of the palace.*)

ANTIGONE: Ismene, dear sister,
   You would think that we had already suffered enough
   For the curse on Oedipus.°

Prologue: Portion of the play explaining the background and current action.   **3. curse on Oedipus:** Oedipus, king of Thebes and the father of Antigone and Ismene, was abandoned by his parents as an infant after the oracle foretold that he would one day kill his father and marry his mother. Rescued by a shepherd and raised by the king of Corinth, Oedipus returned years later to Thebes and unknowingly lived out the oracle's prophecy by killing Laios and marrying Iokaste. After his two sons, Eteocles and Polyneices, killed each other in combat, the throne went to Kreon, Iokaste's brother.

                              I cannot imagine any grief
   That you and I have not gone through. And now —   5
   Have they told you of the new decree of our King
      Kreon?
ISMENE: I have heard nothing: I know
   That two sisters lost two brothers, a double death
   In a single hour; and I know that the Argive army
   Fled in the night; but beyond this, nothing.   10
ANTIGONE: I thought so. And that is why I wanted
     you
   To come out here with me. There is something we
     must do.
ISMENE: Why do you speak so strangely?
ANTIGONE: Listen, Ismene:
   Kreon buried our brother Eteocles   15
   With military honors, gave him a soldier's funeral,
   And it was right that he should; but Polyneices,
   Who fought as bravely and died as miserably, —
   They say that Kreon has sworn
   No one shall bury him, no one mourn for him,   20
   But his body must lie in the fields, a sweet treasure
   For carrion birds to find as they search for food.
   That is what they say, and our good Kreon is
     coming here
   To announce it publicly; and the penalty —
   Stoning to death in the public square!
                     There it is,   25
   And now you can prove what you are:
   A true sister, or a traitor to your family.
ISMENE: Antigone, you are mad! What could I possibly
     do?
ANTIGONE: You must decide whether you will help me
     or not.
ISMENE: I do not understand you. Help you in what?   30
ANTIGONE: Ismene, I am going to bury him. Will you
     come?
ISMENE: Bury him! You have just said the new law
     forbids it.
ANTIGONE: He is my brother. And he is your brother,
     too.

ISMENE: But think of the danger! Think what Kreon
    will do!

35 ANTIGONE: Kreon is not strong enough to stand in my
    way.

ISMENE: Ah sister!
    Oedipus died, everyone hating him
    For what his own search brought to light, his eyes
40   Ripped out by his own hand; and Iocaste died,
    His mother and wife at once: she twisted the cords
    That strangled her life; and our two brothers died,
    Each killed by the other's sword. And we are left:
    But oh, Antigone,
    Think how much more terrible than these
    Our own death would be if we should go against
45   Kreon
    And do what he has forbidden! We are only
        women,
    We cannot fight with men, Antigone!
    The law is strong, we must give in to the law
    In this thing, and in worse. I beg the Dead
50   To forgive me, but I am helpless: I must yield
    To those in authority. And I think it is dangerous
        business
    To be always meddling.

ANTIGONE: If that is what you think,
    I should not want you, even if you asked to come.
    You have made your choice, you can be what you
        want to be.
55   But I will bury him; and if I must die,
    I say that this crime is holy: I shall lie down
    With him in death, and I shall be as dear
    To him as he to me.
               It is the dead,
    Not the living, who make the longest demands:
    We die for ever . . .
60   You may do as you like,
    Since apparently the laws of the gods mean nothing
        to you.

ISMENE: They mean a great deal to me; but I have no
        strength
    To break laws that were made for the public good.

ANTIGONE: That must be your excuse, I suppose. But
    as for me,
    I will bury the brother I love.

65 ISMENE: Antigone,
    I am so afraid for you!

ANTIGONE: You need not be:
    You have yourself to consider, after all.

ISMENE: But no one must hear of this, you must tell no
    one!
    I will keep it a secret, I promise!

ANTIGONE: O tell it! Tell everyone!
70   Think how they'll hate you when it all comes out
    If they learn that you knew about it all the time!

ISMENE: So fiery! You should be cold with fear.

ANTIGONE: Perhaps. But I am doing only what I must.

ISMENE: But can you do it? I say that you cannot.

75 ANTIGONE: Very well: when my strength gives out,
    I shall do no more.

ISMENE: Impossible things should not be tried at all.

ANTIGONE: Go away, Ismene:
    I shall be hating you soon, and the dead will too,
    For your words are hateful. Leave me my foolish
        plan: 80
    I am not afraid of the danger; if it means death,
    It will not be the worst of deaths — death without
        honor.

ISMENE: Go then, if you feel that you must.
    You are unwise,
    But a loyal friend indeed to those who love you.   85

*(Exit into the palace. Antigone goes off, left. Enter the
Chorus.)*

PARODOS° • *Strophe°* 1

CHORUS: Now the long blade of the sun, lying
    Level east to west, touches with glory
    Thebes of the Seven Gates. Open, unlidded
    Eye of golden day! O marching light
    Across the eddy and rush of Dirce's stream,°   5
    Striking the white shields of the enemy
    Thrown headlong backward from the blaze of
        morning!

CHORAGOS:° Polyneices their commander
    Roused them with windy phrases,
    He the wild eagle screaming   10
    Insults above our land,
    His wings their shields of snow,
    His crest their marshalled helms.

Antistrophe° 1

CHORUS: Against our seven gates in a yawning ring
    The famished spears came onward in the night;   15
    But before his jaws were sated with our blood,
    Or pinefire took the garland of our towers,
    He was thrown back, and as he turned, great
        Thebes —
    No tender victim for his noisy power —
    Rose like a dragon behind him, shouting war.   20

CHORAGOS: For God hates utterly
    The bray of bragging tongues;
    And when he beheld their smiling,
    Their swagger of golden helms,
    The frown of his thunder blasted   25
    Their first man from our walls.

Parodos: The song or ode chanted by the Chorus on its entry.
Strophe: Song sung by the Chorus as it danced from stage right
to stage left.   **5. Dirce's stream:** River near Thebes.   **8. Choragos:** Leader of the Chorus.   **Antistrophe:** Song sung by the
Chorus following the Strophe, as it danced back from stage left
to stage right.

Antigone (Martha Henry)
reassures Ismene in the
Repertory Theatre of Lincoln
Center production of *Antigone*
at the Vivian Beaumont
Theatre, directed by John
Hirsch in 1971.

Strophe 2

CHORUS: We heard his shout of triumph high in the air
    Turn to a scream; far out in a flaming arc
    He fell with his windy torch, and the earth struck
        him.
30   And others storming in fury no less than his
    Found shock of death in the dusty joy of battle.
CHORAGOS: Seven captains at seven gates
    Yielded their clanging arms to the god
    That bends the battle-line and breaks it.
35   These two only, brothers in blood,

Face to face in matchless rage,
Mirroring each the other's death
Clashed in long combat.

Antistrophe 2

CHORUS: But now in the beautiful morning of victory
    Let Thebes of the many chariots sing for joy!   40
    With hearts for dancing we'll take leave of war:
    Our temples shall be sweet with hymns of praise,
    And the long nights shall echo with our chorus.

SCENE 1

CHORAGOS: But now at last our new King is coming:
  Kreon of Thebes, Menoikeus' son.
  In this auspicious dawn of his reign
  What are the new complexities
5 That shifting Fate has woven for him?
  What is his counsel? Why has he summoned
  The old men to hear him?

(*Enter Kreon from the palace, center. He addresses the Chorus from the top step.*)

KREON: Gentlemen: I have the honor to inform you that
  our Ship of State, which recent storms have threat-
10 ened to destroy, has come safely to harbor at last,
  guided by the merciful wisdom of Heaven. I have
  summoned you here this morning because I know
  that I can depend upon you: your devotion to King
  Laios was absolute; you never hesitated in your duty
15 to our late ruler Oedipus; and when Oedipus died,
  your loyalty was transferred to his children. Unfortunately, as you know, his two sons, the princes Eteocles and Polyneices, have killed each other in battle;
  and I, as the next in blood, have succeeded to the full
  power of the throne.   20
    I am aware, of course, that no Ruler can expect
  complete loyalty from his subjects until he has been
  tested in office. Nevertheless, I say to you at the very
  outset that I have nothing but contempt for the kind
  of Governor who is afraid, for whatever reason, to   25
  follow the course that he knows is best for the State;
  and as for the man who sets private friendship above
  the public welfare, — I have no use for him, either. I
  call God to witness that if I saw my country headed
  for ruin, I should not be afraid to speak out plainly;   30
  and I need hardly remind you that I would never
  have any dealings with an enemy of the people. No
  one values friendship more highly than I; but we
  must remember that friends made at the risk of
  wrecking our Ship are not real friends at all.   35

Kreon (Philip Bosco), Antigone, and Haimon (David Birney).

These are my principles, at any rate, and that is
why I have made the following decision concerning
the sons of Oedipus: Eteocles, who died as a man
should die, fighting for his country, is to be buried
40   with full military honors, with all the ceremony that
is usual when the greatest heroes die; but his brother
Polyneices, who broke his exile to come back with
fire and sword against his native city and the shrines
of his fathers' gods, whose one idea was to spill
45   the blood of his blood and sell his own people into
slavery — Polyneices, I say, is to have no burial: no
man is to touch him or say the least prayer for
him; he shall lie on the plain, unburied; and the birds
and the scavenging dogs can do with him whatever
50   they like.
    This is my command, and you can see the wisdom
behind it. As long as I am King, no traitor is going to
be honored with the loyal man. But whoever shows
by word and deed that he is on the side of the
55   State, — he shall have my respect while he is living
and my reverence when he is dead.
CHORAGOS: If that is your will, Kreon son of
    Menoikeus,
    You have the right to enforce it: we are yours.
KREON: That is my will. Take care that you do your
    part.
CHORAGOS: We are old men: let the younger ones carry
60   it out.
KREON: I do not mean that: the sentries have been
    appointed.
CHORAGOS: Then what is it that you would have us do?
KREON: You will give no support to whoever breaks
    this law.
CHORAGOS: Only a crazy man is in love with death!
65 KREON: And death it is; yet money talks, and the wisest
    Have sometimes been known to count a few coins
        too many.

(*Enter Sentry from left.*)

SENTRY: I'll not say that I'm out of breath from running,
    King, because every time I stopped to think about
    what I have to tell you, I felt like going back. And all
70   the time a voice kept saying, "You fool, don't you
    know you're walking straight into trouble?"; and
    then another voice: "Yes, but if you let somebody
    else get the news to Kreon first, it will be even worse
    than that for you!" But good sense won out, at least I
75   hope it was good sense, and here I am with a story
    that makes no sense at all; but I'll tell it anyhow,
    because, as they say, what's going to happen's going
    to happen and —
KREON: Come to the point. What have you to say?
80 SENTRY: I did not do it. I did not see who did it.
    You must not punish me for what someone else has
        done.
KREON: A comprehensive defense! More effective,
    perhaps,
    If I knew its purpose. Come: what is it?

SENTRY: A dreadful thing . . . I don't know how to put
    it —
KREON: Out with it!
SENTRY: Well, then;   85
    The dead man —
                    Polyneices —

(*Pause. The Sentry is overcome, fumbles for words.
Kreon waits impassively.*)

                                out there —
                                        someone, —
    New dust on the slimy flesh!

(*Pause. No sign from Kreon.*)

    Someone has given it burial that way, and
    Gone . . .

(*Long pause. Kreon finally speaks with deadly control.*)

KREON: And the man who dared do this?
SENTRY: I swear I
    Do not know! You must believe me!
                                        Listen: 90
    The ground was dry, not a sign of digging, no,
    Not a wheeltrack in the dust, no trace of anyone.
    It was when they relieved us this morning: and one
        of them,
    The corporal, pointed to it.
                            There it was,
    The strangest —
                    Look: 95
    The body, just mounded over with light dust: you
        see?
    Not buried really, but as if they'd covered it
    Just enough for the ghost's peace. And no sign
    Of dogs or any wild animal that had been there.

    And then what a scene there was! Every man of us   100
    Accusing the other: we all proved the other man
        did it.
    We all had proof that we could not have done it.
    We were ready to take hot iron in our hands,
    Walk through fire, swear by all the gods,
    It was not I!   105
    I do not know who it was, but it was not I!

(*Kreon's rage has been mounting steadily, but the Sentry
is too intent upon his story to notice it.*)

    And then, when this came to nothing, someone said
    A thing that silenced us and made us stare
    Down at the ground: you had to be told the news,
    And one of us had to do it! We threw the dice,   110
    And the bad luck fell to me. So here I am,
    No happier to be here than you are to have me:
    Nobody likes the man who brings bad news.
CHORAGOS: I have been wondering, King: can it be
    that the gods have done this?
KREON (*furiously*): Stop!   115
    Must you doddering wrecks

Go out of your heads entirely? "The gods"!
Intolerable!
The gods favor this corpse? Why? How had he
    served them?
120 Tried to loot their temples, burn their images,
Yes, and the whole State, and its laws with it!
Is it your senile opinion that the gods love to honor
    bad men?
A pious thought! —
           No, from the very beginning
There have been those who have whispered
    together,
125 Stiff-necked anarchists, putting their heads together,
Scheming against me in alleys. These are the men,
And they have bribed my own guard to do this
    thing.
(*Sententiously.*) Money!
There's nothing in the world so demoralizing as
    money.
130 Down go your cities,
Homes gone, men gone, honest hearts corrupted,
Crookedness of all kinds, and all for money!
(*To Sentry.*)   But you —
I swear by God and by the throne of God,
The man who has done this thing shall pay for it!
135 Find that man, bring him here to me, or your death
Will be the least of your problems: I'll string you up
Alive, and there will be certain ways to make you
Discover your employer before you die;
And the process may teach you a lesson you seem to
    have missed:
140 The dearest profit is sometimes all too dear:
That depends on the source. Do you understand
    me?
A fortune won is often misfortune.
SENTRY: King, may I speak?
KREON: Your very voice distresses me.
SENTRY: Are you sure that it is my voice, and not your
    conscience?
145 KREON: By God, he wants to analyze me now!
SENTRY: It is not what I say, but what has been done,
    that hurts you.
KREON: You talk too much.
SENTRY: Maybe; but I've done nothing.
KREON: Sold your soul for some silver: that's all you've
    done.
SENTRY: How dreadful it is when the right judge judges
    wrong!
150 KREON: Your figures of speech
May entertain you now; but unless you bring me the
    man,
You will get little profit from them in the end.
          (*Exit Kreon into the palace.*)
SENTRY: "Bring me the man"— !
I'd like nothing better than bringing him the man!
But bring him or not, you have seen the last of me
155   here.
At any rate, I am safe!   (*Exit Sentry.*)

ODE° 1 • *Strophe 1*

CHORUS: Numberless are the world's wonders, but
    none
  More wonderful than man; the stormgray sea
  Yields to his prows, the huge crests bear him high;
  Earth, holy and inexhaustible, is graven
  With shining furrows where his plows have gone   5
  Year after year, the timeless labor of stallions.

Antistrophe 1

  The lightboned birds and beasts that cling to cover,
  The lithe fish lighting their reaches of dim water,
  All are taken, tamed in the net of his mind;
  The lion on the hill, the wild horse windy-maned,   10
  Resign to him; and his blunt yoke has broken
  The sultry shoulders of the mountain bull.

Strophe 2

  Words also, and thought as rapid as air,
  He fashions to his good use; statecraft is his
  And his the skill that deflects the arrows of snow,   15
  The spears of winter rain: from every wind
  He has made himself secure — from all but one:
  In the late wind of death he cannot stand.

Antistrophe 2

  O clear intelligence, force beyond all measure!
  O fate of man, working both good and evil!   20
  When the laws are kept, how proudly his city stands!
  When the laws are broken, what of his city then?
  Never may the anarchic man find rest at my hearth,
  Never be it said that my thoughts are his thoughts.

SCENE 2

(*Reenter Sentry leading Antigone.*)

CHORAGOS: What does this mean? Surely this captive
    woman
  Is the Princess, Antigone. Why should she be taken?
SENTRY: Here is the one who did it! We caught her
  In the very act of burying him. — Where is Kreon?
CHORAGOS: Just coming from the house.

(*Enter Kreon, center.*)

KREON: What has happened? 5
  Why have you come back so soon?
SENTRY (*expansively*):   O King,

Ode: Song sung by the Chorus.

A man should never be too sure of anything:
I would have sworn
That you'd not see me here again: your anger
Frightened me so, and the things you threatened me
10   with;
But how could I tell then
That I'd be able to solve the case so soon?
No dice-throwing this time: I was only too glad to
      come!
Here is this woman. She is the guilty one:
15   We found her trying to bury him.
Take her, then; question her; judge her as you will.
I am through with the whole thing now, and glad of
      it.
    KREON: But this is Antigone! Why have you brought
      her here?
    SENTRY: She was burying him, I tell you!
    KREON (severely):   Is this the truth?
20   SENTRY: I saw her with my own eyes. Can I say more?
    KREON: The details: come, tell me quickly!
    SENTRY: It was like this:
After those terrible threats of yours, King,
We went back and brushed the dust away from the
      body.
The flesh was soft by now, and stinking,
25   So we sat on a hill to windward and kept guard.
No napping this time! We kept each other awake.
But nothing happened until the white round sun
Whirled in the center of the round sky over us:
Then, suddenly,
A storm of dust roared up from the earth, and the
30   sky
Went out, the plain vanished with all its trees
In the stinging dark. We closed our eyes and
      endured.
The whirlwind lasted a long time, but it passed;
And then we looked, and there was Antigone!
35   I have seen
A mother bird come back to a stripped nest, heard
Her crying bitterly a broken note or two
For the young ones stolen. Just so, when this girl
Found the bare corpse, and all her love's work
      wasted,
40   She wept, and cried on heaven to damn the hands
That had done this thing.
                    And then she brought more dust
And sprinkled wine three times for her brother's
      ghost.
We ran and took her at once. She was not afraid,
Not even when we charged her with what she had
      done.
She denied nothing.
45   And this was a comfort to me,
And some uneasiness: for it is a good thing
To escape from death, but it is no great pleasure
To bring death to a friend.
                    Yet I always say
There is nothing so comfortable as your own safe
      skin!

    KREON (slowly, dangerously): And you, Antigone,   50
    You with your head hanging, — do you confess this
      thing?
    ANTIGONE: I do. I deny nothing.
    KREON (to Sentry):   You may go.
                            (Exit Sentry.)
    (To Antigone.) Tell me, tell me briefly:
    Had you heard my proclamation touching this
      matter?
    ANTIGONE: It was public. Could I help hearing it?   55
    KREON: And yet you dared defy the law.
    ANTIGONE: I dared.
It was not God's proclamation. That final Justice
That rules the world below makes no such laws.

Your edict, King, was strong,
But all your strength is weakness itself against   60
The immortal unrecorded laws of God.
They are not merely now: they were, and shall be,
Operative for ever, beyond man utterly.

I knew I must die, even without your decree:
I am only mortal. And if I must die   65
Now, before it is my time to die,
Surely this is no hardship: can anyone
Living, as I live, with evil all about me,
Think Death less than a friend? This death of mine
Is of no importance; but if I had left my brother   70
Lying in death unburied, I should have suffered.
Now I do not.
                  You smile at me. Ah Kreon,
Think me a fool, if you like; but it may well be
That a fool convicts me of folly.
    CHORAGOS: Like father, like daughter: both headstrong,
      deaf to reason!   75
    She has never learned to yield.
    KREON: She has much to learn.
The inflexible heart breaks first, the toughest iron
Cracks first, and the wildest horses bend their necks
At the pull of the smallest curb.
                      Pride? In a slave?
This girl is guilty of a double insolence,   80
Breaking the given laws and boasting of it.
Who is the man here,
She or I, if this crime goes unpunished?
Sister's child, or more than sister's child,
Or closer yet in blood — she and her sister   85
Win bitter death for this!
    (To Servants.)   Go, some of you,
Arrest Ismene. I accuse her equally.
Bring her: you will find her sniffling in the house
      there.

Her mind's a traitor: crimes kept in the dark
Cry for light, and the guardian brain shudders;   90
But how much worse than this
Is brazen boasting of barefaced anarchy!
    ANTIGONE: Kreon, what more do you want than my
      death?

Top: Kreon (F. Murray
Abraham) in a scene from the
1982 New York Shakespeare
Festival production directed by
Joseph Chaikin. Right:
Antigone (Lisa Banes)
steadfastly admitting her guilt.

The Chorus urges Kreon to change his decree before it is too late.

KREON: Nothing.
  That gives me everything.
ANTIGONE: Then I beg you: kill me.
95   This talking is a great weariness: your words
  Are distasteful to me, and I am sure that mine
  Seem so to you. And yet they should not seem so:
  I should have praise and honor for what I have
      done.
  All these men here would praise me
100   Were their lips not frozen shut with fear of you.
  (*Bitterly.*) Ah the good fortune of kings,
  Licensed to say and do whatever they please!
KREON: You are alone here in that opinion.
ANTIGONE: No, they are with me. But they keep their
      tongues in leash.
105   KREON: Maybe. But you are guilty, and they are not.
ANTIGONE: There is no guilt in reverence for the dead.
KREON: But Eteocles — was he not your brother too?

ANTIGONE: My brother too.
KREON: And you insult his memory?
ANTIGONE (*softly*): The dead man would not say that I
      insult it.
KREON: He would: for you honor a traitor as much as
      him.   110
ANTIGONE: His own brother, traitor or not, and equal
      in blood.
KREON: He made war on his country. Eteocles defended
      it.
ANTIGONE: Nevertheless, there are honors due all the
      dead.
KREON: But not the same for the wicked as for the
      just.
ANTIGONE: Ah Kreon, Kreon,   115
  Which of us can say what the gods hold wicked?
KREON: An enemy is an enemy, even dead.
ANTIGONE: It is my nature to join in love, not hate.

KREON (*finally losing patience*): Go join them then; if
            you must have your love,
120   Find it in hell!
CHORAGOS: But see, Ismene comes:

(*Enter Ismene, guarded.*)

         Those tears are sisterly, the cloud
         That shadows her eyes rains down gentle sorrow.
KREON: You too, Ismene,
125   Snake in my ordered house, sucking my blood
         Stealthily — and all the time I never knew
         That these two sisters were aiming at my throne!
                                                    Ismene,
         Do you confess your share in this crime, or deny it?
         Answer me.
130   ISMENE: Yes, if she will let me say so. I am guilty.
      ANTIGONE (*coldly*): No, Ismene. You have no right to
            say so.
         You would not help me, and I will not have you
            help me.
      ISMENE: But now I know what you meant; and I am
            here
         To join you, to take my share of punishment.
      ANTIGONE: The dead man and the gods who rule the
135   dead
         Know whose act this was. Words are not friends.
      ISMENE: Do you refuse me, Antigone? I want to die
            with you:
         I too have a duty that I must discharge to the dead.
      ANTIGONE: You shall not lessen my death by sharing it.
140   ISMENE: What do I care for life when you are dead?
      ANTIGONE: Ask Kreon. You're always hanging on his
            opinions.
      ISMENE: You are laughing at me. Why, Antigone?
      ANTIGONE: It's a joyless laughter, Ismene.
      ISMENE: But can I do nothing?
      ANTIGONE: Yes. Save yourself. I shall not envy you.
         There are those who will praise you; I shall have
145   honor, too.
      ISMENE: But we are equally guilty!
      ANTIGONE: No more, Ismene.
         You are alive, but I belong to Death.
      KREON (*to the Chorus*): Gentlemen, I beg you to
            observe these girls:
         One has just now lost her mind; the other,
150   It seems, has never had a mind at all.
      ISMENE: Grief teaches the steadiest minds to waver,
            King.
      KREON: Yours certainly did, when you assumed guilt
            with the guilty!
      ISMENE: But how could I go on living without her?
      KREON: You are.
         She is already dead.
      ISMENE: But your own son's bride!
      KREON: There are places enough for him to push his
155   plow.
         I want no wicked women for my sons!
      ISMENE: O dearest Haimon, how your father wrongs
            you!

KREON: I've had enough of your childish talk of
            marriage!
CHORAGOS: Do you really intend to steal this girl from
            your son?
KREON: No; Death will do that for me.
CHORAGOS: Then she must die?   160
KREON (*ironically*): You dazzle me.
                         — But enough of this talk!
      (*To Guards.*) You, there, take them away and guard
            them well:
      For they are but women, and even brave men run
      When they see Death coming.
            (*Exeunt° Ismene, Antigone, and Guards.*)

ODE 2 • *Strophe 1*

CHORUS: Fortunate is the man who has never tasted
            God's vengeance!
         Where once the anger of heaven has struck, that
            house is shaken
         For ever: damnation rises behind each child
         Like a wave cresting out of the black northeast,
         When the long darkness under sea roars up   5
         And bursts drumming death upon the windwhipped
            sand.

Antistrophe 1

         I have seen this gathering sorrow from time long
            past
         Loom upon Oedipus' children: generation from
            generation
         Takes the compulsive rage of the enemy god.
         So lately this last flower of Oedipus' line   10
         Drank the sunlight! but now a passionate word
         And a handful of dust have closed up all its beauty.

Strophe 2

            What mortal arrogance
            Transcends the wrath of Zeus?
         Sleep cannot lull him nor the effortless long months 15
         Of the timeless gods: but he is young for ever,
         And his house is the shining day of high Olympos.
            All that is and shall be,
            And all the past, is his.
         No pride on earth is free of the curse of heaven.   20

Antistrophe 2

         The straying dreams of men
            May bring them ghosts of joy:
         But as they drowse, the waking embers burn them;

165. [S.D.] ***Exeunt:*** Latin for "they go out."

Or they walk with fixed eyes, as blind men walk.
But the ancient wisdom speaks for our own time:
   Fate works most for woe
   With Folly's fairest show.
Man's little pleasure is the spring of sorrow.

SCENE 3

CHORAGOS: But here is Haimon, King, the last of all
   your sons.
   Is it grief for Antigone that brings him here,
   And bitterness at being robbed of his bride?

(Enter Haimon.)

KREON: We shall soon see, and no need of diviners.
                   — Son,
   You have heard my final judgment on that girl:
   Have you come here hating me, or have you come
   With deference and with love, whatever I do?
HAIMON: I am your son, father. You are my guide.
   You make things clear for me, and I obey you.
   No marriage means more to me than your
   continuing wisdom.
KREON: Good. That is the way to behave: subordinate
   Everything else, my son, to your father's will.
   This is what a man prays for, that he may get
   Sons attentive and dutiful in his house,
   Each one hating his father's enemies,
   Honoring his father's friends. But if his sons
   Fail him, if they turn out unprofitably,
   What has he fathered but trouble for himself
   And amusement for the malicious?
              So you are right
   Not to lose your head over this woman.
   Your pleasure with her would soon grow cold,
   Haimon,
   And then you'd have a hellcat in bed and
   elsewhere.
   Let her find her husband in Hell!
   Of all the people in this city, only she
   Has had contempt for my law and broken it.

   Do you want me to show myself weak before the
   people?
   Or to break my sworn word? No, and I will not.
   The woman dies.
   I suppose she'll plead "family ties." Well, let her.
   If I permit my own family to rebel,
   How shall I earn the world's obedience?
   Show me the man who keeps his house in hand,
   He's fit for public authority.
              I'll have no dealings
   With lawbreakers, critics of the government:
   Whoever is chosen to govern should be obeyed —
   Must be obeyed, in all things, great and small,
   Just and unjust! O Haimon,
   The man who knows how to obey, and that man
   only,

Knows how to give commands when the time
   comes.
   You can depend on him, no matter how fast
   The spears come: he's a good soldier, he'll stick it
   out.
   Anarchy, anarchy! Show me a greater evil!
   This is why cities tumble and the great houses rain
   down,
   This is what scatters armies!
   No, no: good lives are made so by discipline.
   We keep the laws then, and the lawmakers,
   And no woman shall seduce us. If we must lose,
   Let's lose to a man, at least! Is a woman stronger
   than we?
CHORAGOS: Unless time has rusted my wits,
   What you say, King, is said with point and dignity.
HAIMON *(boyishly earnest)*: Father:
   Reason is God's crowning gift to man, and you are
   right
   To warn me against losing mine. I cannot say —
   I hope that I shall never want to say! — that you
   Have reasoned badly. Yet there are other men
   Who can reason, too; and their opinions might be
   helpful.
   You are not in a position to know everything
   That people say or do, or what they feel:
   Your temper terrifies — everyone
   Will tell you only what you like to hear.
   But I, at any rate, can listen; and I have heard them
   Muttering and whispering in the dark about this girl.
   They say no woman has ever, so unreasonably,
   Died so shameful a death for a generous act:
   "She covered her brother's body. Is this indecent?
   She kept him from dogs and vultures. Is this a
   crime?
   Death? — She should have all the honor that we can
   give her!"

   This is the way they talk out there in the city.
   You must believe me:
   Nothing is closer to me than your happiness.
   What could be closer? Must not any son
   Value his father's fortune as his father does his?
   I beg you, do not be unchangeable:
   Do not believe that you alone can be right.
   The man who thinks that,
   The man who maintains that only he has the power
   To reason correctly, the gift to speak, the soul —
   A man like that, when you know him, turns out
   empty.
   It is not reason never to yield to reason!

   In flood time you can see how some trees bend,
   And because they bend, even their twigs are safe,
   While stubborn trees are torn up, roots and all.
   And the same thing happens in sailing:
   Make your sheet fast, never slacken, — and over
   you go,
   Head over heels and under: and there's your voyage.

Forget you are angry! Let yourself be moved!
I know I am young; but please let me say this:
The ideal condition
Would be, I admit, that men should be right by
    instinct;
90 But since we are all too likely to go astray,
The reasonable thing is to learn from those who can
    teach.
CHORAGOS: You will do well to listen to him, King,
If what he says is sensible. And you, Haimon,
Must listen to your father. — Both speak well.
KREON: You consider it right for a man of my years
95   and experience
To go to school to a boy?
HAIMON: It is not right
If I am wrong. But if I am young, and right,
What does my age matter?
KREON: You think it right to stand up for an anarchist?
100 HAIMON: Not at all. I pay no respect to criminals.
KREON: Then she is not a criminal?
HAIMON: The City would deny it, to a man.
KREON: And the City proposes to teach me how to rule?
HAIMON: Ah. Who is it that's talking like a boy now?
KREON: My voice is the one voice giving orders in this
105   City!
HAIMON: It is no City if it takes orders from one voice.
KREON: The State is the King!
HAIMON: Yes, if the State is a desert.

(*Pause.*)

KREON: This boy, it seems, has sold out to a woman.
HAIMON: If you are a woman: my concern is only for
    you.
KREON: So? Your "concern"! In a public brawl with
110   your father!
HAIMON: How about you, in a public brawl with
    justice?
KREON: With justice, when all that I do is within my
    rights?
HAIMON: You have no right to trample on God's right.
KREON (*completely out of control*): Fool, adolescent
    fool! Taken in by a woman!
115 HAIMON: You'll never see me taken in by anything vile.
KREON: Every word you say is for her!
HAIMON (*quietly, darkly*):   And for you.
And for me. And for the gods under the earth.
KREON: You'll never marry her while she lives.
HAIMON: Then she must die. — But her death will
    cause another.
120 KREON: Another?
Have you lost your senses? Is this an open threat?
HAIMON: There is no threat in speaking to emptiness.
KREON: I swear you'll regret this superior tone of
    yours!
You are the empty one!
HAIMON: If you were not my father,
125   I'd say you were perverse.
KREON: You girl-struck fool, don't play at words with
    me!

HAIMON: I am sorry. You prefer silence.
KREON: Now, by God —
I swear, by all the gods in heaven above us,
You'll watch it, I swear you shall!
(*To the Servants.*)   Bring her out!
Bring the woman out! Let her die before his eyes!   130
Here, this instant, with her bridegroom beside her!
HAIMON: Not here, no; she will not die here, King.
And you will never see my face again.
Go on raving as long as you've a friend to endure
    you.   (*Exit Haimon.*)
CHORAGOS: Gone, gone.   135
Kreon, a young man in a rage is dangerous!
KREON: Let him do, or dream to do, more than a man
    can.
He shall not save these girls from death.
CHORAGOS: These girls?
You have sentenced them both?
KREON: No, you are right.
I will not kill the one whose hands are clean.   140
CHORAGOS: But Antigone?
KREON (*somberly*):   I will carry her far away
Out there in the wilderness, and lock her
Living in a vault of stone. She shall have food,
As the custom is, to absolve the State of her death.
And there let her pray to the gods of hell: 145
They are her only gods:
Perhaps they will show her an escape from death,
Or she may learn,
                        though late,
That piety shown the dead is pity in vain.
                                        (*Exit Kreon.*)

ODE 3 • *Strophe*

CHORUS: Love, unconquerable
Waster of rich men, keeper
Of warm lights and all-night vigil
In the soft face of a girl:
Sea-wanderer, forest-visitor!   5
Even the pure Immortals cannot escape you,
And mortal man, in his one day's dusk,
Trembles before your glory.

Antistrophe

Surely you swerve upon ruin
The just man's consenting heart,   10
As here you have made bright anger
Strike between father and son —
And none has conquered but Love!
A girl's glance working the will of heaven:
Pleasure to her alone who mocks us,   15
Merciless Aphrodite.°

---

16. Aphrodite: Goddess of love and beauty.

SCENE 4

CHORAGOS (*as Antigone enters guarded*): But I can no
    longer stand in awe of this,
    Nor, seeing what I see, keep back my tears.
    Here is Antigone, passing to that chamber
    Where all find sleep at last.

Strophe 1

5 ANTIGONE: Look upon me, friends, and pity me
    Turning back at the night's edge to say
    Good-by to the sun that shines for me no longer;
    Now sleepy Death
    Summons me down to Acheron,° that cold shore:
10   There is no bridesong there, nor any music.
  CHORUS: Yet not unpraised, not without a kind of
    honor,
    You walk at last into the underworld
    Untouched by sickness, broken by no sword.
    What woman has ever found your way to death?

Antistrophe 1

15 ANTIGONE: How often I have heard the story of Niobe,°
    Tantalos' wretched daughter, how the stone
    Clung fast about her, ivy-close: and they say
    The rain falls endlessly
    And sifting soft snow; her tears are never done.
20   I feel the loneliness of her death in mine.
  CHORUS: But she was born of heaven, and you
    Are woman, woman-born. If her death is yours,
    A mortal woman's, is this not for you
    Glory in our world and in the world beyond?

Strophe 2

25 ANTIGONE: You laugh at me. Ah, friends, friends,
    Can you not wait until I am dead? O Thebes,
    O men many-charioted, in love with Fortune,
    Dear springs of Dirce, sacred Theban grove,
    Be witnesses for me, denied all pity,
30   Unjustly judged! and think a word of love
    For her whose path turns
    Under dark earth, where there are no more tears.
  CHORUS: You have passed beyond human daring and
    come at last
    Into a place of stone where Justice sits.
35   I cannot tell
    What shape of your father's guilt appears in this.

---

9. **Acheron:** River in Hades, domain of the dead.   **15. Niobe:**
When Niobe's many children (up to twenty in some accounts)
were slain in punishment for their mother's boastfulness, Niobe
was turned into a stone on Mount Sipylus. Her tears became
the mountain's streams.

Antistrophe 2

ANTIGONE: You have touched it at last: that bridal bed
    Unspeakable, horror of son and mother mingling:
    Their crime, infection of all our family!
    O Oedipus, father and brother!   40
    Your marriage strikes from the grave to murder
    mine.
    I have been a stranger here in my own land:
    All my life
    The blasphemy of my birth has followed me.
  CHORUS: Reverence is a virtue, but strength   45
    Lives in established law: that must prevail.
    You have made your choice,
    Your death is the doing of your conscious hand.

Epode°

ANTIGONE: Then let me go, since all your words are
    bitter,
    And the very light of the sun is cold to me.   50
    Lead me to my vigil, where I must have
    Neither love nor lamentation; no song, but silence.

(*Kreon interrupts impatiently.*)

KREON: If dirges and planned lamentations could put
    off death,
    Men would be singing for ever.
    (*To the Servants.*)   Take her, go!
    You know your orders: take her to the vault   55
    And leave her alone there. And if she lives or dies,
    That's her affair, not ours: our hands are clean.
ANTIGONE: O tomb, vaulted bride-bed in eternal rock,
    Soon I shall be with my own again
    Where Persephone° welcomes the thin ghosts
    underground: 60
    And I shall see my father again, and you, mother,
    And dearest Polyneices —
                     dearest indeed
    To me, since it was my hand
    That washed him clean and poured the ritual wine:
    And my reward is death before my time!   65

    And yet, as men's hearts know, I have done no
    wrong,
    I have not sinned before God. Or if I have,
    I shall know the truth in death. But if the guilt
    Lies upon Kreon who judged me, then, I pray,
    May his punishment equal my own.
CHORAGOS: O passionate heart,   70
    Unyielding, tormented still by the same winds!
KREON: Her guards shall have good cause to regret
    their delaying.
ANTIGONE: Ah! That voice is like the voice of death!

Epode: Song sung by the Chorus while standing still after
singing the strophe and antistrophe.   **60. Persephone:** Abducted by Pluto, god of the underworld, to be his queen.

KREON: I can give you no reason to think you are
    mistaken.
75 ANTIGONE: Thebes, and you my fathers' gods,
    And rulers of Thebes, you see me now, the last
    Unhappy daughter of a line of kings,
    Your kings, led away to death. You will remember
    What things I suffer, and at what men's hands,
80   Because I would not transgress the laws of heaven.
    (*To the Guards, simply.*) Come: let us wait no
      longer.   (*Exit Antigone, left, guarded.*)

ODE 4 • *Strophe 1*

CHORUS: All Danae's beauty was locked away
    In a brazen cell where the sunlight could not come:
    A small room still as any grave, enclosed her.
    Yet she was a princess too,
5   And Zeus in a rain of gold poured love upon her.°
    O child, child,
    No power in wealth or war
    Or tough sea-blackened ships
    Can prevail against untiring Destiny!

Antistrophe 1

10   And Dryas's, son° also, that furious king,
    Bore the god's prisoning anger for his pride:
    Sealed up by Dionysos in deaf stone,
    His madness died among echoes.
    So at the last he learned what dreadful power
15   His tongue had mocked:
    For he had profaned the revels,
    And fired the wrath of the nine
    Implacable Sisters° that love the sound of the flute.

Strophe 2

    And old men tell a half-remembered tale
20   Of horror° where a dark ledge splits the sea
    And a double surf beats on the gray shores:
    How a king's new woman, sick
    With hatred for the queen he had imprisoned,
    Ripped out his two sons' eyes with her bloody
      hands

1–5. All Danae's beauty . . . poured love upon her: Locked
away to prevent the fulfillment of a prophecy that she would
bear a son who would kill her father, Danae was nonetheless
impregnated by Zeus, who came to her in a shower of gold.
The prophecy was fulfilled by the son that came of their union.
10. Dryas's son: King Lycurgus of Thrace, whom Dionysus,
god of wine, caused to be stricken with madness.   **18. Sisters:**
The Muses, nine sister goddesses who presided over poetry and
music, arts and sciences.   **19–20. half-remembered tale of horror:** The second wife of King Phineas blinded the sons of his
first wife, Cleopatra, whom Phineas had imprisoned in a cave.

While grinning Ares° watched the shuttle plunge   25
Four times: four blind wounds crying for revenge,

Antistrophe 2

Crying, tears and blood mingled. — Piteously born,
Those sons whose mother was of heavenly birth!
Her father was the god of the North Wind
And she was cradled by gales,   30
She raced with young colts on the glittering hills
And walked untrammeled in the open light:
But in her marriage deathless Fate found means
To build a tomb like yours for all her joy.

SCENE 5

(*Enter blind Teiresias, led by a boy. The opening speeches
of Teiresias should be in singsong contrast to the realistic lines of Kreon.*)

TEIRESIAS: This is the way the blind man comes,
    Princes, Princes,
    Lockstep, two heads lit by the eyes of one.
KREON: What new thing have you to tell us, old
    Teiresias?
TEIRESIAS: I have much to tell you: listen to the prophet,
    Kreon.
KREON: I am not aware that I have ever failed to listen.   5
TEIRESIAS: Then you have done wisely, King, and ruled
    well.
KREON: I admit my debt to you. But what have you to
    say?
TEIRESIAS: This, Kreon: you stand once more on the
    edge of fate.
KREON: What do you mean? Your words are a kind of
    dread.
TEIRESIAS: Listen, Kreon: 10
    I was sitting in my chair of augury, at the place
    Where the birds gather about me. They were all a-
      chatter,
    As is their habit, when suddenly I heard
    A strange note in their jangling, a scream, a
    Whirring fury; I knew that they were fighting,   15
    Tearing each other, dying
    In a whirlwind of wings clashing. And I was afraid.
    I began the rites of burnt-offering at the altar
    But Hephaistos° failed me: instead of bright flame,
    There was only the sputtering slime of the fat
      thigh-flesh   20
    Melting: the entrails dissolved in gray smoke,
    The bare bone burst from the welter. And no blaze!

    This was a sign from heaven. My boy described it,
    Seeing for me as I see for others.
    I tell you, Kreon, you yourself have brought   25

25. Ares: God of war.   **19. Hephaistos:** God of fire.

This new calamity upon us. Our hearths and altars
Are stained with the corruption of dogs and carrion
    birds
That glut themselves on the corpse of Oedipus's son.
The gods are deaf when we pray to them, their fire
30   Recoils from our offering, their birds of omen
Have no cry of comfort, for they are gorged
With the thick blood of the dead.
                                   O my son,
These are no trifles! Think: all men make mistakes,
But a good man yields when he knows his course is
    wrong,
35   And repairs the evil. The only crime is pride.

Give in to the dead man, then: do not fight with a
    corpse —
What glory is it to kill a man who is dead?
Think, I beg you:
It is for your own good that I speak as I do.
40   You should be able to yield for your own good.
KREON: It seems that prophets have made me their
    especial province.
All my life long
I have been a kind of butt for the dull arrows
Of doddering fortune-tellers!
                              No, Teiresias:
45   If your birds — if the great eagles of God himself
Should carry him stinking bit by bit to heaven,
I would not yield. I am not afraid of pollution:
No man can defile the gods.
                           Do what you will,
Go into business, make money, speculate
50   In India gold or that synthetic gold from Sardis,
Get rich otherwise than by my consent to bury him.
Teiresias, it is a sorry thing when a wise man
Sells his wisdom, lets out his words for hire!
TEIRESIAS: Ah Kreon! Is there no man left in the
    world —
KREON: To do what? — Come, let's have the
55   aphorism!
TEIRESIAS: No man who knows that wisdom outweighs
    any wealth?
KREON: As surely as bribes are baser than any
    baseness.
TEIRESIAS: You are sick, Kreon! You are deathly sick!
KREON: As you say: it is not my place to challenge a
    prophet.
60   TEIRESIAS: Yet you have said my prophecy is for sale.
KREON: The generation of prophets has always loved
    gold.
TEIRESIAS: The generation of kings has always loved
    brass.
KREON: You forget yourself! You are speaking to your
    King.
TEIRESIAS: I know it. You are a king because of me.
65   KREON: You have a certain skill; but you have sold out.
TEIRESIAS: King, you will drive me to words that —
KREON: Say them, say them!

Only remember: I will not pay you for them.
TEIRESIAS: No, you will find them too costly.
KREON: No doubt. Speak:
Whatever you say, you will not change my will.
TEIRESIAS: Then take this, and take it to heart!   70
The time is not far off when you shall pay back
Corpse for corpse, flesh of your own flesh.
You have thrust the child of this world into living
    night,
You have kept from the gods below the child that is
    theirs:
The one in a grave before her death, the other,   75
Dead, denied the grave. This is your crime:
And the Furies° and the dark gods of Hell
Are swift with terrible punishment for you.

Do you want to buy me now, Kreon?

                                   Not many days,
And your house will be full of men and women
    weeping,   80
And curses will be hurled at you from far
Cities grieving for sons unburied, left to rot
Before the walls of Thebes.

These are my arrows, Kreon: they are all for you.

(*To Boy.*) But come, child: lead me home.   85
Let him waste his fine anger upon younger men.
Maybe he will learn at last
To control a wiser tongue in a better head.
                                   (*Exit Teiresias.*)
CHORAGOS: The old man has gone, King, but his
    words
Remain to plague us. I am old, too,   90
But I cannot remember that he was ever false.
KREON: That is true. . . . It troubles me.
Oh it is hard to give in! but it is worse
To risk everything for stubborn pride.
CHORAGOS: Kreon: take my advice.
KREON: What shall I do?   95
CHORAGOS: Go quickly: free Antigone from her vault
And build a tomb for the body of Polyneices.
KREON: You would have me do this!
CHORAGOS: Kreon, yes!
And it must be done at once: God moves
Swiftly to cancel the folly of stubborn men.   100
KREON: It is hard to deny the heart! But I
Will do it: I will not fight with destiny.
CHORAGOS: You must go yourself, you cannot leave it
    to others.
KREON: I will go.
              — Bring axes, servants:
Come with me to the tomb. I buried her, I   105

---

77. Furies: Spirits called on to avenge crimes, especially those against kin.

Will set her free.
                                   Oh quickly!
My mind misgives —
The laws of the gods are mighty, and a man must
    serve them
To the last day of his life!   (*Exit Kreon.*)

PAEAN° • *Strophe 1*

CHORAGOS: God of many names
CHORUS: O Iacchos
                                          son
of Kadmeian Semele
                            O born of the Thunder!
Guardian of the West
                            Regent
of Eleusis' plain
                            O Prince of maenad Thebes
5   and the Dragon Field by rippling Ismenos:°

Antistrophe 1

CHORAGOS: God of many names
CHORUS: the flame of torches
    flares on our hills
                            the nymphs of Iacchos
    dance at the spring of Castalia:°
    from the vine-close mountain
                            come ah come in ivy:
10 *Evohe evohe!*° sings through the streets of Thebes

Strophe 2

CHORAGOS: God of many names
CHORUS: Iacchos of Thebes
    heavenly Child
                            of Semele bride of the Thunderer!
The shadow of plague is upon us:
                                    come
with clement feet
                            oh come from Parnasos
down the long slopes
                            across the lamenting water
15

Paean: A song of praise or prayer.   **1–5. God of many names . . .
rippling Ismenos:** The following is a litany of names for Dionysus (Iacchos): he was son of Zeus ("Thunder") and Semele;
he was honored in secret rites at Eleusis; and he was worshiped
by the Maenads of Thebes. Kadmos, Semele's father, sowed
dragon's teeth in a field beside the river Ismenos from which
sprang warriors who became the first Thebans.   **8. spring of
Castalia:** A spring on Mount Parnassus used by priestesses of
Dionysus in rites of purification.   **10. *Evohe evohe!:*** Cry of the
Maenads to Dionysus.

Antistrophe 2

CHORAGOS: Io Fire! Chorister of the throbbing stars!
    O purest among the voices of the night!
    Thou son of God, blaze for us!
CHORUS: Come with choric rapture of circling Maenads
    Who cry *Io Iacche!*°
                    God of many names!   20

EXODOS°

(*Enter Messenger from left.*)

MESSENGER: Men of the line of Kadmos, you who live
    Near Amphion's citadel,°
                            I cannot say
Of any condition of human life "This is fixed,
This is clearly good, or bad." Fate raises up,
And Fate casts down the happy and unhappy alike: 5
No man can foretell his Fate.
                            Take the case of Kreon:
Kreon was happy once, as I count happiness:
Victorious in battle, sole governor of the land,
Fortunate father of children nobly born.
And now it has all gone from him! Who can say   10
That a man is still alive when his life's joy fails?
He is a walking dead man. Grant him rich,
Let him live like a king in his great house:
If his pleasure is gone, I would not give
So much as the shadow of smoke for all he owns.   15
CHORAGOS: Your words hint at sorrow: what is your
    news for us?
MESSENGER: They are dead. The living are guilty of
    their death.
CHORAGOS: Who is guilty? Who is dead? Speak!
MESSENGER: Haimon.
    Haimon is dead; and the hand that killed him
    Is his own hand.
CHORAGOS: His father's? or his own?   20
MESSENGER: His own, driven mad by the murder his
    father had done.
CHORAGOS: Teiresias, Teiresias, how clearly you saw it
    all!
MESSENGER: This is my news: you must draw what
    conclusions you can from it.
CHORAGOS: But look: Eurydice, our Queen:
    Has she overheard us?   25

(*Enter Eurydice from the palace, center.*)

EURYDICE: I have heard something, friends:
    As I was unlocking the gate of Pallas'° shrine,
    For I needed her help today, I heard a voice
    Telling of some new sorrow. And I fainted

20. *Io Iacche!:* Ritual cry.   **Exodos:** Final scene.   **2. Amphion's citadel:** A name for Thebes.   **27. Pallas:** Pallas Athene,
goddess of wisdom.

30 There at the temple with all my maidens about me.
    But speak again: whatever it is, I can bear it:
    Grief and I are no strangers.
MESSENGER: Dearest Lady,
    I will tell you plainly all that I have seen.
    I shall not try to comfort you: what is the use,
35 Since comfort could lie only in what is not true?
    The truth is always best.
                         I went with Kreon
    To the outer plain where Polyneices was lying,
    No friend to pity him, his body shredded by dogs.
    We made our prayers in that place to Hecate
    And Pluto,° that they would be merciful. And we
40 bathed
    The corpse with holy water, and we brought
    Fresh-broken branches to burn what was left of it,
    And upon the urn we heaped up a towering barrow
    Of the earth of his own land.
                         When we were done, we ran
    To the vault where Antigone lay on her couch of
45 stone.
    One of the servants had gone ahead,
    And while he was yet far off he heard a voice
    Grieving within the chamber, and he came back
    And told Kreon. And as the King went closer,
50 The air was full of wailing, the words lost,
    And he begged us to make all haste. "Am I a
    prophet?"
    He said, weeping, "And must I walk this road,
    The saddest of all that I have gone before?
    My son's voice calls me on. Oh quickly, quickly!
55 Look through the crevice there, and tell me
    If it is Haimon, or some deception of the gods!"

    We obeyed; and in the cavern's farthest corner
    We saw her lying:
    She had made a noose of her fine linen veil
60 And hanged herself. Haimon lay beside her,
    His arms about her waist, lamenting her,
    His love lost under ground, crying out
    That his father had stolen her away from him.

    When Kreon saw him the tears rushed to his eyes
    And he called to him: "What have you done, child?
65 speak to me.
    What are you thinking that makes your eyes so
    strange?
    O my son, my son, I come to you on my knees!"
    But Haimon spat in his face. He said not a word,
    Staring —
                         And suddenly drew his sword
    And lunged. Kreon shrank back, the blade missed;
70 and the boy,
    Desperate against himself, drove it half its length
    Into his own side, and fell. And as he died
    He gathered Antigone close in his arms again,

39–40. Hecate and Pluto: Goddess of witchcraft and sorcery
and King of Hades, the underworld.

    Choking, his blood bright red on her white cheek.
    And now he lies dead with the dead, and she is his   75
    At last, his bride in the house of the dead.
                         (*Exit Eurydice into the palace.*)
CHORAGOS: She has left us without a word. What can
    this mean?
MESSENGER: It troubles me, too; yet she knows what is
    best,
    Her grief is too great for public lamentation,
    And doubtless she has gone to her chamber to weep   80
    For her dead son, leading her maidens in his dirge.

(*Pause.*)

CHORAGOS: It may be so: but I fear this deep silence.
MESSENGER: I will see what she is doing. I will go in.
                         (*Exit Messenger into the palace.*)

(*Enter Kreon with attendants, bearing Haimon's body.*)

CHORAGOS: But here is the king himself: oh look at
    him,
    Bearing his own damnation in his arms.   85
KREON: Nothing you say can touch me any more.
    My own blind heart has brought me
    From darkness to final darkness. Here you see
    The father murdering, the murdered son —
    And all my civic wisdom!   90

    Haimon my son, so young, so young to die,
    I was the fool, not you; and you died for me.
CHORAGOS: That is the truth; but you were late in
    learning it.
KREON: This truth is hard to bear. Surely a god
    Has crushed me beneath the hugest weight of
    heaven,   95
    And driven me headlong a barbaric way
    To trample out the thing I held most dear.

    The pains that men will take to come to pain!

(*Enter Messenger from the palace.*)

MESSENGER: The burden you carry in your hands is
    heavy,
    But it is not all: you will find more in your house. 100
KREON: What burden worse than this shall I find there?
MESSENGER: The Queen is dead.
KREON: O port of death, deaf world,
    Is there no pity for me? And you, Angel of evil,
    I was dead, and your words are death again.   105
    Is it true, boy? Can it be true?
    Is my wife dead? Has death bred death?
MESSENGER: You can see for yourself.

(*The doors are opened and the body of Eurydice is disclosed within.*)

KREON: Oh pity!
    All true, all true, and more than I can bear!   110
    O my wife, my son!
MESSENGER: She stood before the altar, and her heart
    Welcomed the knife her own hand guided,

And a great cry burst from her lips for Megareus°
    dead,
115   And for Haimon dead, her sons; and her last breath
    Was a curse for their father, the murderer of her sons.
    And she fell, and the dark flowed in through her
      closing eyes.
KREON: O God, I am sick with fear.
    Are there no swords here? Has no one a blow for
      me?
MESSENGER: Her curse is upon you for the deaths of
120   both.
KREON: It is right that it should be. I alone am guilty.
    I know it, and I say it. Lead me in,
    Quickly, friends.
    I have neither life nor substance. Lead me in.
CHORAGOS: You are right, if there can be right in so
125   much wrong.
    The briefest way is best in a world of sorrow.

114. Megareus: Son of Kreon and brother of Haimon,
Megareus sacrificed himself in the unsuccessful attack upon
Thebes, believing that his death was necessary to save Thebes.

KREON: Let it come,
    Let death come quickly, and be kind to me.
    I would not ever see the sun again.
CHORAGOS: All that will come when it will; but we,
    meanwhile,   130
    Have much to do. Leave the future to itself.
KREON: All my heart was in that prayer!
CHORAGOS: Then do not pray any more: the sky is deaf.
KREON: Lead me away. I have been rash and foolish.
    I have killed my son and my wife.   135
    I look for comfort; my comfort lies here dead.
    Whatever my hands have touched has come to
      nothing.
    Fate has brought all my pride to a thought of dust.

(*As Kreon is being led into the house, the Choragos
advances and speaks directly to the audience.*)

CHORAGOS: There is no happiness where there is no
    wisdom;
    No wisdom but in submission to the gods.   140
    Big words are always punished,
    And proud men in old age learn to be wise.

COMMENTARIES

Oliver Taplin's emphasis on the audience's emotional state during the performance of a Greek tragedy brings us back to the seminal comments of Aristotle. Tragedies were noted for their capacity to invoke pity and fear in the audience. Taplin helps us understand how an audience's emotional response can clarify our critical view of tragedy.

Jean Anouilh, a major French playwright in the mid-twentieth century, wrote a version of *Antigone* during the Nazi occupation of Paris and much of France. The political content of the play takes on interesting meaning in light of his experience. The excerpt that appears here offers a modern interpretation of the struggle between Antigone and Kreon.

Oliver Taplin (*b. 1943*)
EMOTION AND MEANING IN GREEK TRAGEDY   *1983*

*Scholar Oliver Taplin focuses on one of Aristotle's concerns in his commentary
on tragedy: the emotions aroused by drama. Taplin explores the argument that
devalues an emotional response to tragedy, and then he considers the proposition
that "tragedy is essentially the emotional experience of its audience."*

It seems to me, then, that Gorgias° is right that tragedy is essentially the *emotional experience of its audience*. Whatever it tells us about the world is conveyed by means of these emotions. Plato agreed with Gorgias in this, but he disapproved of the process and regarded it as harmful. Aristotle agreed with him too, but, contrary to Plato, regarded it as beneficial and salutary. Plato's objection was that such emotions are not the province of the highest part of the soul, the intellectual part. This is the forefather of the error made by so many later critics who have not acknowledged the centrality of emotion in the communication of tragedy. They think that if tragedy is essentially an emotional experience, it must be *solely* that; and they think this because they assume that strong emotion is necessarily in opposition to thought, that the psychic activities are mutually exclusive. But is this right? Understanding, reason, learning, moral discrimination; these things are not, in my experience, incompatible with emotion (nor presumably in the experience of Gorgias and Aristotle): What is incompatible is cold insensibility. Whether or not emotion is inimical to such intellectual processes depends on the *circumstances in which it is aroused*.

The characteristic tragic emotions — pity, horror, fascination, indignation, and so forth — are felt in many other situations besides in the theater. Above all we suffer them in the face of the misfortunes of real life, of course. What distinguishes the experience of a great tragedy? For one thing, as already remarked, we feel for the fortunes of people who have no direct personal relation to us: While this does not decrease the intensity of the emotion, it affords us some distance and perspective. We can feel and at the same time observe from outside. But does this distinguish tragedy from other "contrived" emotional experiences (most of them tending to the anti-intellectual), for example an animal hunt, a football match, an encounter group, reading a thriller, or watching a horror movie? Well, the experience of tragedy is by no means a random series of sensations. Our emotional involvement has perspective and context at the same time, and not just in retrospect. Thus the events of the tragedy are in an ordered *sequence*, a sequence which gives shape and comprehensibility to what we feel. And, most important of all, the affairs of the characters which move us are given a moral setting which is argued and explored in the play. They act and suffer within situations of moral conflict, or social, intellectual, and theological conflict. The quality of the tragedy depends *both* on its power to arouse our emotions *and* on the setting of those emotions in a sequence of moral and intellectual complications which is set out and examined. Tragedy evokes our feelings for others, like much else; but it is distinguished by the order and significance it imparts to suffering. So if the audience is not moved, then the tragedy, however intellectual, is a total failure: If its passions are aroused, but in a thoughtless, amorphous way, then it is merely a bad tragedy, sensational, melodramatic.

Thus it is that our emotions in the theater, far from driving out thought and meaning, are indivisible from them: They are simultaneous and mutually dependent. The experience of tragedy can achieve this coherence in a way that the emotional experiences of real life generally cannot because they are too close, too cluttered with detail and partiality, to be seen in perspective. Tragedy makes us feel that we understand life in its tragic aspects. We have the sense that we can better sympathize with and cope with suffering, misfortune, and waste. It is this sense of understanding (not isolated pearls of wisdom) that is the "message" of a tragedy,

---

Gorgias: Greek orator and rhetorician (c. 483–376 B.C.).

that the great playwright imparts. This is well put in T. S. Eliot's° essay "Shakespeare and the Stoicism of Seneca," where he argues that it is the quality of the emotional expression rather than the quality of the philosophy which makes literature great, which makes it "strong, true and informative . . . useful and beneficial in the sense in which poetry is useful and beneficial." "All great poetry," Eliot writes, "gives the illusion of a view of life . . . for every precise emotion tends towards intellectual formulation."

> **T. S. Eliot:** Poet and critic (1888–1965).

Jean Anouilh (1910–1987)
FROM ANTIGONE   1942

TRANSLATED BY LEWIS GALANTIÈRE

Jean Anouilh began writing plays in 1931. Some of his best-known works, in addition to Antigone, *are* Eurydice *(1941),* Orestes *(1942),* Medea *(1946),* Ring Round the Moon *(1947),* The Waltz of the Toreadors *(1951), and* The Lark *(1952), which is about Joan of Arc. Anouilh wrote* Antigone *in 1942 in occupied Paris and produced it with his wife in the title role in February 1944, when the Nazis controlled most of Europe. Kreon (spelled Creon in this excerpt) is more willing to compromise in Anouilh's version of the play, and for that reason some critics saw the play as pro-Nazi. But Anouilh's sympathies were with Antigone, who represented the anti-Nazi view of the Parisian Resistance. Throughout its early run, the play was an inspiration to the patriotic French.*

This excerpt begins when Ismene returns to accept some of the responsibility for Polyneices' burial and continues through the confrontation of Haimon (Haemon in this excerpt) and Kreon to the end of the play.

(*Ismene enters through arch.*)

ISMENE (*distraught*): Antigone!

ANTIGONE (*turns to Ismene*): You, too? What do you want?

ISMENE: Oh, forgive me, Antigone. I've come back. I'll be brave. I'll go with you now.

ANTIGONE: Where will you go with me?

ISMENE (*to Creon*): Creon! If you kill her, you'll have to kill me too.

ANTIGONE: Oh, no, Ismene. Not a bit of it. I die alone. You don't think I'm going to let you die with me after what I've been through? You don't deserve it.

ISMENE: If you die, I don't want to live. I don't want to be left behind, alone.

ANTIGONE: You chose life and I chose death. Now stop blubbering. You had your chance to come with me in the black night, creeping on your hands and knees. You had your chance to claw up the earth with your nails, as I did; to get yourself caught like a thief, as I did. And you refused it.

ISMENE: Not anymore. I'll do it alone tonight.

ANTIGONE (*turns round toward Creon*): You hear that, Creon? The thing is catching! Who knows but that lots of people will catch the disease from me! What are you waiting for? Call in your guards! Come on, Creon! Show a little courage! It only hurts for a minute! Come on, cook!

CREON (*turns toward arch and calls*): Guard!

(*Guards enter through arch.*)

ANTIGONE (*in a great cry of relief*): At last, Creon!

(*Chorus enters through left arch.*)

CREON (*to the Guards*): Take her away! (*Creon goes up on top step.*)

(*Guards grasp Antigone by her arms, turn and hustle her toward the arch, right, and exeunt.° Ismene mimes horror, backs away toward the arch, left, then turns and runs out through the arch. A long pause, as Creon moves slowly downstage.*)

CHORUS (*Behind Creon. Speaks in a deliberate voice*): You are out of your mind, Creon. What have you done?

CREON (*his back to Chorus*): She had to die.

CHORUS: You must not let Antigone die. We shall carry the scar of her death for centuries.

CREON: She insisted. No man on earth was strong enough to dissuade her. Death was her purpose, whether she knew it or not. Polynices was a mere pretext. When she had to give up that pretext, she found another one — that life and happiness were tawdry things and not worth possessing. She was bent upon only one thing: to reject life and to die.

CHORUS: She is a mere child, Creon.

CREON: What do you want me to do for her? Condemn her to live?

HAEMON (*calls from offstage*): Father! (*Haemon enters through arch, right. Creon turns toward him.*)

CREON: Haemon, forget Antigone. Forget her, my dearest boy.

HAEMON: How can you talk like that?

CREON (*grasps Haemon by the hands*): I did everything I could to save her, Haemon. I used every argument. I swear I did. The girl doesn't love you. She could have gone on living for you; but she refused. She wanted it this way; she wanted to die.

HAEMON: Father! The guards are dragging Antigone away! You've got to stop them! (*He breaks away from Creon.*)

CREON (*looks away from Haemon*): I can't stop them. It's too late. Antigone has spoken. The story is all over Thebes. I cannot save her now.

CHORUS: Creon, you must find a way. Lock her up. Say that she has gone out of her mind.

CREON: Everybody will know it isn't so. The nation will say that I am making an exception of her because my son loves her. I cannot.

CHORUS: You can still gain time and get her out of Thebes.

CREON: The mob already knows the truth. It is howling for her blood. I can do nothing.

HAEMON: But, Father, you are master in Thebes!

CREON: I am master under the law. Not above the law.

HAEMON: You cannot let Antigone be taken from me. I am your son!

CREON: I cannot do anything else, my poor boy. She must die and you must live.

HAEMON: Live, you say! Live a life without Antigone? A life in which I am to go on admiring you as you busy yourself about your kingdom, make your persuasive speeches, strike your attitudes? Not without Antigone. I love Antigone. I will not live without Antigone!

CREON: Haemon — you will have to resign yourself to life without Antigone. (*He moves to left of Haemon.*) Sooner or later there comes a day of sorrow in each man's life when he must cease to be a child and take up the burden of manhood. That day has come for you.

HAEMON (*backs away a step*): That giant strength, that courage. That massive god who used to pick me up in his arms and shelter me from shadows and monsters — was that you, Father? Was it of you I stood in awe? Was that man you?

CREON: For God's sake, Haemon, do not judge me! Not you, too!

HAEMON (*pleading now*): This is all a bad dream, Father. You are not yourself. It isn't true that we have been backed up against a wall, forced to surrender. We don't have to say *yes* to this terrible thing. You are still king. You are still the father I revered.

---

exeunt: Latin for "they go out."

You have no right to desert me, to shrink into nothingness. The world will be too bare, I shall be too alone in the world, if you force me to disown you.

CREON: The world *is* bare, Haemon, and you *are* alone. You must cease to think your father all-powerful. Look straight at me. See your father as he is. That is what it means to grow up and be a man.

HAEMON (*stares at Creon for a moment*): I tell you that I will not live without Antigone. (*Turns and goes quickly out through arch.*)

CHORUS: Creon, the boy will go mad.

CREON: Poor boy! He loves her.

CHORUS: Creon, the boy is wounded to death.

CREON: We are all wounded to death.

(*First Guard enters through arch, right, followed by Second and Third Guards pulling Antigone along with them.*)

FIRST GUARD: Sir, the people are crowding into the palace!

ANTIGONE: Creon, I don't want to see their faces. I don't want to hear them howl. You are going to kill me; let that be enough. I want to be alone until it is over.

CREON: Empty the palace! Guards at the gates!

(*Creon quickly crosses toward the arch; exit. Two Guards release Antigone; exeunt behind Creon. Chorus goes out through arch, left. The lighting dims so that only the area about the table is lighted. The cyclorama° is covered with a dark blue color. The scene is intended to suggest a prison cell, filled with shadows and dimly lit. Antigone moves to stool and sits. The First Guard stands upstage. He watches Antigone, and as she sits, he begins pacing slowly downstage, then upstage. A pause.*)

ANTIGONE (*turns and looks at the Guard*): It's you, is it?

GUARD: What do you mean, me?

ANTIGONE: The last human face that I shall see. (*A pause as they look at each other, then Guard paces upstage, turns, and crosses behind table.*) Was it you that arrested me this morning?

GUARD: Yes, that was me.

ANTIGONE: You hurt me. There was no need for you to hurt me. Did I act as if I was trying to escape?

GUARD: Come on now, Miss. It was my business to bring you in. I did it. (*A pause. He paces to and fro upstage. Only the sound of his boots is heard.*)

ANTIGONE: How old are you?

GUARD: Thirty-nine.

ANTIGONE: Have you any children?

GUARD: Yes. Two.

ANTIGONE: Do you love your children?

GUARD: What's that got to do with you? (*A pause. He paces upstage and downstage.*)

ANTIGONE: How long have you been in the Guard?

GUARD: Since the war. I was in the army. Sergeant. Then I joined the Guard.

ANTIGONE: Does one have to have been an army sergeant to get into the Guard?

GUARD: Supposed to be. Either that or on special detail. But when they make you a guard, you lose your stripes.

ANTIGONE (*murmurs*): I see.

GUARD: Yes. Of course, if you're a guard, everybody knows you're something special; they know you're an old N.C.O.° Take pay, for instance. When you're a guard you get your pay, and on top of that you get six months' extra pay, to make sure you don't lose anything by not being a sergeant anymore. And of course you do better than that. You get a house, coal, rations, extras for the wife and kids. If you've got two kids, like me, you draw better than a sergeant.

ANTIGONE (*barely audible*): I see.

---

cyclorama: Curved cloth or wall forming the back of many modern stage settings.
N.C.O.: Noncommissioned officer, usually of a subordinate rank such as sergeant.

GUARD: That's why sergeants, now, they don't like guards. Maybe you noticed they try to make out they're better than us? Promotion, that's what it is. In the army, anybody can get promoted. All you need is good conduct. Now in the Guard, it's slow, and you have to know your business — like how to make out a report and the like of that. But when you're an N.C.O. in the Guard, you've got something that even a sergeant major ain't got. For instance —

ANTIGONE (*breaking him off*): Listen.

GUARD: Yes, Miss.

ANTIGONE: I'm going to die soon.

(*The Guard looks at her for a moment, then turns and moves away.*)

GUARD: For instance, people have a lot of respect for guards, they have. A guard may be a soldier, but he's kind of in the civil service, too.

ANTIGONE: Do you think it hurts to die?

GUARD: How would I know? Of course, if somebody sticks a saber in your guts and turns it round, it hurts.

ANTIGONE: How are they going to put me to death?

GUARD: Well, I'll tell you. I heard the proclamation all right. Wait a minute. How did it go now? (*He stares into space and recites from memory.*) "In order that our fair city shall not be pol-luted with her sinful blood, she shall be im-mured — immured." That means, they shove you in a cave and wall up the cave.

ANTIGONE: Alive?

GUARD: Yes. . . . (*He moves away a few steps.*)

ANTIGONE (*murmurs*): O tomb! O bridal bed! Alone! (*Antigone sits there, a tiny figure in the middle of the stage. You would say she felt a little chilly. She wraps her arms round herself.*)

GUARD: Yes! Outside the southeast gate of the town. In the Cave of Hades. In broad daylight. Some detail, eh, for them that's on the job! First they thought maybe it was a job for the army. Now it looks like it's going to be the Guard. There's an outfit for you! Nothing the Guard can't do. No wonder the army's jealous.

ANTIGONE: A pair of animals.

GUARD: What do you mean, a pair of animals?

ANTIGONE: When the winds blow cold, all they need do is to press close against one another. I am all alone.

GUARD: Is there anything you want? I can send out for it, you know.

ANTIGONE: You are very kind. (*A pause. Antigone looks up at the Guard.*) Yes, there is something I want. I want you to give someone a letter from me, when I am dead.

GUARD: How's that again? A letter?

ANTIGONE: Yes, I want to write a letter; and I want you to give it to someone for me.

GUARD (*straightens up*): Now, wait a minute. Take it easy. It's as much as my job is worth to go handing out letters from prisoners.

ANTIGONE (*removes a ring from her finger and holds it out toward him*): I'll give you this ring if you will do it.

GUARD: Is it gold? (*He takes the ring from her.*)

ANTIGONE: Yes, it is gold.

GUARD (*shakes his head*): Uh-uh. No can do. Suppose they go through my pockets. I might get six months for a thing like that. (*He stares at the ring, then glances off right to make sure that he is not being watched.*) Listen, tell you what I'll do. You tell me what you want to say, and I'll write it down in my book. Then, afterwards, I'll tear out the pages and give them to the party, see? If it's in my handwriting, it's all right.

ANTIGONE (*winces*): In your handwriting? (*She shudders slightly.*) No. That would be awful. The poor darling! In your handwriting.

GUARD (*offers back the ring*): O.K. It's no skin off my nose.

ANTIGONE (*quickly*): Of course, of course. No, keep the ring. But hurry. Time is getting short. Where is your notebook? (*The Guard pockets the ring, takes his notebook and pencil from his pocket, puts his foot up on chair, and rests the notebook on his knee, licks his pencil.*) Ready? (*He nods.*) Write, now. "My darling . . ."

GUARD (*writes as he mutters*): The boyfriend, eh?

ANTIGONE: "My darling. I wanted to die, and perhaps you will not love me anymore . . ."

GUARD (*mutters as he writes*): ". . . will not love me anymore."

ANTIGONE: "Creon was right. It is terrible to die."

GUARD (*repeats as he writes*): ". . . terrible to die."

ANTIGONE: "And I don't even know what I am dying for. I am afraid . . ."

GUARD (*looks at her*): Wait a minute! How fast do you think I can write?

ANTIGONE (*takes hold of herself*): Where are you?

GUARD (*reads from his notebook*): "And I don't even know what I am dying for."

ANTIGONE: No. Scratch that out. Nobody must know that. They have no right to know. It's as if they saw me naked and touched me, after I was dead. Scratch it all out. Just write: "Forgive me."

GUARD (*looks at Antigone*): I cut out everything you said there at the end, and I put down, "Forgive me"?

ANTIGONE: Yes. "Forgive me, my darling. You would all have been so happy except for Antigone. I love you."

GUARD (*finishes the letter*): ". . . I love you." (*He looks at her.*) Is that all?

ANTIGONE: That's all.

GUARD (*straightens up, looks at notebook*): Damn funny letter.

ANTIGONE: I know.

GUARD (*looks at her*): Who is it to? (*A sudden roll of drums begins and continues until after Antigone's exit. The First Guard pockets the notebook and shouts at Antigone.*) O.K. That's enough out of you! Come on!

(*At the sound of the drum roll, Second and Third Guards enter through the arch. Antigone rises. Guards seize her and exeunt with her. The lighting moves up to suggest late afternoon. Chorus enters.*)

CHORUS: And now it is Creon's turn.

(*Messenger runs through the arch, right.*)

MESSENGER: The Queen . . . the Queen! Where is the Queen?

CHORUS: What do you want with the Queen? What have you to tell the Queen?

MESSENGER: News to break her heart. Antigone had just been thrust into the cave. They hadn't finished heaving the last block of stone into place when Creon and the rest heard a sudden moaning from the tomb. A hush fell over us all, for it was not the voice of Antigone. It was Haemon's voice that came forth from the tomb. Everybody looked at Creon; and he howled like a man demented: "Take away the stones! Take away the stones!" The slaves leaped at the wall of stones, and Creon worked with them, sweating and tearing at the blocks with his bleeding hands. Finally a narrow opening was forced, and into it slipped the smallest guard.

   Antigone had hanged herself by the cord of her robe, by the red and golden twisted cord of her robe. The cord was round her neck like a child's collar. Haemon was on his knees, holding her in his arms and moaning, his face buried in her robe. More stones were removed, and Creon went into the tomb. He tried to raise Haemon to his feet. I could hear him begging Haemon to rise to his feet. Haemon was deaf to his father's voice, till suddenly he stood up of his own accord, his eyes dark and burning. Anguish was in his face, but it was the face of a little boy. He stared at his father. Then suddenly he struck him — hard; and he drew his sword. Creon leaped out of range. Haemon went on staring at him, his eyes full of contempt — a glance that was like a knife, and that Creon couldn't escape. The King stood trembling in the far corner of the tomb, and Haemon went on staring. Then, without a word, he stabbed himself and lay down beside Antigone, embracing her in a great pool of blood.

(*A pause as Creon and Page enter through arch on the Messenger's last words. Chorus and the Messenger both turn to look at Creon; then exit the Messenger through curtain.*)

CREON: I have had them laid out side by side. They are together at last, and at peace. Two lovers on the morrow of their bridal. Their work is done.

CHORUS: But not yours, Creon. You have still one thing to learn. Eurydice, the Queen, your wife —

CREON: A good woman. Always busy with her garden, her preserves, her sweaters — those sweaters she never stopped knitting for the poor. Strange, how the poor never stop needing sweaters. One would almost think that was all they needed.

CHORUS: The poor in Thebes are going to be cold this winter, Creon. When the Queen was told of her son's death, she waited carefully until she had finished her row, then put down her knitting calmly — as she did everything. She went up to her room, her lavender-scented room, with its embroidered doilies and its pictures framed in plush; and there, Creon, she cut her throat. She is laid out now in one of those two old-fashioned twin beds, exactly where you went to her one night when she was still a maiden. Her smile is still the same, scarcely a shade more melancholy. And if it were not for that great red blot on the bed linen by her neck, one might think she was asleep.

CREON (*in a dull voice*): She, too. They are all asleep. (*Pause.*) It must be good to sleep.

CHORUS: And now you are alone, Creon.

CREON: Yes, all alone. (*To Page.*) My lad.

PAGE: Sir?

CREON: Listen to me. They don't know it, but the truth is, the work is there to be done, and a man can't fold his arms and refuse to do it. They say it's dirty work. But if we didn't do it, who would?

PAGE: I don't know, sir.

CREON: Of course you don't. You'll be lucky if you never find out. In a hurry to grow up, aren't you?

PAGE: Oh, yes, sir.

CREON: I shouldn't be if I were you. Never grow up if you can help it. (*He is lost in thought as the hour chimes.*) What time is it?

PAGE: Five o clock, sir.

CREON: What have we on at five o'clock?

PAGE: Cabinet meeting, sir.

CREON: Cabinet meeting. Then we had better go along to it.

(*Exeunt Creon and Page slowly through arch, left, and Chorus moves downstage.*)

CHORUS: And there we are. It is quite true that if it had not been for Antigone they would all have been at peace. But that is over now. And they are all at peace. All those who were meant to die have died: those who believed one thing, those who believed the contrary thing, and even those who believed nothing at all, yet were caught up in the web without knowing why. All dead: stiff, useless, rotting. And those who have survived will now begin quietly to forget the dead: they won't remember who was who or which was which. It is all over. Antigone is calm tonight, and we shall never know the name of the fever that consumed her. She has played her part.

(*Three Guards enter, resume their places on steps as at the rise of the curtain, and begin to play cards.*)

A great melancholy wave of peace now settles down upon Thebes, upon the empty palace, upon Creon, who can now begin to wait for his own death. Only the guards are left, and none of this matters to them. It's no skin off their noses. They go on playing cards.

(*Chorus walks toward the arch, left, as the curtain falls.*)

Euripides

Euripides (c. 485–c. 406 B.C.), last of the great Greek tragedians, did not enjoy the personal popularity accorded Aeschylus and Sophocles, possibly because his work criticized Athenian politics and society. Moreover, he was not highly regarded because he broke away from the formality of language and theme of his predecessors.

Euripides was raised in Salamis, the island from which the Greeks decisively defeated the Persians in 480 B.C. This victory heralded the Periclean Age (c. 460–404 B.C.), when Athens enjoyed its greatest power. During that time, however, the Athenians spent almost three decades fighting the Peloponnesian Wars (431–404 B.C.), which drained their energies and treasury. Eventually, they were forced to relinquish their dominance to Sparta. In such an environment, the officials and patriots of Athens were not happy with the work of someone who reminded them of their mistakes and questioned their values.

Euripides is especially noted for shifting the focus of dramatic events from the gods to humans. He valued individual human beings and the working of their wills. Influenced by the teaching of the Sophists, wandering professors who taught argument and philosophy, he agreed with Protagoras's principle "Man is the measure of all things." The ancients sometimes referred to Euripides as the philosopher of the stage.

One aspect of his dramatic critique of Greek culture was an unusual emphasis on women. Medea is the first thoroughly developed female character in Greek drama. She is treated as an independent woman, not as Jason's wife or as someone's mother. She is herself. Athenians, intolerant of foreigners and women, felt both groups to be inferior to Greek aristocratic men. It is no wonder that of the twenty plays Euripides produced at the feasts of Dionysus only five won prizes.

Of his ninety-two plays, eighteen survive — more than twice as many as survive from any other Greek tragedian: *Alcestis* (438), *Medea* (431), *The Children of Heracles* (c. 430), *Hippolytus* (428), *Andromache* (426?), *Hecuba* (c. 424), *Cyclops* (c. 423), *The Suppliants* (c. 422), *Electra* (c. 417), *Heracles* (c. 417), *The Trojan Women* (415), *Helen* (412), *Iphigenia in Taurus* (c. 412), *The Phoenician Women* (c. 412–408), *Ion* (c. 411), *Orestes* (408), *The Bacchae* (405), and *Iphigenia in Aulis* (405). Another play, *Rhesus,* long attributed to Euripides, is now thought to have been written by an anonymous fourth-century B.C. playwright. Ten of Euripides' remaining plays place women at their center.

Euripides continued Aeschylus's innovations in his use of the *skene*. Instead of representing the front of a palace, the *skene* in Euripides' plays sometimes represented a peasant's hut, a rural shrine, or other common structure. He was interested in theatrical devices, especially machines that gave him the opportunity to achieve dramatic effects. He often used the *mekane* — a crane or derrick that lifted actors in or out of the play — to resolve his dramas when his characters found themselves in impossible situations. His choral odes, although beautiful, are sometimes considered detachable from the episodes of dramatic action. Moreover, his dialogue is more colloquial — closer to everyday speech — than is the dialogue found in other Greek tragedies. All these deviations from the dramatic norm emphasize the humanity in his plays and elevate human values over those of the gods.

Eighteen months before his death, Euripides left Athens for the court of King Archelaus in Macedon. His departure may have signaled his dissatisfaction with the politics of Athens, or it may have been prompted by the indifference of Athens to his talents. In any event, his works were performed long after his death, and, ironically, his posthumous popularity dwarfed that of the other tragic playwrights.

MEDEA

Although *Medea* won only last prize at the City Dionysia festival in 431 B.C., behind works by Euphorion, son of Aeschylus, and Sophocles, the play's emotional dimension and Medea's depth of feeling have made her one of the most impressive characters in dramatic fiction.

In his first play, *The Daughters of Pelias* (454 B.C.), Euripides treated part of the well-known legend of Jason and Medea. On the order of his enemy, King Pelias of Iolcus, Jason sailed with the Argonauts to Colchis. There, with the help of Medea's witchcraft, he retrieved the Golden Fleece. Medea returned with Jason to Iolcus, where she convinced Pelias's daughters that they could restore their father's youth if they cut him into pieces and boiled the pieces with magic herbs, as she had done with a ram. When the daughters tried it, however, the treacherous Medea gave them impotent herbs and Pelias died. Jason's Argonauts captured Iolcus, and Medea and Jason escaped to Corinth.

Euripides continued the tale in *Medea*. When the play opens, Jason and Medea are in exile in Corinth. Jason has decided to marry King Creon's daughter Glauke, supposedly to guarantee the safety of the children he has had with Medea. Considering all the sacrifices she has made for Jason, Medea feels betrayed and cast aside for a younger woman. Medea's situation is painful. The Chorus recognizes the legality of Jason's decision to put aside his wife in favor of a younger woman. His motives might be interpreted as plausible and perhaps noble. Medea is Asiatic, a foreigner. By marrying Glauke, Jason will impart noble status on his and Medea's children. By law he can maintain Medea as a concubine along with his wife. Medea knows this, but she rejects Jason's explanations. He assumes that she is merely sexually jealous of Glauke.

The themes of this tragedy are certainly accessible to modern audiences. As the critic G.M.A. Grube has pointed out, "The tragedy of *Medea* — of Love turning to hatred when betrayed, until the woman's whole soul is dominated by a lust for vengeance that overpowers even maternal love — is one which no modern reader should, in its essentials, find difficult to make his own." The modern audience, however, may take pause at Medea's revenge. She plans not only to rid Jason of his young bride but to kill Creon as well. And her vengeance does not stop there: she determines to kill those whom Jason most loves — their two sons.

Exploring Medea's feelings and her awareness of the gravity of her actions sets Euripides' work apart from that of other Greek tragedians. His sympathy for the many tragic heroines he created marks his work from beginning to end. Unlike other playwrights working with the Medea legend, Euripides saves Medea from the punishment of Jason and the people of Corinth. To do this, he uses the *mekane*, in the form of the dragon chariot that lifts her above the *skene* beyond Jason's reach at the end of the play. She leaves him in an agony of grief.

Medea in Performance

Medea has one of the longest and most active production histories in all of drama. Not only did Alexander the Great produce the play in the fourth century B.C., but the Roman playwright Seneca wrote his own version (A.D. 60), with a much less sympathetic Medea. Seneca's Jason is a reasonable man unfairly wronged by a witch. French and English productions and adaptations began in 1553 and have continued to the present. The French playwright Corneille wrote his version in 1634, and an English version of 1756 portrays Medea as insane.

Important modern productions began in the early twentieth century. The American actress Margaret Anglin was a sensation in the 1918 production, which established her as the greatest Medea up to her time. Hans Henny Jahnne adapted *Medea* for a production in Berlin in 1926. According to a review written at the time, Medea was portrayed by an older black actress whose magic potions kept Jason young while she aged. The poisoned robe Medea gave to her young rival had the power to turn the princess into an elderly woman "who gradually [grew] older and older and [decayed] into death and decomposition."

Judith Anderson made the role hers in 1947, in a version by the American poet Robinson Jeffers that played for almost a decade. In the 1982 production with John Gielgud as Jason and Zoë Caldwell as Medea, a much older Judith Anderson played the nurse and received extraordinary reviews. In 1974 Greek actress Irene Papas starred in New York in a colloquial English version. Important productions were staged in Russia in the 1960s. Countee Cullen very successfully produced the play in 1959 with a black Medea. In 1986, an all-male Kabuki version of *Medea* was presented at the Delacorte Theater in Central Park by the Japanese Toho Company under the direction of Yukio Ninagawa. A critic from the *New York Times* described the director's intentions: "Yukio Ninagawa, known for his productions of classical theater as avant-garde spectacle, aims in his work to create a universal theater that fuses the traditions of Japanese and Western culture in an expressive style of its own" (Jennifer Dunning, *New York Times*, Aug. 31, 1986). A *Boston Globe* critic praised the power of the Kabuki production: "This was a Medea of stunning theatrical imagery. Classical Corinthian order was gradually and relentlessly replaced by savage revenge and blood-stained chaos" (Lyn Gardner, *Boston Globe*, Aug. 29, 1986). In April 1994 Diana Rigg was Medea in a production highly praised in both London and New York. She was seen as commanding and powerful in the part, played starkly and simply. The recent production at Dublin's Abbey Theatre, in 2000, used a new translation by Kenneth McLeish and Frederic Raphael and employed a modernized setting that brought the play into the early years of the twenty-first century. Directed by Deborah Warner and starring Fiona Shaw as Medea, this production and Shaw's performance received rave reviews. When the production came to the United States in 2002, a *New York Times* critic summed up the power of this new interpretation: "The miracle of this *Medea* is how completely it integrates its ideas of a latter-day culture of celebrity into a classic text . . . without ever seeming to warp the spirit of the original. . . . Ms. Shaw and Ms. Warner have created one of the most human Medeas ever, precisely because they have refused to simplify her" (Ben Brantley, *New York Times,* Oct. 4, 2002).

Euripides (c. 485–406 B.C.)

MEDEA   *431 B.C.*

TRANSLATED BY PAUL ROCHE

Characters

NURSE
TUTOR *to Medea's sons*
MEDEA, *Asiatic princess*
CHORUS *of Corinthian women*
CREON, *King of Corinth*
JASON, *husband of Medea*
AEGEUS, *King of Athens*
MESSENGER
TWO BOYS, *sons of Medea*
HANDMAIDS *of Medea*
ATTENDANTS AND GUARDS *for Creon and Aegeus*

Time and Setting: *It is midmorning outside Jason's house in Corinth. Ten years have passed since the Argonauts sailed home after finding the Golden Fleece. During that time, Jason and Medea [the Asian bride he brought back with him] have been living modestly in Corinth: models of an unassailable married life of devotion to each other and their children. But the news has just broken that Jason is to marry the daughter of the King of Corinth. [The exit on stage left leads to the town and royal palace, that on the right to the country.]*

[*Enter the Nurse from the house. She is an old woman who has looked after Medea from babyhood. Her face, the only part of her showing from the dark, heavy clothes that envelop her, is puckered with age and distress.*]

PROLOGUE°

NURSE: Why did the winged oars of the Argo°
    ever weave between those gnashing blue
    fjords towards the land of Colchis?
        Why did the pines in the dells of Pelion°
    ever fall to the axe and fill   5
    the rowing hands of heroes sent by Pelias°
    to fetch the Golden Fleece?
        My mistress, Medea, then
    never would have sailed to Iolcus° with its towers
    or been struck to the heart with love of Jason.   10
        She never would have baited Pelias' daughters
    to the murder of their father°

[**Prologue:** Portion of the play explaining the background and current action. (The editor's notes are in brackets.)]   **1. Argo:** The ship in which Jason and his companions sailed on the quest for the Golden Fleece.   **4. Pelion:** A mountain in northern Greece.   **6. Pelias:** When Jason came to claim the kingdom of Iolcus, from which Pelias had expelled Jason's father, Pelias sent Jason to get the Golden Fleece.   **9. Iolcus:** Town from which the Argonauts sailed.   **11–12. She never . . . murder of their father:** Medea, a sorceress by reputation, tricked Pelias's daughters into cutting their father into pieces and boiling them, on the pretext that this would magically restore him to youth. This was her revenge on Pelias, who had murdered Jason's father, Aeson, during Jason's absence on the quest for the Golden Fleece, which was successful.

and be living here in Corinth° now
with her husband and her children . . .
15   Ah, she has merited this city's good opinion,
exile though she came,
and was in everything Jason's perfect foil,
being in marriage that saving thing:
a wife who does not go against her man.

[*With a despairing glance toward the house.*]

20   Now everything has turned to hate,
her passion to a plague.
Jason has betrayed his sons and her,
takes to bed a royal bride
Creon's daughter — the king of Corinth's.
25   Medea, spurned and desolate,
breaks out in oaths,
invokes the solemnest vows,
calls the gods to witness
how Jason has rewarded her.
30   She does not eat,
lies prostrate, slumped in anguish,
wastes away in day-long tears.
Ever since she heard of Jason's perfidy
she has not raised her eyes
35   or looked up from the floor.
She might be a rock or wave of the sea,
for all she heeds of sympathy from friends,
except sometimes to tilt her pale head away
and moan to herself about her father —
40   whom she loved —
and her country and the home she sacrificed°
to journey here
with a man — oh — who so disdains her now.
Yes, now she knows
45   at a terrible first hand
what it is to miss one's native land.

[*She pauses; almost whispers the next words.*]

She hates her sons.
Takes no pleasure in their sight.
I dread to think
50   of what is hatching in her mind.
She is a fierce spirit:
takes no insult lying down.
I know her well. She frightens me:°

13. **be living here in Corinth:** Expelled from the kingdom [of Iolcus], Jason and Medea took refuge in Corinth, a wealthy city and rival of Athens, located on the isthmus between the Peloponnese and Attica.   41. **home she sacrificed:** Medea had helped Jason take the Golden Fleece away from her own father's kingdom.   53. **She frightens me:** [The translator notes that he has omitted four lines bracketed by many editors as doubtful (lines 40–43 in the original Greek text).] Dramatically, they are certainly a mistake: *"I am frightened she will slip / into the palace unawares, / and in the nuptial bedroom / ram a sharp knife into Jason's side, / or even kill the King as well as bridegroom / and get herself a far worse doom."*

a dangerous woman, and
anyone who crosses her   55
will not easily sing a song of triumph.
But here come the boys after their run:
suspecting nothing of a mother's tragedy . . .
Oh, it is true —
unhappy thoughts and youth never go together.   60

[*Enter Tutor with Two Boys, aged about eight and ten. Tutor is an old man, dressed loosely in an ochercolored cloak. The boys are squeezed into shorts and have close-fitting woolen caps on their heads. They hang about in the background, laughing and talking, while the old man advances.*]

TUTOR [*with a half-teasing familiarity*]:   Ah, Nurse!
Faithful old appendage of my Lady's home,
what are you doing here all forlorn,
standing moaning to yourself outside the gates?
Does Medea really want to be left alone?   65
NURSE: Ah, dogged old pedagogue of Jason's sons,
when a master's fortunes are struck down
the heart of a faithful slave is stricken too.
I am plunged in such a depth of grief
I came out here to tell the earth and sky   70
Medea's catastrophe.
TUTOR: What! Has the poor woman not stopped her
      crying yet?
NURSE: Stopped! You amaze me.
Her ordeal, far from halfway done,
hardly has begun.   75
TUTOR: Poor innocent fool — to be quite frank about
      our mistress —
she knows little of the latest blow.
NURSE: Latest? What's that, old man?
Don't keep it from me.
TUTOR: Nothing, nothing . . . I'm sorry I even spoke.   80
NURSE: Come now, we're both slaves here, are we not?
By your own gray beard, do not hold it back . . .
I can keep a secret if I must.
TUTOR: Well, I'd gone to where the old dice-players sit,
near Pirene's sacred fountain,   85
and there I overheard (pretending not to listen)
someone say:
"Creon, this country's king,
is making plans to drive these boys from Corinth —
their mother too"—   90
I don't know if the story's true.
I hope that it is not.
NURSE: No, surely no?
Jason would not let his sons be treated so,
however far he's parted from their mother.   95
TUTOR [*grimly*]: Old loves are left behind by new.
That man is not this house's friend.
NURSE: We're all finished, then —
if we ship this second wave
before we've bailed the first.   100
TUTOR: Now listen —
this is not the time to let our mistress know.

Just keep quiet about it — not a word.
NURSE [*with an anguished glance over her shoulder, in
a whisper*]: Poor little boys,
105   do you hear how much your father's worth to you?
I wish he were . . .

[*Checks herself.*]

no, not dead, he is my master still . . .
but, oh, what an enemy he's proved
to those he should have loved!
110 TUTOR: What human being is not?
Is this news to you,
that every person's dearest neighbor is himself:
some rightly so, some out of greed and selfishness.
This father does not love his sons, but —
115   his new wedding bed.
NURSE: Come along, boys, into the house.
Everything is going to be all right.

[*Dropping her voice.*]

Keep them away as much as you can.
Do not let them near their mother
120 so long as she is in this deadly mood.
Already I have caught her eyes on them:
the eyes of a mad bull.
There's something she is plotting
and her fury won't lie down — this I know —
125   until the lightning strikes and someone's felled.
Let us hope it's enemies, not friends.

[*A long-drawn-out sob — Medea's — is heard from the
house.*]°

MEDEA: I am so unhappy — oh!
·the misery of it! I wish I were dead.
NURSE [*hustling the children toward the door*]:
Listen — there . . . poor children, your mother,
130   Raking her heart up, raking her rage.
Quick, inside: into the house.
Don't come anywhere near her sight.
Don't approach. Beware, watch out
For her savage mood, destructive spleen:
135   Yes and her implacable will.
Off with you now; hurry inside.
Soon, I know, her fury will flare
Out from the slowly gathering cloud.
What will she perpetrate then, I fear —
140 Proud, importunate willful soul —
So bitterly spurned.

[*Exeunt*° *Tutor and Boys.*]

[*A long-suppressed shout is heard from inside: Medea's
voice.*]

---

126. The next 116 lines in the Greek [to the end of the Parodos]
are cast in a different meter, which [the translator] transposed
into the nearest English equivalent. [**141.** (S.D.) *Exeunt:* Latin
for "they go out."]

MEDEA: Oh, what misery! Oh, what pain!
Cursed sons, and a mother for cursing!
Death take you all — you and your father:
The whole house wither.   145
NURSE [*sobbing*]: Oh, how it grieves me!
Why make the sons
share in their father's
Guilt? Oh, why
should *they* be hated?   150
Poor young children, your danger appals me.
Ruthless is the temper of royalty:
Often commanding, seldom commanded;
Terribly slow to forgive and forget.
How much better to live among equals.   155
I want no part of greatness and glory:
Let me decline in a safe old age.
The very name of the "middle way"
Has health in it: is best for man.
Good never comes from overreaching,   160
And when it provokes the gods, it destroys
All the more thoroughly.

PARODOS OR ENTRY SONG

[*The Chorus of Corinthian women enters, full of apprehension and concern for Medea.*]

CHORUS: I heard her voice, I heard her shout,
It was the most unhappy
Woman from Colchis — far from calm yet —
But tell me, old Nurse.
From the porch of the house, it moaned outside.   5
O women, I cannot delight
In the pain of Jason's house:
A house I have loved very well.
NURSE: House there is none: life of it gone.
The master is had . . . by a princess's bed.   10
The mistress in her boudoir pines.
There are no words her friends can find
To touch her disconsolate heart.
MEDEA [*in another spasm*]: Ahhh!
Cleave my brain with a flash from the sky.   15
What good is left for me in living?
Alas! Alas! Come Death, unloose
My life from a life I loathe.

[*Strophe*]°

CHORUS: Listen, O Zeus and Earth and Light
To the stricken tune of this plangent° wife.   20
And you, loveless lady,
What yearning for love on a bed of delight
Could make you hurry to death, the night?
Pray not for that.

[**Strophe:** Song sung by the Chorus as it danced from stage right
to stage left.] **20. plangent:** Lamenting.

25   If your husband has gone to adore
      A new bride in his bed, why, this
      Has often happened before.
      Do not harrow your soul. For Zeus
      Will succor your cause. What use
30   To lessen your life with grief
      For a lost lord?
      MEDEA [*from inside*]: O mighty Themis,° and
          Artemis,° Queen,
      For all the fine vows I bound him with,
      See what my hated husband has done.
35   Grant me to watch him, at last, with his bride,
      Palace and all, crumble in ruin.
      How dare they do to me what they have done!
      O Father, my country, the land I abandoned,
      Flagrantly killing my brother.°
40 NURSE: Hear what she says
          with her cry from the heart
      To Themis and Zeus:
          (goddess of rights
      And he whom mankind
45   makes keeper of vows.)
      Certainly soon
          in no small way
      Her fury will play itself out.

[*Antistrophe*]°

    CHORUS: If she would come out and, face to face,
50   Listen to what we have to say,
          She might let go
      This rampant anger, spite of soul.
      I hope I never fail my friends.
      So go, Nurse, entice her to come:
55   Say we are *with* her: we are her friends.
      Hurry, before she does any harm
          To those inside . . .
      Grief can swell to enormity.
      NURSE [*walking to the door*]: I'll do my best, but am
60   afraid I
      May *not* be able to persuade My Lady; and yet
          I am glad to shoulder the burden;
      Although she glares with a bull-mad gaze
          (Or is it a lioness with her whelps)
65   When anyone comes or speaks or helps.

[*She turns at the door.*]

      Oh, botchers and blunderers! Yes,
      That's what they were, those artists of old:
      Makers of music for life and joy,

For grand celebrations and groaning boards;
But, oh, nothing for sorrow and pain: 70
No music or song on hand-plucked lyre
    For the thing that brings death
And terrible endings to many a home.

Oh, what a blessing is missed
    by having no music for this!   75
What a waste of it, then
    by singing in vain,
When fullness at feasts
    is its own joy and gain.

                    [*Exit Nurse into the house.*]

CHORUS: Deep is her sobbing from depths of pain: 80
    Shrill the news her suffering brings
Of marriage betrayed, a love gone wrong.
    Outraged, she
                importunate prays
    To Themis, the daughter of Zeus:
Keeper of vows, who sailed her through   85
    Those dangerous straits and the night
To Hellas° across the salt of the sea.

FIRST EPISODE

[*Medea enters from the house, colorfully, even opu-
lently, dressed. She is wan and her eyes are red with
weeping, but she is surprisingly calm and in control.*]

MEDEA: Women of Corinth, be indulgent, please:
    I have obeyed you and come out.
        The charge of aloofness — as I know too well —
    is something often leveled
    at both the retiring and the busy man.   5
        He who chooses a quiet life
    has this alleged against him too:
    laziness and lack of spirit.
        Yes, public opinion has most shallow eyes.
        People hate at sight   10
    a harmless human being,
    knowing nothing of the real man.
        I agree, of course,
    that a foreigner should conform,
    adapt to his society . . .   15
    and a citizen is censurable no less
    when too self-centered or uncouth
    to avoid offending his companions.
        Nevertheless, I . . .

[*She breaks off with a pang.*]

    I . . . out of a clear sky   20
    have been struck a blow that breaks my heart.
        My friends, it is over.
        I want to die.
        Life has lost all point.

---

32. **Themis:** Justice. **Artemis:** Guardian of women. Called
Diana by the Romans. 39. **killing my brother:** Medea slew
her brother Absyrtus when she escaped with Jason and tossed
him piecemeal over the side of the ship, knowing that their pursuers would stop to pick the pieces up. [**Antistrophe:** Song
sung by the Chorus following the Strophe, as it danced back
from stage left to stage right.]

87. **Hellas:** Greece.

25   The man who was my life
        — and he knows it too —
        has become for me beneath contempt.

        [*She surveys the women.*]

            Of all the creatures that can feel and think,
        we women are the worst-treated things alive.
30   To begin with,
        we bid the highest price in dowries
        just to buy some man
        to be dictator of our bodies . . .
            How that compounds the wrong!
35   Then there is the terrifying risk:
        Shall we get a good man or a bad?
            Divorce is a disgrace
        (at least for women),
        to repudiate the man, not possible.
40   So, plunged into habits new to her,
        conventions she has never known at home,
        she has to guess like some clairvoyant
        how to handle the man who shares her bed.
            And if we learn our lesson well
45   in this exacting role,
        and our husband does not kick against the marriage
            yoke,
        oh, ours is an enviable life!
            Otherwise, we are better dead.
            When a man gets bored with wife and home,
50   he simply roams abroad,
        relieves the tedium of his spirit:
        turns to a friend or finds his cronies.
            We women, on the other hand,
        turn only to a single man.
55   We live safe at home, they say.
            They do battle with the spear.
            How superficial!
        I had rather stand my ground three times among the
            shields
        than face a childbirth once.
60   Anyway,
        your case and mine are not the same.
            You have your city.
            You have your father's home.
            Life offers you the sweet fellowship of friends.
65   I am alone,
        without a city, wronged by a husband,
        uprooted from a foreign land.
            I have no mother, brother, cousin;
        am without a haven from this storm.
70   So, please, I ask you this:
        if I can find a way to pay my husband back —
        your silence.
            Woman, on the whole, is a timid thing:
        the din of war, the flash of steel, unnerves her;
75   but, wronged in love,
        there is no heart more murderous.
    LEADER: As you wish, Medea.
            You have a score to settle with your lord.
            I do not wonder that you smart . . .

            But, look, I see Creon coming: 80
        this country's king —
        bristling, I dare say, with new decisions.

        [*Enter Creon with attendants. He is a bearded man of
        about sixty, royally but modestly dressed. His face
        wears a look of troubled resolution.*]

    CREON: Go, Medea. Remove yourself.
            Get packing from this land.
            I order you —   85
        you with your black-faced fury
        lowering against your lord.
            And take your brace of offspring with you;
        no dallying either.
            I am here to see this order done,   90
        and until I've pushed you out and over the border,
        I'll not go home.
    MEDEA: So.
            I am lost — crushed utterly.
            My enemies let out the sail,   95
        while I have no place to disembark from doom.
            Nevertheless, hard-pressed as I am,
        I ask you this:
            For what reason, Creon, do you drive me out?
    CREON: Fear: 100
        no need to camouflage the fact;
        I am afraid you'll deal my child some lethal
            blow . . .
        and many things conspire to make me fear.
            You are a woman of some knowledge,
        versed in many an unsavory skill.   105
            Your husband's gone:
        your soul is raw with loss of love . . .
        and now it is reported that you threaten me:
        mean to hurt the father of the bride
        and of course the bride and groom.   110
            That is what I want to guard against —
        an accident.
            Madam, better to be hated now by you
        than soften and pay later with regrets.
    MEDEA [*exchanging a look with the Chorus*]:
            Heaven help me!   115
        My reputation is a curse:
        This is not the only time it has done me lasting
            harm.
            Oh, let the perspicacious man
        keep his children from enlightenment —
        above the general run.   120
            It will earn them only
        the sneer of uselessness
        and the spiteful jealousy of fellow men.
            Bring education to the dolt
        and, far from being accounted wise,   125
        you will yourself be cast as dolt.
            Outshine a pundit of established fame
        and you become a byword of distaste.
            This precisely
        is what I have to face.   130
            Because I have a little knowledge,

some are filled with jealousy,
others think me secretive, and crazy.

 In point of fact, my knowledge
135 does not amount to much.

[*She turns upon Creon eyes pathetic with innocence.*]

 But now I frighten *you:*
do you think I'll strike some death-knell on your
 house?
 No, no: I am not like that.
 Creon, forget your fear:
140 I have no criminal intent against a king.
 For how have *you* wronged me?
 You simply gave your virgin child
to a suitor of your bent.
 No, it is my husband that I hate.
145 You, I think, have acted prudently
and even now I don't begrudge your enterprise
 success.
 Marry them both and blessings on you,
only let me go on living in this land.
 Ill-used though I am, I shall keep quiet:
150 I am overruled.
 CREON: Reassuring talk,
but it chills me to the marrow.
 What are you really hatching in your mind?
 I trust you, Madam,
155 less even than I did before.
 The impassioned woman,
like the impassioned man,
is easier to watch than the crafty and the quiet.
 So, leave, I say, at once,
160 and no speeches, please.
 My mind's made up.
 You are dangerous.
 All your cleverness
shall not keep you here.
165 MEDEA: Please, I beg you — on my knees —
by your fresh young daughter-bride . . .
 CREON: You waste your words.
 I am adamant.
 MEDEA: Will you expel me —
170 heedless of my prayers?
 CREON: I will. For I love you less
than I love my home.
 MEDEA: Ah, home! My own beloved country.
 What memories crowd upon me now!
175 CREON: Exactly: next to my own children,
my country is *my* dearest love as well.
 MEDEA: Love, did you say?
 It is a mighty curse.
 CREON: In my opinion . . . that depends . . .
180 MEDEA: O Zeus, remember
the author of this crime.
 CREON: Go away — you poor deluded thing —
rid me of my troubles.
 MEDEA: The troubles are all mine:
185 I have a glut of them.

CREON [*turning on his heel*]: I'll call the servants:
 They'll put you out by force.
MEDEA [*clinging to him*]: No, not that . . . Creon,
 I have something else . . .
CREON: You seem determined, Madam,   190
 to make a nuisance of yourself.
MEDEA: No, I'll go into banishment . . .
 That is not what I beg you now.
CREON: Then, why not *go*, and let this land be rid of
 you?
MEDEA: Just let me stay this single day   195
to arrange my exodus from here
and make provision for my little sons —
whose father cannot bring himself to care.
 Be kind to them.
 You are a father too: 200
you know what kindly feelings are.
 As for me,
it means nothing to me
whether I stay or go.
 It's them I shed my tears for: 205
their lot is hard.
CREON [*after a tussle with himself*]:
 My soul is not tyrannical enough.
 My heart has often let me down . . .
 So now, Medea,
though I know I take a false step: 210
have it your own way.
 But let me warn you solemnly,
if tomorrow's holy light
sees you and your two children
still inside the borders of this realm,   215
you die.
 Every word of this I mean.
 Now, stay if you must; but one day only . . .
not long enough for you to perpetrate anything I
 dread.
[*Exit Creon.*]
CHORUS: Ill-starred woman,   220
 Oh, what a nightmare of anguish is on you!
 Whom will you turn to? Where will you turn?
 What country, what stranger, what home for a
 haven?
 Who will receive you?
 God has certainly steered you —   225
 Oh, my poor Medea —
 Into a sea-race of sorrows.
MEDEA [*turning on them with the gleam of revenge*]:
 In the center of disasters, yes,
but all is far from lost — make no mistake —
a test awaits the newlyweds,   230
no little ordeal for the happy pair.

[*With a laugh of derision.*]

 Do you think I ever would have toadied to this
 man
if nothing could be got from it, no gain, no tool?
 No, not one syllable,
not a touch with my little finger.   235

The fool!
    He could have scotched me with one stroke,
flung me out;
    instead he lets me stay one extra day,
240   to make three enemies three corpses:
ha! father, daughter, and my husband.

[*She leans toward the Chorus.*]

    Friends,
I can think of several ways to bring their death
        about.
    Which one shall I choose?
245   Shall I set their house of honeymoon alight,
or creep into the nuptial bower
and plunge a sharp knife through their vitals?
    One thing makes me pause:
    if I am caught entering the palace, or red-handed,
250   I die . . . and give my enemies the last laugh.
    No, there is a surer way,
one more direct;
for which I have a natural bent:
death by poison.
255   Yes, that is it.

[*She walks, thinking.*]

    Well, suppose they are dead:
will any city take me in,
will any man afford me home in a country safe for
        living
and shield me from reprisals?
260   No, there is none.
    I must postpone it, therefore, for a while
until some tower of strength appears for me;
then, through trickery and stealth,
I shall proceed with death by poison.
265   What if I'm forced to go before it's done?
    Ah, then I shall seize a sword,
face certain death,
and with my own hands run them through.
    I shall not shrink from such a step,
270   by Hecate,° no: the goddess who abides
in the shrine of my inner hearth —
the one I reverence most of all the gods
and have chosen to abet me.
    Nobody breaks my heart —
275   with impunity.
    Their wedding I'll reduce
to agony and grief:
agony for having met and married,
and grief for having banished me.
280   Good!
    Use your magic to the hilt.
    Plot, Medea, devise your recipes:
advance to the deadly act that tests your courage.

---

270. **Hecate:** Identified with Artemis, and sometimes called Persephone (Roman name Proserpina), she was supposed to preside over magic and witchcraft.

See your present plight:
laughed at by the seed of Sisyphus°   285
because of Jason's match?
    Never.
    Your father was a king:
his father, Helios the Sun . . .
be aware of *that*.   290
    Besides, you are a born woman:
feeble when it comes to the sublime,
marvelously inventive over crime.

FIRST CHORAL ODE°

[*The Chorus sings an ode about the topsy-turvy changing standards of the world. Out of the turmoil will come a new importance for women, and a new reverence. Meanwhile, Medea is a harbinger of female independence and vitality.*]

[*Strophe 1*]

    Back to their fountains
        the sacred rivers are falling;
The cosmos and all morality
        turning to chaos.
The mind of a man is nothing but fraud   5
        and his faith in the gods a delusion.
One day the story will change:
        then shall the glory
        of women resound,
And reverence will come to the race of woman,   10
    Reversing at last the sad
        reputation of ladies.

[*Antistrophe 1*]

    The ballads of ages gone by
        that harped on the falseness
Of women, will cease to be sung . . .   15
    If only Apollo,
Prince of the lyric, had put
    in *our* hearts the invention
Of music and songs for the lyre
Wouldn't I then have raised   20
    up a feminine paean
To answer the epic of men?
Time in the roll of the ages has much to unfold
    Of the fortunes of women no less
        than the fortunes of men.   25

[**285. seed of Sisyphus:** Sisyphus, a king of Corinth, was punished in the otherworld by being made to roll a boulder up a hill. As it approached the top, the boulder would roll back down, creating a never-ending task. To be a descendant of Sisyphus was considered a disgrace by the ancients.]   [**Ode:** Song sung by the Chorus.]

[*Strophe 2*]

So you, Medea, sailing away
    from your father's house,
Threading a passage with heart on fire
    through the jowls of the Euxine
30 Cliffs° to inhabit a strange
    land where your bed is empty of man
(The lover you lost, O heartbroken lady!)
Now are chased from the realm,
    shamed and banned.

[*Antistrophe 2*]

35 The joy of a bond is gone;
    and wide of the world of Hellas,
All shame has flown —
    high in the sky and away.
Bereft of a fatherly home,
40 Where can you sail for a haven against
The storm, unfortunate woman —
    Your bed
Royally quelled by another
    who queens it in your home?

SECOND EPISODE

[*Jason enters from the road that leads to the palace. He is a young-looking man, dressed in the swash-buckling cloak and plumed helmet of a captain in the King's Guards.*]

JASON [*embarrassed and exasperated*]:

So . . . this is not the first time
I have seen irrevocable damage done
by a barbarous rage.
    You could have stayed here,
5 in this land, in this house,
had you submitted quietly to your ruler's plans.
    Instead, you ranted like a lunatic . . .
so now are banished.
    To me your tirade does not mean a thing:
10 go on declaiming what a monster Jason is.
    But when it comes to royalty,
the princess and the king,
count yourself lucky to be only banished.
    I have tried continuously to calm things down;
15 for I should like you to remain.
    But you, Madam,
obstinate° in folly,
have continuously reviled our royalty,
    And so you are banished.
20   Yet, in spite of everything, I come, Medea,
patient to the last with someone I am fond of,
to do what I can to help.

You and the children
need not leave the country penniless
and unprovided for . . .   25
exile drags with it a chain of troubles.
    And hate me though you may,
I cannot bring myself to wish you harm.

MEDEA: You criminal —

an epithet too good for you . . . such inhumanity . . . 30
so you come to me, do you,
you byword of aversion both in heaven and on
    earth,°
to me your own worst enemy?
    This is not courage.
    This is not being brave: 35
to look a victim in the eyes whom you've betrayed —
somebody you loved —
    This is a disease,
and the foulest that a man can have:
you are shameless.   40

[*With the thinnest of smiles.*]

But you have done well to come:
I can unload some venom from my heart
and you can smart to hear it.
    To begin at the beginning,
yes, first things first: 45
I saved your life —
as every son of Greece who stepped on board the
    Argo knows.
    You were sent to yoke
the fire-breathing bulls
and sow the plot of death.   50
    Yes, I saved you, lit up life for you,
when I slew the guardian of the Golden Fleece,
that giant snake which hugged it, sleepless,
coil on coil.
    I deserted my own father and my home 55
to come away with you to Iolcus by Mount Pelion,
full of zeal and very little sense.
    King Pelias, I killed,
a most horrid death —
perpetrated through his daughters —   60
and overturned their home.
    All this for you,
I even bore you sons — you most reprobate man —
just to be discarded for a new bride.
    Had you been childless,   65
this craving for another bedmate
might have been forgiven.
    But no: all faith in vows is shattered.
I am baffled:
    Do you suppose the gods of old no longer rule? 70
    Or is it that mankind
now has different principles —
because your every vow to me, I'm sure you know,
is null and void.

29–30. Euxine Cliffs: On the Black Sea.

32. Editors bracket this line as doubtful.

75   Curse this right hand of mine,
      so often held by yours;
      and these knees of mine —
      sullied to no purpose
      by the grasp of a rotten man.
80   You turned my hopes to lies.
      Come now, tell me frankly —
      as if we were two friends,
      as if you really were prepared to help
      (and I hope the question makes you feel ashamed) —
85   where do I go from here?

      [*With a bitter laugh.*]

      Home to my father, perhaps,
      and my native land,
      both of whom I sacrificed for *you*?
      Or to the poor deprived daughters of Pelias?
90   They would be overjoyed to entertain
      their father's murderer.
      Yes: this is how things stand.
      Among my own friends
      I am an execrated woman.
95   There was no call for me to hurt *them,*
      but now I have a death-feud on my hands —
      and all for you.
      What a reward!
      What a heroine you have made me
100   among the daughters of Hellas!
      Lucky Medea, having *you*:
      such a wonderful husband . . . and so loyal!
      I leave this land displaced, expelled,
      deprived of friends,
105   only my children with me, and alone.
      What a charming record for our new bridegroom
          this:
      "His own sons and the wife who saved him
      are wayside beggars."

      [*She breaks off and looks upward.*]

      O Zeus, what made you give us
110   clear signs for telling
      mere glitter from true gold,
      but when we need to know
      the base metal of a man
      no stamp upon his flesh for telling counterfeit?
115   LEADER: How frightening is resentment
          how difficult to cure,
      When lovers hurl past love
          at one another's hate.
      JASON: I'll have to choose my words
120   with no uncommon skill, it seems . . .
      like a good sailor riding out a storm,
      if I am to sail close-sheeted, Madam,
      through your lashing, dangerous tongue.

      [*Folding his arms.*]

      So, you pile up what you did for me
125   into pinnacles of grace.

      Well, as far as I am concerned,
      it was Aphrodite° and no one else in heaven or earth
      who saved me on my voyage.
      Your cleverness played a part, of course,
      but I could underline, if I wanted to be ungenerous,   130
      how it was infatuation, sheer shooting passion,
      that drove you to save my life.
      I shall not stress the point.
      After all, your service did no harm.
      But this I shall maintain: 135
      that what you gained by saving me
      was far more than you gave.

      [*Holds up a hand to stop Medea from interrupting.*]

      In the first place,
      you have a home in Hellas
      instead of some barbarian land.   140
      You have known justice:
      the benefit of laws which never yield to might;
      have had your talents recognized all over Greece
      and won renown.
      For, were you living at the world's ends,   145
      your name would not be known . . .
      Oh, to me, houses crammed with gold,
      and a sweeter song than Orpheus sang,
      are nothing with no name.
      But, enough discussion of my dangerous voyage: 150
      an argument which *you* provoked.
      Now to your vindictive challenge
      of my royal marriage.
      I'll show you, first, it was an act of common sense,
      secondly, unselfish,   155
      and, finally, a mark of my devotion
      to you and all my family.

      [*Medea gives a gasp of incredulity.*]

      No, be still.
      When I came here from the land of Iolcus,
      frustrations crowding on my trail,   160
      could I, a wretched fugitive,
      have hit upon a greater stroke of luck
      than marriage to the daughter of the king?
      It was not — which cuts you to the quick —
      that I was tired of your attractions   165
      and smitten with a longing for a new wife;
      still less that I was out to multiply my offspring
      (I am quite satisfied with the sons we have);
      no, it was simply that I wanted above all
      to let us live in comfort, not be poor . . .   170
      I know too well
      how the pauper is avoided by his friends.
      I wanted our children to be reared
      in a manner worthy of my ancestry,
      and, begetting others, brothers for your sons,   175
      knit them all together
      into one close and happy family.

      127. Aphrodite: Goddess of love, called Venus by the Romans.

What point was there for *you* to have more
    children?
    My intention was — and it seemed real gain —
180 to help the ones I have,
through those I hope to have.
    Was this such a wicked plan?
    You would not say so,
except through jealousy — that stinging jealousy of
    bed.
185   You women are all the same.
    If your love life goes all right,
everything is fine;
but once crossed in bed,
the liveliest and best that life can offer
190 might as well be wormwood.
    What we poor males really need
is a way of having babies on our own —
no females, please.
    Then the world would be
195 completely trouble free.
LEADER [*sternly*]: Jason, this speech of yours is
    plausible,
But say what you like, it is not right
To sacrifice your wife.
MEDEA [*with cold disdain*]:
My outlook must be very different, then, from
    others.
200   To my mind a hypocrite who is too glib
only multiplies the danger that it puts him in:
the more he glozes° falsehood with his tongue,
the more confident and rash he grows.
    He ends by not being very clever.
205   So, you, toward me —
you'd better drop your specious pleading.
    One simple observation
lays the whole thing flat:
were you not a coward, it was your duty
210 to convince *me*; not go sneaking off to marry.
JASON: And you would have welcomed the suggestion,
    I am sure.
    Why, even now you can't contain your blazing rage.
MEDEA: *That* was not what governed you:
you felt your glory tarnished by an aging oriental
    wife.
215 JASON: Please, please believe me:
    it was nothing to do with women —
my desire to make this match —
but as I have already said
to safeguard you and rear young princes
220 to be brothers to my sons . . .
so make our family solid.
MEDEA [*with a bitter laugh*]:
    Haha! Solid happiness on the grave of love;
Prosperity with a secret sting . . .
    O you gods — not for me — ever.

202. **glozes:** Glosses over.

JASON [*earnestly*]: Please change your prayer to this 225
and make it reasonable:
    "May success not seem to me sad failure,
nor good fortune ever a disaster."
MEDEA: You go on mocking me: *you* have roof and
    shelter.
    I am deserted, flying for my life, alone. 230
JASON: *You* chose it. Blame no one else.
MEDEA: Did I? I was the one who wed and then
    betrayed?
JASON: No: you just swore a heap of filthy curses on
    the king.
MEDEA: Yes, and you shall find that *I* am the curse
that Fate has made to haunt you. 235
JASON: There's no point in talking any more with
    you.

[*Preparing to go.*]

Anything that you or the children want in exile,
let me know; I'd gladly furnish it,
or send letters of introduction for you
to friends abroad who will be kind. 240
    To turn this offer down, Medea,
is nothing short of madness.
    Forget your feelings of resentment:
let yourself be helped.
MEDEA [*spitting out the words*]:
    Not your friends, not your things: 245
I would not touch anything of yours —
how dare you offer it!
    The presents of the wicked are pure poison.
JASON [*flinging his cloak about him*]:
In that case, heaven be my witness:
all my design to help you and your sons 250
is thwarted by your preference for evil.
    Your self-will cuts you off.
    Suffer then accordingly.

[*He begins to go.*]

MEDEA: Go then. Don't waste your passion here:
go to the fresh young virgin you can't wait for . . . 255
    Have her.
        [*As Jason exits, furious and embarrassed.*]
    And God grant
the match you make, you'll long to have unmade.

SECOND CHORAL ODE

[*The women of the Chorus, appalled by what has happened to Medea, speak of the dangers of love and the
sufferings of exile.*]

[*Strophe 1*]

Love is a dangerous thing:
Loving without any limit.

Discredit and loss it can bring . . .
But, oh, if the goddess should visit
5   A love that is modest and right,
No god is so exquisite.
Great lady, aim not at me
Your gold and infallibly
Passion-tipped, poisoned delight.

[*Antistrophe 1*]

10   Stay me with innocent living;
Most beautiful gift of the gods.
Never let Cypris° the fierce
Queen of desire propel
My heart to a dissolute lust
15   From old to a new and another
Bed and a dissonant longing,
But test with a sweet eye for peace
The love-bonds of reverent women.

[*Strophe 2*]

O my country, my home, never let
20   Me lose my state and my city —
Living that desperate loss
so helpless and hard, without pity.
Death: I would bargain with death,
To die such a day to a finish.
25   For nothing is like the sorrow
Or supersedes the sadness
Of losing your native land.

[*Antistrophe 2*]

LEADER: The thing is before my eyes.
Learned from no rumor or lies:
30   Medea without city or friends
Nowhere where pity extends —
Oh, how you must suffer! . . .
Let a man rot in a charmless lot
If he never unshutters his heart
35   To the cleansing esteem of another.
He'll not be my friend: no, never.

THIRD EPISODE

[*Enter Aegeus from the country. He is a man in his early
middle years and dressed in traveling clothes. His open
features — kindly but unimaginative — seem preoccupied. In his retinue are Noblemen and Servants.*]

AEGEUS [*stretching out his hands*]:
Medea, all health and happiness . . .
and one can say a fairer thing when greeting friends?

12. Cypris: Aphrodite, goddess of love.

MEDEA [*wanly*]: Health and happiness to you, good
Aegeus,
wise Pandion's son . . . But where do you stem from?
AEGEUS: I have just left Apollo's ancient oracle at
Delphi.   5
MEDEA: What — a pilgrim there — the nub of the
world of prophecy?
AEGEUS: I went to ask for progeny — for a fruitful seed.
MEDEA [*suddenly interested*]:
In the name of heaven! Have you been childless all
this time?
AEGEUS: Childless, yes — by some design of heaven.   10
MEDEA: But with a wife . . . or have you never married?
AEGEUS: I am married. Yes, I have a wife who shares
my bed.
MEDEA: And what did Apollo say about your having
children?
AEGEUS: Something far too deep for me, a mere mortal,
to unravel.
MEDEA: Am I allowed to know the god's reply?   15
AEGEUS: Certainly. It would take a mind like yours to
fathom.
MEDEA: Tell me . . . what did he say . . . since you are
allowed?
AEGEUS: Why, just this:
"Do not unstopper the wine-skin till . . ."°
MEDEA: Till you've done something — been
somewhere — special?   20
AEGEUS [*baffled*]: Until I'm back at home again.
MEDEA: Then why did you sail in here?
AEGEUS: There is a man called Pittheus, king of
Troezen . . .
MEDEA: Yes, a son of Pelops: a very pious man, they
say.
AEGEUS: I want to ask his help about this oracle.   25
MEDEA: Yes, a clever man, and an expert in such
things.
AEGEUS: And of all my old battle cronies, my favorite.
MEDEA: Well, I hope that all your dreams come true.
AEGEUS: Medea, you look so pale, so sad. What is it?
MEDEA: My husband, Aegeus: he is the world's most
wicked man.   30
AEGEUS: You don't say? . . . Come, tell me all about
your troubles.
MEDEA: He's set up a mistress to queen it in my home.
AEGEUS: Dear me! Would he really do a thing like that?
MEDEA: Yes, yes . . . And I am deposed — the one he
loved.
AEGEUS: Did he fall in love . . . or is he just tired of *you*? 35
MEDEA: In love — Ha — head over heels . . .
flinging all fidelity to the winds.
AEGEUS: Let him get on with it . . . since he's as wicked
as you say he is.
MEDEA: But it was with royalty he fell in love:
a king's daughter.
AEGEUS: Eh? What king's daughter? Please go on.   40

19. "Do not . . . wine-skin": Probably "Do not have sexual
intercourse."

MEDEA: Creon's, king of Corinth.
AEGEUS: In that case, Madam, it *is* serious.
  You have my sympathies.
MEDEA: It is the end. What is more, I am being
    banished.
45 AEGEUS: Banished? This is indeed a crowning blow —
    but by whom?
MEDEA: Creon: he wants to banish me from Corinth.
AEGEUS: And Jason agrees? I find that monstrous.
MEDEA [*with fierce irony*]: Oh, he says he doesn't —
50   but he'll bear it bravely.

[*On her knees.*]

    Aegeus, I beg you,
  by your beard,
  by these knees of yours I clasp,
  pity me, pity my unhappiness.
55   Do not see me banished and alone,
  let me come to Athens, shelter me,
  accept me in your home.
    The gods will pay you back,
  give you the children you so long to have,
60 surround your death with happiness.
    You do not guess how Providence has blessed
      you, meeting me.
  I mean to end your childlessness
  and make your seed bear sons.

[*Almost in a whisper.*]

    I promise it. I know the drugs.
AEGEUS [*impressed*]: Medea, many reasons make me
65   ready
  to acquiesce in your request,
  not least of all the gods;
  then because you've given me — a promise:
  promise of children . . .
70 oh, left to myself, I had all but given up.

[*Gently raising her.*]

    My proposition, then is this:
  get yourself to Athens
  and there, as is incumbent on me,
  I shall do my utmost to protect you.
75   However, I must tell you clearly,
  I cannot take you with me out of Corinth,
  but if you reach my palace on your own,
  there you shall have full sanctuary
  and to no one shall I give you up.
80   So, by your own means you must leave this land:
  I cannot risk offending the Corinthians —
  who are also friends of mine.
MEDEA: As you say . . . but . . .
  if only you could promise it on oath,
85 it would make it all so . . . settled between us.
AEGEUS: Do you not trust me? What is the matter
    now?
MEDEA [*glancing nervously over her shoulders*]:
    I do trust you . . . but . . .
  but I have my enemies.

It isn't only Creon,
there is the house of Pelias too: 90
They'll want to prize me from your territories.
  If you are bound by oath
you will not give me up.
  But if you have only made a promise,
not sworn it to the gods,   95
there is always the chance that sheer diplomacy
will win you to their wishes.
  I have no weapons on my side,
on theirs is wealth and all the weight of royalty.
AEGEUS: You are very provident, Medea.   100
  However, if that is what you want,
I shall not go against it.
  In point of fact,
to swear an oath protects me too:
I can counter those who wish you ill   105
with a clear excuse;
and you of course, are well secured.
  So, name your deities.
MEDEA [*in crystal-cold syllables*]:
  Swear by the Earth on which you tread.
  Swear by the Sun, my father's father dread.   110
  Swear by every god and godhead.
AEGEUS: Yes, but what to do or not to do? Please say.
MEDEA: Never yourself to drive me from your land,
  and if an enemy of mine tries to drag me off,
  never while you live to let me go.   115
AEGEUS: I swear by the Earth and sacred light of the
    Sun
  to abide by the words you have just pronounced.
MEDEA [*relentlessly*]:
  Good . . . but if you break your word — what
      penalty?
AEGEUS: The penalty for sacrilege.

[*They clasp hands in silence.*]

MEDEA: Go now and be glad. All is well.   120
  I shall come to Athens as quickly as I can,
  but first I have some work to do, to carry out a
    plan.

[*As Aegeus is leaving.*]

LEADER: We hope that Hermes, master of journeys,
  Will hasten you home safely to Athens:
  Home to the hope of your heart's desire,   125
    For, Aegeus, you are
    A most magnanimous man.
MEDEA [*wheels round and faces the Chorus*]:
  O Zeus and lady daughter, Justice,
  O resplendent Sun!
  And you my friends,   130
    At last we are on the road to vengeance
  and to our song of triumph. At last there is hope:
  we shall see my enemies put down.
    At the very point my plot could founder,
  this man opens up a port, an anchorage.   135
    So to Athens I shall go
  and moor to her fast towers.

[*She beckons the women closer.*]

    Now I can unfold to you my whole design:
    there is nothing sweet in it, as you will see.
140   I send a servant of my house to Jason
    asking him to come to me.
        He arrives
    I tell him in the softest accents;
    how I now agree;
145   how it all seems for the best:
    his royal marriage, his sacrifice of me;
    everything that he has planned is for the best.
        But I ask him to let my children stay . . .
    with no intention — you understand —
150   of leaving any child of mine in a hostile place
    for those who hate me to maltreat.
        No, this is just a device
    for murdering the daughter of the king.
    I send them there with presents in their hands,
155   presents for the bride — as a kind of plea
    against their banishment —
    yes, a gown of gossamer and a diadem made of
        beaten gold.
    If she takes this finery and puts it on,
    the girl will die in agony
160   and anyone who touches her;
    so deadly are the poisons I shall steep the presents in.
        But now my whole tone changes:
    a sob of pain for the next thing I must do.
        I kill my sons — my own —
165   no one shall snatch them from me.
        And when I have desolated Jason's house beyond
            recall,
    I shall escape from here:
    fly from the murder of my little ones,
    my mission done.
170   People that one hates, my friends,
    must never have the last laugh.
        Well, so be it.
        What good is life to me?
        I have no father, home, defense from danger.
175   Oh, the mistake I made was when I left his house,
    trusting the word of a man from Greece . . .
    but he is going to pay the price.
        Never again alive
    shall he see the sons he had by me,
180   nor any child by this new bride of his —
    poor girl, who has to die a wretched death,
    poisoned by me.
        Let no man think me insignificant or weak:
    I am no meek martyr, no — quite the contrary —
185   relentless an enemy I make;
    though kind enough to friends.
        Such is the genius of my life.
LEADER [*imploringly*]:
    Though you have shared all this in confidence with
        us, Medea,
    and though I long to be of help,
190   we must uphold the laws of life:

and so I say to you: "You must not do it."
MEDEA: There is no other way.
    And though I understand your sentiments,
    you have not been through my agony.
LEADER: But, my lady, to kill your own two sons . . . ?   195
MEDEA: It is the supreme way to hurt my husband.
LEADER: And it makes you the most desolate of
        women.
MEDEA: Be that as it may.
    Argument is now superfluous.

[*She turns to the Nurse, who has entered during the previous dialogue.*]

    Nurse, when I need real loyalty   200
    you are the one I always turn to.
        Go now and fetch Jason here.
        But as you are a woman
    and a faithful servant of this house,
    whisper no syllable of what I plan.   205

        [*Exit Nurse, dragging her feet.*]

THIRD CHORAL ODE

[*The Women of Corinth desperately try to move Medea
from her purpose. Does she imagine Athens, that blessed
land, will welcome a murderess? Surely, she herself will
flinch from the cold-blooded killing of her sons?*]

[*Strophe 1*]

    The people of Athens are blest through the ages,
        Seeds of the all-hallowed gods,
    Born on a soil unravaged and holy,
        They feed on the wide
        Bright pastures of knowledge.   5
    Lightly they walk through the crystal air
    In a land where Harmonia,
        Goldenly fair,
    Once gave birth, they say, to the nine
        Muses, the pure   10
        Maids of Pieria.°

[*Antistrophe 1*]

    And out of the sweetly flowing currents
        Of Cephisus,° they declare,
    Aphrodite sprinkles the land
        And fragrantly breathes   15
        Delicate breezes.

7–11. where Harmonia . . . Maids of Pieria: Harmonia, the
balance of nature, and the genius of the people resulted in the
cultivation of the arts. Pieria was a holy fountain in Boetia
where the nine Muses were supposed to live.   **13. Cephisus:**
An Athenian river.

    Forever she sheds from the stream of her hair,
        Plaited with roses,
    Scented petals; and sends the Loves — the Erotes —
20 To preside with Wisdom over the heart
        And together prepare
        The glories of art.

[*Strophe 2*]

    How then shall a glorious city,
        City of sacred rivers,
25   Host of the salutary guest,
    Kindly take to the killer of children,
    Harbor among them a murderess?
    Think of how you are stabbing your sons.
    Think, too, of the blood you assume.
30 Do not, please, we beg by your knees,
    By everything and every means —
        Murder your children.

[*Antistrophe 2*]

    Where, when, will you find the mind,
        The hand or the callous heart
35   Hardened enough to strike
    These, yours — oh, heartless enough? —
    How then will you see through your gaze
    Swollen with tears as you sight your aim?
    No, no, when your little ones kneel
40 Crying for mercy, you will not
    Find the nerve, never be able,
        To bloody your hands.

FOURTH EPISODE

[*Jason enters with the Nurse behind him. On his face is
written apprehension mixed with hope; on hers, despair.*]

JASON: I have come, Medea, because you asked me.
        I put myself at your disposal
    even though you are against me.
        What, Madam, can I do for you?
MEDEA [*in a small, contrite voice*]:
5   Jason please forgive me for all the things I said.
        Bear lightly with my outbursts, will you,
    if only in remembrance of our great love together.
        I have been arguing with myself,
    have taxed myself severely.
10   "You raving fool," I said,
    "To antagonize those who want to do you good,
    setting yourself against your rulers and your husband.
        His royal marriage
    and his design to bring up brothers for your sons
15 does you the greatest service that he could.
        Why not calm yourself?
        Are *you* suffering because the gods are good?

Have you no children of your own?
    And are you not aware
you came as fugitive with not too many friends?"   20
    Such reflections made me realize
I have been out of my mind, hysterical.
    Now I thank you.
    Now I am convinced
that in securing us this benefit   25
you are the wise one, *I* the fool —
I who should have been your ally
and encouraged you.
    Yes, I should have been at hand to help,
decked the bed, dressed the bride —   30
and been glad to do it . . .
    But we women —
well, we are what we are: let's leave it at that!
    Do not copy us in our perverseness
or try to get your own back, giving tit for tat.   35
    I ask your pardon.
    I admit to being wrong.
    I've thought better of it now.

[*With an upsurge of put-on happiness.*]

    Children, children, come out here,
out of the house.   40

[*The two Boys appear with their Tutor.*]

    Come greet your father, hug him, join with me
in loving, not resenting him.
    Your mother's rancor's over.
    There's peace between us: the fighting's done.
    Come, take his hand.   45

[*As the children run into their father's arms.*]

    O God, what a presentiment!
    What an image looming in the dark!
JASON: My sons, my sons,°
    if only you could go on living, go on loving,
    with your arms stretched out like that to me
        forever . . .   50
MEDEA [*choking*]: It breaks my heart;
    I am far too prone to tears, too full of tears . . .
    it is the sudden ending of my quarrel with your father
    which makes them flow.
    A sight so touching . . .   55
        it overflows.
LEADER: My eyes, too, are stinging,
    but may this be the worst that is to come.
JASON [*gently releasing the Boys*]: I praise you now,
        Medea,
    and I did not blame you then.   60
        It is natural for a woman to be enraged
    when her husband goes off making second marriages.

---

48. To my mind there is no doubt that this line and half the
next (in the Greek) go to Jason, and not Medea as the manuscripts and editors have it. Otherwise, Medea's remark in 93
[930] makes no sense. The attempt to have it correspond to
Jason's wish in 72 [916] does not work. [Translator's note.]

Tokusaburo Arashi as Medea
with her two sons in a
Japanese version of *Medea*
performed at the National
Theatre in London, September
24, 1987.

But now
you are in a better frame of mind
65 and, even if it took a little time,
realize the good points of this plan . . .
the decision is a level-headed woman's.

[*Turning to the children.*]

As for you, my boys,
your father has been far from idle
70 and, heaven willing, he has made
good settlements for you.
In time I shouldn't wonder
if you were not first citizens in Corinth —
along with your new brothers.

[*Laying his hands on their shoulders.*]

75 Grow up now fine fellows.
Your father and a kindly providence
have the rest in hand.

How I look toward the time
when you will be two strapping grown young men,
trampling down my enemies. 80

[*Medea has averted her head and is sobbing. Her feelings, though genuine, are being used by her to further her next move.*]

But, Medea, what is this —
these dewy eyes, these tears;
your white face turned away
as if my words struck pain, not joy?
MEDEA: It is nothing. 85
I was just thinking of our sons.
JASON: Well, be of good heart now:
I shall see them through.
MEDEA: I will do my best . . . it isn't that I don't believe
you,
but you know how women weep. 90

150

JASON: I know, but don't be sad for *them* . . . why
     should you?
MEDEA [*watching the tender look on Jason's face*]:
     I am their mother.
     When you prayed just now
for a long life for your sons,
95   a sudden sadness whispered: "Will this be?"
     Well, that's one item only
of what I had to say.
     The other thing is this:
     Since the king has set his mind
100   on sending me away from Corinth,
and since I've come to recognize that this is best
(for I'd only be an obstacle to you,
living with the royal family here —
who think I am a menace to their house),
105   I shall take myself away, go into banishment.
     But the children, please, I should like *them*
to grow up under your own hand.
     Persuade Creon to let them stay.
JASON [*taken off his guard, but flattered*]:
     I — I am not certain that I can:
110   it'll take a little trying.
MEDEA: But you could ask your wife to beg her father
     to let the two boys stay.
JASON [*reflecting*]: Why not? I think I can get her to
     agree.
MEDEA: Of course you can:
115   if she's the slightest bit like any woman.
     And here *I* can play a useful part.
     I shall send her a present
more ravishingly beautiful, believe me,
than anything this age has seen:
120   a gown of gossamer and a diadem of beaten gold.
     These the boys shall carry them to her.

[*She claps her hands and two Maids appear.*]

     Go quickly, one of you,
and bring the gorgeous presents here.

[*One of the Maids hurries into the house.*]

     What a double delight
125   What a shower of happiness for her
to have you for a hero husband
and now these treasures which were handed down
by my father's father — the glorious Sun.

[*The Maid comes back with two boxes. Medea turns to the Boys.*]

     Boys, take hold of this wedding gift.
130   Carry it to the happy princess-bride.
     Place it in her hands.
     It is not the kind of present she'll despise.
JASON [*as the Boys step forward*]:
     You foolish woman — why empty your hands?
     Do you think a royal wardrobe is in want,
135   or a palace short of gold?
     Keep these things. Don't give them up.

If my wife values me at all,
my mere wish will have more weight than *things*,
I'm sure of that.
MEDEA [*with an onrush of conviction*]: Do not deny me.   140
     Even the gods, they say, succumb to gifts,
and gold is stronger than the strongest wits.
     She is lucky, *she* is blessed, *she* increases.
     This exile I would barter for my babies
not just with gold but with my life.   145

[*Forcing the boxes into the Boys' hands.*]

     Go, my sons, into the halls of wealth;
down on your knees and beg her —
this new wife of your father's, and my mistress —
to let you stay in Corinth.
     Most important of all,   150
see that she takes the precious things
into her own hands.

[*Packing them off.*]

     Quick, now, go. Success be yours.
     Come and tell me the good news.
     Your mother waits with all ears.   155

[*Exeunt the Boys with their Tutor, followed by Jason.*]

FOURTH CHORAL ODE

[*The multimurders are imminent. Woe to the victims! Woe to the murderess!*]

[*Strophe 1*]

     Now has the last hope gone of the children living,
Gone and forever: they walk already to murder.
The bride is taking the golden diadem,
     Is taking the poison and doom.
Over her yellow hair her hands are fitting   5
     The decorated dying.

[*Antistrophe 1*]

     The gorgeousness of the gossamer gown will win,
And the beaten gold of the diadem embrace her.
The bride is decked and ready to meet the dead.
     The trap is lethally set: 10
Doomed miserable woman, doomed to fall in —
     Ineluctably caught by Fate.

[*Strophe 2*]

     And you who are groomed for a murder:
     Son-in-law of a king,
     Jason unsuspecting —   15
Are to bring on your sons a demise, and a death
     On your bride of a hideous kind.
       Unhappy man, how far
       You are falling.

[*Antistrophe 2*]

20   And you the unenviable mother,
                    How I weep for your pain!
                    Killer of children for
            A vengeance of love that has gone, betrayed
                    By your man for another
25   Bride whom he sleeps beside
                    In his wrong.

FIFTH EPISODE

[*The Tutor hurries in from the palace with the two Boys.*]

TUTOR [*breathless with excitement*]: My lady, your
                    boys —
            they won't be banished.
                    And the princess, the bride —
            with her own hands —
5   she took your presents, oh, so gladly . . .
                    Now the children's danger is over!

[*Baffled by Medea's grim reaction.*]

            Well I never! Isn't this good news?
            What so transfixes you?

[*Medea draws in her breath in a muffled cry of pain.*]

TUTOR: What I hear is out of tune with what I say.

[*Medea sighs deeply.*]

10 TUTOR: I thought I brought good news.
            What kind of news, I wonder, have I brought?
    MEDEA: What you have brought, you have brought:
            the fault is not with you.
    TUTOR: Why, my Lady, these shuttered eyes:
15   these tears falling?
    MEDEA: Oh, I am pressed, old friend — hard pressed:
            the gods and my own evil counsels.
    TUTOR: Courage, dear mistress:
            Your sons will always bring you home.
    MEDEA [*in a kind of trance*]:
20   Home? . . . First I must send others there . . . Mercy!
    TUTOR: You are not the only mother to be severed from
                    her sons.
            We have to bear our own humanity — humanely.
    MEDEA [*pressing his hand*]:
            I shall try . . . Now go inside
            and see to what the children need today.
                                    [*Exit Tutor, worried.*]
    MEDEA [*throwing out her arms toward the two
25   Boys*]: My sons, my sons,
            you will have a city and a home
            far from me.
                    I shall be left lonely,
            and you will live without your mother always.
30   For I must go in exile to another land:
            never have my joy in you,
            or see your bright young progress;

never deck your brides, your marriage beds,
or light you radiant to your wedding day.

[*The Boys are now in her arms.*]

            Oh, what a blight my ruthlessness has been!   35
            How useless, little ones,
    my nursing all your growing up!
            How useless all the cares endured:
    the wearying solicitudes,
    the shooting agony of giving you your lives.   40
            And now, how miserably have dwindled
    my innumerable dreams of you:
    your loving comfort when I'm old,
    your own hands dressing me when I am dead —
    a passing every person might desire.   45
            Such sweet fancy vanishes
    and, wrenched from you instead,
    I shall drag my sad life out alone.

[*She cups their faces in her hands in turn.*]

            Your own dear eyes shall miss forever
    your poor mother's face —   50
    your way of life and hers utterly apart.
            Oh, children
    do you let those eyes now stare their fill,
    and your last smiles linger to the last?

[*She turns to the Chorus, panting.*]

            O–h! What shall I do?   55
            My heart dissolves
    when I gaze into their bright irises . . .
            No, I cannot do it.
            Goodbye to my determination.
            I shall take my boys away with me.   60
            Why damage *them* in trying to hurt their father,
    and only hurt myself twice over?
            No, I cannot.
            Goodbye to my decisions.

[*A pause, then she suddenly breaks away from the Boys.*]

            What — what undermines me now?   65
            Do I really mean to let my enemies go,
    to laugh at me?
            Steel yourself, Medea:
    away with this cowardice, these arguments that melt.

[*Almost pushing them.*]

            Go, Boys, into the house.   70

[*She turns to the Chorus grimly.*]

            Anyone whose conscience will not let him stay
    let him look to it: avoid my sacrifice . . .
    this hand of mine shall never falter.

[*Another spasm of emotion grips her, and she runs to the
Boys as they reach the door.*]

    No, no! Stop me, my heart:
    we must not do this thing.   75

Let them go, you stricken woman,
spare your sons.
    Let them live with you in Athens:
they will be your joy.

[*Throwing her arms round them again.*]

80   Ah! Not by all the haunting spirits of the
          underworld,
shall I leave my children for my enemies to
      trample down.
No, never.°

[*With a sharp realization.*]

    But — they have to die —
the whole thing is settled anyway . . .
85   Yes . . . the diadem is on her head . . .
the royal bride at this moment rots,
dying in her gown — I know it.

[*She turns to the Chorus as if to explain her second
impulsive embrace.*]

    You see: the path I have to tread
is unutterably sad,
90 but the one I set these children on
is sadder still . . .
    Therefore I desire to speak with them.

[*Seizing their hands.*]

    Give me your right hands to kiss,
each of you, my little ones —
95 give them to your mother.

[*Covering their hands, their faces, their bodies, in kisses.*]

    How adorable — this hand — and this . . .
These lips — how very much adored!
And this face and form of childhood's
ingenuous nobility . . . how I bless you both . . .
100 not here — beyond . . .
every blessing here your father has despoiled.
    So sweet . . . the mere touch of you:
the bloom of children's skin—so soft . . .
their breath — a perfect balm.

[*Gently releasing them; then almost savagely turning her
back.*]

105   Go, go . . . I cannot look at you.
I am in an agony, and lost.

[*The two Boys, weeping, hurry into the house.*]

    The evil that I do, I understand full well,
But a passion drives me greater than my will.
    Passion is the curse of man:
110   It wreaks the greatest ill.

---

82. [Translator has followed] editors [who] omit lines 1062
and 1063 [of the Greek text] as a melodramatic interpolation:
"*But they have to die, and since they must, / let it be by the
hands of her who gave them life.*"

FIFTH CHORAL ODE

[*If there can be a feminine philosophy of parenthood, is
its honest judgment likely to be that children are worth
it after all?*]

    So often before
Have I gone toward concepts far too tenuous
And come upon questions far too deep
For the race of woman to try to unravel.
Nevertheless, even we women   5
Have a muse of our own, that ushers us in.
(Though, alas, not all) to the world of wisdom.
Perhaps you might find it one in a thousand.
It serves to inspire the talent of ladies,
And makes me able now to proclaim   10
That people without the function of parent
Are happier than begetters of offspring.
The childless man has no way of telling
Whether he misses a curse or a blessing.
Nevertheless, the childless person   15
Certainly misses many a burden.
I mark how the man with children growing
Sweetly at home is worn with worrying:
How to make sure they are properly fed,
How to leave them a livelihood.   20
And then after all to be in the dark:
Were all the worries worth it or not?
Were they a worthy or worthless lot?

    But now let me tell
Of the worst and saddest trait of all.   25
Suppose the children have quite a good life,
Reach their teenhood honest and fine,
What if a fate like Death the cruel
Carries them downward body and soul?
What is the use if after all   30
(On top of all those other ones)
The gods let loose this grief as well . . .
Just for the joy of having sons?

SIXTH EPISODE

[*Medea has been sitting during the Chorus. Now she
leaps up as she catches sight of a man lunging breathlessly toward them from the street: the Messenger.*]

MEDEA: Somebody with news at last, my friends,
    And from the right direction.
        Yes, I see him:
one of Jason's men — panting as he hurries —
    With some tremendous news of bad.   5

[*The Messenger — an official of the Bride's house —
bursts in: hardly able to get his words out.*]

MESSENGER: Run, Medea, run!
    What — you have done . . . is . . . too
      unthinkable . . .

too awful . . .
　　Seize whatever means you can . . .
10　　sailing boat or chariot . . . Escape!
MEDEA: Run? Escape? Is it then so vital?
MESSENGER: Dead . . . They are this minute dead . . .
　　the princess royal with her father —
　　and through your poisons.
15 MEDEA: What a pretty word you bring —
　　my benefactor, my friend forever!
MESSENGER [*recoiling*]: What are you saying, Madam?
　　Are you in your right mind — not unhinged?
　　A king's home a charnel house —
20　　and you rejoice? . . . Are you not afraid?
MEDEA: I have my ready answer too,
　　so don't be hasty, friend,
　　but tell me how they perished.
　　An appalling death
25　　would give me double joy.
MESSENGER [*supports himself against a pillar as he
　　begins to recollect an agonizing experience*]:
　　We were so pleased to see your brace of boys
　　come hand in hand to the bride's house with their
　　　　father:
　　for your ordeal had upset us servants greatly.
　　The rumor went racing through the house
　　that all was well again between your husband and
30　　　　yourself.
　　Some of us kissed the children's hands,
　　kissed their golden tops;
　　and I in my enthusiasm even followed them
　　to the women's wing.
35　　There, the mistress —
　　I mean the one we have to honor now —
　　had eyes so taken up with Jason
　　she did not even see at first
　　the two boys hand in hand.
40　　But when she did,
　　a veil of scorn dropped over her eyes,
　　she turned her lovely face away,
　　bristling at your sons' intrusion.
　　Your husband then began to woo her
45　　from her petulance and girlish tantrums, saying:
　　　　"You must not hate your friends.
　　　　Stop being hurt and turn your head around.
　　　　Consider yours your husband's loved ones.
　　　　Come, won't you take their presents
50　　and beseech your father
　　to let these boys off banishment — just for me?"

[*Pauses and sits down hopelessly on a step.*]

　　When she saw how exquisite the presents were,
　　far from holding out on him,
　　there was nothing she withheld:
55　　but gave in completely to her groom.
　　And hardly had your husband and your children
　　left the house
　　when she took the gorgeous robe and put it on,
　　and placed the golden circlet on her curls,
60　　arranging the ringlets in the brightness of a mirror

and smiling at her own dead image there.
　　Then rising from her stool
she minced off through the halls
on dainty milk white toes,
wildly pleased with what she had received,　　　65
over and over again
running her eyes down the clear sweep to her heels.
　　But all at once
a hideous spectacle took place.
　　Her color changed. She tottered back;　　　70
shuddered in every limb; was able just in time
to fall into a chair and not upon the floor.
　　An old woman there, attending her,
thinking that perhaps the fierce possession of Pan°
or some other power was on her,　　　75
broke into a chant of wonder,
then saw the white froth spuming at her lips,
her eyeballs bulging all askew,
her skin quite leached of blood,
and changed her chanting to a yelp:　　　80
a wail of horror.
　　A maid went dashing to the palace for her father,
another went to tell the fresh-wed groom
what was happening to his bride.
　　The whole house rang with footsteps running.　　　85
　　It took no longer than a sprinter takes
to go the hundred yards,
before the poor girl lay unconscious with her eyelids
　　shut.
Then suddenly she rallied
and gave a curdling shriek,　　　90
fighting off a double nightmare.

[*He pauses, gulps, takes a deep breath.*]

　　The golden diadem that clasped her head
burst into a voracious and uncanny flow of fire,
while the robe of gossamer your children gave her
began to eat her tender flesh away.　　　95
　　Streaming with flame,
she leapt up from her chair and fled,
tossing her mane of hair from side to side,
in a frantic bid to shake the diadem off.
　　But its grip was adamant　　　100
and the golden circlet held.
　　The more she tossed,
the more the fire flowed,
till, overwhelmed with pain,
she sank down to the floor —　　　105
unrecognizable to all except her father —
her calm regard grotesquely twisted,
her sweet symmetry all shattered;
and from the crown of her head in molten clots
fire and blood dripped down together.　　　110
　　The flesh curdled off her bones
like the teardrops congealing out of pines,
inexplicably dissolved by those ravening venoms.

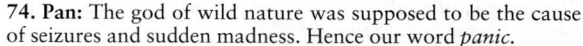

74. Pan: The god of wild nature was supposed to be the cause
of seizures and sudden madness. Hence our word *panic.*

It was curious and horrible to see.
115   No one dared to touch her body:
the warning was too obvious.
          But her father, unawares, poor man,
rushed headlong through the room,
flung himself lamenting on the body,
120   hugged and kissed it, sobbing out:
          "My stricken darling,
what evil power has done this to you,
who has made you dead
and left me, like some ancient tombstone, derelict?
125   O gods! . . . let me die with you, my daughter."
          But . . . but when he stopped . . .
from these outpourings —
these melancholy sobs . . .
and tried to lift his aged carcass up,
130   he found himself stuck fast —
clamped to the flimsy robe
like ivy to a laurel bole.
          A ghastly wrestling match ensued.
          He would try to raise a knee,
135   she would drag him back;
and when he took to force,
his own decrepit flesh
pulled off from the bone.
          At last, exhausted,
140   pathetically unable
to lift himself above the shambles,
he gave his spirit up.
          There they lie, corpse by corpse,
father and young daughter —
145   fit objects for our tears.

[*He rises, swaying.*]

          To you, Medea . . . from me . . .
there are no words to say.
          Retribution? You yourself will know
the best escape . . .
150   though in my esteem — and not just for today —
the whole of life is shadow,
and I would even say:
the people who know best or seem to know,
the subtlest professors,
155   are the very ones who pay the dearest price.

[*Flinging his cloak about him.*]

          A happy human being? Ha, there's no such
               thing . . .
more prosperity, more success in one maybe:
but happier? . . . It does not make one happy.
                                        [*Exit Messenger.*]

LEADER: Justice personified this day
160   has brought on Jason's head
          — oh, we have seen it! —
the richest retribution.
          But it is you we weep for,
poor blighted child of Creon,
165   walking through the gates of death
because you married Jason.

MEDEA [*in clear, cold tones*]:
          Now, friends, to complete this mission with
               dispatch:
to slay my children and hurry from this land.
          I must not dawdle and betray my sons
to much more savage hands than mine to kill.   170
          There's no way out. They have to die.
          And since they must,
let me be the one to cut them down:
the very one who gave them life!

[*She begins her walk to the door, almost like a sleep-walker, talking to herself.*]

          Yes, heart, be steel.   175
          Why vacillate?
          The act is . . .
necessary as it is cruel and hard.
          Come, reluctant hand,
grip the sword — grip it, Medea: 180
cross your borderline of lifelong pain.
          Away this flinching!
          Away this longing:
consign to oblivion the love you had for them —
the children of your flesh.   185
          Even when you kill them they are dear . . .
oh, my sons! . . . I am in despair, despair.

[*Medea, with the Nurse mutely following in tears, passes into the house.*]

SIXTH CHORAL ODE

[*The women pray desperately for something to stop the imminent murder.*]

[*Strophe*]

          Come Earth, come sunshafts of the Sun,
          Behold this woman and withhold her
          From her laying scarlet fingers
          On the children of her blood.
          Gold of your gold are they begotten: 5
          Heinous is to spill this holy
          Ichor in the blood of mortals.
          Curb her, stop her, godborn Light, oh,
          Keep this house from murder! Keep it
          Never haunted by the Furies.°   10

[*Antistrophe*]

          Were those birth pangs wasted bearing:
          Children's birth pangs wasted birth?
          You, my lady, after sailing

10. **Furies:** Ministers of the vengeance of the gods, employed in punishing the guilty on earth as well as in the underworld.

15   Safe between the dark blue clashing
     Gorges, will you hug a rankling
     Hatred to your heart, a loathsome
     Rage for murder and revenge?
     Those that spill the blood of family
     Stain themselves with heaven's anger,
20   Haunt their homes with doom forever.

SEVENTH EPISODE or DENOUEMENT

[*Cries are heard from inside the house.*]

FIRST WOMAN: A shout — listen — a shout from the
        boys.
FIRST BOY: O–h! What can we do? . . .
        Our mother is on us!
SECOND BOY: Brother, brother! . . . We're going to be
        killed.
5   SECOND WOMAN: That murderous relentless woman!
THIRD WOMAN: Shall we break in, snatch them from
        death?
FIRST BOY: Yes, by heaven . . . save us . . . help!
SECOND BOY: We're trapped, cornered . . . now . . . by
        her sword.

[*As the Chorus beat on the barred doors, there are
groans and cries, and presently a trickle of blood oozes
from under the doors. The women watch it, fascinated.*]

CHORUS: Woman of stone, heart of iron,
10   Disconsolate woman, ready to kill
        The seed of your hands with the hand that tilled.
        One other only, one have I known
        Murderously handle the fruit of her womb:
        Ino the maniac, god-driven one,
15   Whom Zeus's wife drove out to roam —°
        Desperate woman goaded to slaughter
        The sons of her flesh, clean against nature.
        She pitched from the precipice into the sea,
        Fell where her foot fell into the ocean,
20   Dashing two infants to death with her own.
        What ghastlier thing is left to be known?

        Women, O women, in love and in pangs,
        What ruin you've brought on us human beings!

[*Jason, breathless, his face twisted with hatred, bursts in
with a troop of servants.*]

JASON: You women standing here outside this house,
25   is that she-ravager, Medea, still at home,
        or has she fled?

[*He waits for a reply, but the women cower before the
door.*]

14–15. **Ino the maniac . . . out to roam:** Ino, a daughter of Cadmus and Harmonia, tried to destroy her two stepchildren so
that her own two children might ascend the throne. Pursued, in
turn, by their father, her husband Athamas, she leapt into the
sea with her two boys. [The account given here] is Euripides'
version.

Deep down in the earth let that woman hide,
or wing into the highest alcoves of the sky,
before she ever saves herself from justice by this
        royal house.
        Does she think that she can kill   30
a princess and a country's king
and vanish with impunity?

[*He strides toward the door.*]

        But it is my sons, not her, I fear for.
        She, she shall be repaid
through her victims.   35
        I have come to save my children's lives
from some enormous retribution by the family of
        the dead
for those enormities their mother did.
LEADER: Jason, you poor optimistic man,
        you still don't know the evils that have come —   40
        or you would not say what you have said.
JASON: What? Does she mean to kill me too?
LEADER: Your sons are dead: murdered by their mother.
JASON [*reeling*]: What — did — you — say?
        Oh, woman — my own wife — you kill me too.   45
LEADER [*as the women form an avenue to the door,
        and Jason sees for the first time the blood
        beginning to trickle down the steps*]:
        Yes. Your children.
        You cannot think of them as being alive.
JASON [*limply*]:
        Where did she kill them . . . here . . . outside,
        or was it in the house?
LEADER: Force these doors   50
        and you will see your children in their blood.
JASON [*drawing his sword in a frenzy*]: Servants, on the
        double,
        break these bolts,
        force the hinges: let me see
        the double homicide,   55
        the murdered dead . . . and the murderess to die.

[*There is a rumbling sound, and out of a cloud above
the house Medea appears in a chariot drawn by dragons. By her side are the dead bodies of the two Boys.*]

MEDEA [*in triumphant disdain*]:
        Why this battering, this beating at the doors?
        Are you looking for their bodies —
and for me who did this thing?
        Save yourself the trouble.   60
        If there's anything you want, then ask.
        But me you shall not lay a hand upon.
        This chariot, the Sun
— my father's father — gave me
to keep me safe against my enemies.   65
JASON [*hissing with revulsion*]:
        You miserable, mephitic° woman!
        Beyond abhorrence —
by me, the gods, the rest of men —

[66. **mephitic:** Foul-smelling.]

Fiona Shaw as Medea with Dylan Denton and Michael Tomer as her sons in the 2002 Abbey Theatre production performed at the Brooklyn Academy of Music.

yet you were the one I married,
not a girl from Greece.
    Oh, I married a tigress,   90
not a woman, not a wife,
and yoked myself to a hater and destroyer:
to a viciousness more fierce than any Tuscan Scylla.°

[*Turning away from the door in a gesture of helplessness.*]

    But why go on?
A million accusations would not make you wince: 95
you are shameless through and through . . .
you — you bloodstained ogress, infanticide . . .
    Hell take you!
    Leave me to mourn my destiny of pain:
my fresh young wedding without joy,   100
my sons begot and reared and lost —
never to be seen alive again.

MEDEA [*with acid imperiousness from the chariot*]:
  How tediously I could rebut you point by point!
    Zeus the Father knows
exactly what you got from me   105
and how you then behaved.
    I would not let you or your royal princess
set our wedded life aside,
make me cheap,
so that you could live in bliss;   110
or let that match-arranger, Creon,
dismiss me from the land without a fight.
    So, call me a tigress if you like,
or a Scylla haunting the Tyrrhenian shore,
I have done what I ought: 115
broken your own heart to the core.

JASON [*wheeling round to face her*]:
  You are in agony too:
  you share my broken life.

MEDEA: It is worth the suffering
        since *you* cannot scoff.   120

JASON: Poor children, what a monster
        fate gave you for a mother!

MEDEA: Poor sons, what a disaster
        your selfish father was!

JASON: It was not *his* right hand   125
        that killed and struck them down.

MEDEA: No, it was his pride
        the lust of his new love.

JASON: You think it right to murder
        just for a thwarted bed.   130

MEDEA: And do you think that a thwarted bed
        is trifling to a woman?

JASON: A modest woman, yes:
        to you the world's worst crime.

MEDEA [*pointing at the dead children*]:
  See, they are no more;   135
        I can hurt you too.

JASON: They'll live, I think,
        in your tormented brain.

93. Tuscan Scylla: A monster that inhabited the straits between Italy and Sicily and snatched sailors off passing ships and devoured them.

70   you could put your own sons to the sword,
the sons you bore,
and kill me too with childlessness . . .
Yet still look upon the sun, see the earth . . .
    Be damned! . . .
    At last I understand
75   what I never understood before,
when I took you from your foreign home to live in
        Greece,
the sheer wickedness of you,
the treachery to your father and the land that reared
        you.
    You are possessed
80   and the gods have unleashed the fiend in you on *me*;
on your own brother, too, cut down in his home
before you came aboard the sweet ship *Argo*'s hull.
    Your work already had begun.
    You married me, bore my sons,
85   and murdered them through jealousy of love.
    No woman in the whole of Hellas
would have dared so much;

MEDEA: The gods know who began
140   this whole calamity.
JASON: Yes, the gods know well
          your pernicious heart.
MEDEA: Hate then: I spurn
          the wormwood from your lips.
145 JASON: As I do yours; so let us
          be rid of one another.
MEDEA: Yes, but on what terms?
          That's also what *I* want.
JASON: Let me have the boys —
150   to mourn and bury them.
MEDEA: Never!
   My own hands shall bury them, they shall be carried
   to the sanctuary of Hera on the Cape,
   where no enemy shall ever do them harm
155 or violate their sepulchre.
      Here in Corinth, the land of Sisyphus,
   I shall inaugurate a solemn festival°
   with rites in perpetuity
   to exorcise this murder.
160   I myself shall go to Athens, land of Erechtheus,
   to live with Aegeus, Pandion's son . . .
   you to a paltry death that fits you well:
   your skull smashed by a fragment of the *Argo*'s hull:
   ironic ending to the saga of your love for me.

THE EXODOS°

[*As the Chorus begin to form for the exodos march, the meter changes. Jason strides into the middle of the arena.*]

JASON: Murder is punished, and you'll be destroyed
      by the avenging phantoms of your children.
MEDEA: What power or divine one is ready to hear
      you:
      perjurer, liar, treacherous guest?

JASON: Vile, vile, murderess of little ones!   5
MEDEA: Go — go and bury your bride.
JASON: Broken I go: bereft of two sons.
MEDEA: You bemoan too soon: wait till you're old.
JASON: Dearest children!
MEDEA: Dear to their mother.   10
JASON: And so she slew them.
MEDEA: To get at your heart.
JASON: You did! You did! How I long to press
   my little children's lips to mine!
MEDEA: Now you are longing, now you call;   15
   you utterly turned from them before.
JASON: For the love of the gods, allow me this:
   to stroke my children's tender skin.
MEDEA: No, you shall not: you waste your words.
JASON [*flinging out his arms*]: Zeus, do you hear how
      I'm at bay,   20
   Dismissed by this ogress, odious woman,
   Tigress besmirched with the blood of her young?
   So I mourn and call on the gods while I may,
   On the powers to witness how you have slain
   My children, and now prevent my hands   25
   From touching them, dead, interring their clay.
   I'd rather they'd never been born to me
   Than have lived to see you destroy them this day.

[*Before the end of these words, Medea, with a cold, vindictive smile, has moved off in the chariot. Jason staggers out of the arena.*]

ENVOI°

CHORUS: Wide is the range of Zeus on Olympus.
   Wide the surprise which the gods can bring:
   What was expected is never perfected,
   What was not, finds a way opened up . . .
   So ended this terrible thing.   5

157. solemn festival: Similar ceremonies were still performed at Corinth in Euripides' time.   [**Exodos:** Final scene.]

[**Envoi:** Concluding remarks.]

COMMENTARIES

John Simon (*b. 1925*)
REVIEW OF *MEDEA*   *1994*

Critic John Simon's review of Medea *focuses on the problems the play presents for modern production and how the director handled them. He is especially interested in the problem, as he views it, of the chorus, reminding us that this modern production reduced the original number from fifteen to three women. However, he also has useful commentary on the dramatic setting and the music and sounds, which help us understand how the play was staged.*

"One must be absolutely modern. This is what Euripides was, as he still is," writes our premier classical scholar, Bernard Knox (with an acknowledged assist from Rimbaud), in his absorbing new book, *Backing Into the Future.* In a letter of May 17, 1948, our still undervalued poet-playwright Robinson Jeffers, who wrote his version of *Medea,* declares, "There is much in any Greek play that would seem dull or absurd to anyone but a classical scholar." Which statement is true? Both.

Any new production of *Medea* must come to grips with the fact that although Euripides speaks as one of us, much of his technique strikes us as dated, though less so than that of his fellow Greek dramatists. This *Medea,* originally produced at London's Almeida Theatre, has many features to its credit, most notably that its director, Jonathan Kent, is aware of this *aporia* (as the Greek would call it) or hot potato (as we would): Euripides today is both necessary and impossible. So Kent pawkily tries to steer a course between these infernal Symplegades (or a rock and a hard place).

The first and worst problem a director of a Greek drama now faces is what to do with the chorus. In the case of *Medea,* Jeffers reduced it to three women, as Grillparzer did before him; Anouilh, in his version, eliminated it altogether. Kent, too, retains three women, but then what? How should they look? Since Paul Brown's costumes here are modern, but with classical Greek overtones, Kent picked something resembling contemporary Greek folk dress, but with distinct echoes of a Melina Mercouri movie. It doesn't look quite right, but what would? Next, how to explain the chorus's very presence? "It is hard to imagine fifteen women standing by while a mother murders her children," wrote Moses Hadas, the late, great classicist. *Three* women standing by doesn't make it much easier. For this, Kent has no solution. But by assigning the roles to three actresses of very different ages and types (the eldest coming across like a man), he achieves a nice, stylized effect — something like the Three Ages of Woman.

The Greek chorus sang and danced; so Kent lets his women do some singing and dancing. For the former, they are usually backed up by an invisible choir, which makes for a bizarre but not uninteresting effect. The dancing, such as it is, is pretty ludicrous, but one admires Kent's guts for risking it at all. And there isn't much of it.

The next problem is what kind of decor to use, other than the standard all-purpose Greek-drama set (Woolworth Hellenic), of which everyone is heartily sick. With the help of his set designer, Peter J. Davison, Kent came up with an imposingly monumental solution, which, along with the scenery for the current *Carousel,* raises the troubling possibility that British set design has way outstripped ours. What we get makes scant sense architecturally but is fiercely theatrical. Two tall, asymmetrical facades intersect at right angles; they are seemingly made of large square bronze sheets, artfully imbricated, with rivets displayed. In the lesser facade, stage right, is an empty doorway revealing some mighty girders. The main facade has, among other things, a picture window that sometimes lights up to reveal, say, Medea a shut-in in her palace, or hovering over her slain children, something the Greeks would never have shown. There is also a functioning, likewise square, onstage well. And in the end, the set does something sensational that you have to see for yourself.

Jonathan Dove's music is, in the spirit of the show, neither modern nor antiquarian, sometimes haunting and sometimes, alas, banal. More interesting sounds are produced by carefully calibrated bangings on the walls. The acting, by a low-profile British cast (save for the star, about whom more anon), is generally solid, distinguished by elocution American actors should envy. The diction of John Turner (Creon) — a tall, imposing man in a fuzzy black greatcoat for which numerous sheep must have been left shivering — is so good I felt virtually impaled by his consonants. I liked Tim Oliver Woodward's Jason, a fellow with one foot in tragedy, the other in trashiness, paltry one moment and deeply pitiable the next.

Diana Rigg's Medea is seldom absolutely right, but always hugely watchable. She, I think, suffers most from the directorial ambivalence: One moment a Mycenean lioness, she turns Mayfair hostess in a twinkling, her tigerish stalking yielding too readily to a kittenish purr. With her back frequently against the wall, her regal figure and darting eyes, she looks part caryatid, part Fury. In this she is superbly abetted by Wayne Dowdeswell's lighting, which uses horizontal and diagonal shafts of light to mesmeric or hallucinatory effect.

And yet Miss Rigg's disciplined and highly cultivated tones, and her fine sense of humor (which she has manifestly been urged to indulge), have a way of making this a thoroughly modern Medea, one eliciting too many knowingly deliberate laughs. Miss Rigg is, rightly, more sensual than her New York predecessors in the role, Judith Anderson and Zoë Caldwell, but they were, rightly, more terrifying. And for all that she looks sexy in red and marmoreal in discreetly blood-spattered white, she seems, like those others, a bit overmature for the role.

All in all, this is a production that deserves to be seen — as well as heard, in Alistair Elliot's wonderfully colloquial yet not unpoetic translation — even if its split personality militates against full impact. It is rich in ideas in its every aspect, including Miss Rigg's performance, and ideas, even intermittently misguided ones, are precious in our theater so habitually short on thought.

Ben Brantley (b. 1955)
REVIEW OF *MEDEA*   *2002*

Fiona Shaw's portrayal of Medea *premiered in Dublin's Abbey Theatre in the summer of 2000. Director Deborah Warner presented audiences with a powerful high-energy version in a new translation. Alan Riding described the London production as "hot" and Shaw as "quivering with passion." Ben Brantley's review of Shaw in the American production at the Brooklyn Academy of Music examines the power and timeliness of the Greek portrait of a woman used and cast aside.*

The word has gone out in Corinth that there's a celebrity in pain in the vicinity. And when the groupies who sniff for blood wounds among the incredibly famous arrive at her house, Medea doesn't disappoint.

There she is, as embodied with a harrowing lack of vanity by the brilliant Fiona Shaw, her recognizable features smudged by unhappiness, her eyes hidden by the formal shield of dark glasses, her mismatched wardrobe a thrown-on hash of running shoes, a cardigan and a little print dress. Why, she might have stepped from those pages of *The National Enquirer* devoted to stars foolish enough to leave home without makeup. The question is: Will she talk to us? Will she let us in on her truly sensational problems?

You bet she will. How satisfying, after all, can revenge be unless you have an audience to reflect it, to magnify it, to turn it into legend? Without their urging, how will you know who you really are?

In the thrilling Abbey Theatre production of Euripides' "Medea," which runs at the Harvey Theater of the Brooklyn Academy of Music through Oct. 12, Greek tragedy's most spectacularly vengeful woman has rematerialized in the dawning years of the 21st century. And it is, to tell the truth, a little frightening to see how comfortably this volcanically uncomfortable woman fits into the world of today.

What Ms. Shaw and the director, Deborah Warner, who collaborated so memorably on their staging of T. S. Eliot's "Waste Land," have achieved here seems so obvious, when you think about it, that you're amazed it hasn't been done before. For this "Medea" homes in on the parallels between the very form of Greek tragedy — with its dialogue between uncommon heroes and heroines and the common folk of the chorus — and an age in which private breakdowns, breakups and humiliations have become public rituals.

Of course if this were the only point of Ms. Warner's "Medea," it wouldn't have turned out to be the most essential ticket of this theater season. This isn't one of those stagings in which a clever concept reduces characters to glossy illustrations.

The miracle of this "Medea" is how completely it integrates its ideas on a latter-day culture of celebrity into a classic text, freshly translated by Kenneth McLeish and Frederic Raphael, without ever seeming to warp the spirit of the original. The anxious perfume that saturates this production is a compound of the passion, terror and existential ambivalence that have plagued humans for as long as they have been able to think.

Ms. Shaw's Medea has little in common with the usual majestically angry sorceress who is guided by one idée fixe: to avenge herself on her husband, Jason, for whom she betrayed her homeland and who has now left her for the young princess of Corinth. There is scant evidence of the commanding icy intellect so elegantly incarnated by Diana Rigg in Jonathan Kent's production of a proto-feminist "Medea" on Broadway in 1994.

It's not that you doubt the intelligence of Ms. Shaw's Medea. But her lacerating misfortunes have broken the circuits of that intelligence, and her responses are a toxic jumble. She seems to wear her nerves outside her skin. Numbness and excruciating pain, shrill anger and mordant, bizarre humor flit across her raw features in disjunctive parade.

Set in a half-finished courtyard littered with children's toys and cinder blocks (the designer is Tom Pye), suggesting a life interrupted, the entire production seems to occur in that heightened, instinct-addling realm that occurs during times of emergency. The evening begins in a state of breathlessness that never really lets up. And as upsetting as much of it is, the show radiates such high theatrical energy and insight that you can't help grinning through most of it.

The first image is of Medea's Nurse (Siobhan McCarthy), represented here as a student au pair type, rushing onto the stage with a handful of knives. She is also, it turns out, carrying bottles of pills. And she proceeds to hide these commonplace household objects, which in this context have suddenly turned threatening.

This interpolated scene is inspired in its banal immediacy, translating abstract terror into specific and familiar physical terms. You can't help feeling like a visitor who has showed up at just the wrong moment. Of course, you keep staring. And if you don't, there's the chorus of five townswomen who emerge from the audience and swarm onto the stage as if to act as your proxy.

They have the feverish look of fans addicted to real-life soap operas, like the kind of people who rushed to the site of Nicole Simpson's murder and stood in line for the trial of Michael C. Skakel. Their relentless talk to Medea, shaped by a sooty mix of empathy and prurience, seems perfectly natural. So, more surprisingly, does Medea's willingness to respond to them.

Then again, as a notorious exile now spurned by even the husband who brought her here, who else does she have to talk to? Besides, as Jason (Jonathan Cake) later says nastily, he and Medea have become people who would "rather be sung about than sing."

This production acutely accents the talk of reputation and fame and its rewards. And you can see that Jason and, in her more befuddled way, Medea are quite keen to put forth their respective versions of their lives together. Medea knows very well she is playing to a crowd and, by extension, to history. She accepts as her due the applause that the chorus gives after she has successfully pleaded with Kreon (Struan Rodger), the king of Crete, to postpone her exile.

If it sounds as if Ms. Shaw's Medea is a smooth spinmeister, then I'm misrepresenting her. What's so mesmerizing and truly frightening about her performance is how cogently she evokes a mind that is anything but clear. This Medea is an all too sensitive instrument played upon by overwhelming forces that come from both without and within.

Among these is simple brute lust. The superb Mr. Cake's vanity-driven Jason may not be his wife's match in ingenuity. But he knows exactly where to touch Medea to turn her into jelly. Their most rancorous arguments are punctuated by perverse sexual sparks that threaten to subdue Medea into passivity. And then the spell is broken, and she emerges all the more addled and angry.

The play's grotesque climax (mercilessly rendered here), in which Medea murders her two sons, does not seem a foregone conclusion. Ms. Shaw and Ms. Warner have created a Medea who isn't even sure herself how she will act from one moment to the next. There are stretches, as Medea rants about her diabolical plans for vengeance, when you think, "Oh, she's just playing," or to use the preferred psychobabble, "acting out."

For this Medea has a wide-ranging mind that, even in abject pain, keeps shifting perspectives on her. Suddenly, without warning, she'll do something like pick up a toy gun and simulate murder with a goofy smile. And she's funny when she's deriding her husband and his bride-to-be, finding the idea of them so unspeakable that she's reduced to making "bleah" and "ick" noises. But the noises also suggest an eloquent woman for whom words are no longer adequate.

When, toward the play's end, a messenger (Derek Hutchinson) arrives to describe the excruciating deaths of Kreon and his daughter, Jason's intended, Ms. Shaw's face goes dead white and still, showing flickers of gratification and just as often of incomprehension that her plan has come to fruition.

And therein lies the real genius of Ms. Shaw's portraiture. Real life seldom affords the tidy motives of murder mysteries or the stark psychological blueprints of novels about serial killers. And the recent spate of reality television serials have confirmed that famous people are never just the cleanly drawn cartoons we would like them to be. Witness the on-camera disintegration of Anna Nicole Smith.

Ms. Shaw and Ms. Warner have created one of the most human Medeas ever, precisely because they have refused to simplify her. Medea's acts may be monstrous, but the woman who performs them is a mass of confused impulses and thwarted drives that elude easy categorization. It is this very blurriness that makes her so vivid, so haunting and so damningly easy to identify with.

Aristophanes

The best known of the Greek comic playwrights, Aristophanes (c. 448–c. 385 B.C.) lived through some of the most difficult times in Athenian history. He watched Athenian democracy fade and decay as factionalism and war took their toll on the strength of the city-state. By the time he died, Athens was caught up in a fierce struggle between supporters of democracy and supporters of oligarchy, government by a small group of leaders.

Aristophanes' plays are democratic in that they appealed to sophisticated and unsophisticated theatergoers alike. Skilled at complex wordplay, he also enjoyed spirited and rowdy comedy. Since his plays were often sharply critical of Athenian policies, his ability to make people laugh was essential to conveying his message. He was a practitioner of what we now call Old Comedy, an irreverent form that ridiculed and insulted prominent people and important institutions. By Aristophanes' time, Old Comedy had become fiercely satirical, especially concerning political matters. Because Aristophanes held strong opinions, he found satire an ideal form for his talents.

Of his more than thirty known plays, only eleven survive. They come from three main periods in his life, beginning, according to legend, when he was a young man, in 427 B.C. *The Acharnians* (425 B.C.), from his first period, focuses on the theme of peace. Dicaeopolis (whose name means "honest" or "good citizen") decides to make a separate peace after the Spartans have ravaged the Acharnian vineyards. The Acharnians vow revenge, but Dicaeopolis explains that peace must begin as an individual decision. Aristophanes saw war as a corporate venture; peacemaking was easier for an individual than for a group or a nation.

The Acharnians was followed by *The Peace* in 421 B.C., just before Sparta and Athens signed a treaty, and it seems clearly to have been written in support of the Athenian peace party, whose power had been growing from the time of *The Acharnians* and whose cause had been aided by that play.

His second period was also dominated by the problems of war. Athens's ill-fated expedition to Sicily in violation of the Treaty of Nicias lies thematically beneath the surface of *The Birds* (414 B.C.), in which some citizens build Cloud-Cuckoo-Land to come between the world of humans and the world of the gods. *Lysistrata* (411 B.C.) is also from this period; its frank antiwar theme is related to the Sicilian wars and to the ultimately devastating Peloponnesian Wars. These were wars fought by Greek city-states in the areas south of Athens, the Peloponnesus. The states had voluntarily contributed money to arm and support Athens against the Persians in 480 B.C. — resulting in the Athenian victory at Salamis. The states later became angry when Pericles, the Athenian leader, demanded that they continue giving contributions, much of which he used to fund the rebuilding of the Acropolis and other civic projects in Athens.

The other Greek city-states felt that Athens was becoming imperialistic and was overreaching itself. War broke out between the city-states in 431 B.C. and lasted for nearly thirty years. These struggles and the difficulties of conducting a costly, long-distance war in Sicily combined eventually to exhaust the Athenian resources of men and funds. Soundly defeated in 405 B.C., Athens surrendered to Sparta in 404. Aristophanes lived to see the Spartan ships at rest in the harbors of Athens's chief port, the Piraeus. And he saw, too, the destruction of the walls of the city, leaving it essentially defenseless.

Aristophanes' third and final period, from 393 B.C. to his death, includes *The Ecclesiazusae* (c. 392 B.C.) (translated as "The Women in Government"), in which women dress as men, find their way into parliament, and pass a new constitution. It is a highly topical play that points to the current situation in Athens and the people's general discontent and anxiety. The last part of *The Plutus,* written five years later, is an allegory about the god of wealth, who is eventually encouraged to make the just wealthy and the unjust poor.

Among the best known of Aristophanes' plays are several whose names refer to the disguises or costumes of the chorus, among them *The Knights, The Wasps,* and *The Frogs. The Frogs* (405 B.C.) is especially interesting for its focus on literary issues. It features a contest in the underworld between Aeschylus, who had been dead more than fifty years, and Euripides, who had just died at a relatively young age. Aristophanes uses the contest to make many enlightening comments about Greek tragedy and the skills of the two authors.

Even in his last period Aristophanes was an innovative force in theater. His last surviving play virtually does away with the chorus as an important character in the action. His later plays resemble modern comedies partly because the chorus does not intrude in the action. His genius helped shape later developments in comedy.

LYSISTRATA

At the time *Lysistrata* was written (411 B.C.), Athens had had a steady diet of war for more than twenty years. Political groups were actively trying to persuade Athenian leaders to discontinue the policies that had alienated Athens from the other city-states that were once its supporters in the Delian League, the group that had funded Athens's struggle against the Persian threat. Aristophanes opposed the imperialist attitudes that conflicted with the democratic spirit of only a generation earlier.

Lysistrata makes it clear that war is the central business of the nation at that time. No sooner is one campaign ended than another begins. The men encountered by the heroine Lysistrata (whose name means "disband the army") on the Acropolis — men who guard the national security and the national treasury — are old and decrepit. The young men are in the field. As Kalonike tells Lysistrata, her man has been away for five months. Such separations were common, and these women are fed up. Lysistrata has gathered the discontented women together to propose a scheme to bring peace and negotiate a treaty.

The scheme is preposterous, but, typical of Old Comedy, its very outrageousness is its source of strength. In time, the idea begins to seem almost reasonable: Lysistrata asks the women to refuse to engage in sex with their husbands until the men stop making war. The women also seize the Acropolis and hold the treasury hostage. Without the national treasury there can be no war. And because they are confident of getting the support of the larger community of women in other nations — who suffer as they do — they do not fear the consequences of their acts.

In amusing scenes generated by this situation Aristophanes pokes fun at both sexes. We hear the gossipy conversation of the women, all of whom arrive late to Lysistrata's meeting. The men are dependent, helpless, ineffectual, and cannot resist the takeover. When the truth begins to settle in, the men solicit their wives' attention with enormous erections protruding beneath their gowns, one example of the exaggerated visual humor Aristophanes counted on. The double meanings in the conversations are also a great source of humor.

The wonderful scene (3) between Myrrhine and her husband Kinesias is predicated on the agony of the husband whose wife constantly promises, and then reneges, to build his sexual excitement to a fever pitch. It is no wonder that Lysistrata can eventually bring the men to sign any treaties she wants.

This heterosexual hilarity is also balanced by a number of homosexual allusions. Kleisthenes, possibly a bisexual Athenian, stands ready to relieve some of the men's sexual discomfort, while Lysistrata admits that if the men do not capitulate, the women will have to satisfy their own needs. Such frankness is typical of Athenian comedy.

Women dominate the action of the play, although we must remember that male actors played women's roles. The women see the stupidity and waste of the war and devise a plan that will end it. Observing that they are the ones who suffer most from the effects of war, the women also note that they pay their taxes in babies. The suffering of women had been a major theme in the tragedies of Euripides, and everyone in Aristophanes' audience would have understood Lysistrata's motivation. The idea that a woman should keep her place is expressed by several characters. And since Athenian audiences would have agreed that women should not meddle in war or government, Aristophanes offered them a fantasy that challenged them on many levels.

Aristophanes praises Lysistrata's ingenuity and her perseverance. When the other women want to give up the plan because of their own sexual needs, she holds firm. She demands that they stand by their resolve. The picture of a strong, independent, intelligent, and capable woman obviously pleased the Athenians because they permitted this play to be performed more than once — an unusual practice. Lysistrata became a recognizable and admirable character in Athenian life.

The following translation of *Lysistrata* has several interesting features. It is composed of scenes, a division not made in the original Greek. The strophe and antistrophe are speeches given by the chorus, probably moving first in one direction and then in the opposite. Instead of having a chorus of elders, as in *Antigone,* Aristophanes uses two choruses — one of men and one of women — that are truly representative of the people: they are as divided and antagonistic as Sophocles' chorus is united and wise. The KORYPHAIOS (leader) of the men's chorus speaks alone, often in opposition to the koryphaios of the women's chorus.

The rhyming patterns of some of the songs are approximated in English, and the sense of dialect is maintained in the speech of Lampito, who represents a kind of country bumpkin. She is very muscular from the workouts that she and all other Spartans engaged in; Aristophanes reveals certain Athenian prejudices toward the Spartans in the scene where Lampito is taunted for her physique.

Lysistrata in Performance

Lysistrata has enjoyed and still enjoys numerous productions, both on college and commercial stages. Because it is a bawdy play, it has sometimes run into trouble. In 1932 the New York police shut down a performance and sent out a warrant for the arrest of "Arthur" Aristophanes. In 1959 Dudley Fitts's translation (used here) was performed at the Phoenix Theater in New York with "women . . . wearing simulated breasts, tipped with sequins, and the ruttish old men stripped down to union suits." Hunter College's 1968 production used rock music, hippie beads, and headbands. Less controversial productions include the first modern version, by Maurice Donnay in Paris (1892), in which Lysistrata takes a general as a lover. The Moscow Art Theater produced a highly acclaimed version in 1923 and brought it to the United States in 1925. That version, modified by Gilbert Seldes (published in book form with illustrations by Picasso), was produced throughout the 1930s. All-black versions of the play have been staged several times since 1938. *Lysistrata* ranks among the favorites of classical drama.

Aristophanes (c. 448–c. 385 B.C.)

LYSISTRATA   *411 B.C.*

TRANSLATED BY DUDLEY FITTS

Persons Represented

LYSISTRATA, ⎫
KALONIKE,   ⎬ *Athenian women*
MYRRHINE,   ⎭
LAMPITO, *a Spartan woman*
CHORUS
COMMISSIONER
KINESIAS, *husband of Myrrhine*
SPARTAN HERALD
SPARTAN AMBASSADOR
A SENTRY
[BABY SON OF KENESIAS
STRATYLLIS
SPARTANS
ATHENIANS]

Scene: *Athens. First, a public square; later, beneath the walls of the Akropolis;° later, a courtyard within the Akropolis.*

Akropolis: Fortress of Athens, sacred to the goddess Athena.

PROLOGUE°

(*Athens; a public square; early morning; Lysistrata alone.*)

LYSISTRATA: If someone had invited them to a
     festival —
  of Bacchos,° say; or to Pan's° shrine, or to
    Aphrodite's°
  over at Kolias — , you couldn't get through the
    streets,
  what with the drums and the dancing. But now,
  not a woman in sight!
               Except — oh, yes!   5

(*Enter Kalonike.*)

Prologue: Portion of the play explaining the background and current action. **2. Bacchos:** (Bacchus) God of wine and the object of wild, orgiastic ritual and celebration; also called Dionysus. **Pan:** God of nature, forests, flocks, and shepherds, depicted as half-man and half-goat. Pan was considered playful and lecherous. **Aphrodite:** Goddess of love.

Here's one of my neighbors, at last. Good
    morning, Kalonike.
KALONIKE: Good morning, Lysistrata.
                                    Darling,
    don't frown so! You'll ruin your face!
LYSISTRATA: Never mind my face.
    Kalonike,
    the way we women behave! Really, I don't blame
10   the men
    for what they say about us.
KALONIKE: No; I imagine they're right.
LYSISTRATA: For example: I call a meeting
    to think out a most important matter — and
    what happens?
    The women all stay in bed!
KALONIKE: Oh, they'll be along.
15   It's hard to get away, you know: a husband, a cook,
    a child . . . Home life can be *so* demanding!
LYSISTRATA: What I have in mind is even more
    demanding.
KALONIKE: Tell me: what is it?
LYSISTRATA: It's big.
KALONIKE: Goodness! *How* big?
LYSISTRATA: Big enough for all of us.
KALONIKE: But we're not all here!
LYSISTRATA: We would be, if *that's* what was up!
20   No, Kalonike,
    this is something I've been turning over for nights,
    long sleepless nights.
KALONIKE: It must be getting worn down, then,
    if you've spent so much time on it.
LYSISTRATA: Worn down or not,
    it comes to this: Only we women can save Greece!
KALONIKE: Only we women? Poor Greece!
25 LYSISTRATA: Just the same,
    it's up to us. First, we must liquidate
    the Peloponnesians —
KALONIKE: Fun, fun!
LYSISTRATA: — and then the Boiotians.°
KALONIKE: Oh! But not those heavenly eels!
LYSISTRATA: You needn't worry.
    I'm not talking about eels. — But here's the point:
30   If we can get the women from those places —
    all those Boiotians and Peloponnesians —
    to join us women here, why, we can save all Greece!
KALONIKE: But dearest Lysistrata!
    How can women do a thing so austere, so
35   political? We belong at home. Our only armor's
    our perfumes, our saffron dresses and
    our pretty little shoes!
LYSISTRATA: Exactly. Those
    transparent dresses, the saffron, the perfume, those
    pretty shoes —
KALONIKE: Oh?
LYSISTRATA: Not a single man would lift
    his spear —

27. **Boiotians:** Crude-mannered inhabitants of Boiotia, which
was noted for its seafood.

KALONIKE: I'll send my dress to the dyer's tomorrow!
LYSISTRATA: — or grab a shield —
KALONIKE: The sweetest little negligee —   40
LYSISTRATA: — or haul out his sword.
KALONIKE: I know where
    I can buy the dreamiest sandals!
LYSISTRATA: Well, so you see. Now, shouldn't
    the women have come?
KALONIKE: Come? They should have *flown*!
LYSISTRATA: Athenians are always late.
                        But imagine!
    There's no one here from the South Shore, or from
    Salamis.   45
KALONIKE: Things are hard over in Salamis, I swear.
    They have to get going at dawn.
LYSISTRATA: And nobody from Acharnai.
    I thought they'd be here hours ago.
KALONIKE: Well, you'll get
    that awful Theagenes woman: she'll be
    a sheet or so in the wind.
                          But look!   50
    Someone at last! Can you see who they are?

(*Enter Myrrhine and other women.*)

LYSISTRATA: They're from Anagyros.
KALONIKE: They certainly are.
    You'd know them anywhere, by the scent.
MYRRHINE: Sorry to be late, Lysistrata.
                        Oh come,
    don't scowl so. Say something!
LYSISTRATA: My dear Myrrhine,   55
    what is there to say? After all,
    you've been pretty casual about the whole thing.
MYRRHINE: Couldn't find
    my girdle in the dark, that's all.
                   But what *is*
    "the whole thing"?
KALONIKE: No, we've got to wait
    for those Boiotians and Peloponnesians.   60
LYSISTRATA: That's more like it. — But, look!
    Here's Lampito!

(*Enter Lampito with women from Sparta.*)

LYSISTRATA: Darling Lampito,
    how pretty you are today! What a nice color!
    Goodness, you look as though you could strangle a
    bull!   65
LAMPITO: Ah think Ah could! It's the work-out
    in the gym every day; and, of co'se that dance of ahs
    where y' kick yo' own tail.
KALONIKE: What an adorable figure!
LAMPITO: Lawdy, when y' touch me lahk that,
    Ah feel lahk a heifer at the altar!
LYSISTRATA: And this young lady?   70
    Where is she from?
LAMPITO: Boiotia. Social-Register type.
LYSISTRATA: Ah. "Boiotia of the fertile plain."
KALONIKE: And if you look,
    you'll find the fertile plain has just been mowed.

LYSISTRATA: And this lady?
LAMPITO: Hagh, wahd, handsome.
75   She comes from Korinth.
KALONIKE: High and wide's the word for it.
LAMPITO: Which one of you
    called this heah meeting, and why?
LYSISTRATA: I did.
LAMPITO: Well, then, tell us:
    What's up?
MYRRHINE: Yes, darling, what *is* on your mind, after
                                                    all?
LYSISTRATA: I'll tell you. — But first, one little question.
MYRRHINE: Well?
LYSISTRATA: It's your husbands. Fathers of your
80   children. Doesn't it bother you
    that they're always off with the Army? I'll stake my
        life,
    not one of you has a man in the house this minute!
KALONIKE: Mine's been in Thrace the last five months,
        keeping an eye
    on that General.
MYRRHINE: Mine's been in Pylos for seven.
LAMPITO: And mahn,
85   whenever he gets a *dis*charge, he goes raht back
    with that li'l ole shield of his, and enlists again!
LYSISTRATA: And not the ghost of a lover to be found!
    From the very day the war began —
                                those Milesians!
    I could skin them alive!
                    — I've not seen so much, even,
90   as one of those leather consolation prizes. —
    But there! What's important is: If I've found a way
    to end the war, are you with me?
MYRRHINE: I should *say* so!
    Even if I have to pawn my best dress and
    drink up the proceeds.
KALONIKE: Me, too! Even if they split me
    right up the middle, like a flounder.
95   LAMPITO: Ah'm shorely with you.
    Ah'd crawl up Taygetos° on mah knees
    if that'd bring peace.
LYSISTRATA: All right, then; here it is:
    Women! Sisters!
    If we really want our men to make peace,
    we must be ready to give up —
100 MYRRHINE: Give up what?
    Quick, tell us!
LYSISTRATA: But *will* you?
MYRRHINE: We will, even if it kills us.
LYSISTRATA: Then we must give up going to bed with
    our men.

(*Long silence.*)

    Oh? So now you're sorry? Won't look at me?
    Doubtful? Pale? All teary-eyed?
                        But come: be frank with me.
    Will you do it, or not? Well? Will you do it?

96. Taygetos: A mountain range.

MYRRHINE: I couldn't. No.   105
    Let the war go on.
KALONIKE: Nor I. Let the war go on.
LYSISTRATA: You, you little flounder,
    ready to be split up the middle?
KALONIKE: Lysistrata, no!
    I'd walk through fire for you — you *know* I
        would! — but don't
    ask us to give up *that*! Why, there's nothing like it!   110
LYSISTRATA: And you?
BOIOTIAN: No. I must say *I'd* rather walk
    through fire.
LYSISTRATA: What an utterly perverted sex we women
    are!
    No wonder poets write tragedies about us.
    There's only one thing we can think of.
                        But you from Sparta:
    if you stand by me, we may win yet! Will you?   115
    It means so much!
LAMPITO: Ah sweah, it means *too* much!
    By the Two Goddesses,° it does! Asking a girl
    to sleep — Heaven knows how long! — in a great
        big bed
    with nobody there but herself! But Ah'll stay with
        you!
    Peace comes first!
LYSISTRATA: Spoken like a true Spartan!   120
KALONIKE: But if —
            oh dear!
                — if we give up what you tell us to,
    will there *be* any peace?
LYSISTRATA: Why, mercy, of course there will!
    We'll just sit snug in our very thinnest gowns,
    perfumed and powdered from top to bottom, and
        those men
    simply won't stand still! And when we say No,   125
    they'll go out of their minds! And there's your peace.
    You can take my word for it.
LAMPITO: Ah seem to remember
    that Colonel Menelaos threw his sword away
    when he saw Helen's breast° all bare.
KALONIKE: But, goodness me!
    What if they just get up and leave us?
LYSISTRATA: In that case   130
    we'll have to fall back on ourselves, I suppose.
    But they won't.
KALONIKE: I must say that's not much help. But
    what if they drag us into the bedroom?
LYSISTRATA: Hang on to the door.
KALONIKE: What if they slap us?
LYSISTRATA: If they do, you'd better give in.
    But be sulky about it. Do I have to teach you how?   135

117. Two Goddesses: A woman's oath referring to Demeter, the earth goddess, and her daughter Persephone, who was associated with seasonal cycles of fertility. **128–29. Colonel Menelaos . . . Helen's breast:** Helen, wife of King Menelaos of Sparta, was abducted by Paris and taken to Troy. The incident led to the Trojan War.

You know there's no fun for men when they have to
  force you.
There are millions of ways of getting them to see
  reason.
Don't you worry: a man
  doesn't like it unless the girl cooperates.
140 KALONIKE: I suppose so. Oh, all right. We'll go along.
LAMPITO: Ah imagine us Spahtans can arrange a peace.
  But you
  Athenians! Why, you're just war-mongerers!
LYSISTRATA: Leave that to me.
  I know how to make them listen.
LAMPITO: Ah don't see how.
  After all, they've got their boats; and there's lots of
    money
  piled up in the Akropolis.
145 LYSISTRATA: The Akropolis? Darling,
  we're taking over the Akropolis today!
  That's the older women's job. All the rest of us
  are going to the Citadel to sacrifice — you
    understand me?
  And once there, we're in for good!
LAMPITO: Whee! Up the rebels!
  Ah can see you're a good strat*ee*gist.
150 LYSISTRATA: Well, then, Lampito,
  what we have to do now is take a solemn oath.
LAMPITO: Say it. We'll sweah.
LYSISTRATA: This is it.
  — But where's our Inner Guard?
                    — Look. Guard: you see this shield?
  Put it down here. Now bring me the victim's
    entrails.
KALONIKE: But the oath?
LYSISTRATA: You remember how in Aischylos'
155   *Seven*°
  they killed a sheep and swore on a shield? Well, then?
KALONIKE: But I don't see how you can swear for
    peace on a shield.
LYSISTRATA: What else do you suggest?
KALONIKE: Why not a white horse?
  We could swear by that.
LYSISTRATA: And where will you get a white horse?
KALONIKE: I never thought of that. *What* can we do?
160 LYSISTRATA: I have it!
  Let's set this big black wine-bowl on the ground
  and pour in a gallon or so of Thasian,° and swear
  not to add one drop of water.
LAMPITO: Ah lahk *that* oath!
LYSISTRATA: Bring the bowl and the wine-jug.
KALONIKE: Oh, what a simply *huge* one!
LYSISTRATA: Set it down. Girls, place your hands on the
165   gift-offering.
  O Goddess of Persuasion! And thou, O Loving-cup!
  Look upon this our sacrifice, and
  be gracious!

155. *Seven:* Aeschylus's *Seven against Thebes,* which deals with
the war between the sons of Oedipus for the throne of Thebes.
162. **Thasian:** Wine from Thasos.

KALONIKE: See the blood spill out. How red and pretty
  it is!
LAMPITO: And Ah must say it smells good.
MYRRHINE: Let me swear first!   170
KALONIKE: No, by Aphrodite, we'll match for it!
LYSISTRATA: Lampito: all of you women: come, touch
    the bowl,
  and repeat after me — remember, this is an oath — :
  I WILL HAVE NOTHING TO DO WITH MY
    HUSBAND OR MY LOVER
KALONIKE: *I will have nothing to do with my husband
    or my lover*   175
LYSISTRATA: THOUGH HE COME TO ME IN
    PITIABLE CONDITION
KALONIKE: *Though he come to me in pitiable condition*
  (Oh Lysistrata! This is killing me!)
LYSISTRATA: IN MY HOUSE I WILL BE
    UNTOUCHABLE
KALONIKE: *In my house I will be untouchable*   180
LYSISTRATA: IN MY THINNEST SAFFRON SILK
KALONIKE: *In my thinnest saffron silk*
LYSISTRATA: AND MAKE HIM LONG FOR ME.
KALONIKE: *And make him long for me.*
LYSISTRATA: I WILL NOT GIVE MYSELF   185
KALONIKE: *I will not give myself*
LYSISTRATA: AND IF HE CONSTRAINS ME
KALONIKE: *And if he constrains me*
LYSISTRATA: I WILL BE COLD AS ICE AND NEVER
    MOVE
KALONIKE: *I will be cold as ice and never move*   190
LYSISTRATA: I WILL NOT LIFT MY SLIPPERS
    TOWARD THE CEILING
KALONIKE: *I will not lift my slippers toward the ceiling*
LYSISTRATA: OR CROUCH ON ALL FOURS LIKE
    THE LIONESS IN THE CARVING
KALONIKE: *Or crouch on all fours like the lioness in
    the carving*
LYSISTRATA: AND IF I KEEP THIS OATH LET ME
    DRINK FROM THIS BOWL   195
KALONIKE: *And if I keep this oath let me drink from
    this bowl*
LYSISTRATA: IF NOT, LET MY OWN BOWL BE
    FILLED WITH WATER.
KALONIKE: *If not, let my own bowl be filled with
    water.*
LYSISTRATA: You have all sworn?
MYRRHINE: We have.
LYSISTRATA: Then thus
  I sacrifice the victim.

(*Drinks largely.*)

KALONIKE: Save some for us!   200
  Here's to you, darling, and to you, and to you!

(*Loud cries offstage.*)

LAMPITO: What's all *that* whoozy-goozy?
LYSISTRATA: Just what I told you.
  The older women have taken the Akropolis.
  Now you, Lampito,

rush back to Sparta. We'll take care of things here.
205   Leave
these girls here for hostages.
                              The rest of you,
up to the Citadel: and mind you push in the bolts.
KALONIKE: But the men? Won't they be after us?
LYSISTRATA: Just you leave
the men to me. There's not fire enough in the world,
210   or threats either, to make me open these doors
except on my own terms.
KALONIKE: I hope not, by Aphrodite!
After all,
we've got a reputation for bitchiness to live up to.
                                        (*Exeunt.*°)

PARODOS:°
CHORAL EPISODE

(*The hillside just under the Akropolis. Enter Chorus of
Old Men with burning torches and braziers; much puffing and coughing.*)

KORYPHAIOS(man):° Forward march, Drakes, old friend:
      never you mind
   that damn big log banging hell down on your back.

Strophe° 1

CHORUS(men): There's this to be said for longevity:
      You see things you thought that you'd never see.
5   Look, Strymodoros, who would have thought it?
         We've caught it —
                        the New Femininity!
   The wives of our bosom, our board, our bed —
   Now, by the gods, they've gone ahead
   And taken the Citadel (Heaven knows why!),
10   Profanèd the sacred statuar-y,
                        And barred the doors,
                        The subversive whores!
KORYPHAIOS(m): Shake a leg there, Philurgos, man: the
      Akropolis or bust!
   Put the kindling around here. We'll build one
      almighty big
15   bonfire for the whole bunch of bitches, every last one;
   and the first we fry will be old Lykon's woman.

Antistrophe° 1

CHORUS(m): They're not going to give me the old horse-
      laugh!

---

205. [S.D.] *Exeunt:* Latin for "they go out."   **Parodos:** The song
or ode chanted by the Chorus on their entry.   **1. Koryphaios:**
Leader of the Chorus; also called *Choragos.* There are two
Choruses and two Koryphaioi, one male and one female.
Strophe: Song sung by the Chorus as it danced from stage right
to stage left.   **Antistrophe:** Song sung by the Chorus following
the Strophe, as it danced back from stage left to stage right.

No, by Demeter, they won't pull this off!
      Think of Kleomenes: even he
      Didn't go free
                        till he brought me his stuff.   20
A good man he was, all stinking and shaggy,
Bare as an eel except for the bag he
Covered his rear with. God, what a mess!
Never a bath in six years, I'd guess.
                              Pure Sparta, man!   25
                              He also ran.
KORYPHAIOS(m): That was a siege, friends! Seventeen
      ranks strong
we slept at the Gate. And shall we not do as much
against these women, whom God and Euripides hate?
If we don't, I'll turn in my medals from Marathon.   30

Strophe 2

CHORUS(m): Onward and upward! A little push,
      And we're there.
   Ouch, my shoulders! I could wish
      For a pair
   Of good strong oxen. Keep your eye   35
      On the fire there, it mustn't die.
                  Akh! Akh!
   The smoke would make a cadaver cough!

Antistrophe 2

   Holy Herakles, a hot spark
      Bit my eye!   40
   Damn this hellfire, damn this work!
      So say I.
   Onward and upward just the same.
   (Laches, remember the Goddess: for shame!)
                  Akh! Akh!   45
   The smoke would make a cadaver cough!
KORYPHAIOS(m): At last (and let us give suitable thanks
      to God
   for his infinite mercies) I have managed to bring
   my personal flame to the common goal. It breathes,
      it lives.
   Now, gentlemen, let us consider. Shall we insert   50
   the torch, say, into the brazier, and thus extract
   a kindling brand? And shall we then, do you think,
   push on to the gate like valiant sheep? On the whole
      yes.
   But I would have you consider this, too: if they —
   I refer to the women — should refuse to open,   55
   what then? Do we set the doors afire
   and smoke them out? At ease, men. Meditate.
   Akh, the smoke! Woof! What we really need
   is the loan of a general or two from the Samos
      Command.°
   At least we've got this lumber off our backs.   60
   That's something. And now let's look to our fire.

---

59. **Samos Command:** Headquarters of the Athenian military.

O Pot, brave Brazier, touch my torch with flame!
Victory, Goddess, I invoke thy name!
Strike down these paradigms of female pride
65 And we shall hang our trophies up inside.

(*Enter Chorus of Old Women on the walls of the Akropolis, carrying jars of water.*)

KORYPHAIOS(woman): Smoke, girls, smoke! There's smoke all over the place!
Probably fire, too. Hurry, girls! Fire! Fire!

Strophe 1

CHORUS(women): Nikodike, run!
Or Kalyke's done
70 To a turn, and poor Kritylla's
Smoked like a ham.
                    Damn
These old men! Are we too late?
I nearly died down at the place
Where we fill our jars:
75   Slaves pushing and jostling —
Such a hustling
I never saw in all my days.

Antistrophe 1

But here's water at last.
Haste, sisters, haste!
80 Slosh it on them, slosh it down,
The silly old wrecks!
                    Sex
Almighty! What they want's
A hot bath? Good. Send one down.
Athena of Athens town,
85   Trito-born!° Helm of Gold!
Cripple the old
Firemen! Help us help them drown!

(*The old men capture a woman, Stratyllis.*)

STRATYLLIS: Let me go! Let me go!
KORYPHAIOS(w):   You walking corpses, have you no shame?
KORYPHAIOS(m):   I wouldn't have believed it!
90 An army of women in the Akropolis!
KORYPHAIOS(w): So we scare you, do we? Grandpa, you've seen
only our pickets yet!
KORYPHAIOS(m):   Hey, Phaidrias!
Help me with the necks of these jabbering hens!
KORYPHAIOS(w): Down with your pots, girls! We'll need both hands
if these antiques attack us!
95 KORYPHAIOS(m):   Want your face kicked in?
KORYPHAIOS(w): Want your balls chewed off?

85. **Trito-born:** Athena, goddess of wisdom, was said to have been born near Lake Tritonis in Libya.

KORYPHAIOS(m):   Look out! I've got a stick!
KORYPHAIOS(w): You lay a half-inch of your stick on Stratyllis,
and you'll never stick again!
KORYPHAIOS(m): Fall apart!
KORYPHAIOS(w):   I'll spit up your guts!
KORYPHAIOS(m):   Euripides! Master!
How well you knew women!
KORYPHAIOS(w):   Listen to him, Rhodippe,   100
up with the pots!
KORYPHAIOS(m):   Demolition of God,
what good are your pots?
KORYPHAIOS(w):   You refugee from the tomb,
what good is your fire?
KORYPHAIOS(m):   Good enough to make a pyre
to barbecue you!
KORYPHAIOS(w):   We'll squizzle your kindling!
KORYPHAIOS(m): You think so?
KORYPHAIOS(w):   Yah! Just hang around a while!   105
KORYPHAIOS(m): Want a touch of my torch?
KORYPHAIOS(w):   It needs a good soaping.
KORYPHAIOS(m): How about you?
KORYPHAIOS(w):   Soap for a senile bridegroom!
KORYPHAIOS(m): Senile? Hold your trap
KORYPHAIOS(w):   Just *you* try to hold it!
KORYPHAIOS(m): The yammer of women!
KORYPHAIOS(w):   Oh is that so?
You're not in the jury room now, you know.   110
KORYPHAIOS(m): Gentlemen, I beg you, burn off that woman's hair!
KORYPHAIOS(w): Let it come down!

(*They empty their pots on the men.*)

KORYPHAIOS(m): What a way to drown!
KORYPHAIOS(w):   Hot, hey?
KORYPHAIOS(m):   Say, enough!
KORYPHAIOS(w): Dandruff
needs watering. I'll make you   115
nice and fresh.
KORYPHAIOS(m):   For God's sake, you,
hold off!

SCENE 1

(*Enter a Commissioner accompanied by four constables.*)

COMMISSIONER: These degenerate women! What a racket of little drums,
what a yapping for Adonis° on every house-top!
It's like the time in the Assembly when I was listening
to a speech — out of order, as usual — by that fool
Demostratos,° all about troops for Sicily,°   5
that kind of nonsense —
                    and there was his wife

2. **Adonis:** Fertility god, loved by Aphrodite.   5. **Demostratos:** Athenian orator and politician.   **Sicily:** Reference to the Sicilian Expedition (415–413 B.C.) in which Athens was decisively defeated.

trotting around in circles howling
Alas for Adonis! —
               and Demostratos insisting
we must draft every last Zakynthian that can walk —
10   and his wife up there on the roof,
drunk as an owl, yowling
Oh weep for Adonis! —
              and that damned ox Demostratos
mooing away through the rumpus. That's what we
    get
for putting up with this wretched woman-business!
KORYPHAIOS^(m): Sir, you haven't heard the half of it.
15   They laughed at us!
Insulted us! They took pitchers of water
and nearly drowned us! We're still wringing out our
    clothes,
for all the world like unhousebroken brats.
COMMISSIONER: Serves you right, by Poseidon!
20   Whose fault is it if these women-folk of ours
get out of hand? We coddle them,
we teach them to be wasteful and loose. You'll see a
    husband
go into a jeweler's. "Look," he'll say,
"jeweler," he'll say, "you remember that gold choker
you made for my wife? Well, she went to a dance
25   last night
and broke the clasp. Now, I've got to go to Salamis,
and can't be bothered. Run over to my house tonight,
will you, and see if you can put it together for her."
Or another one
30   goes to a cobbler — a good strong workman, too,
with an awl that was never meant for child's play.
    "Here,"
he'll tell him, "one of my wife's shoes is pinching
her little toe. Could you come up about noon
and stretch it out for her?"
                    Well, what do you expect?
35   Look at me, for example, I'm a Public Officer,
and it's one of my duties to pay off the sailors.
And where's the money? Up there in the Akropolis!
And those blasted women slam the door in my face!
But what are we waiting for?
               — Look here, constable,
40   stop sniffing around for a tavern, and get us
some crowbars. We'll force their gates! As a matter
    of fact,
I'll do a little forcing myself.

(*Enter Lysistrata, above, with Myrrhine, Kalonike, and the Boiotian.*)

LYSISTRATA: No need of forcing.
Here I am, of my own accord. And all this talk
about locked doors — ! We don't need locked doors,
45   but just the least bit of common sense.
COMMISSIONER: Is that so, ma'am!
                   — Where's my constable?
                        — Constable,
arrest that woman, and tie her hands behind her.
LYSISTRATA: If he touches me, I swear by Artemis

there'll be one scamp dropped from the public pay-
    roll tomorrow!
COMMISSIONER: Well, constable? You're not afraid, I
    suppose? Grab her,   50
two of you, around the middle!
KALONIKE: No, by Pandrosos!°
Lay a hand on her, and I'll jump on you so hard
your guts will come out the back door!
COMMISSIONER: That's what *you* think!
Where's the sergeant? — Here, you: tie up that
    trollop first,
the one with the pretty talk!
MYRRHINE: By the Moon-Goddess,° 55
just try! They'll have to scoop you up with a spoon!
COMMISSIONER: Another one!
                   Officer, seize that woman!
                            I swear
I'll put an end to this riot!
BOIOTIAN: By the Taurian,°
one inch closer, you'll be one screaming bald-head!
COMMISSIONER: Lord, what a mess! And my
    constables seem ineffective.   60
But — women get the best of us? By God, no!
                — Skythians!°
Close ranks and forward march!
LYSISTRATA: "Forward," indeed!
By the Two Goddesses, what's the sense in *that*?
They're up against four companies of women
armed from top to bottom.
COMMISSIONER: Forward, my Skythians! 65
LYSISTRATA: Forward, yourselves, dear comrades!
You grainlettucebeanseedmarket girls!
You garlicandonionbreadbakery girls!
Give it to 'em! Knock 'em down! Scratch 'em!
Tell 'em what you think of 'em!

(*General melee, the Skythians yield.*)

                  — Ah, that's enough! 70
Sound a retreat: good soldiers don't rob the dead.
COMMISSIONER: A nice day *this* has been for the
    police!
LYSISTRATA: Well, there you are. — Did you really
    think we women
would be driven like slaves? Maybe now you'll admit
that a woman knows something about spirit.
COMMISSIONER: Spirit enough, 75
especially spirits in bottles! Dear Lord Apollo!
KORYPHAIOS^(m): Your Honor, there's no use talking to
    them. Words
mean nothing whatever to wild animals like these.
Think of the sousing they gave us! and the water
was not, I believe, of the purest.   80

---

51. Pandrosos: A woman's oath referring to one of the daughters of the founder of Athens. **55. Moon-Goddess:** Artemis, goddess of the hunt and of fertility, daughter of Zeus. **58. Taurian:** Reference to Artemis, who was said to have been worshiped in a cult at Taurica Chersonesos. **61. Skythians:** Athenian archers.

KORYPHAIOS⁽ʷ⁾: You shouldn't have come after us. And
    if you try it again,
    you'll be one eye short! — Although, as a matter of
      fact,
    what I like best is just to stay at home and read,
    like a sweet little bride: never hurting a soul, no,
85   never going out. But if you *must* shake hornets' nests,
    look out for the hornets.

Strophe 1

CHORUS⁽ᵐ⁾: Of all the beasts that God hath wrought
      What monster's worse than woman?
    Who shall encompass with his thought
90   Their guile unending? No man.

    They've seized the Heights, the Rock, the Shrine —
      But to what end? I wot not.
    Sure there's some clue to their design!
      Have you the key? I thought not.
KORYPHAIOS⁽ᵐ⁾: We might question them, I suppose.
95   But I warn you, sir,
    don't believe anything you hear! It would be un-
      Athenian
    not to get to the bottom of this plot.
COMMISSIONER: Very well.
    My first question is this: Why, so help you God,
    did you bar the gates of the Akropolis?
LYSISTRATA: Why?
100   To keep the money, of course. No money, no war.
COMMISSIONER: You think that money's the cause of
    war?
LYSISTRATA: I do.
    Money brought about that Peisandros° business
    and all the other attacks on the State. Well and good!
    They'll not get another cent here!
105 COMMISSIONER: And what will you do?
LYSISTRATA: What a question! From now on, we intend
    to control the Treasury.
COMMISSIONER: Control the Treasury!
LYSISTRATA: Why not? Does that seem strange?
      After all,
    we control our household budgets.
COMMISSIONER: But that's different!
LYSISTRATA: "Different"? What do you mean?
110 COMMISSIONER: I mean simply this:
    it's the Treasury that pays for National Defense.
LYSISTRATA: Unnecessary. We propose to abolish war.
COMMISSIONER: Good God. — And National
    Security?
LYSISTRATA: Leave that to us.
COMMISSIONER: You?
LYSISTRATA: Us.
COMMISSIONER: We're done for, then!
115 LYSISTRATA: Never mind.

103. Peisandros: A politician who plotted against the Athenian
democracy.

We women will save you in spite of yourselves.
COMMISSIONER: What nonsense!
LYSISTRATA: If you like. But you must accept it, like it
    or not.
COMMISSIONER: Why, this is downright subversion!
LYSISTRATA: Maybe it is.
    But we're going to save you, Judge.
COMMISSIONER: I don't *want* to be saved.
LYSISTRATA: Tut. The death-wish. All the more reason.   120
COMMISSIONER: But the idea of women bothering
    themselves about peace and war!
LYSISTRATA: Will you listen to me?
COMMISSIONER: Yes. But be brief, or I'll —
LYSISTRATA: This is no time for stupid threats.
COMMISSIONER: By the gods,
    I can't stand any more!
AN OLD WOMAN: Can't stand? Well, well.
COMMISSIONER: That's enough out of you, you old
    buzzard!   125
    Now, Lysistrata: tell me what you're thinking.
LYSISTRATA: Glad to.
               Ever since this war began
We women have been watching you men, agreeing
    with you,
keeping our thoughts to ourselves. That doesn't mean
we were happy: we weren't, for we saw how things
    were going;   130
but we'd listen to you at dinner
arguing this way and that.
             — Oh you, and your big
Top Secrets! —
         And then we'd grin like little patriots
(though goodness knows we didn't feel like
    grinning) and ask you:
"Dear, did the Armistice come up in Assembly
    today?"   135
And you'd say, "None of your business! Pipe
    down!" you'd say.
And so we would.
AN OLD WOMAN: *I* wouldn't have, by God!
COMMISSIONER: You'd have taken a beating, then!
                          — Go on.
LYSISTRATA: Well, we'd be quiet. But then, you know,
    all at once
you men would think up something worse than ever.   140
Even *I* could see it was fatal. And, "Darling," I'd say,
"have you gone completely mad?" And my husband
    would look at me
and say, "Wife, you've got your weaving to attend
    to.
Mind your tongue, if you don't want a slap.
'War's a man's affair!'"°   145
COMMISSIONER: Good words, and well pronounced.
LYSISTRATA: You're a fool if you think so.
                    It was hard enough
    to put up with all this banquet-hall strategy.

145. 'War's a man's affair!': Quoted from Homer's *Iliad*, VI,
492, Hector's farewell to his wife, Andromache.

150 But then we'd hear you out in the public square:
"Nobody left for the draft-quota here in Athens?"
you'd say; and, "No," someone else would say, "not
a man!"
And so we women decided to rescue Greece.
You might as well listen to us now: you'll have to,
later.
COMMISSIONER: *You* rescue Greece? Absurd.
LYSISTRATA: You're the absurd one.
COMMISSIONER: You expect me to take orders from a
woman?
155   I'd die first!
LYSISTRATA: Heavens, if that's what's bothering you,
take my veil,
here, and wrap it around your poor head.
KALONIKE: Yes
and you can have my market-basket, too.
Go home, tighten your girdle, do the washing, mind
160 your beans! "War's
a woman's affair!"
KORYPHAIOS(w):   Ground pitchers! Close ranks!

Antistrophe

CHORUS(w): This is a dance that I know well,
My knees shall never yield.
Wobble and creak I may, but still
165 I'll keep the well-fought field.
Valor and grace march on before,
Love prods us from behind.
Our slogan is EXCELSIOR,
Our watchword SAVE MANKIND.
KORYPHAIOS(w): Women, remember your grandmothers!
170 Remember
that little old mother of yours, what a stinger she
was!
On, on, never slacken. There's a strong wind astern!
LYSISTRATA: O Eros of delight! O Aphrodite! Kyprian!°
If ever desire has drenched our breasts or dreamed
in our thighs, let it work so now on the men of
175 Hellas°
that they shall tail us through the land, slaves, slaves
to Woman, Breaker of Armies!
COMMISSIONER: And if we do?
LYSISTRATA: Well, for one thing, we shan't have to
watch you
going to market, a spear in one hand, and heaven
knows
what in the other.
180 KALONIKE: Nicely said, by Aphrodite!
LYSISTRATA: As things stand now, you're neither men
nor women.

Armor clanking with kitchen pans and pots —
You sound like a pack of Korybantes!°
COMMISSIONER: A man must do what a man must do.
LYSISTRATA: So I'm told.
But to see a General, complete with Gorgon-shield,   185
jingling along the dock to buy a couple of herrings!
KALONIKE: *I* saw a Captain the other day — lovely
fellow he was,
nice curly hair — sitting on his horse; and — can
you believe it? —
he'd just bought some soup, and was pouring it into
his helmet!
And there was a soldier from Thrace   190
swishing his lance like something out of Euripides,
and the poor fruit-store woman got so scared
that she ran away and let him have his figs free!
COMMISSIONER: All this is beside the point.
                         Will you be so kind
as to tell me how you mean to save Greece?
LYSISTRATA: Of course.   195
Nothing could be simpler.
COMMISSIONER: I assure you, I'm all ears.
LYSISTRATA: Do you know anything about weaving?
Say the yarn gets tangled: we thread it
this way and that through the skein, up and down,
until it's free. And it's like that with war.   200
We'll send our envoys
up and down, this way and that, all over Greece,
until it's finished.
COMMISSIONER: Yarn? Thread? Skein?
Are you out of your mind? I tell you,
war is a serious business.
LYSISTRATA: So serious   205
that I'd like to go on talking about weaving.
COMMISSIONER: All right. Go ahead.
LYSISTRATA: The first thing we have to do
is to wash our yarn, get the dirt out of it.
You see? Isn't there too much dirt here in Athens?
You must wash those men away.
                         Then our spoiled wool —   210
that's like your job-hunters, out for a life
of no work and big pay. Back to the basket,
citizens or not, allies or not,
or friendly immigrants.
                         And your colonies?
Hanks of wool lost in various places. Pull them   215
together, weave them into one great whole,
and our voters are clothed for ever.
COMMISSIONER: It would take a woman
to reduce state questions to a matter of carding and
weaving.
LYSISTRATA: You fool! Who were the mothers whose
sons sailed off
to fight for Athens in Sicily?

220 COMMISSIONER: Enough!
    I beg you, do not call back those memories.
    LYSISTRATA: And then,
      instead of the love that every woman needs,
      we have only our single beds, where we can
        dream
      of our husbands off with the Army.
                                    Bad enough for wives!
225   But what about our girls, getting older every day,
      and older, and no kisses?
    COMMISSIONER: Men get older, too.
    LYSISTRATA: Not in the same sense.
                            A soldier's discharged,
      and he may be bald and toothless, yet he'll find
      a pretty young thing to go to bed with.
                                    But a woman!
230   Her beauty is gone with the first gray hair.
      She can spend her time
      consulting the oracles and the fortune-tellers,
      but they'll never send her a husband.
    COMMISSIONER: Still, if a man can rise to the
        occasion —
235 LYSISTRATA: Rise? Rise, yourself!

(*Furiously.*)

    Go invest in a coffin!
                            You've money enough.
                                    I'll bake you
      a cake for the Underworld.
                            And here's your funeral wreath!

(*She pours water upon him.*)

MYRRHINE: And here's another!

(*More water.*)

KALONIKE: And here's
    my contribution!

(*More water.*)

LYSISTRATA: What are you waiting for?
    All aboard Styx Ferry!
240   Charon's° calling for you!
      It's sailing-time: don't disrupt the schedule!
    COMMISSIONER: The insolence of women! And
        to me!
      No, by God, I'll go back to town and show
      the rest of the Commission what might happen to
        them.   (*Exit Commissioner.*)
    LYSISTRATA: Really, I suppose we should have laid out
245   his corpse
      on the doorstep, in the usual way.
                                    But never mind.
      We'll give him the rites of the dead tomorrow
        morning.

            (*Exit Lysistrata with Myrrhine and Kalonike.*)

240. Charon: The god who ferried the souls of the newly dead
across the river Styx to Hades.

PARABASIS:°
CHORAL EPISODE • Ode° *1*

KORYPHAIOS[(m)]: Sons of Liberty, awake! The day of
        glory is at hand.
CHORUS[(m)]: I smell tyranny afoot, I smell it rising from
        the land.
    I scent a trace of Hippias,° I sniff upon the breeze
    A dismal Spartan hogo that suggests King
        Kleisthenes.°
        Strip, strip for action, brothers!   5
        Our wives, aunts, sisters, mothers
    Have sold us out: the streets are full of godless
        female rages.
    Shall we stand by and let our women confiscate our
        wages?

                                    [*Epirrhema*° 1]
KORYPHAIOS[(m)]: Gentlemen, it's a disgrace to Athens, a
        disgrace
    to all that Athens stands for, if we allow these
        grandmas   10
    to jabber about spears and shields and making
        friends
    with the Spartans. What's a Spartan? Give me a
        wild wolf
    any day. No. They want the Tyranny back, I
        suppose.
    Are we going to take that? No. Let us look like
    the innocent serpent, but be the flower under it,   15
    as the poet sings. And just to begin with,
    I propose to poke a number of teeth
    down the gullet of that harridan over there.

Antode° *1*

KORYPHAIOS[(w)]: Oh, is that so? When you get home,
        your own mamma won't know you!
CHORUS[(w)]: Who do you think we are, you senile
        bravos? Well, I'll show you.   20
    I bore the sacred vessels in my eighth year,° and at ten
    I was pounding out the barley for Athena Goddess;°
        then

Parabasis: Section of the play in which the author presented his
own views through the Koryphaios directly to the audience.
The parabasis in *Lysistrata* is shorter than those in Aristophanes' other works and unusual in that the Koryphaios does not
speak directly for the author.   **Ode:** Song sung by the Chorus.
3. Hippias: An Athenian tyrant.   **4. Kleisthenes:** A bisexual
Athenian.   **Epirrhema:** A part of the parabasis spoken by the
Koryphaios following an ode delivered by his or her half of the
Chorus.   **Antode:** Lyric song sung by half of the Chorus in
response to the Ode sung by the other half.   **21. eighth year:**
Young girls between the ages of seven and eleven served in the
temple of Athena in the Akropolis.   **22. pounding out the bar-
ley for Athena Goddess:** At age ten a girl could be chosen to
grind the sacred grain of Athena.

They made me Little Bear
At the Brauronian Fair;°
25   I'd held the Holy Basket° by the time I was of age,
The Blessed Dry Figs had adorned my plump
decolletage.

[Antepirrhema° 1]
KORYPHAIOS⁽ʷ⁾: A "disgrace to Athens," and I, just at
the moment
I'm giving Athens the best advice she ever had?
Don't I pay taxes to the State? Yes, I pay them
30   in baby boys. And what do you contribute,
you impotent horrors? Nothing but waste: all
our Treasury,° dating back to the Persian Wars,
gone! rifled! And not a penny out of your pockets!
Well, then? Can you cough up an answer to that?
35   Look out for your own gullet, or you'll get a crack
from this old brogan that'll make your teeth see
stars!

Ode 2

CHORUS⁽ᵐ⁾: Oh insolence!
Am I unmanned?
Incontinence!
40   Shall my scarred hand
Strike never a blow
To curb this flow-
ing female curse?

Leipsydrion!°
45   Shall I betray
The laurels won
On that great day?
Come, shake a leg,
Shed old age, beg
50   The years reverse!

[Epirrhema 2]
KORYPHAIOS⁽ᵐ⁾: Give them an inch, and we're done
for! We'll have them
launching boats next and planning naval
strategy,
sailing down on us like so many Artemisias.
Or maybe they have ideas about the cavalry.
55   That's fair enough, women are certainly good
in the saddle. Just look at Mikon's paintings,
all those Amazons wrestling with all those men!
On the whole, a straitjacket's their best uniform.

24. **Brauronian Fair:** A ritual in the cult of Artemis, who is associated with wild beasts, in which young girls dressed up as bears and danced for the goddess.   25. **Holy Basket:** In one ritual to Athena, young girls carried baskets of objects sacred to the goddess.   **Antepirrhema:** The speech delivered by the second Koryphaios after the second half of the Chorus had sung an ode.   32. **Treasury:** Athenian politicians were raiding the funds that were collected by Athens to finance a war against Persia.   44. **Leipsydrion:** A place where Athenian patriots had heroically fought.

Antode 2

CHORUS⁽ʷ⁾: Tangle with me,
And you'll get cramps.   60
Ferocity
's no use now, Gramps!
By the Two,
I'll get through
To you wrecks yet!   65

I'll scramble your eggs,
I'll burn your beans,
With my two legs.
You'll see such scenes
As never yet   70
Your two eyes met.
A curse? You bet!

[Antepirrhema 2]
KORYPHAIOS⁽ʷ⁾: If Lampito stands by me, and that
delicious Theban girl,
Ismenia — what good are *you*? You and your
seven
Resolutions! Resolutions? Rationing Boiotian eels   75
and making our girls go without them at Hekate's°
Feast!
That was statesmanship! And we'll have to put up
with it
and all the rest of your decrepit legislation
until some patriot — God give him strength! —
grabs you by the neck and kicks you off the Rock.   80

SCENE 2

(*Reenter Lysistrata and her lieutenants.*)

KORYPHAIOS⁽ʷ⁾ (*tragic tone*): Great Queen, fair
Architect of our emprise,
Why lookst thou on us with foreboding eyes?
LYSISTRATA: The behavior of these idiotic women!
There's something about the female temperament
that I can't bear!
KORYPHAIOS⁽ʷ⁾:   What in the world do you mean?   5
LYSISTRATA: Exactly what I say.
KORYPHAIOS⁽ʷ⁾: What dreadful thing has happened?
Come, tell us: we're all your friends.
LYSISTRATA: It isn't easy
to say it; yet, God knows, we can't hush it up.
KORYPHAIOS⁽ʷ⁾: Well, then? Out with it!
LYSISTRATA: To put it bluntly,   10
we're dying to get laid.
KORYPHAIOS⁽ʷ⁾:   Almighty God!
LYSISTRATA: Why bring God into it? — No, it's just as
I say.
I can't manage them any longer: they've gone
man-crazy,

76. **Hekate:** Patron of successful wars, object of a Boiotian cult (later associated with sorcery).

they're all trying to get out.
                                        Why, look:
15   one of them was sneaking out the back door
      over there by Pan's cave; another
      was sliding down the walls with rope and tackle;
      another was climbing aboard a sparrow, ready to
         take off
      for the nearest brothel — I dragged *her* back by the
         hair!
      They're all finding some reason to leave.
20   Look there!
      There goes another one.
                              — Just a minute, you!
      Where are you off to so fast?
      FIRST WOMAN: I've got to get home.
      I've a lot of Milesian wool, and the worms are
         spoiling it.
      LYSISTRATA: Oh bother you and your worms! Get back
         inside!
25   FIRST WOMAN: I'll be back right away, I swear I will.
      I just want to get it stretched out on my bed.
      LYSISTRATA: You'll do no such thing. You'll stay
         right here.
      FIRST WOMAN: And my wool?
      You want it ruined?
      LYSISTRATA: Yes, for all I care.
      SECOND WOMAN: Oh dear! My lovely new flax from
         Amorgos —
      I left it at home, all uncarded!
30   LYSISTRATA: Another one!
      And all she wants is someone to card her flax.
      Get back in there!
      SECOND WOMAN: But I swear by the Moon-Goddess
      the minute I get it done, I'll be back!
      LYSISTRATA: I say No.
      If you, why not all the other women as well?
      THIRD WOMAN: O Lady Eileithyia!° Radiant goddess!
35   Thou
         intercessor for women in childbirth! Stay, I pray thee,
         oh stay this parturition. Shall I pollute
         a sacred spot?°
      LYSISTRATA: And what's the matter with *you?*
      THIRD WOMAN: I'm having a baby — any minute now.
      LYSISTRATA: But you weren't pregnant yesterday.
40   THIRD WOMAN: Well, I am today.
      Let me go home for a midwife, Lysistrata:
      there's not much time.
      LYSISTRATA: I never heard such nonsense.
      What's that bulging under your cloak?
      THIRD WOMAN: A little baby boy.
      LYSISTRATA: It certainly isn't. But it's something hollow,
45   like a basin or — Why, it's the helmet of Athena!
      And you said you were having a baby.
      THIRD WOMAN: Well, I am! So there!

      LYSISTRATA: Then why the helmet?
      THIRD WOMAN: I was afraid that my pains
         might begin here in the Akropolis; and I wanted
         to drop my chick into it, just as the dear doves do.
      LYSISTRATA: Lies! Evasions! — But at least one thing's
         clear: 50
         you can't leave the place before your purification.°
      THIRD WOMAN: But I can't stay here in the Akropolis!
         Last night I dreamed
         of the Snake.
      FIRST WOMAN: And those horrible owls, the noise they
         make!
         I can't get a bit of sleep; I'm just about dead.
      LYSISTRATA: You useless girls, that's enough: Let's have
         no more lying.   55
         Of course you want your men. But don't you imagine
         that they want you just as much? I'll give you my
         word,
         their nights must be pretty hard.
                                        Just stick it out!
         A little patience, that's all, and our battle's won.
         I have heard an Oracle. Should you like to hear it? 60
      FIRST WOMAN: An Oracle? Yes, tell us!
      LYSISTRATA: Here is what it says:
         WHEN SWALLOWS SHALL THE HOOPOE SHUN
            AND SPURN HIS HOT DESIRE,
         ZEUS WILL PERFECT WHAT THEY'VE BEGUN
            AND SET THE LOWER HIGHER.   65
      FIRST WOMAN: Does that mean we'll be on top?
      LYSISTRATA: BUT IF THE SWALLOWS SHALL FALL
            OUT
            AND TAKE THE HOOPOE'S BAIT,
         A CURSE MUST MARK THEIR HOUR OF
            DOUBT,
            INFAMY SEAL THEIR FATE.   70
      THIRD WOMAN: I swear, *that* Oracle's all too clear.
      FIRST WOMAN: Oh the dear gods!
      LYSISTRATA: Let's not be downhearted, girls. Back to
         our places!
         The god has spoken. How can we possibly fail him?

         (*Exit Lysistrata with the dissident women.*)

CHORAL EPISODE • *Strophe*

CHORUS(m): I know a little story that I learned way
         back in school
      Goes like this:
      Once upon a time there was a young man — and no
         fool —
      Named Melanion; and his
      One aversion was marriage. He loathed the very
         thought.   5
      So he ran off to the hills, and in a special grot
      Raised a dog, and spent his days
      Hunting rabbits. And it says

---

35. **Eileithyia:** Goddess of childbirth.   37–38. **pollute a sacred spot:** Giving birth on the Akropolis was forbidden because it was sacred ground.

51. **purification:** A ritual cleansing of a woman after childbirth.

10   That he never never never did come home.
It might be called a refuge *from* the womb.
All right,
          all right,
                    all right!
We're as bright as young Melanion, and we hate the
     very sight
Of you women!
A MAN: How about a kiss, old lady?
15   A WOMAN: Here's an onion for your eye!
A MAN: A kick in the guts, then?
A WOMAN: Try, old bristle-tail, just try!
A MAN: Yet they say Myronides
     On hands and knees
20   Looked just as shaggy fore and aft as I!

Antistrophe

CHORUS(w): Well, *I* know a little story, and it's just as
     good as yours.
     Goes like this:
     Once there was a man named Timon — a rough
          diamond, of course,
     And that whiskery face of his
     Looked like murder in the shrubbery. By God, he
25   was a son
     Of the Furies, let me tell you! And what did he do
          but run
     From the world and all its ways,
     Cursing mankind! And it says
     That his choicest execrations as of then
30   Were leveled almost wholly at *old* men.
     All right,
          all right,
                    all right!
     But there's one thing about Timon: he could always
          stand the sight
     of us women.
A WOMAN: How about a crack in the jaw, Pop?
35   A MAN: I can take it, Ma — no fear!
A WOMAN: How about a kick in the face?
A MAN: You'd reveal your old caboose?
A WOMAN: What I'd show,
     I'll have you know,
40   Is an instrument you're too far gone to use.

SCENE 3

(*Reenter Lysistrata.*)

LYSISTRATA: Oh, quick, girls, quick! Come here!
A WOMAN: What is it?
LYSISTRATA: A man.
     A man simply bulging with love.
                         O Kyprian Queen,°
     O Paphian, O Kytherean! Hear us and aid us!

2. Kyprian Queen: Aphrodite.

A WOMAN: Where is this enemy?
LYSISTRATA: Over there, by Demeter's shrine.
A WOMAN: Damned if he isn't. But who *is* he?
MYRRHINE: My husband.   5
     Kinesias.
LYSISTRATA: Oh then, get busy! Tease him! Undermine
     him!
     Wreck him! Give him everything — kissing, tickling,
          nudging,
     whatever you generally torture him with — : give
          him everything
     except what we swore on the wine we would not
          give.
MYRRHINE: Trust me.
LYSISTRATA: I do. But I'll help you get him started.   10
     The rest of you women, stay back.

(*Enter Kinesias.*)

KINESIAS: Oh God! Oh my God!
     I'm stiff from lack of exercise. All I can do to stand
          up.
LYSISTRATA: Halt! Who are you, approaching our lines?
KINESIAS: Me? I.
LYSISTRATA: A man?
KINESIAS: You have eyes, haven't you?
LYSISTRATA: Go away.   15
KINESIAS: Who says so?
LYSISTRATA: Officer of the Day.
KINESIAS: Officer, I beg you,
     by all the gods at once, bring Myrrhine out.
LYSISTRATA: Myrrhine? And who, my good sir, are
     you?
KINESIAS: Kinesias. Last name's Pennison. Her husband.
LYSISTRATA: Oh, of course. I beg your pardon. We're
     glad to see you.   20
     We've heard so much about you. Dearest Myrrhine
     is always talking about Kinesias — never nibbles an
          egg
     or an apple without saying
     "Here's to Kinesias!"
KINESIAS: Do you really mean it?
LYSISTRATA: I do.
     When we're discussing men, she always says   25
     "Well, after all, there's nobody like Kinesias!"
KINESIAS: Good God. — Well, then, please send her
     down here.
LYSISTRATA: And what do *I* get out of it?
KINESIAS: A standing promise.
LYSISTRATA: I'll take it up with her.
                              (*Exit Lysistrata.*)
KINESIAS: But be quick about it!
     Lord, what's life without a wife? Can't eat. Can't
     sleep.   30
     Every time I go home, the place is so empty, so
     insufferably sad. Love's killing me, Oh,
     hurry!

(*Enter Manes, a slave, with Kinesias's baby; the voice of
Myrrhine is heard offstage.*)

MYRRHINE: But of course I love him! Adore him —
                                                    But no,
  he hates love. No. I won't go down.

(*Enter Myrrhine, above.*)

KINESIAS: Myrrhine!
35 Darlingest Myrrhinette! Come down quick!
MYRRHINE: Certainly not.
KINESIAS: Not? But why, Myrrhine?
MYRRHINE: Why? You don't need me.
KINESIAS: Need you? My God, *look* at me!
MYRRHINE: So long!

(*Turns to go.*)

KINESIAS: Myrrhine, Myrrhine, Myrrhine!
  If not for my sake, for our child!

(*Pinches Baby.*)

                              — All right, you: pipe up!
BABY: Mummie! Mummie! Mummie!
40 KINESIAS: You hear that?
  Pitiful, I call it. Six days now
  with never a bath; no food; enough to break your
      heart!
MYRRHINE: My darlingest child! What a father *you*
      acquired!
KINESIAS: At least come down for his sake.
MYRRHINE: I suppose I must.
45 Oh, this mother business!   (*Exit.*)
KINESIAS: How pretty she is! And younger!
  The harder she treats me, the more bothered I get.

(*Myrrhine enters, below.*)

MYRRHINE: Dearest child,
  you're as sweet as your father's horrid. Give me a kiss.
KINESIAS: Now don't you see how wrong it was to get
      involved
50 in this scheming League of women? It's bad
  for us both.
MYRRHINE: Keep your hands to yourself!
KINESIAS: But our house
  going to rack and ruin?
MYRRHINE: I don't care.
KINESIAS: And your knitting
  all torn to pieces by the chickens? Don't you care?
MYRRHINE: Not at all.
55 KINESIAS: And our debt to Aphrodite?
  Oh, *won't* you come back?
MYRRHINE: No. — At least, not until you men
  make a treaty and stop this war.
KINESIAS: Why, I suppose
  that might be arranged.
MYRRHINE: Oh? Well, I suppose
  I might come down then. But meanwhile,
  I've sworn not to.
60 KINESIAS: Don't worry. — Now let's have fun.
MYRRHINE: No! Stop it! I said no!
                              — Although, of course,
  I *do* love you.

KINESIAS: I know you do. Darling Myrrhine:
  come, shall we?
MYRRHINE: Are you out of your mind? In front of the
      child?
KINESIAS: Take him home, Manes.
                              (*Exit Manes with Baby.*)
                              There. He's gone.
                                          Come on!
  There's nothing to stop us now.
MYRRHINE: You devil! But where?   65
KINESIAS: In Pan's cave. What could be snugger than
      that?
MYRRHINE: But my purification before I go back to the
      Citadel?
KINESIAS: Wash in the Klepsydra.°
MYRRHINE: And my oath?
KINESIAS: Leave the oath to me.
  After all, I'm the man.
MYRRHINE: Well . . . if you say so.
                              I'll go find a bed.
KINESIAS: Oh, bother a bed! The ground's good
      enough for me.   70
MYRRHINE: No. You're a bad man, but you deserve
      something better than dirt.   (*Exit Myrrhine.*)
KINESIAS: What a love she is! And how thoughtful!

(*Reenter Myrrhine.*)

MYRRHINE: Here's your bed.
  Now let me get my clothes off.
                              But, good horrors!
  We haven't a mattress.
KINESIAS: Oh, forget the mattress!
MYRRHINE: No.
  Just lying on blankets? Too sordid.
KINESIAS: Give me a kiss.   75
MYRRHINE: Just a second.   (*Exit Myrrhine.*)
KINESIAS: I swear, I'll explode!

(*Reenter Myrrhine.*)

MYRRHINE: Here's your mattress.
  I'll just take my dress off.
                              But look —
  where's our pillow?
KINESIAS: I don't *need* a pillow!
MYRRHINE: Well, *I* do.
                              (*Exit Myrrhine.*)
KINESIAS: I don't suppose even Herakles°
  would stand for this!

(*Reenter Myrrhine.*)

MYRRHINE: There we are. Ups-a-daisy!   80
KINESIAS: So we are. Well, come to bed.
MYRRHINE: But I wonder:
  is everything ready now?
KINESIAS: I can swear to that. Come, darling!

68. Klepsydra: A water clock beneath the walls of the Akropolis. Kinesias's suggestion borders on blasphemy.   **79. Herakles:** Greek hero (Hercules) known for his Twelve Labors.

MYRRHINE: Just getting out of my girdle.
                                      But remember, now,
   what you promised about the treaty.
KINESIAS: Yes, yes, yes!
MYRRHINE: But no coverlet!
85 KINESIAS: Damn it, I'll be your coverlet!
MYRRHINE: Be right back.   (*Exit Myrrhine.*)
KINESIAS: This girl and her coverlets
   will be the death of me.

(*Reenter Myrrhine.*)

MYRRHINE: Here we are. Up you go!
KINESIAS: Up? I've been up for ages.
MYRRHINE: Some perfume?
KINESIAS: No, by Apollo!
MYRRHINE: Yes, by Aphrodite!
90   I don't care whether you want it or not.
                  (*Exit Myrrhine.*)
KINESIAS: For love's sake, hurry!

(*Reenter Myrrhine.*)

MYRRHINE: Here, in your hand. Rub it right in.
KINESIAS: Never cared for perfume.
   And this is particularly strong. Still, here goes.
MYRRHINE: What a nitwit I am! I brought you the
   Rhodian bottle.
95 KINESIAS: Forget it.
MYRRHINE: No trouble at all. You just wait here.
              (*Exit Myrrhine.*)
KINESIAS: God damn the man who invented perfume!

(*Reenter Myrrhine.*)

MYRRHINE: At last! The right bottle!
KINESIAS: I've got the rightest bottle of all,
   and it's right here waiting for you.
   Darling, forget everything else. Do come to bed.
MYRRHINE: Just let me get my shoes off.
100   — And, by the way,
   you'll vote for the treaty?
KINESIAS: I'll think about it.
         (*Myrrhine runs away.*)
   There! That's done it! The damned woman,
   she gets me all bothered, she half kills me,
   and off she runs! What'll I do? Where
   can I get laid?
105   — And you, little prodding pal,
   who's going to take care of *you*? No, you and I
   had better get down to old Foxdog's Nursing Clinic.
CHORUS(m): Alas for the woes of man, alas
      Specifically for you.
110   She's brought you to a pretty pass:
      What are you going to do?
  Split, heart! Sag, flesh! Proud spirit, crack!
  Myrrhine's got you on your back.
KINESIAS: The agony, the protraction!
KORYPHAIOS(m):   Friend,
115   What woman's worth a damn?
   They bitch us all, world without end.
KINESIAS: Yet they're so damned sweet, man!

KORYPHAIOS(m): Calamitous, that's what I say.
   You should have learned that much today.
CHORUS(m): O blessed Zeus, roll womankind   120
    Up into one great ball;
  Blast them aloft on a high wind,
    And once there, let them fall.
  Down, down they'll come, the pretty dears,
  And split themselves on our thick spears.   125
                (*Exit Kinesias.*)

SCENE 4

(*Enter a Spartan Herald.*)

HERALD: Gentlemen, Ah beg you will be so kind
   as to direct me to the Central Committee.
   Ah have a communication.

(*Reenter Commissioner.*)

COMMISSIONER: Are you a man,
   or a fertility symbol?
HERALD: Ah refuse to answer that question!
   Ah'm a certified herald from Spahta, and Ah've come   5
   to talk about an ahmistice.
COMMISSIONER: Then why
   that spear under your cloak?
HERALD: Ah have no speah!
COMMISSIONER: You don't walk naturally, with your
    tunic
   poked out so. You have a tumor, maybe,
   or a hernia?
HERALD: You lost yo' mahnd, man?
COMMISSIONER: Well,   10
   something's up, I can see that. And I don't like it.
HERALD: Colonel, Ah resent this.
COMMISSIONER: So I see. But what *is* it?
HERALD: A staff
   with a message from Spahta.
COMMISSIONER: Oh, I know about those staffs.
   Well, then, man, speak out: How are things in Sparta?
HERALD: Hahd, Colonel, hahd! We're at a standstill.   15
   Cain't seem to think of anything but women.
COMMISSIONER: How curious! Tell me, do you
    Spartans think
   that maybe Pan's to blame?
HERALD: Pan? No, Lampito and her little naked friends.
   They won't let a man come nigh them.   20
COMMISSIONER: How are you handling it?
HERALD: Losing our mahnds,
   if y' want to know, and walking around hunched over
   lahk men carrying candles in a gale.
   The women have swohn they'll have nothing to do
    with us
   until we get a treaty.
COMMISSIONER: Yes. I know.   25
   It's a general uprising, sir, in all parts of Greece.
   But as for the answer —
         Sir: go back to Sparta
   and have them send us your Armistice Commission.

Geraldine James (far left) is Lysistrata in the Old Vic Theatre production in London, 1993.

I'll arrange things in Athens.
                    And I may say
30   that my standing is good enough to make them listen.
HERALD: A man after mah own haht! Seh, Ah thank
    you.   (*Exit Herald.*)

CHORAL EPISODE • *Strophe*

CHORUS(m): Oh these women! Where will you find
    A slavering beast that's more unkind?
        Where's a hotter fire?
    Give me a panther, any day.
5   He's not so merciless as they,
        And panthers don't conspire.

Antistrophe

CHORUS(w): We may be hard, you silly old ass,
    But who brought you to this stupid pass?
        You're the ones to blame.
10   Fighting with us, your oldest friends,
    Simply to serve your selfish ends —
        Really, you have no shame!
KORYPHAIOS(m): No, I'm through with women for ever.

KORYPHAIOS(w):   If you say so.
    Still, you might put some clothes on. You look too
      absurd
    standing around naked. Come, get into this cloak.   15
KORYPHAIOS(m): Thank you; you're right. I merely took
    it off
    because I was in such a temper.
KORYPHAIOS(w):   That's much better.
    Now you resemble a man again.
                Why have you been so horrid?
    And look: there's some sort of insect in your eye.
    Shall I take it out?
KORYPHAIOS(m):   An insect, is it? So that's   20
    what's been bothering me. Lord, yes: take it out!
KORYPHAIOS(w): You might be more polite.
                     — But, heavens!
    What an enormous mosquito!
KORYPHAIOS(m):   You've saved my life.
    That mosquito was drilling an artesian well
    in my left eye.
KORYPHAIOS(w):   Let me wipe   25
    those tears away. — And now: one little kiss?
KORYPHAIOS(m): No, no kisses.
KORYPHAIOS(w): You're so difficult.
KORYPHAIOS(m): You impossible women! How you do
    get around us!

30 The poet was right: Can't live with you, or without
        you.
    But let's be friends.
    And to celebrate, you might join us in an Ode.

Strophe 1

CHORUS[(m and w)]: Let it never be said
        That my tongue is malicious:
35   Both by word and by deed
    I would set an example that's noble and gracious.
        We've had sorrow and care
        Till we're sick of the tune.
        Is there anyone here
40   Who would like a small loan?
            My purse is crammed,
            As you'll soon find;
    And you needn't pay me back if the Peace gets signed.

Strophe 2

        I've invited to lunch
45   Some Karystian rips° —
        An esurient bunch,
    But I've ordered a menu to water their lips.
        I can still make soup
        And slaughter a pig.
50   You're all coming, I hope?
        But a bath first, I beg!
            Walk right up
            As though you owned the place,
    And you'll get the front door slammed to in your face.

SCENE 5

(*Enter Spartan Ambassador, with entourage.*)

KORYPHAIOS[(m)]: The Commission has arrived from
        Sparta.
            How oddly they're walking!
                    Gentlemen, welcome to Athens!
    How is life in Lakonia?
AMBASSADOR: Need we discuss that?
    Simply use your eyes.
CHORUS[(m)]:   The poor man's right:
                    What a sight!
5 AMBASSADOR: Words fail me.
    But come, gentlemen, call in your Commissioners,
    and let's get down to a Peace.
CHORAGOS[(m)]:   The state we're in! Can't bear
    a stitch below the waist. It's a kind of pelvic
    paralysis.

45. **Karystian rips:** The Karystians were allies of Athens but
were scorned for their primitive ways and loose morals.

COMMISSIONER: Won't somebody call Lysistrata? —
                                Gentlemen,
    we're no better off than you.
AMBASSADOR: So I see.   10
A SPARTAN: Seh, do y'all feel a certain strain early in the
    morning?
AN ATHENIAN: I do, sir. It's worse than a strain.
    A few more days, and there's nothing for us but
        Kleisthenes,
    that broken blossom.
CHORAGOS[(m)]:   But you'd better get dressed again.
    You know these people going around Athens with
        chisels   15
    looking for statues of Hermes.°
ATHENIAN: Sir, you are right.
SPARTAN: He certainly is! Ah'll put mah own clothes
    back on.

(*Enter Athenian Commissioners.*)

COMMISSIONER: Gentlemen from Sparta, welcome.
    This is a sorry business.
SPARTAN (*to one of his own group*): Colonel, we got
                dressed just in time. Ah sweah,
    if they'd seen us the way we were, there'd have been
        a new wah   20
    between the states.
COMMISSIONER: Shall we call the meeting to order?
                        Now, Lakonians,
    what's your proposal?
AMBASSADOR: We propose to consider peace.
COMMISSIONER: Good. That's on our minds, too.
                — Summon Lysistrata.
    We'll never get anywhere without her.
AMBASSADOR: Lysistrata?   25
    Summon Lysis-*any*body! Only, summon!
KORYPHAIOS[(m)]:   No need to summon:
    here she is, herself.

(*Enter Lysistrata.*)

COMMISSIONER: Lysistrata! Lion of women!
    This is your hour to be
    hard and yielding, outspoken and shy, austere and
    gentle. You see here   30
    the best brains of Hellas (confused, I admit,
    by your devious charming) met as one man
    to turn the future over to you.
LYSISTRATA: That's fair enough,
    unless you men take it into your heads
    to turn to each other instead of to us. But I'd know   35
    soon enough if you did.
                — Where is Reconciliation?
    Go, some of you: bring her here.
                        (*Exeunt two women.*)

16. **statues of Hermes:** The usual representation of Hermes was
with an erect phallus. Statues of Hermes were scattered
throughout Athens and were attacked by vandals just before
the Sicilian Expedition.

                                                    And now, women,
   lead the Spartan delegates to me: not roughly
   or insultingly, as our men handle them, but gently,
40   politely, as ladies should. Take them by the hand,
   or by anything else if they won't give you their hands.

(The Spartans are escorted over.)

   There. — The Athenians next, by any convenient
   handle.

(The Athenians are escorted.)

   Stand there, please. — Now, all of you, listen to me.

(During the following speech the two women reenter, carrying an enormous statue of a naked girl; this is Reconciliation.)

   I'm only a woman, I know; but I've a mind,
45   and, I think, not a bad one: I owe it to my father
   and to listening to the local politicians.
   So much for that.
                              Now, gentlemen,
   since I have you here, I intend to give you a scolding.
   We are all Greeks.
50   Must I remind you of Thermopylai,° of Olympia,
   of Delphoi? names deep in all our hearts?
   Are they not a common heritage?
                                        Yet you men
   go raiding through the country from both sides,
   Greek killing Greek, storming down Greek cities —
55   and all the time the Barbarian across the sea
   is waiting for his chance!
                                — That's my first point.
AN ATHENIAN: Lord! I can hardly contain myself.
LYSISTRATA: As for you Spartans:
   Was it so long ago that Perikleides°
   came here to beg our help? I can see him still,
   his gray face, his sombre gown. And what did he
60   want?
   An army from Athens. All Messene
   was hot at your heels, and the sea-god splitting your
   land.
   Well, Kimon and his men,
   four thousand strong, marched out and saved all
   Sparta.
   And what thanks do we get? You come back to
65   murder us.
AN ATHENIAN: They're aggressors, Lysistrata!
A SPARTAN: Ah admit it.
   When Ah look at those laigs, Ah sweah Ah'll
   aggress mahself!

LYSISTRATA: And you, Athenians: do you think you're
   blameless?
   Remember that bad time when we were helpless,
   and an army came from Sparta,   70
   and that was the end of the Thessalian menace,
   the end of Hippias and his allies.
                              And that was Sparta,
   and only Sparta; but for Sparta, we'd be
   cringing slaves today, not free Athenians.

(From this point, the male responses are less to Lysistrata than to the statue.)

A SPARTAN: A well shaped speech.
AN ATHENIAN: Certainly it has its points.   75
LYSISTRATA: Why are we fighting each other? With all
   this history
   of favors given and taken, what stands in the way
   of making peace?
AMBASSADOR: Spahta is ready, ma'am,
   so long as we get that place back.
LYSISTRATA: What place, man?
AMBASSADOR: Ah refer to Pylos.
COMMISSIONER: Not a chance, by God!   80
LYSISTRATA: Give it to them, friend.
COMMISSIONER: But — what shall we have to bargain
   with?
LYSISTRATA: Demand something in exchange.
COMMISSIONER: Good idea. — Well, then:
   Cockeville first, and the Happy Hills, and the country
   between the Legs of Megara.
AMBASSADOR: Mah government objects.   85
LYSISTRATA: Overruled. Why fuss about a pair of legs?

(General assent. The statue is removed.)

AN ATHENIAN: I want to get out of these clothes and
   start my plowing.
A SPARTAN: Ah'll fertilize mahn first, by the Heavenly
   Twins!
LYSISTRATA: And so you shall,
   once you've made peace. If you are serious,   90
   go, both of you, and talk with your allies.
COMMISSIONER: Too much talk already. No, we'll
   stand together.
   We've only one end in view. All that we want
   is our women; and I speak for our allies.
AMBASSADOR: Mah government concurs.
AN ATHENIAN: So does Karystos.   95
LYSISTRATA: Good. — But before you come inside
   to join your wives at supper, you must perform
   the usual lustration. Then we'll open
   our baskets for you, and all that we have is yours.
   But you must promise upright good behavior   100
   from this day on. Then each man home with his
   woman!
AN ATHENIAN: Let's get it over with.
A SPARTAN: Lead on. Ah follow.
AN ATHENIAN: Quick as a cat can wink!
                              (Exeunt all but the Choruses.)

50. **Thermopylai:** A narrow pass where, in 480 B.C., an army of three hundred Spartans held out for three days against a superior Persian force.   58. **Perikleides:** Spartan ambassador to Athens who successfully urged Athenians to aid Sparta in quelling a rebellion.

Antistrophe 1

CHORUS(w): Embroideries and
105   Twinkling ornaments and
           Pretty dresses — I hand
       Them all over to you, and with never a qualm.
           They'll be nice for your daughters
           On festival days
110   When the girls bring the Goddess
           The ritual prize.
           Come in, one and all:
           Take what you will.
       I've nothing here so tightly corked that you can't
           make it spill.

Antistrophe 2

115   You may search my house
           But you'll not find
           The least thing of use,
       Unless your two eyes are keener than mine.
           Your numberless brats
120   Are half starved? and your slaves?
           Courage, grandpa! I've lots
           Of grain left, and big loaves.
           I'll fill your guts,
           I'll go the whole hog;
       But if you come too close to me, remember: 'ware
125   the dog!   (*Exeunt Choruses.*)

EXODOS°

(*A Drunken Citizen enters, approaches the gate, and is
halted by a sentry.*)

CITIZEN: Open. The. Door.
SENTRY: Now, friend, just shove along!
       — So you want to sit down. If it weren't such an old
           joke,
       I'd tickle your tail with this torch. Just the sort of
           gag
       this audience appreciates.
   CITIZEN: I. Stay. Right. Here.
5 SENTRY: Get away from there, or I'll scalp you!
           The gentlemen from Sparta
       are just coming back from dinner.

(*Exit Citizen; the general company reenters; the two
Choruses now represent Spartans and Athenians.*)

A SPARTAN: Ah must say,
       Ah never tasted better grub.
AN ATHENIAN: And those Lakonians!
       They're gentlemen, by the Lord! Just goes to show,
       a drink to the wise is sufficient.

COMMISSIONER: And why not?   10
       A sober man's an ass.
   Men of Athens, mark my words: the only efficient
   Ambassador's a drunk Ambassador. Is that clear?
   Look: we go to Sparta,
   and when we get there we're dead sober. The result? 15
   Everyone cackling at everyone else. They make
       speeches;
   and even if we understand, we get it all wrong
   when we file our reports in Athens. But today — !
   Everybody's happy. Couldn't tell the difference
   between *Drink to Me Only* and   20
   The Star-Spangled Athens.
                          What's a few lies,
   washed down in good strong drink?

(*Reenter the Drunken Citizen.*)

SENTRY: God almighty,
       he's back again!
CITIZEN: I. Resume. My. Place.
A SPARTAN (*to an Athenian*): Ah beg yo', seh,
       take yo' instrument in yo' hand and play for us.   25
       Ah'm told
       yo' understand the in*tric*acies of the floot?
       Ah'd lahk to execute a song and dance
       in honor of Athens,
                          and, of cohse, of Spahta.
CITIZEN: Toot. On. Your. Flute.   30

(*The following song is a solo — an aria — accompanied by the flute. The Chorus of Spartans begins a slow
dance.*)

A SPARTAN: O Memory,
       Let the Muse speak once more
       In my young voice. Sing glory.
       Sing Artemision's shore,
       Where Athens fluttered the Persians. *Alalai,*°   35
       Sing glory, that great
       Victory! Sing also
       Our Leonidas and his men,
       Those wild boars, sweat and blood
       Down in a red drench. Then, then   40
       The barbarians broke, though they had stood
       Numberless as the sands before!

       O Artemis,
       Virgin Goddess, whose darts
       Flash in our forests: approve   45
       This pact of peace and join our hearts,
       From this day on, in love.
       Huntress, descend!
LYSISTRATA: All that will come in time.
                          But now, Lakonians,
       take home your wives. Athenians, take yours.   50
       Each man be kind to his woman; and you, women

Exodos: Final scene.

35. *Alalai:* War cry.

be equally kind. Never again, pray God,
shall we lose our way in such madness.
KORYPHAIOS(Athenian):   And now let's dance our joy.

(*From this point the dance becomes general.*)

CHORUS(Athenian): Dance, you Graces
                         Artemis, dance
Dance, Phoibos,° Lord of dancing
55   Dance,
In a scurry of Maenads,° Lord Dionysos
                    Dance, Zeus Thunderer
            Dance, Lady Hera°
Queen of the sky
                Dance, dance, all you gods
Dance witness everlasting of our pact
60 *Evohi Evohe°*
Dance for the dearest
                    the Bringer of Peace
Deathless Aphrodite!
COMMISSIONER: Now let us have another song from
    Sparta.
CHORUS(Spartan): From Taygetos, from Taygetos,
65   Lakonian Muse, come down.

Sing to the Lord Apollo
    Who rules Amyklai Town.

Sing Athena of the House of Brass!°
Sing Leda's Twins,° that chivalry
    Resplendent on the shore   70
Of our Eurotas; sing the girls
    That dance along before:
Sparkling in dust their gleaming feet,
    Their hair a Bacchant fire,
And Leda's daughter, thyrsos° raised,   75
    Leads their triumphant choir.

CHORUS(S and A): *Evohe!*
            Evohai!
                Evohe!
                    We pass
        Dancing
                dancing
                    to greet
Athena of the House of Brass.

---

55. **Phoibos:** Apollo, god of the sun.   56. **Maenads:** Female
worshipers of Bacchus (Dionysus).   57. **Hera:** Wife of Zeus.
60. *Evohi Evohe:* "Come forth! Come forth!" An orgiastic cry
associated with rituals of Bacchus.

68. *House of Brass:* Temple to Athena on the Akropolis of
Sparta.   69. **Leda's Twins:** Leda, raped by Zeus, bore quadru-
plets, two daughters (one of whom was Helen) and two sons.
75. **thyrsos:** A staff twined with ivy and carried by Bacchus and
his followers.

Roman Drama

Indigenous Sources

Roman drama has several sources, not all of them well understood. The first and most literary is Greek drama, but among the more curious are the indigenous sources, which are especially difficult to trace. One such source might be the Etruscans, members of an old and obscure civilization in northern Italy that reached its height in the sixth century B.C. and that the Romans eventually absorbed. The Etruscans had developed an improvised song and dance that was very entertaining. The town of Atella provided another indigenous comic tradition known as the ATELLAN FARCE, a very broad and sometimes coarse popular comedy. Such entertainments may have been acted in open spaces or at fairs, probably not on a stage at first.

The Atellan farce is especially interesting for developments in later Roman drama and world drama. The characters in this farce seem to have been STOCK CHARACTERS, characters who are always recognizable and whose antics are predictable. The most common in the Atellan farce are Maccus the clown; Bucco the stupid, and probably fat, clown; Pappus, the foolish or stubborn old man; and the hunchbacked, wily slave Dossennus. At first these pieces of drama were improvised to a repeatable pattern, often involving a master who tries to get his slave to do his bidding but who somehow ends up being made to look the fool by the cunning slave. When the farces began to develop in Rome, they were written down and played onstage.

The concept of the stock character is associated with the masters of Roman comedy, Plautus and Terence, who often adapted Greek plays and made them their own. The braggart warrior (*miles gloriosus*), a stock character on the Roman stage, reappears in modern plays. The miser has been a mainstay in literature since Roman times and probably is best known today as Scrooge in Dickens's *A Christmas Carol* and as *The Miser* of Molière. The parasite was Roman in origin and can be seen today in numerous television situation comedies. Another Roman invention is the use of identical twins for comic effect. Because it permitted a wide range of comic misunderstandings, this device has been used by many playwrights, including Shakespeare in *The Comedy of Errors*. The Roman use of masks made the twins device much easier to employ than it would be in today's productions.

The Greek Influence

According to legend, in 240 B.C., a slave, Livius Andronicus, presented performances of his Latin translations of a Greek tragedy and a Greek comedy, giving the Romans their first real taste of Greek drama and literature. Livius soon earned his freedom, and his literary career became so firmly established that his translations from the Greek were those read in Rome for more than two hundred years. His translation of the *Odyssey* was the standard text through the time of Cicero (first century B.C.).

Roman comedy derived primarily from the New Comedy of Menander, although it could, like Aristophanes' Old Comedy, sometimes be risqué. Comedy was the most well attended and the most performed of Rome's drama. That is not to say that the Romans produced no tragedies. They did, and the influence of Roman tragedy has been as long-lasting as that of comedy. Still, the Roman people preferred to laugh rather than to feel the pity and terror of tragic emotion.

Just as the Greek plays developed in connection with festivals, the Roman plays became associated with games held several times a year. During the games, performances were offered on an average of five to eleven days. The Megalesian Games took place in early April, in honor of the Great Mother, the goddess Cybele, whose temple stood on the Palatine Hill. In late April the Floral Games were held in front of the temple of Flora on the Aventine Hill. The most important were the Roman Games in September and the Plebeian Games in November.

The Greek drama competitions had no counterpart among the Romans, for whom drama was not the primary entertainment during the festivals. Roman playwrights and actors were hired to put on performances to entertain and divert the impatient audiences who could choose among a variety of spectacles, including gladiator fights, chariot races, and animal baiting. The producer had to please the audience or lose his chance to supply more entertainment.

Roman comedies were sometimes revisions or amalgamations of Greek plays. The themes and characters of Roman tragedies also derived from Greek originals. Figuring often in Roman tragedies was the Trojan War; its characters were reworked into new situations and their agonies reinterpreted.

For costumes the actors wore the Greek tunic (called a CHITON) and a long white cloak or mantle called the PALLIUM. Like the Greeks, the Romans wore low shoes, called the SOCK, for comedy, and shoes with an elevated sole, the BUSKIN, for tragedy. For plays that had a totally Roman setting and narrative, the actors wore the Roman toga. Eventually, Roman actors used traditional Greek masks that immediately identified the characters for the audience. (The question of whether the earliest Roman actors wore masks as well has not been resolved.) The younger Roman characters wore black wigs, older characters wore white wigs, and characters representing slaves wore red wigs.

One of the most intriguing questions concerning Roman plays is the importance of music in the drama. In Greek plays the chorus took most of the responsibility for the music, but in Roman drama actors may have sung their lines, so the Roman plays may have resembled musical comedies. The dialogue in some comedies introduces an interlude of flute playing, indicating that there were times with no actor onstage, no spoken words, and no mimed action, but only a musician to entertain the audience.

The Roman Stage

In the third century B.C. the Romans began building wooden stages that could be taken down quickly and moved as necessary. Eventually, they built stone theaters following Greek plans but varying from the Greek model in a number of important respects. They were built on flat ground, rather than on the hillsides as were the Greek theaters. The influence of the Romans' early wooden stage remained in the permanent buildings in several ways. The Roman stage was elevated, and since there was little or no chorus, the orchestra, in which the chorus moved from place to place, was no longer needed. The SCAENA, or background, against which the action took place, was often three stories tall and was proportionally longer than the Greek *skene* (as in Figure 3). This wide but shallow stage was exploited by the playwrights, who often set their plays on a street with various houses, temples, and other buildings along it.

The space in front of the *scaena* was known as the PROSCAENA, from which the PROSCENIUM ARCH, which frames the stage and separates the actors from the audience, developed much later in the Renaissance. The action took place on

Figure 3. Roman theater at Sabratha, Libya. With the *frons scaena* still in good shape, this photograph shows how the Romans modified the basic Greek design.

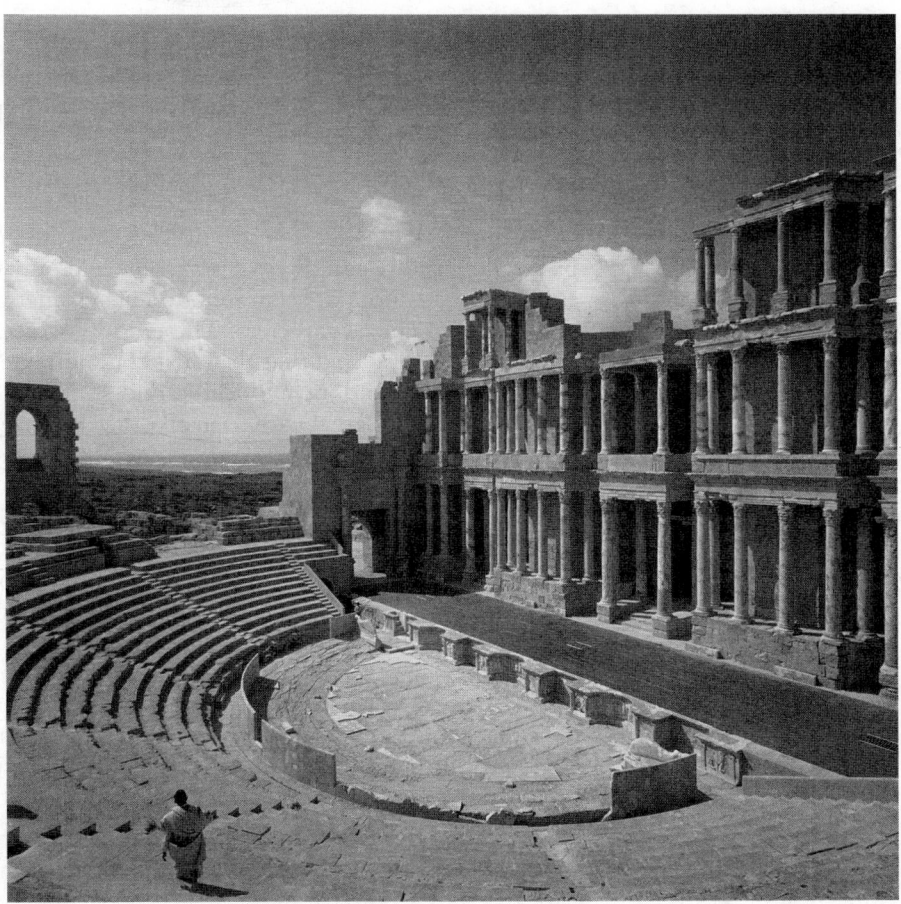

Figure 4. Theater of Marcellus.

the *pulpitum,* behind the *proscaena.* The potential for the proscenium arch is evident in the plan of the Theater of Marcellus (Figure 4), where the sections to the left and the right of the stage (*pulpitum*) already indicate a separation from the audience.

As in the plan of the Theater of Marcellus, the *frons scaena* (the front wall, or façade) usually had three doors (some had only two), which were ordinarily established as doors of separate buildings, sometimes a temple and the others the homes of chief characters. These doors were active "participants" in the drama; it has been said that the most common line heard in a Roman play is a statement that the door is opening and someone is coming in. The standard Roman play takes great care to justify the entrances and exits of its characters, which may indicate that Roman audiences expected more realism in their comedies than did their Greek counterparts.

The *frons scaena,* the front of the theater, not only was several stories high but also was much more architecturally developed than the *skene* of the Greek theater. The typical Roman architectural devices of multiple arches, columns, and pilasters decorated the *scaena,* giving it a stately appearance. Like the Greek theater, the Roman theater used machinery that permitted actors to be moved through the air and to make entrances from the heavens.

The greatest of the Roman dramatists, Plautus and Terence, would have had their plays produced originally on early wooden stages or on Greek stages. The characteristic Roman theater was not created until the period of the empire, more than a hundred years after their deaths. By that time Seneca could have seen his plays produced in the Roman theater, but they may not ever have been produced in Roman times. His plays may have been closet dramas, designed only to be read.

Roman Drama Timeline

DATE	THEATER	POLITICAL	SOCIAL/CULTURAL
800–600 B.C.			**753:** Rome is founded.
600–500			**6th c.:** The Circus Maximus is constructed for chariot races and athletic contests. **509–527:** Roman Republic
500–400			**450:** Roman law is codified in the Twelve Tables.
400–300		**390:** Rome is rebuilt after a Gallic invasion.	
300–200	**3rd c.:** Atellan farce, lively improvised scenarios based on domestic life, is imported from southern Italy to Rome. **240:** Ludi Romani, a festival in honor of Jupiter, incorporates comedy and tragedy for the first time. The festival, established by the elder Tarquin, Etruscan ruler of Rome, already included chariot races, boxing matches, and other popular entertainments. The plays performed at the festival in 240 are probably translations or imitations of Greek plays. **205–184:** Titus Maccius Plautus writes his plays, including *The Twin Menaechmi*.	**272:** Rome conquers central and southern Italy. **264–241:** First Punic War with Carthage **222:** Rome conquers northern Italy. **218–201:** Second Punic War	**c. 300:** Roman consul Appius Claudius Crassus builds the Appian Way, which stretches from Rome to Capua. **287:** Full equality between plebeians and patricians in Rome
200–100	**160:** Publius Terentius Afer (Terence) writes *The Brothers*. **c. 126–c. 62:** Roscius, a popular Roman actor	**195:** Cato the Elder becomes consul and initiates many reforms in urban development and government representation. **149–146:** The Third Punic War. Rome destroys Carthage and Corinth and conquers Greece. **133:** Tiberius Gracchus, Roman reformer, is murdered at the instigation of the Senate.	**186:** Wild animals are exhibited at the Circus Maximus. Contests between wild animals and humans begin shortly hereafter. **106–43:** Cicero, Roman orator **105:** Gladiatorial contests become part of state festivals.

Roman Drama Timeline *(continued)*

DATE	THEATER	POLITICAL	SOCIAL/CULTURAL
100 B.C.–1 A.D.	**1st c.:** Theaters are built throughout the Roman empire. **90:** Vitruvius writes *De Architectura*, a treatise on Roman architecture that discusses theater architecture in Greece and Rome. **55:** The first permanent stone theater is built in Rome.	**69 B.C.:** Cleopatra born. She reigns as queen of Egypt from 51 to 49 and from 48 to her death in 30. **60:** First Triumvirate (Pompey, Crassus, and Julius Caesar) rules Rome. **47:** Herod is appointed King of Judea. **45:** Julius Caesar is declared dictator by Roman Senate. **44:** On the Ides of March Caesar is assassinated. **43–28:** The Second Triumvirate (Antony, Lepidus, and Octavius) rules Rome. **27 B.C.–A.D. 476:** Roman empire **27:** Gaius Octavius, Julius Caesar's grand-nephew, becomes the first emperor of the Roman empire, assuming the name Augustus.	**87–54:** Catullus, Roman poet **70–19:** Virgil (P. Virgilius Maro), poet and author of the *Aeneid* **47:** The library of Ptolemy in Alexandria destroyed by fire; many valuable manuscripts and works of art are lost. **46:** Julius Caesar stages the first *naumachia* (mock sea battle). **43 B.C.–A.D. 17:** Ovid (Publius Ovidius Naso), poet and author of the *Metamorphoses* **22:** Roman pantomime, a predecessor of modern ballet, is introduced by Pylades and Bathyllus. **19:** Horace (65–8 B.C.) writes *Ars Poetica*. **4:** Birth of Jesus
1–100	**4 B.C.–A.D. 65:** Seneca. Dates for his plays, including *Medea,* are unknown. Seneca commits suicide after suffering a decline in power and influence.	**14:** Augustus dies, and his stepson Tiberius becomes emperor. **37:** Tiberius's grand-nephew Gaius Caesar (Caligula) is named emperor. **41:** Caligula is assassi-nated by his own guards; his wife and young daughter are also murdered. Caligula's uncle Claudius is named emperor. **54:** Claudius is allegedly poisoned by his wife, Julia Agrippina. Claudius's stepson Nero is named emperor. **68:** Nero commits suicide. **69:** Vespasian is named emperor. He is succeeded by his son Titus.	**c. 30:** Crucifixion of Jesus **64:** Much of Rome is destroyed by fire. Nero blames the fire on Rome's increasing Christian population and initiates the first large-scale persecution of Christians in Rome. **79:** Mount Vesuvius erupts, destroying Pompeii. **80:** The Colosseum is completed.

Roman Drama Timeline (continued)

DATE	THEATER	POLITICAL	SOCIAL/CULTURAL
100–200	**197–202:** Tertullian writes *De Spectaculis*, denouncing the theater as anti-Christian.	**117:** Hadrian becomes emperor. **120:** Hadrian commissions the building of the Pantheon ("the place of all gods"). **122–126:** Hadrian's Wall is extended across Great Britain. **138:** Hadrian dies and is succeeded by Antonius Pius and then by Marcus Aurelius.	**c. 130–200:** Galen, Roman physicist and pioneer in anatomy and physiology **164–180:** A devastating plague sweeps the Roman empire.
200–300	**c. 300:** Records of earliest religious plays.	Roman citizenship given to every freeborn subject in the empire. Under Roman rule, Carthage regains prominence as a center of culture and commerce. **220:** Goths invade the Balkan Peninsula and Asia Minor. **257:** Goths invade the Black Sea provinces.	
300–400		**313:** Edict of Milan. Emperor Constantine establishes toleration of Christianity. **331:** Emperor Constantine moves the Roman capital from Rome to Constantinople. **360:** Huns invade Europe.	**354–430:** St. Augustine, author of the influential *City of God* and *Confessions* **c. 360:** Scrolls begin to be replaced by books.
400–500		**401–403:** Visigoths invade Italy. **410:** Alaric, king of Visigoths, sacks Rome.	**c. 400:** In part because of the rise of Christianity, state festivals honoring pagan gods cease in Rome. **404:** Gladiatorial contests are abolished. **c. 410:** Experiments with alchemy begin. **523:** Wild animal contests are abolished.

Roman Dramatists
Plautus

All surviving Roman comedy shows the influence of Greek originals. Plautus (254–184 B.C.) is among Rome's most famous playwrights and may have been a member of a troupe that performed Atellan comedy. His middle name is Maccius (a form of Maccus, the clown of the farces), possibly alluding to the role he had habitually played. Tradition has it that he was in the theater for a good while before he began writing comedies. His first plays date from 205 B.C., about thirty-five years after Livius introduced Greek drama to the Romans. No one knows how many plays he wrote, and it has been common to assign many unauthenticated titles to him. About twenty-one plays exist that are thought to be his, the most famous of which are *Amphitryon, The Pot of Gold, The Captives, Curculio, The Braggart Warrior, The Rope,* and *The Twin Menaechmi.*

The last play is probably the best-known Roman comedy. It features Menaechmus from Syracuse, who goes to Epidamnus searching for his lost twin. There he meets people who mistake him for his brother: a cook; a prostitute; Sponge, a typical parasite; and even his brother's wife and father-in-law. The comedy uses all the confusions inherent in mistaken identity.

Plautus (254–184 B.C.)

FROM *THE TWIN MENAECHMI*   *c. 205–184 B.C.*

TRANSLATED BY LIONEL CASSON

The Twin Menaechmi was the first ancient play to be translated into a modern language and put on the stage (1486 in Italy). It has been adapted by numerous modern playwrights, including Shakespeare in *The Comedy of Errors* and, more recently, Rodgers and Hart in *The Boys from Syracuse* (1938), a musical that ran on Broadway for 235 performances. *Boys* has been revived numerous times and is still a popular summer theater play. The following scene from the beginning of act III of *The Twin Menaechmi* shows the parasite Sponge mistaking the identity of Menaechmus of Syracuse for that of his friend Menaechmus of Epidamnus. They have a great go-around over a dress in a typical mixup of the kind that originated with Roman comedies and has been popular in farces and comedies ever since.

ACT III

SPONGE: I'm over thirty now, and never have I ever in all those years pulled a more damned fool stunt than the one I pulled today: There was this town meeting, and *I* had to dive in and come up right in the middle of it. While I'm standing there with my mouth open, Menaechmus sneaks off on me. I'll bet he's gone to his girlfriend. Perfectly willing to leave me behind, too!

(*Paces up and down a few times, shaking his head bitterly. Then, in a rage.*) Damn, damn, damn the fellow who first figured out town meetings! All they do is keep a busy man away from his business. Why don't people pick a panel of men of leisure for this kind of thing? Hold a roll call at each meeting and whoever doesn't answer gets fined on the spot. There are plenty of persons around who need only one meal a day; they don't have business hours to keep because they don't go after dinner invitations or give them out. They're the ones to fuss with town meetings and town elections. If that's how things were run, I wouldn't have lost my lunch today. He sure wanted me along, didn't he? I'll go in, anyway. There's still hope of leftovers to soothe my soul. (*He is about to go up to the door when it suddenly swings open and Menaechmus of Syracuse appears, standing on the threshold with a garland, a little askew, on his head; he is holding the dress and listening to Lovey who is chattering at him from inside. Sponge quickly backs off into a corner.*) What's this I see? Menaechmus — and he's leaving, garland and all! The table's been cleared! I sure came in time — in time to walk him home. Well, I'll watch what his game is, and then I'll go and have a word with him.

MENAECHMUS OF SYRACUSE (*to Lovey inside*): Take it easy, will you! I'll have it back to you today in plenty of time, altered and trimmed to perfection. (*Slyly.*) Believe me, you'll say it's not your dress; you won't know it any more.

SPONGE (*to the audience*): He's bringing the dress to the dressmaker. The dining's done, the drinks are down — and Sponge spent the lunch hour outside. God damn it I'm not the man I think I am if I don't get even with him for this, but really even. You just watch. I'll give it to him, I will.

MENAECHMUS OF SYRACUSE (*closing the door and walking downstage; to the audience, jubilantly*): Good god, no one ever expected less — and got more blessings from heaven in one day than me. I dined, I wined, I wenched, and (*holding up the dress*) made off with this to which, from this moment on, she hereby forfeits all right, title, and interest.

SPONGE (*straining his ears, to the audience*): I can't make out what he's saying from back here. Is that full-belly talking about me and my right title and interest?

MENAECHMUS OF SYRACUSE (*to the audience*): She said I stole it from my wife and gave it to her. I saw she was mistaking me for someone else, so I promptly played it as if she and I were having a hot and heavy affair and began to yes her; I agreed right down the line to everything she said. Well, to make a long story short, I never had it so good for so little.

SPONGE (*clenching his fists, to the audience*): I'm going up to him. I'm itching to give him the works. (*Leaves his corner and strides belligerently toward Menaechmus.*)

MENAECHMUS OF SYRACUSE (*to the audience*): Someone coming up to me. Wonder who it is?

SPONGE (*roaring*): Well! You featherweight, you filth, you slime, you disgrace to the human race, you double-crossing good-for-nothing! What did I ever do to you that you had to ruin my life? You sure gave me the slip downtown a little while ago! You killed off the day all right — and held the funeral feast without me. Me who was coheir under the will! Where do you come off to do a thing like that!

MENAECHMUS OF SYRACUSE (*too pleased with life to lose his temper*): Mister, will you please tell me what business you and I have that gives you the right to use language like that to a stranger here, someone you never saw in your life? You hand me that talk and I'll hand you something you won't like.

SPONGE (*dancing with rage*): God damn it, you already have! I know god damned well you have!

MENAECHMUS OF SYRACUSE (*amused and curious*): What's your name, mister?

SPONGE (*as before*): Still making jokes, eh? As if you don't know my name!

MENAECHMUS OF SYRACUSE: So help me, so far as I know, I never heard of you or saw you till this minute. But I know one thing for sure: whoever you are, you'd better behave yourself and stop bothering me.

SPONGE (*taken aback for a minute*): Menaechmus! Wake up!

MENAECHMUS OF SYRACUSE (*genially*): Believe me, to the best of my knowledge, I am awake.

SPONGE: You don't know me?

MENAECHMUS OF SYRACUSE (*as before*): If I did, I wouldn't say I didn't.

SPONGE (*incredulously*): You don't know your own parasite?

MENAECHMUS OF SYRACUSE: Mister, it looks to me as if you've got bats in your belfry.

SPONGE (*shaken, but not convinced*): Tell me this: Didn't you steal that dress there from your wife today and give it to Lovey?

MENAECHMUS OF SYRACUSE: Good god, no! I don't have a wife, I never gave anything to any Lovey, and I never stole any dress. Are you in your right mind?

SPONGE (*aside, groaning*): A dead loss, the whole affair. (*To Menaechmus.*) But you came out of your house wearing the dress! I saw you myself!

MENAECHMUS OF SYRACUSE (*exploding*): Damn you! You think everybody's a pervert just because you are? I was wearing this dress? Is that what you're telling me?

SPONGE: I most certainly am.

MENAECHMUS OF SYRACUSE: Now you go straight to the one place fit for you! No — get yourself to the lunatic asylum; you're stark-raving mad.

SPONGE (*venomously*): God damn it, there's one thing nobody in the world is going to stop me from doing: I'm telling the whole story, exactly what happened, to your wife this minute. All these insults are going to boomerang back on your own head. Believe you me, you'll pay for eating that whole lunch yourself. (*Dashes into the house of Menaechmus of Epidamnus.*)

MENAECHMUS OF SYRACUSE (*throwing his arms wide, to the audience*): What's going on here? Must everyone I lay eyes on play games with me this way? Wait — I hear the door.

(*The door of Lovey's house opens, and one of her maids comes out holding a bracelet. She walks over to Menaechmus and, as he looks on blankly, hands it to him.*)

MAID: Menaechmus, Lovey says would you please do her a big favor and drop this at the jeweler's on your way? She wants you to give him an ounce of gold and have him make the whole bracelet over.

MENAECHMUS OF SYRACUSE (*with alacrity*): Tell her I'll not only take care of this but anything else she wants taken care of. Anything at all. (*He takes the piece and examines it absorbedly.*)

MAID (*watching him curiously, in surprise*): Don't you know what bracelet it is?

MENAECHMUS OF SYRACUSE: Frankly no — except that it's gold.

MAID: It's the one you told us you stole from your wife's jewel box when nobody was looking.

MENAECHMUS OF SYRACUSE (*forgetting himself, in high dudgeon*): I never did anything of the kind!

MAID: You mean you don't remember it? Well, if that's the case, you give it right back!

MENAECHMUS OF SYRACUSE (*after a few seconds of highly histrionic deep thought*): Wait a second. No, I *do* remember it. Of course — this is the one I gave her. Oh, and there's something else: Where are the armlets I gave her at the same time?

MAID (*puzzled*): You never gave her any armlets.

MENAECHMUS OF SYRACUSE (*quickly*): Right you are. This was all I gave her.

MAID: Shall I tell her you'll take care of it?

MENAECHMUS OF SYRACUSE: By all means, tell her. I'll take care of it, all right. I'll see she gets it back the same time she gets the dress back.

MAID (*going up to him and stroking his cheek*): Menaechmus dear, will you do me a favor too? Will you have some earrings made for me? Drop earrings, please; ten grams of gold in each. (*Meaningfully.*) It'll make me *so* glad to see you every time you come to the house.

MENAECHMUS OF SYRACUSE: Sure. (*With elaborate carelessness.*) Just give me the gold. I'll pay for the labor myself.

MAID: Please, you pay for the gold too. I'll make it up to you afterward.

MENAECHMUS OF SYRACUSE: No, you pay for the gold. I'll make it up to *you* afterward. Double.

MAID: I don't have the money.

MENAECHMUS OF SYRACUSE (*with a great air of magnanimity*): Well, any time you get it, you just let me have it.

MAID (*turning to go*): I'm going in now. Anything I can do for you?

MENAECHMUS OF SYRACUSE: Yes. Tell her I'll see to both things — (*sotto voce, to the audience*) that they get sold as quickly as possible for whatever they'll bring. (*As the maid starts walking toward the door.*) Has she gone in yet? (*Hearing a slam.*) Ah, she's in, the door's closed. (*Jubilantly.*) The lord loves me! I've had a helping hand from heaven! (*Suddenly looks about warily.*) But why hang around when I have the time and chance to get away from this (*jerking his thumb at Lovey's house*) pimping parlor here? Menaechmus! Get a move on, hit the road, forward march! I'll take off this garland and toss it to the left here (*doing so*). Then, if anyone tries to follow me, he'll think I went that way. Now I'll go and see if I can find my servant. I want to let him know all the blessings from heaven I've had.

(*He races off, stage right. The stage is now empty.*)

Terence

Terence (c. 190–159 B.C.) is said to have been a North African slave brought to Rome, where his master realized he was unusually intelligent and gifted. After he was freed, Terence took his place in Roman literary life and produced a body of six plays, all of which still exist: *The Woman of Andros, The Self-Tormentor, The Eunuch, Phormio, The Mother-in-Law,* and *The Brothers.* Terence's plays are notable for including a subplot or secondary action — carefully — and for avoiding the technique of addressing the audience directly.

The Romans preferred Plautus's broad farcical humor to Terence's more carefully plotted, elegantly styled plays. Terence borrowed liberally from Greek sources, often more than one for each of his plays, to develop unusually complicated plots. A manager or producer worked with him on all his plays, and the musician who worked with him was a slave, Flaccus. Terence's productive life was relatively short. He died on a trip to Greece, apparently worrying over a piece of missing luggage said to have contained new plays.

Terence's situation was unusual: he had two wealthy Roman patrons who were interested in seeing the best Greek comedy brought to the Romans. Consequently, they paid for his productions and gave him more support than the average comic playwright could have expected. Terence's dramatic skills developed considerably from the beginning to the end of his work, contrasting sharply with the repetitive nature of Plautus's work. Terence was more than a translator, but he wrote at a time when Romans were interested in emulating the Greeks, and his fidelity to Greek originals was one of his strongest recommendations.

Terence (*c. 190–159 B.C.*)

FROM *THE BROTHERS*   *160 B.C.*

TRANSLATED BY ROBERT GRAVES

The ending of *The Brothers*, generally recognized as Terence's masterpiece and certainly the most influential of his plays, has Demea planning a reversal on his brother, Micio. Micio is a good, easygoing bachelor who wishes well for others. Demea has been a stern father to one of his sons, Ctesipho, and has tried to steer him in a direction other than the one Ctesipho wants to follow. Demea has entrusted the upbringing of his second son, Aeschinus, to his lenient brother, Micio. Both sons deceive both brothers and end up with the women they want rather than the women the brothers want for them. Meanwhile, Demea gives up and turns the tables on Micio, engineering his brother's marriage to Aeschinus's mother-in-law. In the process of all this, Demea decides to adopt the gentle, easygoing ways of his brother and to forsake his former stern behavior.

This play was adapted often in the seventeenth century by Marston, Beaumont and Fletcher, and others. Molière relied on it for his *School for Wives*. At least five plays were adapted from it for the eighteenth-century English stage.

FROM ACT V

MICIO (*to Syrus, within*): My brother ordered it,° say ye! Where is he? . . . Hah, Brother, was it you who ordered this?

DEMEA: Yes, that I did! And in this and all things else I'm ready to do whatever may conduce to the uniting, serving, helping, and the joining together of both families.

AESCHINUS (*to Micio*): Pray, Sir, let it be so!

MICIO: Well, I've nothing to say against it.

DEMEA: Truth, 'tis no more than we are obliged to do. For first, she's your son's mother-in-law . . .

MICIO: What then?

DEMEA: A very virtuous and modest woman . . .

MICIO: So they say indeed.

DEMEA: Not weighed down by years . . .

MICIO: Not yet.

DEMEA: But past child-bearing: a lonesome woman whom nobody esteems . . .

MICIO (*aside*): What the Devil is he at?

DEMEA: . . . Therefore you ought to marry her; and you Aeschinus, should do what you can to bring this about.

MICIO: Who? I marry?

DEMEA: Yes, you.

MICIO: I, prithee?

DEMEA: Yes, you I say.

MICIO: Pho, you are fooling us, surely?

DEMEA (*to Aeschinus*): If thou hast any life in thee, persuade him to it.

AESCHINUS: Dear Father . . .

MICIO (*interrupting*): Blockhead! Dost thou take in earnest what he says?

DEMEA: 'Tis in vain to refuse; it can't be avoided.

MICIO: Pho, you are in your dotage!

AESCHINUS: Good Sir, let me win this one favor.

MICIO (*angrily*): Art out of thy wits, let me alone!

DEMEA: Come, come! Hearken for once to what your son says.

MICIO: Haven't ye played the fool enough yet? Shall I at threescore and five marry an old woman who's ready to drop into the grave? This is your wise counsel, is it?

AESCHINUS: Pray, Sir, do; I've promised you shall.

MICIO: You promised, with a mischief! Promise for thyself, thou chit!

DEMEA: Fie, fie! What if he had begged a greater favor from you?

MICIO: As if there were any greater favor than this!

DEMEA: Pray grant his request.

AESCHINUS: Good Sir, be not so hard-hearted.

DEMEA: Pho, promise him for once!

MICIO: Will ye never leave baiting me?

My brother ordered it: Demea ordered the breaking down of a wall to allow the two families to communicate. In this way Demea imitates the good-naturedness of his brother, Micio, and traps him into marrying Aeschinus's mother-in-law.

AESCHINUS: Not till I've prevailed, Sir.

MICIO: Truth, this is downright forcing a man.

DEMEA: Come, Micio, be good-natured and consent.

MICIO: Though this be the most damned, foolish, ridiculous whim, and the most averse to my nature that could possibly be, yet since you are so extremely set upon it, I'll humor ye for once.

AESCHINUS: That is excellent, I'm obliged to ye beyond measure.

DEMEA (*aside*): Well, what's next? . . . What shall I say next? This is as I'd have it. . . . What's more to be done?

(*To Micio.*)

Ho! There's Hegio our poor kinsman, and nearest relation; in truth, we ought in conscience to do something for him.

MICIO: What, pray?

DEMEA: There's a small plot of land in the suburbs, which you farm out — pray let's give him that to live on.

MICIO: A small one, say ye?

DEMEA: Though it were a great one, you might yet give it to him. He has been as good as a father to Pamphila; he's a very honest man, our kinsman, and you couldn't bestow it better. Besides, Brother, there's a certain proverb (none of my own, I assure you) which you so well and wisely made use of: "That age has always this ill effect of making us more worldly, as well as wiser." We should do well to avoid this scandal. 'Tis a true proverb, Brother, and ought to be held in mind.

MICIO: What's all this? . . . Well, so let it be, if he has need of it.

AESCHINUS: Brave Father, I vow!

DEMEA: Now you are my true brother, both in body and soul.

MICIO: I'm glad of it.

DEMEA (*aside, laughing*): I've stabbed him with his own weapons, i'fack!

(*Enter Syrus, with a pick-axe upon his shoulders.*)

SYRUS (*to Demea*): The job is done as ye ordered, Sir.

DEMEA: Thou art an honest lad. . . . And upon my conscience I think Syrus deserves his freedom.

MICIO: He, his freedom? For what exploit?

DEMEA: O, for a thousand.

SYRUS: O dear Mr. Demea, you are a rare gentleman, edad you are! You know I've looked after the young gentlemen from their cradles. I taught them, advised them, and instructed them all I possibly could.

DEMEA: Nothing more evident! Nay, more than that, he catered for them, pimped for them, and in the morning took care of a debauchee for them. These are no ordinary accomplishments, I can assure ye.

SYRUS: Your worship's very merry.

DEMEA: Besides, he was prime mover in buying this music-girl. It was he who managed the whole intrigue, and 'tis no more than justice to reward him, as an encouragement to others! In short, Aeschinus desires the same thing.

MICIO (*to Aeschinus*): Do you desire it too?

AESCHINUS: Yes, if you please, Sir.

MICIO: Since 'tis so, come hither, Syrus! Thou art a free man.

(*Syrus kneels down, Micio lays his hand on his head, and after that gives him a cuff on the ear.*)

SYRUS (*rising up*): Generously done! A thousand thanks to ye all, and to you, Mr. Demea.

DEMEA: I'm well satisfied.

AESCHINUS: And I too.

SYRUS: I won't question it, Sir. But I wish heartily my joy were more complete, that my poor spouse Phrygia might be made as free as I am.

DEMEA: Truth, she's a mighty good woman.

SYRUS: And your grandson's first foster-mother, too.
DEMEA: Faith, in good earnest, if for that, she deserves her freedom before any woman in the world.
MICIO: What! For that simple service?
DEMEA: Yes, indeed! In fine, I'll pay for her freedom myself.
SYRUS: God's blessing light upon your worship, and grant all your wishes.
MICIO: Syrus, thou hast made a good day's work of it.
DEMEA: Besides, Brother, it would be a deed of charity to lend him a little money to set up in business that he may face the world without fear. I undertake that he'll soon repay it.
MICIO: Not a penny-piece!
AESCHINUS: He's a very honest fellow, Sir.
SYRUS: Upon my word, I'll repay you the loan. Do but trust me!
AESCHINUS: Pray do, Sir.
MICIO: I'll consider the matter with care.
DEMEA: He shall pay ye, I'll see to that.
SYRUS (*to Demea*): Egad, you're the best man alive.
AESCHINUS: And the pleasantest in the world.
MICIO: What's the meaning of this, Brother? How comes this sudden change of humor? Why this gallant squandering and profusion?
DEMEA: I'll tell ye, Brother. These sons of yours don't reckon you a sweet-natured and pleasant man because you live as you should and do what is just and reasonable, but because you fawn upon them, cocker them up, and give them what they'll spend. Now, son Aeschinus, if you are dissatisfied with my course of life, because I wouldn't indulge you in all things, right or wrong, then I'll not trouble my head with you any further. Be free to squander, buy mistresses, and do what you will! But if you wish me to advise ye, and set ye up, and help ye too in matters of which your youth can give ye but little understanding — matters of which you are over-fond, and don't well consider — see, here I'm ready to stand by you.
AESCHINUS: Dear Sir, we commit ourselves wholly to your charge; for you know what's fitting to be done far better than we . . . But what will ye do for my brother Ctesipho?
DEMEA: Why, let him take the music-girl; and so bid adieu to general wenching.
AESCHINUS: That's very reasonable. (*To the spectators.*) Gentlemen, your favor!

(*Exeunt° all.*)

[S.D.] *Exeunt:* Latin for "they go out."

Seneca

The surviving Roman plays come from just three hands: Plautus, Terence, and Seneca (4 B.C.–A.D. 65). The comedies of Plautus are raucous, broad, and farcical; those of Terence are polished and carefully structured. Seneca wrote tragedies that were well known to Elizabethans such as Marlowe and Shakespeare, and it is clear that the Elizabethan Age found SENECAN TRAGEDY to be peculiarly suited to its own temperament.

Senecan tragedies were based on either Greek or Roman themes and included murder, bloodthirsty actions (many of which did not occur on stage but were only described), horror of various kinds, ghosts, and long, bombastic speeches. Signs of Senecan influence can be seen in Elizabethan drama, with its taste for many of these devices; plays like *Hamlet* are notable for ending in a pool of blood, with most of the actors lying dead onstage. The theme of revenge was also prized by Seneca and, later, by the Elizabethans.

Not a professional theater person, Seneca was wealthy and learned, a philosopher active in the government of Emperor Nero's Rome. His plays, most of which were adapted from Euripides, were probably written only to be read, as was common at the time, or perhaps recited, although there is no record of their having been performed. The Roman people thirsted for mime and farce but had much less taste for serious plays.

Ten plays attributed to Seneca exist, nine of which are surely his and one of which is only possibly his. His most famous are *Mad Hercules, The Phoenician Women, Medea, Phaedra, Agamemnon, Thyestes,* and *The Trojan Women.*

Seneca (4 B.C.–A.D. 65)

FROM *THYESTES*

TRANSLATED BY ELLA ISABEL HARRIS

Thyestes, probably adapted from the *Oresteia* of Aeschylus, influenced a number of Elizabethan revenge tragedies, such as Shakespeare's *Hamlet.* The story is gruesome even by modern standards. Thyestes seduces his brother Atreus's wife, and Atreus banishes him. When Atreus summons Thyestes to Atreus's home, he goes suspiciously, hoping to be able to see his children. The banquet Atreus holds for Thyestes seems to signal reconciliation between the brothers. But when it is over, Atreus brings in the heads of Thyestes' children, revealing that Thyestes has just eaten their bodies in the feast.

The second scene from act V — before Thyestes is told about the meal he has eaten — follows in its entirety. It shows Thyestes wrestling with himself in a passion of uncertainty. Thyestes' soliloquy is a psychological study of the effects of grief, care, uncertainty, and fear. Seneca's plays have many such soliloquies, and their revelations of complex emotional states deeply impressed the age of Shakespeare.

ACT V • *Scene II*

(*Thyestes sits alone at the banquet table, half overcome with wine; he tries to sing and be gay, but some premonition of evil weighs upon him.*)

THYESTES (*to himself*): By long grief dulled, put by thy cares, my heart,
    Let fear and sorrow fly and bitter need,
    Companion of thy timorous banishment,
    And shame, hard burden of afflicted souls.
    Whence thou has fallen profits more to know
    Than whither; great is he who with firm step
    Moves on the plain when fallen from the height;
    He who, oppressed by sorrows numberless
    And driven from his realm, with unbent neck
    Carries his burdens, not degenerate
    Or conquered, who stands firm beneath the weight
    Of all his burdens, he is great indeed.
    Now scatter all the clouds of bitter fate,
    Put by all signs of thy unhappy days,
    In happy fortunes show a happy face,
    Forget the old Thyestes. Ah, this vice
    Still follows misery: never to trust

In happy days; though better fortunes come,
Those who have borne afflictions find it hard
To joy in better days. What holds me back,
Forbids me celebrate the festal tide?
What cause of grief, arising causelessly,
Bids me to weep? What art thou that forbids
That I should crown my head with festal wreath?
It does forbid, forbid! Upon my head
The roses languish, and my hair that drips
With ointment rises as with sudden fear,
My face is wet with showers of tears that fall
Unwillingly, and groans break off my song.
Grief loves accustomed tears, the wretched feel
That they must weep. I would be glad to make
Most bitter lamentation, and to wail,
And rend this robe with Tyrian purple dyed.
My mind gives warning of some coming grief,
Presages future ills. The storm that smites
When all the sea is calm weighs heavily
Upon the sailor. Fool! What grief, what storm,
Dost thou conceive? Believe thy brother now.
Be what it may, thou fearest now too late,
Or causelessly. I do not wish to be
Unhappy, but vague terror smites my breast.
No cause is evident and yet my eyes
O'erflow with sudden tears. What can it be,
Or grief, or fear? Or has great pleasure tears?

The surviving Roman plays offer enough variety to give us an idea of what the drama achieved. Like so much of Roman culture, Roman drama rested in the shadow of Greek accomplishments. The Romans were responsible for maintaining the Greek texts, allowing us to see a great deal of their work. Although it may be true that much of the Roman drama that was produced no longer exists, what survives shows variety and high quality.

Medieval Drama

The Role of the Church

The medieval period in Europe (A.D. 476–1500) began with the collapse of Rome, a calamity of such magnitude that the years between then and the beginning of the Crusades in 1095 have been traditionally, if erroneously, called the Dark Ages. Historians used this term to refer to their lack of knowledge about a time in which no great central powers organized society or established patterns of behavior and standards in the arts.

Drama, or at least records of it, all but disappeared. The major institution to profit from the fall of the Roman empire was the Roman Catholic Church, which in the ninth and tenth centuries enjoyed considerable power and influence. Many bishops considered drama a godless activity, a distraction from the piety that the church demanded of its members. During the great age of cathedral building and the great ages of religious painting and religious music — from the seventh century to the thirteenth — drama was not officially approved. Therefore, it is a striking irony that the rebirth of drama in the Western world should have taken place in the heart of the monasteries, developing slowly and inconspicuously until it outgrew its beginnings.

The Church may well have intended nothing more than the simple dramatization of its message. Or it is possible that the people may have craved drama, and the Church's response could have been an attempt to answer their needs. In either event, the Church could never have foreseen the outcome of adding a few moments of drama to the liturgy, the church services. LITURGICAL DRAMA began in the ninth century with TROPES, or embellishments, which were sung during parts of the Mass (the public celebration of the Eucharist). The earliest known example of a trope, called the QUEM QUAERITIS ("Whom seek ye?"), grew out of the Easter Mass and was sung in a monastic settlement in Switzerland called St. Gall:

ANGEL: Whom seek ye in the sepulchre, O ye Christians?
THREE MARYS: Jesus of Nazareth, who was crucified, O ye Angels.
ANGEL: He is not here; he is risen as he has foretold.
    Go, announce that he is risen from the sepulchre.

Some scholars think that in its earliest form this trope was sung by four monks in a dialogue pattern, three monks representing the three Marys at Christ's tomb and the other representing the angel. Tropes like the *Quem Quaeritis* evolved over the years to include a number of participants — monks, nuns, and choirboys in different communities — as the tropes spread from church to church throughout the Continent. These dramatic interpolations never became dramas separate from the Mass itself, although their success and popularity led to experiments with other dramatic sequences centering on moments in the Mass and in the life of Christ. The actors in these pieces did not think of themselves as specialists or professionals; they were simply monks or nuns who belonged to the church. The churchgoers obviously enjoyed the tropes, and more were created, despite the Church's official position on drama.

In the tenth century a nun called Hrotsvitha entertained herself and her fellow nuns with imitations of the Latin dramatist Terence. Although her own subject matter was holy in nature, she realized that Terence was an amusing comic writer with a polished style. She referred to herself as "the strong voice of Gandersheim," her community in Saxony, and said that she had "not hesitated to imitate in my writings a poet whose works are so widely read, my object being to glorify, within the limits of my poor talent, the laudable chastity of Christian virgins." Her plays are very short moral tales, often illustrating moments in the lives of Christian martyred women. As far as is known, these plays do not seem to have gone beyond the nuns' walls; therefore, they had little effect on the drama developing in the period.

Once dramatic scenes were added that took the action outside of the liturgy, it was not long before dramas were being staged outside the church. The Anglo-Norman drama *Adam,* dating from the twelfth century, has explicit stage directions establishing its setting outside the church. The play is to be staged on the west side of the church with a platform extending from the steps. The characters of Adam, Eve, God (called Figura), and the Devil and his assistants are given costumes and extensive dialogue. The dramatic detail in this play implies a considerable development of plot and action, which, despite its theological matter, is plainly too elaborate to be contained within the service of the Mass.

Miracle Plays

Once outside the church, the drama flourished and soon became independent, although its themes continued to be religious and its services were connected with religious festivals. In 1264 Pope Urban IV added to the religious calendar a new, important feast: Corpus Christi, celebrated beginning on the first Thursday after Trinity Sunday, about two months after Easter. The purpose of the feast was to celebrate the doctrine declaring that the body of Christ was real and present in the Host (consecrated bread or wafer) taken by the faithful in the sacrament of Communion.

At first the feast of Corpus Christi was localized in Liège, Belgium. But in the fourteenth and fifteenth centuries it spread through papal decree and became one of the chief feasts of the church. Among other things, it featured a procession and pageant in which the Host was displayed publicly through the streets of a town. Because of the importance and excitement of this feast, entire communities took part in the celebration.

MIRACLE PLAYS on the subject of miracles performed by saints developed late in the twelfth century in both England and on the Continent. Typically, these plays focused on the Virgin Mary and St. Nicholas, both of whom had strong followings (sometimes described as cults) during the medieval period. Mary is often portrayed as helping those in need and danger — often at the last minute. Some of those she saved may have seemed unsavory sinners to a pious audience, but the point was that the saint saved all who truly wished to be saved.

Although they quickly became public entertainments removed from the church building and were popular as Corpus Christi entertainments throughout the fifteenth century, few miracle plays survive in English because King Henry VIII banned them in the middle of the sixteenth century during his reformation of the Church. As a result, they were not performed or preserved.

The craft guilds, professional organizations of workers involved in the same trade — carpenters, wool merchants, and so on — soon began competing with each other in producing plays that could be performed during the feast of Corpus Christi. Most of their plays derived from Bible stories and the life of Christ. Religious guilds, such as the Confrèrie of the Passion, produced plays in Paris and elsewhere on the Continent. Because the Bible is silent on many details of Christ's life, some plays invented new material and illuminated dark areas, thereby satisfying the intense curiosity medieval Christians had about events the Bible omitted.

Mystery Plays

The Church did not ignore drama after it left the church buildings. Since the plays had religious subject matter and could be used to teach the Bible and to model Christian behavior, they remained of considerable value to the Church.

First performed by the clergy, these religious plays dramatized the mystery of Christ's Passion. Later the plays were produced by members of craft guilds, and they became known as CRAFT OR MYSTERY PLAYS. Beginning in the medieval period, the word *mystery* was used to describe a skill or trade known only to a few who apprenticed and mastered its special techniques; it also referred to religious mysteries.

By the fifteenth century, mystery plays and the feast of Corpus Christi were popular almost everywhere in Europe, and in England certain towns produced exceptionally elaborate cycles with unusually complex and ambitious plays. The CYCLES were groups of plays numbering from twenty-four to forty-eight. Four cycles have been preserved: the Chester, York, Towneley (Wakefield), and N-Town cycles, named for their towns of origin. N-Town plays were a generic version of plays that any town could take and use as its own, although the plays were probably written near Lincoln.

The plays were performed again and again during annual holidays and feasts, and the texts were carefully preserved. Some of the plays, such as *The Fall of Lucifer,* are very short. Others are more elaborate in length and complexity and resemble modern plays: *Noah,* from the Wakefield Cycle, which has been produced regularly in recent history; *The Slaughter of Innocents;* and *The Second Shepherds' Pageant,* one of the most entertaining mystery plays.

The producers of the plays often had a sense of appropriateness in their choice of subjects. For example, the Water-Drawers guild sponsored *Noah's Flood,* the Butchers (because they sold "flesh") *Temptation, The Woman Taken in Adultery,* and the Shipwrights *The Building of the Ark.*

Among the best-known mystery plays is the somewhat farcical *The Second Shepherds' Pageant,* which is both funny and serious. It tells of a crafty shepherd named Mak who steals a lamb from his fellow shepherds and takes it home. His wife, Gill, then places it in a cradle and pretends it is her baby. Eventually the shepherds — who suspect Mak from the first — smoke out the fraud and give Mak a blanket-tossing for their trouble. But after they do so, they see a star in the heavens and turn their attention to the birth of baby Jesus, the Lamb of God. They join the Magi and come to pay homage to the Christ Child.

The easy way in which the profane elements of everyday life coexisted with the sacred in medieval times has long interested scholars. *The Second Shepherds' Pageant* virtually breaks into two parts, the first dedicated to the wickedness of Mak and Gill and the horseplay of the shepherds. But once Mak has had his due reward, the play alters in tone and the sense of devotion to Christian teachings becomes uppermost. The fact that the mystery plays moved away from liturgical Latin and to the vernacular (local) language made such a juxtaposition of sacred and profane much more possible.

The dominance of the guilds in producing mystery plays suggests that guilds enjoyed increasing political power and authority. The guilds grew stronger and more influential — probably at the expense of the Church. Some historians have seen this development as crucial to the growing secularization of the Middle Ages.

Morality Plays

MORALITY PLAYS were never part of any cycle but developed independently as moral tales in the late fourteenth or early fifteenth century on the Continent and in England. They do not illustrate moments in the Bible, nor do they describe the life of Christ or the saints. Instead, they describe the lives of people facing the temptations of the world. The plays are careful to present a warning to the unwary that their souls are always in peril, that the devil is on constant watch, and that people must behave properly if they are to be saved.

One feature of morality plays is their reliance on ALLEGORY, a favorite medieval device. Allegory is the technique of giving abstract ideas or values a physical representation. In morality plays, abstractions such as goodness became characters in the drama. In modern times we sometimes use allegory in art, as when we represent justice as a blindfolded woman. Allegorically, justice should act impartially because she does not "see" any distinctions, such as those of rank or privilege, that characterize most people standing before a judge.

The use of allegory permitted medieval dramatists to personify abstract values such as sloth, greed, daintiness, vanity, strength, and hope by making them characters and placing them onstage in action. The dramatist specified symbols, clothing, and gestures appropriate to these abstract figures, thus helping the audience recognize the ideas the characters represented. The use of allegory was an extremely durable technique that was already established in medieval painting, printed books, and books of emblems, in which, for example, sloth would be shown as a man reclining lazily on a bed or greed would be represented as overwhelmingly fat and vanity as a figure completely absorbed in a mirror.

The central problem in the morality play was the salvation of human beings, represented by an individual's struggle to avoid sin and damnation and achieve salvation in the otherworld. As in *Everyman* (c. 1495), a late-medieval play that is the best known of the morality plays, the subjects were usually abstract battles between certain vices and specific virtues for the possession of the human soul, a theme repeated in the Elizabethan age in Marlowe's *Doctor Faustus*.

In many ways the morality play was a dramatized sermon designed to teach a moral lesson. Marked by high seriousness, it was nevertheless entertaining. Using allegory to represent abstract qualities allowed the didactic playwrights to draw clear-cut lines of moral force: Satan was always bad; angels were always good. The allegories were clear, direct, and apparent to all who witnessed the plays.

We do not have much knowledge of the origins of morality plays. Many of them are lost, but some that remain are occasionally performed: *The Pride of Life,* the earliest extant morality play; *The Castle of Perseverance; Wisdom; Mankind;* and *Everyman* are the best known. They all enjoyed a remarkable popularity in the latter part of the medieval period, all the way up to the early Renaissance.

Although Chinese and Japanese drama neither influenced nor was influenced by Western drama in the medieval period, from roughly the late twelfth to the beginning of the seventeenth centuries, it, like Western drama, was connected to temples, shrines, and religious ceremony. During this period Japanese Nō drama developed as a highly refined, deliberate, and ritualized form involving ceremonial dance and music as well as a developed narrative. Centuries later, Nō drama had an influence on Western literature, particularly on writers such as Ezra Pound and playwrights such as W. B. Yeats and Samuel Beckett.

Nō drama developed from a popular form of drama called sarugaku Nō, invented by Kan'ami (1333–1384) in the fourteenth century. The rulers of Japan at that time, shoguns (generals) of the samurai warrior class, enjoyed theater and supported performances of highly sophisticated drama. They preferred sarugaku — "monkey music" — a form that included gymnastic action, music, dance, and a story line. Kan'ami refined sarugaku into sarugaku Nō, a more deliberate and controlled form that elevated the actor and demanded more skill — the word Nō means "skill" — from performers. The refinement Kan'ami brought to the drama was associated with Zen Buddhism, the form of religion favored by the shogun of the period.

Nō drama, which relies on masks, ritual costume, dance, and music, is produced around the world even today. It emerged late in the fourteenth century out of Kan'ami's innovations, but it was his son, Zeami Motokiyo (1363–1443), who developed Nō into a serious form marked by the restraint and control associated with Zen Buddhism. The religious influences on Nō drama emphasized self-control, honorable behavior, and purity of action. Zeami produced a body of drama that can be seen today in the West as well as in the East. *Lady Han (Hanjo)* deals with a realistic situation in which a prostitute falls in love with a traveling captain. Before he leaves they exchange fans on which a painting of the moon will identify them. Such romances were not uncommon, and the emotions portrayed in Nō drama are derived from living experience.

The Medieval Stage

Relatively little commentary survives about the conventions of medieval staging, and some of it is contradictory. We know that in the earliest years — after the tropes developed into full-blown religious scenes acted inside the cathedrals — certain sections of the church were devoted to specific short plays. These areas of the church became known as MANSIONS; each mansion represented a building or physical place known to the audience. The audience moved from one mansion to another, seeing play after play, absorbing the dramatic representation of the events, characters, and locale associated with each mansion.

The tradition of moving from mansion to mansion inside the church carried over into the performances that took place later outside the church. Instead of

Figure 5. Pageant wagon

mansions, wagons with raised stages provided the playing areas. Usually, the wagons remained stationary and the audience moved from one to another. During the guild cycles the pageants would move; the performers would give their plays at several locales so that many people could see them.

According to medieval descriptions, drawings, and reconstructions, a PAGEANT CART could also be simply a flat surface drawn on wheels that had a wagon next to it; these structures touched on their long side. In some cases a figure could descend from an upper area as if from the clouds, or actors could descend from the pageants onto the audience's level to enact a descent into an underworld. The stage was, then, a raised platform visible to the audience below (Figure 5).

A curtain concealed a space, usually inside or below the wagon, for changing costumes. The actors used costumes and props, sometimes very elaborate and expensive, in an effort to make the drama more impressive. Indeed, between the thirteenth and the sixteenth centuries, a number of theatrical effects were developed to please a large audience. For instance, in the morality and mystery plays the devils were often portrayed as frightening, grotesque, and sometimes even comic figures. They became crowd pleasers. A sensational element was developed in some of the plays in the craft cycles, especially those about the lives of the saints and martyrs, in which there were plenty of chances to portray horrifying tortures.

The prop that seems to have pleased the most audiences was a complex machine known as the MOUTH OF HELL or "Hell mouth," usually a large fish-shaped orifice from which smoke and explosions, fueled by gunpowder, belched constantly. The devils took great delight in stuffing their victims into these maws. According to a contemporary account, one of the machines required seventeen men to operate.

The level of realism achieved by medieval plays was at times startling. In addition to visual realism, medieval plays involved a psychological level of participation on the part of both audience and actor. Sometimes they demanded that the actors suffer in accord with the characters they played. Some records attest to characters playing Christ on the cross having to be revived after their hearts stopped, and at least one Judas apparently was hanged just a little too long and had to be resuscitated.

The Actors

In the early days of liturgical drama, the actors in the tropes were monks and choirboys, and in the mystery plays they were drawn from the guilds. At first all the actors were male, but records show that eventually women took important roles.

The demands of more sophisticated plays encouraged the development of a kind of professionalism, although it seems unlikely that players in the cycles could have supported themselves exclusively on their earnings. Special skills became essential for the design and operation of complex stage machines and for the performance of acrobatics that were expected of certain characters, such as devils. As actors developed facility in delivering lines and as writers found ways to incorporate more challenging elements in their plays, a professionalism no doubt arose, even if actors and writers had few opportunities to earn a living on the stage.

By the second half of the sixteenth century, the early Renaissance, groups of wandering actors were producing highly demanding and sophisticated plays, and writers such as Shakespeare were able to join them and make a living. When these professionals secured their own theaters, they had no problems filling them with good drama, with actors, and with an audience.

Dramatic techniques developed in the medieval period were put to good use in the Renaissance theater. For example, the colorful and dramatic devil characters that stalked the mystery plays were transformed into sophisticated villains in Elizabethan drama. The devil Mephistopheles (Mephistophilis) behaves like a smooth Tudor lawyer in Marlowe's *Doctor Faustus;* Iago in *Othello* is suspected of having cloven hooves. Perhaps one important difference is that the Elizabethan devil-villains are truly frightening, since they are so recognizably human in their villainy.

Medieval Drama Timeline

DATE	THEATER	POLITICAL	SOCIAL/CULTURAL
400–500		**476:** The fall of Rome and beginning of the Dark Ages **483–565:** Byzantine Emperor Justinian, author of the Code of Civil Laws	**480–524:** Boëthius, Roman scholar, philosopher, and theologian, is executed for treason.
500–600	**500–1000:** Traveling performers proliferate in Europe.		**570–632:** Muhammed, founder of Islam **590–594:** Devastating plague spreads through Europe and kills half the population.
600–700		Persians take Damascus and Jerusalem.	**636:** Anglo-Saxons are introduced to Christianity. **695:** Jews are persecuted in Spain.
700–800		**768–814:** Charlemagne reigns in France and is crowned Holy Roman Emperor in 800 by Pope Leo III in Rome on Christmas Day. **792:** Beginning of the Viking era in Britain	**c. 710:** Buddhist monasteries in Japan become centers of civilization. **787:** The Council of Nicaea officially rejects iconoclasm.
800–900	**9th c.:** Beginnings of liturgical drama	**843:** Treaty of Verdun divides the Holy Roman Empire into German, French, and Italian kingdoms. **850:** Rurik, a Northman, becomes ruler of Kiev, an important Russian trading post. Trade begins with Constantinople, which remains a commercial and cultural center throughout the Dark Ages.	**c. 800–1000:** *Beowulf,* one of the first long poems written in English **855:** Earliest known attempts at polyphonic music **863:** Cyril and Methodius invent a Slavic alphabet called Cyrillic.
900–1000	**c. 900:** Farces make their first appearance since classical times. **925:** Earliest extant Easter trope **965–975:** Compilation of the *Regularis Concordia* (Monastic Agreement) by Ethelwood, bishop of Winchester, England. The *Regularis Concordia* contains the text of the earliest extant playlet in Europe, with directions for its performance.		**c. 900:** The beginnings of the famous Arabian tales called *A Thousand and One Nights*

Medieval Drama Timeline (continued)

DATE	THEATER	POLITICAL	SOCIAL/CULTURAL
900–1000 (continued)	**970:** Plays of Hrosvitha, a German nun and the first known female playwright. The six plays are modeled on the comedies of Terence but deal with serious religious matters.	**1000:** Leif Ericson, possibly the first European to venture to North America	**975:** Arabic arithmetical notation is brought to Europe by the Arabs. **980–1037:** Avicenna (Ibn Sina), Arab physician and philosopher **990:** Development of systemic musical notation.
1000–1100		**1066:** The Normans conquer Britain. **1086:** Compilation of the *Domesday Book,* a survey of the British economy, population, and land ownership at that time **1096–1099:** First Crusade. Crusaders take Jerusalem from the Arabs.	**1054:** The Great Schism separates Eastern and Western Churches in Europe. **1079–1142:** Peter Abelard, French theologian and philosopher
1100–1200	**12th c.:** Religious plays are first performed outside churches.	**1109–1113:** Anglo-French War **1147–1149:** Second Crusade. Crusaders lose Jerusalem to the Arabs. **1167–1227:** Genghis Khan, founder of Mongol empire **1189–1193:** Third Crusade. Crusaders fail to recapture Jerusalem.	**c. 1125:** Beginnings of French troubadour and trouvère music **1133–1855:** St. Bartholomew's Fair, London, England **1167:** Oxford University is founded.
1200–1300	**13th c.:** Beginnings of Yuan zaju drama in China **1250:** *Easter Play of Muri,* beginnings of German drama **1276–1277:** French poet Adam de la Halle writes *The Play of the Greenwood,* the oldest extant medieval secular drama.	**1202–1204:** Fourth Crusade. Crusaders seize Constantinople. **1212:** Children's Crusade. Thousands of children are sent as crusaders to Jerusalem; most die or are sold as slaves. **1215:** King John of England signs the Magna Carta, guaranteeing habeas corpus, trial by jury, and restrictions on the power of the king. **1224–1227:** Anglo-French War **1228:** Sixth Crusade **1248:** Seventh Crusade	**c. 1202:** Court jesters appear at European courts. **1225:** Guillaume de Lorris writes *Roman de la Rose,* a story of courtly wooing. **1225–1274:** Thomas Aquinas, important Scholastic philosopher **1254–1324:** Marco Polo, Venetian traveler whose accounts of life in China became famous in the West **1264:** First celebration of the feast of Corpus Christi **c. 1282:** Florence emerges as the leading European city of commerce and finance.

DATE	THEATER	POLITICAL	SOCIAL/CULTURAL
1300–1400	**14th c.:** Beginnings of Nō drama in Japan **c. 1385–1450:** *The Second Shepherds' Pageant,* part of the English Wakefield Cycle **1398–1548:** Confrèrie de la Passion at Paris performs religious plays.	**1337:** Hundred Years War begins.	**c. 1302:** Dante's *Divine Comedy* **1304–1374:** Petrarch, Italian poet **1347–1351:** The Black Death kills approximately 75 million people throughout Europe. **1360–1400:** *Piers Plowman* and *Sir Gawain and the Green Knight*: achievements of Middle English literature **1387:** Chaucer's *Canterbury Tales*
1400–1500	**c. 1425:** *The Castle of Perseverance,* English morality play **1429:** Plautus's plays are rediscovered in Italy. **c. 1470:** *Pierre Patheline,* most renowned of medieval French farces **1490:** *Corpus Christi* play of Eger, Bohemia **c. 1495:** *Everyman,* best-known English morality play	**1429:** Joan of Arc's troops resist the British siege of Orleans, an important turning point in the Hundred Years War. **1431:** Joan of Arc is captured and burned as a heretic. **1453:** France wins the Hundred Years War and becomes an important continental power. England abandons the Continent to develop its naval forces. **1481:** Spanish Inquisition **1482–1485:** Reign of Richard III. Richard maintains a company of actors at court, which tours surrounding towns when not needed by His Majesty. **1485–1509:** Reign of Henry VII, first of the Tudor rulers. Like Richard III, Henry maintains a company of actors.	**1400–1455:** Fra Angelico, Italian painter **c. 1406–1469:** Fra Lippo Lippi, Italian painter best known for his frescoes **c. 1430:** Modern English develops from Middle English. **c. 1450:** Gutenberg invents movable type. **1485:** Sir Thomas Malory publishes *Le Morte Darthur,* one of the first books printed in England. **1492:** Columbus sets sail across the Atlantic.
1500–1600	**1527:** Henry VIII builds a House of Revels in which to stage court entertainments. **1548:** Production of plays is forbidden in Paris. **1558:** Elizabeth I forbids performance of all religious plays.	**1509–1547:** Reign of Henry VIII **1534:** Henry VIII breaks with the Roman Catholic Church. Drama is used as a political instrument to attack or defend opposing viewpoints. **1558–1603:** Reign of Elizabeth I	**1509:** Pope Clement V resides at Avignon, beginning the Babylonian Captivity, during which Rome is not the papal seat. **1545–1563:** The Council of Trent is convened by the Catholic Church to solidify its control over expressions of Church doctrine. Medieval religious plays are deemed provocative and controversial.

Hrosvitha

The German nun Hrosvitha (c. 935–1000) (also Hroswitha, Roswitha, Hrotsvit, and Hrotsuit) belonged to the Benedictine convent in Gandersheim, founded in 852. Her name translates to "strong voice," a term she uses to describe herself in her writing. Her voice is that of a learned woman, and today it can be heard as a feminist voice in a time and society that were unquestioningly patriarchal.

Hrosvitha is considered not only the earliest German woman poet but the first woman dramatist in Europe. A Saxon noblewoman, she entered the convent in approximately 959, living with nuns who were themselves of noble birth. The abbey was under the protection of Otto I (912–973), who united a powerful Germany and produced a long-lasting period of peace and development. Otto became the Holy Roman Emperor on February 13, 962. His rule, dubbed the Ottonian Renaissance, favored religion, learning, the arts, and music.

During this period, the abbey at Gandersheim was obligated not to the Church but to the king himself, and Otto eventually released it from his direct governance, permitting it to maintain a law court and to coin money. While such political issues may not have affected Hrosvitha, the fact that the period was one of learning and scholarship was of great importance. Hrosvitha was educated in the liberal arts, beginning with the quadrivium (geometry, arithmetic, music, and astronomy) and continuing with the trivium (grammar, rhetoric, and logic). Her studies were conducted in Latin, the language she used to write her plays. Her education was comparable to that of liberally educated men and of the nuns who lived with her.

Hrosvitha's work is deeply rooted in her religious beliefs. Her religious order meditated on the drama of the lives of Christian saints and especially on their often spectacular martyrdoms. The abbey gave its inhabitants a life of contemplation, removed from the world. But it is also clear that the nuns had the talent, education, and opportunities to write religious tracts and, in the case of Hrosvitha, religious drama. The question of whether Hrosvitha's plays were actually produced is not settled.

Hrosvitha wrote six plays and several other prose and poetic works. The plays reject the temptations of the world in the name of Christ. In *Gallicanus* the title character is promised the hand of Constantia if he wins a specific battle, but Constantia, daughter of the Christian emperor Constantine, has taken a vow of chastity. Eventually, with the aid of saints, Gallicanus converts to Christianity and becomes a martyr. The conversion of an important Roman is the theme of *Callimachus,* and the conversion theme dominates *Paphnutius* and *Abraham. Sapientia* also emphasizes martyrdom. Sapientia's three daughters, whose names translate as Faith, Hope, and Charity, offer a threat to the stability of Emperor Hadrian's rule. They are tortured brutally but survive without pain until Hadrian beheads them. Eventually Sapientia joins her daughters in heavenly bliss, inspiring the local women who have witnessed the events.

DULCITIUS

Dulcitius is probably the second of Hrosvitha's plays. It was rediscovered in 1494 in an eleventh-century manuscript along with her other dramatic works. Its first printing was in 1501 in an edition with woodcuts by Albrecht Dürer, indicating its importance at the time. The play is plainly didactic and was designed to teach a lesson rather than merely to entertain. The lesson, as in all her plays, is a moral one, urging listeners or readers to live a life of purity and virtue in order to celebrate the greatness of God. In this sense, Hrosvitha wrote in the medieval literary tradition of Europe. Her plays are fascinating to the modern reader, however, because she purposely emulated the techniques of the Roman playwright Terence.

She chose Terence as her model because his texts were used in education and therefore widely known in Europe. Moreover, they were amusing comedies written with such great style that they were models of elocution. Hrosvitha admits to imitating Terence, but her motives were subversive. She wished to use the eloquent style of Terence not to entertain her audience with secular amusement and charming courtesans but to honor the virtue of chaste virgins who praised God and Christian virtues.

Dulcitius, a jail governor, lusts after the three virgins Agape, Chionia, and Hirenia (Love, Purity, and Peace). Hrosvitha emphasizes his power, but all his worldly power comes to nothing in the face of the virgins' beliefs. In this sense, Hrosvitha celebrates how the apparent weakness of females in her own society can confound the apparent strength of males. Despite his position and power, Dulcitius's lust cannot be satisfied.

Moreover, the three virgins are problematic not only to Dulcitius but to Emperor Diocletian as well. When Agape tells Diocletian that it is dangerous to offend almighty God, Diocletian asks: "Dangerous to whom?" She responds, "To you and to the state you rule." Hrosvitha therefore not only establishes the power of the virgins but of the Christian religion. Astonishingly, this "new-fangled religion" threatens Rome itself, which is why Diocletian persecuted Christians so brutally during his reign.

The play's short lines, quick realistic dialogue, and carefully focused interaction are recognizably like Terence's. The present translation uses virgules (/) to indicate the end of lines as they were printed in the original Latin. The broad farcical humor of the "miraculous" scene in which Dulcitius embraces pots and pans in the kitchen thinking they are the three virgins — a scene performed while the virgins watch through the crack in the door — is also in the tradition of Roman comedy.

Despite the three virgins' ultimate martyrdom, the play is a comedy. The soldiers and Dulcitius will end up in "Tartarus," while the virgins "will enter the heavenly bridal chamber of the Eternal King." For the devout canonness Hrosvitha, no ending could be happier.

***Dulcitius* in
Performance**

In the opinion of most scholars, the plays of Hrosvitha were not produced but instead read as CLOSET DRAMA. On the other hand, comic scenes such as the one in which Dulcitius blackens his face against the pots and pans have led some theater historians to speculate that the plays were performed by the nuns themselves in the abbey. In any event, *Dulcitius* would not have had a public audience and may not have influenced other medieval drama. It is, however, a remarkable moment in the history of drama. As Hrosvitha tells us: "I, the strong voice of Gandersheim, have not hesitated to imitate in my writings a poet whose works are so widely read, my object being to glorify, within the limits of my poor talent, the laudable chastity of Christian virgins in that self-same form of composition which has been used to describe the shameless acts of licentious women."

Hrosvitha (*c. 935–1000*)

DULCITIUS   *c. 965*

THE MARTYRDOM OF THE HOLY VIRGINS AGAPE, CHIONIA, AND HIRENA

TRANSLATED BY K. M. WILSON

[Characters

DIOCLETIAN
AGAPE   WIFE (OF DULCITIUS)
CHIONIA   SISSINUS
HIRENA   SOLDIERS
DULCITIUS   GUARDS]

The martyrdom of the holy virgins° Agape, Chionia, and Hirena, whom, in the silence of the night, Governor Dulcitius secretly visited, desiring to delight in their embrace. But as soon as he entered, / he became demented / and kissed and hugged the pots and pans, mistaking them for the girls until his face and his clothes were soiled with disgusting black dirt. Afterward Count Sissinus, acting on orders, / was given the girls so he might put them to tortures. / He, too, was deluded miraculously / but finally ordered that Agape and Chionia be burnt and Hirena be slain by an arrow.

DIOCLETIAN: The renown of your free and noble descent / and the brightness of your beauty demand / that you be married to one of the foremost men of my court. This will be done according to our command if you deny Christ° and comply by bringing offerings to our gods.° 5

The martyrdom of the holy virgins: The martyrdom of the three virgins occurred in 290 during Diocletian's persecution of the Christians in Thessalonica.   **5. deny Christ:** Deny the vow of virginity they made in the name of Christ.   **6. our gods:** Gods acknowledged by the Roman empire.

AGAPE: Be free of care, / don't trouble yourself to prepare our wedding / because we cannot be compelled under any duress / to betray Christ's holy name, which we must confess, / nor to stain our virginity.   10
DIOCLETIAN: What madness possesses you? What rage drives you three? /
AGAPE: What signs of our madness do you see? /
DIOCLETIAN: An obvious and great display. /
AGAPE: In what way? /   15
DIOCLETIAN: Chiefly in that renouncing the practices of ancient religion / you follow the useless, new-fangled ways of the Christian superstition. /
AGAPE: Heedlessly you offend the majesty of the omnipotent God. That is dangerous . . .   20
DIOCLETIAN: Dangerous to whom?
AGAPE: To you and to the state you rule. /
DIOCLETIAN: She is mad; remove the fool! /
CHIONIA: My sister is not mad; she rightly reprehended your folly.   25
DIOCLETIAN: She rages even more madly; remove her from our sight and arraign the third girl. /
HIRENA: You will find the third, too, a rebel / and resisting you forever. /
DIOCLETIAN: Hirena, although you are younger in   30 birth, / be greater in worth! /
HIRENA: Show me, I pray, how?
DIOCLETIAN: Bow your neck to the gods, set an example for your sisters, and be the cause for their freedom!
HIRENA: Let those worship idols, Sire, / who wish to incur God's ire. / But I won't defile my head, anointed   35

with royal unguent by debasing myself at the idols' feet.

DIOCLETIAN: The worship of gods brings no dishonor / but great honor. /

40

HIRENA: And what dishonor is more disgraceful, / what disgrace is any more shameful / than when a slave is venerated as a master?

DIOCLETIAN: I don't ask you to worship slaves / but the mighty gods of princes and greats. /

45

HIRENA: Is he not anyone's slave / who, for a price, is up for sale? /

DIOCLETIAN: For her speech so brazen, / to the tortures she must be taken. /

50

HIRENA: This is just what we hope for, this is what we desire, / that for the love of Christ through tortures we may expire. /

DIOCLETIAN: Let these insolent girls / who defy our decrees and words / be put in chains and kept in the squalor of prison until Governor Dulcitius can examine them.

55

DULCITIUS: Bring forth, soldiers, the girls whom you hold sequestered. /

SOLDIERS: Here they are whom you requested. /

60

DULCITIUS: Wonderful, indeed, how beautiful, how graceful, how admirable these little girls are!

SOLDIERS: Yes, they are perfectly lovely.

DULCITIUS: I am captivated by their beauty.

SOLDIERS: That is understandable.

65

DULCITIUS: To draw them to my heart, I am eager. /

SOLDIERS: Your success will be meager. /

DULCITIUS: Why?

SOLDIERS: Because they are firm in faith.

DULCITIUS: What if I sway them by flattery? /

70

SOLDIERS: They will despise it utterly. /

DULCITIUS: What if with tortures I frighten them? /

SOLDIERS: Little will it matter to them. /

DULCITIUS: Then what should be done, I wonder? /

SOLDIERS: Carefully you should ponder. /

75

DULCITIUS: Place them under guard in the inner room of the pantry, where they keep the servants' pots. /

SOLDIERS: Why in that particular spot? /

DULCITIUS: So that I may visit them often at my leisure. /

SOLDIERS: At your pleasure. /

80

DULCITIUS: What do the captives do at this time of night? /

SOLDIERS: Hymns they recite. /

DULCITIUS: Let us go near. /

SOLDIERS: From afar we hear their tinkling little voices clear. /

85

DULCITIUS: Stand guard before the door with your lantern / but I will enter / and satisfy myself in their longed-for embrace. /

SOLDIERS: Enter. We will guard this place. /

90

AGAPE: What is that noise outside the door? /

HIRENA: That wretched Dulcitius coming to the fore. /

CHIONIA: May God protect us!

AGAPE: Amen.

CHIONIA: What is the meaning of this clash of the pots and the pans?

95

HIRENA: I will check. / Come here, please, and look through the crack! /

AGAPE: What is going on?

HIRENA: Look, the fool, the madman base, / he thinks he is enjoying our embrace. /

100

AGAPE: What is he doing?

HIRENA: Into his lap he pulls the utensils, / he embraces the pots and the pans, giving them tender kisses. /

CHIONIA: Ridiculous!

HIRENA: His face, his hands, his clothes, are so soiled, so filthy, that with all the soot that clings to him, he looks like an Ethiopian.

105

AGAPE: It is only right that he should appear in body the way he is in his mind: possessed by the Devil.

HIRENA: Wait! He prepares to leave. Let us watch how he is greeted, / and how he is treated / by the soldiers who wait for him.

110

SOLDIERS: Who is coming out? / A demon without doubt. / Or rather, the Devil himself is he; / let us flee! /

DULCITIUS: Soldiers, where are you taking yourselves in flight? / Stay! Wait! Escort me home with your light! /

115

SOLDIERS: The voice is our master's tone / but the look the Devil's own. / Let us not stay! / Let us run away; the apparition will slay us! /

120

DULCITIUS: I will go to the palace and complain, / and reveal to the whole court the insults I had to sustain. /

DULCITIUS: Guards, let me into the palace; / I must have a private audience. /

GUARDS: Who is this vile and detestable monster covered in torn and despicable rags? Let us beat him, / from the steps let us sweep him; / he must not be allowed to enter.

125

DULCITIUS: Alas, alas, what has happened? Am I not dressed in splendid garments? Don't I look neat and clean? / Yet anyone who looks at my mien / loathes me as a foul monster. To my wife I shall return, / and from her learn / what has happened. But there is my spouse, / with disheveled hair she leaves the house, / and the whole household follows her in tears.

130

135

WIFE: Alas, alas, my Lord Dulcitius, what has happened to you? / You are not sane; the Christians have made a laughing stock out of you. /

DULCITIUS: Now I know at last. I owe this mockery to their witchcraft.

140

WIFE: What upsets me so, what makes me more sad, is that you were ignorant of all that happened to you.

DULCITIUS: I command that those insolent girls be led forth, / and that they be publicly stripped of all their clothes, / so that they experience similar mockery in retaliation for ours. /

145

SOLDIERS: We labor in vain; / we sweat without gain. / Behold, their garments stick to their virginal bodies like skin, / and he who urged us to strip them snores in his seat, / and he cannot be awakened from his

150

sleep. / Let us go to the Emperor and report what has happened.

DIOCLETIAN: It grieves me very much / to hear that Governor Dulcitius has been so greatly deluded, / so greatly insulted, / so utterly humiliated. / But these vile young women shall not boast with impunity of having made a mockery of our gods and those who worship them. I shall direct Count Sissinus to take due vengeance.

155

SISSINUS: Soldiers, where are those insolent girls who are to be tortured?
160
SOLDIERS: They are kept in prison.
SISSINUS: Leave Hirena there, / bring the others here. /
SOLDIERS: Why do you except the one?
SISSINUS: Sparing her youth. Perchance, she may be converted easier, if she is not intimidated by her sisters' presence. /
165
SOLDIERS: That makes sense. /

SOLDIERS: Here are the girls whose presence you requested.
170
SISSINUS: Agape and Chionia, give heed, / and to my council accede! /
AGAPE: We will not give heed. /
SISSINUS: Bring offerings to the gods.
AGAPE: We bring offerings of praise forever / to the true Father eternal, / and to His Son co-eternal, / and also to the Holy Spirit.
175
SISSINUS: This is not what I bid, / but on pain of penalty prohibit. /
AGAPE: You cannot prohibit it; neither shall we ever sacrifice to demons.
180
SISSINUS: Cease this hardness of heart, and make your offerings. But if you persist, / then I shall insist / that you be killed according to the Emperor's orders.
CHIONIA: It is only proper that you should obey the orders of your Emperor, whose decrees we disdain, as you know. For if you wait and try to spare us, then you could be rightfully killed.
185
SISSINUS: Soldiers, do not delay, / take these blaspheming girls away, / and throw them alive into the flames.
190
SOLDIERS: We shall instantly build the pyre you asked for, and we will cast these girls into the raging fire, and thus we'll put an end to these insults at last. /
AGAPE: O Lord, nothing is impossible for Thee; / even the fire forgets its nature and obeys Thee; / but we are weary of delay; / therefore, dissolve the earthly bonds that hold our souls, we pray, / so that as our earthly bodies die, / our souls may sing your praise in Heaven.
195
SOLDIERS: Oh, marvel, oh stupendous miracle! Behold their souls are no longer bound to their bodies, / yet no traces of injury can be found; neither their hair, nor their clothes are burnt by the fire, / and their bodies are not at all harmed by the pyre. /
200
SISSINUS: Bring forth Hirena.

SOLDIERS: Here she is.
205
SISSINUS: Hirena, tremble at the deaths of your sisters and fear to perish according to their example.

HIRENA: I hope to follow their example and expire, / so with them in Heaven eternal joy I may acquire. /
SISSINUS: Give in, give in to my persuasion. /
HIRENA: I will never yield to evil persuasion. /   210
SISSINUS: If you don't yield, I shall not give you a quick and easy death, but multiply your sufferings.
HIRENA: The more cruelly I'll be tortured, / the more gloriously I'll be exalted. /
SISSINUS: You fear no tortures, no pain? / What you   215
abhor, I shall ordain. /
HIRENA: Whatever punishment you design, / I will escape with help Divine. /
SISSINUS: To a brothel you will be consigned, / where   220
your body will be shamefully defiled. /
HIRENA: It is better that the body be dirtied with any stain than that the soul be polluted with idolatry.
SISSINUS: If you are so polluted in the company of harlots, you can no longer be counted among the virginal choir.   225
HIRENA: Lust deserves punishment, but forced compliance the crown. With neither is one considered guilty, / unless the soul consents freely. /
SISSINUS: In vain have I spared her, in vain have I pitied her youth.   230
SOLDIERS: We knew this before; / for on no possible score / can she be moved to adore our gods, nor can she be broken by terror.
SISSINUS: I shall spare her no longer. /
SOLDIERS: Rightly you ponder. /   235
SISSINUS: Seize her without mercy, / drag her with cruelty, / and take her in dishonor to the brothel. /
HIRENA: They will not do it. /
SISSINUS: Who can prohibit it? /
HIRENA: He whose foresight rules the world. /   240
SISSINUS: I shall see . . . /
HIRENA: Sooner than you wish, it will be. /
SISSINUS: Soldiers, be not afraid / of what this blaspheming girl has said. /
SOLDIERS: We are not afraid, / but eagerly follow what   245
you bade. /

SISSINUS: Who are those approaching? How similar they are to the men / to whom we gave Hirena just then. / They are the same. Why are you returning so fast? / Why so out of breath, I ask? /   250
SOLDIERS: You are the one for whom we look. /
SISSINUS: Where is she whom you just took? /
SOLDIERS: On the peak of the mountain.
SISSINUS: Which one?
SOLDIERS: The one close by.   255
SISSINUS: Oh you idiots, dull and blind. / You have completely lost your mind! /
SOLDIERS: Why do you accuse us, / why do you abuse us, / why do you threaten us with menacing voice and face?
SISSINUS: May the gods destroy you! /   260
SOLDIERS: What have we committed? What harm have we done? How have we transgressed against your orders?
SISSINUS: Have I not given the orders that you should take that rebel against the gods to a brothel?   265

SOLDIERS: Yes, so you did command, / and we were eager to fulfill your demand, / but two strangers intercepted us / saying that you sent them to us / to lead Hirena to the mountain's peak.

270 SISSINUS: That's new to me. /

SOLDIERS: We can see. /

SISSINUS: What were they like? /

SOLDIERS: Splendidly dressed and an awe-inspiring sight. /

275 SISSINUS: Did you follow? /

SOLDIERS: We did so. /

SISSINUS: What did they do? /

SOLDIERS: They placed themselves on Hirena's left and right, / and told us to be forthright / and not to hide

280 from you what happened.

SISSINUS: I see a sole recourse, / that I should mount my horse / and seek out those who so freely made sport with us.

SISSINUS: Hmm, I don't know what to do. I am bewil-

285 dered by the witchcraft of these Christians. I keep going around the mountain and keep finding this track / but I neither know how to proceed nor how to find my way back. /

SOLDIERS: We are all deluded by some intrigue; / we are afflicted with a great fatigue; / if you allow this 290 insane person to stay alive, / then neither you nor we shall survive. /

SISSINUS: Anyone among you, / I don't care which, string a bow, and shoot an arrow, and kill that witch! / 295

SOLDIERS: Rightly so. /

HIRENA: Wretched Sissinus, blush for shame, and proclaim your miserable defeat because without the help of weapons, you cannot overcome a tender little virgin as your foe. / 300

SISSINUS: Whatever the shame that may be mine, I will bear it more easily now because I know for certain that you will die.

HIRENA: This is the greatest joy I can conceive, / but for you this is a cause to grieve, / because you shall 305 be damned in Tartarus° for your cruelty, / while I shall receive the martyr's palm and the crown of virginity; / thus I will enter the heavenly bridal chamber of the Eternal King, to whom are all honor and glory in all eternity. / 310

306. **Tartarus:** Hell.

COMMENTARIES

Marla Carlson
READING HROTSVIT'S TORMENTED BODIES   *1998*

> *In this excerpt from an article that appeared in* Theatre Journal, *Marla Carlson reminds us in this brief treatment of* Dulcitius *that the question of physical beauty can be interpreted in several different ways. In the world of Hrosvitha, the pagan emphasis on the physical body must always be seen in relation to the Christian emphasis on the soul. Carlson sees a gender connection between the two.*

In *The Martyrdom of the Holy Virgins Agape, Chionia, and Hirena*, beauty is a transparent sign of virtue. The play (also known as *Dulcitius*) begins with an ironic contrast: the pagan Emperor Diocletian manifests the rage and madness he attributes to the virgins, while they remain impassive. The girls' bodies function as foci of desire but are themselves free from desire. By contrast, the non-Christian men are represented as desiring subjects, which also means they are *subject* to their bodies. Diocletian wants to direct the disposal of the girls in marriage. Governor Dulcitius wants to use and possess them himself, and his desire produces his downfall. After he is blackened in the kitchen by making love to the pots and pans he mistakes for the virgins, Agape observes that now Dulcitius's body corresponds to his mind. On the other side of the balance, although the physical beauty of the girls is a visible manifestation of their virtue, pagan interpreters misread it as a sign of commodity exchange value, beginning with Diocletian's demand that the girls bring offerings to the Roman gods *in order* to be married well (the last thing they'd want!). But while the signs can be misread, Christian virtue cannot be *degraded*. When Dulcitius orders Agape, Chionia, and Hirena stripped for display, their clothes magically adhere to their bodies and cannot be removed. Hirena is threatened with sexual degradation in a brothel and retorts: "Lust deserves punishment, but forced compliance the crown; neither is one considered guilty, / unless the soul consents freely." All the same, God prevents her body from being defiled, and although Agape and Chionia are thrown into a fire and their souls depart at once, their physical bodies remain unharmed. Death is not a sign of pagan power but of God's grace, and at the final Resurrection, the martyr's beautiful body will again serve as the proper sign of the pure soul. In this play, the body — and in particular, its sexual properties — focuses the conflict between Christian female and pagan male.

Sue-Ellen Case (b. 1942)
RE-VIEWING HROTSVIT   *1983*

Sue-Ellen Case not only examines the plays of Hrosvitha but actually produced them. She discusses the feminist issues in the plays and explains the symmetry between Hrosvitha's six plays and the six plays of Terence. She demonstrates the significance of the plays of Hrosvitha for a modern audience.

The Plays

Hrotsvit wrote six plays in response to the six plays of Terence. Her project was to change the roles for women on the stage from negative ones to positive ones. However, critics have traditionally ignored this feminist aspect of her project and concentrated on the Christian context for it. A. Daniel Frankforter, in his article "Sexism and the Search for Thematic Structure of the Plays of Hroswitha of Gandersheim," characterizes the critics' misapprehension of Hrotsvit as stemming from "an asexual (male) perspective" which regards Hrotsvit as "a monk of generation" whose "sex is assumed to have little or no significance . . . her choice of women as chief characters is not seen as crucial to interpretation," and therefore "she emerges as a minor eulogist of ordinary Christian heroes."[1] Frankforter opposes this sexist perspective and finds that if Hrotsvit's project is seen as a revision of the roles for women "what emerges from the six plays . . . is a systematic exploration of each of the opportunities for female integrity possible in the social roles permitted women in Hroswitha's world."[2]

A brief description of roles of women in three of Terence's plays elicits some of the basic roles and attendant social issues Hrotsvit revised. *The Girl from Andros* never appears onstage, though her offstage screams during labor are used for comic development of the plot. Only two women appear onstage: a "sloppy drunken

---

[1]A. Daniel Frankforter, "Sexism and the Search for Thematic Structure of the Plays of Hroswitha of Gandersheim," *International Journal of Women's Studies,* vol. 2, no. 3, p. 225.

[2]Frankforter, p. 226.

slut" who is a midwife from Lesbos and a slave girl who is frightened and manipulated by her witty male counterpart, the slave Davus.[3] This Imperial Comedy centers on the relationship between father and son in which women are assets (ingenues from good families) or liabilities (mercenary courtesans) in the son's economy of obedience to his father and the patriarchal social order. *The Self Tormentor* uses the traditional double plot, centering on two father/son relationships. The double plot engineers male rivalry for the possession of women, completing the portrait of patriarchal economy. Luce Irigaray, a pioneer in feminist theories of morphology, described women's position within this economy: "woman is traditionally use-value for man, exchange value among men. Merchandise, then . . . she is never anything more than the scene of more or less rival exchange between two men."[4] In this play, an interesting piece of women's social history emerges to push the plot to its happy ending. One of the fathers had ordered his wife to kill their baby if it were a girl. The wife did not obey (an act perceived as cowardice and infidelity), and now the girl can be used as marriage material to solve the rivalry between the two sons and reconcile them both with their father's wishes.

The Eunuch was Terence's most popular play in Rome. The central issue in the play is one central to several plays by Hrotsvit — rape. A young man sees a girl cross the marketplace (an apt setting) and falls in love with her because of her beauty. In order to gain entrance to her house, he disguises himself as a eunuch and rapes her. The girl's response is never staged, but it is reported that she sits in torn garments and weeps. Nevertheless, because of his love for her, the young man's crime is forgiven, and he gains the girl in marriage. From these three plays, one can summarize the Classical inheritance Hrotsvit received for women on the stage: they are relatively invisible, their responses are rarely dramatized and most often reported by men, they are manipulated as use value among men in the plot situation, and their best possible ending is marriage — with or without consent.

The most striking difference between the plays of Hrotsvit and those of Terence is that in her plays women are at the center of the action and it is their response to male aggression which determines the development of the plot. Hrotsvit places her heroines in the context of objectification, use, and violence but offers them an alternative. The play *Dulcitius* opens with three young women before the Emperor Diocletian and his soldiers. Diocletian declares the patriarchal edict: "The pure and famous race to which you belong and your own rare beauty make it fitting that you should be wedded to the highest in the court." Beauty and high station are the trap of objectification. In spite of the rank and military power which confronts these young girls, they resist, answering that they have vowed to live in chastity. Angered, the emperor sends them to prison and to the charge of Governor Dulcitius. Dulcitius wants them because of their beauty, but the guards tell him they will resist seduction. He responds "Then I shall woo in another fashion — with torture!" The latent relationship in such a patriarchal society between desire and dominance becomes literal. The stage setting reveals the passive position of the women as prisoners and sets up the alliance between desire and privilege in the role of the Governor. However, the internal power of the women's wishes overcomes

---

[3]Constance Carrier and Douglass Parker, *The Complete Comedies of Terence* (New Brunswick: Rutgers University Press, 1974), p. 21.

[4]Luce Irigaray, "This Sex Which Is Not One," in *New French Feminisms* (New York: Schocken Books, 1981), p. 105.

this material one. A spell overcomes Dulcitius as he enters to rape them, and he makes love to pots and pans, thinking they are the women. Hrotsvit has given a stage metaphor to the objectification of women, as objects are substituted for women, particularly objects associated with their domestic labor. The women watch Dulcitius and giggle. In their laughter and his foolishness as a result of their spell-binding power, the women dominate the rapist. The male dramatic perspective has been reversed.

The play *Callimachus* also centers on rape. In the opening scenes, Callimachus tells Drusiana he loves her because of her beauty. Her response is one of incomprehension: "My beauty? What is my beauty to you?" From a woman's point of view, this is a deep, provocative question, but Callimachus answers it in terms of patriarchal economy: "But little now . . . I hope it might be much before long." Drusiana persists in her refusal, telling Callimachus that even though she is married, she has taken the vow of chastity. He responds that he will use all of his skill and strength to trap her — the motor of Classical plots. Instead, Drusiana asks Christ to help her to die, so she may escape her dilemma. Christ complies with her wish immediately. Women have the power to petition and to succeed. Undaunted by her death, Callimachus enters her tomb to rape the corpse. Hrotsvit has dramatized the essence of the passive victim and of the objectification of patriarchal desire. Unlike Terence, who ultimately resolves it as natural, she has staged it as perverse. Callimachus is killed by a heavenly serpent before he can complete the act (nature is on the side of the heroine) and is later resurrected (along with Drusiana) and converted to her world view. In other words, the plot moves in her direction and is moved by her resolve.

The alternative to patriarchal possession is characterized by Hrotsvit as the vow of chastity. Later periods have regarded this vow as ultimate repression rather than as a declaration of independence. Yet Hrotsvit's solution answers a question posed by Irigaray "What if the goods refuse to go to market? What if they maintained among themselves another kind of trade?"[5] Chastity was the choice available to women to remain outside the patriarchal order of desire. In the case of a nun such as Hrotsvit, the removal into a women's community (perhaps the first separatist collectives) brought the opportunity to be educated and to be an educator. Hrotsvit was what Frankforter calls a "career nun."[6] Given her collective context, Hrotsvit may have been the first woman playwright to write for a community of women. Thus, in writing from a woman's point of view for women to watch, she is involved in an entirely new dramatic dynamic. Yet her identity as a nun has traditionally been cited as the cause of elements of suppression rather than liberation in her works. The patriarchal bias of Freudian analysis perceived her profession as oppression. Rosamond Gilder formulated the case simply: "Hrotsvit gives expression to a vein of sadism which is also associated with certain acts of repression." Gilder elaborates on the psychological mechanism: "Hrotsvit obtained a certain release for her emotional suppressions by elaborating these pictures of carnal dangers and the pitfalls of the flesh."[7] Such a Freudian analysis assigns the responsibility for the victimization of women in the plays to Hrotsvit's repressed sexuality and its resultant fantasies rather than to the patriarchal society in which her characters

[5]Irigaray, p. 110.
[6]Frankforter, p. 226.
[7]Rosamond Gilder, *Enter the Actress* (London: Harrap and Co., 1931), pp. 34–35.

were situated. Perhaps the easiest refutation of such an assertion lies in the fact that Hrotsvit did not invent her own plots. Instead, she worked from materials which were considered historical in her time. For example, the martyrdom and rape of the young women in *Dulcitius* was taken from *The Acts of Christian Martyrs*. The story was recorded in the fourth century, based on historical edicts of Diocletian and records of the trial and punishment of the women. Hrotsvit's project was to dramatize the violence against women recorded in these histories and was in no way to record her own fantasies.

Feminine Morphology and Paphnutius

Since this essay is meant to be merely an exploration of the application of feminist critical technique to the work and role of Hrotsvit, this section will illustrate the application of only one feminist theory of form to a single play — *Paphnutius*. The theory is derived from essays by Irigaray, Hélène Cixous (whose work "The Laugh of the Medusa" is now a classic in feminist studies), and Jane Gallop's book on feminism and psychoanalysis.[8] The source of their ideas lies in a feminist reading of the works of Derrida, Lacan, and Foucault. The basic assumption of these authors is that the dominant cultural form is phallocentrism. This means two things: that the dominant form is organized around a concept of centrality and that the phallus is at the center of all dominant morphology. Because of its centric location, the phallus determines a form based upon phallic privilege, phallic exhibition, and a phallic desire to possess. Therefore, the phallocentric form is both clear (exhibited, as in linear, logical development) and closed (self-possessed — as in beginning, middle, and end).

The alternative form found in women's work is described as contiguous. Irigaray describes it as a "nearness," a form "constantly in the process of weaving itself . . . embracing words and yet casting them off," concerned not with clarity, but with what is "touched upon" (p. 103). Cixous calls it "working the in-between" (p. 254), while Gallop describes it as "the register of touching, nearness, presence, immediacy, contact" (p. 30). It can be elliptical rather than illustrative, fragmentary rather than whole, ambiguous rather than clear, and interrupted rather than complete. The stage society within such a form could never be the plain patriarchy of Terence, with its clear line of power from father to son. Rather, it is a complex society of subtle dependencies which manifest themselves in resonances of one another's changes.

This sense of contiguity is the organizing principle, as well as the subject of the opening scene of the play *Paphnutius*. The play opens on the sadness of Father Paphnutius. When asked by his disciples about its cause, he launches into a medieval discourse on the world as harmonic, proceeding from an explanation of the quadrivium, through a Boethian discussion of music to the organizing principle of concord and discord. The organization of all things is contiguous. Paphnutius describes its residence in "not only, as I have told you, in the combination of body and soul, and in the utterance of the voice, now high, now low, but even in the pulsation of the veins and in the proportion of our members." As the scene proceeds, the disciples ask Paphnutius about his sadness. He replies that it is because of the

---

[8]Hélène Cixous, "The Laugh of the Medusa," in Irigaray, *New French Feminisms;* and Jane Gallop, *The Daughter's Seduction: Feminism and Psychoanalysis* (Ithaca: Cornell University Press, 1982).

whore Thais. The rest of the play is concerned with his work to change her relationship to her own sexuality, her residency in a convent in which she practices self-mortification, and Paphnutius's concluding vision of her transfiguration.

The "contempt with which the learned musical Prologue was regarded for over half a century" originated in an assessment of the Scholastic discourse as mediocre medieval philosophy.[9] The "modern disparagement of the Prologue" rests on the perception that it does not work in the overall construction of the drama.[10] There seems to be no connection between the ideas of music and nature, and the sadness in Paphnutius caused by the whore Thais. The ideas in the prologue seem to be abandoned as the story of Thais unfolds. Yet if one replaces the phallocentric model of form with one of contiguity, the play seems to be tightly constructed. Hrotsvit has begun her play with an exposition of the contiguous dependency among parts of the world. A monk in a distant monastery, who has never seen the whore Thais, can find no peace until the concord between her understanding and her sexuality is restored. The inner dynamics of Thais's personality "touches upon" the surrounding world in which she lives. Paphnutius can find no peace until he has removed this woman from the colonized use of her body in the city to her own repossession of it within a convent. Hrotsvit has merely used the most basic ideas in Scholastic discourse to set up her dramatic situation — to provide the intellectual environment for the personal story. Hrotsvit makes no linear transition from the opening scene to the story because her world is contiguous. Her short scenes suggest rather than explicate, "touch upon" each other rather than develop. In this play, she has replaced the objectified, patriarchal intercourse between men and women which she dramatizes in her Roman settings, with the contiguous resonances of sexual concord which exist between Thais and Paphnutius. When the play is approached from a feminist, rather than phallocentric model of form, it seems a masterpiece rather than a mediocre medieval morality story.

Performance

Hrotsvit's plays were not collected for circulation until the sixteenth century. They were not translated into modern Romance languages until the mid-nineteenth century and not into English until the twentieth century. The relative unavailability of her texts made production before the twentieth century improbable. Yet in the twentieth century, it is important to note that productions of her plays were often by women or in times in which women's issues were important to the theater world. A good example of the latter condition is the production history of Hrotsvit's work in London. The first major production of *Paphnutius* was directed by Edith Craig (daughter of Ellen Terry and sister of Gordon) in London in 1914. The production was by the Pioneer Players, a group founded and directed by Edith Craig, with Ellen Terry playing the role of the abbess in the convent in which Thais was confined. The translation was done by Christopher St. John, a *nom de plume* (indicative practice) for Christabel Marshall. Marshall had recently adapted the suffragette play *How the Vote Was Won* in 1909 and the play *The First Actress* in 1911 — an indication that her interest in the text of Hrotsvit probably came from an interest in a woman playwright. Indeed, there was a movement in London

[9]David Chamberlain, "Musical Learning and Dramatic Action in Hrotsvit's *Pafnutius*," *Studies in Philology*. Fall 1980, p. 319.
[10]Ibid.

theater at that time to be concerned with women's issues — particularly the vote. In 1908, actresses had formed a franchise league to support the suffrage movement, which produced plays about the vote and satires of male chauvinism.[11] The English women did not get the vote until 1928, and the decade of the 1920s was filled with the issue. Within this context, the 1920 production of *Callimachus* at the Art Theatre, the 1924 production of *Paphnutius* at the Maddermarket Theatre, the founding of the Roswitha club in 1926, the new translations by St. John, Waley and Tillyard during the decade, and the cessation of Hrotsvit productions after that decade can be easily understood.

My production of her works in 1982 came as a result of teaching a class on women and theater and becoming familiar with all of the new productions and critical studies evolving from the works of women playwrights and women's theater groups. The first problem in producing Hrotsvit is the obscurity of her name and play titles. The second is the short playing time of her texts. I decided to solve both problems by directing three plays in one evening and creating a title which might attract the Seattle women's community by identifying the plays according to the social roles of their three heroines: "The Virgin (*Dulcitius*), The Whore (*Paphnutius*), and The Desperate One" (*Callimachus*). My choice of production concept was determined by my goal of producing the first woman playwright. In order to emphasize her historical role, I decided to direct the play as a period piece. This introduces another set of difficulties, since the theater has no tradition of staging plays from the early Middle Ages and hence no concept of costumes, sets, or playing style. We took the costumes from mosaics and illuminations around the period and decided on flats, imitating the two-dimensional painting style of the time, with edifices found in Ottonian manuscript illuminations. The playing style was a combination of a classical sense of formal blocking and gestures, combined with intense, personal purpose. A projection screen rose from the back of a steeply raked stage and a processional ramp ran from the front of the stage through the center of the audience. This combination created the feeling of the space in a cathedral. The elevated ramp gave the Saints elevation and dominance. Between the plays, early medieval music was performed. All this allowed a style to emerge which was both an imitation of classical formality and liturgical ceremony.

The context of Christianity and its trappings often created an audience response which was marked in its silent reverence. People seemed afraid to wiggle or whisper. At other times, this same sense turned into an active irreverence, manifested by laughter and something close to jeering. Contemporary staging of a Christian play is complicated to understand. Shakespeare productions have prepared an audience for the Elizabethan world of superstition, and Greek plays have prepared them for the world of pagan mythology, but the relative absence of medieval productions leaves the world of medieval Christianity to be understood by personal opinions about Christianity rather than the sense of it as a historical world view. Thus, for some feminists, the Christianity was seen as offensive and patriarchal. Particularly in these times of the Moral Majority, Hrotsvit's plays seemed to them to be written by an "Uncle Tom" trapped by male values. Many audience members laughed hysterically at the miracles, the voice of God, and the resurrections — seeing them not as stage conventions but as bygone beliefs. Christopher St. John records a similar

[11]Michelene Wandor, *Understudies: Theatre and Sexual Politics* (London: Eyre Methuen, 1981), p. 10.

reaction to the plays in their early London productions, citing a scene in *Calli-machus* "Drusiana's prayer that she might die rather than yield to Callimachus was greeted with shouts of laughter" (p. 159). I think the only solution to this problem lies not in the staging concept of such scenes, but in establishing a familiarity with the playwright and her conventions through productions and an acquaintance with her texts in theater history and criticism classes.

For the actors, this problem translates into ways for them to individually under-stand the dilemma of their characters. The women identified instances of martyr-dom and conviction which meant something to them. These ranged from pictures of concentration camp women, which some of the Jewish women brought to rehearsal, to stories of guerrillas in El Salvador or instances of rape victims who resisted. They did not focus so much on religious experiences, as on sexual ones, political ones, or psychological approaches to their own fears and strengths. The men in the cast resisted identifying with the male aggression and cruelty portrayed by many of the characters. When asked to torment one of the young virgins in a flirtatious manner, they insisted they didn't know how. This identification came slowly, through memories of teasing girls in grade school, to early experiences of seduction and sexual aggression. For the men playing Saints, the problem was in giving focus to the women onstage and learning how to respond to the power of the women in a realistic fashion. This involved investigating their own fears of women's power.

For the actors, one of the most difficult aspects of Hrotsvit's work was her con-tiguous sense of form and her compressed, almost fragmentary sense of a scene. Characters have extremely short speeches of only one or two sentences, com-pressed into scenes of relatively scant dialogue and often no physical action. Fortu-nately, recent productions of plays by such authors as Beckett and Kroetz provided the actors with some experience in this style. The method which seemed most use-ful was to play the entire scene by improvising a long, literal development of its sit-uation and then compress it moment by moment until it played in Hrotsvit's form. One fortunate consequence of this playing style is that the concentration and delib-eration required by the actor, made him or her oblivious to the sometimes raucous audience response.

Finally, the response of the critics illustrated an interesting aspect of viewing the plays. Almost all announcements and reviews of the plays included the words "rape" and "necrophilia" in their titles. One critic pointed out that these plays should make contemporary audiences feel less defensive about violence on TV, since it was already popular in the early Middle Ages. The titles are surprising, since neither the rapes nor the necrophilia ever occur. They are the intentions of the male characters but are foiled by heavenly intervention. The preoccupation by crit-ics with these intentions might suggest that they were watching the male characters more than the females, even though it was not the focus of the text nor of the blocking. In fact, given the staging of resurrections and other such miracles, these dramatic intentions seemed minor parts of the staging. Yet they were the focus of critical reviews. This critical reception points out the necessity for a re-viewing of Hrotsvit from a feminist point of view and underlines the sense that her position and its implications in the world of theater is still long overdue.

Zeami Motokiyo

Zeami Motokiyo (1363–1443) is the genius of Nō drama. His father, Kan'ami (1333–1384), an actor centered near the then-capital of Japan, Kyoto, took a popular form of theater known as sarugaku and began to mold it into something more stylish and more demanding. *Sarugaku* has no English equivalent. This form of drama involved some of the ingredients of contemporary Nō, such as music and movement as well as text. Zeami grew up in a theatrical setting and trained with his father. His life changed completely when Kan'ami was invited to stage a performance of his newly developed sarugaku Nō drama for the ruler of Japan, Yoshimitsu (1358–1408), the hereditary shogun (or leader), in 1374.

Yoshimitsu was then sixteen and Zeami eleven. Yoshimitsu saw Zeami perform in a minor role and insisted that Zeami leave his father and become part of the court. Reportedly Yoshimitsu fell in love with Zeami and they were lovers until Yoshimitsu died. Now that he was part of the shogun's court, Zeami was given a brilliant education and the opportunity to continue his work in drama.

He continued to develop the ideas Kan'ami had begun to put on the stage and is credited with having created what we now think of as the classic form of Nō drama. He shaped the drama into the familiar sections of dance, music, and dialogue, and he created roles that depended less on the actor's ability to represent a character than his ability to connect emotionally with the audience. Zeami described the perfection of an actor's performance in metaphoric terms as "hana," a flower whose beauty is perfect and immediately apparent. As Jin'ichi Konishi has described it: "In Zeami's sense the Flower is an effect resulting from an excellent performance. When the audience is caught up in the actor's performance, we can say that there is Flower. Thus the Flower is everything for the actor, because if he has failed to create it his audience will sooner or later desert him."[1]

Because Zeami's patron was the most powerful figure in Japan, he was able to maintain a theatrical troupe of his own and train his actors as he saw fit. He wrote several treatises on acting, including *Sarugaku dangi,* or *Talks on Sarugaku,* which is read today in several languages.

As the favored figure of the shogun, Zeami was able to address a highly sophisticated audience and demand their keen attention. His work achieves a depth and subtlety that a rural audience might not have appreciated. In English, and with only the text itself to contemplate, we cannot appreciate the full experience of seeing Nō drama. Gesture, silence, movement, and dance, as well as the complexities of music, all combine to make this rich and emotionally moving.

[1]Quoted in Benito Ortolani, *The Japanese Theatre*, rev. ed. (Princeton: Princeton University Press, 1990), p. 122.

One of the principles of Zeami's innovations in Nō is restraint. Gestures are minimal and movements are precise and ritualized to accommodate the roles of the primary characters. Each Nō drama has a set of characters that are easily recognizable by the audience. The *shite* is the primary character, the hero, sometimes described as the "doer." The *tsure* is the companion to the main character, while the *waki* is a character who witnesses the action, sometimes a person connected with the *tsure*. The *wakizure* are associates of the *tsure* and often have little or nothing to say in the drama. The *ai* character sometimes describes the opening situation of the drama or comments extensively between dramatic sections, while the *shite* character changes costumes. Often this character speaks in a dull monotone in order not to distract from the work of the *shite*.

The music of flute and various drums is significant to the drama's action and can be very complex. Likewise, the dance segments of Nō are usually extensive and occasionally interrupt a dialogue in ways that may seem inappropriate or unexpected. The following text cannot adequately represent how these dramas were performed because the dances can be as long as twenty minutes or more. Today performances of Nō dramas are often two hours or so in length, although they were perhaps half that length in medieval times.

Much of the text of Nō drama is sung to music, or *uta*. Stage directions, such as *ageuta* and *sageuta*, point to different kinds of music appropriate to a particular section of the drama. Some text is sung, whereas other sections of text are chanted, a technique that has an extensive history in Japanese theater. These techniques are obviously designed to elevate the text and the action rather than to have it imitate daily life or speech. Nō is formalized and removed from immediate life, although one of Zeami's aesthetic principles, *monomane*, insists on an actor's learning to imitate important aspects of the figures he represents. However, as Ezra Pound explains, "In the Noh we find an art built on the god-dance, or upon some local legend of spiritual apparition, or, later, on gestes of war and feats of acting that is not mimetic."[2]

One of the interesting issues in confronting Nō is that it exists primarily in terms of performance rather than as a written text. The study of Nō as literature is a relatively recent development in Japan, and the translation of the texts of Nō drama into English and other languages has occurred mostly since 1960. Fortunately, Zeami's dramas are rich in literary value and well worth reading carefully.

Today five schools of Nō drama derive from important *shite* actors who have stamped them with their style. In addition five categories of Nō drama encompass all 240 plays in the current repertory (out of the existing two or three thousand). The categories are *waki-no*, plays about the gods; *shura-mono*, plays usually about a ghost samurai warrior; *kazura-mono*, woman plays; *yonbamme-mono*, plays about madness, current events, ghosts, and other subjects; and *kiri nō*, or final plays, usually about demons, monsters, and other nonhuman phantasms. Often a performance of Nō will include plays from all five categories in that order.

---

[2]Ezra Pound and Ernest Fenollosa, *The Classic Noh Theatre of Japan* (New York: New Directions, 1959), p. 4.

Zeami experienced some setbacks late in life. In 1429, he and his most gifted son, Motomasa, were driven from the palace of shogun Yoshinori (1394–1441), thus preventing their involvement in important performances. Motomasa died in 1432. After one of his other sons left the theater to become a Buddhist monk, Zeami was exiled in 1434 to the Sado islands for two years. He eventually returned to Kyoto shortly before he died. His legacy as a playwright and actor was left to a son-in-law, Komparu Zenchiku (1405–c. 1470), a fine dramatic actor and author of some surviving Nō dramas.

LADY HAN (HANJO)

The primary character, or *shite*, in *Lady Han* (c. 1400–1420) is Hanago, a courtesan, or prostitute, in the brothel at the post-station in Nogami, a town on the route to the capital, Kyoto, "far along the highway to the East / where seas have overwhelmed the pine-clad hills / in reproach to one who went away / and never came again." She is referred to as Lady Han in a tone of derision because her situation resembles that of a legendary figure, Han Shōyo, a concubine of a Han dynasty emperor who was cast aside and who pined for her love. The story of Hanago resembles many tales of abandoned love and the longing for a missing lover.

The metaphor of the pine tree, connected to the act of pining for a lover, is intentional and typical of Nō drama. The stage setting for the play features at least one, and usually three, pine trees. Zeami uses them for their emotional value as well as for their appearance. In addition, the metaphor for the moon — both its feminine associations and its associations with lunacy and change — appears in the fans that Hanago and her lover, Captain Yoshida, keep as mementos of each other (as moonflowers on Hanago's fan and as the moon itself on Yoshida's). Because of its connection with madness, this play is in the fourth category of Nō dramas, *yonbamme-mono*. When the Madam chastises Hanago for "mooning over that fan again," Zeami plays on the relationship of fan to moon and to madness and distraction in a manner that is typical of his work.

The story is simple but apparently representative of many such stories connected with the courtesans of the period. It was not uncommon for a traveling man to engage the services of a courtesan and then to fall in love with her. In this play both Hanago and Yoshida wish to connect again but are confounded by circumstances that keep them apart until the end of the drama.

We are introduced primarily to the pain that Hanago suffers. Her suffering is central to the play and to Zeami's concerns because the piece is a study in suffering and therefore a deep examination of human emotion. The fans are the key to discovery; the play ends with Yoshida demanding to see the fan of "that mad girl." When he sees it and she sees his fan, they are reunited, but the resolution of the action is still uncertain.

The general examination of love is also important in the play. Hanago is a courtesan and serves the Madam's wishes, but she reserves for herself the emotion of love, which is not shared with her customers. As a result, she feels bereft when she thinks of Yoshida and his promise to return. She wishes she could avoid loving altogether when she says, "The faithless man! O he is hateful, hateful! / simply pray and let a sacred stream / cleanse you, till you love no more." She continues: "The human heart / truly is a shallow, turbid pool; / and if we, impure, entreat the Gods, / it is no wonder they reject us!"

When the Gentleman asks Hanago to "rave and entertain us," he reveals an attitude that was common enough, confusing the role of the courtesan as entertainer with the madness of the love-lorn woman. Clearly he has little sympathy for her feelings and treats her madness as amusing rather than as pathetic.

The dialogue of the play is primarily in verse. Some of the lines are borrowed from — or resemble closely — the classic poetry known to much of the audience. The question of originality in Nō drama was never a significant issue. It has been said that Nō is a "drama of allusion," and the audience was sophisticated enough to catch the allusions to past literature and history. The poetry of *Lady Han* is rich in metaphor, such as "the moon of truth," "the jewel of love," and the complex interplay of the moon and the fans, all of which intensify and elevate the audience's experience of the drama.

Figure 6. Plan of the Nō stage.

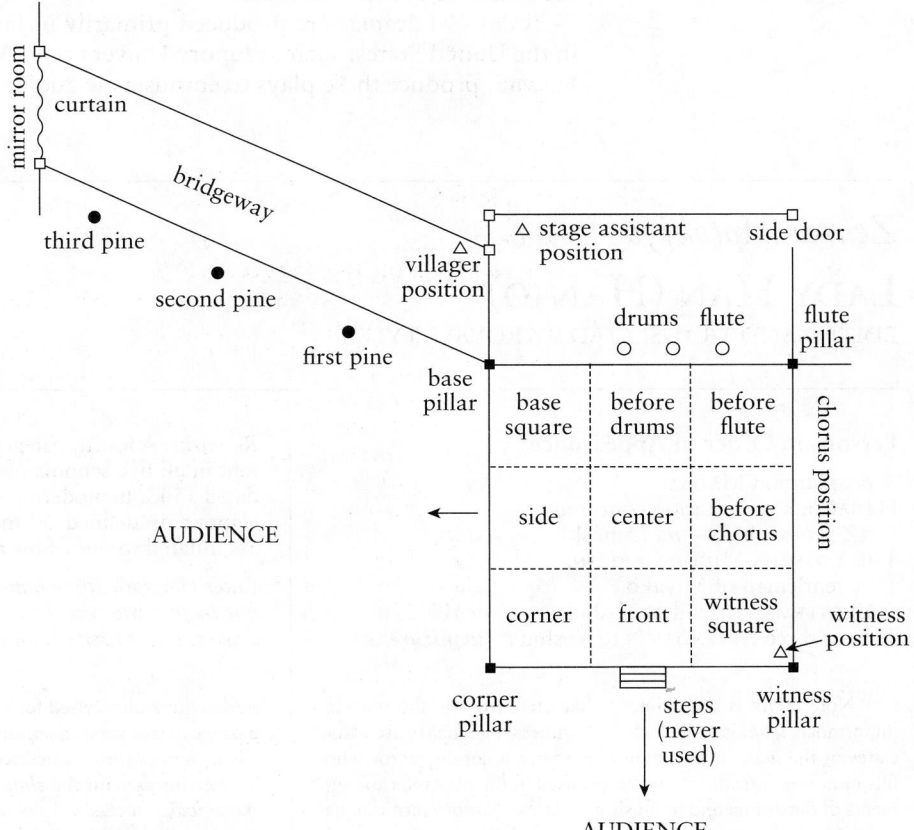

Lady Han in Performance

Lady Han, like all Nō dramas, was performed on a stage that was covered with a roof — even when performed indoors. The diagram in Figure 6 shows the basic plan of the Nō stage. The audience sits before the primary structure, a flat platform with a pitched roof resembling a house. The bridgeway provides the entrance and exit for the actors. The pine trees are traditional and spaced as indicated. The stage directions usually tell actors where to stand in relation to the musical instruments and the nine segments of the stage proper. The "villager position" is usually reserved for the *ai* character (the Madam in this play), who either introduces the action or comments during the interval when the main character is offstage.

Dance is powerfully expressive in *Lady Han*. At one point, early in the play, Hanago performs a *kakeri* tour of the stage. *Kakeri* is a dance performed to hand drum and flute and traditionally represents the pain and suffering of a mad woman. The medieval audience understood the significance of this dance and responded to it appropriately. Later Hanago does a *Jo-no-mai* dance, which is slow, long, and usually performed in three sections. This quiet dance helps us understand Hanago's inner world.

All the actors in Nō are male, including the female characters. The actors wear masks, but they do not attempt to present themselves as especially feminine. The effort at gender illusion was not part of the Nō tradition. Today some women act in Nō dramas, but most are amateurs. Very few professional Nō actresses perform in Japan.

Today Nō dramas are produced primarily in Japan, but several universities in the United States, such as Emory University in Atlanta and the University of Hawaii, produce these plays to enthusiastic audiences.

Zeami Motokiyo (1363–1443)

LADY HAN (HANJO)

EDITED AND TRANSLATED BY ROYALL TYLER

c. 1400–1420

Persons in Order of Appearance*

A post-station MADAM	*ai*
HANAGO, a post-station courtesan (*Zō-anna* or *Ko-omote* mask)	*shite*
THE YOSHIDA MINOR CAPTAIN, a gentleman of Miyako	*tsure*
A GENTLEMAN, friend of Yoshida	*waki*
Two or three ATTENDANTS to Yoshida	*wakizure*

*Note: *Shite* is the primary character; *tsure* is the next in importance; *waki* is a sidekick, or "witness"; *wakizure* are associates of the *waki*; *ai* is a minor character, a commentator who fills in during intervals. Some terms used in the play refer to segments of the drama and to music and dance. *Nanori:* introducing oneself; *sageuta,* verse sung in a low register; *ageuta,* verse sung in a high register; *ashirai,* music to accompany the primary actor;

Remarks: A fourth-category (*yonbamme-mono*) play current in all five schools of Nō. The text translated here is dated 1543. In modern performances, the Yoshida Minor Captain is defined as the *waki* and the Gentleman is assimilated to one of his attendants, the *wakizure*.

Enter Hanago, fan in hand — the standard fan of Nō, and not in fact the one described in the play. She sits before drums. Enter then Madam, to stand in base square.

shidai, quiet music used for an entrance; *mondō,* dialogue; *sashi,* passage in free verse; *issei,* song in a high register; *uta,* song, usually in verse; *kuri,* chanted song in the highest tone; *kuse,* a song by the chorus with the *shite* usually sitting in the center of the stage; *waka,* a classical poem; *noriji,* passage sung with a drum struck with a stick, indicating elevated emotion; *rongi,* rhythmic song by chorus at a critical moment for the *shite.*

MADAM: (*nanori*) You have before you the madam of the inn at Nogami in the province of Mino. One among the many girls in my service, Hanago, has been with me ever since she was small. This Hanago
5　is forever toying with her fan, which has a special meaning for her, and that is why everyone calls her Lady Han. This spring, you see, a gentleman known as the Yoshida Minor Captain spent the night here, on his way down from Miyako towards the East. It
10　was Hanago I had entertain him, and he exchanged fans with her before continuing on his way. Ever since, she has done nothing but stare at his fan. It is no use my telling her to go and entertain a guest: she will not do it. She just stays in her room. Guests are
15　constantly accusing me of providing poor service. That is why I am now going to have Hanago clear out.

Madam steps towards Hanago. (In modern performances, Madam goes to first pine and calls to Hanago, who is not yet on stage.)

(*mondō*) So Hanago, there you are! Time and again lately I have had to speak to you, yet you never listen to a word I say. I have had enough. I will not have
20　you stay in this room a moment longer. Clear out now and go wherever you please. [*Notices Hanago's fan.*] Oh, you make me so angry! Look at you, mooning over that fan again! The very sight of it drives me to distraction! [*Snatches the fan and throws it down.*]
25　Now, clear out, do you hear? Clear out! Clear out!

Exit Madam. Hanago picks up the fan and weeps.

HANAGO: (*kudoki*) O the world does play us false,
　　　　and always will; yet many sorrows
　　　　break her days' swift flow — she whom fate
　　　　bends to be a woman of the stream.[1]
30　(*sageuta*) Now I go wandering,
　　　　knowing nothing of what lies ahead;
　　　　robe wet with weeping,　　　　*Weeps.*
　　(*ageuta*) Nogami I abandon and set
　　　　　　forth　　　　　　　*Slowly rises.*
　　　　Nogami I abandon and set forth
35　　　　along the Ōmi Road[2] — to him, perhaps,
　　　　that cruel man — for since he left,
　　　　dew forever lingers on my sleeves.
　　　　O that I might vanish with my
　　　　　　grief!　　　　　　　*Weeps.*
　　　　O that I might vanish with my grief!

　　　　　　To ashirai music, exit Hanago.
Enter Gentleman, who sits before chorus.
　To shidai music, enter Yoshida and Attendants; they stand along the side of stage. (In modern performances, Gentleman does not appear, his part being taken by an Attendant.)

YOSHIDA and ATTENDANTS:
　(*shidai*) Sad is our farewell to towering Fuji[3]　　40
　　　　sad is our farewell to towering Fuji,
　　　　whose snows we shall praise in Miyako!
YOSHIDA: (*nanori*) I whom you see before you now am the Yoshida Minor Captain. You must know that last spring I travelled down to the East, and that with　45 autumn now so soon upon us, I am making my way back up to Miyako.
YOSHIDA and ATTENDANTS:
　(*ageuta*) Forth from Miyako
　　　　we sallied as the spring mists rose
　　　　we sallied as the spring mists rose,　　　　50
　　　　lingered a while, and now the fall winds
　　　　　　blow,
　　　　sweeping through the gate at Shirakawa,[4]
　　　　whence, in travel wear, we start for home.
　　　　By shore and mountain, on to Mino
　　　　　　province
　　　　we have come, and to the village of Nogami　55
　　　　we have come, and to the village of Nogami.
YOSHIDA: (*mondō*) Are you there, my man? [*An Attendant goes down on one knee.*] Having come so swiftly, we have already reached the inn at Nogami in Mino province. This is where I pledged my love to a young　60 woman whom people quickly dubbed Lady Han. Please go and find out whether she is still here.
ATTENDANT: Sir, I have inquired about Lady Han. It appears that she and the madam had a falling-out, and I am sorry to report that she has left.　　　　65
YOSHIDA: I see. Then perhaps I made too much of what passed between her and me. None the less, make sure that word reaches me in Miyako if Lady Han ever returns.
　(*tsukizerifu*) Having travelled so swiftly, we are al-　70 ready here in Miyako. A certain matter preoccupies me greatly. I will therefore go straight to Tadasu,[5] to pray. All of you, follow me, please!

Yoshida sits on a stool at witness position, while Attendants sit directly on the stage nearby. To issei music, enter Hanago. Her right shoulder is bared to the under-robe and she carries a spray of dwarf bamboo (sasa) stems: these are signs that she is mad. She stops at first pine.

HANAGO: (*sashi*) Where snow is gone,
　　　　the new shoots, love,　　　　　　　75
　　　　upon Kasuga meadow,

---

[1] A prostitute, as in *Eguchi*.
[2] The province of Ōmi, around Lake Biwa, lies between Nogami and Miyako.

[3] Mount Fuji, far beyond Nogami on the road to the East, was naturally a major attraction for a traveller, and had been poetically consecrated as such by its presence on Narihira's path in *Ise monogatari* ('Tales of Ise,' 10th c.).
[4] The Shirakawa Barrier (a tollgate and checkpoint) in Iwashiro province (the present Fukushima Prefecture) was exceedingly famous. No poetic evocation of a journey like this one could fail to mention it.
[5] The name of the sacred wood around the Lower Kamo Shrine, still one of the major shrines of Kyoto. Yoshida will pray to be reunited with Hanago.

spring: slender and few,
    those glimpses I had of you![6]
He was untrue, who took my love with him.
Now day follows day, the months wheel
80   round,
while wearily I listen to the wind,
for no one else will speak to me of him.
Before the banners of the sunset clouds,
I grieve, longing to reach beyond those skies,[7]
85 and lost to any thought of present need.
O Gods, O blessed Buddhas, pity me!
O bring to pass what I so desire!
The Gods of Ashigara and
    Hakone,   *To base square.*
Tamatsushima, Kibune, and Miwa,[8]
90 graciously have vowed to lend their aid
and protect the love of men and women.
Should I address my prayers
    to all of these,   *Kneels in prayer.*
surely they will send an answering boon.
Accept with profound respect obedience renewed . . .[9]

(QUASI-DANCE: *kakeri*)

To music, Hanago performs a kakeri *tour of the stage. Though short, her* kakeri *changes rhythm several times, thus conveying her disturbed state of mind. As text resumes, she is in base square.*

         (*issei*) The lady is in love:
                    everyone knows,
95   and so quickly, too.
CHORUS: *He* never knew,
                    when he first stole my heart.[10]
HANAGO: The faithless man! O he is hateful,
          hateful!   *Weeps.*
100 (*sashi*) Simply pray and let a sacred stream
          cleanse you, till you love no more:[11]
          whoever said that lied. The human heart
          truly is a shallow, turbid pool;

[6]A poem by Mibu no Tadamine, from the imperial collection *Kokinshū* ('Poems Old and New,' 905). Very early in spring, in the time of the Nara court (8th c.), ladies and gentlemen went into the meadows near the Kasuga Shrine to pick new shoots amid the lingering snow, and the occasion became established in poetry. A gentleman might glimpse a lady and fall in love.

[7]From a *Kokinshū* love poem: the words of a woman of humble station who longs for her noble lover in far-off Miyako.

[8]These are all deities of mountains or of the streams that flow from them, and several are associated (like the Kamo Shrine where Yoshida and Hanago finally meet again) with marriage myths.

[9]These opening words of a formula for addressing the gods occur also in *Tatsuta*.

[10]A poem from the imperial collection *Shūishū* ('Poetic Gleanings,' *c.* 1006) by Mibu no Tadamine.

[11]A *Kokinshū* poet cited this method, only to lament that it did not work.

and if we, impure, entreat the Gods,
it is no wonder they reject us!   105
I only know that *he* has not divined
    the tears of love
CHORUS: (*sageuta*) that leave me unconsoled.
O where will my sad journey end?
         (*ageuta*) Only let your heart   110
                    come into accord
                    with the true Way
come into accord with the true Way,
    and you need not pray:
    the Gods will keep you.[12]   115
Even for such as me, the moon of truth
might shine bright and clear, but time
    goes by,
and nothing comes from him, who is unkind.
The jewel of love is mine, yet I must weep
as he withholds it.[13] Ah, what can I do?   120
I only pray we two should share our life.
I only pray we two should share our
    life.   *Prays.*

Gentleman rises.

GENTLEMAN: (*mondō*) You, the mad girl! Why are you
    not raving today? Come, rave and entertain us![14]
HANAGO: You are too cruel! Why, see there!   125
          Those boughs, till now, had looked firm
              enough,
          yet at the wind's touch, one leaf falls.
          For once I have my wits, you gentlemen
          would have me rave. It is you, I think,
          the wild wind turns. That flying autumn leaf 130
          spins my heart away to storms of love.
          O please, do not ask me to rave!
GENTLEMAN: Well, what have you done with Lady Han's
    fan?
HANAGO: You are quite mad! Are you now calling me 135
    Lady Han?
          This fan, you see, was his — that cruel man's
          whose faithlessness I mourn. It was his gift,
          and once I touch it, I cannot put it from me,

[12]An old poem of uncertain origin, often cited in medieval literature.

[13]The 'jewel of love' is, more literally, the 'jewel in the robe' that figures in a parable in the *Lotus Sutra*. It refers to the jewel of Buddha-nature with which all beings are endowed, although most do not know they have it.

[14]This apparently callous utterance is typical of Nō plays that feature a mad person. People hardly distinguished between the ravings of the mad and the antics of entertainers, and it appears that Hanago (who is an entertainer anyway) has been entertaining people here for some time. Women entertainers often travelled the roads in medieval Japan, but if any other kind of woman had done so, alone like Hanago, she probably would have had to pretend she was an entertainer in order to escape notice.

140 though my tears fall like rain.
Ah, I recall the words of an old song:
In Lady Han's chamber, whiteness of an autumn fan;
on the So King's terrace, music of an evening ch'in.[15]

*Hanago takes a few steps forward. Gentleman sits before
Chorus.*

CHORUS: (*uta*) With summer done,
145   the fan and autumn's,
                          pale, pale dews —
                          O, of these two,
                          which will be first to fall?[16]
                   Day and night, upon a desolate bed,
150   I lie alone, downcast and forlorn,
                   from my chamber gazing on
                          the moon.   *Sits at center.*
        (*kuri*) Now the moon has sunk behind Mount Chō,
                   I lift my fan to double for the moon.
HANAGO: Flower petals scatter on brocade:
155 CHORUS: I gather snow and weep for fleeting spring.
HANAGO: (*sashi*) Evening storms and the morning clouds:
                   how could either stir no troubled thoughts?
CHORUS: A bell tolling in the lonely night
                   echoes from the heights of Cockcrow Hill
160   as dawn comes on, urging love away.
HANAGO: O that at least moonlight, slanting in,
CHORUS: might linger on my pillow! Yet it leaves,
                   and, as before, I lie here alone.   *Weeps.*
        (*kuse*) Green the curtains, red the dainty room
165   where he and I lay, our pillows twinned,
                   warm all night under welcoming quilts;
                   but those sweet dreams of bliss fled long ago.
                   Yet he lives and I live. The day must come,
                   so my heart says, when we two shall meet.
                   Might it be soon! O how *they* hastened,
170   too,[17]
                   to whisper each to each enraptured vows
                   to share as birds one wing, as trees one root,
                   there in his fair palace at Ri-san.
                   Whoever could have heard them and
                          passed on,
175   to people even now, what they said then?

Hanago rises and begins to dance.

                   Ah, but my own love promised me
                   he would return before autumn came,

---

[15]A couplet in Chinese included in the *Wakan rōei shū*. The *ch'in* belongs to the zither family, like the Japanese *koto*. Its music here, like the fan, is meant to evoke the whiteness of snow.

[16]A Japanese poem, also from the *Wakan rōei shū*, and attributed elsewhere to Mibu no Tadamine. It suggests that Lady Han was abandoned like a fan in the cool of autumn. The 'dews' are also her tears. The passage below, through the *waka*, alludes repeatedly to lines by Chinese and Japanese poets included in the *Wakan rōei shū* and other such works.

[17]The celebrated lovers Hui-tsung (the T'ang emperor) and Yang Kuei-fei.

---

                   and still the nights go by: so many nights
                   that prove he lied, he with his false heart!
                   I believed him, and he never comes.   180
                   Evenings I spend leaning on the railing,
                   gazing out towards far distant skies.
                   Autumn wind at twilight, rushing gales,
                   chill air from the heights, the late fall storms,
                   all come calling on that pine nearby.   185
                   When will I hear from him, for whom I pine?
HANAGO: At least I have his gift: the fan I hold,
CHORUS: that its breeze might whisper me some word.
                   Yet summer now is past, and through my
                          window
                   the autumn wind sinks, cold. Round Snow,
                          my fan,   190
                   so frosty white, starts me shivering
                   merely to hear its name. O autumn wind,
                   I would quarrel with you.
                   Yet well I know, to meet means to part,
                   and loss follows from past happiness.   195
                   No, I should not blame him or the world.
                   But how can I forget my unloved state?
                   That is all that matters. He is gone,
                   and Lady Han's poor room is desolate.

Hanago pauses a moment near base pillar.

        (*waka*) The painted moon   200

(DANCE: *jo-no-mai*)

She now does a jo-no-mai *dance, or, in many modern
performances, a slightly faster* chū-no-mai. *As the text
resumes, she continues dancing and abstract miming.*

HANAGO: I slip beneath my robe,
                   the fan I hold,
CHORUS: (*noriji*) my bright sleeve, make three —
HANAGO: so pretty, too —
CHORUS: his most earnest vow,   205
HANAGO: to return by fall. Yet suns and moons
CHORUS: in procession pass, while fall winds blow,
HANAGO: and still no word breathes to stir the reeds.[18]
CHORUS: The belling of the stag, shrill insect cries
                   recede and lapse. So too his promise fades. 210
                   Better, then, if he had never made it!
HANAGO: (*uta*) His gift to me, this fan
CHORUS: his gift to me, this fan,
                   with its back and front, is less two-faced
                   than the giver's heart. Oh yes, he lied.   215
                   I shall not see him, nor will my love die
                   I shall not see him, nor will my love
                          die.   *Weeps.*
YOSHIDA: (*mondō*) Are you there, my friend? Please tell
        that mad girl that I wish to see her fan.

*Gentleman rises and turns to Hanago, who is in base
square.*

---

[18]The rustling of the reeds might announce his coming.

220   GENTLEMAN: Come, Lady Han, the gentleman in the palanquin says he wants a look at your fan. Do let him have it.
HANAGO: This fan was my love's parting gift, and that is why I keep it with me always. Oh, it is true,

225   His parting gift:
                              that is my enemy.
                              Were it gone from me,
                              a moment of forgetfulness
                              might even now be mine.[19]

230   (uta) That is my own thought. Yet, all the same, at times I feel him with me.
Then, how I would miss
        my fan!   Turns to Gentleman.
No, I cannot show it to another.

Hides the fan protectively in the fold of her robe and turns away. Gentleman sits.

CHORUS: (rongi) I myself remember well that keepsake
235   and her lover's words, yet do not speak or make her any sign. How could she know?
              Yet, one look, and she will know my fan.
HANAGO: You want a look at it, you say — but why? Why should you require, so urgently,
240   a fan painted with an evening moon? What can your purpose be?
CHORUS: (rongi) Ah, then perhaps you have forgotten all those ardent promises you heard at Nogami, while beside you lay
245   a traveller, to return by fall: do they mean nothing to you now?
HANAGO: Nogami, yes — why, Nogami lies far along the highway to the East

where seas have overwhelmed the pine-clad hills[20]
in reproach to one who went away   250
and never came again.
Are you that man?

Peers at his face. Gentleman takes Yoshida's fan and starts towards her.

CHORUS: (rongi) O do not reprove me with those waves that may have swept the hills, for I am true,
HANAGO: and you, too, preserve a keepsake fan   255

Sits at center and receives Yoshida's fan.

CHORUS: that never leaves my side: a treasured fan
HANAGO: now offered me,
CHORUS: for you to take,
              and examine in the gathering dusk:

Hanago opens the fan, with both hands lifts it reverently, and gazes at it.

              Yes, I glimpse a painting of moonflowers.   260

Takes out her own fan, rises, and gives it to Yoshida. She then sits at center.

              Then why delay? Koremitsu, come, bring me a lamp, that I may see *her* fan![21]

Each, holding an open fan, compares it with the other's. They look into each other's eyes.

              Each in the other's fan knows that lost friend who now is found. For each, these gifts sealed after all the bond of steadfast love   265
              sealed after all the bond of steadfast love.

In base square, Hanago stamps the final beat.

---

[19]A poem from the *Kokinshū,* also quoted in *Pining Wind.*

[20]In a *Kokinshū* poem, a lover swears that if he is ever false, waves will sweep over a mountain named Sue-no-matsuyama ('Pine Mountain of Sue') in the far north of Japan, and the oath became proverbial.
[21]With a last, literary flourish brought on by the mention of 'moonflowers,' Yoshida speaks (through the Chorus) as though he were Prince Genji in the 'Yūgao' chapter of the *Tale of Genji;* for the lady Yūgao sent a maid to offer Genji white moonflowers (*yūgao,* 'evening faces'), which the maid held out to Genji on a fan. Koremitsu, who had escorted Genji to the spot, was his confidant.

THE SECOND SHEPHERDS' PAGEANT

The author of *The Second Shepherds' Pageant* (c. 1385–1450) has not been identified, but his style is distinct enough to permit scholars to cite him simply as the Wakefield Master. His work is so clearly superior to the other writers of mystery pageants that some critics have dubbed him a medieval literary genius. Because he used a distinctive poetic meter and rhyming style, we know that he wrote several other plays in the Wakefield Cycle, including *Noah and the Ark, The First Shepherds' Play, Herod the Great,* and *The Buffeting.* None of the thirty-two plays in the Wakefield Cycle — nor any play in other English cycles — combines the wit, cleverness, farce, and seriousness of *The Second Shepherds' Pageant.*

The Wakefield Cycle is the group of plays performed by the guilds of Wakefield during the Corpus Christi holiday, which falls eight weeks after Easter, in either late May or early June. The performances began at sunrise and continued until late in the evening, usually outdoors in good weather. The plays in all the cycles begin with the creation and continue narrating important biblical moments, such as stories of Abraham, Herod, Julius Caesar, the shepherds at the nativity, the scourging of Christ, and even the hanging of Judas. Sometimes called the Towneley Cycle because the Towneley family owned the fifteenth-century manuscripts, the Wakefield Cycle represented a highly developed tradition that was of considerable economic significance to Wakefield. Large numbers of people came from surrounding towns to see the pageants and therefore represented an important tourist traffic for local inns and businesses. The towns of York, Chester, and Coventry enjoyed the same benefits.

One of the important functions of the mystery plays was their presentation of significant and familiar biblical stories. Much of the medieval audience was illiterate or had limited access to books. Consequently, they learned or reviewed some basic Bible stories from watching these plays. The entertainment value of the plays was considered a secondary issue, although it is plain from *The Second Shepherds' Pageant* that, by the late fifteenth century, audiences were familiar enough with the material that adding a bit of farce tended to energize the drama. It is clear that the Wakefield Master, who seems to have been a minor cleric, fully understood his rural and urban audiences' need for amusement as well as their need for instruction.

In the Wakefield Cycle the same author wrote two Shepherd plays. As far as we can tell, the second play, which is presented here, followed the first. They were the twelfth and thirteenth plays in the cycle of thirty-two. Some scholars have suggested that the first play is a first draft or early version and that *The Second Shepherds' Pageant* is an improved or more fully developed play. The evidence does not support such a view, however, because the story of Mak and Gib, the two shepherds who are at the center of the comic action, are missing from the first play. In addition, some references in the second play to characters in the first play would be meaningless to an audience who had not seen the first play. It is likely that the Wakefield Cycle was a processional cycle, in which the pageant carts carrying the guilds moved from location to location, each guild performing the same play in each locale. The audience in each location, if they stayed through the day, would have seen each play in succession. On the other hand, some evidence suggests that it may have been a stationary cycle, in which the plays would have been performed in succession in a single courtyard or open space to one audience.

If it were a processional cycle, we have no idea which guild would have sponsored *The Second Shepherds' Pageant;* nothing has come down to us to indicate a choice. However, we do know that the town of York began heavily taxing the wool industries in the early fifteenth century, and consequently those industries moved to towns like Wakefield. It may well be that the development of those industries accounts for the plural number of shepherd plays.

The Second Shepherds' Pageant joins together two well-known stories. The more important is the story of the birth of Jesus as witnessed by shepherds in Luke 2.15–20. The second narrative was also familiar from folklore: Mak's story of a shepherd who steals a lamb and tries to pass it off as his baby. The conjunction of these two stories offered the Wakefield Master a great deal of imaginative reinforcement for each narrative line. The metaphor of Jesus as a lamb was extant in Roman times in part because Jesus was offered as a sacrifice for the human race. Representing the lamb as an infant — and connecting that infant to the Christ child — thus helps intensify the concept of Christ's sacrifice. When the shepherds discover Mak's ruse — a process that not only takes some time, but that involves a great deal of humor — they toss Mak in a blanket in what is essentially an act of good humor. In other words, they offer Mak the same kind of charity that Christians associate with the Christ child, and in return, they are invited to be in the presence of the Christ child.

The Second Shepherds' Pageant in Performance

In medieval times, the play was performed by amateurs, ostensibly members of the guild that produced the play. It would probably have been staged on a pageant wagon of the kind shown in Figure 5 (p. 208). Assuming that that the Wakefield Cycle was extant in the early 1400s, it is remarkable to consider that one of the last known early performances of the play was in Tudor times in 1533. This means that the social issues described in the play, the hardships experienced by ordinary folk, and the complaints about taxation and rising prices were all relevant to a later generation.

Today, *The Second Shepherds' Pageant* is a favorite Christmas production at a number of universities. In addition, mystery plays have grown in popularity. The Broomhill Opera of South Africa staged an abbreviated version of the traditional cycle in 2001 and 2002. Merging African drumming and choral music with the traditional plays is intense and highly successful. The York Cycle was staged in the streets of York, England, in 1975, and a selection of nine of the plays was staged again in 1994. The Chester Cycle is staged in Chester every five years, with the most recent performance in 2003 and the next scheduled for 2008. Toronto produced the York Cycle in 1998; the Players of St. Peter put on selections from the mystery plays each December in St. Clement, Eastcheap, London.

Mystery plays such as *The Second Shepherds' Pageant* are still emotionally moving for a large number of people, and today's performances still attract considerable audiences.

Anonymous

THE SECOND SHEPHERDS' PAGEANT

(c. 1385–1450)

EDITED BY A. C. CAWLEY

Characters

COLL, *the First Shepherd*
GIB, *the Second Shepherd*
DAW, *the Third Shepherd*
MAK, *the Sheep-stealer*
GILL, *Mak's Wife*
ANGEL
MARY, *with the Christ-child*

Scene I.   *The open fields*

1 SHEPHERD: Lord, what these weathers are cold! And
     I am ill happed.
   I am near-hand dold, so long have I napped;
   My legs they fold, my fingers are chapped.
   It is not as I would, for I am lapped
5   In sorrow.
   In storms and tempest,
   Now in the east, now in the west,
   Woe is him has never rest
   Mid-day nor morrow!

10   But we sely husbands that walk on the moor,
   In faith, we are near-hands out of the door.
   No wonder, as it stands, if we be poor,
   For the tilth of our lands lies fallow as the floor,
   As ye ken.
15   We are so hammed,
   Fortaxed and rammed,
   We are made hand-tamed
   With these gentlery-men.

Thus they reave us our rest, our Lady them wary!
These men that are lord-fast, they cause the plough
     tarry.   20
That, men say, is for the best; we find it contrary.
Thus are husbands oppressed, in point to miscarry
On live.
Thus hold they us under,
Thus they bring us in blunder;   25
It were great wonder
And ever should we thrive.

For may he get a paint sleeve or a brooch,
     nowadays,
Woe is him that him grieve, or once again-says!
Dare no man him repreve, what mastery he mays;   30
And yet may no man lieve one word that he says —
No letter.
He can make purveyance
With boast and bragance,
And all is through maintenance   35
Of men that are greater.

There shall come a swain as proud as a po;
He must borrow my wain, my plough also;
Then I am full fain to grant ere he go.
Thus live we in pain, anger, and woe   40
By night and day.
He must have, if he langed,
If I should forgang it;

1. How cold this weather is! And I am poorly clad.   2. **near-hand dold:** Nearly numb.   3. **fold:** Give way.   4. **lapped:** Wrapped.   10. But we poor husbandmen.   11. We are nearly homeless.   13. **tilth:** Arable part.   15. **hammed:** Crippled.   16. **Fortaxed and rammed:** Overtaxed and crushed.   17–18. We are reduced to submission by these gentry.

19. They rob us of our rest, our Lady curse them!   20. **lord-fast:** bound to a lord.   22–3. In danger of coming to mortal harm.   25. **blunder:** Trouble.   27. **ever:** If.   28. If he is able to get an embroidered sleeve, i.e. a lord's livery.   29. **again-says:** Gainsays.   30. No man dare reprove him, no matter what force he uses.   31. **lieve:** Believe.   33. He can requisition [our belongings].   34. **bragance:** Bragging.   35. **maintenance:** Support.   37. **po:** Peacock.   42–3. He must have what he wants, even if I have to go without it.

Mak becomes Joseph (Malcolm Storry) and Gill becomes Mary (Avril Carson), while the First Shepherd (Philip McGough) kneels before the manger in the 1978 Royal Shakespeare Company production, adapted by John Barton and titled *The Shepherds' Play,* and directed by David Tucker.

Philip McGough as the First Shepherd, Malcolm Storry as Mak, and Hilton McRae and David Bradley as the other two shepherds in the 1978 Royal Shakespeare Company production.

45 I were better be hanged
    Than once say him nay.

    It does me good, as I walk thus by mine own,
    Of this world for to talk in manner of moan.
    To my sheep will I stalk and harken anon,
    There abide on a balk, or sit on a stone
50 Full soon;
    For I trow, pardie,
    True men if they be,
    We get more company
    Ere it be noon.

    [Enter Second Shepherd]

55 2 SHEP.: Benste and Dominus, what may this bemean?
    Why fares this world thus? Oft have we not seen.
    Lord, these weathers are spitous, and the winds full
        keen,
    And the frosts so hideous they water mine een —
    No lie.
60 Now in dry, now in wet,
    Now in snow, now in sleet,
    When my shoon freeze to my feet
    It is not all easy.

    But as far as I ken, or yet as I go,
65 We sely wedmen dree mickle woe:
    We have sorrow then and then; it falls oft so.
    Silly Copple, our hen, both to and fro
    She cackles;
    But begin she to croak,
70 To groan or to cluck,
    Woe is him our cock,
    For he is in the shackles.

    These men that are wed have not all their will;
    When they are full hard sted, they sigh full still.
75 God wot they are led full hard and full ill;
    In bower nor in bed they say nought theretill.
    This tide
    My part have I fun,
    I know my lesson:
80 Woe is him that is bun,
    For he must abide.
    But now late in our lives — a marvel to me,

    That I think my heart rives such wonders to see;
    What that destiny drives it should so be —
    Some men will have two wives, and some men three 85
    In store;
    Some are woe that have any.
    But so far can I:
    Woe is him that has many,
    For he feels sore.   90

    But, young men, of wooing, for God that you
        bought,
    Be well ware of wedding, and think in your
        thought:
    'Had I wist' is a thing that serveth of nought.
    Mickle still mourning has wedding home brought,
    And griefs,   95
    With many a sharp shower;
    For thou mayst catch in an hour
    That shall sow thee full sour
    As long as thou lives.

    For, as ever read I epistle, I have one to my fere 100
    As sharp as thistle, as rough as a briar.
    She is browed like a bristle, with a sour-loten cheer;
    Had she once wet her whistle, she could sing full
        clear
    Her paternoster.
    She is as great as a whale,   105
    She has a gallon of gall;
    By him that died for us all,
    I would I had run to I had lost her!
1 SHEP.: God look over the raw! Full deafly ye stand.
2 SHEP.: Yea, the devil in thy maw, so tariand!   110
    Saw'st thou awre of Daw?
1 SHEP.:   Yea, on a lea-land
    Heard I him blow. He comes here at hand,
    Not far.
    Stand still.
2 SHEP.:   Why?
1 SHEP.: For he comes, hope I.   115
2 SHEP.: He will make us both a lie,
    But if we beware.

46. **mine own:** Myself.   47. **manner of moan:** Grumble.   49. **balk:** A strip of rough grassland dividing two ploughed portions of a common field.   51. **pardie:** By God.   55. **Benste:** Benedicite (bless us); **Bemean:** Mean.   56. We have not often seen the like.   57. **keen:** Cruel.   58. **een:** Eyes.   64–6. But as far as I know or as my experience goes, we poor married men suffer much woe: we have sorrow time and again.   71. Unhappy is our cock.   74. When they are hard put to it they sigh unceasingly.   76–8. They never answer back. Now I've found out what I have to do.   80. **bun:** Bound (in marriage).   81. **abide:** Remain so.

83. **rives:** Breaks.   84. Whatever destiny compels must come to pass.   87. **woe:** Miserable.   88. **can:** Know.   90. **sore:** Pain.   91. But young men, as for wooing, by God who redeemed you.   92. **Well ware:** Very wary.   93. 'If only I had known' is something that doesn't help you.   94. **Mickle still:** Constant.   96. **sharp:** Pang.   98. What shall grieve you most bitterly.   100. I have one for my mate.   102. She has bristly brows and a sour-looking face.   108. **to:** Till.   109. God save the audience! You stand there as deaf as a post. (The First Shepherd has evidently been trying to attract the other's attention.)   110–12. The devil in your belly for tarrying so long! Have you seen Daw anywhere? . . . Yea, in a fallow field I heard him blow [his horn].   115. **hope:** Think.   116. **make:** Tell.   117. **But if:** Unless.

[*Enter Third Shepherd*]

3 SHEP.: Christ's cross me speed, and Saint Nicholas!
　　　　Thereof had I need; it is worse than it was.
120　Whoso could take heed and let the world pass,
　　　　It is ever in dread and brickle as glass,
　　　　And slithes.
　　　　This world fared never so,
　　　　With marvels mo and mo —
125　Now in weal, now in woe,
　　　　And all thing writhes.

　　　　Was never since Noah's flood such floods seen,
　　　　Winds and rains so rude, and storms so keen:
　　　　Some stammered, some stood in doubt, as I ween.
130　Now God turn all to good! I say as I mean,
　　　　For ponder:
　　　　These floods so they drown,
　　　　Both in fields and in town,
　　　　And bear all down;
135　And that is a wonder.

　　　　We that walk on the nights our cattle to keep,
　　　　We see sudden sights when other men sleep.
　　　　Yet methink my heart lights; I see shrews peep.
　　　　Ye are two all-wights — I will give my sheep
140　A turn.
　　　　But full ill have I meant;
　　　　As I walk on this bent,
　　　　I may lightly repent,
　　　　My toes if I spurn.

145　Ah, sir, God you save, and master mine!
　　　　A drink fain would I have, and somewhat to dine.
1 SHEP.: Christ's curse, my knave, thou art a lither
　　　　hine!
2 SHEP.: What, the boy list rave! Abide unto syne;
　　　　We have made it.
150　Ill thrift on thy pate!
　　　　Though the shrew came late,
　　　　Yet is he in state
　　　　To dine — if he had it.

3 SHEP.: Such servants as I, that sweat and swinks,
155　Eat our bread full dry, and that me forthinks.
　　　　We are oft wet and weary when master-men winks;

Yet come full lately both dinners and drinks.
But nately
Both our dame and our sire,
When we have run in the mire,　　　　　　　　　　160
They can nip at our hire,
And pay us full lately.
But hear my truth, master: for the fare that ye make,
I shall do thereafter — work as I take.
I shall do a little, sir, and among ever lake,　　　　　165
For yet lay my supper never on my stomach
In fields.
Whereto should I threap?
With my staff can I leap;
And men say 'Light cheap　　　　　　　　　　　　　170
Litherly foryields.'

1 SHEP.: Thou wert an ill lad to ride on wooing
　　　　With a man that had but little of spending.
2 SHEP.: Peace, boy, I bade. No more jangling,
　　　　Or I shall make thee full rad, by the heaven's king!　175
　　　　With thy gauds —
　　　　Where are our sheep, boy? — we scorn.
3 SHEP.: Sir, this same day at morn
　　　　I them left in the corn,
　　　　When they rang Lauds.　　　　　　　　　　　　180

　　　　They have pasture good, they cannot go wrong.
1 SHEP.: That is right. By the rood, these nights are
　　　　long!
　　　　Yet I would, ere we yode, one gave us a song.
2 SHEP.: So I thought as I stood, to mirth us among.
3 SHEP.: I grant.　　　　　　　　　　　　　　　185
1 SHEP.: Let me sing the tenory.
2 SHEP.: And I the treble so high.
3 SHEP.: Then the mean falls to me.
　　　　Let see how ye chant.　　　　　　[*They sing.*

Then Mak enters with a cloak covering his tunic.

MAK: Now, Lord, for thy names seven, that made both
　　　　moon and starns　　　　　　　　　　　　190
　　　　Well more than I can neven, thy will, Lord, of me
　　　　tharns.
　　　　I am all uneven; that moves oft my harns.

---

119. *it*, i.e. the world.　120–3. Anyone who could look on and let the world go by [would see that] it is always fearful and as brittle as glass, and slides away (i.e. is transitory). But the world never behaved in this way before.　124. mo: More.　126. writhes: Changes.　129. ween: Fear.　131. ponder: Consider.　138. lights: Grows light; shrews: Rogues.　139. all-wights: Monsters.　139–44. I will turn my sheep away. But I have been ill disposed [to the shepherds]; as I walk on this field, I may stub my toes in easy penance.　147. lither hine: Lazy hind.　148–9. What, the boy is pleased to rave! Wait till later; we have finished it (i.e. our meal).　150. thrift: Luck.　152. in state: Ready.　154. swinks: Toil.　155. forthinks: Displeases.　156. winks: Sleep.

157. lately: Tardily.　158. nately: Thoroughly.　161. They can stint our wages.　163–5. But hear my promise, master: in return for the food you provide, I shall do accordingly — work as I'm paid. I shall do but little, sir, and betweenwhiles play all the time.　168. threap: Haggle.　170–3. 'A cheap bargain repays badly.' . . . You'd be the wrong lad for anyone that 's hard up to take a-wooing with him (cf. *Othello* III. iii. 71).　174–7. Stop your wrangling, or I'll quickly make you, by the king of heaven! We scorn your pranks — where are our sheep, boy?　180. Lauds: The first of the seven canonical offices, usually sung at daybreak.　182. rood: Cross.　183. yode: Went.　184. To gladden us meanwhile.　186. tenory: Tenor.　190–2. Now, Lord, by thy seven names, who made both moon and stars far more than I can name, thy will concerning me, Lord, is lacking. I am all at sixes and sevens; that often unsettles my brain.

Now would God I were in heaven, for there weep
   no bairns
So still.
195 1 SHEP.: Who is that pipes so poor?
MAK: Would God ye wist how I foor!
   Lo, a man that walks on the moor,
   And has not all his will.

2 SHEP.: Mak, where hast thou gone? Tell us tiding.
200 3 SHEP.: Is he come? Then ilkone take heed to his thing.

He takes Mak's cloak from him.

MAK: What! I be a yeoman, I tell you, of the king.
   The self and the same, sond from a great lording,
   And sich.
   Fie on you! Go hence
205   Out of my presence!
   I must have reverence.
   Why, who be ich?

1 SHEP.: Why make ye it so quaint? Mak, ye do wrong.
2 SHEP.: But, Mak, list ye saint? I trow that ye long.
210 3 SHEP.: I trow the shrew can paint, the devil might
   him hang!
MAK: I shall make complaint, and make you all to
   thwang
   At a word,
   And tell even how ye doth.
1 SHEP.: But, Mak, is that sooth?
215   Now take out that Southern tooth,
   And set in a turd!

2 SHEP.: Mak, the devil in your eye! A stroke would I
   lene you.
3 SHEP.: Mak, know ye not me? By God, I could teen
   you.
MAK: God look you all three! Methought I had seen
   you.
   Ye are a fair company.
220 1 SHEP.:   Can ye now mean you?
2 SHEP.: Shrew, peep !
   Thus late as thou goes,
   What will men suppose?
   And thou hast an ill noise
225   Of stealing of sheep.

MAK: And I am true as steel, all men wot;
   But a sickness I feel that holds me full hot:
   My belly fares not well, it is out of estate.
3 SHEP.: Seldom lies the devil dead by the gate.
MAK: Therefore   230
   Full sore am I and ill;
   If I stand stone-still,
   I eat not a needle
   This month and more.

1 SHEP.: How fares thy wife? By my hood, how fares 235
   she?
MAK: Lies waltering — by the rood — by the fire, lo!
   And a house full of brood. She drinks well, too;
   Ill speed other good that she will do!
   But she
   Eats as fast as she can,   240
   And ilk year that comes to man
   She brings forth a lakan —
   And, some years, two

But were I now more gracious, and richer by far,
   I were eaten out of house and of harbour.   245
   Yet is she a foul dowse, if ye come near;
   There is none that trows nor knows a war
   Than ken I.
   Now will ye see what I proffer?
   To give all in my coffer   250
   To-morn at next to offer
   Her head-masspenny.

2 SHEP.: I wot so forwaked is none in this shire;
   I would sleep if I taked less to my hire.
3 SHEP.: I am cold and naked, and would have a fire. 255
1 SHEP.: I am weary, forraked, and run in the mire —
   Wake thou!
2 SHEP.: Nay, I will lie down by.
   For I must sleep, truly.
3 SHEP.: As good a man's son was I   260
   As any of you.

But, Mak, come hither! Between shalt thou lie down.
MAK: Then might I let you bedene of that ye would
   rown,
   No dread.

---

194. **still:** Incessantly. 195. Who is it that cries so piteously? **196. wist:** Knew; **foor:** Fared. **199. tiding:** News. **200. ilkone:** Everyone. **202. sond:** Messenger. **203. sich:** Such like. **208.** Why are you so uppish? **209.** But, Mak, do you want to play the saint? I believe you do. **210. trow:** Believe. **211.** And have you all flogged. **213. doth:** Do. **215.** Southern speech. (Mak has been trying to talk Southern English.) **216. set:** Put. **217. lene:** Give. **218. teen:** Hurt. **219. look:** Save. **220.** Can you remember now? **221. peep:** Pry about. **223. suppose:** Suspect. **224. ill noise:** Reputation. **225. Of:** For.

227. **full hot:** Severely. **228. estate:** Condition. **229.** Seldom lies the devil dead by the roadside, i.e. appearances may be deceptive. **232. needle:** Morsel. **232–3.** May I be turned to stone if I have eaten a morsel. **236. waltering:** Sprawling. **237. brood:** children. **238.** i.e. there is no hope of her doing much else. **241. ilk:** Every. **242. lakan:** Baby. **244. gracious:** Prosperous. **245. harbour:** Home. **246. dowse:** Wench. **247.** There is none who believes [he knows] or [really] knows a worse one. **251–2.** To-morrow at the latest to give all in my coffer as an offering for her soul. **253. forwaked:** Wearied with waking. **254.** Even if I should get less wages. **256. forraked:** Worn out with walking. **257. by:** Nearby. **262. between:** Between us. **263–4.** Then I might keep you from whispering what you want, no doubt.

265   From my top to my toe,   [*He recites a night-spell.*
       Manus tuas commendo,
       Pontio Pilato.
       Christ's cross me speed !

       Now were time for a man that lacks what he would
270   To stalk privily then unto a fold,
       And nimbly to work then, and be not too bold,
       For he might abuy the bargain, if it were told
       At the ending.
       Now were time for to reel;
275   But he needs good counsel
       That fain would fare well,
       And has but little spending.

       But about you a circle, as round as a moon,
       To I have done what I will, till that it be noon,
280   That ye lie stone-still to that I have done;
       And I shall say theretill of good words a fone:
       'On height,
       Over your heads, my hand I lift.
       Out go your eyes! Fordo your sight!'
285   But yet I must make better shift,
       And it be right.

       Lord, what they sleep hard! — that may ye all hear.
       Was I never a shepherd, but now will I lere.
       If the flock be scared, yet shall I nip near.
290   How! draw hitherward! Now mends our cheer
       From sorrow
       A fat sheep, I dare say,
       A good fleece, dare I lay.
       Eft-quit when I may,
295   But this will I borrow.

                    [*He goes home with the sheep.*

Scene II.   *Mak's cottage*

MAK: How, Gill, art thou in? Get us some light.
WIFE: Who makes such din this time of the night?
       I am set for to spin; I hope not I might
       Rise a penny to win, I shrew them on height!
300   So fares
       A housewife that has been,
       To be raised thus between.

       Here may no note be seen
       For such small chares.

MAK: Good wife, open the heck! See'st thou not what I   305
       bring?
WIFE: I may thole thee draw the sneck. Ah, come in,
       my sweeting!
MAK: Yea, thou thar not reck of my long standing.
WIFE: By the naked neck art thou like for to hang.
MAK: Do way!
       I am worthy my meat,   310
       For in a strait can I get
       More than they that swink and sweat
       All the long day.

       Thus it fell to my lot, Gill; I had such grace.
WIFE: It were a foul blot to be hanged for the case.   315
MAK: I have scaped, Jelott, oft as hard a glase.
WIFE: 'But so long goes the pot to the water,' men says,
       'At last
       Comes it home broken.'
MAK: Well know I the token,   320
       But let it never be spoken!
       But come and help fast.
       I would he were flain; I list well eat.
       This twelvemonth was I not so fain of one sheep-
       meat.
WIFE: Come they ere he be slain, and hear the sheep   325
       bleat —
MAK: Then might I be ta'en: that were a cold sweat!
       Go spar
       The gate-door.
WIFE: Yes, Mak,
       For and they come at thy back —
MAK: Then might I buy, for all the pack,   330
       The devil of the war.

WIFE: A good bourd have I spied, since thou canst
       none:
       Here shall we him hide, till they be gone,
       In my cradle. Abide! Let me alone,
       And I shall lie beside in childbed and groan.   335
MAK: Thou red,
       And I shall say thou wast light
       Of a knave-child this night.
WIFE: Now well is me day bright
       That ever was I bred!   340

272–3. For he might pay dearly for it, if it came to a final reckoning.   **274. reel:** Move quickly.   **277. spending:** Money.   **278. circle:** Magic circle.   **281.** And I shall also say a few good words.   **282. height:** High.   **284–7.** 'Lose your power of sight.' But yet I must make better efforts, if things are to come right. Lord, how soundly they sleep!   **288. lere:** Learn.   **289.** Yet I shall grab [a sheep] tightly.   **290–2.** Now a fat sheep shall comfort us.   **294. Eft-quit:** Repay.   **298–304.** I don't think I can earn a penny by getting up [from my spinning], curse them! Any woman who has been a housewife knows what it means to be got up from her work continually. I have no work to show because of such small chores.

305. **heck:** Inner door.   306. I will let you draw the latch. 307. You needn't mind about my standing [outside] so long. 309. **Do way!:** Enough!   310. **meat:** Food.   311. **strait:** Fix. 312. **swink:** Toil.   315. **blot:** Deed.   316. **glase:** Blow. 320. **token:** Portent.   323–4. I wish he were skinned; I am eager to eat. At no time this year have I been so glad of a meal of mutton.   327. **spar:** Fasten.   328. **gate-door:** Outer door.   329. **For:** If.   330–1. Then I may get the devil of a bad time from the whole pack of them.   332. **bourd:** Jest; **canst:** Knowest. 336. **red:** Get ready.   337. **wast light:** Delivered.   338. **knave-child:** Boy.   339–41. I'm happy when I think of the bright day I was born! This is a good method and a cunning trick.

This is a good guise and a far cast;
Yet a woman's advice helps at the last.
I wot never who spies; again go thou fast.
MAK: But I come ere they rise, else blows a cold blast!
345   I will go sleep.
Yet sleep all this meny;
And I shall go stalk privily,
As it had never been I
That carried their sheep.

Scene III.   *The open fields*

350 1 SHEP.: *Resurrex a mortruus!* have hold my hand!
  Judas carnas dominus! I may not well stand:
My foot sleeps, by Jesus, and I walter fastand.
I thought that we laid us full near England.
2 SHEP.: Ah, yea?
355   Lord, what I have slept well!
As fresh as an eel,
As light I me feel
As leaf on a tree.

3 SHEP.: Benste be herein! So me quakes,
360   My heart is out of skin, what-so it makes.
Who makes all this din? So my brow blakes,
To the door will I win. Hark, fellows, wakes!
We were four:
See ye awre of Mak now?
365 1 SHEP.: We were up ere thou.
2 SHEP.: Man, I give God avow
Yet yede he nawre.

3 SHEP.: Methought he was lapped in a wolf-skin.
1 SHEP.: So are many happed now — namely within.
370 3 SHEP.: When we had long napped, methought with a gin
A fat sheep he trapped; but he made no din.
2 SHEP.: Be still!
Thy dream makes thee wood;
It is but phantom, by the rood.
375 1 SHEP.: Now God turn all to good,
If it be his will.
2 SHEP.: Rise, Mak, for shame! Thou liest right long.
MAK: Now Christ's holy name be us among!
What is this? For Saint Jame, I may not well gang!

I trow I be the same. Ah, my neck has lain wrong   380
Enough.   [*They help him to get up.*
Mickle thank! Since yester-even,
Now by Saint Stephen,
I was flayed with a sweven —
My heart out of slough.   385

I thought Gill began to croak and travail full sad,
Well-nigh at the first cock, of a young lad
For to mend our flock. Then be I never glad;
I have tow on my rock more than ever I had.
Ah, my head!   390
A house full of young tharms,
The devil knock out their harns!
Woe is him has many bairns,
And thereto little bread.

I must go home, by your leave, to Gill, as I thought.   395
I pray you look my sleeve, that I steal nought;
I am loath you to grieve or from you take aught.
3 SHEP.: Go forth, ill might thou chieve! Now would I
we sought,
This morn,
That we had all our store.   400
1 SHEP.: But I will go before.
Let us meet.
2 SHEP.:   Where?
3 SHEP.: At the crooked thorn.

Scene IV.   *Mak's cottage*

MAK: Undo this door! Who is here? How long shall I
stand?
WIFE: Who makes such a bere? Now walk in the   405
wenyand!
MAK: Ah, Gill, what cheer? It is I, Mak, your husband.
WIFE: Then may we see here the devil in a band,
Sir Guile!
Lo, he comes with a lote,
As he were holden in the throat.   410
I may not sit at my note
A hand-long while.

MAK: Will ye hear what fare she makes to get her a
glose?

343. Return again quickly [to the others]. **344. else:** Unless. **346. meny:** Company. **350–1.** Bad Latin for "rise from the dead" and "Judas carnate Lord." **352.** I'm tottering with hunger. **354. Ah, yea:?** Oh, really? **355.** How well I have slept! **359. Benste:** Blessing. **359–60.** I tremble so much, my heart is in my mouth, whatever the reason for it. **361. blakes:** Darkens. **362. win:** Go; **wakes!:** Wake up! **364.** Have you seen Mak anywhere? **366–7.** I vow to God he's gone nowhere yet. **369.** Many are covered like that nowadays — especially underneath. **370. gin:** Snare. **373. wood:** Mad. **379.** By Saint James; **gang:** Walk.

380–1. My neck has been lying very crookedly. **384–5.** I was terrified by a dream — I nearly jumped out of my skin. **386. full sad:** Hard. **388. mend:** Increase. **389.** I have more tow on my distaff (i.e. more trouble in store) than I ever had. **391. tharms:** Bellies. **392. harns:** Brains. **395. thought:** Intended. **396. look:** Examine. **398. chieve:** Prosper. **398–400.** Now I want us this morning to see that we have all our stock. **405. bere:** Din; Walk in the waning moon, i.e. at an unlucky time. **407. band:** Noose. **409. lote:** Noise. **410. holden:** Held by. **411. note:** Work. **412. hand-long:** Brief. **413.** Will you listen to the fuss she makes in the hope of excusing herself?

And does naught but lakes, and claws her toes.
415 WIFE: Why, who wanders, who wakes? Who comes,
        who goes?
     Who brews, who bakes? What makes me thus hoarse?
     And then
     It is ruth to behold —
     Now in hot, now in cold,
420 Full woeful is the household
     That wants a woman.

     But what end hast thou made with the herds, Mak?
MAK: The last word that they said when I turned my
        back.
     They would look that they had their sheep, all the
        pack.
425 I hope they will not be well paid when they their
        sheep lack,
     Pardie!
     But how-so the game goes,
     To me they will suppose,
     And make a foul noise,
430 And cry out upon me.

     But thou must do as thou hight.
WIFE: I accord me theretill;
     I shall swaddle him right in my cradle.
     If it were a greater sleight, yet could I help till.
     I will lie down straight. Come hap me.
MAK: I will.
435 WIFE: Behind!
     Come Coll and his marrow,
     They will nip us full narrow.
MAK: But I may cry 'Out, harrow!'
     The sheep if they find.

440 WIFE: Harken ay when they call; they will come anon.
     Come and make ready all, and sing by thine own;
     Sing lullay thou shall, for I must groan,
     And cry out by the wall on Mary and John,
     For sore.
445 Sing lullay on fast,
     When thou hearest at the last;
     And but I play a false cast,
     Trust me no more.

Scene V. *The crooked thorn*

3 SHEP.: Ah, Coll, good morn! Why sleepest thou not?
450 1 SHEP.: Alas, that ever was I born! We have a foul
        blot —

414. lakes: Play. 418. ruth: A pity. 419. i.e., at all times.
421. wants: Lacks. 422. herds: Shepherds. 425. hope:
Think; paid: Pleased. 427. how-so: However. 428. They
will suspect me. 431. hight: Promised; I agree to that. 433.
sleight: Trick; I could still help with it. 434. straight:
Straightaway; hap: Cover. 436. marrow: Mate. 437. full
narrow: Hard. 438. A cry for help. 442. lullay: Lullaby.
444. sore: Pain. 445. fast: Quickly. 447. And if I don't play a
false trick.

A fat wether have we lorn.
3 SHEP.:   Marry, God's forbot!
2 SHEP.: Who should do us that scorn? That were a
     foul spot.
1 SHEP.: Some shrew.
     I have sought with my dogs
     All Horbury shrogs,   455
     And, of fifteen hogs,
     Found I but one ewe.

3 SHEP.: Now trow me, if ye will — by Saint Thomas
        of Kent,
     Either Mak or Gill was at that assent.
1 SHEP.: Peace, man, be still! I saw when he went.   460
     Thou slander'st him ill; thou ought to repent
     Good speed.
2 SHEP.: Now as ever might I thee,
     If I should even here die,
     I would say it were he   465
     That did that same deed.

3 SHEP.: Go we thither, I rede, and run on our feet.
     Shall I never eat bread, the sooth to I wit.
1 SHEP.: Nor drink in my head, with him till I meet.
2 SHEP.: I will rest in no stead till that I him greet,   470
     My brother.
     One I will hight:
     Till I see him in sight,
     Shall I never sleep one night
     There I do another.   475

Scene VI. *Mak's cottage*

3 SHEP.: Will ye hear how they hack? Our sire list
        croon.
1 SHEP.: Heard I never none crack so clear out of tone.
     Call on him.
2 SHEP.:   Mak, undo your door soon!
MAK: Who is it that spake, as it were noon,
     On loft?   480
     Who is that, I say?
3 SHEP.: Good fellows, were it day.
MAK: As far as ye may,
     Good, speak soft,

451. lorn: Lost; God's forbot: God forbid. 452. do us that
scorn: Insult; foul spot: Disgrace. 455. Horbury, near Wakefield; shrugs: Thickets. 456–7. Among fifteen hogs (or young
sheep) I found only a ewe, i.e. the wether was missing. 458.
St. Thomas of Canterbury. 459. Either Mak or Gill was a
party to it. 462. Good speed: Quickly. 463. As I hope to
prosper. 467. rede: Advise. 468. Till I know the truth.
470. stead: Place. 471. *My brother*, a friendly form of
address. 472. One thing I will promise. 475. There: Where.
476. Do you hear them trilling? Our gentleman is pleased to
croon. 477. crack: Bawl; tone: Tune. 478. soon: Immediately. 479–80. Who is it that spoke aloud, as though it were
noon? 482. were it: If only it were. 484. Good: Good sirs.

485   Over a sick woman's head, that is at malease;
         I had liefer be dead ere she had any disease.
      WIFE: Go to another stead! I may not well quease;
         Each foot that ye tread goes thorough my nose
         So high.
490   1 SHEP.: Tell us, Mak, if ye may,
         How fare ye, I say?
      MAK: But are ye in this town to-day?
         Now how fare ye?

         Ye have run in the mire, and are wet yet;
495   I shall make you a fire, if ye will sit.
         A nurse would I hire. Think ye on yet?
         Well quit is my hire — my dream, this is it —
         A season.
         I have bairns, if ye knew,
500   Well more than enew;
         But we must drink as we brew,
         And that is but reason.

         I would ye dined ere ye yode. Methink that ye sweat.
      2 SHEP.: Nay, neither mends our mood drink nor meat.
505   MAK: Why, sir, ails you aught but good?
      3 SHEP.:   Yea, our sheep that we gete
         Are stolen as they yode. Our loss is great.
      MAK: Sirs, drink!
         Had I been there,
         Some should have bought it full sore.
510   1 SHEP.: Marry, some men trow that ye were,
         And that us forthinks.

      2 SHEP.: Mak, some men trows that it should be ye.
      3 SHEP.: Either ye or your spouse, so say we.
      MAK: Now if ye have suspouse to Gill or to me,
515   Come and rip our house, and then may ye see
         Who had her.
         If I any sheep fot,
         Either cow or stot —
         And Gill, my wife, rose not
520   Here since she laid her —

         As I am true and leal, to God here I pray
         That this be the first meal that I shall eat this day.
      1 SHEP.: Mak, as have I sele, advise thee, I say:
         He learned timely to steal that could not say nay.

      WIFE: I swelt!   525
         Out, thieves, from my wones!
         Ye come to rob us for the nonce.
      MAK: Hear ye not how she groans?
         Your hearts should melt.

      WIFE: Out, thieves, from my bairn! Nigh him not there.   530
      MAK: Wist ye how she had farn, your hearts would be
            sore.
         Ye do wrong, I you warn, that thus come before
         To a woman that has farn; but I say no more.
      WIFE: Ah, my middle!
         I pray to God so mild,   535
         If ever I you beguiled,
         That I eat this child
         That lies in this cradle.
      MAK: Peace, woman, for God's pain, and cry not so!
         Thou spillest thy brain, and makest me full woe.   540
      2 SHEP.: I trow our sheep be slain. What find ye two?
      3 SHEP.: All work we in vain; as well may we go.
         But hatters!
         I can find no flesh,
         Hard nor nesh,   545
         Salt nor fresh,
         But two tome platters.

         Quick cattle but this, tame nor wild,
         None, as have I bliss, as loud as he smelled.
      WIFE: No, so God me bless, and give me joy of my child!   550
      1 SHEP.: We have marked amiss; I hold us beguiled.
      2 SHEP.: Sir, don.
         Sir — our Lady him save! —
         Is your child a knave?
      MAK: Any lord might him have,   555
         This child, to his son.

         When he wakens he kips; that joy is to see.
      3 SHEP.: In good time to his hips, and in sely.
         But who were his gossips so soon ready?
      MAK: So fair fall their lips!
      1 SHEP. [*Aside*]:   Hark now, a lie!   560
      MAK: So God them thank,
         Parkin, and Gibbon Waller, I say,
         And gentle John Horne, in good fay —

485–6. Because of a sick woman who is in distress; I had rather die than she should suffer any discomfort.   **487. quease:** Breathe.   **488–9.** Every step you tread goes through my nose so strongly, i.e. goes right through my head.   **496–8.** I would like to hire a nurse. Do you still remember [my dream about a new addition to the family]? I've been paid my wages in full for a while — this is my dream come true.   **500. enew:** Enough.   **503. yode:** Went.   **505.** Why, sir, is anything wrong with you?   **506. gete:** Tend.   **509. full sore:** Paid for.   **511. forthinks:** Displeases.   **512. trows:** Believe.   **514. suspouse:** Suspicion.   **515. rip:** Ransack.   **517. fot:** Fetched.   **518. stot:** Heifer.   **521. leal:** Honest.   **523–4.** Mak, as I hope for happiness, take thought I say: he learned early to steal who could not say no [to another's property].

525. swelt: Feel faint.   **526. wones:** House.   **527.** You come on purpose to rob us.   **530.** Do not go near him there.   **531.** If you knew what she had been through.   **533.** To a woman who has been in labour.   **537. eat:** May eat.   **540. spillest:** Injurest.   **543. hatters!:** Confound it!   **545. nesh:** Soft.   **547. But two tome platters:** Only two empty platters.   **548–9.** Live stock but this (i.e. the 'baby' in the cradle), tame or wild, none [have I found], as I hope to be happy, that smelled as loud as he (i.e. the missing sheep).   **551.** Aimed wrongly, i.e. made a mistake.   **552. don:** Completely.   **554. knave:** Boy.   **557. kips:** Snatches.   **558.** A good and happy future to him.   **559. gossips:** Godparents.   **561.** Good luck to them.   **563.** *John Horne* is the shepherd in the *First Shepherds' Pageant* who quarrels with Gyb about the pasturing of an imaginary flock of sheep; **fay:** Faith.

He made all the garray —
565   With the great shank.
2 SHEP.: Mak, friends will we be, for we are all one.
MAK: We? Now I hold for me, for mends get I none.
    Farewell all three! — all glad were ye gone.
3 SHEP.: Fair words may there be, but love is there
        none
570   This year.   [*They leave the cottage.*
1 SHEP.: Gave ye the child anything?
2 SHEP.: I trow not one farthing.
3 SHEP.: Fast again will I fling;
    Abide ye me there.   [*He returns to the cottage.*

575   Mak, take it to no grief, if I come to thy bairn.
MAK: Nay, thou dost me great reprief, and foul hast
    thou farn.
3 SHEP.: The child will it not grieve, that little day-
        starn.
    Mak, with your leave, let me give your bairn
    But sixpence.
580 MAK: Nay, do way! He sleeps.
3 SHEP.: Methink he peeps.
MAK: When he wakens he weeps.
    I pray you go hence.

3 SHEP.: Give me leave him to kiss, and lift up the
        clout.   [*He glimpses the sheep.*
585   What the devil is this? He has a long snout!
1 SHEP.: He is marked amiss. We wait ill about.
2 SHEP.: Ill-spun weft, iwis, ay comes foul out.
    Aye, so!   [*He recognizes the sheep.*
    He is like to our sheep!
590 3 SHEP.: How, Gib, may I peep?
1 SHEP.: I trow kind will creep
    Where it may not go.

2 SHEP.: This was a quaint gaud and a far cast;
    It was a high fraud.
3 SHEP.:   Yea, sirs, was't.
595   Let burn this bawd and bind her fast.
    A false scold hangs at the last;
    So shalt thou.
    Will ye see how they swaddle
    His four feet in the middle?
600   Saw I never in a cradle
    A horned lad ere now.

MAK: Peace, bid I. What, let be your fare!
    I am he that him begat, and yond woman him bare.
1 SHEP.: What devil shall be hat, Mak? Lo,
    God, Mak's heir!   605
2 SHEP.: Let be all that. Now God give him care,
    I sagh.
WIFE: A pretty child is he
    As sits on a woman's knee;
    A dillydown, pardie,
    To gar a man laugh.   610

3 SHEP.: I know him by the ear-mark; that is a good
        token.
MAK: I tell you, sirs, hark! his nose was broken.
    Since told me a clerk that he was forspoken.
1 SHEP.: This is a false work; I would fain be wroken.
    Get weapon!   615
WIFE: He was taken with an elf,
    I saw it myself;
    When the clock struck twelve,
    Was he forshapen.
2 SHEP.: Ye two are well feft sam in a stead.   620
1 SHEP.: Since they maintain their theft, let do them to
    dead.
MAK: If I trespass eft, gird off my head.
    With you will I be left.
3 SHEP.:   Sirs, do my rede:
    For this trespass
    We will neither ban ne flite,   625
    Fight nor chide,
    But have done as tite,
    And cast him in canvas.

[*They toss Mak in a blanket.*

Scene VII.   *The open fields*

1 SHEP.: Lord, what I am sore, in point for to burst!
    In faith, I may no more; therefore will I rest.   630
2 SHEP.: As a sheep of seven score he weighed in my fist.
    For to sleep aywhere methink that I list.
3 SHEP.: Now I pray you
    Lie down on this green.
1 SHEP.: On these thieves yet I mean.   635
3 SHEP.: Whereto should ye teen?
    Do as I say you.

---

564. garray: Commotion. **565. shank:** Long legs. **566. all one:** Agreed. **567.** For my own part, I'm holding back, for I get no amends. **568.** [I should be] very glad if you were gone. (Probably an aside.) **573.** I will dash back. **575.** Don't take offense. **576.** Nay, you do me great shame, and you have behaved badly. **577. day-starn:** Star. **584. clout:** Cloth. **586–7.** He is misshapen. We do wrong to pry about. . . . Ill-spun weft, indeed, always comes out badly, i.e. what is bred in the bone will come out in the flesh. **591–3.** Nature will creep where it cannot walk, i.e. assert itself in one way or another. . . . This was a clever dodge and a cunning trick.

602. fare: Uproar. **604. hat:** Be called. **605. care:** Sorrow. **606.** I saw [the sheep myself]. **609. dillydown:** Darling. **610. gar:** Make. **613. forspoken:** Bewitched. **614. wroken:** Avenged. **616. with:** By. **619. forshapen:** Transformed. **620.** You two are well endowed together in one place, i.e. are as clever a pair of rascals as ever lived under one roof. **621. dead:** Death. **622. eft:** Again; **gird:** Strike. **623.** I throw myself on your mercy. . . . Take my advice. **625. neither ban ne flite:** Neither curse nor quarrel. **627. as tite:** At once. **632.** I think I would be glad to sleep anywhere. **635. mean:** Think. **636. teen:** Vex yourself.

An Angel sings 'Gloria in excelsis,' and then says:

ANGEL: Rise, herdmen hend, for now is he born
    That shall take from the fiend that Adam had lorn;
640   That warlock to shend, this night is he born.
    God is made your friend now at this morn,
    He behests.
    At Bedlem go see
    There lies that free
645   In a crib full poorly,
    Betwixt two beasts.
    1 SHEP.: This was a quaint steven that ever yet I heard.
    It is a marvel to neven, thus to be scared.
    2 SHEP.: Of God's son of heaven he spoke upward.
650   All the wood on a leven methought that he gard
    Appear.
    3 SHEP.: He spake of a bairn
    In Bedlem, I you warn.
    1 SHEP.: That betokens yond starn;
655   Let us seek him there.

    2 SHEP.: Say, what was his song? Heard ye not how he
    cracked it,
    Three breves to a long?
    3 SHEP.:   Yea, marry, he hacked it:
    Was no crochet wrong, nor no thing that lacked it.
660   1 SHEP.: For to sing us among, right as he knacked it,
    I can.
    2 SHEP.: Let see how ye croon.
    Can ye bark at the moon?
    3 SHEP.: Hold your tongues! Have done!
    1 SHEP.: Hark after, then.   [*Sings.*

665   2 SHEP.: To Bedlem he bade that we should gang;
    I am full adrad that we tarry too long.
    3 SHEP.: Be merry and not sad — of mirth is our song!
    Everlasting glad to meed may we fang
    Without noise.
670   1 SHEP.: Hie we thither forthy,
    If we be wet and weary,
    To that child and that lady;
    We have it not to lose.
    2 SHEP.: We find by the prophecy — let be your din! —
675   Of David and Isay, and more than I min —
    They prophesied by clergy — that in a virgin
    Should he light and lie, to sloken our sin,

And slake it,
Our kind, from woe;
For Isay said so: 680
Ecce virgo
Concipiet a child that is naked.

3 SHEP.: Full glad may we be, and abide that day
    That lovely to see, that all mights may.
    Lord, well were me for once and for ay,   685
    Might I kneel on my knee, some word for to say
    To that child.
    But the angel said
    In a crib was he laid;
    He was poorly arrayed,   690
    Both meek and mild.

1 SHEP.: Patriarchs that have been, and prophets
    beforn,
    They desired to have seen this child that is born.
    They are gone full clean; that have they lorn.
    We shall see him, I ween, ere it be morn,   695
    To token.
    When I see him and feel,
    Then wot I full well
    It is true as steel
    That prophets have spoken: 700

    To so poor as we are that he would appear
    First find, and declare by his messenger.
2 SHEP: Go we now, let us fare; the place is us near.

3 SHEP.: I am ready and yare; go we in fere
    To that bright.   705
    Lord, if thy will be —
    We are lewd all three —
    Thou grant us some kins glee
    To comfort thy wight.

Scene VIII.   *The stable in Bethlehem*

1 SHEP.: Hail, comely and clean; hail, young child!   710
    Hail, maker, as I mean, of a maiden so mild!
    Thou hast waried, I ween, the warlock so wild:
    The false guiler of teen, now goes he beguiled.
    Lo, he merries,

---

638. hend: Gentle.   **640. warlock:** The devil; **shend:** Destroy.
642. behests: Promises.   **643. Bedlem:** Bethlehem.   **644.
There lies that free:** Where lies that noble one.   **647. quaint
steven:** Elegant voice.   **648. neven:** Tell of.   **649. upward:** On
high.   **650–1.** I thought he made the whole wood appear as if
lit up by lightning.   **656. cracked:** Sang.   **657. hacked:**
Trilled.   **658.** No crochet was wrong, and there was nothing
it lacked.   **659. knacked:** Sang.   **665. gang:** Go.   **666. adrad:**
Afraid.   **668–9.** We can get everlasting joy as our reward
without any fuss.   **670. forthy:** Therefore.   **671. If:** Even if.
673. We must not forget it.   **675. Isay:** Isaiah; **min:** Remember.
676. clergy: Learning.   **677. light:** Alight; **sloken:** Quench.

678. slake: Relieve.   **679. kind:** Race.   **681–2.** Behold, a virgin shall conceive.   **684–5.** To see that lovely one who is
almighty. Lord, I would be happy for once and all.   **692.
beforn:** In the past.   **694.** That chance have they lost.   **696.
To token:** As a sign.   **702.** Find [us] first of all, and make
known [his birth] through his messenger.   **704. yare:** Eager; **in
fere:** Together.   **705. bright:** Bright one.   **707. lewd:** Simple.
708–9. Grant us some joyful way of comforting thy child.
710. clean: Pure.   **711. of:** Born of.   **712. waried:** Cursed.
713. The false and malicious deceiver, i.e. the devil.   **714. mer-
ries:** Is merry.

715   Lo, he laughs, my sweeting!
        A well fare meeting!
        I have holden my heting:
        Have a bob of cherries.

        2 SHEP.: Hail, sovereign saviour, for thou hast us
            sought!
720   Hail, freely food and flower, that all thing has
            wrought!
        Hail, full of favour, that made all of nought!
        Hail! I kneel and I cower. A bird have I brought
        To my bairn.
        Hail, little tiny mop!
725   Of our creed thou art crop;
        I would drink on thy cop,
        Little day-starn.

        3 SHEP.: Hail, darling dear, full of Godhead!
        I pray thee be near when that I have need.
730   Hail, sweet is thy cheer! My heart would bleed
        To see thee sit here in so poor weed,
        With no pennies.
        Hail! Put forth thy dall!
        I bring thee but a ball:

        Have and play thee withal,   735
        And go to the tennis.

        MARY: The Father of heaven, God omnipotent,
        That set all on seven, his Son has he sent.
        My name could he neven, and light ere he went.
        I conceived him full even through might, as he   740
            meant;
        And now is he born.
        He keep you from woe! —
        I shall pray him so.
        Tell forth as ye go,
        And min on this morn.   745

        1 SHEP.: Farewell, lady, so fair to behold,
        With thy child on thy knee.
        2 SHEP.:   But he lies full cold.
        Lord, well is me! Now we go, thou behold.
        3 SHEP.: Forsooth, already it seems to be told
        Full oft.   750
        1 SHEP.: What grace we have fun!
        2 SHEP.: Come forth; now are we won!
        3 SHEP.: To sing are we bun:
        Let take on loft.

---

716. well fare: Very fine.   **717.** I have kept my promise.   **718. bob:** Bunch.   **720. food and flower:** Noble child.   **724. mop:** moppet.   **725–6.** You are the head of our faith; I would drink in your cup (i.e. the cup of the eucharist).   **731. weed:** Clothing.   **733. dall:** Hand.

738. That made all the world in seven days.   **739–40.** He named my name and alighted in me before He went. I conceived him indeed through God's might, as His purpose was.   **745. min:** Remembered.   **752. won:** Redeemed.   **753. bun:** Bound.   **754.** Let us begin loudly.

EVERYMAN

This late medieval play may have origins in northern Europe. A Flemish play, *Elckerlijk* ("Everyman"), dates from c. 1495, and the question of whether the English *Everyman* was translated from it or whether it is a translation of *Everyman* has not been settled. Both plays may have had a common origin in an unknown play. The English *Everyman* was produced frequently in the fifteenth and early years of the sixteenth centuries. Its drama was largely theological; its purpose, to reform the audience. One indication that entertainment was not the primary goal of this morality play is its lack of the comic moments found in other plays, such as *The Second Shepherds' Pageant*.

The author of the play may have been a priest. This assumption has long been common because the play has much theological content and offers a moral message of the kind one might expect to hear from the pulpit. The theme of the play is fundamental: the inevitability of death. And for that reason, in part, the play continues to have a universal appeal. Modern productions may not give the audience a suitable medieval chill, but the message of the play is still relevant for everyone.

The medieval reliance on allegory is apparent in the naming of the characters in *Everyman*: Death, Kindred, Cousin, Goods, Knowledge, Strength, Beauty, and Everyman himself. Each character does not just stand for a specific quality; he or she *is* that quality. The allegorical way of thinking derived from the medieval faith that everything in the world had a moral meaning. Morality plays depended on this belief and always articulated setting, characters, and circumstances in terms of their moral value. This was in keeping with the medieval belief that the soul was always in jeopardy and that life was a test of one's moral condition. When Everyman meets a character, the most important information about his or her moral value is communicated instantly in the name of the character. Characters in allegorical plays also reveal themselves through their costumes and props. The character Good Deeds is simply good deeds: there is no need for psychological development because the medieval audience had a full understanding of what good deeds meant and how Good Deeds as a character would behave.

The structure of *Everyman* resembles a journey. Everyman undertakes to see who among all his acquaintances will accompany him on his most important trip: to the grave and the judgment of God Almighty. Seeing life as a journey — or as part of a journey — was especially natural for the medieval mind, which had as models the popular and costly religious pilgrimages to holy shrines and to the Holy Land itself. If life on earth is only part of the journey of the soul, then the morality play helps to put it into clear perspective. This life is not, the play tells us, the most important part of the soul's existence.

At its core, *Everyman* has a profound commercial metaphor: Everyman is called to square accounts with God. The metaphor of accounting appears early in the play, when Everyman talks about his accounts and reckonings as if they appeared in a book that should go with him to heaven. His life will be examined; if he is found wanting, he will go into the fires of hell. If he has lived profitably from a moral viewpoint, he will enjoy life everlasting. The language of the play is heavily loaded with accounting metaphors that identify it as the product of a society quite unlike that of the Greeks or the Romans. Such metaphors suggest that *Everyman* directs its message to middle-class merchants for whom accounting was a significant concept.

Like many sermons, *Everyman* imparts a lesson that its auditors were expected to heed. Hence the key points of the play are repeated at the end by the Doctor. For moderns, didactic plays are sometimes tedious. For the medieval mind, they represented delightful ways of learning important messages.

Everyman in Performance

Very little is known about early productions of *Everyman*. It was produced in Holland and England for seventy-five years beginning in the mid-fifteenth century. The play disappeared from the stage for centuries, finally resurfacing in 1901 in a production under the auspices of the Elizabethan Stage Society in London, directed by William Poel. Poel designed the costumes and set, directed, and played at first the part of Death; when he got older, he played the part of God. Poel produced *Everyman* many times over the next fifteen years.

The 1901 production was followed by a 1902 revival in New York starring Edith Wynne Matthison and produced by Ben Greet, marking the play's first American performance. Greet continued producing *Everyman* for the next thirty-five years in both England and America.

After seeing Poel's production, Max Reinhardt, the legendary German director, decided to produce *Everyman* in Germany. The Austrian poet and playwright Hugo von Hofmannsthal wrote a new German adaptation, *Jedermann,* for Reinhardt. The adaptation features Everyman as a wealthy burgher, and central to the play is an ornate banquet scene in which Death appears. Hofmannsthal's German adaptation marked a shift in emphasis from the simpler and more personal English *Everyman* to the spectacular *Jedermann* that concentrates on a wealthy man's lustful life and his attempts to get into heaven. *Jedermann* was first produced in Berlin on December 1, 1911. In 1913 Reinhardt produced the play in Salzburg, Austria, at the Salzburg Cathedral square, and except for the years of World War II, Reinhardt's version of *Jedermann* has been performed regularly at the annual Salzburg Festival. The critic Brooks Atkinson found Reinhardt's production "nothing short of miraculous." In a review of Reinhardt's 1927 production, the critic Gilbert Gabriel found *Jedermann,* "crammed with splendors for the eye, largesse of bells and uplifting voices for the ear." A reviewer at the 1936 Salzburg Festival production of *Jedermann* wrote that the play "has everything but simplicity."

The popularity of the Reinhardt productions of *Jedermann* paved the way for numerous productions of *Everyman* over the years. In 1936, during the Great Depression in the United States, the WPA (Works Progress Administration) held special Sunday church performances of *Everyman*. Other notable productions include a 1941 *Everyman* in New York performed by refugee actors from Europe, and a 1955 tour with college casts in New England and California. In 1922 a new English adaptation of the German *Jedermann* by Sir

John Martin-Harvey was presented at Stratford-on-Avon. This production toured to London and New York in 1923. In 1936 Sir John's adaptation was performed at the Hollywood Bowl in California with Peggy Wood and Lionel Braham. Long popular with college and community groups, the play continues to be performed around the world.

Anonymous

EVERYMAN

EDITED BY A. C. CAWLEY

c. 1495

Characters

GOD	KNOWLEDGE
MESSENGER	CONFESSION
DEATH	BEAUTY
EVERYMAN	STRENGTH
FELLOWSHIP	DISCRETION
KINDRED	FIVE WITS
COUSIN	ANGEL
GOODS	DOCTOR
GOOD DEEDS	

Here beginneth a treatise how the high Father of Heaven sendeth Death to summon every creature to come and give account of their lives in this world, and is in manner of a moral play.

MESSENGER: I pray you all give your audience,
    And hear this matter with reverence,
    By figure° a moral play:
    The *Summoning of Everyman* called it is,
5   That of our lives and ending shows
    How transitory we be all day.°
    This matter is wondrous precious,
    But the intent of it is more gracious,
    And sweet to bear away.
10   The story saith: Man, in the beginning
    Look well, and take good heed to the ending,
    Be you never so gay!
    Ye think sin in the beginning full sweet,
    Which in the end causeth the soul to weep,
15   When the body lieth in clay.
    Here shall you see how Fellowship and Jollity,
    Both Strength, Pleasure, and Beauty,
    Will fade from thee as flower in May;
    For ye shall hear how our Heaven King
20   Calleth Everyman to a general reckoning:
    Give audience, and hear what he doth say.

                               (Exit.)

(*God speaketh.*)

GOD: I perceive, here in my majesty,
    How that all creatures be to me unkind,°
    Living without dread in worldly prosperity:
    Of ghostly sight° the people be so blind,   25
    Drowned in sin, they know me not for their God;
    In worldly riches is all their mind,
    They fear not my righteousness, the sharp rod.
    My law that I showed, when I for them died,
    They forget clean, and shedding of my blood red;   30
    I hanged between two, it cannot be denied;
    To get them life I suffered to be dead;
    I healed their feet, with thorns hurt was my head.
    I could do no more than I did, truly;
    And now I see the people do clean forsake me: 35
    They use the seven deadly sins damnable,
    As pride, covetise, wrath, and lechery
    Now in the world be made commendable;
    And thus they leave of angels the heavenly
        company.
    Every man liveth so after his own pleasure,   40
    And yet of their life they be nothing sure:
    I see the more that I them forbear
    The worse they be from year to year.
    All that liveth appaireth° fast;
    Therefore I will, in all the haste,   45
    Have a reckoning of every man's person;
    For, and° I leave the people thus alone
    In their life and wicked tempests,
    Verily they will become much worse than beasts;
    For now one would by envy another up eat;   50
    Charity they do all clean forget.
    I hoped well that every man
    In my glory should make his mansion,
    And thereto I had them all elect;
    But now I see, like traitors deject,°   55

---

3. By figure: In form.   **6. all day:** Always.

23. unkind: Ungrateful.   **25. ghostly sight:** Spiritual vision.
44. appaireth: Degenerates.   **47. and:** If.   **55. deject:** Abject.

They thank me not for the pleasure that I to them
   meant,
  Nor yet for their being that I them have lent.
  I proffered the people great multitude of mercy,
  And few there be that asketh it heartily.
60 They be so cumbered with worldly riches
  That needs on them I must do justice,
  On every man living without fear.
  Where art thou, Death, thou mighty messenger?

(*Enter Death.*)

DEATH: Almighty God, I am here at your will,
65 Your commandment to fulfill.
GOD: Go thou to Everyman,
  And show him, in my name,
  A pilgrimage he must on him take,
  Which he in no wise may escape;
70 And that he bring with him a sure reckoning
  Without delay or any tarrying.
                    (*God withdraws.*)
DEATH: Lord, I will in the world go run overall,
  And cruelly outsearch both great and small;
  Every man will I beset that liveth beastly
75 Out of God's laws, and dreadeth not folly.
  He that loveth riches I will strike with my dart,
  His sight to blind, and from heaven to depart° —
  Except that alms be his good friend —
  In hell for to dwell, world without end.
80 Lo, yonder I see Everyman walking.
  Full little he thinketh on my coming;
  His mind is on fleshly lusts and his treasure,
  And great pain it shall cause him to endure
  Before the Lord, Heaven King.

(*Enter Everyman.*)

85 Everyman, stand still! Whither art thou going
  Thus gaily? Hast thou thy Maker forget?
EVERYMAN: Why askest thou?
  Wouldest thou wit?°
DEATH: Yea, sir; I will show you:
90 In great haste I am sent to thee
  From God out of his majesty.
EVERYMAN: What, sent to me?
DEATH: Yea, certainly.
  Though thou have forget him here,
95 He thinketh on thee in the heavenly sphere,
  As, ere we depart, thou shalt know.
EVERYMAN: What desireth God of me?
DEATH: That shall I show thee:
  A reckoning he will needs have
100 Without any longer respite.
EVERYMAN: To give a reckoning longer leisure I crave;
  This blind matter troubleth my wit.
DEATH: On thee thou must take a long journey;
  Therefore thy book of count° with thee thou
    bring,

77. **depart:** Separate.   88. **wit:** Know.   104. **count:** Account.

For turn° again thou cannot by no way.   105
  And look thou be sure of thy reckoning,
  For before God thou shalt answer, and show
  Thy many bad deeds, and good but a few;
  How thou hast spent thy life, and in what wise,
  Before the chief Lord of paradise.   110
  Have ado that we were in that way,°
  For, wit thou well, thou shalt make none attorney.°
EVERYMAN: Full unready I am such reckoning to give.
  I know thee not. What messenger art thou?
DEATH: I am Death, that no man dreadeth,°   115
  For every man I rest,° and no man spareth;
  For it is God's commandment
  That all to me should be obedient.
EVERYMAN: O Death, thou comest when I had thee
    least in mind!
  In thy power it lieth me to save;   120
  Yet of my good° will I give thee, if thou will be kind:
  Yea, a thousand pound shalt thou have,
  And defer this matter till another day.
DEATH: Everyman, it may not be, by no way.
  I set not by gold, silver, nor riches,   125
  Ne by pope, emperor, king, duke, ne princes;
  For, and I would receive gifts great,
  All the world I might get;
  But my custom is clean contrary.
  I give thee no respite. Come hence, and not tarry. 130
EVERYMAN: Alas, shall I have no longer respite?
  I may say Death giveth no warning!
  To think on thee, it maketh my heart sick,
  For all unready is my book of reckoning.
  But twelve year and I might have abiding,°   135
  My counting-book I would make so clear
  That my reckoning I should not need to fear.
  Wherefore, Death, I pray thee, for God's mercy,
  Spare me till I be provided of remedy.
DEATH: Thee availeth not to cry, weep, and pray;   140
  But haste thee lightly that thou were gone that
    journey,°
  And prove thy friends if thou can;
  For, wit thou well, the tide abideth no man,
  And in the world each living creature
  For Adam's sin must die of nature.°   145
EVERYMAN: Death, if I should this pilgrimage take,
  And my reckoning surely make,
  Show me, for saint charity,°
  Should I not come again shortly?
DEATH: No, Everyman; and thou be once there,   150
  Thou mayst never more come here,
  Trust me verily.

105. **turn:** Return.   **111. Have ado . . . that way:** Let us see about making that journey.   **112. none attorney:** No one [your] advocate.   **115. no man dreadeth:** Fears no man.   **116. rest:** Arrest.   **121. good:** Goods.   **135. But twelve year . . . abiding:** If I could stay for just twelve more years.   **141. But haste thee . . . that journey:** But set off quickly on your journey.   **145. of nature:** In the course of nature.   **148. for saint charity:** In the name of holy charity.

EVERYMAN: O gracious God in the high seat celestial,
     Have mercy on me in this most need!
155   Shall I have no company from this vale terrestrial
     Of mine acquaintance, that way me to lead?
DEATH: Yea, if any be so hardy
     That would go with thee and bear thee company.
     Hie thee that thou were gone to God's magnificence,
160   Thy reckoning to give before his presence.
     What, weenest° thou thy life is given thee,
     And thy worldly goods also?
EVERYMAN: I had wend° so, verily.
DEATH: Nay, nay; it was but lent thee;
165   For as soon as thou art go,
     Another a while shall have it, and then go therefro,
     Even as thou has done.
     Everyman, thou art mad! Thou hast thy wits five,
     And here on earth will not amend thy life;
170   For suddenly I do come.
EVERYMAN: O wretched caitiff,° whither shall I flee,
     That I might scape this endless sorrow?
     Now, gentle Death, spare me till to-morrow,
     That I may amend me
175   With good advisement.
DEATH: Nay, thereto I will not consent,
     Nor no man will I respite;
     But to the heart suddenly I shall smite
     Without any advisement.
180   And now out of thy sight I will me hie;
     See thou make thee ready shortly,
     For thou mayst say this is the day
     That no man living may scape away.
                                        (*Exit Death*.)
EVERYMAN: Alas, I may well weep with sighs deep!
185   Now have I no manner of company
     To help me in my journey, and me to keep;
     And also my writing is full unready,
     How shall I do now for to excuse me?
     I would to God I had never be get!°
190   To my soul a full great profit it had be;
     For now I fear pains huge and great.
     The time passeth. Lord, help, that all wrought!
     For though I mourn it availeth nought.
     The day passeth, and is almost ago;°
195   I wot not well what for to do.
     To whom were I best my complaint to make?
     What and I to Fellowship thereof spake,
     And showed him of this sudden chance?
     For in him is all mine affiance;°
200   We have in the world so many a day
     Be good friends in sport and play.
     I see him yonder, certainly.
     I trust that he will bear me company;
     Therefore to him will I speak to ease my sorrow.
205   Well met, good Fellowship, and good morrow!

death is not compassionate

(*Fellowship speaketh*.)

FELLOWSHIP: Everyman, good morrow, by this day!
     Sir, why lookest thou so piteously?
     If any thing be amiss, I pray thee me say,
     That I may help to remedy.
EVERYMAN: Yea, good Fellowship, yea;   210
     I am in great jeopardy.
FELLOWSHIP: My true friend, show to me your mind;
     I will not forsake thee to my life's end,
     In the way of good company.
EVERYMAN: That was well spoken, and lovingly.   215
FELLOWSHIP: Sir, I must needs know your heaviness;°
     I have pity to see you in any distress.
     If any have you wronged, ye shall revenged be,
     Though I on the ground be slain for thee —
     Though that I know before that I should die.   220
EVERYMAN: Verily, Fellowship, gramercy.°
FELLOWSHIP: Tush! by thy thanks I set not a straw.
     Show me your grief, and say no more.
EVERYMAN: If I my heart should to you break,°
     And then you to turn your mind from me,   225
     And would not me comfort when ye hear me speak,
     Then should I ten times sorrier be.
FELLOWSHIP: Sir, I say as I will do indeed.
EVERYMAN: Then be you a good friend at need:
     I have found you true herebefore.   230
FELLOWSHIP: And so ye shall evermore;
     For, in faith, and thou go to hell,
     I will not forsake thee by the way.
EVERYMAN: Ye speak like a good friend; I believe you
          well.
     I shall deserve° it, and I may.   235
FELLOWSHIP: I speak of no deserving, by this day!
     For he that will say, and nothing do,
     Is not worthy with good company to go;
     Therefore show me the grief of your mind,
     As to your friend most loving and kind.   240
EVERYMAN: I shall show you how it is:
     Commanded I am to go a journey,
     A long way, hard and dangerous,
     And give a strait count, without delay,
     Before the high Judge, Adonai.°   245
     Wherefore, I pray you, bear me company,
     As ye have promised, in this journey.
FELLOWSHIP: That is matter indeed.° Promise is duty;
     But, and I should take such a voyage on me,
     I know it well, it should be to my pain;   250
     Also it maketh me afeard, certain.
     But let us take counsel here as well as we can,
     For your words would fear a strong man.
EVERYMAN: Why, ye said if I had need
     Ye would me never forsake, quick ne dead,   255
     Though it were to hell, truly.

---

161. weenest: Suppose.   **163. wend:** Supposed.   **171. caitiff:**
Captive.   **189. be get:** Been born.   **194. ago:** Gone.   **199. af-
fiance:** Trust.

216. heaviness: Sorrow.   **221. gramercy:** Thanks.   **224. break:**
Open.   **235. deserve:** Repay.   **245. Adonai:** Hebrew name for
God.   **248. That is matter indeed:** That is a good reason
indeed [for asking me].

FELLOWSHIP: So I said, certainly,
  But such pleasures be set aside, the sooth to say;
  And also, if we took such a journey,
260 When should we come again?
EVERYMAN: Nay, never again, till the day of doom.
FELLOWSHIP: In faith, then will not I come there!
  Who hath you these tidings brought?
EVERYMAN: Indeed, Death was with me here.
265 FELLOWSHIP: Now, by God that all hath bought,°
  If Death were the messenger,
  For no man that is living to-day
  I will not go that loath journey —
  Not for the father that begat me!
270 EVERYMAN: Ye promised otherwise, pardie.°
FELLOWSHIP: I wot well I said so, truly;
  And yet if thou wilt eat, and drink, and make good
    cheer,
  Or haunt to women the lusty company,°
  I would not forsake you while the day is clear,°
275 Trust me verily.
EVERYMAN: Yea, thereto ye would be ready!
  To go to mirth, solace, and play,
  Your mind will sooner apply,
  Than to bear me company in my long journey.
280 FELLOWSHIP: Now, in good faith, I will not that way.
  But and thou will murder, or any man kill,
  In that I will help thee with a good will.
EVERYMAN: O, that is a simple advice indeed.
  Gentle fellow, help me in my necessity!
285 We have loved long, and now I need;
  And now, gentle Fellowship, remember me.
FELLOWSHIP: Whether ye have loved me or no,
  By Saint John, I will not with thee go.
EVERYMAN: Yet, I pray thee, take the labor, and do so
    much for me
290 To bring me forward, for saint charity,
  And comfort me till I come without the town.
FELLOWSHIP: Nay, and thou would give me a new gown,
  I will not a foot with thee go;
  But, and thou had tarried, I would not have left
    thee so.
295 And as now God speed thee in thy journey,
  For from thee I will depart as fast as I may.
EVERYMAN: Whither away, Fellowship? Will thou
    forsake me?
FELLOWSHIP: Yea, by my fay!° To God I betake° thee.
EVERYMAN: Farewell, good Fellowship; for thee my
    heart is sore.
300 Adieu for ever! I shall see thee no more.
FELLOWSHIP: In faith, Everyman, farewell now at the
    ending;
  For you I will remember that parting is mourning.
                                    (*Exit Fellowship*.)

265. **bought:** Redeemed.   270. **pardie:** By God.   273. **haunt to women the lusty company:** Frequent the lively company of women.   274. **while the day is clear:** Until daybreak. 298. **fay:** Faith.   **betake:** Commend.

EVERYMAN: Alack! shall we thus depart° indeed —
  Ah, Lady, help! — without any more comfort?
  Lo, Fellowship forsaketh me in my most need.   305
  For help in this world whither shall I resort?
  Fellowship herebefore with me would merry make,
  And now little sorrow for me doth he take.
  It is said, "In prosperity men friends may find,
  Which in adversity be full unkind."   310
  Now whither for succor shall I flee,
  Sith° that Fellowship hath forsaken me?
  To my kinsmen I will, truly,
  Praying them to help me in my necessity;
  I believe that they will do so,   315
  For kind will creep where it may not go.°
  I will go say,° for yonder I see them.
  Where be ye now, my friends and kinsmen?

(*Enter Kindred and Cousin.*)

KINDRED: Here be we now at your commandment.
  Cousin, I pray you show us your intent   320
  In any wise, and do not spare.
COUSIN: Yea, Everyman, and to us declare
  If ye be disposed to go anywhither;
  For, wit you well, we will live and die together.
KINDRED: In wealth and woe we will with you hold, 325
  For over his kin a man may be bold.°
EVERYMAN: Gramercy, my friends and kinsmen kind.
  Now shall I show you the grief of my mind:
  I was commanded by a messenger,
  That is a high king's chief officer;   330
  He bade me go a pilgrimage, to my pain,
  And I know well I shall never come again;
  Also I must give a reckoning strait,
  For I have a great enemy° that hath me in wait,°
  Which intendeth me for to hinder.   335
KINDRED: What account is that which ye must render?
  That would I know.
EVERYMAN: Of all my works I must show
  How I have lived and my days spent;
  Also of ill deeds that I have used   340
  In my time, sith life was me lent;
  And of all virtues that I have refused.
  Therefore, I pray you, go thither with me
  To help to make mine account, for saint charity.
COUSIN: What, to go thither? Is that the matter?   345
  Nay, Everyman, I had liefer fast bread and water°
  All this five year and more.
EVERYMAN: Alas, that ever I was bore!
  For now shall I never be merry,
  If that you forsake me.   350

303. **depart:** Part.   312. **Sith:** Since.   316. **for kind will creep where it may not go:** For kinship will creep where it cannot walk; i.e., blood is thicker than water.   317. **say:** Essay, try. 326. **For over his kin . . . may be bold:** For a man may be sure of his kinsfolk.   334. **enemy:** Devil.   **hath me in wait:** Has me under observation.   346. **liefer fast bread and water:** Rather fast on bread and water.

KINDRED: Ah, sir, what ye be a merry man!
    Take good heart to you, and make no moan.
    But one thing I warn you, by Saint Anne —
    As for me, ye shall go alone.
355 EVERYMAN: My Cousin, will you not with me go?
    COUSIN: No, by our Lady! I have the cramp in my toe.
    Trust not to me, for, so God me speed,
    I will deceive you in your most need.
    KINDRED: It availeth not us to tice.°
360   Ye shall have my maid with all my heart;
    She loveth to go to feasts, there to be nice,°
    And to dance, and abroad to start:
    I will give her leave to help you in that journey,
    If that you and she may agree.
    EVERYMAN: Now show me the very effect° of your
365   mind:
    Will you go with me, or abide behind?
    KINDRED: Abide behind? Yea, that will I, and I may!
    Therefore farewell till another day.
                          (*Exit Kindred.*)
    EVERYMAN: How should I be merry or glad?
370   For fair promises men to me make,
    But when I have most need they me forsake.
    I am deceived; that maketh me sad.
    COUSIN: Cousin Everyman, farewell now,
    For verily I will not go with you.
375   Also of mine own an unready reckoning
    I have to account; therefore I make tarrying.
    Now God keep thee, for now I go.
                          (*Exit Cousin.*)
    EVERYMAN: Ah, Jesus, is all come hereto?
    Lo, fair words maketh fools fain;°
380   They promise, and nothing will do, certain.
    My kinsmen promised me faithfully
    For to abide with me steadfastly,
    And now fast away do they flee:
    Even so Fellowship promised me.
385   What friend were best me of to provide?°
    I lose my time here longer to abide.
    Yet in my mind a thing there is:
    All my life I have loved riches;
    If that my Good° now help me might,
390   He would make my heart full light.
    I will speak to him in this distress —
    Where art thou, my Goods and riches?

(*Goods speaks from a corner.*)

GOODS: Who calleth me? Everyman? What! hast thou
    haste?
    I lie here in corners, trussed and piled so high,
395   And in chests I am locked so fast,
    Also sacked in bags. Thou mayst see with thine eye
    I cannot stir; in packs low I lie.
    What would ye have? Lightly° me say.

EVERYMAN: Come hither, Good, in all the haste thou
    may,
    For of counsel I must desire thee.   400
GOODS: Sir, and ye in the world have sorrow or
    adversity,
    That can I help you to remedy shortly.
EVERYMAN: It is another disease that grieveth me;
    In this world it is not, I tell thee so.
    I am sent for, another way to go,   405
    To give a strait count general
    Before the highest Jupiter of all;
    And all my life I have had joy and pleasure in thee,
    Therefore, I pray thee, go with me;
    For, peradventure, thou mayst before God
    Almighty   410
    My reckoning help to clean and purify;
    For it is said ever among
    That money maketh all right that is wrong.
GOODS: Nay, Everyman, I sing another song.
    I follow no man in such voyages;   415
    For, and I went with thee,
    Thou shouldst fare much the worse for me;
    For because on me thou did set thy mind,
    Thy reckoning I have made blotted and blind,
    That shine account thou cannot make truly;   420
    And that hast thou for the love of me.
EVERYMAN: That would grieve me full sore,
    When I should come to that fearful answer.
    Up, let us go thither together.
GOODS: Nay, not so! I am too brittle, I may not
    endure;   425
    I will follow no man one foot, be ye sure.
EVERYMAN: Alas, I have thee loved, and had great
    pleasure
    All my life-days on good and treasure.
GOODS: That is to thy damnation, without leasing,°
    For my love is contrary to the love everlasting;   430
    But if thou had me loved moderately during,
    As to the poor to give part of me,
    Then shouldst thou not in this dolor be,
    Nor in this great sorrow and care.
EVERYMAN: Lo, now was I deceived ere I was ware,   435
    And all I may wite° misspending of time.
GOODS: What, weenest thou that I am thine?
EVERYMAN: I had wend so.
GOODS: Nay, Everyman, I say no.
    As for a while I was lent thee;   440
    A season thou hast had me in prosperity.
    My condition is man's soul to kill;
    If I save one, a thousand I do spill.°
    Weenest thou that I will follow thee?
    Nay, not from this world, verily.   445
EVERYMAN: I had wend otherwise.
GOODS: Therefore to thy soul Good is a thief;
    For when thou art dead, this is my guise —

---

359. **tice:** Entice.   361. **nice:** Wanton.   365. **effect:** Tenor.
379. **fain:** Glad.   385. **me of to provide:** To provide myself with.
389. **Good:** Goods.   398. **Lightly:** Quickly.

429. **without leasing:** Without a lie, i.e., truly.   436. **wite:** Blame.
443. **spill:** Ruin.

Another to deceive in this same wise
450   As I have done thee, and all to his soul's reprief.°
EVERYMAN: O false Good, cursed may thou be,
   Thou traitor to God, that hast deceived me
   And caught me in thy snare!
GOODS: Marry, thou brought thyself in care,
455   Whereof I am glad;
   I must needs laugh, I cannot be sad.
EVERYMAN: Ah, Good, thou hast had long my heartly
      love;
   I gave thee that which should be the Lord's above.
   But wilt thou not go with me indeed?
460   I pray thee truth to say.
GOODS: No, so God me speed!
   Therefore farewell, and have good day.
                                        (Exit Goods.)
EVERYMAN: O, to whom shall I make my moan
   For to go with me in that heavy journey?
465   First Fellowship said he would with me gone;
   His words were very pleasant and gay,
   But afterward he left me alone.
   Then spake I to my kinsmen, all in despair,
   And also they gave me words fair;
470   They lacked no fair speaking,
   But all forsook me in the ending.
   Then went I to my Goods, that I loved best,
   In hope to have comfort, but there had I least;
   For my Goods sharply did me tell
475   That he bringeth many into hell.
   Then of myself I was ashamed,
   And so I am worthy to be blamed;
   Thus may I well myself hate.
   Of whom shall I now counsel take?
480   I think that I shall never speed
   Till that I go to my Good Deed.
   But, alas, she is so weak
   That she can neither go nor speak;
   Yet will I venture on her now.
485   My Good Deeds, where be you?

(Good Deeds speaks from the ground.)

GOOD DEEDS: Here I lie, cold in the ground;
   Thy sins hath me sore bound,
   That I cannot stir.
EVERYMAN: O Good Deeds, I stand in fear!
490   I must you pray of counsel,
   For help now should come right well.°
GOOD DEEDS: Everyman, I have understanding
   That ye be summoned account to make
   Before Messias, of Jerusalem King;
   And you do by me,° that journey with you will I
495   take.
EVERYMAN: Therefore I come to you, my moan to
      make;
   I pray you that ye will go with me.

GOOD DEEDS: I would full fain, but I cannot stand,
      verily.
EVERYMAN: Why, is there anything on you fall?
GOOD DEEDS: Yea, sir, I may thank you of° all;   500
   If ye had perfectly cheered me,
   Your book of count full ready had be.
   Look, the books of your works and deeds eke!°
   Behold how they lie under the feet,
   To your soul's heaviness.   505
EVERYMAN: Our Lord Jesus help me!
   For one letter here I cannot see.
GOOD DEEDS: There is a blind reckoning in time of
      distress.
EVERYMAN: Good Deeds, I pray you help me in this
      need,
   Or else I am for ever damned indeed;   510
   Therefore help me to make reckoning
   Before the Redeemer of all thing,
   That King is, and was, and ever shall.
GOOD DEEDS: Everyman, I am sorry of your fall,
   And fain would I help you, and I were able.   515
EVERYMAN: Good Deeds, your counsel I pray you
      give me.
GOOD DEEDS: That shall I do verily;
   Though that on my feet I may not go,
   I have a sister that shall with you also,
   Called Knowledge, which shall with you abide,   520
   To help you to make that dreadful reckoning.

(Enter Knowledge.)

KNOWLEDGE: Everyman, I will go with thee, and be thy
      guide,
   In thy most need to go by thy side.
EVERYMAN: In good condition I am now in every
      thing,
   And am wholly content with this good thing,   525
   Thanked be God my creator.
GOOD DEEDS: And when she hath brought you there
   Where thou shalt heal thee of thy smart,
   Then go you with your reckoning and your Good
      Deeds together,
   For to make you joyful at heart   530
   Before the blessed Trinity.
EVERYMAN: My Good Deeds, gramercy!
   I am well content, certainly,
   With your words sweet.
KNOWLEDGE: Now go we together lovingly   535
   To Confession, that cleansing river.
EVERYMAN: For joy I weep; I would we were there!
   But, I pray you, give me cognition
   Where dwelleth that holy man, Confession.
KNOWLEDGE: In the house of salvation: 540
   We shall find him in that place,
   That shall us comfort, by God's grace.

(Knowledge takes Everyman to Confession.)

---

450. reprief: Shame.   491. should come right well: Would be
very welcome.   495. by me: As I advise.

500. of: For.   503. eke: Also.

Lo, this is Confession. Kneel down and ask mercy,
For he is in good conceit° with God Almighty.

EVERYMAN: O glorious fountain, that all uncleanness
545   doth clarify,
Wash from me the spots of vice unclean,
That on me no sin may be seen.
I come with Knowledge for my redemption,
Redempt with heart° and full contrition;
550   For I am commanded a pilgrimage to take,
And great accounts before God to make.
Now I pray you, Shrift, mother of salvation,
Help my Good Deeds for my piteous exclamation.

CONFESSION: I know your sorrow well, Everyman.
555   Because with Knowledge ye come to me,
I will you comfort as well as I can,
And a precious jewel I will give thee,
Called penance, voider of adversity;
Therewith shall your body chastised be,
560   With abstinence and perseverance in God's service.
Here shall you receive that scourge of me,
Which is penance strong that ye must endure,
To remember thy Savior was scourged for thee
With sharp scourges, and suffered it patiently;
565   So must thou, ere thou scape that painful pilgrimage.
Knowledge, keep him in this voyage,
And by that time Good Deeds will be with thee.
But in any wise be siker° of mercy,
For your time draweth fast; and° ye will saved be,
570   Ask God mercy, and he will grant truly.
When with the scourge of penance man doth him
      bind,
The oil of forgiveness then shall he find.

EVERYMAN: Thanked be God for his gracious work!
For now I will my penance begin;
575   This hath rejoiced and lighted my heart,
Though the knots be painful and hard within.

KNOWLEDGE: Everyman, look your penance that ye
      fulfill,
What pain that ever it to you be;
And Knowledge shall give you counsel at will
580   How your account ye shall make clearly.

EVERYMAN: O eternal God, O heavenly figure,
O way of righteousness, O goodly vision,
Which descended down in a virgin pure
Because he would every man redeem,
585   Which Adam forfeited by his disobedience:
O blessed Godhead, elect and high divine,
Forgive my grievous offense;
Here I cry thee mercy in this presence.°
O ghostly treasure, O ransomer and redeemer,
590   Of all the world hope and conductor,
Mirror of joy, and founder of mercy,
Which enlumineth heaven and earth thereby,
Hear my clamorous complaint, though it late be;

Receive my prayers, of thy benignity;
Though I be a sinner most abominable,   595
Yet let my name be written in Moses' table.°
O Mary, pray to the Maker of all thing,
Me for to help at my ending;
And save me from the power of my enemy,
For Death assaileth me strongly.   600
And, Lady, that I may by mean of thy prayer
Of your Son's glory to be partner,
By the means of his passion, I it crave;
I beseech you help my soul to save.
Knowledge, give me the scourge of penance;   605
My flesh therewith shall give acquittance:°
I will now begin, if God give me grace.

KNOWLEDGE: Everyman, God give you time and space!
Thus I bequeath you in the hands of our Saviour;
Now may you make your reckoning sure.   610

EVERYMAN: In the name of the Holy Trinity,
My body sore punished shall be:
Take this, body, for the sin of the flesh!

(*Scourges himself.*)

Also° thou delightest to go gay and fresh,
And in the way of damnation thou did me bring,   615
Therefore suffer now strokes and punishing.
Now of penance I will wade the water clear,
To save me from purgatory, that sharp fire.

(*Good Deeds rises from the ground.*)

GOOD DEEDS: I thank God, now I can walk and go,
And am delivered of my sickness and woe.   620
Therefore with Everyman I will go, and not spare;
His good works I will help him to declare.

KNOWLEDGE: Now, Everyman, be merry and glad!
Your Good Deeds cometh now; ye may not be sad.
Now is your Good Deeds whole and sound,   625
Going upright upon the ground.

EVERYMAN: My heart is light, and shall be evermore;
Now will I smite° faster than I did before.

GOOD DEEDS: Everyman, pilgrim, my special friend,
Blessed be thou without end;   630
For thee is preparate the eternal glory.
Ye have me made whole and sound,
Therefore I will bide by thee in every stound.°

EVERYMAN: Welcome, my Good Deeds; now I hear thy
      voice,
I weep for very sweetness of love.   635

KNOWLEDGE: Be no more sad, but ever rejoice;
God seeth thy living in his throne above.
Put on this garment to thy behoof,°

---

544. **conceit:** Esteem.   549. **heart:** Heartfelt.   568. **siker:** Sure.   569. **and:** If.   588. **in this presence:** In the presence of this company.

596. **Moses' table:** Medieval theologians regarded the two tablets given to Moses on Mount Sinai as symbols of baptism and penance. Thus Everyman is asking to be numbered among those who have escaped damnation by doing penance for their sins.   606. **acquittance:** Satisfaction (as part of the sacrament of penance).   614. **Also:** As.   628. **smite:** Strike.   633. **stound:** Trial.   638. **behoof:** Advantage.

Which is wet with your tears,
640   Or else before God you may it miss,
When ye to your journey's end come shall.
EVERYMAN: Gentle Knowledge, what do ye it call?
KNOWLEDGE: It is a garment of sorrow:
From pain it will you borrow;°
645   Contrition it is,
That geteth forgiveness;
It pleaseth God passing well.
GOOD DEEDS: Everyman, will you wear it for your
    heal?°
EVERYMAN: Now blessed be Jesu, Mary's Son,
650   For now have I on true contrition.
And let us go now without tarrying;
Good Deeds, have we clear our reckoning?
GOOD DEEDS: Yea, indeed, I have it here.
EVERYMAN: Then I trust we need not fear;
655   Now, friends, let us not part in twain.
KNOWLEDGE: Nay, Everyman, that will we not, certain.
GOOD DEEDS: Yet must thou lead with thee
Three persons of great might.
EVERYMAN: Who should they be?
660   GOOD DEEDS: Discretion and Strength they hight,°
And thy Beauty may not abide behind.
KNOWLEDGE: Also ye must call to mind
Your Five Wits as for your counsellors.
GOOD DEEDS: You must have them ready at all hours.
665   EVERYMAN: How shall I get them hither?
KNOWLEDGE: You must call them all together,
And they will hear you incontinent.°
EVERYMAN: My friends, come hither and be present,
Discretion, Strength, my Five Wits, and Beauty.

(*Enter Beauty, Strength, Discretion, and Five Wits.*)

670   BEAUTY: Here at your will we be all ready.
What will ye that we should do?
GOOD DEEDS: That ye would with Everyman go,
And help him in his pilgrimage.
Advise you, will ye with him or not in that voyage?
675   STRENGTH: We will bring him all thither,
To his help and comfort, ye may believe me.
DISCRETION: So will we go with him all together.
EVERYMAN: Almighty God, lofed° may thou be!
I give thee laud that I have hither brought
Strength, Discretion, Beauty, and Five Wits. Lack I
680   nought.
And my Good Deeds, with Knowledge clear,
All be in my company at my will here;
I desire no more to my business.
STRENGTH: And I, Strength, will by you stand in
    distress,
685   Though thou would in battle fight on the ground.
FIVE WITS: And though it were through the world
    round,
We will not depart for sweet ne sour.

BEAUTY: No more will I unto death's hour,
Whatsoever thereof befall.
DISCRETION: Everyman, advise you first of all;   690
Go with a good advisement and deliberation.
We all give you virtuous monition°
That all shall be well.
EVERYMAN: My friends, harken what I will tell:
I pray God reward you in his heavenly sphere.   695
Now harken, all that be here,
For I will make my testament
Here before you all present:
In alms half my good I will give with my hands twain
In the way of charity, with good intent,   700
And the other half still shall remain
In queth,° to be returned there it ought to be.°
This I do in despite of the fiend of hell,
To go quit out of his peril°
Ever after and this day.   705
KNOWLEDGE: Everyman, harken what I say:
Go to priesthood, I you advise,
And receive of him in any wise°
The holy sacrament and ointment together.
Then shortly see ye turn again hither;   710
We will all abide you here.
FIVE WITS: Yea, Everyman, hie you that ye ready were.
There is no emperor, king, duke, ne baron,
That of God hath commission
As hath the least priest in the world being;   715
For of the blessed sacraments pure and benign
He beareth the keys, and thereof hath the cure°
For man's redemption — it is ever sure —
Which God for our soul's medicine
Gave us out of his heart with great pine.°   720
Here in this transitory life, for thee and me,
The blessed sacraments seven there be:
Baptism, confirmation, with priesthood good,
And the sacrament of God's precious flesh and blood,
Marriage, the holy extreme unction, and penance;   725
These seven be good to have in remembrance,
Gracious sacraments of high divinity.
EVERYMAN: Fain would I receive that holy body,
And meekly to my ghostly father I will go.
FIVE WITS: Everyman, that is the best that ye can do.   730
God will you to salvation bring,
For priesthood exceedeth all other thing:
To us Holy Scripture they do teach,
And converteth man from sin heaven to reach;
God hath to them more power given   735
Than to any angel that is in heaven.
With five words° he may consecrate,

---

692. **monition:** Forewarning.   702. **queth:** Bequest. **returned there it ought to be:** This line probably refers to restitution, that is, the restoration to its proper owner of unlawfully acquired property.   704. **quit out of his peril:** Free out of his power. 708. **in any wise:** Without fail.   717. **cure:** Charge.   720. **pine:** Suffering.   737. **five words:** *Hoc est enim Corpus meum* ("For this is my body," the words of the consecration of the body of Christ at Mass).

---

644. **borrow:** Release.   648. **heal:** Salvation.   660. **hight:** Are called.   667. **incontinent:** Immediately.   678. **lofed:** Praised.

Scene from the Guthrie Theater
production of *Everyman,* directed by
Robert Benedetti.

God's body in flesh and blood to make,
And handleth his Maker between his hands.
740 The priest bindeth and unbindeth all bands,
Both in earth and in heaven.
Thou ministers all the sacraments seven;
Though we kissed thy feet, thou were worthy;
Thou art surgeon that cureth sin deadly:
745 No remedy we find under God
But all only priesthood.°
Everyman, God gave priests that dignity,

746. **But all only priesthood:** Except only from the priesthood.

And setteth them in his stead among us to be;
Thus be they above angels in degree.

(*Everyman goes to the priest to receive the last sacraments.*)

KNOWLEDGE: If priests be good, it is so, surely.   750
But when Jesus hanged on the cross with great
   smart,
There he gave out of his blessed heart
The same sacrament in great torment:
He sold them not to us, that Lord omnipotent.
Therefore Saint Peter the apostle doth say   755
That Jesu's curse hath all they

Which God their Savior do buy or sell,
Or they for any money do take or tell.°
Sinful priests giveth the sinners example bad;
Their children sitteth by other men's fires, I have
760   heard;
And some haunteth women's company
With unclean life, as lusts of lechery:
These be with sin made blind.
FIVE WITS: I trust to God no such may we find;
765   Therefore let us priesthood honor,
And follow their doctrine for our souls' succor.
We be their sheep, and they shepherds be
By whom we all be kept in surety.
Peace, for yonder I see Everyman come,
770   Which hath made true satisfaction.
GOOD DEEDS: Methink it is he indeed.

(Reenter Everyman.)

EVERYMAN: Now Jesu be your alder speed!°
I have received the sacrament for my redemption,
And then mine extreme unction:
775   Blessed be all they that counselled me to take it!
And now, friends, let us go without longer respite;
I thank God that ye have tarried so long.
Now set each of you on this rood° your hand,
And shortly follow me:
780   I go before there I would be; God be our guide!
STRENGTH: Everyman, we will not from you go
Till ye have done this voyage long.
DISCRETION: I, Discretion, will bide by you also.
KNOWLEDGE: And though this pilgrimage be never so
          strong,°
785   I will never part you fro.
STRENGTH: Everyman, I will be as sure by thee
As ever I did by Judas Maccabee.°

(Everyman comes to his grave.)

EVERYMAN: Alas, I am so faint I may not stand;
My limbs under me doth fold.
790   Friends, let us not turn again to this land,
Not for all the world's gold;
For into this cave must I creep
And turn to earth, and there to sleep.
BEAUTY: What, into this grave? Alas!
795 EVERYMAN: Yea, there shall ye consume, more and less.
BEAUTY: And what, should I smother here?
EVERYMAN: Yea, by my faith, and never more appear.
In this world live no more we shall,
But in heaven before the highest Lord of all.

BEAUTY: I cross out all this;° adieu, by Saint John!   800
I take my cap in my lap,° and am gone.
EVERYMAN: What, Beauty, whither will ye?
BEAUTY: Peace, I am deaf; I look not behind me,
Not and thou wouldest give me all the gold in thy
          chest.   (Exit Beauty.)
EVERYMAN: Alas, whereto may I trust?   805
Beauty goeth fast away from me;
She promised with me to live and die.
STRENGTH: Everyman, I will thee also forsake and
          deny;
Thy game liketh° me not at all.
EVERYMAN: Why, then, ye will forsake me all?   810
Sweet Strength, tarry a little space.
STRENGTH: Nay, sir, by the rood of grace!
I will hie me from thee fast,
Though thou weep till thy heart to-brast.°
EVERYMAN: Ye would ever bide by me, ye said.   815
STRENGTH: Yea, I have you far enough conveyed.
Ye be old enough, I understand,
Your pilgrimage to take on hand;
I repent me that I hither came.
EVERYMAN: Strength, you to displease I am to blame;   820
Yet promise is debt, this ye well wot.
STRENGTH: In faith, I care not.
Thou art but a fool to complain;
You spend your speech and waste your brain.
Go thrust thee into the ground!   (Exit Strength.)   825
EVERYMAN: I had wend surer I should you have found.
He that trusteth in his Strength
She him deceiveth at the length.
Both Strength and Beauty forsaketh me;
Yet they promised me fair and lovingly.   830
DISCRETION: Everyman, I will after Strength be gone;
As for me, I will leave you alone.
EVERYMAN: Why, Discretion, will ye forsake me?
DISCRETION: Yea, in faith, I will go from thee,
For when Strength goeth before   835
I follow after evermore.
EVERYMAN: Yet, I pray thee, for the love of the Trinity,
Look in my grave once piteously.
DISCRETION: Nay, so nigh will I not come;
Farewell, every one!   (Exit Discretion.)   840
EVERYMAN: O, all thing faileth, save God alone —
Beauty, Strength, and Discretion;
For when Death bloweth his blast,
They all run from me full fast.
FIVE WITS: Everyman, my leave now of thee I take;   845
I will follow the other, for here I thee forsake.
EVERYMAN: Alas, then may I wail and weep,
For I took you for my best friend.
FIVE WITS: I will no longer thee keep;
Now farewell, and there an end.   850
                              (Exit Five Wits.)

755–58. Therefore Saint Peter . . . do take or tell: Reference to the sin of simony, the selling of church offices or benefits. tell: Count out, i.e., sell. 772. your alder speed: The helper of you all. 778. rood: Cross. 784. strong: Grievous. 787. Judas Maccabee: Judas Maccabeus, who overcame Syrian domination and won religious freedom for the Jews in 165 B.C., believed that his strength came not from worldly might but from heaven (1 Maccabees 3:19).

800. I cross out all this: I cancel all this, i.e., my promise to stay with you. 801. I take my cap in my lap: Doff my cap [so low that it comes] into my lap. 809. liketh: Pleases. 814. brast: Break.

EVERYMAN: O Jesu, help! All hath forsaken me.

GOOD DEEDS: Nay, Everyman; I will bide with thee.
  I will not forsake thee indeed;
  Thou shalt find me a good friend at need.

EVERYMAN: Gramercy, Good Deeds! Now may I true
855   friends see.
  They have forsaken me, every one;
  I loved them better than my Good Deeds alone.
  Knowledge, will ye forsake me also?

KNOWLEDGE: Yea, Everyman, when ye to Death shall
  go;
860 But not yet, for no manner of danger.

EVERYMAN: Gramercy, Knowledge, with all my heart.

KNOWLEDGE: Nay, yet I will not from hence depart
  Till I see where ye shall become.

EVERYMAN: Methink, alas, that I must be gone
865 To make my reckoning and my debts pay,
  For I see my time is nigh spent away.
  Take example, all ye that this do hear or see,
  How they that I loved best do forsake me,
  Except my Good Deeds that bideth truly.

870 GOOD DEEDS: All earthly things is but vanity:
  Beauty, Strength, and Discretion do man forsake,
  Foolish friends, and kinsmen, that fair spake —
  All fleeth save Good Deeds, and that am I.

EVERYMAN: Have mercy on me, God most mighty;
  And stand by me, thou mother and maid, holy
875 Mary.

GOOD DEEDS: Fear not; I will speak for thee.

EVERYMAN: Here I cry God mercy.

GOOD DEEDS: Short our end, and minish our pain;
  Let us go and never come again.

880 EVERYMAN: Into thy hands, Lord, my soul I
  commend;
  Receive it, Lord, that it be not lost.
  As thou me boughtest, so me defend,
  And save me from the fiend's boast,
  That I may appear with that blessed host
885 That shall be saved at the day of doom.
  In manus tuas, of mights most
  For ever, *commendo spiritum meum.*°

(*He sinks into his grave.*)

KNOWLEDGE: Now hath he suffered that we all shall
  endure;
  The Good Deeds shall make all sure.
  Now hath he made ending;   890
  Methinketh that I hear angels sing,
  And make great joy and melody
  Where Everyman's soul received shall be.

ANGEL: Come, excellent elect spouse, to Jesu!
  Hereabove thou shalt go   895
  Because of thy singular virtue.
  Now the soul is taken the body fro,
  Thy reckoning is crystal-clear.
  Now shalt thou into the heavenly sphere,
  Unto the which all ye shall come   900
  That liveth well before the day of doom.

(*Enter Doctor.*)

DOCTOR: This moral men may have in mind.
  Ye hearers, take it of worth, old and young,
  And forsake Pride, for he deceiveth you in the end;
  And remember Beauty, Five Wits, Strength, and
  Discretion,   905
  They all at the last do every man forsake,
  Save his Good Deeds there doth he take.
  But beware, for and they be small
  Before God, he hath no help at all;
  None excuse may be there for every man.   910
  Alas, how shall he do then?
  For after death amends may no man make,
  For then mercy and pity doth him forsake.
  If his reckoning be not clear when he doth come,
  God will say: "*Ite, maledicti, in ignem eternum.*"°   915
  And he that hath his account whole and sound,
  High in heaven he shall be crowned;
  Unto which place God bring us all thither,
  That we may live body and soul together.
  Thereto help the Trinity!   920
  Amen, say ye, for saint charity.

Thus endeth this moral play of Everyman.

886–87. *In manus tuas . . . commendo spiritum meum:* Into
your hands, most mighty One for ever, I commend my spirit.

915. "*Ite, maledicti, in ignem eternum*": Depart, ye cursed,
into everlasting fire.

Renaissance Drama

The period following the Middle Ages in Europe, from about the fourteenth to the seventeenth centuries, is known as the *Renaissance,* a term meaning "rebirth." In this period a shift away from medieval values and culture was motivated by a revival of classical learning; advances in physics, astronomy, and the biological sciences; the exploration of the "new world" of the Americas; and political and economic developments. This shift was not abrupt, however; it was gradual, like a thaw. It began in the south, in Italy, in the late 1300s and moved northward through the activities of scholars, travelers, performers, and writers, until it reached England sometime late in the 1400s.

The Renaissance built on medieval culture and at the same time developed a secular understanding of the individual in society that eventually transformed this culture, long dominated by the Roman Catholic Church in many spheres — artistic, intellectual, political, as well as spiritual. The transformation was influenced by the work of great writers, scholars, philosophers, and scientists such as Desiderius Erasmus (1466?–1536), Niccolò Machiavelli (1469–1527), Nicolaus Copernicus (1473–1543), Francis Bacon (1561–1626), and Galileo Galilei (1564–1642). In addition, the rise in power of the guilds and the increase in wealth of the successful Italian trading states, which produced large and influential families in cities such as Florence, Venice, Milan, and Genoa, contributed to the erosion of the Church's power.

Italian scholars, following classical models, had begun in the last decades of the fourteenth century to center their studies on human achievements. Such studies, known as the humanities, became the chief concern of the most innovative thinkers of the day. Their interests were well served by the rediscovery of ancient Greek philosophical and scientific texts. Although ancient texts had been preserved in monasteries for centuries, knowledge of them was restricted. A new demand for classical texts, fed by the humanists' focus on ancient models as the source of wisdom and by their return to a liberal arts curriculum established by the Greeks, led to the wide dissemination of the works of Plato, Aristotle, Cicero, and important Greek dramatists during the Renaissance. The achievement of the ancients was an inspiration to Renaissance writers and reaffirmed their conviction that a study of the humanities was the key to transforming the old medieval attitudes into a new, dynamic worldview.

Vitruvius and the Rediscovery of Roman Design

Most medieval Italian theater depended on portable stages, but it was clear in the last decades of the fourteenth century that to present the newly rediscovered Roman or Greek plays, something more closely resembling the original Greek theater would be necessary. Fortunately, *The Ten Books of Architecture* (written c. 16–13 B.C.) of the great Roman architect Vitruvius (first century B.C.) was rediscovered in a manuscript in the monastery of St. Gall in Switzerland. It included detailed plans for the Greek-inspired Roman theater.

Using Vitruvius's designs, the Italians began building stages that were raised platforms with a FRONS SCAENA, the flat front wall used in the Roman theater. The earliest Italian woodcuts show the stages to be relatively simple with pillars supporting a roof or cover. Curtains stretched between the pillars permitted the actors to enter and exit. Usually, three "doors" with names over each indicated the houses of specific characters.

The study of Roman architecture eventually produced, in 1584, one of the wonders of the Renaissance, the Olympic Theater (Teatro Olimpico) in Vicenza, designed by the great Renaissance architect Andrea Palladio (1508–1580), whose interpretation of Roman architecture was so compelling that it influenced architecture all over the world (Figure 7). The Olympic Theater, which has been preserved and is still used for performances, has an orchestra, a semicircular seating area, and a multistory frons scaena. But it also has several vistas of streets constructed in three-dimensional forced perspective running backward from the frons scaena.

The Olympic Theater was built with an essentially conservative design that worked well for Roman plays but not for Renaissance plays. It did not inspire new theater designs. In newer theaters, Italian plays had begun to use scenery and painted backdrops that could be changed to suggest a change in location of the action. Carefully painted backdrops were also effective in increasing illusion: one backdrop could immediately locate an action on a city street, while another could help shift the audience imaginatively to a woodland scene. These innovations proved difficult in the Olympic Theater.

The theory of vanishing-point perspective developed by the architect Filippo Brunelleschi (1377–1446) and published by Leon Battista Alberti in *On Painting* in 1435 helped revolutionize the design of flat theatrical backdrops. Earlier Renaissance painters had had no way to establish a firm sense of perspective on a flat surface, so all three-dimensional objects appeared flat; all space in a landscape or cityscape seemed shortened and unreal. The use of a single vanishing point — in which lines were lightly drawn from the edges of the canvas (or theatrical backdrop) so that they met in a single point in the center — made it possible to show buildings, trees, and figures in their proper proportion to one another (Figure 8). For the first time, Renaissance painters could achieve lifelike illusions on a flat surface. On the other hand, three-dimensional scenery was possible in the Olympic Theater — as well as some others — at this time, and the illusion of reality was thus intensified.

The designer Sebastiano Serlio (1475–1554) used the vanishing-point technique, intensified by receding lines of tiles in the floor and on the painted

ABOVE: Figure 7. Designed by Andrea Palladio, the Teatro Olimpico (begun 1579) in Vicenza, Italy, was the first indoor theater of the Renaissance. The scaena's openings produced an illusion of depth. RIGHT: Figure 8. Perspective setting designed by Baldassare Peruzzi (1481–1536).

backdrop. Serlio established all-purpose settings for comedy, tragedy, and satire. The rigidity of the backdrops for comedy and tragedy — both used a piazza, a small town square, ringed by stone buildings — restricted their use. But the setting for satire was rustic: trees, bushes, a couple of cottages. Until the nineteenth century, European theaters were equipped with sets of backdrops and wingpieces derived from his designs.

The most important and long-lasting development of Italian theater design in the mid-1500s was the PROSCENIUM ARCH, a "frame" that surrounds the stage, permitting the audience to look in on the scene, whether in a room or in a town square. The arch lent a finished touch to the theater, separating the action from the audience and distancing the actors. The proscenium arch is common in most theaters today.

Commedia dell'Arte

Renaissance Italy had two traditions of theater. *Commedia erudita* was learned, almost scholarly, in its interests in Roman staging and Roman plays. COMMEDIA DELL'ARTE was less reverent, more slapstick, and generally more popular. It is difficult, however, to say which was more influential on literature over the years. Each made its contribution.

In terms of acting and storytelling, the influence of the commedia dell'arte is almost unparalleled. The term means "comedy performed by professionals." The actors usually had grown up in performing families that made their living touring the countryside, performing at fairs and on feast days. From the early Renaissance through the eighteenth century, the commedia dell'arte entertained all of Europe and influenced comic theater in every nation.

The essence of commedia dell'arte was improvised scripts. A general narrative outline served as a basis, but the speeches were improvised to a degree (with some reliance on set elements and on experience with performing the same role many times). The principal characters were types who soon became familiar all over Europe: Pantalone, the often magisterial but miserly old man; Arlecchino (Harlequin), the cunning clown. Pulcinella, the Punch of Punch and Judy, and Columbina, the innocent *zanni* (servant characters), began as clowns. They joined a host of other STOCK CHARACTERS such as pedantic lawyers, a braggart captain, and a serving maid. Certain versions of general characters — such as Arlecchino, who began as a simple *zanno* — became famous and were copied in many countries. When Volpone calls Mosca a "zany" near the end of Ben Jonson's *Volpone,* he reminds his audience that his characters are indebted to the *zanni* in commedia dell'arte. Knowing who the characters were even before the play began was a convenience that Renaissance audiences enjoyed.

The youthful lovers in the commedia did not require masks, but the old men, the *zanni,* and other characters all had masks that identified them and made them look, to modern eyes, rather grotesque. These masks survive today in the carnival, in Venice, where the commedia began. Stock characters thrive in popular comedies everywhere. Molière and, much later, Bernard Shaw depended on them. To a large extent, one of comedy's greatest sources of energy lies in the delight that audiences have always taken in stock characters. Today hardly a situation comedy on television could survive without them.

The staging of commedia dell'arte was simple. It often took place in open air, but sometimes indoors in a more formal theatrical setting. Sometimes performers dispensed with the stage altogether and worked in marketplaces. Their scenarios were farcical crowd pleasers filled with buffoonery. They were based on the LAZZO and the BURLA. The *burla* was the general plot for any given performance. *Lazzi* were comic routines something like Abbott and Costello's "Who's on First?" skit. Abbott and Costello developed their routine for burlesque, a form of comedy popular in the first half of the twentieth century centering on broad gags, routines, and running jokes. *Lazzi* were carefully planned to seem to be spontaneous interruptions of the action. Actor Chevy Chase's trademark pratfall as he enters a scene is a descendant of the sixteenth-century *lazzo.*

Elizabethan Drama

The reign of Queen Elizabeth I (1558–1603) is known as the Elizabethan age in England — a period of discovery and prosperity as well as a period of great achievement in the arts, especially drama. Sir Francis Drake and Sir Walter Raleigh adventured across the Atlantic Ocean to the "New World," and England secured its economic future by defeating the invasion attempt of the Spanish Armada in 1588. England had become Protestant in the 1530s — one reason Catholic Spain felt it needed to subdue the nation.

Elizabethan England, especially after the defeat of the Armada, produced one of the great ages of drama, rivaling the great age of Greece. During this period, playwrights such as Thomas Kyd (1558–1594), Christopher Marlowe (1564–1593), William Shakespeare (1564–1616), Ben Jonson (1572–1637), John Marston (1576–1634), John Fletcher (1579–1625), John Webster (1580?–1625?), Thomas Middleton (1580?–1627), and John Ford (1586–1639) drew crowds by the thousands.

That the Elizabethans enjoyed plays with a moral basis is plain from the fact that so much of the great drama of the late 1500s and early 1600s is moral in character. Still, early Elizabethan plays were less obviously moralistic than the then-popular morality plays. They did not aim specifically to teach a moral lesson, although there are many lessons to be learned from Shakespeare and his contemporaries.

During Shakespeare's youth wandering players put on a number of plays from REPERTORY, their stock of perhaps a dozen current plays they could perform. How many players there were or what their source of plays was, we do not know. Much of what we know comes directly from *Hamlet* and the appearance of the players who perform Hamlet's "Mouse-trap." What we learn there tells us that dramatic styles had developed in the English countryside and that theater was thriving.

The First Professional Companies

Although professional players' groups had long been licensed to perform in France and Italy, until the 1570s professional actors — those who had no other trade — did not enjoy favor in England. Such people could be arrested for vagrancy. The law, however, changed, and actors with royal patronage were permitted to perform. The history of theater changed, too. In 1576 James Burbage (father of the famous star of Shakespeare's plays, Richard Burbage) built the first building made specially for plays in England. It was called The Theatre.

Soon there were other theaters: the Swan, the Globe (Figure 9), the Rose, the Fortune, the Hope. The Globe was large enough to accommodate two to three thousand people. Because these theaters were open-air, they could not be used in winter, but all were extraordinarily successful. Shakespeare, who was part owner of the Globe and, later, of the second indoor Blackfriars Theatre, received money from admission fees and from his role as chief playwright. He became rich enough to retire in splendid style to Stratford, his hometown. Few other Elizabethan actors and playwrights had as much of a financial stake in their work as did Shakespeare.

The Elizabethan Theater

The design of the Elizabethan theater is a matter of some speculation. Many of the plays popular before the theaters were built were performed in a square inn yard, with a balcony above. The audience looked out their windows or stood in the yard. One location of the earliest English drama is the Inns of Court, essentially a college for law students in London, where students staged plays. The audience there would have been learned, bright, and imaginative. Indeed, the first English tragedy, *Gorboduc*, by Thomas Sackville and Thomas Norton, was played indoors at the Inner Temple, one of the Inns of Court, in 1562, before Marlowe and Shakespeare were born.

The shape of the early theaters was often octagonal or circular, like the bear pits in which bears, tied to stakes, were baited by dogs for the amusement of the audience. The stage was raised about five feet from the ground with levels of seating in several galleries. Approximately half the area over the stage was roofed and contained machinery to lower actors from the "heavens"; it was painted blue with stars to simulate the sky. Some stages were approximately twenty-five by forty feet. Doors or curtained openings at the back of the stage served for entrances and exits, and at the back of the stage was a special room for costume changes. The stage may have contained a section that was normally curtained but that opened to reveal an interior, such as a bedroom. The existence of this feature is, however, in considerable dispute.

The Elizabethan Audience

The entrance fee to the theaters was a penny, probably the equivalent of five to ten dollars in today's money. For another penny one could take a seat, prob-

Figure 9. A conjectural
reconstruction of the Globe
Theatre, 1599 to 1613.

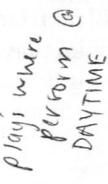

plays where perform @ DAYTIME

A   Main entrance
B   The yard — *ppl stood who couldn't afford a seat*
C   Entrances to lowest gallery
D   Position of entrances to staircase and
    upper galleries
E   Corridor serving the different sections
    of the middle gallery
F   Middle gallery ("Twopenny Rooms")
G   Position of "Gentlemen's Rooms" or
    "Lords' Rooms"
H   The stage
J   The hanging being put up round the
    stage
K   The "hell" under the stage

L   The stage trap leading down to the hell
M   Stage doors
N   Curtained "place behind the stage"
O   Gallery above the stage, used as required
    sometimes by musicians, sometimes by
    spectators, and often as part of the play
P   Backstage area (the tiring-house)
Q   Tiring-house door
R   Dressing-rooms
S   Wardrobe and storage
T   The hut housing the machine for lower-
    ing enthroned gods, etc., to the stage
U   The "heavens"
W   Hoisting the playhouse flag

ably on a bench, in one of the upper galleries. In some theaters more private spaces were available as well. A great many playgoers were satisfied to stand around the stage and were thus nicknamed "groundlings." Hamlet calls them the "understanding gentlemen of the ground." The more academic playwrights, Marlowe and Jonson, used the term to mean those who would not perfectly understand the significance of the plays.

Shakespeare and other Elizabethan playwrights expected a widely diverse audience — from coarse to extraordinarily polished. Shakespeare had the gift, as did Marlowe and even Jonson in his comedies, to appeal to them all. Shakespeare's plays were given in public playhouses open to everyone. They were also given in university theaters, as in the case of *Macbeth;* in indoor private theaters; and in royal command performances. Shakespeare's universality reveals itself in his appeal to many different kinds of people.

Female Characters on the English Stage

Because the theater was considered to be morally questionable, women were not allowed to act on English stages. Boys and young men filled the parts of young female characters such as Juliet, Desdemona, and Ophelia. No contemporary commentator makes any complaint about having to put up with a boy playing the part of Juliet or any of Shakespeare's other love interests, such as Desdemona in *Othello,* Ophelia in *Hamlet,* or even Queen Cleopatra. Older women, such as the Nurse in *Romeo and Juliet,* were played by some of the gifted male character actors of the company.

The Masque

The Elizabethan MASQUE was a special entertainment of royalty. It was a celebration that included a rudimentary plot, a great deal of singing and dancing, and magnificent costumes and lighting. Masques were usually performed only once, often to celebrate a royal marriage. Masque audiences participated in the dances and were usually delighted by complex machinery that lifted or lowered characters from the skies. The masque was devised in Italy in the 1570s by Count Giovanni Bardi, founder of the Florentine Camerata, a Renaissance group of theatergoers sponsored by Lorenzo de' Medici.

The geniuses of the masque are generally considered to have been Ben Jonson and Inigo Jones. Jones was the architect whose Banqueting Hall at Whitehall in London, which still stands, provided the setting for most of the great masques of the seventeenth century. Jonson and Jones worked together from 1605 to 1631 to produce a remarkable body of masques that today resemble the bones of a dinosaur: what we read on the page suggests in only the vaguest way what the presentation must have been like when the masques were mounted.

Because of the expenses of costuming and staging, most masques were too costly to be produced more than once. The royal exchequer was frequently burdened in Queen Elizabeth's time; more so after King James took the throne in 1603. Masque costumes were impressive, the scenery astounding, and the effects amazing. In all of this, the words — which are, after all, at the center of Shakespeare's plays as well as other plays of the period — were of least account. As a result of the emphasis on the machinery and designs — the work of Inigo Jones — Jonson abandoned his partnership in a huff, complaining that he could not compete with the scene painters and carpenters.

The value placed on spectacle in the masques tells us something about the taste of the aristocrats, who enjoyed sumptuous foods, clothes, and amusements. Eventually, audiences of the public theaters hungered for spectacle, too. Their appetite was satisfied by masques inserted in the plays of Marston, Webster, and Shakespeare, whose masque in *The Tempest* is a delightful short tribute to the genre. An added device for achieving spectacular effects onstage was huge storm machines installed in the Globe. Some say that one reason Shakespeare wrote *The Tempest* was to take advantage of the new equipment. Foreign visitors described London theaters as gorgeous places of entertainment far surpassing their own. The quest for more intense spectacle eventually led to disaster in one theater. The Globe actually burned down in 1613 because a cannon in the roof above the stage misfired and brought the house down in real flames.

The royal demand for masques was unaffected. As Francis Bacon said in his essay "On Masques" (1625), "These things are but toys to come amongst such serious observations. But yet, since princes will have such things, it is better they should be graced with elegancy than daubed with cost. Dancing to song is a thing of great state and pleasure."

Spanish Drama

The Spanish developed, independently, a corral, or open theatrical space, resembling the Elizabethan inn yard, in which they produced plays. This development may have been an accident of architecture — because of the widespread need for inns and for places to store horses — that permitted the symmetry of growth of the English Elizabethan and the Spanish Golden Age theaters.

The most important playwright of the Spanish theater was Lope de Vega (1562–1635), who is said to have written twelve hundred plays (seven hundred fifty survive). Many of them are relatively brief, and some resemble the scenarios for the commedia dell'arte. A good number, though, are full-length and impressive works, such as *The Sheep Well, The King, The Greatest Alcalde,* and *The Gardener's Dog.* Pedro Calderón de la Barca (1600–1681) became, on Lope de Vega's death, the reigning Spanish playwright. His *Life Is a Dream* is performed regularly throughout the world. Calderón became a priest in 1651 and wrote religious plays that on rare occasions got him into trouble with the Inquisition, an agency of the Church that searched out and punished heresy. He was especially imaginative in his use of stage machinery and especially gifted in producing philosophical and poetic dialogue.

Renaissance Drama Timeline

DATE	THEATER	POLITICAL	SOCIAL/CULTURAL
1300–1400	**1377–1446:** Filippo Brunelleschi, an Italian architect, develops vanishing-point perspective, which allows theatrical scenery to be drawn in realistic proportions.		**1348–1353:** Boccaccio's *Decameron* becomes a model for Italian prose. **c. 1386–1466:** Donatello, Italian painter and major innovator in Renaissance sculpture
1400–1500	**1414:** Rediscovery of Vitruvius's *De Architectura* (90 B.C.). After its publication in 1486, the treatise significantly influences the development of staging practices.		**1450:** Florence under the Medici family becomes the center of the Renaissance and humanism. **1452–1519:** Leonardo da Vinci, brilliant inventor, architect, musician, and artist **1469–1527:** Niccolò Machiavelli, who writes the political treatise *The Prince* in 1513 and the comedy *Mandragola* between 1513 and 1520 **1473–1543:** Nicolaus Copernicus, founder of modern astronomy
	1495: The Dutch morality play *Elckerlijk* by Peter Dorland van Diest becomes the prototype for the English *Everyman*.	**1494:** The Parliament of Drogheda marks the subservience of Ireland to England.	**1496:** Henry VII commissions Venetian navigator John Cabot (1450–1498) to discover a new trade route to Asia. **1497:** Cabot reaches the east coast of North America. **1497:** Vasco de Gama (c. 1469–1524) rounds the Cape of Good Hope.
1500–1600		**1503:** James IV of Scotland marries Margaret Tudor, daughter of Henry VII.	**1507:** Pope Julius II announces the sale of indulgences to finance the rebuilding of St. Peter's Basilica in Rome.
	1508: Vernacular drama begins in Italy with Ludovico Ariosto's *The Casket*. **1508:** The Hôtel de Bourgogne, a permanent theater building, opens in Paris.		**1509–1564:** John Calvin, Swiss reformer **c. 1509:** A massive slave trade begins in the New World. **1512:** Copernicus's *Commentariolus* states that the earth and other planets turn around the sun. **1514–1564:** Andreas Vesalius, Dutch physician, founder of modern anatomy **1516–1547:** Henry Howard, Earl of Surrey, English poet
	1512: The word *masque* is first used to denote a poetic drama.	**1517:** Martin Luther protests the sale of indulgences by posting his 95 theses on a church door in Wittenberg, Germany, thus launching the Protestant Reformation in Germany.	**1519:** Hernando Cortés enters Tenochtitlán, capital of Mexico; is received by Montezuma, the Aztec ruler; and assumes control of Mexico in 1521.

DATE	THEATER	POLITICAL	SOCIAL/CULTURAL
1500–1600 (continued)	**1550–1650:** Golden Age of Spanish drama. The two principal playwrights are Lope de Vega (1562–1635) and Pedro Calderón de la Barca (1600–1681).	**1534:** Henry VIII (reigned 1509–1547) breaks with the Roman Catholic Church.	**1522:** Luther translates the New Testament into German and translates the Old Testament in 1534.
	1558–1594: Playwright Thomas Kyd, author of *The Spanish Tragedy* (c. 1587)	**1535:** Henry VIII's Act of Supremacy names him head of the Church of England. Sir Thomas More is executed after refusing to comply with the Act.	**1547–1616:** Miguel de Cervantes, author of the novel *Don Quixote* and many plays
	1562: The First English tragedy, *Gorboduc*, is performed at the Inns of Court.	**1547:** Ivan IV (the Terrible) becomes czar of Russia. Moscow is destroyed by fire in the same year.	**c. 1552–1599:** Edmund Spenser, English poet, author of *Faerie Queene*
	1564–1593: Christopher Marlowe, author of *Doctor Faustus* (c. 1588), *Tamburlaine* (1590), and *Edward the Second* (c. 1592)	**1553–1558:** Reign of Mary I of England. The country returns temporarily to Catholicism.	**1554–1586:** Sir Philip Sidney, poet and soldier, author of *An Apology for Poetry*
	1564–1616: William Shakespeare	**1558–1603:** Reign of Elizabeth I in England. Protestantism becomes the religion of the realm. England emerges as a world power.	**1561–1626:** Francis Bacon, English philosopher and statesman
	c. 1568: Formation of the Italian commedia dell'arte company I Gelosi		**1564–1642:** Galileo Galilei, Italian astronomer
	1572–1637: Playwright Ben Jonson, author of *Volpone* (1605) and *Bartholomew Fair* (1614)	**1570:** Japan opens the port of Nagasaki to trade with the West.	**1571–1630:** Johannes Kepler, German astronomer. His laws accurately describe the revolutions of the planets around the sun.
	1574: The Earl of Leicester's Men, the first important acting troupe in London, is licensed.	**1572:** At the Saint Bartholomew's Day Massacre in France, thousands of Protestants are killed.	**1572–1631:** John Donne, English metaphysic poet
	1575: *Gammer Gurton's Needle*, early English farce, author unknown		
	1576: James Burbage builds The Theatre for the public performance of plays. Blackfriars, London's first private theater, is also built.		
	1577: John Northbrooke publishes *A Treatise against Dicing, Dancing, Plays, and Interludes*, one of several tracts attacking the growing professional theater.		**1577:** *Chronicles of England, Scotland and Ireland* is published by Raphael Holinshed and provides Shakespeare with information for his historical plays.
	1580–1627: Playwright Thomas Middleton, author of *A Chaste Maid in Cheapside* (1630) and *The Changeling* (with William Rowley, 1622)		**1580:** Sir Francis Drake, first Englishman to circumnavigate the globe

Renaissance Drama Timeline (continued)

DATE	THEATER	POLITICAL	SOCIAL/CULTURAL
1500–1600 (continued)	**1584:** Completion of the Teatro Olimpico in Vicenza, Italy, designed by architect Andrea Palladio (1508–1580). **1586?–c. 1640:** Playwright John Ford, author of 'Tis Pity She's a Whore (1633) **1593:** London theaters are closed because of a plague and open again in 1594. **1595–1596:** Shakespeare's comedy A Midsummer Night's Dream **1599:** The Globe Theatre is built in London.	**1587:** The Catholic Mary Stuart, queen of Scotland, is executed in England. **1587–1649:** John Winthrop, first governor of the Massachusetts Bay Colony **1588:** The English fleet defeats the Spanish Armada. **1589:** Henry IV of France, first of the Bourbon line **1589:** Russian czar Boris Godunov separates Moscow's church from that in Constantinople. **1595:** The Dutch begin to colonize the East Indies. **1598:** The Edict of Nantes grants French Huguenots freedom of worship, but is revoked in 1685.	**1583:** Sir Philip Sydney's Defence of Poesy argues for literature's importance in teaching morality and virtue. **1596–1650:** René Descartes, French philosopher, mathematician, and scientist
1600–1700	**1600–1601:** Shakespeare's Hamlet **1611–1612:** Shakespeare's The Tempest **1613:** Fire destroys the Globe Theatre. **1633:** The Oberammergau Passion play is first performed in Germany. **1642:** The English Parliament closes the theaters.	**1603:** Death of Elizabeth I. James VI of Scotland, son of Mary Stuart, becomes James I of England. **1605:** The Gunpowder Plot, an attempt to blow up the English Parliament and James I, is uncovered. **1618–1648:** The Thirty Years War is initiated by a Protestant revolt in Bohemia against the authority of the Holy Roman emperor. **1625:** Death of James I. His son becomes Charles I of England. **1630:** John Winthrop founds Boston. **1642:** Civil war begins in England. **1643:** Louis XIV becomes king of France at age four. **1649:** Charles I is beheaded in England, beginning the Commonwealth and Protectorate. **1648:** The Treaty of Westphalia ends the Thirty Years War.	**1600:** Dutch opticians invent the telescope. **1602:** The Dutch East India Company is established to trade with the Far East. **1606–1669:** Rembrandt van Rijn, greatest master of the Dutch school of painting **1607:** Jamestown, Virginia, the first permanent settlement across the Atlantic, is founded. **1608–1674:** John Milton, English poet, author of Paradise Lost **1611:** The King James Bible is published. **1619:** The first slaves from Africa arrive in Virginia. **1620:** The Pilgrims land at Plymouth Rock, Massachusetts. **1626:** Peter Minuit purchases Manhattan Island from native Indian chiefs. **1632–1704:** John Locke, English philosopher, founder of empiricism

Christopher Marlowe

Christopher Marlowe (1564–1593) was born two months before William Shakespeare and in somewhat similar social circumstances. Marlowe's father was a shoemaker; Shakespeare's a glovemaker. But unlike Shakespeare, Marlowe won a scholarship to Cambridge, where he remained six years and began his career as a playwright. His first play, *Tamburlaine,* was finished before he left the university. When it was performed in London it had the benefit of Edward Alleyn, the finest actor of his time, playing the title role.

The son-in-law of Philip Henslowe, who owned the Rose, the Fortune, and the Hope theaters in London, Alleyn was a rhetorical actor with a commanding voice and gestures. His style was perfect for declaiming what Ben Jonson called Marlowe's "Mighty line": his IAMBIC PENTAMETER BLANK VERSE, which moves in stately rhythms and which dominated the Elizabethan stage. Marlowe's blank verse, especially in the emotional moments of Faustus's career — as in his invocation of the devils in act I, scene III — resonates and rolls from the tongue in mighty billows. It has a virtually incantatory effect on the listener, and in a London theater of the time, as spoken by Edward Alleyn, it must have been mesmerizing.

Marlowe also had considerable success as a poet and as a translator of the classics. His version of Ovid's *Amores* is very lively, and his long poem *Hero and Leander* is a dynamic contribution to the poetry of Renaissance humanism. It shows his affection for the classics in a form that Shakespeare also employed: the longer narrative poem.

Marlowe's university scholarship was intended for those studying for the ministry, but instead of entering the ministry, he went up to London in 1587. Some of his friends revealed that his beliefs were close to those of atheism, a charge that in his time could have resulted in death. Fortunately, when he applied for his master's degree and was on the verge of having it denied, Queen Elizabeth intervened on his behalf. Her involvement has made subsequent generations think that he must have been a spy on her behalf during at least some of the time he was in Catholic sections of France.

Partly as a result of his connection with Elizabeth, Marlowe has often been portrayed as a romantic swashbuckler in the heart of complex intrigues. He was also well known to most of the literary people of London: Shakespeare, Sir Walter Raleigh, Francis Bacon, Thomas Kyd, and Thomas Harriot (an astronomer and writer) were all close associates. They and Marlowe were also acquainted with the remarkable magician Dr. John Dee. As members of a group dubbed the School of Night, they met privately to discuss ideas of the occult, alchemy, and skeptic philosophy — subjects that could not easily be talked about in the open.

Marlowe's first play was *Tamburlaine* (1587; in two parts), followed by *The Jew of Malta* (1589) and *Edward the Second* (1592). They are all powerful plays that feature a great tragic character. *The Massacre at Paris* (1593) is based on the St. Bartholomew Day's Massacre in 1573, when some thirty thousand Huguenots — French Protestants — were killed by Catholics in Paris. Marlowe's knowledge of the details of the events seems to have been considerable, although the play itself is not as powerful as his earlier tragedies. *Dido, Queen of Carthage* (1593; with Thomas Nashe) is a typical kind of collaboration of the period. None of these plays, good as they are, come to the level of *Doctor Faustus*, which stands as one of the greatest plays of the Elizabethan age.

Apparently quick to anger, Marlowe was involved in one murder before he himself was murdered over a bar bill at the inn of the Widow Bull in Deptford. He was drinking with an acquaintance, Ingram Frizer, who worked for the great Walsingham family, a patron of Marlowe's. During an argument Marlowe grabbed Frizer from behind, but Frizer broke free and stabbed Marlowe, who died instantly. At the time of Marlowe's death Shakespeare was just beginning his career as a playwright.

DOCTOR FAUSTUS

Doctor Faustus was probably written between 1588 and 1593, shortly before Marlowe died. There is a record of its being readied for the press in 1601, but if that version was printed, no copies survive. The first printed version, now called the A-text, is from 1604; an amplified version, called the B-text, came out in 1616. Neither had been supervised by Marlowe, and to make things more complicated, records indicate that his father-in-law Philip Henslowe paid two writers a substantial sum to add to the original text. What the additions were or what the original text was, we probably will never know.

Current scholarship leads us to believe that the 1616 text, printed here, is actually closer to the original acting version than the 1604 text was. The breaking of the text into five acts and their scenes is a modern convention, as is the supplying of most of the stage directions. The five-act pattern common in classical plays is natural to Elizabethan plays as well.

The influence of the medieval stage is readily apparent in *Doctor Faustus*. The emphasis on the devils, the seven deadly sins, and the terrifying vision of hell in act V is reminiscent of the devils of the mystery plays and their reliance on frightening hell's mouth props. The allusion to medieval theater's tradition of the mansion in Mephistophilis's speech in act V also echoes the basic message of the morality plays:

> Ay, Faustus, now thou hast no hope of heaven;
> Therefore despair. Think only upon hell,
> For that must be thy mansion, there to dwell.

Doctor Faustus differs from the morality plays in one very important way, though. We are never led to think that Faustus would have lived a better or more interesting life if he had restrained his ambition. Faustus is a hero, especially of the romantic sort that strove to achieve great things and challenge the gods. The Elizabethans admired Faustus much more than they condemned him, no matter what moral tags Marlowe might have put in the play to satisfy society's official view of itself.

Among the sources of the play are a medieval folklore tradition connected with the wizard who sold his soul to the devil for greater powers and a German book called *Historia von D. Johan Fausten,* published in 1587. Marlowe may have seen the book or, more likely, may have seen an English translation in 1592 called *The History of the damnable life, and deserved death of Doctor John Faustus.* In either event, the Faust legend goes back to the early medieval period and could have reached Marlowe in any number of ways.

Doctor Faustus is one of the earliest English tragedies. Its hero is in many ways larger than life, and while not a member of the nobility, he is at ease with royalty and clearly superior in intellectual abilities. The richness of the psychological portrayal of Faustus — as well as of Wagner and Mephistophilis — elevates the play from the best earlier efforts of English and European dramatists. Faustus represents an interesting tradition: the University of Wittenberg produced the most important Protestant of the sixteenth century, Martin Luther. His daring — comparable in some ways to Faustus's overreaching — led to the Reformation, one of the most cataclysmic changes in European thought in the Renaissance. Hamlet is also a student at Wittenberg, a fact that gives us insight into the Elizabethan imagination. Wittenberg to the Elizabethans meant fierce intellectual energy and daring.

As in the case of many of Shakespeare's tragedies, *Doctor Faustus* has interludes of comic relief, with the horse coursers who are bilked by Faustus and with other clowns and mechanicals who wonder openly about the terrifying skills of the magician. This linking of magic and comic has annoyed some critics who have agreed with Aristotle that such a mixture is problematic and tends to diffuse the effect of the drama. Actually, in performance the comic scenes are in no way a dilution of effect. They tend to buoy the energy of the play and help us focus anew on the insatiable Faustus.

But *Doctor Faustus* has a modern twist that takes it out of the medieval mold. The Renaissance was a period of expansion, especially the expansion of knowledge. Astronomy was symbolic of the new age: Telescopes were beginning to give Europeans a sense of the vastness and complexity of the universe. When Faustus asks information of Mephistophilis, he begins with questions about the planets and the universe, knowledge of which had long been thought to be somehow secret. Mastering that knowledge was symbolic of mastering the knowledge of the innermost workings of science.

Faustus's quest for knowledge became for some people a Renaissance theme. The magicians referred to in the text, such as Roger Bacon and Cornelius Agrippa, were genuine. Their work was read throughout Europe, and the kinds of magic actions that Faustus aspires to were thought possible. The Elizabethans definitely believed in the presence of spirits, of ghosts, of intervention through witches of the otherworld. *Doctor Faustus* fed the contemporary interest in the occult. Faustus quests for forbidden knowledge; he must sell his soul to the devil to acquire it. His lust for knowledge — he says at the outset that he has dominated all the world of learning available to him — is without bounds.

Many of Marlowe's audience would have seen in Doctor Faustus an allusion to the magus John Dee, who cast the horoscope of Queen Elizabeth. Marlowe knew Dee, on whom the description of Faustus is based. Known throughout Europe for his almost supernormal intellectual capacity, Dee was learned in many sciences. His introduction to the first English edition of Euclid's *Geometry* made him not only respected in Europe but eventually known throughout the New World. Dee's version of Euclid was used at Harvard University until the late 1700s. Because Dee was a wizard, his house at Mortlake was attacked and burned to the ground by frightened peasants while he was abroad. With his house went one of the most impressive personal libraries in Europe.

Faustus was willing to seek forbidden knowledge — in the way Adam and Eve did — at all costs, in full awareness that he risked the loss of his soul. And while Marlowe condemns Faustus to hell and does not save him at the end, we have the feeling — as did Elizabethans — that there is something grand and heroic about Faustus's risk taking. He fails, yes, but he does so in a way that makes mediocre citizens who would never have had his imagination or daring seem pallid and weak. We find ourselves involved in Faustus's struggle.

Dr. Faustus in Performance

Marlowe may not have seen *Doctor Faustus* performed. There are no performance records until 1594, when Philip Henslowe and the Royal Admiral's Men produced the play. Productions were frequent until 1598, and Henslowe's records indicate that the play was extremely popular. The great actor Edward Alleyn portrayed Faustus. Along with several reissuings of printed versions of the play, productions seem to have continued into the early part of the 1600s, when a number of writers were hired at different times to add lines to the original text. After the Restoration in 1660 and the reopening of the theaters, *Doctor Faustus* was again played frequently, with Thomas Betterton in the title role. In the eighteenth century the play was sometimes staged as a farce and in some cases reduced to a puppet show. In the nineteenth century, however, audiences were given the chance to see the play as a serious tragedy, with Sir Henry Irving, one of the greatest of the nineteenth-century actors, performing in London at the Lyceum Theatre in 1885. Twentieth-century performances included a number of amateur productions, including one during wartime by the great director Peter Brook in 1942.

Orson Welles performed the title role in a Works Progress Administration (WPA) production in New York; reviews were mixed. Welles, himself a magician, emphasized the magical elements so that trapdoors and special effects became great moments of entertainment. The Phoenix Theatre's 1964 production in New York continued that tradition, with fireworks accompanying the entrance of the "hot whore." That production emphasized the blackness of the play, with dark sets and glittering dark costumes. At the end of the play, Faustus was faced with the yawning pit of hellfire. Productions of the play were also popular in Germany in the first half of the twentieth century. In his novel *Doctor Faustus*, Thomas Mann saw in the play a metaphor for Germany's having sold its soul to Hitler.

Christopher Marlowe (1564–1593)

THE TRAGICAL HISTORY OF THE LIFE AND DEATH OF DOCTOR FAUSTUS

c. 1593

The Players

THE CHORUS
DOCTOR FAUSTUS
WAGNER, *his student and servant*
VALDES
CORNELIUS
THREE SCHOLARS
AN OLD MAN

POPE ADRIAN
RAYMOND, *King of Hungary*
BRUNO, *the rival Pope*
TWO CARDINALS
THE ARCHBISHOP OF RHEIMS
CHARLES V, *Emperor of Germany*
MARTINO ⎫
FREDERICK ⎬ *Gentlemen of the Emperor's court*
BENVOLIO ⎭
BEELZEBUB
DUKE OF SAXONY
DUKE OF ANHOLT
DUCHESS OF ANHOLT
ROBIN, *the clown, a hostler*
DICK
A VINTNER
A HORSE-COURSER
A CARTER
HOSTESS

GOOD ANGEL
BAD ANGEL
LUCIFER
MEPHISTOPHILIS
PRIDE ⎫
COVETOUSNESS ⎪
ENVY ⎪
WRATH ⎬ *The Seven Deadly Sins*
GLUTTONY ⎪
SLOTH ⎪
LECHERY ⎭
ALEXANDER, THE GREAT
HIS PARAMOUR
DARIUS, *King of Persia*
HELEN OF TROY
TWO CUPIDS
DEVILS, BISHOPS, MONKS, FRIARS, SOLDIERS

Note: Material in brackets has been added by the editor.

The Scene: *Wittenberg, Rome, the Emperor's court at Innsbruck, court of the Duke of Anholt, and the neighboring countryside.*

PROLOGUE

(*Enter Chorus.*)

CHORUS: Not marching in the fields of Trasimene
    Where Mars° did mate° the warlike Carthagens,°
    Nor sporting in the dalliance of love
    In courts of kings where state° is overturned,
    Nor in the pomp of proud audacious deeds   5
    Intends our muse to vaunt his heavenly verse.
    Only this, gentles: we must now perform
    The form of Faustus' fortunes, good or bad.
    And now to patient judgments we appeal,
    And speak for Faustus in his infancy.   10
    Now is he born, of parents base of stock,
    In Germany, within a town called Rhode.
    At riper years to Wittenberg he went,
    Whereas his kinsmen chiefly brought him up.
    So much he profits in divinity,   15
    The fruitful plot of scholarism graced,°
    That shortly he was graced with doctor's name,
    Excelling all whose sweet delight disputes°
    In th'heavenly matters of theology,
    Till swoll'n with cunning of a self-conceit,   20
    His waxen wings did mount above his reach,
    And melting,° heavens conspired his overthrow;
    For, falling to a devilish exercise
    And glutted now with learning's golden gifts,
    He surfeits upon cursèd necromancy.   25
    Nothing so sweet as magic is to him,
    Which he prefers before his chiefest bliss;
    And this the man that in his study sits.

Prologue. 1–2. Trasimene . . . Carthagens: Perhaps an allusion to a lost play about the Carthaginian Hannibal, who achieved one of his greatest victories at Lake Trasimene in 217 B.C. **2. Mars:** Roman god of war. **mate:** Rival, meet in battle. **4. state:** Government. **16. fruitful plot . . . graced:** Adorned the university. **18. whose sweet delight disputes:** Who takes pleasure in disputing. **21–22. waxen wings . . . melting:** Metaphor referring to Icarus's attempt to fly with waxen wings, which melted when he ignored his father's warning and flew too near the sun.

ACT I • *Scene I*

(*Faustus in his study.*)

FAUSTUS: Settle thy studies, Faustus, and begin
    To sound the depth of that thou wilt profess.
    Having commenced,° be a divine in show;
    Yet level° at the end of every art,
5   And live and die in Aristotle's works.
    Sweet Analytics, 'tis thou hast ravished me!
    Bene' disserere est finis logices.°
    Is to dispute well logic's chiefest end?
    Affords this art no greater miracle?
10   Then read no more; thou hast attained that end.
    A greater subject fitteth Faustus' wit!
    Bid *On cay mae on*° farewell, Galen° come.
    Seeing *ubi desinit philosophus ibi incipit medicus,*°
    Be a physician, Faustus; heap up gold,
15   And be eternized for some wondrous cure.
    Summum bonum medicinae sanitas.°
    The end of physic is our body's health.
    Why, Faustus, hast thou not attained that end?
    Is not thy common talk sound aphorisms?
20   Are not thy bills° hung up as monuments,
    Whereby whole cities have escaped the plague,
    And divers desperate maladies been cured?
    Yet art thou still but Faustus and a man.
    Couldst thou make men to live eternally,
25   Or, being dead, raise them to life again,
    Then this profession were to be esteemed.
    Physic, farewell! Where is Justinian?°
    Si una eademque res legatus duobus,   [He reads.]
    Alter rem, alter valorem rei, etc.°
30   A petty case of paltry legacies!
    Exhaereditare filium non potest pater nisi° —
               [He reads.]
    Such is the subject of the Institute
    And universal body of the law.
    This study fits a mercenary drudge
35   Who aims at nothing but external trash,
    Too servile and illiberal for me.

When all is done, divinity is best.
Jerome's Bible,° Faustus, view it well:
Stipendium peccati mors est.° Ha! *Stipendium, etc.*
               [He reads.]
The reward of sin is death. That's hard.   40
Si pecasse negamus, fallimur   [He reads.]
Et nulla est in nobis veritas.°
If we say that we have no sin,
We deceive ourselves, and there's no truth in us.
Why then belike we must sin,   45
And so consequently die.
Ay, we must die an everlasting death.
What doctrine call you this? *Che serà, serà:*
What will be, shall be! Divinity, adieu!
These metaphysics of magicians,   50
And necromantic books are heavenly.
Lines, circles, signs, letters, and characters —
Ay, these are those that Faustus most desires.
O, what a world of profit and delight,
Of power, of honor, of omnipotence   55
Is promised to the studious artisan!
All things that move between the quiet poles
Shall be at my command. Emperors and kings
Are but obeyed in their several provinces,
Nor can they raise the wind or rend the clouds,   60
But his dominion that exceeds in this
Stretcheth as far as doth the mind of man.
A sound magician is a demi-god.
Here try thy brains to get a deity!
Wagner!

(*Enter Wagner.*)

    Commend me to my dearest friends,   65
The German Valdes and Cornelius;
Request them earnestly to visit me.
WAGNER: I will sir.
               (*Exit.*)
FAUSTUS: Their conference will be a greater help to me
    Than all my labors, plod I ne'er so fast.   70

(*Enter the Good Angel and the Evil Angel.*)

GOOD ANGEL: O, Faustus, lay that damnèd book aside,
    And gaze not on it, lest it tempt thy soul
    And heap God's heavy wrath upon thy head.
    Read, read the Scriptures. That is blasphemy.
BAD ANGEL: Go forward, Faustus, in that famous art   75
    Wherein all nature's treasury is contained.
    Be thou on earth as Jove is in the sky,
    Lord and commander of these elements.
               (*Exeunt*° *Angels.*)
FAUSTUS: How am I glutted with conceit° of this!
    Shall I make spirits fetch me what I please,   80

I, I. 3. **commenced:** Taken a degree. 4. **level:** Aim. 7. *Bene' disserere est finis logices:* The end of logic is to dispute well. A tenet of the anti-Aristotelian system introduced at Cambridge when Marlowe was a student there. 12. *On cay mae on:* From Aristotle, being or not being. **Galen:** Greek physician regarded throughout the Middle Ages as a medical authority. 13. *ubi desinit philosophus ibi incipit medicus:* Where the philosopher stops, the doctor begins. 16. *Summum . . . sanitas:* Health is the highest good of the practice of medicine. 20. **bills:** Medical prescriptions. 27. **Justinian:** Roman emperor of Constantinople (527–565), responsible for assembling the Roman law and renowned throughout the Middle Ages as a jurist. 28–29. *Si . . . rei, etc.:* If the same object is willed to two persons, let one have the thing itself and the other its value, etc. This is an incorrect version of one of Justinian's rules. 31. *Exhaereditare . . . nisi —:* The father cannot disinherit the son except —; another of Justinian's rules roughly paraphrased.

38. **Jerome's Bible:** St. Jerome's Vulgate [Latin] translation of the Bible. 39. *Stipendium . . . est:* Translated in line 40 (Rom. 6:23). 41–42. *Si . . . veritas:* Translated in lines 43–44 (1 John 1:8). 78. [S.D.] *Exeunt:* Latin for "they go out." 79. **conceit:** The conception of attaining.

Resolve me of° all ambiguities,
Perform what desperate enterprise I will?
I'll have them fly to India for gold,
Ransack the ocean for orient pearl,
85 And search all corners of the new-found world
For pleasant fruits and princely delicates.
I'll have them read me strange philosophy
And tell the secrets of all foreign kings;
I'll have them wall all Germany with brass
90 And make swift Rhine circle fair Wittenberg.°
I'll have them fill the public schools with silk
Wherewith the students shall be bravely clad.
I'll levy soldiers with the coin they bring
And chase the Prince of Parma from our land
95 And reign sole king of all the provinces.°
Yea, stranger engines for the brunt of war
Than was the fiery keel at Antwerp's bridge°
I'll make my servile spirits to invent.
Come, German Valdes and Cornelius,
                              [He calls within.]
100 And make me blessed with your sage conference!

(Enter Valdes and Cornelius.)

Valdes, sweet Valdes, and Cornelius,
Know that your words have won me at the last
To practice magic and concealed arts;
Yet not your words only, but mine own fantasy
105 That will receive no object, for my head
But ruminates on necromantic skill.
Philosophy is odious and obscure;
Both law and physic are for petty wits;
Divinity is basest of the three,
110 Unpleasant, harsh, contemptible and vile.
'Tis, magic, magic, that hath ravished me.
Then, gentle friends, aid me in this attempt,
And I, that have with subtle syllogisms
Gravelled° the pastors of the German church,
115 And made the flowering pride of Wittenberg
Swarm to my problems° as th'infernal spirits
On sweet Musaeus° when he came to hell,
Will be as cunning as Agrippa was,
Whose shadows° made all Europe honor him.
VALDES: Faustus, these books, thy wit, and our
120   experience
Shall make all nations to canonize us.
As Indian Moors° obey their Spanish lords,

So shall the spirits of every element
Be always serviceable to us three.
Like lions shall they guard us when we please,   125
Like Almain rutters° with their horsemen's staves
Or Lapland giants trotting by our sides,
Sometimes like women or unwedded maids,
Shadowing° more beauty in their airy brows
Than in the white breasts of the queen of love.   130
From Venice shall they drag huge argosies,
And from America the golden fleece
That yearly stuffs old Philip's treasury,
If learnèd Faustus will be resolute.
FAUSTUS: Valdes, as resolute am I in this   135
As thou to live; therefore object it not.
CORNELIUS: The miracles that magic will perform
Will make thee vow to study nothing else.
He that is grounded in astrology,
Enriched with tongues,° well seen in minerals,   140
Hath all the principles magic doth require.
Then doubt not, Faustus, but to be renowned
And more frequented for this mystery
Than heretofore the Delphian oracle.°
The spirits tell me they can dry the sea   145
And fetch the treasure of all foreign wracks,
Yea, all the wealth that our forefathers hid
Within the massy entrails of the earth.
Then tell me, Faustus, what shall we three want?
FAUSTUS: Nothing, Cornelius. O, this cheers my soul!   150
Come, show me some demonstrations magical,
That I may conjure in some lusty grove
And have these joys in full possession.
VALDES: Then haste thee to some solitary grove,
And bear wise Bacon's and Abanus' works,°   155
The Hebrew Psalter, and New Testament;
And whatsoever else is requisite
We will inform thee ere our conference cease.
CORNELIUS: Valdes, first let him know the words of
      art,
And then, all other ceremonies learned,   160
Faustus may try his cunning by himself.
VALDES: First I'll instruct thee in the rudiments,
And then wilt thou be perfecter than I.
FAUSTUS: Then come and dine with me, and after meat
We'll canvass every quiddity° thereof,   165
For ere I sleep I'll try what I can do.
This night I'll conjure, though I die therefore.
                                          (Exeunt.)

81. Resolve me of: Explain to me.   90. Rhine . . . Wittenberg: Wittenberg is actually on the Elbe River, not the Rhine. 95. provinces: The Netherlands.   97. fiery . . . bridge: In April 1584 the Dutch used a fireship to destroy a bridge built across a river by the Prince of Parma in an attempt to blockade Antwerp.   114. Gravelled: Puzzled and amazed.   116. problems: Public disputations.   117. Musaeus: A semimythical Greek poet. Following Virgil, Marlowe has him visit hell like the mythical Orpheus.   118–19. Agrippa . . . shadows: Cornelius Agrippa (1486?–1535), a German physician and student of the occult, was said to have power to raise spirits (shadows) from the dead.   122. Indian Moors: American Indians.

126. Almain rutters: German cavalry.   129. Shadowing: Harboring, sheltering.   140. Enriched with tongues: Fluent in Latin, the language used for communicating with spirits. 144. Delphian oracle: The high priest of Apollo at Delphi who had power to foretell the future. [An oracle is the response of a god to a question asked by one who worships the god. The Delphic Oracle was the chief oracle of Greece, presided over by Apollo.]   155. Bacon's . . . works: Roger Bacon (1214?–1294) and Pietro D'Abano (1250–1316) were famous in the Middle Ages for their feats of magic.   165. quiddity: Essential element (a term from scholastic logic).

Scene II

(*Enter two Scholars.*)

FIRST SCHOLAR: I wonder what's become of Faustus, that
was wont to make our schools ring with *sic probo.*°

(*Enter Wagner.*)

SECOND SCHOLAR: That shall we presently know; here
comes his boy.

5 FIRST SCHOLAR: How now sirrah! Where's thy master?
WAGNER: God in heaven knows.
SECOND SCHOLAR: Why, dost not thou know then?
WAGNER: Yes, I know, but that follows not.
FIRST SCHOLAR: Go to, sirrah! Leave your jesting and
10   tell us where he is.
WAGNER: That follows not by force of argument, which
you, being licentiates,° should stand upon; therefore
acknowledge your error and be attentive.
SECOND SCHOLAR: Then you will not tell us?
15 WAGNER: You are deceived, for I will tell you. Yet if you
were not dunces, you would never ask me such a
question. For is he not *corpus naturale,* and is not
that *mobile?*° Then wherefore should you ask such a
question? But that I am by nature phlegmatic, slow
20   to wrath, and prone to lechery — to love, I would
say — it were not for you to come within forty foot
of the place of execution, although I do not doubt
but to see you both hanged the next sessions. Thus
having triumphed over you, I will set my counte-
25   nance like a precisian° and begin to speak thus:
Truly, my dear brethren, my master is within at dinner with Valdes and Cornelius, as this wine, if it
could speak, would inform your worships. And so,
the Lord bless you, preserve you, and keep you, my
30   dear brethren.

(*Exit.*)

FIRST SCHOLAR: O Faustus, then I fear that which I
have long suspected.
That thou art fall'n into that damnèd art
For which they two are infamous through the
world.
SECOND SCHOLAR: Were he a stranger, not allied
to me,
35   The danger of his soul would make me mourn.
But come, let us go and inform the rector.°
It may be his grave counsel may reclaim him.
FIRST SCHOLAR: I fear me nothing will reclaim
him now.
SECOND SCHOLAR: Yet let us see what we
can do.

(*Exeunt.*)

I, II. 2. *sic probo:* Thus I prove (used in scholastic argument).
12. licentiates: Holders of university degrees.   17–18. *corpus
naturale . . . mobile:* The subject matter of physics, in scholastic terms, was *corpus naturale seu mobile* (natural body in
motion).   25. precisian: Puritan.   36. rector: Head of the university.

Scene III

(*Thunder. Enter [above] Lucifer and four Devils. Enter
Faustus to conjure.*)

FAUSTUS: Now that the gloomy shadow of the night,
Longing to view Orion's drizzling look,
Leaps from th'Antarctic world unto the sky
And dims the welkin° with her pitchy breath,
Faustus begin thine incantations,   5
And try if devils will obey thy hest,
Seeing thou hast prayed and sacrificed to them.
Within this circle is Jehovah's name,
Forward and backward anagrammatized,
Th'abbreviated names of holy saints,   10
Figures of every adjunct to the heavens,
And characters of signs and erring° stars,
By which the spirits are enforced to rise.
Then fear not, Faustus, to be resolute,
And try the utmost magic can perform.   15

(*Thunder.*)

*Sint mihi Dei Acherontis propitii! Valeat numen tri-
plex Jehovae. Ignei, aerii, aquatani spiritus, salvete!
Orientis princeps, Beelzebub, inferni ardentis monar-
cha, et Demogorgon, propitiamus vos, ut appareat et
surgat Mephistophilis. Quid tu moraris? Per Jehovam*   20
*Gehennam, et consecratam aquam quam nunc spargo,
signumque crucis quod nunc facto, et per vota nostra,
ipse nunc surgat nobis dicatus Mephistophilis.*°

(*Enter [Mephistophilis,] a Devil.*)

I charge thee to return and change thy shape;
Thou art too ugly to attend on me.   25
Go, and return an old Franciscan friar;
That holy shape becomes a devil best.

(*Exit Devil.*)

I see there's virtue in my heavenly words.
Who would not be proficient in this art?
How pliant is this Mephistophilis,   30
Full of obedience and humility.
Such is the force of magic and my spells.
Now Faustus, thou art conjurer laureate,
That canst command great Mephistophilis.
Quin redis Mephistophilis fratris imagine.°   35

(*Enter Mephistophilis [dressed like a Franciscan friar].*)

MEPHISTOPHILIS: Now Faustus, what wouldst thou
have me do?

I, III. 4. welkin: Sky.   12. erring: Wandering.   16–23. *Sint . . .
Mephistophilis:* May the gods of Aceron be propitious to me.
Let the triple name of Jehova [the trinity] be gone. Hail spirits
of fire, air, and water. Prince of the East, Beelzebub, monarch of
burning hell, and Demogorgon, we petition you that Mephistophilis may appear and rise. Why do you linger? By Jehova,
Gehenna, and the holy water which I now sprinkle and the sign
of the cross which I now make and by our vows, let Mephistophilis himself now rise to serve us.   35. *Quin . . . imagine:* Return, Mephistophilis, in the shape of a friar.

FAUSTUS: I charge thee wait upon me whilst I live,
    To do whatever Faustus shall command,
    Be it to make the moon drop from her sphere
40   Or the ocean to overwhelm the world.
MEPHISTOPHILIS: I am a servant to great Lucifer
    And may not follow thee without his leave.
    No more than he commands must we perform.
FAUSTUS: Did not he charge thee to appear to me?
MEPHISTOPHILIS: No, I came hither of mine own
45   accord.
FAUSTUS: Did not my conjuring speeches raise thee?
    Speak.
MEPHISTOPHILIS: That was the cause, but yet *per
        accidens,*°
    For when we hear one rack the name of God,
    Abjure the Scriptures and his Savior Christ,
50   We fly in hope to get his glorious soul;
    Nor will we come unless he use such means
    Whereby he is in danger to be damned.
    Therefore the shortest cut for conjuring
    Is stoutly to abjure the Trinity
55   And pray devoutly to the prince of hell.
FAUSTUS: So Faustus hath
    Already done, and holds this principle:
    There is no chief but only Beelzebub,
    To whom Faustus doth dedicate himself.
60   This word "damnation" terrifies not me,
    For I confound hell in Elysium.
    My ghost° be with the old philosophers!
    But leaving these vain trifles of men's souls,
    Tell me what is that Lucifer thy lord?
MEPHISTOPHILIS: Arch-regent and commander of all
65   spirits.
FAUSTUS: Was not that Lucifer an angel once?
MEPHISTOPHILIS: Yes Faustus, and most dearly loved
        of God.
FAUSTUS: How comes it then that he is prince of devils?
MEPHISTOPHILIS: O, by aspiring pride and insolence,
70   For which God threw him from the face of heaven.
FAUSTUS: And what are you that live with Lucifer?
MEPHISTOPHILIS: Unhappy spirits that fell with
        Lucifer,
    Conspired against our God with Lucifer,
    And are for ever damned with Lucifer.
FAUSTUS: Where are you damned?
75 MEPHISTOPHILIS: In hell.
FAUSTUS: How comes it then that thou art out of hell?
MEPHISTOPHILIS: Why this is hell, nor am I out of it.
    Think'st thou that I who saw the face of God
    And tasted the eternal joys of heaven
80   Am not tormented with ten thousand hells
    In being deprived of everlasting bliss?
    O Faustus, leave these frivolous demands
    Which strike a terror to my fainting soul.
FAUSTUS: What, is great Mephistophilis so passionate
85   For being deprivèd of the joys of heaven?

47. cause . . . *per accidens:* The terms are from scholastic logic.
62. ghost: Spirit.

    Learn thou of Faustus' manly fortitude,
    And scorn those joys thou never shalt possess.
    Go bear these tidings to great Lucifer:
    Seeing Faustus hath incurred eternal death
    By desperate thoughts against Jove's deity,   90
    Say he surrenders up to him his soul,
    So he will spare him four and twenty years,
    Letting him live in all voluptuousness,
    Having thee ever to attend on me,
    To give me whatsoever I shall ask,   95
    To tell me whatsoever I demand,
    To slay mine enemies, and aid my friends,
    And always be obedient to my will.
    Go, and return to mighty Lucifer,
    And meet me in my study at midnight,   100
    And then resolve me of thy master's mind.
MEPHISTOPHILIS: I will, Faustus.

                                (*Exit.*)

FAUSTUS: Had I as many souls as there be stars,
    I'd give them all for Mephistophilis.
    By him I'll be great emperor of the world,   105
    And make a bridge thorough the moving air,
    To pass the ocean with a band of men.
    I'll join the hills that bind° the Afric shore,
    And make that country continent to Spain,
    And both contributory to my crown.   110
    The Emperor shall not live but by my leave,
    Nor any potentate of Germany.
    Now that I have obtained what I desire,
    I'll live in speculation of this art
    Till Mephistophilis return again.   115

                                (*Exit.*)

Scene IV

(*Enter Wagner and [Robin,] the Clown.*)

WAGNER: Come hither, sirrah boy.
ROBIN: Boy! O disgrace to my person. Zounds, boy in
    your face! You have seen many boys with such
    pickedevants,° I am sure.
WAGNER: Sirrah, hast thou no comings in?°   5
ROBIN: Yes, and goings out too, you may see, sir.
WAGNER: Alas, poor slave! See how poverty jests in his
    nakedness. I know the villain's out of service, and so
    hungry that I know he would give his soul to the
    devil for a shoulder of mutton, though it were blood-   10
    raw.
ROBIN: Not so neither. I had need to have it well
    roasted, and good sauce to it, if I pay so dear, I can
    tell you.
WAGNER: Sirrah, wilt thou be my man and wait on me,   15
    and I will make thee go like *Qui mihi discipulus?*°

108. bind: Enclose. I, IV. 4. pickedevants: Pointed beards.
5. comings in: Earnings. 16. *Qui mihi discipulus:* Who is my
disciple (the opening words of a Latin poem by William Lyly,
well known to Elizabethan schoolboys).

ROBIN: What, in verse?

WAGNER: No slave; in beaten° silk and staves-acre.°

ROBIN: Staves-acre? That's good to kill vermin. Then,
20   belike, if I serve you I shall be lousy.

WAGNER: Why, so thou shalt be, whether thou dost it or
no; for, sirrah, if thou dost not presently bind thyself
to me for seven years, I'll turn all the lice about thee
into familiars° and make them tear thee in pieces.

25 ROBIN: Nay sir, you may save yourself a labor, for they
are as familiar with me as if they paid for their meat
and drink, I can tell you.

WAGNER: Well, sirrah, leave your jesting and take these
guilders.

30 ROBIN: Yes, marry sir, and I thank you too.

WAGNER: So, now thou art to be at an hour's warning,
whensoever and wheresoever the devil shall fetch
thee.

ROBIN: Here, take your guilders again. I'll none of 'em.

35 WAGNER: Not I. Thou art pressed.° Prepare thyself, for I
will presently raise up two devils to carry thee away.
Banio! Belcher!

ROBIN: Belcher? And Belcher come here, I'll belch him. I
am not afraid of a devil.

(Enter two Devils.)

40 WAGNER: How now, sir? Will you serve me now?

ROBIN: Ay, good Wagner; take away the devil then.

WAGNER: Spirits away! Now, sirrah, follow me.

                                    [Exeunt Devils.]

ROBIN: I will sir. But hark you, master, will you teach me
this conjuring occupation?

45 WAGNER: Ay, sirrah. I'll teach thee to turn thyself to a
dog, or a cat, or a mouse, or a rat, or any thing.

ROBIN: A dog, or a cat, or a mouse, or a rat! O brave
Wagner!

WAGNER: Villain, call me Master Wagner, and see that
50   you walk attentively, and let your right eye be always
diametrally° fixed upon my left heel, that thou may'st
quasi vestigial nostras insistere.°

ROBIN: Well, sir, I warrant you.

                                    (Exeunt.)

ACT II • Scene I

(Enter Faustus in his Study.)

FAUSTUS: Now Faustus must thou needs be damned,
And canst thou not be saved.
What boots° it then to think on God or heaven?
Away with such vain fancies, and despair;
5   Despair in God, and trust in Beelzebub.
Now go not backward; Faustus, be resolute.

Why waver'st thou? O, something soundeth in mine
ear:
"Abjure this magic; turn to God again."
Ay, and Faustus will turn to God again!
To God? He loves thee not.   10
The God thou serv'st is thine own appetite,
Wherein is fixed the love of Beelzebub.
To him I'll build an altar and a church,
And offer lukewarm blood of new-born babes.

(Enter the two Angels.)

BAD ANGEL: Go forward, Faustus, in that famous art.   15

GOOD ANGEL: Sweet Faustus, leave that execrable art.

FAUSTUS: Contrition, prayer, repentance — what of
these?

GOOD ANGEL: O, they are means to bring thee unto
heaven.

BAD ANGEL: Rather illusions, fruits of lunacy,
That make men foolish that do use them most.   20

GOOD ANGEL: Sweet Faustus, think of heaven and
heavenly things.

BAD ANGEL: No Faustus, think of honor and wealth.
                                    (Exeunt Angels.)

FAUSTUS: Wealth? Why, the signory of Emden° shall be
mine.
When Mephistophilis shall stand by me,
What power can hurt me? Faustus thou art safe.   25
Cast no more doubts. Mephistophilis, come
And bring glad tidings from great Lucifer.
Is't not midnight? Come, Mephistophilis.
Veni,° veni, Mephistophile.

(Enter Mephistophilis.)

Now tell me what saith Lucifer, thy lord?   30

MEPHISTOPHILIS: That I shall wait on Faustus whilst
he lives,
So he will buy my service with his soul.

FAUSTUS: Already Faustus hath hazarded that for thee.

MEPHISTOPHILIS: But now thou must bequeath it
solemnly
And write a deed of gift with thine own blood,   35
For that security craves great Lucifer.
If thou deny it, I must back to hell.

FAUSTUS: Stay, Mephistophilis! Tell me what good
Will my soul do thy lord.

MEPHISTOPHILIS: Enlarge his kingdom.

FAUSTUS: Is that the reason why he tempts us thus?   40

MEPHISTOPHILIS: *Solamen miseris socios habuisse
doloris.°*

FAUSTUS: Why, have you any pain that torture others?

MEPHISTOPHILIS: As great as have the human souls of
men.
But tell me, Faustus, shall I have thy soul?

---

18. beaten: Embroidered with metal. **staves-acre:** A plant
used for killing vermin. **24. familiars:** Attendant evil spirits.
35. pressed: Enlisted into service in exchange for money.
51. diametrally: In a straight line. **52. quasi . . . insistere:** As
if to walk in our tracks. **II, I. 3. boots:** Avails.

23. Emden: The chief city of East Friesland near the mouth
of the river Ems, which had considerable trade relations with
Elizabethan England. **29. Veni:** Come. **41. Solamen . . . doloris:** It is a consolation in misery to have a fellow sufferer.

45   And I will be thy slave and wait on thee
      And give thee more than thou hast wit to ask.
FAUSTUS: Ay, Mephistophilis, I'll give it him.
MEPHISTOPHILIS: Then Faustus, stab thy arm
      courageously,
      And bind thy soul that at some certain day
50   Great Lucifer may claim it as his own,
      And then be thou as great as Lucifer.
FAUSTUS: [*stabbing his arm*] Lo, Mephistophilis, for
      love of thee,
      I cut mine arm, and with my proper° blood
      Assure my soul to be great Lucifer's,
55   Chief lord and regent of perpetual night.
      View here this blood that trickles from mine arm,
      And let it be propitious for my wish.
MEPHISTOPHILIS: But Faustus,
      Write it in manner of a deed of gift.
60 FAUSTUS: Ay, so I do. [*He writes.*] But Mephistophilis,
      My blood congeals, and I can write no more.
MEPHISTOPHILIS: I'll fetch thee fire to dissolve it
      straight.

                                                    (*Exit.*)
FAUSTUS: What might the staying of my blood portend?
      Is it unwilling I should write this bill?
65   Why streams it not that I may write afresh?
      "Faustus gives to thee his soul." Ah, there it stayed.
      Why shouldst thou not? Is not thy soul thine own?
      Then write again: "Faustus gives to thee his soul."

(*Enter Mephistophilis with the chafer of fire.*)

MEPHISTOPHILIS: See Faustus, here is fire. Set it on.°
70 FAUSTUS: So. Now the blood begins to clear again.
      Now will I make an end immediately.

                                                 [*He writes.*]
MEPHISTOPHILIS: [*Aside.*] What will not I do to obtain
      his soul?
FAUSTUS: *Consummatum est;*° this bill is ended,
      And Faustus hath bequeathed his soul to Lucifer.
75   But what is this inscription on mine arm?
      Homo fuge!° Whither should I fly?
      If unto God, he'll throw me down to hell.
      My senses are deceived; here's nothing writ.
      O yes, I see it plain. Even here is writ
80   *Homo fuge!* Yet shall not Faustus fly.
MEPHISTOPHILIS: [*Aside.*] I'll fetch him somewhat to
      delight his mind.

                                                    (*Exit.*)

(*Enter Devils, giving crowns and rich apparel to Faustus. They dance and then depart. Enter Mephistophilis.*)

FAUSTUS: What means this show? Speak Mephistophilis.
MEPHISTOPHILIS: Nothing, Faustus, but to delight thy
      mind
      And let thee see what magic can perform.

---

53. proper: Own.   69. Set it on: Set the dish of blood on the
fire.   73. *Consummatum est:* It is completed (the words of Jesus
at his Crucifixion; John 19:30).   76. *Homo fuge:* Fly, man.

FAUSTUS: But may I raise such spirits when I please?   85
MEPHISTOPHILIS: Ay Faustus, and do greater things
      than these.
FAUSTUS: Then, Mephistophilis, receive this scroll,
      A deed of gift of body and of soul,
      But yet conditionally that thou perform
      All covenants and articles between us both.   90
MEPHISTOPHILIS: Faustus, I swear by hell and Lucifer
      To effect all promises between us made.
FAUSTUS: Then hear me read it Mephistophilis.
      On these conditions following:
      First, that Faustus may be a spirit in form and sub-   95
      stance;
      Secondly, that Mephistophilis shall be his servant and
      be at his command;
      Thirdly, that Mephistophilis shall do for him and
      bring him whatsoever;   100
      Fourthly, that he shall be in his chamber or house
      invisible;
      Lastly, that he shall appear to the said John Faustus
      at all times, in what form or shape soever he please: I,
      John Faustus, of Wittenberg, doctor, by these pres-   105
      ents, do give both body and soul to Lucifer, Prince of
      the East, and his minister, Mephistophilis; and fur-
      thermore grant unto them that four and twenty years
      being expired, the articles above written inviolate,
      full power to fetch or carry the said John Faustus,   110
      body and soul, flesh, blood, or goods, into their habi-
      tation wheresoever.
                                   By me, John Faustus.
MEPHISTOPHILIS: Speak Faustus. Do you deliver this as
      your deed?
FAUSTUS: Ay, take it, and the devil give thee good of it.   115
MEPHISTOPHILIS: So now, Faustus, ask me what thou
      wilt.
FAUSTUS: First will I question with thee about hell.
      Tell me, where is the place that men call hell?
MEPHISTOPHILIS: Under the heavens.
FAUSTUS: Ay, so are all things else. But whereabouts?   120
MEPHISTOPHILIS: Within the bowels of these elements,
      Where we are tortured and remain for ever.
      Hell hath no limits, nor is circumscribed
      In one self place, but where we are is hell,
      And where hell is, there must we ever be.   125
      And, to be short, when all the world dissolves
      And every creature shall be purified,
      All places shall be hell that is not heaven.
FAUSTUS: I think hell's a fable.
MEPHISTOPHILIS: Ay, think so still, till experience
      change thy mind.   130
FAUSTUS: Why, dost thou think that Faustus shall be
      damned?
MEPHISTOPHILIS: Ay, of necessity, for here's the scroll
      In which thou hast given thy soul to Lucifer.
FAUSTUS: Ay, and body too. But what of that?
      Think'st thou that Faustus is so fond° to imagine   135

---

135. fond: Foolish.

That after this life there is any pain?
No, these are trifles and mere old wives' tales.
MEPHISTOPHILIS: But I am an instance to prove the
    contrary,
For I tell thee I am damned and now in hell.
140 FAUSTUS: Nay, and this be hell, I'll willingly be
    damned.
What? Sleeping, eating, walking and disputing?
But, leaving off this, let me have a wife,
The fairest maid in Germany,
For I am wanton and lascivious,
145 And cannot live without a wife.
MEPHISTOPHILIS: I prithee, Faustus, talk not of a wife.
FAUSTUS: Nay, sweet Mephistophilis, fetch me one, for
    I will have one.
MEPHISTOPHILIS: Well, Faustus, thou shalt have a
    wife.
Sit there till I come.   [*Exit.*]

(*Enter [Mephistophilis] with a Devil dressed like a
woman, with fireworks.*)

150 FAUSTUS: What sight is this?
MEPHISTOPHILIS: Now Faustus, how dost thou like thy
    wife?
FAUSTUS: Here's a hot whore indeed! No, I'll no wife.
MEPHISTOPHILIS: Marriage is but a ceremonial toy,
And if thou lovest me, think no more of it.
155 I'll cull thee out the fairest courtesans
And bring them every morning to thy bed.
She whom thine eye shall like, thy heart shall have,
Were she as chaste as was Penelope,°
As wise as Saba,° or as beautiful
160 As was bright Lucifer before his fall.
Hold; take this book; peruse it thoroughly.
The iterating of these lines brings gold;
The framing of this circle on the ground
Brings thunder, whirlwinds, storm and lightning.
165 Pronounce this thrice devoutly to thyself,
And men in harness° shall appear to thee,
Ready to execute what thou command'st.
FAUSTUS: Thanks, Mephistophilis, for this sweet book.
This will I keep as chary as my life.

                      (*Exeunt.*)

Scene II

(*Enter Faustus in his study and Mephistophilis.*)

FAUSTUS: When I behold the heavens, then I repent
And curse thee, wicked Mephistophilis,
Because thou hast deprived me of those joys.
MEPHISTOPHILIS: 'Twas thine own seeking, Faustus;
    thank thyself.
5 But think'st thou heaven is such a glorious thing?

158. **Penelope:** The faithful wife of Ulysses in Homer's
Odyssey.   159. **Saba:** The Queen of Sheba.   166. **harness:**
Armor.

I tell thee, Faustus, 'tis not half so fair
As thou, or any man that breathes on earth.
FAUSTUS: How prov'st thou that?
MEPHISTOPHILIS: 'Twas made for man; then he's more
    excellent.
FAUSTUS: If heaven was made for man, 'twas made for
    me.   10
I will renounce this magic and repent.

(*Enter the two Angels.*)

GOOD ANGEL: Faustus repent; yet God will pity thee.
BAD ANGEL: Thou art a spirit;° God cannot pity thee.
FAUSTUS: Who buzzeth in mine ears I am a spirit?
Be I a devil, yet God may pity me;   15
Yea, God will pity me if I repent.
BAD ANGEL: Ay, but Faustus never shall repent.
                      (*Exeunt angels.*)
FAUSTUS: My heart is hardened; I cannot repent.
Scarce can I name salvation, faith, or heaven,
But fearful echoes thunder in mine ears: 20
"Faustus, thou art damned!" Then swords and
    knives,
Poison, guns, halters, and envenomed steel
Are laid before me to dispatch myself;
And long ere this I should have done the deed,
Had not sweet pleasure conquered deep despair.   25
Have not I made blind Homer sing to me
Of Alexander's love and Oenone's death?°
And hath not he, that built the walls of Thebes
With ravishing sound of his melodious harp,°
Made music with my Mephistophilis?   30
Why should I die then, or basely despair?
I am resolved; Faustus shall not repent.
Come, Mephistophilis, let us dispute again
And reason of divine astrology.
Speak; are there many spheres above the moon?   35
Are all celestial bodies but one globe,
As is the substance of this centric earth?
MEPHISTOPHILIS: As are the elements, such are the
    heavens,
Even from the moon unto the empyreal orb,
Mutually folded in each others' spheres,   40
And jointly move upon one axle-tree.
Whose terminè° is termed the world's wide pole;
Nor are the names of Saturn, Mars, or Jupiter
Feigned, but are erring stars.°
FAUSTUS: But have they all
One motion, both *situ et tempore?*°   45

II, II. 13. spirit: Devil.   **27. Alexander's . . . death:** Paris (also
called Alexander) loved the nymph Oenone when he lived as a
shepherd on Mt. Ida. Oenone died of a broken heart when he
left her.   **28–29. he . . . harp:** Amphion, son of Zeus and
Antiope, caused stones to move and the walls of Thebes to be
built simply by playing on the lyre given to him by Hermes.
42. terminè: Limit.   **44. erring stars:** Planets.   **45. *situ et tempore:*** In position (direction of movement) and in the time they
take to revolve about the earth.

MEPHISTOPHILIS: All move from east to west in four
and twenty hours upon the poles of the world, but
differ in their motions upon the poles of the zodiac.
FAUSTUS: These slender questions Wagner can decide.
50   Hath Mephistophilis no greater skill?
Who knows not the double motion of the planets?
That the first is finished in a natural day?
The second thus? Saturn in thirty years?
Jupiter in twelve; Mars in four; the sun, Venus and
55   Mercury in a year, the moon in twenty eight days.
These are freshmen's suppositions. But tell me hath
every sphere a dominion or *intelligentia?*°
MEPHISTOPHILIS: Ay.
FAUSTUS: How many heavens or spheres are there?
60   MEPHISTOPHILIS: Nine — the seven planets, the firma-
ment, and the empyreal heaven.
FAUSTUS: But is there not *coelum igneum, et crystallinum?*°
MEPHISTOPHILIS: No, Faustus, they be but fables.
65   FAUSTUS: Resolve me then in this one question: why are
not conjunctions, oppositions, aspects, eclipses° all at
one time, but in some years we have more, in some
less?
MEPHISTOPHILIS: *Per inaequalem motum respectu*
70   *totius.*°
FAUSTUS: Well, I am answered. Now tell me who made
the world.
MEPHISTOPHILIS: I will not.
FAUSTUS: Sweet Mephistophilis, tell me.
75   MEPHISTOPHILIS: Move me not, Faustus.
FAUSTUS: Villain, have not I bound thee to tell me any
thing?
MEPHISTOPHILIS: Ay, that is not against our kingdom.
This is. Thou art damned. Think thou of hell.
FAUSTUS: Think, Faustus, upon God that made the
80   world.
MEPHISTOPHILIS: Remember this.
                                                        (*Exit.*)
FAUSTUS: Ay, go accursèd spirit to ugly hell.
'Tis thou hast damned distressèd Faustus' soul.
Is't not too late?

(*Enter the two Angels.*)

85   BAD ANGEL: Too late.
GOOD ANGEL: Never too late, if Faustus will repent.
BAD ANGEL: If thou repent, devils will tear thee in
pieces.
GOOD ANGEL: Repent, and they shall never raze thy skin.
                                              (*Exeunt Angels.*)

FAUSTUS: O Christ, my Savior, my Savior,
Help to save distressèd Faustus' soul.   90

(*Enter Lucifer, Beelzebub, and Mephistophilis.*)

LUCIFER: Christ cannot save thy soul, for he is just.
There's none but I have interest in the same.
FAUSTUS: O, what art thou that look'st so terribly?
LUCIFER: I am Lucifer,
And this is my companion prince in hell.   95
FAUSTUS: O, Faustus, they are come to fetch thy soul.
BEELZEBUB: We are come to tell thee thou dost injure us.
LUCIFER: Thou call'st on Christ, contrary to thy
promise.
BEELZEBUB: Thou shouldst not think on God.
LUCIFER: Think on the devil.   100
BEELZEBUB: And his dam too.
FAUSTUS: Nor will I henceforth. Pardon me in this,
And Faustus vows never to look to heaven,
Never to name God, or to pray to him,
To burn his Scriptures, slay his ministers,   105
And make my spirits pull his churches down.
LUCIFER: So shalt thou show thyself an obedient
servant,
And we will highly gratify thee for it.
BEELZEBUB: Faustus, we are come from hell in person to
show thee some pastime. Sit down, and thou shalt   110
behold the Seven Deadly Sins appear to thee in their
own proper shapes and likeness.
FAUSTUS: That sight will be as pleasant to me as Paradise
was to Adam the first day of his creation.
LUCIFER: Talk not of Paradise or creation, but mark the   115
show. Go, Mephistophilis, fetch them in.
                                    [*Exit Mephistophilis.*]

(*Enter the Seven Deadly Sins, [with Mephistophilis, led
by a Piper*].)

BEELZEBUB: Now Faustus, question them of their names
and dispositions.
FAUSTUS: That shall I soon. What art thou, the first?
PRIDE: I am Pride. I disdain to have any parents. I am   120
like to Ovid's flea:° I can creep into every corner of a
wench. Sometimes, like a periwig, I sit upon her
brow. Next, like a necklace, I hang about her neck.
Then, like a fan of feathers, I kiss her lips, and then,
turning myself to a wrought smock, do what I list.   125
But fie, what a smell is here! I'll not speak another
word unless the ground be perfumed and covered
with cloth of Arras.°
FAUSTUS: Thou art a proud knave indeed. What art
thou, the second?   130
COVETOUSNESS: I am Covetousness, begotten of an old
churl in a leather bag, and might I now obtain my
wish, this house, you and all, should turn to gold, that
I might lock you safe into my chest. O my sweet gold!

---

57. dominion or *intelligentia*: Governing angel.   **62–63. *coelum . . . crystallinum*:** The fiery heaven and crystalline sphere
of Ptolemaic astronomy.   **66. conjunctions:** Seeming proximi-
ties of heavenly bodies.   **oppositions:** Divergences of heavenly
bodies.   **aspects:** Any other relations of such bodies to one
another.   **eclipses:** The blottings out of one heavenly body by
another.   **69–70. *Per . . . totius*:** By their unequal movements
in respect to the whole (i.e., the different speeds of the various
planets within the total cosmos).

121. Ovid's flea: The medieval poem *Carmine de Pulice* (Poem
of the Flea) was generally attributed to Ovid.   **128. cloth of
Arras:** Flemish cloth used generally for tapestries.

Emry James (l.) as Mephistophilis and Ian McKellen as Doctor Faustus in the 1974 Royal Shakespeare Company's production of Marlowe's play.

135 FAUSTUS: And what art thou, the third?

ENVY: I am Envy, begotten of a chimney-sweeper and an oyster-wife. I cannot read and therefore wish all books burned. I am lean with seeing others eat. O,
140 that there would come a famine over all the world, that all might die, and I live alone; then thou shouldst see how fat I'd be. But must thou sit and I stand? Come down, with a vengeance.

FAUSTUS: Out envious wretch! But what are thou, the fourth?

145 WRATH: I am Wrath. I had neither father nor mother. I leaped out of a lion's mouth when I was scarce an hour old, and ever since have run up and down the world with this case of rapiers, wounding myself when I could get none to fight withal. I was born in
150 hell, and look to it, for some of you shall be my father.

FAUSTUS: And what are you, the fifth?

GLUTTONY: I am Gluttony. My parents are all dead, and the devil a penny they have left me but a small pen-
155 sion, and that buys me thirty meals a day and ten bevers° — a small trifle to suffice nature. I come of a royal pedigree. My father was a gammon of bacon, and my mother was a hogshead of claret wine. My godfathers were these: Peter Pickled-herring and
160 Martin Martlemas-beef.° But my godmother, O, she was a jolly gentlewoman, and well beloved in every good town and city; her name was Mistress Margery March-beer.° Now Faustus, thou hast heard all my progeny; wilt thou bid me to a supper.

FAUSTUS: Not I. Thou wilt eat up all my victuals.   165

GLUTTONY: Then the devil choke thee.

FAUSTUS: Choke thyself, glutton. What art thou, the sixth?

SLOTH: Heigh ho! I am Sloth. I was begotten on a sunny bank, where I have lain ever since, and you have done 170 me great injury to bring me from thence. Let me be carried thither again by Gluttony and Lechery. Heigh ho! I'll not speak a word more for a king's ransom.

FAUSTUS: And what are you Mistress Minx, the seventh and last?   175

LECHERY: Who, I, sir? I am one that loves an inch of raw mutton° better than an ell of fried stockfish,° and the first letter of my name begins with lechery.

LUCIFER: Away to hell! Away! On piper!

     (*Exeunt the seven Sins [and the Piper].*)

FAUSTUS: O, how this sight doth delight my soul!   180

LUCIFER: But Faustus, in hell is all manner of delight.

FAUSTUS: O, might I see hell and return again safe, how happy were I then!

LUCIFER: Faustus, thou shalt. At midnight I will send for thee. Meanwhile peruse this book and view it 185

---

156. **bevers:** Light snacks taken between regular meals. 160. **Martlemas-beef:** Salted meat hung for the winter on Martinmas, November 11.

163. **March-beer:** A fine ale made in the springtime and aged for two years before being drunk.   176–177. **raw mutton:** Common slang for "whore."   177. **stockfish:** Dried codfish.

thoroughly, and thou shalt turn thyself into what
shape thou wilt.
FAUSTUS: Thanks, mighty Lucifer.
   This will I keep as chary as my life.
190 LUCIFER: Now Faustus, farewell.
FAUSTUS: Farewell, great Lucifer. Come, Mephistophilis.
                            (*Exeunt, several ways.*)

Scene III

(*Enter the Clown,* [*Robin, holding a book*].)

ROBIN: What, Dick, look to the horses there till I come
   again. I have gotten one of Doctor Faustus' conjuring
   books, and now we'll have such knavery as't passes.

(*Enter Dick.*)

DICK: What, Robin, you must come away and walk the
5   horses.
ROBIN: I walk the horses? I scorn't, 'faith. I have other
   matters in hand. Let the horses walk themselves and
   they will. [*He reads.*] *A per se a; t, h, e, the; o per se o;
   deny orgon, gorgon.* Keep further from me, O thou
10   illiterate and unlearned hostler.
DICK: 'Snails,° what hast thou got there? A book? Why,
   thou canst not tell ne'er a word on't.
ROBIN: That thou shalt see presently. Keep out of the
   circle, I say, lest I send you into the hostry with a
15   vengeance.
DICK: That's like, 'faith. You had best leave your foolery, for an my master come, he'll conjure you, 'faith.
ROBIN: My master conjure me? I'll tell thee what: an my
   master come here, I'll clap as fair a pair of horns°
20   on's head as e'er thou sawest in thy life.
DICK: Thou needst not do that, for my mistress hath
   done it.
ROBIN: Ay, there be of us here that have waded as deep
   into matters as other men, if they were disposed to
25   talk.
DICK: A plague take you! I thought you did not sneak up
   and down after her for nothing. But I prithee, tell me
   in good sadness,° Robin, is that a conjuring book?
ROBIN: Do but speak what thou'lt have me to do, and
30   I'll do't. If thou'lt dance naked, put off thy clothes
   and I'll conjure thee about presently. Or if thou'lt go
   but to the tavern with me, I'll give thee white wine,
   red wine, claret wine, sack, muscadine, malmesey
   and whippincrust.° Hold belly, hold, and we'll not
35   pay one penny for it.
DICK: O brave! Prithee let's to it presently, for I am as
   dry as a dog.
ROBIN: Come then, let's away.
                                        (*Exeunt.*)

ACT III • *Prologue*

(*Enter the Chorus.*)

CHORUS: Learnèd Faustus,
   To find the secrets of astronomy
   Graven in the book of Jove's high firmament,
   Did mount him up to scale Olympus' top,
   Where, sitting in a chariot burning bright   5
   Drawn by the strength of yokèd dragons' necks,
   He views the clouds, the planets, and the stars,
   The tropics, zones, and quarters of the sky,
   From the bright circle of the hornèd moon
   Even to the height of *Primum Mobile.*°   10
   And whirling round with this circumference,
   Within the concave compass of the pole,
   From east to west his dragons swiftly glide
   And in eight days did bring him home again.
   Not long he stayed within his quiet house   15
   To rest his bones after his weary toil,
   But new exploits do hale him out again,
   And mounted then upon a dragon's back,
   That with his wings did part the subtle air,
   He now is gone to prove cosmography,°   20
   That measures coasts and kingdoms of the earth,
   And, as I guess, will first arrive at Rome
   To see the Pope and manner of his court
   And take some part of holy Peter's feast,
   The which this day is highly solemnized.   25
                                        (*Exit.*)

Scene I

(*Enter Faustus and Mephistophilis.*)

FAUSTUS: Having now, my good Mephistophilis,
   Passed with delight the stately town of Trier,
   Environed round with airy mountain tops,
   With walls of flint, and deep entrenchèd lakes,°
   Not to be won by any conquering prince;   5
   From Paris next, coasting the realm of France,
   We saw the river Main fall into Rhine,
   Whose banks are set with groves of fruitful vines;
   Then up to Naples, rich Campania,
   Whose buildings fair and gorgeous to the eye,   10
   The streets straight forth and paved with finest brick,
   Quarters the town in four equivalents.
   There saw we learnèd Maro's° golden tomb,
   The way he cut, an English mile in length,
   Through a rock of stone in one night's space.°   15

III, Prologue. 10. *Primum Mobile:* In Ptolemaic astronomy
the outermost sphere of creation, which moves the other
nine spheres.   20. prove cosmography: Explore the universe.
III, I. 4. entrenchèd lakes: Castle moats.   13. Maro: Virgil.
14–15. way . . . space: A tunnel between the bays of Naples
and Baiae, through Mt. Posilipo, was said to have been cut by
Virgil (regarded as a magician in the Middle Ages) by supernatural art.

II, III. 11. 'Snails: By God's nails.   19. horns: The common sign
of a cuckold.   28. sadness: Seriousness.   34. whippincrust:
Possibly a corruption of "hippocras," a highly spiced and
sugared wine.

From thence to Venice, Padua, and the rest,
In midst of which a sumptuous temple stands,
That threats the stars with her aspiring top,
Whose frame is paved with sundry colored stones,
20   And roofed aloft with curious work in gold.°
Thus hitherto hath Faustus spent his time.
But tell me now, what resting-place is this?
Hast thou, as erst I did command,
Conducted me within the walls of Rome?
MEPHISTOPHILIS: I have, my Faustus, and for proof
25   thereof
This is the goodly palace of the Pope;
And 'cause we are no common guests,
I choose his privy chamber for our use.
FAUSTUS: I hope his holiness will bid us welcome.
MEPHISTOPHILIS: All's one, for we'll be bold with his
30   venison.
But now, my Faustus, that thou may'st perceive
What Rome contains for to delight thine eyes,
Know that this city stands upon seven hills
That underprop the groundwork of the same.
35   Just through the midst runs flowing Tiber's stream,
With winding banks that cut it in two parts,
Over the which four stately bridges lean,
That make safe passage to each part of Rome.
Upon the bridge called Ponte Angelo
40   Erected is a castle passing strong,
Where thou shalt see such store of ordinance
As that the double cannons, forged of brass,
Do match the number of the days contained
Within the compass of one complete year;
45   Beside the gates and high pyramidès
That Julius Caesar brought from Africa.°
FAUSTUS: Now, by the kingdoms of infernal rule,
Of Styx, of Acheron, and the fiery lake
Of ever-burning Phlegethon, I swear
50   That I do long to see the monuments
And situation of bright-splendent Rome.
Come, therefore, let's away.
MEPHISTOPHILIS: Nay, stay my Faustus. I know you'd
see the Pope
And take some part of holy Peter's feast,
55   The which, in state and high solemnity,
This day is held through Rome and Italy
In honor of the Pope's triumphant victory.
FAUSTUS: Sweet Mephistophilis, thou pleasest me.
Whilst I am here on earth, let me be cloyed
60   With all things that delight the heart of man.
My four and twenty years of liberty
I'll spend in pleasure and in dalliance,
That Faustus' name, whilst this bright frame doth
stand,
May be admirèd through the furthest land.

MEPHISTOPHILIS: 'Tis well said, Faustus. Come then,
stand by me   65
And thou shalt see them come immediately.
FAUSTUS: Nay, stay, my gentle Mephistophilis,
And grant me my request, and then I go.
Thou know'st within the compass of eight days
We viewed the face of heaven, of earth, and hell.   70
So high our dragons soared into the air,
That looking down, the earth appeared to me
No bigger than my hand in quantity.
There did we view the kingdoms of the world,
And what might please mine eye I there beheld.   75
Then in this show let me an actor be,
That this proud Pope may Faustus' cunning see.
MEPHISTOPHILIS: Let it be so, my Faustus. But, first stay
And view their triumphs° as they pass this way,
And then devise what best contents thy mind   80
By cunning in thine art to cross the Pope
Or dash the pride of this solemnity,
To make his monks and abbots stand like apes
And point like antics at his triple crown,
To beat the beads about the friars' pates   85
Or clap huge horns upon the cardinals' heads,
Or any villainy thou canst devise,
And I'll perform it, Faustus. Hark, they come.
This day shall make thee be admired in Rome.

(*Enter the Cardinals and Bishops, some bearing crosiers,
some the pillars; Monks and Friars singing their procession. Then the Pope, and Raymond, King of Hungary,
with Bruno, led in chains.*)

POPE: Cast down our footstool.
RAYMOND: Saxon Bruno, stoop,   90
Whilst on thy back his holiness ascends
Saint Peter's chair and state pontifical.
BRUNO: Proud Lucifer, that state belongs to me,
But thus I fall to Peter, not to thee.
POPE: To me and Peter shalt thou groveling lie   95
And crouch before the papal dignity.
Sound trumpets then, for thus Saint Peter's heir
From Bruno's back ascends Saint Peter's chair.

(*A flourish while he ascends.*)

Thus, as the gods creep on with feet of wool
Long ere with iron hands they punish men,   100
So shall our sleeping vengeance now arise
And smite with death thy hated enterprise.
Lord Cardinals of France and Padua,
Go forthwith to our holy consistory,
And read amongst the Statutes Decretal°   105
What, by the holy council held at Trent,°
The sacred synod hath decreed for him
That doth assume the papal government

17–20. **In midst . . . gold:** St. Mark's cathedral in Venice.
45–46. **gates . . . Africa:** Before the gates of St. Peter's there still
stands the obelisk that was brought to Rome from Heliopolis
by the Emperor Caligula in the first century A.D.

79. **triumphs:** Spectacular displays.   105. **Statutes Decretal:**
Papal decrees concerning religious doctrine or ecclesiastical law.
106. **council . . . Trent:** The Council of Trent, held by the
Church from 1545 to 1563.

110   Without election and a true consent.
      Away, and bring us word with speed.
FIRST CARDINAL: We go my Lord.

                         (*Exeunt Cardinals.*)

POPE: Lord Raymond.   [*They talk apart.*]
FAUSTUS: Go, haste thee, gentle Mephistophilis,
      Follow the cardinals to the consistory,
115   And as they turn their superstitious books,
      Strike them with sloth and drowsy idleness,
      And make them sleep so sound that in their shapes
      Thyself and I may parley with this Pope,
      This proud confronter of the Emperor,
120   And in despite of all his holiness
      Restore this Bruno to his liberty
      And bear him to the states of Germany.
MEPHISTOPHILIS: Faustus, I go.
FAUSTUS: Dispatch it soon.
125   The Pope shall curse that Faustus came to Rome.
              (*Exeunt Faustus and Mephistophilis.*)
BRUNO: Pope Adrian,° let me have some right of law.
      I was elected by the Emperor.
POPE: We will depose the Emperor for that deed
      And curse the people that submit to him.
130   Both he and thou shalt stand excommunicate
      And interdict from church's privilege
      And all society of holy men.
      He grows too proud in his authority,
      Lifting his lofty head above the clouds,
135   And like a steeple overpeers the church.
      But we'll pull down his haughty insolence,
      And as Pope Alexander, our progenitor,
      Trod on the neck of German Frederick,°
      Adding this golden sentence to our praise,
140   "That Peter's heirs should tread on emperors
      And walk upon the dreadful adder's back,
      Treading the lion and the dragon down
      And fearless spurn the killing basilisk,"°
      So will we quell that haughty schismatic,
145   And by authority apostolical
      Depose him from his regal government.
BRUNO: Pope Julius swore to princely Sigismond,°
      For him and the succeeding popes of Rome,
      To hold the emperors their lawful lords.
150 POPE: Pope Julius did abuse the church's rites,
      And therefore none of his decrees can stand.

126. **Pope Adrian:** Marlowe perhaps means Pope Hadrian IV (1154–1159), who tried to assert his authority over Frederick Barbarossa, the Holy Roman Emperor. What historicity there may be in these scenes at the papal court is badly confused. 137–138. **Pope Alexander . . . Frederick:** Pope Alexander III (1159–1181), successor to Hadrian IV, continued the struggle against Barbarossa, forcing him to acknowledge the papal supremacy at Canossa. 143. **basilisk:** A mythical monster with power to kill by its looks. 147. **Pope Julius . . . Sigismond:** None of the three popes named Julius was contemporary with the Emperor Sigismund (1368–1437). Sigismund did, however, in 1414 summon the Council of Constance, which sought to end the Great Schism (1378–1417), during which the papacy in Rome was challenged by a line of popes in Avignon.

      Is not all power on earth bestowed on us?
      And therefore, though we would, we cannot err.
      Behold this silver belt, whereto is fixed
      Seven golden keys fast sealed with seven seals   155
      In token of our sevenfold power from heaven,
      To bind or loose, lock fast, condemn or judge,
      Resign, or seal, or whatso pleaseth us.
      Then he and thou and all the world shall stoop,
      Or be assurèd of our dreadful curse   160
      To light as heavy as the pains of hell.

(*Enter Faustus and Mephistophilis, like the Cardinals.*)

MEPHISTOPHILIS: Now tell me, Faustus, are we not
      fitted well?
FAUSTUS: Yes, Mephistophilis, and two such cardinals
      Ne'er served a holy pope as we shall do.
      But whilst they sleep within the consistory,   165
      Let us salute his reverend fatherhood.
RAYMOND: Behold, my lord, the cardinals are
      returned.
POPE: Welcome, grave fathers. Answer presently:
      What have our holy council there decreed
      Concerning Bruno and the Emperor,   170
      In quittance of their late conspiracy
      Against our state and papal dignity?
FAUSTUS: Most sacred patron of the church of Rome,
      By full consent of all the synod
      Of priests and prelates it is thus decreed: 175
      That Bruno and the German Emperor
      Be held as Lollards° and bold schismatics
      And proud disturbers of the church's peace.
      And if that Bruno by his own assent,
      Without enforcement of the German peers,   180
      Did seek to wear the triple diadem
      And by your death to climb Saint Peter's chair,
      The Statutes Decretal have thus decreed:
      He shall be straight condemned of heresy
      And on a pile of fagots burned to death.   185
POPE: It is enough. Here, take him to your charge,
      And bear him straight to Ponte Angelo,
      And in the strongest tower enclose him fast.
      Tomorrow, sitting in our consistory
      With all our college of grave cardinals,   190
      We will determine of his life or death.
      Here, take his triple crown along with you,
      And leave it in the church's treasury.
      Make haste again, my good lord cardinals,
      And take our blessing apostolical.   195
MEPHISTOPHILIS: So, so. Was never devil thus blessed
      before.
FAUSTUS: Away, sweet Mephistophilis, be gone.
      The cardinals will be plagued for this anon.

(*Exeunt Faustus and Mephistophilis [with Bruno].*)

POPE: Go presently and bring a banquet forth,
      That we may solemnize Saint Peter's feast,   200

177. **Lollards:** Followers of John Wyclif (1320?–1384), the English reformer.

And with Lord Raymond, King of Hungary,
Drink to our late and happy victory.   (*Exeunt.*)

Scene II

(*A sennet [is sounded] while the banquet is brought in;
and then enter Faustus and Mephistophilis in their own
shapes.*)

MEPHISTOPHILIS: Now, Faustus, come, prepare thyself
          for mirth.
     The sleepy cardinals are hard at hand
     To censure Bruno, that is posted hence,
     And on a proud-paced steed, as swift as thought,
5   Flies o'er the Alps to fruitful Germany,
     There to salute the woeful Emperor.
FAUSTUS: The Pope will curse them for their sloth
          today,
     That slept both Bruno and his crown away.
     But now, that Faustus may delight his mind
10   And by their folly make some merriment,
     Sweet Mephistophilis, so charm me here
     That I may walk invisible to all
     And do whate'er I please unseen of any.
MEPHISTOPHILIS: Faustus, thou shalt. Then kneel down
          presently:
15   *Whilst on thy head I lay my hand*
          And charm thee with this magic wand.
          First wear this girdle; then appear
          Invisible to all are here.
          The planets seven, the gloomy air,
20   *Hell and the Furies'° forkèd hair,*
          Pluto's blue fire, and Hecate's tree,°
          With magic spells so compass thee
          That no eye may thy body see.
     So Faustus. Now, for all their holiness,
25   Do what thou wilt, thou shalt not be discerned.
FAUSTUS: Thanks, Mephistophilis. Now friars take heed
     Lest Faustus make your shaven crowns to bleed.
MEPHISTOPHILIS: Faustus, no more. See where the
          cardinals come.

(*Enter Pope and all the Lords. Enter the Cardinals with
a book.*)

POPE: Welcome, lord cardinals. Come, sit down.
30   Lord Raymond, take your seat. Friars attend,
     And see that all things be in readiness,
     As best beseems this solemn festival.
FIRST CARDINAL: First, may it please your sacred
          holiness
     To view the sentence of the reverend synod
35   Concerning Bruno and the Emperor?
POPE: What needs this question? Did I not tell you
     Tomorrow we would sit i' th' consistory

And there determine of his punishment?
You brought us word even now; it was decreed
That Bruno and the cursèd Emperor   40
Were by the holy council both condemned
For loathèd Lollards and base schismatics.
Then wherefore would you have me view that
     book?
FIRST CARDINAL: Your grace mistakes. You gave us no
     such charge.
RAYMOND: Deny it not. We all are witnesses   45
     That Bruno here was late delivered you,
     With his rich triple crown to be reserved
     And put into the church's treasury.
BOTH CARDINALS: By holy Paul, we saw them not.
POPE: By Peter, you shall die   50
     Unless you bring them forth immediately.
     Hale them to prison. Lade their limbs with
          gyves.°
     False prelates, for this hateful treachery
     Cursed be your souls to hellish misery.

          [*Exeunt the two Cardinals with Attendants.*]

FAUSTUS: So, they are safe. Now, Faustus, to the
          feast.   55
     The Pope had never such a frolic guest.
POPE: Lord Archbishop of Rheims, sit down with us.
ARCHBISHOP: I thank your holiness.
FAUSTUS: Fall to. The devil choke you an you spare.°
POPE: Who's that spoke? Friars look about.   60
FRIAR: Here's nobody, if it like your holiness.
POPE: Lord Raymond, pray fall to. I am beholding
     To the Bishop of Milan for this so rare a present.
FAUSTUS: I thank you, sir.   [*He snatches the dish.*]
POPE: How now? Who snatched the meat from me?   65
     Villains, why speak you not?
     My good Lord Archbishop, here's a most dainty
          dish
     Was sent me from a cardinal in France.
FAUSTUS: I'll have that too.   [*He snatches the dish.*]
POPE: What Lollards do attend our holiness,   70
     That we receive such great indignity?
     Fetch me some wine.
FAUSTUS: Ay, pray do, for Faustus is a-dry.
POPE: Lord Raymond, I drink unto your grace.
FAUSTUS: I pledge your grace.   [*He snatches the cup.*] 75
POPE: My wine gone too? Ye lubbers, look about
     And find the man that doth this villainy,
     Or by our sanctitude, you all shall die.
     I pray, my lords, have patience at this
     Troublesome banquet.   80
ARCHBISHOP: Please it your holiness, I think it be some
     ghost crept out of purgatory, and now is come unto
     your holiness for his pardon.
POPE: It may be so.
     Go then, command our priests to sing a dirge   85

III, II. 20. *Furies:* Spirits called on to avenge crimes, especially crimes against kin.   **21.** *Hecate's tree:* Hecate is the goddess of witchcraft.

52. Lade . . . gyves: Shackle their limbs.   **59. an you spare:** If you hold back.

To lay the fury of this same troublesome ghost.
                                    [*Exit an attendant.*]
    Once again, my lord, fall to.
                                    (*The Pope crosseth himself.*)
FAUSTUS: How now?
    Must every bit be spicèd with a cross?
90 Nay then, take that.   [*He strikes the Pope.*]
POPE: O I am slain. Help me, my lords.
    O come and help to bear my body hence.
    Damned be this soul for ever for this deed.

                        (*Exeunt the Pope and his train.*)

MEPHISTOPHILIS: Now, Faustus, what will you do now?
95 For I can tell you you'll be cursed with bell, book,
    and candle.°
FAUSTUS: Bell, book, and candle; candle, book, and bell,
    Forward and backward, to curse Faustus to hell.

(*Enter the Friars with bell, book, and candle for the
dirge.*)

FIRST FRIAR: Come, brethren, let's about our business
100   with good devotion.   [*They chant.*]
        *Cursed be he that stole his holiness' meat from
        the table.*
            Maledicat Dominus!°
        *Cursed be he that struck his holiness a blow on
        the face.*
            Maledicat Dominus!
        Cursed be he that struck Friar Sandelo a blow on
105   *the pate.*
            Maledicat Dominus!
        Cursed be he that disturbeth our holy dirge.
            Maledicat Dominus!
        Cursed be he that took away his holiness's wine.
110   *Maledicat Dominus! Et omnes sancti.*°
        Amen.

([*Faustus and Mephistophilis*] *beat the Friars, fling fireworks among them, and exeunt.*)

Scene III

(*Enter [Robin,] the clown, and Dick, with a cup.*)

DICK: Sirrah Robin, we were best look that your devil
    can answer the stealing of this same cup, for the vint-
    ner's boy follows us at the hard heels.
ROBIN: 'Tis no matter. Let him come. An he follow us,
5   I'll so conjure him as he was never conjured in his
    life, I warrant him. Let me see the cup.

(*Enter Vintner.*)

DICK: Here 'tis. Yonder he comes. Now, Robin, now or
    never show thy cunning.

95–96. **bell, book, and candle:** Used traditionally in the rite of
excommunication.   102. *Maledicat Dominus:* May the Lord
curse him.   110. *Et omnes sancti:* And all the saints.

VINTNER: O, are you here? I am glad I have found you.
    You are a couple of fine companions. Pray, where's   10
    the cup you stole from the tavern?
ROBIN: How, how? We steal a cup? Take heed what you
    say. We look not like cup stealers, I can tell you.
VINTNER: Never deny's, for I know you have it, and I'll
    search you.   15
ROBIN: Search me? Ay, and spare not. Hold the cup, Dick.
    [*Aside to Dick.*] Come, come, search me, search me.

[*The Vintner searches Robin.*]

VINTNER: [*to Dick*] Come on, sirrah, let me search you
    now.
DICK: Ay, ay, do, do. Hold the cup, Robin. [*Aside to*   20
    Robin.] I fear not your searching. We scorn to steal
    your cups, I can tell you.

[*The Vintner searches Dick.*]

VINTNER: Never outface me for the matter, for sure the
    cup is between you two.
ROBIN: Nay, there you lie. 'Tis beyond us both.   25
VINTNER: A plague take you! I thought 'twas your knav-
    ery to take it away. Come, give it me again.
ROBIN: Ay, much. When? Can you tell? Dick, make me
    a circle, and stand close at my back, and stir not for
    thy life. Vintner, you shall have your cup anon. Say   30
    nothing, Dick, *O per se, O Demogorgon, Belcher
    and Mephistophilis.*

(*Enter Mephistophilis.* [*Exit the Vintner, in fright.*])

MEPHISTOPHILIS: Monarch of hell, under whose black
        survey
    Great potentates do kneel with awful fear,
    Upon whose altars thousand souls do lie,   35
    How am I vexèd by these villains' charms!
    From Constantinople have they brought me now,
    Only for pleasure of these damnèd slaves.
ROBIN: By Lady, sir, you have had a shrewd journey of
    it. Will it please you to take a shoulder of mutton to 40
    supper and a tester° in your purse, and go back again?
DICK: Ay, I pray you heartily, sir, for we called you but in
    jest, I promise you.
MEPHISTOPHILIS: To purge the rashness of this cursèd
        deed,
    First be thou turnèd to this ugly shape,   45
    For apish deeds transformèd to an ape.
ROBIN: O brave, an ape! I pray sir, let me have the carry-
    ing of him about to show some tricks.
MEPHISTOPHILIS: And so thou shalt. Be thou trans-
    formed to a dog, and carry him upon thy back. Away,   50
    be gone!
ROBIN: A dog? That's excellent. Let the maids look well
    to their porridge pots, for I'll into the kitchen pres-
    ently. Come, Dick, come.

            (*Exeunt [Robin and Dick,] the two clowns.*)

III, III. 41. **tester:** Sixpence.

55 MEPHISTOPHILIS: Now with the flames of everburning
    fire,
        I'll wing myself and forthwith fly amain
        Unto my Faustus, to the great Turk's court.

                                                    (*Exit.*)

ACT IV • *Prologue*

(*Enter Chorus.*)

CHORUS: When Faustus had with pleasure ta'en the
        view
        Of rarest things and royal courts of kings,
        He stayed his course and so returnèd home;
        Where such as bare his absence but with grief —
5   I mean his friends and nearest companions —
        Did gratulate his safety with kind words,
        And in their conference of what befell,
        Touching his journey through the world and air,
        They put forth questions of astrology,
10   Which Faustus answered with such learnèd skill
        As they admired and wondered at his wit.
        Now is his fame spread forth in every land.
        Amongst the rest, the Emperor is one —
        Carolus the fifth° — at whose palace now
15   Faustus is feasted 'mongst his noblemen.
        What there he did in trial of his art
        I leave untold, your eyes shall see performed.

                                                    (*Exit.*)

Scene I

(*Enter Martino and Frederick, at several doors.*)

MARTINO: What ho, officers, gentlemen,
        Hie to the presences° to attend the Emperor.
        Good Frederick, see the rooms be voided
        straight;
        His majesty is coming to the hall.
5   Go back, and see the state° in readiness.
FREDERICK: But where is Bruno, our elected Pope,
        That on a fury's back came post from Rome?
        Will not his grace consort the Emperor?
MARTINO: O yes, and with him comes the German
        conjurer,
10   The learnèd Faustus, fame of Wittenberg,
        The wonder of the world for magic art;
        And he intends to show great Carolus
        The race of all his stout progenitors,
        And bring in presence of his majesty
15   The royal shapes and warlike semblances
        Of Alexander° and his beauteous paramour.

IV, Prologue. 14. **Carolus the fifth:** Charles V, King of Spain
(as Charles I from 1516 to 1556) and Holy Roman Emperor
from 1519 to 1556.   IV, I. 2. **presences:** Emperor's chamber.
5. **state:** Throne.   16. **Alexander:** Alexander the Great.

FREDERICK: Where is Benvolio?
MARTINO: Fast asleep, I warrant you.
        He took his rouse with stoups° of Rhenish wine
        So kindly yesternight to Bruno's health
20   That all this day the sluggard keeps his bed.
FREDERICK: See, see, his window's ope. We'll call to
        him.
MARTINO: What ho, Benvolio!

(*Enter Benvolio above at a window, in his nightcap, buttoning.*)

BENVOLIO: What a devil ail you two?
MARTINO: Speak softly, sir, lest the devil hear you,   25
        For Faustus at the court is late arrived,
        And at his heels a thousand furies wait
        To accomplish whatsoever the doctor please.
BENVOLIO: What of this?
MARTINO: Come, leave thy chamber first, and thou
        shalt see   30
        This conjurer perform such rare exploits
        Before the Pope° and royal Emperor
        As never yet was seen in Germany.
BENVOLIO: Has not the Pope enough of conjuring yet?
        He was upon the devil's back late enough,   35
        And if he be so far in love with him,
        I would he would post with him to Rome again.
FREDERICK: Speak, wilt thou come and see this sport?
BENVOLIO: Not I.
MARTINO: Wilt thou stand in thy window and see it
        then?   40
BENVOLIO: Ay, and I fall not asleep i' th' meantime.
MARTINO: The Emperor is at hand, who comes to see
        What wonders by black spells may compassed be.
BENVOLIO: Well, go you attend the Emperor. I am con-
        tent for this once to thrust my head out at a window, 45
        for they say if a man be drunk overnight the devil
        cannot hurt him in the morning. If that be true, I
        have a charm in my head shall control him as well as
        the conjurer, I warrant you.

(*Exit [Frederick, with Martino. Benvolio remains at the
window above].*)

Scene II

(*A sennet [is sounded. Enter] Charles, the German Emperor, Bruno, [the Duke of] Saxony, Faustus, Mephistophilis, Frederick, Martino, and Attendants.*)

EMPEROR: Wonder of men, renowned magician,
        Thrice-learnèd Faustus, welcome to our court.
        This deed of thine, in setting Bruno free
        From his and our professèd enemy,
        Shall add more excellence unto thine art   5

19. **took . . . stoups:** Had a drinking bout with brimming gob-
lets.   32. **the Pope:** Bruno.

Than if by powerful necromantic spells
Thou couldst command the world's obedience.
Forever be beloved of Carolus,
And if this Bruno thou hast late redeemed°
10   In peace possess the triple diadem
And sit in Peter's chair despite of chance,
Thou shalt be famous through all Italy
And honored of the German Emperor.
FAUSTUS: These gracious words, most royal Carolus,
15   Shall make poor Faustus to his utmost power
Both love and serve the German Emperor
And lay his life at holy Bruno's feet.
For proof whereof, if so your grace be pleased,
The doctor stands prepared by power of art
20   To cast his magic charms that shall pierce through
The ebon gates of ever-burning hell,
And hale the stubborn Furies from their caves
To compass whatsoe'er your grace commands.
BENVOLIO: [above] Blood, he speaks terribly, but for all
25   that, I do not greatly believe him. He looks as like a
conjurer as the Pope° to a costermonger.°
EMPEROR: Then, Faustus, as thou late did'st promise us,
We would behold that famous conqueror,
Great Alexander, and his paramour
30   In their true shapes and state majestical,
That we may wonder at their excellence.
FAUSTUS: Your majesty shall see them presently.
Mephistophilis, away,
And with a solemn noise of trumpets' sound
35   Present before this royal Emperor,
Great Alexander and his beauteous paramour.
MEPHISTOPHILIS: Faustus, I will.
                                                              [Exit.]
BENVOLIO: Well, master doctor, an your devils come not
away quickly, you shall have me asleep presently.
40   Zounds, I could eat myself for anger to think I have
been such an ass all this while, to stand gaping after
the devil's governor and can see nothing.
FAUSTUS: I'll make you feel something anon, if my art
fail me not
My lord, I must forewarn your majesty
45   That when my spirits present the royal shapes
Of Alexander and his paramour,
Your grace demand no questions of the king,
But in dumb silence let them come and go.
EMPEROR: Be it as Faustus please; we are content.
50   BENVOLIO: Ay, ay, and I am content too. And thou bring
Alexander and his paramour before the Emperor, I'll
be Actaeon and turn myself to a stag.
FAUSTUS: And I'll play Diana and send you the horns
presently.

([A] sennet [is sounded]. Enter at one [door] the Emperor Alexander, at the other Darius.° They meet [in

combat]. Darius is thrown down; Alexander kills him,
takes off his crown, and, offering to go out, his paramour meets him. He embraceth her and sets Darius'
crown upon her head; and coming back, both salute the
Emperor, who, leaving his state, offers to embrace them,
which Faustus seeing, suddenly stays him. Then trumpets cease and music sounds.)

My gracious lord, you do forget yourself.
These are but shadows, not substantial.   55
EMPEROR: O pardon me. My thoughts are so ravishèd
With sight of this renownèd emperor,
That in mine arms I would have compassed him.
But, Faustus, since I may not speak to them,
To satisfy my longing thoughts at full,   60
Let me this tell thee: I have heard it said
That this fair lady, whilst she lived on earth,
Had on her neck a little wart or mole;
How may I prove that saying to be true?
FAUSTUS: Your majesty may boldly go and see.   65
EMPEROR: Faustus, I see it plain,
And in this sight thou better pleasest me
Than if I gained another monarchy.
FAUSTUS: Away! Be gone!
                                             (Exit show.)
See, see, my gracious lord, what strange beast is yon,   70
that thrusts his head out at window?
EMPEROR: O wondrous sight! See, Duke of Saxony,
Two spreading horns most strangely fastenèd
Upon the head of young Benvolio.
SAXONY: What? Is he asleep or dead?   75
FAUSTUS: He sleeps, my lord, but dreams not of his
horns.
EMPEROR: This sport is excellent. We'll call and wake
him.
What ho, Benvolio!
BENVOLIO: A plague upon you! Let me sleep a while.
EMPEROR: I blame thee not to sleep much, having such a 80
head of thine own.
SAXONY: Look up, Benvolio; 'tis the Emperor calls.
BENVOLIO: The Emperor? Where? O zounds, my head!
EMPEROR: Nay, and thy horns hold, 'tis no matter for
thy head, for that's armed sufficiently.   85
FAUSTUS: Why, how now, sir knight! What, hanged by the
horns? This is most horrible. Fie, fie, pull in your head
for shame. Let not all the world wonder at you.
BENVOLIO: Zounds, doctor, is this your villainy?
FAUSTUS: O say not so, sir. The doctor has no skill,   90
No art, no cunning, to present these lords
Or bring before this royal Emperor
The mighty monarch, warlike Alexander.
If Faustus do it, you are straight resolved
In bold Actaeon's shape to turn a stag.   95
And therefore, my lord, so please your majesty,
I'll raise a kennel of hounds shall hunt him so
As all his footmanship shall scarce prevail
To keep his carcass from their bloody fangs
Ho, Belimote, Argiron, Asterote!   100
BENVOLIO: Hold, hold! Zounds, he'll raise up a kennel of

IV, II. 9. redeemed: Rescued.   26. the Pope: Bruno.   Costermonger: Fruit vendor; a term of contempt.   53. [S.D.] Darius:
King Darius III of Persia (336–330 B.C.), defeated at Granicus
in 334 B.C. by the Greeks under Alexander the Great.

devils, I think, anon. Good, my lord, entreat for me.
'Sblood, I am never able to endure these torments.
EMPEROR: Then, good master doctor,
105   Let me entreat you to remove his horns.
He has done penance now sufficiently.
FAUSTUS: My gracious lord, not so much for injury done
to me, as to delight your majesty with some mirth,
hath Faustus justly requited this injurious° knight;
110   which being all I desire, I am content to remove his
horns. Mephistophilis, transform him.

[*Mephistophilis removes the horns.*]

And hereafter, sir, look you speak; well of scholars.
BENVOLIO: [*aside.*] Speak well of ye? 'Sblood, and scholars be such cuckold makers to clap horns of honest
115   men's heads o' this order, I'll ne'er trust smooth faces
and small ruffs° more. But an I be not revenged for
this, would I might be turned to a gaping oyster and
drink nothing but salt water.
                              [*Exit Benvolio above.*]
EMPEROR: Come, Faustus. While the Emperor lives,
120   In recompense of this thy high desert,
Thou shalt command the state of Germany
And live beloved of mighty Carolus.
                                        (*Exeunt.*)

Scene III

(*Enter Benvolio, Martino, Frederick, and Soldiers.*)

MARTINO: Nay, sweet Benvolio, let us sway thy
        thoughts
From this attempt against the conjurer.
BENVOLIO: Away! You love me not to urge me thus.
Shall I let slip so great an injury,
5   When every servile groom jests at my wrongs
And in their rustic gambols proudly say,
"Benvolio's head was graced with horns today"?
O, may these eyelids never close again
Till with my sword I have that conjurer slain.
10   If you will aid me in this enterprise,
Then draw your weapons and be resolute.
If not, depart. Here will Benvolio die,
But Faustus' death shall quit° my infamy.
FREDERICK: Nay, we will stay with thee, betide what
        may,
15   And kill that doctor if he come this way.
BENVOLIO: Then, gentle Frederick, hie thee to the grove,
And place our servants and our followers
Close in an ambush there behind the trees.
By this, I know, the conjurer is near.
20   I saw him kneel and kiss the Emperor's hand
And take his leave, laden with rich rewards.
Then, soldiers, boldly fight. If Faustus die,
Take you the wealth; leave us the victory.

FREDERICK: Come, soldiers. Follow me unto the grove.
Who kills him shall have gold and endless love.   25

                (*Exit Frederick with the Soldiers.*)

BENVOLIO: My head is lighter than it was by th'horns,
But yet my heart's more ponderous than my head
And pants until I see that conjurer dead.
MARTINO: Where shall we place ourselves, Benvolio?
BENVOLIO: Here will we stay to bide the first assault.   30
O, were that damnèd hell-hound but in place,
Thou soon shouldst see me quit my foul disgrace.

(*Enter Frederick.*)

FREDERICK: Close, close, the conjurer is at hand
And all alone comes walking in his gown.
Be ready then, and strike the peasant down.   35
BENVOLIO: Mine be that honor then. Now, sword,
        strike home.
For horns he gave I'll have his head anon.

(*Enter Faustus with the false head.*)

MARTINO: See, see, he comes.
BENVOLIO: No words! This blow ends all.
Hell take his soul; his body thus must fall.
                              [*He stabs Faustus.*]
FAUSTUS: [*falling*] Oh!   40
FREDERICK: Groan you, master doctor?
BENVOLIO: Break may his heart with groans! Dear
        Frederick, see,
Thus will I end his griefs immediately.
MARTINO: Strike with a willing hand. His head is off.

[*Benvolio strikes off Faustus' false head.*]

BENVOLIO: The devil's dead. The Furies now may
        laugh.   45
FREDERICK: Was this that stern aspèct, that awful
        frown,
Made the grim monarch of infernal spirits
Tremble and quake at his commanding charms?
MARTINO: Was this that damnèd head whose heart
        conspired
Benvolio's shame before the Emperor?   50
BENVOLIO: Ay, that's the head, and here the body lies,
Justly rewarded for his villainies.
FREDERICK: Come, let's devise how we may add more
        shame
To the black scandal of his hated name.
BENVOLIO: First, on his head, in quittance of my
        wrongs,   55
I'll nail huge forkèd horns and let them hang
Within the window where he yoked° me first,
That all the world may see my just revenge.
MARTINO: What use shall we put his beard to?
BENVOLIO: We'll sell it to a chimney-sweeper. It will   60
wear out ten birchen brooms, I warrant you.
FREDERICK: What shall eyes do?

---

109. injurious: Insulting.   **116. small ruffs:** Academic gowns.
IV, III. 13. quit: Pay for.

57. yoked: Placed the horns on.

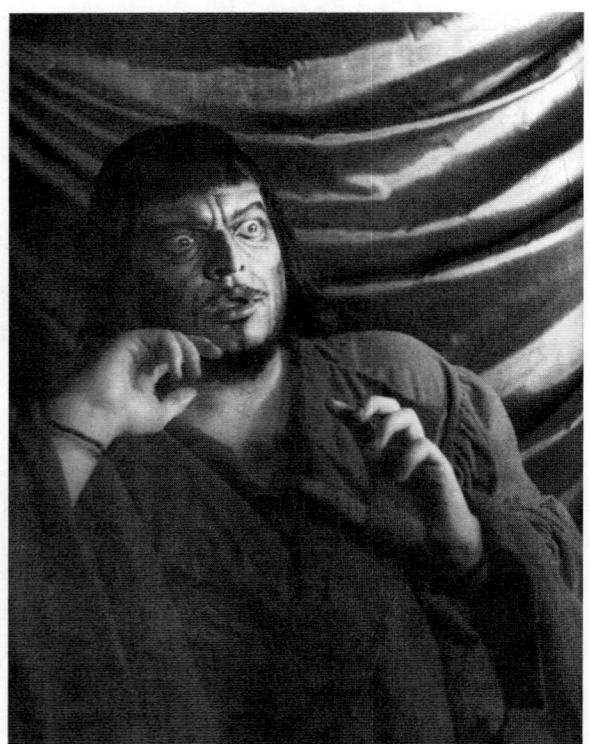

Orson Welles as Faustus in the 1937 Broadway production
of *The Tragical History of Dr. Faustus,* which Welles also
directed.

BENVOLIO: We'll put out his eyes, and they shall serve
   for buttons to his lips to keep his tongue from catch-
65   ing cold.
MARTINO: An excellent policy! And now, sirs, having
   divided him, what shall the body do?

[*Faustus rises.*]

BENVOLIO: Zounds, the devil's alive again.
FREDERICK: Give him his head, for God's sake.
FAUSTUS: Nay, keep it. Faustus will have heads and
70   hands,
   Ay, all your hearts, to recompense this deed.
   Knew you not, traitors, I was limited
   For four-and-twenty years to breathe on earth?
   And had you cut my body with your swords,
75   Or hewed this flesh and bones as small as sand,
   Yet in a minute had my spirit returned,
   And I had breathed a man made free from harm.
   But wherefore do I dally my revenge?
   Asteroth, Belimoth, Mephistophilis!

(*Enter Mephistophilis and other Devils.*)

80   Go, horse these traitors on your fiery backs,
   And mount aloft with them as high as heaven;

Thence pitch them headlong to the lowest hell.
Yet stay. The world shall see their misery,
And hell shall after plague their treachery.
Go, Belimoth, and take this caitiff° hence   85
And hurl him in some lake of mud and dirt.
Take thou this other; drag him through the woods
Amongst the pricking thorns and sharpest briars,
Whilst with my gentle Mephistophilis
This traitor flies unto some steepy rock   90
That, rolling down, may break the villain's bones
As he intended to dismember me.
Fly hence. Dispatch my charge immediately.
FREDERICK: Pity us, gentle Faustus. Save our lives.
FAUSTUS: Away!
FREDERICK: He must needs go that the devil drives.   95

(*Exeunt Spirits with the Knights.*)

(*Enter the ambushed Soldiers.*)

FIRST SOLDIER: Come, sirs, prepare yourselves in
   readiness.
   Make haste to help these noble gentlemen;
   I heard them parley with the conjurer.
SECOND SOLDIER: See where he comes. Dispatch and
   kill the slave.
FAUSTUS: What's here? An ambush to betray my life?   100
   Then, Faustus, try thy skill. Base peasants, stand,
   For lo, these trees remove at my command
   And stand as bulwarks 'twixt yourselves and me,
   To shield me from your hated treachery.
   Yet to encounter this your weak attempt,   105
   Behold an army comes incontinent.°

(*Faustus strikes the door, and enter a Devil playing on a
drum, after him another bearing an ensign, and divers
with weapons, Mephistophilis with fireworks. They set
upon the Soldiers and drive them out.* [*Exit Faustus.*])

Scene IV

(*Enter at several doors Benvolio, Frederick, and Martino, their heads and faces bloody and besmeared with
mud and dirt, all having horns on their heads.*)

MARTINO: What ho, Benvolio!
BENVOLIO: Here! What, Frederick, ho!
FREDERICK: O help me, gentle friend. Where is Martino?
MARTINO: Dear Frederick, here,
   Half smothered in a lake of mud and dirt,   5
   Through which the Furies dragged me by the heels.
FREDERICK: Martino, see! Benvolio's horns again.
MARTINO: O misery! How now, Benvolio?
BENVOLIO: Defend me, heaven. Shall I be haunted° still?
MARTINO: Nay, fear not man; we have not power to
   kill.   10

85. **caitiff:** Despicable wretch.   106. **incontinent:** At once.
IV, IV. 9. **haunted:** (1) Bewitched; (2) hunted, pursued (since he
is a stag).

BENVOLIO: My friends transformèd thus! O hellish
    spite!
  Your heads are all set with horns.
FREDERICK: You hit it right.
  It is your own you mean. Feel on your head.
BENVOLIO: Zounds, horns again!
15 MARTINO: Nay, chafe not man. We all are sped.°
BENVOLIO: What devil attends this damned magician,
  That, spite of spite, our wrongs are doublèd?
FREDERICK: What may we do, that we may hide our
  shames?
BENVOLIO: If we should follow him to work revenge,
20   He'd join long asses' ears to these huge horns,
  And make us laughing-stocks to all the world.
MARTINO: What shall we then do, dear Benvolio?
BENVOLIO: I have a castle joining near these woods,
  And thither we'll repair and live obscure
25   Till time shall alter these our brutish shapes,
  Sith black disgrace hath thus eclipsed our fame,
  We'll rather die with grief than live with shame.
                        (*Exeunt omnes.*°)

Scene v°

(*Enter Faustus and Mephistophilis.*)

FAUSTUS: Now, Mephistophilis, the restless course
  That time doth run with calm and silent foot,
  Shortening my days and thread of vital life,
  Calls for the payment of my latest years.
5   Therefore, sweet Mephistophilis, let us
  Make haste to Wittenberg.
MEPHISTOPHILIS: What, will you go on horseback, or
  on foot?
FAUSTUS: Nay, till I am past this fair and pleasant
  green,
  I'll walk on foot.
                    [*Exit Mephistophilis.*]

(*Enter a Horse-Courser.*°)

10 HORSE-COURSER: I have been all this day seeking one
  Master Fustian.° Mass, see where he is. God save you,
  master doctor.
FAUSTUS: What, horse-courser! You are well met.
HORSE-COURSER: I beseech your worship, accept of
15   these forty dollars.
FAUSTUS: Friend, thou canst not buy so good a horse for
  so small a price. I have no great need to sell him, but
  if thou likest him for ten dollars more, take him,
  because I see thou hast a good mind to him.

HORSE-COURSER: I beseech you, sir, accept of this. I am 20
  a very poor man and have lost very much of late by
  horse-flesh, and this bargain will set me up again.
FAUSTUS: Well, I will not stand with thee.° Give me the
  money.

[*The Horse-Courser gives Faustus money.*]

  Now, sirrah, I must tell you that you may ride him 25
  o'er hedge and ditch, and spare him not. But, do you
  hear? In any case, ride him not into the water.
HORSE-COURSER: How sir? Not into the water? Why,
  will he not drink of all waters?°
FAUSTUS: Yes, he will drink of all waters, but ride him 30
  not into the water — o'er hedge and ditch, or where
  thou wilt, but not into the water. Go, bid the hostler
  deliver him unto you, and remember what I say.
HORSE-COURSER: I warrant you, sir. O joyful day!
  Now am I a man made forever. 35
                             (*Exit.*)
FAUSTUS: What art thou, Faustus, but a man
  condemned to die?
  Thy fatal time draws to a final end.
  Despair doth drive distrust into my thoughts.
  Confound these passions with a quiet sleep.
  Tush! Christ did call the thief upon the cross; 40
  Then rest thee, Faustus, quiet in conceit.°

(*He sits to sleep [in his chair].*)

(*Enter the Horse-Courser, wet.*)

HORSE-COURSER: O what a cozening doctor was this? I
  riding my horse into the water, thinking some hidden
  mystery° had been in the horse, I had nothing under
  me but a little straw and had much ado to escape 45
  drowning. Well, I'll go rouse him and make him give
  me my forty dollars again. Ho, sirrah doctor, you
  cozening scab!° Master doctor, awake and rise, and
  give me my money again, for your horse is turned to
  a bottle° of hay. Master doctor! 50

(*He [tries to wake Faustus, and in doing so] pulls off
his leg.*)

  Alas, I am undone! What shall I do? I have pulled off
  his leg.

[*Faustus awakes.*]

FAUSTUS: O, help, help! The villain hath murdered me.
HORSE-COURSER: Murder or not murder, now he has
  but one leg, I'll outrun him and cast this leg into 55
  some ditch or other.
FAUSTUS: Stop him, stop him, stop him! Ha, ha, ha,
  Faustus hath his leg again, and the horse-courser a
  bundle of hay for his forty dollars.

---

15. sped: provided (with horns). **27.** [S.D.] *Exeunt omnes:*
Latin for "All go out." IV, v. The first eleven lines of this
scene do not appear in all versions of the play, but they provide
a transition to the Horse-Courser episode and remind readers
of Faustus's impending tragedy. **9.** [S.D.] *Horse-Courser:* One
who deals in horses. **11. Fustian:** The perversion of Faustus's
name is a deliberate attempt at humor.

23. stand with thee: Bargain. **29. drink . . . waters:** Be ready
for anything (a common proverb of the time). **41. conceit:**
Thoughts. **44. mystery:** Quality. **48. cozening scab:** Deceitful, contemptible rascal. **50. bottle:** Bundle.

(Enter Wagner.)

60   How now, Wagner, what news with thee?
WAGNER: If it please you, the Duke of Anholt doth earnestly entreat your company and hath sent some of his men to attend you with provision fit for your journey.
65 FAUSTUS: The Duke of Anholt's an honorable gentleman, and one to whom I must be no niggard of my cunning. Come away.

                                                              (Exeunt.)

Scene VI

(Enter [Robin, the] Clown, Dick, [the] Horse-Courser, and a Carter.°)

CARTER: Come, my masters, I'll bring you to the best beer in Europe. What ho, hostess! Where be these whores?

(Enter Hostess.)

HOSTESS: How now, what lack you? What, my old
5   guests, welcome.
ROBIN: Sirrah, Dick, dost thou know why I stand so mute?
DICK: No, Robin; why is't?
ROBIN: I am eighteen pence on the score.° But say noth-
10   ing, see if she have forgotten me.
HOSTESS: Who's this that stands so solemnly by himself? What, my old guest?
ROBIN: O hostess, how do you? I hope my score stands still.°
15 HOSTESS: Ay, there's no doubt of that, for methinks you make no haste to wipe it out.
DICK: Why, hostess, I say, fetch us some beer.
HOSTESS: You shall presently. Look up into th'hall there, ho!

                                                              (Exit.)

20 DICK: Come, sirs, what shall we do now till mine hostess come?
CARTER: Marry, sir, I'll tell you the bravest tale how a conjurer served me. You know Doctor Fauster?
HORSE-COURSER: Ay, a plague take him. Here's some
25   on's have cause to know him. Did he conjure thee too?
CARTER: I'll tell you how he served me. As I was going to Wittenberg t'other day with a load of hay, he met me and asked me what he should give me for as much
30   hay as he could eat. Now, sir, I thinking that a little would serve his turn, bade him take as much as he would for three farthings. So he presently gave me my money and fell to eating; and as I am a cursen°

IV, VI. [S.D.] *Carter:* A person who drives a cart. **9. on the score:** In debt. **13–14. stands still:** Does not go higher. **33. cursen:** Christened.

man, he never left eating till he had eat up all my load of hay.   35
ALL: O monstrous! Eat a whole load of hay!
ROBIN: Yes, yes, that may be, for I have heard of one that has eat a load of logs.
HORSE-COURSER: Now, sirs, you shall hear how villainously he served me. I went to him yesterday to buy a 40
horse of him, and he would by no means sell him under forty dollars. So, sir, because I knew him to be such a horse as would run over hedge and ditch and never tire, I gave him his money. So when I had my horse, Doctor Fauster bade me ride him night and 45
day and spare him no time; but, quoth he, in any case ride him not into the water. Now sir, I thinking the horse had had some rare quality that he would not have me know of, what did I but rid him into a great river, and when I came just in the midst, my 50
horse vanished away, and I sat straddling upon a bottle of hay.
ALL: O brave doctor!
HORSE-COURSER: But you shall hear how bravely I served him for it. I went me home to his house, and 55
there I found him asleep. I kept a hallooing and whooping in his ears, but all could not wake him. I seeing that took him by the leg and never rested pulling till I had pulled me his leg quite off, and now 'tis at home in mine hostry.   60
ROBIN: And has the doctor but one leg then? That's excellent, for one of his devils turned me into the likeness of an ape's face.
CARTER: Some more drink, hostess.
ROBIN: Hark you, we'll into another room and drink a 65
while, and then we'll go seek out the doctor.

                                                              (Exeunt.)

Scene VII

(Enter the Duke of Anholt, his Duchess, Faustus, and Mephistophilis, [Servants and Attendants].)

DUKE: Thanks, master doctor, for these pleasant sights. Nor know I how sufficiently to recompense your great deserts° in erecting that enchanted castle in the air, the sight whereof so delighted me, as nothing in the world could please me more.   5
FAUSTUS: I do think myself, my good lord, highly recompensed in that it pleaseth your grace to think but well of that which Faustus hath performed. But, gracious lady, it may be that you have taken no pleasure in those sights. Therefore, I pray you, tell me what is the 10
thing you most desire to have; be it in the world, it shall be yours. I have heard that great-bellied women do long for things are rare and dainty.
DUCHESS: True, master doctor, and since I find you so kind, I will make known unto you what my heart 15

IV, VII. **3. deserts:** Good deeds.

desires to have. And were it now summer, as it is January, a dead time of the winter, I would request no
better meat than a dish of ripe grapes.

FAUSTUS: This is but a small matter. Go, Mephistophilis,
away!

20

(Exit Mephistophilis.)

Madam I will do more than this for your content.

(Enter Mephistophilis again with the grapes.)

Here; now taste ye these. They should be good, for
they come from a far country, I can tell you.

DUKE: This makes me wonder more than all the rest,
that at this time of year, when every tree is barren of
his fruit, from whence you had these ripe grapes.

25

FAUSTUS: Please it, your grace, the year is divided into
two circles over the whole world, so that when it
is winter with us, in the contrary circle it is likewise summer with them, as in India, Saba,° and such
countries that lie far east, where they have fruit twice
a year. From whence, by means of a swift spirit that I
have, I had these grapes brought, as you see.

30

DUCHESS: And trust me, they are the sweetest grapes
that e'er I tasted.

35

*(The Clown[s, Robin, Dick, the Carter, and the Horse-
Courser,] bounce at the gate within.)*

DUKE: What rude disturbers have we at the gate?
Go, pacify their fury. Set it ope,
And then demand of them what they would have.

[Exit a Servant.]

(They knock again and call out to talk with Faustus.)

[Enter Servant to them.]

SERVANT: Why, how now, masters, what a coil° is there?
What is the reason you disturb the duke.

40

DICK: We have no reason for it; therefore a fig for him.

SERVANT: What, saucy varlets,° dare you be so bold?

HORSE-COURSER: I hope, sir, we have wit enough to be
more bold than welcome.

45

SERVANT: It appears so. Pray be bold elsewhere,
And trouble not the duke.

DUKE: What would they have?

SERVANT: They all cry out to speak with Doctor Faustus.

CARTER: Ay, and we will speak with him.

DUKE: Will you, sir? Commit the rascals.

50

DICK: Commit with us! He were as good commit with
his father as commit with us.

FAUSTUS: I do beseech your grace, let them come in;
They are good subject for a merriment.

DUKE: Do as thou wilt, Faustus. I give thee leave.

FAUSTUS: I thank your grace.

(Enter Robin, Dick, Carter, and Horse-Courser.)

55

Why, how now, my good friends?
'Faith you are too outrageous,° but come near;

---

30. Saba: Sheba.   **39. coil:** Disturbance.   **42. varlets:** Knaves,
rascals.   **56. outrageous:** violent.

I have procured your pardons. Welcome all!

ROBIN: Nay, sir, we will be welcome for our money, and
we will pay for what we take. What ho! Give's half a
dozen of beer here, and be hanged.

60

FAUSTUS: Nay, hark you; can you tell me where you are?

CARTER: Ay, marry can I: we are under heaven.

SERVANT: Ay, but sir sauce-box, know you in what
place?

HORSE-COURSER: Ay, ay, the house is good enough to
drink in. Zounds, fill us some beer, or we'll break all
the barrels in the house and dash out all your brains
with your bottles.

65

FAUSTUS: Be not so furious. Come, you shall have beer.
My lord, beseech you give me leave a while:
I'll gage my credit, 'twill content your grace.

70

DUKE: With all my heart, kind doctor. Please thyself;
Our servants and our court's at thy command.

FAUSTUS: I humbly thank your grace. Then fetch some
beer.

HORSE-COURSER: Ay, marry, there spake a doctor
indeed, and 'faith,
I'll drink a health to thy wooden leg for that word.

75

FAUSTUS: My wooden leg? What dost thou mean by
that?

CARTER: Ha, ha, ha! Dost hear him, Dick? He has
forgot his leg.

HORSE-COURSER: Ay, ay, he does not stand much°
upon that.

FAUSTUS: No, faith; not much upon a wooden leg.

CARTER: Good lord, that flesh and blood should be so
frail with your worship! Do not you remember a
horse-courser you sold a horse to?

80

FAUSTUS: Yes, I remember I sold one a horse.

CARTER: And do you remember you bid he should not
ride into the water?

85

FAUSTUS: Yes, I do very well remember that.

CARTER: And do you remember nothing of your leg?

FAUSTUS: No, in good sooth.

CARTER: Then, I pray, remember your courtesy.°

FAUSTUS: I thank you, sir.

90

CARTER: 'Tis not so much worth. I pray you, tell me one
thing.

FAUSTUS: What's that?

CARTER: Be both your legs bedfellows every night together?

95

FAUSTUS: Wouldst thou make a Colossus° of me, that
thou askest me such questions?

CARTER: No, truly, sir. I would make nothing of you, but
I would fain know that.

(Enter Hostess with drink.)

FAUSTUS: Then, I assure thee, certainly they are.

100

CARTER: I thank you; I am fully satisfied.

---

78. stand much: Make much of (with a quibble).   **89. courtesy:** Curtsy, or leg.   **96. Colossus:** A giant statue said to have
stood with its legs astride at the entrance to the ancient harbor
of Rhodes.

FAUSTUS: But wherefore dost thou ask?

CARTER: For nothing, sir. But methinks you should have a wooden bedfellow of one of 'em.

105 HORSE-COURSER: Why, do you hear, sir; did not I pull off one of your legs when you were asleep?

FAUSTUS: But I have it again, now I am awake. Look you here, sir.

ALL: O horrible! Had the doctor three legs?

110 CARTER: Do you remember, sir, how you cozened me and ate up my load of —

(Faustus charms him dumb.)

DICK: Do you remember how you made me wear an ape's —

[Faustus charms him dumb.]

HORSE-COURSER: You whoreson conjuring scab, do you
115   remember how you cozened me with a ho —

[Faustus charms him dumb.]

ROBIN: Ha' you forgotten me? You think to carry it away° with your *hey-pass* and *re-pass;* do you remember the dog's fa —

[Faustus charms him dumb.]   (Exeunt Clowns.)

HOSTESS: Who pays for the ale? Hear you, master doc-
120   tor, now you have sent away my guests, I pray who shall pay me for my a —

[Faustus charms her dumb.]   (Exit Hostess.)

DUCHESS: My lord,
    We are much beholding to this learnèd man.

DUKE: So are we, madam, which we will recompense
125   With all the love and kindness that we may.
    His artful sport drives all sad thoughts away.
                                              (Exeunt.)

ACT V • Scene I

(*Thunder and lightning. Enter Devils with covered dishes. Mephistophilis leads them into Faustus' study. Then enter Wagner.*)

WAGNER: I think my master means to die shortly.
    He has made his will and given me his wealth,
    His house, his goods, and store of golden plate,
    Besides two thousand ducats ready coined.
5   I wonder what he means. If death were nigh,
    He would not frolic thus. He's now at supper
    With the scholars, where there's such belly-cheer
    As Wagner in his life ne'er saw the like.
    And see where they come; belike the feast is done.
                                              (Exit.)

(*Enter Faustus, Mephistophilis, and two or three Scholars.*)

116–17. carry it away: Come off best.

FIRST SCHOLAR: Master Doctor Faustus, since our con- 10
    ference about fair ladies, which was the beautifulest in all the world, we have determined with ourselves that Helen of Greece was the admirablest lady that ever lived. Therefore, master doctor, if you will do us so much favor as to let us see that peerless dame of 15 Greece, whom all the world admires for majesty, we should think ourselves much beholding unto you.

FAUSTUS: Gentlemen,
    For that I know your friendship is unfeigned,
    And Faustus' custom is not to deny   20
    The just requests of those that wish him well,
    You shall behold that peerless dame of Greece,
    No otherwise for pomp and majesty
    Than when Sir Paris crossed the seas with her
    And brought the spoils to rich Dardania.°   25
    Be silent then, for danger is in words.

(*Music sounds. Mephistophilis brings in Helen; she passeth over the stage.*)

SECOND SCHOLAR: Was this fair Helen, whose admirèd worth
    Made Greece with ten years' war afflict poor Troy?
    Too simple is my wit to tell her praise,
    Whom all the world admires for majesty.   30

THIRD SCHOLAR: No marvel though the angry Greeks pursued
    With ten years' war the rape of such a queen,
    Whose heavenly beauty passeth all compare.

FIRST SCHOLAR: Since we have seen the pride of nature's works
    And only paragon of excellence,   35
    We'll take our leaves and for this blessèd sight
    Happy and blest be Faustus evermore.

FAUSTUS: Gentlemen, farewell; the same wish I to you.
                                      (Exeunt Scholars.)

(*Enter an Old Man.*)

OLD MAN: O gentle Faustus, leave this damnèd art,
    This magic that will charm thy soul to hell   40
    And quite bereave thee of salvation.
    Though thou hast now offended like a man,
    Do not persevere in it like a devil.
    Yet, yet, thou hast an amiable° soul,
    If sin by custom grow not into nature.   45
    Then, Faustus, will repentance come too late;
    Then thou art banished from the sight of heaven.
    No mortal can express the pains of hell.
    It may be this my exhortation
    Seems harsh and all unpleasant; let it not,   50
    For, gentle son, I speak it not in wrath
    Or envy of° thee, but in tender love
    And pity of thy future misery.

V, I. 22–25. peerless dame . . . Dardania: The Greek Helen (the "peerless dame"), wife of Menelaus, was carried off to Troy (Dardania) by Paris, sparking the Trojan War. 44. amiable: Worthy of divine love or grace. 52. envy of: Ill will toward.

55 And so have hope that this my kind rebuke,
    Checking° thy body, may amend thy soul.
FAUSTUS: Where art thou, Faustus? Wretch, what hast
        thou done?
    Damned art thou, Faustus, damned; despair and die!
    Hell claims his right, and with a roaring voice
    Says, "Faustus, come; thine hour is almost come";
60 And Faustus now will come to do thee right.

(*Mephistophilis gives him a dagger.*)

OLD MAN: O stay, good Faustus, stay thy desperate
        steps.
    I see an angel hovers o'er thy head,
    And with a vial full of precious grace
    Offers to pour the same into thy soul.
65 Then call for mercy and avoid despair.
FAUSTUS: Ah, my sweet friend, I feel thy words
    To comfort my distressèd soul.
    Leave me a while to ponder on my sins.
OLD MAN: Faustus, I leave thee, but with grief of heart,
70 Fearing the enemy of thy hapless soul.
                                              (*Exit.*)
FAUSTUS: Accursèd Faustus, where is mercy now?
    I do repent, and yet I do despair.
    Hell strives with grace for conquest in my breast.
    What shall I do to shun the snares of death?
MEPHISTOPHILIS: Thou traitor, Faustus, I arrest thy
75   soul
    For disobedience to my sovereign lord.
    Revolt, or I'll in piecemeal tear thy flesh.
FAUSTUS: I do repent I e'er offended him.
    Sweet Mephistophilis, entreat thy lord
80 To pardon my unjust presumption,
    And with my blood again I will confirm
    The former vow I made to Lucifer.
MEPHISTOPHILIS: Do it then, Faustus, with unfeignèd°
        heart,
    Lest greater dangers do attend thy drift.°

[*Faustus stabs his arm and writes on a paper with his
blood.*]

FAUSTUS: Torment, sweet friend, that base and agèd
85   man
    That durst dissuade me from thy Lucifer,
    With greatest torment that our hell affords.
MEPHISTOPHILIS: His faith is great; I cannot touch his
        soul,
    But what I may afflict his body with
90 I will attempt, which is but little worth.
FAUSTUS: One thing, good servant, let me crave of
        thee
    To glut the longing of my heart's desire —
    That I may have unto my paramour
    That heavenly Helen which I saw of late,
95 Whose sweet embracings may extinguish clear

Those thoughts that do dissuade me from my vow,
    And keep mine oath I made to Lucifer.
MEPHISTOPHILIS: This, or what else my Faustus shall
        desire,
    Shall be performed in twinkling of an eye.

(*Enter Helen again, passing over [the stage] between two
Cupids.*)

FAUSTUS: Was this the face that launched a thousand
        ships   100
    And burnt the topless towers of Ilium?
    Sweet Helen, make me immortal with a kiss.

[*She kisses him.*]

    Her lips suck forth my soul. See where it flies!
    Come, Helen, come, give me my soul again.
    Here will I dwell, for heaven is in these lips,   105
    And all is dross that is not Helena.

[*Enter the Old Man.*]

    I will be Paris, and for love of thee
    Instead of Troy shall Wittenberg be sacked;
    And I will combat with weak Menelaus°
    And wear thy colors on my plumèd crest.   110
    Yea, I will wound Achilles° in the heel
    And then return to Helen for a kiss.
    O, thou art fairer than the evening's air,
    Clad in the beauty of a thousand stars.
    Brighter art thou than flaming Jupiter°   115
    When he appeared to hapless Semele,°
    More lovely than the monarch of the sky
    In wanton Arethusa's azured arms,°
    And none but thou shalt be my paramour.

                          (*Exeunt [all but the Old Man].*)

OLD MAN: Accursèd Faustus, miserable man,   120
    That from thy soul exclud'st the grace of heaven
    And fliest the throne of his tribunal seat!

(*Enter the Devils.*)

    Satan begins to sift me with his pride.
    As in this furnace God shall try my faith,
    My faith, vile hell, shall triumph over thee.   125
    Ambitious fiends, see how the heavens smiles
    At your repulse and laughs your state° to scorn.
    Hence hell, for hence I fly unto my God.
                                              (*Exeunt.*)

---

55. **Checking:** Admonishing.   83. **unfeignèd:** Honest.
84. **drift:** Purpose.

109. **Menelaus:** The husband of Helen of Troy.   111. **Achilles:**
The Greek hero of the Trojan war, wounded in the heel by
Paris.   115. **Jupiter:** Zeus.   116. **Semele:** The daughter of
Cadmus and Harmonia who bore Zeus the child, Dionysus.
117–18. **monarch . . . arms:** Arethusa was a nymph, one of the
Nereids, who governed a fountain on the isle of Ortygia near
Syracuse.   127. **state:** Royal power.

Scene II

(*Thunder. Enter [above] Lucifer, Beelzebub, and Mephistophilis.*)

LUCIFER: Thus from infernal Dis° do we ascend
    To view the subjects of our monarchy,
    Those souls which sin seals the black sons of hell,
    'Mong which as chief, Faustus, we come to thee,
5   Bringing with us lasting damnation
    To wait upon thy soul. The time is come
    Which makes it forfeit.
MEPHISTOPHILIS: And this gloomy night,
    Here in this room will wretched Faustus be.
BEELZEBUB: And here we'll stay
10   To mark him how he doth demean himself.
MEPHISTOPHILIS: How should he, but in desperate
      lunacy?
    Fond worldling, now his heart-blood dries with
      grief;
    His conscience kills it, and his laboring brain
    Begets a world of idle fantasies
15   To over-reach the devil. But all in vain;
    His store of pleasures must be sauced° with pain.
    He and his servant, Wagner, are at hand.
    Both come from drawing Faustus' latest will.
    See where they come.

(*Enter Faustus and Wagner.*)

20 FAUSTUS: Say, Wagner, thou has perused my will;
    How dost thou like it?
WAGNER: Sir, so wondrous well
    As in all humble duty I do yield
    My life and lasting service for your love.

(*Enter the Scholars.*)

FAUSTUS: Gramercies,° Wagner. Welcome, gentlemen.
                    [*Exit Wagner.*]
25 FIRST SCHOLAR: Now, worthy Faustus, methinks your
    looks are changed.
FAUSTUS: Ah, gentlemen!
SECOND SCHOLAR: What ails Faustus?
FAUSTUS: Ah, my sweet chamber-fellow, had I lived with
30   thee, then had I lived still, but now must die eternally.
    Look, sirs; comes he not? Comes he not?
FIRST SCHOLAR: O my dear Faustus, what imports this
    fear?
SECOND SCHOLAR: Is all our pleasure turned to melan-
35   choly?
THIRD SCHOLAR: He is not well with being over-solitary.
SECOND SCHOLAR: If it be so, we'll have physicians, and
    Faustus shall be cured.
THIRD SCHOLAR: 'Tis but a surfeit sir; fear nothing.
40 FAUSTUS: A surfeit of deadly sin that hath damned both
    body and soul.

V, II. **1. Dis:** Hades, or hell. **16. sauced:** Paid for.
24. Gramercies: Thanks.

SECOND SCHOLAR: Yet Faustus, look up to heaven, and
    remember mercy is infinite.
FAUSTUS: But Faustus' offence can ne'er be pardoned.
    The serpent that tempted Eve may be saved, but not 45
    Faustus. Ah gentlemen, hear me with patience and
    tremble not at my speeches. Though my heart pants
    and quivers to remember that I have been a student
    here these thirty years, O, would I had never seen
    Wittenberg, never read book. And what wonders I 50
    have done, all Germany can witness — yea, all the
    world — for which Faustus hath lost both Germany
    and the world, yea heaven itself, heaven the seat of
    God, the throne of the blessed, the kingdom of joy,
    and must remain in hell for ever. Hell, ah hell for 55
    ever! Sweet friends, what shall become of Faustus,
    being in hell for ever?
SECOND SCHOLAR: Yet Faustus, call on God.
FAUSTUS: On God, whom Faustus hath abjured? On
    God, whom Faustus hath blasphemed? Ah, my God, 60
    I would weep, but the devil draws in my tears. Gush
    forth blood instead of tears, yea life and soul. O, he
    stays my tongue! I would lift up my hands, but see,
    they hold 'em; they hold 'em.
ALL: Who, Faustus? 65
FAUSTUS: Why, Lucifer and Mephistophilis. Ah, gentle-
    men, I gave them my soul for my cunning.
ALL: God forbid!
FAUSTUS: God forbade it indeed, but Faustus hath done
    it. For the vain pleasure of four and twenty years 70
    hath Faustus lost eternal joy and felicity. I writ them
    a bill with mine own blood. The date is expired. This
    is the time, and he will fetch me.
FIRST SCHOLAR: Why did not Faustus tell us of this
    before, that divines might have prayed for thee? 75
FAUSTUS: Oft have I thought to have done so, but the
    devil threatened to tear me in pieces if I named God,
    to fetch me, body and soul, if I once gave ear to divin-
    ity. And now 'tis too late. Gentlemen away, lest you
    perish with me. 80
SECOND SCHOLAR: O, what may we do to save Faustus?
FAUSTUS: Talk not of me, but save yourselves and de-
    part.
THIRD SCHOLAR: God will strengthen me; I will stay
    with Faustus. 85
FIRST SCHOLAR: Tempt not God, sweet friend, but let us
    into the next room and there pray for him.
FAUSTUS: Ay, pray for me, pray for me; and what noise
    soever you hear, come not unto me, for nothing can
    rescue me. 90
SECOND SCHOLAR: Pray thou, and we will pray that God
    may have mercy upon thee.
FAUSTUS: Gentlemen, farewell. If I live till morning, I'll
    visit you; if not, Faustus is gone to hell.
ALL: Faustus, farewell. 95
                    (*Exeunt Scholars.*)
MEPHISTOPHILIS: [*above*] Ay, Faustus, now thou hast
    no hope of heaven;
    Therefore despair. Think only upon hell,
    For that must be thy mansion, there to dwell.

FAUSTUS: O thou bewitching fiend, 'twas thy
    temptation
100   Hath robbed me of eternal happiness.
MEPHISTOPHILIS: I do confess it, Faustus, and rejoice.
    'Twas I, that when thou wert i' the way to heaven,
    Damned up thy passage. When thou took'st the book
    To view the Scriptures, then I turned the leaves
105   And led thine eye.
    What, weep'st thou? 'Tis too late. Despair!
      Farewell!
    Fools that will laugh on earth must weep in hell.
                        (*Exit.*)

(*Enter the Good Angel and the Bad Angel at several doors.*)

GOOD ANGEL: Ah, Faustus, if thou hadst given ear to
    me,
    Innumerable joys had followed thee;
    But thou didst love the world.
110 BAD ANGEL: Gave ear to me,
    And now must taste hell's pains perpetually.
GOOD ANGEL: O what will all thy riches, pleasures,
    pomps
    Avail thee now?
BAD ANGEL: Nothing but vex thee more,
    To want in hell, that had on earth such store.

(*Music while the throne descends.*)

115 GOOD ANGEL: O, thou hast lost celestial happiness,
    Pleasures unspeakable, bliss without end.
    Hadst thou affected sweet divinity,
    Hell or the devil had had no power on thee.
    Hadst thou kept on that way, Faustus, behold
120   In what resplendent glory thou hadst sat
    In yonder throne, like those bright shining saints,
    And triumphed over hell. That hast thou lost,
    And now, poor soul, must thy good angel leave thee.

[*The throne ascends.*]

    The jaws of hell are open to receive thee.
                        (*Exit.*)

(*Hell is discovered.*)

BAD ANGEL: Now, Faustus, let thine eyes with horror
125   stare
    Into that vast perpetual torture-house.
    There are the Furies tossing damnèd souls
    On burning forks; their bodies boil in lead.
    There are live quarters broiling on the coals,
130   That ne'er can die. This ever-burning chair
    Is for o'er-tortured souls to rest them in.
    These that are fed with sops of flaming fire
    Were gluttons and loved only delicates
    And laughed to see the poor starve at their gates.
135   But yet all these are nothing; thou shalt see
    Ten thousand tortures that more horrid be.
FAUSTUS: O, I have seen enough to torture me.
BAD ANGEL: Nay, thou must feel them, taste the smart
    of all.

He that loves pleasure must for pleasure fall.
And so I leave thee, Faustus, till anon;   140
Then wilt thou tumble in confusion.

([*Hell disappears.*] *The clock strikes eleven.*)

FAUSTUS: Ah Faustus,
    Now hast thou but one bare hour to live,
    And then thou must be damned perpetually.
    Stand still, you ever-moving spheres of heaven,   145
    That time may cease and midnight never come.
    Fair nature's eye, rise, rise again, and make
    Perpetual day; or let this hour be but
    A year, a month, a week, a natural day,
    That Faustus may repent and save his soul.   150
    O lente, lente currite noctis equi!°
    The stars move still; time runs; the clock will strike;
    The devil will come, and Faustus must be damned.
    O, I'll leap up to my God! Who pulls me down?
    See, see, where Christ's blood streams in the
      firmament!   155
    One drop would save my soul, half a drop! Ah, my
      Christ!
    Rend not my heart for naming of my Christ!
    Yet will I call on him. O, spare me, Lucifer!
    Where is it now? 'Tis gone. And see where God
    Stretcheth out his arm and bends his ireful brows.   160
    Mountains and hills, come, come, and fall on me,
    And hide me from the heavy wrath of God.
    No, no!
    Then will I headlong run into the earth.
    Earth, gape! O no, it will not harbor me!   165
    You stars that reigned at my nativity,
    Whose influence hath allotted death and hell.
    Now draw up Faustus like a foggy mist
    Into the entrails of yon laboring cloud,
    That when you vomit forth into the air,   170
    My limbs may issue from your smoky mouths,
    So that my soul may but ascend to heaven.

(*The watch strikes.*)

    Ah, half the hour is past; 'twill all be past anon.
    O God,
    If thou wilt not have mercy on my soul,   175
    Yet for Christ's sake, whose blood hath ransomed
      me,
    Impose some end to my incessant pain.
    Let Faustus live in hell a thousand years,
    A hundred thousand, and at last be saved.
    O, no end is limited to damnèd souls.   180
    Why wert thou not a creature wanting soul?
    Or why is this immortal that thou hast?
    Ah, Pythagoras' *metempsychosis*,° were that true,
    This soul should fly from me and I be changed
    Into some brutish beast. All beasts are happy,   185

151. O . . . equi: O slowly, slowly; run you horses of night (adapted from Ovid's *Amores*). **183. metempsychosis:** Belief in the transmigration of souls, associated with the Greek philosopher Pythagoras of Samos.

For, when they die
Their souls are soon dissolved in elements,
But mine must live still to be plagued in hell.
Cursed be the parents that engendered me!
190   No, Faustus, curse thyself, curse Lucifer
That hath deprived thee of the joys of heaven.

(*The clock strikes twelve.*)

O, it strikes, it strikes! Now, body, turn to air,
Or Lucifer will bear thee quick° to hell.
O soul, be changed to little water-drops,
195   And fall into the ocean, ne'er be found!

(*Thunder, and enter the Devils.*)

My God, my God, look not so fierce on me!
Adders and serpents, let me breathe a while!
Ugly hell, gape not! Come not, Lucifer!
I'll burn my books! Ah, Mephistophilis!
(*Exeunt [Faustus and Devils].*)

Scene III

(*Enter the Scholars.*)

FIRST SCHOLAR: Come, gentlemen, let us go visit
    Faustus,
For such a dreadful night was never seen
Since first the world's creation did begin.
Such fearful shrieks and cries were never heard.
5   Pray heaven the doctor have escaped the danger.
SECOND SCHOLAR: O help us, heaven! See, here are
    Faustus' limbs,
All torn asunder by the hand of death.

193. quick: Alive.

THIRD SCHOLAR: The devils whom Faustus served
    have torn him thus;
For 'twixt the hours of twelve and one,
    methought
I heard him shriek and call aloud for help,   10
At which self time the house seemed all on fire
With dreadful horror of these damnèd fiends.
SECOND SCHOLAR: Well, gentlemen, though Faustus'
    end be such
As every Christian heart laments to think on,
Yet for he was a scholar, once admired   15
For wondrous knowledge in our German schools,
We'll give his mangled limbs due burial;
And all the students clothed in mourning black,
Shall wait upon° his heavy° funeral.
(*Exeunt.*)

EPILOGUE

(*Enter Chorus.*)

CHORUS: Cut is the branch that might have grown full
    straight,
And burnèd is Apollo's laurel bough
That sometime grew within this learnèd man.
Faustus is gone. Regard his hellish fall,
Whose fiendful fortune may exhort the wise   5
Only to wonder at unlawful things,
Whose deepness doth entice such forward wits
To practice more than heavenly power permits.
[*Exit.*]

Terminat hora diem; terminat author opus.°

V, III. 19. wait upon: Be present at.   heavy: Sorrowful.   Epilogue. 9. *Terminat . . . opus:* The hour ends the day; the author ends his work.

COMMENTARY

Ernst Honigmann (*b. 1927*)
FROM *TEN PROBLEMS IN* DOCTOR FAUSTUS   *1991*

> *Honigmann, a distinguished critic of Shakespeare and Renaissance drama, raises certain questions about first the "togetherness" of Faustus and Mephistophilis and then the rationality of Faustus. If Faustus is a champion of the rational, why does he behave as he does in the face of a self-confessed devil? Some of Honigmann's observations are dependent on either the A-text or the B-text, the two earliest printings of the play. But whichever text one consults, the problems he sees are intriguing.*

How much genuine fellow-feeling is there in this strange relationship? Quite apart from the fact that they both enjoy the same jokes, they address each other affectionately as "my Faustus" and "my Mephostophilis," and Mephostophilis even speaks of "my Faustus" in the latter's absence.

> I'll wing myself and forthwith fly amain
> Unto my Faustus to the great Turk's court.   (B 1179)

If something close to tenderness seems at times to bind them together, let us remember that there is a connection between loving a person and thinking that you own him (or her). True, we note some dramatic irony as well, as when Faustus addresses "my good Mephostophilis" (A 822); and it suits both of them to get on together, so they call each other "sweet Mephostophilis," "sweet friend" and the like (A 696, 1342), to oil the relationship. Yet since they also rage against each other every so often it has the dynamics of a very human relationship — including deception and (on Faustus' part) some self-deception. Mephostophilis, indeed, insofar as he was once an angel and fell with Lucifer, assumes a kind of "older brother" stance in answering Faustus' questions about heaven and hell; he has been through it all himself, he understands Faustus' point of view — does that not beget fellow-feeling? And perhaps even affection? Ben Jonson remembered Faustus and Mephostophilis when he created Volpone and Mosca, including the delicious twist that the servant plans to outwit his master — yet Jonson's rogues strike me as a colder pair, their relationship as largely professional, whereas Faustus and Mephostophilis also interact unprofessionally. Mephostophilis risks losing Faustus' soul by speaking too honestly:

> FAUSTUS: And what are you that live with Lucifer?
> MEPHOST: Unhappy spirits that live with Lucifer,
>   Conspired against our God with Lucifer,
>   And are for ever damned with Lucifer.   (A 314)

We are encouraged to think of Faustus and Mephostophilis as very close — though exactly how close remains a mystery. When they play their pranks on the Pope and others they may even hug or slap each other with delight — or, alternatively, Mephostophilis may signal to us, grimacing, that he has to humour a childish master. The *togetherness* of Faustus and Mephostophilis, in short, has been an issue throughout the play, and probably one that should not be resolved until Faustus' very last utterance, the moment of truth: "ah, Mephostophilis!"

I must not pretend, however, that this central relationship is identical in the two texts — far from it. Two passages in the B-text, not found in A, stress the distance between the two principals, the malignancy of Mephostophilis and his delight in destroying Faustus. These passages, both placed just before the end, suggest that in the B-text Mephostophilis savors his victim's death-agony. First the devils ascend from hell to "mark [Faustus] how he doth demean himself." How should he, exclaims Mephostophilis —

> How should he, but in desperate lunacy?
> Fond worldling, now his heart-blood dries with grief,
> His conscience kills it, and his labouring brain
> Begets a world of idle fantasies
> To overreach the devil — but all in vain.
> His store of pleasures must be sauced with pain.   (B 1906)

All fellow-feeling has vanished. And when the scholars depart, leaving Faustus to his final meditations, Mephostophilis turns on him gleefully —

> MEPHOST: Ay, Faustus, now hast thou no hope of heaven,
>   Therefore despair, think only upon hell!
>   For that must be thy mansion, there to dwell.
> FAUSTUS: O thou bewitching fiend, 'twas thy temptation
>   Hath robbed me of eternal happiness.
> MEPHOST: I do confess it, Faustus, and rejoice . . .   (B 1983)

It makes a difference, too, that in the B-text Mephostophilis remains onstage during Faustus' interview with the scholars, and that in the B-text Mephostophilis "brings in" Helen of Troy, the first time she appears — presumably like a ringmaster or auctioneer, pointing out her special attractions. (Not so in the *Faust-book,* where Faustus tells his friends that he will "bring her into your presence personally": ch. 45.) The Mephostophilis of the A-text has a subtler relationship with Faustus, less devilish, more human.

Mephostophilis, I said, risks losing Faustus' soul by speaking too honestly. Here is another "theological" problem, for which I see no easy solution. Many a rationalist has thought, before and after Marlowe, "I am aware of no convincing evidence for the existence of God, therefore I shall behave as if there is no God." Yet is it rational to go on denying God when you are talking to a self-confessed devil? And when the devil appears to be unshakeable in the conviction that God exists?

> FAUSTUS: Was not that Lucifer an angel once?
> MEPHOST: Yes, Faustus, and most dearly loved of God.   (A 309)

Put the case that *one* of the supernatural beings of the Christo-Hebraic tradition incontrovertibly exists — good angel, bad angel, Lucifer — then there is an inherent likelihood that God "exists" as well. And if a hostile witness, such as Mephostophilis, assures Faustus that God exists, how can a rational man turn his back on God? make war on the Omnipotent? and choose Hell instead? —

> FAUSTUS: Come, I think hell's a fable.
> MEPHOST: Ay, think so still, till experience change thy mind!   (A 574)

Could it be that Faustus is a very confused doctor of divinity? or is Marlowe a very confused dramatist? or am I guilty now of trying to "over-explain"?

Some critics have argued that Faustus deteriorates intellectually in the course of the play, like Milton's Satan, as witnessed by his childish activities in the middle scenes. Alternatively, Chorus' opening statement

> So much he profits in divinity
> That shortly he was graced with doctor's name,
> Excelling all, and sweetly can dispute . . .   (B 16)

may refer to the past, not to Faustus as he now is —

> For, falling to a devilish exercise
> And glutted now with learning's golden gifts
> He surfeits upon cursed necromancy.   (B 23)

Theologians sometimes talk of a "fall before the Fall" (Milton appears to allude to this in Eve's dream before the Fall). Marlowe's Faustus, perhaps, should be seen as fallen, or devil-possessed, before he signs his formal pact — therefore intellectually impaired from the play's beginning. I prefer this explanation because he behaves irrationally from the beginning, already believing in spirits, and Lucifer, but not in God. Marlowe allows us to think of Faustus as something other than the ideal theologian by inserting implicit stage directions in the speech in his study. "Bid *on kai me on* farewell; Galen, come," "Physic farewell; where is Justinian?", "divinity, adieu"— does Faustus simply pick up one book after another? or should he hurl them away, frustrated, with each sarcastic "adieu" and "farewell"? A frightening impulsiveness, breaking out during this first meditation, could help to reconcile us to Faustus' perplexing irrationality. The *Faust-book* offered this possibility: Dr. Faustus "fell into such fantasies and deep cogitations, that . . . sometime he would *throw the Scripture from him*" (ch. I).

William Shakespeare

Despite the fact that Shakespeare wrote some thirty-seven plays, owned part of his theatrical company, acted in plays, and retired a relatively wealthy man in the city of his birth, there is much we do not know about him. His father was a glovemaker with pretensions to being a gentleman; Shakespeare himself had his coat of arms placed on his home, New Place, purchased in part because it was one of the grandest buildings in Stratford. Church records indicate that he was born in April 1564 and died in April 1616, after having been retired from the stage for two or three years. We know that he married Anne Hathaway in 1582, when he was eighteen and she twenty-six; that he had a daughter Susanna and twins, Judith and Hamnet; and that Hamnet, his only son, died at age eleven. Shakespeare has no direct descendants today.

We know very little about his education. We assume that he went to the local grammar school, since as the son of a burgess he was eligible to attend for free. If he did so, he would have received a very strong education based on

The engraving by Martin Droeshout of William Shakespeare appeared in the First Folio Edition, published in 1623.

rhetoric, logic, and classical literature. He would have been exposed to the comedies of Plautus, the tragedies of Seneca, and the poetry of Virgil, Ovid, and a host of other, lesser writers.

A rumor has persisted that he spent some time as a Latin teacher. No evidence exists to suggest that Shakespeare went to a university, although his general learning and knowledge are so extraordinary and broad that generations of scholars have assumed that he may have also gone to the Inns of Court to study law. This cannot be proved, though; thus, some people claim that another person, with considerable university education, must have written his plays. However, no one in the Elizabethan theater had an education of the sort often proposed for Shakespeare. Marlowe and Ben Jonson were the most learned of Elizabethan playwrights, but their work is quite different in character and feeling from that of Shakespeare.

One recent theory about Shakespeare's early years suggests that before going to London to work in theater he belonged to a wandering company of actors much like those who appear in *Hamlet*. It is an ingenious theory and has much to recommend it, among which is explaining how Shakespeare could take the spotlight so quickly as to arouse the anger of more experienced London writers.

Shakespeare did not begin his career writing for the stage but, in the more conventional approach for the age, as a poet. He sought the support of an aristocratic patron, the earl of Southampton. Like many wealthy and polished young courtiers, Southampton felt it a pleasant ornament to sponsor a poet whose works would be dedicated to him. Shakespeare wrote sonnets apparently with Southampton in mind, and, hoping for preferment, the long narrative poems *Venus and Adonis, The Rape of Lucrece,* and *The Phoenix and the Turtle.* However, Southampton eventually decided to become the patron of another poet, John Florio, an Italian who had translated Michel de Montaigne's *Essays.*

Shakespeare's response was to turn to the stage. His first plays were a considerable success: *King Henry VI* in three parts — three full-length plays. Satisfying London's taste for plays that told the history of England's tangled political past, Shakespeare won considerable renown with a lengthy series of plays ranging from *Richard II* through the two parts of *King Henry IV* to *Henry V.* Audiences were delighted; competing playwrights envied him his triumphs. Francis Meres's famous book of the period, *Palladis Tamia: Wit's Treasury,* cites Shakespeare as modern Plautus and Seneca, the best in both comedy and tragedy. Meres says that by 1598 Shakespeare was known for a dozen plays. That his success was firm by this time is demonstrated by his having purchased his large house, New Place, in Stratford in 1597. He could not have done this without financial security.

In the next few years Shakespeare made a number of interesting purchases of property in Stratford; he also made deals with his own theater company to secure the rights to perform in London. These arrangements produced legal records that give us some of the clearest information we have concerning Shakespeare's activities during this period. His company was called the Lord Chamberlain's Men while Queen Elizabeth was alive but was renamed the King's Men by King James in the spring of 1603, less than two months after Elizabeth died. As the King's Men, Shakespeare's company had considerable power and success. Its audience sometimes included King James, as in the first performance of *Macbeth*.

Shakespeare was successful as a writer of histories, comedies, and tragedies. He also wrote in another genre, known as romance. These plays share elements with both comedies and tragedies, and they often depend on supernatural or improbable elements. *Cymbeline, The Winter's Tale,* and *The Tempest* are the best known of Shakespeare's romances. They are late works and have a fascinating complexity.

When Shakespeare died on April 23, 1616, he was buried as a gentleman in the church in which he had been baptized in Stratford-upon-Avon. His will left most of his money and possessions to his two daughters, Judith and Susanna.

A MIDSUMMER NIGHT'S DREAM

A Midsummer Night's Dream (1595–1596) is an early comedy and one of Shakespeare's most beloved works. It is also one of his most imaginative plays, introducing us to the world of fairies and the realm of dreams. Romantic painters, such as Fuseli, have long found in this play a rich store of images that stretch far beyond the limits of the real world of everyday experience.

For Shakespeare the fun of the play is in showing how the world of the fairies intersects with the world of real people, and we can interpret the play as a hint of what would happen if the world of dreams were to cross the world of real experience. The fact that these worlds are more alike than they are different gives Shakespeare the comic basis on which to work. He also finds some new and amusing ways to interpret the device of mistaken identities.

The play is set in Athens, with Duke Theseus about to wed Hippolyta, the queen of the Amazons. Helena and Hermia are young women in love with Demetrius and Lysander, respectively. Demetrius, however, wants to marry Hermia and has the blessing of Hermia's father. Hermia's refusal to follow her father's wishes drives her into the woods, where she is followed by both young men and Helena, who does not want to lose Demetrius.

The four young people find themselves in the world of the fairies, although the humans cannot see the fairies. Puck, an impish sprite, is ordered by Oberon, king of the fairies, to put the juice of a certain flower in Demetrius's eyes so that he will fall in love with Helena. When Puck puts it in Lysander's eyes instead, the plot backfires: Lysander is suddenly in love with Helena, and Hermia is confounded. Oberon has Puck place the same juice in the eyes of Titania, the queen of the fairies, causing her to fall in love with the first creature she sees when she awakes.

That creature is Bottom, the "rude mechanical" (ignorant artisan) whose head has been transformed into an ass's head. Such a trick opens up possibilities for wonderful comic elements. The richness of the illusions that operate onstage constantly draws us to the question of how we ever can know the truth of our own experiences, especially when some of them are dreams whose imaginative power is occasionally overwhelming.

Shakespeare plays here with some of the Aristotelian conventions of the drama, especially Aristotle's view that drama imitates life. One of the great comic devices in *A Midsummer Night's Dream* is the play within a play that Bottom, Quince, Snug, Flute, and Starveling are to put on before Theseus and Hippolyta. They tell the story of Pyramus and Thisby, lovers who lose each other because they misinterpret signs. It is "Merry and tragical! Tedious and brief!" But it is also a wonderful parody of what playwrights — including Shakespeare — often do when operating in the Aristotelian mode. The aim of the play is realism, yet the players are naive and inexperienced in drama; they do their best constantly to remind the audience that it is only a play.

The comic ineptness of the rude mechanicals' play needs no disclaimers of this sort, and the immediate audience — Theseus, Hippolyta, Demetrius, Helena, Lysander, and Hermia — is amused by the ardor of the players. The audience in the theater is also mightily amused at the antics of the mechanicals, which on the surface are simply funny and a wonderful pastiche of artless play-acting.

Beneath the surface, something more serious is going on. Shakespeare is commenting on the entire function of drama in our lives. He constantly reminds us in this play that we are watching an illusion, even an illusion within an illusion, but he also convinces us that illusions teach us a great deal about reality. The real-world setting of *A Midsummer Night's Dream* — Athens — is quite improbable. The mechanicals all have obviously English names and are out of place in an Athenian pastoral setting. The play on the level of Athens is pure fantasy, with even more fantastic goings-on at the level of the fairy world. But fantasy nourishes us. It helps us interpret our own experiences by permitting us to distance ourselves from them and reflect on how they affect others, one of the deepest functions of drama.

As in most comedies, everything turns out exceptionally well. A multiple marriage, one of the delightful conventions of many comedies, ends the drama, and virtually everyone receives what she or he wanted. We are left with a sense of satisfaction because we, too, get our wish about how things should turn out. Puck, one of the greatest of Shakespeare's characters, turns out to be sympathetic and human in his feelings about people. And Bottom, a clown whose origins are certainly Greek and Roman, endears us to him with his generosity and caring toward others. Shakespeare promotes a remarkably warm view of humanity in this play, leaving us with a sense of delight and a glow that is rare even in comedy.

A Midsummer Night's Dream in Performance

A Midsummer Night's Dream has attracted many great directors in modern times, although in the late seventeenth and eighteenth centuries the play was adapted essentially as a vehicle for presenting the world of the fairies. It even became an opera in 1692. Ludwig Tieck engaged Mendelssohn to write incidental music for the play in Berlin in 1843; their production was for many years the most influential post-Shakespearean adaptation. Beerbohm Tree's 1900 production in London's Savoy Theatre included real rabbits and many other highly realistic details; eventually it played to more than 220,000 patrons. After numerous adaptations it was produced by Granville Barker in London from 1912 to 1914 in its original text, and in New York in 1915. The Old Vic's 1954 production was so lavish that it was staged at the Metropolitan Opera House in New York. Peter Brook played down the fairies and explored the play as a study of love. His 1970 production is well remembered for his having placed Oberon and Puck on trapezes set against a stark white background. He also used some costumes and other elements of commedia dell'arte to spark the comedy. (See Barnes's review of the Brook production on p. 349.) The American Repertory Theatre's 1986 Boston production (see photos on pp. 320–21) reflects the approach to staging that the Royal Shakespeare Company has taken in recent years. The themes of love and transformation inspire the players in a way that shows off the brilliance of the play.

A *Midsummer's Night Dream* has been filmed several times. In 1935 both James Cagney and Mickey Rooney starred in a version that has some charm. In 1968 the Royal Shakespeare Company with Diana Rigg produced a somewhat less interesting film. The most recent version with Kevin Kline, Michelle Pfeiffer, and Stanley Tucci received generally good reviews in 1999.

William Shakespeare (1564–1616)
A MIDSUMMER NIGHT'S DREAM   *c. 1596*

[Dramatis Personae

THESEUS, *Duke of Athens*
EGEUS, *father to Hermia*
LYSANDER,
DEMETRIUS, } *in love with Hermia*
PHILOSTRATE, *Master of the Revels to Theseus*

QUINCE, *a carpenter*
SNUG, *a joiner*
BOTTOM, *a weaver*
FLUTE, *a bellows-mender*
SNOUT, *a tinker*
STARVELING, *a tailor*

HIPPOLYTA, *Queen of the Amazons, betrothed to Theseus*
HERMIA, *daughter to Egeus, in love with Lysander*

Note: The text of *A Midsummer Night's Dream* has come down to us in different versions — such as the first quarto, the second quarto, and the first Folio. The copy of the text used here is largely drawn from the first quarto. Passages enclosed in square brackets are taken from one of the other versions.

HELENA, *in love with Demetrius*
OBERON, *King of the Fairies*
TITANIA, *Queen of the Fairies*
PUCK, *or Robin Goodfellow*
PEASEBLOSSOM,
COBWEB,
MOTH, } *fairies*
MUSTARDSEED,
Other FAIRIES *attending their king and queen*
ATTENDANTS *on Theseus and Hippolyta*

Scene: *Athens, and a wood near it.*]

{*ACT I • Scene I*}°

(*Enter Theseus, Hippolyta, [Philostrate,] with others.*)

THESEUS: Now, fair Hippolyta, our nuptial hour
    Draws on apace. Four happy days bring in
    Another moon; but, O, methinks, how slow

I, I. Location: The palace of Theseus.

This old moon wanes! She lingers° my desires
5 Like to a step-dame° or a dowager°
Long withering out a young man's revenue.
HIPPOLYTA: Four days will quickly steep themselves in
night,
Four nights will quickly dream away the time;
And then the moon, like to a silver bow
10 New-bent in heaven, shall behold the night
Of our solemnities.
THESEUS: Go, Philostrate,
Stir up the Athenian youth to merriments,
Awake the pert and nimble spirit of mirth,
Turn melancholy forth to funerals;
15 The pale companion° is not for our pomp.°
[Exit Philostrate.]
Hippolyta, I woo'd thee with my sword,°
And won thy love doing thee injuries;
But I will wed thee in another key,
With pomp, with triumph,° and with reveling.

(Enter Egeus and his daughter Hermia, and Lysander,
and Demetrius.)

20 EGEUS: Happy be Theseus, our renowned Duke!
THESEUS: Thanks, good Egeus. What's the news with
thee?
EGEUS: Full of vexation come I, with complaint
Against my child, my daughter Hermia.
Stand forth, Demetrius. My noble lord,
25 This man hath my consent to marry her.
Stand forth, Lysander. And, my gracious Duke,
This man hath bewitch'd the bosom of my child.
Thou, thou, Lysander, thou hast given her rhymes
And interchang'd love tokens with my child.
30 Thou hast by moonlight at her window sung
With feigning voice verses of feigning° love,
And stol'n the impression of her fantasy,°
With bracelets of thy hair, rings, gauds,° conceits,°
Knacks,° trifles, nosegays, sweetmeats —
messengers
35 Of strong prevailment in unhardened youth.
With cunning hast thou filch'd my daughter's heart,
Turn'd her obedience, which is due to me,
To stubborn harshness. And, my gracious Duke,
Be it so she will not here before your Grace
40 Consent to marry with Demetrius,
I beg the ancient privilege of Athens:
As she is mine, I may dispose of her,

Which shall be either to this gentleman
Or to her death, according to our law
Immediately° provided in that case.   45
THESEUS: What say you, Hermia? Be advis'd, fair maid.
To you your father should be as a god —
One that compos'd your beauties, yea, and one
To whom you are but as a form in wax
By him imprinted and within his power   50
To leave° the figure or disfigure° it.
Demetrius is a worthy gentleman.
HERMIA: So is Lysander.
THESEUS: In himself he is;
But in this kind,° wanting° your father's voice,°
The other must be held the worthier.   55
HERMIA: I would my father look'd but with my eyes.
THESEUS: Rather your eyes must with his judgment look.
HERMIA: I do entreat your Grace to pardon me.
I know not by what power I am made bold,
Nor how it may concern° my modesty,   60
In such a presence here to plead my thoughts;
But I beseech your Grace that I may know
The worst that may befall me in this case,
If I refuse to wed Demetrius.
THESEUS: Either to die the death, or to abjure   65
Forever the society of men.
Therefore, fair Hermia, question your desires,
Know of your youth, examine well your blood,°
Whether, if you yield not to your father's choice,
You can endure the livery° of a nun,   70
For aye° to be in shady cloister mew'd,°
To live a barren sister all your life,
Chanting faint hymns to the cold fruitless moon.
Thrice blessed they that master so their blood
To undergo such maiden pilgrimage,   75
But earthlier happy° is the rose distill'd,
Than that which withering on the virgin thorn
Grows, lives, and dies in single blessedness.
HERMIA: So will I grow, so live, so die, my lord,
Ere I will yield my virgin patent° up   80
Unto his lordship, whose unwished yoke
My soul consents not to give sovereignty.
THESEUS: Take time to pause; and, by the next new
moon —
The sealing-day betwixt my love and me
For everlasting bond of fellowship —   85
Upon that day either prepare to die
For disobedience to your father's will,
Or° else to wed Demetrius, as he would,
Or on Diana's altar° to protest°
For aye austerity and single life.   90

4. lingers: Lengthens, protects. 5. step-dame: Stepmother. dowager: Widow with a jointure or dower [an estate or title from her deceased husband]. 15. companion: Fellow. pomp: Ceremonial magnificence. 16. with my sword: In a military engagement against the Amazons, when Hippolyta was taken captive. 19. triumph: Public festivity. 31. feigning: (1) Counterfeiting, (2) faining, desirous. 32. And . . . fantasy: And made her fall in love with you (imprinting your image on her imagination) by stealthy and dishonest means. 33. gauds: Playthings. conceits: Fanciful trifles. 34. Knacks: Knickknacks.

45. Immediately: Expressly. 51. leave: Leave unaltered. disfigure: Obliterate. 54. kind: Respect. wanting: Lacking voice: Approval. 60. concern: Befit. 68. blood: Passions. 70. livery: Habit. 71. aye: Ever. mew'd: Shut in (said of a hawk, poultry, etc.). 76. earthlier happy: Happier as respects this world. 80. patent: Privilege. 88. Or: Either. 89. Diana's altar: Diana was a virgin goddess. protest: Vow.

DEMETRIUS: Relent, sweet Hermia, and, Lysander, yield
  Thy crazed° title to my certain right.
LYSANDER: You have her father's love, Demetrius;
  Let me have Hermia's. Do you marry him.
95 EGEUS: Scornful Lysander! True, he hath my love,
  And what is mine my love shall render him.
  And she is mine, and all my right of her
  I do estate unto° Demetrius.
LYSANDER: I am, my lord, as well deriv'd° as he,
100   As well possess'd;° my love is more than his;
  My fortunes every way as fairly° rank'd,
  If not with vantage,° as Demetrius';
  And, which is more than all these boasts can be,
  I am belov'd of beauteous Hermia.
105   Why should not I then prosecute my right?
  Demetrius, I'll avouch it to his head,°
  Made love to Nedar's daughter, Helena,
  And won her soul; and she, sweet lady, dotes,
  Devoutly dotes, dotes in idolatry,
110   Upon this spotted° and inconstant man.
THESEUS: I must confess that I have heard so much,
  And with Demetrius thought to have spoke thereof;
  But, being over-full of self-affairs,
  My mind did lose it. But, Demetrius, come,
115   And come, Egeus, you shall go with me;
  I have some private schooling for you both.
  For you, fair Hermia, look you arm° yourself
  To fit your fancies° to your father's will;
  Or else the law of Athens yields you up
120   Which by no means we may extenuate° —
  To death, or to a vow of single life.
  Come, my Hippolyta. What cheer, my love?
  Demetrius and Egeus, go° along.
  I must employ you in some business
125   Against° our nuptial, and confer with you
  Of something nearly that° concerns yourselves.
EGEUS: With duty and desire we follow you.

   (*Exeunt*° [*all but Lysander and Hermia*].)

LYSANDER: How now, my love, why is your cheek so
  pale?
  How chance the roses there do fade so fast?
130 HERMIA: Belike° for want of rain, which I could well
  Beteem° them from the tempest of my eyes.
LYSANDER: Ay me! For aught that I could ever read,
  Could ever hear by tale or history,
  The course of true love never did run smooth;
135   But either it was different in blood° —

HERMIA: O cross,° too high to be enthrall'd to low!
LYSANDER: Or else misgraffed° in respect of years —
HERMIA: O spite, too old to be engag'd to young!
LYSANDER: Or else it stood upon the choice of
  friends° —
HERMIA: O hell, to choose love by another's eyes! 140
LYSANDER: Or, if there were a sympathy in choice,
  War, death, or sickness did lay siege to it,
  Making it momentany° as a sound,
  Swift as a shadow, short as any dream,
  Brief as the lightning in the collied° night, 145
  That, in a spleen,° unfolds° both heaven and earth,
  And ere a man hath power to say "Behold!"
  The jaws of darkness do devour it up.
  So quick° bright things come to confusion.°
HERMIA: If then true lovers have been ever cross'd,° 150
  It stands as an edict in destiny.
  Then let us teach our trial patience,°
  Because it is a customary cross,
  As due to love as thoughts and dreams and sighs,
  Wishes and tears, poor fancy's° followers. 155
LYSANDER: A good persuasion. Therefore, hear me,
  Hermia.
  I have a widow aunt, a dowager
  Of great revenue, and she hath no child.
  From Athens is her house remote seven leagues;
  And she respects° me as her only son. 160
  There, gentle Hermia, may I marry thee,
  And to that place the sharp Athenian law
  Cannot pursue us. If thou lovest me, then,
  Steal forth thy father's house tomorrow night;
  And in the wood, a league without the town, 165
  Where I did meet thee once with Helena
  To do observance to a morn of May,°
  There will I stay for thee.
HERMIA: My good Lysander!
  I swear to thee, by Cupid's strongest bow,
  By his best arrow with the golden head,° 170
  By the simplicity° of Venus' doves,°
  By that which knitteth souls and prospers loves,
  And by that fire which burn'd the Carthage queen,
  When the false Troyan° under sail was seen,

92. **crazed:** Cracked, unsound.   98. **estate unto:** Settle or bestow upon.   99. **deriv'd:** Descended, i.e., "as well born."   100. **possess'd:** Endowed with wealth.   101. **fairly:** Handsomely.   102. **vantage:** Superiority.   106. **head:** Face.   110. **spotted:** Morally stained.   117. **look you arm:** Take care you prepare.   118. **fancies:** Likings, thoughts of love.   120. **extenuate:** Mitigate.   123. **go:** Come.   125. **Against:** In preparation for.   126. **nearly that:** That closely.   127. [S.D.] *Exeunt:* Latin for "they go out."   130. **Belike:** Very likely.   131. **Beteem:** Grant, afford.   135. **blood:** Hereditary station.

136. **cross:** Vexation.   137. **misgraffed:** Ill grafted, badly matched.   139. **friends:** Relatives.   143. **momentany:** Lasting but a moment.   145. **collied:** Blackened (as with coal dust), darkened.   146. **in a spleen:** In a swift impulse in a violent flash.   **unfolds:** Discloses.   149. **quick:** Quickly; or, perhaps, living, alive.   **confusion:** Ruin.   150. **ever cross'd:** Always thwarted.   152. **teach . . . patience:** Teach ourselves patience in this trial.   155. **fancy's:** Amorous passion's.   160. **respects:** Regards.   167. **do . . . May:** Perform the ceremonies of May Day.   170. **best arrow . . . golden head:** Cupid's best gold-pointed arrows were supposed to induce love, his blunt leaden arrows aversion.   171. **simplicity:** Innocence.   **doves:** Those that drew Venus's chariot.   173–74. **by that fire . . . false Troyan:** Dido, Queen of Carthage, immolated herself on a funeral pyre after having been deserted by the Trojan hero Aeneas.

175   By all the vows that ever men have broke,
    In number more than ever women spoke,
    In that same place thou hast appointed me
    Tomorrow truly will I meet with thee.
  LYSANDER: Keep promise, love. Look, here comes
    Helena.

(*Enter Helena.*)

180 HERMIA: God speed fair° Helena, whither away?
  HELENA: Call you me fair? That fair again unsay.
    Demetrius loves your fair.° O happy fair!°
    Your eyes are lodestars,° and your tongue's sweet air°
    More tuneable° than lark to shepherd's ear
185   When wheat is green, when hawthorn buds appear.
    Sickness is catching. O, were favor° so,
    Yours would I catch, fair Hermia, ere I go;
    My ear should catch your voice, my eye your eye,
    My tongue should catch your tongue's sweet melody.
190   Were the world mine, Demetrius being bated,°
    The rest I'd give to be to you translated.°
    O, teach me how you look, and with what art
    You sway the motion° of Demetrius' heart.
  HERMIA: I frown upon him, yet he loves me still.
  HELENA: O that your frowns would teach my smiles
195   such skill!
  HERMIA: I give him curses, yet he gives me love.
  HELENA: O that my prayers could such affection°
    move!°
  HERMIA: The more I hate, the more he follows me.
  HELENA: The more I love, the more he hateth me.
200 HERMIA: His folly, Helena, is no fault of mine.
  HELENA: None, but your beauty. Would that fault were
    mine!
  HERMIA: Take comfort. He no more shall see my face.
    Lysander and myself will fly this place.
    Before the time I did Lysander see,
205   Seem'd Athens as a paradise to me.
    O, then, what graces in my love do dwell,
    That he hath turn'd a heaven unto a hell!
  LYSANDER: Helen, to you our minds we will unfold.
    Tomorrow night, when Phoebe° doth behold
210   Her silver visage in the wat'ry glass,°
    Decking with liquid pearl the bladed grass,
    A time that lovers' flights doth still° conceal,
    Through Athens' gates have we devis'd to steal.
  HERMIA: And in the wood, where often you and I
215   Upon faint° primrose beds were wont to lie,
    Emptying our bosoms of their counsel° sweet,

    There my Lysander and myself shall meet;
    And thence from Athens turn away our eyes,
    To seek new friends and stranger companies.
    Farewell, sweet playfellow. Pray thou for us,   220
    And good luck grant thee thy Demetrius!
    Keep word, Lysander. We must starve our sight
    From lovers' food till morrow deep midnight.
  LYSANDER: I will, my Hermia.   (*Exit Hermia.*)
    Helena, adieu.
    As you on him, Demetrius dote on you!   225
        (*Exit Lysander.*)
  HELENA: How happy some o'er other some can be!°
    Through Athens I am thought as fair as she.
    But what of that? Demetrius thinks not so;
    He will not know what all but he do know.
    And as he errs, doting on Hermia's eyes,   230
    So I, admiring of° his qualities.
    Things base and vile, holding no quantity,°
    Love can transpose to form and dignity.
    Love looks not with the eyes, but with the mind,
    And therefore is wing'd Cupid painted blind.   235
    Nor hath Love's mind of any judgment taste;°
    Wings, and no eyes, figure° unheedy haste.
    And therefore is Love said to be a child,
    Because in choice he is so oft beguil'd.
    As waggish boys in game° themselves forswear,   240
    So the boy Love is perjur'd everywhere.
    For ere Demetrius look'd on Hermia's eyne,°
    He hail'd down oaths that he was only mine;
    And when this hail some heat from Hermia felt,
    So he dissolv'd, and show'rs of oaths did melt.   245
    I will go tell him of fair Hermia's flight.
    Then to the wood will he tomorrow night
    Pursue her; and for this intelligence°
    If I have thanks, it is a dear° expense.°
    But herein mean I to enrich my pain,   250
    To have his sight thither and back again.   (*Exit.*)

{*Scene II*}°

(*Enter Quince the Carpenter, and Snug the Joiner, and Bottom the Weaver, and Flute the Bellows-Mender, and Snout the Tinker, and Starveling the Tailor.*)

QUINCE: Is all our company here?
BOTTOM: You were best to call them generally,° man by man, according to the scrip.°

---

180. **fair:** Fair-complexioned (generally regarded by the Elizabethans as more beautiful than dark-complexioned). 182. **your fair:** Your beauty (even though Hermia is dark-complexioned). **happy fair:** Lucky fair one. 183. **lodestars:** Guiding stars. **air:** Music. 184. **tuneable:** Tuneful, melodious. 186. **favor:** Appearance, looks. 190. **bated:** Excepted. 191. **translated:** Transformed. 193. **motion:** Impulse. 197. **affection:** Passion. **move:** Arouse. 209. **Phoebe:** Diana, the moon. 210. **glass:** Mirror. 212. **still:** Always. 215. **faint:** Pale. 216. **counsel:** Secret thought.

226. **o'er . . . can be:** Can be in comparison to some others. 231. **admiring of:** Wondering at. 232. **holding no quantity:** Unsubstantial, unshapely. 236. **Nor . . . taste:** Nor has Love, which dwells in the fancy or imagination, any *taste* or least bit of judgment or reason. 237. **figure:** Are a symbol of. 240. **game:** Sport, jest. 242. **eyne:** Eyes (old form of plural). 248. **intelligence:** Information. 249. **dear:** Costly. **a dear expense:** A trouble worth taking. I, II. **Location:** Athens. Quince's house(?). 2. **generally:** Bottom's blunder for *individually.* 3. **scrip:** Script, written list.

QUINCE: Here is the scroll of every man's name which is
    thought fit, through all Athens, to play in our in-
    terlude before the Duke and the Duchess on his
    wedding-day at night.

BOTTOM: First, good Peter Quince, say what the play
    treats on, then read the names of the actors, and so
    grow to° a point.

QUINCE: Marry,° our play is "The most lamentable com-
    edy and most cruel death of Pyramus and Thisby."

BOTTOM: A very good piece of work, I assure you, and a
    merry. Now, good Peter Quince, call forth your
    actors by the scroll. Masters, spread yourselves.

QUINCE: Answer as I call you. Nick Bottom, the weaver.

BOTTOM: Ready. Name what part I am for, and proceed.

QUINCE: You, Nick Bottom, are set down for Pyramus.

BOTTOM: What is Pyramus? A lover, or a tyrant?

QUINCE: A lover, that kills himself most gallant for love.

BOTTOM: That will ask some tears in the true perform-
    ing of it. If I do it, let the audience look to their eyes.
    I will move storms; I will condole° in some measure.
    To the rest — yet my chief humor° is for a tyrant. I
    could play Ercles° rarely, or a part to tear a cat° in, to
    make all split.°
      "The raging rocks
    And shivering shocks
    Shall break the locks
      Of prison gates;
    And Phibbus' car°
    Shall shine from far
    And make and mar
      The foolish Fates."
    This was lofty! Now name the rest of the players. This
    is Ercles' vein, a tyrant's vein. A lover is more con-
    doling.

QUINCE: Francis Flute, the bellows-mender.

FLUTE: Here, Peter Quince.

QUINCE: Flute, you must take Thisby on you.

FLUTE: What is Thisby? A wand'ring knight?

QUINCE: It is the lady that Pyramus must love.

FLUTE: Nay, faith, let not me play a woman. I have a
    beard coming.

QUINCE: That's all one.° You shall play it in a mask, and
    you may speak as small° as you will.

BOTTOM: An° I may hide my face, let me play Thisby
    too. I'll speak in a monstrous little voice, "Thisne,
    Thisne!" "Ah Pyramus, my lover dear! Thy Thisby
    dear, and lady dear!"

QUINCE: No, no; you must play Pyramus; and, Flute,
    you Thisby.

BOTTOM: Well, proceed.

QUINCE: Robin Starveling, the tailor.

STARVELING: Here, Peter Quince.

QUINCE: Robin Starveling, you must play Thisby's
    mother. Tom Snout, the tinker.

SNOUT: Here, Peter Quince.

QUINCE: You, Pyramus' father; myself, Thisby's father;
    Snug, the joiner, you, the lion's part; and I hope here
    is a play fitted.

SNUG: Have you the lion's part written? Pray you, if it
    be, give it me, for I am slow of study.

QUINCE: You may do it extempore, for it is nothing but
    roaring.

BOTTOM: Let me play the lion too. I will roar that I will
    do any man's heart good to hear me. I will roar that I
    will make the Duke say, "Let him roar again, let him
    roar again."

QUINCE: An you should do it too terribly, you would
    fright the Duchess and the ladies, that they would
    shriek; and that were enough to hang us all.

ALL: That would hang us, every mother's son.

BOTTOM: I grant you, friends, if you should fright the
    ladies out of their wits, they would have no more dis-
    cretion but to hang us; but I will aggravate° my voice
    so that I will roar you° as gently as any sucking dove;
    I will roar you an 'twere any nightingale.

QUINCE: You can play no part but Pyramus; for Pyra-
    mus is a sweet-fac'd man, a proper° man as one shall
    see in a summer's day, a most lovely gentleman-like
    man. Therefore you must needs play Pyramus.

BOTTOM: Well, I will undertake it. What beard were I
    best to play it in?

QUINCE: Why, what you will.

BOTTOM: I will discharge° it in either your° straw-color
    beard, your orange-tawny beard, your purple-in-
    grain° beard, or your French-crown-color° beard,
    your perfect yellow.

QUINCE: Some of your French crowns° have no hair at
    all, and then you will play barefac'd. But, masters,
    here are your parts. [*He distributes parts.*] And I am
    to entreat you, request you, and desire you, to con°
    them by tomorrow night; and meet me in the palace
    wood, a mile without the town, by moonlight. There
    will we rehearse; for if we meet in the city, we shall be
    dogg'd with company, and our devices° known. In
    the meantime I will draw a bill° of properties, such as
    our play wants. I pray you, fail me not.

BOTTOM: We will meet, and there we may rehearse most
    obscenely° and courageously. Take pains, be perfect;°
    adieu.

---

10. grow to: Come to.   **11. Marry:** A mild oath, originally the name of the Virgin Mary.   **23. condole:** Lament, arouse pity.   **24. humor:** Inclination, whim.   **25. Ercles:** Hercules (the tradition of ranting came from Seneca's *Hercules Furens*).   **tear a cat:** Rant.   **26. make all split:** Cause a stir, bring the house down.   **31. Phibbus' car:** Phoebus's, the sun-god's, chariot.   **45. That's all one:** It makes no difference.   **46. small:** High-pitched.   **47. An:** If.

76. aggravate: Bottom's blunder for *diminish*.   **77. roar you:** Roar for you.   **80. proper:** Handsome.   **86. discharge:** Perform.   **your:** I.e., you know the kind I mean.   **87–88. purple-in-grain:** Dyed a very deep red (from *grain*, the name applied to the dried insect used to make the dye).   **88. French-crown-color:** Color of a French crown, a gold coin.   **90. crowns:** Heads bald from syphilis, the "French disease."   **93. con:** Learn by heart.   **97. devices:** Plans.   **98. bill:** List.   **101. obscenely:** An unintentionally funny blunder, whatever Bottom meant to say.   **perfect:** Letter-perfect in memorizing your parts.

QUINCE: At the Duke's oak we meet.
BOTTOM: Enough. Hold, or cut bow-strings.°

(*Exeunt.*)

{*ACT II • Scene 1*}°

(*Enter a Fairy at one door, and Robin Goodfellow [Puck] at another.*)

PUCK: How now, spirit! Whither wander you?
FAIRY: Over hill, over dale,
   Thorough° bush, thorough brier,
   Over park, over pale,°
5   Thorough flood, thorough fire,
   I do wander every where,
   Swifter than the moon's sphere;
   And I serve the Fairy Queen,
   To dew her orbs° upon the green.
10 The cowslips tall her pensioners° be.
   In their gold coats spots you see;
   Those be rubies, fairy favors,°
   In those freckles live their savors.°
   I must go seek some dewdrops here
15 And hang a pearl in every cowslip's ear.
   Farewell, thou lob° of spirits; I'll be gone.
   Our Queen and all her elves come here anon.°
PUCK: The King doth keep his revels here tonight.
   Take heed the Queen come not within his sight.
20 For Oberon is passing fell° and wrath,°
   Because that she as her attendant hath
   A lovely boy, stolen from an Indian king;
   She never had so sweet a changeling.°
   And jealous Oberon would have the child
25 Knight of his train, to trace° the forests wild.
   But she perforce° withholds the loved boy,
   Crowns him with flowers and makes him all her joy.
   And now they never meet in grove or green,
   By fountain° clear, or spangled starlight sheen,
30 But they do square,° that all their elves for fear
   Creep into acorn-cups and hide them there.
FAIRY: Either I mistake your shape and making quite,
   Or else you are that shrewd° and knavish sprite°
   Call'd Robin Goodfellow. Are not you he
35 That frights the maidens of the villagery,
   Skim milk, and sometimes labor in the quern,°
   And bootless° make the breathless huswife churn,

And sometime make the drink to bear no barm,°
Mislead night-wanderers, laughing at their harm?
Those that Hobgoblin call you and sweet Puck,   40
You do their work, and they shall have good luck.
Are you not he?
PUCK: Thou speakest aright;
   I am that merry wanderer of the night.
   I jest to Oberon and make him smile
   When I a fat and bean-fed horse beguile,   45
   Neighing in likeness of a filly foal;
   And sometime lurk I in a gossip's° bowl,
   In very likeness of a roasted crab,°
   And when she drinks, against her lips I bob
   And on her withered dewlap° pour the ale.   50
   The wisest aunt,° telling the saddest° tale,
   Sometime for three-foot stool mistaketh me;
   Then slip I from her bum, down topples she,
   And "tailor"° cries, and falls into a cough;
   And then the whole quire° hold their hips and
     laugh,   55
   And waxen° in their mirth and neeze° and swear
   A merrier hour was never wasted there.
   But, room, fairy! Here comes Oberon.
FAIRY: And here my mistress. Would that he were
   gone!

(*Enter [Oberon] the King of Fairies at one door, with his train; and [Titania] the Queen at another, with hers.*)

OBERON: Ill met by moonlight, proud Titania.   60
TITANIA: What, jealous Oberon? Fairies, skip hence.
   I have forsworn his bed and company.
OBERON: Tarry, rash wanton.° Am not I thy lord?
TITANIA: Then I must be thy lady; but I know
   When thou hast stolen away from fairy land,   65
   And in the shape of Corin° sat all day,
   Playing on pipes of corn° and versing love
   To amorous Phillida.° Why art thou here,
   Come from the farthest steep° of India,
   But that, forsooth, the bouncing Amazon,   70
   Your buskin'd° mistress and your warrior love,
   To Theseus must be wedded, and you come
   To give their bed joy and prosperity.
OBERON: How canst thou thus for shame, Titania,
   Glance at my credit with Hippolyta,°   75
   Knowing I know thy love to Theseus?
   Didst not thou lead him through the glimmering
     night

---

104. **Hold . . . bow-strings:** An archer's expression not definitely explained, but probably meaning here "keep your promises, or give up the play." **II, 1. Location:** A wood near Athens. 3. **Thorough:** Through. 4. **pale:** Enclosure. 9. **orbs:** Circles, i.e., fairy rings. 10. **pensioners:** Retainers, members of the royal bodyguard. 12. **favors:** Love tokens. 13. **savors:** Sweet smells. 16. **lob:** Country bumpkin. 17. **anon:** At once. 20. **passing fell:** Exceedingly angry. **wrath:** Wrathful. 23. **changeling:** Child exchanged for another by the fairies. 25. **trace:** Range through. 26. **perforce:** Forcibly. 29. **fountain:** Spring. 30. **square:** Quarrel. 33. **shrewd:** Mischievous. **sprite:** Spirit. 36. **quern:** Handmill. 37. **bootless:** In vain.

38. **barm:** Yeast, head on the ale. 47. **gossip's:** Old woman's. 48. **crab:** Crab apple. 50. **dewlap:** Loose skin on neck. 51. **aunt:** Old woman. **saddest:** Most serious. 54. **tailor:** Possibly because she ends up sitting cross-legged on the floor, looking like a tailor. 55. **quire:** Company. 56. **waxen:** Increase. **neeze:** Sneeze. 63. **wanton:** Headstrong creature. 66, 68. **Corin, Phillida:** Conventional names of pastoral lovers. 67. **corn:** Here, oat stalks. 69. **steep:** Mountain range. 71. **buskin'd:** Wearing half-boots called buskins. 75. **Glance . . . Hippolyta:** Make insinuations about my favored relationship with Hippolyta.

From Perigenia,° whom he ravished?
And make him with fair Aegles° break his faith,
80   With Ariadne° and Antiopa?°
TITANIA: These are the forgeries of jealousy;
And never, since the middle summer's spring,°
Met we on hill, in dale, forest, or mead,
By paved° fountain or by rushy° brook,
85   Or in° the beached margent° of the sea,
To dance our ringlets° to the whistling wind,
But with thy brawls thou hast disturb'd our sport.
Therefore the winds, piping to us in vain,
As in revenge, have suck'd up from the sea
90   Contagious° fogs; which falling in the land
Hath every pelting° river made so proud
That they have overborne their continents.°
The ox hath therefore stretch'd his yoke in vain,
The ploughman lost his sweat, and the green corn°
95   Hath rotted ere his youth attain'd a beard;
The fold° stands empty in the drowned field,
And crows are fatted with the murrion° flock;
The nine men's morris° is fill'd up with mud,
And the quaint mazes° in the wanton° green
100   For lack of tread are undistinguishable.
The human mortals want° their winter° here;
No night is now with hymn or carol bless'd.
Therefore° the moon, the governess of floods,
Pale in her anger, washes all the air,
105   That rheumatic diseases° do abound.
And thorough this distemperature° we see
The seasons alter: hoary-headed frosts
Fall in the fresh lap of the crimson rose,
And on old Hiems'° thin and icy crown
110   An odorous chaplet of sweet summer buds
Is, as in mockery, set. The spring, the summer,

78. **Perigenia:** Perigouna, one of Theseus's conquests. (This and the following women are named in Thomas North's translation of Plutarch's *Life of Theseus.*)   79. **Aegles:** Aegle, for whom Theseus deserted Ariadne according to some accounts. 80. **Ariadne:** The daughter of Minos, King of Crete, who helped Theseus escape the labyrinth after killing the Minotaur; later she was abandoned by Theseus.   **Antiopa:** Queen of the Amazons and wife of Theseus; elsewhere identified with Hippolyta, but here thought of as a separate woman.   82. **middle summer's spring:** Beginning of midsummer.   84. **paved:** With pebbled bottom.   **rushy:** Bordered with rushes.   85. **in:** On. **margent:** Edge, border.   86. **ringlets:** Dances in a ring. (See *orbs* in line 9.)   90. **Contagious:** Noxious.   91. **pelting:** Paltry; or striking, moving forcefully.   92. **continents:** Banks that contain them.   94. **corn:** Grain of any kind.   96. **fold:** Pen for sheep or cattle.   97. **murrion:** Having died of the murrain, plague.   98. **nine men's morris:** Portion of the village green marked out in a square for a game played with nine pebbles or pegs.   99. **quaint mazes:** Intricate paths marked out on the village green to be followed rapidly on foot as a kind of contest. **wanton:** Luxuriant.   101. **want:** Lack.   **winter:** Regular winter season; or proper observances of winter, such as the *hymn or carol* in the next line (?).   103. **Therefore:** I.e., as a result of our quarrel.   105. **rheumatic diseases:** Colds, flu, and other respiratory infections.   106. **distemperature:** Disturbance in nature.   109. **Hiems:** The winter god.

The childing° autumn, angry winter, change
Their wonted liveries,° and the mazed° world,
By their increase,° now knows not which is which.
And this same progeny of evils comes   115
From our debate,° from our dissension;
We are their parents and original.°
OBERON: Do you amend it then; it lies in you.
Why should Titania cross her Oberon?
I do but beg a little changeling boy,   120
To be my henchman.°
TITANIA: Set your heart at rest.
The fairy land buys not the child of me.
His mother was a vot'ress° of my order,
And, in the spiced Indian air, by night,
Full often hath she gossip'd by my side,   125
And sat with me on Neptune's yellow sands,
Marking th' embarked traders° on the flood,°
When we have laugh'd to see the sails conceive
And grow big-bellied with the wanton° wind;
Which she, with pretty and with swimming gait,   130
Following — her womb then rich with my young
   squire —
Would imitate, and sail upon the land
To fetch me trifles, and return again,
As from a voyage, rich with merchandise.
But she, being mortal, of that boy did die;   135
And for her sake do I rear up her boy,
And for her sake I will not part with him.
OBERON: How long within this wood intend you stay?
TITANIA: Perchance till after Theseus' wedding-day.
If you will patiently dance in our round°   140
And see our moonlight revels, go with us;
If not, shun me, and I will spare° your haunts.
OBERON: Give me that boy, and I will go with thee.
TITANIA: Not for thy fairy kingdom. Fairies, away!
We shall chide downright, if I longer stay.   145

(*Exeunt [Titania with her train].*)

OBERON: Well, go thy way. Thou shalt not from° this
   grove
Till I torment thee for this injury.
My gentle Puck, come hither. Thou rememb'rest
Since° once I sat upon a promontory,
And heard a mermaid on a dolphin's back   150
Uttering such dulcet and harmonious breath°
That the rude sea grew civil at her song
And certain stars shot madly from their spheres,
To hear the sea-maid's music.
PUCK: I remember.
OBERON: That very time I saw, but thou couldst not,   155

112. **childing:** Fruitful, pregnant.   113. **wonted liveries:** Usual apparel.   **mazed:** Bewildered.   114. **their increase:** Their yield, what they produce.   116. **debate:** Quarrel.   117. **original:** Origin.   121. **henchman:** Attendant, page.   123. **vot'ress:** Female votary; devotee, worshiper.   127. **traders:** Trading vessels.   **flood:** Flood tide.   129. **wanton:** Sportive.   140. **round:** Circular dance.   142. **spare:** Shun.   146. **from:** Go from. 149. **Since:** When.   151. **breath:** Voice, song.

Flying between the cold moon and the earth,
Cupid all° arm'd. A certain aim he took
At a fair vestal° throned by the west,
And loos'd his love-shaft smartly from his bow,
160 As° it should pierce a hundred thousand hearts;
But I might° see young Cupid's fiery shaft
Quench'd in the chaste beams of the wat'ry moon,
And the imperial vot'ress passed on,
In maiden meditation, fancy-free.°
165 Yet mark'd I where the bolt of Cupid fell:
It fell upon a little western flower,
Before milk-white, now purple with love's wound,
And maidens call it love-in-idleness.°
Fetch me that flow'r; the herb I showed thee once.
170 The juice of it on sleeping eyelids laid
Will make or man or° woman madly dote
Upon the next live creature that it sees.
Fetch me this herb, and be thou here again
Ere the leviathan° can swim a league.
175 PUCK: I'll put a girdle round about the earth
In forty° minutes.   [*Exit.*]
OBERON: Having once this juice,
I'll watch Titania when she is asleep,
And drop the liquor of it in her eyes.
The next thing then she waking looks upon,
180 Be it on lion, bear, or wolf, or bull,
On meddling monkey, or on busy ape,
She shall pursue it with the soul of love.
And ere I take this charm from off her sight,
As I can take it with another herb,
185 I'll make her render up her page to me.
But who comes here? I am invisible,
And I will overhear their conference.

(*Enter Demetrius, Helena following him.*)

DEMETRIUS: I love thee not, therefore pursue me not.
Where is Lysander and fair Hermia?
190 The one I'll slay, the other slayeth me.
Thou told'st me they were stol'n unto this wood;
And here am I, and wode° within this wood,
Because I cannot meet my Hermia.
Hence, get thee gone, and follow me no more.
195 HELENA: You draw me, you hard-hearted adamant;°
But yet you draw not iron, for my heart
Is true as steel. Leave° you your power to draw,
And I shall have no power to follow you.

DEMETRIUS: Do I entice you? Do I speak you fair?°
Or, rather, do I not in plainest truth   200
Tell you I do not nor I cannot love you?
HELENA: And even for that do I love you the more.
I am your spaniel; and, Demetrius,
The more you beat me, I will fawn on you.
Use me but as your spaniel, spurn me, strike me,   205
Neglect me, lose me; only give me leave,
Unworthy as I am, to follow you.
What worser place can I beg in your love —
And yet a place of high respect with me —
Than to be used as you use your dog?   210
DEMETRIUS: Tempt not too much the hatred of my
spirit,
For I am sick when I do look on thee.
HELENA: And I am sick when I look not on you.
DEMETRIUS: You do impeach° your modesty too much
To leave the city and commit yourself   215
Into the hands of one that loves you not,
To trust the opportunity of night
And the ill counsel of a desert° place
With the rich worth of your virginity.
HELENA: Your virtue° is my privilege.° For that°   220
It is not night when I do see your face,
Therefore I think I am not in the night;
Nor doth this wood lack worlds of company,
For you in my respect° are all the world.
Then how can it be said I am alone,   225
When all the world is here to look on me?
DEMETRIUS: I'll run from thee and hide me in the
brakes,°
And leave thee to the mercy of wild beasts.
HELENA: The wildest hath not such a heart as you.
Run when you will, the story shall be chang'd: 230
Apollo flies and Daphne holds the chase,°
The dove pursues the griffin,° the mild hind°
Makes speed to catch the tiger — bootless° speed,
When cowardice pursues and valor flies.
DEMETRIUS: I will not stay° thy questions.° Let me go! 235
Or if thou follow me, do not believe
But I shall do thee mischief in the wood.
HELENA: Ay, in the temple, in the town, the field,
You do me mischief. Fie, Demetrius!
Your wrongs do set a scandal on my sex.   240
We cannot fight for love, as men may do;
We should be woo'd and were not made to woo.
                                      [*Exit Demetrius.*]

---

157. all: Fully.   **158. vestal:** Vestal virgin (contains a complimentary allusion to Queen Elizabeth as a votaress of Diana and probably refers to an actual entertainment in her honor at Elvetham in 1591).   **160. As:** As if.   **161. might:** Could.   **164. fancy-free:** Free of love's spell.   **168. love-in-idleness:** Pansy, heartsease.   **171. or . . . or:** Either . . . or.   **174. leviathan:** Sea monster, whale.   **176. forty:** Used indefinitely.   **192. wode:** Mad (pronounced "wood" and often spelled so).   **195. adamant:** Lodestone, magnet (with pun on *hard-hearted*, since adamant was also thought to be the hardest of all stones and was confused with the diamond).   **197. Leave:** Give up.

199. fair: Courteously.   **214. impeach:** Call into question.   **218. desert:** Deserted.   **220. virtue:** Goodness or power to attract.   **privilege:** Safeguard, warrant.   **For that:** Because.   **224. in my respect:** As far as I am concerned.   **227. brakes:** Thickets.   **231. Apollo . . . chase:** In the ancient myth, Daphne fled from Apollo and was saved from rape by being transformed into a laurel tree; here it is the female who *holds the chase*, or pursues, instead of the male.   **232. griffin:** A fabulous monster with the head of an eagle and the body of a lion.   **hind:** Female deer.   **233. bootless:** Fruitless.   **235. stay:** Wait for.   **questions:** Talk or argument.

NEAR RIGHT: Oberon
instructing Puck in the power
of the "little western flower"
in the American Repertory
Theatre's 1986 production.
CENTER: Oberon with Titania
upon his shoulder. FAR RIGHT:
The rude mechanicals:
Moonshine with Lion. BELOW:
Kevin Kline as Bottom, and
Michelle Pfeiffer as Titania,
in a touching moment from
the 1999 film, *William
Shakespeare's A Midsummer
Night's Dream,* directed by
Michael Hoffman.

320

I'll follow thee and make a heaven of hell,
To die upon° the hand I love so well.   [*Exit.*]
OBERON: Fare thee well, nymph. Ere he do leave this
245   grove,
Thou shalt fly him and he shall seek thy love.

(*Enter Puck.*)

Hast thou the flower there? Welcome, wanderer.
PUCK: Ay, there it is.   [*Offers the flower.*]
OBERON: I pray thee, give it me.
I know a bank where the wild thyme blows,°
250   Where oxlips° and the nodding violet grows,
Quite over-canopied with luscious woodbine,°
With sweet musk-roses° and with eglantine.°
There sleeps Titania sometime of the night
Lull'd in these flowers with dances and delight;

244. **upon:** By.   249. **blows:** Blooms.   250. **oxlips:** Flowers
resembling cow-slip and primrose.   251. **woodbine:** Honeysuckle.   252. **musk-roses:** A kind of large, sweet-scented rose.
eglantine: Sweetbriar, another kind of rose.

And there the snake throws° her enamel'd skin,   255
Weed° wide enough to wrap a fairy in.
And with the juice of this I'll streak° her eyes,
And make her full of hateful fantasies.
Take thou some of it, and seek through this grove.
                  [*Gives some love-juice.*]
A sweet Athenian lady is in love   260
With a disdainful youth. Anoint his eyes,
But do it when the next thing he espies
May be the lady. Thou shalt know the man
By the Athenian garments he hath on.
Effect it with some care, that he may prove   265
More fond on° her than she upon her love;
And look thou meet me ere the first cock crow.
PUCK: Fear not, my lord, your servant shall do so.
                          (*Exeunt.*)

255. **throws:** Sloughs off, sheds.   256. **Weed:** Garment.
257. **streak:** Anoint, touch gently.   266. **fond on:** Doting on.

{*Scene II*}°

(*Enter Titania, Queen of Fairies, with her train.*)

TITANIA: Come, now a roundel° and a fairy song;
    Then, for the third part of a minute, hence —
    Some to kill cankers° in the musk-rose buds,
    Some war with rere-mice° for their leathern wings,
5   To make my small elves coats, and some keep back
    The clamorous owl, that nightly hoots and wonders
    At our quaint° spirits. Sing me now asleep.
    Then to your offices and let me rest.

(*Fairies sing.*)

FIRST FAIRY: You spotted snakes with double° tongue,
10   Thorny hedgehogs, be not seen;
    Newts° and blindworms, do no wrong,
        Come not near our fairy queen.
    [*Chorus.*] Philomel,° with melody
        Sing in our sweet lullaby;
15 Lulla, lulla, lullaby, lulla, lulla, lullaby.
        Never harm,
        Nor spell nor charm,
    Come our lovely lady nigh.
    So, good night, with lullaby.
20 FIRST FAIRY: Weaving spiders, come not here;
        Hence, you long-legg'd spinners, hence!
    Beetles black, approach not near;
        Worm nor snail, do no offense.
    [*Chorus.*] Philomel, with melody, etc.
25 SECOND FAIRY: Hence, away! Now all is well.
        One aloof stand sentinel.
                        [*Exeunt Fairies. Titania sleeps.*]

(*Enter Oberon [and squeezes the flower on Titania's eye-lids].*)

OBERON: What thou seest when thou dost wake,
    Do it for thy true-love take;
    Love and languish for his sake.
30 Be it ounce,° or cat, or bear,
    Pard,° or boar with bristled hair,
    In thy eye that shall appear
    When thou wak'st, it is thy dear
    Wake when some vile thing is near.   [*Exit.*]

(*Enter Lysander and Hermia.*)

LYSANDER: Fair love, you faint with wand'ring in the
35   wood;
    And to speak troth,° I have forgot our way.
    We'll rest us, Hermia, if you think it good,

And tarry for the comfort of the day.
HERMIA: Be 't so, Lysander. Find you out a bed,
    For I upon this bank will rest my head.   40
LYSANDER: One turf shall serve as pillow for us both,
    One heart, one bed, two bosoms, and one troth.°
HERMIA: Nay, good Lysander; for my sake, my dear,
    Lie further off yet, do not lie so near.
LYSANDER: O, take the sense, sweet, of my
        innocence!°   45
    Love takes the meaning in love's conference.°
    I mean, that my heart unto yours is knit
    So that but one heart we can make of it;
    Two bosoms interchained with an oath —
    So then two bosoms and a single troth.   50
    Then by your side no bed-room me deny,
    For lying so, Hermia, I do not lie.°
HERMIA: Lysander riddles very prettily.
    Now much beshrew° my manners and my pride
    If Hermia meant to say Lysander lied.   55
    But, gentle friend, for love and courtesy
    Lie further off, in human° modesty;
    Such separation as may well be said
    Becomes a virtuous bachelor and a maid,
    So far be distant; and, good night, sweet friend.   60
    Thy love ne'er alter till thy sweet life end!
LYSANDER: Amen, amen, to that fair prayer, say I,
    And then end life when I end loyalty!
    Here is my bed. Sleep give thee all his rest!
HERMIA: With half that wish the wisher's eyes be
        press'd!°   65
        [*They sleep, separated by a short distance.*]

(*Enter Puck.*)

PUCK: Through the forest have I gone,
    But Athenian found I none
    On whose eyes I might approve°
    This flower's force in stirring love.
    Night and silence. — Who is here?   70
    Weeds of Athens he doth wear.
    This is he, my master said,
    Despised the Athenian maid;
    And here the maiden, sleeping sound,
    On the dank and dirty ground.   75
    Pretty soul! She durst not lie
    Near this lack-love, this kill-courtesy.
    Churl, upon thy eyes I throw
    All the power this charm doth owe.°
                        [*Applies the love-juice.*]
    When thou wak'st, let love forbid   80
    Sleep his seat on thy eyelid.

II, I. **Location:** The wood.   **1. roundel:** Dance in a ring.
3. cankers: Cankerworms.   **4. rere-mice:** Bats.   **7. quaint:**
Dainty.   **9. double:** Forked.   **11. Newts:** water lizards (considered poisonous, as were blindworms — small snakes with
tiny eyes — and spiders).   **13. Philomel:** The nightingale.
(Philomela, daughter of King Pandion, was transformed into a
nightingale, according to Ovid's *Metamorphoses,* after she had
been raped by her sister Procne's husband, Tereus.)
30. ounce: Lynx.   **31. Pard:** Leopard.   **36. troth:** Truth.

42. troth: Faith, troth-plight.   **45. take . . . innocence:** Interpret my intention as innocent.   **46. Love . . . conference:**
When lovers confer, love teaches each lover to interpret the
other's meaning lovingly.   **52. lie:** Tell a falsehood (with a riddling pun on *lie,* recline).   **54. beshrew:** Curse (but mildly
meant).   **57. human:** Courteous.   **65. With . . . press'd:** May
we share your wish, so that your eyes too are *press'd,* closed, in
sleep.   **68. approve:** Test.   **79. owe:** Own.

So awake when I am gone,
For I must now to Oberon.   (*Exit.*)

(*Enter Demetrius and Helena, running.*)

HELENA: Stay, though thou kill me, sweet Demetrius.
DEMETRIUS: I charge thee, hence, and do not haunt me
85   thus.
HELENA: O, wilt thou darkling° leave me? Do not so.
DEMETRIUS: Stay, on thy peril!° I alone will go.
                                                          [*Exit.*]
HELENA: O, I am out of breath in this fond° chase!
    The more my prayer, the lesser is my grace.°
90   Happy is Hermia, wheresoe'er she lies,°
    For she hath blessed and attractive eyes.
    How came her eyes so bright? Not with salt
        tears;
    If so, my eyes are oft'ner wash'd than hers.
    No, no, I am as ugly as a bear;
95   For beasts that meet me run away for fear.
    Therefore no marvel though Demetrius
    Do, as a monster, fly my presence thus.
    What wicked and dissembling glass of mine
    Made me compare with Hermia's sphery eyne?°
100   But who is here? Lysander, on the ground?
    Dead, or asleep? I see no blood, no wound.
    Lysander, if you live, good sir, awake.
LYSANDER [*awaking*]: And run through fire I will for
        thy sweet sake.
    Transparent° Helena! Nature shows art,
105   That through thy bosom makes me see thy heart.
    Where is Demetrius? O, how fit a word
    Is that vile name to perish on my sword!
HELENA: Do not say so, Lysander, say not so.
    What though he love your Hermia? Lord, what
        though?
110   Yet Hermia still loves you. Then be content.
LYSANDER: Content with Hermia? No! I do repent
    The tedious minutes I with her have spent.
    Not Hermia but Helena I love.
    Who will not change a raven for a dove?
115   The will of man is by his reason sway'd,
    And reason says you are the worthier maid.
    Things growing are not ripe until their season;
    So I, being young, till now ripe not° to reason.
    And touching° now the point° of human skill,°
120   Reason becomes the marshal to my will
    And leads me to your eyes, where I o'erlook°
    Love's stories written in love's richest book.
HELENA: Wherefore was I to this keen mockery born?
    When at your hands did I deserve this scorn?
125   Is 't not enough, is 't not enough, young man,
    That I did never, no, nor never can,

Deserve a sweet look from Demetrius' eye,
    But you must flout my insufficiency?
    Good troth,° you do me wrong, good sooth,° you do,
    In such disdainful manner me to woo.   130
    But fare you well. Perforce I must confess
    I thought you lord of° more true gentleness.
    O, that a lady, of° one man refus'd,
    Should of another therefore be abus'd!°   (*Exit.*)
LYSANDER: She sees not Hermia. Hermia, sleep thou
        there,   135
    And never mayst thou come Lysander near!
    For as a surfeit of the sweetest things
    The deepest loathing to the stomach brings,
    Or as the heresies that men do leave
    Are hated most of those they did deceive,   140
    So thou, my surfeit and my heresy,
    Of all be hated, but the most of me!
    And, all my powers, address your love and might
    To honor Helen and to be her knight!   (*Exit.*)
HERMIA [*awaking*]: Help me, Lysander, help me! Do
        thy best   145
    To pluck this crawling serpent from my breast!
    Ay me, for pity! What a dream was here!
    Lysander, look how I do quake with fear.
    Methought a serpent eat° my heart away,
    And you sat smiling at his cruel prey.°   150
    Lysander! What, remov'd? Lysander! Lord!
    What, out of hearing? Gone? No sound, no word?
    Alack, where are you? Speak, an if you hear,
    Speak, of all loves!° I swoon almost with fear.
    No? Then I well perceive you are not nigh.   155
    Either death, or you, I'll find immediately.
                    (*Exit. [Manet°* Titania lying asleep.]*)

{*ACT III • Scene 1*}°

(*Enter the Clowns [Quince, Snug, Bottom, Flute, Snout,
and Starveling].*)

BOTTOM: Are we all met?
QUINCE: Pat, pat; and here's a marvailes° convenient
    place for our rehearsal. This green plot shall be our
    stage, this hawthorn brake° our tiring-house,° and
    we will do it in action as we will do it before the   5
    Duke.
BOTTOM: Peter Quince?
QUINCE: What sayest thou, bully° Bottom?
BOTTOM: There are things in this comedy of Pyramus
    and Thisby that will never please. First, Pyramus   10
    must draw a sword to kill himself, which the ladies
    cannot abide. How answer you that?

---

129. Good troth, good sooth: Indeed, truly.   **132. lord of:** Possessor of.   **gentleness:** Courtesy.   **133. of:** By.   **134. abus'd:** Ill treated.   **149. eat:** Ate (pronounced "et").   **150. prey:** Act of preying.   **154. of all loves:** For all love's sake.   **156.** [S.D.] *Manet:* Latin for "she remains."   **III, I. Location:** Scene continues.   **2. marvailes:** Marvelous.   **4. brake:** Thicket.   **tiring-house:** Attiring area, hence backstage.   **8. bully:** Worthy, jolly, fine fellow.

86. darkling: In the dark.   **87. on thy peril:** On pain of danger to you if you don't obey me and stay.   **88. fond:** Doting.   **89. my grace:** The favor I obtain.   **90. lies:** Dwells.   **99. sphery eyne:** Eyes as bright as stars in their spheres.   **104. Transparent:** (1) Radiant; (2) able to be seen through.   **118. ripe not:** (Am) not ripened.   **119. touching:** Reaching.   **point:** Summit.   **skill:** Judgment.   **121. o'erlook:** Read.

SNOUT: By 'r lakin,° a parlous° fear.

STARVELING: I believe we must leave the killing out,
15   when all is done.°

BOTTOM: Not a whit. I have a device to make all well.
Write me° a prologue; and let the prologue seem to
say, we will do no harm with our swords and that
Pyramus is not kill'd indeed; and, for the more better
20   assurance, tell them that I Pyramus am not Pyramus,
but Bottom the weaver. This will put them out of
fear.

QUINCE: Well, we will have such a prologue, and it shall
be written in eight and six.°

25 BOTTOM: No, make it two more; let it be written in eight
and eight.

SNOUT: Will not the ladies be afeard of the lion?

STARVELING: I fear it, I promise you.

BOTTOM: Masters, you ought to consider with your-
30   selves, to bring in — God shield us! — a lion among
ladies,° is a most dreadful thing. For there is not a
more fearful° wild-fowl than your lion living; and we
ought to look to 't.

SNOUT: Therefore another prologue must tell he is not a
35   lion.

BOTTOM: Nay, you must name his name, and half his
face must be seen through the lion's neck, and he
himself must speak through, saying thus, or to the
same defect:° "Ladies"— or "Fair ladies — I would
40   wish you"— or "I would request you"— or "I
would entreat you — not to fear, not to tremble;
my life for yours.° If you think I come hither as a
lion, it were pity of my life.° No, I am no such thing,
I am a man as other men are." And there indeed let
45   him name his name, and tell them plainly he is Snug
the joiner.

QUINCE: Well, it shall be so. But there is two hard
things: that is, to bring the moonlight into a chamber; for, you know, Pyramus and Thisby meet by
50   moonlight.

SNOUT: Doth the moon shine that night we play our play?

BOTTOM: A calendar, a calendar! Look in the almanac.
Find out moonshine, find out moonshine.

                              [They consult an almanac.]

QUINCE: Yes, it doth shine that night.

55 BOTTOM: Why then may you leave a casement of the
great chamber window, where we play, open, and the
moon may shine in at the casement.

QUINCE: Ay; or else one must come in with a bush of
thorns° and a lantern, and say he comes to disfigure,°
or to present,° the person of Moonshine. Then there   60
is another thing: we must have a wall in the great
chamber; for Pyramus and Thisby, says the story, did
talk through the chink of a wall.

SNOUT: You can never bring in a wall. What say you,
Bottom?   65

BOTTOM: Some man or other must present Wall. And
let him have some plaster, or some loam, or some
rough-cast° about him, to signify wall; and let him
hold his fingers thus, and through that cranny shall
Pyramus and Thisby whisper.   70

QUINCE: If that may be, then all is well. Come, sit down,
every mother's son, and rehearse your parts. Pyramus, you begin. When you have spoken your speech,
enter into that brake, and so every one according to
his cue.   75

(*Enter Robin* [*Puck*].)

PUCK: What hempen° home-spuns have we swagg'ring
    here,
So near the cradle of the Fairy Queen?
What, a play toward?° I'll be an auditor;°
An actor too perhaps, if I see cause.

QUINCE: Speak, Pyramus. Thisby, stand forth.   80

BOTTOM: "Thisby, the flowers of odious savors
    sweet,"—

QUINCE: Odors, odors.

BOTTOM: —"Odors savors sweet;
So hath thy breath, my dearest Thisby dear.
But hark, a voice! Stay thou but here awhile,   85
And by and by I will to thee appear."   (*Exit.*)

PUCK: A stranger Pyramus than e'er played here.°
                                               [*Exit.*]

FLUTE: Must I speak now?

QUINCE: Ay, marry, must you; for you must understand
he goes but to see a noise that he heard, and is to   90
come again.

FLUTE: "Most radiant Pyramus, most lily-white of hue,
Of color like the red rose on triumphant brier,
Most brisky juvenal° and eke° most lovely Jew,°
As true as truest horse that yet would never tire.   95
I'll meet thee, Pyramus, at Ninny's tomb."

QUINCE: "Ninus'° tomb," man. Why, you must not speak
that yet. That you answer to Pyramus. You speak all

100   your part at once, cues and all. Pyramus enter. Your
      cue is past; it is, "never tire."
FLUTE: O —"As true as truest horse, that yet would
      never tire."

[Enter Puck, and Bottom as Pyramus with the ass head.]°

BOTTOM: "If I were fair,° Thisby, I were° only thine."
QUINCE: O monstrous! O strange! We are haunted.
      Pray, masters! Fly, masters! Help!

[Exeunt Quince, Snug, Flute, Snout, and Starveling.]

105 PUCK: I'll follow you, I'll lead you about a round,°
      Through bog, through bush, through brake,
         through brier.
      Sometime a horse I'll be, sometime a hound,
      A hog, a headless bear, sometime a fire,°
      And neigh, and bark, and grunt, and roar, and burn,
110   Like horse, hound, hog, bear, fire, at every turn.
                                (Exit.)

BOTTOM: Why do they run away? This is a knavery of
      them to make me afeard.

(Enter Snout.)

SNOUT: O Bottom, thou art chang'd! What do I see on
      thee?
115 BOTTOM: What do you see? You see an ass-head of your
      own, do you?   *[Exit Snout.]*

(Enter Quince.)

QUINCE: Bless thee, Bottom, bless thee! Thou art trans-
      lated.°   *(Exit.)*
BOTTOM: I see their knavery. This is to make an ass of
120   me, to fright me, if they could. But I will not stir from
      this place, do what they can. I will walk up and down
      here, and I will sing, that they shall hear I am not
      afraid.   *[Sings.]*
      The woosel cock° so black of hue,
125   With orange-tawny bill,
      The throstle° with his note so true,
       The wren with little quill° —
TITANIA *[awaking]*: What angel wakes me from my
      flow'ry bed?
BOTTOM *[sings]*: The finch, the sparrow, and the lark,
130   The plain-song° cuckoo grey,
      Whose note full many a man doth mark,
       And dares not answer nay° —
      For, indeed, who would set his wit to so foolish a
      bird? Who would give a bird the lie,° though he cry
135   "cuckoo" never so?°

101. [S.D.] *with the ass head*: This stage direction, taken from
the Folio, presumably refers to a standard stage property.
102. **fair**: Handsome. **were**: Would be. 105. **about a round**:
Roundabout. 108. **fire**: Will-o'-the-wisp. 117–18. **translated**:
Transformed. 124. **woosel cock**: Male ousel or ouzel, black-
bird. 126. **throstle**: Song thrush. 127. **quill**: Literally, a reed
pipe; hence, the bird's piping song. 130. **plain-song**: Singing
a melody without variations. 132. **dares . . . nay**: Cannot
deny that he is a cuckold. 134. **give . . . lie**: Call the bird a
liar. 135. **never so**: Ever so much.

TITANIA: I pray thee, gentle mortal, sing again.
      Mine ear is much enamored of thy note;
      So is mine eye enthrallèd to thy shape;
      And thy fair virtue's force° perforce doth move me
      On the first view to say, to swear, I love thee.   140
BOTTOM: Methinks, mistress, you should have little rea-
      son for that. And yet, to say the truth, reason and
      love keep little company together nowadays. The
      more the pity that some honest neighbors will not
      make them friends. Nay, I can gleek° upon occasion.   145
TITANIA: Thou art as wise as thou art beautiful.
BOTTOM: Not so, neither. But if I had wit enough to get
      out of this wood, I have enough to serve mine own
      turn.°
TITANIA: Out of this wood do not desire to go.   150
      Thou shalt remain here, whether thou wilt or no.
      I am a spirit of no common rate.°
      The summer still° doth tend upon my state;°
      And I do love thee. Therefore, go with me.
      I'll give thee fairies to attend on thee,   155
      And they shall fetch thee jewels from the deep,
      And sing while thou on pressèd flowers dost sleep.
      And I will purge thy mortal grossness so
      That thou shalt like an airy spirit go.
      Peaseblossom, Cobweb, Moth,° and Mustard-
      seed!   160

(Enter four Fairies [Peaseblossom, Cobweb, Moth, and Mustardseed]).

PEASEBLOSSOM: Ready.
COBWEB: And I.
MOTH: And I
MUSTARDSEED: And I.
ALL: Where shall we go?
TITANIA: Be kind and courteous to this gentleman.
      Hop in his walks and gambol in his eyes;
      Feed him with apricocks and dewberries,   165
      With purple grapes, green figs, and mulberries;
      The honey-bags steal from the humble-bees,
      And for night-tapers crop their waxen thighs
      And light them at the fiery glow-worm's eyes,
      To have my love to bed and to arise;   170
      And pluck the wings from painted butterflies
      To fan the moonbeams from his sleeping eyes.
      Nod to him, elves, and do him courtesies.
PEASEBLOSSOM: Hail, mortal!
COBWEB: Hail!   175
MOTH: Hail!
MUSTARDSEED: Hail!
BOTTOM: I cry your worship's mercy, heartily. I beseech
      your worship's name.

139. **thy . . . force**: The power of your beauty. 145. **gleek**:
Scoff, jest. 148–49. **serve . . . turn**: Answer my purpose.
152. **rate**: Rank, value. 153. **still**: Ever always. **doth . . .
state**: Waits upon me as part of my royal retinue. 160. **Moth**:
Mote, speck. (The two words *moth* and *mote* were pronounced
alike.)

180   COBWEB: Cobweb.
       BOTTOM: I shall desire you of more acquaintance, good
           Master Cobweb. If I cut my finger, I shall make bold
           with you.° Your name, honest gentleman?
       PEASEBLOSSOM: Peaseblossom.
185   BOTTOM: I pray you, commend me to Mistress Squash,°
           your mother, and to Master Peascod,° your father.
           Good Master Peaseblossom, I shall desire you of more
           acquaintance too. Your name, I beseech you, sir?
       MUSTARDSEED: Mustardseed.
190   BOTTOM: Good Master Mustardseed, I know your pa-
           tience° well. That same cowardly, giant-like ox-beef
           hath devour'd many a gentleman of your house. I
           promise you your kindred hath made my eyes water
           ere now. I desire you of more acquaintance, good
195   Master Mustardseed.
       TITANIA: Come wait upon him; lead him to my bower.
           The moon methinks looks with a wat'ry eye;
           And when she weeps,° weeps every little flower,
           Lamenting some enforced° chastity.
200   Tie up my lover's tongue, bring him silently.
                                                       (*Exeunt.*)

{*Scene II*}°

(*Enter* [*Oberon,*] *King of Fairies.*)

       OBERON: I wonder if Titania be awak'd;
           Then, what it was that next came in her eye,
           Which she must dote on in extremity.

([*Enter*] *Robin Goodfellow* [*Puck*].)

           Here comes my messenger. How now, mad spirit?
5   What night-rule° now about this haunted° grove?
       PUCK: My mistress with a monster is in love.
           Near to her close° and consecrated bower,
           While she was in her dull° and sleeping hour,
           A crew of patches,° rude mechanicals,°
10   That work for bread upon Athenian stalls,
           Were met together to rehearse a play
           Intended for great Theseus' nuptial day.
           The shallowest thick-skin of that barren sort,°
           Who Pyramus presented,° in their sport
15   Forsook his scene° and ent'red in a brake.
           When I did him at this advantage take,
           An ass's nole° I fixed on his head.

182–83. If . . . you: Cobwebs were used to stanch bleeding.
185. Squash: Unripe pea pod.   186. Peascod: Ripe pea pod.
190–91. your patience: What you have endured.   198. she
weeps: I.e., she causes dew.   199. enforced: Forced, violated; or, possibly, constrained (since Titania at this moment is
hardly concerned about chastity).   III, II. Location: The
wood.   5. night-rule: Diversion for the night.   haunted:
Much frequented.   7. close: Secret, private.   8. dull: Drowsy.
9. patches: Clowns, fools.   rude mechanicals: Ignorant artisans.   13. barren sort: Stupid company or crew.   14. presented: Acted.   15. scene: Playing area.   17. nole: Noddle,
head.

           Anon his Thisby must be answered,
           And forth my mimic° comes. When they him spy,
           As wild geese that the creeping fowler eye,   20
           Or russet-pated choughs,° many in sort,°
           Rising and cawing at the gun's report,
           Sever° themselves and madly sweep the sky,
           So, at his sight, away his fellows fly;
           And, at our stamp, here o'er and o'er one falls;   25
           He murder cries and help from Athens calls.
           Their sense thus weak, lost with their fears thus
               strong,
           Made senseless things begin to do them wrong,
           For briers and thorns at their apparel snatch;
           Some, sleeves — some, hats; from yielders all things
               catch.   30
           I led them on in this distracted fear
           And left sweet Pyramus translated there,
           When in that moment, so it came to pass,
           Titania wak'd and straightway lov'd an ass.
       OBERON: This falls out better than I could devise.   35
           But hast thou yet latch'd° the Athenian's eyes
           With the love-juice, as I did bid thee do?
       PUCK: I took him sleeping — that is finish'd too —
           And the Athenian woman by his side,
           That, when he wak'd, of force° she must be ey'd.   40

(*Enter Demetrius and Hermia.*)

       OBERON: Stand close. This is the same Athenian.
       PUCK: This is the woman, but not this the man.
                                          [*They stand aside.*]
       DEMETRIUS: O, why rebuke you him that loves you so?
           Lay breath so bitter on your bitter foe.
       HERMIA: Now I but chide; but I should use thee worse,   45
           For thou, I fear, hast given me cause to curse.
           If thou hast slain Lysander in his sleep,
           Being o'er shoes in blood, plunge in the deep,
           And kill me too.
           The sun was not so true unto the day   50
           As he to me. Would he have stolen away
           From sleeping Hermia? I'll believe as soon
           This whole° earth may be bor'd and that the moon
           May through the center creep and so displease
           Her brother's° noontide with th' Antipodes.°   55
           It cannot be but thou has murd'red him;
           So should a murderer look, so dead,° so grim.
       DEMETRIUS: So should the murdered look, and so
               should I,
           Pierc'd through the heart with your stern cruelty.
           Yet you, the murderer, look as bright, as clear,   60
           As yonder Venus in her glimmering sphere.
       HERMIA: What's this to my Lysander? Where is he?
           Ah, good Demetrius, wilt thou give him me?

19. mimic: Burlesque actor.   21. russet-pated choughs: Gray-
headed jackdaws.   in sort: In a flock.   23. Sever: Scatter.
36. latch'd: Moistened, anointed.   40. of force: Perforce.
53. whole: Solid.   55. Her brother's: I.e., the sun's.   th' Antip-
odes: The people on the opposite side of the earth.   57. dead:
Deadly, or deathly pale.

DEMETRIUS: I had rather give his carcass to my hounds.
HERMIA: Out dog! Out cur! Thou driv'st me past the
65   bounds
    Of maiden's patience. Hast thou slain him, then?
    Henceforth be never numb'red among men!
    O, once tell true, tell true, even for my sake!
    Durst thou have look'd upon him being awake,
70 And hast thou kill'd him sleeping? O brave touch!°
    Could not a worm,° an adder, do so much?
    An adder did it, for with doubler tongue
    Than thine, thou serpent, never adder stung.
DEMETRIUS: You spend your passion° on a mispris'd
    mood.°
75 I am not guilty of Lysander's blood,
    Nor is he dead, for aught that I can tell.
HERMIA: I pray thee, tell me then that he is well.
DEMETRIUS: An if I could, what should I get
    therefore?
HERMIA: A privilege never to see me more.
80 And from thy hated presence part I so.
    See me no more, whether he be dead or no.
                                                    (*Exit.*)
DEMETRIUS: There is no following her in this fierce
    vein.
    Here therefore for a while I will remain.
    So sorrow's heaviness doth heavier° grow
85 For debt that bankrupt° sleep doth sorrow owe;
    Which now in some slight measure it will pay,
    If for his tender here I make some stay.°
                                        (*Lie down [and sleep].*)
OBERON: What hast thou done? Thou hast mistaken
    quite
    And laid the love-juice on some true-love's sight.
90 Of thy misprision° must perforce ensue
    Some true love turn'd and not a false turn'd true.
PUCK: Then fate o'er-rules, that, one man holding
    troth,°
    A million fail, confounding oath on oath.°
OBERON: About the wood go swifter than the wind,
95 And Helena of Athens look thou find.
    All fancy-sick° she is and pale of cheer°
    With sighs of love, that cost the fresh blood° dear.
    By some illusion see thou bring her here.
    I'll charm his eyes against she do appear.°

PUCK: I go, I go; look how I go   100
    Swifter than arrow from the Tartar's bow.°
                                                    [*Exit.*]
OBERON: Flower of this purple dye,
    Hit with Cupid's archery.
    Sink in angle of his eye.
            [*Applies love-juice to Demetrius' eyes.*]
    When his love he doth espy,   105
    Let her shine as gloriously
    As the Venus of the sky.
    When thou wak'st, if she be by,
    Beg of her for remedy.

(*Enter Puck.*)

PUCK: Captain of our fairy band,   110
    Helena is here at hand,
    And the youth, mistook by me,
    Pleading for a lover's fee.°
    Shall we their fond pageant° see?
    Lord, what fools these mortals be!   115
OBERON: Stand aside. The noise they make
    Will cause Demetrius to awake.
PUCK: Then will two at once woo one;
    That must needs be sport alone;°
    And those things do best please me   120
    That befall prepost'rously.°
                                        [*They stand aside.*]

(*Enter Lysander and Helena.*)

LYSANDER: Why should you think that I should woo in
    scorn?
    Scorn and derision never come in tears.
    Look when° I vow, I weep; and vows so born,
    In their nativity all truth appears.°   125
    How can these things in me seem scorn to you,
    Bearing the badge° of faith, to prove them true?
HELENA: You do advance° your cunning more and
    more.
    When truth kills truth,° O devilish-holy fray!
    These vows are Hermia's. Will you give her o'er?   130
    Weigh oath with oath, and you will nothing weigh.
    Your vows to her and me, put in two scales
    Will even weigh, and both as light as tales.°
LYSANDER: I had no judgment when to her I swore.
HELENA: Nor none, in my mind, now you give her o'er.   135
LYSANDER: Demetrius loves her, and he loves not you.
DEMETRIUS [*awaking*]: O Helen, goddess, nymph,
    perfect, divine!
    To what, my love, shall I compare thine eyne?

---

70. brave touch: Noble exploit (said ironically).   **71. worm:**
Serpent.   **74. passion:** Violent feelings.   **mispris'd mood:**
Anger based on misconception.   **84. heavier:** (1) Harder to
bear, (2) drowsier.   **85. bankrupt:** Demetrius is saying that
his sleepiness adds to the weariness caused by sorrow.
86–87. Which . . . stay: To a small extent I will be able to "pay
back" and hence find some relief from sorrow, if I pause here
a while (*make some stay*) while sleep "tenders" or offers itself
by way of paying the debt owed to sorrow.   **90. misprision:**
Mistake.   **92. troth:** Faith.   **93. confounding . . . oath:** Inval-
idating one oath with another.   **96. fancy-sick:** Lovesick.
cheer: Face.   **97. sighs . . . blood:** An allusion to the physio-
logical theory that each sigh costs the heart a drop of blood.
99. against . . . appear: In anticipation of her coming.

101. Tartar's bow: Tartars were famed for their skill with the
bow.   **113. fee:** Privilege, reward.   **114. fond pageant:** Foolish exhibition.   **119. alone:** Unequaled.   **121. prepost'rously:**
Out of the natural order.   **124. Look when:** Whenever.
124–25. vows . . . appears: Vows made by one who is weeping
give evidence thereby of their sincerity.   **127. badge:** Identifying device such as that worn on servants' livery.   **128. advance:** Carry forward, display.   **129. truth kills truth:** One of
Lysander's vows must invalidate the other.   **133. tales:** Lies.

Crystal is muddy. O, how ripe in show°
140 Thy lips, those kissing cherries, tempting grow!
That pure congealed white, high Taurus'° snow,
Fann'd with the eastern wind, turns to a crow°
When thou hold'st up thy hand. O, let me kiss
This princess of pure white, this seal° of bliss!
145 HELENA: O spite! O hell! I see you all are bent
To set against me for your merriment.
If you were civil and knew courtesy,
You would not do me thus much injury.
Can you not hate me, as I know you do,
150 But you must join in souls to mock me too?
If you were men, as men you are in show,
You would not use a gentle lady so —
To vow, and swear, and superpraise° my parts,°
When I am sure you hate me with your hearts.
155 You both are rivals, and love Hermia;
And now both rivals, to mock Helena.
A trim° exploit, a manly enterprise,
To conjure tears up in a poor maid's eyes
With your derision! None of noble sort
160 Would so offend a virgin and extort°
A poor soul's patience, all to make you sport.
LYSANDER: You are unkind, Demetrius. Be not so;
For you love Hermia; this you know I know.
And here, with all good will, with all my heart,
165 In Hermia's love I yield you up my part;
And yours of Helena to me bequeath,
Whom I do love and will do till my death.
HELENA: Never did mockers waste more idle breath.
DEMETRIUS: Lysander, keep thy Hermia; I will none.°
170 If e'er I lov'd her, all that love is gone.
My heart to her but as guest-wise sojourn'd,
And now to Helen is it home return'd.
There to remain.
LYSANDER: Helen, it is not so.
DEMETRIUS: Disparage not the faith thou dost not know,
175 Lest, to thy peril, thou aby° it dear.
Look where thy love comes; yonder is thy dear.

(*Enter Hermia.*)

HERMIA: Dark night, that from the eye his° function
takes,
The ear more quick of apprehension makes;
Wherein it doth impair the seeing sense,
180 It pays the hearing double recompense.
Thou art not by mine eye, Lysander, found;
Mine ear, I thank it, brought me to thy sound.
But why unkindly didst thou leave me so?
LYSANDER: Why should he stay, whom love doth press
to go?

HERMIA: What love could press Lysander from my
side?   185
LYSANDER: Lysander's love, that would not let him
bide,
Fair Helena, who more engilds the night
Than all yon fiery oes° and eyes of light.
Why seek'st thou me? Could not this make thee
know,
The hate I bear thee made me leave thee so?   190
HERMIA: You speak not as you think. It cannot be.
HELENA: Lo, she is one of this confederacy!
Now I perceive they have conjoin'd all three
To fashion this false sport, in spite of me.°
Injurious Hermia, most ungrateful maid!   195
Have you conspir'd, have you with these contriv'd°
To bait° me with this foul derision?
Is all the counsel° that we two have shar'd,
The sisters' vows, the hours that we have spent,
When we have chid the hasty-footed time   200
For parting us — O, is all forgot?
All school-days friendship, childhood innocence?
We, Hermia, like two artificial° gods,
Have with our needles created both one flower,
Both on one sampler, sitting on one cushion,   205
Both warbling of one song, both in one key,
As if our hands, our sides, voices, and minds
Had been incorporate. So we grew together,
Like to a double cherry, seeming parted,
But yet an union in partition;   210
Two lovely° berries molded on one stem;
So, with two seeming bodies, but one heart;
Two of the first, like coats in heraldry,
Due but to one and crowned with one crest.°
And will you rent° our ancient love asunder,   215
To join with men in scorning your poor friend?
It is not friendly, 'tis not maidenly.
Our sex, as well as I, may chide you for it,
Though I alone do feel the injury.
HERMIA: I am amazed at your passionate words.   220
I scorn you not. It seems that you scorn me.
HELENA: Have you not set Lysander, as in scorn,
To follow me and praise my eyes and face?
And made your other love, Demetrius,
Who even but now did spurn me with his foot,   225
To call me goddess, nymph, divine and rare,
Precious, celestial? Wherefore speaks he this
To her he hates? And wherefore doth Lysander
Deny your love, so rich within his soul,
And tender° me, forsooth, affection,   230
But by your setting on, by your consent?

---

139. **show:** Appearance. 141. **Taurus:** A lofty mountain range in Asia Minor. 142. **turns to a crow:** Seems black by contrast. 144. **seal:** Pledge. 153. **superpraise:** Overpraise. **parts:** Qualities. 157. **trim:** Pretty, fine (said ironically). 160. **extort:** Twist, torture. 169. **will none:** Wish none of her. 175. **aby:** Pay for. 177. **his:** Its.

188. **oes:** Circles, orbs, stars. 194. **in spite of me:** To vex me. 196. **contriv'd:** Plotted. 197. **bait:** Torment, as one sets on dogs to bait a bear. 198. **counsel:** Confidential talk. 203. **artificial:** Skilled in art or creation. 211. **lovely:** Loving. 213–14. **Two . . . crest:** We have two separate bodies, just as a coat of arms in heraldry can be represented twice on a shield but surmounted by a single crest. 215. **rent:** Rend. 230. **tender:** Offer.

What though I be not so in grace° as you,
So hung upon with love, so fortunate,
But miserable most, to love unlov'd?
235 This you should pity rather than despise.
HERMIA: I understand not what you mean by this.
HELENA: Ay, do! Persever, counterfeit sad° looks,
    Make mouths° upon° me when I turn my back,
    Wink each at other, hold the sweet jest up.
240 This sport, well carried,° shall be chronicled.
    If you have any pity, grace, or manners,
    You would not make me such an argument.°
    But fare ye well. 'Tis partly my own fault,
    Which death, or absence, soon shall remedy.
245 LYSANDER: Stay, gentle Helena; hear my excuse,
    My love, my life, my soul, fair Helena!
HELENA: O excellent!
HERMIA: Sweet, do not scorn her so.
DEMETRIUS: If she cannot entreat,° I can compel.
LYSANDER: Thou canst compel no more than she
        entreat.
    Thy threats have no more strength than her weak
250   prayers.
    Helen, I love thee, by my life, I do!
    I swear by that which I will lose for thee,
    To prove him false that says I love thee not.
DEMETRIUS: I say I love thee more than he can do.
255 LYSANDER: If thou say so, withdraw, and prove it too.
DEMETRIUS: Quick, come!
HERMIA: Lysander, whereto tends all this?
LYSANDER: Away, you Ethiope!°
            [*He tries to break away from Hermia.*]
DEMETRIUS: No, no; he'll
    Seem to break loose; take on as you would follow,
    But yet come not. You are a tame man, go!
LYSANDER: Hang off,° thou cat, thou burr! Vile thing,
260   let loose,
    Or I will shake thee from me like a serpent!
HERMIA: Why are you grown so rude? What change is
        this,
    Sweet love?
LYSANDER: Thy love? Out, tawny Tartar, out!
    Out, loathed med'cine!° O hated potion, hence!
HERMIA: Do you not jest?
265 HELENA: Yes, sooth,° and so do you.
LYSANDER: Demetrius, I will keep my word with thee.
DEMETRIUS: I would I had your bond, for I perceive
    A weak bond° holds you. I'll not trust your word.
LYSANDER: What, should I hurt her, strike her, kill her
        dead?
270 Although I hate her, I'll not harm her so.

HERMIA: What, can you do me greater harm than hate?
    Hate me? Wherefore? O me, what news,° my love?
    Am not I Hermia? Are not you Lysander?
    I am as fair now as I was erewhile.°
    Since night you lov'd me; yet since night you left me.   275
    Why, then you left me — O, the gods forbid! —
    In earnest, shall I say?
LYSANDER: Ay, by my life!
    And never did desire to see thee more.
    Therefore be out of hope, of question, of doubt;
    Be certain, nothing truer. 'Tis no jest   280
    That I do hate thee and love Helena.
HERMIA: O me! You juggler! You cankerblossom!°
    You thief of love! What, have you come by night
    And stol'n my love's heart from him?
HELENA: Fine, i' faith!
    Have you no modesty, no maiden shame,   285
    No touch of bashfulness? What, will you tear
    Impatient answers from my gentle tongue?
    Fie, fie! You counterfeit, you puppet,° you!
HERMIA: Puppet? Why so? Ay, that way goes the game.
    Now I perceive that she hath made compare   290
    Between our statures; she hath urg'd her height,
    And with her personage, her tall personage,
    Her height, forsooth, she hath prevail'd with him.
    And are you grown so high in his esteem,
    Because I am so dwarfish and so low?   295
    How low am I, thou painted maypole? Speak!
    How low am I? I am not yet so low
    But that my nails can reach unto thine eyes.
            [*She flails at Helena but is restrained.*]
HELENA: I pray you, though you mock me, gentlemen,
    Let her not hurt me. I was never curst;°   300
    I have no gift at all in shrewishness;
    I am a right° maid for my cowardice.
    Let her not strike me. You perhaps may think,
    Because she is something° lower than myself,
    That I can match her.
HERMIA: Lower! Hark, again!   305
HELENA: Good Hermia, do not be so bitter with me.
    I evermore did love you, Hermia,
    Did ever keep your counsels, never wrong'd you;
    Save that, in love unto Demetrius,
    I told him of your stealth° unto this wood.   310
    He followed you; for love I followed him.
    But he hath chid me hence and threat'ned me
    To strike me, spurn me, nay, to kill me too.
    And now, so° you will let me quiet go,
    To Athens will I bear my folly back   315
    And follow you no further. Let me go.
    You see how simple and how fond° I am.
HERMIA: Why, get you gone. Who is 't that hinders you?

232. grace: Favor. 237. sad: Grave, serious. 238. mouths:
Maws, faces, grimaces. upon: At. 240. carried: Managed.
242. argument: Subject for a jest. 248. entreat: Succeed by
entreaty. 257. Ethiope: Referring to Hermia's relatively dark
hair and complexion; see also *tawny Tartar* six lines later.
260. Hang off: Let go. 264. med'cine: Poison. 265. sooth:
Truly. 268. weak bond: Hermia's arm (with a pun on *bond*,
oath, in the previous line).

272. what news: What is the matter. 274. erewhile: Just now.
282. cankerblossom: Worm that destroys the flower bud (?).
288. puppet: (1) Counterfeit, (2) dwarfish woman (in reference to Hermia's smaller stature). 300. curst: Shrewish.
302. right: True. 304. something: Somewhat. 310. stealth:
Stealing away. 314. so: If only. 317. fond: Foolish.

HELENA: A foolish heart, that I leave here behind.

HERMIA: What, with Lysander?

320 HELENA: With Demetrius.

LYSANDER: Be not afraid; she shall not harm thee,
    Helena.

DEMETRIUS: No, sir, she shall not, though you take her
    part.

HELENA: O, when she is angry, she is keen and
    shrewd!°

    She was a vixen when she went to school;

325 And though she be but little, she is fierce.

HERMIA: "Little" again! Nothing but "low" and
    "little"!

    Why will you suffer her to flout me thus?

    Let me come to her.

LYSANDER: Get you gone, you dwarf!
    You minimus,° of hind'ring knot-grass° made!

---

323. shrewd: Shrewish.   329. minimus: Diminutive creature.
knot-grass: A weed, an infusion of which was thought to stunt
the growth.

You bead, you acorn!

DEMETRIUS: You are too officious   330
    In her behalf that scorns your services.
    Let her alone. Speak not of Helena;
    Take not her part. For, if thou dost intend°
    Never so little show of love to her,
    Thou shalt aby° it.

LYSANDER: Now she holds me not;   335
    Now follow, if thou dar'st, to try whose right,
    Of thine or mine, is most in Helena.   [Exit.]

DEMETRIUS: Follow? Nay, I'll go with thee, cheek by
    jowl.°

                              [Exit, following Lysander.]

HERMIA: You, mistress, all this coil° is 'long of° you.
    Nay, go not back.°

---

333. intend: Give sign of.   335. aby: Pay for.   338. cheek by
jowl: Side by side.   339. coil: Turmoil, dissension.   'long of:
On account of.   340. go not back: Don't retreat. (Hermia is
again proposing a fight.)

RIGHT: Elizabeth McGovern as Helena in the 1987 New York Shakespeare festival production of *A Midsummer Night's Dream*, directed by A. J. Antoon. LEFT: F. Murray Abraham (left) as Bottom, playing Pyramus.

340 HELENA: I will not trust you, I,
    Nor longer stay in your curst company.
    Your hands than mine are quicker for a fray;
    My legs are longer, though, to run away.   [*Exit.*]
HERMIA: I am amaz'd, and know not what to say.
                  (*Exit.*)
345 OBERON: This is thy negligence. Still thou mistak'st,
    Or else committ'st thy knaveries willfully.
PUCK: Believe me, king of shadows, I mistook.
    Did not you tell me I should know the man
    By the Athenian garments he had on?
350 And so far blameless proves my enterprise
    That I have 'nointed an Athenian's eyes;
    And so far am I glad it so did sort°
    As this their jangling I esteem a sport.
OBERON: Thou see'st these lovers seek a place to fight.
355 Hie therefore, Robin, overcast the night;
    The starry welkin° cover thou anon
    With drooping fog as black as Acheron,°
    And lead these testy rivals so astray
    As° one come not within another's way.
360 Like to Lysander sometime frame thy tongue,
    Then stir Demetrius up with bitter wrong;°

352. **sort:** Turn out.   356. **welkin:** Sky.   357. **Acheron:** River of Hades (here representing Hades itself).   359. **As:** That. 361. **wrong:** Insults.

And sometime rail thou like Demetrius.
And from each other look thou lead them thus,
Till o'er their brows death-counterfeiting sleep
With leaden legs and batty° wings doth creep.   365
Then crush this herb° into Lysander's eye,
                  [*Gives herb.*]
Whose liquor hath this virtuous° property,
To take from thence all error with his° might
And make his eyeballs roll with wonted° sight.
When they next wake, all this derision°   370
Shall seem a dream and fruitless vision,
And back to Athens shall the lovers wend
With league whose date° till death shall never end.
Whiles I in this affair do thee employ,
I'll to my queen and beg her Indian boy;   375
And then I will her charmed eye release
From monster's view, and all things shall be peace.
PUCK: My fairy lord, this must be done with haste,
    For night's swift dragons° cut the clouds full fast,
    And yonder shines Aurora's harbinger,°   380

365. **batty:** Batlike.   366. **this herb:** The antidote (mentioned in II, I, 184) to love-in-idleness.   367. **virtuous:** Efficacious. 368. **his:** Its.   369. **wonted:** Accustomed.   370. **derision:** Laughable business.   373. **date:** Term of existence. 379. **dragons:** Supposed to be yoked to the car of the goddess of night.   380. **Aurora's harbinger:** The morning star, precursor of dawn.

At whose approach, ghosts, wand'ring here and
    there,
Troop home to churchyards. Damnèd spirits all,
That in crossways and floods have burial,°
Already to their wormy beds are gone.
385   For fear lest day should look their shames upon,
They willfully themselves exile from light
And must for aye° consort with black-brow'd night.
OBERON: But we are spirits of another sort.
    I with the Morning's love° have oft made sport,
390   And, like a forester,° the groves may tread
Even till the eastern gate, all fiery-red,
Opening on Neptune with fair blessèd beams,
Turns into yellow gold his salt green streams.
But, notwithstanding, haste; make no delay.
395   We may effect this business yet ere day.   [Exit.]
PUCK: Up and down, up and down,
    I will lead them up and down.
    I am fear'd in field and town.
    Goblin, lead them up and down.
400   Here comes one.

(Enter Lysander.)

LYSANDER: Where art thou, proud Demetrius? Speak
    thou now.
PUCK [mimicking Demetrius]: Here, villain, drawn°
    and ready. Where art thou?
LYSANDER: I will be with thee straight.°
PUCK: Follow me, then,
    To plainer° ground.
        [Lysander wanders about, following the voice.]°

(Enter Demetrius.)

DEMETRIUS: Lysander! Speak again!
405   Thou runaway, thou coward, art thou fled?
Speak! In some bush? Where dost thou hide thy
    head?
PUCK [mimicking Lysander]: Thou coward, art thou
    bragging to the stars,
Telling the bushes that thou look'st for wars,
And wilt not come? Come, recreant;° come, thou
    child,
410   I'll whip thee with a rod. He is defil'd
That draws a sword on thee.
DEMETRIUS: Yea, art thou there?
PUCK: Follow my voice. We'll try° no manhood here.
                              (Exeunt.)

[Lysander returns.]

LYSANDER: He goes before me and still dares me on.
    When I come where he calls, then he is gone.
The villain is much lighter-heel'd than I.   415
I followed fast, but faster he did fly,
That fallen am I in dark uneven way,
And here will rest me. [Lies down.] Come, thou
    gentle day!
For if but once thou show me thy gray light,
I'll find Demetrius and revenge this spite.   [Sleeps.]   420

([Enter] Robin [Puck] and Demetrius.)

PUCK: Ho, ho, ho! Coward, why com'st thou not?
DEMETRIUS: Abide me, if thou dar'st; for well I wot°
    Thou runn'st before me, shifting every place,
And dar'st not stand nor look me in the face.
Where art thou now?
PUCK: Come hither. I am here.   425
DEMETRIUS: Nay, then, thou mock'st me. Thou shalt
    buy° this dear,°
If ever I thy face by daylight see.
Now, go thy way. Faintness constraineth me
To measure out my length on this cold bed.
By day's approach look to be visited.   430
                    [Lies down and sleeps.]

(Enter Helena.)

HELENA: O weary night, O long and tedious night,
    Abate° thy hours! Shine, comforts, from the east,
That I may back to Athens by daylight,
From these that my poor company detest;
And sleep, that sometimes shuts up sorrow's eye,   435
Steal me awhile from mine own company.
                [Lies down and] sleep[s].
PUCK: Yet but three? Come one more;
    Two of both kinds makes up four.
Here she comes, curst and sad.
Cupid is a knavish lad,   440
Thus to make poor females mad.

[Enter Hermia.]

HERMIA: Never so weary, never so in woe,
    Bedabbled with the dew and torn with briers,
I can no further crawl, no further go;
My legs can keep no pace with my desires.   445
Here will I rest me till the break of day.
Heavens shield Lysander, if they mean a fray!
               [Lies down and sleeps.]
PUCK: On the ground
    Sleep sound.
    I'll apply   450
    To your eye,
Gentle lover, remedy.
        [Squeezing the juice on Lysander's eyes.]
    When thou wak'st,
    Thou tak'st

383. crossways . . . burial: Those who had committed suicide
were buried at crossways, with a stake driven through them;
those drowned, i.e., buried in floods or great waters, were condemned to wander disconsolate for want of burial rites.
387. for aye: Forever.   389. Morning's love: Cephalus, a beautiful youth beloved by Aurora; or perhaps the goddess of the
dawn herself.   390. forester: Keeper of a royal forest.
402. drawn: With drawn sword.   403. straight: Immediately.
404. plainer: Smoother.   404. [S.D.] Lysander wanders about:
It is not clearly necessary that Lysander exit at this point; neither exit nor reentrance is indicated in the early texts.
409. recreant: Cowardly wretch.   412. try: Test.

422. wot: Know.   426. buy: Pay for.   dear: Dearly.
432. Abate: Lessen, shorten.

455 True delight
In the sight
Of thy former lady's eye;
And the country proverb known,
That every man should take his own,
460 In your waking shall be shown:
Jack shall have Jill;
Nought shall go ill;
The man shall have his mare again, and all shall be
well.   [*Exit. Manent the four lovers.*]

{*ACT IV • Scene I*}°

(*Enter* [*Titania,*] *Queen of Fairies, and* [*Bottom the*]
Clown, and Fairies; and [*Oberon,*] *the King, behind
them.*)

TITANIA: Come, sit thee down upon this flow'ry bed,
While I thy amiable° cheeks do coy,°
And stick musk-roses in thy sleek smooth head,
And kiss thy fair large ears, my gentle joy.
         [*They recline.*]
5 BOTTOM: Where's Peaseblossom?
PEASEBLOSSOM: Ready.
BOTTOM: Scratch my head, Peaseblossom. Where's
Mounsieur Cobweb?
COBWEB: Ready.
10 BOTTOM: Mounsieur Cobweb, good mounsieur, get you
your weapons in your hand, and kill me a red-hipp'd
humble-bee on the top of a thistle; and, good mounsieur, bring me the honey-bag. Do not fret yourself
too much in the action, mounsieur; and, good moun-
15 sieur, have a care the honey-bag break not; I would
be loath to have you overflown with a honey-bag,
signior. Where's Mounsieur Mustardseed?
MUSTARDSEED: Ready.
BOTTOM: Give me your neaf,° Mounsieur Mustardseed.
20 Pray you, leave your curtsy,° good mounsieur.
MUSTARDSEED: What's your will?
BOTTOM: Nothing, good mounsieur, but to help Cav-
alery° Cobweb° to scratch. I must to the barber's,
mounsieur; for methinks I am marvailes hairy about
25 the face; and I am such a tender ass, if my hair do but
tickle me, I must scratch.
TITANIA: What, wilt thou hear some music, my sweet
love?
BOTTOM: I have a reasonable good ear in music. Let's
30 have the tongs and the bones.°

[*Music: tongs, rural music.*]°
TITANIA: Or say, sweet love, what thou desirest to eat.
BOTTOM: Truly, a peck of provender. I could munch your
good dry oats. Methinks I have a great desire to a
bottle° of hay. Good hay, sweet hay, hath no fellow.°
TITANIA: I have a venturous fairy that shall seek   35
The squirrel's hoard, and fetch thee new nuts.
BOTTOM: I had rather have a handful or two of dried
peas. But, I pray you, let none of your people stir me.
I have an exposition° of sleep come upon me.
TITANIA: Sleep thou, and I will wind thee in my arms.   40
Fairies, be gone, and be all ways° away.
         [*Exeunt fairies.*]
So doth the woodbine the sweet honeysuckle
Gently entwist; the female ivy so
Enrings the barky fingers of the elm.
Oh, how I love thee! How I dote on thee!   45
         [*They sleep.*]

(*Enter Robin Goodfellow* [*Puck*].)

OBERON [*advancing*]: Welcome, good Robin. See'st
thou this sweet sight?
Her dotage now I do begin to pity.
For, meeting her of late behind the wood,
Seeking sweet favors° for this hateful fool,
I did upbraid her and fall out with her.   50
For she his hairy temples then had rounded
With coronet of fresh and fragrant flowers;
And that same dew, which sometime° on the buds
Was wont to swell like round and orient pearls,°
Stood now within the pretty flouriets'° eyes   55
Like tears that did their own disgrace bewail.
When I had at my pleasure taunted her,
And she in mild terms begg'd my patience,
I then did ask of her her changeling child;
Which straight she gave me, and her fairy sent   60
To bear him to my bower in fairy land.
And, now I have the boy, I will undo
This hateful imperfection of her eyes.
And, gentle Puck, take this transformed scalp
From off the head of this Athenian swain,   65
That, he awaking when the other° do,
May all to Athens back again repair,
And think no more of this night's accidents
But as the fierce vexation of a dream.
But first I will release the Fairy Queen.   70
[*Squeezes juice in her eyes.*]
Be as thou wast wont to be;
See as thou wast wont to see.
Dian's bud° o'er Cupid's flower

IV, I. Location: Scene continues. The four lovers are still asleep
onstage. **2. amiable:** Lovely. **coy:** Caress. **19. neaf:** Fist.
20. leave your curtsy: Put on your hat. **22–23. Cavalery:** Cavalier. Form of address for a gentleman. **23. Cobweb:** Seemingly an error, since Cobweb has been sent to bring honey while
Peaseblossom has been asked to scratch. **30. tongs . . . bones:**
Instruments for rustic music. (The tongs were played like a triangle, whereas the bones were held between the fingers and
used as clappers.) [S.D.] *Music . . . music:* This stage direction is added from the Folio.

34. bottle: Bundle. **fellow:** Equal. **39. exposition:** Bottom's word for *disposition.* **41. all ways:** In all directions.
49. favors: I.e., gifts of flowers. **53. sometime:** Formerly.
54. orient pearls: The most beautiful of all pearls, those coming
from the Orient. **55. flouriets':** Flowerets'. **66. other:** Others. **73. Dian's bud:** Perhaps the flower of the *agnus castus* or
chaste-tree, supposed to preserve chastity; or perhaps referring
simply to Oberon's herb by which he can undo the effects of
"Cupid's flower," the love-in-idleness of II, I, 165–68.

Hath such force and blessed power.

75 Now, my Titania, wake you, my sweet queen.
TITANIA [*waking*]: My Oberon! What visions have I
    seen!
    Methought I was enamor'd of an ass.
OBERON: There lies your love.
TITANIA: How came these things to pass?
    O, how mine eyes do loathe his visage now!
80 OBERON: Silence awhile. Robin, take off this head.
    Titania, music call, and strike more dead
    Than common sleep of all these five° the sense.
TITANIA: Music, ho! Music, such as charmeth sleep!
                                               [*Music.*]
    PUCK [*removing the ass's head*]: Now, when thou
        wak'st, with thine own fool's eyes peep.
    OBERON: Sound, music! Come, my queen, take hands
85   with me,
    And rock the ground whereon these sleepers be.
                                               [*Dance.*]
    Now thou and I are new in amity,
    And will tomorrow midnight solemnly°
    Dance in Duke Theseus' house triumphantly
90 And bless it to all fair prosperity.
    There shall the pairs of faithful lovers be
    Wedded, with Theseus, all in jollity.
PUCK: Fairy King, attend, and mark:
    I do hear the morning lark.
95 OBERON: Then, my queen, in silence sad,°
    Trip we after night's shade.
    We the globe can compass soon,
    Swifter than the wand'ring moon.
TITANIA: Come, my lord, and in our flight
100 Tell me how it came this night
    That I sleeping here was found
    With these mortals on the ground.   (*Exeunt.*)
                                         (*Wind horn [within].*)

(*Enter Theseus and all his train; [Hippolyta, Egeus].*)

THESEUS: Go, one of you, find out the forester,
    For now our observation° is perform'd;
105 And since we have the vaward° of the day,
    My love shall hear the music of my hounds.
    Uncouple in the western valley; let them go.
    Dispatch, I say, and find the forester.
                                 [*Exit an Attendant.*]
    We will, fair queen, up to the mountain's top
110 And mark the musical confusion
    Of hounds and echo in conjunction.
HIPPOLYTA: I was with Hercules and Cadmus° once,
    When in a wood of Crete they bay'd° the bear
    With hounds of Sparta.° Never did I hear

Such gallant chiding; for, besides the groves,   115
The skies, the fountains, every region near
Seem'd all one mutual cry. I never heard
So musical a discord, such sweet thunder.
THESEUS: My hounds are bred out of the Spartan kind,
So flew'd,° so sanded;° and their heads are hung   120
With ears that sweep away the morning dew;
Crook-knee'd, and dewlapp'd° like Thessalian bulls;
Slow in pursuit, but match'd in mouth like bells,
Each under each.° A cry° more tuneable°
Was never holla'd to, nor cheer'd with horn,   125
In Crete, in Sparta, nor in Thessaly.
Judge when you hear. [*Sees the sleepers.*] But, soft!
    What nymphs are these?
EGEUS: My lord, this' my daughter here asleep;
    And this, Lysander; this Demetrius is;
    This Helena, old Nedar's Helena.   130
    I wonder of their being here together.
THESEUS: No doubt they rose up early to observe
    The rite of May, and, hearing our intent,
    Came here in grace of our solemnity.°
    But speak, Egeus. Is not this the day   135
    That Hermia should give answer of her choice?
EGEUS: It is, my lord.
THESEUS: Go, bid the huntsmen wake them with their
    horns.
                                 [*Exit an Attendant.*]

(*Shout within. Wind horns. They all start up.*)

    Good morrow, friends. Saint Valentine° is past.
    Begin these wood-birds but to couple now?   140
LYSANDER: Pardon, my lord.   [*They kneel.*]
THESEUS: I pray you all, stand up.
    I know you two are rival enemies;
    How comes this gentle concord in the world,
    That hatred is so far from jealousy
    To sleep by hate and fear no enmity?   145
LYSANDER: My lord, I shall reply amazedly,
    Half sleep, half waking; but as yet, I swear,
    I cannot truly say how I came here.
    But, as I think — for truly would I speak,
    And now I do bethink me, so it is —   150
    I came with Hermia hither. Our intent
    Was to be gone from Athens, where° we might,
    Without° the peril of the Athenian law —
EGEUS: Enough, enough, my lord; you have enough.
    I beg the law, the law, upon his head.   155
    They would have stol'n away; they would, Demetrius,

---

82. **these five:** I.e., the four lovers and Bottom.   88. **solemnly:** Ceremoniously.   95. **sad:** Sober.   104. **observation:** Observance to a morn of May (I, i, 167).   105. **vaward:** Vanguard, i.e., earliest part.   112. **Cadmus:** Mythical founder of Thebes. (This story about him is unknown.)   113. **bay'd:** Brought to bay.   114. **hounds of Sparta:** Breed famous in antiquity for their hunting skill.

120. **So flew'd:** Similarly having large hanging chaps or fleshy covering of the jaw.   **sanded:** Of sandy color.   122. **dewlapp'd:** Having pendulous folds of skin under the neck.   123–24. **match'd . . . under each:** Harmoniously matched in their various cries like a set of bells, from treble down to bass.   124. **cry:** Pack of hounds.   **tuneable:** Well tuned, melodious.   134. **solemnity:** Observance of these same rites of May.   139. **Saint Valentine:** Birds were supposed to choose their mates on St. Valentine's Day.   152. **where:** Wherever; or to where.   153. **Without:** Outside of, beyond.

Thereby to have defeated you and me,
You of your wife and me of my consent,
Of my consent that she should be your wife.

DEMETRIUS: My lord, fair Helen told me of their
160   stealth,
Of this their purpose hither to this wood,
And I in fury hither followed them,
Fair Helena in fancy following me.
But, my good lord, I wot not by what power —
165   But by some power it is — my love to Hermia,
Melted as the snow, seems to me now
As the remembrance of an idle gaud.°
Which in my childhood I did dote upon;
And all the faith, the virtue of my heart,
170   The object and the pleasure of mine eye,
Is only Helena. To her, my lord,
Was I betroth'd ere I saw Hermia,
But like a sickness did I loathe this food;
But, as in health, come to my natural taste,
175   Now I do wish it, love it, long for it,
And will for evermore be true to it.

THESEUS: Fair lovers, you are fortunately met.
Of this discourse we more will hear anon.
Egeus, I will overbear your will;
180   For in the temple, by and by, with us
These couples shall eternally be knit.
And, for° the morning now is something° worn,
Our purpos'd hunting shall be set aside.
Away with us to Athens. Three and three,
185   We'll hold a feast in great solemnity.
Come, Hippolyta.

                [*Exeunt Theseus, Hippolyta, Egeus, and train.*]

DEMETRIUS: These things seem small and
         undistinguishable,
Like far-off mountains turned into clouds.

HERMIA: Methinks I see these things with parted° eye,
When every thing seems double.

190 HELENA: So methinks;
And I have found Demetrius like a jewel,
Mine own, and not mine own.°

DEMETRIUS: Are you sure
That we are awake? It seems to me
That yet we sleep, we dream. Do not you think
195   The Duke was here, and bid us follow him?

HERMIA: Yea, and my father.

HELENA: And Hippolyta.

LYSANDER: And he did bid us follow to the temple.

DEMETRIUS: Why, then, we are awake. Let's follow
         him,
And by the way let us recount our dreams.
                                      [*Exeunt.*]

---

167. idle gaud: Worthless trinket. **182. for:** Since. **something:** Somewhat. **189. parted:** Improperly focused. **191–92. like . . . not mine own:** Like a jewel that one finds by chance and therefore possesses but cannot certainly consider one's own property.

BOTTOM [*awaking*]: When my cue comes, call me, and   200
I will answer. My next is, "Most fair Pyramus."
Heigh-ho! Peter Quince! Flute, the bellows-mender!
Snout, the tinker! Starveling! God's my life, stol'n
hence, and left me asleep! I have had a most rare
vision. I have had a dream, past the wit of man to say   205
what dream it was. Man is but an ass, if he go about°
to expound this dream. Methought I was — there is
no man can tell what. Methought I was — and methought I had — but man is but a patch'd° fool, if he
will offer° to say what me-thought I had. The eye of   210
man hath not heard, the ear of man hath not seen,
man's hand is not able to taste, his tongue to conceive, nor his heart to report, what my dream was. I
will get Peter Quince to write a ballad of this dream.
It shall be call'd "Bottom's Dream," because it hath   215
no bottom; and I will sing it in the latter end of a
play, before the Duke. Peradventure, to make it the
more gracious, I shall sing it at her° death.   [*Exit.*]

{*Scene II*}°

(*Enter Quince, Flute, [Snout, and Starveling].*)

QUINCE: Have you sent to Bottom's house? Is he come
home yet?

STARVELING: He cannot be heard of. Out of doubt he is
transported.°

FLUTE: If he come not, then the play is marr'd. It goes   5
not forward, doth it?

QUINCE: It is not possible. You have not a man in all
Athens able to discharge° Pyramus but he.

FLUTE: No, he hath simply the best wit of any handicraft
man in Athens.   10

QUINCE: Yea, and the best person too; and he is a very
paramour for a sweet voice.

FLUTE: You must say "paragon." A paramour is, God
bless us, a thing of naught.

(*Enter Snug the Joiner.*)

SNUG: Masters, the Duke is coming from the temple,   15
and there is two or three lords and ladies more married. If our sport had gone forward, we had all been
made men.

FLUTE: O sweet bully Bottom! Thus hath he lost sixpence a day° during his life; he could not have scap'd   20
sixpence a day. An the Duke had not given him sixpence a day for playing Pyramus, I'll be hang'd. He
would have deserv'd it. Sixpence a day in Pyramus,
or nothing.

(*Enter Bottom.*)

---

206. go about: Attempt. **209. patch'd:** Wearing motley, i.e., a dress of various colors. **210. offer:** Venture. **218. her:** Thisby's (?). **IV, II. Location:** Athens, Quince's house (?).
4. transported: Carried off by fairies; or, possibly, transformed.
8. discharge: Perform. **19–20. sixpence a day:** As a royal pension.

Stage model of the set for Max Reinhardt's 1913 production of *A Midsummer Night's Dream* at the Deutsches Theater in Berlin. The design called for an entire forest to be built on a stage that revolved as the action shifted.

25   BOTTOM: Where are these lads? Where are these hearts?°
QUINCE: Bottom! O most courageous day! O most happy hour!
BOTTOM: Masters, I am to discourse wonders.° But ask me not what; for if I tell you, I am no true Athenian. I
30   will tell you everything, right as it fell out.
QUINCE: Let us hear, sweet Bottom.
BOTTOM: Not a word of° me. All that I will tell you is, that the Duke hath din'd. Get your apparel together, good strings° to your beards, new ribands° to
35   your pumps, meet presently° at the palace, every man look o'er his part; for the short and the long is, our play is preferr'd.° In any case, let Thisby have clean linen; and let not him that plays the lion pare his nails, for they shall hang out for the lion's claws. And,
40   most dear actors, eat no onions nor garlic, for we are to utter sweet breath; and I do not doubt but to hear them say, it is a sweet comedy. No more words. Away! go, away!   [*Exeunt.*]

25. **hearts:** Good fellows.   28. **am . . . wonders:** Have wonders to relate.   32. **of:** Out of.   34. **strings:** To attach the beards. **ribands:** Ribbons.   35. **presently:** Immediately.   37. **preferr'd:** Selected for consideration.

{*ACT V • Scene 1*}°

(*Enter Theseus, Hippolyta, and Philostrate, [Lords, and Attendants].*)

HIPPOLYTA: 'Tis strange, my Theseus, that° these lovers speak of.
THESEUS: More strange than true. I never may° believe
These antic° fables, nor these fairy toys.°
Lovers and madmen have such seething brains
Such shaping fantasies,° that apprehend   5
More than cool reason ever comprehends.
The lunatic, the lover, and the poet
Are of imagination all compact.°
One sees more devils than vast hell can hold;
That is the madman. The lover, all as frantic,   10
Sees Helen's° beauty in a brow of Egypt.°
The poet's eye, in a fine frenzy rolling,

V, I. **Location:** Athens. The palace of Theseus.   1. **that:** That which.   2. **may:** Can.   3. **antic:** Strange, grotesque (with additional punning sense of *antique,* ancient). **fairy toys:** Trifling stories about fairies.   5. **fantasies:** Imaginations.   8. **compact:** Formed, composed.   11. **Helen's:** Of Helen of Troy, pattern of beauty.   **brow of Egypt:** Face of a gypsy.

Doth glance from heaven to earth, from earth to
  heaven;
And as imagination bodies forth
15 The forms of things unknown, the poet's pen
Turns them to shapes and gives to airy nothing
A local habitation and a name.
Such tricks hath strong imagination
That, if it would but apprehend some joy,
20 It comprehends some bringer° of that joy;
Or in the night, imagining some fear,°
How easy is a bush suppos'd a bear!
HIPPOLYTA: But all the story of the night told over,
And all their minds transfigur'd so together,
25 More witnesseth than fancy's images°
And grows to something of great constancy;°
But, howsoever,° strange and admirable.°

(*Enter lovers: Lysander, Demetrius, Hermia, and Helena.*)

THESEUS: Here come the lovers, full of joy and mirth.
Joy, gentle friends! Joy and fresh days of love
Accompany your hearts!
30 LYSANDER: More than to us
Wait in your royal walks, your board, your bed!
THESEUS: Come now, what masques, what dances shall
  we have,
To wear away this long age of three hours
Between our after-supper and bed-time?
35 Where is our usual manager of mirth?
What revels are in hand? Is there no play,
To ease the anguish of a torturing hour?
Call Philostrate.
PHILOSTRATE: Here, mighty Theseus.
THESEUS: Say, what abridgement° have you for this
  evening?
40 What masque? What music? How shall we beguile
The lazy time, if not with some delight?
PHILOSTRATE: There is a brief° how many sports are
  ripe.
Make choice of which your Highness will see first.
                              [*Giving a paper.*]
THESEUS [*reads*]: "The battle with the Centaurs,° to be
  sung
45 By an Athenian eunuch to the harp."
We'll none of that. That have I told my love,
In glory of my kinsman° Hercules.

[*Reads.*] "The riot of the tipsy Bacchanals,
Tearing the Thracian singer in their rage.""°
That is an old device; and it was play'd   50
When I from Thebes came last a conqueror.
[*Reads.*] "The thrice three Muses mourning for the
  death
Of Learning, late deceas'd in beggary.""°
That is some satire, keen and critical,
Not sorting with° a nuptial ceremony.   55
[*Reads.*] "A tedious brief scene of young Pyramus
And his love Thisby; very tragical mirth."
Merry and tragical? Tedious and brief?
That is, hot ice and wondrous strange° snow.
How shall we find the concord of this discord?   60
PHILOSTRATE: A play there is, my lord, some ten words
  long,
Which is as brief as I have known a play;
But by ten words, my lord, it is too long,
Which makes it tedious. For in all the play
There is not one word apt, one player fitted.   65
And tragical, my noble lord, it is,
For Pyramus therein doth kill himself.
Which, when I saw rehears'd, I must confess,
Made mine eyes water, but more merry tears
The passion of loud laughter never shed.   70
THESEUS: What are they that do play it?
PHILOSTRATE: Hard-handed men that work in Athens
  here,
Which never labor'd in their minds till now,
And now have toil'd° their unbreathed° memories
With this same play, against° your nuptial.   75
THESEUS: And we will hear it.
PHILOSTRATE: No, my noble lord,
It is not for you. I have heard it over,
And it is nothing, nothing in the world;
Unless you can find sport in their intents,
Extremely stretch'd° and conn'd° with cruel pain,   80
To do you service.
THESEUS: I will hear that play;
For never anything can be amiss'
When simpleness and duty tender it.
Go, bring them in; and take your places, ladies.

[*Philostrate goes to summon the players.*]

HIPPOLYTA: I love not to see wretchedness o'ercharg'd°   85
And duty in his service° perishing.
THESEUS: Why, gentle sweet, you shall see no such thing.

20. bringer: Source.   **21. fear:** Object of fear.   **25. More . . .
images:** Testifies to something more substantial than mere
imaginings.   **26. constancy:** Certainty.   **27. howsoever:** In
any case.   **admirable:** A source of wonder.   **39. abridgement:**
Pastime (to abridge or shorten the evening).   **42. brief:** Short
written statement, list.   **44. "battle . . . Centaurs":** Probably
refers to the battle of the Centaurs and the Lapithae, when the
Centaurs attempted to carry off Hippodamia, bride of Theseus's friend Pirothous.   **47. kinsman:** Plutarch's *Life of Theseus* states that Hercules and Theseus were near-kinsmen.
Theseus is referring to a version of the battle of the Centaurs in
which Hercules was said to be present.

48–49. "The riot . . . rage": This was the story of the death of
Orpheus, as told in *Metamorphoses*.   **52–53. "The thrice . . .
beggary":** Possibly an allusion to Spenser's *Teares of the Muses*
(1591), though "satires" deploring the neglect of learning and
the creative arts were common-place.   **55. sorting with:** Befitting.   **59. strange:** Seemingly an error for some adjective that
would contrast with *snow*, just as *hot* contrasts with *ice*.
74. toil'd: Taxed.   **unbreathed:** Unexercised.   **75. against:**
In preparation for.   **80. stretch'd:** Strained.   **conn'd:** Memorized.   **85. wretchedness o'ercharg'd:** Incompetence over-
burdened.   **86. his service:** Its attempt to serve.

HIPPOLYTA: He says they can do nothing in this kind.°
THESEUS: The kinder we, to give them thanks for
nothing.
90   Our sport shall be to take what they mistake;
And what poor duty cannot do, noble respect
Takes it in might, not merit.°
Where I have come, great clerks° have purposed
To greet me with premeditated welcomes;
95   Where I have seen them shiver and look pale,
Make periods in the midst of sentences,
Throttle their practic'd accent° in their fears,
And in conclusion dumbly have broke off,
Not paying me a welcome. Trust me, sweet,
100   Out of this silence yet I pick'd a welcome;
And in the modesty of fearful duty
I read as much as from the rattling tongue
Of saucy and audacious eloquence.
Love, therefore, and tongue-tied simplicity
105   In least° speak most, to my capacity.°

[*Philostrate returns.*]

PHILOSTRATE: So please your Grace, the Prologue° is
address'd.°
THESEUS: Let him approach.   [*Flourish of trumpets.*]

(*Enter the Prologue* [*Quince*].)

PROLOGUE: If we offend, it is with our good will.
That you should think, we come not to offend,
110   But with good will. To show our simple skill,
That is the true beginning of our end.
Consider, then, we come but in despite.
We do not come, as minding° to content you,
Our true intent is. All for your delight
115   We are not here. That you should here repent you,
The actors are at hand; and, by their show,
You shall know all that you are like to know.
THESEUS: This fellow doth not stand upon points.°
LYSANDER: He hath rid his prologue like a rough° colt;
120   he knows not the stop.° A good moral, my lord: it is
not enough to speak, but to speak true.
HIPPOLYTA: Indeed he hath play'd on his prologue like
a child on a recorder;° a sound, but not in government.°
125 THESEUS: His speech was like a tangled chain, nothing°
impair'd, but all disorder'd. Who is next?

(*Enter Pyramus and Thisby, and Wall, and Moonshine,
and Lion.*)

PROLOGUE: Gentles, perchance you wonder at this
show;
But wonder on, till truth make all things plain.
This man is Pyramus, if you would know;
This beauteous lady Thisby is certain.   130
This man, with lime and rough-cast, doth present
Wall, that vile Wall which did these lovers sunder;
And through Wall's chink, poor souls, they are
content
To whisper. At the which let no man wonder.
This man, with lantern, dog, and bush of thorn,   135
Presenteth Moonshine; for, if you will know,
By moonshine did these lovers think no scorn°
To meet at Ninus' tomb, there, there to woo.
This grisly beast, which Lion hight° by name,
The trusty Thisby, coming first by night,   140
Did scare away, or rather did affright;
And, as she fled, her mantle she did fall,°
Which Lion vile with bloody mouth did stain.
Anon comes Pyramus, sweet youth and tall,°
And finds his trusty Thisby's mantle slain;   145
Whereat, with blade, with bloody blameful blade,
He bravely broach'd° his boiling bloody breast.
And Thisby, tarrying in mulberry shade,
His dagger drew, and died. For all the rest,
Let Lion, Moonshine, Wall, and lovers twain   150
At large° discourse, while here they do remain.

(*Exeunt Lion, Thisby, and Moonshine.*)

THESEUS: I wonder if the lion be to speak.
DEMETRIUS: No wonder, my lord. One lion may, when
many asses do.
WALL: In this same interlude it doth befall   155
That I, one Snout by name, present a wall;
And such a wall, as I would have you think,
That had in it a crannied hole or chink,
Through which the lovers, Pyramus and Thisby,
Did whisper often very secretly.   160
This loam, this rough-cast, and this stone doth show
That I am that same wall; the truth is so.
And this the cranny is, right and sinister,°
Through which the fearful lovers are to whisper.
THESEUS: Would you desire lime and hair to speak better?   165
DEMETRIUS: It is the wittiest partition° that ever I heard
discourse, my lord.

[*Pyramus comes forward.*]

THESEUS: Pyramus draws near the wall. Silence!

---

88. kind: Kind of thing.   **92. Takes . . . merit:** Values it for the
effort made rather than for the excellence achieved.
93. clerks: Learned men.   **97. practic'd accent:** Rehearsed
speech; or usual way of speaking.   **105. least:** Saying least.
to my capacity: In my judgment and understanding.
106. Prologue: Speaker of the prologue.   **address'd:** Ready.
113. minding: Intending.   **118. stand upon points:** (1) Heed
niceties or small points, (2) pay attention to punctuation in his
reading. (The humor of Quince's speech is in the blunders of its
punctuation.)   **119. rough:** Unbroken.   **120. stop:** (1) The
stopping of a colt by reining it in, (2) punctuation mark.
123. recorder: A wind instrument like a flute.   **123–24. government:** Control.   **125. nothing:** Not at all.

137. think no scorn: Think it no disgraceful matter.
139. hight: Is called.   **142. fall:** Let fall.   **144. tall:** Courageous.   **147. broach'd:** Stabbed.   **151. At large:** In full, at
length.   **163. right and sinister:** The right side of it and the
left (sinister); or running from right to left, horizontally.
166. partition: (1) Wall, (2) section of a learned treatise or
oration.

PYRAMUS: O grim-look'd° night! O night with hue so
    black!
170 O night, which ever art when day is not!
    O night, O night! Alack, alack, alack,
    I fear my Thisby's promise is forgot.
    And thou, O wall, O sweet, O lovely wall,
    That stand'st between her father's ground and mine,
175 Thou wall, O wall, O sweet and lovely wall,
    Show me thy chink, to blink through with mine eyne!

                [*Wall holds up his fingers.*]

    Thanks, courteous wall. Jove shield thee well for
    this!
    But what see I? No Thisby do I see.
    O wicked wall, through whom I see no bliss!
180 Curs'd be thy stones for thus deceiving me!
THESEUS: The wall, methinks, being sensible,° should
    curse again.
PYRAMUS: No, in truth, sir, he should not. "Deceiving
    me" is Thisby's cue: she is to enter now, and I am to
185 spy her through the wall. You shall see, it will fall pat
    as I told you. Yonder she comes.

(*Enter Thisby.*)

THISBY: O wall, full often hast thou heard my moans,
    For parting my fair Pyramus and me.
    My cherry lips have often kiss'd thy stones,
190 Thy stones with lime and hair knit up in thee.
PYRAMUS: I see a voice. Now will I to the chink,
    To spy an° I can hear my Thisby's face.
    Thisby!
THISBY: My love! Thou art my love, I think.
PYRAMUS: Think what thou wilt, I am thy lover's
195   grace;°
    And, like Limander° am I trusty still.
THISBY: And I like Helen,° till the Fates me kill.
PYRAMUS: Not Shafalus° to Procrus° was so true.
THISBY: As Shafalus to Procrus, I to you.
200 PYRAMUS: O, kiss me through the hole of this vile wall!
THISBY: I kiss the wall's hole, not your lips at all.
PYRAMUS: Wilt thou at Ninny's tomb meet me
    straightway?
THISBY: 'Tide° life, 'tide death, I come without delay.

           [*Exeunt Pyramus and Thisby.*]

WALL: Thus have I, Wall, my part discharged so;
205 And, being done, thus Wall away doth go.   [*Exit.*]
THESEUS: Now is the mural down between the two
    neighbors.
DEMETRIUS: No remedy, my lord, when walls are so
    willful to hear° without warning.°
210 HIPPOLYTA: This is the silliest stuff that ever I heard.

---

169. **grim-look'd:** Grim-looking. 181. **sensible:** Capable of feeling. 192. **an:** If. 195. **lover's grace:** Gracious lover. 196. **Limander:** Blunder for *Leander*. 197. **Helen:** Blunder for *Hero*. 198. **Shafalus, Procrus:** Blunders for *Cephalus* and *Procris*, also famous lovers. 203. **'Tide:** Betide, come. 209. **to hear:** As to hear. **without warning:** Without warning the parents.

THESEUS: The best in this kind° are but shadows;° and
    the worst are no worse, if imagination amend them.
HIPPOLYTA: It must be your imagination then, and not
    theirs.
THESEUS: If we imagine no worse of them than they of 215
    themselves, they may pass for excellent men. Here
    come two noble beasts in, a man and a lion.

(*Enter Lion and Moonshine.*)

LION: You, ladies, you, whose gentle hearts do fear
    The smallest monstrous mouse that creeps on floor,
    May now perchance both quake and tremble here, 220
    When lion rough in wildest rage doth roar.
    Then know that I, as Snug the joiner, am
    A lion fell,° nor else no lion's dam;
    For, if I should as lion come in strife
    Into this place, 'twere pity on my life. 225
THESEUS: A very gentle beast, and of a good conscience.
DEMETRIUS: The very best at a beast, my lord, that e'er I
    saw.
LYSANDER: This lion is a very fox for his valor.°
THESEUS: True; and a goose for his discretion.° 230
DEMETRIUS: Not so, my lord; for his valor cannot carry
    his discretion; and the fox carries the goose.
THESEUS: His discretion, I am sure, cannot carry his
    valor, for the goose carries not the fox. It is well.
    Leave it to his discretion, and let us listen to the 235
    moon.
MOON: This lanthorn° doth the horned moon present —
DEMETRIUS: He should have worn the horns on his
    head.°
THESEUS: He is no crescent, and his horns are invisible 240
    within the circumference.
MOON: This lanthorn doth the horned moon present;
    Myself the man i' th' moon do seem to be.
THESEUS: This is the greatest error of all the rest. The
    man should be put into the lanthorn. How is it else 245
    the man i' th' moon?
DEMETRIUS: He dares not come there for the° candle;
    for, you see, it is already in snuff.°
HIPPOLYTA: I am aweary of this moon. Would he would
    change! 250
THESEUS: It appears, by his small light of discretion, that
    he is in the wane; but yet, in courtesy, in all reason,
    we must stay the time.
LYSANDER: Proceed, Moon.

---

211. **in this kind:** Of this sort. **shadows:** Likenesses, representations. 223. **lion fell:** Fierce lion (with a play on the idea of *lion skin*). 229. **is . . . valor:** His valor consists of craftiness and discretion. 230. **goose . . . discretion:** As discreet as a goose, that is, more foolish than discreet. 237. **lanthorn:** This original spelling may suggest a play on the *horn* of which lanterns were made and also on a cuckold's horns; but the spelling *lanthorn* is not used consistently for comic effect in this play or elsewhere. In V, I, 135, for example, the word is *lantern* in the original. 238–39. **on his head:** As a sign of cuckoldry. 247. **for the:** Because of the. 248. **in snuff:** (1) Offended, (2) in need of snuffing.

255 MOON: All that I have to say is to tell you that the lanthorn is the moon, I, the man in the moon, this thorn-
bush my thorn-bush, and this dog my dog.
DEMETRIUS: Why, all these should be in the lanthorn;
for all these are in the moon. But silence! Here comes
260 Thisby.

(*Enter Thisby.*)

THISBY: This is old Ninny's tomb. Where is my love?
LION [*roaring*]: Oh —   [*Thisby runs off.*]
DEMETRIUS: Well roar'd, Lion.
THESEUS: Well run, Thisby.
265 HIPPOLYTA: Well shone, Moon. Truly, the moon shines
with a good grace.

      [*The Lion shakes Thisby's mantle, and exit.*]

THESEUS: Well mous'd,° Lion.
DEMETRIUS: And then came Pyramus.
LYSANDER: And so the lion vanish'd.

(*Enter Pyramus.*)

PYRAMUS: Sweet Moon, I thank thee for thy sunny
270   beams;
I thank thee, Moon, for shining now so bright;
For, by thy gracious, golden, glittering gleams,
I trust to take of truest Thisby sight.
      But stay, O spite!
275   But mark, poor knight,
What dreadful dole° is here!
      Eyes, do you see?
      How can it be?
O dainty duck! O dear!
280   Thy mantle good,
What, stain'd with blood!
Approach, ye Furies fell!°
      O Fates, come, come,
      Cut thread and thrum;°
285 Quail,° crush, conclude, and quell!°
THESEUS: This passion, and the death of a dear friend,
would go near to make a man look sad.°
HIPPOLYTA: Beshrew my heart, but I pity the man.
PYRAMUS: O wherefore, Nature, didst thou lions frame?
290 Since lion vile hath here deflow'r'd my dear,
Which is — no, no — which was the fairest dame
That liv'd, that lov'd, that lik'd, that look'd with
      cheer.°
      Come, tears, confound,
      Out, sword, and wound
295 The pap of Pyramus;
      Ay, that left pap,
      Where heart doth hop.   [*Stabs himself.*]
Thus die I, thus, thus, thus.

      Now am I dead,
      Now am I fled;   300
My soul is in the sky.
      Tongue, lose thy light;
      Moon, take thy flight.   [*Exit Moonshine.*]
Now die, die, die, die, die.   [*Dies.*]
DEMETRIUS: No die, but an ace,° for him; for he is but 305
one.°
LYSANDER: Less than an ace, man; for he is dead, he is
nothing.
THESEUS: With the help of a surgeon he might yet
recover, and yet prove an ass.°   310
HIPPOLYTA: How chance Moonshine is gone before
Thisby comes back and finds her lover?
THESEUS: She will find him by starlight. Here she comes;
and her passion ends the play.

[*Enter Thisby.*]

HIPPOLYTA: Methinks she should not use a long one for 315
such a Pyramus. I hope she will be brief.
DEMETRIUS: A mote will turn the balance, which Pyra-
mus, which° Thisby, is the better: he for a man God
warr'nt us; she for a woman, God bless us.
LYSANDER: She hath spied him already with those sweet 320
eyes.
DEMETRIUS: And thus she means,° videlicet:°
THISBY: Asleep, my love?
      What, dead, my dove?
      O Pyramus, arise!   325
      Speak, speak. Quite dumb?
Dead, dead? A tomb
Must cover thy sweet eyes.
      These lily lips,
      This cherry nose,   330
These yellow cowslip cheeks,
      Are gone, are gone!
      Lovers, make moan.
His eyes were green as leeks.
      O Sisters Three,°   335
      Come, come to me,
With hands as pale as milk;
      Lay them in gore,
      Since you have shore°
With shears his thread of silk.   340
      Tongue, not a word.
      Come, trusty sword,
Come, blade, my breast imbrue!°   [*Stabs herself.*]
      And farewell, friends.
      Thus Thisby ends.   345
Adieu, adieu, adieu.   [*Dies.*]

---

267. **mous'd:** Shaken.   276. **dole:** Grievous event.   282. **fell:**
Fierce.   284. **thread and thrum:** The warp in weaving and the
loose end of the warp.   285. **Quail:** Overpower.   **quell:** Kill,
destroy.   286–87. **This . . . sad:** If one had other reason to
grieve, one might be sad, but not from this absurd portrayal of
passion.   292. **cheer:** Countenance.

305. **ace:** The side of the die featuring the single pip, or spot.
(The pun is on *die* as a singular of *dice*; Bottom's performance is not worth a whole *die* but rather one single face
of it, one small portion.)   306. **one:** (1) An individual person,
(2) unique.   310. **ass:** With a pun on *ace*.   317–18. **which . . .
which:** Whether . . . or.   322. **means:** Moans, laments.   **videlicet:** To wit.   335. **Sisters Three:** The Fates.   339. **shore:**
Shorn.   343. **imbrue:** Stain with blood.

THESEUS: Moonshine and Lion are left to bury the dead.
DEMETRIUS: Ay, and Wall too.
BOTTOM [*starting up*]: No, I assure you; the wall is
350   down that parted their fathers. Will it please you to
see the epilogue, or to hear a Bergomask dance° between two of our company?
THESEUS: No epilogue, I pray you; for your play needs
no excuse. Never excuse; for when the players are all
355   dead, there need none to be blam'd. Marry, if he that
writ it had play'd Pyramus and hang'd himself in
Thisby's garter, it would have been a fine tragedy;
and so it is, truly, and very notably discharg'd. But,
come, your Bergomask. Let your epilogue alone.
                                [*A dance.*]
360 The iron tongue of midnight hath told° twelve.
Lovers, to bed; 'tis almost fairy time.
I fear we shall outsleep the coming morn
As much as we this night have overwatch'd.°
This palpable-gross° play hath well beguil'd
365 The heavy° gait of night. Sweet friends, to bed.
A fortnight hold we this solemnity,
In nightly revels and new jollity.   (*Exeunt.*)

(*Enter Puck*)

PUCK: Now the hungry lion roars,
    And the wolf behowls the moon;
370 Whilst the heavy ploughman snores,
    All with weary task fordone.°
Now the wasted brands° do glow,
    Whilst the screech-owl, screeching loud,
Puts the wretch that lies in woe
375   In remembrance of a shroud.
Now it is the time of night
    That the graves, all gaping wide,
Every one lets forth his sprite,°
    In the churchway paths to glide.
380 And we fairies, that do run
    By the triple Hecate's° team
From the presence of the sun,
    Following darkness like a dream,
Now are frolic.° Not a mouse
385 Shall disturb this hallowed house.
I am sent with broom before,
To sweep the dust behind° the door.

(*Enter [Oberon and Titania,] King and Queen of Fairies,
with all their train.*)

OBERON: Through the house give glimmering light,
    By the dead and drowsy fire;
Every elf and fairy sprite   390
    Hop as light as bird from brier;
And this ditty, after me,
Sing, and dance it trippingly.
TITANIA: First, rehearse your song by rote,
    To each word a warbling note.   395
Hand in hand, with fairy grace,
Will we sing, and bless this place.
                      [*Song and dance.*]
OBERON: Now, until the break of day,
Through this house each fairy stray.
To the best bride-bed will we,   400
Which by us shall blessed be;
And the issue there create°
Ever shall be fortunate.
So shall all the couples three
Ever true in loving be;   405
And the blots of Nature's hand
Shall not in their issue stand;
Never mole, hare lip, nor scar,
Nor mark prodigious,° such as are
Despised in nativity,   410
Shall upon their children be.
With this field-dew consecrate,°
Every fairy take his gait,°
And each several° chamber bless,
Through this palace, with sweet peace;   415
And the owner of it blest
Ever shall in safety rest.
Trip away; make no stay;
Meet me all by break of day.

        (*Exeunt [Oberon, Titania, and train].*)

PUCK: If we shadows have offended,   420
Think but this, and all is mended,
That you have but slumb'red here°
While these visions did appear.
And this weak and idle theme,
No more yielding but° a dream,   425
Gentles, do not reprehend.
If you pardon, we will mend.
And, as I am an honest Puck,
If we have unearned luck
Now to scape the serpent's tongue,°   430
We will make amends ere long;
Else the Puck a liar call.
So, good night unto you all.
Give me your hands,° if we be friends,
And Robin shall restore amends.   [*Exit.*] 435

---

351. **Bergomask dance:** A rustic dance named for Bergamo,
a province in the state of Venice. 360. **told:** Counted,
struck ("tolled"). 363. **overwatch'd:** Stayed up too late.
364. **palpable-gross:** Obviously crude. 365. **heavy:** Drowsy,
dull. 371. **fordone:** Exhausted. 372. **wasted brands:**
Burned-out logs. 378. **Every . . . sprite:** Every grave lets forth
its ghost. 381. **triple Hecate's:** Hecate ruled in three capacities: as Luna or Cynthia in heaven, as Diana on earth, and as
Proserpina in hell. 384. **frolic:** Merry. 387. **behind:** From
behind. (Robin Goodfellow was a household spirit who helped
good housemaids and punished lazy ones.)

402. **create:** Created. 409. **prodigious:** Monstrous, unnatural.
412. **consecrate:** Consecrated. 413. **take his gait:** Go his way.
414. **several:** Separate. 422. **That . . . here:** That it is a "midsummer night's dream." 425. **No . . . but:** Yielding no more
than. 430. **serpent's tongue:** Hissing. 434. **Give . . . hands:**
Applaud.

COMMENTARIES

Some of the finest critical commentary ever written has been devoted to the works of Shakespeare. From the seventeenth century to the present, critics have taken a considerable interest in the nuances of his work.

In the commentary on *A Midsummer Night's Dream* we find a wide range of responses to the work. Enid Welsford's comments are in a special context, that of the court masque, the rich entertainments that were designed to please royalty. As Welsford explains, *A Midsummer Night's Dream* has many elements of the masque.

In a more specifically feminist observation, critic Linda Bamber shows how assumptions regarding power in a male-female relationship affect our interpretation of the play.

Peter Brook, one of the most notable contemporary directors of Shakespeare and the producer of a landmark production of *A Midsummer Night's Dream* (1970), gives us a director's view of the play. He centers the discussion on love, which in many forms is at the heart of the play. See the review of his production on page 346.

Clive Barnes's review gives us a clear sense of the visual and kinetic details that made Peter Brook's *A Midsummer Night's Dream* one of the most memorable modern stagings of Shakespeare. The use of juggling, acrobats, and trapezes energized the production and underscored the youthful vitality of the characters.

Contemporary reviews of Shakespeare's plays take a very different approach to the plays than do critical studies. The reviewers are concerned first with the actors and their interpretation of the drama. They are then concerned with the director's insights and sense of pacing. In addition to focusing on the title roles, critics also aim to communicate a sense of the dynamics of the production as a whole. Peter Brook's production of *A Midsummer Night's Dream*, for example, was perhaps most startling for its all-white set and backdrop, and for the marvelous scenes staged with principal actors lolling on simple white swings. Critics can give us insight into the staging of the work and the ways in which the staging imparts meaning to the drama.

Enid Welsford (1892–1981)

MASQUE ELEMENTS IN *A MIDSUMMER NIGHT'S DREAM*

1927

Enid Welsford examines A Midsummer Night's Dream *from the point of view of its masquelike qualities. Shakespeare's* The Tempest *includes a masque and has certain scenic qualities that link it to that tradition, and so does* A Midsummer Night's Dream. *Its fantastic costumes and remarkable fairy population could be considered part of the antimasque, a parody of the masque itself. The antimasque often involved masquers dressed in grotesque animal costumes, making a loud racket, and dancing in erratic and fantastic gestures. Meant originally as a contrast to the magnificence of the masque, the antimasque became a favorite of the less conservative masquers.*

The only character study in *A Midsummer Night's Dream* is to be found in the portrayal of Bottom, Theseus, and perhaps Hippolyta. Even in drawing these characters Shakespeare was evidently influenced by the memory of pageants, complimentary speeches, and entertainments addressed by townspeople and humble folk to the Queen or to the nobility. A glance through Nichols's *Public Progresses* shows what innumerable lengthy speeches, what innumerable disguisings and shows, Elizabeth was obliged to bear with gracious demeanor. Her experiences were similar to those of Theseus:

> Where I have come, great clerks have purposed
> To greet me with premeditated welcomes;
> Where I have seen them shiver and look pale,
> Make periods in the midst of sentences,
> Throttle their practic'd accent in their fears,
> And, in conclusion, dumbly have broke off,
> Not paying me a welcome.

One Sunday afternoon, at Kenilworth Castle, Elizabeth and her court whiled away the time by watching the countrypeople at a Brideale and Morris Dance. Their amused kindly tolerance is just that of Theseus and the lovers toward the Athenian workmen. So that even in the most solid and dramatic parts of his play Shakespeare is only giving an idealized version of courtly and country revels and of the people that played a part in them.

In *A Midsummer Night's Dream* Bottom and his companions serve the same purpose as the antimasque in the courtly revels. It is true that Shakespeare's play was written before Ben Jonson had elaborated and defined the antimasque, but from the first grotesque dances were popular, and the principle of contrast was always latent in the masque. There is, however, a great difference between Jonson's and Shakespeare's management of foil and relief. In the antimasque the transition is sudden and the contrast complete, a method of composition effective enough in spectacle and ballet. But in a play, as Shakespeare well knew, the greatest beauty is gained through contrast when the difference is not obvious and striking, but rises out of a deep though unobtrusive resemblance. This could not be better illustrated than by the picture of Titania winding the ass-headed Bottom in her arms. Why is it that this is a pleasing picture, why is it that the rude mechanicals do not, as a matter of fact, disturb or sully Titania's "close and consecrated bower"? Malvolio° in Bottom's place would be repellent, yet Malvolio, regarded superficially, is less violently contrasted to the Fairy Queen than is Nick Bottom. Bottom with his ass's head is grotesquely hideous, and in ordinary life he is crude, raw, and very stupid. We have no reason to suppose that Malvolio was anything but a well-set-up, proper-looking man, spruce, well dressed, the perfect family butler. His mentality too is of a distinctly higher order than Bottom's. He fills a responsible position with

Malvolio: A character in Shakespeare's *Twelfth Night*.

credit, he follows a reasoned line of conduct, he thinks nobly of the soul. Two things alone he lacks (and that is why no self-respecting fey could ever kiss him) — humor and imagination. Malvolio is, therefore, the only character who cannot be included in the final harmony of *Twelfth Night.* Bottom and his fellows did perhaps lack humor (though the interview with the fairies suggests that Bottom had a smack of it), but in its place they possessed unreason. Imagination they did have, of the most simple, primal, childlike kind. It is their artistic ambition that lifts them out of the humdrum world and turns them into Midsummer Dreamers, and we have seen how cunningly Shakespeare extracts from their very stupidity romance and moonshine. But, indeed, grotesqueness and stupidity (of a certain kind) have a kinship with beauty. For these qualities usually imply a measure of spiritual freedom, they lead to at least a temporary relief from the tyranny of reason and from the pressure of the external world. In *A Midsummer Night's Dream* the dominance of the Lord of Misrule is not marked by coarse parody, but by the partial repeal of the laws of cause and effect. By delicate beauty, gentle mockery, and simple romantic foolishness our freedom is gained.

Linda Bamber (b. 1945)
ON *A MIDSUMMER NIGHT'S DREAM*   1982

The question of masculine and feminine is central to A Midsummer Night's Dream. *Much of the action is precipitated by a power struggle between Titania and Oberon, and the young Athenians who rush off to the woods are there because a father has decided to oppose the will of his daughter regarding her marriage. Linda Bamber is a feminist critic interested in examining the centers of power in the play, particularly with an eye for what we accept as the natural order of relationships. She shows that the action of the comedy is essentially tied into questions of gender, which begin to become questions of genre.*

The best example [in Shakespeare] of the relationship between male dominance and the status quo comes in *A Midsummer Night's Dream,* which begins with a rebellion of the feminine against the power of masculine authority. Hermia refuses the man both Aegeus and Theseus order her to marry; her refusal sends us off into the forest, beyond the power of the father and the masculine state. Once in the forest, of course, we find the social situation metaphorically repeated in this world of imagination and nature. The fairy king, Oberon, rules the forest. His rule, too, is troubled by the rebellion of the feminine. Titania has refused to give him her page, the child of a human friend who died in childbirth. But by the end of the story Titania is conquered, the child relinquished, and order restored. Even here the comic upheavals, whether we see them as May games or bad dreams, are associated with an uprising of women. David P. Young has pointed out how firmly this play connects order with masculine dominance and the disruption of order with the rebellion of the feminine:

> It is appropriate that Theseus, as representative of daylight and right reason, should have
> subdued his bride-to-be to the rule of his masculine will. That is the natural order of

things. It is equally appropriate that Oberon, as king of darkness and fantasy, should have lost control of his wife, and that the corresponding natural disorder described by Titania should ensue.[1]

The natural order, the status quo, is for men to rule women. When they fail to do so, we have the exceptional situation, the festive, disruptive, disorderly moment of comedy.

A Midsummer Night's Dream is actually an anomaly among the festive comedies. It is unusual for the forces of the green world to be directed, as they are here, by a masculine figure. Because the green world here is a partial reproduction of the social world, the feminine is reduced to a kind of first cause of the action while a masculine power directs it. In the other festive comedies the feminine Other presides. She does not *command* the forces of the alternative world, as Oberon does, but since she acts in harmony with these forces her will and desire often prevail.

Where are we to bestow our sympathies? On the forces that make for the disruption of the status quo and therefore for the plot? Or on the force that asserts itself against the disruption and reestablishes a workable social order? Of course we cannot choose. We can only say that in comedy we owe our holiday to such forces as the tendency of the feminine to rebel, whereas to the successful reassertion of masculine power we owe our everyday order. Shakespearean comedy endorses both sides. Holiday is, of course, the subject and the analogue of each play; but the plays always end in a return to everyday life. The optimistic reading of Shakespearean comedy says that everyday life is clarified and enriched by our holiday from it; according to the pessimistic reading the temporary subversion of the social order has revealed how much that order excludes, how high a price we pay for it. But whether our return to everyday life is a comfortable one or not, the return itself is the inevitable conclusion to the journey out.

Does this make the comedies sexist? Is the association of women with the disruption of the social order an unconscious and insulting projection? It seems to begin as such; but as the form of Shakespearean comedy develops, the Otherness of the feminine develops into as powerful a force in the drama as the social authority of the masculine Self. For the feminine in Shakespearean comedy begins as a shrew but develops into a comic heroine. The shrew's rebellion directly challenges masculine authority, whereas the comic heroine merely presides over areas of experience to which masculine authority is irrelevant. But the shrew is essentially powerless against the social system, whereas the comic heroine is in alliance with forces that can never be finally overcome. The shrew is defeated by the superior strength, physical and social, of a man, or by women who support the status quo. She provokes a battle of the sexes, and the outcome of this battle, from Shakespeare's point of view, is inevitable. The comic heroine, on the other hand, does not fight the system but merely surfaces, again and again, when and where the social system is temporarily subverted. The comic heroine does not actively resist the social and political hegemony° of the men, but as an irresistible version of the Other she successfully competes for our favor with the (masculine) representatives of the social Self. The development of the feminine from the shrew to the comic heroine indicates a certain consciousness on the author's part of sexual politics; and it indicates

[1]David P. Young, *Something of Great Constancy* (New Haven, CT: Yale UP, 1966), 183.
hegemony: Overriding authority.

a desire, at least, to create conditions of sexual equality within the drama even while reflecting the unequal conditions of men and women in the society at large.

Peter Brook (b. 1925)
The Play Is the Message . . .   *1987*

When a distinguished director becomes a critic, we have the opportunity to understand a play from the point of view of one who has to make the play work in front of an audience. Brook's production of A Midsummer Night's Dream *was a sensation in England and the United States in 1970. It featured absolutely white lighting, white sets, and actors in swings. Brook had analyzed the play in such a fashion that he saw love as its constant concern, "constantly repeated." He concluded that to present the play, the players must embody the concept of love. They must bring to the play their own realization of the play's themes — even to the point of seeing theater anew, like the mechanicals "who are touching an extraordinary world with the tips of their fingers, a world which transcends their daily experience and which fills them with wonder" — the effect of the love they bring to their task.*

People have often asked me: "What is the theme of *A Midsummer Night's Dream*?" There is only one answer to that question, the same as one would give regarding a cup. The quality of a cup is its cupness. I say this by way of introduction, to show that if I lay so much stress on the dangers involved in trying to define the themes of the *Dream* it is because too many productions, too many attempts at visual interpretation are based on preconceived ideas, as if these had to be illustrated in some way. In my opinion we should first of all try to rediscover the play as a living thing; then we shall be able to analyze our discoveries. Once I have finished working on the play, I can begin to produce my theories. It was fortunate that I did not attempt to do so earlier because the play would not have yielded up its secrets.

At the center of the *Dream*, constantly repeated, we find the word "love." Everything comes back to this, even the structure of the play, even its music. The quality the play demands from its performers is to build up an atmosphere of love during the performance itself, so that this abstract idea — for the word "love" is in itself a complete abstraction — may become palpable. The play presents us with forms of love which become less and less blurred as it goes on. "Love" soon begins to resound like a musical scale and little by little we are introduced to its various modes and tones.

Love is, of course, a theme which touches all men. No one, not even the most hardened, the coldest, or the most despairing, is insensitive to it, even if he does not know what love is. Either his practical experience confirms its existence or he suffers from its absence, which is another way of recognizing that it exists. At every moment the play touches something which concerns everyone.

As this is theater, there must be conflicts, so this play about love is also a play about the opposite of love, love and its opposite force. We are brought to realize that love, liberty, and imagination are closely connected. Right at the beginning of the play, for example, the father in a long speech tries to obstruct his daughter's love and we are surprised that such a character, apparently a secondary role, should have so long a speech — until we discover the real importance of his words. What he says not only reflects a generation gap (a father opposing his daughter's love because he had intended her for someone else), it also explains the reasons for his feeling of suspicion toward the young man whom his daughter loves. He describes him as an individual prone to fantasy, led by his imagination — an unpardonable weakness in the father's eyes.

From this starting point we see, as in any of Shakespeare's plays, a confrontation. Here it is between love and its opposing qualities, between fantasy and solid common sense — caught in an endless series of mirrors. As usual, Shakespeare confuses the issue. If we asked someone's opinion on the father's point of view, he might say, for example, that "The father is in the wrong because he is against freedom of the imagination," a very widespread attitude today.

In this way, for most present-day audiences, the girl's father comes over as the classical father figure who misunderstands young people and their flights of fancy. But later on, we discover surprisingly that he is right, because the imaginative world in which this lover lives causes him to behave in a quite disgusting way toward the very same daughter: as soon as a drop of liquid falls into his eyes, acting as a drug which liberates natural tendencies, he not only jilts her but his love is transformed into violent hate. He uses words which might well be borrowed from *Measure for Measure,* denouncing the girl with the kind of vehemence that, in the Middle Ages, led people to burn one another at the stake. Yet at the end of the play we are once more in agreement with the Duke, who rejects the father in the name of love. The young man has now been transformed.

So we observe this game of love in a psychological and metaphysical context; we hear Titania's assertion that the opposition between herself and Oberon is fundamental, primordial. But Oberon's acts deny this, for he perceives that within their opposition a reconciliation is possible.

The play covers an extraordinarily broad range of universal forces and feelings in a mythical world, which suddenly changes, in the last part, into high society. We find ourselves back in the very real palace: and the same Shakespeare who, a few pages earlier, offered us a scene of pure fantasy between Titania and Oberon, where it would be absurd to ask prosaic questions like "Where does Oberon live?" or "When describing a queen like Titania did Shakespeare wish to express political ideas?," now takes us into a precise social environment. We are present at the meeting point of two worlds, that of the workmen and the court, the world of wealth and elegance, and alleged sensitivity, the world of people who have had the leisure to cultivate fine sentiments and are now shown as insensitive and even disgusting in their superior attitude toward the poor.

At the beginning of the court scene we see our former heroes, who have spent the entire play involved in the theme of love, and would no doubt be quite capable of giving academic lectures on the subject, suddenly finding themselves plunged into a context which has apparently nothing to do with love (with their own love, since all their problems have been solved). Now they are in the context of a relationship with each other and with another social class, and they are at a loss. They do not realize that here too scorn eliminates love.

We see how well Shakespeare has situated everything. Athens in the *Dream* resembles our Athens in the sixties: the workmen, as they state in the first scene, are very much afraid of the authorities; if they commit the slightest error they will be hanged, and there is nothing comical about that. Indeed, they risk hanging as soon as they shed their anonymity. At the same time they are irresistibly attracted by the carrot of "sixpence a day" which will enable them to escape poverty. Yet their real motive is neither glory nor adventure nor money (that is made very clear and should guide the actors who perform this scene). Those simple men who have only ever worked with their hands apply to the use of the imagination exactly the same quality of love which traditionally underlies the relationship between a craftsman and his tools. That is what gives these scenes both their strength and their comic quality. These craftsmen make efforts which are grotesque in one sense because they push awkwardness to its limit, but at another level they set themselves to their task with such love that the meaning of their clumsy efforts changes before our eyes.

The spectators can easily decide to adopt the same attitude as the courtiers: to find all this quite simply ridiculous; to laugh with the complacency of people who quite confidently mock the efforts of others. Yet the audience is invited to take a step back: to feel it cannot quite identify with the court, with people who are too grand and too unkind. Little by little, we come to see that the craftsmen, who behave with little understanding but who approach their new job with love, are discovering theater — an imaginary world for them, toward which they instinctively feel great respect. In fact, the "mechanicals" scene is often misinterpreted because the actors forget to look at theater through innocent eyes, they take a professional actor's views of good or bad acting, and in so doing they diminish the mystery and the sense of magic felt by these amateurs, who are touching an extraordinary world with the tips of their fingers, a world which transcends their daily experience and which fills them with wonder.

We see this quite clearly in the part of the boy who plays the girl, Thisby. At first sight this tough lad is irresistibly absurd, but by degrees, through his love for what he is doing, we discover what more is involved. In our production, the actor playing the part is a professional plumber, who only took to acting a short while ago. He well understands what is involved, what it means to feel this nameless and shapeless kind of love. This boy, himself new to theater, acts the part of someone who is new to theater. Through his conviction and his identification we discover that these awkward craftsmen, without knowing it, are teaching us a lesson — or it might be preferable to say that a lesson is being taught us through them. These craftsmen are able to make the connection between love for their trade and for a completely different task, whereas the courtiers are not capable of linking the love about which they talk so well with their simple role as spectators.

Nonetheless, little by little the courtiers become involved, even touched by the play within the play, and if one follows very closely what is there in the text we see that for a moment the situation is completely transformed. One of the central images of the play is a wall, which, at a given moment, vanishes. Its disappearance, to which Bottom draws our attention, is caused by an act of love. Shakespeare is showing us how love can pervade a situation and act as a transforming force.

The *Dream* touches lightly on the fundamental question of the transformations which may occur if certain things are better understood. It requires us to reflect on the nature of love. All the landscapes of love are thrown into relief, and we are given a particular social context through which the other situations can be measured. Through the subtlety of its language the play removes all kinds of barriers. It is therefore not a play which provokes resistance, or creates disturbance in the usual sense. Rival politicians could sit side by side at a performance of *A Midsum-mer Night's Dream* and each leave with the impression that the play fits his point of view perfectly. But if they give it a fine, sensitive attention they cannot fail to perceive a world just like their own, more and more riddled with contradictions and, like their own, waiting for that mysterious force, love, without which harmony will never return.

Clive Barnes (b. 1927)
REVIEW OF *A MIDSUMMER NIGHT'S DREAM*   *1970*

Clive Barnes's review credits the Peter Brook production of A Midsummer Night's Dream *as a landmark. Audiences in Stratford, London, New York, and elsewhere agreed. Brook (b. 1925) emphasized the dramatic spectacle — the sets, costumes, and action — in such a way as to reveal new depths of emotion. The playfulness of the jugglers, acrobats, and those on the trapezes emphasized the joy and youth of the main characters.*

Once in a while, once in a very rare while, a theatrical production arrives that is going to be talked about as long as there is a theater, a production that, for good or ill, is going to exert a major influence on the contemporary stage. Such a production is Peter Brook's staging of Shakespeare's *A Midsummer Night's Dream,* which the Royal Shakespeare Company introduced here tonight.

It is a magnificent production, the most important work yet of the world's most imaginative and inventive director. If Peter Brook had done nothing else but this "Dream" he would have deserved a place in theater history,

Brook has approached the play with a radiant innocence. He has treated the script as if it had just been written and sent to him through the mail. He has staged it with no reference to the past, no reverence for tradition.

He has stripped the play down, asked exactly what it is about. He has forgotten gossamer fairies, sequined eyelids, gauzy veils, and whole forests of Beerbohm-trees.

He sees the play for what it is — an allegory of sensual love, and a magic playground of lost innocence and hidden fears. Love in Shakespeare comes as suddenly as death, and when Shakespeare's people love they are all but consumed with sexual passion.

Brook's first concern is to enchant us — to reveal this magic playground. He has conceived the production as a box of theatrical miracles. It takes place in a pure-white setting. The stage is walled in on three sides and the floor is also white. Ladders lead up the walls and on the top are scaffolds and rostrums from which actors can look down on the playing area like spectators at a bullfight.

The fairy characters — Oberon, Titania, and Puck — are made into acrobats and jugglers. They swing in on trapezes, they amaze us with juggling tricks, Tarzan-like swings across the stage, all the sad deftness of clowns.

Shakespeare's quartet of mingled lovers, now mod kids humming love songs to loosely strummed guitars, are lost in the Venetian woods. The trees are vast metal coils thrown down from the walls on fishing rods, and moving in on unwary lovers like spiraling metallic tendrils. And in this wood of animal desire the noises are not the friendly warblings of fairyland, but the grunts and groans of some primeval jungle.

Sex and sexuality are vital in the play. Oberon and Titania, even when quarreling, kiss with hasty, hungry passion — no shining moon for them — and the lovers seem to be journeying through some inner landscape of their own desires toward maturity.

The sexual relationships — with the wittiest use of phallic symbolism the stage can have ever seen — is stressed between Titania and her Bottom. Yet the carnality of the piece is seen with affectionate tolerance rather than the bitterness the playwright shows in *Troilus and Cressida,* and this tolerance, even playfulness, suffuses the production.

Brook is a magician and he gives us new eyes. Here, for reasons admirably supported by the text, he has Theseus and Hippolyta (that previously rather dull royal couple whose wedding provides the framework for the play) played by the same actors as play Oberon and Titania. At once the play takes on a new and personal dimension. The fairies take on a new humanity, and these human princelings, once so uninteresting, are now endowed with a different mystery, and the gentle, almost sad note on which the play ends has a feeling of human comprehension and godlike compassion to it. It is most moving.

Two other characters take on dual assignments. Philostrate, that court master of ceremonies for Theseus, is also, naturally enough, Puck, and, rather more puzzlingly, Egeus, the angry father of Hermia, whose opposition to her marriage sets off the action, is also Peter Quince, one of the mechanicals. Presumably the purpose is to bring the play within the play more closely into the main structure, for just as Egeus initiates the real action, so Quince initiates the inner play. But it savors of a literary rather than dramatic device.

Puck is the key figure in this version. Looking like a more than usually perky Picasso clown, he bounces through the action with happy amiability, the model of toleration. John Kane plays him delightfully, performing his tricks with a true circus expertise and acting with unaffected delight.

The Theseus/Oberon and Hippolyta/Titania of Alan Howard and Sara Kestelman are special pleasures, and the mechanicals with the terrible tragedy of *Pyramus and Thisbe* are the best I have ever seen, with David Waller's virile Bottom particularly splendid.

But the star of this dream is Peter Brook himself, with his ideas, his theories, and above all his practices. Of course he is helped — first by the samite-white pleasure palace devised by his Los Angeles–based designer, Sally Jacobs, and the richly evocative music and sound score provided by Richard Peaslee. But Mr. Brook is the genius architect of our most substantial pleasure.

He makes it all so fresh and so much fun. After a riotously funny and bawdy courtship of Titania by Bottom, the two leave the stage to, of all wonderful things, Mendelssohn's Wedding March, and all hell breaks loose, with confetti, paper streamers, and Oberon himself flying in urbane mockery across the stage.

And Brook uses everything to hand — he is defiantly eclectic. It is as though he is challenging the world, by saying that there is no such thing as Shakespearean style. If it suits his purpose he will use a little kathakali, a pop song, sparklers borrowed from a toyshop, dramatic candles borrowed from Grotowski. It is all splendid grist to his splendid mill. Shakespeare can be fun, Shakespeare can be immediate, Shakespeare can most richly live.

HAMLET

Hamlet (1600–1601), Shakespeare's boldest, most profound play, is a landmark in the poet's work. It coincides with the new century and the uncertainties of the last years of the old regime, brought to an end by the death of Queen Elizabeth in 1603. Until the very moment of her death, the succession was in doubt, but at her death she indicated that her cousin James of Scotland would take the throne. The new age was in many ways more complicated, more ambiguous, and more democratic than the old. It was also more dangerous because it was more uncertain.

Hamlet returns to a Denmark and a court that he hardly recognizes, to a mother newly wed to his uncle and in many ways not the woman he remembers, and, finally, to a ghostly father who will not rest until the crimes against him are avenged. Like Marlowe's Faustus, Hamlet was a scholar at the University of Wittenberg, where he presumably had studied theology and therefore had a special knowledge of the world of the spirits. Perhaps he studied medicine and law as well. He gives evidence of knowing literature and having a taste for theater, and he is a ready hand with weapons when necessary.

Hamlet is also a melancholic. To the Elizabethan, *melancholic* did not mean depressed, although Hamlet dresses in black and still mourns for his father, even against the wishes of his uncle. The melancholic, rather, was introspective, thoughtful, perhaps world-weary, and possibly a touch sardonic. Above all things, he was an intellectual, a person of wide-ranging knowledge and intelligence, a reliable commentator with a probing mind.

Hamlet's broad intelligence and the penetrating introspection revealed in his soliloquies, such as his famous "To be, or not to be" meditation on suicide, make him a character with more psychological dimension, more "soul," than many people we know in life. In this sense the play is thoroughly modern; it satisfies our modern need to know the interior lives of characters who engage us onstage. Hamlet's range of feeling, his range of felt and expressed emotion, is impressive to any audience.

Hamlet is a revenge tragedy, a type of play that was especially appealing to the Elizabethans. Thomas Kyd's *The Spanish Tragedy* and John Marston's *Antonio's Revenge* are two examples of successful Elizabethan revenge tragedies. Shakespeare had written an earlier play that could be termed a revenge tragedy, *Titus Andronicus,* in 1594. Below are some characteristics of the revenge tragedy.

The revenge of a relative's murder or rape

The revenge of a father by a son or vice versa

The appearance of a ghost

The hesitancy or delay of the hero

Tricks or devices to achieve revenge

The use of real or pretended insanity

Suicide

Political intrigue in a court

An able, scheming villain who is a ruler above the law

Philosophical soliloquies

Sensational use of horror (murder and gore onstage)

All these elements are present in *Hamlet*. But the play has other important qualities as well. The minor characters are developed in unexpected ways. Ophelia, the innocent, loving woman, becomes a touching figure in her own right. Unable to understand the nature of evil in the Danish court and driven to insanity by Hamlet's rejection of her and by her father's murder, she permits herself to sink to a watery death in a stream. Audiences are moved by her songs, her insane ramblings, and her devotion to her father as well as to Hamlet.

Characters such as Gertrude, Hamlet's mother, reveal a richness of psychology that sometimes startles us. Polonius, Ophelia's father, is virtually a stock character — the old, foolish philosopher — but he takes on special significance when he urges Ophelia to spy for him and when he ultimately dies at the hand of Hamlet. As Hamlet says, it was an unnecessary death for a "wretched, rash, intruding fool." But Polonius's son, Laertes, loved his father, and when Laertes returns grief-stricken, he does not hesitate a moment to get his revenge.

Hamlet's hesitancy is linked with his reputation as a melancholic. Because he thinks things through so deeply, he does not act instantly, as does Laertes. Even when the ghost reveals himself as his father and tells him that he has been murdered and must be avenged, Hamlet fears that the apparition might be a dangerous fakery of the devil to lure him to murder.

But Hamlet shows that he can act swiftly — indeed, rashly. His killing of Polonius is a rash act. He thinks the man behind the tapestry in his mother's bedroom is his uncle, since no other man but her husband has any right to be there. When Hamlet is sent to England with Rosencrantz and Guildenstern, he quickly senses a plot, undoes it, leaps aboard a pirate ship, and negotiates his way home with alacrity. This is not the work of a man who cannot act. In the graveyard scene he acts just as impulsively as Laertes would when he leaps into Ophelia's grave.

Hamlet's talents exhibited in his welcoming of the players in act II show him to be an experienced theatergoer, one with some skills onstage. He is also an expert writer; his additions to *The Murder of Gonzago* convert that imaginary play into a "mousetrap" baited to catch the murderer of his father. In early Renaissance paintings the mousetrap is a symbol for Jesus Christ, who catches the devil. The allusion would not have been lost on the Elizabethan audience, who would have seen Hamlet's psychological approach as being quite reasonable.

Emotions are of great importance to Hamlet. He feels deeply and he watches others to see what their feelings are. He knows that their demeanor may not reveal them as they are, so he must learn to be a careful student of behavior. As he tells his mother, "I know not 'seems.'" What seems is only what is apparent; his procedure is always to penetrate the surfaces of things to know their reality, which is why he uses drama as an instrument to penetrate psychological surfaces.

Hamlet in
Performance

Richard Burbage played Hamlet in its original production, which was probably in 1601 but may have been in 1600. He continued playing the part into advanced age. *Hamlet* was staged on an English ship off the coast of Africa in 1607. The first American production was in 1759. When one thinks of productions of the play, one thinks of the great actors who played the role. Their names read like a *Who's Who* of acting: David Garrick (1717–1779), Edmund Kean (1789–1833), William Charles Macready (1793–1873), and Sir Henry Irving (1838–1905) were all identified with the role.

In the twentieth century the two most dominating Hamlets were John Gielgud and Laurence Olivier, who both acted for the Old Vic Theatre. To interpret the part, Olivier studied psychoanalyst Ernest Jones's essay on Hamlet's Oedipus complex. Jones was a disciple of Freud, who discussed Hamlet in his *Interpretation of Dreams* (see Freud's commentary on p. 411). Paul Scofield, in Peter Brook's 1955 production, found the part so challenging that he said playing it "feels like trespassing." Christopher Plummer, Derek Jacobi, and Jonathan Pryce have played the part to acclaim from the 1950s to recent times. Richard Burton also played Hamlet in New York in 1964. Michael Pennington's version for the Royal Shakespeare Company's 1980 production (see photos on p. 384) was well received by both critics and audiences. Pennington felt that the part tested not only one's skill but also one's character. He said, "When things go well you could do three performances a day and still be the last to leave the party, and at other times the part shakes you like a rat."

The major productions in the 1980s alone were astonishingly numerous: Christopher Walken for the American Shakespeare Festival in Stratford, Connecticut (1982); Roger Rees for the Royal Shakespeare Company in Stratford, England (1984); Kevin Kline for the New York Shakespeare Festival (1986); Ingmar Bergman's acclaimed production in Swedish (1988) in Sweden and New York; Daniel Day-Lewis for the National Theatre in London (1989); Austin Pendleton for the Riverside Shakespeare Company in New York (1989).

Franco Zeffirelli cast Mel Gibson in his 1990 film, which presents a credible Hamlet capable of deep emotional outburst. The setting of the film is lavish, and the interaction between Hamlet and Gertrude has a special psychological valence. *Hamlet* had a banner year in 1995 when Liam Neeson played the Danish prince in London and New York to considerable acclaim. That production was marked by a careful deemphasis of the great soliloquies. Ralph Fiennes, in the wake of a film success in *Schindler's List,* played in Edwardian clothes on Broadway, using madness as "a way of acting out." Keanu Reeves, another film actor, performed the part at the Manitoba Theater Center in Winnipeg, Canada. One critic said of Reeves's performance, "His hairstyle changed with his moods." Robert Wilson, known for massive semioperatic productions, played entirely alone, in a production premiered in Houston called *Hamlet: A Monologue.* On his deathbed Hamlet relives his story in flashbacks; he provides critical speeches of other characters himself. Among his efforts at Shakespeare, Kenneth Branagh took the title role in a lavish production of *Hamlet* in 1996. His richly produced Shakespeare films continue to be box office and critical successes. There is no end in sight for creative interpretations of this great play.

Hamlet has been the dream role not only of great actors but of great actresses as well. Sarah Bernhardt played Hamlet in the late nineteenth century, and Eva Le Gallienne, Siobhan McKenna, and Judith Anderson took on the part in the twentieth century. *Hamlet* has also given rise to numerous spin-offs, the best of which is Tom Stoppard's *Rosencrantz and Guildenstern Are Dead* (1967). Heiner Müller's *Hamlet-machine* (1977) is a respected avant-garde version of the play. Lee Blessing's *Fortinbras* (1991) is also an innovative retelling of the play from the point of view of a minor character — except that this character becomes the king. Blessing's success suggests that *Hamlet* is rich enough and inspiring enough to generate numerous further redactions and interpretations. Michael Almereyda's 2000 film version of *Hamlet* starred Ethan Hawke as Hamlet, Sam Shepard as the Ghost, Kyle MacLachlan as Claudius, and Bill Murray as Polonius. It is the most recent of many filmed versions of the play.

William Shakespeare (1564–1616)
HAMLET, PRINCE OF DENMARK   *c. 1600*

[Dramatis Personae

CLAUDIUS, *King of Denmark*
HAMLET, *son to the late King Hamlet, and nephew to the present King*
POLONIUS, *Lord Chamberlain*
HORATIO, *friend to Hamlet*
LAERTES, *son to Polonius*
VOLTIMAND,
CORNELIUS,
ROSENCRANTZ,   } *courtiers*
GUILDENSTERN,
OSRIC,
GENTLEMAN,
PRIEST, OR DOCTOR OF DIVINITY
MARCELLUS,   } *officers*
BERNARDO,
FRANCISCO, *a solider*
REYNALDO, *servant to Polonius*
PLAYERS
TWO CLOWNS, *grave-diggers*
FORTINBRAS, *Prince of Norway*
CAPTAIN
ENGLISH AMBASSADORS

GERTRUDE, *Queen of Denmark, mother to Hamlet*
OPHELIA, *daughter to Polonius*

LORDS, LADIES, OFFICERS, SOLDIERS, SAILORS,
    MESSENGERS, AND OTHER ATTENDANTS
GHOST *of Hamlet's father*

Scene: *Denmark.*]

{*ACT I • Scene 1*}°

(*Enter Bernardo and Francisco, two sentinels,* [*meeting*].)

BERNARDO: Who's there?
FRANCISCO: Nay, answer me.° Stand and unfold
    yourself.
BERNARDO: Long live the King!
FRANCISCO: Bernardo?
BERNARDO: He.   5
FRANCISCO: You come most carefully upon your hour.
BERNARDO: 'Tis now struck twelve. Get thee to bed,
    Francisco.
FRANCISCO: For this relief much thanks. 'Tis bitter
    cold,
    And I am sick at heart.
BERNARDO: Have you had quiet guard?
FRANCISCO: Not a mouse stirring.   10
BERNARDO: Well, good night.
    If you do meet Horatio and Marcellus,
    The rivals° of my watch, bid them make haste.

(*Enter Horatio and Marcellus.*)

Note: The text of *Hamlet* has come down to us in different versions — such as the first quarto, the second quarto, and the first Folio. The copy of the text used here is largely drawn from the second quarto. Passages enclosed in square brackets are taken from one of the other versions, in most cases the first Folio.

I, I. Location: Elsinore castle. A guard platform.   **2. me:** Francisco emphasizes that *he* is the sentry currently on watch.
13. rivals: Partners.

FRANCISCO: I think I hear them. Stand, ho! Who is there?
HORATIO: Friends to this ground.
15 MARCELLUS: And liegemen to the Dane.°
FRANCISCO: Give you° good night.
MARCELLUS: O, farewell, honest soldier.
    Who hath relieved you?
FRANCISCO: Bernardo hath my place.
    Give you good night.   (*Exit Francisco.*)
MARCELLUS: Holla, Bernardo!
BERNARDO: Say,
    What, is Horatio there?
HORATIO: A piece of him.
BERNARDO: Welcome, Horatio. Welcome, good
20   Marcellus.
HORATIO: What, has this thing appear'd again tonight?
BERNARDO: I have seen nothing.
MARCELLUS: Horatio says 'tis but our fantasy,
    And will not let belief take hold of him
25 Touching this dreaded sight, twice seen of us.
    Therefore I have entreated him along
    With us to watch the minutes of this night,
    That if again this apparition come
    He may approve° our eyes and speak to it.
HORATIO: Tush, tush, 'twill not appear.
30 BERNARDO: Sit down awhile,
    And let us once again assail your ears,
    That are so fortified against our story,
    What we have two nights seen.
HORATIO: Well, sit we down,
    And let us hear Bernardo speak of this.
35 BERNARDO: Last night of all,
    When yond same star that's westward from the pole°
    Had made his° course t' illume that part of heaven
    Where now it burns, Marcellus and myself,
    The bell then beating one —

(*Enter Ghost.*)

MARCELLUS: Peace, break thee off! Look where it
40   comes again!
BERNARDO: In the same figure, like the King that's dead.
MARCELLUS: Thou art a scholar.° Speak to it, Horatio.
BERNARDO: Looks 'a° not like the King? Mark it,
    Horatio.
HORATIO: Most like. It harrows me with fear and
    wonder.
BERNARDO: It would be spoke to.
45 MARCELLUS: Speak to it,° Horatio.
HORATIO: What art thou that usurp'st this time of
    night,
    Together with that fair and warlike form
    In which the majesty of buried Denmark°
    Did sometimes° march? By heaven I charge thee
    speak!

MARCELLUS: It is offended.
BERNARDO: See, it stalks away.   50
HORATIO: Stay! Speak, speak. I charge thee, speak.
                              (*Exit Ghost.*)
MARCELLUS: 'Tis gone, and will not answer.
BERNARDO: How now, Horatio? You tremble and look
    pale.
    Is not this something more than fantasy?
    What think you on 't?   55
HORATIO: Before my God, I might not this believe
    Without the sensible° and true avouch
    Of mine own eyes.
MARCELLUS: Is it not like the King?
HORATIO: As thou art to thyself.
    Such was the very armor he had on   60
    When he the ambitious Norway° combated.
    So frown'd he once when, in an angry parle,°
    He smote the sledded° Polacks° on the ice.
    'Tis strange.
MARCELLUS: Thus twice before, and jump° at this dead
    hour,   65
    With martial stalk hath he gone by our watch.
HORATIO: In what particular thought to work I know
    not,
    But, in the gross and scope° of mine opinion,
    This bodes some strange eruption to our state.
MARCELLUS: Good now,° sit down, and tell me, he that
    knows,   70
    Why this same strict and most observant watch
    So nightly toils° the subject° of the land,
    And why such daily cast° of brazen cannon,
    And foreign mart° for implements of war,
    Why such impress° of shipwrights, whose sore task 75
    Does not divide the Sunday from the week.
    What might be toward,° that this sweaty haste
    Doth make the night joint-laborer with the day?
    Who is 't that can inform me?
HORATIO: That can I,
    At least, the whisper goes so. Our last king,   80
    Whose image even but now appear'd to us,
    Was, as you know, by Fortinbras of Norway,
    Thereto prick'd on° by a most emulate° pride,
    Dar'd to the combat; in which our valiant
    Hamlet —
    For so this side of our known world esteem'd
    him —   85
    Did slay this Fortinbras; who, by a seal'd compact,
    Well ratified by law and heraldry,
    Did forfeit, with his life, all those his lands
    Which he stood seiz'd° of, to the conqueror;

---

15. liegemen to the Dane: Men sworn to serve the Danish king.
16. Give you: God give you. **29. approve:** Corroborate.
36. pole: Polestar. **37. his:** Its. **42. scholar:** One learned in
Latin and able to address spirits. **43. 'a:** He. **45. It . . . it:** A
ghost could not speak until spoken to. **48. buried Denmark:**
The buried king of Denmark. **49. sometimes:** Formerly.

57. sensible: Confirmed by the senses. **61. Norway:** King of
Norway. **62. parle:** Parley. **63. sledded:** Traveling on sleds.
Polacks: Poles. **65. jump:** Exactly. **68. gross and scope:**
General view. **70. Good now:** An expression denoting entreaty or expostulation. **72. toils:** Causes to toil. **subject:**
Subjects. **73. cast:** Casting. **74. mart:** Buying and selling.
75. impress: Impressment, conscription. **77. toward:** In
preparation. **83. prick'd on:** Incited. **emulate:** Ambitious.
89. seiz'd: Possessed.

90   Against the° which a moi'ty competent°
      Was gaged° by our king, which had return'd
      To the inheritance of Fortinbras
      Had he been vanquisher, as, by the same comart°
      And carriage° of the article design'd,
95   His fell to Hamlet. Now, sir, young Fortinbras,
      Of unimproved° mettle hot and full,
      Hath in the skirts° of Norway here and there
      Shark'd up° a list of lawless resolutes°
      For food and diet° to some enterprise
100   That hath a stomach° in 't, which is no other —
      As it doth well appear unto our state —
      But to recover of us, by strong hand
      And terms compulsatory, those foresaid lands
      So by his father lost. And this, I take it,
105   Is the main motive of our preparations,
      The source of this our watch, and the chief head°
      Of this post-haste and romage° in the land.
   BERNARDO: I think it be no other but e'en so.
      Well may it sort° that this portentous figure
110   Comes armed through our watch so like the King
      That was and is the question of these wars.
   HORATIO: A mote° it is to trouble the mind's eye.
      In the most high and palmy° state of Rome,
      A little ere the mightiest Julius fell,
115   The graves stood tenantless and the sheeted° dead
      Did squeak and gibber in the Roman streets;
      As° stars with trains of fire and dews of blood,
      Disasters° in the sun; and the moist star°
      Upon whose influence Neptune's° empire stands°
120   Was sick almost to doomsday° with eclipse.
      And even the like precurse° of fear'd events,
      As harbingers° preceding still° the fates
      And prologue to the omen° coming on,
      Have heaven and earth together demonstrated
125   Unto our climatures° and countrymen.

   (Enter Ghost.)

      But soft, behold! Lo where it comes again!
      I'll cross° it, though it blast me. Stay, illusion!
      If thou hast any sound, or use of voice,

      Speak to me!   (It spreads his arms.)
      If there be any good thing to be done   130
      That may to thee do ease and grace to me,
      Speak to me!
      If thou art privy to thy country's fate,
      Which, happily,° foreknowing may avoid,
      O, speak!   135
      Or if thou hast uphoarded in thy life
      Extorted treasure in the womb of earth,
      For which, they say, you spirits oft walk in death,
                                         (The cock crows.)
      Speak of it. Stay, and speak! Stop it, Marcellus.
   MARCELLUS: Shall I strike at it with my partisan?°   140
   HORATIO: Do, if it will not stand.   [They strike at it.]
   BERNARDO: 'Tis here!
   HORATIO: 'Tis here!
   MARCELLUS: 'Tis gone.   [Exit Ghost.]
      We do it wrong, being so majestical,
      To offer it the show of violence;
      For it is, as the air, invulnerable,   145
      And our vain blows malicious mockery.
   BERNARDO: It was about to speak when the cock
         crew.
   HORATIO: And then it started like a guilty thing
      Upon a fearful summons. I have heard,
      The cock, that is the trumpet to the morn,   150
      Doth with his lofty and shrill-sounding throat
      Awake the god of day, and, at his warning,
      Whether in sea or fire, in earth or air,
      Th' extravagant and erring° spirit hies
      To his confine; and of the truth herein   155
      This present object made probation.°
   MARCELLUS: It faded on the crowing of the cock.
      Some say that ever 'gainst° that season comes
      Wherein our Savior's birth is celebrated,
      The bird of dawning singeth all night long,   160
      And then, they say, no spirit dare stir abroad;
      The nights are wholesome, then no planets
         strike,°
      No fairy takes,° nor witch hath power to charm,
      So hallowed and so gracious° is that time.
   HORATIO: So have I heard and do in part believe it. 165
      But, look, the morn, in russet mantle clad,
      Walks o'er the dew of yon high eastward hill.
      Break we our watch up, and by my advice
      Let us impart what we have seen tonight
      Unto young Hamlet; for, upon my life,   170
      This spirit, dumb to us, will speak to him.
      Do you consent we shall acquaint him with it,
      As needful in our loves, fitting our duty?
   MARCELLUS: Let's do 't, I pray, and I this morning know
      Where we shall find him most conveniently.   175
                                         (Exeunt.)°

90. **Against the:** In return for. . . . **moi'ty competent:** Sufficient portion. **91. gaged:** Engaged, pledged. **93. comart:**
Joint bargain (?). **94. carriage:** Import, bearing. **96. unim-
proved:** Not turned to account (?) or untested (?). **97. skirts:**
Outlying regions, outskirts. **98. Shark'd up:** Got together in
haphazard fashion. **resolutes:** Desperadoes. **99. food and
diet:** No pay but their keep. **100. stomach:** Relish of danger.
106. head: Source. **107. romage:** Bustle, commotion.
109. sort: Suit. **112. mote:** Speck of dust. **113. palmy:**
Flourishing. **115. sheeted:** Shrouded. **117. As:** This abrupt
transition suggests that matter is possibly omitted between lines
116 and 117. **118. Disasters:** Unfavorable signs of aspects.
moist star: Moon, governing tides. **119. Neptune:** God of the
sea. **stands:** Depends. **120. sick . . . doomsday:** See Matt.
24:29 and Rev. 6:12. **121. precurse:** Heralding, foreshadowing. **122. harbingers:** Forerunners. **still:** Continually.
123. omen: Calamitous event. **125. climatures:** Regions.
127. cross: Meet, face directly.

134. happily: Haply, perchance. **140. partisan:** Long-handled
spear. **154. extravagant and erring:** Wandering. (The words
have similar meaning.) **156. probation:** Proof. **158. 'gainst:**
Just before. **162. strike:** Exert evil influence. **163. takes:**
Bewitches. **164. gracious:** Full of goodness. **175. [S.D.]**
Exeunt: Latin for "they go out."

{Scene II}°

(*Flourish. Enter Claudius, King of Denmark, Gertrude the Queen, Councilors, Polonius and his son Laertes, Hamlet, cum aliis°* [*including Voltimand and Cornelius*].)

KING: Though yet of Hamlet our dear brother's death
 The memory be green, and that it us befitted
 To bear our hearts in grief and our whole kingdom
 To be contracted in one brow of woe,
5 Yet so far hath discretion fought with nature
 That we with wisest sorrow think on him,
 Together with remembrance of ourselves.
 Therefore our sometime sister, now our queen,
 Th' imperial jointress° to this warlike state,
10 Have we, as 'twere with a defeated joy —
 With an auspicious and a dropping eye,
 With mirth in funeral and with dirge in marriage,
 In equal scale weighing delight and dole —
 Taken to wife. Nor have we herein barr'd
15 Your better wisdoms, which have freely gone
 With this affair along. For all, our thanks.
 Now follows that you know° young Fortinbras,
 Holding a weak supposal° of our worth,
 Or thinking by our late dear brother's death
20 Our state to be disjoint and out of frame,
 Colleagued with° this dream of his advantage,°
 He hath not fail'd to pester us with message
 Importing° the surrender of those lands
 Lost by his father, with all bands° of law,
25 To our most valiant brother. So much for him.
 Now for ourself and for this time of meeting.
 Thus much the business is: we have here writ
 To Norway, uncle of young Fortinbras —
 Who, impotent and bed-rid, scarcely hears
30 Of this his nephew's purpose — to suppress
 His° further gait° herein, in that the levies,
 The lists, and full proportions are all made
 Out of his subject;° and we here dispatch
 You, good Cornelius, and you, Voltimand,
35 For bearers of this greeting to old Norway,
 Giving to you no further personal power
 To business with the King, more than the scope
 Of these delated° articles allow. [*Gives a paper.*]
 Farewell, and let your haste commend your duty.
CORNELIUS, VOLTIMAND: In that, and all things, will
40 we show our duty.
KING: We doubt it nothing. Heartily farewell.

     [*Exit Voltimand and Cornelius.*]

And now, Laertes, what's the news with you?
 You told us of some suit; what is 't, Laertes?
 You cannot speak of reason to the Dane°
 And lose your voice.° What wouldst thou beg,
  Laertes,   45
 That shall not be my offer, not thy asking?
 The head is not more native° to the heart,
 The hand more instrumental° to the mouth,
 Than is the throne of Denmark to thy father.
 What wouldst thou have, Laertes?
LAERTES: My dread lord, 50
 Your leave and favor to return to France,
 From whence though willingly I came to Denmark
 To show my duty in your coronation,
 Yet now I must confess, that duty done,
 My thoughts and wishes bend again toward France 55
 And bow them to your gracious leave and pardon.°
KING: Have you your father's leave? What says
  Polonius?
POLONIUS: H'ath, my lord, wrung from me my slow
  leave
 By laborsome petition, and at last
 Upon his will I seal'd my hard° consent.   60
 I do beseech you, give him leave to go.
KING: Take thy fair hour, Laertes. Time be thine,
 And thy best graces spend it at thy will!
 But now, my cousin° Hamlet, and my son —
HAMLET: A little more than kin, and less than kind.° 65
KING: How is it that the clouds still hang on you?
HAMLET: Not so, my lord. I am too much in the sun.°
QUEEN: Good Hamlet, cast thy nighted color off,
 And let thine eye look like a friend on Denmark.
 Do not forever with thy veiled° lids   70
 Seek for thy noble father in the dust.
 Thou know'st 'tis common,° all that lives must die,
 Passing through nature to eternity.
HAMLET: Ay, madam, it is common.
QUEEN: If it be,
 Why seems it so particular with thee?   75
HAMLET: Seems, madam! Nay, it is. I know not "seems."
 'Tis not alone my inky cloak, good mother,
 Nor customary suits of solemn black,
 Nor windy suspiration of forc'd breath,
 No, nor the fruitful° river in the eye,   80
 Nor the dejected havior of the visage,

I, II. **Location:** The castle. [S.D.] *cum aliis*: With others. **9. jointress:** Woman possessed of a joint tenancy of an estate. **17. know:** Be informed (that). **18. weak supposal:** Low estimate. **21. Colleagued with:** Joined to, allied with. **dream . . . advantage:** Illusory hope of success. **23. Importing:** Pertaining to. **24. bands:** Contracts. **31. His:** Fortinbras's. **gait:** Proceeding. **31–33. in that . . . subject:** Since the levying of troops and supplies is drawn entirely from the King of Norway's own subjects. **38. delated:** Detailed. (Variant of *dilated*.)

44. the Dane: The Danish king. **45. lose your voice:** Waste your speech. **47. native:** Closely connected, related. **48. instrumental:** Serviceable. **56. leave and pardon:** Permission to depart. **60. hard:** Reluctant. **64. cousin:** Any kin not of the immediate family. **65. A little . . . kind:** Closer than an ordinary nephew (since I am stepson), and yet more separated in natural feeling (with pun on *kind*, meaning affectionate and natural, lawful). This line is often read as an aside, but it need not be. **67. sun:** The sunshine of the King's royal favor (with pun on *son*). **70. veiled:** Downcast. **72. common:** Of universal occurrence. (But Hamlet plays on the sense of *vulgar* in line 74.) **80. fruitful:** Abundant.

Together with all forms, moods, shapes of grief,
That can denote me truly. These indeed seem,
For they are actions that a man might play.
85 But I have that within which passes show;
These but the trappings and the suits of woe.
KING: 'Tis sweet and commendable in your nature,
    Hamlet,
To give these mourning duties to your father.
But you must know your father lost a father,
90 That father lost, lost his, and the survivor bound
In filial obligation for some term
To do obsequious° sorrow. But to persever°
In obstinate condolement° is a course
Of impious stubbornness. 'Tis unmanly grief.
95 It shows a will most incorrect to heaven,
A heart unfortified, a mind impatient,
An understanding simple and unschool'd.
For what we know must be and is as common
As any the most vulgar thing to sense,°
100 Why should we in our peevish opposition
Take it to heart? Fie, 'tis a fault to heaven,
A fault against the dead, a fault to nature,
To reason most absurd, whose common theme
Is death of fathers, and who still hath cried,
105 From the first corse° till he that died today,
"This must be so." We pray you, throw to earth
This unprevailing° woe, and think of us
As of a father; for let the world take note,
You are the most immediate° to our throne,
110 And with no less nobility of love
Than that which dearest father bears his son
Do I impart toward you. For your intent
In going back to school in Wittenberg,°
It is most retrograde° to our desire,
115 And we beseech you, bend you° to remain
Here in the cheer and comfort of our eye,
Our chiefest courtier, cousin, and our son.
QUEEN: Let not thy mother lose her prayers, Hamlet.
I pray thee stay with us, go not to Wittenberg.
120 HAMLET: I shall in all my best obey you, madam.
KING: Why, 'tis a loving and a fair reply.
Be as ourself in Denmark. Madam, come.
This gentle and unforc'd accord of Hamlet
Sits smiling to my heart, in grace whereof
125 No jocund° health that Denmark drinks today
But the great cannon to the clouds shall tell,
And the King's rouse° the heaven shall bruit again,°
Respeaking earthly thunder.° Come away.

(*Flourish. Exeunt all but Hamlet.*)

HAMLET: O, that this too too sullied° flesh would melt,   130
Thaw, and resolve itself into a dew!
Or that the Everlasting had not fix'd
His canon° 'gainst self-slaughter! O God, God,
How weary, stale, flat, and unprofitable
Seem to me all the uses of this world!
Fie on 't, ah, fie! 'Tis an unweeded garden   135
That grows to seed. Things rank and gross in
    nature
Possess it merely.° That it should come to this!
But two months dead — nay, not so much, not two.
So excellent a king, that was to° this
Hyperion° to a satyr; so loving to my mother   140
That he might not beteem° the winds of heaven
Visit her face too roughly. Heaven and earth,
Must I remember? Why, she would hang on him
As if increase of appetite had grown
By what it fed on, and yet, within a month —   145
Let me not think on 't. Frailty, thy name is
    woman! —
A little month, or ere those shoes were old
With which she followed my poor father's body,
Like Niobe,° all tears, why she, even she —
O God, a beast, that wants discourse of reason,°   150
Would have mourn'd longer — married with my
    uncle,
My father's brother, but no more like my father
Than I to Hercules. Within a month,
Ere yet the salt of most unrighteous tears
Had left the flushing in her galled° eyes,   155
She married. O, most wicked speed, to post
With such dexterity to incestuous° sheets!
It is not nor it cannot come to good.
But break, my heart, for I must hold my tongue.

(*Enter Horatio, Marcellus, and Bernardo.*)

HORATIO: Hail to your lordship!
HAMLET: I am glad to see you well.   160
    Horatio! — or I do forget myself.
HORATIO: The same, my lord, and your poor servant
    ever.
HAMLET: Sir, my good friend; I'll change° that name
    with you.
    And what make° you from Wittenberg, Horatio?
    Marcellus?   165

92. obsequious: Suited to obsequies or funerals. persever: Persevere. 93. condolement: Sorrowing. 99. As . . . sense: As the most ordinary experience. 105. corse: Corpse. 107. unprevailing: Unavailing. 109. most immediate: Next in succession. 113. Wittenberg: Famous German university founded in 1502. 114. retrograde: Contrary. 115. bend you: Incline yourself. 125. jocund: Merry. 127. rouse: Draft of liquor. bruit again: Loudly echo. 128. thunder: Of trumpet and kettledrum sounded when the King drinks, see I, iv, 8–12.

129. sullied: Defiled. (The early quartos read *sallied*, the Folio *solid*.) 132. canon: Law. 137. merely: Completely. 139. to: In comparison to. 140. Hyperion: Titan sun-god, father of Helios. 141. beteem: Allow. 149. Niobe: Tantalus's daughter, Queen of Thebes, who boasted that she had more sons and daughters than Leto; for this, Apollo and Artemis, children of Leto, slew her fourteen children. She was turned by Zeus into a stone that continually dropped tears. 150. wants . . . reason: Lacks the faculty of reason. 155. galled: Irritated, inflamed. 157. incestuous: In Shakespeare's day, the marriage of a man like Claudius to his deceased brother's wife was considered incestuous. 163. change: Exchange (i.e., the name of friend). 164. make: Do.

MARCELLUS: My good lord.

HAMLET: I am very glad to see you. [*To Bernardo.*]
    Good even, sir. —
    But what, in faith, make you from Wittenberg?

HORATIO: A truant disposition, good my lord.

170 HAMLET: I would not hear your enemy say so,
    Nor shall you do my ear that violence
    To make it truster of your own report
    Against yourself. I know you are no truant.
    But what is your affair in Elsinore?
175   We'll teach you to drink deep ere you depart.

HORATIO: My lord, I came to see your father's
    funeral.

HAMLET: I prithee do not mock me, fellow student;
    I think it was to see my mother's wedding.

HORATIO: Indeed, my lord, it followed hard° upon.

HAMLET: Thrift, thrift, Horatio! The funeral bak'd
180   meats
    Did coldly furnish forth the marriage tables.
    Would I had met my dearest° foe in heaven
    Or° ever I had seen that day, Horatio!
    My father! — Methinks I see my father.

HORATIO: Where, my lord?

185 HAMLET: In my mind's eye, Horatio.

HORATIO: I saw him once. 'A° was a goodly king.

HAMLET: 'A was a man, take him for all in all,
    I shall not look upon his like again.

HORATIO: My lord, I think I saw him yesternight.

190 HAMLET: Saw? Who?

HORATIO: My lord, the King your father.

HAMLET: The King my father?

HORATIO: Season your admiration° for a while
    With an attent° ear, till I may deliver,
    Upon the witness of these gentlemen,
    This marvel to you.

195 HAMLET: For God's love, let me hear!

HORATIO: Two nights together had these gentlemen,
    Marcellus and Bernardo, on their watch,
    In the dead waste and middle of the night,
    Been thus encount'red. A figure like your father,
200   Armed at point° exactly, cap-a-pe,°
    Appears before them, and with solemn march
    Goes slow and stately by them. Thrice he walk'd
    By their oppress'd and fear-surprised eyes
    Within his truncheon's° length, whilst they,
        distill'd
205   Almost to jelly with the act° of fear,
    Stand dumb and speak not to him. This to me
    In dreadful secrecy impart they did,
    And I with them the third night kept the watch,
    Where, as they had delivered, both in time,
210   Form of the thing, each word made true and good,

    The apparition comes. I knew your father;
    These hands are not more like.

HAMLET: But where was this?

MARCELLUS: My lord, upon the platform where we
    watch.

HAMLET: Did you not speak to it?

HORATIO: My lord, I did,
    But answer made it none. Yet once methought   215
    It lifted up it° head and did address
    Itself to motion, like as it would speak;
    But even then the morning cock crew loud,
    And at the sound it shrunk in haste away,
    And vanish'd from our sight.

HAMLET: 'Tis very strange.   220

HORATIO: As I do live, my honor'd lord, 'tis true,
    And we did think it writ down in our duty
    To let you know of it.

HAMLET: Indeed, indeed, sirs. But this troubles me.
    Hold you the watch tonight?

ALL: We do, my lord.   225

HAMLET: Arm'd, say you?

ALL: Arm'd, my lord.

HAMLET: From top to toe?

ALL: My lord, from head to foot.

HAMLET: Then saw you not his face?

HORATIO: O, yes, my lord. He wore his beaver° up.   230

HAMLET: What, looked he frowningly?

HORATIO: A countenance more
    In sorrow than in anger.

HAMLET: Pale or red?

HORATIO: Nay, very pale.

HAMLET: And fix'd his eyes upon you?

HORATIO: Most constantly.

HAMLET: I would I had been there.

HORATIO: It would have much amaz'd you.   235

HAMLET: Very like, very like. Stay'd it long?

HORATIO: While one with moderate haste might tell° a
    hundred.

MARCELLUS, BERNARDO: Longer, longer.

HORATIO: Not when I saw 't.

HAMLET: His beard was grizzl'd, — no?

HORATIO: It was, as I have seen it in his life,   240
    A sable silver'd.°

HAMLET: I will watch tonight.
    Perchance 'twill walk again.

HORATIO: I warr'nt it will.

HAMLET: If it assume my noble father's person,
    I'll speak to it, though hell itself should gape
    And bid me hold my peace. I pray you all,   245
    If you have hitherto conceal'd this sight,
    Let it be tenable° in your silence still,
    And whatsomever else shall hap tonight,
    Give it an understanding, but no tongue.
    I will requite your loves. So, fare you well.   250

---

179. hard: Close.   **182. dearest:** Direst.   **183. Or:** Ere, before.
186. 'A: He.   **192. Season your admiration:** Restrain your
astonishment.   **193. attent:** Attentive.   **200. at point:** Completely.   **cap-a-pe:** From head to foot.   **204. truncheon:** Officer's staff.   **205. act:** Action, operation.

216. it: Its.   **230. beaver:** Visor on the helmet.   **237. tell:**
Count.   **241. sable silver'd:** Black mixed with white.
247. tenable: Held tightly.

Upon the platform, 'twixt eleven and twelve,
I'll visit you.
ALL: Our duty to your honor.
HAMLET: Your loves, as mine to you. Farewell.
                    (*Exeunt [all but Hamlet]*.)
My father's spirit in arms! All is not well.
I doubt° some foul play. Would the night were
255   come!
Till then sit still, my soul. Foul deeds will rise,
Though all the earth o'erwhelm them, to men's eyes.
                                    (*Exit*.)

{*Scene III*}°

(*Enter Laertes and Ophelia, his sister.*)

LAERTES: My necessaries are embark'd. Farewell.
    And, sister, as the winds give benefit
    And convoy is assistant,° do not sleep
    But let me hear from you.
OPHELIA: Do you doubt that?
5 LAERTES: For Hamlet, and the trifling of his favor,
    Hold it a fashion and a toy in blood,°
    A violet in the youth of primy° nature,
    Forward,° not permanent, sweet, not lasting,
    The perfume and suppliance° of a minute —
    No more.
OPHELIA: No more but so?
10 LAERTES: Think it no more.
    For nature crescent° does not grow alone
    In thews° and bulk, but, as this temple° waxes,
    The inward service of the mind and soul
    Grows wide withal.° Perhaps he loves you now,
15 And now no soil° nor cautel° doth besmirch
    The virtue of his will;° but you must fear,
    His greatness weigh'd,° his will is not his own.
    [For he himself is subject to his birth.]
    He may not, as unvalued persons do,
20 Carve° for himself; for on his choice depends
    The safety and health of this whole state,
    And therefore must his choice be circumscrib'd
    Unto the voice and yielding° of that body
    Whereof he is the head. Then if he says he loves
        you,
25 It fits your wisdom so far to believe it
    As he in his particular act and place
    May give his saying deed,° which is no further

Than the main voice of Denmark goes withal.
Then weigh what loss your honor may sustain
If with too credent° ear you list° his songs,   30
Or lose your heart, or your chaste treasure open
To his unmaster'd importunity.
Fear it, Ophelia, fear it, my dear sister,
And keep you in the rear of your affection,
Out of the shot° and danger of desire.   35
The chariest° maid is prodigal enough
If she unmask her beauty to the moon.
Virtue itself scapes not calumnious strokes.
The canker galls° the infants of the spring
Too oft before their buttons° be disclos'd,°   40
And in the morn and liquid dew° of youth
Contagious blastments° are most imminent.
Be wary then; best safety lies in fear.
Youth to itself rebels, though none else near.
OPHELIA: I shall the effect of this good lesson keep   45
    As watchman to my heart. But, good my brother,
    Do not, as some ungracious pastors do,
    Show me the steep and thorny way to heaven,
    Whiles, like a puff'd° and reckless libertine,
    Himself the primrose path of dalliance treads,   50
    And recks° not his own rede.°

(*Enter Polonius.*)

LAERTES: O, fear me not.
    I stay too long. But here my father comes.
    A double blessing is a double° grace;
    Occasion° smiles upon a second leave.
POLONIUS: Yet here, Laertes? Aboard, aboard, for
        shame!   55
    The wind sits in the shoulder of your sail,
    And you are stay'd for. There — my blessing with
        thee!
    And these few precepts in thy memory
    Look thou character.° Give thy thoughts no tongue
    Nor any unproportion'd thought his° act.   60
    Be thou familiar,° but by no means vulgar.°
    Those friends thou hast, and their adoption tried,°
    Grapple them to thy soul with hoops of steel,
    But do not dull thy palm with entertainment
    Of each new-hatch'd, unfledg'd courage.° Beware   65
    Of entrance to a quarrel, but, being in,
    Bear't that° th' opposed may beware of thee.
    Give every man thy ear, but few thy voice;
    Take each man's censure,° but reserve thy judgment.

---

255. **doubt:** Suspect. **I, III. Location:** Polonius's chambers.
3. **convoy is assistant:** Means of conveyance are available.
6. **toy in blood:** Passing amorous fancy. 7. **primy:** In its prime,
springtime. 8. **Forward:** Precocious. 9. **suppliance:** Supply,
filler. 11. **crescent:** Growing, waxing. 12. **thews:** Bodily
strength. **temple:** Body. 14. **Grows wide withal:** Grows
along with it. 15. **soil:** Blemish. **cautel:** Deceit. 16. **will:**
Desire. 17. **greatness weigh'd:** High position considered.
20. **Carve:** Choose pleasure. 23. **voice and yielding:** Assent,
approval. 27. **deed:** Effect.

30. **credent:** Credulous. **list:** Listen to. 35. **shot:** Range.
36. **chariest:** Most scrupulously modest. 39. **canker galls:**
Cankerworm destroys. 40. **buttons:** Buds. **disclos'd:**
Opened. 41. **liquid dew:** Time when dew is fresh. 42. **blast-
ments:** Blights. 49. **puff'd:** Bloated. 51. **recks:** Heeds.
rede: Counsel. 53. **double:** I.e., Laertes has already bidden his
father good-bye. 54. **Occasion:** Opportunity. 59. **character:**
Inscribe. 60. **his:** Its. 61. **familiar:** Sociable. **vulgar:** Common. 62. **tried:** Tested. 65. **courage:** Young man of spirit.
67. **Bear't that:** Manage it so that. 69. **censure:** Opinion,
judgment.

70   Costly thy habit as thy purse can buy,
      But not express'd in fancy; rich, not gaudy,
      For the apparel oft proclaims the man,
      And they in France of the best rank and station
      Are of a most select and generous chief° in that.
75   Neither a borrower nor a lender be,
      For loan oft loses both itself and friend,
      And borrowing dulleth edge of husbandry.°
      This above all: to thine own self be true,
      And it must follow, as the night the day,
80   Thou canst not then be false to any man.
      Farewell. My blessing season° this in thee!
LAERTES: Most humbly do I take my leave, my lord.
POLONIUS: The time invests° you. Go, your servants
      tend.°
LAERTES: Farewell, Ophelia, and remember well
85   What I have said to you.
OPHELIA: 'Tis in my memory lock'd,
      And you yourself shall keep the key of it.
LAERTES: Farewell.   (*Exit Laertes.*)
POLONIUS: What is 't, Ophelia, he hath said to you?
OPHELIA: So please you, something touching the Lord
90   Hamlet.
POLONIUS: Marry,° well bethought.
      'Tis told me he hath very oft of late
      Given private time to you, and you yourself
      Have of your audience been most free and
          bounteous.
95   If it be so — as so 'tis put on° me,
      And that in way of caution — I must tell you
      You do not understand yourself so clearly
      As it behooves my daughter and your honor.
      What is between you? Give me up the truth.
OPHELIA: He hath, my lord, of late made many
100   tenders°
      Of his affection to me.
POLONIUS: Affection? Pooh! You speak like a green
          girl,
      Unsifted° in such perilous circumstance.
      Do you believe his tenders, as you call them?
105 OPHELIA: I do not know, my lord, what I should think.
POLONIUS: Marry, I will teach you. Think yourself a
          baby
      That you have ta'en these tenders° for true pay,
      Which are not sterling.° Tender° yourself more
          dearly,
      Or — not to crack the wind° of the poor phrase,
110   Running it thus — you'll tender me a fool.°

OPHELIA: My lord, he hath importun'd me with
      love
      In honorable fashion.
POLONIUS: Ay, fashion° you may call it. Go to, go to.
OPHELIA: And hath given countenance° to his speech,
      my lord,
      With almost all the holy vows of heaven.   115
POLONIUS: Ay, springes° to catch woodcocks.° I do
      know,
      When the blood burns, how prodigal the soul
      Lends the tongue vows. These blazes,
          daughter,
      Giving more light than heat, extinct in both
      Even in their promise, as it is a-making,   120
      You must not take for fire. From this time
      Be something scanter of your maiden presence.
      Set your entreatments° at a higher rate
      Than a command to parle.° For Lord Hamlet,
      Believe so much in him° that he is young,   125
      And with a larger tether may he walk
      Than may be given you. In few,° Ophelia,
      Do not believe his vows, for they are brokers,°
      Not of that dye° which their investments° show,
      But mere implorators° of unholy suits,   130
      Breathing° like sanctified and pious bawds,
      The better to beguile. This is for all:
      I would not, in plain terms, from this time forth
      Have you so slander° any moment leisure
      As to give words or talk with the Lord Hamlet.   135
      Look to 't, I charge you. Come your ways.
OPHELIA: I shall obey, my lord.   (*Exeunt.*)

{*Scene IV*}°

(*Enter Hamlet, Horatio, and Marcellus.*)

HAMLET: The air bites shrewdly; it is very cold.
HORATIO: It is a nipping and an eager air.
HAMLET: What hour now?
HORATIO: I think it lacks of twelve.
MARCELLUS: No, it is struck.
HORATIO: Indeed? I heard it not.
      It then draws near the season   5
      Wherein the spirit held his wont to walk.

---

74. **generous chief:** Noble eminence (?).   77. **husbandry:** Thrift.   81. **season:** Mature.   83. **invests:** Besieges. . . . **tend:** Attend, wait.   91. **Marry:** By the Virgin Mary (a mild oath).   95. **put on:** Impressed on, told to.   100. **tenders:** Offers.   103. **Unsifted:** Untried.   107. **tenders:** With added meaning here of *promises to pay*.   108. **sterling:** Legal currency.   **Tender:** Hold.   109. **crack the wind:** Run it until it is broken, winded.   110. **tender me a fool:** (1) Show yourself to me as a fool, (2) show me up as a fool, (3) present me with a grandchild (*fool* was a term of endearment for a child).

113. **fashion:** Mere form, pretense.   114. **countenance:** Credit, support.   116. **springes:** Snares.   **woodcocks:** Birds easily caught; here used to connote gullibility.   123. **entreatments:** Negotiations for surrender (a military term).   124. **parle:** Discuss terms with the enemy. (Polonius urges his daughter, in the metaphor of military language, not to meet with Hamlet and consider giving in to him merely because he requests an interview.)   125. **so . . . him:** This much concerning him.   127. **In few:** Briefly.   128. **brokers:** Go-betweens, procurer[s]   129. **dye:** Color or sort.   **investments:** Clothes (i.e., they a[re] not what they seem).   130. **mere implorators:** Out-[and-] out solicitors.   131. **Breathing:** Speaking.   134. **sl[ander:]** Bring disgrace or reproach upon.   **I, IV. Location:** Th[e] platform.

(A flourish of trumpets, and two pieces° go off [within].)

What does this mean, my lord?

HAMLET: The King doth wake° tonight and takes his
    rouse,°

Keeps wassail,° and the swagg'ring up-spring° reels;

10 And as he drains his draughts of Rhenish° down,

The kettle-drum and trumpet thus bray out

The triumph of his pledge.°

HORATIO: Is it a custom?

HAMLET: Ay, marry, is 't,

But to my mind, though I am native here

15 And to the manner° born, it is a custom

More honor'd in the breach than the observance.°

This heavy-headed revel east and west°

Makes us traduc'd and tax'd of° other nations.

They clepe° us drunkards, and with swinish phrase°

20 Soil our addition;° and indeed it takes

From our achievements, though perform'd at
    height,°

The pith and marrow of our attribute.

So, oft it chances in particular men,

That for some vicious mole of nature° in them,

25 As in their birth — wherein they are not guilty,

Since nature cannot choose his° origin —

By the o'ergrowth of some complexion,°

Oft breaking down the pales° and forts of reason,

Or by some habit that too much o'er-leavens°

30 The form of plausive° manners, that these men,

Carrying, I say, the stamp of one defect,

Being nature's livery,° or fortune's star,°

Their virtues else, be they as pure as grace,

As infinite as man may undergo,

35 Shall in the general censure take corruption

From that particular fault. The dram of eale°

Doth all the noble substance of a doubt°

To his own scandal.°

(Enter Ghost.)

HORATIO: Look, my lord, it comes!

HAMLET: Angels and ministers of grace defend us!

Be thou a spirit of health° or goblin damn'd,   40

Bring with thee airs from heaven or blasts from
    hell,

Be thy intents wicked or charitable,

Thou com'st in such a questionable° shape

That I will speak to thee. I'll call thee Hamlet,

King, father, royal Dane. O, answer me!   45

Let me not burst in ignorance, but tell

Why thy canoniz'd° bones, hearsed° in death,

Have burst their cerements;° why the sepulcher

Wherein we saw thee quietly interr'd

Hath op'd his ponderous and marble jaws   50

To cast thee up again. What may this mean,

That thou, dead corse, again in complete steel

Revisits thus the glimpses of the moon,°

Making night hideous, and we fools of nature°

So horridly to shake our disposition   55

With thoughts beyond the reaches of our souls?

Say, why is this? Wherefore? What should we do?

               ([Ghost] beckons [Hamlet].)

HORATIO: It beckons you to go away with it,

As if it some impartment° did desire

To you alone.

MARCELLUS: Look with what courteous action   60

It waves you to a more removed ground.

But do not go with it.

HORATIO: No, by no means.

HAMLET: It will not speak. Then I will follow it.

HORATIO: Do not, my lord.

HAMLET: Why, what should be the fear?

I do not set my life at a pin's fee,°   65

And for my soul, what can it do to that,

Being a thing immortal as itself?

It waves me forth again. I'll follow it.

HORATIO: What if it tempt you toward the flood, my
    lord

Or to the dreadful summit of the cliff   70

That beetles o'er° his° base into the sea,

And there assume some other horrible form

Which might deprive your sovereignty of reason,°

And draw you into madness? Think of it.

The very place puts toys of desperation,°   75

Without more motive, into every brain

That looks so many fathoms to the sea

And hears it roar beneath.

HAMLET: It waves me still.

Go on, I'll follow thee.

---

6. [S.D.] *pieces*: I.e., of ordnance, cannon. **8. wake**: Stay awake and hold revel. **rouse**: Carouse, drinking bout. **9. wassail**: Carousal. **up-spring**: Wild German dance. **10. Rhenish**: Rhine wine. **12. triumph . . . pledge**: His feat in draining the wine in a single draft. **15. manner**: Custom (of drinking). **16. More . . . observance**: Better neglected than followed. **17. east and west**: I.e., everywhere. **18. tax'd of**: Censured by. **19. clepe**: Call. **with swinish phrase**: By calling us swine. addition: Reputation. **21. at height**: Outstandingly. of nature: Natural blemish in one's constitution. complexion: Humor (i.e., one of the four ought to determine temperament). s of a fortification). **29. o'er-hout (as yeast works in dough). re's livery**: Endowment from ced by fortune. **36. dram of 37. of a doubt**: A famous crux, ut or often dout, i.e., often erase nteract. **38. To . . . scandal**: To erprise.

40. **of health**: Of spiritual good. **43. questionable**: Inviting question or conversation. **47. canoniz'd**: Buried according to the canons of the church. **hearsed**: Coffined. **48. cerements**: Grave-clothes. **53. glimpses of the moon**: Earth by night. **54. fools of nature**: Mere men, limited to natural knowledge. **59. impartment**: Communication. **65. fee**: Value. **71. beetles o'er**: Overhangs threateningly. **his**: Its. **73. deprive . . . reason**: Take away the rule of reason over your mind. **75. toys of desperation**: Fancies of desperate acts, i.e., suicide.

MARCELLUS: You shall not go, my lord.
                                        [*They try to stop him.*]
80   HAMLET: Hold off your hands!
     HORATIO: Be rul'd, you shall not go.
     HAMLET: My fate cries out,
        And makes each petty artery° in this body
        As hardy as the Nemean lion's° nerve.°
        Still am I call'd. Unhand me, gentlemen.
85   By heaven, I'll make a ghost of him that lets° me!
        I say, away! Go on. I'll follow thee.
                                (*Exeunt Ghost and Hamlet.*)
     HORATIO: He waxes desperate with imagination.
     MARCELLUS: Let's follow. 'Tis not fit thus to obey him.
     HORATIO: Have after. To what issue° will this come?
     MARCELLUS: Something is rotten in the state of
90   Denmark.
     HORATIO: Heaven will direct it.°
     MARCELLUS: Nay, let's follow him. (*Exeunt.*)

{*Scene V*}°

(*Enter Ghost and Hamlet.*)

HAMLET: Whither wilt thou lead me? Speak. I'll go no
           further.
GHOST: Mark me.
HAMLET: I will.
GHOST: My hour is almost come,
     When I to sulph'rous and tormenting flames
     Must render up myself.
HAMLET: Alas, poor ghost!
5   GHOST: Pity me not, but lend thy serious hearing
     To what I shall unfold.
HAMLET: Speak. I am bound to hear.
GHOST: So art thou to revenge, when thou shalt hear.
HAMLET: What?
10   GHOST: I am thy father's spirit,
     Doom'd for a certain term to walk the night,
     And for the day confin'd to fast° in fires,
     Till the foul crimes° done in my days of nature
     Are burnt and purg'd away. But that° I am forbid
15   To tell the secrets of my prison-house,
     I could a tale unfold whose lightest word
     Would harrow up thy soul, freeze thy young blood,
     Make thy two eyes, like stars, start from their
           spheres,°
     Thy knotted and combined locks° to part,
20   And each particular hair to stand an end,°

Like quills upon the fearful porpentine.°
But this eternal blazon° must not be
To ears of flesh and blood. List, list, O, list!
If thou didst ever thy dear father love —
HAMLET: O God!   25
GHOST: Revenge his foul and most unnatural murder.
HAMLET: Murder?
GHOST: Murder most foul, as in the best it is,
     But this most foul, strange, and unnatural.
HAMLET: Haste me to know 't, that I, with wings as
           swift   30
     As meditation or the thoughts of love,
     May sweep to my revenge.
GHOST: I find thee apt;
     And duller shouldst thou be than the fat weed
     That roots itself in ease on Lethe° wharf,°
     Wouldst thou not stir in this. Now, Hamlet, hear.   35
     'Tis given out that, sleeping in my orchard,
     A serpent stung me. So the whole ear of Denmark
     Is by a forged process° of my death
     Rankly abus'd.° But know, thou noble youth,
     The serpent that did sting thy father's life   40
     Now wears his crown.
HAMLET: O my prophetic soul!
     My uncle!
GHOST: Ay, that incestuous, that adulterate° beast,
     With witchcraft of his wits, with traitorous gifts —
     O wicked wit and gifts, that have the power   45
     So to seduce! — won to his shameful lust
     The will of my most seeming-virtuous queen.
     O Hamlet, what a falling-off was there!
     From me, whose love was of that dignity
     That it went hand in hand even with the vow   50
     I made to her in marriage, and to decline
     Upon a wretch whose natural gifts were poor
     To those of mine!
     But virtue, as it never will be moved,
     Though lewdness court it in a shape of heaven,°   55
     So lust, though to a radiant angel link'd,
     Will sate itself in a celestial bed,
     And prey on garbage.
     But, soft, methinks I scent the morning air.
     Brief let me be. Sleeping within my orchard,   60
     My custom always of the afternoon,
     Upon my secure° hour thy uncle stole,
     With juice of cursed hebona° in a vial,
     And in the porches of my ears did pour
     The leprous° distillment, whose effect   65
     Holds such an enmity with blood of man

---

82. artery: Sinew.   **83. Nemean lion:** One of the monsters slain by Hercules in his twelve labors.   **nerve:** Sinew   **85. lets:** Hinders.   **89. issue:** Outcome.   **91. it:** The outcome.   **I, v. Location:** The battlements of the castle.   **12. fast:** Do penance. **13. crimes:** Sins.   **14. But that:** Were it not that.   **18. spheres:** Eye sockets, here compared to the orbits or transparent revolving spheres in which, according to Ptolemaic astronomy, the heavenly bodies were fixed.   **19. knotted . . . locks:** Hair neatly arranged and confined.   **20. an end:** On end.

21. fearful porpentine: Frightened porcupine.   **22. eternal blazon:** Revelation of the secrets of eternity.   **34. Lethe:** The river of forgetfulness in Hades.   **wharf:** Bank.   **38. forged process:** Falsified account.   **39. abus'd:** Deceived.   **43. adulterate:** Adulterous.   **55. shape of heaven:** Heavenly form. **62. secure:** Confident, unsuspicious.   **63. hebona:** Poison. (The word seems to be a form of *ebony*, though it is thought perhaps to be related to *henbane*, a poison, or to *ebenus*, yew.) **65. leprous:** Causing leprosy-like disfigurement.

That swift as quicksilver it courses through
The natural gates and alleys of the body,
And with a sudden vigor it doth posset°
70 And curd, like eager° droppings into milk,
The thin and wholesome blood. So did it mine,
And a most instant tetter° bark'd° about,
Most lazar-like,° with vile and loathsome crust,
All my smooth body.
75 Thus was I, sleeping, by a brother's hand
Of life, of crown, of queen, at once dispatch'd,°
Cut off even in the blossoms of my sin,
Unhous'led,° disappointed,° unanel'd,°
No reck'ning made, but sent to my account
80 With all my imperfections on my head.
O, horrible! O, horrible, most horrible!
If thou hast nature° in thee, bear it not.
Let not the royal bed of Denmark be
A couch for luxury° and damned incest.
85 But, howsomever thou pursues this act,
Taint not thy mind, nor let thy soul contrive
Against thy mother aught. Leave her to heaven
And to those thorns that in her bosom lodge,
To prick and sting her. Fare thee well at once.
90 The glow-worm shows the matin° to be near,
And 'gins to pale his uneffectual fire.°
Adieu, adieu, adieu! Remember me.   [*Exit.*]
HAMLET: O all you host of heaven! O earth! What
    else?
    And shall I couple° hell? O fie! Hold, hold, my
    heart,
95 And you, my sinews, grow not instant old,
But bear me stiffly up. Remember thee!
Ay, thou poor ghost, whiles memory holds a seat
In this distracted globe.° Remember thee!
Yea, from the table° of my memory
100 I'll wipe away all trivial fond° records,
All saws° of books, all forms,° all pressures° past
That youth and observation copied there,
And thy commandment all alone shall live
Within the book and volume of my brain,
105 Unmix'd with baser matter. Yes, by heaven!
O most pernicious woman!
O villain, villain, smiling, damned villain!
My tables — meet it is I set it down,
That one may smile, and smile, and be a villain.
110 At least I am sure it may be so in Denmark.
                                            [*Writing.*]

So, uncle, there you are. Now to my word;
It is "Adieu, adieu! Remember me."
I have sworn 't.

(*Enter Horatio and Marcellus.*)

HORATIO: My lord, my lord!
MARCELLUS: Lord Hamlet!
HORATIO: Heavens secure him!
HAMLET: So be it!   115
MARCELLUS: Illo, ho, ho, my lord!
HAMLET: Hillo, ho, ho,° boy! Come, bird, come.
MARCELLUS: How is 't, my noble lord?
HORATIO: What news, my lord?
HAMLET: O, wonderful!
HORATIO: Good my lord, tell it.
HAMLET: No, you will reveal it.   120
HORATIO: Not I, my lord, by heaven.
MARCELLUS: Nor I, my lord.
HAMLET: How say you, then, would heart of man once
    think it?
    But you'll be secret?
HORATIO, MARCELLUS: Ay, by heaven, my lord.
HAMLET: There's never a villain dwelling in all
    Denmark
    But he's an arrant° knave.   125
HORATIO: There needs no ghost, my lord, come from
    the grave
    To tell us this.
HAMLET: Why, right, you are in the right.
And so, without more circumstance° at all,
I hold it fit that we shake hands and part,
You, as your business and desire shall point you —   130
For every man hath business and desire,
Such as it is — and for my own poor part,
Look you, I'll go pray.
HORATIO: These are but wild and whirling words, my
    lord.
HAMLET: I am sorry they offend you, heartily;   135
    Yes, faith, heartily.
HORATIO: There's no offense, my lord.
HAMLET: Yes, by Saint Patrick,° but there is, Horatio,
And much offense too. Touching this vision here,
It is an honest° ghost, that let me tell you.
For your desire to know what is between us,   140
O'ermaster 't as you may. And now, good friends
As you are friends, scholars, and soldiers,
Give me one poor request.
HORATIO: What is 't, my lord? We will.
HAMLET: Never make known what you have seen
    tonight.   145
HORATIO, MARCELLUS: My lord, we will not.

---

69. **posset:** Coagulate, curdle. 70. **eager:** Sour, acid. 72. **tetter:** Eruption of scabs. **bark'd:** Covered with a rough covering, like bark on a tree. 73. **lazar-like:** Leper-like. 76. **dispatch'd:** Suddenly deprived. 78. **Unhous'led:** Without having received the sacrament [of Holy Communion]. **disappointed:** Unready (spiritually) for the last journey. **unanel'd:** Without having received extreme unction. 82. **nature:** The promptings of a son. 84. **luxury:** Lechery. 90. **matin:** Morning. 91. **uneffectual fire:** Cold light. 94. **couple:** Add. 98. **globe:** Head. 99. **table:** Writing tablet. 100. **fond:** Foolish. 101. **saws:** Wise sayings. **forms:** Images. **pressures:** Impressions stamped.

117. **Hillo, ho, ho:** A falconer's call to a hawk in air. Hamlet is playing upon Marcellus's *Illo,* i.e., *halloo.* 125. **arrant:** Thoroughgoing. 128. **circumstance:** Ceremony. 137. **Saint Patrick:** The keeper of purgatory and patron saint of all blunders and confusion. 139. **honest:** I.e., a real ghost and not an evil spirit.

HAMLET: Nay, but swear 't.
HORATIO: In faith,
    My lord, not I.
MARCELLUS: Nor I, my lord, in faith.
HAMLET: Upon my sword.°   [*Holds out his sword.*]
MARCELLUS: We have sworn, my lord, already.
HAMLET: Indeed, upon my sword, indeed.
                              (*Ghost cries under the stage.*)
150 GHOST: Swear.
    HAMLET: Ha, ha, boy, say'st thou so? Art thou there,
        truepenny?°
        Come on, you hear this fellow in the cellarage.
        Consent to swear.
    HORATIO: Propose the oath, my lord.
    HAMLET: Never to speak of this that you have seen,
155   Swear by my sword.
    GHOST [*beneath*]: Swear.
    HAMLET: Hic et ubique?° Then we'll shift our ground.
                              [*He moves to another spot.*]
        Come hither, gentlemen,
        And lay your hands again upon my sword.
160   Swear by my sword
        Never to speak of this that you have heard.
    GHOST [*beneath*]: Swear by his sword.
    HAMLET: Well said, old mole! Canst work i' th' earth
        so fast?
        A worthy pioner!° Once more remove, good friends.
                              [*Moves again.*]
    HORATIO: O day and night, but this is wondrous
165   strange!
    HAMLET: And therefore as a stranger give it welcome.
        There are more things in heaven and earth, Horatio,
        Than are dreamt of in your philosophy.°
        But come;
170   Here, as before, never, so help you mercy,
        How strange or odd soe'er I bear myself —
        As I perchance hereafter shall think meet
        To put an antic° disposition on —
        That you, at such times seeing me, never shall,
175   With arms encumb'red° thus, or this headshake,
        Or by pronouncing of some doubtful phrase,
        As "Well, well, we know," or "We could, an if° we
        would,"
        Or "If we list° to speak," or "There be, an if they
        might,"
        Or such ambiguous giving out,° to note°
180   That you know aught of me — this do swear,
        So grace and mercy at your most need help you.
    GHOST [*beneath*]: Swear.   [*They swear.*]

HAMLET: Rest, rest, perturbed spirit! So, gentlemen,
    With all my love I do commend me to you;
    And what so poor a man as Hamlet is   185
    May do, t' express his love and friending to you,
    God willing, shall not lack. Let us go in together,
    And still° your fingers on your lips, I pray.
    The time is out of joint. O cursed spite,
    That ever I was born to set it right!   190
                      [*They wait for him to leave first.*]
    Nay, come, let's go together.   (*Exeunt.*)

{ACT II • Scene 1}°

(*Enter old Polonius, with his man* [*Reynaldo*].)

POLONIUS: Give him this money and these notes,
    Reynaldo.
REYNALDO: I will, my lord.
POLONIUS: You shall do marvel's° wisely, good
    Reynaldo,
    Before you visit him, to make inquire
    Of his behavior.
REYNALDO: My lord, I did intend it.   5
POLONIUS: Marry, well said, very well said. Look you,
    sir,
    Inquire me first what Danskers° are in Paris,
    And how, and who, what means,° and where they
    keep,°
    What company, at what expense; and finding
    By this encompassment° and drift° of question   10
    That they do know my son, come you more nearer
    Than your particular demands will touch it.°
    Take° you, as 'twere, some distant knowledge of him,
    As thus, "I know his father and his friends,
    And in part him." Do you mark this, Reynaldo?   15
REYNALDO: Ay, very well, my lord.
POLONIUS: "And in part him, but," you may say, "not
    well.
    But, if 't be he I mean, he's very wild,
    Addicted so and so," and there put on° him
    What forgeries° you please — marry, none so rank   20
    As may dishonor him, take heed of that,
    But, sir, such wanton,° wild, and usual slips,
    As are companions noted and most known
    To youth and liberty.
REYNALDO: As gaming, my lord.
POLONIUS: Ay, or drinking, fencing, swearing,   25
    Quarreling, drabbing° — you may go so far.

---

148. **sword:** The hilt in the form of a cross.   151. **truepenny:**
Honest old fellow.   157. **Hic et ubique:** Here and everywhere
(Latin).   164. **pioner:** Pioneer, digger, miner.   168. **your philosophy:** This subject called "natural philosophy" or "science"
that people talk about.   173. **antic:** Fantastic.   175. **encumb-
b'red:** Folded or entwined.   177. **an if:** If.   178. **list:** Were
inclined.   179. **giving out:** Profession of knowledge.   **note:**
Give a sign, indicate.

188. **still:** Always. II, I. **Location:** Polonius's chambers.
3. **marvel's:** Marvelous(ly).   7. **Danskers:** Danes.   8. **what
means:** What wealth (they have).   **keep:** Dwell.   10. **encom-
passment:** Roundabout talking.   **drift:** Gradual approach or
course.   11–12. **come . . . it:** You will find out more this
way than by asking pointed questions (particular demands).
13. **Take:** Assume, pretend.   19. **put on:** Impute to.   20. **forgeries:** Invented tales.   22. **wanton:** Sportive, unrestrained.
26. **drabbing:** Whoring.

REYNALDO: My lord, that would dishonor him.
POLONIUS: Faith, no, as you may season° it in the
      charge.
      You must not put another scandal on him
30   That he is open to incontinency;°
      That's not my meaning. But breathe his faults so
          quaintly°
      That they may seem the taints of liberty,°
      The flash and outbreak of a fiery mind,
      A savageness in unreclaimed° blood,
      Of general assault.°
35 REYNALDO: But, my good lord —
POLONIUS: Wherefore should you do this?
REYNALDO: Ay, my lord,
      I would know that.
POLONIUS: Marry, sir, here's my drift,
      And, I believe, it is a fetch of wit.°
      You laying these slight sullies on my son,
40   As 'twere a thing a little soil'd i' th' working,°
      Mark you,
      Your party in converse,° him you would
          sound,°
      Having ever° seen in the prenominate crimes°
      The youth you breathe° of guilty, be assur'd
45   He closes with you in this consequence:°
      "Good sir," or so, or "friend," or "gentleman,"
      According to the phrase or the addition°
      Of man and country.
REYNALDO: Very good, my lord.
POLONIUS: And then, sir, does 'a this —'a does — what
      was I about to say?
50   By the mass, I was about to say something.
      Where did I leave?
REYNALDO: At "closes in the consequence."
POLONIUS: At "closes in the consequence," ay,
      marry.
      He closes thus: "I know the gentleman;
      I saw him yesterday, or th' other day,
      Or then, or then, with such, or such, and, as you
55   say,
      There was 'a gaming, there o'ertook in 's rouse,°
      There falling out° at tennis," or perchance,
      "I saw him enter such a house of sale,"
      Videlicet,° a brothel, or so forth. See you now,
60   Your bait of falsehood takes this carp° of truth;
      And thus do we of wisdom and of reach,°

      With windlasses° and with assays of bias,°
      By indirections find directions° out.
      So by my former lecture and advice
      Shall you my son. You have me, have you not?   65
REYNALDO: My lord, I have.
POLONIUS: God buy ye; fare ye well.
REYNALDO: Good my lord.
POLONIUS: Observe his inclination in yourself.°
REYNALDO: I shall, my lord.
POLONIUS: And let him ply° his music.
REYNALDO: Well, my lord.   70
POLONIUS: Farewell.   (Exit Reynaldo.)

(Enter Ophelia.)

                  How now, Ophelia, what's the matter?
OPHELIA: O, my lord, my lord, I have been so
      affrighted!
POLONIUS: With what, i' th' name of God?
OPHELIA: My lord, as I was sewing in my closet,°
      Lord Hamlet, with his doublet° all unbrac'd,°   75
      No hat upon his head, his stockings fouled,
      Ungart'red, and down-gyved to his ankle,°
      Pale as his shirt, his knees knocking each other,
      And with a look so piteous in purport
      As if he had been loosed out of hell   80
      To speak of horrors — he comes before me.
POLONIUS: Mad for thy love?
OPHELIA: My lord, I do not know,
      But truly I do fear it.
POLONIUS: What said he?
OPHELIA: He took me by the wrist and held me hard.
      Then goes he to the length of all his arm,   85
      And, with his other hand thus o'er his brow
      He falls to such perusal of my face
      As 'a would draw it. Long stay'd he so.
      At last, a little shaking of mine arm
      And thrice his head thus waving up and down,   90
      He rais'd a sigh so piteous and profound
      As it did seem to shatter all his bulk°
      And end his being. That done, he lets me go,
      And, with his head over his shoulder turn'd,
      He seem'd to find his way without his eyes,   95
      For out o' doors he went without their helps,
      And, to the last, bended their light on me.
POLONIUS: Come, go with me. I will go seek the King.
      This is the very ecstasy° of love
      Whose violent property° fordoes° itself   100

28. season: Temper, soften. 30. incontinency: Habitual loose behavior. 31. quaintly: Delicately, ingeniously. 32. taints of liberty: Faults resulting from freedom. 34. unreclaimed: Untamed. 35. general assault: Tendency that assails all unrestrained youth. 38. fetch of wit: Clever trick. 40. soil'd i' th' working: Shopworn. 42. converse: Conversation. sound: Sound out. 43. Having ever: If he has ever. prenominate crimes: Before-mentioned offenses. 44. breathe: Speak. 45. closes . . . consequence: Follows your lead in some fashion as follows. 47. addition: Title. 56. o'ertook in 's rouse: Overcome by drink. 57. falling out: Quarreling. 59. Videlicet: Namely. 60. carp: A fish. 61. reach: Capacity, ability.

62. windlasses: Circuitous paths (literally, circuits made to head off the game in hunting). assays of bias: Attempts through indirection (like the curving path of the bowling ball, which is biased or weighted to one side). 63. directions: The way things really are. 68. in yourself: In your own person (as well as by asking questions). 70. let him ply: See that he continues to study. 74. closet: Private chamber. 75. doublet: Close-fitting jacket. unbrac'd: Unfastened. 77. down-gyved to his ankle: Fallen to the ankles (like gyves or fetters). 92. bulk: Body. 99. ecstasy: Madness. 100. property: Nature. fordoes: Destroys.

And leads the will to desperate undertakings
As oft as any passion under heaven
That does afflict our natures. I am sorry.
What, have you given him any hard words of late?
105 OPHELIA: No, my good lord, but, as you did
       command,
    I did repel his letters and denied
    His access to me.
POLONIUS: That hath made him mad.
    I am sorry that with better heed and judgment
    I had not quoted° him. I fear'd he did but trifle
    And meant to wrack thee; but, beshrew my
110   jealousy!°
    By heaven, it is as proper to our age°
    To cast beyond° ourselves in our opinions
    As it is common for the younger sort
    To lack discretion. Come, go we to the King.
    This must be known, which, being kept close,°
115   might move
    More grief to hide than hate to utter love.°
    Come.   (*Exeunt.*)

{*Scene II*}°

(*Flourish. Enter King and Queen, Rosencrantz, and
Guildenstern* [*with others*].)

KING: Welcome, dear Rosencrantz and Guildenstern.
    Moreover that° we much did long to see you,
    The need we have to use you did provoke
    Our hasty sending. Something have you heard
5   Of Hamlet's transformation — so call it,
    Sith° nor th' exterior nor° the inward man
    Resembles that° it was. What it should be,
    More than his father's death, that thus hath put him
    So much from th' understanding of himself,
10 I cannot dream of. I entreat you both
    That, being of so young days° brought up with him,
    And sith so neighbor'd to his youth and havior,
    That you vouchsafe your rest° here in our court
    Some little time, so by your companies
15 To draw him on to pleasures, and to gather
    So much as from occasion you may glean,
    Whether aught to us unknown afflicts him thus,
    That, open'd,° lies within our remedy.
QUEEN: Good gentlemen, he hath much talk'd of you
20 And sure I am two men there is not living

To whom he more adheres. If it will please you
To show us so much gentry° and good will
As to expend your time with us awhile
For the supply and profit° of our hope,
Your visitation shall receive such thanks   25
As fits a king's remembrance.
ROSENCRANTZ: Both your Majesties
    Might, by the sovereign power you have of us,
    Put your dread pleasures more into command
    Than to entreaty.
GUILDENSTERN: But we both obey,
    And here give up ourselves in the full bent°   30
    To lay our service freely at your feet,
    To be commanded.
KING: Thanks, Rosencrantz and gentle Guildenstern.
QUEEN: Thanks, Guildenstern and gentle Rosencrantz.
    And I beseech you instantly to visit   35
    My too much changed son. Go, some of you,
    And bring these gentlemen where Hamlet is.
GUILDENSTERN: Heavens make our presence and our
       practices
    Pleasant and helpful to him!
QUEEN: Ay, amen!
                 (*Exeunt Rosencrantz and Guildenstern
                 [with some Attendants].*)

(*Enter Polonius.*)

POLONIUS: Th' ambassadors from Norway, my good
       lord,   40
    Are joyfully return'd.
KING: Thou still° hast been the father of good news.
POLONIUS: Have I, my lord? I assure my good liege
    I hold my duty, as I hold my soul,
    Both to my God and to my gracious king;   45
    And I do think, or else this brain of mine
    Hunts not the trail of policy so sure
    As it hath us'd to do, that I have found
    The very cause of Hamlet's lunacy.
KING: O, speak of that! That do I long to hear.   50
POLONIUS: Give first admittance to th' ambassadors.
    My news shall be the fruit° to that great feast.
KING: Thyself do grace to them, and bring them in.
                                   (*Exit Polonius.*)
    He tells me, my dear Gertrude, he hath found
    The head and source of all your son's distemper. 55
QUEEN: I doubt° it is no other but the main,°
    His father's death, and our o'erhasty marriage.

(*Enter Ambassadors* [*Voltimand and Cornelius, with
Polonius*].)

KING: Well, we shall sift him. — Welcome, my good
       friends!
    Say, Voltimand, what from our brother Norway?

---

109. **quoted:** Observed.   110. **beshrew my jealousy:** A plague
upon my suspicious nature.   111. **proper . . . age:** Characteristic of us (old) men.   112. **cast beyond:** Overshoot, miscalcu-
late.   115. **close:** Secret.   115–16. **might . . . love:** Might
cause more grief (to others) by hiding the knowledge of Hamlet's strange behavior to Ophelia than hatred by telling it.
II, ii. Location: The castle.   2. **Moreover that:** Besides the fact
that.   6. **Sith:** Since.   **nor . . . nor:** Neither . . . nor.   7. **that:**
What.   11. **of . . . days:** From such early youth.   13. **vouchsafe your rest:** Please to stay.   18. **open'd:** Revealed.

22. **gentry:** Courtesy.   24. **supply and profit:** Aid and successful outcome.   30. **in . . . bent:** To the utmost degree of our
capacity.   42. **still:** Always.   52. **fruit:** Dessert.   56. **doubt:**
Fear, suspect.   **main:** Chief point, principal concern.

60 VOLTIMAND: Most fair return of greetings and desires.
        Upon our first,° he sent out to suppress
        His nephew's levies, which to him appear'd
        To be a preparation 'gainst the Polack,
        But, better look'd into, he truly found
65   It was against your Highness. Whereat griev'd
        That so his sickness, age, and impotence
        Was falsely borne in hand,° sends out arrests
        On Fortinbras, which he, in brief, obeys,
        Receives rebuke from Norway, and in fine°
70   Makes vow before his uncle never more
        To give th' assay° of arms against your Majesty.
        Whereon old Norway, overcome with joy,
        Gives him three score thousand crowns in annual
            fee,
        And his commission to employ those soldiers,
75   So levied as before, against the Polack,
        With an entreaty, herein further shown,
                                    [Giving a paper.]
        That it might please you to give quiet pass
        Through your dominions for this enterprise,
        On such regards of safety and allowance°
        As therein are set down.
80 KING: It likes° us well;
        And at our more consider'd° time we'll read,
        Answer, and think upon this business.
        Meantime we thank you for your well-took labor.
        Go to your rest; at night we'll feast together.
        Most welcome home!   (Exeunt Ambassadors.)
85 POLONIUS: This business is well ended.
        My liege, and madam, to expostulate°
        What majesty should be, what duty is,
        Why day is day, night night, and time is time,
        Were nothing but to waste night, day, and time.
90   Therefore, since brevity is the soul of wit,°
        And tediousness the limbs and outward flourishes,
        I will be brief. Your noble son is mad.
        Mad call I it, for, to define true madness,
        What is 't but to be nothing else but mad?
        But let that go.
95 QUEEN: More matter, with less art.
    POLONIUS: Madam, I swear I use no art at all.
        That he is mad, 'tis true; 'tis true 'tis pity,
        And pity 'tis 'tis true — a foolish figure,°
        But farewell it, for I will use no art.
100   Mad let us grant him, then, and now remains
        That we find out the cause of this effect,
        Or rather say, the cause of this defect,
        For this effect defective comes by cause.°

    Thus it remains, and the remainder thus.
    Perpend.°   105
    I have a daughter — have while she is mine —
    Who, in her duty and obedience, mark,
    Hath given me this. Now gather, and surmise.
    [Reads the letter.] "To the celestial and my soul's
        idol,
    the most beautified Ophelia"—   110
    That's an ill phrase, a vile phrase; "beautified" is a
        vile
    phrase. But you shall hear. Thus: [Reads.]
    "In her excellent white bosom, these, etc."
QUEEN: Came this from Hamlet to her?
POLONIUS: Good madam, stay awhile; I will be
        faithful.   115
                                             [Reads.]

    "Doubt° thou the stars are fire,
        Doubt that the sun doth move,
    Doubt truth to be a liar,
        But never doubt I love.
    O dear Ophelia, I am ill at these numbers.° I have   120
    not art to reckon° my groans. But that I love thee
    best, O most best, believe it. Adieu.
            Thine evermore, most dear lady, whilst this
                machine° is to him, Hamlet."
    This in obedience hath my daughter shown me,   125
    And, more above,° hath his solicitings,
    As they fell out° by time, by means, and place,
    All given to mine ear.
KING: But how hath she
    Receiv'd his love?
POLONIUS: What do you think of me?
KING: As of a man faithful and honorable.   130
POLONIUS: I would fain prove so. But what might you
        think,
    When I had seen this hot love on the wing —
    As I perceiv'd it, I must tell you that,
    Before my daughter told me — what might you,
    Or my dear Majesty your Queen here, think,   135
    If I had play'd the desk or table-book,°
    Or given my heart a winking,° mute and dumb,
    Or look'd upon this love with idle sight?°
    What might you think? No, I went round° to work,
    And my young mistress thus I did bespeak:°   140
    "Lord Hamlet is a prince, out of thy star;°
    This must not be." And then I prescripts gave her,
    That she should lock herself from his resort,
    Admit no messengers, receive no tokens.

---

61. **Upon our first:** At our first words on the business.
67. **borne in hand:** Deluded, taken advantage of.   69. **in fine:**
In the end.   71. **assay:** Trial.   79. **On . . . allowance:** With such
pledges of safety and provisos.   80. **likes:** Pleases.   81. **consider'd:** Suitable for deliberation.   86. **expostulate:** Expound.
90. **wit:** Sound sense or judgment.   98. **figure:** Figure of speech.
103. **For . . . cause:** I.e., for this defective behavior, this madness has a cause.

105. **Perpend:** Consider.   116. **Doubt:** Suspect, question.
120. **ill . . . numbers:** Unskilled at writing verses.   121. **reckon:**
(1) Count, (2) number metrically, scan.   124. **machine:** Body.
126. **more above:** Moreover.   127. **fell out:** Occurred.
136. **play'd . . . table-book:** Remained shut up, concealing the
information.   137. **winking:** Closing of the eyes.   138. **with
idle sight:** Complacently or uncomprehendingly.   139. **round:**
Roundly, plainly.   140. **bespeak:** Address.   141. **out of thy
star:** Above your sphere, position.

145 Which done, she took the fruits of my advice;
And he, repelled — a short tale to make —
Fell into a sadness, then into a fast,
Thence to a watch,° thence into a weakness,
Thence to a lightness,° and, by this declension,°
150 Into the madness wherein now he raves,
And all we mourn for.
KING: Do you think this?
QUEEN: It may be, very like.
POLONIUS: Hath there been such a time — I would fain
       know that —
That I have positively said "'Tis so,"
When it prov'd otherwise?
155 KING: Not that I know.
POLONIUS [*pointing to his head and shoulder*]: Take
       this from this, if this be otherwise.
If circumstances lead me, I will find
Where truth is hid, though it were hid indeed
Within the center.°
KING: How may we try it further?
POLONIUS: You know, sometimes he walks four hours
160   together
Here in the lobby.
QUEEN: So he does indeed.
POLONIUS: At such a time I'll loose my daughter to
       him.
Be you and I behind an arras° then.
Mark the encounter. If he love her not
165 And be not from his reason fall'n thereon,°
Let me be no assistant for a state,
But keep a farm and carters.
KING: We will try it.

(*Enter Hamlet [reading on a book].*)

QUEEN: But look where sadly the poor wretch comes
       reading.
POLONIUS: Away, I do beseech you both, away.
I'll board° him presently.

       (*Exeunt King and Queen [with Attendants].*)

170   O, give me leave.
How does my good Lord Hamlet?
HAMLET: Well, God-a-mercy.°
POLONIUS: Do you know me, my lord?
HAMLET: Excellent well. You are a fishmonger.°
175 POLONIUS: Not I, my lord.
HAMLET: Then I would you were so honest a man.
POLONIUS: Honest, my lord?
HAMLET: Ay, sir. To be honest, as this world goes, is to
       be one man pick'd out of ten thousand.

POLONIUS: That's very true, my lord.   180
HAMLET: For if the sun breed maggots in a dead dog, be-
       ing a good kissing carrion° — Have you a daughter?
POLONIUS: I have, my lord.
HAMLET: Let her not walk i' th' sun.° Conception° is a
       blessing, but as your daughter may conceive, friend,   185
       look to 't.
POLONIUS [*aside*]: How say you by that? Still harping on
       my daughter. Yet he knew me not at first; 'a said I
       was a fishmonger. 'A is far gone. And truly in my
       youth I suff'red much extremity for love, very near   190
       this. I'll speak to him again. — What do you read,
       my lord?
HAMLET: Words, words, words.
POLONIUS: What is the matter,° my lord?
HAMLET: Between who?   195
POLONIUS: I mean, the matter that you read, my lord.
HAMLET: Slanders, sir, for the satirical rogue says here
       that old men have gray beards, that their faces are
       wrinkled, their eyes purging° thick amber and plum-
       tree gum, and that they have a plentiful lack of wit,   200
       together with most weak hams. All which, sir, though
       I most powerfully and potently believe, yet I hold it
       not honesty° to have it thus set down, for you your-
       self, sir, shall grow old as I am, if like a crab you
       could go backward.   205
POLONIUS [*aside*]: Though this be madness, yet there is
       method in 't. — Will you walk out of the air, my lord?
HAMLET: Into my grave.
POLONIUS: Indeed, that's out of the air. [*Aside.*] How
       pregnant° sometimes his replies are! A happiness°   210
       that often madness hits on, which reason and sanity
       could not so prosperously° be deliver'd of. I will
       leave him, [and suddenly contrive the means of meet-
       ing between him] and my daughter. — My honorable
       lord, I will most humbly take my leave of you.   215
HAMLET: You cannot, sir, take from me any thing that I
       will more willingly part withal — except my life,
       except my life, except my life.

(*Enter Guildenstern and Rosencrantz.*)

POLONIUS: Fare you well, my lord.
HAMLET: These tedious old fools!°   220
POLONIUS: You go to seek the Lord Hamlet; there he is.
ROSENCRANTZ [*to Polonius*]: God save you, sir!
                                        [*Exit Polonius.*]

GUILDENSTERN: My honor'd lord!
ROSENCRANTZ: My most dear lord!

---

148. watch: State of sleeplessness.   **149. lightness:** Light-head-edness.   **declension:** Decline, deterioration.   **159. center:** Middle point of the earth (which is also the center of the Ptole-maic universe).   **163. arras:** Hanging, tapestry.   **165. thereon:** On that account.   **170. board:** Accost.   **172. God-a-mercy:** Thank you.   **174. fishmonger:** Fish merchant (with connota-tion of *bawd, procurer*[?]).

182. good kissing carrion: A good piece of flesh for kissing, or for the sun to kiss.   **184. i' th' sun:** With additional im-plication of the sunshine of princely favors.   **Conception:** (1) Understanding, (2) pregnancy.   **194. matter:** Substance (but Hamlet plays on the sense of *basis for a dispute*).   **199. purg-ing:** Discharging.   **203. honesty:** Decency.   **210. pregnant:** Full of meaning.   **happiness:** Felicity of expression.   **212. pros-perously:** Successfully.   **220. old fools:** I.e., old men like Polonius.

225 HAMLET: My excellent good friends! How dost thou, Guildenstern? Ah, Rosencrantz! Good lads, how do you both?

ROSENCRANTZ: As the indifferent° children of the earth.

GUILDENSTERN: Happy in that we are not over-happy.
230   On Fortune's cap we are not the very button.

HAMLET: Nor the soles of her shoe?

ROSENCRANTZ: Neither, my lord.

HAMLET: Then you live about her waist, or in the middle of her favors?

235 GUILDENSTERN: Faith, her privates° we.

HAMLET: In the secret parts of Fortune? O, most true; she is a strumpet.° What news?

ROSENCRANTZ: None, my lord, but the world's grown honest.

240 HAMLET: Then is doomsday near. But your news is not true. [Let me question more in particular. What have you, my good friends, deserv'd at the hands of Fortune that she sends you to prison hither?

GUILDENSTERN: Prison, my lord?

HAMLET: Denmark's a prison.   245

ROSENCRANTZ: Then is the world one.

HAMLET: A goodly one, in which there are many confines,° wards,° and dungeons, Denmark being one o' th' worst.

ROSENCRANTZ: We think not so, my lord.   250

HAMLET: Why then 'tis none to you, for there is nothing either good or bad but thinking makes it so. To me it is a prison.

ROSENCRANTZ: Why then, your ambition makes it one. 'Tis too narrow for your mind.   255

HAMLET: O God, I could be bounded in a nutshell and count myself a king of infinite space, were it not that I have bad dreams.

GUILDENSTERN: Which dreams indeed are ambition, for the very substance of the ambitious° is merely the   260
shadow of a dream.

HAMLET: A dream itself is but a shadow.

ROSENCRANTZ: Truly, and I hold ambition of so airy and light a quality that it is but a shadow's shadow.

228. **indifferent:** Ordinary.   235. **privates:** Close acquaintances (with sexual pun on *private parts*).   237. **strumpet:** Prostitute (a common epithet for indiscriminate Fortune, see line 497 p. 374).

247–48. **confines:** Places of confinement.   248. **wards:** Cells. 260. **the very . . . ambitious:** That seemingly very substantial thing which the ambitious pursue.

LEFT: Hamlet returns to Denmark. Left to right, Voltemand (Jeremy Geidt), Gertrude (Christine Estabrook), Claudius (Mark Metcalf), Hamlet (Mark Rylance), and Laertes (Derek Smith) in the 1991 American Repertory Theatre production of *Hamlet,* directed by Ron Daniels. RIGHT: The dumb-show sequence with Candy Buckley as the Player Queen.

265 HAMLET: Then are our beggars bodies,° and our monarchs and outstretch'd° heroes the beggars' shadows. Shall we to th' court? For, by my fay,° I cannot reason.

ROSENCRANTZ, GUILDENSTERN: We'll wait upon° you.

270 HAMLET: No such matter. I will not sort° you with the rest of my servants, for, to speak to you like an honest man, I am most dreadfully attended.°] But, in the beaten way° of friendship, what make° you at Elsinore?

275 ROSENCRANTZ: To visit you, my lord, no other occasion.

HAMLET: Beggar that I am, I am even poor in thanks; but I thank you, and sure, dear friends, my thanks are too dear a halfpenny.° Were you not sent for? Is it your own inclining? Is it a free visitation? Come,
280 come, deal justly with me. Come, come; nay, speak.

GUILDENSTERN: What should we say, my lord?

HAMLET: Why, anything, but to th' purpose. You were sent for; and there is a kind of confession in your looks which your modesties have not craft enough to
285 color. I know the good King and Queen have sent for you.

ROSENCRANTZ: To what end, my lord?

HAMLET: That you must teach me. But let me conjure° you, by the rights of our fellowship, by the consonancy of our youth,° by the obligation of our ever-   290
preserv'd love, and by what more dear a better proposer° could charge° you withal, be even° and direct with me, whether you were sent for, or no?

ROSENCRANTZ [*aside to Guildenstern*]: What say you?

HAMLET [*aside*]: Nay then, I have an eye of° you. — If   295
you love me, hold not off.

GUILDENSTERN: My lord, we were sent for.

HAMLET: I will tell you why; so shall my anticipation prevent your discovery,° and your secrecy to the King and Queen molt no feather.° I have of late — but   300
wherefore I know not — lost all my mirth, forgone all custom of exercises; and indeed it goes so heavily with my disposition that this goodly frame, the earth, seems to me a sterile promontory; this most excellent canopy, the air, look you, this brave° o'erhanging fir-   305
mament, this majestical roof fretted° with golden fire, why, it appeareth nothing to me but a foul and

265. bodies: Solid substances rather than shadows (since beggars are not ambitious).   **266. outstretch'd:** (1) Far-reaching in their ambition, (2) elongated as shadows.   **267. fay:** Faith.   **269. wait upon:** Accompany, attend.   **270. sort:** Class, associate.   **272. dreadfully attended:** Waited upon in slovenly fashion.   **273. beaten way:** Familiar path.   **make:** Do.   **278. dear a halfpenny:** Expensive at the price of a halfpenny, i.e., of little worth.

288. conjure: Adjure, entreat.   **289–90. consonancy of our youth:** The fact that we are of the same age.   **291–92. better proposer:** More skillful propounder.   **292. charge:** Urge.   **even:** Straight, honest.   **295. of:** On.   **299. prevent your discovery:** Forestall your disclosure.   **300. molt no feather:** Not diminish in the least.   **305. brave:** Splendid.   **306. fretted:** Adorned (with fret-work, as in a vaulted ceiling).

pestilent congregation of vapors. What a piece of
work is a man! How noble in reason, how infinite in
310   faculties, in form and moving how express° and admirable, in action how like an angel, in apprehension
how like a god! The beauty of the world, the paragon
of animals! And yet, to me, what is this quintessence°
of dust? Man delights not me — no, nor woman nei-
315   ther, though by your smiling you seem to say so.

ROSENCRANTZ: My lord, there was no such stuff in my
thoughts.

HAMLET: Why did you laugh then, when I said "man
delights not me"?

320   ROSENCRANTZ: To think, my lord, if you delight not in
man, what lenten entertainment° the players shall receive from you. We coted° them on the way, and
hither are they coming, to offer you service.

HAMLET: He that plays the king shall be welcome; his
325   Majesty shall have tribute of me. The adventurous
knight shall use his foil and target,° the lover shall
not sigh gratis, the humorous man° shall end his part
in peace, [the clown shall make those laugh whose
lungs are tickle o' th' sere°], and the lady shall say her
330   mind freely, or the blank verse shall halt° for 't. What
players are they?

ROSENCRANTZ: Even those you were wont to take such
delight in, the tragedians of the city.

HAMLET: How chances it they travel? Their residence,°
335   both in reputation and profit, was better both ways.

ROSENCRANTZ: I think their inhibition° comes by the
means of the innovation.°

HAMLET: Do they hold the same estimation they did
when I was in the city? Are they so follow'd?

340   ROSENCRANTZ: No, indeed, are they not.

[HAMLET: How comes it? Do they grow rusty?

ROSENCRANTZ: Nay, their endeavor keeps in the
wonted° pace. But there is, sir, an aery° of children,
little eyases,° that cry out on the top of question,°
345   and are most tyrannically° clapp'd for 't. These are
now the fashion, and so berattle° the common

stages° — so they call them — that many wearing
rapiers° are afraid of goose-quills° and dare scarce
come thither.

HAMLET: What, are they children? Who maintains 'em?   350
How are they escoted?° Will they pursue the quality°
no longer than they can sing?° Will they not say
afterwards, if they should grow themselves to com-
mon° players — as it is most like, if their means are
no better — their writers do them wrong, to make   355
them exclaim against their own succession?°

ROSENCRANTZ: Faith, there has been much to do° on
both sides, and the nation holds it no sin to tarre°
them to controversy. There was, for a while, no
money bid for argument° unless the poet and the   360
player went to cuffs in the question.°

HAMLET: Is 't possible?

GUILDENSTERN: O, there has been much throwing about
of brains.

HAMLET: Do the boys carry it away?°   365

ROSENCRANTZ: Ay, that they do, my lord — Hercules
and his load° too.°]

HAMLET: It is not very strange, for my uncle is King of
Denmark, and those that would make mouths° at
him while my father liv'd, give twenty, forty, fifty, a   370
hundred ducats° apiece for his picture in little.°
'Sblood,° there is something in this more than natural, if philosophy could find it out.

(A flourish [of trumpets within].)

GUILDENSTERN: There are the players.

HAMLET: Gentlemen, you are welcome to Elsinore. Your   375
hands, come then. Th' appurtenance of welcome is
fashion and ceremony. Let me comply° with you in
this garb,° lest my extent° to the players, which, I tell
you, must show fairly outwards,° should more appear
like entertainment° than yours. You are welcome.   380
But my uncle-father and aunt-mother are deceiv'd.

GUILDENSTERN: In what, my dear lord?

---

310. **express:** Well-framed (?), exact (?).   313. **quintessence:**
The fifth essence of ancient philosophy, beyond earth, water,
air, and fire, supposed to be the substance of the heavenly bodies and to be latent in all things.   321. **lenten entertainment:**
Meager reception (appropriate to Lent).   322. **coted:** Overtook and passed beyond.   326. **foil and target:** Sword and
shield.   327. **humorous man:** Eccentric character, dominated
by one trait or "humor."   329. **tickle o' th' sere:** Easy on the
trigger, ready to laugh easily. (*Sere* is part of a gunlock.)
330. **halt:** Limp.   334. **residence:** Remaining in one place, i.e.,
in the city.   336. **inhibition:** Formal prohibition (from acting
plays in the city).   337. **innovation:** I.e., the new fashion in
satirical plays performed by boy actors in the "private" theaters; or possibly a political uprising; or the strict limitations set
on the theater in London in 1600.   343. **wonted:** Usual.
aery: Nest.   344. **eyases:** Young hawks.   **cry . . . question:**
Speak shrilly, dominating the controversy (in decrying the public theaters).   345. **tyrannically:** Outrageous.   346. **berattle:**
Berate.

346–47. **common stages:** Public theaters.   347–48. **many
wearing rapiers:** Many men of fashion, who were afraid to
patronize the common players for fear of being satirized by the
poets who wrote for the children.   348. **goose-quills:** Pens of
satirists.   351. **escoted:** Maintained.   **quality:** (Acting) profession.   352. **no longer . . . sing:** Only until their voices
change.   353–54. **common:** Regular, adult.   356. **succession:**
Future careers.   357. **to do:** Ado.   358. **tarre:** Set on (as
dogs).   360. **argument:** Plot for a play.   361. **went . . . question:** Came to blows in the play itself.   365. **carry it away:** Win
the day.   366–67. **Hercules . . . load:** Thought to be an allusion to the sign of the Globe Theatre, which was Hercules bearing the world on his shoulder.   341–67. **How . . . load too:**
The passage, omitted from the early quartos, alludes to the so-
called War of the Theatres, 1599–1602, the rivalry between
the children companies and the adult actors.   369. **mouths:**
Faces.   371. **ducats:** Gold coins.   **in little:** In miniature.
372. **'Sblood:** By His (God's, Christ's) blood.   377. **comply:**
Observe the formalities of courtesy.   378. **garb:** Manner.   **my
extent:** The extent of my showing courtesy.   379. **show fairly
outwards:** Look cordial to outward appearances.   380. **entertainment:** A (warm) reception.

HAMLET: I am but mad north-north-west.° When the wind is southerly I know a hawk from a handsaw.°

(*Enter Polonius.*)

385 POLONIUS: Well be with you, gentlemen!
HAMLET: Hark you, Guildenstern, and you too; at each ear a hearer. That great baby you see there is not yet out of his swaddling-clouts.°
ROSENCRANTZ: Happily° he is the second time come to

390 them; for they say an old man is twice a child.
HAMLET: I will prophesy he comes to tell me of the players; mark it. — You say right, sir, o' Monday morning, 'twas then indeed.
POLONIUS: My lord, I have news to tell you.

395 HAMLET: My lord, I have news to tell you. When Roscius° was an actor in Rome —
POLONIUS: The actors are come hither, my lord.
HAMLET: Buzz,° buzz!
POLONIUS: Upon my honor —

400 HAMLET: Then came each actor on his ass —
POLONIUS: The best actors in the world, either for tragedy, comedy, history, pastoral, pastoral-comical, historical-pastoral, tragical-historical, tragical-comical-historical-pastoral, scene individable,° or poem

405 unlimited.° Seneca° cannot be too heavy, nor Plautus° too light. For the law of writ and the liberty,° these are the only men.
HAMLET: O Jephthah, judge of Israel,° what a treasure hadst thou!

410 POLONIUS: What a treasure had he, my lord?
HAMLET: Why,
"One fair daughter, and no more,
The which he loved passing° well."
POLONIUS [*aside*]: Still on my daughter.

415 HAMLET: Am I not i' th' right, old Jephthah?
POLONIUS: If you call me Jephthah, my lord, I have a daughter that I love passing well.
HAMLET: Nay, that follows not.
POLONIUS: What follows, then, my lord?

420 HAMLET: Why,
"As by lot, God wot,"°
and then, you know,

"It came to pass, as most like° it was."
The first row° of the pious chanson° will show you more, for look where my abridgement° comes.   425

(*Enter the Players.*)

You are welcome, masters; welcome, all. I am glad to see thee well. Welcome, good friends. O, old friend! Why, thy face is valanc'd° since I saw thee last. Com'st thou to beard° me in Denmark? What, my young lady° and mistress? By 'r lady, your ladyship is   430 nearer to heaven than when I saw you last, by the altitude of a chopine.° Pray God your voice, like a piece of uncurrent° gold, be not crack'd within the ring.° Masters, you are all welcome. We'll e'en to 't like French falconers, fly at anything we see. We'll   435 have a speech straight.° Come, give us a taste of your quality; come, a passionate speech.
FIRST PLAYER: What speech, my good lord?
HAMLET: I heard thee speak me a speech once, but it was never acted, or, if it was, not above once, for the   440 play, I remember, pleas'd not the million; 'twas caviary to the general.° But it was — as I receiv'd it, and others, whose judgments in such matters cried in the top of° mine — an excellent play, well digested in the scenes, set down with as much modesty as   445 cunning.° I remember one said there were no sallets° in the lines to make the matter savory, nor no matter in the phrase that might indict° the author of affection, but call'd it an honest method, as wholesome as sweet, and by very much more handsome than fine.°   450 One speech in 't I chiefly lov'd: 'twas Aeneas' tale to Dido, and thereabout of it especially when he speaks of Priam's slaughter.° If it live in your memory, begin at this line: let me see, let me see —
"The rugged Pyrrhus,° like th' Hyrcanian beast"° —   455
'Tis not so. It begins with Pyrrhus:
"The rugged Pyrrhus, he whose sable° arms,

---

383. **north-north-west:** Only partly, at times.   384. **hawk, handsaw:** Mattock (or *hack*) and a carpenter's cutting tool respectively; also birds, with a play on *hernshaw* or heron.   388. **swaddling-clouts:** Cloths in which to wrap a newborn baby.   389. **Happily:** Haply, perhaps.   396. **Roscius:** A famous Roman actor who died in 62 B.C.   398. **Buzz:** An interjection used to denote stale news.   404. **scene individable:** A play observing the unity of place.   404–05. **poem unlimited:** A play disregarding the unities of time and place.   405. **Seneca:** Writer of Latin tragedies.   405–06. **Plautus:** Writer of Latin comedy.   406. **law . . . liberty:** Dramatic composition both according to rules and without rules, i.e., "classical" and "romantic" dramas.   408. **Jephthah . . . Israel:** Jephthah had to sacrifice his daughter; see Judges 11. Hamlet goes on to quote from a ballad on the theme.   413. **passing:** Surpassingly.   421. **wot:** Knows.

423. **like:** Likely, probable.   424. **row:** Stanza.   **chanson:** Ballad, song.   425. **my abridgement:** Something that cuts short my conversation; also, a diversion.   428. **valanc'd:** Fringed (with a beard).   429. **beard:** Confront (with obvious pun).   430. **young lady:** Boy playing women's parts.   432. **chopine:** Thick-soled shoe of Italian fashion.   433. **uncurrent:** Not passable as lawful coinage.   433–34. **crack'd . . . ring:** Changed from adolescent to male voice, no longer suitable for women's roles. (Coins featured rings enclosing the sovereign's head; if the coin was cracked within this ring, it was unfit for currency.)   436. **straight:** At once.   442. **caviary to the general:** Caviar to the multitude, i.e., a choice dish too elegant for coarse tastes.   443–44. **cried in the top of:** Spoke with greater authority than.   446. **cunning:** Skill.   **sallets:** Salad, i.e., spicy improprieties.   448. **indict:** Convict.   450. **fine:** Elaborately ornamented, showy.   453. **Priam's slaughter:** The slaying of the ruler of Troy, when the Greeks finally took the city.   455. **Pyrrhus:** A Greek hero in the Trojan War, also known as Neoptolemus, son of Achilles.   **Hyrcanian beast:** I.e., the tiger. (See Virgil, *Aeneid*, IV, 266; compare the whole speech with Marlowe's *Dido Queen of Carthage*, II, I, 214 ff.)   457. **sable:** Black (for reasons of camouflage during the episode of the Trojan horse).

Black as his purpose, did the night resemble
When he lay couched in the ominous horse,°
460 Hath now this dread and black complexion smear'd
With heraldry more dismal.° Head to foot
Now is he total gules,° horridly trick'd°
With blood of fathers, mothers, daughters, sons,
Bak'd and impasted° with the parching streets,°
465 That lend a tyrannous and a damned light
To their lord's° murder. Roasted in wrath and fire,
And thus o'er-sized° with coagulate gore,
With eyes like carbuncles, the hellish Pyrrhus
Old grandsire Priam seeks."
470 So proceed you.
POLONIUS: 'Fore God, my lord, well spoken, with good
accent and good discretion.
FIRST PLAYER: "Anon he finds him
Striking too short at Greeks. His antique sword,
Rebellious to his arm, lies where it falls,
475 Repugnant° to command. Unequal match'd,
Pyrrhus at Priam drives, in rage strikes wide,
But with the whiff and wind of his fell° sword
Th' unnerved father falls. [Then senseless Ilium,°]
Seeming to feel this blow, with flaming top
480 Stoops to his° base, and with a hideous crash
Takes prisoner Pyrrhus' ear. For, lo! His sword,
Which was declining on the milky head
Of reverend Priam, seem'd i' th' air to stick.
So as a painted° tyrant Pyrrhus stood,
485 And, like a neutral to his will and matter,°
Did nothing.
But, as we often see, against° some storm,
A silence in the heavens, the rack° stand still,
The bold winds speechless, and the orb below
490 As hush as death, anon the dreadful thunder
Doth rend the region,° so, after Pyrrhus' pause,
Aroused vengeance sets him new a-work,
And never did the Cyclops'° hammers fall
On Mars's armor forg'd for proof eterne°
495 With less remorse than Pyrrhus' bleeding sword
Now falls on Priam.
Out, out, thou strumpet Fortune! All you gods,
In general synod,° take away her power!
Break all the spokes and fellies° from her wheel,

And bowl the round nave° down the hill of
heaven,
As low as to the fiends!"   500
POLONIUS: This is too long.
HAMLET: It shall to the barber's with your beard. —
Prithee say on. He's for a jig° or a tale of bawdry, or
he sleeps. Say on, come to Hecuba.°   505
FIRST PLAYER: "But who, ah woe! had seen the
mobled° queen"—
HAMLET: "The mobled queen?"
POLONIUS: That's good. "Mobled queen" is good.
FIRST PLAYER: "Run barefoot up and down, threat'ning
the flames
With bisson rheum,° a clout° upon that head   510
Where late the diadem stood, and for a robe,
About her lank and all o'er-teemed° loins,
A blanket, in the alarm of fear caught up —
Who this had seen, with tongue in venom steep'd,
'Gainst Fortune's state° would treason have
pronounc'd.°   515
But if the gods themselves did see her then
When she saw Pyrrhus make malicious sport
In mincing with his sword her husband's limbs,
The instant burst of clamor that she made,
Unless things mortal move them not at all,   520
Would have made milch° the burning eyes of
heaven,
And passion in the gods."
POLONIUS: Look whe'er° he has not turn'd his color and
has tears in 's eyes. Prithee, no more.
HAMLET: 'Tis well; I'll have thee speak out the rest of 525
this soon. Good my lord, will you see the players well
bestow'd?° Do you hear, let them be well us'd, for
they are the abstract° and brief chronicles of the
time. After your death you were better have a bad
epitaph than their ill report while you live.   530
POLONIUS: My lord, I will use them according to their
desert.
HAMLET: God's bodkin,° man, much better! Use every
man after his desert, and who shall scape whipping?
Use them after your own honor and dignity. The less 535
they deserve, the more merit is in your bounty. Take
them in.
POLONIUS: Come, sirs.
HAMLET: Follow him, friends. We'll hear a play tomorrow. [*As they start to leave, Hamlet detains the First* 540
Player.] Dost thou hear me, old friend? Can you play
the Murder of Gonzago?
FIRST PLAYER: Ay, my lord.

---

459. ominous horse: Trojan horse, by which the Greeks gained access to Troy.   **461. dismal:** Ill-omened.   **462. gules:** Red (a heraldic term).   **trick'd:** Adorned, decorated.   **464. impasted:** Crusted, like a thick paste.   **with . . . streets:** By the parching heat of the streets (because of the fires everywhere). **466. their lord's:** Priam's.   **467. o'er-sized:** Covered as with size or glue.   **475. Repugnant:** Disobedient, resistant.   **477. fell:** Cruel.   **478. senseless Ilium:** Insensate Troy.   **480. his:** Its. **484. painted:** Painted in a picture.   **485. like . . . matter:** As though poised indecisively between his intention and its fulfillment.   **487. against:** Just before.   **488. rack:** Mass of clouds. **491. region:** Sky.   **493. Cyclops:** Giant armor makers in the smithy of Vulcan.   **494. proof eterne:** Eternal resistance to assault.   **498. synod:** Assembly.   **499. fellies:** Pieces of wood forming the rim of a wheel.

500. nave: Hub.   **504. jig:** Comic song and dance often given at the end of a play.   **505. Hecuba:** Wife of Priam. **506. mobled:** Muffled.   **510. bisson rheum:** Blinding tears. **clout:** Cloth.   **512. o'er-teemed:** Worn out with bearing children.   **515. state:** Rule, managing.   **pronounc'd:** Proclaimed. **521. milch:** Milky moist with tears.   **523. whe'er:** Whether. **527. bestow'd:** Lodged.   **528. abstract:** Summary account. **533. God's bodkin:** By God's (Christ's) little body, *bodykin* (not to be confused with *bodkin*, dagger).

HAMLET: We'll ha 't tomorrow night. You could, for
545   need, study a speech of some dozen or sixteen lines,
       which I would set down and insert in 't, could you
       not?
FIRST PLAYER: Ay, my lord.
HAMLET: Very well. Follow that lord, and look you
550   mock him not. — My good friends, I'll leave you till
       night. You are welcome to Elsinore.
                          (*Exeunt Polonius and Players.*)
ROSENCRANTZ: Good my lord!
                          (*Exeunt [Rosencrantz and Guildenstern].*)
HAMLET: Ay, so, God buy you. — Now I am alone.
       O, what a rogue and peasant slave am I!
555   Is it not monstrous that this player here,
       But in a fiction, in a dream of passion,
       Could force his soul so to his own conceit°
       That from her working all his visage wann'd,°
       Tears in his eyes, distraction in his aspect,
560   A broken voice, and his whole function suiting
       With forms to his conceit?° And all for nothing!
       For Hecuba!
       What's Hecuba to him, or he to Hecuba,
       That he should weep for her? What would he do,
565   Had he the motive and the cue for passion
       That I have? He would drown the stage with tears
       And cleave the general ear with horrid speech,
       Make mad the guilty and appall the free,°
       Confound the ignorant, and amaze indeed
570   The very faculties of eyes and ears. Yet I,
       A dull and muddy-mettled° rascal, peak,°
       Like John-a-dreams,° unpregnant of° my cause,
       And can say nothing — no, not for a king
       Upon whose property° and most dear life
575   A damn'd defeat was made. Am I a coward?
       Who calls me villain? Breaks my pate across?
       Plucks off my beard, and blows it in my face?
       Tweaks me by the nose? Gives me the lie° i' th'
          throat,
       As deep as to the lungs? Who does me this?
580   Ha, 'swounds, I should take it; for it cannot be
       But I am pigeon-liver'd,° and lack gall
       To make oppression bitter, or ere this
       I should have fatted all the region kites°
       With this slave's offal. Bloody, bawdy villain!
585   Remorseless, treacherous, lecherous, kindless° villain!
       [O, vengeance!]
       Why, what an ass am I! This is most brave,
       That I, the son of a dear father murder'd,

Prompted to my revenge by heaven and hell,
Must, like a whore, unpack my heart with words,   590
And fall a-cursing, like a very drab,°
A stallion! Fie upon 't, foh! About,° my brains!
Hum, I have heard
That guilty creatures sitting at a play
Have by the very cunning of the scene   595
Been struck so to the soul that presently°
They have proclaim'd their malefactions;
For murder, though it have no tongue, will speak
With most miraculous organ. I'll have these players
Play something like the murder of my father   600
Before mine uncle. I'll observe his looks;
I'll tent° him to the quick. If 'a do blench,°
I know my course. The spirit that I have seen
May be the devil, and the devil hath power
T' assume a pleasing shape; yea, and perhaps   605
Out of my weakness and my melancholy,
As he is very potent with such spirits,°
Abuses° me to damn me. I'll have grounds
More relative° than this. The play's the thing
Wherein I'll catch the conscience of the King.   610
                                      (*Exit.*)

{*ACT III* • *Scene 1*}°

(*Enter King, Queen, Polonius, Ophelia, Rosencrantz,
Guildenstern, Lords.*)

KING: And can you, by no drift of conference,°
       Get from him why he puts on this confusion,
       Grating so harshly all his days of quiet
       With turbulent and dangerous lunacy?
ROSENCRANTZ: He does confess he feels himself
          distracted,   5
       But from what cause 'a will by no means speak.
GUILDENSTERN: Nor do we find him forward° to be
          sounded,°
       But with a crafty madness keeps aloof
       When we would bring him on to some confession
       Of his true state.
QUEEN: Did he receive you well?   10
ROSENCRANTZ: Most like a gentleman.
GUILDENSTERN: But with much forcing of his
          disposition.°
ROSENCRANTZ: Niggard of question,° but of our
          demands
       Most free in his reply.

---

557. **conceit:** Conception.   558. **wann'd:** Grew pale.
560–61. **his whole . . . conceit:** His whole being responded with
actions to suit his thought.   568. **free:** Innocent.   571. **muddy-
mettled:** Dull-spirited.   **peak:** Mope, pine.   572. **John-a-
dreams:** Sleepy dreaming idler.   **unpregnant of:** Not quickened
by.   574. **property:** The crown; perhaps also character, quality.
578. **Gives me the lie:** Calls me a liar.   581. **pigeon-liver'd:** The
pigeon or dove was popularly supposed to be mild because it
secreted no gall.   583. **region kites:** Kites (birds of prey) of the
air, from the vicinity.   585. **kindless:** Unnatural.

591. **drab:** Prostitute.   592. **stallion:** Prostitute (male or female). (Many editors follow the Folio reading of *scullion*.)
About: About it, to work.   596. **presently:** At once.
602. **tent:** Probe.   **blench:** Quail, flinch.   607. **spirits:**
Humors (of melancholy).   608. **Abuses:** Deludes.   609. **relative:** Closely related, pertinent.   **III, 1. Location:** The castle.
1. **drift of conference:** Direction of conversation.   7. **forward:**
Willing.   **sounded:** Tested deeply.   12. **disposition:** Inclination.   13. **question:** Conversation.

Most Famous Silliy?

QUEEN: Did you assay° him
15 To any pastime?
ROSENCRANTZ: Madam, it so fell out that certain players
    We o'er-raught° on the way. Of these we told him,
    And there did seem in him a kind of joy
    To hear of it. They are here about the court,
20 And, as I think, they have already order
    This night to play before him.
POLONIUS: 'Tis most true,
    And he beseech'd me to entreat your Majesties
    To hear and see the matter.
KING: With all my heart, and it doth much content me
25 To hear him so inclin'd.
    Good gentlemen, give him a further edge,°
    And drive his purpose into these delights.
ROSENCRANTZ: We shall, my lord.

            (*Exeunt Rosencrantz and Guildenstern.*)

KING: Sweet Gertrude, leave us too,
    For we have closely° sent for Hamlet hither,
30 That he, as 'twere by accident, may here
    Affront° Ophelia.
    Her father and myself, [lawful espials,°]
    Will so bestow ourselves that seeing, unseen,
    We may of their encounter frankly judge,
35 And gather by him, as he is behav'd,
    If 't be th' affliction of his love or no
    That thus he suffers for.
QUEEN: I shall obey you.
    And for your part, Ophelia, I do wish
    That your good beauties be the happy cause
40 Of Hamlet's wildness. So shall I hope your virtues
    Will bring him to his wonted way again,
    To both your honors.
OPHELIA: Madam, I wish it may.
                    [*Exit Queen.*]
POLONIUS: Ophelia, walk you here. — Gracious,° so
    please you,
    We will bestow ourselves. [*To Ophelia.*] Read on
    this book,   [*Gives her a book.*]
45 That show of such an exercise° may color°
    Your loneliness. We are oft to blame in this —
    'Tis too much prov'd° — that with devotion's visage
    And pious action we do sugar o'er
    The devil himself.
50 KING [*aside*]: O, 'tis too true!
    How smart a lash that speech doth give my
        conscience!
    The harlot's cheek, beautied with plast'ring art,
    Is not more ugly to° the thing° that helps it

Than is my deed to my most painted word.
    O heavy burden!   55
POLONIUS: I hear him coming. Let's withdraw, my lord.
                [*King and Polonius withdraw.°*]

(*Enter Hamlet.* [*Ophelia pretends to read a book.*])

HAMLET: To be, or not to be, that is the question:
    Whether 'tis nobler in the mind to suffer
    The slings and arrows of outrageous fortune,
    Or to take arms against a sea of troubles,   60
    And by opposing end them. To die, to sleep —
    No more — and by a sleep to say we end
    The heart-ache and the thousand natural shocks
    That flesh is heir to. 'Tis a consummation
    Devoutly to be wish'd. To die, to sleep;   65
    To sleep, perchance to dream. Ay, there's the rub,°
    For in that sleep of death what dreams may come
    When we have shuffled° off this mortal coil,°
    Must give us pause. There's the respect°
    That makes calamity of so long life.°   70
    For who would bear the whips and scorns of time,
    Th' oppressor's wrong, the proud man's contumely,°
    The pangs of despis'd° love, the law's delay,
    The insolence of office,° and the spurns°
    That patient merit of th' unworthy takes,   75
    When he himself might his quietus° make
    With a bare bodkin?° Who would fardels° bear,
    To grunt and sweat under a weary life,
    But that the dread of something after death,
    The undiscover'd country from whose bourn°   80
    No traveler returns, puzzles the will,
    And makes us rather bear those ills we have
    Than fly to others that we know not of?
    Thus conscience does make cowards of us all
    And thus the native hue° of resolution   85
    Is sicklied o'er with the pale cast° of thought,
    And enterprises of great pitch° and moment°
    With this regard° their currents° turn awry,
    And lose the name of action. — Soft you now,
    The fair Ophelia. Nymph, in thy orisons°   90
    Be all my sins remb'red.
OPHELIA: Good my lord,
    How does your honor for this many a day?
HAMLET: I humbly thank you; well, well, well.
OPHELIA: My lord, I have remembrances of yours,

14. **assay:** Try to win.   17. **o'er-raught:** Overtook and passed. 26. **edge:** Incitement.   29. **closely:** Privately.   31. **Affront:** Confront, meet.   32. **espials:** Spies.   43. **Gracious:** Your Grace (i.e., the King).   45. **exercise:** Act of devotion. (The book she reads is one of devotion.)   **color:** Give a plausible appearance to.   47. **too much prov'd:** Too often shown to be true, too often practiced.   53. **to:** Compared to.   **thing:** I.e., the cosmetic.

56. [s.d.] **withdraw:** The King and Polonius may retire behind an arras. The stage directions specify that they "enter" again near the end of the scene.   66. **rub:** Literally, an obstacle in the game of bowls.   68. **shuffled:** Sloughed, cast. **coil:** Turmoil.   69. **respect:** Consideration.   70. **of . . . life:** So long-lived.   72. **contumely:** Insolent abuse.   73. **despis'd:** Rejected.   74. **office:** Officialdom.   **spurns:** Insults.   76. **quietus:** Acquittance; here, death.   77. **bodkin:** Dagger.   **fardels:** Burdens.   80. **bourn:** Boundary.   85. **native hue:** Natural color, complexion.   86. **cast:** Shade of color.   87. **pitch:** Height (as of a falcon's flight).   **moment:** Importance.   88. **regard:** Respect, consideration.   **currents:** Courses.   90. **orisons:** Prayers.

95 That I have longed long to re-deliver.
I pray you, now receive them. [*Offers tokens.*]
HAMLET: No, not I, I never gave you aught.
OPHELIA: My honor'd lord, you know right well you did,
And with them words of so sweet breath compos'd
100 As made these things more rich. Their perfume lost,
Take these again, for to the noble mind
Rich gifts wax poor when givers prove unkind.
There, my lord. [*Gives tokens.*]
HAMLET: Ha, ha! Are you honest?°
105 OPHELIA: My lord?
HAMLET: Are you fair?°
OPHELIA: What means your lordship?
HAMLET: That if you be honest and fair, your honesty°
should admit no discourse° to your beauty.
110 OPHELIA: Could beauty, my lord, have better commerce° than with honesty?
HAMLET: Ay, truly, for the power of beauty will sooner
transform honesty from what it is to a bawd than the
force of honesty can translate beauty into his like-
115 ness. This was sometime° a paradox,° but now the
time° gives it proof. I did love you once.
OPHELIA: Indeed, my lord, you made me believe so.
HAMLET: You should not have believ'd me, for virtue
cannot so inoculate° our old stock but we shall relish
120 of it.° I lov'd you not.
OPHELIA: I was the more deceiv'd.
HAMLET: Get thee to a nunn'ry.° Why wouldst thou be a
breeder of sinners? I am myself indifferent honest;°
but yet I could accuse me of such things that it were
125 better my mother had not borne me: I am very proud,
revengeful, ambitious, with more offenses at my
beck° than I have thoughts to put them in, imagination to give them shape, or time to act them in. What
should such fellows as I do crawling between earth
130 and heaven? We are arrant knaves, all; believe none
of us. Go thy ways to a nunn'ry. Where's your father?
OPHELIA: At home, my lord.
HAMLET: Let the doors be shut upon him, that he may
play the fool nowhere but in 's own house.
135 Farewell.
OPHELIA: O, help him, you sweet heavens!
HAMLET: If thou dost marry, I'll give thee this plague for
thy dowry: be thou as chaste as ice, as pure as snow,
thou shalt not escape calumny. Get thee to a nunn'ry,
140 farewell. Or, if thou wilt needs marry, marry a fool,

for wise men know well enough what monsters° you°
make of them. To a nunn'ry, go, and quickly too.
Farewell.
OPHELIA: Heavenly powers, restore him!
HAMLET: I have heard of your paintings too, well 145
enough. God hath given you one face, and you make
yourselves another. You jig,° and amble, and you
lisp, you nickname God's creatures, and make your
wantonness your ignorance.° Go to, I'll no more on
't; it hath made me mad. I say, we will have no moe 150
marriage. Those that are married already — all but
one — shall live. The rest shall keep as they are. To a
nunn'ry, go. (*Exit.*)
OPHELIA: O, what a noble mind is here o'erthrown!
The courtier's, soldier's, scholar's, eye, tongue, sword, 155
Th' expectancy and rose of the fair state,°
The glass of fashion and the mold of form,°
Th' observ'd of all observers,° quite, quite down!
And I, of ladies most deject and wretched,
That suck'd the honey of his music vows, 160
Now see that noble and most sovereign reason,
Like sweet bells jangled, out of time and harsh,
That unmatch'd form and feature of blown° youth
Blasted with ecstasy.° O, woe is me,
T' have seen what I have seen, see what I see! 165

(*Enter King and Polonius.*)

KING: Love? His affections do not that way tend;
Nor what he spake, though it lack'd form a little,
Was not like madness. There's something in his soul,
O'er which his melancholy sits on brood,
And I do doubt° the hatch and the disclose° 170
Will be some danger; which for to prevent,
I have in quick determination
Thus set it down: he shall with speed to England,
For the demand of° our neglected tribute.
Haply the seas and countries different 175
With variable° objects shall expel
This something-settled° matter in his heart,
Whereon his brains still beating puts him thus
From fashion of himself.° What think you on 't?
POLONIUS: It shall do well. But yet do I believe 180
The origin and commencement of his grief
Sprung from neglected love. — How now, Ophelia?
You need not tell us what Lord Hamlet said;

---

104. **honest:** (1) Truthful; (2) chaste. 106. **fair:** (1) Beautiful; (2) just, honorable. 108. **your honesty:** Your chastity. 109. **discourse:** Familiar dealings. 110–11. **commerce:** Dealings. 115. **sometime:** Formerly. **paradox:** A view opposite to commonly held opinion. 115–16. **the time:** The present age. 119. **inoculate:** Graft, be engrafted to. 119–20. **but . . . it:** That we do not still have about us a taste of the old stock; i.e., retain our sinfulness. 122. **nunn'ry:** (1) Convent, (2) brothel. 123. **indifferent honest:** Reasonably virtuous. 127. **beck:** Command.

141. **monsters:** An allusion to the horns of a cuckold. **you:** You women. 147. **jig:** Dance and sing affectedly and wantonly. 148–49. **make . . . ignorance:** Excuse your affection on the grounds of your ignorance. 156. **Th' expectancy . . . state:** The hope and ornament of the kingdom made fair (by him). 157. **The glass . . . form:** The mirror of fashion and the pattern of courtly behavior. 158. **observ'd . . . observers:** The center of attention and honor in the court. 163. **blown:** Blooming. 164. **ecstasy:** Madness. 170. **doubt:** Fear. **disclose:** Disclosure. 174. **For . . . of:** To demand. 176. **variable:** Various. 177. **something-settled:** Somewhat settled. 179. **From . . . himself:** Out of his natural manner.

185
We heard it all. — My lord, do as you please,
But, if you hold it fit, after the play
Let his queen mother all alone entreat him
To show his grief. Let her be round° with him;
And I'll be plac'd, so please you, in the ear
Of all their conference. If she find him not,

190
To England send him, or confine him where
Your wisdom best shall think.

KING: It shall be so.
Madness in great ones must not unwatch'd go.

(*Exeunt.*)

{*Scene II*}°

(*Enter Hamlet and three of the Players.*)

HAMLET: Speak the speech, I pray you, as I pronounc'd
it to you, trippingly on the tongue. But if you mouth
it, as many of our players° do, I had as lief the town-
crier spoke my lines. Nor do not saw the air too

5
much with your hand, thus, but use all gently; for in
the very torrent, tempest, and, as I may say, whirlwind of your passion, you must acquire and beget a
temperance that may give it smoothness. O, it
offends me to the soul to hear a robustious° periwig-

10
pated° fellow tear a passion to tatters, to very rags, to
split the ears of the groundlings,° who for the most
part are capable of° nothing but inexplicable dumb-
shows and noise. I would have such a fellow whipp'd
for o'er-doing Termagant.° It out-herods Herod.°

15
Pray you, avoid it.

FIRST PLAYER: I warrant your honor.

HAMLET: Be not too tame neither, but let your own discretion be your tutor. Suit the action to the word, the
word to the action, with this special observance, that

20
you o'erstep not the modesty of nature. For anything
so o'erdone is from° the purpose of playing, whose
end, both at the first and now, was and is, to hold, as
't were, the mirror up to nature, to show virtue her
feature, scorn her own image, and the very age and

25
body of the time his° form and pressure.° Now this
overdone, or come tardy off,° though it makes the
unskillful laugh, cannot but make the judicious

grieve, the censure of which one° must in your
allowance o'erweigh a whole theater of others. O,
there be players that I have seen play, and heard oth-   30
ers praise, and that highly, not to speak it profanely,
that, neither having th' accent of Christians nor the
gait of Christian, pagan, nor man, have so strutted
and bellow'd that I have thought some of nature's
journeymen° had made men and not made them   35
well, they imitated humanity so abominably.

FIRST PLAYER: I hope we have reform'd that indiffer-
ently° with us, sir.

HAMLET: O, reform it altogether. And let those that play
your clowns speak no more than is set down for   40
them; for there be of them° that will themselves
laugh, to set on some quantity of barren° spectators
to laugh too, though in the mean time some necessary question of the play be then to be consider'd.
That's villainous, and shows a most pitiful ambition   45
in the fool that uses it. Go, make you ready.

[*Exeunt Players.*]

(*Enter Polonius, Guildenstern, and Rosencrantz.*)

How now, my lord? Will the King hear this piece of
work?

POLONIUS: And the Queen too, and that presently.°

HAMLET: Bid the players make haste.   50

[*Exit Polonius.*]

Will you two help to hasten them?

ROSENCRANTZ: Ay, my lord.   (*Exeunt they two.*)

HAMLET: What ho, Horatio!

(*Enter Horatio.*)

HORATIO: Here, sweet lord, at your service.

HAMLET: Horatio, thou art e'en as just a man
As e'er my conversation cop'd withal.°   55

HORATIO: O, my dear lord —

HAMLET: Nay, do not think I flatter;
For what advancement may I hope from thee
That no revenue hast but thy good spirits,
To feed and clothe thee? Why should the poor be
flatter'd?
No, let the candied° tongue lick absurd pomp,   60
And crook the pregnant° hinges of the knee
Where thrift° may follow fawning. Dost thou hear?
Since my dear soul was mistress of her choice
And could of men distinguish her election,
Sh' hath seal'd thee for herself, for thou hast been   65
As one, in suff'ring all, that suffers nothing,
A man that Fortune's buffets and rewards
Hast ta'en with equal thanks; and blest are those

---

187. round: Blunt. **III, II. Location:** The castle. **3. our players:** Indefinite use; i.e., *players nowadays.* **9. robustious:** Violent, boisterous. **9–10. periwig-pated:** Wearing a wig. **11. groundlings:** Spectators who paid least and stood in the yard of the theater. **12. capable of:** Susceptible of being influenced by. **14. Termagant:** A god of the Saracens; a character in the St. Nicholas play, where one of his worshipers, leaving him in charge of goods, returns to find them stolen; whereupon he beats the god or idol, which howls vociferously. **Herod:** Herod of Jewry. (A character in *The Slaughter of the Innocents* and other cycle plays. The part was played with great noise and fury.) **21. from:** Contrary to. **25. his:** Its. **pressure:** Stamp, impressed character. **26. come tardy off:** Inadequately done.

28. the censure . . . one: The judgment of even one of whom. **35. journeymen:** Laborers not yet masters in their trade. **37–38. indifferently:** Tolerably. **41. of them:** Some among them. **42. barren:** I.e., of wit. **49. presently:** At once. **55. my . . . withal:** My contact with people provided opportunity for encounter with. **60. candied:** Sugared, flattering. **61. pregnant:** Compliant. **62. thrift:** Profit.

Whose blood° and judgment are so well
   commeddled°
70 That they are not a pipe for Fortune's finger
To sound what stop° she please. Give me that
   man
That is not passion's slave, and I will wear him
In my heart's core, ay, in my heart of heart,
As I do thee. — Something too much of this. —
75 There is a play tonight before the King.
One scene of it comes near the circumstance
Which I have told thee of my father's death.
I prithee, when thou seest that act afoot,
Even with the very comment of thy soul°
80 Observe my uncle. If his occulted° guilt
Do not itself unkennel in one speech,
It is a damned° ghost that we have seen,
And my imaginations are as foul
As Vulcan's stithy.° Give him heedful note,
85 For I mine eyes will rivet to his face,
And after we will both our judgments join
In censure of his seeming.°
HORATIO: Well, my lord.
If 'a steal aught the whilst this play is playing,
And scape detecting, I will pay the theft.

([*Flourish.*] *Enter trumpets and kettledrums, King, Queen, Polonius, Ophelia, [Rosencrantz, Guildenstern, and other Lords, with Guards carrying torches].*)

90 HAMLET: They are coming to the play. I must be idle. Get
   you a place.   [*The King, Queen, and courtiers sit.*]
KING: How fares our cousin Hamlet?
HAMLET: Excellent, i' faith, of the chameleon's dish:°
   I eat the air, promise-cramm'd. You cannot feed ca-
95   pons so.
KING: I have nothing with° this answer, Hamlet. These
   words are not mine.°
HAMLET: No, nor mine now. [*To Polonius.*] My lord,
   you played once i' th' university, you say?
100 POLONIUS: That did I, my lord; and was accounted a
   good actor.
HAMLET: What did you enact?
POLONIUS: I did enact Julius Caesar. I was killed i' th'
   Capitol; Brutus kill'd me.
105 HAMLET: It was a brute part of him to kill so capital a
   calf there. Be the players ready?
ROSENCRANTZ: Ay, my lord; they stay upon your
   patience.

QUEEN: Come hither, my dear Hamlet, sit by me.
HAMLET: No, good mother, here's metal more attractive. 110
POLONIUS [*to the King*]: O, ho, do you mark that?
HAMLET: Lady, shall I lie in your lap?
   [*Lying down at Ophelia's feet.*]
OPHELIA: No, my lord.
[HAMLET: I mean, my head upon your lap?
OPHELIA: Ay, my lord.] 115
HAMLET: Do you think I meant country° matters?
OPHELIA: I think nothing, my lord.
HAMLET: That's a fair thought to lie between maids' legs.
OPHELIA: What is, my lord?
HAMLET: Nothing. 120
OPHELIA: You are merry, my lord.
HAMLET: Who, I?
OPHELIA: Ay, my lord.
HAMLET: O God, your only jig-maker.° What should a
   man do but be merry? For look you how cheerfully 125
   my mother looks, and my father died within 's° two
   hours.
OPHELIA: Nay, 'tis twice two months, my lord.
HAMLET: So long? Nay then, let the devil wear black for
   I'll have a suit of sables.° O heavens! Die two months 130
   ago, and not forgotten yet? Then there's hope a great
   man's memory may outlive his life half a year. But,
   by 'r lady, 'a must build churches, then, or else shall
   'a suffer not thinking on,° with the hobby-horse,
   whose epitaph is "For, O, for, O, the hobby-horse is 135
   forgot."°

(*The trumpets sound. Dumb show follows.*)

(*Enter a King and a Queen [very lovingly]; the Queen embracing him, and he her. [She kneels and makes show of protestation unto him.] He takes her up, and declines his head upon her neck. He lies him down upon a bank of flowers. She, seeing him asleep, leaves him. Anon comes in another man, takes off his crown, kisses it, pours poison in the sleeper's ears, and leaves him. The Queen returns; finds the King dead, makes passionate action. The Poisoner, with some three or four, come in again, seem to condole with her. The dead body is carried away. The Poisoner woos the Queen with gifts; she seems harsh awhile but in the end accepts love.*)
   [*Exeunt.*]

OPHELIA: What means this, my lord?
HAMLET: Marry, this' miching mallecho;° it means
   mischief.

---

69. **blood:** Passion. **commeddled:** Commingled. 71. **stop:** Hole in a wind instrument for controlling the sound. 79. **very . . . soul:** Inward and sagacious criticism. 80. **occulted:** Hidden. 82. **damned:** In league with Satan. 84. **stithy:** Smithy, place of stiths (anvils). 87. **censure of his seeming:** Judgment of his appearance or behavior. 93. **chameleon's dish:** Chameleons were supposed to feed on air. Hamlet deliberately misinterprets the King's *fares* as *feeds.* By his phrase *eat the air* he also plays on the idea of feeding himself with the promise of succession, of being the *heir.* 96. **have . . . with:** Make nothing of. 97. **are not mine:** Do not respond to what I asked.

116. **country:** With a bawdy pun. 124. **only jig-maker:** Very best composer of jigs (song and dance). 126. **within 's:** Within this. 130. **suit of sables:** Garments trimmed with the fur of the sable and hence suited for a wealthy person, not a mourner (with a pun on *sable* black). 134. **suffer . . . on:** Undergo oblivion. 135–36. **"For . . . forgot":** Verse of a song occurring also in *Love's Labor's Lost,* III, i, 30. The hobby-horse was a character made up to resemble a horse, appearing in the Morris dance and such May-game sports. This song laments the disappearance of such customs under pressure from the Puritans. 138. **this' miching mallecho:** This is sneaking mischief.

140   OPHELIA: Belike° this show imports the argument° of
      the play.

      (*Enter Prologue.*)

      HAMLET: We shall know by this fellow. The players can-
      not keep counsel;° they'll tell all.
      OPHELIA: Will 'a tell us what this show meant?
145   HAMLET: Ay, or any show that you will show him. Be
      not you° asham'd to show, he'll not shame to tell you
      what it means.
      OPHELIA: You are naught, you are naught.° I'll mark the
      play.
150   PROLOGUE: For us, and for our tragedy,
      Here stooping° to your clemency,
      We beg your hearing patiently.   [*Exit.*]
      HAMLET: Is this a prologue, or the posy of a ring?°
      OPHELIA: 'Tis brief, my lord.
155   HAMLET: As woman's love.

      (*Enter [two Players as] King and Queen.*)

      PLAYER KING: Full thirty times hath Phoebus' cart°
      gone round
      Neptune's salt wash° and Tellus'° orbed ground,
      And thirty dozen moons with borrowed° sheen
      About the world have times twelve thirties been,
160   Since love our hearts and Hymen° did our hands
      Unite commutual° in most sacred bands.
      PLAYER QUEEN: So many journeys may the sun and
      moon
      Make us again count o'er ere love be done!
      But, woe is me, you are so sick of late,
165   So far from cheer and from your former state,
      That I distrust you. Yet, though I distrust,°
      Discomfort you, my lord, it nothing° must.
      For women's fear and love hold quantity;°
      In neither aught, or in extremity.
170   Now, what my love is, proof° hath made you know,
      And as my love is siz'd, my fear is so.
      Where love is great, the littlest doubts are fear;
      Where little fears grow great, great love grows
      there.
      PLAYER KING: Faith, I must leave thee, love, and
      shortly too;
175   My operant° powers their functions leave to do.°
      And thou shalt live in this fair world behind,
      Honor'd, belov'd; and haply one as kind
      For husband shalt thou —

PLAYER QUEEN: O, confound the rest!
      Such love must needs be treason in my breast.
      In second husband let me be accurst!   180
      None wed the second but who kill'd the first.
      HAMLET: Wormwood, wormwood.
      PLAYER QUEEN: The instances° that second marriage
      move°
      Are base respects of thrift,° but none of love.
      A second time I kill my husband dead,   185
      When second husband kisses me in bed.
      PLAYER KING: I do believe you think what now you
      speak,
      But what we do determine oft we break.
      Purpose is but the slave to memory,°
      Of violent birth, but poor validity,°   190
      Which now, like fruit unripe, sticks on the tree,
      But fall unshaken when they mellow be.
      Most necessary 'tis that we forget
      To pay ourselves what to ourselves is debt.°
      What to ourselves in passion we propose,   195
      The passion ending, doth the purpose lose.
      The violence of either grief or joy
      Their own enactures° with themselves destroy.
      Where joy most revels, grief doth most lament;
      Grief joys, joy grieves, on slender accident.   200
      This world is not for aye,° nor 'tis not strange
      That even our loves should with our fortunes
      change;
      For 'tis a question left us yet to prove,
      Whether love lead fortune, or else fortune love.
      The great man down, you mark his favorite flies;   205
      The poor advanc'd makes friends of enemies.
      And hitherto doth love on fortune tend;
      For who not needs° shall never lack a friend,
      And who in want° a hollow friend doth try,°
      Directly seasons him° his enemy.   210
      But, orderly to end where I begun,
      Our wills and fates do so contrary run
      That our devices still° are overthrown;
      Our thoughts are ours, their ends° none of our own.
      So think thou wilt no second husband wed,   215
      But die thy thoughts when thy first lord is dead.
      PLAYER QUEEN: Nor earth to me give food, nor heaven
      light,
      Sport and repose lock from me day and night,
      To desperation turn my trust and hope,
      An anchor's cheer° in prison be my scope!°   220

---

140. **Belike:** Probably.   **argument:** Plot.   143. **counsel:** Secret.
145–46. **Be not you:** If you are not.   148. **naught:** Indecent.
151. **stooping:** Bowing.   153. **posy . . . ring:** Brief motto in
verse inscribed in a ring.   156. **Phoebus' cart:** The sun god's
chariot.   157. **salt wash:** The sea.   **Tellus:** Goddess of the
earth, of the *orbed ground.*   158. **borrowed:** Reflected.
160. **Hymen:** God of matrimony.   161. **commutual:** Mutually.
166. **distrust:** Am anxious about.   167. **nothing:** Not at all.
168. **hold quantity:** Keep proportion with one another.
170. **proof:** Experience.   175. **operant:** Active.   **leave to do:**
Cease to perform.

183. **instances:** Motives.   **move:** Motivate.   184. **base . . .
thrift:** Ignoble considerations of material prosperity.   189. **Purpose . . . memory:** Our good intentions are subject to forgetfulness.   190. **validity:** Strength, durability.   193–94. **Most . . .
debt:** It's inevitable that in time we forget the obligations we have
imposed on ourselves.   198. **enactures:** Fulfillments.   201. **aye:**
Ever.   208. **who not needs:** He who is not in need (of wealth).
209. **who in want:** He who is in need.   **try:** Test (his generosity).
210. **seasons him:** Ripens him into.   213. **devices still:** Intentions
continually.   214. **ends:** Results.   220. **anchor's cheer:** Anchor-
ite's or hermit's fare.   **my scope:** The extent of my happiness.

Each opposite° that blanks° the face of joy
Meet what I would have well and it destroy!
Both here and hence° pursue me lasting strife,
If, once a widow, ever I be wife!

225 HAMLET: If she should break it now!
PLAYER KING: 'Tis deeply sworn. Sweet, leave me here
      awhile;
My spirits grow dull, and fain I would beguile
The tedious day with sleep.   [*Sleeps.*]
PLAYER QUEEN: Sleep rock thy brain,
230 And never come mischance between us twain!
                                               [*Exit.*]
HAMLET: Madam, how like you this play?
QUEEN: The lady doth protest too much, methinks.
HAMLET: O, but she'll keep her word.
KING: Have you heard the argument?° Is there no of-
235   fense in 't?
HAMLET: No, no, they do but jest, poison in jest; no of-
      fense i' th' world.
KING: What do you call the play?
HAMLET: "The Mouse-trap." Marry, how? Tropically.°
240 This play is the image of a murder done in Vienna.
      Gonzago is the Duke's name; his wife, Baptista. You
      shall see anon. 'Tis a knavish piece of work, but what
      of that? Your Majesty, and we that have free° souls, it
      touches us not. Let the gall'd jade° winch,° our with-
245   ers° are unwrung.°

(*Enter Lucianus.*)

This is one Lucianus, nephew to the King.
OPHELIA: You are as good as a chorus,° my lord.
HAMLET: I could interpret between you and your love, if
      I could see the puppets dallying.°
250 OPHELIA: You are keen, my lord, you are keen.
HAMLET: It would cost you a groaning to take off mine
      edge.
OPHELIA: Still better, and worse.°
HAMLET: So° you mistake° your husbands. Begin, mur-
255   derer, leave thy damnable faces, and begin. Come,
      the croaking raven doth bellow for revenge.
LUCIANUS: Thoughts black, hands apt, drugs fit, and
      time agreeing,

Confederate season,° else no creature seeing,
Thou mixture rank, of midnight weeds collected,   260
With Hecate's ban° thrice blasted, thrice infected,
Thy natural magic and dire property
On wholesome life usurp immediately.
            [*Pours the poison into the sleeper's ears.*]
HAMLET: 'A poisons him i' th' garden for his estate. His
      name's Gonzago. The story is extant, and written in   265
      very choice Italian. You shall see anon how the mur-
      derer gets the love of Gonzago's wife.
                                          [*Claudius rises.*]
OPHELIA: The King rises.
[HAMLET: What, frighted with false fire?°]
QUEEN: How fares my lord?   270
POLONIUS: Give o'er the play.
KING: Give me some light. Away!
POLONIUS: Lights, lights, lights!

            (*Exeunt all but Hamlet and Horatio.*)

HAMLET: "Why, let the strucken deer go weep,
      The hart ungalled° play.   275
For some must watch,° while some must sleep;
      Thus runs the world away."°
Would not this,° sir, and a forest of feathers° — if the
      rest of my fortunes turn Turk with° me — with two
      Provincial roses° on my raz'd° shoes, get me a fellow-   280
      ship in a cry of players?°
HORATIO: Half a share.
HAMLET: A whole one, I.
      "For thou dost know, O Damon dear,
      This realm dismantled° was   285
Of Jove himself, and now reigns here
      A very, very — pajock."°
HORATIO: You might have rhym'd.
HAMLET: O good Horatio, I'll take the ghost's word for
      a thousand pound. Didst perceive?   290
HORATIO: Very well, my lord.
HAMLET: Upon the talk of pois'ning?
HORATIO: I did very well note him.
HAMLET: Ah, ha! Come, some music! Come, the re-
      corders!°   295

---

222. **opposite:** Adverse thing. **blanks:** Causes to blanch or grow pale. 223. **hence:** In the life hereafter. 234. **argument:** Plot. 239. **Tropically:** Figuratively. (The first quarto reading, *trapically,* suggests a pun on *trap* in *Mouse-trap.*) 243. **free:** Guiltless. 244. **gall'd jade:** Horse whose hide is rubbed by saddle or harness. **winch:** Wince. 244–45. **withers:** The part between the horse's shoulder blades. 245. **unwrung:** Not rubbed sore. 247. **chorus:** In many Elizabethan plays the forthcoming action was explained by an actor known as the "chorus"; at a puppet show the actor who spoke the dialogue was known as an "interpreter," as indicated by the lines follow-ing. 249. **dallying:** With sexual suggestion, continued in *keen,* i.e., sexually aroused, *groaning,* i.e., moaning in pregnancy, and *edge,* i.e., sexual desire or impetuosity. 253. **Still . . . worse:** More keen-witted and less decorous. 254. **So:** Even thus (in marriage). **mistake:** Mistake, take erringly, false-heartedly.

259. **Confederate season:** The time and occasion conspiring (to assist the murderer). 261. **Hecate's ban:** The curse of Hecate, the goddess of witchcraft. 269. **false fire:** The blank discharge of a gun loaded with powder but not shot. 275. **ungalled:** Unafflicted. 276. **watch:** Remain awake. 274–77. **Why . . . away:** Probably from an old ballad, with allusion to the popular belief that a wounded deer retires to weep and die; cf. *As You Like It,* II, i, 66. 278. **this:** The play. **feathers:** Allusion to the plumes that Elizabethan actors were fond of wearing. 279. **turn Turk with:** Turn renegade against, go back on. 280. **Provincial roses:** Rosettes of ribbon like the roses of a part of France. **raz'd:** With ornamental slashing. 280–81. **fellowship . . . players:** Partnership in a theatrical company. 285. **dismantled:** Stripped, divested. 287. **pajock:** Peacock, a bird with a bad reputation (here substituted for the obvious rhyme-word *ass*). 295. **recorders:** Wind instruments like the flute.

"For if the King like not the comedy,
Why then, belike, he likes it not, perdy"°
Come, some music!

(Enter Rosencrantz and Guildenstern.)

GUILDENSTERN: Good my lord, vouchsafe me a word
300   with you.

HAMLET: Sir, a whole history.

GUILDENSTERN: The King, sir —

HAMLET: Ay, sir, what of him?

GUILDENSTERN: Is in his retirement marvelous dis-
305   temp'red.

HAMLET: With drink, sir?

GUILDENSTERN: No, my lord, with choler.°

HAMLET: Your wisdom should show itself more richer
to signify this to the doctor, for for me to put him to
310   his purgation would perhaps plunge him into more
choler.

GUILDENSTERN: Good my lord, put your discourse into
some frame° and start not so wildly from my affair.

HAMLET: I am tame, sir. Pronounce.

315   GUILDENSTERN: The Queen, your mother, in most great
affliction of spirit, hath sent me to you.

HAMLET: You are welcome.

GUILDENSTERN: Nay, good my lord, this courtesy is not
of the right breed. If it shall please you to make me a
320   wholesome answer, I will do your mother's commandment; if not, your pardon° and my return shall
be the end of my business.

HAMLET: Sir, I cannot.

ROSENCRANTZ: What, my lord?

325   HAMLET: Make you a wholesome answer; my wit's dis-
eas'd. But, sir, such answer as I can make, you
shall command, or rather, as you say, my mother. Therefore no more, but to the matter. My mother, you
say —

330   ROSENCRANTZ: Then thus she says: your behavior hath
struck her into amazement and admiration.°

HAMLET: O wonderful son, that can so stonish a
mother! But is there no sequel at the heels of this
mother's admiration? Impart.

335   ROSENCRANTZ: She desires to speak with you in her
closet,° ere you go to bed.

HAMLET: We shall obey, were she ten times our mother.
Have you any further trade with us?

ROSENCRANTZ: My lord, you once did love me.

340   HAMLET: And do still, by these pickers and stealers.°

ROSENCRANTZ: Good my lord, what is your cause of distemper? You do surely bar the door upon your own
liberty, if you deny your griefs to your friend.

HAMLET: Sir, I lack advancement.

ROSENCRANTZ: How can that be, when you have the   345
voice of the King himself for your succession in
Denmark?

HAMLET: Ay, sir, but "While the grass grows"° — the
proverb is something° musty.

(Enter the Players with recorders.)

O, the recorders! Let me see one. [*He takes a re-*   350
corder.] To withdraw° with you: why do you go about
to recover the wind° of me, as if you would drive me
into a toil?°

GUILDENSTERN: O, my lord, if my duty be too bold, my
love is too unmannerly.°   355

HAMLET: I do not well understand that. Will you play
upon this pipe?

GUILDENSTERN: My lord, I cannot.

HAMLET: I pray you.

GUILDENSTERN: Believe me, I cannot.   360

HAMLET: I do beseech you.

GUILDENSTERN: I know no touch of it, my lord.

HAMLET: It is as easy as lying. Govern these ventages°
with your fingers and thumb, give it breath with your
mouth, and it will discourse most eloquent music.   365
Look you, these are the stops.

GUILDENSTERN: But these cannot I command to any
utt'rance of harmony; I have not the skill.

HAMLET: Why, look you now, how unworthy a thing
you make of me! You would play upon me, you   370
would seem to know my stops, you would pluck out
the heart of my mystery, you would sound me from
my lowest note to the top of my compass,° and there
is much music, excellent voice, in this little organ,°
yet cannot you make it speak. 'Sblood, do you think I   375
am easier to be play'd on than a pipe? Call me what
instrument you will, though you can fret° me, you
cannot play upon me.

(Enter Polonius.)

God bless you, sir!

POLONIUS: My lord, the Queen would speak with you,   380
and presently.°

HAMLET: Do you see yonder cloud that's almost in
shape of a camel?

POLONIUS: By th' mass, and 'tis like a camel, indeed.

HAMLET: Methinks it is like a weasel.   385

POLONIUS: It is back'd like a weasel.

---

297. **perdy:** A corruption of the French *par dieu,* by God.
307. **choler:** Anger. (But Hamlet takes the word in its more
basic humors sense of *bilious disorder.*)   313. **frame:** Order.
321. **pardon:** Permission to depart.   331. **admiration:** Wonder.
336. **closet:** Private chamber.   340. **pickers and stealers:**
Hands (so called from the catechism, "to keep my hands from
picking and stealing").

348. **While . . . grows:** The rest of the proverb is "the silly
horse starves"; Hamlet may not live long enough to succeed to
the kingdom.   349. **something:** Somewhat.   351. **withdraw:**
Speak privately.   352. **recover the wind:** Get the windward
side.   353. **toil:** Snare.   354–55. **if . . . unmannerly:** If I am
using an unmannerly boldness, it is my love that occasions it.
363. **ventages:** Stops of the recorder.   373. **compass:** Range
(of voice).   374. **organ:** Musical instrument.   377. **fret:** Irri-
tate (with a quibble on *fret* meaning the piece of wood, gut,
or metal that regulates the fingering on an instrument).
381. **presently:** At once.

HAMLET: Or like a whale?

POLONIUS: Very like a whale.

HAMLET: Then I will come to my mother by and by.°

390 [*Aside.*] They fool me° to the top of my bent.° — I will come by and by.

POLONIUS: I will say so.   [*Exit.*]

HAMLET: "By and by" is easily said. Leave me, friends.

[*Exeunt all but Hamlet.*]

'Tis now the very witching time° of night,

395 When churchyards yawn and hell itself breathes out
Contagion to this world. Now could I drink hot
    blood,
And do such bitter business as the day
Would quake to look on. Soft, now to my mother.
O heart, lose not thy nature! Let not ever

400 The soul of Nero° enter this firm bosom.
Let me be cruel, not unnatural;
I will speak daggers to her, but use none.
My tongue and soul in this be hypocrites:
How in my words somever° she be shent,°

405 To give them seals° never, my soul, consent!

(*Exit.*)

{*Scene III*}°

(*Enter King, Rosencrantz, and Guildenstern.*)

KING: I like him not, nor stands it safe with us
To let his madness range. Therefore prepare you.
I your commission will forthwith dispatch,°
And he to England shall along with you.

5 The terms° of our estate° may not endure
Hazard so near 's as doth hourly grow
Out of his brows.°

GUILDENSTERN: We will ourselves provide.
Most holy and religious fear it is
To keep those many many bodies safe

10 That live and feed upon your Majesty.

ROSENCRANTZ: The single and peculiar° life is bound
With all the strength and armor of the mind
To keep itself from noyance,° but much more
That spirit upon whose weal depends and rests

15 The lives of many. The cess° of majesty
Dies not alone, but like a gulf° doth draw
What's near it with it; or it is a messy wheel

Fix'd on the summit of the highest mount,
To whose huge spokes ten thousand lesser things
Are mortis'd and adjoin'd, which, when it falls,   20
Each small annexment, petty consequence,
Attends° the boist'rous ruin. Never alone
Did the King sigh, but with a general groan.

KING: Arm° you, I pray you, to this speedy voyage,
For we will fetters put about this fear,   25
Which now goes too free-footed.

ROSENCRANTZ: We will haste us.

(*Exeunt Gentlemen [Rosencrantz
and Guildenstern].*)

(*Enter Polonius.*)

POLONIUS: My lord, he's going to his mother's closet.
Behind the arras° I'll convey myself
To hear the process.° I'll warrant she'll tax him
    home,°
And, as you said, and wisely was it said,   30
'Tis meet that some more audience than a mother,
Since nature makes them partial, should o'erhear
The speech, of vantage.° Fare you well, my liege.
I'll call upon you ere you go to bed,
And tell you what I know.

KING: Thanks, dear my lord.   35

(*Exit [Polonius].*)

O, my offense is rank, it smells to heaven;
It hath the primal eldest curse° upon 't,
A brother's murder. Pray can I not,
Though inclination be as sharp as will.°
My stronger guilt defeats my strong intent,   40
And, like a man to double business bound,
I stand in pause where I shall first begin,
And both neglect. What if this cursed hand
Were thicker than itself with brother's blood,
Is there not rain enough in the sweet heavens   45
To wash it white as snow? Whereto serves mercy
But to confront the visage of offense?°
And what's in prayer but this twofold force,
To be forestalled° ere we come to fall,
Or pardon'd being down? Then I'll look up;   50
My fault is past. But, O, what form of prayer
Can serve my turn? "Forgive me my foul
    murder"?
That cannot be, since I am still possess'd
Of those effects for which I did the murder,
My crown, mine own ambition, and my queen.   55

---

389. by and by: Immediately.   **390. fool me:** Make me play the fool.   **top of my bent:** Limit of my ability or endurance (literally, the extent to which a bow may be bent).   **394. witching time:** Time when spells are cast and evil is abroad.   **400. Nero:** Murderer of his mother, Agrippina.   **404. How . . . somever:** However much by my words.   **shent:** Rebuked.   **405. give them seals:** Confirm them with deeds.   **III, III. Location:** The castle.   **3. dispatch:** Prepare, cause to be drawn up.   **5. terms:** Condition, circumstances.   **our estate:** My royal position.   **7. brows:** Effronteries, threatening frowns (?), brain (?).   **11. single and peculiar:** Individual and private.   **13. noyance:** Harm.   **15. cess:** Decease.   **16. gulf:** Whirlpool.

22. Attends: Participates in.   **24. Arm:** Prepare.   **28. arras:** Screen of tapestry placed around the walls of household apartments. (On the Elizabethan stage, the arras was presumably over a door or discovery space in the tiring-house façade.)   **29. process:** Proceedings.   **tax him home:** Reprove him severely.   **33. of vantage:** From an advantageous place.   **37. primal eldest curse:** The curse of Cain, the first murderer; he killed his brother Abel.   **39. Though . . . will:** Though my desire is as strong as my determination.   **46–47. Whereto . . . offense:** For what function does mercy serve other than to undo the effects of sin?   **49. forestalled:** Prevented (from sinning).

FAR LEFT: Michael Pennington as
Hamlet. NEAR LEFT: A scene from the
Royal Shakespeare Company's 1980
production. BELOW LEFT: Hamlet,
played by Kenneth Branagh, duels
Laertes, played by Michael Maloney.
Branagh directed this 1996 film.
RIGHT: The grave-digger holds up
Yorick's skull as Hamlet and Horatio
(Tom Wilkinson) look on. BELOW
RIGHT: Carol Royle as Ophelia with
Hamlet in the nunnery scene.

May one be pardon'd and retain th' offense?
In the corrupted currents° of this world
Offense's gilded hand° may shove by justice,
And oft 'tis seen the wicked prize° itself
60   Buys out the law. But 'tis not so above.
There is no shuffling,° there the action lies°
In his° true nature, and we ourselves compell'd,
Even to the teeth and forehead° of our faults,
To give in evidence. What then? What rests?°
65   Try what repentance can. What can it not?
Yet what can it, when one cannot repent?
O wretched state! O bosom black as death!
O limed° soul, that, struggling to be free,
Art more engag'd!° Help, angels! Make assay.°
70   Bow, stubborn knees, and heart with strings of steel,
Be soft as sinews of the new-born babe!
All may be well.

                                        [He kneels.]

(Enter Hamlet [with sword drawn].)

HAMLET: Now might I do it pat,° now 'a is a-praying;
And now I'll do 't. And so 'a goes to heaven;
75   And so am I reveng'd. That would be scann'd:°
A villain kills my father, and for that,
I, his sole son, do this same villain send
To heaven.
Why, this is hire and salary, not revenge.
80   'A took my father grossly,° full of bread,°
With all his crimes broad blown,° as flush° as May;
And how his audit° stands who knows save
    heaven?
But in our circumstance and course° of thought,
'Tis heavy with him. And am I then reveng'd,
85   To take him in the purging of his soul,
When he is fit and season'd for his passage?
No!
Up, sword, and know thou a more horrid hent.°

                                        [Puts up his sword.]

When he is drunk asleep, or in his rage,
90   Or in th' incestuous pleasure of his bed,
At game a-swearing, or about some act
That has no relish of salvation in 't —
Then trip him, that his heels may kick at heaven,
And that his soul may be as damn'd and black

As hell, whereto it goes. My mother stays.   95
This physic° but prolongs thy sickly days.   (Exit.)
KING: My words fly up, my thoughts remain
    below.
Words without thoughts never to heaven go.

                                        (Exit.)

{Scene IV}°

(Enter [Queen] Gertrude and Polonius.)

POLONIUS: 'A will come straight. Look you lay° home
    to him.
Tell him his pranks have been too broad° to bear
    with,
And that your Grace hath screen'd and stood
    between
Much heat° and him. I'll sconce° me even here.
Pray you, be round° [with him.   5
HAMLET (within): Mother, mother, mother!]
QUEEN: I'll warrant you, fear me not.
Withdraw, I hear him coming.

                [Polonius hides behind the arras.]

(Enter Hamlet.)

HAMLET: Now, mother, what's the matter?
QUEEN: Hamlet, thou hast thy father° much offended.   10
HAMLET: Mother, you have my father much offended.
QUEEN: Come, come, you answer with an idle° tongue.
HAMLET: Go, go, you question with a wicked tongue.
QUEEN: Why, how now, Hamlet?
HAMLET: What's the matter now?
QUEEN: Have you forgot me?
HAMLET: No, by the rood,° not so: 15
You are the Queen, your husband's brother's wife
And — would it were not so! — you are my mother.
QUEEN: Nay, then, I'll set those to you that can speak.
HAMLET: Come, come, and sit you down; you shall not
    budge.
You go not till I set you up a glass   20
Where you may see the inmost part of you.
QUEEN: What wilt thou do? Thou wilt not murder me?
    Help, ho!
POLONIUS [behind]: What, ho! Help!
HAMLET [drawing]: How now? A rat? Dead, for a
    ducat, dead!   25
                [Makes a pass through the arras.]
POLONIUS [behind]: O, I am slain! [Falls and dies.]
QUEEN: O me, what hast thou done?
HAMLET: Nay, I know not. Is it the King?
QUEEN: O, what a rash and bloody deed is this!

---

57. **currents:** Courses.   58. **gilded hand:** Hand offering gold
as a bribe.   59. **wicked prize:** Prize won by wickedness.
61. **shuffling:** Escape by trickery.   **the action lies:** The accusation is made manifest, comes up for consideration (a legal
metaphor).   62. **his:** Its.   63. **teeth and forehead:** Face to face,
concealing nothing.   64. **rests:** Remains.   68. **limed:** Caught
as with birdlime, a sticky substance used to ensnare birds.
69. **engag'd:** Embedded.   **assay:** Trial.   73. **pat:** Opportunely.
75. **would be scann'd:** Needs to be looked into.   80. **grossly:**
Not spiritually prepared.   **full of bread:** Enjoying his worldly
pleasures. (See Ezek. 16:49.)   81. **crimes broad blown:** Sins
in full bloom.   **flush:** Lusty.   82. **audit:** Account.   83. **in . . .
course:** As we see it in our mortal situation.   88. **know . . .
hent:** Await to be grasped by me on a more horrid occasion.

96. **physic:** Purging (by prayer).   **III, IV. Location:** The queen's
private chamber.   1. **lay:** Thrust (i.e., reprove him soundly).
2. **broad:** Unrestrained.   4. **Much heat:** The king's anger.
sconce: Ensconce, hide.   5. **round:** Blunt.   10. **thy father:**
Your stepfather, Claudius.   12. **idle:** Foolish.   15. **rood:** Cross.

HAMLET: A bloody deed — almost as bad, good
    mother,
30   As kill a king, and marry with his brother.
QUEEN: As kill a king!
HAMLET: Ay, lady, it was my word.
    [*Parts the arras and discovers Polonius.*]
    Thou wretched, rash, intruding fool, farewell!
    I took thee for thy better. Take thy fortune.
    Thou find'st to be too busy is some danger. —
35   Leave wringing of your hands. Peace, sit you down,
    And let me wring your heart, for so I shall,
    If it be made of penetrable stuff,
    If damned custom° have not braz'd° it so
    That it be proof° and bulwark against sense.°
QUEEN: What have I done, that thou dar'st wag thy
40   tongue
    In noise so rude against me?
HAMLET: Such an art
    That blurs the grace and blush of modesty,
    Calls virtue hypocrite, takes off the rose
    From the fair forehead of an innocent love
45   And sets a blister° there, makes marriage-vows
    As false as dicers' oaths. O, such a deed
    As from the body of contraction° plucks
    The very soul, and sweet religion° makes
    A rhapsody° of words. Heaven's face does glow
50   O'er this solidity and compound mass
    With heated visage, as against the doom,
    Is thought-sick at the act.°
QUEEN   Ay me, what act,
    That roars so loud and thunders in the index?°
HAMLET: Look here, upon this picture, and on this,
55   The counterfeit presentment° of two brothers.
    [*Shows her two likenesses.*]
    See, what a grace was seated on this brow:
    Hyperion's° curls, the front° of Jove himself,
    An eye like Mars, to threaten and command,
    A station° like the herald Mercury
60   New-lighted on a heaven-kissing hill —
    A combination and a form indeed,
    Where every god did seem to set his seal,
    To give the world assurance of a man.
    This was your husband. Look you now, what
    follows:
65   Here is your husband, like a mildew'd ear,°
    Blasting his wholesome brother. Have you eyes?
    Could you on this fair mountain leave to feed,

And batten° on this moor?° Ha, have you eyes?
You cannot call it love, for at your age
The heyday° in the blood is tame, it's humble,   70
And waits upon the judgment, and what judgment
Would step from this to this? Sense,° sure, you
    have,
Else could you not have motion, but sure that sense
Is apoplex'd,° for madness would not err,
Nor sense to ecstasy was ne'er so thrall'd   75
But it reserv'd some quantity of choice
To serve in such a difference. What devil was 't
That thus hath cozen'd° you at hoodman-blind?°
Eyes without feeling, feeling without sight,
Ears without hands or eyes, smelling sans° all,   80
Or but a sickly part of one true sense
Could not so mope.°
O shame, where is thy blush? Rebellious hell,
If thou canst mutine° in a matron's bones,
To flaming youth let virtue be as wax,   85
And melt in her own fire. Proclaim no shame
When the compulsive ardor gives the charge,
Since frost itself as actively doth burn,
And reason panders will.°
QUEEN: O Hamlet, speak no more!   90
    Thou turn'st mine eyes into my very soul,
    And there I see such black and grained° spots
    As will not leave their tinct.°
HAMLET: Nay, but to live
    In the rank sweat of an enseamed° bed,
    Stew'd in corruption, honeying and making love   95
    Over the nasty sty —
QUEEN: O, speak to me no more.
    These words, like daggers, enter in my ears.
    No more, sweet Hamlet!
HAMLET: A murderer and a villain,
    A slave that is not twentieth part the tithe°   100
    Of your precedent° lord, a vice° of kings,
    A cutpurse of the empire and the rule,
    That from a shelf the precious diadem stole,
    And put it in his pocket!
QUEEN: No more!   105

---

38. **damned custom:** Habitual wickedness.   **braz'd:** Brazened, hardened.   39. **proof:** Armor.   **sense:** Feeling.   45. **sets a blister:** Brands as a harlot.   47. **contraction:** The marriage contract.   48. **religion:** Religious vows.   49. **rhapsody:** Senseless string.   49–52. **Heaven's . . . act:** Heaven's face flushes with anger to look down upon this solid world, this compound mass, with hot face as though the day of doom were near, and is thought-sick at the deed (i.e., Gertrude's marriage).   53. **index:** Table of contents, prelude, or preface.   55. **counterfeit presentment:** Portrayed representation.   57. **Hyperion:** The sun god.   **front:** Brow.   59. **station:** Manner of standing.   65. **ear:** I.e., of grain.

68. **batten:** Gorge.   **moor:** Barren upland.   70. **heyday:** State of excitement.   72. **Sense:** Perception through the five senses (the functions of the middle or sensible soul).   74. **apoplex'd:** Paralyzed. (Hamlet goes on to explain that without such a paralysis of will, mere madness would not so err, nor would the five senses so enthrall themselves to *ecstasy* or lunacy; even such deranged states of mind would be able to make the obvious choice between Hamlet Senior and Claudius.)   78. **cozen'd:** Cheated.   **hoodman-blind:** Blindman's bluff.   80. **sans:** Without.   82. **mope:** Be dazed, act aimlessly.   84. **mutine:** Mutiny.   86–89. **Proclaim . . . will:** Call it no shameful business when the compelling ardor of youth delivers the attack, i.e., commits lechery, since the frost of advanced age burns with as active a fire of lust and reason perverts itself by fomenting lust rather than restraining it.   92. **grained:** Dyed in grain, indelible.   93. **tinct:** Color.   94. **enseamed:** Laden with grease.   100. **tithe:** Tenth part.   101. **precedent:** Former (i.e., the elder Hamlet).   **vice:** Buffoon (a reference to the vice of the morality plays).

(*Enter Ghost [in his nightgown].*)

HAMLET: A king of shreds and patches° —
  Save me, and hover o'er me with your wings,
  You heavenly guards! What would your gracious
    figure?
QUEEN: Alas, he's mad!
110 HAMLET: Do you not come your tardy son to chide,
  That, laps'd in time and passion,° lets go by
  Th' important° acting of your dread command?
  O, say!
GHOST: Do not forget. This visitation
115 Is but to whet thy almost blunted purpose.
  But, look, amazement° on thy mother sits.
  O, step between her and her fighting soul!
  Conceit° in weakest bodies strongest works.
  Speak to her, Hamlet.
HAMLET: How is it with you, lady?
120 QUEEN: Alas, how is 't with you,
  That you do bend your eye on vacancy,
  And with th' incorporal° air do hold discourse?
  Forth at your eyes your spirits wildly peep,
  And, as the sleeping soldiers in th' alarm,
125 Your bedded° hair, like life in excrements,°
  Start up and stand an° end. O gentle son,
  Upon the heat and flame of thy distemper
  Sprinkle cool patience. Whereon do you look?
HAMLET: On him, on him! Look you how pale he
    glares!
130 His form and cause conjoin'd,° preaching to stones,
  Would make them capable.° — Do not look upon
    me,
  Lest with this piteous action you convert
  My stern effects.° Then what I have to do
  Will want true color° — tears perchance for blood.
135 QUEEN: To whom do you speak this?
HAMLET: Do you see nothing there?
QUEEN: Nothing at all, yet all that is I see.
HAMLET: Nor did you nothing hear?
QUEEN: No, nothing but ourselves.
140 HAMLET: Why, look you there, look how it steals away!
  My father, in his habit° as he lived!
  Look, where he goes, even now, out at the portal!
                                    (*Exit Ghost.*)
QUEEN: This is the very coinage of your brain.
  This bodiless creation ecstasy°
145 Is very cunning in.

HAMLET: Ecstasy?
  My pulse, as yours, doth temperately keep time,
  And makes as healthful music. It is not madness
  That I have utter'd. Bring me to the test,
  And I the matter will reword, which madness   150
  Would gambol° from. Mother, for love of grace,
  Lay not that flattering unction° to your soul
  That not your trespass but my madness speaks.
  It will but skin and film the ulcerous place,
  Whiles rank corruption, mining° all within,   155
  Infects unseen. Confess yourself to heaven,
  Repent what's past, avoid what is to come,
  And do not spread the compost° on the weeds
  To make them ranker. Forgive me this my virtue;°
  For in the fatness° of these pursy° times   160
  Virtue itself of vice must pardon beg,
  Yea, curb° and woo for leave° to do him good.
QUEEN: O Hamlet, thou hast cleft my heart in twain.
HAMLET: O, throw away the worser part of it,
  And live the purer with the other half.   165
  Good night. But go not to my uncle's bed;
  Assume a virtue, if you have it not.
  That monster, custom, who all sense doth eat,°
  Of habits devil,° is angel yet in this,
  That to the use of actions fair and good   170
  He likewise gives a frock or livery°
  That aptly is put on. Refrain tonight,
  And that shall lend a kind of easiness
  To the next abstinence; the next more easy;
  For use° almost can change the stamp of nature,   175
  And either°. . . the devil, or throw him out
  With wondrous potency. Once more, good night;
  And when you are desirous to be bless'd,°
  I'll blessing beg of you. For this same lord,
                       [*Pointing to Polonius.*]
  I do repent; but heaven hath pleas'd it so   180
  To punish me with this, and this with me,
  That I must be their scourge and minister.°
  I will bestow° him, and will answer well
  The death I gave him. So, again, good night.
  I must be cruel only to be kind.   185

---

106. **shreds and patches:** Motley, the traditional costume of the clown or fool.   111. **laps'd . . . passion:** Having allowed time to lapse and passion to cool.   112. **important:** Importunate, urgent.   116. **amazement:** Distraction.   118. **Conceit:** Imagination.   122. **incorporal:** Immaterial.   125. **bedded:** Laid in smooth layers. **excrements:** Outgrowths.   126. **an:** On.   130. **His . . . conjoin'd:** His appearance joined to his cause for speaking.   131. **capable:** Receptive.   132–33. **convert . . . effects:** Divert me from my stern duty.   134. **want true color:** Lack plausibility so that (with a play on the normal sense of *color*) I shall shed tears instead of blood.   141. **habit:** Dress.   144. **ecstasy:** Madness.

151. **gambol:** Skip away.   152. **unction:** Ointment.   55. **mining:** Working under the surface.   158. **compost:** Manure.   159. **this my virtue:** My virtuous talk in reproving you.   160. **fatness:** Grossness. **pursy:** Short-winded, corpulent.   162. **curb:** Bow, bend the knee. **leave:** Permission.   168. **who . . . eat:** Who consumes all proper or natural feeling.   169. **Of habits devil:** Devil-like in prompting evil habits.   171. **livery:** An outer appearance, a customary garb (and hence a predisposition easily assumed in time of stress).   175. **use:** Habit.   176. **And either:** A defective line usually emended by inserting the word *master* after *either*, following the fourth quarto and early editors.   178. **be bless'd:** Become blessed, i.e., repentant.   182. **their scourge and minister:** Agent of heavenly retribution. (By *scourge*, Hamlet also suggests that he himself will eventually suffer punishment in the process of fulfilling heaven's will.)   183. **bestow:** Stow, dispose of.

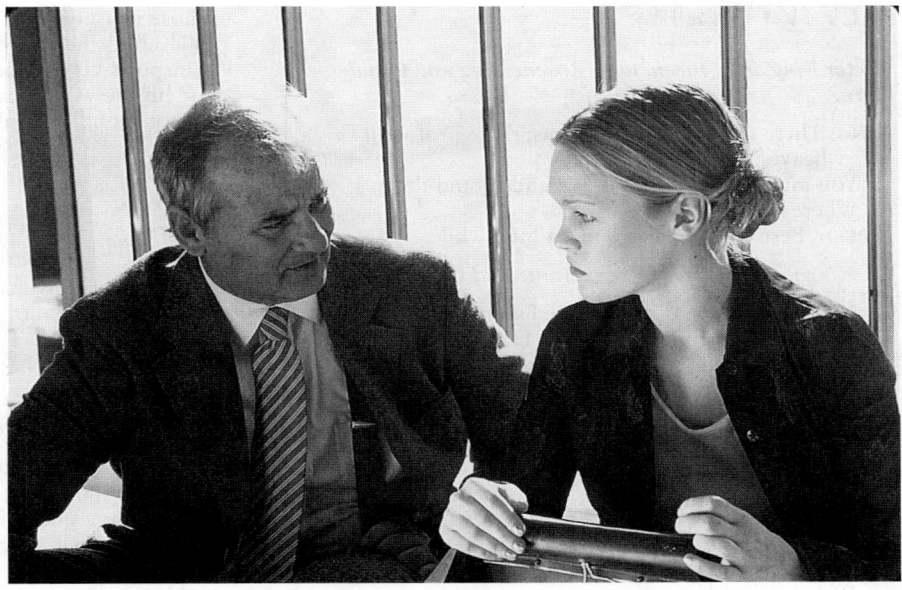

Bill Murray as Polonius and Julia Stiles as Ophelia in Michael Almereyda's 2000 film adaptation of *Hamlet*, which also starred Ethan Hawke as Hamlet, Sam Shepard as the Ghost of Hamlet's father, and Kyle MacLachlan as Claudius.

    Thus bad begins and worse remains behind.°
    One word more, good lady.
QUEEN: What shall I do?
HAMLET: Not this, by no means, that I bid you do:
    Let the bloat° king tempt you again to bed,
190   Pinch wanton on your cheek, call you his mouse,
    And let him, for a pair of reechy° kisses,
    Or paddling in your neck with his damn'd fingers,
    Make you to ravel all this matter out,
    That I essentially am not in madness,
195   But mad in craft. 'Twere good° you let him know,
    For who that's but a queen, fair, sober, wise,
    Would from a paddock,° from a bat, a gib,°
    Such dear concernings° hide? Who would do so?
    No, in despite of sense and secrecy,
200   Unpeg the basket° on the house's top,
    Let the birds fly, and, like the famous ape,°
    To try conclusions,° in the basket creep
    And break your own neck down.
QUEEN: Be thou assur'd, if words be made of breath,
205   And breath of life, I have no life to breathe
    What thou hast said to me.

HAMLET: I must to England; you know that?
QUEEN: Alack,
    I had forgot. 'Tis so concluded on.
HAMLET: There's letters seal'd, and my two school-
      fellows,
    Whom I will trust as I will adders fang'd,   210
    They bear the mandate; they must sweep my way,°
    And marshal me to knavery. Let it work.
    For 'tis the sport to have the enginer°
    Hoist with° his own petar,° and 't shall go hard
    But I will delve one yard below their mines,°   215
    And blow them at the moon. O, 'tis most sweet,
    When in one line two crafts° directly meet.
    This man shall set me packing.°
    I'll lug the guts into the neighbor room.
    Mother, good night indeed. This counselor   220
    Is now most still, most secret, and most grave,
    Who was in life a foolish prating knave.
    Come, sir, to draw toward an end° with you.
    Good night, mother.

      (*Exeunt* [*severally, Hamlet dragging in Polonius*].)

---

186. behind: To come.   189. bloat: Bloated.   191. reechy: Dirty, filthy.   195. good: Said ironically; also the following eight lines.   197. paddock: Toad.   gib: Tomcat.   198. dear concernings: Important affairs.   200. Unpeg the basket: Open the cage, i.e., let out the secret.   201. famous ape: In a story now lost.   202. conclusions: Experiments (in which the ape apparently enters a cage from which birds have been released and then tries to fly out of the cage as they have done, falling to his death).

211. sweep my way: Go before me.   213. enginer: Constructor of military contrivances.   214. Hoist with: Blown up by. petar: Petard, an explosive used to blow in a door or make a breach.   215. mines: Tunnels used in warfare to undermine the enemy's emplacements; Hamlet will countermine by going under their mines.   217. crafts: Acts of guile, plots.   218. set me packing: Set me to making schemes, and set me to lugging (him) and, also, send me off in a hurry.   223. draw . . . end: Finish up (with a pun on *draw,* pull).

{*ACT IV • Scene I*}°

(*Enter King and Queen, with Rosencrantz and Guilden-stern.*)

KING: There's matter in these sighs, these profound heaves
  You must translate; 'tis fit we understand them.
  Where is your son?
QUEEN: Bestow this place on us a little while.

  [*Exeunt Rosencrantz and Guildenstern.*]

5   Ah, mine own lord, what have I seen tonight!
KING: What, Gertrude? How does Hamlet?
QUEEN: Mad as the sea and wind when both contend
  Which is the mightier. In his lawless fit,
  Behind the arras hearing something stir,
10 Whips out his rapier, cries, "A rat, a rat!"
  And, in this brainish apprehension,° kills
  The unseen good old man.
KING: O heavy deed!
  It had been so with us, had we been there.
  His liberty is full of threats to all —
15 To you yourself, to us, to everyone.
  Alas, how shall this bloody deed be answer'd?
  It will be laid to us, whose providence°
  Should have kept short,° restrain'd, and out of haunt°
  This mad young man. But so much was our love
20 We would not understand what was most fit,
  But, like the owner of a foul disease,
  To keep it from divulging,° let it feed
  Even on the pith of life. Where is he gone?
QUEEN: To draw apart the body he hath kill'd,
25 O'er whom his very madness, like some ore°
  Among a mineral° of metals base,
  Shows itself pure: 'a weeps for what is done.
KING: O Gertrude, come away!
  The sun no sooner shall the mountains touch
30 But we will ship him hence, and this vile deed
  We must, with all our majesty and skill,
  Both countenance and excuse. Ho, Guildenstern!

(*Enter Rosencrantz and Guildenstern.*)

  Friends both, go join you with some further aid.
  Hamlet in madness hath Polonius slain,
35 And from his mother's closet hath he dragg'd him.
  Go seek him out; speak fair, and bring the body
  Into the chapel. I pray you, haste in this.

  [*Exeunt Rosencrantz and Guildenstern.*]

  Come, Gertrude, we'll call up our wisest friends
  And let them know both what we mean to do
40 And what's untimely done° . . . .

IV, I. **Location:** The castle.   **11. brainish apprehension:** Head-strong conception.   **17. providence:** Foresight.   **18. short:** On a short tether.   **out of haunt:** Secluded.   **22. divulging:** Becoming evident.   **25. ore:** Vein of gold.   **26. mineral:** Mine.
40. And . . . done: A defective line; conjectures as to the missing words include *so, haply, slander* (Capell and others); *for, haply, slander* (Theobald and others).

  Whose whisper o'er the world's diameter,°
  As level° as the cannon to his blank,°
  Transports his pois'ned shot, may miss our name,
  And hit the woundless° air. O, come away!
45 My soul is full of discord and dismay.   (*Exeunt.*)

{*Scene II*}°

(*Enter Hamlet.*)

HAMLET: Safely stow'd.
[ROSENCRANTZ, GUILDENSTERN (*within*): Hamlet! Lord Hamlet!]
HAMLET: But soft, what noise? Who calls on Hamlet?
  O, here they come.   5

(*Enter Rosencrantz and Guildenstern.*)

ROSENCRANTZ: What have you done, my lord, with the dead body?
HAMLET: Compounded it with dust, whereto 'tis kin.
ROSENCRANTZ: Tell us where 'tis, that we may take it thence
  And bear it to the chapel.
HAMLET: Do not believe it.   10
ROSENCRANTZ: Believe what?
HAMLET: That I can keep your counsel and not mine own. Besides, to be demanded of° a sponge, what replication° should be made by the son of a king?
ROSENCRANTZ: Take you me for a sponge, my lord?   15
HAMLET: Ay, sir, that soaks up the King's countenance,° his rewards, his authorities. But such officers do the King best service in the end. He keeps them, like an ape an apple, in the corner of his jaw, first mouth'd, to be last swallow'd. When he needs what you have 20 glean'd, it is but squeezing you, and, sponge, you shall be dry again.
ROSENCRANTZ: I understand you not, my lord.
HAMLET: I am glad of it. A knavish speech sleeps in° a foolish ear.   25
ROSENCRANTZ: My lord, you must tell us where the body is, and go with us to the King.
HAMLET: The body is with the King, but the King is not with the body.° The King is a thing —
GUILDENSTERN: A thing, my lord?   30
HAMLET: Of nothing.° Bring me to him. [Hide fox, and all after.°]   (*Exeunt.*)

---

41. diameter: Extent from side to side.   **42. As level:** With as direct aim.   **blank:** White spot in the center of a target.   **44. woundless:** Invulnerable.   IV, II. **Location:** The castle.   **13. demanded of:** Questioned by.   **14. replication:** Reply.   **16. countenance:** Favor.   **24. sleeps in:** Has no meaning to.   **29. The . . . body:** Perhaps alludes to the legal commonplace of "the king's two bodies," which drew a distinction between the sacred office of kingship and the particular mortal who possessed it at any given time.   **31. Of nothing:** Of no account.   **31–32. Hide . . . after:** An old signal cry in the game of hide-and-seek, suggesting that Hamlet now runs away from them.

{*Scene III*}°

(*Enter King, and two or three.*)

KING: I have sent to seek him, and to find the body.
How dangerous is it that this man goes loose!
Yet must not we put the strong law on him.
He's lov'd of the distracted° multitude,
Who like not in their judgment, but their eyes,
And where 'tis so, th' offender's scourge° is weigh'd,°
But never the offense. To bear° all smooth and even,
This sudden sending him away must seem
Deliberate pause.° Diseases desperate grown
By desperate appliance are reliev'd,
Or not at all.

(*Enter Rosencrantz, [Guildenstern,] and all the rest.*)

                How now? What hath befall'n?
ROSENCRANTZ: Where the dead body is bestow'd, my
    lord,
    We cannot get from him.
KING: But where is he?
ROSENCRANTZ: Without, my lord; guarded, to know
    your pleasure.
KING: Bring him before us.
ROSENCRANTZ: Ho! Bring in the lord.

(*They enter [with Hamlet].*)

KING: Now, Hamlet, where's Polonius?
HAMLET: At supper.
KING: At supper? Where?
HAMLET: Not where he eats, but where 'a is eaten. A
    certain convocation of politic worms° are e'en at
    him. Your worm is your only emperor for diet.° We
    fat all creatures else to fat us, and we fat ourselves for
    maggots. Your fat king and your lean beggar is but
    variable service,° two dishes, but to one table —
    that's the end.
KING: Alas, alas!
HAMLET: A man may fish with the worm that hath eat°
    of a king, and eat of the fish that hath fed of that
    worm.
KING: What dost thou mean by this?
HAMLET: Nothing but to show you how a king may go a
    progress° through the guts of a beggar.
KING: Where is Polonius?
HAMLET: In heaven. Send thither to see. If your messen-
    ger find him not there, seek him i' th' other place
    yourself. But if indeed you find him not within this
    month, you shall nose him as you go up the stairs
    into the lobby.

KING [*to some Attendants*]: Go seek him there.
HAMLET: 'A will stay till you come.
                                    [*Exit Attendants.*]
KING: Hamlet, this deed, for thine especial safety. —   40
    Which we do tender,° as we dearly° grieve
    For that which thou hast done — must send thee
        hence
    [With fiery quickness.] Therefore prepare thyself.
    The bark° is ready, and the wind at help,   45
    Th' associates tend,° and everything is bent°
    For England.
HAMLET: For England!
KING: Ay, Hamlet.
HAMLET: Good.   50
KING: So is it, if thou knew'st our purposes.
HAMLET: I see a cherub° that sees them. But, come, for
    England! Farewell, dear mother.
KING: Thy loving father, Hamlet.
HAMLET: My mother. Father and mother is man and   55
    wife, man and wife is one flesh, and so, my mother.
    Come, for England!   (*Exit.*)
KING: Follow him at foot;° tempt him with speed
    aboard.
    Delay it not; I'll have him hence tonight.
    Away! For everything is seal'd and done   60
    That else leans on° th' affair. Pray you, make haste.

                    [*Exeunt all but the King.*]

And, England,° if my love thou hold'st at aught —
As my great power thereof may give thee sense,
Since yet thy cicatrice° looks raw and red
After the Danish sword, and thy free awe°   65
Pays homage to us — thou mayst not coldly set°
Our sovereign process,° which imports at full,
By letters congruing° to that effect,
The present° death of Hamlet. Do it, England,
For like the hectic° in my blood he rages,   70
And thou must cure me. Till I know 'tis done,
Howe'er my haps,° my joys were ne'er begun.
                                            (*Exit.*)

{*Scene IV*}°

(*Enter Fortinbras with his Army over the stage.*)

FORTINBRAS: Go, captain, from me greet the Danish
    king.
    Tell him that, by his license,° Fortinbras
    Craves the conveyance° of a promis'd march

IV, III. Location: The castle.   **4. distracted:** Fickle, unstable.
6. scourge: Punishment.   **weigh'd:** Taken into consideration.
7. bear: Manage.   **9. Deliberate pause:** Carefully considered
action.   **20. politic worms:** Crafty worms (suited to a master
spy like Polonius).   **21. diet:** Food, eating (with perhaps a
punning reference to the Diet of Worms, a famous convoca-
tion held in 1521).   **24. variable service:** Different courses of a
single meal.   **27. eat:** Eaten (pronounced "et").   **32. progress:**
Royal journey of state.   **42. tender:** Regard, hold dear.   **dearly:** Intensely.   **45. bark:**
Sailing vessel.   **46. tend:** Wait.   **bent:** In readiness.
52. cherub: Cherubim are angels of knowledge.   **58. at foot:**
Close behind, at heel.   **61. leans on:** Bears upon, is related to.
62. England: King of England.   **64. cicatrice:** Scar.   **65. free
awe:** Voluntary show of respect.   **66. set:** Esteem.
67. process: Command.   **68. congruing:** Agreeing.
69. present: Immediate.   **70. hectic:** Persistent fever.
72. haps: Fortunes.   **IV, IV. Location:** The coast of Denmark.
2. license: Permission.   **3. conveyance:** Escort, convoy.

Over his kingdom. You know the rendezvous.
5   If that his Majesty would aught with us,
We shall express our duty in his eye;°
And let him know so.
CAPTAIN: I will do 't, my lord.
FORTINBRAS: Go softly° on.   [*Exeunt all but the
Captain.*]

(*Enter Hamlet, Rosencrantz, [Guildenstern,] etc.*)

HAMLET: Good sir, whose powers° are these?
10 CAPTAIN: They are of Norway, sir.
HAMLET: How purposed, sir, I pray you?
CAPTAIN: Against some part of Poland.
HAMLET: Who commands them, sir?
CAPTAIN: The nephew to old Norway, Fortinbras.
15 HAMLET: Goes it against the main° of Poland, sir,
Or for some frontier?
CAPTAIN: Truly to speak, and with no addition,°
We go to gain a little patch of ground
That hath in it no profit but the name.
20 To pay° five ducats, five, I would not farm it;°
Nor will it yield to Norway or the Pole
A ranker° rate, should it be sold in fee.°
HAMLET: Why, then the Polack never will defend it.
CAPTAIN: Yes, it is already garrison'd.
HAMLET: Two thousand souls and twenty thousand
25   ducats
Will not debate the question of this straw.°
This is th' imposthume° of much wealth and
peace,
That inward breaks, and shows no cause without
Why the man dies. I humbly thank you, sir.
CAPTAIN: God buy you, sir.   [*Exit.*]
30 ROSENCRANTZ: Will 't please you go, my lord?
HAMLET: I'll be with you straight. Go a little before.

[*Exit all except Hamlet.*]

How all occasions do inform against° me,
And spur my dull revenge! What is a man,
If his chief good and market of° his time
35 Be but to sleep and feed? A beast, no more.
Sure he that made us with such large discourse,°
Looking before and after, gave us not
That capability and god-like reason
To fust° in us unus'd. Now, whether it be
40 Bestial oblivion,° or some craven scruple
Of thinking too precisely on th' event° —
A thought which, quarter'd, hath but one part
wisdom
And ever three parts coward — I do not know

Why yet I live to say "This thing's to do,"
Sith° I have cause and will and strength and means   45
To do 't. Examples gross° as earth exhort me:
Witness this army of such mass and charge°
Led by a delicate and tender prince,
Whose spirit, with divine ambition puff'd
Makes mouths° at the invisible event,   50
Exposing what is mortal and unsure
To all that fortune, death, and danger dare,
Even for an egg-shell. Rightly to be great
Is not to stir without great argument,
But greatly to find quarrel in a straw   55
When honor's at the stake. How stand I then,
That have a father kill'd, a mother stain'd,
Excitements of° my reason and my blood,
And let all sleep, while, to my shame, I see
The imminent death of twenty thousand men,   60
That, for a fantasy° and trick° of fame,
Go to their graves like beds, fight for a plot°
Whereon the numbers cannot try the cause,°
Which is not tomb enough and continent°
To hide the slain? O, from this time forth,   65
My thoughts be bloody, or be nothing worth!

(*Exit.*)

{*Scene V*}°

(*Enter Horatio, [Queen] Gertrude, and a Gentleman.*)

QUEEN: I will not speak with her.
GENTLEMAN: She is importunate, indeed distract.
Her mood will needs be pitied.
QUEEN: What would she have?
GENTLEMAN: She speaks much of her father, says she
hears
There's tricks° i' th' world, and hems, and beats her
heart,°   5
Spurns enviously at straws,° speaks things in doubt°
That carry but half sense. Her speech is nothing,
Yet the unshaped use° of it doth move
The hearers to collection;° they yawn° at it,
And botch° the words up fit to their own thoughts, 10
Which, as her winks and nods and gestures yield°
them,
Indeed would make one think there might be
thought,°
Though nothing sure, yet much unhappily.

6. eye: Presence. 8. softly: Slowly. 9. powers: Forces.
15. main: Main part. 17. addition: Exaggeration. 20. To
pay: I.e., for a yearly rental of. farm it: Take a lease of it.
22. ranker: Higher. in fee: Fee simple, outright.
26. debate . . . straw: Settle this trifling matter.
27. imposthume: Abscess. 32. inform against: Denounce,
betray; take shape against. 34. market of: Profit of compensation for. 36. discourse: Power of reasoning. 39. fust: Grow
moldy. 40. oblivion: Forgetfulness. 41. event: Outcome.

45. Sith: Since. 46. gross: Obvious. 47. charge: Expense.
50. Makes mouths: Makes scornful faces. 58. Excitements of:
Promptings by. 61. fantasy: Fanciful caprice. trick: Trifle.
62. plot: I.e., of ground. 63. Whereon . . . cause: On which
there is insufficient room for the soldiers needed to engage in a
military contest. 64. continent: Receptacle, container. IV, v.
Location: The castle. 5. tricks: Deceptions. heart: Breast.
6. Spurns . . . straws: Kicks spitefully, takes offense at trifles.
in doubt: Obscurely. 8. unshaped use: Distracted manner.
9. collection: Inference, a guess at some sort of meaning.
yawn: Wonder, grasp. 10. botch: Patch. 11. yield: Delivery,
bring forth (her words). 12. thought: Conjectured.

HORATIO: 'twere good she were spoken with, for she
    may strew
15 Dangerous conjectures in ill-breeding° minds.
QUEEN: Let her come in.   [*Exit Gentlemen.*]
  [*Aside.*] To my sick soul, as sin's true nature is,
  Each toy° seems prologue to some great amiss.°
  So full of artless jealousy is guilt,
20 It spills itself in fearing to be spilt.°

(*Enter Ophelia* [*distracted*]*.*)

OPHELIA: Where is the beauteous majesty of Denmark?
QUEEN: How now, Ophelia?
OPHELIA (*she sings*): "How should I your true love
    know
    From another one?
25 By his cockle hat° and staff,
    And his sandal shoon."°
QUEEN: Alas, sweet lady, what imports this song?
OPHELIA: Say you? Nay, pray you, mark.
  "He is dead and gone, lady,   (*Song.*)
30   He is dead and gone;
  At his head a grass-green turf,
    At his heels a stone."
  O, ho!
QUEEN: Nay, but Ophelia —
35 OPHELIA: Pray you mark.
  [*Sings.*] "White his shroud as the mountain
    snow"—

(*Enter King.*)

QUEEN: Alas, look here, my lord.
OPHELIA: "Larded° all with flowers   (*Song.*)
  Which bewept to the ground did not go
40   With true-love showers."
KING: How do you, pretty lady?
OPHELIA: Well, God 'ild° you! They say the owl° was a
  baker's daughter. Lord, we know what we are, but
  know not what we may be. God be at your table!
45 KING: Conceit° upon her father.
OPHELIA: Pray let's have no words of this; but when
  they ask you what it means, say you this:
  "Tomorrow is Saint Valentine's° day.   (*Song.*)
    All in the morning betime,
50 And I a maid at your window,
    To be your Valentine.
  Then up he rose, and donn'd his clo'es,
    And dupp'd° the chamber-door,

  Let in the maid, that out a maid
    Never departed more."   55
KING: Pretty Ophelia!
OPHELIA: Indeed, la, without an oath, I'll make an end
  on 't:
  [*Sings.*] "By Gis° and by Saint Charity,
    Alack, and fie for shame!
  Young men will do 't, if they come to 't;   60
    By Cock,° they are to blame.
  Quoth she, 'Before you tumbled me,
    You promised me to wed.' "
  He answers:
  " 'So would I ha' done, by yonder sun,   65
    An thou hadst not come to my bed.' "
KING: How long hath she been thus?
OPHELIA: I hope all will be well. We must be patient, but
  I cannot choose but weep, to think they would lay
  him i' th' cold ground. My brother shall know of it; 70
  and so I thank you for your good counsel. Come, my
  coach! Good night, ladies; good night, sweet ladies;
  good night, good night.
                      [*Exit.*]
KING: Follow her close; give her good watch, I pray
  you.   [*Exit Horatio.*] 75
  O, this is the poison of deep grief; it springs
  All from her father's death — and now behold!
  O Gertrude, Gertrude,
  When sorrows come, they come not single spies,°
  But in battalions. First, her father slain;   80
  Next, your son gone, and he most violent author
  Of his own just remove; the people muddied,°
  Thick and unwholesome in their thoughts and
    whispers,
  For good Polonius' death; and we have done but
    greenly,°
  In hugger-mugger° to inter him; poor Ophelia   85
  Divided from herself and her fair judgment,
  Without the which we are pictures, or mere beasts;
  Last, and as much containing as all these,
  Her brother is in secret come from France,
  Feeds on his wonder, keeps himself in clouds,°   90
  And wants° not buzzers° to infect his ear
  With pestilent speeches of his father's death,
  Wherein necessity, of matter beggar'd,°
  Will nothing stick our person to arraign
  In ear and ear.° O my dear Gertrude, this,   95
  Like to a murd'ring-piece,° in many places
  Gives me superfluous death.   (*A noise within.*)
[QUEEN: Alack, what noise is this?]

---

15. ill-breeding: Prone to suspect the worst. **18. toy:** Trifle.
amiss: Calamity. **19–20. So . . . spilt:** Guilt is so full of suspicion that it unskillfully betrays itself in fearing betrayal.
25. cockle hat: Hat with cockleshell stuck in it as a sign that the
wearer had been a pilgrim to the shrine of St. James of Com-
postella in Spain. **26. shoon:** Shoes. **38. Larded:** Decorated.
42. God 'ild: God yield or reward. **owl:** Refers to a legend
about a baker's daughter who was turned into an owl for refusing Jesus bread. **45. Conceit:** Brooding. **48. Valentine's:**
This song alludes to the belief that the first girl seen by a man
on the morning of this day was his valentine or true love.
53. dupp'd: Opened.

59. Gis: Jesus. **62. Cock:** A perversion of *God* in oaths.
79. spies: Scouts sent in advance of the main force. **82. muddied:** Stirred up, confused. **84. greenly:** Imprudently, foolishly. **85. hugger-mugger:** Secret haste. **90. in clouds:** i.e., of
suspicion and rumor. **91. wants:** Lacks. **buzzers:** Gossipers,
informers. **93. of matter beggar'd:** Unprovided with facts.
95. Will . . . and ear: Will not hesitate to accuse my (royal) person in everybody's ears. **96. murd'ring-piece:** Cannon loaded
so as to scatter its shot.

KING: Attend!
100   Where are my Switzers?° Let them guard the door.

(*Enter a Messenger.*)

         What is the matter?
MESSENGER: Save yourself, my lord!
      The ocean, overpeering of his list,°
      Eats not the flats° with more impiteous° haste
      Than young Laertes, in a riotous head,°
105   O'erbears your officers. The rabble call him lord,
      And, as° the world were now but to begin,
      Antiquity forgot, custom not known,
      The ratifiers and props° of every word,°
      They cry, "Choose we! Laertes shall be king!"
110   Caps, hands, and tongues applaud it to the clouds,
      "Laertes shall be king, Laertes king!"
                                  (*A noise within.*)
QUEEN: How cheerfully on the false trail they cry!
      O, this is counter,° you false Danish dogs!

(*Enter Laertes with others.*)

KING: The doors are broke.
LAERTES: Where is this King? Sirs, stand you all
115   without.
ALL: No, let's come in.
LAERTES: I pray you, give me leave.
ALL: We will, we will.
                        [*They retire without the door.*]
LAERTES: I thank you. Keep the door. O thou vile king,
      Give me my father!
QUEEN: Calmly, good Laertes.
                        [*She tries to hold him back.*]
LAERTES: That drop of blood that's calm proclaims me
120   bastard,
      Cries cuckold to my father, brands the harlot
      Even here, between the chaste unsmirched brow
      Of my true mother.
KING: What is the cause, Laertes,
      That thy rebellion looks so giant-like?
125   Let him go, Gertrude. Do not fear our° person.
      There's such divinity doth hedge a king
      That treason can but peep to what it would,°
      Acts little of his will.° Tell me, Laertes,
      Why thou art thus incens'd. Let him go, Gertrude.
      Speak, man.
LAERTES: Where is my father?
130   KING: Dead.
QUEEN: But not by him.
KING: Let him demand his fill.

LAERTES: How came he dead? I'll not be juggled with.
      To hell, allegiance! Vows, to the blackest devil!
      Conscience and grace, to the profoundest pit!
      I dare damnation. To this point I stand,   135
      That both the worlds I give to negligence,°
      Let come what comes, only I'll be reveng'd
      Most throughly° for my father.
KING: Who shall stay you?
LAERTES: My will, not all the world's.°
      And for my means, I'll husband them so well,   140
      They shall go far with little.
KING: Good Laertes,
      If you desire to know the certainty
      Of your dear father, is 't writ in your revenge
      That, swoopstake,° you will draw both friend and
         foe,
      Winner and loser?   145
LAERTES: None but his enemies.
KING: Will you know them then?
LAERTES: To his good friends thus wide I'll ope my arms,
      And, like the kind life-rend'ring pelican,°
      Repast° them with my blood.
KING: Why, now you speak
      Like a good child and a true gentleman.   150
      That I am guiltless of your father's death,
      And am most sensibly° in grief for it,
      It shall as level° to your judgment 'pear
      As day does to your eye.
                  (*A noise within:*) "Let her come in."
LAERTES: How now? What noise is that?   155

(*Enter Ophelia.*)

      O heat, dry up my brains! Tears seven times salt
      Burn out the sense and virtue° of mine eye!
      By heaven, thy madness shall be paid with weight°
      Till our scale turn the beam.° O rose of May!
      Dear maid, kind sister, sweet Ophelia!   160
      O heavens, is 't possible a young maid's wits
      Should be as mortal as an old man's life?
      [Nature is fine in° love, and where 'tis fine,
      It sends some precious instance° of itself
      After the thing it loves.°]   165
OPHELIA: "They bore him barefac'd on the bier;
                                           (*Song.*)

      [Hey non nonny, nonny, hey nonny,]
      And in his grave rain'd many a tear"—
      Fare you well, my dove!

---

100. **Switzers:** Swiss guards, mercenaries.   102. **overpeering of his list:** Overflowing its shore.   103. **flats:** Flatlands near shore. **impiteous:** Pitiless.   104. **head:** Armed force.   106. **as:** As if. 108. **ratifiers and props:** Refer to *antiquity* and *custom*. **word:** Promise.   113. **counter:** A hunting term meaning to follow the trail in a direction opposite to that which the game has taken.   125. **fear our:** Fear for my.   127. **can . . . would:** Can only glance; as from far off or through a barrier, at what it would intend.   128. **Acts . . . will:** (But) performs little of what it intends.

136. **both . . . negligence:** Both this world and the next are of no consequence to me.   138. **throughly:** Thoroughly.   139. **My will . . . world's:** I'll stop (*stay*) when my will is accomplished, not for anyone else's.   144. **swoopstake:** Literally, taking all stakes on the gambling table at once, i.e., indiscriminately; *draw* is also a gambling term.   148. **pelican:** Refers to the belief that the female pelican fed its young with its own blood. 149. **Repast:** Feed.   152. **sensibly:** Feelingly.   153. **level:** Plain. 157. **virtue:** Faculty, power.   158. **paid with weight:** Repaid, avenged equally or more.   159. **beam:** Crossbar of a balance. 163. **fine in:** Refined by.   164. **instance:** Token. 165. **After . . . loves:** Into the grave, along with Polonius.

LAERTES: Hadst thou thy wits, and didst persuade°
170   revenge,
      It could not move thus.
OPHELIA: You must sing "A-down a-down,
      And you call him a-down-a."
      O, how the wheel° becomes it! It is the false steward°
175   that stole his master's daughter.
LAERTES: This nothing's more than matter.°
OPHELIA: There's rosemary,° that's for remembrance;
      pray you, love, remember. And there is pansies,° that's
      for thoughts.
180 LAERTES: A document° in madness, thoughts and remem-
      brance fitted.
OPHELIA: There's fennel° for you, and columbines.°
      There's rue° for you, and here's some for me; we may
      call it herb of grace o' Sundays. You may wear your
185   rue with a difference.° There's a daisy.° I would give
      you some violets,° but they wither'd all when my
      father died. They say 'e made a good end —
      [Sings.] "For bonny sweet Robin is all my joy."
LAERTES: Thought° and affliction, passion, hell itself,
190   She turns to favor° and to prettiness.
OPHELIA: "And will 'a not come again? (Song.)
      And will 'a not come again?
         No, no, he is dead,
         Go to thy death-bed,
195   He never will come again.

      "His beard was as white as snow,
      All flaxen was his poll.°
         He is gone, he is gone,
         And we cast away moan.
200   God 'a' mercy on his soul!"
      And of all Christians' souls, I pray God. God buy you.
                                                      [Exit.]
LAERTES: Do you see this, O God?
KING: Laertes, I must commune with your grief,
      Or you deny me right. Go but apart,
205   Make choice of whom your wisest friends you will,
      And they shall hear and judge 'twixt you and me.
      If by direct or by collateral° hand
      They find us touch'd,° we will our kingdom give,
      Our crown, our life, and all that we call ours,

To you in satisfaction; but if not,   210
Be you content to lend your patience to us,
And we shall jointly labor with your soul
To give it due content.
LAERTES: Let this be so.
   His means of death, his obscure funeral —
   No trophy,° sword, nor hatchment° o'er his bones,   215
   No noble rite nor formal ostentation° —
   Cry to be heard, as 'twere from heaven to earth,
   That I must call 't in question.
KING: So you shall;
   And where th' offense is, let the great ax fall.
   I pray you go with me.   (Exeunt.) 220

{*Scene VI*}°

(*Enter Horatio and others.*)

HORATIO: What are they that would speak with me?
GENTLEMAN: Seafaring men, sir. They say they have let-
   ters for you.
HORATIO: Let them come in.   [*Exit Gentleman.*]
   I do not know from what part of the world   5
   I should be greeted, if not from lord Hamlet.

(*Enter Sailors.*)

FIRST SAILOR: God bless you sir.
HORATIO: Let him bless thee too.
FIRST SAILOR: 'A shall, sir, an 't please him. There's a letter for you, sir — it came from th' ambassador that   10
   was bound for England — if your name be Horatio,
   as I am let to know it is.   [*Gives letter.*]
HORATIO [*reads*]: "Horatio, when thou shalt have overlook'd this, give these fellows some means° to the
   King; they have letters for him. Ere we were two days 15
   old at sea, a pirate of very warlike appointment° gave
   us chase. Finding ourselves too slow of sail, we put
   on a compell'd valor, and in the grapple I boarded
   them. On the instant they got clear of our ship, so I
   alone became their prisoner. They have dealt with me   20
   like thieves of mercy,° but they knew what they did: I
   am to do a good turn for them. Let the King have the
   letters I have sent, and repair thou to me with as
   much speed as thou wouldest fly death. I have words
   to speak in thine ear will make thee dumb; yet are   25
   they much too light for the bore° of the matter. These
   good fellows will bring thee where I am. Rosencrantz
   and Guildenstern hold their course for England. Of
   them I have much to tell thee. Farewell.
                  He that thou knowest thine, Hamlet."   30
   Come, I will give you way for these your letters,
   And do 't the speedier that you may direct me
   To him from whom you brought them.   (*Exeunt.*)

170. persuade: Argue cogently for. **174. wheel:** Spinning wheel as accompaniment to the song, or refrain. **false steward:** The story is unknown. **176. This . . . matter:** This seeming nonsense is more meaningful than sane utterance. **177. rosemary:** Used as a symbol of remembrance both at weddings and at funerals. **178. pansies:** Emblems of love and courtship; perhaps from French *pensées*, thoughts. **180. document:** Instruction, lesson. **182. fennel:** Emblem of flattery. **columbines:** Emblems of unchastity (?) or ingratitude (?). **183. rue:** Emblem of repentance; when mingled with holy water, it was known as *herb of grace*. **185. with a difference:** Suggests that Ophelia and the queen have different causes of sorrow and repentance; perhaps with a play on *rue* in the sense of ruth, pity. **daisy:** Emblem of dissembling, faithlessness. **186. violets:** Emblems of faithfulness. **189. Thought:** Melancholy. **190. favor:** Grace. **197. poll:** Head. **207. collateral:** Indirect. **208. us touch'd:** Me implicated.

215. trophy: Memorial. **hatchment:** Tablet displaying the armorial bearings of a deceased person. **216. ostentation:** Ceremony. **IV, VI. Location:** The castle. **14. means:** Means of access. **16. appointment:** Equipage. **21. thieves of mercy:** Merciful thieves. **26. bore:** Caliber, i.e., importance.

{*Scene VII*}°

(*Enter King and Laertes.*)

KING: Now must your conscience my acquittance seal,°
  And you must put me in your heart for friend,
  Sith you have heard, and with a knowing ear,
  That he which hath your noble father slain
5 Pursued my life.
LAERTES: It well appears. But tell me
  Why you proceeded not against these feats°
  So criminal and so capital° in nature,
  As by your safety, greatness, wisdom, all things else,
  You mainly° were stirr'd up.
KING: O, for two special reasons,
10 Which may to you, perhaps, seem much unsinew'd,°
  But yet to me th' are strong. The Queen his mother
  Lives almost by his looks, and for myself —
  My virtue or my plague, be it either which —
  She's so conjunctive° to my life and soul
15 That, as the star moves not but in his sphere,°
  I could not but by her. The other motive,
  Why to a public count° I might not go,
  Is the great love the general gender° bear him,
  Who, dipping all his faults in their affection,
20 Would, like the spring° that turneth wood to stone,
  Convert his gyves° to graces, so that my arrows,
  Too slightly timber'd° for so loud° a wind,
  Would have reverted to my bow again
  And not where I had aim'd them.
25 LAERTES: And so have I a noble father lost,
  A sister driven into desp'rate terms,°
  Whose worth, if praises may go back° again,
  Stood challenger on mount° of all the age
  For her perfections. But my revenge will come.
KING: Break not your sleeps for that. You must not
30   think
  That we are made of stuff so flat and dull
  That we can let our beard be shook with danger
  And think it pastime. You shortly shall hear more.
  I lov'd your father, and we love ourself;
35 And that, I hope, will teach you to imagine —

(*Enter a Messenger with letters.*)

[How now? What news?]

MESSENGER: [Letters, my lord, from Hamlet:]
  These to your Majesty, this to the Queen.
                                    [*Gives letters.*]
KING: From Hamlet? Who brought them?
MESSENGER: Sailors, my lord, they say; I saw them not.
  They were given me by Claudio. He receiv'd them   40
  Of him that brought them.
KING: Laertes, you shall hear them.
  Leave us.   [*Exit Messenger.*]
[*Reads.*] "High and mighty, you shall know I am set
  naked° on your kingdom. Tomorrow shall I beg leave
  to see your kingly eyes, when I shall, first asking your   45
  pardon° thereunto, recount the occasion of my sud-
  den and more strange return.   Hamlet."
  What should this mean? Are all the rest come back?
  Or is it some abuse,° and no such thing?
LAERTES: Know you the hand?
KING: 'Tis Hamlet's character.° "Naked!"   50
  And in a postscript here, he says "alone."
  Can you devise° me?
LAERTES: I am lost in it, my lord. But let him come.
  It warms the very sickness in my heart
  That I shall live and tell him to his teeth,   55
  "Thus didst thou."
KING: If it be so, Laertes —
  As how should it be so? How otherwise?° —
  Will you be ruled by me?
LAERTES: Ay, my lord,
  So° you will not o'errule me to a peace.
KING: To thine own peace. If he be now returned,   60
  As checking at° his voyage, and that he means
  No more to undertake it, I will work him
  To an exploit, now ripe in my device,
  Under the which he shall not choose but fall;
  And for his death no wind of blame shall breathe,   65
  But even his mother shall uncharge the practice°
  And call it accident.
LAERTES: My lord, I will be rul'd,
  The rather if you could devise it so
  That I might be the organ.°
KING: It falls right.
  You have been talk'd of since your travel much,   70
  And that in Hamlet's hearing, for a quality
  Wherein, they say, you shine. Your sum of parts°
  Did not together pluck such envy from him
  As did that one, and that, in my regard,
  Of the unworthiest siege.°   75
LAERTES: What part is that, my lord?

IV, VII. **Location:** The castle.   **1. my acquittance seal:** Confirm
or acknowledge my innocence.   **6. feats:** Acts.   **7. capital:**
Punishable by death.   **9. mainly:** Greatly.   **10. unsinew'd:**
Weak.   **14. conjunctive:** Closely united.   **15. sphere:** The hollow sphere in which, according to Ptolemaic astronomy, the
planets moved.   **17. count:** Account, reckoning.   **18. general
gender:** Common people.   **20. spring:** A spring with such a
concentration of lime that it coats a piece of wood with lime-
stone, in effect gilding it.   **21. gyves:** Fetters (which, gilded by
the people's praise, would look like badges of honor).
22. slightly timber'd: Light.   **loud:** Strong.   **26. terms:** State,
condition.   **27. go back:** Recall Ophelia's former virtues.
28. on mount: On high.

44. naked: Destitute, unarmed, without following.   **46. pardon:** Permission.   **49. abuse:** Deceit.   **50. character:** Handwriting.   **52. devise:** Explain to.   **57. As . . . otherwise:** How
can this (Hamlet's return) be true? Yet how otherwise than true
(since we have the evidence of his letter).   **59. So:** Provided
that.   **61. checking at:** Turning aside from (like a falcon leaving the quarry to fly at a chance bird).   **66. uncharge the practice:** Acquit the stratagem of being a plot.   **69. organ:** Agent,
instrument.   **72. Your . . . parts:** All your other virtues.
75. unworthiest siege: Least important rank.

KING: A very riband in the cap of youth,
　　Yet needful too, for youth no less becomes
　　The light and careless livery that it wears
80　Than settled age his sables° and his weeds,°
　　Importing health° and graveness. Two months since
　　Here was a gentleman of Normandy.
　　I have seen myself, and serv'd against, the French,
　　And they can well° on horseback, but this gallant
85　Had witchcraft in 't; he grew unto his seat,
　　And to such wondrous doing brought his horse
　　As had he been incorps'd and demi-natured°
　　With the brave beast. So far he topp'd° my thought
　　That I, in forgery° of shapes and tricks,
　　Come short of what he did.
90　LAERTES:　　　　　　　　　A Norman was 't?
　　KING: A Norman.
　　LAERTES: Upon my life, Lamord.
　　KING:　　　　　　　　　The very same.
　　LAERTES: I know him well. He is the brooch° indeed
　　And gem of all the nation.
95　KING: He made confession° of you,
　　And gave you such a masterly report
　　For art and exercise in your defense,
　　And for your rapier most especial,
　　That he cried out, 'twould be a sight indeed,
　　If one could match you. The scrimers° of their
100　　nation,
　　He swore, had neither motion, guard, nor eye,
　　If you oppos'd them. Sir, this report of his
　　Did Hamlet so envenom with his envy
　　That he could nothing do but wish and beg
105　Your sudden coming o'er to play° with you.
　　Now, out of this —
　　LAERTES:　　　　　　What out of this, my lord?
　　KING: Laertes, was your father dear to you?
　　Or are you like the painting of a sorrow,
　　A face without a heart?
　　LAERTES:　　　　　　Why ask you this?
110　KING: Not that I think you did not love your father,
　　But that I know love is begun by time,°
　　And that I see, in passages of proof,°
　　Time qualifies° the spark and fire of it.
　　There lives within the very flame of love
115　A kind of wick or snuff° that will abate it,
　　And nothing is at a like goodness still,°
　　For goodness, growing to a plurisy,°
　　Dies in his own too much.° That° we would do,

We should do when we would; for this "would"
　　changes
And hath abatements° and delays as many　　120
As there are tongues, are hands, are accidents,°
And then this "should" is like a spendthrift's sigh,°
That hurts by easing.° But, to the quick o' th' ulcer;
Hamlet comes back. What would you undertake
To show yourself your father's son in deed　　125
More than in words?
LAERTES:　　　　　To cut his throat i' th' church!
KING: No place, indeed, should murder sanctuarize;°
　　Revenge should have no bounds. But, good Laertes,
　　Will you do this,° keep close within your chamber.
　　Hamlet return'd shall know you are come home.　　130
　　We'll put on those° shall praise your excellence
　　And set a double varnish on the fame
　　The Frenchman gave you, bring you in fine°
　　　together,
　　And wager on your heads. He, being remiss,°
　　Most generous,° and free from all contriving,　　135
　　Will not peruse the foils, so that, with ease,
　　Or with a little shuffling, you may choose
　　A sword unbated,° and in a pass of practice°
　　Requite him for your father.
LAERTES:　　　　　　I will do 't.
　　And for that purpose I'll anoint my sword.　　140
　　I bought an unction° of a mountebank°
　　So mortal that, but dip a knife in it,
　　Where it draws blood no cataplasm° so rare,
　　Collected from all simples° that have virtue
　　Under the moon, can save the thing from death　　145
　　That is but scratch'd withal. I'll touch my point
　　With this contagion, that, if I gall° him slightly,
　　It may be death.
KING:　　　　　Let's further think of this,
　　Weigh what convenience both of time and means
　　May fit us to our shape.° If this should fail,　　150
　　And that our drift look through our bad
　　　performance,°
　　'Twere better not assay'd. Therefore this project
　　Should have a back or second, that might hold
　　If this did blast in proof.° Soft, let me see.
　　We'll make a solemn wager on your cunnings —　　155

80. **sables:** Rich robes furred with sable. **weeds:** Garments.
81. **Importing health:** Indicating prosperity. 84. **can well:** Are
skilled. 87. **incorps'd and demi–natur'd:** Of one body and
nearly of one nature (like the centaur). 88. **topp'd:** Surpassed.
89. **forgery:** Invention. 93. **brooch:** Ornament. 95. **confession:** Admission of superiority. 100. **scrimers:** Fencers.
105. **play:** Fence. 111. **begun by time:** Subject to change.
112. **passages of proof:** Actual instances. 113. **qualifies:**
Weakens. 115. **snuff:** The charred part of a candlewick.
116. **nothing . . . still:** Nothing remains at a constant level of
perfection. 117. **plurisy:** Excess, plethora. 118. **in . . .
much:** Of its own excess. **That:** That which.

120. **abatements:** Diminutions. 121. **accidents:** Occurrences,
incidents. 122. **spendthrift's sigh:** An allusion to the belief
that each sigh cost the heart a drop of blood. 123. **hurts by
easing:** Costs the heart blood even while it affords emotional
relief. 127. **sanctuarize:** Protect from punishment (alludes to
the right of sanctuary with which certain religious places were
invested). 129. **Will you do this:** If you wish to do this.
131. **put on those:** Instigate those who. 133. **in fine:** Finally.
134. **remiss:** Negligently unsuspicious. 135. **generous:** Noble-
minded. 138. **unbated:** Not blunted, having no button.
pass of practice: Treacherous thrust. 141. **unction:** Ointment.
mountebank: Quack doctor. 143. **cataplasm:** Plaster or poul-
tice. 144. **simples:** Herbs. 147. **gall:** Graze, wound.
150. **shape:** Part that we propose to act. 151. **drift . . . performance:** i.e., intention be disclosed by our bungling. 154. **blast
in proof:** Burst in the test (like a cannon).

I ha 't!
When in your motion you are hot and dry —
As° make your bouts more violent to that end —
And that he calls for drink, I'll have prepar'd him
160   A chalice for the nonce,° whereon but sipping,
If he by chance escape your venom'd stuck,°
Our purpose may hold there. [*A cry within.*] But
        stay, what noise?

(*Enter Queen.*)

QUEEN: One woe doth tread upon another's heel,
        So fast they follow. Your sister's drowned, Laertes.
165   LAERTES: Drown'd! O, where?
QUEEN: There is a willow grows askant° the brook
        That shows his hoar° leaves in the glassy stream;
        Therewith fantastic garlands did she make
        Of crow-flowers, nettles, daisies, and long purples°
170   That liberal° shepherds give a grosser name,
        But our cold° maids do dead men's fingers call them.
        There on the pendent boughs her crownet° weeds
        Clamb'ring to hang, an envious sliver° broke,
        When down her weedy° trophies and herself
175   Fell in the weeping brook. Her clothes spread wide,
        And mermaid-like awhile they bore her up,
        Which time she chanted snatches of old lauds,°
        As one incapable° of her own distress,
        Or like a creature native and indued°
180   Unto that element. But long it could not be
        Till that her garments, heavy with their drink,
        Pull'd the poor wretch from her melodious lay
        To muddy death.
LAERTES: Alas, then she is drown'd?
QUEEN: Drown'd, drown'd.
185   LAERTES: Too much of water hast thou, poor Ophelia,
        And therefore I forbid my tears. But yet
        It is our trick;° nature her custom holds,
        Let shame say what it will. [*He weeps.*] When these
            are gone,
        The woman will be out.° Adieu, my lord.
190   I have a speech of fire, that fain would blaze,
        But that this folly drowns it.   (*Exit.*)
KING: Let's follow, Gertrude.
        How much I had to do to calm his rage!
        Now fear I this will give it start again;
        Therefore let's follow.   (*Exeunt.*)

158. As: And you should. 160. nonce: Occasion.
161. stuck: Thrust (from *stoccado*, a fencing term).
166. askant: Aslant. 167. hoar: White or gray. 169. long
purples: Early purple orchids. 170. liberal: Free-spoken.
171. cold: Chaste. 172. crownet: Made into a chaplet or
coronet. 173. envious sliver: Malicious branch.
174. weedy: I.e., of plants. 177. lauds: Hymns. 178. incapable: Lacking capacity to apprehend. 179. indued: Adapted
by nature. 187. It is our trick: Weeping is our natural way
(when sad). 188–89. When . . . out: When my tears are all
shed, the woman in me will be expended, satisfied.

{*ACT V • Scene 1*}°

(*Enter two Clowns*° [*with spades, etc.*])

FIRST CLOWN: Is she to be buried in Christian burial
    when she willfully seeks her own salvation?
SECOND CLOWN: I tell thee she is; therefore make her
    grave straight.° The crowner° hath sat on her, and
    finds it Christian burial.   5
FIRST CLOWN: How can that be, unless she drown'd her-
    self in her own defense?
SECOND CLOWN: Why, 'tis found so.
FIRST CLOWN: It must be "se offendendo";° it cannot
    be else. For here lies the point: if I drown myself   10
    wittingly, it argues an act, and an act hath three
    branches — it is to act, to do, and to perform.
    Argal,° she drown'd herself wittingly.
SECOND CLOWN: Nay, but hear you, goodman delver —
FIRST CLOWN: Give me leave. Here lies the water; good.   15
    Here stands the man; good. If the man go to this
    water, and drown himself, it is, will he,° nill he, he
    goes, mark you that. But if the water come to him
    and drown him, he drowns not himself. Argal, he
    that is not guilty of his own death shortens not his   20
    own life.
SECOND CLOWN: But is this law?
FIRST CLOWN: Ay, marry, is 't — crowner's quest° law.
SECOND CLOWN: Will you ha' the truth on 't? If this had
    not been a gentlewoman, she should have been   25
    buried out o' Christian burial.
FIRST CLOWN: Why, there thou say'st.° And the more
    pity that great folk should have count'nance° in this
    world to drown or hang themselves, more than their
    even-Christen.° Come, my spade. There is no ancient   30
    gentlemen but gard'ners, ditchers, and grave-makers.
    They hold up Adam's profession.
SECOND CLOWN: Was he a gentleman?
FIRST CLOWN: 'A was the first that ever bore arms.
[SECOND CLOWN: Why, he had none.   35
FIRST CLOWN: What, art a heathen? How dost thou
    understand the Scripture? The Scripture says "Adam
    digg'd." Could he dig without arms?] I'll put another
    question to thee. If thou answerest me not to the pur-
    pose, confess thyself° —   40
SECOND CLOWN: Go to.
FIRST CLOWN: What is he that builds stronger than
    either the mason, the shipwright, or the carpenter?
SECOND CLOWN: The gallows-maker, for that frame
    outlives a thousand tenants.   45

V, I. Location: A churchyard. [S.D.] *Clowns*: Rustics.
4. straight: Straightway, immediately. crowner: Coroner.
9. se offendendo: A comic mistake for *se defendendo*, term used
in verdicts of justifiable homicide. 13. Argal: Corruption of
ergo, therefore. 17. will he: Will he not. 23. quest: Inquest.
27. there thou say'st: That's right. 28. count'nance: Privilege.
30. even-Christen: Fellow Christian. 40. confess thyself: The
saying continues, "and be hanged."

FIRST CLOWN: I like thy wit well, in good faith. The gallows does well, but how does it well? It does well to those that do ill. Now thou dost ill to say the gallows is built stronger than the church. Argal, the gallows may do well to thee. To 't again, come.

SECOND CLOWN: "Who builds stronger than a mason, a shipwright, or a carpenter?"

FIRST CLOWN: Ay, tell me that, and unyoke.°

SECOND CLOWN: Marry, now I can tell.

FIRST CLOWN: To 't.

SECOND CLOWN: Mass,° I cannot tell.

(Enter Hamlet and Horatio [at a distance].)

FIRST CLOWN: Cudgel thy brains no more about it, for your dull ass will not mend his pace with beating; and, when you are ask'd this question next, say "a grave-maker." The houses he makes lasts till doomsday. Go, get thee in, and fetch me a stoup° of liquor.

[Exit Second Clown. First Clown digs.]
(Song.)

"In youth, when I did love, did love,°
    Methought it was very sweet,
To contract — O — the time for — a — my behove,°
    O, methought there — a — was nothing — a —
        meet."°

HAMLET: Has this fellow no feeling of his business, that 'a sings at grave-making?

HORATIO: Custom hath made it in him a property of easiness.°

HAMLET: 'Tis e'en so. The hand of little employment hath the daintier sense.°
(Song.)

FIRST CLOWN: "But age, with his stealing steps,
    Hath claw'd me in his clutch,
And hath shipped me into the land,°
    As if I had never been such."
[Throws up a skull.]

HAMLET: That skull had a tongue in it, and could sing once. How the knave jowls° it to the ground, as if 'twere Cain's jaw-bone, that did the first murder! This might be the pate of a politician,° which this ass now o'erreaches,° one that would circumvent God, might it not?

HORATIO: It might, my lord.

HAMLET: Or of a courtier, which could say "Good morrow, sweet lord! How dost thou, sweet lord?" This might be my Lord Such-a-one, that prais'd my Lord Such-a-one's horse when 'a meant to beg it, might it not?

HORATIO: Ay, my lord.

HAMLET: Why, e'en so, and now my Lady Worm's, chapless,° and knock'd about the mazzard° with a sexton's spade. Here's fine revolution,° an° we had the trick to see 't. Did these bones cost no more the breeding,° but to play at loggats° with them? Mine ache to think on 't.
(Song.)

FIRST CLOWN: "A pick-axe, and a spade, a spade,
    For and° a shrouding sheet;
O, a pit of clay for to be made
    For such a guest is meet."
[Throws up another skull.]

HAMLET: There's another. Why may not that be the skull of a lawyer? Where be his quiddities° now, his quillities,° his cases, his tenures,° and his tricks? Why does he suffer this mad knave now to knock him about the sconce° with a dirty shovel, and will not tell him of his action of battery? Hum! This fellow might be in 's time a great buyer of land, with his statutes, his recognizances,° his fines, his double° vouchers,° his recoveries.° [Is this the fine of his fines, and the recovery of his recoveries,] to have his fine pate full of fine dirt?° Will his vouchers vouch him no more of his purchases, and double [ones too], than the length and breadth of a pair of indentures?° The very conveyances° of his lands will scarcely lie in this box,° and must th' inheritor° himself have no more, ha?

HORATIO: Not a jot more, my lord.

HAMLET: Is not parchment made of sheep-skins?

HORATIO: Ay, my lord, and of calf-skins too.

---

53. unyoke: After this great effort you may unharness the team of your wits. **56. Mass:** By the Mass. **61. stoup:** Two-quart measure. **62. In . . . love:** This and the two following stanzas, with nonsensical variations, are from a poem attributed to Lord Vaux and printed in *Tottel's Miscellany* (1557). The O and *a* (for "ah") seemingly are the grunts of the digger. **64. To contract . . . behove:** To make a betrothal agreement for my benefit (?). **65. meet:** Suitable, i.e., more suitable. **68–69. property of easiness:** Something he can do easily and without thinking. **71. daintier sense:** More delicate sense of feeling. **74. into the land:** Toward my grave (?) (but note the lack of rhyme in *steps, land*). **77. jowls:** Dashes. **79. politician:** Schemer, plotter. **80. o'erreaches:** Circumvents, gets the better of (with a quibble on the literal sense).

89–90. chapless: Having no lower jaw. **90. mazzard:** Head (literally, a drinking vessel). **91. revolution:** Change. **an:** If. **92–93. the breeding:** In the breeding, raising. **93. loggats:** A game in which pieces of hardwood are thrown to lie as near as possible to a stake. **96. For and:** And moreover. **100. quiddities:** Subtleties, quibbles (from Latin *quid,* a thing). **100–01. quillities:** Verbal niceties, subtle distinctions (variation of *quiddities*). **101. tenures:** The holding of a piece of property or office, or the conditions or period of such holding. **103. sconce:** Head. **106. statutes, recognizances:** Legal documents guaranteeing a debt by attaching land and property. **106–07. fines, recoveries:** Ways of converting entailed estates into "fee simple" or freehold. **106. double:** Signed by two signatories. **107. vouchers:** Guarantees of the legality of a title to real estate. **107–09. fine of his fines . . . fine pate . . . fine dirt:** End of his legal maneuvers . . . elegant head . . . minutely sifted dirt. **111. pair of indentures:** Legal document drawn up in duplicate on a single sheet and then cut apart on a zigzag line so that each pair was uniquely matched. (Hamlet may refer to two rows of teeth, or dentures.) **112. conveyances:** Deeds. **113. this box:** The skull. **inheritor:** Possessor, owner.

HAMLET: They are sheep and calves which seek out assurance in that.° I will speak to this fellow. — Whose grave's this, sirrah?°

120

FIRST CLOWN: Mine, sir.

[Sings.] "O, a pit of clay for to be made
[For such a guest is meet]."

HAMLET: I think it be thine, indeed, for thou liest in 't.

125

FIRST CLOWN: You lie out on 't, sir, and therefore 'tis not yours. For my part, I do not lie in 't, yet it is mine.

HAMLET: Thou dost lie in 't, to be in 't and say it is thine. 'Tis for the dead, not for the quick;° therefore thou liest.

130

FIRST CLOWN: 'Tis a quick lie, sir; 'twill away again from me to you.

HAMLET: What man dost thou dig it for?

FIRST CLOWN: For no man, sir.

HAMLET: What woman, then?

135

FIRST CLOWN: For none, neither.

HAMLET: Who is to be buried in 't?

FIRST CLOWN: One that was a woman, sir, but, rest her soul, she's dead.

HAMLET: How absolute° the knave is! We must speak by the card,° or equivocation° will undo us. By the Lord, Horatio, this three years I have taken note of it: the age is grown so pick'd° that the toe of the peasant comes so near the heel of the courtier, he galls his kibe.° How long hast thou been a grave-maker?

140

145

FIRST CLOWN: Of all the days i' th' year, I came to 't that day that our last king Hamlet overcame Fortinbras.

HAMLET: How long is that since?

FIRST CLOWN: Cannot you tell that? Every fool can tell that. It was that very day that young Hamlet was born — he that is mad, and sent into England.

150

HAMLET: Ay, marry, why was he sent into England?

FIRST CLOWN: Why, because 'a was mad. 'A shall recover his wits there, or, if 'a do not, 'tis no great matter there.

HAMLET: Why?

155

FIRST CLOWN: 'Twill not be seen in him there. There the men are as mad as he.

HAMLET: How came he mad?

FIRST CLOWN: Very strangely, they say.

HAMLET: How strangely?

160

FIRST CLOWN: Faith, e'en with losing his wits.

HAMLET: Upon what ground?

FIRST CLOWN: Why, here in Denmark. I have been sexton here, man and boy, thirty years.

HAMLET: How long will a man lie i' th' earth ere he rot?

165

FIRST CLOWN: Faith, if 'a be not rotten before 'a die — as we have many pocky° corses [now-a-days], that

will scarce hold the laying in — 'a will last you some eight year or nine year. A tanner will last you nine year.

HAMLET: Why he more than another?

170

FIRST CLOWN: Why, sir, his hide is so tann'd with his trade that 'a will keep out water a great while, and your water is a sore decayer of your whoreson dead body. [Picks up a skull.] Here's a skull now hath lain you° i' th' earth three and twenty years.

175

HAMLET: Whose was it?

FIRST CLOWN: A whoreson mad fellow's it was. Whose do you think it was?

HAMLET: Nay, I know not.

FIRST CLOWN: A pestilence on him for a mad rogue! 'A pour'd a flagon of Rhenish° on my head once. This same skull, sir, was Yorick's skull, the King's jester.

180

HAMLET: This?

FIRST CLOWN: E'en that.

HAMLET: [Let me see.] [Takes the skull.] Alas, poor Yorick! I knew him, Horatio, a fellow of infinite jest, of most excellent fancy. He hath borne me on his back a thousand times; and now, how abhorr'd in my imagination it is! My gorge rises at it. Here hung those lips that I have kiss'd I know not how oft. Where be your gibes now? Your gambols, your songs, your flashes of merriment that were wont to set the table on a roar? Not one now, to mock your own grinning? Quite chap-fall'n?° Now get you to my lady's chamber, and tell her, let her paint an inch thick, to this favor° she must come; make her laugh at that. Prithee, Horatio, tell me one thing.

185

190

195

HORATIO: What's that, my lord?

HAMLET: Dost thou think Alexander look'd o' this fashion i' th' earth?

200

HORATIO: E'en so.

HAMLET: And smelt so? Pah! [Puts down the skull.]

HORATIO: E'en so, my lord.

HAMLET: To what base uses we may return, Horatio! Why may not imagination trace the noble dust of Alexander, till 'a find it stopping a bung-hole?

205

HORATIO: 'twere to consider too curiously,° to consider so.

HAMLET: No, faith, not a jot, but to follow him thither with modesty° enough, and likelihood to lead it. [As thus]: Alexander died, Alexander was buried, Alexander returneth to dust; the dust is earth; of earth we make loam;° and why of that loam, whereto he was converted, might they not stop a beer-barrel?

210

Imperious° Caesar, dead and turn'd to clay,
Might stop a hole to keep the wind away.
O, that that earth which kept the world in awe

215

---

119. **assurance in that:** Safety in legal parchments.   120. **sirrah:** Term of address to inferiors.   128. **quick:** Living.   139. **absolute:** Positive, decided.   139–40. **by the card:** By the mariner's card on which the points of the compass were marked, i.e., with precision.   140. **equivocation:** Ambiguity in the use of terms.   142. **pick'd:** Refined, fastidious.   143–44. **galls his kibe:** Chafes the courtier's chilblain (a swelling or sore caused by cold).   166. **pocky:** Rotten, diseased (literally, with the pox, or syphilis).

174–75. **lain you:** Lain.   181. **Rhenish:** Rhine wine.   194. **chap-fall'n:** (1) Lacking the lower jaw; (2) dejected.   196. **favor:** Aspect, appearance.   207. **curiously:** Minutely.   210. **modesty:** Moderation.   213. **loam:** Clay mixture for brickmaking or other clay use.   215. **Imperious:** Imperial.

Should patch a wall t' expel the winter's flaw!°
But soft, but soft awhile! Here comes the King.

(*Enter King, Queen, Laertes, and the Corse [of Ophelia, in procession, with Priest, Lords etc.].*)

220   The Queen, the courtiers. Who is this they follow?
And with such maimed rites? This doth betoken
The corse they follow did with desp'rate hand
Fordo it° own life. 'Twas of some estate.°
Couch° we awhile, and mark.

                    [*He and Horatio conceal themselves.*
                    Ophelia's body is taken to the grave.]

225   LAERTES: What ceremony else?
HAMLET [*to Horatio*]: That is Laertes, a very noble
    youth. Mark.
LAERTES: What ceremony else?
PRIEST: Her obsequies have been as far enlarg'd
    As we have warranty. Her death was doubtful,
230   And, but that great command o'ersways the order,
She should in ground unsanctified been lodg'd
Till the last trumpet. For° charitable prayers,
Shards,° flints, and pebbles should be thrown on her.
Yet here she is allow'd her virgin crants,°
235   Her maiden strewments,° and the bringing home
Of bell and burial.°
LAERTES: Must there no more be done?
PRIEST: No more be done.
We should profane the service of the dead
To sing a requiem and such rest to her
As to peace-parted souls.
240   LAERTES: Lay her i' th' earth,
And from her fair and unpolluted flesh
May violets° spring! I tell thee, churlish priest,
A minist'ring angel shall my sister be
When thou liest howling!
HAMLET [*to Horatio*]:   What, the fair Ophelia!
QUEEN [*scattering flowers*]: Sweets to the sweet!
245   Farewell.
I hoped thou shouldst have been my Hamlet's wife.
I thought thy bride-bed to have deck'd, sweet maid,
And not have strew'd thy grave.
LAERTES: O, treble woe
Fall ten times treble on that cursed head
250   Whose wicked deed thy most ingenious sense°
Depriv'd thee of! Hold off the earth awhile,
Till I have caught her once more in mine arms.

         [*Leaps into the grave and embraces Ophelia.*]

Now pile your dust upon the quick and dead,
Till of this flat a mountain you have made

T 'o'ertop old Pelion,° or the skyish head   255
Of blue Olympus.°
HAMLET [*coming forward*]: What is he whose grief
Bears such an emphasis, whose phrase of sorrow
Conjures the wand'ring stars,° and makes them stand
Like wonder-wounded hearers? This is I,   260
Hamlet the Dane.°
LAERTES: The devil take thy soul!

                     [*Grappling with him.*]

HAMLET: Thou pray'st not well.
I prithee, take thy fingers from my throat;
For, though I am not splenitive° and rash,
Yet have I in me something dangerous,   265
Which let thy wisdom fear. Hold off thy hand.
KING: Pluck them asunder.
QUEEN: Hamlet, Hamlet!
ALL: Gentlemen!
HORATIO: Good my lord, be quiet.

           [*Hamlet and Horatio are parted.*]

HAMLET: Why, I will fight with him upon this theme
Until my eyelids will no longer wag.   270
QUEEN: O my son, what theme?
HAMLET: I lov'd Ophelia. Forty thousand brothers
Could not with all their quantity of love
Make up my sum. What wilt thou do for her?
KING: O, he is mad, Laertes.   275
QUEEN: For love of God, forbear him.
HAMLET: 'Swounds,° show me what thou' do.
Woo 't° weep? Woo 't fight? Woo 't fast? Woo 't tear
    thyself?
Woo 't drink up eisel?° Eat a crocodile?
I'll do 't. Dost thou come here to whine?   280
To outface me with leaping in her grave?
Be buried quick° with her, and so will I.
And, if thou prate of mountains, let them throw
Millions of acres on us, till our ground,
Singeing his pate° against the burning zone,°   285
Make Ossa° like a wart! Nay, an thou 'lt mouth,°
I'll rant as well as thou.
QUEEN: This is mere° madness,
And thus a while the fit will work on him;
Anon, as patient as the female dove
When that her golden couplets° are disclos'd,°   290
His silence will sit drooping.
HAMLET: Hear you, sir.
What is the reason that you use me thus?

---

218. **flaw:** Gust of wind.   223. **Fordo it:** Destroy its.   **estate:** Rank.   224. **Couch:** Hide, lurk.   232. **For:** In place of.
233. **Shards:** Broken bits of pottery.   234. **crants:** Garland.
235. **strewments:** Traditional strewing of flowers.
235–36. **bringing . . . burial:** Laying to rest of the body in consecrated ground, to the sound of the bell.   242. **violets:** See IV, v, 186 and note.   250. **ingenious sense:** Mind endowed with finest qualities.

255, 256. **Pelion, Olympus:** Mountains in the north of Thessaly; see also *Ossa* at line 286.   259. **wand'ring stars:** Planets.
261. **the Dane:** This title normally signifies the king, see I, i, 15 and note.   264. **splenitive:** Quick-tempered.   277. **'Swounds:** By His (Christ's) wounds.   278. **Woo 't:** Wilt thou.
279. **eisel:** Vinegar.   282. **quick:** Alive.   285. **his pate:** Its head, i.e., top.   **burning zone:** Sun's orbit.   286. **Ossa:** Another mountain in Thessaly. (In their war against the Olympian gods, the giants attempted to heap Ossa, Pelion, and Olympus on one another to scale heaven.)   **mouth:** Rant.   287. **mere:** Utter.   290. **golden couplets:** Two baby pigeons, covered with yellow down.   **disclos'd:** Hatched.

I lov'd you ever. But it is no matter.
Let Hercules himself do what he may,
295   The cat will mew, and dog will have his day.°
KING: I pray thee, good Horatio, wait upon him.

(*Exit Hamlet and Horatio.*)

[*To Laertes.*] Strengthen your patience in° our last
      night's speech;
We'll put the matter to the present push.° —
Good Gertrude, set some watch over your son. —
300   This grave shall have a living° monument.
An hour of quiet shortly shall we see;
Till then, in patience our proceeding be.   (*Exeunt.*)

{*Scene II*}°

(*Enter Hamlet and Horatio.*)

HAMLET: So much for this, sir; now shall you see the
      other.°
   You do remember all the circumstance?
HORATIO: Remember it, my lord!
HAMLET: Sir, in my heart there was a kind of
      fighting
5   That would not let me sleep. Methought I lay
   Worse than the mutines° in the bilboes.° Rashly,°
   And prais'd be rashness for it — let us know,°
   Our indiscretion sometime serves us well
   When our deep plots do pall,° and that should
      learn° us
10   There's a divinity that shapes our ends,
   Rough-hew° them how we will —
HORATIO: That is most certain.
HAMLET: Up from my cabin,
   My sea-gown scarf'd about me, in the dark
   Grop'd I to find out them, had my desire,
15   Finger'd° their packet, and in fine° withdrew
   To mine own room again, making so bold,
   My fears forgetting manners, to unseal
   Their grand commission; where I found, Horatio —
   Ah, royal knavery! — an exact command,
20   Larded° with many several sorts of reasons
   Importing° Denmark's health and England's too,
   With, ho, such bugs° and goblins in my life,°
   That, on the supervise,° no leisure bated,°

No, not to stay the grinding of the axe,
My head should be struck off.
HORATIO: Is 't possible?   25
HAMLET: Here's the commission; read it at more
      leisure.   [*Gives document.*]
   But wilt thou hear now how I did proceed?
HORATIO: I beseech you.
HAMLET: Being thus benetted round with villainies,
   Or I could make a prologue to my brains,   30
   They had begun the play.° I sat me down,
   Devis'd a new commission, wrote it fair.°
   I once did hold it, as our statists° do,
   A baseness° to write fair, and labor'd much
   How to forget that learning, but, sir, now   35
   It did me yeoman's° service. Wilt thou know
   Th' effect° of what I wrote?
HORATIO: Ay, good my lord.
HAMLET: An earnest conjuration from the King,
   As England was his faithful tributary,
   As love between them like the palm might flourish,   40
   As peace should still her wheaten garland° wear
   And stand a comma° 'tween their amities,
   And many such-like as's° of great charge,°
   That, on the view and knowing of these contents,
   Without debasement further, more or less,   45
   He should those bearers put to sudden death,
   Not shriving time° allow'd.
HORATIO: How was this seal'd?
HAMLET: Why, even in that was heaven ordinant.°
   I had my father's signet° in my purse,
   Which was the model of that Danish seal;   50
   Folded the writ up in the form of th' other,
   Subscrib'd° it, gave 't th' impression,° plac'd it safely,
   The changeling° never known. Now, the next day
   Was our sea-fight, and what to this was sequent
   Thou knowest already.   55
HORATIO: So Guildenstern and Rosencrantz go to 't.
HAMLET: [Why, man, they did make love to this
      employment.]
   They are not near my conscience. Their defeat
   Does by their own insinuation° grow.
   'Tis dangerous when the baser nature comes   60
   Between the pass° and fell° incensed points
   Of mighty opposites.
HORATIO: Why, what a king is this!

294–95. **Let . . . day:** Despite any blustering attempts at interference every person will sooner or later do what he must do.
297. **in:** By recalling. 298. **present push:** Immediate test.
300. **living:** Lasting; also refers (for Laertes' benefit) to the plot
against Hamlet. V, II. Location: The castle. 1. **see the other:**
Hear the other news. 6. **mutines:** Mutineers. **bilboes:** Shackles. **Rashly:** On impulse (this adverb goes with lines 12ff.).
7. **know:** Acknowledge. 9. **pall:** Fail. **learn:** Teach.
11. **Rough-hew:** Shape roughly. 15. **Finger'd:** Pilfered,
pinched. **in fine:** Finally, in conclusion. 20. **Larded:**
Enriched. 21. **Importing:** Relating to. 22. **bugs:** Bugbears,
hobgoblins. **in my life:** To be feared if I were allowed to live.
23. **supervise:** Reading. **leisure bated:** Delay allowed.

30–31. **Or . . . play:** Before I could consciously turn my brain
to the matter, it had started working on a plan. (*Or* means *ere*.)
32. **fair:** In a clear hand. 33. **statists:** Statesmen. 34. **baseness:** Lower-class trait. 36. **yeoman's:** Substantial, workman-
like. 37. **effect:** Purport. 41. **wheaten garland:** Symbolic of
fruitful agriculture, of peace. 42. **comma:** Indicating continuity, link. 43. **as's:** (1) The "whereases" of formal document,
(2) asses. **charge:** (1) Import, (2) burden. 47. **shriving time:**
Time for confession and absolution. 48. **ordinant:** Directing.
49. **signet:** Small seal. 52. **Subscrib'd:** Signed. **impression:**
With a wax seal. 53. **changeling:** The substituted letter (literally, a fairy child substituted for a human one). 59. **insinuation:** Interference. 61. **pass:** Thrust. **fell:** Fierce.

HAMLET: Does it not, think thee, stand° me now
     upon —
     He that hath killed my king and whor'd my mother,
65   Popp'd in between th' election° and my hopes,
     Thrown out his angle° for my proper° life,
     And with such coz'nage° — is 't not perfect
          conscience
     [To quit° him with this arm? And is 't not to be
          damn'd
     To let this canker° of our nature come
70   In further evil?
HORATIO: It must be shortly known to him from
          England
     What is the issue of the business there.
HAMLET: It will be short. The interim is mine,
     And a man's life 's no more than to say "One."°
75   But I am very sorry, good Horatio,
     That to Laertes I forgot myself,
     For by the image of my cause I see
     The portraiture of his. I'll court his favors.
     But, sure, the bravery° of his grief did put me
     Into a tow'ring passion.
80 HORATIO: Peace, who comes here?]

(Enter a Courtier [Osric].)

OSRIC: Your lordship is right welcome back to Denmark.
HAMLET: I humbly thank you, sir. [*To Horatio.*] Dost
     know this water-fly?
HORATIO: No, my good lord.
85 HAMLET: Thy state is the more gracious, for 'tis a vice to
     know him. He hath much land, and fertile. Let a
     beast be lord of beasts, and his crib shall stand at the
     King's mess.° 'Tis a chough,° but, as I say, spacious in
     the possession of dirt.
90 OSRIC: Sweet lord, if your lordship were at leisure, I
     should impart a thing to you from his Majesty.
HAMLET: I will receive it, sir, with all diligence of spirit.
     Put your bonnet to his right use; 'tis for the head.
OSRIC: I thank your lordship, it is very hot.
95 HAMLET: No, believe me, 'tis very cold; the wind is
     northerly.
OSRIC: It is indifferent° cold, my lord, indeed.
HAMLET: But yet methinks it is very sultry and hot for
     my complexion.°
100 OSRIC: Exceedingly, my lord; it is very sultry, as
     'twere — I cannot tell how. My lord, his Majesty
     bade me signify to you that 'a has laid a great wager
     on your head. Sir, this is the matter —

HAMLET: I beseech you, remember —
     [*Hamlet moves him to put on his hat.*]
OSRIC: Nay, good my lord; for my ease,° in good faith. 105
     Sir, here is newly come to court Laertes — believe
     me, an absolute gentleman, full of most excellent
     differences,° of very soft society° and great show-
     ing.° Indeed, to speak feelingly° of him, he is the
     card° or calendar° of gentry,° for you shall find in him 110
     the continent of what part° a gentleman would see.
HAMLET: Sir, his definement° suffers no perdition° in
     you, though, I know, to divide him inventorially°
     would dozy° th' arithmetic of memory, and yet
     but yaw° neither° in respect of° his quick sail. But, 115
     in the verity of extolment,° I take him to be a soul of
     great article,° and his infusion° of such dearth and
     rareness,° as, to make true diction° of him, his
     semblable° is his mirror, and who else would trace°
     him, his umbrage,° nothing more. 120
OSRIC: Your lordship speaks most infallibly of him.
HAMLET: The concernancy,° sir? Why do we wrap the
     gentleman in our more rawer breath?°
OSRIC: Sir?
HORATIO: Is 't not possible to understand in another 125
     tongue?° You will do 't,° sir, really.
HAMLET: What imports the nomination° of this gentle-
     man?
OSRIC: Of Laertes?
HORATIO [*to Hamlet*]: His purse is empty already; all 's 130
     golden words are spent.
HAMLET: Of him, sir.
OSRIC: I know you are not ignorant —
HAMLET: I would you did, sir; yet, in faith, if you did, it
     would not much approve° me. Well, sir? 135

---

63. **stand:** Become incumbent.   65. **election:** The Danish
monarch was "elected" by a small number of high-
ranking electors.   66. **angle:** Fishing line.   **proper:** Very.
67. **coz'nage:** Trickery.   68. **quit:** Repay.   69. **canker:** Ulcer.
74. **a man's . . . "One":** To take a man's life requires no more
than to count to one as one duels.   79. **bravery:** Bravado.
86–88. **Let . . . mess:** If a man, no matter how beastlike, is as
rich in possessions as Osric, he may eat at the king's table.
88. **chough:** Chattering jackdaw.   97. **indifferent:** Somewhat.
99. **complexion:** Temperament.

105. **for my ease:** A conventional reply declining the invitation
to put his hat back on.   108. **differences:** Special qualities.
soft society: Agreeable manners.   108–09. **great showing:** Distinguished appearance.   109. **feelingly:** With just perception.
110. **card:** Chart, map.   **calendar:** Guide.   **gentry:** Good
breeding.   111. **the continent . . . part:** One who contains in
him all the qualities (a *continent* is that which contains).
112. **definement:** Definition. (Hamlet proceeds to mock Osric
by using his lofty diction back at him.)   **perdition:** Loss,
diminution.   113. **divide him inventorially:** Enumerate his
graces.   114. **dozy:** Dizzy.   115. **yaw:** To move unsteadily
(said of a ship).   **neither:** For all that.   **in respect of:** In comparison with.   116. **in . . . extolment:** In true praise (of him).
117. **article:** Moment or importance.   **infusion:** Essence, character imparted by nature.   117–18. **dearth and rareness:**
Rarity.   118. **make true diction:** Speak truly.   119. **sem-
blable:** Only true likeness.   **who . . . trace:** Any other person
who would wish to follow.   120. **umbrage:** Shadow.
122. **concernancy:** Import, relevance.   123. **breath:** Speech.
125–26. **to understand . . . tongue:** For Osric to understand
when someone else speaks in his manner. (Horatio twits Osric
for not being able to understand the kind of flowery speech he
himself uses when Hamlet speaks in such a vein.)   126. **You
will do 't:** You can if you try.   127. **nomination:** Naming.
135. **approve:** Commend.

OSRIC: You are not ignorant of what excellence Laertes
is —

HAMLET: I dare not confess that, lest I should compare°
with him in excellence; but to know a man well were
140   to know himself.°

OSRIC: I mean, sir, for his weapon; but in the imputation
laid on him by them,° in his meed° he's unfellow'd.°

HAMLET: What's his weapon?

OSRIC: Rapier and dagger.

145   HAMLET: That's two of his weapons — but well.

OSRIC: The King, sir, hath wager'd with him six Barbary
horses, against the which he has impawn'd,° as I take
it, six French rapiers and poniards, with their
assigns,° as girdle, hangers,° and so. Three of the car-
150   riages,° in faith, are very dear to fancy,° very respon-
sive° to the hilts, most delicate° carriages, and of very
liberal conceit.°

HAMLET: What call you the carriages?

HORATIO [to Hamlet]: I knew you must be edified by the
155   margent° ere you had done.

OSRIC: The carriages, sir, are the hangers.

HAMLET: The phrase would be more germane to the
matter if we could carry a cannon by our sides; I
would it might be hangers till then. But, on: six
160   Barb'ry horses against six French swords, their
assigns, and three liberal-conceited carriages; that's
the French bet against the Danish. Why is this
impawn'd, as you call it?

OSRIC: The King, sir, hath laid,° sir, that in a dozen
165   passes° between yourself and him, he shall not
exceed you three hits. He hath laid on twelve for
nine, and it would come to immediate trial, if your
lordship would vouchsafe the answer.

HAMLET: How if I answer no?

170   OSRIC: I mean, my lord, the opposition of your person
in trial.

HAMLET: Sir, I will walk here in the hall. If it please his
Majesty, it is the breathing time° of day with me. Let
the foils be brought, the gentleman willing, and the
175   King hold his purpose, I will win for him an I can;
if not, I will gain nothing but my shame and the odd
hits.

OSRIC: Shall I deliver you so?

HAMLET: To this effect, sir — after what flourish your
nature will.   180

OSRIC: I commend my duty to your lordship.

HAMLET: Yours, yours. [Exit Osric.] He does well to
commend it himself; there are no tongues else for 's
turn.

HORATIO: This lapwing° runs away with the shell on his   185
head.

HAMLET: 'A did comply, sir, with his dug,° before 'a
suck'd it. Thus has he — and many more of the same
breed that I know the drossy° age dotes on — only
got the tune° of the time and, out of an habit of   190
encounter,° a kind of yesty° collection,° which carries
them through and through the most fann'd and win-
now'd° opinions; and do but blow them to their trial,
the bubbles are out.°

(Enter a Lord.)

LORD: My lord, his Majesty commended him to you by   195
young Osric, who brings back to him that you attend
him in the hall. He sends to know if your pleasure
hold to play with Laertes, or that you will take longer
time.

HAMLET: I am constant to my purposes; they follow the   200
King's pleasure. If his fitness speaks,° mine is ready;
now or whensoever, provided I be so able as now.

LORD: The King and Queen and all are coming down.

HAMLET: In happy time.°

LORD: The Queen desires you to use some gentle enter-   205
tainment° to Laertes before you fall to play.

HAMLET: She well instructs me.   [Exit Lord.]

HORATIO: You will lose, my lord.

HAMLET: I do not think so. Since he went into France, I
have been in continual practice; I shall win at the   210
odds. But thou wouldst not think how ill all's here
about my heart; but it is no matter.

HORATIO: Nay, good my lord —

HAMLET: It is but foolery, but it is such a kind of gain-
giving,° as would perhaps trouble a woman.   215

HORATIO: If your mind dislike anything, obey it. I will
forestall their repair hither, and say you are not fit.

HAMLET: Not a whit, we defy augury. There is special
providence in the fall of a sparrow. If it be now, 'tis
not to come; if it be not to come, it will be now, if it 220

---

138. compare: Seem to compete.   **139–40. but . . . himself:**
For, to recognize excellence in another man, one must know
oneself.   **141–42. imputation . . . them:** Reputation given him
by others.   **142. meed:** Merit.   **unfellow'd:** Unmatched.
147. impawn'd: Staked, wagered.   **149. assigns:** Appurte-
nances.   **hangers:** Straps on the sword belt (*girdle*) from which
the sword hung.   **149–50. carriages:** An affected way of saying *hangers;* literally, gun-carriages.   **150. dear to fancy:** Fan-
cifully designed, tasteful.   **150–51. responsive:** Corresponding
closely, matching.   **151. delicate:** I.e., in workmanship.
152. liberal conceit: Elaborate design.   **155. margent:** Margin
of a book, place for explanatory notes.   **164. laid:** Wagered.
165. passes: Bouts. (The odds of the betting are hard to explain.
Possibly the king bets that Hamlet will win at least five out of
twelve, at which point Laertes raises the odds against himself
by betting he will win nine.)   **173. breathing time:** Exercise
period.

185. lapwing: A bird that draws intruders away from its nest
and was thought to run about when newly hatched with its
head in the shell; a seeming reference to Osric's hat.
187. comply . . . dug: Observe ceremonious formality toward
his mother's teat.   **189. drossy:** Frivolous.   **190. tune:** Temper, mood, manner of speech.   **190–91. habit of encounter:**
Demeanor of social intercourse.   **191. yesty:** Yeasty, frothy.
collection: i.e., of current phrases.   **192–93. fann'd and win-
now'd:** Select and refined.   **193–94. blow . . . out:** Put them to
the test, and their ignorance is exposed.   **201. If . . . speaks:** If
his readiness answers to the time.   **204. In happy time:** A
phrase of courtesy indicating acceptance.   **206. entertainment:**
Greeting.   **214–15. gain-giving:** Misgiving.

be not now, yet it will come. The readiness is all.
Since no man of aught he leaves knows what is 't to
leave betimes,° let be.

*(A table prepar'd. [Enter] trumpets, drums, and Officers
with cushions; King, Queen, [Osric,] and all the State;
foils, daggers, [and wine borne in;] and Laertes.)*

KING: Come, Hamlet, come, and take this hand from
    me.
        [The King puts Laertes' hand into Hamlet's.]
HAMLET: Give me your pardon, sir. I have done you
225   wrong,
    But pardon 't, as you are a gentleman.
    This presence° knows,
    And you must needs have heard, how I am punish'd
    With a sore distraction. What I have done
230   That might your nature, honor, and exception°
    Roughly awake, I here proclaim was madness.
    Was 't Hamlet wrong'd Laertes? Never Hamlet.
    If Hamlet from himself be ta'en away,
    And when he's not himself does wrong Laertes,
235   Then Hamlet does it not, Hamlet denies it.
    Who does it, then? His madness. If 't be so,
    Hamlet is of the faction that is wrong'd;
    His madness is poor Hamlet's enemy.
    [Sir, in this audience,]
240   Let my disclaiming from a purpos'd evil
    Free me so far in your most generous thoughts
    That I have shot my arrow o'er the house
    And hurt my brother.
LAERTES: I am satisfied in nature,°
    Whose motive in this case should stir me most
245   To my revenge. But in my terms of honor
    I stand aloof, and will no reconcilement
    Till by some elder masters of known honor
    I have a voice° and precedent of peace
    To keep my name ungor'd. But till that time,
250   I do receive your offer'd love like love,
    And will not wrong it.
HAMLET: I embrace it freely,
    And will this brothers' wager frankly play.
    Give us the foils. Come on.
LAERTES: Come, one for me.
HAMLET: I'll be your foil,° Laertes. In mine ignorance
255   Your skill shall, like a star i' th' darkest night,
    Stick fiery off° indeed.
LAERTES: You mock me, sir.
HAMLET: No, by this hand.
KING: Give them the foils, young Osric. Cousin Hamlet,
    You know the wager?
HAMLET: Very well, my lord.
260   Your Grace has laid the odds o' th' weaker side.

222–23. **what . . . betimes:** What is the best time to leave it.
227. **presence:** Royal assembly.   230. **exception:** Disapproval.
243. **in nature:** As to my personal feelings.   248. **voice:**
Authoritative pronouncement.   254. **foil:** Thin metal background which sets a jewel off (with pun on the blunted rapier
for fencing).   256. **Stick fiery off:** Stand out brilliantly.

KING: I do not fear it; I have seen you both.
    But since he is better'd,° we have therefore odds.
LAERTES: This is too heavy, let me see another.
           [Exchanges his foil for another.]
HAMLET: This likes me well. These foils have all a length?
           [They prepare to play.]
OSRIC: Ay, my good lord.   265
KING: Set me the stoups of wine upon that table.
    If Hamlet give the first or second hit,
    Or quit° in answer of the third exchange,
    Let all the battlements their ordnance fire.
    The King shall drink to Hamlet's better breath,   270
    And in the cup an union° shall he throw,
    Richer than that which four successive kings
    In Denmark's crown have worn. Give me the cups,
    And let the kettle° to the trumpet speak,
    The trumpet to the cannoneer without,   275
    The cannons to the heavens, the heaven to earth,
    "Now the King drinks to Hamlet." Come, begin.
           (Trumpets the while.)
    And you, the judges, bear a wary eye.
HAMLET: Come on sir.
LAERTES: Come, my lord.   *[They play. Hamlet scores* 280
                                   a hit.]
HAMLET: One.
LAERTES: No.
HAMLET: Judgment.
OSRIC: A hit, a very palpable hit.
           (Drum, trumpets, and shot. Flourish.
                 A piece goes off.)
LAERTES: Well, again.
KING: Stay, give me drink. Hamlet, this pearl is thine. 285
    [He throws a pearl in Hamlet's cup and drinks.]
    Here's to thy health. Give him the cup.
HAMLET: I'll play this bout first, set it by awhile.
    Come. *[They play.]* Another hit; what say you?
LAERTES: A touch, a touch. I do confess 't.
KING: Our son shall win.
QUEEN: He's fat,° and scant of breath. 290
    Here, Hamlet, take my napkin,° rub thy brows.
    The Queen carouses° to thy fortune, Hamlet.
HAMLET: Good madam!
KING: Gertrude, do not drink.
QUEEN: I will, my lord; I pray you pardon me.   295
                               [Drinks.]
KING [*aside*]: It is the pois'ned cup. It is too late.
HAMLET: I dare not drink yet, madam; by and by.
QUEEN: Come, let me wipe thy face.
LAERTES [*to King*]: My lord, I'll hit him now.
KING: I do not think 't.
LAERTES [*aside*]: And yet it is almost against my
    conscience.   300

---

262. **is better'd:** Has improved; is the odds-on favorite.
268. **quit:** Repay (with a hit).   271. **union:** Pearl (so called,
according to Pliny's *Natural History*, IX, because pearls are
unique, never identical).   274. **kettle:** Kettledrum.   290. **fat:**
Not physically fit, out of training.   291. **napkin:** Handkerchief.
292. **carouses:** Drinks a toast.

HAMLET: Come, for the third Laertes. You do but dally.
 I pray you, pass with your best violence;
 I am afeard you make a wanton of me.°
LAERTES: Say you so? Come on.   [*They play.*]
305 OSRIC: Nothing, neither way.
LAERTES: Have at you now!

> [*Laertes wounds Hamlet; then, in scuffling,*
> *they change rapiers,° and Hamlet wounds*
> *Laertes.*]

KING: Part them! They are incens'd.
HAMLET: Nay, come, again.   [*The Queen falls.*]
OSRIC: Look to the Queen there, ho!
HORATIO: They bleed on both sides. How is it, my lord?
OSRIC: How is 't, Laertes?
LAERTES: Why, as a woodcock° to mine own springe,°
310   Osric;
 I am justly kill'd with mine own treachery.
HAMLET: How does the Queen?
KING: She swoons to see them bleed.
QUEEN: No, no, the drink, the drink — O my dear
     Hamlet —
 The drink, the drink! I am pois'ned.   [*Dies.*]
315 HAMLET: O villainy! Ho, let the door be lock'd!
 Treachery! Seek it out.   [*Laertes falls.*]
LAERTES: It is here, Hamlet. Hamlet, thou art slain.
 No med'cine in the world can do thee good;
 In thee there is not half an hour's life.
320 The treacherous instrument is in thy hand,
 Unbated° and envenom'd. The foul practice
 Hath turn'd itself on me. Lo, here I lie,
 Never to rise again. Thy mother's pois'ned.
 I can no more. The King, the King's to blame.
HAMLET: The point envenom'd too? Then, venom, to
325   thy work.   [*Stabs the King.*]
ALL: Treason! Treason!
KING: O, yet defend me, friends; I am but hurt.
HAMLET: Here, thou incestuous, murd'rous, damned
     Dane,

> [*He forces the King to drink*
> *the poisoned cup.*]

 Drink off this potion. Is thy union° here?
 Follow my mother.   [*King dies.*]
330 LAERTES: He is justly serv'd.
 It is a poison temper'd° by himself.
 Exchange forgiveness with me, noble Hamlet.
 Mine and my father's death come not upon thee,
 Nor thine on me!   [*Dies.*]

HAMLET: Heaven make thee free of it! I follow thee.   335
 I am dead, Horatio. Wretched Queen, adieu!
 You that look pale and tremble at this chance,
 That are but mutes° or audience to this act,
 Had I but time — as this fell° sergeant,° Death,
 Is strict in his arrest — O, I could tell you —   340
 But let it be. Horatio, I am dead;
 Thou livest. Report me and my cause aright
 To the unsatisfied.
HORATIO: Never believe it.
 I am more an antique Roman° than a Dane.
 Here's yet some liquor left.

> [*He attempts to drink from the poisoned cup.*
> *Hamlet prevents him.*]

HAMLET: As th' art a man,   345
 Give me the cup! Let go! By heaven, I'll ha 't.
 O God, Horatio, what a wounded name,
 Things standing thus unknown, shall I leave behind
     me!
 If thou didst ever hold me in thy heart,
 Absent thee from felicity awhile,   350
 And in this harsh world draw thy breath in pain
 To tell my story.

> (*A march afar off* [*and a volley within*].)

               What warlike noise is this?
OSRIC: Young Fortinbras, with conquest come from
     Poland,
 To the ambassadors of England gives
 This warlike volley.
HAMLET: O, I die, Horatio!   355
 The potent poison quite o'ercrows° my spirit.
 I cannot live to hear the news from England,
 But I do prophesy th' election lights
 On Fortinbras. He has my dying voice.°
 So tell him, with th' occurrents° more and less   360
 Which have solicited° — the rest is silence.   [*Dies.*]
HORATIO: Now cracks a noble heart. Good night,
     sweet prince;
 And flights of angels sing thee to thy rest!

> [*March within.*]

 Why does the drum come hither?

(*Enter Fortinbras, with the* [*English*] *Ambassadors* [*with*
drum, colors, and attendants].)

FORTINBRAS: Where is this sight?
HORATIO: What is it you would see?   365
 If aught of woe or wonder, cease your search.
FORTINBRAS: This quarry° cries on havoc.° O proud
     Death.
 What feast is toward° in thine eternal cell,

---

303. **make . . . me:** Treat me like a spoiled child, holding back to give me an advantage.   306. [s.D.] ***in scuffling, they change rapiers:*** This stage direction occurs in the Folio. According to a widespread stage tradition, Hamlet receives a scratch, realizes that Laertes' sword is unbated, and accordingly forces an exchange.   310. **woodcock:** A bird, a type of stupidity or as a decoy.   **springe:** Trap, snare.   321. **Unbated:** Not blunted with a button.   329. **union:** Pearl (see line 271; with grim puns on the word's other meanings: marriage, shared death[?]).   331. **temper'd:** Mixed.

338. **mutes:** Silent observers.   339. **fell:** Cruel.   **sergeant:** Sheriff's officer.   344. **Roman:** It was the Roman custom to follow masters in death.   356. **o'ercrows:** Triumphs over.   359. **voice:** Vote.   360. **occurrents:** Events, incidents.   361. **solicited:** Moved, urged.   367. **quarry:** Heap of dead.   **cries on havoc:** Proclaims a general slaughter.   368. **toward:** In preparation.

That thou so many princes at a shot
So bloodily hast struck?

370 FIRST AMBASSADOR: The sight is dismal;
And our affairs from England come too late.
The ears are senseless that should give us hearing,
To tell him his commandment is fulfill'd,
That Rosencrantz and Guildenstern are dead.
Where should we have our thanks?

375 HORATIO: Not from his° mouth,
Had it th' ability of life to thank you.
He never gave commandment for their death.
But since, so jump° upon this bloody question,°
You from the Polack wars, and you from England,

380 Are here arriv'd, give order that these bodies
High on a stage° be placed to the view,
And let me speak to th' yet unknowing world
How these things came about. So shall you hear
Of carnal, bloody, and unnatural acts,

385 Of accidental judgments,° casual° slaughters,
Of deaths put on° by cunning and forc'd cause,
And, in this upshot, purposes mistook
Fall'n on th' inventors' heads. All this can I
Truly deliver.

FORTINBRAS: Let us haste to hear it,
And call the noblest to the audience.   390
For me, with sorrow I embrace my fortune.
I have some rights of memory° in this kingdom,
Which now to claim my vantage° doth invite me.

HORATIO: Of that I shall have also cause to speak,
And from his mouth whose voice will draw on
more.°   395
But let this same be presently° perform'd,
Even while men's minds are wild, lest more
mischance
On° plots and errors happen.

FORTINBRAS: Let four captains
Bear Hamlet, like a soldier, to the stage,
For he was likely, had he been put on,°   400
To have prov'd most royal; and, for his passage,°
The soldiers' music and the rite of war
Speak loudly for him.
Take up the bodies. Such a sight as this
Becomes the field,° but here shows much amiss.   405
Go, bid the soldiers shoot.

(*Exeunt [marching, bearing off the dead bodies;
a peal of ordnance is shot off].*)

375. **his:** Claudius's.   378. **jump:** Precisely.   **question:** Dispute.   381. **stage:** Platform.   385. **judgments:** Retributions.
casual: Occurring by chance.   386. **put on:** Instigated.
392. **of memory:** Traditional, remembered.

393. **vantage:** Presence at this opportune moment.
395. **voice . . . more:** Vote will influence still others.
396. **presently:** Immediately.   398. **On:** On the basis of.
400. **put on:** Invested in royal office and so put to the test.
401. **passage:** Death.   405. **field:** I.e., of battle.

COMMENTARIES

The modern era of Shakespeare criticism probably begins with Samuel Taylor Coleridge, whose lectures on Shakespeare were instrumental in helping a generation of early-nineteenth-century theatergoers take the playwright seriously. Coleridge, adapting the ideas of the German romantic critic Friedrich Schlegel, reached a wide and generally popular audience. His work centers on the character of Hamlet and his problems in the play, examining how Hamlet reveals himself both to us and to himself.

Sigmund Freud sees in *Hamlet* the seeds of the Oedipus complex that he had already identified in Sophocles' *Oedipus Rex*. The question of how one psychoanalyzes a literary character is perhaps best raised in Freud's essay. Later, a follower of Freud, Ernest Jones, wrote an entire book on Hamlet, analyzing him from the psychoanalytic perspective.

T. S. Eliot, speaking as a careful and noted student of Elizabethan and Jacobean drama, begins to point out some of the difficulties he sees with *Hamlet*. It is fascinating to see how great poets such as Coleridge and Eliot can approach the same play from such diverse points of view.

Samuel Taylor Coleridge (1772–1834)
ON *HAMLET*   *1812*

*Samuel Taylor Coleridge was the first modern English critic of Shakespeare to de-
velop influential readings of the great plays. He visited atheneums and lyceums (institutions promoting learning) on both sides of the Atlantic delivering his lectures
on Shakespeare, and his interpretations stimulated a new age of thoughtful criticism. His lecture on* Hamlet *includes a careful reading of difficult lines, but it also
centers on questions of the relationship of Shakespeare to his creation. Further, the
mental state of Hamlet becomes of central interest to Coleridge and a basis of
much of his observation.*

The seeming inconsistencies in the conduct and character of Hamlet have long
exercised the conjectural ingenuity of critics; and, as we are always loath to suppose that the cause of defective apprehension is in ourselves, the mystery has been
too commonly explained by the very easy process of setting it down as in fact inexplicable, and by resolving the phenomenon into a misgrowth or *lusus* of the capricious and irregular genius of Shakespeare. The shallow and stupid arrogance of
these vulgar and indolent decisions I would fain do my best to expose. I believe the
character of Hamlet may be traced to Shakespeare's deep and accurate science in
mental philosophy. Indeed, that this character must have some connection with the
common fundamental laws of our nature may be assumed from the fact that Hamlet has been the darling of every country in which the literature of England has been
fostered. In order to understand him, it is essential that we should reflect on the
constitution of our own minds. Man is distinguished from the brute animals in proportion as thought prevails over sense: but in the healthy processes of the mind, a
balance is constantly maintained between the impressions from outward objects
and the inward operations of the intellect: — for if there be an overbalance in the
contemplative faculty, man thereby becomes the creature of mere meditation, and
loses his natural power of action. Now one of Shakespeare's modes of creating
characters is to conceive any one intellectual or moral faculty in morbid excess, and
then to place himself, Shakespeare, thus mutilated or diseased, under given circumstances. In Hamlet he seems to have wished to exemplify the moral necessity of a
due balance between our attention to the objects of our senses, and our meditation
on the workings of our minds, — an *equilibrium* between the real and the imaginary worlds. In Hamlet this balance is disturbed: his thoughts, and the images of
his fancy, are far more vivid than his actual perceptions, and his very perceptions,
instantly passing through the *medium* of his contemplations, acquire, as they pass,
a form and a color not naturally their own. Hence we see a great, an almost enormous, intellectual activity, and a proportionate aversion to real action, consequent
upon it, with all its symptoms and accompanying qualities. This character Shakespeare places in circumstances, under which it is obliged to act on the spur of the
moment: — Hamlet is brave and careless of death; but he vacillates from sensibility, and procrastinates from thought, and loses the power of action in the energy of
resolve. Thus it is that this tragedy presents a direct contrast to that of Macbeth;
the one proceeds with the utmost slowness, the other with a crowded and breathless rapidity.

The effect of this overbalance of the imaginative power is beautifully illustrated in the everlasting broodings and superfluous activities of Hamlet's mind, which, unseated from its healthy relation, is constantly occupied with the world within, and abstracted from the world without, — giving substance to shadows, and throwing a mist over all commonplace actualities. It is the nature of thought to be indefinite; — definiteness belongs to external imagery alone. Hence it is that the sense of sublimity arises, not from the sight of an outward object, but from the beholder's reflection upon it; — not from the sensuous impression, but from the imaginative reflex. Few have seen a celebrated waterfall without feeling something akin to disappointment: it is only subsequently that the image comes back full into the mind, and brings with it a train of grand or beautiful associations. Hamlet feels this; his senses are in a state of trance, and he looks upon external things as hieroglyphics. His soliloquy —

Oh! that this too, too solid flesh would melt, &c.

springs from that craving after the indefinite — for that which is not — which most easily besets men of genius; and the self-delusion common to this temper of mind is finely exemplified in the character which Hamlet gives of himself: —

    — It can not be
But I am pigeon-livered, and lack gall
To make oppression bitter.

He mistakes the seeing his chains for the breaking of them, delays action till action is of no use, and dies the victim of mere circumstance and accident.[. . .]

    Act I, scene IV. The unimportant conversation with which this scene opens is a proof of Shakespeare's minute knowledge of human nature. It is a well-established fact, that on the brink of any serious enterprise, or event of moment, men almost invariably endeavor to elude the pressure of their own thoughts by turning aside to trivial objects and familiar circumstances: thus this dialogue on the platform begins with remarks on the coldness of the air, and inquiries, obliquely connected, indeed, with the expected hour of the visitation, but thrown out in a seeming vacuity of topics, as to the striking of the clock and so forth. The same desire to escape from the impending thought is carried on in Hamlet's account of, and moralizing on, the Danish custom of wassailing: he runs off from the particular to the universal, and in his repugnance to personal and individual concerns, escapes, as it were, from himself in generalizations, and smothers the impatience and uneasy feelings of the moment in abstract reasoning. Besides this, another purpose is answered; — for by thus entangling the attention of the audience in the nice distinctions and parenthetical sentences of this speech of Hamlet's, Shakespeare takes them completely by surprise on the appearance of the Ghost, which comes upon them in all the suddenness of its visionary character. Indeed, no modern writer would have dared, like Shakespeare, to have preceded this last visitation by two distinct appearances, — or could have contrived that the third should rise upon the former two in impressiveness and solemnity of interest.

    But in addition to all the other excellences of Hamlet's speech concerning the wassail-music — so finely revealing the predominant idealism, the ratiocinative° meditativeness, of his character — it has the advantage of giving nature and probability to the impassioned continuity of the speech instantly directed to the Ghost.

ratiocinative: Reasoned.

The *momentum* had been given to his mental activity; the full current of the thoughts and words had set in, and the very forgetfulness, in the fervor of his augmentation, of the purpose for which he was there, aided in preventing the appearance from benumbing the mind. Consequently, it acted as a new impulse, — a sudden stroke which increased the velocity of the body already in motion, whilst it altered the direction. The copresence of Horatio, Marcellus, and Bernardo is most judiciously contrived; for it renders the courage of Hamlet and his impetuous eloquence perfectly intelligible. The knowledge, — the unthought of consciousness, — the sensation, — of human auditors — of flesh and blood sympathists — acts as a support and a stimulation of *a tergo,* while the front of the mind, the whole consciousness of the speaker, is filled, yea, absorbed, by the apparition. Add too, that the apparition itself has by its previous appearances been brought nearer to a thing of this world. This accrescence° of objectivity in a Ghost that yet retains all its ghostly attributes and fearful subjectivity, is truly wonderful.

Act I, scene v. Hamlet's speech: —

O all you host of heaven! O earth! What else?
And shall I couple hell? —

I remember nothing equal to this burst unless it be the first speech of Prometheus in the Greek drama, after the exit of Vulcan and the two Afrites. But Shakespeare alone could have produced the vow of Hamlet to make his memory a blank of all maxims and generalized truths, that "observation had copied there,"— followed immediately by the speaker noting down the generalized fact,

That one may smile, and smile, and be a villain!

MARCELLUS: Hillo, ho, ho, my lord!
HAMLET: Hillo, ho, ho, boy! come bird, come, &c.

This part of the scene after Hamlet's interview with the Ghost has been charged with an improbable eccentricity. But the truth is that after the mind has been stretched beyond its usual pitch and tone, it must either sink into exhaustion and inanity, or seek relief by change. It is thus well known, that persons conversant in deeds of cruelty contrive to escape from conscience by connecting something of the ludicrous with them, and by inventing grotesque terms and a certain technical phraseology to disguise the horror of their practices. Indeed, paradoxical as it may appear, the terrible by a law of the human mind always touches on the verge of the ludicrous. Both arise from the perception of something out of the common order of things — something, in fact, out of its place; and if from this we can abstract danger, the uncommonness will alone remain, and the sense of the ridiculous be excited. The close alliance of these opposites — they are not contraries — appears from the circumstance, that laughter is equally the expression of extreme anguish and horror as of joy: as there are tears of sorrow and tears of joy, so is there a laugh of terror and a laugh of merriment. These complex causes will naturally have produced in Hamlet the disposition to escape from his own feelings of the overwhelming and supernatural by a wild transition to the ludicrous, — a sort of cunning bravado, bordering on the flights of delirium. For you may, perhaps, observe that Hamlet's wildness is but half false; he plays that subtle trick of pretending to act only when he is very near really being what he acts.

accrescence: Accumulation or concentration.

Sigmund Freud (1856–1939)
HAMLET'S SCRUPLES   *1900–1930°*

*Sigmund Freud was the most celebrated psychiatrist of the twentieth century.
He was especially interested in Greek myth, as his comments on* Oedipus Rex *suggest.* Hamlet *was another play that took on mythic proportions for him, in part
because Freud saw in Hamlet the operation of his famous theory of the Oedipus
complex. In the following excerpt Freud examines the events of the play that bear
on his theory.*

Another of the great creations of tragic poetry, Shakespeare's *Hamlet,* has its
roots in the same soil as *Oedipus Rex.* But the changed treatment of the same material reveals the whole difference in the mental life of these two widely separated
epochs of civilization: the secular advance of repression in the emotional life of
mankind. In the *Oedipus* the child's wishful fantasy that underlies it is brought into
the open and realized as it would be in a dream. In *Hamlet* it remains repressed;
and — just as in the case of a neurosis — we only learn of its existence from its
inhibiting consequences. Strangely enough, the overwhelming effect produced by
the more modern tragedy has turned out to be compatible with the fact that people
have remained completely in the dark as to the hero's character. The play is built up
on Hamlet's hesitations over fulfilling the task of revenge that is assigned to him;
but its text offers no reasons or motives for these hesitations and an immense variety of attempts at interpreting them have failed to produce a result. According to
the view which was originated by Goethe and is still the prevailing one today,
Hamlet represents the type of man whose power of direct action is paralyzed by an
excessive development of his intellect. (He is "sicklied o'er with the pale cast of
thought.") According to another view, the dramatist has tried to portray a patho-
logically irresolute character which might be classed as neurasthenic.° The plot of
the drama shows us, however, that Hamlet is far from being represented as a person incapable of taking any action. We see him doing so on two occasions: first in a
sudden outburst of temper, when he runs his sword through the eavesdropper
behind the arras, and secondly in a premeditated and even crafty fashion, when,
with all the callousness of a Renaissance prince, he sends the two courtiers to the
death that had been planned for himself. What is it, then, that inhibits him in fulfilling the task set him by his father's ghost? The answer, once again, is that it is the
peculiar nature of the task. Hamlet is able to do anything — except take vengeance
on the man who did away with his father and took that father's place with his
mother, the man who shows him the repressed wishes of his own childhood realized. Thus the loathing which should drive him on to revenge is replaced in him by
self-reproaches, by scruples of conscience, which remind him that he himself is literally no better than the sinner whom he is to punish. Here I have translated into
conscious terms what was bound to remain unconscious in Hamlet's mind; and if
anyone is inclined to call him a hysteric, I can only accept the fact as one that is

---

1900–1930: Freud's *Interpretation of Dreams,* from which this excerpt is taken, was first published in 1900 and updated regularly by Freud through eight editions. This passage is taken from
the eighth edition, published in 1930.
   neurasthenic: One who suffers from fatigue, loss of energy, and feelings of inadequacy.

implied by my interpretation. The distaste for sexuality expressed by Hamlet in his conversation with Ophelia fits in very well with this: the same distaste which was destined to take possession of the poet's mind more and more during the years that followed, and which reached its extreme expression in *Timon of Athens*. For it can of course only be the poet's own mind which confronts us in Hamlet. I observe in a book on Shakespeare by Georg Brandes (1896) a statement that *Hamlet* was written immediately after the death of Shakespeare's father (in 1601), that is, under the immediate impact of his bereavement and, as we may well assume, while his childhood feelings about his father had been freshly revived. It is known, too, that Shakespeare's own son who died at an early age bore the name of "Hamnet," which is identical with "Hamlet." Just as *Hamlet* deals with the relation of a son to his parents, so *Macbeth* (written at approximately the same period) is concerned with the subject of childlessness. But just as all neurotic symptoms, and, for that matter, dreams, are capable of being "overinterpreted" and indeed need to be if they are to be fully understood, so all genuinely creative writings are the product of more than a single motive and more than a single impulse in the poet's mind, and are open to more than a single interpretation. In what I have written I have only attempted to interpret the deepest layer of impulses in the mind of the creative writer.

T. S. Eliot (1888–1965)
HAMLET AND HIS PROBLEMS   1934

Not only a leading poet of the twentieth-century modernist period, T. S. Eliot also produced extremely interesting criticism of Elizabethan literature. His several collections of essays have in some cases defined important critical terms that later readers have used to gain insight into great writers. One of those terms is developed here: the objective correlative, which Eliot feels is missing in Hamlet. *His argument is provocative and revealing.*

Few critics have ever admitted that *Hamlet* the play is the primary problem, and Hamlet the character only secondary. And Hamlet the character has had an especial temptation for that most dangerous type of critic: the critic with a mind which is naturally of the creative order, but which through some weakness in creative power exercises itself in criticism instead. These minds often find in Hamlet a vicarious existence for their own artistic realization. Such a mind had Goethe, who made of Hamlet a Werther; and such had Coleridge who made of Hamlet a Coleridge; and probably neither of these men in writing about Hamlet remembered that his first business was to study a work of art. The kind of criticism that Goethe and Coleridge produced, in writing of Hamlet, is the most misleading kind possible. For they both possessed unquestionable critical insight, and both make their critical aberrations the more plausible by the substitution — of their own Hamlet for Shakespeare's — which their creative gift effects. We should be thankful that Walter Pater° did not fix his attention on this play.

Walter Pater: English writer and critic (1839–1894). His writings were often overelaborate.

Two writers of our time, Mr. J. M. Robertson and Professor Stoll of the University of Minnesota, have issued small books which can be praised for moving in the other direction. Mr. Stoll performs a service in recalling to our attention the labors of the critics of the seventeenth and eighteenth centuries, observing that

> they knew less about psychology than more recent Hamlet critics, but they were nearer in spirit to Shakespeare's art; and as they insisted on the importance of the effect of the whole rather than on the importance of the leading character, they were nearer, in their old-fashioned way, to the secret of dramatic art in general.

Qua work of art, the work of art cannot be interpreted; there is nothing to interpret; we can only criticize it according to standards, in comparison to other works of art; and for "interpretation" the chief task is the presentation of relevant historical facts which the reader is not assumed to know. Mr. Robertson points out, very pertinently, how critics have failed in their "interpretation" of *Hamlet* by ignoring what ought to be very obvious: that *Hamlet* is a stratification, that it represents the efforts of a series of men, each making what he could out of the work of his predecessors. The *Hamlet* of Shakespeare will appear to us very differently if, instead of treating the whole action of the play as due to Shakespeare's design, we perceive his *Hamlet* to be superposed upon much cruder material which persists even in the final form.

We know that there was an older play by Thomas Kyd, that extraordinary dramatic (if not poetic) genius who was in all probability the author of two plays so dissimilar as the *Spanish Tragedy* and *Arden of Feversham;* and what this play was like we can guess from three clues: from the *Spanish Tragedy* itself, from the tale of Belleforest upon which Kyd's *Hamlet* must have been based, and from a version acted in Germany in Shakespeare's lifetime which bears strong evidence of having been adapted from the earlier, not from the later, play. From these three sources it is clear that in the earlier play the motive was a revenge motive simply; that the action or delay is caused, as in the *Spanish Tragedy,* solely by the difficulty of assassinating a monarch surrounded by guards; and that the "madness" of Hamlet was feigned in order to escape suspicion, and successfully. In the final play of Shakespeare, on the other hand, there is a motive which is more important than that of revenge, and which explicitly "blunts" the latter; the delay in revenge is unexplained on grounds of necessity or expediency; and the effect of the "madness" is not to lull but to arouse the king's suspicion. The alteration is not complete enough, however, to be convincing. Furthermore, there are verbal parallels so close to the *Spanish Tragedy* as to leave no doubt that in places Shakespeare was merely *revising* the text of Kyd. And finally there are unexplained scenes — the Polonius-Laertes and the Polonius-Reynaldo scenes — for which there is little excuse; these scenes are not in the verse style of Kyd, and not beyond doubt in the style of Shakespeare. These Mr. Robertson believes to be scenes in the original play of Kyd reworked by a third hand, perhaps Chapman,° before Shakespeare touched the play. And he concludes, with very strong show of reason, that the original play of Kyd was, like certain other revenge plays, in two parts of five acts. The upshot of Mr. Robertson's examination is, we believe, irrefragable: that Shakespeare's *Hamlet,* so far as it is Shakespeare's, is a play dealing with the effect of a mother's guilt upon her son, and that Shakespeare was unable to impose this motive successfully upon the "intractable" material of the old play.

Chapman: George Chapman (1559?–1634), Elizabethan poet and playwright.

Of the intractability there can be no doubt. So far from being Shakespeare's masterpiece, the play is most certainly an artistic failure. In several ways the play is puzzling, and disquieting as is none of the others. Of all the plays it is the longest and is possibly the one on which Shakespeare spent most pains; and yet he has left in it superfluous and inconsistent scenes which even hasty revision should have noticed. The versification is variable. Lines like

> Look, the morn, in russet mantle clad,
> Walks o'er the dew of yon high eastern hill,

are of the Shakespeare of *Romeo and Juliet.* The lines in act V, scene II,

> Sir, in my heart there was a kind of fighting
> That would not let me sleep . . .
> Up from my cabin,
> My sea-gown scarf'd about me, in the dark
> Grop'd I to find out them: had my desire;
> Finger'd their packet;

are of his quite mature. Both workmanship and thought are in an unstable position. We are surely justified in attributing the play, with that other profoundly interesting play of "intractable" material and astonishing versification, *Measure for Measure,* to a period of crisis, after which follow the tragic successes which culminate in *Coriolanus. Coriolanus* may be not as "interesting" as *Hamlet,* but it is, with *Antony and Cleopatra,* Shakespeare's most assured artistic success. And probably more people have thought *Hamlet* a work of art because they found it interesting, than have found it interesting because it is a work of art. It is the *Mona Lisa* of literature.

The grounds of *Hamlet's* failure are not immediately obvious. Mr. Robertson is undoubtedly correct in concluding that the essential emotion of the play is the feeling of a son toward a guilty mother:

> [Hamlet's] tone is that of one who has suffered tortures on the score of his mother's degradation. . . . The guilt of a mother is an almost intolerable motive for drama, but it had to be maintained and emphasized to supply a psychological solution, or rather a hint of one.

This, however, is by no means the whole story. It is not merely the "guilt of a mother" that cannot be handled as Shakespeare handled the suspicion of Othello, the infatuation of Antony, or the pride of Coriolanus. The subject might conceivably have expanded into a tragedy like these, intelligible, self-complete, in the sunlight. *Hamlet,* like the sonnets, is full of some stuff that the writer could not drag to light, contemplate, or manipulate into art. And when we search for this feeling, we find it, as in the sonnets, very difficult to localize. You cannot point to it in the speeches; indeed, if you examine the two famous soliloquies you see the versification of Shakespeare, but a content which might be claimed by another, perhaps by the author of the *Revenge of Bussy d'Ambois,°* act V, scene I. We find Shakespeare's Hamlet not in the action, not in any quotations that we might select, so much as in an unmistakable tone which is unmistakably not in the earlier play.

Revenge of Bussy d'Ambois: Tragedy (1610–1611) by George Chapman, dealing with the reluctance of Clement d'Ambois to avenge his brother's death.

The only way of expressing emotion in the form of art is by finding an "objective correlative"; in other words, a set of objects, a situation, a chain of events which shall be the formula of that *particular* emotion; such that when the external facts, which must terminate in sensory experience, are given, the emotion is immediately evoked. If you examine any of Shakespeare's more successful tragedies, you will find this exact equivalence; you will find that the state of mind of Lady Macbeth walking in her sleep has been communicated to you by a skillful accumulation of imagined sensory impressions; the words of Macbeth on hearing of his wife's death strike us as if, given the sequence of events, these words were automatically released by the last event in the series. The artistic "inevitability" lies in this complete adequacy of the external to the emotion; and this is precisely what is deficient in *Hamlet*. Hamlet (the man) is dominated by an emotion which is inexpressible, because it is in *excess* of the facts as they appear. And the supposed identity of Hamlet with his author is genuine to this point: that Hamlet's bafflement at the absence of objective equivalent to his feelings is a prolongation of the bafflement of his creator in the face of his artistic problem. Hamlet is up against the difficulty that his disgust is occasioned by his mother, but that his mother is not an adequate equivalent for it; his disgust envelops and exceeds her. It is thus a feeling which he cannot understand; he cannot objectify it, and it therefore remains to poison life and obstruct action. None of the possible actions can satisfy it; and nothing that Shakespeare can do with the plot can express Hamlet for him. And it must be noticed that the very nature of the *données* of the problem precludes objective equivalence. To have heightened the criminality of Gertrude would have been to provide the formula for a totally different emotion in Hamlet; it is just *because* her character is so negative and insignificant that she arouses in Hamlet the feeling which she is incapable of representing.

The "madness" of Hamlet lay to Shakespeare's hand; in the earlier play a simple ruse, and to the end, we may presume, understood as a ruse by the audience. For Shakespeare it is less than madness and more than feigned. The levity of Hamlet, his repetition of phrase, his puns, are not part of a deliberate plan of dissimulation, but a form of emotional relief. In the character Hamlet it is the buffoonery of an emotion which can find no outlet in action; in the dramatist it is the buffoonery of an emotion which he cannot express in art. The intense feeling, ecstatic or terrible, without an object or exceeding its object, is something which every person of sensibility has known; it is doubtless a subject of study for pathologists. It often occurs in adolescence: the ordinary person puts these feelings to sleep, or trims down his feelings to fit the business world; the artist keeps them alive by his ability to intensify the world to his emotions. The Hamlet of Laforgue° is an adolescent; the Hamlet of Shakespeare is not, he has not that explanation and excuse. We must simply admit that here Shakespeare tackled a problem which proved too much for him. Why he attempted it at all is an insoluble puzzle; under compulsion of what experience he attempted to express the inexpressibly horrible, we cannot ever know. We need a great many facts in his biography; and we should like to know whether, and when, and after or at the same time as what personal experience, he read Montaigne's *Apologie de Raimond Sebond*. We should have, finally, to know something which is by hypothesis unknowable, for we assume it to be an experience which, in the manner indicated, exceeded the facts. We should have to understand things which Shakespeare did not understand himself.

Laforgue: Jules Laforgue (1860–1887), French poet who was an important influence on Eliot.

OTHELLO

Othello was one of Shakespeare's most popular plays, produced frequently in his lifetime and throughout the seventeenth century. Although the date of composition is uncertain, we do know that the earliest recorded production was November 1, 1604, in the old Banqueting Hall at the court of King James I and his wife, Anne of Denmark. This detail is interesting because it coincides with the later production — during the same winter season and at the same theater — of Ben Jonson's *Masque of Blackness,* which was specifically commissioned by Queen Anne so that she could "paint herself black" along with the ladies in her retinue.

There seems to have been a vogue for blackness in England at the time. A great many Moors — the term, as Shakespeare and others of his time use it, means a dark-skinned person from Africa — were living in England at the end of Queen Elizabeth's reign and the beginning of King James's, the period of both performances. Though her government had given Moors "full diplomatic recognition" as a gesture of thanks for their conquest of England's enemy Spain, in 1601 Queen Elizabeth was so alarmed by the number of blacks in England that she appointed a foreign merchant to transport them from the kingdom. In 1604 a delegation of Arabs visited London, and their customs and style caused some stir, both of admiration and concern. While the color black was symbolically associated by white people with the devil and moral turpitude, and the practice of slavery was already advanced, a number of black African noblemen had traveled to England, and some had returned to Africa as translators and intermediaries in trading expeditions.

Aaron, a Moor in Shakespeare's *Titus Andronicus* (1594), was dark-skinned and a villain. Early on, however, Shakespeare represents black characters in other entertainments as noble. He establishes the noble birth and character of Othello, for instance, who tells us, "I am black" (III, iii, 263). The character of Othello, a general of the Venetian forces, derives from an early Italian story by Geraldi Cinthio published in 1566 in Italian and 1584 in French. Shakespeare might have read either one. He adapted the story, adding new characters, reinterpreting the action, and completely reimagining Othello, Desdemona, and Iago.

The setting, Venice, was exotic for Elizabethan audiences, but it was appropriate for establishing a character who was unusual and something of "the other," as, for example, Shylock was in the earlier *Merchant of Venice* (1596–1597). It was especially felicitous a choice of setting for Othello's generalship because the Venetian republic, by law, had to have a foreigner as general of the armies. No one in the play disputes Othello's leadership and soldiership — not even Iago.

While the play makes great use of the contrasts of black and white, light and dark, evening and day, both to establish mood and to imply moral values, the central action is not devoted to issues relative to Othello's race. The opening scenes reveal that Brabantio, Desdemona's father, and Iago, Othello's ensign, are capable of racial slurs. But each speaks out of anger and disappointment. The official governors of Venice never once imply racial inequity, nor do they condone any disrespect for Othello. Indeed, they support him in his marriage once they hear Desdemona indicate her willing choice of Othello as her mate.

The dramatic action centers on Iago's bitter disappointment at having been passed over for promotion in favor of Cassio, whom he regards as an inexperienced boy. Cassio is well enough regarded by Othello and others to end the play as governor of Mauritania, the country in northwest Africa that was settled by Berbers and from which the name Moors is derived. Even if Cassio was preferred because he was the intermediary between Othello and Desdemona, and even though he has the weakness of sometimes being an unsoldierly drunk, he proves more worthy than the villainous Iago, who virtually personifies the devil. At the end of the play, Othello, understanding how terribly he has been betrayed, wishes to look at Iago's foot to see if, like the devil's, it is cleft.

In some productions of the play, Iago almost steals the show. His soliloquies indicating how he will manipulate the characters to achieve his evil ends are so powerful as to chill an audience. He seems to be the force driving the action, while Othello struggles like a fly in the web of his deceit. Yet Othello is the great character in the drama. He rises majestically to deliver some of the greatest speeches Shakespeare ever wrote. Eventually, his initial innocence is replaced by rage and anger. Iago purposely infects Othello with jealousy, implying that his young, new wife Desdemona is dallying with Cassio. He offers "ocular proof" but proof that would not be convincing if Othello were not anxious to be convinced. Iago moves Othello from a contented man — a soldier at peace with himself — to a deracinated jealous husband.

Watching the progress of that action rivets the audience. Seeing how the villain Iago improvises at every turn to take advantage of each opportunity to present false "evidence" fascinates audience and reader alike. Ironically, the symbolism of blackness is reversed in Iago, whose inner soul is dark and hell bound, while Othello is led to commit a heinous crime whose horror he ultimately recognizes. He pays with his own death by his own hand. Our sympathy is with him at the end of the play, despite his moments of frightening anger and horror. He has been used by a lesser man, and what has permitted him to be deceived — as interpreted by some critics — is his essential innocence and goodness.

Among the patterns of imagery in the play, those connected with animals — such as the pig, the barbary horse, and the black ram — support Iago's efforts to emphasize Othello's bestiality. When he claims that Othello and Desdemona are "making the beast with two backs," he wishes to enlist Brabantio's aid in humiliating Othello and perhaps damaging his reputation with the Duke of Venice. The careful manipulation of this imagery helps Iago forward his plan even before he knows what it is.

Othello himself stands as one of the towering figures in Shakespeare's works, challenging actors in his own day and in ours. Desdemona may be faulted for her willfulness in marrying without her father's knowledge or permission — at the time a grave infraction. But the audience forgives her if only because it is obvious that nothing she could have said would have convinced her father to look kindly on Othello as a son-in-law. And while passion is at the core of the play, it may not have been passion alone that caused her to act as she did.

Othello in Performance

The first recorded production of *Othello* was November 1604 at the court of King James. But public performances probably were held at the Globe Theatre sometime that year or the following. Although no reliable performance records are available, we know that the play was produced by Shakespeare's company, The King's Men, both at the Globe in April 1610 and in Oxford in September of the same year. It was performed again in 1629, 1635, and 1636. It was popular in the eighteenth and nineteenth centuries as well as in the twentieth century and is among Shakespeare's most produced plays.

The first Othello was Richard Burbage, Shakespeare's finest actor in one of his finest roles. He wore Elizabethan clothes with no special effort to adopt a Moorish costume. We have no record of his makeup, and the only eyewitness account describes him as a "grieved Moor." However, judging from the tradition maintained up to 1709, when we have a portrait of Othello, we can assume he was played as a black man. The play enjoyed such popularity that it constantly attracted the most gifted actors of the day.

The nineteenth century produced several notable Othellos, but it also saw the beginning of a trend in which Othello became "tawny" rather than black. He became what was then known as a "white Moor." Edmund Kean, the greatest actor of his day, portrayed Othello in this fashion to extraordinary acclaim. The first black actor to play Othello was Ira Aldridge, an American on the London stage in the nineteenth century.

In modern times, two productions stand out as milestones: Paul Robeson's in New York in 1943–1944 and Laurence Olivier's in London in 1964. Robeson was known as a great singer but had performed onstage in Eugene O'Neill's *The Emperor Jones* prior to *Othello*. His physical presence on stage was striking in every way, especially when linked with his commanding voice. Martin Wine describes him as the "outstanding 'romantic' Othello of our time," by which he means a sympathetic and moving Othello. The Broadway production played for more performances than nearly any American production of Shakespeare up to that time. James Earl Jones, who played the role many years later, was in the audience and felt that Robeson's command of the concept of honor was singular and has never been approached since.

Laurence Olivier had himself made up not just as a black man but as a black African. Some critics were impressed by the achievement, but others felt it was still difficult to accept the idea of a white actor in the part. Yet Olivier's version was taut, powerful, and one of his greatest achievements. He took comfort in the fact that Shakespeare wrote the role for a white actor and did not worry over the shift in tradition. Martin Wine described his performance as "the most controversial" performance of our time. Olivier's interpretation was of an egotistical Othello, one who was tormented by neurotic tendencies and even a touch of paranoia. Olivier's Othello was less a man of the Renaissance than a man of modern times.

Most modern productions have made use of effective lighting, emphasizing the opening darkness of the drama. They also make use of simple staging, using archways effectively and suggestions of buildings, ships and sails, and sometimes Moorish architectural details.

William Shakespeare (1564–1616)
OTHELLO THE MOOR OF VENICE

1604

The Names of the Actors

OTHELLO, THE MOOR
BRABANTIO, [*a Venetian senator,*] *father to Desdemona*
CASSIO, *an honorable lieutenant* [*to Othello*]
IAGO, [*Othello's ancient,*] *a villain*
RODERIGO, *a gulled gentleman*
DUKE OF VENICE
SENATORS [*of Venice*]
MONTANO, *governor of Cyprus*
LODOVICO AND GRATIANO, [*kinsmen to Brabantio,*]
    two noble Venetians
SAILORS
CLOWNS
DESDEMONA, *wife to Othello*
EMILIA, *wife to Iago*
BIANCA, *a courtesan*
[MESSENGER, HERALD, OFFICERS, VENETIAN
    GENTLEMEN, MUSICIANS, ATTENDANTS

Scene: Venice and Cyprus]

ACT I • *Scene 1*

A street in Venice.

Enter Roderigo and Iago.

RODERIGO: Tush, never tell me! I take it much
        unkindly
    That thou, Iago, who hast had my purse
    As if the strings were thine, shouldst know of this.°
IAGO: 'Sblood,° but you'll not hear me!
5   If ever I did dream of such a matter,
    Abhor me.
RODERIGO: Thou told'st me thou didst hold him in thy
        hate.
IAGO: Despise me if I do not. Three great ones of the
        city,
    In personal suit to make me his lieutenant,
10   Off-capped to him;° and, by the faith of man,
    I know my price; I am worth no worse a place.
    But he, as loving his own pride and purposes,
    Evades them with a bombast circumstance.°
    Horribly stuffed with epithets of war;
15   [And, in conclusion,]
    Nonsuits° my mediators; for, "Certes," says he,

I, i. 3. **this:** I.e., Desdemona's elopement. 5. **'Sblood:** By God's blood. 10. **him:** I.e., Othello. 13. **a bombast circumstance:** Pompous circumlocution. 16. **Nonsuits:** Rejects.

"I have already chose my officer."
    And what was he?
    Forsooth, a great arithmetician,°
    One Michael Cassio, a Florentine   20
    (A fellow almost damned in a fair wife°)
    That never set a squadron in the field,
    Nor the division of a battle knows
    More than a spinster; unless the bookish theoric,
    Wherein the togèd consuls can propose   25
    As masterly as he. Mere prattle without practice
    Is all his soldiership. But he, sir, had th' election;
    And I (of whom his eyes had seen the proof
    At Rhodes, at Cyprus, and on other grounds
    Christian and heathen) must be belee'd and calmed° 30
    By debitor and creditor; this counter-caster,°
    He, in good time, must his lieutenant be,
    And I — God bless the mark! — his Moorship's
        ancient.°
RODERIGO: By heaven, I rather would have been his
        hangman.
IAGO: Why, there's no remedy; 'tis the curse of service. 35
    Preferment goes by letter and affection,°
    And not by old gradation, where each second
    Stood heir to th' first. Now, sir, be judge yourself,
    Whether I in any just term am affined°
    To love the Moor.
RODERIGO: I would not follow him then.   40
IAGO: O, sir, content you;
    I follow him to serve my turn upon him.
    We cannot all be masters, nor all masters
    Cannot be truly followed. You shall mark
    Many a duteous and knee-crooking knave   45
    That, doting on his own obsequious bondage,
    Wears out his time, much like his master's ass,
    For naught but provender; and when he's old,
        cashiered.°
    Whip me such honest knaves! Others there are
    Who, trimmed° in forms and visages of duty,   50
    Keep yet their hearts attending on themselves;
    And, throwing but shows of service on their lords,
    Do well thrive by them, and when they have lined
        their coats,
    Do themselves homage. These fellows have some
        soul;

---

19. **arithmetician:** Theoretician. 21. **almost . . . wife:** (An obscure allusion; Cassio is unmarried, but see IV, i, 115–16). 30. **belee'd and calmed:** Left in the lurch. 31. **counter-caster:** Bookkeeper. 33. **ancient:** Ensign. 36. **affection:** Favoritism. 39. **affined:** Obliged. 48. **cashiered:** Turned off. 50. **trimmed:** Dressed up.

55   And such a one do I profess myself. For, sir,
      It is as sure as you are Roderigo,
      Were I the Moor, I would not be Iago.
      In following him, I follow but myself;
      Heaven is my judge, not I for love and duty,
60   But seeming so, for my peculiar end;
      For when my outward action doth demonstrate
      The native act and figure of my heart°
      In compliment extern,° 'tis not long after
      But I will wear my heart upon my sleeve
65   For daws to peck at; I am not what I am.
RODERIGO: What a full fortune does the thick-lips°
          owe°
      If he can carry't thus!
IAGO: Call up her father,
      Rouse him. Make after him, poison his delight,
      Proclaim him in the streets. Incense her kinsmen,
70   And though he in a fertile climate dwell,
      Plague him with flies; though that his joy be joy,
      Yet throw such changes of vexation on't
      As it may lose some color.
RODERIGO: Here is her father's house. I'll call aloud.
75 IAGO: Do, with like timorous° accent and dire yell
      As when, by night and negligence, the fire
      Is spied in populous cities.
RODERIGO: What, ho, Brabantio! Signior Brabantio,
          ho!
IAGO: Awake! What, ho, Brabantio! Thieves! thieves!
          thieves!
80   Look to your house, your daughter, and your bags!
      Thieves! thieves!

Brabantio at a window.°

BRABANTIO (*above*): What is the reason of this terrible
          summons?
      What is the matter there?
RODERIGO: Signior, is all your family within?
IAGO: Are your doors locked?
85 BRABANTIO: Why, wherefore ask you this?
IAGO: Zounds, sir, y' are robbed! For shame, put on
          your gown!
      Your heart is burst; you have lost half your soul.
      Even now, now, very now, an old black ram
      Is tupping your white ewe. Arise, arise!
90   Awake the snorting° citizens with the bell.
      Or else the devil will make a grandsire of you.
      Arise, I say!
BRABANTIO: What, have you lost your wits?
RODERIGO: Most reverend signior, do you know my
          voice?
95 BRABANTIO: Not I. What are you?
RODERIGO: My name is Roderigo.

BRABANTIO: The worser welcome!
      I have charged thee not to haunt about my doors.
      In honest plainness thou hast heard me say
      My daughter is not for thee; and now, in madness,
      Being full of supper and distemp'ring draughts,   100
      Upon malicious knavery dost thou come
      To start my quiet.
RODERIGO: Sir, sir, sir —
BRABANTIO: But thou must needs be sure
      My spirit and my place have in them power   105
      To make this bitter to thee.
RODERIGO: Patience, good sir.
BRABANTIO: What tell'st thou me of robbing? This is
          Venice;
      My house is not a grange.°
RODERIGO: Most grave Brabantio,
      In simple and pure soul I come to you.
IAGO: Zounds, sir, you are one of those that will not   110
      serve God if the devil bid you. Because we come to do
      you service, and you think we are ruffians, you'll
      have your daughter covered with a Barbary horse;
      you'll have your nephews° neigh to you; you'll have
      coursers for cousins, and gennets for germans.°   115
BRABANTIO: What profane wretch art thou?
IAGO: I am one, sir, that comes to tell you your daughter
      and the Moor are now making the beast with two
      backs.
BRABANTIO: Thou are a villain.
IAGO: You are — a senator.   120
BRABANTIO: This thou shalt answer. I know thee,
          Roderigo.
RODERIGO: Sir, I will answer anything. But I beseech
          you,
      If't be your pleasure and most wise consent,
      As partly I find it is, that your fair daughter,
      At this odd-even° and dull watch o' th' night,   125
      Transported, with no worse nor better guard
      But with a knave of common hire, a gondolier,
      To the gross clasps of a lascivious Moor —
      If this be known to you, and your allowance,°
      We then have done you bold and saucy wrongs;   130
      But if you know not this, my manners tell me
      We have your wrong rebuke. Do not believe
      That, from the sense° of all civility,
      I thus would play and trifle with your reverence.
      Your daughter, if you have not given her leave,   135
      I say again, hath made a gross revolt,
      Tying her duty, beauty, wit, and fortunes
      In an extravagant and wheeling° stranger
      Of here and everywhere. Straight satisfy yourself.
      If she be in her chamber, or your house,   140
      Let loose on me the justice of the state
      For thus deluding you.

---

62. The . . . heart: What I really believe and intend.   **63. compliment extern:** Outward appearance.   **66. thick-lips:** An Elizabethan epithet for blacks, including Moors.   **owe:** Own.
75. timorous: Terrifying.   [S.D.] ***Brabantio at a window:*** (Added from quarto).   **90. snorting:** Snoring.

108. grange: Isolated farmhouse.   **114. nephews:** I.e., grandsons.
115. gennets for germans: Spanish horses for near kinsmen.
125. odd-even: Between night and morning.   **129. allowance:** Approval.   **133. from the sense:** In violation.   **138. extravagant and wheeling:** Expatriate and roving.

BRABANTIO: Strike on the tinder, ho!
  Give me a taper! Call up all my people!
  This accident° is not unlike my dream.
145 Belief of it oppresses me already.
  Light, I say! light!   *Exit [above].*
IAGO: Farewell, for I must leave you.
  It seems not meet, nor wholesome to my place,
  To be produced — as, if I stay, I shall —
  Against the Moor. For I do know the state,
150 However this may gall him with some check,°
  Cannot with safety cast° him; for he's embarked
  With such loud reason to the Cyprus wars,
  Which even now stand in act,° that for their souls
  Another of his fathom° they have none
155 To lead their business; in which regard,
  Though I do hate him as I do hell-pains,
  Yet, for necessity of present life,
  I must show out a flag and sign of love,
  Which is indeed but sign. That you shall surely find
    him,
160 Lead to the Sagittary° the raisèd search;
  And there will I be with him. So farewell.   *Exit.*

*Enter [below] Brabantio in his nightgown,° and Servants
with torches.*

BRABANTIO: It is too true an evil. Gone she is;
  And what's to come of my despisèd time
  Is naught but bitterness. Now, Roderigo,
165 Where didst thou see her? — O unhappy girl! —
  With the Moor, say'st thou? — Who would be a
    father? —
  How didst thou know 'twas she! — O, she deceives
    me
  Past thought! — What said she to you? — Get moe°
    tapers!
  Raise all my kindred! — Are they married, think
    you?
170 RODERIGO: Truly I think they are.
BRABANTIO: O heaven! How got she out? O treason of
    the blood!
  Fathers, from hence trust not your daughters' minds
  By what you see them act. Is there not charms
  By which the property° of youth and maidhood
175 May be abused? Have you not read, Roderigo,
  Of some such thing?
RODERIGO: Yes, sir, I have indeed.
BRABANTIO: Call up my brother. — O, would you had
    had her! —
  Some one way, some another. — Do you know
  Where we may apprehend her and the Moor?
180 RODERIGO: I think I can discover him, if you please
  To get good guard and go along with me.
BRABANTIO: I pray you lead on. At every house I'll call;

I may command at most. — Get weapons, ho!
And raise some special officers of night. —
On, good Roderigo; I'll deserve° your pains.   185
                        Exeunt.

Scene II

Before the lodgings of Othello.

Enter Othello, Iago, and Attendants with torches.

IAGO: Though in the trade of war I have slain men,
  Yet do I hold it very stuff o' th' conscience
  To do no contrived murther. I lack iniquity
  Sometimes to do me service. Nine or ten times
  I had thought t' have yerked° him here under the
    ribs.   5
OTHELLO: 'Tis better as it is.
IAGO: Nay, but he prated,
  And spoke such scurvy and provoking terms
  Against your honor
  That with the little godliness I have
  I did full hard forbear him. But I pray you, sir,   10
  Are you fast° married? Be assured of this,
  That the magnifico° is much beloved,
  And hath in his effect a voice potential°
  As double° as the Duke's. He will divorce you,
  Or put upon you what restraint and grievance   15
  The law, with all his might to enforce it on,
  Will give him cable.
OTHELLO: Let him do his spite.
  My services which I have done the signiory°
  Shall out-tongue his complaints. 'Tis yet to
    know° —
  Which, when I know that boasting is an honor,   20
  I shall promulgate — I fetch my life and being
  From men of royal siege;° and my demerits°
  May speak unbonneted to as proud a fortune
  As this that I have reached.° For know, Iago,
  But that I love the gentle Desdemona,   25
  I would not my unhousèd° free condition
  Put into circumscription and confine
  For the sea's worth. But look what lights come
    yond?
IAGO: Those are the raisèd father and his friends.
  You were best go in.
OTHELLO: Not I; I must be found.   30
  My parts, my title, and my perfect soul°
  Shall manifest me rightly. Is it they?
IAGO: By Janus, I think no.

---

144. **accident:** Occurrence.   150. **check:** Reprimand.   151. **cast:**
Discharge.   153. **stand in act:** Are going on.   154. **fathom:**
Capacity.   160. **Sagittary:** An inn.   [S.D.] *nightgown:* Dress-
ing gown.   168. **moe:** More.   174. **property:** Nature.

185. **deserve:** Show gratitude for.   I, II. 5. **yerked:** Stabbed.
11. **fast:** Securely.   12. **magnifico:** Grandee (Brabantio).
13. **potential:** Powerful.   14. **double:** Doubly influential.
18. **signiory:** Venetian government.   19. **yet to know:** Still
not generally known.   22. **siege:** Rank.   **demerits:** Deserts.
24. **May speak . . . reached:** Are equal, I modestly assert, to
those of Desdemona's family.   26. **unhousèd:** Unrestrained.
31. **perfect soul:** Stainless conscience.

Enter Cassio, with torches, Officers.

OTHELLO: The servants of the Duke, and my
    lieutenant.
35   The goodness of the night upon you, friends!
    What is the news?
CASSIO: The Duke does greet you, general;
    And he requires your haste-post-haste appearance
    Even on the instant.
OTHELLO: What's the matter, think you?
CASSIO: Something from Cyprus, as I may divine.
40   It is a business of some heat. The galleys
    Have sent a dozen sequent° messengers
    This very night at one another's heels,
    And many of the consuls, raised and met,
    Are at the Duke's already. You have been hotly
      called for;
45   When, being not at your lodging to be found,
    The Senate hath sent about three several quests
    To search you out.
OTHELLO: 'Tis well I am found by you.
    I will but spend a word here in the house,
    And go with you.   *[Exit]*
CASSIO: Ancient, what makes he here?
50 IAGO: Faith, he to-night hath boarded a land carack.°
    If it prove lawful prize, he's made for ever.
CASSIO: I do not understand.
IAGO: He's married.
CASSIO: To who?

[Enter Othello.]

IAGO: Marry, to — Come, captain, will you go?
OTHELLO: Have
    with you.
CASSIO: Here comes another troop to seek for you.

Enter Brabantio, Roderigo, and others with lights and weapons.

55 IAGO: It is Brabantio. General, be advised.
    He comes to bad intent.
OTHELLO: Holla! stand there!
RODERIGO: Signior, it is the Moor.
BRABANTIO: Down with him, thief!

[They draw on both sides.]

IAGO: You, Roderigo! Come, sir, I am for you.
OTHELLO: Keep up° your bright swords, for the dew
    will rust them.
60   Good signior, you shall more command with years
    Than with your weapons.
BRABANTIO: O thou foul thief, where hast thou stowed
    my daughter?
    Damned as thou art, thou hast enchanted her!
    For I'll refer me to all things of sense,
65   If she in chains of magic were not bound,
    Whether a maid so tender, fair, and happy,

So opposite to marriage that she shunned
The wealthy curlèd darlings of our nation,
Would ever have, t' incur a general mock,
Run from her guardage to the sooty bosom   70
Of such a thing as thou — to fear, not to delight.
Judge me the world if 'tis not gross in sense°
That thou hast practiced on her with foul charms,
Abused her delicate youth with drugs or minerals
That weaken motion.° I'll have't disputed on;   75
'Tis probable, and palpable to thinking.
I therefore apprehend and do attach° thee
For an abuser of the world, a practicer
Of arts inhibited and out of warrant.
Lay hold upon him. If he do resist,   80
Subdue him at his peril.
OTHELLO: Hold your hands,
    Both you of my inclining and the rest.
    Were it my cue to fight, I should have known it
    Without a prompter. Where will you that I go
    To answer this your charge?
BRABANTIO: To prison, till fit time   85
    Of law and course of direct session°
    Call thee to answer.
OTHELLO: What if I do obey?
    How may the Duke be therewith satisfied,
    Whose messengers are here about my side
    Upon some present business of the state   90
    To bring me to him?
OFFICER: 'Tis true, most worthy signior.
    The Duke's in council, and your noble self
    I am sure is sent for.
BRABANTIO: How? The Duke in council?
    In this time of the night? Bring him away.
    Mine's not an idle° cause. The Duke himself,   95
    Or any of my brothers of the state,
    Cannot but feel this wrong as 'twere their own;
    For if such actions may have passage free,
    Bondslaves and pagans shall our statesmen be.
                          Exeunt.

Scene III

The Venetian Senate Chamber.

Enter Duke and Senators, set at a table, with lights and Attendants.

DUKE: There is no composition° in these news
    That gives them credit.
1. SENATOR: Indeed they are disproportioned.
    My letters say a hundred and seven galleys.
DUKE: And mine a hundred forty.
2. SENATOR: And mine two hundred.
    But though they jump° not on a just account —   5

41. **sequent:** Consecutive. 50. **carack:** Treasure ship. 59. **Keep up:** I.e., sheath.

72. **gross in sense:** Obvious. 75. **motion:** Perception. 77. **attach:** Arrest. 86. **direct session:** Regular trial. 95. **idle:** Trifling. I, III. 1. **composition:** Consistency. 5. **jump:** Agree.

As in these cases where the aim° reports
'Tis oft with difference — yet do they all confirm
A Turkish fleet, and bearing up to Cyprus.
DUKE: Nay, it is possible enough to judgment.
10   I do not so secure me° in the error
But the main article° I do approve°
In fearful sense.
SAILOR (*within*):   What, ho! what, ho! what, ho!
OFFICER: A messenger from the galleys.

Enter Sailor.

DUKE: Now, what's the business?
SAILOR: The Turkish preparation makes for Rhodes.
15   So was I bid report here to the state
By Signior Angelo.
DUKE: How say you by this change?
1. SENATOR: This cannot be
By no assay° of reason. 'Tis a pageant
To keep us in false gaze.° When we consider
20   Th' importancy of Cyprus to the Turk,
And let ourselves again but understand
That, as it more concerns the Turk than Rhodes,
So may he with more facile question bear° it,
For that it stands not in such warlike brace,°
25   But altogether lacks th' abilities
That Rhodes is dressed in — if we make thought of
this,
We must not think the Turk is so unskillful
To leave that latest which concerns him first,
Neglecting an attempt of ease and gain
30   To wake and wage° a danger profitless.
DUKE: Nay, in all confidence, he's not for Rhodes.
OFFICER: Here is more news.

Enter a Messenger.

MESSENGER: The Ottomites, reverend and gracious,
Steering with due course toward the isle of Rhodes,
35   Have there injointed them with an after fleet.
1. SENATOR: Ay, so I thought. How many, as you guess?
MESSENGER: Of thirty sail; and now they do restem°
Their backward course, bearing with frank
appearance
Their purposes toward Cyprus, Signior Montano,
40   Your trusty and most valiant servitor,
With his free duty recommends you thus,
And prays you to believe him.
DUKE: 'Tis certain then for Cyprus.
Marcus Luccicos,° is not he in town?
45   1. SENATOR: He's now in Florence.
DUKE: Write from us to him; post, post-haste dispatch.
1. SENATOR: Here comes Brabantio and the valiant
Moor.

6. **aim:** Conjecture.   10. **so secure me:** Take such comfort.
11. **article:** Substance. **approve:** Accept.   18. **assay:** Test.
19. **in false gaze:** Looking the wrong way.   23. **with . . .
bear:** More easily capture.   24. **brace:** Posture of defense.
30. **wake and wage:** Rouse and risk.   37. **restem:** Steer again.
44. **Marcus Luccicos:** (Presumably a Venetian envoy).

Enter Brabantio, Othello, Cassio, Iago, Roderigo, and
Officers.

DUKE: Valiant Othello, we must straight employ you
Against the general enemy Ottoman.

[*To Brabantio.*]

I did not see you. Welcome, gentle signior.   50
We lacked your counsel and your help to-night.
BRABANTIO: So did I yours. Good your grace, pardon
me.
Neither my place, nor aught I heard of business,
Hath raised me from my bed; nor doth the general
care
Take hold on me; for my particular grief   55
Is of so floodgate° and o'erbearing nature
That it engluts° and swallows other sorrows,
And it is still itself.
DUKE: Why, what's the matter?
BRABANTIO: My daughter! O, my daughter!
ALL: Dead?
BRABANTIO: Ay, to me.
She is abused, stol'n from me, and corrupted   60
By spells and medicines bought of mountebanks;
For nature so prepost'rously to err,
Being not deficient,° blind, or lame of sense,
Sans witchcraft could not.
DUKE: Whoe'er he be that in this foul proceeding   65
Hath thus beguiled your daughter of herself,
And you of her, the bloody book of law
You shall yourself read in the bitter letter
After your own sense; yea, though our proper° son
Stood in your action.°
BRABANTIO: Humbly I thank your grace.   70
Here is the man — this Moor, whom now, it seems,
Your special mandate for the state affairs
Hath hither brought.
ALL: We are very sorry for't.
DUKE [*to Othello*]: What, in your own part, can you
say to this?
BRABANTIO: Nothing, but this is so.   75
OTHELLO: Most potent, grave, and reverend signiors,
My very noble, and approved° good masters,
That I have ta'en away this old man's daughter,
It is most true; true I have married her.
The very head and front of my offending   80
Hath this extent, no more. Rude° am I in my
speech,
And little blessed with the soft phrase of peace;
For since these arms of mine had seven years' pith°
Till now some nine moons wasted, they have used
Their dearest action in the tented field;   85
And little of this great world can I speak
More than pertains to feats of broil and battle;

56. **floodgate:** Torrential.   57. **engluts:** Devours.   63. **deficient:** Feeble-minded.   69. **our proper:** My own.   70. **Stood
in your action:** Were accused by you.   77. **approved:** Tested by
experience.   81. **Rude:** Unpolished.   83. **pith:** Strength.

And therefore little shall I grace my cause
In speaking for myself. Yet, by your gracious
    patience,
90   I will a round° unvarnished tale deliver
Of my whole course of love — what drugs, what
    charms,
What conjuration, and what mighty magic
(For such proceeding am I charged withal)
I won his daughter.
BRABANTIO: A maiden never bold;
95   Of spirit so still and quiet that her motion
Blushed° at herself; and she — in spite of nature,
Of years, of country, credit, everything —
To fall in love with what she feared to look on!
It is a judgment maimed and most imperfect
100   That will confess perfection so could err
Against all rules of nature, and must be driven
To find out practices° of cunning hell
Why this should be. I therefore vouch° again
That with some mixtures pow'rful o'er the blood,°
105   Or with some dram, conjured to this effect,
He wrought upon her.
DUKE: To vouch this is no proof,
Without more certain and more overt test
Than these thin habits° and poor likelihoods
Of modern seeming° do prefer against him.
110   1. SENATOR: But, Othello, speak.
Did you by indirect and forcèd° courses
Subdue and poison this young maid's affections?
Or came it by request, and such fair question°
As soul to soul affordeth?
OTHELLO: I do beseech you,
115   Send for the lady to the Sagittary
And let her speak of me before her father.
If you do find me foul in her report,
The trust, the office, I do hold of you
Not only take away, but let your sentence
Even fall upon my life.
120   DUKE: Fetch Desdemona hither.
OTHELLO: Ancient, conduct them; you best know the
    place.

          Exit [Iago, with] two or three [Attendants].

And till she come, as truly as to heaven
I do confess the vices of my blood,
So justly to your grave ears I'll present
125   How I did thrive in this fair lady's love,
And she in mine.
DUKE: Say it, Othello.
OTHELLO: Her father loved me, oft invited me;
Still° questioned me the story of my life
130   From year to year — the battles, sieges, fortunes

That I have passed.
I ran it through, even from my boyish days
To th' very moment that he bade me tell it.
Wherein I spoke of most disastrous chances,
Of moving accidents by flood and field;   135
Of hairbreadth scapes i' th' imminent deadly
    breach;
Of being taken by the insolent foe
And sold to slavery; of my redemption thence
And portance° in my travels' history;
Wherein of anters° vast and deserts idle,   140
Rough quarries, rocks, and hills whose heads touch
    heaven,
It was my hint° to speak — such was the process;
And of the Cannibals that each other eat,
The Anthropophagi,° and men whose heads
Do grow beneath their shoulders. This to hear   145
Would Desdemona seriously incline;
But still the house affairs would draw her thence;
Which ever as she could with haste dispatch,
She'ld come again, and with a greedy ear
Devour up my discourse. Which I observing,   150
Took once a pliant° hour, and found good means
To draw from her a prayer of earnest heart
That I would all my pilgrimage dilate,°
Whereof by parcels° she had something heard,
But not intentively.° I did consent,   155
And often did beguile her of her tears
When I did speak of some distressful stroke
That my youth suffered. My story being done,
She gave me for my pains a world of sighs.
She swore, i' faith, 'twas strange, 'twas passing
    strange;   160
'Twas pitiful, 'twas wondrous pitiful.
She wished she had not heard it; yet she wished
That heaven had made her such a man. She thanked
    me;
And bade me, if I had a friend that loved her,
I should but teach him how to tell my story,   165
And that would woo her. Upon this hint° I spake.
She loved me for the dangers I had passed,
And I loved her that she did pity them.
This only is the witchcraft I have used.
Here comes the lady. Let her witness it.   170

Enter Desdemona, Iago, Attendants.

DUKE: I think this tale would win my daughter too.
    Good Brabantio,
Take up this mangled matter at the best.
Men do their broken weapons rather use
Than their bare hands.
BRABANTIO: I pray you hear her speak. 175

---

90. round: Plain.   **95–96. her motion Blushed:** Her own emotions caused her to blush.   **102. practices:** Plots.   **103. vouch:** Assert.   **104. blood:** Passions.   **108. thin habits:** Slight appearances.   **109. modern seeming:** Everyday supposition.   **111. forcèd:** Violent.   **113. question:** Conversation.   **129. Still:** Continually.

139. portance: Behavior.   **140. anters:** Caves.   **142. hint:** Occasion.   **144. Anthropophagi:** Man-eaters.   **151. pliant:** Propitious.   **153. dilate:** Recount in full.   **154. parcels:** Portions.   **155. intentively:** With full attention.   **166. hint:** Opportunity.

If she confess that she was half the wooer,
Destruction on my head if my bad blame
Light on the man! Come hither, gentle mistress.
Do you perceive in all this noble company
Where most you owe obedience?

180 DESDEMONA: My noble father,
I do perceive here a divided duty.
To you I am bound for life and education;°
My life and education both do learn me
How to respect you: you are the lord of duty;

185 I am hitherto your daughter. But here's my husband;
And so much duty as my mother showed
To you, preferring you before her father,
So much I challenge° that I may profess
Due to the Moor my lord.

BRABANTIO: God be with you! I have done.
190 Please it your grace, on to the state affairs.
I had rather to adopt a child than get° it.
Come hither, Moor.
I here do give thee that with all my heart
Which, but thou hast already, with all my heart

195 I would keep from thee. For your sake,° jewel,
I am glad at soul I have no other child;
For thy escape° would teach me tyranny,
To hang clogs on them. I have done, my lord.

DUKE: Let me speak like yourself° and lay a sentence°
200 Which, as a grise° or step, may help these lovers
[Into your favor.]
When remedies are past, the griefs are ended
By seeing the worst, which late on hopes depended.
To mourn a mischief that is past and gone

205 Is the next way to draw new mischief on.
What cannot be preserved when fortune takes,
Patience her injury a mock'ry makes.
The robbed that smiles steals something from the
   thief;
He robs himself that spends a bootless grief.

210 BRABANTIO: So let the Turk of Cyprus us beguile:
We lose it not so long as we can smile.
He bears the sentence well that nothing bears
But the free comfort which from thence he hears;
But he bears both the sentence and the sorrow

215 That to pay grief must of poor patience borrow.
These sentences, to sugar, or to gall,
Being strong on both sides, are equivocal.
But words are words. I never yet did hear
That the bruisèd heart was piercèd through the ear.

220 Beseech you, now to the affairs of state.

DUKE: The Turk with a most mighty preparation makes
for Cyprus. Othello, the fortitude° of the place is best
known to you; and though we have there a substitute of most allowed° sufficiency, yet opinion,° a more

sovereign mistress of effects, throws a more safer   225
voice on you. You must therefore be content to slub-
ber° the gloss of your new fortunes with this more
stubborn and boist'rous expedition.

OTHELLO: The tyrant custom, most grave senators,
Hath made the flinty and steel couch of war   230
My thrice-driven bed of down. I do agnize
A natural and prompt alacrity
I find in hardness;° and do undertake
These present wars against the Ottomites.
Most humbly, therefore, bending to your state,   235
I crave fit disposition for my wife,
Due reference of place, and exhibition,°
With such accommodation and besort°
As levels° with her breeding.

DUKE: If you please,
Be't at her father's.

BRABANTIO: I will not have it so.   240

OTHELLO: Nor I.

DESDEMONA: Nor I. I would not there reside,
To put my father in impatient thoughts
By being in his eye. Most gracious Duke,
To my unfolding lend your prosperous° ear,   245
And let me find a charter in your voice,
T' assist my simpleness.°

DUKE: What would you, Desdemona?

DESDEMONA: That I did love the Moor to live with
   him,
My downright violence, and storm of fortunes,   250
May trumpet to the world. My heart's subdued
Even to the very quality of my lord.
I saw Othello's visage in his mind,
And to his honors and his valiant parts
Did I my soul and fortunes consecrate.   255
So that, dear lords, if I be left behind,
A moth of peace, and he go to the war,
The rites for which I love him are bereft me,
And I a heavy interim shall support
By his dear absence. Let me go with him.   260

OTHELLO: Let her have your voice.
Vouch with me, heaven, I therefore beg it not
To please the palate of my appetite,
Not to comply with heat° — the young affects°
In me defunct — and proper satisfaction;   265
But to be free and bounteous to her mind;
And heaven defend your good souls that you think
I will your serious and great business scant
When she is with me. No, when light-winged toys
Of feathered Cupid seel° with wanton dullness   270
My speculative and officed instruments,°

---

182. **education:** Upbringing.   189. **challenge:** Claim the right.
191. **get:** Beget.   195. **For your sake:** Because of you.   197. **escape:** Escapade.   199. **like yourself:** As you should.   **sentence:**
Maxim.   200. **grise:** Step.   222. **fortitude:** Fortification.
224. **allowed:** Acknowledged.   **opinion:** Public opinion.

227. **slubber:** Sully.   231–33. **agnize . . . hardness:** Recognize
in myself a natural and easy response to hardship.   237. **exhibition:** Allowance of money.   238. **besort:** Suitable company.
239. **levels:** Corresponds.   245. **prosperous:** Favorable.
247. **simpleness:** Lack of skill.   264. **heat:** Passions.   **young
affects:** Tendencies of youth.   270. **seel:** Blind.   271. **My . . .
instruments:** My perceptive and responsible faculties.

That° my disports corrupt and taint my business,
Let housewives make a skillet of my helm,
And all indign° and base adversities
275 Make head against my estimation!°
Duke: Be it as you shall privately determine,
Either for her stay or going. Th' affair cries haste,
And speed must answer it.
1. Senator: You must away to-night.
Othello: With all my heart.
280 Duke: At nine i' th' morning here we'll meet again.
Othello, leave some officer behind,
And he shall our commission bring to you,
With such things else of quality and respect
As doth import° you.
Othello: So please your grace, my ancient;
285 A man he is of honesty and trust
To his conveyance I assign my wife,
With what else needful your good grace shall
think
To be sent after me.
Duke: Let it be so.
Good night to every one.
      [To Brabantio.]   And, noble signior,
290 If virtue no delighted° beauty lack,
Your son-in-law is far more fair than black.
1. Senator: Adieu, brave Moor. Use Desdemona well.
Brabantio: Look to her, Moor, if thou hast eyes to see:
She has deceived her father, and may thee.

            Exeunt [Duke, Senators, Officers, etc.].

295 Othello: My life upon her faith! — Honest Iago,
My Desdemona must I leave to thee.
I prithee let thy wife attend on her,
And bring them after in the best advantage.°
Come, Desdemona. I have but an hour
300 Of love, of worldly matters and direction,
To spend with thee. We must obey the time.

            Exit Moor and Desdemona.

Roderigo: Iago, —
Iago: What say'st thou, noble heart?
Roderigo: What will I do, think'st thou?
305 Iago: Why, go to bed and sleep.
Roderigo: I will incontinently° drown myself.
Iago: If thou dost, I shall never love thee after. Why,
thou silly gentleman!
Roderigo: It is silliness to live when to live is torment;
310 and then have we a prescription to die when death is
our physician.
Iago: O villainous! I have looked upon the world for
four times seven years; and since I could distinguish
betwixt a benefit and an injury, I never found man
315 that knew how to love himself. Ere I would say I

would drown myself for the love of a guinea hen, I
would change my humanity with a baboon.
Roderigo: What should I do? I confess it is my shame
to be so fond, but it is not in my virtue to amend it.
Iago: Virtue? a fig! 'Tis in ourselves that we are thus or   320
thus. Our bodies are our gardens, to which our wills
are gardeners; so that if we will plant nettles or sow
lettuce, set hyssop and weed up thyme, supply it with
one gender° of herbs or distract it with many —
either to have it sterile with idleness or manured with   325
industry — why, the power and corrigible authority°
of this lies in our wills. If the balance of our lives had
not one scale of reason to poise° another of sensuality, the blood and baseness° of our natures would
conduct us to most preposterous conclusions. But we   330
have reason to cool our raging motions,° our carnal
strings, our unbitted° lusts; whereof I take this that
you call love to be a sect or scion.°
Roderigo: It cannot be.
Iago: It is merely a lust of the blood and a permission of   335
the will. Come, be a man! Drown thyself? Drown
cats and blind puppies! I have professed me thy
friend, and I confess me knit to thy deserving with
cables of perdurable toughness. I could never better
stead thee than now. Put money in thy purse. Follow   340
thou the wars; defeat thy favor° with an usurped
beard. I say, put money in thy purse. It cannot be that
Desdemona should long continue her love to the
Moor — put money in thy purse — nor he his to her.
It was a violent commencement in her, and thou shalt   345
see an answerable sequestration° — put but money
in thy purse. These Moors are changeable in their
wills — fill thy purse with money. The food that to
him now is as luscious as locusts shall be to him
shortly as bitter as coloquintida.° She must change   350
for youth: when she is sated with his body, she will
find the error of her choice. [She must have change,
she must.] Therefore put money in thy purse. If thou
wilt needs damn thyself, do it a more delicate way
than drowning. Make° all the money thou canst. If   355
sanctimony and a frail vow betwixt an erring° barbarian and a supersubtle Venetian be not too hard
for my wits and all the tribe of hell, thou shalt enjoy
her. Therefore make money. A pox of drowning thyself! 'Tis clean out of the way. Seek thou rather to   360
be hanged in compassing thy joy than to be drowned
and go without her.
Roderigo: Wilt thou be fast to my hopes, if I depend on
the issue?
Iago: Thou art sure of me. Go, make money. I have told   365
thee often, and I retell thee again and again, I hate the

---

272. **That:** So that.   274. **indign:** Unworthy.   275. **estimation:** Reputation.   284. **import:** Concern.   290. **delighted:**
Delightful.   298. **in the best advantage:** At the best opportunity.   306. **incontinently:** Forthwith.

324. **gender:** Species.   326. **corrigible authority:** Corrective
power.   328. **poise:** Counterbalance.   329. **blood and baseness:** Animal instincts.   331. **motions:** Appetites.   332. **unbit-
ted:** Uncontrolled.   333. **sect or scion:** Offshoot, cutting.
341. **defeat thy favor:** Spoil thy appearance.   346. **sequestra-
tion:** Estrangement.   350. **coloquintida:** A medicine.
355. **Make:** Raise.   356. **erring:** Wandering.

Moor. My cause is hearted;° thine hath no less rea-
son. Let us be conjunctive in our revenge against him.
If thou canst cuckold him, thou dost thyself a plea-
370   sure, me a sport. There are many events in the womb
of time, which will be delivered. Traverse,° go, pro-
vide thy money! We will have more of this tomorrow.
Adieu.
RODERIGO: Where shall we meet i' th' morning?
375 IAGO: At my lodging.
RODERIGO: I'll be with thee betimes.
IAGO: Go to, farewell — Do you hear, Roderigo?
[RODERIGO: What say you?
IAGO: No more of drowning, do you hear?
380 RODERIGO: I am changed.
IAGO: Go to, farewell. Put money enough in your
purse.]
RODERIGO: I'll sell all my land.   *Exit.*
IAGO: Thus do I ever make my fool my purse;
For I mine own gained knowledge should profane
385 If I would time expend with such a snipe°
But for my sport and profit. I hate the Moor;
And it is thought abroad that 'twixt my sheets
H'as done my office. I know not if't be true;
But I, for mere suspicion in that kind,
390 Will do as if for surety. He holds me well;°
The better shall my purpose work on him.
Cassio's a proper man. Let me see now:
To get his place, and to plume up° my will
In double knavery — How, how? — Let's see: —
395 After some time, to abuse Othello's ears
That he is too familiar with his wife.
He hath a person and a smooth dispose°
To be suspected — framed to make women false.
The Moor is of a free° and open nature
400 That thinks men honest that but seem to be so;
And will as tenderly be led by th' nose
As asses are.
I have't! It is engend'red! Hell and night
Must bring this monstrous birth to the world's light.
                       Exit.

ACT II • *Scene* I

An open place in Cyprus, near the harbor.

Enter Montano and two Gentlemen.

MONTANO: What from the cape can you discern at sea?
1. GENTLEMAN: Nothing at all: it is a high-wrought
flood.
I cannot 'twixt the heaven and the main
Descry a sail.
5 MONTANO: Methinks the wind hath spoke aloud at land;

A fuller blast ne'er shook our battlements.
If it hath ruffianed so upon the sea,
What ribs of oak, when mountains melt on them,
Can hold the mortise?° What shall we hear of this?
2. GENTLEMAN: A segregation° of the Turkish fleet.   10
For do but stand upon the foaming shore,
The chidden billow seems to pelt the clouds;
The wind-shaked surge, with high and monstrous
mane,
Seems to cast water on the burning Bear
And quench the Guards° of th' ever-fixèd pole.°   15
I never did like molestation° view
On the enchafèd flood.
MONTANO: If that the Turkish fleet
Be not ensheltered and embayed, they are drowned;
It is impossible to bear it out.

Enter a third Gentleman.

3. GENTLEMAN: News, lads! Our wars are done.   20
The desperate tempest hath so banged the Turks
That their designment halts.° A noble ship of Venice
Hath seen a grievous wrack and sufferance°
On most part of their fleet.
MONTANO: How? Is this true?
3. GENTLEMAN: The ship is here put in,   25
A Veronesa;° Michael Cassio,
Lieutenant to the warlike Moor Othello,
Is come on shore; the Moor himself at sea,
And is in full commission here for Cyprus.
MONTANO: I am glad on't. 'Tis a worthy governor.   30
3. GENTLEMAN: But his same Cassio, though he speak
of comfort
Touching the Turkish loss, yet he looks sadly
And prays the Moor be safe, for they were parted
With foul and violent tempest.
MONTANO: Pray heaven he be;
For I have served him, and the man commands   35
Like a full soldier. Let's to the seaside, ho!
As well to see the vessel that's come in
As to throw out our eyes for brave Othello,
Even till we make the main and th' aerial blue
An indistinct regard.°
3. GENTLEMAN: Come, let's do so;   40
For every minute is expectancy
Of more arrivance.

Enter Cassio.

CASSIO: Thanks, you the valiant of this warlike isle,
That so approve the Moor! O, let the heavens
Give him defense against the elements,   45
For I have lost him on a dangerous sea!
MONTANO: Is he well shipped?

---

367. **My cause is hearted:** My heart is in it.   371. **Traverse:** Forward march.   385. **snipe:** Fool.   390. **well:** In high regard.
393. **plume up:** Gratify.   397. **dispose:** Manner.   399. **free:**
Frank.

II, I. 9. **hold the mortise:** Hold their joints together.   10. **segregation:** Scattering.   15. **Guards:** Stars near the North Star.
pole: Polestar.   16. **molestation:** Tumult.   22. **designment halts:**
Plan is crippled.   23. **sufferance:** Disaster.   26. **Veronesa:**
Ship furnished by Verona.   40. **An indistinct regard:** Indistinguishable.

CASSIO: His bark is stoutly timbered, and his pilot
    Of very expert and approved allowance;
50   Therefore my hopes, not surfeited to death,°
    Stand in bold cure.°
      (*Within.*)   A sail, a sail, a sail!

Enter a messenger.

CASSIO: What noise?
MESSENGER: The town is empty; on the brow o' th' sea
    Stand ranks of people, and they cry "A sail!"
55 CASSIO: My hopes do shape him for the governor.

A shot.

2. GENTLEMAN: They do discharge their shot of
    courtesy:
    Our friends at least.
CASSIO: I pray you, sir, go forth
    And give us truth who 'tis that is arrived.
2. GENTLEMAN: I shall.   *Exit.*
MONTANO: But, good lieutenant, is your general
60   wived?
CASSIO: Most fortunately. He hath achieved a maid
    That paragons° description and wild fame;
    One that excels the quirks° of blazoning° pens,
    And in th' essential vesture of creation
    Does tire the ingener.°

Enter Second Gentleman.

65   How now? Who has put in?
2. GENTLEMAN: 'Tis one Iago, ancient to the general.
CASSIO: H'as had most favorable and happy speed:
    Tempests themselves, high seas, and howling winds,
    The guttered° rocks and congregated sands,
70   Traitors ensteeped° to clog the guiltless keel,
    As having sense of beauty, do omit
    Their mortal° natures, letting go safely by
    The divine Desdemona.
MONTANO: What is she?
CASSIO: She that I spake of, our great captain's captain,
75   Left in the conduct of the bold Iago,
    Whose footing° here anticipates our thoughts
    A se'nnight's° speed. Great Jove, Othello guard,
    And swell his sail with thine own pow'rful breath,
    That he may bless this bay with his tall ship,
80   Make love's quick pants in Desdemona's arms,
    Give renewed fire to our extinct spirits,
    [And bring all Cyprus comfort!]

Enter Desdemona, Iago, Roderigo, and Emilia [with Attendants].

        O, behold!

    The riches of the ship is come on shore!
    You men of Cyprus, let her have your knees.°
    Hail to thee, lady! and the grace of heaven,   85
    Before, behind thee, and on every hand,
    Enwheel thee round!
DESDEMONA: I thank you, valiant Cassio.
    What tidings can you tell me of my lord?
CASSIO: He is not yet arrived; nor know I aught
    But that he's well and will be shortly here.   90
DESDEMONA: O but I fear! How lost you company?
CASSIO: The great contention of the sea and skies
    Parted our fellowship.
      (*Within.*)   A sail, a sail! [*A shot.*]
                  But hark. A sail!
2. GENTLEMAN: They give their greeting to the citadel;
    This likewise is a friend.
CASSIO: See for the news.   95

        [*Exit Gentleman.*]

    Good ancient, you are welcome.
    [*To Emilia.*]   Welcome, mistress. —
    Let it not gall your patience, good Iago,
    That I extend my manners. 'Tis my breeding
    That gives me this bold show of courtesy.

[*Kisses Emilia.*°]

IAGO: Sir, would she give you so much of her lips   100
    As of her tongue she oft bestows on me,
    You would have enough.
DESDEMONA: Alas, she has no speech!
IAGO: In faith, too much.
    I find it still when I have list to sleep.
    Marry, before your ladyship, I grant,   105
    She puts her tongue a little in her heart
    And chides with thinking.
EMILIA: You have little cause to say so.
IAGO: Come on, come on! You are pictures out of
    doors,
    Bells in your parlors, wildcats in your kitchens,   110
    Saints in your injuries, devils being offended,
    Players in your housewifery,° and housewives° in
    your beds.
DESDEMONA: O, fie upon thee, slanderer!
IAGO: Nay, it is true, or else I am a Turk:
    You rise to play, and go to bed to work.   115
EMILIA: You shall not write my praise.
IAGO: No, let me out.
DESDEMONA: What wouldst thou write of me, if thou
    shouldst praise me?
IAGO: O gentle lady, do not put me to't,
    For I am nothing if not critical.
DESDEMONA: Come on, assay.° — There's one gone to
    the harbor?   120

---

50. **surfeited to death:** Overindulged. 51. **in bold cure:** A good chance of fulfillment. 62. **paragons:** Surpasses. 63. **quirks:** Ingenuities. **blazoning:** Describing. 64–65. **And . . . ingener:** Merely to describe her as God made her exhausts her praiser. 69. **guttered:** Jagged. 70. **ensteeped:** Submerged. 72. **mortal:** Deadly. 76. **footing:** Landing. 77. **se'nnight's:** Week's.

84. **knees:** I.e., kneeling. [S.D.] *Kisses Emilia:* (Kissing was a common Elizabethan form of social courtesy). 112. **housewifery:** Housekeeping. **housewives:** Hussies. 120. **assay:** Try.

IAGO: Ay, madam.

DESDEMONA: I am not merry; but I do beguile
    The thing I am by seeming otherwise. —
    Come, how wouldst thou praise me?

125 IAGO: I am about it; but indeed my invention
    Comes from my pate as birdlime° does from
        freize° —
    It plucks out brains and all. But my Muse labors,
    And thus she is delivered:
    If she be fair and wise, fairness and wit —
130 The one's for use, the other useth it.

DESDEMONA: Well praised! How if she be black° and
    witty?

IAGO: If she be black, and thereto have a wit,
    She'll find a white that shall her blackness fit.

DESDEMONA: Worse and worse!

135 EMILIA: How if fair and foolish?

IAGO: She never yet was foolish that was fair,
    For even her folly° helped her to an heir.

DESDEMONA: These are old fond° paradoxes to make
    fools laugh i' th' alehouse. What miserable praise
140 hast thou for her that's foul° and foolish?

IAGO: There's none so foul, and foolish thereunto,
    But does foul pranks which fair and wise ones do.

DESDEMONA: O heavy ignorance! Thou praisest the
    worst best. But what praise couldst thou bestow on a
145 deserving woman indeed — one that in the authority
    of her merit did justly put on the vouch° of very mal-
    ice itself?

IAGO: She that was ever fair, and never proud;
    Had tongue at will, and yet was never loud;
150 Never lacked gold, and yet went never gay;
    Fled from her wish, and yet said "Now I may";
    She that, being ang'red, her revenge being nigh,
    Bade her wrong stay, and her displeasure fly;
    She that in wisdom never was so frail
155 To change the cod's head for the salmon's tail;°
    She that could think, and ne'er disclose her mind;
    See suitors following, and not look behind:
    She was a wight (if ever such wight were) —

DESDEMONA: To do what?

160 IAGO: To suckle fools and chronicle small beer.°

DESDEMONA: O most lame and impotent conclusion!
    Do not learn of him, Emilia, though he be thy hus-
    band. How say you, Cassio? Is he not a most profane
    and liberal° counsellor?

165 CASSIO: He speaks home,° madam. You may relish him
    more in the soldier than in the scholar.

IAGO [aside]: He takes her by the palm. Ay, well said,
    whisper! With as little a web as this will I ensnare as
    great a fly as Cassio. Ay, smile upon her, do! I will
    gyve thee in thine own courtship.° — You say true; 170
    'tis so, indeed! — If such tricks as these strip you out
    of your lieutenantry, it had been better you had not
    kissed your three fingers so oft — which now again
    you are most apt to play the sir° in. Very good! well
    kissed! an excellent courtesy! 'Tis so, indeed. Yet 175
    again your fingers to your lips? Would they were
    clyster pipes° for your sake! (*Trumpet within.*) The
    Moor! I know his trumpet.

CASSIO: 'Tis truly so.

DESDEMONA: Let's meet him and receive him.   180

CASSIO: Lo, where he comes.

Enter Othello and Attendants.

OTHELLO: O my fair warrior!

DESDEMONA: My dear Othello!

OTHELLO: It gives me wonder great as my content
    To see you here before me. O my soul's joy!
    If after every tempest come such calms,   185
    May the winds blow till they have wakened death!
    And let the laboring bark climb hills of seas
    Olympus-high, and duck again as low
    As hell's from heaven! If it were now to die,
    'Twere now to be most happy;° for I fear   190
    My soul hath her content so absolute
    That not another comfort like to this
    Succeeds in unknown fate.

DESDEMONA: The heavens forbid
    But that our loves and comforts should increase
    Even as our days do grow.

OTHELLO: Amen to that, sweet powers! 195
    I cannot speak enough of this content;
    It stops me here; it is too much of joy.
    And this, and this, the greatest discords be

They kiss.

    That e'er our hearts shall make!

IAGO [aside]:   O, you are well
        tuned now!
    But I'll set down° the pegs that make this music, 200
    As honest as I am.

OTHELLO: Come, let us to the castle.
    News, friends! Our wars are done; the Turks are
        drowned.
    How does my old acquaintance of this isle? —
    Honey, you shall be well desired° in Cyprus;
    I have found great love amongst them. O my sweet, 205
    I prattle out of fashion, and I dote
    In mine own comforts. I prithee, good Iago,
    Go to the bay and disembark my coffers.
    Bring thou the master° to the citadel;

126. **birdlime:** A sticky paste. **freize:** Rough cloth.
131. **black:** Brunette. 137. **folly:** Wantonness. 138. **fond:**
Foolish. 140. **foul:** Ugly. 146. **put on the vouch:** Compel
the approval. 155. **To . . . tail:** I.e., to exchange the good for
the poor but expensive. 160. **chronicle small beer:** Keep petty
household accounts. 164. **profane and liberal:** Worldly and
licentious. 165. **home:** Bluntly.

170. **gyve . . . courtship:** Manacle you by means of your
courtly manners. 174. **sir:** Courtly gentleman. 177. **clyster
pipes:** Syringes. 190. **happy:** Fortunate. 200. **set down:**
Loosen. 204. **well desired:** Warmly welcomed. 209. **master:**
Ship captain.

Sir Laurence Olivier as Othello and
Maggie Smith as Desdemona in a tense
moment in his National Theatre
production of *Othello* in London, 1964.

John Douglas Thomas as Othello and
Jennifer Mudge Tucker as Desdemona in
the Trinity Repertory production of
Othello, Providence, Rhode Island, 1998.

210 He is a good one, and his worthiness
Does challenge° much respect. — Come,
Desdemona,
Once more well met at Cyprus.

Exit Othello [with all but Iago and Roderigo].

IAGO: [*to an Attendant, who goes out*]: Do thou meet
me presently at the harbor. [*To Roderigo.*] Come
215 hither. If thou be'st valiant (as they say base men
being in love have then a nobility in their natures
more than is native to them), list me. The lieutenant
to-night watches on the court of guard.° First, I must
tell thee this: Desdemona is directly in love with him.
220 RODERIGO: With him? Why, 'tis not possible.
IAGO: Lay thy finger thus,° and let thy soul be instructed.
Mark me with what violence she first loved the
Moor, but for bragging and telling her fantastical
lies; and will she love him still for prating? Let not
225 thy discreet heart think it. Her eye must be fed; and
what delight shall she have to look on the devil?
When the blood is made dull with the act of sport,
there should be, again to inflame it, and to give satiety a fresh appetite, loveliness in favor, sympathy in
230 years, manners, and beauties; all which the Moor is
defective in. Now for want of these required conveniences,° her delicate tenderness will find itself
abused, begin to heave the gorge,° disrelish and
abhor the Moor. Very nature will instruct her in it
235 and compel her to some second choice. Now, sir, this
granted — as it is a most pregnant° and unforced
position — who stands so eminent in the degree of
this fortune as Cassio does? A knave very voluble; no
further conscionable° than in putting on the mere
240 form of civil and humane° seeming for the better
compassing of his salt° and most hidden loose affection? Why, none! why, none! A slipper° and subtle
knave; a finder-out of occasions; that has an eye can
stamp and counterfeit advantages, though true advan-
245 tage never present itself; a devilish knave! Besides,
the knave is handsome, young, and hath all those
requisites in him that folly and green minds look
after. A pestilent complete knave! and the woman
hath found him already.
250 RODERIGO: I cannot believe that in her; she's full of
most blessed condition.°
IAGO: Blessed fig's-end! The wine she drinks is made of
grapes. If she had been blessed, she would never have
loved the Moor. Blessed pudding! Didst thou not see
255 her paddle with the palm of his hand? Didst not
mark that?
RODERIGO: Yes, that I did; but that was but courtesy.

IAGO: Lechery, by this hand! an index and obscure
prologue to the history of lust and foul thoughts.
260 They met so near with their lips that their breaths
embraced together. Villainous thoughts, Roderigo!
When these mutualities° so marshal the way, hard at
hand comes the master and main exercise, th' incor-
porate° conclusion. Pish! But, sir, be you ruled by me:
265 I have brought you from Venice. Watch you to-night;
for the command, I'll lay't upon you. Cassio knows
you not. I'll not be far from you: do you find some
occasion to anger Cassio, either by speaking too
loud, or tainting° his discipline, or from what other
270 course you please which the time shall more favorably minister.
RODERIGO: Well.
IAGO: Sir, he's rash and very sudden in choler,° and haply
with his truncheon may strike at you. Provoke him
275 that he may; for even out of that will I cause these of
Cyprus to mutiny; whose qualification° shall come
into no true taste° again but by the displanting of
Cassio. So shall you have a shorter journey to your
desires by the means I shall then have to prefer°
280 them; and the impediment most profitably removed
without the which there were no expectation of our
prosperity.
RODERIGO: I will do this if you can bring it to any
opportunity.
285 IAGO: I warrant thee. Meet me by and by at the citadel; I
must fetch his necessaries ashore. Farewell.
RODERIGO: Adieu.   *Exit.*
IAGO: That Cassio loves her, I do well believe't;
That she loves him, 'tis apt° and of great credit.
290 The Moor, howbeit that I endure him not,
Is of a constant, loving, noble nature,
And I dare think he'll prove to Desdemona
A most dear husband. Now I do love her too;
Not out of absolute lust, though peradventure
295 I stand accountant° for as great a sin,
But partly led to diet° my revenge,
For that I do suspect the lusty Moor
Hath leaped into my seat; the thought whereof
Doth, like a poisonous mineral, gnaw my inwards;
300 And nothing can or shall content my soul
Till I am evened with him, wife for wife;
Or failing so, yet that I put the Moor
At least into a jealousy so strong
That judgment cannot cure. Which thing to do,
305 If this poor trash of Venice, whom I trash°
For° his quick hunting, stand the putting on,°
I'll have our Michael Cassio on the hip,°

211. **challenge:** Deserve.   218. **court of guard:** Headquarters.
221. **thus:** I.e., on your lips.   231–32. **conveniences:** Compati-
bilities.   233. **heave the gorge:** Be nauseated.   236. **pregnant:**
Evident.   239. **conscionable:** Conscientious.   240. **humane:**
Polite.   241. **salt:** Lecherous.   242. **slipper:** Slippery.
251. **condition:** Character.

262. **mutualities:** Exchanges.   263–64. **incorporate:** Carnal.
269. **tainting:** Discrediting.   273. **sudden in choler:** Violent in
anger.   276. **qualification:** Appeasement.   277. **true taste:**
Satisfactory state.   279. **prefer:** Advance.   289. **apt:** Probable.
295. **accountant:** Accountable.   296. **diet:** Feed.   305. **I trash:**
I weight down (in order to keep under control).   306. **For:** In
order to develop.   **stand the putting on:** Responds to my incit-
ing.   307. **on the hip:** At my mercy.

Abuse him to the Moor in the rank garb°
(For I fear Cassio with my nightcap too),
310 Make the Moor thank me, love me, and reward me
For making him egregiously an ass
And practicing upon° his peace and quiet
Even to madness. 'Tis here, but yet confused:
Knavery's plain face is never seen till used.   *Exit.*

Scene II

A street in Cyprus.

Enter Othello's Herald, with a proclamation.

HERALD: It is Othello's pleasure, our noble and valiant
general, that, upon certain tidings now arrived,
importing the mere perdition° of the Turkish fleet,
every man put himself into triumph; some to dance,
5 some to make bonfires, each man to what sport and
revels his addiction leads him. For, besides these beneficial news, it is the celebration of his nuptial. So
much was his pleasure should be proclaimed. All
offices° are open, and there is full liberty of feasting
10 from the present hour of five till the bell have told
eleven. Heaven bless the isle of Cyprus and our noble
general Othello!   *Exit.*

Scene III

The Cyprian Castle.

Enter Othello, Desdemona, Cassio, and Attendants.

OTHELLO: Good Michael, look you to the guard tonight.
    Let's teach ourselves that honorable stop,
    Not to outsport discretion.
CASSIO: Iago hath direction what to do;
5   But not withstanding, with my personal eye
    Will I look to't.
OTHELLO: Iago is most honest.
    Michael, good night. To-morrow with your earliest
    Let me have speech with you.
    [To Desdemona.]   Come, my dear love.
    The purchase made, the fruits are to ensue;
10   That profit's yet to come 'tween me and you. —
    Good night.

         Exit [Othello with Desdemona and Attendants].

Enter Iago.

CASSIO: Welcome, Iago. We must to the watch.
IAGO: Not this hour, lieutenant; 'tis not yet ten o' th'
clock. Our general cast° us thus early for the love of

his Desdemona; who let us not therefore blame. He   15
hath not yet made wanton the night with her, and she
is sport for Jove.
CASSIO: She's a most exquisite lady.
IAGO: And, I'll warrant her, full of game.
CASSIO: Indeed, she's a most fresh and delicate creature.   20
IAGO: What an eye she has! Methinks it sounds a parley
to provocation.
CASSIO: An inviting eye; and yet methinks right modest.
IAGO: And when she speaks, is it not an alarum to love?
CASSIO: She is indeed perfection.   25
IAGO: Well, happiness to their sheets! Come, lieutenant,
I have a stoup° of wine, and here without are a brace
of Cyprus gallants that would fain have a measure to
the health of black Othello.
CASSIO: Not to-night, good Iago. I have very poor and   30
unhappy brains for drinking; I could well wish cour-
tesy would invent some other custom of entertain-
ment.
IAGO: O, they are our friends. But one cup! I'll drink for
you.   35
CASSIO: I have drunk but one cup to-night, and that was
craftily qualified° too; and behold what innovation°
it makes here. I am unfortunate in the infirmity and
dare not task my weakness with any more.
IAGO: What, man! 'Tis a night of revels: the gallants de-   40
sire it.
CASSIO: Where are they?
IAGO: Here at the door; I pray you call them in.
CASSIO: I'll do't, but it dislikes me.   *Exit.*
IAGO: If I can fasten but one cup upon him   45
    With that which he hath drunk to-night already,
    He'll be as full of quarrel and offense
    As my young mistress' dog. Now my sick fool
        Roderigo,
    Whom love hath turned almost the wrong side out,
    To Desdemona hath to-night caroused   50
    Potations pottle-deep;° and he's to watch.
    Three lads of Cyprus — noble swelling spirits,
    That hold their honors in a wary distance,°
    The very elements° of this warlike isle —
    Have I to-night flustered with flowing cups,   55
    And they watch too. Now, 'mongst this flock of
        drunkards
    Am I to put our Cassio in some action
    That may offend the isle.

*Enter Cassio, Montano, and Gentlemen [; Servants fol-
lowing with wine].*

                      But here they come.
    If consequence do but approve my dream,
    My boat sails freely, both with wind and stream.   60
CASSIO: 'Fore God, they have given me a rouse° already.

---

308. rank garb: Gross manner.   312. practicing upon: Plotting against.   II, II. 3. mere perdition: Complete destruction.
9. offices: Kitchens and storerooms.   II, III. 14. cast: Dismissed.

27. stoup: Two-quart tankard.   37. qualified: Diluted.   innovation: Disturbance.   51. pottle-deep: Bottoms up.   53. That
. . . distance: Very sensitive about their honor.   54. very elements: True representatives.   61. rouse: Bumper.

MONTANO: Good faith, a little one; not past a pint, as I
  am a soldier.
IAGO: Some wine, ho!
  [*Sings.*]
65   And let me the canakin clink, clink;
    And let me the canakin clink
      A soldier's a man;
      A life's but a span,
    Why then, let a soldier drink.
70   Some wine, boys!
CASSIO: 'Fore God, an excellent song!
IAGO: I learned it in England, where indeed they are most
  potent in potting. Your Dane, your German, and your
  swag-bellied Hollander — Drink, ho! — are nothing
75 to your English.
CASSIO: Is your Englishman so expert in his drinking?
IAGO: Why, he drinks you with facility your Dane dead
  drunk; he sweats not to overthrow your Almain; he
  gives your Hollander a vomit ere the next pottle can
80 be filled.
CASSIO: To the health of our general!
MONTANO: I am for it, lieutenant, and I'll do you
  justice.
IAGO: O sweet England!
  [*Sings.*]
85   King Stephen was a worthy peer;
      His breeches cost him but a crown;
    He held 'em sixpence all too dear,
      With that he called the tailor lown.°
    He was a wight of high renown,
90   And thou art but of low degree.
    'Tis pride that pulls the country down;
      Then take thine auld cloak about thee.
    Some wine, ho!
CASSIO: 'Fore God, this is a more exquisite song than
95 the other.
IAGO: Will you hear't again?
CASSIO: No, for I hold him to be unworthy of his place
  that does those things.° Well, God's above all; and
  there be souls must be saved, and there be souls must
100 not be saved.
IAGO: It's true, good lieutenant.
CASSIO: For mine own part — no offense to the general,
  nor any man of quality — I hope to be saved.
IAGO: And so do I too, lieutenant.
105 CASSIO: Ay but, by your leave, not before me. The lieutenant is to be saved before the ancient. Let's have no
  more of this; let's to our affairs. — God forgive us
  our sins! — Gentlemen, let's look to our business. Do
  not think, gentlemen, I am drunk. This is my ancient;
110 this is my right hand, and this is my left. I am not
  drunk now. I can stand well enough, and I speak well
  enough.
ALL: Excellent well!
CASSIO: Why, very well then. You must not think then
115 that I am drunk.   *Exit.*

88. **lown:** Rascal.   98. **does . . . things:** I.e., behaves in this
fashion.

MONTANO: To th' platform, masters. Come, let's set the
  watch.
IAGO: You see this fellow that is gone before.
  He's a soldier fit to stand by Caesar
  And give direction; and do but see his vice.
  'Tis to his virtue a just equinox,°   120
  The one as long as th' other. 'Tis pity of him.
  I fear the trust Othello puts him in,
  On some odd time of his infirmity,
  Will shake this island.
MONTANO: But is he often thus?
IAGO: 'Tis evermore his prologue to his sleep: 125
  He'll watch the horologe a double set°
  If drink rock not his cradle.
MONTANO: It were well
  The general were put in mind of it.
  Perhaps he sees it not, or his good nature
  Prizes the virtue that appears in Cassio   130
  And looks not on his evils. Is not this true?

Enter Roderigo.

IAGO [*aside to him*]: How now, Roderigo?
  I pray you after the lieutenant, go!   *Exit Roderigo.*
MONTANO: And 'tis great pity that the noble Moor
  Should hazard such a place as his own second   135
  With one of an ingraft° infirmity.
  It were an honest action to say
  So to the Moor.
IAGO: Not I, for this fair island!
  I do love Cassio well and would do much
  To cure him of this evil.
    (*Within:* Help! help!)
                But hark! What noise?   140

Enter Cassio, driving in Roderigo.

CASSIO: Zounds, you rogue! you rascal!
MONTANO: What's the matter, lieutenant?
CASSIO: A knave to
  teach me my duty?
  I'll beat the knave into a twiggen° bottle.
RODERIGO: Beat me?
CASSIO: Dost thou prate, rogue?

[*Strikes him.*]

MONTANO: Nay, good lieutenant!

[*Stays him.*]

  I pray you, sir, hold your hand.
CASSIO: Let me go, sir,   145
  Or I'll knock you o'er the mazzard.°
MONTANO: Come, come,
  you're drunk!
CASSIO: Drunk?

They fight.

120. **just equinox:** Exact equivalent.   126. **watch . . . set:** Stay
awake twice around the clock.   136. **ingraft:** I.e., ingrained.
143. **twiggen:** Wicker-covered.   146. **mazzard:** Head.

IAGO [*aside to Roderigo*]: Away, I say! Go out and cry
      a mutiny!   *Exit Roderigo.*
   Nay, good lieutenant. God's will, gentlemen!
   Help, ho! — lieutenant — sir — Montano — sir —
150   Help, masters! — Here's a goodly watch indeed!

A bell rung.

   Who's that which rings the bell? Diablo, ho!
   The town will rise.° God's will, lieutenant, hold!
   You'll be shamed for ever.

Enter Othello and Gentlemen with weapons.

OTHELLO: What is the matter here?
MONTANO: Zounds, I bleed still. I am hurt to th' death.
      He dies.
155 OTHELLO: Hold for your lives!
IAGO: Hold, hold! Lieutenant — sir — Montano —
      gentlemen!
   Have you forgot all sense of place and duty?
   Hold! The general speaks to you. Hold, for shame!
OTHELLO: Why, how now ho? From whence ariseth
      this?
160   Are we turned Turks, and to ourselves do that
   Which heaven hath forbid the Ottomites?
   For Christian shame put by this barbarous brawl!
   He that stirs next to carve for° his own rage
   Holds his soul light; he dies upon his motion.
165   Silence that dreadful bell! It frights the isle
   From her propriety.° What is the matter, masters?
   Honest Iago, that looks dead with grieving,
   Speak. Who began this? On thy love, I charge thee.
IAGO: I do not know. Friends all, but now, even now,
170   In quarter,° and in terms like bride and groom
   Devesting them for bed; and then, but now —
   As if some planet had unwitted men —
   Swords out, and tilting one at other's breast
   In opposition bloody. I cannot speak
175   Any beginning to this peevish odds,°
   And would in action glorious I had lost
   Those legs that brought me to a part of it!
OTHELLO: How comes it, Michael, you are thus
      forgot?
CASSIO: I pray you pardon me; I cannot speak.
OTHELLO: Worthy Montano, you were wont to be
180   civil;
   The gravity and stillness of your youth
   The world hath noted, and your name is great
   In months of wisest censure.° What's the matter
   That you unlace° your reputation thus
185   And spend your rich opinion° for the name
   Of a night-brawler? Give me answer to it.
MONTANO: Worthy Othello, I am hurt to danger.
   Your officer, Iago, can inform you,

While I spare speech, which something now
      offends° me,
Of all that I do know; nor know I aught   190
By me that's said or done amiss this night,
Unless self-charity be sometimes a vice,
And to defend ourselves it be a sin
When violence assails us.
OTHELLO: Now, by heaven,
   My blood° begins my safer guides to rule,   195
   And passion, having my best judgment collied,°
   Assays° to lead the way. If I once stir
   Or do but lift this arm, the best of you
   Shall sink in my rebuke. Give me to know
   How this foul rout began, who set it on;   200
   And he that is approved in° this offense,
   Though he had twinned with me, both at a birth,
   Shall lose me. What! in a town of war,
   Yet wild, the people's hearts brimful of fear,
   To manage° private and domestic quarrel?   205
   In night, and on the court and guard of safety?
   'Tis monstrous. Iago, who began't?
MONTANO: If partially affined, or leagued in office,°
   Thou dost deliver more or less than truth,
   Thou art no soldier.
IAGO: Touch me not so near.   210
   I had rather have this tongue cut from my mouth
   Than it should do offense to Michael Cassio;
   Yet I persuade myself, to speak the truth
   Shall nothing wrong him. This it is, general.
   Montano and myself being in speech,   215
   There comes a fellow crying out for help,
   And Cassio following him with determined sword
   To execute° upon him. Sir, this gentleman
   Steps in to Cassio and entreats his pause.
   Myself the crying fellow did pursue,   220
   Lest by his clamor — as it so fell out —
   The town might fall in fright. He, swift of foot,
   Outran my purpose; and I returned then rather
   For that I heard the clink and fall of swords,
   And Cassio high in oath;° which till to-night   225
   I ne'er might say before. When I came back —
   For this was brief — I found them close together
   At blow and thrust, even as again they were
   When you yourself did part them.
   More of this matter cannot I report;   230
   But men are men; the best sometimes forget.
   Though Cassio did some little wrong to him,
   As men in rage strike those that wish them best,
   Yet surely Cassio I believe received
   From him that fled some strange indignity,   235
   Which patience could not pass.°

---

152. rise: Grow riotous.   163. carve for: Indulge.   166. propriety: Proper self.   170. quarter: Friendliness.   175. peevish
odds: Childish quarrel.   183. censure: Judgment.   184. un-
lace: Undo.   185. rich opinion: High reputation.

189. offends: Pains.   195. blood: Passion.   196. collied:
Darkened.   197. Assays: Tries.   201. approved in: Proved
guilty of.   205. manage: Carry on.   208. partially . . . office:
Prejudiced by comradeship or official relations.   218. execute:
Work his will.   225. high in oath: Cursing.   236. pass: Pass
over, ignore.

OTHELLO: I know, Iago,
Thy honesty and love doth mince this matter,
Making it light to Cassio. Cassio, I love thee;
But never more be officer of mine.

Enter Desdemona, attended.

240   Look if my gentle love be not raised up!
I'll make thee an example.
DESDEMONA: What's the matter?
OTHELLO: All's well now, sweeting; come away to bed.

[*To Montano.*]

Sir, for your hurts, myself will be your surgeon.
Lead him off.

[*Montano is led off.*]

245   Iago, look with care about the town
And silence those whom this vile brawl distracted.°
Come, Desdemona; 'tis the soldiers' life
To have their balmy slumbers waked with strife.

Exit [with all but Iago and Cassio].

IAGO: What, are you hurt, lieutenant?
250   CASSIO: Ay, past all surgery.
IAGO: Marry, God forbid!
CASSIO: Reputation, reputation, reputation! O, I have
lost my reputation! I have lost the immortal part of
myself, and what remains is bestial. My reputation,
255   Iago, my reputation!
IAGO: As I am an honest man, I thought you had received some bodily wound. There is more sense in
that than in reputation. Reputation is an idle and
most false imposition; oft got without merit and lost
260   without deserving. You have lost no reputation at all
unless you repute yourself such a loser. What, man!
there are ways to recover° the general again. You are
but now cast in his mood° — a punishment more in
policy than in malice, even so as one would beat his
265   offenseless dog to affright an imperious lion. Sue to
him again, and he's yours.
CASSIO: I will rather sue to be despised than to deceive
so good a commander with so slight, so drunken,
and so indiscreet an officer. Drunk! and speak par-
270   rot!° and squabble! swagger! swear! and discourse
fustian° with one's own shadow! O thou invisible
spirit of wine, if thou hast no name to be known by,
let us call thee devil!
IAGO: What was he that you followed with your sword?
275   What had he done to you?
CASSIO: I know not.
IAGO: Is't possible?
CASSIO: I remember a mass of things, but nothing distinctly; a quarrel, but nothing wherefore. O God, that
280   men should put an enemy in their mouths to steal

away their brains! that we should with joy, pleas-
ance, revel, and applause° transform ourselves into
beasts!
IAGO: Why, but you are now well enough. How came   285
you thus recovered?
CASSIO: It hath pleased the devil drunkenness to give
place to the devil wrath. One unperfectness shows
me another, to make me frankly despise myself.
IAGO: Come, you are too severe a moraler. As the time,   290
the place, and the condition of this country stands, I
could heartily wish this had not so befall'n; but since
it is as it is, mend it for your own good.
CASSIO: I will ask him for my place again: he shall tell
me I am a drunkard! Had I as many mouths as   295
Hydra,° such an answer would stop them all. To be
now a sensible man, by and by a fool, and presently a
beast! O strange! Every inordinate cup is unblest,
and the ingredient° is a devil.
IAGO: Come, come, good wine is a good familiar crea-   300
ture if it be well used. Exclaim no more against it.
And, good lieutenant, I think you think I love you.
CASSIO: I have well approved° it, sir. I drunk!
IAGO: You or any man living may be drunk at some
time, man. I'll tell you what you shall do. Our gen-   305
eral's wife is now the general. I may say so in this
respect, for that he hath devoted and given up himself to the contemplation, mark, and denotement of
her parts and graces. Confess yourself freely to her;
importune her help to put you in your place again.   310
She is of so free,° so kind, so apt, so blessed a disposition she holds it a vice in her goodness not to do
more than she is requested. This broken joint between you and her husband entreat her to splinter;°
and my fortunes against any lay° worth naming, this   315
crack of your love shall grow stronger than it was
before.
CASSIO: You advise me well.
IAGO: I protest, in the sincerity of love and honest kindness.
CASSIO: I think it freely; and betimes in the morning will   320
I beseech the virtuous Desdemona to undertake for
me. I am desperate of my fortunes if they check me
here.
IAGO: You are in the right. Good night, lieutenant; I must
to the watch.   325
CASSIO: Good night, honest Iago.   *Exit Cassio.*
IAGO: And what's he then that says I play the villain,
When this advice is free I give and honest,
Probal° to thinking, and indeed the course
To win the Moor again? For 'tis most easy   330
Th' inclining Desdemona to subdue°
In an honest suit; she's framed as fruitful

---

246. **distracted:** Excited. 262. **recover:** Regain favor with.
263. **in his mood:** Dismissed because of his anger. 269–70. **parrot:** Meaningless phrases. 271. **fustian:** Bombastic nonsense.

282. **applause:** Desire to please. 295. **Hydra:** Monster with
many heads. 298. **ingredient:** Contents. 302. **approved:**
Proved. 310. **free:** Bounteous. 313. **splinter:** Bind up with
splints. 314. **lay:** Wager. 329. **Probal:** Probable. 331. **subdue:** Persuade.

As the free elements. And then for her
To win the Moor — were't to renounce his baptism,
335 All seals and symbols of redeemèd sin —
His soul is so enfettered to her love
That she may make, unmake, do what she list,
Even as her appetite shall play the god
With his weak function. How am I then a villain
340 To counsel Cassio to this parallel° course,
Directly to his good? Divinity° of hell!
When devils will the blackest sins put on,°
They do suggest at first with heavenly shows,
As I do now. For whiles this honest fool
345 Plies Desdemona to repair his fortunes,
And she for him pleads strongly to the Moor,
I'll pour this pestilence into his ear,
That she repeals him° for her body's lust;
And by how much she strives to do him good,
350 She shall undo her credit with the Moor.
So will I turn her virtue into pitch,
And out of her own goodness make the net
That shall enmesh them all.

Enter Roderigo.

                        How, now, Roderigo?
RODERIGO: I do follow here in the chase, not like a
355   hound that hunts, but one that fills up the cry.° My
money is almost spent; I have been to-night exceedingly well cudgelled; and I think the issue will be — I
shall have so much experience for my pains; and so,
with no money at all, and a little more wit, return
360   again to Venice.
IAGO: How poor are they that have not patience!
What wound did ever heal but by degrees?
Thou know'st we work by wit, and not by
   witchcraft;
And wit depends on dilatory time.
365 Does't not go well? Cassio hath beaten thee,
And thou by that small hurt hast cashiered Cassio.°
Though other things grow fair against the sun,
Yet fruits that blossom first will first be ripe.
Content thyself awhile. By the mass, 'tis morning!
370 Pleasure and action make the hours seem short.
Retire thee; go where thou art billeted.
Away, I say! Thou shalt know more hereafter.
Nay, get thee gone!   *Exit Roderigo.*
            Two things are to be done:
My wife must move for Cassio to her mistress;
375 I'll set her on;
Myself the while to draw the Moor apart
And bring him jump° when he may Cassio find
Soliciting his wife. Ay, that's the way!
Dull no device by coldness and delay.   *Exit.*

---

340. parallel: Corresponding. 341. Divinity: Theology.
342. put on: Incite. 348. repeals him: Seeks his recall.
355. cry: Pack. 366. cashiered Cassio: Maneuvered Cassio's
discharge. 377. jump: At the exact moment.

ACT III • *Scene I*

Before the chamber of Othello and Desdemona.

Enter Cassio, with Musicians and the Clown.

CASSIO: Masters, play here, I will content° your pains:
   Something that's brief; and bid "Good morrow,
   general."

[*They play.*]

CLOWN: Why, masters, ha' your instruments been in
   Naples,° that they speak i' th' nose thus?
MUSICIAN: How, sir, how?   5
CLOWN: Are these, I pray you, called wind instruments?
MUSICIAN: Ay, marry, are they, sir.
CLOWN: O, thereby hangs a tail.
MUSICIAN: Whereby hangs a tail, sir?
CLOWN: Marry, sir, by many a wind instrument that I   10
   know. But, masters, here's money for you; and the
   general so likes your music that he desires you, for
   love's sake, to make no more noise with it.
MUSICIAN: Well, sir, we will not.
CLOWN: If you have any music that may not be heard,   15
   to't again: but, as they say, to hear music the general
   does not greatly care.
MUSICIAN: We have none such, sir.
CLOWN: Then put up your pipes in your bag, for I'll
   away. Go, vanish into air, away!   20

                Exit Musician [*with his fellows*].

CASSIO: Dost thou hear, my honest friend?
CLOWN: No, I hear not your honest friend. I hear you.
CASSIO: Prithee keep up thy quillets.° There's a poor
   piece of gold for thee. If the gentlewoman that at-
   tends the general's wife be stirring, tell her there's one 25
   Cassio entreats her a little favor of speech. Wilt thou
   do this?
CLOWN: She is stirring sir. If she will stir hither, I shall
   seem to notify unto her.
CASSIO: [*Do, good my friend.*]   *Exit Clown.*

Enter Iago.

                        In happy time,° Iago.   30
IAGO: You have not been abed then?
CASSIO: Why, no; the day had broke
   Before we parted. I have made bold, Iago,
   To send in to your wife: my suit to her
   Is that she will to virtuous Desdemona   35
   Procure me some access.
IAGO: I'll send her to you presently;
   And I'll devise a mean to draw the Moor
   Out of the way, that your converse and
      business
   May be more free.

III, I. 1. content: Reward. 4. Naples: (Notorious for its association with venereal disease). 23. quillets: Quips. 30. In
happy time: Well met.

CASSIO: I humbly thank you for't.   *Exit [Iago].*
40   I never knew
    A Florentine° more kind and honest.

Enter Emilia.

EMILIA: Good morrow, good lieutenant. I am sorry
    For your displeasure: but all will sure be well.
    The general and his wife are talking of it,
45 And she speaks for you stoutly. The Moor replied
    That he you hurt is of great fame in Cyprus
    And great affinity,° and that in wholesome wisdom
    He might not but refuse you; but he protests he
        loves you,
    And needs no other suitor but his likings
50 [To take the safest occasion° by the front°]
    To bring you in again.
CASSIO: Yet I beseech you,
    If you think fit, or that it may be done,
    Give me advantage of some brief discourse
    With Desdemona alone.
EMILIA: Pray you come in.
55 I will bestow you where you shall have time
    To speak your bosom° freely.
CASSIO: I am much bound to you.

                                        Exeunt.

Scene II

The castle.

Enter Othello, Iago, and Gentlemen.

OTHELLO: These letters give, Iago, to the pilot
    And by him do my duties to the Senate.
    That done, I will be walking on the works;°
    Repair there to me.
IAGO: Well, my good lord, I'll do't.
5 OTHELLO: This fortification, gentlemen, shall we see't?
GENTLEMEN: We'll wait upon your lordship.   *Exeunt.*

Scene III

The castle grounds.

Enter Desdemona, Cassio, and Emilia.

DESDEMONA: Be thou assured, good Cassio, I will do
    All my abilities in thy behalf.
EMILIA: Good madam, do. I warrant it grieves my
        husband
    As if the cause were his.
DESDEMONA: O, that's an honest fellow. Do not doubt,
5   Cassio,

    But I will have my lord and you again
    As friendly as you were.
CASSIO: Bounteous madam,
    Whatever shall become of Michael Cassio,
    He's never anything but your true servant.
DESDEMONA: I know't; I thank you. You do love my
        lord;   10
    You have known him long; and be you well assured
    He shall in strangeness° stand no farther off
    Than in a politic distance.°
CASSIO: Ay, but, lady,
    That policy may either last so long,
    Or feed upon such nice and waterish diet,°   15
    Or breed itself so out of circumstance,
    That, I being absent, and my place supplied,
    My general will forget my love and service.
DESDEMONA: Do not doubt° that; before Emilia here
    I give thee warrant of thy place. Assure thee,   20
    If I do vow a friendship, I'll perform it
    To the last article. My lord shall never rest;
    I'll watch him tame° and talk him out of patience;
    His bed shall seem a school, his board a shrift;°
    I'll intermingle everything he does   25
    With Cassio's suit. Therefore be merry, Cassio,
    For thy solicitor shall rather die
    Than give thy cause away.

Enter Othello and Iago [at a distance].

EMILIA: Madam, here comes my lord.
CASSIO: Madam, I'll take my leave.   30
DESDEMONA: Why, stay, and hear me speak.
CASSIO: Madam, not now: I am very ill at ease,
    Unfit for mine own purposes.
DESDEMONA: Well, do your discretion.   *Exit Cassio.*
IAGO: Ha! I like not that.
OTHELLO: What dost thou say?   35
IAGO: Nothing, my lord; or if — I know not what.
OTHELLO: Was not that Cassio parted from my wife?
IAGO: Cassio, my lord? No, sure, I cannot think it,
    That he would steal away so guilty-like,
    Seeing your coming.
OTHELLO: I do believe 'twas he.   40
DESDEMONA: How now, my lord?
    I have been talking with a suitor here,
    A man that languishes in your displeasure.
OTHELLO: What is't you mean?
DESDEMONA: Why, your lieutenant, Cassio. Good my
        lord,   45
    If I have any grace or power to move you,
    His present° reconciliation take;
    For if he be not one that truly loves you,
    That errs in ignorance, and not in cunning,

---

41. Florentine: I.e., even a Florentine (like Cassio; Iago was
a Venetian). **47. affinity:** Family connections. **50. occasion:**
Opportunity. **front:** Forelock. **56. your bosom:** Your
inmost thoughts. **III, II. 3. works:** Fortifications.

III, III. 12. strangeness: Aloofness. **13. Than . . . distance:**
Than wise policy requires. **15. Or . . . diet:** Or be continued for
such slight reasons. **19. doubt:** Fear. **23. watch him tame:**
Keep him awake until he gives in. **24. shrift:** Confessional.
47. present: Immediate.

50   I have no judgment in an honest face,
        I prithee call him back.
    OTHELLO: Went he hence now?
    DESDEMONA: Yes, faith; so humbled
        That he hath left part of his grief with me
        To suffer with him. Good love, call him back.
    OTHELLO: Not now, sweet Desdemon; some other
55   time.
    DESDEMONA: But shall't be shortly?
    OTHELLO: The sooner, sweet, for you.
    DESDEMONA: Shall't be to-night at supper?
    OTHELLO: No, not to-night.
    DESDEMONA: To-morrow dinner then?
    OTHELLO: I shall not dine at home;
        I meet the captains at the citadel.
    DESDEMONA: Why then, to-morrow night, or Tuesday
60   morn,
        On Tuesday noon or night, or Wednesday morn.
        I prithee name the time, but let it not
        Exceed three days. I' faith, he's penitent;
        And yet his trespass, in our common reason
65   (Save that, they say, the wars must make examples
        Out of their best), is not almost° a fault
        T' incur a private check.° When shall he come?
        Tell me, Othello. I wonder in my soul
        What you could ask me that I should deny
70   Or stand so mamm'ring on.° What? Michael
            Cassio,
        That came a-wooing with you, and so many a
            time,
        When I have spoke of you dispraisingly,
        Hath ta'en your part — to have so much to do
        To bring him in? By'r Lady, I could do much —
    OTHELLO: Prithee no more. Let him come when he
75   will!
        I will deny thee nothing.
    DESDEMONA: Why, this is not a boon;
        'Tis as I should entreat you wear your gloves,
        Or feed on nourishing dishes, or keep you warm,
        Or sue to you to do a peculiar profit
80   To your own person. Nay, when I have a suit
        Wherein I mean to touch your love indeed,
        It shall be full of poise and difficult weight,
        And fearful° to be granted.
    OTHELLO: I will deny thee nothing!
        Whereon I do beseech thee grant me this,
85   To leave me but a little to myself.
    DESDEMONA: Shall I deny you? No. Farewell, my lord.
    OTHELLO: Farewell, my Desdemon: I'll come to thee
            straight.
    DESDEMONA: Emilia, come. — Be as your fancies teach
            you;
        Whate'er you be, I am obedient. *Exit [with Emilia].*
90 OTHELLO: Excellent wretch!° Perdition catch my soul

        But I do love thee! and when I love thee not,
        Chaos is come again.
    IAGO: My noble lord —
    OTHELLO: What dost thou say, Iago?
    IAGO: Did Michael Cassio, when you wooed my lady,
        Know of your love?   95
    OTHELLO: He did, from first to last. Why dost thou
            ask?
    IAGO: But for a satisfaction of my thought;
        No further harm.
    OTHELLO: Why of thy thought, Iago?
    IAGO: I did not think he had been acquainted with her.
    OTHELLO: O, yes, and went between us° very oft.   100
    IAGO: Indeed?
    OTHELLO: Indeed? Ay, indeed! Discern'st thou aught in
            that?
        Is he not honest?
    IAGO: Honest, my lord?
    OTHELLO: Honest. Ay, honest.
    IAGO: My lord, for aught I know.
    OTHELLO: What dost thou think?
    IAGO: Think, my lord?
    OTHELLO: Think, my lord? 105
        By heaven, he echoes me,
        As if there were some monster in his thought
        Too hideous to be shown. Thou dost mean
            something:
        I heard thee say even now, thou lik'st not that,
        When Cassio left my wife. What didst not like?   110
        And when I told thee he was of my counsel
        In my whole course of wooing, thou cried'st
            "Indeed?"
        And didst contract and purse thy brow together,
        As if thou then hadst shut up in thy brain
        Some horrible conceit.° If thou dost love me,   115
        Show me thy thought.
    IAGO: My lord, you know I love you.
    OTHELLO: I think thou dost;
        And, for I know thou'rt full of love and honesty
        And weigh'st thy words before thou giv'st them
            breath,
        Therefore these stops of thine fright me the more; 120
        For such things in a false disloyal knave
        Are tricks of custom; but in a man that's just
        They are close dilations, working from the heart
        That passion cannot rule.°
    IAGO: For Michael Cassio,
        I dare be sworn I think that he is honest.   125
    OTHELLO: I think so too.
    IAGO: Men should be what they seem;
        Or those that be not, would they might seem none!°
    OTHELLO: Certain, men should be what they seem.
    IAGO: Why then, I think Cassio's an honest man.

66. **not almost:** Hardly. 67. **a private check:** Even a private
reprimand. 70. **mamm'ring on:** Hesitating about. 83. **fear-**
ful: Dangerous. 90. **wretch:** (A term of endearment).

100. **went . . . us:** (I.e., as messenger). 115. **conceit:** Fancy.
123–24. **close dilations . . . rule:** Secret emotions which well up
in spite of restraint. 127. **seem none:** I.e., not pretend to be
men when they are really monsters.

130 OTHELLO: Nay, yet there's more in this.
    I prithee speak to me as to thy thinkings,
    As thou dost ruminate, and give thy worst of
      thoughts
    The worst of words.
  IAGO: Good my lord, pardon me:
    Though I am bound to every act of duty,
135 I am not bound to that all slaves are free to.°
    Utter my thoughts? Why, say they are vile and false,
    As where's that palace whereinto foul things
    Sometimes intrude not? Who has a breast so pure
    But some uncleanly apprehensions
140 Keep leets and law days,° and in Sessions sit
    With meditations lawful?
  OTHELLO: Thou dost conspire against thy friend, Iago,
    If thou but think'st him wronged, and mak'st his ear
    A stranger to thy thoughts.
  IAGO: I do beseech you —
145 Though I perchance am vicious in my guess
    (As I confess it is my nature's plague
    To spy into abuses, and oft my jealousy°
    Shapes faults that are not), that your wisdom yet
    From one that so imperfectly conjects°
150 Would take no notice, nor build yourself a trouble
    Out of his scattering and unsure observance.
    It were not for your quiet nor your good,
    Nor for my manhood, honesty, and wisdom,
    To let you know my thoughts.
  OTHELLO: What dost thou mean?
155 IAGO: Good name in man and woman, dear my lord,
    Is the immediate° jewel of their souls.
    Who steals my purse steals trash; 'tis something,
      nothing;
    'Twas mine, 'tis his, and has been slave to
      thousands;
    But he that filches from me my good name
160 Robs me of that which not enriches him
    And makes me poor indeed.
  OTHELLO: By heaven, I'll know thy thoughts!
  IAGO: You cannot, if my heart were in your hand;
    Nor shall not whilst 'tis in my custody.
  OTHELLO: Ha!
165 IAGO: O, beware, my lord, of jealousy!
    It is the green-eyed monster, which doth mock°
    The meat it feeds on. That cuckold lives in bliss
    Who, certain of his fate, loves not his wronger;
    But O, what damnèd minutes tells he o'er
170 Who dotes, yet doubts — suspects, yet strongly loves!
  OTHELLO: O misery!
  IAGO: Poor and content is rich, and rich enough;
    But riches fineless° is as poor as winter
    To him that ever fears he shall be poor.

    Good God, the souls of all my tribe defend   175
    From jealousy!
  OTHELLO: Why, why is this?
    Think'st thou I'ld make a life of jealousy,
    To follow still the changes of the moon
    With fresh suspicions? No! To be once in doubt
    Is once to be resolved. Exchange me for a goat   180
    When I shall turn the business of my soul
    To such exsufflicate and blown° surmises,
    Matching this inference. 'Tis not to make me jealous
    To say my wife is fair, feeds well, loves company,
    Is free of speech, sings, plays, and dances;   185
    Where virtue is, these are more virtuous.
    Nor from mine own weak merits will I draw
    The smallest fear or doubt of her revolt,°
    For she had eyes, and chose me. No, Iago;
    I'll see before I doubt; when I doubt, prove;   190
    And on the proof there is no more but this —
    Away at once with love or jealousy!
  IAGO: I am glad of this; for now I shall have reason
    To show the love and duty that I bear you
    With franker spirit. Therefore, as I am bound,   195
    Receive it from me. I speak not yet of proof.
    Look at your wife; observe her well with Cassio;
    Wear your eyes thus, not jealous nor secure:°
    I would not have your free and noble nature,
    Out of self-bounty,° be abused. Look to't.   200
    I know our country disposition well:
    In Venice they do let God see the pranks
    They dare not show their husbands; their best
      conscience
    Is not to leave't undone, but keep't unknown.
  OTHELLO: Dost thou say so?   205
  IAGO: She did deceive her father, marrying you;
    And when she seemed to shake and fear your looks,
    She loved them most.
  OTHELLO: And so she did.
  IAGO: Why, go to then!
    She that, so young, could give out such a seeming
    To seel° her father's eyes up close as oak° —   210
    He thought 'twas witchcraft — but I am much to
      blame.
    I humbly do beseech you of your pardon
    For too much loving you.
  OTHELLO: I am bound to thee for ever.
  IAGO: I see this hath a little dashed your spirits.
  OTHELLO: Not a jot, not a jot.
  IAGO: I' faith, I fear it has.   215
    I hope you will consider what is spoke
    Comes from my love. But I do see y' are moved.
    I am to pray you not to strain my speech
    To grosser issues° nor to larger reach
    Than to suspicion.   220

---

135. bound . . . free to: Bound to tell that which even slaves are allowed to keep to themselves.   **140. leets and law days:** Sittings of the courts.   **147. jealousy:** Suspicion.   **149. conjects:** Conjectures.   **156. immediate:** Nearest the heart.   **166. mock:** Play with, like a cat with mouse.   **173. fineless:** Unlimited.

182. exsufflicate and blown: Spat out and flyblown.   **188. revolt:** Unfaithfulness.   **198. secure:** Overconfident.   **200. selfbounty:** Natural goodness.   **210. seel:** Close.   **oak:** Oak grain.   **219. To grosser issues:** To mean something more monstrous.

Laurence Fishburne, Othello,
and Kenneth Branagh, Iago, in
Oliver Parker's 1995 film
version of *Othello*.

OTHELLO: I will not.

IAGO: Should you do so, my lord,
My speech should fall into such vile success°
As my thoughts aim not at. Cassio's my worthy
    friend —
My lord, I see y' are moved.

OTHELLO: No, not much moved:
225 I do not think but Desdemona's honest.°

IAGO: Long live she so! and long live you to think so!

OTHELLO: And yet, how nature erring from itself —

IAGO: Ay, there's the point! as (to be bold with you)
Not to affect many proposèd matches
230 Of her own clime, complexion, and degree,
Whereto we see in all things nature tends —
Foh! one may smell in such a will most rank,
Foul disproportions, thought unnatural —
But pardon me — I do not in position°
235 Distinctly speak of her; though I may fear
Her will, recoiling° to her better judgment,
May fall to match° you with her country forms,
And happily° repent.

OTHELLO: Farewell, farewell!
If more thou dost perceive, let me know more.
240 Set on thy wife to observe. Leave me, Iago.

IAGO: My lord, I take my leave.   [*Going.*]

OTHELLO: Why did I marry? This honest creature
    doubtless
Sees and knows more, much more, than he unfolds.

IAGO [*returns*]: My lord, I would I might entreat your
    honor
To scan this thing no further: leave it to time.   245
Although 'tis fit that Cassio have his place,
For sure he fills it up with great ability,
Yet, if you please to hold off a while,
You shall by that perceive him and his means.
Note if your lady strain his entertainment°   250
With any strong or vehement importunity;
Much will be seen in that. In the mean time
Let me be thought too busy° in my fears
(As worthy cause I have to fear I am)
And hold her free,° I do beseech your honor.   255

OTHELLO: Fear not my government.°

IAGO: I once more take my leave.   *Exit.*

OTHELLO: This fellow's of exceeding honesty,
And knows all qualities,° with a learnèd spirit
Of° human dealings. If I do prove her haggard,°   260
Though that her jesses° were my dear heartstrings,
I'd whistle her off and let her down the wind
To prey at fortune.° Haply, for I am black
And have not those soft parts of conversation°
That chamberers° have, or for I am declined   265
Into the vale of years — yet that's not much —

222. **vile success**: Evil outcome. 225. **honest**: Chaste.
234. **position**: Definite assertion. 236. **recoiling**: Reverting.
237. **fall to match**: Happen to compare. 238. **happily**: Haply,
perhaps.

250. **strain his entertainment**: Urge his recall. 253. **busy**:
Meddlesome. 255. **hold her free**: Consider her guiltless.
256. **government**: Self-control. 259. **qualities**: Natures.
259–60. **learned spirit Of**: Mind informed about. 260. **haggard**: A wild hawk. 261. **jesses**: Thongs for controlling a
hawk. 262–63. **whistle . . . fortune**: Turn her out and let her
take care of herself. 264. **soft . . . conversation**: Ingratiating
manners. 265. **chamberers**: Courtiers.

She's gone. I am abused, and my relief
Must be to loathe her. O curse of marriage,
That we can call these delicate creatures ours,
270 And not their appetites! I had rather be a toad
And live upon the vapor of a dungeon
Than keep a corner in the thing I love
For others' uses. Yet 'tis the plague of great ones;°
Prerogatived° are they less than the base.
275 'Tis destiny unshunnable, like death.
Even then this forkèd plague° is fated to us
When we do quicken.° Look where she comes.

Enter Desdemona and Emilia.

If she be false, O, then heaven mocks itself!
I'll not believe't.
DESDEMONA: How now, my dear Othello?
280   Your dinner, and the generous° islanders
By you invited, do attend your presence.
OTHELLO: I am to blame.
DESDEMONA: Why do you speak so faintly?
Are you not well?
OTHELLO: I have a pain upon my forehead, here.
DESDEMONA: Faith, that's with watching;° 'twill away
285   again.
Let me but bind it hard, within this hour
It will be well.
OTHELLO: Your napkin° is too little;

*[He pushes the handkerchief from him, and it falls un-
noticed.]*

Let it° alone. Come, I'll go in with you.
DESDEMONA: I am very sorry that you are not well.

Exit [with Othello].

290 EMILIA: I am glad I have found this napkin;
This was her first remembrance from the Moor,
My wayward husband hath a hundred times
Wooed me to steal it; but she so loves the token
(For he conjured her she should ever keep it)
295   That she reserves it evermore about her
To kiss and talk to. I'll have the work ta'en out°
And give't Iago.
What he will do with it heaven knows, not I;
I nothing but to please his fantasy.°

Enter Iago.

300 IAGO: How now? What do you here alone?
EMILIA: Do not you chide; I have a thing for you.
IAGO: A thing for me? It is a common thing —
EMILIA: Ha?
IAGO: To have a foolish wife.

EMILIA: O, is that all? What will you give me now   305
For that same handkerchief?
IAGO: What handkerchief?
EMILIA: What handkerchief!
Why, that the Moor first gave to Desdemona;
That which so often you did bid me steal.
IAGO: Hast stol'n it from her?   310
EMILIA: No, faith; she let it drop by negligence,
And to th' advantage,° I, being here, took't up.
Look, here it is.
IAGO: A good wench! Give it me.
EMILIA: What will you do with't, that you have been so
earnest
To have me filch it?
IAGO: Why, what is that to you?   315

[Snatches it.]

EMILIA: If it be not for some purpose of import,°
Give't me again. Poor lady, she'll run mad
When she shall lack it.
IAGO: Be not acknown on't;° I have use for it.
Go, leave me.   *Exit Emilia.* 320
I will in Cassio's lodgings lose this napkin
And let him find it. Trifles light as air
Are to the jealous confirmations strong
As proofs of holy writ. This may do something.
The Moor already changes with my poison: 325
Dangerous conceits° are in their nature poisons,
Which at the first are scarce found to distaste,
But with a little act upon the blood
Burn like the mines of sulphur.

Enter Othello.

                                I did say so.
Look where he comes! Not poppy nor mandragora,° 330
Nor all the drowsy syrups of the world,
Shall ever med'cine thee to that sweet sleep
Which thou owedst yesterday.
OTHELLO: Ha! ha! false to me?
IAGO: Why, how now, general? No more of that!
OTHELLO: Avaunt! be gone! Thou hast set me on the
rack.   335
I swear 'tis better to be much abused
Than but to know't a little.
IAGO: How now, my lord?
OTHELLO: What sense had I of her stol'n hours of lust?
I saw't not, thought it not, it harmed not me;
I slept the next night well, fed well, was free° and
merry;   340
I found not Cassio's kisses on her lips
He that is robbed, not wanting° what is stol'n,
Let him not know't, and he's not robbed at all.
IAGO: I am sorry to hear this.

---

273. **great ones:** Prominent men. 274. **Prerogatived:** Privileged. 276. **forkèd plague:** I.e., horns of a cuckold. 277. **do
quicken:** Are born. 280. **generous:** Noble. 285. **watching:**
Working late. 287. **napkin:** Handkerchief. 288. **it:** I.e., his
forehead. 296. **work ta'en out:** Pattern copied. 299. **fantasy:** Whim.

312. **to th' advantage:** Opportunely. 316. **import:** Importance. 319. **Be . . . on't:** Do not acknowledge it. 326. **conceits:**
Ideas. 330. **mandragora:** A narcotic. 340. **free:** Carefree.
342. **wanting:** Missing.

345 OTHELLO: I had been happy if the general camp,
         Pioneers° and all, had tasted her sweet body,
         So I had nothing known. O, now for ever
         Farewell the tranquil mind! farewell content!
         Farewell the plumèd troop, and the big° wars
350   That make ambition virtue! O, farewell!
         Farewell the neighing steed and the shrill trump,
         The spirit-stirring drum, th' ear-piercing fife,
         The royal banner, and all quality,
         Pride, pomp, and circumstance° of glorious war!
355   And O you mortal engines° whose rude throats
         Th' immortal Jove's dread clamors counterfeit,°
         Farewell! Othello's occupation's gone!
    IAGO: Is't possible, my lord?
    OTHELLO: Villain, be sure thou prove my love a
         whore!
360   Be sure of it; give me the ocular proof;
         Or, by the worth of mine eternal soul,
         Thou hadst been better have been born a dog
         Than answer my waked wrath!
    IAGO: Is't come to this?
    OTHELLO: Make me to see't; or at the least so prove it
365   That the probation° bear no hinge nor loop
         To hang a doubt on — or woe upon thy life!
    IAGO: My noble lord —
    OTHELLO: If thou dost slander her and torture me,
         Never pray more; abandon all remorse;
370   On horror's head horrors accumulate;
         Do deeds to make heaven weep, all earth amazed;
         For nothing canst thou to damnation add
         Greater than that.
    IAGO: O grace! O heaven forgive me!
         Are you a man? Have you a soul or sense? —
375   God b' wi' you! take mine office. O wretched fool,
         That liv'st to make thine honesty a vice!
         O monstrous world! Take note, take note, O world,
         To be direct and honest is not safe.
         I thank you for this profit;° and from hence
380   I'll love no friend, sith love breeds such offense.
    OTHELLO: Nay, stay. Thou shouldst be honest.
    IAGO: I should be wise; for honesty's a fool
         And loses that it works for.
    OTHELLO: By the world,
         I think my wife be honest, and think she is not;
385   I think that thou art just, and think thou art not.
         I'll have some proof. Her name, that was as fresh
         As Dian's visage, is now begrimed and black
         As mine own face. If there be cords, or knives,
         Poison, or fire, or suffocating streams,
390   I'll not endure it. Would I were satisfied!°
    IAGO: I see, sir, you are eaten up with passion:
         I do repent me that I put it to you.
         You would be satisfied?

OTHELLO: Would? Nay, I will.
    IAGO: And may; but how? how satisfied, my lord?
         Would you, the supervisor,° grossly gape on?   395
         Behold her topped?
    OTHELLO: Death and damnation! O!
    IAGO: It were a tedious difficulty, I think,
         To bring them to that prospect. Damn them then,
         If ever mortal eyes do see them bolster°
         More than their own! What then? How then?   400
         What shall I say? Where's satisfaction?
         It is impossible you should see this,
         Were they as prime° as goats, as hot as monkeys,
         As salt° as wolves in pride,° and fools as gross
         As ignorance made drunk. But yet, I say,   405
         If imputation and strong circumstances
         Which lead directly to the door of truth
         Will give you satisfaction, you may have't.
    OTHELLO: Give me a living reason she's disloyal.
    IAGO: I do not like the office.   410
         But sith I am ent'red in this cause so far,
         Pricked to't by foolish honesty and love,
         I will go on. I lay with Cassio lately,
         And being troubled with a raging tooth,
         I could not sleep.   415
         There are a kind of men so loose of soul
         That in their sleeps will mutter their affairs.
         One of this kind is Cassio.
         In sleep I heard him say, "Sweet Desdemona,
         Let us be wary, let us hide our loves!"   420
         And then, sir, would he gripe and wring my
             hand,
         Cry "O sweet creature!" and then kiss me hard,
         As if he plucked up kisses by the roots
         That grew upon my lips; then laid his leg
         Over my thigh, and sighed, and kissed, and then   425
         Cried "Cursèd fate that gave thee to the Moor!"
    OTHELLO: O monstrous! monstrous!
    IAGO: Nay, this was but
         his dream.
    OTHELLO: But this denoted a foregone conclusion;°
         'Tis a shrewd doubt,° though it be but a dream.
    IAGO: And this may help to thicken other proofs   430
         That do demonstrate thinly.
    OTHELLO: I'll tear her all to pieces!
    IAGO: Nay, but be wise. Yet we see nothing done;
         She may be honest yet. Tell me but this —
         Have you not sometimes seen a handkerchief
         Spotted with strawberries in your wife's hand?   435
    OTHELLO: I gave her such a one; 'twas my first gift.
    IAGO: I know not that; but such a handkerchief —
         I am sure it was your wife's — did I to-day
         See Cassio wipe his beard with.
    OTHELLO: If it be that —

---

346. Pioneers: Sappers, laborers.   349. big: Stately.   354. circumstance: Pageantry.   355. mortal engines: Deadly artillery.
356. counterfeit: Imitate.   365. probation: Proof.   379. profit:
Profitable lesson.   390. satisfied: Completely informed.

395. supervisor: Spectator.   399. bolster: Lie together.
403. prime: Lustful.   404. salt: Lecherous.   pride: Heat.
428. foregone conclusion: Previous experience.   429. a
shrewd doubt: Cursedly suspicious.

440 IAGO: If it be that, or any that was hers,
It speaks against her with the other proofs.
OTHELLO: O, that the slave had forty thousand lives!
One is too poor, too weak for my revenge.
Now do I see 'tis true. Look here, Iago:
445 All my fond love thus do I blow to heaven.
'Tis gone.
Arise, black vengeance, from the hollow hell!
Yield up, O love, thy crown and hearted throne
To tyrannous hate! Swell, bosom, with thy
fraught,°
For 'tis of aspics'° tongues!
450 IAGO: Yet be content.
OTHELLO: O, blood, blood, blood!
IAGO: Patience, I say. Your mind perhaps may
change.
OTHELLO: Never, Iago. Like to the Pontic sea,°
Whose icy current and compulsive course
455 Ne'er feels retiring ebb, but keeps due on
To the Propontic and the Hellespont,
Even so my bloody thoughts, with violent pace,
Shall ne'er look back, ne'er ebb to humble love,
Till that a capable° and wide revenge
Swallow them up.
460 (*He kneels.*) Now, by yond marble heaven,
In the due reverence of a sacred vow
I here engage my words.
IAGO: Do not rise yet.

(*Iago kneels.*)

Witness, you ever-burning lights above,
You elements that clip° us round about,
465 Witness that here Iago doth give up
The execution° of his wit,° hands, heart
To wronged Othello's service! Let him command,
And to obey shall be in me remorse,°
What bloody business ever.

[*They rise.*]

OTHELLO: I greet thy love,
Not with vain thanks but with acceptance
470 bounteous,
And will upon the instant put thee to't.
Within these three days let me hear thee say
That Cassio's not alive.
IAGO: My friend is dead; 'tis done at your request.
475 But let her live.
OTHELLO: Damn her, lewd minx! O, damn her! damn
her!
Come, go with me apart. I will withdraw
To furnish me with some swift means of death
For the fair devil. Now art thou my lieutenant.
480 IAGO: I am your own forever. *Exeunt.*

Scene IV

The environs of the castle.

Enter Desdemona, Emilia, and Clown.

DESDEMONA: Do you know, sirrah, where Lieutenant
Cassio lies?°
CLOWN: I dare not say he lies anywhere.
DESDEMONA: Why, man?
CLOWN: He's a soldier, and for me to say a soldier lies is   5
stabbing.
DESDEMONA: Go to. Where lodges he?
CLOWN: To tell you where he lodges is to tell you where
I lie.
DESDEMONA: Can anything be made of this?   10
CLOWN: I know not where he lodges; and for me to
devise a lodging, and say he lies here or he lies there,
were to lie in mine own throat.
DESDEMONA: Can you enquire him out, and be edified
by report?   15
CLOWN: I will catechize the world for him; that is, make
questions, and by them answer.
DESDEMONA: Seek him, bid him come hither. Tell him I
have moved° my lord on his behalf and hope all will
be well.   20
CLOWN: To do this is within the compass of man's wit,
and therefore I'll attempt the doing of it. *Exit.*
DESDEMONA: Where should I lose that handkerchief,
Emilia?
EMILIA: I know not, madam.   25
DESDEMONA: Believe me, I had rather have lost my
purse
Full of crusadoes,° and but my noble Moor
Is true of mind, and made of no such baseness
As jealous creatures are, it were enough
To put him to ill thinking.
EMILIA: Is he not jealous?   30
DESDEMONA: Who? he? I think the sun where he was
born
Drew all such humors° from him.

Enter Othello.

EMILIA: Look where he comes.
Desdemona: I will not leave him now till Cassio
Be called to him — How is't with you, my lord?
OTHELLO: Well, my good lady. [*Aside.*] O, hardness to
dissemble! —   35
How do you, Desdemona?
DESDEMONA: Well, my good lord.
OTHELLO: Give me your hand. This hand is moist, my
lady.
DESDEMONA: It yet hath felt no age nor known no
sorrow.
OTHELLO: This argues fruitfulness and liberal heart.

---

449. **fraught:** Burden. 450. **aspics:** Deadly poisonous snakes.
453. **Pontic sea:** Black Sea. 459. **capable:** All-embracing.
464. **clip:** Encompass. 466. **execution:** Activities. **wit:**
Mind. 468. **remorse:** Pity.

III, IV. 2. **lies:** Lives, lodges. 19. **moved:** Made proposals to.
27. **crusadoes:** Portuguese gold coins. 32. **humors:** Inclinations.

40   Hot, hot, and moist. This hand of yours requires
      A sequester° from liberty, fasting and prayer,
      Much castigation, exercise devout;
      For here's a young and sweating devil here
      That commonly rebels. 'Tis a good hand,
      A frank one.
45 DESDEMONA: You may, indeed, say so;
      For 'twas that hand that gave away my heart.
    OTHELLO: A liberal hand! The hearts of old gave
          hands;
      But our new heraldry° is hands, not hearts.
    DESDEMONA: I cannot speak of this. Come now, your
          promise!
50 OTHELLO: What promise, chuck?
    DESDEMONA: I have sent to bid Cassio come speak
          with you.
    OTHELLO: I have a salt and sorry rheum° offends me.
      Lend me thy handkerchief.
    DESDEMONA: Here, my lord.
    OTHELLO: That which I gave you.
    DESDEMONA: I have it not about me.
    OTHELLO: Not?
    DESDEMONA: No, faith, my lord.
55 OTHELLO: That's a fault.
      That handkerchief
      Did an Egyptian° to my mother give.
      She was a charmer,° and could almost read
      The thoughts of people. She told her, while she kept
          it,
60   'Twould make her amiable° and subdue my father
      Entirely to her love; but if she lost it
      Or made a gift of it, my father's eye
      Should hold her loathèd, and his spirits should hunt
      After new fancies. She, dying, gave it me,
65   And bid me, when my fate would have me wive;
      To give it her. I did so; and take heed on't;
      Make it a darling like your precious eye.
      To lose't or give't away were such perdition°
      As nothing else could match.
    DESDEMONA: Is't possible?
70 OTHELLO: 'Tis true. There's magic in the web of it.
      A sibyl that had numb'red in the world
      The sun to course two hundred compasses,°
      In her prophetic fury sewed the work;
      The worms were hallowed that did breed the silk;
75   And it was dyed in mummy° which the skillful
      Conserved of maidens' hearts.
    DESDEMONA: I' faith? Is't true?
    OTHELLO: Most veritable. Therefore look to't well.
    DESDEMONA: Then would to God that I had never
          seen't!

OTHELLO: Ha! Wherefore?
DESDEMONA: Why do you speak so startingly and
      rash?   80
OTHELLO: Is't lost? Is't gone? Speak, is it out o' th'
      way?
DESDEMONA: Heaven bless us!
OTHELLO: Say you?
DESDEMONA: It is not lost. But what an if it were?
OTHELLO: How?   85
DESDEMONA: I say it is not lost.
OTHELLO: Fetch't, let me see't!
DESDEMONA: Why, so I can, sir; but I will not now.
   This is a trick to put° me from my suit:
   Pray you let Cassio be received again.
OTHELLO: Fetch me the handkerchief! My mind
      misgives.   90
DESDEMONA: Come, come!
   You'll never meet a more sufficient man.
OTHELLO: The handkerchief!
[DESDEMONA: I pray talk me of Cassio.
OTHELLO: The handkerchief!]
DESDEMONA: A man that all his time°
   Hath founded his good fortunes on your love,   95
   Shared dangers with you —
OTHELLO: The handkerchief!
DESDEMONA: I' faith, you are to blame.
OTHELLO: Zounds!   Exit Othello.
EMILIA: Is not this man jealous?   100
DESDEMONA: I ne'er saw this before.
   Sure there's some wonder in this
      handkerchief;
   I am most unhappy in the loss of it.
EMILIA: 'Tis not a year or two shows us a man.
   They are all but stomachs, and we all but food;   105
   They eat us hungerly, and when they are full,
   They belch us.

Enter Iago and Cassio.

                    Look you — Cassio and my husband!
IAGO: There is no other way; 'tis she must do't.
   And lo the happiness!° Go and importune her.
DESDEMONA: How now, good Cassio? What's the news
      with you?   110
CASSIO: Madam, my former suit. I do beseech you
   That by your virtuous means I may again
   Exist, and be a member of his love
   Whom I with all the office of my heart
   Entirely honor. I would not be delayed.   115
   If my offense be of such mortal kind
   That neither service past, nor present sorrows,
   Nor purposed merit in futurity,
   Can ransom me into his love again,
   But to know so must be my benefit.   120
   So shall I clothe me in a forced content,

---

41. **sequester:** Removal.   48. **heraldry:** Heraldic symbolism.
52. **salt . . . rheum:** Distressing head cold.   57. **Egyptian:** Gypsy.
58. **charmer:** Sorceress.   60. **amiable:** Lovable.   68. **perdi-**
tion: Disaster.   72. **compasses:** Annual rounds.   75. **mummy:**
A drug made from mummies.

88. **put:** Divert.   94. **all . . . time:** During his whole career.
109. **happiness:** Good luck.

And shut myself up in° some other course,
To fortune's alms.
DESDEMONA: Alas, thrice-gentle Cassio!
My advocation° is not now in tune.
125 My lord is not my lord; nor should I know him,
Were he in favor° as in humor altered.
So help me every spirit sanctified
As I have spoken for you all my best
And stood within the blank° of his displeasure
130 For my free speech! You must a while be patient.
What I can do I will; and more I will
Than for myself I dare. Let that suffice you.
IAGO: Is my lord angry?
EMILIA: He went hence but now,
And certainly in strange unquietness.
135 IAGO: Can he be angry? I have seen the cannon
When it hath blown his ranks into the air
And, like the devil, from his very arm
Puffed his own brother — and is he angry?
Something of moment then. I will go meet him.
140 There's matter in't indeed if he be angry.
DESDEMONA: I prithee do so.   *Exit [Iago].*
                    Something sure of state,°
Either from Venice or some unhatched practice°
Made demonstrable here in Cyprus to him,
Hath puddled° his clear spirit; and in such cases
145 Men's natures wrangle with inferior things,
Though great ones are their object. 'Tis even so;
For let our finger ache, and it endues°
Our other, healthful members even to a sense
Of pain. Nay, we must think men are not gods,
150 Nor of them look for such observancy
As fits the bridal. Beshrew me much, Emilia,
I was, unhandsome warrior° as I am,
Arraigning his unkindness with my soul;°
But now I find I had suborned the witness,
155 And he's indicted falsely.
EMILIA: Pray heaven it be state matters, as you
    think,
And no conception nor no jealous toy°
Concerning you.
DESDEMONA: Alas the day! I never gave him cause.
160 EMILIA: But jealous souls will not be answered so;
They are not ever jealous for the cause,
But jealous for they're jealous. 'Tis a monster
Begot upon itself,° born on itself.
DESDEMONA: Heaven keep that monster from Othello's
    mind!

EMILIA: Lady, amen.   165
DESDEMONA: I will go seek him. Cassio, walk here
    about:
If I do find him fit, I'll move your suit
And seek to effect it to my uttermost.
CASSIO: I humbly thank your ladyship.

            Exeunt Desdemona and Emilia.
Enter Bianca.

BIANCA: Save you, friend Cassio!
CASSIO: What make you from home?   170
How is't with you, my most fair Bianca?
I' faith, sweet love, I was coming to your house.
BIANCA: And I was going to your lodging, Cassio.
What, keep a week away? seven days and nights?
Eightscore eight hours? and lovers' absent hours,   175
More tedious than the dial° eightscore times?
O weary reck'ning!
CASSIO: Pardon me, Bianca:
I have this while with leaden thoughts been pressed;
But I shall in a more continuate° time
Strike off this score of absence. Sweet Bianca,   180

[Gives her Desdemona's handkerchief.]

Take me this work out.°
BIANCA: O Cassio, whence came this?
This is some token from a newer friend.
To the felt absence now I feel a cause.
Is't come to this? Well, well.
CASSIO: Go to, woman!
Throw your vile guesses in the devil's teeth,   185
From whence you have them. You are jealous now
That this is from some mistress, some
    remembrance.
No, by my faith, Bianca.
BIANCA: Why, whose is it?
CASSIO: I know not, sweet; I found it in my chamber.
I like the work° well; ere it be demanded,   190
As like enough it will, I'd have it copied.
Take it and do't, and leave me for this time.
BIANCA: Leave you? Wherefore?
CASSIO: I do attend here on the general
And think it no addition, nor my wish,   195
To have him see me womaned.
BIANCA: Why, I pray you?
CASSIO: Not that I love you not.
BIANCA: But that you do not love me!
I pray you bring me on the way a little,
And say if I shall see you soon at night.
CASSIO: 'Tis but a little way that I can bring you,   200
For I attend here; but I'll see you soon.
BIANCA: 'Tis very good. I must be circumstanced.°
                    Exeunt.

ACT IV • Scene I

The environs of the castle.

Enter Othello and Iago.

IAGO: Will you think so?
OTHELLO: Think so, Iago?
IAGO: What,
    To kiss in private?
OTHELLO: An unauthorized kiss.
IAGO: Or to be naked with her friend in bed
    An hour or more, not meaning any harm?
5 OTHELLO: Naked in bed, Iago, and not mean harm?
    It is hypocrisy against the devil.°
    They that mean virtuously, and yet do so,
    The devil their virtue tempts, and they tempt
        heaven.
IAGO: So they do nothing, 'tis a venial slip.
10   But if I give my wife a handkerchief —
OTHELLO: What then?
IAGO: Why, then 'tis hers, my lord; and being hers,
    She may, I think, bestow't on any man.
OTHELLO: She is protectress of her honor too;
15   May she give that?
IAGO: Her honor is an essence that's not seen;
    They have it very oft that have it not.
    But for the handkerchief —
OTHELLO: By heaven, I would most gladly have forgot
        it!
20 Thou said'st — O, it comes o'er my memory
    As doth the raven o'er the infected° house,
    Boding to all! — he had my handkerchief.
IAGO: Ay, what of that?
OTHELLO: That's not so good now.
IAGO: What
    If I had said I had seen him do you wrong?
25 Or heard him say — as knaves be such abroad
    Who having, by their own importunate suit,
    Or voluntary dotage of some mistress,
    Convincèd or supplied° them, cannot choose
    But they must blab —
OTHELLO: Hath he said anything?
30 IAGO: He hath, my lord; but be you well assured,
    No more than he'll unswear.
OTHELLO: What hath he said?
IAGO: Faith, that he did — I know not what he did.
OTHELLO: What? what?
IAGO: Lie —
OTHELLO: With her?
35 IAGO: With her, on her; what you will.
OTHELLO: Lie with her? lie on her? — We say lie on
    her when they belie her. — Lie with her! Zounds,
    that's fulsome. — Handkerchief — confessions —
    handkerchief! — To confess, and be hanged for his

labor — first to be hanged, and then to confess! 40
I tremble at it. Nature would not invest herself in
such shadowing passion without some instruction.°
It is not words that shakes me thus. — Pish! Noses,
ears, and lips? Is't possible? — Confess? — Handkerchief? — O devil!   45

(*Falls in a trance.*)

IAGO: Work on,
    My med'cine, work! Thus credulous fools are
        caught,
    And many worthy and chaste dames even thus,
    All guiltless, meet reproach. — What, ho! my lord!
    My lord, I say! Othello!

Enter Cassio.

                                How now, Cassio?   50
CASSIO: What's the matter?
IAGO: My lord is fall'n into an epilepsy.
    This is his second fit; he had one yesterday.
CASSIO: Rub him about the temples.
IAGO: No, forbear.
    The lethargy° must have his quiet course.   55
    If not, he foams at mouth, and by and by
    Breaks out to savage madness. Look, he stirs.
    Do you withdraw yourself a little while.
    He will recover straight. When he is gone,
    I would on great occasion speak with you.   60
                                [*Exit Cassio.*]
    How is it, general? Have you not hurt your head?
OTHELLO: Dost thou mock me?
IAGO: I mock you? No, by heaven.
    Would you would bear your fortune like a man!
OTHELLO: A hornèd man's° a monster and a beast.
IAGO: There's many a beast then in a populous city, 65
    And many a civil monster.
OTHELLO: Did he confess it?
IAGO: Good sir, be a man.
    Think every bearded fellow that's but yoked
    May draw with you. There's millions now alive
    That nightly lie in those unproper° beds   70
    Which they dare swear peculiar:° your case is better.
    O, 'tis the spite of hell, the fiend's arch-mock,
    To lip a wanton in a secure° couch,
    And to suppose her chaste! No, let me know;
    And knowing what I am, I know what she shall be. 75
OTHELLO: O, thou art wise! 'Tis certain.
IAGO: Stand you
        awhile apart;
    Confine yourself but in a patient list.°
    Whilst you were here, o'erwhelmèd with your
        grief —

IV, I. 6. hypocrisy . . . devil: I.e., feigned sin instead of feigned
virtue.   21. infected: Plague-stricken.   28. Convincèd or supplied: Overcome or gratified.

41–42. Nature . . . instruction: My natural faculties would not
be so overcome by passion without reason.   55. lethargy:
Coma.   64. hornèd man: Cuckold.   70. unproper: Not exclusively their own.   71. peculiar: Exclusively their own.
73. secure: Free from fear of rivalry.   77. in a patient list:
Within the limits of self-control.

A passion most unsuiting such a man —
80   Cassio came hither. I shifted him away
And laid good 'scuse upon your ecstasy,°
Bade him anon return, and here speak with me;
The which he promised. Do but encave° yourself
And mark the fleers, the gibes, and notable scorns
85   That dwell in every region of his face;
For I will make him tell the tale anew —
Where, how, how oft, how long ago, and when
He hath, and is again to cope° your wife.
I say, but mark his gesture. Marry, patience!
90   Or I shall say y'are all in all in spleen,°
And nothing of a man.
OTHELLO: Dost thou hear, Iago?
I will be found most cunning in my patience;
But — dost thou hear? — most bloody.
IAGO: That's not amiss:
But yet keep time in all. Will you withdraw?

[*Othello retires.*]

95   Now will I question Cassio of Bianca,
A huswife° that by selling her desires
Buys herself bread and clothes. It is a creature
That dotes on Cassio, as 'tis the strumpet's plague
To beguile many and be beguiled by one.
100   He, when he hears of her, cannot refrain
From the excess of laughter. Here he comes.

Enter Cassio.

As he shall smile, Othello shall go mad;
And his unbookish° jealousy must conster°
Poor Cassio's smiles, gestures, and light behavior
105   Quite in the wrong. How do you now, lieutenant?
CASSIO: The worser that you give me the addition°
Whose want even kills me.
IAGO: Ply Desdemona well, and you are sure on't.
Now, if this suit lay in Bianca's power,
How quickly should you speed!
110   CASSIO: Alas, poor caitiff!°
OTHELLO: Look how he laughs already!
IAGO: I never knew a woman love man so.
CASSIO: Alas, poor rogue! I think, i' faith, she loves me.
OTHELLO: Now he denies it faintly, and laughs it out.
IAGO: Do you hear, Cassio?
115   OTHELLO: Now he importunes him
To tell it o'er. Go to! Well said, well said!
IAGO: She gives out that you shall marry her.
Do you intend it?
CASSIO: Ha, ha, ha!
120   OTHELLO: Do you triumph, Roman? Do you triumph?
CASSIO: I marry her? What, a customer?° Prithee bear
some charity to my wit; do not think it so unwhole-
some. Ha, ha, ha!

OTHELLO: So, so, so, so! They laugh that win!
IAGO: Faith, the cry goes that you shall marry her.   125
CASSIO: Prithee say true.
IAGO: I am a very villain else.
OTHELLO: Have you scored me?° Well.
CASSIO: This is the monkey's own giving out. She is per-
suaded I will marry her out of her own love and flat-   130
tery, not out of my promise.
OTHELLO: Iago beckons° me; now he begins the story.
CASSIO: She was here even now; she haunts me in every
place. I was t' other day talking on the sea bank with
certain Venetians, and thither comes the bauble,°   135
and, by this hand, she falls me thus about my neck —
OTHELLO: Crying "O dear Cassio!" as it were. His gesture imports it.
CASSIO: So hangs, and lolls, and weeps upon me; so
shakes and pulls me! Ha, ha, ha!   140
OTHELLO: Now he tells how she plucked him to my
chamber. O, I see that nose of yours, but not that dog
I shall throw it to.
CASSIO: Well, I must leave her company.

Enter Bianca.

IAGO: Before me! Look where she comes.   145
CASSIO: 'Tis such another fitchew!° marry, a perfumed
one. What do you mean by this haunting of me?
BIANCA: Let the devil and his dam haunt you! What did
you mean by that same handkerchief you gave me
even now? I was a fine fool to take it. I must take out   150
the whole work? A likely piece of work that you
should find it in your chamber and know not who
left it there! This is some minx's token, and I must
take out the work? There! Give it your hobby-horse.°
Wheresoever you had it, I'll take out no work on't.   155
CASSIO: How now, my sweet Bianca? How now? how
now?
OTHELLO: By heaven, that should be my handkerchief!
BIANCA: An you'll come to supper to-night, you may; an
you will not, come when you are next prepared for.   160
                                                        Exit.
IAGO: After her, after her!
CASSIO: Faith, I must; she'll rail in the street else.
IAGO: Will you sup there?
CASSIO: Yes, I intend so.
IAGO: Well, I may chance to see you; for I would very   165
fain speak with you.
CASSIO: Prithee come. Will you?
IAGO: Go to! say no more.   *Exit Cassio.*
OTHELLO [*comes forward*]: How shall I murder him,
Iago?   170
IAGO: Did you perceive how he laughed at his vice?°
OTHELLO: O Iago!
IAGO: And did you see the handkerchief?
OTHELLO: Was that mine?

81. **ecstasy:** Trance.   83. **encave:** Conceal.   88. **cope:** Meet.
90. **all in all in spleen:** Wholly overcome by your passion.
96. **huswife:** Hussy.   103. **unbookish:** Uninstructed.   **conster:**
Construe, interpret.   106. **addition:** Title.   110. **caitiff:** Wretch.
121. **customer:** Prostitute.

128. **scored me:** Settled my account (?).   132. **beckons:** Signals.   135. **bauble:** Plaything.   146. **fitchew:** Polecat (slang for
whore).   154. **hobby-horse:** Harlot.   171. **vice:** I.e., vicious
conduct.

175 IAGO: Yours, by this hand! And to see how he prizes° the
        foolish woman your wife! She gave it him, and he
        hath giv'n it his whore.
    OTHELLO: I would have him nine years a-killing — A
        fine woman! a fair woman! a sweet woman!
180 IAGO: Nay, you must forget that.
    OTHELLO: Ay, let her rot, and perish, and be damned to-
        night; for she shall not live. No, my heart is turned to
        stone; I strike it, and it hurts my hand. O, the world
        hath not a sweeter creature! She might lie by an
185   emperor's side and command him tasks.
    IAGO: Nay, that's not your way.
    OTHELLO: Hang her! I do but say what she is. So deli-
        cate with her needle! an admirable musician! O, she
        will sing the savageness out of a bear! Of so high and
190   plenteous wit and invention° —
    IAGO: She's the worse for all this.
    OTHELLO: O, a thousand thousand times! And then, of
        so gentle a condition!°
    IAGO: Ay, too gentle.
195 OTHELLO: Nay, that's certain. But yet the pity of it, Iago!
        O Iago, the pity of it, Iago!
    IAGO: If you are so fond over her iniquity, give her
        patent° to offend; for if it touch not you, it comes
        near nobody.
200 OTHELLO: I will chop her into messes! Cuckold me!
    IAGO: O, 'tis foul in her.
    OTHELLO: With mine officer!
    IAGO: That's fouler.
    OTHELLO: Get me some poison, Iago, this night. I'll not
205   expostulate with her, lest her body and beauty unpro-
        vide° my mind again. This night, Iago!
    IAGO: Do it not with poison. Strangle her in her bed,
        even the bed she hath contaminated.
    OTHELLO: Good, good! The justice of it pleases. Very
210   good!
    IAGO: And for Cassio, let me be his undertaker,° you
        shall hear more by midnight.
    OTHELLO: Excellent good!

    A trumpet.

        What trumpet is that same?
    IAGO: I warrant something from Venice.

    Enter Lodovico, Desdemona, and Attendants.

215   'Tis Lodovico.
        This comes from the Duke; and see, your wife is
            with him.
    LODOVICO: God save you, worthy general!
    OTHELLO: With all my
        heart, sir.
    LODOVICO: The Duke and senators of Venice greet
        you.

    [*Gives him a letter.*]

    OTHELLO: I kiss the instrument of their pleasures.

    [*Opens the letter and reads.*]

    DESDEMONA: And what's the news, good cousin
        Lodovico?   220
    IAGO: I am very glad to see you, signior.
        Welcome to Cyprus.
    LODOVICO: I thank you. How does Lieutenant
        Cassio?
    IAGO: Lives, sir.
    DESDEMONA: Cousin, there's fall'n between him and
        my lord
        An unkind breach; but you shall make all well.   225
    OTHELLO: Are you sure of that?
    DESDEMONA: My lord?
    OTHELLO [*reads*]: "This fail you not to do, as you
        will — "
    LODOVICO: He did not call; he's busy in the paper.
        Is there division 'twixt thy lord and Cassio?   230
    DESDEMONA: A most unhappy one. I would do much
        T' atone° them, for the love I bear to Cassio.
    OTHELLO: Fire and brimstone!
    DESDEMONA: My lord?
    OTHELLO: Are you wise?
    DESDEMONA: What, is he angry?
    LODOVICO: May be the letter
        moved him;
        For, as I think, they do command him home,   235
        Deputing Cassio in his government.
    DESDEMONA: By my troth, I am glad on't.
    OTHELLO: Indeed?
    DESDEMONA: My lord?
    OTHELLO: I am glad to see you mad.°
    DESDEMONA: Why, sweet Othello —
    OTHELLO: Devil!

    [*Strikes her.*]

    DESDEMONA: I have not deserved this.   240
    LODOVICO: My lord, this would not be believed in
        Venice,
        Though I should swear I saw't. 'Tis very much.
        Make her amends; she weeps.
    OTHELLO: O devil, devil!
        If that the earth could teem° with woman's tears,
        Each drop she falls would prove a crocodile.°   245
        Out of my sight!
    DESDEMONA: I will not stay to offend you.
                                              [*Going.*]
    LODOVICO: Truly, an obedient lady.
        I do beseech your lordship call her back.
    OTHELLO: Mistress!
    DESDEMONA: My lord?
    OTHELLO: What would you with her, sir?   250
    LODOVICO: Who? I, my lord?

---

175. prizes: Values.   190. invention: Imagination.   193. condition: Disposition.   198. patent: License.   205. unprovide:
Disarm.   211. be his undertaker: Undertake to deal with him.

232. atone: Reconcile.   238. mad: I.e., waggish.   244. teem:
Breed.   245. crocodile: (Crocodiles were supposed to shed
hypocritical tears to lure men to destruction).

Paul Robeson in the 1930 London production of *Othello*.

Paul Robeson as Othello in the 1943 New York production, directed by Margaret Webster.

OTHELLO: Ay! You did wish that I would make her
    turn.
  Sir, she can turn, and turn, and yet go on
  And turn again; and she can weep, sir, weep;
255 And she's obedient; as you say, obedient,
  Very obedient. — Proceed you in your tears. —
  Concerning this, sir — O well-painted passion!° —
  I am commanded home. — Get you away;
  I'll send for you anon. — Sir, I obey the mandate
260 And will return to Venice. — Hence, avaunt!

                        [*Exit Desdemona.*]

  Cassio shall have my place. And, sir, to-night
  I do entreat that we may sup together.
  You are welcome, sir, to Cyprus — Goats and
    monkeys!
                                      Exit.

LODOVICO: Is this the noble Moor whom our full
    Senate
265 Call all in all sufficient? Is this the nature
  Whom passion could not shake? whose solid virtue
  The shot of accident nor dart of chance
  Could neither graze nor pierce?
IAGO: He is much changed.
LODOVICO: Are his wits safe? Is he not light of brain?
270 IAGO: He's that he is; I may not breathe my censure.
  What he might be — if what he might he is not —
  I would to heaven he were!
LODOVICO: What, strike his wife?
IAGO: Faith, that was not so well; yet would I knew
  That stroke would prove the worst!
LODOVICO: Is it his use?°
275 Or did the letters work upon his blood
  And new-create this fault?
IAGO: Alas, alas!
  It is not honesty in me to speak
  What I have seen and known. You shall observe
    him,
  And his own courses will denote him so
280 That I may save my speech. Do but go after
  And mark how he continues.
LODOVICO: I am sorry that I am deceived in him.
                                    Exeunt.

Scene II

Within the castle.

Enter Othello and Emilia.

OTHELLO: You have seen nothing then?
EMILIA: Nor ever heard, nor ever did suspect.
OTHELLO: Yes, you have seen Cassio and she together.
EMILIA: But then I saw no harm, and then I heard
5   Each syllable that breath made up between them.
OTHELLO: What, did they never whisper?

257. **passion:** Grief.   274. **use:** Custom.

EMILIA: Never, my lord.
OTHELLO: Nor send you out o' th' way?
EMILIA: Never.
OTHELLO: To fetch her fan, her gloves, her mask, nor
    nothing?
EMILIA: Never, my lord.   10
OTHELLO: That's strange.
EMILIA: I durst, my lord, to wager she is honest,
  Lay down my soul at stake. If you think other,
  Remove your thought; it doth abuse your bosom.°
  If any wretch have put this in your head,   15
  Let heaven requite it with the serpent's curse!°
  For if she be not honest, chaste, and true,
  There's no man happy; the purest of their wives
  Is foul as slander.
OTHELLO: Bid her come hither. Go.
                              Exit Emilia.
  She says enough; yet she's a simple bawd   20
  That cannot say as much. This is a subtle whore,
  A closet lock and key of villainous secrets;
  And yet she'll kneel and pray; I have seen her do't.

Enter Desdemona and Emilia.

DESDEMONA: My lord, what is your will?
OTHELLO: Pray, chuck,
    come hither.
DESDEMONA: What is your pleasure?
OTHELLO: Let me see your eyes.   25
  Look in my face.
DESDEMONA: What horrible fancy's this?
OTHELLO [*to Emilia*]: Some of your function, mistress.
  Leave procreants° alone and shut the door;
  Cough or cry hem if anybody come.
  Your mystery, your mystery!° Nay, dispatch!   30
                              Exit Emilia.

DESDEMONA: Upon my knees, what doth your speech
    import?
  I understand a fury in your words,
  [But not the words.]
OTHELLO: Why, what art thou?
DESDEMONA: Your wife, my lord;
    your true
  And loyal wife.
OTHELLO: Come, swear it, damn thyself;   35
  Lest, being like one of heaven,° the devils
    themselves
  Should fear to seize thee. Therefore be double-
    damned —
  Swear thou art honest.°
DESDEMONA: Heaven doth truly know it.
OTHELLO: Heaven truly knows that thou art false as
    hell.

IV, II. 14. **abuse . . . bosom:** Deceive your heart.   16. **serpent's curse:** (Cf. Genesis 3:14).   28. **procreants:** Mating couples.   30. **mystery:** Trade, occupation.   36. **being . . . heaven:** Looking like an angel.   38. **honest:** Chaste.

DESDEMONA: To whom, my lord? With whom? How
40   am I false?
OTHELLO: Ah, Desdemona! away! away! away!
DESDEMONA: Alas the heavy day! Why do you weep?
    Am I the motive of these tears, my lord?
    If haply you my father do suspect
45   An instrument° of this your calling back,
    Lay not your blame on me. If you have lost him,
    Why, I have lost him too.
OTHELLO: Had it pleased heaven
    To try me with affliction, had they rained
    All kinds of sores and shames on my bare head,
50   Steeped me in poverty to the very lips,
    Given to captivity me and my utmost hopes,
    I should have found in some place of my soul
    A drop of patience. But, alas, to make me
    A fixèd figure for the time of scorn°
55   To point his slow unmoving finger at!
    Yet could I bear that too; well, very well.
    But there where I have garnered up my heart,
    Where either I must live or bear no life,
    The fountain from the which my current runs
60   Or else dries up — to be discarded thence,
    Or keep it as a cistern for foul toads
    To knot and gender in — turn thy complexion
    there,°
    Patience, thou young and rose-lipped cherubin!
    Ay, there look grim as hell!
65 DESDEMONA: I hope my noble lord esteems me honest.
OTHELLO: O, ay; as summer flies are in the shambles,°
    That quicken° even with blowing. O thou weed,
    Who art so lovely fair, and smell'st so sweet,
    That the sense aches at thee, would thou hadst ne'er
    been born!
DESDEMONA: Alas, what ignorant sin have I
70   committed?
OTHELLO: Was this fair paper, this most goodly book,
    Made to write "whore" upon? What committed?
    Committed? O thou public commoner!°
    I should make very forges of my cheeks
75   That would to cinders burn up modesty,
    Did I but speak thy deeds. What committed?
    Heaven stops the nose at it, and the moon winks;°
    The bawdy wind, that kisses all it meets,
    Is hushed within the hollow mine of earth
80   And will not hear it. What committed?
    Impudent strumpet!
DESDEMONA: By heaven, you do me wrong!
OTHELLO: Are not you a strumpet?
DESDEMONA: No, as I am a Christian!
    If to preserve this vessel for my lord
    From any other foul unlawful touch
85   Be not to be a strumpet, I am none.

---

45. **An instrument:** To be the cause. 54. **time of scorn:** Scornful world. 62. **turn thy complexion there:** Change thy color at that point. 66. **shambles:** Slaughterhouse. 67. **quicken:** Come to life. 73. **commoner:** Harlot. 77. **winks:** Closes her eyes.

OTHELLO: What, not a whore?
DESDEMONA: No, as I shall be saved!
OTHELLO: Is't possible?
DESDEMONA: O, heaven forgive us!
OTHELLO: I cry you mercy° then.
    I took you for that cunning whore of Venice
    That married with Othello. — [*Calling.*] You,
    mistress,   90
    That have the office opposite to Saint Peter
    And keep the gate of hell!

Enter Emilia.

                   You, you, ay, you!
    We have done our course; there's money for your
    pains:
    I pray you turn the key, and keep our counsel. *Exit.*
EMILIA: Alas, what does this gentleman conceive?   95
    How do you, madam? How do you, my good lady?
DESDEMONA: Faith, half asleep.°
EMILIA: Good madam, what's the matter with my lord?
DESDEMONA: With who?
EMILIA: Why, with my lord, madam.   100
DESDEMONA: Who is thy lord?
EMILIA: He that is yours, sweet lady.
DESDEMONA: I have none. Do not talk to me, Emilia.
    I cannot weep; nor answer have I none
    But what should go by water. Prithee to-night
    Lay on my bed my wedding sheets, remember;   105
    And call thy husband hither.
EMILIA: Here's a change indeed!
                         Exit.
DESDEMONA: 'Tis meet I should be used so, very meet.
    How have I been behaved, that he might stick
    The small'st opinion° on my least misuse?°

Enter Iago and Emilia.

IAGO: What is your pleasure, madam? How is't with
    you?   110
DESDEMONA: I cannot tell. Those that do teach young
    babes
    Do it with gentle means and easy tasks:
    He might have chid me so; for, in good faith,
    I am a child to chiding.
IAGO: What is the matter, lady?
EMILIA: Alas, Iago, my lord hath so bewhored her,   115
    Thrown such despite and heavy terms upon her
    As true hearts cannot bear.
DESDEMONA: Am I that name, Iago?
IAGO: What name, fair lady?
DESDEMONA: Such as she said my lord did say I was.
EMILIA: He called her whore. A beggar in his drink   120
    Could not have laid such terms upon his callet.°
IAGO: Why did he so?
DESDEMONA: I do not know; I am sure I am none such.

---

88. **cry you mercy:** Beg your pardon. 97. **half asleep:** I.e., stunned. 109. **small'st opinion:** Least suspicion. **least misuse:** Slightest misconduct. 121. **callet:** Whore.

IAGO: Do not weep, do not weep. Alas the day!
125 EMILIA: Hath she forsook so many noble matches,
    Her father and her country, and her friends,
    To be called whore? Would it not make one weep?
DESDEMONA: It is my wretched fortune.
IAGO: Beshrew him for't!
    How comes this trick° upon him?
DESDEMONA: Nay, heaven doth know.
130 EMILIA: I will be hanged if some eternal villain,
    Some busy and insinuating rogue,
    Some cogging, cozening° slave, to get some office,
    Have not devised this slander. I'll be hanged else.
IAGO: Fie, there is no such man! It is impossible.
135 DESDEMONA: If any such there be, heaven pardon him!
EMILIA: A halter pardon him! and hell gnaw his bones!
    Why should he call her whore? Who keeps her
       company?
    What place? what time? what form? what likelihood?
    The Moor 's abused by some most villainous knave,
140   Some base notorious knave, some scurvy fellow.
    O heaven, that such companions° thou 'dst unfold,°
    And put in every honest hand a whip
    To lash the rascals naked through the world
    Even from the east to th' west!
IAGO: Speak within door.°
145 EMILIA: O, fie upon them! Some such squire he was
    That turned your wit the seamy side without
    And made you to suspect me with the Moor.
IAGO: You are a fool. Go to.
DESDEMONA: Alas, Iago,
    What shall I do to win my lord again?
150   Good friend, go to him; for, by this light of heaven,
    I know not how I lost him. Here I kneel:
    If e'er my will did trespass 'gainst his love
    Either in discourse° of thought or actual deed,
    Or that mine eyes, mine ears, or any sense
155   Delighted them in any other form,
    Or that I do not yet, and ever did,
    And ever will (though he do shake me off
    To beggarly divorcement) love him dearly,
    Comfort forswear° me! Unkindness may do much;
160   And his unkindness may defeat° my life,
    But never taint my love. I cannot say "whore."
    It does abhor me now I speak the word;
    To do the act that might the addition earn
    Not the world's mass of vanity could make me.
165 IAGO: I pray you be content. 'Tis but his humor.
    The business of the state does him offense,
    [And he does chide with you.]
DESDEMONA: If 'twere no other —
IAGO: 'Tis but so, I warrant.

[*Trumpets within.*]

Hark how these instruments summon you to supper.
The messengers of Venice stay the meat: 170
Go in, and weep not. All things shall be well.

    Exeunt Desdemona and Emilia.

Enter Roderigo.

    How now, Roderigo?
RODERIGO: I do not find that thou deal'st justly with me.
IAGO: What in the contrary?
RODERIGO: Every day thou daff'st me with some   175
    device,° Iago, and rather, as it seems to me now,
    keep'st from me all conveniency° than suppliest me
    with the least advantage of hope. I will indeed no
    longer endure it; nor am I yet persuaded to put up in
    peace what already I have foolishly suffered.   180
IAGO: Will you hear me, Roderigo?
RODERIGO: Faith, I have heard too much; for your
    words and performances are no kin together.
IAGO: You charge me most unjustly.
RODERIGO: With naught but truth. I have wasted myself   185
    out of my means. The jewels you have had from me
    to deliver to Desdemona would half have corrupted a
    votarist.° You have told me she hath received them,
    and returned me expectations and comforts of sud-
    den respect° and acquaintance; but I find none.   190
IAGO: Well, go to; very well.
RODERIGO: Very well! go to! I cannot go to, man; nor
    'tis not very well. By this hand, I say 'tis very scurvy,
    and begin to find myself fopped° in it.
IAGO: Very well.   195
RODERIGO: I tell you 'tis not very well. I will make my-
    self known to Desdemona. If she will return me my
    jewels, I will give over my suit and repent my unlaw-
    ful solicitation; if not, assure yourself I will seek satis-
    faction of you.   200
IAGO: You have said now.
RODERIGO: Ay, and said nothing but what I protest in-
    tendment of doing.
IAGO: Why, now I see there's mettle in thee; and even
    from this instant do build on thee a better opinion   205
    than ever before. Give me thy hand, Roderigo. Thou
    has taken against me a most just exception; but yet I
    protest I have dealt most directly° in thy affair.
RODERIGO: It hath not appeared.
IAGO: I grant indeed it hath not appeared, and your   210
    suspicion is not without wit and judgment. But,
    Roderigo, if thou hast that in thee indeed which I
    have greater reason to believe now than ever, I mean
    purpose, courage, and valor, this night show it. If
    thou the next night following enjoy not Desdemona,   215
    take me from this world with treachery and devise
    engines for° my life.

---

129. trick: Freakish behavior.   **132. cogging, cozening:** Cheating, defrauding.   **141. companions:** Rogues.   **unfold:** Expose. **144. within door:** With restraint.   **153. discourse:** Course. **159. Comfort forswear:** Happiness forsake.   **160. defeat:** Destroy.

175–76. thou . . . device: You put me off with some trick. **177. conveniency:** Favorable opportunities.   **188. votarist:** Nun.   **190. sudden respect:** Immediate notice.   **194. fopped:** Duped.   **208. directly:** Straightforwardly.   **217. engines for:** Plots against.

RODERIGO: Well, what is it? Is it within reason and com-
    pass?
220 IAGO: Sir, there is especial commission come from
    Venice to depute Cassio in Othello's place.
RODERIGO: Is that true? Why, then Othello and Desde-
    mona return again to Venice.
IAGO: O, no; he goes into Mauritania and takes away
225 with him the fair Desdemona, unless his abode be lin-
    gered here° by some accident; wherein none can be
    so determinate° as the removing of Cassio.
RODERIGO: How do you mean removing of him?
IAGO: Why, by making him uncapable of Othello's
230 place — knocking out his brains.
RODERIGO: And that you would have me to do?
IAGO: Ay, if you dare do yourself a profit and a right. He
    sups to-night with a harlotry, and thither will I go to
    him. He knows not yet of his honorable fortune. If
235 you will watch his going thence, which I will fashion
    to fall out between twelve and one, you may take
    him at your pleasure. I will be near to second your
    attempt, and he shall fall between us. Come, stand
    not amazed at it, but go along with me. I will show
240 you such a necessity in his death that you shall think
    yourself bound to put it on him. It is now high sup-
    per time, and the night grows to waste. About it!
RODERIGO: I will hear further reason for this.
IAGO: And you shall be satisfied.   *Exeunt.*

Scene III

Within the castle.

*Enter Othello, Lodovico, Desdemona, Emilia, and
Attendants.*

LODOVICO: I do beseech you, sir, trouble yourself no
    further.
OTHELLO: O, pardon me; 'twill do me good to walk.
LODOVICO: Madam, good night. I humbly thank your
    ladyship.
DESDEMONA: Your honor is most welcome.
OTHELLO: Will you
    walk, sir?
5   O, Desdemona —
DESDEMONA: My lord?
OTHELLO: Get you to bed on th' instant; I will be
    returned forthwith. Dismiss your attendant there.
    Look 't be done.
10 DESDEMONA: I will, my lord.

            Exit [Othello, with Lodovico and Attendants].

EMILIA: How goes it now? He looks gentler than he
    did.
DESDEMONA: He says he will return incontinent.°

He hath commanded me to go to bed,
And bade me to dismiss you.
EMILIA: Dismiss me?
DESDEMONA: It was his bidding; therefore, good
    Emilia,   15
    Give me my nightly wearing, and adieu.
    We must not now displease him.
EMILIA: I would you had never seen him!
DESDEMONA: So would not I. My love doth so approve
    him
    That even his stubbornness,° his checks,° his
        frowns —   20
    Prithee unpin me — have grace and favor in them.
EMILIA: I have laid those sheets you bade me on the bed.
DESDEMONA: All's one. Good faith, how foolish are
    our minds!
    If I do die before thee, prithee shroud me
    In one of those same sheets.
EMILIA: Come, come! You talk.   25
DESDEMONA: My mother had a maid called Barbary.
    She was in love; and he she loved proved mad°
    And did forsake her. She had a song of "Willow";
    An old thing 'twas; but it expressed her fortune,
    And she died singing it. That song to-night   30
    Will not go from my mind; I have much to do
    But to go hang my head all at one side
    And sing it like poor Barbary. Prithee dispatch.
EMILIA: Shall I go fetch your nightgown?°
DESDEMONA: No, unpin me here.   35
    This Lodovico is a proper man.
EMILIA: A very handsome man.
DESDEMONA: He speaks well.
EMILIA: I know a lady in Venice would have walked
    barefoot to Palestine for a touch of his nether lip.   40
DESDEMONA (*sings*):
    "The poor soul sat sighing by a sycamore tree
    Sing all a green willow;
    Her hand on her bosom, her head on her knee,
    Sing willow, willow, willow.
    The fresh streams ran by her and murmured her
        moans;   45
    Sing willow, willow, willow;
    Her salt tears fell from her, and soft'ned the
        stones" —
    Lay by these.
    "Sing willow, willow, willow" —
    Prithee hie thee;° he'll come anon.   50
    "Sing all a green willow must be my garland.
    Let nobody blame him; his scorn I approve" —
    Nay, that's not next. Hark! who is 't that knocks?
EMILIA: It's the wind.
DESDEMONA (*sings*):
    "I call my love false love; but what said he then?   55
    Sing willow, willow, willow:

225–26. abode . . . here: Stay here be extended.   227. deter-
minate: Effective.   IV, III. 12. incontinent: At once.

20. stubbornness: Roughness.   checks: Rebukes.   27. mad:
Wild, faithless.   34. nightgown: Dressing gown.   50. hie thee:
Hurry.

If I court moe women, you'll couch with moe
   men."
So get thee gone; good night. Mine eyes do itch.
Doth that bode weeping?
EMILIA: 'Tis neither here nor there.
DESDEMONA: I have heard it said so. O, these men,
60   these men!
Dost thou in conscience think — tell me, Emilia —
That there be women do abuse their husbands
In such gross kind?
EMILIA: There be some such, no question.
DESDEMONA: Wouldst thou do such a deed for all the
   world?
EMILIA: Why, would not you?
65 DESDEMONA: No, by this heavenly light!
EMILIA: Nor I neither by this heavenly light.
   I might do't as well i' th' dark.
DESDEMONA: Wouldst thou do such a deed for all the
   world?
70 EMILIA: The world's a huge thing; it is a great price for a
   small vice.
DESDEMONA: In troth, I think thou wouldst not.
EMILIA: In troth, I think I should; and undo't when I had
   done it. Marry, I would not do such a thing for a
75   joint-ring,° nor for measures of lawn, nor for gowns,
   petticoats, nor caps, nor any petty exhibition;° but,
   for all the whole world — 'Ud's pity! who would not
   make her husband a cuckold to make him a monarch? I should venture purgatory for't.
80 DESDEMONA: Beshrew me if I would do such a wrong
   For the whole world.
EMILIA: Why, the wrong is but a wrong i' th' world; and
   having the world for your labor, 'tis a wrong in your
   own world, and you might quickly make it right.
85 DESDEMONA: I do not think there is any such woman.
EMILIA: Yes, a dozen; and as many to th' vantage° as
   Would store° the world they played for.
   But I do think it is their husbands' faults
   If wives do fall. Say that they slack their duties
90   And pour our treasures into foreign laps;
   Or else break out in peevish° jealousies,
   Throwing restraint upon us; or say they strike us,
   Or scant our former having° in despite —
   Why, we have galls;° and though we have some
     grace,
95   Yet have we some revenge. Let husbands know
   Their wives have sense like them. They see, and
     smell,
   And have their palates both for sweet and sour,
   As husbands have. What is it that they do
   When they change us for others? Is it sport?
100   I think it is. And doth affection breed it?
   I think it doth. Is't frailty that thus errs?

It is so too. And have not we affections,
Desires for sport, and frailty, as men have?
Then let them use us well; else let them know,
The ills we do, their ills instruct us so.   105
DESDEMONA: Good night, good night. God me such
   usage° send,
Not to pick bad from bad, but by bad mend!
                    Exeunt.

ACT V • *Scene I*

A street in Cyprus.

Enter Iago and Roderigo.

IAGO: Here, stand behind this bulk;° straight will he
   come.
   Wear thy good rapier bare, and put it home.
   Quick, quick! Fear nothing; I'll be at thy elbow.
   It makes us, or it mars us — think on that,
   And fix most firm thy resolution.   5
RODERIGO: Be near at hand; I may miscarry in't.
IAGO: Here, at thy hand. Be bold, and take thy stand.

[Stands aside.]

RODERIGO: I have no great devotion to the deed,
   And yet he hath given me satisfying reasons.
   'Tis but a man gone. Forth my sword! He dies!   10
IAGO: I have rubbed this young quat° almost to the
   sense,°
   And he grows angry. Now whether he kill Cassio,
   Or Cassio him, or each do kill the other,
   Every way makes my gain. Live Roderigo,
   He calls me to a restitution large   15
   Of gold and jewels that I bobbed° from him
   As gifts to Desdemona.
   It must not be. If Cassio do remain,
   He hath a daily beauty in his life
   That makes me ugly; and besides, the Moor   20
   May unfold me to him; there stand I in much peril.
   No, he must die. Be't so! I hear him coming.

Enter Cassio.

RODERIGO: I know his gait. 'Tis he. Villain, thou diest!

[Makes a pass at Cassio.]

CASSIO: That thrust had been mine enemy indeed
   But that my coat° is better than thou know'st.   25
   I will make proof of thine.

[Draws, and wounds Roderigo.]

RODERIGO: O, I am slain!

*[Iago darts from concealment behind Cassio,
   wounds him in the leg, and exits.]*

---

75. **joint-ring:** Ring made in separable halves.   76. **exhibition:** Gift.   86. **to th' vantage:** Besides.   87. **store:** Populate.
91. **peevish:** Senseless.   93. **having:** Allowance.   94. **galls:**
Spirits to resent.

106. **usage:** Habits.   **V, I. 1. bulk:** Projecting shop-front.
11. **quat:** Pimple. **sense:** Quick.   16. **bobbed:** Swindled.
25. **coat:** Undershirt of mail.

CASSIO: I am maimed for ever. Help, ho! Murder!
    murder!

[*Falls.*]
Enter Othello.

OTHELLO: The voice of Cassio. Iago keeps his word.
RODERIGO: O, villain that I am!
OTHELLO: It is even so.
30 CASSIO: O, help, ho! light! a surgeon!
OTHELLO: 'Tis he. O brave Iago, honest and just,
    That hast such noble sense of thy friend's wrong!
    Thou teachest me. Minion,° your dear lies dead,
    And your unblest fate hies.° Strumpet, I come.
    Forth of my heart those charms, thine eyes, are
35   blotted.
    Thy bed, lust-stained, shall with lust's blood be
    spotted.   *Exit Othello.*

Enter Lodovico and Gratiano.

CASSIO: What, ho? No watch? No passage?° Murder!
    murder!
GRATIANO: 'Tis some mischance. The cry is very
    direful.
CASSIO: O, help!
40 LODOVICO: Hark!
RODERIGO: O wretched villain!
LODOVICO: Two or three groan. It is a heavy° night.
    These may be counterfeits. Let's think't unsafe
    To come in to the cry without more help.
45 RODERIGO: Nobody come? Then shall I bleed to death.
LODOVICO: Hark!

Enter Iago, with a light.

GRATIANO: Here's one comes in his shirt, with light
    and weapons.
IAGO: Who's there? Whose noise is this that cries on°
    murder?
LODOVICO: We do not know.
IAGO: Did not you hear a cry?
CASSIO: Here, here! For heaven's sake, help me!
IAGO: What's
50   the matter?
GRATIANO: This is Othello's ancient, as I take it.
LODOVICO: The same indeed, a very valiant fellow.
IAGO: What are you here that cry so grievously?
CASSIO: Iago? O, I am spoiled, undone by villains!
55   Give me some help.
IAGO: O me, lieutenant! What villains have done this?
CASSIO: I think that one of them is hereabout
    And cannot make° away.
IAGO: O treacherous villains!

[*To Lodovico and Gratiano.*]

    What are you there? Come in, and give some help.

RODERIGO: O, help me here!   60
CASSIO: That's one of them.
IAGO: O murd'rous slave! O villain!

[*Stabs Roderigo.*]

RODERIGO: O damned Iago! O inhuman dog!
IAGO: Kill men i' th' dark? — Where be these bloody
    thieves? —
    How silent is this town! — Ho! murder! murder! —
    What may you be? Are you of good or evil?   65
LODOVICO: As you shall prove us, praise us.
IAGO: Signior Lodovico?
LODOVICO: He, sir.
IAGO: I cry you mercy. Here's Cassio hurt by villains.
GRATIANO: Cassio?   70
IAGO: How is't, brother?
CASSIO: My leg is cut in two.
IAGO: Marry,° heaven forbid!
    Light, gentlemen. I'll bind it with my shirt.

Enter Bianca.

BIANCA: What is the matter, ho? Who is't that cried?
IAGO: Who is't that cried?   75
BIANCA: O my dear Cassio! my sweet Cassio!
    O Cassio, Cassio, Cassio!
IAGO: O notable strumpet! — Cassio, may you suspect
    Who they should be that have thus mangled you?
CASSIO: No.   80
GRATIANO: I am sorry to find you thus. I have been to
    seek you.
IAGO: Lend me a garter. So. O for a chair°
    To bear him easily hence!
BIANCA: Alas, he faints! O Cassio, Cassio, Cassio!
IAGO: Gentlemen all, I do suspect this trash   85
    To be a party in this injury. —
    Patience a while, good Cassio. — Come, come!
    Lend me a light. Know we this face or no?
    Alas, my friend and my dear countryman
    Roderigo? No — Yes, sure. — O heaven, Roderigo!   90
GRATIANO: What, of Venice?
IAGO: Even he, sir. Did you know him?
GRATIANO: Know him? Ay.
IAGO: Signior Gratiano? I cry your gentle pardon.
    These bloody accidents must excuse my manners
    That so neglected you.
GRATIANO: I am glad to see you.   95
IAGO: How do you, Cassio? — O, a chair, a chair!
GRATIANO: Roderigo?
IAGO: He, he, 'tis he!

[*A chair brought in.*]

    O, that's well said;° the chair.
    Some good man bear him carefully from hence.   100
    I'll fetch the general's surgeon. [*To Bianca.*] For you,
    mistress,

---

33. Minion: Mistress.   **34. hies:** Hurries on.   **37. passage:**
Passersby.   **42. heavy:** Cloudy, dark.   **48. cries on:** Raises the
cry of.   **58. make:** Get.

72. Marry: (From "By Mary").   **82. chair:** Litter.   **99. well
said:** Well done.

Save you your labor. — He that lies slain here,
Cassio,
  Was my dear friend. What malice was between you?
CASSIO: None in the world; nor do I know the man.
IAGO [*to Bianca*]: What, look you pale? — O, bear him
105   out o' th' air.

               [*Cassio and Roderigo are borne off.*]

  Stay you, good gentlemen. — Look you pale,
    mistress? —
  Do you perceive the gastness° of her eye? —
  Nay, if you stare, we shall hear more anon.
  Behold her well; I pray you look upon her.
110 Do you see, gentlemen? Nay, guiltiness will speak.
  Though tongues were out of use.

Enter Emilia.

EMILIA: 'Las, what's the matter? What's the matter,
    husband?
IAGO: Cassio hath here been set on in the dark
  By Roderigo, and fellows that are scaped.
115 He's almost slain, and Roderigo dead.
EMILIA: Alas, good gentlemen! alas, good Cassio!
IAGO: This is the fruits of whoring. Prithee, Emilia,
  Go know of Cassio where he supped to-night.

[*To Bianca.*]

  What, do you shake at that?
BIANCA: He supped at my house; but I therefore shake
120 not.
IAGO: O, did he so? I charge you go with me.
EMILIA: Fie, fie upon thee, strumpet!
BIANCA: I am no strumpet, but of life as honest°
  As you that thus abuse me.
EMILIA: As I? Foh! fie upon thee!
125 IAGO: Kind gentlemen, let's go see poor Cassio dressed.

[*To Bianca.*]

  Come, mistress, you must tell 's another tale.
  Emilia, run you to the citadel
  And tell my lord and lady what hath happed.

                   [*Exit Emilia.*]

  Will you go on afore?   *Exeunt* [*all but Iago*].
          This is the night
130 That either makes me or fordoes° me quite.   [*Exit.*]

Scene II

A bedchamber in the castle.

Desdemona [*asleep*] *in her bed. Enter Othello with a light.*

OTHELLO: It is the cause, it is the cause,° my soul.
  Let me not name it to you, you chaste stars!

It is the cause. Yet I'll not shed her blood,
Nor scar that whiter skin of hers than snow,
And smooth as monumental alabaster.   5
Yet she must die, else she'll betray more men.
Put out the light, and then put out the light.
If I quench thee, thou flaming minister,°
I can again thy former light restore,
Should I repent me; but once put out thy light,   10
Thou cunning'st pattern of excelling nature,
I know not where is that Promethean heat°
That can thy light relume.° When I have plucked the
  rose,
I cannot give it vital growth again;
It needs must wither. I'll smell thee on the tree.   15

(*He kisses her.*)

  O balmy breath, that dost almost persuade
Justice to break her sword! One more, one more!
Be thus when thou art dead, and I will kill thee,
And love thee after. One more, and that's the last!
So sweet was ne'er so fatal. I must weep,   20
But they are cruel tears. This sorrow's heavenly;
It strikes where it doth love. She wakes.
DESDEMONA: Who's there? Othello?
OTHELLO: Ay, Desdemona.
DESDEMONA: Will you come to bed, my lord?
OTHELLO: Have you prayed to-night, Desdemon?
DESDEMONA: Ay,
  my lord.   25
OTHELLO: If you bethink yourself of any crime°
  Unreconciled as yet to heaven and grace,
  Solicit for it straight.
DESDEMONA: Alack, my lord, what may you mean by
  that?
OTHELLO: Well, do it, and be brief; I will walk by.   30
  I would not kill thy unprepared spirit.
  No, heaven forfend!° I would not kill thy soul.
DESDEMONA: Talk you of killing?
OTHELLO: Ay, I do.
DESDEMONA: Then heaven
  Have mercy on me!
OTHELLO: Amen, with all my heart!
DESDEMONA: If you say so, I hope you will not kill me. 35
OTHELLO: Hum!
DESDEMONA: And yet I fear you; for you're fatal then
  When your eyes roll so. Why I should fear I know
    not,
  Since guiltiness I know not; but yet I feel I fear.
OTHELLO: Think on thy sins.
DESDEMONA: They are loves I bear to you. 40
OTHELLO: Ay, and for that thou diest.
DESDEMONA: That death 's unnatural that kills for
  loving.
  Alas, why gnaw you so your nether lip?
  Some bloody passion shakes your very frame.

---

107. **gastness:** Terror. 123. **honest:** Chaste. 130. **fordoes:**
Destroys. **V, II. 1. cause:** Cause of justice.

8. **minister:** Servant. 12. **Promethean heat:** Divine fire. 13. **relume:** Relight. 26. **crime:** Sin. 32. **forfend:** Forbid.

45 These are portents,° but yet I hope, I hope,
They do not point on me.
OTHELLO: Peace and be still!
DESDEMONA: I will so. What's the matter?
OTHELLO: That handkerchief which I so loved and
     gave thee
Thou gav'st to Cassio.
DESDEMONA: No, by my life and soul!
Send for the man and ask him.
50 OTHELLO: Sweet soul, take heed,
Take heed of perjury; thou art on thy deathbed.
DESDEMONA: Ay, but not yet to die.
OTHELLO: Yes, presently.°
Therefore confess thee freely of thy sin;
For to deny each article with oath
55 Cannot remove nor choke the strong conception°
That I do groan withal. Thou art to die.
DESDEMONA: Then Lord have mercy on me!
OTHELLO: I say amen.
DESDEMONA: And have you mercy too! I never did
Offend° you in my life; never loved Cassio
60 But with such general warranty of heaven
As I might love. I never gave him token.
OTHELLO: By heaven, I saw my handkerchief in's hand!
O perjured woman! thou dost stone my heart,°
And mak'st me call what I intend to do
65 A murder, which I thought a sacrifice.
I saw the handkerchief.
DESDEMONA: He found it then.
I never gave it him. Send for him hither.
Let him confess a truth.
OTHELLO: He hath confessed.
DESDEMONA: What, my lord?
OTHELLO: That he hath used thee.
DESDEMONA: How? Unlawfully?
70 OTHELLO: Ay.
DESDEMONA: He will not say so.
OTHELLO: No, his mouth is stopped.
Honest Iago hath ta'en order° for't.
DESDEMONA: O, my fear interprets. What, is he dead?
OTHELLO: Had all his hairs been lives, my great
     revenge
75 Had stomach for them all.
DESDEMONA: Alas, he is betrayed, and I undone!
OTHELLO: Out, strumpet! Weep'st thou for him to my
     face?
DESDEMONA: O, banish me, my lord, but kill me not!
OTHELLO: Down, strumpet!
80 DESDEMONA: Kill me to-morrow; let me live to-night!
OTHELLO: Nay, if you strive —
DESDEMONA: But half an hour!
OTHELLO: Being done, there is no pause.
DESDEMONA: But while I say one prayer!
OTHELLO: It is too late.

---

45. **portents:** Signs of impending violence. **52. presently:** At once. **55. conception:** Belief. **59. Offend:** Wrong. **63. stone my heart:** Turn my heart to stone. **72. ta'en order:** Taken measures.

(Smothers her.)

[DESDEMONA: O Lord, Lord, Lord!]

Emilia at the door.

EMILIA (*calls within*): My lord, my lord! What, ho! my
     lord, my lord!   85
OTHELLO: What noise is this? Not dead? not yet quite
     dead?
I that am cruel am yet merciful;
I would not have thee linger in thy pain.
So, so.
EMILIA (*within*): What, ho! my lord, my lord!
OTHELLO: Who's there?   90
EMILIA (*within*): O, good my lord, I would speak a
     word with you!
OTHELLO: Yes, 'tis Emilia. — By and by.° — She's
     dead. —
'Tis like she comes to speak of Cassio's death.
The noise was here. Ha! no more moving?
Still as the grave. — Shall she come in? Were't
     good! —   95
I think she stirs again. No. — What's best to do?
If she come in, she'll sure speak to my wife.
My wife! my wife! what wife! I have no wife.
O, insupportable! O heavy hour!
Methinks it should be now a huge eclipse   100
Of sun and moon, and that th' affrighted globe
Should yawn° at alteration.
EMILIA (*within*):   I do beseech you
That I may speak with you, O good my lord!
OTHELLO: I had forgot thee. O, come in, Emilia.
Soft, by and by. — Let me the curtains draw. —   105

[*Closes the bed-curtains.*]

Where art thou?

[*Opens the door.*]
Enter Emilia.
                              What's the matter with thee now?
EMILIA: O my good lord, yonder's foul murder done!
OTHELLO: What? Now?
EMILIA: But now, my lord.
OTHELLO: It is the very error° of the moon.   110
She comes more nearer earth than she was wont
And makes men mad.
EMILIA: Cassio, my lord, hath killed a young Venetian
Called Roderigo.
OTHELLO: Roderigo killed?
And Cassio killed?
EMILIA: No, Cassio is not killed.   115
OTHELLO: Not Cassio killed? Then murder's out of
     tune,
And sweet revenge grows harsh.
DESDEMONA: O, falsely, falsely murdered?

---

92. **By and by:** Just a moment (addressed to Emilia). 102. **yawn:** Open, as in an earthquake. 110. **error:** Straying off course.

EMILIA: O, Lord!
    what cry is that?
OTHELLO: That? What?
120 EMILIA: Out and alas! that was my lady's voice.
    Help! help, ho! help! O lady, speak again!
    Sweet Desdemona! O sweet mistress, speak!
DESDEMONA: A guiltless death I die.
EMILIA: O, who hath done this deed?
125 DESDEMONA: Nobody — I myself. Farewell.
    Commend° me to my kind lord. O, farewell!

(*She dies.*)

OTHELLO: Why, how should she be murd'red?
EMILIA: Alas,
    who knows?
OTHELLO: You heard her say herself, it was not I.
EMILIA: She said so. I must needs report the truth.
130 OTHELLO: She's like a liar gone to burning hell!
    'Twas I that killed her.
EMILIA: O, the more angel she,
    And you the blacker devil!
OTHELLO: She turned to folly, and she was a whore.
EMILIA: Thou dost belie her, and thou art a devil.
OTHELLO: She was false as water.°
EMILIA: Thou art rash as fire
135   to say
    That she was false. O, she was heavenly true!
OTHELLO: Cassio did top her. Ask thy husband else.
    O, I were damned beneath all depth in hell
    But that I did proceed upon just grounds
140   To this extremity. Thy husband knew it all.
EMILIA: My husband?
OTHELLO: Thy husband.
EMILIA: That she was false to wedlock?
OTHELLO: Ay, with Cassio. Nay, had she been true,
145   If heaven would make me such another world
    Of one entire and perfect chrysolite,°
    I'ld not have sold her for it.
EMILIA: My husband?
OTHELLO: Ay 'twas he that told me first.
    An honest man he is, and hates the slime
    That sticks on filthy deeds.
150 EMILIA: My husband?
OTHELLO: What needs this iterance,° woman? I say thy
    husband.
EMILIA: O mistress, villainy hath made mocks with
    love!
    My husband say that she was false?
OTHELLO: He, woman.
    I say, thy husband. Dost understand the word?
155   My friend, thy husband; honest, honest Iago.
EMILIA: If he say so, may his pernicious soul
    Rot half a grain a day! he lies to th' heart.
    She was too fond of her most filthy bargain.
OTHELLO: Ha!

EMILIA: Do thy worst. 160
    This deed of thine is no more worthy heaven
    Than thou wast worthy her.
OTHELLO: Peace, you were best.
EMILIA: Thou hast not half the power to do me harm
    As I have to be hurt.° O gull! O dolt!
    As ignorant as dirt! thou hast done a deed — 165
    I care not for thy sword; I'll make thee known,
    Though I lost twenty lives. Help! help! Ho! help!
    The Moor hath killed my mistress! Murder!
    murder!

Enter Montano, Gratiano, Iago, and others.

MONTANO: What is the matter? How now, general?
EMILIA: O, are you come, Iago? You have done well, 170
    That men must lay their murders on your neck.
GRATIANO: What is the matter?
EMILIA: Disprove this villain, if thou be'st a man.
    He says thou told'st him that his wife was false.
    I know thou didst not; thou'rt not such a villain. 175
    Speak, for my heart is full.
IAGO: I told him what I thought, and told no more
    Than what he found himself was apt and true.
EMILIA: But did you ever tell him she was false?
IAGO: I did. 180
EMILIA: You told a lie, an odious damnèd lie!
    Upon my soul, a lie! a wicked lie!
    She false with Cassio? Did you say with Cassio?
IAGO: With Cassio, mistress. Go to, charm° your
    tongue.
EMILIA: I will not charm my tongue; I am bound to
    speak: 185
    My mistress here lies murdered in her bed —
ALL: O heavens forfend!
EMILIA: And your reports have set the murder on.
OTHELLO: Nay, stare not, masters. It is true indeed.
GRATIANO: 'Tis a strange truth. 190
MONTANO: O monstrous act!
EMILIA: Villainy, villainy, villainy!
    I think upon't — I think I smell't! — O villainy!
    I thought so then. — I'll kill myself for grief. —
    O villainy, villainy!
IAGO: What, are you mad? I charge you get you home. 195
EMILIA: Good gentlemen, let me have leave to speak.
    'Tis proper I obey him, but not now.
    Perchance, Iago, I will ne'er go home.
OTHELLO: O! O! O!   (*Falls on the bed.*)
EMILIA: Nay, lay thee down and roar!
    For thou hast killed the sweetest innocent 200
    That e'er did lift up eye.
OTHELLO: O, she was foul!

[*Rises.*]

    I scarce did know you, uncle. There lies your niece,
    Whose breath, indeed, these hands have newly
    stopped.

126. Commend: Remember.   135. water: (Which is yielding).
146. chrysolite: (Precious topaz).   151. iterance: Repetition.

164. to be hurt: To endure hurt.   184. charm: Cast a spell on.

I know this act shows° horrible and grim.
GRATIANO: Poor Desdemon! I am glad thy father's
205   dead.
Thy match was mortal to him, and pure grief
Shore his old thread in twain. Did he live now,
This sight would make him do a desperate turn;°
Yea, curse his better angel from his side,
210   And fall to reprobation.°
OTHELLO: 'Tis pitiful; but yet Iago knows
That she with Cassio hath the act of shame
A thousand times committed. Cassio confessed it;
And she did gratify° his amorous works
215   With that recognizance° and pledge of love
Which I first gave her. I saw it in his hand.
It was a handkerchief, an antique token
My father gave my mother.
EMILIA: O God! O heavenly God!
IAGO: Zounds, hold your peace!
220 EMILIA: 'Twill out, 'twill out! I peace?
No, I will speak as liberal as the north,°
Let heaven and men and devils, let them all,
All, all, cry shame against me, yet I'll speak.
IAGO: Be wise, and get you home.
EMILIA: I will not.

[*Iago draws and threatens Emilia.*]

GRATIANO: Fie!
225   Your sword upon a woman?
EMILIA: O thou dull Moor, that handkerchief thou
      speak'st of
I found by fortune, and did give my husband;
For often with a solemn earnestness —
More than indeed belonged to such a trifle —
He begged of me to steal't.
230 IAGO: Villainous whore!
EMILIA: She give it Cassio? No, alas, I found it,
And I did give't my husband.
IAGO: Filth, thou liest!
EMILIA: By heaven, I do not, I do not, gentlemen.
O murd'rous coxcomb! what should such a fool
Do with so good a wife?
235 OTHELLO: Are there no stones° in heaven
But what serves for the thunder? Precious villain!

The Moor runs at Iago [*but is disarmed by Montano*].
Iago kills his wife.

GRATIANO: The woman falls. Sure he hath killed his
      wife.
EMILIA: Ay, ay. O, lay me by my mistress' side.
                              Exit Iago.
GRATIANO: He's gone, but his wife's killed.
MONTANO: 'Tis a notorious° villain. Take you this
240   weapon,

Which I have here recovered from the Moor.
Come, guard the door without. Let him not pass,
But kill him rather. I'll after that same villain,
For 'tis a damnèd slave.

      Exit [*Montano, with all but Othello and Emilia*].

OTHELLO: I am not valiant neither;
But every puny whipster° gets my sword.   245
But why should honor outlive honesty?
Let it go all.
EMILIA: What did thy song bode, lady?
Hark, canst thou hear me? I will play the swan,
And die in music. [*Sings.*] "Willow, willow, willow."
Moor, she was chaste. She loved thee, cruel Moor: 250
So come my soul to bliss as I speak true.
So speaking as I think, alas, I die.

(*She dies.*)

OTHELLO: I have another weapon in this chamber;
It is a sword of Spain, the ice brook's° temper.
O, here it is. — Uncle, I must come forth.   255
GRATIANO (*within*): If thou attempt it, it will cost thee
      dear.
Thou hast no weapon, and perforce must suffer.
OTHELLO: Look in upon me then and speak with me,
Or, naked° as I am, I will assault thee.

[*Enter Gratiano.*]

GRATIANO: What is the matter?
OTHELLO: Behold, I have a weapon;   260
A better never did itself sustain
Upon a soldier's thigh. I have seen the day
That with this little arm and this good sword
I have made my way through more impediments
Than twenty times your stop.° But O vain boast!   265
Who can control his fate? 'Tis not so now.
Be not afraid, though you do see me weaponed.
Here is my journey's end, here is my butt,°
And very seamark° of my utmost sail:
Do you go back dismayed? 'Tis a lost° fear.   270
Man but a rush° against Othello's breast,
And he retires. Where should Othello go?
Now, how dost thou look now? O ill-starred
      wench!
Pale as thy smock! When we shall meet at compt,°
This look of thine will hurl my soul from heaven,   275
And fiends will snatch at it. Cold, cold, my girl?
Even like thy chastity.
O cursèd, cursèd slave! Whip me, ye devils,
From the possession of this heavenly sight!
Blow me about in winds! roast me in sulphur!   280

205. **shows:** Appears. 208. **turn:** Act. 210. **reprobation:** Rejection by God, damnation. 214. **gratify:** Reward. 215. **recognizance:** Token. 221. **liberal as the north:** Unchecked as the north wind blows. 235. **stones:** Bolts like those used for thunderbolts. 240. **notorious:** Notable.

245. **puny whipster:** Whippersnapper. 254. **ice brook:** I.e., a Spanish blade, tempered in cold running water. 259. **naked:** Disarmed. 265. **stop:** Power to stop. 268. **butt:** Limit. 269. **seamark:** Beacon, destination. 270. **lost:** Wasted. 271. **Man but a rush:** Wield only a reed. 274. **compt:** Final accounting, Last Judgment.

Wash me in steep-down gulfs of liquid fire!
Oh Desdemon! dead Desdemon! dead! Oh! Oh!

Enter Lodovico, Montano, Iago [as prisoner], and Offi-cers; Cassio in a chair.

LODOVICO: Where is this rash and most unfortunate
    man?
OTHELLO: That's he that was Othello. Here I am.
285 LODOVICO: Where is that viper? Bring the villain forth.
OTHELLO: I look down towards his feet° — but that's a
    fable.
    If that thou be'st a devil, I cannot kill thee.

[Wounds Iago.]

LODOVICO: Wrench his sword from him.

[Othello is disarmed.]

IAGO: I bleed, sir, but not killed.
OTHELLO: I am not sorry neither. I'ld have thee live;
290   For in my sense, 'tis happiness to die.
LODOVICO: O thou Othello that wert once so good,
    Fall'n in the practice° of a damnèd slave,
    What shall be said to thee?
OTHELLO: Why, anything;
    An honorable murderer, if you will;
295   For naught did I in hate, but all in honor.
LODOVICO: This wretch hath part confessed his
    villainy.
    Did you and he consent in° Cassio's death?
OTHELLO: Ay.
CASSIO: Dear general, I never gave you cause.
300 OTHELLO: I do believe it, and I ask your pardon.
    Will you, I pray, demand that demi-devil
    Why he hath thus ensnared my soul and body?
IAGO: Demand me nothing. What you know, you
    know.
    From this time forth I never will speak word.
LODOVICO: What, not to pray?
305 GRATIANO: Torments will ope your lips.
OTHELLO: Well, thou dost best.
LODOVICO: Sir, you shall understand what hath
    befall'n,
    Which, as I think, you know not. Here is a letter
    Found in the pocket of the slain Roderigo;
310   And here another. The one of them imports
    The death of Cassio to be undertook
    By Roderigo.
OTHELLO: O villain!
CASSIO: Most heathenish and most gross!
LODOVICO: Now here's another discontented paper
315   Found in the pocket too; and this, it seems,
    Roderigo mean t' have sent this damnèd villain;
    But that, belike, Iago in the nick°
    Came in and satisfied him.

OTHELLO: O thou pernicious caitiff! —
    How came you, Cassio, by that handkerchief
    That was my wife's?
CASSIO: I found it in my chamber;   320
    And he himself confessed but even now
    That there he dropped it for a special purpose
    Which wrought to his desire.
OTHELLO: O fool! fool! fool!
CASSIO: There is besides in Roderigo's letter,
    How he upbraids Iago that he made him   325
    Brave me upon the watch; whereon it came
    That I was cast;° and even but now he spake,
    After long seeming dead — Iago hurt him,
    Iago set him on.
LODOVICO: You must forsake this room and go with
    us.   330
    Your power and your command is taken off,
    And Cassio rules in Cyprus. For this slave,
    If there be any cunning cruelty
    That can torment him much and hold him long,
    It shall be his. You shall close prisoner rest   335
    Till that the nature of your fault be known
    To the Venetian state. Come, bring away.
OTHELLO: Soft you! a word or two before you go.
    I have done the state some service, and they
        know't.
    No more of that. I pray you, in your letters,   340
    When you shall these unlucky° deeds relate,
    Speak of me as I am. Nothing extenuate,
    Nor set down aught in malice. Then must you
        speak
    Of one that loved not wisely, but too well;
    Of one not easily jealous, but, being wrought,   345
    Perplexed° in the extreme; of one whose hand,
    Like the base Judean,° threw a pearl away
    Richer than all his tribe; of one whose subdued°
        eyes,
    Albeit unusèd to the melting mood,
    Drop tears as fast as the Arabian trees   350
    Their med'cinable gum. Set you down this.
    And say besides that in Aleppo once,
    Where a malignant and a turbaned Turk
    Beat a Venetian and traduced the state,
    I took by th' throat the circumcisèd dog   355
    And smote him — thus.

(He stabs himself.)

LODOVICO: O bloody period!°
GRATIANO: All that's spoke is marred.
OTHELLO: I kissed thee ere I killed thee. No way but
    this,
    Killing myself, to die upon a kiss.

(He [falls upon the bed and] dies.)

286. I . . . feet: I.e., to see if they are cloven, like the Devil's.
292. practice: Plot.   297. consent in: Agree upon.   317. nick:
Nick of time.

327. cast: Dismissed.   341. unlucky: Fatal.   346. Perplexed:
Distracted.   347. Judean: Judas Iscariot (?) (quarto reads "In-
dian").   348. subdued: I.e., conquered by grief.   357. period:
Ending.

CASSIO: This did I fear, but thought he had no
360   weapon;
       For he was great of heart.
   LODOVICO [*to Iago*]:   O Spartan dog,
       More fell° than anguish, hunger, or the sea!
       Look on the tragic loading of this bed.
       This is thy work. The object poisons sight;
365   Let it be hid.° Gratiano, keep the house,

362. fell: Cruel.   **365. Let it be hid:** I.e., draw the bed curtains.

And seize upon° the fortunes of the Moor,
For they succeed on you. To you, lord governor,
Remains the censure° of this hellish villain,
The time, the place, the torture. O, enforce it!
Myself will straight aboard, and to the state   370
This heavy act with heavy heart relate.

                                    Exeunt.

366. seize upon: Take legal possession of.   **368. censure:** Judicial sentence.

COMMENTARIES

The great Shakespeare critic A. C. Bradley examines Othello's character in a portion of his series of lectures on the play. His approach is to probe Othello's essential nature, beginning with the premise that Othello is not by nature jealous but that Iago makes him so. Virginia Mason Vaughan offers insights into the way in which one of the greatest nineteenth-century English actors prepared for the role and what he felt he had to trim from the text in order to satisfy midcentury audiences. John Holstrom's review of Laurence Olivier's singular performance in the newly founded Royal Shakespeare Company in 1964 is mixed. He praises Olivier but complains of the ensemble around him. This review touches on the ways in which even a memorable performance can be marred by a questionable production.

A. C. Bradley (1851–1935)
OTHELLO'S CHARACTER   *1904*

Among his distinguished lectures on Shakespearean tragedy, A. C. Bradley meditated on the essential nature of Othello. He sees him as a relatively simple man, especially in contrast to Iago, whom Bradley sees as more highly charged and luminous in the play. But what he sees in Othello is nobility, the same nobility that scores of theatergoers have seen on stages throughout the world.

The character of Othello is comparatively simple, but, as I have dwelt on the prominence of intrigue and accident in the play, it is desirable to show how essentially the success of Iago's plot is connected with this character. Othello's description of himself as

   one not easily jealous, but, being wrought,
Perplexed in the extreme,

is perfectly just. His tragedy lies in this — that his whole nature was indisposed to jealousy and yet was such that he was unusually open to deception and, if once wrought to passion, likely to act with little reflection, with no delay, and in the most decisive manner conceivable.

Let me first set aside a mistaken view. I do not mean the ridiculous notion that Othello was jealous by temperament, but the idea, which has some little plausibility, that the play is primarily a study of a noble barbarian, who has become a Christian and has imbibed some of the civilization of his employers, but who retains beneath the surface the savage passions of his Moorish blood and also the suspiciousness regarding female chastity common among Oriental peoples, and that the last three Acts depict the outburst of these original feelings through the thin crust of Venetian culture. It would take too long to discuss this idea,[1] and it would perhaps be useless to do so, for all arguments against it must end in an appeal to the reader's understanding of Shakespeare. If he thinks it is like Shakespeare to look at things in this manner; that he had a historical mind and occupied himself with problems of "Kulturgeschichte"; that he labored to make his Romans perfectly Roman, to give a correct view of the Britons in the days of Lear or Cymbeline, to portray in Hamlet a stage of the moral consciousness not yet reached by the people around him, the reader will also think this interpretation of *Othello* probable. To me it appears hopelessly un-Shakespearean. I could as easily believe that Chaucer meant the Wife of Bath for a study of the peculiarities of Somersetshire. I do not mean that Othello's race is a matter of no account. It has, as we shall presently see, its importance in the play. It makes a difference to our idea of him; it makes a difference to the action and catastrophe. But in regard to the essentials of his character it is not important; and if anyone had told Shakespeare that no Englishman would have acted like the Moor and had congratulated him on the accuracy of his racial psychology, I am sure he would have laughed.

Othello is, in one sense of the word, by far the most romantic figure among Shakespeare's heroes; and he is so partly from the strange life of war and adventure which he has lived from childhood. He does not belong to our world, and he seems to enter it we know not whence — almost as if from wonderland. There is something mysterious in his descent from men of royal siege; in his wanderings in vast deserts and among marvelous peoples; in his tales of magic handkerchiefs and prophetic Sibyls; in the sudden vague glimpses we get of numberless battles and sieges in which he has played the hero and has borne a charmed life; even in chance references to his baptism, his being sold to slavery, his sojourn in Aleppo.

And he is not merely a romantic figure; his own nature is romantic. He has not, indeed, the meditative or speculative imagination of Hamlet; but in the strictest sense of the word he is more poetic than Hamlet. Indeed, if one recalls Othello's most famous speeches — those that begin, "Her father loved me," "O now for ever," "Never, Iago," "Had it pleased Heaven," "It is the cause," "Behold, I have a weapon," "Soft you, a word or two before you go" — and if one places side by side with these speeches an equal number by any other hero, one will not doubt that Othello is the greatest poet of them all. There is the same poetry in his casual phrases — like "These nine moons wasted," "Keep up your bright swords, for the dew will rust them," "You chaste stars," "It is a sword of Spain, the ice-brook's

---

[1]The reader who is tempted by it should, however, first ask himself whether Othello does act like a barbarian or like a man who, though wrought almost to madness, does "all in honour."

temper," "It is the very error of the moon"— and in those brief expressions of intense feeling which ever since have been taken as the absolute expression, like

> If it were now to die,
> 'Twere now to be most happy; for, I fear,
> My soul hath her content so absolute
> That not another comfort like to this
> Succeeds in unknown fate,

or

> If she be false, O then heaven mocks itself,
> I'll not believe it;

or

> No, my heart is turned to stone; I strike it, and it hurts
>   my hand,

or

> But yet the pity of it, Iago! O Iago, the pity of it, Iago!

or

> O thou weed,
> Who are so lovely fair and smell'st so sweet
> That the sense aches at thee, would thou hadst ne'er been
>   born.

And this imagination, we feel, has accompanied his whole life. He has watched with a poet's eye the Arabian trees dropping their med'cinable gum, and the Indian throwing away his chance-found pearl; and has gazed in a fascinated dream at the Pontic sea rushing, never to return, to the Propontic and the Hellespont; and has felt as no other man ever felt (for he speaks of it as none other ever did) the poetry of the pride, pomp, and circumstance of glorious war.

So he comes before us, dark and grand, with a light upon him from the sun where he was born; but no longer young, and now grave, self-controlled, steeled by the experience of countless perils, hardships, and vicissitudes, at once simple and stately in bearing and in speech, a great man naturally modest but fully conscious of his worth, proud of his services to the State, unawed by dignitaries and unelated by honors, secure, it would seem, against all dangers from without and all rebellion from within. And he comes to have his life crowned with the final glory of love, a love as strange, adventurous and romantic as any passage of his eventful history, filling his heart with tenderness and his imagination with ecstasy. For there is no love, not that of Romeo in his youth, more steeped in imagination than Othello's.

The sources of danger in this character are revealed but too clearly by the story. In the first place, Othello's mind, for all its poetry, is very simple. He is not observant. His nature tends outward. He is quite free from introspection and is not given to reflection. Emotion excites his imagination, but it confuses and dulls his intellect. On this side he is the very opposite of Hamlet, with whom, however, he shares a great openness and trustfulness of nature. In addition, he has little experience of the corrupt products of civilized life and is ignorant of European women.

In the second place, for all his dignity and massive calm (and he has greater dignity than any other of Shakespeare's men), he is by nature full of the most vehement passion. Shakespeare emphasizes his self-control, not only by the wonderful pictures of the First Act, but by references to the past. Lodovico, amazed at his violence, exclaims:

> Is this the noble Moor whom our full Senate
> Call all in all sufficient? Is this the nature
> Whom passion could not shake? whose solid virtue
> The shot of accident nor dart of chance
> Could neither graze nor pierce?

Iago, who has here no motive for lying, asks:

> Can he be angry? I have seen the cannon
> When it hath blown his ranks into the air,
> And, like the devil, from his very arm
> Puffed his own brother — and can he be angry?[2]

This, and other aspects of his character, are best exhibited by a single line — one of Shakespeare's miracles — the words by which Othello silences in a moment the night brawl between his attendants and those of Brabantio:

> Keep up your bright swords, for the dew will rust them.

And the same self-control is strikingly shown where Othello endeavors to elicit some explanation of the fight between Cassio and Montano. Here, however, there occur ominous words, which make us feel how necessary was this self-control, and make us admire it the more:

> Now, by heaven,
> My blood begins my safer guides to rule,
> And passion, having my best judgment collied,
> Assays to lead the way.

We remember these words later, when the sun of reason is "collied," blackened and blotted out in total eclipse.

Lastly, Othello's nature is all of one piece. His trust, where he trusts, is absolute. Hesitation is almost impossible to him. He is extremely self-reliant, and decides and acts instantaneously. If stirred to indignation, as "in Aleppo once," he answers with one lightning stroke. Love, if he loves, must be to him the heaven where either he must live or bear no life. If such a passion as jealousy seizes him, it will swell into a well-nigh uncontrollable flood. He will press for immediate conviction or immediate relief. Convinced, he will act with the authority of a judge and the swiftness of a man in mortal pain. Undeceived, he will do like execution on himself.

This character is so noble, Othello's feelings and actions follow so inevitably from it and from the forces brought to bear on it, and his sufferings are so heartrending that he stirs, I believe, in most readers a passion of mingled love and pity which they feel for no other hero in Shakespeare and to which not even Mr. Swinburne can do more than justice. Yet there are some critics and not a few readers who cherish a grudge against him. They do not merely think that in the later stages of his temptation he showed a certain obtuseness and that, to speak pedantically, he acted with unjustifiable precipitance and violence; no one, I sup-

---

[2] For the actor, then, to represent him as violently angry when he cashiers Cassio is an utter mistake.

pose, denies that. But even when they admit that he was not of a jealous temper, they consider that he *was* "easily jealous"; they seem to think that it was inexcusable in him to feel any suspicion of his wife at all; and they blame him for never suspecting Iago or asking him for evidence. I refer to this attitude of mind chiefly in order to draw attention to certain points in the story. It comes partly from mere inattention (for Othello did suspect Iago and did ask him for evidence); partly from a misconstruction of the text which makes Othello appear jealous long before he really is so; and partly from failure to realize certain essential facts. I will begin with these.

(1) Othello, we have seen, was trustful and thorough in his trust. He put entire confidence in the honesty of Iago, who had not only been his companion in arms but, as he believed, had just proved his faithfulness in the matter of the marriage. This confidence was misplaced, and we happen to know it; but it was no sign of stupidity in Othello. For his opinion of Iago was the opinion of practically everyone who knew him: and that opinion was that Iago was before all things "honest," his very faults being those of excess in honesty. This being so, even if Othello had not been trustful and simple, it would have been quite unnatural in him to be unmoved by the warnings of so honest a friend, warnings offered with extreme reluctance and manifestly from a sense of a friend's duty.[3] *Any* husband would have been troubled by them.

(2) Iago does not bring these warnings to a husband who had lived with a wife for months and years and knew her like his sister or his bosom friend. Nor is there any ground in Othello's character for supposing that, if he had been such a man, he would have felt and acted as he does in the play. But he was newly married; in the circumstances he cannot have known much of Desdemona before his marriage; and further he was conscious of being under the spell of a feeling which can give glory to the truth but can also give it to a dream.

(3) This consciousness in any imaginative man is enough, in such circumstances, to destroy his confidence in his powers of perception. In Othello's case, after a long and most artful preparation, there now comes, to reinforce its effect, the suggestions that he is not an Italian, nor even a European; that he is totally ignorant of the thoughts and the customary morality of Venetian women;[4] that he had himself seen in Desdemona's deception of her father how perfect an actress she could be. As he listens in horror, for a moment at least the past is revealed to him in a new and dreadful light, and the ground seems to sink under his feet. These suggestions are followed by a tentative but hideous and humiliating insinuation of what his honest and much-experienced friend fears may be the true explanation of Desdemona's rejection of acceptable suitors and of her strange, and naturally temporary, preference for a black man. Here Iago goes too far. He sees something in Othello's face that frightens him, and he breaks off. Nor does this idea take any hold of Othello's mind. But it is not surprising that his utter powerlessness to repel it on the ground of knowledge of his wife, or even of that instinctive interpretation

[3]It is important to observe that, in his attempt to arrive at the facts about Cassio's drunken misdemeanor, Othello had just had an example of Iago's unwillingness to tell the whole truth where it must injure a friend. No wonder he feels in the temptation scene that "this honest creature doubtless Sees and knows more, much more, than he unfolds."

[4]To represent that Venetian women do not regard adultery so seriously as Othello does, and again that Othello would be wise to accept the situation like an Italian husband, is one of Iago's most artful and most maddening devices.

of character which is possible between persons of the same race,[5] should complete his misery, so that he feels he can bear no more, and abruptly dismisses his friend (III, iii, 238).

Now I repeat that *any* man situated as Othello was would have been disturbed by Iago's communications, and I add that many men would have been made wildly jealous. But up to this point, where Iago is dismissed, Othello, I must maintain, does not show jealousy. His confidence is shaken, he is confused and deeply troubled, he feels even horror; but he is not yet jealous in the proper sense of that word. In his soliloquy (III, iii, 258 ff.) the beginning of this passion may be traced; but it is only after an interval of solitude, when he has had time to dwell on the idea presented to him, and especially after statements of fact, not mere general grounds of suspicion, are offered, that the passion lays hold of him. Even then, however, and indeed to the very end, he is quite unlike the essentially jealous man, quite unlike Leontes. No doubt the thought of another man's possessing the woman he loves is intolerable to him; no doubt the sense of insult and the impulse of revenge are at times most violent; and these are the feelings of jealousy proper. But these are not the chief or the deepest source of Othello's suffering. It is the wreck of his faith and his love. It is the feeling,

> If she be false, oh then Heaven mocks itself;

the feeling,

> O Iago, the pity of it, Iago!

the feeling,

> But there where I have garner'd up my heart,
> Where either I must live, or bear no life;
> The fountain from the which my current runs,
> Or else dries up — to be discarded thence. . . .

You will find nothing like this in Leontes.

Up to this point, it appears to me, there is not a syllable to be said against Othello. But the play is a tragedy, and from this point we may abandon the ungrateful and undramatic task of awarding praise and blame. When Othello, after a brief interval, reenters (III, iii, 330), we see at once that the poison has been at work, and "burns like the mines of sulphur."

> Look where he comes! Not poppy, nor mandragora,
> Nor all the drowsy syrups of the world,
> Shall ever medicine thee to that sweet sleep
> Which thou owedst yesterday.

He is "on the rack," in an agony so unbearable that he cannot endure the sight of Iago. Anticipating the probability that Iago has spared him the whole truth, he feels that in that case his life is over and his "occupation gone" with all its glories. But he has not abandoned hope. The bare possibility that his friend is deliberately deceiv-

[5]If the reader has ever chanced to see an African violently excited, he may have been startled to observe how completely at a loss he was to interpret those bodily expressions of passion which in a fellow countryman he understands at once, and in a European foreigner with somewhat less certainty. The effect of difference in blood in increasing Othello's bewilderment regarding his wife is not sufficiently realized. The same effect has to be remembered in regard to Desdemona's mistakes in dealing with Othello in his anger.

ing him — though such a deception would be a thing so monstrously wicked that he can hardly conceive it credible — is a kind of hope. He furiously demands proof, ocular proof. And when he is compelled to see that he is demanding an impossibility he still demands evidence. He forces it from the unwilling witness, and hears the maddening tale of Cassio's dream. It is enough. And if it were not enough, has he not sometimes seen a handkerchief spotted with strawberries in his wife's hand? Yes, it was his first gift to her.

> I know not that; but such a handkerchief —
> I am sure it was your wife's — did I to-day
> See Cassio wipe his beard with.

"If it be that," he answers — but what need to test the fact? The "madness of revenge" is in his blood, and hesitation is a thing he never knew. He passes judgment and controls himself only to make his sentence a solemn vow.

The Othello of the Fourth Act is Othello in his fall. His fall is never complete, but he is much changed. Toward the close of the temptation scene he becomes at times most terrible, but his grandeur remains almost undiminished. Even in the following scene (III, iv), where he goes to test Desdemona in the matter of the handkerchief and receives a fatal confirmation of her guilt, our sympathy with him is hardly touched by any feeling of humiliation. But in the Fourth Act "Chaos has come." A slight interval of time may be admitted here. It is but slight; for it was necessary for Iago to hurry on, and terribly dangerous to leave a chance for a meeting of Cassio with Othello; and his insight into Othello's nature taught him that his plan was to deliver blow on blow, and never to allow his victim to recover from the confusion of the first shock. Still there is a slight interval; and when Othello reappears we see at a glance that he is a changed man. He is physically exhausted, and his mind is dazed. He sees everything blurred through a mist of blood and tears. He has actually forgotten the incident of the handkerchief and has to be reminded of it. When Iago, perceiving that he can now risk almost any lie, tells him that Cassio has confessed his guilt, Othello, the hero who has seemed to us only second to Coriolanus in physical power, trembles all over; he mutters disjointed words; a blackness suddenly intervenes between his eyes and the world; he takes it for the shuddering testimony of nature to the horror he has just heard, and he falls senseless to the ground. When he recovers it is to watch Cassio, as he imagines, laughing over his shame. It is an imposition so gross, and should have been one so perilous, that Iago would never have ventured it before. But he is safe now. The sight only adds to the confusion of intellect the madness of rage; and a ravenous thirst for revenge, contending with emotions of infinite longing and regret, conquers them. The delay till nightfall is torture to him. His self-control has wholly deserted him, and he strikes his wife in the presence of the Venetian envoy. He is so lost to all sense of reality that he never asks himself what will follow the deaths of Cassio and his wife. An ineradicable instinct of justice, rather than any last quiver of hope, leads him to question Emilia; but nothing could convince him now, and there follows the dreadful scene of accusation; and then, to allow us the relief of burning hatred and burning tears, the interview of Desdemona with Iago, and that last talk of hers with Emilia, and her last song.

But before the end there is again a change. The supposed death of Cassio (v, i) satiates the thirst for vengeance. The Othello who enters the bedchamber with the words,

> It is the cause, it is the cause, my soul,

is not the man of the Fourth Act. The deed he is bound to do is no murder, but a sacrifice. He is to save Desdemona from herself, not in hate but in honor; in honor, and also in love. His anger has passed; a boundless sorrow has taken its place; and

> this sorrow's heavenly:
> It strikes where it doth love.

Even when, at the sight of her apparent obduracy, and at the hearing of words which by a crowning fatality can only reconvince him of her guilt, these feelings give way to others, it is to righteous indignation they give way, not to rage; and, terribly painful as this scene is, there is almost nothing here to diminish the admiration and love which heighten pity. And pity itself vanishes, and love and admiration alone remain, in the majestic dignity and sovereign ascendancy of the close. Chaos has come and gone; and the Othello of the Council Chamber and the quay of Cyprus has returned or a greater and nobler Othello still. As he speaks those final words in which all the glory and agony of his life — long ago in India and Arabia and Aleppo, and afterward in Venice, and now in Cyprus — seem to pass before us, like the pictures that flash before the eyes of a drowning man, a triumphant scorn for the fetters of the flesh and the littleness of all the lives that must survive him sweeps our grief away, and when he dies upon a kiss the most painful of all tragedies leaves us for the moment free from pain, and exulting in the power of "love and man's unconquerable mind."

Virginia Mason Vaughan (b. 1947)
MACREADY'S OTHELLO   *1994*

In her discussion of Othello's *performance history, Virginia Mason Vaughan describes one of the greatest Shakespearean actors of the mid-nineteenth century. William Charles Macready (1793–1873) was born in England and performed in London and throughout the United States. His care in producing* Othello, *including his willingness to edit out sensitive lines, gives us an interesting insight into the history of the play's production.*

Alan Downer, Macready's biographer, describes the tragedian's acting methods: "In the study and rehearsal of a part, Macready searched for character traits which an audience would recognize as natural, and by the skillful use of pause, transition, and colloquialism strove to convey the poet's meaning."[1] One technique was the "Macready pause," a slight hesitation within the speech in imitation of a natural speaking voice. Macready used these pauses to make Othello seem more realistic. On 1 November 1836, he recorded: "I think I acted Othello well with considerable spirit, and more *pause* than I generally allow myself, which is an undoubted

---

[1]Alan Downer, *The Eminent Tragedian: William Charles Macready* (Cambridge: Harvard University Press, 1966), p. 80. See also Bertram Joseph, *The Tragic Actor* (London: Routledge and Kegan Paul, 1959), pp. 284–320, for a discussion of Macready's acting style and the traits of his competitors, including Vandenhoff, Phelps, and Kean.

improvement."[2] Again, on 7 November: "Acted Othello, not exactly well, but again derived great benefit from *taking time* between my sentences."[3] Macready also used specific stage business to achieve what he thought would be a more natural effect. Downer observes, for example, that "To further contribute to the reality of the senate scene in *Othello* he played with his back to the audience."[4]

The productions Macready mounted at Covent Garden and Drury Lane demonstrate his meticulousness over scenic design and costume. George Ellis prepared watercolor drawings of costumes and scenery from the Covent Garden *Othello* for Charles Kean; seven scenic drawings, now in the Folger Shakespeare Library,[5] show careful attention to detail. The first is a wash of the Rialto that was also used for *The Merchant of Venice,* complete with bridge, canal, gondola, and Renaissance buildings in the background. The second scene is the citadel of Famagusta on the isle of Cyprus. It consists of three layers: the front panel shows the castle wall and cannons pointing out to sea; the middle panel portrays a castle turret, while the back panel opens to a prospect across the harbor. The third scene is a gateway leading from outside the castle to the inside. The drunken revels of *Othello,* act II, scene III, would be staged before these gates. The fourth watercolor is an ornate chamber in the castle, suitable for the temptation scene, the fifth an antechamber in the castle, ornamented with carved scrolled walls. The sixth set is a piazza outside an Italian Renaissance building, flanked by columns. Last, of course, is the bedchamber. The bed, hidden in the center back alcove, is ornately decked with labial curtains. At first the bed's upstage location seems to marginalize Desdemona, but three sets of brightly colored curtains draped above lure the eye inward toward the recess. The entire set, in contrast to the grim action of the murder, is brightly colored in shades of blue, pink, and yellow.

Macready's elaborate scenery was symptomatic of his efforts to produce Shakespeare in historically accurate settings. Shattuck demonstrates the tragedian's meticulous attention to historical detail when he produced *King John.*[6] This concern was not confined to the history plays, however. For *Othello* accuracy meant realistic scenes from Renaissance Venice (the Rialto, bridge, canal, gondolas, and Doge's Palace) and Cyprus (the citadel at Famagusta). Though they were painted after the fact, these watercolors demonstrate the extravagant beauty of Macready's 1837 Covent Garden *Othello,* a beauty that set a high standard for subsequent spectacular, historically based productions.

Macready's quest for scenic harmony included detailed attention to costumes. For London productions no expense was spared. Watercolor sketches of the Covent Garden costumes[7] are just as detailed and colorful as the scenic designs. They too may have been used, where appropriate, in *The Merchant of Venice.* Brabantio wears a red robe trimmed with ermine over a black doublet. Gratiano, in

---

[2]William Charles Macready, *The Diaries of William Charles Macready,* ed. William Toynbee (London: Chapman and Hall, Ltd., 1912), v. 1, p. 354.

[3]Ibid., p. 357.

[4]Downer, *Eminent Tragedian,* p. 75.

[5]The promptbooks described below are listed in Charles H. Shattuck's *The Shakespeare Promptbooks: A Descriptive Catalogue* (Urbana: University of Illinois Press, 1965). This particular promptbook, Folger 14, is listed in Shattuck as no. 26 (p. 359).

[6]See Charles H. Shattuck, *William Charles Macready's King John* (Urbana: University of Illinois Press, 1962).

[7]Folger Promptbook 15, Shattuck 27. (See note 5 above.)

contrast, appears in a black robe with red doublet. Othello's red tunic is fringed with gold to match his gold cape. Iago is dressed in a buff doublet with a green vest and gold trim. He wears red hose and black shoes. Later, he changes to buff leggings and a blue jacket. Cassio is foppish. He sports a plumed hat, green vest, and a gold doublet slashed to show red beneath. Lodovico is more decorous in silver and blue, with hat, cape, doublet, and hose. Montano wears a long white gown trimmed in red with a gold sash. The Venetian guard appears in sixteenth-century armor, while servants are appareled in rough brown jackets and doublets. White lace signifies Desdemona's purity, whereas black (with a red underskirt) suggests Emilia's earthiness. Tissue of gold or silver bespeaks an exalted station.

Red, black, gold, white, and blue — the colors create that harmonious effect Macready so cherished. Othello's red aligned him with the Venetian Senators, figures of law and authority. Emilia's red petticoat picks up the color scheme, but her scarlet indicates easy virtue. Each scene is chromatically planned, even the bed curtains' labial folds — the shapes and colors, like the acting, should suggest the emotions represented onstage.

The grandeur of Macready's Covent Garden *Othello* is best conveyed by the Senate Council scene (I, iii). Macready's promptbook notes:

> The Senators are discov'd seated on an elevated platform, up the sides, and aX the back of the stage. Ten in Red Gowns- / including the Duke-Gratiano-and Brabantio / aX at back- Thirty- / including Lodovico / - in Black Gowns, with large open ermin'd sleeves, -at sides R & L. - The Duke's seat is slightly elevated above the others.- The Secretary is seated, - writing, and faces the duke.[8]

This scene was the culmination of Macready's search in *Othello* productions for historical accuracy; this was the Doge and his Council as he envisioned it from historical research and his own visits to Venice. Macready even covered the walls of the Doge's Hall with Titians and Tintorettos.[9] He was pleased with the result: his diary of 16 October 1837 exudes that "The Council of Forty was a scene of beautiful effect, one of the most real things I ever saw."[10]

Productions in the provinces and the United States could never be this elaborate, but traveling stars could carry their costumes with them; the Moor, at least, could be seen in appropriate splendor. Even through the swamps of Georgia, from Savannah to Mobile, Macready carted mammoth trunks of resplendent costumes so that he could represent his characters as he envisioned them.

Costumes aside, Macready's careful preparation was often wasted when he left London to play with provincial casts or journeyed to the backwoods of America. Although he was a difficult, egocentric man who often upstaged his fellow actors, as Kean had before him, one can sympathize with the meticulous actor faced with inadequate theatres and poorly prepared casts. In Liverpool, 31 January 1850, Macready found that "The Roderigo, Mr. Brown was *drunk*!"[11] Later that year in

---

[8]Folger Promptbook 13, Shattuck 25.

[9]Julie Hankey, Ed., *Othello* by William Shakespeare (Bristol: Bristol Classical Press, 1987), p. 153.

[10]William Charles Macready, *Macready's Reminiscences: and Selections from His Diaries and Letters,* ed. Sir Frederick Pollock (New York: Harper & Brothers, 1875), p. 416.

[11]Toynbee, *Diaries,* vol. II, p. 446.

Birmingham, Macready acted with an Othello who "actually *belaboured* [him] in the third act; it was so bad that at last [he] was obliged to resist the gentleman's 'corporal chastisement' and decline his shaking and pummelling!"[12] Perhaps such treatment was Macready's just punishment for rough handling of Desdemonas like Helena Faucit Martin. The wonder is that the perfectionist Macready could act at all with provincial and American casts too reluctant to rehearse and rather short on theatrical talent.

That Macready traveled from city to city, cast to cast, and performed Shakespeare's *Othello* night after night testifies to the uniformity of mid-nineteenth-century productions. As manager at Covent Garden and Drury Lane, Macready supervised his ideal *Othello*, a carefully designed performance in which scenery, costumes, blocking, and acting created a harmonious experience. In the provinces or outside New York and Philadelphia, the council scene might have two Senators instead of forty, but the blocking was substantially the same. So was the text.

A collation of the 1839 Macready acting edition with its predecessors — Mrs. Inchbald's (ca. 1808), Kemble's (1814), and Oxberry's (based on Edmund Kean's performances, 1819) — shows that Macready's Covent Garden *Othello* was somewhat more chaste and sensitive to the delicate feelings of his audiences than his predecessors'. Like Oxberry, but unlike Kemble and Inchbald, Macready's Iago makes no reference to "making the beast with two backs." Macready's Senate scene is by design much grander, requiring forty Senators rather than his predecessors' seven. Othello's cannibals and anthropophagi are quietly eliminated in keeping with the hero's dignity. On the Cyprus quay Macready drops Iago's reference to wives as "Players in your housewifery and housewives in your beds" (II, i, 111). Iago's observation that Othello "hath not yet made wanton the night with her . . ." (II, ii, 16) is also removed. Instead of "Happiness to their sheets!" Iago cries, "Happiness to them!" In the temptation scene, lines 463 to 467 are cut, whereas Inchbald and Kemble had retained them. Macready and Oxberry also root out the kisses from Cassio's dream. The major cuts from the eighteenth century — clown, Bianca, fit, willow song scene — persist. Macready's fastidiousness climaxes in act IV, scene ii, where he removes "Oh thou weed . . . That the sense aches at thee" (67–69) and "Was this fair paper . . . made to write whore upon" (71–72). He also substitutes the tame "one" for "strumpet" and "whore." In the next scene, Desdemona is not allowed to ask for her nightly apparel. Macready restores the original "Let me the curtains draw" (V, ii, 105), probably in reference to stage business. Hankey notes contemporary accounts of Macready's "thrilling effect" of thrusting his dark face through the curtains at Emilia's knock.[13] He closes the play — as Kean had done in performance — with Othello's last words.

Macready's purified text drops, in other words, all references to sheets, beds, going to bed, adultery, and sex. The bed behind half-closed curtains perhaps symbolizes the hidden sexuality underlying the play. While nothing remains in the revised language to offend a Victorian, the subject — adultery — was indeed salacious. Yet *Othello* was popular among all audiences, and no one apparently condemned the plot as immoral.

---

[12]Ibid., p. 463.
[13]Hankey, *Othello*, p. 317.

John Holstrom

GOING IT ALONE: A REVIEW OF OLIVIER'S OTHELLO   *1964*

Laurence Olivier has been considered one of the greatest Othellos of our time, but in this review John Holstrom finds fault with the production. He is careful to note that Olivier's portrayal of Othello is "a towering success," but he does so in the context of condemning most of the rest of the production. Holstrom makes us aware that for the play to work well, the cast must be balanced and equal to the measure of Othello himself.

There are differing opinions about foils. I don't mean those fencing things, or the wrappings of chocolate bars, but the setting of unobtrusive nonprecious metal into which a jewel is sunk, to shine the brighter against its dull background. This, in theatrical terms, was the view of those actor-managers (a dying if not dead race now) who surrounded themselves with a weak, untalented company so that they could shine out alone, without fear of distracting competition.

Others, however, believe that a precious stone is made more brilliant, not less, by being set in fine silver; others again have been made painfully aware that the effect of a great virtuoso performance on the stage is not heightened but cheapened by unworthy support from the rest of the cast. Acting isn't a finished form like plastic art. It has to be born again each time the curtain rises. The dynamism of a performance depends on intermeshing with a rhythm established by the lesser cogs; its character depends on relationships.

So I feel bitterly disappointed that when a theatrical jewel of great price — the long-awaited Olivier Othello, no less — finally comes our way, it should have been set in so feebly uninspired a production (by John Dexter, incredibly enough) and such a dreary, characterless cast that its power is lamed, its brilliance made to look suspect and its imaginative flights too often left to crash from their trapezes.

Sir Laurence has been quoted as saying, a few years back, that one of the reasons he hadn't attempted Othello was unwillingness to black up and sweat blood only to have the show stolen by some brilliant young fellow playing Iago. True enough, this can happen. Iago is infinitely the easier and more rewarding part, and it's rare (though it has been managed) for an actor not to be pretty striking in it. But Olivier is no fool. Having decided to do it, he wouldn't let vanity or insecurity betray him into doing an actor-manager on us, when *Othello* was at stake. This one knows. And yet the net result, at the National Theatre, has been as bad as if he had.

Essentially, make no mistake about it, his Othello is a towering success. Its lines are drawn as bravely and clearly as only a master can. This is a humorous, coolly intelligent Moor, quick to detect any false note, who could only be blinded to Iago's treachery by the deepest trust in him. He must lean on Iago with the absolute reliance many great officers have had in their serjeant-majors. Iago must therefore be a man with a different but entirely convincing mask for Othello, Cassio, Roderigo, Emilia, all the people he's intricately involved with. He must gaze into Othello's eyes with the passionate, worried devotion of a great hound. He must equally convince everyone else that he has their welfare at heart, come what may.

And at the National Theatre, what Iago do we get? We get a good little character actor called Frank Finlay, who has been puffed-up by the Royal Court claque into a thoroughly bad leading one. In Northern character parts, like Willie Mossop in *Hobson's Choice,* Finlay is admirable. As Stogumber in *Saint Joan* he was a pain. As Iago he is a national disaster, because he's giving no support at all to what would have been (but isn't) the greatest Othello of our day. Finlay's Iago is as nonexistent as Errol John's Othello was in the same building a year ago. Buff-jerkined, he lopes busily about the stage with a constant flow of neat, overelaborate gesture. He orates with flexed eyeballs and tirelessly bared teeth, spitting out each word with equal emphasis, like a punch-drunk Methodist preacher who's past caring what, if anything, it means. It's as crude, boring, and perfunctory an Iago as we'll see for a while: and the tragedy is that it gives Olivier nothing to play against and thus makes him seem sometimes unconvincing, sometimes artificial.

For this Othello, a highly wrought conception, desperately needs support. Olivier starts at a low pitch, with slightly thickened voice, working lightly and gracefully towards the sentiment and later the troubled guts of the part. In the marvelous temptation scene, he instantly registers a flicker of unease about the vanishing Cassio, but defers actual seriousness till audaciously late in the scene, holding the most delicate balance between joking and credence, keeping Iago's insinuations at bay in a kind of ironic game. He is also a Christian Othello, with a cross on his chest, and it's only when his control snaps that he tears the cross off and prays ("Now by yond marble heaven") as a Mohammedan. The epileptic fit remains a threat, nearly recurring more than once after the actual swoon. The great Propontic speeches are half-chanted, almost like Grand Opera, and it's here most of all that Olivier, supported by no sort of grandeur or passion in the rest, seems overcalculated in his isolation. The end is touchingly and beautifully done, with a return to the earlier poise and tenderness.

It could have been great. With even an averagely good Iago it probably would have been. And with a decent production and a fine Iago — the best in recent memory have been Richard Burton's rock-solid beast and Leo McKern's magnificent creation wasted on poor Errol John last year — it would have been something to tell our grandchildren about. But when all's said, this is a first attempt, not a last. Olivier is in his prime. Burton and McKern are still around, and so is Vladek Sheybal, that marvellous Pole who in spite of his accent would probably be the best Iago of all. As for the National Theatre Company, only six months old, it's already time for a ruthless shake-up.

One word of praise to Maggie Smith for a Desdemona of considerable dignity and delicacy. Her face, perhaps, is too ineradicably sly, and the mournful little voice, so perfect in comedy, is sometimes a problem in tragedy. But she was sweetly serious, besides sporting a most wringable neck.

A Cultural Casebook

The Issue of Race and Othello

Abdul El-Ouahed Ben Messasud, Moorish Ambassador to Queen Elizabeth I (reigned 1558–1603). Oil on panel. Artist unknown.

By the sixteenth century, Elizabethan England had already inherited the seeds of racial prejudice. Explorers and adventurers of the fourteenth and fifteenth centuries had written of distant, culturally exotic nations whose inhabitants were dark-skinned. In Shakespeare's time, enough Africans lived in London and in other large coastal towns that theater audiences would have had some contact with black people. Late in her reign, the strong presence of Africans in England provoked Queen Elizabeth to order some of them sent back to Africa. Understanding his times, Shakespeare knew that his audience would be prejudiced against Othello — just as certain characters in the play itself are prejudiced. He crafted his play to stimulate conflicting emotional responses in his audience — creating the black Othello as a noble, grand, and imposing figure whose flaw, jealousy, and his willingness to trust his white officer, Iago, combine to seal his fate. Playing with his audience's notion of good and evil and black and white, Shakespeare confronts Renaissance racism with irony.

Some early critics disputed whether Shakespeare had in mind a "tawny" Moor or a "black" Moor for the title character. While the nineteenth-century stage preferred a light-skinned Othello, twentieth-century versions preferred a black Othello, usually with a black actor playing the role. Some great Othellos have been performed by white actors with the reasoning that Shakespeare wrote the part for Richard Burbage, who was white and one of the greatest actors of his day. Today the role is usually reserved for black actors, with a number of outstanding performances by Moses Gunn, James Earl Jones, and others.

The documents compiled here help us to consider *Othello* in the context of racial prejudice, both in Shakespeare's time and our own. Sir John Mandeville's *Travels,* dating 1357, demonstrates that early reports about the existence of black civilizations had reached Europe. Ethiopians were known to the English and referred to as Moors. Around the time of the first performance of *Othello,* an Arab delegation in London drew attention with its exotic fashions and styles. By the time *Othello* was performed, the English audience would have understood from general knowledge and experience what a "dark-visaged" man — either from north or central Africa — would have looked like.

Sir John Mandeville attempted to explain the nature of both Egypt and neighboring Ethiopia. He maintained that the inhabitants had been turned black by the heat of the sun. Much later, Richard Eden translated a travel book by Peter Martyr written in 1530. The single paragraph included in this casebook indicates that blacks were already present in Quarequa, a mountainous region of Haiti and the Dominican Republic. Eden theorizes that these black inhabitants were the descendants of seafaring Africans who were blown off course and landed in the Caribbean.

A Muslim convert to Christianity, Leo Africanus (as he became known to Europeans) wrote *A Geographical Historie of Africa* in 1550. It was expanded and revised for an English audience by John Pory in 1600. The book was a popular treatise that answered the needs of the curious to learn about Africa. In a sometimes fanciful fashion, it describes regions and nations as well as peoples, customs, and religious practices.

In "Othello and Color Prejudice," G. K. Hunter, a distinguished modern Shakespeare scholar, asserts that "Shakespeare intended his hero to be a black man." Hunter clarifies this statement with reference to other Renaissance works and writers. Margaret Webster, who directed the great performance of Paul Robeson in *Othello* in 1943, discusses the question of race in the play from the perspective of the mid-twentieth century. Her focus is on Desdemona as much as on Othello. Peter Marks reviewed Patrick Stewart (of *Star Trek* fame) in a 1997–1998 production that had an all-black cast except for Stewart's portrayal of Othello. Marks felt that the result "tends to take the racial issue off the table." Whether that is the case or not, we should attempt to know as much as we can about the prejudices and understandings of Shakespeare's time as well as those of our own in regard to *Othello*.

In addition to the material in this Casebook, we should refer to Ben Jonson's *Masque of Blackness,* which follows. It was commissioned by Queen Anne for the court of King James I and was performed the same year and in the same theater as *Othello.* In some ways Jonson's *Masque* can be seen as a commentary on the age and perhaps on *Othello.*

Sir John Mandeville (c. 1300–1372)
FROM *MANDEVILLE'S TRAVELS*   1357
TRANSLATED FROM THE FRENCH BY COTTON TITUS

Mandeville's Travels, *written in France in 1357, was one of the most popular travel books of the late Middle Ages and early Renaissance. Some of it is fantasy; some of it is gathered from the travels of many people. Othello's line concerning "men whose heads / Do grow beneath their shoulders" (I, III, 144–45) comes from this well-known book. The excerpts here point to contemporary views of Africans available to Shakespeare.*

And between Egypt and Nubia it hath well a twelve journeys of desert. And men of Nubia be Christian, but they be black as the Moors for great heat of the sun.

In Egypt there be five provinces; one that hight° Sa'id, that other that hight Damanhur, another Rosetta that is an isle in Nile, another Alexandria, and another the land of Damietta. That city was wont to be right strong, but it was twice won of the Christian men. And therefore after that the Saracens beat down the walls, and with the walls and the towers thereof the Saracens made another city more far from the sea and cleped it the New Damietta, so that now no man dwelleth at the rather town of Damietta. At that city of Damietta is one of the havens of Egypt. And at Alexandria is that other, that is a full strong city, but there is no water to drink but if it come by conduit from Nile that entereth into their cisterns; and whoso stopped that water from them, they might not endure there. In Egypt there be but few fortlets or castles because that the country is so strong of himself.

Note of a Marvel

At the deserts of Egypt was a worthy man that was an holy hermit,[1] and there met with him a monster; that is to say, a monster is a thing deformed against kind both of man or of beast or of anything else, and that is cleped° a monster. And this

hight: Is called.
[1] St. Anthony or St. Paul the Hermit.
cleped: Named.

monster that met with this holy hermit was as it had been a man that had two horns trenchant on his forehead, and he had a body like a man to the navel, and beneath he had the body like a goat. And the hermit asked him what he was, and the monster answered him and said he was a deadly creature such as God had formed and dwelled in those deserts in purchasing his sustenance; and besought the hermit that he would pray God for him, the which that came from Heaven for to save all mankind, and was born of a maiden, and suffered passion and death, as we well know, by whom we live and be. And yet is the head with the two horns of that monster at Alexandria for a marvel.

In Egypt is the city of Heliopolis, that is to say the city of the sun. In that city there is a temple made round after the shape of the Temple of Jerusalem. The priests of that temple have all their writings under the date of the fowl that is cleped Phoenix, and there is none but one in all the world. And he cometh to burn himself upon the altar of that temple at the end of five hundred year, for so long he liveth. And at the five hundred years' end the priests array their altar honestly and put thereupon spices and sulphur vif and other things that will burn lightly, and the bird Phoenix cometh and burneth himself to ashes. And the first day next after men find in the ashes a worm; and the second day next after men find a bird quick and perfect; and the third day next after he flieth his way. And so there is no more birds of that kind in all the world but it alone, and truly that is a great miracle of God. And men may well liken that bird unto God because that there is no God but one, and also that Our Lord arose from death to life the third day.[. . .]

Beside the land of Chaldea is the land of Amazonia, that is the land of Feminia. And in that realm is all women and no man, not as some men say that men may not live there but for because that the women will not suffer no men amongst them to be their sovereigns. For sometime there was a king in that country, and men married as in other countries. And so befell that the king had war with them of Scythia, the which king hight Scolopitus, that was slain in battle and all the good blood of his realm. And when the queen and all the other noble ladies saw that they were all widows, and that all the royal blood was lost, they armed them and as creatures out of wit they slew all the men of the country that were left, for they would that all the women were widows as the queen and they were.

And from that time hitherwards they never would suffer man to dwell amongst them longer than seven days and seven nights, nor that no child that were male should dwell amongst them longer than he were nourished and then sent to his father. And when they will have any company of man, then they draw them towards the lands marching next to them. And then they have their loves that use them, and they dwell with them an eight days or ten, and then go home again. And if they have any knave child, they keep it a certain time and then send it to the father when he can go alone and eat by himself, or else they slay it. And if it be a female, they do away that one pap with an hot iron. And if it be a woman of great lineage, they do away the left pap that they may the better bear a shield. And if it be a woman on foot, they do away the right pap for to shoot with bow Turkish, for they shoot well with bows.

In that land they have a queen that governeth all that land, and all they be obedient to her. And always they make their queen by election that is most worthy in arms, for they be right good warriors and orped° and wise, noble, and worthy. And they go often time insold to help of other kings in their wars for gold and silver as

orped: Valiant.

other soldiers do, and they maintain themselves right vigorously. This land of Amazonia is an isle all environed with the sea save in two places where be two entries. And beyond that water dwell the men that be their paramours and their loves, where they go to solace them when they will.

Beside Amazonia is the land of *terra Margine,* that is a great country and a full delectable. And for the goodness of the country King Alexander let first make there the city of Alexandria (and yet he made twelve cities of the same name), but that city is now cleped Seleucia.

And from that other coast of Chaldea toward the south is Ethiopia, a great country that stretcheth to the end of Egypt. Ethiopia is departed into two principal parts, and that is in the east part and in the meridional part, the which part meridional is cleped Mauretania. And the folk of that country be black enough and more black than in the other part, and they be cleped Moors. In that part is a well that in the day it is so cold that no man may drink thereof, and in the night it is so hot that no man may suffer his hand therein. And beyond that part toward the south to pass by the Sea Ocean is a great land and a great country, but men may not dwell there for the fervent burning of the sun, so is it passing hot in that country. In Ethiopia all the rivers and all the waters be troubled, and they be some deal salt for the great heat that is there.

And the folk of that country be lightly drunk and have but little appetite to meat. And they have commonly the flux of the womb, and they live not long. In Ethiopia be many diverse folk. And Ethiopia is cleped Cusis. In that country be folk that have but one foot, and they go so blithe that it is marvel, and the foot is so large that it shadoweth all the body against the sun when they will lie and rest them. In Ethiopia, when the children be young and little, they be all yellow, and when that they wax of age that yellowness turneth to be all black. In Ethiopia is the city of Savah and the land of the which one of the three kings that presented Our Lord in Bethlehem was king of.

Richard Eden (1521?–1576)
FROM *DECADES OF THE NEW WORLD*   1555

Around 1555, Richard Eden translated the work of Peter Martyr, written originally in 1530. Eden added his own material to Martyr's book and produced a popular "introduction" to the New World. In this excerpt he comments on black inhabitants of a mountainous region of Hispaniola (now Haiti and the Dominican Republic), whom he assumes arrived in the New World by accident.

There is a region not past two days journey distant from *Quarequa,* in which they found only black Moors: and those exceeding fierce and cruel. They suppose that in time past certain black moors sailed thither out of *Aethiopia* to rob: and that by shipwreck or some other chance, they were driven to those mountains. Th[e] inhabitants of *Quarequa* live in continual war and debate with these black men.

Leo Africanus (c. 1485–c. 1554)
and John Pory (1572–1635)
FROM *A GEOGRAPHICAL HISTORIE OF AFRICA*   1550, 1600

The travel accounts of Leo Africanus, born al-Hasan ibn Muhammad al-Wazzān Al-Zayyātī, were widely read in Elizabethan England. Most important in shaping the Elizabethans' impressions of Africans was his work, A Geographical Historie of Africa (1550), which was revised and expanded by another traveler, John Pory, in 1600. The first two excerpts that follow are by Pory, who emphasizes certain negative features of north African outlaws. Africanus, born in Granada, explains later in his account that he owes his birth to Africa, and balances the picture by stressing the civility, liberality, and fidelity of the Moors inhabiting the desert of Libya.

The People of Cafri, Part of the Lower Ethiopia

The people of this place called in the Arabian tongue Cafri, Cafres, or Cafates, that is to say, lawless or outlaws, are for the most part exceeding black of color, which very thing may be a sufficient argument, that the sun is not the sole or chief cause of their blackness; for in diverse other countries where the heat thereof is far more scorching and intolerable, there are tawny, brown, yellowish, ash-colored, and white people; so that the cause thereof seemeth rather to be of an hereditary quality transfused from the parents, than the intemperance of an hot climate, though it also may be some furtherance thereunto. The Hollanders in the year 1595, entering the harbor of Saint Bras, somewhat to the east of Cabo das Agulhas, had conversation and truck with some of these Cafres, whom they found to be a stout and valiant people, but very base and contemptible in their behavior and apparel, being clad in ox and sheeps skins, wrapped about their shoulders with the hairy sides inward, in form of a mantle. Their weapons are a kind of small slender darts or pikes, some whereof are headed with some kind of metal, the residue being unheaded, and hardened only at the points with fire. They cover their private parts with a sheeps tail, which is bound up before and behind with a girdle. Their home-beasts are, like those of Spaine, very well limbed and proportioned. Their sheep are great and fair, not having any wool on their backs, but a kind of harsh hair like goats. Other particulars by them observed, for brevitys sake, I omit.

The Kingdom of Damut

The kingdom of Damut (as *Sanutus* affirmeth) doth border upon the kingdom of Xoa, and is enclosed on either side with the lake of Barcena, and the land of Zanguebar. Howbeit others place Damut between the kingdoms of Vangue and Goiame toward the west, which opinion seemeth most probable. This country aboundeth with gold, ginger, grapes, corn, and beasts of all sorts. The slaves of this kingdom are much esteemed, and are commonly sold throughout all Arabia, Persia, and Egypt, where they prove most valiant soldiers. The greater part of the people of Damut are Gentiles, and the residue Christians, who have certain monasteries. In this kingdom is that exceeding high and dreadful mountain (having one narrow passage only to ascend by), whither the *Prete* sendeth his nobles which are convicted of any heinous crime, to suffer ignominious death with hunger and cold. About the fountains of Nilus some say, that there are Amazones or women-warriors, most valiant and redoubted, which use bows and arrows, and live under the government of a Queen: as likewise the people called Cafri or Cafates, being as black as pitch, and of a mighty stature, and (as some think) descended of the Jewes; but now they are idolators, and most deadly enemies to the Christians; for they make continual assaults upon the Abassins, despoiling them both of life and goods: but all the day-time they lie lurking in mountains, woods, and deep valleys.

The Manners and Customs of the African People, which Inhabit the Desert of Libya

The women of this nation be gross, corpulent, and of a swart complexion. They are fattest upon their breast and paps, but slender about the girdle-stead. Very civil they are, after their manner, both in speech and gestures: sometimes they will accept of a kiss; but whoso tempteth them farther, putteth his own life in hazard. For by reason of jealousy you may see them daily one to be the death and destruction of another, and that in such savage and brutish manner, that in this case they will show no compassion at all. And they seem to be more wise in this behalf than divers of our people for they will by no means match themselves unto an harlot. The liberality of this people hath at all times been exceeding great. And when any travelers may pass through their dry and desert territories, they will never repair to their tents, neither will they themselves travel upon the common highway. And if any caravan or multitude of merchants will pass those deserts, they are bound to pay certain custom unto the prince of the said people, namely, for every camels load a piece of cloth worth a ducat. Upon a time I remember that traveling in the company of certain merchants over the desert by them called Araoan, it was our chance there to meet with the prince of Zanaga; who, after he had received his due custom, invited the said company of merchants, for their recreation, to go and abide with him in his tents four or five days. Howbeit, because his tents were too far out of our way, and for that we should have wandered farther than we thought good, esteeming it more convenient for us to hold on our direct course, we refused his gentle offer, and for his courtesy gave him great thanks. But nor being satisfied therewith, he commanded that our camels should proceed on forward, but the merchants he carried along with him, and gave them very sumptuous entertainment of his place of abode. Where we were no sooner arrived, but this good prince caused camels of all kinds and ostriches, which he had hunted and taken by the way, to be killed for his household provision. Howbeit we requested him not to make such daily slaughters of his camels; affirming moreover, that we never used to eat the flesh of a geld camel, but when all other victuals failed us. Whereunto he answered, that he should deal uncivilly, if he welcomed so worthy and so seldom-seen guests with the killing of small cattle only. Wherefore he wished us to fall to such provision as was set before us. Here might you have seen great plenty of roasted and sodden flesh: their roasted ostriches were brought to the table in wicker platters, being seasoned with sundry kinds of herbs and spices. Their bread made of Mill and panicke was of a most savory and pleasant taste: and always at the end of dinner or supper we had plenty of dates and great store of milk served in. Yea, this bountiful and noble prince, that he might sufficiently show how welcome we were unto him, would together with his nobility always bear us company: howbeit we ever dined and supped apart by our selves. Moreover he caused certain religious and most learned men to come unto our banquet; who, all the time we remained with the said prince, used not to eat any bread at all, but fed only upon flesh and milk. Whereat we being somewhat amazed, the good prince gently told us, that they all were born in such places whereas no kind of grain would grow: howbeit that himself, for the entertainment of strangers, had great plenty of corn laid up in store. Wherefore he bad us to be of good cheer, saying that he would eat only of such things as his own native soil afforded: affirming moreover, that bread was yet in use among them at their feast of passover, and at other feasts also, whereupon they used to offer sacrifice. And thus we remained with him for the space of two days; all which time, what wonderful and magnificent cheer we had made us, would seem incredible to report. But the third day, being desirous to take our leave, the prince accompanied us to that place where we overtook our camels and company sent before. And this I dare most deeply take mine oath on, that we spent the said prince ten times more, than our custom which he received came to. We thought it not amiss here to set down this history, to declare in some sort the courtesy and liberality of the said nation. Neither could the prince aforesaid understand our language nor we his; but all our speech to and fro was made by an interpreter. And this which we have here recorded as touching this nation, is likewise to be understood of the other four nations above mentioned, which are dispersed over the residue of the Numidian deserts.

The Commendable Actions and Virtues of the Africans

Those Arabians which inhabit in Barbarie or upon the coast of the Mediterran sea, are greatly addicted unto the study of good arts and sciences: and those things which concern their law and religion are esteemed by them in the first place. Moreover they have been heretofore most studious of the Mathematics, of Philosophy, and of Astrology: but these arts (as it is aforesaid) were four hundred years ago, utterly destroyed and taken away by the chief professors of their law. The inhabitants of cities do most religiously observe and reverence those things which appertain unto their religion: yea they honor those doctors and priests, of whom they learn their law, as if they were petty-gods. Their Churches they frequent very diligently, to the end they may repeat certain prescript and formal prayers; most superstitiously persuading themselves that the same day wherein they make their prayers, it is not lawful for them to wash certain of their members, when as at other times they will wash their whole bodies. Whereof we will (by Gods help) discourse more at large in the second Book of this present treatise, when we shall fall into the mentioning of *Mahumet* and of his religion. Moreover those which inhabit Barbarie are of great cunning & dexterity for building & for mathematical inventions, which a man may easily conjecture by their artificial works. Most honest people they are, and destitute of all fraud and guile; not only embracing all simplicity and truth, but also practicing the same throughout the whole course of their lives: albeit certain Latin authors, which have written of the same regions, are far otherwise of opinion. Likewise they are most strong and valiant people, especially those which dwell upon the mountains. They keep their covenant most faithfully; insomuch that they had rather die than break promise. No nation in the world is so subject unto jealousy; for they will rather lease their lives, than put up any disgrace in the behalf of their women. So desirous they are of riches and honor, that therein no other people can go beyond them. They travel in a manner over the whole world to exercise traffic. For they are continually to be seen in Aegypt, in Aethiopia, in Arabia, Persia, India, and Turkie: and whithersoever they go, they are most honorably esteemed of: for none of them will possess any art, unless he hath attained unto great exactness and perfection therein. They have always been much delighted with all kind of civility and modest behavior: and it is accounted heinous among them for any man to utter in company, any bawdy or unseemly word. They have always in mind this sentence of a grave author; Give place to thy superior. If any youth in presence of his father, his uncle, or any other of his kindred, doth sing or talk aught of love matters, he is deemed to be worthy of grievous punishment. Whatsoever lad or youth there lighteth by chance into any company which discourseth of love, no sooner heareth nor understandeth what their talk tendeth unto, but immediately he withdraweth himself from among them. These are the things which we thought most worthy of relation as concerning the civility, humanity, and upright dealing of the Barbarians: let us now proceed unto the residue. Those Arabians which dwell in tents, that is to say, which bring up cattle, are of a more liberal and civil disposition: to wit, they are in their kind as devout, valiant, patient, courteous, hospitable, and as honest in life and conversation as any other people. They be most faithful observers of their word and promise; insomuch that the people, which before we said to dwell in the mountains, are greatly stirred up with emulation of their virtues. Howbeit the said mountainers, both for learning, for virtue, and for religion, are thought much inferior to the Numidians, albeit they have little or no knowledge at all in natural philosophy. They are reported likewise to be most skilful warriors, to be valiant, and exceeding lovers and practicers of all humanity. Also, the Moors and Arabians inhabiting Libya are somewhat civil of behavior, being plain dealers, void of dissimulation, favorable to strangers, and lovers of simplicity. Those which we before named white, or tawny Moors, are steadfast in friendship: as likewise, they indifferently and favorably esteem of other nations: and wholly endeavor themselves in this one thing, namely, that they may lead a most pleasant and jocund life. Moreover they maintain most learned professors of liberal arts, and such men are most devout in their religion. Neither is there any people in all Africa that lead a more happy and honorable life.

G. K. Hunter (b. 1920)
FROM "OTHELLO AND COLOR PREJUDICE"   1978

In attempting to determine Shakespeare's motives in portraying Othello as a black Moor, G. K. Hunter, a professor at Yale University, has examined the evidence suggesting the associations an Elizabethan audience would have made with the color black. In this excerpt he establishes the common color prejudice that would have been present in Shakespeare's audience and implies that Shakespeare consciously worked against it.

It is generally admitted today that Shakespeare was a practical man of the theater: however careless he may have been about maintaining consistency for the exact *reader* of his plays, he was not likely to introduce a theatrical novelty which would only puzzle his audience; it does not seem wise, therefore, to dismiss his theatrical innovations as if they were unintentional. The blackness of Othello is a case in point. Shakespeare largely modified the story he took over from Cinthio: he made a tragic hero out of Cinthio's passionate and bloody lover; he gave him a royal origin, a Christian baptism, a romantic *bravura* of manner, and, most impor-

[Read as the British Academy Shakespeare Lecture, 19 April 1967. First published in *The Proceedings of the British Academy*, liii (1967).]

tant of all, an orotund magnificence of diction. Yet, changing all this, he did not change his color and so produced a daring theatrical novelty — a black hero for a white community — a novelty which remains too daring for many recent theatrical audiences. Shakespeare cannot merely have carried over the color of Othello by being too lazy or too uninterested to meddle with it; for no actor, spending the time in "blacking-up," and hence no producer, could be indifferent to such an innovation, especially in that age, devoted to "imitation" and hostile to "originality." In fact, the repeated references to Othello's color in the play and the wider net of images of dark and light spread across the diction, show that Shakespeare was not only not unaware of the implication of his hero's color but was indeed intensely aware of it as one of the primary factors in his play.[1] I am therefore assuming in this lecture that the blackness of Othello has a theatrical purpose, and I intend to try to suggest what it was possible for that purpose to have been.

Shakespeare intended his hero to be a black man — that much I take for granted;[2] what is unknown is what the idea of a black man suggested to Shakespeare, and what reaction the appearance of a black man on the stage was calculated to produce. It is fairly certain, however, that some modern reactions are not likely to have been shared by the Elizabethans. The modern theater-going European intellectual, with a background of cultivated superiority to "color problems" in other continents, would often choose to regard Othello as a fellow man and to watch the story — which could so easily be reduced to its headline level: "sheltered white girl errs: said, 'Color does not matter' "— with a sense of freedom from such prejudices. But this lofty fair-mindedness may be too lofty for Shakespeare's play and not take the European any nearer the Othello of Shakespeare than the lady from Maryland quoted in the Furness New Variorum edition: "In studying the play of *Othello*, I have always *imagined* its hero a white man." Both views, that the color of Othello does not matter and that it matters too much to be tolerable, err, I suggest, by oversimplifying. Shakespeare was clearly deliberate in keeping Othello's color; and it is obvious that he counted on some positive audience reaction to this color; but it is equally obvious that he did not wish the audience to dismiss Othello as a stereotype.[. . .]

Modern rationalizations about "color" tend to be different from those of the Middle Ages and Renaissance. We are powerfully aware of the relativism of viewpoints; we distinguish easily between different racial cultures; and explicit arguments about the mingling of the races usually begin at the economic and social level and only move to questions of God's providence at the lunatic fringe.

The Elizabethans also had a powerful sense of the economic threat posed by the foreign groups they had daily contact with — Flemings or Frenchmen — but they had little or no continuous contact with "Moors" and no sense of economic threat from them. This did not mean, however, that they had no racial or color prejudice. They had, to start with, the basic common man's attitude that all foreigners are curious and inferior — the more foreign the more inferior, in the sense of the proverb quoted by Purchas: "Three Moors to a Portuguese; three Portuguese to an Englishman."[3] They had also the basic and ancient sense that black is the color of

---

[1]See R. B. Heilman, "More Fair Than Black: Light and Dark in *Othello*," *Essays in Criticism*, i (1951), 313–35.

[2]I ignore the many treatises devoted to proving that he was of tawny or sunburnt color. These are, however, very worthy of study, as documents of prejudice.[. . .]

[3]See M. P. Tilley, *A Dictionary of Proverbs* (1950), M. 1132.

sin and death, "the badge of hell, the hue of dungeons, and the school of night" (as Shakespeare himself says).[4] This supposition is found all over the world (even in darkest Africa)[5] from the earliest to the latest times; which suggests a response to the basic antinomy of day and night. Certainly in the West there is a continuous and documented cultural tradition depending on it.[6][. . .]

An extreme example of this status of the Moor appears in the report of the pageant for the baptism of Prince Henry in 1594. It had been arranged that a lion should pull the triumphal car; but the lion could not be used, so a Moor was substituted.[7]

Renaissance scepticism and the voyages of discovery might seem, at first sight, to have destroyed the ignorance on which such thoughtless equations of black men and devils depended. But this does not prove to have been so. The voyagers brought back some accurate reports of black and heathen; but they often saw, or said they saw, what they expected to see — the marvels of the East.[8] In any case the vocabulary at their disposal frustrated any attempt at scientific discrimination. The world was still seen largely, in terms of vocabulary, as a network of religious names. The word "Moor" had no clear racial status. Elizabethan authors describe "Moors" as existing all over the globe. We hear of "Mores of Malabar" from Spenser,[9] of Moors in Malacca from James Lancaster,[10] of Moors in Guinea from Eden,[11] of Moors in Ethiopia from Lodge,[12] of Moors in Fukien from Willes,[13] of Moors in America from Marlowe[14] and sundry others. There seem to be Moors everywhere; but only everywhere, we should note, in that outer circuit of non-Christian lands where the saving grace of Jerusalem is weakest in its whitening power. Throughout the Elizabethan period there seems to remain considerable confusion whether the Moor is a human being or a monster. In the "plat" of the perished play of *Tamar Cam* (1592) we are told of an entry of "Tartars, Geates, Amozins, Nagars, ollive cullord moores, Canniballs, Hermophrodites, Pigmies," etc. — a characteristic medley.[15] In *Volpone* we are given a list of the undesirables

---

[4]*Love's Labour's Lost*, IV, III, 250 f.

[5]See V. W. Turner, "Colour Classification in Ndembu Ritual," *Anthropological Approaches to the Study of Religion,* ed. M. Banton (1966); Arthur Leib, "The Mystical Significance of Colours in . . . Madagascar," *Folk-lore,* lvii (1946), 128–33; Joan Westcott, "The Sculpture and Myths of Eshu-Elegba, the Yoruba Trickster," *Africa,* xxxii (1962).

[6]See E. Hoffman-Krayer and H. Bächtold-Stäubli, *Handwörterbuch des deutschen Aberglaubens* [1927], s.v. Schwartz.

[7]See *A True Reportary of the Baptisme of Frederik Henry, Prince of Scotland* (1594) (S.T.C. 13163).

[8]See R. Wittkower, "Marvels of the East," *Journal of the Warburg and Courtauld Institutes,* v (1942), 159–97.[. . .]

[9]*Faerie Queene,* VI, VII, 43.

[10]R. Hakluyt, *Principal Navigations* (Glasgow, 1903–1905 edition), vi. 399.

[11]Peter Martyr Anglerius, tr. R. Eden, *The History of Travel* (1577), fl. 348v.

[12]*Works* (Hunterian Society), ii. 52.

[13]Hakluyt, vi. 321 (where it is quite clear that "Moorish" means "Mahomedan."

[14]*Doctor Faustus* (*Works,* ed. C. F. Tucker Brooke, p. 150). Compare the "black Indians" in A. Brewer's *The Lovesick King* (Bang's Materialien [1907], 952 f.) and in B. Googe's *The Popish Kingdom* (translated from H. Kirchmeyer) (1570) — 1880 ed., p. 39 — and the "African Indians" in *Sir Thomas Stukeley* (1596) — Tudor Facsimile Texts, 2169.

[15]*Henslowe Papers,* ed. W. W. Greg (1907), p. 148. Compare the "Negro-Tartars" in *Gesta Grayorum* (M.S.R. 46) and the "Negarian Tartars" (ibid. 52).

that Volpone has coupled with to produce his Fool, Dwarf, and Hermaphrodite. The supposed parents are described as

> beggars,
> Gipsies and Jews and black-moors.[16]

The geographical vagueness of these authors does not mean, however, that they are vague in their sense of an antithetical relationship between "Moors" (wherever they live) and civilized white Christians. The first meaning given to the word "Moor" in *O.E.D.* is "Mahomedan" (with examples up to 1629); but in many of the examples this seems to mean no more than "infidel," non-Christian. The pressure that defines the word is more negative than positive. Like *Barbarian* and *Gentile* (or *Wog*) it was a word for "people not like us,"[17] so signaled by color. The word *Gentile* itself had still the religious sense of *Pagan,* and the combined phrase "Moors and Gentiles" is used regularly to represent the religious gamut of non-Christian possibilities (see *O.E.D.* for examples). Similarly, *Barbary* was not simply a place in Africa, but also the unclearly located home of Barbarism, as in Chaucer (Franklin's Tale, 1451, Man of Law's Tale, 183).

I have suggested above that the discoveries of the voyagers contributed little to Renaissance scientific or nontheological explanations of the world. And this was particularly true of the problems raised by the black-skinned races. No scientific explanation of black skins had ever been achieved, though doctors had long disputed it. Lodovicus Caelius Rhodiginus in his *Lectionum Antiquarum libri XXX* (1620) can cite column after column of authorities; but all without conclusive answers. We hear among the latest reports of Africa collected in T. Astley's *New General Collection of Voyages* (1745) that the blackness of the Negro is "a Topic that has given Rise to numberless Conjectures and great Disputes among the Learned in Europe" (ii, 269). Sir Thomas Browne in three essays in his *Pseudodoxia Epidemica* (VI, x–xii) not only declared that the subject was "amply and satisfactorily discussed as we know by no man" but proceeded to remedy this by way of amplitude rather than satisfactoriness. The theological explanation was left in possession of the field. Adam and Eve, it was assumed, were white; it follows that the creation of the black races can only be ascribed to some subsequent *fiat.* The two favorite possibilities were the cursing of Cain and the cursing of Ham or Cham and his posterity — and sometimes these two were assumed to be different expressions of the same event; at least one might allege, with Sir Walter Ralegh, that "the sonnes of Cham did possesse the vices of the sonnes of Cain."[18] The Cham explanation had the great advantage that "the threefold world" of tradition could be described in terms of the three sons of Noah — Japhet having produced the Europeans, Shem the Asiatics, while the posterity of Ham occupied Africa, or, in a more sophisticated version, "the Meridionall or southern partes of the world both in Asia and Africa"[19] — sophisticated, we should notice, without altering the basic theological assumption that Cham's posterity were banished to the most uncomfortable part of the globe, and a foretaste of the Hell to come. This geographical

[16]Ben Jonson, *Volpone,* I, v, 44 f.
[17]So that "Wogs begin at Calais," etc.
[18]*The History of the World,* I, VI, 2.
[19]A. Willet, *Hexapla in Genesin* (1605), p. 119.

assumption fitted in with the wisdom that the etymological doctors had in the Middle Ages been able to glean from the name *Ham* — defined as "*Cham: calidus, et ipse ex praesagio futuri cognominatus est. Posteritas enim eius eam terrae partem possedit quae vicino sole calentior est.*"[20] When this is linked to the other point made in relation to the Cham story — that his posterity were cursed to be slaves[21] — one can see how conveniently and plausibly such a view fitted the facts and desires found in the early navigators. Azurara, the chronicler of Prince Henry the Navigator's voyages, tells us that it was natural to find blackamoors as the slaves of lighter skinned men:

> these blacks were Moors (i.e. Mahomedans) like the others, though their slaves, in accordance with ancient custom which I believe to have been because of the curse which, after the Deluge, Noah laid upon his son Cain [*sic*], cursing him in this way: that his race should be subject to all the other races in the world. And from his race these blacks are descended.[22]

The qualities of the "Moors" who appear on the Elizabethan stage are hardly at all affected by Elizabethan knowledge of real Moors from real geographical locations, and, given the literary modes available, this is hardly surprising. It is true that the first important Moor-role — that of Muly Hamet in Peele's *The Battle of Alcazar* (c. 1589) — tells the story of a real man (with whom Queen Elizabeth had a treaty) in a real historical situation. But the dramatic focus that Peele manages to give to his Moorish character is largely dependent on the devil and underworld associations he can suggest for him — making him call up "Fiends, Fairies, hags that fight in beds of steel" and causing him to show more acquaintance with the geography of hell than with that of Africa. Aaron in *Titus Andronicus* is liberated from even such slender ties as associate Muly Hamet with geography. Aaron is in the play as the representative of a world of generalized barbarism, which is Gothic in Tamora and Moorish in Aaron, and unfocused in both. The purpose of the play is served by a general opposition between Roman order and Barbarian disorder. Shakespeare has the doubtful distinction of making explicit here (perhaps for the first time in English literature) the projection of black wickedness in terms of negro sexuality. The relationship between Tamora and Aaron is meant, clearly enough, to shock our normal sensibilities and their black baby is present as an emblem of disorder. In this respect, as in most others, Eleazer in *Lust's Dominion* (c. 1600) — the third pre-Othello stage-Moor — is copied from Aaron. The location of this play (Spain) gives a historically plausible excuse to present the devil in his favorite human form —"that of a Negro or Moor," but does not really use the locale to establish any racial points.

These characters provide the dominant images that must have been present in the minds of Shakespeare's original audience when they entered the Globe to see a play called *The Moor of Venice* — an expectation of pagan devilry set against white Christian civilization — excessive civilization perhaps in Venice, but civilization at least "like us." Even those who knew Cinthio's story of the Moor of Venice could not have had very different expectations, which may be summed up from the

---

[20]Isidore of Seville, *Etymologiae*, VII, vi, 17. (*Patrologia Latina*, lxxxii, col. 276.)
[21]See St Ambrose, *Comment. in epist. ad Philippenses* (*P.L.* xvii, col. 432). [. . .]
[22]*Discovery and Conquest of Guinea* (Hakluyt Society, XCV [1896], 54).

story told by Bandello (III, xxi) in which a master beats his Moorish servant, and the servant in revenge rapes and murders his wife and children.[23] Bandello draws an illuminating moral:

> By this I intend it to appear that a man should not be served by this sort of slave; for they are seldom found faithful, and at best they are full of filth, unclean, and stink all the time like goats. But all this is as nothing put beside the savage cruelty that reigns in them.

It is in such terms that the play opens. We hear from men like us of a man not like us, of "his Moorship," "the Moor," "the thick-lips," "an old black ram," "a Barbary horse," "the devil," of "the gross clasps of a lascivious Moor." The sexual fear and disgust that lie behind so much racial prejudice are exposed for our derisive expectations to fasten upon them. And we are at this point bound to agree with these valuations, for no alternative view is revealed. There is, of course, a certain comic *brio* which helps to distance the whole situation, and neither Brabantio, nor Iago nor Roderigo can wholly command our identification. None the less we are drawn on to await the entry of a traditional Moor figure, the kind of person we came to the theatre expecting to find.

When the second scene begins, however, it is clear that Shakespeare is bent to ends other than the fulfilment of these expectations. The Iago/Roderigo relationship of I, i, is repeated in the Iago/Othello relationship of the opening of I, ii; but Othello's response to the real-seeming circumstance with which Iago lards his discourse is very different from the hungrily self-absorbed questionings of Roderigo. Othello draws on an inward certainty about himself, a radiant clarity about his own well-founded moral position. This is no "lascivious Moor," but a great Christian gentleman, against whom Iago's insinuations break like water against granite. Not only is Othello a Christian, moreover; he is the leader of Christendom in the last and highest sense in which Christendom existed as a viable entity, crusading against the "black pagans." He is to defend Cyprus against the Turk, "hellish horseleaches of Christian blood."[24] It was the fall of Cyprus which produced the alliance of Lepanto, and we should associate Othello with the emotion that Europe continued to feel — till well after the date of *Othello* — about that victory and about Don John of Austria.

Shakespeare has presented to us a traditional view of what Moors are like, i.e., gross, disgusting, inferior, carrying the symbol of their damnation on their skin; and has caught our overeasy assent to such assumptions in the grip of a guilt which associates us and our assent with the white man representative of such views in the play — Iago. Othello acquires the glamour of an innocent man that *we* have wronged, and an admiration stronger than he could have achieved by virtue plainly represented:

> . . . as these black masks
> Proclaim an enshield beauty ten times louder
> Than beauty could, displayed.

---

[23]M. Bandello, *Novelle,* Book III, novel xxi, derived from Pontanus (Opera, i, 25, b), and translated by F. Belleforest, *Histoires tragiques.* The story was apparently Englished in ballad form, in 1569, 1570, and again in 1624, 1675. See E. Hyder Rollins, "Analytical Index" (*Studies in Philology,* xxi [1924]), item 2542: "a strange petyful novell Dyscoursynge of a noble Lorde and his lady with thayre ij cheldren executed by a blacke morryon."

[24]Hakluyt, *Principal Navigations* (1903–5 ed.), V. 122.

(Is it an accident that Shakespeare wrote these lines from *Measure for Measure* in approximately the same year as he wrote *Othello*?) Iago is a "civilized" man; but where, for the "inferior" Othello, appearance and reality, statement and truth are linked indissolubly, civilization for Iago consists largely of a capacity to manipulate appearances and probabilities:

> For when my outward action doth demonstrate
> The native act and figure of my heart
> In compliment extern, 'tis not long after
> But I will wear my heart upon my sleeve
> For daws to peck at: I am not what I am.

Othello may be "the devil" in appearance: but it is the "fair" Iago who gives birth to the dark realities of sin and death in the play:

> It is engender'd. Hell and night
> Must bring this monstrous birth to the world's light

The relationship between these two is developed in terms of appearance and reality. Othello controls the reality of action; Iago the "appearance" of talk about action; Iago the Italian is isolated (even from his wife), envious, enigmatic (even to himself), self-centered; Othello the "extravagant and wheeling stranger" is surrounded and protected by a network of duties, obligations, esteems, pious to his father-in-law, deferential to his superiors, kind to his subordinates, loving to his wife. To sum up, assuming that *soul* is reality and *body* is appearance, we may say that Iago is the white man with the black soul while Othello is the black man with the white soul. Long before Blake's little black boy had said

> I am black, but oh my soul is white.
> White as an angel is the English child,
> But I am black as if bereaved of light.

and before Kipling's Gunga Din:

> An' for all 'is dirty 'ide
> 'E was white, clear white inside . . .
> You're a better man than I am, Gunga Din!

Othello had represented the guilty awareness of Europe that the "foreigner type" is only the type we do not know, whose foreignness vanishes when we have better acquaintance; that the prejudicial foreign appearance may conceal a vision of truth, as Brabantio is told:

> If virtue no delighted beauty lack
> Your son-in-law is far more fair than black.

This reality of fairness in Othello provides a principal function for Desdemona in the play. Her love is of a spiritual intensity, of a strong simplicity equal to that of Othello himself, and pierces without effort beyond appearance, into reality:

> I saw Othello's visage in his mind.

Her love is a daring act of faith, beyond reason or social propriety. Like Beauty in the fairytale she denies the beastly (or devilish) appearance to proclaim her allegiance to the invisible reality. And she does so throughout the play, even when the case for the appearance seems most strong and when Iago's power over appearances rides highest. Even when on the point of death at Othello's hands, she gives testimony to her faith (martyr in the true sense of the word):

> Commend me to my *kind* lord.

Othello is then a play which manipulates our sympathies, supposing that we will have brought to the theater a set of careless assumptions about "Moors." It assumes also that we will find it easy to abandon these as the play brings them into focus and identifies them with Iago, draws its elaborate distinction between the external appearance of devilishness and the inner reality.

Margaret Webster (1905–1972)
SHAKESPEARE WITHOUT TEARS   *1942*

Margaret Webster directed the notable Broadway performance of Othello *with Paul Robeson in 1943–1944. In this excerpt from her memoirs, she comments on the question of race and its importance to the play. She focuses on Desdemona and her motives in marrying a black man whom her father could not accept. Webster connects this important detail to Othello's "acceptance of the possibility of Desdemona's infidelity."*

The question of Othello's race is of paramount importance to the play. There has been much controversy as to Shakespeare's intention. It is improbable that he troubled himself greatly with ethnological exactness. The Moor, to an Elizabethan, was a blackamoor, an African, an Ethiopian. Shakespeare's other Moor, Aaron, in *Titus Andronicus,* is specifically black; he has thick lips and a fleece of woolly hair. The Prince of Morocco in *The Merchant of Venice* bears "the shadowed livery of the burnished sun," and even Portia recoils from his "complexion" which he himself is at great pains to excuse.

Othello is repeatedly described, both by himself and others, as black; not pale beige, but black; and for a century and a half after the play's first presentation he was so represented on the stage. But after this the close consideration of nice minds began to discern something not quite ladylike about Desdemona's marrying a black man with thick lips. They cannot have been more horrified than Brabantio, her father, who thought that only witchcraft could have caused "nature so preposterously to err," or more convinced of the disastrous outcome of such a match than Iago, who looked upon it as nothing but a "frail vow between an erring Barbarian and a supersubtle Venetian," and declared, with his invincible cynicism, that "when she is sated with his body, she will find the error of her choice: She must have change; she must!"

It is very apparent, and vital to the play, that Othello himself was very conscious of these same considerations and quiveringly aware of what the judgment of the world would be upon his marriage. It is one of the most potent factors in his acceptance of the possibility of Desdemona's infidelity. And she herself loses much in the quality of her steadfastness and courage if it be supposed that she simply married against her father's wishes a man who chanced to be a little darker than his fellows, instead of daring a marriage which would cause universal condemnation among the ladies of polite society. To scamp this consideration in the play is to deprive

Ron Canada as Iago and Patrick Stewart as Othello, in the Shakespeare Theater's 1997–1998 production of *Othello* in Washington, D.C., directed by Jude Kelly. In this version Stewart played Othello with an otherwise all-black cast.

Othello of his greatest weakness, Desdemona of her highest strength, Iago of his skill and judgment, Emilia of a powerful factor in her behavior both to her master and her mistress, and Venice itself of an arrogance in toleration which was one of the principal hallmarks of its civilization — a civilization which frames, first and last, the soaring emotions of the play.

After these three tragedies, Shakespeare will never again take us into so passion-tossed a world, never set his actors to release themselves so fully from the normal restraints of polite behavior, never pound his audience into submission by the relentless power of words. He will give us a jealous man in Leontes, an ambitious one in Octavius, an embittered outcast in Timon, but it will not be the sacrificial jealousy of Othello, the haunted ambition of Macbeth, or the madness of Lear. Nothing that happens in the later plays will carry us beyond the sphere where reason is still a comfortable guide. Nor will man ever again cry with such anguish to the stars to shield him from the unbearable responsibility of the world he has fashioned. The theatre will revert to its normal self, its walls solid and comfortably bounding the two hours' traffic of make-believe. There will be plenty of technical problems to be faced. *Antony and Cleopatra* especially will call for a width and range of vision; many of the plays to come will need adroit and lavish handling. But never again will the hearts of players and audience be so swept with the mystery of life and the bitter release of death.

Ben Jonson

Known primarily as a writer of comedies such as *Every Man in His Humor* (1598) and *Every Man out of His Humor* (1599) in the reign of Elizabeth I, Jonson's most interesting plays were performed during the reign (called the Jacobean period) of her successor, King James I. *Volpone* (1606) and *The Alchemist* (1610) stand today as Jonson's most often produced plays. Both are broad comedies: *Volpone* plays on the foxiness of a dying man who is anxious to see which of his heirs is worthy, and *The Alchemist* is a satire on the wiliness of con men who pretend to know how to transmute base metal into gold. All of these plays were highly regarded in Jacobean times. In addition to his comedies, Jonson's tragedies *Sejanus* (1603) and *Catiline* (1611) earned him the description of "best in tragedy" from a contemporary who maintained a diary devoted to his experiences in the theater.

Jonson led an exciting life. Born after his father died, he was placed in the Westminster School at the expense of its master, William Camden, author of the famous survey *Britannia*. There Jonson learned Latin and Greek but he himself said that instead of attending a university, he practiced his trade. Because Jonson's stepfather was a bricklayer, it has been assumed that Jonson learned that trade. He eventually grew tired of bricklaying and managed to get a job as an actor. In 1598, while a member of Philip Henslowe's theater, he killed a fellow actor in a brawl. He claimed self-defense and was granted "benefit of clergy," which was accorded those who could read and translate a Latin passage, but as punishment he carried a brand on his thumb from Tyburn, the place of execution and punishment, for the rest of his life.

For Jonson the stage was a way of making a living. He aspired to be a pure poet and was accorded great honor in his lifetime by other poets. But he could not, even with the patronage of important noblemen, eke out a sufficient living writing only poetry. Jonson was imprisoned in Elizabeth's reign for writing an offensive play, *The Isle of Dogs* (1597), and in the early years of King James's reign, which began on March 24, 1603, play writing continued to be dangerous. Toward the end of 1605, Jonson teamed with George Chapman and William Marston to write *Eastward Ho!,* a comedy that ridiculed the Scots (James I was a Scot). Jonson and Chapman were imprisoned, but Jonson eventually contacted enough important people to secure his release, probably in October, claiming that the few offensive lines had been written by Marston, who had fled London to avoid prison. Then in November the great Gunpowder Plot — remembered today with bonfires on November 5, Guy Fawkes Day — cast a dangerous shadow over him. Led by the Catholic conspirator Guy Fawkes, the Gunpowder Plot was a plan to kill the king, his advisors, and all members of the hierarchy of the Church and Parliament. Guy Fawkes's use of the pseudonym John Johnson, together with Jonson's conversion to Catholicism, may have resulted in the playwright's becoming a suspect. Luckily, he was well known in James's court and was able to demonstrate his loyalty and innocence.

For most of his life Jonson made his living by writing for the public stage, but he was by no means always successful. Although many of his plays are today regarded as among the most important of the late Renaissance, tastes changed during his lifetime, and by the end of his life he found himself no longer in vogue.

Jonson won considerable acclaim as a writer in the court of James I and Queen Anne. He composed entertainments and masques designed to be associated with important state occasions. The masque was a dramatic form that enjoyed great popularity for close to a century and a half. It was restricted to the entertainment and participation of royalty and courtiers. As its name implies, characters were sometimes masked to represent abstract ideas such as Blackness or Beauty or mythic characters such as Albion, an allegory for England itself.

Inigo Jones (1573–1652), brought to court by Queen Anne, collaborated with Jonson to make the Jacobean masque a dazzling spectacle. Jones was a painter and architect who had traveled abroad and returned to England with members of Anne's court when Anne ascended the British throne. He was responsible for designing costumes, scenery, special effects, and lighting. He introduced Italian theater machinery and techniques into his entertainments. The Jacobean masque was elaborate, sensational, and so enormously expensive that it is said to have contributed to the impoverishment of the crown inherited by James's successor, Charles I.

THE MASQUE OF BLACKNESS

Apparently dissatisfied with Samuel Daniel, the poet and writer who had produced the first masque for her court, Queen Anne turned to Ben Jonson and asked him to create a masque in which she and some of her court ladies could paint themselves black and pretend to be Moors. The source for her inspiration is unclear, but she may have encountered African emissaries in London or otherwise been aware of the presence of numerous Africans in London. During the later years of her reign, Queen Elizabeth felt there were too many black Africans in London and ordered them sent abroad. James does not seem to have followed her example.

The Masque of Blackness was the first of Ben Jonson's many masques. It was performed January 6, 1605, in the same theater and around the same time as *Othello*. Inigo Jones's machinery impressed the audience, which included foreign emissaries, such as the Venetian and Spanish ambassadors. Sir Dudley Carleton, present at the performance, was not pleased that the queen and her attendants had painted themselves black. He feared that kissing the hands of the masquers might blacken his face. He may have been familiar with earlier royal entertainments in which black characters were represented with long black gloves and black cloth masks.

Jonson's opening description of the setting is extensive because in masques the costumes and imaginative figures took on great importance. But his text is also ingenious. Given the assignment to produce a masque for blackamoors, he invented the conceit that "the Ethiops were as fair / As other dames, now black with black despair." Hence, the narrative moves these figures toward recovering their original brightness by seeking a nation whose name ends in *"-tania"* and residing there for thirteen days. Their journey takes them to Mauretania, Lusitania, and Aquitania, but none of those nations can avail them. Finally, Britannia fulfills their desire, and the masque ends with the prospect of their remaining another twelve nights.

The daughters of Niger are described as beautiful women, all the more beautiful because of their black skin and hair, but in Jonson's masque they encounter a Eurocentric point of view expressed by "some few / Poor brainsick men" who convince them that they should be "fair." The word "fair" in Elizabethan English means primarily beautiful, but it also means light in color. The point of the masque is to emphasize the beauty of the daughters (who are played by the queen and her attendants) and to restore them to their original fairness.

One important feature of the masque is the representation of figures in an allegorical fashion. In other words, Oceanus is not a psychologically real character but a figure who represents the ocean. Niger is the river, Aethiopia the nation. All the characters in the masque follow this pattern. When the queen and her attendants dance (line 302), they assume allegorical identities. The queen is Euphoris, or Happiness, and her symbol is a "golden tree laden with fruit." The dance that the queen and her attendants perform is the highlight of the masque, and the courtiers who participated felt it to be a joyful and exciting occasion.

The Masque of Blackness, like all Jacobean masques, was a multimedia event, like a modern "happening." The lines of dialogue are carefully crafted, and the narrative suitably dramatic. But it is the music, the song, the dance, and the machinery of the setting — the rocking and moving seashell and the sudden appearances of characters — that make the masque successful and impressive. As far as we know, masques such as this were not performed more than once or twice, partly because of expense and partly because of the demand for novelty in a relatively small court.

The speaking characters were played by professional actors, but all the other roles were drawn from the court. That way the poetry could be heard and the drama maintained without stressing the courtiers, who would have had, with very few exceptions, no aspirations toward the stage.

The Masque of Blackness in Performance

Since the masque is preeminently a performance piece, we must credit the spectacle over the poetry and dialogue. Even Jonson, early in his collaboration, pays homage to Inigo Jones's innovations in the masque. Sir Dudley Carleton, who was present at the performance in the old banqueting house, had much to say about it. His comments help us imagine the scene:

> On Twelfth-Day . . . at night, we had the Queen's masque in the Banqueting House, or rather her pageant. There was a great engine at the lower end of the room, which had motion, and in it were the images of sea horses, with other terrible fishes, which were ridden by Moors; the indecorum was, that there was all fish and no water. At the further end was a great shell in the form of a scallop, wherein were four seats; on

Inigo Jones, Costume for a Nymph, Daughter of Niger. Jonson described the masquers: "The attire of [the] *Masquers* was alike, in all, without difference: the colors, *azure,* and *silver*; (their hair thick, and curled upright in tresses, like *Pyramids*), but returned on the top with a scroll and antique dressing of feathers, and jewels interlaced with ropes of pearl. And, for the front, ear, neck, and wrists, the ornament was of the most choice and orient pearl; best setting off from the black."

the lowest sat the Queen with my lady Bedford; on the rest were placed the ladies . . . their apparel was rich, but too courtesan-like for such great ones. Instead of vizards, their faces, and arms up to elbows, were painted black, which was disguise sufficient, for they were hard to be known; *but it became them nothing so well as their own red and white, and you cannot imagine a more ugly sight than a troop of lean-cheeked Moors.* The Spanish and Venetian Ambassadors were both present, and sat by the King in state; at which Monsieur Beaumont [the French ambassador] quarrels so extremely that he saith the whole court is Spanish . . . the night's work was concluded with a banquet in the great chamber, which was so seriously assaulted that down went tables and trestles before one bit was touched.

Masques are occasionally performed today but in nothing like their original form. The costs for the *Masque of Blackness* exceeded £3,000, a fortune of hundreds of thousands of dollars in today's money.

Ben Jonson (1572–1637)
THE MASQUE OF BLACKNESS

List of Characters

OCEANUS
NIGER
AETHIOPIA
TRITONS, SEA-MAIDS, NYMPHS, THE DAUGHTERS OF
   NIGER, *and* OCEANIAE

The honor and splendor of these spectacles was such in the performance as, could those hours have lasted, this of mine now had been a most unprofitable work. But, when it is the fate even of the greatest and most
5 absolute° births to need and borrow a life of posterity, little had been done to the study of magnificence° in these° if presently with the rage of the people, who, as a part of greatness, are privileged by custom to deface their carcases,° the spirits had also perished. In duty,
10 therefore, to that majesty who gave them their authority and grace, and, no less than the most royal of predecessors, deserves eminent celebration for these solemnities, I add this later hand to redeem them° as well from ignorance as envy, two common evils, the one of censure, the
15 other of oblivion.
Pliny, Solinus, Ptolemy, and of late Leo the African, remember° unto us a river in Ethiopia famous by the name of Niger, of which the people were called *Nigritae*, now Negroes, and are the blackest nation of the world.
20 This river taketh spring out of a certain lake,° eastward, and after a long race falleth into the western ocean. Hence, because it was her majesty's will to have them° blackamores at first, the invention° was derived by me, and presented thus.

25 *First, for the scene, was drawn a Landtschap° consisting of small woods, and here and there a void place filled with huntings;° which falling,° an artificial sea was seen to shoot forth, as if it flowed to the land, raised with waves which seemed to move, and in some places*
30 *the billow to break, as imitating that orderly disorder which is common in nature. In front of this sea were placed six tritons in moving and sprightly actions, their* upper parts human, save that their hairs were blue, as partaking of the sea color, their desinent° parts fish, mounted above their heads, and all varied in disposi-
35 tion.° From their backs were borne out certain light pieces of taffeta as if carried by the wind, and their music made out of wreathed shells. Behind these a pair of sea-maids, for song, were as conspicuously seated; between which two great sea-horses, as big as the life, put
40 forth themselves, the one mounting aloft and writhing his head from the other, which seemed to sink forwards (so intended for variation, and that the figure behind might come off better); upon their backs Oceanus and Niger were advanced.
45
Oceanus presented in a human form, the color of his flesh blue, and shadowed° with a robe of sea-green; his head grey and horned, as he is described by the ancients; his beard of the like mixed color. He was garlanded with algae, or sea-grass, and in his hand a trident.
50
Niger in form and color of an Ethiop, his hair and rare° beard curled, shadowed with a blue and bright mantle; his front,° neck and wrists adorned with pearl; and crowned with an artificial wreath of cane and paper-rush.°
55
These induced° the masquers, which were twelve nymphs, Negroes, and the daughters of Niger, attended by so many of the Oceaniae,° which were their light-bearers.
The masquers were placed in a great concave shell
60 like mother of pearl, curiously° made to move on those waters and rise with the billow; the top thereof was stuck with a chevron of lights which, indented to the proportion of the shell, struck a glorious beam upon them as they were seated one above another; so that
65 they were all seen, but in an extravagant° order.
On sides of the shell did swim six huge sea-monsters, varied in their shape and dispositions,° bearing on their backs the twelve torch-bearers, who were planted there in several greces,° so as the backs of some were seen,
70 some in purfle,° or side, others in face; and all having their lights burning out of whelks or murex shells.
The attire of the masquers was alike in all, without difference: the colors, azure and silver; their hair thick and curled upright in tresses, like pyramids, but returned
75

---

5. **absolute:** Perfect; here, noble.   6. **magnificence:** According to Aristotle, the virtue of monarchs.   7. **these:** I.e., masques.
7–9. **people . . . carcases:** At the end of the masque, the audience was traditionally permitted to tear down the scenery and plunder the decorations.   13. **them:** The "spirits" of line 9.
17. **remember:** Mention.   20. **lake:** Lake Chad.   22. **them:** The masquers.   **invention:** Device of the masque.   25. **Landtschap:** Landscape.   27. **huntings:** Animals hunting their prey. **which falling:** The landscape-curtain was released from above, and fell to the floor in front of the stage to reveal the scene.

34. **desinent:** Terminal.   35–36. **disposition:** Arrangement.
47. **shadowed:** Covered.   52. **rare:** Thin.   53. **front:** Forehead.
55. **paper-rush:** Papyrus.   56. **induced:** Brought in.   58. **Oceaniae:** Sea nymphs, daughters of Oceanus.   61. **curiously:** Artfully.   66. **extravagant:** (1) Unusual; (2) moving about in an extraordinary way.   68. **dispositions:** Positions.   70. **greces:** Steps.   71. **purfle:** Profile.

on the top with a scroll and antique dressing of feathers
and jewels interlaced with ropes of pearl. And for the
front,° ear, neck and wrists, the ornament was of the
most choice and orient pearl, best setting off from the
80 *black.*

   For the light-bearers, sea-green, waved about the
skirts with gold and silver; their hair loose and flowing,
garlanded with sea-grass, and that stuck with branches
of coral.
85   *These thus presented,° the scene behind seemed a*
vast sea, and united with this that flowed forth, from
the termination or horizon of which (being the level of
the state,° which was placed in the upper end of the
hall) was drawn, by the lines of perspective, the whole
90 *work shooting downwards from the eye; which deco-*
rum made it more conspicuous, and caught the eye afar
off with a wandering beauty. To which was added an
obscure and cloudy night-piece that made the whole set
off. So much for the bodily part, which was of Master
95 *Inigo Jones° his design and act.*

   By this,° one of the tritons, with the two sea-maids,
began to sing to the others' loud music, their voices
being a tenor and two trebles.°

SONG:
   Sound, sound aloud
100   The welcome of the orient flood
   Into the west;
   Fair Niger, son to great Oceanus,
   Now honored thus,
   With all his beauteous race,
105   Who, though but black in face,
   Yet are they bright,
   And full of life and light,
   To prove that beauty best
   Which not the color but the feature°
110   Assures unto the creature.
OCEANUS: Be silent now the ceremony's done,
   And Niger, say, how comes it, lovely son,
   That thou, the Ethiop's river, so far east,
   Art seen to fall into th'extremest west
115   Of me, the king of floods, Oceanus,
   And in mine empire's heart salute me thus?
   My ceaseless current now amazèd stands
   To see thy labor through so many lands
   Mix thy fresh billow with my brackish stream,
120   And in thy sweetness stretch thy diadem
   To these far distant and unequalled skies,
   This squarèd circle of celestial bodies.°
NIGER: Divine Oceanus, 'tis not strange at all
   That, since the immortal souls of creatures mortal

Mix with their bodies, yet reserve forever   125
A power of separation, I should sever
My fresh streams from thy brackish, like things
   fixed,
Though with thy powerful saltness thus far mixed.
Virtue, though chained to earth, will still live free,
And hell itself must yield to industry.°   130
OCEANUS: But what's the end of thy herculean labors
   Extended to these calm and blessèd shores?
NIGER: To do a kind and careful father's part,
   In satisfying every pensive heart
   Of these my daughters, my most lovèd birth: 135
   Who, though they were the first formed dames of
      earth,
   And in whose sparkling and refulgent eyes
   The glorious sun did still delight to rise;
   Though he — the best judge and most formal cause°
   Of all dames' beauties — in their firm hues draws   140
   Signs of his fervent'st love, and thereby shows
   That in their black° the perfect'st beauty grows,
   Since the fixed color of their curlèd hair,
   Which is the highest grace of dames most fair,
   No cares, no age can change, or there display   145
   The fearful tincture of abhorrèd grey,
   Since Death herself (herself being pale and blue)
   Can never alter their most faithful hue;
   All which are arguments to prove how far
   Their beauties conquer in great beauty's war,   150
   And more, how near divinity they be
   That stand from passion or decay so free.
   Yet since the fabulous voices of some few
   Poor brainsick men, styled poets here with you,
   Have with such envy of their graces sung   155
   The painted beauties other empires sprung,
   Letting their loose and wingèd fictions fly
   To infect all climates, yea, our purity;
   As of one Phaëton,° that fired the world,
   And that before his heedless flames were hurled   160
   About the globe, the Ethiops were as fair
   As other dames, now black with black despair;
   And in respect of their complexions changed,
   Are eachwhere since for luckless creatures ranged.
   Which when my daughters heard, as women are   165
   Most jealous of their beauties, fear and care
   Possessed them° whole; yea, and believing them,
   They wept such ceaseless tears into my stream
   That it hath thus far overflowed his shore
   To seek them patience, who have since e'ermore   170
   As the sun riseth charged his burning throne

---

78. **front:** Forehead.   85. **presented:** Having been presented.
87–88. **level . . . state:** Height of the royal throne.   95. **Inigo
Jones (1573–1652):** Architect and stage designer, Jonson's
collaborator throughout his career as court masque writer.
96. **this:** This time.   98. **trebles:** Sopranos.   109. **feature:**
Form.   122. **squarèd . . . bodies:** I.e., heavenly bodies perfectly transformed into an earthly realm.

130. **hell . . . industry:** From Horace, Odes I, iii, 36: "herculean effort overcame hell"; alluded to in the next line.
139. **formal cause:** Creator of the form or essence; Aristotelian
terminology.   142. **black:** Synonymous with ugly in Elizabethan English.   159. **Phaëton:** Son of Phoebus Apollo, the
sun god. He was allowed to drive the chariot of the sun, but
could not control the horses, and Zeus destroyed him lest he set
the world afire.   167. **them:** The poets. (Jonson)

With volleys of revilings, 'cause he shone
On their scorched cheeks with such intemperate
      fires,
And other dames made queens of all desires.
175 To frustrate which strange error oft I sought,
Though most in vain, against a settled thought
As women's are, till they confirmed at length
By miracle what I with so much strength
Of argument resisted; else they feigned:
180 For in the lake where their first spring they gained,
As they sat cooling their soft limbs one night,
Appeared a face all circumfused with light —
And sure they saw't, for Ethiops never dream —
Wherein they might decipher through the stream
185 These words:

That they a land must forthwith seek
Whose termination, of the Greek,
Sounds -tania; where bright Sol,° that heat
Their bloods, doth never rise or set,
190 But in his journey passeth by,
And leaves that climate of the sky
To comfort of a greater light,
Who forms all beauty with his sight.

In search of this have we three princedoms passed
195 That speak out -tania in their accents last;
Black Mauretania° first, and secondly
Swarth° Lusitania;° next we did descry
Rich Aquitania,° and yet cannot find
The place unto these longing nymphs designed.°
200 Instruct and aid me, great Oceanus:
What land is this that now appears to us?
OCEANUS: This land that lifts into the temperate air
His snowy cliff is Albion° the fair,
So called of Neptune's son, who ruleth here;
205 For whose dear guard, myself four thousand year,
Since old Deucalion's° days, have walked the round
About his empire, proud to see him crowned
Above my waves.

At this the moon was discovered in the upper part of
210 *the house, triumphant in a silver throne made in figure*
of a pyramis.° Her garments white and silver, the dress-
ing of her head antique, and crowned with a luminary,
or sphere of light, which striking on the clouds, and
heightened with silver, reflected as natural clouds do by
215 *the splendor of the moon. The heaven about her was*
vaulted with blue silk and set with stars of silver which
had in them their several lights burning. The sudden
sight of which made Niger to interrupt Oceanus with
this present° passion.

188. **Sol:** The sun.   196. **Mauretania:** The land of the Moors, including modern Morocco and part of Algeria.   197. **Swarth:** Swarthy. **Lusitania:** Portugal and western Spain. 198. **Aquitania:** Southwestern France.   199. **designed:** Indicated.   203. **Albion:** Traditional poetic name for England. 206. **Deucalion:** A Greek Noah, survivor of the universal flood. 211. **pyramis:** Pyramid.   219. *present:* Immediate.

NIGER: O see, our silver star! 220
Whose pure, auspicious light greets us thus far!
Great Aethiopia,° goddess of our shore,
Since with particular worship we adore
Thy general brightness, let particular grace
Shine on my zealous daughters: show the place 225
Which long their longings urged their eyes to see.
Beautify them, which long have deified thee.
AETHIOPIA: Niger, be glad; resume thy native cheer.
Thy daughters' labors have their period° here,
And so thy errors.° I was that bright face 230
Reflected by the lake, in which thy race
Read mystic lines; which skill Pythagoras
First taught to men by a reverberate° glass.°
This blessèd isle doth with that -tania end,
Which there they saw inscribed, and shall extend 235
Wished satisfaction to their best desires.
Britannia, which the triple world° admires,
This isle hath now recovered for her name,°
Where reign those beauties that with so much fame
The sacred muses' sons have honorèd, 240
And from bright Hesperus° to Eos° spread.
With that great name Britannia, this blessed isle
Hath won her ancient dignity and style,°
A world divided from the world, and tried
The abstract of it in his general pride.° 245
For were the world with all his wealth a ring,
Britannia, whose new name° makes all tongues sing,
Might be a diamond worthy to enchase° it,
Ruled by a sun that to this height doth grace it,
Whose beams shine day and night, and are of force 250
To blanch an Ethiop, and revive a corse.°
His light sciential° is, and, past mere nature,
Can salve the rude defects of every creature.
Call forth thy honored daughters, then,
And let them, 'fore the Britain men, 255
Indent° the land with those pure traces°
They flow with in their native graces.
Invite them boldly to the shore;
Their beauties shall be scorched no more;
This sun is temperate, and refines 260
All things on which his radiance shines.

222. **Aethiopia:** The moon goddess.   229. **period:** End. 230. **errors:** With a quibble on "wanderings."   233. **reverberate:** Reflecting.   232–33. **Pythagoras . . . glass:** Pythagoras was supposedly able to reflect messages onto the moon by writing in blood on a mirror.   237. **triple world:** Heaven, earth, and the underworld.   238. **recovered . . . name:** See line 247 and gloss.   241. **Hesperus:** Evening, the west. **Eos:** Dawn, the east.   243. **style:** Characterization.   244–45. **tried . . . pride:** Experienced the ideal of it through England's own pride in herself. "His" refers to England, despite "her" two lines earlier.   247. **new name:** The name Great Britain was coined when James VI of Scotland became king also of England and Wales in 1604. It was not officially adopted, however, until 1707.   248. **enchase:** Set in.   251. **corse:** Corpse.   252. **sciential:** Endowed with the powers of science.   256. **Indent:** Leave footprints on.   **traces:** Footsteps.

265 *Here the tritons sounded, and they danced on shore, every couple as they advanced severally presenting their fans, in one of which were inscribed their mixed names, in the other a mute hieroglyphic expressing their mixed qualities. (Which manner of symbol I rather chose than imprese,° as well for strangeness as relishing of antiquity, and more applying to that original doctrine of sculpture which the Egyptians are said first to have* 270 *brought from the Ethiopians.)*

The names		The symbols
The queen	*Euphoris*°	A golden tree° laden with fruit.
	1.	
Countess of Bedford	*Aglaia*°	
275 Lady Herbert	*Diaphane*°	The figure icosa-hedron° of crystal.
	2.	
Countess of Derby	*Eucampse*°	
Lady Rich	*Ocyte*°	A pair of naked feet in a river.°
	3.	
280 Countess of Suffolk	*Kathare*°	
Lady Bevill	*Notis*°	The salamander° simple.
	4.	
Lady Effingham	*Psychrote*°	
Lady Elizabeth	*Glycyte*°	A cloud full of
285 Howard		rain,° dropping.
	5.	
Lady Susan de Vere	*Malacia*°	
Lady Wroth	*Baryte*°	An urn, sphered with wine.°
	6.	
Lady Walsingham	*Periphere*°	

290   The names of the Oceaniae were: *Doris, Petraea, Ocyrhoe, Cydippe, Glauce, Tyche, Beroe, Acaste, Clytia, Ianthe, Lycoris, Plexaure.*

---

267. **imprese:** Emblems.   272. *Euphoris:* Abundance.   **golden tree:** Symbol of fertility.   274. *Aglaia:* Splendor.   275. *Diaphane:* Transparent.   276. **icosahedron:** A twenty-sided figure symbolizing water.   277. *Eucampse:* Flexibility.   278. **Ocyte:** Swiftness.   279. **naked . . . river:** Symbolizing purity. 280. *Kathare:* Spotless.   281. *Notis:* Moisture.   **salamander:** Which is not harmed by fire and can extinguish it.   283. **Psychrote:** Coldness.   284. *Glycyte:* Sweetness.   284–85. **cloud . . . rain:** Symbolizing education.   286. *Malacia:* Delicacy. 287. *Baryte:* Weight.   287–88. **urn . . . wine:** Obscure, but the whole symbolizes the globe of earth.   289. *Periphere:* Revolving, circular.

Their own single dance ended, as they were about to make choice of their men, one from the sea was heard to call 'em with this charm, sung by a tenor voice.   295

SONG:

    Come away, come away,
      We grow jealous of your stay;
    If you do not stop your ear,
      We shall have more cause to fear
      Sirens of the land, than they   300
      To doubt the sirens of the sea.

Here they danced with their men several measures° and corantos.° All which ended, they were again accited° to sea with a song of two trebles,° whose cadences were iterated by a double echo from several parts of the land.   305

SONG:

           Daughters of the subtle flood,
           Do not let earth longer entertain you;
1ST ECHO: Let earth longer entertain you.
2ND ECHO: Longer entertain you.
           'Tis to them enough of good   310
           That you give this little hope to gain you.
1ST ECHO: Give this little hope to gain you.
2ND ECHO: Little hope to gain you.
           If they love,
             You shall quickly see;   315
           For when to flight you move,
           They'll follow you, the more you flee.
1ST ECHO: Follow you, the more you flee.
2ND ECHO: The more you flee.
           If not, impute it each to other's matter;   320
           They are but earth —
1ST ECHO: But earth,
2ND ECHO: Earth —
           And what you vowed was water.
1ST ECHO: And what you vowed was water.   325
2ND ECHO: You vowed was water.
AETHIOPIA: Enough, bright nymphs, the night grows old,
    And we are grieved we cannot hold
    You longer light; but comfort take.
    Your father only to the lake   330
    Shall make return; yourselves, with feasts,
    Must here remain the Ocean's guests.
    Nor shall this veil the sun hath cast
    Above your blood more summers last;
    For which, you shall observe these rites: 335
    Thirteen times thrice, on thirteen nights
    (So often as I fill my sphere
    With glorious light throughout the year),
    You shall, when all things else do sleep
    Save your chaste thoughts, with reverence steep   340

---

302. *measures:* Slow dances.   303. *corantos:* Dances with a running or gliding step.   *accited:* Summoned.   304. *trebles:* Sopranos.

Your bodies in that purer brine
And wholesome dew called rosmarine;°
Then with that soft and gentler° foam,
Of which the ocean yet yields some,
345 Whereof bright Venus, beauty's queen,
Is said to have begotten been,
You shall your gentler limbs o'er-lave,
And for your pains perfection have;
So that, this night, the year gone round,°
350 You do again salute this ground,
And in the beams of yond' bright sun
Your faces dry, and all is done.

*At which, in a dance they returned to the sea, where
they took their shell, and with this full song went out.*

---

342. rosmarine: Sea dew.   **343. gentler:** Very gentle.   **349. year
. . . round:** The sequel, however, was not produced until 1608.

SONG:
Now Dian° with her burning face   355
    Declines apace,
    By which our waters know
    To ebb, that late did flow.
Back seas, back nymphs, but with a forward grace
    Keep, still, your reverence to the place;   360
And shout with joy of favor you have won
    In sight of Albion, Neptune's son.

*So ended the first masque, which, beside the singular
grace of music and dances, had that success in the nobility of performance as nothing needs to the illustration*   365
but the memory by whom it was personated.

---

355. Dian: The moon.

COMMENTARY

Eldred Jones (b. 1925)
AFRICA IN ENGLISH MASQUE AND PAGEANTRY   1965

In his book, Othello's Countrymen (1965), *Eldred Jones offers an extensive
review of the appearance of Africans in English entertainments. While the heyday
of the masque form is brief, it offered numerous opportunities to portray Africans
even before Ben Jonson's* Masque of Blackness. *What Jones demonstrates is that
the traditions and attitudes depicted in the masques were deeply ingrained in
English culture. Jonson relied on tradition as he developed his material.*

The English masque had only a short vogue. From its emergence as a distinct art
form with a name of its own, to its disappearance as a significant form, the period
stretches over less than a century and a half. Reckoning from the days when by the
combined efforts of Ben Jonson and Inigo Jones the masque rose to its final form,
the period shrinks to a little over three decades. But, from its earliest beginnings to
its disappearance, figures from Africa frequently contributed to the splendor and
strangeness of both the spectacle and the poetry of the masque. Like the form itself,
these African figures were at first vague and ill-defined, bearing little relevance to
any overall theme, and frequently having no connection with Africa except in
name. But later, as the masque took a settled form, they became more defined and
more deliberately related both to their supposed place of origin and to the themes
of the masques in which they appeared. For instance, figures which in the earliest

masques would have been described as "Moors" or "Blackamoors" appear in Jonson's *Masque of Blacknesse* as the "Daughters of Niger" against a background of both ancient and modern authorities: "Pliny, Solinus, Ptolemy, and of late Leo the African."

Whatever may have been the character or the strength of the stimulus which the English masque undoubtedly received from Renaissance Italy, certain of its features are to be found in activities which had been part of English life since medieval times. The dance was the nucleus around which the other features of the masque came to be established, and dancing, especially the dance called "Morisce" or "Morisco," had been an essential part of English medieval village festivals from earliest times. One of the customs associated with Morris dancing was the blackening of the faces of the participants. This tradition of blackening was also a feature of other popular activities in medieval England. The folk processions, the sword dance and the folk drama, all show an employment of the grotesque of which blackening was only one feature.

One of the most interesting characters in the medieval mummers play was the king of Egypt, who had a black face and who was accepted by tradition as the father of St. George. The devils in the mystery plays were also usually portrayed as black, and indeed some local traditions required all the participants in the mummers play to have black faces. The term "Moriscoe" (with its associations with "Moor" and "Morocco") and the king of Egypt also suggest a possible link between the English medieval dramatic tradition and Africa.

The practice of blackening was transferred to the more sophisticated court "disguisings" of the sixteenth century. In the earliest surviving description of a courtly festivity which involved blackening, the terms "Egipcians," "Moreskoes," and "blacke Moors" appear. In this masquelike performance in 1510, Henry VIII and the Earl of Essex had come in "appareled after Turkey fashion," while "the torchebearers were appareyled in Crymosyn satyne and grene, lyke Moreskoes, their faces blacke. . . ." Later in the same proceedings, six ladies also appeared "their heads rouled in plesauntes and typpers lyke the Egipcians, embroudered with gold. Their faces, neckes, armes and handes, covered with fyne plesaunce blacke . . . so that the same ladies seemed to be nigrost [sic] or blacke Mores." In this festivity, as in earlier entertainments of this kind, the black characters were merely decorative. The strangeness of their appearance had an exotic impact, and that was all that was required at that time. But it was this tradition which, continuing, made Queen Anne request Ben Jonson to make the characters in his masque of 1605 "Black-mores at first."

The Elizabethan outdoor pageant also frequently employed "Moors," and here again this use seems to have been linked with the use of grotesque characters in the medieval pageant. A king of Moors appeared in a pageant undertaken by the London drapers in 1522, and a surviving list of expenses in connection with it gives some indication of his function. The relevant entry records

> payment of 5s. to John Wakelyn, for playing the king of Moors, (the company finding him his apparell, his stage, and wyld fire).

Robert Withington, who notes this entry, draws the interesting conclusion that the "wyld fire" seems to connect the king of Moors here with the "wild man" or "green man" whose function in medieval pageantry was to clear a way through the crowd for the procession by using "wyld-fire" or fireworks. The king of Moors seems then to have crept into the later "procession" or "entertainment" as a grotesque character, to compel the crowds back by his strange appearance and his use of fireworks. (Individual items of the king's costume suggest that his appearance was spectacular: "the said king's girdle, his garland or turban of white feathers and black satin, sylver paper for his shoes, &c. .") In later outdoor pageants this crude function was refined so that the "Moor" or "king of Moors" appeared as a principal speaking character, often acting as the Presenter. In George Peele's pageant of 1585, for instance, the Presenter is described as "him that rid on a luzern before the Pageant, apparelled like a Moor." In Middleton's *Triumph of Truth* (1613) and Anthony Munday's *Chrysanaleia* (1616) similarly important functions were reserved for a Moor.

The popularity of Moors in masques can be judged by the number of references in surviving records either to masques specifically called masques of Moors, or to masques involving such characters, during the reigns of Edward VI, Elizabeth, and James I. The charges for a "Masque of Young Moors" given during Shrovetide 1547, in which King Edward took part, make very interesting reading, for they give illuminating information about the costuming of these characters. The blackening was effected through the use of black gloves, nether stockings, and face masks. These items are mentioned in the long list of charges: "To Rychard Lees of London mercer for viij yards d. of black vellett for gloves above thelbow for mores . . ."; "To hughe Eston the kynges hosyer for the makyng of xiiij peyres of nether stockes of lether black for mores"; a payment to "Nycholas modena straynger . . . for the trymyng Coloring and lyning of xvj vezars or maskes for moores." Some attempt was made to disguise the hair by giving the Moors "Cappes made with Cowrse budge." The elaborate costumes included "belles to hange at the skyrtes of the mores garments" and "dartes with brode heddes and ffethers of sylver. . . ." During the same reign, the accounts show that there was a masque involving Moors on 6 January 1551 and a masque of female Moors at Christmas 1551.

The accounts relating to the reign of Philip and Mary do not refer to any Moors in masques. In view of the apparent popularity of Moors in masques during Edward's reign, and the fact that a year after Elizabeth's accession they seem to have resumed their popularity and continued to hold it up to and during the reign of James I, this seems to indicate a significant temporary change of taste. One is led to speculate on whether portrayals of Moors were suspended out of deference to Philip, who, having had closer dealings with Moors, may have felt touchier on the subject than English monarchs.

Whatever the reasons were for the disappearance of Moors from masques during the reign of Philip and Mary, they reappeared in all their grandeur soon after Queen Elizabeth's accession. An inventory (dated 27 April 1560) of the wardrobe of the Office of the Revels refers to a masque of six Barbarians, and a masque of six Moors. The masque of Barbarians was performed on 1 January 1560, according to a note in the inventory, while the masque of Moors whose date is less certain is placed by E. K. Chambers on 29 January 1559.

There are no more references to masques involving African characters until 1579. (The records of the intervening years are either lost or are very incomplete.) But even this one masque referred to was not performed, although a Willyam Lyzard was paid "for patorns for the mores maske that should have served on Shrovetuesday." There are no other references to masques with Africans in Queen Elizabeth's reign.

Before we encounter our next Africans in masques, early in the reign of James I, a remarkable transformation had taken place. The masque had borrowed from the pageants and processions the use of poetry, and this new form had been employed by the gentlemen of the Inns of Court in their *Gesta Grayorum* (1595). Thus when the masque emerges under James I it emerges as a new form, a form worthy to engage the minds of serious poets. For a short while the English masque flourished as a serious art.

Queen Anne, who was to take a leading part in Ben Jonson's first court masque, expressed a wish "to have them [the masquers] Black-mores at first." This was not in itself a strange request. Now, however, more was involved than mere dressing-up. There had to be a poetic theme which would justify the introduction of black characters. It was therefore logical that Jonson should choose an African theme. His masquers thus emerged as "twelve Nymphs, Negro's, and the daughters of Niger . . ." since Negroes were "the blackest nation of the world." Niger himself was "in forme and colour of an Aethiope; his haire, and rare beard curled. . . ."

Around these characters Jonson weaves an ingenious story, using, whenever he so required, the fictions of the ancients to augment the fruits of his own imagination. The result is an engaging fable. The daughters of Niger had suddenly discovered, while reading Ovid, that they were not, after all, the most beautiful creatures in the world, and that their present color was the result of Phaeton's action:

> And, that, before his heedlesse flames were hurld
> About the Globe, the Aethiopes were as faire,
> As other Dames . . .

The now disillusioned and distracted girls cursed the sun for disfiguring them ("A custome of the Aethiopes, notable in Herod[otus] and Diod[orus] Sic[ulus]. See Plinie Nat. Hist. Lib. 5, cap. 8," adds a helpful Jonson) until they saw in a vision ("for Aethiopes never dreame") that they would recover their beauty if they traveled to a land with the termination "Tania." After passing through " 'blacke Mauritania, Swarth Lusitania and Rich Aquitania," they arrive in Britannia, the end of their quest. Here the beams of a "Sunne" (James),

> are of force
> To blanch an Aethiope, and revive a Cor's [sic].

All they had to do was to bathe thirteen nights in the ocean, and they would gain whiteness and beauty.

Jonson, once he had hit on the idea of black characters, wove both the poetry and, in so far as he controlled Inigo Jones, costume and scenery around them. The costumes and setting were carefully based on pale colors — silver and azure — with "jewells interlaced with ropes of pearle . . . best setting off from the black." The poetry is shot through with contrasts — light and darkness, black and white, death and life, the sun and the moon, and, by total implication, Africa and Europe. Niger's daughters for instance are thus described:

> Who, though but blacke in face,
> Yet, are they bright,
> And full of life and light.

In what must have been a *tour de force* in Elizabethan ears, Niger maintains that the black complexion is the most beautiful:

That, in their black, the prefectst beauty growes;
Since the fix't colour of their curled haire,
(Which is the highest grace of dames most faire)
No cares, no age can change; or there display
The fearefull tincture of abhorred *Gray*;
Since *Death* her selfe (her selfe being pale and blue)
Can never alter their most faithfull hiew.

Nothing as intricately harmonized as *The Masque of Blacknesse* had been attempted in the masque form before. It is a perfect blend of matter and manner; in it the extravagance which was germane to the masque is controlled by a disciplined imagination. This opinion was obviously not shared by Sir Dudley Carleton, whose comments on this presentation are preserved for us. Sir Dudley's criticisms of the scenery, that "there was all Fish and no Water," and of the apparel —"to light and Curtizan-light [sic] for such great ones"— show a literal rather than a literary mind. He, however, notes an interesting detail, namely that the masquers used paint (and not the usual velvet masks) to disguise their complexions:

> Instead of Vizzards, their Faces and Arms up to the Elbows, were painted black, which was Disguise sufficient, for they were hard to be known; but it became them nothing so well as their red and white, and you cannot imagine a more ugly Sight, then a Troop of lean-cheek'd Moors.

The thirteen days promised in *The Masque of Blacknesse* ran into three years before the daughters of Niger, by then washed white, were to return to the stage in *The Masque of Beauty,* which was presented in 1608.

Pedro Calderón de la Barca

Calderón is one of Spain's greatest poets and dramatists of the Golden Age — the early and mid-seventeenth century. This was a time when Lope de Vega (1562–1635) dominated the stage and fashioned the form of the popular drama as a three-act structure, with the opening act establishing the issues and characters, the second act developing the conflict, and the third act resolving the problems raised by the drama. Lope established the form of the *comedia* (tragicomic social drama) in his *The New Art of Play Writing* (1609). Calderón followed Lope's structure.

The Golden Age also produced Spain's greatest painters — El Greco (1541–1614), Murillo (1617–1682), and Velásquez (1599–1660). The activity and significance of art in this period may be underscored by noting that during most of this period, King Philip IV brought artists to court and provided them with studios. Velásquez painted many portraits of King Philip, who visited his studio daily. Likewise, the theater was nurtured by the court throughout this period. Lope was the first court playwright; when he died in 1635, Calderón took his place.

Calderón came from a well-to-do family ruled by a difficult and tyrannical father. He went first to the University of Alcalá and then to the university at Salamanca, where he studied law and probably theology. He changed his original plan to become a priest and began writing plays in 1623. Apparently the king or perhaps the powerful prime minister, Olivares, became aware of his work and brought him into the court circle, giving him the opportunity to produce a variety of plays. Despite the fact that Spain's power and wealth were eroding rapidly, Philip's court maintained a strenuous program of lavish entertainment. Some historians have seen this behavior as an escapist refusal to believe that most of the immense wealth in gold and silver brought back twice yearly from the Americas was already mortgaged on wars, insurrections, and entertainment. Not long after Calderón died, the nation was virtually bankrupt.

The opportunities afforded him at court made it possible for Calderón to produce elaborate entertainments, especially after Olivares built a new court suitable for more brilliant productions in 1634. The old court, the Alcázar, was dark, small, and depressing. The new court was large, elegant, and expressive. It demanded a steady stream of entertainments.

The popular stage was often an open-air theater similar to the Elizabethan theater of Shakespeare's time. Scenery was minimal, costumes rarely more than suggestions, and lighting natural. Plays were put on in the afternoon at 3 o'clock in the summer and at 2 o'clock in the winter. But at court lighting was provided by candles and oil lamps, scenic backgrounds were possible, and costuming was imaginative.

In Calderón's remarkable output as a playwright he may have produced as many as a hundred one-act religious plays for the feast of Corpus Christi. These *auto sacramentales* are allegorical plays, usually about saints' lives and similar to medieval miracle plays. Some of these plays were widely admired, such as *The Constant Prince* (1629), about the martyrdom of Portuguese prince Ferdinand; *The Wonder-Working Magician* (1637), about a Faust character; and *The Two Lovers of Heaven* (1640). Nearly eighty of these plays survive.

Calderón wrote many secular dramas as well as *zarzuelas*, a form that combined music, dance, and drama and that developed into his operas, in which the dialogue is set to music. Among his most important secular plays are *The Surgeon of His Honor* (1635), *Life Is a Dream* (1635), *The Mayor of Zalamea* (1640), and *Daughter of the Air* (1653). Each of these plays is powerful, but *Life Is a Dream* has become the longest-lived and the most often produced of his plays. He wrote it in his favorite baroque style — *Gongorism,* named for an earlier baroque poet, Luis de Góngora y Argote (1561–1627), whose style is marked by references to mythology, stylistic excesses, and complexity of language and thought. In translation many of these stylistic effects are lost, although *Life Is a Dream* is marked by complexity of thought even in English.

In 1651 Calderón took religious orders and retired from the popular stage, but he continued to write for the court. He eventually became an honorary chaplain to Philip and spent much of his time at court in Madrid even while officially assigned to Toledo.

LIFE IS A DREAM

The central action of *Life Is a Dream* is the conversion, or "rebirth," of Prince Segismund. The action of the subplot is the recovery of Rosaura's honor after her seduction by the foreign duke Astolfo. These two strands of action intertwine when Rosaura helps Segismund begin to understand the true nature of the world, and he helps her regain her honor once he is recognized by the people of Poland as the true heir of his father.

Life Is a Dream, often called Spain's *Hamlet,* is one of Calderón's philosophical plays. It centers on self-discovery and the untrustworthiness of illusion. Like Hamlet, Segismund spends part of the second act of the play trying to decide the truth of his experiences: Were they real, or were they a dream? Is life real or a dream? The concept of life as a dream comes from eastern thought and was commonly discussed in the seventeenth century. Skepticism — the reluctance to believe in the knowledge gathered by the senses — was widespread in this age. Both Shakespeare and Calderón were influenced by the revival of classical skepticism, and both examined experience in an effort to discover truth.

When the play opens, Segismund is imprisoned and baffled at his lack of freedom. He does not know that his horoscope predicted at his birth that he would grow up to be a tyrant who would conquer his father, King Basil. As a result Basil placed him in a prison with Clotaldo as his guard and tutor. But the aging Basil, concerned with the succession of his throne, has second thoughts and suspects that the horoscope might be wrong. He releases Segismund to observe his behavior: if he seems tyrannical, he will be reimprisoned and told that his moments of freedom were a dream; if he is prudent, he will inherit the crown.

Rosaura arrives searching for Astolfo, the man who wronged her. She is disguised as a man and is present when Basil experiments with freeing Segismund. Segismund behaves tyrannically, doing what he wants when he wants with no thought for anyone else. He is in a sense a "natural" man because he had not been socialized in a normal family or in normal surroundings. But before he is returned to prison, he falls in love with Rosaura, and his love for her begins the process of his conversion.

Once returned to prison, Segismund believes his experience of freedom was a dream until he reflects on Rosaura. His memory of her begins to convince him that he truly experienced freedom after all. Ultimately, the people resist the imposition of a foreign king, Astolfo, Duke of Muscovy, and storm the prison to free Segismund. He is a changed man who realizes that he must temper his desires and consider other people's feelings. At the head of an army, he defeats his father, Basil. When his father bows before him, he in turn bows before his father, thus demonstrating his allegiance and his conversion from a wrathful tyrant. Rosaura is a central part of Segismund's metamorphosis. She may be an allegorical representation of beauty, feminine (and therefore civilizing) beauty, or humanity. Segismund pledges to help her recover her honor. Prince Astolfo is revealed as a seducer, and Segismund is a wiser and more compassionate person.

Life Is a Dream in Performance

Like *Hamlet,* Calderón's *Life Is a Dream* has been produced often since its first appearance in 1635. Ironically, modern productions in Spain are infrequent because the Spanish are reluctant to tamper with the original verse, which is difficult and unusual. On the other hand, Federico García Lorca produced it in Spain in 1932 respecting the conventions of classic Spanish theater. The Teatro Español produced a full version in 1982. Productions in other parts of the world have, since the first English version in London in 1899, been frequent and interesting. Among the several modern New York versions was the 1981 production directed by María Irene Fornés. Ann Bogart did a highly praised "pictorially 'Spanish'" production in Cambridge, Massachusetts, in 1989 using Edwin Honig's translation. José Rivera's somewhat vaudevillean adaptation appeared in Hartford in 1998 and in New York in 2000, titled *Sueño.*

Another recent production was that by the Royal Lyceum Theatre Company of Scotland at the Brooklyn Academy of Music in 1999. This was a high-energy, powerful drama concentrating on the pain and bewilderment of Segismund, who appeared much of the time bearing a large chain, symbolic of his imprisonment. The stage was simple: a twenty-five-foot circle of broken stones over which hung a huge picture-frame mirror tilted to show only part of the action and to mirror the reality of the stage action in an unreal way throughout. The director, Calixto Bieito, from Barcelona, compressed the action into one two-hour act, relying for clarity on some long speeches of exposition and explanation. He also included two Spanish musicians singing Flamenco songs and beating Flamenco rhythms in the background — a haunting accompaniment. As in most modern productions, Clifford's translation attempted to make the language fresh for its own time rather than emulate the archaisms and poetic complexities of the original. John Clifford's translation was not literal but poetic and approximate.

Pedro Calderón de la Barca (1600–1681)

LIFE IS A DREAM   *1635*
TRANSLATED BY ROY CAMPBELL

Dramatis Personae

BASIL, *King of Poland*
SEGISMUND, *Prince*
ASTOLFO, *Duke of Muscovy*
CLOTALDO, *old man*
CLARION, *a comical servant*
ROSAURA, *a lady*
STELLA, *a princess*
Soldiers, guards, musicians, servants, retinues, women

The scene is laid in the court of Poland, a nearby fortress, and the open country.

ACT I

(*On one side a craggy mountain: on the other a rude tower whose base serves as a prison for Segismund. The door facing the spectators is open. The action begins at nightfall.*)

(*Rosaura, dressed as a man, appears on the rocks climbing down to the plain: behind her comes Clarion.*)

ROSAURA: You headlong hippogriff who match the gale
  In rushing to and fro, you lightning-flicker
  Who give no light, you scaleless fish, you bird
  Who have no coloured plumes, you animal
5 Who have no natural instinct, tell me whither
  You lead me stumbling through this labyrinth
  Of naked crags! Stay here upon this peak
  And be a Phaëthon to the brute-creation!
  For I, pathless save only for the track
10 The laws of destiny dictate for me,
  Shall, blind and desperate, descend this height

Whose furrowed brows are frowning at the sun.
How rudely, Poland, you receive a stranger
(Hardly arrived, but to be treated hardly)
And write her entry down in blood with thorns.   15
My plight attests this well, but after all,
Where did the wretchèd ever pity find?
CLARION: Say *two* so wretchèd. Don't you leave me out
  When you complain! If we two sallied out
  From our own country, questing high adventure,   20
  And after so much madness and misfortune
  Are still two here, and were two when we fell
  Down those rough crags — shall I not be offended
  To share the trouble yet forego the credit?
ROSAURA: I did not give you shares in my complaint   25
  So as not to rob you of the right to sorrow
  Upon your own account. There's such relief
  In venting grief that a philosopher
  Once said that sorrows should not be bemoaned
  But sought for pleasure.
CLARION: Philosopher?   30
  I call him a long-bearded, drunken sot
  And would they'd cudgelled him a thousand blows
  To give him something worth his while lamenting!
  But, madam, what should we do, by ourselves,
  On foot and lost at this late hour of day,   35
  Here on this desert mountain far away —
  The sun departing after fresh horizons?
ROSAURA: Clarion, how can I answer, being both
  The partner of your plight and your dilemma?
CLARION: Would anyone believe such strange events?   40
ROSAURA: If there my sight is not deceived by fancy,
  In the last timid light that yet remains
  I seem to see a building.
CLARION: Either my hopes
  Are lying or I see the signs myself.

ROSAURA: Between the towering crags, there stands so
45   small
    A royal palace that the lynx-eyed sun
    Could scarce perceive it at midday, so rude
    In architecture that it seems but one
    Rock more down-toppled from the sun-kissed crags
    That form the jaggèd crest.
50 CLARION: Let's go closer,
    For we have stared enough: it would be better
    To let the inmates make us welcome.
ROSAURA: See:
    The door, or, rather, that funereal gap,
    Is yawning wide — whence night itself seems born,
55   Flowing out from its black, rugged centre.

(A sound of chains is heard.)

CLARION: Heavens! What's that I hear?
ROSAURA: I have become
    A block immovable of ice and fire.
CLARION: Was that a little chain? Why, I'll be
    hanged
    If that is not the clanking ghost of some
60   Past galley-slave — my terror proves it is!
SEGISMUND: Oh, miserable me! Unhappy me!
ROSAURA: How sad a cry that is! I fear new trials
    And torments.
CLARION: It's a fearful sound.
ROSAURA: Oh, come,
    My Clarion, let us fly from suffering!
65 CLARION: I'm in such sorry trim, I've not the spirit
    Even to run away.
ROSAURA: And if you had,
    You'd not have seen that door, not known of it.
    When one's in doubt, the common saying goes
    One walks between two lights.
CLARION: I'm the reverse.
    It's not that way with me.
70 ROSAURA: What then disturbs you?
CLARION: I walk in doubt between two darknesses.
ROSAURA: Is not that feeble exhalation there
    A light? That pallid star whose fainting tremors,
    Pulsing a doubtful warmth of glimmering rays,
75   Make even darker with its spectral glow
    That gloomy habitation? Yes! because
    By its reflection (though so far away)
    I recognise a prison, grim and sombre,
    The sepulchre of some poor living carcase.
80   And, more to wonder at, a man lies there
    Clothed in the hides of savage beasts, with limbs
    Loaded with fetters, and a single lamp
    For company. So, since we cannot flee,
    Let us stay here and listen to his plaint
    And what his sorrows are.
85 SEGISMUND: Unhappy me!
    Oh, miserable me! You heavens above,
    I try to think what crime I've done against you
    By being born. Although to have been born,
    I know, is an offence, and with just cause
90   I bear the rigours of your punishment:

Since to be born is man's worst crime. But yet
I long to know (to clarify my doubts)
What greater crime, apart from being born,
Can thus have earned my greater chastisement.
Aren't others born like me? And yet they seem   95
To boast a freedom that I've never known.
The bird is born, and in the hues of beauty
Clothed with its plumes, yet scarce has it become
A feathered posy — or a flower with wings —
When through ethereal halls it cuts its way,   100
Refusing the kind shelter of its nest.
And I, who have more soul than any bird,
Must have less liberty?
The beast is born, and with its hide bright-painted,
In lovely tints, has scarce become a spangled   105
And starry constellation (thanks to the skilful
Brush of the Painter) than its earthly needs
Teach it the cruelty to prowl and kill,
The monster of its labyrinth of flowers.
Yet I, with better instincts than a beast,   110
Must have less liberty?
The fish is born, the birth of spawn and slime,
That does not even live by breathing air.
No sooner does it feel itself a skiff
Of silver scales upon the wave than swiftly   115
It roves about in all directions taking
The measure of immensity as far
As its cold blood's capacity allows.
Yet I, with greater freedom of the will,
Must have less liberty?   120
The brook is born, and like a snake unwinds
Among the flowers. No sooner, silver serpent,
Does it break through the blooms than it regales
And thanks them with its music for their kindness,
Which opens to its course the majesty   125
Of the wide plain. Yet I, with far more life,
Must have less liberty?
This fills me with such passion, I become
Like the volcano Etna, and could tear
Pieces of my own heart out of my breast!   130
What law, justice, or reason can decree
That man alone should never know the joys
And be alone excepted from the rights
God grants a fish, a bird, a beast, a brook?
ROSAURA: His words have filled me full of fear and
    pity.   135
SEGISMUND: Who is it overheard my speech? Clotaldo?
CLARION: Say "yes!"
ROSAURA: It's only a poor wretch, alas,
    Who in these cold ravines has overheard
    Your sorrows.
SEGISMUND: Then I'll kill you.

(Seizes her.)

    So as to leave no witness of my frailty.   140
    I'll tear you into bits with these strong arms!
CLARION: I'm deaf. I wasn't able to hear that.
ROSAURA: If you were human born, it is enough
    That I should kneel to you for you to spare me.

SEGISMUND: Your voice has softened me, your presence
145   halted me,
     And now, confusingly, I feel respect
     For you. Who are you? Though here I have learned
     So little of the world, since this grim tower
     Has been my cradle and my sepulchre;
150 And though since I was born (if you can say
     I really have been born) I've only seen
     This rustic desert where in misery
     I dwell alone, a living skeleton,
     An animated corpse; and though till now,
155 I never spoke, save to one man who hears
     My griefs and through whose converse I have heard
     News of the earth and of the sky; and though,
     To astound you more, and make you call me
     A human monster, I dwell here, and am
160 A man of the wild animals, a beast
     Among the race of men; and though in such
     Misfortune, I have studied human laws,
     Instructed by the birds, and learned to measure
     The circles of the gentle stars, you only
165 Have curbed my furious rage, amazed my vision,
     And filled with wonderment my sense of hearing.
     Each time I look at you, I feel new wonder!
     The more I see of you, the more I long
     To go on seeing more of you. I think
170 My eyes are dropsical, to go on drinking
     What it is death for them to drink, because
     They go on drinking that which I am dying
     To see and that which, seen, will deal me death.
     Yet let me gaze on you and die, since I
175 Am so bewitched I can no longer think
     What not seeing you would do to me — the sight
     Itself being fatal! that would be more hard
     Than dying, madness, rage, and fiercest grief:
     It would be life — worst fate of all because
180 The gift of life to such a wretchèd man
     Would be the gift of death to happiness!
ROSAURA: Astonished as I look, amazed to hear,
     I know not what to say nor what to ask.
     All I can say is that heaven guided me
185 Here to be comforted, if it is comfort
     To see another sadder than oneself.
     They say a sage philosopher of old,
     Being so poor and miserable that he
     Lived on the few plain herbs he could collect,
190 One day exclaimed: "Could any man be poorer
     Or sadder than myself?"— when, turning round,
     He saw the very answer to his words.
     For there another sage philosopher
     Was picking up the scraps he'd thrown away.
195 I lived cursing my fortune in this world
     And asked within me: "Is there any other
     Suffers so hard a fate?" Now out of pity
     You've given me the answer. For within me
     I find upon reflection that my griefs
200 Would be as joys to you and you'd receive them
     To give you pleasure. So if they perchance
     In any measure may afford relief,

     Listen attentively to my misfortune
     And take what is left over for yourself.
     I am . . .   205
CLOTALDO (*Within*): Guards of the tower! You
          sluggards
     Or cowards, you have let two people pass
     Into the prison bounds . . .
ROSAURA: Here's more confusion!
SEGISMUND: That is Clotaldo, keeper of my prison.
     Are my misfortunes still not at an end?   210
CLOTALDO: Come. Be alert, and either seize or slay
          them
     Before they can resist!
VOICES (*Within*):   Treason! Betrayal!
CLARION: Guards of the tower who let us pass
          unhindered,
     Since there's a choice, to seize us would be simpler.

(*Enter Clotaldo with soldiers. He holds a pistol and they
all wear masks.*)

CLOTALDO (*Aside to the soldiers*):
     Cover your faces, all! It's a precaution   215
     Imperative that nobody should know us
     While we are here.
CLARION: What's this? A masquerade?
CLOTALDO: O you, who ignorantly passed the bounds
     And limits of this region, banned to all —
     Against the king's decree which has forbidden   220
     That any should find out the prodigy
     Hidden in these ravines — yield up your weapons
     Or else this pistol, like a snake of metal,
     Will spit the piercing venom of two shots
     With scandalous assault upon the air.   225
SEGISMUND: Tyrannic master, ere you harm these people
     Let my life be the spoil of these sad bonds
     In which (I swear it by Almighty God)
     I'll sooner rend myself with hands and teeth
     Amid these rocks than see them harmed and mourn   230
     Their suffering.
CLOTALDO: Since you know, Segismund,
     That your misfortunes are so huge that, even
     Before your birth, you died by heaven's decree,
     And since you know these walls and binding chains
     Are but the brakes and curbs to your proud frenzies,   235
     What use is it to bluster?

(*To the guards.*)

                              Shut the door
     Of this close prison! Hide him in its depths!
SEGISMUND: Ah, heavens, how justly you denied me
          freedom!
     For like a Titan I would rise against you,
     Pile jasper mountains high on stone foundations   240
     And climb to burst the windows of the sun!
CLOTALDO: Perhaps you suffer so much pain today
     Just to forestall that feat.
ROSAURA: Now that I see
     How angry pride offends you, I'd be foolish
     Not to plead humbly at your feet for life.   245

ABOVE: John Ortiz as Segismund hangs over Rosaura (Michi Barall) and Clarion (Jan Leslie Hardin), who contemplate the significance of his imprisonment. From José Rivera's Hartford Stage Company 1998 production of *Sueño*. The visual impact of this scene recollects Leonardo da Vinci's drawing of the "measure of man" as well as emblems of the crucifixion. RIGHT TOP: Segismund (John Ortiz) in prison holding his symbolic chains while Rosaura looks on in José Rivera's production of *Sueño* at the Hartford Stage. RIGHT BOTTOM: George Anton as Segismund in Calixto Bieito's Royal Lyceum Theatre production of *Life Is a Dream* at the Brooklyn Academy of Music, October 1999. The chains he carries symbolize his imprisonment and his torment.

Be moved by me to pity. It would be
Notoriously harsh that neither pride
Nor humbleness found favour in your eyes!
CLARION: And if neither Humility nor Pride
    Impress you (characters of note who act   250
    And motivate a thousand mystery plays)
    Let me, here, who am neither proud nor humble,
    But merely something halfway in between,
    Plead to you both for shelter and for aid.
CLOTALDO: Ho, there!
SOLDIER: Sir?
CLOTALDO: Take their weapons. Bind
    their eyes   255
So that they cannot see the way they're led.
ROSAURA: This is my sword. To nobody but you
    I yield it, since you're, after all, the chief.
    I cannot yield to one of meaner rank.
CLARION: My sword is such that I will freely give it   260
    To the most mean and wretched.

(*To one soldier.*)

                        Take it, you!
ROSAURA: And if I have to die, I'll leave it to you
    In witness of your mercy. It's a pledge
    Of great worth and may justly be esteemed
    For someone's sake who wore it long ago.   265
CLOTALDO (*Apart*): Each moment seems to bring me
    new misfortune!
ROSAURA: Because of that, I ask you to preserve
    This sword with care. Since if inconstant Fate
    Consents to the remission of my sentence,
    It has to win me honour. Though I know not   270
    The secret that it carries, I do know
    It has got one — unless I trick myself —
    And prize it just as the sole legacy
    My father left me.
CLOTALDO: Who then was your father?
ROSAURA: I never knew.
CLOTALDO: And why have you come here?   275
ROSAURA: I came to Poland to avenge a wrong.
CLOTALDO (*Apart*):
    Sacred heavens!

(*On taking the sword he becomes very perturbed.*)

               What's this? Still worse and worse.
    I am perplexed and troubled with more fears.

(*Aloud.*)

    Tell me: who gave that sword to you?
ROSAURA: A woman.
CLOTALDO: Her name?
ROSAURA: A secret I am forced to keep.   280
CLOTALDO: What makes you think this sword contains
    a secret?
ROSAURA: That she who gave it to me said: "Depart
    To Poland. There with subtlety and art
    Display it so that all the leading people
    And noblemen can see you wearing it,   285
    And I know well that there's a lord among them

Who will both shelter you and grant you favour."
But, lest he should be dead, she did not name him.
CLOTALDO (*Aside*): Protect me, heavens! What is this I
    hear?
290 I cannot say if real or imagined
But here's the sword I gave fair Violante
In token that, whoever in the future
Should come from her to me wearing this sword,
Would find in me a tender father's love.
295 Alas, what can I do in such a pass,
When he who brings the sword to win my favour
Brings it to find his own red death instead
Arriving at my feet condemned already?
What strange perplexity! How hard a fate!
300 What an inconstant fortune to be plagued with!
This is my son not only by all signs
But also by the promptings of my heart,
Since, seeing him, my heart seems to cry out
To him, and beat its wings, and, though unable
305 To break the locks, behaves as one shut in,
Who, hearing noises in the street outside,
Cranes from the window-ledge. Just so, not knowing
What's really happening, but hearing sounds,
My heart runs to my eyes which are its windows
310 And out of them flows into bitter tears.
Protect me, heaven! What am I to do?
To take him to the king is certain death.
To hide him is to break my sacred oath
And the strong law of homage. From one side
315 Love of one's own, and from the other loyalty —
Call me to yield. Loyalty to my king
(Why do I doubt?) comes before life and honour.
Then live my loyalty, and let him die!
When I remember, furthermore, he came
320 To avenge an injury — a man insulted
And unavenged is in disgrace. My son
Therefore he is not, nor of noble blood.
But if some danger has mischanced, from which
No one escapes, since honour is so fragile
325 That any act can smash it, and it takes
A stain from any breath of air, what more
Could any nobleman have done than he,
Who, at the cost of so much risk and danger,
Comes to avenge his honour? Since he's so brave
330 He is my son, and my blood's in his veins.
And so betwixt the one doubt and the other,
The most important mean between extremes
Is to go to the king and tell the truth —
That he's my son, to kill, if so he wishes.
335 Perhaps my loyalty thus will move his mercy
And if I thus can merit a live son
I'll help him to avenge his injury.
But if the king prove constant in his rigour
And deal him death, he'll die in ignorance
That I'm his father.

(*Aloud to Rosaura and Clarion.*)

340   Come then, strangers, come!
And do not fear that you have no companions

In your misfortunes, since, in equal doubt,
Tossed between life and death, I cannot guess
Which is the greater evil or the less.

(*A hall at the royal palace, in court.*)

(*Enter Astolfo and soldiers at one side: from the other
side Princess Stella and ladies. Military music and salvos.*)

ASTOLFO: To greet your excellent bright beams   345
As brilliant as a comet's rays,
The drums and brasses mix their praise
With those of fountains, birds, and streams.
With sounds alike, in like amaze,
Your heavenly face each voice salutes,   350
Which puts them in such lively fettle,
The trumpets sound like birds of metal,
The songbirds play like feathered flutes.
And thus they greet you, fair señora —
The salvos, as their queen, the brasses,   355
As to Minerva when she passes,
The songbirds to the bright Aurora,
And all the flowers and leaves and grasses
As doing homage unto Flora,
Because you come to cheat the day   360
Which now the night has covered o'er —
Aurora in your spruce array,
Flora in peace, Pallas in war,
But in my heart the queen of May.
STELLA: If human voice could match with acts   365
You would have been unwise to say
Hyperboles that a few facts
May well refute some other day
Confounding all this martial fuss
With which I struggle daringly,   370
Since flatteries you proffer thus
Do not accord with what I see.
Take heed that it's an evil thing
And worthy of a brute accursed,
Loud praises with your mouth to sing   375
When in your heart you wish the worst.
ASTOLFO: Stella, you have been badly misinformed
If you doubt my good faith. Here let me beg you
To listen to my plea and hear me out.
The third Eugtorgius died, the King of Poland.   380
Basil, his heir, had two fair sisters who
Bore you, my cousin, and myself. I would not
Tire you with all that happened here. You know
Clorilene was our mother who enjoys,
Under a better reign, her starry throne.   385
She was the elder. Lovely Recisunda
(Whom may God cherish for a thousand years!)
The younger one, my mother and your aunt,
Was wed in Muscovy. Now to return:
Basil has yielded to the feebleness   390
Of age, loves learnèd study more than women,
Has lost his wife, is childless, will not marry.
And so it comes that you and I both claim
The heirdom of the realm. You claim that you
Were daughter to the elder daughter. I   395

Say that my being born a man, although
Son of the younger daughter, gives me title
To be preferred. We've told the king, our uncle,
Of both of our intentions. And he answered
400 That he would judge between our rival claims,
For which the time and place appointed was
Today and here. For that same reason I
Have left my native Muscovy. With that
Intent I come — not seeking to wage war
405 But so that you might thus wage war on me!
May Love, wise god, make true what people say
(Your "people" is a wise astrologer)
By settling this through your being chosen queen —
Queen and my consort, sovereign of my will;
410 My uncle crowning you, for greater honour;
Your courage conquering, as it deserves;
My love applauding you, its emperor!
STELLA: To such chivalrous gallantry, my breast
Cannot hold out. The imperial monarchy
415 I wish were mine only to make it yours —
Although my love is not quite satisfied
That you are to be trusted since your speech
Is somewhat contradicted by that portrait
You carry in the locket round your neck.
420 ASTOLFO: I'll give you satisfaction as to that.

(*Drums*.)

But these loud instruments will not permit it
That sound the arrival of the king and council.

(*Enter King Basil with his following*.)

STELLA: Wise Thales . . .
ASTOLFO: Learned Euclid . . .
STELLA: Among the signs . . .
ASTOLFO: Among the stars . . .
STELLA: Where you preside in power . . .
425 ASTOLFO: Where you reside . . .
STELLA: And plot their paths . . .
ASTOLFO: And trace their fiery trails . . .
STELLA: Describing . . .
ASTOLFO: . . . Measuring and judging them . . .
STELLA: Please read my stars that I, in humble
      bonds . . .
ASTOLFO: Please read them, so that I in soft
      embraces . . .
STELLA: May twine as ivy to this tree!
430 ASTOLFO: May find
Myself upon my knees before these feet!
BASIL: Come and embrace me, niece and nephew. Trust
      me,
Since you're both loyal to my loving precepts,
And come here so affectionately both —
435 In nothing shall I leave you cause to cavil,
And both of you as equals will be treated.
The gravity of what I have to tell
Oppresses me, and all I ask of you
Is silence: the event itself will claim
440 Your wonderment. So be attentive now,
Belovèd niece and nephew, illustrious courtiers,

Relatives, friends, and subjects! You all know
That for my learning I have merited
The surname of The Learnèd, since the brush
Of great Timanthes, and Lisippus' marbles —   445
Stemming oblivion (consequence of time) —
Proclaimed me to mankind Basil the Great.
You know the science that I most affect
And most esteem is subtle mathematics
(By which I forestall time, cheat fame itself)   450
Whose office is to show things gradually.
For when I look my tables up and see,
Present before me, all the news and actions
Of centuries to come, I gain on Time —
Since Time recounts whatever I have said   455
After I say it. Those snowflaking haloes,
Those canopies of crystal spread on high,
Lit by the sun, cut by the circling moon,
Those diamond orbs, those globes of radiant crystal
Which the bright stars adorn, on which the signs   460
Parade in blazing excellence, have been
My chiefest study all through my long years.
They are the volumes on whose adamantine
Pages, bound up in sapphire, heaven writes,
In lines of burnished gold and vivid letters,   465
All that is due to happen, whether adverse
Or else benign. I read them in a flash,
So quickly that my spirit tracks their movements —
Whatever road they take, whatever goal
They aim at. Would to heaven that before   470
My genius had been the commentary
Writ in their margins, or the index to
Their pages, that my life had been the rubble,
The ruin, and destruction of their wrath,
And that my tragedy in them had ended,   475
Because, to the unlucky, even their merit
Is like a hostile knife, and he whom knowledge
Injures is but a murderer to himself.
And this I say myself, though my misfortunes
Say it far better, which, to marvel at,   480
I beg once more for silence from you all.
With my late wife, the queen, I had a son,
Unhappy son, to greet whose birth the heavens
Wore themselves out in prodigies and portents.
Ere the sun's light brought him live burial   485
Out of the womb (for birth resembles death)
His mother many times, in the delirium
And fancies of her sleep, saw a fierce monster
Bursting her entrails in a human form,
Born spattered with her lifeblood, dealing death,   490
The human viper of this century!
The day came for his birth, and every presage
Was then fulfilled, for tardily or never
Do the more cruel ones prove false. At birth
His horoscope was such that the bright sun,   495
Stained in its blood, entered ferociously
Into a duel with the moon above.
The whole earth seemed a rampart for the strife
Of heaven's two lights, who — though not hand-to-
      hand —

500 Fought light-to-light to gain the mastery!
The worst eclipse the sun has ever suffered
Since Christ's own death horrified earth and sky.
The whole earth overflowed with conflagrations
So that it seemed the final paroxysm
505 Of existence. The skies grew dark. Buildings shook.
The clouds rained stones. The rivers ran with
    blood.
In this delirious frenzy of the sun,
Thus, Segismund was born into the world,
Giving a foretaste of his character
510 By killing his own mother, seeming to speak thus
By his ferocity: "I am a man,
Because I have begun now to repay
All kindnesses with evil." To my studies
I went forthwith, and saw in all I studied
515 That Segismund would be the most outrageous
Of all men, the most cruel of all princes,
And impious of all monarchs, by whose acts
The kingdom would be torn up and divided
So as to be a school of treachery
520 And an academy of vices. He,
Risen in fury, amidst crimes and horrors,
Was born to trample me (with shame I say it)
And make of my grey hairs his very carpet.
Who is there but believes an evil Fate?
525 And more if he discovers it himself,
For self-love lends its credit to our studies.
So I, believing in the Fates, and in
The havoc that their prophecies predestined,
Determined to cage up this newborn tiger
530 To see if on the stars we sages have
Some power. I gave out that the prince had died
Stillborn, and, well-forewarned, I built a tower
Amidst the cliffs and boulders on yon mountains
Over whose tops the light scarce finds its way,
535 So stubbornly their obelisks and crags
Defend the entry to them. The strict laws
And edicts that I published then (declaring
That nobody might enter the forbidden
Part of the range) were passed on that account.
540 There Segismund lives to this day, a captive,
Poor and in misery, where, save Clotaldo,
His guardian, none have seen or talked to him.
The latter has instructed him in all
Branches of knowledge and in the Catholic faith,
545 Alone the witness of his misery.
There are three things to be considered now:
Firstly, Poland, that I love you greatly,
So much that I would free you from the oppression
And servitude of such a tyrant king.
550 He would not be a kindly ruler who
Would put his realm and homeland in such danger.
The second fact that I must bear in mind
Is this: that to deny my flesh and blood
The rights which law, both human and divine,
Concedes, would not accord with Christian
555   charity,
For no law says that, to prevent another

Being a tyrant, I may be one myself,
And if my son's a tyrant, to prevent him
From doing outrage, I myself should do it.
Now here's the third and last point I would speak
    of,   560
Namely, how great an error it has been
To give too much belief to things predicted,
Because, even if his inclination should
Dictate some headlong, rash precipitancies,
They may perhaps not conquer him entirely,   565
For the most accursèd destiny, the most
Violent inclination, the most impious
Planet — all can but influence, not force,
The free will which man holds direct from God.
And so, between one motive and another   570
Vacillating discursively, I hit
On a solution that will stun you all.
I shall tomorrow, but without his knowing
He is my son — your king — place Segismund
(For that's the name with which he was baptised) 575
Here on my throne, beneath my canopy,
Yes, in my very place, that he may govern you
And take command. And you must all be here
To swear him fealty as his loyal subjects.
Three things may follow from this test, and these 580
I'll set against the three which I proposed.
The first is that should the prince prove prudent,
Stable, and benign — thus giving the lie
To all that prophecy reports of him —
Then you'll enjoy in him your rightful ruler   585
Who was so long a courtier of the mountains
And neighbour to the beasts. Here is the second:
If he prove proud, rash, cruel, and outrageous,
And with a loosened rein gallop unheeding
Across the plains of vice, I shall have done   590
My duty, and fulfilled my obligation
Of mercy. If I then re-imprison him,
That's incontestably a kingly deed —
Not cruelty but merited chastisement.
The third thing's this: that if the prince should be 595
As I've described him, then — by the love I feel
For you, my vassals — I shall give you worthier
Rulers to wear the sceptre and the crown;
Because your king and queen will be my nephew
And niece, each with an equal right to rule,   600
Each gaining the inheritance he merits,
And joined in faith of holy matrimony.
This I command you as a king, I ask you
As a kind father, as a sage I pray you,
As an experienced old man I tell you,   605
And (if it's true, as Spanish Seneca
Says, that the king is slave unto his nation)
This, as a humble slave, I beg of you.
ASTOLFO: If it behoves me to reply (being
The person most involved in this affair)   610
Then, in the name of all, let Segismund
Appear! It is enough that he's your son!
ALL: Give us our prince: we want him for our king!
BASIL: Subjects, I thank you for your kindly favour.

615   Accompany these, my two Atlases,
        Back to their rooms. Tomorrow you shall see him.
    ALL: Long live the great King Basil! Long live Basil!

(*Exeunt all, accompanying Stella and Astolfo. The King
remains.*)

(*Enter Clotaldo with Rosaura and Clarion.*)

CLOTALDO: May I have leave to speak, sire?
BASIL: Oh, Clotaldo!
    You're very welcome.
CLOTALDO: Thus to kneel before you
620   Is always welcome, sire — yet not today
    When sad and evil Fate destroys the joy
    Your presence normally concedes.
BASIL: What's wrong?
CLOTALDO: A great misfortune, sire, has come upon me
    Just when I should have met it with rejoicing.
BASIL: Continue.
625 CLOTALDO: Sire, this beautiful young man
    Who inadvertently and daringly
    Came to the tower, wherein he saw the prince,
    Is my . . .
BASIL: Do not afflict yourself, Clotaldo.
    Had it not been just now, I should have minded,
630   I must confess. But I've revealed the secret,
    And now it does not matter if he knows it.
    Attend me afterwards. I've many things
    To tell you. You in turn have many things
    To do for me. You'll be my minister,
635   I warn you, in the most momentous action
    The world has ever seen. These prisoners, lest you
    Should think I blame your oversight, I'll pardon.
                                  (*Exit.*)

CLOTALDO: Long may you live, great sire! A thousand
       years!

(*Aside.*)

    Heaven improves our fates. I shall not tell him
640   Now that he is my son, since it's not needed
    Till he's avenged.

(*Aloud.*)

    Strangers, you may go free.
ROSAURA: Humbly I kiss your feet.
CLARION: Whilst I'll just *miss* them —
    Old friends will hardly quibble at one letter.
645 ROSAURA: You've granted me my life, sir. I remain
    Your servant and eternally your debtor.
CLOTALDO: No! It was not your life I gave you. No!
    Since any wellborn man who, unavenged,
    Nurses an insult does not live at all.
650   And seeing you have told me that you came
    For that sole reason, it was not life I spared —
    Life in disgrace is not a life at all.

(*Aside.*)

    I see this spurs him.
ROSAURA: Freely I confess it —
    Although you spared my life, it was no life.

655 But I will wipe my honour's stain so spotless
    That after I have vanquished all my dangers
    Life well may seem a shining gift from you.
CLOTALDO: Take here your burnished steel: 'twill be
       enough,
    Bathed in your enemies' red blood, to right you.
    For steel that once was mine (I mean of course 660
    Just for the time I've had it in my keeping)
    Should know how to avenge you.
ROSAURA: Now, in your name I gird it on once more
    And on it I will swear to take revenge
    Although my foe were even mightier. 665
CLOTALDO: Is he so powerful?
ROSAURA: So much so that . . .
    Although I have no doubt in your discretion . . .
    I say no more because I'd not estrange
    Your clemency.
CLOTALDO: You would have won me had you told me,
       since 670
    That would prevent me helping him.

(*Aside.*)

    If only I could discover who he is!
ROSAURA: So that you'll not think that I value lightly
    Such confidence, know that my adversary
    Is no less than Astolfo, Duke of Muscovy. 675
CLOTALDO (*Aside*): (I hardly can withstand the grief it
      gives me
    For it is worse than aught I could imagine!
    Let us inquire of him some further facts.)

(*Aloud.*)

    If you were born a Muscovite, your ruler
    Could never have affronted you. Go back 680
    Home to your country. Leave this headstrong valour.
    It will destroy you.
ROSAURA: Though he's been my prince,
    I know that he has done me an affront.
CLOTALDO: Even though he slapped your face, that's
       no affront.

(*Aside.*)

    O heavens!
ROSAURA: My insult was far deeper!
CLOTALDO: Tell it: 685
    Since nothing I imagine could be deeper.
ROSAURA: Yes. I will tell it, yet, I know not why,
    With such respect I look upon your face,
    I venerate you with such true affection,
    With such high estimation do I weigh you, 690
    That I scarce dare to tell you — these men's clothes
    Are an enigma, not what they appear.
    So now you know. Judge if it's no affront
    That here Astolfo comes to wed with Stella
    Although betrothed to me. I've said enough. 695

                    (*Exeunt Rosaura and Clarion.*)

CLOTALDO: Here! Listen! Wait! What mazed
    confusion!

It is a labyrinth wherein the reason
Can find no clue. My family honour's injured.
The enemy's all powerful. I'm a vassal
700   And she's a woman. Heavens! Show a path
Although I don't believe there is a way!
There's nought but evil bodings in the sky.
The whole world is a prodigy, say I.

ACT II

(*A Hall in the Royal Palace.*)

(*Enter Basil and Clotaldo.*)

CLOTALDO: All has been done according to your
        orders.
BASIL: Tell me, Clotaldo, how it went?
CLOTALDO: Why, thus:
    I took to Segismund a calming drug
    Wherein are mixed herbs of especial virtue,
5   Tyrannous is their overpowering strength,
    Which seize and steal and alienate man's gift
    Of reasoning, thus making a live corpse
    Of him. His violence evaporated
    With all his faculties and senses too.
10   There is no need to prove it's possible
    Because experience teaches us that medicine
    Is full of natural secrets, that there is no
    Animal, plant, or stone that has not got
    Appointed properties. If human malice
15   Explores a thousand poisons which deal death,
    Who then can doubt, that being so, that other
    Poisons, less violent, cause only sleep?
    But (leaving that doubt aside, as proven false
    By every evidence) hear then the sequel:
20   I went down into Segismund's close prison
    Bearing the drink wherein, with opium,
    Henbane and poppies had been mixed. With him
    I talked a little while of the humanities,
    In which dumb Nature has instructed him,
25   The mountains and the heavens and the stars,
    In whose divine academies he learned
    Rhetoric from the birds and the wild creatures.
    To lift his spirit to the enterprise
    Which you require of him, I chose for subject
30   The swiftness of a stalwart eagle, who,
    Deriding the base region of the wind,
    Rises into the sphere reserved for fire,
    A feathered lightning, an untethered comet.
    Then I extolled such lofty flight and said:
35   "After all, he's the king of birds, and so
    Takes precedence, by right, over the rest."
    No more was needful for, in taking up
    Majesty for his subject, he discoursed
    With pride and high ambition, as his blood
40   Naturally moves, incites, and spurs him on
    To grand and lofty things, and so he said
    That in the restless kingdom of the birds
    There should be those who swear obedience, too!

"In this, my miseries console me greatly,
Because if I'm a vassal here, it's only   45
By force, and not by choice. Of my own will
I would not yield in rank to any man."
Seeing that he grew furious — since this touched
The theme of his own griefs — I gave the potion
And scarcely had it passed from cup to breast   50
Before he yielded all his strength to slumber.
A chill sweat ran through all his limbs and veins.
Had I not known that this was mere feigned death
I would have thought him dead. Then came the men
To whom you've trusted this experiment,   55
Who placed him in a coach and brought him here
To your own rooms, where all things were
        prepared
In royalty and grandeur as befitting
His person. In your own bed they have laid him
Where, when the torpor wanes, they'll do him
        service   60
As if he were Your Majesty himself.
All has been done as you have ordered it,
And if I have obeyed you well, my lord,
I'd beg a favour (pardon me this freedom) —
To know what your intention is in thus   65
Transporting Segismund here to the palace.
BASIL: Your curiosity is just, Clotaldo,
    And yours alone I'll satisfy. The star
    Which governs Segismund, my son, in life,
    Threatens a thousand tragedies and woes.   70
    And now I wish to see whether the stars
    (Which never lie — and having shown to us
    So many cruel signs seem yet more certain)
    May yet be brought to moderate their sentence,
    Whether by prudence charmed or valour won,   75
    For man does have the power to rule his stars.
    I would examine this, bringing him here
    Where he may know he is my son, and make
    Trial of his talent. If magnanimously
    He conquers and controls himself, he'll reign,   80
    But if he proves a tyrant and is cruel,
    Back to his chains he'll go. Now, you will ask,
    Why did we bring him sleeping in this manner
    For the experiment? I'll satisfy you,
    Down to the smallest detail, with my answer.   85
    If he knows that he is my son today,
    And if tomorrow he should find himself
    Once more reduced to prison, to misery,
    He would despair entirely, knowing truly
    Who, and whose son, he is. What consolation   90
    Could he derive, then, from his lot? So I
    Contrive to leave an exit for such grief,
    By making him believe it was a dream.
    By these means we may learn two things at once:
    First, his character — for he will really be   95
    Awake in all he thinks and all his actions;
    Second, his consolation — which would be
    (If he should wake in prison on the morrow,
    Although he saw himself obeyed today)
    That he might understand he had been dreaming,   100

And he will not be wrong, for in this world,
Clotaldo, all who live are only dreaming.
CLOTALDO: I've proofs enough to doubt of your
    success,
But now it is too late to remedy it.
105 From what I can make out, I think he's wakened
And that he's coming this way, by the sound.
BASIL: I shall withdraw. You, as his tutor, go
And guide him through his new bewilderments
By answering his queries with the truth.
110 CLOTALDO: You give me leave to tell the truth of it?
BASIL: Yes, because knowing all things, he may find
    Known perils are the easiest to conquer.
                                        (*Exit Basil.*)

(*Enter Clarion.*)

CLARION: It cost me four whacks to get here so quickly.
    I caught them from a red-haired halberdier
115 Sprouting a ginger beard over his livery,
    And I've come to see what's going on.
    No windows give a better view than those
    A man brings with him in his head, not asking
    For tickets of admission or paid seats,
120 Since at all functions, festivals, or feasts
    He looks out with the same nice self-composure.
CLOTALDO (*Aside*): Here's Clarion who's the servant of
        that person —
    That trader in woes, importer from Poland
    Of my disgrace.

(*Aloud.*)

                    Come, Clarion, what news?
125 CLARION: Item the first: encouraged by the fact
    Your clemency's disposed to venge her insult,
    Rosaura has resumed her proper clothing.
CLOTALDO: That's right: it's less indecorous and bold.
CLARION: Item: she's changed her name, and given out
    That she's your niece. And now they've made so
130   much
    Of her that she's been raised to maid of honour
    To the unique and only princess, Stella.
CLOTALDO: That's right: her honour stands to my
        account.
CLARION: Indeed she merely bides the time till you
135 Will settle all accounts about her honour.
CLOTALDO: Biding the time is wise, for in the end
    It's Time that's going to settle all accounts!
CLARION: Item: that she's attended like a queen,
    Because they take her for your niece. Item:
140 That I, who trudged along with her, am dying
    Of hunger. Nobody remembers me,
    Nor yet remembers that I'm like my name
    And (should I sound my Clarion) could tell
    All to the king and Stella and Astolfo.
145 For I am both a Clarion and a servant —
    Two things which ill-accord with secrecy.
    If silence should, by chance, let slip my hand,
    Then there's a chorus which would fit me well:
    "Dawn-breaking Clarion plays no better tune!"

CLOTALDO: You've reason for complaint. I'll satisfy it   150
    If you'll but serve me . . .
CLARION: Hush, here's Segismund!

(*Enter musicians, singing, and servants arraying Segismund, who seems amazed.*)

SEGISMUND: Heavens above! What's this that I am
        seeing?
    I wonder at it all, with naught of fear!
    But with a mighty doubt, I disbelieve it!
    I? — in a sumptuous palace? I — encircled   155
    With rich brocades and silks? I — overwhelmed
    With servants in such brilliant liveries?
    I — to awake in such a gorgeous bed?
    I — in the middle of so many footmen
    Who clothe me in rich garments? I'm awake: 160
    It would be false to take this for a dream.
    Am I not Segismund? Heavens! disabuse me
    If I'm mistaken. Say, what could have happened
    In my imagination while I slept —
    That I should find myself in such a place?   165
    But why should I worry, whatever it was?
    I'll let myself be served and entertained —
    Befall what may.
FIRST SERVANT (*Aside to Second Servant and Clarion*):
                    He's very melancholy!
SECOND SERVANT: Who would not be, considering all
        that's happened
    To him?
CLARION: I would not be!
SECOND SERVANT: You, speak to him.   170
FIRST SERVANT: Shall they begin to sing again?
SEGISMUND: Why, no,
    I would not have them sing.
SECOND SERVANT: You're so distraught,
    I wish you entertained.
SEGISMUND: My griefs are such
    That no mere voices can amuse me now —
    Only the martial music pleased my mind.   175
CLOTALDO: Your Highness, mighty prince, give me
        your hand
    To kiss. I'm glad to be the first to offer
    Obedience at your feet.
SEGISMUND (*Aside*):   This is Clotaldo.
    How is it he, that tyrannised my thralldom,
    Should now be treating me with such respect?   180

(*Aloud.*)

    Tell me what's happening all around me here.
CLOTALDO: With the perplexities of your new state,
    Your reason will encounter many doubts,
    But I shall try to free you from them all
    (If that may be) because you now must know   185
    You are hereditary Prince of Poland.
    If you have been withdrawn from public sight
    Under restraint, it was in strict obedience
    To Fate's inclemency, which will permit
    A thousand woes to fall upon this empire   190
    The moment that you wear the sovereign's crown.

But trusting that you'll prudently defeat
Your own malignant stars (since they can be
Controlled by magnanimity) you've been
195   Brought to this palace from the tower you knew
Even while your soul was yielded up to sleep.
My lord the king, your father, will be coming
To see you, and from him you'll learn the rest.
SEGISMUND: Then, vile, infamous traitor, what have I
200   To know more than this fact of who I am,
To show my pride and power from this day onward?
How have you played your country such a treason
As to deny me, against law and right,
The rank which is my own?
CLOTALDO: Unhappy me!
SEGISMUND: You were a traitor to the law, a flattering
205   liar
To your own king, and cruel to myself.
And so the king, the law, and I condemn you,
After such fierce misfortunes as I've borne,
To die here by my hands.
SECOND SERVANT: My lord!
SEGISMUND: Let none
210   Get in the way. It is in vain. By God!
If you intrude, I'll throw you through the window.
SECOND SERVANT: Clotaldo, fly!
CLOTALDO: Alas, poor Segismund!
That you should show such pride, all unaware
That you are dreaming this.
                             (*Exit.*)
SECOND SERVANT: Take care! Take care!
SEGISMUND: Get out!
215   SECOND SERVANT: He was obeying the king's orders.
SEGISMUND: In an injustice, no one should obey
The king, and I'm his prince.
SECOND SERVANT: He had no right
To look into the rights and wrongs of it.
SEGISMUND: You must be mad to answer back at me.
CLARION: The prince is right. It's you who're in the
220   wrong!
SECOND SERVANT: Who gave you right to speak?
CLARION: I simply took it.
SEGISMUND: And who are you?
CLARION: I am the go-between,
And in this art I think I am a master —
Since I'm the greatest jackanapes alive.
SEGISMUND (*To Clarion*):
225   In all this new world, you're the only one
Of the whole crowd who pleases me.
CLARION: Why, my lord,
I am the best pleaser of Segismunds
That ever was: ask anybody here!

(*Enter Astolfo.*)

ASTOLFO: Blessèd the day, a thousand times, my prince,
230   On which you landed here on Polish soil
To fill with so much splendour and delight
Our wide horizons, like the break of day!
For you arise as does the rising sun

Out of the rugged mountains, far away.
Shine forth then! And although so tardily   235
You bind the glittering laurels on your brows,
The longer may they last you still unwithered.
SEGISMUND: God save you.
ASTOLFO: That you do not know me, sir,
Is some excuse for greeting me without
The honour due to me. I am Astolfo   240
The Duke of Muscovy. You are my cousin.
We are of equal rank.
SEGISMUND: Then if I say,
"God save you," do I not display good feeling?
But since you take such note of who you are,
The next time that I see you, I shall say   245
"God save you *not*," if you would like that better.
SECOND SERVANT (*To Astolfo*):
Your Highness, make allowance for his breeding
Amongst the mountains. So he deals with all.

(*To Segismund.*)

Astolfo does take precedence, Your Highness —
SEGISMUND: I have no patience with the way he came   250
To make his solemn speech, then put his hat on!
SECOND SERVANT: He's a grandee!
SEGISMUND: I'm grander than grandees!
SECOND SERVANT: For all that, there should be respect
    between you,
More than among the rest.
SEGISMUND: And who told you
To mix in my affairs?   255

(*Enter Stella.*)

STELLA: Many times welcome to Your Royal Highness,
Now come to grace the dais that receives him
With gratitude and love. Long may you live
August and eminent, despite all snares,
And count your life by centuries, not years!   260
SEGISMUND (*Aside to Clarion*):
Now tell me, who's this sovereign deity
At whose divinest feet Heaven lays down
The fleece of its aurora in the east?
CLARION: Sir, it's your cousin Stella.
SEGISMUND: She were better
Named "sun" than "star"!

(*To Stella.*)

                    Though your speech was fair, 265
Just to have seen you and been conquered by you
Suffices for a welcome in itself.
To find myself so blessed beyond my merit
What can I do but thank you, lovely Stella,
For you could add more brilliance and delight   270
To the most blazing star? When you get up
What work is left the sun to do? O give me
Your hand to kiss, from out whose cup of snow
The solar horses drink the fires of day!
STELLA: Be a more gentle courtier.
ASTOLFO: I am lost.   275

SECOND SERVANT: I know Astolfo's hurt. I must divert
    him.

(*To Segismund.*)

    Sir, you should know that thus to woo so boldly
    Is most improper. And, besides, Astolfo . . .
SEGISMUND: Did I not tell you not to meddle with me?
SECOND SERVANT: I only say what's just.
SEGISMUND: All this annoys me.
280   Nothing seems just to me but what I want.
SECOND SERVANT: Why, sir, I heard you say that no
      obedience
    Or service should be lent to what's unjust.
SEGISMUND: You also heard me say that I would throw
    Anyone who annoys me from that balcony.
SECOND SERVANT: With men like me you cannot do
285   such things.
SEGISMUND: No? Well, by God, I'll have to prove it
    then!

(*He takes him in his arms and rushes out, followed by
many, to return soon after.*)

ASTOLFO: What on earth have I seen? Can it be true?
STELLA: Go, all, and stop him!
SEGISMUND (*Returning*):   From the balcony
    He's fallen in the sea. How strange it seems!
290 ASTOLFO: Measure your acts of violence, my lord:
    From crags to palaces, the distance is
    As great as that between man and the beasts.
SEGISMUND: Well, since you are for speaking out so
      boldly,
    Perhaps one day you'll find that on your shoulders
295   You have no head to place your hat upon.
                           (*Exit Astolfo.*)

(*Enter Basil.*)

BASIL: What's happened here?
SEGISMUND: Nothing at all. A man
    Wearied me, so I threw him in the sea.
CLARION (*To Segismund*):
    Be warned. That is the king.
BASIL: On the first day,
    So soon, your coming here has cost a life?
300 SEGISMUND: He said I couldn't: so I won the bet.
BASIL: It grieves me, Prince, that, when I hoped to see
      you
    Forewarned, and overriding Fate, in triumph
    Over your stars, the first thing I should see
    Should be such rigour — that your first deed here
305   Should be a grievous homicide. Alas!
    With what love, now, can I offer my arms,
    Knowing your own have learned to kill already?
    Who sees a dirk, red from a mortal wound,
    But does not fear it? Who can see the place
310   Soaking in blood, where late a man was murdered,
    But even the strongest must respond to nature?
    So in your arms seeing the instrument
    Of death, and looking on a blood-soaked place,

    I must withdraw myself from your embrace,
    And though I thought in loving bonds to bind   315
    Your neck, yet fear withholds me from your arms.
SEGISMUND: Without your loving arms I can sustain
    Myself as usual. That such a loving father
    Could treat me with such cruelty, could thrust me
    From his side ungratefully, could rear me   320
    As a wild beast, could hold me for a monster,
    And pray that I were dead, that such a father
    Withholds his arms from winding round my neck,
    Seems unimportant, seeing that he deprives
    Me of my very being as a man.   325
BASIL: Would to heaven I had never granted it,
    For then I never would have heard your voice,
    Nor seen your outrages.
SEGISMUND: Had you denied
    Me being, then I would not have complained,
    But that you took it from me when you gave it —   330
    That is my quarrel with you. Though to give
    Is the most singular and noble action,
    It is the basest action if one gives
    Only to take away.
BASIL: How well you thank me
    For being raised from pauper to a prince!   335
SEGISMUND: In this what is there I should thank you
      for?
    You tyrant of my will! If you are old
    And feeble, and you die, what can you give me
    More than what is my own by right of birth?
    You are my father and my king, therefore   340
    This grandeur comes to me by natural law.
    Therefore, despite my present state, I'm not
    Indebted to you, rather can I claim
    Account of all those years in which you robbed me
    Of life and being, liberty, and honour.   345
    You ought to thank me that I press no claim
    Since you're my debtor, even to bankruptcy.
BASIL: Barbarous and outrageous brute! The
      heavens
    Have no fulfilled their prophecy: I call
    Them to bear witness to your pride. Although   350
    You know now, disillusioned, who you are,
    And see yourself where you take precedence,
    Take heed of this I say: be kind and humble
    Since it may be that you are only dreaming,
    Although it seems to you you're wide-awake.   355
                           (*Exit Basil.*)
SEGISMUND: Can I perhaps be dreaming, though I
      seem
    So wide-awake? No: I am not asleep,
    Since I can touch, and realise what I
    Have been before, and what I am today.
    And if you even now relented, Father,   360
    There'd be no cure since I know who I am
    And you cannot, for all your sighs and groans,
    Cheat me of my hereditary crown.
    And if I was submissive in my chains
    Before, then I was ignorant of what I am,   365

Which I now know (and likewise know that I
Am partly man but partly beast as well).

(*Enter Rosaura in woman's clothing.*)

ROSAURA (*Aside*): I came in Stella's train. I am afraid
 Of meeting with Astolfo, since Clotaldo
370 Says he must not know who I am, not see me,
 Because (he says) it touches on my honour.
 And well I trust Clotaldo since I owe him
 The safety of my life and honour both.
CLARION: What pleases you, and what do you admire
375 Most, of the things you've seen here in the world?
SEGISMUND: Why, nothing that I could not have
  foreseen —
 Except the loveliness of women! Once,
 I read among the books I had out there
 That who owes God most grateful contemplation
380 Is Man: who is himself a tiny world.
 But I think who owes God more grateful study
 Is Woman — since she is a tiny heaven,
 Having as much more beauty than a man
 As heaven than earth. And even more, I say,
385 If she's the one that I am looking at.
ROSAURA (*Aside*): That is the prince. I'll go.
SEGISMUND: Stop! Woman! Wait!
 Don't join the sunset with the breaking day
 By fading out so fast. If east and west
 Should clash like that, the day would surely suffer
390 A syncope. But what is this I see?
ROSAURA: What I am looking at I doubt, and yet
 Believe.
SEGISMUND (*Aside*): This beauty I have seen before.
ROSAURA (*Aside*): This pomp and grandeur I have seen
  before
 Cooped in a narrow dungeon.
395 SEGISMUND (*Aside*):   I have found
 My life at last.

 (*Aloud.*)

      Woman (for that sole word
 Outsoars all wooing flattery of speech
 From one that is a man), woman, who are you?
 If even long before I ever saw you
400 You owed me adoration as your prince,
 How much the more should you be conquered by
  me
 Now I recall I've seen you once before!
 Who are you, beauteous woman?
ROSAURA (*Aside*):   I'll pretend.

 (*Aloud.*)

 In Stella's train, I am a luckless lady.
SEGISMUND: Say no such thing. You are the sun from
405 which
 The minor star that's Stella draws its life,
 Since she receives the splendour of your rays.
 I've seen how in the kingdom of sweet odours,
 Commander of the squadrons of the flowers,
410 The rose's deity presides, and is

Their empress by divine right of her beauty.
 Among the precious stones which can be listed
 In the academy of mines, I've seen
 The diamond much preferred above the rest,
 And crowned their emperor, for shining brightest. 415
 In the revolving empire of the stars
 The morning star takes pride among the others.
 In their perfected spheres, when the sun calls
 The planets to his council, he presides
 And is the very oracle of day. 420
 Then if among stars, gems, planet, and flowers
 The fairest are exalted, why do you
 Wait on a lesser beauty than yourself
 Who are, in greater excellence and beauty,
 The sun, the morning star, the diamond, and the
  rose! 425

(*Enter Clotaldo, who remains by the stage-curtain.*)

CLOTALDO (*Aside*):
 I wish to curb him, since I brought him up.
 But, what is this?
ROSAURA: I reverence your favour,
 And yet reply, rhetorical, with silence,
 For when one's mind is clumsy and untaught,
 He answers best who does not speak at all. 430
SEGISMUND: Stay! Do not go! How can you wish to go
 And leave me darkened by my doubts?
ROSAURA: Your Highness,
 I beg your leave to go.
SEGISMUND: To go so rudely
 Is not to beg my leave but just to take it.
ROSAURA: But if you will not grant it, I must take it. 435
SEGISMUND: That were to change my courtesy to
  rudeness.
 Resistance is like venom to my patience.
ROSAURA: But even if this deadly, raging venom
 Should overcome your patience, yet you dare not
 And could not treat me with dishonour, sir. 440
SEGISMUND: Why, just to see then if I can, and dare
  to —
 You'll make me lose the fear I bear your beauty,
 Since the impossible is always tempting
 To me. Why, only now I threw a man
 Over this balcony who said I couldn't: 445
 And so to find out if I can or not
 I'll throw your honour through the window too.
CLOTALDO (*Aside*):
 He seems determined in this course. Oh, heavens!
 What's to be done that for a second time
 My honour's threatened by a mad desire? 450
ROSAURA: Then with good reason it was prophesied
 Your tyranny would wreak this kingdom
 Outrageous scandals, treasons, crimes, and deaths.
 But what can such a creature do as you
 Who are not even a man, save in the name — 455
 Inhuman, barbarous, cruel, and unbending
 As the wild beasts amongst whom you were nursed?
SEGISMUND: That you should not insult me in this way
 I spoke to you most courteously, and thought

460 I'd thereby get my way; but if you curse me thus
     Even when I am speaking gently, why,
     By the living God, I'll really give you cause.
     Ho there! Clear out, the lot of you, at once!
     Leave her to me! Close all the doors upon us.
     Let no one enter!

                    (*Exeunt Clarion and other attendants.*)

465 ROSAURA: I am lost . . . I warn you . . .
     SEGISMUND: I am a tyrant and you plead in vain.
     CLOTALDO (*Aside*):
          Oh, what a monstrous thing! I must restrain him
          Even if I die for it.

     (*Aloud.*)

                         Sir! Wait! Look here!
     SEGISMUND: A second time you have provoked my
               anger,
470   You feeble, mad old man! Do you prize lightly
          My wrath and rigour that you've gone so far?
     CLOTALDO: Brought by the accents of her voice, I
               came
          To tell you you must be more peaceful
          If still you hope to reign, and warn you that
475   You should not be so cruel, though you rule —
          Since this, perhaps, is nothing but a dream.
     SEGISMUND: When you refer to disillusionment
          You rouse me near to madness. Now you'll see,
          Here as I kill you, if it's truth or dreaming!

     (*As he tries to pull out his dagger, Clotaldo restrains him
     and throws himself on his knees before him.*)

     CLOTALDO: It's thus I'd save my life: and hope to do
480   so —
     SEGISMUND: Take your presumptuous hand from off
               this steel.
     CLOTALDO: Till people come to hold your rage and
               fury
          I shall not let you go.
     ROSAURA: O heavens!
     SEGISMUND: Loose it,

     (*They struggle.*)

          I say, or else — you interfering fool —
485   I'll crush you to your death in my strong arms!
     ROSAURA: Come quickly! Here's Clotaldo being killed!
                                              (*Exit.*)

     (*Astolfo appears as Clotaldo falls on the floor, and the
     former stands between Segismund and Clotaldo.*)

     ASTOLFO: Why, what is this, most valiant prince?
          What? Staining
          Your doughty steel in such old, frozen blood?
          For shame! For shame! Sheathe your illustrious
               weapon!
490 SEGISMUND: When it is stained in his infamous blood!
     ASTOLFO: At my feet here he has found sanctuary
          And there he's safe, for it will serve him well.
     SEGISMUND: Then serve me well by dying, for like this

     I will avenge myself for your behaviour
     In trying to annoy me first of all.   495
     ASTOLFO: To draw in self-defense offends no king,
          Though in his palace.

     (*Astolfo draws his sword and they fight.*)

     CLOTALDO (*To Astolfo*): Do not anger him!

     (*Enter Basil, Stella, and attendants.*)

     BASIL: Hold! Hold! What's this? Fighting with naked
          swords?
     STELLA (*Aside*): It is Astolfo! How my heart misgives
          me!   500
     BASIL: Why, what has happened here?
     ASTOLFO: Nothing, my Lord,
          Since you've arrived.

     (*Both sheathe their swords.*)

     SEGISMUND: Much, though you *have* arrived.
          I tried to kill the old man.
     BASIL: Had you no
          Respect for those white hairs?
     CLOTALDO: Sire, since they're only
          Mine, as you well can see, it does not matter!   505
     SEGISMUND: It is in vain you'd have me hold white hairs
          In such respect, since one day you may find
          Your own white locks prostrated at my feet
          For still I have not taken vengeance on you
          For the foul way in which you had me reared.   510
                                              (*Exit.*)

     BASIL: Before that happens you will sleep once more
          Where you were reared, and where what's happened
               may
          Seem just a dream (being mere earthly glory).

     (*All save Astolfo and Stella leave.*)

     ASTOLFO: How seldom does prediction fail, when evil!
          How oft, foretelling good! Exact in harm,   515
          Doubtful in benefit! Oh, what a great
          Astrologer would be one who foretold
          Nothing but harms, since there's no doubt at all
          That they are always due! In Segismund
          And me the case is illustrated clearly.   520
          In him, crimes, cruelties, deaths, and disasters
          Were well predicted, since they all came true.
          But in my own case, to predict for me
          (As I foresaw beholding rays which cast
          The sun into the shade and outface heaven)   525
          Triumphs and trophies, happiness and praise,
          Was false — and yet was true: it's only just
          That when predictions start with promised favours
          They should end in disdain.
     STELLA: I do not doubt
          Your protestations are most heartfelt; only   530
          They're not for me, but for another lady
          Whose portrait you were wearing round your neck
          Slung in a locket when you first arrived.
          Since it is so, she only can deserve
          These wooing flatteries. Let her repay you   535

For in affairs of love, flatteries and vows
Made for another are mere forged credentials.

(*Rosaura enters but waits by the curtain.*)

ROSAURA (*Aside*): Thanks be to God, my troubles are
    near ended!
    To judge from what I see, I've naught to fear.
540 ASTOLFO: I will expel that portrait from my breast
    To make room for the image of your beauty
    And keep it there. For there where Stella is
    Can be no room for shade, and where the sun is
    No place for any star. I'll fetch the portrait.

(*Aside.*)

545   Forgive me, beautiful Rosaura, that,
    When absent, men and women seldom keep
    More faith than this.
                           (*Exit.*)

(*Rosaura comes forward.*)

ROSAURA (*Aside*): I could not hear a word. I was afraid
    That they would see me.
STELLA: Oh, Astrea!
ROSAURA: My lady!
550 STELLA: I am delighted that you came. Because
    To you alone would I confide a secret.
ROSAURA: Thereby you greatly honour me, your
    servant.
STELLA: Astrea, in the brief time I have known you
    I've given you the latchkey of my will.
555   For that, and being who you are, I'll tell you
    A secret which I've very often hidden
    Even from myself.
ROSAURA: I am your slave.
STELLA: Then, briefly:
    Astolfo, who's my cousin (the word cousin
560   Suffices, since some things are plainly said
    Even by thinking them), is to wed me
    If Fortune thus can wipe so many cares
    Away with one great joy. But I am troubled
    In that, the day he first came here, he carried
    A portrait of a lady round his neck.
565   I spoke to him about it courteously.
    He was most amiable, he loves me well,
    And now he's gone for it. I am embarrassed
    That he should give it me himself. Wait here,
    And tell him to deliver it to you.
570   Do not say more. Since you're discreet and fair:
    You'll surely know just what love is.
                          (*Exit.*)
ROSAURA: Great heavens!
    How I wish that I did not! For who could be
    So prudent or so skilful as would know
    What to advise herself in such a case?
575   Lives there a person on this earth today
    Who's more beset by the inclement stars,
    Who has more cares besieging him, or fights
    So many dire calamities at once?
    What can I do in such bewilderment

Wherein it seems impossible to find   580
Relief or comfort? Since my first misfortune
No other thing has chanced or happened to me
But was a new misfortune. In succession
Inheritors and heirs of their own selves
(Just like the Phoenix, his own son and father)   585
Misfortunes reproduce themselves, are born,
And live by dying. In their sepulchre
The ashes they consume are hot forever.
A sage once said misfortunes must be cowards
Because they never dare to walk alone   590
But come in crowds. I say they are most valiant
Because they always charge so bravely on
And never turn their backs. Who charges with them
May dare all things because there is no fear
That they'll ever desert him; and I say it   595
Because in all my life I never once
Knew them to leave me, nor will they grow tired
Of me till, wounded and shot through and through
By Fate, I fall into the arms of death.
Alas, what can I do in this dilemma?   600
If I reveal myself, then old Clotaldo,
To whom I owe my life, may take offence,
Because he told me to await the cure
And mending of my honour in concealment.
If I don't tell Astolfo who I am   605
And he detects me, how can I dissimulate?
Since even if I say I am not I,
The voice, the language, and the eyes will falter,
Because the soul will tell them that they lie.
What shall I do? It is in vain to study   610
What I should do, when I know very well
That, whatsoever way I choose to act,
When the time comes I'll do as sorrow bids,
For no one has control over his sorrows.
Then since my soul dares not decide its actions   615
Let sorrow fill my cup and let my grief
Reach its extremity and, out of doubts
And vain appearances, once and for all
Come out into the light — and Heaven shield me!

(*Enter Astolfo.*)

ASTOLFO: Here, lady, is the portrait . . . but . . . great
    God!   620
ROSAURA: Why does Your Highness halt, and stare
    astonished?
ASTOLFO: Rosaura! Why, to see you here!
ROSAURA: Rosaura?
    Sir, you mistake me for some other lady.
    I am Astrea, and my humble station
    Deserves no perturbation such as yours.   625
ASTOLFO: Enough of this pretence, Rosaura, since
    The soul can never lie. Though as Astrea
    I see you now, I love you as Rosaura.
ROSAURA: Not having understood Your Highness'
    meaning
    I can make no reply except to say   630
    That Stella (who might be the star of Venus)
    Told me to wait here and to tell you from her

To give to me the portrait you were fetching
(Which seems a very logical request)
635   And I myself will take it to my lady.
Thus Stella bids: even the slightest things
Which do me harm are governed by some star.
ASTOLFO: Even if you could make a greater effort
How poorly you dissimulate, Rosaura!
640   Tell your poor eyes they do not harmonise
With your own voice, because they needs must
jangle
When the whole instrument is out of tune.
You cannot match the falsehood of your words
With the sincerity of what you're feeling.
645 ROSAURA: All I can say is — that I want the portrait.
ASTOLFO: As you require a fiction, with a fiction
I shall reply. Go and tell Stella this:
That I esteem her so, it seems unworthy
Only to send the counterfeit to her
650   And that I'm sending her the original.
And you, take the original along with you,
Taking yourself to her.
ROSAURA: When a man starts
Forth on a definite task, resolved and valiant,
Though he be offered a far greater prize
655   Than what he seeks, yet he returns with failure
If he returns without his task performed.
I came to get that portrait. Though I bear
The original with me, of greater value,
I would return in failure and contempt
660   Without the copy. Give it me, Your Highness,
Since I cannot return without it.
ASTOLFO: But
If I don't give it you, how can you do so?
ROSAURA: Like this, ungrateful man! I'll take it from
you.

(*She tries to wrest it from him.*)

ASTOLFO: It is in vain.
ROSAURA: By God, it shall not come
Into another woman's hands!
665 ASTOLFO: You're terrifying!
ROSAURA: And you're perfidious!
ASTOLFO: Enough, my dear
Rosaura!
ROSAURA: I, your dear? You lie, you villain!

(*They are both clutching the portrait.*)

(*Enter Stella.*)

STELLA: Astrea and Astolfo, what does this mean?
ASTOLFO (*Aside*): Here's Stella.
ROSAURA (*Aside*):   Love, grant me the
strength to win
My portrait.

(*To Stella.*)

670   If you want to know, my lady,
What this is all about, I will explain.
ASTOLFO (*To Rosaura, aside*):
What do you mean?

ROSAURA: You told me to await
Astolfo here and ask him for a portrait
On your behalf. I waited here alone
And as one thought suggests another thought,   675
Thinking of portraits, I recalled my own
Was here inside my sleeve. When one's alone,
One is diverted by a foolish trifle
And so I took it out to look at it.
It slipped and fell, just as Astolfo here,   680
Bringing the portrait of the other lady,
Came to deliver it to you as promised.
He picked my portrait up, and so unwilling
Is he to give away the one you asked for,
Instead of doing so, he seized upon   685
The other portrait which is mine alone
And will not give it back though I entreated
And begged him to return it. I was angry
And tried to snatch it back. That's it he's holding,
And you can see yourself if it's not mine.   690
STELLA: Let go the portrait.

(*She snatches it from him.*)

ASTOLFO: Madam!
STELLA: The draughtsman
Was not unkind to truth.
ROSAURA: Is it not mine?
STELLA: Why, who could doubt it?
ROSAURA: Ask him for the other.
STELLA: Here, take your own, Astrea. You may leave us.
ROSAURA (*Aside*): Now I have got my portrait, come
what will.   695
                                                    (*Exit.*)
STELLA: Now give me up the portrait that I asked for
Although I'll see and speak to you no more.
I do not wish to leave it in your power
Having been once so foolish as to beg it.
ASTOLFO (*Aside*): Now how can I get out of this foul
trap?   700

(*To Stella.*)

Beautiful Stella, though I would obey you,
And serve you in all ways, I cannot give you
The portrait, since . . .
STELLA: You are a crude, coarse villain
And ruffian of a wooer. For the portrait —
I do not want it now, since, if I had it,   705
It would remind me I had asked you for it.
                                                    (*Exit.*)

ASTOLFO: Listen! Look! Wait! Let me explain!

(*Aside.*)

                                                  Oh, damn
Rosaura! How the devil did she get
To Poland for my ruin and her own?

(*The prison of Segismund in the tower.*)

(*Segismund lying on the ground loaded with fetters and
clothed in skins as before. Clotaldo, two attendants, and
Clarion.*)

CLOTALDO: Here you must leave him — since his
710   reckless pride
        Ends here today where it began.
ATTENDANT: His chain
        I'll rivet as it used to be before.
CLARION: O Prince, you'd better not awake too soon
        To find how lost you are, how changed your fate,
715   And that your fancied glory of an hour
        Was but a shade of life, a flame of death!
CLOTALDO: For one who knows so well to wield his
        tongue
        It's fit a worthy place should be provided
        With lots of room and lots of time to argue.
720   This is the fellow that you have to seize

(*To the attendants.*)

        And that's the room in which you are to lock him.

(*Points to the nearest cell.*)

CLARION: Why me?
CLOTALDO: Because a Clarion who knows
        Too many secrets must be kept in gaol —
        A place where even clarions are silent.
725 CLARION: Have I, by chance, wanted to kill my father
        Or thrown an Icarus from a balcony?
        Am I asleep or dreaming? To what end
        Do you imprison me?
CLOTALDO: You're Clarion.
CLARION: Well, say I swear to be a cornet now,
730   A silent one, a wretched instrument . . . ?

(*They hustle him off.*)

(*Clotaldo remains.*)

(*Enter Basil, wearing a mask.*)

BASIL: Clotaldo.
CLOTALDO: Sire . . . and is it thus alone
        Your Majesty has come?
BASIL: Vain curiosity
        To see what happens here to Segismund.
CLOTALDO: See where he lies, reduced to misery!
735 BASIL: Unhappy prince! Born at a fatal moment!
        Come waken him, now he has lost his strength
        With all the opium he's drunk.
CLOTALDO: He's stirring
        And talking to himself.
BASIL: What is he dreaming?
        Let's listen now.
SEGISMUND: He who chastises tyrants
740   Is a most pious prince . . . Now let Clotaldo
        Die by my hand . . . my father kiss my feet . . .
CLOTALDO: He threatens me with death!
BASIL: And me with insult
        And cruelty.
CLOTALDO: He'd take my life away.
BASIL: And he'd humiliate me at his feet.
SEGISMUND (*Still in a dream*):
745   Throughout the expanse of this world's theatre
        I'll show my peerless valour, let my vengeance

Be wreaked, and the Prince Segismund be seen
To triumph — over his father . . . but, alas!

(*Awakening.*)

        Where am I?
BASIL (*To Clotaldo*): Since he must not see me here,   750
        I'll listen further off. You know your cue.

(*Retires to one side.*)

SEGISMUND: Can this be I? Am I the same who,
        chained
        And long imprisoned, rose to such a state?
        Are you not still my sepulchre and grave,
        You dismal tower? God! What things I have
        dreamed!   755
CLOTALDO (*Aside*): Now I must go to him to
        disenchant him.

(*Aloud.*)

        Awake already?
SEGISMUND: Yes: it was high time.
CLOTALDO: What? Do you have to spend all day
        asleep?
        Since I was following the eagle's flight
        With tardy discourse, have you still lain here   760
        Without awaking?
SEGISMUND: No. Nor even now
        Am I awake. It seems I've always slept,
        Since, if I've dreamed what I've just seen and heard
        Palpably and for certain, then I am dreaming
        What I see now — nor is it strange I'm tired,   765
        Since what I, sleeping, see, tells me that I
        Was dreaming when I thought I was awake.
CLOTALDO: Tell me your dream.
SEGISMUND: That's if it *was* a dream!
        No, I'll not tell you what I dreamed; but what
        I lived and saw, Clotaldo, I *will* tell you.   770
        I woke up in a bed that might have been
        The cradle of the flowers, woven by Spring.
        A thousand nobles, bowing, called me Prince,
        Attiring me in jewels, pomp, and splendour.
        My equanimity you turned to rapture   775
        Telling me that I was the Prince of Poland.
CLOTALDO: I must have got a fine reward!
SEGISMUND: Not so:
        For as a traitor, twice, with rage and fury,
        I tried to kill you.
CLOTALDO: Such cruelty to me?
SEGISMUND: I was the lord of all, on all I took revenge,   780
        Except I loved one woman . . . I believe
        That *that* was true, though all the rest has faded.
                              (*Exit Basil.*)
CLOTALDO (*Aside*): I see the king was moved, to hear
        him speak.

(*Aloud.*)

        Talking of eagles made you dream of empires,
        But even in your dreams it's good to honour   785
        Those who have cared for you and brought you up.

For Segismund, even in dreams, I warn you
Nothing is lost by trying to do good.

(*Exit.*)

SEGISMUND: That's true, and therefore let us subjugate
790   The bestial side, this fury and ambition,
Against the time when we may dream once more,
As certainly we shall, for this strange world
Is such that but to live here is to dream.
And now experience shows me that each man
795   Dreams what he is until he is awakened.
The king dreams he's a king and in this fiction
Lives, rules, administers with royal pomp.
Yet all the borrowed praises that he earns
Are written in the wind, and he is changed
800   (How sad a fate!) by death to dust and ashes.
What man is there alive who'd seek to reign
Since he must wake into the dream that's death.
The rich man dreams his wealth which is his care
And woe. The poor man dreams his sufferings.
805   He dreams who thrives and prospers in this life.
He dreams who toils and strives. He dreams who
        injures,
Offends, and insults. So that in this world
Everyone dreams the thing he is, though no one
Can understand it. I dream I am here,
810   Chained in these fetters. Yet I dreamed just now
I was in a more flattering, lofty station.
What is this life? A frenzy, an illusion,
A shadow, a delirium, a fiction.
The greatest good's but little, and this life
815   Is but a dream, and dreams are only dreams.

ACT III

(*The tower.*)

(*Enter Clarion.*)

CLARION: I'm held in an enchanted tower, because
Of all I know. What would they do to me
For all I don't know, since — for all I know —
They're killing me by starving me to death.
5   O that a man so hungry as myself
Should live to die of hunger while alive!
I am so sorry for myself that others
May well say "I can well believe it," since
This silence ill accords with my name "Clarion,"
10   And I just can't shut up. My fellows here?
Spiders and rats — fine feathered songsters those!
My head's still ringing with a dream of fifes
And trumpets and a lot of noisy humbug
And long processions as of penitents
15   With crosses, winding up and down, while some
Faint at the sight of blood besmirching others.
But now to tell the truth, I am in prison.
For knowing secrets, I am kept shut in,
Strictly observed as if I were a Sunday,
20   And feeling sadder than a Tuesday, where
I neither eat nor drink. They say a secret

Is sacred and should be as strictly kept
As any saint's day on the calendar.
Saint Secret's Day for me's a working day
Because I'm never idle then. The penance   25
I suffer here is merited, I say:
Because being a lackey, I was silent,
Which, in a servant, is a sacrilege.

(*A noise of drums and trumpets.*)

FIRST SOLDIER (*Within*):
Here is the tower in which he is imprisoned.
Smash in the door and enter, everybody!   30
CLARION: Great God! They've come to seek me. That
    is certain
Because they say I'm here. What can they want?

(*Enter several soldiers.*)

FIRST SOLDIER: Go in.
SECOND SOLDIER: He's here!
CLARION: No, he's not here!
ALL THE SOLDIERS: Our lord!
CLARION: What, are they drunk?
FIRST SOLDIER: You are our rightful prince.
We do not want and never shall allow   35
A stranger to supplant our trueborn prince.
Give us your feet to kiss!
ALL THE SOLDIERS: Long live the prince!
CLARION: Bless me, if it's not real! In this strange
    kingdom
It seems the custom, everyday, to take
Some fellow and to make him prince and then   40
Shut him back in this tower. That *must* be it!
So I must play my role.
ALL THE SOLDIERS: Give us your feet.
CLARION: I can't. They're necessary. After all
What sort of use would be a footless prince?
SECOND SOLDIER: All of us told your father, as one
    man,   45
We want no prince of Muscovy but you!
CLARION: You weren't respectful to my father? Shame!
FIRST SOLDIER: It was our loyalty that made us tell him.
CLARION: If it was loyalty, you have my pardon.
SECOND SOLDIER: Restore your empire. Long live
    Segismund!   50
CLARION (*Aside*): That is the name they seem to give to
    all
These counterfeited princes.

(*Enter Segismund.*)

SEGISMUND: Who called Segismund?
CLARION (*Aside*): I seem to be a hollow sort of prince.
FIRST SOLDIER: Which of you's Segismund?
SEGISMUND: I am.
SECOND SOLDIER (*To Clarion*):   Then, why,
Rash fool, did you impersonate the prince   55
Segismund?
CLARION: What? I, Segismund? Yourselves
Be-Segismunded me without request.
All yours was both the rashness and the folly.

FIRST SOLDIER: Prince Segismund, whom we acclaim
    our lord,
60 Your father, great King Basil, in his fear
    That heaven would fulfil a prophecy
    That one day he would kneel before your feet
    Wishes now to deprive you of the throne
    And give it to the Duke of Muscovy.
65 For this he called a council, but the people
    Discovered his design and knowing, now,
    They have a native king, will have no stranger.
    So scorning the fierce threats of destiny,
    We've come to seek you in your very prison,
70 That aided by the arms of the whole people,
    We may restore you to the crown and sceptre,
    Taking them from the tyrant's grasp. Come, then:
    Assembling here, in this wide desert region,
    Hosts of plebeians, bandits, and freebooters,
75 Acclaim you king. Your liberty awaits you!
    Hark to its voice!

(*Shouts within.*)

            Long life to Segismund!
SEGISMUND: Once more, you heavens will that I should
    dream
    Of grandeur, once again, 'twixt doubts and shades,
    Behold the majesty of pomp and power
80 Vanish into the wind, once more you wish
    That I should taste the disillusion and
    The risk by which all human power is humbled,
    Of which all human power should live aware.
    It must not be. I'll not be once again
85 Put through my paces by my fortune's stars.
    And since I know this life is all a dream,
    Depart, vain shades, who feign, to my dead senses,
    That you have voice and body, having neither!
    I want no more feigned majesty, fantastic
90 Display, no void illusions, that one gust
    Can scatter like the almond tree in flower,
    Whose rosy buds, without advice or warning,
    Dawn in the air too soon and then, as one,
    Are all extinguished, fade, and fall, and wither
95 In the first gust of wind that comes along!
    I know you well. I know you well by now.
    I know that all that happens in yourselves
    Happens as in a sleeping man. For me
    There are no more delusions and deceptions
100 Since I well know this life is all a dream.
SECOND SOLDIER: If you think we are cheating, just
    sweep
    Your gaze along these towering peaks, and see
    The hosts that wait to welcome and obey you.
SEGISMUND: Already once before I've seen such crowds
105 Distinctly, quite as vividly as these:
    And yet it was a dream.
SECOND SOLDIER: No great event
    Can come without forerunners to announce it
    And this is the real meaning of your dream.
SEGISMUND: Yes, you say well. It was the fore-
    announcement

And just in case it was correct, my soul,   110
(Since life's so short) let's dream the dream anew!
But it must be attentively, aware
That we'll awake from pleasure in the end.
Forewarned of that, the shock's not so abrupt,
The disillusion's less. Evils anticipated   115
Lose half their sting. And armed with this
    precaution —
That power, even when we're sure of it, is borrowed
And must be given back to its true owner —
We can risk anything and dare the worst.
Subjects, I thank you for your loyalty.   120
In me you have a leader who will free you,
Bravely and skilfully, from foreign rule.
Sound now to arms, you'll soon behold my valour.
Against my father I must march and bring
Truth from the stars. Yes: he must kneel to me.   125

(*Aside.*)

But yet, since I may wake before he kneels,
Perhaps I'd better not proclaim what may not
    happen.
ALL: Long live Segismund!

(*Enter Clotaldo.*)

CLOTALDO: Gracious heavens! What is
    This riot here?
SEGISMUND: Clotaldo!
CLOTALDO: Sir!

(*Aside.*)

                     He'll prove
    His cruelty on me.
CLARION: I bet he throws him   130
    Over the mountain.
CLOTALDO: At your royal feet
    I kneel, knowing my penalty is death.
SEGISMUND: Rise, rise, my foster father, from the
    ground,
    For you must be the compass and the guide
    In which I trust. You brought me up, and I   135
    Know what I owe your loyalty. Embrace me!
CLOTALDO: What's that you say?
SEGISMUND: I know I'm in a dream,
    But I would like to act well, since good actions,
    Even in a dream, are not entirely lost.
CLOTALDO: Since doing good is now to be your glory,   140
    You will not be offended that I too
    Should do what's right. You march against your
    father!
    I cannot give you help against my king.
    Here at your feet, my lord, I plead for death.
SEGISMUND (*Aloud*): Villain!

(*Aside.*)

                But let us suffer this annoyance.   145
Though my rage would slay him, yet he's loyal.
A man does not deserve to die for that.
How many angry passions does this leash

150　　Restrain in me, this curb of knowing well
　　　　That I must wake and find myself alone!
　　SECOND SOLDIER: All this fine talk, Clotaldo, is a cruel
　　　　Spurn of the public welfare. We are loyal
　　　　Who wish our own prince to reign over us.
　　CLOTALDO: Such loyalty, after the king were dead,
155　　Would honour you. But while the king is living
　　　　He is our absolute, unquestioned lord.
　　　　There's no excuse for subjects who oppose
　　　　His sovereignty in arms.
　　FIRST SOLDIER:　　　　　　　We'll soon see well
　　　　Enough, Clotaldo, what this loyalty
　　　　Is worth.
160　CLOTALDO:　　You would be better if you had some.
　　　　It is the greatest prize.
　　SEGISMUND:　　　　　　　Peace, peace, I pray you.
　　CLOTALDO: My lord!
　　SEGISMUND:　　　　　Clotaldo, if your feelings
　　　　Are truly thus, go you, and serve the king;
　　　　That's prudence, loyalty, and common sense.
165　　But do not argue here with anyone
　　　　Whether it's right or wrong, for every man
　　　　Has his own honour.
　　CLOTALDO:　　　　　　Humbly I take my leave.
　　　　　　　　　　　　　　　　　　　　　　　(*Exit.*)
　　SEGISMUND: Now sound the drums and march in rank
　　　　　　and order
　　　　Straight to the palace.
　　ALL:　　　　　　　　Long live Segismund!
170　SEGISMUND: Fortune, we go to reign! Do not awake me
　　　　If I am dreaming! Do not let me fall
　　　　Asleep if it is true! To act with virtue
　　　　Is what matters, since if this proves true,
　　　　That truth's sufficient reason in itself;
175　　If not, we win us friends against the time
　　　　When we at last awake.

(*A room in the Royal Palace.*)

(*Enter Basil and Astolfo.*)

　　BASIL: Whose prudence can rein in a bolting horse?
　　　　Who can restrain a river's pride, in spate?
　　　　Whose valour can withstand a crag dislodged
180　　And hurtling downwards from a mountain peak?
　　　　All these are easier by far than to hold back
　　　　A crowd's proud fury, once it has been roused.
　　　　It has two voices, both proclaiming war,
　　　　And you can hear them echoing through the
　　　　　　mountains,
185　　Some shouting "Segismund," others "Astolfo."
　　　　The scene I set for swearing of allegiance
　　　　Lends but an added horror to this strife:
　　　　It has become the back cloth to a stage
　　　　Where Fortune plays out tragedies in blood.
190　ASTOLFO: My lord, forget the happiness and wealth
　　　　You promised me from your most blessèd hand.
　　　　If Poland, which I hope to rule, refuses
　　　　Obedience to my right, grudging me honour,
　　　　It is because I've got to earn it first.

　　　　Give me a horse, that I with angry pride　　　195
　　　　May match the thunder in my voice and ride
　　　　To strike, like lightning, terror far and wide.
　　　　　　　　　　　　　　　　　　(*Exit Astolfo.*)
　　BASIL: No remedy for what's infallible!
　　　　What is foreseen is perilous indeed!
　　　　If something has to be, there's no way out;　　200
　　　　In trying to evade it, you but court it.
　　　　This law is pitiless and horrible.
　　　　Thinking one can evade the risk, one meets it:
　　　　My own precautions have been my undoing,
　　　　And I myself have quite destroyed my kingdom.　205

(*Enter Stella.*)

　　STELLA: If you, my lord, in person do not try
　　　　To curb the vast commotion that has started
　　　　In all the streets between the rival factions,
　　　　You'll see your kingdom, swamped in waves of
　　　　　crimson,
　　　　Swimming in its own blood, with nothing left　　210
　　　　But havoc, dire calamity, and woe.
　　　　So frightful is the damage to your empire
　　　　That, seen, it strikes amazement; heard, despair.
　　　　The sun's obscured, the very winds are hindered.
　　　　Each stone is a memorial to the dead.　　　　　215
　　　　Each flower springs from a grave while every building
　　　　Appears a mausoleum, and each soldier
　　　　A premature and walking skeleton.

(*Enter Clotaldo.*)

　　CLOTALDO: Praise be to God, I reach your feet alive!
　　BASIL: Clotaldo! What's the news of Segismund?　　220
　　CLOTALDO: The crowd, a headstrong monster blind
　　　　　　with rage,
　　　　Entered his dungeon tower and set him free.
　　　　He, now exalted for the second time,
　　　　Conducts himself with valour, boasting how
　　　　He will bring down the truth out of the stars.　225
　　BASIL: Give me a horse, that I myself, in person,
　　　　May vanquish such a base, ungrateful son!
　　　　For I, in the defence of my own crown,
　　　　Shall do by steel what science failed to do.
　　　　　　　　　　　　　　　　　　　　　(*Exit.*)
　　STELLA: I'll be Bellona to your Sun, and try　　　230
　　　　To write my name next yours in history.
　　　　I'll ride as though I flew on outstretched wings
　　　　That I may vie with Pallas.
　　　　　　　　　　　　　　　　　　(*Exit.*)

(*Enter Rosaura, holding back Clotaldo.*)

　　ROSAURA: I know that all is war, Clotaldo, yet
　　　　Although your valour calls you to the front,　　235
　　　　First hear me out. You know quite well that I
　　　　Arrived in Poland poor and miserable,
　　　　Where, shielded by your valour, I found mercy.
　　　　You told me to conceal myself, and stay
　　　　Here in the palace, hiding from Astolfo.　　　　240
　　　　He saw me in the end, and so insulted
　　　　My honour that (although he saw me clearly)

He nightly speaks with Stella in the garden.
I have the key to it and I will show you
245 How you can enter there and end my cares.
Thus bold, resolved, and strong, you can recover
My honour, since you're ready to avenge me
By killing him.
CLOTALDO: It's true that I intended,
Since first I saw you (having heard your tale)
250 With my own life to rectify your wrongs.
The first step that I took was bid you dress
According to your sex, for fear Astolfo
Might see you as you were, and deem you
          wanton.
I was devising how we could recover
255 Your honour (so much did it weigh on me)
Even though we had to kill him. (A wild plan —
Though since he's not my king, I would not flinch
From killing him.) But then, when suddenly
Segismund tried to kill me, it was he
260 Who saved my life with his surpassing valour.
Consider: how can I requite Astolfo
With death for giving me my life so bravely,
And when my soul is full of gratitude?
So torn between the two of you I stand —
265 Rosaura, whose life I saved, and Astolfo,
Who saved my life. What's to be done? Which
          side
To take, and whom to help, I cannot judge.
What I owe you in that I gave you life
I owe to him in that he gave me life.
270 And so there is no course that I can take
To satisfy my love. I am a person
Who has to act, yet suffer either way.
ROSAURA: I should not have to tell so brave a man
That if it is nobility to give,
275 It's baseness to receive. That being so
You owe no gratitude to him, admitting
That it was he who gave you life, and you
Who gave me life, since he forced you to take
A meaner role, and through me you assumed
280 A generous role. So you should side with me:
My cause is so far worthier than his own
As giving is than taking.
CLOTALDO: Though nobility
Is with the giver, it is gratitude
That dwells with the receiver. As a giver
285 I have the name of being generous:
Then grant me that of being grateful too
And let me earn the title and be grateful,
As I am liberal, giving or receiving.
ROSAURA: You granted me my life, at the same time
290 Telling me it was worthless, since dishonoured,
And therefore was no life. Therefore from you
I have received no life at all. And since
You should be liberal first and grateful after
(Since so you said yourself) I now entreat you
295 Give me the life, the life you never gave me!
As giving magnifies the most, give first
And then be grateful after, if you will!

CLOTALDO: Won by your argument, I will be
          liberal.
Rosaura, I shall give you my estate
And you shall seek a convent, there to live. 300
This measure is a happy thought, for, see,
Fleeing a crime, you find a sanctuary.
For when the empire's threatened with disasters
And is divided thus, I, born a noble,
Am not the man who would augment its woes. 305
So with this remedy which I have chosen
I remain loyal to the kingdom, generous
To you, and also grateful to Astolfo.
And thus I choose the course that suits you best.
Were I your father, what could I do more? 310
ROSAURA: Were you my father, then I would accept
The insult. Since you are not, I refuse.
CLOTALDO: What do you hope to do then?
ROSAURA: Kill the duke!
CLOTALDO: A girl who never even knew her father
Armed with such courage?
ROSAURA: Yes.
CLOTALDO: What spurs you on? 315
ROSAURA: My good name.
CLOTALDO: In Astolfo you will find . . .
ROSAURA: My honour rides on him and strikes him
          down!
CLOTALDO: Your king, too, Stella's husband!
ROSAURA: Never, never
Shall that be, by almighty God, I swear!
CLOTALDO: Why, this is madness!
ROSAURA: Yes it is!
CLOTALDO: Restrain it. 320
ROSAURA: That I cannot.
CLOTALDO: Then you are lost forever!
ROSAURA: I know it!
CLOTALDO: Life and honour both together!
ROSAURA: I well believe it!
CLOTALDO: What do you intend?
ROSAURA: My death.
CLOTALDO: This is despair and desperation.
ROSAURA: It's honour.
CLOTALDO: It is nonsense.
ROSAURA: It is valour. 325
CLOTALDO: It's frenzy.
ROSAURA: Yes, it's anger! Yes, it's fury!
CLOTALDO: In short you cannot moderate your
          passion?
ROSAURA: No.
CLOTALDO: Who is there to help you?
ROSAURA: I, myself.
CLOTALDO: There is no cure?
ROSAURA: There is no cure!
CLOTALDO: Think well
If there's not some way out . . .
ROSAURA: Some other way 330
To do away with me . . .
          (*Exit.*)

CLOTALDO: If you are lost,
My daughter, let us both be lost together!

(*In the country.*)

(*Enter Segismund clothed in skins. Soldiers marching. Clarion. Drums beating.*)

SEGISMUND: If Rome, today, could see me here,
    renewing
    Her olden triumphs, she might laugh to see
335   A wild beast in command of mighty armies,
    A wild beast, to whose fiery aspirations
    The firmament were all too slight a conquest!
    But stoop your flight, my spirit. Do not thus
    Be puffed to pride by these uncertain plaudits
340   Which, when I wake, will turn to bitterness
    In that I won them only to be lost.
    The less I value them, the less I'll miss them.

(*A trumpet sounds.*)

CLARION: Upon a rapid courser (pray excuse me,
    Since if it comes to mind I must describe it)
345   In which it seems an atlas was designed
    Since if its body is earth, its soul is fire
    Within its breast, its foam appears the sea,
    The wind its breath, and chaos its condition,
    Since in its soul, its foam, its breath and flesh,
350   It seems a monster of fire, earth, sea, and wind,
    Upon the horse, all of a patchwork colour,
    Dappled, and rushing forward at the will
    Of one who plies the spur, so that it flies
    Rather than runs — see how a woman rides
    Boldly into your presence.°
355 SEGISMUND: Her light blinds me.
CLARION: Good God! Why, here's Rosaura!
SEGISMUND: It is heaven
    That has restored her to my sight once more.

(*Enter Rosaura with sword and dagger in riding costume.*)

ROSAURA: Generous Segismund, whose majesty
    Heroically rises in the lustre
360   Of his great deeds out of his night of shadows,
    And as the greatest planet, in the arms
    Of his aurora, lustrously returns
    To plants and roses, over hills and seas,
    When, crowned with gold, he looks abroad,
        dispersing
365   Radiance, flashing his rays, bathing the summits,
    And broidering the fringes of the foam,
    So may you dawn upon the world, bright sun
    Of Poland, that a poor unhappy woman
    May fall before your feet and beg protection
370   Both as a woman and unfortunate —
    Two things that must oblige you, sire, as one
    Who prize yourself as valiant, each of them
    More than suffices for your chivalry.
    Three times you have beheld me now, three times
375   Been ignorant of who I am, because

351–55. **Upon a . . . presence:** Clarion's speech is a parody of exaggerated style including Calderón's. [R.C.]

Three times you saw me in a different clothing.
The first time you mistook me for a man,
Within that rigorous prison, where your hardships
Made mine seem pleasure. Next time, as a woman,
You saw me, when your pomp and majesty   380
Were as a dream, a phantasm, a shade.
The third time is today when, as a monster
Of both the sexes, in a woman's costume
I bear a soldier's arms. But to dispose you
The better to compassion, hear my story.   385
My mother was a noble in the court
Of Moscow, who, since most unfortunate,
Must have been beautiful. Then came a traitor
And cast his eyes on her (I do not name him,
Not knowing who he is). Yet I deduce   390
That he was valiant too from my own valour,
Since he gave form to me — and I could wish
I had been born in pagan times, that I might
Persuade myself he was some god of those
Who rain in showers of gold, turn into swans   395
Or bulls, for Danaës, Ledas, or Europas.
That's strange: I thought I was just rambling on
By telling old perfidious myths, yet find
I've told you how my mother was cajoled.
Oh, she was beautiful as no one else   400
Has been, but was unfortunate like all.
He swore to wed her (that's an old excuse)
And this trick reached so nearly to her heart
That thought must weep, recalling it today.
The tyrant left her only with his sword   405
As Aeneas left Troy. I sheathed its blade here
Upon my thigh, and I will bare it too
Before the ending of this history.
Out of this union, this poor link which neither
Could bind the marriage nor handcuff the crime,   410
Myself was born, her image and her portrait,
Not in her beauty, but in her misfortune,
For mine's the same. That's all I need to say.
The most that I can tell you of myself
Is that the man who robbed me of the spoils   415
And trophies of my honour is Astolfo.
Alas! to name him my heart rages so
(As hearts will do when men name enemies).
Astolfo was my faithless and ungrateful
Lord, who (quite forgetful of our happiness,   420
Since of a past love even the memory fades)
Came here to claim the throne and marry Stella
For she's the star who rises as I set.
It's hard to credit that a star should sunder
Lovers the stars had made comfortable!   425
So hurt was I, so villainously cheated,
That I became mad, brokenhearted, sick,
Half wild with grief, and like to die, with all
Hell's own confusion ciphered on my mind
Like Babel's incoherence. Mutely I told   430
My griefs (since woes and griefs declare themselves
Better than can the mouth, by their effects),
When, with my mother (we were by ourselves),
She broke the prison of my pent-up sorrows

435 And from my breast they all rushed forth in troops.
I felt no shyness, for in knowing surely
That one to whom one's errors are recounted
Has also been an ally in her own,
One finds relief and rest, since bad example
440 Can sometimes serve for a good purpose too.
She heard my plaint with pity, and she tried
To palliate my sorrows with her own.
How easily do judges pardon error
When they've offended too! An example,
445 A warning, in herself, she did not trust
To idleness, or the slow cure of time,
Nor try to find a remedy for her honour
In my misfortunes, but, with better counsel,
She bade me follow him to Poland here
450 And with prodigious gallantry persuade him
To pay the debt to honour that he owes me.
So that it would be easier to travel,
She bade me don male clothing, and took down
This ancient sword which I am wearing now.
455 Now it is time that I unsheathe the blade
As I was bid, for, trusting in its sign,
She said: "Depart to Poland, show this sword
That all the nobles may behold it well,
And it may be that one of them will take
460 Pity on you, and counsel you, and shield you."
I came to Poland and, you will remember,
Entered your cave. You looked at me in wonder.
Clotaldo passionately took my part
To plead for mercy to the king, who spared me,
465 Then, when he heard my story, bade me change
Into my own clothes and attend on Stella,
There to disturb Astolfo's love and stop
Their marriage. Again you saw me in woman's dress
And were confused by the discrepancy.
470 But let's pass to what's new: Clotaldo, now
Persuaded that Astolfo must, with Stella,
Come to the throne, dissuades me from my purpose,
Against the interests of my name and honour.
But seeing you, O valiant Segismund,
475 Are claiming your revenge, now that the heavens
Have burst the prison of your rustic tower,
(Wherein you were the tiger of your sorrows,
The rock of sufferings and direful pains)
And sent you forth against your sire and country,
480 I come to aid you, mingling Dian's silks
With the hard steel of Pallas. Now, strong Captain,
It well behoves us both to stop this marriage —
Me, lest my promised husband should be wed,
You, lest, when their estates are joined, they weigh
485 More powerfully against your victory.
I come, as a mere woman, to persuade you
To right my shame; but, as a man, I come
To help you battle for your crown. As woman,
To melt your heart, here at your feet I fall;
490 But, as a man, I come to serve you bravely
Both with my person and my steel, and thus,
If you today should woo me as a woman,
Then I should have to kill you as a man would

In honourable service of my honour;
Since I must be three things today at once —   495
Passionate, to persuade you: womanly,
To ply you with my woes: manly, to gain
Honour in battle.
SEGISMUND: Heavens! If it is true I'm dreaming,
Suspend my memory, for in a dream
So many things could not occur. Great heavens!   500
If I could only come free of them all!
Or never think of any! Who ever felt
Such grievous doubts? If I but dreamed that triumph
In which I found myself, how can this woman
Refer me to such sure and certain facts?   505
Then all of it was true and not a dream.
But if it be the truth, why does my past life
Call it a dream? This breeds the same confusion.
Are dreams and glories so alike, that fictions
Are held for truths, realities for lies?   510
Is there so little difference in them both
That one should question whether what one sees
And tastes is true or false? What? Is the copy
So near to the original that doubt
Exists between them? Then if that is so,   515
And grandeur, power, majesty, and pomp,
Must all evaporate like shades at morning,
Let's profit by it, this time, to enjoy
That which we only can enjoy in dreams.
Rosaura's in my power: my soul adores her beauty. 520
Let's take the chance. Let love break every law
On which she has relied in coming here
And kneeling, trustful, prostrate at my feet.
This is a dream. If so, dream pleasures now
Since they must turn to sorrows in the end!   525
But with my own opinions, I begin
Once again to convince myself. Let's think.
If it is but vainglory and a dream,
Who for mere human vainglory would lose
True glory? What past blessing is not merely   530
A dream? Who has known heroic glories,
That deep within himself, as he recalls them,
Has never doubted that they might be dreams?
But if this all should end in disenchantment,
Seeing that pleasure is a lovely flame   535
That's soon converted into dust and ashes
By any wind that blows, then let us seek
That which endures in thrifty, lasting fame
In which no pleasures sleep, nor grandeurs dream.
Rosaura's without honour. In a prince   540
It's worthier to restore it than to steal it.
I shall restore it, by the living God,
Before I win my throne! Let's shun the danger
And fly from the temptation which is strong!
Then sound to arms!   545

(*To a soldier.*)

Today I must give battle before darkness
Buries the rays of gold in green-black waves!
ROSAURA: My lord! Alas, you stand apart, and offer
No word of pity for my plight. How is it

550   You neither hear nor see me nor even yet
      Have turned your face on me?
SEGISMUND: Rosaura, for your
         honour's sake
      I must be cruel to you, to be kind.
      My voice must not reply to you because
      My honour must reply to you. I am silent
555   Because my deeds must speak to you alone.
      I do not look at you since, in such straits,
      Having to see your honour is requited,
      I must not see your beauty.
                              (*Exit with soldiers.*)

ROSAURA: What strange enigma's this? After such
         trouble
560   Still to be treated with more doubtful riddles!

(*Enter Clarion.*)

CLARION: Madam, may you be visited just now?
ROSAURA: Why, Clarion, where have you been all this
         time?
CLARION: Shut in the tower, consulting cards
      About my death: "to be or not to be."
      And it was a near thing.
ROSAURA: Why?
565   CLARION: Because I know
      The secret who you are: in fact, Clotaldo . . .

(*Drums.*)

      But hush what noise is that?
ROSAURA: What can it be?
CLARION: From the beleaguered palace a whole
         squadron
      Is charging forth to harry and defeat
      That of fierce Segismund.
570   ROSAURA: Why, what a coward
      Am I, not to be at his side, the terror
      And scandal of the world, while such fierce strife
      Presses all round in lawless anarchy.
                                        (*Exit.*)

VOICES OF SOME: Long live our king!
VOICES OF OTHERS: Long live our liberty!
575   CLARION: Long live both king and liberty. Yes, live!
      And welcome to them both! I do not worry.
      In all this pother, I behave like Nero
      Who never grieved at what was going on.
      If I had anything to grieve about
580   It would be me, myself. Well hidden here,
      Now, I can watch the sport that's going on.
      This place is safe and hidden between crags,
      And since death cannot find me here, two figs for
         death!

(*He hides. Drums and the clash of arms are heard.*)

(*Enter Basil, Clotaldo, and Astolfo, fleeing.*)

BASIL: Was ever king so hapless as myself
      Or father more ill used?
585   CLOTALDO: Your beaten army
      Rush down, in all directions, in disorder.
ASTOLFO: The traitors win!

BASIL: In battles such as these
      Those on the winning side are ever "loyal,"
      And traitors the defeated. Come, Clotaldo,
      Let's flee from the inhuman cruelty   590
      Of my fierce son!

(*Shots are fired within. Clarion falls wounded.*)

CLARION: Heavens, save me!
ASTOLFO: Who is this
      Unhappy soldier bleeding at our feet?
CLARION: I am a most unlucky man who, wishing
      To guard myself from death, have sought it out
      By fleeing from it. Shunning it, I found it,   595
      Because, to death, no hiding-place is secret.
      So you can argue that whoever shuns it
      Most carefully runs into it the quickest.
      Turn, then, once more into the thick of battle:
      There is more safety there amidst the fire   600
      And clash of arms than here on this secluded
      Mountain, because no hidden path is safe
      From the inclemency of Fate; and so,
      Although you flee from death, yet you may find it
      Quicker than you expect, if God so wills.   605

(*He falls dead.*)

BASIL: "If God so wills". . . With what strange
         eloquence
      This corpse persuades our ignorance and error
      To better knowledge, speaking from the mouth
      Of its fell wound, where the red liquid flowing
      Seems like a bloody tongue which teaches us   610
      That the activities of man are vain
      When they are pitted against higher powers.
      For I, who wished to liberate my country
      From murder and sedition, gave it up
      To the same ills from which I would have saved it. 615
CLOTALDO: Though Fate, my lord, knows every path,
         and finds
      Him whom it seeks even in the midst of crags
      And thickets, it is not a Christian judgment
      To say there is no refuge from its fury.
      A prudent man can conquer Fate itself.   620
      Though you are not exempted from misfortune,
      Take action to escape it while you can!
ASTOLFO: Clotaldo speaks as one mature in
         prudence,
      And I as one in valour's youthful prime.
      Among the thickets of this mount is hidden   625
      A horse, the very birth of the swift wind.
      Flee on him, and I'll guard you in the rear.
BASIL: If it is God's will I should die, or if
      Death waits here for my coming, I will seek
      Him out today, and meet him face to face.   630

(*Enter Segismund, Stella, Rosaura, soldiers, and their
train.*)

A SOLDIER: Amongst the thickets of this mountain
      The king is hiding.
SEGISMUND: Seek him out at once!

Leave no foot of the summit unexplored
But search from stem to stem and branch to branch!
CLOTALDO: Fly, sir!
BASIL: What for?
ASTOLFO: What do you mean to do?
BASIL: Astolfo, stand aside!
CLOTALDO: What is your wish?
BASIL: To take a cure I've needed for sometime.

(To Segismund.)

    If you have come to seek me, here I am.

(Kneeling.)

    Your father, prince, kneels humbly at your feet.
640   The white snow of my hair is now your carpet.
Tread on my neck and trample on my crown!
Lay low and drag my dignity in dust!
Take vengeance on my honour! Make a slave
Of me and, after all I've done to thwart them,
645   Let Fate fulfil its edict and claim homage
And Heaven fulfil its oracles at last!
SEGISMUND: Illustrious court of Poland, who have been
The witnesses of such unwonted wonders,
Attend to me, and hear your prince speak out.
What Heaven decrees and God writes with his
650   finger
(Whose prints and ciphers are the azure leaves
Adorned with golden lettering of the stars)
Never deceives nor lies. They only lie
Who seek to penetrate the mystery
655   And, having reached it, use it to ill purpose.
My father, who is here to evade the fury
Of my proud nature, made me a wild beast:
So, when I, by my birth of gallant stock,
My generous blood, and inbred grace and valour,
660   Might well have proved both gentle and forbearing,
The very mode of life to which he forced me,
The sort of bringing up I had to bear
Sufficed to make me savage in my passions.
What a strange method of restraining them!
665   If one were to tell any man: "One day
You will be killed by an inhuman monster,"
Would it be the best method he could choose
To wake that monster when it was asleep?
Or if they told him: "That sword which you're
     wearing
670   Will be your death," what sort of cure were it
To draw it forth and aim it at his breast?
Or if they told him: "Deep blue gulfs of water
Will one day be your sepulchre and grave
Beneath a silver monument of foam,"
675   He would be mad to hurl himself in headlong
When the sea highest heaved its showy mountains
And crystalline sierras plumed with spray.
The same has happened to the king as to him
Who wakes a beast which threatens death, to him
680   Who draws a naked sword because he fears it,
To him who dives into the stormy breakers.

Though my ferocious nature (hear me now)
Was like a sleeping beast, my inborn rage
A sheathèd sword, my wrath a quiet ripple,
Fate should not be coerced by man's injustice —   685
This rouses more resentment. So it is
That he who seeks to tame his fortune must
Resort to moderation and to measure.
He who foresees an evil cannot conquer it.
Thus in advance, for though humility   690
Can overcome it, this it can do only
When the occasion's there, for there's no way
To dodge one's fate and thus evade the issue.
Let this strange spectacle serve as example —
This prodigy, this horror, and this wonder,   695
Because it is no less than one, to see,
After such measures and precautions taken
To thwart it, that a father thus should kneel
At his son's feet, a kingdom thus be shattered.
This was the sentence of the heavens above,   700
Which he could not evade, much though he tried.
Can I, younger in age, less brave, and less
In science than the king, conquer that fate?

(To the King.)

    Sire, rise, give me your hand, now that the
     heavens
Have shown you that you erred as to the method   705
To vanquish them. Humbly I kneel before you
And offer you my neck to tread upon.
BASIL: Son, such a great and noble act restores you
Straight to my heart. Oh, true and worthy prince!
You have won both the laurel and the palm.   710
Crown yourself with your deeds! For you *have*
     conquered!
ALL: Long live Segismund! Long live Segismund!
SEGISMUND: Since I have other victories to win,
The greatest of them all awaits me now:
To conquer my own self. Astolfo, give   715
Your hand here to Rosaura, for you know
It is a debt of honour and must be paid.
ASTOLFO: Although, it's true, I owe some
     obligations —
She does not know her name or who she is,
It would be base to wed a woman who . . .   720
CLOTALDO: Hold! Wait! Rosaura's of as noble stock
As yours, Astolfo. In the open field
I'll prove it with my sword. She is my daughter
And that should be enough.
ASTOLFO: What do you say?
CLOTALDO: Until I saw her married, righted,
     honoured,   725
I did not wish for it to be discovered.
It's a long story but she is my daughter.
ASTOLFO: That being so, I'm glad to keep my word.
SEGISMUND: And now, so that the princess Stella
     here
Will not remain disconsolate to lose   730
A prince of so much valour, here I offer

My hand to her, no less in birth and rank.
Give me your hand.
STELLA: I gain by meriting
So great a happiness.
SEGISMUND: And now, Clotaldo,
735   So long so loyal to my father, come
To my arms. Ask me anything you wish.
FIRST SOLDIER: If thus you treat a man who never
        served you,
What about me who led the revolution
And brought you from your dungeon in the tower?
What will you give me?
740   SEGISMUND: That same tower and dungeon
From which you never shall emerge till death.
No traitor is of use after his treason.

BASIL: All wonder at your wisdom!
ASTOLFO: What a change
Of character!
ROSAURA: How wise and prudent!
SEGISMUND: Why
Do you wonder? Why do you marvel, since   745
It was a dream that taught me and I still
Fear to wake up once more in my close dungeon?
Though that may never happen, it's enough
To dream it might, for thus I came to learn
That all our human happiness must pass   750
Away like any dream, and I would here
Enjoy it fully ere it glide away,
Asking (for noble hearts are prone to pardon)
Pardon for faults in the actors or the play.

COMMENTARIES

Michael Billington (b. 1939)
REVIEW OF THE 1998 EDINBURGH FESTIVAL
PRODUCTION OF *LIFE IS A DREAM*   1998

Billington's review of the play emphasizes the energy and excitement created on stage. But it also emphasizes the optimism inherent in the play, the thought that even one as isolated and brutalized as Segismundo (Segismund) could discover in himself the qualities needed to change his life.

The marriage of foreign and native talent doesn't always work. But the Edinburgh Festival, along with the Barbican Centre, has had the bright idea of inviting a Catalan director-designer team, Calixto Bieito and Carles Pujol, to stage Calderón's 1635 masterpiece, *Life Is a Dream,* in John Clifford's new translation with a British multiracial cast. The result is sensational.

For a start Calderón's play ushers us into a strange, labyrinthine world, one that deals both with the illusory nature of existence and the possibility of change. The story itself concerns a Polish prince, Segismundo, who has been kept imprisoned since birth in a dark tower. The reason? His father Basilio's fear of a prediction that his son would usurp his throne. And, when the savage Segismundo is briefly released, he fulfils Basilio's worst fears by committing rape and murder. But although he is quickly bunged back in the tower, Segismundo is once more set free by an uprising. This time, however, he behaves not like a bestial tyrant but with enlightened wisdom: defeating his father in battle, he forgives him and forges reconciliation.

Like all great plays, Calderón's work looks both backwards and forwards. *Oedipus Rex* comes to mind in the prophecy that ironically rebounds on those who seek to avoid it: the reduction of Segismundo, through social isolation, to animalistic savagery, also suggests Sophocles's *Philoctetes*. But the hero's belief, after his brief restoration to power, that "life's an illusion, a shadow, a fiction" prefigures Pirandello. And even his conclusion that our existence is no more than "empty air" has a touch of Borges and Beckett.

Yet what is extraordinary about the play is its optimism. Segismundo, not surprisingly, harps on the idea that life is a waking dream, that power, wealth, and pleasure are all illusory. Yet Calderón, far from drawing the conclusion that Camus later came to in *The Myth of Sisyphus* that all man's actions are therefore "senseless, absurd, useless," argues the exact opposite. He emerges as an apostle of change and a champion of free will. We may all be shadows, but, Calderón suggests, evil can still be defeated. As a message, it is a refreshing antidote to the arid determinism of the absurd.

The play emerges as a mix of magic realism and phantasmagoric ritual; and that shifting quality is perfectly caught by Bieito and his codesigner, Pujol. The stage itself is a circular cinder-track. Above it hovers a giant mirror which at first accurately reflects the characters. It is then tilted crazily to suggest the disordered world of Segismundo's prince-for-a-day tyranny. Finally, it is angled so the audience sees itself, a reminder that we are watching a theatrical spectacle and that we are as much role-players as anyone on the stage.

The Catalan team, including costume-designer Merce Paloma, also brings out the play's political implications. Dress is modern, so that Segismundo's paternalistic jailer sports a military uniform and his father a vivid, multicolored robe. On one level, the play becomes a parable about fascism and a world in which brutal solitary confinement is followed by equally arbitrary release.

The modernity of the message is also visible in the acting. George Anton plays the imprisoned prince with a ruthless lack of sentimentality. He is an angular, desperate, animalistic figure who, on release from prison, instantly hurls an old retainer out of the window, dives under the skirts of the king's niece for some inappropriate sex, and curls up on the throne to play cards with Sylvester McCoy's anarchic clown.

The production is least successful in handling the complex subplot: one in which the heroine, Rosaura, returns from Moscow in male attire to recover her lover and, in the process, rediscovers her long-lost father. This is no fault of the Irish actress, Olwen Fouere, who has a genuinely androgynous quality that enables her to shift shape ending "as a kind of monster carrying man's weapons but wearing women's clothes." The blame lies largely with Calderón, who gives Rosaura an outrageously long speech that cries out to be cut.

But this is still a notable occasion in which John Clifford's translation reclaims a Spanish masterpiece for the modern stage. There was once a bad Oxford production of the play that was rudely dubbed *Life's a Scream*. On this occasion, Calderón's vision of the illusion of existence is caught with painterly precision.

Ed Morales

REVIEW OF JOSÉ RIVERA'S PRODUCTION OF *SUEÑO*   1998

In this extensive discussion of José Rivera's adaptation of Life Is a Dream, *Morales examines the reasoning behind Rivera's reworking of Calderón's language and Rivera's emphasis on the philosophical issues that lie beneath the surface of the play. Morales also gives us some insight into the challenges faced by a modern producer of a seventeenth-century drama, especially in light of the ways in which both the theater and its audiences have changed.*

Sueño, José Rivera's adaptation of Calderón de la Barca's classic *La Vida es Sueño (Life Is a Dream),* starts out impressively enough. When John Ortiz's hirsute, muscular, and scantily clad body appears onstage suspended in midair by long red ropes, Hartford Stage Company audiences can't help but hold their collective breath and expect a wild theatrical ride. Ortiz plays Segismundo, the son of a Spanish monarch held in a dungeon because of his original sin — killing his mother in childbirth — but about to be freed from his misery to have a go at his birthright as a ruler. The sharp contrast between his captivity and deliverance causes Segismundo to blur the line between reality and dreams, and allows Calderón to explore the big philosophical questions (What is existence? *Is* life a dream, and if so, who is dreaming *us*? God?) that have made *La Vida es Sueño* so enduring. However, it's hard not to wonder what kind of resonance these issues can have for a twentieth-century audience, when a good chunk of reality is virtual or simulated.

At first glance, *Sueño*'s theatrical strategy seems to be a variation on what might be called the New York Shakespeare Festival style of reinventing the classics. The characters engage in a contemporary sassiness; they draw out some of the contemporaneous subtext from seventeenth-century situations; and traditionally cross-dressed roles are augmented by nontraditionally cross-dressed ones. But on closer inspection, Rivera's *Sueño* proves to be a true adaptation, not a recontextualization; there are no TV sets or gang paraphernalia in this production. The costumes are faithful to their origins in Spain. Indeed, it's not the surface aspects of the production that offer a contemporary spin on Calderón's metaphysical musings: it is the *language* that has been changed, shifting from the baroque Spanish verse of the 1600s to the contemporary rhythms of America at the end of the twentieth century.

From Segismundo's opening soliloquies, where he proclaims himself "a storm of chemical responses pretending to have a soul," Rivera has reclaimed Calderón's florid use of metaphor and made it his own, spiced with science, sarcasm, and sweetness. "I wanted to find the language Calderón would have used if he was a forty-two-year-old playwright living in California," the theater and television writer says on the phone from his home in Los Angeles. That blending of the contemporary and the antiquated can have some surprising results. For instance, when Segismundo says he is "God's wild virus," you can feel all the implications of imagined or real modern-day plagues while simultaneously acknowledging their roots in an empire engaged in conquering a New World.

Rivera was not only faced with the task of reinventing Calderón's language, but also the challenge of making the play, which is long on plot and short on characterization, "actable." By doing case studies of people who had experienced long-term isolation, Rivera was able to create a realistic psychological profile for Segismundo and enliven his character with appropriate behavior, particularly in the early scenes between him and Rosaura (Michi Barall), a young noblewoman bent on revenge. Long monologues were replaced with short, snappy, almost sit-com-esque interactions, a possible by-product of the time Rivera has done in Hollywood. (The writer professes to have given up television work, particularly since the demise of *Eerie, Indiana,* a series he created that some claim was too smart to remain on the air.)

In this way, the wordplay between Lord Astolfo (Damian Young) and Princess Estrella (Alene Dawson) — two scheming nobles who have their eyes on the throne — is one of the highlights of the production. "Flowers are dishrags compared to you," carps Astolfo in his parodic wooing of a noblewoman in line to succeed the reigning monarch. "Helen? A slutbox. . . . Aphrodite? Maggot poop." Young and Jan Leslie Harding, in her drag interpretation of Rosaura's clownish manservant Clarin (the character is traditionally played by a male), provide comic relief from the dark antics Segismundo engages in when he's given a chance to prove he might be worthy of nobility.

By showcasing these underlying comedic moments, *Sueño* moves away from the tragically cerebral aura that traditionally surrounds Calderón's work. Nevertheless, the play's dramatic impact is reinvigorated by Rivera's commitment to updating its contextual underpinnings. In the post-Freud era, there are echoes of the Oedipus complex in Segismundo's attacks on his father Basilio's kingship. Perhaps more important, their relationship strongly resembles the one between Prospero and Caliban in *The Tempest.* Segismundo is portrayed as a vulgar, uneducated beast, an id looking to inflict severe psychological, as well as physical, pain. Basilio, on the other hand, seems to be uncertain about his moral imperative: he is vaguely aware of his own complicity in the brutal conquest of the New World. Even as he obsesses over a lunar eclipse (the evil omen that marks the birth of his son), another spherical object, the Aztec calendar, lurks center stage for much of the play.

For Rivera, this zigzagging between the old and the new in some ways mirrors the ambivalence of the Hispanic phenomenon, and may explain Latino interest in the Hartford Stage production. (The fact that the theatre coordinated a major community relations drive didn't hurt either.) According to Rivera, while Hispanics may not feel directly connected to Spain, they still relate to intrinsic elements of the culture. "There's this code of honor that we all seem to be struggling with," muses Rivera. "Being Latino in the U.S. is like being caught in the middle between tradition and nontradition. But we have come to feel comfortable with contradiction."

While Rivera's rewrite may make Calderón's work more accessible and contemporary, *Sueño* has even more profound implications. Instead of saying, "If the Fates decree that now's your time to die / There's nothing you can do," Clarin declares, "If God wants your ass, he's going to get your ass." While the change works as humor, these lines are also helping Rivera establish the idea that the presence of mortal life is no longer just an extension of the proof of the existence of God. "In the original, Segismundo gets attached to the idea that if everything is a dream, the dreamer must be God," says Rivera. "What my version is trying to say is that the idea of God is unreliable."

In transferring Calderón's psyche into his own, Rivera is making a statement about American reality and the way it represents the difference between Old World and New World thinking. The romantic pairings that climax the original — Astolfo-Rosaura and Segismundo-Estrella — are reversed. Rosaura turns her back on nobility and urges Segismundo to join her in a quest for free will and the overturning of the rigid class structures of Europe. It's a moment that brings out an idea buried in Calderón's text, that a New World is about to begin. In José Rivera's own sly and spiritual way, *Sueño* carries the enormous implication that we're on the verge of that kind of history happening all over again.

Matt Wolf
THE *HAMLET* OF SPAIN, IN A FEVERED STAGING   1999

Matt Wolf reviews the 1999 London production of Life Is a Dream, *connecting the play to Calderón's near-contemporary, William Shakespeare. In certain ways Wolf sees Segismundo as a version of Hamlet. Like Hamlet, Segismundo quests for the truth and is never sure he has found it. And like Hamlet, Segismundo has been denied a portion of his birthright.*

Imagine a play that suggests Shakespeare — particularly *Hamlet* or *The Tempest* — filtered through a Pirandellian prism, with an enormous gilt-edged mirror suspended forbiddingly above the action and a gravel-strewn set providing its own aural soundscape.

That is one way of describing the production of *Life Is a Dream* that the Royal Lyceum Theater Company of Scotland will present on Tuesday at the Brooklyn Academy of Music. The Spanish director Calixto Bieito's fevered staging of the defining seventeenth-century play by Pedro Calderón de la Barca will have six performances at the Harvey Theater as part of the 1999 Next Wave Festival.

In Spain, Calderón's play enjoys something of the status of *Hamlet,* with which it shares an interest in man at his most self-avowedly anguished. Indeed, professing in John Clifford's contemporary translation that "humankind's greatest crime is to be born," Calderón's antiheroic prince, Segismundo (played by George Anton), recalls the racked metaphysician that is Shakespeare's Danish prince.

Segismundo has been sequestered from birth in a tower because of fears by his father, the king, Basilio (Jeffery Kissoon), that his son will rise up against him. The prince is then briefly released upon adulthood, only to be imprisoned once more, a caged animal capable, we discover later, of very real mercy.

And though he finds a vengeful ally of sorts in Rosaura (Olwen Fouere), the spurned lover whose separate fate provides the main subplot, Segismundo ends the play a free and potentially noble man — if, that is, freedom and nobility mean anything in the elision between wakefulness and sleep that is the true terrain of *Life Is a Dream.*

"What I love about it is it's a very questioning play," said Mr. Clifford, the translator, from his home in Edinburgh. "It's asking fundamental questions, starting with, 'What are we doing here?'" (His translation, he said, draws less from the accepted 1635 text than from an earlier published version dating to 1630.)

Mr. Bieito's production was first seen at the 1998 Edinburgh International Festival, where several critics found it a high point of the theater program ("The two hours pass like, well, a dream," wrote Charles Spencer in the *Daily Telegraph*). After a hiatus, the production toured last month to London as part of the Barbican International Theater Event (BITE '99) season.

His aim, Mr. Bieito said after the London opening, was to invigorate anew a play barely known in Britain or the United States, notwithstanding its affinities to the Elizabethans as well as to countless modernist writers, including Pirandello and Ionesco.

"For me, it was easier to work in Britain," said Mr. Bieito, thirty-five, of a rare directing assignment away from Barcelona, where he has lived since he was fifteen. Among his credits back home: a Catalan-language version in 1997 of the Broadway musical *Company*, whose songs include the very appropriately titled "Barcelona."

"In Spain," said the director, who doubles as his own designer (with Carles Pujol), "you have all the pressure all the time of tradition, of people thinking what *Life Is a Dream* must be." But in Scotland, he said, "I was freed to do the play and to renew it. Classical theater must not be classical, it must be fresh."

The result is a multicultural staging defiantly un-British in its impetuousness and vigor, especially coming from a writer who, Mr. Clifford said, "has an unfortunate reputation as a rigid Catholic theologian."

And Graham Sheffield, the Barbican's artistic director, said, "Calixto seems to have made the play modern without sacrificing its traditional roots; its physicality is frightening."

The play's animalistic passions more often than not fall to Mr. Anton, thirty-four, a Scot who spends much of the evening raising his voice and shedding his clothes as he charts Segismundo's journey from a Caliban figure to a Prospero of sorts.

The actor compared Mr. Bieito to a boxing coach. "When you were in the ring, as it were, he was hot," Mr. Anton said of his director. "He'd be at your side going, 'Quieter, quieter,' and then, 'Punch, punch, punch.'"

That may be because, said Mr. Kissoon, the performer, the director "wants to wake us up."

Late Seventeenth- and Eighteenth-Century Drama

The Restoration: Rebirth of Drama

Theater in England continued to thrive after Shakespeare's death, with a host of successful playwrights, including John Webster (1580?–1638?), Francis Beaumont (c. 1584–1616) and his collaborator John Fletcher (1579–1625), Philip Massinger (1583–1640), Thomas Middleton (1580–1627), John Ford (1586–c. 1655), and James Shirley (1596–1666). All these playwrights were busy working independently or in collaboration. Fletcher, chosen successor to Shakespeare at the Globe, furnished the theater with as many as four plays a year. But in 1642 long-standing religious and political conflicts between King Charles I and Parliament finally erupted into civil war, with the Parliament, under the influence of Puritanism, eventually winning.

The Puritans were religious extremists with narrow, specific values. They were essentially an emerging merchant class of well-to-do citizens who viewed the aristocracy as wastrels. Theater for them was associated with both the aristocracy and the low life. Theatergoing was synonymous with wasting time, the theaters were often a focus for immoral activity, and the neighborhoods around the theaters were as unsavory as any in England. Under the Puritan government, all theaters in England were closed for almost twenty years. When the new king, Charles II, was crowned in 1660, those that had not been converted to other uses had become completely outmoded.

As a young prince, Charles, with his mother and brother, had been sent to the Continent in the early stages of the civil war. When his father, Charles I, was beheaded, the future king and his family were in France, where they were in a position to see the remarkable achievements of French comedy and French classical tragedy. Charles II developed a taste for theater that accompanied him back to England. And when he returned in triumph to usher in the exciting and swashbuckling period known as the Restoration, he permitted favorites to build new theaters.

Theater on the Continent: Neoclassicism

Interaction among the leading European countries — England, Spain, and France — was sporadic at best in the seventeenth century because of intermittent wars among the nations, yet the development of theater in all three countries took similar turns throughout the early 1600s.

By the 1630s, the French were aware of Spanish achievements in the theater; Pierre Corneille (1606–1684), who emerged as France's leading playwright of the time, adapted a Spanish story by de Castro that became one of his most important plays, *Le Cid*.

By the time Charles II took up residence in France in the 1640s, the French had developed a suave, polished, and intellectually demanding approach to drama. Corneille and the neoclassicists were part of a large movement in European culture and the arts that tried to codify and emulate the achievement of the ancients. Qualities such as harmony, symmetry, balance in everything structural, and clear moral themes were most in evidence. Because NEOCLASSICISM valued thought over feeling, the thematic material in neoclassical drama was very important. That material was sometimes political, reflecting the values of Augustan Rome — 27 B.C. to A.D. 17 — when Caesar Augustus lived and when it was appropriate to think in terms of subordinating the self to the interests of the state. Neoclassical dramatists focused on honor, moral integrity, self-sacrifice, and heroic political subjects.

One school of critics held playwrights strictly to the Aristotelian concepts of the unities of time, place, character, and action. These "rules critics" demanded a perfect observance of the unities — that is, they wanted a play to have one plot, a single action that takes place in one day, and a single setting. In most cases the plays that satisfied them are now often thought of as static, cold, limited, and dull. Their perfection is seen today as rigid and emotionally icy.

Corneille's work did not please such critics, and they turned to a much younger competitor, Jean Racine (1639–1699), who brought the tradition of French tragedy to its fullest. Most of his plays are on classical subjects, beginning in 1667 with *Andromache,* continuing with *Britannicus* (1669), *Iphigenia* (1674), and *Mithridate* (1673), and ending in 1677 with his most famous and possibly best play, *Phaedra*.

Phaedra is a deeply passionate, moral play centering on the love of Phaedra for her stepson, Hippolytus. Venus is responsible for her incestuous love — which is the playwright's way of saying that Phaedra is impelled by the gods or by destiny, almost against her will.

The French stage, unlike the English, never substituted boys for female roles, and so plays such as *Phaedra* were opportunities for brilliant actresses. Phaedra, in particular, dominates the stage — she is a commanding and infinitely complex figure. It is no wonder that this play was a favorite of Sarah Bernhardt (1844–1923), one of France's greatest actresses.

French Comedy: Molière

At the same time that Racine commanded the tragic stage, Jean Baptiste Poquelin (1622–1673), known as Molière, began his dominance of the comic stage. He was aware of Racine's achievements and applauded them strongly. His career started with a small theater company that spent most of its time touring the countryside beyond Paris. When the company settled in Paris, its plays were influenced by some of the stock characters and situations of the commedia dell'arte, but they also began to reflect Molière's own genius for composition.

Seeing the company in 1658, King Louis XIV found it so much to his liking that he installed it in a theater and demanded to see more of its work. From that time on, Molière wrote, produced, and acted in one comedy after another, most of which have become part of the permanent repertoire of the French stage. Plays such as *The Misanthrope* (1666), *The Miser* (1669), *The Bourgeois Gentleman* (1670), *The Imaginary Invalid* (1673), and his satire on the theme of religious hypocrisy, *Tartuffe* (1669), are also staged all over the world.

Theater in England: Restoration Comedy

When the theaters reopened in England in the 1660s, they needed new plays. Times and tastes had changed, England had suffered enormous upheaval, and the Puritan-dominated, theater-darkened past was quickly undone. The new age wanted glitter, excitement, sensuality, and dramatic dazzle. Audiences wanted upbeat comedies that poked fun at the stuffed shirts of society and at old-fashioned institutions and fashions.

Several important physical changes took effect immediately. The new stages were in indoor theaters using artificial light. They could be operated year-round, and the price for seats varied according to location. The middle-priced seats were in the pit before the proscenium-arched stage (Figure 10). The first-level boxes against the walls were most expensive, while the lowest-priced seats were in the upper ranges of the balconies.

The new indoor theaters were generally adapted from spaces designed for courtly events. They were rectangular, often twice as long as they were wide, and usually lighted by candles in chandeliers. The proscenium frame around the stage appeared in the new theaters. Eventually, movable scenery and changeable painted backdrops helped the playwrights create their illusions, although some plays of the period could easily be performed on a bare stage.

Once English women were permitted to take part in theater, actresses appeared who commanded the stage immediately. The actresses of the period were bright, witty, and charming and were often the most important draw for seventeenth-century audiences. Nell Gwynne (1650–1687), one of the most famous actresses of her day and mistress to Charles II, became a legend of the English stage.

Among England's notable playwrights from 1660 through the eighteenth century were Aphra Behn (1640–1689), the first professional woman playwright on the English stage and author of *The Rover*, one of the most frequently performed plays of the period; William Wycherley (1640–1716), whose *The Plain Dealer*, indebted to Molière, and *The Country Wife* are regarded as his best work; William Congreve (1670–1729), whose *The Way of the World* is justly famous; and Richard Brinsley Sheridan (1751–1816), whose *School for Scandal* is still bright, lively, and engaging for modern audiences. Other important playwrights whose work is still performed are George Farquhar (1678–1707), especially known for *The Beaux Stratagem* (1707), John Gay (1685–1732), whose *Beggar's Opera* has been revived constantly since its first performance in 1728, and Oliver Goldsmith (1730–1774), author of *She Stoops to Conquer* (1773).

John Dryden (1631–1700), perhaps the most highly regarded English playwright from 1664 to 1677, collaborated in adaptations of Shakespeare's plays, but he became popular for his heroic dramas in rhymed verse: *The Indian Queen* (1664), its sequel *The Indian Emperor* (1665), *Tyrannick Love* (1669), and the two-part, ten-act *The Conquest of Granada* (1670). Montezuma is at the center of the first two plays; *Tyrannick Love* concerns the martyrdom

Figure 10. Conjectural reconstruction of an early Restoration theater. By Peter Kahn, Cornell University.

of St. Catherine by the Roman emperor, Maximin. *The Conquest of Granada* focuses on internal conflicts among the Moors fighting for survival in Spain. Almanzor, the main character, is considered one of Dryden's most accomplished creations. *Aureng-Zebe* (1675), his last effort in heroic rhymed drama, focuses on Aureng-Zebe, emperor of India and among the most rational and moral of his characters. Its plot and love complications are extremely dense and its mood somewhat melancholy. Today the heroic plays of the 1660s resemble high-style melodramas, but they were enormously popular in their time.

Dryden was also successful writing comedies such as *The Wild Gallant* (1663) and *The Rival Ladies* (1664). His tragicomedies were popular in his time and represent some of his most imaginative dramatic efforts. *Marriage à-la-Mode* (1672) is still highly regarded, especially for Dryden's songs. Among his experiments in opera is a version of Milton's *Paradise Lost* that he called *The State of Innocence and the Fall of Man* (1677) in which he rhymed some of Milton's blank verse. This work was never performed, although it remains a curiosity of the age. Dryden is also to be noted for his critical writing on drama, such as his famous *Of Dramatick Poesie* (1668) and *Of Heroick Plays* (1672), which laid down the theory behind his dramas and opened the questions of dramatic practice for examination.

Marriages of convenience are often the target of Restoration playwrights. The aristocratic attitude toward marriage usually centered on the union of "suitable" mates whose families were of the same social level and who were financially attractive to one another. Consequently, sometimes impoverished gentlemen of good name would seek out wealthy women and vice versa. The grounds for marriage were sometimes based on love but more often on financial or social convenience. As a result, conflicts in choosing marriage partners often involved elaborate dealings between parents and children, as in Oliver Goldsmith's comic play, *She Stoops to Conquer*. It is not until the end of the eighteenth century that the sentimental comedy appears, introducing recognizable emotional responses that appear to moderns as normal. Aristocratic attitudes toward marriage are evident in drama as late as the end of the nineteenth century, as in Oscar Wilde's *The Importance of Being Earnest*.

The English playwrights produced a wide range of comedy, drawing on their understanding of the audience's desire for bright, gay, and witty entertainment. The comedies of the period came to be known in the twentieth century as COMEDIES OF MANNERS because they reveal the foibles of the society that watched them. Society enjoyed laughing at itself. Although some of the English drama of the eighteenth century developed a moralistic tone and was often heavily classical, the earlier RESTORATION COMEDIES were less interested in reforming the society than in capitalizing on its faults.

Eighteenth-Century Drama

Eighteenth-century Europe absorbed much of the spirit of France and the French neoclassicists. England, like other European countries, began to see the effects of neoclassicism in the arts and literature. Emulation of classical art and classical values was common throughout Europe, and critics established standards of excellence in the arts to guarantee quality.

The most famous name in eighteenth-century English drama is David Garrick (1717–1779), the legendary actor and manager of the Drury Lane Theatre. The theaters, including his own, often reworked French drama and earlier English and Italian drama, but they began to develop a new SENTIMENTAL COMEDY to balance the neoclassical heroic tragedies of the period. It was a comedy in which the emotions of the audience were played on, manipulated, and exploited to arouse sympathy for the characters in the play.

Sentimental comedy flourished after 1720, but Colley Cibber (1671–1757) is sometimes credited with beginning the sentimental comedy with his *Love's Last Shift* (1696). The play centers on Loveless, who wanders from his marriage only to find that his wife has disguised herself as a prostitute to win him back. As in all sentimental comedies, what the audience most wants is what it gets: a certain amount of tears, a contrasting amount of laughter, and a happy ending. Cibber was especially well known as an actor for his portrayal of fops, his way of poking satiric fun at his own society and its pretensions.

Sir Richard Steele (1672–1729) wrote one of the best-known sentimental comedies, *The Conscious Lovers* (1722). Steele's coauthor of *The Spectator,* Joseph Addison (1672–1719), also distinguished himself with his contribution to the heroic tragedy of the age, the long neoclassical *Cato* (1713). It was considered to be the finest example of the moral heroic style. Today it is not a playable drama because the action is too slow, the speeches too long, and the theme too obscure, although it is a perfect model of what the age preferred in heroic tragedy. George Lillo (1693–1739) in *The London Merchant* (1731) produced a bourgeois tragedy in which the main character was from the middle class. It was one of the most frequently produced plays of its time.

The audiences at the time enjoyed bright, amusing comedies that often criticized wayward youth, overprotective parents, dishonest financial dealings, and social expectations. Their taste in tragedies veered toward a moralizing heroism that extolled the ideals of dedication to the values of the community and self-sacrifice on the part of the hero.

Drama in Japan

During the period of the Tokugawa shogunate (1603–1868), Japan attempted to seal itself off from the Western world. Although the Portuguese had a trading facility in Nagasaki, their influence was limited in range and scope. The great playwrights and actors of the Tokugawa period in Edo (Tokyo), Kyoto, and Osaka were generally unaware of traditions of Western drama, and in some cases they had never read or seen a foreign play.

Although Japan was essentially a military dictatorship at the time, the period was peaceful and prosperous, with a rising merchant middle class that demanded entertainment representing their own values and interests. The shogun, or leader, was a warrior, and the warrior class — the samurai — had much to say about the forms of entertainment available. They were interested in theater in part because with peacetime came leisure time and the opportunity for indulgence. The gay district or "floating world" of Kyoto permitted prostitution and various theatrical and circus-like entertainments for men. It was in this atmosphere that traditions of kabuki theater and puppet theater flourished.

Kabuki began from a dance performed in 1603 by a woman entertainer named Okuni, whose popularity was such that she developed numerous imitators, especially prostitutes who danced kabuki in order to attract customers. The dance was enlarged with sketches from contemporary life accompanied by a popular three-stringed instrument called a *shamisen*. The role of the *shamisen* musician in kabuki plays was to establish the rhythms of speech and help stimulate the emotions of the audience. Kabuki quickly drew important actors who used elaborate makeup and brilliant costumes to perform multiact plays over an entire day.

After women were banned from the stage in 1629, men performed all the parts in kabuki plays. Audiences found kabuki exciting because it was designed to stimulate the masses. This popular entertainment form narrated stories of contemporary life and sometimes permitted people to grumble about inequities they perceived in their own society. Kabuki also produced a generation of highly gifted actors, many from the samurai class, who became a draw in their own right.

Partly because the actors became difficult and demanding, some of the important playwrights of the time, including Chikamatsu Monzaemon (1653–1725), turned to the *jōruri* or puppet plays. Unlike actors, puppets made no demands on authors and never stole the show. They were also versatile enough to create remarkably subtle expressions of emotion, thought, and action. Some plays were produced in both kabuki and *jōruri* forms, but because incredible special effects were possible with puppets — effects that could not be achieved with actors — *jōruri* theater flourished in the early eighteenth century.

Chikamatsu, the greatest of Japanese playwrights, was born into a samurai family that had little influence in society. He drifted into kabuki theater and now enjoys the reputation of being Japan's first professional playwright. His early plays were for particularly important kabuki actors. He specialized in history plays, which were popular because they educated people not only about their own history, but also about faraway places. His domestic plays, especially his tragedies, which are primarily puppet plays, are more frequently produced today in part because their subjects — middle-class suffering and emotional longing — seem more modern to us. *The Love Suicides at Sonezaki*, one of a series of love suicide plays, was so influential as to help cause the entire genre to be banned.

During this period, kabuki acting and stagecraft developed quickly, with highly stylized masks, extraordinary costumes, and complex sets. Eventually, complex stage machinery — trap doors and revolving stages — made the drama all the more interesting. The puppet stage depended on a chanter who recited the lines of all the characters and sometimes the narrator. Eventually, puppets operated by a single person gave way to more complex three-person puppets requiring unusual coordination and skill and producing subtle expressions and effects. Today both forms of theater still exist in Japan and have been performed throughout the world.

Late Seventeenth- and Eighteenth-Century Drama Timeline

DATE	THEATER	POLITICAL	SOCIAL/CULTURAL
1600–1700	**1603:** Okuni creates the first kabuki dance.	**1603:** Beginning of the Tokugawa shogunate in Edo, Japan. A long period of peace.	**1606–1669:** Rembrandt van Rijn, Dutch painter
	1606–1684: French playwright Pierre Corneille, author of *Le Cid* (1636)	**1605:** Gun Powder Plot in London; execution of Guy Fawkes	**1608–1674:** John Milton, English author
	1622–1673: Molière (born Jean Baptiste Poquelin), French dramatist and actor, author of *The Misanthrope* (1666), *Tartuffe* (1667), and *The Learned Ladies* (1672)		**1610:** Galileo's first observations through a telescope
			1620: Voyage of the Mayflower
			1628: William Harvey describes the circulation of blood.
	c. 1634–1691: Sir George Etherege, author of *Love in a Tub* and *The Man of Mode* (1676)		**1631–1700:** John Dryden, English author and playwright
	1635–1710: Thomas Betterton, perhaps the Restoration's most important actor		**1633:** John Donne's *Poems*, the complete collection of his poetry, is published.
			1637: René Descartes's *Discourse on Method*, exploration of mathematics and laws
	1639–1699: Jean Racine, French playwright, author of *Phaedre* (1677)		**1638:** Anne Hutchinson is expelled from the Massachusetts Bay Colony and founds Rhode Island.
	1640–1689: Aphra Behn, first professional woman playwright in the English theater, author of *The Rover* (1677–1680)	**1642:** Beginning of the English Civil War _parliament_ **1643:** Louis XIV becomes _def. King Charles I_ king of France at age four.	
			1645: Gian Lorenzo Bernini begins his "Ecstasy of St. Theresa."
	1650–1687: Nell Gwynne, English actress and mistress of Charles II	**1649:** King Charles I of England is beheaded by Parliament.	**1650:** Anne Bradstreet publishes *The Tenth Muse*, first collection of poetry from the New World.
	1656: First use of Italianate scenery in England in a production of *The Siege of Rhodes*, designed by John Webb	**1655:** Oliver Cromwell prohibits Anglican church services and divides England into eleven districts governed by major-generals.	
	1658: Molière's troupe, the Illustre Théâtre, is invited to perform at the court of King Louis XIV. The company is subsequently given permission to remain in Paris, as the Troupe de Monsieur, and allowed to use the Petit Bourbon for public performances.	**1658:** Cromwell dissolves Parliament.	
	1660: Theatrical activity resumes in London (after being halted in 1642) when King Charles II issues patents to Thomas Killigrew and William Davenant. Women are permitted on the English stage for the first time.	**1660:** Restoration of the English monarchy and end of the Commonwealth. Charles II, son of the executed Charles I, is crowned.	**1660:** Samuel Pepys begins his diary. **1660:** Dutch Boers settle on the Cape of Good Hope. **1661–1731:** Daniel Defoe, English author

Late Seventeenth- and Eighteenth-Century Drama Timeline (continued)

DATE	THEATER	POLITICAL	SOCIAL/CULTURAL
1600–1700 (continued)	**1664:** Japanese playwright Fukui Yagozaemon writes *The Outcast's Revenge*, the first full-length kabuki play. **1670–1729:** William Congreve, author of *Love for Love* (1695) and *The Way of the World* (1700) **1680:** The Comédie-Française, the first national theater, opens in Paris. **1695–1715:** Proliferation of female playwrights in England. Thirty-seven new plays by women are produced on the London stage during this period by playwrights such as Mary Pix (1666–1706), Susanna Centlivre (c. 1670–1723), Mary Delarivière Manley (c. 1672–1724), and Catharine Trotter (1679–1749). **1698:** Jeremy Collier's *A Short View of the Immorality and Profaneness of the English Stage*, the most effective of several attacks on the theater published at the turn of the century	**1664:** The British annex New Amsterdam and rename it New York. **1682:** Louis XIV moves the French court to Versailles. **1682–1725:** Peter the Great reigns as czar of Russia and calls for political and cultural reforms. **1685:** Louis XIV revokes the Edict of Nantes, and persecution of the Huguenots (French Protestants) ensues. **1688:** William of Orange invades England with the encouragement of prominent Protestants, who fear James II's Catholicism. James flees to France and then England. William III and Mary II (daughter of James II) are crowned in 1689. **1690:** An Irish uprising in favor of James II is suppressed by William III at the Battle of the Boyne. **1697:** The last remains of Mayan civilization destroyed by the Spanish.	**1664–1666:** Isaac Newton (1642–1727), English mathematician and physicist, discovers the law of universal gravitation and begins to develop calculus. **1665:** Plague devastates London. **1666:** Great Fire of London **1685–1750:** J. S. Bach, German composer **1687:** Isaac Newton publishes *Mathematical Principles*. **1688–1704:** Alexander Pope, English poet **1692:** Salem witchcraft trials **1694–1778:** François Marie Arouet de Voltaire, French author often described as the embodiment of the Enlightenment
1700–1800	**1703:** Chikamatsu creates the genre of love suicide plays with *The Love Suicides at Sonezaki*. **1707–1793:** Carlo Goldoni, Italian playwright, author of *The Servant of Two Masters* (1743) **1717–1779:** David Garrick, greatest English actor of the eighteenth century and owner and manager of the Drury Lane Theatre in London **1720–1806:** Carlo Gozzi, Italian playwright, author of *King Stag* (1762) and *Turandot* (1762)	**1703:** Peter the Great lays the foundation for St. Petersburg. **1707:** The Act of Union unites Scotland and England, which become Great Britain. **1714:** The House of Hanover begins its rule of Great Britain with the accession of George I. **1715:** Louis XIV, France's Sun King, dies.	**1703–1758:** Jonathan Edwards, American theologian **1709–1784:** Samuel Johnson, English literary critic, scholar, poet, and lexicographer **1720:** First serialization of novels in newspapers **1724:** Emmanuel Kant, German metaphysics philosopher

Late Seventeenth- and Eighteenth-Century Drama Timeline (continued)

DATE	THEATER	POLITICAL	SOCIAL/CULTURAL
1700–1800 (continued)	**1728:** John Gay (1685–1732) writes *The Beggar's Opera*, arguably the most popular English play of the eighteenth century.		**1726:** Jonathan Swift writes *Gulliver's Travels*.
	1730–1774: Oliver Goldsmith, author of *The Vicar of Wakefield*, *The Deserted Village*, and *She Stoops to Conquer*		**1732:** Covent Garden opera house opens in London.
	1729–1781: Gotthold Ephraim Lessing, Germany's first important playwright, author of *Minna von Barnhelm* (1767) and *Emilia Galotti* (1772)		**1732:** Franz Josef Haydn, prolific Austrian composer
	1737: The Licensing Act in England prohibits the performance of any play not previously licensed by the Lord Chamberlain. A number of such laws regulating theatrical activity are enacted throughout the eighteenth century.	**1740:** Frederick the Great introduces freedom of press and worship in Prussia.	**1742:** Cotton factories are established in Birmingham and Northampton, England.
			1746–1828: Francisco de Goya, Spanish painter and political cartoonist
	1749–1832: Johann Wolfgang von Goethe, German writer. His early works include the play *Götz von Berlichingen* (1773) and the novel *The Sorrows of Young Werther* (1774).	**1756–1763:** Frederick begins the Seven Years War pitting Prussia and Great Britain against Russia, Austria, and France.	**1751:** Dennis Diderot, French writer and philosopher, publishes the first volume of his *Encyclopédie*.
			1756–1791: Wolfgang Amadeus Mozart, Austrian classical composer
	1751–1816: Richard Brinsley Sheridan, playwright and statesman, author of *The School for Scandal* (1777)	**1762:** Catherine the Great (b. 1729) becomes empress of Russia after overthrowing her husband, Peter III; she reigns until her death in 1796.	**1757–1827:** William Blake, Romantic poet and artist, author of *Songs of Innocence* and *Songs of Experience*
	1762: English actor-manager David Garrick prohibits audience members from sitting on the stage.	**1763:** The Treaty of Paris ends the Seven Years War. Prussia emerges as an important European power. France loses many colonial possessions.	**1759–1797:** Mary Wollstonecraft, English writer and early feminist, author of *Vindication of the Rights of Woman* (1792)
		1765: British Parliament passes the Stamp Act. Nine colonies draw up a declaration of rights and liberties.	**1762:** The Sorbonne library opens in Paris.
	c. 1769: Spectators are banned from sitting on the stage in Paris.	**1766:** Catherine the Great grants freedom of worship in Russia.	
		1776: U.S. Declaration of Independence	

Molière

Molière (1622–1673, born Jean Baptiste Poquelin) came from a family attached to the glittering court of King Louis XIV, the Sun King. His father had purchased an appointment to the king, and as a result the family was familiar with the exciting court life of Paris, although not on intimate terms with the courtiers who surrounded the king. Molière's father was a furnisher and upholsterer to the king; the family, while well-to-do and enjoying some power, was still apart from royalty and the privileged aristocracy.

Molière's education was exceptional. He went to Jesuit schools and spent more than five years at Collège de Clermont, which he left in 1641 having studied both the humanities and philosophy. His knowledge of philosophy was unusually deep, and his background in the classics was exceptionally strong. He also took a law degree in 1641 at Orléans, but never practiced. His father's dream was that his son should inherit his appointment as furnisher to the king, thereby guaranteeing himself a comfortable future.

That, however, was not to be. Instead of following the law, Molière decided at the last minute to abandon his secure future, change his name so as not to scandalize his family, and take up a career in the theater. He began by joining a company of actors run by the Béjart family. They established a theater based in Paris called the Illustre Théâtre. It was run by Madeleine Béjart, with whom Molière had a professional and personal relationship until she died in 1672. Eventually, Molière began writing plays but only after he had worked extensively as an actor.

The famed commedia dell'arte actor Tiberio Fiorillo, known as Scaramouche, was a close friend of Molière and perhaps responsible for Molière's choice of a career in theater. Scaramouche may have been part of the Illustre Théâtre, or he may have acted in it on occasion. Unfortunately, the Illustre Théâtre lasted only a year. It was one of several Parisian theatrical groups, and none of them prospered.

The company went bankrupt in 1644, and Molière, forced to leave Paris for about thirteen years, played in the provinces and remote towns. Before leaving Paris he had to be bailed out of debtors' prison. What was left of the Béjart group merged with another company on tour, and Molière became director of that company. During this time he suffered most of the indignities typical of the traveling life, including impoverishment.

In October 1658 Louis XIV saw Molière's troupe acting in one of his comedies at the Louvre. The royal court was so impressed with what it saw that the king gave him the use of a theater. Molière's work remained immensely popular and controversial. He acted in his own plays, produced his own plays, and wrote a succession of major works that are still favorites.

Because other companies envied his success and favor with the king, a number of "scandals" arose around some of his plays. The first play to invite controversy was *The School for Wives* (1662), in which Arnolphe reacts in horror to the infidelities he sees in the wives all around him. He decides that his wife-to-be must be raised far from the world, where she will be ignorant of the way-ward lives of the Parisians. A man who intends to seduce her tells Arnolphe (not knowing who he is) how he will get her out of Arnolphe's grasp. The play is highly comic, but groups of theatergoers protested that it was immoral and scandalous. In response Molière wrote *Criticism of the School for Wives* (1663), in which the debate over the play is enacted.

One of Molière's most popular plays, *Tartuffe* (written in 1664), concerns a religious hypocrite who weasels his way into a noble household and then goes about trying to seduce its mistress. Molière envisioned the religious con man as his target in this play, and the name *Tartuffe* became shorthand for a religious hypocrite. The name still implies hypocrisy in France.

A French church group, the Society of the Holy Sacrament, thought it was being portrayed in the title role and protested that the play was immoral and offensive. The society's condemnation of the play effectively prevented it from being performed. Molière tried rewriting *Tartuffe,* but the society would not approve its production.

In 1669 the Society of the Holy Sacrament was dissolved in a restructuring of the French church, and *Tartuffe* was finally permitted to be played to large audiences. Theatergoers loved the play and found great amusement in the sly, lecherous rogue who completely beguiles Orgon, the man who thinks Tartuffe is a great saint and who introduces him into his household. In most modern productions Tartuffe is played broadly, almost as a caricature or a clown. Audiences find him amusing, scabrous, and irresistible. They usually find the play irresistible, as well, because it involves crafty maneuvering onstage and complicated deceptions.

Among Molière's other successes are *The Miser* (1668), *The Bourgeois Gentleman* (1670), and his final play, *The Imaginary Invalid* (1673). Molière had a bad cough for most of the last decade of his life, which onstage he often made to seem the cough of the character he was playing. But Molière was gen-uinely ill; he died on stage, playing the title role of *The Imaginary Invalid.*

THE MISANTHROPE

The Misanthrope (1666) in its own age was not the most successful of Molière's plays, but it has certainly been one of the most produced of all the plays in his canon. Typical of his work, it derives from a close and careful observation of French life and manners. Recently, English-language audiences have been able to savor this play in Richard Wilbur's superb translation, which catches the sharpness of the French wit and the elegance of the verse — both hallmarks of French seventeenth-century drama.

In one sense the play is based on the type of improbability that marks Greek New Comedy. It portrays the romance of two very different people, Alceste, the misanthrope who speaks his mind and brashly tells people what he thinks of them, and Célimène, the coquette who rarely says what she thinks but who enjoys the attention of many suitors. She enjoys society and her capacity to dominate it. Alceste cannot abide society and its superficialities. At the end of the play he resolves to leave it.

A revelation in the play is that while Alceste and Célimène are different on the surface, beneath the surface they are similar. They are both extreme types who behave extremely. Célimène carries coquetry to great lengths, leading on as many men as possible. Alceste is the epitome of a misanthrope, refusing to flatter people just to make them feel good. He says that he must tell the truth, and he does — even when it hurts, perhaps especially when it hurts. For him to fall in love with a coquette who must deceive those around her to keep herself at the center of attention is a wonderful comic irony. But beneath that irony lies the thought that Alceste himself may have flaws that are the opposite of Célimène's.

The ending of *The Misanthrope,* which avoids the marriage of the protagonists (a more typical ending of comedies), may have contributed to the disappointment of its initial audiences. Another comic playwright would have brought the two lovers together. But Molière chose a more complex and, for some, a less satisfying ending. While two secondary characters marry, the main characters — Alceste and Célimène — agree to disagree and decide to live separately after all. Molière leaves his audience simply hoping that the two will change their minds. But as the play ends, the audience has no real reason to expect that they will.

This is a very French drama. The society is elegant, formal, and mannered. Molière knows every character and reveals each one totally. The surface elegance of the verse is such that the manners of the society seem polished, artificial, and ritualistic without being especially deceptive. The deception in this play is not at the center of things nor does the play depend on mix-ups and misapprehensions for its success. This in itself gives us a rather intriguing hint about Molière's intentions. The theme of honesty is at the play's center, but it is no simple thing to decide, in a social situation such as these characters enjoy, exactly how honest honesty should be or when honesty is the best policy. Alceste has one view and Célimène has another.

Molière enjoys pitting the values of Célimène and Alceste against one another, but it is clear that he does not want to offer sweeping or simple solutions to their conflict. Instead, he is content to leave his audience thinking and wondering.

The Misanthrope in Performance

The first full production of *The Misanthrope* was on June 4, 1666, with Molière as Alceste and his wife as Célimène. Most of the players who joined them were aware that Alceste was modeled after Molière himself and that Molière was poking fun at himself and his marriage. Molière made the part more comical than serious. The French national theater, Comédie-Française, records some fifteen hundred performances of the play between 1680 and 1960, making it one of the most performed of all French comedies. Late in the eighteenth century, actors began playing Alceste as a serious character, as he is played today.

The first important American production in English was by Richard Mansfield, who acted the part of Alceste in New York in 1905. The reviews noted that "his embodiment of Alceste is vibrant with pain. . . . He smiles, but it is always the smile of bitterness." Richard Wilbur's verse translation played in the tiny Theatre East in New York in 1956 while the original rhymed French version with a French company played simultaneously at the Winter Garden on Broadway. Both productions were very successful. Wilbur's version has since played virtually all over America, with several productions in New York in the 1960s, 70s, and 80s. The West Side Repertory Theater performed it in modern black tie and tails in 1991, with James Jacobus as Alceste. *The Misanthrope* has also had innumerable college productions since Wilbur's translation, which has, at least in the United States, become the standard version.

Tony Harrison also translated the play for the British National Theatre in 1975 with Alec McCowan as Alceste and Diana Rigg as Célimène. Reviews were mixed, but the play was said to have "the brilliance of a tiara of diamonds."

Molière [*Jean Baptiste Poquelin*] (1622–1673)

THE MISANTHROPE

1666

TRANSLATED BY RICHARD WILBUR

Characters

ALCESTE, *in love with Célimène*
PHILINTE, *Alceste's friend*
ORONTE, *in love with Célimène*
CÉLIMÈNE, *Alceste's beloved*
ÉLIANTE, *Célimène's cousin*
ARSINOÉ, *a friend of Célimène's*
ACASTE }
CLITANDRE } *Marquesses*
BASQUE, *Célimène's servant*
A GUARD *of the Marshalsea*
DUBOIS, *Alceste's valet*

The scene throughout is in Célimène's house at Paris.

ACT I • *Scene 1* [*Philinte, Alceste.*]

PHILINTE: Now, what's got into you?
ALCESTE (*seated*):   Kindly leave me alone.
PHILINTE: Come, come, what is it? This lugubrious
    tone . . .
ALCESTE: Leave me, I said; you spoil my solitude.
PHILINTE: Oh, listen to me, now, and don't be rude.
ALCESTE: I choose to be rude, Sir, and to be hard of
5   hearing.
PHILINTE: These ugly moods of yours are not
    endearing;

Friends though we are, I really must insist . . .
ALCESTE (*abruptly rising*): Friends? Friends, you say?
    Well, cross me off your list.
    I've been your friend till now, as you well know;
    But after what I saw a moment ago   10
    I tell you flatly that our ways must part.
    I wish no place in a dishonest heart.
PHILINTE: Why, what have I done, Alceste? Is this quite
    just?
ALCESTE: My God, you ought to die of self-disgust.
    I call your conduct inexcusable, Sir,   15
    And every man of honor will concur.
    I see you almost hug a man to death,
    Exclaim for joy until you're out of breath,
    And supplement these loving demonstrations
    With endless offers, vows, and protestations;   20
    Then when I ask you "Who was that?" I find
    That you can barely bring his name to mind!
    Once the man's back is turned, you cease to love
    him,
    And speak with absolute indifference of him!
    By God, I say it's base and scandalous   25
    To falsify the heart's affections thus;
    If I caught myself behaving in such a way,
    I'd hang myself for shame, without delay.
PHILINTE: It hardly seems a hanging matter to me;
    I hope that you will take it graciously   30
    If I extend myself a slight reprieve,

And live a little longer, by your leave.
ALCESTE: How dare you joke about a crime so grave?
PHILINTE: What crime? How else are people to behave?
35 ALCESTE: I'd have them be sincere, and never part
       With any word that isn't from the heart.
   PHILINTE: When someone greets us with a show of
          pleasure,
       It's but polite to give him equal measure,
       Return his love the best that we know how,
40   And trade him offer for offer, vow for vow.
   ALCESTE: No, no, this formula you'd have me follow,
       However fashionable, is false and hollow,
       And I despise the frenzied operations
       Of all these barterers of protestations,
45   These lavishers of meaningless embraces
       These utterers of obliging commonplaces,
       Who court and flatter everyone on earth
       And praise the fool no less than the man of worth.
       Should you rejoice that someone fondles you,
50   Offers his love and service, swears to be true,
       And fills your ears with praises of your name,
       When to the first damned fop he'll say the same?
       No, no: no self-respecting heart would dream
       Of prizing so promiscuous an esteem;
55   However high the praise, there's nothing worse
       Than sharing honors with the universe.
       Esteem is founded on comparison:
       ⌐To honor all men is to honor none.⌐
       Since you embrace this indiscriminate vice
60   Your friendship comes at far too cheap a price;
       I spurn the easy tribute of a heart
       Which will not set the worthy man apart:
       I choose, Sir, to be chosen; and in fine,
       The friend of mankind is no friend of mine.
65 PHILINTE: But in polite society, custom decrees
       That we show certain outward courtesies . . .
   ALCESTE: Ah, no! we should condemn with all our
          force
       Such false and artificial intercourse.
       Let men behave like men; let them display
70   Their inmost hearts in everything they say;
       Let the heart speak, and let our sentiments
       Not mask themselves in silly compliments.
   PHILINTE: In certain cases it would be uncouth
       And most absurd to speak the naked truth;
75   With all respect for your exalted notions,
       It's often best to veil one's true emotions.
       Wouldn't the social fabric come undone
       If we were wholly frank with everyone?
       Suppose you met with someone you couldn't bear;
80   Would you inform him of it then and there?
   ALCESTE: Yes.
   PHILINTE: Then you'd tell old Emilie it's pathetic
       The way she daubs her features with cosmetic
       And plays the gay coquette at sixty-four?
   ALCESTE: I would.
   PHILINTE: And you'd call Dorilas a bore,
85   And tell him every ear at court is lame
       From hearing him brag about his noble name?

ALCESTE: Precisely.
PHILINTE: Ah, you're joking.
ALCESTE: Au contraire.°
       In this regard there's none I'd choose to spare.
       All are corrupt; there's nothing to be seen
       In court or town but aggravates my spleen.°   90
       I fall into deep gloom and melancholy
       When I survey the scene of human folly,
       Finding on every hand base flattery,
       Injustice, fraud, self-interest, treachery. . . .
       Ah, it's too much; mankind has grown so base,   95
       I mean to break with the whole human race.
   PHILINTE: This philosophic rage is a bit extreme;
       You've no idea how comical you seem;
       Indeed, we're like those brothers in the play
       Called School for Husbands,° one of whom was
          prey . . .   100
   ALCESTE: Enough, now! None of your stupid similes.
   PHILINTE: Then let's have no more tirades, if you
          please.
       The world won't change, whatever you say or do;
       And since plain speaking means so much to you,
       I'll tell you plainly that by being frank   105
       You've earned the reputation of a crank,
       And that you're thought ridiculous when you rage
       And rant against the manners of the age.
   ALCESTE: So much the better; just what I wish to hear.
       No news could be more grateful to my ear.   110
       All men are so detestable in my eyes,
       I should be sorry if they thought me wise.
   PHILINTE: Your hatred's very sweeping, is it not?
   ALCESTE: Quite right: I hate the whole degraded lot.
   PHILINTE: Must all poor human creatures be embraced, 115
       Without distinction, by your vast distaste?
       Even in these bad times, there are surely a few . . .
   ALCESTE: No, I include all men in one dim view:
       Some men I hate for being rogues: the others
       I hate because they treat the rogues like brothers, 120
       And, lacking a virtuous scorn for what is vile,
       Receive the villain with a complaisant smile.
       Notice how tolerant people choose to be
       Toward that bold rascal who's at law with me.
       His social polish can't conceal his nature,   125
       One sees at once that he's a treacherous creature;
       No one could possibly be taken in
       By those soft speeches and that sugary grin.
       The whole world knows the shady means by
          which
       The low-brow's grown so powerful and rich,   130
       And risen to a rank so bright and high
       That virtue can but blush, and merit sigh.

87. *Au contraire*: On the contrary.   90. spleen: A body organ
thought to be the seat of melancholy, one of the four humors of
medieval physiology.   100. *School for Husbands*: A play by
Molière (1661) in which two brothers, Sganarelle and Ariste,
are guardians of two orphan girls. Sganarelle hopes to marry
one of the girls, Isabelle, but she frees herself by trickery from
his domineering ways and marries someone else.

Whenever his name comes up in conversation,
None will defend his wretched reputation;
135 Call him knave, liar, scoundrel, and all the rest,
Each head will nod, and no one will protest.
And yet his smirk is seen in every house,
He's greeted everywhere with smiles and bows,
And when there's any honor that can be got
140 By pulling strings, he'll get it, like as not.
My God! It chills my heart to see the ways
Men come to terms with evil nowadays
Sometimes, I swear, I'm moved to flee and find
Some desert land unfouled by humankind.
145 PHILINTE: Come, let's forget the follies of the times
And pardon mankind for its petty crimes;
Let's have an end of rantings and of railings,
And show some leniency toward human failings.
This world requires a pliant rectitude;
150 Too stern a virtue makes one stiff and rude;
Good sense views all extremes with detestation,
And bids us to be noble in moderation.
The rigid virtues of the ancient days
Are not for us; they jar with all our ways
155 And ask of us too lofty a perfection.
Wise men accept their times without objection,
And there's no greater folly, if you ask me,
Than trying to reform society.
Like you, I see each day a hundred and one
160 Unhandsome deeds that might be better done,
But still, for all the faults that meet my view,
I'm never known to storm and rave like you.
I take men as they are, or let them be,
And teach my soul to bear their frailty;
165 And whether in court or town, whatever the scene,
My phlegm's° as philosophic as your spleen.
ALCESTE: This phlegm which you so eloquently
commend,
Does nothing ever rile it up, my friend?
Suppose some man you trust should treacherously
170 Conspire to rob you of your property,
And do his best to wreck your reputation?
Wouldn't you feel a certain indignation?
PHILINTE: Why, no. These faults of which you so
complain
Are part of human nature, I maintain,
175 And it's no more a matter for disgust
That men are knavish, selfish and unjust,
Than that the vulture dines upon the dead,
And wolves are furious, and apes ill-bred.
ALCESTE: Shall I see myself betrayed, robbed, torn to
bits,
180 And not . . . Oh, let's be still and rest our wits.
Enough of reasoning, now. I've had my fill.
PHILINTE: Indeed, you would do well, Sir, to be still.
Rage less at your opponent, and give some thought
To how you'll win this lawsuit that he's brought.
185 ALCESTE: I assure you I'll do nothing of the sort.

166. **phlegm:** In medieval physiology, the humor thought to be cold and moist and to cause sluggishness.

PHILINTE: Then who will plead your case before the
court?
ALCESTE: Reason and right and justice will plead for
me.
PHILINTE: Oh, Lord. What judges do you plan to see?
ALCESTE: Why, none. The justice of my cause is clear.
PHILINTE: Of course, man; but there's politics to
fear . . .   190
ALCESTE: No, I refuse to lift a hand. That's flat.
I'm either right, or wrong.
PHILINTE: Don't count on that.
ALCESTE: No, I'll do nothing.
PHILINTE: Your enemy's influence
Is great, you know . . .
ALCESTE: That makes no difference.
PHILINTE: It will; you'll see.
ALCESTE: Must honor bow to guile?   195
If so, I shall be proud to lose the trial.
PHILINTE: Oh, really . . .
ALCESTE: I'll discover by this case
Whether or not men are sufficiently base
And impudent and villainous and perverse
To do me wrong before the universe.   200
PHILINTE: What a man!
ALCESTE: Oh, I could wish, whatever the cost,
Just for the beauty of it, that my trial were lost.
PHILINTE: If people heard you talking so, Alceste,
They'd split their sides. Your name would be a jest.
ALCESTE: So much the worse for jesters.
PHILINTE: May I enquire   205
Whether this rectitude you so admire,
And these hard virtues you're enamored of
Are qualities of the lady whom you love?
It much surprises me that you, who seem
To view mankind with furious disesteem,   210
Have yet found something to enchant your eyes
Amidst a species which you so despise.
And what is more amazing, I'm afraid,
Is the most curious choice your heart has made.
The honest Éliante is fond of you,   215
Arsinoé, the prude, admires you too;
And yet your spirit's been perversely led
To choose the flighty Célimène instead,
Whose brittle malice and coquettish ways
So typify the manners of our days.   220
How is it that the traits you most abhor
Are bearable in this lady you adore?
Are you so blind with love that you can't find them?
Or do you contrive, in her case, not to mind them?
ALCESTE: My love for that young widow's not the kind   225
That can't perceive defects; no, I'm not blind.
I see her faults, despite my ardent love,
And all I see I fervently reprove.
And yet I'm weak; for all her falsity,
That woman knows the art of pleasing me,   230
And though I never cease complaining of her,
I swear I cannot manage not to love her.
Her charm outweighs her faults; I can but aim
To cleanse her spirit in my love's pure flame.

235   PHILINTE: That's no small task; I wish you all success.
            You think then that she loves you?
        ALCESTE: Heavens, yes!
            I wouldn't love her did she not love me.
        PHILINTE: Well, if her taste for you is plain to see,
            Why do these rivals cause you such despair?
240   ALCESTE: True love, Sir, is possessive, and cannot bear
            To share with all the world. I'm here today
            To tell her she must send that mob away.
        PHILINTE: If I were you, and had your choice to make,
            Éliante, her cousin, would be the one I'd take;
245   That honest heart, which cares for you alone,
            Would harmonize far better with your own.
        ALCESTE: True, true: each day my reason tells me so;
            But reason doesn't rule in love, you know.
        PHILINTE: I fear some bitter sorrow is in store;
250   This love . . .

Scene II [*Oronte, Alceste, Philinte.*]

ORONTE (*to Alceste*): The servants told me at the door
            That Éliante and Célimène were out,
            But when I heard, dear Sir, that you were about,
            I came to say, without exaggeration,
5   That I hold you in the vastest admiration,
            And that it's always been my dearest desire
            To be the friend of one I so admire.
            I hope to see my love of merit requited,
            And you and I in friendship's bond united.
10   I'm sure you won't refuse — if I may be frank —
            A friend of my devotedness — and rank.

(*During this speech of Oronte's Alceste is abstracted
and seems unaware that he is being spoken to. He only
breaks off his reverie when Oronte says:*)

            It was for you, if you please, that my words were
                intended.
        ALCESTE: For me, Sir?
        ORONTE: Yes, for you. You're not offended?
        ALCESTE: By no means. But this much surprises me . . .
15   The honor comes most unexpectedly . . .
        ORONTE: My high regard should not astonish you;
            The whole world feels the same. It is your due.
        ALCESTE: Sir . . .
        ORONTE: Why, in all the State there isn't one
            Can match your merits; they shine, Sir, like the sun.
        ALCESTE: Sir . . .
20   ORONTE: You are higher in my estimation
            Than all that's most illustrious in the nation.
        ALCESTE: Sir . . .
        ORONTE: If I lie, may heaven strike me dead!
            To show you that I mean what I have said,
            Permit me, Sir, to embrace you most sincerely,
25   And swear that I will prize our friendship dearly.
            Give me your hand. And now, Sir, if you choose,
            We'll make our vows.
        ALCESTE: Sir . . .
        ORONTE: What! You refuse?

ALCESTE: Sir, it's a very great honor you extend:
            But friendship is a sacred thing, my friend;
            It would be profanation to bestow   30
            The name of friend on one you hardly know.
            All parts are better played when well-rehearsed
            Let's put off friendship, and get acquainted first.
            We may discover it would be unwise
            To try to make our natures harmonize.   35
        ORONTE: By heaven! You're sagacious to the core;
            This speech has made me admire you even more.
            Let time, then, bring us closer day by day;
            Meanwhile, I shall be yours in every way.
            If, for example, there should be anything   40
            You wish at court, I'll mention it to the King.
            I have his ear, of course; it's quite well known
            That I am much in favor with the throne.
            In short, I am your servant. And now, dear friend,
            Since you have such fine judgment, I intend   45
            To please you, if I can, with a small sonnet
            I wrote not long ago. Please comment on it,
            And tell me whether I ought to publish it.
        ALCESTE: You must excuse me, Sir; I'm hardly fit
            To judge such matters.
        ORONTE: Why not?
        ALCESTE: I am. I fear,   50
            Inclined to be unfashionably sincere.
        ORONTE: Just what I ask; I'd take no satisfaction
            In anything but your sincere reaction.
            I beg you not to dream of being kind.
        ALCESTE: Since you desire it, Sir, I'll speak my mind.   55
        ORONTE: *Sonnet.* It's a sonnet. . . . *Hope.* . . . The
                poem's addressed
            To a lady who wakened hopes within my breast.
            Hope . . . this is not the pompous sort of thing,
            Just modest little verses, with a tender ring.
        ALCESTE: Well, we shall see.
        ORONTE: *Hope* . . . I'm anxious to hear   60
            Whether the style seems properly smooth and clear,
            And whether the choice of words is good or bad.
        ALCESTE: We'll see, we'll see.
        ORONTE: Perhaps I ought to add
            That it took me only a quarter-hour to write it.
        ALCESTE: The time's irrelevant, Sir: kindly recite it.   65
        ORONTE (*reading*): Hope comforts us awhile, 'tis true,
            Lulling our cares with careless laughter,
            And yet such joy is full of rue,
            My Phyllis, if nothing follows after.
        PHILINTE: I'm charmed by this already; the style's
                delightful.   70
        ALCESTE (*sotto voce,° to Philinte*): How can you say
                that? Why, the thing is frightful.
        ORONTE: Your fair face smiled on me awhile,
            But was it kindness so to enchant me?
            'Twould have been fairer not to smile,
            If hope was all you meant to grant me.   75
        PHILINTE: What a clever thought! How handsomely
                you phrase it!

71. [S.D.] *sotto voce:* In a soft voice or stage whisper.

ALCESTE (*sotto voce, to Philinte*): You know the thing
    is trash. How dare you praise it?
ORONTE: If it's to be my passion's fate
    Thus everlastingly to wait,
80   Then death will come to set me free:
    For death is fairer than the fair;
    Phyllis, to hope is to despair
    When one must hope eternally.
PHILINTE: The close is exquisite — full of feeling and
    grace.
ALCESTE (*sotto voce, aside*): Oh, blast the close; you'd
85   better close your face
    Before you send your lying soul to hell.
PHILINTE: I can't remember a poem I've liked so well.
ALCESTE (*sotto voce, aside*): Good Lord!
ORONTE (*to Philinte*):   I fear you're
    flattering me a bit.
PHILINTE: Oh, no!
ALCESTE (*sotto voce, aside*): What else d'you call it, you
    hypocrite?
ORONTE (*to Alceste*): But you, Sir, keep your promise
90   now: don't shrink
    From telling me sincerely what you think.
ALCESTE: Sir, these are delicate matters; we all desire
    To be told that we've the true poetic fire.
    But once, to one whose name I shall not mention
95   I said, regarding some verse of his invention,
    That gentlemen should rigorously control
    That itch to write which often afflicts the soul;
    That one should curb the heady inclination
    To publicize one's little avocation
100   And that in showing off one's works of art
    One often plays a very clownish part.
ORONTE: Are you suggesting in a devious way
    That I ought not . . .
ALCESTE: Oh, that I do not say.
    Further, I told him that no fault is worse
105   Than that of writing frigid, lifeless verse,
    And that the merest whisper of such a shame
    Suffices to destroy a man's good name.
ORONTE: D'you mean to say my sonnet's dull and
    trite?
ALCESTE: I don't say that. But I went on to cite
110   Numerous cases of once-respected men
    Who came to grief by taking up the pen.
ORONTE: And am I like them? Do I write so poorly?
ALCESTE: I don't say that. But I told this person,
    "Surely
    You're under no necessity to compose;
115   Why you should wish to publish, heaven knows.
    There's no excuse for printing tedious rot
    Unless one writes for bread, as you do not.
    Resist temptation, then, I beg of you;
    Conceal your pastimes from the public view;
120   And don't give up, on any provocation,
    Your present high and courtly reputation,
    To purchase at a greedy printer's shop
    The name of silly author and scribbling fop."
    These were the points I tried to make him see.

ORONTE: I sense that they are also aimed at me,   125
    But now — about my sonnet — I'd like to be told . . .
ALCESTE: Frankly, that sonnet should be pigeonholed.
    You've chosen the worst models to imitate.
    The style's unnatural. Let me illustrate:
    For example, Your fair face smiled on me awhile,   130
    Followed by, 'Twould have been fairer not to smile!
    Or this: such joy is full of rue;
    Or this: For death is fairer than the fair;
    Or, Phyllis, to hope is to despair
    When one must hope eternally!   135
    This artificial style, that's all the fashion,
    Has neither taste, nor honesty, nor passion;
    It's nothing but a sort of wordy play,
    And nature never spoke in such a way.
    What, in this shallow age, is not debased?   140
    Our fathers, though less refined, had better taste;
    I'd barter all that men admire today
    For one old love song I shall try to say:
    If the King had given me for my own
    Paris, his citadel,   145
    And I for that must leave alone
    Her whom I love so well,
    I'd say then to the Crown,
    Take back your glittering town;
    My darling is more fair, I swear,   150
    My darling is more fair.
    The rhyme's not rich, the style is rough and old,
    But don't you see that it's the purest gold
    Beside the tinsel nonsense now preferred,
    And that there's passion in its every word?   155
    If the King had given me for my own
    Paris, his citadel,
    And I for that must leave alone
    Her whom I love so well,
    I'd say then to the Crown,   160
    Take back your glittering town;
    My darling is more fair, I swear,
    My darling is more fair.
    There speaks a loving heart. (*To Philinte.*) You're
    laughing, eh?
    Laugh on, my precious wit. Whatever you say,   165
    I hold that song's worth all the bibelots°
    That people hail today with ah's and oh's.
ORONTE: And I maintain my sonnet's very good.
ALCESTE: It's not at all surprising that you should.
    You have your reasons; permit me to have mine   170
    For thinking that you cannot write a line.
ORONTE: Others have praised my sonnet to the skies.
ALCESTE: I lack their art of telling pleasant lies.
ORONTE: You seem to think you've got no end of wit.
ALCESTE: To praise your verse, I'd need still more of it.   175
ORONTE: I'm not in need of your approval, Sir.
ALCESTE: That's good; you couldn't have it if you were.
ORONTE: Come now, I'll lend you the subject of my
    sonnet;
    I'd like to see you try to improve upon it.

166. bibelots: Trinkets.

ALCESTE: I might, by chance, write something just as
180   shoddy;
        But then I wouldn't show it to everybody.
ORONTE: You're most opinionated and conceited.
ALCESTE: Go find your flatterers, and be better treated.
ORONTE: Look here, my little fellow, pray watch your
        tone.
ALCESTE: My great big fellow, you'd better watch your
185   own.
PHILINTE (*stepping between them*): Oh, please, please,
        gentlemen! This will never do.
ORONTE: The fault is mine, and I leave the field to you.
        I am your servant, Sir, in every way.
ALCESTE: And I, Sir, am your most abject valet.

Scene III [*Philinte, Alceste.*]

PHILINTE: Well, as you see, sincerity in excess
        Can get you into a very pretty mess;
        Oronte was hungry for appreciation. . . .
ALCESTE: Don't speak to me.
PHILINTE: What?
ALCESTE: No more conversation.
PHILINTE: Really, now . . .
ALCESTE: Leave me alone.
PHILINTE: If I . . .
5   ALCESTE: Out of my sight!
PHILINTE: But what . . .
ALCESTE: I won't listen.
PHILINTE: But . . .
ALCESTE: Silence!
PHILINTE: Now, it is polite . . .
ALCESTE: By heaven, I've had enough. Don't follow
        me.
PHILINTE: Ah, you're just joking. I'll keep you
        company.

ACT II • Scene I [*Alceste, Célimène.*]

ALCESTE: Shall I speak plainly, Madam? I confess
        Your conduct gives me infinite distress,
        And my resentment's grown too hot to smother.
        Soon, I foresee, we'll break with one another.
5   If I said otherwise, I should deceive you;
        Sooner or later, I shall be forced to leave you,
        And if I swore that we shall never part
        I should misread the omens of my heart.
CÉLIMÈNE: You kindly saw me home, it would appear,
10   So as to pour invectives in my ear.
ALCESTE: I've no desire to quarrel. But I deplore
        Your inability to shut the door
        On all these suitors who beset you so.
        There's what annoys me, if you care to know.
15 CÉLIMÈNE: Is it my fault that all these men pursue me?
        Am I to blame if they're attracted to me?
        And when they gently beg an audience,
        Ought I to take a stick and drive them hence?

ALCESTE: Madam, there's no necessity for a stick;
        A less responsive heart would do the trick.   20
        Of your attractiveness I don't complain;
        But those your charms attract, you then detain
        By a most melting and receptive manner,
        And so enlist their hearts beneath your banner.
        It's the agreeable hopes which you excite   25
        That keep these lovers round you day and night;
        Were they less liberally smiled upon,
        That sighing troop would very soon be gone.
        But tell me, Madam, why it is that lately
        This man Clitandre interests you so greatly?   30
        Because of what high merits do you deem
        Him worthy of the honor of your esteem?
        Is it that your admiring glances linger
        On the splendidly long nail of his little finger?
        Or do you share the general deep respect   35
        For the blond wig he chooses to affect?
        Are you in love with his embroidered hose?
        Do you adore his ribbons and his bows?
        Or is it that this paragon bewitches
        Your tasteful eye with his vast German breeches? 40
        Perhaps his giggle, or his falsetto voice,
        Makes him the latest gallant of your choice?
CÉLIMÈNE: You're much mistaken to resent him so.
        Why I put up with him you surely know:
        My lawsuit's very shortly to be tried,   45
        And I must have his influence on my side.
ALCESTE: Then lose your lawsuit, Madam, or let it
        drop;
        Don't torture me by humoring such a fop.
CÉLIMÈNE: You're jealous of the whole world, Sir.
ALCESTE: That's true,
        Since the whole world is well-received by you.   50
CÉLIMÈNE: That my good nature is so unconfined
        Should serve to pacify your jealous mind;
        Were I to smile on one, and scorn the rest,
        Then you might have some cause to be distressed.
ALCESTE: Well, if I mustn't be jealous, tell me, then, 55
        Just how I'm better treated than other men.
CÉLIMÈNE: You know you have my love. Will that not
        do?
ALCESTE: What proof have I that what you say is true?
CÉLIMÈNE: I would expect, Sir, that my having said it
        Might give the statement a sufficient credit.   60
ALCESTE: But how can I be sure that you don't tell
        The selfsame thing to other men as well?
CÉLIMÈNE: What a gallant speech! How flattering to
        me!
        What a sweet creature you make me out to be!
        Well then, to save you from the pangs of doubt,   65
        All that I've said I hereby cancel out;
        Now, none but yourself shall make a monkey of
        you:
        Are you content?
ALCESTE: Why, why am I doomed to love you?
        I swear that I shall bless the blissful hour
        When this poor heart's no longer in your power!   70
        I make no secret of it: I've done my best

To exorcise this passion from my breast
But thus far all in vain; it will not go;
It's for my sins that I must love you so.
CÉLIMÈNE: Your love for me is matchless, Sir; that's
75   clear.
ALCESTE: Indeed, in all the world it has no peer;
Words can't describe the nature of my passion,
And no man ever loved in such a fashion.
CÉLIMÈNE: Yes, it's a brand-new fashion, I agree:
80   You show your love by castigating me,
And all your speeches are enraged and rude.
I've never been so furiously wooed.
ALCESTE: Yet you could calm that fury, if you chose.
Come, shall we bring our quarrels to a close?
85   Let's speak with open hearts, then, and begin . . .

Scene II [*Célimène, Alceste, Basque.*]

CÉLIMÈNE: What is it?
BASQUE: Acaste is here.
CÉLIMÈNE: Well, send him in.

Scene III [*Célimène, Alceste.*]

ALCESTE: What! Shall we never be alone at all?
You're always ready to receive a call,
And you can't bear, for ten ticks of the clock,
Not to keep open house for all who knock.
5   CÉLIMÈNE: I couldn't refuse him: he'd be most put out.
ALCESTE: Surely that's not worth worrying about.
CÉLIMÈNE: Acaste would never forgive me if he guessed
That I consider him a dreadful pest.
ALCESTE: If he's a pest, why bother with him then?
10   CÉLIMÈNE: Heavens! One can't antagonize such men;
Why, they're the chartered gossips of the court,
And have a say in things of every sort.
One must receive them, and be full of charm;
They're no great help, but they can do you harm,
15   And though your influence be ever so great,
They're hardly the best people to alienate.
ALCESTE: I see, dear lady, that you could make a case
For putting up with the whole human race;
These friendships that you calculate so nicely . . .

Scene IV [*Alceste, Célimène, Basque.*]

BASQUE: Madam, Clitandre is here as well.
ALCESTE: Precisely.
CÉLIMÈNE: Where are you going?
ALCESTE: Elsewhere.
CÉLIMÈNE: Stay.
ALCESTE: No, no.
CÉLIMÈNE: Stay, Sir.
ALCESTE: I can't.
CÉLIMÈNE: I wish it.
ALCESTE: No, I must go.

I beg you, Madam, not to press the matter;
You know I have no taste for idle chatter.   5
CÉLIMÈNE: Stay. I command you.
ALCESTE: No, I cannot stay.
CÉLIMÈNE: Very well; you have my leave to go away.

Scene V [*Éliante, Philinte, Acaste, Clitandre, Alceste, Célimène, Basque.*]

ÉLIANTE (*to Célimène*): The Marquesses have kindly
come to call.
Were they announced?
CÉLIMÈNE: Yes. Basque, bring chairs for all.

(*Basque provides the chairs and exits.*)

(*To Alceste.*) You haven't gone?
ALCESTE: No; and I shan't depart
Till you decide who's foremost in your heart.
CÉLIMÈNE: Oh, hush.
ALCESTE: It's time to choose; take them, or me.   5
CÉLIMÈNE: You're mad.
ALCESTE: I'm not, as you shall shortly see.
CÉLIMÈNE: Oh?
ALCESTE: You'll decide.
CÉLIMÈNE: You're joking now, dear friend.
ALCESTE: No, no; you'll choose; my patience is at an
end.
CLITANDRE: Madam, I come from court, where poor
Cléonte
Behaved like a perfect fool, as is his wont.   10
Has he no friend to counsel him, I wonder,
And teach him less unerringly to blunder?
CÉLIMÈNE: It's true, the man's a most accomplished
dunce;
His gauche behavior charms the eye at once;
And every time one sees him, on my word,   15
His manner's grown a trifle more absurd.
ACASTE: Speaking of dunces, I've just now conversed
With old Damon, who's one of the very worst;
I stood a lifetime in the broiling sun
Before his dreary monologue was done.   20
CÉLIMÈNE: Oh, he's a wondrous talker, and has the
power
To tell you nothing hour after hour:
If, by mistake, he ever came to the point,
The shock would put his jawbone out of joint.
ÉLIANTE (*to Philinte*): The conversation takes its usual
turn,   25
And all our dear friends' ears will shortly burn.
CLITANDRE: Timante's a character, Madam.
CÉLIMÈNE: Isn't he, though?
A man of mystery from top to toe,
Who moves about in a romantic mist
On secret missions which do not exist.   30
His talk is full of eyebrows and grimaces;
How tired one gets of his momentous faces;
He's always whispering something confidential

Which turns out to be quite inconsequential;
35 Nothing's too slight for him to mystify;
He even whispers when he says "good-by."
ACASTE: Tell us about Géralde.
CÉLIMÈNE: That tiresome ass.
He mixes only with the titled class,
And fawns on dukes and princes, and is bored
40 With anyone who's not at least a lord.
The man's obsessed with rank, and his discourses
Are all of hounds and carriages and horses;
He uses Christian names with all the great,
And the word Milord, with him, is out of date.
45 CLITANDRE: He's very taken with Bélisc, I hear.
CÉLIMÈNE: She is the dreariest company, poor dear.
Whenever she comes to call, I grope about
To find some topic which will draw her out,
But, owing to her dry and faint replies,
50 The conversation wilts, and droops, and dies.
In vain one hopes to animate her face
By mentioning the ultimate commonplace;
But sun or shower, even hail or frost
Are matters she can instantly exhaust.
55 Meanwhile her visit, painful though it is,
Drags on and on through mute eternities,
And though you ask the time, and yawn, and
yawn,
She sits there like a stone and won't be gone.
ACASTE: Now for Adraste.
CÉLIMÈNE: Oh, that conceited elf
60 Has a gigantic passion for himself;
He rails against the court, and cannot bear it
That none will recognize his hidden merit;
All honors given to others give offense
To his imaginary excellence.
65 CLITANDRE: What about young Cléon? His house,
they say,
Is full of the best society, night and day.
CÉLIMÈNE: His cook has made him popular, not he:
It's Cléon's table that people come to see.
ÉLIANTE: He gives a splendid dinner, you must admit.
70 CÉLIMÈNE: But must he serve himself along with it?
For my taste, he's a most insipid dish
Whose presence sours the wine and spoils the fish.
PHILINTE: Damis, his uncle is admired no end.
What's your opinion, Madam?
CÉLIMÈNE: Why, he's my friend.
75 PHILINTE: He seems a decent fellow, and rather clever.
CÉLIMÈNE: He works too hard at cleverness,
however.
I hate to see him sweat and struggle so
To fill his conversation with *bons mots.*°
Since he's decided to become a wit
80 His taste's so pure that nothing pleases it;
He scolds at all the latest books and plays,
Thinking that wit must never stoop to praise,
That finding fault's a sign of intellect,

---

78. ***bons mots:*** Clever remarks, witticisms.

That all appreciation is abject,
And that by damning everything in sight   85
One shows oneself in a distinguished light.
He's scornful even of our conversations:
Their trivial nature sorely tries his patience;
He folds his arms, and stands above the battle,
And listens sadly to our childish prattle.   90
ACASTE: Wonderful, Madam! You've hit him off
precisely.
CLITANDRE: No one can sketch a character so nicely.
ALCESTE: How bravely, Sirs, you cut and thrust
at all
These absent fools, till one by one they fall:
But let one come in sight, and you'll at once   95
Embrace the man you lately called a dunce,
Telling him in a tone sincere and fervent
How proud you are to be his humble servant.
CLITANDRE: Why pick on us? *Madame's* been speaking,
Sir.
And you should quarrel, if you must, with her.   100
ALCESTE: No, no, by God, the fault is yours, because
You lead her on with laughter and applause,
And make her think that she's the more delightful
The more her talk is scandalous and spiteful.
Oh, she would stoop to malice far, far less   105
If no such claque approved her cleverness.
It's flatterers like you whose foolish praise
Nourishes all the vices of these days.
PHILINTE: But why protest when someone ridicules
Those you'd condemn, yourself, as knaves or
fools?   110
CÉLIMÈNE: Why, Sir? Because he loves to make a
fuss.
You don't expect him to agree with us,
When there's an opportunity to express
His heaven-sent spirit of contrariness?
What other people think, he can't abide;   115
Whatever they say, he's on the other side;
He lives in deadly terror of agreeing;
'Twould make him seem an ordinary being.
Indeed, he's so in love with contradiction,
He'll turn against his most profound conviction,   120
And with a furious eloquence deplore it,
If only someone else is speaking for it.
ALCESTE: Go on, dear lady, mock me as you please;
You have your audience in ecstasies.
PHILINTE: But what she says is true: you have a way 125
Of bridling at whatever people say;
Whether they praise or blame, your angry spirit
Is equally unsatisfied to hear it.
ALCESTE: Men, Sir, are always wrong, and that's the
reason
That righteous anger's never out of season;   130
All that I hear in all their conversation
Is flattering praise or reckless condemnation.
CÉLIMÈNE: But . . .
ALCESTE: No, no, Madam, I am forced to state
That you have pleasures which I deprecate,

135 And that these others, here, are much to blame
     For nourishing the faults which are your shame.
CLITANDRE: I shan't defend myself, Sir; but I vow
     I'd thought this lady faultless until now.
ACASTE: I see her charms and graces, which are many;
140 But as for faults, I've never noticed any.
ALCESTE: I see them, Sir; and rather than ignore them,
     I strenuously criticize her for them.
     The more one loves, the more one should object
     To every blemish, every least defect.
145 Were I this lady, I would soon get rid
     Of lovers who approved of all I did,
     And by their slack indulgence and applause
     Endorsed my follies and excused my flaws.
CÉLIMÈNE: If all hearts beat according to your
          measure,
150 The dawn of love would be the end of pleasure;
     And love would find its perfect consummation
     In ecstasies of rage and reprobation.
ÉLIANTE: Love, as a rule, affects men otherwise
     And lovers rarely love to criticize.
155 They see their lady as a charming blur,
     And find all things commendable in her.
     If she has any blemish, fault, or shame,
     They will redeem it by a pleasing name.
     The pale-faced lady's lily-white, perforce;
160 The swarthy one's a sweet brunette, of course;
     The spindly lady has a slender grace;
     The fat one has a most majestic pace;
     The plain one, with her dress in disarray
     They classify as *beauté négligée;*°
165 The hulking one's a goddess in their eyes,
     The dwarf, a concentrate of Paradise;
     The haughty lady has a noble mind;
     The mean one's witty, and the dull one's kind;
     The chatterbox has liveliness and verve,
170 The mute one has a virtuous reserve.
     So lovers manage, in their passion's cause,
     To love their ladies even for their flaws.
ALCESTE: But I still say . . .
CÉLIMÈNE: I think it would be nice
     To stroll around the gallery once or twice.
     What! You're not going, Sirs?
175 CLITANDRE AND ACASTE: No, Madam, no.
ALCESTE: You seem to be in terror lest they go.
     Do what you will, Sirs; leave, or linger on,
     But I shan't go till after you are gone.
ACASTE: I'm free to linger, unless I should perceive
180 *Madame* is tired, and wishes me to leave.
CLITANDRE: And as for me, I needn't go today
     Until the hour of the King's *coucher.*°
CÉLIMÈNE (*to Alceste*): You're joking, surely?
ALCESTE: Not in the
          least; we'll see
     Whether you'd rather part with them, or me.

164. *beauté négligée:* Slovenly beauty.   182. the King's *coucher:*
The King's bedtime, a ceremonial occasion.

Scene VI [*Alceste, Célimène, Éliante, Acaste,
Philinte, Clitandre, Basque.*]

BASQUE (*to Alceste*): Sir, there's a fellow here who bids
     me state
     That he must see you, and that it can't wait.
ALCESTE: Tell him that I have no such pressing affairs.
BASQUE: It's a long tailcoat that this fellow wears,
     With gold all over.
CÉLIMÈNE (*to Alceste*):   You'd best go down and see.
     Or — have him enter.   5

Scene VII [*Alceste, Célimène, Éliante, Acaste,
Philinte, Clitandre, Guard.*]

ALCESTE (*confronting the Guard*):   Well, what do you
          want with me?
     Come in. Sir.
GUARD: I've a word, Sir, for your ear.
ALCESTE: Speak it aloud, Sir; I shall strive to hear.
GUARD: The Marshals have instructed me to say
     You must report to them without delay.   5
ALCESTE: Who? Me, Sir?
GUARD: Yes, Sir; you.
ALCESTE: But what do they want?
PHILINTE (*to Alceste*): To scotch your silly quarrel with
     Oronte.
CÉLIMÈNE (*to Philinte*): What quarrel?
PHILINTE: Oronte and he have
          fallen out
     Over some verse he spoke his mind about;
     The Marshals wish to arbitrate the matter.   10
ALCESTE: Never shall I equivocate or flatter!
PHILINTE: You'd best obey their summons; come, let's
     go.
ALCESTE: How can they mend our quarrel, I'd like to
          know?
     Am I to make a cowardly retraction,
     And praise those jingles to his satisfaction?   15
     I'll not recant; I've judged that sonnet rightly.
     It's bad.
PHILINTE: But you might say so more politely . . .
ALCESTE: I'll not back down; his verses make me sick.
PHILINTE: If only you could be more politic!
     But come, let's go.
ALCESTE: I'll go, but I won't unsay   20
     A single word.
PHILINTE: Well, let's be on our way.
ALCESTE: Till I am ordered by my lord the King
     To praise that poem, I shall say the thing
     Is scandalous, by God, and that the poet
     Ought to be hanged for having the nerve to show it.   25

(*To Clitandre and Acaste, who are laughing.*)

     By heaven, Sirs, I really didn't know
     That I was being humorous.

Scene from the Williamstown Theatre Festival's 1973 production of *The Misanthrope*, directed by Austin Pendleton.

CÉLIMÈNE: Go, Sir, go;
  Settle your business.
ALCESTE: I shall, and when I'm through,
  I shall return to settle things with you.

ACT III • Scene 1 [Clitandre, Acaste.]

CLITANDRE: Dear Marquess, how contented you
      appear;
  All things delight you, nothing mars your cheer.
  Can you, in perfect honesty, declare
  That you've a right to be so debonair?
5 ACASTE: By Jove, when I survey myself, I find
  No cause whatever for distress of mind.
  I'm young and rich; I can in modesty
  Lay claim to an exalted pedigree;
  And owing to my name and my condition
10 I shall not want for honors and position.
  Then as to courage, that most precious trait,
  I seem to have it, as was proved of late
  Upon the field of honor, where my bearing,
  They say, was very cool and rather daring.
15 I've wit, of course; and taste in such perfection
  That I can judge without the least reflection,

And at the theater, which is my delight,
Can make or break a play on opening night,
And lead the crowd in hisses or bravos,
And generally be known as one who knows.   20
I'm clever, handsome, gracefully polite;
My waist is small, my teeth are strong and white;
As for my dress, the world's astonished eyes
Assure me that I bear away the prize.
I find myself in favor everywhere,   25
Honored by men, and worshiped by the fair;
And since these things are so, it seems to me
I'm justified in my complacency.
CLITANDRE: Well, if so many ladies hold you dear,
  Why do you press a hopeless courtship here?   30
ACASTE: Hopeless, you say? I'm not the sort of fool
  That likes his ladies difficult and cool.
  Men who are awkward, shy, and peasantish
  May pine for heartless beauties, if they wish,
  Grovel before them, bear their cruelties,   35
  Woo them with tears and sighs and bended knees,
  And hope by dogged faithfulness to gain
  What their poor merits never could obtain.
  For men like me, however, it makes no sense
  To love on trust, and foot the whole expense.   40
  Whatever any lady's merits be,

I think, thank God, that I'm as choice as she;
That if my heart is kind enough to burn
For her, she owes me something in return;
45   And that in any proper love affair
The partners must invest an equal share.
CLITANDRE: You think, then, that our hostess favors
    you?
ACASTE: I've reason to believe that that is true.
CLITANDRE: How did you come to such a mad
    conclusion?
50   You're blind, dear fellow. This is sheer delusion.
ACASTE: All right, then: I'm deluded and I'm blind.
CLITANDRE: Whatever put the notion in your mind?
ACASTE: Delusion.
CLITANDRE: What persuades you that you're right?
ACASTE: I'm blind.
CLITANDRE: But have you any proofs to cite?
ACASTE: I tell you I'm deluded.
55   CLITANDRE: Have you, then,
Received some secret pledge from Célimène?
ACASTE: Oh, no: she scorns me.
CLITANDRE: Tell me the truth, I beg.
ACASTE: She just can't bear me.
CLITANDRE: Ah, don't pull my leg.
Tell me what hope she's given you, I pray.
60   ACASTE: I'm hopeless, and it's you who win the day.
She hates me thoroughly, and I'm so vexed
I mean to hang myself on Tuesday next.
CLITANDRE: Dear Marquess, let us have an armistice
And make a treaty. What do you say to this?
65   If ever one of us can plainly prove
That Célimène encourages his love,
The other must abandon hope, and yield,
And leave him in possession of the field.
ACASTE: Now, there's a bargain that appeals to me;
70   With all my heart, dear Marquess, I agree.
But hush.

Scene II [*Célimène, Acaste, Clitandre.*]

CÉLIMÈNE: Still here?
CLITANDRE: 'Twas love that stayed our feet.
CÉLIMÈNE: I think I heard a carriage in the street.
Whose is it? D'you know?

Scene III [*Célimène, Acaste, Clitandre, Basque.*]

BASQUE: Arsinoé is here, *Madame*.
CÉLIMÈNE: Arsinoé, you say? Oh, dear.
BASQUE: Éliante is entertaining her below.
CÉLIMÈNE: What brings the creature here, I'd like to
    know?
5   ACASTE: They say she's dreadfully prudish, but in fact
I think her piety . . .
CÉLIMÈNE: It's all an act.
At heart she's worldly, and her poor success
In snaring men explains her prudishness.

It breaks her heart to see the beaux and gallants
Engrossed by other women's charms and talents,   10
And so she's always in a jealous rage
Against the faulty standards of the age.
She lets the world believe that she's a prude
To justify her loveless solitude,
And strives to put a brand of moral shame   15
On all the graces that she cannot claim.
But still she'd love a lover; and Alceste
Appears to be the one she'd love the best.
His visits here are poison to her pride;
She seems to think I've lured him from her side   20
And everywhere, at court or in the town,
The spiteful, envious woman runs me down.
In short, she's just as stupid as can be,
Vicious and arrogant in the last degree,
And . . .   25

Scene IV [*Arsinoé, Célimène, Clitandre, Acaste.*]

CÉLIMÈNE: Ah! What happy chance has brought you
    here?
I've thought about you ever so much, my dear.
ARSINOÉ: I've come to tell you something you should
    know.
CÉLIMÈNE: How good of you to think of doing so!

(*Clitandre and Acaste go out, laughing.*)

Scene V [*Arsinoé, Célimène.*]

ARSINOÉ: It's just as well those gentlemen didn't tarry.
CÉLIMÈNE: Shall we sit down?
ARSINOÉ: That won't be necessary.
Madam, the flame of friendship ought to burn
Brightest in matters of the most concern,
And as there's nothing which concerns us more   5
Than honor, I have hastened to your door
To bring you, as your friend, some information
About the status of your reputation.
I visited, last night, some virtuous folk,
And, quite by chance, it was of you they spoke;   10
There was, I fear, no tendency to praise
Your light behavior and your dashing ways.
The quantity of gentlemen you see
And your by now notorious coquetry
Were both so vehemently criticized   15
By everyone, that I was much surprised.
Of course, I needn't tell you where I stood;
I came to your defense as best I could,
Assured them you were harmless, and declared
Your soul was absolutely unimpaired.   20
But there are some things, you must realize,
One can't excuse, however hard one tries,
And I was forced at last into conceding
That your behavior, Madam, is misleading,
That it makes a bad impression, giving rise   25

To ugly gossip and obscene surmise,
And that if you were more *overtly* good,
You wouldn't be so much misunderstood.
Not that I think you've been unchaste — no! no!
30   The saints preserve me from a thought so low!
But mere good conscience never did suffice:
One must avoid the outward show of vice.
Madam, you're too intelligent, I'm sure,
To think my motives anything but pure
35   In offering you this counsel — which I do
Out of a zealous interest in you.
    CÉLIMÈNE: Madam, I haven't taken you amiss;
I'm very much obliged to you for this;
And I'll at once discharge the obligation
40   By telling you about *your* reputation.
You've been so friendly as to let me know
What certain people say of me, and so
I mean to follow your benign example
By offering you a somewhat similar sample.
45   The other day, I went to an affair
And found some most distinguished people there
Discussing piety, both false and true.
The conversation soon came round to you.
Alas! Your prudery and bustling zeal
50   Appeared to have a very slight appeal.
Your affectation of a grave demeanor,
Your endless talk of virtue and of honor,
The aptitude of your suspicious mind
For finding sin where there is none to find,
55   Your towering self-esteem, that pitying face
With which you contemplate the human race,
Your sermonizings and your sharp aspersions
On people's pure and innocent diversions —
All these were mentioned, Madam, and, in fact,
60   Were roundly and concertedly attacked.
"What good," they said, "are all these outward
        shows,
When everything belies her pious pose?
She prays incessantly, but then, they say,
She beats her maids and cheats them of their pay;
65   She shows her zeal in every holy place,
But still she's vain enough to paint her face;
She holds that naked statues are immoral,
But with a naked *man* she'd have no quarrel."
Of course, I said to everybody there
70   That they were being viciously unfair;
But still they were disposed to criticize you,
And all agreed that someone should advise you
To leave the morals of the world alone,
And worry rather more about your own.
They felt that one's self-knowledge should be
75   great
Before one thinks of setting others straight;
That one should learn the art of living well
Before one threatens other men with hell,
And that the Church is best equipped, no doubt,
80   To guide our souls and root our vices out.
Madam, you're too intelligent, I'm sure,
To think my motives anything but pure

In offering you this counsel — which I do
Out of a zealous interest in you.
ARSINOÉ: I dared not hope for gratitude, but I   85
Did not expect so acid a reply;
I judge, since you've been so extremely tart,
That my good counsel pierced you to the heart.
CÉLIMÈNE: Far from it, Madam. Indeed, it seems to me
We ought to trade advice more frequently.   90
One's vision of oneself is so defective
That it would be an excellent corrective.
If you are willing, Madam, let's arrange
Shortly to have another frank exchange
In which we'll tell each other, *entre nous,*°   95
What you've heard tell of me, and I of you.
ARSINOÉ: Oh, people never censure you, my dear;
It's me they criticize. Or so I hear.
CÉLIMÈNE: Madam, I think we either blame or praise
According to our taste and length of days.   100
There is a time of life for coquetry,
And there's a season, too, for prudery.
When all one's charms are gone, it is, I'm sure,
Good strategy to be devout and pure:
It makes one seem a little less forsaken.   105
Some day, perhaps, I'll take the road you've taken:
Time brings all things. But I have time aplenty,
And see no cause to be a prude at twenty.
ARSINOÉ: You give your age in such a gloating tone
That one would think I was an ancient crone;   110
We're not so far apart, in sober truth,
That you can mock me with a boast of youth!
Madam, you baffle me. I wish I knew
What moves you to provoke me as you do.
CÉLIMÈNE: For my part, Madam, I should like to know   115
Why you abuse me everywhere you go.
Is it my fault, dear lady, that your hand
Is not, alas, in very great demand?
If men admire me, if they pay me court
And daily make me offers of the sort   120
You'd dearly love to have them make to you,
How can I help it? What would you have me do?
If what you want is lovers, please feel free
To take as many as you can from me.
ARSINOÉ: Oh, come. D'you think the world is losing
        sleep   125
Over the flock of lovers which you keep,
Or that we find it difficult to guess
What price you pay for their devotedness?
Surely you don't expect us to suppose
Mere merit could attract so many beaux?   130
It's not your virtue that they're dazzled by;
Nor is it virtuous love for which they sigh.
You're fooling no one, Madam; the world's not
        blind;
There's many a lady heaven has designed
To call men's noblest, tenderest feelings out,   135
Who has no lovers dogging her about;
From which it's plain that lovers nowadays

---

95. *entre nous:* Between ourselves.

Must be acquired in bold and shameless ways,
And only pay one court for such reward
140   As modesty and virtue can't afford.
Then don't be quite so puffed up, if you please,
About your tawdry little victories;
Try, if you can, to be a shade less vain,
And treat the world with somewhat less disdain.
145   If one were envious of your amours,
One soon could have a following like yours;
Lovers are no great trouble to collect
If one prefers them to one's self-respect.
CÉLIMÈNE: Collect them then, my dear; I'd love to see
150   You demonstrate that charming theory;
Who knows, you might . . .
ARSINOÉ: Now, Madam, that will do;
It's time to end this trying interview.
My coach is late in coming to your door,
Or I'd have taken leave of you before.
CÉLIMÈNE: Oh, please don't feel that you must rush
155   away;
I'd be delighted, Madam, if you'd stay.
However, lest my conversation bore you,
Let me provide some better company for you;
This gentleman, who comes most apropos,
160   Will please you more than I could do, I know.

Scene VI [*Alceste, Célimène, Arsinoé.*]

CÉLIMÈNE: Alceste, I have a little note to write
Which simply must go out before tonight;
Please entertain *Madame*; I'm sure that she
Will overlook my incivility.

Scene VII [*Alceste, Arsinoé.*]

ARSINOÉ: Well, Sir, our hostess graciously contrives
For us to chat until my coach arrives;
And I shall be forever in her debt
For granting me this little *tête-à-tête.*°
5   We women very rightly give our hearts
To men of noble character and parts,
And your especial merits, dear Alceste
Have roused the deepest sympathy in my breast.
Oh, how I wish they had sufficient sense
10   At court, to recognize your excellence!
They wrong you greatly, Sir. How it must hurt you
Never to be rewarded for your virtue!
ALCESTE: Why, Madam, what cause have I to feel
        aggrieved?
What great and brilliant thing have I achieved?
15   What service have I rendered to the King
That I should look to him for anything?
ARSINOÉ: Not everyone who's honored by the State
Has done great services. A man must wait

4. *tête-à-tête*: French for "head-to-head," in private conversation.

Till time and fortune offer him the chance.
Your merit, Sir, is obvious at a glance,   20
And . . .
ALCESTE: Ah, forget my merit; I am not neglected.
The court, I think, can hardly be expected
To mine men's souls for merit, and unearth
Our hidden virtues and our secret worth.
ARSINOÉ: *Some* virtues, though, are far too bright to
        hide;   25
Yours are acknowledged, Sir, on every side.
Indeed, I've heard you warmly praised of late
By persons of considerable weight.
ALCESTE: This fawning age has praise for everyone,
And all distinctions, Madam, are undone.   30
All things have equal honor nowadays,
And no one should be gratified by praise.
To be admired, one only need exist,
And every lackey's on the honors list.
ARSINOÉ: I only wish, Sir, that you had your eye   35
On some position at court, however high;
You'd only have to hint at such a notion
For me to set the proper wheels in motion
I've certain friendships I'd be glad to use
To get you any office you might choose.   40
ALCESTE: Madam, I fear that any such ambition
Is wholly foreign to my disposition.
The soul God gave me isn't of the sort
That prospers in the weather of a court.
It's all too obvious that I don't possess   45
The virtues necessary for success.
My one great talent is for speaking plain;
I've never learned to flatter or to feign;
And anyone so stupidly sincere
Had best not seek a courtier's career.   50
Outside the court, I know, one must dispense
With honors, privilege, and influence;
But still one gains the right, foregoing these,
Not to be tortured by the wish to please.
One needn't live in dread of snubs and slights,   55
Nor praise the verse that every idiot writes,
Nor humor silly Marquesses, nor bestow
Politic sighs on Madam So-and-So.
ARSINOÉ: Forget the court, then; let the matter rest.
But I've another cause to be distressed   60
About your present situation, Sir.
It's to your love affair that I refer.
She whom you love, and who pretends to love you,
Is, I regret to say, unworthy of you.
ALCESTE: Why, Madam? Can you seriously intend   65
To make so grave a charge against your friend?
ARSINOÉ: Alas, I must. I've stood aside too long
And let that lady do you grievous wrong;
But now my debt to conscience shall be paid:
I tell you that your love has been betrayed.   70
ALCESTE: I thank you, Madam; you're extremely kind.
Such words are soothing to a lover's mind.
ARSINOÉ: Yes, though she *is* my friend, I say again
You're very much too good for Célimène.
She's wantonly misled you from the start.   75

ALCESTE: You may be right; who knows another's heart?
   But ask yourself if it's the part of charity
   To shake my soul with doubts of her sincerity.
ARSINOÉ: Well, if you'd rather be a dupe than doubt
      her,
80   That's your affair. I'll say no more about her.
ALCESTE: Madam, you know that doubt and vague
         suspicion
   Are painful to a man in my position;
   It's most unkind to worry me this way
   Unless you've some real proof of what you say.
85 ARSINOÉ: Sir, say no more: all doubts shall be removed,
   And all that I've been saying shall be proved.
   You've only to escort me home, and there
   We'll look into the heart of this affair.
   I've ocular evidence which will persuade you
90   Beyond a doubt, that Célimène's betrayed you.
   Then, if you're saddened by that revelation,
   Perhaps I can provide some consolation.

ACT IV • Scene I [*Éliante, Philinte.*]

PHILINTE: Madam, he acted like a stubborn child
   I thought they never would be reconciled;
   In vain we reasoned, threatened, and appealed;
   He stood his ground and simply would not yield.
5   The Marshals, I feel sure have never heard
   An argument so splendidly absurd.
   "No, gentlemen," said he, "I'll not retract.
   His verse is bad: extremely bad, in fact.
   Surely it does the man no harm to know it.
10   Does it disgrace him, not to be a poet?
   A gentleman may be respected still,
   Whether he writes a sonnet well or ill.
   That I dislike his verse should not offend him;
   In all that touches honor, I commend him;
15   He's noble, brave, and virtuous — but I fear
   He can't in truth be called a sonneteer.
   I'll gladly praise his wardrobe; I'll endorse
   His dancing, or the way he sits a horse;
   But, gentlemen, I cannot praise his rhyme.
20   In fact, it ought to be a capital crime
   For anyone so sadly unendowed
   To write a sonnet, and read the thing aloud."
   At length he fell into a gentler mood
   And, striking a concessive attitude,
25   He paid Oronte the following courtesies:
   "Sir, I regret that I'm so hard to please,
   And I'm profoundly sorry that your lyric
   Failed to provoke me to a panegyric."°
   After these curious words, the two embraced
30   And then the hearing was adjourned — in haste.
ÉLIANTE: His conduct has been very singular lately;
   Still, I confess that I respect him greatly.
   The honesty in which he takes such pride
   Has — to my mind — its noble, heroic side.

28. panegyric: Elaborate praise.

In this false age, such candor seems outrageous;   35
   But I could wish that it were more contagious.
PHILINTE: What most intrigues me in our friend Alceste
   Is the grand passion that rages in his breast.
   The sullen humors he's compounded of
   Should not, I think, dispose his heart to love;   40
   But since they do, it puzzles me still more
   That he should choose your cousin to adore.
ÉLIANTE: It does, indeed, belie the theory
   That love is born of gentle sympathy,
   And that the tender passion must be based   45
   On sweet accords of temper and of taste.
PHILINTE: Does she return his love, do you suppose?
ÉLIANTE: Ah, that's a difficult question, Sir. Who
      knows?
   How can we judge the truth of her devotion?
   Her heart's a stranger to its own emotion.   50
   Sometimes it thinks it loves, when no love's there;
   At other times it loves quite unaware.
PHILINTE: I rather think Alceste is in for more
   Distress and sorrow than he's bargained for;
   Were he of my mind, Madam, his affection   55
   Would turn in quite a different direction,
   And we would see him more responsive to
   The kind regard which he receives from you.
ÉLIANTE: Sir, I believe in frankness, and I'm inclined
   In matters of the heart, to speak my mind.   60
   I don't oppose his love for her; indeed,
   I hope with all my heart that he'll succeed,
   And were it in my power, I'd rejoice
   In giving him the lady of his choice.
   But if, as happens frequently enough   65
   In love affairs, he meets with a rebuff —
   If Célimène should grant some rival's suit —
   I'd gladly play the role of substitute;
   Nor would his tender speeches please me less
   Because they'd once been made without success.   70
PHILINTE: Well, Madam, as for me, I don't oppose
   Your hopes in this affair; and heaven knows
   That in my conversations with the man
   I plead your cause as often as I can.
   But if those two should marry, and so remove   75
   All chance that he will offer you his love,
   Then I'll declare my own, and hope to see
   Your gracious favor pass from him to me.
   In short, should you be cheated of Alceste,
   I'd be most happy to be second best.   80
ÉLIANTE: Philinte, you're teasing.
PHILINTE: Ah, Madam, never fear;
   No words of mine were ever so sincere
   And I shall live in fretful expectation
   Till I can make a fuller declaration.

Scene II [*Alceste, Éliante, Philinte.*]

ALCESTE: Avenge me, Madam! I must have satisfaction,
   Or this great wrong will drive me to distraction!
ÉLIANTE: Why, what's the matter? What's upset you so?

ALCESTE: Madam, I've had a mortal, mortal blow.
5   If Chaos repossessed the universe,
       I swear I'd not be shaken any worse.
       I'm ruined. . . . I can say no more. . . . My soul . . .
ÉLIANTE: Do try, Sir, to regain your self-control.
ALCESTE: Just heaven! Why were so much beauty and
         grace
10   Bestowed on one so vicious and so base?
ÉLIANTE: Once more, Sir, tell us
ALCESTE: My world has gone to wrack:
       I'm — I'm betrayed; she's stabbed me in the back:
       Yes, Célimène (who would have thought it of her?)
       Is false to me, and has another lover.
ÉLIANTE: Are you quite certain? Can you prove these
15   things?
PHILINTE: Lovers are prey to wild imaginings
         And jealous fancies. No doubt there's some
         mistake. . . .
ALCESTE: Mind your own business, Sir, for heaven's
         sake.
         (To Éliante.) Madam, I have the proof that you
         demand
20   Here in my pocket, penned by her own hand.
       Yes, all the shameful evidence one could want
       Lies in this letter written to Oronte —
       Oronte! whom I felt sure she couldn't love,
       And hardly bothered to be jealous of.
25 PHILINTE: Still, in a letter, appearances may deceive;
         This may not be so bad as you believe.
ALCESTE: Once more I beg you, Sir, to let me be;
       Tend to your own affairs; leave mine to me.
ÉLIANTE: Compose yourself; this anguish that you
         feel . . .
30 ALCESTE: Is something, Madam, you alone can heal.
       My outraged heart, beside itself with grief,
       Appeals to you for comfort and relief.
       Avenge me on your cousin, whose unjust
       And faithless nature has deceived my trust;
35   Avenge a crime your pure soul must detest.
ÉLIANTE: But how, Sir?
ALCESTE: Madam, this heart within my breast
       Is yours; pray take it; redeem my heart from her,
       And so avenge me on my torturer.
       Let her be punished by the fond emotion,
40   The ardent love, the bottomless devotion,
       The faithful worship which this heart of mine
       Will offer up to yours as to a shrine.
ÉLIANTE: You have my sympathy, Sir, in all you suffer;
         Nor do I scorn the noble heart you offer;
45   But I suspect you'll soon be mollified
       And this desire for vengeance will subside.
       When some belovèd hand has done us wrong
       We thirst for retribution — but not for long;
       However dark the deed that she's committed,
50   A lovely culprit's very soon acquitted.
       Nothing's so stormy as an injured lover,
       And yet no storm so quickly passes over.
ALCESTE: No, Madam, no — this is no lovers' spat;
       I'll not forgive her, it's gone too far for that;

My mind's made up; I'll kill myself before   55
I waste my hopes upon her any more.
Ah, here she is. My wrath intensifies.
I shall confront her with her tricks and lies,
And crush her utterly, and bring you then
A heart no longer slave to Célimène.   60

Scene III [*Célimène, Alceste.*]

ALCESTE (*aside*): Sweet heaven, help me to control my
         passion.
CÉLIMÈNE (*aside*): Oh, Lord. (*To Alceste.*) Why stand
         there staring in that fashion?
       And what d'you mean by those dramatic sighs,
       And that malignant glitter in your eyes?
ALCESTE: I mean that sins which cause the blood to
         freeze   5
       Look innocent beside your treacheries;
       That nothing Hell's or Heaven's wrath could do
       Ever produced so bad a thing as you.
CÉLIMÈNE: Your compliments were always sweet and
         pretty.
ALCESTE: Madam, it's not the moment to be witty.   10
       No, blush and hang your head; you've ample
         reason,
       Since I've the fullest evidence of your treason.
       Ah, this is what my sad heart prophesied;
       Now all my anxious fears are verified;
       My dark suspicion and my gloomy doubt   15
       Divined the truth, and now the truth is out.
       For all your trickery, I was not deceived;
       It was my bitter stars that I believed.
       But don't imagine that you'll go scot-free;
       You shan't misuse me with impunity.   20
       I know that love's irrational and blind;
       I know the heart's not subject to the mind,
       And can't be reasoned into beating faster;
       I know each soul is free to choose its master;
       Therefore had you but spoken from the heart,   25
       Rejecting my attention from the start,
       I'd have no grievance, or at any rate
       I could complain of nothing but my fate.
       Ah, but so falsely to encourage me —
       That was a treason and a treachery   30
       For which you cannot suffer too severely,
       And you shall pay for that behavior dearly.
       Yes, now I have no pity, not a shred;
       My temper's out of hand, I've lost my head
       Shocked by the knowledge of your double-
         dealings,   35
       My reason can't restrain my savage feelings;
       A righteous wrath deprives me of my senses,
       And I won't answer for the consequences.
CÉLIMÈNE: What does this outburst mean? Will you
         please explain?
       Have you, by any chance, gone quite insane?   40
ALCESTE: Yes, yes, I went insane the day I fell
       A victim to your black and fatal spell,

Thinking to meet with some sincerity
Among the treacherous charms that beckoned me.
CÉLIMÈNE: Pooh. Of what treachery can you
45   complain?
ALCESTE: How sly you are, how cleverly you feign!
    But you'll not victimize me any more.
    Look: here's a document you've seen before.
    This evidence, which I acquired today,
50   Leaves you, I think, without a thing to say.
CÉLIMÈNE: Is this what sent you into such a fit?
ALCESTE: You should be blushing at the sight of it.
CÉLIMÈNE: Ought I to blush? I truly don't see why.
ALCESTE: Ah, now you're being bold as well as sly;
55   Since there's no signature, perhaps you'll claim . . .
CÉLIMÈNE: I wrote it, whether or not it bears my name.
ALCESTE: And you can view with equanimity
    his proof of your disloyalty to me!
CÉLIMÈNE: Oh, don't be so outrageous and extreme.
60 ALCESTE: You take this matter lightly, it would seem.
    Was it no wrong to me, no shame to you,
    That you should send Oronte this *billet-doux*?°
CÉLIMÈNE: Oronte! Who said it was for him?
ALCESTE: Why, those
    Who brought me this example of your prose.
65   But what's the difference? If you wrote the letter
    To someone else, it pleases me no better.
    My grievance and your guilt remain the same.
CÉLIMÈNE: But need you rage, and need I blush for
        shame,
    If this was written to a *woman* friend?
70 ALCESTE: Ah! Most ingenious. I'm impressed no end;
    And after that incredible evasion
    Your guilt is clear. I need no more persuasion.
    How dare you try so clumsy a deception?
    D'you think I'm wholly wanting in perception?
75   Come, come, let's see how brazenly you'll try
    To bolster up so palpable a lie:
    Kindly construe this ardent closing section
    As nothing more than sisterly affection!
    Here, let me read it. Tell me, if you dare to,
    That this is for a woman . . .
80 CÉLIMÈNE: I don't dare to.
    What right have you to badger and berate me,
    And so high-handedly interrogate me?
ALCESTE: Now, don't be angry; all I ask of you
    Is that you justify a phrase or two . . .
85 CÉLIMÈNE: No, I shall not. I utterly refuse,
    And you may take those phrases as you choose.
ALCESTE: Just show me how this letter could be meant
    For a woman's eyes, and I shall be content.
CÉLIMÈNE: No, no, it's for Oronte; you're perfectly
        right.
90   I welcome his attentions with delight,
    I prize his character and his intellect
    And everything is just as you suspect.
    Come, do your worst now; give your rage free rein;
    But kindly cease to bicker and complain.

62. *billet-doux:* Love letter.

ALCESTE (*aside*): Good God! Could anything be more
        inhuman?   95
    Was ever a heart so mangled by a woman?
    When I complain of how she has betrayed me,
    She bridles, and commences to upbraid me!
    She tries my tortured patience to the limit;
    She won't deny her guilt; she glories in it!   100
    And yet my heart's too faint and cowardly
    To break these chains of passion, and be free,
    To scorn her as it should, and rise above
    This unrewarded, mad, and bitter love.
    (*To Célimène.*) Ah, traitress, in how confident a
        fashion   105
    You take advantage of my helpless passion,
    And use my weakness for your faithless charms
    To make me once again throw down my arms!
    But do at least deny this black transgression;
    Take back that mocking and perverse confession;   110
    Defend this letter and your innocence,
    And I, poor fool, will aid in your defense.
    Pretend, pretend, that you are just and true,
    And I shall make myself believe in you.
CÉLIMÈNE: Oh, stop it. Don't be such a jealous dunce,   115
    Or I shall leave off loving you at once.
    Just why should I *pretend*? What could impel me
    To stoop so low as that? And kindly tell me
    Why, if I loved another, I shouldn't merely
    Inform you of it, simply and sincerely!   120
    I've told you where you stand, and that admission
    Should altogether clear me of suspicion;
    After so generous a guarantee
    What right have you to harbor doubts of me?
    Since women are (from natural reticence)   125
    Reluctant to declare their sentiments,
    And since the honor of our sex requires
    That we conceal our amorous desires,
    Ought any man for whom such laws are broken
    To question what the oracle has spoken?   130
    Should he not rather feel an obligation
    To trust that most obliging declaration?
    Enough, now. Your suspicions quite disgust me;
    Why should I love a man who doesn't trust me?
    I cannot understand why I continue,   135
    Fool that I am, to take an interest in you.
    I ought to choose a man less prone to doubt,
    And give you something to be vexed about.
ALCESTE: Ah, what a poor enchanted fool I am;
    These gentle words, no doubt, were all a sham,   140
    But destiny requires me to entrust
    My happiness to you, and so I must.
    I'll love you to the bitter end, and see
    How false and treacherous you dare to be.
CÉLIMÈNE: No, you don't really love me as you ought.   145
ALCESTE: I love you more than can be said or thought;
    Indeed, I wish you were in such distress
    That I might show my deep devotedness.
    Yes, I could wish that you were wretchedly poor,
    Unloved, uncherished, utterly obscure;   150
    That fate had set you down upon the earth

Without possessions, rank, or gentle birth;
Then, by the offer of my heart, I might
Repair the great injustice of your plight;
155   I'd raise you from the dust, and proudly prove
The purity and vastness of my love.
CÉLIMÈNE: This is a strange benevolence indeed!
God grant that I may never be in need. . . .
Ah, here's Monsieur Dubois in quaint disguise.

Scene IV [*Célimène, Alceste, Dubois.*]

ALCESTE: Well, why this costume? Why those frightened
eyes?
What ails you?
DUBOIS: Well, Sir, things are most mysterious.
ALCESTE: What do you mean?
DUBOIS: I fear they're very serious.
ALCESTE: What?
DUBOIS: Shall I speak more loudly?
ALCESTE: Yes; speak out.
DUBOIS: Isn't there someone here, Sir?
5   ALCESTE: Speak, you lout!
Stop wasting time.
DUBOIS: Sir, we must slip away.
ALCESTE: How's that?
DUBOIS: We must decamp without delay.
ALCESTE: Explain yourself.
DUBOIS: I tell you we must fly.
ALCESTE: What for?
DUBOIS: We mustn't pause to say good-by.
ALCESTE: Now what d'you mean by all of this, you
10   clown?
DUBOIS: I mean, Sir, that we've got to leave this town.
ALCESTE: I'll tear you limb from limb and joint from
joint
If you don't come more quickly to the point.
DUBOIS: Well, Sir, today a man in a black suit,
15   Who wore a black and ugly scowl to boot,
Left us a document scrawled in such a hand
As even Satan couldn't understand.
It bears upon your lawsuit, I don't doubt;
But all hell's devils couldn't make it out.
20   ALCESTE: Well, well, go on. What then? I fail to see
How this event obliges us to flee.
DUBOIS: Well, Sir, an hour later, hardly more,
A gentleman who's often called before
Came looking for you in an anxious way.
25   Not finding you, he asked me to convey
(Knowing I could be trusted with the same)
The following message. . . . Now, what *was* his
name?
ALCESTE: Forget his name, you idiot. What did he say?
DUBOIS: Well, it was one of your friends, Sir, anyway.
30   He warned you to begone, and he suggested
That if you stay, you may well be arrested.
ALCESTE: What? Nothing more specific? Think, man,
think!
DUBOIS: No, Sir. He had me bring him pen and ink,

And dashed you off a letter which, I'm sure,
Will render things distinctly less obscure.   35
ALCESTE: Well — let me have it!
CÉLIMÈNE: What *is* this all about?
ALCESTE: God knows; but I have hopes of finding out.
How long am I to wait, you blitherer?
DUBOIS: (*after a protracted search for the letter*):
I must have left it on your table, Sir.
ALCESTE: I ought to . . .
CÉLIMÈNE: No, no, keep your self-control;   40
Go find out what's behind his rigmarole.
ALCESTE: It seems that fate, no matter what I do,
Has sworn that I may not converse with you;
But, Madam, pray permit your faithful lover
To try once more before the day is over.   45

ACT V • *Scene I* [*Alceste, Philinte.*]

ALCESTE: No, it's too much. My mind's made up, I tell
you.
PHILINTE: Why should this blow, however hard,
compel you . . .
ALCESTE: No, no, don't waste your breath in argument;
Nothing you say will alter my intent;
This age is vile, and I've made up my mind   5
To have no further commerce with mankind.
Did not truth, honor, decency, and the laws
Oppose my enemy and approve my cause?
My claims were justified in all men's sight;
I put my trust in equity and right;   10
Yet, to my horror and the world's disgrace,
Justice is mocked, and I have lost my case!
A scoundrel whose dishonesty is notorious
Emerges from another lie victorious!
Honor and right condone his brazen fraud,   15
While rectitude and decency applaud!
Before his smirking face, the truth stands charmed,
And virtue conquered, and the law disarmed!
His crime is sanctioned by a court decree!
And not content with what he's done to me,   20
The dog now seeks to ruin me by stating
That I composed a book now circulating,
A book so wholly criminal and vicious
That even to speak its title is seditious!
Meanwhile Oronte, my rival, lends his credit   25
To the same libelous tale, and helps to spread it!
Oronte! a man of honor and of rank,
With whom I've been entirely fair and frank;
Who sought me out and forced me, willy-nilly,
To judge some verse I found extremely silly;   30
And who, because I properly refused
To flatter him, or see the truth abused,
Abets my enemy in a rotten slander!
There's the reward of honesty and candor!
The man will hate me to the end of time   35
For failing to commend his wretched rhyme!
And not this man alone, but all humanity
Do what they do from interest and vanity;

40 They prate of honor, truth, and righteousness,
   But lie, betray, and swindle nonetheless.
   Come then: man's villainy is too much to bear;
   Let's leave this jungle and this jackal's lair.
   Yes! treacherous and savage race of men,
   You shall not look upon my face again.

45 PHILINTE: Oh, don't rush into exile prematurely;
   Things aren't as dreadful as you make them, surely.
   It's rather obvious, since you're still at large,
   That people don't believe your enemy's charge.
   Indeed, his tale's so patently untrue

50 That it may do more harm to him than you.

   ALCESTE: Nothing could do that scoundrel any harm:
   His frank corruption is his greatest charm,
   And, far from hurting him, a further shame
   Would only serve to magnify his name.

55 PHILINTE: In any case, his bald prevarication
   Has done no injury to your reputation,
   And you may feel secure in that regard.
   As for your lawsuit, it should not be hard
   To have the case reopened, and contest
   This judgment . . .

60 ALCESTE: No, no, let the verdict rest.
   Whatever cruel penalty it may bring,
   I wouldn't have it changed for anything.
   It shows the times' injustice with such clarity
   That I shall pass it down to our posterity

65 As a great proof and signal demonstration
   Of the black wickedness of this generation.
   It may cost twenty thousand francs; but I
   Shall pay their twenty thousand, and gain thereby
   The right to storm and rage at human evil,

70 And send the race of mankind to the devil.

   PHILINTE: Listen to me . . .

   ALCESTE: Why? What can you possibly say?
   Don't argue, Sir; your labor's thrown away.
   Do you propose to offer lame excuses
   For men's behavior and the times' abuses?

75 PHILINTE: No, all you say I'll readily concede:
   This is a low, conniving age, indeed;
   Nothing but trickery prospers nowadays,
   And people ought to mend their shabby ways.
   Yes, man's a beastly creature; but must we then

80 Abandon the society of men?
   Here in the world, each human frailty
   Provides occasion for philosophy,
   And that is virtue's noblest exercise;
   If honesty shone forth from all men's eyes,

85 If every heart were frank and kind and just,
   What could our virtues do but gather dust
   (Since their employment is to help us bear
   The villainies of men without despair)?
   A heart well-armed with virtue can endure . . .

90 ALCESTE: Sir, you're a matchless reasoner, to be sure;
   Your words are fine and full of cogency;
   But don't waste time and eloquence on me.
   My reason bids me go, for my own good.
   My tongue won't lie and flatter as it should;

95 God knows what frankness it might next commit,
   And what I'd suffer on account of it.
   Pray let me wait for Célimène's return
   In peace and quiet. I shall shortly learn,
   By her response to what I have in view,
   Whether her love for me is feigned or true.   100

   PHILINTE: Till then, let's visit Éliante upstairs.

   ALCESTE: No, I am too weighed down with somber
   cares.
   Go to her, do; and leave me with my gloom
   Here in the darkened corner of this room.

   PHILINTE: Why, that's no sort of company, my friend; 105
   I'll see if Éliante will not descend.

Scene II [*Célimène, Oronte, Alceste.*]

ORONTE: Yes, Madam, if you wish me to remain
   Your true and ardent lover, you must deign
   To give me some more positive assurance.
   All this suspense is quite beyond endurance.
   If your heart shares the sweet desires of mine,   5
   Show me as much by some convincing sign;
   And here's the sign I urgently suggest:
   That you no longer tolerate Alceste,
   But sacrifice him to my love, and sever
   All your relations with the man forever.   10

   CÉLIMÈNE: Why do you suddenly dislike him so?
   You praised him to the skies not long ago.

   ORONTE: Madam, that's not the point. I'm here to find
   Which way your tender feelings are inclined.
   Choose, if you please, between Alceste and me,   15
   And I shall stay or go accordingly.

   ALCESTE (*emerging from the corner*): Yes, Madam,
   choose; this gentleman's demand
   Is wholly just, and I support his stand.
   I too am true and ardent; I too am here
   To ask you that you make your feelings clear.   20
   No more delays, now; no equivocation;
   The time has come to make your declaration.

   ORONTE: Sir, I've no wish in any way to be
   An obstacle to your felicity.

   ALCESTE: Sir, I've no wish to share her heart with you; 25
   That may sound jealous, but at least it's true.

   ORONTE: If, weighing us, she leans in your
   direction . . .

   ALCESTE: If she regards you with the least affection . . .

   ORONTE: I swear I'll yield her to you there and then.

   ALCESTE: I swear I'll never see her face again.   30

   ORONTE: Now, Madam, tell us what we've come to
   hear.

   ALCESTE: Madam, speak openly and have no fear.

   ORONTE: Just say which one is to remain your lover.

   ALCESTE: Just name one name, and it will all be over.

   ORONTE: What! Is it possible that you're undecided?   35

   ALCESTE: What! Can your feelings possibly be divided?

   CÉLIMÈNE: Enough: this inquisition's gone too far:
   How utterly unreasonable you are!
   Not that I couldn't make the choice with ease,
   My heart has no conflicting sympathies   40

I know full well which one of you I favor,
And you'd not see me hesitate or waver.
But how can you expect me to reveal
So cruelly and bluntly what I feel?
45 I think it altogether too unpleasant
To choose between two men when both are present;
One's heart has means more subtle and more kind
Of letting its affections be divined,
Nor need one be uncharitably plain
50 To let a lover know he loves in vain.
ORONTE: No, no, speak plainly; I for one can stand it.
I beg you to be frank.
ALCESTE: And I demand it.
The simple truth is what I wish to know,
And there's no need for softening the blow.
55 You've made an art of pleasing everyone,
But now your days of coquetry are done:
You have no choice now, Madam, but to choose,
For I'll know what to think if you refuse;
I'll take your silence for a clear admission
60 That I'm entitled to my worst suspicion.
ORONTE: I thank you for this ultimatum, Sir.
And I may say I heartily concur.
CÉLIMÈNE: Really, this foolishness is very wearing:
Must you be so unjust and overbearing?
65 Haven't I told you why I must demur?
Ah, here's Éliante; I'll put the case to her.

Scene III [*Éliante, Philinte, Célimène, Oronte,
Alceste.*]

CÉLIMÈNE: Cousin, I'm being persecuted here
By these two persons, who, it would appear,
Will not be satisfied till I confess
Which one I love the more, and which the less,
5 And tell the latter to his face that he
Is henceforth banished from my company.
Tell me, has ever such a thing been done?
ÉLIANTE: You'd best not turn to me; I'm not the one
To back you in a matter of this kind:
10 I'm all for those who frankly speak their mind.
ORONTE: Madam, you'll search in vain for a defender.
ALCESTE: You're beaten, Madam, and may as well
surrender.
ORONTE: Speak, speak, you must; and end this awful
strain.
ALCESTE: Or don't, and your position will be plain.
15 ORONTE: A single word will close this painful scene.
ALCESTE: But if you're silent, I'll know what you mean.

Scene IV [*Arsinoé, Célimène, Éliante, Alceste,
Philinte, Acaste, Clitandre, Oronte.*]

ACASTE (*to Célimène*): Madam, with all due deference,
we two
Have come to pick a little bone with you.

CLITANDRE (*to Oronte and Alceste*): I'm glad you're
present, Sirs, as you'll soon learn,
Our business here is also your concern.
ARSINOÉ (*to Célimène*): Madam, I visit you so soon
again   5
Only because of these two gentlemen,
Who came to me indignant and aggrieved
About a crime too base to be believed.
Knowing your virtue, having such confidence in it,
I couldn't think you guilty for a minute,   10
In spite of all their telling evidence;
And, rising above our little difference
I've hastened here in friendship's name to see
You clear yourself of this great calumny.
ACASTE: Yes, Madam, let us see with what
composure   15
You'll manage to respond to this disclosure.
You lately sent Clitandre this tender note.
CLITANDRE: And this one, for Acaste, you also
wrote.
ACASTE (*to Oronte and Alceste*): You'll recognize this
writing, Sirs, I think;
The lady is so free with pen and ink   20
That you must know it all too well, I fear.
But listen: this is something you should hear.

"How absurd you are to condemn my lightheart-
edness in society, and to accuse me of being happiest
in the company of others. Nothing could be more   25
unjust; and if you do not come to me instantly and
beg pardon for saying such a thing, I shall never forgive you as long as I live. Our big bumbling friend the
Viscount . . ."

What a shame that he's not here.   30

"Our big bumbling friend the Viscount, whose
name stands first in your complaint, is hardly a man
to my taste; and ever since the day I watched him
spend three-quarters of an hour spitting into a well,
so as to make circles in the water, I have been unable 35
to think highly of him. As for the little Marquess . . ."

In all modesty, gentlemen, that is I.

"As for the little Marquess, who sat squeezing my
hand for such a long while yesterday, I find him in all   40
respects the most trifling creature alive; and the only
things of value about him are his cape and his sword.
As for the man with the green ribbons . . ."

(*To Alceste.*) It's your turn now, Sir.

"As for the man with the green ribbons, he   45
amuses me now and then with his bluntness and his
bearish ill-humor; but there are many times indeed
when I think him the greatest bore in the world. And
as for the sonneteer . . ."

50   (*To Oronte.*) Here's your helping.

"And as for the sonneteer, who has taken it into
his head to be witty, and insists on being an author in
the teeth of opinion, I simply cannot be bothered to
listen to him, and his prose wearies me quite as much
55   as his poetry. Be assured that I am not always so well-
entertained as you suppose; that I long for your
company, more than I dare to say, at all these entertainments to which people drag me; and that the
presence of those one loves is the true and perfect
60   seasoning to all one's pleasures."

CLITANDRE: And now for me.

"Clitandre, whom you mention, and who so
pesters me with his saccharine speeches, is the last
man on earth for whom I could feel any affection. He
65   is quite mad to suppose that I love him, and so are
you, to doubt that you are loved. Do come to your
senses; exchange your suppositions for his; and visit
me as often as possible, to help me bear the annoyance of his unwelcome attentions."

70   It's sweet character that these letters show,
And what to call it, Madam, you well know.
Enough. We're off to make the world acquainted
With this sublime self-portrait that you've painted.
ACASTE: Madam, I'll make you no farewell oration;
75   No, you're not worthy of my indignation.
Far choicer hearts than yours, as you'll discover,
Would like this little Marquess for a lover.

Scene V [*Célimène, Éliante, Arsinoé, Alceste, Oronte, Philinte.*]

ORONTE: So! After all those loving letters you wrote,
You turn on me like this, and cut my throat!
And your dissembling, faithless heart, I find,
Has pledged itself by turns to all mankind!
5   How blind I've been! But now I clearly see;
I thank you, Madam, for enlightening me.
My heart is mine once more, and I'm content;
The loss of it shall be your punishment.
(*To Alceste.*) Sir, she is yours; I'll seek no more to stand
10   Between your wishes and this lady's hand.

Scene VI [*Célimène, Éliante, Arsinoé, Alceste, Philinte.*]

ARSINOÉ (*to Célimène*): Madam, I'm forced to speak. I'm far too stirred
To keep my counsel, after what I've heard.
I'm shocked and staggered by your want of morals.

It's not my way to mix in others' quarrels;
But really, when this fine and noble spirit,   5
This man of honor and surpassing merit,
Laid down the offering of his heart before you,
How *could* you . . .
ALCESTE: Madam, permit me, I implore you,
To represent myself in this debate.
Don't bother, please, to be my advocate.   10
My heart, in any case, could not afford
To give your services their due reward;
And if I chose, for consolation's sake,
Some other lady, 'twould not be you I'd take.
ARSINOÉ: What makes you think you could, Sir? And how dare you   15
Imply that I've been trying to ensnare you?
If you can for a moment entertain
Such flattering fancies, you're extremely vain.
I'm not so interested as you suppose
In Célimène's discarded gigolos.   20
Get rid of that absurd illusion, do.
Women like me are not for such as you.
Stay with this creature, to whom you're so attached;
I've never seen two people better matched.

Scene VII [*Célimène, Éliante, Alceste, Philinte.*]

ALCESTE (*to Célimène*): Well, I've been still throughout this exposé,
Till everyone but me has said his say.
Come, have I shown sufficient self-restraint?
And may I now . . .
CÉLIMÈNE: Yes, make your just complaint.
Reproach me freely, call me what you will;   5
You've every right to say I've used you ill.
I've wronged you, I confess it; and in my shame
I'll make no effort to escape the blame.
The anger of those others I could despise;
My guilt toward you I sadly recognize.   10
Your wrath is wholly justified, I fear
I know how culpable I must appear,
I know all things bespeak my treachery,
And that, in short, you've grounds for hating me.
Do so; I give you leave.
ALCESTE: Ah, traitress — how,   15
How should I cease to love you, even now?
Though mind and will were passionately bent
On hating you, my heart would not consent.
(*To Éliante and Philinte.*) Be witness to my madness, both of you;
See what infatuation drives one to;   20
But wait; my folly's only just begun,
And I shall prove to you before I'm done
How strange the human heart is, and how far
From rational we sorry creatures are.
(*To Célimène.*) Woman, I'm willing to forget your shame,   25

And clothe your treacheries in a sweeter name;
I'll call them youthful errors, instead of crimes,
And lay the blame on these corrupting times.
My one condition is that you agree
30 To share my chosen fate, and fly with me
To that wild, trackless, solitary place
In which I shall forget the human race.
Only by such a course can you atone
For those atrocious letters; by that alone
35 Can you remove my present horror of you,
And make it possible for me to love you.
CÉLIMÈNE: What! *I* renounce the world at my young
    age,
And die of boredom in some hermitage?
ALCESTE: Ah, if you really loved me as you ought,
40 You wouldn't give the world a moment's
    thought;
Must you have me, and all the world beside?
CÉLIMÈNE: Alas, at twenty one is terrified
Of solitude. I fear I lack the force
And depth of soul to take so stern a course.
45 But if my hand in marriage will content you,
Why, there's a plan which I might well consent to,
And . . .
ALCESTE: No, I detest you now. I could excuse
Everything else, but since you thus refuse
50 To love me wholly, as a wife should do,
And see the world in me, as I in you,
Go! I reject your hand, and disenthrall
My heart from your enchantments, once for all.

Scene VIII [*Éliante, Alceste, Philinte.*]

ALCESTE (*to Éliante*): Madam, your virtuous beauty
    has no peer;
Of all this world you only are sincere;
I've long esteemed you highly, as you know;
Permit me ever to esteem you so,
And if I do not now request your hand,   5
Forgive me, Madam, and try to understand.
I feel unworthy of it; I sense that fate
Does not intend me for the married state,
That I should do you wrong by offering you
My shattered heart's unhappy residue,   10
And that in short . . .
ÉLIANTE: Your argument's well taken:
Nor need you fear that I shall feel forsaken.
Were I to offer him this hand of mine,
Your friend Philinte, I think, would not decline.
PHILINTE: Ah, Madam, that's my heart's most
    cherished goal,   15
For which I'd gladly give my life and soul.
ALCESTE (*to Éliante and Philinte*): May you be true to
    all you now profess,
And so deserve unending happiness.
Meanwhile, betrayed and wronged in everything,
I'll flee this bitter world where vice is king,   20
And seek some spot unpeopled and apart
Where I'll be free to have an honest heart.
PHILINTE: Come, Madam, let's do everything we can
To change the mind of this unhappy man.

COMMENTARY

Lionel Gossman (b. 1929)
ALCESTE'S LOVE FOR CÉLIMÈNE   1963

What underlies Alceste's unlikely infatuation with Célimène? Gossman suggests that Alceste is playing to the very people of fashion whom he affects to look down on; consequently, he must conceal the real reasons for his love.

In reality, Alceste's love for Célimène is neither super-rational (above all reason and all explanation) nor irrational (below all reason and explanation). It is quite simply a peculiar and contradictory fascination which goes by the name of love in the vocabulary of the Alcestes of the world. It *can* be explained, and the explanation reveals that far from being the sincere and spontaneous being he says he is, Alceste is as calculating as anyone else.

It is precisely because Célimène is the most sought after and *worldly* of women (to all *appearances* the most unsuitable for Alceste) that he falls in love with her. It is not Célimène that Alceste loves or desires. She is irrelevant *as a person* to his "love." It is the world that he seeks to reach and possess through her. To have at his feet this woman whom all the world admires and courts would be to win the recognition of the world for himself. Alceste's love is entirely mediated by those very "gens à la mode"° for whom he so loudly protests his contempt. He "loves" Célimène because she has what he wants — the admiration of the world — and cannot admit he wants, without at the same time admitting that he is not the free, frank, and independent person he wants to be admired as. The object of his desire is thus also his unavowed rival, and this *for the very same reason* that she is the object of his desire. While he protests his love for Célimène, Alceste must therefore conceal the real reason for this love by affecting to deplore her participation in the "false" society of the *gens à la mode* and to despise her charms and her popularity. The final break with Célimène strikingly illustrates the ambiguity that characterizes Alceste's entire relationship with her from the beginning. Alceste calls on witnesses to observe how superior and disinterested his love is compared to the love of the elegant suitors who have abandoned Célimène, while at the same time he affirms before them his own contempt for it as unworthy of him:

> *Vous voyez* ce que peut une indigne tendresse,
> Et je vous fais tous deux *témoins* de ma foiblesse.
> Mais, à vous dire vrai, ce n'est pas encor tout,
> Et *vous allez me voir* la pousser jusqu'au bout,
> *Montrer* que c'est à tort que sages on nous nomme,
> Et que dans tous les coeurs il est toujours de l'homme.
> [V, VII, 19–24][1]

Having once proved how different his love is from that of Célimène's frivolous and calculating suitors, however, Alceste is only too quick to use her unwillingness to follow him to his desert as an excuse to drop her. Célimène without her suitors can have no attraction for Alceste.

Those who fall for Alceste's argument about the irrationality of passion are his dupes. Alceste cannot accept in the front rank of his own consciousness, or admit to others, that his whole life is pure posturing before others, that he who claims to be sincere and spontaneous is as preoccupied with the public as anybody and as mediated by it as those whom he charges with acting parts for others. Is he not, after all, the only person in the world who does not posture, whose emotions spring directly from the heart and who speaks nothing but what he really thinks and feels? Alceste uses the myth of the irrationality of passion to hide from others and from himself a character that is every bit as cold and ungenerous as the characters of those he criticizes for their coldness and lack of generosity.[. . .]

Alceste's life is in an important sense a life not of participation but of demonstration. This is one way in which he differs from the tragic heroes of Racine. The scandalous contradiction between the ideal and the real, between being and appearance, between the world of absolute values and the world of contingent opportunities is at the heart of seventeenth-century tragedy. There is never any danger, however, that Alceste will share in the somber destinies of Racine's heroes. His

---

"**gens à la mode**": Fashionable people.
[1]V, IV, 1751–56 of original text; italics added by Gossman.

world is far removed from theirs. He does not stake his destiny, as Junie or Andromaque or Monime° does, on living an authentic life in a world of inauthenticity. The inauthenticity of the world is not a menace to him; on the contrary, it is the very source of all his satisfactions. It provides the basis for his own superiority and he spends his time not in a real struggle to reach authenticity, but in endless efforts to have his superiority recognized by the very world of inauthenticity which he affects to detest. The absence of value in the world becomes, with Alceste, a matter for personal self-congratulation. Far from threatening his existence, the world of lies and deceit founds it. He exhausts himself in theatrical gestures, because all his wrestling with the ideal and the real, all his disgust with the world's falseness, however painfully experienced subjectively, is, objectively viewed, nothing but vain, ineffectual, and deeply inauthentic posturing. He does not really suffer because life is full of pretense and selfishness, because men have made their lives so vain and stupid. He suffers because he cannot bear to be like others and because others refuse him the adulation which he wants from them.[. . .]

Alceste acts the part of an absolute, but no one accepts his absoluteness: He loses his lawsuit, he fails to make Célimène submit to him, and he is laughed at by the world at large. He is an absolute in the world of his own conceptualizing alone, and thither he withdraws to decide for himself the fate of all his battles. The desert to which Alceste has always thought of withdrawing and to which he makes as if to withdraw at the end of the comedy is the world of his own mind. In it there is nothing to contradict his absoluteness, but there is unfortunately nothing to confirm it either. Alceste's difficulty is that his absoluteness can be experienced as real only with reference to others. Withdrawal to the desert cannot therefore be a final solution. It can only be an *act*, just as his rejection of Philinte at the beginning of the play was an act. This withdrawal requires an audience to watch it; and this hermit seeks not to escape but to be pursued. Alceste's withdrawal is simply a pose. And this is the very marrow of Molière's play. Alceste literally *joue la comédie*.° He is perpetually play-acting, whether we think of his passion for Célimène or of his passion for justice, and in this respect he resembles Molière's other comic heroes.

Junie . . . Andromaque . . . Monime: Characters in plays by Racine.
joue la comédie: Plays a sham part; play-acts.

Aphra Behn

Although not technically the first English woman playwright or the first woman to earn a living by her pen, Aphra Behn (c. 1640–1689) was the first notably successful woman playwright. She wrote twenty plays, several novels, among them *Oroonoko* (c. 1688), and *Poems on Several Occasions* (1684). She also published translations and edited volumes of poetry.

Behn grew up in an England governed by the Puritan Commonwealth. Throughout the 1650s Oliver Cromwell was Protector, and the theaters were closed. The Puritans were, in her eyes, dull, hypocritical, and repressive. Her allegiance was with the Stuarts, whose King Charles I was beheaded by order of Parliament in 1649. His sons, Charles and James, were forced into exile on the Continent, along with many Stuart courtiers, such as the gallants who appear in *The Rover*. When Charles II was restored to the throne in 1660, the period known as the Restoration began. Behn was twenty years old.

Very little is known of her, and much of that is guesswork based on her writing. For example, *Oroonoko* is a novel set in Surinam, which was a British colony when she visited there with members of her family in 1663–1664. Her father, who had been appointed lieutenant-general of Surinam, died, and she returned to London. She married Mr. Behn, possibly a Dutch merchant in England, who died two years later. She seems to have been persuaded by the writer and theater manager Thomas Killigrew to become an English spy in Antwerp. She was residing there when the great fire of 1666 destroyed most of London. Her services were so little valued that she was not paid and ended up for a brief time in debtors' prison when she returned to England.

Once out of prison, she took advantage of her friendship with Thomas Betterton, who belonged to a theater company at Lincoln's Inn Fields. He played the lead in her first play, *The Forced Marriage* (1670), which ran successfully for six nights. The record for the first run of a play was thirteen nights. In 1670 Behn reached a mostly courtly audience, those politically aligned with Charles II or somehow involved in court politics.

Behn succeeded again with *The Amorous Prince* in 1671. Those first two plays were wholly original, but she quickly resorted to the Shakespearean device of adapting the work of others. Like Shakespeare, she made considerable changes and constantly improved the material she borrowed. After the success of *The Rover* (1677), she was accused of plagiarism and answered the charge in the Postscript to the play. She did borrow some characters and details from Thomas Killigrew's *Thomaso; or, The Wanderer*, a closet drama, or play intended to be read, not staged (1654; published 1664); but, as she says in her Postscript, no one would have taken notice if her play were not so successful — and written by a woman. Playwrights commonly adapted earlier material because they had to produce many plays in a short time to earn a meager living.

The theme of her first play, loveless and unhappy marriages arranged by families, recurs throughout Behn's work. All we know about her own marriage is that it was brief; she did not remarry despite having long-term relationships. But she concerned herself with the fate of women in her society. A young woman could not hope to marry if she were not a virgin. Once she was married, a woman's property became her husband's, and her legal identity was melded with his. Consequently, she was at her husband's mercy since she had no recourse in law against any of his excesses.

However, the alternative to marriage was considered worse. If a woman was seduced, and people found out, she could expect to lose her status and forsake marriage. As a result, she would be forced to earn her own living, a harsh prospect since women were not given the same education as men and could not take part in any of the professions. One fate of many such women was to become prostitutes. In the meantime men pursued their goal of seduction, as they do in *The Rover* and other Behn plays, with no thought given to the welfare of the women they seduced. Furthermore, they frequently threatened women with rape if the women were uncompliant. The theme of rape echoes through Behn's plays. By necessity Behn had to appeal to a predominantly male audience, but even so she expresses some of her deeper concerns for the welfare of her sex. She exposes the unfairness and pain of arranged marriages and portrays women as complex and intelligent. Her work seems to reflect the influence of Shakespeare's female characters, such as Helena and Hermia in *A Midsummer Night's Dream* and Beatrice in *Much Ado about Nothing*.

Behn's plays include *Abdelazer* (1676), *The Town Fop* (1676), *The Lucky Chance* (1686), and *The Emperor of the Moon* (1687). Her last play, *The Widow Ranter* (1689), produced posthumously, was a failure. But it is an interesting portrait of the settlement of the Virginias, based on her experience in the New World. The prefaces to Behn's plays treat important issues, such as the unequal education of women. She points out, however, that in playwriting the lack of education in Greek and Latin is no handicap. She reminds her readers that Shakespeare and Jonson did very well with limited education, and that "gownmen" (scholars) talked incessantly and to little account. What was needed for the stage was experience and a good ear, and Aphra Behn had both.

THE ROVER; OR, THE BANISHED CAVALIERS

The English rakes who swagger through this play are displaced Royalist cavaliers who lived perilously in exile during the Puritan interregnum of the 1650s as they awaited the restoration of Charles II to the throne. Their concerns in Naples are warlike and lusty. Their frequent dueling delighted the audiences of 1677 and caused *The Rover* to be one of Behn's best-received plays. Beneath the brawling, however, is a more serious struggle between the sexes.

It is pre-Lenten carnival time in Naples, when all the people dress in masquerade. The players in *The Rover* disguise themselves — Hellena as a gypsy or a page, Belvile as Antonio, the others in costumes that make them unrecognizable — from the first act to the last. Such masquerading permits the young men and women to meet and talk without supervision. Among the characters, the most stable are Florinda and Belvile, who love each other from the beginning and who end up married despite the objections of Florinda's brother Pedro and their father, who has promised Florinda to Don Vincentio, a wealthy old man.

Behn's favorite theme of arranged or forced marriage thus surfaces quickly in this play, and much of the action involves its circumvention. A related theme also develops quickly: forcible rape. The Cavaliers, or rakes, treat women of lower social class as if they were whores. In this play Florinda faces rape not once but twice. First Willmore, the Rover, treats her as "an errant harlot" and forces her to scream "rape" (III, v). When Frederick and Belvile intervene, Willmore explains that he was drunk and not to blame. Florinda's second close call comes with Blunt. When she runs into his apartment to escape discovery on the street, Blunt decides to avenge his disgrace at the hands of Lucetta by raping Florinda — thus punishing the entire sex for his mishandling. This time Frederick, without knowing who Florinda is, decides both to help Blunt and to rape her as well. When she gives them a ring that reveals her to be an aristocrat, a woman of quality, Frederick says, "'twould anger us vilely to be trussed up for a rape upon a maid of quality, when we only believe we ruffle a harlot" (IV, v, 150–53).

These scenes are painful from our modern perspective and must have been even more so to women in Behn's audience. Part of her purpose, though, is to point out that men treated women differently according to class. Aristocrats such as these cavaliers were sometimes willfully brutal toward women in a lower class. Behn builds sympathy for Florinda and, by extension, for all women who are treated viciously by men. It is conceivable that some men in the audiences of Behn's day might not have been conscious of her purpose, since they may have approved of behavior such as Blunt's and Frederick's.

Like Florinda, the other female characters in *The Rover* face obstacles with wit and resourcefulness, but not all the women are successful. Behn's portrait of the courtesan Angellica is laced with irony. Against her will and better judgment, Angellica finds herself falling in love with Willmore. When she takes Willmore as a lover without demanding from him the usual thousand crowns, her handmaid Moretta watches in horror, realizing that her mistress is giving away something she would normally sell at a dear price. Angellica is smitten by Willmore — just as Hellena is smitten by the same rover — but once Willmore enjoys Angellica's pleasures, he dismisses her from his mind. Angellica the courtesan knows that this is the way men relate to women. But Angellica the woman, who gave Willmore her "virgin heart," is as deceived as any woman could be.

Hellena, promised to the church as a nun by her father, begins the play revealing her plans to avoid the convent at all costs. Her brother Pedro does not say so, but he seems to expect that when she is in the convent he will have access to the 300,000 crowns her uncle has bequeathed her. Pedro attempts to force Hellena to "marry" the church in the same way that he attempts to force Florinda to marry a man she does not love. Neither sister will have any of it.

The play centers more on the success of Florinda and Hellena than it does on Belvile or Willmore. Hellena, by virtue of her wit — which is equal to Willmore's — and her understanding of social realities, forces Willmore to submit to her will. He is all for making love, but she demands that Hymen, the god of marriage, be invoked before their lovemaking. When he tells her that she should be content with love and not demand marriage, she replies, "What shall I get? A cradle full of noise and mischief, with a pack of repentance at my back?" (V, 514–16) She is more than his match. The play ends with Florinda, Hellena, and Valeria all winning the husbands of their choice on their own terms.

The Rover; or, The Banished Cavaliers in Performance

King Charles II attended the March 24, 1677, production of *The Rover*, and successive royal performances were commanded before different monarchs in 1724 and 1729. Some seventy performances of the play took place between 1700 and 1725, and even more were recorded between 1726 and 1760. However, after 1790 the play was not produced for many decades.

Today's productions indicate a modern understanding of the play's feminist themes and its subtle wit-play between the sexes. The Folger Theater Group in Washington, D.C., produced the work in 1982, playing it broadly for its humor. Critics praised the play for its vitality but complained that the production overdid the "business"— stage gestures, movement, and action — and the actors did not clearly deliver their lines. Christopher Reeve played Willmore in the Williamstown Theater production in 1987, with Kate Burton as Florinda. The director, John Rubinstein, moved the setting from Naples to the West Indies. One of the most interesting, although not wholly satisfying, productions was in 1986 by the Royal Shakespeare Company. Jeremy Irons played Willmore and Imogen Stubbs played Hellena. The director, John Barton, adapted the text using the earlier source play *Thomaso; or, The Wanderer* by Thomas Killigrew. Critics of the Royal Shakespeare production were struck by the modernity of Behn's play.

THE ROVER; OR, THE BANISHED CAVALIERS

PROLOGUE

Wits, like physicians, never can agree,
When of a different society.
And Rabel's drops° were never more cried down
By all the learned doctors of the town,
5   Than a new play whose author is unknown.
Nor can those doctors with more malice sue
(And powerful purses) the dissenting few,
Than those, with an insulting pride, do rail
At all who are not of their own cabal.°
10   If a young poet hit your humor right,
You judge him then out of revenge and spite.
So amongst men there are ridiculous elves,
Who monkeys hate for being too like themselves.
So that the reason of the grand debate
15   Why wit so oft is damned when good plays take,
Is that you censure as you love, or hate.
      Thus like a learned conclave poets sit,
Catholic° judges both of sense and wit,
And damn or save as they themselves think fit.
20   Yet those who to others' faults are so severe,
Are not so perfect but themselves may err.
Some write correct, indeed, but then the whole
(Bating° their own dull stuff i'th' play) is stole:
As bees do suck from flowers their honeydew,
25   So they rob others striving to please you.
      Some write their characters genteel and fine,
But then they do so toil for every line,
That what to you does easy seem, and plain,
Is the hard issue of their laboring brain.
30   And some th' effects of all their pains, we see,
Is but to mimic good extempore.°
Others, by long converse about the town,
Have wit enough to write a lewd lampoon,
But their chief skill lies in a bawdy song.
35   In short, the only wit that's now in fashion,
Is but the gleanings of good conversation.
As for the author of this coming play,
I asked him what he thought fit I should say
In thanks for your good company today:
40   He called me fool, and said it was well known
You came not here for our sakes, but your own.

New plays are stuffed with wits, and with deboches,°
That crowd and sweat like cits° in May-Day°
   coaches.°

WRITTEN BY A PERSON OF QUALITY

The Actors' Names

[Men]
DON ANTONIO, *the Viceroy's son*
DON PEDRO, *a noble Spaniard, his friend*
BELVILE, *an English colonel in love with Florinda*
WILLMORE, *the Rover*
FREDERICK, *an English gentleman, and friend to Belvile
   and Blunt*
BLUNT, *an English country gentleman*
STEPHANO, *servant to Don Pedro*
PHILIPPO, *Lucetta's gallant*
SANCHO, *pimp to Lucetta*
BISKEY and SEBASTIAN, *two bravos° to Angellica*
OFFICER and SOLDIERS
[DIEGO,] *Page to Don Antonio*

[Women]
FLORINDA, *sister to Don Pedro*
HELLENA, *a gay young woman designed for a nun, and
   sister to Florinda*
VALERIA, *a kinswoman to Florinda*
ANGELLICA BIANCA, *a famous courtesan*
MORETTA, *her woman*
CALLIS, *governess to Florinda and Hellena*
LUCETTA, *a jilting wench*
SERVANTS, other MASQUERADERS, MEN and WOMEN

The Scene: *Naples, in Carnival time.*

ACT I • *Scene 1*

(*A Chamber. Enter Florinda and Hellena.*)

FLORINDA: What an impertinent thing is a young girl
   bred in a nunnery! How full of questions! Prithee no
   more, Hellena; I have told thee more than thou
   understand'st already.

---

3. **Rabel's drops:** A patent medicine.   9. **cabal:** A small, secret
political group.   18. **Catholic:** Having broad tastes or interests.
23. **Bating:** Leaving out.   31. **extempore:** A performance given
without a script or rehearsal.

42. **deboches:** Orgies, debauches.   43. **cits:** Residents of cities.
May-Day: May 1, celebrated as a spring festival.   **coaches:**
Carriages on parade during a May Day celebration.   44. **[The
Actors' Names] bravos:** Villains, adventurers.

5 HELLENA: The more's my grief. I would fain know as much as you, which makes me so inquisitive; nor is't enough I know you're a lover, unless you tell me too who 'tis you sigh for.

FLORINDA: When you're a lover I'll think you fit for a

10 secret of that nature.

HELLENA: 'Tis true, I never was a lover yet, but I begin to have a shrewd guess what 'tis to be so, and fancy it very pretty to sigh, and sing, and blush, and wish, and dream and wish, and long and wish to see the

15 man, and when I do, look pale and tremble, just as you did when my brother brought home the fine English colonel to see you. What do you call him? Don Belvile?

FLORINDA: Fie, Hellena.

20 HELLENA: That blush betrays you. I am sure 'tis so. Or is it Don Antonio the Viceroy's son? Or perhaps the rich old Don Vincentio, whom my father designs you for a husband? Why do you blush again?

FLORINDA: With indignation; and how near soever my

25 father thinks I am to marrying that hated object, I shall let him see I understand better what's due to my beauty, birth, and fortune, and more to my soul, than to obey those unjust commands.

HELLENA: Now hang me, if I don't love thee for that

30 dear disobedience. I love mischief strangely, as most of our sex do who are come to love nothing else. But tell me, dear Florinda, don't you love that fine *Anglese*?° For I vow, next to loving him myself, 'twill please me most that you do so, for he is so gay and so

35 handsome.

FLORINDA: Hellena, a maid designed for a nun ought not to be so curious in a discourse of love.

HELLENA: And dost thou think that ever I'll be a nun? Or at least till I'm so old I'm fit for nothing else?

40 Faith no, sister; and that which makes me long to know whether you love Belvile, is because I hope he has some mad companion or other that will spoil my devotion. Nay, I'm resolved to provide myself this Carnival, if there be e'er a handsome proper fellow of

45 my humor above ground,° though I ask first.

FLORINDA: Prithee be not so wild.

HELLENA: Now you have provided yourself of a man you take no care of poor me. Prithee tell me, what dost thou see about me that is unfit for love? Have I

50 not a world of youth? A humor gay? A beauty passable? A vigor desirable? Well shaped? Clean limbed? Sweet breathed? And sense enough to know how all these ought to be employed to the best advantage? Yes, I do and will; therefore lay aside your hopes of

55 my fortune by my being a devote,° and tell me how you came acquainted with this Belvile. For I perceive you knew him before he came to Naples.

FLORINDA: Yes, I knew him at the siege of Pamplona; he was then a colonel of French horse,° who when the town was ransacked, nobly treated my brother and

60 myself, preserving us from all insolences. And I must own, besides great obligations, I have I know not what that pleads kindly for him about my heart, and will suffer no other to enter. But see, my brother.

(Enter Don Pedro, Stephano with a masking habit,° and Callis.)

PEDRO: Good morrow, sister. Pray when saw you your

65 lover Don Vincentio?

FLORINDA: I know not, sir. Callis, when was he here? For I consider it so little I know not when it was.

PEDRO: I have a command from my father here to tell you you ought not to despise him, a man of so vast a

70 fortune, and such a passion for you. — Stephano, my things.

(Puts on his masking habit.)

FLORINDA: A passion for me? 'Tis more than e'er I saw, or he had a desire should be known. I hate Vincentio, sir, and I would not have a man so dear to me as my

75 brother follow the ill customs of our country and make a slave of his sister. And, sir, my father's will I'm sure you may divert.

PEDRO: I know not how dear I am to you, but I wish only to be ranked in your esteem equal with the English

80 colonel Belvile. Why do you frown and blush? Is there any guilt belongs to the name of that cavalier?

FLORINDA: I'll not deny I value Belvile. When I was exposed to such dangers as the licensed lust of common soldiers threatened when rage and conquest

85 flew through the city, then Belvile, this criminal for my sake, threw himself into all dangers to save my honor. And will you not allow him my esteem?

PEDRO: Yes, pay him what you will in honor, but you must consider Don Vincentio's fortune, and the join-

90 ture° he'll make you.

FLORINDA: Let him consider my youth, beauty, and fortune, which ought not to be thrown away on his age and jointure.

PEDRO: 'Tis true, he's not so young and fine a gentleman

95 as that Belvile. But what jewels will that cavalier present you with? Those of his eyes and heart?

HELLENA: And are not those better than any Don Vincentio has brought from the Indies?

PEDRO: Why, how now! Has your nunnery breeding

100 taught you to understand the value of hearts and eyes?

HELLENA: Better than to believe Vincentio's deserve value from any woman. He may perhaps increase her bags, but not her family.°

---

33. *Anglese*: The English colonel Belvile.   45. above ground: In the real world (i.e., outside the convent).   55. devote: Nun.

59. of French horse: In the French cavalry.   64. [S.D.] *masking habit*: Costume for the Carnival masquerades.   90–91. jointure: An estate given by a husband to a wife in lieu of her dowry.   103–04. increase her bags . . . family: Give her material goods but not enhance her family's standing.

105   PEDRO: This is fine! Go! Up to your devotion! You are
      not designed for the conversation of lovers.
      HELLENA (*aside*): Nor saints yet a while, I hope. — Is't
      not enough you make a nun of me, but you must cast
      my sister away too, exposing her to a worse confine-
110   ment than a religious life?
      PEDRO: The girl's mad! It is a confinement to be carried
      into the country to an ancient villa belonging to the
      family of the Vincentios these five hundred years, and
      have no other prospect than that pleasing one of see-
115   ing all her own that meets her eyes: a fine air, large
      fields, and gardens where she may walk and gather
      flowers?
      HELLENA: When, by moonlight? For I am sure she dares
      not encounter with the heat of the sun; that were a
120   task only for Don Vincentio and his Indian breeding,
      who loves it in the dog days.° And if these be her
      daily divertissements,° what are those of the night?
      To lie in a wide moth-eaten bed-chamber with furni-
      ture in fashion in the reign of King Sancho the First;°
125   the bed, that which his forefathers lived and died in.
      PEDRO: Very well.
      HELLENA: This apartment, new furbrushed° and fitted
      out for the young wife, he out of freedom makes his
      dressing room; and being a frugal and a jealous cox-
130   comb,° instead of a valet to uncase° his feeble car-
      cass, he desires you to do that office. Signs of favor,
      I'll assure you, and such as you must not hope for
      unless your woman be out of the way.
      PEDRO: Have you done yet?
135   HELLENA: That honor being past, the giant stretches
      itself, yawns and sighs a belch or two loud as a mus-
      ket, throws himself into bed, and expects you in his
      foul sheets; and ere you can get yourself undressed,
      calls you with a snore or two. And are not these fine
140   blessings to a young lady?
      PEDRO: Have you done yet?
      HELLENA: And this man you must kiss, nay you must
      kiss none but him too, and nuzzle through his beard
      to find his lips. And this you must submit to for
145   threescore years, and all for a jointure.
      PEDRO: For all your character of Don Vincentio, she is
      as like to marry him as she was before.
      HELLENA: Marry Don Vincentio! Hang me, such a wed-
      lock would be worse than adultery with another man.
150   I had rather see her in the *Hostel de Dieu*,° to waste
      her youth there in vows, and be a handmaid to lazars°
      and cripples, than to lose it in such a marriage.
      PEDRO: You have considered, sister, that Belvile has no
      fortune to bring you to; banished his country, de-
155   spised at home, and pitied abroad.
      HELLENA: What then? The Viceroy's son is better than

that old Sir Fifty. Don Vincentio! Don Indian! He
thinks he's trading to Gambo° still, and would barter
himself — that bell and bauble — for your youth
and fortune.   160
PEDRO: Callis, take her hence and lock her up all this
Carnival, and at Lent she shall begin her everlasting
penance in a monastery.
HELLENA: I care not; I had rather be a nun than be
obliged to marry as you would have me if I were de-   165
signed for't.
PEDRO: Do not fear the blessing of that choice. You shall
be a nun.
HELLENA (*aside*): Shall I so? You may chance to be mistaken in my way of devotion. A nun! Yes, I am like to   170
make a fine nun! I have an excellent humor for a
grate!° No, I'll have a saint of my own to pray to
shortly, if I like any that dares venture on me.
PEDRO: Callis, make it your business to watch this wild-
cat. — As for you, Florinda, I've only tried you all   175
this while and urged my father's will; but mine is that
you would love Antonio: He is brave and young, and
all that can complete the happiness of a gallant maid.
This absence of my father will give us opportunity to
free you from Vincentio by marrying here, which you   180
must do tomorrow.
FLORINDA: Tomorrow!
PEDRO: Tomorrow, or 'twill be too late. 'Tis not my
friendship to Antonio which makes me urge this, but
love to thee and hatred to Vincentio; therefore resolve   185
upon tomorrow.
FLORINDA: Sir, I shall strive to do as shall become your
sister.
PEDRO: I'll both believe and trust you. Adieu.

                (*Exeunt*° *Pedro and Stephano.*)

HELLENA: As becomes his sister! That is to be as resolved   190
your way as he is his.

(*Hellena goes to Callis.*)

FLORINDA: I ne'er till now perceived my ruin near.
I've no defense against Antonio's love,
For he has all the advantages of nature,
The moving arguments of youth and fortune.   195
HELLENA: But hark you, Callis, you will not be so cruel
to lock me up indeed, will you?
CALLIS: I must obey the commands I have. Besides, do
you consider what a life you are going to lead?
HELLENA: Yes, Callis, that of a nun; and till then I'll be in-   200
debted a world of prayers to you if you'll let me now
see what I never did, the divertissements of a Carnival.
CALLIS: What, go in masquerade? 'Twill be a fine farewell to the world, I take it. Pray what would you do
there?   205
HELLENA: That which all the world does, as I am told:

---

121. **dog days:** The hot days of summer.   122. **divertissements:**
Amusements.   124. **King Sancho the First:** King of Spain,
probably Sancho I of Castile (970–1035).   127. **new fur-**
brushed: Refurbished.   129–30. **coxcomb:** Conceited person,
fop.   130. **uncase:** Disrobe.   150. *Hostel de Dieu*: Hospital
operated by a group of nuns.   151. **lazars:** Lepers.

158. **Gambo:** British colony in West Africa.   172. **grate:** The
grille covering the windows in a convent (i.e., the convent).
189. [S.D.] *Exeunt:* Latin for "they go out."

Be as mad as the rest and take all innocent freedoms.
Sister, you'll go too, will you not? Come, prithee be
not sad. We'll outwit twenty brothers if you'll be
210 ruled by me. Come, put off this dull humor with your
clothes, and assume one as gay and as fantastic as the
dress my cousin Valeria and I have provided, and let's
ramble.

FLORINDA: Callis, will you give us leave to go?

215 CALLIS (aside): I have a youthful itch of going myself. —
Madam, if I thought your brother might not know it,
and I might wait on you; for by my troth I'll not trust
young girls alone.

FLORINDA: Thou seest my brother's gone already, and
220 thou shalt attend and watch us.

(Enter Stephano.)

STEPHANO: Madam, the habits are come, and your
cousin Valeria is dressed and stays for you.

FLORINDA (aside): 'Tis well. I'll write a note, and if I
chance to see Belvile and want an opportunity to
225 speak to him, that shall let him know what I've
resolved in favor of him.

HELLENA: Come, let's in and dress us.   (Exeunt.)

Scene II

(A long street. Enter Belvile, melancholy; Blunt and
Frederick.)

FREDERICK: Why, what the devil ails the colonel, in a
time when all the world is gay to look like mere Lent
thus? Hadst thou been long enough in Naples to
have been in love, I should have sworn some such
5 judgment had befallen thee.

BELVILE: No, I have made no new amours since I came
to Naples.

FREDERICK: You have left none behind you in Paris?

BELVILE: Neither.

10 FREDERICK: I cannot divine the cause then, unless the
old cause, the want of money.

BLUNT: And another old cause, the want of a wench.
Would not that revive you?

BELVILE: You are mistaken, Ned.

15 BLUNT: Nay, 'adsheartlikins,° then thou'rt past cure.

FREDERICK: I have found it out: Thou hast renewed thy
acquaintance with the lady that cost thee so many
sighs at the siege of Pamplona — pox on't, what d'ye
call her — her brother's a noble Spaniard, nephew to
20 the dead general. Florinda. Ay, Florinda. And will
nothing serve thy turn but that damned virtuous
woman, whom on my conscience thou lov'st in spite
too, because thou seest little or no possibility of gaining her.

25 BELVILE: Thou art mistaken; I have int'rest enough in
that lovely virgin's heart to make me proud and vain,

were it not abated by the severity of a brother, who,
perceiving my happiness —

FREDERICK: Has civilly forbid thee the house?

BELVILE: 'Tis so, to make way for a powerful rival, the   30
Viceroy's son, who has the advantage of me in being
a man of fortune, a Spaniard, and her brother's
friend; which gives him liberty to make his court,
whilst I have recourse only to letters and distant
looks from her window, which are as soft and kind as   35
those which heaven sends down on penitents.

BLUNT: Heyday! 'Adsheartlikins, simile! By this light the
man is quite spoiled. Fred, what the devil are we made
of that we cannot be thus concerned for a wench?
'Adsheartlikins, our Cupids are like the cooks of the   40
camp: They can roast or boil a woman, but they have
none of the fine tricks to set 'em off; no hogoes° to
make the sauce pleasant and the stomach sharp.

FREDERICK: I dare swear I have had a hundred as young,
kind, and handsome as this Florinda; and dogs eat   45
me if they were not as troublesome to me i'th' morning as they were welcome o'er night.

BLUNT: And yet I warrant he would not touch another
woman if he might have her for nothing.

BELVILE: That's thy joy, a cheap whore.   50

BLUNT: Why, 'adsheartlikins, I love a frank soul. When
did you ever hear of an honest woman that took a
man's money? I warrant 'em good ones. But gentlemen, you may be free; you have been kept so poor
with parliaments and protectors that the little stock   55
you have is not worth preserving. But I thank my
stars I had more grace than to forfeit my estate by
cavaliering.

BELVILE: Methinks only following the court should be
sufficient to entitle 'em to that.   60

BLUNT: 'Adsheartlikins, they know I follow it to do it
no good, unless they pick a hole in my coat for lending you money now and then, which is a greater
crime to my conscience, gentlemen, than to the commonwealth.   65

(Enter Willmore.)

WILLMORE: Ha! Dear Belvile! Noble colonel!

BELVILE: Willmore! Welcome ashore, my dear rover!
What happy wind blew us this good fortune?

WILLMORE: Let me salute my dear Fred, and then command me. — How is't, honest lad?   70

FREDERICK: Fair, sir, the old compliment, infinitely the
better to see my dear mad Willmore again. Prithee,
why camest thou ashore? And where's the Prince?°

WILLMORE: He's well, and reigns still lord of the wat'ry
element. I must aboard again within a day or two,   75
and my business ashore was only to enjoy myself a
little this Carnival.

BELVILE: Pray know our new friend, sir; he's but bashful, a raw traveler, but honest, stout, and one of us.

---

15. 'adsheartlikins: Expostulation equivalent to "As God loves
us."

42. hogoes: Relishes.   **73. Prince:** Charles II, in exile on the
Continent during the reign of Cromwell.

(*Embraces Blunt.*)

80 WILLMORE: That you esteem him gives him an int'rest here.

BLUNT: Your servant, sir.

WILLMORE: But well, faith, I'm glad to meet you again in a warm climate, where the kind sun has its godlike

85 power still over the wine and women. Love and mirth are my business in Naples, and if I mistake not the place, here's an excellent market for chapmen° of my humor.

BELVILE: See, here be those kind merchants of love you

90 look for.

(*Enter several men in masking habits, some playing on music, others dancing after; women dressed like courtesans, with papers pinned on their breasts, and baskets of flowers in their hands.*)

BLUNT: 'Adsheartlikins, what have we here?

FREDERICK: Now the game begins.

WILLMORE: Fine pretty creatures! May a stranger have leave to look and love? What's here? "Roses for every

95 month"? (*Reads the papers.*)

BLUNT: Roses for every month? What means that?

BELVILE: They are, or would have you think they're courtesans, who here in Naples are to be hired by the month.

100 WILLMORE: Kind and obliging to inform us, pray where do these roses grow? I would fain plant some of 'em in a bed of mine.

WOMAN: Beware such roses, sir.

WILLMORE: A pox of fear: I'll be baked with thee

105 between a pair of sheets, and that's thy proper still; so I might but strew such roses over me and under me. Fair one, would you would give me leave to gather at your bush this idle month; I would go near to make somebody smell of it all the year after.

110 BELVILE: And thou hast need of such a remedy, for thou stink'st of tar and ropes' ends like a dock or pesthouse.

(*The Woman puts herself into the hands of a man and exeunt.*)

WILLMORE: Nay, nay, you shall not leave me so.

BELVILE: By all means use no violence here.

WILLMORE: Death! Just as I was going to be damnably

115 in love, to have her led off! I could pluck that rose out of his hand, and even kiss the bed the bush grew in.

FREDERICK: No friend to love like a long voyage at sea.

BLUNT: Except a nunnery, Fred.

WILLMORE: Death! But will they not be kind? Quickly

120 be kind? Thou know'st I'm no tame sigher, but a rampant lion of the forest.

(*Advances from the farther end of the scenes two men dressed all over with horns° of several sorts, making grimaces at one another, with papers pinned on their backs.*)

BELVILE: Oh the fantastical rogues, how they're dressed! 'Tis a satire against the whole sex.

WILLMORE: Is this a fruit that grows in this warm coun-

125 try?

BELVILE: Yes, 'tis pretty to see these Italians start, swell, and stab at the word cuckold, and yet stumble at horns on every threshold.

WILLMORE: See what's on their back. (*Reads.*) "Flowers

130 of every night." Ah, rogue! And more sweet than roses of every month! This is a gardener of Adam's own breeding.

(*They dance.*)

BELVILE: What think you of these grave people? Is a wake in Essex half so mad or extravagant?

135 WILLMORE: I like their sober grave way; 'tis a kind of legal authorized fornication, where the men are not chid° for't, nor the women despised, as amongst our dull English. Even the monsieurs° want that part of good manners.

140 BELVILE: But here in Italy, a monsieur is the humblest best-bred gentleman: Duels are so baffled by bravos that an age shows not one but between a Frenchman and a hangman, who is as much too hard for him on the Piazza as they are for a Dutchman on the New

145 Bridge. But see, another crew.

(*Enter Florinda, Hellena, and Valeria, dressed like gypsies; Callis and Stephano, Lucetta, Philippo, and Sancho in masquerade.*)

HELLENA: Sister, there's your Englishman, and with him a handsome proper fellow. I'll to him, and instead of telling him his fortune, try my own.

WILLMORE: Gypsies, on my life. Sure these will prattle if

150 a man cross their hands.° (*Goes to Hellena.*) — Dear, pretty, and, I hope, young devil, will you tell an amorous stranger what luck he's like to have?

HELLENA: Have a care how you venture with me, sir, lest I pick your pocket, which will more vex your English

155 humor than an Italian fortune will please you.

WILLMORE: How the devil cam'st thou to know my country and humor?

HELLENA: The first I guess by a certain forward impudence, which does not displease me at this time; and

160 the loss of your money will vex you because I hope you have but very little to lose.

WILLMORE: Egad, child, thou'rt i'th' right; it is so little I dare not offer it thee for a kindness. But cannot you divine what other things of more value I have about

165 me that I would more willingly part with?

HELLENA: Indeed no, that's the business of a witch, and I am but a gypsy yet. Yet without looking in your hand, I have a parlous° guess 'tis some foolish heart you mean, an inconstant English heart, as little worth

170 stealing as your purse.

---

87. **chapmen:** Merchants, in this case merchants of love.
121. [S.D.] *horns:* Emblem of the cuckold, a man whose wife is unfaithful.   137. **chid:** Chided, reproached.   138. **monsieurs:** Frenchmen.
150. **cross their hands:** Cross their hands with silver: pay them to tell his fortune.   168. **parlous:** Dangerously cunning, clever (from *perilous*).

WILLMORE: Nay, then thou dost deal with the devil, that's certain. Thou hast guessed as right as if thou hadst been one of that number it has languished for. I find you'll be better acquainted with it, nor can you take it
175 in a better time; for I am come from sea, child, and Venus not being propitious to me in her own element,° I have a world of love in store. Would you would be good-natured and take some on't° off my hands.

HELLENA: Why, I could be inclined that way, but for a
180 foolish vow I am going to make to die a maid.

WILLMORE: Then thou art damned without redemption, and as I am a good Christian, I ought in charity to divert so wicked a design. Therefore prithee, dear creature, let me know quickly when and where I shall
185 begin to set a helping hand to so good a work.

HELLENA: If you should prevail with my tender heart, as I begin to fear you will, for you have horrible loving eyes, there will be difficulty in't that you'll hardly undergo for my sake.

190 WILLMORE: Faith, child, I have been bred in dangers, and wear a sword that has been employed in a worse cause than for a handsome kind woman. Name the danger; let it be anything but a long siege, and I'll undertake it.

HELLENA: Can you storm?

195 WILLMORE: Oh, most furiously.

HELLENA: What think you of a nunnery wall? For he that wins me must gain that first.

WILLMORE: A nun! Oh, now I love thee for't! There's no sinner like a young saint. Nay, now there's no deny-
200 ing me; the old law had no curse to a woman like dying a maid: Witness Jeptha's daughter.°

HELLENA: A very good text this, if well handled; and I perceive, Father Captain, you would impose no severe penance on her who were inclined to console
205 herself before she took orders.°

WILLMORE: If she be young and handsome.

HELLENA: Ay, there's it. But if she be not —

WILLMORE: By this hand, child, I have an implicit faith, and dare venture on thee with all faults. Besides, 'tis
210 more meritorious to leave the world when thou hast tasted and proved the pleasure on't. Then 'twill be a virtue in thee, which now will be pure ignorance.

HELLENA: I perceive, good Father Captain, you design only to make me fit for heaven. But if, on the con-
215 trary, you should quite divert me from it, and bring me back to the world again, I should have a new man to seek, I find. And what a grief that will be; for when I begin, I fancy I shall love like anything; I never tried yet.

WILLMORE: Egad, and that's kind! Prithee, dear crea-
220 ture, give me credit for a heart, for faith, I'm a very honest fellow. Oh, I long to come first to the banquet of love! And such a swinging appetite I bring. Oh, I'm impatient. Thy lodging, sweetheart, thy lodging, or I'm a dead man!
225
HELLENA: Why must we be either guilty of fornication or murder if we converse with you men? And is there no difference between leave to love me, and leave to lie with me?

WILLMORE: Faith, child, they were made to go together.
230
LUCETTA (pointing to Blunt): Are you sure this is the man?

SANCHO: When did I mistake your game?

LUCETTA: This is a stranger, I know by his gazing; if he be brisk he'll venture to follow me, and then, if I
235 understand my trade, he's mine. He's English, too, and they say that's a sort of good-natured loving people, and have generally so kind an opinion of themselves that a woman with any wit may flatter 'em into any sort of fool she pleases.
240
(She often passes by Blunt and gazes on him; he struts and cocks, and walks and gazes on her.)

BLUNT: 'Tis so, she is taken; I have beauties which my false glass° at home did not discover.

FLORINDA (aside): This woman watches me so, I shall get no opportunity to discover myself to him, and so miss the intent of my coming. — [To Belvile.] But as I
245 was saying, sir, by this line you should be a lover. (Looking in his hand.)

BELVILE: I thought how right you guessed: All men are in love, or pretend to be so. Come, let me go; I'm weary of this fooling.   (Walks away.)

FLORINDA: I will not, sir, till you have confessed whether
250 the passion that you have vowed Florinda be true or false.

(She holds him; he strives to get from her.)

BELVILE: Florinda!   (Turns quick toward her.)

FLORINDA: Softly.

BELVILE: Thou hast nam'd one will fix me here forever.
255
FLORINDA: She'll be disappointed then, who expects you this night at the garden gate. And if you fail not, as — (Looks on Callis, who observes 'em.) Let me see the other hand — you will go near to do, she vows to die or make you happy.
260
BELVILE: What canst thou mean?

FLORINDA: That which I say. Farewell.

(Offers to go.)

BELVILE: O charming sibyl,° stay; complete that joy which as it is will turn into distraction! Where must I be? At the garden gate? I know it. At night, you say?
265 I'll sooner forfeit heaven than disobey.

(Enter Don Pedro and other maskers, and pass over the stage.)

176. Venus . . . element: Venus, the goddess of love, was supposedly born from the foam of the sea.   178. on't: Of it.
201. Jeptha's daughter: To fulfill a vow, Jeptha sacrificed his only child, a virgin daughter, whom he allowed to go off to the mountains for two months to "bewail" her virginity before he killed her. "And it became a custom in Israel that the daughters of Israel went year by year to lament the daughter of Jeptha . . . four days in the year" (Judges 11:39–40).   205. took orders: Entered the convent.

242. false glass: Lying mirror.   263. sibyl: A female prophet; fortune-teller.

CALLIS: Madam, your brother's here.

FLORINDA: Take this to instruct you farther.

(*Gives him a letter, and goes off.*)

FREDERICK: Have a care, sir, what you promise; this may
270   be a trap laid by her brother to ruin you.

BELVILE: Do not disturb my happiness with doubts.

(*Opens the letter.*)

WILLMORE: My dear pretty creature, a thousand bless-
    ings on thee! Still in this habit, you say? And after
    dinner at this place?

275 HELLENA: Yes, if you will swear to keep your heart and
    not bestow it between this and that.

WILLMORE: By all the little gods of love, I swear; I'll
    leave it with you, and if you run away with it, those
    deities of justice will revenge me.

(*Exeunt all the women [except Lucetta].*)

280 FREDERICK: Do you know the hand?

BELVILE: 'Tis Florinda's.
    All blessings fall upon the virtuous maid.

FREDERICK: Nay, no idolatry; a sober sacrifice I'll allow
    you.

285 BELVILE: Oh friends, the welcom'st news! The softest
    letter! Nay, you shall all see it. And could you now be
    serious, I might be made the happiest man the sun
    shines on!

WILLMORE: The reason of this mighty joy?

290 BELVILE: See how kindly she invites me to deliver her
    from the threatened violence of her brother. Will you
    not assist me?

WILLMORE: I know not what thou mean'st, but I'll make
    one at any mischief where a woman's concerned. But
295   she'll be grateful to us for the favor, will she not?

BELVILE: How mean you?

WILLMORE: How should I mean? Thou know'st there's
    but one way for a woman to oblige me.

BELVILE: Do not profane; the maid is nicely virtuous.

300 WILLMORE: Who, pox, then she's fit for nothing but a
    husband. Let her e'en go, colonel.

FREDERICK: Peace, she's the colonel's mistress, sir.

WILLMORE: Let her be the devil; if she be thy mistress,
    I'll serve her. Name the way.

305 BELVILE: Read here this postscript. (*Gives him a letter.*)

WILLMORE (*reads*): "At ten at night, at the garden gate,
    of which, if I cannot get the key, I will contrive a
    way over the wall. Come attended with a friend or
    two."— Kind heart, if we three cannot weave a string
310   to let her down a garden wall, 'twere pity but the
    hangman wove one for us all.

FREDERICK: Let her alone for that; your woman's wit,
    your fair kind woman, will outtrick a broker or a
    Jew, and contrive like a Jesuit° in chains. But see,
315   Ned Blunt is stolen out after the lure of a damsel.

(*Exeunt Blunt and Lucetta.*)

BELVILE: So, he'll scarce find his way home again unless
    we get him cried by the bellman in the market place.
    And 'twould sound prettily: "A lost English boy of
    thirty."

FREDERICK: I hope 'tis some common crafty sinner, one   320
    that will fit him. It may be she'll sell him for Peru:°
    The rogue's sturdy, and would work well in a mine.
    At least I hope she'll dress him for our mirth, cheat
    him of all, then have him well-favoredly banged, and
    turned out at midnight.   325

WILLMORE: Prithee what humor is he of, that you wish
    him so well?

BELVILE: Why, of an English elder brother's humor: edu-
    cated in a nursery, with a maid to tend him till fifteen,
    and lies with his grandmother till he's of age; one that   330
    knows no pleasure beyond riding to the next fair, or
    going up to London with his right worshipful father
    in parliament time, wearing gay clothes, or making
    honorable love to his lady mother's laundry maid;
    gets drunk at a hunting match, and ten to one then   335
    gives some proofs of his prowess. A pox upon him,
    he's our banker, and has all our cash about him; and
    if he fail, we are all broke.

FREDERICK: Oh, let him alone for that matter; he's of a
    damned stingy quality that will secure our stock. I   340
    know not in what danger it were indeed if the jilt
    should pretend she's in love with him, for 'tis a kind
    believing coxcomb; otherwise, if he part with more
    than a piece of eight,° geld° him — for which offer he
    may chance to be beaten if she be a whore of the first   345
    rank.

BELVILE: Nay, the rogue will not be easily beaten; he's
    stout enough. Perhaps if they talk beyond his capac-
    ity he may chance to exercise his courage upon some
    of them, else I'm sure they'll find it as difficult to beat   350
    as to please him.

WILLMORE: 'Tis a lucky devil to light upon so kind a
    wench!

FREDERICK: Thou hadst a great deal of talk with thy
    little gypsy; couldst thou do no good upon her? For   355
    mine was hardhearted.

WILLMORE: Hang her, she was some damned honest
    person of quality, I'm sure, she was so very free and
    witty. If her face be but answerable to her wit and
    humor, I would be bound to constancy this month to   360
    gain her. In the meantime, have you made no kind
    acquaintance since you came to town? You do not
    use to be honest° so long, gentlemen.

FREDERICK: Faith, love has kept us honest: We have
    been all fir'd with a beauty newly come to town, the   365
    famous Paduana° Angellica Bianca.

WILLMORE: What, the mistress of the dead Spanish
    general?

314. Jew . . . Jesuit: Anti-Semitic and anti-Catholic attitudes of the time portrayed Jews and Jesuits as cunning and not worthy of trust.

321. sell him for Peru: Sell him as a slave. **344. piece of eight:** Spanish money. **geld:** Castrate. **363. honest:** Sexually inactive. **366. Paduana:** Angellica was born in Padua, Italy.

BELVILE: Yes, she's now the only ador'd beauty of all
370   the youth in Naples, who put on all their charms to
        appear lovely in her sight: Their coaches, liveries, and
        themselves all gay as on a monarch's birthday to
        attract the eyes of this fair charmer, while she has
        the pleasure to behold all languish for her that see
375   her.
FREDERICK: 'Tis pretty to see with how much love the
        men regard her, and how much envy the women.
WILLMORE: What gallant has she?
BELVILE: None; she's exposed to sale, and four days in
380   the week she's yours, for so much a month.
WILLMORE: The very thought of it quenches all manner
        of fire in me. Yet prithee, let's see her.
BELVILE: Let's first to dinner, and after that we'll pass the
        day as you please. But at night ye must all be at my
385   devotion.
WILLMORE: I will not fail you.   [*Exeunt.*]

ACT II • *Scene 1*

(*The long street. Enter Belvile and Frederick in masking
habits, and Willmore in his own clothes, with a vizard°
in his hand.*)

WILLMORE: But why thus disguised and muzzled?
BELVILE: Because whatever extravagances we commit in
        these faces, our own may not be obliged to answer
        'em.
5   WILLMORE: I should have changed my eternal buff,°
        too; but no matter, my little gypsy would not have
        found me out then. For if she should change hers, it is
        impossible I should know her unless I should hear her
        prattle. A pox on't, I cannot get her out of my head.
10   Pray heaven, if ever I do see her again, she prove
        damnably ugly, that I may fortify myself against her
        tongue.
BELVILE: Have a care of love, for o' my conscience she
        was not of a quality to give thee any hopes.
15 WILLMORE: Pox on 'em, why do they draw a man in
        then? She has played with my heart so, that 'twill
        never lie still till I have met with some kind wench
        that will play the game out with me. Oh, for my arms
        full of soft, white, kind woman — such as I fancy
20   Angellica.
BELVILE: This is her house, if you were but in stock to
        get admittance. They have not dined yet; I perceive
        the picture is not out.°

(*Enter Blunt.*)

WILLMORE: I long to see the shadow of the fair sub-
25   stance; a man may gaze on that for nothing.

BLUNT: Colonel, thy hand. And thine, Fred. I have been
        an ass, a deluded fool, a very coxcomb from my birth
        till this hour, and heartily repent my little faith.
BELVILE: What the devil's the matter with thee, Ned?
BLUNT: Oh, such a mistress, Fred! Such a girl!   30
WILLMORE: Ha! Where?
FREDERICK: Ay, where?
BLUNT: So fond, so amorous, so toying, and so fine! And
        all for sheer love, ye rogue! Oh, how she looked and
        kissed! And soothed my heart from my bosom! I can-   35
        not think I was awake, and yet methinks I see and
        feel her charms still. Fred, try if she have not left the
        taste of her balmy kisses upon my lips. (*Kisses him.*)
BELVILE: Ha! Ha! Ha!
WILLMORE: Death, man, where is she?   40
BLUNT: What a dog was I to stay in dull England so
        long! How have I laughed at the colonel when he
        sighed for love! But now the little archer° has re-
        venged him! And by this one dart I can guess at all his
        joys, which then I took for fancies, mere dreams and   45
        fables. Well, I'm resolved to sell all in Essex and plant
        here forever.
BELVILE: What a blessing 'tis, thou hast a mistress thou
        dar'st boast of; for I know thy humor is rather to
        have a proclaimed clap than a secret amour.   50
WILLMORE: Dost know her name?
BLUNT: Her name? No, 'adsheartlikins. What care I for
        names? She's fair, young, brisk and kind, even to rav-
        ishment! And what a pox care I for knowing her by
        any other title?   55
WILLMORE: Didst give her anything?
BLUNT: Give her? Ha! Ha! Ha! Why, she's a person of
        quality. That's a good one! Give her? 'Adsheartlikins,
        dost think such creatures are to be bought? Or are we
        provided for such a purchase? Give her, quoth ye?   60
        Why, she presented me with this bracelet for the toy
        of a diamond I used to wear. No, gentlemen, Ned
        Blunt is not everybody. She expects me again tonight.
WILLMORE: Egad, that's well; we'll all go.
BLUNT: Not a soul! No, gentlemen, you are wits; I am a   65
        dull country rogue, I.
FREDERICK: Well, sir, for all your person of quality, I
        shall be very glad to understand your purse be se-
        cure; 'tis our whole estate at present, which we are
        loath to hazard in one bottom.° Come sir, unlade.   70
BLUNT: Take the necessary trifle useless now to me, that
        am beloved by such a gentlewoman. 'Adsheartlikins,
        money! Here, take mine too.
FREDERICK: No, keep that to be cozened,° that we may
        laugh.   75
WILLMORE: Cozened? Death! Would I could meet with
        one that would cozen me of all the love I could spare
        tonight.
FREDERICK: Pox, 'tis some common whore, upon my life.

II, I. [S.D.] *vizard*: Face mask.   **5. buff:** Military coat made of
buff (leather).   **23. picture is not out:** Hanging her picture outside the house is a sign that she is open for business. (See lines
111–12 later in the scene.)

43. little archer: Cupid.   **70. hazard in one bottom:** Keep in
one place, as in the hold (bottom) of a ship.   **74. cozened:**
Cheated.

80 BLUNT: A whore? Yes, with such clothes, such jewels, such a house, such furniture, and so attended! A whore!

BELVILE: Why yes, sir, they are whores, though they'll neither entertain you with drinking, swearing, or
85 bawdry; are whores in all those gay clothes and right° jewels; are whores with those great houses richly furnished with velvet beds, store of plate,° handsome attendance, and fine coaches; are whores, and errant° ones.

90 WILLMORE: Pox on't, where do these fine whores live?

BELVILE: Where no rogues in office, ycleped° constables, dare give 'em laws, nor the wine-inspired bullies of the town break their windows; yet they are whores though this Essex calf° believe 'em persons of quality.

95 BLUNT: 'Adsheartlikins, y'are all fools. There are things about this Essex calf that shall take with the ladies, beyond all your wit and parts. This shape and size, gentlemen, are not to be despised; my waist, too, tolerably long, with other inviting signs that shall be
100 nameless.

WILLMORE: Egad, I believe he may have met with some person of quality that may be kind to him.

BELVILE: Dost thou perceive any such tempting things about him that should make a fine woman, and of
105 quality, pick him out from all mankind to throw away her youth and beauty upon; nay, and her dear heart, too? No, no, Angellica has raised the price too high.

WILLMORE: May she languish for mankind till she die,
110 and be damned for that one sin alone.

(*Enter two Bravos and hang up a great picture of Angellica's against the balcony, and two little ones at each side of the door.*)

BELVILE: See there the fair sign to the inn where a man may lodge that's fool enough to give her price.

(*Willmore gazes on the picture.*)

BLUNT: 'Adsheartlikins, gentlemen, what's this?

BELVILE: A famous courtesan, that's to be sold.

115 BLUNT: How? To be sold? Nay, then I have nothing to say to her. Sold! What impudence is practiced in this country; with what order and decency whoring's established here by virtue of the Inquisition!° Come, let's be gone; I'm sure we're no chapmen for this
120 commodity.

FREDERICK: Thou art none, I'm sure, unless thou couldst have her in thy bed at a price of a coach in the street.

WILLMORE: How wondrous fair she is! A thousand crowns a month? By heaven, as many kingdoms were

too little! A plague of this poverty, of which I ne'er   125
complain but when it hinders my approach to beauty which virtue ne'er could purchase.

                                    (*Turns from the picture.*)

BLUNT: What's this? (*Reads.*) "A thousand crowns a month"! 'Adsheartlikins, here's a sum! Sure 'tis a mistake. — [*To one of the Bravos.*] Hark you, friend,   130
does she take or give so much by the month?

FREDERICK: A thousand crowns! Why, 'tis a portion for the Infanta!°

BLUNT: Hark ye, friends, won't she trust?°

BRAVO: This is a trade, sir, that cannot live by credit.   135

(*Enter Don Pedro in masquerade, followed by Stephano.*)

BELVILE: See, here's more company; let's walk off a while.

                        (*Exeunt English,° Pedro reads.*)

PEDRO: Fetch me a thousand crowns; I never wished to buy this beauty at an easier rate. (*Passes off.*)

(*Enter Angellica and Moretta in the balcony, and draw a silk curtain.*)

ANGELLICA: Prithee, what said those fellows to thee?

BRAVO: Madam, the first were admirers of beauty only,   140
but no purchasers; they were merry with your price and picture, laughed at the sum, and so passed off.

ANGELLICA: No matter, I'm not displeased with their rallying; their wonder feeds my vanity, and he that wishes but to buy gives me more pride than he that   145
gives my price can make my pleasure.

BRAVO: Madam, the last I knew through all his disguises to be Don Pedro, nephew to the general, and who was with him in Pamplona.

ANGELLICA: Don Pedro? My old gallant's nephew?   150
When his uncle died he left him a vast sum of money; it is he who was so in love with me at Padua, and who used to make the general so jealous.

MORETTA: Is this he that used to prance before our window, and take such care to show himself an amorous   155
ass? If I am not mistaken, he is the likeliest man to give your price.

ANGELLICA: The man is brave and generous, but of a humor so uneasy and inconstant that the victory over his heart is as soon lost as won; a slave that can add   160
little to the triumph of the conqueror. But inconstancy's the sin of all mankind, therefore I'm resolved that nothing but gold shall charm my heart.

MORETTA: I'm glad on't; 'tis only interest that women of our profession ought to consider, though I wonder   165
what has kept you from that general disease of our sex so long; I mean, that of being in love.

ANGELLICA: A kind but sullen star under which I had the happiness to be born. Yet I have had no time for love; the bravest and noblest of mankind have purchased   170

---

86. right: Real.   **87. plate:** Silverware.   **89. errant:** Unmitigated.   **91. ycleped:** Past participle of *clepe*: called.   **94. Essex calf:** Derogatory term meaning "fool," referring to Essex, England, Blunt's home.   **118. Inquisition:** The Spanish Inquisition (1478–1834) forced prostitutes out of Spain and into neighboring countries.

132–33. portion for the Infanta: Dowry for the Spanish princess.
134. trust: Extend credit for payment.   **136. [S.D.]** *English:* All the English characters.

Ann Reinking and Edward Hermann
in the Williamstown Theatre
Festival's 1987 production of *The
Rover,* directed by John Rubinstein.

my favors at so dear a rate, as if no coin but gold
were current with our trade. But here's Don Pedro
again; fetch me my lute, for 'tis for him or Don Antonio the Viceroy's son that I have spread my nets.

(*Enter at one door Don Pedro, Stephano; Don Antonio
and Diego [his page] at the other door, with people following him in masquerade, antically attired, some with
music. They both go up to the picture.*)

175   ANTONIO: A thousand crowns! Had not the painter flattered her, I should not think it dear.
PEDRO: Flattered her? By heaven, he cannot. I have seen
the original, nor is there one charm here more than
adorns her face and eyes; all this soft and sweet, with
180   a certain languishing air that no artist can represent.

ANTONIO: What I heard of her beauty before had fired
my soul, but this confirmation of it has blown it to a
flame.
PEDRO: Ha!
PAGE: Sir, I have known you throw away a thousand   185
crowns on a worse face, and though y'are near your
marriage, you may venture a little love here; Florinda
will not miss it.
PEDRO (*aside*): Ha! Florinda! Sure 'tis Antonio.
ANTONIO: Florinda! Name not those distant joys; there's   190
not one thought of her will check my passion here.
PEDRO [*aside*]: Florinda scorned! (*A noise of a lute
above.*) And all my hopes defeated of the possession
of Angellica! (*Antonio gazes up.*) Her injuries, by
heaven, he shall not boast of!   195

(Song to a lute above.)

SONG
[I]
When Damon first began to love
He languished in a soft desire,
And knew not how the gods to move,
To lessen or increase his fire.
200   *For Caelia in her charming eyes*
Wore all love's sweets, and all his cruelties.

II
But as beneath a shade he lay,
Weaving of flowers for Caelia's hair,
She chanced to lead her flock that way,
205   *And saw the am'rous shepherd there.*
She gazed around upon the place,
And saw the grove, resembling night,
To all the joys of love invite,
Whilst guilty smiles and blushes dressed her face.
210   *At this the bashful youth all transport grew,*
And with kind force he taught the virgin how
To yield what all his sighs could never do.

(*Angellica throws open the curtains and bows to Antonio, who pulls off his vizard and bows and blows up kisses. Pedro, unseen, looks in's face. [The curtains close.]*)

ANTONIO: By heaven, she's charming fair!
PEDRO (*aside*): 'Tis he, the false Antonio!
ANTONIO (*to the Bravo*): Friend, where must I pay my
215   off'ring of love?
My thousand crowns I mean.
PEDRO: That off'ring I have designed to make,
And yours will come too late.
ANTONIO: Prithee begone; I shall grow angry else,
220   And then thou art not safe.
PEDRO: My anger may be fatal, sir, as yours,
And he that enters here may prove this truth.
ANTONIO: I know not who thou art, but I am sure
thou'rt worth my killing, for aiming at Angellica.
(*They draw and fight.*)

(*Enter Willmore and Blunt, who draw and part 'em.*)

225   BLUNT: 'Adsheartlikins, here's fine doings.
WILLMORE: Tilting for the wench, I'm sure. Nay, gad, if
that would win her I have as good a sword as the best
of ye. Put up, put up, and take another time and
place, for this is designed for lovers only.
(*They all put up.*)
PEDRO: We are prevented; dare you meet me tomorrow
230   on the Molo?°
For I've a title to a better quarrel,
That of Florinda, in whose credulous heart
Thou'st made an int'rest, and destroyed my hopes.
ANTONIO: Dare!
235   I'll meet thee there as early as the day.

230. Molo: Wharf.

PEDRO: We will come thus disguised, that whosoever
chance to get the better, he may escape unknown.
ANTONIO: It shall be so.

(*Exeunt Pedro and Stephano.*)

— Who should this rival be? Unless the English
colonel, of whom I've often heard Don Pedro speak.   240
It must be he, and time he were removed who lays a
claim to all my happiness.

(*Willmore, having gazed all this while on the picture[s], pulls down a little one.*)

WILLMORE: This posture's loose and negligent;
The sight on't would beget a warm desire
In souls whom impotence and age had chilled.   245
This must along with me.
BRAVO: What means this rudeness, sir? Restore the
picture.
ANTONIO: Ha! Rudeness committed to the fair Angel-
lica! — Restore the picture, sir.   250
WILLMORE: Indeed I will not, sir.
ANTONIO: By heaven, but you shall.
WILLMORE: Nay, do not show your sword; if you do, by
this dear beauty, I will show mine too.
ANTONIO: What right can you pretend to't?   255
WILLMORE: That of possession, which I will maintain.
You, perhaps, have a thousand crowns to give for the
original.
ANTONIO: No matter, sir, you shall restore the picture.

(*[The curtains open.] Angellica and Moretta above.*)

ANGELLICA: Oh, Moretta, what's the matter?   260
ANTONIO: Or leave your life behind.
WILLMORE: Death! You lie; I will do neither.

(*They fight. The Spaniards join with Antonio, Blunt laying on like mad.*)

ANGELLICA: Hold, I command you, if for me you fight.

(*They leave off and bow.*)

WILLMORE [*aside*]: How heavenly fair she is! Ah, plague
of her price!   265
ANGELLICA: You sir, in buff, you that appear a soldier,
that first began this insolence —
WILLMORE: 'Tis true, I did so, if you call it insolence for
a man to preserve himself. I saw your charming picture and was wounded; quite through my soul each   270
pointed beauty ran; and wanting a thousand crowns
to procure my remedy, I laid this little picture to my
bosom, which, if you cannot allow me, I'll resign.
ANGELLICA: No, you may keep the trifle.
ANTONIO: You shall first ask me leave, and this.   275

(*Fight again as before.*)

(*Enter Belvile and Frederick, who join with the English.*)

ANGELLICA: Hold! Will you ruin me? — Biskey! Sebastian! Part 'em!
(*The Spaniards are beaten off.*)

MORETTA: Oh, madam, we're undone. A pox upon that rude fellow; he's set on to ruin us. We shall never see good days again till all these fighting poor rogues are sent to the galleys.

(Enter Belvile, Blunt, Frederick, and Willmore with's shirt bloody.)

BLUNT: 'Adsheartlikins, beat me at this sport and I'll ne'er wear sword more.

BELVILE *(to Willmore)*: The devil's in thee for a mad fellow; thou art always one at an unlucky adventure. Come, let's be gone whilst we're safe, and remember these are Spaniards, a sort of people that know how to revenge an affront.

FREDERICK: You bleed! I hope you are not wounded.

WILLMORE: Not much. A plague on your dons; if they fight no better they'll ne'er recover Flanders.° What the devil was't to them that I took down the picture?

BLUNT: Took it! 'Adsheartlikins, we'll have the great one too; 'tis ours by conquest. Prithee help me up and I'll pull it down.

ANGELLICA *[to Willmore]*: Stay, sir, and ere you affront me farther let me know how you durst commit this outrage. To you I speak, sir, for you appear a gentleman.

WILLMORE: To me, madam? — Gentlemen, your servant.

(Belvile stays him.°)

BELVILE: Is the devil in thee? Dost know the danger of ent'ring the house of an incensed courtesan?

WILLMORE: I thank you for your care, but there are other matters in hand, there are, though we have no great temptation. Death! Let me go!

FREDERICK: Yes, to your lodging if you will, but not in here. Damn these gay harlots; by this hand I'll have as sound and handsome a whore for a patacoon.° Death, man, she'll murder thee!

WILLMORE: Oh, fear me not. Shall I not venture where a beauty calls? A lovely charming beauty! For fear of danger? When, by heaven, there's none so great as to long for her whilst I want money to purchase her.

FREDERICK: Therefore 'tis loss of time unless you had the thousand crowns to pay.

WILLMORE: It may be she may give a favor; at least I shall have the pleasure of saluting her when I enter and when I depart.

BELVILE: Pox, she'll as soon lie with thee as kiss thee, and sooner stab than do either. You shall not go.

ANGELLICA: Fear not, sir, all I have to wound with is my eyes.

BLUNT: Let him go. 'Adsheartlikins, I believe the gentlewoman means well.

BELVILE: Well, take thy fortune; we'll expect you in the next street. Farewell, fool, farewell.

WILLMORE: Bye, colonel.   *(Goes in.)*

FREDERICK: The rogue's stark mad for a wench.

(Exeunt.)

Scene II

(A fine chamber. Enter Willmore, Angellica, and Moretta.)

ANGELLICA: Insolent sir, how durst you pull down my picture?

WILLMORE: Rather, how durst you set it up to tempt poor am'rous mortals with so much excellence, which I find you have but too well consulted by the unmerciful price you set upon't. Is all this heaven of beauty shown to move despair in those that cannot buy? And can you think th'effects of that despair should be less extravagant than I have shown?

ANGELLICA: I sent for you to ask my pardon, sir, not to aggravate your crime. I thought I should have seen you at my feet imploring it.

WILLMORE: You are deceived. I came to rail at you, and rail such truths too, as shall let you see the vanity of that pride which taught you how to set such price on sin.
For such it is whilst that which is love's due
Is meanly bartered for.

ANGELLICA: Ha! Ha! Ha! Alas, good captain, what pity 'tis your edifying doctrine will do no good upon me. Moretta, fetch the gentleman a glass,° and let him survey himself to see what charms he has. — *(Aside, in a soft tone.)* And guess my business.

MORETTA: He knows himself of old: I believe those breeches and he have been acquainted ever since he was beaten at Worcester.°

ANGELLICA: Nay, do not abuse the poor creature.

MORETTA: Good weather-beaten corporal, will you march off? We have no need of your doctrine, though you have of our charity. But at present we have no scraps; we can afford no kindness for God's sake. In fine, sirrah, the price is too high i'th' mouth° for you, therefore troop, I say.

WILLMORE: Here, good forewoman of the shop, serve me and I'll be gone.

MORETTA: Keep it to pay your laundress; your linen stinks of the gun room. For here's no selling by retail.

WILLMORE: Thou hast sold plenty of thy stale ware at a cheap rate.

MORETTA: Ay, the more silly kind heart I, but this is an age wherein beauty is at higher rates. In fine, you know the price of this.

WILLMORE: I grant you 'tis here set down, a thousand crowns a month. Pray, how much may come to my

291. ne'er recover Flanders: In 1659 the Spanish gave Flanders, which had been part of the Spanish Netherlands, to France as settlement to end a war.   300. [S.D.] *stays him:* Keeps him from leaving.   308. patacoon: Portuguese or Spanish coin of small denomination.

21. glass: Mirror.   26. Worcester: Charles II was routed by Cromwell at Worcester in 1651 and was forced into exile on the Continent.   32. high i'th' mouth: High.

45   share for a pistole?° Bawd, take your black lead° and
      sum it up, that I may have a pistole's worth of this
      vain gay thing, and I'll trouble you no more.
      MORETTA: Pox on him, he'll fret me to death! Abomin-
      able fellow, I tell thee we only sell by the whole
50   piece.
      WILLMORE: 'Tis very hard, the whole cargo or nothing.
      Faith, madam, my stock will not reach it; I cannot be
      your chapman. Yet I have countrymen in town, mer-
      chants of love like me; I'll see if they'll put in for a
55   share. We cannot lose much by it, and what we have
      no use for, we'll sell upon the Friday's mart at "Who
      gives more?"— I am studying, madam, how to pur-
      chase you, though at present I am unprovided of
      money.
60   ANGELLICA (aside): Sure this from any other man would
      anger me; nor shall he know the conquest he has
      made. — Poor angry man, how I despise this railing.
      WILLMORE: Yes, I am poor. But I'm a gentleman,
      And one that scorns this baseness which you practice.
65   Poor as I am I would not sell myself,
      No, not to gain your charming high-prized person.
      Though I admire you strangely for your beauty,
      Yet I contemn your mind.
      And yet I would at any rate enjoy you;
70   At your own rate; but cannot. See here
      The only sum I can command on earth:
      I know not where to eat when this is gone.
      Yet such a slave I am to love and beauty
      This last reserve I'll sacrifice to enjoy you.
75   Nay, do not frown, I know you're to be bought,
      And would be bought by me. By me,
      For a meaning trifling sum, if I could pay it down.
      Which happy knowledge I will still repeat,
      And lay it to my heart: It has a virtue in't,
      And soon will cure those wounds your eyes have
80   made.
      And yet, there's something so divinely powerful
         there —
      Nay, I will gaze, to let you see my strength.

(Holds her, looks on her, and pauses and sighs.)

      By heav'n, bright creature, I would not for the world
      Thy fame were half so fair as is thy face.

(Turns her away from him.)

      ANGELLICA (aside): His words go through me to the
85   very soul. —
      If you have nothing else to say to me —
      WILLMORE: Yes, you shall hear how infamous you are —
      For which I do not hate thee —
      But that secures my heart, and all the flames it feels
90   Are but so many lusts:
      I know it by their sudden bold intrusion.
      The fire's impatient and betrays; 'tis false.

44–45. how much . . . pistole: How much will my pistole (a
Spanish coin) buy?   **45. black lead:** Pencil.

      For had it been the purer flame of love,
      I should have pined and languished at your feet,
      Ere found the impudence to have discovered it.   95
      I now dare stand your scorn and your denial.
      MORETTA: Sure she's bewitched, that she can stand thus
      tamely and hear his saucy railing. — Sirrah, will you
      be gone?
      ANGELLICA (to Moretta): How dare you take this lib-   100
      erty! Withdraw! — Pray tell me, sir, are not you
      guilty of the same mercenary crime? When a lady is
      proposed to you for a wife, you never ask how fair,
      discreet, or virtuous she is, but what's her fortune;
      which, if but small, you cry "She will not do my busi- 105
      ness," and basely leave her, though she languish for
      you. Say, is not this as poor?
      WILLMORE: It is a barbarous custom, which I will scorn
      to defend in our sex, and do despise in yours.
      ANGELLICA: Thou'rt a brave fellow! Put up thy gold,
         and know,   110
      That were thy fortune as large as is thy soul,
      Thou shouldst not buy my love
      Couldst thou forget those mean effects of vanity
      Which set me out to sale,
      And as a lover prize my yielding joys.   115
      Canst thou believe they'll be entirely thine,
      Without considering they were mercenary?
      WILLMORE: I cannot tell, I must bethink me first.
         (Aside.) Ha! Death, I'm going to believe her.
      ANGELLICA: Prithee confirm that faith, or if thou canst
         not,   120
      Flatter me a little: 'Twill please me from thy mouth.
      WILLMORE (aside): Curse on thy charming tongue!
         Dost thou return
         My feigned contempt with so much subtlety? —
      Thou'st found the easiest way into my heart,
      Though I yet know that all thou say'st is false.   125

(Turning from her in rage.)

      ANGELLICA: By all that's good, 'tis real;
      I never loved before, though oft a mistress.
      Shall my first vows be slighted?
      WILLMORE (aside): What can she mean?
      ANGELLICA (in an angry tone): I find you cannot credit
         me.   130
      WILLMORE: I know you take me for an errant ass,
      An ass that may be soothed into belief,
      And then be used at pleasure;
      But, madam, I have been so often cheated
      By perjured, soft, deluding hypocrites,   135
      That I've no faith left for the cozening sex,
      Especially for women of your trade.
      ANGELLICA: The low esteem you have of me perhaps
      May bring my heart again:
      For I have pride that yet surmounts my love.   140

(She turns with pride; he holds her.)

      WILLMORE: Throw off this pride, this enemy to bliss,
      And show the power of love: 'Tis with those arms
      I can be only vanquished, made a slave.

ANGELLICA: Is all my mighty expectation vanished?
145　No, I will not hear thee talk; thou hast a charm
　　In every word that draws my heart away,
　　And all the thousand trophies I designed
　　Thou hast undone. Why art thou soft?
　　Thy looks are bravely rough, and meant for war.
150　Couldst thou not storm on still?
　　I then perhaps had been as free as thou.
WILLMORE (aside): Death, how she throws her fire
　　　about my soul! —
　　Take heed, fair creature, how you raise my hopes,
　　Which once assumed pretends to all dominion:
155　There's not a joy thou hast in store
　　I shall not then command.
　　For which I'll pay you back my soul, my life!
　　Come, let's begin th'account this happy minute!
ANGELLICA: And will you pay me then the price I ask?
WILLMORE: Oh, why dost thou draw me from an
160　awful worship,
　　By showing thou art no divinity.
　　Conceal the fiend, and show me all the angel!
　　Keep me but ignorant, and I'll be devout
　　And pay my vows forever at this shrine.

(Kneels and kisses her hand.)

165　ANGELLICA: The pay I mean is but thy love for mine.
　　Can you give that?
WILLMORE: Entirely. Come, let's withdraw where I'll
　　renew my vows, and breathe 'em with such ardor
　　thou shalt not doubt my zeal.
170　ANGELLICA: Thou hast a power too strong to be resisted.

(Exeunt Willmore and Angellica.)

MORETTA: Now my curse go with you! Is all our project
　　fallen to this? To love the only enemy to our trade?
　　Nay, to love such a shameroon;° a very beggar; nay, a
　　pirate beggar, whose business is to rifle and be gone;
175　a no-purchase, no-pay tatterdemalion,° and English
　　picaroon;° a rogue that fights for daily drink, and
　　takes a pride in being loyally lousy? Oh, I could curse
　　now, if I durst. This is the fate of most whores.
　　Trophies, which from believing fops we win,
180　Are spoils to those who cozen us again.   [Exit.]

ACT III • Scene I

(A street. Enter Florinda, Valeria, Hellena, in antic° different dresses from what they were in before; Callis attending.)

FLORINDA: I wonder what should make my brother in so
　　ill a humor? I hope he has not found out our ramble
　　this morning.

HELLENA: No, if he had, we should have heard on't at
　　both ears, and have been mewed up° this afternoon,   5
　　which I would not for the world should have happened. Hey ho, I'm as sad as a lover's lute.
VALERIA: Well, methinks we have learnt this trade of
　　gypsies as readily as if we had been bred upon the
　　road to Loretto;° and yet I did so fumble when I told   10
　　the stranger his fortune that I was afraid I should
　　have told my own and yours by mistake. But methinks Hellena has been very serious ever since.
FLORINDA: I would give my garters she were in love, to be
　　revenged upon her for abusing me. How is't, Hellena?   15
HELLENA: Ah, would I had never seen my mad monsieur. And yet, for all your laughing, I am not in love.
　　And yet this small acquaintance, o' my conscience,
　　will never out of my head.
VALERIA: Ha! Ha! Ha! I laugh to think how thou art fit-   20
　　ted with a lover, a fellow that I warrant loves every
　　new face he sees.
HELLENA: Hum, he has not kept his word with me here,
　　and may be taken up. That thought is not very pleasant to me. What the deuce should this be now that I   25
　　feel?
VALERIA: What is't like?
HELLENA: Nay, the Lord knows, but if I should be
　　hanged I cannot choose but be angry and afraid
　　when I think that mad fellow should be in love with   30
　　anybody but me. What to think of myself I know not:
　　Would I could meet with some true damned gypsy,
　　that I might know my fortune.
VALERIA: Know it! Why there's nothing so easy: Thou
　　wilt love this wand'ring inconstant till thou find'st   35
　　thyself hanged about his neck, and then be as mad to
　　get free again.
FLORINDA: Yes, Valeria, we shall see her bestride his
　　baggage horse and follow him to the campaign.
HELLENA: So, so, now you are provided for there's no   40
　　care taken of poor me. But since you have set my
　　heart a-wishing, I am resolved to know for what, I
　　will not die of the pip,° so I will not.
FLORINDA: Art thou mad to talk so? Who will like thee
　　well enough to have thee, that hears what a mad   45
　　wench thou art?
HELLENA: Like me? I don't intend every he that likes me
　　shall have me, but he that I like. I should have stayed
　　in the nunnery still if I had liked my lady abbess as
　　well as she liked me. No, I came thence not, as my   50
　　wise brother imagines, to take an eternal farewell of
　　the world, but to love and to be beloved; and I will be
　　beloved, or I'll get one of your men, so I will.
VALERIA: Am I put into° the number of lovers?

---

173. **shameroon:** Shameful person. 175. **tatterdemalion:**
Ragamuffin. 176. **picaroon:** Wandering rogue. III, I. [S.D.]
antic: Absurd, ludicrous, strange.

5. **mewed up:** Shut in, imprisoned. 10. **Loretto:** Loreto is an
Italian town on the Adriatic coast, a destination for pilgrims
visiting the cottage of the Virgin Mary. 43. **pip:** A disease of
poultry and birds, applied vaguely, usually humorously, to various ailments in humans. 54. **Am I put into:** Do you include
me among?

55 HELLENA: You? Why, coz, I know thou'rt too good-
natured to leave us in any design; thou wouldst venture a cast° though thou comest off a loser, especially
with such a gamester. I observed your man, and your
willing ear incline that way; and if you are not a
60   lover, 'tis an art soon learnt — that I find.   (*Sighs.*)
FLORINDA: I wonder how you learnt to love so easily. I
had a thousand charms to meet my eyes and ears ere I
could yield, and 'twas the knowledge of Belvile's
merit, not the surprising person, took my soul. Thou
65   art too rash, to give a heart at first sight.
HELLENA: Hang your considering lover! I never thought
beyond the fancy that 'twas a very pretty, idle, silly
kind of pleasure to pass one's time with: to write little
soft nonsensical billets,° and with great difficulty and
70   danger receive answers in which I shall have my
beauty praised, my wit admired, though little or
none, and have the vanity and power to know I am
desirable. Then I have the more inclination that way
because I am to be a nun, and so shall not be sus-
75   pected to have any such earthly thoughts about me;
but when I walk thus — and sigh thus — they'll
think my mind's upon my monastery, and cry, "How
happy 'tis she's so resolved." But not a word of man.
FLORINDA: What a mad creature's this!
80 HELLENA: I'll warrant, if my brother hears either of you
sigh, he cries gravely, "I fear you have the indiscretion to be in love, but take heed of the honor of our
house, and your own unspotted fame"; and so he
conjures on till he has laid the soft winged god in
85   your hearts, or broke the bird's nest.° But see, here
comes your lover, but where's my inconstant? Let's
step aside, and we may learn something.

(*Go aside.*)

(*Enter Belvile, Frederick, and Blunt.*)

BELVILE: What means this! The picture's taken in.
BLUNT: It may be the wench is good-natured, and will be
90   kind gratis.° Your friend's a proper handsome fellow.
BELVILE: I rather think she has cut his throat and is fled;
I am mad he should throw himself into dangers. Pox
on't, I shall want him, too, at night. Let's knock and
ask for him.
95 HELLENA: My heart goes a-pit, a-pat, for fear 'tis my
man they talk of.

(*Knock; Moretta above.*)

MORETTA: What would you have?
BELVILE: Tell the stranger that entered here about two
hours ago that his friends stay here for him.
100 MORETTA: A curse upon him for Moretta: Would he
were at the devil! But he's coming to you.

(*Enter Willmore.*)

HELLENA: Ay, ay 'tis he. Oh, how this vexes me!

BELVILE: And how and how, dear lad, has fortune
smiled? Are we to break her windows, or raise up
altars to her, hah?   105
WILLMORE: Does not my fortune sit triumphant on my
brow? Dost not see the little wanton god there all gay
and smiling? Have I not an air about my face and
eyes that distinguish me from the crowd of common
lovers? By heaven, Cupid's quiver has not half so   110
many darts as her eyes! Oh, such a *bona roba!*° To
sleep in her arms is lying *in fresco,*° all perfumed air
about me.
HELLENA (*aside*): Here's fine encouragement for me to
fool on!   115
WILLMORE: Hark'ee, where didst thou purchase that
rich Canary° we drank today? Tell me, that I may
adore the spigot and sacrifice to the butt.° The juice
was divine; into which I must dip my rosary, and
then bless all things that I would have bold or fortu-   120
nate.
BELVILE: Well, sir, let's go take a bottle and hear the
story of your success.
FREDERICK: Would not French wine do better?
WILLMORE: Damn the hungry balderdash!° Cheerful   125
sack° has a generous virtue in't inspiring a successful
confidence, gives eloquence to the tongue and vigor
to the soul, and has in a few hours completed all my
hopes and wishes! There's nothing left to raise a new
desire in me. Come, let's be gay and wanton. And,   130
gentlemen, study; study what you want, for here are
friends that will supply gentlemen. [*Jingles gold.*]
Hark what a charming sound they make! 'Tis he and
she gold whilst here, and shall beget new pleasures
every moment.   135
BLUNT: But hark'ee, sir, you are not married, are you?
WILLMORE: All the honey of matrimony but none of the
sting, friend.
BLUNT: 'Adsheartlikins, thou'rt a fortunate rogue!
WILLMORE: I am so, sir: let these inform you! Ha, how   140
sweetly they chime! Pox of poverty: It makes a man a
slave, makes wit and honor sneak. My soul grew lean
and rusty for want of credit.
BLUNT: 'Adsheartlikins, this I like well; it looks like my
lucky bargain! Oh, how I long for the approach of   145
my squire, that is to conduct me to her house again.
Why, here's two provided for!
FREDERICK: By this light, y'are happy men.
BLUNT: Fortune is pleased to smile on us, gentlemen, to
smile on us.   150

(*Enter Sancho and pulls down Blunt by the sleeve; they
go aside.*)

SANCHO: Sir, my lady expects you. She has removed all
that might oppose your will and pleasure, and is impatient till you come.

56–57. **venture a cast:** Throw the dice.   69. **billets:** Brief letters, notes.   84–85. **laid . . . bird's nest:** Ruined your chances.
90. **gratis:** Free of charge.

111. *bona roba:* A courtesan.   112. *in fresco:* In the fresh air out
of doors.   117. **Canary:** A light sweet wine from the Canary
Islands.   118. **butt:** Large wine cask.   125. **hungry balderdash:**
Cheap mixture of liquor.   126. **sack:** Dry white Spanish wine.

BLUNT: Sir, I'll attend you. — Oh the happiest rogue! I'll
155   take no leave, lest they either dog me or stay me.
                                        (*Exit with Sancho.*)
BELVILE: But then the little gypsy is forgot?
WILLMORE: A mischief on thee for putting her into my
       thoughts! I had quite forgot her else, and this night's
       debauch had drunk her quite down.
160 HELLENA: Had it so, good captain!

(*Claps him on the back.*)

WILLMORE (*aside*): Ha! I hope she did not hear me!
HELLENA: What, afraid of such a champion?
WILLMORE: Oh, you're a fine lady of your word, are you
       not? To make a man languish a whole day —
165 HELLENA: In tedious search of me.
WILLMORE: Egad, child, thou'rt in the right. Hadst thou
       seen what a melancholy dog I have been ever since I
       was a lover, how I have walked the streets like a
       Capuchin,° with my hands in my sleeves — faith,
170   sweetheart, thou wouldst pity me.
HELLENA [*aside*]: Now if I should be hanged I can't be
       angry with him, he dissembles so heartily. — Alas,
       good captain, what pains you have taken; now were I
       ungrateful not to reward so true a servant.
175 WILLMORE: Poor soul, that's kindly said; I see thou
       barest a conscience. Come then, for a beginning
       show me thy dear face.
HELLENA: I'm afraid, my small acquaintance, you have
       been staying that swinging stomach you boasted of
180   this morning. I then remember my little collation°
       would have gone down with you without the sauce
       of a handsome face. Is your stomach so queasy now?
WILLMORE: Faith, long fasting, child, spoils a man's
       appetite. Yet if you durst treat, I could so lay about
185   me still —
HELLENA: And would you fall to before a priest says
       grace?
WILLMORE: O fie, fie, what an old out-of-fashioned
       thing hast thou named? Thou couldst not dash me
190   more out of countenance shouldst thou show me an
       ugly face.

(*Whilst he is seemingly courting Hellena, enter Angellica, Moretta, Biskey, and Sebastian, all in masquerade.
Angellica sees Willmore and stares.*)

ANGELLICA: Heavens, 'tis he! And passionately fond to
       see another woman!
MORETTA: What could you less expect from such a
195   swaggerer?
ANGELLICA: Expect? As much as I paid him: a heart
          entire,
       Which I had pride enough to think when'er I gave,
       It would have raised the man above the vulgar,
       Made him all soul, and that all soft and constant.
200 HELLENA: You see, captain, how willing I am to be
       friends with you, till time and ill luck make us lovers;
       and ask you the question first rather than put your

---

169. **Capuchin:** Franciscan monk.   180. **collation:** Snack.

---

modesty to the blush by asking me. For alas, I know
       you captains are such strict men, and such severe
       observers of your vows to chastity, that 'twill be hard 205
       to prevail with your tender conscience to marry a
       young willing maid.
WILLMORE: Do not abuse me, for fear I should take thee
       at thy word and marry thee indeed, which I'm sure
       will be revenge sufficient.   210
HELLENA: O' my conscience, that will be our destiny,
       because we are both of one humor: I am as incon-
       stant as you, for I have considered, captain, that a
       handsome woman has a great deal to do whilst her
       face is good. For then is our harvest-time to gather   215
       friends, and should I in these days of my youth catch
       a fit of foolish constancy, I were undone: 'tis loitering
       by daylight in our great journey. Therefore, I declare
       I'll allow but one year for love, one year for indiffer-
       ence, and one year for hate; and then go hang your- 220
       self, for I profess myself the gay, the kind, and the
       inconstant. The devil's in't if this won't please you!
WILLMORE: Oh, most damnably. I have a heart with a
       hole quite through it too; no prison mine, to keep a
       mistress in.   225
ANGELLICA (*aside*): Perjured man! How I believe thee
       now!
HELLENA: Well, I see our business as well as humors are
       alike: yours to cozen as many maids as will trust you,
       and I as many men as have faith. See if I have not as 230
       desperate a lying look as you can have for the heart
       of you. (*Pulls off her vizard; he starts.*) How do you
       like it, captain?
WILLMORE: Like it! By heaven, I never saw so much
       beauty! Oh, the charms of those sprightly black eyes! 235
       That strangely fair face, full of smiles and dimples!
       Those soft round melting cherry lips and small even
       white teeth! Not to be expressed, but silently adored!
       [*She replaces her mask.*] Oh, one look more, and strike
       me dumb, or I shall repeat nothing else till I'm mad.   240

(*He seems to court her to pull off her vizard; she refuses.*)

ANGELLICA: I can endure no more. Nor is it fit to inter-
       rupt him, for if I do, my jealousy has so destroyed my
       reason I shall undo him. Therefore I'll retire, and you,
       Sebastian (*to one of her Bravos*), follow that woman
       and learn who 'tis; while you (*to the other Bravo*) tell 245
       the fugitive I would speak to him instantly.   (*Exit.*)

(*This while Florinda is talking to Belvile, who stands
sullenly; Frederick courting Valeria.*)

VALERIA [*to Belvile*]: Prithee, dear stranger, be not so
       sullen, for though you have lost your love you see my
       friend frankly offers you hers to play with in the
       meantime.   250
BELVILE: Faith, madam, I am sorry I can't play at her
       game.
FREDERICK [*to Valeria*]: Pray leave your intercession and
       mind your own affair. They'll better agree apart: He's
       a modest sigher in company, but alone no woman   255
       'scapes him.

FLORINDA [*aside*]: Sure he does but rally. Yet, if it should be true? I'll tempt him farther. — Believe me, noble stranger, I'm no common mistress. And for a little
260 proof on't, wear this jewel.° Nay, take it, sir, 'tis right, and bills of exchange may sometimes miscarry.

BELVILE: Madam, why am I chose out of all mankind to be the object of your bounty?

VALERIA: There's another civil question asked.

265 FREDERICK [*aside*]: Pox of's modesty; it spoils his own markets and hinders mine.

FLORINDA: Sir, from my window I have often seen you, and women of my quality have so few opportunities for love that we ought to lose none.

270 FREDERICK [*to Valeria*]: Ay, this is something! Here's a woman! When shall I be blest with so much kindness from your fair mouth? — (*Aside to Belvile*.) Take the jewel, fool!

BELVILE: You tempt me strangely, madam, every way —

275 FLORINDA (*aside*): So, if I find him false, my whole repose is gone.

BELVILE: And but for a vow I've made to a very fair lady, this goodness had subdued me.

FREDERICK [*aside to Belvile*]: Pox on't, be kind, in pity
280 to me be kind. For I am to thrive here but as you treat her friend.

HELLENA: Tell me what you did in yonder house, and I'll unmask.

WILLMORE: Yonder house? Oh, I went to a — to —
285 why, there's a friend of mine lives there.

HELLENA: What, a she or a he friend?

WILLMORE: A man, upon honor, a man. A she friend? No, no, madam, you have done my business, I thank you.

290 HELLENA: And was't your man friend that had more darts in's eyes than Cupid carries in's whole budget of arrows?

WILLMORE: So —

HELLENA: "Ah, such a *bona roba*! To be in her arms is
295 lying *in fresco,* all perfumed air about me." Was this your man friend too?

WILLMORE: So —

HELLENA: That gave you the he and the she gold, that begets young pleasures?

300 WILLMORE: Well, well, madam, then you can see there are ladies in the world that will not be cruel. There are, madam, there are.

HELLENA: And there be men, too, as fine, wild, inconstant fellows as yourself. There be, captain, there be,
305 if you go to that now. Therefore, I'm resolved —

WILLMORE: Oh!

HELLENA: To see your face no more —

WILLMORE: Oh!

HELLENA: Till tomorrow.

310 WILLMORE: Egad, you frighted me.

HELLENA: Nor then neither, unless you'll swear never to see that lady more.

260. **jewel**: A locket with her picture in it.

WILLMORE: See her! Why, never to think of womankind again.

HELLENA: Kneel and swear.   315

(*Kneels, she gives him her hand.*)

WILLMORE: I do, never to think, to see, to love, nor lie, with any but thyself.

HELLENA: Kiss the book.

WILLMORE: Oh, most religiously.   (*Kisses her hand.*)

HELLENA: Now what a wicked creature am I, to damn a   320
proper fellow.

CALLIS (*to Florinda*): Madam, I'll stay no longer: 'tis e'en dark.

FLORINDA [*to Belvile*]: However, sir, I'll leave this with you, that when I'm gone you may repent the oppor-   325
tunity you have lost by your modesty.

(*Gives him the jewel, which is her picture, and exit.
He gazes after her.*)

WILLMORE [*to Hellena*]: 'Twill be an age till tomorrow, and till then I will most impatiently expect you. Adieu, my dear pretty angel.

(*Exeunt all the women.*)

BELVILE: Ha! Florinda's picture! 'Twas she herself. What   330
a dull dog was I! I would have given the world for one minute's discourse with her.

FREDERICK: This comes of your modesty. Ah, pox o' your vow; 'twas ten to one but we had lost the jewel by't.

BELVILE: Willmore, the blessed'st opportunity lost!   335
Florinda, friends, Florinda!

WILLMORE: Ah, rogue! Such black eyes! Such a face! Such a mouth! Such teeth! And so much wit!

BELVILE: All, all, and a thousand charms besides.

WILLMORE: Why, dost thou know her?   340

BELVILE: Know her! Ay, ay, and a pox take me with all my heart for being so modest.

WILLMORE: But hark'ee, friend of mine, are you my rival? And have I been only beating the bush all this while?

BELVILE: I understand thee not. I'm mad! See here —   345

(*Shows the picture.*)

WILLMORE: Ha! Whose picture's this? 'Tis a fine wench!

FREDERICK: The colonel's mistress, sir.

WILLMORE: Oh, oh, here. (*Gives the picture back.*) I thought't had been another prize. Come, come, a bottle will set thee right again.   350

BELVILE: I am content to try, and by that time 'twill be late enough for our design.

WILLMORE: Agreed.
      Love does all day the soul's great empire keep,
      But wine at night lulls the soft god asleep.   355

(*Exeunt.*)

Scene II

(*Lucetta's house. Enter Blunt and Lucetta with a light.*)

LUCETTA: Now we are safe and free: no fears of the coming home of my old jealous husband, which made me

a little thoughtful when you came in first. But now
love is all the business of my soul.

5 BLUNT: I am transported! — (*Aside.*) Pox on't, that I
had but some fine things to say to her, such as lovers
use. I was a fool not to learn of Fred a little by heart
before I came. Something I must say. 'Adsheartlikins,
sweet soul, I am not used to compliment, but I'm an

10 honest gentleman, and thy humble servant.

LUCETTA: I have nothing to pay for so great a favor, but
such a love as cannot but be great, since at first sight
of that sweet face and shape it made me your absolute captive.

15 BLUNT (*aside*): Kind heart, how prettily she talks! Egad,
I'll show her husband a Spanish trick: Send him out
of the world and marry her; she's damnably in love
with me, and will ne'er mind settlements,° and so
there's that saved.

20 LUCETTA: Well, sir, I'll go and undress me, and be with
you instantly.

BLUNT: Make haste then, for 'adsheartlikins, dear soul,
thou canst not guess at the pain of a longing lover
when his joys are drawn within the compass of a few

25 minutes.

LUCETTA: You speak my sense, and I'll make haste to
prove it.   (*Exit.*)

BLUNT: 'Tis a rare girl, and this one night's enjoyment
with her will be worth all the days I ever passed in

30 Essex. Would she would go with me into England,
though to say truth, there's plenty of whores already.
Put a pox on 'em, they are such mercenary prodigal
whores that they want such a one as this, that's free
and generous, to give 'em good examples. Why, what

35 a house she has, how rich and fine!

(*Enter Sancho.*)

SANCHO: Sir, my lady has sent me to conduct you to her
chamber.

BLUNT: Sir, I shall be proud to follow. — (*Aside.*) Here's
one of her servants too; 'adsheartlikins, by this garb

40 and gravity he might be a justice of peace in Essex,
and is but a pimp here.

(*Exeunt.*)

Scene III

(*The scene changes to a chamber with an alcove bed in't,
a table, etc.; Lucetta in bed. Enter Sancho and Blunt,
who takes the candle of Sancho at the door.*)

SANCHO: Sir, my commission reaches no farther.
BLUNT: Sir, I'll excuse your compliment.
                                          [*Exit Sancho.*]
— What, in bed, my sweet mistress?
LUCETTA: You see, I still outdo you in kindness.
5 BLUNT: And thou shalt see what haste I'll make to quit
scores. Oh, the luckiest rogue!

18. will ne'er mind settlements: Won't require the gifts of property usually settled on a wife after marriage.

(*He undresses himself.*)

LUCETTA: Should you be false or cruel now —
BLUNT: False! 'Adsheartlikins, what dost thou take me
for, a Jew? An insensible heathen? A pox of thy old
jealous husband: An° he were dead, egad, sweet soul, 10
it should be none of my fault if I did not marry thee.
LUCETTA: It never should be mine.
BLUNT: Good soul! I'm the fortunatest dog!
LUCETTA: Are you not undressed yet?
BLUNT: As much as my impatience will permit.   15

(*Goes toward the bed in his shirt, drawers, etc.*)

LUCETTA: Hold, sir, put out the light; it may betray us
else.
BLUNT: Anything; I need no other light but that of thine
eyes. — (*Aside.*) 'Adsheartlikins, there I think I had it.

(*Puts out the candle; the bed descends; he gropes about
to find it.*)

Why, why, where am I got? What, not yet? Where are 20
you, sweetest? — Ah, the rogue's silent now. A pretty
love-trick this; how she'll laugh at me anon! — You
need not, my dear rogue, you need not! I'm all on fire
already; come, come, now call me, in pity. — Sure
I'm enchanted! I have been round the chamber, and 25
can find neither woman nor bed. I locked the door;
I'm sure she cannot go that way, or if she could, the
bed could not. — Enough, enough, my pretty wanton; do not carry the jest too far! (*Lights on a trap,
and is let down.*) — Ha! Betrayed! Dogs! Rogues! 30
Pimps! Help! Help!

(*Enter Lucetta, Philippo, and Sancho with a light.*)

PHILIPPO: Ha! Ha! Ha! He's dispatched finely.
LUCETTA: Now, sir, had I been coy, we had missed of this
booty.
PHILIPPO: Nay, when I saw 'twas a substantial fool, I 35
was mollified. But when you dote upon a serenading
coxcomb, upon a face, fine clothes, and a lute, it
makes me rage.
LUCETTA: You know I was never guilty of that folly, my
dear Philippo, but with yourself. But come, let's see 40
what we have got by this.
PHILIPPO: A rich coat; sword and hat; these breeches,
too, are well lined! See here, a gold watch! A purse —
Ha! Gold! At least two hundred pistoles! A bunch of
diamond rings, and one with the family arms! A gold 45
box, with a medal of his king, and his lady mother's
picture! These were sacred relics, believe me. See, the
waistband of his breeches have a mine of gold — old
queen Bess's!° We have a quarrel to her ever since
eighty-eight,° and may therefore justify the theft: The 50
Inquisition might have committed it.
LUCETTA: See, a bracelet of bowed gold! These his sisters
tied about his arm at parting. But well, for all this, I

10. An: If.   48–49. old queen Bess's: Queen Elizabeth I (reigned
1558–1603).   50. eighty-eight: The year the Spanish Armada
was defeated by the English (1588).

55 fear his being a stranger may make a noise and hinder our trade with them hereafter.

PHILIPPO: That's our security: He is not only a stranger to us, but to the country too. The common shore° into which he is descended, thou know'st, conducts him into another street, which this light will hinder
60 him from ever finding again. He knows neither your name, nor that of the street where your house is; nay, nor the way to his own lodgings.

LUCETTA: And art thou not an unmerciful rogue, not to afford him one night for all this? I should not have
65 been such a Jew.

PHILIPPO: Blame me not, Lucetta, to keep as much of thee as I can to myself. Come, that thought makes me wanton; let's to bed. — Sancho, lock up these.

This is the fleece which fools do bear,
70 *Designed for witty men to shear.*   (*Exeunt.*)

Scene IV

(*The scene changes, and discovers Blunt creeping out of a common shore; his face, etc., all dirty.*)

BLUNT (*climbing up*): Oh, Lord, I am got out at last, and, which is a miracle, without a clue. And now to damning and cursing! But if that would ease me, where shall I begin? With my fortune, myself, or the
5 quean° that cozened me? What a dog was I to believe in woman! Oh, coxcomb! Ignorant conceited coxcomb! To fancy she could be enamored with my person! At first sight enamored! Oh, I'm a cursed puppy! 'Tis plain, fool was writ upon my forehead! She per-
10 ceived it; saw the Essex calf there. For what allurements could there be in this countenance, which I can endure because I'm acquainted with it. Oh dull, silly dog, to be thus soothed into a cozening! Had I been drunk, I might fondly have credited the young quean;
15 but as I was in my right wits to be thus cheated, confirms it: I am a dull believing English country fop. But my comrades! Death and the devil, there's the worst of all! Then a ballad will be sung tomorrow on the Prado,° to a lousy tune of the enchanted squire and
20 the annihilated damsel. But Fred — that rogue — and the colonel will abuse me beyond all Christian patience. Had she left me my clothes, I have a bill of exchange at home would have saved my credit. But now all hope is taken from me. Well, I'll home, if I
25 can find the way, with this consolation: that I am not the first kind believing coxcomb; but there are, gallants, many such good natures amongst ye.

And though you've better arts to hide your follies,
'Adsheartlikins, y'are all as errant cullies.°

(*Exit.*)

---

57. **common shore:** Sewer. 5. **quean:** Harlot, tramp.
18–19. **ballad . . . Prado:** A song satirizing him will be sung on the Prado, a fashionable promenade in Madrid, for common amusement. 29. *cullies:* A cully is one easily fooled; a simpleton.

Scene V

(*Scene: the garden in the night. Enter Florinda in an undress,° with a key and a little box.*)

FLORINDA: Well, thus far I'm in my way to happiness. I have got myself free from Callis; my brother too, I find by yonder light, is got into his cabinet,° and thinks not of me; I have by good fortune got the key of the garden back door. I'll open it to prevent 5 Belvile's knocking: A little noise will now alarm my brother. Now am I as fearful as a young thief. (*Unlocks the door.*) Hark! What noise is that? Oh, 'twas the wind that played amongst the boughs. Belvile stays long, methinks; it's time. Stay, for fear of 10 a surprise, I'll hide these jewels in yonder jasmine.

(*She goes to lay down the box.*)

(*Enter Willmore, drunk.*)

WILLMORE: What the devil is become of these fellows Belvile and Frederick? They promised to stay at the next corner for me, but who the devil knows the corner of a full moon? Now, whereabouts am I? Ha, 15 what have we here? A garden! A very convenient place to sleep in. Ha! What has God sent us here? A female! By this light, a woman! I'm a dog if it be not a very wench!

FLORINDA: He's come! Ha! Who's there? 20

WILLMORE: Sweet soul, let me salute thy shoestring.

FLORINDA [*aside*]: 'Tis not my Belvile. Good heavens, I know him not! — Who are you, and from whence come you?

WILLMORE: Prithee, prithee, child, not so many hard 25 questions! Let it suffice I am here, child. Come, come kiss me.

FLORINDA: Good gods! What luck is mine?

WILLMORE: Only good luck, child, parlous° good luck. Come hither. —'Tis a delicate shining wench. By this 30 hand, she's perfumed, and smells like any nosegay. — Prithee, dear soul, let's not play the fool and lose time — precious time. For as Gad shall save me, I'm as honest a fellow as breathes, though I'm a little disguised° at present. Come, I say. Why, thou mayst be 35 free with me: I'll be very secret. I'll not boast who 'twas obliged me, not I; for hang me if I know thy name.

FLORINDA: Heavens! What a filthy beast is this!

WILLMORE: I am so, and thou ought'st the sooner to lie 40 with me for that reason. For look you, child, there will be no sin in't, because 'twas neither designed nor premeditated: 'Tis pure accident on both sides. That's a certain thing now. Indeed, should I make love to you, and you vow fidelity, and swear and lie till you 45 believed and yielded — that were to make it willful fornication, the crying sin of the nation. Thou art,

---

III, v. [S.D.] *undress:* Undergarment. 3. **cabinet:** Private room.
29. **parlous:** Excessively, with pun on *perilous*. 34–35. **disguised:** I.e., by liquor.

therefore, as thou art a good Christian, obliged in
conscience to deny me nothing. Now, come be kind
50   without any more idle prating.
FLORINDA: Oh, I am ruined! Wicked man, unhand me!
WILLMORE: Wicked? Egad, child, a judge, were he
young and vigorous, and saw those eyes of thine,
would know 'twas they gave the first blow, the first
55   provocation. Come, prithee let's lose no time, I say.
This is a fine convenient place.
FLORINDA: Sir, let me go, I conjure° you, or I'll call out.
WILLMORE: Ay, ay, you were best to call witness to see
how finely you treat me. Do!
60   FLORINDA: I'll cry murder, rape, or anything, if you do
not instantly let me go!
WILLMORE: A rape? Come, come, you lie, you baggage, you lie. What! I'll warrant you would fain have
the world believe now that you are not so forward as
65   I. No, not you. Why at this time of night was your
cobweb door set open, dear spider, but to catch flies?
Ha! Come, or I shall be damnably angry. Why, what
a coil° is here!
FLORINDA: Sir, can you think —
70   WILLMORE: That you would do't for nothing? Oh, oh, I
find what you would be at. Look here, here's a pistole
for you. Here's a work indeed! Here, take it, I say!
FLORINDA: For heaven's sake, sir, as you're a gentleman —
75   WILLMORE: So now, now, she would be wheedling me
for more! What, you will not take it then? You are
resolved you will not? Come, come, take it or I'll put
it up again, for look ye, I never give more. Why, how
now, mistress, are you so high i'th' mouth a pistole
80   won't down with you? Ha! Why, what a work's here!
In good time! Come, no struggling to be gone. But an
y'are good at a dumb wrestle, I'm for ye. Look ye,
I'm for ye.   (She struggles with him.)

(Enter Belvile and Frederick.)

BELVILE: The door is open. A pox of this mad fellow!
85   I'm angry that we've lost him; I durst have sworn he
had followed us.
FREDERICK: But you were so hasty, colonel, to be gone.
FLORINDA: Help! Help! Murder! Help! Oh, I am ruined!
BELVILE: Ha! Sure that's Florinda's voice! (Comes up to
90   them.) A man! — Villain, let go that lady!

(A noise; Willmore turns and draws; Frederick interposes.)

FLORINDA: Belvile! Heavens! My brother too is coming,
and 'twill be impossible to escape. Belvile, I conjure
you to walk under my chamber window, from
whence I'll give you some instructions what to do.
95   This rude man has undone us.   (Exit.)
WILLMORE: Belvile!

(Enter Pedro, Stephano, and other servants, with lights.)

PEDRO: I'm betrayed! Run, Stephano, and see if Florinda
be safe.
(Exit Stephano.)

(They fight, and Pedro's party beats 'em out.)

— So, whoe'er they be, all is not well. I'll to Florinda's chamber.   (Going out, meets Stephano.)   100
STEPHANO: You need not, sir: The poor lady's fast
asleep, and thinks no harm. I would not awake her,
sir, for fear of frighting her with your danger.
PEDRO: I'm glad she's there. — Rascals, how came the
garden door open?   105
STEPHANO: That question comes too late, sir. Some of
my fellow servants masquerading, I'll warrant.
PEDRO: Masquerading! A lewd custom to debauch our
youth! There's something more in this than I imagine.
(Exeunt.)

Scene VI

(Scene changes to the street. Enter Belvile in rage, Frederick holding him, Willmore melancholy.)

WILLMORE: Why, how the devil should I know Florinda?
BELVILE: Ah, plague of your ignorance! If it had not been
Florinda, must you be a beast? A brute? A senseless
swine?
WILLMORE: Well, sir, you see I am endued° with pa-   5
tience: I can bear. Though egad, y'are very free with
me, methinks. I was in good hopes the quarrel would
have been on my side, for so uncivilly interrupting
me.
BELVILE: Peace, brute, whilst thou'rt safe. Oh, I'm dis-   10
tracted!
WILLMORE: Nay, nay, I'm an unlucky dog, that's certain.
BELVILE: Ah, curse upon the star that ruled my birth, or
whatsoever other influence that makes me still so
wretched.   15
WILLMORE: Thou break'st my heart with these complaints. There is no star in fault, no influence but
sack, the cursed sack I drunk.
FREDERICK: Why, how the devil came you so drunk?
WILLMORE: Why, how the devil came you so sober?   20
BELVILE: A curse upon his thin skull, he was always
beforehand that way.
FREDERICK: Prithee, dear colonel, forgive him; he's sorry
for his fault.
BELVILE: He's always so after he has done a mischief. A   25
plague on all such brutes!
WILLMORE: By this light, I took her for an errant harlot.
BELVILE: Damn your debauched opinion! Tell me, sot,
hadst thou so much sense and light about thee to distinguish her woman, and couldst not see something   30
about her face and person to strike an awful reverence into thy soul?

---

57. conjure: Entreat, implore.   68. coil: Noisy disturbance.   5. endued: Endowed.

WILLMORE: Faith no, I considered her as mere a woman
     as I could wish.
35 BELVILE: 'Sdeath, I have no patience. Draw, or I'll kill
     you!
   WILLMORE: Let that alone till tomorrow, and if I set not
     all right again, use your pleasure.
   BELVILE: Tomorrow! Damn it,
40   The spiteful light will lead me to no happiness.
     Tomorrow is Antonio's, and perhaps
     Guides him to my undoing. Oh, that I could meet
     This rival, this powerful fortunate!
   WILLMORE: What then?
45 BELVILE: Let thy own reason, or my rage, instruct thee.
   WILLMORE: I shall be finely informed then, no doubt.
     Hear me, colonel, hear me; show me the man and I'll
     do his business.
   BELVILE: I know him no more than thou, or if I did I
50   should not need thy aid.
   WILLMORE: This you say is Angellica's house; I prom-
     ised the kind baggage to lie with her tonight.

                                   (*Offers to go in.*)

(*Enter Antonio and his Page. Antonio knocks on the hilt
of's sword.*)

ANTONIO: You paid the thousand crowns I directed?
   PAGE: To the lady's old woman, sir, I did.
55 WILLMORE: Who the devil have we here?
   BELVILE: I'll now plant myself under Florinda's window,
     and if I find no comfort there, I'll die.

                          (*Exeunt Belvile and Frederick.*)
(*Enter Moretta.*)

MORETTA: Page?
   PAGE: Here's my lord.
60 WILLMORE: How is this? A picaroon going to board my
     frigate? — Here's one chase gun for you!

(*Drawing his sword, justles Antonio, who turns and
draws. They fight; Antonio falls.*)

MORETTA: Oh, bless us! We're all undone!

(*Runs in and shuts the door.*)

PAGE: Help! Murder!

(*Belvile returns at the noise of fighting.*)

BELVILE: Ha! The mad rogue's engaged in some unlucky
65   adventure again.

(*Enter two or three Masqueraders.*)

MASQUERADER: Ha! A man killed!
   WILLMORE: How, a man killed? Then I'll go home to
     sleep.

(*Puts up and reels out. Exeunt Masqueraders another
way.*)

BELVILE: Who should it be? Pray heaven the rogue is
70   safe, for all my quarrel to him.

(*As Belvile is groping about, enter an Officer and six
Soldiers.*)

SOLDIER: Who's there?
   OFFICER: So, here's one dispatched. Secure the mur-
     derer.
   BELVILE: Do not mistake my charity for murder! I came
     to his assistance!   (*Soldiers sieze on Belvile.*)   75
   OFFICER: That shall be tried, sir. St. Jago! Swords drawn
     in the Carnival time!   (*Goes to Antonio.*)
   ANTONIO: Thy hand, prithee.
   OFFICER: Ha! Don Antonio! Look well to the villain
     there. — How is it, sir?   80
   ANTONIO: I'm hurt.
   BELVILE: Has my humanity made me a criminal?
   OFFICER: Away with him!
   BELVILE: What a curst chance is this!

                          (*Exeunt soldiers with Belvile.*)

ANTONIO [*aside*]: This is the man that has set upon me   85
     twice. — (*To the officer.*) Carry him to my apartment
     till you have further orders from me.
                                   (*Exit Antonio, led.*)

ACT IV • *Scene 1*

(*A fine room. Discovers Belvile as by dark alone.*)

BELVILE: When shall I be weary of railing on fortune,
     who is resolved never to turn with smiles upon me?
     Two such defeats in one night none but the devil and
     that mad rogue could have contrived to have plagued
     me with. I am here a prisoner. But where, heaven   5
     knows. And if there be murder done, I can soon
     decide the fate of a stranger in a nation without
     mercy. Yet this is nothing to the torture my soul bows
     with when I think of losing my fair, my dear
     Florinda. Hark, my door opens. A light! A man, and   10
     seems of quality. Armed, too! Now shall I die like a
     dog, without defense.

(*Enter Antonio in a nightgown, with a light; his arm in a
scarf, and a sword under his arm. He sets the candle on
the table.*)

ANTONIO: Sir, I come to know what injuries I have done
     you, that could provoke you to so mean an action as
     to attack me basely without allowing time for my   15
     defense?
   BELVILE: Sir, for a man in my circumstances to plead
     innocence would look like fear. But view me well,
     and you will find no marks of coward on me, nor
     anything that betrays that brutality you accuse me   20
     with.
   ANTONIO: In vain, sir, you impose upon my sense. You
     are not only he who drew on me last night, but yes-
     terday before the same house, that of Angellica. Yet
     there is something in your face and mien° that makes   25
     me wish I were mistaken.

---

25. mien: Demeanor, appearance.

BELVILE: I own I fought today in the defense of a friend of mine with whom you, if you're the same, and your party were first engaged. Perhaps you think this

30 crime enough to kill me; but if you do, I cannot fear you'll do it basely.

ANTONIO: No sir, I'll make you fit for a defense with this.   (*Gives him the sword.*)

BELVILE: This gallantry surprises me, nor know I how to

35 use this present, sir, against a man so brave.

ANTONIO: You shall not need. For know, I come to snatch you from a danger that is decreed against you: perhaps your life, or long imprisonment. And 'twas with so much courage you offended, I cannot see you

40 punished.

BELVILE: How shall I pay this generosity?

ANTONIO: It had been safer to have killed another than have attempted me. To show your danger, sir, I'll let you know my quality: And 'tis the Viceroy's son whom

45 you have wounded.

BELVILE: The Viceroy's son! — (*Aside.*) Death and confusion! Was this plague reserved to complete all the rest? Obliged by° him, the man of all the world I would destroy!

50 ANTONIO: You seem disordered, sir.

BELVILE: Yes, trust me, I am, and 'tis with pain that man receives such bounties who wants the power to pay 'em back again.

ANTONIO: To gallant spirits 'tis indeed uneasy, but you

55 may quickly overpay me, sir.

BELVILE (*aside*): Then I am well. Kind heaven, but set us even, that I may fight with him and keep my honor safe. — Oh, I'm impatient, sir, to be discounting the mighty debt I owe you. Command me quickly.

60 ANTONIO: I have a quarrel with a rival, sir, about the maid we love.

BELVILE (*aside*): Death, 'tis Florinda he means! That thought destroys my reason, and I shall kill him.

ANTONIO: My rival, sir, is one has all the virtues man

65 can boast of —

BELVILE (*aside*): Death, who should this be?

ANTONIO: He challenged me to meet him on the Molo as soon as day appeared, but last night's quarrel has made my arm unfit to guide a sword.

70 BELVILE: I apprehend you, sir. You'd have me kill the man that lays a claim to the maid you speak of. I'll do't. I'll fly to do't!

ANTONIO: Sir, do you know her?

BELVILE: No, sir, but 'tis enough she is admired by you.

75 ANTONIO: Sir, I shall rob you of the glory on't, for you must fight under my name and dress.

BELVILE: That opinion must be strangely obliging that makes you think I can personate the brave Antonio, whom I can but strive to imitate.

80 ANTONIO: You say too much to my advantage. Come, sir, the day appears that calls you forth. Within, sir, is the habit.°   (*Exit Antonio.*)

BELVILE: Fantastic fortune, thou deceitful light, That cheats the wearied traveler by night, Though on a precipice each step you tread,   85 I am resolved to follow where you lead.   (*Exit.*)

Scene II

(*The Molo. Enter Florinda and Callis in masks, with Stephano.*)

FLORINDA (*aside*): I'm dying with my fears: Belvile's not coming as I expected under my window makes me believe that all those fears are true. — Canst thou not tell with whom my brother fights?

STEPHANO: No, madam, they were both in masquerade.   5 I was by when they challenged one another, and they had decided the quarrel then, but were prevented by some cavaliers; which made 'em put it off till now. But I am sure 'tis about you they fight.

FLORINDA (aside): Nay, then, 'tis with Belvile, for what 10 other lover have I that dares fight for me except Antonio, and he is too much in favor with my brother. If it be he, for whom shall I direct my prayers to heaven?

STEPHANO: Madam, I must leave you, for if my master see me, I shall be hanged for being your conductor. I 15 escaped narrowly for the excuse I made for you last night i'th' garden.

FLORINDA: I'll reward thee for't. Prithee, no more.
                                    (*Exit Stephano.*)

(*Enter Don Pedro in his masking habit.*)

PEDRO: Antonio's late today; the place will fill, and we may be prevented.   (*Walks about.*)   20

FLORINDA (*aside*): Antonio? Sure I heard amiss.

PEDRO: But who will not excuse a happy lover When soft fair arms confine the yielding neck, And the kind whisper languishingly breathes "Must you be gone so soon?"   25 Sure I had dwelt forever on her bosom — But stay, he's here.

(*Enter Belvile dressed in Antonio's clothes.*)

FLORINDA [*aside*]: 'Tis not Belvile; half my fears are vanished.

PEDRO: Antonio!   30

BELVILE (*aside*): This must be he. — You're early, sir; I do not use to be outdone this way.

PEDRO: The wretched, sir, are watchful, and 'tis enough you've the advantage of me in Angellica.

BELVILE (*aside*): Angellica! Or° I've mistook my man, or 35 else Antonio! Can he forget his interest in Florinda and fight for common prize?

PEDRO: Come, sir, you know our terms.

BELVILE (*aside*): By heaven, not I. — No talking; I am ready, sir.   40

(*Offers to fight; Florinda runs in.*)

---

48. Obliged by: Favored by.   **82. habit:** Antonio's clothing.

35. Or: Either.

FLORINDA (*to Belvile*): Oh, hold! Whoever you be, I do
   conjure you hold! If you strike here, I die!
PEDRO: Florinda!
BELVILE: Florinda imploring for my rival!
45 PEDRO: Away; this kindness is unseasonable.

(*Puts her by; they fight; she runs in just as Belvile dis-
arms Pedro.*)

FLORINDA: Who are you, sir, that dares deny my prayers?
BELVILE: Thy prayers destroy him; if thou wouldst pre-
   serve him, do that thou'rt unacquainted with, and
   curse him.
                                   (*She holds him.*)
50 FLORINDA: By all you hold most dear, by her you love,
   I do conjure you, touch him not.
BELVILE: By her I love?
   See, I obey, and at your feet resign
   The useless trophy of my victory.

(*Lays his sword at her feet.*)

55 PEDRO: Antonio, you've done enough to prove you love
   Florinda.
BELVILE: Love Florinda! Does heaven love adoration,
   prayer, or penitence? Love her? Here, sir, your sword
   again.

(*Snatches up the sword and gives it to him.*)

60   Upon this truth I'll fight my life away.
PEDRO: No, you've redeemed my sister, and my friendship.

(*He gives him Florinda, and pulls off his vizard to show
his face, and puts it on again.*)

BELVILE: Don Pedro!
PEDRO: Can you resign your claims to other women,
65   and give your heart entirely to Florinda?
BELVILE: Entire, as dying saints' confessions are!
   I can delay my happiness no longer:
   This minute let me make Florinda mine.
PEDRO: This minute let it be. No time so proper: This
70   night my father will arrive from Rome, and possibly
   may hinder what we purpose.
FLORINDA: O, heavens! This minute?

(*Enter Masqueraders and pass over.*)

BELVILE: Oh, do not ruin me!
PEDRO: The place begins to fill, and that we may not be
75   observed, do you walk off to St. Peter's church,
   where I will meet you and conclude your happiness.
BELVILE: I'll meet you there. — (*Aside.*) If there be no
   more saints' churches in Naples.
FLORINDA: Oh, stay, sir, and recall your hasty doom!
80   Alas, I have not yet prepared my heart
   To entertain so strange a guest.
PEDRO: Away; this silly modesty is assumed too late.
BELVILE: Heaven, madam, what do you do?
FLORINDA: Do? Despise the man that lays a tyrant's
   claim
85   To what he ought to conquer by submission.

BELVILE: You do not know me. Move a little this way.
                                   (*Draws her aside.*)
FLORINDA: Yes, you may force me even to the altar,
   But not the holy man that offers there
   Shall force me to be thine.

(*Pedro talks to Callis this while.*)

BELVILE: Oh, do not lose so blest an opportunity!   90

(*Pulls off his vizard.*)

   See, 'tis your Belvile, not Antonio,
   Whom your mistaken scorn and anger ruins.
FLORINDA: Belvile!
   Where was my soul it could not meet thy voice,
   And take this knowledge in.   95

(*As they are talking, enter Willmore, finely dressed, and
Frederick.*)

WILLMORE: No intelligence? No news of Belvile yet?
   Well, I am the most unlucky rascal in nature. Ha! Am
   I deceived, or is it he? Look, Fred! 'Tis he, my dear
   Belvile!

(*Runs and embraces him; Belvile's vizard falls out on's
hand.*)

BELVILE: Hell and confusion seize thee!   100
PEDRO: Ha! Belvile! I beg your pardon, sir.

(*Takes Florinda from him.*)

BELVILE: Nay, touch her not. She's mine by conquest, sir;
   I won her by my sword.
WILLMORE: Didst thou so? And egad, child, we'll keep
   her by the sword.   105

(*Draws on Pedro; Belvile goes between.*)

BELVILE: Stand off!
   Thou'rt so profanely lewd, so curst by heaven,
   All quarrels thou espousest must be fatal.
WILLMORE: Nay, an you be so hot, my valor's coy,
   And shall be courted when you want it next.   110
                                   (*Puts up his sword.*)
BELVILE (*to Pedro*): You know I ought to claim a
   victor's right,
   But you're the brother to divine Florinda,
   To whom I'm such a slave. To purchase her
   I durst not hurt the man she holds so dear.
PEDRO: 'Twas by Antonio's, not by Belvile's
   sword   115
   This question should have been decided, sir.
   I must confess much to your bravery's due,
   Both now and when I met you last in arms;
   But I am nicely punctual in my word,
   As men of honor ought, and beg your pardon: 120
   For this mistake another time shall clear.

(*Aside to Florinda as they are going out.*)

   — This was some plot between you and Belvile,
   But I'll prevent you.
                            [*Exeunt Pedro and Florinda.*]

(*Belvile looks after her and begins to walk up and down in rage.*)

WILLMORE: Do not be modest now and lose the woman.
125   But if we shall fetch her back so —
BELVILE: Do not speak to me!
WILLMORE: Not speak to you? Egad, I'll speak to you, and will be answered, too.
BELVILE: Will you, sir?
130   WILLMORE: I know I've done some mischief, but I'm so dull a puppy that I'm the son of a whore if I know how or where. Prithee inform my understanding.
BELVILE: Leave me, I say, and leave me instantly!
WILLMORE: I will not leave you in this humor, nor till I
135   know my crime.
BELVILE: Death, I'll tell you, sir —

(*Draws and runs at Willmore; he runs out, Belvile after him; Frederick interposes.*)

(*Enter Angellica, Moretta, and Sebastian.*)

ANGELLICA: Ha! Sebastian, is that not Willmore? Haste! haste and bring him back.

[*Exit Sebastian.*]

FREDERICK [*aside*]: The colonel's mad: I never saw him
140   thus before. I'll after 'em lest he do some mischief, for I am sure Willmore will not draw on him.   (*Exit.*)
ANGELLICA: I am all rage! My first desires defeated! For one for aught he knows that has no Other merit than her quality,
145   Her being Don Pedro's sister. He loves her! I know 'tis so. Dull, dull, insensible, He will not see me now, though oft invited, And broke his word last night. False perjured man! He that but yesterday fought for my favors,
150   And would have made his life a sacrifice To've gained one night with me, Must now be hired and courted to my arms.
MORETTA: I told you what would come on't, but Moretta's an old doting fool. Why did you give him
155   five hundred crowns, but to set himself out for other lovers? You should have kept him poor if you had meant to have had any good from him.
ANGELLICA: Oh, name not such mean trifles! Had I given Him all my youth has earned from sin,
160   I had not lost a thought nor sigh upon't. But I have given him my eternal rest, My whole repose, my future joys, my heart! My virgin heart, Moretta! Oh, 'tis gone!
MORETTA: Curse on him, here he comes. How fine she
165   has made him, too.

(*Enter Willmore and Sebastian; Angellica turns and walks away.*)

WILLMORE: How now, turned shadow? Fly when I pursue, and follow when I fly? (*Sings.*)
Stay, gentle shadow of my dove,
    And tell me ere I go,

Whether the substance may not prove   170
    A fleeting thing like you.

(*As she turns she looks on him.*)

There's a soft kind look remaining yet.
ANGELLICA: Well, sir, you may be gay: All happiness, all joys pursue you still. Fortune's your slave, and gives you every hour choice of new hearts and beauties, till   175
you are cloyed° with the repeated bliss which others vainly languish for. But know, false man, that I shall be revenged.

(*Turns away in rage.*)

WILLMORE: So, gad, there are of those faint-hearted lovers, whom such a sharp lesson next their hearts   180
would make as impotent as fourscore.° Pox o' this whining; my business is to laugh and love. A pox on't, I hate your sullen lover: A man shall lose as much time to put you in humor now as would serve to gain a new woman.   185
ANGELLICA: I scorn to cool that fire I cannot raise, Or do the drudgery of your virtuous mistress.
WILLMORE: A virtuous mistress? Death, what a thing thou hast found out for me! Why, what the devil should I do with a virtuous woman, a sort of ill-   190
natured creatures that take a pride to torment a lover. Virtue is but an infirmity in woman, a disease that renders even the handsome ungrateful; whilst the ill-favored, for want of solicitations and address, only fancy themselves so. I have lain with a woman of   195
quality who has all the while been railing at whores.
ANGELLICA: I will not answer for your mistress's virtue, Though she be young enough to know no guilt; And I could wish you would persuade my heart 'Twas the two hundred thousand crowns you courted.   200
WILLMORE: Two hundred thousand crowns! What story's this? What trick? What woman, ha?
ANGELLICA: How strange you make it. Have you forgot the creature you entertained on the Piazzo last night?   205
WILLMORE (*aside*): Ha! My gypsy worth two hundred thousand crowns! Oh, how I long to be with her! Pox, I knew she was of quality.
ANGELLICA: False man! I see my ruin in thy face. How many vows you breathed upon my bosom   210
Never to be unjust. Have you forgot so soon?
WILLMORE: Faith, no; I was just coming to repeat 'em. But here's a humor indeed would make a man a saint. — (*Aside.*) Would she would be angry enough to leave me, and command me not to wait on her.   215

(*Enter Hellena dressed in man's clothes.*)

HELLENA: This must be Angellica: I know it by her mumping° matron here. Ay, ay, 'tis she. My mad captain's with her, too, for all his swearing. How this

---

176. **cloyed:** Full to bursting.   181. **as fourscore:** As an eighty-year-old.   217. **mumping:** Moping.

unconstant humor makes me love him! — Pray, good
220   grave gentlewoman, is not this Angellica?
MORETTA: My too young sir, it is. — [*Aside.*] I hope 'tis
one from Don Antonio.   (*Goes to Angellica.*)
HELLENA (*aside*): Well, something I'll do to vex him for
this.
225 ANGELLICA: I will not speak with him. Am I in humor to
receive a lover?
WILLMORE: Not speak with him? Why, I'll be gone, and
wait your idler minutes. Can I show less obedience to
the thing I love so fondly?
(*Offers to go.*)
230 ANGELLICA: A fine excuse this! Stay —
WILLMORE: And hinder your advantage? Should I repay
your bounties so ungratefully?
ANGELLICA [*to Hellena*]: Come hither, boy. —
[*To Willmore.*] That I may let you see
235   How much above the advantages you name
I prize one minute's joy with you.
WILLMORE (*impatient to be gone*): Oh, you destroy me
with this endearment. — [*Aside.*] Death, how shall
I get away? — Madam, 'twill not be fit I should be
240   seen with you. Besides, it will not be convenient. And
I've a friend — that's dangerously sick.
ANGELLICA: I see you're impatient. Yet you shall stay.
WILLMORE (*aside*): And miss my assignation with my
gypsy.

(*Walks about impatiently; Moretta brings Hellena, who
addresses herself to Angellica.*)

245 HELLENA: Madam,
You'll hardly pardon my intrusion
When you shall know my business,
And I'm too young to tell my tale with art;
But there must be a wondrous store of goodness
250   Where so much beauty dwells.
ANGELLICA: A pretty advocate, whoever sent thee.
Prithee proceed.

(*To Willmore, who is stealing off.*)

— Nay, sir, you shall not go.
WILLMORE (*aside*): Then I shall lose my dear gypsy for-
ever. Pox on't, she stays me out of spite.
255 HELLENA: I am related to a lady, madam,
Young, rich, and nobly born, but has the fate
To be in love with a young English gentleman.
Strangely she loves him, at first sight she loved him,
But did adore him when she heard him speak;
260   For he, she said, had charms in every word
That failed not to surprise, to wound and conquer.
WILLMORE (*aside*): Ha! Egad, I hope this concerns me.
ANGELLICA (*aside*): 'Tis my false man he means. Would
he were gone:
This praise will raise his pride, and ruin me.
(*To Willmore.*) — Well,
265   Since you are so impatient to be gone,
I will release you, sir.
WILLMORE (*aside*): Nay, then I'm sure 'twas me he
spoke of: This cannot be the effects of kindness in

her. — No, Madam, I've considered better on't, and
will not give you cause of jealousy.   270
ANGELLICA: But sir, I've business that —
WILLMORE: This shall not do; I know 'tis but to try me.
ANGELLICA: Well, to your story, boy. — (*Aside.*) Though
'twill undo me.
HELLENA: With this addition to his other beauties,   275
He won her unresisting tender heart.
He vowed, and sighed, and swore he loved her
dearly;
And she believed the cunning flatterer,
And thought herself the happiest maid alive.
Today was the appointed time by both   280
To consummate their bliss:
The virgin, altar, and the priest were dressed;
And whilst she languished for th'expected
bridegroom,
She heard he paid his broken vows to you.
WILLMORE (*aside*): So, this is some dear rogue that's in 285
love with me, and this way lets me know it. Or, if
it be not me, he means someone whose place I may
supply.
ANGELLICA: Now I perceive
The cause of thy impatience to be gone,   290
And all the business of this glorious dress.
WILLMORE: Damn the young prater; I know not what
he means.
HELLENA: Madam,
In your fair eyes I read too much concern   295
To tell my further business.
ANGELLICA: Prithee, sweet youth, talk on: Thou mayst
perhaps
Raise here a storm that may undo my passion,
And then I'll grant thee anything.
HELLENA: Madam, 'tis to entreat you (oh
unreasonable)   300
You would not see this stranger.
For if you do, she vows you are undone;
Though nature never made a man so excellent,
And sure he 'ad been a god, but for inconstancy.
WILLMORE (*aside*): Ah, rogue, how finely he's instructed! 305
'Tis plain, some woman that has seen me *en passant.*°
ANGELLICA: Oh, I shall burst with jealousy! Do you
know the man you speak of?
HELLENA: Yes, madam, he used to be in buff and scarlet.
ANGELLICA (*to Willmore*): Thou false as hell, what canst 310
thou say to this?
WILLMORE: By heaven —
ANGELLICA: Hold, do not damn thyself —
HELLENA: Nor hope to be believed.

(*He walks about; they follow.*)

ANGELLICA: Oh perjured man!   315
Is't thus you pay my generous passion back?
HELLENA: Why would you, sir, abuse my lady's faith?
ANGELLICA: And use me so unhumanely.
HELLENA: A maid so young, so innocent —

306. *en passant:* In passing.

320 WILLMORE: Ah, young devil!
     ANGELLICA: Dost thou not know thy life is in my
        power?
     HELLENA: Or think my lady cannot be revenged?
     WILLMORE (*aside*): So, so, the storm comes finely on.
     ANGELLICA: Now thou art silent: Guilt has struck thee
325   dumb.
        Oh, hadst thou still been so, I'd lived in safety.

(*She turns away and weeps.*)

     WILLMORE (*aside to Hellena*): Sweetheart, the lady's
        name and house — quickly! I'm impatient to be with
        her.

(*Looks toward Angellica to watch her turning, and as
she comes towards them he meets her.*)

330 HELLENA (*aside*): So, now is he for another woman.
     WILLMORE: The impudent'st young thing in nature:
        I cannot persuade him out of his error, madam.
     ANGELLICA: I know he's in the right; yet thou'st a
        tongue
        That would persuade him to deny his faith.

(*In rage walks away.*)

335 WILLMORE (*said softly to Hellena*): Her name, her
        name, dear boy!
     HELLENA: Have you forgot it, sir?
     WILLMORE (*aside*): Oh, I perceive he's not to know I am
        a stranger to his lady. — Yes, yes, I do know, but I
340   have forgot the — (*Angellica turns.*) — By heaven,
        such early confidence I never saw.
     ANGELLICA: Did I not charge you with this mistress,
        sir?
        Which you denied, though I beheld your perjury.
        This little generosity of thine has rendered back my
        heart.   (*Walks away.*)
345 WILLMORE (*to Hellena*): So, you have made sweet work
        here, my little mischief. Look your lady be kind and
        good-natured now, or I shall have but a cursed bar-
        gain on't. (*Angellica turns toward them.*) — The
        rogue's bred up to mischief; art thou so great a fool
350   to credit him?
     ANGELLICA: Yes, I do, and you in vain impose upon me.
        Come hither, boy. Is not this he you spake of?
     HELLENA: I think it is. I cannot swear, but I vow he has
        just such another lying lover's look.

(*Hellena looks in his face; he gazes on her.*)

355 WILLMORE (*aside*): Ha! Do I not know that face? By
        heaven, my little gypsy! What a dull dog was I: Had I
        but looked that way I'd known her. Are all my hopes
        of a new woman banished? — Egad, if I do not fit
        thee for this, hang me. — [*To Angellica.*] Madam, I
360   have found out the plot.
     HELLENA [*aside*]: Oh lord, what does he say? Am I dis-
        covered now?
     WILLMORE: Do you see this young spark here?
     HELLENA [*aside*]: He'll tell her who I am.
365 WILLMORE: Who do you think this is?

HELLENA [*aside*]: Ay, ay, he does know me. — Nay, dear
   captain, I am undone if you discover me.
WILLMORE: Nay, nay, no cogging;° she shall know what
   a precious mistress I have.
HELLENA: Will you be such a devil?   370
WILLMORE: Nay, nay, I'll teach you to spoil sport you
   will not make. — This small ambassador comes not
   from a person of quality, as you imagine and he says,
   but from a very errant gypsy: the talking'st, prating'st, canting'st little animal thou ever saw'st.   375
ANGELLICA: What news you tell me, that's the thing I
   mean.
HELLENA (*aside*): Would I were well off the place! If ever
   I go a-captain-hunting again —
WILLMORE: Mean that thing? That gypsy thing? Thou   380
   mayst as well be jealous of thy monkey or parrot as
   of her. A German motion° were worth a dozen of her,
   and a dream were a better enjoyment — a creature of
   a constitution fitter for heaven than man.
HELLENA (*aside*): Though I'm sure he lies, yet this vexes 385
   me.
ANGELLICA: You are mistaken: she's a Spanish woman
   made up of no such dull materials.
WILLMORE: Materials? Egad, an she be made of any
   that will either dispense or admit of love, I'll be   390
   bound to continence.
HELLENA (*aside to him*): Unreasonable man, do you
   think so?
WILLMORE: You may return, my little brazen head, and
   tell your lady, that till she be handsome enough to be 395
   beloved, or I dull enough to be religious, there will be
   small hopes of me.
ANGELLICA: Did you not promise, then, to marry her?
WILLMORE: Not I, by heaven.
ANGELLICA: You cannot undeceive my fears and tor-   400
   ments, till you have vowed you will not marry her.
HELLENA (*aside*): If he swears that, he'll be revenged on
   me indeed for all my rogueries.
ANGELLICA: I know what arguments you'll bring against
   me: fortune and honor.   405
WILLMORE: Honor! I tell you, I hate it in your sex;
   and those that fancy themselves possessed of that
   foppery are the most impertinently troublesome of
   all womankind, and will transgress nine command-
   ments to keep one. And to satisfy your jealousy, I   410
   swear —
HELLENA (*aside to him*): Oh, no swearing, dear captain.
WILLMORE: If it were possible I should ever be inclined
   to marry, it should be some kind young sinner: one
   that has generosity enough to give a favor hand-   415
   somely to one that can ask it discreetly, one that has
   wit enough to manage an intrigue of love. Oh, how
   civil such a wench is to a man that does her the honor
   to marry her.
ANGELLICA: By heaven, there's no faith in anything he   420
   says.

(*Enter Sebastian.*)

368. **cogging:** Fawning, coaxing.   382. **motion:** Puppet show.

SEBASTIAN: Madam, Don Antonio —

ANGELLICA: Come hither.

HELLENA [*aside*]: Ha! Antonio! He may be coming
425   hither, and he'll certainly discover me. I'll therefore
retire without a ceremony.   (*Exit Hellena.*)

ANGELLICA: I'll see him. Get my coach ready.

SEBASTIAN: It waits you, madam.

WILLMORE [*aside*]: This is lucky. — What, madam, now
430   I may be gone and leave you to the enjoyment of my
rival?

ANGELLICA: Dull man, that canst not see how ill, how
poor,
That false dissimulation looks. Be gone,
And never let me see thy cozening face again,
435   Lest I relapse and kill thee.

WILLMORE: Yes, you can spare me now. Farewell, till
you're in better humor. — [*Aside.*] I'm glad of this
release. Now for my gypsy:
For though to worse we change, yet still we find
440   New joys, new charms, in a new miss that's kind.
                                          (*Exit Willmore.*)

ANGELLICA: He's gone, and in this ague° of my soul
The shivering fit returns.
Oh, with what willing haste he took his leave,
As if the longed-for minute were arrived
445   Of some blest assignation.
In vain I have consulted all my charms,
In vain this beauty prized, in vain believed
My eyes could kindle any lasting fires;
I had forgot my name, my infamy,
450   And the reproach that honor lays on those
That dare pretend a sober passion here.
Nice reputation, though it leave behind
More virtues than inhabit where that dwells,
Yet that once gone, those virtues shine no more.
455   Then since I am not fit to be beloved,
I am resolved to think on a revenge
On him that soothed° me thus to my undoing.
                                          (*Exeunt.*)

Scene III

(*A street. Enter Florinda and Valeria in habits different
from what they have been seen in.*)

FLORINDA: We're happily escaped, and yet I tremble
still.

VALERIA: A lover, and fear? Why, I am but half an one,
and yet I have courage for any attempt. Would Hel-
5   lena were here: I would fain have had her as deep in
this mischief as we; she'll fare but ill else, I doubt.

FLORINDA: She pretended a visit to the Augustine nuns;
but I believe some other design carried her out; pray
heaven we light on her. Prithee, what didst do with
10   Callis?

VALERIA: When I saw no reason would do good on her, I
followed her into the wardrobe, and as she was looking for something in a great chest, I toppled her in by
the heels, snatched the key of the apartment where
you were confined, locked her in, and left her bawl-   15
ing for help.

FLORINDA: 'Tis well you resolve to follow my fortunes,
for thou darest never appear at home again after such
an action.

VALERIA: That's according as the young stranger and I   20
shall agree. But to our business. I delivered your note
to Belvile when I got out under pretense of going to
mass. I found him at his lodging, and believe me it
came seasonably, for never was man in so desperate a
condition. I told him of your resolution of making   25
your escape today if your brother would be absent
long enough to permit you; if not, to die rather than
be Antonio's.

FLORINDA: Thou should'st have told him I was confined
to my chamber upon my brother's suspicion that the   30
business on the Molo was a plot laid between him
and I.

VALERIA: I said all this, and told him your brother was
now gone to his devotion; and he resolves to visit
every church till he find him, and not only undeceive   35
him in that, but caress him so as shall delay his return
home.

FLORINDA: Oh heavens! He's here, and Belvile with him,
too.

(*They put on their vizards.*)

(*Enter Don Pedro, Belvile, Willmore; Belvile and Don
Pedro seeming in serious discourse.*)

VALERIA: Walk boldly by them, and I'll come at a dis-   40
tance, lest he suspect us.

(*She walks by them and looks back on them.*)

WILLMORE: Ha! A woman, and of excellent mien!

PEDRO: She throws a kind look back on you.

WILLMORE: Death, 'tis a likely wench and that kind
look shall not be cast away. I'll follow her.   45

BELVILE: Prithee do not.

WILLMORE: Do not? By heavens, to the antipodies,°
with such an invitation.

(*She goes out, and Willmore follows her.*)

BELVILE: 'Tis a mad fellow for a wench.

(*Enter Frederick.*)

FREDERICK: Oh, colonel, such news!   50

BELVILE: Prithee what?

FREDERICK: News that will make you laugh in spite of
fortune.

BELVILE: What, Blunt has had some damned trick put
upon him? Cheated, banged, or clapped?°   55

FREDERICK: Cheated, sir, rarely cheated of all but his shirt and drawers; the unconscionable whore too turned him out before consummation, so that, tra-versing the streets at midnight, the watch found him in this *fresco* and conducted him home. By heaven, 'tis such a sight, and yet I durst as well been hanged as laughed at him or pity him: He beats all that do but ask him a question, and is in such an humor.

PEDRO: Who is't has met with this ill usage, sir?

BELVILE: A friend of ours whom you must see for mirth's sake. — (*Aside.*) I'll employ him to give Florinda time for an escape.

PEDRO: What is he?

BELVILE: A young countryman of ours, one that has been educated at so plentiful a rate he yet ne'er knew the want of money; and 'twill be a great jest to see how simply he'll look without it. For my part, I'll lend him none: And the rogue know not how to put on a borrowing face and ask first, I'll let him see how good 'tis to play our parts whilst I play his. Prithee, Fred, do you go home and keep him in that posture till we come.   (*Exeunt.*)

(*Enter Florinda from the farther end of the scene, look-ing behind her.*)

FLORINDA: I am followed still. Ha! My brother too advancing this way! Good heavens defend me from being seen by him!   (*She goes off.*)

(*Enter Willmore, and after him Valeria, at a little dis-tance.*)

WILLMORE: Ah, there she sails! She looks back as she were willing to be boarded; I'll warrant her prize.°

(*He goes out, Valeria following.*)

(*Enter Hellena, just as he goes out, with a page.*)

HELLENA: Ha, is not that my captain that has a woman in chase? 'Tis not Angellica. — Boy, follow those people at a distance, and bring me an account where they go in.   (*Exit Page.*)
— I'll find his haunts, and plague him everywhere. Ha! My brother!

(*Belvile, Willmore, Pedro cross the stage; Hellena runs off.*)

Scene IV

(*Scene changes to another street. Enter Florinda.*)

FLORINDA: What shall I do? My brother now pursues me. Will no kind power protect me from his tyranny? Ha! Here's a door open; I'll venture in, since nothing can be worse than to fall into his hands. My life and honor are at stake, and my necessity has no choice.   (*She goes in.*)

82. warrant her prize: Consider her worthy of pursuing.

(*Enter Valeria, Hellena's Page peeping after Florinda.*)

PAGE: Here she went in; I shall remember this house.
                (*Exit Boy.*)

VALERIA: This is Belvile's lodging, she's gone in as readily as if she knew it. Ha! Here's that mad fellow again; I dare not venture in. I'll watch my opportunity.
                (*Goes aside.*)

(*Enter Willmore, gazing about him.*)

WILLMORE: I have lost her hereabouts. Pox on't, she must not 'scape me so.   (*Goes out.*)

Scene V

(*Scene changes to Blunt's chamber, discovers him sitting on a couch in his shirt and drawers, reading.*)

BLUNT: So, now my mind's a little at peace, since I have resolved revenge. A pox on this tailor, though, for not bringing home the clothes I bespoke. And a pox of all poor cavaliers: A man can never keep a spare suit for 'em, and I shall have these rogues come in and find me naked, and then I'm undone. But I'm resolved to arm myself: The rascals shall not insult over me too much. (*Puts on an old rusty sword and buff belt.*) Now, how like a morris dancer° I am equipped! A fine ladylike whore to cheat me thus without affording me a kind-ness for my money! A pox light on her, I shall never be reconciled to the sex more; she has made me as faith-less as a physician, as uncharitable as a churchman, and as ill-natured as a poet. Oh, how I'll use all wom-ankind hereafter! What would I give to have one of 'em within my reach now! Any mortal thing in petti-coats, kind fortune, send me, and I'll forgive thy last night's malice. — Here's a cursed book, too — a warning to all young travelers — that can instruct me how to prevent such mischiefs now 'tis too late. Well, 'tis a rare convenient thing to read a little now and then, as well as hawk and hunt.

                (*Sits down again and reads.*)

(*Enter to him Florinda.*)

FLORINDA: This house is haunted, sure: 'Tis well fur-nished, and no living thing inhabits it. Ha! A man! Heavens, how he's attired! Sure 'tis some rope dancer, or fencing master. I tremble now for fear, and yet I must venture now to speak to him. — Sir, if I may not interrupt your meditations —

                (*He starts up and gazes.*)

BLUNT: Ha, what's here? Are my wishes granted? And is not that a she creature? 'Adsheartlikins, 'tis. — What wretched thing art thou, ha?

FLORINDA: Charitable sir, you've told yourself already

IV, v, 9. morris dancer: The morris dance is a lively dance per-formed by men wearing costumes and bells.

what I am: a very wretched maid, forced by a strange
unlucky accident to seek a safety here, and must be
35   ruined if you do not grant it.

BLUNT: Ruined! Is there any ruin so inevitable as that
which now threatens thee? Dost thou know, miserable woman, into what den of mischiefs thou art
fallen; what abyss of confusion, ha? Dost not see
40   something in my looks that frights thy guilty soul,
and makes thee wish to change that shape of woman
for any humble animal, or devil? For those were safer
for thee, and less mischievous.

FLORINDA: Alas, what mean you, sir? I must confess,
45   your looks have something in 'em makes me fear, but
I beseech you, as you seem a gentleman, pity a harmless virgin that takes your house for sanctuary.

BLUNT: Talk on, talk on; and weep, too, till my faith so
return. Do, flatter me out of my senses again. A
50   harmless virgin with a pox; as much one as t'other,
'adsheartlikins. Why, what the devil, can I not be safe
in my house for you, not in my chamber? Nay, not
even being naked too cannot secure me? This is an
impudence greater than has invaded me yet. Come,
55   no resistance.   (*Pulls her rudely.*)

FLORINDA: Dare you be so cruel?

BLUNT: Cruel? 'Adsheartlikins, as a galley slave, or a
Spanish whore. Cruel? Yes, I will kiss and beat thee
all over, kiss and see thee all over; thou shalt lie with
60   me too, not that I care for the enjoyment, but to let
thee see I have ta'en deliberated malice to thee, and
will be revenged on one whore for the sins of another.
I will smile and deceive thee; flatter thee, and beat
thee; embrace thee and rob thee, as she did me; fawn
65   on thee, and strip thee stark naked; then hang thee
out at my window by the heels, with a paper of scurvy
verses fastened to thy breast in praise of damnable
women. Come, come, along.

FLORINDA: Alas, sir, must I be sacrificed for the crimes
70   of the most infamous of my sex? I never understood
the sins you name.

BLUNT: Do, persuade the fool you love him, or that, one
of you can be just or honest; tell me I was not an easy
coxcomb, or any strange impossible tale: It will be
75   believed sooner than thy false showers or protestations. A generation of damned hypocrites! To flatter
my very clothes from my back! Dissembling witches!
Are these the returns you make an honest gentleman
that trusts, believes, and loves you? But if I be not
80   even with you — Come along, or I shall — (*Pulls her
again.*)

(*Enter Frederick.*)

FREDERICK: Ha, what's here to do?

BLUNT: 'Adsheartlikins, Fred, I am glad thou art come,
to be a witness of my dire revenge.

FREDERICK: What's this, a person of quality too, who is
85   upon the ramble° to supply the defects of some grave
impotent husband?

---

85. **upon the ramble:** Rambling, wandering.

BLUNT: No, this has another pretense: Some very unfortunate accident brought her hither, to save a life pursued by I know not who or why, and forced to take
sanctuary here at fool's haven. 'Adsheartlikins, to me   90
of all mankind for protection? Is the ass to be cajoled
again, think ye? No, young one, no prayers or tears
shall mitigate my rage; therefore prepare for both my
pleasures of enjoyment and revenge. For I am resolved to make up my loss here on thy body: I'll take   95
it out in kindness and in beating.

FREDERICK: Now, mistress of mine, what do you think
of this?

FLORINDA: I think he will not, dares not be so barbarous.

FREDERICK: Have a care, Blunt, she fetched a deep sigh;   100
she is enamored with thy shirt and drawers. She'll
strip thee even of that; there are of her calling such
unconscionable baggages and such dexterous thieves,
they'll flea° a man and he shall ne'er miss his skin till
he feels the cold. There was a countryman of ours   105
robbed of a row of teeth whilst he was a-sleeping,
which the jilt made him buy again when he waked.
You see, lady, how little reason we have to trust you.

BLUNT: 'Adsheartlikins, why this is most abominable!

FLORINDA: Some such devils there may be, but by all   110
that's holy, I am none such. I entered here to save a
life in danger.

BLUNT: For no goodness, I'll warrant her.

FREDERICK: Faith, damsel, you had e'en confessed the
plain truth, for we are fellows not to be caught twice   115
in the same trap. Look on that wreck: a tight vessel
when he set out of haven, well trimmed and laden.
And see how a female picaroon of this island of
rogues has shattered him, and canst thou hope for
any mercy?   120

BLUNT: No, no, gentlewoman, come along; 'adsheartlikins, we must be better acquainted. — We'll both
lie with her, and then let me alone to bang her.

FREDERICK: I'm ready to serve you in matters of revenge
that has a double pleasure in't.   125

BLUNT: Well said. — You hear, little one, how you are
condemned by public vote to the bed within; there's
no resisting your destiny, sweetheart.

(*Pulls her.*)

FLORINDA: Stay, sir. I have seen you with Belvile, an
English cavalier. For his sake, use me kindly. You   130
know him, sir.

BLUNT: Belvile? Why yes, sweeting, we do know Belvile,
and wish he were with us now. He's a cormorant at
whore and bacon:° He'd have a limb or two of thee,
my virgin pullet. But 'tis no matter; we'll leave him   135
the bones to pick.

FLORINDA: Sir, if you have any esteem for that Belvile, I
conjure you to treat me with more gentleness; he'll
thank you for the justice.

FREDERICK: Hark'ee, Blunt, I doubt we are mistaken in   140
this matter.

---

104. **flea:** Strip off the skin (flay).   133–34. **cormorant . . .
bacon:** Glutton for sex.

FLORINDA: Sir, if you find me not worth Belvile's care, use me as you please. And that you may think I merit better treatment than you threaten, pray take this
145   present.

(*Gives him a ring; he looks on it.*)

BLUNT: Hum, a diamond! Why, 'tis a wonderful virtue now that lies in this ring, a mollifying virtue. 'Adsheartlikins, there's more persuasive rhetoric in't than all her sex can utter.
150   FREDERICK: I begin to suspect something, and 'twould anger us vilely to be trussed up for a rape upon a maid of quality, when we only believe we ruffle a harlot.
BLUNT: Thou art a credulous fellow, but 'adsheartlikins, I have no faith yet. Why, my saint prattled as par-
155   lously as this does; she gave me a bracelet, too, a devil on her! But I sent my man to sell it today for necessaries, and it proved as counterfeit as her vows of love.
FREDERICK: However, let it reprieve her till we see
160   Belvile.
BLUNT: That's hard, yet I will grant it.

(*Enter a Servant.*)

SERVANT: Oh, sir, the colonel is just come in with his new friend and a Spaniard of quality, and talks of having you to dinner with 'em.
165   BLUNT: 'Adsheartlikins, I'm undone! I would not see 'em for the world. Hark'ee, Fred, lock up the wench in your chamber.
FREDERICK: Fear nothing, madam: Whate'er he threatens, you are safe whilst in my hands.

(*Exeunt Frederick and Florinda.*)

170   BLUNT: And sirrah, upon your life, say I am not at home, or that I'm asleep, or — or — anything. Away; I'll prevent their coming this way.

(*Locks the door, and exeunt.*)

ACT V

(*Blunt's chamber. After a great knocking as at his chamber door, enter Blunt softly crossing the stage, in his shirt and drawers as before.*)

[VOICES] (*call within*): Ned! Ned Blunt! Ned Blunt!
BLUNT: The rogues are up in arms. 'Adsheartlikins, this villainous Frederick has betrayed me: They have heard of my blessed fortune.
5   [VOICES] (*and knocking within*): Ned Blunt! Ned! Ned!
BELVILE [*within*]: Why, he's dead, sir, without dispute dead; he has not been seen today. Let's break open the door. Here, boy —
BLUNT: Ha, break open the door? 'Adsheartlikins, that
10   mad fellow will be as good as his word.
BELVILE [*within*]: Boy, bring something to force the door.

(*A great noise within, at the door again.*)

BLUNT: So, now must I speak in my own defense, I'll try what rhetoric will do. — Hold, hold! What do you mean, gentlemen, what do you mean?
BELVILE (*within*): Oh, rogue, art alive? Prithee open the   15
door and convince us.
BLUNT: Yes, I am alive, gentlemen, but at present a little busy.
BELVILE (*within*): How, Blunt grown a man of business? Come, come, open and let's see this miracle.   20
BLUNT: No, no, no, no, gentlemen, 'tis no great business. But — I am — at — my devotion. 'Adsheartlikins, will you not allow a man time to pray?
BELVILE (*within*): Turned religious? A greater wonder than the first! Therefore open quickly, or we shall   25
unhinge, we shall.
BLUNT [*aside*]: This won't do. — Why hark'ee, colonel, to tell you the truth, I am about a necessary affair of life: I have a wench with me. You apprehend me? — The devil's in't if they be so uncivil as to disturb me   30
now.
WILLMORE [*within*]: How, a wench? Nay then, we must enter and partake. No resistance. Unless it be your lady of quality, and then we'll keep our distance.
BLUNT: So, the business is out.   35
WILLMORE [*within*]: Come, come, lend's more hands to the door. Now heave, all together. (*Breaks open the door.*) So, well done, my boys.

(*Enter Belvile [and his Page], Willmore, Frederick, and Pedro. Blunt looks simply, they all laugh at him; he lays his hand on his sword, and comes up to Willmore.*)

BLUNT: Hark'ee, sir, laugh out your laugh quickly, d'ye hear, and be gone. I shall spoil your sport else, 'adsheartlikins, sir. I shall. The jest has been carried on   40
too long. — (*Aside.*) A plague upon my tailor!
WILLMORE: 'Sdeath, how the whore has dressed him! Faith, sir, I'm sorry.
BLUNT: Are you so, sir? Keep't to yourself then, sir, I   45
advise you, d'ye hear, for I can as little endure your pity as his mirth.

(*Lays his hand on's sword.*)

BELVILE: Indeed, Willmore, thou wert a little too rough with Ned Blunt's mistress. Call a person of quality whore, and one so young, so handsome, and so elo-   50
quent? Ha, ha, he.
BLUNT: Hark'ee, sir, you know me, and know I can be angry. Have a care, for 'adsheartlikins, I can fight, too, I can, sir. Do you mark me? No more.
BELVILE: Why so peevish, good Ned? Some disappoint-   55
ments, I'll warrant. What, did the jealous count, her husband, return just in the nick?
BLUNT: Or the devil, sir. (*They laugh.*) D'ye laugh? Look ye settle me a good sober countenance, and that quickly, too, or you shall know Ned Blunt is not —   60
BELVILE: Not everybody, we know that.
BLUNT: Not an ass to be laughed at, sir.
WILLMORE: Unconscionable sinner! To bring a lover so near his happiness — a vigorous passionate lover —

65 and then not only cheat him of his movables, but his very desires, too.

BELVILE: Ah, sir, a mistress is a trifle with Blunt; he'll have a dozen the next time he looks abroad. His eyes have charms not to be resisted; there needs no more
70 than to expose that taking person to the view of the fair, and he leads 'em all in triumph.

PEDRO: Sir, though I'm a stranger to you, I am ashamed at the rudeness of my nation; and could you learn who did it, would assist you to make an example of
75 'em.

BLUNT: Why ay, there's one speaks sense now, and handsomely. And let me tell you, gentlemen, I should not have showed myself like a jack pudding° thus to have made you mirth, but that I have revenge within my
80 power. For know, I have got into my possession a female, who had better have fallen under any curse than the ruin I design her. 'Adsheartlikins, she assaulted me here in my own lodgings, and had doubtless committed a rape upon me, had not this sword
85 defended me.

FREDERICK: I know not that, but o' my conscience thou had ravished her, had she not redeemed herself with a ring. Let's see't, Blunt.

(*Blunt shows the ring.*)

BELVILE [*aside*]: Ha! The ring I gave Florinda when we
90 exchanged our vows! — Hark'ee, Blunt —

(*Goes to whisper to him.*)

WILLMORE: No whispering, good colonel, there's a woman in the case. No whispering.

BELVILE [*aside to Blunt*]: Hark'ee, fool, be advised, and conceal both the ring and the story for your reputa-
95 tion's sake. Do not let people know what despised cullies we English are; to be cheated and abused by one whore, and another rather bribe thee than be kind to thee, is an infamy to our nation.

WILLMORE: Come, come, where's the wench? We'll see
100 her; let her be what she will, we'll see her.

PEDRO: Ay, ay, let us see her. I can soon discover whether she be of quality, or for your diversion.

BLUNT: She's in Fred's custody.

WILLMORE: Come, come, the key —

(*To Frederick, who gives him the key; they are going.*)

105 BELVILE [*aside*]: Death, what shall I do? — Stay, gentlemen. — [*Aside.*] Yet if I hinder 'em, I shall discover all. — Hold, let's go one at once.° Give me the key.

WILLMORE: Nay, hold there, colonel, I'll go first.

FREDERICK: Nay, no dispute, Ned and I have the propri-
110 ety of her.

WILLMORE: Damn propriety! Then we'll draw cuts. (*Belvile goes to whisper [to] Willmore.*) Nay, no corruption, good colonel. Come, the longest sword carries her.

78. **jack pudding:** Clown.   107. **one at once:** One after the other.

(*They all draw, forgetting Don Pedro, being a Spaniard, had the longest.*)

BLUNT: I yield up my interest to you, gentlemen, and 115
that will be revenge sufficient.

WILLMORE (*to Pedro*): The wench is yours. — [*Aside.*] Pox of his Toledo,° I had forgot that.

FREDERICK: Come, sir, I'll conduct you to the lady.

(*Exeunt Frederick and Pedro.*)

BELVILE (*aside*): To hinder him will certainly discover 120
her. — Dost know, dull beast, what mischief thou hast done?

(*Willmore walking up and down, out of humor.*)

WILLMORE: Ay, ay, to trust our fortune to lots! A devil on't, 'twas madness, that's the truth on't.

BELVILE: Oh, intolerable sot — 125

(*Enter Florinda running, masked, Pedro after her; Willmore gazing round her.*)

FLORINDA (*aside*): Good heaven defend me from discovery!

PEDRO: 'Tis but in vain to fly me; you're fallen to my lot.

BELVILE [*aside*]: Sure she's undiscovered yet, but now I fear there is no way to bring her off. 130

WILLMORE [*aside*]: Why, what a pox, is not this my woman, the same I followed but now?

(*Pedro talking to Florinda, who walks up and down.*)

PEDRO: As if I did not know ye, and your business here.

FLORINDA (*aside*): Good heaven, I fear he does indeed!

PEDRO: Come, pray be kind; I know you meant to be so 135
when you entered here, for these are proper gentlemen.

WILLMORE: But sir, perhaps the lady will not be imposed upon: She'll choose her man.

PEDRO: I am better bred than not to leave her choice 140
free.

(*Enter Valeria, and is surprised at sight of Don Pedro.*)

VALERIA (*aside*): Don Pedro here! There's no avoiding him.

FLORINDA (*aside*): Valeria! Then I'm undone.

VALERIA (*to Pedro, running to him*): Oh, I have found 145
you, sir! The strangest accident — if I had breath — to tell it.

PEDRO: Speak! Is Florinda safe? Hellena well?

VALERIA: Ay, ay, sir. Florinda is safe. — [*Aside.*] From any fears of you. 150

PEDRO: Why, where's Florinda? Speak!

VALERIA: Ay, where indeed, sir; I wish I could inform you. But to hold you no longer in doubt —

FLORINDA (*aside*): Oh, what will she say?

VALERIA: She's fled away in the habit — of one of her 155
pages, sir. But Callis thinks you may retrieve her yet,

118. **Toledo:** His sword, which won the draw, was made in Toledo, Spain.

if you make haste away. She'll tell you, sir, the rest. — (*Aside.*) If you can find her out.

PEDRO: Dishonorable girl, she has undone my aim. — [*To Belvile.*] Sir, you see my necessity of leaving you, and I hope you'll pardon it. My sister, I know, will make her flight to you, and if she do, I shall expect she should be rendered back.

BELVILE: I shall consult my love and honor, sir.

(*Exit Pedro.*)

FLORINDA (*to Valeria*): My dear preserver, let me embrace thee.

WILLMORE: What the devil's all this?

BLUNT: Mystery, by this light.

VALERIA: Come, come, make haste and get yourselves married quickly, for your brother will return again.

BELVILE: I'm so surprised with fears and joys, so amazed to find you here in safety, I can scarce persuade my heart into a faith of what I see.

WILLMORE: Hark'ee, colonel, is this that mistress who has cost you so many sighs, and me so many quarrels with you?

BELVILE: It is. — [*To Florinda.*] Pray give him the honor of your hand.

WILLMORE: Thus it must be received, then. (*Kneels and kisses her hand.*) And with it give your pardon, too.

FLORINDA: The friend to Belvile may command me anything.

WILLMORE (*aside*): Death, would I might; 'tis a surprising beauty.

BELVILE: Boy, run and fetch a father instantly.

(*Exit Boy.*)

FREDERICK: So, now do I stand like a dog, and have not a syllable to plead my own cause with. By this hand, madam, I was never thoroughly confounded before, nor shall I ever more dare look up with confidence, till you are pleased to pardon me.

FLORINDA: Sir, I'll be reconciled to you on one condition: that you'll follow the example of your friend in marrying a maid that does not hate you, and whose fortune, I believe, will not be unwelcome to you.

FREDERICK: Madam, had I no inclinations that way, I should obey your kind commands.

BELVILE: Who, Fred marry? He has so few inclinations for womankind that had he been possessed of paradise he might have continued there to this day, if no crime but love could have disinherited him.

FREDERICK: Oh, I do not use to boast of my intrigues.

BELVILE: Boast! Why, thou cost nothing but boast. And I dare swear, wert thou as innocent from the sin of the grape as thou art from the apple, thou might'st yet claim that right in Eden which our first parents lost by too much loving.

FREDERICK: I wish this lady would think me so modest a man.

VALERIA: She would be sorry then, and not like you half so well. And I should be loath to break my word with you, which was, that if your friend and mine agreed, it should be a match between you and I.

(*She gives him her hand.*)

FREDERICK: Bear witness, colonel, 'tis a bargain.

(*Kisses her hand.*)

BLUNT (*to Florinda*): I have a pardon to beg, too; but 'adsheartlikins, I am so out of countenance that I'm a dog if I can say anything to purpose.

FLORINDA: Sir, I heartily forgive you all.

BLUNT: That's nobly said, sweet lady. — Belvile, prithee present her her ring again, for I find I have not courage to approach her myself.

(*Gives him the ring; he gives it to Florinda.*)

(*Enter Boy.*)

BOY: Sir, I have brought the father that you sent for.

[*Exit Boy.*]

BELVILE: 'Tis well. And now, my dear Florinda, let's fly to complete that mighty joy we have so long wished and sighed for. — Come, Fred, you'll follow?

FREDERICK: Your example, sir, 'twas ever my ambition in war, and must be so in love.

WILLMORE: And must not I see this juggling° knot tied?

BELVILE: No, thou shalt do us better service and be our guard, lest Don Pedro's sudden return interrupt the ceremony.

WILLMORE: Content; I'll secure this pass.

(*Exeunt Belvile, Florinda, Frederick, and Valeria.*)

(*Enter Boy.*)

BOY (*to Willmore*): Sir, there's a lady without would speak to you.

WILLMORE: Conduct her in; I dare not quit my post.

BOY [*to Blunt*]: And sir, your tailor waits you in your chamber.

BLUNT: Some comfort yet: I shall not dance naked at the wedding.

(*Exeunt Blunt and Boy.*)

(*Enter again the Boy, conducting in Angellica in a masking habit and a vizard. Willmore runs to her.*)

WILLMORE [*aside*]: This can be none but my pretty gypsy. — Oh, I see you can follow as well as fly. Come, confess thyself the most malicious devil in nature; you think you have done my business with Angellica —

ANGELLICA: Stand off, base villain!

(*She draws a pistol and holds it to his breast.*)

WILLMORE: Ha, 'tis not she! Who art thou, and what's thy business?

ANGELLICA: One thou hast injured, and who comes to kill thee for't.

WILLMORE: What the devil canst thou mean?

ANGELLICA: By all my hopes to kill thee —

(*Holds still the pistol to his breast; he going back, she following still.*)

WILLMORE: Prithee, on what acquaintance? For I know thee not.

227. **juggling:** Based on trickery or deception.

ANGELLICA: Behold this face so lost to thy
    remembrance,   (*Pulls off her vizard.*)
        And then call all thy sins about thy soul
255   And let 'em die with thee.
    WILLMORE: Angellica!
    ANGELLICA: Yes, traitor! Does not thy guilty blood run
        shivering through thy veins? Hast thou no horror at
        this sight, that tells thee thou hast not long to boast
260   thy shameful conquest?
    WILLMORE: Faith, no, child. My blood keeps its old
        ebbs and flows still, and that usual heat too, that
        could oblige thee with a kindness, had I but opportu-
        nity.
265 ANGELLICA: Devil! Dost wanton with my pain? Have at
        thy heart!
    WILLMORE: Hold, dear virago!° Hold thy hand a little; I
        am not now at leisure to be killed. Hold and hear
        me. — (*Aside.*) Death, I think she's in earnest.
270 ANGELLICA (*aside, turning from him*): Oh, if I take not
        heed, my coward heart will leave me to his mercy. —
        What have you, sir, to say? — But should I hear thee,
        thoud'st talk away all that is brave about me, and I
        have vowed thy death by all that's sacred.

(*Follows him with the pistol to his breast.*)

275 WILLMORE: Why then, there's an end of a proper hand-
        some fellow, that might 'a lived to have done good
        service yet. That's all I can say to't.
    ANGELLICA (*pausingly*): Yet — I would give thee time
        for — penitence.
280 WILLMORE: Faith, child, I thank God I have ever took
        care to lead a good, sober, hopeful life, and am of a
        religion that teaches me to believe I shall depart in
        peace.
    ANGELLICA: So will the devil! Tell me,
285   How many poor believing fools thou hast undone?
        How many hearts thou hast betrayed to ruin?
        Yet these are little mischiefs to the ills
        Thou'st taught mine to commit: Thou'st taught it
            love.
    WILLMORE: Egad, 'twas shrewdly hurt the while.
290 ANGELLICA: Love, that has robbed it of its unconcern,
        Of all that pride that taught me how to value it.
        And in its room
        A mean submissive passion was conveyed,
        That made me humbly bow, which I ne'er did
295   To anything but heaven.
        Thou, perjured man, didst this; and with thy
            oaths,
        Which on thy knees thou didst devoutly make,
        Softened my yielding heart, and then I was a slave.
        Yet still had been content to've worn my chains,
300   Worn 'em with vanity and joy forever,
        Hadst thou not broke those vows that put them on.
        'Twas then I was undone.

(*All this while follows him with the pistol to his breast.*)

267. virago: A woman of great stature, strength, and courage.

WILLMORE: Broke my vows? Why, where hast thou
    lived? Amongst the gods? For I never heard of mortal
    man that has not broke a thousand vows.   305
ANGELLICA: Oh, impudence!
WILLMORE: Angellica, that beauty has been too long
    tempting, not to have made a thousand lovers lan-
    guish; who, in the amorous fever, no doubt have
    sworn like me. Did they all die in that faith, still   310
    adoring? I do not think they did.
ANGELLICA: No, faithless man; had I repaid their vows,
    as I did shine, I would have killed the ingrateful that
    had abandoned me.
WILLMORE: This old general has quite spoiled thee: 315
    Nothing makes a woman so vain as being flattered.
    Your old lover ever supplies the defects of age with
    intolerable dotage, vast charge, and that which you
    call constancy; and attributing all this to your own
    merits, you domineer, and throw your favors in's   320
    teeth, upbraiding him still with the defects of age,
    and cuckold him as often as he deceives your expec-
    tations. But the gay, young, brisk lover, that brings
    his equal fires, and can give you dart for dart, you'll
    find will be as nice as you sometimes.   325
ANGELLICA: All this thou'st made me know, for which I
        hate thee.
    Had I remained in innocent security,
    I should have thought all men were born my slaves,
    And worn my power like lightning in my eyes,
    To have destroyed at pleasure when offended.   330
    But when love held the mirror, the undeceiving
        glass
    Reflected all the weakness of my soul, and made me
        know
    My richest treasure being lost, my honor,
    All the remaining spoil could not be worth
    The conqueror's care or value.   335
    Oh, how I fell, like a long-worshiped idol,
    Discovering all the cheat.
    Would not the incense and rich sacrifice
    Which blind devotion offered at my altars
    Have fallen to thee?   340
    Why wouldst thou then destroy my fancied power?
WILLMORE: By heaven, thou'rt brave, and I admire
        thee strangely.
    I wish I were that dull, that constant thing
    Which thou wouldst have, and nature never meant
        me.
    I must, like cheerful birds, sing in all groves,   345
    And perch on every bough,
    Billing the next kind she that flies to meet me;
    Yet, after all, could build my nest with thee,
    Thither repairing when I'd loved my round,
    And still reserve a tributary flame.   350
    To gain your credit, I'll pay you back your charity,
    And be obliged for nothing but for love.

(*Offers her a purse of gold.*)

ANGELLICA: Oh, that thou wert in earnest!
    So mean a thought of me

355 Would turn my rage to scorn, and I should pity
    thee,
  And give thee leave to live;
  Which for the public safety of our sex,
  And my own private injuries, I dare not do.
  Prepare —   (Follows still, as before.)
360   I will no more be tempted with replies.
WILLMORE: Sure —
ANGELLICA: Another word will damn thee! I've heard thee talk too long.

(She follows him with the pistol ready to shoot; he retires, still amazed. Enter Don Antonio, his arm in a scarf, and lays hold on the pistol.)

ANTONIO: Ha! Angellica!
365 ANGELLICA: Antonio! What devil brought thee hither?
ANTONIO: Love and curiosity, seeing your coach at door. Let me disarm you of this unbecoming instrument of death. (Takes away the pistol.) Amongst the number of your slaves was there not one worthy the honor to
370 have fought your quarrel? — [To Willmore.] Who are you, sir, that are so very wretched to merit death from her?
WILLMORE: One, sir, that could have made a better end of an amorous quarrel without you, than with you.
375 ANTONIO: Sure 'tis some rival. Ha! The very man took down her picture yesterday; the very same that set on me last night! Blessed opportunity —

(Offers to shoot him.)

ANGELLICA: Hold, you're mistaken, sir.
ANTONIO: By heaven, the very same! — Sir, what pre-
380 tensions have you to this lady?
WILLMORE: Sir, I do not use to be examined, and am ill at all disputes but this —

(Draws; Antonio offers to shoot.)

ANGELLICA (to Willmore): Oh, hold! You see he's armed with certain death.
  — And you, Antonio, I command you hold,
385 By all the passion you've so lately vowed me.

(Enter Don Pedro, sees Antonio, and stays.)

PEDRO (aside): Ha! Antonio! And Angellica!
ANTONIO: When I refuse obedience to your will,
  May you destroy me with your mortal hate.
  By all that's holy, I adore you so,
390   That even my rival, who has charms enough
  To make him fall a victim to my jealousy,
  Shall live; nay, and have leave to love on still.
PEDRO (aside): What's this I hear?
ANGELLICA (pointing to Willmore): Ah thus, 'twas thus he talked, and I believed.
395 Antonio, yesterday
  I'd not have sold my interest in his heart
  For all the sword has won and lost in battle.
  — But now, to show my utmost of contempt,
  I give thee life; which, if thou wouldst preserve,
400   Live where my eyes may never see thee more.

Live to undo someone whose soul may prove
So bravely constant to revenge my love.

(Goes out. Antonio follows, but Pedro pulls him back.)

PEDRO: Antonio, stay.
ANTONIO: Don Pedro!
405 PEDRO: What coward fear was that prevented thee from meeting me this morning on the Molo?
ANTONIO: Meet thee?
PEDRO: Yes, me; I was the man that dared thee to't.
ANTONIO: Hast thou so often seen me fight in war, to
410 find no better cause to excuse my absence? I sent my sword and one to do thee right, finding myself uncapable to use a sword.
PEDRO: But 'twas Florinda's quarrel that we fought, and you, to show how little you esteemed her, sent me
415 your rival, giving him your interest. But I have found the cause of this affront, and when I meet you fit for the dispute, I'll tell you my resentment.
ANTONIO: I shall be ready, sir, ere long, to do you reason.   (Exit Antonio.)
420 PEDRO: If I could find Florinda, now whilst my anger's high, I think I should be kind, and give her to Belvile in revenge.
WILLMORE: Faith, sir, I know not what you would do, but I believe the priest within has been so kind.
425 PEDRO: How? My sister married?
WILLMORE: I hope by this time he is, and bedded too, or he has not my longings about him.
PEDRO: Dares he do this? Does he not fear my power?
WILLMORE: Faith, not at all; if you will go in and thank
430 him for the favor he has done your sister, so; if not, sir, my power's greater in this house than yours: I have a damned surly crew here that will keep you till the next tide, and then clap you on board for prize. My ship lies but a league off the Molo, and we shall show
435 your donship a damned Tramontana° rover's trick.

(Enter Belvile.)

BELVILE: This rogue's in some new mischief. Ha! Pedro returned!
PEDRO: Colonel Belvile, I hear you have married my sister.
BELVILE: You have heard truth then, sir.
440 PEDRO: Have I so? Then, sir, I wish you joy.
BELVILE: How?
PEDRO: By this embrace I do, and I am glad on't.
BELVILE: Are you in earnest?
PEDRO: By our long friendship and my obligations to
445 thee, I am; the sudden change I'll give you reasons for anon. Come, lead me to my sister, that she may know I now approve her choice.

(Exit Belvile with Pedro.)

(Willmore goes to follow them. Enter Hellena, as before in boy's clothes, and pulls him back.)

435. **Tramontana:** Region of Italy north of the Alps.

WILLMORE: Ha! My gypsy! Now a thousand blessings
on thee for this kindness. Egad, child, I was e'en in
despair of ever seeing thee again; my friends are all
provided for within, each man his kind woman.

HELLENA: Ha! I thought they had served me some such
trick!

WILLMORE: And I was e'en resolved to go aboard, and
condemn myself to my lone cabin, and the thoughts
of thee.

HELLENA: And could you have left me behind? Would
you have been so ill natured?

WILLMORE: Why, 'twould have broke my heart, child.
But since we are met again, I defy foul weather to
part us.

HELLENA: And would you be a faithful friend now, if a
maid should trust you?

WILLMORE: For a friend I cannot promise: Thou art of a
form so excellent, a face and humor too good for
cold dull friendship. I am parlously afraid of being in
love, child; and you have not forgotten how severely
you have used me?

HELLENA: That's all one; such usage you must still look
for: to find out all your haunts, to rail at you to all
that love you, till I have made you love only me in
your own defense, because nobody else will love you.

WILLMORE: But hast thou no better quality to recommend thyself by?

HELLENA: Faith, none, captain. Why, twill be the greater
charity to take me for thy mistress. I am a lone child,
a kind of orphan lover, and why I should die a maid,
and in a captain's hands too, I do not understand.

WILLMORE: Egad, I was never clawed away with broad-
sides from any female before. Thou hast one virtue I
adore — good nature. I hate a coy demure mistress,
she's as troublesome as a colt, I'll break none. No,
give me a mad mistress when mewed, and in flying,
one I dare trust upon the wing, that whilst she's kind
will come to the lure.°

HELLENA: Nay, as kind as you will, good captain, whilst
it lasts. But let's lose no time.

WILLMORE: My time's as precious to me as thine can be.
Therefore, dear creature, since we are so well agreed,
let's retire to my chamber; and if ever thou wert
treated with such savory love! Come, my bed's prepared for such a guest all clean and sweet as thy fair
self. I love to steal a dish and a bottle with a friend,
and hate long graces. Come, let's retire and fall to.

HELLENA: 'Tis but getting my consent, and the business
is soon done. Let but old gaffer Hymen° and his
priest say amen to's, and I dare lay my mother's
daughter by as proper a fellow as your father's son,
without fear or blushing.

WILLMORE: Hold, hold, no bug words,° child. Priest
and Hymen? Prithee add a hangman to 'em to make

up the consort. No, no, we'll have no vows but love,
child, nor witness but the lover: The kind deity
enjoins naught but love and enjoy. Hymen and priest
wait still upon portion and jointure; love and beauty
have their own ceremonies. Marriage is as certain a
bane to love as lending money is to friendship. I'll
neither ask nor give a vow, though I could be content
to turn gypsy and become a left-handed bridegroom
to have the pleasure of working that great miracle of
making a maid a mother, if you durst venture. 'Tis
upse gypsy° that, and if I miss I'll lose my labor.

HELLENA: And if you do not lose, what shall I get? A
cradle full of noise and mischief, with a pack of
repentance at my back? Can you teach me to weave
incle° to pass my time with? 'Tis upse gypsy that, too.

WILLMORE: I can teach thee to weave a true love's knot
better.

HELLENA: So can my dog.

WILLMORE: Well, I see we are both upon our guards,
and I see there's no way to conquer good nature but
by yielding. Here, give me thy hand: One kiss, and I
am thine.

HELLENA: One kiss! How like my page he speaks! I am
resolved you shall have none, for asking such a
sneaking sum. He that will be satisfied with one kiss
will never die of that longing. Good friend single-
kiss, is all your talking come to this? A kiss, a
caudle!° Farewell, captain single-kiss.

(*Going out; he stays her.*)

WILLMORE: Nay, if we part so, let me die like a bird
upon a bough, at the sheriff's charge. By heaven,
both the Indies shall not buy thee from me. I adore
thy humor and will marry thee, and we are so of one
humor it must be a bargain. Give me thy hand.
(*Kisses her hand.*) And now let the blind ones, love
and fortune, do their worst.

HELLENA: Why, god-a-mercy, captain!

WILLMORE: But hark'ee: the bargain is now made, but is
it not fit we should know each other's names, that
when we have reason to curse one another hereafter,
and people ask me who 'tis I give to the devil, I may
at least be able to tell what family you came of?

HELLENA: Good reason, captain, and where I have
cause, as I doubt not but I shall have plentiful, that I
may know at whom to throw my — blessings, I
beseech ye your name.

WILLMORE: I am called Robert the Constant.

HELLENA: A very fine name! Pray was it your faulkner°
or butler that christened you? Do they not use to
whistle when they call you?

WILLMORE: I hope you have a better, that a man may
name without crossing himself — you are so merry
with mine.

484–86. **flying . . . lure:** I.e., one who will be faithful as long as
that doesn't interfere with her wishes. **497. Hymen:** God of
marriage. **501. bug words:** Words that inspire fear.

513. **upse gypsy:** Gypsy fashion. **517. incle:** Linen yarn or
tape. **530. caudle:** A warm drink made of gruel and wine or
ale, sweetened and spiced, given to the sick. **549. faulkner:**
Falconer, trainer of hawks.

555 HELLENA: I am called Hellena the Inconstant.

(*Enter Pedro, Belvile, Florinda, Frederick, Valeria.*)

PEDRO: Ha! Hellena!

FLORINDA: Hellena!

HELLENA: The very same. Ha! My brother! Now, captain, show your love and courage; stand to your arms
560 and defend me bravely, or I am lost forever.

PEDRO: What's this I hear? False girl, how came you
hither, and what's your business? Speak!

(*Goes roughly to her.*)

WILLMORE: Hold off, sir; you have leave to parley° only.

(*Puts himself between.*)

HELLENA: I had e'en as good tell it, as you guess it. Faith,
565 brother, my business is the same with all living creatures of my age: to love and be beloved — and here's
the man.

PEDRO: Perfidious maid, hast thou deceived me too;
deceived thyself and heaven?

570 HELLENA: 'Tis time enough to make my peace with that;
Be you but kind, let me alone with heaven.

PEDRO: Belvile, I did not expect this false play from you.
Was't not enough you'd gain Florinda, which I pardoned, but your lewd friends too must be enriched
575 with the spoils of a noble family?

BELVILE: Faith, sir, I am as much surprised at this as you
can be. Yet, sir, my friends are gentlemen, and ought
to be esteemed for their misfortunes, since they have
the glory to suffer with the best of men and kings.
580 'Tis true, he's a rover of fortune, yet a prince aboard
his little wooden world.

PEDRO: What's this to the maintenance of a woman of
her birth and quality?

WILLMORE: Faith, sir, I can boast of nothing but a
585 sword which does me right where'er I come, and has
defended a worse cause than a woman's, and since I
loved her before I either knew her birth or name, I
must pursue my resolution and marry her.

PEDRO: And is all your holy intent of becoming a nun
590 debauched into a desire of man?

HELLENA: Why, I have considered the matter, brother,
and find the three hundred thousand crowns my
uncle left me, and you cannot keep from me, will be
better laid out in love than in religion, and turn to as
595 good an account. Let most voices carry it: for heaven
or the captain?

ALL CRY: A captain! A captain!

HELLENA: Look ye, sir, 'tis a clear case.

PEDRO: Oh, I am mad! — (*Aside.*) If I refuse, my life's in
600 danger. — Come, there's one motive induces me.
Take her; I shall now be free from fears of her honor.
Guard it you now, if you can; I have been a slave to't
long enough.   (*Gives her to him.*)

WILLMORE: Faith, sir, I am of a nation that are of opinion a woman's honor is not worth guarding when she 605
has a mind to part with it.

HELLENA: Well said, captain.

PEDRO (*to Valeria*): This was your plot, mistress, but I
hope you have married one that will revenge my
quarrel to you.   610

VALERIA: There's no altering destiny, sir.

PEDRO: Sooner than a woman's will; therefore I forgive
you all, and wish you may get my father's pardon as
easily, which I fear.

(*Enter Blunt dressed in a Spanish habit, looking very
ridiculous; his Man adjusting his band.*)

MAN: 'Tis very well, sir.   615

BLUNT: Well, sir! 'Adsheartlikins, I tell you 'tis damnable
ill, sir. A Spanish habit! Good Lord! Could the devil
and my tailor devise no other punishment for me but
the mode of a nation I abominate?

BELVILE: What's the matter, Ned?   620

BLUNT: Pray view me round, and judge.

                                                   (*Turns round.*)

BELVILE: I must confess thou art a kind of an odd figure.

BLUNT: In a Spanish habit with a vengeance! I had rather
be in the Inquisition for Judaism° than in this doublet
and breeches; a pillory were an easy collar to this,   625
three handfuls high; and these shoes, too, are worse
than the stocks, with the sole an inch shorter than my
foot. In fine, gentlemen, methinks I look like a bag of
bays° stuffed full of fool's flesh.

BELVILE: Methinks 'tis well, and makes thee look e'en   630
cavalier. Come, sir, settle your face and salute our
friends. Lady —

BLUNT (*to Hellena*): Ha! Sayst thou so, my little rover?
Lady, if you be one, give me leave to kiss your hand,
and tell you, 'adsheartlikins, for all I look so, I am   635
your humble servant. A pox of my Spanish habit!
(*Music is heard to play.*)

WILLMORE: Hark! What's this?

(*Enter Boy.*)

BOY: Sir, as the custom is, the gay people in masquerade,
who make every man's house their own, are coming
up.   640

(*Enter several men and women in masking habits, with
music; they put themselves in order and dance.*)

BLUNT: 'Adsheartlikins, would 'twere lawful to pull off
their false faces, that I might see if my doxy° were not
amongst 'em.

BELVILE (*to the maskers*): Ladies and gentlemen, since
you are come so *a propos,*° you must take a small   645
collation with us.

---

563. parley: Speak or discuss.

624. Inquisition for Judaism: The Spanish Inquisition, which
persecuted heretics, Jews, and Muslims.   628–29. bag of bays:
Spices wrapped in cloth and used for flavoring in cooking.
642. doxy: Mistress, prostitute.   645. *a propos:* In a timely
fashion; appropriately.

WILLMORE (*to Hellena*): Whilst we'll to the good man
    within, who stays to give us a cast of his office.°
    Have you no trembling at the near approach?
650 HELLENA: No more than you have in an engagement or
    a tempest.
WILLMORE: Egad, thou'rt a brave girl, and I admire thy
    love and courage.
       Lead on; no other dangers they can dread,
655   *Who venture in the storms o'th' marriage bed.*
                                  (*Exeunt.*)

EPILOGUE

    The banished cavaliers! A roving blade!
    A popish carnival! A masquerade!
    The devil's in't if this will please the nation
    In these our blessed times of reformation,
5   When conventickling° is so much in fashion.
    And yet —
    That mutinous tribe less factions do beget,
    Than your continual differing in wit.
    Your judgment's, as your passion's, a disease:
10   Nor muse nor miss your appetite can please;
    You're grown as nice as queasy consciences,
    Whose each convulsion, when the spirit moves,
    Damns everything that maggot° disapproves.
       With canting° rule you would the stage refine,
15   And to dull method all our sense confine.
    With th'insolence of commonwealths you rule,
    Where each gay fop and politic grave fool
    On monarch wit impose, without control.
    As for the last, who seldom sees a play,
20   Unless it be the old Blackfriars° way;
    Shaking his empty noddle o'er bamboo,°
    He cries, "Good faith, these plays will never do!
    Ah, sir, in my young days, what lofty wit,
    What high-strained scenes of fighting there were writ.
25   These are slight airy toys. But tell me, pray,
    What has the House of Commons done today?"
    Then shows his politics, to let you see
    Of state affairs he'll judge as notably
    As he can do of wit and poetry.
30   The younger sparks, who hither do resort,
    Cry,
    "Pox o' your genteel things! Give us more sport'!

Damn me, I'm sure 'twill never please the court."
    Such fops are never pleased, unless the play
Be stuffed with fools as brisk and dull as they.   35
Such might the half-crown spare, and in a glass
At home behold a more accomplished ass.
Where they may set their cravats, wigs, and faces,
And practice all their buffoonry grimaces.
See how this huff becomes, this damny,° stare,   40
Which they at home may act because they dare,
But must with prudent caution do elsewhere.
Oh that our Nokes, or Tony Lee,° could show
A fop but half so much to th' life as you.

POSTSCRIPT

This play had been sooner in print, but for a report
about the town (made by some either very malicious
or very ignorant) that 'twas *Thomaso*° altered; which
made the booksellers fear some trouble from the proprietor of that admirable play, which indeed has wit 5
enough to stock a poet, and is not to be pieced or
mended by any but the excellent author himself. That
I have stolen some hints from it, may be a proof that
I valued it more than to pretend to alter it, had I the
dexterity of some poets, who are not more expert in 10
stealing than in the art of concealing, and who even
that way outdo the Spartan boys.° I might have
appropriated all to myself; but I, vainly proud of my
judgment, hang out the sign of Angellica (the only
stolen object) to give notice where a great part of the 15
wit dwelt; though if the *Play of the Novella*° were as
well worth remembering as *Thomaso*, they might
(bating° the name) have as well said I took it from
thence. I will only say the plot and business (not to
boast on't) is my own; as for the words and charac- 20
ters, I leave the reader to judge and compare 'em with
Thomaso, to whom I recommend the great entertainment of reading it. Though had this succeeded ill, I
should have had no need of imploring that justice
from the critics, who are naturally so kind to any that 25
pretend to usurp their dominion, especially of our
sex: They would doubtless have given me the whole
honor on't. Therefore I will only say in English what
the famous Vergil does in Latin: I make verses, and
others have the fame. 30

---

648. stays . . . office: The priest waits to perform his office, i.e.,
to marry them. **5. conventickling:** A pun. A conventicle was a
secret meeting of religious dissenters (those who were not members of the Church of England). **13. maggot:** Conscience.
14. canting: Hypocritical. **20. Blackfriars:** The Blackfriars
Theatre (1576–1655), considered old-fashioned in Behn's time.
21. o'er bamboo: Over a cane, implying old age.

40. damny: Damn me. **43. Nokes . . . Lee:** The best low comedians of the day. James Nokes performed in Thomas Betterton's company. **3. *Thomaso*:** Thomas Killigrew's *Thomaso;
or, The Wanderer* (1654; published 1664). **12. Spartan boys:**
Those who hid in the Trojan horse. **16. *Play of the Novella*:**
The Novella (1632) by Richard Brome, from which Behn borrowed several ideas. **18. bating:** Excepting.

COMMENTARIES

Virginia Woolf (1882–1941)
ON APHRA BEHN   *1929*

> *Virginia Woolf was a leading experimental writer of fiction in the first half of the twentieth century. She is known for the novels* Mrs. Dalloway *(1925),* To the Lighthouse *(1927), and* Orlando *(1928) and for her essays, including* A Room of One's Own *(1929), from which this excerpt comes. Woolf was one of the first modern commentators to call attention to the extraordinary achievement of Aphra Behn.*

With Mrs. Behn we turn a very important corner on the road. We leave behind, shut up in their parks among their folios, those solitary great ladies who wrote without audience or criticism, for their own delight alone. We come to town and rub shoulders with ordinary people in the streets. Mrs. Behn was a middle-class woman with all the plebeian virtues of humor, vitality, and courage; a woman forced by the death of her husband and some unfortunate adventures of her own to make her living by her wits. She had to work on equal terms with men. She made, by working very hard, enough to live on. The importance of that fact outweighs anything that she actually wrote, even the splendid "A Thousand Martyrs I Have Made," or "Love in Fantastic Triumph Sat," for here begins the freedom of the mind, or rather the possibility that in the course of time the mind will be free to write what it likes. For now that Aphra Behn had done it, girls could go to their parents and say, You need not give me an allowance; I can make money by my pen. Of course the answer for many years to come was, Yes, by living the life of Aphra Behn! Death would be better! and the door was slammed faster than ever. That profoundly interesting subject, the value that men set upon women's chastity and its effect upon their education, here suggests itself for discussion, and might provide an interesting book if any student at Girton or Newnham cared to go into the matter. Lady Dudley, sitting in diamonds among the midges of a Scottish moor, might serve for frontispiece. Lord Dudley, the *Times* said when Lady Dudley died the other day, "a man of cultivated taste and many accomplishments, was benevolent and bountiful, but whimsically despotic. He insisted upon his wife's wearing full dress, even at the remotest shooting-lodge in the Highlands; he loaded her with gorgeous jewels," and so on, "he gave her everything — always excepting any measure of responsibility." Then Lord Dudley had a stroke and she nursed him and ruled his estates with supreme competence for ever after. That whimsical despotism was in the nineteenth century too.

But to return. Aphra Behn proved that money could be made by writing at the sacrifice, perhaps, of certain agreeable qualities; and so by degrees writing became not merely a sign of folly and a distracted mind, but was of practical importance. A husband might die, or some disaster overtake the family. Hundreds of women began as the eighteenth century drew on to add to their pin money, or to come to the rescue of their families by making translations or writing the innumerable bad novels which have ceased to be recorded even in textbooks, but are to be picked up in the fourpenny boxes in the Charing Cross Road. The extreme activity of mind which showed itself in the later eighteenth century among women — the talking, and the meeting, the writing of essays on Shakespeare, the translating of the classics — was founded on the solid fact that women could make money by writing. Money dignifies what is frivolous if unpaid for. It might still be well to sneer at "blue stockings with an itch for scribbling," but it could not be denied that they could put money in their purses. Thus, towards the end of the eighteenth century a change came about which, if I were rewriting history, I should describe more fully and think of greater importance than the Crusades or the Wars of the Roses. The middle-class woman began to write. For if *Pride and Prejudice* matters, and *Middlemarch* and *Vilette* and *Wuthering Heights* matter, then it matters far more than I can prove in an hour's discourse that women generally, and not merely the lonely aristocrat shut up in her country house among her folios and her flatterers, took to writing. Without those forerunners, Jane Austen and the Brontës and George Eliot could no more have written than Shakespeare could have written without Marlowe, or Marlowe without Chaucer, or Chaucer without those forgotten poets who paved the ways and tamed the natural savagery of the tongue. For masterpieces are not single and solitary births; they are the outcome of many years of thinking in common, of thinking by the body of the people, so that the experience of the mass is behind the single voice. Jane Austen should have laid a wreath upon the grave of Fanny Burney, and George Eliot done homage to the robust shade of Eliza Carter — the valiant old woman who tied a bell to her bedstead in order that she might wake early and learn Greek. All women together ought to let flowers fall upon the tomb of Aphra Behn, which is, most scandalously but rather appropriately, in Westminster Abbey,° for it was she who earned them the right to speak their minds. It is she — shady and amorous as she was — who makes it not quite fantastic for me to say to you tonight: Earn five hundred a year by your wits.

Westminster Abbey: The burial place in London of British royalty as well as distinguished citizens, including, in the Poets' Corner, famous writers.

Elaine Hobby (b. 1956)
COURTSHIP AND MARRIAGE IN *THE ROVER*   1989

Elaine Hobby closely examines The Rover *to help us understand the conventions of romantic love in Aphra Behn's work. Her essay is especially enlightening on the questions of marriage and rape and on the differences in the viewpoints of men and women characters in the play. Hobby notes the complexities implied in the characterization of Angellica, the courtesan.*

Commonly, Behn's plays feature at least two pairs of young lovers, whose attitudes to love and marriage serve as contrasting strategies in courtship. A common pattern is that of the "constant couple," who remain true to one another, and finally marry, despite parental opposition and, usually, confusions over one another's true identity and conduct. These lovers are not, however, idyllically well matched or perfectly happy. In *The Rover*, Florinda and Belvile are just such a constant couple. From the beginning they are in love with one another, and resolved to accept no other partner. Except for her stubbornness on this one issue, Florinda is all quiet obedience, failing to argue her case against an arranged marriage. Her passivity is no ideal. Twice in the course of the play she narrowly escapes being raped by the friends of her beloved, and on each occasion is only saved because her obvious high social class causes her attackers to hesitate, fearing retribution from her relatives. The second of these incidents is a nightmare scene where, seeking refuge in Blunt's house, she is regarded by him as the perfect target for his revenge against all women (and Lucetta in particular) for making fun of him. When Frederick, the play's great upholder of patriarchal morality, arrives, the two men agree to rape her.

> BLUNT: We'll both lie with her, and then let me alone to bang her.
> FREDERICK: I'm ready to serve you in matters of revenge that has a double pleasure in't.
> (IV, v, 123–26)

In a world where men can choose to rape a woman, any woman, for spite, there is no safety for the romantic heroine. In Behn's plays, as in her novels, rape or the threat of it is shown to be an almost routine masculine strategy to bully and manipulate women. In *The Amorous Prince*, Frederick threatens to rape Laura at knifepoint to humble her for scorning him, and in the same play Silvio threatens to rape his "sister" Cleonte. Sir Timothy Tawdrey in *The Town-Fopp,* when threatening to rape Phillis, tells her that old patriarchal lie: that all women want to be forcibly taken. Phillis's fate is the most terrible of all. Having no economic choices (like Philadelphia in Behn's novel *The Unfortunate Happy Lady*), she has no option but to marry her would-be rapist.

Setting out with a theme of courtship and marriage, Behn writes about rape and prostitution, constructing scenarios that show how closely connected these fates are for women. Where Florinda's reliance on "true love" for her salvation twice brings her to the brink of being raped, the courtesan Angellica Bianca in the same play is betrayed by her final inability to escape from the tempting lies of romance. Early in the play, she makes a cool assessment of women's position, explaining that she had opted to sell her body for the solid return of financial reward, rather than trusting to illusory male fidelity: "Nothing but gold shall charm my heart" (II, 1, 163). She knows, too, that marriage for money is a no less mercenary affair than prostitution. Disaster arrives, however, because she has seriously misjudged the power structure of her society. She arrives in town hoping to captivate either the viceroy's son Don Antonio, or Don Pedro, the nephew of her deceased "protector." Had she been married to her old lover, Don Pedro would have been her kin, and had some social duty to support her. As it is, she is left to live on her wits and her transitory physical charms. When Willmore, the "rover" of the title, finally rejects her in favor of the wealthy virgin Hellena, she is forced to recognize that her chosen independence was illusory. In a world where men make the rules, her only salable item is her virginity. Having sold that in the wrong market, she is damned.

When Angellica falls hopelessly for the feckless Willmore, she wants to believe that love and romance can be dissociated from social and economic structures, that "true love" in her world can be above financial considerations. She calls on him to see things her way and, blinded by this desire, does not recognize that he is using her for his pleasure.

> ANGELLICA: Thou'rt a brave fellow! Put up thy gold, and know,
> That were thy fortune large as is thy soul,
> Thou shouldst not buy my love
> Couldst thou forget these mean effects of vanity
> Which set me out to sale,
> And as a lover prize my yielding joys.
> Canst thou believe they'll be entirely thine,
> Without considering they were mercenary?   (II, ii, 110–17)

In the course of the play, Willmore's repeated answer to this is a resounding "No." Having worshiped her beauty, tasted the pleasures of her body, and spent her money to attract a wealthier woman, he leaves her for a better catch.

Angellica is a troubling and uncomfortable figure in the play, disrupting the wit and airiness of scenes between Hellena and Willmore and undercutting the conventional "happy ending" of true lovers united. Realizing she has been betrayed by Willmore despite giving him "My virgin heart . . . Oh! 'tis gone!" (IV, ii, 163) she plots her revenge "for the public safety of our sex" (V, 357). Trapping him at gunpoint she decides, however, to let him live: he is not worth the trouble of an execution: "But now, to show my utmost of contempt, / I give thee life" (V, 398–99). Through Willmore, she has learned that male protestations of devotion, and all their courtly love rhetoric, are for them just a game. There is no true power, no safety, for women.[. . .]

In many of Behn's plays, men's obsessions with their courtship conventions prevent them from understanding the women they address. Romance is a male invention, and women are jeopardized and often betrayed if they believe such declarations of undying passion. The task for the witty heroine who is at the center of many of Behn's plays, as Hellena is in *The Rover*, is to discover as much as possible about her man's true intentions, beneath his courtly facade. Willmore refers to both Angellica and to Hellena as his "angel" in high-flown rhetoric, but where Angellica is briefly fooled by this worship, Hellena is quite clear-sighted about the limit of his commitment. As far as possible, she takes control of her situation, disguising herself and playing parts, testing out and then capturing the man she has chosen. Disguised, she watches him court and promise fidelity to Angellica, and in a bitter but witty scene mocks him, throwing back at him the overblown promises she has heard him make (III, i). She has no interest in traditional courtship rituals, thinking them "a very pretty, idle, silly kind of pleasure to pass one's time with" (III, i, 67–68), but she is not deceived by Willmore's forthright arguments in favor of unfettered sensuality. She knows already what Angellica shows the audience: Marriage is a necessity for women, otherwise, as she challenges Willmore, "What shall I get? A cradle full of noise and mischief, with a pack of repentance at my back?" (V, 514–16).

She gets her man, but it is a tawdry victory and the audience knows it, with Angellica there to remind them. Willmore has shown himself to be insensitive, capricious, and dangerous to women, and there is no reason to imagine that he will be faithful to Hellena for longer than the month that he originally resolves to sacrifice to gain her. In *The Second Part of the Rover*, where Willmore again chooses between two women (and this time chooses the prostitute), it is revealed in passing that Hellena had died at sea within three months of the marriage.

The world of courtship and marriage depicted by Behn in these plays is a bleak one. Bright, witty women like Hellena use daring and imagination in a desperate attempt to evade the arranged marriages or confinements to nunneries destined them by their families. They race against time, trying their best to negotiate when all power lies in others' hands. None of the dashing young blades they choose and test out are admirable characters, but they seem preferable to a fool like Haunce van Ezel (in *The Dutch Lover*) or an odious tyrant like Octavio (in *The Feign'd Curtizans*). Woven in with the wit and humor, music and spectacle, are hard, sober women's truths about the debauchery of the Restoration court and its acolytes. Armed with wit and driven by necessity, like her heroines, Aphra Behn succeeded in dramatizing in marketable form the dilemmas that faced her and her sisters.

Chikamatsu Monzaemon

Generally regarded as the most significant Japanese playwright, Chikamatsu Monzaemon (1653–1725) was born in the province of Echizen into a minor samurai family. His family name was Sugimori, but he changed it when he began writing plays. In his lifetime — during the celebrated Tokugawa shogunate (1603–1868) — hundreds of thousands of samurai did not serve the shogun or a *daimyo,* or master. Chikamatsu was among those called *rōnin,* samurai who lived without a master and who were therefore without a clear direction. Trained as warriors, the samurai, supported by the farmer class in Japan during the extended peace of the period, had little to do. Some of them left the samurai class and, like Chikamatsu, changed their names and went into theater or into some form of business.

The class structure of Japan at this time consisted essentially of peasant farmers, the samurai, the nobility, and merchants. (Some commentators add a class of artisans.) During the late seventeenth and eighteenth centuries, the merchants grew into a wealthy class and often held power over the nobility through debts and other obligations. Chikamatsu was especially interesting because he experienced life as part of the samurai class, but also appears to have been connected with a Buddhist monastery as a youth. He may have taken his pseudonym from the Chikamatsu temple at which he stayed for some time. At age nineteen, he became a page in a noble family and experienced palace life. Some sources suggest that he was employed by nobleman Ogimachi Kimmochi (1653–1733), who wrote puppet plays; others suggest he worked for Lord Ichijo Eikan, a connoisseur of puppet plays. Regardless, it was probably this experience that propelled Chikamatsu to give up his position and become Japan's first professional playwright. In essence, Chikamatsu had personal experience in three of the four primary classes in Japanese culture.

Unfortunately, we do not know a great deal about Chikamatsu. We do not know which was his first play, nor do we know how many plays he wrote. Estimates run from 130 to 140 plays, the majority of which are *jōruri* or puppet plays and the rest kabuki plays using live actors.

Kabuki, whose linguistic root implies subversive behavior, began with a dance in the "floating world," or gay quarter of Kyoto. This was an area licensed for the entertainment of samurai and nobles and permitting prostitution and many forms of entertainment for men, including theater. If we think of Nō drama as refined and religious at heart, we can think of kabuki as profane and appealing to the masses. Its beginning was in 1603 in the dances of a woman named Okuni. Scholar James Brandon, an expert on classical Japanese theater, says of kabuki, "it was the rock entertainment of the 17th century. Okuni performed the first Japanese plays of contemporary urban life: numerous painted screens and scrolls show her outrageously garbed as a handsome young warrior, exotic Christian rosary draped on her bosom, conducting an assignation with a prostitute."[1] Eventually, prostitutes took up the practice of kabuki in narrative plays that were sometimes based on current events and that used live actors aiming at an essentially realistic theater. In 1629, the authorities eventually cracked down and banned women actors, giving rise to the highly specialized *onnagata,* male actors who represented women on stage.

Chikamatsu was most renowned for his puppet plays, but early in his career he also wrote for the kabuki theater. At that time puppet plays were known as *jōruri,* but the more common term today is *bunraku.* Both forms of theater, kabuki and bunraku, are performed in Japan and elsewhere today. Chikamatsu's earliest plays were probably written for the puppet theater in 1683. The puppet theater relied on chanters — virtuoso speakers with highly trained voices — to deliver the lines of the characters. One of the greatest chanters of this period, Takemoto Gidayū (1651–1714), is known to have produced a number of Chikamatsu's earliest plays, among them *Kagekiyo Victorious* (1686).

Chikamatsu's early kabuki plays seem to have been inspired by especially popular actors, among them the brilliant Sakata Tōjūrō (1647–1709). One problem with kabuki actors in the late seventeenth century was that many grew arrogant and difficult. They developed a cult of personality as strong as our contemporary film star system, resulting in a drama that focused not on the play itself but on the presence of the actor.

The puppet theater had the advantage of eliminating this complication. In addition, during the early part of the eighteenth century, the drama that was possible with puppets was similar to what is possible today with computer-generated imagery (CGI) in animated and live-action films. Impossible situations could be enacted with puppets: caesarian operations, quick transformations, dismemberments, and more. At the time when Chikamatsu wrote *jōruri* plays, each puppet was operated by a single person, usually dressed in black (as they are today) so as to permit the puppets to seem to be acting on their own. Each puppet head was painted in such a way that signaled to the audience that it was either a good or a villainous figure. Chikamatsu went beyond these limitations, however, and created characters of some moral ambiguity and considerable complexity.

His works are usually divided into history plays and domestic plays, often domestic tragedies. The most successful of his history plays is *The Battles of Coxinga* (1715), set in China. Because Japan was essentially sealed off from foreigners and no Japanese were allowed to travel at this time, the foreign setting added to its appeal. Chikamatsu also invented the successful genre called *shinjū-mono,* or love-suicide play. *The Love Suicides at Sonezaki* (1703) was the first of a series of love-suicide plays written by Chikamatsu as well as other playwrights of the time. It was based on an actual event that constituted a minor scandal only weeks before he produced his play. He refined the genre in several more plays, *The Love Suicides at the Women's Temple* (1708) and the unusually modern and complex *The Love Suicides at Amijima* (c. 1720).

The genre was so popular that it became a societal threat. In response to these plays, a great many people committed their own love-suicides, and conse-

---

[1]James Brandon, *The Cambridge Guide to Asian Theatre* (Cambridge: Cambridge University Press, 1993), p. 147.

quently the authorities banned all such plays in 1722. (Curiously, a similar cult of suicide developed in Europe after the publication of Goethe's *The Sorrows of Young Werther* [1774].)

After 1705 Chikamatsu moved to Osaka, where he was the resident playwright for Gidayū's puppet theater until his death in 1725. His work matured, and his subtle and complex use of language, especially rhyme patterns and puns, established him as one of Japan's greatest writers. He is noted for a technique known as the "pivot-word" — a word that has a double meaning, functioning one way in the beginning of a line and in another way in the rest of the line. His skill as a poet makes reading his plays almost as rewarding as seeing them enacted.

THE LOVE SUICIDES AT SONEZAKI

Sonezaki shinjū is the first of the *shinjū-mono,* or love-suicide plays. Chikamatsu wrote some dozen such plays himself, and other playwrights contributed their own. Taken from a current event, the story is direct and moving. Tokubei falls in love with Ohatsu, a young prostitute whose freedom he cannot afford to buy. In desperation, Tokubei sees only one way out of their dilemma, suicide.

In this play, Chikamatsu explores a number of interesting issues. It was not uncommon for a visitor to the floating world to fall in love with a courtesan. Japanese society maintained a clear double standard: men were permitted to enjoy the favors of prostitutes in the licensed areas, while their wives were threatened with execution if they committed adultery. In some plays a brother and father approved the killing of an unfaithful woman by her husband. Wives who maintained silence in face of such activity were praised. Those who complained or grew jealous were often divorced, and once divorced they were ruined. Prostitutes were unmarried entertainers whose job was to attract the attention of men and to please them. They were owned by the establishments they served and could be purchased for a high price.

One of the first things one notices about *The Love Suicides at Sonezaki* is that the characters are essentially part of what we would think of today as the middle class. The play is a representational drama, a domestic tragedy, that attempts to present characters speaking as they would if they were encountered in actual society. Tokubei works for a company that sells soy sauce. The villain Kuheiji is a powerful oil merchant. One of Ohatsu's customers is a "country bumpkin." What Chikamatsu reveals is the potential of ordinary people for experiencing powerful emotions. It would take another 150 years for such serious middle-class drama to appear on European stages.

The play is also interesting because it respects the Aristotelian unities even though Chikamatsu could have known nothing of Aristotle, or of any foreign play. The action takes place in a twenty-four-hour period, the characters develop clearly and consistently, and there is no sub-plot. As a result, the play seems modern to the Western reader.

Unfortunately, because it was connected with a specific current event, this play and other *shinjū* plays fell out of favor only a few years after the ban. Moreover, after Chikamatsu's death the puppet theater developed much more technically advanced production values. The development of three-person puppets permitted more surprising effects and more subtle and amazing movements that required considerable coordination among the puppeteers. Chikamatsu's plays were sometimes rewritten to take advantage of these and other developments, such as a revolving stage (about a century before a similar development in Europe). Therefore, most of the current texts of the plays have the marks of a modern rewriting. In the text given here, however, Chikamatsu's 1703 version, except for a brief introductory passage, appears as it was originally played.

Because the chanter controls the dialogue in the puppet play, he also acts as a narrator commenting on and forwarding the action. The narrator chants some of the most beautiful poetry in the third scene. A passage known as the *michiyuki,* or "lovers' journey," offers Chikamatsu the opportunity to raise the level of diction and explore the emotions implied in the action of lovers journeying toward their death. It begins,

Farewell to this world, and to the night farewell.
We who walk the road to death, to what should we be likened?
To the frost by the road that leads to the graveyard,
Vanishing with each step we take ahead:
How sad is this dream of a dream!

The conjunction of religion, Amida Buddhism, in this and other plays that have at their root an erotic content, is not unusual. Most of the better kabuki plays treated religion as important. Ohatsu and Tokubei end *The Love Suicides at Sonezaki* with a sense of religious assurance that may seem odd to Western audiences. At the heart of this play and other love-suicide dramas is the conflict of two important values of Japanese society: *giri,* the obligations one has to family and society, and *ninjō,* the personal human feelings to which one responds. Like yin and yang, these elements must be balanced. If one worries only about obligation to others and ignores emotion, one can miss important life experiences. If one is dominated only by personal emotion and desire, society itself will suffer. In this play Tokubei is torn by his obligation to his master and his feelings for Ohatsu. In addition he is humiliated by the clever Kuheiji and loses his honor. Ohatsu realizes the situation Tokubei is in and proposes a way out for them both. The narrator, obviously moved by the lovers' situation, sees them as moving toward paradise.

One of the details that makes this play seem so modern, especially in relation to European plays of the eighteenth century, is its emphasis on money. Tokubei seems naïve in lending his money even to a good friend, considering what is at stake. But it is the forfeit of the money by Kuheiji's cleverness that drives Tokubei to the play's ultimate resolution. One way or another, Tokubei seems doomed because of the considerable sum of money he has received from his master.

The Love Suicides at Sonezaki in Performance

A key element of all *jōruri* puppet plays is the musician, who plays a three-string instrument called the *shamisen*. Performers on this instrument were successful entertainers before they combined with chanters and puppets, and even today the musician has a prominent role in both kabuki and bunraku (puppet) productions. The chanter stands or sits to the side of the stage, and the handlers of the puppets are usually in a lowered section of the stage so they remain inconspicuous. In modern performances, the handlers are often dressed in absolute black, including face masks, and from a slight distance they are almost unnoticeable. The puppets are elaborate and capable of expressing considerable emotion, especially in conjunction with the shamisen musician.

The stage itself has grown wider since Chikamatsu's age, but it still relies on painted scenery and realistic representation of the various locations of the drama. *The Love Suicides at Sonezaki* has also been performed as a kabuki play with living actors, usually wearing masks and elaborate costumes, as is true of a number of important puppet plays. Contemporary productions of puppet plays, both those of Chikamatsu and other playwrights, take advantage of the scale of large Western theaters, a development that was adopted largely after World War II. These plays are remarkably effective in those spaces.

Chikamatsu Monzaemon (1653–1725)

THE LOVE SUICIDES AT SONEZAKI   *1703*

TRANSLATED BY DONALD KEENE

Cast of Characters

TOKUBEI, *aged 25, employee of a dealer in soy sauce*
KUHEIJI, *an oil merchant*
HOST *of Temma House*
CHŌZŌ, *an apprentice*
CUSTOMER *of Ohatsu*
TOWNSMEN
OHATSU, *aged 19, a courtesan*
HOSTESS
COURTESANS
SERVANTS

Scene One: The grounds of the Ikudama Shrine in Osaka. Time: May 21, 1703.

NARRATOR:
This graceful young man has served many springs
With the firm of Hirano in Uchihon Street;
He hides the passion that burns in his breast
Lest word escape and the scandal spread.
He drinks peach wine, a cup at a time,
And combs with care his elegant locks.
"Toku" he is called, and famed for his taste,
But now, his talents buried underground,
He works as a clerk, his sleeves stained with oil,

A slave to his sweet remembrances of love.
Today he makes the rounds of his clients
With a lad who carries a cask of soy:
They have reached the shrine of Ikudama.
A woman's voice calls from a bench inside a refreshment stand.
OHATSU: Tokubei — that's you, isn't it?
NARRATOR: She claps her hands, and Tokubei nods in recognition.
TOKUBEI: Chōzō, I'll be following later. Make the rounds of the temples in Tera Street and the uptown mansions, and then return to the shop. Tell them that I'll be back soon. Don't forget to call on the dyer's in Azuchi Street and collect the money he owes us. And stay away from Dōtombori.
NARRATOR: He watches as long as the boy remains in sight, then lifts the bamboo blinds.
TOKUBEI: Ohatsu — what's the matter?
NARRATOR: He starts to remove his bamboo hat.
OHATSU: Please keep your hat on just now. I have a customer from the country today who's making a pilgrimage to all thirty-three temples of Kwannon. He's been boasting that he intends to spend the whole day drinking. At the moment he's gone off to hear the impersonators' show, but if he returns and finds us

together, there might be trouble. All the chair-bearers know you. It's best you keep your face covered.

But to come back to us. Lately you haven't written me a word. I've been terribly worried but, not knowing what the situation might be in your shop, I couldn't very well write you. I must have called a hundred times at the Tamba House, but they hadn't any news of you either. Somebody — yes, it was Taichi, the blind musician — asked his friends, and they said you'd gone back to the country. I couldn't believe it was true. You've really been too cruel. Didn't you even want to ask about me? Perhaps you hoped things would end that way, but I've been sick with worry. If you think I'm lying, feel this swelling!

NARRATOR: She takes his hand and presses it to her breast, weeping reproachful and entreating tears, exactly as if they were husband and wife. Man though he is, he also weeps.

TOKUBEI: You're right, entirely right, but what good would it have done to tell you and make you suffer? I've been going through such misery that I couldn't be more distracted if Bon, New Year, the Ten Nights, and every other feast in the calendar came all at once. My mind's been in a turmoil, and my finances in chaos. To tell the truth, I went up to Kyoto to raise some money, among other things. It's a miracle I'm still alive. If they make my story into a three-act play, I'm sure the audiences will weep.

NARRATOR: Words fail and he can only sigh.

OHATSU: And is this the comic relief of your tragedy? Why couldn't you have trusted me with your worries when you tell me even trivial little things? You must've had some reason for hiding. Why don't you take me into your confidence?

NARRATOR: She leans over his knee. Bitter tears soak her handkerchief.

TOKUBEI: Please don't cry or be angry with me. I wasn't hiding anything, but it wouldn't have helped to involve you. At any rate, my troubles have largely been settled, and I can tell you the whole story now.

My master has always treated me with particular kindness because I'm his nephew. For my part, I've served him with absolute honesty. There's never been a penny's discrepancy in the accounts. It's true that recently I used his name when I bought on credit a bolt of Kaga silk to make into a summer kimono, but that's the one and only time, and if I have to raise the money on the spot, I can always sell back the kimono without taking a loss. My master has been so impressed by my honesty that he proposed I marry his wife's niece with a dowry of two *kamme*,° and promised to set me up in business. That happened last year, but how could I shift my affections when I have you? I didn't give his suggestion a second thought, but in the meantime my mother — she's really my stepmother — conferred with my master, keeping it a secret from me. She went back to the

country with the two *kamme* in her clutches. Fool that I am, I never dreamt what had happened.

The trouble began last month when they tried to force me to marry. I got angry and said, "Master, you surprise me. You know how unwilling I am to get married, and yet you've inveigled my old mother into giving her consent. You've gone too far, master. I can't understand the mistress's attitude either. If I took as my wife this young lady whom I've always treated with the utmost deference and accepted her dowry in the bargain, I'd spend my whole life dancing attendance on my wife. How could I ever assert myself? I've refused once, and even if my father were to return from his grave, the answer would still be no."

The master was furious that I should have answered so bluntly. His voice shook with rage. "I know your real reasons. You're involved with Ohatsu, or whatever her name is, from the Temma House in Dōjima. That's why you seem so averse to my wife's niece. Very well — after what's been said, I'm no longer willing to give you the girl, and since there's to be no wedding, return the money. Settle without fail by the twenty-second of the month and clear your business accounts. I'll chase you from Osaka and never let you set foot here again!"

I too have my pride as a man. "Right you are!" I answered, and rushed off to my village. But my so-called mother wouldn't let the money from her grip, not if this world turned into the next. I went to Kyoto, hoping to borrow the money from the wholesale soy sauce dealers in the Fifth Ward. I've always been on good terms with them. But, as ill luck would have it, they had no money to spare. I retraced my steps to the country, and this time, with the intercession of the whole village, I managed to extract the money from my mother. I intended to return the dowry immediately and settle things for once and for all. But if I can't remain in Osaka, how shall I be able to meet you?

My bones may be crushed to powder, my flesh be torn away, and I may sink, an empty shell, in the slime of Shijimi River. Let that happen if it must, but if I am parted from you, what shall I do?

NARRATOR: He weeps, suffocated by his grief. Ohatsu, holding back the welling tears of sympathy, strengthens and comforts him.

OHATSU: How you've suffered! And when I think that it's been because of me, I feel happy, sad, and most grateful all at once. But please, show more courage. Pull yourself together. Your uncle may have forbidden you to set foot in Osaka again, but you haven't committed robbery or arson. I'll think of some way to keep you here. And if a time should come when we can no longer meet, did our promises of love hold only for this world? Others before us have chosen reunion through death. To die is simple enough — none will hinder and none be hindered on the journey to the Mountain of Death and the River of Three Ways.

kamme: A considerable sum of money.

NARRATOR: Ohatsu falters among these words of encouragement, choked by tears. She resumes.

OHATSU: The twenty-second is tomorrow. Return the money early, since you must return it anyway. Try to get in your master's good graces again.

TOKUBEI: I want to, and I'm impatient to return the money, but on the thirteenth of the month Kuheiji the oil merchant — I think you know him — begged me desperately for the money. He said he needed it only for one day, and promised to return it by the morning of the eighteenth. I decided to lend him the money since I didn't need it until the twenty-second, and it was for a friend close as a brother. He didn't get in touch with me on the eighteenth or nineteenth. Yesterday he was out and I couldn't see him. I intended to call on him this morning, but I've spent it making the rounds of my customers in order to wind up my business by tomorrow. I'll go to him this evening and settle everything. He's a man of honor and he knows my predicament. I'm sure nothing will go wrong. Don't worry. Oh — look there, Ohatsu!

NARRATOR:
"Hatsuse is far away,
Far too is Naniwa-dera:
So many temples are renowned
For the sound of their bells,
Voices of the Eternal Law.
If, on an evening in spring,
You visit a mountain temple
You will see . . ."
At the head of a band of revelers

TOKUBEI: Kuheiji! That's a poor performance! You've no business running off on excursions when you haven't cleared up your debt with me. Today we'll settle our account.

NARRATOR: He grasps Kuheiji's arm and restrains him. Kuheiji's expression is dubious.

KUHEIJI: What are you talking about, Tokubei? These people with me are all residents of the ward. We've had a meeting in Ueshio Street to raise funds for a pilgrimage to Ise. We've drunk a little saké, but we're on our way home now. What do you mean by grabbing my arm? Don't be rowdy!

NARRATOR: He removes his wicker hat and glares at Tokubei.

TOKUBEI: I'm not being rowdy. All I ask is that you return the two *kamme* of silver I lent you on the thirteenth, which you were supposed to repay on the eighteenth.

NARRATOR: Before he can finish speaking, Kuheiji bursts out laughing.

KUHEIJI: Are you out of your mind, Tokubei? I can't remember having borrowed a penny from you in all the years I've known you. Don't make any accusations which you'll regret.

NARRATOR: He shakes himself free. His companions also remove their hats. Tokubei pales with astonishment.

TOKUBEI: Don't say that, Kuheiji! You came to me in tears, saying that you couldn't survive your monthly bills, and I thought that this was the kind of emergency for which we'd been friends all these years. I lent you the money as an act of generosity, though I needed it desperately myself. I told you that I didn't even require a receipt, but you insisted on putting your seal to one, for form's sake. You made me write out a promissory note and you sealed it. Don't try to deny it, Kuheiji!

NARRATOR: Tokubei rebukes him heatedly.

KUHEIJI: What's that? I'd like to see the seal.

TOKUBEI: Do you think I'm afraid to show you?

NARRATOR: He produces the paper from his wallet.

TOKUBEI: If these gentlemen are from the ward, I am sure that they will recognize your seal. Will you still dispute it?

NARRATOR: When he unfolds the paper and displays it, Kuheiji claps his hands in recollection.

KUHEIJI: Yes, it's my seal all right. Oh, Tokubei, I never thought you'd do such a thing, not even if you were starving and forced to eat dirt. On the tenth of the month I lost a wallet containing the seal. I advertised for it everywhere, but without success, so as of the sixteenth of this month, as I've informed these gentlemen, I've changed my seal. Could I have affixed the seal I lost on the tenth to a document on the thirteenth? No — what happened was that you found my wallet, wrote the promissory note, and affixed my seal. Now you're trying to extort money from me — that makes you a worse criminal than a forger. You'd do better, Tokubei, to commit out-and-out robbery. You deserve to have your head cut off, but for old times' sake, I'll forgive you. Let's see if you can make any money out of this!

NARRATOR: He throws the note in Tokubei's face and glares at him fiercely in an extraordinary display of feigned innocence. Tokubei, furious, cries aloud.

TOKUBEI: You've been damned clever. You've put one over on me. I'm dishonored. What am I to do? Must I let you take my money brazenly from me? You've planned everything so cleverly that even if I go to court, I'm sure to lose. I'll take back my money with my fists! See here! I'm Tokubei of the Hirano-ya, a man of honor. Do you follow me? I'm not a man to trick a friend out of his money the way you have. Come on!

NARRATOR: He falls on Kuheiji.

KUHEIJI: You impudent little apprentice! I'll knock the insolence out of you!

NARRATOR: He seizes the front of Tokubei's kimono and they grapple, trading blows and shoves. Ohatsu rushes barefoot to them.

OHATSU (*to townsmen*): Please everybody, stop the fight! He's a friend of mine. Where are the chairbearers? Why don't they do something? Tokubei's being beaten!

NARRATOR: She writhes in anguish, but is helpless. Her customer, country bumpkin that he is, bundles her forcibly into a palanquin.

CUSTOMER: It won't do for you to get hurt.

OHATSU: Please wait just a moment! Oh, I'm so unhappy!

NARRATOR: The palanquin is rushed off, leaving only the echoes of her weeping voice.

Tokubei is alone; Kuheiji has five companions. Men rush out from the nearby booths and drive them all with sticks to the lotus pond. Who tramples Tokubei? Who beats him? There is no way to tell. His hair is disheveled, his sash undone. He stumbles and falls to this side and that.

TOKUBEI: Kuheiji, you swine! Do you think I'll let you escape alive?

NARRATOR: He staggers about searching for Kuheiji, but he has fled and vanished. Tokubei falls heavily in his tracks and, weeping bitterly, he cries aloud.

TOKUBEI (to bystanders): I feel humiliated and ashamed that you've seen me this way. There was not a false word in my accusation. I've always treated Kuheiji like a brother, and when he begged me for the money, saying he'd never forget it as long as he lived, I lent it to him, sure that he'd do the same for me, though the money was precious as life, and I knew that without it tomorrow, the twenty-first, I'd have to kill myself. He made me write the note in my own hand, then put his seal to it. But it was a seal which he had already reported as lost, and now he's turned the accusations against me! It's mortifying, infuriating — to be kicked and beaten this way, dishonored and forced to my knees. It would've been better if I had died while smashing and biting him!

NARRATOR: He strikes the ground and gnashes his teeth, clenches his fists and moans, a sight to stir compassion.

TOKUBEI: There's no point in my talking this way. Before three days have passed I, Tokubei, will make amends by showing all Osaka the purity at the bottom of my heart.

NARRATOR: The meaning of these words is later known.

TOKUBEI: I'm sorry to have bothered you all. Please forgive me.

NARRATOR: He speaks his apologies, picks up his battered hat and puts it on. His face, downcast in the sinking rays of the sun, is clouded by tears that engulf him. Dejectedly he leaves, a sight too pitiful to behold.

Scene Two: Inside the Temma House. Time: Evening of the same day.

NARRATOR:
The breezes of love are all-pervasive
By Shijimi River, where love-drowned guests
Like empty shells, bereft of their senses,
Wander the dark ways of love
Lit each night by burning lanterns,
Fireflies that glow in the four seasons,
Stars that shine on rainy nights.

By Plum Bridge, blossoms show even in summer.
Rustics on a visit, city connoisseurs,
All journey the varied roads of love,
Where adepts wander and novices play:
What a lively place this New Quarter is!

But alas for Ohatsu of the Temma House — even after she returns the day's events still weigh on her. She cannot swallow the day's saké, she feels on edge. As she sits weeping, some courtesans from the neighboring houses and other friends come for a little chat.

FIRST COURTESAN: Have you heard, Ohatsu? They say that Toku was given a thrashing for something bad he did. Is it true?

SECOND COURTESAN: No, my customer told me that Toku was trampled to death.

NARRATOR: They say he was fettered for fraud or trussed for counterfeiting a seal. Not one decent thing have they to report: every expression of sympathy makes their visit the more painful.

OHATSU: No, please, not another word. The more I hear, the worse my breast pains me. I'm sure I'll be the first to die. I wish I were dead already.

NARRATOR: She can only weep. But amidst her tears she happens to look outside and catches a glimpse of Tokubei, a pathetic figure wearing a wicker hat, even at night. Her heart leaps, and she wants to run to him, but in the sitting room are the master and his wife, and by the entrance stands the cook, while in the kitchen a maid is hovering: with so many sharp eyes watching, she cannot do as she pleases.

OHATSU: I feel terribly depressed. I think I'll step outside for a moment.

NARRATOR: She slips out softly.

OHATSU: What happened? I've heard rumors of every sort about you. They've driven me out of my mind with worry.

NARRATOR: She thrusts her face under the brim of his wicker hat and weeps in secret, soundless, painful tears. He too is lost in tears.

TOKUBEI: I've been made the victim of a clever plot, as no doubt you've heard, and the more I struggle, the worse off I am. Everything has turned against me now. I can't survive this night. I've made up my mind to it.

NARRATOR: As he whispers, voices are heard from within.

VOICES: Come inside, Ohatsu. There's enough gossip about you as it is.

OHATSU: There — did you hear? We can't go on talking. Do as I show you.

NARRATOR: She hides him under the train of her mantle. He crawls behind her to the garden door, where he slips beneath the porch at the step. Ohatsu sits by the entrance and, pulling the tobacco tray to her, lights her pipe. She assumes an air of unconcern.

At this moment Kuheiji and a couple of his loud-mouthed friends burst in, accompanied by a blind musician.

KUHEIJI: Hello, girls. You're looking lonesome. Would you like me for a customer? Hello there, host. I haven't seen you in ages.

NARRATOR: He strides arrogantly into the room.

HOST: Bring a tobacco tray and some saké cups.

NARRATOR: He makes the customary fuss over the guests.

KUHEIJI: No, don't bother about saké. We were drinking before we came. I have something to tell you. Tokubei, the number one customer of your Ohatsu, found a seal I'd lost and tried to cheat me out of two *kamme* in silver with a forged note. The facts were too much for him, and he finally met with some unpleasantness from which he was lucky to escape alive. His reputation has been ruined. Be on your guard if he comes here again. Everybody will tell you that I speak the truth, so even if Tokubei tells you the exact opposite, don't believe him for a moment. You'd do best not to let him in at all. Sooner or later he's bound to end up on the gallows.

NARRATOR: He pours out his words convincingly. Tokubei, underneath the porch, gnashes his teeth and trembles with rage. Ohatsu, afraid that he may reveal himself, calms him with her foot, calms him gently. The host is loath to answer yes or no, for Tokubei's a customer of long standing.

HOST: Well, then, how about some soup?

NARRATOR: Covering his confusion, he leaves the room. Ohatsu, weeping bitterly, exclaims.

OHATSU: You needn't try your clever words on me. Tokubei and I have been intimate for years. We've told each other our inmost secrets. He hasn't a particle of deceit in him, the poor boy. His generosity has been his undoing. He's been tricked, but he hasn't the evidence to prove it. After what has happened Tokubei has no choice but to kill himself. I wish I knew whether or not he was resolved to die.

NARRATOR: She pretends to be talking to herself, but with her foot she questions him. He nods, and taking her ankle, passes it across his throat, to let her know that he is bent on suicide.

OHATSU: I knew it. I knew it. No matter how long one lives, it comes to the same thing. Only death can wipe out the disgrace.

NARRATOR: Kuheiji is startled by her words.

KUHEIJI: What is Ohatsu talking about? Why should Tokubei kill himself? Well, if he kills himself, I'll take good care of you after he is gone! I think you've fallen for me too!

OHATSU: That's most generous of you, I'm sure. But would you object if, by way of thanks for your kindness, I killed you? Could I go on living even a moment if separated from Toku? Kuheiji, you dirty thief! Anyone hearing your silly lies can only suspect you. I'm sure that Toku intends to die with me, as I with him.

NARRATOR: She taps with her foot, and Tokubei, weeping, takes it in his hands and reverently touches it to his forehead. He embraces her knees and sheds tears

of love. She too can hardly conceal her emotions. Though no word is spoken, answering each other heart to heart, they silently weep. That no one knows makes it sadder still.

Kuheiji feels uncomfortable.

KUHEIJI: The wind's against us today. Let's get out of here. The whores in this place are certainly peculiar — they seem to have an aversion for customers like ourselves with plenty of money to spend. Let's stop at the Asa House and have a drink there. We'll rattle around a couple of gold pieces, then go home to bed. Oh — my wallet is so heavy I can hardly walk.

NARRATOR: Spewing forth all manner of abuse, they noisily depart. The host and his wife call to the servants.

HOST: It's time to put out the lights for the night. Lay out beds for the guests who are staying on. Ohatsu, you sleep upstairs. Get to bed early.

OHATSU (to herself): Master, mistress, I shall probably never see you again. Farewell. Farewell to all the servants too.

NARRATOR: Thus inwardly taking leave, she goes to her bedchamber. Later they will learn that this was a parting for life; how pitiful the foolish hearts of men who do not realize the truth in time!

HOST: See that the fire is out under the kettle. Don't let the mice get at the relishes.

NARRATOR: They shut the place and bar the gate. Hardly have their heads touched their pillows than all are snoring merrily. So short is the night that before they've had a chance to dream, two o'clock in the morning has come. Ohatsu is dressed for death, a black cloak dark as the ways of love thrown over her kimono of spotless white. She tiptoes to the staircase and looks down. Tokubei shows his face from under the porch. He beckons, nods, points, communicating his intent without a word. Below the stairs a servant girl is sleeping. A hanging lantern brightly shines. Ohatsu in desperation attaches her fan to a palm-leaf broom, and from the second step of the staircase attempts in vain to extinguish the flame. At last, by stretching every inch, she puts it out, only to tumble suddenly down the stairs. The lamp is out, and in the darkness the servant girl turns in her sleep. Trembling, the lovers grope for each other — a fearful moment. The host awakens in his room to the back.

HOST: What was that noise just now? Servants! The night lamp has gone out. Get up and light it!

NARRATOR: The servant girl, aroused, sleepily rubs her eyes and gets up from bed stark naked.

SERVANT: I can't find the flint box.

NARRATOR: She wanders about the room searching, and Ohatsu, faint with terror, dodges this way and that to avoid her. At last she catches Tokubei's hand, and softly they creep to the entranceway. They unfasten the latch, but the hinges creak, and frightened by the noise, they hesitate. Just then the maid begins to strike the flints; they time their actions to the rasping sound, and with each rasp open the door farther until, huddled together and their sleeves twisted round them, they pass through the door one after the other, feeling as though they tread on a tiger's tail. They exchange glances and cry out for joy, happy that they are to die — a painful, heart-rending sight. The life left them now is as brief as sparks that fly from blocks of flint.

Scene Three: The journey from Dōjima to the Sonezaki Shrine.

NARRATOR:
Farewell to this world, and to the night farewell.
We who walk the road to death, to what should we
   be likened?
To the frost by the road that leads to the graveyard,
Vanishing with each step we take ahead:
How sad is this dream of a dream!

TOKUBEI:
Ah, did you count the bell? Of the seven strokes
That mark the dawn, six have sounded.
The remaining one will be the last echo
We shall hear in this life.

OHATSU:
It will echo the bliss of nirvana.

NARRATOR:
Farewell, and not to the bell alone —
They look a last time on the grass, the trees, the sky.
The clouds, the river go by unmindful of them;
The Dipper's bright reflection shines in the water.

TOKUBEI:
Let's pretend that Umeda Bridge
Is the bridge the magpies built
Across the Milky Way, and make a vow
To be husband and wife stars for eternity.

OHATSU:
I promise. I'll be your wife forever.

NARRATOR:
They cling together — the river waters
Will surely swell with the tears they shed.
Across the river, in a teahouse upstairs,
Some revelers, still not gone to bed,
Are loudly talking under blazing lamps —
No doubt gossiping about the good or bad
Of this year's crop of lovers' suicides;
Their hearts sink to hear these voices.

TOKUBEI:
How strange! but yesterday, even today,
We spoke as if such things did not concern us.
Tomorrow we shall figure in their gossip.
If the world will sing about us, let it sing.

NARRATOR:
This is the song that now they hear.
   "I'm sure you'll never have me for your wife,
      I know my love means nothing to you . . ."
Yes, for all our love, for all our grieving,
Our lives, our lots, have not been as we wished.
Never, until this very day, have we known

A single night of heart's relaxation —
Instead, the tortures of an ill-starred love.
   "What is this bond between us?
   I cannot forget you.
   But you would shake me off and go —
   I'll never let you!
   Kill me with your hands, then go.
   I'll never release you!"
   So she said in tears.

OHATSU:
Of all the many songs, that one, tonight!

TOKUBEI:
Who is it singing? We who listen

BOTH:
Suffer the ordeal of those before us.

NARRATOR:
They cling to each other, weeping bitterly.
Any other night would not matter
If tonight were only a little longer,
But the heartless summer night, as is its wont,
Breaks as cockcrows hasten their last hour.

TOKUBEI:
It will be worse if we wait for dawn.
Let us die in the wood of Tenjin.

NARRATOR:
He leads her by the hand.
At Umeda Embankment, the night ravens.

TOKUBEI:
Tomorrow our bodies may be their meal.

OHATSU:
It's strange, this is your unlucky year
Of twenty-five, and mine of nineteen.
It's surely proof how deep are our ties
That we who love each other are cursed alike.
All the prayers I have made for this world
To the gods and to the Buddha, I here and now
Direct to the future: in the world to come
May we be reborn on the same lotus!

NARRATOR:
One hundred eight the beads her fingers tell
On her rosary;° tears increase the sum.
No end to her grief, but the road has an end:
Their minds are numbed, the sky is dark, the wind
   still,
They have reached the thick wood of Sonezaki.
   Shall it be here, shall it be there? When they brush the grass, the falling dew vanishes even quicker than their lives, in this uncertain world a lightning flash — or was it something else?

OHATSU: I'm afraid. What was that now?

TOKUBEI: That was a human spirit. I thought we alone would die tonight, but someone else has preceded us. Whoever it may be, we'll have a companion on the journey to the Mountain of Death. *Namu Amida Butsu. Namu Amida Butsu.*°

rosary: A Buddhist rosary. ***Namu Amida Butsu:*** Calling the name of the Amida Buddha, an incarnation of Siddhartha Gautama, with sincerity should grant the individual eternal life in The Pure Land — hence Pure Land Buddhism.

NARRATOR: She weeps helplessly.

OHATSU: To think that others are dying tonight too! How heartbreaking!

NARRATOR: Man though he is, his tears fall freely.

TOKUBEI: Those two spirits flying together — do you suppose they belong to anyone else? They must be yours and mine!

OHATSU: Those two spirits? Then, are we dead already?

TOKUBEI: Normally, if we saw a spirit, we'd knot our clothes and murmur prayers to keep our souls with us, but now we hurry towards our end, hoping instead our two souls will find the same dwelling. Do not mistake the way, do not lose me!

NARRATOR: They embrace, flesh to flesh, then fall to the ground and weep — how pitiful they are! Their strings of tears unite like entwining branches, or the pine and palm that grow from a single trunk, a symbol of eternal love. Here the dew of their unhappy lives will at last settle.

TOKUBEI: Let this be the spot.

NARRATOR: He unfastens the sash of his cloak. Ohatsu removes her tear-stained outer robe, and throws it on the palm tree; the frond might now serve as a broom to sweep away the sad world's dust. Ohatsu takes a razor from her sleeve.

OHATSU: I had this razor prepared in case we were overtaken on the way and separated. I was determined not to forfeit our name as lovers. How happy I am that we are to die together as we hoped!

TOKUBEI: How wonderful of you to have thought of that! I am so confident in our love that I have no fears even about death. And yet it would be unfortunate if because of the pain we are to suffer people said that we looked ugly in death. Let us secure our bodies to this twin-trunked tree and die immaculately! We will become an unparalleled example of a lovers' suicide.

OHATSU: Yes, let us do that.

NARRATOR: Alas! She little thought she thus would use her light blue undersash! She draws it taut, and with her razor slashes it through.

OHATSU: The sash is cut, but you and I will never be torn apart.

NARRATOR: She sits, and he binds her twice, thrice to the tree, firmly so that she will not stir.

TOKUBEI: Is it tight?

OHATSU: Very tight.

NARRATOR: She looks at her husband, and he at her — they burst into tears.

BOTH: This is the end of our unhappy lives!

TOKUBEI: No I mustn't give way to grief.

NARRATOR: He lifts his head and joins his hands in prayer.

TOKUBEI: My parents died when I was a boy, and I grew up thanks to the efforts of my uncle, who was my master. It disgraces me to die without repaying his kindness. Instead I shall cause him trouble which will last even after my death. Please forgive my sins.

Soon I shall see my parents in the other world. Father, Mother, welcome me there!

NARRATOR: He weeps. Ohatsu also joins her hands.

OHATSU: I envy you. You say you will meet your parents in the world of the dead. My father and mother are in this world and in good health. I wonder when I shall see them again. I heard from them this spring, but I haven't seen them since the beginning of last autumn. Tomorrow, when word reaches the village of our suicides, how unhappy they will be! Now I must bid farewell for this life to my parents, my brothers and sisters. If at least my thoughts can reach you, please appear before me, if only in dreams. Dear Mother, beloved Father!

NARRATOR: She sobs and wails aloud. Her husband also cries out and sheds incessant tears in all too understandable emotion.

OHATSU: We could talk forever, but it serves no purpose. Kill me, kill me quickly!

NARRATOR: She hastens the moment of death.

TOKUBEI: I'm ready.

NARRATOR: He swiftly draws his dagger.

TOKUBEI: The moment has come. *Namu Amida. Namu Amida.*

NARRATOR: But when he tries to bring the blade against the skin of the woman he's loved, and held and slept with so many months and years, his eyes cloud over, his hand shakes. He tries to steady his weakening resolve, but still he trembles, and when he thrusts, the point misses. Twice or thrice the flashing blade deflects this way and that until a cry tells it has struck her throat.

TOKUBEI: *Namu Amida. Namu Amida. Namu Amida Butsu.*

NARRATOR: He twists the blade deeper and deeper, but the strength has left his arm. When he sees her weaken, he stretches forth his hands. The last agonies of death are indescribable.

TOKUBEI: Must I lag behind you? Let's draw our last breaths together.

NARRATOR: He thrusts and twists the razor in his throat, until it seems the handle or the blade must snap. His eyes grow dim, and his last painful breath is drawn away at its appointed hour. No one is there to tell the tale, but the wind that blows through Sonezaki Wood transmits it, and high and low alike gather to pray for these lovers who beyond a doubt will in the future attain Buddhahood. They have become models of true love.

A Cross-Cultural Casebook

Kabuki, Jōruri, and Bunraku Theater

Two characters in a 1986 kabuki performance.

Kabuki theater is distinguished by its use of actors in extravagant costumes and distinctive masks or makeup. The masks or makeup usually establish their roles in the drama, which is a narrative often associated with recent events involving people similar to those in the audience. Despite its highly stylized presentation, kabuki aspired to a certain level of realism. Jōruri are puppet plays — now referred to as bunraku. However, bunraku, which is still performed in Japan and abroad, uses different and more complex puppets than were available to the early jōruri playwrights. Jōruri plays are usually divided into history plays and domestic plays, with both forms achieving considerable popularity in the early eighteenth century.

During Japan's Tokugawa shogunate, one period stands out as a golden age of literature, drama, and art. The Genroku period technically lasted only a short time, from 1688 to 1704, but because it was such a grand era commentators extend the period to the 1740s. During this period, kabuki developed to a full-scale actors' theater with many theaters and an enthusiastic audience from all sectors of society. The puppet, or jōruri, theater flourished in this time as well, producing some curious cross-over effects: kabuki actors borrowed movements associated with puppets when they enacted jōruri plays.

During the Genroku period, the "floating world" established itself as a world of pleasure, licensed for all kinds of entertainment — from outdoor dances, acrobatics, magic acts, and theater, to bath houses, tea houses, and brothels. Prostitution was licensed in specific areas of the three major cities, Edo, Kyoto, and Osaka. For most men, prostitution was one of the primary reasons for visiting the "floating world." Prostitutes were ranked according to their beauty and desirability. Only a few achieved the top rank, but those who did commanded considerable sums and reserved the right to ignore customers they did not fancy. The most famous of the courtesans were sometimes involved in scandals and became well known for their successes.

Female prostitution was not exclusive to the "floating world." Catamites, male prostitutes, and boy prostitutes were plentiful. Before the 1629 ban on women on stage, some plays were labeled yū jō kabuki — prostitute kabuki — plays in which the actresses were noted prostitutes. Wakashu kabuki, with boy prostitutes aged eleven to fifteen, developed soon after. When women were prohibited from the stage, male actors specialized in female roles and became known as *onnagata* (female impersonators).

The widespread tolerance of prostitution in the licensed areas must be seen as an integral part of the atmosphere that surrounded the kabuki and jōruri plays, many of which are charged with erotic content. Shakespeare's plays were also put on in an atmosphere of what we might consider gross entertainment, particularly in relation to bear baiting with large hounds, a popular delight of the time. In the eighteenth century, the "floating world" was explicitly set aside for the pleasure of men. Wives were expected to tolerate the absence of their husbands and to avoid not only complaint but also any trace of jealousy that might make their husbands uneasy.

Japan during this time was essentially a dictatorship, with the shogun in Edo ruling with an eye on maintaining power, peace, and stability in the society. The Tokugawa period (1603–1868) achieved its goals for more than 250 years. It effectively sealed off Japan from most of the West (only a few traders and travelers were admitted). Consequently, when Japan was opened to the West, its society suffered a shock and extraordinarily rapid change. The "floating world" of the Tokugawa period may have been an important contribution to maintaining a stable society during that time.

The following essays offer some insights into the age and the artistry of its theater. A description of the social circumstances of the Genroku period is central to scholar Jacob Raz's essay on "The Golden Age." Raz helps us understand the cultural background of the period in an effort to position the drama more clearly. He emphasizes the rise of the influence of the merchant class, and thus a new middle class that placed high value on money over other concerns, on the drama that they expected would represent their interests. At the same time, his discussion gives us a sense of the range of styles current in both kabuki and jōruri.

Faubion Bowers not only helps us understand the appeal of the puppet theater, he also gives us a synopsis of Chikamatsu's history play *Kokusenya* (*The Battles of Coxinga*). He shows us, too, the nature of the interrelationship of kabuki and jōruri.

Tsururo Ando offers us a brief discussion of Chikamatsu, with a clear analysis of the special contributions he made to the structure of Japanese drama, both kabuki and jōruri.

A discussion of the theater buildings of the period is at the heart of Donald H. Shively's essay on the theater. In the process he offers some insight into the kinds of entertainment that were popular in the minor entertainment areas in Kyoto, which at one time had been Japan's primary city. Earle Ernst provides us with diagrams of the development of the kabuki stage from 1600 to the early eighteenth century.

Benito Ortolani discusses the social background of both kabuki and jōruri, emphasizing the role that various social classes play in their approach to dramatic entertainment. His essay offers a clear view of the age and the intersection of the art of drama and the culture that produced it.

Jacob Raz (b. 1950)
THE GENROKU PERIOD — THE GOLDEN AGE   1983

Professor Jacob Raz teaches in the East Asian Studies department at Tel Aviv University in Israel. He has studied in Waseda University in Japan and specializes in Japanese theater. He teaches both Japanese aesthetics and Zen Buddhism. In this essay, he offers us a clear view of the Genroku period, the historical period that is usually thought of as the golden age of Japanese drama.

Most of the forms, conventions and player and audience attitudes in the kabuki theatre were shaped in the Genroku period. During this period models were formed for later generations, and its influence created the mature kabuki, forging the art that exists today. It is therefore convenient, for our discussion, to use this era to describe Edo audience attitudes and relations with players, even if some of the processes mentioned here came into full development later.

The cultural background of the Genroku period has often been discussed by Western scholars; here I shall briefly survey a few points that are directly related to the main discussion.

During this period the rise of the merchants and the decline of the samurai reached new extremes. The former could afford anything they wanted, while the latter had to swallow their pride when conducting the humiliating exchange of rice for money. Art — including poetry, literature, colour printing, puppet-theatre and others — flourished. Human rights were still denied to most of the people; the only liberty (and this, too, was permanently persecuted) was the liberty to pursue pleasure. Tastes were refined, and the commoners provided the models and inspiration for the arts. Learning among the commoners spread remarkably, and a tendency to imitate the upper classes and their Confucian values is strongly evident.

This increased tensions, which had actually arisen before but were strongly felt now: tension between the economic power of the commoners and the lack of political outlets for this power; tension between the hostile feelings for the upper classes and the natural snobbish tendency to imitate them; tension between the pleasure-seeking atmosphere and the many government restrictions.

By this time the characters of the three urban centres — Edo, Ōsaka and Kyōto — had already reached full maturity; the differences between the military, young town of Edo, the commercial Ōsaka, and the traditional Kyōto were clearly reflected in their respective arts, theatres, and audience tastes. Edo was where the government sat, the military class concentrated, and the control of the bakufu[1] was mostly felt. It had a history of less than one hundred years. People flowed into the town from all over the country, forming a unique, rough, untraditional, sometimes anti-traditional citizenry. Intercourse with the samurai was stronger than in Ōsaka or Kyōto. Gradually the Edoites developed a character which was summed up by the nickname 'Edokko' — a person who is rough, sharp, tends to be argumentative, "a kind of Cockney . . . critical, slangy and cheeky."

Kyōto was not as dynamic as Edo in its changes and population growth; her citizens were more polished, still under the atmosphere of the numerous temples and shrines, the Imperial Court, and the long aristocratic tradition. They were gentle and refined, and had an ear and an eye for delicacy and subtlety in art.

The Ōsakans were the wealthiest and, of all the three centres were perhaps the most free from government controls and samurai influence. Ōsaka was, however, an old town exhibiting a respect for tradition not unlike Kyōto's. Her people, too, were gentler and more polished than the arrogant Edoites. The differences among the three centres still exist and the distinctions are valid, to a certain extent, even now. The similarities between Ōsaka and Kyōto made them a relatively homogeneous centre, named by the Japanese *Kamigata*. Thus two main centres — Kamigata and Edo — were formed during the Genroku period, and they might be compared, with reservations, to the eighteenth century bourgeoisie of Europe and the new culture of America.

Thus two main kinds of audience were gradually formed, and two forms or styles of theatre were created to respond to these audiences and their tastes. Thus the Edo audiences directly affected the development of the *aragoto* — the rough acting style of the actor Danjūrō, and the Kamigata audiences cultivated the gentler, more realistic acting style called *nuregoto* or *wagoto*. The onnagata (female

---

[1]**Bakufu:** Literally, "tent government." It means government by the military.

impersonator) was also a product of the Kamigata area. No wonder that the noisy, brash, energetic style of the aragoto pleased Edo audiences but was often rejected by Kamigata audiences. Edo actors exploited themes that might afford them opportunities to please their audience in the aragoto style — that is, historical stories and heroic figures; Kamigata actors used more domestic themes, centering on the lives of the commoners.

The puppet-theatre reached unprecedented heights of success during the Genroku era, attracting the best playwrights and story-tellers of the day. As time passed, these playwrights would turn to kabuki and, with the help of the writers, players themselves would adopt the plays written for puppets. The popularity of the puppet-theatre was so great that the adaptations were not only literary. Actors shaped their acting style after the movements of the puppets; even the puppetish element in the acting style of kabuki is strong.

After the 1680's, when the theatre was no longer aimed at male audiences, more and more women, wives of merchants as well as ladies-in-waiting from the samurai class, would attend the theatre. The latter usually came disguised; we can see them in contemporary paintings and prints with head covers among the spectators. The presence of women in the audience changed the atmosphere in the theatre as well as its standards. For men the theatre was only part of their entertainment. They had available to them a wide range of pleasures in the gay quarters — tea-houses, bath-houses, brothels, the company of the elegant oiran,[2] the streets, and the theatres. The world of the *yūri*, the gay quarter, was theirs; they were its customers, its patrons and its dictators.

The women of the Genroku period (and actually throughout the Edo period) had very limited opportunities for entertainment. Usually confined to their homes, seeing their husbands going out to have a good time, their only place for escape, refreshment and pleasure was the theatre. In a sense, the theatre of Genroku had the same function for women that onna kabuki and wakashu kabuki had held for the men of the early seventeenth century. It provided them with a free erotic world, a romantic place of license and dreams occupied by charming and admired actors.

Many love affairs took place between female members of the audience and players. The most famous was the Ejima-Ikushima affair, which hastened the end of the theatre to which the actor Ikushima belonged. This affair, which itself served as a subject for plays, shows many of the typical phenomena of the period, so it might be useful to relate it briefly. There are numerous, often contradictory accounts of the affair, but it may be summed up as follows.

Ejima, a high-ranking lady-in-waiting, was known for her passion for kabuki actors. In 1713 she attended a play at the Yamamura-za, one of the four permanent theatres of Edo. During the performance, she invited the actors to her box, which was occupied also by several of her friends, and held a gay party there, the details of which are not entirely clear. After the performance, a love affair developed between her and the actor Ikushima (there were previous attempts on her part to approach several actors, who had refused). Their secret meetings are said to have been held at the theatre manager's house. In 1714 Ejima was on her way back from some religious duties she had performed at the Zōjōji temple, accompanied by some hundred attendants. Instead of returning to the palace, the whole company

[2]**Oiran:** Highest class of prostitutes.

went out of its way to visit the Yamamura-za, and another gay and noisy party was held, which is said to have disrupted the performance.

The government could not overlook such behaviour and immediately reacted. Ejima and her brother were exiled, and another brother was executed, being, as a brother, responsible for his sister's behaviour according to the Confucian code. Ikushima, the manager, and several actors were exiled to a different place, and the court maids were put under arrest. The four theatres of Edo were closed and the Yamamura-za was torn down and closed for good. Later, the three were permitted to reopen and became the three permanent theatres of Edo; needless to say, they were now under the most stringent restrictions.

Bakufu attempts to 'protect' the audience from the evil influence of the actors had begun long before and took many forms. One was to restrict the theatres and the actors' residence to limited areas near the gay quarters. Another seems to have been a kind of propaganda written by official writers and educators of the time against the players and the new fashion, spreading rapidly among the Genroku people, of imitating actors. Ogyū Sorai, a scholar and adviser to the shogun, wrote:

> People are easily influenced by the behaviour of actors and prostitutes. Recently there has been a tendency for even high-ranking people to use the argot of actors and prostitutes. This habit has become a kind of fashion, and people think that those who do not use such words and phrases are rustics. I am ashamed that this is so. Such a tendency will result in the collapse of the social order. It is therefore necessary to segregate actors and prostitutes from ordinary society.[3]

The scholar had every reason to worry, from the government point of view. Society widely imitated actors, who had previously imitated it. In the past, the actors who had played women's roles endeavoured to shape their style after high-born or courtesans, who in turn modelled their appearance and behaviour on those of court ladies. Now, as one of the contemporary writers said, the ladies themselves imitated the actors and formed their manners after them. Kimonos, wigs and many articles of dress and accessories used by famous onnagata players were copied by the women of Edo. Actors dictated the fashion of their audience. Characters from the plays were imitated by the people and the dandies of the day; the language and style of the stage affected the behaviour of the spectators; fabric patterns and designs which are still known as Genroku originated in the theatre and the gay quarters. Theatres and courtesans also served as the most popular models for painters and writers. Thus in the bakufu's futile attempts to dictate the standards of behaviour of the commoners, the Confucian laws had two powerful competitors: the actor and the courtesan.

As a reaction to this sensuous, colourful influence of the actor on his audience, another contemporary scholar writes about the ideal aims of the kabuki theatre:

> In general, kabuki plays should be a mirror reflecting good and evil. Seeing a play performed on the stage, the audience should be aware that a subject should work hard for the sake of his feudal lord, a child should be obedient to its parents, a woman should be loyal to her husband, a mother-in-law should be kind to her daughter-in-law, a stepmother should be kinder to her stepchild than to her own child, a stepchild should be obedient to its stepmother, brothers and sisters should have friendly relations, friends should

---

[3]Quoted in Ernst Earle, *Kabuki Theatre*, New York: Oxford University Press, 1956, p. 6.

be frank and avoid hypocrisy. Thus the audience should learn how to live by seeing plays performed on the stage by skilful actors. But nowadays most people consider plays only as entertainment and forget their true function. Spectators discuss the beauty of things on the stage and actors think it most important to display their beauty.[4]

To be sure, this attitude was shared by several of the kabuki people themselves, as we can see in Namiki Gohei's (one of the outstanding playwrights of the eighteenth century) words in his *Battle of the Geisha* (1796): "No matter how young you are, you should not consider a play only as entertainment. The theatre aims at encouraging good and rebuking evil. In other words, it is a way of studying life. You should appreciate the moral precepts expressed in a play and apply them to your daily activities."[5]

These quotations are from the post-Genroku era. Needless to say, audiences of the Genroku era or any other period did not come to the theatre to be educated, nor did actors play in order to preach Confucianism on stage. The theatre did influence daily life, but in aspects other than ethical or intellectual.

The actors of the time were interested in artistic problems and in their relationship with their audience. It may be helpful, therefore, to examine briefly some of the opinions expressed by the actors concerning the attitude that the actor should have towards his audience. The quotations are taken mainly from the *Yakusha rongo* (or *Yakusha banashi*), an anthology of the teachings of the great actors of the Genroku period.[6]

[4] Tamenaga Icho's "A Primer of the Kabuki" (1762), quoted in *Kabuki Theater,* p. 215.
[5] Quoted ibid., ibid.
[6] *Yakusha rongo* or *Yakusha banashi,* published in 1776. Published in print in 1906 in *Shin gunsho ruijū* (10 vols), vol. 3, and from then on in various forms. I have used the English translation by Charles J. Dunn and Bunzō Torigoe (who edited and annotated it as well), *The Actors' Analects* (*Yakusha Rongo*), 1969.

Faubion Bowers 1917–1999
RETURN TO THE PUPPETS

1952

Faubion Bowers taught at Hosei University in Tokyo before World War II (1940–41). When war broke out, he trained as an interpreter for U.S. troops and acted as interpreter for General Douglas MacArthur, who directed the occupation of Japan in 1945. Bowers became associated with Japanese theater in the postwar period and is credited with having saved kabuki drama. His essay here explains some of the appeal of jōruri drama.

The puppet theatre was an older historical development than Kabuki. It had attracted many meritorious playwrights who wanted to avoid the constant difficulties of writing for arrogant Kabuki actors. With the deaths of Sakata Tojuro and Danjuro I, some of Kabuki's vitality disappeared. The puppet theatre began to dominate the theatrical scene. It gained such popularity that Kabuki, in order to continue, was forced to borrow its material and adapt it. From this time onward, the interchange between Kabuki and the puppets increased steadily.

It was Danjuro himself who in the year of his death, 1717, made the first direct borrowing from the Osaka puppets. He made over Chikamatsu's historical play *Kokusenya*[1] into a Kabuki play, and played the leading role, the hero Watonai, in *aragoto*[2] style. This was an important moment in theatre history for Japan. It was the first time that a well-written puppet play had been used in the Kabuki theatre. It was also a wedding of Osaka's and Edo's best talents.

The play *Kokusenya*, written in 1715, casts an interesting light on Japan's attitude towards China at the time. It is still performed today in its weird costumes — Japanese versions of Chinese costumes of the period.

The story is as follows:

The Ming Dynasty in China has been overthrown. The Ming princess, Sendan, flees to Japan. There she is saved by a gallant hero named Watonai. Watonai's father was Roikkan, an old retainer of the Chinese Ming Emperor. His mother was Japanese. Watonai and his parents return to China in order to restore the Ming Dynasty.

The chief Chinese general of the anti-Ming faction is called Kanki, and has pledged himself to the invading Tatar king. His wife, Kinshojo, is Roikkan's own daughter and Watonai's sister. The family ask her to help their cause. She is to plead with her husband to assist them in restoring the Ming Dynasty. Watonai waits on the bank of the Yellow River to learn the answer as to whether she is successful in persuading her husband. The agreed-upon signal is that if the husband refuses, she will drop powdered rouge from the castle window into the river water.

As Watonai waits, he sees the river turn red. He then forces his way into the castle singlehanded, only to find that Kinshojo has killed herself. The dilemma of choosing between her family and her husband was too much for her. The coloring in the river was not the signal, but her life's blood. Watonai's mother kills herself in grief over the daughter's death.

General Kanki, much moved by his wife's intensity of feeling, resolves to enter the war on the side of Watonai. Together they defeat the Tatar army and restore the Ming Dynasty.

A still closer connection between the puppets and Kabuki was started in the same year as the performance of *Kokusenya*, by the appearance in Edo of Tachi-matsu Hachirobei, the puppeteer. He gained fame there not only for his skill in manipulating the dolls, but also by teaching some of the Kabuki actors how to move, particularly when playing soft love roles. His gentle movements of the puppets had contributed substantially to Chikamatsu's popularity in Osaka.

The Takemoto-Za puppet theatre, first established at the end of the 17th century, had by the first half of the 18th century reached a fantastic degree of popularity in Osaka. In competition, a rival puppet theatre, the Toyotake-Za, set up operation across the street. This new theatre started as the result of a quarrel. Toyotake Wakadayu, a disciple and protege of the *joruri* singer, Takemoto Gidayu, fell out with his master, probably over his ambition to have more leading roles to sing and recite. Toyotake Wakadayu quit the Takemoto-Za, and taking with him Ki-no-Kaion (1663–1742) as chief writer, established his own theatre. A curious vying for popularity between the two theatres ensued. If Chikamatsu had a success at the Takemoto-Za, Ki-no-Kaion followed with a play on a similar theme at the

[1]**Kokusenya:** The Battles at Coxinga.
[2]**aragoto:** Rough style.

Toyotake-Za. Although this does not speak well for Ki-no-Kaion's inventiveness, his excellence as a craftsman, judging from his surviving plays, cannot be denied. Both theatres prospered side by side for many years.

The years 1723 and 1724 saw the retirement from writing of both Chikamatsu and Ki-no-Kaion. Following in their wake, a large number of excellent writers appeared. The chief writers for the Takemoto-Za and the Toyotake-Za, respectively, were Takeda Izumo (1691–1756) and Nishizawa Ippu (1665–1731). These successors had as additional work the duty of managing the theatres. The heaviness of these non-writing tasks and resultant lack of time for writing precipitated the custom among playwrights of "joint compositions" (*gassaku joruri*). Texts were no longer the responsibility of one playwright. The chief writer worked with his confrères and students to produce a single play. *The Chronicle of the Alphabetical Rise and Fall* (*Hiragana Seisuiki*) written around 1739, is the combined effort of as many as five men: Takeda Izumo, his son Takeda Koizumo, Namiki Senryu, Miyoshi Shoraku, and Asada Kahei.

The theatres of Japan until the 19th century opened at dawn and closed when darkness came. As a result, programs and plays were of great length. In addition, programs changed every two weeks on the average. To write such long plays, a large number of writers were needed. The practice of joint composition was both necessary and practical. Each act in Japanese drama includes three parts: *kuchi* (mouth), *naka* (middle), and *kiri* (cut), (the Jo-Ha-Kyu formula); and each of these parts is equivalent in length to an act of Western drama. Although plays were usually written in five acts, this actually meant a possible fifteen acts in our sense of the word. Such massive dramatic structures could not possibly have come from a single pen, nor could a consistent standard of excellence be maintained. Subsequently uneven and inferior acts were dropped from the repertoire of Kabuki and puppet companies. The custom of performing excerpts from these long plays came into being.

Posterity has suffered from this habit of performing segments of plays. Many passages and texts have completely disappeared and cannot now be reconstructed. In recent times the parts performed are sometimes so truncated that without extensive program notes or considerable prior theatrical experience it is impossible to follow the gist of the play. This abbreviation is partly excusable because of the fact that there is a tremendous amount of repetition in classical plays of Japan. In the old days, throughout the entire day spectators drifted in and out of the theatres. It was customary for the plays to begin each act with a recapitulation of the story of the preceding action. These are now deleted because modern audiences give less divided attention. Also, as the repertoire became more familiar and traditional, many among the audience began to know the plays by heart.

Tsuruo Ando (1908–1969)
THE PLAYWRIGHT CHIKAMATSU   1970

Japanese author Tsuruo Ando gives us a concise assessment of Chikamatsu's achievement in the puppet theater. In his book Bunraku, *from which this piece is excerpted, Ando discusses the early development of jōruri as well as the role of important chanters, such as Gidayu and his theater, the Takemoto-za, for which Chikamatsu wrote.*

The success of Gidayu-bushi[1] depended to a large extent upon the competence and artistic taste of the narrators, their *shamisen* accompanists, and the puppeteers — and upon their ability to work together — but the creators of the works they performed must not be forgotten. The most successful of these was Chikamatsu Monzaemon (1653–1724).

Chikamatsu was the second son of Sugimori, a member of the Echizen clan. In 1675 he became playwright for Uji Kaga-no-jo's troupe at Shijo in Kyoto. Later, as we have already noted, he was appointed main playwright for Gidayu's troupe in Osaka. He also wrote many plays for the famous Osaka Kabuki actor Sakata Tojuro I. Most celebrated among his works are the double-suicide pieces (*shinju-mono*), which exerted a great influence on Japanese drama in general.

Chikamatsu's achievements were many but possibly the most important of them was the creation of a five-act dramatic form which in later years became the standard for both Gidayu-bushi and Kabuki. The oldest *ko-joruri* play was *The Twelve-Step Book* (Junidan Soshi), which had set the precedent for twelve acts. But this form was very cumbersome, and the technical and dramatic advances that had been made by the time Chikamatsu arrived on the scene demanded a stronger dramatic structure.

Chikamatsu's new five-act form for period pieces (*jidai-mono*) allowed for the logical spacing out of the basic dramatic structure of introduction, development, and climax. Each act also has the same type of development, with three parts called *kuchi, naka,* and *kiri.* As we have observed before, the *kiri* is even to this day considered the most important and difficult part of each act and is always performed by an experienced narrator.

The first act of a five-act play always opens in a formal or ceremonial setting such as a palace or the front of a temple or a shrine — a setting which lends weight to the piece. The act introduces the characters of the play, usually deals with some incident in the life of the villain, and almost always ends with the hero's being chased off by the villain, who is followed by someone who is going to help the hero win. Thus the viewer is led on a merry chase into the rest of the story.

The second act is not particularly important or interesting. Its basic purpose is to give more details about the situation.

The third act is such an important part of a play that during the middle and later part of the Edo period, when plays were written by groups of writers, the most skillful and famous one among the group was always chosen to write the third act. It contains the action — the most important part of the development of the story.

The fourth act always begins with a *michiyuki* (literally, "road-going"). This is the most poetic and dancelike scene of the play. It shows the characters of the play on their way to some important destination which in some way or other always means an important change in their lives. It tells in almost sung narration and beautiful dancelike movement of the thoughts, reminiscences, hopes, and fears of the person or persons traveling. The scenery always depicts some beautiful stretch of forest, mountain, or seashore and is always set in the season most appropriate to the mood of the traveler or travelers. This fourth act provides artistic beauty and a relaxed atmosphere after the violent action and tension of the third act.

The fifth act brings the play to an end, always with utter defeat for the villain and glorious triumph for the hero.

---

[1]**Gidayu-bushi:** The style of chanting developed by Takemoto Gidayu, with whom Chikamatsu worked.

RIGHT: A close look at a
bunraku puppet, with its
puppeteer in back of it.
BELOW: Puppeteers dressed
in black perform with their
bunraku puppets.

This form of dramaturgy is in evidence throughout the history of *joruri* and Kabuki after Chikamatsu. Actual division of the acts and scenes is sometimes different, but the basic structure never changes.

In addition to the five-act system for period and historical pieces, Chikamatsu developed a three-act system for plays concerning contemporary life (*sewa-mono*) — a system based on the Noh dramaturgy of Zeami called *jo-ha-kyu* (introduction, development, climax). The *jo* section or first act is an easy, gentle introduction; the *ha* section or second act is the development section, which is full of delicate and detailed rhythms at a faster tempo; and the *kyu* section or third act climaxes and ends the piece in a brilliant *presto* tempo. This technique originated in Gagaku, an ancient form of court music.

Chikamatsu used the *jo-ha-kyu* structure in his *sewa-mono*,[2] the most famous of which are his double-suicide pieces, not only for the overall composition but within each act as well. Thus he was able to reach great heights of poetic beauty and to develop an almost musical overall rhythm. This structure is so important to all classical Japanese dramaturgy and performance techniques that without a feeling for it a play or a performance is very flat and uninteresting.

The two forms of dramaturgy developed by Chikamatsu brought about a radical change in the history of Japanese drama which is felt to this day.

Chikamatsu was also particularly good at characterization. His characters run the whole gamut from peasant to priest to aristocrat, and he covered every period of history from the prehistoric legendary age of the gods right up through to his own day. His sense of period and his understanding of humanity were so superior that all of Japanese history and its various heroes and villains, as well as all those in between, live even for us today.

The skill and beauty of Chikamatsu's language is beyond compare. His great love for and understanding of human beings lends a natural, settled atmosphere to his works. His clean, clear view of history enabled him to write with ease of expression no matter which period he chose. Especially in his contemporary *sewa-mono* pieces, his portrayal of customs and the social atmosphere was always sensitive and correct. Again, he was always on the side of the underdog.

Chikamatsu died at the age of seventy-one in November 1724, ten years after Gidayu I (Chikugo-no-jo). Today, some two and a half centuries later, his plays are a living legacy both in Bunraku and in Kabuki.

[2]**sewa-mono:** Domestic plays.

Donald H. Shively (b. 1921)
THE DEVELOPMENT OF THEATER BUILDINGS   1978

Professor emeritus at the University of California–Berkeley, Donald Shively discusses the development of the kabuki theater from 1600, beginning with the theater of Nō drama, through its use of revolving stages in 1830. The experience of the audience was altered dramatically by the changes in theater design, especially the hanamichi, *a runway that took the actor into the audience while still maintaining his distance from both the main action and the onlookers.*

The earliest kabuki performances, as noted, were staged in rudimentary enclosures which could be hastily constructed if subscription *nō* stages were not already available in the amusement quarters at the edge of the cities. From about 1617 Kyoto began issuing licenses to operate theaters. As was true of houses of prostitution, the theaters were increasingly restricted to certain quarters of the city. In Kyoto they were clustered in the area of Shijō, just east of the river, and although as many as seven licenses were issued by 1669, it is not clear how many were in operation at one time.[1] This concentration parallels the establishment of the large prostitution quarters at Shimabara, several miles to the southwest, in 1641. The Shijō theater area and riverbank was a large amusement center in which kabuki was one of many dozens of diversions. There were smaller playhouses, puppet theaters, and a number of wayside entertainers who recited tales from military epics, the *Taiheiki* and *Heike monogatari*. There were fortune-tellers, dentists, *sumō* wrestlers, jugglers, and tightrope walkers. There were sideshows exhibiting such freaks as the female giant and the armless woman archer. There were exotic animals — tigers, bears, porcupines, eagles and peacocks, performing monkeys and dancing dogs. Teahouses, restaurants, and refreshment stands lined the streets. Paintings of the period show these establishments crowded together, thronged with people of every description.[2]

Edo performances of women's kabuki and youths' kabuki took place as early as 1617 in the Yoshiwara and the nearby amusement area of Nakabashi. The first theater to be licensed was the Saruwaka-za in Nakabashi in 1624, later renamed Nakamura-za, which continued to operate at a succession of locations until 1893. It serves as a particularly remarkable example of the exercise of an hereditary license to operate a theater. This and later kabuki theaters were ordered to move from time to time and finally, after the Meireki fire of 1657 forced the Yoshiwara far outside the city, were restricted to Sakai-chō and Kobiki-chō and shortly limited to four in number. The Tokugawa government continued to follow a policy of treating the prostitution and theater quarters as parallel concerns. When the theater quarters burned in 1841, nearly two centuries later, they were ordered to move to Saruwaka-chō in Asakusa, close by the Yoshiwara. In Osaka too, where the issuing of regular licenses to theaters followed the Edo precedent, they were restricted from the 1660s to Dōtombori and Horie.

With the issuing of licenses permitting the construction of permanent theaters, the buildings became gradually more substantial. The mat fence was replaced by solid board walls, and a row of boxes (*sajiki*) was built along the two sides of the parquet (*doma*) for spectators who required more comfort and privacy. Later boxes were added at the rear of the parquet. City officials, seeking to keep kabuki a simple form of entertainment, forbade the construction of roofs over the parquet. But resourceful theater owners devised a method of stretching mats across the par-

[1] Dōmoto Kansei (Yatarō) *Kamigata engeki shi* (Tokyo: Shun'yōdō, 1934), p. 41; Takano Tatsuyuki, *Nihon engeki shi* (Tokyo: Tōkyō-dō, 1948), II: 265–269. Dōmoto believes that seven theaters were licensed as early as 1624, but Takano's opinion that this did not happen until 1669–1670 seems more probable.

[2] There are many illustrations of the scene at the Shijō riverbank, including performances of *onna kabuki, wakashu kabuki,* and a variety of sideshows in screen paintings of the second quarter of the seventeenth century, as in Kondō Ichitarō, *Japanese Genre Painting: The Lively Art of Renaissance Japan,* trans. R. A. Miller (Tokyo: Charles E. Tuttle Co., 1961), plates 4, 66–71, pp. 22 and 24; also Kikuchi Sadao et al., eds., *Kinsei fūzoku zukan* (Tokyo: Mainichi Shimbunsha, 1974), II:109; and Kyoto Kokuritsu Hakubutsukan, comp., *Rakuchū rakugai zu* (Tokyo: Kadokawa Shoten, 1966), unnumbered plates at back.

quet to serve as makeshift shelters which provided shade from the sun and protection against light showers. Over a period of two centuries the theater buildings became gradually more elaborate and comfortable as the authorities made concessions, alternating between a resigned attitude and a stricter policy of sumptuary regulation.

Set back slightly from the street so as not to obstruct traffic, the theater facade was dominated by a tower on which ornamental spears were mounted to indicate possession of an official license. This spear (or drum) tower was draped with a cloth bunting featuring the large design of the theater's crest. The Nakamura-za first used the wheeling crane (*maizuru*) design. The Ichimura-za chose a rounded crane within an octagon.[3] Most theaters placed large billboards on the tower, the center board announcing in bold characters the name of the proprietor, those on either side the names of leading actors. Lower billboards, typically four in number if the offering was a four-act play, gave the titles of each act. From the 1720s a tableau from each act was painted above the title.

Before these signs stood low platforms where barkers waved their fans to attract the attention of passersby and entice them into the theater. In addition to the cruder techniques of whistling and calling to onlookers, they would attempt to draw a crowd by staging impersonations of the leading actors, imitating their voices as they recited tantalizing lines from the play, and parodying their characteristic poses and gestures. Contemporary paintings record the remarkably exuberant commitment of these *kido geisha* (entrance performers) to their task.[4]

The early theaters had only one entrance, located in the center of the building under the drum tower. It was a small opening with a high threshold which the customer had to step over while ducking under a low overhead. Aptly called the mouse-entrance (*nezumi kido*), it was a holdover from the enclosures used for subscription *nō* and was presumably designed to make it difficult for anyone to slip in quickly without paying. As the theaters grew larger in the eighteenth century, an entrance was provided on each side of the drum tower for admission to the parquet. The stoop entrance was abandoned and a short curtain (*noren*) hung across the top of the doorway, as is customary in Japanese shops. Tickets were purchased outside and other fees paid within for the rental of a reed mat (*hanjō*) and a length of smoldering cord to light one's pipe. On each side of the front of the building an entrance was added for guests going to boxes in order to avoid jostling by the plebs. Inside, stairs led to the upper level of boxes.

The price of tickets ranged widely between the cheapest and the best seats. In 1714, boxes in Edo theaters commanded 1200 *mon,* single spaces 200 *mon.* Parquet tickets averaged 64 *mon.* When space was available, single-act tickets were sold for 12 *mon.* Rental of a mat was 6 *mon* additional.[5] These prices increased rather steadily through much of the Tokugawa period, probably following the general inflationary trend, but exacerbated at certain times by the escalating salaries of

[3]The use of the crane became taboo in 1690 because the word for crane (*tsuru*) was used by the shōgun Tsunayoshi in his daughter's name, Tsuruhime. Thereafter the Nakamura-za used a gingko leaf design and the Ichimura-za changed its crest to an orange-tree design. Suda Atsuo, *Nihon gekijō shi no kenkyū* (Tokyo: Sagami Shobō, 1957), p. 330.
[4]The six-fold screen (Tokyo National Museum) of the Nakamura-za with its new ginko-leaf crest and stage, attributed to Hishikawa Moronobu (d. 1694), appears in Kondō, plate 76 (identified inexplicably as the Morita-za); Gunji (1969), plate 416; and Suwa Haruo, *Kabuki kaika* (Tokyo: Kadokawa Shoten, 1970), plate 58.
[5]Takano, II:242–243.

the star actors. Attending a major theater was not cheap. The cost of a box seat in 1828 was 1 *ryō* 2 *bu,* the equivalent of 3 bales (*hyō*) of rice or a servant's salary for three or four months. When a performance was popular, the price of tickets rose abruptly.[6]

While the Nakamura-za in Edo provides a detailed illustration of the physical design of a theater, it should be noted that no two were identical. Theaters were, moreover, periodically rebuilt, for fires frequently ravaged Edo. In the 1690s the outer dimensions of the Nakamura-za were 71.5 feet by 97.5 feet, or 6,971 square feet.[7] At its largest in 1809, it measured 80 feet by 138.5 feet, or 11,080 square feet.[8] The structure remained a fraction the size of the present Kabuki-za in Tokyo which has 39,000 square feet of space on the ground floor, seating 1,078 people, approximately the same number as the Tokugawa structure. But the modern building has five floors with 120,000 square feet of floor space and accommodates an additional 1,522 people on the mezzanine and balconies.[9] The Nakamura-za of 1720 had a row of boxes along the two sides and across the back. Although only one tier was allowed at that time, by 1724 a second tier of boxes had been added. It was repeatedly forbidden to hang bamboo blinds across the front of the boxes and to install screens or other partitions which would provide privacy for the occupants. However, a number of paintings from this period show such items in use, partially concealing from the gaze of the populace ladies-in-waiting of the shogun's or daimyo's households, members of the Buddhist clergy, and rich merchants.[10]

The parquet (*doma*) of the Nakamura-za, 52 feet wide and 82.4 feet deep in 1720, had a capacity of 800 persons. Later, the front half with its better seats was divided into partitions (*masu*) not quite five feet square which narrowly accommodated seven or eight people.[11] Rear parquet space was unreserved. The last back seats, called the *ōmukō* (greatly beyond) were so far from the stage that they were also known as the "deaf gallery." Thus including boxes and the cheapest parquet seats the theater held about 1,200.[12] Operating policy was to crowd in as many as possible. According to a book of 1703: "The people came in pushing and jostling, and eight persons sat knee over knee on a mat. It is very pleasant to see them pressed together like human *sushi.*"[13]

By the early eighteenth century, wooden roofs occasionally sheltered part of the pit, although not officially sanctioned until 1724. Thereafter tile roofs were recommended to decrease the danger of fire from flying embers. Even after the theaters added roofs, artificial lighting remained proscribed because of the danger to the

---

[6]Gunji (1956), pp. 62–63; Gunji (1969), pp. 51–52. Only the large theaters of the three cities are discussed in this chapter, but there were also small, low-priced theaters known as *miyachi shibai* located on temple grounds, which were permitted to give performances for one hundred days during the year. Gunji (1956), pp. 38–42.

[7]Suda, p. 328.

[8]Zushi Yoshihiko, *Nihon no gekijō kaiko* (Tokyo: Sagami Shobō, 1947), p. 61. The largest Kyoto theaters seem to have been somewhat larger, at least in 1689 when one measured 106 by 196 feet, over 20,000 square feet. Suda, p. 330.

[9]Yoshida Teruji, ed., *Kabuki-za* (Tokyo: Kabuki-za Shuppanbu, 1951), p. 324.

[10]Zushi, p. 60; Suda, pp. 331–333; Takano, II:341. Three-tiered boxes are mentioned in 1701, but this perhaps means two tiers raised above the floor, allowing space underneath. Suda, p. 331.

[11]From 1772, wooden partitions replaced ropes to divide the *masu,* and later the size of the *masu* was reduced until finally there was space for only four people. Suda, 339.

[12]Takano, II:343; Iizuka Tomoichirō, *Kabuki gairon* (Tokyo: Hakubunkan, 1928), p. 469; Gunji (1969), p. 50.

[13]*"(Kyō-Ōsaka) Yakusha hyōban iro jamisen,"* in *Kabuki hyōbanki shūsei* (Tokyo: Iwanami Shoten, 1973), III:327a; Takano, II:343.

wooden structure from the open flame of oil lamps and candles. Performances, expected to end about 5 P.M., depended on natural light from windows with translucent paper-covered *shōji* installed on both sides of the theater behind or above the upper row of boxes.[14]

Dressing rooms, located directly behind the stage, were built in two stories by the 1670s. Before the end of the century the Morita-za in Edo added a third level.[15] This section of the building was built high to take as little ground space as necessary from the stage and parquet. A passageway leading to the dressing room section was constructed behind the boxes. Though intended for use by actors to gain access to the end of the runway (*hanamichi*), it was soon traveled by actors summoned to boxes or patrons visiting dressing rooms.[16] The usual arrangement called for baths and quarters for musicians, writers, and *wakashu* on the first floor, *onnagata* on the second, and players of men's roles on the third. A large rehearsal area also occupied the third level. Leading players had individual dressing rooms, although partitions had not received official sanction.[17]

The early kabuki stage basically recreated the square *nō* stage with pillars in the four corners supporting a thatched roof. The main platform had two narrow appendages, one to the right used by the chorus in the *nō*, the other at the rear for the musicians. Off the left of the stage a "bridge" (*hashigakari*) for entrances and exits extended back at an oblique angle with a railing on each side and a long roof. These features of the *nō* stage were gradually modified in the kabuki theater, although it is surprising how long they persisted. The stage itself was only nineteen feet square at the outset. Rather than alter its design, more space was gained by greatly widening the bridge and eliminating its handrails. It then emerged as a secondary performing area, a rectangle set back slightly from the main stage. A platform was appended to the front of the stage (*tsuke-butai*) which jutted into the audience. Though these changes were not completed until the first decades of the eighteenth century, some stages had already become quite large. That of the Nakamura-za measured 32.5 feet by 37.7 feet in 1724. Not until 1796, however, was the roof over the main stage eliminated.[18]

One of the most distinctive inventions of the kabuki theater is the *hanamichi*, a five-foot-wide runway which extends from the left side of the stage to the rear of the audience. It is used for more dramatic entrances and exits and as an occasional pivot of activity. Its origins are unclear. The more obvious assumption, that it began as a second *hashigakari* directed through the audience, appears to be incorrect. Perhaps as early as the 1650s a small platform was attached to the stage slightly left of center where members of the audience placed gifts (*hana*) of money or goods for their favorite actors. These were called *hana* because the gift was attached to a flower (*hana*) branch. Such a platform appears in a drawing of the Nakamura-za in 1687.[19] By 1724, at least, the *hanamichi* was a runway 52 feet long, set at an oblique angle, probably ending toward the rear end of the row of boxes on the left side of the hall. Although the word *hanamichi* may originally have meant "a path for gifts," by the 1720s and perhaps several decades earlier, it was

[14]Suda, p. 333.
[15]Suda, p. 327.
[16]Suda, pp. 327, 329.
[17]Suda, pp. 335, 345.
[18]Suda, p. 337. The present Kabuki-za stage is 77 feet by 95 feet.
[19]Suda, p. 329. There is some evidence that it was used as part of the stage by 1668. Iizuka, p. 421; Takano, II:361–363.

Perspective view of Kyogen play stage by artist Okumura Masanobu.

used primarily as an extension of the stage. Woodblock prints of the next decade show actors standing or seated upon it. Occasionally a small platform called the *nanori-dai* was added about the midway point where an actor could stand almost dead center of the parquet to announce the name and pedigree (*nanori*) of the character he was portraying. After 1780 another narrower runway was sometimes erected on the right side of the hall. Perhaps as a result, the main *hanamichi* was set at right angles to the stage, parallel to its narrower companion.[20]

Most of the physical features of the theater discussed on the preceding pages are illustrated in a woodblock print by Okumura Masanobu (1686–1764) of the Ichimura-za in Edo in 1744. The *nō* stage with its roof and front pillars, the appended *hashigakari* stage right and *tsuke-butai* stage front and the *hanamichi* are clearly evident. There is a raised walk (*ayumi*) across the hall for easier access by customers and vendors to the front part of the pit. A tea and a food vendor pass through the audience. The stage curtain is drawn to stage right. Boxes of the first tier were known as quail boxes (*uzura sajiki*) because their wooden bars made them resemble crates for keeping quail. The second tier of boxes retained eaves from the days, a few decades earlier, when there was no roof over the pit. Sliding doors of translucent paper let in daylight above the boxes.[21]

[20]Suda, pp. 337–341.

[21]The pillar at stage left bears the name of the play, *Nanakusa wakayagi Soga*, followed by the name of the theater, Ichimura-za. The other pillar gives the name of the scene, "Yaoya Oshichi kyōdai biraki." On the beam joining the pillars we see that the Ichimura-za has reclaimed its crane crest. On stage beside her shop counter stands the vegetable dealer (*yaoya*) Oshichi, played

Artist Utagawa Toyokuni III's woodblock print of an eighteenth-century stage, with the galleries at the edges of the stage and the two balconies, the arhat dais and the yoshino.

In such a theater the play moved easily into the audience. The tiers of boxes at the front of the hall were alongside the stage. Later in the eighteenth century a low balcony intruded behind the left corner of the stage (stage right). Known as the *rakandai* (arhat dais), its tightly lined-up spectators hovered over the stage like the five hundred arhats of a Buddhist painting. A seventeen-syllable satirical poem (*senryū*) observes: "The five hundred went home, having seen the actors' backs." A second balcony inevitably grew above this. It was called *tsūten* (passing through to heaven), or Yoshino (a mountain district noted for cherry blossoms), as its perspective barely penetrated the artificial cherry blossoms suspended from the ceiling of the hall. A woodblock print of the last decades of the Tokugawa period shows the plebs, crammed in these galleries at the edge of the stage, watching gleefully, mouths agape, as the actors perform, almost within reach.[22] When the play was a great success, the management, not impervious to the potential boon, seated customers on the stage itself. This practice is recorded by the satirical poems: "A big hit — the action is performed in a six-foot square," and "Spectators and actors are lined up together — a big hit."[23] With an audience thus gathered on three sides of the performers and cheap balcony seating available over one corner of the stage, no concept of a platform-framing proscenium arch emerged.

---

by Segawa Kikujirō in this performance of the first month of 1744. Kichizō, played by Onoe Kikugorō, approaches on the *hanamsichi.* A stage attendant waves his fan to quiet the audience. This print is an example of the Western-style perspective picture (*ukie,* "floating picture") which came into vogue about 1736. Yoshida Teruji, *Kabuki-e no kenkyū* (Tokyo: Ryokuen Shobō, 1936, 1963), pp. 98–101. The print is in the collection of the Atami Bijutsu-kan.

[22]Detail of a print of a theater interior by Utagawa Toyokuni III (1786–1864), in the collection of the Waseda Daigaku Engeki Hakubutsukan (The Tsubouchi Memorial Theatre Museum, Waseda University). The entire print is reproduced in Gunji (1969), plate 448.

[23]Gunji (1956), pp. 59–60.

Earle Ernst

THE EVOLUTION OF THE KABUKI STAGE   *1974*

Earle Ernst is professor emeritus at the University of Hawaii, where a theater has been named for him. The diagrams shown in Figures 11 and 12 offer us a sense of the design of the kabuki stage with its primary elements clearly defined. Ernst's drawings, from his book on kabuki theater, offer us a view of the innovations made over time to the structure of the stage on which the drama was performed.

Figure 11. EVOLUTION OF THE KABUKI STAGE (I)

I c. 1600

II c. 1700

III c. 1710

A	Curtained entrance *(agemaku)*	O	"Hurry"-door *(okubyō-guchi)*
D	*Daijinbashira*	RS	Rear stage *(atoza)*
F	Forestage *(tsukebutai)*	S	Stage proper *(honbutai)*
H	"Bridge" *(hashigakari)*	W	*Waki-za*
M	*Metsukebashira*		

Figure 12. EVOLUTION OF THE KABUKI STAGE (II)

IV c. 1780

V c. 1830

A	Curtained entrance (*agemaku*)	M	*Metsukebashira*
B	Boxes (*sajiki*)	N	Nanoridai
D	*Daijinbashira*	O	"Hurry"-door (*okubyō-guchi*)
DC	Draw curtain (*hikimaku*)	P	Pre-forestage (*harigashi*))
F	Forestage (*tsukebutai*)	R	Revolving stage (*mawari-butai*)
H	"Bridge" (*hashigakari*)	S	Stage proper (*honbutai*)
HA	*Hanamichi*	T	Trap-lift
I	Inner revolving stage	TH	Temporary *hanamichi*
	(*janomemawashi*)	X	*Rakandai*

Benito Ortolani (b. 1928)
BACKGROUND OF KABUKI AND JŌRURI   1995

Professor emeritus at Brooklyn College, Benito Ortolani has written about Japanese theater as well as the playwright Luigi Pirandello. He is the editor of the International Bibliography of Theatre. *His discussion of the social circumstances surrounding kabuki and jōruri is thorough and distinct and offers some insight into the characters who appear in the plays.*

The history of Edo's theatrical splendor under the Tokugawa regime (1603–1868) has been the subject of several studies by Japanese and western authors, especially since World War II. The wealth of information available makes it possible to reconstruct a rather accurate picture of the complex and fascinating *kabuki* and *jōruri* worlds. Especially important are those studies that relate these genres to the phenomenal development of the new middle class in Edo and Osaka, the big Japanese cities that shared with Kyoto, and eventually took over from it, the leadership of theatrical fashion.

All authors agree that *kabuki* and *jōruri* are the typical theatrical expressions of the Tokugawa culture as it developed in the urban milieu, where the merchants played the main role in their fluctuating and ambiguous position of energetic economic leadership in the face of socio-political oppression. The large theatres supplied the townspeople with the only places for regular gatherings where "their" world could be collectively celebrated — a showplace for their economic success, their licentious fantasies, and daring fashions, as well as for the venting of their veiled criticism of forbidden topics and of their masked aspirations for social recognition.

When the Tokugawa world collapsed, *kabuki* and *jōruri* kept alive a memory and nostalgia for a past that was rapidly disappearing and dissolving into a new westernized society. Just as *bugaku*[1] remained alive at the price of crystallizing into a theatrical monument to the aristocratic court society of the Nara and Heian periods[2]; just as the *nō* paid the same price of crystallization to preserve the taste and refinement of the Ashikaga *samurai* society; just so did *kabuki* and *jōruri* become a frozen monument to the tastes and moods of the Tokugawa merchant middle-class.

Political Background

Kabuki was born as an explosion of lust for life and extravagance celebrating the end of over a century of political chaos, interminable civil wars among ever-changing alliances of feudal lords, ever-recurring devastations, reprisals, and death, under an all-pervading feeling of fear, instability, and insecurity. Peace resulted from the successful leadership of three generals who managed to bring the divided country under a unified, iron-handed, military rule. The two leaders who had started this unifying process, Oda Nobunaga and Toyotomi Hideyoshi, did not achieve a lasting peace: it was only Tokugawa Ieyasu who stopped the bloodbath and quieted social unrest. He is the creator of the system that succeeded in maintaining peace and stability for two and a half centuries — and at the same time

[1]**bugaku:** Court dance for an aristocratic audience.
[2]**Nara and Heian periods:** 710–1185.

determined the parameters of development of the unique Tokugawa society, thoroughly isolated from the rest of the world, and extraordinarily punctilious in its control of a hierarchical organization of each aspect of public and private life.

The theatre was no exception. Probably in no other epoch or place in the world has the theatre been the object of so many decrees of the supreme authority, of abolitions, restrictions, and regulations affecting every detail: regulations prescribed sites of theatre construction, the materials permissible for constructing the roofs of theatre buildings, the areas in which actors were allowed to live and move freely, access by the actors to the theatre's boxes, the kind of clothes the actors were allowed to wear and the precise type of hat they were ordered to wear whenever outside their territory, permission regarding the performance of certain types of dances within *kabuki* presentations, permission for theatres to operate following major scandals, including minutiae which may appear embarrassing to a modern reader, such as prohibiting female impersonators from using public facilities reserved for ladies.

The Tokugawa castle in Edo became the nucleus of the largest metropolis of Japan. Edo, the present-day Tokyo, functioned as the actual capital of the empire. In the grounds now occupied by the imperial palace in Tokyo, the Tokugawa rulers set up their court, completely independent from that of the emperor, who was left undisturbed and powerless — a nominal ruler in a nominal capital, Kyoto. The fortress of Tokugawa power was surrounded by the quarters of a permanent army of hundreds of thousands of *samurai* and their families — a continuous austere and oppressive reminder of the military dictatorship that dominated every aspect of Japanese life. It was outside the gloomy atmosphere of those barracks-lined quarters, and precisely in the colorful and lively off-limits red light districts, that Edo was to become the new theatre capital of Japan. As far as theatrical life is concerned for Japan, Edo eventually became, and Tokyo still is, the counterpart of Paris for France, London for England, and New York for the United States.

The establishment of the Tokugawa order did not happen without protest among the *samurai* themselves and without the appearance of opposition groups, among which the *kabuki mono* provide a most interesting occurrence — very much like the British "punk" phenomenon of the seventies and early eighties. They acquire a special meaning in the context of the study of *kabuki*'s background, because they explain the general association that both audiences and government had with the word *kabuki* at the beginning of the Tokugawa era. The verb *kabuku*, used since the middle ages with the meaning of "to slant," or "to tilt," had acquired, by the beginning of the Tokugawa era, a slang usage for any anti-establishment action that defied the conventions and the proper rules of behavior. The *kabuki mono* were therefore people who expressed their anti-conformism through a series of protests against the established order, which ranged from highly unusual ways of dressing to shocking hairdos and extravagantly decorated, enormous swords, and up to four-foot-long tobacco pipes. Like today's motorcycle gangs they would roam the streets and oftentimes engage in acts of violence and riots, flaunting their revolt against all conventions and decency, by performing such acts as playing the flute with one's anus.

The bulk of *kabuki mono* was formed of masterless *samurai,* but youngsters of important *samurai* families, even of *daimyō,*[3] had joined the gangs, in some cases

[3]**daimyo:** Samurai masters.

giving a definite political color to violent actions with potential revolutionary implications, and warnings of allegiance to traditional Tokugawa enemies. The execution of a *kabuki mono* in 1612 by a Tokugawa officer provoked the assassination of the officer by the *kabuki* "brothers" of the executed youth. The ensuing search by the authorities led to the discovery of a secret document with 500 signatures of *kabuki mono* which included sons of important *daimyō*. It is no wonder that Ieyasu acted swiftly and executed a large number of the dangerous rebels who were trying to subvert the very foundation of his new order. The fashion of rebellion against convention was adopted, in addition, by a group of court nobles in 1607 who then also received the name of *kabuki mono*: in women's clothing they entered the innermost quarters of the residence where the ladies of the imperial court lived and violated the sacred taboo of a place where men were strictly forbidden, right in the heart of the imperial palace. The scandal ended with the execution of the culprits and the exile of the complacent ladies.

To the Tokugawa regime *kabuki* meant subversion and heresy, something immoral and dangerous, but in the folk mentality the daring and sometimes heroic behavior of a few major *kabuki mono* leaders became the stuff of legend which was celebrated in songs, tales, and on the stages of the very first *kabuki* shows, while their eccentric fashions became popular all over Japan, even in the remotest villages.

In their obsession for providing political stability and avoiding at all costs a return to chaos, Ieyasu and his immediate successors enforced a strict policy of social stability, which in many ways affected the very life and development of the theatre. The new social order and the ethical values upon which it was built became the reference frame for all plays, making it necessary for western readers to study this frame of reference to understand the plays. Of course, many elements belonged to already widely accepted principles and to an already existing social *status quo;* new, however, were the enormous stress placed on the unconditional loyalty to superior authority, the thoroughness of the indoctrination, and the rigidity of the application of the principles at all costs and at all levels of society.

The Tokugawa took over from the old Chinese Confucian theories — adapted for their purposes of imposing a *samurai* dominated structure — the division of society into four classes: warrior-administrators (*samurai*) peasants (*nōmin*) artisans (*kōjin*) and merchants (*shōmin*). The hierarchy was not based on intelligence, preparation, wealth, or capacity, but determined by the interests of the dominating *samurai* class. The farmers provided the bushels of rice, that is, the income of the *samurai;* the artisans made swords and other weapons, the vital companions of the military class. Principles that may be considered unrealistic and reactionary even for seventeenth-century Japan were made to prevail — such as the absolute predominance of a military aristocracy that was useless and ill-prepared for peace purposes and the idea that, at the bottom of the social pyramid, below the farmers and the artisans, were the merchants, deemed a non-productive class making profits on already finished products without producing any themselves. Outside the four classes that made up the quasi-totality of the population remained the small but rather important groups of the old court nobility (*kuge*) around the emperor in Kyoto, which now was reduced to purely ceremonial functions; the *shaji,* that is, the clerical officials of Buddhism and Shinto; and, at the bottom of the social pyramid, the outcastes (*semmin*) among whom were such despised categories of people as prostitutes and *kabuki* actors.

Samurai and *Kabuki*

The social classes were far from constituting homogeneous groups. Many *kabuki* and *jōruri* plays present the distress of *samurai* fallen in disgrace and living among merchants, often concealing their true identity. To the *samurai* belonged such different people as the most powerful man in the country, the Shogun himself, powerful and rich feudal lords, high state employees and poor foot soldiers, who hardly had anything more than their pride and their swords. There was a complicated hierarchical ranking among the feudal lords, the government employees, and so forth. Hierarchy pervaded all classes, including the outcastes and the underworld. It was impossible to escape from it, as much as it was impossible not to belong to some group which would be held responsible for the actions of each of its members; thus were created the premises for such frequently seen extreme dramatic situations as where individuals are torn between contrasting allegiances, and are painfully conscious of the consequences of their actions for the whole family or group. The highpoint of this system of "collective responsibility" was introduced by the Tokugawa governor in Kyoto with a 1603 law which divided all citizens into groups of ten, and made all ten responsible for any crime committed by any member of that group.

From the very beginning the government of the Shogun adopted a policy of suspicion and restrictions against *kabuki*. The same characteristics that had given the name *kabuki* to the *kabuki mono* must have influenced both audiences and government to identify the new show by the same term. In the eyes of the shogunate early *kabuki* was another form of rebellious non-conformism, perverse in its eroticism, transvestism, outrageous costumes, and hybrid mixture of religious elements with licentious contents. Moreover, in its initial phases, *kabuki* became a source of frequent riots involving outcastes, townspeople, and, to the dismay of government officials, also *samurai*. The petty *samurai*, deprived in the peaceful society of any meaningful military function, were among the first to fill their idle time by constant attendance at both *kabuki* and puppet shows, although in disguise because of the off-limits locales at which such entertainments took place.

Besides the several ranks of *samurai* in the active service of either the Shogun or of about two hundred *daimyō* existing at the beginning of the seventeenth century, hundreds of thousands of *rōnin* (masterless *samurai*) became an unexpected element of social mobility within the apparently unshakeable stability of the system. The long wars had multiplied the number of *samurai* deprived of a lord, and therefore of an official position and a steady income. Many *rōnin* were forced by necessity to take jobs considered unworthy of a *samurai*, and concealed their shame under a false name — a popular situation in *kabuki* and *jōruri* plays. Among such *rōnin* were the famous forty-seven *samurai* who dared to challenge the authority of the Shogun in order to revenge the death of their master, and who became national heroes of a sort, inspiring the most famous play in the puppet and *kabuki* repertoire, the *Chūshingura*. An unproven but persistent tradition presents a *rōnin*, Nagoya Sanza (previously a *samurai* in the service of the Christian *daimyō* Gamo Ujisato) as the lover and main collaborator of the famous dancer Okuni, the legendary founder of *kabuki*. The historical truth about Nagoya Sanza will probably never be established, but if not Sanza, certainly other masterless *samurai* joined the outcastes in the despised occupation of *kabuki* actor. This explains the origin of illustrious *samurai* family names (such as Nakamura, Ichikawa, or Onoe) for dynasties of *kabuki* actors, in spite of the official laws that deprived outcastes of the right to a family name.

Artist Shunko Katsukawa's
(1743–1812) depiction of a
kabuki actor in the warrior-
like thunder god pose.

Peasants and *Kabuki*   In the official hierarchy of the Tokugawa society the peasants were ranked after the *samurai,* a tribute to their economic importance in an agricultural society which still recognized a bushel of rice as the measure of wealth. The peasants constituted about 80% of the total population, alone carried the burden of taxation, and, in the great majority of cases, lived in a state of quasi-servitude to the land and the feudal lord, without the right to move away from their fields or choose a different occupation in the cities. Peasants in general did not occupy a position of importance in *kabuki* plays and had very little to do with the organization of the *kabuki* world. However, the reality of a lively amateur *kabuki* in several rural centers, and, even more, of the puppet theatre in numerous villages has been underestimated and almost completely neglected by non-Japanese scholars, who obviously have been more impressed by the rich historical materials about the major performers and the large theatres of the major cities. In general, the heroes of the *kabuki* world are chosen from among the *samurai* and merchants, and the lowly peasants are presented as narrow-minded, petty, cowardly, and comically foolish.

Merchants and *Kabuki*   The Tokugawa peace favored an enormous increase in trade and the development of organized production of large quantities of goods required by cities that ranged among the world's most populous of the time. Wealth accumulated in the hands of merchants. They created a tight capitalistic system, favored by the traditional idea that only land could be taxed, leaving the enormous profits of trade tax-free. Some merchants, especially those who secured monopolies of vital products, could compete in wealth with the most powerful *daimyō.* Many *samurai* ended up owing money to the bankers of the new economy, which was rapidly shifting from its agricultural foundation to money and credit transactions. Socially inferior in the official society, the merchants found in the "floating world" of the red light districts — glittering with tea-houses, *kabuki* theatres, and every type of entertainment — an island where social distinction did not count and only cash decided the issues. No wonder then that rich merchants spent enormous amounts of money as generous patrons of that world. Wealth attracted all kinds of artists, who transformed the red light districts into the very centers of a new, colorful, highly original culture, evidently much more worldly than the one which gave birth to the *nō*. The greatest novelist of the Tokugawa period, Ihara Saikaku (1642–1693, who also wrote the *jōruri* play *Koyomi,* The Calendar) made life in the red light districts the main theme of his masterpieces. The masters of *ukiyo-e* wood-block prints multiplied the images of celebrated *kabuki* actors and women of pleasure. In no other nation's dramatic literature — nor in that of Japan in other periods — do brothels and courtesans appear in so great a number of plays, obviously mirroring the new cultural importance of the red light districts in which actors and theatre buildings were confined by law. Success in the arts depended now no longer on the *samurai,* but on the favor of the rich merchants and the ticket-buying townspeople who frequently visited the red light districts. Accordingly, playwrights, actors, musicians, puppeteers, painters, and all other providers of entertainment created a world of fantasy to please the taste of the new patrons. Even the *samurai* world was projected on the stage in the light of that fantasy, and appeared quite different from the somber reality of daily military life and from the sophisticated understatement of Zen-inspired simplicity that had characterized the *nō;* a gaudy, colorful immediacy of overstatement became typical of *kabuki* and *jōruri.*

Both *nō* and *kabuki* are unique and genuine expressions of the Japanese spirit and culture. They mirror, however, taste and ideals of different social classes, in profoundly different environments and epochs.

Outcastes and *Kabuki*

The word *geijutsu* today has the meaning of "art" with all its metaphysical and "dignified" implications. During the Tokugawa period, however, it was used — without any aura of dignity or respect — to indicate the performances of professional entertainers, sometimes with a meaning equivalent to "tricks." Actors formed a special group among the outcastes, and are referred to in several Japanese sources together with the other groups of outcastes such as *eta, semmin,* and *hinin.* This sociological bias is extremely important to understand the history of *kabuki.* The actors were called *kawaramono* (people of the riverbed) or, with a sense of contempt, beggars of the riverbed (*kawara kojiki*). They were submitted to humiliating restrictions of movement and places where they were allowed to live, of people they could mix with, and were even forced to wear a wicker hat as a sign of their despised profession whenever they left their territory. The habit of naming actors and prostitutes together in all official documents originated in the real connection between the two professions at the beginning of *kabuki.* Wealth, success, and fame, connected with a respectable moral life, did not change the social stigma of one's being a "beggar from the river bed" even when "squatting on brocaded mats," but these attributes did establish the premises for changes which slowly took place after the Tokugawa period. A stigma kept hanging over *kabuki* actors for a long time, even after they were officially "emancipated" at the beginning of the Meiji period.[4]

With great popularity a few successful performers reached yearly incomes comparable to the astronomical figures paid to movie stars nowadays. They could afford an extremely luxurious life, and were the object almost of a cult, comparable to the delirium of rock fans for superstars like Elvis Presley or, more recently, Madonna. *Kabuki* fans would fight for a sign of their idols' friendship, send expensive presents, and mourn their deaths with incredible manifestations of public grief. The process of advanced westernization eventually swept away most of the social stigma. Famous *kabuki* actors are now in a position comparable to stars of other show business genres. The Japanese government has bestowed upon a few *kabuki* actors the official recognition as "living cultural treasure," a great honor reserved for the best masters of the major traditional arts.

---

[4]Meiji period: 1868–1912.

Oliver Goldsmith

Oliver Goldsmith (1728–1774) was born in County Longford, Ireland, where he spent most of his first twenty-three years. Because his father was a clergyman, Goldsmith seemed destined for the church. After a very undistinguished undergraduate career at Trinity College, Dublin (B.A. 1750), however, he was forced to wait two years before applying for a clerical position, whereupon he was turned down for being unqualified. In his youth, Goldsmith was not a well-directed person, nor did he apply himself well in anything that might have led to a steady income. In 1752, he accepted the help of an uncle and went to Edinburgh to study medicine. He then went to Leyden, in the Netherlands, to continue his medical studies, but no universities in Leyden or nearby sites record him as a student. In 1755 he spent the better part of a year traveling — on foot, with very little money — in Germany, Switzerland, and Italy. He practiced medicine for a short time when he returned to England, but his patients usually lacked the ability to pay him. He applied to be a ship's doctor, but was rejected again as unqualified. Eventually, he became a teacher in a school, a job he hated. He also seems to have given some thought to studying law, but nothing came of that.

Goldsmith's writing career began almost accidentally, when he accepted a job writing "criticisms," reviews of various kinds for a journal called *Monthly Review*. He began to see that there was considerable demand for books from English publishers and that it might be possible to earn a living as a hack writer. Because he was fluent in French, he was able to translate a number of French books and to write a commentary on Voltaire, a writer he admired. He undertook a number of projects for various publishers and, after writing a series of "Chinese Letters" — social commentary supposedly from the point of view of a Chinese man in London — came to the notice of a number of writers and artists.

Among those who became his friend were Sir Joshua Reynolds, the great painter, who did a portrait of him, and Samuel Johnson, the reigning literary figure of the day and author of the *Dictionary*. In 1762, Johnson found Goldsmith about to be thrown into the street by his landlord for nonpayment of back rent. He asked Goldsmith if he had any manuscript that might be sold for money, and after consideration Goldsmith gave him the manuscript for the novel *The Vicar of Wakefield*. Johnson sold it immediately for sixty pounds, a considerable sum of money, and put Goldsmith back on his feet.

The novel did not appear in print for four years because the publisher who bought it was not convinced it would sell. As it turned out, he was right. It did not turn a profit until Goldsmith died twelve years later, but *The Vicar of Wakefield* eventually found an audience and stands now as one of the finest novels of the period, one of the few still read widely today.

Unfortunately, Goldsmith could not live easily on the income from his work, even though he solicited subscriptions for a number of anthologies and an eight-volume history of animals called *The Roman History*. He turned to writing for the stage because he thought it might pay better, and possibly because he had come to know David Garrick, the greatest actor of the time and the manager of an important theater. Garrick was part of Samuel Johnson's circle and naturally came in contact with Goldsmith. The first play Goldsmith offered was *The Good-Natured Man* (1768), performed at Covent Garden. It was a success, running for nine evenings. He eventually earned some four hundred pounds, which was a considerable sum at the time. But typically, he overspent in outfitting a new place and found himself soon in debt, a condition that persisted throughout his life.

In 1770 Goldsmith published a poem, "The Deserted Village," that describes a fictional village, Auburn (probably modeled on his own village, Lissoy), altered forever by the industrial revolution. Before the mid-eighteenth century, people could make a living working at home. Villages were self-sustaining because local crafts were preferred and life was simple. Communities were warm and supportive. With the coming of large factories and machines that did the work of artisans, all that changed. The villages emptied, and the row-houses and slums associated with factories and the industrial revolution developed in their place.

"The Deserted Village," like *The Vicar of Wakefield*, is read and valued even more in today's world, at a time when issues take on considerable importance. From a modern perspective, "The Deserted Village" may even be considered a "green" poem. Goldsmith, whose reputation had grown by the time he wrote this poem, was paid a hundred pounds for "The Deserted Village." In considerable haste, he wrote the lives of several prominent figures, among them *The Life of Henry St. John, Lord Viscount Bolingbroke*, also published in 1770. The next year he published *The History of England from the Earliest Times to the Death of George II*. These projects were hasty and often inaccurate, but they found an audience and kept him alive.

In 1773 he managed to get *She Stoops to Conquer* accepted for the stage. This was no easy feat. He expected David Garrick to produce it, but Garrick was lukewarm and worried that the play might not appeal to an audience. At this time Garrick, like most of the theater-owners of the time, was producing sentimental plays that elicited a soap-opera-like response from the audience: weeping followed by false reassurances. Indeed, it was because of the craze for sentimental plays that Goldsmith fashioned *She Stoops to Conquer* as a kind of antidote. Eventually, Garrick gave the play to an assistant named Colman, who produced it even though he had little or no confidence in its success. Even the cast was difficult. Some actors refused their parts; others grumbled and complained. Nevertheless, the play ran for twelve days — a long run for the period — and Goldsmith earned more than five hundred pounds. On the tenth day was a performance by royal command: the king and queen attended and were delighted by the raucous comedy.

One year later, Goldsmith died from an untreated bladder infection. He is said to have relied on a useless patent medicine rather than seeking a doctor's advice. He died having achieved something that makes him unique in English literature: he is the author of a novel, poem, and play that have all withstood the test of time and are read with pleasure more than two hundred years after their original publication.

Goldsmith was known personally as a man with numerous quirks. He wrote with such ease that even Samuel Johnson expressed envy, but he spoke so poorly that some people thought he was simpleminded. He also envied the success of others, especially those of lesser talents. He was a heavy drinker, but he was also regarded as a good friend. When he died, James Boswell, Samuel Johnson's biographer, was reminded that Goldsmith was a very great man, whatever his faults. Goldsmith is buried in Westminster Abbey with an epitaph by Johnson.

SHE STOOPS TO CONQUER

The basis of the play, in which Hardcastle's home is mistaken for a country inn, is often considered preposterous on the ground that nothing of this sort could ever happen. However, Goldsmith recalled a time in his youth when he had some money in his pocket and decided, as he was traveling, to stay at an inn the way gentlemen did. At the time, he was around fifteen. He asked the advice of a local person who decided to play a trick by telling Goldsmith that Squire Featherstone's house was an inn. Goldsmith's manner was similar to that of Hastings and Marlow in the play; because he was such a young fellow behaving in such a high-minded manner, Featherstone decided to play along with the joke and boarded and fed him. Only later did Goldsmith discover the truth.

Of course, this is only one of the unlikely circumstances in the play. Critics have long pointed to the improbabilities as defects in the comedy, but for more than two centuries audiences have never worried about them and often have never noticed them. The fact that Mrs. Hardcastle wants her son Tony Lumpkin to marry his cousin Constance Neville just so that Miss Neville's inheritance of jewelry will stay in the family is one unlikely situation. Another is that Marlow is able to converse freely and openly with women of low station, especially women of pleasure, but that he cannot say a word to a "modest woman" without stuttering and stumbling. Most unlikely is the journey, in the fifth act, in which Tony Lumpkin takes his mother and Miss Neville on a ruinous ride around the country, through mud-holes and swamps, only to end up in his mother's garden — which she does not recognize, thinking she is forty miles away. The crowning touch, however, is Kate Hardcastle's awareness of Marlow's problem with women and her masquerade as a house maid — a result of her father's insistence that she dress simply in the evening — as a means of untying his tongue. He "makes love" to her without realizing who she is, then denies he has done so to her father and his own, only to discover, much to his shock, that the "house maid" who had grown so much in his estimation is the daughter of the house and therefore eligible for marriage. For her part, Kate Hardcastle delights in having found a man with experience and spirit, rather than "one of the most bashful and reserved young fellows in all the world."

The play is built on a foundation of misunderstandings, but it also depends on a system of contrasts that begins with the opening scene. Hardcastle prefers everything to be simple and old, while his family longs for change and fashion. The contrast of the refined city ways of Hastings and Marlow with the country ways of Squire Hardcastle and the extremely rural views of Tony Lumpkin offer innumerable opportunities for humor. And in typical fashion, the sparks from the town are deceived by the rural bumpkins, who end up having the upper hand.

The success of the play depends on these ingredients, but in performance the part of Tony Lumpkin has become one of the great jewels of the stage, almost on a par with Shakespeare's Sir John Falstaff. He has been played with astonishing success again and again since the play's first performances. The role is almost always played in a manner that lets the audience in on all the jokes. Tony Lumpkin is a comic figure for all time.

She Stoops to Conquer in Performance

Few of those involved with the first production in 1773 had much faith in its success. Goldsmith himself had not determined the final title of the play until the night of the first performance. He had intended to call it *The Old House, a New Inn*, but that did not please the producer. He then settled on the subtitle *The Mistakes of a Night* and only at the last minute came up with *She Stoops to Conquer*, which now seems the most appropriate title. The first production was, for its time, a considerable success. Twelve nights was a long run in 1773, and Goldsmith was warmed by the knowledge that the king had requested a royal performance for the tenth night.

Performances of *She Stoops to Conquer* have been especially plentiful in recent years, but it is probably safe to say that there has not been a decade since 1773 in which the play has not been produced somewhere in the English-speaking world. Among recent performances is the Abbey Theatre's production in Dublin in July 2003. The reviews cited a vigorous and comic production and a considerable success. The Pearl Theatre on St. Marks Place in New York City produced the play in 2002. In December of that same year, the National Theatre in London produced the play in the Lyttleton Theatre. Max Stafford-Clark, the legendary director of the Royal Court theater, produced the play with his Out of Joint theater company. One of the remarkable conjunctions was that the production was in repertory with April De Angelis' play, *A Laughing Matter*, using the same actors as those in Goldsmith's play and a cast of characters that included Samuel Johnson, Oliver Goldsmith, James Boswell, Edmund Burke, Joshua Reynolds, David Garrick, Peg Woffington, and many more figures from the period.

Numerous productions of the play have graced the stages of universities from MIT in Massachusetts to Simon Fraser University in Canada. The play works well enough to sustain itself in amateur as well as professional productions, and its humor, improbable or not, seems destined to remain current.

Oliver Goldsmith (1728–1774)

She Stoops to Conquer or the Mistakes of a Night

Dramatis Personæ

Men

Sir Charles Marlow
Young Marlow (*his Son*)
Hardcastle
Hastings
Tony Lumpkin
Diggory

Women

Mrs. Hardcastle
Miss Hardcastle
Miss Neville
Maid
Landlord, Servants &c., &c.

ACT I

Scene, A Chamber *in an old-fashioned* House

Enter Mrs. Hardcastle and Mr. Hardcastle

MRS. HARDCASTLE: I vow, Mr. Hardcastle, you're very particular. Is there a creature in the whole country, but ourselves, that does not take a trip to town now and then, to rub off the rust a little? There's the two Miss Hoggs, and our neighbour, Mrs. Grigsby, go to take a month's polishing every winter.

HARDCASTLE: Ay, and bring back vanity and affectation to last them the whole year. I wonder why London cannot keep its own fools at home. In my time, the follies of the town crept slowly among us, but now they travel faster than a stage-coach. Its fopperies come down, not only as inside passengers, but in the very basket.

MRS. HARDCASTLE: Ay, *your* times were fine times, indeed; you have been telling us of *them* for many a long year. Here we live in an old rumbling mansion, that looks for all the world like an inn, but that we never see company. Our best visitors are old Mrs. Oddfish, the curate's wife, and little Cripplegate, the lame dancing-master: And all our entertainment your old stories of Prince Eugene and the Duke of Marlborough. I hate such old-fashioned trumpery.

HARDCASTLE: And I love it. I love every thing that's old: old friends, old times, old manners, old books, old wine; and, I believe, Dorothy (*Taking her hand*) you'll own I have been pretty fond of an old wife.

MRS. HARDCASTLE: Lord, Mr. Hardcastle, you're for ever at your Dorothy's and your old wife's. You may be a Darby, but I'll be no Joan, I promise you. I'm not so old as you'd make me, by more than one good year. Add twenty to twenty, and make money of that.

HARDCASTLE: Let me see; twenty added to twenty, makes just fifty and seven.

MRS. HARDCASTLE: It's false, Mr. Hardcastle: I was but twenty when I was brought to bed of Tony, that I had by Mr. Lumpkin, my first husband; and he's not come to years of discretion yet.

HARDCASTLE: Nor ever will, I dare answer for him. Ay, you have taught *him* finely.

MRS. HARDCASTLE: No matter, Tony Lumpkin has a good fortune. My son is not to live by his learning. I don't think a boy wants much learning to spend fifteen hundred a year.

HARDCASTLE: Learning, quotha! A mere composition of tricks and mischief.

MRS. HARDCASTLE: Humour, my dear: nothing but humour. Come, Mr. Hardcastle, you must allow the boy a little humour.

HARDCASTLE: I'd sooner allow him an horse-pond. If burning the footmens shoes, frighting the maids, and worrying the kittens, be humour, he has it. It was but yesterday he fastened my wig to the back of my chair, and when I went to make bow, I popt my bald head in Mrs. Frizzle's face.

MRS. HARDCASTLE: And am I to blame? The poor boy was always too sickly to do any good. A school would be his death. When he comes to be a little stronger, who knows what a year or two's Latin may do for him?

HARDCASTLE: Latin for him! A cat and fiddle. No, no, the ale-house and the stable are the only schools he'll ever go to.

MRS. HARDCASTLE: Well, we must not snub the poor boy now, for I believe we shan't have him long among us. Any body that looks in his face may see he's consumptive.

HARDCASTLE: Ay, if growing too fat be one of the symptoms.

MRS. HARDCASTLE: He coughs sometimes.

HARDCASTLE: Yes, when his liquor goes the wrong way.

MRS. HARDCASTLE: I'm actually afraid of his lungs.

HARDCASTLE: And truly so am I; for he sometimes whoops like a speaking trumpet — (*Tony hallooing behind the Scenes*) — O there he goes — A very consumptive figure, truly.

Enter Tony, crossing the Stage

MRS. HARDCASTLE: Tony, where are you going, my charmer? Won't you give papa and I a little of your company, lovee?

TONY: I'm in haste, mother, I cannot stay.

MRS. HARDCASTLE: You shan't venture out this raw evening, my dear: You look most shockingly.

TONY: I can't stay, I tell you. The Three Pigeons expects me down every moment. There's some fun going forward.

HARDCASTLE: Ay; the ale-house, the old place: I thought so.

MRS. HARDCASTLE: A low, paltry set of fellows.

TONY: Not so low, neither. There's Dick Muggins the exciseman, Jack Slang the horse doctor, Little Aminadab that grinds the music box, and Tom Twist that spins the pewter platter.

MRS. HARDCASTLE: Pray, my dear, disappoint them for one night at least.

TONY: As for disappointing *them*, I should not much mind; but I can't abide to disappoint *myself*.

MRS. HARDCASTLE (*detaining him*): You shan't go.

TONY: I will, I tell you.

MRS. HARDCASTLE: I say you shan't.

TONY: We'll see which is strongest, you or I.

[*Exit, hauling her out.*

Hardcastle solus°

HARDCASTLE: Ay, there goes a pair that only spoil each other. But is not the whole age in a combination to drive sense and discretion out of doors? There's my pretty darling Kate; the fashions of the times have almost infected her too. By living a year or two in town, she is as fond of gauze, and French frippery, as the best of them.

Enter Miss Hardcastle

HARDCASTLE: Blessings on my pretty innocence! Drest out as usual, my Kate. Goodness! What a quantity of superfluous silk hast thou got about thee, girl! I could never teach the fools of this age, that the indigent world could be cloathed out of the trimmings of the vain.

MISS HARDCASTLE: You know our agreement, Sir. You allow me the morning to receive and pay visits, and to dress in my own manner; and in the evening, I put on my housewife's dress to please you.

HARDCASTLE: Well, remember, I insist on the terms of our agreement; and, by the bye, I believe I shall have occasion to try your obedience this very evening.

MISS HARDCASTLE: I protest, Sir, I don't comprehend your meaning.

HARDCASTLE: Then to be plain with you, Kate, I expect the young gentleman I have chosen to be your husband from town this very day. I have his father's letter, in which he informs me his son is set out, and that he intends to follow himself shortly after.

solus: Alone.

MISS HARDCASTLE: Indeed! I wish I had known something of this before. Bless me, how shall I behave? It's a thousand to one I shan't like him; our meeting will be so formal, and so like a thing of business, that I shall find no room for friendship or esteem.

HARDCASTLE: Depend upon it, child, I'll never controul your choice; but Mr. Marlow, whom I have pitched upon, is the son of my old friend, Sir Charles Marlow, of whom you have heard me talk so often. The young gentleman has been bred a scholar, and is designed for an employment in the service of his country. I am told he's a man of an excellent understanding.

MISS HARDCASTLE: Is he?

HARDCASTLE: Very generous.

MISS HARDCASTLE: I believe I shall like him.

HARDCASTLE: Young and brave.

MISS HARDCASTLE: I'm sure I shall like him.

HARDCASTLE: And very handsome.

MISS HARDCASTLE: My dear Papa, say no more (*Kissing his hand*) he's mine, I'll have him.

HARDCASTLE: And, to crown all, Kate, he's one of the most bashful and reserved young fellows in all the world.

MISS HARDCASTLE: Eh! you have frozen me to death again. That word, reserved, has undone all the rest of his accomplishments. A reserved lover, it is said, always makes a suspicious husband.

HARDCASTLE: On the contrary, modesty seldom resides in a breast that is not enriched with nobler virtues. It was the very feature in his character that first struck me.

MISS HARDCASTLE: He must have more striking features to catch me, I promise you. However, if he be so young, so handsome, and so every thing, as you mention, I believe he'll do still. I think I'll have him.

HARDCASTLE: Ay, Kate, but there is still an obstacle. It is more than an even wager, he may not have *you*.

MISS HARDCASTLE: My dear papa, why will you mortify one so? — Well, if he refuses, instead of breaking my heart at his indifference, I'll only break my glass for its flattery, Set my cap to some newer fashion, and look out for some less difficult admirer.

HARDCASTLE: Bravely resolved! In the mean time I'll go prepare the servants for his reception; as we seldom see company they want as much training as a company of recruits the first day's muster.   [*Exit.*

Miss Hardcastle sola°

MISS HARDCASTLE: Lud,° this news of Papa's puts me all in a flutter. Young, handsome; these he put last; but I put them foremost. Sensible, good-natured; I like all that. But then reserved, and sheepish, that's much against him. Yet can't he be cured of his timidity, by being taught to be proud of his wife? Yes, and can't I — But I vow I'm disposing of the husband, before I have secured the lover.

sola: Alone.   **Lud:** Lord.

Jane Wood as Mrs. Hardcastle in the 2002 Out of Joint production of *She Stoops to Conquer,* directed by Max Stafford–Clark, at the Lyttleton Theatre in London.

Enter Miss Neville

MISS HARDCASTLE: I'm glad you're come, Neville, my dear. Tell me, Constance, how do I look this evening? Is there any thing whimsical about me? Is it one of my well looking days, child? Am I in face to day?

MISS NEVILLE: Perfectly, my dear. Yet now I look again — bless me! — sure no accident has happened among the canary birds or the gold fishes. Has your brother or the cat been meddling? Or has the last novel been too moving?

MISS HARDCASTLE: No; nothing of all this. I have been threatened — I can scarce get it out — I have been threatened with a lover.

MISS NEVILLE: And his name ——

MISS HARDCASTLE: Is Marlow.

MISS NEVILLE: Indeed!

MISS HARDCASTLE: The son of Sir Charles Marlow.

MISS NEVILLE: As I live, the most intimate friend of Mr. Hastings, *my* admirer. They are never asunder. I believe you must have seen him when we lived in town.

MISS HARDCASTLE: Never.

MISS NEVILLE: He's a very singular character, I assure you. Among women of reputation and virtue, he is the modestest man alive; but his acquaintance give him a very different character among creatures of another stamp: you understand me?

MISS HARDCASTLE: An odd character, indeed. I shall never be able to manage him. What shall I do? Pshaw, think no more of him, but trust to occurrences for success. But how goes on your own affair my dear, has my mother been courting you for my brother Tony, as usual?

MISS NEVILLE: I have just come from one of our agreeable tête-à-têtes.° She has been saying a hundred tender things, and setting off her pretty monster as the very pink of perfection.

MISS HARDCASTLE: And her partiality is such, that she actually thinks him so. A fortune like your's is no small temptation. Besides, as she has the sole management of it, I'm not surprized to see her unwilling to let it go out of the family.

MISS NEVILLE: A fortune like mine, which chiefly consists in jewels, is no such mighty temptation. But at any rate if my dear Hastings be but constant, I make no doubt to be too hard for her at last. However, I let her suppose that I am in love with her son, and she never once dreams that my affections are fixed upon another.

MISS HARDCASTLE: My good brother holds out stoutly. I could almost love him for hating you so.

MISS NEVILLE: It is a good natured creature at bottom, and I'm sure would wish to see me married to any body but himself. But my aunt's bell rings for our afternoon's walk through the improvements. Allons. Courage is necessary, as our affairs are critical.

MISS HARDCASTLE: Would it were bed time and all were well.

[*Exeunt.*°

tête-à-têtes: Face-to-face conversations.
Exeunt: They leave. (Plural form of *exit.*)

Scene, An Alehouse Room. Several shabby fellows, with Punch and Tobacco. Tony at the head of the Table, a little higher than the rest: A mallet in his hand.

OMNES: Hurrea, hurrea, hurrea, bravo.
FIRST FELLOW: Now, gentlemen, silence for a song. The 'Squire is going to knock himself down for a song.
OMNES: Ay, a song, a song.
TONY: Then I'll sing you, gentlemen, a song I made upon this ale-house, the Three Pigeons.

SONG

Let school-masters puzzle their brain,
  With grammar, and nonsense, and learning;
Good liquor, I stoutly maintain,
  Gives genus *a better discerning.*
Let them brag of their Heathenish Gods,
  Their Lethes, their Styxes, and Stygians;
Their Quis, and their Quæs, and their Quods,°
  They're all but a parcel of Pigeons.
                    Toroddle, toroddle, toroll.

When Methodist preachers come down,
  A preaching that drinking is sinful,
I'll wager the rascals a crown,
  They always preach best with a skinful.
But when you come down with your pence,
  For a slice of their scurvy religion,
I'll leave it to all men of sense,
  But you, my good friend, are the pigeon.
                    Toroddle, toroddle, toroll.

Then come, put the jorum about,
  And let us be merry and clever,
Our hearts and our liquors are stout,
  Here's the Three Jolly Pigeons for ever.
Let some cry up woodcock or hare,
  Your bustards, your ducks, and your widgeons;
But of all the birds in the air,
  Here's a health to the Three Jolly Pigeons.
                    Toroddle, toroddle, toroll.

OMNES: Bravo, bravo.
FIRST FELLOW: The 'Squire has got spunk in him.
SECOND FELLOW: I loves to hear him sing, bekeays he never gives us nothing that's *low.*
THIRD FELLOW: O damn anything that's *low,* I cannot bear it.
FOURTH FELLOW: The genteel thing is the genteel thing at any time. If so be that a gentleman bees in a con-catenation accordingly.
THIRD FELLOW: I like the maxum of it, Master Muggins. What, tho' I am obliged to dance a bear, a man may be a gentleman for all that. May this be my poison if my bear ever dances but to the very genteelest of tunes. Water Parted, or the minuet in Ariadne.

SECOND FELLOW: What a pity it is the 'Squire is not come to his own. It would be well for all the publicans within ten miles round of him.
TONY: Ecod,° and so it would, Master Slang. I'd then show what it was to keep choice of company.
SECOND FELLOW: O, he takes after his own father for that. To be sure old 'Squire Lumpkin was the finest gentleman I ever set my eyes on. For winding the streight horn, or beating a thicket for a hare, or a wench he never had his fellow. It was a saying in the place, that he kept the best horses, dogs, and girls in the whole county.
TONY: Ecod, and when I'm of age I'll be no bastard I promise you. I have been thinking of Bett Bouncer and the miller's grey mare to begin with. But come, my boys, drink about and be merry, for you pay no reckoning. Well Stingo, what's the matter?

Enter Landlord

LANDLORD: There be two gentlemen in a post-chaise at the door. They have lost their way upo' the forest; and they are talking something about Mr. Hardcastle.
TONY: As sure as can be one of them must be the gentleman that's coming down to court my sister. Do they seem to be Londoners?
LANDLORD: I believe they may. They look woundily like Frenchmen.
TONY: Then desire them to step this way, and I'll set them right in a twinkling. (*Exit Landlord.*) Gentleman as they mayn't be good enough company for you, step down for a moment, and I'll be with you in the squeezing of a lemon.
                                    [*Exeunt Mob.*

Tony solus

TONY: Father-in-law has been calling me whelp, and hound, this half year. Now, if I pleased, I could be so revenged upon the old grumbletonian. But then I'm afraid — afraid of what! I shall soon be worth fifteen hundred a year, and let him frighten me out of that if he can.

Enter Landlord, conducting Marlow and Hastings

MARLOW: What a tedious uncomfortable day have we had of it! We were told it was but forty miles across the country, and we have come above threescore.
HASTINGS: And all Marlow, from that unaccountable reserve of yours, that would not let us enquire more frequently on the way.
MARLOW: I own, Hastings, I am unwilling to lay myself under an obligation to every one I meet: and often, stand the chance of an unmannerly answer.
HASTINGS: At present, however, we are not likely to receive any answer.
TONY: No offence, gentlemen. But I'm told you have been enquiring for one Mr. Hardcastle, in these parts. Do you know what part of the country you are in?

Quis . . . Quods: Latin; this, that, and those.

Ecod: Ye gods.

HASTINGS: Not in the least Sir, but should thank you for information.

TONY: Nor the way you came?

HASTINGS: No, Sir; but if you can inform us ——

TONY: Why, gentlemen, if you know neither the road you are going, nor where you are, nor the road you came, the first thing I have to inform is, that — You have lost your way.

MARLOW: We wanted no ghost to tell us that.

TONY: Pray, gentlemen, may I be so bold as to ask the place from whence you came?

MARLOW: That's not necessary towards directing us where we are to go.

TONY: No offence; but question for question is all fair, you know. Pray, gentlemen, is not this same Hardcastle a cross-grain'd, old-fashion'd, whimsical fellow with an ugly face, a daughter, and a pretty son?

HASTINGS: We have not seen the gentleman, but he has the family you mention.

TONY: The daughter, a tall trapesing, trolloping, talkative maypole —— The son, a pretty, well-bred, agreeable youth, that every body is fond of.

MARLOW: Our information differs in this. The daughter is said to be well-bred and beautiful; the son, an aukward booby, reared up, and spoiled at his mother's apron-string.

TONY: He-he-hem — Then, gentlemen, all I have to tell you is, that you won't reach Mr. Hardcastle's house this night, I believe.

HASTINGS: Unfortunate!

TONY: It's a damn'd long, dark, boggy, dirty, dangerous way. Stingo, tell the gentlemen the way to Mr. Hardcastle's; (*Winking upon the Landlord*) Mr. Hardcastle's, of Quagmire Marsh, you understand me.

LANDLORD: Master Hardcastle's! Lock-a-daisy, my masters, you're come a deadly deal wrong! When you came to the bottom of the hill, you should have cross'd down Squash-lane.

MARLOW: Cross down Squash-lane!

LANDLORD: Then you were to keep streight forward, 'till you came to four roads.

MARLOW: Come to where four roads meet!

TONY: Ay; but you must be sure to take only one of them.

MARLOW: O Sir, you're facetious.

TONY: Then keeping to the right, you are to go sideways till you come upon Crack-skull common: there you must look sharp for the track of the wheel, and go forward, 'till you come to farmer Murrain's barn. Coming to the farmer's barn, you are to turn to the right, and then to the left, and then to the right about again, till you find out the old mill ——

MARLOW: Zounds, man! we could as soon find out the longitude!°

HASTINGS: What's to be done, Marlow?

MARLOW: This house promises but a poor reception; though, perhaps the Landlord can accommodate us.

longitude: An unsolved problem at the time the play was first produced.

LANDLORD: Alack master, we have but one spare bed in the whole house.

TONY: And to my knowledge, that's taken up by three lodgers already. (*After a pause, in which the rest seem disconcerted*) I have hit it. Don't you think, Stingo, our landlady could accommodate the gentlemen by the fire-side, with —— three chairs and a bolster?

HASTINGS: I hate sleeping by the fire-side.

MARLOW: And I detest your three chairs and a bolster.

TONY: You do, do you? — then let me see — what — if you go on a mile further, to the Buck's Head; the old Buck's Head on the hill, one of the best inns in the whole county?

HASTINGS: Oho! so we have escaped an adventure for this night, however.

LANDLORD (*apart to Tony*): Sure, you ben't sending them to your father's as an inn, be you?

TONY: Mum, you fool you. Let *them* find that out. (*To them*) You have only to keep on streight forward, till you come to a large old house by the road side. You'll see a pair of large horns over the door. That's the sign. Drive up the yard, and call stoutly about you.

HASTINGS: Sir, we are obliged to you. The servants can't miss the way?

TONY: No, no: But I tell you though, the landlord is rich, and going to leave off business; so he wants to be thought a Gentleman, saving your presence, he! he! he! He'll be for giving you his company, and ecod if you mind him, he'll persuade you that his mother was an alderman, and his aunt a justice of the peace.

LANDLORD: A troublesome old blade to be sure; but a keeps as good wines and beds as any in the whole country.

MARLOW: Well, if he supplies us with these, we shall want no further connexion. We are to turn to the right, did you say?

TONY: No, no; streight forward. I'll just step myself, and shew you a piece of the way. (*To the landlord*) Mum.

LANDLORD: Ah, bless your heart, for a sweet, pleasant —— damn'd mischievous son of a whore.

[*Exeunt.*

ACT II

SCENE, *An old-fashioned* HOUSE

Enter Hardcastle, followed by three or four awkward Servants

HARDCASTLE: Well, I hope you're perfect in the table exercise I have been teaching you these three days. You all know your posts and your places, and can shew that you have been used to good company, without ever stirring from home.

OMNES: Ay, ay.

HARDCASTLE: When company comes, you are not to pop out and stare, and then run in again, like frighted rabbits in a warren.

OMNES: No, no.

HARDCASTLE: You, Diggory, whom I have taken from the barn, are to make a shew at the side-table; and you, Roger, whom I have advanced from the plough, are to place yourself behind *my* chair. But you're not to stand so, with your hands in your pockets. Take your hands from your pockets, Roger; and from your head, you blockhead you. See how Diggory carries his hands. They're a little too stiff, indeed, but that's no great matter.

DIGGORY: Ay, mind how I hold them. I learned to hold my hands this way, when I was upon drill for the militia. And so being upon drill ——

HARDCASTLE: You must not be so talkative, Diggory. You must be all attention to the guests. You must hear us talk, and not think of talking; you must see us drink, and not think of drinking; you must see us eat, and not think of eating.

DIGGORY: By the laws, your worship, that's perfectly unpossible. Whenever Diggory sees yeating going forward, ecod he's always wishing for a mouthful himself.

HARDCASTLE: Blockhead! Is not a belly-full in the kitchen as good as a belly-full in the parlour? Stay your stomach with that reflection.

DIGGORY: Ecod I thank your worship, I'll make a shift to stay my stomach with a slice of cold beef in the pantry.

HARDCASTLE: Diggory, you are too talkative. Then if I happen to say a good thing, or tell a good story at table, you must not all burst out a-laughing, as if you made part of the company.

DIGGORY: Then ecod your worship must not tell the story of Ould Grouse in the gun-room: I can't help laughing at that — he! he! he! — for the soul of me. We have laughed at that these twenty years — ha! ha! ha!

HARDCASTLE: Ha! ha! ha! The story is a good one. Well, honest Diggory, you may laugh at that — but still remember to be attentive. Suppose one of the company should call for a glass of wine, how will you behave? A glass of wine, Sir, if you please (*to* Diggory) — Eh, why don't you move?

DIGGORY: Ecod, your worship, I never have courage till I see the eatables and drinkables brought upo' the table, and then I'm as bauld as a lion.

HARDCASTLE: What, will no body move?

FIRST SERVANT: I'm not to leave this pleace.

SECOND SERVANT: I'm sure it's no pleace of mine.

THIRD SERVANT: Nor mine, for sartain.

DIGGORY: Wauns, and I'm sure it canna be mine.

HARDCASTLE: You numbskulls! and so while, like your betters, you are quarrelling for places, the guests must be starved. O you dunces! I find I must begin all over again. — But don't I hear a coach drive into the yard? To your posts you blockheads. I'll go in the mean time and give my old friend's son a hearty reception at the gate.

[*Exit Hardcastle.*

DIGGORY: By the elevens, my pleace is gone quite out of my head.

ROGER: I know that my pleace is to be every where.

FIRST SERVANT: Where the devil is mine?

SECOND SERVANT: My pleace is to be no where at all; and so Ize go about my business.

[*Exeunt Servants, running about as if frighted, different ways.*

Enter Servants with Candles, shewing in Marlow and Hastings

SERVANT: Welcome, gentlemen, very welcome. This way.

HASTINGS: After the disappointments of the day, welcome once more, Charles, to the comforts of a clean room and a good fire. Upon my word, a very well-looking house; antique but creditable.

MARLOW: The usual fate of a large mansion. Having first ruined the master by good housekeeping, it at last comes to levy contributions as an inn.

HASTINGS: As you say, we passengers are to be taxed to pay all these fineries. I have often seen a good side-board, or a marble chimney-piece, tho' not actually put in the bill, enflame a reckoning confoundedly.

MARLOW: Travellers, George, must pay in all places. The only difference is, that in good inns, you pay dearly for luxuries; in bad inns, you are fleeced and starved.

HASTINGS: You have lived pretty much among them. In truth, I have been often surprized, that you who have seen so much of the world, with your natural good sense, and your many opportunities, could never yet acquire a requisite share of assurance.

MARLOW: The Englishman's malady. But tell me, George, where could I have learned that assurance you talk of? My life has been chiefly spent in a college, or an inn, in seclusion from that lovely part of the creation that chiefly teach men confidence. I don't know that I was ever familiarly acquainted with a single modest woman — except my mother — But among females of another class you know —

HASTINGS: Ay, among them you are impudent enough of all conscience.

MARLOW: They are of *us*, you know.

HASTINGS: But in the company of women of reputation I never saw such an ideot, such a trembler; you look for all the world as if you wanted an opportunity of stealing out of the room.

MARLOW: Why man that's because I *do* want to steal out of the room. Faith, I have often formed a resolution to break the ice, and rattle away at any rate. But I don't know how, a single glance from a pair of fine eyes has totally overset my resolution. An impudent fellow may counterfeit modesty, but I'll be hanged if a modest man can ever counterfeit impudence.

HASTINGS: If you could but say half the fine things to them that I have heard you lavish upon the bar-maid of an inn, or even a college bed-maker —

MARLOW: Why, George, I can't say fine things to them. They freeze, they petrify me. They may talk of a comet, or a burning mountain, or some such bagatelle. But to me, a modest woman, drest out in all her finery, is the most tremendous object of the whole creation.

HASTINGS: Ha! ha! ha! At this rate, man, how can you ever expect to marry!

MARLOW: Never, unless as among kings and princes, my bride were to be courted by proxy. If, indeed, like an Eastern bridegroom, one were to be introduced to a wife he never saw before, it might be endured. But to go through all the terrors of a formal courtship, together with the episode of aunts, grandmothers and cousins, and at last to blurt out the broad staring question, of, *madam will you marry me?* No, no, that's a strain much above me I assure you.

HASTINGS: I pity you. But how do you intend behaving to the lady you are come down to visit at the request of your father?

MARLOW: As I behave to all other ladies. Bow very low. Answer yes, or no, to all her demands — But for the rest, I don't think I shall venture to look in her face, till I see my father's again.

HASTINGS: I'm surprized that one who is so warm a friend can be so cool a lover.

MARLOW: To be explicit, my dear Hastings, my chief inducement down was to be instrumental in forwarding your happiness, not my own. Miss Neville loves you, the family don't know you, as my friend you are sure of a reception, and let honour do the rest.

HASTINGS: My dear Marlow! But I'll suppress the emotion. Were I a wretch, meanly seeking to carry off a fortune, you should be the last man in the world I would apply to for assistance. But Miss Neville's person is all I ask, and that is mine, both from her deceased father's consent, and her own inclination.

MARLOW: Happy man! You have talents and art to captivate any woman. I'm doom'd to adore the sex, and yet to converse with the only part of it I despise. This stammer in my address, and this aukward prepossessing visage of mine, can never permit me to soar above the reach of a milliner's 'prentice, or one of the dutchesses of Drury-lane. Pshaw! this fellow here to interrupt us.

Enter Hardcastle

HARDCASTLE: Gentlemen, once more you are heartily welcome. Which is Mr. Marlow? Sir, you're heartily welcome. It's not my way, you see, to receive my friends with my back to the fire. I like to give them a hearty reception in the old stile at my gate. I like to see their horses and trunks taken care of.

MARLOW (*aside*): He has got our names from the servants already. (*To Him.*) We approve your caution and hospitality, Sir. (*To Hastings.*) I have been thinking, George, of changing our travelling dresses in the morning. I am grown confoundedly ashamed of mine.

HARDCASTLE: I beg, Mr. Marlow, you'll use no ceremony in this house.

HASTINGS: I fancy, George, you're right: the first blow is half the battle. I intend opening the campaign with the white and gold.

HARDCASTLE: Mr. Marlow — Mr. Hastings — gentlemen — pray be under no constraint in this house. This is Liberty-hall, gentlemen. You may do just as you please here.

MARLOW: Yet, George, if we open the campaign too fiercely at first, we may want ammunition before it is over. I think to reserve the embroidery to secure a retreat.

HARDCASTLE: Your talking of a retreat, Mr. Marlow, puts me in mind of the Duke of Marlborough, when we went to besiege Denain. He first summoned the garrison.

MARLOW: Don't you think the *ventre dor*° waistcoat will do with the plain brown?

HARDCASTLE: He first summoned the garrison, which might consist of about five thousand men ——

HASTINGS: I think not: Brown and yellow mix but very poorly.

HARDCASTLE: I say, gentlemen, as I was telling you, he summoned the garrison, which might consist of about five thousand men ——

MARLOW: The girls like finery.

HARDCASTLE: Which might consist of about five thousand men, well appointed with stores, ammunition, and other implements of war. Now, says the Duke of Marlborough to George Brooks, that stood next to him — You must have heard of George Brooks; I'll pawn my Dukedom, says he, but I take that garrison without spilling a drop of blood. So ——

MARLOW: What, my good friend, if you gave us a glass of punch in the mean time, it would help us to carry on the siege with vigour.

HARDCASTLE: Punch, Sir! (*Aside*) This is the most unaccountable kind of modesty I ever met with.

MARLOW: Yes, Sir, Punch. A glass of warm punch, after our journey, will be comfortable. This is Liberty-Hall, you know.

HARDCASTLE: Here's Cup, Sir.

MARLOW (*aside*): So this fellow, in his Liberty-hall, will only let us have just what he pleases.

HARDCASTLE (*taking the Cup*): I hope you'll find it to your mind. I have prepared it with my own hands, and I believe you'll own the ingredients are tolerable. Will you be so good as to pledge me, Sir? Here, Mr. Marlow, here is our better acquaintance.   [*drinks.*

MARLOW (*aside*): A very impudent fellow this! but he's a character, and I'll humour him a little. Sir, my service to you.   [*drinks.*

HASTINGS (*aside*): I see this fellow wants to give us his company, and forgets that he's an innkeeper, before he has learned to be a gentleman.

MARLOW: From the excellence of your cup, my old friend, I suppose you have a good deal of business in this part of the country. Warm work, now and then, at elections, I suppose.

---

ventre dor: Gold stomach.

HARDCASTLE: No, Sir, I have long given that work over. Since our betters have hit upon the expedient of electing each other, there's no business *for us that sell ale.*

HASTINGS: So, then you have no turn for politics, I find.

HARDCASTLE: Not in the least. There was a time, indeed, I fretted myself about the mistakes of government, like other people; but finding myself every day grow more angry, and the government growing no better, I left it to mend itself. Since that, I no more trouble my head about *Heyder Ally, Ally Cawn,* than about *Ally Croaker.°* Sir, my service to you.

HASTINGS: So that with eating above stairs, and drinking below, with receiving your friends within, and amusing them without, you lead a good pleasant bustling life of it.

HARDCASTLE: I do stir about a great deal, it's certain. Half the differences of the parish are adjusted in this very parlour.

MARLOW (*after drinking*): And you have an argument in your cup, old gentleman, better than any in Westminster-hall.

HARDCASTLE: Ay, young gentleman, that, and a little philosophy.

MARLOW (*aside*): Well, this is the first time I ever heard of an innkeeper's philosophy.

HASTINGS: So then, like an experienced general, you attack them on every quarter. If you find their reason manageable, you attack it with your philosophy; if you find they have no reason, you attack them with this. Here's your health, my philosopher. (*drinks*)

HARDCASTLE: Good, very good, thank you; ha, ha. Your Generalship puts me in mind of Prince Eugene, when he fought the Turks at the battle of Belgrade. You shall hear.

MARLOW: Instead of the battle of Belgrade, I believe it's almost time to talk about supper. What has your philosophy got in the house for supper?

HARDCASTLE: For supper, Sir! (*Aside*) Was ever such a request to a man in his own house!

MARLOW: Yes, Sir, supper, Sir; I begin to feel an appetite. I shall make devilish work to-night in the larder, I promise you.

HARDCASTLE (*aside*): Such a brazen dog sure never my eyes beheld. (*To him*) Why really, Sir, as for supper I can't well tell. My Dorothy, and the cook maid, settle these things between them. I leave these kind of things entirely to them.

MARLOW: You do, do you?

HARDCASTLE: Entirely. By-the-bye, I believe they are in actual consultation upon what's for supper this moment in the kitchen.

MARLOW: Then I beg they'll admit *me* as one of their privy council. It's a way I have got. When I travel, I always chuse to regulate my own supper. Let the cook be called. No offence I hope, Sir.

Heyder . . . Croaker: Heyder Ali and Ali Khan were Indian potentates. "Ally Croaker" is an Irish song that ends with "oh, the inconstant Ally Croaker / Oh, the inconstant Ally, Ally Croaker."

HARDCASTLE: O no, Sir, none in the least; yet, I don't know how: our Bridget, the cook maid, is not very communicative upon these occasions. Should we send for her, she might scold us all out of the house.

HASTINGS: Let's see your list of the larder then. I ask it as a favour. I always match my appetite to my bill of fare.

MARLOW (*to Hardcastle, who looks at them with surprise*): Sir, he's very right, and it's my way too.

HARDCASTLE: Sir, you have a right to command here. Here, Roger, bring us the bill of fare for to night's supper. I believe it's drawn out. Your manner, Mr. Hastings, puts me in mind of my uncle, Colonel Wallop. It was a saying of his, that no man was sure of his supper till he had eaten it.

HASTINGS (*aside*): All upon the high ropes! His uncle a Colonel! We shall soon hear of his mother being a justice of peace. But let's hear the bill of fare.

MARLOW (*perusing*): What's here? For the first course; for the second course; for the desert. The devil, Sir, do you think we have brought down the whole Joiners Company, or the Corporation of Bedford, to eat up such a supper? Two or three little things, clean and comfortable, will do.

HASTINGS: But, let's hear it.

MARLOW (*reading*): For the first course at the top, a pig, and pruin sauce.

HASTINGS: Damn your pig, I say.

MARLOW: And damn your pruin sauce, say I.

HARDCASTLE: And yet, gentlemen, to men that are hungry, pig, with pruin sauce is very good eating.

MARLOW: At the bottom, a calve's tongue and brains.

HASTINGS: Let your brains be knock'd out, my good Sir; I don't like them.

MARLOW: Or you may clap them on a plate by themselves. I do.

HARDCASTLE (*aside*): Their impudence confounds me. (*To them*) Gentlemen, you are my guests, make what alterations you please. Is there any thing else you wish to retrench or alter, gentlemen?

MARLOW: Item. A pork pie, a boiled rabbet and sausages, a florentine, a shaking pudding, and a dish of tiff — taff — taffety cream!

HASTINGS: Confound your made dishes, I shall be as much at a loss in this house as at a green and yellow dinner at the French ambassador's table. I'm for plain eating.

HARDCASTLE: I'm sorry, gentlemen, that I have nothing you like, but if there be any thing you have a particular fancy to ——

MARLOW: Why, really, Sir, your bill of fare is so exquisite, that any one part of it is full as good as another. Send us what you please. So much for supper. And now to see that our beds are air'd, and properly taken care of.

HARDCASTLE: I entreat you'll leave all that to me. You shall not stir a step.

MARLOW: Leave that to you! I protest, Sir, you must excuse me, I always look to these things myself.

HARDCASTLE: I must insist, Sir, you'll make yourself easy on that head.

MARLOW: You see I'm resolved on it. (*Aside*) A very troublesome fellow this, as ever I met with.

HARDCASTLE: Well, Sir, I'm resolved at least to attend you. (*Aside*) This may be modern modesty, but I never saw any thing look so like old-fashioned impudence.
[*Exeunt Marlow and Hardcastle.*

Hastings solus

HASTINGS: So I find this fellow's civilities begin to grow troublesome. But who can be angry at those assiduities which are meant to please him. Ha! what do I see? Miss Neville, by all that's happy!

Enter Miss Neville

MISS NEVILLE: My dear Hastings! To what unexpected good fortune? to what accident am I to ascribe this happy meeting?

HASTINGS: Rather let me ask the same question, as I could never have hoped to meet my dearest Constance at an inn.

MISS NEVILLE: An inn! sure you mistake! my aunt, my guardian, lives here. What could induce you to think this house an inn?

HASTINGS: My friend Mr. Marlow, with whom I came down, and I, have been sent here as to an inn, I assure you. A young fellow whom we accidentally met at a house hard by directed us hither.

MISS NEVILLE: Certainly it must be one of my hopeful cousin's tricks, of whom you have heard me talk so often, ha! ha! ha! ha!

HASTINGS: He whom your aunt intends for you? He of whom I have such just apprehensions?

MISS NEVILLE: You have nothing to fear from him, I assure you. You'd adore him if you knew how heartily he despises me. My aunt knows it too, and has undertaken to court me for him, and actually begins to think she has made a conquest.

HASTINGS: Thou dear dissembler! You must know, my Constance, I have just seized this happy opportunity of my friend's visit here to get admittance into the family. The horses that carried us down are now fatigued with their journey, but they'll soon be refreshed; and then if my dearest girl will trust in her faithful Hastings, we shall soon be landed in France, where even among slaves the laws of marriage are respected.

MISS NEVILLE: I have often told you, that though ready to obey you, I yet should leave my little fortune behind with reluctance. The greatest part of it was left me by my uncle, the India Director, and chiefly consists in jewels. I have been for some time persuading my aunt to let me wear them. I fancy I'm very near succeeding. The instant they are put into my possession you shall find me ready to make them and myself yours.

HASTINGS: Perish the baubles! Your person is all I desire. In the meantime, my friend Marlow must not be let into his mistake. I know the strange reserve of his temper is such, that if abruptly informed of it, he would instantly quit the house before our plan was ripe for execution.

MISS NEVILLE: But how shall we keep him in the deception? Miss Hardcastle is just returned from walking; what if we still continue to deceive him? — This, this way ——
[*They confer.*

Enter Marlow

MARLOW: The assiduities of these good people tease me beyond bearing. My host seems to think it ill manners to leave me alone, and so he claps not only himself, but his old-fashioned wife on my back. They talk of coming to sup with us too; and then, I suppose, we are to run the gauntlet thro' all the rest of the family. — What have we got here! —

HASTINGS: My dear Charles! Let me congratulate you! — The most fortunate accident! — Who do you think is just alighted?

MARLOW: Cannot guess.

HASTINGS: Our mistresses, boy, Miss Hardcastle and Miss Neville. Give me leave to introduce Miss Constance Neville to your acquaintance. Happening to dine in the neighbourhood, they called, on their return to take fresh horses, here. Miss Hardcastle has just stept into the next room, and will be back in an instant. Wasn't it lucky? eh!

MARLOW (*aside*): I have just been mortified enough of all conscience, and here comes something to complete my embarrassment.

HASTINGS: Well! but wasn't it the most fortunate thing in the world?

MARLOW: Oh! yes. Very fortunate — a most joyful encounter —— But our dresses, George, you know, are in disorder —— What if we should postpone the happiness 'till to-morrow? —— To-morrow at her own house —— It will be every bit as convenient —— And rather more respectful —— To-morrow let it be. [*offering to go.*]

MISS NEVILLE: By no means, Sir. Your ceremony will displease her. The disorder of your dress will shew the ardour of your impatience. Besides, she knows you are in the house, and will permit you to see her.

MARLOW: O! the devil! how shall I support it? Hem! hem! Hastings, you must not go. You are to assist me, you know. I shall be confoundedly ridiculous. Yet, hang it! I'll take courage. Hem!

HASTINGS: Pshaw man! it's but the first plunge, and all's over. She's but a woman, you know.

MARLOW: And of all women, she that I dread most to encounter!

Enter Miss Hardcastle as returned from walking, a Bonnet, &c.

HASTINGS (*introducing them*): Miss Hardcastle, Mr. Marlow, I'm proud of bringing two persons of such merit together, that only want to know, to esteem each other.

MISS HARDCASTLE (*aside*): Now, for meeting my modest gentleman with a demure face, and quite in his own manner. (*After a pause, in which he appears very uneasy and disconcerted*) I'm glad of your safe arrival, Sir —— I'm told you had some accidents by the way.

MARLOW: Only a few, madam. Yes, we had some. Yes, Madam, a good many accidents, but should be sorry — Madam — or rather glad of any accidents — that are so agreeably concluded. Hem!

HASTINGS (*to him*): You never spoke better in your whole life. Keep it up, and I'll insure you the victory.

MISS HARDCASTLE: I'm afraid you flatter, Sir. You that have seen so much of the finest company can find little entertainment in an obscure corner of the country.

MARLOW (*gathering courage*): I have lived, indeed, in the world, Madam; but I have kept very little company. I have been but an observer upon life, Madam, while others were enjoying it.

MISS NEVILLE: But that, I am told, is the way to enjoy it at last.

HASTINGS (*to him*): Cicero never spoke better. Once more, and you are confirm'd in assurance for ever.

MARLOW (*to him*): Hem! Stand by me then, and when I'm down, throw in a word or two to set me up again.

MISS HARDCASTLE: An observer, like you, upon life, were, I fear, disagreeably employed, since you must have had much more to censure than to approve.

MARLOW: Pardon me, Madam. I was always willing to be amused. The folly of most people is rather an object of mirth than uneasiness.

HASTINGS (*to him*): Bravo, bravo. Never spoke so well in your whole life. Well, Miss Hardcastle, I see that you and Mr. Marlow are going to be very good company. I believe our being here will but embarrass the interview.

MARLOW: Not in the least, Mr. Hastings. We like your company of all things. (*To him*) Zounds! George, sure you won't go? How can you leave us?

HASTINGS: Our presence will but spoil conversation, so we'll retire to the next room. (*To him*) You don't consider, man, that we are to manage a little tête-à-tête of our own.

[*Exeunt.*

MISS HARDCASTLE (*after a pause*): But you have not been wholly an observer, I presume, Sir: The ladies I should hope have employed some part of your addresses.

MARLOW (*relapsing into timidity*): Pardon me, Madam, I — I — I — as yet have studied — only — to — deserve them.

MISS HARDCASTLE: And that some say is the very worst way to obtain them.

MARLOW: Perhaps so, madam. But I love to converse only with the more grave and sensible part of the sex. —— But I'm afraid I grow tiresome.

MISS HARDCASTLE: Not at all Sir; there is nothing I like so much as grave conversation myself; I could hear it for ever. Indeed I have often been surprized how a man of *sentiment* could ever admire those light airy pleasures, where nothing reaches the heart.

MARLOW: It's — a — disease — of the mind, madam. In the variety of tastes there must be some who, wanting a relish for — um — a — um.

MISS HARDCASTLE: I understand you, Sir. There must be some, who wanting a relish for refined pleasures, pretend to despise what they are incapable of tasting.

MARLOW: My meaning, madam, but infinitely better expressed. And I can't help observing — a ——

MISS HARDCASTLE (*aside*): Who could ever suppose this fellow impudent upon some occasions. (*To him*) You were going to observe, Sir ——

MARLOW: I was observing, madam —— I protest, madam, I forget what I was going to observe.

MISS HARDCASTLE (*aside*): I vow and so do I. (*To him*) You were observing, Sir, that in this age of hypocrisy — something about hypocrisy, Sir.

MARLOW: Yes, madam. In this age of hypocrisy there are few who upon strict enquiry do not — a — a — a ——

MISS HARDCASTLE: I understand you perfectly, Sir.

MARLOW (*aside*): Egad! and that's more than I do myself.

MISS HARDCASTLE: You mean that in this hypocritical age there are few that do not condemn in public what they practise in private, and think they pay every debt to virtue when they praise it.

MARLOW: True, madam; those who have most virtue in their mouths, have least of it in their bosoms. But I'm sure I tire you, madam.

MISS HARDCASTLE: Not in the least, Sir; there's something so agreeable and spirited in your manner, such life and force —— pray, Sir, go on.

MARLOW: Yes, madam. I was saying —— that there are some occasions —— when a total want of courage, madam, destroys all the —— and puts us —— upon a —— a —— a ——

MISS HARDCASTLE: I agree with you entirely, a want of courage upon some occasions assumes the appearance of ignorance, and betrays us when we most want to excel. I beg you'll proceed.

MARLOW: Yes, madam. Morally speaking, madam —— But I see Miss Neville expecting us in the next room. I would not intrude for the world.

MISS HARDCASTLE: I protest, Sir, I never was more agreeably entertained in all my life. Pray go on.

MARLOW: Yes, madam. I was —— But she beckons us to join her. Madam, shall I do myself the honour to attend you?

MISS HARDCASTLE: Well then, I'll follow.

MARLOW (*aside*): This pretty, smooth dialogue has done for me.   [*Exit.*

Miss Hardcastle sola

MISS HARDCASTLE: Ha! ha! ha! Was there ever such a sober sentimental interview? I'm certain he scarce look'd in my face the whole time. Yet the fellow, but for his unaccountable bashfulness, is pretty well too.

He has good sense, but then so buried in his fears, that it fatigues one more than ignorance. If I could teach him a little confidence, it would be doing somebody that I know of a piece of service. But who is that somebody? — that, faith, is a question I can scarce answer.

[*Exit.*

Enter Tony and Miss Neville, followed by Mrs. Hardcastle and Hastings

TONY: What do you follow me for, cousin Con? I wonder you're not ashamed to be so very engaging.

MISS NEVILLE: I hope, cousin, one may speak to one's own relations, and not be to blame.

TONY: Ay, but I know what sort of a relation you want to make me though; but it won't do. I tell you, cousin Con, it won't do, so I beg you'll keep your distance, I want no nearer relationship.

[*She follows coqueting him to the back scene.*

MRS. HARDCASTLE: Well! I vow, Mr. Hastings, you are very entertaining. There's nothing in the world I love to talk of so much as London, and the fashions, though I was never there myself.

HASTINGS: Never there! You amaze me! From your air and manner, I concluded you had been bred all your life either at Ranelagh, St. James's, or Tower Wharf.

MRS. HARDCASTLE: O! Sir, you're only pleased to say so. We Country persons can have no manner at all. I'm in love with the town, and that serves to raise me above some of our neighbouring rustics; but who can have a manner, that has never seen the Pantheon, the Grotto Gardens, the Borough, and such places where the Nobility chiefly resort? All I can do, is to enjoy London at second-hand. I take care to know every tête-à-tête from the Scandalous Magazine, and have all the fashions as they come out, in a letter from the two Miss Rickets of Crooked-lane. Pray how do you like this head, Mr. Hastings?

HASTINGS: Extremely elegant and degagée,° upon my word, Madam. Your Friseur is a Frenchman, I suppose?

MRS. HARDCASTLE: I protest I dressed it myself from a print in the Ladies Memorandum-book for the last year.

HASTINGS: Indeed. Such a head in a side-box, at the Playhouse, would draw as many gazers as my Lady May'ress at a City Ball.

MRS. HARDCASTLE: I vow, since inoculation began, there is no such thing to be seen as a plain woman; so one must dress a little particular or one may escape in the crowd.

HASTINGS: But that can never be your case, Madam, in any dress. (*Bowing*)

MRS. HARDCASTLE: Yet, what signifies *my* dressing when I have such a piece of antiquity by my side as Mr. Hardcastle: all I can say will never argue down a single button from his cloaths. I have often wanted

degagée: Free and easy.

him to throw off his great flaxen wig, and where he was bald, to plaister it over like my Lord Pately, with powder.

HASTINGS: You are right, Madam; for, as among the ladies there are none ugly, so among the men there are none old.

MRS. HARDCASTLE: But what do you think his answer was? Why, with his usual Gothic vivacity, he said I only wanted him to throw off his wig to convert it into a tête for my own wearing.

HASTINGS: Intolerable! At your age you may wear what you please, and it must become you.

MRS. HARDCASTLE: Pray, Mr. Hastings, what do you take to be the most fashionable age about town?

HASTINGS: Some time ago, forty was all the mode; but I'm told the ladies intend to bring up fifty for the ensuing winter.

MRS. HARDCASTLE: Seriously. Then I shall be too young for the fashion.

HASTINGS: No lady begins now to put on jewels till she's past forty. For instance, Miss there, in a polite circle, would be considered as a child, as a mere maker of samplers.

MRS. HARDCASTLE: And yet Mrs. Niece thinks herself as much a woman, and is as fond of jewels as the oldest of us all.

HASTINGS: Your niece, is she? And that young gentleman, a brother of yours, I should presume?

MRS. HARDCASTLE: My son, Sir. They are contracted to each other. Observe their little sports. They fall in and out ten times a day, as if they were man and wife already. (*To them*) Well Tony, child, what soft things are you saying to your cousin Constance this evening?

TONY: I have been saying no soft things; but that it's very hard to be followed about so. Ecod! I've not a place in the house now that's left to myself but the stable.

MRS. HARDCASTLE: Never mind him, Con, my dear. He's in another story behind your back.

MISS NEVILLE: There's something generous in my cousin's manner. He falls out before faces to be forgiven in private.

TONY: That's a damned confounded —— crack.

MRS. HARDCASTLE: Ah! he's a sly one. Don't you think they're like each other about the mouth, Mr. Hastings? The Blenkinsop mouth to a T. They're of a size too. Back to back, my pretties, that Mr. Hastings may see you. Come Tony.

TONY: You had as good not make me, I tell you.

(*Measuring.*)

MISS NEVILLE: O lud! he has almost cracked my head.

MRS. HARDCASTLE: O the monster! For shame, Tony. You a man, and behave so!

TONY: If I'm a man, let me have my fortin. Ecod! I'll not be made a fool of no longer.

MRS. HARDCASTLE: Is this, ungrateful boy, all that I'm to get for the pains I have taken in your education? I that have rock'd you in your cradle, and fed that pretty mouth with a spoon! Did not I work that waistcoat to make you genteel? Did not I prescribe for you every day, and weep while the receipt was operating?

TONY: Ecod! you had reason to weep, for you have been dosing me ever since I was born. I have gone through every receipt in the complete huswife ten times over; and you have thoughts of coursing me through *Quincy°* next spring. But, Ecod! I tell you, I'll not be made a fool of no longer.

MRS. HARDCASTLE: Wasn't it all for your good, viper? Wasn't it all for your good?

TONY: I wish you'd let me and my good alone then. Snubbing this way when I'm in spirits. If I'm to have any good, let it come of itself; not to keep dinging it, dinging it into one so.

MRS. HARDCASTLE: That's false; I never see you when you're in spirits. No, Tony, you then go to the alehouse or kennel. I'm never to be delighted with your agreeable, wild notes, unfeeling monster!

TONY: Ecod! Mamma, your own notes are the wildest of the two.

MRS. HARDCASTLE: Was ever the like? But I see he wants to break my heart, I see he does.

HASTINGS: Dear Madam, permit me to lecture the young gentleman a little. I'm certain I can persuade him to his duty.

MRS. HARDCASTLE: Well! I must retire. Come, Constance, my love. You see, Mr. Hastings, the wretchedness of my situation: Was ever poor woman so plagued with a dear, sweet, pretty, provoking, undutiful boy.

[*Exeunt Mrs. Hardcastle and Miss Neville.*

HASTINGS, TONY

TONY (*singing*): *There was a young man riding by, and fain would have his will. Rang do didlo dee.* Don't mind her. Let her cry. It's the comfort of her heart. I have seen her and sister cry over a book for an hour together, and they said, they liked the book the better the more it made them cry.

HASTINGS: Then you're no friend to the ladies, I find, my pretty young gentleman?

TONY: That's as find 'um.

HASTINGS: Not to her of your mother's chusing, I dare answer? And yet she appears to me a pretty well-tempered girl.

TONY: That's because you don't know her as well as I. Ecod! I know every inch about her; and there's not a more bitter cantanckerous toad in all Christendom.

HASTINGS (*aside*): Pretty encouragement this for a lover!

TONY: I have seen her since the height of that. She has as many tricks as a hare in a thicket, or a colt the first day's breaking.

HASTINGS: To me she appears sensible and silent!

TONY: Ay, before company. But when she's with her playmates she's as loud as a hog in a gate.

Quincy: Author of *Pharmacopaeia,* a book of medical remedies.

HASTINGS: But there is a meek modesty about her that charms me.

TONY: Yes, but curb her never so little, she kicks up, and you're flung in a ditch.

HASTINGS: Well, but you must allow her a little beauty. — Yes, you must allow her some beauty.

TONY: Bandbox! She's all a made up thing, mun. Ah! could you but see Bet Bouncer of these parts, you might then talk of beauty. Ecod, she has two eyes as black as sloes, and cheeks as broad and red as a pulpit cushion. She'd make two of she.

HASTINGS: Well, what say you to a friend that would take this bitter bargain off your hands?

TONY: Anon?

HASTINGS: Would you thank him that would take Miss Neville and leave you to happiness and your dear Betsy?

TONY: Ay; but where is there such a friend, for who would take *her*?

HASTINGS: I am he. If you but assist me, I'll engage to whip her off to France, and you shall never hear more of her.

TONY: Assist you! Ecod I will, to the last drop of my blood. I'll clap a pair of horses to your chaise that shall trundle you off in a twinkling, and may be get you a part of her fortin beside, in jewels, that you little dream of.

HASTINGS: My dear squire, this looks like a lad of spirit.

TONY: Come along then, and you shall see more of my spirit before you have done with me. (*Singing*) *We are the boys that fears no noise where the thundering cannons roar.*

[*Exeunt.*

ACT III

Enter Hardcastle solus

HARDCASTLE: What could my old friend Sir Charles mean by recommending his son as the modestest young man in town? To me he appears the most impudent piece of brass that ever spoke with a tongue. He has taken possession of the easy chair by the fire-side already. He took off his boots in the parlour, and desired me to see them taken care of. I'm desirous to know how his impudence affects my daughter. — She will certainly be shocked at it.

Enter Miss Hardcastle, plainly dress'd

HARDCASTLE: Well, my Kate, I see you have changed your dress as I bid you; and yet, I believe, there was no great occasion.

MISS HARDCASTLE: I find such a pleasure, Sir, in obeying your commands, that I take care to observe them without ever debating their propriety.

HARDCASTLE: And yet, Kate, I sometimes give you some cause, particularly when I recommended my *modest* gentleman to you as a lover to-day.

MISS HARDCASTLE: You taught me to expect something extraordinary, and I find the original exceeds the description.

HARDCASTLE: I was never so surprized in my life! He has quite confounded all my faculties!

MISS HARDCASTLE: I never saw any thing like it: And a man of the world, too!

HARDCASTLE: Ay, he learned it all abroad, — what a fool was I, to think a young man could learn modesty by travelling. He might as soon learn wit at a masquerade.

MISS HARDCASTLE: It seems all natural to him.

HARDCASTLE: A good deal assisted by bad company and a French dancing-master.

MISS HARDCASTLE: Sure you mistake, papa! a French dancing-master could never have taught him that timid look, — that aukward address, — that bashful manner ——

HARDCASTLE: Whose look? whose manner? child!

MISS HARDCASTLE: Mr. Marlow's: his meauvaise honte, his timidity struck me at the first sight.

HARDCASTLE: Then your first sight deceived you; for I think him one of the most brazen first sights that ever astonished my senses.

MISS HARDCASTLE: Sure, Sir, you rally! I never saw any one so modest.

HARDCASTLE: And can you be serious! I never saw such a bouncing swaggering puppy since I was born. Bully Dawson was but a fool to him.

MISS HARDCASTLE: Surprizing! He met me with a respectful bow, a stammering voice, and a look fixed on the ground.

HARDCASTLE: He met me with a loud voice, a lordly air, and a familiarity that made my blood freeze again.

MISS HARDCASTLE: He treated me with diffidence and respect; censured the manners of the age; admired the prudence of girls that never laughed; tired me with apologies for being tiresome; then left the room with a bow, and, madam, I would not for the world detain you.

HARDCASTLE: He spoke to me as if he knew me all his life before. Asked twenty questions, and never waited for an answer. Interrupted my best remarks with some silly pun, and when I was in my best story of the Duke of Marlborough and Prince Eugene, he asked if I had not a good hand at making punch. Yes, Kate, he ask'd your father if he was a maker of punch!

MISS HARDCASTLE: One of us must certainly be mistaken.

HARDCASTLE: If he be what he has shewn himself, I'm determined he shall never have my consent.

MISS HARDCASTLE: And if he be the sullen thing I take him, he shall never have mine.

HARDCASTLE: In one thing then we are agreed — to reject him.

MISS HARDCASTLE: Yes. But upon conditions. For if you should find him less impudent, and I more presuming; if you find him more respectful, and I more importunate — I don't know — the fellow is well enough for a man — Certainly we don't meet many such at a horse race in the country.

HARDCASTLE: If we should find him so —— But that's impossible. The first appearance has done my business. I'm seldom deceived in that.

MISS HARDCASTLE: And yet there may be many good qualities under that first appearance.

HARDCASTLE: Ay, when a girl finds a fellow's outside to her taste, she then sets about guessing the rest of his furniture. With her, a smooth face stands for good sense, and a genteel figure for every virtue.

MISS HARDCASTLE: I hope, Sir, a conversation begun with a compliment to my good sense won't end with a sneer at my understanding?

HARDCASTLE: Pardon me, Kate. But if young Mr. Brazen can find the art of reconciling contradictions, he may please us both, perhaps.

MISS HARDCASTLE: And as one of us must be mistaken, what if we go to make further discoveries?

HARDCASTLE: Agreed. But depend on't I'm in the right.

MISS HARDCASTLE: And depend on't I'm not much in the wrong.   [*Exeunt.*

Enter Tony running in with a Casket

TONY: Ecod! I have got them. Here they are. My Cousin Con's necklaces, bobs and all. My mother shan't cheat the poor souls out of their fortune neither. O! my genus, is that you?

Enter Hastings

HASTINGS: My dear friend, how have you managed with your mother? I hope you have amused her with pretending love for your cousin, and that you are willing to be reconciled at last? Our horses will be refreshed in a short time, and we shall soon be ready to set off.

TONY: And here's something to bear your charges by the way. (*Giving the casket*) Your sweetheart's jewels. Keep them, and hang those, I say, that would rob you of one of them.

HASTINGS: But how have you procured them from your mother?

TONY: Ask me no questions, and I'll tell you no fibs. I procured them by the rule of thumb. If I had not a key to every drawer in mother's bureau, how could I go to the ale-house so often as I do? An honest man may rob himself of his own at any time.

HASTINGS: Thousands do it every day. But to be plain with you; Miss Neville is endeavouring to procure them from her aunt this very instant. If she succeeds, it will be the most delicate way at least of obtaining them.

TONY: Well, keep them, till you know how it will be. But I know how it will be well enough, she'd as soon part with the only sound tooth in her head.

HASTINGS: But I dread the effects of her resentment, when she finds she has lost them.

TONY: Never you mind her resentment, leave *me* to manage that. I don't value her resentment the bounce of a cracker. Zounds! here they are. Morrice, Prance.   [*Exit Hastings.*

Miriam Margolyes as Mrs. Hardcastle and David Essex as Tony Lumpkin in director Peter Hall's 1993 production of *She Stoops to Conquer* at the Queen's Theatre in London.

Tony, Mrs. Hardcastle, Miss Neville

MRS. HARDCASTLE: Indeed, Constance, you amaze me. such a girl as you want jewels? It will be time enough for jewels, my dear, twenty years hence, when your beauty begins to want repairs.

MISS NEVILLE: But what will repair beauty at forty, will certainly improve it at twenty, Madam.

MRS. HARDCASTLE: Yours, my dear, can admit of none. That natural blush is beyond a thousand ornaments. Besides, child, jewels are quite out at present. Don't you see half the ladies of our acquaintance, my lady Killdaylight, and Mrs. Crump, and the rest of them, carry their jewels to town, and bring nothing but Paste and Marcasites back?

MISS NEVILLE: But who knows, Madam, but somebody that shall be nameless would like me best with all my little finery about me?

MRS. HARDCASTLE: Consult your glass, my dear, and then see, if with such a pair of eyes, you want any better sparklers. What do you think, Tony, my dear, does your cousin Con want any jewels, in your eyes, to set off her beauty?

TONY: That's as thereafter may be.

MISS NEVILLE: My dear aunt, if you knew how it would oblige me.

MRS. HARDCASTLE: A parcel of old-fashioned rose and table-cut things. They would make you look like the court of king Solomon at a puppet-shew. Besides, I believe I can't readily come at them. They may be missing, for aught I know to the contrary.

TONY (*apart to Mrs. Hardcastle*): Then why don't you tell her so at once, as she's so longing for them. Tell her they're lost. It's the only way to quiet her. Say they're lost, and call me to bear witness.

MRS. HARDCASTLE (*apart to Tony*): You know, my dear, I'm only keeping them for you. So if say I they're gone, you'll bear me witness, will you? He! he! he!

TONY: Never fear me. Ecod! I'll say I saw them taken out with my own eyes.

MISS NEVILLE: I desire them but for a day, Madam. Just to be permitted to shew them as relicks, and then they may be lock'd up again.

MRS. HARDCASTLE: To be plain with you, my dear Constance; if I could find them, you should have them. They're missing, I assure you. Lost, for aught I know; but we must have patience wherever they are.

MISS NEVILLE: I'll not believe it; this is but a shallow pretence to deny me. I know they're too valuable to be so slightly kopt, and as you are to answer for the loss.

MRS. HARDCASTLE: Don't be alarm'd, Constance. If they be lost, I must restore an equivalent. But my son knows they are missing, and not to be found.

TONY: That I can bear witness to. They are missing, and not to be found, I'll take my oath on't.

MRS. HARDCASTLE: You must learn resignation, my dear; for tho' we lose our fortune, yet we should not lose our patience. See me, how calm I am.

MISS NEVILLE: Ay, people are generally calm at the misfortunes of others.

MRS. HARDCASTLE: Now, I wonder a girl of your good sense should waste a thought upon such trumpery. We shall soon find them; and, in the mean time, you shall make use of my garnets till your jewels be found.

MISS NEVILLE: I detest garnets.

MRS. HARDCASTLE: The most becoming things in the world to set off a clear complexion. You have often seen how well they look upon me. You *shall* have them.   [*Exit.*

MISS NEVILLE: I dislike them of all things. You shan't stir. — Was ever any thing so provoking to mislay my own jewels, and force me to wear her trumpery.

TONY: Don't be a fool. If she gives you the garnets, take what you can get. The jewels are your own already. I have stolen them out of her bureau, and she does not know it. Fly to your spark, he'll tell you more of the matter. Leave me to manage *her*.

MISS NEVILLE: My dear cousin.

TONY: Vanish. She's here, and has missed them already. Zounds! how she fidgets and spits about like a Catharine wheel.

Enter Mrs. Hardcastle

MRS. HARDCASTLE: Confusion! thieves! robbers! We are cheated, plundered, broke open, undone.

TONY: What's the matter, what's the matter, mamma? I hope nothing has happened to any of the good family!

MRS. HARDCASTLE: We are robbed. My bureau has been broke open, the jewels taken out, and I'm undone.

TONY: Oh! is that all? Ha, ha, ha. By the laws, I never saw it better acted in my life. Ecod, I thought you was ruin'd in earnest, ha, ha, ha.

MRS. HARDCASTLE: Why, boy, I *am* ruined in earnest. My bureau has been broke open, and all taken away.

TONY: Stick to that; ha, ha, ha; stick to that. I'll bear witness, you know, call me to bear witness.

MRS. HARDCASTLE: I tell you, Tony, by all that's precious, the jewels are gone, and I shall be ruin'd for ever.

TONY: Sure I know they're gone, and I am to say so.

MRS. HARDCASTLE: My dearest Tony, but hear me. They're gone, I say.

TONY: By the laws, mamma, you make me for to laugh, ha, ha. I know who took them well enough, ha, ha, ha.

MRS. HARDCASTLE: Was there ever such a blockhead, that can't tell the difference between jest and earnest. I tell you I'm not in jest, booby.

TONY: That's right, that's right: You must be in a bitter passion, and then nobody will suspect either of us. I'll bear witness that they are gone.

MRS. HARDCASTLE: Was there ever such a cross-grain'd brute, that won't hear me! Can you bear witness that you're no better than a fool? Was ever poor woman so beset with fools on one hand, and thieves on the other!

TONY: I can bear witness to that.

MRS. HARDCASTLE: Bear witness again, you blockhead, you, and I'll turn you out of the room directly. My poor niece, what will become of *her*! Do you laugh, you unfeeling brute, as if you enjoy'd my distress?

TONY: I can bear witness to that.

MRS. HARDCASTLE: Do you insult me, monster? I'll teach you to vex your mother, I will.

TONY: I can bear witness to that.

[*He runs off, she follows him.*

Enter Miss Hardcastle and Maid

MISS HARDCASTLE: What an unaccountable creature is that brother of mine, to send them to the house as an inn, ha, ha. I don't wonder at his impudence.

MAID: But what is more, madam, the young gentleman as you passed by in your present dress, ask'd me if you were the bar maid? He mistook you for the bar maid, madam.

MISS HARDCASTLE: Did he? Then as I live I'm resolved to keep up the delusion. Tell me, Pimple, how do you like my present dress? Don't you think I look something like Cherry° in the Beaux Stratagem?

MAID: It's the dress, madam, that every lady wears in the country, but when she visits or receives company.

MISS HARDCASTLE: And are you sure he does not remember my face or person?

MAID: Certain of it.

MISS HARDCASTLE: I vow I thought so; for though we spoke for some time together, yet his fears were such, that he never once looked up during the interview. Indeed, if he had, my bonnet would have kept him from seeing me.

MAID: But what do you hope from keeping him in his mistake?

MISS HARDCASTLE: In the first place, I shall be *seen*, and that is no small advantage to a girl who brings her face to market. Then I shall perhaps make an acquaintance, and that's no small victory gained over one who never addresses any but the wildest of her sex. But my chief aim is to take my gentleman off his guard, and like an invisible champion of romance examine the giant's force before I offer to combat.

MAID: But you are sure you can act your part, and disguise your voice, so that he may mistake that, as he has already mistaken your person?

MISS HARDCASTLE: Never fear me. I think I have got the true bar cant. — Did your honour call? —— Attend the Lion there. —— Pipes and tobacco for the Angel. — The Lamb has been outrageous this half hour.

MAID: It will do, madam. But he's here.

[*Exit Maid.*

Enter Marlow

MARLOW: What a bawling in every part of the house; I have scarce a moment's repose. If I go to the best room, there I find my host and his story. If I fly to the gallery, there we have my hostess with her curtesy down to the ground. I have at last got a moment to myself, and now for recollection. [*Walks and muses.*

MISS HARDCASTLE: Did you call, Sir? did your honour call?

MARLOW (*musing*): As for Miss Hardcastle, she's too grave and sentimental for me.

MISS HARDCASTLE: Did your honour call?

[*She still places herself before him, he turning away.*

Cherry: The landlord's daughter in George Farquhar's *Beaux' Stratagem* (1707), a favorite Restoration comedy.

MARLOW: No, child. (*Musing*) Besides from the glimpse I had of her, I think she squints.

MISS HARDCASTLE: I'm sure, Sir, I heard the bell ring.

MARLOW: No. no. (*Musing*) I have pleased my father, however, by coming down, and I'll to-morrow please myself by returning.

[*Taking out his tablets, and perusing.*

MISS HARDCASTLE: Perhaps the other gentleman called, Sir?

MARLOW: I tell you, no.

MISS HARDCASTLE: I should be glad to know, Sir. We have such a parcel of servants.

MARLOW: No, no, I tell you. (*Looks full in her face*) Yes, child, I think I did call. I wanted —— I wanted —— I vow, child, you are vastly handsome!

MISS HARDCASTLE: O la, Sir, you'll make one asham'd.

MARLOW: Never saw a more sprightly malicious eye. Yes, yes, my dear, I did call. Have you got any of your — a — what d'ye call it in the house?

MISS HARDCASTLE: No, Sir, we have been out of that these ten days.

MARLOW: One may call in this house, I find, to very little purpose. Suppose I should call for a taste, just by way of trial, of the nectar of your lips; perhaps I might be disappointed in that too.

MISS HARDCASTLE: Nectar! nectar! that's a liquor there's no call for in these parts. French, I suppose. We keep no French wines here, Sir.

MARLOW: Of true English growth, I assure you.

MISS HARDCASTLE: Then it's odd I should not know it. We brew all sorts of wines in this house, and I have lived here these eighteen years.

MARLOW: Eighteen years! Why one would think, child, you kept the bar before you were born. How old are you?

MISS HARDCASTLE: O! Sir, I must not tell my age. They say women and music should never be dated.

MARLOW: To guess at this distance, you can't be much above forty. (*Approaching*) Yet nearer I don't think so much. (*Approaching*) By coming close to some women they look younger still; but when we come very close indeed. (*Attempting to kiss her*)

MISS HARDCASTLE: Pray, Sir, keep your distance. One would think you wanted to know one's age as they do horses, by mark of mouth.

MARLOW: I protest, child, you use me extremely ill. If you keep me at this distance, how is it possible you and I can be ever acquainted?

MISS HARDCASTLE: And who wants to be acquainted with you? I want no such acquaintance, not I. I'm sure you did not treat Miss Hardcastle that was here awhile ago in this obstropalous manner. I'll warrant me, before her you look'd dash'd, and kept bowing to the ground, and talk'd, for all the world, as if you was before a justice of peace.

MARLOW (*aside*): Egad! she has hit it, sure enough. (*To her*) In awe of her, child? Ha! ha! ha! A mere, aukward, squinting thing, no, no. I find you don't know

me. I laugh'd, and rallied her a little; but I was unwilling to be too severe. No, I could not be too severe, *curse me*!

MISS HARDCASTLE: O! then, Sir, you are a favourite, I find, among the ladies?

MARLOW: Yes, my dear, a great favourite. And yet, hang me, I don't see what they find in me to follow. At the Ladies Club in town I'm called their agreeable Rattle. Rattle, child, is not my real name, but one I'm known by. My name is Solomons. Mr. Solomons, my dear, at your service. (*Offering to salute her*)

MISS HARDCASTLE: Hold, sir; you were introducing me to your club, not to yourself. And you're so great a favourite there you say?

MARLOW: Yes, my dear. There's Mrs. Mantrap, Lady Betty Blackleg, the Countess of Sligo, Mrs. Langhorns, old Miss Biddy Buckskin, and your humble servant, keep up the spirit of the place.

MISS HARDCASTLE: Then it's a very merry place, I suppose.

MARLOW: Yes, as merry as cards, suppers, wine, and old women can make us.

MISS HARDCASTLE: And their agreeable Rattle, ha! ha! ha!

MARLOW (*aside*): Egad! I don't quite like this chit. She looks knowing, methinks. You laugh, child!

MISS HARDCASTLE: I can't but laugh to think what time they all have for minding their work or their family.

MARLOW (*aside*): All's well, she don't laugh at me. (*To her*) Do *you* ever work, child?

MISS HARDCASTLE: Ay, sure. There's not a screen or a quilt in the whole house but what can bear witness to that.

MARLOW: Odso! Then you must shew me your embroidery. I embroider and draw patterns myself a little. If you want a judge of your work you must apply to me.   [*Seizing her hand.*

MISS HARDCASTLE: Ay, but the colours don't look well by candle light. You shall see all in the morning.

[*Struggling.*

MARLOW: And why not now, my angel? Such beauty fires beyond the power of resistance. —— Pshaw! the father here! My old luck: I never nick'd seven that I did not throw ames ace three times following.

[*Exit Marlow.*

Enter Hardcastle, who stands in surprize

HARDCASTLE: So, madam! So I find *this* is your *modest* lover. This is your humble admirer that kept his eyes fixed on the ground, and only ador'd at humble distance. Kate, Kate, art thou not asham'd to deceive your father so?

MISS HARDCASTLE: Never trust me, dear papa, but he's still the modest man I first took him for, you'll be convinced of it as well as I.

HARDCASTLE: By the hand of my body, I believe his impudence is infectious! Didn't I see him seize your hand? Didn't I see him hawl you about like a milk maid? and now you talk of his respect and his modesty, forsooth!

MISS HARDCASTLE: But if I shortly convince you of his modesty, that he has only the faults that will pass off with time, and the virtues that will improve with age, I hope you'll forgive him.

HARDCASTLE: The girl would actually make one run mad! I tell you I'll not be convinced. I am convinced. He has scarcely been three hours in the house, and he has already encroached on all my prerogatives. You may like his impudence, and call it modesty. But my son-in-law, madam, must have very different qualifications.

MISS HARDCASTLE: Sir, I ask but this night to convince you.

HARDCASTLE: You shall not have half the time, for I have thoughts of turning him out this very hour.

MISS HARDCASTLE: Give me that hour then, and I hope to satisfy you.

HARDCASTLE: Well, an hour let it be then. But I'll have no trifling with your father. All fair and open, do you mind me?

MISS HARDCASTLE: I hope, Sir, you have ever found that I considered your commands as my pride; for your kindness is such, that my duty as yet has been inclination.   [*Exeunt.*

ACT IV

Enter Hastings and Miss Neville

HASTINGS: You surprise me! Sir Charles Marlow expected here this night? Where have you had your information?

MISS NEVILLE: You may depend upon it. I just saw his letter to Mr. Hardcastle, in which he tells him he intends setting out a few hours after his son.

HASTINGS: Then, my Constance, all must be completed before he arrives. He knows me; and should he find me here, would discover my name, and perhaps my designs, to the rest of the family.

MISS NEVILLE: The jewels, I hope, are safe.

HASTINGS: Yes, yes. I have sent them to Marlow, who keeps the keys of our baggage. In the meantime, I'll go to prepare matters for our elopement. I have had the Squire's promise of a fresh pair of horses; and, if I should not see him again, will write him further directions.   [*Exit.*

MISS NEVILLE: Well! success attend you. In the meantime, I'll go amuse my aunt with the old pretence of a violent passion for my cousin. ——   [*Exit.*

Enter Marlow, followed by a Servant

MARLOW: I wonder what Hastings could mean by sending me so valuable a thing as a casket to keep for him, when he knows the only place I have is the seat of a post-coach at an Inn-door. Have you deposited the casket with the landlady, as I ordered you? Have you put it into her own hands?

SERVANT: Yes, your honour.

MARLOW: She said she'd keep it safe, did she?

SERVANT: Yes, she said she'd keep it safe enough; she asked me how I came by it? and she said she had a great mind to make me give an account of myself.
                                                    [*Exit Servant.*

MARLOW: Ha! ha! ha! They're safe however. What an unaccountable set of beings have we got amongst! This little bar-maid though runs in my head most strangely, and drives out the absurdities of all the rest of the family. She's mine, she must be mine, or I'm greatly mistaken.

Enter Hastings

HASTINGS: Bless me! I quite forgot to tell her that I intended to prepare at the bottom of the garden. Marlow here, and in spirits too!

MARLOW: Give me joy, George! Crown me, shadow me with laurels! Well, George, after all, we modest fellows don't want for success among the women.

HASTINGS: Some women you mean. But what success has your honour's modesty been crowned with now, that it grows so insolent upon us?

MARLOW: Didn't you see the tempting, brisk, lovely little thing that runs about the house with a bunch of keys to its girdle?

HASTINGS: Well! and what then?

MARLOW: She's mine, you rogue you. Such fire, such motion, such eyes, such lips —— but egad! she would not let me kiss them though.

HASTINGS: But are you sure, so very sure of her?

MARLOW: Why man, she talk'd of shewing me her work above-stairs, and I am to improve the pattern.

HASTINGS: But how can *you*, Charles, go about to rob a woman of her honour?

MARLOW: Pshaw! pshaw! we all know the honour of the bar-maid of an inn. I don't intend to *rob* her, take my word for it, there's nothing in this house, I shan't honestly *pay* for.

HASTINGS: I believe the girl has virtue.

MARLOW: And if she has, I should be the last man in the world that would attempt to corrupt it.

HASTINGS: You have taken care, I hope, of the casket I sent you to lock up? It's in safety?

MARLOW: Yes, yes. It's safe enough. I have taken care of it. But how could you think the seat of a post-coach at an Inn-door a place of safety? Ah! numbskull! I have taken better precautions for you than you did for yourself. —— I have ——

HASTINGS: What!

MARLOW: I have sent it to the landlady to keep for you.

HASTINGS: To the landlady!

MARLOW: The landlady.

HASTINGS: You did.

MARLOW: I did. She's to be answerable for its forthcoming, you know.

HASTINGS: Yes, she'll bring it forth with a witness.

MARLOW: Wasn't I right? I believe you'll allow that I acted prudently upon this occasion?

HASTINGS (*aside*): He must not see my uneasiness.

MARLOW: You seem a little disconcerted though, methinks. Sure nothing has happened?

HASTINGS: No, nothing. Never was I in better spirits in all my life. And so you left it with the landlady, who, no doubt, very readily undertook the charge?

MARLOW: Rather too readily. For she not only kept the casket; but, thro' her great precaution, was going to keep the messenger too. Ha! ha! ha!

HASTINGS: He! he! he! They're safe however.

MARLOW: As a guinea in a miser's purse.

HASTINGS (*aside*): So now all hopes of fortune are at an end, and we must set off without it. (*To him*) Well, Charles, I'll leave you to your meditations on the pretty bar-maid, and, he! he! he! may you be as successful for yourself as you have been for me.   [*Exit.*

MARLOW: Thank ye, George! I ask no more. Ha! ha! ha!

Enter Hardcastle

HARDCASTLE: I no longer know my own house. It's turned all topsey-turvey. His servants have got drunk already. I'll bear it no longer, and yet, from my respect for his father, I'll be calm. (*To him*) Mr. Marlow, your servant. I'm your very humble servant. (*Bowing low*)

MARLOW: Sir, your humble servant. (*Aside*) What's to be the wonder now?

HARDCASTLE: I believe, Sir, you must be sensible, Sir, that no man alive ought to be more welcome than your father's son, Sir. I hope you think so?

MARLOW: I do, from my soul, Sir. I don't want much intreaty. I generally make my father's son welcome wherever he goes.

HARDCASTLE: I believe you do, from my soul, Sir. But tho' I say nothing to your own conduct, that of your Servants is insufferable. Their manner of drinking is setting a very bad example in this house, I assure you.

MARLOW: I protest, my very good Sir, that's no fault of mine. If they don't drink as they ought *they* are to blame. I ordered them not to spare the cellar. I did, I assure you. (*To the side scene*) Here, let one of my servants come up. (*To him*) My positive directions were, that as I did not drink myself, they should make up for my deficiencies below.

HARDCASTLE: Then they had your orders for what they do! I'm satisfied!

MARLOW: They had, I assure [you]. You shall hear from one of themselves.

Enter Servant, drunk

MARLOW: You, Jeremy! Come forward, sirrah! What were my orders? Were you not told to drink freely, and call for what you thought fit, for the good of the house?

HARDCASTLE (*aside*): I begin to lose my patience.

JEREMY: Please your honour, liberty and Fleet-street for ever! Tho' I'm but a servant, I'm as good as another man. I'll drink for no man before supper, Sir, dammy! Good liquor will sit upon a good supper, but a good supper will not sit upon —— hiccup —— upon my conscience, Sir.

MARLOW: You see, my old friend, the fellow is as drunk as he can possibly be. I don't know what you'd have more, unless you'd have the poor devil soused in a beer-barrel.

HARDCASTLE: Zounds! He'll drive me distracted if I contain myself any longer. Mr. Marlow. Sir; I have submitted to your insolence for more than four hours, and I see no likelihood of its coming to an end. I'm now resolved to be master here, Sir, and I desire that you and your drunken pack may leave my house directly.

MARLOW: Leave your house! — Sure, you jest, my good friend! What, when I'm doing what I can to please you.

HARDCASTLE: I tell you, Sir, you don't please me; so I desire you'll leave my house.

MARLOW: Sure, you cannot be serious! At this time o'night, and such a night. You only mean to banter me?

HARDCASTLE: I tell you, Sir, I'm serious; and, now that my passions are rouzed, I say this house is mine, Sir; this house is mine, and I command you to leave it directly.

MARLOW: Ha! ha! ha! A puddle in a storm. I shan't stir a step, I assure you. (*In a serious tone*) This your house, fellow! It's my house. This is my house. Mine, while I chuse to stay. What right have you to bid me leave this house, Sir? I never met with such impudence, curse me, never in my whole life before.

HARDCASTLE: Nor I, confound me if ever I did. To come to my house, to call for what he likes, to turn me out of my own chair, to insult the family, to order his servants to get drunk, and then to tell me *This house is mine, Sir.* By all that's impudent, it makes me laugh. Ha! ha! ha! Pray, Sir, (*Bantering*) as you take the house, what think you of taking the rest of the furniture? There's a pair of silver candlesticks, and there's a fire-screen, and here's a pair of brazen nosed bellows, perhaps you may take a fancy to them?

MARLOW: Bring me your bill, Sir, bring me your bill, and let's make no more words about it.

HARDCASTLE: There are a set of prints too. What think you of the rake's progress for your own apartment?

MARLOW: Bring me your bill, I say; and I'll leave you and your infernal house directly.

HARDCASTLE: Then there's a mahogany table, that you may see your own face in.

MARLOW: My bill, I say.

HARDCASTLE: I had forgot the great chair, for your own particular slumbers, after a hearty meal.

MARLOW: Zounds! bring me my bill, I say, and let's hear no more on't.

HARDCASTLE: Young man, young man, from your father's letter to me, I was taught to expect a well-bred modest man, as a visitor here, but now I find him no better than a coxcomb and a bully; but he will be down here presently, and shall hear more of it. [*Exit.*

MARLOW: How's this! Sure, I have not mistaken the house! Every thing looks like an inn. The servants cry, coming. The attendance is aukward; the bar-maid too to attend us. But she's here, and will further inform me. Whither so fast, child. A word with you.

Enter Miss Hardcastle

MISS HARDCASTLE: Let it be short, then. I'm in a hurry. (*Aside*) (I believe he begins to find out his mistake, but it's too soon quite to undeceive him.)

MARLOW: Pray, child, answer me one question. What are you, and what may your business in this house be?

MISS HARDCASTLE: A relation of the family, Sir.

MARLOW: What. A poor relation?

MISS HARDCASTLE: Yes, Sir. A poor relation appointed to keep the keys, and to see that the guests want nothing in my power to give them.

MARLOW: That is, you act as the bar-maid of this inn.

MISS HARDCASTLE: Inn. O law — What brought that in your head. One of the best families in the county keep an inn. Ha, ha, ha, old Mr. Hardcastle's house an inn.

MARLOW: Mr. Hardcastle's house! Is this house Mr. Hardcastle's house, child!

MISS HARDCASTLE: Ay, sure. Whose else should it be.

MARLOW: So then all's out, and I have been damnably imposed on. O, confound my stupid head, I shall be laugh'd at over the whole town. I shall be stuck up in caricatura in all the print-shops. The Dullissimo Maccaroni. To mistake this house of all others for an inn, and my father's old friend for an inn-keeper. What a swaggering puppy must he take me for. What a silly puppy do I find myself. There again, may I be hang'd, my dear, but I mistook you for the bar-maid.

MISS HARDCASTLE: Dear me! dear me! I'm sure there's nothing in my *behaviour* to put me upon a level with one of that stamp.

MARLOW: Nothing, my dear, nothing. But I was in for a list of blunders, and could not help making you a subscriber. My stupidity saw every thing the wrong way. I mistook your assiduity for assurance, and your simplicity for allurement. But its over — This house I no more shew *my* face in!

MISS HARDCASTLE: I hope, Sir, I have done nothing to disoblige you. I'm sure I should be sorry to affront any gentleman who has been so polite, and said so many civil things to me. I'm sure I should be sorry (*Pretending to cry*) if he left the family upon my account. I'm sure I should be sorry, people said any thing amiss, since I have no fortune but my character.

MARLOW (*aside*): By heaven, she weeps. This is the first mark of tenderness I ever had from a modest woman, and it touches me; (*To her*) Excuse me, my lovely girl, you are the only part of the family I leave with reluctance. But to be plain with you, the difference of our birth, fortune and education, make an honourable connexion impossible; and I can never harbour a

thought of seducing simplicity that trusted in my honour, or bringing ruin upon one whose only fault was being too lovely.

MISS HARDCASTLE (*aside*): Generous man! I now begin to admire him. (*To him*) But I'm sure my family is as good as Miss Hardcastle's, and though I'm poor, that's no great misfortune to a contented mind, and, until this moment, I never thought that it was bad to want fortune.

MARLOW: And why now, my pretty simplicity?

MISS HARDCASTLE: Because it puts me at a distance from one, that if I had a thousand pound I would give it all to.

MARLOW (*aside*): This simplicity bewitches me, so that if I stay I'm undone. I must make one bold effort, and leave her. (*To her*) Your partiality in my favour, my dear, touches me most sensibly, and were I to live for myself alone, I could easily fix my choice. But I owe too much to the opinion of the world, too much to the authority of a father, so that — I can scarcely speak it — it affects me. Farewell. [*Exit.*

MISS HARDCASTLE: I never knew half his merit till now. He shall not go, if I have power or art to detain him. I'll still preserve the character in which I stoop'd to conquer, but will undeceive my papa, who, perhaps, may laugh him out of his resolution. [*Exit.*

Enter Tony, Miss Neville

TONY: Ay, you may steal for yourselves the next time. I have done my duty. She has got the jewels again, that's a sure thing; but she believes it was all a mistake of the servants.

MISS NEVILLE: But, my dear cousin, sure you won't forsake us in this distress. If she in the least suspects that I am going off, I shall certainly be locked up, or sent to my aunt Pedigree's, which is ten times worse.

TONY: To be sure, aunts of all kinds are damn'd bad things. But what can I do? I have got you a pair of horses that will fly like Whistlejacket, and I'm sure you can't say but I have courted you nicely before her face. Here she comes, we must court a bit or two more, for fear she should suspect us.

[*They retire, and seem to fondle.*

Enter Mrs. Hardcastle

MRS. HARDCASTLE: Well, I was greatly fluttered, to be sure. But my son tells me it was all a mistake of the servants. I shan't be easy, however, till they are fairly married, and then let her keep her own fortune. But what do I see! Fondling together, as I'm alive. I never saw Tony so sprightly before. Ah! have I caught you, my pretty doves! What, billing, exchanging stolen glances, and broken murmurs. Ah!

TONY: As for murmurs, mother, we grumble a little now and then, to be sure. But there's no love lost between us.

MRS. HARDCASTLE: A mere sprinkling, Tony, upon the flame, only to make it burn brighter.

MISS NEVILLE: Cousin Tony promises to give us more of his company at home. Indeed, he shan't leave us any more. It won't leave us cousin Tony, will it?

TONY: O! it's a pretty creature. No I'd sooner leave my horse in a pound, than leave you when you smile upon one so. Your laugh makes you so becoming.

MISS NEVILLE: Agreeable cousin! Who can help admiring that natural humour, that pleasant, broad, red, thoughtless, (*Patting his cheek*) ah! it's a bold face.

MRS. HARDCASTLE: Pretty innocence.

TONY: I'm sure I always lov'd cousin Con's hazle eyes, and her pretty long fingers, that she twists this way and that, over the haspicholls, like a parcel of bobbins.

MRS. HARDCASTLE: Ah, he would charm the bird from the tree. I was never so happy before. My boy takes after his father, poor Mr. Lumpkin, exactly. The jewels, my dear Con, shall be your's incontinently. You shall have them. Isn't he a sweet boy, my dear? You shall be married to-morrow, and we'll put off the rest of his education, like Dr. Drowsy's sermons, to a fitter opportunity.

Enter Diggory

DIGGORY: where's the 'Squire? I have got a letter for your worship.

TONY: Give it to my mamma. She reads all my letters first.

DIGGORY: I had orders to deliver it into your own hands.

TONY: Who does it come from?

DIGGORY: Your worship mun ask that o' the letter itself.

TONY: I could wish to know, tho'. (*Turning the letter, and gazing on it.*)

MISS NEVILLE (*aside*): Undone, undone. A letter to him from Hastings. I know the hand. If my aunt sees it, we are ruined for ever. I'll keep her employ'd a little if I can. (*To Mrs. Hardcastle*) But I have not told you, Madam, of my cousin's smart answer just now to Mr. Marlow. We so laugh'd — You must know, Madam — this way a little, for he must not hear us.

[*They confer.*

TONY (*still gazing*): A damn'd cramp piece of penmanship, as ever I saw in my life. I can read your printhand very well. But here there are such handles, and shanks, and dashes, that one can scarce tell the head from the tail. *To Anthony Lumpkin, Esquire.* It's very odd, I can read the outside of my letters, where my own name is, well enough. But when I come to open it, it's all — buzz. That's hard, very hard; for the inside of the letter is always the cream of the correspondence.

MRS. HARDCASTLE: Ha, ha, ha. Very well, very well. And so my son was too hard for the philosopher.

MISS NEVILLE: Yes, Madam; but you must hear the rest, Madam. A little more this way, or he may hear us. You'll hear how he puzzled him again.

MRS. HARDCASTLE: He seems strangely puzzled now himself, methinks.

TONY (*still gazing*): A damned up and down hand, as if it was disguised in liquor. (*Reading*) *Dear Sir.* Ay, that's

that. Then there's an *M*, and a *T*, and an *S*, but whether the next be an *izzard* or an *R*, confound me, I cannot tell.

MRS. HARDCASTLE: What's that, my dear. Can I give you any assistance?

MISS NEVILLE: Pray, aunt, let me read it. No body reads a cramp hand better than I. (*Twitching the letter from her*) Do you know who it is from?

TONY: Can't tell, except from Dick Ginger the feeder.

MISS NEVILLE: Ay, so it is, (*Pretending to read*) Dear 'Squire, Hoping that you're in health, as I am at this present. The gentlemen of the Shake bag club has cut the gentlemen of goose-green quite out of feather. The odds — um — odd battle — um — long fighting — um here, here, it's all about cocks, and fighting; it's of no consequence, here, put it up, put it up.

[*Thrusting the crumpled letter upon him.*

TONY: But I tell you, Miss, it's of all the consequence in the world. I would not lose the rest of it for a guinea. Here, mother, do you make it out. Of no consequence!

[*Giving Mrs. Hardcastle the letter.*

MRS. HARDCASTLE: How's this! (*Reads*) Dear 'Squire, I'm now waiting for Miss Neville, with a post-chaise and pair, at the bottom of the garden, but I find my horses yet unable to perform the journey. I expect you'll assist us with a pair of fresh horses, as you promised. Dispatch is necessary, as the *hag* (ay the hag) your mother, will otherwise suspect us. Your's, Hastings. Grant me patience. I shall run distracted. My rage choaks me.

MISS NEVILLE: I hope, Madam, you'll suspend your resentment for a few moments, and not impute to me any impertinence, or sinister design that belongs to another.

MRS. HARDCASTLE (*curtseying very low*): Fine spoken, Madam, you are most miraculously polite and engaging, and quite the very pink of curtesy and circumspection, Madam. (*Changing her tone*) And you, you great ill-fashioned oaf, with scarce sense enough to keep your mouth shut. Were you too join'd against me? But I'll defeat all your plots in a moment. As for you, Madam, since you have got a pair of fresh horses ready, it would be cruel to disappoint them. So, if you please, instead of running away with your spark, prepare, this very moment, to run off with *me.* Your old aunt Pedigree will keep you secure, I'll warrant me. You too, Sir, may mount your horse, and guard us upon the way. Here, Thomas, Roger, Diggory, I'll shew you, that I wish you better than you do yourselves.   [*Exit.*

MISS NEVILLE: So now I'm completely ruined.

TONY: Ay, that's a sure thing.

MISS NEVILLE: What better could be expected from being connected with such a stupid fool, and after all the nods and signs I made him.

TONY: By the laws, Miss, it was your own cleverness, and not my stupidity, that did your business. You were so nice and so busy with your Shake-bags and

Goose-greens, that I thought you could never be making believe.

Enter Hastings

HASTINGS: So, Sir, I find by my servant, that you have shewn my letter, and betray'd us. Was this well done, young gentleman?
TONY: Here's another. Ask Miss there who betray'd you. Ecod, it was her doing, not mine.

Enter Marlow

MARLOW: So I have been finely used here among you. Rendered contemptible, driven into ill manners, despised, insulted, laugh'd at.
TONY: Here's another. We shall have old Bedlam broke loose presently.
MISS NEVILLE: And there, Sir, is the gentleman to whom we all owe every obligation.
MARLOW: What can I say to him, a mere boy, an ideot, whose ignorance and age are a protection.
HASTINGS: A poor contemptible booby, that would but disgrace correction.
MISS NEVILLE: Yet with cunning and malice enough to make himself merry with all our embarrassments.
HASTINGS: An insensible cub.
MARLOW: Replete with tricks and mischief.
TONY: Baw! damme, but I'll fight you both one after the other, —— with baskets.°
MARLOW: As for him, he's below resentment. But your conduct, Mr. Hastings, requires an explanation. You knew of my mistakes, yet would not undeceive me.
HASTINGS: Tortured as I am with my own disappointments, is this a time for explanations? It is not friendly, Mr. Marlow.
MARLOW: But, Sir —
MISS NEVILLE: Mr. Marlow, we never kept on your mistake, till it was too late to undeceive you. Be pacified.

Enter Servant

SERVANT: My mistress desires you'll get ready immediately, Madam. The horses are putting to. Your hat and things are in the next room. We are to go thirty miles before morning.
                                                      [*Exit Servant.*
MISS NEVILLE: Well, well; I'll come presently.
MARLOW (*to Hastings*): Was it well done, Sir, to assist in rendering me ridiculous? To hang me out for the scorn of all my acquaintance. Depend upon it, Sir, I shall expect an explanation.
HASTINGS: Was it well done, Sir, if you're upon that subject, to deliver what I entrusted to yourself, to the care of another, Sir?
MISS NEVILLE: Mr. Hastings. Mr. Marlow. Why will you increase my distress by this groundless dispute? I implore, I entreat you ——

baskets: Old-fashioned swords.

Enter Servant

SERVANT: Your cloak, Madam. My mistress is impatient.
MISS NEVILLE: I come. Pray be pacified. If I leave you thus, I shall die with apprehension.

Enter Servant

SERVANT: Your fan, muff, and gloves, Madam. The horses are waiting.
MISS NEVILLE: O, Mr. Marlow! if you knew what a scene of constraint and ill-nature lies before me, I'm sure it would convert your resentment into pity.
MARLOW: I'm so distracted with a variety of passions, that I don't know what I do. Forgive me, Madam. George, forgive me. You know my hasty temper, and should not exasperate it.
HASTINGS: The torture of my situation is my only excuse.
MISS NEVILLE: Well, my dear Hastings, if you have that esteem for me that I think, that I am sure you have, your constancy for three years will but encrease the happiness of our future connection. If —
MRS. HARDCASTLE (*within*): Miss Neville. Constance, why Constance, I say.
MISS NEVILLE: I'm coming. Well, constancy. Remember, constancy is the word.   [*Exit.*
HASTINGS: My heart! How can I support this. To be so near happiness, and such happiness.
MARLOW (*to Tony*): You see now, young gentleman the effects of your folly. What might be amusement to you, is here disappointment, and even distress.
TONY (*from a reverie*): Ecod, I have hit it. It's here. Your hands. Yours and yours, my poor Sulky. My boots there, ho. Meet me two hours hence at the bottom of the garden; and if you don't find Tony Lumpkin a more good-natur'd fellow than you thought for, I'll give you leave to take my best horse, and Bet Bouncer into the bargain. Come along. My boots, ho!
                                                      [*Exeunt.*

ACT V

SCENE, *Continues*

Enter Hastings and Servant

HASTINGS: You saw the Old Lady and Miss Neville drive off, you say.
SERVANT: Yes, your honour. They went off in a post coach, and the young 'Squire went on horseback. They're thirty miles off by this time.
HASTINGS: Then all my hopes are over.
SERVANT: Yes, Sir. Old Sir Charles is arrived. He and the old Gentleman of the house have been laughing at Mr. Marlow's mistake this half hour. They are coming this way.
HASTINGS: Then I must not be seen. So now to my fruitless appointment at the bottom of the garden. This is about the time.   [*Exit.*

Enter Sir Charles and Hardcastle

HARDCASTLE: Ha, ha, ha. The peremptory tone in which he sent forth his sublime commands.

SIR CHARLES: And the reserve with which I suppose he treated all your advances.

HARDCASTLE: And yet he might have seen something in me above a common inn-keeper, too.

SIR CHARLES: Yes, Dick, but he mistook you for an uncommon innkeeper, ha, ha, ha.

HARDCASTLE: Well, I'm in too good spirits to think of anything but joy. Yes, my dear friend, this union of our families will make our personal friendships hereditary; and tho' my daughter's fortune is but small ——

SIR CHARLES: Why, Dick, will you talk of fortune to *me*. My son is possessed of more than a competence already, and can want nothing but a good and virtuous girl to share his happiness and encrease it. If they like each other, as you say they do ——

HARDCASTLE: *If,* man. I tell you they *do* like each other. My daughter as good as told me so.

SIR CHARLES: But girls are apt to flatter themselves, you know.

HARDCASTLE: I saw him grasp her hand in the warmest manner, myself; and here he comes to put you out of your *iffs,* I warrant him.

Enter Marlow

MARLOW: I come, Sir, once more, to ask pardon for my strange conduct. I can scarce reflect on my insolence without confusion.

HARDCASTLE: Tut, boy, a trifle. You take it too gravely. An hour or two's laughing with my daughter will set all to rights again. She'll never like you the worse for it.

MARLOW: Sir, I shall be always proud of her approbation.

HARDCASTLE: Approbation is but a cold word, Mr. Marlow; if I am not deceived, you have something more than approbation thereabouts. You take me.

MARLOW: Really, Sir, I have not that happiness.

HARDCASTLE: Come, boy, I'm an old fellow, and know what's what, as well as you that are younger. I know what has past between you; but mum.

MARLOW: Sure, Sir, nothing has past between us but the most profound respect on my side, and the most distant reserve on her's. You don't think, Sir, that my impudence has been past upon all the rest of the family.

HARDCASTLE: Impudence! No, I don't say that — Not quite impudence — Though girls like to be play'd with, and rumpled a little too, sometimes. But she has told no tales, I assure you.

MARLOW: I never gave her the slightest cause.

HARDCASTLE: Well, well, I like modesty in its place well enough. But this is over-acting, young gentleman. You *may* be open. Your father and I will like you the better for it.

MARLOW: May I die, Sir, if I ever ——

HARDCASTLE: I tell you, she don't dislike you; and as I'm sure you like her ——

MARLOW: Dear Sir — I protest, Sir ——

HARDCASTLE: I see no reason why you should not be joined as fast as the parson can tie you.

MARLOW: But hear me, Sir ——

HARDCASTLE: Your father approves the match, I admire it, every moment's delay will be doing mischief, so ——

MARLOW: But why won't you hear me? By all that's just and true, I never gave Miss Hardcastle the slightest mark of my attachment, or even the most distant hint to suspect me of affection. We had but one interview, and that was formal, modest and uninteresting.

HARDCASTLE (*aside*): This fellow's formal modest impudence is beyond bearing.

SIR CHARLES: And you never grasp'd her hand, or made any protestations!

MARLOW: As heaven is my witness, I came down in obedience to your commands. I saw the lady without emotion, and parted without reluctance. I hope you'll exact no further proofs of my duty, nor prevent me from leaving a house in which I suffer so many mortifications.   [*Exit.*

SIR CHARLES: I'm astonish'd at the air of sincerity with which he parted.

HARDCASTLE: And I'm astonish'd at the deliberate intrepidity of his assurance.

SIR CHARLES: I dare pledge my life and honour upon his truth.

HARDCASTLE: Here comes my daughter, and I would stake my happiness upon her veracity.

Enter Miss Hardcastle

HARDCASTLE: Kate, come hither, child. Answer us sincerely, and without reserve; has Mr. Marlow made you any professions of love and affection?

MISS HARDCASTLE: The question is very abrupt, Sir! But since you require unreserved sincerity, I think he has.

HARDCASTLE (*to Sir Charles*): You see.

SIR CHARLES: And pray, madam, have you and my son had more than one interview?

MISS HARDCASTLE: Yes, Sir, several.

HARDCASTLE (*to Sir Charles*): You see.

SIR CHARLES: But did he profess any attachment?

MISS HARDCASTLE: A lasting one.

SIR CHARLES: Did he talk of love?

MISS HARDCASTLE: Much, Sir.

SIR CHARLES: Amazing! And all this formally?

MISS HARDCASTLE: Formally.

HARDCASTLE: Now, my friend, I hope you are satisfied.

SIR CHARLES: And how did he behave, madam?

MISS HARDCASTLE: As most profest admirers do. Said some civil things of my face, talked much of his want of merit, and the greatness of mine; mentioned his heart, gave a short tragedy speech, and ended with pretended rapture.

SIR CHARLES: Now I'm perfectly convinced, indeed. I know his conversation among women to be modest and submissive. This forward canting ranting manner by no means describes him, and I am confident, he never sat for the picture.

MISS HARDCASTLE: Then what, Sir, if I should convince you to your face of my sincerity? If you and my papa, in about half an hour, will place yourselves behind that screen, you shall hear him declare his passion to me in person.

SIR CHARLES: Agreed. And if I find him what you describe, all my happiness in him must have an end.

[*Exit.*

MISS HARDCASTLE: And if you don't find him what I describe — I fear my happiness must never have a beginning.

[*Exeunt.*

SCENE *changes to the Back of the Garden*

Enter Hastings

HASTINGS: What an ideot am I, to wait here for a fellow, who probably takes a delight in mortifying me. He never intended to be punctual, and I'll wait no longer. What do I see. It is he, and perhaps with news of my Constance.

Enter Tony, booted and spattered

HASTINGS: My honest 'Squire! I now find you a man of your word. This looks like friendship.

TONY: Ay, I'm your friend, and the best friend you have in the world, if you knew but all. This riding by night, by the bye, is cursedly tiresome. It has shook me worse than the basket of a stage-coach.

HASTINGS: But how? Where did you leave your fellow-travellers? Are they in safety? Are they housed?

TONY: Five and twenty miles in two hours and a half is no such bad driving. The poor beasts have smoaked for it: Rabbet me, but I'd rather ride forty miles after a fox, than ten with such *varment.*

HASTINGS: Well, but where have you left the ladies? I die with impatience.

TONY: Left them? Why, where should I leave them, but where I found them?

HASTINGS: This is a riddle.

TONY: Riddle me this, then. What's that goes round the house, and round the house, and never touches the house?

HASTINGS: I'm still astray.

TONY: Why, that's it, mon. I have led them astray. By jingo, there's not a pond or slough within five miles of the place but they can tell the taste of.

HASTINGS: Ha, ha, ha, I understand; you took them in a round, while they supposed themselves going forward. And so you have at last brought them home again.

TONY: You shall hear. I first took them down Feather-bed-lane, where we stuck fast in the mud. I then rattled them crack over the stones of Up-and-down Hill — I then introduc'd them to the gibbet on Heavy-tree Heath, and from that, with a circumbendibus, I fairly lodged them in the horsepond at the bottom of the garden.

HASTINGS: But no accident, I hope.

TONY: No, no. Only mother is confoundedly frightened. She thinks herself forty miles off. She's sick of the journey, and the cattle can scarce crawl. So if your own horses be ready, you may whip off with cousin, and I'll be bound that no soul here can budge a foot to follow you.

HASTINGS: My dear friend, how can I be grateful?

TONY: Ay, now its dear friend, noble 'Squire. Just now, it was all ideot, cub, and run me through the guts. Damn *your* way of fighting, I say. After we take a knock in this part of the country, we kiss and be friends. But if you had run me through the guts, then I should be dead, and you might go kiss the hangman.

HASTINGS: The rebuke is just. But I must hasten to relieve Miss Neville; if you keep the old lady employed, I promise to take care of the young one.

[*Exit Hastings.*

TONY: Never fear me. Here she comes. Vanish. She's got from the pond, and draggled up to the waist like a mermaid.

Enter Mrs. Hardcastle

MRS. HARDCASTLE: Oh, Tony, I'm killed. Shook. Battered to death. I shall never survive it. That last jolt that laid us against the quickset hedge has done my business.

TONY: Alack, mamma, it was all your own fault. You would be for running away by night, without knowing one inch of the way.

MRS. HARDCASTLE: I wish we were at home again. I never met so many accidents in so short a journey. Drench'd in the mud, overturn'd in a ditch, stuck fast in a slough, jolted to a jelly, and at last to lose our way. Whereabouts do you think we are, Tony?

TONY: By my guess we should be upon Crackskull common, about forty miles from home.

MRS. HARDCASTLE: O lud! O lud! the most notorious spot in all the country. We only want a robbery to make a complete night on't.

TONY: Don't be afraid, mama, don't be afraid. Two of the five that kept here are hanged, and the other three may not find us. Don't be afraid. Is that a man that's galloping behind us? No; it's only a tree. Don't be afraid.

MRS. HARDCASTLE: The fright will certainly kill me.

TONY: Do you see anything like a black hat moving behind the thicket?

MRS. HARDCASTLE: O death!

TONY: No, it's only a cow. Don't be afraid, mama; don't be afraid.

MRS. HARDCASTLE: As I'm alive, Tony, I see a man coming towards us. Ah! I'm sure on't. If he perceives us, we are undone.

TONY (*aside*): Father-in-law, by all that's unlucky, come to take one of his night walks. (*To her*) Ah, it's a highwayman, with pistils as long as my arm. A damn'd ill-looking fellow.

MRS. HARDCASTLE: Good heaven defend us! He approaches.

TONY: Do you hide yourself in that thicket, and leave me to manage him. If there be any danger I'll cough and cry hem. When I cough be sure to keep close.

[*Mrs. Hardcastle hides behind a tree in the back scene.*]

Enter Hardcastle

HARDCASTLE: I'm mistaken, or I heard voices of people in want of help. Oh, Tony, is that you? I did not expect you so soon back. Are your mother and her charge in safety?

TONY: Very safe, Sir, at my aunt Pedigree's. Hem.

MRS. HARDCASTLE (*from behind*): Ah death! I find there's danger.

HARDCASTLE: Forty miles in three hours; sure, that's too much, my youngster.

TONY: Stout horses and willing minds make short journeys, as they say. Hem.

MRS. HARDCASTLE (*from behind*): Sure he'll do the dear boy no harm.

HARDCASTLE: But I heard a voice here; I should be glad to know from whence it came?

TONY: It was I, Sir, talking to myself, Sir. I was saying that forty miles in four hours was very good going. Hem. As to be sure it was. Hem. I have got a sort of cold by being out in the air. We'll go in, if you please. Hem.

HARDCASTLE: But if you talk'd to yourself, you did not answer yourself. I am certain I heard two voices, and am resolved (*Raising his voice*) to find the other out.

MRS. HARDCASTLE (*from behind*): Oh! he's coming to find me out. Oh!

TONY: What need you go, Sir, if I tell you? Hem. I'll lay down my life for the truth — hem — I'll tell you all, Sir.

[*Detaining him.*]

HARDCASTLE: I tell you I will not be detained. I insist on seeing. It's in vain to expect I'll believe you.

MRS. HARDCASTLE (*running forward from behind*): O lud, he'll murder my poor boy, my darling. Here, good gentleman, whet your rage upon me. Take my money, my life, but spare that young gentleman, spare my child, if you have any mercy.

HARDCASTLE: My wife! as I'm a Christian. From whence can she come, or what does she mean!

MRS. HARDCASTLE (*kneeling*): Take compassion on us, good Mr. Highwayman. Take our money, our watches, all we have, but spare our lives. We will never bring you to justice, indeed we won't, good Mr. Highwayman.

HARDCASTLE: I believe the woman's out of her senses. What, Dorothy, don't you know *me*?

MRS. HARDCASTLE: Mr. Hardcastle, as I'm alive! My fears blinded me. But who, my dear, could have expected to meet you here, in this frightful place, so far from home. What has brought you to follow us?

HARDCASTLE: Sure, Dorothy, you have not lost your wits! So far from home, when you are within forty yards of your own door! (*To him*) This is one of your old tricks, you graceless rogue you. (*To her*) Don't you know the gate, and the mulberry-tree; and don't you remember the horsepond, my dear?

MRS. HARDCASTLE: Yes, I shall remember the horse-pond as long as I live; I have caught my death in it. (*To Tony*) And is it to you, you graceless varlet, I owe all this? I'll teach you to abuse your mother, I will.

TONY: Ecod, mother, all the parish says you have spoil'd me, and so you may take the fruits on't.

MRS. HARDCASTLE: I'll spoil you, I will.

[*Follows him off the stage. Exit.*]

HARDCASTLE: There's morality, however, in his reply.

[*Exit.*]

Enter Hastings and Miss Neville

HASTINGS: My dear Constance, why will you deliberate thus? If we delay a moment, all is lost for ever. Pluck up a little resolution, and we shall soon be out of the reach of her malignity.

MISS NEVILLE: I find it impossible. My spirits are so sunk with the agitations I have suffered, that I am unable to face any new danger. Two or three years' patience will at last crown us with happiness.

HASTINGS: Such a tedious delay is worse than inconstancy. Let us fly, my charmer. Let us date our happiness from this very moment. Perish fortune. Love and content will encrease what we possess beyond a monarch's revenue. Let me prevail.

MISS NEVILLE: No, Mr. Hastings; no. Prudence once more comes to my relief, and I will obey its dictates. In the moment of passion, fortune may be despised, but it ever produces a lasting repentance. I'm resolved to apply to Mr. Hardcastle's compassion and justice for redress.

HASTINGS: But tho' he had the will, he has not the power to relieve you.

MISS NEVILLE: But he has influence, and upon that I am resolved to rely.

HASTINGS: I have no hopes. But since you persist, I must reluctantly obey you.   [*Exeunt.*]

SCENE *Changes*

Enter Sir Charles and Miss Hardcastle

SIR CHARLES: What a situation am I in! If what you say appears, I shall then find a guilty son. If what he says be true, I shall then lose one that, of all others, I most wished for a daughter.

MISS HARDCASTLE: I am proud of your approbation, and to shew I merit it, if you place yourselves as I directed, you shall hear his explicit declaration. But he comes.

SIR CHARLES: I'll to your father, and keep him to the appointment.   [*Exit Sir Charles.*]

Enter Marlow

MARLOW: Tho' prepared for setting out, I come once more to take leave, nor did I, till this moment, know the pain I feel in the separation.

MISS HARDCASTLE (*in her own natural manner*): I believe these sufferings cannot be very great, Sir, which you can so easily remove. A day or two longer, perhaps, might lessen your uneasiness, by shewing the little value of what you think proper to regret.

MARLOW (*aside*): This girl every moment improves upon me. (*To her*) It must not be, Madam. I have already trifled too long with my heart. My very pride begins to submit to my passion. The disparity of education and fortune, the anger of a parent, and the contempt of my equals, begin to lose their weight; and nothing can restore me to myself, but this painful effort of resolution.

MISS HARDCASTLE: Then go, Sir. I'll urge nothing more to detain you. Tho' my family be as good as her's you came down to visit, and my education, I hope, not inferior, what are these advantages without equal affluence? I must remain contented with the slight approbation of imputed merit; I must have only the mockery of your addresses, while all your serious aims are fix'd on fortune.

Enter Hardcastle and Sir Charles from behind

SIR CHARLES: Here, behind this screen.

HARDCASTLE: Ay, ay, make no noise. I'll engage my Kate covers him with confusion at last.

MARLOW: By heavens, Madam, fortune was ever my smallest consideration. Your beauty at first caught my eye; for who could see that without emotion? But every moment that I converse with you, steals in some new grace, heightens the picture, and gives it stronger expression. What at first seem'd rustic plainness, now appears refin'd simplicity. What seem'd forward assurance, now strikes me as the result of courageous innocence, and conscious virtue.

SIR CHARLES: What can it mean! He amazes me!

HARDCASTLE: I told you how it would be. Hush!

MARLOW: I am now determined to stay, Madam, and I have too good an opinion of my father's discernment, when he sees you, to doubt his approbation.

MISS HARDCASTLE: No, Mr. Marlow, I will not, cannot detain you. Do you think I could suffer a connexion, in which there is the smallest room for repentance? Do you think I would take the mean advantage of a transient passion, to load you with confusion? Do you think I could ever relish that happiness, which was acquired by lessening your's?

MARLOW: By all that's good, I can have no happiness but what's in your power to grant me. Nor shall I ever feel repentance, but in not having seen your merits before. I will stay, even contrary to your wishes; and tho' you should persist to shun me, I will make my respectful assiduities atone for the levity of my past conduct.

MISS HARDCASTLE: Sir, I must entreat you'll desist. As our acquaintance began, so let it end, in indifference. I might have given an hour or two to levity; but, seriously, Mr. Marlow, do you think I could ever submit to a connexion, where *I* must appear mercenary, and *you* imprudent? Do you think I could ever catch at the confident addresses of a secure admirer?

MARLOW (*kneeling*): Does this look like security? Does this look like confidence? No, Madam, every moment that shews me your merit, only serves to encrease my diffidence and confusion. Here let me continue ——

SIR CHARLES: I can hold it no longer. Charles, Charles, how hast thou deceived me! Is this your indifference, your uninteresting conversation!

HARDCASTLE: Your cold contempt; your formal interview. What have you to say now?

MARLOW: That I'm all amazement! What can it mean!

HARDCASTLE: It means that you can say and unsay things at pleasure. That you can address a lady in private, and deny it in public; that you have one story for us, and another for my daughter.

MARLOW: Daughter! — this lady your daughter!

HARDCASTLE: Yes, Sir, my only daughter. My Kate, whose else should she be?

MARLOW: Oh, the devil.

MISS HARDCASTLE: Yes, Sir, that very identical tall squinting lady you were pleased to take me for. (*Curtseying*) She that you addressed as the mild, modest, sentimental man of gravity, and the bold forward agreeable Rattle of the Ladies Club; ha, ha, ha.

MARLOW: Zounds, there's no bearing this; it's worse than death.

MISS HARDCASTLE: In which of your characters, Sir, will you give us leave to address you? As the faultering gentleman, with looks on the ground, that speaks just to be heard, and hates hypocrisy; or the loud confident creature, that keeps it up with Mrs. Mantrap, and old Miss Biddy Buckskin, till three in the morning; ha, ha, ha.

MARLOW: Oh, curse on my noisy head. I never attempted to be impudent yet, that I was not taken down. I must be gone.

HARDCASTLE: By the hand of my body, but you shall not. I see it was all a mistake, and I am rejoiced to find it. You shall not, Sir, I tell you. I know she'll forgive you. Won't you forgive him, Kate? We'll all forgive you. Take courage, man.

[*They retire, she tormenting him to the back Scene.*]

Enter Mrs. Hardcastle, Tony

MRS. HARDCASTLE: So, so, they're gone off. Let them go, I care not.

HARDCASTLE: Who gone?

MRS. HARDCASTLE: My dutiful niece and her gentleman, Mr. Hastings, from Town. He who came down with our modest visitor here.

SIR CHARLES: Who, my honest George Hastings? As worthy a fellow as lives, and the girl could not have made a more prudent choice.

HARDCASTLE: Then, by the hand of my body, I'm proud of the connexion.

MRS. HARDCASTLE: Well, if he has taken away the lady, he has not taken her fortune, that remains in this family to console us for her loss.

HARDCASTLE: Sure, Dorothy, you would not be so mercenary?

MRS. HARDCASTLE: Ay, that's my affair, not your's. But you know if your son, when of age, refuses to marry his cousin, her whole fortune is then at her own disposal.

HARDCASTLE: Ay, but he's not of age, and she has not thought proper to wait for his refusal.

Enter Hastings and Miss Neville

MRS. HARDCASTLE (*aside*): What, returned so soon. I begin not to like it.

HASTINGS (*to Hardcastle*): For my late attempt to fly off with your niece, let my present confusion be my punishment. We are now come back, to appeal from your justice to your humanity. By her father's consent, I first paid her my addresses, and our passions were first founded in duty.

MISS NEVILLE: Since his death, I have been obliged to stoop to dissimulation to avoid oppression. In an hour of levity, I was ready even to give up my fortune to secure my choice. But I'm now recover'd from the delusion, and hope from your tenderness what is denied me from a nearer connexion.

MRS. HARDCASTLE: Pshaw, pshaw, this is all but the whining end of a modern novel.

HARDCASTLE: Be it what it will, I'm glad they're come back to reclaim their due. Come hither, Tony boy. Do you refuse this lady's hand whom I now offer you?

TONY: What signifies my refusing? You know I can't refuse her till I'm of age, father.

HARDCASTLE: While I thought concealing your age boy was likely to conduce to your improvement, I concurred with your mother's desire to keep it secret. But since I find she turns it to a wrong use, I must now declare, you have been of age these three months.

TONY: Of age! Am I of age, father?

HARDCASTLE: Above three months.

TONY: Then you'll see the first use I'll make of my liberty. (*Taking Miss Neville's hand*) Witness all men by these presents, that I, Anthony Lumpkin, Esquire, of BLANK place, refuse you, Constantia Neville, spinster, of no place at all, for my true and lawful wife. So Constance Neville may marry whom she pleases, and Tony Lumpkin is his own man again.

SIR CHARLES: O brave 'Squire.

HASTINGS: My worthy friend.

MRS. HARDCASTLE: My undutiful offspring.

MARLOW: Joy, my dear George, I give you joy sincerely. And could I prevail upon my little tyrant here to be less arbitrary, I should be the happiest man alive, if you would return me the favour.

HASTINGS (*to Miss Hardcastle*): Come, madam, you are now driven to the very last scene of all your contrivances. I know you like him, I'm sure he loves you, and you must and shall have him.

HARDCASTLE (*joining their hands*): And I say so too. And Mr. Marlow, if she makes as good a wife as she has a daughter, I don't believe you'll ever repent your bargain. So now to supper, to-morrow we shall gather all the poor of the parish about us, and the Mistakes of the Night shall be crowned with a merry morning; so boy take her; as you have been mistaken in the mistress, my wish is, that you may never be mistaken in the wife.

EPILOGUE
By J. CRADOCK, Esq.
To be spoken in the character of TONY LUMPKIN

Well — now all's ended — and my comrades gone,
Pray what becomes of *mother's nonly son?*
A hopeful blade! — in town I'll fix my station,
And try to make a bluster in the nation.
As for my cousin Neville, I renounce her,
Off — in a crack — I'll carry big Bett Bouncer.
Why should not I in the great world appear?
I soon shall have a thousand pounds a year;
No matter what a man may here inherit,
In London — 'gad, they've some regard for spirit.
I see the horses prancing up the streets,
And big Bet Bouncer, bobs to all she meets;
Then hoikes to jiggs and pastimes ev'ry night —
Not to the plays — they say it a'n't polite,
To Sadler's-Wells perhaps, or Operas go,
And once by chance, to the roratorio.
Thus here and there, for ever up and down,
We'll set the fashions too, to half the town;
And then at auctions — money ne'er regard,
Buy pictures like the great, ten pounds a yard:
Zounds, we shall make these London gentry say,
We know what's damn'd genteel, as well as they.

Nineteenth-Century Drama through the Turn of the Twentieth Century

Technical Innovations

Technically, theaters changed more during the period between 1800 and 1900 than in any comparable earlier period. The introduction of gas jets early in the century had a major effect. Now, light could be dimmed or raised as needed; the house could be gradually and entirely darkened. With gaslight onstage, selective lighting contributed to the emotional effect of plays and allowed actors to move deeper into the stage instead of playing important scenes on the apron. With the advent of elaborate scenery, as in the Drottningholm Theater in Sweden, lighting devices were often placed behind the proscenium pillars and scenery so that actors were more visible when they stood within the proscenium. The changes did not take place overnight, but as new theaters were built in the early nineteenth century (and as older theaters were refurbished) the apron shrank and the front doors leading to it disappeared. That change reinforced the nineteenth-century practice of treating the proscenium opening as the imaginary "fourth wall" of a room. The elaborate framing of Chicago's Auditorium (1889, Figure 13) allowed for complex lighting systems as well as the framing of the proscenium, which acts as a "window" into the dramatic action.

Numerous other technical innovations were introduced into the new theaters, such as London's Drury Lane Theatre, which was rebuilt in 1812. Highly sophisticated machinery lifted actors from below the stage, and flies or fly galleries above the stage permitted scene changes and other dramatic alterations and effects. The technical resources of the modern theaters in Europe were extraordinary by midcentury.

Romantic Drama

The lighting and architectural changes were complex and uneven, but they accompanied changes in styles of acting, styles of plays, and the content of plays. Early-nineteenth-century English Romantic poets produced a variety of plays espousing a new philosophy of the individual, a philosophy of democracy, and a cry for personal liberation, but unfortunately their plays failed to capture the popular stage. William Wordsworth's *The Borderers* (1796–1797), concerning political struggles on the border between England and Scotland,

Figure 13. Elaborately decorated proscenium arch. Auditorium, Chicago, 1889.

was a failure. A relatively recent production (1989) at Yale University revealed its static, declamatory nature. Even a play with an inherently dramatic subject such as *The Fall of Robespierre* (1794) by Robert Southey and Samuel Taylor Coleridge — concerning the violent excesses of the French Revolution of 1789 — could not stir popular audiences. John Keats wrote *Otho the Great* (1819) about a tenth-century dispute between brothers and a father and son. He hoped that the great actor and producer Edmund Kean would want to produce the play, but Kean declined. Percy Bysshe Shelley wrote *The Cenci* (1819) when he was in Italy, hoping it would be produced on the English stage, but it was banned by the censors. The style of Shelley's play has been compared with John Webster's *The Dutchess of Malfi* (1613); its themes include violent death and insanity. George Gordon, Lord Byron, wrote several plays that had admirers but were not successful. *Manfred* (1817) is a CLOSET DRAMA — a play meant to be read, not produced. It presents a powerful portrait of a brooding intellect that could, in some ways, be compared with Hamlet. Allardyce Nicoll, the British drama historian and critic, has said of this and other Romantic plays that "audiences and readers familiar with *Lear* and *Macbeth* and *Othello* could not be expected to feel a thrill of wonder and delight in the contemplation of works so closely akin to these in general aim and yet so far removed from them in freshness of imaginative power."

French and German Romantic dramatists were more successful than their English counterparts. Johann Wolfgang von Goethe (1749–1832), one of Germany's most important playwrights, produced a number of successful plays in the late eighteenth century. Then came his masterpiece, *Faust* (1808, 1832), in two parts, with a scope and grandeur of concept that challenged the theaters of his day. The play opens in heaven, with Mephistopheles presenting his plan for tempting Faust; Faust signs over his soul to Mephistopheles in return for one moment of perfect joy. Faust was willing to risk all in his efforts to live life to its fullest, and despite his sins he was admired as a hero. Faust's self-analytic individualism, marked by a love of excess and a capacity for deep feeling and frightening intensity, has fascinated the German mind ever since Goethe rediscovered him. His development of Faust as a psychologically complex character contrasts with Christopher Marlowe's version in *Doctor Faustus*.

Another important force in German theater was Johann Cristoph Friedrich von Schiller (1759–1805), whose early play *The Robbers* (1781) was written when he was twenty-two. This still-popular (and still-produced) play reminds English audiences of the legend of Robin Hood since its hero, Karl von Moor, is a robber admirable for his generosity and seriousness. His adversary is his evil brother, who dominates the castle, the emblem of local repressive political power. Schiller was a highly successful playwright throughout the late eighteenth century. In the early nineteenth century he produced several popular historical plays such as *Maria Stuart* (1800) on Scotland's Queen Mary, the ill-fated cousin of Queen Elizabeth I. *The Maid of Orleans* (1801) told the story of Joan of Arc, the French heroine who led her army to victory only to be burned at the stake to satisfy political and religious exigencies. Both plays evoke deep sympathy for their heroines and both have been noted for their sentimentality. His last play, *William Tell* (1804), like *The Robbers*, tells the story of a heroic individual's fight against the oppressive forces of an evil baron. Schiller made the story of William Tell universal, and his theatrical successes were soon known throughout Europe and the Americas.

In France, the Romantic tragedy held sway for some time in the 1830s. Victor Hugo (1802–1885) had a great success in *Hernani* (1830), although critics and writers who insisted on classical rules were so disturbed by its innovation that they made disturbances in the theater. They attended only to jeer the pardon of Hernani, an outlaw, by Don Carlos, king of Spain. At the end Hernani and Donna Sol, his loved one, drink a poison so as to die together because they could not live together. Alexandre Dumas (1802–1879), soon to be famous as a novelist, produced a number of successful, influential plays, among them *Henry III and His Court* (1829) and *The Tower of Nesle* (1832).

Melodrama

MELODRAMA developed in Germany and France in the mid- and late eighteenth century. The *melo* in *melodrama* means "song"; incidental music was a hallmark of melodrama. In England certain regulations separated Covent Garden, Drury Lane, and the Haymarket — the three "major" theaters with exclusive licenses to produce spoken drama — from the "minor" theaters, which had to produce musical plays such as burlettas, which resembled our comic operettas. Eventually, the minor theaters began to produce plays with spoken dialogue and accompanying music, heralding a new, popular style. Melodrama proved to be one of the most durable innovations of the late eighteenth century.

In Germany, August Friedrich Ferdinand von Kotzebue (1761–1819) and in France Guilbert de Pixérécourt (1773–1844), who coined the term *melodrama*, began developing the melodramatic play. Many of these dramas used background music that altered according to the mood of the scene, a tradition that continues today in films and on television. Nineteenth-century melodramas featured familiar crises: the virtuous maiden fallen into the hands of an unscrupulous landlord; the father who, lamenting over a portrait of his dead wife, discovers that he is speaking to his — until then — lost daughter. Nineteenth-century melodramas had well-defined heroes, heroines, and villains. The plots were filled with surprises and unlikely twists designed to amaze and delight the audience. Most of the plays were explicitly sentimental, depending on a strong emotional appeal with clear-cut and relatively decisive endings.

Though not popular later on, the plays of Kotzebue and Pixérécourt pleased their contemporary audiences and helped establish melodrama as a dominant style for the first six decades of the nineteenth century. Kotzebue published thirty-six plays (twenty-two were produced) and enjoyed an immense popularity in England and the United States. Translated into several languages, his works influenced later popular playwrights, who admired his ability to invent and resolve complex plot situations. An example of the ending of *La-Peyrouse* (1798) may provide a taste of the mode. The hero, cast ashore on a desert island, falls in love with the "savage" Malvina. When he rejoins his wife, Adelaide, he is presented with the problem of what to do with Malvina. Here is the women's solution:

> MALVINA (*turning affectionately, yet with trembling to Adelaide*): I have prayed for thee, and for myself — let us be sisters!
> ADELAIDE: Sisters! (*She remains some moments lost in thought.*) Sisters! Sweet girl, you have awakened a consoling idea in my bosom! Yes, we will be sisters, and this man shall be our brother! Share him we cannot, nor can either possess him singly. (*With enthusiasm.*) We, the sisters, will inhabit one hut, he shall dwell in another. We will educate our children, he shall assist us both — by day we will make but one family, at night we will separate — how say you? will you consent? . . . (*Extending her arms to La-Peyrouse.*) A sisterly embrace!

In France Pixérécourt produced a similar and highly successful drama that pleased his audiences. Not everyone was pleased, however. Goethe resigned his office from the Weimar Court Theatre when Pixérécourt's *The Dog of Montargis* was produced in 1816 because he did not want to be associated with any play that had a dog as its hero.

Not all these plays have been forgotten. Alexandre Dumas's *La Dame aux camélias* (Camille) was a theatrical hit in 1852 and has remained popular ever since, inspiring the Verdi opera *La Traviata* (1853) and revivals and adaptations up to the present, including the British playwright Pam Gems's feminist version (1987), starring Kathleen Turner. Based on a woman Dumas knew in

Paris, it is the story of a wealthy young man who falls in love with a courtesan, Marguerite Gauthier. Like Angellica in *The Rover,* she has manipulated men throughout her life, but now she is truly in love with Armand. The young man's father opposes the match, but even he is moved by the majesty of their love. Eventually, the father faces Marguerite and convinces her that if she really loves his son, she will let him go since their union can bring nothing but harm to Armand. She then fabricates a contempt for Armand and dismisses him, broken-hearted. Later, after they have been separated and she has fallen deathly ill, Armand learns the truth and rushes to her. On her deathbed Armand professes his love as she dies in his arms.

In the United States, George Aiken produced another long-lasting and influential drama, *Uncle Tom's Cabin* (1852), based on Harriet Beecher Stowe's novel. Stowe, a prominent northern abolitionist, poured all her anger at slavery into her novel. Aiken's stage version played for three hundred nights in its first production and across the nation more than a quarter of a million times. Some of its characters — Uncle Tom, Little Eva, Sambo, Topsy, and Simon Legree — live on in the popular imagination, but despite the contemporary interest in Stowe and in this play, the paternalistic subtitle, "Life among the Lowly," marks its era.

The Well-Made Play

Early in the nineteenth century, a Frenchman with an unusual theatrical gift for pleasing popular audiences began a career that spanned fifty successful years. Eugène Scribe (1791–1861) may have produced as many as four or five hundred plays. He employed collaborators and mined novels and stories for his plots, producing tragedies, comedies, opera libretti, and vaudeville one-act pieces. He quickly determined that the plot held the attention of the audience and that rambling character studies were of lesser interest. Consequently, he developed a formula for dramatic action and made sure that all his works fit into it. The result was the creation of a "factory" for making plays. Among the elements of Scribe's formula were the following:

1. A careful exposition telling the audience what the situation is, usually including one or more secrets to be revealed later.
2. Surprises, such as letters to be opened at a critical moment and identities to be revealed later.
3. Suspense that builds steadily throughout the play, usually sustained by cliff-hanging situations and characters who miss each other by way of carefully timed entrances and exits. At critical moments, characters lose important papers or misplace identifying jewelry, for instance.
4. A CLIMAX late in the play when the secrets are revealed and the hero confronts his antagonists and succeeds.
5. A DENOUEMENT, the resolution of the drama when all the loose ends are drawn together and explanations are made that render all the action plausible.

It should be evident from this description that the WELL-MADE PLAY still thrives, not only on the stage but also in films and on television. Scribe's emphasis on plot was sensational for his time, and his success was unrivaled; however, none of his plays has survived in contemporary performance. Only one, *Adrienne*

Lecouvreur (1849), the story of a famous actress poisoned by a rival, is mentioned by critics as interesting because of its depth of characterization. Scribe was superficial and brilliant — a winning combination in theater at the time. He had numerous imitators and prepared the way for later developments in theater.

The Rise of Realism

Technical changes in theaters during the latter part of the nineteenth century continued at a rapid pace. When limelight was added to gas, the result was bright, intense lighting onstage; in the last decades of the century electric light heralded a new era in lighting design. Good lighting generally demanded detailed and authentic scenery; the dreamy light produced by gas often hid imperfections that were now impossible to disguise. The new Madison Square Theater (1879) in New York City was built with elevators that allowed its stage, complete with detailed and realistic scenery as well as actors, to be raised into position. European theaters had developed similar capacities.

In the 1840s accurate period costumes began to be the norm for historical plays. In the Elizabethan theater, contemporary clothing had been worn onstage, but by the mid-1800s costume designers were researching historical periods and producing costumes that aimed at historical accuracy.

In addition to offering lifelike scenery, lighting, and costumes, the theaters of the latter part of the century also featured plays whose circumstances and language were recognizable, contemporary, and believable. Even the sentimental melodramas seemed more realistic than productions of *King Lear* or *Macbeth,* plays that were still popular. The work of Scribe, including his historical plays, used a relatively prosaic everyday language. The situations may not seem absolutely lifelike to our eyes, but in their day they prepared the way for realism.

Changes in philosophy also contributed to the development of a realistic drama. Émile Zola (1840–1902) preached a doctrine of NATURALISM, demanding that drama avoid the artificiality of convoluted plot and urging a drama of natural, lifelike action. He intended his work to help change social conditions in France. His naturalistic novel *Nana* (1880) focused on a courtesan whose life came to a terrifying end. The play *Thérèse Raquin* (1873), based on Zola's novel of the same name, told the story of a woman and her lover who murder her husband and then commit suicide out of a sense of mutual guilt. There are no twists, surprises, or even much suspense in the play. Zola's subjects seem to have been uniformly grim, and naturalism became associated with the darker side of life.

REALISM, which avoided mechanical "clockwork" plots with their artificially contrived conclusions, began in the later years of the eighteenth century (some scholars claim to see evidence of it even earlier, in the work of Thomas Middleton) and progressed steadily to the end of the nineteenth century. In the realistic plays of Henrik Ibsen (1828–1906) and August Strindberg (1849–1912), the details of the setting, the costuming, and the circumstances of the action were so fully realized as to convince audiences that they were listening in on life itself. (See Figure 14 for an example of a realistic stage setting.)

In Britain, Oscar Wilde (1854–1900), poet, novelist, and playwright, offered an alternative to both melodrama and realistic drama near the end of the cen-

Figure 14. Realistic setting in a 1941 production of Anton Chekhov's *The Cherry Orchard*.

tury. Wilde had spent much of his literary life promoting the philosophy of art for art's sake. He asserted that the pleasure of poetry was in its sounds, images, and thoughts. Poetry and drama did not serve religious, political, social, or even personal goals. For Wilde, art served itself. He was such a brilliant conversationalist that the Irish poet-playwright W. B. Yeats declared him the only person he ever heard who spoke complete, rounded sentences that sounded as if he had written and polished them the night before. His witticisms were often barbed and vicious but always incisive and perceptive. He became famous for his bright, witty comedies. *The Importance of Being Earnest* (1895), sometimes wrongly accused of being about nothing, is the most often performed. It is an unsentimental, witty, and sometimes brittle comedy that dissects English upper-class attitudes that most of his audience would have taken for granted.

Wilde competed with numerous comic playwrights in England and abroad, such as the enormously successful Arthur Wing Pinero (1855–1934) and W. S. Gilbert (1836–1911) in England and Georges Feydeau (1862–1921) in France. None, though, could manage the unusual combination of wit and seriousness that marks Wilde's achievement. Another important competitor was another Irish playwright (Wilde was also Irish), Bernard Shaw (1856–1950), whose plays were also comic and serious, such as *Arms and the Man* (1894), *You Never Can Tell* (1898), and *Pygmalion* (1913). But Shaw is probably best known for his plays of ideas — plays in which an underlying idea or principle drives the action — such as *Mrs. Warren's Profession* (1898), *Man and Superman* (1903), and *Major Barbara* (1905).

After a disappointing beginning as a playwright, Anton Chekhov (1860–1904) worked with the Moscow Arts Theatre under the directorship of Konstantin Stanislavski (1865–1938), one of the most influential figures in modern Western drama. Stanislavski emphasized "inner realism" by having the actor become the character even in situations off stage by developing improvisational experiences to let the actor explore the character in situations other than those within the play. The Stanislavski Method helped the actor become the part, rather than just play the part. Chekhov and Stanislavski worked together to produce Chekhov's plays at a time when Chekhov felt himself a failure as a dramatist.

The first production of Chekhov's *The Seagull* (1896), his sixth major staged play, was a failure. Stanislavski convinced Chekhov to give it to his company to produce, resulting in an important triumph. Chekhov then reworked an earlier play into *Uncle Vanya* (1899) for Stanislavski, and it, too, was a hit. *Three Sisters* (1901) was not successful in its first performances, but it later became known as one of Chekhov's finest works. His last play, *The Cherry Orchard* (1904), was put on by Stanislavski's company and has become one of the most important works of twentieth-century drama. Chekhov died of a heart attack soon after the play's first production. Today Chekhov's legacy continues, with all his major plays staged throughout the world. Thus one of the most important nineteenth-century writers led the way to new developments in twentieth-century drama that are still evident today on the stage as well as in films and on television.

Nineteenth-Century Drama Timeline

DATE	THEATER	POLITICAL	SOCIAL/CULTURAL
1700–1800	**1759–1805:** Friedrich von Schiller, German playwright, author of *The Robbers* (1781) and *Maria Stuart* (1800)		**1770–1827:** Ludwig van Beethoven, German composer
	1761–1819: August Friedrich Ferdinand von Kotzebue, German playwright and one of the early developers of melodrama	**1775:** The American War of Independence begins at Concord, Massachusetts.	**1775–1817:** Jane Austen, English novelist
	1767–1787: *Sturm und Drang* period in German drama featuring the work of Goethe, Schiller, and others who rebelled against eighteenth-century rationalism	**1776:** The Declaration of Independence is signed. **1783:** Peace of Versailles: Britain recognizes the independence of the United States. **1789:** French revolutionaries storm the Bastille as the French revolution sweeps over French society.	
	1773: The Swedish National Theater is established in Stockholm.		**1792–1822:** Percy Bysshe Shelley, English Romantic poet
	1773–1844: Guilbert de Pixérécourt, French playwright generally credited with originating the melodrama	**1793:** Louis XVI and his queen, Marie Antoinette, are guillotined. The reign of terror, a purge instituted by the revolutionary government of France, claims 35,000 lives in one year.	**1793:** Eli Whitney (1765–1825) invents the cotton gin. **1795:** British forces occupy the Cape of Good Hope. **1795–1821:** John Keats, English Romantic poet
	1791–1861: Eugène Scribe, French playwright, developer of the "well-made" play, author of *Adrienne Lecouvreur* (1849)	**1799:** Napoleon Bonaparte overthrows the Directory of France, the moderate government that replaced the government of terror.	**1798:** *Lyrical Ballads* is published by Wordsworth and Coleridge. **1799–1837:** Alexander Pushkin, Russian poet
1800–1900	**1806–1872:** Edwin Forrest, America's first great native-born actor	**1803:** The Louisiana Purchase doubles the area of the United States. **1804:** Napoleon I (1769–1821) declares himself emperor of France.	**1802–1885:** Victor Hugo, French novelist **1803–1882:** Ralph Waldo Emerson, American Transcendental philosopher, clergyman, and author
	1808 and 1832: German writer Johann Wolfgang von Goethe (1749–1832) produces his masterpiece, *Faust* (in two parts).	**1805:** Admiral Horatio Nelson's victory over Napoleon at Trafalgar establishes the supremacy of British naval forces.	**1805:** Gas lighting is introduced in Great Britain.
	1809–1852: Nikolai Gogol, Russian playwright, author of *The Inspector General* (1836)	**1811–1820:** The Regency period: George, Prince of Wales, acts as regent for George III, who was declared insane.	**1809–1852:** Louis Braille, French inventor of reading system for the blind
	1813–1837: Georg Büchner, German playwright, author of *Danton's Death* (1835) and *Woyzeck* (1836)	**1812:** The United States declares war on Britain. **1814:** Treaty of Ghent ends the War of 1812; Britain is defeated.	**1812–1870:** Charles Dickens, English novelist

Nineteenth-Century Drama Timeline (continued)

DATE	THEATER	POLITICAL	SOCIAL/CULTURAL
1800–1900 (continued)	**1816:** Chestnut Street Theater in Philadelphia is the first theater to illuminate its stage with gas lighting.	**1815:** Napoleon is decisively defeated at the Battle of Waterloo.	**1816–1855:** Charlotte Brontë, English novelist
	1822–1890: Dion Boucicault, Irish American actor and writer of popular melodramas, among them *The Octoroon* (1859) and *The Colleen Bawn* (1860)	**1818:** Shaka ascends the Zulu throne in Southern Africa and initiates a period of military reform; he is assassinated in 1828.	**1817–1862:** Henry David Thoreau, American Transcendental writer and naturalist
		1820: Accession of George IV	**1820–1906:** Susan B. Anthony, American leader of the women's suffrage movement
	1828–1906: Henrik Ibsen, Norwegian playwright. Among his best-known works are *A Doll House* (1879) and *Hedda Gabler* (1890).	**1820:** The Missouri Compromise admits Maine as a free state and Missouri as a slave state.	**1821–1881:** Fyodor Dostoevsky, Russian novelist
		1821: Mexico declares its independence.	**1828–1910:** Leo Tolstoy, Russian novelist and philosopher
	1830: *Hernani*, by the French novelist and playwright Victor Hugo (1802–1885), traditionally marks the beginning of French romanticism.	**1823:** The Monroe Doctrine closes the American continent to European colonization.	**1830–1886:** Emily Dickinson, American poet
			1831: William Lloyd Garrison (1805–1879), American abolitionist, founds the *Liberator*.
	1837: William Charles Macready (1793–1873), an English actor, is the first to use the limelight (or Drummond light), a prototype of the spotlight.	**1837:** Queen Victoria begins her sixty-four-year reign in Great Britain.	**1833–1897:** Johannes Brahms, German composer
		1839: Beginning of the First opium War between Britain and China. The war ends in 1842 with the Treaty of Nanjing, which turns over Hong Kong to Britain and opens several Chinese ports to Western trade.	**1839:** Louis Daguerre (1789–1851) invents the daguerreotype, an early type of photograph.
	1840–1902: Émile Zola, French writer and promoter of naturalism in literature. Among his works is the novel (also a play) *Thérèse Raquin* (1873).		**1840–1893:** Peter Ilyich Tchaikovsky, Russian composer
			1843–1916: Henry James, American realist novelist
			1844: The telegraph is used for the first time.
			1845: Frederick Douglass (c. 1817–1895), African American abolitionist, publishes *Narrative of the Life of Frederick Douglass.*
		1846–1848: Mexican War over the United States' annexation of Texas. The Treaty of Guadalupe Hidalgo (1848) cedes Texas to the United States.	**1845–1849:** The great potato famine in Ireland kills nearly a million Irish; 1,600,000 immigrate to the United States.
	1849: The Astor Place Riot in New York is a result of the rivalry between the actors William Charles Macready and Edwin Forrest; twenty-two people are killed.		**1848:** The First U.S. Women's Rights Convention is held in Seneca Falls, N.Y.
			1848: California gold rush
	1849–1923: Sarah Bernhardt, French performer, perhaps the greatest actress of the nineteenth century		**1848:** Karl Marx, German political philosopher, writes *The Communist Manifesto*, with Friedrich Engels.
	1849–1912: August Strindberg, Swedish playwright. Among his works are *Miss Julie* (1888) and *The Dream Play* (1902).	**1852:** Napoleon III declares himself emperor of France and rules until 1871.	**1850:** Tennyson succeeds Wordsworth as poet laureate of Great Britain.
			1851: Herman Melville (1819–1891) publishes *Moby Dick*.
			1852: Harriet Beecher Stowe (1811–1896) publishes *Uncle Tom's Cabin*.

Nineteenth-Century Drama Timeline (continued)

DATE	THEATER	POLITICAL	SOCIAL/CULTURAL
1800–1900 (continued)	**1854–1900:** Oscar Wilde, Irish writer. His plays include *A Woman of No Importance* (1893) and *The Importance of Being Earnest* (1895). **1856–1950:** Bernard Shaw, Irish playwright. Among his works are *Mrs. Warren's Profession* (1898), *Major Barbara* (1905), and *Pygmalion* (1912). **1860–1904:** Anton Chekhov, Russian writer, author of *The Seagull* (1896) and *The Cherry Orchard* (1903) **1870–1900:** Golden Age of Peking (Beijing) Opera **1871–1896:** Gilbert and Sullivan write their comic operas, among them *H.M.S. Pinafore* (1878) and *The Pirates of Penzance* (1879). **1876:** Opening of Richard Wagner's Festival Theater in Bayreuth, Germany. Among his works is the four-part *Der Ring des Nibelungen* (1853–1874). **1881:** The Savoy Theatre is the first theater in London to be completely illuminated by electric light. **1887:** Théâtre Libre is founded in Paris by André Antoine to pursue naturalism in subject matter and staging. **1890–1930:** Vaudeville becomes one of the most popular forms of entertainment in the United States. **1896:** The first revolving stage is installed by Karl Lautenschlager at the Residenz Theater in Munich. **1898:** The Moscow Art Theatre is founded under the direction of Konstantin Stanislavsky and Vladimir Nemirovich-Danchenko.	**1857:** Czar Alexander II begins emancipation of serfs in Russia. **1860:** Abraham Lincoln is elected president. South Carolina secedes from the Union. **1861:** Italy is unified under Victor Emmanuel II. **1861–1865:** The Civil War is fought in the United States. **1862:** Otto von Bismarck is appointed prime minister of Prussia. **1865:** Abraham Lincoln is assassinated by the actor John Wilkes Booth at Ford's Theatre in Washington, D.C. **1869:** The Suez Canal opens. **1870–1871:** Franco-Prussian War **1871:** The German Empire is founded under Kaiser Wilhelm I. **1876:** At the Battle of the Little Bighorn, the Sioux defeat General George Custer's troops. **1885:** The Congo becomes a personal possession of King Leopold II of Belgium. **1890:** The Battle of Wounded Knee ends the American Indians' wars of resistance; two hundred Indians are killed by the U.S. Army. **1898:** The Spanish-American War. Cuban patriots demand independence and receive the military support of the United States. The 1898 Treaty of Paris gives Puerto Rico, Guam, the Philippines, and Cuba to the United States. **1899–1902:** The Boer War (South African War) ends British supremacy in South Africa.	**1854–1856:** Scottish explorer David Livingstone crosses Africa. **1859:** Charles Darwin (1809–1882) publishes *On the Origin of Species by Natural Selection.* **1860s:** Louis Pasteur (1822–1895), French chemist, develops pasteurization. **1865–1939:** William Butler Yeats, Irish poet and playwright **1869:** The first transcontinental railroad in the United States is completed. **1869–1959:** Frank Lloyd Wright, preeminent American architect **1876:** Alexander Graham Bell (1847–1922) invents the telephone. **1877:** Thomas Edison (1847–1931) invents the phonograph. **1879:** Thomas Edison invents the lightbulb. **1898–1976:** Paul Robeson, African American singer, actor, and civil rights activist

Henrik Ibsen

Using the new style of realism, Henrik Ibsen (1828–1906) slowly and painfully became the most influential modern dramatist. Subjects that had been ignored on the stage became the center of his work. But his rise to fame was anything but direct. His family was extremely poor, and as a youth he worked in a drugstore in Grimstad, a seaport town in Norway. At seventeen he had an illegitimate child with a servant girl. At twenty-one he wrote his first play, in verse. In 1850, at the age of twenty-two, he left Grimstad for Oslo (then called Christiana) to become a student, but within a year he joined the new National Theater and stayed for six years, writing and directing.

In the 1850s he wrote numerous plays that did not bring him recognition: *St. John's Eve* (1853), *Lady Inger of Østraat* (1855), *Olaf Liljekrans* (1857),

Henrik Ibsen at age sixty-eight, seventeen years after the first production of *A Doll House*. He was the most influential playwright in Europe when this photograph was taken in 1896.

700

and *The Vikings at Helgeland* (1857). In the early 1860s, with a wife and daughter to support, he went through a period of serious self-doubt and despair, and his first play in five years, *Love's Comedy* (1862), was turned down for performance. Eventually he got a job with the Christiana Theater and had a rare success with *The Pretenders* (1864), a historical play about thirteenth-century warriors vying for the vacant throne of Norway.

His breakthrough came with the publication in 1866 of the verse play *Brand,* which was written to be read and not performed. (It was first produced in 1885.) It is the portrait of a clergyman who takes the strictures of religion so seriously that he rejects the New Testament doctrine of love and accepts the Old Testament doctrine of the will of God. He destroys himself in the process and ends the play on a mountaintop in the Ice Church, facing an avalanche about to kill him. Out of the clouds comes the answer to his questions of whether love or will achieves salvation: "He is the God of Love." *Brand* made Ibsen famous. He followed it with another successful closet drama, *Peer Gynt* (1867), about a character, quite unlike Brand, who avoids the rigors of morality and ends up unable to know if he has been saved or condemned.

Despite these successes, Ibsen still struggled for recognition. It was not until 1877 that he had his first success in a play that experimented with the new realistic style of drama: *The Pillars of Society,* which probed behind the hypocrisies of Karsten Bernick, a merchant who prospers by all manner of double-dealing and betrayal of his relatives. Eventually, he admits his crimes but, instead of being punished, is welcomed back into society and is more successful than ever. This play gave Ibsen a reputation in Germany, where it was frequently performed, and prepared him for his great successes. *A Doll House* (1879), which he wrote in Italy, came two years later. It was more fully realistic in style than *The Pillars of Society* and, while immensely successful in Scandinavia, did not become widely known elsewhere for another ten years.

His next play, *Ghosts* (1881), was denounced violently because it dared to treat a subject that had been taboo on the stage: syphilis. *Ghosts* introduced a respectable family, the Alvings, who harbor the secret that their late father contracted the disease and passed it on to Oswald, his son. In addition, the theme of incest is suggested in the presence of Alving's illegitimate daughter, Regina, who falls in love with Oswald. This kind of material was so foreign to the late-nineteenth-century stage that Ibsen was vilified and isolated by the literary community in Norway. He chose exile for a time in Rome, Amalfi, and Munich.

Ibsen's last years were filled with activity. He wrote some of his best-known plays in rapid succession: *An Enemy of the People* (1882), *The Wild Duck* (1884), *Hedda Gabler* (1890), *The Master Builder* (1892), and *John Gabriel Borkman* (1896). In 1891 he returned to live in Norway, where he died fifteen years later.

The most influential European dramatist in the late nineteenth century, Ibsen inspired emerging writers in the United States, Ireland, and many other nations. But his full influence was not felt until the early decades of the twentieth century, when other writers were able to spread the revolutionary doctrine that was implied in realism as practiced by Ibsen and Strindberg. Being direct, honest, and unsparing in treating character and theme became the normal mode of serious drama after Ibsen.

A DOLL HOUSE

Once Henrik Ibsen found his voice as a realist playwright, he began to develop plays centering on social problems and the problems of the individual struggling against the demands of society. In *A Doll House* (1879) he focused on the repression of women. It was a subject that deeply offended conservatives and was very much on the minds of progressive and liberal Scandinavians. It was therefore a rather daring theme. The play opens with the dutiful, eager wife Nora Helmer twittering like a lark and pattering like a squirrel, pleasing her husband, Torvald. Helmer is consumed with propriety. As far as he is concerned, Nora is only a woman, an empty-headed ornament in a house designed to keep his life functioning smoothly.

Nora is portrayed as a macaroon-eating, sweet-toothed creature looking for ways to please her husband. When she reveals that she borrowed the money that took them to Italy for a year to save her husband's life, she shows us that she is made of much stronger stuff than anyone has given her credit for. Yet the manner in which she borrowed the money is technically criminal because she had to forge her father's signature, and she now finds herself at the mercy of the lender, Nils Krogstad.

From a modern perspective, Nora's action seems daring and imaginative rather than merely illegal and surreptitious. Torvald Helmer's moralistic position is to us essentially stifling. He condemns Nora's father for a similar failure

LEFT: For this 1906 production of Ibsen's *The Wild Duck,* the director, André Antoine, had the set constructed of Norwegian pine to achieve a high degree of realism. ABOVE: Edvard Munch's 1906 stage design for Max Reinhardt's production of Ibsen's *Ghosts* at the Kammerspiele in Berlin. Although *Ghosts* (1881) was written in Ibsen's realistic style, Munch's expressionistic lines and shadows seem to reflect the tendencies in Ibsen's late plays to move beyond realism to a more dreamlike structure.

to secure proper signatures, just as he condemns Nils Krogstad for doing the same. He condemns people for their crimes without considering their circumstances or motives. He is moralistic rather than moral.

The atmosphere of the Helmer household is oppressive. Everything is set up to amuse Torvald, and he lacks any awareness that other people might be his equal. Early in the play Ibsen establishes Nora's longings: she explains that to pay back her loan she has had to take in copying work, and, rather than resent her labor, she observes that it made her feel wonderful, the way a man must feel. Ibsen said that his intention in the play was not primarily to promote the emancipation of women; it was to establish, as Ibsen's biographer Michael Meyer says, "that the primary duty of anyone was to find out who he or she really was and to become that person."

However, the play from the first was seen as addressing the problems of women, especially married women who were treated as their husbands' property. When the play was first performed, the slam of the door at Nora's leaving was much louder than it is today. It was shocking to late-nineteenth-century society, which took Torvald Helmer's attitudes for granted. The first audiences probably were split in their opinions about Nora's actions. As Meyer reminds us, "No play had ever before contributed so momentously to the social debate, or been so widely and furiously discussed among people who were not normally interested in theatrical or even artistic matters." Although the critics in Copenhagen (where the play was first produced) and London were very negative, the audiences were filled with curiosity and flocked to the theaters to see the play.

What the audiences saw was that once Nora is awakened, the kind of life Torvald imagines for her is death to Nora. Torvald cannot see how his self-absorbed concern and fear for his own social standing reveal his limitations and selfishness. Nora sees immediately the limits of his concern, and her only choice is to leave him so that she can grow morally and spiritually.

What she does and where she goes have been a matter of speculation since the play was first performed. Ibsen refused to encourage any specific conjecture. It is enough that she has the courage to leave. But the ending of the play bothered audiences as well as critics, and it was performed in Germany in 1880 with a happy ending that Ibsen himself wrote to forestall anyone else from doing so. The first German actress to play the part insisted that she would personally never leave her children and therefore would not do the play as written. In the revised version, instead of leaving, Nora is led to the door of her children's room and falls weeping as the curtain goes down. The so-called happy-ending version was played for a while in England and elsewhere. No one was satisfied with this ending, and eventually the play reverted to its original form.

Through the proscenium arch of the theater in Ibsen's day audiences were permitted to eavesdrop on themselves, since Ibsen clearly was analyzing their own mores. In a way the audience was looking at a dollhouse; but instead of containing miniature furniture and miniature people, it contained replicas of those watching. That very sense of intimacy, made possible by the late-nineteenth-century theater, heightened the intensity of the play.

A Doll House in Performance

A Doll House was first produced in the Royal Theatre, Copenhagen, in December 1879. Despite its immediate popular success in Scandinavia and Germany, two years passed before the play appeared elsewhere and ten years before it appeared in England and America in a complete and accurate text. Further, the early German version (February 1880), with Hedwig Niemann-Raabe as Nora, had to be revised with a happy ending because the actress refused to play the original ending. Fortunately, the "happy ending," in which Nora does not leave home, was not successful and Niemann-Raabe eventually played the part as written. An adaptation, also with the happy ending, titled *The Child Wife,* was produced in Milwaukee in 1882. While the first professional London production of the play in 1889 found favor with the public, it was attacked in the press for being "unnatural, immoral and, in its concluding scene, essentially undramatic." Among other things, Ibsen was being condemned for not providing a vibrant plot.

Among the play's memorable performances was Ethel Barrymore's version in New York in 1905. Barrymore was praised for a brilliant interpretation of "the child wife." Ruth Gordon played the part to acclaim in 1937, as did Claire Bloom in 1971 on the stage and in 1973 in film. Jane Fonda played the role in Joseph Losey's film version of 1973. The Norwegian actress Liv Ullmann performed the role in Lincoln Center in 1975 and was praised as "the most enchanting," the "most honest" Nora that the critic Walter Kerr had seen. Other critics were less kind, but it was a successful run. One of the most riveting of modern productions starred Janet McTeer in Anthony Page's revival of *A Doll House.* This production began in London in 1997 and transferred to New York for a Broadway run the same year. Ben Brantley of the *New York Times* said of it, "Nothing can prepare you for the initial shock of Ms.

McTeer's performance, which transforms the passive Nora Helmer, Ibsen's childlike plaything of a wife, into an electric, even aggressive presence" revealing "previously hidden nuances in Ibsen's landmark work." This production was faithful to the production values of Ibsen's original, using an essentially Victorian-era setting with period costumes. McTeer's energy transformed the play and gave Nora a new dimension that made the audience feel that she would do better than merely survive when she left her home. The play is performed regularly in college and regional theaters in the United States and elsewhere.

Henrik Ibsen (1828–1906)

A DOLL HOUSE

1879

TRANSLATED BY ROLF FJELDE

The Characters

TORVALD HELMER, *a lawyer*
NORA, *his wife*
DR. RANK
MRS. LINDE
NILS KROGSTAD, *a bank clerk*
THE HELMERS' THREE SMALL CHILDREN
ANNE-MARIE, *their nurse*
HELENE, *a maid*
A DELIVERY BOY

The action takes place in Helmer's residence.

ACT I

(*A comfortable room, tastefully but not expensively furnished. A door to the right in the back wall leads to the entryway; another to the left leads to Helmer's study. Between these doors, a piano. Midway in the left-hand wall a door, and further back a window. Near the window a round table with an armchair and a small sofa. In the right-hand wall, toward the rear, a door, and nearer the foreground a porcelain stove with two armchairs and a rocking chair beside it. Between the stove and the side door, a small table. Engravings on the walls. An*

As Fjelde explains in his foreword to the translation, he does not use the possessive "A Doll's House" because "the house is not Nora's, as the possessive implies." Fjelde believes that Ibsen includes Torvald with Nora in the original title, "for the two of them at the play's opening are still posing like the little marzipan bride and groom atop the wedding cake."

étagère° with china figures and other small art objects; a small bookcase with richly bound books; the floor carpeted; a fire burning in the stove. It is a winter day.)

(*A bell rings in the entryway; shortly after we hear the door being unlocked. Nora comes into the room, humming happily to herself; she is wearing street clothes and carries an armload of packages, which she puts down on the table to the right. She has left the hall door open, and through it a Delivery Boy is seen holding a Christmas tree and a basket, which he gives to the Maid who let them in.*)

NORA: Hide the tree well, Helene. The children mustn't get a glimpse of it till this evening, after it's trimmed. (*To the Delivery Boy, taking out her purse.*) How much?

DELIVERY BOY: Fifty, ma'am.

NORA: There's a crown. No, keep the change. (*The Boy thanks her and leaves. Nora shuts the door. She laughs softly to herself while taking off her street things. Drawing a bag of macaroons from her pocket, she eats a couple, then steals over and listens at her husband's study door.*) Yes, he's home. (*Hums again as she moves to the table right.*)

HELMER (*from the study*): Is that my little lark twittering out there?

NORA (*busy opening some packages*): Yes, it is.

HELMER: Is that my squirrel rummaging around?

NORA: Yes!

HELMER: When did my squirrel get in?

NORA: Just now. (*Putting the macaroon bag in her pocket and wiping her mouth.*) Do come in, Torvald, and see what I've bought.

[S.D.] **étagère:** Cabinet with shelves.

Pet name

belittling

HELMER: Can't be disturbed. (*After a moment he opens the door and peers in, pen in hand.*) Bought, you say? All that there? Has the little spendthrift been out throwing money around again?

NORA: Oh, but Torvald, this year we really should let ourselves go a bit. It's the first Christmas we haven't had to economize.

HELMER: But you know we can't go squandering.

NORA: Oh yes, Torvald, we can squander a little now. Can't we? Just a tiny, wee bit. Now that you've got a big salary and are going to make piles and piles of money.

HELMER: Yes — starting New Year's. But then it's a full three months till the raise comes through.

NORA: Pooh! We can borrow that long.

HELMER: Nora! (*Goes over and playfully takes her by the ear.*) Are your scatterbrains off again? What if today I borrowed a thousand crowns, and you squandered them over Christmas week, and then on New Year's Eve a roof tile fell on my head, and I lay there —

NORA (*putting her hand on his mouth*): Oh! Don't say such things!

HELMER: Yes, but what if it happened — then what?

NORA: If anything so awful happened, then it just wouldn't matter if I had debts or not.

HELMER: Well, but the people I'd borrowed from?

NORA: Them? Who cares about them! They're strangers.

HELMER: Nora, Nora, how like a woman! No, but seriously, Nora, you know what I think about that. No debts! Never borrow! Something of freedom's lost — and something of beauty, too — from a home that's founded on borrowing and debt. We've made a brave stand up to now, the two of us; and we'll go right on like that the little while we have to.

NORA (*going toward the stove*): Yes, whatever you say, Torvald.

HELMER (*following her*): Now, now, the little lark's wings mustn't droop. Come on, don't be a sulky squirrel. (*Taking out his wallet.*) Nora, guess what I have here.

NORA (*turning quickly*): Money!

HELMER: There, see. (*Hands her some notes.*) Good grief, I know how costs go up in a house at Christmastime.

NORA: Ten — twenty — thirty — forty. Oh, thank you, Torvald; I can manage no end on this.

HELMER: You really will have to.

NORA: Oh yes, I promise I will! But come here so I can show you everything I bought. And so cheap! Look, new clothes for Ivar here — and a sword. Here a horse and a trumpet for Bob. And a doll and a doll's bed here for Emmy; they're nothing much, but she'll tear them to bits in no time anyway. And here I have dress material and handkerchiefs for the maids. Old Anne-Marie really deserves something more.

HELMER: And what's in that package there?

NORA (*with a cry*): Torvald, no! You can't see that till tonight!

HELMER: I see. But tell me now, you little prodigal, what have you thought of for yourself?

NORA: For myself? Oh, I don't want anything at all.

HELMER: Of course you do. Tell me just what — within reason — you'd most like to have.

NORA: I honestly don't know. Oh, listen, Torvald —

HELMER: Well?

NORA (*fumbling at his coat buttons, without looking at him*): If you want to give me something, then maybe you could — you could —

HELMER: Come on, out with it.

NORA (*hurriedly*): You could give me money, Torvald. No more than you think you can spare; then one of these days I'll buy something with it.

HELMER: But Nora —

NORA: Oh, please, Torvald darling, do that! I beg you, please. Then I could hang the bills in pretty gilt paper on the Christmas tree. Wouldn't that be fun?

HELMER: What are those little birds called that always fly through their fortunes?

NORA: Oh yes, spendthrifts; I know all that. But let's do as I say, Torvald; then I'll have time to decide what I really need most. That's very sensible, isn't it?

HELMER (*smiling*): Yes, very — that is, if you actually hung onto the money I give you, and you actually used it to buy yourself something. But it goes for the house and for all sorts of foolish things, and then I only have to lay out some more.

NORA: Oh, but Torvald —

HELMER: Don't deny it, my dear little Nora. (*Putting his arm around her waist.*) Spendthrifts are sweet, but they use up a frightful amount of money. It's incredible what it costs a man to feed such birds.

NORA: Oh, how can you say that! Really, I save everything I can.

HELMER (*laughing*): Yes, that's the truth. Everything you can. But that's nothing at all.

NORA (*humming, with a smile of quiet satisfaction*): Hm, if you only knew what expenses we larks and squirrels have, Torvald.

HELMER: You're an odd little one. Exactly the way your father was. You're never at a loss for scaring up money; but the moment you have it, it runs right out through your fingers; you never know what you've done with it. Well, one takes you as you are. It's deep in your blood. Yes, these things are hereditary, Nora.

NORA: Ah, I could wish I'd inherited many of Papa's qualities.

HELMER: And I couldn't wish you anything but just what you are, my sweet little lark. But wait; it seems to me you have a very — what should I call it? — a very suspicious look today —

NORA: I do?

HELMER: You certainly do. Look me straight in the eye.

NORA (*looking at him*): Well?

HELMER (*shaking an admonitory finger*): Surely my sweet tooth hasn't been running riot in town today, has she?

NORA: No. Why do you imagine that?

HELMER: My sweet tooth really didn't make a little detour through the confectioner's?

NORA: No, I assure you, Torvald —

HELMER: Hasn't nibbled some pastry?

NORA: No, not at all.

HELMER: Not even munched a macaroon or two?

NORA: No, Torvald, I assure you, really —

HELMER: There, there now. Of course I'm only joking.

NORA (*going to the table, right*): You know I could never think of going against you.

HELMER: No, I understand that; and you *have* given me your word. (*Going over to her.*) Well, you keep your little Christmas secrets to yourself, Nora darling. I expect they'll come to light this evening, when the tree is lit.

NORA: Did you remember to ask Dr. Rank?

HELMER: No. But there's no need for that, it's assumed he'll be dining with us. All the same, I'll ask him when he stops by here this morning. I've ordered some fine wine. Nora, you can't imagine how I'm looking forward to this evening.

NORA: So am I. And what fun for the children, Torvald!

HELMER: Ah, it's so gratifying to know that one's gotten a safe, secure job, and with a comfortable salary. It's a great satisfaction, isn't it?

NORA: Oh, it's wonderful!

HELMER: Remember last Christmas? Three whole weeks before, you shut yourself in every evening till long after midnight, making flowers for the Christmas tree, and all the other decorations to surprise us. Ugh, that was the dullest time I've ever lived through.

NORA: It wasn't at all dull for me.

HELMER (*smiling*): But the outcome *was* pretty sorry, Nora.

NORA: Oh, don't tease me with that again. How could I help it that the cat came in and tore everything to shreds.

HELMER: No, poor thing, you certainly couldn't. You wanted so much to please us all, and that's what counts. But it's just as well that the hard times are past.

NORA: Yes, it's really wonderful.

HELMER: Now I don't have to sit here alone, boring myself, and you don't have to tire your precious eyes and your fair little delicate hands —

NORA (*clapping her hands*): No, is it really true, Torvald, I don't have to? Oh, how wonderfully lovely to hear! (*Taking his arm.*) Now I'll tell you just how I've thought we should plan things. Right after Christmas — (*The doorbell rings.*) Oh, the bell. (*Straightening the room up a bit.*) Somebody would have to come. What a bore!

HELMER: I'm not at home to visitors, don't forget.

MAID (*from the hall doorway*): Ma'am, a lady to see you —

NORA: All right, let her come in.

MAID (*to Helmer*): And the doctor's just come too.

HELMER: Did he go right to my study?

MAID: Yes, he did.

(*Helmer goes into his room. The Maid shows in Mrs. Linde, dressed in traveling clothes, and shuts the door after her.*)

MRS. LINDE (*in a dispirited and somewhat hesitant voice*): Hello, Nora.

NORA (*uncertain*): Hello —

MRS. LINDE: You don't recognize me.

NORA: No, I don't know — but wait, I think — (*Exclaiming.*) What! Kristine! Is it really you?

MRS. LINDE: Yes, it's me.

NORA: Kristine! To think I didn't recognize you. But then, how could I? (*More quietly.*) How you've changed, Kristine!

MRS. LINDE: Yes, no doubt I have. In nine — ten long years.

NORA: Is it so long since we met! Yes, it's all of that. Oh, these last eight years have been a happy time, believe me. And so now you've come in to town, too. Made the long trip in the winter. That took courage.

MRS. LINDE: I just got here by ship this morning.

NORA: To enjoy yourself over Christmas, of course. Oh, how lovely! Yes, enjoy ourselves, we'll do that. But take your coat off. You're not still cold? (*Helping her.*) There now, let's get cozy here by the stove. No, the easy chair there! I'll take the rocker here. (*Seizing her hands.*) Yes, now you have your old look again; it was only in that first moment. You're a bit more pale, Kristine — and maybe a bit thinner.

MRS. LINDE: And much, much older, Nora.

NORA: Yes, perhaps a bit older; a tiny, tiny bit; not much at all. (*Stopping short; suddenly serious.*) Oh, but thoughtless me, to sit here, chattering away. Sweet, good Kristine, can you forgive me?

MRS. LINDE: What do you mean, Nora?

NORA (*softly*): Poor Kristine, you've become a widow.

MRS. LINDE: Yes, three years ago.

NORA: Oh, I knew it, of course; I read it in the papers. Oh, Kristine, you must believe me; I often thought of writing you then, but I kept postponing it, and something always interfered.

MRS. LINDE: Nora dear, I understand completely.

NORA: No, it was awful of me, Kristine. You poor thing, how much you must have gone through. And he left you nothing?

MRS. LINDE: No.

NORA: And no children?

MRS. LINDE: No.

NORA: Nothing at all, then?

MRS. LINDE: Not even a sense of loss to feed on.

NORA (*looking incredulously at her*): But Kristine, how could that be?

MRS. LINDE (*smiling wearily and smoothing her hair*): Oh, sometimes it happens, Nora.

NORA: So completely alone. How terribly hard that must be for you. I have three lovely children. You can't see them now; they're out with the maid. But now you must tell me everything —

[handwritten note: thinks she has it all at this point, especially in comparison to Kristine]

MRS. LINDE: No, no, no, tell me about yourself.

NORA: No, you begin. Today I don't want to be selfish. I want to think only of you today. But there is something I must tell you. Did you hear of the wonderful luck we had recently?

MRS. LINDE: No, what's that?

NORA: My husband's been made manager in the bank, just think!

MRS. LINDE: Your husband? How marvelous!

NORA: Isn't it? Being a lawyer is such an uncertain living, you know, especially if one won't touch any cases that aren't clean and decent. And of course Torvald would never do that, and I'm with him completely there. Oh, we're simply delighted, believe me! He'll join the bank right after New Year's and start getting a huge salary and lots of commissions. From now on we can live quite differently — just as we want. Oh, Kristine, I feel so light and happy! Won't it be lovely to have stacks of money and not a care in the world?

MRS. LINDE: Well, anyway, it would be lovely to have enough for necessities.

NORA: No, not just for necessities, but stacks and stacks of money!

MRS. LINDE (*smiling*): Nora, Nora, aren't you sensible yet? Back in school you were such a free spender.

NORA (*with a quiet laugh*): Yes, that's what Torvald still says. (*Shaking her finger.*) But "Nora, Nora" isn't as silly as you all think. Really, we've been in no position for me to go squandering. We've had to work, both of us.

MRS. LINDE: You too?

NORA: Yes, at odd jobs — needlework, crocheting, embroidery, and such — (*casually*) and other things too. You remember that Torvald left the department when we were married? There was no chance of promotion in his office, and of course he needed to earn more money. But that first year he drove himself terribly. He took on all kinds of extra work that kept him going morning and night. It wore him down, and then he fell deathly ill. The doctors said it was essential for him to travel south.

MRS. LINDE: Yes, didn't you spend a whole year in Italy?

NORA: That's right. It wasn't easy to get away, you know. Ivar had just been born. But of course we had to go. Oh, that was a beautiful trip, and it saved Torvald's life. But it cost a frightful sum, Kristine.

MRS. LINDE: I can well imagine.

NORA: Four thousand, eight hundred crowns it cost. That's really a lot of money.

MRS. LINDE: But it's lucky you had it when you needed it.

NORA: Well, as it was, we got it from Papa.

MRS. LINDE: I see. It was just about the time your father died.

NORA: Yes, just about then. And, you know, I couldn't make that trip out to nurse him. I had to stay here, expecting Ivar any moment, and with my poor sick Torvald to care for. Dearest Papa, I never saw him

again, Kristine. Oh, that was the worst time I've known in all my marriage.

MRS. LINDE: I know how you loved him. And then you went off to Italy?

NORA: Yes. We had the means now, and the doctors urged us. So we left a month after.

MRS. LINDE: And your husband came back completely cured?

NORA: Sound as a drum!

MRS. LINDE: But — the doctor?

NORA: Who?

MRS. LINDE: I thought the maid said he was a doctor, the man who came in with me.

NORA: Yes, that was Dr. Rank — but he's not making a sick call. He's our closest friend, and he stops by at least once a day. No, Torvald hasn't had a sick moment since, and the children are fit and strong, and I am, too. (*Jumping up and clapping her hands.*) Oh, dear God, Kristine, what a lovely thing to live and be happy! But how disgusting of me — I'm talking of nothing but my own affairs. (*Sits on a stool close by Kristine, arms resting across her knees.*) Oh, don't be angry with me! Tell me, is it really true that you weren't in love with your husband? Why did you marry him, then?

MRS. LINDE: My mother was still alive, but bedridden and helpless — and I had my two younger brothers to look after. In all conscience, I didn't think I could turn him down.

NORA: No, you were right there. But was he rich at the time?

MRS. LINDE: He was very well off, I'd say. But the business was shaky, Nora. When he died, it all fell apart, and nothing was left.

NORA: And then — ?

MRS. LINDE: Yes, so I had to scrape up a living with a little shop and a little teaching and whatever else I could find. The last three years have been like one endless workday without a rest for me. Now, it's over, Nora. My poor mother doesn't need me, for she's passed on. Nor the boys, either; they're working now and can take care of themselves.

NORA: How free you must feel —

MRS. LINDE: No — only unspeakably empty. Nothing to live for now. (*Standing up anxiously.*) That's why I couldn't take it any longer out in that desolate hole. Maybe here it'll be easier to find something to do and keep my mind occupied. If I could only be lucky enough to get a steady job, some office work —

NORA: Oh, but Kristine, that's so dreadfully tiring, and you already look so tired. It would be much better for you if you could go off to a bathing resort.

MRS. LINDE (*going toward the window*): I have no father to give me travel money, Nora.

NORA (*rising*): Oh, don't be angry with me.

MRS. LINDE (*going to her*): Nora dear, don't you be angry with me. The worst of my kind of situation is all the bitterness that's stored away. No one to work for, and yet you're always having to snap up your opportunities. You have to live; and so you grow self-ish. When you told me the happy change in your lot, do you know I was delighted less for your sakes than for mine?

NORA: How so? Oh, I see. You think maybe Torvald could do something for you.

MRS. LINDE: Yes, that's what I thought.

NORA: And he will, Kristine! Just leave it to me; I'll bring it up so delicately — find something attractive to humor him with. Oh, I'm so eager to help you.

MRS. LINDE: How very kind of you, Nora, to be so concerned over me — doubly kind, considering you really know so little of life's burdens yourself.

NORA: I — ? I know so little — ?

MRS. LINDE (*smiling*): Well, my heavens — a little needlework and such — Nora, you're just a child.

NORA (*tossing her head and pacing the floor*): You don't have to act so superior.

MRS. LINDE: Oh?

NORA: You're just like the others. You all think I'm incapable of anything serious —

MRS. LINDE: Come now —

NORA: That I've never had to face the raw world.

MRS. LINDE: Nora dear, you've just been telling me all your troubles.

NORA: Hm! Trivial! (*Quietly.*) I haven't told you the big thing.

MRS. LINDE: Big thing? What do you mean?

NORA: You look down on me so, Kristine, but you shouldn't. You're proud that you worked so long and hard for your mother.

MRS. LINDE: I don't look down on a soul. But it is true: I'm proud — and happy, too — to think it was given to me to make my mother's last days almost free of care.

NORA: And you're also proud thinking of what you've done for your brothers.

MRS. LINDE: I feel I've a right to be.

NORA: I agree. But listen to this, Kristine — I've also got something to be proud and happy for.

MRS. LINDE: I don't doubt it. But whatever do you mean?

NORA: Not so loud. What if Torvald heard! He mustn't, not for anything in the world. Nobody must know, Kristine. No one but you.

MRS. LINDE: But what is it, then?

NORA: Come here. (*Drawing her down beside her on the sofa.*) It's true — I've also got something to be proud and happy for. I'm the one who saved Torvald's life.

MRS. LINDE: Saved — ? Saved how?

NORA: I told you about the trip to Italy. Torvald never would have lived if he hadn't gone south —

MRS. LINDE: Of course; your father gave you the means —

NORA (*smiling*): That's what Torvald and all the rest think, but —

MRS. LINDE: But — ?

NORA: Papa didn't give us a pin. I was the one who raised the money.

MRS. LINDE: You? That whole amount?

NORA: Four thousand, eight hundred crowns. What do you say to that?

MRS. LINDE: But Nora, how was it possible? Did you win the lottery?

NORA (*disdainfully*): The lottery? Pooh! No art to that.

MRS. LINDE: But where did you get it from then?

NORA (*humming, with a mysterious smile*): Hmm, tra-la-la-la.

MRS. LINDE: Because you couldn't have borrowed it.

NORA: No? Why not?

MRS. LINDE: A wife can't borrow without her husband's consent.

NORA (*tossing her head*): Oh, but a wife with a little business sense, a wife who knows how to manage —

MRS. LINDE: Nora, I simply don't understand —

NORA: You don't have to. Whoever said I *borrowed* the money? I could have gotten it other ways. (*Throwing herself back on the sofa.*) I could have gotten it from some admirer or other. After all, a girl with my ravishing appeal —

MRS. LINDE: You lunatic.

NORA: I'll bet you're eaten up with curiosity, Kristine.

MRS. LINDE: Now listen here, Nora — you haven't done something indiscreet?

NORA (*sitting up again*): Is it indiscreet to save your husband's life?

MRS. LINDE: I think it's indiscreet that without his knowledge you —

NORA: But that's the point: He mustn't know! My Lord, can't you understand? He mustn't ever know the close call he had. It was to *me* the doctors came to say his life was in danger — that nothing could save him but a stay in the south. Didn't I try strategy then! I began talking about how lovely it would be for me to travel abroad like other young wives; I begged and I cried; I told him please to remember my condition, to be kind and indulge me; and then I dropped a hint that he could easily take out a loan. But at that, Kristine, he nearly exploded. He said I was frivolous, and it was his duty as man of the house not to indulge me in whims and fancies — as I think he called them. Aha, I thought, now you'll just have to be saved — and that's when I saw my chance.

MRS. LINDE: And your father never told Torvald the money wasn't from him?

NORA: No, never. Papa died right about then. I'd considered bringing him into my secret and begging him never to tell. But he was too sick at the time — and then, sadly, it didn't matter.

MRS. LINDE: And you've never confided in your husband since?

NORA: For heaven's sake, no! Are you serious? He's so strict on that subject. Besides — Torvald, with all his masculine pride — how painfully humiliating for him if he ever found out he was in debt to me. That would just ruin our relationship. Our beautiful, happy home would never be the same.

MRS. LINDE: Won't you ever tell him?

NORA (*thoughtfully, half smiling*): Yes — maybe sometime years from now, when I'm no longer so attractive. Don't laugh! I only mean when Torvald loves me less than now, when he stops enjoying my dancing and dressing up and reciting for him. Then it might be wise to have something in reserve — (*Breaking off.*) How ridiculous! That'll never happen — Well, Kristine, what do you think of my big secret? I'm capable of something too, hm? You can imagine, of course, how this thing hangs over me. It really hasn't been easy meeting the payments on time. In the business world there's what they call quarterly interest and what they call amortization, and these are always so terribly hard to manage. I've had to skimp a little here and there, wherever I could, you know. I could hardly spare anything from my house allowance, because Torvald has to live well. I couldn't let the children go poorly dressed; whatever I got for them, I felt I had to use up completely — the darlings!

MRS. LINDE: Poor Nora, so it had to come out of your own budget, then?

NORA: Yes, of course. But I was the one most responsible, too. Every time Torvald gave me money for new clothes and such, I never used more than half; always bought the simplest, cheapest outfits. It was a godsend that everything looks so well on me that Torvald never noticed. But it did weigh me down at times, Kristine. It *is* such a joy to wear fine things. You understand.

MRS. LINDE: Oh, of course.

NORA: And then I found other ways of making money. Last winter I was lucky enough to get a lot of copying to do. I locked myself in and sat writing every evening till late in the night. Ah, I was tired so often, dead tired. But still it was wonderful fun, sitting and working like that, earning money. It was almost like being a man.

MRS. LINDE: But how much have you paid off this way so far?

NORA: That's hard to say, exactly. These accounts, you know, aren't easy to figure. I only know that I've paid out all I could scrape together. Time and again I haven't known where to turn. (*Smiling.*) Then I'd sit here dreaming of a rich old gentleman who had fallen in love with me —

MRS. LINDE: What! Who is he?

NORA: Oh, really! And that he'd died, and when his will was opened, there in big letters it said, "All my fortune shall be paid over in cash, immediately, to that enchanting Mrs. Nora Helmer."

MRS. LINDE: But Nora dear — who *was* this gentleman?

NORA: Good grief, can't you understand? The old man never existed; that was only something I'd dream up time and again whenever I was at my wits' end for money. But it makes no difference now; the old fossil can go where he pleases for all I care; I don't need him or his will — because now I'm free. (*Jumping up.*) Oh, how lovely to think of that, Kristine! Care-

free! To know you're carefree, utterly carefree; to be able to romp and play with the children, and to keep up a beautiful, charming home — everything just the way Torvald likes it! And think, spring is coming, with big blue skies. Maybe we can travel a little then. Maybe I'll see the ocean again. Oh yes, it *is* so marvelous to live and be happy!

(*The front doorbell rings.*)

MRS. LINDE (*rising*): There's the bell. It's probably best that I go.

NORA: No, stay. No one's expected. It must be for Torvald.

MAID (*from the hall doorway*): Excuse me, ma'am — there's a gentleman here to see Mr. Helmer, but I didn't know — since the doctor's with him —

NORA: Who is the gentleman?

KROGSTAD (*from the doorway*): It's me, Mrs. Helmer.

(*Mrs. Linde starts and turns away toward the window.*)

NORA (*stepping toward him, tense, her voice a whisper*): You? What is it? Why do you want to speak to my husband?

KROGSTAD: Bank business — after a fashion. I have a small job in the investment bank, and I hear now your husband is going to be our chief —

NORA: In other words, it's —

KROGSTAD: Just dry business, Mrs. Helmer. Nothing but that.

NORA: Yes, then please be good enough to step into the study. (*She nods indifferently as she sees him out by the hall door, then returns and begins stirring up the stove.*)

MRS. LINDE: Nora — who was that man?

NORA: That was a Mr. Krogstad — a lawyer.

MRS. LINDE: Then it really was him.

NORA: Do you know that person?

MRS. LINDE: I did once — many years ago. For a time he was a law clerk in our town.

NORA: Yes, he's been that.

MRS. LINDE: How he's changed.

NORA: I understand he had a very unhappy marriage.

MRS. LINDE: He's a widower now.

NORA: With a number of children. There now, it's burning. (*She closes the stove door and moves the rocker a bit to one side.*)

MRS. LINDE: They say he has a hand in all kinds of business.

NORA: Oh? That may be true; I wouldn't know. But let's not think about business. It's so dull.

(*Dr. Rank enters from Helmer's study.*)

RANK (*still in the doorway*): No, no, really — I don't want to intrude, I'd just as soon talk a little while with your wife. (*Shuts the door, then notices Mrs. Linde.*) Oh, beg pardon. I'm intruding here too.

NORA: No, not at all. (*Introducing him.*) Dr. Rank, Mrs. Linde.

RANK: Well now, that's a name much heard in this

house. I believe I passed the lady on the stairs as I came.

MRS. LINDE: Yes, I take the stairs very slowly. They're rather hard on me.

RANK: Uh-hm, some touch of internal weakness?

MRS. LINDE: More overexertion, I'd say.

RANK: Nothing else? Then you're probably here in town to rest up in a round of parties?

MRS. LINDE: I'm here to look for work.

RANK: Is that the best cure for overexertion?

MRS. LINDE: One has to live, Doctor.

RANK: Yes, there's a common prejudice to that effect.

NORA: Oh, come on, Dr. Rank — you really do want to live yourself.

RANK: Yes, I really do. Wretched as I am, I'll gladly prolong my torment indefinitely. All my patients feel like that. And it's quite the same, too, with the morally sick. Right at this moment there's one of those moral invalids in there with Helmer —

MRS. LINDE (*softly*): Ah!

NORA: Who do you mean?

RANK: Oh, it's a lawyer, Krogstad, a type you wouldn't know. His character is rotten to the root — but even he began chattering all-importantly about how he had to *live*.

NORA: Oh? What did he want to talk to Torvald about?

RANK: I really don't know. I only heard something about the bank.

NORA: I didn't know that Krog — that this man Krogstad had anything to do with the bank.

RANK: Yes, he's gotten some kind of berth down there. (*To Mrs. Linde.*) I don't know if you also have, in your neck of the woods, a type of person who scuttles about breathlessly, sniffing out hints of moral corruption, and then maneuvers his victim into some sort of key position where he can keep an eye on him. It's the healthy these days that are out in the cold.

MRS. LINDE: All the same, it's the sick who most need to be taken in.

RANK (*with a shrug*): Yes, there we have it. That's the concept that's turning society into a sanatorium.

(*Nora, lost in her thoughts, breaks out into quiet laughter and claps her hands.*)

RANK: Why do you laugh at that? Do you have any real idea of what society is?

NORA: What do I care about dreary old society? I was laughing at something quite different — something terribly funny. Tell me, Doctor — is everyone who works in the bank dependent now on Torvald?

RANK: Is that what you find so terribly funny?

NORA (*smiling and humming*): Never mind, never mind! (*Pacing the floor.*) Yes, that's really immensely amusing: that we — that Torvald has so much power now over all those people. (*Taking the bag out of her pocket.*) Dr. Rank, a little macaroon on that?

RANK: See here, macaroons! I thought they were contraband here.

NORA: Yes, but these are some that Kristine gave me.

MRS. LINDE: What? I — ?

NORA: Now, now, don't be afraid. You couldn't possibly know that Torvald had forbidden them. You see, he's worried they'll ruin my teeth. But hmp! Just this once! Isn't that so, Dr. Rank? Help yourself! (*Puts a macaroon in his mouth.*) And you too, Kristine. And I'll also have one, only a little one — or two, at the most. (*Walking about again.*) Now I'm really tremendously happy. Now's there's just one last thing in the world that I have an enormous desire to do.

RANK: Well! And what's that?

NORA: It's something I have such a consuming desire to say so Torvald could hear.

RANK: And why can't you say it?

NORA: I don't dare. It's quite shocking.

MRS. LINDE: Shocking?

RANK: Well, then it isn't advisable. But in front of us you certainly can. What do you have such a desire to say so Torvald could hear?

NORA: I have such a huge desire to say — to hell and be damned!

RANK: Are you crazy?

MRS. LINDE: My goodness, Nora!

RANK: Go on, say it. Here he is.

NORA (*hiding the macaroon bag*): Shh, shh, shh!

(*Helmer comes in from his study, hat in hand, overcoat over his arm.*)

NORA (*going toward him*): Well, Torvald dear, are you through with him?

HELMER: Yes, he just left.

NORA: Let me introduce you — this is Kristine, who's arrived here in town.

HELMER: Kristine — ? I'm sorry, but I don't know —

NORA: Mrs. Linde, Torvald dear. Mrs. Kristine Linde.

HELMER: Of course. A childhood friend of my wife's, no doubt?

MRS. LINDE: Yes, we knew each other in those days.

NORA: And just think, she made the long trip down here in order to talk with you.

HELMER: What's this?

MRS. LINDE: Well, not exactly —

NORA: You see, Kristine is remarkably clever in office work, and so she's terribly eager to come under a capable man's supervision and add more to what she already knows —

HELMER: Very wise, Mrs. Linde.

NORA: And then when she heard that you'd become a bank manager — the story was wired out to the papers — then she came in as fast as she could and — Really, Torvald, for my sake you can do a little something for Kristine, can't you?

HELMER: Yes, it's not at all impossible. Mrs. Linde, I suppose you're a widow?

MRS. LINDE: Yes.

HELMER: Any experience in office work?

MRS. LINDE: Yes, a good deal.

HELMER: Well, it's quite likely that I can make an opening for you —

NORA (*clapping her hands*): You see, you see!

HELMER: You've come at a lucky moment, Mrs. Linde.

MRS. LINDE: Oh, how can I thank you?

HELMER: Not necessary. (*Putting his overcoat on.*) But today you'll have to excuse me —

RANK: Wait, I'll go with you. (*He fetches his coat from the hall and warms it at the stove.*)

NORA: Don't stay out long, dear.

HELMER: An hour; no more.

NORA: Are you going too, Kristine?

MRS. LINDE (*putting on her winter garments*): Yes, I have to see about a room now.

HELMER: Then perhaps we can all walk together.

NORA (*helping her*): What a shame we're so cramped here, but it's quite impossible for us to —

MRS. LINDE: Oh, don't even think of it! Good-bye, Nora dear, and thanks for everything.

NORA: Good-bye for now. Of course you'll be back this evening. And you too, Dr. Rank. What? If you're well enough? Oh, you've got to be! Wrap up tight now.

(*In a ripple of small talk the company moves out into the hall; children's voices are heard outside on the steps.*)

NORA: There they are! There they are! (*She runs to open the door. The children come in with their nurse, Anne-Marie.*) Come in, come in! (*Bends down and kisses them.*) Oh, you darlings — ! Look at them, Kristine. Aren't they lovely!

RANK: No loitering in the draft here.

HELMER: Come, Mrs. Linde — this place is unbearable now for anyone but mothers.

(*Dr. Rank, Helmer, and Mrs. Linde go down the stairs. Anne-Marie goes into the living room with the children. Nora follows, after closing the hall door.*)

NORA: How fresh and strong you look. Oh, such red cheeks you have! Like apples and roses. (*The children interrupt her throughout the following.*) And it was so much fun? That's wonderful. Really? You pulled both Emmy and Bob on the sled? Imagine, all together! Yes, you're a clever boy, Ivar. Oh, let me hold her a bit, Anne-Marie. My sweet little doll baby! (*Takes the smallest from the nurse and dances with her.*) Yes, yes, Mama will dance with Bob as well. What? Did you throw snowballs? Oh, if I'd only been there! No, don't bother, Anne-Marie — I'll undress them myself. Oh yes, let me. It's such fun. Go in and rest; you look half frozen. There's hot coffee waiting for you on the stove. (*The nurse goes into the room to the left. Nora takes the children's winter things off, throwing them about, while the children talk to her all at once.*) Is that so? A big dog chased you? But it didn't bite? No, dogs never bite little, lovely doll babies. Don't peek in the packages, Ivar! What is it? Yes, wouldn't you like to know. No, no, it's an ugly something. Well? Shall we play? What shall we play? Hide-and-seek? Yes, let's play hide-and-seek. Bob must hide first. I must? Yes, let me hide first. (*Laughing and shouting, she and the chil-*

dren play in and out of the living room and the adjoining room to the right. At last Nora hides under the table. The children come storming in, search, but cannot find her, then hear her muffled laughter, dash over to the table, lift the cloth up and find her. Wild shouting. She creeps forward as if to scare them. More shouts. Meanwhile, a knock at the hall door; no one has noticed it. Now the door half opens, and Krogstad appears. He waits a moment; the game goes on.*)

KROGSTAD: Beg pardon, Mrs. Helmer —

NORA (*with a strangled cry, turning and scrambling to her knees*): Oh! What do you want?

KROGSTAD: Excuse me. The outer door was ajar; it must be someone forgot to shut it —

NORA (*rising*): My husband isn't home, Mr. Krogstad.

KROGSTAD: I know that.

NORA: Yes — then what do you want here?

KROGSTAD: A word with you.

NORA: With — ? (*To the children, quietly.*) Go in to Anne-Marie. What? No, the strange man won't hurt Mama. When he's gone, we'll play some more. (*She leads the children into the room to the left and shuts the door after them. Then, tense and nervous:*) You want to speak to me?

KROGSTAD: Yes, I want to.

NORA: Today? But it's not yet the first of the month —

KROGSTAD: No, it's Christmas Eve. It's going to be up to you how merry a Christmas you have.

NORA: What is it you want? Today I absolutely can't —

KROGSTAD: We won't talk about that till later. This is something else. You do have a moment to spare, I suppose?

NORA: Oh yes, of course — I do, except —

KROGSTAD: Good. I was sitting over at Olsen's Restaurant when I saw your husband go down the street —

NORA: Yes?

KROGSTAD: With a lady.

NORA: Yes. So?

KROGSTAD: If you'll pardon my asking: Wasn't that lady a Mrs. Linde?

NORA: Yes.

KROGSTAD: Just now come into town?

NORA: Yes, today.

KROGSTAD: She's a good friend of yours?

NORA: Yes, she is. But I don't see —

KROGSTAD: I also knew her once.

NORA: I'm aware of that.

KROGSTAD: Oh? You know all about it. I thought so. Well, then let me ask you short and sweet: Is Mrs. Linde getting a job in the bank?

NORA: What makes you think you can cross-examine me, Mr. Krogstad — you, one of my husband's employees? But since you ask, you might as well know — yes, Mrs. Linde's going to be taken on at the bank. And I'm the one who spoke for her Mr. Krogstad. Now you know.

KROGSTAD: So I guessed right.

NORA (*pacing up and down*): Oh, one does have a tiny

bit of influence, I should hope. Just because I am a woman, don't think it means that — When one has a subordinate position, Mr. Krogstad, one really ought to be careful about pushing somebody who — hm —

KROGSTAD: Who has influence?

NORA: That's right.

KROGSTAD (*in a different tone*): Mrs. Helmer, would you be good enough to use your influence on my behalf?

NORA: What? What do you mean?

KROGSTAD: Would you please make sure that I keep my subordinate position in the bank?

NORA: What does that mean? Who's thinking of taking away your position?

KROGSTAD: Oh, don't play the innocent with me. I'm quite aware that your friend would hardly relish the chance of running into me again; and I'm also aware now whom I can thank for being turned out.

NORA: But I promise you —

KROGSTAD: Yes, yes, yes, to the point: There's still time, and I'm advising you to use your influence to prevent it. *threat?*

NORA: But Mr. Krogstad, I have absolutely no influence.

KROGSTAD: You haven't? I thought you were just saying —

NORA: You shouldn't take me so literally. I! How can you believe that I have any such influence over my husband?

KROGSTAD: Oh, I've known your husband from our student days. I don't think the great bank manager's more steadfast than any other married man.

NORA: You speak insolently about my husband, and I'll show you the door.

KROGSTAD: The lady has spirit.

NORA: I'm not afraid of you any longer. After New Year's, I'll soon be done with the whole business.

KROGSTAD (*restraining himself*): Now listen to me, Mrs. Helmer. If necessary, I'll fight for my little job in the bank as if it were life itself.

NORA: Yes, so it seems.

KROGSTAD: It's not just a matter of income; that's the least of it. It's something else — All right, out with it! Look, this is the thing. You know, just like all the others, of course, that once, a good many years ago, I did something rather rash.

NORA: I've heard rumors to that effect.

KROGSTAD: The case never got into court; but all the same, every door was closed in my face from then on. So I took up those various activities you know about. I had to grab hold somewhere; and I dare say I haven't been among the worst. But now I want to drop all that. My boys are growing up. For their sakes, I'll have to win back as much respect as possible here in town. That job in the bank was like the first rung in my ladder. And now your husband wants to kick me right back down in the mud again.

NORA: But for heaven's sake, Mr. Krogstad, it's simply not in my power to help you.

KROGSTAD: That's because you haven't the will to — but I have the means to make you.

NORA: You certainly won't tell my husband that I owe you money?

KROGSTAD: Hm — what if I told him that?

NORA: That would be shameful of you. (*Nearly in tears.*) This secret — my joy and my pride — that he should learn it in such a crude and disgusting way — learn it from you. You'd expose me to the most horrible unpleasantness —

KROGSTAD: Only unpleasantness?

NORA (*vehemently*): But go on and try. It'll turn out the worse for you, because then my husband will really see what a crook you are, and then you'll never be able to hold your job.

KROGSTAD: I asked if it was just domestic unpleasantness you were afraid of?

NORA: If my husband finds out, then of course he'll pay what I owe at once, and then we'd be through with you for good.

KROGSTAD (*a step closer*): Listen, Mrs. Helmer — you've either got a very bad memory, or else no head at all for business. I'd better put you a little more in touch with the facts.

NORA: What do you mean?

KROGSTAD: When your husband was sick, you came to me for a loan of four thousand, eight hundred crowns.

NORA: Where else could I go?

KROGSTAD: I promised to get you that sum —

NORA: And you got it.

KROGSTAD: I promised to get you that sum, on certain conditions. You were so involved in your husband's illness, and so eager to finance your trip, that I guess you didn't think out all the details. It might just be a good idea to remind you. I promised you the money on the strength of a note I drew up.

NORA: Yes, and that I signed.

KROGSTAD: Right. But at the bottom I added some lines for your father to guarantee the loan. He was supposed to sign down there.

NORA: Supposed to? He did sign.

KROGSTAD: I left the date blank. In other words, your father would have dated his signature himself. Do you remember that?

NORA: Yes, I think —

KROGSTAD: Then I gave you the note for you to mail to your father. Isn't that so?

NORA: Yes.

KROGSTAD: And naturally you sent it at once — because only some five, six days later you brought me the note, properly signed. And with that, the money was yours.

NORA: Well, then; I've made my payments regularly, haven't I?

KROGSTAD: More or less. But — getting back to the point — those were hard times for you then, Mrs. Helmer.

NORA: Yes, they were.

KROGSTAD: Your father was very ill, I believe.

NORA: He was near the end.

threat - blackmail

Krogstad is Nora's loaner

KROGSTAD: He died soon after?

NORA: Yes.

KROGSTAD: Tell me, Mrs. Helmer, do you happen to recall the date of your father's death? The day of the month, I mean.

NORA: Papa died the twenty-ninth of September.

KROGSTAD: That's quite correct; I've already looked into that. And now we come to a curious thing — (*taking out a paper*) which I simply cannot comprehend.

NORA: Curious thing? I don't know —

KROGSTAD: This is the curious thing: that your father co-signed the note for your loan three days after his death.

NORA: How — ? I don't understand.

KROGSTAD: Your father died the twenty-ninth of September. But look. Here your father dated his signature October second. Isn't that curious, Mrs. Helmer? (*Nora is silent.*) Can you explain it to me? (*Nora remains silent.*) It's also remarkable that the words "October second" and the year aren't written in your father's hand, but rather in one that I think I know. Well, it's easy to understand. Your father forgot perhaps to date his signature, and then someone or other added it, a bit sloppily, before anyone knew of his death. There's nothing wrong in that. It all comes down to the signature. And there's no question about *that*, Mrs. Helmer. It really *was* your father who signed his own name here, wasn't it?

NORA (*after a short silence, throwing her head back and looking squarely at him*): No, it wasn't. *I* signed Papa's name.

TOP: Nora (Claire Bloom) is troubled as Helmer (Donald Madden) kisses her in Patrick Garland's 1971 production. RIGHT: Helmer, Nora, and Mrs. Linde (Patricia Elliott) discuss the possibility of finding a suitable job for Mrs. Linde in the bank. FAR RIGHT: Krogstad (Robert Gerringer) explains the seriousness of her actions to Nora.

KROGSTAD: Wait, now — are you fully aware that this is a dangerous confession?

NORA: Why? You'll soon get your money.

KROGSTAD: Let me ask you a question — why didn't you send the paper to your father?

NORA: That was impossible. Papa was so sick. If I'd asked him for his signature, I also would have had to tell him what the money was for. But I couldn't tell him, sick as he was, that my husband's life was in danger. That was just impossible.

KROGSTAD: Then it would have been better if you'd given up the trip abroad.

NORA: I couldn't possibly. The trip was to save my husband's life. I couldn't give that up.

KROGSTAD: But didn't you ever consider that this was a fraud against me?

NORA: I couldn't let myself be bothered by that. You weren't any concern of mine. I couldn't stand you, with all those cold complications you made, even though you knew how badly off my husband was.

KROGSTAD: Mrs. Helmer, obviously you haven't the vaguest idea of what you've involved yourself in. But I can tell you this: It was nothing more and nothing worse that I once did — and it wrecked my whole reputation.

NORA: You? Do you expect me to believe that you ever acted bravely to save your wife's life?

KROGSTAD: Laws don't inquire into motives.

NORA: Then they must be very poor laws.

KROGSTAD: Poor or not — if I introduce this paper in court, you'll be judged according to law.

NORA: This I refuse to believe. A daughter hasn't a right to protect her dying father from anxiety and care? A wife hasn't a right to save her husband's life? I don't know much about laws, but I'm sure that somewhere in the books these things are allowed. And you don't know anything about it — you who practice the law? You must be an awful lawyer, Mr. Krogstad.

KROGSTAD: Could be. But business — the kind of business we two are mixed up in — don't you think I know about that? All right. Do what you want now. But I'm telling you *this:* If I get shoved down a second time, you're going to keep me company. (*He bows and goes out through the hall.*)

NORA (*pensive for a moment, then tossing her head*): Oh, really! Trying to frighten me! I'm not so silly as all that. (*Begins gathering up the children's clothes, but soon stops.*) But — ? No, but that's impossible! I did it out of love.

THE CHILDREN (*in the doorway, left*): Mama, that strange man's gone out the door.

NORA: Yes, yes, I know it. But don't tell anyone about the strange man. Do you hear? Not even Papa!

THE CHILDREN: No, Mama. But now will you play again?

NORA: No, not now.

THE CHILDREN: Oh, but Mama, you promised.

NORA: Yes, but I can't now. Go inside; I have too much to do. Go in, go in, my sweet darlings. (*She herds them gently back in the room and shuts the door after them. Settling on the sofa, she takes up a piece of embroidery and makes some stitches, but soon stops abruptly.*) No! (*Throws the work aside, rises, goes to the hall door and calls out.*) Helene! Let me have the tree in here. (*Goes to the table, left, opens the table drawer, and stops again.*) No, but that's utterly impossible!

MAID (*with the Christmas tree*): Where should I put it, ma'am?

NORA: There. The middle of the floor.

MAID: Should I bring anything else?

NORA: No, thanks. I have what I need.

(*The Maid, who has set the tree down, goes out.*)

NORA (*absorbed in trimming the tree*): Candles here — and flowers here. That terrible creature! Talk, talk, talk! There's nothing to it at all. The tree's going to be lovely. I'll do anything to please you Torvald. I'll sing for you, dance for you —

(*Helmer comes in from the hall, with a sheaf of papers under his arm.*)

NORA: Oh! You're back so soon?

HELMER: Yes. Has anyone been here?

NORA: Here? No.

HELMER: That's odd. I saw Krogstad leaving the front door.

NORA: So? Oh yes, that's true. Krogstad was here a moment.

HELMER: Nora, I can see by your face that he's been here, begging you to put in a good word for him.

NORA: Yes.

HELMER: And it was supposed to seem like your own idea? You were to hide it from me that he'd been here. He asked you that, too, didn't he?

NORA: Yes, Torvald, but —

HELMER: Nora, Nora, and you could fall for that? Talk with that sort of person and promise him anything? And then in the bargain, tell me an untruth.

NORA: An untruth — ?

HELMER: Didn't you say that no one had been here? (*Wagging his finger.*) My little songbird must never do that again. A songbird needs a clean beak to warble with. No false notes. (*Putting his arm about her waist.*) That's the way it should be, isn't it? Yes, I'm sure of it. (*Releasing her.*) And so, enough of that. (*Sitting by the stove.*) Ah, how snug and cozy it is here. (*Leafing among his papers.*)

NORA (*busy with the tree, after a short pause*): Torvald!

HELMER: Yes.

NORA: I'm so much looking forward to the Stenborgs' costume party, day after tomorrow.

HELMER: And I can't wait to see what you'll surprise me with.

NORA: Oh, that stupid business!

HELMER: What?

NORA: I can't find anything that's right. Everything seems so ridiculous, so inane.

HELMER: So my little Nora's come to *that* recognition?

NORA (*going behind his chair, her arms resting on its back*): Are you very busy, Torvald?

HELMER: Oh —

NORA: What papers are those?

HELMER: Bank matters.

NORA: Already?

HELMER: I've gotten full authority from the retiring management to make all necessary changes in personnel and procedure. I'll need Christmas week for that. I want to have everything in order by New Year's.

NORA: So that was the reason this poor Krogstad —

HELMER: Hm.

NORA (*still leaning on the chair and slowly stroking the nape of his neck*): If you weren't so very busy, I would have asked you an enormous favor, Torvald.

HELMER: Let's hear. What is it?

NORA: You know, there isn't anyone who has your good taste — and I want so much to look well at the cos-

tume party. Torvald, couldn't you take over and decide what I should be and plan my costume?

HELMER: Ah, is my stubborn little creature calling for a lifeguard?

NORA: Yes, Torvald, I can't get anywhere without your help.

HELMER: All right — I'll think it over. We'll hit on something.

NORA: Oh, how sweet of you. (*Goes to the tree again. Pause.*) Aren't the red flowers pretty — ? But tell me, was it really such a crime that this Krogstad committed?

HELMER: Forgery. Do you have any idea what that means?

NORA: Couldn't he have done it out of need?

HELMER: Yes, or thoughtlessness, like so many others. I'm not so heartless that I'd condemn a man categorically for just one mistake.

NORA: No, of course not, Torvald!

HELMER: Plenty of men have redeemed themselves by openly confessing their crimes and taking their punishment.

NORA: Punishment — ?

HELMER: But now Krogstad didn't go that way. He got himself out by sharp practices, and that's the real cause of his moral breakdown.

NORA: Do you really think that would — ?

HELMER: Just imagine how a man with that sort of guilt in him has to lie and cheat and deceive on all sides, has to wear a mask even with the nearest and dearest he has, even with his own wife and children. And with the children, Nora — that's where it's most horrible.

NORA: Why?

HELMER: Because that kind of atmosphere of lies infects the whole life of a home. Every breath the children take in is filled with the germs of something degenerate.

NORA (*coming closer behind him*): Are you sure of that?

HELMER: Oh, I've seen it often enough as a lawyer. Almost everyone who goes bad early in life has a mother who's a chronic liar.

NORA: Why just — the mother?

HELMER: It's usually the mother's influence that's dominant, but the father's works in the same way, of course. Every lawyer is quite familiar with it. And still this Krogstad's been going home year in, year out, poisoning his own children with lies and pretense; that's why I call him morally lost. (*Reaching his hands out toward her.*) So my sweet little Nora must promise me never to plead his cause. Your hand on it. Come, come, what's this? Give me your hand. There, now. All settled. I can tell you it'd be impossible for me to work alongside of him. I literally feel physically revolted when I'm anywhere near such a person.

NORA (*withdraws her hand and goes to the other side of the Christmas tree*): How hot it is here! And I've got so much to do.

HELMER (*getting up and gathering his papers*): Yes, and I have to think about getting some of these read through before dinner. I'll think about your costume, too. And something to hang on the tree in gilt paper, I may even see about that. (*Putting his hand on her head.*) Oh you, my darling little songbird. (*He goes into his study and closes the door after him.*)

NORA (*softly, after a silence*): Oh, really! It isn't so. It's impossible. It must be impossible.

ANNE-MARIE (*in the doorway left*): The children are begging so hard to come in to Mama.

NORA: No, no, no, don't let them in to me! You stay with them, Anne-Marie.

ANNE-MARIE: Of course, ma'am. (*Closes the door.*)

NORA (*pale with terror*): Hurt my children — ! Poison my home? (*A moment's pause; then she tosses her head.*) That's not true. Never. Never in all the world.

ACT II

(*Same room. Beside the piano the Christmas tree now stands stripped of ornament, burned-down candle stubs on its ragged branches. Nora's street clothes lie on the sofa. Nora, alone in the room, moves restlessly about; at last she stops at the sofa and picks up her coat.*)

NORA (*dropping the coat again*): Someone's coming! (*Goes toward the door, listens.*) No — there's no one. Of course — nobody's coming today, Christmas Day — or tomorrow, either. But maybe — (*Opens the door and looks out.*) No, nothing in the mailbox. Quite empty. (*Coming forward.*) What nonsense! He won't do anything serious. Nothing terrible could happen. It's impossible. Why, I have three small children.

(*Anne-Marie, with a large carton, comes in from the room to the left.*)

ANNE-MARIE: Well, at last I found the box with the masquerade clothes.

NORA: Thanks. Put it on the table.

ANNE-MARIE (*does so*): But they're all pretty much of a mess.

NORA: Ahh! I'd love to rip them in a million pieces!

ANNE-MARIE: Oh, mercy, they can be fixed right up. Just a little patience.

NORA: Yes, I'll go get Mrs. Linde to help me.

ANNE-MARIE: Out again now? In this nasty weather? Miss Nora will catch cold — get sick.

NORA: Oh, worse things could happen — How are the children?

ANNE-MARIE: The poor mites are playing with their Christmas presents, but —

NORA: Do they ask for me much?

ANNE-MARIE: They're so used to having Mama around, you know.

NORA: Yes, but Anne-Marie, I *can't* be together with them as much as I was.

[handwritten: Nora neglects children - strange]

ANNE-MARIE: Well, small children get used to anything.

NORA: You think so? Do you think they'd forget their mother if she was gone for good? [handwritten: ? gone for good / foreshadow?]

ANNE-MARIE: Oh, mercy — gone for good!

NORA: Wait, tell me. Anne-Marie — I've wondered so often — how could you ever have the heart to give your child over to strangers?

ANNE-MARIE: But I had to, you know, to become little Nora's nurse.

NORA: Yes, but how could you *do* it?

ANNE-MARIE: When I could get such a good place? A girl who's poor and who's gotten in trouble is glad enough for that. Because that slippery fish, he didn't do a thing for me, you know.

NORA: But your daughter's surely forgotten you.

ANNE-MARIE: Oh, she certainly has not. She's written to me, both when she was confirmed and when she was married.

NORA (*clasping her about the neck*): You old Anne-Marie, you were a good mother for me when I was little.

ANNE-MARIE: Poor little Nora, with no other mother but me.

NORA: And if the babies didn't have one, then I know that you'd — What silly talk! (*Opening the carton.*) Go in to them. Now I'll have to — Tomorrow you can see how lovely I'll look.

ANNE-MARIE: Oh, there won't be anyone at the party as lovely as Miss Nora. (*She goes off into the room, left.*)

NORA (*begins unpacking the box, but soon throws it aside*): Oh, if I dared to go out. If only nobody would come. If only nothing would happen here while I'm out. What craziness — nobody's coming. Just don't think. This muff — needs a brushing. Beautiful gloves, beautiful gloves. Let it go. Let it go! One, two, three, four, five, six — (*With a cry.*) Oh, there they are! (*Poises to move toward the door, but remains irresolutely standing. Mrs. Linde enters from the hall, where she has removed her street clothes.*)

NORA: Oh, it's you, Kristine. There's no one else out there? How good that you've come.

MRS. LINDE: I hear you were up asking for me.

NORA: Yes, I just stopped by. There's something you really can help me with. Let's get settled on the sofa. Look, there's going to be a costume party tomorrow evening at the Stenborgs' right above us, and now Torvald wants me to go as a Neapolitan peasant girl and dance the tarantella that I learned in Capri.

MRS. LINDE: Really, are you giving a whole performance?

NORA: Torvald says yes, I should. See, here's the dress. Torvald had it made for me down there; but now it's all so tattered that I just don't know —

MRS. LINDE: Oh, we'll fix that up in no time. It's nothing more than the trimmings — they're a bit loose here and there. Needle and thread? Good, now we have what we need.

NORA: Oh, how sweet of you!

MRS. LINDE (*sewing*): So you'll be in disguise tomorrow, Nora. You know what? I'll stop by then for a moment and have a look at you all dressed up. But listen, I've absolutely forgotten to thank you for that pleasant evening yesterday.

NORA (*getting up and walking about*): I don't think it was as pleasant as usual yesterday. You should have come to town a bit sooner, Kristine — Yes, Torvald really knows how to give a home elegance and charm.

MRS. LINDE: And you do, too, if you ask me. You're not your father's daughter for nothing. But tell me, is Dr. Rank always so down in the mouth as yesterday?

NORA: No, that was quite an exception. But he goes around critically ill all the time — tuberculosis of the spine, poor man. You know, his father was a disgusting thing who kept mistresses and so on — and that's why the son's been sickly from birth.

MRS. LINDE (*lets her sewing fall to her lap*): But my dearest Nora, how do you know about such things?

NORA (*walking more jauntily*): Hmp! When you've had three children, then you've had a few visits from — from women who know something of medicine, and they tell you this and that.

MRS. LINDE (*resumes sewing; a short pause*): Does Dr. Rank come here every day?

NORA: Every blessed day. He's Torvald's best friend from childhood, and *my* good friend, too. Dr. Rank almost belongs to this house.

MRS. LINDE: But tell me — is he quite sincere? I mean, doesn't he rather enjoy flattering people?

NORA: Just the opposite. Why do you think that?

MRS. LINDE: When you introduced us yesterday, he was proclaiming that he'd often heard my name in this house; but later I noticed that your husband hadn't the slightest idea who I really was. So how could Dr. Rank — ?

NORA: But it's all true, Kristine. You see, Torvald loves me beyond words, and, as he puts it, he'd like to keep me all to himself. For a long time he'd almost be jealous if I even mentioned any of my old friends back home. So of course I dropped that. But with Dr. Rank I talk a lot about such things because he likes hearing about them.

MRS. LINDE: Now listen, Nora; in many ways you're still like a child. I'm a good deal older than you, with a little more experience. I'll tell you something: You ought to put an end to all this with Dr. Rank.

NORA: What should I put an end to?

MRS. LINDE: Both parts of it, I think. Yesterday you said something about a rich admirer who'd provide you with money —

NORA: Yes, one who doesn't exist — worse luck. So?

MRS. LINDE: Is Dr. Rank well off?

NORA: Yes, he is.

MRS. LINDE: With no dependents?

NORA: No, no one. But —

MRS. LINDE: And he's over here every day?

NORA: Yes, I told you that.

MRS. LINDE: How can a man of such refinement be so grasping?

NORA: I don't follow you at all.

MRS. LINDE: Now don't try to hide it, Nora. You think I can't guess who loaned you the forty-eight hundred crowns?

NORA: Are you out of your mind? How could you think such a thing! A friend of ours, who comes here every single day. What an intolerable situation that would have been!

MRS. LINDE: Then it really wasn't him.

NORA: No, absolutely not. It never even crossed my mind for a moment — And he had nothing to lend in those days; his inheritance came later.

MRS. LINDE: Well, I think that was a stroke of luck for you, Nora dear.

NORA: No, it never would have occurred to me to ask Dr. Rank — Still, I'm quite sure that if I had asked him —

MRS. LINDE: Which you won't, of course.

NORA: No, of course not. I can't see that I'd ever need to. But I'm quite positive that if I talked to Dr. Rank —

MRS. LINDE: Behind your husband's back?

NORA: I've got to clear up this other thing; *that's* also behind his back. I've *got* to clear it all up.

MRS. LINDE: Yes, I was saying that yesterday, but —

NORA (*pacing up and down*): A man handles these problems so much better than a woman —

MRS. LINDE: One's husband does, yes.

NORA: Nonsense. (*Stopping.*) When you pay everything you owe, then you get your note back, right?

MRS. LINDE: Yes, naturally.

NORA: And can rip it into a million pieces and burn it up — that filthy scrap of paper!

MRS. LINDE (*looking hard at her, laying her sewing aside, and rising slowly*): Nora, you're hiding something from me.

NORA: You can see it in my face?

MRS. LINDE: Something's happened to you since yesterday morning. Nora, what is it?

NORA (*hurrying toward her*): Kristine! (*Listening.*) Shh! Torvald's home. Look, go in with the children a while. Torvald can't bear all this snipping and stitching. Let Anne-Marie help you.

MRS. LINDE (*gathering up some of the things*): All right, but I'm not leaving here until we've talked this out. (*She disappears into the room, left, as Torvald enters from the hall.*)

NORA: Oh, how I've been waiting for you, Torvald dear.

HELMER: Was that the dressmaker?

NORA: No, that was Kristine. She's helping me fix up my costume. You know, it's going to be quite attractive.

HELMER: Yes, wasn't that a bright idea I had?

NORA: Brilliant! But then wasn't I good as well to give in to you?

HELMER: Good — because you give in to your husband's judgment? All right, you little goose, I know you didn't mean it like that. But I won't disturb you. You'll want to have a fitting, I suppose.

NORA: And you'll be working?

HELMER: Yes. (*Indicating a bundle of papers.*) See. I've been down to the bank. (*Starts toward his study.*)

NORA: Torvald.

HELMER (*stops*): Yes.

NORA: If your little squirrel begged you, with all her heart and soul, for something — ?

HELMER: What's that?

NORA: Then would you do it?

HELMER: First, naturally, I'd have to know what it was.

NORA: Your squirrel would scamper about and do tricks, if you'd only be sweet and give in.

HELMER: Out with it.

NORA: Your lark would be singing high and low in every room —

HELMER: Come on, she does that anyway.

NORA: I'd be a wood nymph and dance for you in the moonlight.

HELMER: Nora — don't tell me it's that same business from this morning?

NORA (*coming closer*): Yes, Torvald, I beg you, please!

HELMER: And you actually have the nerve to drag that up again?

NORA: Yes, yes, you've got to give in to me; you *have* to let Krogstad keep his job in the bank.

HELMER: My dear Nora, I've slated his job for Mrs. Linde.

NORA: That's awfully kind of you. But you could just fire another clerk instead of Krogstad.

HELMER: This is the most incredible stubbornness! Because you go and give an impulsive promise to speak up for him, I'm expected to —

NORA: That's not the reason, Torvald. It's for your own sake. That man does writing for the worst papers; you said it yourself. He could do you any amount of harm. I'm scared to death of him —

HELMER: Ah, I understand. It's the old memories haunting you.

NORA: What do you mean by that?

HELMER: Of course, you're thinking about your father.

NORA: Yes, all right. Just remember how those nasty gossips wrote in the papers about Papa and slandered him so cruelly. I think they'd have had him dismissed if the department hadn't sent you up to investigate, and if you hadn't been so kind and openminded toward him.

HELMER: My dear Nora, there's a notable difference between your father and me. Your father's official career was hardly above reproach. But mine is; and I hope it'll stay that way as long as I hold my position.

NORA: Oh, who can ever tell what vicious minds can invent? We could be so snug and happy now in our quiet, carefree home — you and I and the children, Torvald! That's why I'm pleading with you so —

HELMER: And just by pleading for him you make it impossible for me to keep him on. It's already known at the bank that I'm firing Krogstad. What if it's rumored around now that the new bank manager was vetoed by his wife —

NORA: Yes, what then — ?

HELMER: Oh yes — as long as our little bundle of stubbornness gets her way — ! I should go and make myself ridiculous in front of the whole office — give people the idea I can be swayed by all kinds of outside pressure. Oh, you can bet I'd feel the effects of that soon enough! Besides — there's something that rules Krogstad right out at the bank as long as I'm the manager.

NORA: What's that?

HELMER: His moral failings I could maybe overlook if I had to —

NORA: Yes, Torvald, why not?

HELMER: And I hear he's quite efficient on the job. But he was a crony of mine back in my teens — one of those rash friendships that crop up again and again to embarrass you later in life. Well, I might as well say it straight out: We're on a first-name basis. And that tactless fool makes no effort at all to hide it in front of others. Quite the contrary — he thinks that entitles him to take a familiar air around me, and so every other second he comes booming out with his, "Yes, Torvald!" and "Sure thing, Torvald!" I tell you, it's been excruciating for me. He's out to make my place in the bank unbearable.

NORA: Torvald, you can't be serious about all this.

HELMER: Oh no? Why not?

NORA: Because these are such petty considerations.

HELMER: What are you saying? Petty? You think I'm petty!

NORA: No, just the opposite, Torvald dear. That's exactly why —

HELMER: Never mind. You call my motives petty; then I might as well be just that. Petty! All right! We'll put a stop to this for good. (*Goes to the hall door and calls.*) Helene!

NORA: What do you want?

HELMER (*searching among his papers*): A decision. (*The Maid comes in.*) Look here; take this letter; go out with it at once. Get hold of a messenger and have him deliver it. Quick now. It's already addressed. Wait, here's some money.

MAID: Yes, sir. (*She leaves with the letter.*)

HELMER (*straightening his papers*): There, now, little Miss Willful.

NORA (*breathlessly*): Torvald, what was that letter?

HELMER: Krogstad's notice.

NORA: Call it back, Torvald! There's still time. Oh, Torvald, call it back! Do it for my sake — for your sake, for the children's sake! Do you hear, Torvald; do it! You don't know how this can harm us.

HELMER: Too late.

NORA: Yes, too late.

HELMER: Nora, dear, I can forgive you this panic, even though basically you're insulting me. Yes, you are! Or isn't it an insult to think that *I* should be afraid of a courtroom hack's revenge? But I forgive you anyway, because this shows so beautifully how much you love me. (*Takes her in his arms.*) This is the way it should be, my darling Nora. Whatever comes, you'll see: When it really counts, I have strength and courage enough as a man to take on the whole weight myself.

NORA (*terrified*): What do you mean by that?

HELMER: The whole weight, I said.

NORA (*resolutely*): No, never in all the world.

HELMER: Good. So we'll share it, Nora, as man and wife. That's as it should be. (*Fondling her.*) Are you happy now? There, there, there — not these frightened dove's eyes. It's nothing at all but empty fantasies — Now you should run through your tarantella and practice your tambourine. I'll go to the inner office, and shut both doors, so I won't hear a thing; you can make all the noise you like. (*Turning in the doorway.*) And when Rank comes, just tell him where he can find me. (*He nods to her and goes with his papers into the study, closing the door.*)

NORA (*standing as though rooted, dazed with fright, in a whisper*): He really could do it. He will do it. He'll do it in spite of everything. No, not that, never, never! Anything but that! Escape! A way out — (*The doorbell rings.*) Dr. Rank! Anything but that! *Anything*, whatever it is! (*Her hands pass over her face, smoothing it; she pulls herself together, goes over and opens the hall door. Dr. Rank stands outside, hanging his fur coat up. During the following scene, it begins getting dark.*)

NORA: Hello, Dr. Rank. I recognized your ring. But you mustn't go in to Torvald yet; I believe he's working.

RANK: And you?

NORA: For you, I always have an hour to spare — you know that. (*He has entered, and she shuts the door after him.*)

RANK: Many thanks. I'll make use of these hours while I can.

NORA: What do you mean by that? While you can?

RANK: Does that disturb you?

NORA: Well, it's such an odd phrase. Is anything going to happen?

RANK: What's going to happen is what I've been expecting so long — but I honestly didn't think it would come so soon.

NORA (*gripping his arm*): What is it you've found out? Dr. Rank, you have to tell me!

RANK (*sitting by the stove*): It's all over with me. There's nothing to be done about it.

NORA (*breathing easier*): Is it you — then — ?

RANK: Who else? There's no point in lying to one's self. I'm the most miserable of all my patients, Mrs. Helmer. These past few days I've been auditing my internal accounts. Bankrupt! Within a month I'll probably be laid out and rotting in the churchyard.

NORA: Oh, what a horrible thing to say.

RANK: The thing itself is horrible. But the worst of it is all the other horror before it's over. There's only one final examination left; when I'm finished with that, I'll know about when my disintegration will begin. There's something I want to say. Helmer with his sen-

sitivity has such a sharp distaste for anything ugly. I don't want him near my sickroom.

NORA: Oh, but Dr. Rank —

RANK: I won't have him in there. Under no condition. I'll lock my door to him — As soon as I'm completely sure of the worst, I'll send you my calling card marked with a black cross, and you'll know then the wreck has started to come apart.

NORA: No, today you're completely unreasonable. And I wanted you so much to be in a really good humor.

RANK: With death up my sleeve? And then to suffer this way for somebody else's sins. Is there any justice in that? And in every single family, in some way or another, this inevitable retribution of nature goes on —

NORA (*her hands pressed over her ears*): Oh, stuff! Cheer up! Please — be gay!

RANK: Yes, I'd just as soon laugh at it all. My poor, innocent spine, serving time for my father's gay army days.

NORA (*by the table, left*): He was so infatuated with asparagus tips and pâté de foie gras, wasn't that it?

RANK: Yes — and with truffles.

NORA: Truffles, yes. And then with oysters, I suppose?

RANK: Yes, tons of oysters, naturally.

NORA: And then the port and champagne to go with it. It's so sad that all these delectable things have to strike at our bones.

RANK: Especially when they strike at the unhappy bones that never shared in the fun.

NORA: Ah, that's the saddest of all.

RANK (*looks searchingly at her*): Hm.

NORA (*after a moment*): Why did you smile?

RANK: No, it was you who laughed.

NORA: No, it was you who smiled, Dr. Rank!

RANK (*getting up*): You're even a bigger tease than I'd thought.

NORA: I'm full of wild ideas today.

RANK: That's obvious.

NORA (*putting both hands on his shoulders*): Dear, dear Dr. Rank, you'll never die for Torvald and me.

RANK: Oh, that loss you'll easily get over. Those who go away are soon forgotten.

NORA (*looks fearfully at him*): You believe that?

RANK: One makes new connections, and then —

NORA: Who makes new connections?

RANK: Both you and Torvald will when I'm gone. I'd say you're well under way already. What was that Mrs. Linde doing here last evening?

NORA: Oh, come — you can't be jealous of poor Kristine?

RANK: Oh yes, I am. She'll be my successor here in the house. When I'm down under, that woman will probably —

NORA: Shh! Not so loud. She's right in there.

RANK: Today as well. So you see.

NORA: Only to sew on my dress. Good gracious, how unreasonable you are. (*Sitting on the sofa.*) Be nice now, Dr. Rank. Tomorrow you'll see how beautifully

I'll dance; and you can imagine then that I'm dancing only for you — yes, and of course for Torvald, too — that's understood. (*Takes various items out of the carton.*) Dr. Rank, sit over here and I'll show you something.

RANK (*sitting*): What's that?

NORA: Look here. Look.

RANK: Silk stockings.

NORA: Flesh-colored. Aren't they lovely? Now it's so dark here, but tomorrow — No, no, no, just look at the feet. Oh well, you might as well look at the rest.

RANK: Hm —

NORA: Why do you look so critical? Don't you believe they'll fit?

RANK: I've never had any chance to form an opinion on that.

NORA (*glancing at him a moment*): Shame on you. (*Hits him lightly on the ear with the stockings.*) That's for you. (*Puts them away again.*)

RANK: And what other splendors am I going to see now?

NORA: Not the least bit more, because you've been naughty. (*She hunts a little and rummages among her things.*)

RANK (*after a short silence*): When I sit here together with you like this, completely easy and open, then I don't know — I simply can't imagine — whatever would have become of me if I'd never come into this house.

NORA (*smiling*): Yes, I really think you feel completely at ease with us.

RANK (*more quietly, staring straight ahead*): And then to have to go away from it all —

NORA: Nonsense, you're not going away.

RANK (*his voice unchanged*): — and not even be able to leave some poor show of gratitude behind, scarcely a fleeting regret — no more than a vacant place that anyone can fill.

NORA: And if I asked you now for — No —

RANK: For what?

NORA: For a great proof of your friendship —

RANK: Yes, yes?

NORA: No, I mean — for an exceptionally big favor —

RANK: Would you really, for once, make me so happy?

NORA: Oh, you haven't the vaguest idea what it is.

RANK: All right, then tell me.

NORA: No, but I can't, Dr. Rank — it's all out of reason. It's advice and help, too — and a favor —

RANK: So much the better. I can't fathom what you're hinting at. Just speak out. Don't you trust me?

NORA: Of course. More than anyone else. You're my best and truest friend, I'm sure. That's why I want to talk to you. All right, then, Dr. Rank: There's something you can help me prevent. You know how deeply, how inexpressibly dearly Torvald loves me; he'd never hesitate a second to give up his life for me.

RANK (*leaning close to her*): Nora — do you think he's the only one —

NORA (*with a slight start*): Who — ?

RANK: Who'd gladly give up his life for you.

NORA (*heavily*): I see.

RANK: I swore to myself you should know this before I'm gone. I'll never find a better chance. Yes, Nora, now you know. And also you know now that you can trust me beyond anyone else.

NORA (*rising, natural and calm*): Let me by.

RANK (*making room for her, but still sitting*): Nora —

NORA (*in the hall doorway*): Helene, bring the lamp in. (*Goes over to the stove.*) Ah, dear Dr. Rank, that was really mean of you.

RANK (*getting up*): That I've loved you just as deeply as somebody else? Was *that* mean?

NORA: No, but that you came out and told me. That was quite unnecessary —

RANK: What do you mean? Have you known — ?

(*The Maid comes in with the lamp, sets it on the table, and goes out again.*)

RANK: Nora — Mrs. Helmer — I'm asking you: Have you known about it?

NORA: Oh, how can I tell what I know or don't know? Really, I don't know what to say — Why did you have to be so clumsy, Dr. Rank! Everything was so good.

RANK: Well, in any case, you now have the knowledge that my body and soul are at your command. So won't you speak out?

NORA (*looking at him*): After that?

RANK: Please, just let me know what it is.

NORA: You can't know anything now.

RANK: I have to. You mustn't punish me like this. Give me the chance to do whatever is humanly possible for you.

NORA: Now there's nothing you can do for me. Besides, actually, I don't need any help. You'll see — it's only my fantasies. That's what it is. Of course! (*Sits in the rocker, looks at him, and smiles.*) What a nice one you are, Dr. Rank. Aren't you a little bit ashamed, now that the lamp is here?

RANK: No, not exactly. But perhaps I'd better go — for good?

NORA: No, you certainly can't do that. You must come here just as you always have. You know Torvald can't do without you.

RANK: Yes, but *you?*

NORA: You know how much I enjoy it when you're here.

RANK: That's precisely what threw me off. You're a mystery to me. So many times I've felt you'd almost rather be with me than with Helmer.

NORA: Yes — you see, there are some people that one loves most and other people that one would almost prefer being with.

RANK: Yes, there's something to that.

NORA: When I was back home, of course I loved Papa most. But I always thought it was so much fun when I could sneak down to the maids' quarters, because they never tried to improve me, and it was always so amusing, the way they talked to each other.

RIGHT: Cheryl Campbell as Nora in the 1981–1982 Royal Shakespeare Company production of *A Doll House.* FAR RIGHT: Nora and Torvald (Stephen Moore).

Nora is a bit children in nature
• plays w/ children
• jumping/ clapping !

RANK: Aha, so it's their place that I've filled.
NORA (*jumping up and going to him*): Oh, dear, sweet Dr. Rank, that's not what I meant at all. But you can understand that with Torvald it's just the same as with Papa —

(*The Maid enters from the hall.*)

MAID: Ma'am — please! (*She whispers to Nora and hands her a calling card.*)
NORA (*glancing at the card*): Ah! (*Slips it into her pocket.*)
RANK: Anything wrong?
NORA: No, no, not at all. It's only some — it's my new dress —
RANK: Really? But — there's your dress.
NORA: Oh, that. But this is another one — I ordered it — Torvald mustn't know —
RANK: Ah, now we have the big secret.
NORA: That's right. Just go in with him — he's back in the inner study. Keep him there as long as —
RANK: Don't worry. He won't get away. (*Goes into the study.*)
NORA (*to the Maid*): And he's standing waiting in the kitchen?
MAID: Yes, he came up by the back stairs.
NORA: But didn't you tell him somebody was here?
MAID: Yes, but that didn't do any good.
NORA: He won't leave?

MAID: No, he won't go till he's talked with you, ma'am.
NORA: Let him come in, then — but quietly. Helene, don't breathe a word about this. It's a surprise for my husband.
MAID: Yes, yes, I understand — (*Goes out.*)
NORA: This horror — it's going to happen. No, no, no, it can't happen, it mustn't. (*She goes and bolts Helmer's door. The Maid opens the hall door for Krogstad and shuts it behind him. He is dressed for travel in a fur coat, boots, and a fur cap.*)
NORA (*going toward him*): Talk softly. My husband's home.
KROGSTAD: Well, good for him.
NORA: What do you want?
KROGSTAD: Some information.
NORA: Hurry up, then. What is it?
KROGSTAD: You know, of course, that I got my notice.
NORA: I couldn't prevent it, Mr. Krogstad. I fought for you to the bitter end, but nothing worked.
KROGSTAD: Does your husband's love for you run so thin? He knows everything I can expose you to, and all the same he dares to —
NORA: How can you imagine he knows anything about this?
KROGSTAD: Ah, no — I can't imagine it either, now. It's not at all like my fine Torvald Helmer to have so much guts —

NORA: Mr. Krogstad, I demand respect for my husband!

KROGSTAD: Why, of course — all due respect. But since the lady's keeping it so carefully hidden, may I presume to ask if you're also a bit better informed than yesterday about what you've actually done?

NORA: More than you ever could teach me.

KROGSTAD: Yes, I *am* such an awful lawyer.

NORA: What is it you want from me?

KROGSTAD: Just a glimpse of how you are, Mrs. Helmer. I've been thinking about you all day long. A cashier, a night-court scribbler, a — well, a type like me also has a little of what they call a heart, you know.

NORA: Then show it. Think of my children.

KROGSTAD: Did you or your husband ever think of mine? But never mind. I simply wanted to tell you that you don't need to take this thing too seriously. For the present, I'm not proceeding with any action.

NORA: Oh no, really! Well — I knew that.

KROGSTAD: Everything can be settled in a friendly spirit. It doesn't have to get around town at all; it can stay just among us three.

NORA: My husband must never know anything of this.

KROGSTAD: How can you manage that? Perhaps you can pay me the balance?

NORA: No, not right now.

KROGSTAD: Or you know some way of raising the money in a day or two?

NORA: No way that I'm willing to use.

KROGSTAD: Well, it wouldn't have done you any good, anyway. If you stood in front of me with a fistful of bills, you still couldn't buy your signature back.

NORA: Then tell me what you're going to do with it.

KROGSTAD: I'll just hold onto it — keep it on file. There's no outsider who'll even get wind of it. So if you've been thinking of taking some desperate step —

NORA: I have.

KROGSTAD: Been thinking of running away from home —

NORA: I have!

KROGSTAD: Or even of something worse —

NORA: How could you guess that?

KROGSTAD: You can drop those thoughts.

NORA: How could you guess I was thinking of *that*?

KROGSTAD: Most of us think about *that* at first. I thought about it too, but I discovered I hadn't the courage —

NORA (*lifelessly*): I don't either.

KROGSTAD (*relieved*): That's true, you haven't the courage? You too?

NORA: I don't have it — I don't have it.

KROGSTAD: It would be terribly stupid, anyway. After that first storm at home blows out, why, then — I have here in my pocket a letter for your husband —

NORA: Telling everything?

KROGSTAD: As charitably as possible.

NORA (*quickly*): He mustn't ever get that letter. Tear it up. I'll find some way to get money.

KROGSTAD: Beg pardon, Mrs. Helmer, but I think I just told you —

NORA: Oh, I don't mean the money I owe you. Let me know how much you want from my husband, and I'll manage it.

KROGSTAD: I don't want any money from your husband.

NORA: What do you want, then?

KROGSTAD: I'll tell you what. I want to recoup, Mrs. Helmer; I want to get on in the world — and there's where your husband can help me. For a year and a half I've kept myself clean of anything disreputable — all that time struggling with the worst conditions; but I was satisfied, working my way up step by step. Now I've been written right off, and I'm just not in the mood to come crawling back. I tell you, I want to move on. I want to get back in the bank — in a better position. Your husband can set up a job for me —

NORA: He'll never do that!

KROGSTAD: He'll do it. I know him. He won't dare breathe a word of protest. And once I'm in there together with him, you just wait and see! Inside of a year, I'll be the manager's right-hand man. It'll be Nils Krogstad, not Torvald Helmer, who runs the bank.

NORA: You'll never see the day!

KROGSTAD: Maybe you think you can —

NORA: I have the courage now — for *that*.

KROGSTAD: Oh, you don't scare me. A smart, spoiled lady like you —

NORA: You'll see; you'll see!

KROGSTAD: Under the ice, maybe? Down in the freezing, coal-black water? There, till you float up in the spring, ugly unrecognizable, with your hair falling out —

NORA: You don't frighten me.

KROGSTAD: Nor do you frighten me. One doesn't do these things, Mrs. Helmer. Besides what good would it be? I'd still have him safe in my pocket.

NORA: Afterwards? When I'm no longer — ?

KROGSTAD: Are you forgetting that *I'll* be in control then over your final reputation? (*Nora stands speechless, staring at him.*) Good; now I've warned you. Don't do anything stupid. When Helmer's read my letter, I'll be waiting for his reply. And bear in mind that it's your husband himself who's forced me back to my old ways. I'll never forgive him for that. Goodbye, Mrs. Helmer. (*He goes out through the hall.*)

NORA (*goes to the hall door, opens it a crack, and listens*): He's gone. Didn't leave the letter. Oh no, no, that's impossible too! (*Opening the door more and more.*) What's that? He's standing outside — not going downstairs. He's thinking it over? Maybe he'll — ? (*A letter falls in the mailbox; then Krogstad's footsteps are heard, dying away down a flight of stairs. Nora gives a muffled cry and runs over toward the sofa table. A short pause.*) In the mailbox. (*Slips warily over to the hall door.*) It's lying there. Torvald, Torvald — now we're lost!

MRS. LINDE (*entering with the costume from the room, left*): There now, I can't see anything else to mend. Perhaps you'd like to try —

NORA (*in a hoarse whisper*): Kristine, come here.

MRS. LINDE (*tossing the dress on the sofa*): What's wrong? You look upset.

NORA: Come here. See that letter? There! Look — through the glass in the mailbox.

MRS. LINDE: Yes, yes, I see it.

NORA: That letter's from Krogstad —

MRS. LINDE: Nora — it's Krogstad who loaned you the money!

NORA: Yes, and now Torvald will find out everything.

MRS. LINDE: Believe me, Nora, it's best for both of you.

NORA: There's more you don't know. I forged a name.

MRS. LINDE: But for heaven's sake — ?

NORA: I only want to tell you that, Kristine, so that you can be my witness.

MRS. LINDE: Witness? Why should I — ?

NORA: If I should go out of my mind — it could easily happen —

MRS. LINDE: Nora!

NORA: Or anything else occurred — so I couldn't be present here —

MRS. LINDE: Nora, Nora, you aren't yourself at all!

NORA: And someone should try to take on the whole weight, all of the guilt, you follow me —

MRS. LINDE: Yes, of course, but why do you think — ?

NORA: Then you're the witness that it isn't true, Kristine. I'm very much myself; my mind right now is perfectly clear; and I'm telling you: Nobody else has known about this; I alone did everything. Remember that.

MRS. LINDE: I will. But I don't understand all this.

NORA: Oh, how could you ever understand it? It's the miracle now that's going to take place.

MRS. LINDE: The miracle?

NORA: Yes, the miracle. But it's so awful, Kristine. It mustn't take place, not for anything in the world.

MRS. LINDE: I'm going right over and talk with Krogstad.

NORA: Don't go near him; he'll do you some terrible harm!

MRS. LINDE: There was a time once when he'd gladly have done anything for me.

NORA: He?

MRS. LINDE: Where does he live?

NORA: Oh, how do I know? Yes. (*Searches in her pocket.*) Here's his card. But the letter, the letter — !

HELMER (*from the study, knocking on the door*): Nora!

NORA (*with a cry of fear*): Oh! What is it? What do you want?

HELMER: Now, now, don't be so frightened. We're not coming in. You locked the door — are you trying on the dress?

NORA: Yes, I'm trying it. I'll look just beautiful, Torvald.

MRS. LINDE (*who has read the card*): He's living right around the corner.

NORA: Yes, but what's the use? We're lost. The letter's in the box.

MRS. LINDE: And your husband has the key?

NORA: Yes, always.

MRS. LINDE: Krogstad can ask for his letter back unread; he can find some excuse —

NORA: But it's just this time that Torvald usually —

MRS. LINDE: Stall him. Keep him in there. I'll be back as quick as I can. (*She hurries out through the hall entrance.*)

NORA (*goes to Helmer's door, opens it, and peers in*): Torvald!

HELMER (*from the inner study*): Well — does one dare set foot in one's own living room at last? Come on, Rank, now we'll get a look — (*In the doorway.*) But what's this?

NORA: What, Torvald dear?

HELMER: Rank had me expecting some grand masquerade.

RANK (*in the doorway*): That was my impression, but I must have been wrong.

NORA: No one can admire me in my splendor — not till tomorrow.

HELMER: But Nora dear, you look so exhausted. Have you practiced too hard?

NORA: No, I haven't practiced at all yet.

HELMER: You know, it's necessary —

NORA: Oh, it's absolutely necessary, Torvald. But I can't get anywhere without your help. I've forgotten the whole thing completely. *helpless act!*

HELMER: Ah, we'll soon take care of that.

NORA: Yes, take care of me, Torvald, please! Promise me that? Oh, I'm so nervous. That big party — You must give up everything this evening for me. No business — don't even touch your pen. Yes? Dear Torvald, promise?

HELMER: It's a promise. Tonight I'm totally at your service — you little helpless thing. Hm — but first there's one thing I want to — (*Goes toward the hall door.*)

NORA: What are you looking for?

HELMER: Just to see if there's any mail.

NORA: No, no, don't do that, Torvald!

HELMER: Now what?

NORA: Torvald, please. There isn't any.

HELMER: Let me look, though. (*Starts out. Nora, at the piano, strikes the first notes of the tarantella. Helmer, at the door, stops.*) Aha!

NORA: I can't dance tomorrow if I don't practice with you.

HELMER (*going over to her*): Nora dear, are you really so frightened?

NORA: Yes, so terribly frightened. Let me practice right now; there's still time before dinner. Oh, sit down and play for me, Torvald. Direct me. Teach me, the way you always have.

HELMER: Gladly, if it's what you want. (*Sits at the piano.*)

NORA (*snatches the tambourine up from the box, then a long, varicolored shawl, which she throws around herself, whereupon she springs forward and cries out*): Play for me now! Now I'll dance!

(*Helmer plays and Nora dances. Rank stands behind Helmer at the piano and looks on.*)

HELMER (*as he plays*): Slower. Slow down.

NORA: Can't change it.

HELMER: Not so violent, Nora!

NORA: Has to be just like this.

HELMER (*stopping*): No, no, that won't do at all.

NORA (*laughing and swinging her tambourine*): Isn't that what I told you?

RANK: Let me play for her.

HELMER (*getting up*): Yes, go on. I can teach her more easily then.

(*Rank sits at the piano and plays, Nora dances more and more wildly. Helmer has stationed himself by the stove and repeatedly gives her directions; she seems not to hear them; her hair loosens and falls over her shoulders; she does not notice, but goes on dancing. Mrs. Linde enters.*)

MRS. LINDE (*standing dumbfounded at the door*): Ah — !

NORA (*still dancing*): See what fun, Kristine!

HELMER: But Nora darling, you dance as if your life were at stake.

NORA: And it is.

HELMER: Rank, stop! This is pure madness. Stop it, I say!

(*Rank breaks off playing, and Nora halts abruptly.*)

HELMER (*going over to her*): I never would have believed it. You've forgotten everything I taught you.

NORA (*throwing away the tambourine*): You see for yourself.

HELMER: Well, there's certainly room for instruction here.

NORA: Yes, you see how important it is. You've got to teach me to the very last minute. Promise me that, Torvald?

HELMER: You can bet on it.

NORA: You mustn't, either today or tomorrow, think about anything else but me; you mustn't open any letters — or the mailbox —

HELMER: Ah, it's still the fear of that man —

NORA: Oh yes, yes, that too.

HELMER: Nora, it's written all over you — there's already a letter from him out there.

NORA: I don't know. I guess so. But you mustn't read such things now; there mustn't be anything ugly between us before it's all over.

RANK (*quietly to Helmer*): You shouldn't deny her.

HELMER (*putting his arm around her*): The child can have her way. But tomorrow night, after you've danced —

NORA: Then you'll be free.

MAID (*in the doorway, right*): Ma'am, dinner is served.

NORA: We'll be wanting champagne, Helene.

MAID: Very good, ma'am. (*Goes out.*)

HELMER: So — a regular banquet, hm?

NORA: Yes, a banquet — champagne till daybreak! (*Calling out.*) And some macaroons, Helene. Heaps of them — just this once.

HELMER (*taking her hands*): Now, now, now — no hysterics. Be my own little lark again.

NORA: Oh, I will soon enough. But go on in — and you, Dr. Rank. Kristine, help me put up my hair.

RANK (*whispering, as they go*): There's nothing wrong — really wrong, is there?

HELMER: Oh, of course not. It's nothing more than this childish anxiety I was telling you about. (*They go out, right.*)

NORA: Well?

MRS. LINDE: Left town.

NORA: I could see by your face.

MRS. LINDE: He'll be home tomorrow evening. I wrote him a note.

NORA: You shouldn't have. Don't try to stop anything now. After all, it's a wonderful joy, this waiting here for the miracle.

MRS. LINDE: What is it you're waiting for?

NORA: Oh, you can't understand that. Go in to them; I'll be along in a moment.

(*Mrs. Linde goes into the dining room. Nora stands a short while as if composing herself; then she looks at her watch.*)

NORA: Five. Seven hours to midnight. Twenty-four hours to the midnight after, and then the tarantella's done. Seven and twenty-four? Thirty-one hours to live.

HELMER (*in the doorway, right*): What's become of the little lark?

NORA (*going toward him with open arms*): Here's your lark!

ACT III

(*Same scene. The table, with chairs around it, has been moved to the center of the room. A lamp on the table is lit. The hall door stands open. Dance music drifts down from the floor above. Mrs. Linde sits at the table, absently paging through a book, trying to read, but apparently unable to focus her thoughts. Once or twice she pauses, tensely listening for a sound at the outer entrance.*)

MRS. LINDE (*glancing at her watch*): Not yet — and there's hardly any time left. If only he's not — (*Listening again.*) Ah, there it is. (*She goes out in the hall and cautiously opens the outer door. Quiet footsteps are heard on the stairs. She whispers.*) Come in. Nobody's here.

KROGSTAD (*in the doorway*): I found a note from you at home. What's back of all this?

MRS. LINDE: I just *had* to talk to you.

KROGSTAD: Oh? And it just *had* to be here in this house?

MRS. LINDE: At my place it was impossible; my room hasn't a private entrance. Come in, we're all alone. The maid's asleep, and the Helmers are at the dance upstairs.

KROGSTAD (*entering the room*): Well, well, the Helmers are dancing tonight? Really?

MRS. LINDE: Yes, why not?

KROGSTAD: How true — why not?

MRS. LINDE: All right, Krogstad, let's talk.

KROGSTAD: Do we two have anything more to talk about?

MRS. LINDE: We have a great deal to talk about.

KROGSTAD: I wouldn't have thought so.

MRS. LINDE: No, because you've never understood me, really.

KROGSTAD: Was there anything more to understand — except what's all too common in life? A calculating woman throws over a man the moment a better catch comes by.

MRS. LINDE: You think I'm so thoroughly calculating? You think I broke it off lightly?

KROGSTAD: Didn't you?

MRS. LINDE: Nils — is that what you really thought?

KROGSTAD: If you cared, then why did you write me the way you did?

MRS. LINDE: What else could I do? If I had to break off with you, then it was my job as well to root out everything you felt for me.

KROGSTAD (*wringing his hands*): So that was it. And this — all this, simply for money!

MRS. LINDE: Don't forget I had a helpless mother and two small brothers. We couldn't wait for you, Nils; you had such a long road ahead of you then.

KROGSTAD: That may be; but you still hadn't the right to abandon me for somebody else's sake.

MRS. LINDE: Yes — I don't know. So many, many times I've asked myself if I did have that right.

KROGSTAD (*more softly*): When I lost you, it was as if all the solid ground dissolved from under my feet. Look at me; I'm a half-drowned man now, hanging onto a wreck.

MRS. LINDE: Help may be near.

KROGSTAD: It was near — but then you came and blocked it off.

MRS. LINDE: Without my knowing it, Nils. Today for the first time I learned that it's you I'm replacing at the bank.

KROGSTAD: All right — I believe you. But now that you know, will you step aside?

MRS. LINDE: No, because that wouldn't benefit you in the slightest.

KROGSTAD: Not "benefit" me, hm! I'd step aside anyway.

MRS. LINDE: I've learned to be realistic. Life and hard, bitter necessity have taught me that.

KROGSTAD: And life's taught me never to trust fine phrases.

MRS. LINDE: Then life's taught you a very sound thing. But you do have to trust in actions, don't you?

KROGSTAD: What does that mean?

MRS. LINDE: You said you were hanging on like a half-drowned man to a wreck.

KROGSTAD: I've good reason to say that.

MRS. LINDE: I'm also like a half-drowned woman on a wreck. No one to suffer with; no one to care for.

KROGSTAD: You made your choice.

MRS. LINDE: There wasn't any choice then.

KROGSTAD: So — what of it?

MRS. LINDE: Nils, if only we two shipwrecked people could reach across to each other.

KROGSTAD: What are you saying?

MRS. LINDE: Two on one wreck are at least better off than each on his own.

KROGSTAD: Kristine!

MRS. LINDE: Why do you think I came into town?

KROGSTAD: Did you really have some thought of me?

MRS. LINDE: I have to work to go on living. All my born days, as long as I can remember, I've worked, and it's been my best and my only joy. But now I'm completely alone in the world; it frightens me to be so empty and lost. To work for yourself — there's no joy in that. Nils, give me something — someone to work for.

KROGSTAD: I don't believe all this. It's just some hysterical feminine urge to go out and make a noble sacrifice.

MRS. LINDE: Have you ever found me to be hysterical?

KROGSTAD: Can you honestly mean this? Tell me — do you know everything about my past?

MRS. LINDE: Yes.

KROGSTAD: And you know what they think I'm worth around here.

MRS. LINDE: From what you were saying before, it would seem that with me you could have been another person.

KROGSTAD: I'm positive of that.

MRS. LINDE: Couldn't it happen still?

KROGSTAD: Kristine — you're saying this in all seriousness? Yes, you are! I can see it in you. And do you really have the courage, then — ?

MRS. LINDE: I need to have someone to care for, and your children need a mother. We both need each other. Nils, I have faith that you're good at heart — I'll risk everything together with you.

KROGSTAD (*gripping her hands*): Kristine, thank you, thank you — Now I know I can win back a place in their eyes. Yes — but I forgot —

MRS. LINDE (*listening*): Shh! The tarantella. Go now! Go on!

KROGSTAD: Why? What is it?

MRS. LINDE: Hear the dance up there? When that's over, they'll be coming down.

KROGSTAD: Oh, then I'll go. But — it's all pointless. Of course, you don't know the move I made against the Helmers.

MRS. LINDE: Yes, Nils, I know.

KROGSTAD: And all the same, you have the courage to — ?

MRS. LINDE: I know how far despair can drive a man like you.

KROGSTAD: Oh, if I only could take it all back.

MRS. LINDE: You easily could — your letter's still lying in the mailbox.

KROGSTAD: Are you sure of that?

MRS. LINDE: Positive. But —

KROGSTAD (*looks at her searchingly*): Is that the meaning of it, then? You'll save your friend at any price. Tell me straight out. Is that it?

MRS. LINDE: Nils — anyone who's sold herself for somebody else once isn't going to do it again.

KROGSTAD: I'll demand my letter back.

MRS. LINDE: No, no.

KROGSTAD: Yes, of course. I'll stay here till Helmer comes down; I'll tell him to give me my letter again — that it only involves my dismissal — that he shouldn't read it —

MRS. LINDE: No, Nils, don't call the letter back.

KROGSTAD: But wasn't that exactly why you wrote me to come here?

MRS. LINDE: Yes, in that first panic. But it's been a whole day and night since then, and in that time I've seen such incredible things in this house. Helmer's got to learn everything; this dreadful secret has to be aired; those two have to come to a full understanding; all these lies and evasions can't go on.

KROGSTAD: Well, then, if you want to chance it. But at least there's one thing I can do, and do right away —

MRS. LINDE (*listening*): Go now, go, quick! The dance is over. We're not safe another second.

KROGSTAD: I'll wait for you downstairs.

MRS. LINDE: Yes, please do; take me home.

KROGSTAD: I can't believe it; I've never been so happy. (*He leaves by way of the outer door; the door between the room and the hall stays open.*)

MRS. LINDE (*straightening up a bit and getting together her street clothes*): How different now! How different! Someone to work for, to live for — a home to build. Well, it is worth the try! Oh, if they'd only come! (*Listening.*) Ah, there they are. Bundle up. (*She picks up her hat and coat. Nora's and Helmer's voices can be heard outside; a key turns in the lock, and Helmer brings Nora into the hall almost by force. She is wearing the Italian costume with a large black shawl about her; he has on evening dress, with a black domino open over it.*)

NORA (*struggling in the doorway*): No, no, no, not inside! I'm going up again. I don't want to leave so soon.

HELMER: But Nora dear —

NORA: Oh, I beg you, please, Torvald. From the bottom of my heart, *please* — only an hour more!

HELMER: Not a single minute, Nora darling. You know our agreement. Come on, in we go; you'll catch cold out here. (*In spite of her resistance, he gently draws her into the room.*)

MRS. LINDE: Good evening.

NORA: Kristine!

HELMER: Why, Mrs. Linde — are you here so late?

MRS. LINDE: Yes, I'm sorry, but I did want to see Nora in costume.

NORA: Have you been sitting here, waiting for me?

MRS. LINDE: Yes. I didn't come early enough; you were all upstairs; and then I thought I really couldn't leave without seeing you.

HELMER (*removing Nora's shawl*): Yes, take a good look. She's worth looking at, I can tell you that, Mrs. Linde. Isn't she lovely?

MRS. LINDE: Yes, I should say —

HELMER: A dream of loveliness, isn't she? That's what everyone thought at the party, too. But she's horribly stubborn — this sweet little thing. What's to be done with her? Can you imagine, I almost had to use force to pry her away.

NORA: Oh, Torvald, you're going to regret you didn't indulge me, even for just a half hour more.

HELMER: There, you see. She danced her tarantella and got a tumultuous hand — which was well earned, although the performance may have been a bit too naturalistic — I mean it rather overstepped the proprieties of art. But never mind — what's important is, she made a success, an overwhelming success. You think I could let her stay on after that and spoil the effect? Oh no; I took my lovely little Capri girl — my capricious little Capri girl, I should say — took her under my arm; one quick tour of the ballroom, a curtsy to every side, and then — as they say in novels — the beautiful vision disappeared. An exit should always be effective, Mrs. Linde, but that's what I can't get Nora to grasp. Phew, It's hot in here. (*Flings the domino on a chair and opens the door to his room.*) Why's it dark in here? Oh yes, of course. Excuse me. (*He goes in and lights a couple of candles.*)

NORA (*in a sharp, breathless whisper*): So?

MRS. LINDE (*quietly*): I talked with him.

NORA: And — ?

MRS. LINDE: Nora — you must tell your husband everything.

NORA (*dully*): I knew it.

MRS. LINDE: You've got nothing to fear from Krogstad, but you have to speak out.

NORA: I won't tell.

MRS. LINDE: Then the letter will.

NORA: Thanks, Kristine. I know now what's to be done. Shh!

HELMER (*reentering*): Well, then, Mrs. Linde — have you admired her?

MRS. LINDE: Yes, and now I'll say good night.

HELMER: Oh, come, so soon? Is this yours, this knitting?

MRS. LINDE: Yes, thanks. I nearly forgot it.

HELMER: Do you knit, then?

MRS. LINDE: Oh yes.

HELMER: You know what? You should embroider instead.

MRS. LINDE: Really? Why?

HELMER: Yes, because it's a lot prettier. See here, one holds the embroidery so, in the left hand, and then one guides the needle with the right — so — in an easy, sweeping curve — right?

MRS. LINDE: Yes, I guess that's —

HELMER: But, on the other hand, knitting — it can never be anything but ugly. Look, see here, the arms tucked in, the knitting needles going up and down — there's something Chinese about it. Ah, that was really a glorious champagne they served.

MRS. LINDE: Yes, good night, Nora, and don't be stubborn anymore.

HELMER: Well put, Mrs. Linde!

MRS. LINDE: Good night, Mr. Helmer.

HELMER (*accompanying her to the door*): Good night, good night. I hope you get home all right. I'd be very happy to — but you don't have far to go. Good night, good night. (*She leaves. He shuts the door after her and returns.*) There, now, at last we got her out the door. She's a deadly bore, that creature.

NORA: Aren't you pretty tired, Torvald?

HELMER: No, not a bit.

NORA: You're not sleepy?

HELMER: Not at all. On the contrary, I'm feeling quite exhilarated. But you? Yes, you really look tired and sleepy.

NORA: Yes, I'm very tired. Soon now I'll sleep.

HELMER: See! You see! I was right all along that we shouldn't stay longer.

NORA: Whatever you do is always right.

HELMER (*kissing her brow*): Now my little lark talks sense. Say, did you notice what a time Rank was having tonight?

NORA: Oh, was he? I didn't get to speak with him.

HELMER: I scarcely did either, but it's a long time since I've seen him in such high spirits. (*Gazes at her a moment, then comes nearer her.*) Hm — it's marvelous, though, to be back home again — to be completely alone with you. Oh, you bewitchingly lovely young woman!

NORA: Torvald, don't look at me like that!

HELMER: Can't I look at my richest treasure? At all that beauty that's mine, mine alone — completely and utterly.

NORA (*moving around to the other side of the table*): You mustn't talk to me that way tonight.

HELMER (*following her*): The tarantella is still in your blood. I can see — and it makes you even more enticing. Listen. The guests are beginning to go. (*Dropping his voice.*) Nora — it'll soon be quiet through this whole house.

NORA: Yes, I hope so.

HELMER: You do, don't you, my love? Do you realize — when I'm out at a party like this with you — do you know why I talk to you so little, and keep such a distance away; just send you a stolen look now and then — you know why I do it? It's because I'm imagining then that you're my secret darling, my secret young bride-to-be, and that no one suspects there's anything between us.

NORA: Yes, yes; oh, yes, I know you're always thinking of me.

HELMER: And then when we leave and I place the shawl over those fine young rounded shoulders — over that wonderful curving neck — then I pretend that you're my young bride, that we're just coming from the wedding, that for the first time I'm bringing you into my house — that for the first time I'm alone with you — completely alone with you, your trembling young beauty! All this evening I've longed for nothing but you. When I saw you turn and sway in the tarantella — my blood was pounding till I couldn't stand it — that's why I brought you down here so early —

NORA: Go away, Torvald! Leave me alone. I don't want all this.

HELMER: What do you mean? Nora, you're teasing me. You will, won't you? Aren't I your husband — ?

(*A knock at the outside door.*)

NORA (*startled*): What's that?

HELMER (*going toward the hall*): Who is it?

RANK (*outside*): It's me. May I come in a moment?

HELMER (*with quiet irritation*): Oh, what does he want now? (*Aloud.*) Hold on. (*Goes and opens the door.*) Oh, how nice that you didn't just pass us by!

RANK: I thought I heard your voice, and then I wanted so badly to have a look in. (*Lightly glancing about.*) Ah, me, these old familiar haunts. You have it snug and cozy in here, you two.

HELMER: You seemed to be having it pretty cozy upstairs, too.

RANK: Absolutely. Why shouldn't I? Why not take in everything in life? As much as you can, anyway, and as long as you can. The wine was superb —

HELMER: The champagne especially.

RANK: You noticed that too? It's amazing how much I could guzzle down.

NORA: Torvald also drank a lot of champagne this evening.

RANK: Oh?

NORA: Yes, and that always makes him so entertaining.

RANK: Well, why shouldn't one have a pleasant evening after a well-spent day?

HELMER: Well spent? I'm afraid I can't claim that.

RANK (*slapping him on the back*): But I can, you see!

NORA: Dr. Rank, you must have done some scientific research today.

RANK: Quite so.

HELMER: Come now — little Nora talking about scientific research!

NORA: And can I congratulate you on the results?

RANK: Indeed you may.

NORA: Then they were good?

RANK: The best possible for both doctor and patient — certainty.

NORA (*quickly and searchingly*): Certainty?

RANK: Complete certainty. So don't I owe myself a gay evening afterwards?

NORA: Yes, you're right, Dr. Rank.

HELMER: I'm with you — just so long as you don't have to suffer for it in the morning.

RANK: Well, one never gets something for nothing in life.

NORA: Dr. Rank — are you very fond of masquerade parties?

RANK: Yes, if there's a good array of odd disguises —

NORA: Tell me, what should we two go as at the next masquerade?

HELMER: You little featherhead — already thinking of the next!

RANK: We two? I'll tell you what: You must go as Charmed Life —

HELMER: Yes, but find a costume for that!

RANK: Your wife can appear just as she looks every day.

HELMER: That was nicely put. But don't you know what you're going to be?

RANK: Yes, Helmer, I've made up my mind.

HELMER: Well?

RANK: At the next masquerade I'm going to be invisible.

HELMER: That's a funny idea.

RANK: They say there's a hat — black, huge — have you never heard of the hat that makes you invisible? You put it on, and then no one on earth can see you.

HELMER (*suppressing a smile*): Ah, of course.

RANK: But I'm quite forgetting what I came for. Helmer, give me a cigar, one of the dark Havanas.

HELMER: With the greatest pleasure. (*Holds out his case.*)

RANK: Thanks. (*Takes one and cuts off the tip.*)

NORA (*striking a match*): Let me give you a light.

RANK: Thank you. (*She holds the match for him; he lights the cigar.*) And now good-bye.

HELMER: Good-bye, good-bye, old friend.

NORA: Sleep well, Doctor.

RANK: Thanks for that wish.

NORA: Wish me the same.

RANK: You? All right, if you like — Sleep well. And thanks for the light. (*He nods to them both and leaves.*)

HELMER (*his voice subdued*): He's been drinking heavily.

NORA (*absently*): Could be. (*Helmer takes his keys from his pocket and goes out in the hall.*) Torvald — what are you after?

HELMER: Got to empty the mailbox; it's nearly full. There won't be room for the morning papers.

NORA: Are you working tonight?

HELMER: You know I'm not. Why — what's this? Someone's been at the lock.

NORA: At the lock — ?

HELMER: Yes, I'm positive. What do you suppose — ? I can't imagine one of the maids — ? Here's a broken hairpin. Nora, it's yours —

NORA (*quickly*): Then it must be the children —

HELMER: You'd better break them of that. Hm, hm — well, opened it after all. (*Takes the contents out and*

ACT III

calls into the kitchen.) Helene! Helene, would you put out the lamp in the hall. (*He returns to the room, shutting the hall door, then displays the handful of mail.*) Look how it's piled up. (*Sorting through them.*) Now what's this?

NORA (*at the window*): The letter! Oh, Torvald, no!

HELMER: Two calling cards — from Rank.

NORA: From Dr. Rank?

HELMER (*examining them*): "Dr. Rank, Consulting Physician." They were on top. He must have dropped them in as he left.

NORA: Is there anything on them?

HELMER: There's a black cross over the name. See? That's a gruesome notion. He could almost be announcing his own death.

NORA: That's just what he's doing.

HELMER: What! You've heard something? Something he's told you?

NORA: Yes. That when those cards came, he'd be taking his leave of us. He'll shut himself in now and die.

HELMER: Ah, my poor friend! Of course I knew he wouldn't be here much longer. But so soon — And then to hide himself away like a wounded animal.

NORA: If it has to happen, then it's best it happens in silence — don't you think so, Torvald?

HELMER (*pacing up and down*): He's grown right into our lives. I simply can't imagine him gone. He with his suffering and loneliness — like a dark cloud setting off our sunlit happiness. Well, maybe it's best this way. For him, at least. (*Standing still.*) And maybe for us too, Nora. Now we're thrown back on each other, completely. (*Embracing her.*) Oh you, my darling wife, how can I hold you close enough? You know what, Nora — time and again I've wished you were in some terrible danger, just so I could stake my life and soul and everything, for your sake.

NORA (*tearing herself away, her voice firm and decisive*): Now you must read your mail, Torvald.

HELMER: No, no, not tonight. I want to stay with you, dearest.

NORA: With a dying friend on your mind?

HELMER: You're right. We've both had a shock. There's ugliness between us — these thoughts of death and corruption. We'll have to get free of them first. Until then — we'll stay apart.

NORA (*clinging about his neck*): Torvald — good night! Good night!

HELMER (*kissing her on the cheek*): Good night, little songbird. Sleep well, Nora. I'll be reading my mail now. (*He takes the letters into his room and shuts the door after him.*)

NORA (*with bewildered glances, groping about, seizing Helmer's domino, throwing it around her, and speaking in short, hoarse, broken whispers*): Never see him again. Never, never. (*Putting her shawl over her head.*) Never see the children either — them, too. Never, never. Oh, the freezing black water! The depths — down — Oh, I wish it were over — He has it now; he's reading it — now. Oh no, no, not yet.

Torvald, good-bye, you and the children — (*She starts for the hall; as she does, Helmer throws open his door and stands with an open letter in his hand.*)

HELMER: Nora!

NORA (*screams*): Oh — !

HELMER: What is this? You know what's in this letter?

NORA: Yes, I know. Let me go! Let me out!

HELMER (*holding her back*): Where are you going?

NORA (*struggling to break loose*): You can't save me, Torvald!

HELMER (*slumping back*): True! Then it's true what he writes? How horrible! No, no, it's impossible — it can't be true.

NORA: It *is* true. I've loved you more than all this world.

HELMER: Ah, none of your slippery tricks.

NORA (*taking one step toward him*): Torvald — !

HELMER: What *is* this you've blundered into!

NORA: Just let me loose. You're not going to suffer for my sake. You're not going to take on my guilt.

HELMER: No more playacting. (*Locks the hall door.*) You stay right here and give me a reckoning. You understand what you've done? Answer! You understand?

NORA (*looking squarely at him, her face hardening*): Yes. I'm beginning to understand everything now.

HELMER (*striding about*): Oh, what an awful awakening! In all these eight years — she who was my pride and joy — a hypocrite, a liar — worse, worse — a criminal! How infinitely disgusting it all is! The shame! (*Nora says nothing and goes on looking straight at him. He stops in front of her.*) I should have suspected something of the kind. I should have known. All your father's flimsy values — Be still! All your father's flimsy values have come out in you. No religion, no morals, no sense of duty — Oh, how I'm punished for letting him off! I did it for your sake, and you repay me like this.

NORA: Yes, like this.

HELMER: Now you've wrecked all my happiness — ruined my whole future. Oh, it's awful to think of. I'm in a cheap little grafter's hands; he can do anything he wants with me, ask for anything, play with me like a puppet — and I can't breathe a word. I'll be swept down miserably into the depths on account of a featherbrained woman.

NORA: When I'm gone from this world, you'll be free.

HELMER: Oh, quit posing. Your father had a mess of those speeches too. What good would that ever do me if you were gone from this world, as you say? Not the slightest. He can still make the whole thing known; and if he does, I could be falsely suspected as your accomplice. They might even think that I was behind it — that I put you up to it. And all that I can thank you for — you that I've coddled the whole of our marriage. Can you see now what you've done to me?

NORA (*icily calm*): Yes.

HELMER: It's so incredible, I just can't grasp it. But we'll have to patch up whatever we can. Take off the shawl. I said, take it off! I've got to appease him somehow or other. The thing has to be hushed up at any cost. And as for you and me, it's got to seem like everything between us is just as it was — to the outside world, that is. You'll go right on living in this house, of course. But you can't be allowed to bring up the children; I don't dare trust you with them — Oh, to have to say this to someone I've loved so much! Well, that's done with. From now on happiness doesn't matter; all that matters is saving the bits and pieces, the appearance — (*The doorbell rings. Helmer starts.*) What's that? And so late. Maybe the worst — ? You think he'd — ? Hide, Nora! Say you're sick. (*Nora remains standing motionless. Helmer goes and opens the door.*)

MAID (*half dressed, in the hall*): A letter for Mrs. Helmer.

HELMER: I'll take it. (*Snatches the letter and shuts the door.*) Yes, it's from him. You don't get it; I'm reading it myself.

NORA: Then read it.

HELMER (*by the lamp*): I hardly dare. We may be ruined, you and I. But — I've got to know. (*Rips open the letter, skims through a few lines, glances at an enclosure, then cries out joyfully.*) Nora! (*Nora looks inquiringly at him.*) Nora! Wait — better check it again — Yes, yes, it's true. I'm saved. Nora, I'm saved!

NORA: And I?

HELMER: You too, of course. We're both saved, both of us. Look. He's sent back your note. He says he's sorry and ashamed — that a happy development in his life — oh, who cares what he says! Nora, we're saved! No one can hurt you. Oh, Nora, Nora — but first, this ugliness all has to go. Let me see — (*Takes a look at the note.*) No, I don't want to see it; I want the whole thing to fade like a dream. (*Tears the note and both letters to pieces, throws them into the stove and watches them burn.*) There — now there's nothing left — He wrote that since Christmas Eve you — Oh, they must have been three terrible days for you, Nora.

NORA: I fought a hard fight.

HELMER: And suffered pain and saw no escape but — No, we're not going to dwell on anything unpleasant. We'll just be grateful and keep on repeating: It's over now, it's over! You hear me, Nora? You don't seem to realize — it's over. What's it mean — that frozen look? Oh, poor little Nora, I understand. You can't believe I've forgiven you. But I have, Nora; I swear I have. I know that what you did, you did out of love for me.

NORA: That's true.

HELMER: You loved me the way a wife ought to love her husband. It's simply the means that you couldn't judge. But you think I love you any the less for not knowing how to handle your affairs? No, no — just lean on me; I'll guide you and teach you. I wouldn't be a man if this feminine helplessness didn't make you twice as attractive to me. You mustn't mind

those sharp words I said — that was all in the first confusion of thinking my world had collapsed. I've forgiven you, Nora; I swear I've forgiven you.

NORA: My thanks for your forgiveness. (*She goes out through the door, right.*)

HELMER: No, wait — (*Peers in.*) What are you doing in there?

NORA (*inside*): Getting out of my costume.

HELMER (*by the open door*): Yes, do that. Try to calm yourself and collect your thoughts again, my frightened little songbird. You can rest easy now; I've got wide wings to shelter you with. (*Walking about close by the door.*) How snug and nice our home is, Nora. You're safe here; I'll keep you like a hunted dove I've rescued out of a hawk's claws. I'll bring peace to your poor, shuddering heart. Gradually it'll happen, Nora; you'll see. Tomorrow all this will look different to you; then everything will be as it was. I won't have to go on repeating I forgive you; you'll feel it for yourself. How can you imagine I'd ever conceivably want to disown you — or even blame you in any way? Ah, you don't know a man's heart, Nora. For a man there's something indescribably sweet and satisfying in knowing he's forgiven his wife — and forgiven her out of a full and open heart. It's as if she belongs to him in two ways now: In a sense he's given her fresh into the world again, and she's become his wife and his child as well. From now on that's what you'll be to me — you little, bewildered, helpless thing. Don't be afraid of anything, Nora; just open your heart to me, and I'll be conscience and will to you both — (*Nora enters in her regular clothes.*) What's this? Not in bed? You've changed your dress?

NORA: Yes, Torvald, I've changed my dress.

HELMER: But why now, so late?

NORA: Tonight I'm not sleeping.

HELMER: But Nora dear —

NORA (*looking at her watch*): It's still not so very late. Sit down, Torvald; we have a lot to talk over. (*She sits at one side of the table.*)

HELMER: Nora — what is this? That hard expression —

NORA: Sit down. This'll take some time. I have a lot to say.

HELMER (*sitting at the table directly opposite her*): You worry me, Nora. And I don't understand you.

NORA: No, that's exactly it. You don't understand me. And I've never understood you either — until tonight. No, don't interrupt. You can just listen to what I say. We're closing out accounts, Torvald.

HELMER: How do you mean that?

NORA (*after a short pause*): Doesn't anything strike you about our sitting here like this?

HELMER: What's that?

NORA: We've been married now eight years. Doesn't it occur to you that this is the first time we two, you and I, man and wife, have ever talked seriously together?

HELMER: What do you mean — seriously?

NORA: In eight whole years — longer even — right from

our first acquaintance, we've never exchanged a serious word on any serious thing.

HELMER: You mean I should constantly go and involve you in problems you couldn't possibly help me with?

NORA: I'm not talking of problems. I'm saying that we've never sat down seriously together and tried to get to the bottom of anything.

HELMER: But dearest, what good would that ever do you?

NORA: That's the point right there: You've never understood me. I've been wronged greatly, Torvald — first by Papa, and then by you.

HELMER: What! By us — the two people who've loved you more than anyone else?

NORA (shaking her head): You never loved me. You've thought it fun to be in love with me, that's all.

HELMER: Nora, what a thing to say!

NORA: Yes, it's true now, Torvald. When I lived at home with Papa, he told me all his opinions, so I had the same ones too; or if they were different I hid them, since he wouldn't have cared for that. He used to call me his doll-child, and he played with me the way I played with my dolls. Then I came into your house —

HELMER: How can you speak of our marriage like that?

NORA (unperturbed): I mean, then I went from Papa's hands into yours. You arranged everything to your own taste, and so I got the same taste as you — or I pretended to; I can't remember. I guess a little of both, first one, then the other. Now when I look back, it seems as if I'd lived here like a beggar — just from hand to mouth. I've lived by doing tricks for you, Torvald. But that's the way you wanted it. It's a great sin what you and Papa did to me. You're to blame that nothing's become of me.

HELMER: Nora, how unfair and ungrateful you are! Haven't you been happy here?

NORA: No, never. I thought so — but I never have.

HELMER: Not — not happy!

NORA: No, only lighthearted. And you've always been so kind to me. But our home's been nothing but a playpen. I've been your doll-wife here, just as at home I was Papa's doll-child. And in turn the children have been my dolls. I thought it was fun when you played with me, just as they thought it fun when I played with them. That's been our marriage, Torvald.

HELMER: There's some truth in what you're saying — under all the raving exaggeration. But it'll all be different after this. Playtime's over; now for the schooling.

NORA: Whose schooling — mine or the children's?

HELMER: Both yours and the children's, dearest.

NORA: Oh, Torvald, you're not the man to teach me to be a good wife to you.

HELMER: And you can say that?

NORA: And I — how am I equipped to bring up children?

HELMER: Nora!

NORA: Didn't you say a moment ago that that was no job to trust me with?

HELMER: In a flare of temper! Why fasten on that?

NORA: Yes, but you were so very right. I'm not up to the job. There's another job I have to do first. I have to try to educate myself. You can't help me with that. I've got to do it alone. And that's why I'm leaving you now.

HELMER (jumping up): What's that?

NORA: I have to stand completely alone, if I'm ever going to discover myself and the world out there. So I can't go on living with you.

HELMER: Nora, Nora!

NORA: I want to leave right away. Kristine should put me up for the night —

HELMER: You're insane! You've no right! I forbid you!

NORA: From here on, there's no use forbidding me anything. I'll take with me whatever is mine. I don't want a thing from you, either now or later.

HELMER: What kind of madness is this!

NORA: Tomorrow I'm going home — I mean, home where I came from. It'll be easier up there to find something to do.

HELMER: Oh, you blind, incompetent child!

NORA: I must learn to be competent, Torvald.

HELMER: Abandon your home, your husband, your children! And you're not even thinking what people will say.

NORA: I can't be concerned about that. I only know how essential this is.

HELMER: Oh, it's outrageous. So you'll run out like this on your most sacred vows.

NORA: What do you think are my most sacred vows?

HELMER: And I have to tell you that! Aren't they your duties to your husband and children?

NORA: I have other duties equally sacred.

HELMER: That isn't true. What duties are they?

NORA: Duties to myself.

HELMER: Before all else, you're a wife and a mother.

NORA: I don't believe in that anymore. I believe that before all else, I'm a human being, no less than you — or anyway, I ought to try to become one. I know the majority thinks you're right, Torvald, and plenty of books agree with you, too. But I can't go on believing what the majority says, or what's written in books. I have to think over these things myself and try to understand them.

HELMER: Why can't you understand your place in your own home? On a point like that, isn't there one everlasting guide you can turn to? Where's your religion?

NORA: Oh, Torvald, I'm really not sure what religion is.

HELMER: What — ?

NORA: I only know what the minister said when I was confirmed. He told me religion was this thing and that. When I get clear and away by myself, I'll go into that problem too. I'll see if what the minister said was right, or, in any case, if it's right for me.

HELMER: A young woman your age shouldn't talk like that. If religion can't move you, I can try to rouse your conscience. You do have some moral feeling? Or, tell me — has that gone too?

NORA: It's not easy to answer that, Torvald. I simply don't know. I'm all confused about these things. I just know I see them so differently from you. I find out for one thing, that the law's not at all what I'd thought — but I can't get it through my head that the law is fair. A woman hasn't a right to protect her dying father or save her husband's life! I can't believe that.

HELMER: You talk like a child. You don't know anything of the world you live in.

NORA: No, I don't. But now I'll begin to learn for myself. I'll try to discover who's right, the world or I.

HELMER: Nora, you're sick; you've got a fever. I almost think you're out of your head.

NORA: I've never felt more clearheaded and sure in my life.

HELMER: And — clearheaded and sure — you're leaving your husband and children?

NORA: Yes.

HELMER: Then there's only one possible reason.

NORA: What?

HELMER: You no longer love me.

NORA: No. That's exactly it.

HELMER: Nora! You can't be serious!

NORA: Oh, this is so hard, Torvald — you've been so kind to me always. But I can't help it. I don't love you anymore.

HELMER (*struggling for composure*): Are you also clearheaded and sure about that?

NORA: Yes, completely. That's why I can't go on staying here.

HELMER: Can you tell me what I did to lose your love?

NORA: Yes, I can tell you. It was this evening when the miraculous thing didn't come — then I knew you weren't the man I'd imagined.

HELMER: Be more explicit; I don't follow you.

NORA: I've waited now so patiently eight long years — for, my Lord, I know miracles don't come every day. Then this crisis broke over me, and such a certainty filled me: *Now* the miraculous event would occur. While Krogstad's letter was lying out there, I never for an instant dreamed that you could give in to his terms. I was so utterly sure you'd say to him: Go on, tell your tale to the whole wide world. And when he'd done that —

HELMER: Yes, what then? When I'd delivered my own wife into shame and disgrace — !

NORA: When he'd done that, I was so utterly sure that you'd step forward, take the blame on yourself and say: I am the guilty one.

HELMER: Nora — !

NORA: You're thinking I'd never accept such a sacrifice from you? No, of course not. But what good would my protests be against you? That was the miracle I was waiting for, in terror and hope. And to stave that off, I would have taken my life.

HELMER: I'd gladly work for you day and night, Nora — and take on pain and deprivation. But there's no one who gives up honor for love.

Janet McTeer as Nora Helmer in Anthony Page's production of *A Doll House* at the Belasco Theater on Broadway, 1997. McTeer's interpretation of the role electrified audiences who, according to Ben Brantley, found "previously hidden nuances in Ibsen's landmark work."

NORA: Millions of women have done just that.

HELMER: Oh, you think and talk like a silly child.

NORA: Perhaps. But you neither think nor talk like the man I could join myself to. When your big fright was over — and it wasn't from any threat against me, only for what might damage you — when all the danger was past, for you it was just as if nothing had happened. I was exactly the same, your little lark, your doll, that you'd have to handle with double care now that I'd turned out so brittle and frail. (*Gets up.*) Torvald — in that instant it dawned on me that for eight years I've been living here with a stranger, and that I'd even conceived three children — oh, I can't stand the thought of it! I could tear myself to bits.

HELMER (*heavily*): I see. There's a gulf that's opened between us — that's clear. Oh, but Nora, can't we bridge it somehow?

NORA: The way I am now, I'm no wife for you.

HELMER: I have the strength to make myself over.

NORA: Maybe — if your doll gets taken away.

HELMER: But to part! To part from you! No, Nora, no — I can't imagine it.

NORA (*going out, right*): All the more reason why it has to be. (*She reenters with her coat and a small overnight bag, which she puts on a chair by the table.*)

HELMER: Nora, Nora, not now! Wait till tomorrow.

NORA: I can't spend the night in a strange man's room.

HELMER: But couldn't we live here like brother and sister —

NORA: You know very well how long that would last. (*Throws her shawl about her.*) Good-bye, Torvald. I won't look in on the children. I know they're in better hands than mine. The way I am now, I'm no use to them.

HELMER: But someday, Nora — someday — ?

NORA: How can I tell? I haven't the least idea what'll become of me.

HELMER: But you're my wife, now and wherever you go.

NORA: Listen, Torvald — I've heard that when a wife deserts her husband's house just as I'm doing, then the law frees him from all responsibility. In any case, I'm freeing you from being responsible. Don't feel yourself bound, any more than I will. There has to be absolute freedom for us both. Here, take your ring back. Give me mine.

HELMER: That too?

NORA: That too.

HELMER: There it is.

NORA: Good. Well, now it's all over. I'm putting the keys here. The maids know all about keeping up the house — better than I do. Tomorrow, after I've left town, Kristine will stop by to pack up everything that's mine from home. I'd like those things shipped up to me.

HELMER: Over! All over! Nora, won't you ever think about me?

NORA: I'm sure I'll think of you often, and about the children and the house here.

HELMER: May I write you?

NORA: No — never. You're not to do that.

HELMER: Oh, but let me send you —

NORA: Nothing. Nothing.

HELMER: Or help you if you need it.

NORA: No. I accept nothing from strangers.

HELMER: Nora — can I never be more than a stranger to you?

NORA (*picking up the overnight bag*): Ah, Torvald — it would take the greatest miracle of all —

HELMER: Tell me the greatest miracle!

NORA: You and I both would have to transform ourselves to the point that — Oh, Torvald, I've stopped believing in miracles.

HELMER: But I'll believe. Tell me! Transform ourselves to the point that — ?

NORA: That our living together could be a true marriage. (*She goes out down the hall.*)

HELMER (*sinks down on a chair by the door, face buried in his hands*): Nora! Nora! (*Looking about and rising.*) Empty. She's gone. (*A sudden hope leaps in him.*) The greatest miracle — ?

(*From below, the sound of a door slamming shut.*)

COMMENTARIES

Ibsen wrote about his own work, both in his letters to producers and actors and in his notes describing the development of his plays. Such notes reveal his concern, his insights as he wrote the plays, and his motives. Sometimes what he says about the plays does not completely square with modern interpretations. On the other hand, he explains in his notes that the circumstances of women in modern society were much on his mind when he was working on *A Doll House.*

Ibsen's "Notes for the Modern Tragedy" is remarkable for suggesting a separate sensibility (spiritual law) for men and for women. His observations about the society in which women live — and in which Nora is confounded — sound as if they could have been written a century later than they were. When

Bernard Shaw wrote his comments on *A Doll House,* the play was a popular shocker; Shaw's observations were designed to help audiences interpret the play's actions more carefully. He is one of the earliest critics of the play, and one must remember while reading Shaw that some productions of the play changed the ending to make it happy. Muriel C. Bradbrook's discussion of *A Doll House* focuses on the moral bankruptcy of Nora's situation, which is to say the situation of all wives of the period.

Henrik Ibsen (1828–1906)
NOTES FOR THE MODERN TRAGEDY   *1878*

TRANSLATED BY A. G. CHATER

Ibsen's first notes for A Doll House *were jotted down on October 19, 1878. They show that his thinking on the relations between men and women was considerably sophisticated and that the material for the play had been gestating. His comments indicate that the essentially male society he knew was one of his central concerns in the play.*

There are two kinds of spiritual law, two kinds of conscience, one in man and another, altogether different, in woman. They do not understand each other; but in practical life the woman is judged by man's law, as though she were not a woman but a man.

The wife in the play ends by having no idea of what is right or wrong; natural feeling on the one hand and belief in authority on the other have altogether bewildered her.

A woman cannot be herself in the society of the present day, which is an exclusively masculine society, with laws framed by men and with a judicial system that judges feminine conduct from a masculine point of view.

She has committed forgery, and she is proud of it; for she did it out of love for her husband, to save his life. But this husband with his commonplace principles of honor is on the side of the law and looks at the question from the masculine point of view.

Spiritual conflicts. Oppressed and bewildered by the belief in authority, she loses faith in her moral right and ability to bring up her children. Bitterness. A mother in modern society, like certain insects who go away and die when she has done her duty in the propagation of the race. Love of life, of home, of husband and children and family. Now and then a womanly shaking off of her thoughts. Sudden return of anxiety and terror. She must bear it all alone. The catastrophe approaches, inexorably, inevitably. Despair, conflict, and destruction.

(Krogstad has acted dishonorably and thereby become well-to-do; now his prosperity does not help him, he cannot recover his honor.)

Bernard Shaw (1856–1950)
A DOLL'S HOUSE   *1891*

One of the first English men of letters to pay close attention to Ibsen's work was
Bernard Shaw. While beginning to write his own plays, Shaw also spent time in the
theater as a critic. His landmark book The Quintessence of Ibsenism *(1891; rev. ed.*
1913), in which this comment on A Doll House appears, is a thorough discussion
not only of the individual plays that Ibsen had produced but also of their implica-
tion for future literature. Shaw saw the significance of the new realism and its
implications for the audiences of the late nineteenth century. He saw, too, that
Ibsen's brand of realism would have an effect on the beliefs of his audiences, that
Ibsen's drama was a drama of important ideas. In the following excerpt Shaw is
especially sensitive to the feminist issues that are at the heart of the play, and he
pays close attention to Nora's character development.

Unfortunately, *Pillars of Society*, as a propagandist play, is disabled by the circumstance that the hero, being a fraudulent hypocrite in the ordinary police-court
sense of the phrase, would hardly be accepted as a typical pillar of society by the
class he represents. Accordingly, Ibsen took care next time to make his idealist irre-
proachable from the standpoint of the ordinary idealist morality. In the famous
Doll's House, the pillar of society who owns the doll is a model husband, father,
and citizen. In his little household, with the three darling children and the affectionate little wife, all on the most loving terms with one another, we have the sweet
home, the womanly woman, the happy family life of the idealist's dream. Mrs.
Nora Helmer is happy in the belief that she has attained a valid realization of all
these illusions; that she is an ideal wife and mother; and that Helmer is an ideal
husband who would, if the necessity arose, give his life to save her reputation. A
few simply contrived incidents disabuse her effectually on all these points. One of
her earliest acts of devotion to her husband has been the secret raising of a sum of
money to enable him to make a tour which was necessary to restore his health. As
he would have broken down sooner than go into debt, she has had to persuade him
that the money was a gift from her father. It was really obtained from a moneylender, who refused to make her the loan unless she induced her father to endorse
the promissory note. This being impossible, as her father was dying at the time, she
took the shortest way out of the difficulty by writing the name herself, to the entire
satisfaction of the moneylender, who, though not at all duped, knew that forged
bills are often the surest to be paid. Since then she has slaved in secret at scrivener's
work until she has nearly paid off the debt.

At this point Helmer is made manager of the bank in which he is employed; and
the moneylender, wishing to obtain a post there, uses the forged bill to force Nora
to exert her influence with Helmer on his behalf. But she, having a hearty contempt
for the man, cannot be persuaded by him that there was any harm in putting her
father's name on the bill, and ridicules the suggestion that the law would not recognize that she was right under the circumstances. It is her husband's own contemptuous denunciation of a forgery formerly committed by the moneylender himself
that destroys her self-satisfaction and opens her eyes to her ignorance of the serious
business of the world to which her husband belongs: the world outside the home he

shares with her. When he goes on to tell her that commercial dishonesty is generally to be traced to the influence of bad mothers, she begins to perceive that the happy way in which she plays with the children, and the care she takes to dress them nicely, are not sufficient to constitute her a fit person to train them. To redeem the forged bill, she resolves to borrow the balance due upon it from an intimate friend of the family. She has learnt to coax her husband into giving her what she asks by appealing to his affection for her: that is, by playing all sorts of pretty tricks until he is wheedled into an amorous humor. This plan she has adopted without thinking about it, instinctively taking the line of least resistance with him. And now she naturally takes the same line with her husband's friend. An unexpected declaration of love from him is the result; and it at once explains to her the real nature of the domestic influence she has been so proud of.

All her illusions about herself are now shattered. She sees herself as an ignorant and silly woman, a dangerous mother, and a wife kept for her husband's pleasure merely; but she clings all the harder to her illusion about him: he is still the ideal husband who would make any sacrifice to rescue her from ruin. She resolves to kill herself rather than allow him to destroy his own career by taking the forgery on himself to save her reputation. The final disillusion comes when he, instead of at once proposing to pursue this ideal line of conduct when he hears of the forgery, naturally enough flies into a vulgar rage and heaps invective on her for disgracing him. Then she sees that their whole family life has been a fiction: their home a mere doll's house in which they have been playing at ideal husband and father, wife and mother. So she leaves him then and there and goes out into the real world to find out its reality for herself, and to gain some position not fundamentally false, refusing to see her children again until she is fit to be in charge of them, or to live with him until she and he become capable of a more honorable relation to one another. He at first cannot understand what has happened, and flourishes the shattered ideals over her as if they were as potent as ever. He presents the course most agreeable to him — that of her staying at home and avoiding a scandal — as her duty to her husband, to her children, and to her religion; but the magic of these disguises is gone; and at last even he understands what has really happened, and sits down alone to wonder whether that more honorable relation can ever come to pass between them.

Muriel C. Bradbrook (1909–1993)
A DOLL'S HOUSE: IBSEN THE MORALIST   *1948*

In her important study of Ibsen, Ibsen: The Norwegian, *Muriel C. Bradbrook discusses all the important plays, but she reserves a special place for* A Doll House. *In her analysis she suggests that Nora slowly discovers the fundamental bankruptcy of her marriage. Bradbrook calls it "eight years' prostitution." She also shows the true extent of Torvald's possessiveness and immaturity. As Bradbrook says, the true moment of recognition — in the Greek tragic sense — occurs when Nora sees both herself and Torvald in their true nature. Bradbrook also helps us see the full implication of Nora's leaving her home. She can never hope again for the comforts she has enjoyed as Torvald's wife.*

Poor Nora, living by playing her tricks like a little pet animal, sensing how to manage Torvald by those pettinesses in his character she does not know she knows of, is too vulnerably sympathetic to find her life-work in reading John Stuart Mill. At the end she still does not understand the strange world in which she has done wrong by forging a signature. She does understand that she has lived by what Virginia Woolf called "the slow waterlogged sinking of her will into his." And this picture is built up for her and for us by the power of structural implication, a form of writing particularly suited to drama, where the latent possibilities of a long stretch of past time can be thrown into relief by a crisis. In *A Doll's House,* the past is not only lighted up by the present, as a transparency might be lit up with a lamp; the past is changed by the present so that it becomes a different thing. Nora's marriage becomes eight years' prostitution, as she gradually learns the true nature of her relations with Torvald and the true nature of Torvald's feelings for her.

In Act I, no less than six different episodes bring out the war that is secretly waged between his masculine dictatorship and her feminine wiles:

Her wheedling him for money with a simple transference: "Let us do as *you* suggest. . . ."

Her promise to Christine: "Just leave it to me: I will broach the matter very cleverly." She is evidently habituated to and aware of her own technique.

Her description of how she tried to coax Torvald into taking the holiday and how she was saving up the story of the bond "for when I am no longer as good-looking as I am now." She knows the precarious nature of her hold.

Her method of asking work for Christine by putting Christine also into a (completely bogus) position of worshiping subservience to Torvald.

Her boast to Krogstad about her influence. Whilst this may be a justifiable triumph over her tormentor, it is an unconscious betrayal of Torvald (witness his fury in Act II at the idea of being thought uxorious).

After this faceted exposition, the treatment grows much broader. Nora admits Torvald's jealousy: Yet she flirts with Rank, aware but not acknowledging the grounds of her control. The pressure of implication remains constant throughout: It is comparable with the effect of a dialect, coloring all that is said. To take a few lines at random from the dialogue of Nora and Rank in Act II:

> NORA (*putting her hand on his shoulder*): Dear, dear Dr. Rank! Death mustn't take you away from Torvald and me. [Nora is getting demonstrative as she senses Rank's responsiveness, and her hopes of obtaining a loan from him rise. Hence her warmth of feeling, purely seductive.]
>
> RANK: It is a loss you will easily recover from. Those who are gone away are soon forgotten. [Poor Rank is reminded by that "Torvald and me" how little he really counts to Nora.]
>
> NORA (*anxiously*): Do you believe that? [Rank has awakened her thoughts of what may happen if *she* has to go away.]

Her methods grow more desperate — the open appeal to Torvald to keep Krogstad and the frantic expedient of the tarantella. In the last act her fate is upon her; yet in spite of all her terror and Torvald's tipsy amorousness, she still believes in his chivalry and devotion. This extraordinary self-deception is perhaps the subtlest and most telling implication of all. Practice had left her theory unshaken: So when the crash comes, she cries, "I have been living with a strange man," yet it was but the kind of man her actions had always implied him to be. Her vanity had completely prevented her from recognizing what she was doing, even though she had become such an expert at doing it.

Torvald is more gradually revealed. In the first act he appears indulgent, perhaps a trifle inclined to nag about the macaroons and to preach, but virtually a more efficient David Copperfield curbing a rather better-trained Dora. In the second act, his resentment and his pleasure alike uncover the deeper bases of his dominance. His anger at the prospect of being thought under his wife's influence and his fury at the imputation of narrow-mindedness show that it is really based on his own cowardice, the need for something weaker to bully: This is confirmed when he gloats over Nora's panic as evidence of her love for him, and over her agitation in the tarantella ("you little helpless thing!"). His love of order and his fastidiousness, when joined to such qualities, betray a set personality; and the last act shows that he has neither control nor sympathy on the physical level. But he is no fool, and his integrity is not all cowardice. Doubtless, debt or forgery really was abhorrent to him.

The climax of the play comes when Nora sees Torvald and sees herself: It is an *anagnorisis,* a recognition. Her life is cored like an apple. For she has had no life apart from this. Behind the irrelevant program for self-education there stands a woman, pitifully inexperienced, numbed by emotional shock, but with a newfound will to face what has happened, to accept her bankruptcy, as, in a very different way, Peer Gynt had at last accepted his.

"Yes, I am beginning to understand. . . ." she says. "What you did," observes the now magnanimous Torvald, "you did out of love for me." "That is true," says Nora: And she calls him to a "settling of accounts," not in any spirit of hostility but in an attempt to organize vacancy. "I have made nothing of my life. . . . I must stand quite alone . . . it is necessary to me . . ." That is really the program. *Ainsi tout leur a craqué dans les mains.*°

The spare and laminated speech gains its effect by inference and riddle. But these are the characteristic virtues of Norse. Irony is its natural weapon. Ibsen was working with the grain of the language. It was no accident that it fell to a Norwegian to take that most finely tooled art, the drama, and bring it to a point and precision so nice that literally not a phrase is without its direct contribution to the structure. The unrelenting cohesion of *A Doll's House* is perhaps, like that of the *Oedipus the King,* too hard on the playgoer; he is allowed no relief. Nora cannot coo to her baby without saying: "My sweet little *baby doll!*" or play with her children without choosing, significantly, *Hide and Seek.* Ibsen will not allow the smallest action to escape from the psychopathology of everyday life. However, a play cannot be acted so that every moment is tense with significance, and, in practice, an actor, for the sake of light and shade, will probably slur some of Ibsen's points, deliberately or unconsciously. The tension between the characters is such that the slightest movement of one sets all the others quivering. But this is partly because they are seen with such detachment, like a clear-cut intaglio. The play is, above all, articulated.

That is not to say that it is the mere dissection of a problem. Perhaps Rank and Mrs. Linde would have been more subtly wrought into the action at a later date; but the tight control kept over Nora and Torvald does not mean that they can be

Ainsi . . . mains: Thus everything has shattered in their hands.

exhausted by analysis or staled by custom. They are so far in advance of the characters of *Pillars of Society* that they are capable of the surprising yet inevitable development that marks the character conceived "in the round," the character that is, in Ibsen's phrase, fully "seen."

Consider, for example, Torvald's soliloquy whilst Nora is taking off her masquerade dress. It recalls at one moment Dickens's most unctuous hypocrites — "Here I will protect you like a hunted dove that I have saved from the claws of the hawk!"— at another Meredith's Willoughby Patterne° —"Only be frank and open with me and I will be both will and conscience to you"— yet from broadest caricature to sharpest analysis, it remains the self-glorified strut of the one character, the bank clerk in his pride, cousin to Peer Gynt, that typical Norwegian, and to Hjalmer Ekdal, the toiling breadwinner of the studio.

Whilst the Ibsenites might have conceded that Torvald is Art, they would probably have contended that Nora is Truth. Nora, however, is much more than a Revolting Wife. She is not a sour misanthropist or a fighting suffragette, but a lovely young woman who knows that she still holds her husband firmly infatuated after eight years of marriage. . . .

In leaving her husband Nora is seeking a fuller life as a human being. She is emancipating herself. Yet the seeking itself is also a renunciation, a kind of death — "I must stand alone." No less than Falk, or the hero of *On the Vidda*, she gives up something that has been her whole life. She is as broken as Torvald in the end: But she is a strong character and he is a weak one. In the "happy ending" which Ibsen reluctantly allowed to be used, it was the sight of the children that persuaded her to stay, and unless it is remembered that leaving Torvald means leaving the children, the full measure of Nora's decision cannot be taken. An actress gets her chance to make this point in the reply to Torvald's plea that Nora should stay for the children's sake.

It should be remembered, too, that the seriousness of the step she takes is lost on the present generation. She was putting herself outside society, inviting insult, destitution, and loneliness. She went out into a very dark night.

Willoughby Patterne: The protagonist in George Meredith's novel *The Egoist* (1879), an arrogant aristocrat who lacks awareness of the needs and desires of the women in his life.

August Strindberg

The Swedish playwright August Strindberg (1849–1912) wrote fifty-eight plays, more than a dozen novels, and more than a hundred short stories, all collected now in fifty-five volumes. Much of the time he was producing this astonishing body of work, he was the victim of persistent paranoia, suffered the destruction of three marriages, and lived through a major nervous breakdown.

He was a man of enormous complexity whose work has traditionally been broken into two parts. The first comprises the work he wrote up to 1894, which includes *The Father* (1877), *Miss Julie* (1888), *The Creditors* (1889), and other naturalistic plays; the second comprises work he wrote after 1897, including *To Damascus* (1898–1901), *There Are Crimes and Crimes* (1899), *Easter* and *The Dance of Death* (both 1901), *A Dream Play* (1902), and *Ghost Sonata* (1907). These are largely expressionist plays. EXPRESSIONISM disregarded the strict demands of naturalism to present a "slice of life" without artistic shaping of plot and resolution. Instead, expressionist drama used materials that resembled dreams — or nightmares — and focused on symbolic actions and a subjective interpretation of the world. Strindberg's later drama is often symbolic, taut, and psychological. His novel *Inferno* (1897) not only marks the transition between his early and late work; it gives this period of his life its name. Strindberg's *Inferno* period was a time of madness and paranoic behavior that virtually redirected his life for more than three years. During this time he was convinced that the secrets of life were wrapped in the occult, and his energies went into alchemical experiments and studies of cabalistic lore.

The first period of his dramatic career began with *Master Olof* (1872), a historical drama that he chose to write in prose, which he felt was a more natural medium than verse, the convention for such plays at the time. The play was turned down, and he rewrote it in verse in 1876. It was rejected for a second time by the Royal Dramatic Theater but was finally produced the following year. At that time, Strindberg recorded: "In 1877 Antoine opened his Théâtre Libre in Paris, and *Thérèse Raquin*, although nothing but an adapted novel, became the dominant model. It was the powerful theme and the concentrated form that showed innovation, although the unity of time was not yet observed, and curtain falls were retained. It was then I wrote my dramas: *Lady Julie, The Father,* and *Creditors.*" *Thérèse Raquin*, Émile Zola's naturalistic play, inspired Strindberg to move further toward his own interpretation of naturalism, which is perhaps most evident in *Miss Julie*. Strindberg was more subjective in his approach to naturalism, less scientific and deterministic, than Zola. Whereas Zola's approach might be described as "photographic" realism, Strindberg's was more selective and impressionistic but no less honest and true. He saw his characters operating out of "a whole series of deeply buried motives." They were not necessarily the product of their biology or their social circumstances, as the naturalists of Zola's stripe sometimes implied. Yet Strindberg saw clearly that class distinctions helped determine the behavior of many people. He seemed to accept the view that people were not created by their class but rather belonged to their class because of the kind of people they were. Strindberg probed deeply into the psychology of his characters, whose emotional lives, rather than outward social qualities, determined their actions.

Strindberg is often described as a woman-hater, a misogynist. For periods of his life he seems to have been misogynistic, but he was nonetheless extremely contradictory in both behavior and belief. There is no simple way to talk about Strindberg's attitude toward women. On the one hand, he is conventional in his thinking that women belong in the home. On the other hand, he married a highly successful actress, Siri von Essen. As he said in a letter in 1895, "Woman is to me the earth and all its glory, the bond that binds, and of all the evil the worst evil I have seen is the female sex." A decade later in *A Blue Book,* he wrote, "When I approach a woman as a lover, I look up to her, I see something of the mother in her, and this I respect. I assume a subordinate position, become childish and puerile and actually am subordinate, like most men. . . . I put her on a pedestal." As in many things, including his attitude toward dramatic techniques and style, Strindberg is a mass of contradictions and complexities of the sort sometimes associated with genius.

MISS JULIE

Miss Julie, the daughter of a count, and Jean, the count's valet, come from strikingly different social backgrounds. In ordinary circumstances, they might not have been on friendly terms, much less have become lovers, as they do. But the count is away, and Miss Julie and Jean are drawn into a sexual liaison marked by a struggle for dominance and control. Miss Julie's fiancé has been disposed of before the play begins because he refused to debase himself slavishly to her will. She is a free spirit, but her breeding is suspect because her mother, like her, took a lover and defied the count. Miss Julie's mother rebelled against her husband and punished him by burning their house down after the insurance expired. As further punishment and abasement, she humiliated the count by arranging to have her lover loan him the money to rebuild the house. Thus, Miss Julie's heritage is one of independence, rebellion, and unorthodoxy.

Under her mother's tutelage, Miss Julie was raised to manipulate men, but she cannot accept them totally. She also seems to feel a mixture of contempt for herself as a woman along with her contempt for men. In his preface to the play, Strindberg says that Julie is a modern "man-hating half-woman" who sells herself for honors of various kinds. (See the commentary on p. 759.)

The play has a mysterious quality. It takes place on Midsummer Eve, when lovers reveal themselves to one another and when almost anything can happen. In primitive fertility rites it was a time associated with sexual awakening. The cook, Kristine, mentions that it is the feast of St. John and alludes to his beheading for spurning Salome's advances. Jean (French for John) in one tense moment of the play beheads Julie's pet bird as a sign of the violence pent up in him. This incident foreshadows Miss Julie's death.

The fairy-tale quality that creeps into the play — as in *A Midsummer Night's Dream,* set on the same day — may seem out of place in a realistic drama, but it is profoundly compelling. It is also typical of Strindberg, who often uses symbolism to suggest a dream quality and deepen the significance of the action. (Dreams are a part of reality that modern playwrights have taken great pains to explore.)

The count himself, Julie's father, never appears in the play, but his presence is always ominous and intense, again much as in a fairy tale. Jean tells Miss Julie that he would willingly kill himself if the count were to order it. Kristine, like a witch, demands retribution because she was spurned by Jean, who was once her lover. Near the end of the play she prevents Julie and Jean from running away from the count by impounding the horses in the stable, thus wreaking her revenge on both of them.

Although Julie may be seen as the princess, Jean has very little claim to being Prince Charming of the play, especially since he has little strength of character. He feels superior to his station as a valet, and Strindberg in his preface refers to him as a nobleman. However, like Kristine, he is coarse beneath his outwardly polished appearance. His highest ambition is to be the proprietor of a first-class hotel, a prospect he wants to share with Julie.

One of the most striking passages in the play is the story Jean tells Julie almost reluctantly. He tries to explain to her what it feels like to be "down below," where she has never been. When he was a boy, he thought of the apple trees in her father's garden as part of the "Garden of Eden, guarded by angry angels." He entered this enchanted place with his mother to weed onions and wandered into the outhouse — a building like a Turkish pavilion whose function he could not guess. While he was exploring it, he heard someone coming and had to exit beneath the outhouse and hide himself under a pile of weeds and "wet dirt that stank." From his hiding place he saw Julie in a pink dress and white stockings. He rushed to the millpond and jumped in to wash the filth off himself. Ironically, only a few moments after he tells her this story, he calls her a whore, and she, in response, says, "Oh, God in heaven, end my wretched life! Take me away from the filth I'm sinking into! Save me! Save me!"

Miss Julie falls under the power of her lover and cannot redirect her life; she sinks deeper and deeper into "filth." She has few choices at the end of the play, and the conclusion to *Miss Julie* is swift. The contrast between the willfulness of Julie and the caution of Jean makes their situation especially desperate. When Julie leaves at the end of the play to seal her fate, we sense the terrible weight of their society's values. Those values are symbolized by the return of the count and the expectations he had of Julie's behavior while he was gone.

Miss Julie in Performance

The first planned professional production of *Miss Julie* was canceled at the last minute by censors in Copenhagen on March 1, 1889. Although the play was performed privately on March 14, 1889, in Copenhagen University's Students' Union, it was not performed professionally in Stockholm until 1906. Some important early productions of the play were in Paris in Antoine's distinguished

Théâtre Libre in 1893 and in Berlin in Max Reinhardt's Kleine Theater in 1904. Reinhardt produced seventeen of Strindberg's plays and was one of his great champions. In 1907 Strindberg produced the play in his own Intimate Theatre in Stockholm, where it ran intermittently for 134 showings. He even arranged a special performance for Bernard Shaw. The first London production was in 1912, but since the 1930s it has been revived many times, with many distinguished actors in all three major roles.

Among the notable modern productions is the Old Vic's 1966 version directed by Michael Elliott, with Maggie Smith and Albert Finney starring. The Baxter Theatre of Johannesburg, South Africa, produced the play in 1985 with the black actor John Kani as Jean and the white Afrikaner actress Sandra Prinsloo as Julie. Some white audiences considered that casting outrageous. The sensational Ingmar Bergman production at the Brooklyn Academy of Music in 1991 stretched the play to two hours and made it more of a domestic tragedy — as John Simon said, "more like us, more believable, and, therefore, more terrifying."

Filmed at least five times, *Miss Julie* has been televised as well. It is one of the most produced modern plays.

August Strindberg (1849–1912)

MISS JULIE

1888

TRANSLATED BY HARRY G. CARLSON

Characters

MISS JULIE, *25 years old*
JEAN, *her father's valet, 30 years old*
KRISTINE, *her father's cook, 35 years old*

(*The action takes place in the Count's kitchen on midsummer eve.*)

Setting: (*A large kitchen, the ceiling and side walls of which are hidden by draperies. The rear wall runs diagonally from down left to up right. On the wall down left are two shelves with copper, iron, and pewter utensils; the shelves are lined with scalloped paper. Visible to the right is most of a set of large, arched glass doors, through which can be seen a fountain with a statue of Cupid, lilac bushes in bloom, and the tops of some Lombardy poplars. At down left is the corner of a large tiled stove; a portion of its hood is showing. At right, one end of the servants' white pine dining table juts out; several chairs stand around it. The stove is decorated with birch branches; juniper twigs are strewn on the floor. On the end of the table stands a large Japanese spice jar, filled with lilac blossoms. An ice box, a sink, and a washstand. Above the door is an old-fashioned bell on a spring; to the left of the door, the mouthpiece of a speaking tube is visible.*)

(*Kristine is frying something on the stove. She is wearing a light-colored cotton dress and an apron. Jean enters. He is wearing livery and carries a pair of high riding boots with spurs, which he puts down on the floor where they can be seen by the audience.*)

JEAN: Miss Julie's crazy again tonight; absolutely crazy!

KRISTINE: So you finally came back?

JEAN: I took the Count to the station and when I returned past the barn I stopped in for a dance. Who do I see but Miss Julie leading off the dance with the gamekeeper! But as soon as she saw me she rushed over to ask me for the next waltz. And she's been waltzing ever since — I've never seen anything like it. She's crazy!

KRISTINE: She always has been, but never as bad as the last two weeks since her engagement was broken off.

JEAN: Yes, I wonder what the real story was there. He was a gentleman, even if he wasn't rich. Ah! These people have such romantic ideas. (*Sits at the end of the table.*) Still, it's strange, isn't it? I mean that she'd rather stay home with the servants on midsummer eve instead of going with her father to visit relatives?

KRISTINE: She's probably embarrassed after that row with her fiancé.

JEAN: Probably! He gave a good account of himself, though. Do you know how it happened, Kristine? I saw it, you know, though I didn't let on I had.

KRISTINE: No! You saw it?

JEAN: Yes, I did. ——— That evening they were out near the stable, and she was "training" him — as she called it. Do you know what she did? She made him jump over her riding crop, the way you'd teach a dog to jump. He jumped twice and she hit him each time. But the third time he grabbed the crop out of her hand, hit her with it across the cheek, and broke it in pieces. Then he left.

KRISTINE: So, that's what happened! I can't believe it!

JEAN: Yes, that's the way it went! ——— What have you got for me that's tasty, Kristine?

KRISTINE (*serving him from the pan*): Oh, it's only a piece of kidney I cut from the veal roast.

JEAN (*smelling the food*): Beautiful! That's my favorite *délice.*° (*Feeling the plate.*) But you could have warmed the plate!

KRISTINE: You're fussier than the Count himself, once you start! (*She pulls his hair affectionately.*)

JEAN (*angry*): Stop it, leave my hair alone! You know I'm touchy about that.

KRISTINE: Now, now, it's only love, you know that. (*Jean eats. Kristine opens a bottle of beer.*)

JEAN: Beer? On midsummer eve? No thank you! I can do better than that. (*Opens a drawer in the table and takes out a bottle of red wine with yellow sealing wax.*) See that? Yellow seal! Give me a glass! A wine glass! I'm drinking this *pur.*°

KRISTINE (*returns to the stove and puts on a small saucepan*): God help the woman who gets you for a husband! What a fussbudget.

JEAN: Nonsense! You'd be damned lucky to get a man like me. It certainly hasn't done you any harm to have people call me your sweetheart. (*Tastes the wine.*) Good! Very good! Just needs a little warming. (*Warms the glass between his hands.*) We bought this in Dijon. Four francs a liter, not counting the cost of the bottle, or the customs duty. ——— What are you cooking now? It stinks like hell!

KRISTINE: Oh, some slop Miss Julie wants to give Diana.

JEAN: Watch your language, Kristine. But why should you have to cook for that damn mutt on midsummer eve? Is she sick?

KRISTINE: Yes, she's sick! She sneaked out with the gatekeeper's dog — and now there's hell to pay. Miss Julie won't have it!

JEAN: Miss Julie has too much pride about some things and not enough about others, just like her mother was. The Countess was most at home in the kitchen and the cowsheds, but a *one*-horse carriage wasn't elegant enough for her. The cuffs of her blouse were

dirty, but she had to have her coat of arms on her cufflinks. ——— And Miss Julie won't take proper care of herself either. If you ask me, she just isn't refined. Just now, when she was dancing in the barn, she pulled the gamekeeper away from Anna and made him dance with her. *We* wouldn't behave like that, but that's what happens when aristocrats pretend they're common people — they get *common!* ——— But she is quite a woman! Magnificent! What shoulders, and what — et cetera!

KRISTINE: Oh, don't overdo it! I've heard what Clara says, and she dresses her.

JEAN: Ha, Clara! You're all jealous of each other! I've been out riding with her. . . . And the way she dances!

KRISTINE: Listen, Jean! You're going to dance with me, when I'm finished here, aren't you?

JEAN: Of course I will.

KRISTINE: Promise?

JEAN: Promise? When I say I'll do something, I do it! By the way, the kidney was very good. (*Corks the bottle.*)

JULIE (*in the doorway to someone outside*): I'll be right back! You go ahead for now! (*Jean sneaks the bottle back into the table drawer and gets up respectfully. Miss Julie enters and crosses to Kristine by the stove.*) Well? Is it ready? (*Kristine indicates that Jean is present.*)

JEAN (*gallantly*): Are you ladies up to something secret?

JULIE (*flicking her handkerchief in his face*): None of your business!

JEAN: Hmm! I like the smell of violets!

JULIE (*coquettishly*): Shame on you! So you know about perfumes, too? You certainly know how to dance. Ah, ah! No peeking! Go away.

JEAN (*boldly but respectfully*): Are you brewing up a magic potion for midsummer eve? Something to prophesy by under a lucky star, so you'll catch a glimpse of your future husband!

JULIE (*caustically*): You'd need sharp eyes to see him! (*To Kristine.*) Pour out half a bottle and cork it well. ——— Come and dance a schottische° with me, Jean . . .

JEAN (*hesitating*): I don't want to be impolite to anyone, and I've already promised this dance to Kristine . . .

JULIE: Oh, she can have another one — can't you, Kristine? Won't you lend me Jean?

KRISTINE: It's not up to me, ma'am. (*To Jean.*) If the mistress is so generous, it wouldn't do for you to say no. Go on, Jean, and thank her for the honor.

JEAN: To be honest, and no offense intended, I wonder whether it's wise for you to dance twice running with the same partner, especially since these people are quick to jump to conclusions . . .

JULIE (*flaring up*): What's that? What sort of conclusions? What do you mean?

JEAN (*submissively*): If you don't understand, ma'am, I must speak more plainly. It doesn't look good to play favorites with your servants. . . .

---

délice: Delight.   *pur*: Pure; the first drink from the bottle.

schottische: A Scottish round dance resembling a polka.

JULIE: Play favorites! What an idea! I'm astonished! As mistress of the house, I honor your dance with my presence. And when I dance, I want to dance with someone who can lead, so I won't look ridiculous.

JEAN: As you order, ma'am! I'm at your service!

JULIE (*gently*): Don't take it as an order! On a night like this we're all just ordinary people having fun, so we'll forget about rank. Now, take my arm! ——— Don't worry, Kristine! I won't steal your sweetheart! (*Jean offers his arm and leads Miss Julie out.*)

Mime

(*The following should be played as if the actress playing Kristine were really alone. When she has to, she turns her back to the audience. She does not look toward them, nor does she hurry as if she were afraid they would grow impatient. Schottische music played on a fiddle sounds in the distance. Kristine hums along with the music. She clears the table, washes the dishes, dries them, and puts them away. She takes off her apron. From a table drawer she removes a small mirror and leans it against the bowl of lilacs on the table. She lights a candle, heats a hairpin over the flame, and uses it to set a curl on her forehead. She crosses to the door and listens, then returns to the table. She finds the handkerchief Miss Julie left behind, picks it up, and smells it. Then, preoccupied, she spreads it out, stretches it, smoothes out the wrinkles, and folds it into quarters, and so forth.*)

JEAN (*enters alone*): God, she really *is* crazy! What a way to dance! Everybody's laughing at her behind her back. What do you make of it, Kristine?

KRISTINE: Ah! It's that time of the month for her, and she always gets peculiar like that. Are you going to dance with me now?

JEAN: You're not mad at me, are you, for leaving . . . ?

KRISTINE: Of course not! ——— Why should I be, for a little thing like that? Besides, I know my place . . .

JEAN (*puts his arm around her waist*): You're a sensible girl, Kristine, and you'd make a good wife . . .

JULIE (*entering; uncomfortably surprised; with forced good humor*): What a charming escort — running away from his partner.

JEAN: On the contrary, Miss Julie. Don't you see how I rushed back to the partner I abandoned!

JULIE (*changing her tone*): You know, you're a superb dancer! ——— But why are you wearing livery on a holiday? Take it off at once!

JEAN: Then I must ask you to go outside for a moment. You see, my black coat is hanging over here . . . (*Gestures and crosses right.*)

JULIE: Are you embarrassed about changing your coat in front of me? Well, go in your room then. Either that or stay and I'll turn my back.

JEAN: With your permission, ma'am! (*He crosses right. His arm is visible as he changes his jacket.*)

JULIE (*to Kristine*): Tell me, Kristine — you two are so close — . Is Jean your fiancé?

KRISTINE: Fiancé? Yes, if you wish. We can call him that.

JULIE: What do you mean?

KRISTINE: You had a fiancé yourself, didn't you? So . . .

JULIE: Well, we were properly engaged . . .

KRISTINE: But nothing came of it, did it? (*Jean returns dressed in a frock coat and bowler hat.*)

JULIE: *Très gentil, monsieur Jean! Très gentil!*

JEAN: *Vous voulez plaisanter, madame!*

JULIE: *Et vous voulez parler français!*° Where did you learn that?

JEAN: In Switzerland, when I was wine steward in one of the biggest hotels in Lucerne!

JULIE: You look like a real gentleman in that coat! *Charmant!*° (*Sits at the table.*)

JEAN: Oh, you're flattering me!

JULIE (*offended*): Flattering you?

JEAN: My natural modesty forbids me to believe that you would really compliment someone like me, and so I took the liberty of assuming that you were exaggerating, which polite people call flattering.

JULIE: Where did you learn to talk like that? You must have been to the theater often.

JEAN: Of course. And I've done a lot of traveling.

JULIE: But you come from here, don't you?

JEAN: My father was a farmhand on the district attorney's estate nearby. I used to see you when you were little, but you never noticed me.

JULIE: No! Really?

JEAN: Sure. I remember one time especially . . . but I can't talk about that.

JULIE: Oh, come now! Why not? Just this once!

JEAN: No, I really couldn't, not now. Some other time, perhaps.

JULIE: Why some other time? What's so dangerous about now?

JEAN: It's not dangerous, but there are obstacles. ——— Her, for example. (*Indicating Kristine, who has fallen asleep in a chair by the stove.*)

JULIE: What a pleasant wife she'll make! She probably snores, too.

JEAN: No, she doesn't, but she talks in her sleep.

JULIE (*cynically*): How do *you* know?

JEAN (*audaciously*): I've heard her! (*Pause, during which they stare at each other.*)

JULIE: Why don't you sit down?

JEAN: I couldn't do that in your presence.

JULIE: But if I order you to?

JEAN: Then I'd obey.

JULIE: Sit down, then. ——— No, wait. Can you get me something to drink first?

JEAN: I don't know what we have in the ice box. I think there's only beer.

JULIE: Why do you say "only"? My tastes are so simple I

Très gentil . . . français!: Very pleasing, Mr. Jean! Very pleasing. You would trifle with me, madam! And you want to speak French!   *Charmant!*: Charming!

prefer beer to wine. (*Jean takes a bottle of beer from the ice box and opens it. He looks for a glass and a plate in the cupboard and serves her.*)

JEAN: Here you are, ma'am.

JULIE: Thank you. Won't you have something yourself?

JEAN: I'm not partial to beer, but if it's an order . . .

JULIE: An order? ——— Surely a gentleman can keep his lady company.

JEAN: You're right, of course. (*Opens a bottle and gets a glass.*)

JULIE: Now, drink to my health! (*He hesitates.*) What? A man of the world — and shy?

JEAN (*in mock romantic fashion, he kneels and raises his glass*): Skål to my mistress!

JULIE: Bravo! ——— Now kiss my shoe, to finish it properly. (*Jean hesitates, then boldly seizes her foot and kisses it lightly.*) Perfect! You should have been an actor.

JEAN (*rising*): That's enough now, Miss Julie! Someone might come in and see us.

JULIE: What of it?

JEAN: People talk, that's what! If you knew how their tongues were wagging just now at the dance, you'd . . .

JULIE: What were they saying? Tell me! ——— Sit down!

JEAN (*sits*): I don't want to hurt you, but they were saying things ——— suggestive things, that, that . . . well, you can figure it out for yourself! You're not a child. If a woman is seen drinking alone with a man — let alone a servant — at night — then . . .

JULIE: Then what? Besides, we're not alone. Kristine is here.

JEAN: Asleep!

JULIE: Then I'll wake her up. (*Rising.*) Kristine! Are you asleep? (*Kristine mumbles in her sleep.*)

JULIE: Kristine! ——— She certainly can sleep!

KRISTINE (*in her sleep*): The Count's boots are brushed — put the coffee on — right away, right away — uh, huh — oh!

JULIE (*grabbing Kristine's nose*): Will you wake up!

JEAN (*severely*): Leave her alone — let her sleep!

JULIE (*sharply*): What?

JEAN: Someone who's been standing over a stove all day has a right to be tired by now. Sleep should be respected . . .

JULIE (*changing her tone*): What a considerate thought — it does you credit — thank you! (*Offering her hand.*) Come outside and pick some lilacs for me! (*During the following, Kristine awakens and shambles sleepily off right to bed.*)

JEAN: Go with you?

JULIE: With me!

JEAN: We couldn't do that! Absolutely not!

JULIE: I don't understand. Surely you don't imagine . . .

JEAN: No, I don't, but the others might.

JULIE: What? That I've fallen in love with a servant?

JEAN: I'm not a conceited man, but such things happen — and for these people, nothing is sacred.

JULIE: I do believe you're an aristocrat!

JEAN: Yes, I am.

JULIE: And I'm stepping down . . .

JEAN: Don't step down, Miss Julie, take my advice. No one'll believe you stepped down voluntarily. People will always say you fell.

JULIE: I have a higher opinion of people than you. Come and see! ——— Come! (*She stares at him broodingly.*)

JEAN: You're very strange, do you know that?

JULIE: Perhaps! But so are you! ——— For that matter, everything is strange. Life, people, everything. Like floating scum, drifting on and on across the water, until it sinks down and down! That reminds me of a dream I have now and then. I've climbed up on top of a pillar. I sit there and see no way of getting down. I get dizzy when I look down, and I must get down, but I don't have the courage to jump. I can't hold on firmly, and I long to be able to fall, but I don't fall. And yet I'll have no peace until I get down, no rest unless I get down, down on the ground! And if I did get down to the ground, I'd want to be under the earth . . . Have you ever felt anything like that?

JEAN: No. I dream that I'm lying under a high tree in a dark forest. I want to get up, up on top, and look out over the bright landscape, where the sun is shining, and plunder the bird's nest up there, where the golden eggs lie. And I climb and climb, but the trunk's so thick and smooth, and it's so far to the first branch. But I know if I just reached that first branch, I'd go right to the top, like up a ladder. I haven't reached it yet, but I will, even if it's only in a dream!

JULIE: Here I am chattering with you about dreams. Come, let's go out! Just into the park! (*She offers him her arm, and they start to leave.*)

JEAN: We'll have to sleep on nine midsummer flowers, Miss Julie, to make our dreams come true! (*They turn at the door. Jean puts his hand to his eye.*)

JULIE: Did you get something in your eye?

JEAN: It's nothing — just a speck — it'll be gone in a minute.

JULIE: My sleeve must have brushed against you. Sit down and let me help you. (*She takes him by the arm and seats him. She tilts his head back and with the tip of a handkerchief tries to remove the speck.*) Sit still, absolutely still! (*She slaps his hand.*) Didn't you hear me? ——— Why, you're trembling; the big, strong man is trembling! (*Feels his biceps.*) What muscles you have!

JEAN (*warning*): Miss Julie!

JULIE: Yes, *monsieur* Jean.

JEAN: *Attention! Je ne suis qu'un homme!*°

JULIE Will you sit still! ——— There! Now it's gone! Kiss my hand and thank me.

JEAN (*rising*): Miss Julie, listen to me! ——— Kristine has gone to bed! ——— Will you listen to me!

JULIE: Kiss my hand first!

***Attention! Je ne suis qu'un homme!*:** Watch out! I am only a man!

JEAN: Listen to me!

JULIE: Kiss my hand first!

JEAN: All right, but you've only yourself to blame!

JULIE: For what?

JEAN: For what? Are you still a child at twenty-five? Don't you know that it's dangerous to play with fire?

JULIE: Not for me. I'm insured.

JEAN (*boldly*): No, you're not! But even if you were, there's combustible material close by.

JULIE: Meaning you?

JEAN: Yes! Not because it's me, but because I'm young ——

JULIE: And handsome — what incredible conceit! A Don Juan perhaps! Or a Joseph!° Yes, that's it, I do believe you're a Joseph!

JEAN: Do you?

JULIE: I'm almost afraid so. (*Jean boldly tries to put his arm around her waist and kiss her. She slaps his face.*) How dare you?

JEAN: Are you serious or joking?

JULIE: Serious.

JEAN: Then so was what just happened. You play games too seriously, and that's dangerous. Well, I'm tired of games. You'll excuse me if I get back to work. I haven't done the Count's boots yet and it's long past midnight.

JULIE: Put the boots down!

JEAN: No! It's the work I have to do. I never agreed to be your playmate, and never will. It's beneath me.

JULIE: You're proud.

JEAN: In certain ways, but not in others.

JULIE: Have you ever been in love?

JEAN: We don't use that word, but I've been fond of many girls, and once I was sick because I couldn't have the one I wanted. That's right, sick, like those princes in the Arabian Nights — who couldn't eat or drink because of love.

JULIE: Who was she? (*Jean is silent.*) Who was she?

JEAN: You can't force me to tell you that.

JULIE: But if I ask you as an equal, as a — friend! Who was she?

JEAN: You!

JULIE (*sits*): How amusing . . .

JEAN: Yes, if you like! It was ridiculous! —— You see, that was the story I didn't want to tell you earlier. Maybe I will now. Do you know how the world looks from down below? —— Of course you don't. Neither do hawks and falcons, whose backs we can't see because they're usually soaring up there above us. I grew up in a shack with seven brothers and sisters and a pig, in the middle of a wasteland, where there wasn't a single tree. But from our window I could see the tops of apple trees above the wall of your father's garden. That was the Garden of Eden, guarded by angry angels with flaming swords.

Don Juan . . . Joseph: Don Juan in Spanish legend is a seducer of women; in Genesis, Joseph resists the advances of Potiphar's wife.

All the same, the other boys and I managed to find our way to the Tree of Life. —— Now you think I'm contemptible, I suppose.

JULIE: Oh, all boys steal apples.

JEAN: You say that, but you think I'm contemptible anyway. Oh well! One day I went into the Garden of Eden with my mother, to weed the onion beds. Near the vegetable garden was a small Turkish pavilion in the shadow of jasmine bushes and over-grown with honeysuckle. I had no idea what it was used for, but I'd never seen such a beautiful building. People went in and came out again, and one day the door was left open. I sneaked close and saw walls covered with pictures of kings and emperors, and red curtains with fringes at the windows — now you know the place I mean. I —— (*Breaks off a sprig of lilac and holds it in front of Miss Julie's nose.*) —— I'd never been inside the manor house, never seen anything except the church — but this was more beautiful. From then on, no matter where my thoughts wandered, they returned — there. And gradually I got a longing to experience, just once, the full pleasure of — *enfin*,° I sneaked in, saw, and marveled! But then I heard someone coming! There was only one exit for ladies and gentlemen, but for me there was another, and I had no choice but to take it! (*Miss Julie, who has taken the lilac sprig, lets it fall on the table.*) Afterwards, I started running. I crashed through a raspberry bush, flew over a strawberry patch, and came up onto the rose terrace. There I caught sight of a pink dress and a pair of white stockings — it was you. I crawled under a pile of weeds, and I mean under — under thistles that pricked me and wet dirt that stank. And I looked at you as you walked among the roses, and I thought: If it's true that a thief can enter heaven and be with the angels, then why can't a farm-hand's son here on God's earth enter the manor house garden and play with the Count's daughter?

JULIE (*romantically*): Do you think all poor children would have thought the way you did?

JEAN (*at first hesitant, then with conviction*): If *all* poor — yes — of course. Of course!

JULIE: It must be terrible to be poor!

JEAN (*with exaggerated suffering*): Oh, Miss Julie! Oh! —— A dog can lie on the Countess's sofa, a horse can have his nose patted by a young lady's hand, but a servant —— (*Changing his tone.*) —— oh, I know — now and then you find one with enough stuff in him to get ahead in the world, but how often? —— Anyhow, do you know what I did then? —— I jumped in the millstream with my clothes on, was pulled out, and got a beating. But the following Sunday, when my father and all the others went to my grandmother's, I arranged to stay home. I scrubbed myself with soap and water, put on my best clothes, and went to church so that I could see you! I saw you and returned home, determined to

enfin: Finally.

die. But I wanted to die beautifully and pleasantly, without pain. And then I remembered that it was dangerous to sleep under an elder bush. We had a big one, and it was in full flower. I plundered its treasures and bedded down under them in the oat bin. Have you ever noticed how smooth oats are? — and soft to the touch, like human skin . . . ! Well, I shut the lid and closed my eyes. I fell asleep and woke up feeling very sick. But I didn't die, as you can see. What was I after? ——— I don't know. There was no hope of winning you, of course. ——— You were a symbol of the hopelessness of ever rising out of the class in which I was born.

JULIE: You're a charming storyteller. Did you ever go to school?

JEAN: A bit, but I've read lots of novels and been to the theater often. And then I've listened to people like you talk — that's where I learned most.

JULIE: Do you listen to what we say?

JEAN: Naturally! And I've heard plenty, too, driving the carriage or rowing the boat. Once I heard you and a friend . . .

JULIE: Oh? ——— What did you hear?

JEAN: I'd better not say. But I was surprised a little. I couldn't imagine where you learned such words. Maybe at bottom there isn't such a great difference between people as we think.

JULIE: Shame on you! We don't act like you when we're engaged.

JEAN (*staring at her*): Is that true? ——— You don't have to play innocent with me, Miss . . .

JULIE: The man I gave my love to was a swine.

JEAN: That's what you all say — afterwards.

JULIE: All?

JEAN: I think so. I know I've heard that phrase before, on similar occasions.

JULIE: What occasions?

JEAN: Like the one I'm talking about. The last time . . .

JULIE (*rising*): Quiet! I don't want to hear any more!

JEAN: That's interesting — that's what *she* said, too. Well, if you'll excuse me, I'm going to bed.

JULIE (*gently*): To bed? On midsummer eve?

JEAN: Yes! Dancing with the rabble out there doesn't amuse me much.

JULIE: Get the key to the boat and row me out on the lake. I want to see the sun come up.

JEAN: Is that wise?

JULIE: Are you worried about your reputation?

JEAN: Why not? Why should I risk looking ridiculous and getting fired without a reference, just when I'm trying to establish myself. Besides, I think I owe something to Kristine.

JULIE: So, now it's Kristine . . .

JEAN: Yes, but you, too. ——— Take my advice, go up and go to bed!

JULIE: Am I to obey you?

JEAN: Just this once — for your own good! Please! It's very late. Drowsiness makes people giddy and liable to lose their heads! Go to bed! Besides — unless I'm mistaken — I hear the others coming to look for me. And if they find us together, you'll be lost!

(*The Chorus approaches, singing.*)

The swineherd found his true love
a pretty girl so fair,
The swineherd found his true love
but let the girl beware.

For then he saw the princess
the princess on the golden hill,
but then saw the princess,
so much fairer still.

So the swineherd and the princess
they danced the whole night through,
and he forgot his first love,
to her he was untrue.

And when the long night ended,
and in the light of day, of day,
the dancing too was ended,
and the princess could not stay.

Then the swineherd lost his true love,
and the princess grieves him still,
and never more she'll wander
from atop the golden hill.

JULIE: I know all these people and I love them, just as they love me. Let them come in and you'll see.

JEAN: No, Miss Julie, they don't love you. They take your food, but they spit on it! Believe me! Listen to them, listen to what they're singing! ——— No. don't listen to them!

JULIE (*listening*): What are they singing?

JEAN: It's a dirty song! About you and me!

JULIE: Disgusting! Oh! How deceitful! ———

JEAN: The rabble is always cowardly! And in a battle like this, you don't fight; you can only run away!

JULIE: Run away? But where? We can't go out — or into Kristine's room.

JEAN: True. But there's my room. Necessity knows no rules. Besides, you can trust me. I'm your friend and I respect you.

JULIE: But suppose — suppose they look for you in there?

JEAN: I'll bolt the door, and if anyone tries to break in, I'll shoot! ——— Come! (*On his knees.*) Come!

JULIE (*urgently*): Promise me. . . ?

JEAN: I swear! (*Miss Julie runs off right. Jean hastens after her.*)

Ballet

(*Led by a fiddler, the servants and farm people enter, dressed festively, with flowers in their hats. On the table they place a small barrel of beer and a keg of schnapps, both garlanded. Glasses are brought out, and the drink-*

ing starts. A dance circle is formed and "The Swineherd and the Princess" is sung. When the dance is finished, everyone leaves, singing.)

(Miss Julie enters alone. She notices the mess in the kitchen, wrings her hands, then takes out her powder puff and powders her nose.)

JEAN (*enters, agitated*): There, you see? And you heard them. We can't possibly stay here now, you know that.

JULIE: Yes, I know. But what can we do?

JEAN: Leave, travel, far away from here.

JULIE: Travel? Yes, but where?

JEAN: To Switzerland, to the Italian lakes. Have you ever been there?

JULIE: No. Is it beautiful?

JEAN: Oh, an eternal summer — oranges growing everywhere, laurel trees, always green . . .

JULIE: But what'll we do there?

JEAN: I'll open a hotel — with first-class service for first-class people.

JULIE: Hotel?

JEAN: That's the life, you know. Always new faces, new languages. No time to worry or be nervous. No hunting for something to do — there's always work to be done: bells ringing night and day, train whistles blowing, carriages coming and going, and all the while gold rolling into the till! That's the life!

JULIE: Yes, it sounds wonderful. But what'll I do?

JEAN: You'll be mistress of the house: the jewel in our crown! With your looks . . . and your manner — oh — success is guaranteed! It'll be wonderful! You'll sit in your office like a queen and push an electric button to set your slaves in motion. The guests will file past your throne and timidly lay their treasures before you. ——— You have no idea how people tremble when they get their bill. ——— I'll salt the bills° and you'll sweeten them with your prettiest smile. ——— Let's get away from here ——— (*Takes a timetable out of his pocket.*) ——— Right away, on the next train! ——— We'll be in Malmö six-thirty tomorrow morning, Hamburg at eight-forty; from Frankfort to Basel will take a day, then on to Como by way of the St. Gotthard Tunnel, in, let's see, three days. Three days!

JULIE: That's all very well! But Jean — you must give me courage! ——— Tell me you love me! Put your arms around me!

JEAN (*hesitating*): I want to — but I don't dare. Not in this house, not again. I love you — never doubt that — you don't doubt it, do you, Miss Julie?

JULIE (*shy; very feminine*): "Miss!"——— Call me Julie! There are no barriers between us anymore. Call me Julie!

JEAN (*tormented*): I can't! There'll always be barriers between us as long as we stay in this house. ——— There's the past and there's the Count. I've never met anyone I had such respect for. ——— When I see his gloves lying on a chair, I feel small. ——— When I

salt the bills: Inflate or pad the bills.

hear that bell up there ring, I jump like a skittish horse. ——— And when I look at his boots standing there so stiff and proud, I feel like bowing! (*Kicking the boots.*) Superstitions and prejudices we learned as children — but they can easily be forgotten. If I can just get to another country, a republic, people will bow and scrape when they see my livery — *they'll* bow and scrape, you hear, not me! I wasn't born to cringe. I've got stuff in me, I've got character, and if I can only grab onto that first branch, you watch me climb! I'm a servant today, but next year I'll own my own hotel. In ten years I'll have enough to retire. Then I'll go to Rumania and be decorated. I could — mind you I said *could* — end up a count!

JULIE: Wonderful, wonderful!

JEAN: Ah, in Rumania you just buy your title, and so you'll be a countess after all. My countess!

JULIE: But I don't care about that — that's what I'm putting behind me! Show me you love me, otherwise — otherwise, what am I?

JEAN: I'll show you a thousand times — afterwards! Not here! And whatever you do, no emotional outbursts, or we'll both be lost! We must think this through coolly, like sensible people. (*He takes out a cigar, snips the end, and lights it.*) You sit there, and I'll sit here. We'll talk as if nothing happened.

JULIE (*desperately*): Oh, my God! Have you no feelings?

JEAN: Me? No one has more feelings than I do, but I know how to control them.

JULIE: A little while ago you could kiss my shoe — and now!

JEAN (*harshly*): Yes, but that was before. Now we have other things to think about.

JULIE: Don't speak harshly to me!

JEAN: I'm not — just sensibly! We've already done one foolish thing, let's not have any more. The Count could return any minute, and by then we've got to decide what to do with our lives. What do you think of my plans for the future? Do you approve?

JULIE: They sound reasonable enough. I have only one question: For such a big undertaking you need capital — do you have it?

JEAN (*chewing on the cigar*): Me? Certainly! I have my professional expertise, my wide experience, and my knowledge of languages. That's capital enough, I should think!

JULIE: But all that won't even buy a train ticket.

JEAN: That's true. That's why I'm looking for a partner to advance me the money.

JULIE: Where will you find one quickly enough?

JEAN: That's up to you, if you want to come with me.

JULIE: But I can't; I have no money of my own. (*Pause.*)

JEAN: Then it's all off . . .

JULIE: And . . .

JEAN: Things stay as they are.

JULIE: Do you think I'm going to stay in this house as your lover? With all the servants pointing their fingers at me? Do you imagine I can face my father after this? No! Take me away from here, away from

Helen Mirren as Miss Julie in a 1971 production of
Strindberg's play.

shame and dishonor ——— Oh, what have I done!
My God, my God! (*She cries.*)

JEAN: Now, don't start that old song! ——— What have
you done? The same as many others before you.

JULIE (*screaming convulsively*): And now you think I'm
contemptible! ——— I'm falling, I'm falling!

JEAN: Fall down to my level and I'll lift you up again.

JULIE: What terrible power drew me to you? The attraction of the weak to the strong? The falling to the rising? Or was it love? Was this love? Do you know
what love is?

JEAN: Me? What do you take me for? You don't think
this was my first time, do you?

JULIE: The things you say, the thoughts you think!

JEAN: That's the way I was taught, and that's the way I
am! Now don't get excited and don't play the grand
lady, because we're in the same boat now! ———
Come on, Julie, I'll pour you a glass of something

special! (*He opens a drawer in the table, takes out a
wine bottle, and fills two glasses already used.*)

JULIE: Where did you get that wine?

JEAN: From the cellar.

JULIE: My father's burgundy!

JEAN: That'll do for his son-in-law, won't it?

JULIE: And I drink beer! Beer!

JEAN: That only shows I have better taste.

JULIE: Thief!

JEAN: Planning to tell?

JULIE: Oh, oh! Accomplice of a common thief! Was I
drunk? Have I been walking in a dream the whole
evening? Midsummer eve! A time of innocent fun!

JEAN: Innocent, eh?

JULIE (*pacing back and forth*): Is there anyone on earth
more miserable than I am at this moment?

JEAN: Why should you be? After such a conquest? Think
of Kristine in there. Don't you think she has feelings,
too?

JULIE: I thought so awhile ago, but not any more. No, a
servant is a servant . . .

JEAN: And a whore is a whore!

JULIE (*on her knees, her hands clasped*): Oh, God in
heaven, end my wretched life! Take me away from
the filth I'm sinking into! Save me! Save me!

JEAN: I can't deny I feel sorry for you. When I lay in that
onion bed and saw you in the rose garden, well . . . I'll
be frank . . . I had the same dirty thoughts all boys
have.

JULIE: And you wanted to die for me!

JEAN: In the oat bin? That was just talk.

JULIE: A lie, in other words!

JEAN (*beginning to feel sleepy*): More or less! I got the
idea from a newspaper story about a chimney sweep
who curled up in a firewood bin full of lilacs because
he got a summons for not supporting his illegitimate
child . . .

JULIE: So, that's what you're like . . .

JEAN: I had to think of something. And that's the kind of
story women always go for.

JULIE: Swine!

JEAN: *Merde!*

JULIE: And now you've seen the hawk's back . . .

JEAN: Not exactly its *back* . . .

JULIE: And I was to be the first branch . . .

JEAN: But the branch was rotten . . .

JULIE: I was to be the sign on the hotel . . .

JEAN: And I the hotel . . .

JULIE: Sit at your desk, entice your customers, pad their
bills . . .

JEAN: That I'd do myself . . .

JULIE: How can anyone be so thoroughly filthy?

JEAN: Better clean up then!

JULIE: You lackey, you menial, stand up, when I speak to
you!

JEAN: Menial's strumpet, lackey's whore, shut up and
get out of here! Who are you to lecture me on coarseness? None of my kind is ever as coarse as you were
tonight. Do you think one of your maids would

throw herself at a man the way you did? Have you ever seen any girl of my class offer herself like that? I've only seen it among animals and streetwalkers.

JULIE (*crushed*): You're right. Hit me, trample on me. I don't deserve any better. I'm worthless. But help me! If you see any way out of this, help me, Jean, please!

JEAN (*more gently*): I'd be lying if I didn't admit to a sense of triumph in all this, but do you think that a person like me would have dared even to look at someone like you if you hadn't invited it? I'm still amazed . . .

JULIE: And proud . . .

JEAN: Why not? Though I must say it was too easy to be really exciting.

JULIE: Go on, hit me, hit me harder!

JEAN (*rising*): No! Forgive me for what I've said! I don't hit a man when he's down, let alone a woman. I can't deny though, that I'm pleased to find out that what looked so dazzling to us from below was only tinsel, that the hawk's back was only gray, after all, that the lovely complexion was only powder, that those polished fingernails had black edges, and that a dirty handkerchief is still dirty, even if it smells of perfume . . . ! On the other hand, it hurts me to find out that what I was striving for wasn't finer, more substantial. It hurts me to see you sunk so low that you're inferior to your own cook. It hurts like watching flowers beaten down by autumn rains and turned into mud.

JULIE: You talk as if you were already above me.

JEAN: I am. You see, I could make you a countess, but you could never make me a count.

JULIE: But I'm the child of a count — something you could never be!

JEAN: That's true. But I could be the father of counts — if . . .

JULIE: But you're a thief. I'm not.

JEAN: There are worse things than being a thief! Besides, when I'm working in a house, I consider myself sort of a member of the family, like one of the children. And you don't call it stealing when a child snatches a berry off a full bush. (*His passion is aroused again.*) Miss Julie, you're a glorious woman, much too good for someone like me! You were drinking and you lost your head. Now you want to cover up your mistake by telling yourself that you love me! You don't. Maybe there was a physical attraction — but then your love is no better than mine. —— I could never be satisfied to be no more than an animal to you, and I could never arouse real love in you.

JULIE: Are you sure of that?

JEAN: You're suggesting it's possible —— Oh, I could fall in love with you, no doubt about it. You're beautiful, you're refined —— (*approaching and taking her hand*) —— cultured, lovable when you want to be, and once you start a fire in a man, it never goes out. (*Putting his arm around her waist.*) You're like hot, spicy wine, and one kiss from you . . . (*He tries to lead her out, but she slowly frees herself.*)

JULIE: Let me go!? —— You'll never win me like that.

JEAN: *How* then? —— Not like that? Not with caresses and pretty speeches. Not with plans about the future or rescue from disgrace! *How* then?

JULIE: How? How? I don't know! —— I have no idea! —— I detest you as I detest rats, but I can't escape from you.

JEAN: Escape with me!

JULIE (*pulling herself together*): Escape? Yes, we must escape! —— But I'm so tired. Give me a glass of wine? (*Jean pours the wine. She looks at her watch.*) But we must talk first. We still have a little time. (*She drains the glass, then holds it out for more.*)

JEAN: Don't drink so fast. It'll go to your head.

JULIE: What does it matter?

JEAN: What does it matter? It's vulgar to get drunk! What did you want to tell me?

JULIE: We must escape! But first we must talk, I mean I must talk. You've done all the talking up to now. You told about your life, now I want to tell about mine, so we'll know all about each other before we go off together.

JEAN: Just a minute! Forgive me! If you don't want to regret it afterwards, you'd better think twice before revealing any secrets about yourself.

JULIE: Aren't you my friend?

JEAN: Yes, sometimes! But don't rely on me.

JULIE: You're only saying that. —— Besides, everyone already knows my secrets. —— You see, my mother was a commoner — very humble background. She was brought up believing in social equality, women's rights, and all that. The idea of marriage repelled her. So, when my father proposed, she replied that she would never become his wife, but he could be her lover. He insisted that he didn't want the woman he loved to be less respected than he. But his passion ruled him, and when she explained that the world's respect meant nothing to her, he accepted her conditions.

But now his friends avoided him and his life was restricted to taking care of the estate, which couldn't satisfy him. I came into the world — against my mother's wishes, as far as I can understand. She wanted to bring me up as a child of nature, and, what's more, to learn everything a boy had to learn, so that I might be an example of how a woman can be as good as a man. I had to wear boy's clothes and learn to take care of horses, but I was never allowed in the cowshed. I had to groom and harness the horses and go hunting — and even had to watch them slaughter animals — that was disgusting! On the estate men were put on women's jobs and women on men's jobs — with the result that the property became run down and we became the laughingstock of the district. Finally, my father must have awakened from his trance because he rebelled and changed everything his way. My parents were then married quietly. Mother became ill — I don't know what illness it was — but she often had convulsions, hid in the attic and in the garden, and sometimes stayed out all night. Then came the great fire, which you've heard about. The house, the stables, and the cowshed all burned down, under very curious circumstances, suggesting arson, because the accident happened the day after the insurance had expired. The quarterly premium my father sent in was delayed because of a messenger's carelessness and didn't arrive in time. (*She fills her glass and drinks.*)

JEAN: Don't drink any more!

JULIE: Oh, what does it matter. —— We were left penniless and had to sleep in the carriages. My father had no idea where to find money to rebuild the house because he had so slighted his old friends that they had forgotten him. Then my mother suggested that he borrow from a childhood friend of hers, a brick manufacturer who lived nearby. Father got the loan without having to pay interest, which surprised him. And that's how the estate was rebuilt. —— (*Drinks again.*) Do you know who started the fire?

JEAN: The Countess, your mother.

JULIE: Do you know who the brick manufacturer was?

JEAN: Your mother's lover?

JULIE: Do you know whose money it was?

JEAN: Wait a moment — no, I don't.

JULIE: It was my mother's.

JEAN: You mean the Count's, unless they didn't sign an agreement when they were married.

JULIE: They didn't. —— My mother had a small inheritance which she didn't want under my father's control, so she entrusted it to her — friend.

JEAN: Who stole it!

JULIE: Exactly! He kept it. —— All this my father found out, but he couldn't bring it to court, couldn't repay his wife's lover, couldn't prove it was his wife's money! It was my mother's revenge for being forced into marriage against her will. It nearly drove him to suicide — there was a rumor that he tried with a pistol, but failed. So, he managed to live through it and my mother had to suffer for what she'd done. You can imagine that those were a terrible five years for me. I loved my father, but I sided with my mother because I didn't know the circumstances. I learned from her to hate men — you've heard how she hated the whole male sex — and I swore to her I'd never be a slave to any man.

JEAN: But you got engaged to that lawyer.

JULIE: In order to make him my slave.

JEAN: And he wasn't willing?

JULIE: He was willing, all right, but I wouldn't let him. I got tired of him.

JEAN: I saw it — out near the stable.

JULIE: What did you see?

JEAN: I saw — how he broke off the engagement.

JULIE: That's a lie! I was the one who broke it off. Has he said that he did? That swine . . .

JEAN: He was no swine, I'm sure. So, you hate men, Miss Julie?

JULIE: Yes! —— Most of the time! But sometimes — when the weakness comes, when passion burns! Oh, God, will the fire never die out?

JEAN: Do you hate me, too?

JULIE: Immeasurably! I'd like to have you put to death, like an animal . . .

JEAN: I see — the penalty for bestiality — the woman gets two years at hard labor and the animal is put to death. Right?

JULIE: Exactly!

JEAN: But there's no prosecutor here — and no animal. So, what'll we do?

JULIE: Go away!

JEAN: To torment each other to death?

JULIE: No! To be happy for — two days, a week, as long as we can be happy, and then — die . . .

JEAN: Die? That's stupid! It's better to open a hotel!

JULIE (*without listening*): —— on the shore of Lake Como, where the sun always shines, where the laurels are green at Christmas and the oranges glow.

JEAN: Lake Como is a rainy hole, and I never saw any oranges outside the stores. But tourists are attracted there because there are plenty of villas to be rented out to lovers, and that's a profitable business. —— Do you know why? Because they sign a lease for six months — and then leave after three weeks!

JULIE (*naively*): Why after three weeks?

JEAN: They quarrel, of course! But they still have to pay the rent in full! And so you rent the villas out again. And that's the way it goes, time after time. There's never a shortage of love — even if it doesn't last long!

JULIE: You don't want to die with me?

JEAN: I don't want to die at all! For one thing, I like living, and for another, I think suicide is a crime against the Providence which gave us life.

JULIE: You believe in God? *You?*

JEAN: Of course I do. And I go to church every other Sunday. —— To be honest, I'm tired of all this, and I'm going to bed.

JULIE: Are you? And do you think I can let it go at that? A man owes something to the woman he's shamed.

JEAN (*taking out his purse and throwing a silver coin on the table*): Here! I don't like owing anything to anybody.

JULIE (*pretending not to notice the insult*): Do you know what the law states . . .

JEAN: Unfortunately the law doesn't state any punishment for the woman who seduces a man!

JULIE (*as before*): Do you see any way out but to leave, get married, and then separate?

JEAN: Suppose I refuse such a *mésalliance?*°

JULIE: *Mésalliance* . . .

JEAN: Yes, for me! You see, I come from better stock than you. There's no arsonist in my family.

JULIE: How do you know?

JEAN: You can't prove otherwise. We don't keep charts

---

mésalliance: Misalliance or mismatch, especially regarding relative social status.

on our ancestors — there's just the police records! But I've read about your family. Do you know who the founder was? He was a miller who let the king sleep with his wife one night during the Danish War. I don't have any noble ancestors like that. I don't have any noble ancestors at all, but I could become one myself.

JULIE: This is what I get for opening my heart to someone unworthy, for giving my family's honor . . .

JEAN: Dishonor! ——— Well, I told you so: When people drink, they talk, and talk is dangerous!

JULIE: Oh, how I regret it! ——— How I regret it! ——— If you at least loved me.

JEAN: For the last time ——— what do you want? Shall I cry; shall I jump over your riding crop? Shall I kiss you and lure you off to Lake Como for three weeks, and then God knows what. . . ? What shall I do? What do you want? This is getting painfully embarrassing! But that's what happens when you stick your nose in women's business. Miss Julie! I see that you're unhappy. I know you're suffering, but I can't understand you. We don't have such romantic ideas; there's not this kind of hate between us. Love is a game we play when we get time off from work, but we don't have all day and night, like you. I think you're sick, really sick. Your mother was crazy, and her ideas have poisoned your life.

JULIE: Be kind to me. At least now you're talking like a human being.

JEAN: Be human yourself, then. You spit on me, and you won't let me wipe myself off ———

JULIE: Help me! Help me! Just tell me what to do, where to go!

JEAN: In God's name, if I only knew myself!

JULIE: I've been crazy, out of my mind, but isn't there any way out?

JEAN: Stay here and keep calm! No one knows anything!

JULIE: Impossible! The others know and Kristine knows.

JEAN: No they don't, and they'd never believe a thing like that!

JULIE (hesitantly): But — it could happen again!

JEAN: That's true!

JULIE: And then?

JEAN (frightened): Then? ——— Why didn't I think about that? Yes, there is only one thing to do — get away from here! Right away! I can't come with you, then we'd be finished, so you'll have to go alone — away — anywhere!

JULIE: Alone? ——— Where? ——— I can't do that!

JEAN: You must! And before the Count gets back! If you stay, you know what'll happen. Once you make a mistake like this, you want to continue because the damage has already been done. . . . Then you get bolder and bolder — until finally you're caught! So leave! Later you can write to the Count and confess everything — except that it was me! He'll never guess who it was, and he's not going to be eager to find out, anyway.

JULIE: I'll go if you come with me.

JEAN: Are you out of your head? Miss Julie runs away with her servant! In two days it would be in the newspapers, and that's something your father would never live through.

JULIE: I can't go and I can't stay! Help me! I'm so tired, so terribly tired. ——— Order me! Set me in motion — I can't think or act on my own . . .

JEAN: What miserable creatures you people are! You strut around with your noses in the air as if you were the lords of creation! All right, I'll order you. Go upstairs and get dressed! Get some money for the trip, and then come back down!

JULIE (in a half-whisper): Come up with me!

JEAN: To your room? ——— Now you're crazy again! (Hesitates for a moment.) No! Go, at once! (Takes her hand to lead her out.)

JULIE (as she leaves): Speak kindly to me, Jean!

JEAN: An order always sounds unkind — now you know how it feels. (Jean, alone, sighs with relief. He sits at the table, takes out a notebook and pencil, and begins adding up figures, counting aloud as he works. He continues in dumb show until Kristine enters, dressed for church. She is carrying a white tie and shirt front.)

KRISTINE: Lord Jesus, what a mess! What have you been up to?

JEAN: Oh, Miss Julie dragged everybody in here. You mean you didn't hear anything? You must have been sleeping soundly.

KRISTINE: Like a log.

JEAN: And dressed for church already?

KRISTINE: Of course! You remember you promised to come with me to communion today!

JEAN: Oh, yes, that's right. ——— And you brought my things. Come on, then! (He sits down. Kristine starts to put on his shirt front and tie. Pause. Jean begins sleepily.) What's the gospel text for today?

KRISTINE: On St. John's Day? — the beheading of John the Baptist, I should think!

JEAN: Ah, that'll be a long one, for sure. ——— Hey, you're choking me! ——— Oh, I'm sleepy, so sleepy!

KRISTINE: Yes, what have you been doing, up all night? Your face is absolutely green.

JEAN: I've been sitting here gabbing with Miss Julie.

KRISTINE: She has no idea what's proper, that one! (Pause.)

JEAN: You know, Kristine . . .

KRISTINE: What?

JEAN: It's really strange when you think about it. ——— Her!

KRISTINE: What's so strange?

JEAN: Everything! (Pause.)

KRISTINE (looking at the half-empty glasses standing on the table): Have you been drinking together, too?

JEAN: Yes.

KRISTINE: Shame on you! ——— Look me in the eye!

JEAN: Well?

KRISTINE: Is it possible? Is it possible?

JEAN (thinking it over for a moment): Yes, it is.

KRISTINE: Ugh! I never would have believed it! No, shame on you, shame!

JEAN: You're not jealous of her, are you?

KRISTINE: No, not of her! If it had been Clara or Sofie I'd have scratched your eyes out! ——— I don't know why, but that's the way I feel. ——— Oh, it's disgusting!

JEAN: Are you angry at her, then?

KRISTINE: No, at you! That was an awful thing to do, awful! Poor girl! ——— No, I don't care who knows it — I won't stay in a house where we can't respect the people we work for.

JEAN: Why should we respect them?

KRISTINE: You're so clever, you tell me! Do you want to wait on people who can't behave decently? Do you? You disgrace yourself that way, if you ask me.

JEAN: But it's a comfort to know they aren't any better than us.

KRISTINE: Not for me. If they're no better, what do we have to strive for to better ourselves. ——— And think of the Count! Think of him! As if he hasn't had enough misery in his life! Lord Jesus! No, I won't stay in this house any longer! ——— And it had to be with someone like you! If it had been that lawyer, if it had been a real gentleman . . .

JEAN: What do you mean?

KRISTINE: Oh, you're all right for what you are, but there are men and gentlemen, after all! ——— No, this business with Miss Julie I can never forget. She was so proud, so arrogant with men, you wouldn't have believed she could just go and give herself — and to someone like you! And she was going to have poor Diana shot for running after the gatekeepers' mutt! ——— Yes, I'm giving my notice, I mean it — I won't stay here any longer. On the twenty-fourth of October, I leave!

JEAN: And then?

KRISTINE: Well, since the subject has come up, it's about time you looked around for something since we're going to get married, in any case.

JEAN: Where am I going to look? I couldn't find a job like this if I was married.

KRISTINE: No, that's true. But you can find work as a porter or as a caretaker in some government office. The state doesn't pay much, I know, but it's secure, and there's a pension for the wife and children . . .

JEAN (grimacing): That's all very well, but it's a bit early for me to think about dying for a wife and children. My ambitions are a little higher than that.

KRISTINE: Your ambitions, yes! Well, you have obligations, too! Think about them!

JEAN: Don't start nagging me about obligations. I know what I have to do! (Listening for something outside.) Besides, this is something we have plenty of time to think over. Go and get ready for church.

KRISTINE: Who's that walking around up there?

JEAN: I don't know, unless it's Clara.

KRISTINE (going): You don't suppose it's the Count, who came home without us hearing him?

JEAN (frightened): The Count? No, I don't think so. He'd have rung.

KRISTINE (going): Well, God help us! I've never seen anything like this before. (The sun has risen and shines through the treetops in the park. The light shifts gradually until it slants in through the windows. Jean goes to the door and signals. Miss Julie enters, dressed in travel clothes and carrying a small bird cage, covered with a cloth, which she places on a chair.)

JULIE: I'm ready now.

JEAN: Shh! Kristine is awake.

JULIE (very nervous during the following): Does she suspect something?

JEAN: She doesn't know anything. But my God, you look awful!

JULIE: Why? How do I look?

JEAN: You're pale as a ghost and — excuse me, but your face is dirty.

JULIE: Let me wash up then. ——— (She goes to the basin and washes her hands and face.) Give me a towel! ——— Oh ——— the sun's coming up.

JEAN: Then the goblins will disappear.

JULIE: Yes, there must have been goblins out last night! ——— Jean, listen, come with me! I have some money now.

JEAN (hesitantly): Enough?

JULIE: Enough to start with. Come with me! I just can't travel alone on a day like this — midsummer day on a stuffy train — jammed in among crowds of people staring at me. Eternal delays at every station, while I'd wish I had wings. No, I can't, I can't! And then there'll be memories, memories of midsummer days when I was little. The church — decorated with birch leaves and lilacs; dinner at the big table with relatives and friends, the afternoons in the park, dancing, music, flowers, and games. Oh, no matter how far we travel, the memories will follow in the baggage car, with remorse and guilt!

JEAN: I'll go with you — but right away, before it's too late. Right this minute!

JULIE: Get dressed, then! (Picking up the bird cage.)

JEAN: But no baggage! It would give us away!

JULIE: No, nothing! Only what we can have in the compartment with us.

JEAN (has taken his hat): What've you got there? What is it?

JULIE: It's only my greenfinch. I couldn't leave her behind.

JEAN: What? Bring a bird cage with us? You're out of your head! Put it down!

JULIE: It's the only thing I'm taking from my home — the only living being that loves me, since Diana was unfaithful. Don't be cruel! Let me take her!

JEAN: Put the cage down, I said! ——— And don't talk so loudly — Kristine will hear us!

JULIE: No, I won't leave her in the hands of strangers! I'd rather you killed her.

JEAN: Bring the thing here, then, I'll cut its head off!

JULIE: Oh! But don't hurt her! Don't . . . no, I can't.

JEAN: Bring it here! I can!

JULIE (*taking the bird out of the cage and kissing it*): Oh, my little Serena, must you die and leave your mistress?

JEAN: Please don't make a scene! Your whole future is at stake! Hurry up! (*He snatches the bird from her, carries it over to the chopping block, and picks up a meat cleaver. Miss Julie turns away.*) You should have learned how to slaughter chickens instead of how to fire pistols. (*He chops off the bird's head.*) Then you wouldn't feel faint at the sight of blood.

JULIE (*screaming*): Kill me, too! Kill me! You, who can slaughter an innocent animal without blinking an eye! Oh, how I hate, how I detest you! There's blood between us now! I curse the moment I set eyes on you! I curse the moment I was conceived in my mother's womb!

JEAN: What good does cursing do? Let's go!

JULIE (*approaching the chopping block, as if drawn against her will*): No, I don't want to go yet. I can't . . . until I see . . . Shh! I hear a carriage ——— (*She listens, but her eyes never leave the cleaver and the chopping block.*) Do you think I can't stand the sight of blood? You think I'm so weak . . . Oh — I'd like to see your blood and your brains on a chopping block! ——— I'd like to see your whole sex swimming in a sea of blood, like my little bird . . . I think I could drink from your skull! I'd like to bathe my feet in your open chest and eat your heart roasted whole! ——— You think I'm weak. You think I love you because my womb craved your seed. You think I want to carry your spawn under my heart and nourish it with my blood — bear your child and take your name! By the way, what is your family name? I've never heard it. ——— Do you have one? I was to be Mrs. Bootblack — or Madame Pigsty. ——— You dog, who wears my collar, you lackey, who bears my coat of arms on your buttons — do I have to share you with my cook, compete with my own servant? Oh! Oh! Oh! ——— You think I'm a coward who wants to run away! No, now I'm staying — and let the storm break! My father will come home . . . to find his desk broken open . . . and his money gone! Then he'll ring — that bell . . . twice for his valet — and then he'll send for the police . . . and then I'll tell everything! Everything! Oh, what a relief it'll be to have it all end — if only it will end! ——— And then he'll have a stroke and die . . . That'll be the end of all of us — and there'll be peace . . . quiet . . . eternal rest! ——— And then our coat of arms will be broken against his coffin — the family title extinct — but the valet's line will go on in an orphanage . . . win laurels in the gutter, and end in jail!

JEAN: There's the blue blood talking! Very good, Miss Julie! Just don't let that miller out of the closet! (*Kristine enters, dressed for church, with a psalm-book in her hand.*)

JULIE (*rushing to Kristine and falling into her arms, as if seeking protection*): Help me, Kristine! Help me against this man!

KRISTINE (*unmoved and cold*): What a fine way to behave on a Sunday morning! (*Sees the chopping block.*) And look at this mess! ——— What does all this mean? Why all this screaming and carrying on?

JULIE: Kristine! You're a woman and my friend! Beware of this swine!

JEAN (*uncomfortable*): While you ladies discuss this, I'll go in and shave. (*Slips off right.*)

JULIE: You must listen to me so you'll understand!

KRISTINE: No, I could never understand such disgusting behavior! Where are you off to in your traveling clothes? ——— And he had his hat on. ——— Well? ——— Well? ———

JULIE: Listen to me, Kristine! Listen, and I'll tell you everything ———

KRISTINE: I don't want to hear it . . .

JULIE: But you must listen to me . . .

KRISTINE: What about? If it's about this silliness with Jean, I'm not interested, because it's none of my business. But if you're thinking of tricking him into running out, we'll soon put a stop to that!

JULIE (*extremely nervous*): Try to be calm now, Kristine, and listen to me! I can't stay here, and neither can Jean — so we must go away . . .

KRISTINE: Hm, hm!

JULIE (*brightening*): You see, I just had an idea ——— What if all three of us go — abroad — to Switzerland and start a hotel together? ——— I have money, you see — and Jean and I could run it — and I thought you, you could take care of the kitchen . . . Wouldn't that be wonderful? ——— Say yes! And come with us, and then everything will be settled! ——— Oh, do say yes! (*Embracing Kristine and patting her warmly.*)

KRISTINE (*coolly, thoughtfully*): Hm, hm!

JULIE (*presto tempo*):° You've never traveled, Kristine. ——— You must get out and see the world. You can't imagine how much fun it is to travel by train — always new faces — new countries. ——— And when we get to Hamburg, we'll stop off at the zoo — you'll like that. ——— and then we'll go to the theater and the opera — and when we get to Munich, dear, there we have museums, with Rubens and Raphael, the great painters, as you know. ——— You've heard of Munich, where King Ludwig lived — the king who went mad. ——— And then we'll see his castles — they're still there and they're like castles in fairy tales. ——— And from there it isn't far to Switzerland — and the Alps. ——— Imagine — the Alps have snow on them even in the middle of summer! ——— And oranges grow there and laurel trees that are green all year round ——— (*Jean can be seen in the wings right, sharpening his razor on a strop which he holds with his teeth and his left hand. He*

---

presto tempo: At a rapid pace.

listens to the conversation with satisfaction, nodding now and then in approval. Miss Julie continues tempo prestissimo.)° And then we'll start a hotel — and I'll be at the desk, while Jean greets the guests . . . does the shopping . . . writes letters. ——— You have no idea what a life it'll be — the train whistles blowing and the carriages arriving and the bells ringing in the rooms and down in the restaurant. ——— And I'll make out the bills — and I know how to salt them! . . . You'll never believe how timid travelers are when they have to pay their bills! ——— And you — you'll be in charge of the kitchen. ——— Naturally, you won't have to stand over the stove yourself. ——— And since you're going to be seen by people, you'll have to wear beautiful clothes. ——— And you, with your looks — no, I'm not flattering you — one fine day you'll grab yourself a husband! ——— You'll see! ——— A rich Englishman — they're so easy to ——— (*Slowing down.*) ——— catch — and then we'll get rich — and build ourselves a villa on Lake Como. ——— It's true it rains there a little now and then, but ——— (*Dully.*) ——— the sun has to shine sometimes — although it looks dark — and then . . . of course we could always come back home again ——— (*Pause.*) ——— here — or somewhere else ———

KRISTINE: Listen, Miss Julie, do you believe all this?

JULIE (*crushed*): Do I believe it?

KRISTINE: Yes!

JULIE (*wearily*): I don't know. I don't believe in anything anymore. (*She sinks down on the bench and cradles her head in her arms on the table.*) Nothing! Nothing at all!

KRISTINE (*turning right to where Jean is standing*): So, you thought you'd run out!

JEAN (*embarrassed; puts the razor on the table*): Run out? That's no way to put it. You hear Miss Julie's plan, and even if she is tired after being up all night, it's still a practical plan.

KRISTINE: Now you listen to me! Did you think I'd work as a cook for that . . .

JEAN (*sharply*): You watch what you say in front of your mistress! Do you understand?

KRISTINE: Mistress!

JEAN: Yes!

KRISTINE: Listen to him! Listen to him!

JEAN: Yes, you listen! It'd do you good to listen more and talk less! Miss Julie is your mistress. If you despise her, you have to despise yourself for the same reason!

KRISTINE: I've always had enough self-respect ———

JEAN: ——— to be able to despise other people!

KRISTINE: ——— to stop me from doing anything that's beneath me. You can't say that the Count's cook has been up to something with the groom or the swineherd! Can you?

tempo prestissimo: At a very rapid pace.

JEAN: No, you were lucky enough to get hold of a gentleman!

KRISTINE: Yes, a gentleman who sells the Count's oats from the stable.

JEAN: You should talk — taking a commission from the grocer and bribes from the butcher.

KRISTINE: What?

JEAN: And you say you can't respect your employers any longer. You, you, you!

KRISTINE: Are you coming to church with me, now? You could use a good sermon after your fine deed!

JEAN: No, I'm not going to church today. You'll have to go alone and confess what you've been up to.

KRISTINE: Yes, I'll do that, and I'll bring back enough forgiveness for you, too. The Savior suffered and died on the Cross for all our sins, and if we go to Him with faith and a penitent heart, He takes all our sins on Himself.

JEAN: Even grocery sins?

JULIE: And do you believe that, Kristine?

KRISTINE: It's my living faith, as sure as I stand here. It's the faith I learned as a child, Miss Julie, and kept ever since. "Where sin abounded, grace did much more abound!"

JULIE: Oh, if I only had your faith. If only . . .

KRISTINE: Well, you see, we can't have it without God's special grace, and that isn't given to everyone ———

JULIE: Who is it given to then?

KRISTINE: That's the great secret of the workings of grace, Miss Julie, and God is no respecter of persons, for the last shall be the first . . .

JULIE: Then He does respect the last.

KRISTINE (*continuing*): . . . and it is easier for a camel to go through the eye of a needle, than for a rich man to enter the Kingdom of God. That's how it is, Miss Julie! Anyhow, I'm going now — alone, and on the way I'm going to tell the groom not to let any horses out, in case anyone wants to leave before the Count gets back! ——— Goodbye! (*Leaves.*)

JEAN: What a witch! ——— And all this because of a greenfinch! ———

JULIE (*dully*): Never mind the greenfinch! ——— Can you see any way out of this? Any end to it?

JEAN (*thinking*): No!

JULIE: What would you do in my place?

JEAN: In your place? Let's see — as a person of position, as a woman who had — fallen. I don't know — wait, now I know.

JULIE (*taking the razor and making a gesture*): You mean like this?

JEAN: Yes! But — understand — *I* wouldn't do it! That's the difference between us!

JULIE: Because you're a man and I'm a woman? What sort of difference is that?

JEAN: The usual difference — between a man and a woman.

JULIE (*with the razor in her hand*): I want to, but I can't! ——— My father couldn't either, the time he should have done it.

JEAN: No, he shouldn't have! He had to revenge himself first.

JULIE: And now my mother is revenged again, through me.

JEAN: Didn't you ever love your father, Miss Julie?

JULIE: Oh yes, deeply, but I've hated him, too. I must have done so without realizing it! It was he who brought me up to despise my own sex, making me half woman, half man. Whose fault is what's happened? My father's, my mother's, my own? My own? I don't have anything that's my own. I don't have a single thought that I didn't get from my father, not an emotion that I didn't get from my mother, and this last idea — that all people are equal — I got that from my fiancé. ——— That's why I called him a swine! How can it be my fault? Shall I let Jesus take on the blame, the way Kristine does? ——— No, I'm too proud to do that and too sensible — thanks to my father's teachings. ——— And as for someone rich not going to heaven, that's a lie. But Kristine won't get in — how will she explain the money she has in the savings bank? Whose fault is it? ——— What does it matter whose fault it is? I'm still the one who has to bear the blame, face the consequences . . .

JEAN: Yes, but . . . (*The bell rings sharply twice. Miss Julie jumps up. Jean changes his coat.*) The Count is back! Do you suppose Kristine — (*He goes to the speaking tube, taps the lid, and listens.*)

JULIE: He's been to his desk!

JEAN: It's Jean, sir! (*Listening; the audience cannot hear the Count's voice.*) Yes, sir! (*Listening.*) Yes, sir! Right away! (*Listening.*) At once, sir! (*Listening.*) I see, in half an hour!

JULIE (*desperately frightened*): What did he say? Dear Lord, what did he say?

JEAN: He wants his boots and his coffee in half an hour.

JULIE: So, in half an hour! Oh, I'm so tired. I'm not able to do anything. I can't repent, can't run away, can't stay, can't live — can't die! Help me now! Order me, and I'll obey like a dog! Do me this last service, save my honor, save his name! You know what I *should* do, but don't have the will to . . . You will it, you order me to do it!

JEAN: I don't know why ——— but now I can't either ——— I don't understand. ——— It's as if this coat made it impossible for me to order you to do anything. ——— And now, since the Count spoke to me — I — I can't really explain it — but — ah, it's the damn lackey in me! ——— I think if the Count came down here now — and ordered me to cut my throat, I'd do it on the spot.

JULIE: Then pretend you're he, and I'm you! ——— You gave such a good performance before when you knelt at my feet. ——— You were a real nobleman. ——— Or — have you ever seen a hypnotist in the theater? (*Jean nods.*) He says to his subject: "Take the broom," and he takes it. He says: "Sweep," and he sweeps ———

JEAN: But the subject has to be asleep.

JULIE (*ecstatically*): I'm already asleep. ——— The whole room is like smoke around me . . . and you look like an iron stove . . . shaped like a man in black, with an tall hat — and your eyes glow like coals when the fire is dying — and your face is a white patch, like ashes ——— (*The sunlight has reached the floor and now shines on Jean.*) ——— it's so warm and good ——— (*She rubs her hands as if warming them before a fire.*) ——— and bright — and so peaceful!

JEAN (*taking the razor and putting it in her hand*): Here's the broom! Go now while it's bright — out to the barn — and . . . (*Whispers in her ear.*)

JULIE (*awake*): Thank you. I'm going now to rest! But just tell me — that those who are first can also receive the gift of grace. Say it, even if you don't believe it.

JEAN: The first? No, I can't ——— But wait — Miss Julie — now I know! You're no longer among the first — you're now among — the last!

JULIE: That's true. ——— I'm among the very last. I'm the last one of all! Oh! ——— But now I can't go! ——— Tell me once more to go!

JEAN: No, now I can't either! I can't!

JULIE: And the first shall be the last!

JEAN: Don't think, don't think! You're taking all my strength from me, making me a coward. ——— What was that? I thought the bell moved! ——— No! Shall we stuff paper in it? ——— To be so afraid of a bell! ——— But it isn't just a bell. There's someone behind it — a hand sets it in motion — and something else sets the hand in motion. ——— Maybe if you cover your ears — cover your ears! But then it rings even louder! rings until someone answers. ——— And then it's too late! And then the police come — and — then ——— (*The bell rings twice loudly. Jean flinches, then straightens up.*) It's horrible! But there's no other way! ——— Go! (*Miss Julie walks firmly out through the door.*)

COMMENTARY

August Strindberg (1849–1912)
FROM THE PREFACE TO *MISS JULIE*   1888
TRANSLATED BY HARRY G. CARLSON

> *Strindberg's preface sets out his intentions in writing* Miss Julie, *a play concerned with the problem of "social climbing or falling, of higher or lower, better or worse, man or woman." He discusses the struggle for dominance between Miss Julie and Jean, and characterizes Miss Julie as a woman forced to "wreak vengeance" on herself.*

Miss Julie is a modern character. Not that the man-hating half-woman has not existed in all ages but because now that she has been discovered, she has come out in the open to make herself heard. The half-woman is a type who pushes her way ahead, selling herself nowadays for power, decorations, honors, and diplomas, as formerly she used to do for money. The type implies a retrogressive step in evolution, an inferior species who cannot endure. Unfortunately, they are able to pass on their wretchedness; degenerate men seem unconsciously to choose their mates from among them. And so they breed, producing an indeterminate sex for whom life is a torture. Fortunately, the offspring go under either because they are out of harmony with reality or because their repressed instincts break out uncontrollably or because their hopes of achieving equality with men are crushed. The type is tragic, revealing the drama of a desperate struggle against Nature, tragic as the romantic heritage now being dissipated by naturalism, which has a contrary aim: happiness, and happiness belongs only to the strong and skillful species.

But Miss Julie is also: a relic of the old warrior nobility now giving way to a new nobility of nerve and intellect, a victim of her own flawed constitution, a victim of the discord caused in a family by a mother's "crime," a victim of the delusions and conditions of her age — and together these are the equivalent of the concept of Destiny, or Universal Law, of antiquity. Guilt has been abolished by the naturalist, along with God, but the consequences of an action — punishment, imprisonment or the fear of it — that he cannot erase, for the simple reason that they remain, whether he pronounces acquittal or not. Those who have been injured are not as kind and understanding as an unscathed outsider can afford to be. Even if her father felt constrained not to seek revenge, his daughter would wreak vengeance upon herself, as she does here, out of an innate or acquired sense of honor, which the upper classes inherit — from where? From barbarism, from the ancient Aryan home of the race, from medieval chivalry. It is a beautiful thing, but nowadays a hindrance to the survival of the race. It is the nobleman's harikari, which compels him to slit open his own stomach when someone insults him and which survives in a modified form in the duel, that privilege of the nobility. That is why Jean, the servant, lives, while Miss Julie cannot live without honor. The slave's advantage over the nobleman is that he lacks this fatal preoccupation with honor. But in all of us Aryans there is something of the nobleman, or a Don Quixote. And so we sympathize with the suicide, whose act means a loss of honor. We are noblemen enough to be pained when we see the mighty fallen and as superfluous as a corpse, yes, even if the fallen should rise again and make amends through an honorable act. The servant Jean is a race-founder, someone in whom the process of differentiation can be detected. Born the son of a tenant farmer, he has educated himself in the things a gentleman should know. He has been quick to learn, has finely developed senses (smell, taste, sight) and a feeling for what is beautiful. He is already moving up in the world and is not embarrassed about using other people's help. He is alienated from his fellow servants, despising them as parts of a past he has already put behind him. He fears and flees them because they know his secrets, pry into his intentions, envy his rise, and look forward eagerly to his fall. Hence his dual, indecisive nature, vacillating between sympathy for people in high social positions and hatred for those who currently occupy those positions. He is an aristocrat, as he himself says, has learned the secrets of good society, is polished on the surface but coarse beneath, wears a frock coat tastefully but without any guarantee that his body is clean.

He has respect for Miss Julie, but is afraid of Kristine because she knows his dangerous secrets. He is sufficiently callous not to let the night's events disturb his plans for the future. With both a slave's brutality and a master's lack of squeamishness, he can see blood without fainting and shake off misfortune easily. Consequently, he comes through the struggle unscathed and will probably end up an innkeeper. And even if *he* does not become a Rumanian count, his son will become a university student and possibly a county police commissioner. . . .

Apart from the fact that Jean is rising in the world, he is superior to Miss Julie because he is a man. Sexually, he is an aristocrat because of his masculine strength, his more keenly developed senses, and his capacity for taking the initiative. His sense of inferiority is mostly due to the social circumstances in which he happens to be living, and he can probably shed it along with his valet's jacket.

His slave mentality expresses itself in the fearful respect he has for the Count (the boots) and his religious superstition; but he respects the Count mainly as the occupant of the kind of high position to which he himself aspires; and the respect remains even after he has conquered the daughter of the house and seen how empty the lovely shell was.

I do not believe that love in any "higher" sense can exist between two people of such different natures, and so I have Miss Julie's love as something she fabricates in order to protect and excuse herself; and I have Jean suppose himself capable of loving her under other social circumstances. I think it is the same with love as with the hyacinth, which must take root in darkness *before* it can produce a sturdy flower. Here a flower shoots up, blooms, and goes to seed all at once, and that is why it dies so quickly.

Oscar Wilde

Oscar Fingal O'Flahertie Wills Wilde (1854–1900) was born to a famous eye surgeon who maintained a home in Dublin's most exclusive neighborhood. Wilde's mother, known by her literary name, Speranza, was noted for collecting Irish folk stories in the western hills in the late 1870s. Her work was important to later literature, but it was especially important for its timing, since most of the storytellers in Ireland were gone by the turn of the century.

Wilde was a brilliant classics scholar at Trinity College, Dublin, where his tutor was the legendary Mahaffy, who later traveled with him in France. After Trinity, he went to Magdalen College, Oxford, where he took a distinguished degree. Among his influences in Oxford was Slade Professor of Art John Ruskin, with whom Wilde had long walks and talks. Ruskin had published important books on northern Gothic art and on Italian art, especially the art of Venice. Art was one of Wilde's primary passions, especially decoration and the decorative arts. He agreed with Walter Pater, a contemporary art critic, that art must best serve the needs of art. He felt, for example, that poetry did not serve religious, political, social, or biographical goals. Its ends were aesthetic and its pleasures were in its sounds, images, and thoughts.

Partly because of his brilliance and partly because he was one of the age's greatest conversationalists, he was soon in the company of the famous and amusing people of his generation. Some of his conversational gift is apparent in his plays.

By his own admission, his life was marked by an overindulgence in sensuality: "What paradox was to me in the sphere of thought, perversity became to me in the sphere of passion." He married Constance Lloyd in 1884 and soon had two sons. But by 1891 he had already had several homosexual liaisons, one of which was to bring him to ruin. His relationship with the much younger Lord Alfred Douglas ended with Douglas's father, the marquis of Queensberry, publicly denouncing Wilde as a sodomite. Wilde sued for libel but lost. As a result, in 1895 he was tried for sodomy, convicted, and sentenced to two years' hard labor. Wilde's actions have been seen as self-destructive, but they are also consistent with his efforts to force society to examine its own hypocrisy. Unfortunately, his efforts in court and prison ruined him, and he died in exile in Paris three years after his release.

His best-known novel, *The Picture of Dorian Gray* (1890; expanded 1891), is the story of a young man whose sensual life eats away at him and eventually destroys him. The novel's failure when it was first published led Wilde to try the stage, where he was a signal success. Remarkably, all his plays were written in the period between 1891 and his imprisonment in 1895. Most of his plays — *Salomé* (1891), *Lady Windermere's Fan* (1892), *A Woman of No Importance* (1893), *An Ideal Husband* (1895), and *The Importance of Being Earnest* (1895) — rank as witty, insightful, and sharp commentaries on the upper-class British society he knew best. They owe a great deal to eighteenth-century comedies, such as William Congreve's *The Way of the World*. But they also owe a great deal to British and European farces and comedies of his own time, many of which he seems to have studied closely. Unlike those plays — many have never been published and no longer exist — Wilde's are still funny and still seem pertinent even though the class he criticized has long vanished.

The Importance of Being Earnest was a remarkable success when it opened at the St. James's Theatre on Valentine's Day 1895, but it closed in two months after fewer than one hundred performances when the scandal of Wilde's conviction became public. Wilde's reputation as playwright was made and broken in a matter of a few years, and it was not restored until after his death.

THE IMPORTANCE OF BEING EARNEST

The play was originally written in four acts, but because the producer requested it be cut, Wilde reworked it into three acts, agreeing that the excisions made the play stronger. Its subtitle, *A Trivial Comedy for Serious People,* has prompted commentators to think of the play as farcical fluff, a play about little or nothing that is nonetheless profoundly amusing. The *New York Times* commented after its first U.S. opening, "The thing is as slight in structure and as devoid of purpose as a paper balloon, but it is extraordinarily funny." Recent critics have challenged this view on the grounds that its subject matter centers on the questions of identity and reality. One current view is that its surfaces are slight but that beneath the surface is a commentary on a society that judges things only by appearance.

The primary characters are Algernon Moncrieff and Jack Worthing, young gentlemen of marriageable age. Among the women are Algernon's cousin Gwendolen Fairfax, who adores the name Ernest and is in love with Jack; Lady Bracknell, her mother; and Cecily Cardew, Jack's ward. Bunbury, referred to by Algernon, seems to be a character, but is instead an invention. He is a convenience for Algernon, a country friend whose illnesses Algernon uses to avoid social events he dislikes, such as Lady Bracknell's dinners. Jack, who lives in the country, has created a similar figure to help him escape to town — an imaginary brother Ernest. In town, Jack pretends to be Ernest; and all his town acquaintances, including Algernon and Gwendolen, know Jack by that name.

The similarities with Restoration comedies are striking. The question of marriage is central in the play, and attitudes toward marriage in Wilde's social class are among the targets of his satire. When Lady Bracknell probes into Jack Worthing's background, she discovers the distressing news about his family "line": Jack is a foundling who had been left in a handbag in Victoria Station. His family "line" is the Brighton Line. Gwendolen could also have stepped from a Restoration comedy. She is determined to have Jack Worthing, and when he seems sluggish about proposing she prompts him, offering a critique of his proposal by telling him he seems inexperienced at it.

The play owes perhaps even more to the farces of the 1880s and 1890s and a great deal to the well-made play of Eugène Scribe and his successors. Critics often compare Wilde to Alexandre Dumas, the author of *La Dame aux camélias* (*Camille*), because both writers fashioned their plays with a considerable degree of artificiality, planting information in the first act that would prove the solution to problems in the last act. They also play with questions of identity, disguise, and revelation at the last minute in much the way Wilde does here when he reveals the identity of Ernest.

In melodramas and well-made plays, the revelation at the end was not that the potential husband had the right name so much as that he had the right background: he was an aristocrat and not the commoner he seemed to be. Wilde has fun with this convention and many others. In an instant, he ridicules the trick of revealing the hero to be "marriageable" because of his birth by emphasizing the triviality of a name. Yet names are of great importance (as Shakespeare tells us in *Romeo and Juliet*), and the earnestness implied in Ernest is one ingredient that helps Jack Worthing succeed.

Critic Kerry Powell has demonstrated that almost every device in *The Importance of Being Earnest* was drawn from a contemporary farce or comedy. The device of the child lost in a piece of luggage was used in *The Lost Child* (1863), and *The Foundling* (1894) actually takes place in Brighton. The name Bunbury and the concept of "Bunburying" come from *The Godpapa* (1891). Even the device of baptism was used in *Crimes and Christening* (1891). Wilde was adept at taking the theater conventions his audience was most familiar with and using them to his own ends — to entertain his audience, but at the same time to help him put an extra edge on his satire.

The Importance of Being Earnest in Performance

After the first production closed down in 1895, the play was revived in London in 1898 and 1902, but an even more successful production in 1909 saw 324 performances. The benchmark for a truly successful play in those days seems to have been one hundred performances, and Wilde would have felt vindicated by the 1909 production, had he lived to see it. *The Importance of Being Earnest* has been produced so often in Great Britain and the United States that only a few productions can be taken into account here. The first New York production was in 1902. John Gielgud and Edith Evans played in the 1939 London production and then again in 1942. In 1947 Gielgud played in New York with Clifton Webb and Estelle Winwood. The reviews were especially strong, calling the play "as insolently monocled in manner and as killingly high-toned in language as mischievous tomfoolery can make it."

The play inspired at least five musicals between 1927 and 1984. The 1979 production at Stratford, Ontario, was called "a perfect play in a perfect production." An unsuccessful production by the Berlin Play Actors in 1987 used all men and relied on insights drawn from transvestite performers, but it was badly received. University productions of the play are fairly common, although, like the Yale Repertory production in 1986, they are not always able to pull off the comic demands of the play's exacting language. The original four-act version of the play, discovered in 1977 in the New York Public Library, was produced in Ohio in the John Carroll University's Marinello Theater in 1985. It was more a curiosity than a triumph. The 1993 production at the Aldwych in London received great praise for its dazzling sets that "matched Wilde's word pictures with bold stage pictures." Maggie Smith played Lady Bracknell.

The play is a witty tour de force of language. Its surfaces gleam, and the best productions play it straight. A contemporary spate of films has made Wilde's work available to a wide audience.

Oscar Wilde (1854–1900)

THE IMPORTANCE OF BEING EARNEST   1895
A TRIVIAL COMEDY FOR SERIOUS PEOPLE

The Persons of the Play

JOHN WORTHING, J.P., *of the Manor House, Woolton, Hertfordshire*
ALGERNON MONCRIEFF, *his friend*
REV. CANON CHASUBLE, D.D., *rector of Woolton*
MERRIMAN, *butler to Mr. Worthing*
LANE, *Mr. Moncrieff's manservant*
LADY BRACKNELL
HON. GWENDOLEN FAIRFAX, *her daughter*
CECILY CARDEW, *John Worthing's ward*
MISS PRISM, *her governess*

The Scenes of the Play

Act I: *Algernon Moncrieff's Flat in Half Moon Street, W.*
Act II: *The Garden at the Manor House, Woolton*
Act III: *Morning Room at the Manor House, Woolton*

ACT I

(*Scene: Morning room in Algernon's flat in Half Moon Street. The room is luxuriously and artistically furnished. The sound of a piano is heard in the adjoining room. Lane is arranging afternoon tea on the table, and after the music has ceased, Algernon enters.*)

ALGERNON: Did you hear what I was playing, Lane?
LANE: I didn't think it polite to listen, sir.
ALGERNON: I'm sorry for that, for your sake. I don't play accurately — anyone can play accurately — but I play with wonderful expression. As far as the piano is concerned, sentiment is my forte. I keep science for Life.
LANE: Yes, sir.

ALGERNON: And, speaking of the science of Life, have you got the cucumber sandwiches cut for Lady Bracknell?
LANE: Yes, sir.   (*Hands them on a salver.*)
ALGERNON (*inspects them, takes two, and sits down on the sofa*): Oh! — by the way, Lane, I see from your book that on Thursday night, when Lord Shoreham and Mr. Worthing were dining with me, eight bottles of champagne are entered as having been consumed.
LANE: Yes, sir; eight bottles and a pint.
ALGERNON: Why is it that at a bachelor's establishment the servants invariably drink the champagne? I ask merely for information.
LANE: I attribute it to the superior quality of the wine, sir. I have often observed that in married households the champagne is rarely of a first-rate brand.
ALGERNON: Good heavens! Is marriage so demoralizing as that?
LANE: I believe it *is* a very pleasant state, sir. I have had very little experience of it myself up to the present. I have only been married once. That was in consequence of a misunderstanding between myself and a young person.
ALGERNON (*languidly*): I don't know that I am much interested in your family life, Lane.
LANE: No, sir; it is not a very interesting subject. I never think of it myself.
ALGERNON: Very natural, I am sure. That will do, Lane, thank you.
LANE: Thank you, sir.   (*Lane goes out.*)
ALGERNON: Lane's views on marriage seem somewhat lax. Really, if the lower orders don't set us a good example, what on earth is the use of them? They seem, as a class, to have absolutely no sense of moral responsibility. belittling

(*Enter Lane.*)

LANE: Mr. Ernest Worthing.

(*Enter Jack. Lane goes out.*)

ALGERNON: How are you, my dear Ernest? What brings you up to town?

JACK: Oh, pleasure, pleasure! What else should bring one anywhere? Eating as usual, I see, Algy!

ALGERNON (*stiffly*): I believe it is customary in good society to take some slight refreshment at five o'clock. Where have you been since last Thursday?

JACK (*sitting down on the sofa*): In the country.

ALGERNON: What on earth do you do there?

JACK (*pulling off his gloves*): When one is in town one amuses oneself. When one is in the country one amuses other people. It is excessively boring.

ALGERNON: And who are the people you amuse?

JACK (*airily*): Oh, neighbors, neighbors.

ALGERNON: Got nice neighbors in your part of Shropshire?

JACK: Perfectly horrid! Never speak to one of them.

ALGERNON: How immensely you must amuse them! (*Goes over and takes sandwich.*) By the way, Shropshire is your county, is it not?

JACK: Eh? Shropshire? Yes, of course. Hallo! Why all these cups? Why cucumber sandwiches? Why such reckless extravagance in one so young? Who is coming to tea?

ALGERNON: Oh! merely Aunt Augusta and Gwendolen.

JACK: How perfectly delightful!

ALGERNON: Yes, that is all very well; but I am afraid Aunt Augusta won't quite approve of your being here.

JACK: May I ask why?

ALGERNON: My dear fellow, the way you flirt with Gwendolen is perfectly disgraceful. It is almost as bad as the way Gwendolen flirts with you.

JACK: I am in love with Gwendolen. I have come up to town expressly to propose to her.

ALGERNON: I thought you had come up for pleasure? — I call that business.

JACK: How utterly unromantic you are!

ALGERNON: I really don't see anything romantic in proposing. It is very romantic to be in love. But there is nothing romantic about a definite proposal. Why, one may be accepted. One usually is, I believe. Then the excitement is all over. The very essence of romance is uncertainty. If ever I get married, I'll certainly try to forget the fact.

JACK: I have no doubt about that, dear Algy. The Divorce Court was specially invented for people whose memories are so curiously constituted.

ALGERNON: Oh! there is no use speculating on that subject. Divorces are made in heaven — (*Jack puts out his hand to take a sandwich. Algernon at once interferes.*) Please don't touch the cucumber sandwiches. They are ordered specially for Aunt Augusta. (*Takes one and eats it.*)

JACK: Well, you have been eating them all the time.

ALGERNON: That is quite a different matter. She is my aunt. (*Takes plate from below.*) Have some bread and butter. The bread and butter is for Gwendolen. Gwendolen is devoted to bread and butter.

JACK (*advancing to table and helping himself*): And very good bread and butter it is too.

ALGERNON: Well, my dear fellow, you need not eat as if you were going to eat it all. You behave as if you were married to her already. You are not married to her already, and I don't think you ever will be.

JACK: Why on earth do you say that?

ALGERNON: Well, in the first place, girls never marry the men they flirt with. Girls don't think it right.

JACK: Oh, that is nonsense!

ALGERNON: It isn't. It is a great truth. It accounts for the extraordinary number of bachelors that one sees all over the place. In the second place, I don't give my consent.

JACK: Your consent!

ALGERNON: My dear fellow, Gwendolen is my first cousin. And before I allow you to marry her, you will have to clear up the whole question of Cecily. (*Rings bell.*)

JACK: Cecily! What on earth do you mean? What do you mean, Algy, by Cecily? I don't know anyone of the name of Cecily.

(*Enter Lane.*)

ALGERNON: Bring me that cigarette case Mr. Worthing left in the smoking room the last time he dined here.

LANE: Yes, sir. (*Lane goes out.*)

JACK: Do you mean to say you have had my cigarette case all this time? I wish to goodness you had let me know. I have been writing frantic letters to Scotland Yard about it. I was very nearly offering a large reward.

ALGERNON: Well, I wish you would offer one. I happen to be more than usually hard up.

JACK: There is no good offering a large reward now that the thing is found.

(*Enter Lane with the cigarette case on a salver. Algernon takes it at once. Lane goes out.*)

ALGERNON: I think that is rather mean of you, Ernest, I must say. (*Opens case and examines it.*) However, it makes no matter, for, now that I look at the inscription inside, I find that the thing isn't yours after all.

JACK: Of course it's mine. (*Moving to him.*) You have seen me with it a hundred times, and you have no right whatsoever to read what is written inside. It is a very ungentlemanly thing to read a private cigarette case.

ALGERNON: Oh! it is absurd to have a hard-and-fast rule about what one should read and what one shouldn't. More than half of modern culture depends on what one shouldn't read.

JACK: I am quite aware of the fact, and I don't propose to discuss modern culture. It isn't the sort of thing one should talk of in private. I simply want my cigarette case back.

ALGERNON: Yes; but this isn't your cigarette case. This cigarette case is a present from someone of the name of Cecily, and you said you didn't know anyone of that name.

JACK: Well, if you want to know, Cecily happens to be my aunt.

ALGERNON: Your aunt!

JACK: Yes. Charming old lady she is, too. Lives at Tunbridge Wells. Just give it back to me, Algy.

ALGERNON (*retreating to back of sofa*): But why does she call herself little Cecily if she is your aunt and lives at Tunbridge Wells? (*Reading.*) "From little Cecily with her fondest love."

JACK (*moving to sofa and kneeling upon it*): My dear fellow, what on earth is there in that? Some aunts are tall, some aunts are not tall. That is a matter that surely an aunt may be allowed to decide for herself. You seem to think that every aunt should be exactly like your aunt! That is absurd! For heaven's sake give me back my cigarette case.
(*Follows Algernon round the room.*)

ALGERNON: Yes. But why does your aunt call you her uncle? "From little Cecily, with her fondest love to her dear Uncle Jack." There is no objection, I admit, to an aunt being a small aunt, but why an aunt, no matter what her size may be, should call her own nephew her uncle, I can't quite make out. Besides, your name isn't Jack at all; it is Ernest.

JACK: It isn't Ernest; it's Jack.

ALGERNON: You have always told me it was Ernest. I have introduced you to everyone as Ernest. You answer to the name of Ernest. You look as if your name was Ernest. You are the most earnest looking person I ever saw in my life. It is perfectly absurd your saying that your name isn't Ernest. It's on your cards. Here is one of them (*taking it from case*) "Mr. Ernest Worthing, B.4, The Albany." I'll keep this as a proof that your name is Ernest if ever you attempt to deny it to me, or to Gwendolen, or to anyone else.
(*Puts the card in his pocket.*)

JACK: Well, my name is Ernest in town and Jack in the country, and the cigarette case was given to me in the country.

ALGERNON: Yes, but that does not account for the fact that your small Aunt Cecily, who lives at Tunbridge Wells, calls you her dear uncle. Come, old boy, you had much better have the thing out at once.

JACK: My dear Algy, you talk exactly as if you were a dentist. It is very vulgar to talk like a dentist when one isn't a dentist. It produces a false impression.

ALGERNON: Well, that is exactly what dentists always do. Now, go on! Tell me the whole thing. I may mention that I have always suspected you of being a confirmed and secret Bunburyist; and I am quite sure of it now.

JACK: Bunburyist? What on earth do you mean by a Bunburyist?

ALGERNON: I'll reveal to you the meaning of that incomparable expression as soon as you are kind enough to inform me why you are Ernest in town and Jack in the country.

JACK: Well, produce my cigarette case first.

ALGERNON: Here it is. (*Hands cigarette case.*) Now produce your explanation, and pray make it improbable.
(*Sits on sofa.*)

JACK: My dear fellow, there is nothing improbable about my explanation at all. In fact it's perfectly ordinary. Old Mr. Thomas Cardew, who adopted me when I was a little boy, made me in his will guardian to his granddaughter, Miss Cecily Cardew. Cecily, who addresses me as her uncle from motives of respect that you could not possibly appreciate, lives at my place in the country under the charge of her admirable governess, Miss Prism.

ALGERNON: Where is that place in the country, by the way?

JACK: That is nothing to you, dear boy. You are not going to be invited — I may tell you candidly that the place is not in Shropshire.

ALGERNON: I suspected that, my dear fellow! I have Bunburyed all over Shropshire on two separate occasions. Now, go on. Why are you Ernest in town and Jack in the country?

JACK: My dear Algy, I don't know whether you will be able to understand my real motives. You are hardly serious enough. When one is placed in the position of guardian, one has to adopt a very high moral tone on all subjects. It's one's duty to do so. And as a high moral tone can hardly be said to conduce very much to either one's health or one's happiness, in order to get up to town I have always pretended to have a younger brother of the name of Ernest, who lives in the Albany, and gets into the most dreadful scrapes. That, my dear Algy, is the whole truth pure and simple.

ALGERNON: The truth is rarely pure and never simple. Modern life would be very tedious if it were either and modern literature a complete impossibility!

JACK: That wouldn't be at all a bad thing.

ALGERNON: Literary criticism is not your forte, my dear fellow. Don't try it. You should leave that to people who haven't been at a university. They do it so well in the daily papers. What you really are is a Bunburyist. I was quite right in saying you were a Bunburyist. You are one of the most advanced Bunburyists I know.

JACK: What on earth do you mean?

ALGERNON: You have invented a very useful younger brother called Ernest, in order that you may be able to come up to town as often as you like. I have invented an invaluable permanent invalid called Bunbury, in order that I may be able to go down into the country whenever I choose. Bunbury is perfectly invaluable. If it wasn't for Bunbury's extraordinary bad health, for instance, I wouldn't be able to dine with you at Willis's tonight, for I have been really engaged to Aunt Augusta for more than a week.

JACK: I haven't asked you to dine with me anywhere tonight.

ALGERNON: I know. You are absurdly careless about sending out invitations. It is very foolish of you. Nothing annoys people so much as not receiving invitations.

JACK: You had much better dine with your Aunt Augusta.

ALGERNON: I haven't the smallest intention of doing anything of the kind. To begin with, I dined there on Monday, and once a week is quite enough to dine with one's own relations. In the second place, whenever I do dine there I am always treated as a member of the family, and sent down with° either no woman at all, or two. In the third place, I know perfectly well whom she will place me next to, tonight. She will place me next Mary Farquhar, who always flirts with her own husband across the dinner table. That is not very pleasant. Indeed, it is not even decent — and that sort of thing is enormously on the increase. The amount of women in London who flirt with their own husbands is perfectly scandalous. It looks so bad. It is simply washing one's clean linen in public. Besides, now that I know you to be a confirmed Bunburyist I naturally want to talk to you about Bunburying. I want to tell you the rules.

JACK: I'm not a Bunburyist at all. If Gwendolen accepts me, I am going to kill my brother, indeed I think I'll kill him in any case. Cecily is a little too much interested in him. It is rather a bore. So I am going to get rid of Ernest. And I strongly advise you to do the same with Mr. — with your invalid friend who has the absurd name.

ALGERNON: Nothing will induce me to part with Bunbury, and if you ever get married, which seems to me extremely problematic, you will be very glad to know Bunbury. A man who marries without knowing Bunbury has a very tedious time of it.

JACK: That is nonsense. If I marry a charming girl like Gwendolen, and she is the only girl I ever saw in my life that I would marry, I certainly won't want to know Bunbury.

ALGERNON: Then your wife will. You don't seem to realize, that in married life three is company and two is none.

JACK (sententiously): That, my dear young friend, is the theory that the corrupt French drama has been propounding for the last fifty years.

ALGERNON: Yes; and that the happy English home has proved in half the time.

JACK: For heaven's sake, don't try to be cynical. It's perfectly easy to be cynical.

ALGERNON: My dear fellow, it isn't easy to be anything nowadays. There's such a lot of beastly competition about. (The sound of an electric bell is heard.) Ah! that must be Aunt Augusta. Only relatives, or creditors, ever ring in that Wagnerian° manner. Now, if I

get her out of the way for ten minutes, so that you can have an opportunity for proposing to Gwendolen, may I dine with you tonight at Willis's?

JACK: I suppose so, if you want to.

ALGERNON: Yes, but you must be serious about it. I hate people who are not serious about meals. It is so shallow of them.

(Enter Lane.)

LANE: Lady Bracknell and Miss Fairfax.

(Algernon goes forward to meet them. Enter Lady Bracknell and Gwendolen.)

LADY BRACKNELL: Good afternoon, dear Algernon, I hope you are behaving very well.

ALGERNON: I'm feeling very well, Aunt Augusta.

LADY BRACKNELL: That's not quite the same thing. In fact the two things rarely go together.

(Sees Jack and bows to him with icy coldness.)

ALGERNON (to Gwendolen): Dear me, you are smart!

GWENDOLEN: I am always smart! Aren't I, Mr. Worthing?

JACK: You're quite perfect, Miss Fairfax.

GWENDOLEN: Oh! I hope I am not that. It would leave no room for developments, and I intend to develop in many directions.

(Gwendolen and Jack sit down together in the corner.)

LADY BRACKNELL: I'm sorry if we are a little late Algernon, but I was obliged to call on dear Lady Harbury. I hadn't been there since her poor husband's death. I never saw a woman so altered; she looks quite twenty years younger. And now I'll have a cup of tea, and one of those nice cucumber sandwiches you promised me.

ALGERNON: Certainly, Aunt Augusta.

(Goes over to tea table.)

LADY BRACKNELL: Won't you come and sit here, Gwendolen?

GWENDOLEN: Thanks, Mama, I'm quite comfortable where I am.

ALGERNON (picking up empty plate in horror): Good heavens! Lane! Why are there no cucumber sandwiches? I ordered them specially.

LANE (gravely): There were no cucumbers in the market this morning, sir. I went down twice.

ALGERNON: No cucumbers?

LANE: No, sir. Not even for ready money.

ALGERNON: That will do, Lane, thank you.

LANE: Thank you, sir.   (Goes out.)

ALGERNON: I am greatly distressed, Aunt Augusta, about there being no cucumbers, not even for ready money.

LADY BRACKNELL: It really makes no matter, Algernon. I had some crumpets with Lady Harbury, who seems to me to be living entirely for pleasure now.

ALGERNON: I hear her hair has turned quite gold from grief.

sent down with: Assigned a woman to escort into the dining room for dinner. **Wagnerian:** Referring to the operas of Richard Wagner (1813–1883), whose music was popularly thought to be loud.

LADY BRACKNELL: It certainly has changed its color. From what cause I, of course, cannot say. (*Algernon crosses and hands tea.*) Thank you. I've quite a treat for you tonight, Algernon. I am going to send you down with Mary Farquhar. She is such a nice woman, and so attentive to her husband. It's delightful to watch them.

ALGERNON: I am afraid, Aunt Augusta, I shall have to give up the pleasure of dining with you tonight after all.

LADY BRACKNELL (*frowning*): I hope not, Algernon. It would put my table completely out. Your uncle would have to dine upstairs. Fortunately he is accustomed to that.

ALGERNON: It is a great bore, and, I need hardly say, a terrible disappointment to me, but the fact is I have just had a telegram to say that my poor friend Bunbury is very ill again. (*Exchanges glances with Jack.*) They seem to think I should be with him.

LADY BRACKNELL: It is very strange. This Mr. Bunbury seems to suffer from curiously bad health.

ALGERNON: Yes; poor Bunbury is a dreadful invalid.

LADY BRACKNELL: Well, I must say, Algernon, that I think it is high time that Mr. Bunbury made up his mind whether he was going to live or to die. This shilly-shallying with the question is absurd. Nor do I in any way approve of the modern sympathy with invalids. I consider it morbid. Illness of any kind is hardly a thing to be encouraged in others. Health is the primary duty of life. I am always telling that to your poor uncle, but he never seems to take much notice — as far as any improvement in his ailments goes. I should be much obliged if you would ask Mr. Bunbury, from me, to be kind enough not to have a relapse on Saturday, for I rely on you to arrange my music for me. It is my last reception, and one wants something that will encourage conversation, particularly at the end of the season when everyone has practically said whatever they had to say, which, in most cases, was probably not much.

ALGERNON: I'll speak to Bunbury, Aunt Augusta, if he is still conscious, and I think I can promise you he'll be all right by Saturday. Of course the music is a great difficulty. You see, if one plays good music, people don't listen, and if one plays bad music people don't talk. But I'll run over the program I've drawn out, if you will kindly come into the next room for a moment.

LADY BRACKNELL: Thank you, Algernon. It is very thoughtful of you. (*Rising, and following Algernon.*) I'm sure the program will be delightful, after a few expurgations. French songs I cannot possibly allow. People always seem to think that they are improper, and either look shocked, which is vulgar, or laugh, which is worse. But German sounds a thoroughly respectable language, and indeed, I believe is so. Gwendolen, you will accompany me.

GWENDOLEN: Certainly, Mama.

(*Lady Bracknell and Algernon go into the music room. Gwendolen remains behind.*)

JACK: Charming day it has been, Miss Fairfax.

GWENDOLEN: Pray don't talk to me about the weather Mr. Worthing. Whenever people talk to me about the weather, I always feel quite certain that they mean something else. And that makes me so nervous.

JACK: I do mean something else.

GWENDOLEN: I thought so. In fact, I am never wrong.

JACK: And I would like to be allowed to take advantage of Lady Bracknell's temporary absence —

GWENDOLEN: I would certainly advise you to do so. Mama has a way of coming back suddenly into a room that I have often had to speak to her about.

JACK (*nervously*): Miss Fairfax, ever since I met you I have admired you more than any girl — I have ever met since — I met you.

GWENDOLEN: Yes, I am quite aware of the fact. And I often wish that in public, at any rate, you had been more demonstrative. For me you have always had an irresistible fascination. Even before I met you I was far from indifferent to you. (*Jack looks at her in amazement.*) We live, as I hope you know Mr. Worthing, in an age of ideals. The fact is constantly mentioned in the more expensive monthly magazines, and has reached the provincial pulpits I am told: And my ideal has always been to love someone of the name of Ernest. There is something in that name that inspires absolute confidence. The moment Algernon first mentioned to me that he had a friend called Ernest, I knew I was destined to love you.

JACK: You really love me, Gwendolen?

GWENDOLEN: Passionately!

JACK: Darling! You don't know how happy you've made me.

GWENDOLEN: My own Ernest!

JACK: But you don't mean to say that you couldn't love me if my name wasn't Ernest?

GWENDOLEN: But your name is Ernest.

JACK: Yes, I know it is. But supposing it was something else? Do you mean to say you couldn't love me then?

GWENDOLEN (*glibly*): Ah! that is clearly a metaphysical speculation, and like most metaphysical speculations has very little reference at all to the actual facts of real life, as we know them.

JACK: Personally, darling, to speak quite candidly, I don't much care about the name of Ernest — I don't think the name suits me at all.

GWENDOLEN: It suits you perfectly. It is a divine name. It has a music of its own. It produces vibrations.

JACK: Well, really, Gwendolen, I must say that I think there are lots of other much nicer names. I think Jack, for instance, a charming name.

GWENDOLEN: Jack? — No, there is very little music in the name Jack, if any at all, indeed. It does not thrill. It produces absolutely no vibrations — I have known several Jacks, and they all, without exception, were more than usually plain. Besides, Jack is a notorious domesticity for John! And I pity any woman who is married to a man called John. She would probably never be allowed to know the entrancing pleasure of a single moment's solitude. The only really safe name is Ernest.

JACK: Gwendolen, I must get christened at once — I mean we must get married at once. There is no time to be lost.

GWENDOLEN: Married, Mr. Worthing?

JACK (*astounded*): Well — surely. You know that I love you, and you led me to believe, Miss Fairfax that you were not absolutely indifferent to me.

GWENDOLEN: I adore you. But you haven't proposed to me yet. Nothing has been said at all about marriage. The subject has not even been touched on.

JACK: Well — may I propose to you now?

GWENDOLEN: I think it would be an admirable opportunity. And to spare you any possible disappointment, Mr. Worthing, I think it only fair to tell you quite frankly beforehand that I am fully determined to accept you.

JACK: Gwendolen!

GWENDOLEN: Yes, Mr. Worthing, what have you got to say to me?

JACK: You know what I have got to say to you.

GWENDOLEN: Yes, but you don't say it.

JACK: Gwendolen, will you marry me?

(*Goes on his knees.*)

GWENDOLEN: Of course I will, darling. How long you have been about it! I am afraid you have had very little experience in how to propose.

JACK: My own one, I have never loved anyone in the world but you.

GWENDOLEN: Yes, but men often propose for practice. I know my brother Gerald does. All my girlfriends tell me so. What wonderfully blue eyes you have, Ernest! They are quite, quite blue. I hope you will always look at me just like that, especially when there are other people present.

(*Enter Lady Bracknell.*)

LADY BRACKNELL: Mr. Worthing! Rise, sir, from this semirecumbent posture. It is most indecorous.

GWENDOLEN: Mama! (*He tries to rise; she restrains him.*) I must beg you to retire. This is no place for you. Besides, Mr. Worthing has not quite finished yet.

LADY BRACKNELL: Finished what, may I ask?

GWENDOLEN: I am engaged to Mr. Worthing, Mama.

(*They rise together.*)

LADY BRACKNELL: Pardon me, you are not engaged to anyone. When you do become engaged to someone, I, or your father, should his health permit him, will inform you of the fact. An engagement should come on a young girl as a surprise, pleasant or unpleasant, as the case may be. It is hardly a matter that she could be allowed to arrange for herself — And now I have a few questions to put to you, Mr. Worthing. While I am making these inquiries, you, Gwendolen, will wait for me below in the carriage.

GWENDOLEN (*reproachfully*): Mama!

LADY BRACKNELL: In the carriage, Gwendolen! (*Gwendolen goes to the door. She and Jack blow kisses to each other behind Lady Bracknell's back. Lady Bracknell looks vaguely about as if she could not understand what the noise was. Finally turns round.*) Gwendolen, the carriage!

GWENDOLEN: Yes, Mama.

(*Goes out, looking back at Jack.*)

LADY BRACKNELL (*sitting down*): You can take a seat, Mr. Worthing.

(*Looks in her pocket for notebook and pencil.*)

JACK: Thank you, Lady Bracknell, I prefer standing.

LADY BRACKNELL (*pencil and notebook in hand*): I feel bound to tell you that you are not down on my list of eligible young men, although I have the same list as the dear Duchess of Bolton has. We work together, in fact. However, I am quite ready to enter your name, should your answers be what a really affectionate mother requires. Do you smoke?

JACK: Well, yes, I must admit I smoke.

LADY BRACKNELL: I am glad to hear it. A man should always have an occupation of some kind. There are far too many idle men in London as it is. How old are you?

JACK: Twenty-nine.

LADY BRACKNELL: A very good age to be married at. I have always been of opinion that a man who desires to get married should know either everything or nothing. Which do you know?

JACK (*after some hesitation*): I know nothing, Lady Bracknell.

LADY BRACKNELL: I am pleased to hear it. I do not approve of anything that tampers with natural ignorance. Ignorance is like a delicate exotic fruit; touch it and the bloom is gone. The whole theory of modern education is radically unsound. Fortunately in England, at any rate, education produces no effect whatsoever. If it did, it would prove a serious danger to the upper classes, and probably lead to acts of violence in Grosvenor Square. What is your income?

JACK: Between seven and eight thousand a year.

LADY BRACKNELL (*makes a note in her book*): In land, or in investments?

JACK: In investments, chiefly.

LADY BRACKNELL: That is satisfactory. What between the duties expected of one during one's lifetime, and the duties exacted from one after one's death, land has ceased to be either a profit or a pleasure. It gives one position, and prevents one from keeping it up. That's all that can be said about land.

JACK: I have a country house with some land, of course, attached to it, about fifteen hundred acres, I believe; but I don't depend on that for my real income. In fact, as far as I can make out, the poachers are the only people who make anything out of it.

LADY BRACKNELL: A country house! How many bedrooms? Well, that point can be cleared up afterwards. You have a town house, I hope? A girl with a simple, unspoiled nature, like Gwendolen, could hardly be expected to reside in the country.

JACK: Well, I own a house in Belgrave Square, but it is let by the year to Lady Bloxham. Of course, I can get it back whenever I like, at six months' notice.

LADY BRACKNELL: Lady Bloxham? I don't know her.

JACK: Oh, she goes about very little. She is a lady considerably advanced in years.

LADY BRACKNELL: Ah, nowadays that is no guarantee of respectability of character. What number in Belgrave Square?

JACK: 149.

LADY BRACKNELL (*shaking her head*): The unfashionable side. I thought there was something. However, that could easily be altered.

JACK: Do you mean the fashion, or the side?

LADY BRACKNELL (*sternly*): Both, if necessary, I presume. What are your politics?

JACK: Well, I am afraid I really have none. I am a Liberal Unionist.

LADY BRACKNELL: Oh, they count as Tories. They dine with us. Or come in the evening, at any rate. Now to minor matters. Are your parents living?

JACK: I have lost both my parents.

LADY BRACKNELL: Both? To lose one parent may be regarded as a misfortune — to lose *both* seems like carelessness. Who was your father? He was evidently a man of some wealth. Was he born in what the Radical papers call the purple of commerce, or did he rise from the ranks of the aristocracy?

JACK: I am afraid I really don't know. The fact is, Lady Bracknell, I said I had lost my parents. It would be nearer the truth to say that my parents seem to have lost me — I don't actually know who I am by birth. I was — well, I was found.

LADY BRACKNELL: Found!

JACK: The late Mr. Thomas Cardew, an old gentleman of a very charitable and kindly disposition, found me, and gave me the name of Worthing, because he happened to have a first-class ticket for Worthing in his pocket at the time. Worthing is a place in Sussex. It is a seaside resort.

LADY BRACKNELL: Where did the charitable gentleman who had a first-class ticket for this seaside resort find you?

JACK (*gravely*): In a handbag.

LADY BRACKNELL: A handbag?

JACK (*very seriously*): Yes, Lady Bracknell. I was in a handbag — a somewhat large, black leather handbag, with handles to it — an ordinary handbag in fact.

LADY BRACKNELL: In what locality did this Mr. James, or Thomas, Cardew come across this ordinary handbag?

JACK: In the cloakroom at Victoria Station. It was given to him in mistake for his own.

LADY BRACKNELL: The cloakroom at Victoria Station?

JACK: Yes. The Brighton line.

LADY BRACKNELL: The line is immaterial. Mr. Worthing, I confess I feel somewhat bewildered by what you have just told me. To be born, or at any rate bred, in a handbag, whether it had handles or not, seems to me to display a contempt for the ordinary decencies of family life that reminds one of the worst excesses of the French Revolution. And I presume you know what that unfortunate movement led to? As for the particular locality in which the handbag was found, a cloakroom at a railway station might serve to conceal a social indiscretion — has probably, indeed, been used for that purpose before now — but it could hardly be regarded as an assured basis for a recognized position in good society.

JACK: May I ask you then what you would advise me to do? I need hardly say I would do anything in the world to ensure Gwendolen's happiness.

LADY BRACKNELL: I would strongly advise you, Mr. Worthing, to try and acquire some relations as soon as possible, and to make a definite effort to produce at any rate one parent of either sex, before the season is quite over.

JACK: Well, I don't see how I could possibly manage to do that. I can produce the handbag at any moment. It is in my dressing room at home. I really think that should satisfy you, Lady Bracknell.

LADY BRACKNELL: Me, sir! What has it to do with me? You can hardly imagine that I and Lord Bracknell would dream of allowing our only daughter — a girl brought up with the utmost care — to marry into a cloakroom, and form an alliance with a parcel? Good morning, Mr. Worthing!

(*Lady Bracknell sweeps out in majestic indignation.*)

JACK: Good morning! (*Algernon, from the other room, strikes up the Wedding March. Jack looks perfectly furious, and goes to the door.*) For goodness' sake don't play that ghastly tune, Algy! How idiotic you are!

(*The music stops, and Algernon enters cheerily.*)

ALGERNON: Didn't it go off all right, old boy? You don't mean to say Gwendolen refused you? I know it is a way she has. She is always refusing people. I think it is most ill-natured of her.

JACK: Oh, Gwendolen is as right as a trivet. As far as she is concerned, we are engaged. Her mother is perfectly unbearable. Never met such a Gorgon° — I don't really know what a Gorgon is like, but I am quite sure that Lady Bracknell is one. In any case, she is a monster, without being a myth, which is rather unfair. I beg your pardon, Algy, I suppose I shouldn't talk about your own aunt in that way before you.

ALGERNON: My dear boy, I love hearing my relations abused. It is the only thing that makes me put up with them at all. Relations are simply a tedious pack of people, who haven't got the remotest knowledge

Gorgon: In Greek myth, one of three very ugly sisters who had, among other characteristics, serpents for hair.

of how to live, nor the smallest instinct about when to die.

JACK: Oh, that is nonsense!

ALGERNON: It isn't!

JACK: Well, I won't argue about the matter. You always want to argue about things.

ALGERNON: That is exactly what things were originally made for.

JACK: Upon my word, if I thought that, I'd shoot myself — (*A pause.*) You don't think there is any chance of Gwendolen becoming like her mother in about a hundred and fifty years, do you Algy?

ALGERNON: All women become like their mothers. That is their tragedy. No man does. That's his.

JACK: Is that clever?

ALGERNON: It is perfectly phrased! and quite as true as any observation in civilized life should be.

JACK: I am sick to death of cleverness. Everybody is clever nowadays. You can't go anywhere without meeting clever people. The thing has become an absolute public nuisance. I wish to goodness we had a few fools left.

ALGERNON: We have.

JACK: I should extremely like to meet them. What do they talk about?

ALGERNON: The fools? Oh! about the clever people, of course.

JACK: What fools!

ALGERNON: By the way, did you tell Gwendolen the truth about your being Ernest in town, and Jack in the country?

JACK (*in a very patronizing manner*): My dear fellow, the truth isn't quite the sort of thing one tells to a nice sweet refined girl. What extraordinary ideas you have about the way to behave to a woman!

ALGERNON: The only way to behave to a woman is to make love to her if she is pretty, and to someone else if she is plain.

JACK: Oh, that is nonsense.

ALGERNON: What about your brother? What about the profligate Ernest?

JACK: Oh, before the end of the week I shall have got rid of him. I'll say he died in Paris of apoplexy. Lots of people die of apoplexy, quite suddenly, don't they?

ALGERNON: Yes, but it's hereditary, my dear fellow. It's a sort of thing that runs in families. You had much better say a severe chill.

JACK: You are sure a severe chill isn't hereditary, or anything of that kind?

ALGERNON: Of course it isn't!

JACK: Very well, then. My poor brother Ernest is carried off suddenly in Paris, by a severe chill. That gets rid of him.

ALGERNON: But I thought you said that — Miss Cardew was a little too much interested in your poor brother Ernest? Won't she feel his loss a good deal?

JACK: Oh, that is all right. Cecily is not a silly romantic girl, I am glad to say. She has got a capital appetite,

goes long walks, and pays no attention at all to her lessons.

ALGERNON: I would rather like to see Cecily.

JACK: I will take very good care you never do. She is excessively pretty, and she is only just eighteen.

ALGERNON: Have you told Gwendolen yet that you have an excessively pretty ward who is only just eighteen?

JACK: Oh! one doesn't blurt these things out to people. Cecily and Gwendolen are perfectly certain to be extremely great friends. I'll bet you anything you like that half an hour after they have met, they will be calling each other sister.

ALGERNON: Women only do that when they have called each other a lot of other things first. Now, my dear boy, if we want to get a good table at Willis's, we really must go and dress. Do you know it is nearly seven?

JACK: (*irritably*): Oh! it always is nearly seven.

ALGERNON: Well, I'm hungry.

JACK: I never knew you when you weren't —

ALGERNON: What shall we do after dinner? Go to a theater?

JACK: Oh, no! I loathe listening.

ALGERNON: Well, let us go to the Club?

JACK: Oh, no! I hate talking.

ALGERNON: Well, we might trot round to the Empire° at ten?

JACK: Oh, no! I can't bear looking at things. It is so silly.

ALGERNON: Well, what shall we do?

JACK: Nothing!

ALGERNON: It is awfully hard work doing nothing. However, I don't mind hard work where there is no definite object of any kind.

(*Enter Lane.*)

LANE: Miss Fairfax.

(*Enter Gwendolen. Lane goes out.*)

ALGERNON: Gwendolen, upon my word!

GWENDOLEN: Algy, kindly turn your back. I have something very particular to say to Mr. Worthing.

ALGERNON: Really, Gwendolen, I don't think I can allow this at all.

GWENDOLEN: Algy, you always adopt a strictly immoral attitude towards life. You are not quite old enough to do that.

(*Algernon retires to the fireplace.*)

JACK: My own darling!

GWENDOLEN: Ernest, we may never be married. From the expression on Mama's face I fear we never shall. Few parents nowadays pay any regard to what their children say to them. The old-fashioned respect for the young is fast dying out. Whatever influence I ever had over Mama, I lost at the age of three. But although she may prevent us from becoming man and wife, and I may marry someone else, and marry often,

Empire: Empire Theatre, a London music hall that was also a rendezvous for prostitutes.

Scene from the Huntington Theatre Company's 1994 production of *The Importance of Being Earnest*.

nothing that she can possibly do can alter my eternal devotion to you.

JACK: Dear Gwendolen!

GWENDOLEN: The story of your romantic origin, as related to me by Mama, with unpleasing comments, has naturally stirred the deeper fibers of my nature. Your Christian name has an irresistible fascination. The simplicity of your character makes you exquisitely incomprehensible to me. Your town address at the Albany I have. What is your address in the country?

JACK: The Manor House, Woolton, Hertfordshire.

(*Algernon, who has been carefully listening, smiles to himself, and writes the address on his shirt cuff. Then picks up the Railway Guide.*)

GWENDOLEN: There is a good postal service, I suppose? It may be necessary to do something desperate. That of course will require serious consideration. I will communicate with you daily.

JACK: My own one!

GWENDOLEN: How long do you remain in town?

JACK: Till Monday.

GWENDOLEN: Good! Algy, you may turn round now.

ALGERNON: Thanks, I've turned round already.

GWENDOLEN: You may also ring the bell.

JACK: You will let me see you to your carriage, my own darling?

GWENDOLEN: Certainly.

JACK (*to Lane, who now enters*): I will see Miss Fairfax out.

LANE: Yes, sir.   (*Jack and Gwendolen go off.*)

(*Lane presents several letters on a salver to Algernon. It is to be surmised that they are bills, as Algernon, after looking at the envelopes, tears them up.*)

ALGERNON: A glass of sherry, Lane.

LANE: Yes, sir.

ALGERNON: Tomorrow, Lane, I'm going Bunburying.

LANE: Yes, sir.

ALGERNON: I shall probably not be back till Monday. You can put up my dress clothes, my smoking jacket, and all the Bunbury suits —

LANE: Yes, sir.   (*Handing sherry.*)

ALGERNON: I hope tomorrow will be a fine day, Lane.

LANE: It never is, sir.

ALGERNON: Lane, you're a perfect pessimist.

LANE: I do my best to give satisfaction, sir.

(*Enter Jack. Lane goes off.*)

JACK: There's a sensible, intellectual girl! the only girl I ever cared for in my life. (*Algernon is laughing immoderately.*) What on earth are you so amused at?

ALGERNON: Oh, I'm a little anxious about poor Bunbury, that is all.

JACK: If you don't take care, your friend Bunbury will get you into a serious scrape some day.

ALGERNON: I love scrapes. They are the only things that are never serious.

JACK: Oh, that's nonsense, Algy. You never talk anything but nonsense.

ALGERNON: Nobody ever does.

(*Jack looks indignantly at him, and leaves the room. Algernon lights a cigarette, reads his shirt cuff, and smiles.*)

ACT II

(*Scene: Garden at the Manor House. A flight of gray stone steps leads up to the house. The garden, an old-fashioned one, full of roses. Time of year, July. Basket chairs, and a table covered with books, are set under a large yew tree. Miss Prism discovered seated at the table. Cecily is at the back watering flowers.*)

MISS PRISM (*calling*): Cecily, Cecily! Surely such a utilitarian occupation as the watering of flowers is rather Moulton's duty than yours? Especially at a moment when intellectual pleasures await you. Your German grammar is on the table. Pray open it at page fifteen. We will repeat yesterday's lesson.

CECILY (*coming over very slowly*): But I don't like German. It isn't at all a becoming language. I know perfectly well that I look quite plain after my German lesson.

MISS PRISM: Child, you know how anxious your guardian is that you should improve yourself in every way. He laid particular stress on your German, as he was leaving for town yesterday. Indeed, he always lays stress on your German when he is leaving for town.

CECILY: Dear Uncle Jack is so very serious! Sometimes he is so serious that I think he cannot be quite well.

MISS PRISM (*drawing herself up*): Your guardian enjoys the best of health, and his gravity of demeanor is especially to be commended in one so comparatively young as he is. I know no one who has a higher sense of duty and responsibility.

CECILY: I suppose that is why he often looks a little bored when we three are together.

MISS PRISM: Cecily! I am surprised at you. Mr. Worthing has many troubles in his life. Idle merriment and triviality would be out of place in his conversation. You must remember his constant anxiety about that unfortunate young man his brother.

CECILY: I wish Uncle Jack would allow that unfortunate young man, his brother, to come down here some-

times. We might have a good influence over him, Miss Prism. I am sure you certainly would. You know German, and geology, and things of that kind influence a man very much.

(*Cecily begins to write in her diary.*)

MISS PRISM (*shaking her head*): I do not think that even I could produce any effect on a character that according to his own brother's admission is irretrievably weak and vacillating. Indeed I am not sure that I would desire to reclaim him. I am not in favor of this modern mania for turning bad people into good people at a moment's notice. As a man sows so let him reap. You must put away your diary, Cecily. I really don't see why you should keep a diary at all.

CECILY: I keep a diary in order to enter the wonderful secrets of my life. If I didn't write them down I should probably forget all about them.

MISS PRISM: Memory, my dear Cecily, is the diary that we all carry about with us.

CECILY: Yes, but it usually chronicles the things that have never happened, and couldn't possibly have happened. I believe that Memory is responsible for nearly all the three-volume novels that Mudie sends us.

MISS PRISM: Do not speak slightingly of the three-volume novel, Cecily. I wrote one myself in earlier days.

CECILY: Did you really, Miss Prism? How wonderfully clever you are! I hope it did not end happily? I don't like novels that end happily. They depress me so much.

MISS PRISM: The good ended happily, and the bad unhappily. That is what Fiction means.

CECILY: I suppose so. But it seems very unfair. And was your novel ever published?

MISS PRISM: Alas! no. The manuscript unfortunately was abandoned. I use the word in the sense of lost or mislaid. To your work, child, these speculations are profitless.

CECILY (*smiling*): But I see dear Dr. Chasuble coming up through the garden.

MISS PRISM (*rising and advancing*): Dr. Chasuble! This is indeed a pleasure.

(*Enter Canon Chasuble.*)

CHASUBLE: And how are we this morning? Miss Prism, you are, I trust, well?

CECILY: Miss Prism has just been complaining of a slight headache. I think it would do her so much good to have a short stroll with you in the park, Dr. Chasuble.

MISS PRISM: Cecily, I have not mentioned anything about a headache.

CECILY: No, dear Miss Prism, I know that, but I felt instinctively that you had a headache. Indeed I was thinking about that, and not about my German lesson, when the Rector came in.

CHASUBLE: I hope, Cecily, you are not inattentive.

CECILY: Oh, I am afraid I am.

CHASUBLE: That is strange. Were I fortunate enough to be Miss Prism's pupil, I would hang upon her lips.

(*Miss Prism glares.*) I spoke metaphorically. — My metaphor was drawn from bees. Ahem! Mr. Worthing, I suppose, has not returned from town yet?

MISS PRISM: We do not expect him till Monday afternoon.

CHASUBLE: Ah yes, he usually likes to spend his Sunday in London. He is not one of those whose sole aim is enjoyment, as, by all accounts, that unfortunate young man his brother seems to be. But I must not disturb Egeria° and her pupil any longer.

MISS PRISM: Egeria? My name is Laetitia, Doctor.

CHASUBLE (*bowing*): A classical allusion merely, drawn from the Pagan authors. I shall see you both no doubt at Evensong?

MISS PRISM: I think, dear Doctor, I will have a stroll with you. I find I have a headache after all, and a walk might do it good.

CHASUBLE: With pleasure, Miss Prism, with pleasure. We might go as far as the schools and back.

MISS PRISM: That would be delightful. Cecily, you will read your Political Economy in my absence. The chapter on the Fall of the Rupee° you may omit. It is somewhat too sensational. Even these metallic problems have their melodramatic side.

(*Goes down the garden with Dr. Chasuble.*)

CECILY (*picks up books and throws them back on table*): Horrid Political Economy! Horrid Geography! Horrid, horrid German!

(*Enter Merriman with a card on a salver.*)

MERRIMAN: Mr. Ernest Worthing has just driven over from the station. He has brought his luggage with him.

CECILY (*takes the card and reads it*): "Mr. Ernest Worthing, B.4, The Albany, W." Uncle Jack's brother! Did you tell him Mr. Worthing was in town?

MERRIMAN: Yes, Miss. He seemed very much disappointed. I mentioned that you and Miss Prism were in the garden. He said he was anxious to speak to you privately for a moment.

CECILY: Ask Mr. Ernest Worthing to come here. I suppose you had better talk to the housekeeper about a room for him.

MERRIMAN: Yes, Miss. (*Merriman goes off.*)

CECILY: I have never met any really wicked person before. I feel rather frightened. I am so afraid he will look just like everyone else.

(*Enter Algernon, very gay and debonair.*)

He does!

ALGERNON (*raising his hat*): You are my little cousin Cecily, I'm sure.

CECILY: You are under some strange mistake. I am not little. In fact, I believe I am more than usually tall for my age (*Algernon is rather taken aback.*) But I am

your cousin Cecily. You, I see from your card, are Uncle Jack's brother, my cousin Ernest, my wicked cousin Ernest.

ALGERNON: Oh! I am not really wicked at all, Cousin Cecily. You mustn't think that I am wicked.

CECILY: If you are not, then you have certainly been deceiving us all in a very inexcusable manner. I hope you have not been leading a double life, pretending to be wicked and being really good all the time. That would be hypocrisy.

ALGERNON (*looks at her in amazement*): Oh! Of course I have been rather reckless.

CECILY: I am glad to hear it.

ALGERNON: In fact, now you mention the subject, I have been very bad in my own small way.

CECILY: I don't think you should be so proud of that, though I am sure it must have been very pleasant.

ALGERNON: It is much pleasanter being here with you.

CECILY: I can't understand how you are here at all. Uncle Jack won't be back till Monday afternoon.

ALGERNON: That is a great disappointment. I am obliged to go up by the first train on Monday morning. I have a business appointment that I am anxious — to miss.

CECILY: Couldn't you miss it anywhere but in London?

ALGERNON: No: the appointment is in London.

CECILY: Well, I know, of course, how important it is not to keep a business engagement, if one wants to retain any sense of the beauty of life, but still I think you had better wait till Uncle Jack arrives. I know he wants to speak to you about your emigrating.

ALGERNON: About my what?

CECILY: Your emigrating. He has gone up to buy your outfit.

ALGERNON: I certainly wouldn't let Jack buy my outfit. He has no taste in neckties at all.

CECILY: I don't think you will require neckties. Uncle Jack is sending you to Australia.

ALGERNON: Australia! I'd sooner die.

CECILY: Well, he said at dinner on Wednesday night, that you would have to choose between this world, the next world, and Australia.

ALGERNON: Oh, well! The accounts I have received of Australia and the next world are not particularly encouraging. This world is good enough for me, Cousin Cecily.

CECILY: Yes, but are you good enough for it?

ALGERNON: I'm afraid I'm not that. That is why I want you to reform me. You might make that your mission, if you don't mind, Cousin Cecily.

CECILY: I'm afraid I've no time, this afternoon.

ALGERNON: Well, would you mind my reforming myself this afternoon?

CECILY: It is rather quixotic° of you. But I think you should try.

ALGERNON: I will. I feel better already.

CECILY: You are looking a little worse.

Egeria: Roman goddess of water. Fall of the Rupee: Reference to the Indian rupee, whose steady deflation between 1873 and 1893 caused the Indian governments finally to close the mints.

quixotic: Foolishly impractical, from the idealistic hero of Cervantes' *Don Quixote*.

ALGERNON: That is because I am hungry.

CECILY: How thoughtless of me. I should have remembered that when one is going to lead an entirely new life, one requires regular and wholesome meals. Won't you come in?

ALGERNON: Thank you. Might I have a buttonhole° first? I never have any appetite unless I have a buttonhole first.

CECILY: A Maréchal Niel?°

ALGERNON: No, I'd sooner have a pink rose.

CECILY: Why?   (Cuts a flower.)

ALGERNON: Because you are like a pink rose, Cousin Cecily.

CECILY: I don't think it can be right for you to talk to me like that. Miss Prism never says such things to me.

ALGERNON: Then Miss Prism is a shortsighted old lady. (Cecily puts the rose in his buttonhole.) You are the prettiest girl I ever saw.

CECILY: Miss Prism says that all good looks are a snare.

ALGERNON: They are a snare that every sensible man would like to be caught in.

CECILY: Oh! I don't think I would care to catch a sensible man. I shouldn't know what to talk to him about.

(They pass into the house. Miss Prism and Dr. Chasuble return.)

MISS PRISM: You are too much alone, dear Dr. Chasuble. You should get married. A misanthrope I can understand — a womanthrope, never!

CHASUBLE (with a scholar's shudder): Believe me, I do not deserve so neologistic a phrase. The precept as well as the practice of the Primitive Church was distinctly against matrimony.

MISS PRISM (sententiously): That is obviously the reason why the Primitive Church has not lasted up to the present day. And you do not seem to realize, dear Doctor, that by persistently remaining single, a man converts himself into a permanent public temptation. Men should be more careful; this very celibacy leads weaker vessels astray.

CHASUBLE: But is a man not equally attractive when married?

MISS PRISM: No married man is ever attractive except to his wife.

CHASUBLE: And often, I've been told, not even to her.

MISS PRISM: That depends on the intellectual sympathies of the woman. Maturity can always be depended on. Ripeness can be trusted. Young women are green. (Dr. Chasuble starts.) I spoke horticulturally. My metaphor was drawn from fruits. But where is Cecily?

CHASUBLE: Perhaps she followed us to the schools.

(Enter Jack slowly from the back of the garden. He is dressed in the deepest mourning, with crepe hatband and black gloves.)

MISS PRISM: Mr. Worthing!

CHASUBLE: Mr. Worthing?

buttonhole: Boutonniere.   Maréchal Niel: A yellow rose.

MISS PRISM: This is indeed a surprise. We did not look for you till Monday afternoon.

JACK (shakes Miss Prism's hand in a tragic manner): I have returned sooner than I expected. Dr. Chasuble, I hope you are well?

CHASUBLE: Dear Mr. Worthing, I trust this garb of woe does not betoken some terrible calamity?

JACK: My brother.

MISS PRISM: More shameful debts and extravagance?

CHASUBLE: Still leading his life of pleasure?

JACK (shaking his head): Dead!

CHASUBLE: Your brother Ernest dead?

JACK: Quite dead.

MISS PRISM: What a lesson for him! I trust he will profit by it.

CHASUBLE: Mr. Worthing, I offer you my sincere condolence. You have at least the consolation of knowing that you were always the most generous and forgiving of brothers.

JACK: Poor Ernest! He had many faults, but it is a sad, sad blow.

CHASUBLE: Very sad indeed. Were you with him at the end?

JACK: No. He died abroad, in Paris, in fact. I had a telegram last night from the manager of the Grand Hotel.

CHASUBLE: Was the cause of death mentioned?

JACK: A severe chill, it seems.

MISS PRISM: As a man sows, so shall he reap.

CHASUBLE (raising his hand): Charity, dear Miss Prism, charity! None of us are perfect. I myself am peculiarly susceptible to drafts. Will the interment take place here?

JACK: No. He seemed to have expressed a desire to be buried in Paris.

CHASUBLE: In Paris! (Shakes his head.) I fear that hardly points to any very serious state of mind at the last. You would no doubt wish me to make some slight allusion to this tragic domestic affliction next Sunday. (Jack presses his hand convulsively.) My sermon on the meaning of the manna in the wilderness can be adapted to almost any occasion, joyful, or, as in the present case, distressing. (All sigh.) I have preached it at harvest celebrations, christenings, confirmations, on days of humiliation and festal days. The last time I delivered it was in the Cathedral, as a charity sermon on behalf of the Society for the Prevention of Discontent among the Upper Orders. The Bishop, who was present, was much struck by some of the analogies I drew.

JACK: Ah! that reminds me, you mentioned christenings I think, Dr. Chasuble? I suppose you know how to christen all right? (Dr. Chasuble looks astounded.) I mean, of course, you are continually christening, aren't you?

MISS PRISM: It is, I regret to say, one of the Rector's most constant duties in this parish. I have often spoken to the poorer classes on the subject. But they don't seem to know what thrift is.

CHASUBLE: But is there any particular infant in whom you are interested, Mr. Worthing? Your brother was, I believe, unmarried, was he not?

JACK: Oh yes.

MISS PRISM (*bitterly*): People who live entirely for pleasure usually are.

JACK: But it is not for any child, dear Doctor. I am very fond of children. No! the fact is, I would like to be christened myself, this afternoon, if you have nothing better to do.

CHASUBLE: But surely, Mr. Worthing, you have been christened already?

JACK: I don't remember anything about it.

CHASUBLE: But have you any grave doubts on the subject?

JACK: I certainly intend to have. Of course I don't know if the thing would bother you in any way, or if you think I am a little too old now.

CHASUBLE: Not at all. The sprinkling, and, indeed, the immersion of adults is a perfectly canonical practice.

JACK: Immersion!

CHASUBLE: You need have no apprehensions. Sprinkling is all that is necessary, or indeed I think advisable. Our weather is so changeable. At what hour would you wish the ceremony performed?

JACK: Oh, I might trot round about five if that would suit you.

CHASUBLE: Perfectly, perfectly! In fact I have two similar ceremonies to perform at that time. A case of twins that occurred recently in one of the outlying cottages on your own estate. Poor Jenkins the carter, a most hardworking man.

JACK: Oh! I don't see much fun in being christened along with other babies. It would be childish. Would half-past five do?

CHASUBLE: Admirably! Admirably! (*Takes out watch.*) And now, dear Mr. Worthing, I will not intrude any longer into a house of sorrow. I would merely beg you not to be too much bowed down by grief. What seem to us bitter trials are often blessings in disguise.

MISS PRISM: This seems to me a blessing of an extremely obvious kind.

(*Enter Cecily from the house.*)

CECILY: Uncle Jack! Oh, I am pleased to see you back. But what horrid clothes you have got on! Do go and change them.

MISS PRISM: Cecily!

CHASUBLE: My child! my child!

(*Cecily goes towards Jack; he kisses her brow in a melancholy manner.*)

CECILY: What is the matter, Uncle Jack? Do look happy! You look as if you had toothache, and I have got such a surprise for you. Who do you think is in the dining room? Your brother!

JACK: Who?

CECILY: Your brother Ernest. He arrived about half an hour ago.

JACK: What nonsense! I haven't got a brother.

CECILY: Oh, don't say that. However badly he may have behaved to you in the past he is still your brother. You couldn't be so heartless as to disown him. I'll tell him to come out. And you will shake hands with him, won't you, Uncle Jack?

(*Runs back into the house.*)

CHASUBLE: These are very joyful tidings.

MISS PRISM: After we had all been resigned to his loss, his sudden return seems to me peculiarly distressing.

JACK: My brother is in the dining room? I don't know what it all means. I think it is perfectly absurd.

(*Enter Algernon and Cecily hand in hand. They come slowly up to Jack.*)

JACK: Good heavens!   (*Motions Algernon away.*)

ALGERNON: Brother John, I have come down from town to tell you that I am very sorry for all the trouble I have given you, and that I intend to lead a better life in the future.

(*Jack glares at him and does not take his hand.*)

CECILY: Uncle Jack, you are not going to refuse your own brother's hand?

JACK: Nothing will induce me to take his hand. I think his coming down here disgraceful. He knows perfectly well why.

CECILY: Uncle Jack, do be nice. There is some good in everyone. Ernest has just been telling me about his poor invalid friend Mr. Bunbury whom he goes to visit so often. And surely there must be much good in one who is kind to an invalid, and leaves the pleasures of London to sit by a bed of pain.

JACK Oh! he has been talking about Bunbury has he?

CECILY: Yes, he has told me all about poor Mr. Bunbury, and his terrible state of health.

JACK: Bunbury! Well, I won't have him talk to you about Bunbury or about anything else. It is enough to drive one perfectly frantic.

ALGERNON: Of course I admit that the faults were all on my side. But I must say that I think that Brother John's coldness to me is peculiarly painful. I expected a more enthusiastic welcome, especially considering it is the first time I have come here.

CECILY: Uncle Jack, if you don't shake hands with Ernest I will never forgive you.

JACK: Never forgive me?

CECILY: Never, never, never!

JACK: Well, this is the last time I shall ever do it.

(*Shakes hands with Algernon and glares.*)

CHASUBLE: It's pleasant, is it not, to see so perfect a reconciliation? I think we might leave the two brothers together.

MISS PRISM: Cecily, you will come with us.

CECILY: Certainly, Miss Prism. My little task of reconciliation is over.

CHASUBLE: You have done a beautiful action today, dear child.

MISS PRISM: We must not be premature in our judgments.
CECILY: I feel very happy.   (*They all go off.*)
JACK: You young scoundrel, Algy, you must get out of this place as soon as possible. I don't allow any Bunburying here.

(*Enter Merriman.*)

MERRIMAN: I have put Mr. Ernest's things in the room next to yours, sir. I suppose that is all right?
JACK: What?
MERRIMAN: Mr. Ernest's luggage, sir. I have unpacked it and put it in the room next to your own.
JACK: His luggage?
MERRIMAN: Yes, sir. Three portmanteaus, a dressing case, two hatboxes, and a large luncheon basket.
ALGERNON: I am afraid I can't stay more than a week this time.
JACK: Merriman, order the dog cart at once. Mr. Ernest has been suddenly called back to town.
MERRIMAN: Yes, sir.   (*Goes back into the house.*)
ALGERNON: What a fearful liar you are, Jack. I have not been called back to town at all.
JACK: Yes, you have.
ALGERNON: I haven't heard anyone call me.
JACK: Your duty as a gentleman calls you back.
ALGERNON: My duty as a gentleman has never interfered with my pleasures in the smallest degree.
JACK: I can quite understand that.
ALGERNON: Well, Cecily is a darling.
JACK: You are not to talk of Miss Cardew like that. I don't like it.
ALGERNON: Well, I don't like your clothes. You look perfectly ridiculous in them. Why on earth don't you go up and change? It is perfectly childish to be in deep mourning for a man who is actually staying for a whole week in your house as a guest. I call it grotesque.
JACK: You are certainly not staying with me for a whole week as a guest or anything else. You have got to leave — by the four-five train.
ALGERNON: I certainly won't leave you so long as you are in mourning. It would be most unfriendly. If I were in mourning you would stay with me, I suppose. I should think it very unkind if you didn't.
JACK: Well, will you go if I change my clothes?
ALGERNON: Yes, if you are not too long. I never saw anybody take so long to dress, and with such little result.
JACK: Well, at any rate, that is better than being always overdressed as you are.
ALGERNON: If I am occasionally a little overdressed, I make up for it by being always immensely overeducated.
JACK: Your vanity is ridiculous, your conduct an outrage, and your presence in my garden utterly absurd. However, you have got to catch the four-five, and I hope you will have a pleasant journey back to town. This Bunburying, as you call it, has not been a great success for you.
                              (*Goes into the house.*)

ALGERNON: I think it has been a great success. I'm in love with Cecily, and that is everything.

(*Enter Cecily at the back of the garden. She picks up the can and begins to water the flowers.*)

But I must see her before I go, and make arrangements for another Bunbury. Ah, there she is.
CECILY: Oh, I merely came back to water the roses. I thought you were with Uncle Jack.
ALGERNON: He's gone to order the dog cart for me.
CECILY: Oh, is he going to take you for a nice drive?
ALGERNON: He's going to send me away.
CECILY: Then have we got to part?
ALGERNON: I am afraid so. It's a very painful parting.
CECILY: It is always painful to part from people whom one has known for a very brief space of time. The absence of old friends one can endure with equanimity. But even a momentary separation from anyone to whom one has just been introduced is almost unbearable.
ALGERNON: Thank you.

(*Enter Merriman.*)

MERRIMAN: The dog cart is at the door, sir.

(*Algernon looks appealingly at Cecily.*)

CECILY: It can wait, Merriman — for — five minutes.
MERRIMAN: Yes, miss.   (*Exit Merriman.*)
ALGERNON: I hope, Cecily, I shall not offend you if I state quite frankly and openly that you seem to me to be in every way the visible personification of absolute perfection.
CECILY: I think your frankness does you great credit, Ernest. If you will allow me I will copy your remarks into my diary.
            (*Goes over to table and begins writing in diary.*)
ALGERNON: Do you really keep a diary? I'd give anything to look at it. May I?
CECILY: Oh no. (*Puts her hand over it.*) You see, it is simply a very young girl's record of her own thoughts and impressions, and consequently meant for publication. When it appears in volume form I hope you will order a copy. But pray, Ernest, don't stop. I delight in taking down from dictation. I have reached "absolute perfection." You can go on. I am quite ready for more.
ALGERNON (*somewhat taken aback*): Ahem! Ahem!
CECILY: Oh, don't cough, Ernest. When one is dictating one should speak fluently and not cough. Besides, I don't know how to spell a cough.

(*Writes as Algernon speaks.*)

ALGERNON (*speaking very rapidly*): Cecily, ever since I first looked upon your wonderful and incomparable beauty, I have dared to love you wildly, passionately, devotedly, hopelessly.
CECILY: I don't think that you should tell me that you love me wildly, passionately, devotedly, hopelessly. Hopelessly doesn't seem to make much sense, does it?
ALGERNON: Cecily!

(Enter Merriman.)

MERRIMAN: The dog cart is waiting, sir.

ALGERNON: Tell it to come round next week, at the same hour.

MERRIMAN *(looks at Cecily, who makes no sign)*: Yes, sir.   *(Merriman retires.)*

CECILY: Uncle Jack would be very much annoyed if he knew you were staying on till next week, at the same hour.

ALGERNON: Oh, I don't care about Jack. I don't care for anybody in the whole world but you. I love you, Cecily. You will marry me, won't you?

CECILY: You silly boy! Of course. Why, we have been engaged for the last three months.

ALGERNON: For the last three months?

CECILY: Yes, it will be exactly three months on Thursday.

ALGERNON: But how did we become engaged?

CECILY: Well, ever since dear Uncle Jack first confessed to us that he had a younger brother who was very wicked and bad, you of course have formed the chief topic of conversation between myself and Miss Prism. And of course a man who is much talked about is always very attractive. One feels there must be something in him after all. I daresay it was foolish of me, but I fell in love with you, Ernest.

ALGERNON: Darling! And when was the engagement actually settled?

CECILY: On the 14th of February last. Worn out by your entire ignorance of my existence, I determined to end the matter one way or the other, and after a long struggle with myself I accepted you under this dear old tree here. The next day I bought this little ring in your name, and this is the little bangle with the true lovers' knot I promised you always to wear.

ALGERNON: Did I give you this? It's very pretty, isn't it?

CECILY: Yes, you've wonderfully good taste, Ernest. It's the excuse I've always given for your leading such a bad life. And this is the box in which I keep all your dear letters.

(Kneels at table, opens box, and produces letters tied up with blue ribbon.)

ALGERNON: My letters! But my own sweet Cecily, I have never written you any letters.

CECILY: You need hardly remind me of that, Ernest. I remember only too well that I was forced to write your letters for you. I wrote always three times a week, and sometimes oftener.

ALGERNON: Oh, do let me read them, Cecily!

CECILY: Oh, I couldn't possibly. They would make you far too conceited. *(Replaces box.)* The three you wrote me after I had broken off the engagement are so beautiful, and so badly spelled, that even now I can hardly read them without crying a little.

ALGERNON: But was our engagement ever broken off?

CECILY: Of course it was. On the 22nd of last March. You can see the entry if you like. *(Shows diary.)* "Today I broke off my engagement with Ernest. I feel it is better to do so. The weather still continues charming."

ALGERNON: But why on earth did you break it off? What had I done? I had done nothing at all. Cecily, I am very much hurt indeed to hear you broke it off. Particularly when the weather was so charming.

CECILY: It would hardly have been a really serious engagement if it hadn't been broken off at least once. But I forgave you before the week was out.

ALGERNON *(crossing to her, and kneeling)*: What a perfect angel you are, Cecily.

CECILY: You dear romantic boy. *(He kisses her; she puts her fingers through his hair.)* I hope your hair curls naturally, does it?

ALGERNON: Yes, darling, with a little help from others.

CECILY: I am so glad.

ALGERNON: You'll never break off our engagement again, Cecily?

CECILY: I don't think I could break it off now that I have actually met you. Besides, of course, there is the question of your name.

ALGERNON *(nervously)*: Yes, of course.

CECILY: You must not laugh at me, darling, but it had always been a girlish dream of mine to love someone whose name was Ernest. *(Algernon rises, Cecily also.)* There is something in that name that seems to inspire absolute confidence. I pity any poor married woman whose husband is not called Ernest.

ALGERNON: But, my dear child, do you mean to say you could not love me if I had some other name?

CECILY: But what name?

ALGERNON: Oh, any name you like — Algernon — for instance —

CECILY: But I don't like the name of Algernon.

ALGERNON: Well, my own dear, sweet, loving little darling, I really can't see why you should object to the name of Algernon. It is not at all a bad name. In fact, it is rather an aristocratic name. Half of the chaps who get into the Bankruptcy Court are called Algernon. But seriously, Cecily — *(moving to her)* — if my name was Algy, couldn't you love me?

CECILY *(rising)*: I might respect you, Ernest, I might admire your character, but I fear that I should not be able to give you my undivided attention.

ALGERNON: Ahem! Cecily! *(Picking up hat.)* Your Rector here is, I suppose, thoroughly experienced in the practice of all the rites and ceremonials of the Church?

CECILY: Oh yes. Dr. Chasuble is a most learned man. He has never written a single book, so you can imagine how much he knows.

ALGERNON: I must see him at once on a most important christening — I mean on most important business.

CECILY: Oh!

ALGERNON: I shan't be away more than half an hour.

CECILY: Considering that we have been engaged since February the 14th, and that I only met you today for the first time, I think it is rather hard that you should leave me for so long a period as half an hour. Couldn't you make it twenty minutes?

ALGERNON: I'll be back in no time.

(*Kisses her and rushes down the garden.*)

CECILY: What an impetuous boy he is! I like his hair so much. I must enter his proposal in my diary.

(*Enter Merriman.*)

MERRIMAN: A Miss Fairfax has just called to see Mr. Worthing. On very important business Miss Fairfax states.

CECILY: Isn't Mr. Worthing in his library?

MERRIMAN: Mr. Worthing went over in the direction of the Rectory some time ago.

CECILY: Pray ask the lady to come out here; Mr. Worthing is sure to be back soon. And you can bring tea.

MERRIMAN: Yes, miss.   (*Goes out.*)

CECILY: Miss Fairfax! I suppose one of the many good elderly women who are associated with Uncle Jack in some of his philanthropic work in London. I don't quite like women who are interested in philanthropic work. I think it is so forward of them.

(*Enter Merriman.*)

MERRIMAN: Miss Fairfax.

(*Enter Gwendolen. Exit Merriman.*)

CECILY (*advancing to meet her*): Pray let me introduce myself to you. My name is Cecily Cardew.

GWENDOLEN: Cecily Cardew? (*Moving to her and shaking hands.*) What a very sweet name! Something tells me that we are going to be great friends. I like you already more than I can say. My first impressions of people are never wrong.

CECILY: How nice of you to like me so much after we have known each other such a comparatively short time. Pray sit down.

GWENDOLEN (*still standing up*): I may call you Cecily, may I not?

CECILY: With pleasure!

GWENDOLEN: And you will always call me Gwendolen, won't you?

CECILY: If you wish.

GWENDOLEN: Then that is all quite settled, is it not?

CECILY: I hope so.

(*A pause. They both sit down together.*)

GWENDOLEN: Perhaps this might be a favorable opportunity for my mentioning who I am. My father is Lord Bracknell. You have never heard of Papa, I suppose?

CECILY: I don't think so.

GWENDOLEN: Outside the family circle, Papa, I am glad to say, is entirely unknown. I think that is quite as it should be. The home seems to me to be the proper sphere for the man. And certainly once a man begins to neglect his domestic duties he becomes painfully effeminate, does he not? And I don't like that. It makes men so very attractive. Cecily, Mama, whose views on education are remarkably strict, has brought me up to be extremely shortsighted; it is part of her system, so do you mind my looking at you through my glasses?

CECILY: Oh! not at all, Gwendolen. I am very fond of being looked at.

GWENDOLEN (*after examining Cecily carefully through a lorgnette*): You are here on a short visit I suppose?

CECILY: Oh no! I live here.

GWENDOLEN (*severely*): Really? Your mother, no doubt, or some female relative of advanced years, resides here also?

CECILY: Oh no! I have no mother, nor, in fact, any relations.

GWENDOLEN: Indeed?

CECILY: My dear guardian, with the assistance of Miss Prism, has the arduous task of looking after me.

GWENDOLEN: Your guardian?

CECILY: Yes, I am Mr. Worthing's ward.

GWENDOLEN: Oh! It is strange he never mentioned to me that he had a ward. How secretive of him! He grows more interesting hourly. I am not sure, however, that the news inspires me with feelings of unmixed delight. (*Rising and going to her.*) I am very fond of you, Cecily; I have liked you ever since I met you! But I am bound to state that now that I know that you are Mr. Worthing's ward, I cannot help expressing a wish you were — well just a little older than you seem to be — and not quite so very alluring in appearance. In fact, if I may speak candidly —

CECILY: Pray do! I think that whenever one has anything unpleasant to say, one should always be quite candid.

GWENDOLEN: Well, to speak with perfect candor, Cecily, I wish that you were fully forty-two, and more than usually plain for your age. Ernest has a strong upright nature. He is the very soul of truth and honor. Disloyalty would be as impossible to him as deception. But even men of the noblest possible moral character are extremely susceptible to the influence of the physical charms of others. Modern, no less than Ancient History, supplies us with many most painful examples of what I refer to. If it were not so, indeed, History would be quite unreadable.

CECILY: I beg your pardon, Gwendolen, did you say Ernest?

GWENDOLEN: Yes.

CECILY: Oh, but it is not Mr. Ernest Worthing who is my guardian. It is his brother — his elder brother.

GWENDOLEN (*sitting down again*): Ernest never mentioned to me that he had a brother.

CECILY: I am sorry to say they have not been on good terms for a long time.

GWENDOLEN: Ah! that accounts for it. And now that I think of it I have never heard any man mention his brother. The subject seems distasteful to most men. Cecily, you have lifted a load from my mind. I was growing almost anxious. It would have been terrible if any cloud had come across a friendship like ours, would it not? Of course you are quite, quite sure that it is not Mr. Ernest Worthing who is your guardian?

CECILY: Quite sure. (*A pause.*) In fact, I am going to be his.

GWENDOLEN (*inquiringly*): I beg your pardon?

CECILY (*rather shy and confidingly*): Dearest Gwendolen, there is no reason why I should make a secret of it to you. Our little county newspaper is sure to chronicle the fact next week. Mr. Ernest Worthing and I are engaged to be married.

GWENDOLEN (*quite politely, rising*): My darling Cecily, I think there must be some slight error. Mr. Ernest Worthing is engaged to me. The announcement will appear in the *Morning Post* on Saturday at the latest.

CECILY (*very politely, rising*): I am afraid you must be under some misconception. Ernest proposed to me exactly ten minutes ago.   (*Shows diary.*)

GWENDOLEN (*examines diary through her lorgnette carefully*): It is certainly very curious, for he asked me to be his wife yesterday afternoon at 5:30. If you would care to verify the incident, pray do so. (*Produces diary of her own.*) I never travel without my diary. One should always have something sensational to read in the train. I am so sorry, dear Cecily, if it is any disappointment to you, but I am afraid *I* have the prior claim.

CECILY: It would distress me more than I can tell you, dear Gwendolen, if it caused you any mental or physical anguish, but I feel bound to point out that since Ernest proposed to you he clearly has changed his mind.

GWENDOLEN (*meditatively*): If the poor fellow has been entrapped into any foolish promise I shall consider it my duty to rescue him at once, and with a firm hand.

CECILY (*thoughtfully and sadly*): Whatever unfortunate entanglement my dear boy may have got into, I will never reproach him with it after we are married.

GWENDOLEN: Do you allude to me, Miss Cardew, as an entanglement? You are presumptuous. On an occasion of this kind it becomes more than a moral duty to speak one's mind. It becomes a pleasure.

CECILY: Do you suggest, Miss Fairfax, that I entrapped Ernest into an engagement? How dare you? This is no time for wearing the shallow mask of manners. When I see a spade I call it a spade.

GWENDOLEN (*satirically*): I am glad to say that I have never seen a spade. It is obvious that our social spheres have been widely different.

(*Enter Merriman, followed by the Footman. He carries a salver, tablecloth, and plate stand. Cecily is about to retort. The presence of the servants exercises a restraining influence, under which both girls chafe.*)

MERRIMAN: Shall I lay tea here as usual, miss?

CECILY (*sternly, in a calm voice*): Yes, as usual.

(*Merriman begins to clear table and lay cloth. A long pause. Cecily and Gwendolen glare at each other.*)

GWENDOLEN: Are there many interesting walks in the vicinity, Miss Cardew?

CECILY: Oh! Yes! a great many. From the top of one of the hills quite close one can see five counties.

GWENDOLEN: Five counties! I don't think I should like that. I hate crowds.

CECILY (*sweetly*): I suppose that is why you live in town?

(*Gwendolen bites her lip, and beats her foot nervously with her parasol.*)

GWENDOLEN (*looking round*): Quite a well-kept garden this is, Miss Cardew.

CECILY: So glad you like it, Miss Fairfax.

GWENDOLEN: I had no idea there were any flowers in the country.

CECILY: Oh, flowers are as common here, Miss Fairfax, as people are in London.

GWENDOLEN: Personally I cannot understand how anybody manages to exist in the country, if anybody who is anybody does. The country always bores me to death.

CECILY: Ah! This is what the newspapers call agricultural depression, is it not? I believe the aristocracy are suffering very much from it just at present. It is almost an epidemic amongst them, I have been told. May I offer you some tea, Miss Fairfax?

GWENDOLEN (*with elaborate politeness*): Thank you. (*Aside.*) Detestable girl! But I require tea!

CECILY (*sweetly*): Sugar?

GWENDOLEN (*superciliously*): No, thank you. Sugar is not fashionable anymore.

(*Cecily looks angrily at her, takes up the tongs, and puts four lumps of sugar into the cup.*)

CECILY (*severely*): Cake or bread and butter?

GWENDOLEN (*in a bored manner*): Bread and butter, please. Cake is rarely seen at the best houses nowadays.

CECILY (*cuts a very large slice of cake, and puts it on the tray*): Hand that to Miss Fairfax.

(*Merriman does so, and goes out with Footman. Gwendolen drinks the tea and makes a grimace. Puts down cup at once, reaches out her hand to the bread and butter, looks at it, and finds it is cake. Rises in indignation.*)

GWENDOLEN: You have filled my tea with lumps of sugar, and though I asked most distinctly for bread and butter, you have given me cake. I am known for the gentleness of my disposition, and the extraordinary sweetness of my nature, but I warn you, Miss Cardew, you may go too far.

CECILY (*rising*): To save my poor, innocent, trusting boy from the machinations of any other girl there are no lengths to which I would not go.

GWENDOLEN: From the moment I saw you I distrusted you. I felt that you were false and deceitful. I am never deceived in such matters. My first impressions of people are invariably right.

CECILY: It seems to me, Miss Fairfax, that I am trespassing on your valuable time. No doubt you have many other calls of a similar character to make in the neighborhood.

(*Enter Jack.*)

GWENDOLEN (*catching sight of him*): Ernest! My own Ernest!

JACK: Gwendolen! Darling! (*Offers to kiss her.*)

GWENDOLEN (*drawing back*): A moment! May I ask if you are engaged to be married to this young lady? (*Points to Cecily.*)

JACK (*laughing*): To dear little Cecily! Of course not! What could have put such an idea into your pretty little head?

GWENDOLEN: Thank you. You may! (*Offers her cheek.*)

CECILY (*very sweetly*): I knew there must be some misunderstanding, Miss Fairfax. The gentleman whose arm is at present round your waist is my dear guardian, Mr. John Worthing.

GWENDOLEN: I beg your pardon?

CECILY: This is Uncle Jack.

GWENDOLEN (*receding*): Jack! Oh!

(*Enter Algernon.*)

CECILY: Here is Ernest.

ALGERNON (*goes straight over to Cecily without noticing anyone else*): My own love! (*Offers to kiss her.*)

CECILY (*drawing back*): A moment, Ernest! May I ask you — are you engaged to be married to this young lady?

ALGERNON (*looking round*): To what young lady? Good heavens! Gwendolen!

CECILY: Yes! to good heavens, Gwendolen, I mean to Gwendolen.

ALGERNON (*laughing*): Of course not! What could have put such an idea into your pretty little head?

CECILY: Thank you. (*Presenting her cheek to be kissed.*) You may. (*Algernon kisses her.*)

GWENDOLEN: I felt there was some slight error, Miss Cardew. The gentleman who is now embracing you is my cousin, Mr. Algernon Moncrieff.

CECILY (*breaking away from Algernon*): Algernon Moncrieff! Oh!

(*The two girls move towards each other and put their arms round each other's waists as if for protection.*)

CECILY: Are you called Algernon?

ALGERNON: I cannot deny it.

CECILY: Oh!

GWENDOLEN: Is your name really John?

JACK (*standing rather proudly*): I could deny it if I liked. I could deny anything if I liked. But my name certainly is John. It has been John for years.

CECILY (*to Gwendolen*): A gross deception has been practiced on both of us.

GWENDOLEN: My poor wounded Cecily!

CECILY: My sweet wronged Gwendolen!

GWENDOLEN (*slowly and seriously*): You will call me sister, will you not?

(*They embrace. Jack and Algernon groan and walk up and down.*)

CECILY (*rather brightly*): There is just one question I would like to be allowed to ask my guardian.

GWENDOLEN: An admirable idea! Mr. Worthing, there is just one question I would like to be permitted to put to you. Where is your brother Ernest? We are both engaged to be married to your brother Ernest, so it is a matter of some importance to us to know where your brother Ernest is at present.

JACK (*slowly and hesitatingly*): Gwendolen — Cecily — it is very painful for me to be forced to speak the truth. It is the first time in my life that I have ever been reduced to such a painful position, and I am really quite inexperienced in doing anything of the kind. However I will tell you quite frankly that I have no brother Ernest. I have no brother at all. I never had a brother in my life, and I certainly have not the smallest intention of ever having one in the future.

CECILY (*surprised*): No brother at all?

JACK (*cheerily*): None!

GWENDOLEN (*severely*): Had you never a brother of any kind?

JACK (*pleasantly*): Never. Not even of any kind.

GWENDOLEN: I am afraid it is quite clear, Cecily, that neither of us is engaged to be married to anyone.

CECILY: It is not a very pleasant position for a young girl suddenly to find herself in. Is it?

GWENDOLEN: Let us go into the house. They will hardly venture to come after us there.

CECILY: No, men are so cowardly, aren't they?

(*They retire into the house with scornful looks.*)

JACK: This ghastly state of things is what you call Bunburying, I suppose?

ALGERNON: Yes, and a perfectly wonderful Bunbury it is. The most wonderful Bunbury I have ever had in my life.

JACK: Well, you've no right whatsoever to Bunbury here.

ALGERNON: That is absurd. One has a right to Bunbury anywhere one chooses. Every serious Bunburyist knows that.

JACK: Serious Bunburyist! Good heavens!

ALGERNON: Well, one must be serious about something, if one wants to have any amusement in life. I happen to be serious about Bunburying. What on earth you are serious about I haven't got the remotest idea. About everything, I should fancy. You have such an absolutely trivial nature.

JACK: Well, the only small satisfaction I have in the whole of this wretched business is that your friend Bunbury is quite exploded. You won't be able to run down to the country quite so often as you used to do, dear Algy. And a very good thing too.

ALGERNON: Your brother is a little off color, isn't he, dear Jack? You won't be able to disappear to London quite so frequently as your wicked custom was. And not a bad thing either.

JACK: As for your conduct towards Miss Cardew, I must say that your taking in a sweet, simple, innocent girl like that is quite inexcusable. To say nothing of the fact that she is my ward.

ALGERNON: I can see no possible defense at all for your deceiving a brilliant, clever, thoroughly experienced young lady like Miss Fairfax. To say nothing of the fact that she is my cousin.

JACK: I wanted to be engaged to Gwendolen, that is all. I love her.

ALGERNON: Well, I simply wanted to be engaged to Cecily. I adore her.

JACK: There is certainly no chance of your marrying Miss Cardew.

ALGERNON: I don't think there is much likelihood, Jack, of you and Miss Fairfax being united.

JACK: Well, that is no business of yours.

ALGERNON: If it was my business, I wouldn't talk about it. (*Begins to eat muffins.*) It is very vulgar to talk about one's business. Only people like stockbrokers do that, and then merely at dinner parties.

JACK: How you can sit there, calmly eating muffins when we are in this horrible trouble. I can't make out. You seem to me to be perfectly heartless.

ALGERNON: Well, I can't eat muffins in an agitated manner. The butter would probably get on my cuffs. One should always eat muffins quite calmly. It is the only way to eat them.

JACK: I say it's perfectly heartless your eating muffins at all, under the circumstances.

ALGERNON: When I am in trouble, eating is the only thing that consoles me. Indeed, when I am in really great trouble, as anyone who knows me intimately will tell you, I refuse everything except food and drink. At the present moment I am eating muffins because I am unhappy. Besides, I am particularly fond of muffins. (*Rising.*)

JACK (*rising*): Well, that is no reason why you should eat them all in that greedy way.

(*Takes muffins from Algernon.*)

ALGERNON (*offering tea cake*): I wish you would have tea cake instead. I don't like tea cake.

JACK: Good heavens! I suppose a man may eat his own muffins in his own garden.

ALGERNON: But you have just said it was perfectly heartless to eat muffins.

JACK: I said it was perfectly heartless of you, under the circumstances. That is a very different thing.

ALGERNON: That may be, but the muffins are the same. (*He seizes the muffin dish from Jack.*)

JACK: Algy, I wish to goodness you would go.

ALGERNON: You can't possibly ask me to go without having some dinner. It's absurd. I never go without my dinner. No one ever does, except vegetarians and people like that. Besides I have just made arrangements with Dr. Chasuble to be christened at a quarter to six under the name of Ernest.

JACK: My dear fellow, the sooner you give up that nonsense the better. I made arrangements this morning with Dr. Chasuble to be christened myself at 5:30, and I naturally will take the name of Ernest. Gwendolen would wish it. We can't both be christened Ernest. It's absurd. Besides, I have a perfect right to be christened if I like. There is no evidence at all that I ever have been christened by anybody. I should think it extremely probable I never was, and so does Dr. Chasuble. It is entirely different in your case. You have been christened already.

ALGERNON: Yes, but I have not been christened for years.

JACK: Yes, but you have been christened. That is the important thing.

ALGERNON: Quite so. So I know my constitution can stand it. If you are not quite sure about your ever having been christened, I must say I think it rather dangerous your venturing on it now. It might make you very unwell. You can hardly have forgotten that someone very closely connected with you was very nearly carried off this week in Paris by a severe chill.

JACK: Yes, but you said yourself that a severe chill was not hereditary.

ALGERNON: It usen't to be, I know — but I daresay it is now. Science is always making wonderful improvements in things.

JACK (*picking up the muffin dish*): Oh, that is nonsense; you are always talking nonsense.

ALGERNON: Jack, you are at the muffins again! I wish you wouldn't. There are only two left. (*Takes them.*) I told you I was particularly fond of muffins.

JACK: But I hate tea cake.

ALGERNON: Why on earth then do you allow tea cake to be served up for your guests? What ideas you have of hospitality!

JACK: Algernon! I have already told you to go. I don't want you here. Why don't you go!

ALGERNON: I haven't quite finished my tea yet! and there is still one muffin left.

(*Jack groans, and sinks into a chair. Algernon still continues eating.*)

ACT III

(*Scene: Morning room at the Manor House. Gwendolen and Cecily are at the window, looking out into the garden.*)

GWENDOLEN: The fact that they did not follow us at once into the house, as anyone else would have done, seems to me to show that they have some sense of shame left.

CECILY: They have been eating muffins. That looks like repentance.

GWENDOLEN (*after a pause*): They don't seem to notice us at all. Couldn't you cough?

CECILY: But I haven't got a cough.

GWENDOLEN: They're looking at us. What effrontery!

CECILY: They're approaching. That's very forward of them.

GWENDOLEN: Let us preserve a dignified silence.

CECILY: Certainly. It's the only thing to do now.

(*Enter Jack followed by Algernon. They whistle some dreadful popular air from a British opera.*)

GWENDOLEN: This dignified silence seems to produce an unpleasant effect.

CECILY: A most distasteful one.

GWENDOLEN: But we will not be the first to speak.

CECILY: Certainly not.

GWENDOLEN: Mr. Worthing, I have something very particular to ask you. Much depends on your reply.

CECILY: Gwendolen, your common sense is invaluable. Mr. Moncrieff, kindly answer me the following question. Why did you pretend to be my guardian's brother?

ALGERNON: In order that I might have an opportunity of meeting you.

CECILY (*to Gwendolen*): That certainly seems a satisfactory explanation, does it not?

GWENDOLEN: Yes, dear, if you can believe him.

CECILY: I don't. But that does not affect the wonderful beauty of his answer.

GWENDOLEN: True. In matters of grave importance, style, not sincerity is the vital thing. Mr. Worthing, what explanation can you offer to me for pretending to have a brother? Was it in order that you might have an opportunity of coming up to town to see me as often as possible?

JACK: Can you doubt it, Miss Fairfax?

GWENDOLEN: I have the gravest doubts upon the subject. But I intend to crush them. This is not the moment for German skepticism. (*Moving to Cecily.*) Their explanations appear to be quite satisfactory, especially Mr. Worthing's. That seems to me to have the stamp of truth upon it.

CECILY: I am more than content with what Mr. Moncrieff said. His voice alone inspires one with absolute credulity.

GWENDOLEN: Then you think we should forgive them?

CECILY: Yes. I mean no.

GWENDOLEN: True! I had forgotten. There are principles at stake that one cannot surrender. Which of us should tell them? The task is not a pleasant one.

CECILY: Could we not both speak at the same time?

GWENDOLEN: An excellent idea! I nearly always speak at the same time as other people. Will you take the time from me?

CECILY: Certainly.

(*Gwendolen beats time with uplifted finger.*)

GWENDOLEN and CECILY (*speaking together*): Your Christian names are still an insuperable barrier. That is all!

JACK and ALGERNON (*speaking together*): Our Christian names! Is that all? But we are going to be christened this afternoon.

GWENDOLEN (*to Jack*): For my sake you are prepared to do this terrible thing?

JACK: I am!

CECILY (*to Algernon*): To please me you are ready to face this fearful ordeal?

ALGERNON: I am!

GWENDOLEN: How absurd to talk of the equality of the sexes! Where questions of self-sacrifice are concerned, men are infinitely beyond us.

JACK: We are! (*Clasps hands with Algernon.*)

CECILY: They have moments of physical courage of which we women know absolutely nothing.

GWENDOLEN (*to Jack*): Darling!

ALGERNON (*to Cecily*): Darling!

(*They fall into each other's arms.*)

(*Enter Merriman. When he enters he coughs loudly, seeing the situation.*)

MERRIMAN: Ahem! Ahem! Lady Bracknell!

JACK: Good heavens!

(*Enter Lady Bracknell. The couples separate, in alarm. Exit Merriman.*)

LADY BRACKNELL: Gwendolen! What does this mean?

GWENDOLEN: Merely that I am engaged to be married to Mr. Worthing, Mama.

LADY BRACKNELL: Come here. Sit down. Sit down immediately. Hesitation of any kind is a sign of mental decay in the young, of physical weakness in the old. (*Turns to Jack.*) Apprised, sir, of my daughter's sudden flight by her trusty maid, whose confidence I purchased by means of a small coin, I followed her at once by a luggage train. Her unhappy father is, I am glad to say, under the impression that she is attending a more than usually lengthy lecture by the University Extension Scheme on the influence of a permanent income on thought. I do not propose to undeceive him. Indeed I have never undeceived him on any question. I would consider it wrong. But of course, you will clearly understand that all communication between yourself and my daughter must cease immediately from this moment. On this point, as indeed on all points, I am firm.

JACK: I am engaged to be married to Gwendolen, Lady Bracknell!

LADY BRACKNELL: You are nothing of the kind, sir. And now, as regards Algernon! — Algernon!

ALGERNON: Yes, Aunt Augusta.

LADY BRACKNELL: May I ask if it is in this house that your invalid friend Mr. Bunbury resides?

ALGERNON (*stammering*): Oh! No! Bunbury doesn't live here. Bunbury is somewhere else at present. In fact, Bunbury is dead.

LADY BRACKNELL: Dead! When did Mr. Bunbury die? His death must have been extremely sudden.

ALGERNON (*airily*): Oh! I killed Bunbury this afternoon. I mean poor Bunbury died this afternoon.

LADY BRACKNELL: What did he die of?

ALGERNON: Bunbury? Oh, he was quite exploded.

LADY BRACKNELL: Exploded! Was he the victim of a revolutionary outrage? I was not aware that Mr. Bunbury was interested in social legislation. If so, he is well punished for his morbidity.

ALGERNON: My dear Aunt Augusta, I mean he was found out! The doctors found out that Bunbury could not live, that is what I mean — so Bunbury died.

Eric Stoltz and Schuyler Grant propose a toast in the Irish Repertory Theatre's 1996 production of *The Importance of Being Earnest.*

LADY BRACKNELL: He seems to have had great confidence in the opinion of his physicians. I am glad, however, that he made up his mind at the last to some definite course of action, and acted under proper medical advice. And now that we have finally got rid of this Mr. Bunbury, may I ask, Mr. Worthing, who is that young person whose hand my nephew Algernon is now holding in what seems to me a peculiarly unnecessary manner?

JACK: That lady is Miss Cecily Cardew, my ward.

(*Lady Bracknell bows coldly to Cecily.*)

ALGERNON: I am engaged to be married to Cecily, Aunt Augusta.

LADY BRACKNELL: I beg your pardon?

CECILY: Mr. Moncrieff and I are engaged to be married, Lady Bracknell.

LADY BRACKNELL (*with a shiver, crossing to the sofa and sitting down*): I do not know whether there is anything peculiarly exciting in the air of this particular part of Hertfordshire, but the number of engagements that go on seems to me considerably above the proper average that statistics have laid down for our guidance. I think some preliminary inquiry on my part would not be out of place. Mr. Worthing, is Miss Cardew at all connected with any of the larger railway stations in London? I merely desire information. Until yesterday I had no idea that there were any families or persons whose origin was a Terminus.

(*Jack looks perfectly furious, but restrains himself.*)

JACK (*in a clear, cold voice*): Miss Cardew is the granddaughter of the late Mr. Thomas Cardew of 149, Belgrave Square, S.W.; Gervase Park, Dorking, Surrey; and the Sporran, Fifeshire, N.B.

LADY BRACKNELL: That sounds not unsatisfactory. Three addresses always inspire confidence, even in tradesmen. But what proof have I of their authenticity?

JACK: I have carefully preserved the Court Guides of the period. They are open to your inspection, Lady Bracknell.

LADY BRACKNELL (*grimly*): I have known strange errors in that publication.

JACK: Miss Cardew's family solicitors are Messrs. Markby, Markby, and Markby.

LADY BRACKNELL: Markby, Markby, and Markby? A firm of the very highest position in their profession. Indeed I am told that one of the Mr. Markbys is occasionally to be seen at dinner parties. So far I am satisfied.

JACK (*very irritably*): How extremely kind of you, Lady Bracknell! I have also in my possession, you will be pleased to hear, certificates of Miss Cardew's birth, baptism, whooping cough, registration, vaccination, confirmation, and the measles; both the German and the English variety.

LADY BRACKNELL: Ah! A life crowded with incident I see; though perhaps somewhat too exciting for a young girl. I am not myself in favor of premature experiences. (*Rises, looks at her watch.*) Gwendolen! the time approaches for our departure. We have not a moment to lose. As a matter of form, Mr. Worthing, I had better ask you if Miss Cardew has any little fortune?

JACK: Oh! about a hundred and thirty thousand pounds in the Funds. That is all. Good-bye, Lady Bracknell. So pleased to have seen you.

LADY BRACKNELL (*sitting down again*): A moment, Mr. Worthing. A hundred and thirty thousand pounds! And in the Funds! Miss Cardew seems to me a most attractive young lady, now that I look at her. Few girls of the present day have any really solid qualities, any of the qualities that last, and improve with time. We live, I regret to say, in an age of surfaces. (*To Cecily.*) Come over here, dear. (*Cecily goes across.*) Pretty child! your dress is sadly simple, and your hair seems almost as Nature might have left it. But we can soon alter all that. A thoroughly experienced French maid produces a really marvelous result in a very brief space of time. I remember recommending one to young Lady Lancing, and after three months her own husband did not know her.

JACK (*aside*): And after six months nobody knew her.

LADY BRACKNELL (*glares at Jack for a few moments. Then bends, with a practiced smile, to Cecily*): Kindly turn round, sweet child. (*Cecily turns completely round.*) No, the side view is what I want. (*Cecily presents her profile.*) Yes, quite as I expected. There are distinct social possibilities in your profile. The two weak points in our age are its want of principle and its want of profile. The chin a little higher, dear. Style largely depends on the way the chin is worn. They are worn very high, just at present. Algernon!

ALGERNON: Yes, Aunt Augusta!

LADY BRACKNELL: There are distinct social possibilities in Miss Cardew's profile.

ALGERNON: Cecily is the sweetest, dearest, prettiest girl in the whole world. And I don't care twopence about social possibilities.

LADY BRACKNELL: Never speak disrespectfully of Society, Algernon. Only people who can't get into it do that. (*To Cecily.*) Dear child, of course you know that Algernon has nothing but his debts to depend upon. But I do not approve of mercenary marriages. When I married Lord Bracknell I had no fortune of any kind. But I never dreamed for a moment of allowing that to stand in my way. Well, I suppose I must give my consent.

ALGERNON: Thank you, Aunt Augusta.

LADY BRACKNELL: Cecily, you may kiss me!

CECILY (*kisses her*): Thank you, Lady Bracknell.

LADY BRACKNELL: You may also address me as Aunt Augusta for the future.

CECILY: Thank you, Aunt Augusta.

LADY BRACKNELL: The marriage, I think, had better take place quite soon.

ALGERNON: Thank you, Aunt Augusta.

CECILY: Thank you, Aunt Augusta.

LADY BRACKNELL: To speak frankly, I am not in favor of long engagements. They give people the opportunity of finding out each other's character before marriage, which I think is never advisable.

JACK: I beg your pardon for interrupting you, Lady Bracknell, but this engagement is quite out of the question. I am Miss Cardew's guardian, and she cannot marry without my consent until she comes of age. That consent I absolutely decline to give.

LADY BRACKNELL: Upon what grounds may I ask? Algernon is an extremely, I may almost say an ostentatiously, eligible young man. He has nothing, but he looks everything. What more can one desire?

JACK: It pains me very much to have to speak frankly to you, Lady Bracknell, about your nephew, but the fact is that I do not approve at all of his moral character. I suspect him of being untruthful.

(*Algernon and Cecily look at him in indignant amazement.*)

LADY BRACKNELL: Untruthful! My nephew Algernon? Impossible! He is an Oxonian.°

JACK: I fear there can be no possible doubt about the matter. This afternoon, during my temporary absence in London on an important question of romance, he obtained admission to my house by means of the false pretense of being my brother. Under an assumed name he drank, I've just been informed by my butler, an entire pint bottle of my Perrier-Jouët, Brut, '89; a wine I was specially reserving for myself. Continuing his disgraceful deception, he succeeded in the course of the afternoon in alienating the affections of my only ward. He subsequently stayed to tea, and devoured every single muffin. And what makes his conduct all the more heartless is, that he was perfectly well aware from the first that I have no brother, that I never had a brother, and that I don't intend to have a brother, not even of any kind. I distinctly told him so myself yesterday afternoon.

LADY BRACKNELL: Ahem! Mr. Worthing, after careful consideration I have decided entirely to overlook my nephew's conduct to you.

JACK: That is very generous of you, Lady Bracknell. My own decision, however, is unalterable. I decline to give my consent.

LADY BRACKNELL (*to Cecily*): Come here, sweet child. (*Cecily goes over.*) How old are you, dear?

CECILY: Well, I am really only eighteen, but I always admit to twenty when I go to evening parties.

Oxonian: Educated at Oxford University.

LADY BRACKNELL: You are perfectly right in making some slight alteration. Indeed, no woman should ever be quite accurate about her age. It looks so calculating — (*In a meditative manner.*) Eighteen but admitting to twenty at evening parties. Well, it will not be very long before you are of age and free from the restraints of tutelage. So I don't think your guardian's consent is, after all, a matter of any importance.

JACK: Pray excuse me, Lady Bracknell, for interrupting you again, but it is only fair to tell you that according to the terms of her grandfather's will Miss Cardew does not come legally of age till she is thirty-five.

LADY BRACKNELL: That does not seem to me to be a grave objection. Thirty-five is a very attractive age. London society is full of women of the very highest birth who have, of their own free choice, remained thirty-five for years. Lady Dumbleton is an instance in point. To my own knowledge she has been thirty-five ever since she arrived at the age of forty, which was many years ago now. I see no reason why our dear Cecily should not be even still more attractive at the age you mention than she is at present. There will be a large accumulation of property.

CECILY: Algy, could you wait for me till I was thirty-five?

ALGERNON: Of course I could, Cecily. You know I could.

CECILY: Yes, I felt it instinctively, but I couldn't wait all that time. I hate waiting even five minutes for anybody. It always makes me rather cross. I am not punctual myself, I know, but I do like punctuality in others, and waiting, even to be married, is quite out of the question.

ALGERNON: Then what is to be done, Cecily?

CECILY: I don't know, Mr. Moncrieff.

LADY BRACKNELL: My dear Mr. Worthing, as Miss Cardew states positively that she cannot wait till she is thirty-five — a remark which I am bound to say seems to me to show a somewhat impatient nature — I would beg of you to reconsider your decision.

JACK: But my dear Lady Bracknell, the matter is entirely in your own hands. The moment you consent to my marriage with Gwendolen, I will most gladly allow your nephew to form an alliance with my ward.

LADY BRACKNELL (*rising and drawing herself up*): You must be quite aware that what you propose is out of the question.

JACK: Then a passionate celibacy is all that any of us can look forward to.

LADY BRACKNELL: That is not the destiny I propose for Gwendolen. Algernon, of course, can choose for himself. (*Pulls out her watch.*) Come, dear; (*Gwendolen rises*) we have already missed five, if not six, trains. To miss any more might expose us to comment on the platform.

(*Enter Dr. Chasuble.*)

CHASUBLE: Everything is quite ready for the christenings.

LADY BRACKNELL: The christenings, sir! Is not that somewhat premature?

CHASUBLE (*looking rather puzzled, and pointing to Jack and Algernon*): Both these gentlemen have expressed a desire for immediate baptism.

LADY BRACKNELL: At their age? The idea is grotesque and irreligious! Algernon, I forbid you to be baptized. I will not hear of such excesses. Lord Bracknell would be highly displeased if he learned that that was the way in which you wasted your time and money.

CHASUBLE: Am I to understand then that there are to be no christenings at all this afternoon?

JACK: I don't think that, as things are now, it would be of much practical value to either of us, Dr. Chasuble.

CHASUBLE: I am grieved to hear such sentiments from you, Mr. Worthing. They savor of the heretical views of the Anabaptists,° views that I have completely refuted in four of my unpublished sermons. However, as your present mood seems to be one peculiarly secular, I will return to the church at once. Indeed, I have just been informed by the pew opener that for the last hour and a half Miss Prism has been waiting for me in the vestry.

LADY BRACKNELL (*starting*): Miss Prism! Did I hear you mention a Miss Prism?

CHASUBLE: Yes, Lady Bracknell. I am on my way to join her.

LADY BRACKNELL: Pray allow me to detain you for a moment. This matter may prove to be one of vital importance to Lord Bracknell and myself. Is this Miss Prism a female of repellent aspect, remotely connected with education?

CHASUBLE (*somewhat indignantly*): She is the most cultivated of ladies, and the very picture of respectability.

LADY BRACKNELL: It is obviously the same person. May I ask what position she holds in your household?

CHASUBLE (*severely*): I am a celibate, madam.

JACK (*interposing*): Miss Prism, Lady Bracknell, has been for the last three years Miss Cardew's esteemed governess and valued companion.

LADY BRACKNELL: In spite of what I hear of her, I must see her at once. Let her be sent for.

CHASUBLE (*looking off*): She approaches; she is nigh.

(*Enter Miss Prism hurriedly.*)

MISS PRISM: I was told you expected me in the vestry, dear Canon. I have been waiting for you there for an hour and three-quarters.

(*Catches sight of Lady Bracknell who has fixed her with a stony glare. Miss Prism grows pale and quails. She looks anxiously round as if desirous to escape.*)

LADY BRACKNELL (*in a severe, judicial voice*): Prism! (*Miss Prism bows her head in shame.*) Come here, Prism! (*Miss Prism approaches in a humble manner.*) Prism! Where is that baby? (*General consternation. The Canon starts back in horror. Algernon*

Anabaptists: A religious sect beginning in the sixteenth century and advocating adult baptism and church membership by adults only.

and Jack pretend to be anxious to shield Cecily and Gwendolen from hearing the details of a terrible public scandal.) Twenty-eight years ago, Prism, you left Lord Bracknell's house, Number 104, Upper Grosvenor Street, in charge of a perambulator that contained a baby, of the male sex. You never returned. A few weeks later, through the elaborate investigations of the Metropolitan police, the perambulator was discovered at midnight, standing by itself in a remote corner of Bayswater. It contained the manuscript of a three-volume novel of more than usually revolting sentimentality. (*Miss Prism starts in involuntary indignation.*) But the baby was not there! (*Everyone looks at Miss Prism.*) Prism! Where is that baby?   (*A pause.*)

MISS PRISM: Lady Bracknell, I admit with shame that I do not know. I only wish I did. The plain facts of the case are these. On the morning of the day you mention, a day that is forever branded on my memory, I prepared as usual to take the baby out in its perambulator. I had also with me a somewhat old, but capacious handbag in which I had intended to place the manuscript of a work of fiction that I had written during my few unoccupied hours. In a moment of mental abstraction, for which I never can forgive myself, I deposited the manuscript in the bassinette, and placed the baby in the handbag.

JACK (*who has been listening attentively*): But where did you deposit the handbag?

MISS PRISM: Do not ask me, Mr. Worthing.

JACK: Miss Prism, this is a matter of no small importance to me. I insist on knowing where you deposited the handbag that contained that infant.

MISS PRISM: I left it in the cloakroom of one of the larger railway stations in London.

JACK: What railway station?

MISS PRISM (*quite crushed*): Victoria. The Brighton line.
                              (*Sinks into a chair.*)

JACK: I must retire to my room for a moment. Gwendolen, wait here for me.

GWENDOLEN: If you are not too long, I will wait here for you all my life.

                    (*Exit Jack in great excitement.*)

CHASUBLE: What do you think this means, Lady Bracknell?

LADY BRACKNELL: I dare not even suspect, Dr. Chasuble. I need hardly tell you that in families of high position strange coincidences are not supposed to occur. They are hardly considered the thing.

(*Noises heard overhead as if someone was throwing trunks about. Everyone looks up.*)

CECILY: Uncle Jack seems strangely agitated.

CHASUBLE: Your guardian has a very emotional nature.

LADY BRACKNELL: This noise is extremely unpleasant. It sounds as if he was having an argument. I dislike arguments of any kind. They are always vulgar, and often convincing.

CHASUBLE (*looking up*): It has stopped now.
                    (*The noise is redoubled.*)

LADY BRACKNELL: I wish he would arrive at some conclusion.

GWENDOLEN: This suspense is terrible. I hope it will last.

(*Enter Jack with a handbag of black leather in his hand.*)

JACK (*rushing over to Miss Prism*): Is this the handbag, Miss Prism? Examine it carefully before you speak. The happiness of more than one life depends on your answer.

MISS PRISM (*calmly*): It seems to be mine. Yes, here is the injury it received through the upsetting of a Gower Street omnibus in younger and happier days. Here is the stain on the lining caused by the explosion of a temperance beverage, an incident that occurred at Leamington. And here, on the lock, are my initials. I had forgotten that in an extravagant mood I had had them placed there. The bag is undoubtedly mine. I am delighted to have it so unexpectedly restored to me. It has been a great inconvenience being without it all these years.

JACK (*in a pathetic voice*): Miss Prism, more is restored to you than this handbag. I was the baby you placed in it.

MISS PRISM (*amazed*): You?

JACK (*embracing her*): Yes — mother!

MISS PRISM (*recoiling in indignant astonishment*): Mr. Worthing! I am unmarried!

JACK: Unmarried! I do not deny that is a serious blow. But after all, who has the right to cast a stone against one who has suffered? Cannot repentance wipe out an act of folly? Why should there be one law for men, and another for women? Mother, I forgive you.
(*Tries to embrace her again.*)

MISS PRISM (*still more indignant*): Mr. Worthing, there is some error. (*Pointing to Lady Bracknell.*) There is the lady who can tell you who you really are.

JACK (*after a pause*): Lady Bracknell, I hate to seem inquisitive, but would you kindly inform me who I am?

LADY BRACKNELL: I am afraid that the news I have to give you will not altogether please you. You are the son of my poor sister, Mrs. Moncrieff, and consequently Algernon's elder brother.

JACK: Algy's elder brother! Then I have a brother after all. I knew I had a brother! I always said I had a brother! Cecily, — how could you have ever doubted that I had a brother. (*Seizes hold of Algernon.*) Dr. Chasuble, my unfortunate brother. Miss Prism, my unfortunate brother. Gwendolen, my unfortunate brother. Algy, you young scoundrel, you will have to treat me with more respect in the future. You have never behaved to me like a brother in all your life.

ALGERNON: Well, not till today, old boy, I admit. I did my best, however, though I was out of practice.
                              (*Shakes hands.*)

GWENDOLEN (*to Jack*): My own! But what own are you? What is your Christian name, now that you have become someone else?

JACK: Good heavens! — I had quite forgotten that point. Your decision on the subject of my name is irrevocable, I suppose?

GWENDOLEN: I never change, except in my affections.

CECILY: What a noble nature you have, Gwendolen!

JACK: Then the question had better be cleared up at once. Aunt Augusta, a moment. At the time when Miss Prism left me in the handbag, had I been christened already?

LADY BRACKNELL: Every luxury that money could buy, including christening, had been lavished upon you by your fond and doting parents.

JACK: Then I was christened! That is settled. Now, what name was I given? Let me know the worst.

LADY BRACKNELL: Being the eldest son you were naturally christened after your father.

JACK (*irritably*): Yes, but what was my father's Christian name?

LADY BRACKNELL (*meditatively*): I cannot at the present moment recall what the General's Christian name was. But I have no doubt he had one. He was eccentric, I admit. But only in later years. And that was the result of the Indian climate, and marriage, and indigestion, and other things of that kind.

JACK: Algy! Can't you recollect what our father's Christian name was?

ALGERNON: My dear boy, we were never even on speaking terms. He died before I was a year old.

JACK: His name would appear in the Army Lists of the period, I suppose, Aunt Augusta?

LADY BRACKNELL: The General was essentially a man of peace, except in his domestic life. But I have no doubt his name would appear in any military directory.

JACK: The Army Lists of the last forty years are here. These delightful records should have been my constant study. (*Rushes to bookcase and tears the books out.*) M. Generals — Mallam, Maxbohm, Magley, what ghastly names they have — Markby, Migsby, Mobbs, Moncrieff! Lieutenant 1840, Captain, Lieutenant-Colonel, Colonel, General 1869, Christian names, Ernest John. (*Puts book very quietly down and speaks quite calmly.*) I always told you, Gwendolen, my name was Ernest, didn't I? Well, it is Ernest after all. I mean it naturally is Ernest.

LADY BRACKNELL: Yes, I remember now that the General was called Ernest. I knew I had some particular reason for disliking the name.

GWENDOLEN: Ernest! My own Ernest! I felt from the first that you could have no other name!

JACK: Gwendolen, it is a terrible thing for a man to find out suddenly that all his life he has been speaking nothing but the truth. Can you forgive me?

GWENDOLEN: I can. For I feel that you are sure to change.

JACK: My own one!

CHASUBLE (*to Miss Prism*): Laetitia! (*Embraces her.*)

MISS PRISM (*enthusiastically*): Frederick! At last!

ALGERNON: Cecily! (*Embraces her.*) At last!

JACK: Gwendolen! (*Embraces her.*) At last!

LADY BRACKNELL: My nephew, you seem to be displaying signs of triviality.

JACK: On the contrary, Aunt Augusta, I've now realized for the first time in my life the vital Importance of Being Earnest.

COMMENTARIES

Peter Raby (b. 1939)
An Unpublished Letter from Oscar Wilde
on *The Importance of Being Earnest*
1991

Peter Raby introduces an 1894 letter from Oscar Wilde describing the plot of the play to his friend George Alexander. Wilde was under enormous financial pressure at the time and was eager to have his play produced. What we see in this letter is the human, vulnerable side of a witty, ironic comic playwright.

The full text of Oscar Wilde's first version of *The Importance of Being Earnest* has been lost for many years. Wilde sent it to George Alexander in July 1894, before leaving for a two-month holiday with his family in Worthing. He was desperate for money. Every encounter with Lord Alfred Douglas cost him more: he was overdrawn at the bank, and, so he claims in the letter, he had to bear the expenses of his mother's household as well as his own

Wilde's output during 1894 was astonishing: he completed *An Ideal Husband,* wrote the contrasting *A Florentine Tragedy* and most of *La Sainte Courtisane,* and embarked on an entirely new genre in *Earnest.* The more tumultuous and complex his private life, the more productive he became. He was in frequent correspondence with a number of producers and managers during the course of the year: with John Hare and Lewis Waller over *An Ideal Husband,* with Charles Frohman and Albert Palmer in New York in connection with a number of properties, both existing and unwritten, and with Dion Boucicault, who was producing *Lady Windermere's Fan* in Australia. Frohman, who controlled the American rights to *Lady Windermere's Fan,* was negotiating for *An Ideal Husband.* The year before, he had invited Wilde to write him a new play, perhaps a "modern *School for Scandal* style of play"; Wilde's American agent, the "brilliant delightful" Elizabeth Marbury, wrote to Wilde in July from Paris with details of Frohman's latest offer, which included an option on his next modern comedy. Albert Palmer was also angling for a comedy "with no real serious interest."

Completed plays and royalties were no longer enough to keep Wilde's finances buoyant. He turned his gift for story-telling to advantage in the form of the scenario. Alexander, generous and approachable, and the producer of Wilde's first great theatrical success, *Lady Windermere's Fan,* had expressed an interest in the new comedy. Wilde seems to have dashed off the *Earnest* scenario more to secure a £150 advance than because he thought the play right for a romantic actor of modern and costume pieces. (In fact, having received the advance, he rapidly backpedalled, suggesting the piece was too farcical, and sending Alexander a more suitable scenario from Worthing, something "strong" and serious, which Frank Harris eventually turned into *Mr and Mrs Daventry.*)

There are many stages between the outline of *Earnest* and the script which was played at the St James's Theatre on February 14, 1895, while the Marquess of Queensberry prowled around the building, unable to gain admission, and when Wilde's world was on the point of disintegration. There are some manuscript pages in a notebook in the Clark Library, at the University of California in Los Angeles, containing notes and scraps of dialogue, for example:

> Beautiful name — Ernest, I couldn't love anybody who wasn't called Ernest —
> Oh! don't say that Gwendolen. It sounds perfectly heartless of you — why should love be dependent on the action of an irresponsible godfather. Is a man's whole fortune to depend on the font. I am told that there was a moment when my father contemplated calling me John —

Another fragment seems to encapsulate a sharply visualized image:

> Gwen: Leave the room, Mamma. This is no place for you.
> Duchess: Mr Worthing rise from this semi-recumbent posture — it is most unbefitting.

The future Lady Bracknell springs fully armed from that one phrase. Indeed, the women characters — Prism, Gwendolen, Duchess — are throughout more vividly delineated in these early phases.

From these fragments, the play grew into a four-act version, with a brace of butlers named after Wilde's publishers, a gardener, and an ominous solicitor. There followed a collection of names with geographical or personal associations: Lancing, Shoreham, Bracknell, Blaxam, Bunbury, Maxbohm, Cardew. (Cicely Cardew, daughter of friends of Wilde, was born in 1893; her uncle was a director of the London and South East Railway, and the Cardew engine hauled the evening boat-train to Newhaven.) By Christmas, the new play had been promised to Charles Wyndham. When Alexander found he had a failure on his hands in Henry James's *Guy Domville*, Wyndham agreed to concede his rights in *Earnest*, provided Wilde wrote him an original play before completing yet another for Alexander. Alexander persuaded Wilde to compress *Earnest* into three acts (which was the form of the original scenario he had been shown). Wilde resisted for a little, but trusted Alexander's judgment; the play, he told Ada Leverson, "must go like a pistol shot." Wilde wanted to attend rehearsals, as he had for his previous London openings, but Douglas, "so beautiful is his nature," declined. Instead, Wilde accompanied Douglas on a final Bunbury to Algeria, returning alone for the final rehearsals of this play.

The following letter was described in Sotheby's Sale Catalogue for July 1933, under item 608, one of a number of Wilde's letters to her husband sold by Lady Alexander. The catalogue provided a synopsis, and reproduced one section. The text is taken from papers at the Clark Library. These are typewritten copies of letters from Wilde to Alexander, marked for inclusion in A.E.W. Mason's study, *Sir George Alexander and the St James's Theatre*, which was published in 1935. Mason wrote to Vyvyan Holland's solicitors, asking for permission to print excerpts, and bracketing those passages he wished to include: these papers are, most probably, Mason's originals. Mason printed only brief extracts from the opening and the last two paragraphs, and his book is the source for the extract printed in Sir Rupen Hart-Davis's edition of Wilde's *Letters*. So far as I am aware, the full letter has not been published before. It is reproduced here by permission of Mr Merlin Holland and the Clark Library (the letter is © Merlin Holland):

16, Tite Street,
S.W.

My dear Aleck,

Thanks for your letter. There really is nothing more to tell you about the comedy beyond what I said already. I mean that the real charm of the play, if it is to have charm, must be in the dialogue. The plot is slight, but, I think, adequate.

Act I. Evening party. 10 p.m.

Lord Alfred Rufford's rooms in Mayfair. Arrives from country Bertram Ashton his friend: a man of 25 or 30 years of age: his great friend.

Rufford asks him about his life. He tells him that he has a ward, etc. very young and pretty. That in the country he has to be serious, etc. that he comes to town to enjoy himself, and has invented a fictitious younger brother of the name of George — to whom all his misdeeds are put down. Rufford is deeply interested about the ward.

Guests arrive: the Duchess of Selby and her daughter, Lady Maud Rufford, with whom the guardian is in love — fin-de-siècle talk, a lot of guests — the guardian proposes to Lady Maud on his knees — enter Duchess —

Lady Maud. "Mamma, this is no place for you."

Scene: Duchess enquires for *her son Lord Alfred Rufford*: servant comes in with note to say that Lord Alfred has been suddenly called away to the country. Lady Maud vows eternal fidelity to the guardian whom she only knows under the name of *George* Ashton.

(P.S. The disclosure of the guardian of his double life is occasioned by Lord Alfred saying to him "You left your handkerchief here the last time you were up" (or cigarette case). The guardian takes it — the Lord A. says but "why, dear George, is it marked Bertram — who is Bertram Ashton?" Guardian discloses plot.)

Act II

The guardian's home — pretty cottage. Mabel Harbord, his ward, and her governess, Miss Prism, Governess of course dragon of propriety. Talk about the profligate George: maid comes in to say "Mr. George Ashton." — governess protests against his admission. Mabel insists. Enter Lord Alfred. Falls in love with ward at once. He is reproached with his bad life, etc. Expressed great repentance. They go to garden.

Enter guardian: Mabel comes in: "I have a great surprise for you — your brother is here" — Guardian, of course, denies having a brother. Mabel says "You cannot disown your own brother, whatever he has done." — and brings in Lord Alfred. Scene: also scene between two men alone. Finally Lord Alfred arrested for debt contracted by guardian: guardian delighted. Mabel, however, makes him forgive his brother and pay up. Guardian looks over bills and scolds Lord Alfred for profligacy.

Miss Prism backs the guardian up. Guardian then orders his brother out of the house. Mabel intercedes, and brother remains. Miss Prism has designs on the guardian — matrimonial — she is 40 at least — she believes he is proposing to her and accepts him — his consternation.

Act III. Mabel and the false brother. He proposes, and is accepted.

When Mabel is alone, Lady Maud, who only knows the guardian under the name of George, arrives alone. She tells Mabel she is engaged to George — scene naturally. Mabel retires: enter George, he kisses his sister naturally. Enter Mabel and sees them. Explanations, of course. Mabel breaks off the match on the ground that there is nothing to reform in George: she only consented to marry him because she thought he was bad and wanted guidance — He promises to be a bad husband — so as to give her an opportunity of making him a better man; she is a little mollified.

Enter guardian: he is reproached also by Lady Maud for his respectable life in the country: a J.P.: a county-councillor: a churchwarden: a philanthropist: a good example. He appeals to his life in London: she is mollified, on condition that he never lives in the country: the country is demoralising: it makes you respectable. "The simple fare at the Savoy: the quiet life in Piccadilly: the solitude of Mayfair is what you need, etc."

Enter Duchess in pursuit of her daughter — objects to both matches. Miss Prism, who had in early days been governess to the Duchess, sets it all right, without intending to do so — everything ends happily.

Result   Curtain

Author called.

Cigarette called.

Manager called.

———————————————

Royalties for a year for author.

———————————————

Manager credited with writing the play. He consoles himself for the slander with bag of red gold.

———————————————

Fireworks

Of course this scenario is open to alterations: the third act, after entrance of Duchess, will have to be elaborated: also, the local doctor, or clergyman, must be brought in, in the play, for Prism.

Well, I think an amusing thing with lots of fun and wit might be made. If you think so, too, and care to have the refusal of it — do let me know — and send me £150. If, when the play is finished, you think it too slight — not serious enough — of course you have the £150 back — I want to go away and write it — and it could be ready in October — as I have nothing else to do — and Palmer is anxious to have a play from me for the States "with no real serious interest"— just a comedy.

In the meanwhile, my dear Aleck, I am so pressed for money, that I don't know what to do. Of course I am extravagant, but a great deal of my worries comes from the fact that I have had for three years to keep up two establishments — my dear Mother's as well as my own — like many Irish ladies she never gets her jointure° paid — small though it is — and naturally it falls on me — this is of course *quite private* but for these years I have had two houses on my shoulders — and of course, am extravagant besides — you have always been a good wise friend to me — so think what you can do.

Kind regards to Mrs. Aleck.

Ever,

OSCAR

jointure: A widow's portion of her husband's estate.

Peter Raby (b. 1939)
THE ORIGINS OF *THE IMPORTANCE OF BEING EARNEST*   1994

In this article, Peter Raby provides some insight into the origins of the play. Wilde wrote quickly, using material that was about him — including names of towns such as Worthing for his characters — so that one has the impression he reflected his environment in his work. However, it is also plain that Wilde lived at such a level that he had considerable need for the money his new farcical comedy was to provide.

Wilde, as the negotiations with Alexander[1] reveal, was acutely conscious of embarking on a new field with this play, referring to it as "farcical comedy" and, to another correspondent, as "quite nonsensical." Its first working title was "The Guardian," and the manuscript notebook in the Clark Library, which also contains speeches for *A Woman of No Importance,* seems to be an attempt at expanding aspects of the first scenario. Even at this early stage, some of the key names had shifted — indeed, only Miss Prism, of all the named characters, retains the same name from scenario to first performance, which gives her an unexpectedly high profile within the play's development. Lady Maud Rufford has become Lady Gwendolen; her mother retains the rank of Duchess; more significantly, Bertram/George Ashton, repeatedly referred to as "Guardian" in the scenario, has been transformed into Mr. Worthing. The importance of his Christian name is now central:

> LADY G: Beautiful name — Ernest. I couldn't love anybody who wasn't called Ernest —
> Oh! don't say that Gwendolen. it sounds perfectly heartless of you — why shd. love be dependent on the action of an irresponsible godfather. Is a man's whole fortune to depend on the font. I am told there was a moment when my father contemplated calling me John —
> How very cruel of him!
> I could love you under any other name —
> Could you love me if my name was Jane? or Maria?
> Devotedly —
> Then you have no sense of romance. Those are not names meant for moonlight.
> cd. you not love me if my name was Geoffrey —
> I might respect you, but love wd. be out of the question — Geoffrey! too straightforward. I cd forgive anything in my husband except passion for telling the truth. That wd. make married life unbearable.

The obsession with the name, and so with form, lies at the play's core, alongside the art of lying, which alone can make married life bearable. Two other quotations from these notes reinforce the theme. On the third page, detached from the dialogue, at an angle and underscored, is the phrase: "Mr. Bunbury — always ill —"; and on the fourth, the following resonant exchange, expanded from the scenario:

> GWEN: Leave the room, Mamma. This is no place for you.
> DUCHESS: Mr. Worthing rise from this semirecumbent posture — it is most unbefitting[2]

---

[1]**George Alexander (1858–1918):** English actor and manager of the St. James Theatre. He commissioned *Lady Windermere's Fan* from Wilde.

[2]AMS Notebook, William Andrews Clark Library, Los Angeles.

All the evidence points to Wilde constructing *The Importance of Being Earnest* with great rapidity and zest, incorporating material which lay conveniently at hand — names, incidents, circumstances — into an outline, and more crucially a tone and manner, which had already taken shape in his mind. The choice of the Sussex seaside resort of Worthing for the guardian's borrowed name follows his habit of incorporating place-names into the comedy he was composing (Hunstanton, Goring). Worthing was particularly apposite for a "serious," propertied Justice of the Peace, following the convention of English comedy of manners. Other neighboring seaside villages to surface in the final text are Lancing and Shoreham. The train journey which John Worthing's benefactor, Thomas Cardew, was about to embark on when he was mistakenly handed the black leather handbag was the very journey from Victoria Station on the Brighton line which Wilde would have taken with his family, who on this occasion included a "horrid ugly Swiss governess."[3]

Other names make links with contrasting aspects of Wilde's life. The guardian's great friend of the scenario was "Lord Alfred Rufford," a name Wilde had already used in the final version of *A Woman of No Importance.* This may have struck Wilde as too blatant a glance at Lord Alfred Douglas; Algernon Moncrieff, Scottish and aristocratic in sound, was more circumspect. (There are several Moncrieffs in the Army List of 1894, including one serving General, stationed in Dublin, of whom Wilde may have heard.) The Douglas connection remains through the character who moved from the Duchess of Selby via Lady Brancaster to Lady Bracknell, Bracknell being the Berkshire home of Douglas's mother, the Marchioness of Queensberry. Wilde's circle of homosexual friends is glanced at obliquely through a number of references. The name Ernest itself has been fully discussed in this context, most recently by Joseph Bristow.[4] "Lady Bloxham" commemorates Jack Bloxam, the editor of the *Chameleon,* in which Wilde's "Phrases and Philosophies for the Use of the Young" was published. B4 the Albany, Jack's London address, echoes the residence of Wilde's friend George Ives. There may, too, be another submerged reference, this time to Robbie Ross, in the name of Miss Cardew's family solicitors, "Markby, Markby, and Markby." There was, in fact, an old-established firm of London solicitors which incorporated the name of Markby. The firm had no dealings with Wilde, but Ross was friendly with one of the managing clerks and would call in to the office to see him. Wilde was not primarily creating a private reference but selecting brilliantly from a set of possibilities to create a particular resonance. Markby, Markby, and Markby conveys an air of respectability, indeed gentility, far removed from the less salubrious solicitors of the four-act version, Gribsby and Parker, in which "Gribsby" has the ring of a particularly ruthless, Dickensian kind of lawyer.

In one version, "Gribsby" had been "Hubbard." Wilde's meticulous care to achieve precisely the right name is recorded in an anecdote of Coulson Kernahan. Kernahan was correcting the proofs of *The Picture of Dorian Gray* and recalls Wilde cross-questioning him: "There's a picture framer — a mere tradesman — in my story, isn't there?" On hearing that he had called him Ashton, Wilde replied: "Ashton is a gentleman's name. And I've given it — God forgive me — to a tradesman!

---

[3]*Letters of Oscar Wilde,* ed. Rupert Hart-Davis (London, 1962), 360.
[4]*The Importance of Being Earnest and Related Writings,* ed. Joseph Bristow (London, 1992), 18–20.

It must be changed to Hubbard. Hubbard positively smells of the tradesman!"[5] Having hit on names which seemed especially apt, Wilde would use them repeatedly, at least, as with these two, in drafts. He would occasionally use a name as a private act of revenge. Max Beerbohm recorded that the names of Wilde's publishers, Lane and Matthews, with whom he was in dispute during the autumn of 1894, were both brought into service as manservant and butler, before Wilde relented at least in the case of Matthews, who became Merriman. There may, too, be a personal dimension to the Bunbury joke. Kerry Powell has drawn attention to the farce *Godpapa,* which included a character called Bunbury with an imaginary ailment.[6] Charles Brookfield was the coauthor of the farce and played Bunbury. Wilde disliked Brookfield, who had mocked him in the travesty *The Poet and the Puppets*: it would have given Wilde a particular pleasure to have infiltrated Brookfield surreptitiously into his own travesty and to have disposed of him so finally and satisfactorily.

Wilde's social ear was acute. The names of the two singleminded girls in his play are finely differentiated. Gwendolen Fairfax carries a certain weight and crisp urbanity, appropriate for Lady Bracknell's daughter, while Jack's ward, Cicely Cardew, has a musical lightness about it. Wilde was an undergraduate at Magdalen with two of the Cardew family. Miss Cecily Cardew was born in 1893, and Wilde reportedly promised, when staying with the Cardews at their country house, that he would name the heroine of his next play after her. (The Victorians would have pronounced "Cecily" as "Cicely," as was done in Nicholas Hytner's 1993 production at the Aldwych Theatre, London.) The Cardew connection may even have prompted Wilde's inventive use of the cloakroom at Victoria Station, for Christopher Baldock Cardew was a director of the London and South East Railway. On the other hand, it may simply have been a dimension of Wilde's genius to create artful fictions that uncannily but surreally echoed life.

Wilde's work is relentlessly self-referential. It also contrives to reflect, shadow, and finally subvert a wide range of contemporary plays. The parallels and motifs which Powell has set out in *Oscar Wilde and the Theatre of the 1890s* draw attention both to Wilde's affinities with an astonishing range of near-contemporary farce and to the specific example of Lestocq and Robson's *The Foundling*, which shared not only a number of common features with *The Importance of Being Earnest* but also a New York producer, Charles Frohman. *The Foundling* opened at Terry's on August 30, 1894. The time-scale is tight, and it cannot be established that Wilde saw a performance: he claimed he did not have the rail-fare to London before his luncheon at the Garrick with Alexander. The date on the typescript draft of Acts III and IV, September 19th, suggests completion some days before. The *Morning Post* of August 31, 1894, reported in its review that Dick Pennell, the hopeful bridegroom and Jack Worthing counterpart, is informed "that he is really a foundling, having been discovered, as a baby, in a bedroom of a hotel at Margate," whereupon Mrs Cotton, the girl's mother, declares that "he shall not be allowed to marry her daughter until he can satisfy her that his parentage is at least respectable." By the time Wilde had composed his first complete draft, he had an excellent opportu-

[5]Coulson Kernahan, *In Good Company: Some Personal Recollections of Swinburne, Lord Roberts, Watts-Dunton, Oscar Wilde, Edward Whymper, S. J. Stone and Stephen Philips* (London, 1917), 213.

[6]Kerry Powell, *Oscar Wilde and the Theatre of the 1890s* (Cambridge, 1990), 127.

nity to see *The Foundling* without traveling to London. One of the few communications from this period which can be dated precisely, a telegram to Ada Leverson, puts Wilde and Douglas in Worthing on September 22. On September 20, *The Foundling* was acted at the Brighton Theatre, Brighton being the actual setting of this seaside farce. A fortnight later, the more serious but near-farcical episode of Douglas's illness would be enacted at Brighton's Grand Hotel.

Wilde offered a brilliant and versatile synthesis of the genre of farcical comedy, as though he had been steeped in it all his life rather than coming to it as a new experiment. It is not an imitation but a subversion which at the same time develops it into a distinct and continuously surprising new form. The mood of hard-edged gaiety which infuses it is one which he was struggling to recapture in his own life. Telling Douglas about his luncheon with Gladys de Grey, with Reggie Lister and Aleck Yorke, he commented wistfully: "They want me to go to Paris with them on Thursday: they say one wears flannels and straw hats and dines in the Bois, but, of course, I have no money, as usual, and can't go."[7] This is the yearning of Ernest-in-town. But Wilde's earlier life was full of such impromptu outings, and a glance through some of the letters of his Oxford years reveals experiences which he seems to have drawn upon for the Bunbury-in-the-country scenes. Traveling to his uncle's Lincolnshire rectory, he accepted a lift from the station in a neighbor's dog-cart, and examined schools in geography and played lawn tennis, and argued with his uncle, who revenged himself "by preaching on Rome in the morning, and on humility in the evening";[8] and then, after the triumph of his First, he went to stay with Frank Miles at Bingham Rectory, where he played more lawn tennis, and ate strawberries, and where he found the four Miles daughters: "all very pretty indeed, one of them who is writing at the other side of the table quite lovely." The idyll, though, is not sufficiently like art or literature to be entirely perfect: "A wonderful garden with such white lilies and rose walks; only there are no serpents or apples it would be quite Paradise."[9] With *The Importance of Being Earnest,* Wilde constructed the glittering, uncompromising idyll of his last great fiction, with a full complement of apples and serpents.

In this artificially constructed world, at once like and unlike both farcical comedy and society, everyone invents what they desire, and everyone finally acquires it. Each character is resourcefully creative: diaries, three-volume novels, sermons, visiting cards, lists of eligible young men form the fabricated evidence which gives credibility to their fictions. Jack invents Ernest, Algernon impersonates him: Cecily and Gwendolen respond to the challenge, and the double fiction becomes reality, within the artificial world of the play. The emphasis on names, that apparently trivial pun which so irritated Sidney Grundy, turns out to be important after all. Form and style, not sincerity, are dominant, and, as Wilde predicted in his initial scenario, "everything ends happily." But the charm of the dialogue has all the practiced artifice of experience, and the serpent's irony makes itself felt in every phrase and cadence.

[7]*Letters of Oscar Wilde,* 358.
[8]*Letters of Oscar Wilde,* 14.
[9]*Letters of Oscar Wilde,* 16–17.

Anton Chekhov

Anton Chekhov (1860–1904) spent most of his childhood in relative poverty. His family managed to set up its household in Moscow after years spent in remote Taganrog, six hundred miles to the south. He studied medicine in Moscow and eventually received his degree. Though he practiced medicine most of his life, he said that if medicine was his wife, literature was his mistress. His earliest literary efforts were for the purpose of relieving his family's poverty, but it was not long before he earned more from writing than from medicine. By 1896 he had written more than three hundred short stories, most of them published in newspapers. Many of them are classics.

His first theatrical works, apart from his short farces, were not successful. *Ivanov* (1887–1889), rushed to production, was a failure, but its revised 1889 version, reflecting much of his personal life, was successful. *The Wood Demon* (1889), also a failure, helped Chekhov eventually produce his great plays: *The Seagull* (1896); *Uncle Vanya* (1897); *Three Sisters* (1901); and his last, *The Cherry Orchard* (1903). These plays essentially reshaped modern drama, creating a style that critic Richard Peace describes as a "subtle blend of naturalism and symbolism."

The Seagull attracted the attention of the Moscow Art Theatre. The play was not a success in its first production in 1896, but two years later it became one of the theater's triumphs. Konstantin Stanislavsky, the great Russian director and actor, played Trigorin, the lead character, but Chekhov felt that he was overacting. They often had disagreements about the playwright's work, but the Moscow Art Theatre supported Chekhov fully.

The surfaces of Chekhov's plays are so lifelike that at times one feels his dramatic purposes are submerged, and to an extent that is true. Chekhov is the master of the SUBTEXT, a technique in which the surface of the dialogue seems innocuous or meandering, but deeper meanings are implied. Madame Ranevskaya's musings about her childhood in act I of *The Cherry Orchard* contrast with the purposeful dialogue of Lopakhin. Her long speeches in act III talking about the "millstone" she loves in Paris are also meanderings, but they reveal an idealistic character doomed to suffer at the hands of a new generation of realists who have no time for her ramblings and sentimentalism.

Because Chekhov's subtexts are always present, to read his work requires close attention. One must constantly probe, analyze, ask what is implied by what is being said. Chekhov resists "explaining" his plays by having key characters give key thematic speeches. Instead, the meaning builds slowly. Our understanding of what a situation or circumstance finally means will change as we read and as we gather more understanding of the subtleties veiled by surfaces.

Chekhov's style is remarkable for its clarity; its surface is direct, simple, and effective. Even his short stories have a clear dramatic center, and the characters he chose to observe are exceptionally modern in that they are not heroes, nor villains. The dramatic concept of a larger-than-life Oedipus or of *Hamlet*'s devilish Claudius is nowhere to be seen in his work. Chekhov's characters are limited, recognizable, and in many ways completely ordinary.

Chekhov's genius was in showing such characters' ambitions, pain, and successes. He was quite aware of important social changes taking place in Russia; the old aristocratic classes, who once owned serfs, were being reduced to a genteel impoverishment, while the children of former slaves were beginning to succeed in business and real estate ventures. Since Chekhov's grandfather had been a serf who bought his freedom in 1841, it is likely that Chekhov was especially supportive of such social change; we see evidence of that in his best plays.

THE CHERRY ORCHARD

The Cherry Orchard (1903), premiered on Chekhov's birthday, January 17, in 1904. The Moscow Art Theatre performance was directed by Konstantin Stanislavsky, an actor-director who pioneered a new method of realistic acting. (Stanislavsky is still read and admired the world over. His techniques were modified in the United States and form the basis of METHOD ACTING.) For the subtle effects that Chekhov wanted, however, he found Stanislavsky too stagey, flamboyant, and melodramatic. They argued hotly over what should happen in his plays, and often Stanislavsky prevailed.

One argument was over whether *The Cherry Orchard* was a tragedy. Chekhov steadfastly called it a comedy, but Stanislavsky saw the ruin of Madame Ranevskaya and the destruction of the cherry orchard as tragic. Chekhov perhaps saw it the same way, but he also considered its potential as the beginning of a new, more realistic life for Madame Ranevskaya and her brother Gayev. Their impracticality was an important cause of their having lost their wealth and estate.

How audiences interpret Lopakhin depends on how they view the ambition of the new class of businessmen whose zeal, work, and cleverness earn them the estates that previously they could have hoped only to work on. Social change is fueled by money, which replaces an inherited aristocracy with ambitious moneymakers who earn the power to force changes on the old, less flexible aristocrats. In Russia massive social change was eventually effected by revolution and the institution of communism. But *The Cherry Orchard* shows that change would have come to Russia in any event.

Perhaps Chekhov's peasant blood helped him see the play as more of a comedy than a tragedy, even though he portrays the characters with greater complexity than we might expect in comedy. Lopakhin is not a simple, unsympathetic character; Trofimov is not a simple dreamer. We need to look closely at what they do and why they do it. For example, when thinking about preserving the beauties of the cherry orchard, Trofimov reminds people that all of Russia is an orchard, that the world is filled with beautiful places. Such a view makes it difficult for him to feel nostalgia for aristocratic privilege.

Trofimov sounds a striking note about the practice of slavery in Russia. He tells Madame Ranevskaya and Gayev that they are living on credit, that they must repay debts to the Russian people. The cherry orchard is beautiful because each tree represents the soul of a serf. The beautiful class of people to which the impractical Madame Ranevskaya belongs owes its beauty and grace to the institution of slavery, and soon the note will be presented for payment. The sound of the breaking string in act I, repeated at the end of the play, is Chekhov's way of symbolizing the losses and changes represented in the play.

Madame Ranevskaya, however, cannot change. Her habits of mind are fully formed before the play begins; nothing that Lopakhin can say will help change her. Even though she knows she is dangerously in debt, she gives a gold coin to a beggar. *Noblesse oblige* — the duty of the upper class to help the poor — is still part of her ethos, even if it also involves her own ruin.

A sense of tragedy is apparent in Madame Ranevskaya's feelings and her helplessness. She seems incapable of transforming herself, no matter how much she may wish to change. We see her as a victim of fate, a fate that is formed by her expectations and training. But the play also contains comic and nonsensical moments, as, for example, in the byplay of Varya, Yasha, and Yepikhodov over a game of billiards in act III. In his letters Chekhov mentions that the play is happy and frivolous, "in places even a farce."

The Cherry Orchard in Performance

Since its first production in 1904, *The Cherry Orchard* has played to responsive audiences in Europe and abroad. It was produced in London in 1911, Berlin in 1919, and New York in 1923 (in Russian). Eva Le Gallienne produced it in New York in her English version in 1928. In 1968 she directed the play with Uta Hagen as Madame Ranevskaya. Tyrone Guthrie directed it at the Old Vic in 1933 and again in 1941. John Gielgud, Peggy Ashcroft, Judy Dench, and Dorothy Tutin performed in a powerful and well-reviewed version in London in 1961. When Joseph Papp produced an all-black *Cherry Orchard* in 1973, James Earl Jones was praised as a powerful Lopakhin.

Andrei Serban's 1977 production for Joseph Papp at Lincoln Center in New York was praised for its extraordinary stage effects. According to the reviewer at *Time* magazine,

> Serban's best images effectively magnify the play's conflict between the old order and the bright new world that is its doom: a frieze of peasants laboring beneath modern telegraph wires, a group of aristocrats watching the setting sun silhouette a factory on the horizon.

The American playwright Jean Claude van Italie has revised the text for contemporary audiences. His version, produced at the John Drew Theater of Guild Hall in East Hampton in July 1985, was directed by Elinor Renfield. Amanda Plummer played Anya and Joanna Merlin played Madame Ranevskaya. Peter Brook's 1987 New York production, with Brian Dennehy as a notable Lopakhin, had little scenery beyond a great number of Oriental rugs. It was played without intermissions at breakneck speed. *New York Times* critic Frank Rich said of it, "On this director's magic carpets, *The Cherry Orchard* flies." Other modern treatments of Chekhov's plays include Michael Picardie's adaptation of *The Cherry Orchard* to South Africa and Brian Friel's adaptation to Ireland. Mustapha Matura's *Trinidad Sisters* (1988) moves *Three Sisters* to Trinidad, demonstrating in part the universal appeal of Chekhov's plays. In 1997 Galina Volchek staged a Russian-language version in the Martin Beck Theater on Broadway. Critic Peter Marks said the play was "communicated vividly."

Anton Chekhov (1860–1904)

THE CHERRY ORCHARD

1903

TRANSLATED BY ANN DUNNIGAN

Characters

RANEVSKAYA, LYUBOV ANDREYEVNA, *a landowner*
ANYA, *her daughter, seventeen years old*
VARYA, *her adopted daughter, twenty-four years old*
GAYEV, LEONID ANDREYEVICH, *Madame Ranevskaya's brother*
LOPAKHIN, YERMOLAI ALEKSEYEVICH, *a merchant*
TROFIMOV, PYOTR SERGEYEVICH, *a student*
SEMYONOV-PISHCHIK, BORIS BORISOVICH, *a landowner*
CHARLOTTA IVANOVNA, *a governess*
YEPIKHODOV, SEMYON PANTELEYEVICH, *a clerk*
DUNYASHA, *a maid*
FIRS, *an old valet, eighty-seven years old*
YASHA, *a young footman*
A STRANGER
THE STATIONMASTER
A POST OFFICE CLERK
GUESTS, SERVANTS

The action takes place on Madame Ranevskaya's estate.

ACT I

(*A room that is still called the nursery. One of the doors leads into Anya's room. Dawn; the sun will soon rise. It is May, the cherry trees are in bloom, but it is cold in the orchard; there is a morning frost. The windows in the room are closed. Enter Dunyasha with a candle, and Lopakhin with a book in his hand.*)

LOPAKHIN: The train is in, thank God. What time is it?
DUNYASHA: Nearly two. (*Blows out the candle.*) It's already light.
LOPAKHIN: How late is the train, anyway? A couple of hours at least. (*Yawns and stretches.*) I'm a fine one! What a fool I've made of myself! Came here on purpose to meet them at the station, and then overslept. . . . Fell asleep in the chair. It's annoying. . . . You might have waked me.
DUNYASHA: I thought you had gone. (*Listens.*) They're coming now, I think!

LOPAKHIN (*listens*): No . . . they've got to get the luggage and one thing and another. (*Pause.*) Lyubov Andreyevna has lived abroad for five years, I don't know what she's like now. . . . She's a fine person. Sweet-tempered, simple. I remember when I was a boy of fifteen, my late father — he had a shop in the village then — gave me a punch in the face and made my nose bleed. . . . We had come into the yard here for some reason or other, and he'd had a drop too much. Lyubov Andreyevna — I remember as if it were yesterday — still young, and so slender, led me to the washstand in this very room, the nursery. "Don't cry, little peasant," she said, "it will heal in time for your wedding. . . ." (*Pause.*) Little peasant . . . my father was a peasant, it's true, and here I am in a white waistcoat and tan shoes. Like a pig in a pastry shop. . . . I may be rich, I've made a lot of money, but if you think about it, analyze it, I'm a peasant through and through. (*Turning pages of the book.*) Here I've been reading this book, and I didn't understand a thing. Fell asleep over it. (*Pause.*)
DUNYASHA: The dogs didn't sleep all night: They can tell that their masters are coming.
LOPAKHIN: What's the matter with you, Dunyasha, you're so . . .
DUNYASHA: My hands are trembling. I'm going to faint.
LOPAKHIN: You're much too delicate, Dunyasha. You dress like a lady, and do your hair like one, too. It's not right. You should know your place.

(*Enter Yepikhodov with a bouquet, he wears a jacket and highly polished boots that squeak loudly. He drops the flowers as he comes in.*)

YEPIKHODOV (*picking up the flowers*): Here, the gardener sent these. He says you're to put them in the dining room. (*Hands the bouquet to Dunyasha.*)
LOPAKHIN: And bring me some kvas.°
DUNYASHA: Yes, sir. (*Goes out.*)
YEPIKHODOV: There's a frost this morning — three degrees — and the cherry trees are in bloom. I cannot

kvas: A Russian beer.

approve of our climate. (*Sighs.*) I cannot. Our climate is not exactly conducive. And now, Yermolai Alekseyevich, permit me to append: The day before yesterday I bought myself a pair of boots, which, I venture to assure you, squeak so that it's quite infeasible. What should I grease them with?

LOPAKHIN: Leave me alone. You make me tired.

YEPIKHODOV: Every day some misfortune happens to me. But I don't complain, I'm used to it, I even smile.

(*Dunyasha enters, serves Lopakhin the kvas.*)

YEPIKHODOV: I'm going. (*Stumbles over a chair and upsets it.*) There! (*As if in triumph.*) Now you see, excuse the expression . . . the sort of circumstance, incidentally. . . . It's really quite remarkable! (*Goes out.*)

DUNYASHA: You know, Yermolai Alekseyich, I have to confess that Yepikhodov has proposed to me.

LOPAKHIN: Ah!

DUNYASHA: And I simply don't know. . . . He's a quiet man, but sometimes, when he starts talking, you can't understand a thing he says. It's nice, and full of feeling, only it doesn't make sense. I sort of like him. He's madly in love with me. But he's an unlucky fellow: Every day something happens to him. They tease him about it around here; they call him Two-and-twenty Troubles.

LOPAKHIN (*listening*): I think I hear them coming . . .

DUNYASHA: They're coming! What's the matter with me? I'm cold all over.

LOPAKHIN: They're really coming. Let's go and meet them. Will she recognize me? It's five years since we've seen each other.

DUNYASHA (*agitated*): I'll faint this very minute . . . oh, I'm going to faint!

(*Two carriages are heard driving up to the house. Lopakhin and Dunyasha go out quickly. The stage is empty. There is a hubbub in the adjoining rooms. Firs hurriedly crosses the stage leaning on a stick. He has been to meet Lyubov Andreyevna and wears old fashioned livery and a high hat. He mutters something to himself, not a word of which can be understood. The noise offstage grows louder and louder. A voice: "Let's go through here. . . ." Enter Lyubov Andreyevna, Anya, Charlotta Ivanovna with a little dog on a chain, all in traveling dress; Varya wearing a coat and kerchief; Gayev, Semyonov-Pishchik, Lopakhin, Dunyasha with a bundle and parasol; servants with luggage — all walk through the room.*)

ANYA: Let's go this way. Do you remember, Mama, what room this is?

LYUBOV ANDREYEVNA: (*joyfully, through tears*): The nursery!

VARYA: How cold it is! My hands are numb. (*To Lyubov Andreyevna.*) Your rooms, both the white one and the violet one, are just as you left them, Mama.

LYUBOV ANDREYEVNA: The nursery . . . my dear, lovely nursery. . . . I used to sleep here when I was little. . . . (*Weeps.*) And now, like a child, I . . . (*Kisses her brother, Varya, then her brother again.*) Varya hasn't changed; she still looks like a nun. And I recognized Dunyasha. . . . (*Kisses Dunyasha.*)

GAYEV: The train was two hours late. How's that? What kind of management is that?

CHARLOTTA (*to Pishchik*): My dog even eats nuts.

PISHCHIK (*amazed*): Think of that now!

(*They all go out except Anya and Dunyasha.*)

DUNYASHA: We've been waiting and waiting for you. . . . (*Takes off Anya's coat and hat.*)

ANYA: I didn't sleep for four nights on the road . . . now I feel cold.

DUNYASHA: It was Lent when you went away, there was snow and frost then, but now? My darling! (*Laughs and kisses her.*) I've waited so long for you, my joy, my precious . . . I must tell you at once, I can't wait another minute. . . .

ANYA (*listlessly*): What now?

DUNYASHA: The clerk, Yepikhodov, proposed to me just after Easter.

ANYA: You always talk about the same thing. . . . (*Straightening her hair.*) I've lost all my hairpins. . . . (*She is so exhausted she can hardly stand.*)

DUNYASHA: I really don't know what to think. He loves me — he loves me so!

ANYA (*looking through the door into her room, tenderly*): My room, my windows . . . it's just as though I'd never been away. I am home! Tomorrow morning I'll get up and run into the orchard. . . . Oh, if I could only sleep! I didn't sleep during the entire journey, I was so tormented by anxiety.

DUNYASHA: Pyotr Sergeich arrived the day before yesterday.

ANYA (*joyfully*): Petya!

DUNYASHA: He's asleep in the bathhouse, he's staying there. "I'm afraid of being in the way," he said. (*Looks at her pocket watch.*) I ought to wake him up, but Varvara Mikhailovna told me not to. "Don't you wake him," she said.

(*Enter Varya with a bunch of keys at her waist.*)

VARYA: Dunyasha, coffee, quickly . . . Mama's asking for coffee.

DUNYASHA: This very minute. (*Goes out.*)

VARYA: Thank God, you've come! You're home again. (*Caressing her.*) My little darling has come back! My pretty one is here!

ANYA: I've been through so much.

VARYA: I can imagine!

ANYA: I left in Holy Week, it was cold then. Charlotta never stopped talking and doing her conjuring tricks the entire journey. Why did you saddle me with Charlotta?

VARYA: You couldn't have traveled alone, darling. At seventeen!

ANYA: When we arrived in Paris, it was cold, snowing. My French is awful. . . . Mama was living on the fifth floor, and when I got there, she had all sorts of Frenchmen and ladies with her, and an old priest with a little book, and it was full of smoke, dismal.

Suddenly I felt sorry for Mama, so sorry. I took her head in my arms and held her close and couldn't let her go. Afterward she kept hugging me and crying. . . .

VARYA (*through her tears*): Don't talk about it, don't talk about it. . . .

ANYA: She had already sold her villa near Mentone, and she had nothing left, nothing. And I hadn't so much as a kopeck left, we barely managed to get there. But Mama doesn't understand! When we had dinner in a station restaurant, she always ordered the most expensive dishes and tipped each of the waiters a ruble. Charlotta is the same. And Yasha also ordered a dinner, it was simply awful. You know, Yasha is Mama's footman; we brought him with us.

VARYA: I saw the rogue.

ANYA: Well, how are things? Have you paid the interest?

VARYA: How could we?

ANYA: Oh, my God, my God!

VARYA: In August the estate will be put up for sale.

ANYA: My God!

(*Lopakhin peeps in at the door and moos like a cow.*)

LOPAKHIN: Moo-o-o! (*Disappears.*)

VARYA (*through her tears*): What I couldn't do to him! (*Shakes her fist.*)

ANYA (*embracing Varya, softly*): Varya, has he proposed to you? (*Varya shakes her head.*) But he loves you. . . . Why don't you come to an understanding, what are you waiting for?

VARYA: I don't think anything will ever come of it. He's too busy, he has no time for me . . . he doesn't even notice me. I've washed my hands of him, it makes me miserable to see him. . . . Everyone talks of our wedding, they all congratulate me, and actually there's nothing to it — it's all like a dream. . . . (*In a different tone.*) You have a brooch like a bee.

ANYA (*sadly*): Mama bought it. (*Goes into her own room; speaks gaily, like a child.*) In Paris I went up in a balloon!

VARYA: My darling is home! My pretty one has come back!

(*Dunyasha has come in with the coffeepot and prepares coffee.*)

VARYA (*stands at the door of Anya's room*): You know, darling, all day long I'm busy looking after the house, but I keep dreaming. If we could marry you to a rich man I'd be at peace. I could go into a hermitage, then to Kiev, to Moscow, and from one holy place to another. . . . I'd go on and on. What a blessing!

ANYA: The birds are singing in the orchard. What time is it?

VARYA: It must be after two. Time you were asleep, darling. (*Goes into Anya's room.*) What a blessing!

(*Yasha enters with a lap robe and a traveling bag.*)

YASHA (*crosses the stage mincingly*): May one go through here?

DUNYASHA: A person would hardly recognize you, Yasha. Your stay abroad has done wonders for you.

YASHA: Hm. . . . And who are you?

DUNYASHA: When you left here I was only that high — (*indicating with her hand*). I'm Dunyasha, Fyodor Kozoyedov's daughter. You don't remember?

YASHA: Hm. . . . A little cucumber! (*Looks around, then embraces her; she cries out and drops a saucer. He quickly goes out.*)

VARYA (*in a tone of annoyance, from the doorway*): What's going on here?

DUNYASHA (*tearfully*): I broke a saucer.

VARYA: That's good luck.

ANYA: We ought to prepare Mama: Petya is here. . . .

VARYA: I gave orders not to wake him.

ANYA (*pensively*): Six years ago Father died, and a month later brother Grisha drowned in the river . . . a pretty little seven-year-old boy. Mama couldn't bear it and went away . . . went without looking back. . . . (*Shudders.*) How I understand her, if she only knew! (*Pause.*) And Petya Trofimov was Grisha's tutor, he may remind her. . . .

(*Enter Firs wearing a jacket and a white waistcoat.*)

FIRS (*goes to the coffeepot, anxiously*): The mistress will have her coffee here. (*Puts on white gloves.*) Is the coffee ready? (*To Dunyasha, sternly.*) You! Where's the cream?

DUNYASHA: Oh, my goodness! (*Quickly goes out.*)

FIRS (*fussing over the coffeepot*): Ah, what an addlepate! (*Mutters to himself.*) They've come back from Paris. . . . The master used to go to Paris . . . by carriage. . . . (*Laughs.*)

VARYA: What is it, Firs?

FIRS: If you please? (*Joyfully.*) My mistress has come home! At last! Now I can die. . . . (*Weeps with joy.*)

(*Enter Lyubov Andreyevna, Gayev, and Semyonov-Pishchik, the last wearing a sleeveless peasant coat of fine cloth and full trousers. Gayev, as he comes in, goes through the motions of playing billiards.*)

LYUBOV ANDREYEVNA: How does it go? Let's see if I can remember . . . cue ball into the corner! Double the rail to center table.

GAYEV: Cut shot into the corner! There was a time, sister, when you and I used to sleep here in this very room, and now I'm fifty-one, strange as it may seem. . . .

LOPAKHIN: Yes, time passes.

GAYEV: How's that?

LOPAKHIN: Time, I say, passes.

GAYEV: It smells of patchouli here.

ANYA: I'm going to bed. Good night, Mama. (*Kisses her mother.*)

LYUBOV ANDREYEVNA: My precious child. (*Kisses her hands.*) Are you glad to be home? I still feel dazed.

ANYA: Good night, Uncle.

GAYEV (*kisses her face and hands*): God bless you. How like your mother you are! (*To his sister.*) At her age you were exactly like her, Lyuba.

(*Anya shakes hands with Lopakhin and Pishchik and goes out, closing the door after her.*)

LYUBOV ANDREYEVNA: She's exhausted.

PISHCHIK: Must have been a long journey.

VARYA: Well, gentlemen? It's after two, high time you were going.

LYUBOV ANDREYEVNA (*laughs*): You haven't changed, Varya. (*Draws Varya to her and kisses her.*) I'll just drink my coffee and then we'll all go. (*Firs places a cushion under her feet.*) Thank you, my dear. I've got used to coffee. I drink it day and night. Thanks, dear old man. (*Kisses him.*)

VARYA: I'd better see if all the luggage has been brought in.

LYUBOV ANDREYEVNA: Is this really me sitting here? (*Laughs.*) I feel like jumping about and waving my arms. (*Buries her face in her hands.*) What if it's only a dream! God knows I love my country, love it dearly. I couldn't look out the train window, I was crying so! (*Through tears.*) But I must drink my coffee. Thank you, Firs, thank you, my dear old friend. I'm so glad you're still alive.

FIRS: The day before yesterday.

GAYEV: He's hard of hearing.

LOPAKHIN: I must go now, I'm leaving for Kharkov about five o'clock. It's so annoying! I wanted to have a good look at you, and have a talk. You're as splendid as ever.

PISHCHIK (*breathing heavily*): Even more beautiful. . . . Dressed like a Parisienne. . . . There goes my wagon, all four wheels!

LOPAKHIN: Your brother here, Leonid Andreich, says I'm a boor, a moneygrubber, but I don't mind. Let him talk. All I want is that you should trust me as you used to, and that your wonderful, touching eyes should look at me as they did then. Merciful God! My father was one of your father's serfs, and your grandfather's, but you yourself did so much for me once, that I've forgotten all that and love you as if you were my own kin — more than my kin.

LYUBOV ANDREYEVNA: I can't sit still, I simply cannot. (*Jumps up and walks about the room in great excitement.*) I cannot bear this joy. . . . Laugh at me, I'm silly. . . . My dear little bookcase . . . (*kisses bookcase*) my little table . . .

GAYEV: Nurse died while you were away.

LYUBOV ANDREYEVNA (*sits down and drinks coffee*): Yes, God rest her soul. They wrote me.

GAYEV: And Anastasy is dead. Petrushka Kosoi left me and is now with the police inspector in town. (*Takes a box of hard candies from his pocket and begins to suck one.*)

PISHCHIK: My daughter, Dashenka . . . sends her regards . . .

LOPAKHIN: I wish I could tell you something very pleasant and cheering. (*Glances at his watch.*) I must go directly, there's no time to talk, but . . . well, I'll say it in a couple of words. As you know, the cherry orchard is to be sold to pay your debts. The auction is set for August twenty-second, but you need not worry, my dear, you can sleep in peace, there is a way out. This is my plan. Now, please listen! Your estate is only twenty versts° from town, the railway runs close by, and if the cherry orchard and the land along the river were cut up into lots and leased for summer cottages, you'd have, at the very least, an income of twenty-five thousand a year.

GAYEV: Excuse me, what nonsense!

LYUBOV ANDREYEVNA: I don't quite understand you, Yermolai Alekseich.

LOPAKHIN: You will get, at the very least, twenty-five rubles a year for a two-and-a-half-acre lot, and if you advertise now, I guarantee you won't have a single plot of ground left by autumn, everything will be snapped up. In short, I congratulate you, you are saved. The site is splendid, the river is deep. Only, of course, the ground must be cleared . . . you must tear down all the old outbuildings, for instance, and this house, which is worthless, cut down the old cherry orchard —

LYUBOV ANDREYEVNA: Cut it down? Forgive me, my dear, but you don't know what you are talking about. If there is one thing in the whole province that is interesting, not to say remarkable, it's our cherry orchard.

LOPAKHIN: The only remarkable thing about this orchard is that it is very big. There's a crop of cherries every other year, and then you can't get rid of them, nobody buys them.

GAYEV: This orchard is even mentioned in the *Encyclopedia.*

LOPAKHIN (*glancing at his watch*): If we don't think of something and come to a decision, on the twenty-second of August the cherry orchard, and the entire estate, will be sold at auction. Make up your minds! There is no other way out, I swear to you. None whatsoever.

FIRS: In the old days, forty or fifty years ago, the cherries were dried, soaked, marinated, and made into jam, and they used to —

GAYEV: Be quiet, Firs.

FIRS: And they used to send cartloads of dried cherries to Moscow and Kharkov. And that brought in money! The dried cherries were soft and juicy in those days, sweet, fragrant. . . . They had a method then . . .

LYUBOV ANDREYEVNA: And what has become of that method now?

FIRS: Forgotten. Nobody remembers. . . .

PISHCHIK: How was it in Paris? What's it like there? Did you eat frogs?

LYUBOV ANDREYEVNA: I ate crocodiles.

PISHCHIK: Think of that now!

LOPAKHIN: There used to be only the gentry and the peasants living in the country, but now these summer people have appeared. All the towns, even the smallest ones, are surrounded by summer cottages. And it is safe to say that in another twenty years these people will multiply enormously. Now the summer resident only drinks tea on his porch, but it may well

---

versts: A verst is approximately equal to a kilometer, a little more than half a mile.

be that he'll take to cultivating his acre and then your cherry orchard will be a happy, rich, luxuriant —
GAYEV (*indignantly*): What nonsense!

(*Enter Varya and Yasha.*)

VARYA: There are two telegrams for you, Mama. (*Picks out a key and with a jingling sound opens an old-fashioned bookcase.*) Here they are.
LYUBOV ANDREYEVNA: From Paris. (*Tears up the telegrams without reading them.*) That's all over. . . .
GAYEV: Do you know, Lyuba, how old this bookcase is? A week ago I pulled out the bottom drawer, and what do I see? Some figures burnt into it. The bookcase was made exactly a hundred years ago. What do you think of that? Eh? We could have celebrated its jubilee. It's an inanimate object, but nevertheless, for all that, it's a bookcase.
PISHCHIK: A hundred years . . . think of that now!
GAYEV: Yes . . . that is something. . . . (*Feeling the bookcase.*) Dear, honored bookcase. I salute thy existence, which for over one hundred years has served the glorious ideals of goodness and justice; thy silent appeal to fruitful endeavor, unflagging in the course of a hundred years, tearfully sustaining through generations of our family, courage and faith in a better future, and fostering in us ideals of goodness and social consciousness. . . .

(*A pause.*)

LOPAKHIN: Yes . . .
LYUBOV ANDREYEVNA: You are the same as ever, Lyonya.
GAYEV (*somewhat embarrassed*): Carom into the corner, cut shot to center table.
LOPAKHIN (*looks at his watch*): Well, time for me to go.
YASHA (*hands medicine to Lyubov Andreyevna*): Perhaps you will take your pills now.
PISHCHIK: Don't take medicaments, dearest lady, they do neither harm nor good. Let me have them, honored lady. (*Takes the pillbox, shakes the pills into his hand, blows on them, puts them into his mouth and washes them down with kvas.*) There!
LYUBOV ANDREYEVNA (*alarmed*): Why, you must be mad!
PISHCHIK: I've taken all the pills.
LOPAKHIN: What a glutton!

(*Everyone laughs.*)

FIRS: The gentleman stayed with us during Holy Week . . . ate half a bucket of pickles. . . . (*Mumbles.*)
LYUBOV ANDREYEVNA: What is he saying?
VARYA: He's been muttering like that for three years now. We've grown used to it.
YASHA: He's in his dotage.

(*Charlotta Ivanovna, very thin, tightly laced, in a white dress with a lorgnette at her belt, crosses the stage.*)

LOPAKHIN: Forgive me, Charlotta Ivanovna, I haven't had a chance to say how do you do to you. (*Tries to kiss her hand.*)

CHARLOTTA (*pulls her hand away*): If I permit you to kiss my hand you'll be wanting to kiss my elbow next, then my shoulder.
LOPAKHIN: I have no luck today. (*Everyone laughs.*) Charlotta Ivanovna, show us a trick!
LYUBOV ANDREYEVNA: Charlotta, show us a trick!
CHARLOTTA: No. I want to sleep. (*Goes out.*)
LOPAKHIN: In three weeks we'll meet again. (*Kisses Lyubov Andreyevna's hand.*) Good-bye till then. Time to go. (*To Gayev.*) Good-bye. (*Kisses Pishchik.*) Good-bye. (*Shakes hands with Varya, then with Firs and Yasha.*) I don't feel like going. (*To Lyubov Andreyevna.*) If you make up your mind about the summer cottages and come to a decision, let me know; I'll get you a loan of fifty thousand or so. Think it over seriously.
VARYA (*angrily*): Oh, why don't you go!
LOPAKHIN: I'm going, I'm going. (*Goes out.*)
GAYEV: Boor. Oh, pardon. Varya's going to marry him, he's Varya's young man.
VARYA: Uncle dear, you talk too much.
LYUBOV ANDREYEVNA: Well, Varya, I shall be very glad. He's a good man.
PISHCHIK: A man, I must truly say . . . most worthy. . . . And my Dashenka . . . says, too, that . . . says all sorts of things. (*Snores but wakes up at once.*) In any case, honored lady, oblige me . . . a loan of two hundred and forty rubles . . . tomorrow the interest on my mortgage is due. . . .
VARYA (*in alarm*): We have nothing, nothing at all!
LYUBOV ANDREYEVNA: I really haven't any money.
PISHCHIK: It'll turn up. (*Laughs.*) I never lose hope. Just when I thought everything was lost, that I was done for, lo and behold — the railway line ran through my land . . . and they paid me for it. And before you know it, something else will turn up, if not today — tomorrow. . . . Dashenka will win two hundred thousand . . . she's got a lottery ticket.
LYUBOV ANDREYEVNA: The coffee is finished, we can go to bed.
FIRS (*brushing Gayev's clothes, admonishingly*): You've put on the wrong trousers again. What am I to do with you?
VARYA (*softly*): Anya's asleep. (*Quietly opens the window.*) The sun has risen, it's no longer cold. Look, Mama dear, what wonderful trees! Oh, Lord, the air! The starlings are singing!
GAYEV (*opens another window*): The orchard is all white. You haven't forgotten, Lyuba? That long avenue there that runs straight — straight as a stretched-out strap; it gleams on moonlight nights. Remember? You've not forgotten?
LYUBOV ANDREYEVNA (*looking out the window at the orchard*): Oh, my childhood, my innocence! I used to sleep in this nursery, I looked out from here into the orchard, happiness awoke with me each morning, it was just as it is now, nothing has changed. (*Laughing with joy.*) All, all white! Oh, my orchard! After the dark, rainy autumn and the cold winter, you are

young again, full of happiness, the heavenly angels have not forsaken you. . . . If I could cast off this heavy stone weighing on my breast and shoulders, if I could forget my past!

GAYEV: Yes, and the orchard will be sold for our debts, strange as it may seem. . . .

LYUBOV ANDREYEVNA: Look, our dead mother walks in the orchard . . . in a white dress! (*Laughs with joy.*) It is she!

GAYEV: Where?

VARYA: God be with you, Mama dear.

LYUBOV ANDREYEVNA: There's no one there, I just imagined it. To the right, as you turn to the summerhouse, a slender white sapling is bent over . . . it looks like a woman.

(*Enter Trofimov wearing a shabby student's uniform and spectacles.*)

LYUBOV ANDREYEVNA: What a wonderful orchard! The white masses of blossoms, the blue sky —

TROFIMOV: Lyubov Andreyevna! (*She looks around at him.*) I only want to pay my respects, then I'll go at once. (*Kisses her hand ardently.*) I was told to wait until morning, but I hadn't the patience.

(*Lyubov Andreyevna looks at him, puzzled.*)

VARYA (*through tears*): This is Petya Trofimov.

TROFIMOV: Petya Trofimov, I was Grisha's tutor. . . . Can I have changed so much?

(*Lyubov Andreyevna embraces him, quietly weeping.*)

GAYEV (*embarrassed*): There, there, Lyuba.

VARYA (*crying*): Didn't I tell you, Petya, to wait till tomorrow?

LYUBOV ANDREYEVNA: My Grisha . . . my little boy . . . Grisha . . . my son. . . .

VARYA: What can we do, Mama dear? It's God's will.

TROFIMOV (*gently, through tears*): Don't, don't. . . .

LYUBOV ANDREYEVNA (*quietly weeping*): My little boy dead, drowned. . . . Why? Why, my friend? (*In a lower voice.*) Anya is sleeping in there, and I'm talking loudly . . . making all this noise. . . . But Petya, why do you look so bad? Why have you grown so old?

TROFIMOV: A peasant woman in the train called me a mangy gentleman.

LYUBOV ANDREYEVNA: You were just a boy then, a charming little student, and now your hair is thin — and spectacles! Is it possible you are still a student? (*Goes toward the door.*)

TROFIMOV: I shall probably be an eternal student.

LYUBOV ANDREYEVNA (*kisses her brother, then Varya*): Now, go to bed. . . . You've grown older too, Leonid.

PISHCHIK (*follows her*): Well, seems to be time to sleep. . . . Oh, my gout! I'm staying the night. Lyubov Andreyevna, my soul, tomorrow morning . . . two hundred and forty rubles. . . .

GAYEV: He keeps at it.

PISHCHIK: Two hundred and forty rubles . . . to pay the interest on my mortgage.

LYUBOV ANDREYEVNA: I have no money, my friend.

PISHCHIK: My dear, I'll pay it back. . . . It's a trifling sum.

LYUBOV ANDREYEVNA: Well, all right, Leonid will give it to you. . . . Give it to him, Leonid.

GAYEV: Me give it to him! . . . Hold out your pocket!

LYUBOV ANDREYEVNA: It can't be helped, give it to him. . . . He needs it. . . . He'll pay it back.

(*Lyubov Andreyevna, Trofimov, Pishchik, and Firs go out. Gayev, Varya, and Yasha remain.*)

GAYEV: My sister hasn't yet lost her habit of squandering money. (*To Yasha.*) Go away, my good fellow, you smell of the henhouse.

YASHA (*with a smirk*): And you, Leonid Andreyevich, are just the same as ever.

GAYEV: How's that? (*To Varya.*) What did he say?

VARYA: Your mother has come from the village; she's been sitting in the servants' room since yesterday, waiting to see you. . . .

YASHA: Let her wait, for God's sake!

VARYA: Aren't you ashamed?

YASHA: A lot I need her! She could have come tomorrow. (*Goes out.*)

VARYA: Mama's the same as ever, she hasn't changed a bit. She'd give away everything, if she could.

GAYEV: Yes. . . . (*A pause.*) If a great many remedies are suggested for a disease, it means that the disease is incurable. I keep thinking, racking my brains, I have many remedies, a great many, and that means in effect, that I have none. It would be good to receive a legacy from someone, good to marry our Anya to a very rich man, good to go to Yaroslav and try our luck with our aunt, the Countess. She is very, very rich, you know.

VARYA (*crying*): If only God would help us!

GAYEV: Stop bawling. Auntie's very rich, but she doesn't like us. In the first place, sister married a lawyer, not a nobleman . . . (*Anya appears in the doorway.*) She married beneath her, and it cannot be said that she has conducted herself very virtuously. She is good, kind, charming, and I love her dearly, but no matter how much you allow for extenuating circumstances, you must admit she leads a sinful life. You feel it in her slightest movement.

VARYA (*in a whisper*): Anya is standing in the doorway.

GAYEV: What? (*Pause.*) Funny, something got into my right eye . . . I can't see very well. And Thursday, when I was in the district court . . .

(*Anya enters.*)

VARYA: Why aren't you asleep, Anya?

ANYA: I can't get to sleep. I just can't.

GAYEV: My little one! (*Kisses Anya's face and hands.*) My child. . . . (*Through tears.*) You are not my niece, you are my angel, you are everything to me. Believe me, believe . . .

ANYA: I believe you, Uncle. Everyone loves you and respects you, but, Uncle dear, you must keep quiet, just keep quiet. What were you saying just now about my mother, about your own sister? What made you say that?

GAYEV: Yes, yes. . . . (*Covers his face with her hand.*) Really, it's awful! My God! God help me! And today I made a speech to the bookcase . . . so stupid! And it was only when I had finished that I realized it was stupid.

VARYA: It's true, Uncle dear, you ought to keep quiet. Just don't talk, that's all.

ANYA: If you could keep from talking, it would make things easier for you, too.

GAYEV: I'll be quiet. (*Kisses Anya's and Varya's hands.*) I'll be quiet. Only this is about business. On Thursday I was in the district court, well, a group of us gathered together and began talking about one thing and another, this and that, and it seems it might be possible to arrange a loan on a promissory note to pay the interest at the bank.

VARYA: If only God would help us!

GAYEV: On Tuesday I'll go and talk it over again. (*To Varya.*) Stop bawling. (*To Anya.*) Your mama will talk to Lopakhin; he, of course, will not refuse her. . . . And as soon as you've rested, you will go to Yaroslav to the Countess, your great-aunt. In that way we shall be working from three directions — and our business is in the hat. We'll pay the interest, I'm certain of it. . . . (*Puts a candy in his mouth.*) On my honor, I'll swear by anything you like, the estate shall not be sold. (*Excitedly.*) By my happiness, I swear it! Here's my hand on it, call me a worthless, dishonorable man if I let it come to auction! I swear by my whole being!

ANYA (*a calm mood returns to her, she is happy*): How good you are, Uncle, how clever! (*Embraces him.*) Now I am at peace! I'm at peace! I'm happy!

(*Enter Firs.*)

FIRS (*reproachfully*): Leonid Andreich, have you no fear of God? When are you going to bed?

GAYEV: Presently, presently. Go away, Firs. I'll . . . all right, I'll undress myself. Well, children, bye-bye. . . . Details tomorrow, and now go to sleep. (*Kisses Anya and Varya.*) I am a man of the eighties. . . . They don't think much of that period today, nevertheless, I can say that in the course of my life I have suffered not a little for my convictions. It is not for nothing that the peasant loves me. You have to know the peasant! You have to know from what —

ANYA: There you go again, Uncle!

VARYA: Uncle dear, do be quiet.

FIRS (*angrily*): Leonid Andreich!

GAYEV: I'm coming, I'm coming. . . . Go to bed. A clean double rail shot to center table. . . . (*Goes out; Firs hobbles after him.*)

ANYA: I'm at peace now. I would rather not go to Yaroslav, I don't like my great-aunt, but still, I'm at peace, thanks to Uncle. (*She sits down.*)

VARYA: We must get some sleep. I'm going now. Oh, something unpleasant happened while you were away. In the old servants' quarters, as you know, there are only the old people: Yefimushka, Polya, Yevstignei, and, of course, Karp. They began letting in all sorts of rogues to spend the night — I didn't say anything. But then I heard they'd been spreading a rumor that I'd given an order for them to be fed nothing but dried peas. Out of stinginess, you see. . . . It was all Yevstignei's doing. . . . Very well, I think, if that's how it is, you just wait. I send for Yevstignei . . . (*yawning*) he comes. . . . "How is it, Yevstignei," I say, "that you could be such a fool. . . ." (*Looks at Anya.*) She's fallen asleep. (*Takes her by the arm.*) Come to your little bed. . . . Come along. (*Leading her.*) My little darling fell asleep. Come. . . . (*They go.*)

(*In the distance, beyond the orchard, a shepherd is playing on a reed pipe. Trofimov crosses the stage and, seeing Varya and Anya, stops.*)

VARYA: Sh! She's asleep . . . asleep. . . . Come along, darling.

ANYA (*softly, half-asleep*): I'm so tired. . . . Those bells . . . Uncle . . . dear . . . Mama and Uncle . . .

VARYA: Come, darling, come along. (*They go into Anya's room.*)

TROFIMOV (*deeply moved*): My sunshine! My spring!

ACT II

(*A meadow. An old, lopsided, long-abandoned little chapel; near it a well, large stones that apparently were once tombstones, and an old bench. A road to the Gayev manor house can be seen. On one side, where the cherry orchard begins, tall poplars loom. In the distance a row of telegraph poles, and far, far away, on the horizon, the faint outline of a large town, which is visible only in very fine, clear weather. The sun will soon set. Charlotta, Yasha, and Dunyasha are sitting on the bench; Yepikhodov stands near playing something sad on the guitar. They are all lost in thought. Charlotta wears an old forage cap; she has taken a gun from her shoulder and is adjusting the buckle on the sling.*)

CHARLOTTA (*reflectively*): I haven't got a real passport, I don't know how old I am, but it always seems to me that I'm quite young. When I was a little girl, my father and mother used to travel from one fair to another giving performances — very good ones. And I did the *salto mortale*° and all sorts of tricks. Then when Papa and Mama died, a German lady took me to live with her and began teaching me. Good. I grew up and became a governess. But where I come from and who I am — I do not know. . . . Who my parents were — perhaps they weren't even married — I don't know. (*Takes a cucumber out of her pocket and eats it.*) I don't know anything. (*Pause.*) One wants so much to talk, but there isn't anyone to talk to . . . I have no one.

salto mortale: Somersault.

YEPIKHODOV (*plays the guitar and sings*): "What care I for the clamorous world, what's friend or foe to me?". . . . How pleasant it is to play a mandolin!

DUNYASHA: That's a guitar, not a mandolin. (*Looks at herself in a hand mirror and powders her face.*)

YEPIKHODOV: To a madman, in love, it is a mandolin. . . . (*Sings.*) "Would that the heart were warmed by the flame of requited love . . ."

(*Yasha joins in.*)

CHARLOTTA: How horribly these people sing! . . . Pfui! Like jackals!

DUNYASHA (*to Yasha*): Really, how fortunate to have been abroad!

YASHA: Yes, to be sure. I cannot but agree with you there. (*Yawns, then lights a cigar.*)

YEPIKHODOV: It stands to reason. Abroad everything has long since been fully constituted.

YASHA: Obviously.

YEPIKHODOV: I am a cultivated man, I read all sorts of remarkable books, but I am in no way able to make out my own inclinations, what it is I really want, whether, strictly speaking, to live or to shoot myself; nevertheless, I always carry a revolver on me. Here it is. (*Shows revolver.*)

CHARLOTTA: Finished. Now I'm going. (*Slings the gun over her shoulder.*) You're a very clever man, Yepikhodov, and quite terrifying; women must be mad about you. Brrr! (*Starts to go.*) These clever people are all so stupid, there's no one for me to talk to. . . . Alone, always alone, I have no one . . . and who I am, and why I am, nobody knows. . . . (*Goes out unhurriedly.*)

YEPIKHODOV: Strictly speaking, all else aside, I must state regarding myself, that fate treats me unmercifully, as a storm does a small ship. If, let us assume, I am mistaken, then why, to mention a single instance, do I wake up this morning, and there on my chest see a spider of terrifying magnitude? . . . Like that. (*Indicates with both hands.*) And likewise, I take up some kvas to quench my thirst, and there see something in the highest degree unseemly, like a cockroach. (*Pause.*) Have you read Buckle?° (*Pause.*) If I may trouble you, Avdotya Fyodorovna, I should like to have a word or two with you.

DUNYASHA: Go ahead.

YEPIKHODOV: I prefer to speak with you alone. . . . (*Sighs.*)

DUNYASHA (*embarrassed*): Very well . . . only first bring me my little cape . . . you'll find it by the cupboard. . . . It's rather damp here. . . .

YEPIKHODOV: Certainly, ma'am . . . I'll fetch it, ma'am. . . . Now I know what to do with my revolver. . . . (*Takes the guitar and goes off playing it.*)

YASHA: Two-and-twenty Troubles! Between ourselves, a stupid fellow. (*Yawns.*)

DUNYASHA: God forbid that he should shoot himself. (*Pause.*) I've grown so anxious, I'm always worried. I was only a little girl when I was taken into the master's house, and now I'm quite unused to the simple life, and my hands are white as can be, just like a lady's. I've become so delicate, so tender and ladylike, I'm afraid of everything. . . . Frightfully so. And, Yasha, if you deceive me, I just don't know what will become of my nerves.

YASHA (*kisses her*): You little cucumber! Of course, a girl should never forget herself. What I dislike above everything is when a girl doesn't conduct herself properly.

DUNYASHA: I'm passionately in love with you, you're educated, you can discuss anything. (*Pause.*)

YASHA (*yawns*): Yes. . . . As I see it, it's like this: If a girl loves somebody, that means she's immoral. (*Pause.*) Very pleasant smoking a cigar in the open air. . . . (*Listens.*) Someone's coming this way. . . . It's the masters. (*Dunyasha impulsively embraces him.*) You go home, as if you'd been to the river to bathe; take that path, otherwise they'll see you and suspect me of having a rendezvous with you. I can't endure that sort of thing.

DUNYASHA (*with a little cough*): My head is beginning to ache from your cigar. . . . (*Goes out.*)

(*Yasha remains, sitting near the chapel. Lyubov Andreyevna, Gayev, and Lopakhin enter.*)

LOPAKHIN: You must make up your mind once and for all — time won't stand still. The question, after all, is quite simple. Do you agree to lease the land for summer cottages or not? Answer in one word: Yes or no? Only one word!

LYUBOV ANDREYEVNA: Who is it that smokes those disgusting cigars out here? (*Sits down.*)

GAYEV: Now that the railway line is so near, it's made things convenient. (*Sits down.*) We went to town and had lunch . . . cue ball to the center! I feel like going to the house first and playing a game.

LYUBOV ANDREYEVNA: Later.

LOPAKHIN: Just one word! (*Imploringly.*) Do give me an answer!

GAYEV (*yawning*): How's that?

LYUBOV ANDREYEVNA (*looks into her purse*): Yesterday I had a lot of money, and today there's hardly any left. My poor Varya tries to economize by feeding everyone milk soup, and in the kitchen the old people get nothing but dried peas, while I squander money foolishly. . . . (*Drops the purse, scattering gold coins.*) There they go. . . . (*Vexed.*)

YASHA: Allow me, I'll pick them up in an instant. (*Picks up the money.*)

LYUBOV ANDREYEVNA: Please do, Yasha. And why did I go to town for lunch? . . . That miserable restaurant of yours with its music, and tablecloths smelling of soap. . . . Why drink so much, Lyonya? Why eat so much? Why talk so much? Today in the restaurant again you talked too much, and it was all so pointless. About the seventies, about the decadents. And to whom? Talking to waiters about the decadents!

Buckle: Thomas Henry Buckle (1821–1862) was a radical historian who formulated a scientific basis for history emphasizing the interrelationship of climate, food production, population, and wealth.

LOPAKHIN: Yes.

GAYEV (*waving his hand*): I'm incorrigible, that's evident. . . . (*Irritably to Yasha.*) Why do you keep twirling about in front of me?

YASHA (*laughs*): I can't help laughing when I hear your voice.

GAYEV (*to his sister*): Either he or I —

LYUBOV ANDREYEVNA: Go away, Yasha, run along.

YASHA (*hands Lyubov Andreyevna her purse*): I'm going, right away. (*Hardly able to contain his laughter.*) This very instant. . . . (*Goes out.*)

LOPAKHIN: That rich man, Deriganov, is prepared to buy the estate. They say he's coming to the auction himself.

LYUBOV ANDREYEVNA: Where did you hear that?

LOPAKHIN: That's what they're saying in town.

LYUBOV ANDREYEVNA: Our aunt in Yaroslav promised to send us something, but when and how much, no one knows.

LOPAKHIN: How much do you think she'll send? A hundred thousand? Two hundred?

LYUBOV ANDREYEVNA: Oh . . . ten or fifteen thousand, and we'll be thankful for that.

LOPAKHIN: Forgive me, but I have never seen such frivolous, such queer, unbusinesslike people as you, my friends. You are told in plain language that your estate is to be sold, and it's as though you don't understand it.

ABOVE: The spare set in Ron Daniel's 1993 production of *The Cherry Orchard* at the American Repertory Theatre highlights the characters' emotional isolation. RIGHT: Claire Bloom as Madame Ranevskaya.

LYUBOV ANDREYEVNA: But what are we to do? Tell us what to do.

LOPAKHIN: I tell you every day. Every day I say the same thing. Both the cherry orchard and the land must be leased for summer cottages, and it must be done now, as quickly as possible — the auction is close at hand. Try to understand! Once you definitely decide on the cottages, you can raise as much money as you like, and then you are saved.

LYUBOV ANDREYEVNA: Cottages, summer people — forgive me, but it's so vulgar.

GAYEV: I agree with you, absolutely.

LOPAKHIN: I'll either burst into tears, start shouting, or fall into a faint! I can't stand it! You've worn me out! (*To Gayev.*) You're an old woman!

GAYEV: How's that?

LOPAKHIN: An old woman! (*Starts to go.*)

LYUBOV ANDREYEVNA (*alarmed*): No, don't go, stay, my dear. I beg you. Perhaps we'll think of something!

LOPAKHIN: What is there to think of?

LYUBOV ANDREYEVNA: Don't go away, please. With you here it's more cheerful somehow. . . . (*Pause.*) I keep expecting something to happen, like the house caving in on us.

GAYEV (*in deep thought*): Double rail shot into the corner. . . . Cross table to the center. . . .

LYUBOV ANDREYEVNA: We have sinned so much. . . .

LOPAKHIN: What sins could you have —

GAYEV (*puts a candy into his mouth*): They say I've eaten up my entire fortune in candies. . . . (*Laughs.*)

LYUBOV ANDREYEVNA: Oh, my sins. . . . I've always squandered money recklessly, like a madwoman, and I married a man who did nothing but amass debts. My husband died from champagne — he drank terribly — then, to my sorrow, I fell in love with another man, lived with him, and just at that time — that was my first punishment, a blow on the head — my little boy was drowned . . . here in the river. And I went abroad, went away for good, never to return, never to see this river. . . . I closed my eyes and ran, beside myself, and *he* after me . . . callously, without pity. I bought a villa near Mentone, because he fell ill there, and for three years I had no rest, day or night. The sick man wore me out, my soul dried up. Then last year, when the villa was sold to pay my debts, I went to Paris, and there he stripped me of everything, and left me for another woman; I tried to poison myself. . . . So stupid, so shameful. . . . And suddenly I felt a longing for Russia, for my own country, for my little girl. . . . (*Wipes away her tears.*) Lord, Lord, be merciful, forgive my sins! Don't punish me anymore! (*Takes a telegram out of her pocket.*) This came today from Paris. . . . He asks my forgiveness, begs me to return. . . . (*Tears up telegram.*) Do I hear music? (*Listens.*)

GAYEV: That's our famous Jewish band. You remember, four violins, a flute, and double bass.

LYUBOV ANDREYEVNA: It's still in existence? We ought to send for them sometime and give a party.

LOPAKHIN (*listens*): I don't hear anything. . . . (*Sings softly.*) "The Germans, for pay, will turn Russians into Frenchmen, they say." (*Laughs.*) What a play I saw yesterday at the theater — very funny!

LYUBOV ANDREYEVNA: There was probably nothing funny about it. Instead of going to see plays you ought to look at yourselves a little more often. How drab your lives are, how full of futile talk!

LOPAKHIN: That's true. I must say, this life of ours is stupid. . . . (*Pause.*) My father was a peasant, an idiot; he understood nothing, taught me nothing; all he did was beat me when he was drunk, and always with a stick. As a matter of fact, I'm as big a blockhead and idiot as he was. I never learned anything, my handwriting's disgusting, I write like a pig — I'm ashamed to have people see it.

LYUBOV ANDREYEVNA: You ought to get married, my friend.

LOPAKHIN: Yes . . . that's true.

LYUBOV ANDREYEVNA: To our Varya. She's a nice girl.

LOPAKHIN: Yes.

LYUBOV ANDREYEVNA: She's a girl who comes from simple people, works all day long, but the main thing is she loves you. Besides, you've liked her for a long time now.

LOPAKHIN: Well? I've nothing against it. . . . She's a good girl. (*Pause.*)

GAYEV: I've been offered a place in the bank. Six thousand a year. . . . Have you heard?

LYUBOV ANDREYEVNA: How could you! You stay where you are. . . .

(*Firs enters carrying an overcoat.*)

FIRS (*to Gayev*): If you please, sir, put this on, it's damp.

GAYEV (*puts on the overcoat*): You're a pest, old man.

FIRS: Never mind. . . . You went off this morning without telling me. (*Looks him over.*)

LYUBOV ANDREYEVNA: How you have aged, Firs!

FIRS: What do you wish, madam?

LOPAKHIN: She says you've grown very old!

FIRS: I've lived a long time. They were arranging a marriage for me before your papa was born. . . . (*Laughs.*) I was already head footman when the emancipation came. At that time I wouldn't consent to my freedom, I stayed with the masters. . . . (*Pause.*) I remember, everyone was happy, but what they were happy about, they themselves didn't know.

LOPAKHIN: It was better in the old days. At least they flogged them.

FIRS (*not hearing*): Of course. The peasants kept to the masters, the masters kept to the peasants; but now they have all gone their own ways, you can't tell about anything.

GAYEV: Be quiet, Firs. Tomorrow I must go to town. I've been promised an introduction to a certain general who might let us have a loan.

LOPAKHIN: Nothing will come of it. And you can rest assured, you won't even pay the interest.

LYUBOV ANDREYEVNA: He's raving. There is no such general.

(*Enter Trofimov, Anya, and Varya.*)

GAYEV: Here come our young people.

ANYA: There's Mama.

LYUBOV ANDREYEVNA (*tenderly*): Come, come along, my darlings. (*Embraces Anya and Varya.*) If you only knew how I love you both! Sit here beside me — there, like that.

(*They all sit down.*)

LOPAKHIN: Our eternal student is always with the young ladies.

TROFIMOV: That's none of your business.

LOPAKHIN: He'll soon be fifty, but he's still a student.

TROFIMOV: Drop your stupid jokes.

LOPAKHIN: What are you so angry about, you queer fellow?

TROFIMOV: Just leave me alone.

LOPAKHIN (*laughs*): Let me ask you something: What do you make of me?

TROFIMOV: My idea of you, Yermolai Alekseich, is this: You're a rich man, you will soon be a millionaire. Just as the beast of prey, which devours everything that crosses its path, is necessary in the metabolic process, so are you necessary.

(*Everyone laughs.*)

VARYA: Petya, you'd better tell us something about the planets.

LYUBOV ANDREYEVNA: No, let's go on with yesterday's conversation.

TROFIMOV: What was it about?

GAYEV: About the proud man.

TROFIMOV: We talked a long time yesterday, but we didn't get anywhere. In the proud man, in your sense of the word, there's something mystical. And you may be right from your point of view, but if you look at it simply, without being abstruse, why even talk about pride? Is there any sense in it if, physiologically, man is poorly constructed, if, in the vast majority of cases, he is coarse, ignorant, and profoundly unhappy? We should stop admiring ourselves. We should just work, and that's all.

GAYEV: You die, anyway.

TROFIMOV: Who knows? And what does it mean — to die? It may be that man has a hundred senses, and at his death only the five that are known to us perish, and the other ninety-five go on living.

LYUBOV ANDREYEVNA: How clever you are, Petya!

LOPAKHIN (*ironically*): Terribly clever!

TROFIMOV: Mankind goes forward, perfecting its powers. Everything that is now unattainable will some day be comprehensible and within our grasp, only we must work, and help with all our might those who are seeking the truth. So far, among us here in Russia, only a very few work. The great majority of the intelligentsia that I know seek nothing, do nothing, and as yet are incapable of work. They call themselves the intelligentsia, yet they belittle their servants, treat the peasants like animals, are wretched students, never read anything serious, and do absolutely nothing; they only talk about science and know very little about art. They all look serious, have grim expressions, speak of weighty matters, and philosophize; and meanwhile anyone can see that the workers eat abominably, sleep without pillows, thirty or forty to a room, and everywhere there are bedbugs, stench, dampness, and immorality. . . . It's obvious that all our fine talk is merely to delude ourselves and others. Show me the day nurseries they are always talking about — and where are the reading rooms? They only write about them in novels, but in reality they don't exist. There is nothing but filth, vulgarity, asiaticism.° . . . I'm afraid of those very serious countenances, I don't like them, I'm afraid of serious conversations. We'd do better to remain silent.

LOPAKHIN: You know, I get up before five in the morning, and I work from morning to night; now, I'm always handling money, my own and other people's, and I see what people around me are like. You have only to start doing something to find out how few honest, decent people there are. Sometimes, when I can't sleep, I think: "Lord, Thou gavest us vast forests, boundless fields, broad horizons, and living in their midst we ourselves ought truly to be giants. . . ."

LYUBOV ANDREYEVNA: Now you want giants! They're good only in fairy tales, otherwise they're frightening.

(*Yepikhodov crosses at the rear of the stage, playing the guitar.*)

LYUBOV ANDREYEVNA (*pensively*): There goes Yepikhodov . . .

ANYA (*pensively*): There goes Yepikhodov . . .

GAYEV: The sun has set, ladies and gentlemen.

TROFIMOV: Yes.

GAYEV (*in a low voice, as though reciting*): Oh, Nature, wondrous Nature, you shine with eternal radiance, beautiful and indifferent; you, whom we call mother, unite within yourself both life and death, giving life and taking it away. . . .

VARYA (*beseechingly*): Uncle dear!

ANYA: Uncle, you're doing it again!

TROFIMOV: You'd better cue ball into the center.

GAYEV: I'll be silent, silent.

(*All sit lost in thought. The silence is broken only by the subdued muttering of Firs. Suddenly a distant sound is heard, as if from the sky, like the sound of a snapped string mournfully dying away.*)

LYUBOV ANDREYEVNA: What was that?

LOPAKHIN: I don't know. Somewhere far off in a mine shaft a bucket's broken loose. But somewhere very far away.

GAYEV: It might be a bird of some sort . . . like a heron.

asiaticism: Trofimov, expressing a common prejudice of the time, refers to Asian apathy.

TROFIMOV: Or an owl . . .

LYUBOV ANDREYEVNA (*shudders*): It's unpleasant somehow. . . . (*Pause.*)

FIRS: The same thing happened before the troubles: An owl hooted and the samovar hissed continually.

GAYEV: Before what troubles?

FIRS: Before the emancipation.

LYUBOV ANDREYEVNA: Come along, my friends, let us go, evening is falling. (*To Anya.*) There are tears in your eyes — what is it, my little one?

(*Embraces her.*)

ANYA: It's all right, Mama. It's nothing.

TROFIMOV: Someone is coming.

(*A Stranger appears wearing a shabby white forage cap and an overcoat. He is slightly drunk.*)

STRANGER: Permit me to inquire, can I go straight through here to the station?

GAYEV: You can. Follow the road.

STRANGER: I am deeply grateful to you. (*Coughs.*) Splendid weather. . . . (*Reciting.*) "My brother, my suffering brother . . . come to the Volga, whose groans". . . (*To Varya.*) Mademoiselle, will you oblige a hungry Russian with thirty kopecks?

(*Varya, frightened, cries out.*)

LOPAKHIN (*angrily*): There's a limit to everything.

LYUBOV ANDREYEVNA (*panic-stricken*): Here you are — take this. . . . (*Fumbles in her purse.*) I have no silver. . . . Never mind, here's a gold piece for you. . . .

STRANGER: I am deeply grateful to you. (*Goes off.*)

(*Laughter.*)

VARYA (*frightened*): I'm leaving . . . I'm leaving. . . . Oh, Mama, dear, there's nothing in the house for the servants to eat, and you give him a gold piece!

LYUBOV ANDREYEVNA: What's to be done with such a silly creature? When we get home I'll give you all I've got. Yermolai Alekseyevich, you'll lend me some more!

LOPAKHIN: At your service.

LYUBOV ANDREYEVNA: Come, my friends, it's time to go. Oh, Varya, we have definitely made a match for you. Congratulations!

VARYA (*through tears*): Mama, that's not something to joke about.

LOPAKHIN: "Aurelia, get thee to a nunnery . . ."°

GAYEV: Look, my hands are trembling: It's a long time since I've played a game of billiards.

LOPAKHIN: "Aurelia, O Nymph, in thy orisons, be all my sins remember'd!"

LYUBOV ANDREYEVNA: Let us go, my friends, it will soon be suppertime.

"**Aurelia . . . nunnery**": From Hamlet's famous line rejecting Ophelia (Lopakhin's next line is also from Shakespeare's *Hamlet*).

VARYA: He frightened me. My heart is simply pounding.

LOPAKHIN: Let me remind you, ladies and gentlemen: On the twenty-second of August the cherry orchard is to be sold. Think about that! — Think!

(*All go out except Trofimov and Anya.*)

ANYA (*laughs*): My thanks to the stranger for frightening Varya, now we are alone.

TROFIMOV: Varya is so afraid we might suddenly fall in love with each other that she hasn't left us alone for days. With her narrow mind she can't understand that we are above love. To avoid the petty and the illusory, which prevent our being free and happy — that is the aim and meaning of life. Forward! We are moving irresistibly toward the bright star that burns in the distance! Forward! Do not fall behind, friends!

ANYA (*clasping her hands*): How well you talk! (*Pause.*) It's marvelous here today!

TROFIMOV: Yes, the weather is wonderful.

ANYA: What have you done to me, Petya, that I no longer love the cherry orchard as I used to? I loved it so tenderly, it seemed to me there was no better place on earth than our orchard.

TROFIMOV: All Russia is our orchard. It is a great and beautiful land, and there are many wonderful places in it. (*Pause.*) Just think, Anya: Your grandfather, your great-grandfather, and all your ancestors were serf-owners, possessors of living souls. Don't you see that from every cherry tree, from every leaf and trunk, human beings are peering out at you? Don't you hear their voices? To possess living souls — that has corrupted all of you, those who lived before and you who are living now, so that your mother, you, your uncle, no longer perceive that you are living in debt, at someone else's expense, at the expense of those whom you wouldn't allow to cross your threshold. . . . We are at least two hundred years behind the times, we have as yet absolutely nothing, we have no definite attitude toward the past, we only philosophize, complain of boredom, or drink vodka. Yet it's quite clear that to begin to live we must first atone for the past, be done with it, and we can atone for it only by suffering, only by extraordinary, unceasing labor. Understand this, Anya.

ANYA: The house we live in hasn't really been ours for a long time, and I shall leave it, I give you my word.

TROFIMOV: If you have the keys of the household, throw them into the well and go. Be as free as the wind.

ANYA (*in ecstasy*): How well you put that!

TROFIMOV: Believe me, Anya, believe me! I am not yet thirty, I am young, still a student, but I have already been through so much! As soon as winter comes, I am hungry, sick, worried, poor as a beggar, and — where has not fate driven me! Where have I not been? And yet always, every minute of the day and night, my soul was filled with inexplicable premonitions. I have a premonition of happiness, Anya, I can see it . . .

ANYA: The moon is rising.

(*Yepikhodov is heard playing the same melancholy song on the guitar. The moon rises. Somewhere near the poplars Varya is looking for Anya and calling: "Anya, where are you?"*)

TROFIMOV: Yes, the moon is rising. (*Pause.*) There it is — happiness . . . it's coming, nearer and nearer, I can hear its footsteps. And if we do not see it, if we do not recognize it, what does it matter? Others will see it.

VARYA'S VOICE: Anya! Where are you?

TROFIMOV: That Varya again! (*Angrily.*) It's revolting!

ANYA: Well? Let's go down to the river. It's lovely there.

TROFIMOV: Come on. (*They go.*)

VARYA'S VOICE: Anya! Anya!

ACT III

(*The drawing room, separated by an arch from the ball-room. The chandelier is lighted. The Jewish band that was mentioned in act II is heard playing in the hall. It is evening. In the ballroom they are dancing a grand rond. The voice of Semyonov-Pishchik: "Promenade à une paire!"° They all enter the drawing room: Pishchik and Charlotta Ivanovna are the first couple, Trofimov and Lyubov Andreyevna the second, Anya and the Post-Office Clerk the third, Varya and the Stationmaster the fourth, etc. Varya, quietly weeping, dries her tears as she dances. Dunyasha is in the last couple. As they cross the drawing room Pishchik calls: "Grand rond, balancez!" and "Les cavaliers à genoux et remerciez vos dames!"° Firs, wearing a dress coat, brings in a tray with seltzer water. Pishchik and Trofimov come into the drawing room.*)

PISHCHIK: I'm a full-blooded man, I've already had two strokes, and dancing's hard work for me, but as they say, "If you run with the pack, you can bark or not, but at least wag your tail." At that, I'm as strong as a horse. My late father — quite a joker he was, God rest his soul — used to say, talking about our origins, that the ancient line of Semyonov-Pishchik was descended from the very horse that Caligula had seated in the Senate.° . . . (*Sits down.*) But the trouble is — no money! A hungry dog believes in nothing but meat. . . . (*Snores but wakes up at once.*) It's the same with me — I can think of nothing but money. . . .

TROFIMOV: You know, there really is something equine about your figure.

PISHCHIK: Well, a horse is a fine animal. . . . You can sell a horse.

(*There is the sound of a billiard game in the next room. Varya appears in the archway.*)

"*Promenade à une paire!*": French for "Walk in pairs!" "*Grand rond . . . dames!*": Instructions in the dance: "Large circle!" and "Gentlemen, kneel down and thank your ladies!" **Caligula . . . Senate:** Caligula (A.D. 12–41), a cavalry soldier, was Roman emperor (A.D. 37–41).

TROFIMOV (*teasing her*): Madame Lopakhina! Madame Lopakhina!

VARYA (*angrily*): Mangy gentleman!

TROFIMOV: Yes, I am a mangy gentleman, and proud of it!

VARYA (*reflecting bitterly*): Here we've hired musicians, and what are we going to pay them with? (*Goes out.*)

TROFIMOV (*to Pishchik*): If the energy you have expended in the course of your life trying to find money to pay interest had gone into something else, ultimately, you might very well have turned the world upside down.

PISHCHIK: Nietzsche . . . the philosopher . . . the greatest, most renowned . . . a man of tremendous intellect . . . says in his works that it is possible to forge banknotes.

TROFIMOV: And have you read Nietzsche?

PISHCHIK: Well . . . Dashenka told me. I'm in such a state now that I'm just about ready for forging. . . . The day after tomorrow I have to pay three hundred and ten rubles . . . I've got a hundred and thirty. . . . (*Feels in his pocket, grows alarmed.*) The money is gone! I've lost the money! (*Tearfully.*) Where is my money? (*Joyfully.*) Here it is, inside the lining. . . . I'm all in a sweat. . . .

(*Lyubov Andreyevna and Charlotta Ivanovna come in.*)

LYUBOV ANDREYEVNA (*humming a* Lezginka):° Why does Leonid take so long? What is he doing in town? (*To Dunyasha.*) Dunyasha, offer the musicians some tea.

TROFIMOV: In all probability, the auction didn't take place.

LYUBOV ANDREYEVNA: It was the wrong time to have the musicians, the wrong time to give a dance. . . . Well, never mind. . . . (*Sits down and hums softly.*)

CHARLOTTA (*gives Pishchik a deck of cards*): Here's a deck of cards for you. Think of a card.

PISHCHIK: I've thought of one.

CHARLOTTA: Now shuffle the pack. Very good. And now, my dear Mr. Pishchik, hand it to me. *Eins, zwei, drei!*° Now look for it — it's in your side pocket.

PISHCHIK (*takes the card out of his side pocket*): The eight of spades — absolutely right! (*Amazed.*) Think of that, now!

CHARLOTTA (*holding the deck of cards in the palm of her hand, to Trofimov*): Quickly, tell me, which card is on top?

TROFIMOV: What? Well, the queen of spades.

CHARLOTTA: Right! (*To Pishchik.*) Now which card is on top?

PISHCHIK: The ace of hearts.

CHARLOTTA: Right! (*Claps her hands and the deck of cards disappears.*) What lovely weather we're having today! (*A mysterious feminine voice, which seems to come from under the floor, answers her: "Oh, yes,*

Lezginka: A lively Russian tune for a dance.   *Eins, zwei, drei!:* "One, two, three" (German).

splendid weather, madam.") You are so nice, you're my ideal. . . . (*The voice: "And I'm very fond of you, too, madam."*)

STATIONMASTER (*applauding*): Bravo, Madame Ventriloquist!

PISHCHIK (*amazed*): Think of that, now! Most enchanting Charlotta Ivanovna . . . I am simply in love with you. . . .

CHARLOTTA: In love? (*Shrugs her shoulders.*) Is it possible that you can love? *Guter Mensch, aber schlechter Musikant.*°

TROFIMOV (*claps Pishchik on the shoulder*): You old horse, you!

CHARLOTTA: Attention, please! One more trick. (*Takes a lap robe from a chair.*) Here's a very fine lap robe; I should like to sell it. (*Shakes it out.*) Doesn't anyone want to buy it?

PISHCHIK (*amazed*): Think of that, now!

CHARLOTTA: *Eins, zwei, drei!* (*Quickly raises the lap robe, behind it stands Anya, who curtsies, runs to her mother, embraces her, and runs back into the ballroom amid the general enthusiasm.*)

LYUBOV ANDREYEVNA (*applauding*): Bravo, bravo!

CHARLOTTA: Once again! *Eins, zwei, drei.* (*Raises the lap robe; behind it stands Varya, who bows.*)

PISHCHIK (*amazed*): Think of that, now!

CHARLOTTA: The end! (*Throws the robe at Pishchik, makes a curtsy, and runs out of the room.*)

PISHCHIK (*hurries after her*): The minx! . . . What a woman! What a woman! (*Goes out.*)

LYUBOV ANDREYEVNA: And Leonid still not here. What he is doing in town so long, I do not understand! It must be all over by now. Either the estate is sold, or the auction didn't take place — but why keep us in suspense so long!

VARYA (*trying to comfort her*): Uncle has bought it, I am certain of that.

TROFIMOV (*mockingly*): Yes.

VARYA: Great-aunt sent him power of attorney to buy it in her name and transfer the debt. She's doing it for Anya's sake. And I am sure, with God's help, Uncle will buy it.

LYUBOV ANDREYEVNA: Our great-aunt in Yaroslav sent fifteen thousand to buy the estate in her name — she doesn't trust us — but that's not even enough to pay the interest. (*Covers her face with her hands.*) Today my fate will be decided, my fate . . .

TROFIMOV (*teasing Varya*): Madame Lopakhina!

VARYA (*angrily*): Eternal student! Twice already you've been expelled from the university.

LYUBOV ANDREYEVNA: Why are you so cross, Varya? If he teases you about Lopakhin, what of it? Go ahead and marry Lopakhin if you want to. He's a nice man, he's interesting. And if you don't want to, don't. Nobody's forcing you, my pet.

Guter Mensch, aber schlechter Musikant: "Good man, but poor musician" (German).

VARYA: To be frank, Mama dear, I regard this matter seriously. He is a good man, I like him.

LYUBOV ANDREYEVNA: Then marry him. I don't know what you're waiting for!

VARYA: Mama, I can't propose to him myself. For the last two years everyone's been talking to me about him; everyone talks, but he is either silent or he jokes. I understand. He's getting rich, he's absorbed in business, he has no time for me. If I had some money, no matter how little, if it were only a hundred rubles, I'd drop everything and go far away. I'd go into a nunnery.

TROFIMOV: A blessing!

VARYA (*to Trofimov*): A student ought to be intelligent! (*In a gentle tone, tearfully.*) How homely you have grown, Petya, how old! (*To Lyubov Andreyevna, no longer crying.*) It's just that I cannot live without work, Mama. I must be doing something every minute.

(*Yasha enters.*)

YASHA (*barely able to suppress his laughter*): Yepikhodov has broken a billiard cue! (*Goes out.*)

VARYA: But why is Yepikhodov here? Who gave him permission to play billiards? I don't understand these people. . . . (*Goes out.*)

LYUBOV ANDREYEVNA: Don't tease her, Petya. You can see she's unhappy enough without that.

TROFIMOV: She's much too zealous, always meddling in other people's affairs. All summer long she's given Anya and me no peace — afraid a romance might develop. What business is it of hers? Besides, I've given no occasion for it, I am far removed from such banality. We are above love!

LYUBOV ANDREYEVNA: And I suppose I am beneath love. (*In great agitation.*) Why isn't Leonid here? If only I knew whether the estate had been sold or not! The disaster seems to me so incredible that I don't even know what to think, I'm lost. . . . I could scream this very instant . . . I could do something foolish. Save me, Petya. Talk to me, say something. . . .

TROFIMOV: Whether or not the estate is sold today — does it really matter? That's all done with long ago; there's no turning back, the path is overgrown. Be calm, my dear. One must not deceive oneself; at least once in one's life one ought to look the truth straight in the eye.

LYUBOV ANDREYEVNA: What truth? You can see where there is truth and where there isn't, but I seem to have lost my sight, I see nothing. You boldly settle all the important problems, but tell me, my dear boy, isn't it because you are young and have not yet had to suffer for a single one of your problems? You boldly look ahead, but isn't it because you neither see nor expect anything dreadful, since life is still hidden from your young eyes? You're bolder, more honest, deeper than we are, but think about it, be just a little bit magnanimous, and spare me. You see, I was born here, my mother and father lived here, and my grandfather. I love this house, without the cherry orchard my life has no meaning for me, and if it must be sold, then sell me with the orchard. . . . (*Embraces Trofimov and kisses him on the forehead.*) And my son was drowned here. . . . (*Weeps.*) Have pity on me, you good, kind man.

TROFIMOV: You know I feel for you with all my heart.

LYUBOV ANDREYEVNA: But that should have been said differently, quite differently. . . . (*Takes out her handkerchief and a telegram falls to the floor.*) My heart is heavy today, you can't imagine. It's so noisy here, my soul quivers at every sound, I tremble all over, and yet I can't go to my room. When I am alone the silence frightens me. Don't condemn me, Petya . . . I love you as if you were my own. I would gladly let you marry Anya, I swear it, only you must study, my dear, you must get your degree. You do nothing, fate simply tosses you from place to place — it's so strange. . . . Isn't that true? Isn't it? And you must do something about your beard, to make it grow somehow. . . . (*Laughs.*) You're so funny!

TROFIMOV (*picks up the telegram*): I have no desire to be an Adonis.°

LYUBOV ANDREYEVNA: That's a telegram from Paris. I get them every day. One yesterday, one today. That wild man has fallen ill again, he's in trouble again. . . . He begs my forgiveness, implores me to come, and really, I ought to go to Paris to be near him. Your face is stern, Petya, but what can one do, my dear? What am I to do? He is ill, he's alone and unhappy, and who will look after him there, who will keep him from making mistakes, who will give him his medicine on time? And why hide it or keep silent, I love him, that's clear. I love him, love him. . . . It's a millstone round my neck, I'm sinking to the bottom with it, but I love that stone, I cannot live without it. (*Presses Trofimov's hand.*) Don't think badly of me, Petya, and don't say anything to me, don't say anything. . . .

TROFIMOV (*through tears*): For God's sake, forgive my frankness: You know that he robbed you!

LYUBOV ANDREYEVNA: No, no, no, you mustn't say such things! (*Covers her ears.*)

TROFIMOV: But he's a scoundrel! You're the only one who doesn't know it! He's a petty scoundrel, a nonentity —

LYUBOV ANDREYEVNA (*angry, but controlling herself*): You are twenty-six or twenty-seven years old, but you're still a schoolboy!

TROFIMOV: That may be!

LYUBOV ANDREYEVNA: You should be a man, at your age you ought to understand those who love. And you ought to be in love yourself. (*Angrily.*) Yes, yes! It's not purity with you, it's simply prudery, you're a ridiculous crank, a freak —

TROFIMOV (*horrified*): What is she saying!

LYUBOV ANDREYEVNA: I am above love! You're not above love, you're just an addlepate, as Firs would say. Not to have a mistress at your age!

TROFIMOV (*in horror*): This is awful! What is she saying! . . . (*Goes quickly toward the ballroom.*) This is awful . . . I can't . . . I won't stay here. . . . (*Goes out, but immediately returns.*) All is over between us! (*Goes out to the hall.*)

LYUBOV ANDREYEVNA (*calls after him*): Petya, wait! You absurd creature, I was joking! Petya!

(*In the hall there is the sound of someone running quickly downstairs and suddenly falling with a crash. Anya and Varya scream, but a moment later laughter is heard.*)

LYUBOV ANDREYEVNA: What was that?

(*Anya runs in.*)

ANYA (*laughing*): Petya fell down the stairs! (*Runs out.*)

LYUBOV ANDREYEVNA: What a funny boy that Petya is!

(*The Stationmaster stands in the middle of the ballroom and recites A. Tolstoy's° "The Sinner." Everyone listens to him, but he has no sooner spoken a few lines than the sound of a waltz is heard from the hall and the recitation is broken off. They all dance. Trofimov, Anya, Varya, and Lyubov Andreyevna come in from the hall.*)

LYUBOV ANDREYEVNA: Come, Petya . . . come, you pure soul . . . please, forgive me. . . . Let's dance. . . . (*They dance.*)

(*Anya and Varya dance. Firs comes in, puts his stick by the side door. Yasha also comes into the drawing room and watches the dancers.*)

YASHA: What is it, grandpa?

FIRS: I don't feel well. In the old days, we used to have generals, barons, admirals, dancing at our balls, but now we send for the post office clerk and the stationmaster, and even they are none too eager to come. Somehow I've grown weak. The late master, their grandfather, dosed everyone with sealing wax, no matter what ailed them. I've been taking sealing wax every day for twenty years or more, maybe that's what's kept me alive.

YASHA: You bore me, grandpa. (*Yawns.*) High time you croaked.

FIRS: Ah, you . . . addlepate! (*Mumbles.*)

(*Trofimov and Lyubov Andreyevna dance from the ballroom into the drawing room.*)

LYUBOV ANDREYEVNA: *Merci.* I'll sit down a while. (*Sits.*) I'm tired.

(*Anya comes in.*)

ANYA (*excitedly*): There was a man in the kitchen just now saying that the cherry orchard was sold today.

Adonis: From Greek myth, a beautiful young man.

A. Tolstoy: Aleksey Konstantinovich Tolstoy (1817–1875), Russian novelist, dramatist, and poet.

LYUBOV ANDREYEVNA: Sold to whom?

ANYA: He didn't say. He's gone. (*Dances with Trofimov; they go into the ballroom.*)

YASHA: That was just some old man babbling. A stranger.

FIRS: Leonid Andreich is not back yet, still hasn't come. And he's wearing the light, between-seasons overcoat; like enough he'll catch cold. Ah, when they're young they're green.

LYUBOV ANDREYEVNA: This is killing me. Yasha, go and find out who it was sold to.

YASHA: But that old man left long ago. (*Laughs.*)

LYUBOV ANDREYEVNA (*slightly annoyed*): Well, what are you laughing at? What are you so happy about?

YASHA: That Yepikhodov is very funny! Hopeless! Two-and-twenty Troubles.

LYUBOV ANDREYEVNA: Firs, if the estate is sold, where will you go?

FIRS: Wherever you tell me to go, I'll go.

LYUBOV ANDREYEVNA: Why do you look like that? Aren't you well? You ought to go to bed.

FIRS: Yes. . . . (*With a smirk.*) Go to bed, and without me who will serve, who will see to things? I'm the only one in the whole house.

YASHA (*to Lyubov Andreyevna*): Lyubov Andreyevna! Permit me to make a request, be so kind! If you go back to Paris again, do me the favor of taking me with you. It is positively impossible for me to stay here. (*Looking around, then in a low voice.*) There's no need to say it, you can see for yourself, it's an uncivilized country, the people have no morals, and the boredom! The food they give us in the kitchen is unmentionable, and besides, there's this Firs who keeps walking about mumbling all sorts of inappropriate things. Take me with you, be so kind!

(*Enter Pishchik.*)

PISHCHIK: May I have the pleasure of a waltz with you, fairest lady? (*Lyubov Andreyevna goes with him.*) I really must borrow a hundred and eighty rubles from you, my charmer . . . I really must. . . . (*Dancing.*) Just a hundred and eighty rubles. . . . (*They pass into the ballroom.*)

YASHA (*softly sings*): "Wilt thou know my soul's unrest . . ."

(*In the ballroom a figure in a gray top hat and checked trousers is jumping about, waving its arms; there are shouts of "Bravo, Charlotta Ivanovna!"*)

DUNYASHA (*stopping to powder her face*): The young mistress told me to dance — there are lots of gentlemen and not enough ladies — but dancing makes me dizzy, and my heart begins to thump. Firs Nikolayevich, the post office clerk just said something to me that took my breath away.

(*The music grows more subdued.*)

FIRS: What did he say to you?

DUNYASHA: "You," he said, "are like a flower."

YASHA (*yawns*): What ignorance. . . . (*Goes out.*)

DUNYASHA: Like a flower. . . . I'm such a delicate girl, I just adore tender words.

FIRS: You'll get your head turned.

(*Enter Yepikhodov.*)

YEPIKHODOV: Avdotya Fyodorovna, you are not desirous of seeing me. . . . I might almost be some sort of insect. (*Sighs.*) Ah, life!

DUNYASHA: What is it you want?

YEPIKHODOV: Indubitably, you may be right. (*Sighs.*) But, of course, if one looks at it from a point of view, then, if I may so express myself, and you will forgive my frankness, you have completely reduced me to a state of mind. I know my fate, every day some misfortune befalls me, but I have long since grown accustomed to that; I look upon my fate with a smile. But you gave me your word, and although I —

DUNYASHA: Please, we'll talk about it later, but leave me in peace now. Just now I'm dreaming. . . . (*Plays with her fan.*)

YEPIKHODOV: Every day a misfortune, and yet, if I may so express myself, I merely smile, I even laugh.

(*Varya enters from the ballroom.*)

VARYA: Are you still here, Semyon? What a disrespectful man you are, really! (*To Dunyasha.*) Run along, Dunyasha. (*To Yepikhodov.*) First you play billiards and break a cue, then you wander about the drawing room as though you were a guest.

YEPIKHODOV: You cannot, if I may so express myself, penalize me.

VARYA: I am not penalizing you, I'm telling you. You do nothing but wander from one place to another, and you don't do your work. We keep a clerk, but for what, I don't know.

YEPIKHODOV (*offended*): Whether I work, or wander about, or eat, or play billiards, these are matters to be discussed only by persons of discernment, and my elders.

VARYA: You dare say that to me! (*Flaring up.*) You dare? You mean to say I have no discernment? Get out of here! This instant!

YEPIKHODOV (*intimidated*): I beg you to express yourself in a more delicate manner.

VARYA (*beside herself*): Get out, this very instant! Get out! (*He goes to the door, she follows him.*) Two-and-twenty Troubles! Don't let me set eyes on you again!

YEPIKHODOV (*goes out, his voice is heard behind the door*): I shall lodge a complaint against you!

VARYA: Oh, you're coming back? (*Seizes the stick left near the door by Firs.*) Come, come on. . . . Come, I'll show you. . . . Ah, so you're coming, are you? Then take that — (*Swings the stick just as Lopakhin enters.*)

LOPAKHIN: Thank you kindly.

VARYA (*angrily and mockingly*): I beg your pardon.

LOPAKHIN: Not at all. I humbly thank you for your charming reception.

VARYA: Don't mention it. (*Walks away, then looks back and gently asks.*) I didn't hurt you, did I?

LOPAKHIN: No, it's nothing. A huge bump coming up, that's all.

(*Voices in the ballroom: "Lopakhin has come! Yermolai Alekseich!" Pishchik enters.*)

PISHCHIK: As I live and breathe! (*Kisses Lopakhin.*) There is a whiff of cognac about you, dear soul. And we've been making merry here, too.

(*Enter Lyubov Andreyevna.*)

LYUBOV ANDREYEVNA: Is that you, Yermolai Alekseich? What kept you so long? Where's Leonid?

LOPAKHIN: Leonid Andreich arrived with me, he's coming . . .

LYUBOV ANDREYEVNA (*agitated*): Well, what happened? Did the sale take place? Tell me!

LOPAKHIN (*embarrassed, fearing to reveal his joy*): The auction was over by four o'clock. . . . We missed the train, had to wait till half past nine. (*Sighing heavily.*) Ugh! My head is swimming. . . .

(*Enter Gayev; he carries his purchases in one hand and wipes away his tears with the other.*)

LYUBOV ANDREYEVNA: Lyonya, what happened? Well, Lyonya? (*Impatiently, through tears.*) Be quick, for God's sake!

GAYEV (*not answering her, simply waves his hand. To Firs, weeping*): Here, take these. . . . There's anchovies, Kerch herrings. . . . I haven't eaten anything all day. . . . What I have been through! (*The click of billiard balls is heard through the open door to the billiard room, and Yasha's voice: "Seven and eighteen!" Gayev's expression changes, he is no longer weeping.*) I'm terribly tired. Firs, help me change. (*Goes through the ballroom to his own room, followed by Firs.*)

PISHCHIK: What happened at the auction? Come on, tell us!

LYUBOV ANDREYEVNA: Is the cherry orchard sold?

LOPAKHIN: It's sold.

LYUBOV ANDREYEVNA: Who bought it?

LOPAKHIN: I bought it. (*Pause.*)

(*Lyubov Andreyevna is overcome; she would fall to the floor if it were not for the chair and table near which she stands. Varya takes the keys from her belt and throws them on the floor in the middle of the drawing room and goes out.*)

LOPAKHIN: I bought it! Kindly wait a moment, ladies and gentlemen, my head is swimming. I can't talk. . . . (*Laughs.*) We arrived at the auction, Deriganov was already there. Leonid Andreich had only fifteen thousand, and straight off Deriganov bid thirty thousand over and above the mortgage. I saw how the land lay, so I got into the fight and bid forty. He bid forty-five. I bid fifty-five. In other words, he kept raising it by five thousand, and I by ten. Well, it

finally came to an end. I bid ninety thousand above the mortgage, and it was knocked down to me. The cherry orchard is now mine! Mine! (*Laughs uproariously.*) Lord! God in heaven! The cherry orchard is mine! Tell me I'm drunk, out of my mind, that I imagine it. . . . (*Stamps his feet.*) Don't laugh at me! If my father and my grandfather could only rise from their graves and see all that has happened, how their Yermolai, their beaten, half-literate Yermolai, who used to run about barefoot in winter, how that same Yermolai has bought an estate, the most beautiful estate in the whole world! I bought the estate where my father and grandfather were slaves, where they weren't even allowed in the kitchen. I'm asleep, this is just some dream of mine, it only seems to be. . . . It's the fruit of your imagination, hidden in the darkness of uncertainty. . . . (*Picks up the keys, smiling tenderly.*) She threw down the keys, wants to show that she's not mistress here anymore. . . . (*Jingles the keys.*) Well, no matter. (*The orchestra is heard tuning up.*) Hey, musicians, play, I want to hear you! Come on, everybody, and see how Yermolai Lopakhin will lay the ax to the cherry orchard, how the trees will fall to the ground! We're going to build summer cottages and our grandsons and great-grandsons will see a new life here. . . . Music! Strike up!

(*The orchestra plays. Lyubov Andreyevna sinks into a chair and weeps bitterly.*)

LOPAKHIN (*reproachfully*): Why didn't you listen to me, why? My poor friend, there's no turning back now. (*With tears.*) Oh, if only all this could be over quickly, if somehow our discordant, unhappy life could be changed!

PISHCHIK (*takes him by the arm; speaks in an undertone*): She's crying. Let's go into the ballroom, let her be alone. . . . Come on. . . . (*Leads him into the ballroom.*)

LOPAKHIN: What's happened? Musicians, play so I can hear you! Let everything be as I want it! (*Ironically.*) Here comes the new master, owner of the cherry orchard! (*Accidentally bumps into a little table, almost upsetting the candelabrum.*) I can pay for everything! (*Goes out with Pishchik.*)

(*There is no one left in either the drawing room or the ballroom except Lyubov Andreyevna, who sits huddled up and weeping bitterly. The music plays softly. Anya and Trofimov enter hurriedly. Anya goes to her mother and kneels before her. Trofimov remains in the doorway of the ballroom.*)

ANYA: Mama! . . . Mama, you're crying! Dear, kind, good Mama, my beautiful one, I love you . . . I bless you. The cherry orchard is sold, it's gone, that's true, true, but don't cry, Mama, life is still before you, you still have your good, pure soul. . . . Come with me, come, darling, we'll go away from here! . . . We'll plant a new orchard, more luxuriant than this one. You will see it and understand; and joy, quiet, deep joy, will sink into your soul, like the evening sun, and you will smile, Mama! Come, darling, let us go. . . .

ACT IV

(*The scene is the same as act I. There are neither curtains on the windows nor pictures on the walls, and only a little furniture piled up in one corner, as if for sale. There is a sense of emptiness. Near the outer door, at the rear of the stage, suitcases, traveling bags, etc., are piled up. Through the open door on the left the voices of Varya and Anya can be heard. Lopakhin stands waiting. Yasha is holding a tray with little glasses of champagne. In the hall, Yepikhodov is tying up a box. Offstage, at the rear, there is a hum of voices. It is the peasants who have come to say good-bye. Gayev's voice: "Thanks, brothers, thank you."*)

YASHA: The peasants have come to say good-bye. In my opinion, Yermolai Alekseich, peasants are good-natured, but they don't know much.

(*The hum subsides. Lyubov Andreyevna enters from the hall with Gayev. She is not crying, but she is pale, her face twitches, and she cannot speak.*)

GAYEV: You gave them your purse, Lyuba. That won't do! That won't do!

LYUBOV ANDREYEVNA: I couldn't help it! I couldn't help it! (*They both go out.*)

LOPAKHIN (*in the doorway, calls after them*): Please, do me the honor of having a little glass at parting. I didn't think of bringing champagne from town, and at the station I found only one bottle. Please! What's the matter, friends, don't you want any? (*Walks away from the door.*) If I'd known that, I wouldn't have bought it. Well, then I won't drink any either. (*Yasha carefully sets the tray down on a chair.*) At least you have a glass, Yasha.

YASHA: To those who are departing! Good luck! (*Drinks.*) This champagne is not the real stuff, I can assure you.

LOPAKHIN: Eight rubles a bottle. (*Pause.*) It's devilish cold in here.

YASHA: They didn't light the stoves today; it doesn't matter, since we're leaving. (*Laughs.*)

LOPAKHIN: Why are you laughing?

YASHA: Because I'm pleased.

LOPAKHIN: It's October, yet it's sunny and still outside, like summer. Good for building. (*Looks at his watch, then calls through the door.*) Bear in mind, ladies and gentlemen, only forty-six minutes till train time! That means leaving for the station in twenty minutes. Better hurry up!

(*Trofimov enters from outside wearing an overcoat.*)

TROFIMOV: Seems to me it's time to start. The carriages are at the door. What the devil has become of my rubbers? They're lost. (*Calls through the door.*) Anya, my rubbers are not here. I can't find them.

LOPAKHIN: I've got to go to Kharkov. I'm taking the same train you are. I'm going to spend the winter in Kharkov. I've been hanging around here with you, and I'm sick and tired of loafing. I can't live without work, I don't know what to do with my hands; they dangle in some strange way, as if they didn't belong to me.

TROFIMOV: We'll soon be gone, then you can take up your useful labors again.

LOPAKHIN: Here, have a little drink.

TROFIMOV: No, I don't want any.

LOPAKHIN: So you're off for Moscow?

TROFIMOV: Yes, I'll see them into town, and tomorrow I'll go to Moscow.

LOPAKHIN: Yes. . . . Well, I expect the professors haven't been giving any lectures: They're waiting for you to come!

TROFIMOV: That's none of your business.

LOPAKHIN: How many years is it you've been studying at the university?

TROFIMOV: Can't you think of something new? That's stale and flat. (*Looks for his rubbers.*) You know we'll probably never see each other again, so allow me to give you one piece of advice at parting: Don't wave your arms about! Get out of that habit — of arm-waving. And another thing, building cottages and counting on the summer residents in time becoming independent farmers — that's just another form of arm-waving. Well, when all's said and done, I'm fond of you anyway. You have fine, delicate fingers, like an artist; you have a fine delicate soul.

LOPAKHIN (*embraces him*): Good-bye, my dear fellow. Thank you for everything. Let me give you some money for the journey, if you need it.

TROFIMOV: What for? I don't need it.

LOPAKHIN: But you haven't any!

TROFIMOV: I have. Thank you. I got some money for a translation. Here it is in my pocket. (*Anxiously.*) But where are my rubbers?

VARYA (*from the next room*): Here, take the nasty things! (*Flings a pair of rubbers onto the stage.*)

TROFIMOV: What are you so cross about, Varya? Hm. . . . But these are not my rubbers.

LOPAKHIN: In the spring I sowed three thousand acres of poppies, and now I've made forty thousand rubles clear. And when my poppies were in bloom, what a picture it was! So, I'm telling you, I've made forty thousand, which means I'm offering you a loan because I can afford to. Why turn up your nose? I'm a peasant — I speak bluntly.

TROFIMOV: Your father was a peasant, mine was a pharmacist — which proves absolutely nothing. (*Lopakhin takes out his wallet.*) No, don't — even if you gave me two hundred thousand I wouldn't take it. I'm a free man. And everything that is valued so highly and held so dear by all of you, rich and poor alike, has not the slightest power over me — it's like a feather floating in the air. I can get along without you, I can pass you by, I'm strong and proud.

Mankind is advancing toward the highest truth, the highest happiness attainable on earth, and I am in the front ranks!

LOPAKHIN: Will you get there?

TROFIMOV: I'll get there. (*Pause.*) I'll either get there or I'll show others the way to get there.

(*The sound of axes chopping down trees is heard in the distance.*)

LOPAKHIN: Well, good-bye, my dear fellow. It's time to go. We turn up our noses at one another, but life goes on just the same. When I work for a long time without stopping, my mind is easier, and it seems to me that I, too, know why I exist. But how many there are in Russia, brother, who exist nobody knows why. Well, it doesn't matter, that's not what makes the wheels go round. They say Leonid Andreich has taken a position in the bank, six thousand a year. . . . Only, of course, he won't stick it out, he's too lazy. . . .

ANYA (*in the doorway*): Mama asks you not to start cutting down the cherry orchard until she's gone.

TROFIMOV: Yes, really, not to have had the tact . . . (*Goes out through the hall.*)

LOPAKHIN: Right away, right away. . . . Ach, what people. . . . (*Follows Trofimov out.*)

ANYA: Has Firs been taken to the hospital?

YASHA: I told them this morning. They must have taken him.

ANYA (*to Yepikhodov, who is crossing the room*): Semyon Panteleich, please find out if Firs has been taken to the hospital.

YASHA (*offended*): I told Yegor this morning. Why ask a dozen times?

YEPIKHODOV: It is my conclusive opinion that the venerable Firs is beyond repair; it's time he was gathered to his fathers. And I can only envy him. (*Puts a suitcase down on a hatbox and crushes it.*) There you are! Of course! I knew it! (*Goes out.*)

YASHA (*mockingly*): Two-and-twenty Troubles!

VARYA (*through the door*): Has Firs been taken to the hospital?

ANYA: Yes, he has.

VARYA: Then why didn't they take the letter to the doctor?

ANYA: We must send it on after them. . . . (*Goes out.*)

VARYA (*from the adjoining room*): Where is Yasha? Tell him his mother has come to say good-bye to him.

YASHA (*waves his hand*): They really try my patience.

(*Dunyasha has been fussing with the luggage; now that Yasha is alone she goes up to him.*)

DUNYASHA: You might give me one little look, Yasha. You're going away . . . leaving me. . . . (*Cries and throws herself on his neck.*)

YASHA: What's there to cry about? (*Drinks champagne.*) In six days I'll be in Paris again. Tomorrow we'll take the express, off we go, and that's the last you'll see of us. I can hardly believe it. *Vive la France!* This place is not for me, I can't live here. . . . It can't be helped.

I've had enough of this ignorance — I'm fed up with it. (*Drinks champagne.*) What are you crying for? Behave yourself properly, then you won't cry.

DUNYASHA (*looks into a small mirror and powders her face*): Send me a letter from Paris. You know, I loved you, Yasha, how I loved you! I'm such a tender creature, Yasha!

YASHA: Here they come. (*Busies himself with the luggage, humming softly.*)

(*Enter Lyubov Andreyevna, Gayev, Charlotta Ivanovna.*)

GAYEV: We ought to be leaving. There's not much time now. (*Looks at Yasha.*) Who smells of herring?

LYUBOV ANDREYEVNA: In about ten minutes we should be getting into the carriages. (*Glances around the room.*) Good-bye, dear house, old grandfather. Winter will pass, spring will come, and you will no longer be here, they will tear you down. How much these walls have seen! (*Kisses her daughter warmly.*) My treasure, you are radiant, your eyes are sparkling like two diamonds. Are you glad? Very?

ANYA: Very! A new life is beginning, Mama!

GAYEV (*cheerfully*): Yes, indeed, everything is all right now. Before the cherry orchard was sold we were all worried and miserable, but afterward, when the question was finally settled once and for all, everybody calmed down and felt quite cheerful. . . . I'm in a bank now, a financier . . . cue ball into the center . . . and you, Lyuba, say what you like, you look better, no doubt about it.

LYUBOV ANDREYEVNA: Yes. My nerves are better, that's true. (*Her hat and coat are handed to her.*) I sleep well. Carry out my things, Yasha, it's time. (*To Anya.*) My little girl, we shall see each other soon. . . . I shall go to Paris and live there on the money your great-aunt sent to buy the estate — long live Auntie! — but that money won't last long.

ANYA: You'll come back soon, Mama, soon . . . won't you? I'll study hard and pass my high school examinations, and then I can work and help you. We'll read all sorts of books together, Mama . . . Won't we? (*Kisses her mother's hand.*) We'll read in the autumn evenings, we'll read lots of books, and a new and wonderful world will open up before us. . . . (*Dreaming.*) Mama, come back. . . .

LYUBOV ANDREYEVNA: I'll come, my precious. (*Embraces her.*)

(*Enter Lopakhin, Charlotta Ivanovna is softly humming a song.*)

GAYEV: Happy Charlotta: She's singing!

CHARLOTTA (*picks up a bundle and holds it like a baby in swaddling clothes*): Bye, baby, bye. . . . (*A baby's crying is heard, "Wah! Wah!"*) Be quiet, my darling, my dear little boy. (*"Wah! Wah!"*) I'm so sorry for you! (*Throws the bundle down.*) You will find me a position, won't you? I can't go on like this.

LOPAKHIN: We'll find something, Charlotta Ivanovna, don't worry.

GAYEV: Everyone is leaving us, Varya's going away . . . all of a sudden nobody needs us.

CHARLOTTA: I have nowhere to go in town. I must go away. (*Hums.*) It doesn't matter . . .

(*Enter Pishchik.*)

LOPAKHIN: Nature's wonder!

PISHCHIK (*panting*): Ugh! Let me catch my breath. . . . I'm exhausted. . . . My esteemed friends. . . . Give me some water. . . .

GAYEV: After money, I suppose? Excuse me, I'm fleeing from temptation. . . . (*Goes out.*)

PISHCHIK: It's a long time since I've been to see you . . . fairest lady. . . . (*To Lopakhin*) So you're here. . . . Glad to see you, you intellectual giant. . . . Here . . . take it . . . four hundred rubles . . . I still owe you eight hundred and forty . . .

LOPAKHIN (*shrugs his shoulders in bewilderment*): I must be dreaming. . . . Where did you get it?

PISHCHIK: Wait . . . I'm hot. . . . A most extraordinary event. Some Englishmen came to my place and discovered some kind of white clay on my land. (*To Lyubov Andreyevna*) And four hundred for you . . . fairest, most wonderful lady. . . . (*Hands her the money.*) The rest later. (*Takes a drink of water.*) Just now a young man in the train was saying that a certain . . . great philosopher recommends jumping off roofs. . . . "Jump!" he says, and therein lies the whole problem. (*In amazement.*) Think of that, now! . . . Water!

LOPAKHIN: Who were those Englishmen?

PISHCHIK: I leased them the tract of land with the clay on it for twenty-four years. . . . And now, excuse me, I have no time . . . I must be trotting along . . . I'm going to Znoikov's . . . to Kardamanov's . . . I owe everybody. (*Drinks.*) Keep well . . . I'll drop in on Thursday . . .

LYUBOV ANDREYEVNA: We're just moving into town, and tomorrow I go abroad . . .

PISHCHIK: What? (*Alarmed.*) Why into town? That's why I see the furniture . . . suitcases. . . . Well, never mind. . . . (*Through tears.*) Never mind. . . . Men of the greatest intellect, those Englishmen. . . . Never mind. . . . Be happy . . . God will help you. . . . Never mind. . . . Everything in this world comes to an end. . . . (*Kisses Lyubov Andreyevna's hand.*) And should the news reach you that my end has come, just remember this old horse, and say: "There once lived a certain Semyonov-Pishchik, God rest his soul." . . . Splendid weather. . . . Yes. . . . (*Goes out greatly disconcerted, but immediately returns and speaks from the doorway.*) Dashenka sends her regards. (*Goes out.*)

LYUBOV ANDREYEVNA: Now we can go. I am leaving with two things on my mind. First — that Firs is sick. (*Looks at her watch.*) We still have about five minutes. . . .

ANYA: Mama, Firs has already been taken to the hospital. Yasha sent him there this morning.

LYUBOV ANDREYEVNA: My second concern is Varya. She's used to getting up early and working, and now, with no work to do, she's like a fish out of water. She's grown pale and thin, and cries all the time, poor girl. . . . (*Pauses.*) You know very well, Yermolai Alekseich, that I dreamed of marrying her to you, and everything pointed to your getting married. (*Whispers to Anya, who nods to Charlotta, and they both go out.*) She loves you, you are fond of her, and I don't know — I don't know why it is you seem to avoid each other. I can't understand it!

LOPAKHIN: To tell you the truth, I don't understand it myself. The whole thing is strange, somehow. . . . If there's still time, I'm ready right now. . . . Let's finish it up — and *basta*,° but without you I feel I'll never be able to propose to her.

LYUBOV ANDREYEVNA: Splendid! After all, it only takes a minute. I'll call her in at once. . . .

LOPAKHIN: And we even have the champagne. (*Looks at the glasses.*) Empty! Somebody's already drunk it. (*Yasha coughs.*) That's what you call lapping it up.

LYUBOV ANDREYEVNA (*animatedly*): Splendid! We'll leave you. . . . Yasha, *allez!*° I'll call her. . . . (*At the door.*) Varya, leave everything and come here. Come! (*Goes out with Yasha.*)

LOPAKHIN (*looking at his watch*): Yes. . . . (*Pause.*)

(*Behind the door there is smothered laughter and whispering; finally Varya enters.*)

VARYA (*looking over the luggage for a long time*): Strange, I can't seem to find it . . .

LOPAKHIN: What are you looking for?

VARYA: I packed it myself, and I can't remember . . . (*Pause.*)

LOPAKHIN: Where are you going now, Varya Mikhailovna?

VARYA: I? To the Ragulins'. . . . I've agreed to go there to look after the house . . . as a sort of housekeeper.

LOPAKHIN: At Yashnevo? That would be about seventy versts from here. (*Pause.*) Well, life in this house has come to an end. . . .

VARYA (*examining the luggage*): Where can it be? . . . Perhaps I put it in the trunk. . . . Yes, life in this house has come to an end . . . there'll be no more . . .

LOPAKHIN: And I'm off for Kharkov . . . by the next train. I have a lot to do. I'm leaving Yepikhodov here . . . I've taken him on.

VARYA: Really!

LOPAKHIN: Last year at this time it was already snowing, if you remember, but now it's still and sunny. It's cold though. . . . About three degrees of frost.

VARYA: I haven't looked. (*Pause.*) And besides, our thermometer's broken. (*Pause.*)

(*A voice from the yard calls: "Yermolai Alekseich!"*)

LOPAKHIN (*as if he had been waiting for a long time for the call*): Coming! (*Goes out quickly.*)

---

basta: Italian for "enough."   *allez!*: French for "go!"

(*Varya sits on the floor, lays her head on a bundle of clothes, and quietly sobs. The door opens and Lyubov Andreyevna enters cautiously.*)

LYUBOV ANDREYEVNA: Well? (*Pause.*) We must be going.

VARYA (*no longer crying, dries her eyes*): Yes, it's time, Mama dear. I can get to the Ragulins' today, if only we don't miss the train.

LYUBOV ANDREYEVNA (*in the doorway*): Anya, put your things on!

(*Enter Anya, then Gayev and Charlotta Ivanovna. Gayev wears a warm overcoat with a hood. The servants and coachmen come in. Yepikhodov bustles about the luggage.*)

LYUBOV ANDREYEVNA: Now we can be on our way.

ANYA (*joyfully*): On our way!

GAYEV: My friends, my dear, cherished friends! Leaving this house forever, can I pass over in silence, can I refrain from giving utterance, as we say farewell, to those feelings that now fill my whole being —

ANYA (*imploringly*): Uncle!

VARYA: Uncle dear, don't!

GAYEV (*forlornly*): Double the rail off the white to center table . . . yellow into the side pocket. . . . I'll be quiet. . . .

(*Enter Trofimov, then Lopakhin.*)

TROFIMOV: Well, ladies and gentlemen, it's time to go!

LOPAKHIN: Yepikhodov, my coat!

LYUBOV ANDREYEVNA: I'll sit here just one more minute. It's as though I had never before seen what the walls of this house were like, what the ceilings were like, and now I look at them hungrily, with such tender love . . .

GAYEV: I remember when I was six years old, sitting on this windowsill on Whitsunday, watching my father going to church . . .

LYUBOV ANDREYEVNA: Have they taken all the things?

LOPAKHIN: Everything, I think. (*Puts on his overcoat.*) Yepikhodov, see that everything is in order.

YEPIKHODOV (*in a hoarse voice*): Rest assured, Yermolai Alekseich!

LOPAKHIN: What's the matter with your voice?

YEPIKHODOV: Just drank some water . . . must have swallowed something.

YASHA (*contemptuously*): What ignorance!

LYUBOV ANDREYEVNA: When we go — there won't be a soul left here. . . .

LOPAKHIN: Till spring.

VARYA (*pulls an umbrella out of a bundle as though she were going to hit someone; Lopakhin pretends to be frightened*): Why are you — I never thought of such a thing!

TROFIMOV: Ladies and gentlemen, let's get into the carriages — it's time now! The train will soon be in!

VARYA: Petya, there they are — your rubbers, by the suitcase. (*Tearfully.*) And what dirty old things they are!

TROFIMOV (*putting on his rubbers*): Let's go, ladies and gentlemen!

GAYEV (*extremely upset, afraid of bursting into tears*): The train . . . the station. . . . Cross table to the center, double the rail . . . on the white into the corner.

LYUBOV ANDREYEVNA: Let us go!

GAYEV: Are we all here? No one in there? (*Locks the side door on the left.*) There are some things stored in there, we must lock up. Let's go!

ANYA: Good-bye, house! Good-bye, old life!

TROFIMOV: Hail to the new life! (*Goes out with Anya.*)

(*Varya looks around the room and slowly goes out. Yasha and Charlotta with her dog go out.*)

LOPAKHIN: And so, till spring. Come along, my friends. . . . Till we meet! (*Goes out.*)

(*Lyubov Andreyevna and Gayev are left alone. As though they had been waiting for this, they fall onto each other's necks and break into quiet, restrained sobs, afraid of being heard.*)

GAYEV (*in despair*): My sister, my sister. . . .

LYUBOV ANDREYEVNA: Oh, my dear, sweet, lovely orchard! . . . My life, my youth, my happiness, good-bye! . . . Good-bye!

ANYA'S VOICE (*gaily calling*): Mama!

TROFIMOV'S VOICE (*gay and excited*): Aa-oo!

LYUBOV ANDREYEVNA: One last look at these walls, these windows. . . . Mother loved to walk about in this room. . . .

GAYEV: My sister, my sister!

ANYA'S VOICE: Mama!

TROFIMOV'S VOICE: Aa-oo!

LYUBOV ANDREYEVNA: We're coming! (*They go out.*)

(*The stage is empty. There is the sound of doors being locked, then of the carriages driving away. It grows quiet. In the stillness there is the dull thud of an ax on a tree, a forlorn, melancholy sound. Footsteps are heard. From the door on the right Firs appears. He is dressed as always in a jacket and white waistcoat, and wears slippers. He is ill.*)

FIRS (*goes to the door and tries the handle*): Locked. They have gone. . . . (*Sits down on the sofa.*) They've forgotten me. . . . Never mind. . . . I'll sit here awhile. . . . I expect Leonid Andreich hasn't put on his fur coat and has gone off in his overcoat. (*Sighs anxiously.*) And I didn't see to it. . . . When they're young, they're green! (*Mumbles something which cannot be understood.*) I'll lie down awhile. . . . There's no strength left in you, nothing's left, nothing. . . . Ach, you . . . addlepate! (*Lies motionless.*)

(*A distant sound is heard that seems to come from the sky, the sound of a snapped string mournfully dying away. A stillness falls, and nothing is heard but the thud of the ax on a tree far away in the orchard.*)

COMMENTARIES

Anton Chekhov (1860–1904)

FROM *LETTERS OF ANTON CHEKOV*   *1888–1903*

TRANSLATED BY MICHAEL HENRY HEIM WITH SIMON KARLINSKY

Chekhov, like Ibsen, was an inveterate letter writer. In letters to family members and colleagues, he wrote quite frankly about his hopes, expectations, and difficulties regarding his work. Chekhov's letters concerning his purpose as an artist and his play The Cherry Orchard *give us some insight into the anxieties and hopes that Chekhov had for his work. His awareness of the difficulties he faced in his writing helps us understand how his plays developed into complex and demanding works.*

October 4, 1888

The people I fear are those who look for tendentiousness between the lines and are determined to see me as either liberal or conservative. I am neither liberal, nor conservative, nor gradualist, nor monk, nor indifferentist. I should like to be a free artist and nothing else. That is why I cultivate no particular predilection for policemen, butchers, scientists, writers, or the younger generation. I look upon tags and labels as prejudices. My holy of holies is the human body, health, intelligence, talent, inspiration, love and the most absolute freedom imaginable, freedom from violence and lies.

November 25, 1892

Keep in mind that the writers we call eternal or simply good, the writers who intoxicate us, have one highly important trait in common: They are moving towards something definite and beckon you to follow, and you feel with your entire being, not only with your mind, that they have a certain goal, like the ghost of Hamlet's father, which had a motive for coming and stirring Hamlet's imagination. Depending on their caliber, some have immediate goals — the abolition of serfdom, the liberation of one's country, politics, beauty, or simply vodka . . . — while the goals of others are more remote — God, life after death, the happiness of mankind, etc. The best of them are realistic and describe life as it is, but because each line is saturated with the consciousness of its goal, you feel life as it should be in addition to life as it is, and you are captivated by it. But what about us? Us! We describe life as it is and stop dead right there. We wouldn't lift a hoof if you lit into us with a whip. We have neither immediate nor remote goals, and there is an emptiness in our souls. We have no politics, we don't believe in revolution, there is no God, we're not afraid of ghosts, and I personally am not even afraid of death or blindness. If you want nothing, hope for nothing, and fear nothing, you cannot be an artist.

To K. S. Stanislavsky°
Yalta. Oct. 30, 1903

When I was writing Lopakhin, I thought of it as a part for you. If for any reason you don't care for it, take the part of Gayev. Lopakhin is a merchant, of course, but he is a very decent person in every sense. He must behave with perfect decorum, like an educated man, with no petty ways or tricks of any sort, and it seemed to me this part, the central one of the play, would come out brilliantly in your hands. . . . In choosing an actor for the part you must remember that Varya, a serious and religious girl, is in love with Lopakhin; she wouldn't be in love with a mere money-grubber. . . .

To Vl. I. Nemirovich-Danchenko°
Yalta. Nov. 2, 1903

. . . Pishchik is a Russian, an old man, worn out by the gout, age, and satiety; stout, dressed in a sleeveless undercoat (à la Simov [an actor in the Moscow Art Theatre]), boots without heels. Lopakhin — a white waistcoat, yellow shoes; when walking, swings his arms, a broad stride, thinks deeply while walking, walks as if on a straight line. Hair not short, and therefore often throws back his head; while in thought he passes his hand through his beard, combing it from the back forward, i.e., from the neck toward the mouth. Trofimov, I think, is clear. Varya — black dress, wide belt.

Three years I spent writing "The Cherry Orchard," and for three years I have been telling you that it is necessary to invite an actress for the role of Lyubov Andreyevna. And now you see you are trying to solve a puzzle that won't work out.

To K. S. Alekseyev (Stanislavsky)
Yalta. Nov. 5, 1903

The house in the play is two-storied, a large one. But in the third act does it not speak of a stairway leading down? Nevertheless, this third act worries me. . . . N. has it that the third act takes place in "some kind of hotel"; . . . evidently I made an error in the play. The action does not pass in "some kind of hotel," but in a *drawing-room*. If I mention a hotel in the play, which I cannot now doubt, after Vl. Iv.'s [Nemirovich-Danchenko] letter, please telegraph me. We must correct it; we cannot issue it thus, with grave errors distorting its meaning.

The house must be large, solid; wooden (like Aksakov's, which, I think, S. T. Morozov has seen) or stone, it is all the same. It is very old and imposing; country residents do not take such houses; such houses are usually wrecked and the material employed for the construction of a country house. The furniture is ancient, stylish, solid; ruin and debt have not affected the surroundings.

When they buy such a house, they reason thus: it is cheaper and easier to build a new and smaller one than to repair this old one.

Your shepherd played well. That was most essential.

K. S. Stanislavsky: Konstantin Stanislavsky (1863–1938), director with the Moscow Art Theatre, which produced most of Chekhov's plays.
Vl. I. Nemirovich-Danchenko: Vladimir Ivanovich Nemirovich-Danchenko (1858–1943), novelist and codirector of the Moscow Art Theatre.

Maxim Gorky (1868–1936)
FROM *RECOLLECTIONS*   *1921*

TRANSLATED BY KATHERINE MANSFIELD

Alexei Maximovitch Pyeshkov changed his name to Maxim Gorky, which in Russian means "Maxim the Bitter." His childhood and early years gave him great reason for bitterness because he was raised by a brutal grandfather who regularly beat Maxim and his mother. Once, when Maxim was eight, he attacked his grandfather with a bread knife for beating his frail and sick mother. Gorky spent many years tramping through Russia and became a writer of the common people. He was introduced to the Moscow Art Theatre by Chekhov, and his first play, The Lower Depths *(1902), starred Chekhov's wife, Olga Knipper. It was a mercilessly realistic portrait of the homeless, impoverished castaways of Russian life. It established Gorky as a major dramatist, and after the Russian revolution he became the most revered of Soviet writers.*

Reading Anton Chekhov's stories, one feels oneself in a melancholy day of late autumn, when the air is transparent and the outline of naked trees, narrow houses, grayish people, is sharp. Everything is strange, lonely, motionless, helpless. The horizon, blue and empty, melts into the pale sky, and its breath is terribly cold upon the earth, which is covered with frozen mud. The author's mind, like the autumn sun, shows up in hard outline the monotonous roads, the crooked streets, the little squalid houses in which tiny, miserable people are stifled by boredom and laziness and fill the houses with an unintelligible, drowsy bustle. . . .

Here is the lachrymose Ranevskaya and the other owners of *The Cherry Orchard,* egotistical like children, with the flabbiness of senility. They missed the right moment for dying; they whine, seeing nothing of what is going on around them, understanding nothing, parasites without the power of again taking root in life. The wretched little student, Trofimov, speaks eloquently of the necessity of working — and does nothing but amuse himself, out of sheer boredom, with stupid mockery of Varya, who works ceaselessly for the good of idlers. . . .

There passes before one a long file of men and women, slaves of their love, of their stupidity and idleness, of their greed for the good things of life; there walk the slaves of the dark fear of life; they straggle anxiously along, filling life with incoherent words about the future, feeling that in the present there is no place for them.

At moments out of the gray mass of them one hears the sound of a shot: Ivanov [in *Ivanov*] or Treplev [in *The Seagull*] has guessed what he ought to do and has died.

Many of them have nice dreams of how pleasant life will be in three hundred years, but it occurs to none of them to ask themselves who will make life pleasant if we only dream.

In front of that dreary, gray crowd of helpless people there passed a great, wise, and observant man; he looked at all these dreary inhabitants of his country, and, with a sad smile, with a tone of gentle but deep reproach, with anguish in his face and in his heart, in a beautiful and sincere voice, he said to them:

"You live badly, my friends. It is shameful to live like that."

Virginia Woolf (1882–1941)
ON THE CHERRY ORCHARD

Virginia Woolf was one of the most important experimental writers of fiction in the first half of the twentieth century. Her best-known works include Mrs. Dalloway *(1925),* To the Lighthouse *(1927),* Orlando *(1928),* A Room of One's Own *(1930), and* The Waves *(1931). In addition to these landmark works, she wrote a large number of essays and commentaries, not to mention letters that have now been gathered into five large volumes. Her insight into literature is always keen and original. Her approach, for instance, to a 1920 production of* The Cherry Orchard *is through language. She is naturally sensitive to careful use of language, and it is therefore important for her to observe that out of the apparently disjointed use of sentences comes extraordinary drama. She ends her commentary with an interesting comparison that delves into the realm of music — or, more properly, into an imaginative realm in which the theatergoers themselves are musical instruments.*

It is, as a rule, when a critic does not wish to commit himself or to trouble himself, that he refers to atmosphere. And, given time, something might be said in greater detail of the causes which produced this atmosphere — the strange dislocated sentences, each so erratic and yet cutting out the shape so firmly, of the realism, of the humor, of the artistic unity. But let the word atmosphere be taken literally to mean that Chekhov has contrived to shed over us a luminous vapor in which life appears as it is, without veils, transparent and visible to the depths. Long before the play was over, we seemed to have sunk below the surface of things and to be feeling our way among submerged but recognizable emotions. "I have no proper passport. I don't know how old I am; I always feel I am still young"— how the words go sounding on in one's mind — how the whole play resounds with such sentences, which reverberate, melt into each other, and pass far away out beyond everything! In short, if it is permissible to use such vague language, I do not know how better to describe the sensation at the end of *The Cherry Orchard*, than by saying that it sends one into the street feeling like a piano played upon at last, not in the middle only but all over the keyboard and with the lid left open so that the sound goes on.

John Corbin (1870–1959)
REVIEW OF THE CHERRY ORCHARD

After brief praise for the Russian-language production of the Moscow Players, John Corbin's review centers itself entirely on an analysis of the play. Clearly, he sees the main characters as feckless and wasteful and has little sympathy for them. On the other hand, he sees in Lopakhin a man of industry and progress. His interpretation may well depend on the emphasis of the postrevolutionary Russian players, whose sympathies would certainly not have aligned with aristocrats.

The Moscow players proceeded last night from the lower depths of Gorky to the high comedy of Tchekhoff, revealing new artistic resources. Stanislavsky, Olga Knipper-Tchekhova, Moskvin, Leonidoff and half a dozen others entered with consummate ease into a rich variety of new characterizations. The stage management was less signal in its effects, but no less perfect. Yet for some reason *The Cherry Orchard* failed to stir the audience, even the Russian portion of it, as did *The Lower Depths* and even *Tsar Fyodor.*

This is a play of comedy values both high and light. The milieu is that of the ancient landed aristocracy, beautifully symbolized by an orchard of cherry trees in full bloom which surrounds the crumbling manor house. Quite obviously, these amiable folks have fallen away from the pristine vigor of their race.

The middle-aged brother and sister who live together are unconscious, irreclaimable spendthrifts, both of their shrinking purses and of their waning lives. With a little effort, one is made to feel, even with a modicum of mental concentration, calamity could be averted. But that is utterly beyond their vacuous and futile amiability; so their estate is sold over their heads and the leagues of gay cherry trees are felled to make way for suburban villas.

Beneath the graceful, easy-going surface of the play one feels rather than perceives a criticism on the Russia of two decades ago. Here is a woman of truly Slavic instability, passing with a single gesture from heartbreak to the gayety of a moment, from acutely maternal grief for an only child long dead to weak doting on a Parisian lover who is faithless to her and yet has power to hold her and batten on her bounty. Here is a man whose sentiment for the home of his ancestors breaks forth in fluent declaiming, quasi-poetic and quasi-philosophic, yet who cannot lift a finger to avert financial disaster.

In the entire cast only one person has normal human sense. Lopakhin is the son of a serf who has prospered in freedom. He is loyal enough to the old masters, dogging their footsteps with good advice. But in the end it is he who buys the estate and fells the cherry trees for the villas of an industrial population. It is as if Tchekhoff saw in the new middle class the hope of a disenchanted yet sounder and more progressive Russia. The war has halted that movement, but indications are not lacking that it is already resuming.

With such a theme developed by the subtly masterful act of Tchekhoff there is scope for comedy acting of the highest quality. It is more than likely that the company seized every opportunity and improved upon it. But to any one who does not understand Russian, judgment in such a matter is quite impossible. Where effects are to be achieved only by the subtlest intonation, the most delicate phrasing, it fares ill with those whose entire vocabulary is da, da.

As an example of the art of the most distinguished company that has visited our shores in modern memory, this production of *The Cherry Orchard* is abundantly worth seeing. The play in itself is of interest as the masterpiece of the man who, with Gorky, has touched the pinnacle of modern Russian comedy. But if some Moscovite should rise up and tell us that in any season our own stage produces casts as perfect and ensembles as finely studied in detail, it would be quite possible to believe him.

Peter Brook (b. 1925)
ON CHEKHOV

Peter Brook has established himself as one of the most distinguished directors of recent years. He was educated at Oxford University and has been a director of the Royal Shakespeare Company in England. In 1987 he directed The Cherry Orchard *at the Brooklyn Academy of Music. Some of his thoughts as he prepared to direct the play are presented here, showing his awareness of Chekhov's "film sense" in a play that was written just as film was emerging as a popular form. He is also aware of Chekhov's personal vision of death and sees it expressed in the circumstances of the play.*

Chekhov always looked for what's natural; he wanted performances and productions to be as limpid as life itself. Chekhov's writing is extremely concentrated, employing a minimum of words; in a way, it is similar to Pinter or Beckett. As with them, it is construction that counts, rhythm, the purely theatrical poetry that comes not from beautiful words but from the right word at the right moment. In the theater, someone can say "yes" in such a way that the "yes" is no longer ordinary — it can become a beautiful word, because it is the perfect expression of what cannot be expressed in any other way. With Chekhov, periods, commas, points of suspension are all of a fundamental importance, as fundamental as the "pauses" precisely indicated by Beckett. If one fails to observe them, one loses the rhythm and tensions of the play. In Chekhov's work, the punctuation represents a series of coded messages which record characters' relationships and emotions, the moments at which ideas come together or follow their own course. The punctuation enables us to grasp what the words conceal.

Chekhov is like a perfect filmmaker. Instead of cutting from one image to another — perhaps from one place to another — he switches from one emotion to another just before it gets too heavy. At the precise moment when the spectator risks becoming too involved in a character, an unexpected situation cuts across: Nothing is stable. Chekhov portrays individuals and a society in a state of perpetual change, he is the dramatist of life's movement, simultaneously smiling and serious, amusing and bitter — completely free from the "music," the Slav "nostalgia" that Paris nightclubs still preserve. He often stated that his plays were comedies — this was the central issue of his conflict with Stanislavsky.

But it's wrong to conclude that *The Cherry Orchard* should be performed as a vaudeville. Chekhov is an infinitely detailed observer of the human comedy. As a doctor, he knew the meaning of certain kinds of behavior, how to discern what was essential, to expose what he diagnosed. Although he shows tenderness and an attentive sympathy, he never sentimentalizes. One doesn't imagine a doctor shedding tears over the illnesses of his patients. He learns how to balance compassion with distance.

In Chekhov's work, death is omnipresent — he knew it well — but there is nothing negative or unsavory in its presence. The awareness of death is balanced with a desire to live. His characters possess a sense of the present moment, and the need to taste it fully. As in great tragedies, one finds a harmony between life and death.

Chekhov died young, having traveled, written, and loved enormously, having taken part in the events of his day, in great schemes of social reform. He died shortly after asking for some champagne, and his coffin was transported in a wagon bearing the inscription "Fresh Oysters." His awareness of death, and of the precious moments that could be lived, endow his work with a sense of the relative: in other words, a viewpoint from which the tragic is always a bit absurd.

In Chekhov's work, each character has its own existence: not one of them resembles another, particularly in *The Cherry Orchard,* which presents a microcosm of the political tendencies of the time. There are those who believe in social transformations, others attached to a disappearing past. None of them can achieve satisfaction or plenitude, and seen from outside, their existences might well appear empty, senseless. But they all burn with intense desires. They are not disillusioned, quite the contrary: In their own ways, they are all searching for a better quality of life, emotionally and socially. Their drama is that society — the outside world — blocks their energy. The complexity of their behavior is not indicated in the words, it emerges from the mosaic construction of an infinite number of details. What is essential is to see that these are not plays about lethargic people. They are hyper-vital people in a lethargic world, forced to dramatize the minutest happening out of a passionate desire to live. They have not given up.

Bernard Shaw

The Irish playwright Bernard Shaw[1] (1856–1950) was astonishing not only for the range of his writing but also for the length and vigor of his life. He was a public figure for most of his days, with an especially keen ability to catch public attention and to make his presence felt. His early work was devoted to criticism in newspapers and then to a series of fairly successful novels. He began writing plays in his late thirties; once he began, he realized that he had discovered his vocation, and he went on to write more than fifty. Some of them, such as *Arms and the Man* (1894), *Candida* (1897), *Mrs. Warren's Profession* (1898), *Man and Superman* (1901–1903), *Major Barbara* (1905), *Pygmalion* (1913), *Heartbreak House* (1919), and *St. Joan* (1923), are among the most performed plays by any English-language writer of his time.

Shaw's gift of analysis and philosophical reflection created in his works a new kind of drama that has sometimes been named for him — Shavian. The term implies a deep interest in ideas rather than in character and a propensity for elaborate discourse between characters who represent different points of view. Shaw assumed that drama should amuse and entertain, but of much greater importance was his didactic motive. Drama should teach a lesson about something of great moral importance.

This is not to say that Shaw was unable to be entertaining. Some of his comedies, still played today, are bright and witty. *You Never Can Tell* (1898), a comedy about male-female relationships whose main character is a dentist, and *Pygmalion*, a comedy in which a man teaches a cockney girl how to speak with an upper-class accent with unexpected results, are both funny plays. *Pygmalion* was redone as a musical, *My Fair Lady,* and has been Shaw's most financially successful play.

Still, Shaw was basically a philosophical writer. His plays can usually be seen as having a specific theme on which the characters constantly discourse. Whether it is on the relation of England to Ireland, on the state of the medical profession, on genetics and propagation, or on poverty, Shaw always focused on an issue and even commented that Shakespeare's shortcoming was that his plays have no message.

Shaw frequently wrote elaborate and lengthy prefaces to his published plays. In his prefaces, Shaw takes time to explain — and fully explore — the messages of his plays. He discusses the questions of genetic planning and the improvement of the race in his preface to *Man and Superman*; in the preface to *Candida* he discusses the relationship of pity to love.

Shaw's lifelong socialism affected his work and his thinking, and he himself was a socialist politician for a short period. Consequently, it is not uncommon to see political concerns expressed and debated in his plays.

---

[1]Shaw was born George Bernard Shaw and is sometimes referred to as GBS. He disliked the name George and preferred to be addressed as Bernard Shaw.

Shaw's political ideas were shaped by his concern for economics as a discipline, beginning in 1882. In 1884 he joined the Fabian Society, established a year earlier as a group to study and promote socialism, and remained active until 1911. Fabianism, unlike Marxism or communism, believed that society need not be destroyed by revolution but could become an instrument of socialist reform. For this reason Fabianism was known as evolutionary socialism. *Fabian Essays* (1889), which Shaw edited, was used by study groups that sprouted up throughout Great Britain to spread Fabian socialist ideas through politics, religion, and society. The result of the movement was the organization of a new political party, the Labor Party (1893), which still exists. The socialist government of Britain in the 1960s and 1970s was a direct outgrowth of Fabian theories.

While Shaw studied economics, he grew to believe that all social values were built on an economic base. He developed this idea in his Fabian essays and maintained it throughout his plays. He also maintained a presence as a critic of theater and accepted Ibsen as a major playwright when most London critics found Ibsen's work unacceptable. Shaw's *Quintessence of Ibsenism* (1891; revised after Ibsen's death in 1913) is still a useful commentary on that playwright's work. (See an excerpt from *The Quintessence of Ibsenism* on pp. 736–37.)

MRS. WARREN'S PROFESSION

Shaw once described this play as being in "my most odious vein." It was written in 1894 and inspired by Janet Achurch, the actress who played Nora in Ibsen's *A Doll House*. Achurch told Shaw the story of a play she was writing based on Guy de Maupassant's short story "Yvette." Shaw adopted the idea and hoped that when he finished his play, Achurch would play Vivie, the heroine. Shaw owed a great deal to other playwrights who had touched on similar themes — although none as directly as Shaw — but his story of a mother-daughter relationship in which the mother was a prostitute was original in that it proposed a "new woman" for the heroine, Vivie, and refused to permit Mrs. Warren to express shame for her professional decisions. This was a highly daring play for its time.

Indeed, the play had only two private performances in London in 1902 before it premiered in the United States in 1905. The play was banned or protested in several cities, especially after its first performances. By the time it was given its first public performances in London in 1926, Shaw had lost interest in the play and simply felt it was too late in production. The Comédie-Française considered it too amoral to produce as late as 1955, which demonstrates that Shaw hit a nerve that was not limited to the reactions of his own day.

The form of the play is essentially conventional for its time, although Shaw consciously employed techniques of Henrik Ibsen, whom he admired enough to have written the seminal study *The Quintessence of Ibsenism* (1891). He had learned from Ibsen how to address social issues directly and how to produce a female character whose ambiguities intrigue an audience. Ibsen's emphasis on the "new woman" — the independent woman who could make her own decisions and her own way — is evident in *Mrs. Warren's Profession*.

The men in the play are generally dependent on the women. Mrs. Warren has a good business sense and has used the capital provided her by Sir George Crofts so well that Crofts need no longer worry about his own welfare. In one sense he is a kept man, living on the earnings of a woman. The Reverend Samuel Gardner has converted from a roué and former client of Mrs. Warren to an overly pious churchman worried about his reputation. His son, Frank, may or may not be a brother to Vivie, and while the play ends with Vivie declaring that she doesn't care if he is her brother or not, the theme of incest seems underdeveloped. Yet Shaw felt it was an essential ingredient of the play. Frank plans not to work, is shiftless and indolent, and would be content to be supported by Vivie and her mother's money just as Crofts is content to bask in the security provided by Mrs. Warren.

The underlying theme of economic opportunities for women drives this play. The Victorians felt that prostitution, widespread in England, was one of the most serious social diseases of the time. But Shaw is keen enough in his analysis of English social life to realize that prostitutes were often forced into the profession because the alternatives were even worse. Mrs. Warren explains to Vivie in act 2 that she watched her two half-sisters follow the path of respectability: "One of them worked in a whitelead factory twelve hours a day for nine shillings a week until she died of lead poisoning. She only expected to get her hands a little paralyzed; but she died. The other was always held up to us as a model because she married a Government laborer in the Deptford victualling yard, and kept his room and the three children neat and tidy on eighteen shillings a week — until he took to drink."

The unrespectable sisters, Liz and Mrs. Warren, followed "the life" and ended up in control of their own situation. Liz, retired in a cathedral town, is emblematic of the height of respectability. Vivie is in a position to reject her mother's life as well as Croft's offer of marriage and wealth and Frank's offer of marriage and love. But she is in this position because her mother provided her with a man's education at Cambridge. She describes herself as a "wrangler" — a term meaning an honors student in mathematics but also implying achievement in debate. This position was formerly available only to men (as Praed implies when he says nothing like that happened "in my day").

Vivie ends the play in the secure knowledge that she will succeed in the law profession and that the limited options available to her mother will never be her only options. Vivie, then, is heroic, and the play comic in form.

Mrs. Warren's Profession in Performance

Mrs. Warren's Profession was produced privately in London on January 5, 1902, at the New Lyric Theater. On October 27, 1902, it was produced at the Hyperion Theater in New Haven, Connecticut, its first American production. H. Granville Barker, a distinguished actor and writer, played the part of Frank, and Fanny Brough was Mrs. Warren. It was performed again in New York in 1905 with the well-known actor, Richard Mansfield, but the police commissioner closed the play for "offending public decency." A special court hearing in 1906 proclaimed the play "not pleasant" but did not declare it indecent.

After performances in Berlin (1907) and Glasgow (1913), the play's first public performance in England took place in Birmingham in 1925, when the British censors finally cleared the play of charges of indecency. It ran in London at the Strand Theatre in 1926 for eighty-six performances.

John Loder and Estelle Winwood played Crofts and Mrs. Warren off-Broadway in 1950 for twenty-eight performances. Ruth Gordon and Lynn Redgrave played Mrs. Warren and Vivie in a 1976 New York Shakespeare Festival production in Lincoln Center that lasted for sixty-nine performances. Edward Herrmann played Frank, and Milo O'Shea played Reverend Gardner. Current productions of the play abound. The Irish Classical Theater Co. in Buffalo, New York, staged a well-received performance in April 2003. That same year, the celebrated British director Peter Hall chose Brenda Blethyn for the lead in the London West End production at the Strand Theatre. The reviews praised Blethyn and the rest of the cast, but they especially honored Shaw for attacking hypocrisy. Former fashion model Twiggy Lawson played Mrs. Warren in a Wiltshire, England, production in July 2003. These contemporary productions demonstrate the validity of Shaw's views.

Bernard Shaw (1856–1950)
MRS. WARREN'S PROFESSION
1898

Characters

VIVIE WARREN
PRAED
MRS WARREN
SIR GEORGE CROFTS
FRANK GARDNER
REVEREND SAMUEL GARDNER

ACT I

Summer afternoon in a cottage garden on the eastern slope of a hill a little south of Haslemere in Surrey. Looking up the hill, the cottage is seen in the left hand corner of the garden, with its thatched roof and porch, and a large latticed window to the left of the porch. Farther back a little wing is built out, making an angle with the right side wall. From the end of this wing a paling curves across and forward, completely shutting in the garden, except for a gate on the right. The common rises uphill beyond the paling to the sky line. Some folded canvas garden chairs are leaning against the side bench in the porch. A lady's bicycle is propped against the wall, under the window. A little to the right of the porch a hammock is slung from two posts. A big canvas umbrella, stuck in the ground, keeps the sun off the hammock, in which a young lady lies reading and making notes, her head towards the cottage and her feet towards the gate. In front of the hammock, and within reach of her hand, is a common kitchen chair, with a pile of serious-looking books and a supply of writing paper upon it.

A gentleman walking on the common comes into sight from behind the cottage. He is hardly past middle age, with something of the artist about him, unconventionally but carefully dressed, and clean-shaven except for a moustache, with an eager, susceptible face and very amiable and considerate manners. He has silky black hair, with waves of grey and white in it. His eyebrows are white, his moustache black. He seems not certain of his way. He looks over the paling; takes stock of the place; and sees the young lady.

THE GENTLEMAN (*taking off his hat*): I beg your pardon. Can you direct me to Hindhead View — Mrs Alison's?

THE YOUNG LADY (*glancing up from her book*): This is Mrs Alison's. (*She resumes her work.*)

THE GENTLEMAN: Indeed! Perhaps — may I ask are you Miss Vivie Warren?

THE YOUNG LADY (*sharply, as she turns on her elbow to get a good look at him*): Yes.

THE GENTLEMAN (*daunted and conciliatory*): I'm afraid I appear intrusive. My name is Praed. (*Vivie at once throws her books upon the chair, and gets out of the hammock.*) Oh, pray dont let me disturb you.

VIVIE (*striding to the gate and opening it for him*): Come in, Mr Praed. (*He comes in.*) Glad to see you. (*She proffers her hand and takes his with a resolute and hearty grip. She is an attractive specimen of the sensible, able, highly educated young middle-class Englishwoman. Age 22. Prompt, strong, confident, self-possessed. Plain, business-like dress, but not dowdy. She wears a chatelaine at her belt, with a fountain pen and a paper knife among its pendants.*)

PRAED: Very kind of you indeed, Miss Warren. (*She shuts the gate with a vigorous slam: he passes in to the middle of the garden, exercising his fingers, which are slightly numbed by her greeting.*) Has your mother arrived?

VIVIE (*quickly, evidently scenting aggression*): Is she coming?

PRAED (*surprised*): Didnt you expect us?

VIVIE: No.

PRAED: Now, goodness me, I hope Ive not mistaken the day. That would be just like me, you know. Your mother arranged that she was to come down from London and that I was to come over from Horsham to be introduced to you.

VIVIE (*not at all pleased*): Did she? Hm! My mother has rather a trick of taking me by surprise — to see how I behave myself when she's away, I suppose. I fancy I shall take my mother very much by surprise one of these days, if she makes arrangements that concern me without consulting me beforehand. She hasnt come.

PRAED (*embarrassed*): I'm really very sorry.

VIVIE (*throwing off her displeasure*): It's not your fault, Mr Praed, is it? And I'm very glad youve come, believe me. You are the only one of my mother's friends I have asked her to bring to see me.

PRAED (*relieved and delighted*): Oh, now this is really very good of you, Miss Warren!

VIVIE: Will you come indoors; or would you rather sit out here whilst we talk?

PRAED: It will be nicer out here, dont you think?

VIVIE: Then I'll go and get you a chair. (*She goes to the porch for a garden chair.*)

PRAED (*following her*): Oh, pray, pray! Allow me. (*He lays hands on the chair.*)

VIVIE (*letting him take it*): Take care of your fingers: theyre rather dodgy things, those chairs. (*She goes across to the chair with the books on it; pitches them into the hammock; and brings the chair forward with one swing.*)

PRAED (*who has just unfolded his chair*): Oh, now do let me take that hard chair! I like hard chairs.

VIVIE: So do I. (*She sits down.*) Sit down, Mr Praed. (*This invitation she gives with genial peremptoriness, his anxiety to please her clearly striking her as a sign of weakness of character on his part.*)

PRAED: By the way, though, hadnt we better go to the station to meet your mother?

VIVIE (*coolly*): Why? She knows the way. (*Praed hesitates, and then sits down in the garden chair, rather disconcerted.*) Do you know, you are just like what I expected. I hope you are disposed to be friends with me.

PRAED (*again beaming*): Thank you, my dear Miss Warren: thank you. Dear me! I'm so glad your mother hasnt spoilt you!

VIVIE: How?

PRAED: Well, in making you too conventional. You know, my dear Miss Warren, I am a born anarchist. I hate authority. It spoils the relations between parent and child — even between mother and daughter. Now I was always afraid that your mother would strain her authority to make you very conventional. It's such a relief to find that she hasnt.

VIVIE: Oh! have I been behaving unconventionally?

PRAED: Oh no: oh dear no. At least not conventionally unconventionally, you understand. (*She nods. He goes on, with a cordial outburst.*) But it was so charming of you to say that you were disposed to be friends with me! You modern young ladies are splendid — perfectly splendid!

VIVIE (*dubiously*): Eh? (*Watching him with dawning disappointment as to the quality of his brains and character.*)

PRAED: When I was your age, young men and women were afraid of each other: there was no good fellowship — nothing real — only gallantry copied out of novels, and as vulgar and affected as it could be. Maidenly reserve! — gentlemanly chivalry! — always saying no when you meant yes! — simple purgatory for shy and sincere souls!

VIVIE: Yes, I imagine there must have been a frightful waste of time — especially women's time.

PRAED: Oh, waste of life, waste of everything. But things are improving. Do you know, I have been in a positive state of excitement about meeting you ever since your magnificent achievements at Cambridge — a thing unheard of in my day. It was perfectly splendid, your tieing with the third wrangler.° Just the right place, you know. The first wrangler is always a dreamy, morbid fellow, in whom the thing is pushed to the length of a disease.

VIVIE: It doesnt pay. I wouldnt do it again for the same money.

PRAED (*aghast*): The same money!

VIVIE: I did it for £50. Perhaps you dont know how it was. Mrs Latham, my tutor at Newnham, told my mother that I could distinguish myself in the mathematical tripos° if I went in for it in earnest. The papers were full just then of Phillipa Summers beating the senior wrangler — you remember about it; and nothing would please my mother but that I should do the same thing. I said flatly that it was not worth my while to face the grind since I was not

---

wrangler: An honors student in mathematics. The term also implies achievement in debate.   **tripos:** An examination for the B.A. degree with honors at Cambridge University.

going in for teaching; but I offered to try for fourth wrangler or thereabouts for £50. She closed with me at that, after a little grumbling; and I was better than my bargain. But I wouldnt do it again for that. £200 would have been nearer the mark.

PRAED (*much damped*): Lord bless me! Thats a very practical way of looking at it.

VIVIE: Did you expect to find me an unpractical person?

PRAED: No, no. But surely it's practical to consider not only the work these honors cost, but also the culture they bring.

VIVIE: Culture! My dear Mr Praed: do you know what the mathematical tripos means? It means grind, grind, grind for six to eight hours a day at mathematics, and nothing but mathematics. I'm supposed to know something about science; but I know nothing except the mathematics it involves. I can make calculations for engineers, electricians, insurance companies, and so on; but I know next to nothing about engineering or electricity or insurance. I dont even know arithmetic well. Outside mathematics, lawn-tennis, eating, sleeping, cycling, and walking, I'm a more ignorant barbarian than any woman could possibly be who hadnt gone in for the tripos.

PRAED (*revolted*): What a monstrous, wicked, rascally system! I knew it! I felt at once that it meant destroying all that makes womanhood beautiful.

VIVIE: I dont object to it on that score in the least. I shall turn it to very good account, I assure you.

PRAED: Pooh! In what way?

VIVIE: I shall set up in chambers in the City and work at actuarial calculations and conveyancing. Under cover of that I shall do some law, with one eye on the Stock Exchange all the time. Ive come down here by myself to read law — not for a holiday, as my mother imagines. I hate holidays.

PRAED: You make my blood run cold. Are you to have no romance, no beauty in your life?

VIVIE: I dont care for either, I assure you.

PRAED: You cant mean that.

VIVIE: Oh yes I do. I like working and getting paid for it. When I'm tired of working, I like a comfortable chair, a cigar, a little whisky, and a novel with a good detective story in it.

PRAED (*in a frenzy of repudiation*): I dont believe it. I am an artist; and I cant believe it: I refuse to believe it. (*Enthusiastically.*) Ah, my dear Miss Warren, you havnt discovered yet, I see, what a wonderful world art can open up to you.

VIVIE: Yes I have. Last May I spent six weeks in London with Honoria Fraser. Mamma thought we were doing a round of sightseeing together; but I was really at Honoria's chambers in Chancery Lane every day, working away at actuarial calculations for her, and helping her as well as a greenhorn could. In the evenings we smoked and talked, and never dreamt of going out except for exercise. And I never enjoyed myself more in my life. I cleared all my expenses, and got initiated into the business without a fee into the bargain.

PRAED: But bless my heart and soul, Miss Warren, do you call that trying art?

VIVIE: Wait a bit. That wasnt the beginning. I went up to town on an invitation from some artistic people in Fitzjohn's Avenue: one of the girls was a Newnham chum. They took me to the National Gallery, to the Opera, and to a concert where the band played all the evening — Beethoven and Wagner and so on. I wouldnt go through that experience again for anything you could offer me. I held out for civility's sake until the third day; and then I said, plump out, that I couldnt stand any more of it, and went off to Chancery Lane. Now you know the sort of perfectly splendid modern young lady I am. How do you think I shall get on with my mother?

PRAED (*startled*): Well, I hope — er —

VIVIE: It's not so much what you hope as what you believe, that I want to know.

PRAED: Well, frankly, I am afraid your mother will be a little disappointed. Not from any shortcoming on your part — I dont mean that. But you are so different from her ideal.

VIVIE: What is her ideal like?

PRAED: Well, you must have observed, Miss Warren, that people who are dissatisfied with their own bringing up generally think that the world would be all right if everybody were to be brought up quite differently. Now your mother's life has been — er — I suppose you know —

VIVIE: I know nothing. (*Praed is appalled. His consternation grows as she continues.*) Thats exactly my difficulty. You forget, Mr. Praed, that I hardly know my mother. Since I was a child I have lived in England, at school or college, or with people paid to take charge of me. I have been boarded out all my life; and my mother has lived in Brussels or Vienna and never let me go to her. I only see her when she visits England for a few days. I dont complain: it's been very pleasant; for people have been very good to me; and there has always been plenty of money to make things smooth. But dont imagine I know anything about my mother. I know far less than you do.

PRAED (*very ill at ease*): In that case — (*He stops, quite at a loss. Then, with a forced attempt at gaiety*) But what nonsense we are talking! Of course you and your mother will get on capitally. (*He rises, and looks abroad at the view.*) What a charming little place you have here!

VIVIE (*unmoved*): If you think you are doing anything but confirming my worst suspicions by changing the subject like that, you must take me for a much greater fool than I hope I am.

PRAED: Your worst suspicions! Oh, pray dont say that. Now dont.

VIVIE: Why wont my mother's life bear being talked about?

PRAED: Pray think, Miss Vivie. It is natural that I should have a certain delicacy in talking to my old friend's daughter about her behind her back. You will have plenty of opportunity of talking to her about it when she comes. (*Anxiously*) I wonder what is keeping her.

VIVIE: No: she wont talk about it either. (*Rising*) However, I wont press you. Only, mind this, Mr Praed. I strongly suspect there will be a battle royal when my mother hears of my Chancery Lane project.

PRAED (*ruefully*): I'm afraid there will.

VIVIE: I shall win the battle, because I want nothing but my fare to London to start there to-morrow earning my own living by devilling° for Honoria. Besides, I have no mysteries to keep up; and it seems she has. I shall use that advantage over her if necessary.

PRAED (*greatly shocked*): Oh no! No, pray. Youd not do such a thing.

VIVIE: Then tell me why not.

PRAED: I really cannot. I appeal to your good feeling. (*She smiles at his sentimentality.*) Besides, you may be too bold. Your mother is not to be trifled with when she's angry.

VIVIE: You cant frighten me, Mr Praed. In that month at Chancery Lane I had opportunities of taking the measure of one or two women very like my mother, who came to consult Honoria. You may back me to win. But if I hit harder in my ignorance than I need, remember that it is you who refuse to enlighten me. Now, let us drop the subject. (*She takes her chair and replaces it near the hammock with the same vigorous swing as before.*)

PRAED (*taking a desperate resolution*): One word, Miss Warren. I had better tell you. It's very difficult; but —

(*Mrs Warren and Sir George Crofts arrive at the gate. Mrs Warren is a woman between 40 and 50, good-looking, showily dressed in a brilliant hat and a gay blouse fitting tightly over her bust and flanked by fashionable sleeves. Rather spoiled and domineering, but, on the whole, a genial and fairly presentable old black-guard of a woman.*

Crofts is a tall, powerfully-built man of about 50, fashionably dressed in the style of a young man. Nasal voice, reedier than might be expected from his strong frame. Clean-shaven, bulldog jaws, large flat ears, and thick neck, gentlemanly combination of the most brutal types of city man, sporting man, and man about town.)

VIVIE: Here they are. (*Coming to them as they enter the garden.*) How do, mater. Mr Praed's been here this half hour, waiting for you.

MRS WARREN: Well, if youve been waiting, Praddy, it's your own fault: I thought youd have had the gumption to know I was coming by the 3:10 train. Vivie: put your hat on, dear: youll get sunburnt. Oh, I forgot to introduce you. Sir George Crofts: my little Vivie.

(*Crofts advances to Vivie with his most courtly manner. She nods, but makes no motion to shake hands.*)

CROFTS: May I shake hands with a young lady whom I have known by reputation very long as the daughter of one of my oldest friends?

VIVIE (*who has been looking him up and down sharply*): If you like. (*She takes his tenderly proffered hand and gives it a squeeze that makes him open his eyes; then turns away, and says to her mother.*) Will you come in, or shall I get a couple more chairs? (*She goes into the porch for the chairs.*)

MRS WARREN: Well, George, what do you think of her?

CROFTS (*ruefully*): She has a powerful fist. Did you shake hands with her, Praed?

PRAED: Yes: it will pass off presently.

CROFTS: I hope so. (*Vivie reappears with two more chairs. He hurries to her assistance.*) Allow me.

MRS WARREN (*patronizingly*): Let Sir George help you with the chairs, dear.

VIVIE (*almost pitching the two into his arms*): Here you are. (*She dusts her hands and turns to Mrs Warren.*) Youd like some tea, wouldnt you?

MRS WARREN (*sitting in Praed's chair and fanning herself*): I'm dying for a drop to drink.

VIVIE: I'll see about it. (*She goes into the cottage. Sir George has by this time managed to unfold a chair and plant it beside Mrs Warren, on her left. He throws the other on the grass and sits down, looking dejected and rather foolish, with the handle of his stick in his mouth. Praed, still very uneasy, fidgets about the garden on their right.*)

MRS WARREN (*to Praed, looking at Crofts*): Just look at him, Praddy: he looks cheerful, dont he? He's been worrying my life out these three years to have that little girl of mine shewn to him; and now that Ive done it, he's quite out of countenance. (*Briskly.*) Come! sit up, George; and take your stick out of your mouth. (*Crofts sulkily obeys.*)

PRAED: I think, you know — if you dont mind my saying so — that we had better get out of the habit of thinking of her as a little girl. You see she has really distinguished herself; and I'm not sure, from what I have seen of her, that she is not older than any of us.

MRS WARREN (*greatly amused*): Only listen to him, George! Older than any of us! Well, she has been stuffing you nicely with her importance.

PRAED: But young people are particularly sensitive about being treated in that way.

MRS WARREN: Yes; and young people have to get all that nonsense taken out of them, and a good deal more besides. Dont you interfere, Praddy. I know how to treat my own child as well as you do. (*Praed, with a grave shake of his head, walks up the garden with his hands behind his back. Mrs Warren pretends to laugh, but looks after him with perceptible concern. Then she whispers to Crofts*) Whats the matter with him? What does he take it like that for?

CROFTS (*morosely*): Youre afraid of Praed.

MRS WARREN: What! Me! Afraid of dear old Praddy! Why, a fly wouldnt be afraid of him.

CROFTS: Youre afraid of him.

---

devilling: To aid a professional (such as a lawyer or literary person) without fee or monetary recognition. This would constitute an apprenticeship.

MRS WARREN (*angry*): I'll trouble you to mind your own business, and not try any of your sulks on me. I'm not afraid of you, anyhow. If you cant make yourself agreeable, youd better go home. (*She gets up, and, turning her back on him, finds herself face to face with Praed.*) Come, Praddy, I know it was only your tender-heartedness. Youre afraid I'll bully her.

PRAED: My dear Kitty: you think I'm offended. Dont imagine that: pray dont. But you know I often notice things that escape you; and though you never take my advice, you sometimes admit afterwards that you ought to have taken it.

MRS WARREN: Well, what do you notice now?

PRAED: Only that Vivie is a grown woman. Pray, Kitty, treat her with every respect.

MRS WARREN (*with genuine amazement*): Respect! Treat my own daughter with respect! What next, pray!

VIVIE (*appearing at the cottage door and calling to Mrs Warren*): Mother: will you come up to my room and take your bonnet off before tea?

MRS WARREN: Yes, dearie. (*She laughs indulgently at Praed and pats him on the cheek as she passes him on her way to the porch. She follows Vivie into the cottage.*)

CROFTS (*furtively*): I say, Praed.

PRAED: Yes.

CROFTS: I want to ask you a rather particular question.

PRAED: Certainly. (*He takes Mrs Warren's chair and sits close to Crofts.*)

CROFTS: Thats right: they might hear us from the window. Look here: did Kitty ever tell you who that girl's father is?

PRAED: Never.

CROFTS: Have you any suspicion of who it might be?

PRAED: None.

CROFTS (*not believing him*): I know, of course, that you perhaps might feel bound not to tell if she had said anything to you. But it's very awkward to be uncertain about it now that we shall be meeting the girl every day. We dont exactly know how we ought to feel towards her.

PRAED: What difference can that make? We take her on her own merits. What does it matter who her father was?

CROFTS (*suspiciously*): Then you know who he was?

PRAED (*with a touch of temper*): I said no just now. Did you not hear me?

CROFTS: Look here, Praed. I ask you as a particular favor. If you do know (*movement of protest from Praed*) — I only say, if you know, you might at least set my mind at rest about her. The fact is, I feel attracted towards her. Oh, dont be alarmed: it's quite an innocent feeling. Thats what puzzles me about it. Why, for all I know, *I* might be her father.

PRAED: You! Impossible! Oh no, nonsense!

CROFTS (*catching him up cunningly*): You know for certain that I'm not?

PRAED: I know nothing about it, I tell you, any more than you. But really, Crofts — oh no, it's out of the question. Theres not the least resemblance.

CROFTS: As to that, theres no resemblance between her and her mother that I can see. I suppose she's not your daughter, is she?

PRAED (*He meets the question with an indignant stare; then recovers himself with an effort and answers gently and gravely*): Now listen to me, my dear Crofts. I have nothing to do with that side of Mrs Warren's life, and never had. She has never spoken to me about it; and of course I have never spoken to her about it. Your delicacy will tell you that a handsome woman needs some friends who are not — well, not on that footing with her. The effect of her own beauty would become a torment to her if she could not escape from it occasionally. You are probably on much more confidential terms with Kitty than I am. Surely you can ask her the question yourself.

CROFTS (*rising impatiently*): I have asked her, often enough. But she's so determined to keep the child all to herself that she would deny that it ever had a father if she could. No: theres nothing to be got out of her — nothing that one can believe, anyhow. I'm thoroughly uncomfortable about it, Praed.

PRAED (*rising also*): Well, as you are, at all events, old enough to be her father, I dont mind agreeing that we both regard Miss Vivie in a parental way, as a young girl whom we are bound to protect and help. All the more, as the real father, whoever he was, was probably a black-guard. What do you say?

CROFTS (*aggressively*): I'm no older than you, if you come to that.

PRAED: Yes you are, my dear fellow: you were born old. I was born a boy: Ive never been able to feel the assurance of a grown-up man in my life.

MRS WARREN (*calling from within the cottage*): Praddee! George! Tea-ea-ea-ea!

CROFTS (*hastily*): She's calling us. (*He hurries in. Praed shakes his head bodingly, and is following slowly when he is hailed by a young gentleman who has just appeared on the common, and is making for the gate. He is a pleasant, pretty, smartly dressed, and entirely good-for-nothing young fellow, not long turned 20, with a charming voice and agreeably disrespectful manners. He carries a very light sporting magazine rifle.*)

THE YOUNG GENTLEMAN: Hallo! Praed!

PRAED: Why, Frank Gardner! (*Frank comes in and shakes hands cordially.*) What on earth are you doing here?

FRANK: Staying with my father.

PRAED: The Roman father?

FRANK: He's rector here. I'm living with my people this autumn for the sake of economy. Things came to a crisis in July: the Roman father had to pay my debts. He's stony broke in consequence; and so am I. What are you up to in these parts? Do you know the people here?

PRAED: Yes: I'm spending the day with a Miss Warren.

FRANK (*enthusiastically*): What! Do you know Vivie? Isnt she a jolly girl! I'm teaching her to shoot — you see (*shewing the rifle*)! I'm so glad she knows you: youre just the sort of fellow she ought to know. (*He *smiles, and raises the charming voice almost to a singing tone as he exclaims.*) It's ever so jolly to find you here, Praed. Aint it now?

PRAED: I'm an old friend of her mother's. Mrs Warren brought me over to make her daughter's acquaintance.

FRANK: The mother! Is she here?

PRAED: Yes — inside, at tea.

MRS WARREN (*calling from within*): Prad-dee-ee-ee-eee! The tea-cake'll be cold.

PRAED (*calling*): Yes, Mrs Warren. In a moment. Ive just met a friend here.

MRS WARREN: A what?

PRAED (*louder*): A friend.

MRS WARREN: Bring him up.

PRAED: All right. (*To Frank.*) Will you accept the invitation?

FRANK (*incredulous, but immensely amused*): Is that Vivie's mother?

PRAED: Yes.

FRANK: By Jove! What a lark! Do you think she'll like me?

PRAED: Ive no doubt youll make yourself popular, as usual. Come in and try (*moving towards the house*).

FRANK: Stop a bit. (*Seriously.*) I want to take you into my confidence.

PRAED: Pray dont. It's only some fresh folly, like the barmaid at Redhill.

FRANK: It's ever so much more serious than that. You say youve only just met Vivie for the first time?

PRAED: Yes.

FRANK (*rhapsodically*): Then you can have no idea what a girl she is. Such character! Such sense! And her cleverness! Oh, my eye, Praed, but I can tell you she is clever! And the most loving little heart that —

CROFTS (*putting his head out of the window*): I say, Praed: what are you about? Do come along. (*He disappears.*)

FRANK: Hallo! Sort of chap that would take a prize at a dog show, aint he? Who's he?

PRAED: Sir George Crofts, an old friend of Mrs Warren's. I think we had better come in.

(*On their way to the porch they are interrupted by a call from the gate. Turning, they see an elderly clergyman looking over it.*)

THE CLERGYMAN (*calling*): Frank!

FRANK: Hello! (*To Praed.*) The Roman father. (*To the clergyman.*) Yes, gov'nor: all right: presently. (*To Praed.*) Look here, Praed: youd better go in to tea. I'll join you directly.

PRAED: Very good. (*He raises his hat to the clergyman, who acknowledges the salute distantly. Praed goes into the cottage. The clergyman remains stiffly outside the gate, with his hands on the top of it. The Rev. Samuel Gardner, a beneficed clergyman of the Established Church, is over 50. He is a pretentious, booming, noisy person, hopelessly asserting himself as a father and a clergyman without being able to command respect in either capacity.*)

REV. SAMUEL: Well, sir. Who are your friends here, if I may ask?

FRANK: Oh, it's all right, gov'nor! Come in.

REV. SAMUEL: No, sir; not until I know whose garden I am entering.

FRANK: It's all right. It's Miss Warren's.

REV. SAMUEL: I have not seen her at church since she came.

FRANK: Of course not: she's a third wrangler — ever so intellectual! — took a higher degree than you did; so why should she go to hear you preach?

REV. SAMUEL: Dont be disrespectful, sir.

FRANK: Oh, it dont matter: nobody hears us. Come in. (*He opens the gate, unceremoniously pulling his father with it into the garden.*) I want to introduce you to her. She and I get on rattling well together: she's charming. Do you remember the advice you gave me last July, gov'nor?

REV. SAMUEL (*severely*): Yes. I advised you to conquer your idleness and flippancy, and to work your way into an honorable profession and live on it and not upon me.

FRANK: No: thats what you thought of afterwards. What you actually said was that since I had neither brains nor money, I'd better turn my good looks to account my marrying somebody with both. Well, look here. Miss Warren has brains: you cant deny that.

REV. SAMUEL: Brains are not everything.

FRANK: No, of course not: theres the money —

REV. SAMUEL (*interrupting him austerely*): I was not thinking of money, sir. I was speaking of higher things — social position, for instance.

FRANK: I dont care a rap about that.

REV. SAMUEL: But I do, sir.

FRANK: Well, nobody wants you to marry her. Anyhow, she has what amounts to a high Cambridge degree; and she seems to have as much money as she wants.

REV. SAMUEL (*sinking into a feeble vein of humor*): I greatly doubt whether she has as much money as you will want.

FRANK: Oh, come: I havnt been so very extravagant. I live ever so quietly; I dont drink; I dont bet much; and I never go regularly on the razzle-dazzle as you did when you were my age.

REV. SAMUEL (*booming hollowly*): Silence, sir.

FRANK: Well, you told me yourself, when I was making ever such an ass of myself about the barmaid at Redhill, that you once offered a woman £50 for the letters you wrote to her when —

REV. SAMUEL (*terrified*): Sh-sh-sh, Frank, for Heaven's sake! (*He looks round apprehensively. Seeing no one within earshot he plucks up courage to boom again, but more subduedly.*) You are taking an ungentlemanly advantage of what I confided to you for your own good, to save you from an error you would have repented all your life long. Take warning by your father's follies, sir; and dont make them an excuse for your own.

FRANK: Did you ever hear the story of the Duke of Wellington and his letters?

REV. SAMUEL: No, sir; and I dont want to hear it.

FRANK: The old Iron Duke didnt throw away £50 — not he. He just wrote: "My dear Jenny: Publish and be damned! Yours affectionately, Wellington." Thats what you should have done.

REV. SAMUEL (*piteously*): Frank, my boy: when I wrote those letters I put myself into that woman's power. When I told you about her I put myself, to some extent, I am sorry to say, in your power. She refused my money with these words, which I shall never forget: "Knowledge is power," she said; "and I never sell power." Thats more than twenty years ago; and she has never made use of her power or caused me a moment's uneasiness. You are behaving worse to me than she did, Frank.

FRANK: Oh yes I dare say! Did you ever preach at her the way you preach at me every day?

REV. SAMUEL (*wounded almost to tears*): I leave you, sir. You are incorrigible. (*He turns towards the gate.*)

FRANK (*utterly unmoved*): Tell them I shant be home to tea, will you, gov'nor, like a good fellow? (*He goes towards the cottage door and is met by Vivie coming out, followed by Praed, Crofts, and Mrs Warren.*)

VIVIE (*to Frank*): Is that your father, Frank? I do so want to meet him.

FRANK: Certainly. (*Calling after his father*) Gov'nor. (*The Rev Samuel turns at the gate, fumbling nervously at his hat. Praed comes down the garden on the opposite side, beaming in anticipation of civilities. Crofts prowls about near the hammock, poking it with his stick to make it swing. Mrs Warren halts on the threshold, staring hard at the clergyman.*) Let me introduce — my father: Miss Warren.

VIVIE (*going to the clergyman and shaking his hand*): Very glad to see you here, Mr Gardner. Let me introduce everybody. Mr Gardner — Mr Frank Gardner — Mr Praed — Sir George Crofts, and — (*As the men are raising their hats to one another, Vivie is interrupted by an exclamation from her mother, who swoops down on the Reverend Samuel.*)

MRS WARREN: Why, it's Sam Gardner, gone into the church! Dont you know us, Sam? This is George Crofts, as large as life and twice as natural. Dont you remember me?

REV. SAMUEL (*very red*): I really — er —

MRS WARREN: Of course you do. Why, I have a whole album of your letters still: I came across them only the other day.

REV. SAMUEL (*miserably confused*): Miss Vavasour, I believe.

MRS WARREN (*correcting him quickly in a loud whisper*): Tch! Nonsense — Mrs. Warren: dont you see my daughter there?

ACT II

(*Inside the cottage after nightfall. Looking eastward from within instead of westward from without, the latticed window, with its curtains drawn, is now seen in the middle of the front wall of the cottage, with the porch door to the left of it. In the left-hand side wall is the door leading to the wing. Farther back against the same wall is a dresser with a candle and matches on it, and Frank's rifle standing beside them, with the barrel resting in the plate-rack. In the centre a table stands with a lighted lamp on it. Vivie's books and writing materials are on a table to the right of the window, against the wall. The fireplace is on the right, with a settle: there is no fire. Two of the chairs are set right and left of the table.*

The cottage door opens, showing a fine starlit night without; and Mrs Warren, her shoulders wrapped in a shawl borrowed from Vivie, enters, followed by Frank. She has had enough of walking, and gives a gasp of relief as she unpins her hat; takes it off; sticks the pin through the crown; and puts it on the table.)

MRS WARREN: O Lord! I dont know which is the worst of the country, the walking or the sitting at home with nothing to do. I could do a whisky and soda now very well, if only they had such a thing in this place.

FRANK (*helping her to take off her shawl, and giving her shoulders the most delicate possible little caress with his fingers as he does so*): Perhaps Vivie's got some.

MRS WARREN (*glancing back at him for an instant from the corner of her eye as she detects the pressure*): Nonsense! What would a young girl like her be doing with such things! Never mind: it dont matter. (*She throws herself wearily into a chair at the table.*) I wonder how she passes her time here! I'd a good deal rather be in Vienna.

FRANK: Let me take you there. (*He folds the shawl neatly; hangs it on the back of the other chair; and sits down opposite Mrs Warren.*)

MRS WARREN: Get out! I'm beginning to think youre a chip of the old block.

FRANK: Like the gov'nor, eh?

MRS WARREN: Never you mind. What do you know about such things? Youre only a boy.

FRANK: Do come to Vienna with me? It'd be ever such larks.

MRS WARREN: No, thank you. Vienna is no place for you — at least not until youre a little older. (*She nods at him to emphasize this piece of advice. He makes a mock-piteous face, belied by his laughing eyes. She looks at him; then rises and goes to him.*) Now, look here, little boy (*taking his face in her hands and turning it up to her*): I know you through and through by your likeness to your father, better than you know yourself. Dont you go taking any silly ideas into your head about me. Do you hear?

FRANK (*gallantly wooing her with his voice*): Cant help it, my dear Mrs Warren: it runs in the family. (*She pretends to box his ears; then looks at the pretty, laughing, upturned face for a moment, tempted. At last she kisses him, and immediately turns away, out of patience with herself.*)

MRS WARREN: There! I shouldnt have done that. I am wicked. Never you mind, my dear: it's only a motherly kiss. Go and make love to Vivie.

FRANK: So I have.

MRS WARREN (*turning on him with a sharp note of alarm in her voice*): What!

FRANK: Vivie and I are ever such chums.

MRS WARREN: What do you mean? Now see here: I wont have any young scamp tampering with my little girl. Do you hear? I wont have it.

FRANK (*quite unabashed*): My dear Mrs Warren: dont you be alarmed. My intentions are honorable — ever so honorable; and your little girl is jolly well able to take care of herself. She dont need looking after half so much as her mother. She aint so handsome, you know.

MRS WARREN (*taken aback by his assurance*): Well, you have got a nice, healthy two inches thick of cheek all over you. I dont know where you got it — not from your father, anyhow. (*Voices and footsteps in the porch.*) Sh! I hear the others coming in. (*She sits down hastily.*) Remember: youve got your warning. (*The Rev. Samuel comes in, followed by Crofts.*) Well, what became of you two? And wheres Praddy and Vivie?

CROFTS (*putting his hat on the settle and his stick in the chimney corner*): They went up the hill. We went to the village. I wanted a drink. (*He sits down on the settle, putting his legs up along the seat.*)

MRS WARREN: Well, she oughtnt to go off like that without telling me. (*To Frank*) Get your father a chair, Frank: where are your manners? (*Frank springs up and gracefully offers his father his chair; then takes another from the wall and sits down at the table, in the middle, with his father on his right and Mrs Warren on his left.*) George: where are you going to stay to-night? You cant stay here. And whats Praddy going to do?

CROFTS: Gardner'll put me up.

MRS WARREN: Oh, no doubt youve taken care of yourself! But what about Praddy?

CROFTS: Dont know. I suppose he can sleep at the inn.

MRS WARREN: Havnt you room for him, Sam?

REV. SAMUEL: Well, er — you see, as rector here, I am not free to do as I like exactly. Er — what is Mr Praed's social position?

MRS WARREN: Oh, he's all right: he's an architect. What an old stick-in-the-mud you are, Sam!

FRANK: Yes, it's all right, gov'nor. He built that place down in Monmouthshire for the Duke of Beaufort — Tintern Abbey they call it. You must have heard of it. (*He winks with lightning smartness at Mrs Warren, and regards his father blandly.*)

REV. SAMUEL: Oh, in that case, of course we shall only be too happy. I suppose he knows the Duke of Beaufort personally.

FRANK: Oh, ever so intimately! We can stick him in Georgina's old room.

MRS WARREN: Well, thats settled. Now if those two would only come in and let us have supper. Theyve no right to stay out after dark like this.

CROFTS (*aggressively*): What harm are they doing you?

MRS WARREN: Well, harm or not, I dont like it.

FRANK: Better not wait for them, Mrs Warren. Praed will stay out as long as possible. He has never known before what it is to stray over the heath on a summer night with my Vivie.

CROFTS (*sitting up in some consternation*): I say, you know. Come!

REV. SAMUEL (*startled out of his professional manner into real force and sincerity*): Frank, once for all, its out of the question. Mrs Warren will tell you that its not to be thought of.

CROFTS: Of course not.

FRANK (*with enchanting placidity*): Is that so, Mrs Warren?

MRS WARREN (*reflectively*): Well, Sam, I dont know. If the girl wants to get married, no good can come of keeping her unmarried.

REV. SAMUEL (*astounded*): But married to him! — your daughter to my son! Only think: it's impossible.

CROFTS: Of course it's impossible. Dont be a fool, Kitty.

MRS WARREN (*nettled*): Why not? Isnt my daughter good enough for your son?

REV. SAMUEL: But surely, my dear Mrs Warren, you know the reason —

MRS WARREN (*defiantly*): I know no reasons. If you know any, you can tell them to the lad, or to the girl, or to your congregation, if you like.

REV. SAMUEL (*helplessly*): You know very well that I couldnt tell anyone the reasons. But my boy will believe me when I tell him there are reasons.

FRANK: Quite right, Dad: he will. But has your boy's conduct ever been influenced by your reasons?

CROFTS: You cant marry her; and thats all about it. (*He gets up and stands on the hearth, with his back to the fireplace, frowning determinedly.*)

MRS WARREN (*turning on him sharply*): What have you got to do with it, pray?

FRANK (*with his prettiest lyrical cadence*): Precisely what I was going to ask, myself, in my own graceful fashion.

CROFTS (*to Mrs Warren*): I suppose you dont want to marry the girl to a man younger than herself and without either a profession or twopence to keep her on. Ask Sam, if you dont believe me. (*To the Rev. Samuel.*) How much more money are you going to give him?

REV. SAMUEL: Not another penny. He has had his patrimony; and he spent the last of it in July. (*Mrs Warren's face falls.*)

CROFTS (*watching her*): There! I told you. (*He resumes his place on the settle and puts up his legs on the seat again, as if the matter were finally disposed of.*)

FRANK (*plaintively*): This is ever so mercenary. Do you suppose Miss Warren's going to marry for money? If we love one another —

MRS WARREN: Thank you. Your love's a pretty cheap commodity, my lad. If you have no means of keeping a wife, that settles it: you cant have Vivie.

FRANK (*much amused*): What do you say, gov'nor, eh?

REV. SAMUEL: I agree with Mrs Warren.

FRANK: And good old Crofts has already expressed his opinion.

CROFTS (*turning angrily on his elbow*): Look here: I want none of your cheek.

FRANK (*pointedly*): I'm ever so sorry to surprise you, Crofts; but you allowed yourself the liberty of speaking to me like a father a moment ago. One father is enough, thank you.

CROFTS (*contemptuously*): Yah! (*He turns away again.*)

FRANK (*rising*): Mrs Warren: I cannot give my Vivie up, even for your sake.

MRS WARREN (*muttering*): Young scamp!

FRANK (*continuing*): And as you no doubt intend to hold out other prospects to her, I shall lose no time in placing my case before her. (*They stare at him; and he begins to declaim gracefully*)

He either fears his fate too much,
Or his deserts are small,
That dares not put it to the touch
To gain or lose it all.

(*The cottage door opens whilst he is reciting; and Vivie and Praed come in. He breaks off. Praed puts his hat on the dresser. There is an immediate improvement in the company's behaviour. Crofts takes down his legs from the settle and pulls himself together as Praed joins him at the fireplace. Mrs Warren loses her ease of manner and takes refuge in querulousness.*)

MRS WARREN: Wherever you have been, Vivie?

VIVIE (*taking off her hat and throwing it carelessly on the table*): On the hill.

MRS WARREN: Well, you shouldnt go off like that without letting me know. How could I tell what had become of you — and night coming on too!

VIVIE (*going to the door of the inner room and opening it, ignoring her mother*): Now, about supper? We shall be rather crowded in here, I'm afraid.

MRS WARREN: Did you hear what I said, Vivie?

VIVIE (*quietly*): Yes, mother. (*Reverting to the supper difficulty.*) How many are we? (*Counting.*) One, two, three, four, five, six. Well, two will have to wait until the rest are done: Mrs Allison has only plates and knives for four.

PRAED: Oh, it doesnt matter about me. I —

VIVIE: You have had a long walk and are hungry, Mr Praed: you shall have your supper at once. I can wait myself. I want one person to wait with me. Frank: are you hungry?

FRANK: Not the least in the world — completely off my peck, in fact.

MRS WARREN (*to Crofts*): Neither are you, George. You can wait.

CROFTS: Oh, hang it, Ive eaten nothing since tea-time. Cant Sam do it?

FRANK: Would you starve my poor father?

REV. SAMUEL (*testily*): Allow me to speak for myself, sir. I am perfectly willing to wait.

VIVIE (*decisively*): Theres no need. Only two are wanted. (*She opens the door of the inner room.*) Will you take my mother in, Mr Gardner. (*The Rev. Samuel takes Mrs Warren; and they pass into the next room. Praed and Crofts follow. All except Praed clearly disapprove of the arrangement, but do not know how to resist it. Vivie stands at the door looking in at them.*) Can you squeeze past to that corner, Mr Praed: it's rather a tight fit. Take care of your coat against the white-wash — thats right. Now, are you all comfortable?

PRAED (*within*): Quite, thank you.

MRS WARREN (*within*): Leave the door open, dearie. (*Frank looks at Vivie; then steals to the cottage door and softly sets it wide open.*) Oh Lor, what a draught! Youd better shut it, dear. (*Vivie shuts it promptly. Frank noiselessly shuts the cottage door.*)

FRANK (*exulting*): Aha! Got rid of em. Well, Vivvums: what do you think of my governor?

VIVIE (*preoccupied and serious*): Ive hardly spoken to him. He doesnt strike me as being a particularly able person.

FRANK: Well, you know, the old man is not altogether such a fool as he looks. You see, he's rector here; and in trying to live up to it he makes a much bigger ass of himself than he really is. No, the gov'nor aint so bad, poor old chap; and I dont dislike him as much as you might expect. He means well. How do you think youll get on with him?

VIVIE (*rather grimly*): I dont think my future life will be much concerned with him, or with any of that old circle of my mother's, except perhaps Praed. What do you think of my mother?

FRANK: Really and truly?

VIVIE: Yes, really and truly.

FRANK: Well, she's ever so jolly. But she's rather a caution, isnt she? And Crofts! Oh, my eye, Crofts!

VIVIE: What a lot, Frank!

FRANK: What a crew!

VIVIE (*with intense contempt for them*): If I thought that I was like that — that I was going to be a waster, shifting along from one meal to another with no purpose, and no character, and no grit in me, I'd open an artery and bleed to death without one moment's hesitation.

FRANK: Oh no, you wouldnt. Why should they take any grind when they can afford not to? I wish I had their luck. No: what I object to is their form. It isnt the thing: it's slovenly, ever so slovenly.

VIVIE: Do you think your form will be any better when youre as old as Crofts, if you dont work?

FRANK: Of course I do — ever so much better. Vivvums mustnt lecture: her little boy's incorrigible. (*He attempts to take her face caressingly in his hands.*)

VIVIE (*striking his hands down sharply*): Off with you: Vivvums is not in a humor for petting her little boy this evening.

FRANK: How unkind!

VIVIE (*stamping at him*): Be serious. I'm serious.

FRANK: Good. Let us talk learnedly. Miss Warren: do you know that all the most advanced thinkers are agreed that half the diseases of modern civilization are due to starvation of the affections in the young. Now, *I —*

VIVIE (*cutting him short*): You are getting tiresome. (*She opens the inner door*) Have you room for Frank there? He's complaining of starvation.

MRS WARREN (*within*): Of course there is (*clatter of knives and glasses as she moves the things on the table.*) Here: theres room now beside me. Come along, Mr Frank.

FRANK (*aside to Vivie, as he goes*): Her little boy will be ever so even with his Vivvums for this. (*He goes into the other room.*)

MRS WARREN (*within*): Here, Vivie: come on you too, child. You must be famished. (*She enters, followed by Crofts, who holds the door open for Vivie with marked deference. She goes out without looking at him; and he shuts the door after her.*) Why, George, you cant be done: youve eaten nothing.

CROFTS: Oh, all I wanted was a drink. (*He thrusts his hands in his pockets, and begins prowling about the room, restless and sulky.*)

MRS WARREN: Well, I like enough to eat. But a little of that cold beef and cheese and lettuce goes a long way. (*With a sigh of only half repletion she sits down lazily at the table.*)

CROFTS: What do you go encouraging that young pup for?

MRS WARREN (*on the alert at once*): Now see here, George: what are you up to about that girl? Ive been watching your way of looking at her. Remember: I know you and what your looks mean.

CROFTS: Theres no harm in looking at her, is there?

MRS WARREN: I'd put you out and pack you back to London pretty soon if I saw any of your nonsense. My girl's little finger is more to me than your whole body and soul. (*Crofts receives this with a sneering grin. Mrs Warren, flushing a little at her failure to impose on him in the character of a theatrically devoted mother, adds in a lower key*) Make your mind easy: the young pup has no more chance than you have.

CROFTS: Maynt a man take an interest in a girl?

MRS WARREN: Not a man like you.

CROFTS: How old is she?

MRS WARREN: Never you mind how old she is.

CROFTS: Why do you make such a secret of it?

MRS WARREN: Because I choose.

CROFTS: Well, I'm not fifty yet; and my property is as good as ever it was —

MRS WARREN (*interrupting him*): Yes; because youre as stingy as youre vicious.

CROFTS (*continuing*): And a baronet isnt to be picked up every day. No other man in my position would put up with you for a mother-in-law. Why shouldnt she marry me?

MRS WARREN: You!

CROFTS: We three could live together quite comfortably.

I'd die before her and leave her a bouncing widow with plenty of money. Why not? It's been growing in my mind all the time Ive been walking with that fool inside there.

MRS WARREN (*revolted*): Yes: it's the sort of thing that would grow in your mind. (*He halts in his prowling; and the two look at one another, she steadfastly, with a sort of awe behind her contemptuous disgust: he stealthily, with a carnal gleam in his eye and a loose grin, tempting her.*)

CROFTS (*suddenly becoming anxious and urgent as he sees no sign of sympathy in her*): Look here, Kitty: youre a sensible woman: you neednt put on any moral airs. I'll ask no more questions; and you need answer none. I'll settle the whole property on her; and if you want a cheque for yourself on the wedding day, you can name any figure you like — in reason.

MRS WARREN: So it's come to that with you, George, like all the other worn out old creatures!

CROFTS (*savagely*): Damn you! (*She rises and turns fiercely on him; but the door of the inner room is opened just then; and the voices of the others are heard returning. Crofts, unable to recover his presence of mind, hurries out of the cottage. The clergyman comes back.*)

REV. SAMUEL (*looking round*): Where is Sir George?

MRS WARREN: Gone out to have a pipe. (*She goes to the fireplace, turning her back on him to compose herself. The clergyman goes to the table for his hat. Meanwhile Vivie comes in, followed by Frank, who collapses into the nearest chair with an air of extreme exhaustion. Mrs Warren looks round at Vivie and says, with her affectation of maternal patronage even more forced than usual.*) Well, dearie: have you had a good supper?

VIVIE: You know what Mrs Alison's suppers are. (*She turns to Frank and pets him.*) Poor Frank! was all the beef gone? did it get nothing but bread and cheese and ginger beer? (*Seriously, as if she had done quite enough trifling for one evening.*) Her butter is really awful. I must get some down from the stores.

FRANK: Do, in Heaven's name!

(*Vivie goes to the writing-table and makes a memorandum to order the butter. Praed comes in from the inner room, putting up his handkerchief, which he has been using as a napkin.*)

REV. SAMUEL: Frank, my boy: it is time for us to be thinking of home. Your mother does not know yet that we have visitors.

PRAED: I'm afraid we're giving trouble.

FRANK: Not the least in the world, Praed: my mother will be delighted to see you. She's a genuinely intellectual, artistic woman; and she sees nobody here from one year's end to another except the gov'nor; so you can imagine how jolly dull it pans out for her. (*To the Rev. Samuel.*) Youre not intellectual or artistic, are you, pater? So take Praed home at once; and I'll stay here and entertain Mrs Warren. Youll pick up

Crofts in the garden. He'll be excellent company for the bull-pup.

PRAED (*taking his hat from the dresser, and coming close to Frank*): Come with us, Frank. Mrs Warren has not seen Miss Vivie for a long time; and we have prevented them from having a moment together yet.

FRANK (*quite softened, and looking at Praed with romantic admiration*): Of course: I forgot. Ever so thanks for reminding me. Perfect gentleman, Praddy. Always were — my ideal through life. (*He rises to go, but pauses a moment between the two older men, and puts his hand on Praed's shoulder.*) Ah, if you had only been my father instead of this unworthy old man! (*He puts his other hand on his father's shoulder.*)

REV. SAMUEL (*blustering*): Silence, sir, silence: you are profane.

MRS WARREN (*laughing heartily*): You should keep him in better order, Sam. Good-night. Here: take George his hat and stick with my compliments.

REV. SAMUEL (*taking them*): Good-night. (*They shake hands. As he passes Vivie he shakes hands with her also and bids her good-night. Then, in booming command, to Frank*) Come along, sir, at once. (*He goes out. Meanwhile Frank has taken his cap from the dresser and his rifle from the rack. Praed shakes hands with Mrs Warren and Vivie and goes out, Mrs Warren accompanying him idly to the door and looking out after him as he goes across the garden. Frank silently begs a kiss from Vivie; but she, dismissing him with a stern glance, takes a couple of books and some paper from the writing-table, and sits down with them at the middle table, so as to have the benefit of the lamp.*)

FRANK (*at the door, taking Mrs Warren's hand*): Good-night, dear Mrs Warren. (*He squeezes her hand. She snatches it away, her lips tightening, and looks more than half disposed to box his ears. He laughs mischievously and runs off, clapping-to° the door behind him.*)

MRS WARREN (*coming back to her place at the table, opposite Vivie, resigning herself to an evening of boredom now that the men are gone*): Did you ever in your life hear anyone rattle on so? Isnt he a tease? (*She sits down.*) Now that I think of it, dearie, dont you go encouraging him. I'm sure he's a regular good-for-nothing.

VIVIE: Yes: I'm afraid poor Frank is a thorough good-for-nothing. I shall have to get rid of him; but I shall feel sorry for him, though he's not worth it, poor lad. That man Crofts does not seem to me to be good for much either, is he?

MRS WARREN (*galled by Vivie's cool tone*): What do you know of men, child, to talk that way about them? Youll have to make up your mind to see a good deal of Sir George Crofts, as he's a friend of mine.

clapping-to: Slamming.

VIVIE (*quite unmoved*): Why? Do you expect that we shall be much together — you and I, I mean?

MRS WARREN (*staring at her*): Of course — until youre married. Youre not going back to college again.

VIVIE: Do you think my way of life would suit you? I doubt it.

MRS WARREN: Your way of life! What do you mean?

VIVIE (*cutting a page of her book with the paper knife on her chatelaine*): Has it really never occurred to you, mother, that I have a way of life like other people?

MRS WARREN: What nonsense is this youre trying to talk? Do you want to shew your independence, now that youre a great little person at school? Dont be a fool, child.

VIVIE (*indulgently*): Thats all you have to say on the subject, is it, mother?

MRS WARREN (*puzzled, then angry*): Dont you keep on asking me questions like that. (*Violently*) Hold your tongue. (*Vivie works on, losing no time, and saying nothing.*) You and your way of life, indeed! What next? (*She looks at Vivie again. No reply.*) Your way of life will be what I please, so it will. (*Another pause.*) Ive been noticing these airs in you ever since you got that tripos or whatever you call it. If you think I'm going to put up with them youre mistaken; and the sooner you find it out, the better. (*Muttering*) All I have to say on the subject, indeed! (*Again raising her voice angrily.*) Do you know who youre speaking to, Miss?

VIVIE (*looking across at her without raising her head from her book*): No. Who are you? What are you?

MRS WARREN (*rising breathless*): You young imp!

VIVIE: Everybody knows my reputation, my social standing, and the profession I intend to pursue. I know nothing about you. What is that way of life which you invite me to share with you and Sir George Crofts, pray?

MRS WARREN: Take care. I shall do something I'll be sorry for after, and you too.

VIVIE (*putting aside her books with cool decision*): Well, let us drop the subject until you are better able to face it. (*Looking critically at her mother*) You want some good walks and a little lawn tennis to set you up. You are shockingly out of condition: you were not able to manage twenty yards uphill to-day without stopping to pant; and your wrists are mere rolls of fat. Look at mine. (*She holds out her wrists.*)

MRS WARREN (*after looking at her helplessly, begins to whimper*): Vivie —

VIVIE (*springing up sharply*): Now pray dont begin to cry. Anything but that. I really cannot stand whimpering. I will go out of the room if you do.

MRS WARREN (*piteously*): Oh, my darling, how can you be so hard on me? Have I no rights over you as your mother?

VIVIE: Are you my mother?

MRS WARREN (*appalled*): Am I your mother! Oh, Vivie!

VIVIE: Then where are our relatives — my father — our family friends? You claim the rights of a mother:

right to call me fool and child; to speak to me as no woman in authority over me at college dare speak to me; to dictate my way of life; and to force on me the acquaintance of a brute whom anyone can see to be the most vicious sort of London man about town. Before I give myself the trouble to resist such claims, I may as well find out whether they have any real existence.

MRS WARREN (*distracted, throwing herself on her knees*): Oh no, no. Stop, stop. I am your mother: I swear it. Oh, you cant mean to turn on me — my own child: it's not natural. You believe me, dont you? Say you believe me.

VIVIE: Who was my father?

MRS WARREN: You dont know what youre asking. I cant tell you.

VIVIE (*determinedly*): Oh yes you can, if you like. I have a right to know; and you know very well that I have that right. You can refuse to tell me, if you please; but if you do, you will see the last of me to-morrow morning.

MRS WARREN: Oh, it's too horrible to hear you talk like that. You wouldnt — you couldnt leave me.

VIVIE (*ruthlessly*): Yes, without a moment's hesitation, if you trifle with me about this. (*Shivering with disgust.*) How can I feel sure that I may not have the contaminated blood of that brutal waster in my veins?

MRS WARREN: No, no. On my oath it's not he, nor any of the rest that you have ever met. I'm certain of that, at least. (*Vivie's eyes fasten sternly on her mother as the significance of this flashes on her.*)

VIVIE (*slowly*): You are certain of that, at least. Ah! You mean that that is all you are certain of. (*Thoughtfully.*) I see. (*Mrs Warren buries her face in her hands.*) Dont do that, mother: you know you dont feel it a bit. (*Mrs Warren takes down her hands and looks up deplorably at Vivie, who takes out her watch and says*) Well, that is enough for to-night. At what hour would you like breakfast? Is half-past eight too early for you?

MRS WARREN (*wildly*): My God, what sort of woman are you?

VIVIE (*coolly*): The sort the world is mostly made of, I should hope. Otherwise I dont understand how it gets its business done. Come (*taking her mother by the wrist, and pulling her up pretty resolutely*): pull yourself together. Thats right.

MRS WARREN (*querulously*): Youre very rough with me, Vivie.

VIVIE: Nonsense. What about bed? It's past ten.

MRS WARREN (*passionately*): Whats the use of my going to bed? Do you think I could sleep?

VIVIE: Why not? I shall.

MRS WARREN: You! youve no heart. (*She suddenly breaks out vehemently in her natural tongue — the dialect of a woman of the people — with all her affectations of maternal authority and conventional manners gone, and an overwhelming inspiration of true conviction and scorn in her.*) Oh, I wont bear it: I

wont put up with the injustice of it. What right have you to set yourself up above me like this? You boast of what you are to me — to me, who gave you the chance of being what you are. What chance had I? Shame on you for a bad daughter and a stuck-up prude!

VIVIE (*cool and determined, but no longer confident; for her replies, which have sounded convincingly sensible and strong to her so far, now begin to ring rather woodenly and even priggishly against the new tone of her mother*): Dont think for a moment I set myself above you in any way. You attacked me with the conventional authority of a mother: I defended myself with the conventional superiority of a respectable woman. Frankly, I am not going to stand any of your nonsense; and when you drop it I shall not expect you to stand any of mine. I shall always respect your right to your own opinions and your own way of life.

MRS WARREN: My own opinions and my own way of life! Listen to her talking! Do you think I was brought up like you — able to pick and choose my own way of life? Do you think I did what I did because I liked it, or thought it right, or wouldnt rather have gone to college and been a lady if I'd had the chance?

VIVIE: Everybody has some choice, mother. The poorest girl alive may not be able to choose between being Queen of England or Principal of Newnham; but she can choose between ragpicking and flowerselling, according to her taste. People are always blaming their circumstances for what they are. I dont believe in circumstances. The people who get on in this world are the people who get up and look for the circumstances they want, and, if they cant find them, make them.

MRS WARREN: Oh, it's easy to talk, very easy, isnt it? Here! — would you like to know what my circumstances were?

VIVIE: Yes: you had better tell me. Wont you sit down?

MRS WARREN: Oh, I'll sit down: dont you be afraid. (*She plants her chair farther forward with brazen energy, and sits down. Vivie is impressed in spite of herself.*) D'you know what your gran'mother was?

VIVIE: No.

MRS WARREN: No, you dont. I do. She called herself a widow and had a fried-fish shop down by the Mint, and kept herself and four daughters out of it. Two of us were sisters: that was me and Liz; and we were both good-looking and well made. I suppose our father was a well-fed man: mother pretended he was a gentleman; but I dont know. The other two were only half sisters — undersized, ugly, starved looking, hard working, honest poor creatures: Liz and I would have half-murdered them if mother hadnt half-murdered us to keep our hands off them. They were the respectable ones. Well, what did they get by their respectability? I'll tell you. One of them worked in a white-lead factory twelve hours a day for nine shillings a week until she died of lead poisoning. She only expected to get her hands a little paralyzed; but she died. The other was always held up to us as a model because she married a Government laborer in the Deptford victualling yard, and kept his room and the three children neat and tidy on eighteen shillings a week — until he took to drink. That was worth being respectable for, wasnt it?

VIVIE (*now thoughtfully attentive*): Did you and your sister think so?

MRS WARREN: Liz didnt, I can tell you: she had more spirit. We both went to a church school — that was part of the ladylike airs we gave ourselves to be superior to the children that knew nothing and went nowhere — and we stayed there until Liz went out one night and never came back. I know the schoolmistress thought I'd soon follow her example; for the clergyman was always warning me that Lizzie'd end by jumping off Waterloo Bridge. Poor fool: that was all he knew about it! But I was more afraid of the whitelead factory than I was of the river; and so would you have been in my place. That clergyman got me a situation as scullery maid in a temperance restaurant where they sent out for anything you liked. Then I was waitress; and then I went to the bar at Waterloo station — fourteen hours a day serving drinks and washing glasses for four shillings a week and my board. That was considered a great promotion for me. Well, one cold, wretched night, when I was so tired I could hardly keep myself awake, who should come up for a half of Scotch but Lizzie, in a long fur cloak, elegant and comfortable, with a lot of sovereigns in her purse.

VIVIE (*grimly*): My aunt Lizzie!

MRS WARREN: Yes; and a very good aunt to have, too. She's living down at Winchester now, close to the cathedral, one of the most respectable ladies there — chaperones girls at the county ball, if you please. No river for Liz, thank you! You remind me of Liz a little: she was a first-rate business woman — saved money from the beginning — never let herself look too like what she was — never lost her head or threw away a chance. When she saw I'd grown up good-looking she said to me across the bar "What are you doing there, you little fool? wearing out your health and your appearance for other people's profit!" Liz was saving money then to take a house for herself in Brussels; and she thought we two could save faster than one. So she lent me some money and gave me a start; and I saved steadily and first paid her back, and then went into business with her as her partner. Why shouldnt I have done it? The house in Brussels was real high class — a much better place for a woman to be in than the factory where Anne Jane got poisoned. None of our girls were ever treated as I was treated in the scullery of that temperance place, or at the Waterloo bar, or at home. Would you have had me stay in them and become a worn out old drudge before I was forty?

VIVIE (*intensely interested by this time*): No; but why did you choose that business? Saving money and good management will succeed in any business.

MRS WARREN: Yes, saving money. But where can a woman get the money to save in any other business? Could you save out of four shillings a week and keep yourself dressed as well? Not you. Of course, if youre a plain woman and cant earn anything more; or if you have a turn for music, or the stage, or newspaper-writing: thats different. But neither Liz nor I had any turn for such things: all we had was our appearance and our turn for pleasing men. Do you think we were such fools as to let other people trade in our good looks by employing us as shopgirls, or barmaids, or waitresses, when we could trade in them ourselves and get all the profits instead of starvation wages? Not likely.

VIVIE: You were certainly quite justified — from the business point of view.

MRS WARREN: Yes; or any other point of view. What is any respectable girl brought up to do but to catch some rich man's fancy and get the benefit of his money by marrying him? — as if a marriage ceremony could make any difference in the right or wrong of the thing! Oh, the hypocrisy of the world makes me sick! Liz and I had to work and save and calculate just like other people; elseways we should be as poor as any good-for-nothing, drunken waster of a woman that thinks her luck will last for ever. (*With great energy.*) I despise such people: theyve no character; and if theres a thing I hate in a woman, it's want of character.

VIVIE: Come now, mother: frankly! Isnt it part of what you call character in a woman that she should greatly dislike such a way of making money?

MRS WARREN: Why, of course. Everybody dislikes having to work and make money; but they have to do it all the same. I'm sure Ive often pitied a poor girl, tired out and in low spirits, having to try to please some man that she doesnt care two straws for — some half-drunken fool that thinks he's making himself agreeable when he's teasing and worrying and disgusting a woman so that hardly any money could pay her for putting up with it. But she has to bear with disagreeables and take the rough with the smooth, just like a nurse in a hospital or anyone else. It's not work that any woman would do for pleasure, goodness knows; though to hear the pious people talk you would suppose it was a bed of roses.

VIVIE: Still you consider it worth while. It pays.

MRS WARREN: Of course it's worth while to a poor girl, if she can resist temptation and is good-looking and well conducted and sensible. It's far better than any other employment open to her. I always thought that oughtnt to be. It cant be right, Vivie, that there shouldnt be better opportunities for women. I stick to that: it's wrong. But it's so, right or wrong; and a girl must make the best of it. But of course its not worth while for a lady. If you took to it youd be a fool; but I should have been a fool if I'd taken to anything else.

VIVIE (*more and more deeply moved*): Mother: suppose we were both as poor as you were in those wretched old days, are you quite sure that you wouldnt advise me to try the Waterloo bar, or marry a laborer, or even go into the factory?

MRS WARREN (*indignantly*): Of course not. What sort of mother do you take me for! How could you keep your self-respect in such starvation and slavery? And whats a woman worth? whats life worth? without self-respect! Why am I independent and able to give my daughter a first-rate education, when other women

BELOW: Vivie, played by Kate Goehring, listens to her mother, Mariette Hartley, reveal her secret in Bernard Shaw's *Mrs. Warren's Profession* at the Huntington Theatre, Boston, 1999.
RIGHT: Vivie and her mother console each other in *Mrs. Warren's Profession*, Huntington Theatre, Boston, 1999.

that had just as good opportunities are in the gutter? Because I always knew how to respect myself and control myself. Why is Liz looked up to in a cathedral town? The same reason. Where would we be now if we'd minded the clergyman's foolishness? Scrubbing floors for one and sixpence a day and nothing to look forward to but the workhouse infirmary. Dont you be led astray by people who dont know the world, my girl. The only way for a woman to provide for herself decently is for her to be good to some man that can afford to be good to her. If she's in his own station of life, let her make him marry her; but if she's far beneath him she cant expect it — why should she? It wouldnt be for her own happiness. Ask any lady in London society that has daughters; and she'll tell you the same, except that I tell you straight and she'll tell you crooked. Thats all the difference.

VIVIE (*fascinated, gazing at her*): My dear mother: you are a wonderful woman — you are stronger than all England. And are you really and truly not one wee bit doubtful — or — or — ashamed?

MRS WARREN: Well, of course, dearie, it's only good manners to be ashamed of it: it's expected from a woman. Women have to pretend to feel a great deal that they dont feel. Liz used to be angry with me for plumping out the truth about it. She used to say that when every woman could learn enough from what was going on in the world before her eyes, there was no need to talk about it to her. But then Liz was such a perfect lady! She had the true instinct of it; while I was always a bit of a vulgarian. I used to be so pleased when you sent me your photographs to see that you were growing up like Liz: youve just her ladylike, determined way. But I cant stand saying one thing when everyone knows I mean another. Whats the use in such hypocrisy? If people arrange the world that way for women, theres no good pretending that it's arranged the other way. I never was a bit ashamed really. I consider that I had a right to be proud that we managed everything so respectably, and never had a word against us, and that the girls were so well taken care of. Some of them did very well: one of them married an ambassador. But of course now I darent talk about such things: whatever would they think of us! (*She yawns.*) Oh dear! I do believe I'm getting sleepy after all. (*She stretches herself lazily, thoroughly relieved by her explosion, and placidly ready for her night's rest.*)

VIVIE: I believe it is I who will not be able to sleep now. (*She goes to the dresser and lights the candle. Then she extinguishes the lamp, darkening the room a good deal.*) Better let in some fresh air before locking up. (*She opens the cottage door, and finds that it is broad moonlight.*) What a beautiful night! Look! (*She draws aside the curtains of the window. The landscape is seen bathed in the radiance of the harvest moon rising over Blackdown.*)

MRS WARREN (*with a perfunctory glance at the scene*): Yes, dear; but take care you dont catch your death of cold from the night air.

VIVIE (*contemptuously*): Nonsense.

MRS WARREN (*querulously*): Oh yes: everything I say is nonsense, according to you.

VIVIE (*turning to her quickly*): No: really that is not so, mother. You have got completely the better of me tonight, though I intended it to be the other way. Let us be good friends now.

MRS WARREN (*shaking her head a little ruefully*): So it has been the other way. But I suppose I must give in to it. I always got the worst of it from Liz; and now I suppose it'll be the same with you.

VIVIE: Well, never mind. Come: good-night, dear old mother. (*She takes her mother in her arms.*)

MRS WARREN (*fondly*): I brought you up well, didnt I, dearie?

VIVIE: You did.

MRS WARREN: And youll be good to your poor old mother for it, wont you?

VIVIE: I will, dear. (*Kissing her*) Good-night.

MRS WARREN (*with unction*): Blessings on my own dearie darling — a mother's blessing! (*She embraces her daughter protectingly, instinctively looking upward as if to call down a blessing.*)

ACT III

(*In the Rectory garden next morning, with the sun shining and the birds in full song. The garden wall has a five-barred wooden gate, wide enough to admit a carriage, in the middle. Beside the gate hangs a bell on a coiled spring, communicating with a pull outside. The carriage drive comes down the middle of the garden and then swerves to its left, where it ends in a little gravelled circus opposite the Rectory porch. Beyond the gate is seen the dusty high road, parallel with the wall, bounded on the farther side by a strip of turf and an unfenced pine wood. On the lawn, between the house and the drive, is a clipped yew tree, with a garden bench in its shade. On the opposite side the garden is shut in by a box hedge; and there is a sundial on the turf, with an iron chair near it. A little path leads off through the box hedge, behind the sundial.*

Frank, seated on the chair near the sundial, on which he has placed the morning papers, is reading the Standard. *His father comes from the house, red-eyed and shivery, and meets Frank's eye with misgiving.*)

FRANK (*looking at his watch*): Half past eleven. Nice hour for a rector to come down to breakfast!

REV. SAMUEL: Dont mock, Frank: dont mock. I am a little — er — (*Shivering*) —

FRANK: Off colour?

REV. SAMUEL (*repudiating the expression*): No, sir: unwell this morning. Wheres your mother?

FRANK: Dont be alarmed: she's not here. Gone to town by the 11.13 with Bessie. She left several messages for you. Do you feel equal to receiving them now, or shall I wait till youve breakfasted?

REV. SAMUEL: I have breakfasted, sir. I am surprised at your mother going to town when we have people staying with us. Theyll think it very strange.

FRANK: Possibly she has considered that. At all events, if Crofts is going to stay here, and you are going to sit up every night with him until four, recalling the incidents of your fiery youth, it is clearly my mother's duty, as a prudent housekeeper, to go up to the stores and order a barrel of whisky and a few hundred siphons.

REV. SAMUEL: I did not observe that Sir George drank excessively.

FRANK: You were not in a condition to, gov'nor.

REV. SAMUEL: Do you mean to say that *I* —

FRANK (*calmly*): I never saw a beneficed clergyman less sober. The anecdotes you told about your past career were so awful that I really dont think Praed would have passed the night under your roof if it hadnt been for the way my mother and he took to one another.

REV. SAMUEL: Nonsense, sir. I am Sir George Crofts' host. I must talk to him about something; and he has only one subject. Where is Mr Praed now?

FRANK: He is driving my mother and Bessie to the station.

REV. SAMUEL: Is Crofts up yet?

FRANK: Oh, long ago. He hasnt turned a hair: he's in much better practice than you — has kept it up ever since, probably. He's taken himself off somewhere to smoke. (*Frank resumes his paper. The Rev. Samuel turns disconsolately towards the gate; then comes back irresolutely.*)

REV. SAMUEL: Er — Frank.

FRANK: Yes.

REV. SAMUEL: Do you think the Warrens will expect to be asked here after yesterday afternoon?

FRANK: Theyve been asked already. Crofts informed us at breakfast that you told him to bring Mrs Warren and Vivie over here to-day, and to invite them to make this house their home. It was after that communication that my mother found she must go to town by the 11.13 train.

REV. SAMUEL (*with despairing vehemence*): I never gave any such invitation. I never thought of such a thing.

FRANK (*compassionately*): How do you know, gov'nor, what you said and thought last night? Hallo! heres Praed back again.

PRAED (*coming in through the gate*): Good morning.

REV. SAMUEL: Good morning. I must apologize for not having met you at breakfast. I have a touch of — of —

FRANK: Clergyman's sore throat, Praed. Fortunately not chronic.

PRAED (*changing the subject*): Well, I must say your house is in a charming spot here. Really most charming.

REV. SAMUEL: Yes: it is indeed. Frank will take you for a walk, Mr Praed, if you like. I'll ask you to excuse me: I must take the opportunity to write my sermon while Mrs Gardner is away and you are all amusing yourselves. You wont mind, will you?

PRAED: Certainly not. Dont stand on the slightest ceremony with me.

REV. SAMUEL: Thank you. I'll — er — er — (*He stammers his way to the porch and vanishes into the house.*)

PRAED (*sitting down on the turf near Frank, and hugging his ankles*): Curious thing it must be writing a sermon every week.

FRANK: Ever so curious, if he did it. He buys em. He's gone for some soda water.

PRAED: My dear boy: I wish you would be more respectful to your father. You know you can be so nice when you like.

FRANK: My dear Praddy: you forget that I have to live with the governor. When two people live together — it dont matter whether theyre father and son, husband and wife, brother and sister — they cant keep up the polite humbug which comes so easy for ten minutes on an afternoon call. Now the governor, who unites to many admirable domestic qualities the irresoluteness of a sheep and the pompousness and aggressiveness of a jackass —

PRAED: No, pray, pray, my dear Frank, remember! He is your father.

FRANK: I give him due credit for that. But just imagine his telling Crofts to bring the Warrens over here! He must have been ever so drunk. You know, my dear Praddy, my mother wouldnt stand Mrs Warren for a moment. Vivie mustnt come here until she's gone back to town.

PRAED: But your mother doesnt know anything about Mrs Warren, does she?

FRANK: I dont know. Her journey to town looks as if she did. Not that my mother would mind in the ordinary way: she has stuck like a brick to lots of women who had got into trouble. But they were all nice women. Thats what makes the real difference. Mrs Warren, no doubt, has her merits; but she's ever so rowdy; and my mother simply wouldnt put up with her. So — hallo! (*This exclamation is provoked by the reappearance of the clergyman, who comes out of the house in haste and dismay.*)

REV. SAMUEL: Frank: Mrs Warren and her daughter are coming across the heath with Crofts: I saw them from the study windows. What am I to say about your mother?

FRANK (*jumping up energetically*): Stick on your hat and go out and say how delighted you are to see them; and that Frank's in the garden; and that mother and Bessie have been called to the bedside of a sick relative, and were ever so sorry they couldnt stop; and that you hope Mrs Warren slept well; and — and — say any blessed thing except the truth, and leave the rest to Providence.

REV. SAMUEL: But how are we to get rid of them afterwards?

FRANK: Theres no time to think of that now. Here! (*He*

bounds into the porch and returns immediately with a clerical felt hat, which he claps on his father's head.) Now: off with you. Praed and I'll wait here, to give the thing an unpremeditated air. (*The clergyman, dazed but obedient, hurries off through the gate. Praed gets up from the turf, and dusts himself.*)

FRANK: We must get that old lady back to town somehow, Praed. Come! honestly, dear Praddy, do you like seeing them together — Vivie and the old lady?

PRAED: Oh, why not?

FRANK (*his teeth on edge*): Dont it make your flesh creep ever so little? — that wicked old devil, up to every villainy under the sun, I'll swear, and Vivie — ugh!

PRAED: Hush, pray. Theyre coming. (*The clergyman and Crofts are seen coming along the road, followed by Mrs Warren and Vivie walking affectionately together.*)

FRANK: Look: she actually has her arm round the old woman's waist. It's her right arm: she began it. She's gone sentimental, by God! Ugh! ugh! Now do you feel the creeps? (*The clergyman opens the gate; and Mrs Warren and Vivie pass him and stand in the middle of the garden looking at the house. Frank, in an ecstasy of dissimulation, turns gaily to Mrs Warren, exclaiming*) Ever so delighted to see you, Mrs Warren. This quiet old rectory garden becomes you perfectly.

MRS WARREN: Well, I never! Did you hear that, George? He says I look well in a quiet old rectory garden.

REV. SAMUEL (*still holding the gate for Crofts, who loafs through it, heavily bored*): You look well everywhere, Mrs Warren.

FRANK: Bravo, gov'nor! Now look here: lets have an awful jolly time of it before lunch. First lets see the church. Everyone has to do that. It's a regular old thirteenth century church, you know: the gov'nor's ever so fond of it, because he got up a restoration fund and had it completely rebuilt six years ago. Praed will be able to show its points.

REV. SAMUEL (*mooning hospitably at them*): I shall be pleased, I'm sure, if Sir George and Mrs Warren really care about it.

MRS WARREN: Oh, come along and get it over. Itll do George good: I'll lay he doesnt trouble church much.

CROFTS (*turning back towards the gate*): Ive no objection.

REV. SAMUEL: Not that way. We go through the fields, if you dont mind. Round here. (*He leads the way by the little path through the box hedge.*)

CROFTS: Oh, all right. (*He goes with the parson. Praed follows with Mrs Warren. Vivie does not stir, but watches them until they have gone, with all the lines of purpose in her face marking it strongly.*)

FRANK: Aint you coming?

VIVIE: No. I want to give you a warning, Frank. You were making fun of my mother just now when you said that about the rectory garden. That is barred in future. Please treat my mother with as much respect as you treat your own.

FRANK: My dear Viv: she wouldnt appreciate it. She's not like my mother: the same treatment wouldnt do for both cases. But what on earth has happened to you? Last night we were perfectly agreed as to your mother and her set. This morning I find you attitudinizing sentimentally with your arm round your parent's waist.

VIVIE (*flushing*): Attitudinizing!

FRANK: That was how it struck me. First time I ever saw you do a second-rate thing.

VIVIE (*controlling herself*): Yes, Frank: there has been a change; but I dont think it a change for the worse. Yesterday I was a little prig.

FRANK: And to-day?

VIVIE (*wincing; then looking at him steadily*): To-day I know my mother better than you do.

FRANK: Heaven forbid!

VIVIE: What do you mean?

FRANK: Viv: theres a freemasonry among thoroughly immoral people that you know nothing of. Youve too much character. Thats the bond between your mother and me: thats why I know her better than youll ever know her.

VIVIE: You are wrong: you know nothing about her. If you knew the circumstances against which my mother had to struggle —

FRANK (*adroitly finishing the sentence for her*): I should know why she is what she is, shouldnt I? What difference would that make? Circumstances or no circumstances, Viv, you wont be able to stand your mother.

VIVIE (*very angry*): Why not?

FRANK: Because she's an old wretch, Viv. If you ever put your arm round her waist in my presence again, I'll shoot myself there and then as a protest against an exhibition which revolts me.

VIVIE: Must I choose between dropping your acquaintance and dropping my mother's?

FRANK (*gracefully*): That would put the old lady at ever such a disadvantage. No, Viv: your infatuated little boy will have to stick to you in any case. But he's all the more anxious that you shouldnt make mistakes. It's no use, Viv: your mother's impossible. She may be a good sort; but she's a bad lot, a very bad lot.

VIVIE (*hotly*): Frank — ! (*He stands his ground. She turns away and sits down on the bench under the yew tree, struggling to recover her self-command. Then she says*) Is she to be deserted by all the world because she's what you call a bad lot? Has she no right to live?

FRANK: No fear of that, Viv: she wont ever be deserted. (*He sits on the bench beside her.*)

VIVIE: But I am to desert her, I suppose.

FRANK (*babyishly, lulling her and making love to her with his voice*): Mustnt go live with her. Little family group of mother and daughter wouldnt be a success. Spoil our little group.

VIVIE (*falling under the spell*): What little group?

FRANK: The babes in the wood: Vivie and little Frank. (*He slips his arm round her waist and nestles against her like a weary child.*) Lets go and get covered up with leaves.

VIVIE (*rythmically, rocking him like a nurse*): Fast asleep, hand in hand, under the trees.

FRANK: The wise little girl with her silly little boy.

VIVIE: The dear little boy with his dowdy little girl.

FRANK: Ever so peaceful, and relieved from the imbecility of the little boy's father and the questionableness of the little girl's —

VIVIE (*smothering the word against her breast*): Sh-sh-sh-sh! little girl wants to forget all about her mother. (*They are silent for some moments, rocking one another. Then Vivie wakes up with a shock, exclaiming*) What a pair of fools we are! Come: sit up. Gracious! your hair. (*She smooths it.*) I wonder do all grown up people play in that childish way when nobody is looking. I never did it when I was a child.

FRANK: Neither did I. You are my first playmate. (*He catches her hand to kiss it, but checks himself to look round first. Very unexpectedly, he sees Crofts emerging from the box hedge.*) Oh damn!

VIVIE: Why damn, dear?

FRANK (*whispering*): Sh! Here's this brute Crofts. (*He sits farther away from her with an unconcerned air.*)

VIVIE: Dont be rude to him, Frank. I particularly wish to be polite to him. It will please my mother. (*Frank makes a wry face.*)

CROFTS: Could I have a few words with you, Miss Vivie?

VIVIE: Certainly.

CROFTS (*to Frank*): Youll excuse me, Gardner. Theyre waiting for you in the church, if you dont mind.

FRANK (*rising*): Anything to oblige you, Crofts — except church. If you want anything, Vivie, ring the gate bell, and a domestic will appear. (*He goes into the house with unruffled suavity.*)

CROFTS (*watching him with a crafty air as he disappears, and speaking to Vivie with an assumption of being on privileged terms with her*): Pleasant young fellow that, Miss Vivie. Pity he has no money, isnt it?

VIVIE: Do you think so?

CROFTS: Well, whats he to do? No profession, no property. Whats he good for?

VIVIE: I realize his disadvantages, Sir George.

CROFTS (*a little taken aback at being so precisely interpreted*): Oh, it's not that. But while we're in this world we're in it; and money's money. (*Vivie does not answer.*) Nice day, isnt it?

VIVIE (*with scarcely veiled contempt for this effort at conversation*): Very.

CROFTS (*with brutal good humor, as if he liked her pluck*): Well, thats not what I came to say. (*Affecting frankness*) Now listen, Miss Vivie. I'm quite aware that I'm not a young lady's man.

VIVIE: Indeed, Sir George?

CROFTS: No; and to tell you the honest truth I dont want to be either. But when I say a thing I mean it; when I feel sentiment I feel it in earnest; and what I value I pay hard money for. Thats the sort of man I am.

VIVIE: It does you great credit, I'm sure.

CROFTS: Oh, I dont mean to praise myself. I have my faults, Heaven knows: no man is more sensible of that than I am. I know I'm not perfect: thats one of the advantages of being a middle-aged man; for I'm not a young man, and I know it. But my code is a simple one, and, I think, a good one. Honor between man and man; fidelity between man and woman; and no cant about this religion or that religion, but an honest belief that things are making for good on the whole.

VIVIE (*with biting irony*): "A power, not ourselves, that makes for righteousness," eh?

CROFTS (*taking her seriously*): Oh, certainly, not ourselves, of course. You understand what I mean. (*He sits down beside her, as one who has found a kindred spirit.*) Well, now as to practical matters. You may have an idea that Ive flung my money about; but I havnt: I'm richer to-day than when I first came into the property. Ive used my knowledge of the world to invest my money in ways that other men have overlooked; and whatever else I may be, I'm a safe man from the money point of view.

VIVIE: It's very kind of you to tell me all this.

CROFTS: Oh well, come, Miss Vivie: you neednt pretend you dont see what I'm driving at. I want to settle down with a Lady Crofts. I suppose you think me very blunt, eh?

VIVIE: Not at all: I am much obliged to you for being so definite and business-like. I quite appreciate the offer: the money, the position, Lady Crofts, and so on. But I think I will say no, if you dont mind. I'd rather not. (*She rises, and strolls across to the sundial to get out of his immediate neighborhood.*)

CROFTS (*not at all discouraged, and taking advantage of the additional room left him on the seat to spread himself comfortably, as if a few preliminary refusals were part of the inevitable routine of courtship*): I'm in no hurry. It was only just to let you know in case young Gardner should try to trap you. Leave the question open.

VIVIE (*sharply*): My no is final. I wont go back from it. (*She looks authoritatively at him. He grins; leans forward with his elbows on his knees to prod with his stick at some unfortunate insect in the grass; and looks cunningly at her. She turns away impatiently.*)

CROFTS: I'm a good deal older than you — twenty-five years — quarter of a century. I shant live for ever; and I'll take care that you shall be well off when I'm gone.

VIVIE: I am proof against even that inducement, Sir George. Dont you think youd better take your answer? There is not the slightest chance of my altering it.

CROFTS (*rising, after a final slash at a daisy, and beginning to walk to and fro*): Well, no matter. I could tell you some things that would change your mind fast enough; but I wont, because I'd rather win you by honest affection. I was a good friend to your mother:

ask her whether I wasnt. She'd never have made the money that paid for your education if it hadnt been for my advice and help, not to mention the money I advanced her. There are not many men would have stood by her as I have. I put not less than £40,000 into it, from first to last.

VIVIE (*staring at him*): Do you mean to say you were my mother's business partner?

CROFTS: Yes. Now just think of all the trouble and the explanations it would save if we were to keep the whole thing in the family, so to speak. Ask your mother whether she'd like to have to explain all her affairs to a perfect stranger.

VIVIE: I see no difficulty, since I understand that the business is wound up, and the money invested.

CROFTS (*stopping short, amazed*): Wound up! Wind up a business thats paying 35 per cent in the worst years! Not likely. Who told you that?

VIVIE (*her color quite gone*): Do you mean that it is still —? (*She stops abruptly, and puts her hand on the sundial to support herself. Then she gets quickly to the iron chair and sits down.*) What business are you talking about?

CROFTS: Well, the fact is it's not what would be considered exactly a high-class business in my set — the county set, you know — our set it will be if you think better of my offer. Not that theres any mystery about it: dont think that. Of course you know by your mother's being in it that it's perfectly straight and honest. Ive known her for many years; and I can say of her that she'd cut off her hands sooner than touch anything that was not what it ought to be. I'll tell you all about it if you like. I dont know whether youve found in travelling how hard it is to find a really comfortable private hotel.

VIVIE (*sickened, averting her fate*): Yes: go on.

CROFTS: Well, thats all it is. Your mother has a genius for managing such things. We've got two in Brussels, one in Berlin, one in Vienna, and two in Buda-Pesth. Of course there are others besides ourselves in it; but we hold most of the capital; and your mother's indispensable as managing director. Youve noticed, I daresay, that she travels a good deal. But you see you cant mention such things in society. Once let out the word hotel and everybody says you keep a public-house. You wouldnt like people to say that of your mother, would you? Thats why we're so reserved about it. By the bye, youll keep it to yourself, wont you? Since it's been a secret so long, it had better remain so.

VIVIE: And this is the business you invite me to join me in?

CROFTS: Oh no. My wife shant be troubled with business. Youll not be in it more than youve always been.

VIVIE: *I* always been! What do you mean?

CROFTS: Only that youve always lived on it. It paid for your education and the dress you have on your back. Dont turn up your nose at business, Miss Vivie; where would your Newnhams and Girtons be without it?

VIVIE (*rising, almost beside herself*): Take care. I know what this business is.

CROFTS (*starting, with a suppressed oath*): Who told you?

VIVIE: Your partner — my mother.

CROFTS (*black with rage*): The old — (*Vivie looks quickly at him. He swallows the epithet and stands swearing and raging foully to himself. But he knows that his cue is to be sympathetic. He takes refuge in generous indignation.*) She ought to have had more consideration for you. *I'd* never have told you.

VIVIE: I think you would probably have told me when we were married: it would have been a convenient weapon to break me in with.

CROFTS (*quite sincerely*): I never intended that. On my word as a gentleman I didnt.

(*Vivie wonders at him. Her sense of the irony of his protest cools and braces her. She replies with contemptuous self-possession.*)

VIVIE: It does not matter. I suppose you understand that when we leave here to-day our acquaintance ceases.

CROFTS: Why? Is it for helping your mother?

VIVIE: My mother was a very poor woman who had no reasonable choice but to do as she did. You were a rich gentleman; and you did the same for the sake of 35 per cent. You are a pretty common sort of scoundrel, I think. That is my opinion of you.

CROFTS (*after a stare — not at all displeased, and much more at his ease on these frank terms than on their former ceremonious ones*): Ha, ha, ha, ha! Go it, little missie, go it: it doesnt hurt me and it amuses you. Why the devil shouldnt I invest my money that way? I take the interest on my capital like other people: I hope you dont think I dirty my own hands with the work. Come: you wouldnt refuse the acquaintance of my mother's cousin the Duke of Belgravia because some of the rents he gets are earned in queer ways. You wouldnt cut the Archbishop of Canterbury, I suppose, because the Ecclesiastical Commissioners have a few publicans and sinners among their tenants. Do you remember your Crofts scholarship at Newnham? Well, that was founded by my brother the M.P. He gets his 22 per cent out of a factory with 600 girls in it, and not one of them getting wages enough to live on. How d'ye suppose most of them manage? Ask your mother. And do you expect me to turn my back on 35 per cent when all the rest are pocketing what they can, like sensible men? No such fool! If youre going to pick and choose your acquaintances on moral principles, youd better clear out of this country, unless you want to cut yourself out of all decent society.

VIVIE (*conscience stricken*): You might go on to point out that I myself never asked where the money I spent came from. I believe I am just as bad as you.

CROFTS (*greatly reassured*): Of course you are; and a very good thing too! What harm does it do after all? (*Rallying her jocularly*) So you dont think me such a scoundrel now you come to think it over. Eh?

VIVIE: I have shared profits with you; and I admitted you just now to the familiarity of knowing what I think of you.

CROFTS (*with serious friendliness*): To be sure you did. You wont find me a bad sort; I dont go in for being superfine intellectually; but Ive plenty of honest human feeling; and the old Crofts breed comes out in a sort of instinctive hatred of anything low, in which I'm sure youll sympathize with me. Believe me, Miss Vivie, the world isnt such a bad place as the croakers make out. So long as you dont fly openly in the face of society, society doesnt ask any inconvenient questions; and it makes precious short work of the cads who do. There are no secrets better kept than the secrets that everybody guesses. In the society I can introduce you to, no lady or gentleman would so far forget themselves as to discuss my business affairs or your mother's. No man can offer you a safer position.

VIVIE (*studying him curiously*): I suppose you really think youre getting on famously with me.

CROFTS: Well, I hope I may flatter myself that you think better of me than you did at first.

VIVIE (*quietly*): I hardly find you worth thinking about at all now. (*She rises and turns towards the gate, pausing on her way to contemplate him and say almost gently, but with intense conviction*) When I think of the society that tolerates you, and the laws that protect you — when I think of how helpless nine out of ten young girls would be in the hands of you and my mother — the unmentionable woman and her capitalist bully —

CROFTS (*livid*): Damn you!

VIVIE: You need not. I am among the damned already.

(*She raises the latch of the gate to open it and go out. He follows her and puts his hand heavily on the top bar to prevent its opening.*)

CROFTS (*panting with fury*): Do you think I'll put up with this from you, you young devil, you?

VIVIE (*unmoved*): Be quiet. Some one will answer the bell. (*Without flinching a step she strikes the bell with the back of her hand. It clangs harshly; and he starts back involuntarily. Almost immediately Frank appears at the porch with his rifle.*)

FRANK (*with cheerful politeness*): Will you have the rifle, Viv; or shall I operate?

VIVIE: Frank: have you been listening?

FRANK: Only for the bell, I assure you; so that you shouldnt have to wait. I think I showed great insight into your character, Crofts.

CROFTS: For two pins I'd take that gun from you and break it across your head.

FRANK (*stalking him cautiously*): Pray dont. I'm ever so careless in handling firearms. Sure to be a fatal accident, with a reprimand from the coroner's jury for my negligence.

VIVIE: Put the rifle away, Frank: it's quite unnecessary.

FRANK: Quite right, Viv. Much more sportsmanlike to catch him in a trap. (*Crofts, understanding the insult, makes a threatening movement.*) Crofts: there are fifteen cartridges in the magazine here; and I am a dead shot at the present distance and at an object of your size.

CROFTS: Oh, you neednt be afraid. I'm not going to touch you.

FRANK: Ever so magnanimous of you under the circumstances! Thank you.

CROFTS: I'll just tell you this before I go. It may interest you, since youre so fond of one another. Allow me, Mister Frank, to introduce you to your half-sister, the eldest daughter of the Reverend Samuel Gardner. Miss Vivie: Your half-brother. Good morning. (*He goes out through the gate and along the road.*)

FRANK (*after a pause of stupefaction, raising the rifle*): Youll testify before the coroner that it's an accident, Viv. (*He takes aim at the retreating figure of Crofts. Vivie seizes the muzzle and pulls it round against her breast.*)

VIVIE: Fire now. You may.

FRANK (*dropping his end of the rifle hastily*): Stop! take care. (*She lets it go. It falls on the turf.*) Oh, youve given your little boy such a turn. Suppose it had gone off — ugh! (*He sinks on the garden seat, overcome.*)

VIVIE: Suppose it had: do you think it would not have been a relief to have some sharp physical pain tearing through me?

FRANK (*coaxingly*): Take it ever so easy, dear Viv. Remember: even if the rifle scared that fellow into telling the truth for the first time in his life, that only makes us the babes in the wood in earnest. (*He holds out his arms to her.*) Come and be covered up with leaves again.

VIVIE (*with a cry of disgust*): Ah, not that, not that. You make all my flesh creep.

FRANK: Why, whats the matter?

VIVIE: Good-bye. (*She makes for the gate.*)

FRANK (*jumping up*): Hallo! Stop! Viv! Viv! (*She turns in the gateway*) Where are you going to? Where shall we find you?

VIVIE: At Honoria Fraser's chambers, 67 Chancery Lane, for the rest of my life. (*She goes off quickly in the opposite direction to that taken by Crofts.*)

FRANK: But I say — wait — dash it! (*He runs after her.*)

ACT IV

(*Honoria Fraser's chambers in Chancery Lane. An office at the top of New Stone Buildings, with a plate-glass window, distempered walls, electric light, and a patent stove. Saturday afternoon. The chimneys of Lincoln's Inn and the western sky beyond are seen through the window. There is a double writing-table in the middle of the room, with a cigar box, ash pans, and a portable electric reading lamp almost snowed up in heaps of papers and books. This table has knee holes and chairs right and left and is very untidy. The clerk's desk, closed*) *and tidy, with its high stool, is against the wall, near a door communicating with the inner rooms. In the opposite wall is the door leading to the public corridor. Its upper panel is of opaque glass, lettered in black on the outside, "Fraser and Warren." A baize screen hides the corner between this door and the window.*

Frank, in a fashionable light-colored coaching suit, with his stick, gloves, and white hat in his hands, is pacing up and down the office. Somebody tries the door with a key.)

FRANK (*calling*): Come in. It's not locked.

(*Vivie comes in, in her hat and jacket. She stops and stares at him.*)

VIVIE (*sternly*): What are you doing here?

FRANK: Waiting to see you. Ive been here for hours. Is this the way you attend to your business? (*He puts his hat and stick on the table, and perches himself with a vault on the clerk's stool, looking at her with every appearance of being in a specially restless, teasing, flippant mood.*)

VIVIE: Ive been away exactly twenty minutes for a cup of tea. (*She takes off her hat and jacket and hangs them up behind the screen.*) How did you get in?

FRANK: The staff had not left when I arrived. He's gone to play cricket on Primrose Hill. Why dont you employ a woman, and give your sex a chance?

VIVIE: What have you come for?

FRANK (*springing off the stool and coming close to her*): Viv: lets go and enjoy the Saturday half-holiday somewhere, like the staff. What do you say to Richmond, and then a music hall, and a jolly supper?

VIVIE: Cant afford it. I shall put in another six hours work before I go to bed.

FRANK: Cant afford it, cant we? Aha! Look here. (*He takes out a handful of sovereigns and makes them chink.*) Gold, Viv, gold!

VIVIE: Where did you get it?

FRANK: Gambling, Viv, gambling. Poker.

VIVIE: Pah! It's meaner than stealing it. No: I'm not coming. (*She sits down to work at the table, with her back to the glass door, and begins turning over the papers.*)

FRANK (*remonstrating piteously*): But, my dear Viv, I want to talk to you ever so seriously.

VIVIE: Very well: sit down in Honoria's chair and talk here. I like ten minutes chat after tea. (*He murmurs.*) No use groaning: I'm inexorable. (*He takes the opposite seat disconsolately.*) Pass that cigar box, will you?

FRANK (*pushing the cigar box across*): Nasty womanly habit. Nice men dont do it any longer.

VIVIE: Yes: they object to the smell in the office; and weve had to take to cigarets. See! (*She opens the box and takes out a cigaret, which she lights. She offers him one; but he shakes his head with a wry face. She settles herself comfortably in her chair, smoking.*) Go ahead.

FRANK: Well, I want to know what youve done — what arrangements youve made.

VIVIE: Everything was settled twenty minutes after I arrived here. Honoria has found the business too much for her this year; and she was on the point of sending for me and proposing a partnership when I walked in and told her I hadnt a farthing in the world. So I installed myself and packed her off for a fortnight's holiday. What happened at Haslemere when I left?

FRANK: Nothing at all. I said youd gone to town on particular business.

VIVIE: Well?

FRANK: Well, either they were too flabbergasted to say anything, or else Crofts had prepared your mother. Anyhow, she didnt say anything; and Crofts didnt say anything; and Praddy only stared. After tea they got up and went; and Ive not seen them since.

VIVIE (*nodding placidly with one eye on a wreath of smoke*): Thats all right.

FRANK (*looking round disparagingly*): Do you intend to stick in this confounded place?

VIVIE (*blowing the wreath decisively away, and sitting straight up*): Yes. These two days have given me back all my strength and self-possession. I will never take a holiday again as long as I live.

FRANK (*with a very wry face*): Mps! You look quite happy — and as hard as nails.

VIVIE (*grimly*): Well for me that I am!

FRANK (*rising*): Look here, Viv: we must have an explanation. We parted the other day under a complete misunderstanding.

VIVIE (*putting away the cigaret*): Well: clear it up.

FRANK: You remember what Crofts said?

VIVIE: Yes.

FRANK: That revelation was supposed to bring about a complete change in the nature of our feeling for one another. It placed us on the footing of brother and sister.

VIVIE: Yes.

FRANK: Have you ever had a brother?

VIVIE: No.

FRANK: Then you dont know what being brother and sister feels like? Now I have lots of sisters: Jessie and Georgina and the rest. The fraternal feeling is quite familiar to me; and I assure you my feeling for you is not the least in the world like it. The girls will go their way; I will go mine; and we shant care if we never see one another again. Thats brother and sister. But as to you, I cant be easy if I have to pass a week without seeing you. Thats not brother and sister. It's exactly what I felt an hour before Crofts made his revelation. In short, dear Viv, it's love's young dream.

VIVIE (*bitingly*): The same feeling, Frank, that brought your father to my mother's feet. Is that it?

FRANK (*revolted*): I very strongly object, Viv, to have my feelings compared to any which the Reverend Samuel is capable of harboring; and I object still more to a comparison of you to your mother. Besides, I dont believe the story. I have taxed my father with it, and obtained from him what I consider tantamount to a denial.

VIVIE: What did he say?

FRANK: He said he was sure there must be some mistake.

VIVIE: Do you believe him?

FRANK: I am prepared to take his word as against Crofts'.

VIVIE: Does it make any difference? I mean in your imagination or conscience; for of course it makes no real difference.

FRANK (*shaking his head*): None whatever to me.

VIVIE: Nor to me.

FRANK (*staring*): But this is ever so surprising! I thought our whole relations were altered in your imagination and conscience, as you put it, the moment those words were out of that brute's muzzle.

VIVIE: No: it was not that. I didnt believe him. I only wish I could.

FRANK: Eh?

VIVIE: I think brother and sister would be a very suitable relation for us.

FRANK: You really mean that?

VIVIE: Yes. It's the only relation I care for, even if we could afford any other. I mean that.

FRANK (*raising his eyebrows like one on whom a new light has dawned, and speaking with quite an effusion of chivalrous sentiment*): My dear Viv: why didnt you say so before? I am ever so sorry for persecuting you. I understand, of course.

VIVIE (*puzzled*): Understand what?

FRANK: Oh, I'm not a fool in the ordinary sense — only in the Scriptural sense of doing all the things the wise man declared to be folly, after trying them himself on the most extensive scale. I see I am no longer Vivvum's little boy. Dont be alarmed: I shall never call you Vivvums again — at least unless you get tired of your new little boy, whoever he may be.

VIVIE: My new little boy!

FRANK (*with conviction*): Must be a new little boy. Always happens that way. No other way, in fact.

VIVIE: None that you know of, fortunately for you.

(*Someone knocks at the door.*)

FRANK: My curse upon yon caller, whoe'er he be!

VIVIE: It's Praed. He's going to Italy and wants to say good-bye. I asked him to call this afternoon. Go and let him in.

FRANK: We can continue our conversation after his departure for Italy. I'll stay him out. (*He goes to the door and opens it.*) How are you, Praddy. Delighted to see you. Come in. (*Praed, dressed for travelling, comes in, in high spirits, excited by the beginning of his journey.*)

PRAED: How do you do, Miss Warren. (*She presses his hand cordially, though a certain sentimentality in his high spirits jars on her.*) I start in an hour from Holborn Viaduct. I wish I could persuade you to try Italy.

VIVIE: What for?

PRAED: Why, to saturate yourself with beauty and romance, of course. (*Vivie, with a shudder, turns her chair to the table, as if the work waiting for her there*

were a consolation and support to her. Praed sits opposite to her. Frank places a chair just behind Vivie, and drops lazily and carelessly into it, talking at her over his shoulder.)

FRANK: No use, Praddy. Viv is a little Philistine. She is indifferent to my romance, and insensible to my beauty.

VIVIE: Mr Praed: once for all, there is no beauty and no romance in life for me. Life is what it is; and I am prepared to take it as it is.

PRAED (*enthusiastically*): You will not say that if you come to Verona and on to Venice. You will cry with delight at living in such a beautiful world.

FRANK: This is most eloquent, Praddy. Keep it up.

PRAED: Oh, I assure you I have cried — I shall cry again, I hope — at fifty! At your age, Miss Warren, you would not need to go so far as Verona. Your spirits would absolutely fly up at the mere sight of Ostend. You would be charmed with the gaiety, the vivacity, the happy air of Brussels. (*Vivie recoils*) Whats the matter?

FRANK: Hallo, Viv!

VIVIE (*to Praed, with deep reproach*): Can you find no better example of your beauty and romance than Brussels to talk to me about?

PRAED (*puzzled*): Of course it's very different from Verona. I dont suggest for a moment that —

VIVIE (*bitterly*): Probably the beauty and romance come to much the same in both places.

PRAED (*completely sobered and much concerned*): My dear Miss Warren: I — (*looking enquiringly at Frank*) Is anything the matter?

FRANK: She thinks your enthusiasm frivolous, Praddy. She's had ever such a serious call.

VIVIE (*sharply*): Hold your tongue, Frank. Dont be silly.

FRANK (*calmly*): Do you call this good manners, Praed?

PRAED (*anxious and considerate*): Shall I take him away, Miss Warren? I feel sure we have disturbed you at your work. (*He is about to rise.*)

VIVIE: Sit down: I'm not ready to go back to work yet. You both think I have an attack of nerves. Not a bit of it. But there are two subjects I want dropped, if you dont mind. One of them (*to Frank*) is love's young dream in any shape or form: the other (*to Praed*) is the romance and beauty of life, especially as exemplified by the gaiety of Brussels. You are welcome to any illusions you may have left on these subjects: I have none. If we three are to remain friends, I must be treated as a woman of business, permanently single (*to Frank*) and permanently unromantic (*to Praed*).

FRANK: I also shall remain permanently single until you change your mind. Praddy: change the subject. Be eloquent about something else.

PRAED (*diffidently*): I'm afraid theres nothing else in the world that I can talk about. The Gospel of Art is the only one I can preach. I know Miss Warren is a great devotee of the Gospel of Getting On; but we cant discuss that without hurting your feelings, Frank, since you are determined not to get on.

FRANK: Oh, dont mind my feelings. Give me some improving advice by all means: it does me ever so much good. Have another try to make a successful man of me, Viv. Come: lets have it all: energy, thrift, foresight, self-respect, character. Dont you hate people who have no character, Viv?

VIVIE (*wincing*): Oh, stop, stop: let us have no more of that horrible cant. Mr Praed: if there are really only those two gospels in the world, we had better all kill ourselves; for the same taint is in both, through and through.

FRANK (*looking critically at her*): There is a touch of poetry about you to-day, Viv, which has hitherto been lacking.

PRAED (*remonstrating*): My dear Frank: arnt you a little unsympathetic?

VIVIE (*merciless to herself*): No: it's good for me. It keeps me from being sentimental.

FRANK (*bantering her*): Checks your strong natural propensity that way, dont it?

VIVIE (*almost hysterically*): Oh yes: go on: dont spare me. I was sentimental for one moment in my life — beautifully sentimental — by moonlight; and now —

FRANK (*quickly*): I say, Viv: take care. Dont give yourself away.

VIVIE: Oh, do you think Mr Praed does not know all about my mother? (*Turning on Praed*) You had better have told me that morning, Mr Praed. You are very old fashioned in your delicacies, after all.

PRAED: Surely it is you who are a little old fashioned in your prejudices, Miss Warren. I feel bound to tell you, speaking as an artist, and believing that the most intimate human relationships are far beyond and above the scope of the law, that though I know that your mother is an unmarried woman, I do not respect her the less on that account. I respect her more.

FRANK (*airily*): Hear, hear!

VIVIE (*staring at him*): Is that all you know?

PRAED: Certainly that is all.

VIVIE: Then you neither of you know anything. Your guesses are innocence itself compared to the truth.

PRAED (*startled and indignant, preserving his politeness with an effort*): I hope not. (*More emphatically*) I hope not, Miss Warren. (*Frank's face shows that he does not share Praed's incredulity. Vivie utters an exclamation of impatience. Praed's chivalry droops before their conviction. He adds, slowly*) If there is anything worse — that is, anything else — are you sure you are right to tell us, Miss Warren?

VIVIE: I am sure that if I had the courage I should spend the rest of my life in telling it to everybody — in stamping and branding it into them until they felt their share in its shame and horror as I feel mine. There is nothing I despise more than the wicked convention that protects these things by forbidding a woman to mention them. And yet I cant tell you. The two infamous words that describe what my mother is are ringing in my ears and struggling on my tongue; but I cant utter them: my instinct is too strong for me.

(*She buries her face in her hands. The two men, astonished, stare at one another and then at her. She raises her head again desperately and takes a sheet of paper and a pen.*) Here: let me draft you a prospectus.

FRANK: Oh, she's mad. Do you hear, Viv, mad. Come: pull yourself together.

VIVIE: You shall see. (*She writes.*) "Paid up capital: not less than £40,000 standing in the name of Sir George Crofts, Baronet, the chief shareholder." What comes next? — I forget. Oh yes: "Premises at Brussels, Berlin, Vienna and Buda-Pesth. Managing director: Mrs Warren"; and now dont let us forget her qualifications: the two words. There! (*She pushes the paper to them.*) Oh, no: dont read it: dont! (*She snatches it back and tears it to pieces; then seizes her head in her hands and hides her face on the table. Frank, who has watched the writing carefully over her shoulder, and opened his eyes very widely at it, takes a card from his pocket; scribbles a couple of words; and silently hands it to Praed, who looks at it with amazement. Frank then remorsefully stoops over Vivie.*)

FRANK (*whispering tenderly*): Viv, dear: thats all right. I read what you wrote: so did Praddy. We understand. And we remain, as this leaves us at present, yours ever so devotedly. (*Vivie slowly raises her head.*)

PRAED: We do indeed, Miss Warren. I declare you are the most splendidly courageous woman I ever met. (*This sentimental compliment braces Vivie. She throws it away from her with an impatient shake, and forces herself to stand up, though not without some support from the table.*)

FRANK: Dont stir, Viv, if you dont want to. Take it easy.

VIVIE: Thank you. You can always depend on me for two things, not to cry and not to faint. (*She moves a few steps towards the door of the inner rooms, and stops close to Praed to say*) I shall need much more courage than that when I tell my mother that we have come to the parting of the ways. Now I must go into the next room for a moment to make myself neat again, if you dont mind.

PRAED: Shall we go away?

VIVIE: No: I'll be back presently. Only for a moment.

(*She goes into the other room, Praed opening the door for her.*)

PRAED: What an amazing revelation! I'm extremely disappointed in Crofts: I am indeed.

FRANK: I'm not in the least. I feel he's perfectly accounted for at last. But what a facer for me, Praddy! I cant marry her now.

PRAED (*sternly*): Frank! (*The two look at one another, Frank unruffled, Praed deeply indignant.*) Let me tell you, Gardner, that if you desert her now you will behave very despicably.

FRANK: Good old Praddy! Ever chivalrous! But you mistake: it's not the moral aspect of the case: it's the money aspect. I really cant bring myself to touch the old woman's money now.

PRAED: And was that what you were going to marry on?

FRANK: What else? *I* havnt any money, nor the smallest turn for making it. If I married Viv now she would have to support me; and I should cost her more than I am worth.

PRAED: But surely a clever, bright fellow like you can make something by your own brains.

FRANK: Oh yes, a little. (*He takes out his money again.*) I made all that yesterday — in an hour and a half. But I made it in a highly speculative business. No, dear Praddy: even if Jessie and Georgina marry millionaires and the governor dies after cutting them off with a shilling, I shall have only four hundred a year. And he wont die until he's three score and ten: he hasnt originality enough. I shall be on short allowance for the next twenty years. No short allowance for Viv, if I can help it. I withdraw gracefully and leave the field to the gilded youth of England. So thats settled. I shant worry her about it: I'll just send her a little note after we're gone. She'll understand.

PRAED (*grasping his hand*): Good fellow, Frank! I heartily beg your pardon. But must you never see her again?

FRANK: Never see her again! Hang it all, be reasonable. I shall come along as often as possible, and be her brother. I can not understand the absurd consequences you romantic people expect from the most ordinary transactions. (*A knock at the door.*) I wonder who this is. Would you mind opening the door? If it's a client it will look more respectable than if I appeared.

PRAED: Certainly. (*He goes to the door and opens it. Frank sits down in Vivie's chair to scribble a note.*) My dear Kitty: come in, come in.

(*Mrs Warren comes in, looking apprehensively round for Vivie. She has done her best to make herself matronly and dignified. The brilliant hat is replaced by a sober bonnet, and the gay blouse covered by a costly black silk mantle. She is pitiably anxious and ill at ease — evidently panic-stricken.*)

MRS WARREN (*to Frank*): What! Youre here, are you?

FRANK (*turning in his chair from his writing, but not rising*): Here, and charmed to see you. You come like a breath of spring.

MRS WARREN: Oh, get out with your nonsense. (*In a low voice*) Wheres Vivie?

(*Frank points expressively to the door of the inner room, but says nothing.*)

MRS WARREN (*sitting down suddenly and almost beginning to cry*): Praddy: wont she see me, dont you think?

PRAED: My dear Kitty: dont distress yourself. Why should she not?

MRS WARREN: Oh, you never can see why not: youre too amiable. Mr Frank: did she say anything to you?

FRANK (*folding his note*): She must see you, if (*very expressively*) you wait until she comes in.

MRS WARREN (*frightened*): Why shouldnt I wait?

(*Frank looks quizzically at her; puts his note carefully on the ink-bottle, so that Vivie cannot fail to find it when next she dips her pen; then rises and devotes his attention entirely to her.*)

FRANK: My dear Mrs Warren: suppose you were a sparrow — ever so tiny and pretty a sparrow hopping in the roadway — and you saw a steam roller coming in your direction, would you wait for it?

MRS WARREN: Oh, dont bother me with your sparrows. What did she run away from Haslemere like that for?

FRANK: I'm afraid she'll tell you if you wait until she comes back.

MRS WARREN: Do you want me to go away?

FRANK: No. I always want you to stay. But I advise you to go away.

MRS WARREN: What! And never see her again!

FRANK: Precisely.

MRS WARREN (*crying again*): Praddy: dont let him be cruel to me. (*She hastily checks her tears and wipes her eyes.*) She'll be so angry if she sees Ive been crying.

FRANK (*with a touch of real compassion in his airy tenderness*): You know that Praddy is the soul of kindness, Mrs Warren. Praddy: what do you say? Go or stay?

PRAED (*to Mrs Warren*): I really should be very sorry to cause you unnecessary pain; but I think perhaps you had better not wait. The fact is — (*Vivie is heard at the inner door.*)

FRANK: Sh! Too late. She's coming.

MRS WARREN: Dont tell her I was crying. (*Vivie comes in. She stops gravely on seeing Mrs Warren, who greets her with hysterical cheerfulness.*) Well, dearie. So here you are at last.

VIVIE: I am glad you have come: I want to speak to you. You said you were going, Frank, I think.

FRANK: Yes. Will you come with me, Mrs Warren? What do you say to a trip to Richmond, and the theatre in the evening? There is safety in Richmond. No steam roller there.

VIVIE: Nonsense, Frank. My mother will stay here.

MRS WARREN (*scared*): I dont know: perhaps I'd better go. We're disturbing you at your work.

VIVIE (*with quiet decision*): Mr Praed: please take Frank away. Sit down, mother. (*Mrs Warren obeys helplessly.*)

PRAED: Come, Frank. Good-bye, Miss Vivie.

VIVIE (*shaking hands*): Good-bye. A pleasant trip.

PRAED: Thank you: thank you. I hope so.

FRANK (*to Mrs Warren*): Good-bye: youd ever so much better have taken my advice. (*He shakes hands with her. Then airily to Vivie*) Bye-bye, Viv.

VIVIE: Good-bye. (*He goes out gaily without shaking hands with her. Praed follows. Vivie, composed and extremely grave, sits down in Honoria's chair, and waits for her mother to speak. Mrs Warren, dreading a pause, loses no time in beginning.*)

MRS WARREN: Well, Vivie, what did you go away like that for without saying a word to me? How could you do such a thing! And what have you done to poor George? I wanted him to come with me; but he shuffled out of it. I could see that he was quite afraid of you. Only fancy: he wanted me not to come. As if (*trembling*) I should be afraid of you, dearie. (*Vivie's gravity deepens.*) But of course I told him it was all settled and comfortable between us, and that we were on the best of terms. (*She breaks down.*) Vivie: whats the meaning of this? (*She produces a paper from an envelope; comes to the table; and hands it across.*) I got it from the bank this morning.

VIVIE: It is my month's allowance. They sent it to me as usual the other day. I simply sent it back to be placed to your credit, and asked them to send you the lodgment receipt. In future I shall support myself.

MRS WARREN (*not daring to understand*): Wasnt it enough? Why didnt you tell me? (*With a cunning gleam in her eye*) I'll double it: I was intending to double it. Only let me know how much you want.

VIVIE: You know very well that that has nothing to do with it. From this time I go my own way in my own business and among my own friends. And you will go yours. (*She rises*) Good-bye.

MRS WARREN (*appalled*): Good-bye?

VIVIE: Yes: good-bye. Come: dont let us make a useless scene: you understand perfectly well. Sir George Crofts has told me the whole business.

MRS WARREN (*angrily*): Silly old — (*She swallows an epithet, and turns white at the narrowness of her escape from uttering it.*) He ought to have his tongue cut out. But I explained it all to you; and you said you didnt mind.

VIVIE (*steadfastly*): Excuse me: I do mind. You explained how it came about. That does not alter it.

(*Mrs Warren, silenced for a moment, looks forlornly at Vivie, who waits like a statue, secretly hoping that the combat is over. But the cunning expression comes back into Mrs Warren's face; and she bends across the table, sly and urgent, half whispering*)

MRS WARREN: Vivie: do you know how rich I am?

VIVIE: I have no doubt you are very rich.

MRS WARREN: But you dont know all that that means: youre too young. It means a new dress every day; it means theatres and balls every night; it means having the pick of all the gentlemen in Europe at your feet; it means a lovely house and plenty of servants; it means the choicest of eating and drinking; it means everything you like, everything you want, everything you can think of. And what are you here? A mere drudge, toiling and moiling early and late for your bare living and two cheap dresses a year. Think over it. (*Soothingly*) Youre shocked, I know. I can enter into your feelings; and I think they do you credit; but trust me, nobody will blame you: you may take my word for that. I know what young girls are; and I know youll think better of it when youve turned it over in your mind.

VIVIE: So thats how it's done, is it? You must have said all that to many a woman, mother, to have it so pat.

MRS WARREN (*passionately*): What harm am I asking you to do? (*Vivie turns away contemptuously. Mrs Warren follows her desperately*) Vivie: listen to me: you dont understand: youve been taught wrong on purpose: you dont know what the world is really like.

VIVIE (*arrested*): Taught wrong on purpose! What do you mean?

MRS WARREN: I mean that youre throwing away all your chances for nothing. You think that people are what they pretend to be — that the way you were taught at school and college to think right and proper is the way things really are. But it's not: it's all only a pretence, to keep the cowardly, slavish common run of people quiet. Do you want to find that out, like other women, at forty, when youve thrown yourself away and lost your chances; or wont you take it in good time now from your own mother, that loves you and swears to you that it's truth — gospel truth? (*Urgently*) Vivie: the big people, the clever people, the managing people, all know it. They do as I do, and think what I think. I know plenty of them. I know them to speak to, to introduce you to, to make friends of for you. I dont mean anything wrong: thats what you dont understand: your head is full of ignorant ideas about me. What do the people that taught you know about life or about people like me? When did they ever meet me, or speak to me, or let anyone tell them about me? — the fools! Would they ever have done anything for you if I hadnt paid them? Havnt I told you that I want you to be respectable? Havnt I brought you up to be respectable? And how can you keep it up without my money and my influence and Lizzie's friends? Cant you see that youre cutting your own throat as well as breaking my heart in turning your back on me?

VIVIE: I recognise the Crofts philosophy of life, mother. I heard it all from him that day at the Gardners'.

MRS WARREN: You think I want to force that played-out old sot on you! I dont, Vivie: on my oath I dont.

VIVIE: It would not matter if you did: you would not succeed. (*Mrs Warren winces, deeply hurt by the implied indifference towards her affectionate intention. Vivie, neither understanding this nor concerning herself about it, goes on calmly*) Mother: you dont at all know the sort of person I am. I dont object to Crofts more than to any other coarsely built man of his class. To tell you the truth, I rather admire him for being strong-minded enough to enjoy himself in his own way and make plenty of money instead of living the usual shooting, hunting, dining-out, tailoring, loafing life of his set merely because all the rest do it. And I'm perfectly aware that if I'd been in the same circumstances as my aunt Liz, I'd have done

exactly what she did. I dont think I'm more prejudiced or straitlaced than you: I think I'm less. I'm certain I'm less sentimental. I know very well that
fashionable morality is all a pretence, and that if I
took your money and devoted the rest of my life to
spending it fashionably, I might be as worthless and
vicious as the silliest woman could possibly want to
be without having a word said to me about it. But I
dont want to be worthless. I shouldnt enjoy trotting
about the park to advertize my dressmaker and carriage builder, or being bored at the opera to show off
a shop windowful of diamonds.

MRS WARREN (*bewildered*): But —

VIVIE: Wait a moment: Ive not done. Tell me why you
continue your business now that you are independent of it. Your sister, you told me, has left all that
behind her. Why dont you do the same?

MRS WARREN: Oh, it's all very easy for Liz: she likes
good society, and has the air of being a lady. Imagine
me in a cathedral town! Why, the very rooks in the
trees would find me out even if I could stand the dul-
ness of it. I must have work and excitement, or I
should go melancholy mad. And what else is there
for me to do? The life suits me: I'm fit for it and
not for anything else. If I didnt do it somebody else
would; so I dont do any real harm by it. And then it
brings in money; and I like making money. No: it's
no use: I cant give it up — not for anybody. But
what need you know about it? I'll never mention it.
I'll keep Crofts away. I'll not trouble you much: you
see I have to be constantly running about from one
place to another. Youll be quit of me altogether when
I die.

VIVIE: No. I am my mother's daughter. I am like you: I
must have work, and must make more money than I
spend. But my work is not your work, and my way
not your way. We must part. It will not make much
difference to us: instead of meeting one another for
perhaps a few months in twenty years, we shall never
meet: thats all.

MRS WARREN (*her voice stifled in tears*): Vivie: I meant
to have been more with you: I did indeed.

VIVIE: It's no use, mother: I am not to be changed by a
few cheap tears and entreaties any more than you
are, I dare say.

MRS WARREN (*wildly*): Oh, you call a mother's tears
cheap.

VIVIE: They cost you nothing; and you ask me to give
you the peace and quietness of my whole life in exchange for them. What use would my company be to
you if you could get it? What have we two in common that could make either of us happy together?

MRS WARREN (*lapsing recklessly into her dialect*): We're
mother and daughter. I want my daughter. Ive a right
to you. Who is to care for me when I'm old? Plenty
of girls have taken to me like daughters and cried at
leaving me; but I let them all go because I had you to
look forward to. I kept myself lonely for you. Youve

no right to turn on me now and refuse to do your
duty as a daughter.

VIVIE (*jarred and antagonized by the echo of the slums
in her mother's voice*): My duty as a daughter! I
thought we should come to that presently. Now once
for all, mother, you want a daughter and Frank wants
a wife. I dont want a mother; and I dont want a husband. I have spared neither Frank nor myself in sending him about his business. Do you think I will spare
you?

MRS WARREN (*violently*): Oh, I know the sort you are —
no mercy for yourself or anyone else. *I* know. My
experience has done that for me anyhow: I can tell
the pious, canting, hard, selfish woman when I meet
her. Well, keep yourself to yourself: *I* dont want you.
But listen to this. Do you know what I would do with
you if you were a baby again — aye, as sure as there's
a Heaven above us?

VIVIE: Strangle me, perhaps.

MRS WARREN: No: I'd bring you up to be a real daughter to me, and not what you are now, with your pride
and your prejudices and the college education you
stole from me — yes, stole: deny it if you can: what
was it but stealing? I'd bring you up in my own house,
so I would.

VIVIE (*quietly*): In one of your own houses.

MRS WARREN (*screaming*): Listen to her! listen to how
she spits on her mother's grey hairs! Oh, may you live
to have your own daughter tear and trample on you
as you have trampled on me. And you will: you will.
No woman ever had luck with a mother's curse on
her.

VIVIE: I wish you wouldnt rant, mother. It only hardens
me. Come: I suppose I am the only young woman
you ever had in your power that you did good to.
Dont spoil it all now.

MRS WARREN: Yes, Heaven forgive me, it's true; and you
are the only one that ever turned on me. Oh, the
injustice of it, the injustice, the injustice! I always
wanted to be a good woman. I tried honest work;
and I was slave-driven until I cursed the day I ever
heard of honest work. I was a good mother; and
because I made my daughter a good woman she turns
me out as if I was a leper. Oh, if I only had my life to
live over again! I'd talk to that lying clergyman in the
school. From this time forth, so help me Heaven in
my last hour, I'll do wrong and nothing but wrong.
And I'll prosper on it.

VIVIE: Yes: it's better to choose your line and go through
with it. If I had been you, mother, I might have done
as you did; but I should not have lived one life and
believed in another. You are a conventional woman
at heart. That is why I am bidding you good-bye
now. I am right, am I not?

MRS WARREN (*taken aback*): Right to throw away all
my money!

VIVIE: No: right to get rid of you? I should be a fool not
to? Isnt that so?

MRS WARREN (*sulkily*): Oh well, yes, if you come to that, I suppose you are. But Lord help the world if everybody took to doing the right thing! And now I'd better go than stay where I'm not wanted. (*She turns to the door.*)

VIVIE (*kindly*): Wont you shake hands?

MRS WARREN (*after looking at her fiercely for a moment with a savage impulse to strike her*): No, thank you. Good-bye.

VIVIE (*matter-of-factly*): Good-bye. (*Mrs Warren goes out, slamming the door behind her. The strain on Vivie's face relaxes; her grave expression breaks up into one of joyous content; her breath goes out in a half sob, half laugh of intense relief. She goes buoyantly to her place at the writing-table; pushes the electric lamp out of the way; pulls over a great sheaf of papers; and is in the act of dipping her pen in the ink when she finds Frank's note. She opens it unconcernedly and reads it quickly, giving a little laugh at some quaint turn of expression in it.*) And good-bye, Frank. (*She tears the note up and tosses the pieces into the wastepaper basket without a second thought. Then she goes at her work with a plunge, and soon becomes absorbed in her figures.*)

COMMENTARIES

Theatre Magazine

A CONTEMPORARY REACTION TO *MRS. WARREN'S PROFESSION*   *1906*

This attack on the play, along with Shaw's response to the Court of Special Sessions in New York, which cleared the play of indecency, gives us a good idea of how many "proper" New Yorkers reacted to the subject matter Shaw felt important to present to audiences. It was printed in Theatre Magazine *in 1906.*

Two judges, with a third one dissenting, in the Court of Special Sessions in New York City, have acquitted Arnold Daly of violating Section 385 of the Penal Code in having produced George Bernard Shaw's play, *Mrs. Warren's Profession*. This section provides against any indecent and suggestive act on the part of any performer. The decision is on a technical point. Mr. Shaw may get such comfort from it as he can, but he will find that no technique, either of Law or Art, can cure defects of material and substance. If he retains the right to produce, the public will retain the right to reject, and may exercise it. It may be that no court can take into consideration, in passing upon a given play, the entire philosophy and all the blatant flauntings of it in his various plays, publications, and utterances. But the public can. It can take care of itself. Statutes and codes are not needed for every offense. Here is a pseudo-anarchist who believes in no family tie (except for himself, perhaps), who proclaims free love, who preaches the seduction of our daughters by wholesale, not by means of wine suppers and "delicate" attentions, but by a false philosophy of specious half-truths; and, if anybody is swept into the dustbin, it will not be the American public. If Mr. Shaw is under a delusion to the contrary, his delusion of grandeur may not be technically amenable to the law of the courts, but it will be to the law of public opinion.

Mr. Shaw lost no time in rushing into print directly he learned of the decision. Few authors understand the value of sensational newspaper advertising so well as he. This is what was cabled in his name to the New York *Sun*:

> The main thing is that the decision states that the exposure of the social evil may lead to social reform. Whatever other comments the Court passed does not matter to me so long as that principle is admitted. According to one paper the Court deems the play disgusting. I shall continue to write similar disgusting things until some definite good is achieved.
>
> The entire blame for the agitation against *Mrs. Warren's Profession* lies in the hands of the New York critics. Their stupidity, inhumanity and scurrilous and obscene language in dealing with the play drove the poor, wretched little Police Commissioner to steps he was reluctant to take. No words of mine are adequate to describe my feelings toward these critics. They should all be gathered in a dustpan and thrown into a dust heap. Had they any sense of decency, they would make a barefooted pilgrimage somewhere or shoot themselves, but I don't suppose they will.
>
> I do not consider the decision of the Court complete unless it contains a recommendation for the imprisonment of all the editors and critics of the New York press who were responsible for bringing about this agitation. The remainder of my life will be devoted to forcing home their disgraceful attitude in the matter. With thousands of women in New York under the adverse influences with which I deal, they had a splendid opportunity of aiding the work, but their stupidity was too great to permit them to see other than sensational phases. In their ostrichlike dullness they imagine they know more about the subject than I do, but when I say a thing is so no sane person will accept their word against mine.
>
> The most scandalous lie they told was that *Mrs. Warren's Profession* was written for the purpose of making money. Any intelligent manager will tell you that a play which is dependent on pornographic situations is doomed to failure. For a week, perhaps, weak, degenerate debauchees may pay extravagant prices to see such a piece and then it is finished. The impression was spread in America that *Mrs. Warren's Profession* was a piece of that character. Its production cost me $5,000 out of my own pocket, besides injuring the receipts of other plays of mine on tour. Yet those who spent money to see *Mrs. Warren's Profession* in the hope of satisfying their mental lasciviousness have my most profound pity in their disappointment. They must hold me guilty of taking their money under false pretenses.

The only statement of any real interest in the foregoing effusion is that the production of *Mrs. Warren's Profession* cost Mr. Shaw $5,000 out of his own pocket. That may explain the willingness of managers and actors to experiment with these queer plays.

New York Times
EFFORTS AT CENSORSHIP OF
MRS. WARREN'S PROFESSION   1905–1906

The names in the series of articles written about the play in the New York Times *in 1905 and 1906 became famous. McAdoo was a police commissioner, and Anthony Comstock was a campaigner for decency who sought every opportunity to uphold "public morality." Justice Olmsted was later associated with prohibition. These articles give us a clear view of the controversy surrounding the play and the difficulties that Shaw felt in trying to protect Arnold Daly, who truly risked being charged with wrongdoing. This is a typical effort at censorship of significant literature.*

Comstock At It Again

Warns Arnold Daly against Playing Mrs. Warren's Profession

October 25, 1905

Copies of this interesting correspondence between Anthony Comstock of the Society for the Suppression of Vice, who has strong views as to the value of the works of George Bernard Shaw, and Arnold Daly, the actor, who is about to produce a new play by Mr. Shaw, entitled *Mrs. Warren's Profession,* came to the *New York Times* last night. Here they are:

Society for the Suppression of Vice

New York, Oct. 20, 1905

Mr. Arnold Daly:

Dear Sir: I am informed that it is your intention to put upon the stage one of Bernard Shaw's filthy products, entitled *Mrs. Warren's Profession.* I also understand that this play has been suppressed in London.

In order that you may not plead ignorance as to the laws and in the interpretation of the laws of this State, I beg to call your attention to the following decision made by the Appellate Division in the case of *People vs. Dorris.* [Here Mr. Comstock quotes the decision.]

There are many other decisions besides this, but the language is so explicit in this case, and as it is the utterance of the Appellate Division of the Supreme Court of this State, in this district, it seems to me sufficient.

Yours very truly,

ANTHONY COMSTOCK,
Secretary

New York, Oct. 21, 1905

Mr. Anthony Comstock, Secretary Society for Suppression of Vice,
142 Nassau St., New York City:

Dear Sir:

You call *Mrs. Warren's Profession* a "filthy" play. I cannot believe that you have read it; but, if so, your use of adjective is decorative, but not descriptive.

It is a strong sermon and a great moral lesson, and I cordially invite you to come to the Garrick Theatre on Wednesday or Thursday of next week, when I will be pleased to have you see a rehearsal of it.

Yours truly,

ARNOLD DALY

Shaw to Comstock: You Can't Scare Me

As to Daly, Believes a Rest in Prison Would Do Him Good

October 27, 1905

Special Cable to the New York Times [*Copyright, 1905*] LONDON, Oct. 26 — "Well, what is it now?" demanded George Bernard Shaw as, backed up to his grate fire, he received me this morning in his charming home, Adelphi Terrace.

I showed him a telegram to the effect that Anthony Comstock had warned Arnold Daly under threat of criminal prosecution not to produce Shaw's play, *Mrs. Warren's Profession.*

Shaw at once assumed that Comstock's warning was tantamount to a threat to imprison Daly, and commented on it in that sense. He said:

> You tell me Anthony Comstock threatens to put Arnold Daly in prison if he produces *Mrs. Warren's Profession,* and ask me what I have to say.
>
> Do you remember the classic telegram sent by Lord Clanricarde to his tenants in Ireland? "If you think you can intimidate me by shooting my agent you are very much mistaken."
>
> Well, all I can say is if Comstock thinks he can intimidate me by imprisoning Daly he does not quite know his man. Let him imprison Daly, by all means. A few months' rest and quiet would do Daly a great deal of good, and the scandal of his imprisonment would completely defeat Comstock's attempt to hide the fact that Mrs. Warren's "profession" exists because libertines pay women well to be evil, and often show them affection and respect, whilst pious people pay them infamously and drudge their bodies and souls to death at honest labor. [. . .]

Shaw's Play Stopped; The Manager Arrested

McAdoo Calls the Piece Revolting and Indecent — Warrants for the Players — Tickets Still on Sale Late in the Day, Notwithstanding Condemnation by the Press

November 1, 1905

Police Commissioner McAdoo took steps yesterday which stopped the further presentation at the Garrick Theatre of *Mrs. Warren's Profession,* George Bernard Shaw's play. Mr. McAdoo saw the performance on Monday night, and the first thing he did when he reached his office yesterday morning was to report to Mayor McClellan that the production was "revolting, indecent, and nauseating where it was not boring."

After talking with the Mayor, Mr. McAdoo wrote to Arnold Daly, ex-Senator Reynolds, who is said to be the owner of the theatre, and Samuel W. Gumpertz, its manager, telling them that he would prevent a second performance and arrest those participating therein. Later a warrant was issued by Magistrate Whitman calling for the arrest of Mr. Reynolds, Mr. Gumpertz, Mr. Daly, and the other actors and actresses in the cast, which was served by Inspector Brooks in person.

Mr. Gumpertz was arraigned in Jefferson Market Court. He was paroled upon his own recognizance until this morning at 11 o'clock.

The warrant charged a violation of that section of the Penal Code which relates to "offending public decency." Before his parole Mr. Gumpertz promised to be present this morning and to have the others named in the warrant, or such of them as were able to appear, in readiness for the hearing. He also said there would be no further performances for the present.

Shortly before the arrest of Mr. Gumpertz, but long after the receipt of Commissioner McAdoo's letter, the sale of tickets at the box office was stopped and the following notice was posted on the door of the theatre:

> Further performance of *Mrs. Warren's Profession* will be abandoned, owing to the universal condemnation of the press.
>
> ARNOLD DALY.
>
> Theatre closed to-night. Will reopen to-morrow night with *Candida,* original cast.

The Court Approves Bernard Shaw's Play

Mrs. Warren's Profession, *Legally Not Indecent, Justices Say* — *"Repellent Things" in it* — *But They May Do Good* — *Justice Olmsted Says That without Advertising It Wouldn't Last*

July 7, 1906

Bernard Shaw's play, *Mrs. Warren's Profession,* has successfully passed the censorship of Special Sessions. The Justices call the play "not pleasant," and declare it fraught with "shock producers" and "repellent things," but say that it is not indecent in the eyes of the law. They add, indeed, that it may become a medium of much needed social reforms.

These characterizations are made in a decision handed down yesterday by the court in the case of the people against Arnold Daly, the actor, and Samuel Gompertz, his manager, whose acquittal is ordered. Messrs. Daly and Gompertz were arrested on the evening of Oct. 20 last at the close of the opening performance of the play at the Garrick Theatre. They were tried in the Court of Special Sessions on April 19. Information was also lodged against Chrystal Herne and Mary Shaw, two of the actresses who appeared in the play.

The prevailing opinion in the case is written by Justice Olmsted, with Justice Wyatt concurring. Justice McAvoy dissented, but wrote no opinion. Justice Olmsted enters into an elaborate analysis of the theme of *Mrs. Warren's Profession,* and in some instances handles the author very much as a theatrical critic would on a first night. Here is the opinion in part:

> The complaining police officer, who was the sole witness, testified to no indecent or suggestive act on the part of the performer. The court is called upon on this state of fact to decide whether the language of the prompt book as spoken on the stage was a public nuisance per se because offensive to public decency. There is nothing in the words them-

selves, nor in any particular phrase or expression, which can be said to be indecent and the court is compelled to resort to the theme and motive of the play to find the indecency complained of. The theme is not a pleasant one.

Justice Olmsted then analyses the theme. This part is rather hard on Bernard Shaw. The Justice says:

> The dramatist has in this play used old and hackneyed materials, the common tool of scores of other playwrights, but he has used them more boldly — so boldly in fact that their tendency is to surprise and shock the audience. It must be said for him that he has in this play made vice less attractive than many other dramatists whose plays have never received the censorious attention of the police.
>
> The suggestion that the clergyman in the play is the father of Mrs. Warren's daughter, with the situation which makes the clergyman's acknowledged son a suitor for the daughter's hand, is another of the dramatist's shock producers, and there are other repellent things both in the play and in its characters: in fact, there is so little that is attractive in the drama that it is safe to predict that without the preliminary sensational advertisement of this proposed production its life on the boards would be short.

Justice Olmsted cites precedents to show that the test of criminality under the opinions of the higher courts is "whether a production is naturally calculated to excite in the spectator impure imagination and whether the other incidents and qualities, however attractive, are merely accessory to this as the primary or main purpose of the representation."

To the question whether Bernard Shaw's play in its essence is moral or immoral Justice Olmsted replies:

> If virtue does not receive its usual reward in this play, vice at least is presented in an odious light and its votaries are punished. The attack on social conditions is one which might result in effecting some needed social reforms. The court cannot refrain from suggesting, however, that the reforming influence of the play in this regard is minimized by the method of the attack.

In conclusion Justice Olmsted says:

> While the court may hold decided opinion regarding the fitness of this play as a stage production, when it comes to consider the question of criminality of the acts of these defendants in publicly producing it, it must make application of the principle of law laid down by the Court of Appeals as the test of criminality.
>
> Making such application in the case at bar, it appears that instead of exciting impure imagination in the mind of the spectator, that which is really excited is disgust; that the unlovely, the repellent, the disgusting in the play are merely accessories to the main purpose of the drama, which is an attack on certain social conditions relating to the employment of women which the dramatist believes, as do many others with him, should be reformed.
>
> Tried by this rule, the play does not come within the inhibition of the statute, and the defendants are acquitted.

Bernard Shaw (1856–1950)
PLAYS UNPLEASANT: *MRS. WARREN'S PROFESSION*   1898

Shaw included Mrs. Warren's Profession *in a group of three plays he titled "unpleasant." He explains in this excerpt from one of his prefaces (1898) that the subjects of these plays are not to be taken lightly by an audience out for an evening of fun but are serious and meant to be considered carefully.*

In *Mrs Warren's Profession* I have gone straight at the fact that, as Mrs Warren puts it, "the only way for a woman to provide for herself decently is for her to be good to some man that can afford to be good to her." There are some questions on which I am, like most Socialists, an extreme Individualist. I believe that any society which desires to found itself on a high standard of integrity of character in its units should organize itself in such a fashion as to make it possible too for all men and all women to maintain themselves in reasonable comfort by their industry without selling their affections and their convictions. At present we not only condemn women as a sex to attach themselves to "breadwinners," licitly or illicitly, on pain of heavy privation and disadvantage; but we have great prostitute classes of men: for instance, dramatists and journalists, to whom I myself belong, not to mention the legions of lawyers, doctors, clergymen, and platform politicians who are daily using their highest faculties to belie their real sentiments: a sin compared to which that of a woman who sells the use of her person for a few hours is too venial to be worth mentioning; for rich men without conviction are more dangerous in modern society than poor women without chastity. Hardly a pleasant subject this!

I must, however, warn my readers that my attacks are directed against themselves, not against my stage figures. They cannot too thoroughly understand that the guilt of defective social organization does not lie alone on the people who actually work the commercial makeshifts which the defects make inevitable, and who often, like Sartorius and Mrs Warren, display valuable executive capacities and even high moral virtues in their administration, but with the whole body of citizens whose public opinion, public action, and public contribution as ratepayers alone can replace Sartorius's slums with decent dwellings, Charteris's intrigues with reasonable marriage contracts, and Mrs Warren's profession with honorable industries guarded by a humane industrial code and a "moral minimum" wage.

Bernard Shaw (1856–1950)
FROM THE PREFACE TO *MRS. WARREN'S PROFESSION*   1902

Most of Shaw's prefaces to his plays address the issues of the plays themselves. This preface concentrates on the efforts of authorities to censor the play and prevent its production. Shaw gives us his views on censorship and on the public attitudes that viewed the play as threatening to public morality. However, he also goes on to comment on the issues of prostitution in the late nineteenth century and its relationship to the society that sustained it. As he puts it, even his supportive critics would not see themselves as responsible for the existence of the Mrs. Warrens among them.

The Author's Apology

Mrs Warren's Profession has been performed at last, after a delay of only eight years; and I have once more shared with Ibsen the triumphant amusement of startling all but the strongest-headed of the London theater critics clean out of the practice of their profession. No author who has ever known the exultation of sending the Press into an hysterical tumult of protest, of moral panic, of involuntary and frantic confession of sin, of a horror of conscience in which the power of distinguishing between the work of art on the stage and the real life of the spectator is confused and overwhelmed, will ever care for the stereotyped compliments which every successful farce or melodrama elicits from the newspapers. Give me that critic who rushed from my play to declare furiously that Sir George Crofts ought to be kicked. What a triumph for the actor, thus to reduce a jaded London journalist to the condition of the simple sailor in the Wapping gallery, who shouts execrations at Iago and warnings to Othello not to believe him! But dearer still than such simplicity is that sense of the sudden earthquake shock to the foundations of morality which sends a pallid crowd of critics into the street shrieking that the pillars of society are cracking and the ruin of the State at hand. Even the Ibsen champions of ten years ago remonstrate with me just as the veterans of those brave days remonstrated with them. Mr Grein, the hardy iconoclast who first launched my plays on the stage alongside *Ghosts* and *The Wild Ducks*, exclaims that I have shattered his ideals. Actually his ideals! What would Dr. Relling say? And Mr William Archer himself disowns me because I "cannot touch pitch without wallowing in it." Truly my play must be more needed than I knew; and yet I thought I knew how little the others know.

Do not suppose, however, that the consternation of the Press reflects any consternation among the general public. Anybody can upset the theater critics, in a turn of the wrist, by substituting for the romantic commonplaces of the stage the moral commonplaces of the pulpit, the platform, or the library. Play *Mrs Warren's Profession* to an audience of clerical members of the Christian Social Union and of women well experienced in Rescue, Temperance, and Girls' Club work, and no moral panic will arise: every man and woman present will know that as long as poverty makes virtue hideous and the spare pocket-money of rich bachelordom makes vice dazzling, their daily hand-to-hand fight against prostitution with prayer and persuasion, shelters and scanty alms, will be a losing one. There was a time when they were able to urge that though "the white-lead factory where Anne Jane was poisoned" may be a far more terrible place than Mrs Warren's house, yet hell is still more dreadful. Nowadays they no longer believe in hell; and the girls among whom they are working know that they did not believe in it, and would laugh at them if they did. So well have the rescuers learnt that Mrs Warren's defense of herself and indictment of society is the thing that most needs saying, that those who know me personally reproach me, not for writing this play, but for wasting my energies on "pleasant plays" for the amusement of frivolous people, when I can build up such excellent stage sermons on their own work. *Mrs Warren's Profession* is the one play of mine which I could submit to a censorship without doubt of the result; only, it must not be the censorship of the minor theater critic, nor of an innocent court official like the King's Reader of Plays, much less of people who consciously profit by Mrs Warren's profession, or who personally make use of it, or who hold the widely whispered view that it is an indispensable safety-valve for the protection of domestic virtue, or, above all, who are smitten with a sentimental affection for our fallen sister, and would "take her up tenderly, lift her with care, fashioned so slenderly, young, and *so* fair." Nor am I prepared to accept the verdict of the medical gentlemen who would compulsorily examine and register Mrs Warren, whilst leaving Mrs Warren's patrons, especially her military patrons, free to destroy her health and anybody else's without fear of reprisals. But I should be quite content to have my play judged by, say, a joint committee of the Central Vigilance Society and the Salvation Army. And the sterner moralists the members of the committee were, the better.[. . .]

I now come to those critics who, intellectually baffled by the problem in *Mrs Warren's Profession,* have made a virtue of running away from it. I will illustrate their method by a quotation from Dickens, taken from the fifth chapter of *Our Mutual Friend.*

> "Hem!" began Wegg. "This, Mr Boffin and Lady, is the first chapter of the first wol-lume of the *Decline and Fall of* ———" here he looked hard at the book, and stopped.
> "What's the matter, Wegg?"
> "Why, it comes into my mind, do you know, sir," said Wegg with an air of insinuating frankness (having first again looked hard at the book), "that you made a little mistake this morning, which I had meant to set you right in; only something put it out of my head. I think you said Rooshan Empire, sir?"
> "It is Rooshan; ain't it, Wegg?"
> "No, sir. Roman. Roman."
> "What's the difference, Wegg?"
> "The difference, sir?" Mr Wegg was faltering and in danger of breaking down, when a bright thought flashed upon him. "The difference, sir? There you place me in a difficulty, Mr Boffin. Suffice it to observe, that the difference is best postponed to some other occasion when Mrs Boffin does not honour us with her company. In Mrs Boffin's presence, sir, we had better drop it."
> Mr Wegg thus came out of his disadvantage with quite a chivalrous air, and not only that, but by dint of repeating with a manly delicacy, "In Mrs Boffin's presence, sir, we had better drop it!" turned the disadvantage on Boffin, who felt that he had committed himself in a very painful manner.

I am willing to let Mr Wegg drop it on these terms, provided I am allowed to mention here that *Mrs Warren's Profession* is a play for women; that it was written for women; that it has been performed and produced mainly through the determination of women that it should be performed and produced; that the enthusiasm of women made its first performance excitingly successful; and that not one of these women had any inducement to support it except their belief in the timeliness and the power of the lesson the play teaches. Those who were "surprised to see ladies present" were men; and when they proceeded to explain that the journals they represented could not possibly demoralize the public by describing such a play, their editors cruelly devoted the space saved by their delicacy to an elaborate and respectful account of the progress of a young lord's attempt to break the bank at Monte Carlo. A few days sooner Mrs Warren would have been crowded out of their papers by an exceptionally abominable police case. [. . .]

My old Independent Theater manager, Mr Grein, besides that reproach to me for shattering his ideals, complains that Mrs Warren is not wicked enough, and names several romancers who would have clothed her black soul with all the terrors of tragedy. I have no doubt they would; but if you please, my dear Mr. Grein, that is just what I did not want to do. Nothing would please our sanctimonious British public more than to throw the whole guilt of Mrs Warren's profession on Mrs Warren herself. Now the whole aim of my play is to throw that guilt on the

British public itself. You may remember that when he produced my first play, *Widowers' Houses*, exactly the same misunderstanding arose. When the virtuous young gentleman rose up in wrath against the slum landlord, the slum landlord very effectually shewed him that slums are the product, not of individual Harpagons, but of the indifference of virtuous young gentlemen to the condition of the city they live in, provided they live at the west end of it on money earned by somebody else's labor. The notion that prostitution is created by the wickedness of Mrs Warren is as silly as the notion — prevalent, nevertheless, to some extent in Temperance circles — that drunkenness is created by the wickedness of the publican. Mrs Warren is not a whit a worse woman than the reputable daughter who cannot endure her. Her indifference to the ultimate social consequences of her means of making money, and her discovery of that means by the ordinary method of taking the line of least resistance to getting it, are too common in English society to call for any special remark. Her vitality, her thrift, her energy, her outspokenness, her wise care of her daughter, and the managing capacity which has enabled her and her sister to climb from the fried fish shop down by the Mint to the establishments of which she boasts, are all high English social virtues. Her defense of herself is so overwhelming that it provokes the *St James's Gazette* to declare that "the tendency of the play is wholly evil" because "it contains one of the boldest and most specious defenses of an immoral life for poor women that has ever been penned." Happily the *St James's Gazette* here speaks in its haste. Mrs Warren's defense of herself is not only bold and specious, but valid and unanswerable. But it is no defense at all of the vice which she organizes. It is no defense of an immoral life to say that the alternative offered by society collectively to poor women is a miserable life, starved, overworked, fetid, ailing, ugly. Though it is quite natural and *right* for Mrs Warren to choose what is, according to her lights, the least immoral alternative, it is none the less infamous of society to offer such alternatives. [For the alternatives offered are not morality and immorality, but two sorts of immorality. The man who cannot see that starvation, overwork, dirt, and disease are as immoral as prostitution — that they are the vices and crimes of a nation, and not merely its misfortunes — is (to put it as politely as possible) a hopelessly Private Person]

The notion that Mrs Warren must be a fiend is only an example of the violence and passion which the slightest reference to sex rouses in undisciplined minds, and which makes it seem natural to our lawgivers to punish silly and negligible indecencies with a ferocity unknown in dealing with, for example, ruinous financial swindling. Had my play been entitled *Mr Warren's Profession*, and Mr Warren been a bookmaker, nobody would have expected me to make him a villain as well. Yet gambling is a vice, and bookmaking an institution, for which there is absolutely nothing to be said. The moral and economic evil done by trying to get other people's money without working for it (and this is the essence of gambling) is not only enormous but uncompensated. There are no two sides to the question of gambling, no circumstances which force us to tolerate it lest its suppression lead to worse things, no consensus of opinion among responsible classes, such as magistrates and military commanders, that it is a necessity, no Athenian records of gambling made splendid by the talents of its professors, no contention that instead of violating morals it only violates a legal institution which is in many respects oppressive and unnatural, no possible plea that the instinct on which it is founded is a vital one. Prostitution can confuse the issue with all these excuses: gambling has none of them. Consequently, if Mrs Warren must needs be a demon, a bookmaker must be a cacodemon. Well, does anybody who knows the sporting world really believe that bookmakers are worse than their neighbors? On the contrary, they have to be a good deal better; for in that world nearly everybody whose social rank does not exclude such an occupation would be a bookmaker if he could; but the strength of character required for handling large sums of money and for strict settlements and unflinching payment of losses is so rare that successful bookmakers are rare too. It may seem that at least public spirit cannot be one of a bookmaker's virtues; but I can testify from personal experience that excellent public work is done with money subscribed by bookmakers. It is true that there are abysses in bookmaking: for example, welshing. Mr Grein hints that there are abysses in Mrs Warren's profession also. So there are in every profession: the error lies in supposing that every member of them sounds these depths. I sit on a public body which prosecutes Mrs Warren zealously; and I can assure Mr Grein that she is often leniently dealt with because she has conducted her business "respectably" and held herself above its vilest branches. The degrees in infamy are as numerous and as scrupulously observed as the degrees in the peerage: the moralist's notion that there are depths at which the moral atmosphere ceases is as delusive as the rich man's notion that there are no social jealousies or snobberies among the very poor. No: had I drawn Mrs Warren as a fiend in human form, the very people who now rebuke me for flattering her would probably be the first to deride me for deducing character logically from occupation instead of observing it accurately in society.

One critic is so enslaved by this sort of logic that he calls my portraiture of the Reverend Samuel Gardner an attack on religion. According to this view Subaltern Iago is an attack on the army, Sir John Falstaff an attack on knighthood, and King Claudius an attack on royalty. Here again the clamor for naturalness and human feeling, raised by so many critics when they are confronted by the real thing on the stage, is really a clamor for the most mechanical and superficial sort of logic. The dramatic reason for making the clergyman what Mrs Warren calls "an old stick-in-the-mud," whose son, in spite of much capacity and charm, is a cynically worthless member of society, is to set up a mordant contrast between him and the woman of infamous profession, with her well brought-up, straightforward, hardworking daughter. The critics who have missed the contrast have doubtless observed often enough that many clergymen are in the Church through no genuine calling, but simply because, in circles which can command preferment, it is the refuge of "the fool of the family"; and that clergymen's sons are often conspicuous reactionists against the restraints imposed on them in childhood by their father's profession. These critics must know, too, from history if not from experience, that women as unscrupulous as Mrs Warren have distinguished themselves as administrators and rulers, both commercially and politically. But both observation and knowledge are left behind when journalists go to the theater. Once in their stalls, they assume that it is "natural" for clergymen to be saintly, for soldiers to be heroic, for lawyers to be hard-hearted, for sailors to be simple and generous, for doctors to perform miracles with little bottles, and for Mrs Warren to be a beast and a demon. All this is not only not natural, but not dramatic. A man's profession only enters into the drama of his life when it comes into conflict with his nature. The result of this conflict is tragic in Mrs Warren's case, and comic in the clergyman's case (at least we are savage enough to laugh at it); but in both cases it is illogical, and in both cases natural. I repeat, the critics who accuse me of sacrificing nature to logic are so sophisticated by their profession that to them logic is nature, and nature absurdity.

A CULTURAL CASEBOOK

The "Woman Question" in the Late Nineteenth Century

The "woman question" was central to great controversy that swept throughout Europe and the United States during the nineteenth century and brought the circumstances of women to the attention of society. Prior to the industrial revolution, women worked side by side with men in the fields or in home-based industries. With the creation of a moneyed class made possible by the fruits of factory labor, however, women similar to Ibsen's Nora Helmer sought economic independence. Although wealthy and newly middle-class women were considered "angels of the house"—responsible for managing the household, supervising the children, and supporting their husband's efforts—eventually these women began to see the limitations of their role. As the philosopher John Stuart Mill put it, women were expected to be willing slaves, but some of them, like Nora in Ibsen's *A Doll House,* rebelled.

Ibsen's Nora Helmer and Strindberg's Miss Julie offer views into the opportunities for women in the age. Marriage is the key to Nora's sense of self and satisfaction until she realizes how little her efforts to save her husband are appreciated. For Miss Julie, romance is not synonymous with marriage, but she realizes, too, that her virtue, once spent, can no longer give her power over men such as Jean. These plays demonstrate the limits of women's power in the second half of the nineteenth century.

The limited legal status of married women was increasingly unsatisfactory to wives during the latter part of the nineteenth century, and laws were passed to help them retain control over some of their own property as distinct from their husbands' property. Because divorce was difficult or impossible, separation usually ended in the ostracism of the woman. Many women in this era worked for reform, and several of the dramas of Ibsen and other Scandinavian writers argued for better treatment of women in society.

The economic limitations imposed on women were severe. Women of the upper-middle classes were expected not to work at all, whereas women of the lower classes living in cities had few choices. Women who did factory work risked injury and disease. As Mrs. Warren eloquently explains in Shaw's *Mrs. Warren's Profession,* even late in the nineteenth century, factory women aged quickly, had no job security, were dispensable, and often ended badly. One alternative was the choice made by Mrs. Warren, who avoided the early death of her sister Jane, victim of lead poisoning in a factory, by becoming a prostitute and then a madam.

In the Victorian era prostitution remained an almost universal fact of life. It enjoyed licensing in some places and toleration and graft in others. In England, the Contagious Diseases Acts, instituted between 1860 and 1870, supposedly protected sailors and other military personnel from venereal disease. The laws required all prostitutes in military regions to be examined by appointed officials. Prostitutes adjudged "sick" were confined in hospitals with little or no hope of being released. Politically active women who had been at the forefront of the equal rights movement and the quest for the vote were outraged at this unequal treatment of the participants in the act of prostitution. Eventually, their protests forced the government to repeal the Contagious Diseases Acts.

Some of the following documents point out the economic and social issues involved in prostitution in the period. Descriptions from brothel directories reveal the widely accepted "business" of running a brothel. Madams, "landladies" of the brothels, were managers who had risen from the ranks, and their number was not large, as Barbara Meil Hobson explains in "Successful Madams." The small number of madams who actually achieved financial independence is a point to remember when considering the achievement of Mrs. Warren in Shaw's play.

As this collection of documents attests, the debate over the "woman question" was conducted in the houses of Parliament, in the daily newspapers of many nations, and in the essays, dramas, and writings of authors such as August Strindberg. The plays of Ibsen, Strindberg, Shaw, and other writers of the period must be seen against the backdrop of the struggle for women's rights.

John Stuart Mill (1806–1873)
ON THE SUBJECTION OF WOMEN   *1869*

John Stuart Mill was an important philosopher in the mid-nineteenth century. He held to a philosophy of utilitarianism, which stressed the usefulness of actions and principles. His views on the subjection of women note that the superior strength of men had been turned into principles of law and behavior as if women were meant to be subjugated. According to Mill, women have been forced into wrongful submission.

From the very earliest twilight of human society, every woman (owing to the value attached to her by men, combined with her inferiority in muscular strength) was found in a state of bondage to some man. Laws and systems of polity always begin by recognizing the relations they find already existing between individuals. They convert what was a mere physical fact into a legal right, give it the sanction of society, and principally aim at the substitution of public and organized means of asserting and protecting these rights, instead of the irregular and lawless conflict of physical strength. Those who had already been compelled to obedience became in this manner legally bound to it.

All causes, social and natural, combine to make it unlikely that women should be collectively rebellious to the power of men. They are so far in a position different from all other subject classes, that their masters require something more from them than actual service. Men do not want solely the obedience of women, they want their sentiments. All men, except the most brutish, desire to have, in the woman most nearly connected with them, not a forced slave but a willing one, not a slave merely, but a favorite. They have therefore put everything in practice to enslave their minds. The masters of all other slaves rely, for maintaining obedience, on fear; either fear of themselves, or religious fears. The masters of women wanted more than simple obedience, and they turned the whole force of education to effect their purpose. All women are brought up from the very earliest years in the belief that their ideal of character is the very opposite to that of men; not self-will, and government by self-control, but submission, and yielding to the control of others. All the moralities tell them that it is the duty of women, and all the current sentimentalities that it is their nature, to live for others; to make complete abnegation of themselves, and to have no life but in their affections. And by their affections are meant the only ones they are allowed to have — those to the men with whom they are connected, or to the children who constitute an additional and indefeasible tie between them and a man. When we put together three things — first, the natural attraction between opposite sexes; secondly, the wife's entire dependence on the husband, every privilege or pleasure she has being either his gift, or depending entirely on his will; and lastly, that the principal object of human pursuit, consideration, and all objects of social ambition, can in general be sought or obtained by her only through him, it would be a miracle if the object of being attractive to men had not become the polar star of feminine education and formation of character. And, this great means of influence over the minds of women having been acquired, an instinct of selfishness made men avail themselves of it to the utmost as a means of holding women in subjection, by representing to them meekness, submissiveness, and resignation of all individual will into the hands of a man, as an essential part of sexual attractiveness. What is now called the nature of women is an eminently artificial thing — the result of forced repression in some directions, unnatural stimulation in others.

August Strindberg (1849–1912)
THE WOMAN QUESTION: WOMEN'S RIGHTS   *1884*

TRANSLATED FROM THE SWEDISH BY MARY SANDBACH

Though he eventually developed a reputation as a misogynist, the playwright August Strindberg published a forward-looking book on marriage early in his career. He was married to the actress Siri von Essen and living in Switzerland when he wrote The Last Word on the Woman Question *(1883). But it was hardly his last word on the subject. The very next year he wrote the novel* Getting Married. *The following excerpt is from the preface to part 1 of that work. Feminism had been a growing movement in Scandinavia and elsewhere, and while Strindberg's views may seem compatible with feminist ideals, he wrote the following declaration of women's rights in a state of irritation. He was apparently sick and tired of the woman question by 1884.*

Meanwhile, under present conditions, it is both impossible and harmful to detach the Woman Question from its context. Woman's desire for emancipation is identical with man's restless longing for freedom. Let us therefore liberate man from his prejudices, and we shall see that the emancipation of women will follow. But we must work together for our objective as friends, not as enemies. The woman of the future, be it a nearer or a more distant future, shall have an indisputable right to demand certain things and, in order to dispel the suspicion that I entertain reactionary ideas, I will now set these out under the following heading:

Woman's Rights

Which the laws of nature would grant her, but of which, thanks to our perverse social system (and not as a result of male tyranny), she has been deprived.

1. The right to the same education as men. I cannot too often repeat that by this I do not mean to imagine that she will be raised to man's level by learning all the unnecessary things with which he now has to stuff himself. Posterity, which will put an end to the difference between elementary and secondary schools, which will put an end to matriculation, and all other examinations, will one day feel obliged to establish a single civic examination which everyone will take, and which will replace confirmation. This examination will be the same for men and women, and will only require those examined to have a thorough knowledge of the arts of reading, writing, and arithmetic, a knowledge of the laws of their country, a knowledge of their civic rights and duties, and also of one living language. He who wants after that to learn what Cicero thought of Lucius Sulla, and what Moses intended to do with the children of Israel may do so, that is if he has time for such luxuries, for posterity will demand that every citizen shall support himself by bodily toil as nature intended.

2. Boys and girls shall attend the same schools, so that both sexes learn to know each other early in life. Things will not then be as they are today, when boys imagine that girls are angels, and girls that boys are knights. In this way we shall avoid all the silent sins of fantasy and precocity, for they are a result of the way in which the sexes are isolated.

3. The girl shall have the same freedom to "run wild" and choose what company she pleases.

4. There shall be complete equality between the sexes, which will do away with that revolting form of hypocrisy called gallantry, or politeness to ladies. A girl will not expect a boy to get up and give her his seat, for that is the hallmark of the subservient slave; and a brother will not get into the habit of expecting his sister to make his bed, or sew on his shirt buttons, for these are things he must do for himself.

5. Woman shall have the vote. In the future, when her confirmation consists of an examination in the laws that govern the community in which she lives, and when this community is obliged to present an annual report to its members, as companies do today, a woman will be just as well able to decide for whom or for what she will vote as a man.

6. Woman shall be eligible for all occupations, which should not be any more difficult to arrange under self-government than it is today when, inconsequently enough, she can become the monarch. Self-government will not be the same as government by professionals, but will be more like local government, that is a commission which can be performed in leisure moments. Is anyone wiser and better suited to govern than an old mother, who has learned through motherhood and running a household both how to rule and how to administrate? (Our forefathers had such a veneration for the wisdom of older women that they believed them to possess supernatural knowledge.)

7. This measure will mean that the moral code will become less rigid, and the law less strict, for a mother has learned to be more tolerant than anyone, and no one knows better than she how patient and how unexacting you must be with the erring children of man.

8. Woman shall be exempt from military service. Anyone who regards this as unjust should take into consideration the fact that nature exacts compensation from her in the form of heavy maternal duties. For that matter military service will not in future be regarded as particularly glorious. It will simply be a duty.

9. By a just distribution of the combined riches of nature the community of the future will ensure that all who are born receive sustenance and instruction. Marriage as a guarantee for these advantages will therefore become unnecessary. Man and wife will conclude a contract, verbal or written, for a union of any length they may decide, which they will have the right to dissolve when they please, without reference to law or gospel. It is true that this will not prevent a situation in which two males want to possess the same female, but the struggle will be less cruel, and the female will be the one to choose, — which is not the case at present — for no one in future will be obliged to marry for money or position, as neither of these things will exist. Selection will therefore be natural, and consequently the race will improve.

So much for the woman of the future and marriage. But there are things we can do to make reasonable improvements in the married state under present conditions. These are:

1. That boys and girls shall be allowed to mix more freely.

2. That the education of boys shall be simplified, so that it will not be unjust if the education of girls is simplified too.

3. The girl (like the boy) shall no longer be forced to learn so much about the past, but she shall be obliged to acquaint herself with the way in which society is governed today.

4. She may be given the vote at the earliest possible moment.

5. False gallantry will cease of itself, and men and women will associate together as men do now. But things shall not be as at present, when men have all male banquets, which end with a toast to the ladies, while the latter sit at home eating porridge and milk.

6. Civil marriage shall be introduced, and this will make divorce easier. Not that it is likely to become more frequent, but easier divorce will make the bonds feel less irksome, and will disabuse the man of the idea that he owns the woman. Children will still hold married couples together, unless the circumstances are very difficult.

Civil marriage would do away with the horrible legal ruling that necessitates warnings by the clergy, or obligatory "desertion."

7. The paragraphs in our laws about a husband's rights as a guardian shall be rescinded.

8. A woman shall come of age at eighteen without any reservations.

9. Deeds of settlement and the judicial division of property shall be obligatory on all married couples.

10. A woman (when her education is the same as that given to men) shall have the right to fill any post and practice any profession she pleases. (But if two million women were let loose on the labor market at the moment the result would be ruthless competition. Here — under present conditions — we must perhaps condescend to an inconsistency, unless by any chance, a surplus of labor accelerated the adoption of the new social system.)

11. When he marries a man shall be obliged to take out a life insurance policy, so that in the event of his death, his wife and children will not be left destitute. This is more especially his duty if he takes a woman away from a gainful occupation.

12. A woman shall keep her own name. She shall not have the right to take her husband's title in its feminine form, for a title under present conditions is a possession, often expensively acquired, and worth money. This proviso is necessary if there is to be equality, and it will prevent many women from being tempted to buy a title with their wealth. Boys shall take their father's name, and girls their mother's.

13. Separate bedrooms shall be the rule from the beginning. For a practice so offensive to "decency" as a common bedchamber brings its own punishment, and gives rise to confusion, distaste, satiety, and even worse things in a relationship. This rule will make a woman's position freer, and will give her the right to possess her own body.

14. If a woman is solely her husband's wife, and the mother of his children and has no independent occupation, she shall receive an allowance for clothes and recreation. She shall not have a salary, or receive clothes as presents, for which she has to say thank you. Moreover, she shall have the *right* to pay for her amusements herself, even when she is out with her husband, and thus be spared from always being *treated*.

15. If a married woman is gainfully occupied and does not run her own home, she shall be obliged to contribute from her earnings as much to the household as her husband does. If she also works in her home she shall be allowed to keep what she earns, for her work at home will thus come to be regarded as an extra contribution, and not as now, as the services rendered by a slave.

Johan Thorsten Sellin (1897–1994)
MARRIAGE AND DIVORCE IN SWEDEN   *1922*

Johan Thorsten Sellin discusses the rights of Swedish women in marriage before the sweeping changes invoked by the law of 1920. Prior to that time the wife was essentially at the mercy of her husband's decisions. She was bound to obey her husband's wishes on virtually all important issues, and her children were her husband's to educate or train as he liked. A wife's limitations were established under law.

Before the law of 1920 went into effect, the status of the wife, as far as the law was concerned, was, in spite of improvements, rather unfavorable in many respects, giving unmistakable evidence of the double standard, which the present law has succeeded in abolishing. She, first of all, followed her husband's estate in life; if he for some reason or other became poor, she was obliged to accept this fact with resignation, even though he might have been the cause of the poverty. Her husband's nationality was hers, and the choice of domicile was in his hands. Her only right to refuse to live where he determined to live depended on whether or not his decision would cause her life to be placed in jeopardy, expose her to injustice, or force her to move abroad. In the last mentioned case, she could refuse to comply with his wishes only if his business at the time of the marriage was not likely to take him abroad or if he was not appointed to some official position which necessitated foreign residence.

A wife was in duty bound to expend her energies and efforts for her family and her home, in accordance with her husband's wishes. This meant that she could not accept outside work without his permission, unless the needs of the family made it imperative. Although the law gave him no power to compel her to follow his wishes, he could refuse to support her or could ask the clergy to "warn" her, the first step toward separation from bed and board. With her husband's permission[1] she could conduct a business or engage in other profitable employment, but if he were legally disqualified to engage in business (due to official position as custom officer, public prosecutor, or tax collector) she shared his disability, even though she may have had his permission. If she failed to heed her husband's refusal, she could be fined like any other individual who conducted a business without license. When she worked lawfully, i.e., with her husband's permission, her earnings belonged to her, although it is not certain that what she purchased with these earnings became hers to do with as she chose.

A married mother had nothing to say in the bringing up of her own children, i.e., the law gave her no such right. Her husband was their guardian until they reached majority, chose their life's work, and gave away his daughters in marriage. If he abused his guardianship, the court could appoint someone else guardian, but in no instance could the mother be so appointed while the family remained undisrupted. She was thereby classified with "feeble-minded persons, heavy debtors, spendthrifts, enemies of the child, persons not yet twenty-five years of age, or so old and crippled that he cannot discharge his duties as guardian, etc." Only in case the husband went insane, deserted his wife, or for other reasons was unable to exercise his guardianship could she be substituted, and if he died, she took his place as guardian of her children — until she remarried. In case husband and wife belonged to different religious faiths, the former decided in which faith the children should be brought up.

As a rule, all the property of the spouses was joint, since in the majority of marriages no private property or income existed. Of this joint property the husband was the sole manager. His administrative powers extended even to his wife's private property, with the exception of her private real property. He decided upon the amount to be spent for the household expenses, for the education of

---

[1]The industrial and commercial acts of 1846 prohibited a woman to engage in business without her husband's permission and security.

the children, and even for his wife's personal needs. The latter had no right to demand anything from her husband, except necessities, even though she may have been the source of the entire family fortune. Most important of all, perhaps, was the fact that no matter how he managed the joint property, he owed his wife no accounting.

Richard Panofsky (b. 1943)
A NINETEENTH-CENTURY HUSBAND'S LETTER TO HIS WIFE

1844

Richard Panofsky, a professor at the University of Massachusetts at Dartmouth, has provided a translated letter from a man named Marcus (1807–1865) to his wife Ulrike (1816–1888). The couple and their six children lived in nineteenth-century Hamburg, Germany. The letter establishes the conditions under which Marcus would take his wife back into his house after she had left him and the children. It also establishes exactly what he expects of his wife. According to Panofsky, Ulrike returned.

June 23, 1844

Dear Wife,

You have sinned greatly — and maybe I too; but this much is certain: Adam sinned after Eve had already sinned. So it is with us; you, alone, carry the guilt of all the misfortune which, however, I helped to enlarge later by my behavior. Listen now, since I still believe certain things to be necessary in order that we may have a peaceful life. If we want not only to be content for a day but forever, you will have to follow my wishes. So examine yourself and determine if you are strong enough to conquer your false ambitions and your stubbornness to submit to all the conditions, the fulfillment of which I cannot ignore. Every sensible person will tell you that all I ask of you is what is easily understood. If you insist on remaining stubborn, then do not return to my house, for you will never be happy with me; your husband, children, and the entire city threaten indifference or even contempt.

But if you decide to act *sensibly* and *correctly,* that is *justly* and *kindly,* then be certain that many in the world will envy you.

I am including here the paper which I read to you in front of the rabbi; ask anyone in your residence if the wishes expressed by me are not quite reasonable, and are of a kind to which every wife can agree for the welfare of domestic happiness. In any case, act in a way you think best.

When you decide to return, write to tell me on which day and hour you depart from Berlin and give me your itinerary whether by way of Kuestrin and Pinne or by way of Wollstein. I will then meet you at Wollstein or Pinne. I expect you will bring Solomon with you.

Don't travel unprepared. If you need money, ask your father.

May God enlighten your heart and mind.

I remain your so far unhappy,

[MARCUS]

Greetings to my parents, brothers, and sisters; also your brother. Show them what you wish, this letter, the enclosure, whatever you want. The children are fortunately healthy.

If you want to return with joy and peace, write me by return mail. In that case, I would rather send you a carriage. Maybe Madam Fraenkel will come along. . . .

[*Enclosure*]

My wife promises — for which every wife is obligated to her husband — to follow my wishes in everything and to strictly obey my orders. It is already self-evident that our marital relations have often been disturbed by the fact that my wife does not follow my wishes but believes herself to be entitled to act on her own, even if this is totally against my orders. In order not to have to remind my wife every second what my wishes are regarding homemaking and public conduct — wishes which I have often expressed — I want to make here a few rules which shall serve as a code of conduct. A home is best run if the work for each hour is planned ahead of time, if possible.

Servants get up no later than 5:00 A.M. in summer and 6:00 A.M. in winter, the children an hour later. The cook prepares breakfast. The nursemaid puts out clothes for every child, prepares water and sponge, cleans the combs, etc. The cook should stay in the kitchen unless there is time to clean the rooms. At least once a week the rooms should be cleaned whenever possible, but not all on the same day.

Every Wednesday, the people in the house should do a laundry. Every last Wednesday in the month, there shall be a large laundry with an outside washerwoman. At least every Monday, the seamstress shall come into the house to fix what is necessary.

Every Thursday or Friday, bread is baked for the week; I think it is best to buy grain and have it ground, but to knead it at home.

Every Friday special bread (Barches) should be bought for the evening meal.

The kitchen list will be prepared and discussed every Thursday evening, jointly, by me and my wife; but my wish is to be decisive.

After this, provisions are to be bought every Friday at the market. For this purpose, my wife, herself, will go to the market on Fridays, accompanied by a servant; she can substitute a special woman who does errands (*Faktorfrau*) if she wishes, but not a servant.

All expenditures have to be written down daily and punctually.

The children receive a bath every Thursday evening. The children's clothes must be kept in a specially appointed chest, with a separate compartment for each child with the child's name upon it. The boys' suits and girls' dresses are to be kept separately. To keep used laundry, there must be a hamper easily accessible. Equally important is the food storage box in which provisions are kept in order, locked and safe from vermin.

The kitchen should be kept in order. Once a week all woodwork and copper must be scoured. The lights and lamps have to be cleaned daily. Toward servants, one has to be strict and just. Therefore, one should not call them names which aren't suitable for a decent wife. One should give them enough nourishing food. Disobedience and obstinacy are to be referred to me.

My wife will never make visits in my absence. However, she should visit the synagogue every Saturday — at least once a month; also she should go for a walk with the children at least once a week.

Helen Watterson Moody (1859–1928)
WHAT IT MEANS TO BE A WIFE   *1899*

The Ladies Home Journal, *by no means a radical magazine in 1899, attempted to show wives how to best serve their husbands and themselves. Helen Watterson Moody, a frequent contributor to the* Journal, *emphasizes methods by which a wife can "Keep Love Secure."*

When a woman marries she assumes two new sets of relations — those of sentiment, through which she becomes the loving, faithful companion of one man and the mother of his children, and the economic relation, through which she becomes one of the great conserving and distributing agents of the world. Since I shall speak of these last two conditions later, I will now only consider that one sentimental relation whose beauty and holiness, if rightly assumed, give foundation to all the rest — that of wifehood.

Marriage is, or should be, primarily a relation of sentiment, yet the happiness of married life is decided by quite other things than sentiment — sturdy and steady moral qualities, good sense, and fair executive ability. I think the recognition of the fact that, though love is the supreme thing in married life, love alone is not enough, always comes to a newly married couple with a sense of surprise.

The Only Way to Keep Love Secure

In the first months of married life, love is so sufficient, and loving so simple, that there seems no other need in life. But by-and-by, when care begins to shadow them, when duties present themselves, and, strangely enough, conflict with each other, when convictions clash and tastes differ, then both husband and wife begin to realize that back of love must stand what I have called "steady and sturdy moral qualities" — justice, patience, honesty, and sincerity, and magnanimity. Indeed, on these depends the very continuance of love in marriage, for it is not possible to go on loving unless that is found which is worthy of love. I say this advisedly. I know the world is full of men and women who think, either because they like to think so, or sadly, because they must, that one can love where one does not respect. It seems to me that this does not ennoble one's ideal of love. One may pity, may have an infinite yearning tenderness over what one cannot respect, but love is of royal birth and recognizes only what is as royal as itself. The way, then, to keep love secure in married life is not so much to be anxiously watching and guarding lest it should escape, or crying that love has spread its wings because the first holiday romance is replaced by graver feeling, but by living along simply and honestly and frankly together, on a high plane, looking most and always toward "whatsoever things are true, whatsoever things are honest, whatsoever things are just, whatsoever things are pure, whatsoever things are lovely, whatsoever things are of good report." Then Love will be not a captive, but a most willing guest.

Marriage Is a Serious and Steady Occupation

That is why I say that the real happiness of married life depends largely upon the personal character that is put into it. Next in importance I place sound, good sense; and I mean by this that underlying sense of proportion by which one is able to discriminate the insignificant, the passing, the unimportant, from the grave, the permanent, the important — that capacity for steady, balancing thought which keeps one from impulsive words and rash deeds. A woman who is blessed with good sense does not consider at the start that marriage is a role to be skillfully and successfully enacted, or a grand frolic of which she is to be the admired and indulged center, or a mere incident in a life crowded with other activities. She knows that marriage is a serious and steady vocation, and that the true wife is one who enters marriage not thinking how much she can get out of it, but how much she can put into it. It is this larger conception of marriage which makes women dwell by their own firesides in sweet content with what is commonly called the "narrow limits of home," knowing well that no true home is narrow since it must give cover to "the whole primal mysteries of life — food, raiment, and work to earn them withal: love and marriage, birth and death, right-doing and wrong-doing — all these commonplaces of humanity which are most divine because they are most commonplace."

The way to make home a wide place to dwell in, is to bring a wide personality to dwell in it. Any home is just as wide as the maker, and can be no wider. When a woman understands this she is able to keep her head steady and her heart undisturbed over newspaper sketches about other women, in which each one of them is made to do the most remarkable and entirely unnecessary combination of things. [. . .]

Married Women Can Find Time If They Will

When I hear a married woman lament the lack of wide opportunities in her life I find myself wondering, in a kind of daze, what she means. If I inquire particularly, I usually discover that by lack of opportunities she means either the time for study and self-cultivation which she deeply desires, or else an opportunity for public activity and recognition. Well, both of these are good in their proper places, and there are few wives who will not be able to find some hours in the week to give to either one or the other. I suspect that in the case of those women who say they actually do not get time for study or music, or for an occasional club meeting, the trouble lies in the fact that they do not want to enough. For be sure of this, that in the long run a man or a woman usually finds time in life to do the thing that he or she wants to do most. A woman may desire the opportunity for self-culture and growth, but if she in her heart really prefers an hour of neighborhood gossip, or a piece of drawn linen for her luncheon table, or a vulgar profusion in the menu she offers her guests, she will have these and not the study. If, on the other hand, the intellectual quickening that comes from communion with big and earnest minds be the one thing in life that she feels she must have, be sure that in some degree she will have it — not enough of it, possibly, to satisfy her, but enough to make her life richer, because she will make her living less complex in order that she may have it.

RIGHT: Scene in a brothel, from the *National Police Gazette,* July 26, 1879. (© Collection of The New-York Historical Society)
BELOW: A scene from Hogarth's *Harlot's Progress:* A madam welcomes a newly arrived woman who will soon become part of the establishment. One of her customers looks on eagerly.

Flora Tristan (1803–1844)

LONDON JOURNAL: PROSTITUTES IN LONDON . . . ALL THE STREETS ARE FULL OF THEM   *1842*

TRANSLATED FROM THE FRENCH BY JEAN HAWKES

Flora Tristan, a French feminist, visited London often. Her journal was published in France in 1840 and translated into English in 1842. Among her many observations, her comments on the prostitutes of London establish the fact of their presence in remarkable numbers. Waterloo Bridge remained a notorious site for plying the trade of prostitution both in the late nineteenth century and afterward. Tristan's detailed account implies a deep sympathy for the women involved.

There are so many prostitutes in London that one sees them everywhere at any time of day; all the streets are full of them, but at certain times they flock in from outlying districts in which most of them live, and mingle with the crowds in theaters and public places. It is rare for them to take men home; their landlords would object, and besides their lodgings are unfit. They take their "captures" to the houses reserved for their trade. . . .

Between seven and eight o'clock one evening, accompanied by two friends armed with canes, I went to take a look at the new suburb which lies on either side of the long broad thoroughfare called Waterloo Road at the end of Waterloo Bridge. This neighborhood is almost entirely inhabited by prostitutes and people who live off prostitution; it is courting danger to go there alone at night. It was a hot summer evening; in every window and doorway women were laughing and joking with their protectors. Half dressed, some of them *naked to the waist,* they were a revolting sight, and the criminal, cynical expressions of their companions filled me with apprehension. These men are for the most part very good looking — young, vigorous, and well made — but their coarse and common air marks them as animals whose sole instinct is to satisfy their appetites. . . .

We went on our way and explored all the streets in the vicinity of Waterloo Road, then we sat upon the bridge to watch the women of the neighborhood flock past, as they do every night between the hours of eight and nine, on their way to the West End, where they ply their trade all through the night and return home between eight and nine in the morning. They infest the promenades and any other place where people gather, such as the approaches to the Stock Exchange, the various public buildings and the theaters, which they invade as soon as entry is reduced to half price. . . . After the play they move on to the "finishes"; these are squalid taverns or vast resplendent gin-palaces where people go to spend what remains of the night. . . .

I had heard descriptions of the debauchery to be seen at finishes, but could never bring myself to believe them. Now I was in London for the fourth time with the firm resolve to discover everything for myself. I determined to overcome my repugnance and go in person to one of these finishes. . . . The same friends who had accompanied me to the Waterloo Road again offered to be my guides. . . .

From the outside these "gin-palaces" with their carefully fastened shutters seem to be quietly slumbering; but no sooner has the doorkeeper admitted you by the little door reserved for the initiates than you are dazzled by the light of a thousand gas lamps. Upstairs there is a spacious salon divided down the middle; in one half there is a row of tables separated one from the other by wooden screens, as in all English restaurants. . . . In the other half there is a dais where the prostitutes parade in all their finery; seeking to arouse the men with their glances and remarks. . . .

Towards midnight the regular clients begin to arrive; several finishes are frequented by men in high society, and this is where the cream of the aristocracy gather. At first the young noblemen recline on the sofas, smoking and exchanging pleasantries with the women; then, when they have drunk enough for the fumes of champagne and Madeira to go to their heads, the illustrious scions of the English nobility, the very honorable members of Parliament remove their coats, untie their cravats, take off their waistcoats and braces, and proceed to set up their private boudoir in a public place. Why not make themselves at home, since they are paying out so much money for the right to display their contempt. . . . The orgy rises to a crescendo; between four and five o'clock in the morning it reaches its height.

At this point it takes a good deal of courage to remain in one's seat, a mute spectator of all that takes place. What a worthy use these English lords make of their immense fortunes! How fine and generous they are when they have lost the use of their reason and offer fifty, even a hundred guineas to a prostitute if she will lend herself to all the obscenities that drunkenness engenders. . . .

For in a finish there is no lack of entertainment. One of the favorite sports is to *ply a woman with drink* until she falls dead drunk upon the floor, then to make her swallow a draught compounded of *vinegar, mustard, and pepper;* this invariably throws the poor creature into horrible convulsions, and her spasms and contortions provoke the *honorable company* to gales of laughter and infinite amusement. Another diversion much appreciated at these fashionable gatherings is to empty the contents of the nearest glass upon the women as they lie insensible on the ground. I have seen satin dresses of no recognizable color, only a confused mass of stains; wine, brandy, beer, tea, coffee, cream, etc. . . . daubed all over them in a thousand fantastic shapes. . . . The air is heavy with the noxious odors of food, drink, tobacco, and others more fetid still which seize you by the throat, grip your temples in a vice, and make your senses reel: it is indescribably horrible! . . . However, this life, which continues relentlessly night after night, is the prostitute's sole hope of a fortune, for she has no hold on the Englishman when he is sober. *The sober Englishman is chaste to the point of prudery.*

It is usually between seven and eight o'clock in the morning when people leave the finish. The servants go out to look for cabs, and anyone still on his feet gathers up his clothes and returns home; as for the rest, the pot-boys dress them in the first garments that come to hand, bundle them into a cab, and tell the cabman where to deliver them. Often nobody knows their address; then they are deposited in the cellar and left to sleep in the straw. This place is known as the drunkards hole, and there they stay until they have recovered their wits sufficiently to say where they wish to be taken.

A LETTER TO THE *TIMES* (LONDON) FROM A PROSTITUTE

1858

After a concerted effort on the part of prominent London citizens to reduce prostitution in London, a prostitute who referred to herself as "one of that abandoned sisterhood" came forth with the following letter filled with suggestions about how to improve the circumstances of the prostitute and her customers. She hopes to avoid the "persecution" of individuals while London attempts to deal with a vice it considers a nuisance.

Sir:

Certain Persons have, as you know, commenced a crusade against London Prostitutes, and, if one of that abandoned sisterhood may presume to address you, grant me your attention.

The precept and example set me by parents, now, thank God, in their graves; the education likewise "thrown away" upon me, and my subsequent experience as a governess in a highly respectable family, were not necessary to the conviction that the class among which I may be numbered consists of outcasts whose undisguised pursuit is an offense to the laws of God and man.

I know that we are cut off from the moral, social, and religious worlds. . . . We need not be told of our ruin and degradation, because we never "fall" without being alive to the fact. A woman seduced may forgive her wrongs . . . it is impossible for her to forget what she is; society will not permit her to do so. . . . Do not suppose, then, that I would attempt to defend what transpires nightly in the Haymarket, in Coventry Street, or wherever women of my caste congregate. I do not ask you to countenance anything of the kind. No, Sir, give "Vice its own image" and do your duty.

But, while you yourself refrain from going a step too far, pray give a warning to others. It is one thing to put down a nuisance. It is another to persecute individuals. I will anticipate much that may fairly be said, and admit that if I live avowedly in defiance of those regulations which the community has established as essential to its well being. . . . I must expect to be checked in such openly vicious courses, for I believe the liberty of the subject should end where injustice to others begins. But pray tell those good gentlemen who are bent on "putting us down," that theirs is not only a delicate, but a difficult undertaking, and they should be careful lest they have more to answer for than they dream of in their philosophy.

The vice of London, Sir, is seen to float upon its surface; let it pass as the weed on its way to the ocean. If it accumulates so as to become offensive, disperse it. If it is otherwise annoying and cannot conveniently be avoided, deal with it accordingly.

Appoint commissioners who are fitted for the office, intelligent, respectable, and responsible gentlemen, and make it worth their while to devote themselves entirely to the reduction of the scandal complained of. Empower these officials to have us taken up and punished for riot or impropriety of any kind. But let not the "pelting petty officer," the ignorant constable of a few shillings a week, and it may be an unfeeling and unthinking brute, interfere with us as he will. Recollect it was man who made us what we are. It is man who pays for the finery, the rouge, and the gin . . . it is man who, when we apply ourselves to industry and honesty, employs us upon starvation wages; and if man had his way, and women's nature were not superior to his, there would be no virtue extant. Say, then, is it for man to persecute even the most profligate among us?

Pray, Sir, think of this, and tell those gentlemen whose speeches I read to act upon it. They may be husbands and fathers . . . and I allow for their parental solicitude. But if they be Christians they will imitate one who said, "Go, and sin no more," and not "move on," "anywhere, anywhere, out of the world."

Your humble servant,

ONE MORE UNFORTUNATE

Barbara Meil Hobson
SUCCESSFUL MADAMS
1987

In this brief excerpt Hobson describes prostitutes who became "successful entrepreneurs" and achieved positions similar to that of Mrs. Warren in Bernard Shaw's play. However, very few prostitutes ever became financially independent. Mrs. Warren is remarkable for her success, not for her profession.

On the other hand, the image of the prostitute as someone who accumulates savings from her trade, wisely invests her capital, and obtains a small fortune was not very realistic either. We know of some famous successful madams at the turn of

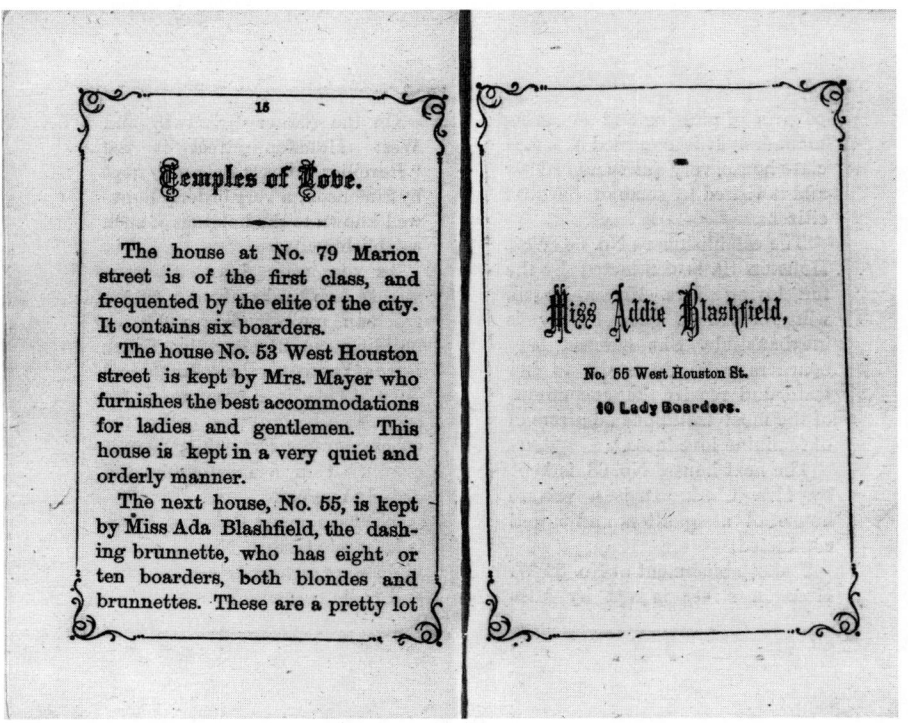

The Gentleman's Directory, Temples of Love, address listings, 1870. Published directories such as this one informed men where to find the best brothels. Even newspapers carried discreet advertisements when prostitutes changed houses so they would not lose their regular clientele. (© Collection of The New-York Historical Society)

the century, including the Everleigh sisters, who operated gilded palaces of vice in Chicago, and Nell Kimball, the famous "queen" of Storeyville. They were the successful entrepreneurs of the demimonde, and they even published their memoirs.

What little we know of typical prostitutes' futures suggests that few women achieved upward economic mobility through prostitution. The nineteenth-century police registers tell us that women in regulated prostitution were most likely to reenter traditional working class occupations. [. . .] The fees Swedish prostitutes had to pay for medical examinations, the percentages madams took for room and board, and the expenses for dress and cosmetics did not leave very much money for savings. Prostitutes in the high-class brothels in nineteenth-century American cities were paid high prices for their sexual services. But madams usually took 50 percent of a prostitute's receipts, and expenses were high. In addition, prostitutes in many of these cities had to take a cut from their earnings for police protection. Research on nineteenth-century St. Paul documents that career paths within prostitution were limited. Only four out of sixty-one brothel prostitutes listed in official records became madams, a revealing statistic in a city where prostitution was aboveboard — unofficially licensed.

Drama in the Early and Mid-Twentieth Century

The realist tradition in drama had certain EXPRESSIONIST qualities evident in the symbolic actions in Strindberg's *Miss Julie* and certain romantic fantasies in later plays of Ibsen. But the surfaces of the plays appear realistic, consisting of a sequence of events that we might imagine happening in real life. The subject matter is also in the tradition of naturalism because it is drawn from life and not beautified or toned down for the middle-class audience.

But in the early to mid-twentieth century realistic drama took a new turn, incorporating distortions of reality that border on the unreal or *surreal*. From the time of Anton Chekhov in 1903 to Samuel Beckett in the 1950s, drama exploited the possibilities of realism, antirealism, and the poetic expansion of expressionism.

The Heritage of Realism

In the late nineteenth century realism was often perceived as too severe for an audience that had loved melodrama. Realistic plays forced comfortable audiences to observe psychological and physical problems that their status as members of the middle class usually allowed them to avoid. Audiences often protested loudly at this painful experience.

Early in the twentieth century, Susan Glaspell (1876–1948) began writing plays for the pleasure of having them read in her own living room in Province-town, Massachusetts. *Trifles* (1916) told the story of a murdered husband in a deadpan fashion without alluding directly to the abusive nature of the husband and the ultimate resistance of the wife. The play may be said to be realistic on the surface, but its deep structure is symbolic and its indirectness implies an experimental attitude toward the writing of plays.

The technique of realism could, however, be adapted for many different purposes, and eventually realism was reshaped to satisfy middle-class sensibilities by commercial playwrights, who produced popular, pleasant plays. By the 1920s in Europe and the 1930s in America, theatergoing audiences expected plays to be realistic. Even the light comedies dominating the commercial stage were in a more or less realistic mode. Anything that disturbed the illusion of realism was thought to be a flaw.

Reactions to the comfortable use of realistic techniques were numerous, especially after World War I. One extreme reaction was that of DADAISM. Through the Dadaists' chief propagandist, Tristan Tzara (1896–1963), the group promoted an art that was essentially enigmatic and incoherent to the average person. That was its point. The Dadaists blamed World War I on sensible, middle-class people who were logical and well intentioned but never questioned convention. The brief plays that were performed in many Dadaist clubs in Europe often featured actors speaking simultaneously so that nothing they said could be understood. The purpose was to confound the normal expectations of theatergoers.

Other developments were also making it possible for playwrights to experiment and move away from a strict reliance on "comfortable" realism. By World War I motion pictures began to make melodramatic entertainment available to most people in the world. Even when films were silent, they relied on techniques that had been common on the nineteenth-century stage. Their growing domination of popular dramatic entertainment provided an outlet for the expectations of middle-class audiences and freed more imaginative playwrights to experiment and develop in different directions.

Realism and Myth

The incorporation of myth in drama offered new opportunities to expand the limits of realism. Sigmund Freud's theories of psychoanalysis at the turn of the century stimulated a new interest in myth and dreams as a psychological link between people. Freud studied Greek myths for clues to the psychic state of his patients, and he published a number of commentaries on Greek plays and on *Hamlet*. (See excerpts on pp. 100–103 and pp. 411–12.) The psychologist Carl Jung, a follower of Freud who eventually split with him, helped give a powerful impetus to the interest in dreams and the symbolism of myth by suggesting that all members of a culture share an inborn knowledge of the basic myths of the culture. Jung postulated a collective unconscious, a repository of mythic material in the mind that all humans inherit as part of their birthright. This theory gave credence to the power of myth in everyday life; along with Freud's theories, it is one of the most important ideas empowering drama and other art forms in the twentieth century. Playwrights who used elements of myth in their plays produced a poetic form of realism that deals with a level of truth common to all humans.

Myth and Culture

Some non-European drama depends on interpretation of local myth in relation to the culture or cultures that produce it. Wole Soyinka's background as a Nigerian familiar with Yoruba culture and myth, along with his formal education in England, prepared him for a career that expanded the horizons of drama for both Nigerian and European audiences.

Soyinka's experimentation has spanned two traditions — modern European theater and modern ritual theater of the Yoruba people of Nigeria. Traditional Yoruba drama develops from religious celebrations and annual festivals and includes music and dance. Soyinka's plays, including *The Strong Breed* (1962), concern themselves with African traditions and issues, but they often also explore mythic forces that link European and African cultures. His plays have been produced throughout the world and have demonstrated the universality of the community and the anxiety of the individual it sometimes breeds. Soyinka has also written critical studies on Yoruba tragedy and has interpreted, translated, and produced Greek tragedy.

Poetic Realism

The Abbey Theatre in Dublin, which functioned with distinction from the turn of the century, produced major works by John Millington Synge, W. B. Yeats, Sean O'Casey, and Lady Gregory. Lady Gregory's peasant plays concentrated on the charming, the amusing, and occasionally the grotesque. She tried to represent the dialect she heard in the west of Ireland, a dialect that was distinctive, poetic, and colorful. She also took advantage of local Irish myths and used some of them for her most powerful plays, such as *Dervorgilla* and *Grania,* both portraits of passionate women from Irish legend and myth.

John Millington Synge, like Lady Gregory, was interested in the twin forces of myth and peasant dialects. His plays are difficult to fit into a realist mold, although their surfaces are sometimes naturalistic. Some audiences reacted violently to his portrayals of peasant life because they were unflattering. Synge's plays were sometimes directly connected with ancient Irish myth, as in *Deirdre of the Sorrows* (1910), which concerns a willful Irish princess who runs off with a young warrior and his brothers on the eve of her wedding to an old king. The story ends sadly for Deirdre, and she is regarded as a fated heroine, almost a Greek figure. Synge's most popular one-act play, *Riders to the Sea* (1904), reveals his gift for emulating the Irish way of speaking English in Ireland's western county of Mayo. His creation of peasant dialogue remains one of his most important contributions to modern drama.

In the United States, Eugene O'Neill, influenced by Strindberg, experimented with realism, first by presenting stark, powerful plays that disturbed his audiences. *The Hairy Ape* (1922) portrayed a primitive coal stoker on a passenger liner who awakened base emotions in the more refined passengers. In *The Emperor Jones* (1921) O'Neill produced the first important American expressionist play. The shifting scenery, created by lighting, was dreamlike and at times frightening. The experience of the play reflected the frightening psychic experiences of the main character, Brutus Jones.

O'Neill also experimented with more poetic forms of realism. In *Desire under the Elms* (1924), he explores the myth of Phaedra — centering on her incestuous love for her husband's son — but sets it in rural New England on a rock-hard farm. In the tradition of realism, the play treats unpleasant themes: sons' distrust of their father and their dishonoring him, lust between a son and his stepmother, and the murder of a baby to "prove" love. But it is not simply realistic. Without its underpinning of myth, the play would be sordid, but the myth helps us see that fate operates even today, not in terms of messages from the gods but rather in terms of messages from our hearts and bodies. Lust is a force in nature that drives and destroys.

Meanwhile, in Fascist Spain, Federico García Lorca, also a poetic realist, was uncovering dark emotional centers of the psyche in his *House of Bernarda Alba* (1936), which explores erotic forces repressed and then set loose. Lorca was opposed to Fascism and was murdered by a Fascist agent. His plays reveal a bleakness of spirit that helps us imagine the darkness — moral and psychological — that enveloped Europe in the 1940s.

Social Realism

Ten years after *Desire under the Elms* enjoyed popularity, a taste for plays based on SOCIAL REALISM developed. This was realism with a political conscience. Because the world was in the throes of a depression that reduced many people to destitution and homelessness, drama began to aim at awakening governments to the consequences of unbridled capitalism and the depressions that freewheeling economies produced.

Plays like Jack Kirkland's *Tobacco Road* (1933), adapted from Erskine Caldwell's novel, presented a grim portrait of rural poverty in America. Sidney Kingsley's *Dead End* (1935) portrayed the lives of virtually homeless boys on the Lower East Side of Manhattan. In the same year Maxwell Anderson produced a verse tragedy, *Winterset,* with gangsters and gangsterism at its core. Also in 1935 Clifford Odets produced *Waiting for Lefty,* an openly leftist labor drama. These plays' realist credentials lay primarily in their effort to show audiences portraits of life that might shock their middle-class sensibilities.

Realism and Expressionism

O'Neill's later plays shed the underpinnings of myth and developed a powerful realistic style as seen in *The Iceman Cometh* (1939), set in a dingy bar filled with patrons living on the edge, listening to Theodor Hickman (Hickey) and Harry Hope give their philosophy of life. At this time he also wrote a haunting one-act play, *Hughie* (1941), set in a shabby hotel lobby late at night. In it, Erie Smith, a small-time gambler, shares his views of life with the hotel night manager, Charlie Hughes. The play is simple but intense and moving. One of O'Neill's greatest plays, *Long Day's Journey into Night,* written in 1941 but not published or produced until 1956, took him in a new direction. For the first time, he began an analysis of his own tortured family background, which included alcoholism and drug addiction. The play was so searing and painful that he sequestered it with Random House, instructing publisher Bennett Cerf not to publish it until twenty-five years after his death. O'Neill's wife, however, broke the will and had the play produced. It has since become the vehicle for some of the best performances of the latter part of the twentieth century.

After Eugene O'Neill's experiments, later American dramatists looked for new ways to expand the resources of realism while retaining its power. The use of EXPRESSIONISM — often poetic in language and effect — was one solution that appealed to both Tennessee Williams and Arthur Miller. Expressionism developed in the first and second decades of the twentieth century. The movement began in Germany and was influenced by some of Strindberg's work. Because expressionism takes many forms, there is no simple way to define the term except to see it as an alternative to realistic drama. Instead of having realistic sets, the stage may sometimes be barren or flooded with light or draped. Characters sometimes become symbolic; dialogue is often sharp, abrupt, enigmatic. The German theater saw its earliest developments in Frank Wedekind, whose first play, *Spring Awakening,* which explored sexual repression, abandoned a naturalistic style. Wedekind's work influenced later German playwrights such as George Kaiser, Ernst Toller, Erwin Piscator, and Bertolt Brecht, whose *Threepenny Opera* (1928) incorporated some of the hallmarks of expressionism, such as a music-hall atmosphere and broadly drawn characters.

Later American playwrights modified the characteristics of expressionism; they melded expressionist elements, such as fantastic sets and highly poetic dic-

Figure 15. Expressionistic setting in Arthur Miller's *Death of a Salesman.*

tion, with a relatively realistic style. Tennessee Williams's *The Glass Menagerie* (1944) and Arthur Miller's *Death of a Salesman* (1949) both use expressionist techniques. Williams's poetic stage directions make clear that he is drawing on nonrealistic dramatic devices. He describes the scene as "memory and . . . therefore nonrealistic." He calls for an interior "rather dim and poetic," and he uses a character who also steps outside the staged action to serve as a narrator — one who "takes whatever license with dramatic convention as is convenient to his purposes." As the narrator tells his story, the walls of the building seem to melt away, revealing the inside of a house and the lives and fantasies of his mother and sister, both caught in their own distorted visions of life.

Arthur Miller's original image for *Death of a Salesman* was the inside of Willy Loman's mind; Jo Mielziner's expressionist set represented his idea as a cross-section of Loman's house. As the action in one room concluded, lights went up to begin action in another (Figure 15). This evocative staging influenced the production of numerous plays by later writers. In the original set, a scrim, or gauze screen, was painted with branches and leaves. When this scrim was lit from the front for memory scenes, the set was transformed to evoke an earlier time when the sons were boys.

Miller used expressionist techniques to create the hallucinatory sequences when Willy talks with Ben, the man who walked into the jungle poor and walked out a millionaire, and when Biff recalls seeing Willy with the woman in Boston.

While expressionism made some inroads in American theater, the techniques of realism persisted and developed. Lorraine Hansberry's *A Raisin in the Sun* (1959) uses basically realistic staging and dialogue to portray the difficulties of the members of one family in reaching for opportunity to overcome poverty. For Williams and Miller, expressionism offered a way to bring other worlds to bear on the staged action — the worlds of dream and fantasy. Hansberry does not use the expressionist techniques of Miller. Her only exotic touch is the visit of the African young man, Asagai, who offers a moment of cultural counterpoint. Hansberry's realism is essentially conservative.

Antirealism

Surrealism (literally, "beyond realism") in the early twentieth century was based originally on an interpretation of experience not through the lucid mind of the waking person but through the mind of the dreamer, the unconscious mind that Freud described. Surrealism augmented or, for some playwrights, supplanted realism and became a means of distorting reality for emotional purposes.

When Pirandello's six characters come onstage looking for their author in *Six Characters in Search of an Author* (1921), no one believes that they are characters rather than actors. Pirandello's play is an examination of the realities we take for granted in drama. He turns the world of expectation in drama upside down. He reminds us that what we assume to be real is always questionable: we cannot be sure of anything; we must presume that things are true, and in some cases we must take them on faith.

Pirandello's philosophy dominated his stories, plays, and novels. His questioning of the certainty of human knowledge was designed to undermine his audience's faith in an absolute reality. Modern physicists have concurred with philosophers, ancient and modern, who question everyday reality. Pirandello was influenced by the modern theories of relativity that physicists were developing, and he found in them validation of his own attack on certainty.

Epic Theater

Bertolt Brecht (1898–1956) began writing plays just after World War I. He was a political dramatist who rejected the theater of his day, which valued the realistic "well-made play," in which all the parts fit perfectly together and function like a machine. His feeling was that such plays were too mechanical, like a "clockwork mouse."

Exploring the style of his predecessor Irwin Piscator, Brecht developed EPIC THEATER. The term implies a sequence of actions or episodes of the kind found in Homer's *Iliad*. In epic theater the sense of dramatic illusion is constantly voided by reminders from the stage that one is watching a play. Stark, harsh lighting, blank stages, placards announcing changes of scenes, bands playing music onstage, and long, discomfiting pauses make it impossible for an audience to become totally immersed in a realistic illusion. Brecht, offering a genuine alternative to realistic drama, wanted the audience to analyze the play's thematic content rather than to sit back and be entertained. He believed that realistic drama convinced audiences that the play's vision of reality described not just things as they are but things as they must be. Such drama, Brecht asserted, helped maintain the social problems that they portrayed by reinforcing, rather than challenging, their realities.

Brecht's *Mother Courage* (written in 1939 and produced in 1941) is an antiwar drama staged early in World War II. The use of song, an unreal setting, and an unusual historical perspective (the Thirty Years' War in the seventeenth century) help to achieve the "defamiliarization" that Brecht thought drama ought to produce in its audiences. The techniques of epic theater in *Galileo* (1938–1939) and *The Good Woman of Setzuan* (1943) — a study of the immoralities that prosper under capitalism — were imitated by playwrights in the 1950s. Hardly a major play in that period is free of Brecht's influence.

Eugène Ionesco (1909–1994) is said to have been the first of the postwar absurdist dramatists, with his production of *The Bald Soprano* and *The Lesson* (both in 1951). Ionesco called them "anti-plays" because they avoided the normal causal relationship of actions and realistic expectations of conventional drama.

Absurdist Drama

The critic Martin Esslin coined the term THEATER OF THE ABSURD when describing the work of Samuel Beckett (1906–1989), the Irish playwright whose dramas often dispense with almost everything that makes the well-made play well made. Some of his plays have no actors onstage — amplified breathing is the only hint of human presence in one case. Some have little or no plot; others have no words. His theater is minimalist, offering a stage reality that seems cut to the bone, without the usual realistic devices of plot, character development, and intricate setting.

The theater of the absurd assumes that the world is meaningless, that meaning is a human concept, and that individuals must create significance and not rely on institutions or traditions to provide it. The absurdist movement grew out of EXISTENTIALISM, a postwar French philosophy demanding that the individual face the emptiness of the universe and create meaning in a life that has no essential meaning within itself. *Waiting for Godot* (1952) captured the modern imagination and established a landmark in absurdist drama.

In *Waiting for Godot* two tramps, Vladimir and Estragon, meet near a tree where they expect Godot to arrive to talk with them. The play has two acts that both end with a small boy explaining that Godot cannot come today but will come tomorrow. Godot is not coming, and the tramps who wait for Godot will wait forever. While they wait they entertain themselves with vaudeville routines and eventually are met by a rich man, Pozzo, and his slave, Lucky. Lucky, on the command "Think, pig," speaks in a stream of garbled phrases that evoke Western philosophy and religion but that remain meaningless. Pozzo and Lucky have no interest in joining Vladimir and Estragon in waiting for Godot. They leave the two alone, waiting — afraid to leave for fear of missing Godot, but uncertain that Godot will ever arrive.

Beckett seems to be saying that in an absurd world such gestures are necessary to create the sense of significance that people need to live. His characters' awareness of an audience and his refusal to create a drama in which an audience can "lose" itself in a comfortable surface of realistic illusion are all, in their own way, indebted to Brecht.

Beckett's *Krapp's Last Tape* (1958) places some extraordinary limitations on performance. Krapp is the only person onstage throughout the play, and his dialogues are with tapes of himself made many years before. The situation is absurd, but as Beckett reveals to us, the absurd has its own complexities, and situations such as Krapp's can sustain complex interpretations. Beckett expects his audience to analyze the drama, not merely be entertained.

The illusion of reality is shed almost entirely in *Endgame* (1957). Hamm cannot move. His parents, both legless, are in trashcans onstage. Clov performs all the play's movement on a barren, cellarlike stage.

Beckett's *Happy Days* (1961) is generally thought to be his most optimistic play. Winnie, who talks almost nonstop throughout, seems mired in trivia and the details of everyday life. Yet, she can pause for philosophical observations on the nature of her existence and position herself thoughtfully in regard to the world. In the first act she is buried in a mound of earth up to her waist, and in the second act she is buried up to her neck, but her positive attitude intensifies. She is doing the best she can. Willy, her husband, hardly says a word and does not begin to act until the last minute of the play, at which time his action is ambiguous. *Happy Days*, while similar to Beckett's other absurdist plays, still intrigues audiences in the twenty-first century. It speaks to the hopeful among us, but it also offers a view of life that is far from sugar coated. It is absurd in the sense that it does not offer an easy answer to the questions raised by the limitations of Winnie's and Willy's existence.

The great plays of this period reflect the values of the cultures from which they spring. They make comments on life in the modern world and question the values that the culture takes for granted. The drama of this part of the twentieth century is a drama of examination.

Early and Mid-Twentieth-Century Drama Timeline

DATE	THEATER	POLITICAL	SOCIAL/CULTURAL
1850–1900	**1854–1931:** David Belasco, American producer. Belasco uses pictorial realism in staging and creates "stars" on the New York stage. **1862–1928:** Adolphe Appia, influential Swiss designer **1871–1909:** John Millington Synge, Irish playwright, author of *Riders to the Sea* (1904) and *The Playboy of the Western World* (1907) **1872–1966:** Edward Gordon Craig, influential English theatrical designer **1873–1943:** Max Reinhardt, Austrian director, producer, and theorist **1880–1964:** Sean O'Casey, Irish playwright, author of *Juno and the Paycock* (1924) and *The Plough and the Stars* (1926) **1887–1954:** Robert Edmond Jones, revolutionary American scenic designer **1888–1953:** Eugene O'Neill, American playwright. Among his works are *Desire under the Elms* (1924), *Mourning Becomes Electra* (1931), and *Long Day's Journey into Night* (1941). **1898–1956:** Bertolt Brecht, German playwright, author of *The Threepenny Opera* (1928), *Mother Courage* (1941), and *The Good Woman of Setzuan* (1943) **1898:** The Irish Literary Society is founded by W. B. Yeats (1865–1939) and Lady Augusta Gregory (1863–1935). The group leads the way in creating an indigenous Irish theater.	**1857:** Sepoy mutiny in India against British officers **1860–65:** Civil War in the United States **1867:** Dominion of Canada formed **1868–1912:** Meiji period in Japan **1871:** Feudalism in Japan ends. **1889:** First Japanese Constitution is enacted. **1895:** China is defeated in war by Japan. Korea becomes independent. **1898:** Boer War in South Africa **1898:** Spanish-American War. Cuba is freed from Spain.	**1853:** U.S. Navy arrives in Tokyo Bay to negotiate a trade treaty. **1861:** Russia emancipates its serfs. **1863:** U.S. Emancipation Proclamation frees slaves. **1869:** The Suez Canal opens. **1876:** General George Custer's troops are destroyed at Little Big Horn by Sioux-Cheyennes. **1880–1914:** All of Africa (except Ethiopia) is rapidly colonized by European and Turkish authorities.

DATE	THEATER	POLITICAL	SOCIAL/CULTURAL
1900–1950	**1904:** The Abbey Theatre, evolved from the Irish Literary Society founded by Yeats and Lady Gregory, opens in Dublin.	**1900:** The Boxer Rebellion attempts to curtail Western commercial interests in China.	**1900–1971:** Louis Armstrong, African American jazz trumpet player
	1905–1984: Lillian Hellman, American playwright, author of *The Children's Hour* (1934) and *The Little Foxes* (1939). Other important American female playwrights of the period include Rachel Crothers (1876–1958), Zona Gale (1874–1938), and Susan Glaspell (1876–1948).	**1901:** Queen Victoria of Great Britain dies and is succeeded by her son Edward VII.	**1900:** Sigmund Freud (1856–1939) writes *The Interpretation of Dreams.*
		1904–1905: Russo-Japanese War. Russia is defeated, and Japan emerges as a world power.	**1901:** Ragtime music becomes popular in the United States.
		1905: The Sinn Fein party is founded in Dublin.	**1903:** Wilbur and Orville Wright's first flight
			1905: The first movie theater in the United States opens in New York City.
	1906–1989: Samuel Beckett, Irish playwright who wrote some of his plays in French. Among his works are *Waiting for Godot* (1952) and *Endgame* (1957).		**1905–1914:** More than 10 million immigrants arrive in the United States.
			1906: An earthquake and subsequent fire ravage San Francisco.
			1907: Picasso's (1881–1973) *Les Demoiselles d'Avignon* is significant to cubism movement in art.
	1911–1983: Tennessee Williams, American playwright, author of *The Glass Menagerie* (1944), *A Streetcar Named Desire* (1947), and *Cat on a Hot Tin Roof* (1955)		**1908:** Henry Ford (1863–1947) designs the Model T.
			1910: W. E. B. DuBois (1868–1963), African American civil rights leader and author, establishes the NAACP.
		1912: Sun Yat Sen is elected president of the Republic of China and founds the Kuomintang.	**1912:** The ocean liner *Titanic* sinks, killing 1,513 passengers.
	1915: Arthur Miller, American playwright, born. Among his works are *Death of a Salesman* (1949) and *The Crucible* (1953).		**1913:** Niels Bohr (1885–1962) formulates his theory of atomic structure.
		1914: World War I begins with the assassination of Austrian Archduke Franz Ferdinand in Sarajevo.	**1914:** The Panama Canal is completed.
	1915: George Cram Cook, Eugene O'Neill, and Susan Glaspell found the Provincetown Players in Provincetown, Massachusetts.		**1915:** D. W. Griffith's film *The Birth of a Nation* is released.
		1916: The Easter Rising in Ireland is suppressed by the British.	**c. 1916:** Albert Einstein (1879–1955) formulates his theory of relativity.
	1917: J. L. Williams's *Why Marry?* receives the first Pulitzer Prize for drama.	**1917:** The Russian Revolution overthrows the czar and establishes Bolshevik control under V. I. Lenin.	**1916:** Jazz music evolves in New Orleans, Chicago, and New York City.
	1918: Formation of the Theater Guild in New York City	**1919:** The Treaty of Versailles formally ends World War I.	**1918:** Influenza epidemic kills 22 million people worldwide by 1922.
	1919: Actors Equity Association is officially recognized as a union in the United States.	**1920:** The Nineteenth Amendment grants American women the right to vote.	**1919:** The Bauhaus, an influential school of art and architecture, is established by Walter Gropius in Germany.
	1920: Théâtre National Populaire is founded in Paris.	**1921:** Southern Ireland becomes the independent Republic of Ireland.	**1920:** Prohibition begins in the United States.
			1933: Prohibition is repealed.

Early and Mid-Twentieth-Century Drama Timeline (continued)

DATE	THEATER	POLITICAL	SOCIAL/CULTURAL
1900–1950 (continued)	**1921:** Italian playwright Luigi Pirandello (1867–1936) writes *Six Characters in Search of an Author*.	**1921:** Ku Klux Klan activities become violent throughout southern United States.	
	1923–1924: Moscow Art Theater visits the United States for the first time.	**1921:** Sacco and Vanzetti, Italian anarchists, are sentenced to death in the United States.	**1922:** T. S. Eliot (1888–1965) publishes *The Waste Land*.
		1922: Fascist dictator Benito Mussolini gains power in Italy.	**1922:** James Joyce (1882–1941) publishes *Ulysses*.
			1923: George Gershwin (1898–1937) performs *Rhapsody in Blue*.
		1924–1972: J. Edgar Hoover, director of the Federal Bureau of Investigation	**1925:** F. Scott Fitzgerald (1896–1940) publishes *The Great Gatsby*.
		1925: Adolf Hitler reorganizes the Nazi Party and publishes volume 1 of *Mein Kampf*.	**1925:** Margaret Sanger (1883–1966) organizes the first international birth control conference.
	1927: Neil Simon born. His plays include *The Odd Couple* (1965), *Chapter Two* (1979), and *Biloxi Blues* (1984).	**1928:** The Kellogg-Briand Pact, outlawing war, is signed in Paris by 65 states.	**1920s:** Harlem Renaissance: African American literature, music, and art flourish in New York City. Langston Hughes (1902–1967), Zora Neale Hurston (1901–1960), Jean Toomer (1894–1967), and many others publish.
		c. 1928: Joseph Stalin comes to power in the Soviet Union.	**1925:** John T. Scopes, schoolteacher, is tried for violating a Tennessee law that prohibits the teaching of the theory of evolution.
	1930–1965: Lorraine Hansberry, African American playwright, author of *A Raisin in the Sun* (1959)	**1929:** The U.S. stock market crash begins the Great Depression.	**1926:** Ernest Hemingway (1899–1961) publishes *The Sun Also Rises*.
	1930: María Irene Fornés, Cuban playwright, born. Among her works are *Fefu and Her Friends* (1977) and *The Conduct of Life* (1985).	**1933:** New Deal economic reforms attempt to provide recovery from the Depression.	**1926:** Duke Ellington's (1899–1974) first records appear.
	1931: The Group Theatre is founded by Harold Clurman, Cheryl Crawford, and Lee Strasberg and operates for ten years.	**1933:** Adolf Hitler comes to power in Germany. German labor unions and political parties other than the Nazi Party are suppressed. Nazis erect their first concentration camp; persecution of Jews begins in Germany.	**1927:** *The Jazz Singer* is the first "talkie" movie.
			1927: Charles Lindbergh (1902–1974) makes the first solo nonstop transatlantic flight.
	1934: Wole Soyinka, Nigerian playwright, born. His works include *The Strong Breed* (1962) and *A Play of Giants* (1985).	**1935:** Roosevelt signs the U.S. Social Security Act.	**1927:** Virginia Woolf (1882–1941), English novelist, publishes *To the Lighthouse*.
	1934: Socialist realism is declared the official artistic policy in Soviet theater.	**1935:** The Nuremberg laws in Nazi Germany deprive German Jews of their citizenship and civil rights.	**1929:** William Faulkner (1897–1962) publishes *The Sound and the Fury*.
	1935: The American plays *Dead End* by Sidney Kingsley, *Winterset* by Maxwell Anderson, and *Waiting for Lefty* by Clifford Odets are produced.	**1935–1936:** Italy's conquest of Ethiopia	**1931:** Robert Frost (1874–1963) wins the Pulitzer Prize for *Collected Poems*.
		1936: Chiang Kai-shek declares war on Japan.	**1931:** The Empire State Building in New York City is completed.
			1932: Aldous Huxley (1894–1963) publishes *Brave New World*.

DATE	THEATER	POLITICAL	SOCIAL/CULTURAL
1900–1950 (continued)	**1935–1939:** The Federal Theatre Project operates in the United States under the auspices of the Works Progress Administration. **1936:** Federico García Lorca, Spanish playwright, writes *The House of Bernarda Alba*. **1937:** Peter Stein, influential German director, born. Among his important productions are *Peer Gynt* (1971) and the *Oresteia* (1980). **1938:** Antonín Artaud, French playwright and theorist, writes *The Theater and Its Double*.	**1936–1939:** Civil War in Spain results in Generalissimo Franco's consolidation of power. **1939:** Germany invades Poland. **1939:** Great Britain and France declare war on Germany and its allies. **1940:** Germany invades France. **1941:** Japan attacks Pearl Harbor, and the United States enters World War II. **1942:** Germany begins killing Jews and others in gas chambers. **1942:** The U.S. Army interns Japanese Americans in prison camps. **1944:** Allies liberate France. **1945:** Hitler commits suicide in Berlin, and Germany signs an unconditional surrender.	**1937:** Amelia Earhart (1897–1937), the first woman to fly across the Atlantic, vanishes over the Pacific Ocean. **1938:** Joe Louis (1914–1981), African American heavyweight boxer, defeats German Max Schmeling. **1943:** Penicillin is first used in the treatment of chronic diseases. **1940s:** The era of great musical theater begins in the United States, featuring the songs of Cole Porter (1891–1964), Richard Rodgers (1902–1979), and Oscar Hammerstein (1895–1960), among many others.
	1946: The Living Theatre is founded by Judith Malina and Julian Beck. **1947:** The Actors Studio is founded in New York City by Robert Lewis, Elia Kazan, and Cheryl Crawford. Lee Strasberg assumes control by 1948. **1947:** Beginning of the regional theater movement in the United States. Margo Jones opens an arena theater in Dallas, Nina Vance founds the Alley Theatre in Houston, and the Arena Stage opens in 1949 in Washington, D.C. **1949:** The Berliner Ensemble is founded in East Berlin.	**1945:** The United States drops atomic bombs on Hiroshima and Nagasaki, Japan. **1946:** Juan Perón is elected president of Argentina. **1947:** India proclaims independence and is divided into Pakistan and India. **1948:** The Republic of Israel is proclaimed by Jewish leaders in Palestine. **1948:** Indian leader Mahatma Gandhi is assassinated. **1949:** Mao Zedong announces the establishment of the People's Republic of China. **1949:** The North Atlantic Treaty Organization allies Canada, Western Europe, and the United States. **1949:** The apartheid system is established in South Africa.	**1947:** Jackie Robinson (1919–1972) becomes the first African American to sign a contract with a major league baseball club.

John Millington Synge

John Millington Synge (1871–1909) was one of the brilliant discoveries of the Irish Literary Renaissance, which was largely the product of Lady Gregory and William Butler Yeats, the codirectors of the Abbey Theatre in Dublin. The Abbey ranks as one of the most influential and successful national theaters in European history. From 1904 to the present, it has been devoted to producing plays by Irish writers, some of whom have gone on to be ranked among the greatest of their age. Besides Synge, Bernard Shaw, Lady Gregory, Yeats, Sean O'Casey, and Brian Friel are among the many whose names still loom impressively as having contributed to the reputation of the Abbey.

Synge was gifted in languages, with a degree in German from Trinity College, Dublin. Also a violinist, he went to Paris to study music and live the bohemian life of the artist. It was there in 1896 that Yeats and Lady Gregory met him, persuading him to return to Ireland and write plays for what was to become the Abbey. They convinced him to spend time in the Aran Islands, the wildest part of Ireland. Yeats felt the Arans were an important source of the literary energy of the nation because the Islanders' colorful language sounded like English filtered through Irish Gaelic.

Synge wrote a number of important plays within less than ten years. Most of them remain in the repertory of modern drama: *In the Shadow of the Glen* (1903), *Riders to the Sea* (1904), *The Well of the Saints* (1905), *The Tinker's Wedding* (1907), *The Playboy of the Western World* (1907), and *Deirdre of the Sorrows* (1910). With the exception of *The Tinker's Wedding*, which is so anticlerical that it has never been given a production at the Abbey, they are all still regularly produced there.

Synge was not always a popular playwright in Ireland. He felt that he faithfully represented peasant ways, but his Dublin audiences often protested that he insulted the Irish. Synge's kind of realism, while not especially harsh or critical, was an unvarnished view of the west of Ireland. The Abbey audiences wanted an idealized portrait of their countrymen and countrywomen, not straightforward and sometimes embarrassing portraits such as the one Synge offered them in *The Playboy of the Western World*. That play caused riots in the Abbey Theatre when first performed because of its nationalistic elements, its gritty, honest portrayal of country people, and for its use of "indecent" language. Regarding this last, supposedly his use of the image of "chosen females standing in their shifts" — shifts referring to women's slips or chemises — incensed audiences.

Synge was shocked at the uproar; he had never expected his play to stimulate such a response. The question of realism was probably not on Synge's mind at all. *Playboy* is less a realistic play than is *Riders to the Sea,* and both are rooted not in any effort to force the audience to look at life as it is really lived but rather in the mythic and symbolic forces that underlie everyone's experiences of heroism, life, and death. The deep roots of both plays are in Irish myth and the Christian religion. Synge was amazed to think that audiences ignored those important aspects and that they focused on other, less significant issues.

Synge's early death robbed world drama of a figure who certainly would have been among the greatest writers of the century. As it is, his work is remarkable; but in his last play, *Deirdre of the Sorrows,* which he never finished, we can see the promise of a body of work that would have taken its place with the best plays of our time.

Riders to the Sea

Riders to the Sea (1904) was the first success that Synge produced for the Abbey Theatre. In some ways it is still one of the most impressive plays to come out of the Irish Literary Renaissance. It is a one-act play, which the Abbey found congenial for its early programs, but its brevity in no way diminishes its power.

The play is set in the west of Ireland, the part least touched by English influence. Aran Islanders speak both Gaelic and English, but their English is marked with a very expressive and idiosyncratic flavor, which Synge tries to replicate in this play. The syntax of Synge's peasants benefits from his musician's ear as well as from his having lived in an inn in Wicklow, where he eavesdropped on the local Irish kitchen girls speaking naturally and unaffectedly.

Riders to the Sea owes much of its power to the local speech and the local way of life portrayed faithfully in the play. In his preface to *The Playboy of the Western World,* Synge credits Irish writers with the advantage of listening "for a few years more" to a language that is "rich as a nut." Maurya's long speeches at the end of *Riders to the Sea* are filled with the rhythms of the sea and the agony of someone who has suffered as much as the world can demand. Even the speeches of the lesser characters have an extraordinarily expressive flavor.

The drama depicts the sufferings of a superstitious peasant woman, yet it contains the same kinds of intensity of dramatic action found in Greek tragedies. It maintains a unity of time, place, character, and action, as well as an intense sense of fate and impending doom. Synge may well have begun developing a new genre of folk tragedy, just as Arthur Miller later began developing a genre of middle-class tragedy in *Death of a Salesman. Riders to the Sea* is permeated by a sense of fate; and Maurya, whose name is remarkably close in sound to *moira,* the Greek word for "fate," senses the inevitability of the premature death of her last son on the sea. The feeling of inevitability is heightened by the discussion between the daughters about the son Michael, who has been feared lost at sea, by their identification of his sock that was recovered from the sea, and by the willful insistence of the last son, Bartley, to ride the mares across the sea to the mainland, knowingly risking his life. (In fact, men did swim their animals from the islands to the mainland, and they often went out to meet the large boats that came near. Even today those waters are difficult, and Aran Islanders still use the same black curraghs their ancestors used to ferry themselves, their goods, and their livestock between the mainland and their homes.) Maurya's horrifying vision of Michael and Bartley on the mares confirms her premonitions and fears. It also provides an element of supernatural intensity.

Perhaps because of its tragic Greek pattern, *Riders to the Sea* has a mythic force. The sense of destiny that Maurya feels is built into her life. Her sense of resignation and deep faith help her grow in our imagination and give her a heroic dimension. Synge's approach to realism is much different from Ibsen's or Chekhov's. It is more elemental, based on the spiritual life of the folk as expressed in the eloquence of their language.

Riders to the Sea
in Performance

All of Synge's plays were written for the early Abbey Theatre, founded in 1904 by Lady Gregory and W. B. Yeats to perform Irish plays. At that time all performances were in Molesworth Hall, leased facilities. Synge's *In the Shadow of the Glen* was one of the first plays to be performed by the company, then known as the Irish National Theatre. The play opened in October 1903, coinciding with an Irish holiday, Samhain (pronounced *sow-in*). Although controversial, it was a success. *Riders to the Sea* was Synge's second play, produced in Molesworth Hall in February 1904. At this time the Abbey had already attracted some excellent actors. Bartley was played by W. G. Fay, who was instrumental in shaping the Abbey. Sarah Allgood, destined to become a standard player in American films in the 1930s and 1940s, played Cathleen. The production was well received by press and public.

Riders to the Sea has usually been paired with other Irish plays in production. The Abbey Theatre Company still produces the play regularly and often takes it on tour. One of the most memorable tours was in 1957 when the Abbey brought the play to the tiny Theatre East in New York. Despite the theater's small size, the effect of the play, which had not been seen in an Abbey performance in the United States since 1911, was electrifying. The finest Irish actress of the age, Siobhan McKenna, played Maurya.

Riders to the Sea enjoys frequent production by both high school and college students. Its brevity and power make it a strong vehicle for amateur productions.

John Millington Synge (1871–1909)
RIDERS TO THE SEA

1904

Persons in the Play

MAURYA (*an old woman*)
BARTLEY (*her son*)
CATHLEEN (*her daughter*)
NORA (*a younger daughter*)
MEN *and* WOMEN

Scene: *An Island off the West of Ireland.*

(*Cottage kitchen, with nets, oilskins, spinning wheel, some new boards standing by the wall, etc. Cathleen, a girl of about twenty, finishes kneading cake, and puts it down in the pot-oven by the fire; then wipes her hands, and begins to spin at the wheel. Nora, a young girl, puts her head in at the door.*)

NORA (*in a low voice*): Where is she?

CATHLEEN: She's lying down, God help her, and may be sleeping, if she's able.

(*Nora comes in softly and takes a bundle from under her shawl.*)

CATHLEEN (*spinning the wheel rapidly*): What is it you have?

NORA: The young priest is after bringing them. It's a shirt and a plain stocking were got off a drowned man in Donegal.

(*Cathleen stops her wheel with a sudden movement, and leans out to listen.*)

NORA: We're to find out if it's Michael's they are, some time herself will be down looking by the sea.

CATHLEEN: How would they be Michael's, Nora? How would he go the length of that way to the far north?

NORA: The young priest says he's known the like of it. "If it's Michael's they are," says he, "you can tell herself he's got a clean burial by the grace of God, and if they're not his, let no one say a word about them, for she'll be getting her death," says he, "with crying and lamenting."

(*The door which Nora half closed is blown open by a gust of wind.*)

CATHLEEN (*looking out anxiously*): Did you ask him would he stop Bartley going this day with the horses to the Galway fair?

NORA: "I won't stop him," says he, "but let you not be afraid. Herself does be saying prayers half through the night, and the Almighty God won't leave her destitute," says he, "with no son living."

CATHLEEN: Is the sea bad by the white rocks, Nora?

NORA: Middling bad, God help us. There's a great roaring in the west, and it's worse it'll be getting when the tide's turned to the wind. (*She goes over to the table with the bundle.*) Shall I open it now?

CATHLEEN: Maybe she'd wake up on us, and come in before we'd done. (*Coming to the table.*) It's a long time we'll be, and the two of us crying.

NORA (*goes to the inner door and listens*): She's moving about on the bed. She'll be coming in a minute.

CATHLEEN: Give me the ladder, and I'll put them up in the turf-loft, the way she won't know of them at all, and maybe when the tide turns she'll be going down to see would he be floating from the east.

(*They put the ladder against the gable of the chimney; Cathleen goes up a few steps and hides the bundle in the turf-loft. Maurya comes from the inner room.*)

MAURYA (*looking up at Cathleen and speaking querulously*): Isn't it turf enough you have for this day and evening?

CATHLEEN: There's a cake baking at the fire for a short space (*throwing down the turf*) and Bartley will want it when the tide turns if he goes to Connemara.

(*Nora picks up the turf and puts it round the pot-oven.*)

MAURYA (*sitting down on a stool at the fire*): He won't go this day with the wind rising from the south and west. He won't go this day, for the young priest will stop him surely.

NORA: He'll not stop him, mother, and I heard Eamon Simon and Stephen Pheety and Colum Shawn saying he would go.

MAURYA: Where is he itself?

NORA: He went down to see would there be another boat sailing in the week, and I'm thinking it won't be long till he's here now, for the tide's turning at the green head, and the hooker's tacking from the east.

CATHLEEN: I hear some one passing the big stones.

NORA (*looking out*): He's coming now, and he in a hurry.

BARTLEY (*comes in and looks round the room. Speaking sadly and quietly*): Where is the bit of new rope, Cathleen, was bought in Connemara?

CATHLEEN (*coming down*): Give it to him, Nora; it's on a nail by the white boards. I hung it up this morning, for the pig with the black feet was eating it.

NORA (*giving him a rope*): Is that it, Bartley?

MAURYA: You'd do right to leave that rope, Bartley, hanging by the boards. (*Bartley takes the rope.*) It will be wanting in this place, I'm telling you, if Michael is washed up tomorrow morning, or the

900

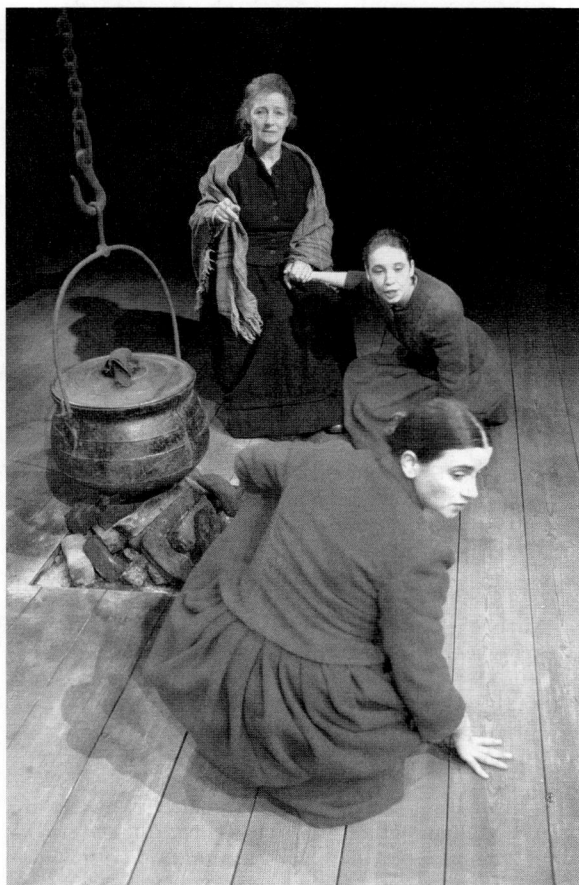

The fateful first scene of *Riders to the Sea* in the 1998 Royal Shakespeare Company / The Other Place production directed by John Crowley. Mairead McKinley (foreground) and Aislinn Mangan (background) play the daughters, Cathleen and Nora. Stella McCusker plays their mother, Maurya.

next morning, or any morning in the week, for it's a deep grave we'll make him by the grace of God.

BARTLEY (*beginning to work with the rope*): I've no halter the way I can ride down on the mare, and I must go now quickly. This is the one boat going for two weeks or beyond it, and the fair will be a good fair for horses I heard them saying below.

MAURYA: It's a hard thing they'll be saying below if the body is washed up and there's no man in it to make the coffin, and I after giving a big price for the finest white boards you'd find in Connemara.

(*She looks round at the boards.*)

BARTLEY: How would it be washed up, and we after looking each day for nine days, and a strong wind blowing a while back from the west and south?

MAURYA: If it wasn't found itself, that wind is raising the sea, and there was a star up against the moon, and it rising in the night. If it was a hundred horses, or a thousand horses you had itself, what is the price of a thousand horses against a son where there is one son only?

BARTLEY (*working at the halter, to Cathleen*): Let you go down each day, and see the sheep aren't jumping in on the rye, and if the jobber comes you can sell the pig with the black feet if there is a good price going.

MAURYA: How would the like of her get a good price for a pig?

BARTLEY (*to Cathleen*): If the west wind holds with the last bit of the moon let you and Nora get up weed enough for another cock for the kelp. It's hard set we'll be from this day with no one in it but one man to work.

MAURYA: It's hard set we'll be surely the day you're drownd'd with the rest. What way will I live and the girls with me, and I an old woman looking for the grave?

(*Bartley lays down the halter, takes off his old coat, and puts on a newer one of the same flannel.*)

BARTLEY (*to Nora*): Is she coming to the pier?

NORA (*looking out*): She's passing the green head and letting fall her sails.

BARTLEY (*getting his purse and tobacco*): I'll have half an hour to go down, and you'll see me coming again in two days, or in three days, or maybe in four days if the wind is bad.

MAURYA (*turning round to the fire, and putting her shawl over her head*): Isn't it a hard and cruel man won't hear a word from an old woman, and she holding him from the sea?

CATHLEEN: It's the life of a young man to be going on the sea, and who would listen to an old woman with one thing and she saying it over?

BARTLEY (*taking the halter*): I must go now quickly. I'll ride down on the red mare, and the gray pony'll run behind me. . . . The blessing of God on you.

(*He goes out.*)

MAURYA (*crying out as he is in the door*): He's gone now, God spare us, and we'll not see him again. He's gone now, and when the black night is falling I'll have no son left me in the world.

CATHLEEN: Why wouldn't you give him your blessing and he looking round in the door? Isn't it sorrow enough is on every one in this house without your sending him out with an unlucky word behind him, and a hard word in his ear?

(*Maurya takes up the tongs and begins raking the fire aimlessly without looking round.*)

NORA (*turning toward her*): You're taking away the turf from the cake.

CATHLEEN (*crying out*): The Son of God forgive us, Nora, we're after forgetting his bit of bread.

(*She comes over to the fire.*)

NORA: And it's destroyed he'll be going till dark night, and he after eating nothing since the sun went up.

CATHLEEN (*turning the cake out of the oven*): It's destroyed he'll be, surely. There's no sense left on any person in a house where an old woman will be talking forever.

(*Maurya sways herself on her stool.*)

CATHLEEN (*cutting off some of the bread and rolling it in a cloth; to Maurya*): Let you go down now to the spring well and give him this and he passing. You'll see him then and the dark word will be broken, and you can say "God speed you," the way he'll be easy in his mind.

MAURYA (*taking the bread*): Will I be in it as soon as himself?

CATHLEEN: If you go now quickly.

MAURYA (*standing up unsteadily*): It's hard set I am to walk.

CATHLEEN (*looking at her anxiously*): Give her the stick, Nora, or maybe she'll slip on the big stones.

NORA: What stick?

CATHLEEN: The stick Michael brought from Connemara.

MAURYA (*taking a stick Nora gives her*): In the big world the old people do be leaving things after them for their sons and children, but in this place it is the young men do be leaving things behind for them that do be old.

(*She goes out slowly. Nora goes over to the ladder.*)

CATHLEEN: Wait, Nora, maybe she'd turn back quickly. She's that sorry, God help her, you wouldn't know the thing she'd do.

NORA: Is she gone round by the bush?

CATHLEEN (*looking out*): She's gone now. Throw it down quickly, for the Lord knows when she'll be out of it again.

NORA (*getting the bundle from the loft*): The young priest said he'd be passing tomorrow, and we might go down and speak to him below if it's Michael's they are surely.

CATHLEEN (*taking the bundle*): Did he say what way they were found?

NORA (*coming down*): "There were two men," says he, "and they rowing round with poteen before the cocks crowed, and the oar of one of them caught the body, and they passing the black cliffs of the north."

CATHLEEN (*trying to open the bundle*): Give me a knife, Nora, the string's perished with the salt water, and there's a black knot on it you wouldn't loosen in a week.

NORA (*giving her a knife*): I've heard tell it was a long way to Donegal.

CATHLEEN (*cutting the string*): It is surely. There was a man in here a while ago — the man sold us that knife — and he said if you set off walking from the rocks beyond, it would be seven days you'd be in Donegal.

NORA: And what time would a man take, and he floating?

(*Cathleen opens the bundle and takes out a bit of a stocking. They look at them eagerly.*)

CATHLEEN (*in a low voice*): The Lord spare us, Nora! isn't it a queer hard thing to say if it's his they are surely?

NORA: I'll get his shirt off the hook the way we can put the one flannel on the other. (*She looks through some clothes hanging in the corner.*) It's not with them, Cathleen, and where will it be?

CATHLEEN: I'm thinking Bartley put it on him in the morning, for his own shirt was heavy with the salt in it (*pointing to the corner*). There's a bit of a sleeve was of the same stuff. Give me that and it will do.

(*Nora brings it to her and they compare the flannel.*)

CATHLEEN: It's the same stuff, Nora; but if it is itself aren't there great rolls of it in the shops of Galway, and isn't it many another man may have a shirt of it as well as Michael himself?

NORA (*who has taken up the stocking and counted the stitches, crying out*): It's Michael, Cathleen, it's Michael; God spare his soul, and what will herself say when she hears this story, and Bartley on the sea?

CATHLEEN (*taking the stocking*): It's a plain stocking.

NORA: It's the second one of the third pair I knitted, and I put up three score stitches, and I dropped four of them.

CATHLEEN (*counts the stitches*): It's that number is in it. (*Crying out.*) Ah, Nora, isn't it a bitter thing to think of him floating that way to the far north, and no one to keen him but the black hags that do be flying on the sea?

NORA (*swinging herself round, and throwing out her arms on the clothes*): And isn't it a pitiful thing when there is nothing left of a man who was a great rower and fisher, but a bit of an old shirt and a plain stocking?

CATHLEEN (*after an instant*): Tell me is herself coming, Nora? I hear a little sound on the path.

NORA (*looking out*): She is, Cathleen. She's coming up to the door.

CATHLEEN: Put these things away before she'll come in. Maybe it's easier she'll be after giving her blessing to Bartley, and we won't let on we've heard anything the time he's on the sea.

NORA (*helping Cathleen to close the bundle*): We'll put them here in the corner.

(*They put them into a hole in the chimney corner. Cathleen goes back to the spinning wheel.*)

NORA: Will she see it was crying I was?

CATHLEEN: Keep your back to the door the way the light'll not be on you.

(*Nora sits down at the chimney corner, with her back to the door. Maurya comes in very slowly, without looking at the girls, and goes over to her stool at the other side of the fire. The cloth with the bread is still in her hand. The girls look at each other, and Nora points to the bundle of bread.*)

CATHLEEN (*after spinning for a moment*): You didn't give him his bit of bread?

(*Maurya begins to keen softly, without turning round.*)

CATHLEEN: Did you see him riding down?

(*Maurya goes on keening.*)

CATHLEEN (*a little impatiently*): God forgive you; isn't it a better thing to raise your voice and tell what you seen, than to be making lamentation for a thing that's done? Did you see Bartley, I'm saying to you.

MAURYA (*with a weak voice*): My heart's broken from this day.

CATHLEEN (*as before*): Did you see Bartley?

MAURYA: I seen the fearfulest thing.

CATHLEEN (*leaves her wheel and looks out*): God forgive you; he's riding the mare now over the green head, and the gray pony behind him.

MAURYA (*starts, so that her shawl falls back from her head and shows her white tossed hair. With a frightened voice*): The gray pony behind him.

CATHLEEN (*coming to the fire*): What is it ails you, at all?

MAURYA (*speaking very slowly*): I've seen the fearfulest thing any person has seen, since the day Bride Dara seen the dead man with the child in his arms.

CATHLEEN AND NORA: Uah.

(*They crouch down in front of the old woman at the fire.*)

NORA: Tell us what it is you seen.

MAURYA: I went down to the spring well, and I stood there saying a prayer to myself. Then Bartley came along, and he riding on the red mare with the gray pony behind him. (*She puts up her hands, as if to hide something from her eyes.*) The Son of God spare us, Nora!

CATHLEEN: What is it you seen?

MAURYA: I seen Michael himself.

CATHLEEN (*speaking softly*): You did not, mother. It wasn't Michael you seen, for his body is after being found in the far north, and he's got a clean burial by the grace of God.

MAURYA (*a little defiantly*): I'm after seeing him this day, and he riding and galloping. Bartley came first on the red mare; and I tried to say "God speed you," but something choked the words in my throat. He went by quickly; and "the blessing of God on you," says he, and I could say nothing. I looked up then, and I crying, at the gray pony, and there was Michael upon it — with fine clothes on him, and new shoes on his feet.

CATHLEEN (*begins to keen*): It's destroyed we are from this day. It's destroyed, surely.

NORA: Didn't the young priest say the Almighty God wouldn't leave her destitute with no son living?

MAURYA (*in a low voice, but clearly*): It's little the like of him knows of the sea. . . . Bartley will be lost now, and let you call in Eamon and make me a good coffin out of the white boards, for I won't live after them. I've had a husband, and a husband's father, and six sons in this house — six fine men, though it was a hard birth I had with every one of them and they coming to the world — and some of them were found and some of them were not found, but they're gone now the lot of them. . . . There were Stephen, and Shawn, were lost in the great wind, and found after in the Bay of Gregory of the Golden Mouth, and carried up the two of them on the one plank, and in by that door.

(*She pauses for a moment, the girls start as if they heard something through the door that is half open behind them.*)

NORA (*in a whisper*): Did you hear that, Cathleen? Did you hear a noise in the northeast?

CATHLEEN (*in a whisper*): There's some one after crying out by the seashore.

MAURYA (*continues without hearing anything*): There was Sheamus and his father, and his own father again, were lost in a dark night, and not a stick or sign was seen of them when the sun went up. There was Patch after was drowned out of a curagh° that turned over. I was sitting here with Bartley, and he a baby, lying on my two knees, and I seen two women, and three women, and four women coming in, and they crossing themselves, and not saying a word. I looked out then, and there were men coming after them, and they holding a thing in the half of a red sail, and water dripping out of it — it was a dry day, Nora — and leaving a track to the door.

(*She pauses again with her hand stretched out toward the door. It opens softly and old women begin to come in, crossing themselves on the threshold, and kneeling down in front of the stage with red petticoats over their heads.*)

MAURYA (*half in a dream, to Cathleen*): Is it Patch or Michael, or what is it at all?

CATHLEEN: Michael is after being found in the far north, and when he is found there how could he be here in this place?

MAURYA: There does be a power of young men floating round in the sea, and what way would they know if it was Michael they had, or another man like him, for when a man is nine days in the sea, and the wind blowing, it's hard set his own mother would be to say what man was it.

CATHLEEN: It's Michael, God spare him, for they're after sending us a bit of his clothes from the far north.

(*She reaches out and hands Maurya the clothes that belonged to Michael. Maurya stands up slowly and takes them in her hands. Nora looks out.*)

curagh: A small boat with a hide- or tarpaulin-covered frame.

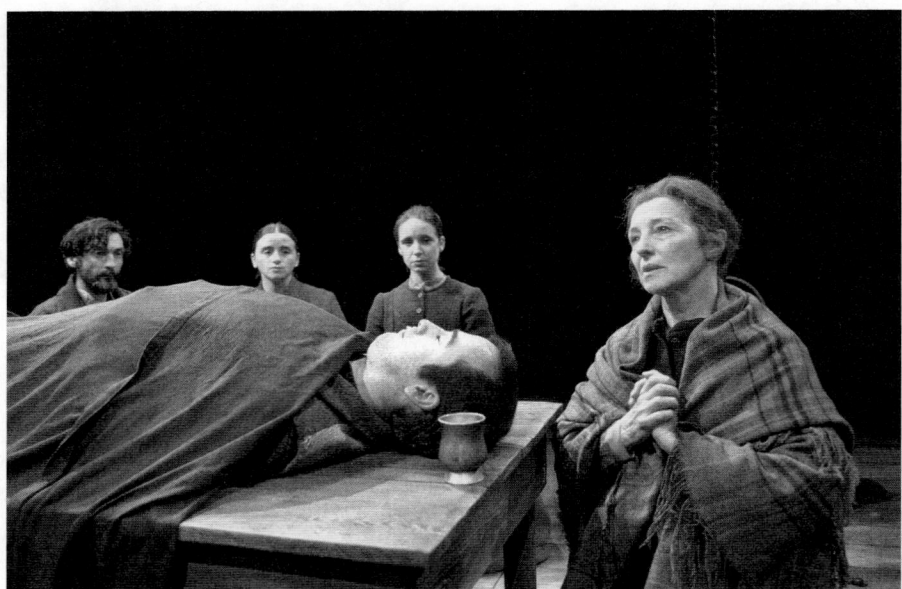

Maurya (Stella McCusker) mourns the death of her last son, Bartley (Stephen Kennedy).

NORA: They're carrying a thing among them and there's water dripping out of it and leaving a track by the big stones.

CATHLEEN (*in a whisper to the women who have come in*): Is it Bartley it is?

ONE OF THE WOMEN: It is surely, God rest his soul.

(*Two younger women come in and pull out the table. Then men carry in the body of Bartley, laid on a plank, with a bit of a sail over it, and lay it on the table.*)

CATHLEEN (*to the women, as they are doing so*): What way was he drowned?

ONE OF THE WOMEN: The gray pony knocked him into the sea, and he was washed out where there is a great surf on the white rocks.

(*Maurya has gone over and knelt down at the head of the table. The women are keening softly and swaying themselves with a slow movement. Cathleen and Nora kneel at the other end of the table. The men kneel near the door.*)

MAURYA (*raising her head and speaking as if she did not see the people around her*): They're all gone now, and there isn't anything more the sea can do to me. . . . I'll have no call now to be up crying and praying when the wind breaks from the south, and you can hear the surf is in the east, and the surf is in the west, making a great stir with the two noises, and they hitting one on the other. I'll have no call now to be going down and getting Holy Water in the dark nights after Samhain,° and I won't care what way the

Samhain: Feast of All Saints, November 1.

sea is when the other women will be keening. (*To Nora.*) Give me the Holy Water, Nora, there's a small sup still on the dresser.

(*Nora gives it to her.*)

MAURYA (*drops Michael's clothes across Bartley's feet, and sprinkles the Holy Water over him*): It isn't that I haven't prayed for you, Bartley, to the Almighty God. It isn't that I haven't said prayers in the dark night till you wouldn't know what I'll be saying; but it's a great rest I'll have now, and it's time surely. It's a great rest I'll have now, and great sleeping in the long nights after Samhain, if it's only a bit of wet flour we do have to eat, and maybe a fish that would be stinking.

(*She kneels down again, crossing herself, and saying prayers under her breath.*)

CATHLEEN (*to an old man*): Maybe yourself and Eamon would make a coffin when the sun rises. We have fine white boards herself bought, God help her, thinking Michael would be found, and I have a new cake you can eat while you'll be working.

THE OLD MAN (*looking at the boards*): Are there nails with them?

CATHLEEN: There are not, Colum; we didn't think of the nails.

ANOTHER MAN: It's a great wonder she wouldn't think of the nails, and all the coffins she's seen made already.

CATHLEEN: It's getting old she is, and broken.

(*Maurya stands up again very slowly and spreads out the pieces of Michael's clothes beside the body, sprinkling them with the last of the Holy Water.*)

NORA (*in a whisper to Cathleen*): She's quiet now and easy; but the day Michael was drowned you could hear her crying out from this to the spring well. It's fonder she was of Michael, and would any one have thought that?

CATHLEEN (*slowly and clearly*): An old woman will be soon tired with anything she will do, and isn't it nine days herself is after crying and keening, and making great sorrow in the house?

MAURYA (*puts the empty cup mouth downward on the table, and lays her hands together on Bartley's feet*): They're all together this time, and the end is come. May the Almighty God have mercy on Bartley's soul, and on Michael's soul, and on the souls of Sheamus and Patch, and Stephen and Shawn (*bending her head*); and may He have mercy on my soul, Nora, and on the soul of every one is left living in the world.

(*She pauses, and the keen rises a little more loudly from the women, then sinks away.*)

MAURYA (*continuing*): Michael has a clean burial in the far north, by the grace of the Almighty God. Bartley will have a fine coffin out of the white boards, and a deep grave surely. What more can we want than that? No man at all can be living forever, and we must be satisfied.

(*She kneels down again and the curtain falls slowly.*)

COMMENTARY

John Millington Synge (1871–1909)
FROM *THE ARAN ISLANDS*   *1907*

> *For several weeks a year from 1898 to 1902, Synge traveled to the Aran Islands, off the west coast of Ireland near Galway. He spent part of his time learning Gaelic and part of it keeping a journal. He wrote mostly about his experiences in this remote part of Ireland, so distant from Dublin civilization that Synge sometimes felt he was in a time warp. This excerpt, published in 1907 but written before* Riders to the Sea, *portrays the people he met on the Aran Islands. Synge said he learned how people speak on the islands in part from overhearing servant girls, such as those he describes here, talking among themselves in the kitchen beneath his room. His musical training allowed him to catch the intonations of English as it was spoken by native Gaelic speakers.*

I am settled at last on Inishmaan in a small cottage with a continual drone of Gaelic coming from the kitchen that opens into my room.

Early this morning the man of the house came over for me with a four-oared curagh° — that is, a curagh with four rowers and four oars on either side, as each man uses two — and we set off a little before noon.

It gave me a moment of exquisite satisfaction to find myself moving away from civilization in this rude canvas canoe of a model that has served primitive races since men first went on the sea.

We had to stop for a moment at a hulk that is anchored in the bay, to make some arrangements for the fish-curing of the middle island, and my crew called out as

curagh: Small boat in the general shape of a canoe.

soon as we were within earshot that they had a man with them who had been in France a month from this day.

When we started again, a small sail was run up in the bow, and we set off across the sound with a leaping oscillation that had no resemblance to the heavy movement of a boat.

The sail is only used as an aid, so the men continued to row after it had gone up, and as they occupied the four cross-seats I lay on the canvas at the stern and the frame of slender laths, which bent and quivered as the waves passed under them.

When we set off it was a brilliant morning of April, and the green, glittering waves seemed to toss the canoe among themselves, yet as we drew nearer this island a sudden thunderstorm broke out behind the rocks we were approaching, and lent a momentary tumult to this still vein of the Atlantic.

We landed at a small pier, from which a rude track leads up to the village between small fields and bare sheets of rock like those in Aranmor. The youngest son of my boatman, a boy of about seventeen, who is to be my teacher and guide, was waiting for me at the pier and guided me to his house, while the men settled the curagh and followed slowly with my baggage.

My room is at one end of the cottage, with a boarded floor and ceiling, and two windows opposite each other. Then there is the kitchen with earth floor and open rafters, and two doors opposite each other opening into the open air, but no windows. Beyond it there are two small rooms of half the width of the kitchen with one window apiece.

The kitchen itself, where I will spend most of my time, is full of beauty and distinction. The red dresses of the women who cluster round the fire on their stools give a glow of almost Eastern richness, and the walls have been toned by the turf-smoke to a soft brown that blends with the grey earth-colour of the floor. Many sorts of fishing-tackle, and the nets and oilskins of the men, are hung upon the walls or among the open rafters; and right overhead, under the thatch, there is a whole cowskin from which they make pampooties.°

Every article on these islands has an almost personal character, which gives this simple life, where all art is unknown, something of the artistic beauty of medieval life. The curaghs and spinning-wheels, the tiny wooden barrels that are still much used in the place of earthenware, the homemade cradles, churns, and baskets, are all full of individuality, and being made from materials that are common here, yet to some extent peculiar to the island, they seem to exist as a natural link between the people and the world that is about them.

The simplicity and unity of the dress increases in another way the local air of beauty. The women wear red petticoats and jackets of the island wool stained with madder, to which they usually add a plaid shawl twisted round their chests and tied at the back. When it rains they throw another petticoat over their heads with the waistband round their faces, or, if they are young, they use a heavy shawl like those worn in Galway. Occasionally other wraps are worn, and during the thunderstorm I arrived in I saw several girls with men's waistcoats buttoned round their bodies. Their skirts do not come much below the knee, and show their powerful legs in the heavy indigo stockings with which they are all provided.

The men wear three colours: the natural wool, indigo, and a grey flannel that is woven of alternate threads of indigo and the natural wool. In Aranmor many of the

pampooties: Soft slippers of sealskin or rawhide.

younger men have adopted the usual fisherman's jersey, but I have only seen one on this island.

As flannel is cheap — the women spin the yarn from the wool of their own sheep, and it is then woven by a weaver in Kilronan for fourpence a yard — the men seem to wear an indefinite number of waistcoats and woollen drawers one over the other. They are usually surprised at the lightness of my own dress, and one old man I spoke to for a minute on the pier, when I came ashore, asked me if I was not cold with "my little clothes."

As I sat in the kitchen to dry the spray from my coat, several men who had seen me walking up came in to talk to me, usually murmuring on the threshold, "The blessing of God on this place," or some similar words.

The courtesy of the old woman of the house is singularly attractive, and though I could not understand much of what she said — she has no English — I could see with how much grace she motioned each visitor to a chair, or stool, according to his age, and said a few words to him till he drifted into our English conversation.

For the moment my own arrival is the chief subject of interest, and the men who come in are eager to talk to me.

Some of them express themselves more correctly than the ordinary peasant, others use the Gaelic idioms continually and substitute "he" or "she" for "it," as the neuter pronoun is not found in modern Irish.

A few of the men have a curiously full vocabulary, others know only the commonest words in English, and are driven to ingenious devices to express their meaning. Of all the subjects we can talk of war seems their favourite, and the conflict between America and Spain° is causing a great deal of excitement. Nearly all the families have relations who had to cross the Atlantic, and all eat of the flour and bacon that is brought from the United States, so they have a vague fear that "if anything happened to America," their own island would cease to be habitable.

Foreign languages are another favourite topic, and as these men are bilingual they have a fair notion of what it means to speak and think in many different idioms. Most of the strangers they see on the islands are philological students, and the people have been led to conclude that linguistic studies, particularly Gaelic studies, are the chief occupation of the outside world.

"I have seen Frenchmen, and Danes, and Germans," said one man, "and there does be a power of Irish books along with them, and they reading them better than ourselves. Believe me there are few rich men now in the world who are not studying the Gaelic."

They sometimes ask me the French for simple phrases, and when they have listened to the intonation for a moment, most of them are able to reproduce it with admirable precision.

No one who has not lived for weeks among these grey clouds and seas can realize the joy with which the eye rests on the red dresses of the women, especially when a number of them are to be found together, as happened early this morning.

I heard that the young cattle were to be shipped for a fair on the mainland, which is to take place in a few days, and I went down on the pier, a little after dawn, to watch them.

conflict between America and Spain: Spanish-American War, 1898.

The bay was shrouded in the greys of coming rain, yet the thinness of the cloud threw a silvery light on the sea, and an unusual depth of blue to the mountains of Connemara.

As I was going across the sandhills one dun-sailed hooker° glided slowly out to begin her voyage, and another beat up to the pier. Troops of red cattle, driven mostly by the women, were coming up from several directions, forming, with the green of the long tract of grass that separates the sea from the rocks, a new unity of colour.

The pier itself was crowded with bullocks and a great number of the people. I noticed one extraordinary girl in the throng who seemed to exert an authority on all who came near her. Her curiously-formed nostrils and narrow chin gave her a witch-like expression, yet the beauty of her hair and skin made her singularly attractive.

When the empty hooker was made fast its deck was still many feet below the level of the pier, so the animals were slung down by a rope from the mast-head, with much struggling and confusion. Some of them made wild efforts to escape, nearly carrying their owners with them into the sea, but they were handled with wonderful dexterity, and there was no mishap.

When the open hold was filled with young cattle, packed as tightly as they could stand, the owners with their wives or sisters, who go with them to prevent extravagance in Galway, jumped down on the deck, and the voyage was begun. Immediately afterwards a rickety old hooker beat up with turf° from Connemara, and while she was unlading all the men sat along the edge of the pier and made remarks upon the rottenness of her timber till the owners grew wild with rage.

The tide was now too low for more boats to come to the pier, so a move was made to a strip of sand towards the southeast, where the rest of the cattle were shipped through the surf. Here the hooker was anchored about eighty yards from the shore, and a curagh was rowed round to tow out the animals. Each bullock was caught in its turn and girded with a sling of rope by which it could be hoisted on board. Another rope was fastened to the horns and passed out to a man in the stern of the curagh. Then the animal was forced down through the surf and out of its depth before it had much time to struggle. Once fairly swimming, it was towed out to the hooker and dragged on board in a half-drowned condition.

The freedom of the sand seemed to give a stronger spirit of revolt, and some of the animals were only caught after a dangerous struggle. The first attempt was not always successful, and I saw one three-year-old lift two men with his horns, and drag another fifty yards along the sand by his tail before he was subdued.

While this work was going on a crowd of girls and women collected on the edge of the cliff and kept shouting down a confused babble of satire and praise.

When I came back to the cottage I found that among the women who had gone to the mainland was a daughter of the old woman's, and that her baby of about nine months had been left in the care of its grandmother.

As I came in she was busy getting ready my dinner, and old Pat Dirane, who usually comes at this hour, was rocking the cradle. It is made of clumsy wicker-work, with two pieces of rough wood fastened underneath to serve as rockers, and all the time I am in my room I can hear it bumping on the floor with extraordinary vio-

hooker: A commercial fishing boat.
turf: Peat used for fuel.

lence. When the baby is awake it sprawls on the floor, and the old woman sings it a variety of inarticulate lullabies that have much musical charm.

Another daughter, who lives at home, has gone to the fair also, so the old woman has both the baby and myself to take care of as well as a crowd of chickens that live in a hole beside the fire. Often when I want tea, or when the old woman goes for water, I have to take my own turn at rocking the cradle.

Susan Glaspell

Susan Glaspell (1876–1948) is an important figure in early twentieth-century American drama. Through her influence, serious theater began to thrive in an environment used to musicals, sentimental comedies, and fashionable revivals. She was born in Davenport, Iowa, to Irish immigrant parents and grew up writing. After graduating from Drake University, she took a job as a reporter and by 1901 had become a full-time writer. Her first novel, *The Glory of the Conquered: The Story of a Great Love,* published in 1909, earned her enough to spend a year in Paris. *The Visioning,* which followed in 1911, was set on an army base and presented a less sentimentalized world than did her first book. She published her first collection of stories, *Lifted Masks,* in 1912. Her best novel, *Fidelity,* was published in 1915, after she had returned to the United States.

In 1908 Glaspell first met her future husband, George Cram (Jig) Cook, a traveled intellectual and Harvard graduate who was teaching at Iowa University. After the initial meeting, Cook eventually married someone else, but five years later was divorced. Following Glaspell's return from Europe in 1913, they were reintroduced by mutual friends; they now felt that they had been fated for each other. They settled on Cape Cod and, with Mary Heaton Vorse, founded the Provincetown Players. The theater company became a highly influential platform for a number of important American writers, such as Djuna Barnes, Edna Ferber, and Edna St. Vincent Millay. Eugene O'Neill, a prominent member of the Provincetown Players, played roles in Glaspell's works, including *Trifles* (1916). Her earliest play — first produced in her living room, and then moved to the Provincetown Playhouse — was *Suppressed Desires* (1915), a spoof on the rage for using Freudian theories to explain everyday life. In a letter to the *New York Times* (February 13, 1920) she said that the play "is having fun with the people who went off their heads about psychoanalysis — went 'bugs'— when this subject reached the first circle in New York to know of it."

Glaspell's one-act plays, including *Close the Book* (1917), *A Woman's Honor* (1918), and *Tickless Time* (1919), were collected in 1920. Her first full-length play, *Bernice* (1919), centered on interpreting the character of a dead woman. Its success led to another full-length play, *The Verge* (1921), about a woman who tries to make a new reality around herself and begins with creating new kinds of plants. Some critics saw the protagonist as an admirable new woman; others saw her as neurotic. *The Inheritors* (1921), also a full-length drama, focuses on the third-generation inheritors of a Midwestern college who clash because one family has liberal views and one has conservative views. Her last play, winner of the Pulitzer Prize, was *Alison's House* (1930), based on the life of Emily Dickinson. The latter part of Glaspell's life was spent writing fiction, concentrating on four novels set in the Midwest about the struggles of women to maintain their ideals and values.

Jig Cook, a writer himself, and a partner in many of Glaspell's ventures, spent the last two years of his life living in Delphi, Greece, in the manner of the peasants living on Mount Parnassus near the temple of Apollo. He died in 1924, and when Glaspell returned to the United States she wrote a memoir of their life together called *The Road to the Temple*. In 1925 she broke with the Provincetown Players, who had moved in directions she did not approve of under the directorship of Eugene O'Neill. O'Neill tried to mollify Glaspell, but she never accepted his use of the theater company she and her husband had cofounded. When she died in 1948, she and O'Neill were essentially unreconciled.

TRIFLES

Trifles (1916) was apparently written as a companion piece for Eugene O'Neill's first produced play, the one-act *Bound East for Cardiff*. The two were put together to make a complete evening presentation. In one sense *Trifles* is a murder mystery, but in another it is a critique of the gender-rigid attitudes of the officials whose responsibility it is to investigate the death of John Wright. Its main character, Minnie Foster Wright, is never presented, only described as a sweet woman who loved to sing when she was young but who married a man who slowly stifled her joy in living.

The setting of the play is a kitchen where the women, Mrs. Peters and Mrs. Hale, remain throughout the action. They examine the condition of the room and by extension, the condition of Minnie Foster Wright. The men, examining the crime scene, the upstairs bedroom, spend much of the time offstage. They feel that they are examining the important evidence; yet when they return with their findings, they are unable to understand what led to the death of John Wright, who to them seems quite a normal farmer.

The women, however, by examining the messy condition of the kitchen, the state of Minnie's preserves, and the quilt she was working on, begin to understand the motive behind Wright's murder. When they get to the dead body of the songbird Minnie had valued, they understand things in a way that the men cannot. The men observe that women are concerned with trifles, things of no importance. But the truth is that the women understand the fate of Minnie Foster Wright and John Wright in a way that would be almost impossible for the men, given their sense of what is significant and what is a trifle.

In many ways the play is a study of gender differences and the way men's expectations and their sense of reality can distort the truth and deform a woman's life. In 1917 Glaspell wrote a short story, using all the same material, called "A Jury of Her Peers," implying that the only peers of Minnie Foster Wright would be women like Mrs. Hale and Mrs. Peters. In 1917, however, women could not vote and in most states could not serve on juries.

Trifles in Performance

The original production included Eugene O'Neill among its cast members and received a positive response, but after Glaspell's death most of her work fell out of fashion. *Trifles* was neglected until the early 1960s, when feminist interest helped revive her plays. Teacher and writer Sylvan Barnet included the play in his drama anthology, helping to bring it to the attention of contemporary viewers. Now produced most often by school and college groups, the play enjoys considerable popularity.

Susan Glaspell (1876–1948)

TRIFLES

1916

Characters

GEORGE HENDERSON, *county attorney*
HENRY PETERS, *sheriff*
LEWIS HALE, *a neighboring farmer*
MRS. PETERS
MRS. HALE

Scene: *The kitchen in the now abandoned farmhouse of John Wright, a gloomy kitchen, and left without having been put in order — the walls covered with a faded wall paper. Down right is a door leading to the parlor. On the right wall above this door is a built-in kitchen cupboard with shelves in the upper portion and drawers below. In the rear wall at right, up two steps is a door opening onto stairs leading to the second floor. In the rear wall at left is a door to the shed and from there to the outside. Between these two doors is an old-fashioned black iron stove. Running along the left wall from the shed door is an old iron sink and sink shelf, in which is set a hand pump. Downstage of the sink is an uncurtained window. Near the window is an old wooden rocker. Center stage is an unpainted wooden kitchen table with straight chairs on either side. There is a small chair down right. Unwashed pans under the sink, a loaf of bread outside the breadbox, a dish towel on the table — other signs of incompleted work. At the rear the shed door opens and the Sheriff comes in followed by the County Attorney and Hale. The Sheriff and Hale are men in middle life, the County Attorney is a young man; all are much bundled up and go at once to the stove. They are followed by the two women — the Sheriff's wife, Mrs. Peters, first: she is a slight wiry woman, a thin nervous face. Mrs. Hale is larger and would ordinarily be called more comfortable looking, but she is disturbed now and looks fearfully about as she enters. The women have come in slowly, and stand close together near the door.*

COUNTY ATTORNEY (*at stove rubbing his hands*): This feels good. Come up to the fire, ladies.

MRS. PETERS (*after taking a step forward*): I'm not — cold.

SHERIFF (*unbuttoning his overcoat and stepping away from the stove to right of table as if to mark the beginning of official business*): Now, Mr. Hale, before we move things about, you explain to Mr. Henderson just what you saw when you came here yesterday morning.

COUNTY ATTORNEY (*crossing down to left of the table*): By the way, has anything been moved? Are things just as you left them yesterday?

SHERIFF (*looking about*): It's just about the same. When it dropped below zero last night I thought I'd better send Frank out this morning to make a fire for us — (*sits right of center table*) no use getting pneumonia with a big case on, but I told him not to touch anything except the stove — and you know Frank.

COUNTY ATTORNEY: Somebody should have been left here yesterday.

SHERIFF: Oh — yesterday. When I had to send Frank to Morris Center for that man who went crazy — I want you to know I had my hands full yesterday. I knew you could get back from Omaha by today and as long as I went over everything here myself ———

COUNTY ATTORNEY: Well, Mr. Hale, tell just what happened when you came here yesterday morning.

HALE (*crossing down to above table*): Harry and I had started to town with a load of potatoes. We came along the road from my place and as I got here I said, "I'm going to see if I can't get John Wright to go in with me on a party telephone." I spoke to Wright about it once before and he put me off, saying folks talked too much anyway, and all he asked was peace and quiet — I guess you know about how much he talked himself; but I thought maybe if I went to the house and talked about it before his wife, though I said to Harry that I didn't know as what his wife wanted made much difference to John ———

COUNTY ATTORNEY: Let's talk about that later, Mr. Hale. I do want to talk about that, but tell now just what happened when you got to the house.

HALE: I didn't hear or see anything; I knocked at the door, and still it was all quiet inside. I knew they must be up, it was past eight o'clock. So I knocked again, and I thought I heard someone say, "Come in." I wasn't sure, I'm not sure yet, but I opened the door — this door (*indicating the door by which the two women are still standing*) and there in that rocker — (*pointing to it*) sat Mrs. Wright. (*They all look at the rocker down left.*)

COUNTY ATTORNEY: What — was she doing?

HALE: She was rockin' back and forth. She had her apron in her hand and was kind of — pleating it.

COUNTY ATTORNEY: And how did she — look?

HALE: Well, she looked queer.

COUNTY ATTORNEY: How do you mean — queer?

HALE: Well, as if she didn't know what she was going to do next. And kind of done up.

COUNTY ATTORNEY (*takes out notebook and pencil and sits left of center table*): How did she seem to feel about your coming?

HALE: Why, I don't think she minded — one way or other. She didn't pay much attention. I said, "How do, Mrs. Wright, it's cold, ain't it?" And she said, "Is it?"— and went on kind of pleating at her apron. Well, I was surprised: she didn't ask me to come up to the stove, or to set down, but just sat there, not even looking at me, so I said, "I want to see John." And then she — laughed. I guess you would call it a laugh. I thought of Harry and the team outside, so I said a little sharp: "Can't I see John?" "No," she says, kind o' dull like. "Ain't he home?" says I. "Yes," says she, "he's home." "Then why can't I see him?" I asked her, out of patience. "'Cause he's dead," says she. "*Dead?*" says I. She just nodded her head, not getting a bit excited, but rockin' back and forth. "Why — where is he?" says I, not knowing what to say. She just pointed upstairs — like that. (*Himself pointing to the room above.*) I started for the stairs, with the idea of going up there. I walked from there to here — then I says, "Why, what did he die of?" "He died of a rope round his neck," says she, and just went on pleatin' at her apron. Well, I went out and called Harry. I thought I might — need help. We went upstairs and there he was lyin'———

COUNTY ATTORNEY: I think I'd rather have you go into that upstairs, where you can point it all out. Just go on now with the rest of the story.

HALE: Well, my first thought was to get that rope off. It looked . . . (*stops: his face twitches*) . . . but Harry, he went up to him, and he said, "No, he's dead all right, and we'd better not touch anything." So we went right back downstairs. She was still sitting that same way. "Has anybody been notified?" I asked. "No," says she, unconcerned. "Who did this, Mrs. Wright?" said Harry. He said it businesslike — and she stopped pleatin' of her apron. "I don't know," she says. "You don't *know?*" says Harry. "No," says she. "Weren't you sleepin' in the bed with him?" says Harry. "Yes," says she, "but I was on the inside." "Somebody slipped a rope round his head and strangled him and you didn't wake up?" says Harry. "I didn't wake up," she said after him. We must 'a' looked as if we didn't see how that could be, for after a minute she said, "I sleep sound." Harry was going to ask her more questions but I said maybe we ought to let her tell her story first to the coroner, or the sheriff, so Harry went fast as he could to Rivers' place, where there's a telephone.

COUNTY ATTORNEY: And what did Mrs. Wright do when she knew that you had gone for the coroner?

HALE: She moved from the rocker to that chair over there (*pointing to a small chair in the down right corner*) and just sat there with her hands held together and looking down. I got a feeling that I ought to make some conversation, so I said I had come in to see if John wanted to put in a telephone, and at that she started to laugh, and then she stopped and looked at me — scared. (*The County Attorney, who has had his notebook out, makes a note.*) I dunno, maybe it wasn't scared. I wouldn't like to say it was. Soon Harry got back, and then Dr. Lloyd came and you, Mr. Peters, and so I guess that's all I know that you don't.

COUNTY ATTORNEY (*rising and looking around*): I guess we'll go upstairs first — and then out to the barn and around there. (*To the Sheriff.*) You're convinced that there was nothing important here — nothing that would point to any motive?

SHERIFF: Nothing here but kitchen things. (*The County Attorney, after again looking around the kitchen, opens the door of a cupboard closet in right wall. He brings a small chair from right — gets on it and looks on a shelf. Pulls his hand away, sticky.*)

COUNTY ATTORNEY: Here's a nice mess. (*The women draw nearer up to center.*)

MRS. PETERS (*to the other woman*): Oh, her fruit; it did freeze. (*To the Lawyer.*) She worried about that when it turned so cold. She said the fire'd go out and her jars would break.

SHERIFF (*rises*): Well, can you beat the woman! Held for murder and worryin' about her preserves.

COUNTY ATTORNEY (*getting down from chair*): I guess before we're through she may have something more serious than preserves to worry about. (*Crosses down right center.*)

HALE: Well, women are used to worrying over trifles. (*The two women move a little closer together.*)

COUNTY ATTORNEY (*with the gallantry of a young politician*): And yet, for all their worries, what would we do without the ladies? (*The women do not unbend. He goes below the center table to the sink, takes a dipperful of water from the pail, and pouring it into a basin, washes his hands. While he is doing this the Sheriff and Hale cross to cupboard, which they inspect. The County Attorney starts to wipe his hands on the roller towel, turns it for a cleaner place.)* Dirty towels! (*Kicks his foot against the pans under the sink.)* Not much of a housekeeper, would you say, ladies?

MRS. HALE (*stiffly*): There's a great deal of work to be done on a farm.

COUNTY ATTORNEY: To be sure. And yet (*with a little bow to her*) I know there are some Dickson County farmhouses which do not have such roller towels. (*He gives it a pull to expose its full-length again.*)

MRS. HALE: Those towels get dirty awful quick. Men's hands aren't always clean as they might be.

COUNTY ATTORNEY: Ah, loyal to your sex, I see. But you and Mrs. Wright were neighbors. I suppose you were friends, too.

MRS. HALE (*shaking her head*): I've not seen much of her of late years. I've not been in this house — it's more than a year.

COUNTY ATTORNEY (*crossing to women up center*): And why was that? You didn't like her?

MRS. HALE: I liked her all well enough. Farmer's wives have their hands full, Mr. Henderson. And then ——

COUNTY ATTORNEY: Yes —— ?

MRS. HALE (*looking about*): It never seemed a very cheerful place.

COUNTY ATTORNEY: No — it's not cheerful. I shouldn't say she had the homemaking instinct.

MRS. HALE: Well, I don't know as Wright had, either.

COUNTY ATTORNEY: You mean that they didn't get on very well?

MRS. HALE: No, I don't mean anything. But I don't think a place'd be any cheerfuller for John Wright's being in it.

COUNTY ATTORNEY: I'd like to talk more of that a little later. I want to get the lay of things upstairs now. (*He goes past the women to up right where the steps lead to a stair door.*)

SHERIFF: I suppose anything Mrs. Peters does'll be all right. She was to take in some clothes for her, you know, and a few little things. We left in such a hurry yesterday.

COUNTY ATTORNEY: Yes, but I would like to see what you take, Mrs. Peters, and keep an eye out for anything that might be of use to us.

MRS. PETERS: Yes, Mr. Henderson. (*The men leave by up right door to stairs. The women listen to the men's steps on the stairs, then look about the kitchen.*)

MRS. HALE (*crossing left to sink*): I'd hate to have men coming into my kitchen, snooping around and criticizing. (*She arranges the pans under sink which the lawyer had shoved out of place.*)

MRS. PETERS: Of course it's no more than their duty. (*Crosses to cupboard up right.*)

MRS. HALE: Duty's all right, but I guess that deputy sheriff that came out to make the fire might have got

a little of this on. (*Gives the roller towel a pull.*) Wish I'd thought of that sooner. Seems mean to talk about her for not having things slicked up when she had to come away in such a hurry. (*Crosses right to Mrs. Peters at cupboard.*)

MRS. PETERS (*who has been looking through cupboard, lifts one end of towel that covers a pan*): She had bread set. (*Stands still.*)

MRS. HALE (*eyes fixed on a loaf of bread beside the breadbox, which is on a low shelf of the cupboard*): She was going to put this in there. (*Picks up loaf, abruptly drops it. In a manner of returning to familiar things.*) It's a shame about her fruit. I wonder if it's all gone. (*Gets up on chair and looks.*) I think there's some here that's all right, Mrs. Peters. Yes — here; (*holding it toward the window*) this is cherries, too. (*Looking again.*) I declare I believe that's the only one. (*Gets down, jar in hand. Goes to the sink and wipes it off on the outside.*) She'll feel awful bad after all her hard work in the hot weather. I remember the afternoon I put up my cherries last summer. (*She puts the jar on the big kitchen table, center of the room. With a sigh, is about to sit down in the rocking chair. Before she is seated realizes what chair it is; with a slow look at it, steps back. The chair which she has touched rocks back and forth. Mrs. Peters moves to center table and they both watch the chair rock for a moment or two.*)

MRS. PETERS (*shaking off the mood which the empty rocking chair has evoked. Now in a businesslike manner she speaks*): Well I must get those things from the front room closet. (*She goes to the door at the right but, after looking into the other room, steps back.*) You coming with me, Mrs. Hale? You could help me carry them. (*They go in the other room; reappear, Mrs. Peters carrying a dress, petticoat, and skirt, Mrs. Hale following with a pair of shoes.*) My, it's cold in there. (*She puts the clothes on the big table and hurries to the stove.*)

MRS. HALE (*right of center table examining the skirt*): Wright was close. I think maybe that's why she kept so much to herself. She didn't even belong to the Ladies' Aid. I suppose she felt she couldn't do her part, and then you don't enjoy things when you feel shabby. I heard she used to wear pretty clothes and be lively, when she was Minnie Foster, one of the town girls singing in the choir. But that — oh, that was thirty years ago. This all you want to take in?

MRS. PETERS: She said she wanted an apron. Funny thing to want, for there isn't much to get you dirty in jail, goodness knows. But I suppose just to make her feel more natural. (*Crosses to cupboard.*) She said they was in the top drawer in this cupboard. Yes, here. And then her little shawl that always hung behind the door. (*Opens stair door and looks.*) Yes, here it is. (*Quickly shuts door leading upstairs.*)

MRS. HALE (*abruptly moving toward her*): Mrs. Peters?

MRS. PETERS: Yes, Mrs. Hale? (*At up right door.*)

MRS. HALE: Do you think she did it?

MRS. PETERS (*in a frightened voice*): Oh, I don't know.

MRS. HALE: Well, I don't think she did. Asking for an apron and her little shawl. Worrying about her fruit.

MRS. PETERS (*starts to speak, glances up, where footsteps are heard in the room above. In a low voice*): Mr. Peters says it looks bad for her. Mr. Henderson is awful sarcastic in a speech and he'll make fun of her sayin' she didn't wake up.

MRS. HALE: Well, I guess John Wright didn't wake when they was slipping that rope under his neck.

MRS. PETERS (*crossing slowly to table and placing shawl and apron on table with other clothing*): No, it's strange. It must have been done awful crafty and still. They say it was such a — funny way to kill a man, rigging it all up like that.

MRS. HALE (*crossing to left of Mrs. Peters at table*): That's just what Mr. Hale said. There was a gun in the house. He says that's what he can't understand.

MRS. PETERS: Mr. Henderson said coming out that what was needed for the case was a motive: something to show anger, or — sudden feeling.

MRS. HALE (*who is standing by the table*): Well, I don't see any signs of anger around here. (*She puts her hand on the dish towel, which lies on the table, stands looking down at table, one-half of which is clean, the other half messy.*) It's wiped to here. (*Makes a move as if to finish work, then turns and looks at loaf of bread outside the breadbox. Drops towel. In that voice of coming back to familiar things.*) Wonder how they are finding things upstairs. (*Crossing below table to down right.*) I hope she had it a little more red-up° up there. You know, it seems kind of *sneaking*. Locking her up in town and then coming out here and trying to get her own house to turn against her!

MRS. PETERS: But, Mrs. Hale, the law is the law.

MRS. HALE: I s'pose 'tis. (*Unbuttoning her coat.*) Better loosen up your things, Mrs. Peters. You won't feel them when you go out. (*Mrs. Peters takes off her fur tippet, goes to hang it on chair back left of table, stands looking at the work basket on floor near down left window.*)

MRS. PETERS: She was piecing a quilt. (*She brings the large sewing basket to the center table and they look at the bright pieces, Mrs. Hale above the table and Mrs. Peters left of it.*)

MRS. HALE: It's a log cabin pattern. Pretty, isn't it? I wonder if she was goin' to quilt it or just knot it? (*Footsteps have been heard coming down the stairs. The Sheriff enters followed by Hale and the County Attorney.*)

SHERIFF: They wonder if she was going to quilt it or just knot it! (*The men laugh, the women look abashed.*)

COUNTY ATTORNEY (*rubbing his hands over the stove*): Frank's fire didn't do much up there, did it? Well, let's go out to the barn and get that cleared up. (*The men go outside by up left door.*)

red-up: (slang) Ready for company.

MRS. HALE (*resentfully*): I don't know as there's anything so strange, our takin' up our time with little things while we're waiting for them to get the evidence. (*She sits in chair right of table smoothing out a block with decision.*) I don't see as it's anything to laugh about.

MRS. PETERS (*apologetically*): Of course they've got awful important things on their minds. (*Pulls up a chair and joins Mrs. Hale at the left of the table.*)

MRS. HALE (*examining another block*): Mrs. Peters, look at this one. Here, this is the one she was working on, and look at the sewing! All the rest of it has been so nice and even. And look at this! It's all over the place! Why, it looks as if she didn't know what she was about! (*After she has said this they look at each other, then start to glance back at the door. After an instant Mrs. Hale has pulled at a knot and ripped the sewing.*)

MRS. PETERS: Oh, what are you doing, Mrs. Hale?

MRS. HALE (*mildly*): Just pulling out a stitch or two that's not sewed very good. (*Threading a needle.*) Bad sewing always made me fidgety.

MRS. PETERS (*with a glance at the door, nervously*): I don't think we ought to touch things.

MRS. HALE: I'll just finish up this end. (*Suddenly stopping and leaning forward.*) Mrs. Peters?

MRS. PETERS: Yes, Mrs. Hale?

MRS. HALE: What do you suppose she was so nervous about?

MRS. PETERS: Oh — I don't know. I don't know as she was nervous. I sometimes sew awful queer when I'm just tired. (*Mrs. Hale starts to say something, looks at Mrs. Peters, then goes on sewing.*) Well, I must get these things wrapped up. They may be through sooner than we think. (*Putting apron and other things together.*) I wonder where I can find a piece of paper, and string. (*Rises.*)

MRS. HALE: In that cupboard, maybe.

MRS. PETERS (*crosses right looking in cupboard*): Why, here's a bird-cage. (*Holds it up.*) Did she have a bird, Mrs. Hale?

MRS. HALE: Why, I don't know whether she did or not — I've not been here for so long. There was a man around last year selling canaries cheap, but I don't know as she took one; maybe she did. She used to sing real pretty herself.

MRS. PETERS (*glancing around*): Seems funny to think of a bird here. But she must have had one, or why would she have a cage? I wonder what happened to it?

MRS. HALE: I s'pose maybe the cat got it.

MRS. PETERS: No, she didn't have a cat. She's got that feeling some people have about cats — being afraid of them. My cat got in her room and she was real upset and asked me to take it out.

MRS. HALE: My sister Bessie was like that. Queer, ain't it?

MRS. PETERS (*examining the cage*): Why, look at this door. It's broke. One hinge is pulled apart. (*Takes a step down to Mrs. Hale's right.*)

Mrs. Hale (Sarah Einerson) and Mrs. Peters (Mary-Margaret Pyeatt) discovering the truth about the dead songbird in the 2000 Echo Theater production of Susan Glaspell's *Trifles,* performed in Dallas, Texas, and directed by Ellen Locy. The production was an entry in Dallas' second annual Festival of Independent Theatres (FIT).

MRS. HALE (*looking too*): Looks as if someone must have been rough with it.

MRS. PETERS: Why, yes. (*She brings the cage forward and puts it on the table.*)

MRS. HALE (*glancing toward up left door*): I wish if they're going to find any evidence they'd be about it. I don't like this place.

MRS. PETERS: But I'm awful glad you came with me, Mrs. Hale. It would be lonesome for me sitting here alone.

MRS. HALE: It would, wouldn't it? (*Dropping her sewing.*) But I tell you what I do wish, Mrs. Peters. I wish I had come over sometimes when *she* was here. I — (*looking around the room*) — wish I had.

MRS. PETERS: But of course you were awful busy, Mrs. Hale — your house and your children.

MRS. HALE (*rises and crosses left*): I could've come. I stayed away because it weren't cheerful — and that's

why I ought to have come. I — (*looking out left window*) — I've never liked this place. Maybe it's because it's down in a hollow and you don't see the road. I dunno what it is, but it's a lonesome place and always was. I wish I had come over to see Minnie Foster sometimes. I can see now — (*Shakes her head.*)

MRS. PETERS (*left of table and above it*): Well, you mustn't reproach yourself, Mrs. Hale. Somehow we just don't see how it is with other folks until — something turns up.

MRS. HALE: Not having children makes less work — but it makes a quiet house, and Wright out to work all day, and no company when he did come in. (*Turning from window.*) Did you know John Wright, Mrs. Peters?

MRS. PETERS: Not to know him; I've seen him in town. They say he was a good man.

MRS. HALE: Yes — good; he didn't drink, and kept his word as well as most, I guess, and paid his debts. But he was a hard man, Mrs. Peters. Just to pass the time of day with him — (*Shivers.*) Like a raw wind that gets to the bone. (*Pauses, her eye falling on the cage.*) I should think she would 'a' wanted a bird. But what do you suppose went with it?

MRS. PETERS: I don't know, unless it got sick and died. (*She reaches over and swings the broken door, swings it again, both women watch it.*)

MRS. HALE: You weren't raised round here, were you? (*Mrs. Peters shakes her head.*) You didn't know — her?

MRS. PETERS: Not till they brought her yesterday.

MRS. HALE: She — come to think of it, she was kind of like a bird herself — real sweet and pretty, but kind of timid and — fluttery. How — she — did — change. (*Silence: then as if struck by a happy thought and relieved to get back to everyday things. Crosses right above Mrs. Peters to cupboard, replaces small chair used to stand on to its original place down right.*) Tell you what, Mrs. Peters, why don't you take the quilt in with you? It might take up her mind.

MRS. PETERS: Why, I think that's a real nice idea, Mrs. Hale. There couldn't possibly be any objection to it could there? Now, just what would I take? I wonder if her patches are in here — and her things. (*They look in the sewing basket.*)

MRS. HALE (*crosses to right of table*): Here's some red. I expect this has got sewing things in it. (*Brings out a fancy box.*) What a pretty box. Looks like something somebody would give you. Maybe her scissors are in here. (*Opens box. Suddenly puts her hand to her nose.*) Why ——— (*Mrs. Peters bends nearer, then turns her face away.*) There's something wrapped up in this piece of silk.

MRS. PETERS: Why, this isn't her scissors.

MRS. HALE (*lifting the silk*): Oh, Mrs. Peters — it's ——— (*Mrs. Peters bends closer.*)

MRS. PETERS: It's the bird.

MRS. HALE: But, Mrs. Peters — look at it! Its neck! Look at its neck! It's all — other side *to.*

MRS. PETERS: Somebody — wrung — its — neck. (*Their eyes meet. A look of growing comprehension, of horror. Steps are heard outside. Mrs. Hale slips box under quilt pieces, and sinks into her chair. Enter Sheriff and County Attorney. Mrs. Peters steps down left and stands looking out of window.*)

COUNTY ATTORNEY (*as one turning from serious things to little pleasantries*): Well, ladies, have you decided whether she was going to quilt it or knot it? (*Crosses to center above table.*)

MRS. PETERS: We think she was going to — knot it. (*Sheriff crosses to right of stove, lifts stove lid, and glances at fire, then stands warming hands at stove.*)

COUNTY ATTORNEY: Well, that's interesting, I'm sure. (*Seeing the bird-cage.*) Has the bird flown?

MRS. HALE (*putting more quilt pieces over the box*): We think the — cat got it.

COUNTY ATTORNEY (*preoccupied*): Is there a cat? (*Mrs. Hale glances in a quick covert way at Mrs. Peters.*)

MRS. PETERS (*turning from window takes a step in*): Well, not *now*. They're superstitious, you know. They leave.

COUNTY ATTORNEY (*to Sheriff Peters, continuing an interrupted conversation*): No sign at all of anyone having come from the outside. Their own rope. Now let's go up again and go over it piece by piece. (*They start upstairs.*) It would have to have been someone who knew just the ——— (*Mrs. Peters sits down left of table. The two women sit there not looking at one another, but as if peering into something and at the same time holding back. When they talk now it is in the manner of feeling their way over strange ground, as if afraid of what they are saying, but as if they cannot help saying it.*)

MRS. HALE (*hesistatively and in hushed voice*): She liked the bird. She was going to bury it in that pretty box.

MRS. PETERS (*in a whisper*): When I was a girl — my kitten — there was a boy took a hatchet, and before my eyes — and before I could get there ——— (*Covers her face an instant.*) If they hadn't held me back I would have — (*catches herself, looks upstairs where steps are heard, falters weakly*) — hurt him.

MRS. HALE (*with a slow look around her*): I wonder how it would seem never to have had any children around. (*Pause.*) No, Wright wouldn't like the bird — a thing that sang. She used to sing. He killed that, too.

MRS. PETERS (*moving uneasily*): We don't know who killed the bird.

MRS. HALE: I knew John Wright.

MRS. PETERS: It was an awful thing was done in this house that night, Mrs. Hale. Killing a man while he slept, slipping a rope around his neck that choked the life out of him.

MRS. HALE: His neck. Choked the life out of him. (*Her hand goes out and rests on the bird-cage.*)

MRS. PETERS (*with rising voice*): We don't know who killed him. We don't *know*.

MRS. HALE (*her own feelings not interrupted*): If there'd been years and years of nothing, then a bird to sing to you, it would be awful — still, after the bird was still.

MRS. PETERS (*something within her speaking*): I know what stillness is. When we homesteaded in Dakota, and my first baby died — after he was two years old, and me with no other then ———

MRS. HALE (*moving*): How soon do you suppose they'll be through looking for the evidence?

MRS. PETERS: I know what stillness is. (*Pulling herself back.*) The law has got to punish crimes, Mrs. Hale.

MRS. HALE (*not as if answering that*): I wish you'd seen Minnie Foster when she wore a white dress with blue ribbons and stood up there in the choir and sang. (*A look around the room.*) Oh, I *wish* I'd come over here once in a while! That was a crime! That was a crime! Who's going to punish that?

MRS. PETERS (*looking upstairs*): We mustn't — take on.

MRS. HALE: I might have known she needed help! I know how things can be — for women. I tell you, it's queer, Mrs. Peters. We live close together and we live far apart. We all go through the same things — it's all just a different kind of the same thing. (*Brushes her eyes, noticing the jar of fruit, reaches out for it.*) If I was you I wouldn't tell her her fruit was gone. Tell her it *ain't*. Tell her it's all right. Take this in to prove it to her. She — she may never know whether it was broke or not.

MRS. PETERS (*takes the jar, looks about for something to wrap it in; takes petticoat from the clothes brought from the other room, very nervously begins winding this around the jar. In a false voice*): My, it's a good thing the men couldn't hear us. Wouldn't they just laugh! Getting all stirred up over a little thing like a — dead canary. As if that could have anything to do with — with — wouldn't they *laugh*! (*The men are heard coming downstairs.*)

MRS. HALE (*under her breath*): Maybe they would — maybe they wouldn't.

COUNTY ATTORNEY: No, Peters, it's all perfectly clear except a reason for doing it. But you know juries when it comes to women. If there was some definite thing. (*Crosses slowly to above table. Sheriff crosses down right. Mrs. Hale and Mrs. Peters remain seated at either side of table.*) Something to show — something to make a story about — a thing that would connect up with this strange way of doing it ——— (*The women's eyes meet for an instant. Enter Hale from outer door.*)

HALE (*remaining by door*): Well, I've got the team around. Pretty cold out there.

COUNTY ATTORNEY: I'm going to stay awhile by myself. (*To the Sheriff.*) You can send Frank out for me, can't you? I want to go over everything. I'm not satisfied that we can't do better.

SHERIFF: Do you want to see what Mrs. Peters is going to take in? (*The Lawyer picks up the apron, laughs.*)

COUNTY ATTORNEY: Oh, I guess they're not very dangerous things the ladies have picked out. (*Moves a few things about, disturbing the quilt pieces which cover the box. Steps back.*) No, Mrs. Peters doesn't need supervising. For that matter a sheriff's wife is married to the law. Ever think of it that way, Mrs. Peters?

MRS. PETERS: Not — just that way.

SHERIFF (*chuckling*): Married to the law. (*Moves to down right door to the other room.*) I just want you to come in here a minute, George. We ought to take a look at these windows.

COUNTY ATTORNEY (*scoffingly*): Oh, windows!

SHERIFF: We'll be right out, Mr. Hale. (*Hale goes outside. The Sheriff follows the County Attorney into the room. Then Mrs. Hale rises, hands tight together, looking intensely at Mrs. Peters, whose eyes make a slow turn, finally meeting Mrs. Hale's. A moment Mrs. Hale holds her, then her own eyes point the way to where the box is concealed. Suddenly Mrs. Peters throws back quilt pieces and tries to put the box in the bag she is carrying. It is too big. She opens box, starts to take bird out, cannot touch it, goes to pieces, stands there helpless. Sound of a knob turning in the other room. Mrs. Hale snatches the box and puts it in the pocket of her big coat. Enter County Attorney and Sheriff, who remains down right.*)

COUNTY ATTORNEY (*crosses to up left door facetiously*): Well, Henry, at least we found out that she was not going to quilt it. She was going to — what is it you call it, ladies?

MRS. HALE (*standing center below table facing front, her hand against her pocket*): We call it — knot it, Mr. Henderson.

COMMENTARY

Christine Dymkowski (b. 1950)

ON THE EDGE: THE PLAYS OF SUSAN GLASPELL   1988

Christine Dymkowski sees Trifles *as a play that occupies the edge — the marginalized space reserved for women. The male figures in the play assume that their interests are central to the murder investigation, whereas Glaspell demonstrates that the most significant issues in the investigation are on the edge of men's attention, where they can never see them.*

The paradoxically central nature of the edge informs Glaspell's theatrical methods and themes. Her first play, *Trifles* (1916), illustrates its use in several ways, the irony of the title already having been noted. The plot revolves around the visit to a farmhouse by County Attorney Henderson and Sheriff Peters to investigate the murder of John Wright; they are accompanied by the farmer who discovered the murder and, almost incidentally, by the farmer's and sheriff's wives. The men's assumption is that Minnie Wright, already in custody for the crime, has killed her husband, and they are there to search the house for clues to a motive. The audience undoubtedly sees them as protagonists at the start of the play.

The stage directions immediately call attention to the women's marginality: the men, "much bundled up" against the freezing cold, "go at once to the stove" in the Wrights' kitchen, while the women who follow them in do so "slowly, and stand close together near the door." The separateness of the female and male worlds is thus immediately established visually and then reinforced by the dialogue:

> MRS. PETERS (*to the other woman*): Oh, her fruit; it did freeze. (*To the Lawyer.*) She worried about that when it turned so cold. . . .
>
> SHERIFF: Well, can you beat the women [*sic*]! Held for murder and worryin' about her preserves.

COUNTY ATTORNEY: I guess before we're through she may have something more serious
than preserves to worry about.

HALE: Well, women are used to worrying over trifles.

(*The two women move a little closer together.*)

Not surprisingly, the women are relegated to the kitchen, while the men's attention
turns to the rest of the house, particularly the bedroom where the crime was committed: "You're convinced that there was nothing important here — nothing that
would point to any motive," Henderson asks Peters, and is assured that there is
"Nothing here but kitchen things." However, while the men view the kitchen as
marginal to their purpose, the drama stays centered there where the women are:
contrary to expectation, it becomes the central focus of the play.

Ironically, it is the kitchen that holds the clues to the desperation and loneliness
of Minnie's life and yields the women the answers for which the men search in vain;
moreover, the understanding that they do reach goes beyond the mere solving of
the crime to a redefinition of what the crime was. Mrs. Hale blames herself for a
failure of imagination: "Oh, I *wish* I'd come over here once in a while! That was a
crime! That was a crime! Who's going to punish that? . . . I might have known she
needed help! I know how things can be — for women. I tell you, it's queer, Mrs.
Peters. We live close together and we live far apart. We all go through the same
things — it's all just a different kind of the same thing." The empathy both women
feel for Minnie leads them to suppress the evidence they have found, patiently
enduring the men's condescension instead of competing with them on their own
ground. Conventional moral values are overturned, just as the expected form of the
murder mystery is ignored: the play differentiates between justice and law and
shows that the traditional "solution" is no such thing.

Just as Glaspell sets the play in the seemingly marginal kitchen, she makes the
absent Minnie Wright its focus, a tactic she was to use again in *Bernice* and *Alison's
House;* although noted by critics, this use of an absent central character has not
received much comment. It is yet another way in which Glaspell makes central the
apparently marginal — indeed, in stage terms, the nonexistent.

Luigi Pirandello

Luigi Pirandello (1867–1936) was an Italian short-story writer and novelist, a secondary school teacher, and finally a playwright. His life was complicated by business failures that wiped out his personal income and threw his wife into a psychological depression that Pirandello quite bluntly described as madness. Out of his acquaintance with madness — he remained with his wife for fourteen years after she lost touch with reality — Pirandello claimed to have developed much of his attitude toward the shifting surfaces of appearances.

Pirandello's short stories and novels show the consistent pattern of his plays: a deep examination of what we know to be real and a questioning of our confidence in our beliefs. His novel *Shoot* (1915) questions the surfaces of cinema reality, which contemporary Italy had embraced with great enthusiasm. His relentless examination of the paradoxes of experience has given him a reputation for pessimism. He himself said, "I think of life as a very sad piece of buffoonery," and he insisted that people bear within them a deep need to deceive themselves "by creating a reality . . . which . . . is discovered to be vain and illusory."

For most of his early career Pirandello was not a popular playwright in Italy, and therefore much of his dramatic work was first performed abroad. In 1923 he was known as an important novelist and came to the attention of Benito Mussolini (1883–1945), the Fascist dictator of Italy. Pirandello joined the Italian Fascist party as a means of establishing the National Art Theatre in Rome, which enjoyed considerable state support. When asked why he was a Fascist, he said, "I am a Fascist because I am an Italian." After Pirandello won the Nobel prize for literature in 1934, one account has him breaking with Fascism entirely over the Italian invasion of Ethiopia, while another account has him giving over his Nobel medal to be melted down for the Ethiopian campaign. Like some of his dramas, his behavior seems to have profound uncertainties that persist to this day.

Pirandello's influence in modern theater resulted from his experimentation with the concept of realism that dominated drama from the time of Strindberg and Ibsen. The concept of the imaginary "fourth wall" of the stage through which the audience observed the action of characters in their living rooms had become the norm in theater. Pirandello, however, questioned all thought of norms by bringing the very idea of reality under philosophical scrutiny. His questioning helped playwrights around the world expand their approaches to theater in the early part of the twentieth century. Pirandello was one of the first, and one of the best, experimentalists.

SIX CHARACTERS IN SEARCH OF AN AUTHOR

Pirandello's play is part of a trilogy: *Six Characters in Search of an Author* (1921), *Each in His Own Way* (1924), and *Tonight We Improvise* (1930). These plays all examine the impossibility of knowing reality. There is no objective truth to know, Pirandello tells us, and what we think of as reality is totally subjective, something that each of us maintains independently of other people and that none of us can communicate. We are, in other words, apart, sealed into our own limited world.

These ideas were hardly novel. Playwrights had dealt with them before, even during the Elizabethan age, at a time when — because of the Protestant Reformation — the absolute systems of reality promoted by the Roman Catholic Church had crumbled. Pirandello's plays were also produced during a period — the 1920s — when his culture was uncertain, frightened, and still reeling in shock from the destruction of World War I. In this depressed time, Pirandello's audience saw in his work a reflection of their own dispirited, fearful selves.

In a sense, *Six Characters in Search of an Author* is about the relationship between art and life, and especially about the relationship between drama and life. The premise of the play is absurd. In the middle of a rehearsal of a Pirandello play, several characters appear and request that an author be present to cobble them into a play. The stage manager assumes that they are presenting themselves as actors to be in a play, but they explain that they are not actors. They are real characters. This implies a paradox that characters are independent of the actors who play them (we are used to the characters being only on paper). When they demand actors to represent them, we know that one limit of impossibility has been reached.

The characters who appear are, in a sense, types: a father, a mother, a stepdaughter, a son, two silent figures — the boy and the child — and, finally, a milliner, Madame Pace. They share the stage with the actors of the company, who are rehearsing the Pirandello play *Mixing It Up*. The six characters have been abandoned by their creator, the author who has absconded, leaving them in search of a substitute. The stepdaughter, late in the play, surmises that their author abandoned them "in a fit of depression, of disgust for the ordinary theater as the public knows it and likes it."

Pirandello uses his characters and their situation to comment on the life of the theater in the 1920s, and he also uses them to begin a series of speculations on the relationship of a public to the actors they see in plays, the characters the actors play, and the authors who create them. To an extent, the relationship between an author and his or her characters always implies a metaphor for the relationship between a creator and all creation. It is tempting to think of Samuel Beckett years later in his *Waiting for Godot* imagining an "author" having abandoned his creations because they failed to satisfy him. The six characters — or creations — who invade the stage in Pirandello's play have a firm sense of themselves and their actions. They bring with them a story — as all characters in plays do — and they invite the manager to participate in their stories, just as characters invite audiences to become one with their narratives.

One of the more amusing scenes depicts the characters' reactions to seeing actors play their parts. Since they are "real" characters, they have the utmost authority in knowing how their parts should be played, and they end up laughing at the inept efforts of the actors in act II. When the manager disputes with them, wondering why they protest so vigorously, they explain that they want to make sure the truth is told. The truth: the concept seems so simple on the surface, but in the situation that Pirandello has conceived, it is loaded with complexities that the stage manager cannot fathom.

By the time the question of truth has been raised, the manager has begun to get a sense of the poignancy of the story that these characters have to tell. He has also begun to see that he must let them continue to tell their story — except that they are not telling it, they are living it. When the climax of their story is reached in the last moments of the play, the line between what is acted and what is lived onstage has become almost completely blurred. When the play ends, it is difficult to know what has truly occurred and what has truly been acted out.

Six Characters in Search of an Author has endured because it still rings true in its examination of the relationship between art and life, illusion and reality. The very word *illusion* is rejected by the characters — as characters they are part of the illusion of reality. They reject the thought that they are literature, asserting, "This is Life, this is passion!"

Six Characters in Search of an Author in Performance

The first production of *Six Characters in Search of an Author* in Rome in May 1921 resulted in a riot that threatened the author and his daughter. The calmer London production in March 1922 in the Kingsway Theatre garnered positive reviews, and the audiences, although at times puzzled, were responsive to what the *Christian Science Monitor* called "one of the freshest and most original productions seen for a long time." The first production in New York was directed by Brock Pemberton at the Princess Theater in October 1922 with the distinguished American actress Florence Eldridge as the stepdaughter. One newspaper critic said, "Pirandello turns a powerful microscope on the dramatist's mental workshop — the modus operandi of play production — and after having destroyed our illusion, like a prestidigitator who shows us how a trick is done, expects us to believe in him."

Pirandello directed the play in Italian in London in 1925, and despite the audience's general inability to understand the language, the New Oxford Theatre was filled for every night of its run. He brought the company to the United States after the British censor determined that the play was "unsuitable for English audiences" and closed the play in London. It was not officially licensed for performance in England again until 1928.

Revivals of the play have been numerous. Three productions in New York in the 1930s preceded revivals in 1948 and 1955. London saw productions in February 1932 and November 1950. By the 1930s audience confusion had simmered down, and in 1932 one London critic declared, "Repetition cannot dull the brilliance of the play's attack on theatrical shams." Sir Ralph Richardson performed in London's West End in 1963. In 1955, Tyrone Guthrie's Phoenix Theater used a translation and adaptation by Guthrie and Michael Wager. The production was not successful, although critics liked the translation. Robert Brustein received extraordinary praise for his American Repertory Theatre (ART) production in 1985. Instead of having the six characters interrupt a Pirandello play, they interrupt the rehearsal of a Molière play, *Sganarelle*, which has roots in Italian commedia dell'arte, and which had been a highly successful ART production. This self-reference — in Pirandellian fashion — helped to blur the line between the realities on and off the stage. Boston critic Kevin Kelly said of the performance, "Brustein immediately links the paradox in Pirandello's theme about reality in illusion / illusion in reality to . . . the pragmatic fantasy of theater itself."

Luigi Pirandello (1867–1936)

SIX CHARACTERS IN SEARCH OF AN AUTHOR   *1921*
A COMEDY IN THE MAKING

TRANSLATED BY EDWARD STORER

Characters of the Comedy in the Making

THE FATHER
THE MOTHER
THE STEPDAUGHTER
THE SON
THE BOY } *do not speak*
THE CHILD }
MADAME PACE

Actors of the Company

THE MANAGER
LEADING LADY
LEADING MAN
SECOND LADY LEAD
L'INGÉNUE
JUVENILE LEAD
OTHER ACTORS AND ACTRESSES
PROPERTY MAN
PROMPTER
MACHINIST
MANAGER'S SECRETARY
DOOR-KEEPER
SCENE SHIFTERS

Scene: *Daytime. The stage of a theater.*

(N.B.: *The Comedy is without acts or scenes. The performance is interrupted once, without the curtain being lowered, when the Manager and the chief characters withdraw to arrange a scenario. A second interruption of the action takes place when, by mistake, the stage hands let the curtain down.*)

ACT I

(*The spectators will find the curtain raised and the stage as it usually is during the daytime. It will be half dark, and empty, so that from the beginning the public may have the impression of an impromptu performance.*)

(*Prompter's box and a small table and chair for the Manager.*)

(*Two other small tables and several chairs scattered about as during rehearsals.*)

(*The Actors and Actresses of the company enter from the back of the stage: first one, then another, then two together; nine or ten in all. They are about to rehearse a Pirandello play:* Mixing It Up. *Some of the company move off toward their dressing rooms. The Prompter, who has the "book" under his arm, is waiting for the Manager in order to begin the rehearsal.*)

(*The Actors and Actresses, some standing, some sitting, chat and smoke. One perhaps reads a paper; another cons his part.*)

(*Finally, the Manager enters and goes to the table prepared for him. His Secretary brings him his mail, through which he glances. The Prompter takes his seat, turns on a light, and opens the "book."*)

THE MANAGER (*throwing a letter down on the table*): I can't see. (*To Property Man.*) Let's have a little light, please!

PROPERTY MAN: Yes, sir, yes, at once. (*A light comes down on to the stage.*)

THE MANAGER (*clapping his hands*): Come along! Come along! Second act of "Mixing It Up." (*Sits down.*)

(*The Actors and Actresses go from the front of the stage to the wings, all except the three who are to begin the rehearsal.*)

THE PROMPTER (*reading the "book"*): "Leo Gala's house. A curious room serving as dining-room and study."

THE MANAGER (*to Property Man*): Fix up the old red room.

PROPERTY MAN (*noting it down*): Red set. All right!

THE PROMPTER (*continuing to read from the "book"*): "Table already laid and writing desk with books and papers. Bookshelves. Exit rear to Leo's bedroom. Exit left to kitchen. Principal exit to right."

THE MANAGER (*energetically*): Well, you understand: The principal exit over there; here, the kitchen. (*Turning to actor who is to play the part of Socrates.*) You make your entrances and exits here. (*To Property Man.*) The baize doors at the rear, and curtains.

PROPERTY MAN (*noting it down*): Right!

PROMPTER (*reading as before*): "When the curtain rises, Leo Gala, dressed in cook's cap and apron, is busy beating an egg in a cup. Philip, also dressed as a cook, is beating another egg. Guidi Venanzi is seated and listening."

LEADING MAN (*to Manager*): Excuse me, but must I absolutely wear a cook's cap?

THE MANAGER (*annoyed*): I imagine so. It says so there anyway. (*Pointing to the "book."*)

LEADING MAN: But it's ridiculous!

THE MANAGER (*jumping up in a rage*): Ridiculous? Ridiculous? Is it my fault if France won't send us any more good comedies, and we are reduced to putting on Pirandello's works, where nobody understands anything, and where the author plays the fool with us all? (*The Actors grin. The Manager goes to Leading Man and shouts.*) Yes sir, you put on the cook's cap and beat eggs. Do you suppose that with all this egg-beating business you are on an ordinary stage? Get that out of your head. You represent the shell of the eggs you are beating! (*Laughter and comments among the Actors.*) Silence! and listen to my explanations, please! (*To Leading Man.*) "The empty form of reason without the fullness of instinct, which is blind."— You stand for reason, your wife is instinct. It's a mixing up of the parts, according to which you

who act your own part become the puppet of yourself. Do you understand?

LEADING MAN: I'm hanged if I do.

THE MANAGER: Neither do I. But let's get on with it. It's sure to be a glorious failure anyway. (*Confidentially.*) But I say, please face three-quarters. Otherwise, what with the abstruseness of the dialogue, and the public that won't be able to hear you, the whole thing will go to hell. Come on! come on!

PROMPTER: Pardon sir, may I get into my box? There's a bit of a draft.

THE MANAGER: Yes, yes, of course!

(*At this point, the Door-Keeper has entered from the stage door and advances toward the Manager's table, taking off his braided cap. During this maneuver, the Six Characters enter, and stop by the door at back of stage, so that when the Door-Keeper is about to announce their coming to the Manager, they are already on the stage. A tenuous light surrounds them, almost as if irradiated by them — the faint breath of their fantastic reality.*)

(*This light will disappear when they come forward toward the actors. They preserve, however, something of the dream lightness in which they seem almost suspended; but this does not detract from the essential reality of their forms and expressions.*)

(*He who is known as the Father is a man of about 50: hair, reddish in color, thin at the temples; he is not bald, however, thick mustaches, falling over his still fresh mouth, which often opens in an empty and uncertain smile. He is fattish, pale; with an especially wide forehead. He has blue, oval-shaped eyes, very clear and piercing. Wears light trousers and a dark jacket. He is alternatively mellifluous and violent in his manner.*)

(*The Mother seems crushed and terrified as if by an intolerable weight of shame and abasement. She is dressed in modest black and wears a thick widow's veil of crepe. When she lifts this, she reveals a waxlike face. She always keeps her eyes downcast.*)

(*The Stepdaughter is dashing, almost impudent, beautiful. She wears mourning too, but with great elegance. She shows contempt for the timid half-frightened manner of the wretched Boy (14 years old, and also dressed in black); on the other hand, she displays a lively tenderness for her little sister, the Child (about four), who is dressed in white, with a black silk sash at the waist.*)

(*The Son (22) is tall, severe in his attitude of contempt for the Father, supercilious and indifferent to the Mother. He looks as if he had come on the stage against his will.*)

DOOR-KEEPER (*cap in hand*): Excuse me, sir . . .

THE MANAGER (*rudely*): Eh? What is it?

DOOR-KEEPER (*timidly*): These people are asking for you, sir.

THE MANAGER (*furious*): I am rehearsing, and you know perfectly well no one's allowed to come in during rehearsals! (*Turning to the Characters.*) Who are you, please? What do you want?

THE FATHER (*coming forward a little, followed by the

others who seem embarrassed): As a matter of fact . . . we have come here in search of an author . . .

THE MANAGER (*half angry, half amazed*): An author? What author?

THE FATHER: Any author, sir.

THE MANAGER: But there's no author here. We are not rehearsing a new piece.

THE STEPDAUGHTER (*vivaciously*): So much the better, so much the better! We can be your new piece.

AN ACTOR (*coming forward from the others*): Oh, do you hear that?

THE FATHER (*to Stepdaughter*): Yes, but if the author isn't here . . . (*To Manager.*) unless you would be willing . . .

THE MANAGER: You are trying to be funny.

THE FATHER: No, for Heaven's sake, what are you saying? We bring you a drama, sir.

THE STEPDAUGHTER: We may be your fortune.

THE MANAGER: Will you oblige me by going away? We haven't time to waste with mad people.

THE FATHER (*mellifluously*): Oh sir, you know well that life is full of infinite absurdities, which, strangely enough, do not even need to appear plausible, since they are true.

THE MANAGER: What the devil is he talking about?

THE FATHER: I say that to reverse the ordinary process may well be considered a madness: that is, to create credible situations, in order that they may appear true. But permit me to observe that if this be madness, it is the sole *raison d'être*° of your profession, gentlemen. (*The Actors look hurt and perplexed.*)

THE MANAGER (*getting up and looking at him*): So our profession seems to you one worthy of madmen then?

THE FATHER: Well, to make seem true that which isn't true . . . without any need . . . for a joke as it were . . . Isn't that your mission, gentlemen: to give life to fantastic characters on the stage?

THE MANAGER (*interpreting the rising anger of the Company*): But I would beg you to believe, my dear sir, that the profession of the comedian is a noble one. If today, as things go, the playwrights give us stupid comedies to play and puppets to represent instead of men, remember we are proud to have given life to immortal works here on these very boards! (*The Actors, satisfied, applaud their Manager.*)

THE FATHER (*interrupting furiously*): Exactly, perfectly, to living beings more alive than those who breathe and wear clothes: beings less real perhaps, but truer! I agree with you entirely. (*The Actors look at one another in amazement.*)

THE MANAGER: But what do you mean? Before, you said . . .

THE FATHER: No, excuse me, I meant it for you, sir, who were crying out that you had no time to lose with madmen, while no one better than yourself knows that nature uses the instrument of human fantasy in order to pursue her high creative purpose.

THE MANAGER: Very well, — but where does all this take us?

THE FATHER: Nowhere! It is merely to show you that one is born to life in many forms, in many shapes, as tree, or as stone, as water, as butterfly, or as woman. So one may also be born a character in a play.

THE MANAGER (*with feigned comic dismay*): So you and these other friends of yours have been born characters?

THE FATHER: Exactly, and alive as you see! (*Manager and Actors burst out laughing.*)

THE FATHER (*hurt*): I am sorry you laugh, because we carry in us a drama, as you can guess from this woman here veiled in black.

THE MANAGER (*losing patience at last and almost indignant*): Oh, chuck it! Get away please! Clear out of here! (*To Property Man.*) For Heaven's sake, turn them out!

THE FATHER (*resisting*): No, no, look here, we . . .

THE MANAGER (*roaring*): We come here to work, you know.

LEADING ACTOR: One cannot let oneself be made such a fool of.

THE FATHER (*determined, coming forward*): I marvel at your incredulity, gentlemen. Are you not accustomed to see the characters created by an author spring to life in yourselves and face each other? Just because there is no "book" (*pointing to the Prompter's box*) which contains us, you refuse to believe . . .

THE STEPDAUGHTER (*advances toward Manager, smiling and coquettish*): Believe me, we are really six most interesting characters, sir; sidetracked however.

THE FATHER: Yes, that is the word! (*To Manager all at once.*) In the sense, that is, that the author who created us alive no longer wished, or was no longer able, materially to put us into a work of art. And this was a real crime, sir, because he who has had the luck to be born a character can laugh even at death. He cannot die. The man, the writer, the instrument of the creation will die, but his creation does not die. And to live for ever, it does not need to have extraordinary gifts or to be able to work wonders. Who was Sancho Panza? Who was Don Abbondio?° Yet they live eternally because — live germs as they were — they had the fortune to find a fecundating matrix, a fantasy which could raise and nourish them: make them live for ever!

THE MANAGER: That is quite all right. But what do you want here, all of you?

THE FATHER: We want to live.

THE MANAGER (*ironically*): For Eternity?

THE FATHER: No, sir, only for a moment . . . in you.

AN ACTOR: Just listen to him!

LEADING LADY: They want to live, in us . . . !

JUVENILE LEAD (*pointing to the Stepdaughter*): I've no objection, as far as that one is concerned!

raison d'être: French for "reason to exist."

Sancho Panza . . . Don Abbondio: Memorable characters in novels: the squire in Cervantes's *Don Quixote* and the priest in Manzoni's *I Promessi Sposi* (*The Betrothed*), respectively.

THE FATHER: Look here! look here! The comedy has to be made. (*To the Manager.*) But if you and your actors are willing, we can soon concert it among ourselves.

THE MANAGER (*annoyed*): But what do you want to concert? We don't go in for concerts here. Here we play dramas and comedies!

THE FATHER: Exactly! That is just why we have come to you.

THE MANAGER: And where is the "book"?

THE FATHER: It is in us! (*The Actors laugh.*) The drama is in us, and we are the drama. We are impatient to play it. Our inner passion drives us on to this.

THE STEPDAUGHTER (*disdainful, alluring, treacherous full of impudence*): My passion, sir! Ah, if you only knew! My passion for him! (*Points to the Father and makes a pretense of embracing him. Then she breaks out into a loud laugh.*)

THE FATHER (*angrily*): Behave yourself! And please don't laugh in that fashion.

THE STEPDAUGHTER: With your permission, gentlemen, I, who am a two months orphan, will show you how I can dance and sing. (*Sings and then dances Prenez garde à Tchou-Tchin-Tchou.*)

Les chinois sont un peuple malin,
De Shangaî à Pékin,
Ils ont mis des écriteaux partout:
Prenez garde à Tchou-Tchin-Tchou.°

ACTORS AND ACTRESSES: Bravo! Well done! Tip-top!

THE MANAGER: Silence! This isn't a café concert, you know! (*Turning to the Father in consternation.*) Is she mad?

THE FATHER: Mad? No, she's worse than mad.

THE STEPDAUGHTER (*to Manager*): Worse? Worse? Listen! Stage this drama for us at once! Then you will see that at a certain moment I . . . when this little darling here. . . . (*Takes the Child by the hand and leads her to the Manager.*) Isn't she a dear? (*Takes her up and kisses her.*) Darling! Darling! (*Puts her down again and adds feelingly.*) Well, when God suddenly takes this dear little child away from that poor mother there; and this imbecile here (*seizing hold of the Boy roughly and pushing him forward*) does the stupidest things, like the fool he is, you will see me run away. Yes, gentlemen, I shall be off. But the moment hasn't arrived yet. After what has taken place between him and me (*indicates the Father with a horrible wink*) I can't remain any longer in this society, to have to witness the anguish of this mother here for that fool. . . . (*Indicates the Son.*) Look at him! Look at him! See how indifferent, how frigid he is, because he is the legitimate son. He despises me, despises him (*pointing to the Boy*), despises this baby

---

Prenez . . . Tchou: This French popular song is an adaptation of "Chu-Chin-Chow," an old Broadway show tune. "The Chinese are a sly people; / From Shanghai to Peking, / They've stuck up warning signs: / Beware of Tchou-Tchin-Tchou." (The words are funnier in French because *chou* means "cabbage.")

here; because . . . we are bastards. (*Goes to the Mother and embraces her.*) And he doesn't want to recognize her as his mother — she who is the common mother of us all. He looks down upon her as if she were only the mother of us three bastards. Wretch! (*She says all this very rapidly, excitedly. At the word "bastards" she raises her voice, and almost spits out the final "Wretch!"*)

THE MOTHER (*to the Manager, in anguish*): In the name of these two little children, I beg you. . . . (*She grows faint and is about to fall.*) Oh God!

THE FATHER (*coming forward to support her as do some of the Actors*): Quick, a chair, a chair for this poor widow!

THE ACTORS: Is it true? Has she really fainted?

THE MANAGER: Quick, a chair! Here!

(*One of the Actors brings a chair, the others proffer assistance. The Mother tries to prevent the Father from lifting the veil which covers her face.*)

THE FATHER: Look at her! Look at her!

THE MOTHER: No, no; stop it please!

THE FATHER (*raising her veil*): Let them see you!

THE MOTHER (*rising and covering her face with her hands, in desperation*): I beg you, sir, to prevent this man from carrying out his plan which is loathsome to me.

THE MANAGER (*dumbfounded*): I don't understand at all. What is the situation? (*To the Father.*) Is this lady your wife?

THE FATHER: Yes, gentlemen: my wife!

THE MANAGER: But how can she be a widow if you are alive? (*The Actors find relief for their astonishment in a loud laugh.*)

THE FATHER: Don't laugh! Don't laugh like that, for Heaven's sake. Her drama lies just here in this: she has had a lover, a man who ought to be here.

THE MOTHER (*with a cry*): No! No!

THE STEPDAUGHTER: Fortunately for her, he is dead. Two months ago as I said. We are in mourning, as you see.

THE FATHER: He isn't here, you see, not because he is dead. He isn't here — look at her a moment and you will understand — because her drama isn't a drama of the love of two men for whom she was incapable of feeling anything except possibly a little gratitude — gratitude not for me but for the other. She isn't a woman, she is a mother, and her drama — powerful, sir, I assure you — lies, as a matter of fact, all in these four children she has had by two men.

THE MOTHER: I had them? Have you got the courage to say that I wanted them? (*To the Company.*) It was his doing. It was he who gave me that other man, who forced me to go away with him.

THE STEPDAUGHTER: It isn't true.

THE MOTHER (*startled*): Not true, isn't it?

THE STEPDAUGHTER: No, it isn't true, it just isn't true.

THE MOTHER: And what can you know about it?

THE STEPDAUGHTER: It isn't true. Don't believe it. (*To Manager.*) Do you know why she says so? For that fellow there. (*Indicates the Son.*) She tortures herself, destroys herself on account of the neglect of that son there, and she wants him to believe that if she abandoned him when he was only two years old, it was because he (*indicates the Father*) made her do so.

THE MOTHER (*vigorously*): He forced me to it, and I call God to witness it. (*To the Manager.*) Ask him (*indicates Husband*) if it isn't true. Let him speak. You (*to Daughter*) are not in a position to know anything about it.

THE STEPDAUGHTER: I know you lived in peace and happiness with my father while he lived. Can you deny it?

THE MOTHER: No, I don't deny it. . . .

THE STEPDAUGHTER: He was always full of affection and kindness for you. (*To the Boy, angrily.*) It's true, isn't it? Tell them! Why don't you speak, you little fool?

THE MOTHER: Leave the poor boy alone. Why do you want to make me appear ungrateful, daughter? I don't want to offend your father. I have answered him that I didn't abandon my house and my son through any fault of mine, nor from any wilful passion.

THE FATHER: It is true. It was my doing.

LEADING MAN (*to the Company*): What a spectacle!

LEADING LADY: We are the audience this time.

JUVENILE LEAD: For once, in a way.

THE MANAGER (*beginning to get really interested*): Let's hear them out. Listen!

THE SON: Oh yes, you're going to hear a fine bit now. He will talk to you of the Demon of Experiment.

THE FATHER: You are a cynical imbecile. I've told you so already a hundred times. (*To the Manager.*) He tries to make fun of me on account of this expression which I have found to excuse myself with.

THE SON (*with disgust*): Yes, phrases! phrases!

THE FATHER: Phrases! Isn't everyone consoled when faced with a trouble or fact he doesn't understand, by a word, some simple word, which tells us nothing and yet calms us?

THE STEPDAUGHTER: Even in the case of remorse. In fact, especially then.

THE FATHER: Remorse? No, that isn't true. I've done more than use words to quiet the remorse in me.

THE STEPDAUGHTER: Yes, there was a bit of money too. Yes, yes, a bit of money. There were the hundred lire he was about to offer me in payment, gentlemen. . . . (*Sensation of horror among the Actors.*)

THE SON (*to the Stepdaughter*): This is vile.

THE STEPDAUGHTER: Vile? There they were in a pale blue envelope on a little mahogany table in the back of Madame Pace's shop. You know Madame Pace — one of those ladies who attract poor girls of good family into their ateliers, under the pretext of their selling *robes et manteaux.*°

THE SON: And he thinks he has bought the right to tyrannize over us all with those hundred lire he was going to pay; but which, fortunately — note this, gentlemen — he had no chance of paying.

robes et manteaux: French for "dresses and capes."

THE STEPDAUGHTER: It was a near thing, though, you know! (*Laughs ironically.*)

THE MOTHER (*protesting*): Shame, my daughter, shame!

THE STEPDAUGHTER: Shame indeed! This is my revenge! I am dying to live that scene . . . The room . . . I see it . . . Here is the window with the mantles exposed, there the divan, the looking-glass, a screen, there in front of the window the little mahogany table with the blue envelope containing one hundred lire. I see it. I see it. I could take hold of it. . . . But you, gentlemen, you ought to turn your backs now: I am almost nude, you know. But I don't blush: I leave that to him. (*Indicating Father.*)

THE MANAGER: I don't understand this at all.

THE FATHER: Naturally enough. I would ask you, sir, to exercise your authority a little here, and let me speak before you believe all she is trying to blame me with. Let me explain.

THE STEPDAUGHTER: Ah yes, explain it in your own way.

THE FATHER: But don't you see that the whole trouble lies here? In words, words. Each one of us has within him a whole world of things, each man of us his own special world. And how can we ever come to an understanding if I put in the words I utter the sense and value of things as I see them; while you who listen to me must inevitably translate them according to the conception of things each one of you has within himself. We think we understand each other, but we never really do. Look here! This woman (*indicating the Mother*) takes all my pity for her as a specially ferocious form of cruelty.

THE MOTHER: But you drove me away.

THE FATHER: Do you hear her? I drove her away! She believes I really sent her away.

THE MOTHER: You know how to talk, and I don't but, believe me, sir (*to Manager*), after he had married me . . . who knows why? . . . I was a poor insignificant woman. . . .

THE FATHER: But, good Heavens! it was just for your humility that I married you. I loved this simplicity in you. (*He stops when he sees she makes signs to contradict him, opens his arms wide in sign of desperation, seeing how hopeless it is to make himself understood.*) You see she denies it. Her mental deafness, believe me, is phenomenal, the limit: (*touches his forehead*) deaf, deaf, mentally deaf! She has plenty of feeling. Oh yes, a good heart for the children; but the brain — deaf, to the point of desperation — !

THE STEPDAUGHTER: Yes, but ask him how his intelligence has helped us.

THE FATHER: If we could see all the evil that may spring from good, what should we do? (*At this point the Leading Lady, who is biting her lips with rage at seeing the Leading Man flirting with the Stepdaughter, comes forward and speaks to the Manager.*)

LEADING LADY: Excuse me, but are we going to rehearse today?

MANAGER: Of course, of course; but let's hear them out.

JUVENILE LEAD: This is something quite new.

L'INGÉNUE: Most interesting!

LEADING LADY: Yes, for the people who like that kind of thing. (*Casts a glance at Leading Man.*)

THE MANAGER (*to Father*): You must please explain yourself quite clearly. (*Sits down.*)

THE FATHER: Very well then: listen! I had in my service a poor man, a clerk, a secretary of mine, full of devotion, who became friends with her. (*Indicating the Mother.*) They understood one another, were kindred souls in fact, without, however, the least suspicion of any evil existing. They were incapable even of thinking of it.

THE STEPDAUGHTER: So he thought of it — for them!

THE FATHER: That's not true. I meant to do good to them — and to myself, I confess, at the same time. Things had come to the point that I could not say a word to either of them without their making a mute appeal, one to the other, with their eyes. I could see them silently asking each other how I was to be kept in countenance, how I was to be kept quiet. And this, believe me, was just about enough of itself to keep me in a constant rage, to exasperate me beyond measure.

THE MANAGER: And why didn't you send him away then — this secretary of yours?

THE FATHER: Precisely what I did, sir. And then I had to watch this poor woman drifting forlornly about the house like an animal without a master, like an animal one has taken in out of pity.

THE MOTHER: Ah yes. . . !

THE FATHER (*suddenly turning to the Mother*): It's true about the son anyway, isn't it?

THE MOTHER: He took my son away from me first of all.

THE FATHER: But not from cruelty. I did it so that he should grow up healthy and strong by living in the country.

THE STEPDAUGHTER (*pointing to him ironically*): As one can see.

THE FATHER (*quickly*): Is it my fault if he has grown up like this? I sent him to a wet nurse in the country, a peasant, as *she* did not seem to me strong enough, though she is of humble origin. That was, anyway, the reason I married her. Unpleasant all this may be, but how can it be helped? My mistake possibly, but there we are! All my life I have had these confounded aspirations towards a certain moral sanity. (*At this point the Stepdaughter bursts into a noisy laugh.*) Oh, stop it! Stop it! I can't stand it.

THE MANAGER: Yes, please stop it, for Heaven's sake.

THE STEPDAUGHTER: But imagine moral sanity from him, if you please — the client of certain ateliers like that of Madame Pace!

THE FATHER: Fool! That is the proof that I am a man! This seeming contradiction, gentlemen, is the strongest proof that I stand here a live man before you. Why, it is just for this very incongruity in my nature that I have had to suffer what I have. I could not live by the side of that woman (*indicating the Mother*) any longer; but not so much for the boredom she inspired me with as for the pity I felt for her.

THE MOTHER: And so he turned me out — .

THE FATHER: — well provided for! Yes, I sent her to that man, gentlemen . . . to let her go free of me.

THE MOTHER: And to free himself.

THE FATHER: Yes, I admit it. It was also a liberation for me. But great evil has come of it. I meant well when I did it, and I did it more for her sake than mine. I swear it. (*Crosses his arms on his chest; then turns suddenly to the Mother.*) Did I ever lose sight of you until that other man carried you off to another town, like the angry fool he was? And on account of my pure interest in you . . . my pure interest, I repeat, that had no base motive in it . . . I watched with the tenderest concern the new family that grew up around her. She can bear witness to this. (*Points to the Stepdaughter.*)

THE STEPDAUGHTER: Oh yes, that's true enough. When I was a kiddie so so high, you know, with plaits over my shoulders and knickers longer than my skirts, I used to see him waiting outside the school for me to come out. He came to see how I was growing up.

THE FATHER: This is infamous, shameful!

THE STEPDAUGHTER: No. Why?

THE FATHER: Infamous! infamous! (*Then excitedly to Manager, explaining.*) After she (*indicating the Mother*) went away, my house seemed suddenly empty. She was my incubus, but she filled my house. I was like a dazed fly alone in the empty rooms. This boy here (*indicating the Son*) was educated away from home, and when he came back, he seemed to me to be no more mine. With no mother to stand between him and me, he grew up entirely for himself, on his own, apart, with no tie of intellect or affection binding him to me. And then — strange but true — I was driven, by curiosity at first and then by some tender sentiment, towards her family, which had come into being through my will. The thought of her began gradually to fill up the emptiness I felt all around me. I wanted to know if she were happy in living out the simple daily duties of life. I wanted to think of her as fortunate and happy because far away from the complicated torments of my spirit. And so, to have proof of this, I used to watch that child coming out of school.

THE STEPDAUGHTER: Yes, yes. True. He used to follow me in the street and smiled at me, waved his hand, like this. I would look at him with interest, wondering who he might be. I told my mother, who guessed at once. (*The Mother agrees with a nod.*) Then she didn't want to send me to school for some days; and when I finally went back, there he was again — looking so ridiculous — with a paper parcel in his hands. He came close to me, caressed me, and drew out a fine straw hat from the parcel, with a bouquet of flowers — all for me!

THE MANAGER: A bit discursive this, you know!

THE SON (*contemptuously*): Literature! Literature!

Scene from the 1985 American Repertory Theatre production of *Six Characters in Search of an Author*, directed by Robert Brustein.

THE FATHER: Literature indeed! This is life, this is passion!

THE MANAGER: It may be, but it won't act.

THE FATHER: I agree. This is only the part leading up. I don't suggest this should be staged. She (*pointing to the Stepdaughter*), as you see, is no longer the flapper with plaits down her back —

THE STEPDAUGHTER: — and knickers showing below the skirt!

THE FATHER: The drama is coming now, sir; something new, complex, most interesting.

THE STEPDAUGHTER: As soon as my father died . . .

THE FATHER: — there was absolute misery for them. They came back here, unknown to me. Through her stupidity! (*Pointing to the Mother.*) It is true she can barely write her own name; but she could anyhow have got her daughter to write to me that they were in need . . .

THE MOTHER: And how was I to divine all this sentiment in him?

THE FATHER: That is exactly your mistake, never to have guessed any of my sentiments.

THE MOTHER: After so many years apart, and all that had happened . . .

THE FATHER: Was it my fault if that fellow carried you away? It happened quite suddenly, for after he had obtained some job or other, I could find no trace of them; and so, not unnaturally, my interest in them dwindled. But the drama culminated unforeseen and violent on their return, when I was impelled by my miserable flesh that still lives. . . . Ah! what misery, what wretchedness is that of the man who is alone and disdains debasing *liaisons!* Not old enough to do without women, and not young enough to go and look for one without shame. Misery? It's worse than misery; it's a horror; for no woman can any longer give him love; and when a man feels this. . . . One ought to do without, you say? Yes, yes, I know. Each of us when he appears before his fellows is clothed in a certain dignity. But every man knows what unconfessable things pass within the secrecy of his own heart. One gives way to the temptation, only to rise from it again, afterwards, with a great eagerness to reestablish one's dignity, as if it were a tombstone to place on the grave of one's shame, and a monument to hide and sign the memory of our weaknesses. Everybody's in the same case. Some folks haven't the courage to say certain things, that's all!

THE STEPDAUGHTER: All appear to have the courage to do them though.

THE FATHER: Yes, but in secret. Therefore, you want more courage to say these things. Let a man but speak these things out, and folks at once label him a cynic. But it isn't true. He is like all the others, better indeed, because he isn't afraid to reveal with the light of the intelligence the red shame of human bestiality on which most men close their eyes so as not to see it.

Woman — for example, look at her case! She turns tantalizing inviting glances on you. You seize her. No sooner does she feel herself in your grasp than she closes her eyes. It is the sign of her mission, the sign by which she says to man: "Blind yourself, for I am blind."

THE STEPDAUGHTER: Sometimes she can close them no

more: when she no longer feels the need of hiding her shame to herself, but dry-eyed and dispassionately, sees only that of the man who has blinded himself without love. Oh, all these intellectual complications make me sick, disgust me — all this philosophy that uncovers the beast in man, and then seeks to save him, excuse him . . . I can't stand it, sir. When a man seeks to "simplify" life bestially, throwing aside every relic of humanity, every chaste aspiration, every pure feeling, all sense of ideality, duty, modesty, shame . . . then nothing is more revolting and nauseous than a certain kind of remorse — crocodiles' tears, that's what it is.

THE MANAGER: Let's come to the point. This is only discussion.

THE FATHER: Very good, sir! But a fact is like a sack which won't stand up when it's empty. In order that it may stand up, one has to put into it the reason and sentiment which have caused it to exist. I couldn't possibly know that after the death of that man, they had decided to return here, that they were in misery, and that she (*pointing to the Mother*) had gone to work as a modiste,° and at a shop of the type of that of Madame Pace.

THE STEPDAUGHTER: A real high-class modiste, you must know, gentlemen. In appearance, she works for the leaders of the best society; but she arranges matters so that these elegant ladies serve her purpose . . . without prejudice to other ladies who are . . . well . . . only so so.

THE MOTHER: You will believe me, gentlemen, that it never entered my mind that the old hag offered me work because she had her eye on my daughter.

THE STEPDAUGHTER: Poor mamma! Do you know, sir, what that woman did when I brought her back the work my mother had finished? She would point out to me that I had torn one of my frocks, and she would give it back to my mother to mend. It was I who paid for it, always I; while this poor creature here believed she was sacrificing herself for me and these two children here, sitting up at night sewing Madame Pace's robes.

THE MANAGER: And one day you met there . . .

THE STEPDAUGHTER: Him, him. Yes sir, an old client. There's a scene for you to play! Superb!

THE FATHER: She, the Mother arrived just then . . .

THE STEPDAUGHTER (*treacherously*): Almost in time!

THE FATHER (*crying out*): No, in time! in time! Fortunately I recognized her . . . in time. And I took them back home with me to my house. You can imagine now her position and mine; she, as you see her; and I who cannot look her in the face.

THE STEPDAUGHTER: Absurd! How can I possibly be expected — after that — to be a modest young miss, a fit person to go with his confounded aspirations for "a solid moral sanity"?

THE FATHER: For the drama lies all in this — in the con-

science that I have, that each one of us has. We believe this conscience to be a single thing, but it is many-sided. There is one for this person, and another for that. Diverse consciences. So we have this illusion of being one person for all, of having a personality that is unique in all our acts. But it isn't true. We perceive this when, tragically perhaps, in something we do, we are as it were, suspended, caught up in the air on a kind of hook. Then we perceive that all of us was not in that act, and that it would be an atrocious injustice to judge us by that action alone, as if all our existence were summed up in that one deed. Now do you understand the perfidy of this girl? She surprised me in a place, where she ought not to have known me, just as I could not exist for her; and she now seeks to attach to me a reality such as I could never suppose I should have to assume for her in a shameful and fleeting moment of my life. I feel this above all else. And the drama, you will see, acquires a tremendous value from this point. Then there is the position of the others . . . his. . . . (*Indicating the Son.*)

THE SON (*shrugging his shoulders scornfully*): Leave me alone! I don't come into this.

THE FATHER: What? You don't come into this?

THE SON: I've got nothing to do with it, and don't want to have; because you know well enough I wasn't made to be mixed up in all this with the rest of you.

THE STEPDAUGHTER: We are only vulgar folk! He is the fine gentleman. You may have noticed, Mr. Manager, that I fix him now and again with a look of scorn while he lowers his eyes — for he knows the evil he has done me.

THE SON (*scarcely looking at her*): I?

THE STEPDAUGHTER: You! you! I owe my life on the streets to you. Did you or did you not deny us, with your behavior, I won't say the intimacy of home, but even that mere hospitality which makes guests feel at their ease? We were intruders who had come to disturb the kingdom of your legitimacy. I should like to have you witness, Mr. Manager, certain scenes between him and me. He says I have tyrannized over everyone. But it was just his behavior which made me insist on the reason for which I had come into the house, — this reason he calls "vile"— into his house, with my mother who is his mother too. And I came as mistress of the house.

THE SON: It's easy for them to put me always in the wrong. But imagine, gentlemen, the position of a son, whose fate it is to see arrive one day at his home a young woman of impudent bearing, a young woman who inquires for his father, with whom who knows what business she has. This young man has then to witness her return bolder than ever, accompanied by that child there. He is obliged to watch her treat his father in an equivocal and confidential manner. She asks for money of him in a way that lets one suppose he must give it to her, *must*, do you understand, because he has every obligation to do so.

---

modiste: A person who makes fashionable clothing for women.

THE FATHER: But I have, as a matter of fact, this obligation. I owe it to your mother.

THE SON: How should I know? When had I ever seen or heard of her? One day there arrive with her (*indicating Stepdaughter*) that lad and this baby here. I am told: "This is *your* mother too, you know." I divine from her manner (*indicating Stepdaughter again*) why it is they have come home. I had rather not say what I feel and think about it. I shouldn't even care to confess to myself. No action can therefore be hoped for from me in this affair. Believe me, Mr. Manager, I am an "unrealized" character, dramatically speaking; and I find myself not at all at ease in their company. Leave me out of it, I beg you.

THE FATHER: What? It is just because you are so that . . .

THE SON: How do you know what I am like? When did you ever bother your head about me?

THE FATHER: I admit it. I admit it. But isn't that a situation in itself? This aloofness of yours which is so cruel to me and to your mother, who returns home and sees you almost for the first time grown up, who doesn't recognize you but knows you are her son. . . . (*Pointing out the Mother to the Manager.*) See, she's crying!

THE STEPDAUGHTER (*angrily, stamping her foot*): Like a fool!

THE FATHER (*indicating Stepdaughter*): She can't stand him, you know. (*Then referring again to the Son.*) He says he doesn't come into the affair, whereas he is really the hinge of the whole action. Look at that lad who is always clinging to his mother, frightened and humiliated. It is on account of this fellow here. Possibly his situation is the most painful of all. He feels himself a stranger more than the others. The poor little chap feels mortified, humiliated at being brought into a home out of charity as it were. (*In confidence.*) He is the image of his father. Hardly talks at all. Humble and quiet.

THE MANAGER: Oh, we'll cut him out. You've no notion what a nuisance boys are on the stage. . . .

THE FATHER: He disappears soon, you know. And the baby too. She is the first to vanish from the scene. The drama consists finally in this: when that mother reenters my house, her family born outside of it, and shall we say superimposed on the original, ends with the death of the little girl, the tragedy of the boy and the flight of the elder daughter. It cannot go on, because it is foreign to its surroundings. So after much torment, we three remain: I, the mother, that son. Then, owing to the disappearance of that extraneous family, we too find ourselves strange to one another. We find we are living in an atmosphere of mortal desolation which is the revenge, as he (*indicating Son*) scornfully said of the Demon of Experiment, that unfortunately hides in me. Thus, sir, you see when faith is lacking, it becomes impossible to create certain states of happiness, for we lack the necessary humility. Vaingloriously, we try to substitute ourselves for this faith, creating thus for the rest of the world a reality which we believe after their fashion, while, actually, it doesn't exist. For each one of us has his own reality to be respected before God, even when it is harmful to one's very self.

THE MANAGER: There is something in what you say. I assure you all this interests me very much. I begin to think there's the stuff for a drama in all this, and not a bad drama either.

THE STEPDAUGHTER (*coming forward*): When you've got a character like me . . .

THE FATHER (*shutting her up, all excited to learn the decision of the Manager*): You be quiet!

THE MANAGER (*reflecting, heedless of interruption*): It's new . . . hem . . . yes. . . .

THE FATHER: Absolutely new!

THE MANAGER: You've got a nerve though, I must say, to come here and fling it at me like this . . .

THE FATHER: You will understand, sir, born as we are for the stage . . .

THE MANAGER: Are you amateur actors then?

THE FATHER: No, I say born for the stage, because . . .

THE MANAGER: Oh, nonsense. You're an old hand, you know.

THE FATHER: No sir, no. We act that role for which we have been cast, that role which we are given in life. And in my own case, passion itself, as usually happens, becomes a trifle theatrical when it is exalted.

THE MANAGER: Well, well, that will do. But you see, without an author. . . . I could give you the address of an author if you like . . .

THE FATHER: No, no. Look here! You must be the author.

THE MANAGER: I? What are you talking about?

THE FATHER: Yes, you, you! Why not?

THE MANAGER: Because I have never been an author: that's why.

THE FATHER: Then why not turn author now? Everybody does it. You don't want any special qualities. Your task is made much easier by the fact that we are all here alive before you. . . .

THE MANAGER: It won't do.

THE FATHER: What? When you see us live our drama. . . .

THE MANAGER: Yes, that's all right. But you want someone to write it.

THE FATHER: No, no. Someone to take it down, possibly, while we play it, scene by scene! It will be enough to sketch it out at first, and then try it over.

THE MANAGER: Well . . . I am almost tempted. It's a bit of an idea. One might have a shot at it.

THE FATHER: Of course. You'll see what scenes will come out of it. I can give you one, at once . . .

THE MANAGER: By Jove, it tempts me. I'd like to have a go at it. Let's try it out. Come with me to my office. (*Turning to the Actors.*) You are at liberty for a bit, but don't step out of the theater for long. In a quarter of an hour, twenty minutes, all back here again! (*To the Father.*) We'll see what can be done. Who knows if we don't get something really extraordinary out of it?

THE FATHER: There's no doubt about it. They (*indicating the Characters*) had better come with us too, hadn't they?

THE MANAGER: Yes, yes. Come on! come on! (*Moves away and then turning to the Actors.*) Be punctual, please! (*Manager and the Six Characters cross the stage and go off. The other Actors remain, looking at one another in astonishment.*)

LEADING MAN: Is he serious? What the devil does he want to do?

JUVENILE LEAD: This is rank madness.

THIRD ACTOR: Does he expect to knock up a drama in five minutes?

JUVENILE LEAD: Like the improvisers!

LEADING LADY: If he thinks I'm going to take part in a joke like this. . . .

JUVENILE LEAD: I'm out of it anyway.

FOURTH ACTOR: I should like to know who they are. (*Alludes to Characters.*)

THIRD ACTOR: What do you suppose? Madmen or rascals!

JUVENILE LEAD: And he takes them seriously!

L'INGÉNUE: Vanity! He fancies himself as an author now.

LEADING MAN: It's absolutely unheard of. If the stage has come to this . . . well I'm . . .

FIFTH ACTOR: It's rather a joke.

THIRD ACTOR: Well, we'll see what's going to happen next.

(*Thus talking, the Actors leave the stage, some going out by the little door at the back, others retiring to their dressing rooms.*)

(*The curtain remains up.*)

(*The action of the play is suspended for twenty minutes.*)

ACT II

(*The stage call-bells ring to warn the company that the play is about to begin again.*)

(*The Stepdaughter comes out of the Manager's office along with the Child and the Boy. As she comes out of the office, she cries: — *)

Nonsense! nonsense! Do it yourselves! I'm not going to mix myself up in this mess. (*Turning to the Child and coming quickly with her on to the stage.*) Come on, Rosetta, let's run!

(*The Boy follows them slowly, remaining a little behind and seeming perplexed.*)

THE STEPDAUGHTER (*stops, bends over the Child and takes the latter's face between her hands*): My little darling! You're frightened, aren't you? You don't know where we are, do you? (*Pretending to reply to a question of the Child.*) What is the stage? It's a place, baby, you know, where people play at being serious, a place where they act comedies. We've got to act a comedy now, dead serious, you know; and

you're in it also, little one. (*Embraces her, pressing the little head to her breast, and rocking the Child for a moment.*) Oh darling, darling, what a horrid comedy you've got to play! What a wretched part they've found for you! A garden . . . a fountain . . . look . . . just suppose, kiddie, it's here. Where, you say? Why, right here in the middle. It's all pretense you know. That's the trouble, my pet: it's all make-believe here. It's better to imagine it though, because if they fix it up for you, it'll only be painted cardboard, painted cardboard for the rockery, the water, the plants. . . . Ah, but I think a baby like this one would sooner have a make-believe fountain than a real one, so she could play with it. What a joke it'll be for the others! But for you, alas! not quite such a joke: you who are real, baby dear, and really play by a real fountain that is big and green and beautiful, with ever so many bamboos around it that are reflected in the water, and a whole lot of little ducks swimming about. . . . No, Rosetta, no, your mother doesn't bother about you on account of that wretch of a son there. I'm in the devil of a temper, and as for that lad. . . . (*Seizes Boy by the arm to force him to take one of his hands out of his pockets.*) What have you got there? What are you hiding? (*Pulls his hand out of his pocket, looks into it, and catches the glint of a revolver.*) Ah! where did you get this? (*The Boy, very pale in the face, looks at her, but does not answer.*) Idiot! If I'd been in your place, instead of killing myself, I'd have shot one of those two, or both of them: father and son.

(*The Father enters from the office, all excited from his work. The Manager follows him.*)

THE FATHER: Come on, come on dear! Come here for a minute! We've arranged everything. It's all fixed up.

THE MANAGER (*also excited*): If you please, young lady, there are one or two points to settle still. Will you come along?

THE STEPDAUGHTER (*following him toward the office*): Ouff! what's the good, if you've arranged everything.

(*The Father, Manager, and Stepdaughter go back into the office again [off] for a moment. At the same time, the Son, followed by the Mother, comes out.*)

THE SON (*looking at the three entering office*): Oh this is fine, fine! And to think I can't even get away!

(*The Mother attempts to look at him, but lowers her eyes immediately when he turns away from her. She then sits down. The Boy and the Child approach her. She casts a glance again at the Son, and speaks with humble tones, trying to draw him into conversation.*)

THE MOTHER: And isn't my punishment the worst of all? (*Then seeing from the Son's manner that he will not bother himself about her.*) My God! Why are you so cruel? Isn't it enough for one person to support all this torment? Must you then insist on others seeing it also?

THE SON (*half to himself, meaning the Mother to hear, however*): And they want to put it on the stage! If there was at least a reason for it! He thinks he has got at the meaning of it all. Just as if each one of us in every circumstance of life couldn't find his own explanation of it! (*Pauses.*) He complains he was discovered in a place where he ought not to have been seen, in a moment of his life which ought to have remained hidden and kept out of the reach of that convention which he has to maintain for other people. And what about my case? Haven't I had to reveal what no son ought ever to reveal: how father and mother live and are man and wife for themselves quite apart from that idea of father and mother which we give them? When this idea is revealed, our life is then linked at one point only to that man and that woman; and as such it should shame them, shouldn't it?

(*The Mother hides her face in her hands. From the dressing rooms and the little door at the back of the stage the Actors and Stage Manager return, followed by the Property Man and the Prompter. At the same moment, the Manager comes out of his office, accompanied by the Father and the Stepdaughter.*)

THE MANAGER: Come on, come on, ladies and gentlemen! Heh! you there, machinist!

MACHINIST: Yes sir?

THE MANAGER: Fix up the parlor with the floral decorations. Two wings and a drop with a door will do. Hurry up!

(*The Machinist runs off at once to prepare the scene and arranges it while the Manager talks with the Stage Manager, the Property Man, and the Prompter on matters of detail.*)

THE MANAGER (*to Property Man*): Just have a look, and see if there isn't a sofa or a divan in the wardrobe . . .

PROPERTY MAN: There's the green one.

THE STEPDAUGHTER: No no! Green won't do. It was yellow, ornamented with flowers — very large! and most comfortable!

PROPERTY MAN: There isn't one like that.

THE MANAGER: It doesn't matter. Use the one we've got.

THE STEPDAUGHTER: Doesn't matter? It's most important!

THE MANAGER: We're only trying it now. Please don't interfere. (*To Property Man.*) See if we've got a shop window — long and narrowish.

THE STEPDAUGHTER: And the little table! The little mahogany table for the pale blue envelope!

PROPERTY MAN (*to Manager*): There's that little gilt one.

THE MANAGER: That'll do fine.

THE FATHER: A mirror.

THE STEPDAUGHTER: And the screen! We must have a screen. Otherwise how can I manage?

PROPERTY MAN: That's all right, Miss. We've got any amount of them.

THE MANAGER (*to the Stepdaughter*): We want some clothes pegs too, don't we?

THE STEPDAUGHTER: Yes, several, several!

THE MANAGER: See how many we've got and bring them all.

PROPERTY MAN: All right!

(*The Property Man hurries off to obey his orders. While he is putting the things in their places, the Manager talks to the Prompter and then with the Characters and the Actors.*)

THE MANAGER (*to Prompter*): Take your seat. Look here: this is the outline of the scenes, act by act. (*Hands him some sheets of paper.*) And now I'm going to ask you to do something out of the ordinary.

PROMPTER: Take it down in shorthand?

THE MANAGER (*pleasantly surprised*): Exactly! Can you do shorthand?

PROMPTER: Yes, a little.

THE MANAGER: Good! (*Turning to a Stage Hand.*) Go and get some paper from my office, plenty, as much as you can find.

(*The Stage Hand goes off and soon returns with a handful of paper which he gives to the Prompter.*)

THE MANAGER (*to Prompter*): You follow the scenes as we play them, and try and get the points down, at any rate the most important ones. (*Then addressing the Actors.*) Clear the stage, ladies and gentlemen! Come over here (*pointing to the left*) and listen attentively.

LEADING LADY: But, excuse me, we . . .

THE MANAGER (*guessing her thought*): Don't worry! You won't have to improvise.

LEADING MAN: What have we to do then?

THE MANAGER: Nothing. For the moment you just watch and listen. Everybody will get his part written out afterwards. At present we're going to try the thing as best we can. They're going to act now.

THE FATHER (*as if fallen from the clouds into the confusion of the stage*): We? What do you mean, if you please, by a rehearsal?

THE MANAGER: A rehearsal for them. (*Points to the Actors.*)

THE FATHER: But since we are the characters . . .

THE MANAGER: All right: "characters" then, if you insist on calling yourselves such. But here, my dear sir, the characters don't act. Here the actors do the acting. The characters are there, in the "book" (*pointing toward Prompter's box*) — when there is a "book"!

THE FATHER: I won't contradict you; but excuse me, the actors aren't the characters. They want to be, they pretend to be, don't they? Now if these gentlemen here are fortunate enough to have us alive before them . . .

THE MANAGER: Oh, this is grand! You want to come before the public yourselves then?

THE FATHER: As we are. . . .

THE MANAGER: I can assure you it would be a magnificent spectacle!

LEADING MAN: What's the use of us here anyway then?

THE MANAGER: You're not going to pretend that you can

act? It makes me laugh! (*The Actors laugh.*) There, you see, they are laughing at the notion. But, by the way, I must cast the parts. That won't be difficult. They cast themselves. (*To the Second Lady Lead.*) You play the Mother. (*To the Father.*) We must find her a name.

THE FATHER: Amalia, sir.

THE MANAGER: But that is the real name of your wife. We don't want to call her by her real name.

THE FATHER: Why ever not, if it is her name? . . . Still, perhaps, if that lady must . . . (*Makes a slight motion of the hand to indicate the Second Lady Lead.*) I see this woman here (*means the Mother*) as Amalia. But do as you like. (*Gets more and more confused.*) I don't know what to say to you. Already, I begin to hear my own words ring false, as if they had another sound . . .

THE MANAGER: Don't you worry about it. It'll be our job to find the right tones. And as for her name, if you want her Amalia, Amalia it shall be; and if you don't like it, we'll find another! For the moment though, we'll call the characters in this way: (*To Juvenile Lead.*) You are the Son. (*To the Leading Lady.*) You naturally are the Stepdaughter. . . .

THE STEPDAUGHTER (*excitedly*): What? what? I, that woman there? (*Bursts out laughing.*)

THE MANAGER (*angry*): What is there to laugh at?

LEADING LADY (*indignant*): Nobody has ever dared to laugh at me. I insist on being treated with respect; otherwise I go away.

THE STEPDAUGHTER: No, no, excuse me . . . I am not laughing at you. . . .

THE MANAGER (*to Stepdaughter*): You ought to feel honored to be played by . . .

LEADING LADY (*at once, contemptuously*): "That woman there". . .

THE STEPDAUGHTER: But I wasn't speaking of you, you know. I was speaking of myself — whom I can't see at all in you! That is all. I don't know . . . but . . . you . . . aren't in the least like me. . . .

THE FATHER: True. Here's the point. Look here, sir, our temperaments, our souls. . . .

THE MANAGER: Temperament, soul, be hanged! Do you suppose the spirit of the piece is in you? Nothing of the kind!

THE FATHER: What, haven't we our own temperaments, our own souls?

THE MANAGER: Not at all. Your soul or whatever you like to call it takes shape here. The actors give body and form to it, voice and gesture. And my actors — I may tell you — have given expression to much more lofty material than this little drama of yours, which may or may not hold up on the stage. But if it does, the merit of it, believe me, will be due to my actors.

THE FATHER: I don't dare contradict you, sir, but, believe me, it is a terrible suffering for us who are as we are, with these bodies of ours, these features to see. . . .

THE MANAGER (*cutting him short and out of patience*):

Good heavens! The make-up will remedy all that, man, the make-up. . . .

THE FATHER: Maybe. But the voice, the gestures . . .

THE MANAGER: Now, look here! On the stage, you as yourself, cannot exist. The actor here acts you, and that's an end to it!

THE FATHER: I understand. And now I think I see why our author who conceived us as we are, all alive, didn't want to put us on the stage after all. I haven't the least desire to offend your actors. Far from it! But when I think that I am to be acted by . . . I don't know by whom. . . .

LEADING MAN (*on his dignity*): By me, if you've no objection!

THE FATHER (*humbly, mellifluously*): Honored, I assure you, sir. (*Bows.*) Still, I must say that try as this gentleman may, with all his good will and wonderful art, to absorb me into himself. . . .

LEADING MAN: Oh chuck it! "Wonderful art!" Withdraw that, please!

THE FATHER: The performance he will give, even doing his best with make-up to look like me. . . .

LEADING MAN: It will certainly be a bit difficult! (*The Actors laugh.*)

THE FATHER: Exactly! It will be difficult to act me as I really am. The effect will be rather — apart from the make-up — according as to how he supposes I am, as he senses me — if he does sense me — and not as I inside of myself feel myself to be. It seems to me then that account should be taken of this by everyone whose duty it may become to criticize us. . . .

THE MANAGER: Heavens! The man's starting to think about the critics now! Let them say what they like. It's up to us to put on the play if we can. (*Looking around.*) Come on! come on! Is the stage set? (*To the Actors and Characters.*) Stand back — stand back! Let me see, and don't let's lose any more time! (*To the Stepdaughter.*) Is it all right as it is now?

THE STEPDAUGHTER: Well, to tell the truth, I don't recognize the scene.

THE MANAGER: My dear lady, you can't possibly suppose that we can construct that shop of Madame Pace piece by piece here? (*To the Father.*) You said a white room with flowered wallpaper, didn't you?

THE FATHER: Yes.

THE MANAGER: Well then. We've got the furniture right more or less. Bring that little table a bit further forward. (*The Stage Hands obey the order. To Property Man.*) You go and find an envelope, if possible, a pale blue one; and give it to that gentleman. (*Indicates Father.*)

PROPERTY MAN: An ordinary envelope?

MANAGER AND FATHER: Yes, yes, an ordinary envelope.

PROPERTY MAN: At once, sir. (*Exit.*)

THE MANAGER: Ready, everyone! First scene — the Young Lady. (*The Leading Lady comes forward.*) No, no, you must wait. I meant her. (*Indicating the Stepdaughter.*) You just watch —

THE STEPDAUGHTER (*adding at once*): How I shall play it, how I shall live it! . . .

LEADING LADY (*offended*): I shall live it also, you may be sure, as soon as I begin!

THE MANAGER (*with his hands to his head*): Ladies and gentlemen, if you please! No more useless discussions! Scene I: the Young Lady with Madame Pace: Oh! (*Looks around as if lost.*) And this Madame Pace, where is she?

THE FATHER: She isn't with us, sir.

THE MANAGER: Then what the devil's to be done?

THE FATHER: But she is alive too.

THE MANAGER: Yes, but where is she?

THE FATHER: One minute. Let me speak! (*Turning to the Actresses.*) If these ladies would be so good as to give me their hats for a moment. . . .

THE ACTRESSES (*half surprised, half laughing, in chorus*): What? Why? Our hats? What does he say?

THE MANAGER: What are you going to do with the ladies' hats? (*The Actors laugh.*)

THE FATHER: Oh nothing. I just want to put them on these pegs for a moment. And one of the ladies will be so kind as to take off her mantle. . . .

THE ACTORS: Oh, what d'you think of that? Only the mantle? He must be mad.

SOME ACTRESSES: But why? Mantles as well?

THE FATHER: To hang them up here for a moment. Please be so kind, will you?

THE ACTRESSES (*taking off their hats, one or two also their cloaks, and going to hang them on the racks*): After all, why not? There you are! This is really funny. We've got to put them on show.

THE FATHER: Exactly; just like that, on show.

THE MANAGER: May we know why?

THE FATHER: I'll tell you. Who knows if, by arranging the stage for her, she does not come here herself, attracted by the very articles of her trade? (*Inviting the Actors to look toward the exit at back of stage.*) Look! Look!

(*The door at the back of stage opens and Madame Pace enters and takes a few steps forward. She is a fat, oldish woman with puffy oxygenated hair. She is rouged and powdered with a comical elegance in black silk. Round her waist is a long silver chain from which hangs a pair of scissors. The Stepdaughter runs over to her at once amid the stupor of the Actors.*)

THE STEPDAUGHTER (*turning toward her*): There she is! There she is!

THE FATHER (*radiant*): It's she! I said so, didn't I! There she is!

THE MANAGER (*conquering his surprise, and then becoming indignant*): What sort of a trick is this?

LEADING MAN (*almost at the same time*): What's going to happen next?

JUVENILE LEAD: Where does she come from?

L'INGÉNUE: They've been holding her in reserve, I guess.

LEADING LADY: A vulgar trick!

THE FATHER (*dominating the protests*): Excuse me, all of you! Why are you so anxious to destroy in the name of a vulgar, commonplace sense of truth, this reality which comes to birth attracted and formed by the magic of the stage itself, which has indeed more right to live here than you, since it is much truer than you — if you don't mind my saying so? Which is the actress among you who is to play Madame Pace? Well, here is Madame Pace herself. And you will allow, I fancy, that the actress who acts her will be less true than this woman here, who is herself in person. You see my daughter recognized her and went over to her at once. Now you're going to witness the scene!

(*But the scene between the Stepdaughter and Madame Pace has already begun despite the protest of the Actors and the reply of the Father. It has begun quietly, naturally, in a manner impossible for the stage. So when the Actors, called to attention by the Father, turn round and see Madame Pace, who has placed one hand under the Stepdaughter's chin to raise her head, they observe her at first with great attention, but hearing her speak in an unintelligible manner their interest begins to wane.*)

THE MANAGER: Well? well?

LEADING MAN: What does she say?

LEADING LADY: One can't hear a word.

JUVENILE LEAD: Louder! Louder please!

THE STEPDAUGHTER (*leaving Madame Pace, who smiles a Sphinx-like smile, and advancing toward the Actors*): Louder? Louder? What are you talking about? These aren't matters which can be shouted at the top of one's voice. If I have spoken them out loud, it was to shame him and have my revenge. (*Indicates Father.*) But for Madame it's quite a different matter.

THE MANAGER: Indeed? indeed? But here, you know people have got to make themselves heard, my dear. Even we who are on the stage can't hear you. What will it be when the public's in the theater? And anyway, you can very well speak up now among yourselves, since we shan't be present to listen to you as we are now. You've got to pretend to be alone in a room at the back of a shop where no one can hear you.

(*The Stepdaughter coquettishly and with a touch of malice makes a sign of disagreement two or three times with her finger.*)

THE MANAGER: What do you mean by no?

THE STEPDAUGHTER (*sotto voce,° mysteriously*): There's someone who will hear us if she (*indicating Madame Pace*) speaks out loud.

THE MANAGER (*in consternation*): What? Have you got someone else to spring on us now? (*The Actors burst out laughing.*)

THE FATHER: No, no sir. She is alluding to me. I've got to

---

sotto voce: In a soft voice or stage whisper.

be here — there behind that door, in waiting; and Madame Pace knows it. In fact, if you will allow me, I'll go there at once, so I can be quite ready. (*Moves away.*)

THE MANAGER (*stopping him*): No! wait! wait! We must observe the conventions of the theater. Before you are ready . . .

THE STEPDAUGHTER (*interrupting him*): No, get on with it at once! I'm just dying, I tell you, to act this scene. If he's ready, I'm more than ready.

THE MANAGER (*shouting*): But, my dear young lady, first of all, we must have the scene between you and this lady. . . . (*Indicates Madame Pace.*) Do you understand?

THE STEPDAUGHTER: Good Heavens! She's been telling me what you know already: that mama's work is badly done again, that the material's ruined; and that if I want her to continue to help us in our misery I must be patient. . . .

MADAME PACE (*coming forward with an air of great importance*): Yes indeed, sir, I no wanta take advantage of her, I no wanta be hard. . . .

(*Note: Madame Pace is supposed to talk in a jargon half Italian, half English.*)

THE MANAGER (*alarmed*): What? What? She talks like that? (*The Actors burst out laughing again.*)

THE STEPDAUGHTER (*also laughing*): Yes yes, that's the way she talks, half English, half Italian! Most comical it is!

MADAME PACE: Itta seem not verra polite gentlemen laugha atta me eeff I trya best speaka English.

THE MANAGER: *Diamine!*° Of course! Of course! Let her talk like that! Just what we want. Talk just like that, Madame, if you please! The effect will be certain. Exactly what was wanted to put a little comic relief into the crudity of the situation. Of course she talks like that! Magnificent!

THE STEPDAUGHTER: Magnificent? Certainly! When certain suggestions are made to one in language of that kind, the effect is certain, since it seems almost a joke. One feels inclined to laugh when one hears her talk about an "old signore" "who wanta talka nicely with you." Nice old signore, eh, Madame?

MADAME PACE: Not so old my dear, not so old! And even if you no like him, he won't make any scandal!

THE MOTHER (*jumping up amid the amazement and consternation of the Actors, who had not been noticing her. They move to restrain her*): You old devil! You murderess!

THE STEPDAUGHTER (*running over to calm her Mother*): Calm yourself, Mother, calm yourself! Please don't. . . .

THE FATHER (*going to her also at the same time*): Calm yourself! Don't get excited! Sit down now!

THE MOTHER: Well then, take that woman away out of my sight!

Diamine!: Italian for "Well, I'll be damned!"

THE STEPDAUGHTER (*to Manager*): It is impossible for my mother to remain here.

THE FATHER (*to Manager*): They can't be here together. And for this reason, you see: that woman there was not with us when we came. . . . If they are on together, the whole thing is given away inevitably, as you see.

THE MANAGER: It doesn't matter. This is only a first rough sketch — just to get an idea of the various points of the scene, even confusedly. . . . (*Turning to the Mother and leading her to her chair.*) Come along, my dear lady, sit down now, and let's get on with the scene. . . .

(*Meanwhile, the Stepdaughter, coming forward again, turns to Madame Pace.*)

THE STEPDAUGHTER: Come on, Madame, come on!

MADAME PACE (*offended*): No, no, *grazie*. I do not do anything witha your mother present.

THE STEPDAUGHTER: Nonsense! Introduce this "old signore" who wants to talk nicely to me. (*Addressing the Company imperiously.*) We've got to do this scene one way or another, haven't we? Come on! (*To Madame Pace.*) You can go!

MADAME PACE: Ah yes! I go'way! I go'way! Certainly! (*Exits furious.*)

THE STEPDAUGHTER (*to the Father*): Now you make your entry. No, you needn't go over there. Come here. Let's suppose you've already come in. Like that, yes! I'm here with bowed head, modest like. Come on! Out with your voice! Say "Good morning, Miss" in that peculiar tone, that special tone. . . .

THE MANAGER: Excuse me, but are you the Manager, or am I? (*To the Father, who looks undecided and perplexed.*) Get on with it, man! Go down there to the back of the stage. You needn't go off. Then come right forward here.

(*The Father does as he is told, looking troubled and perplexed at first. But as soon as he begins to move, the reality of the action affects him, and he begins to smile and to be more natural. The Actors watch intently.*)

THE MANAGER (*sotto voce, quickly to the Prompter in his box*): Ready! ready! Get ready to write now.

THE FATHER (*coming forward and speaking in a different tone*): Good afternoon, Miss!

THE STEPDAUGHTER (*head bowed down slightly, with restrained disgust*): Good afternoon!

THE FATHER (*looks under her hat which partly covers her face. Perceiving she is very young, he makes an exclamation, partly of surprise, partly of fear lest he compromise himself in a risky adventure*): Ah . . . but . . . ah . . . I say . . . this is not the first time that you have come here, is it?

THE STEPDAUGHTER (*modestly*): No sir.

THE FATHER: You've been here before, eh? (*Then seeing her nod agreement.*) More than once? (*Waits for her to answer, looks under her hat, smiles, and then says:*) Well then, there's no need to be so shy, is there? May I take off your hat?

THE STEPDAUGHTER (*anticipating him and with veiled disgust*): No sir . . . I'll do it myself. (*Takes it off quickly.*)

(*The Mother, who watches the progress of the scene with the Son and the other two children who cling to her, is on thorns; and follows with varying expressions of sorrow, indignation, anxiety, and horror the words and actions of the other two. From time to time she hides her face in her hands and sobs.*)

THE MOTHER: Oh, my God, my God!

THE FATHER (*playing his part with a touch of gallantry*): Give it to me! I'll put it down. (*Takes hat from her hands.*) But a dear little head like yours ought to have a smarter hat. Come and help me choose one from the stock, won't you?

L'INGÉNUE (*interrupting*): I say . . . those are our hats you know.

THE MANAGER (*furious*): Silence! silence! Don't try and be funny, if you please. . . . We're playing the scene now, I'd have you notice. (*To the Stepdaughter.*) Begin again, please!

THE STEPDAUGHTER (*continuing*): No thank you, sir.

THE FATHER: Oh, come now. Don't talk like that. You must take it. I shall be upset if you don't. There are some lovely little hats here; and then — Madame will be pleased. She expects it, anyway, you know.

THE STEPDAUGHTER: No, no! I couldn't wear it!

THE FATHER: Oh, you're thinking about what they'd say at home if they saw you come in with a new hat? My dear girl, there's always a way round these little matters, you know.

THE STEPDAUGHTER (*all keyed up*): No, it's not that. I couldn't wear it because I am . . . as you see . . . you might have noticed . . .

(*Showing her black dress.*)

THE FATHER: . . . in mourning! Of course: I beg your pardon: I'm frightfully sorry. . . .

THE STEPDAUGHTER (*forcing herself to conquer her indignation and nausea*): Stop! Stop! It's I who must thank you. There's no need for you to feel mortified or specially sorry. Don't think any more of what I've said. (*Tries to smile.*) I must forget that I am dressed so. . . .

THE MANAGER (*interrupting and turning to the Prompter*): Stop a minute! Stop! Don't write that down. Cut out that last bit. (*Then to the Father and Stepdaughter.*) Fine! it's going fine! (*To the Father only.*) And now you can go on as we arranged. (*To the Actors.*) Pretty good that scene, where he offers her the hat, eh?

THE STEPDAUGHTER: The best's coming now. Why can't we go on?

THE MANAGER: Have a little patience! (*To the Actors.*) Of course, it must be treated rather lightly.

LEADING MAN: Still, with a bit of go in it!

LEADING LADY: Of course! It's easy enough! (*To Leading Man.*) Shall you and I try it now?

LEADING MAN: Why, yes! I'll prepare my entrance. (*Exit in order to make his entrance.*)

THE MANAGER (*to Leading Lady*): See here! The scene between you and Madame Pace is finished. I'll have it written out properly after. You remain here . . . oh, where are you going?

LEADING LADY: One minute. I want to put my hat on again. (*Goes over to hatrack and puts her hat on her head.*)

THE MANAGER: Good! You stay here with your head bowed down a bit.

THE STEPDAUGHTER: But she isn't dressed in black.

LEADING LADY: But I shall be, and much more effectively than you.

THE MANAGER (*to Stepdaughter*): Be quiet please, and watch! You'll be able to learn something. (*Clapping his hands.*) Come on! come on! Entrance, please!

(*The door at rear of stage opens, and the Leading Man enters with the lively manner of an old gallant. The rendering of the scene by the Actors from the very first words is seen to be quite a different thing, though it has not in any way the air of a parody. Naturally, the Stepdaughter and the Father, not being able to recognize themselves in the Leading Lady and the Leading Man, who deliver their words in different tones and with a different psychology, express, sometimes with smiles, sometimes with gestures, the impression they receive.*)

LEADING MAN: Good afternoon, Miss . . .

THE FATHER (*at once unable to contain himself*): No! no!

(*The Stepdaughter, noticing the way the Leading Man enters, bursts out laughing.*)

THE MANAGER (*furious*): Silence! And you, please, just stop that laughing. If we go on like this, we shall never finish.

THE STEPDAUGHTER: Forgive me, sir but it's natural enough. This lady (*indicating Leading Lady*) stands there still; but if she is supposed to be me, I can assure you that if I heard anyone say "Good afternoon" in that manner and in that tone, I should burst out laughing as I did.

THE FATHER: Yes, yes, the manner, the tone . . .

THE MANAGER: Nonsense! Rubbish! Stand aside and let me see the action.

LEADING MAN: If I've got to represent an old fellow who's coming into a house of an equivocal character . . .

THE MANAGER: Don't listen to them, for Heaven's sake! Do it again! It goes fine. (*Waiting for the Actors to begin again.*) Well?

LEADING MAN: Good afternoon, Miss.

LEADING LADY: Good afternoon.

LEADING MAN (*imitating the gesture of the Father when he looked under the hat, and then expressing quite clearly first satisfaction and then fear*): Ah, but . . . I say . . . this is not the first time that you have come here, is it?

THE MANAGER: Good, but not quite so heavily. Like

this. (*Acts himself.*) "This isn't the first time that you have come here"... (*To Leading Lady.*) And you say: "No, sir."

LEADING LADY: No, sir.

LEADING MAN: You've been here before, more than once.

THE MANAGER: No, no, stop! Let her nod "yes" first. "You've been here before, eh?" (*The Leading Lady lifts up her head slightly and closes her eyes as though in disgust. Then she inclines her head twice.*)

THE STEPDAUGHTER (*unable to contain herself*): Oh my God! (*Puts a hand to her mouth to prevent herself from laughing.*)

THE MANAGER (*turning round*): What's the matter?

THE STEPDAUGHTER: Nothing, nothing!

THE MANAGER (*to Leading Man*): Go on!

LEADING MAN: You've been here before, eh? Well then, there's no need to be so shy, is there? May I take off your hat?

(*The Leading Man says this last speech in such a tone and with such gestures that the Stepdaughter, though she has her hand to her mouth, cannot keep from laughing.*)

LEADING LADY (*indignant*): I'm not going to stop here to be made a fool of by that woman there.

LEADING MAN: Neither am I! I'm through with it!

THE MANAGER (*shouting to Stepdaughter*): Silence! for once and all, I tell you!

THE STEPDAUGHTER: Forgive me! forgive me!

THE MANAGER: You haven't any manners: that's what it is! You go too far.

THE FATHER (*endeavoring to intervene*): Yes, it's true, but excuse her . . .

THE MANAGER: Excuse what? It's absolutely disgusting.

THE FATHER: Yes, sir, but believe me, it has such a strange effect when . . .

THE MANAGER: Strange? Why strange? Where is it strange?

THE FATHER: No, sir; I admire your actors — this gentleman here, this lady; but they are certainly not us!

THE MANAGER: I should hope not. Evidently they cannot be you, if they are actors.

THE FATHER: Just so: actors! Both of them act our parts exceedingly well. But, believe me, it produces quite a different effect on us. They want to be us, but they aren't, all the same.

THE MANAGER: What is it then anyway?

THE FATHER: Something that is . . . that is theirs — and no longer ours . . .

THE MANAGER: But naturally, inevitably, I've told you so already.

THE FATHER: Yes, I understand . . . I understand . . .

THE MANAGER: Well then, let's have no more of it! (*Turning to the Actors.*) We'll have the rehearsals by ourselves, afterwards, in the ordinary way. I never could stand rehearsing with the author present. He's never satisfied! (*Turning to Father and Stepdaughter.*) Come on! Let's get on with it again; and try and see if you can't keep from laughing.

THE STEPDAUGHTER: Oh, I shan't laugh any more. There's a nice little bit coming from me now: you'll see.

THE MANAGER: Well then: when she says "Don't think any more of what I've said, I must forget, etc.," you (*addressing the Father*) come in sharp with "I understand"; and then you ask her . . .

THE STEPDAUGHTER (*interrupting*): What?

THE MANAGER: Why she is in mourning.

THE STEPDAUGHTER: Not at all! See here: when I told him that it was useless for me to be thinking about my wearing mourning, do you know how he answered me? "Ah well," he said, "then let's take off this little frock."

THE MANAGER: Great! Just what we want, to make a riot in the theater!

THE STEPDAUGHTER: But it's the truth!

THE MANAGER: What does that matter? Acting is our business here. Truth up to a certain point, but no further.

THE STEPDAUGHTER: What do you want to do then?

THE MANAGER: You'll see, you'll see! Leave it to me.

THE STEPDAUGHTER: No sir! What you want to do is to piece together a little romantic sentimental scene out of my disgust, out of all the reasons, each more cruel and viler than the other, why I am what I am. He is to ask me why I'm in mourning; and I'm to answer with tears in my eyes, that it is just two months since papa died. No sir, no! He's got to say to me, as he did say, "Well, let's take off this little dress at once." And I, with my two months' mourning in my heart, went there behind that screen, and with these fingers tingling with shame . . .

THE MANAGER (*running his hands through his hair*): For Heaven's sake! What are you saying?

THE STEPDAUGHTER (*crying out excitedly*): The truth! The truth!

THE MANAGER: It may be. I don't deny it, and I can understand all your horror; but you must surely see that you can't have this kind of thing on the stage. It won't go.

THE STEPDAUGHTER: Not possible, eh? Very well! I'm much obliged to you — but I'm off.

THE MANAGER: Now be reasonable! Don't lose your temper!

THE STEPDAUGHTER: I won't stop here! I won't! I can see you fixed it all up with him in your office. All this talk about what is possible for the stage . . . I understand! He wants to get at his complicated "cerebral drama," to have his famous remorses and torments acted; but I want to act my part, *my part!*

THE MANAGER (*annoyed, shaking his shoulders*): Ah! Just *your* part! But, if you will pardon me, there are other parts than yours: His (*indicating the Father*) and hers (*indicating the Mother*)! On the stage you can't have a character becoming too prominent and overshadowing all the others. The thing is to pack them all into a neat little framework and then act what is actable. I am aware of the fact that everyone has his own interior life which he wants very much to put forward. But the difficulty lies in this fact: to set out just so much as is necessary for the stage, taking the other characters into consideration, and at the same time hint at the unrevealed interior life of each. I am willing to admit, my dear young lady, that from your point of view it would be a fine idea if each character could tell the public all his troubles in a nice monologue or a regular one hour lecture. (*Good humoredly.*) You must restrain yourself, my dear, and in your own interest, too; because this fury of yours, this exaggerated disgust you show, may make a bad impression, you know. After you have confessed to me that there were others before him at Madame Pace's and more than once . . .

THE STEPDAUGHTER (*bowing her head, impressed*): It's true. But remember those others mean him for me all the same.

THE MANAGER (*not understanding*): What? The others? What do you mean?

THE STEPDAUGHTER: For one who has gone wrong, sir, he who was responsible for the first fault is responsible for all that follow. He is responsible for my faults, was, even before I was born. Look at him, and see if it isn't true!

THE MANAGER: Well, well! And does the weight of so much responsibility seem nothing to you? Give him a chance to act it, to get it over!

THE STEPDAUGHTER: How? How can he act all his "noble remorses," all his "moral torments," if you want to spare him the horror of being discovered one day — after he had asked her what he did ask her — in the arms of her, that already fallen woman, that child, sir, that child he used to watch come out of school? (*She is moved.*)

(*The Mother at this point is overcome with emotion and breaks out into a fit of crying. All are touched. A long pause.*)

THE STEPDAUGHTER (*as soon as the Mother becomes a little quieter, adds resolutely and gravely*): At present, we are unknown to the public. Tomorrow, you will act us as you wish, treating us in your own manner. But do you really want to see drama, do you want to see it flash out as it really did?

THE MANAGER: Of course! That's just what I do want, so I can use as much of it as is possible.

THE STEPDAUGHTER: Well then, ask that Mother there to leave us.

THE MOTHER (*changing her low plaint into a sharp cry*): No! No! Don't permit, it, sir, don't permit it!

THE MANAGER: But it's only to try . . .

THE MOTHER: I can't bear it. I can't.

THE MANAGER: But since it has happened already . . . I don't understand!

THE MOTHER: It's taking place now. It happens all the time. My torment isn't a pretended one. I live and feel every minute of my torture. Those two children there — have you heard them speak? They can't speak anymore. They cling to me to keep my torment

actual and vivid for me. But for themselves, they do not exist, they aren't anymore. And she (*indicating the Stepdaughter*) has run away, she has left me, and is lost. If I now see her here before me, it is only to renew for me the tortures I have suffered for her too.

THE FATHER: The eternal moment! She (*indicating the Stepdaughter*) is here to catch me, fix me, and hold me eternally in the stocks for that one fleeting and shameful moment of my life. She can't give it up! And you, sir, cannot either fairly spare me . . .

THE MANAGER: I never said I didn't want to act it. It will form, as a matter of fact, the nucleus of the whole first act right up to her surprise. (*Indicates the Mother.*)

THE FATHER: Just so! This is my punishment: the passion in all of us that must culminate in her final cry.

THE STEPDAUGHTER: I can hear it still in my ears. It's driven me mad, that cry! — You can put me on as you like; it doesn't matter. Fully dressed, if you like — provided I have at least the arm bare; because, standing like this (*she goes close to the Father and leans her head on his breast*) with my head so, and my arms round his neck, I saw a vein pulsing in my arm here; and then, as if that live vein had awakened disgust in me, I closed my eyes like this, and let my head sink on his breast. (*Turning to the Mother.*) Cry out, mother! Cry out! (*Buries head in Father's breast, and with her shoulders raised as if to prevent her hearing the cry, adds in tones of intense emotion.*) Cry out as you did then!

THE MOTHER (*coming forward to separate them*): No! My daughter, my daughter! (*And after having pulled her away from him.*) You brute! you brute! She is my daughter! Don't you see she's my daughter?

THE MANAGER (*walking backward toward footlights*): Fine! fine! Damned good! And then, of course — curtain!

THE FATHER (*going toward him excitedly*): Yes, of course, because that's the way it really happened.

THE MANAGER (*convinced and pleased*): Oh, yes, no doubt about it. Curtain here, curtain!

(*At the reiterated cry of the Manager, the Machinist lets the curtain down, leaving the Manager and the Father in front of it before the footlights.*)

THE MANAGER: The darned idiot! I said "curtain" to show the act should end there, and he goes and lets it down in earnest. (*To the Father, while he pulls the curtain back to go on to the stage again.*) Yes, yes, it's all right. Effect certain! That's the right ending. I'll guarantee the first act at any rate.

ACT III

(*When the curtain goes up again, it is seen that the stage hands have shifted the bit of scenery used in the last part and have rigged up instead at the back of the stage a drop, with some trees, and one or two wings. A portion of a fountain basin is visible. The Mother is sitting on the right with the two children by her side. The Son is on the same side, but away from the others. He seems bored, angry, and full of shame. The Father and the Stepdaughter are also seated toward the right front. On the other side (left) are the Actors, much in the positions they occupied before the curtain was lowered. Only the Manager is standing up in the middle of the stage, with his hand closed over his mouth, in the act of meditating.)*

THE MANAGER (*shaking his shoulders after a brief pause*): Ah yes: the second act! Leave it to me, leave it all to me as we arranged, and you'll see! It'll go fine!

THE STEPDAUGHTER: Our entry into his house (*indicates Father*) in spite of him . . . (*Indicates the Son.*)

THE MANAGER (*out of patience*): Leave it to me, I tell you!

THE STEPDAUGHTER: Do let it be clear, at any rate, that it is in spite of my wishes.

THE MOTHER (*from her corner, shaking her head*): For all the good that's come of it . . .

THE STEPDAUGHTER (*turning toward her quickly*): It doesn't matter. The more harm done us, the more remorse for him.

THE MANAGER (*impatiently*): I understand! Good Heavens! I understand! I'm taking it into account.

THE MOTHER (*supplicatingly*): I beg you, sir, to let it appear quite plain that for conscience' sake I did try in every way . . .

THE STEPDAUGHTER (*interrupting indignantly and continuing for the Mother*): . . . to pacify me, to dissuade me from spiting him. (*To Manager.*) Do as she wants: satisfy her, because it is true! I enjoy it immensely. Anyhow, as you can see, the meeker she is, the more she tries to get at his heart, the more distant and aloof does he become.

THE MANAGER: Are we going to begin this second act or not?

THE STEPDAUGHTER: I'm not going to talk any more now. But I must tell you this: you can't have the whole action take place in the garden, as you suggest. It isn't possible!

THE MANAGER: Why not?

THE STEPDAUGHTER: Because he (*indicates the Son again*) is always shut up alone in his room. And then there's all the part of that poor dazed-looking boy there which takes place indoors.

THE MANAGER: Maybe! On the other hand, you will understand — we can't change scenes three or four times in one act.

LEADING MAN: They used to once.

THE MANAGER: Yes, when the public was up to the level of that child there.

LEADING LADY: It makes the illusion easier.

THE FATHER (*irritated*): The illusion! For Heaven's sake, don't say illusion. Please don't use that word, which is particularly painful for . . .

THE MANAGER (*astounded*): And why, if you please?

THE FATHER: It's painful, cruel, really cruel; and you ought to understand that.

THE MANAGER: But why? What ought we to say then? The illusion, I tell you, sir, which we've got to create for the audience. . . .

THE LEADING MAN: With our acting.

THE MANAGER: The illusion of a reality.

THE FATHER: I understand; but you, perhaps, do not understand us. Forgive me! You see . . . here for you and your actors, the thing is only — and rightly so . . . a kind of game. . . .

THE LEADING LADY (*interrupting indignantly*): A game! We're not children here, if you please! We are serious actors.

THE FATHER: I don't deny it. What I mean is the game, or play, of your art, which has to give, as the gentleman says, a perfect illusion of reality.

THE MANAGER: Precisely — !

THE FATHER: Now, if you consider the fact that we (*indicates himself and the other five Characters*), as we are, have no other reality outside of this illusion. . . .

THE MANAGER (*astonished, looking at his Actors, who are also amazed*): And what does that mean?

THE FATHER (*after watching them for a moment with a wan smile*): As I say, sir, that which is a game of art for you is our sole reality. (*Brief pause. He goes a step or two nearer the Manager and adds.*) But not only for us, you know, by the way. Just you think it over well. (*Looks him in the eyes.*) Can you tell me who you are?

THE MANAGER (*perplexed, half-smiling*): What? Who am I? I am myself.

THE FATHER: And if I were to tell you that that isn't true, because you and I . . . ?

THE MANAGER: I should say you were mad — ! (*The Actors laugh.*)

THE FATHER: You're quite right to laugh: because we are all making believe here. (*To Manager.*) And you can therefore object that it's only for a joke that that gentleman there (*indicates the Leading Man*), who naturally is himself, has to be me, who am on the contrary myself — this thing you see here. You see I've caught you in a trap! (*The Actors laugh.*)

THE MANAGER (*annoyed*): But we've had all this over once before. Do you want to begin again?

THE FATHER: No, no! That wasn't my meaning! In fact, I should like to request you to abandon this game of art (*looking at the Leading Lady as if anticipating her*) which you are accustomed to play here with your actors, and to ask you seriously once again: who are you?

THE MANAGER (*astonished and irritated, turning to his Actors*): If this fellow here hasn't got a nerve! A man who calls himself a character comes and asks me who I am!

THE FATHER (*with dignity, but not offended*): A character, sir, may always ask a man who he is. Because a character has really a life of his own, marked with his especial characteristics; for which reason he is always "somebody." But a man — I'm not speaking of you now — may very well be "nobody."

THE MANAGER: Yes, but you are asking these questions of me, the boss, the manager! Do you understand?

THE FATHER: But only in order to know if you, as you really are now, see yourself as you once were with all the illusions that were yours then, with all the things both inside and outside of you as they seemed to you — as they were then indeed for you. Well, sir, if you think of all those illusions that mean nothing to you now, of all those things which don't even *seem* to you to exist anymore, while once they *were* for you, don't you feel that — I won't say these boards — but the very earth under your feet is sinking away from you when you reflect that in the same way this *you* as you feel it today — all this present reality of yours — is fated to seem a mere illusion to you tomorrow?

THE MANAGER (*without having understood much, but astonished by the specious argument*): Well, well! And where does all this take us anyway?

THE FATHER: Oh, nowhere! It's only to show you that if we (*indicating the Characters*) have no other reality beyond the illusion, you too must not count overmuch on your reality as you feel it today, since, like that of yesterday, it may prove an illusion for you tomorrow.

THE MANAGER (*determining to make fun of him*): Ah, excellent! Then you'll be saying next that you, with this comedy of yours that you brought here to act, are truer and more real than I am.

THE FATHER (*with the greatest seriousness*): But of course, without doubt!

THE MANAGER: Ah, really?

THE FATHER: Why, I thought you'd understand that from the beginning.

THE MANAGER: More real than I?

THE FATHER: If your reality can change from one day to another. . . .

THE MANAGER: But everyone knows it can change. It is always changing, the same as anyone else's.

THE FATHER (*with a cry*): No, sir, not ours! Look here! That is the very difference! Our reality doesn't change: it can't change! It can't be other than what it is, because it is already fixed for ever. It's terrible. Ours is an immutable reality which should make you shudder when you approach us if you are really conscious of the fact that your reality is a mere transitory and fleeting illusion, taking this form today and that tomorrow, according to the conditions, according to your will, your sentiments, which in turn are controlled by an intellect that shows them to you today in one manner and tomorrow . . . who knows how? . . . Illusions of reality represented in this fatuous comedy of life that never ends, nor can ever end! Because if tomorrow it were to end . . . then why, all would be finished.

THE MANAGER: Oh for God's sake, will you *at least* finish with this philosophizing and let us try and shape this comedy which you yourself have brought me here? You argue and philosophize a bit too much, my dear sir. You know you seem to me almost, al-

most . . . (*Stops and looks him over from head to foot.*) Ah, by the way, I think you introduced yourself to me as a — what shall . . . we say — a "character," created by an author who did not afterward care to make a drama of his own creations.

THE FATHER: It is the simple truth, sir.

THE MANAGER: Nonsense! Cut that out, please! None of us believes it, because it isn't a thing, as you must recognize yourself, which one can believe seriously. If you want to know, it seems to me you are trying to imitate the manner of a certain author whom I heartily detest — I warn you — although I have unfortunately bound myself to put on one of his works. As a matter of fact, I was just starting to rehearse it, when you arrived. (*Turning to the Actors.*) And this is what we've gained — out of the frying-pan into the fire!

THE FATHER: I don't know to what author you may be alluding, but believe me I feel what I think; and I seem to be philosophizing only for those who do not think what they feel, because they blind themselves with their own sentiment. I know that for many people this self-blinding seems much more "human"; but the contrary is really true. For man never reasons so much and becomes so introspective as when he suffers, since he is anxious to get at the cause of his sufferings, to learn who has produced them, and whether it is just or unjust that he should have to bear them. On the other hand, when he is happy, he takes his happiness as it comes and doesn't analyze it, just as if happiness were his right. The animals suffer without reasoning about their sufferings. But take the case of a man who suffers and begins to reason about it. Oh no! it can't be allowed! Let him suffer like an animal, and then — ah yes, he is "human"!

THE MANAGER: Look here! Look here! You're off again, philosophizing worse than ever.

THE FATHER: Because I suffer, sir! I'm not philosophizing: I'm crying aloud the reason of my sufferings.

THE MANAGER (*makes brusque movement as he is taken with a new idea*): I should like to know if anyone has ever heard of a character who gets right out of his part and perorates and speechifies as you do. Have you ever heard of a case? I haven't.

THE FATHER: You have never met such a case, sir, because authors, as a rule, hide the labor of their creations. When the characters are really alive before their author, the latter does nothing but follow them in their action, in other words, in the situations which they suggest to him; and he has to will them the way they will themselves — for there's trouble if he doesn't. When a character is born, he acquires at once such an independence, even of his own author, that he can be imagined by everybody even in many other situations where the author never dreamed of placing him; and so he acquires for himself a meaning which the author never thought of giving him.

THE MANAGER: Yes, yes, I know this.

THE FATHER: What is there then to marvel at in us?

Imagine such a misfortune for characters as I have described to you: to be born of an author's fantasy, and be denied life by him; and then answer me if these characters left alive, and yet without life, weren't right in doing what they did do and are doing now, after they have attempted everything in their power to persuade him to give them their stage life. We've all tried him in turn, I, she (*indicating the Stepdaughter*) and she (*indicating the Mother*).

THE STEPDAUGHTER: It's true. I too have sought to tempt him, many, many times, when he has been sitting at his writing table, feeling a bit melancholy, at the twilight hour. He would sit in his armchair too lazy to switch on the light, and all the shadows that crept into his room were full of our presence coming to tempt him. (*As if she saw herself still there by the writing table, and was annoyed by the presence of the Actors.*) Oh, if you would only go away, go away and leave us alone — mother here with that son of hers — I with that child — that boy there always alone — and then I with him (*just hints at the Father*) — and then I alone, alone . . . in those shadows! (*Makes a sudden movement as if in the vision she has of herself illuminating those shadows she wanted to seize hold of herself.*) Ah! my life! my life! Oh, what scenes we proposed to him — and I tempted him more than any of the others!

THE FATHER: Maybe. But perhaps it was your fault that he refused to give us life: because you were too insistent, too troublesome.

THE STEPDAUGHTER: Nonsense! Didn't he make me so himself? (*Goes close to the Manager to tell him as if in confidence.*) In my opinion he abandoned us in a fit of depression, of disgust for the ordinary theater as the public knows it and likes it.

THE SON: Exactly what it was, sir; exactly that!

THE FATHER: Not at all! Don't believe it for a minute. Listen to me! You'll be doing quite right to modify, as you suggest, the excesses both of this girl here, who wants to do too much, and of this young man, who won't do anything at all.

THE SON: No, nothing!

THE MANAGER: You too get over the mark occasionally, my dear sir, if I may say so.

THE FATHER: I? When? Where?

THE MANAGER: Always! Continuously! Then there's this insistence of yours in trying to make us believe you are a character. And then too, you must really argue and philosophize less, you know, much less.

THE FATHER: Well, if you want to take away from me the possibility of representing the torment of my spirit which never gives me peace, you will be suppressing me: that's all. Every true man, sir, who is a little above the level of the beasts and plants does not live for the sake of living, without knowing how to live; but he lives so as to give a meaning and a value of his own to life. For me this is *everything*. I cannot give up this, just to represent a mere fact as she (*indicating the Stepdaughter*) wants. It's all very well for

her, since her "vendetta" lies in the "fact." I'm not going to do it. It destroys my *raison d'être*.

THE MANAGER: Your *raison d'être*! Oh, we're going ahead fine! First she starts off, and then you jump in. At this rate, we'll never finish.

THE FATHER: Now, don't be offended! Have it your own way — provided, however, that within the limits of the parts you assign us each one's sacrifice isn't too great.

THE MANAGER: You've got to understand that you can't go on arguing at your own pleasure. Drama is action, sir, action and not confounded philosophy.

THE FATHER: All right. I'll do just as much arguing and philosophizing as everybody does when he is considering his own torments.

THE MANAGER: If the drama permits! But for Heaven's sake, man, let's get along and come to the scene.

THE STEPDAUGHTER: It seems to me we've got too much action with our coming into his house. (*Indicating Father.*) You said, before, you couldn't change the scene every five minutes.

THE MANAGER: Of course not. What we've got to do is to combine and group up all the facts in one simultaneous, close-knit action. We can't have it as you want, with your little brother wandering like a ghost from room to room, hiding behind doors and meditating a project which — what did you say it did to him?

THE STEPDAUGHTER: Consumes him, sir, wastes him away!

THE MANAGER: Well, it may be. And then at the same time, you want the little girl there to be playing in the garden . . . one in the house, and the other in the garden; isn't that it?

THE STEPDAUGHTER: Yes, in the sun, in the sun! That is my only pleasure: to see her happy and careless in the garden after the misery and squalor of the horrible room where we all four slept together. And I had to sleep with her — I, do you understand? — with my vile contaminated body next to hers; with her holding me fast in her loving little arms. In the garden, whenever she spied me, she would run to take me by the hand. She didn't care for the big flowers, only the little ones; and she loved to show me them and pet me.

THE MANAGER: Well then, we'll have it in the garden. Everything shall happen in the garden; and we'll group the other scenes there. (*Calls a Stage Hand.*) Here, a backcloth with trees and something to do as a fountain basin. (*Turning round to look at the back of the stage.*) Ah, you've fixed it up. Good! (*To Stepdaughter.*) This is just to give an idea, of course. The Boy, instead of hiding behind the doors, will wander about here in the garden, hiding behind the trees. But it's going to be rather difficult to find a child to do that scene with you where she shows you the flowers. (*Turning to the Boy.*) Come forward a little, will you please? Let's try it now! Come along! come along! (*Then seeing him come shyly forward, full of fear and looking lost.*) It's a nice business, this lad here.

What's the matter with him? We'll have to give him a word or two to say. (*Goes close to him, puts a hand on his shoulders, and leads him behind one of the trees.*) Come on! come on! Let me see you a little! Hide here . . . yes, like that. Try and show your head just a little as if you were looking for someone. . . . (*Goes back to observe the effect, when the Boy at once goes through the action.*) Excellent! fine! (*Turning to Stepdaughter.*) Suppose the little girl there were to surprise him as he looks round, and run over to him, so we could give him a word or two to say?

THE STEPDAUGHTER: It's useless to hope he will speak, as long as that fellow there is here. . . . (*Indicates the Son.*) You must send him away first.

THE SON (*jumping up*): Delighted! Delighted! I don't ask for anything better. (*Begins to move away.*)

THE MANAGER (*at once stopping him*): No! No! Where are you going? Wait a bit!

(*The Mother gets up alarmed and terrified at the thought that he is really about to go away. Instinctively she lifts her arms to prevent him, without, however, leaving her seat.*)

THE SON (*to Manager, who stops him*): I've got nothing to do with this affair. Let me go, please! Let me go!

THE MANAGER: What do you mean by saying you've got nothing to do with this?

THE STEPDAUGHTER (*calmly, with irony*): Don't bother to stop him: he won't go away.

THE FATHER: He has to act the terrible scene in the garden with his mother.

THE SON (*suddenly resolute and with dignity*): I shall act nothing at all. I've said so from the very beginning. (*To the Manager.*) Let me go!

THE STEPDAUGHTER (*going over to the Manager*): Allow me? (*Puts down the Manager's arm which is restraining the Son.*) Well, go away then, if you want to! (*The Son looks at her with contempt and hatred. She laughs and says.*) You see, he can't, he can't go away! He is obliged to stay here, indissolubly bound to the chain. If I, who fly off when that happens which has to happen because I can't bear him — if I am still here and support that face and expression of his, you can well imagine that he is unable to move. He has to remain here, has to stop with that nice father of his, and that mother whose only son he is. (*Turning to the Mother.*) Come on, mother, come along! (*Turning to Manager to indicate her.*) You see, she was getting up to keep him back. (*To the Mother, beckoning her with her hand.*) Come on, come on! (*Then to Manager.*) You can imagine how little she wants to show these actors of yours what she really feels; but so eager is she to get near him that. . . . There, you see? She is willing to act her part. (*And in fact, the Mother approaches him; and as soon as the Stepdaughter has finished speaking, opens her arms to signify that she consents.*)

THE SON (*suddenly*): No! no! If I can't go away, then I'll stop here; but I repeat: I act nothing!

THE FATHER (*to Manager excitedly*): You can force him, sir.

THE SON: Nobody can force me.

THE FATHER: I can.

THE STEPDAUGHTER: Wait a minute, wait . . . First of all, the baby has to go to the fountain. . . . (*Runs to take the Child and leads her to the fountain.*)

THE MANAGER: Yes, yes of course; that's it. Both at the same time.

(*The Second Lady Lead and the Juvenile Lead at this point separate themselves from the group of Actors. One watches the Mother attentively; the other moves about studying the movements and manner of the Son whom he will have to act.*)

THE SON (*to Manager*): What do you mean by both at the same time? It isn't right. There was no scene between me and her. (*Indicates the Mother.*) Ask her how it was!

THE MOTHER: Yes, it's true. I had come into his room. . . .

THE SON: Into my room, do you understand? Nothing to do with the garden.

THE MANAGER: It doesn't matter. Haven't I told you we've got to group the action?

THE SON (*observing the Juvenile Lead studying him*): What do you want?

THE JUVENILE LEAD: Nothing! I was just looking at you.

THE SON (*turning toward the Second Lady Lead*): Ah! she's at it too: to re-act her part! (*Indicating the Mother.*)

THE MANAGER: Exactly! And it seems to me that you ought to be grateful to them for their interest.

THE SON: Yes, but haven't you yet perceived that it isn't possible to live in front of a mirror which not only freezes us with the image of ourselves, but throws our likeness back at us with a horrible grimace?

THE FATHER: That is true, absolutely true. You must see that.

THE MANAGER (*to Second Lady Lead and Juvenile Lead*): He's right! Move away from them!

THE SON: Do as you like. I'm out of this!

THE MANAGER: Be quiet, you, will you? And let me hear your mother! (*To Mother.*) You were saying you had entered. . . .

THE MOTHER: Yes, into his room, because I couldn't stand it any longer. I went to empty my heart to him of all the anguish that tortures me. . . . But as soon as he saw me come in. . . .

THE SON: Nothing happened! There was no scene. I went away, that's all! I don't care for scenes!

THE MOTHER: It's true, true. That's how it was.

THE MANAGER: Well now, we've got to do this bit between you and him. It's indispensable.

THE MOTHER: I'm ready . . . when you are ready. If you could only find a chance for me to tell him what I feel here in my heart.

THE FATHER (*going to Son in a great rage*): You'll do this for your mother, for your mother, do you understand?

THE SON (*quite determined*): I do nothing!

THE FATHER (*taking hold of him and shaking him*): For God's sake, do as I tell you! Don't you hear your mother asking you for a favor? Haven't you even got the guts to be a son?

THE SON (*taking hold of the Father*): No! No! And for God's sake stop it, or else. . . . (*General agitation. The Mother, frightened, tries to separate them.*)

THE MOTHER (*pleading*): Please! please!

THE FATHER (*not leaving hold of the Son*): You've got to obey, do you hear?

THE SON (*almost crying from rage*): What does it mean, this madness you've got? (*They separate.*) Have you no decency, that you insist on showing everyone our shame? I won't do it! I won't! And I stand for the will of our author in this. He didn't want to put us on the stage, after all!

THE MANAGER: Man alive! You came here . . .

THE SON (*indicating Father*): He did! I didn't!

THE MANAGER: Aren't you here now?

THE SON: It was his wish, and he dragged us along with him. He's told you not only the things that did happen, but also things that have never happened at all.

THE MANAGER: Well, tell me then what did happen. You went out of your room without saying a word?

THE SON: Without a word, so as to avoid a scene!

THE MANAGER: And then what did you do?

THE SON: Nothing . . . walking in the garden. . . . (*Hesitates for a moment with expression of gloom.*)

THE MANAGER (*coming closer to him, interested by his extraordinary reserve*): Well, well . . . walking in the garden. . . .

THE SON (*exasperated*): Why on earth do you insist? It's horrible!

(*The Mother trembles, sobs, and looks toward the fountain.*)

THE MANAGER (*slowly observing the glance and turning toward the Son with increasing apprehension*): The baby?

THE SON: There in the fountain. . . .

THE FATHER (*pointing with tender pity to the Mother*): She was following him at the moment. . . .

THE MANAGER (*to the Son anxiously*): And then you. . . .

THE SON: I ran over to her; I was jumping in to drag her out when I saw something that froze my blood . . . the boy standing stock still, with eyes like a madman's, watching his little drowned sister, in the fountain! (*The Stepdaughter bends over the fountain to hide the Child. She sobs.*) Then. . . . (*A revolver shot rings out behind the trees where the Boy is hidden.*)

THE MOTHER (*with a cry of terror runs over in that direction together with several of the Actors amid general confusion*): My son! My son! (*Then amid the cries and exclamations one hears her voice.*) Help! Help!

THE MANAGER (*pushing the Actors aside while they lift up the Boy and carry him off*): Is he really wounded?

SOME ACTORS: He's dead! dead!

OTHER ACTORS: No, no, it's only make-believe, it's only pretense!

THE FATHER (*with a terrible cry*): Pretense? Reality, sir, reality!

THE MANAGER: Pretense? Reality? To hell with it all! Never in my life has such a thing happened to me. I've lost a whole day over these people, a whole day!

COMMENTARY

John Corbin (1870–1959)
REVIEW OF *SIX CHARACTERS IN SEARCH OF AN AUTHOR*   1922

Corbin's review of the distinguished 1922 New York production of Six Characters in Search of an Author *reminds us how much the audiences loved the play. They stood clapping long after the last curtain. Florence Eldridge, who became famous for her role, is given relatively little attention here. Corbin instead focused his comments on the complexity of the play's comic premise.*

Philosophical fooling and shrewd criticism on the art of the theatre mingle in the Italian play which Brock Pemberton is presenting in translation at the Princess.

Imagine a playwright whose creative mind is haunted by six characters, the persons of a harrowing family drama, all urging insistently that they be given full and subtly shaded representation in the theatre. That is the normal condition of authentic creation; but as art consists in rigid elimination as well as in delicate emphasis, many of the aspirations of the six for self-expression have to be denied. Imagine next that the subject of their suffering is not sympathetic to the public, and that the only true and significant outcome is undramatic — not moving and inspiring, but static. That very often happens when a dramatist takes his real inspiration from life as it is actually lived, and in the supreme court of the manager's office he is nonsuited. There is no play.

But there are characters more live and vital than most of those that see the footlights. Imagine, finally, that these characters, still longing to live out their lives on the scene, go out in search of a more obliging author — and find a stage manager who has a company but no new play, only the stock stuff of a world somewhat deficient in new inspiration. Recognizing raw materials of interest and power, the enterprising business man undertakes to supply the place of the author. It seems to him a positive windfall to be relieved of that insistent and obnoxious incident of production. He will allow the six characters to live out their own lives while a secretary takes down the dialogue and his company stands by preparing to assume the parts. Magnificent!

Those who look upon ordinary rehearsals as a madhouse will receive illumination. Instead of a single author, long subdued in misery, the manager has his six orphans to contend with. The actors of his company, accustomed to have parts ruthlessly adapted to their personalities, are confronted each with a fury of unreason, demanding the absolute. For these characters, though the shadows of a dream, are "real" in the sense of being raw vitality unshaped to the necessities of art and the practical ends of the theatre. In the turmoil that ensues there is much satire on the foibles of player folk and managers and no little philosophy of dramatic art and dramatic criticism.

Margaret Wycherly is Mother in the roving dramatis personae and lends to the character genuine imagination and emotional power. Moffat Johnston is the garrulous father, eagerly philosophic and disquisitional. Florence Eldridge is the stepdaughter, overflowing with eager youth and charm. Throughout the production is able and highly competent. The audience last night, largely composed of folk of the theatre, rose to the novelty and humor of the idea and lingered long in applause after the brief three acts were over.

What the public will say to this rather slender and technical satire remains to be seen, but already it may be said that the season is indebted to Mr. Pemberton for one more exploration of strange fields and pastures new.

Federico García Lorca

Federico García Lorca (1898–1936) lived through some of the most troubling times of modern Spain. He was born in the countryside near Granada, and maintained a lifelong love of the Spanish village and country people. His father was a wealthy farmer, and his mother was a teacher who encouraged his early love of literature, art, and music. Lorca's talents were extraordinary. A fine pianist, he counted among his friends some of Spain's greatest musicians, including Manuel de Falla. Lorca painted throughout his life and maintained a close friendship with Salvador Dalí. His career in the university was not especially distinguished, but as a student he became famous for readings of his own poetry. He produced an early play, *The Butterfly's Evil Spell,* in 1920, the year before he published his first book of poems. His political leanings throughout his life were liberal and reformist, but his early years were spent living under a Spanish dictatorship. General elections ended Spain's monarchy and established the Second Spanish Republic in 1931, but Fascist leaders, notably Francisco Franco, began agitating for control. Standing for a free republic and prominent as a leftist, Lorca was killed suddenly and without explanation by Franco's forces in 1936, just two days before the start of the Spanish Civil War.

Lorca's dramatic work had developed steadily. His second play, *The Girl Who Waters the Sweet Basil Flower and the Inquisitive Prince* (1923), was a puppet show. Lorca, who especially enjoyed this form of drama, had bought his own puppet theater when he was fifteen. He designed the sets, and Manuel de Falla provided the music. Unfortunately, the manuscript for this play has been lost. Text for another puppet play of the same period, *The Billy-Club Puppets,* does exist, as do copies of some later dramatic sketches: *Buster Keaton's Promenade* (1926), which takes off on Buster Keaton's film character, and *The Public* (1933), one of several experimental surrealist plays. His first real success was *Mariana Pineda* (1927), produced in Granada. After suffering a personal crisis, perhaps connected to his growing awareness of his homosexuality, Lorca spent a year in New York, from which experience he wrote *The Poet in New York,* published — much later — in 1940.

Lorca returned to Spain and produced a number of plays in the early 1930s, such as *The Shoemaker's Prodigious Wife* (1930), *The Love of Don Perlimplin with Belisa in the Garden* (1933), and *Doña Rosita, the Spinster* (1935), the last of his plays to be produced during his lifetime. His three most important plays are generally referred to as folk tragedies: *Blood Wedding* (1933) and *Yerma* (1934) were produced in Madrid, and *The House of Bernarda Alba* was produced in Buenos Aires in 1945. These three plays were influenced by a great Spanish actress and producer, Margarita Xirgu, for whom the title role of Yerma was created.

Lorca's reputation flourished after the end of World War II, but because Spain's Fascist government continued until Franco's death in 1975, Lorca's work could not be produced in his native country until the 1980s. His gift was in combining poetry, music, original set designs, and a sense of the language of the country people who inspired his work. He had a feel for the pagan forces that informed the country people and aimed to show their creative power in everyday life. He celebrated instinctive, primitive religious feeling, the joy of living, the sexual energy of the universe, and the fullness of life.

THE HOUSE OF BERNARDA ALBA

Lorca diverged from his earlier poetic style when he created this play, subtitled "a drama about women in the villages of Spain." He is on record as having said, "Not a drop of poetry! Reality! Realism!" Supposed to be as realistic and detailed as a "photographic document," the play pointed to some of the harsher realities of life for women in rural Spain. Indeed, only women appear in the play. Pepe el Romano, a young handsome man, betrothed to Angustias, Bernarda's eldest daughter (apparently for her money), is mentioned often but never appears. In the beginning of the third act, a stallion making loud sounds in his stall represents the symbolic force of sex in nature. Bernarda Alba demands that the stallion be freed before it brings the walls down, but at the same time she determines to keep her daughters hidden away in her house and under her thumb. The focus of the play is on Bernarda Alba's determination to preserve her dignity in her village. She wants to make sure that no one talks about her family disparagingly; she must keep up appearances even at the risk of smothering the sexual energies of her five daughters.

When the play opens, Bernarda's second husband has just died, and she declares that the household shall mourn for eight years. Her daughters would be shut in and not see a man for any of that time. However, since Angustias has her own money from her father, Bernarda's first husband, she is courted by Pepe el Romano. At the same time Pepe secretly expresses his true affection to Angustias's sister Adela, who is much closer to him in age and who would be a more suitable wife. Bernarda, however, is adamant about the period of mourning and eventually chases Pepe away with a shotgun after discovering that he has given in to his desires.

This is a play about the tyranny of Bernarda over her daughters. It portrays her desire to be respected in the community at all costs, even the cost of living a lie. It is also a play about "Women without men." Some critics have seen in the prisonlike atmosphere (note the constant reference to bars) a suggestion of the religious convent and the sexual repression it implies. The Cistercians, known as Bernardas, were an order of nuns familiar to Lorca. But Lorca is exploring a number of powerful forces in life: the power of the family and tradition, the power of religion and its strictures of moral behavior, the power of economic necessity and the way it distorts lives, and the power of a political force that maintains itself through absolute authority. Most of these forces were evident in the Spain Lorca knew throughout his life. From 1932 much of his time was spent traveling with, and writing for, a government-sponsored touring company, La Barraca, that put on classic Spanish plays in remote towns around the nation. He had plenty of opportunity to observe everyday life in rural Spain. This play reveals some of its nature.

The House of Bernarda Alba in Performance

The first production of the play, in 1945, was in Buenos Aires, which Lorca visited shortly before he died, impressing those he met with his genius. South America has long found his work important; Lorca's play was produced in various South American countries long before it appeared in Spain. Eric Bentley staged a minimalist production of the play at the Abbey Theatre in Dublin in 1950, with Peggy Hayes as Bernarda and Angela Newmann as Adela. He describes this production in his *In Search of Theater* (1953), saying, "Ireland and Spain are two of the remaining vestiges of Catholic-peasant civilization. Lorca's play springs from this civilization, gives it amazingly full expression, and is a bitter rejection of it."

The play was given a limited production in Paris in the Studio des Champs-Élysées in 1946, employing a fine set with stark white walls and black wrought-iron bars across the windows. A New York production at the ANTA Playhouse lasted for seventeen performances in January 1951. Bentley had earlier speculated that the play would be very difficult to communicate to 1950s London or New York audiences, and he seems to have been correct. It was produced in New York again by Teatro Hispano, directed by Max Ferra, in early 1972. Bernarda was played by the Cuban actress Ofelia González. Numerous productions in Europe followed; one of the most powerful was in 1986 at the Lyric Theatre in Hammersmith, London, directed by Nuria Espert. The sets and the lighting served to intensify the sense of overwhelming heat from the Andalusian sun. Paul Preston, in his review in the *Times Literary Supplement,* said, "Glenda Jackson's Bernarda is as stiff-backed as the most humourless prison governor or mother superior, dominating her brood with snarling sarcasm and fulminating looks." Joan Plowright played a powerful Poncia, but Patricia Hayes, as Bernarda's mother, was singled out for a stunning performance: "wearing muslin rags over white flesh like a feverish and ecstatic moth" (Michael Ratcliffe in the *Observer*). The play moved into the West End (London's Broadway) to the Globe Theatre in 1987 with the same cast. Among the most recent productions is the 1993 production in Northern Ireland at the adventurous women's company, the Charabanc Theatre Company. Lynne Parker adapted and directed the play to exceptional reviews, and the production toured twenty towns throughout Ireland and Northern Ireland before settling in at the Project Arts Centre in Dublin. The reviews of the production celebrated its excellence and explored the women's issues in the drama. The Orange Tree Theatre in Richmond, which is billed as "London's only theatre in the round," staged a very well reviewed production in March–April 2003. Auriol Smith directed a translation that she and Rebecca Morahan had done. Lynn Farley played Bernarda Alba.

Federico García Lorca (1898–1936)

THE HOUSE OF BERNARDA ALBA   *1936*
A DRAMA ABOUT WOMEN IN THE VILLAGES OF SPAIN
TRANSLATED BY JAMES GRAHAM-LUJÁN AND RICHARD L. O'CONNELL

Characters

BERNARDA (*age 60*)
MARÍA JOSEFA, *Bernarda's Mother* (*age 80*)
ANGUSTIAS, *Bernarda's Daughter* (*age 39*)
MAGDALENA, *Bernarda's Daughter* (*age 30*)
AMELIA, *Bernarda's Daughter* (*age 27*)
MARTIRIO, *Bernarda's Daughter* (*age 24*)
ADELA, *Bernarda's Daughter* (*age 20*)
A MAID (*age 50*)
LA PONCIA, *A Maid* (*age 60*)
PRUDENCIA (*age 50*)
WOMEN IN MOURNING

The writer states that these Three Acts are intended as a photographic document.

ACT 1

(*A very white room in Bernarda Alba's house. The walls are white. There are arched doorways with jute curtains tied back with tassels and ruffles. Wicker chairs. On the walls, pictures of unlikely landscapes full of nymphs or legendary kings.*
It is summer. A great brooding silence fills the stage. It is empty when the curtain rises. Bells can be heard tolling outside.)

FIRST SERVANT (*entering*): The tolling of those bells hits me right between the eyes.
PONCIA (*she enters, eating bread and sausage*): More than two hours of mumbo jumbo. Priests are here from all the towns. The church looks beautiful. At the first responsory for the dead, Magdalena fainted.
FIRST SERVANT: She's the one who's left most alone.
PONCIA: She's the only one who loved her father. Ay! Thank God we're alone for a little. I came over to eat.
FIRST SERVANT: If Bernarda sees you . . . !
PONCIA: She's not eating today so she'd just as soon we'd all die of hunger! Domineering old tyrant! But she'll be fooled! I opened the sausage crock.
FIRST SERVANT (*with an anxious sadness*): Couldn't you give me some for my little girl, Poncia?
PONCIA: Go ahead! And take a fistful of peas too. She won't know the difference today.
VOICE (*within*): Bernarda!
PONCIA: There's the grandmother! Isn't she locked up tight?

FIRST SERVANT: Two turns of the key.
PONCIA: You'd better put the cross-bar up too. She's got the fingers of a lock-picker!
VOICE (*within*): Bernarda!
PONCIA (*shouting*): She's coming! (*to the servant*) Clean everything up good. If Bernarda doesn't find things shining, she'll pull out the few hairs I have left.
SERVANT: What a woman!
PONCIA: Tyrant over everyone around her. She's perfectly capable of sitting on your heart and watching you die for a whole year without turning off that cold little smile she wears on her wicked face. Scrub, scrub those dishes!
SERVANT: I've got blood on my hands from so much polishing of everything.
PONCIA: She's the cleanest, she's the decentest, she's the highest everything! A good rest her poor husband's earned!

(*The bells stop.*)

SERVANT: Did all the relatives come?
PONCIA: Just hers. His people hate her. They came to see him dead and make the sign of the cross over him; that's all.
SERVANT: Are there enough chairs?
PONCIA: More than enough. Let them sit on the floor. When Bernarda's father died people stopped coming under this roof. She doesn't want them to see her in her "domain." Curse her!
SERVANT: She's been good to you.
PONCIA: Thirty years washing her sheets. Thirty years eating her leftovers. Nights of watching when she had a cough. Whole days peeking through a crack in the shutters to spy on the neighbors and carry her the tale. Life without secrets one from the other. But in spite of that — curse her! May the "pain of the piercing nail" strike her in the eyes.
SERVANT: Poncia!
PONCIA: But I'm a good watchdog! I bark when I'm told and bite beggars' heels when she sics me on 'em. My sons work in her fields — both of them already married, but one of these days I'll have enough.
SERVANT: And then. . . ?
PONCIA: Then I'll lock myself up in a room with her and spit in her face — a whole year. "Bernarda, here's for this, that and the other!" Till I leave her — just like a lizard the boys have squashed. For that's what she

949

is — she and her whole family! Not that I envy her her life. Five girls are left her, five ugly daughters — not counting Angustias the eldest, by her first husband, who has money — the rest of them, plenty of eyelets to embroider, plenty of linen petticoats, but bread and grapes when it comes to inheritance!

SERVANT: Well, *I'd* like to have what they've got!

PONCIA: All we have is our hands and a hole in God's earth.

SERVANT: And that's the only earth they'll ever leave to us — to us who have nothing!

PONCIA (*at the cupboard*): This glass has some specks.

SERVANT: Neither soap nor rag will take them off.

(*The bells toll.*)

PONCIA: The last prayer! I'm going over and listen. I certainly like the way our priest sings. In the Pater Noster his voice went up, and up — like a pitcher filling with water little by little. Of course, at the end his voice cracked, but it's glorious to hear it. No, there never was anybody like the old Sacristan — Tronchapinos. At my mother's Mass, may she rest in peace, he sang. The walls shook — and when he said "Amen," it was as if a wolf had come into the church.

(*Imitating him.*)

A-a-a-a-men!

(*She starts coughing.*)

SERVANT: Watch out — you'll strain your windpipe!

PONCIA: I'd rather strain something else!

(*Goes out laughing.*)
(*The servant scrubs. The bells toll.*)

SERVANT (*imitating the bells*): Dong, dong, dong. Dong, dong, dong. May God forgive him!

BEGGAR WOMAN (*at the door, with a little girl*): Blesséd be God!

SERVANT: Dong, dong, dong. I hope he waits many years for us! Dong, dong, dong.

BEGGAR (*loudly, a little annoyed*): Blesséd be God!

SERVANT (*annoyed*): Forever and ever!

BEGGAR: I came for the scraps.

(*The bells stop tolling.*)

SERVANT: You can go right out the way you came in. Today's scraps are for me.

BEGGAR: But you have somebody to take care of you — and my little girl and I are all alone!

SERVANT: Dogs are alone too, and they live.

BEGGAR: They always give them to me.

SERVANT: Get out of here! Who let you in anyway? You've already tracked up the place.

(*The beggar woman and little girl leave. The servant goes on scrubbing.*)

Floors finished with oil, cupboards, pedestals, iron beds — but us servants, we can suffer in silence — and live in mud huts with a plate and a spoon. I hope someday not a one will be left to tell it.

(*The bells sound again.*)

Yes, yes — ring away. Let them pelt you in a coffin with gold inlay and brocade to carry it on — you're no less dead than I'll be, so take what's coming to you, Antonio María Benavides — stiff in your broadcloth suit and your high boots — take what's coming to you! You'll never again lift my skirts behind the corral door!

(*From the rear door, two by two, women in mourning with large shawls and black skirts and fans, begin to enter. They come in slowly until the stage is full.*)

SERVANT (*breaking into a wail*): Oh, Antonio María Benavides, now you'll never see these walls, nor break bread in this house again! I'm the one who loved you most of all your servants.

(*Pulling her hair.*)

Must I love on after you've gone? Must I go on living?

(*The two hundred women finish coming in, and Bernarda and her five daughters enter. Bernarda leans on a cane.*)

BERNARDA (*to the servant*): Silence!

SERVANT (*weeping*): Bernarda!

BERNARDA: Less shrieking and more work. You should have had all this cleaner for the wake. Get out. This isn't your place.

(*The servant goes off crying.*)

The poor are like animals — they seem to be made of different stuff.

FIRST WOMAN: The poor feel their sorrows too.

BERNARDA: But they forget them in front of a plateful of peas.

FIRST GIRL (*timidly*): Eating is necessary for living.

BERNARDA: At your age one doesn't talk in front of older people.

WOMAN: Be quiet, child.

BERNARDA: I've never taken lessons from anyone. Sit down.

(*They sit down. Pause. Loudly.*)

Magdalena, don't cry. If you want to cry, get under your bed. Do you hear me?

SECOND WOMAN (*to Bernarda*): Have you started to work the fields?

BERNARDA: Yesterday.

THIRD WOMAN: The sun comes down like lead.

FIRST WOMAN: I haven't known heat like this for years.

(*Pause. They all fan themselves.*)

BERNARDA: Is the lemonade ready?

PONCIA: Yes, Bernarda.

(*She brings in a large tray full of little white jars which she distributes.*)

BERNARDA: Give the men some.

PONCIA: They're already drinking in the patio.

BERNARDA: Let them get out the way they came in. I don't want them walking through here.

A GIRL (*to Angustias*): Pepe el Romano was with the men during the service.

ANGUSTIAS: There he was.

BERNARDA: His mother was there. She saw his mother. Neither she nor I saw Pepe . . .

GIRL: I thought . . .

BERNARDA: The one who *was* there was Darajalí, the widower. Very close to your Aunt. We all of us saw him.

SECOND WOMAN (*aside, in a low voice*): Wicked, worse than wicked woman!

THIRD WOMAN: A tongue like a knife!

BERNARDA: Women in church shouldn't look at any man but the priest — and him only because he wears skirts. To turn your head is to be looking for the warmth of corduroy.

FIRST WOMAN: Sanctimonious old snake!

PONCIA (*between her teeth*): Itching for a man's warmth.

BERNARDA (*beating with her cane on the floor*): Blesséd be God!

ALL (*crossing themselves*): Forever blesséd and praised.

BERNARDA: Rest in peace with holy company at your head.

ALL: Rest in peace!

BERNARDA: With the Angel Saint Michael, and his sword of justice.

ALL: Rest in peace!

BERNARDA: With the key that opens, and the hand that locks.

ALL: Rest in peace!

BERNARDA: With the most blesséd, and the little lights of the field.

ALL: Rest in peace!

BERNARDA: With our holy charity, and all souls on land and sea.

ALL: Rest in peace!

BERNARDA: Grant rest to your servant, Antonio María Benavides, and give him the crown of your blesséd glory.

ALL: Amen.

BERNARDA (*she rises and chants*): *Requiem aeternam donat eis domine.*

ALL (*standing and chanting in the Gregorian fashion*): *Et lux perpetua luce ab eis.*°

(*They cross themselves.*)

FIRST WOMAN: May you have health to pray for his soul. (*They start filing out.*)

THIRD WOMAN: You won't lack loaves of hot bread.

SECOND WOMAN: Nor a roof for your daughters.

(*They are all filing in front of Bernarda and going out. Angustias leaves by the door to the patio.*)

Requiem aeternam . . . ab eis: Eternal rest grant to him, O Lord. And let perpetual light shine on him.

FOURTH WOMAN: May you go on enjoying your wedding wheat.

PONCIA (*she enters, carrying a money bag*): From the men — this bag of money for Masses.

BERNARDA: Thank them — and let them have a glass of brandy.

GIRL (*to Magdalena*): Magdalena . . .

BERNARDA (*to Magdalena, who is starting to cry*): Sh-h-h-h!

(*She beats with her cane on the floor.*)

(*All the women have gone out.*)

BERNARDA (*to the women who have just left*): Go back to your houses and criticize everything you've seen! I hope it'll be many years before you pass under the archway of my door again.

PONCIA: You've nothing to complain about. The whole town came.

BERNARDA: Yes, to fill my house with the sweat from their wraps and the poison of their tongues.

AMELIA: Mother, don't talk like that.

BERNARDA: What other way is there to talk about this curséd village with no river — this village full of wells where you drink water always fearful it's been poisoned?

PONCIA: Look what they've done to the floor!

BERNARDA: As though a herd of goats had passed through.

(*Poncia cleans the floor.*)

Adela, give me a fan.

ADELA: Take this one.

(*She gives her a round fan with green and red flowers.*)

BERNARDA (*throwing the fan on the floor*): Is that the fan to give to a widow? Give me a black one and learn to respect your father's memory.

MARTIRIO: Take mine.

BERNARDA: And you?

MARTIRIO: I'm not hot.

BERNARDA: Well, look for another, because you'll need it. For the eight years of mourning, not a breath of air will get in this house from the street. We'll act as if we'd sealed up doors and windows with bricks. That's what happened in my father's house — and in my grandfather's house. Meantime, you can all start embroidering your hope-chest linens. I have twenty bolts of linen in the chest from which to cut sheets and coverlets. Magdalena can embroider them.

MAGDALENA: It's all the same to me.

ADELA (*sourly*): If you don't want to embroider them — they can go without. That way yours will look better.

MAGDALENA: Neither mine nor yours. I know I'm not going to marry. I'd rather carry sacks to the mill. Anything except sit here day after day in this dark room.

BERNARDA: That's what a woman is for.

MAGDALENA: Cursed be all women.

BERNARDA: In this house you'll do what I order. You

can't run with the story to your father any more. Needle and thread for women. Whiplash and mules for men. That's the way it has to be for people who have certain obligations.

(*Adela goes out.*)

VOICE: Bernarda! Let me out!

BERNARDA (*calling*): Let her out now!

(*The first servant enters.*)

FIRST SERVANT: I had a hard time holding her. In spite of her eighty years, your mother's strong as an oak.

BERNARDA: It runs in the family. My grandfather was the same way.

SERVANT: Several times during the wake I had to cover her mouth with an empty sack because she wanted to shout out to you to give her dishwater to drink at least, and some dogmeat, which is what she says you feed her.

MARTIRIO: She's mean!

BERNARDA (*to servant*): Let her get some fresh air in the patio.

SERVANT: She took her rings and the amethyst earrings out of the box, put them on, and told me she wants to get married.

(*The daughters laugh.*)

BERNARDA: Go with her and be careful she doesn't get near the well.

SERVANT: You don't need to be afraid she'll jump in.

BERNARDA: It's not that — but the neighbors can see her there from their windows.

(*The servant leaves.*)

MARTIRIO: We'll go change our clothes.

BERNARDA: Yes, but don't take the kerchiefs from your heads.

(*Adela enters.*)

And Angustias?

ADELA (*meaningfully*): I saw her looking out through the cracks of the back door. The men had just gone.

BERNARDA: And you, what were *you* doing at the door?

ADELA: I went there to see if the hens had laid.

BERNARDA: But the men had already gone!

ADELA (*meaningfully*): A group of them were still standing outside.

BERNARDA (*furiously*): Angustias! Angustias!

ANGUSTIAS (*entering*): Did you want something?

BERNARDA: For what — and at whom — were you looking?

ANGUSTIAS: Nobody.

BERNARDA: Is it decent for a woman of your class to be running after a man the day of her father's funeral? Answer me! Whom were you looking at?

(*Pause.*)

ANGUSTIAS: I . . .

BERNARDA: Yes, you!

ANGUSTIAS: Nobody.

BERNARDA: Soft! Honeytongue!

(*She strikes her.*)

PONCIA (*running to her*): Bernarda, calm down!

(*She holds her. Angustias weeps.*)

BERNARDA: Get out of here, all of you!

(*They all go out.*)

PONCIA: She did it not realizing what she was doing — although it's bad, of course. It really disgusted me to see her sneak along to the patio. Then she stood at the window listening to the men's talk, which, as usual, was not the sort one should listen to.

BERNARDA: That's what they come to funerals for. (*With curiosity.*) What were they talking about?

PONCIA: They were talking about Paca la Roseta. Last night they tied her husband up in a stall, stuck her on a horse behind the saddle, and carried her away to the depths of the olive grove.

BERNARDA: And what did she do?

PONCIA: She? She was just as happy — they say her breasts were exposed and Maximiliano held on to her as if he were playing a guitar. Terrible!

BERNARDA: And what happened?

PONCIA: What had to happen. They came back almost at daybreak. Paca la Roseta with her hair loose and a wreath of flowers on her head.

BERNARDA: She's the only bad woman we have in the village.

PONCIA: Because she's not from here. She's from far away. And those who went with her are the sons of outsiders too. The men from here aren't up to a thing like that.

BERNARDA: No, but they like to see it, and talk about it, and suck their fingers over it.

PONCIA: They were saying a lot more things.

BERNARDA (*looking from side to side with a certain fear*): What things?

PONCIA: I'm ashamed to talk about them.

BERNARDA: And my daughter heard them?

PONCIA: Of course!

BERNARDA: That one takes after her Aunts: white and mealy-mouthed and casting sheep's eyes at any little barber's compliment. Oh, what one has to go through and put up with so people will be decent and not too wild!

PONCIA: It's just that your daughters are of an age when they ought to have husbands. Mighty little trouble they give you. Angustias must be much more than thirty now.

BERNARDA: Exactly thirty-nine.

PONCIA: Imagine. And she's never had a beau . . .

BERNARDA (*furiously*): None of them has ever had a beau and they've never needed one! They get along very well.

PONCIA: I didn't mean to offend you.

BERNARDA: For a hundred miles around there's no one

good enough to come near them. The men in this town are not of their class. Do you want me to turn them over to the first shepherd?

PONCIA: You should have moved to another town.

BERNARDA: That's it. To sell them!

PONCIA: No, Bernarda, to change. . . . Of course, any place else, they'd be the poor ones.

BERNARDA: Hold your tormenting tongue!

PONCIA: One can't even talk to you. Do we, or do we not share secrets?

BERNARDA: We do not. You're a servant and I pay you. Nothing more.

PONCIA: But . . .

FIRST SERVANT (*entering*): Don Arturo's here. He's come to see about dividing the inheritance.

BERNARDA: Let's go. (*to the servant*) You start white-washing the patio. (*to La Poncia*) And you start putting all the dead man's clothes away in the chest.

PONCIA: We could give away some of the things.

BERNARDA: Nothing — not a button even! Not even the cloth we covered his face with.

(*She goes out slowly, leaning on her cane. At the door she turns to look at the two servants. They go out. She leaves.*)

(*Amelia and Martirio enter.*)

AMELIA: Did you take the medicine?

MARTIRIO: For all the good it'll do me.

AMELIA: But you took it?

MARTIRIO: I do things without any faith, but like clock-work.

AMELIA: Since the new doctor came you look livelier.

MARTIRIO: I feel the same.

AMELIA: Did you notice? Adelaida wasn't at the funeral.

MARTIRIO: I know. Her sweetheart doesn't let her go out even to the front doorstep. Before, she was gay. Now, not even powder on her face.

AMELIA: These days a girl doesn't know whether to have a beau or not.

MARTIRIO: It's all the same.

AMELIA: The whole trouble is all these wagging tongues that won't let us live. Adelaida has probably had a bad time.

MARTIRIO: She's afraid of our mother. Mother is the only one who knows the story of Adelaida's father and where he got his lands. Everytime she comes here, Mother twists the knife in the wound. Her father killed his first wife's husband in Cuba so he could marry her himself. Then he left her there and went off with another woman who already had one daughter, and then he took up with this other girl, Adelaida's mother, and married her after his second wife died insane.

AMELIA: But why isn't a man like that put in jail?

MARTIRIO: Because men help each other cover up things like that and no one's able to tell on them.

AMELIA: But Adelaida's not to blame for any of that.

MARTIRIO: No. But history repeats itself. I can see that everything is a terrible repetition. And she'll have the same fate as her mother and grandmother — both of them wife to the man who fathered her.

AMELIA: What an awful thing!

MARTIRIO: It's better never to look at a man. I've been afraid of them since I was a little girl. I'd see them in the yard, yoking the oxen and lifting grain sacks, shouting and stamping, and I was always afraid to grow up for fear one of them would suddenly take me in his arms. God has made me weak and ugly and has definitely put such things away from me.

AMELIA: Don't say that! Enrique Humanas was after you and he liked you.

MARTIRIO: That was just people's ideas! One time I stood in my nightgown at the window until daybreak because he let me know through his shepherd's little girl that he was going to come, and he didn't. It was all just talk. Then he married someone else who had more money than I.

AMELIA: And ugly as the devil.

MARTIRIO: What do men care about ugliness? All they care about is lands, yokes of oxen, and a submissive bitch who'll feed them.

AMELIA: Ay!

(*Magdalena enters.*)

MAGDALENA: What are you doing?

MARTIRIO: Just here.

AMELIA: And you?

MAGDALENA: I've been going through all the rooms. Just to walk a little, and look at Grandmother's needle-point pictures — the little woolen dog, and the black man wrestling with the lion — which we liked so much when we were children. Those were happier times. A wedding lasted ten days and evil tongues weren't in style. Today people are more refined. Brides wear white veils, just as in the cities, and we drink bottled wine, but we rot inside because of what people might say.

MARTIRIO: Lord knows what went on then!

AMELIA (*to Magdalena*): One of your shoelaces has come untied.

MAGDALENA: What of it?

AMELIA: You'll step on it and fall.

MAGDALENA: One less!

MARTIRIO: And Adela?

MAGDALENA: Ah! She put on the green dress she made to wear for her birthday, went out to the yard, and began shouting: "Chickens! Chickens, look at me!" I had to laugh.

AMELIA: If Mother had only seen her!

MAGDALENA: Poor little thing! She's the youngest one of us and still has her illusions. I'd give something to see her happy.

(*Pause. Angustias crosses the stage, carrying some towels.*)

ANGUSTIAS: What time is it?

MAGDALENA: It must be twelve.

ANGUSTIAS: So late?

AMELIA: It's about to strike.

(*Angustias goes out.*)

MAGDALENA (*meaningfully*): Do you know what?

(*Pointing after Angustias.*)

AMELIA: No.

MAGDALENA: Come on!

MARTIRIO: I don't know what you're talking about!

MAGDALENA: Both of you know it better than I do, always with your heads together, like two little sheep, but not letting anybody else in on it. I mean about Pepe el Romano!

MARTIRIO: Ah!

MAGDALENA (*mocking her*): Ah! The whole town's talking about it. Pepe el Romano is coming to marry Angustias. Last night he was walking around the house and I think he's going to send a declaration soon.

MARTIRIO: I'm glad. He's a good man.

AMELIA: Me too. Angustias is well off.

MAGDALENA: Neither one of you is glad.

MARTIRIO: Magdalena! What do you mean?

MAGDALENA: If he were coming because of Angustias' looks, for Angustias as a woman, I'd be glad too, but he's coming for her money. Even though Angustias is our sister, we're her family here and we know she's old and sickly, and always has been the least attractive one of us! Because if she looked like a dressed-up stick at twenty, what can she look like now, now that she's forty?

MARTIRIO: Don't talk like that. Luck comes to the one who least expects it.

AMELIA: But Magdalena's right after all! Angustias has all her father's money; she's the only rich one in the house and that's why, now that Father's dead and the money will be divided, they're coming for her.

MAGDALENA: Pepe el Romano is twenty-five years old and the best looking man around here. The natural thing would be for him to be after you, Amelia, or our Adela, who's twenty — not looking for the least likely one in this house, a woman who, like her father, talks through her nose.

MARTIRIO: Maybe he likes that!

MAGDALENA: I've never been able to bear your hypocrisy.

MARTIRIO: Heavens!

(*Adela enters.*)

MAGDALENA: Did the chickens see you?

ADELA: What did you want me to do?

AMELIA: If Mother sees you, she'll drag you by your hair!

ADELA: I had a lot of illusions about this dress. I'd planned to put it on the day we were going to eat watermelons at the well. There wouldn't have been another like it.

MARTIRIO: It's a lovely dress.

ADELA: And one that looks very good on me. It's the best thing Magdalena's ever cut.

MAGDALENA: And the chickens, what did they say to you?

ADELA: They presented me with a few fleas that riddled my legs.

(*They laugh.*)

MARTIRIO: What you can do is dye it black.

MAGDALENA: The best thing you can do is give it to Angustias for her wedding with Pepe el Romano.

ADELA (*with hidden emotion*): But Pepe el Romano . . .

AMELIA: Haven't you heard about it?

ADELA: No.

MAGDALENA: Well, now you know!

ADELA: But it can't be!

MAGDALENA: Money can do anything.

ADELA: Is that why she went out after the funeral and stood looking through the door?

(*Pause.*)

And that man would . . .

MAGDALENA: Would do anything.

(*Pause.*)

MARTIRIO: What are you thinking, Adela?

ADELA: I'm thinking that this mourning has caught me at the worst moment of my life for me to bear it.

MAGDALENA: You'll get used to it.

ADELA (*bursting out, crying with rage*): I will not get used to it! I can't be locked up. I don't want my skin to look like yours. I don't want my skin's whiteness lost in these rooms. Tomorrow I'm going to put on my green dress and go walking in the streets. I want to go out!

(*The first servant enters.*)

MAGDALENA (*in a tone of authority*): Adela!

SERVANT: The poor thing! How she misses her father. . . .

(*She goes out.*)

MARTIRIO: Hush!

AMELIA: What happens to one will happen to all of us.

(*Adela grows calm.*)

MAGDALENA: The servant almost heard you.

SERVANT (*entering*): Pepe el Romano is coming along at the end of the street.

(*Amelia, Martirio and Magdalena run hurriedly.*)

MAGDALENA: Let's go see him!

(*They leave rapidly.*)

SERVANT (*to Adela*): Aren't you going?

ADELA: It's nothing to me.

SERVANT: Since he has to turn the corner, you'll see him better from the window of your room.

(*The servant goes out. Adela is left on the stage, standing doubtfully; after a moment, she also leaves rapidly, going toward her room. Bernarda and La Poncia come in.*)

BERNARDA: Damned portions and shares.

PONCIA: What a lot of money is left to Angustias!

BERNARDA: Yes.

PONCIA: And for the others, considerably less.

BERNARDA: You've told me that three times now, when you know I don't want it mentioned! Considerably less; a lot less! Don't remind me any more.

(*Angustias comes in, her face heavily made up.*)

Angustias!

ANGUSTIAS: Mother.

BERNARDA: Have you dared to powder your face? Have you dared to wash your face on the day of your father's death?

ANGUSTIAS: He wasn't my father. Mine died a long time ago. Have you forgotten that already?

BERNARDA: You owe more to this man, father of your sisters, than to your own. Thanks to him, your fortune is intact.

ANGUSTIAS: We'll have to see about that first!

BERNARDA: Even out of decency! Out of respect!

ANGUSTIAS: Let me go out, mother!

BERNARDA: Let you go out? After I've taken that powder off your face, I will. Spineless! Painted hussy! Just like your aunts!

(*She removes the powder violently with her handkerchief.*)

Now get out!

PONCIA: Bernarda, don't be so hateful!

BERNARDA: Even though my mother is crazy, I still have my five senses and I know what I'm doing.

(*They all enter.*)

MAGDALENA: What's going on here?

BERNARDA: Nothing's "going on here"!

MAGDALENA (*to Angustias*): If you're fighting over the inheritance, you're the richest one and can hang on to it all.

ANGUSTIAS: Keep your tongue in your pocketbook!

BERNARDA (*beating on the floor*): Don't fool yourselves into thinking you'll sway me. Until I go out of this house feet first I'll give the orders for myself and for you!

(*Voices are heard and María Josefa, Bernarda's mother, enters. She is very old and has decked out her head and breast with flowers.*)

MARÍA JOSEFA: Bernarda, where is my mantilla? Nothing, nothing of what I own will be for any of you. Not my rings nor my black moiré dress. Because not a one of you is going to marry — not a one. Bernarda, give me my necklace of pearls.

BERNARDA (*to the servant*): Why did you let her get in here?

SERVANT (*trembling*): She got away from me!

MARÍA JOSEFA: I ran away because I want to marry — I want to get married to a beautiful manly man from the shore of the sea. Because here the men run from women.

BERNARDA: Hush, hush, Mother!

MARÍA JOSEFA: No, no — I won't hush. I don't want to see these single women, longing for marriage, turning their hearts to dust; and I want to go to my home town. Bernarda, I want a man to get married to and be happy with!

BERNARDA: Lock her up!

MARÍA JOSEFA: Let me go out, Bernarda!

(*The servant seizes María Josefa.*)

BERNARDA: Help her, all of you!

(*They all grab the old woman.*)

MARÍA JOSEFA: I want to get away from here! Bernarda! To get married by the shore of the sea — by the shore of the sea!

(*Quick curtain.*)

ACT 2

(*A white room in Bernarda's house. The doors on the left lead to the bedrooms. Bernarda's daughters are seated on low chairs, sewing. Magdalena is embroidering. La Poncia is with them.*)

ANGUSTIAS: I've cut the third sheet.

MARTIRIO: That one goes to Amelia.

MAGDALENA: Angustias, shall I put Pepe's initials here too?

ANGUSTIAS (*dryly*): No.

MAGDALENA (*calling, from off stage to Adela*): Adela, aren't you coming?

AMELIA: She's probably stretched out on the bed.

PONCIA: Something's wrong with that one. I find her restless, trembling, frightened — as if a lizard were between her breasts.

MARTIRIO: There's nothing, more or less, wrong with her than there is with all of us.

MAGDALENA: All of us except Angustias.

ANGUSTIAS: I feel fine, and anybody who doesn't like it can pop.

MAGDALENA: We all have to admit the nicest things about you are your figure and your tact.

ANGUSTIAS: Fortunately, I'll soon be out of this hell.

MAGDALENA: Maybe you won't get out!

MARTIRIO: Stop this talk!

ANGUSTIAS: Besides, a good dowry is better than dark eyes in one's face!

MAGDALENA: All you say just goes in one ear and out the other.

AMELIA (*to La Poncia*): Open the patio door and see if we can get a bit of a breeze.

(*La Poncia opens the door.*)

MARTIRIO: Last night I couldn't sleep because of the heat.

The women stand as witnesses in a scene from *The House of Bernarda Alba* directed by Julia Robinson at the Alba Tomi Theatre in New York in 1987.

AMELIA: Neither could I.

MAGDALENA: I got up for a bit of air. There was a black storm cloud and a few drops even fell.

PONCIA: It was one in the morning and the earth seemed to give off fire. I got up too. Angustias was still at the window with Pepe.

MAGDALENA (*with irony*): That late? What time did he leave?

ANGUSTIAS: Why do you ask, if you saw him?

AMELIA: He must have left about one-thirty.

ANGUSTIAS: Yes. How did you know?

AMELIA: I heard him cough and heard his mare's hoofbeats.

PONCIA: But I heard him leave around four.

ANGUSTIAS: It must have been someone else!

PONCIA: No, I'm sure of it!

AMELIA: That's what it seemed to me, too.

MAGDALENA: That's very strange!

(*Pause.*)

PONCIA: Listen, Angustias, what did he say to you the first time he came by your window?

ANGUSTIAS: Nothing. What should he say? Just talked.

MARTIRIO: It's certainly strange that two people who never knew each other should suddenly meet at a window and be engaged.

ANGUSTIAS: Well, I didn't mind.

AMELIA: I'd have felt very strange about it.

ANGUSTIAS: No, because when a man comes to a window he knows, from all the busybodies who come and go and fetch and carry, that he's going to be told "yes."

MARTIRIO: All right, but he'd have to ask you.

ANGUSTIAS: Of course!

AMELIA (*inquisitively*): And how did he ask you?

ANGUSTIAS: Why, no way: — "You know I'm after you. I need a good, well brought up woman, and that's you — if it's agreeable."

AMELIA: These things embarrass me!

ANGUSTIAS: They embarrass me too, but one has to go through it!

PONCIA: And did he say anything more?

ANGUSTIAS: Yes, he did all the talking.

MARTIRIO: And you?

ANGUSTIAS: I couldn't have said a word. My heart was almost coming out of my mouth. It was the first time I'd ever been alone at night with a man.

MAGDALENA: And such a handsome man.

ANGUSTIAS: He's not bad looking!

PONCIA: Those things happen among people who have an idea how to do things, who talk and say and move their hand. The first time my husband, Evaristo the Short-tailed, came to my window . . . Ha! Ha! Ha!

AMELIA: What happened?

PONCIA: It was very dark. I saw him coming along and as he went by he said, "Good evening." "Good evening," I said. Then we were both silent for more than half an hour. The sweat poured down my body. Then Evaristo got nearer and nearer as if he wanted to squeeze in through the bars and said in a very low voice —"Come here and let me feel you!"

(*They all laugh. Amelia gets up, runs, and looks through the door.*)

AMELIA: Ay, I thought mother was coming!
MAGDALENA: What she'd have done to us!

(*They go on laughing.*)

AMELIA: Sh-h-h! She'll hear us.
PONCIA: Then he acted very decently. Instead of getting some other idea, he went to raising birds, until he died. You aren't married but it's good for you to know, anyway, that two weeks after the wedding a man gives up the bed for the table, then the table for the tavern, and the woman who doesn't like it can just rot, weeping in a corner.
AMELIA: You liked it.
PONCIA: I learned how to handle him!
MARTIRIO: Is it true that you sometimes hit him?
PONCIA: Yes, and once I almost poked out one of his eyes!
MAGDALENA: All women ought to be like that!
PONCIA: I'm one of your mother's school. One time I don't know what he said to me, and then I killed all his birds — with the pestle!

(*They laugh.*)

MAGDALENA: Adela, child! Don't miss this.
AMELIA: Adela!

(*Pause.*)

MAGDALENA: I'll go see!

(*She goes out.*)

PONCIA: That child is sick!
MARTIRIO: Of course. She hardly sleeps!
PONCIA: What *does* she do, then?
MARTIRIO: How do I know what she does?
PONCIA: You probably know better than we do, since you sleep with just a wall between you.
ANGUSTIAS: Envy gnaws on people.
AMELIA: Don't exaggerate.
ANGUSTIAS: I can tell it in her eyes. She's getting the look of a crazy woman.
MARTIRIO: Don't talk about crazy women. This is one place you're not allowed to say that word.

(*Magdalena and Adela enter.*)

MAGDALENA: Didn't you say she was asleep?
ADELA: My body aches.
MARTIRIO (*with a hidden meaning*): Didn't you sleep well last night?
ADELA: Yes.
MARTIRIO: Then?
ADELA (*loudly*): Leave me alone. Awake or asleep, it's no affair of yours. I'll do whatever I want to with my body.
MARTIRIO: I was just concerned about you!
ADELA: Concerned? — curious! Weren't you sewing? Well, continue! I wish I were invisible so I could pass through a room without being asked where I was going!
SERVANT (*entering*): Bernarda is calling you. The man with the laces is here.

(*All but Adela and La Poncia go out, and as Martirio leaves, she looks fixedly at Adela.*)

ADELA: Don't look at me like that! If you want, I'll give you my eyes, for they're younger, and my back to improve that hump you have, but look the other way when I go by.
PONCIA: Adela, she's your sister, and the one who most loves you besides!
ADELA: She follows me everywhere. Sometimes she looks in my room to see if I'm sleeping. She won't let me breathe, and always, "Too bad about that face!" "Too bad about that body! It's going to waste!" But I won't let that happen. My body will be for whomever I choose.
PONCIA (*insinuatingly, in a low voice*): For Pepe el Romano, no?
ADELA (*frightened*): What do you mean?
PONCIA: What I said, Adela!
ADELA: Shut up!
PONCIA (*loudly*): Don't you think I've noticed?
ADELA: Lower your voice.
PONCIA: Then forget what you're thinking about!
ADELA: What do you know?
PONCIA: We old ones can see through walls. Where do you go when you get up at night?
ADELA: I wish you were blind!
PONCIA: But my head and hands are full of eyes, where something like this is concerned. I couldn't possibly guess your intentions. Why did you sit almost naked at your window, and with the light on and the window open, when Pepe passed by the second night he came to talk with your sister?
ADELA: That's not true!
PONCIA: Don't be a child! Leave your sister alone. And if you like Pepe el Romano, keep it to yourself.

(*Adela weeps.*)

Besides, who says you can't marry him? Your sister Angustias is sickly. She'll die with her first child. Narrow waisted, old — and out of my experience I can tell you she'll die. Then Pepe will do what all widowers do in these parts: he'll marry the youngest and most beautiful, and that's you. Live on that hope, forget him, anything; but don't go against God's law.
ADELA: Hush!
PONCIA: I won't hush!
ADELA: Mind your own business. Snooper, traitor!
PONCIA: I'm going to stick to you like a shadow!
ADELA: Instead of cleaning the house and then going to bed and praying for the dead, you root around like an old sow about goings on between men and women — so you can drool over them.
PONCIA: I keep watch; so people won't spit when they pass our door.
ADELA: What a tremendous affection you've suddenly conceived for my sister.
PONCIA: I don't have any affection for any of you. I

want to live in a decent house. I don't want to be dirtied in my old age!

ADELA: Save your advice. It's already too late. For I'd
leap not over you, just a servant, but over my mother
to put out this fire I feel in my legs and my mouth.
What can you possibly say about me? That I lock
myself in my room and will not open the door? That
I don't sleep? I'm smarter than you! See if you can
catch the hare with your hands.

PONCIA: Don't defy me, Adela, don't defy me! Because I
can shout, light lamps, and make bells ring.

ADELA: Bring four thousand yellow flares and set them
about the walls of the yard. No one can stop what
has to happen.

PONCIA: You like him that much?

ADELA: That much! Looking in his eyes I seem to drink
his blood in slowly.

PONCIA: I won't listen to you.

ADELA: Well, you'll have to. I've been afraid of you. But
now I'm stronger than you!

(*Angustias enters.*)

ANGUSTIAS: Always arguing!

PONCIA: Certainly. She insists that in all this heat I have
to go bring her I don't know what from the store.

ANGUSTIAS: Did you buy me the bottle of perfume?

PONCIA: The most expensive one. And the face powder. I
put them on the table in your room.

(*Angustias goes out.*)

ADELA: And be quiet!

PONCIA: We'll see!

(*Martirio and Amelia enter.*)

MARTIRIO (*to Adela*): Did you see the laces?

AMELIA: Angustias', for her wedding sheets, are beautiful.

ADELA (*to Martirio, who is carrying some lace*): And
these?

MARTIRIO: They're for me. For a nightgown.

ADELA (*with sarcasm*): One needs a sense of humor
around here!

MARTIRIO (*meaningfully*): But only for me to look at. I
don't have to exhibit myself before anybody.

PONCIA: No one ever sees us in our nightgowns.

MARTIRIO (*meaningfully, looking at Adela*): Sometimes
they don't! But I love nice underwear. If I were rich,
I'd have it made of Holland Cloth. It's one of the few
tastes I've left.

PONCIA: These laces are beautiful for babies caps and
christening gowns. I could never afford them for my
own. Now let's see if Angustias will use them for
hers. Once she starts having children, they'll keep her
running night and day.

MAGDALENA: I don't intend to sew a stitch on them.

AMELIA: And much less bring up some stranger's children. Look how our neighbors across the road are —
making sacrifices for four brats.

PONCIA: They're better off than you. There at least they

laugh and you can hear them fight.

MARTIRIO: Well, you go work for them, then.

PONCIA: No, fate has sent me to this nunnery!

(*Tiny bells are heard distantly as though through several
thicknesses of wall.*)

MAGDALENA: It's the men going back to work.

PONCIA: It was three o'clock a minute ago.

MARTIRIO: With this sun!

ADELA (*sitting down*): Ay! If only we could go out in the
fields too!

MAGDALENA (*sitting down*): Each class does what it has
to!

MARTIRIO (*sitting down*): That's it!

AMELIA (*sitting down*): Ay!

PONCIA: There's no happiness like that in the fields right
at this time of year. Yesterday morning the reapers
arrived. Forty or fifty handsome young men.

MAGDALENA: Where are they from this year?

PONCIA: From far, far away. They came from the mountains! Happy! Like weathered trees! Shouting and
throwing stones! Last night a woman who dresses in
sequins and dances, with an accordion, arrived, and
fifteen of them made a deal with her to take her to the
olive grove. I saw them from far away. The one who
talked with her was a boy with green eyes — tight
knit as a sheaf of wheat.

AMELIA: Really?

ADELA: Are you sure?

PONCIA: Years ago another one of those women came
here, and I myself gave my eldest son some money so
he could go. Men need things like that.

ADELA: Everything's forgiven *them*.

AMELIA: To be born a woman's the worst possible punishment.

MAGDALENA: Even our eyes aren't our own.

(*A distant song is heard, coming nearer.*)

PONCIA: There they are. They have a beautiful song.

AMELIA: They're going out to reap now.

CHORUS:

The reapers have set out
Looking for ripe wheat;
They'll carry off the hearts
Of any girls they meet.

(*Tambourines and carrañacas are heard. Pause. They all
listen in the silence cut by the sun.*)

AMELIA: And they don't mind the sun!

MARTIRIO: They reap through flames.

ADELA: How I'd like to be a reaper so I could come and
go as I pleased. Then we could forget what's eating us
all.

MARTIRIO: What do you have to forget?

ADELA: Each one of us has something.

MARTIRIO (*intensely*): Each one!

PONCIA: Quiet! Quiet!

CHORUS (*very distantly*):

Throw wide your doors and windows,

*You girls who live in the town
The reaper asks you for roses
With which to deck his crown.*
PONCIA: What a song!
MARTIRIO (*with nostalgia*):
*Throw wide your doors and windows,
You girls who live in the town.*
ADELA (*passionately*):
*The reaper asks you for roses
With which to deck his crown.*

(*The song grows more distant.*)

PONCIA: Now they're turning the corner.
ADELA: Let's watch them from the window of my room.
PONCIA: Be careful not to open the shutters too much because they're likely to give them a push to see who's looking.

(*The three leave. Martirio is left sitting on the low chair with her head between her hands.*)

AMELIA (*drawing near her*): What's wrong with you?
MARTIRIO: The heat makes me feel ill.
AMELIA: And it's no more than that?
MARTIRIO: I was wishing it were November, the rainy days, the frost — anything except this unending summertime.
AMELIA: It'll pass and come again.
MARTIRIO: Naturally.

(*Pause.*)

What time did you go to sleep last night?
AMELIA: I don't know. I sleep like a log. Why?
MARTIRIO: Nothing. Only I thought I heard someone in the yard.
AMELIA: Yes?
MARTIRIO: Very late.
AMELIA: And weren't you afraid?
MARTIRIO: No. I've heard it other nights.
AMELIA: We'd better watch out! Couldn't it have been the shepherds?
MARTIRIO: The shepherds come at six.
AMELIA: Maybe a young, unbroken mule?
MARTIRIO (*to herself, with double meaning*): That's it! That's it. An unbroken little mule.
AMELIA: We'll have to set a watch.
MARTIRIO: No. No. Don't say anything. It may be I've just imagined it.
AMELIA: Maybe.

(*Pause. Amelia starts to go.*)

MARTIRIO: Amelia!
AMELIA (*at the door*): What?

(*Pause.*)

MARTIRIO: Nothing.

(*Pause.*)

AMELIA: Why did you call me?

(*Pause.*)

MARTIRIO: It just came out. I didn't mean to.

(*Pause.*)

AMELIA: Lie down for a little.
ANGUSTIAS (*she bursts in furiously, in a manner that makes a great contrast with previous silence*): Where's that picture of Pepe I had under my pillow? Which one of you has it?
MARTIRIO: No one.
AMELIA: You'd think he was a silver St. Bartholomew.°
ANGUSTIAS: Where's the picture?

(*Poncia, Magdalena and Adela enter.*)

ADELA: What picture?
ANGUSTIAS: One of you has hidden it from me.
MAGDALENA: Do you have the effrontery to say that?
ANGUSTIAS: I had it in my room, and now it isn't there.
MARTIRIO: But couldn't it have jumped out into the yard at midnight? Pepe likes to walk around in the moonlight.
ANGUSTIAS: Don't joke with me! When he comes I'll tell him.
PONCIA: Don't do that! Because it'll turn up.

(*Looking at Adela.*)

ANGUSTIAS: I'd like to know which one of you has it.
ADELA (*looking at Martirio*): Somebody has it! But not me!
MARTIRIO (*with meaning*): Of course not you!
BERNARDA (*entering with her cane*): What scandal is this in my house in the heat's heavy silence? The neighbors must have their ears glued to the walls.
ANGUSTIAS: They've stolen my sweetheart's picture!
BERNARDA (*fiercely*): Who? Who?
ANGUSTIAS: They have!
BERNARDA: Which one of you?

(*Silence.*)

Answer me!

(*Silence.*) (*To La Poncia.*)

Search their rooms! Look in their beds. This comes of not tying you up with shorter leashes. But I'll teach you now! (*to Angustias*) Are you sure?
ANGUSTIAS: Yes.
BERNARDA: Did you look everywhere?
ANGUSTIAS: Yes, Mother.

(*They all stand in an embarrassed silence.*)

BERNARDA: At the end of my life — to make me drink the bitterest poison a mother knows. (*to Poncia*) Did you find it?
PONCIA: Here it is.
BERNARDA: Where did you find it?
PONCIA: It was . . .
BERNARDA: Say it! Don't be afraid.
PONCIA (*wonderingly*): Between the sheets in Martirio's bed.

silver St. Bartholomew: A medallion used for good fortune.

BERNARDA (*to Martirio*): Is that true?

MARTIRIO: It's true.

BERNARDA (*advancing on her, beating her with her cane*): You'll come to a bad end yet, you hypocrite! Trouble maker!

MARTIRIO (*fiercely*): Don't hit me, Mother!

BERNARDA: All I want to!

MARTIRIO: If I let you! You hear me? Get back!

PONCIA: Don't be disrespectful to your mother!

ANGUSTIAS (*holding Bernarda*): Let her go, please!

BERNARDA: Not even tears in your eyes.

MARTIRIO: I'm not going to cry just to please you.

BERNARDA: Why did you take the picture?

MARTIRIO: Can't I play a joke on my sister? What else would I want it for?

ADELA (*leaping forward, full of jealousy*): It wasn't a joke! You never liked to play jokes. It was something else bursting in her breast — trying to come out. Admit it openly now.

MARTIRIO: Hush, and don't make me speak; for if I should speak the walls would close together one against the other with shame.

ADELA: An evil tongue never stops inventing lies.

BERNARDA: Adela!

MAGDALENA: You're crazy.

AMELIA: And you stone us all with your evil suspicions.

MARTIRIO: But some others do things more wicked!

ADELA: Until all at once they stand forth stark naked and the river carries them along.

BERNARDA: Spiteful!

ANGUSTIAS: It's not my fault Pepe el Romano chose me!

ADELA: For your money.

ANGUSTIAS: Mother!

BERNARDA: Silence!

MARTIRIO: For your fields and your orchards.

MAGDALENA: That's only fair.

BERNARDA: Silence, I say! I saw the storm coming but I didn't think it'd burst so soon. Oh, what an avalanche of hate you've thrown on my heart! But I'm not old yet — I have five chains for you, and this house my father built, so not even the weeds will know of my desolation. Out of here!

(*They go out. Bernarda sits down desolately. La Poncia is standing close to the wall. Bernarda recovers herself, and beats on the floor.*)

I'll have to let them feel the weight of my hand! Bernarda, remember your duty!

PONCIA: May I speak?

BERNARDA: Speak. I'm sorry you heard. A stranger is always out of place in a family.

PONCIA: What I've seen, I've seen.

BERNARDA: Angustias must get married right away.

PONCIA: Certainly. We'll have to get her away from here.

BERNARDA: Not her, him!

PONCIA: Of course. He's the one to get away from here. You've thought it all out.

BERNARDA: I'm not thinking. These are things that shouldn't and can't be thought out. I give orders.

PONCIA: And you think he'll be satisfied to go away?

BERNARDA (*rising*): What are you imagining now?

PONCIA: He will, of course, marry Angustias.

BERNARDA: Speak up! I know you well enough to see that your knife's out for me.

PONCIA: I never knew a warning could be called murder.

BERNARDA: Have you some "warning" for me?

PONCIA: I'm not making any accusations, Bernarda. I'm only telling you to open your eyes and you'll see.

BERNARDA: See what?

PONCIA: You've always been smart, Bernarda. You've seen other people's sins a hundred miles away. Many times I've thought you could read minds. But, your children are your children, and now you're blind.

BERNARDA: Are you talking about Martirio?

PONCIA: Well, yes — about Martirio . . .

(*With curiosity.*)

I wonder why she hid the picture?

BERNARDA (*shielding her daughter*): After all, she says it was a joke. What else could it be?

PONCIA (*scornfully*): Do you believe that?

BERNARDA (*sternly*): I don't merely believe it. It's so!

PONCIA: Enough of this. We're talking about your family. But if we were talking about your neighbor across the way, what would it be?

BERNARDA: Now you're beginning to pull the point of the knife out.

PONCIA (*always cruelly*): No, Bernarda. Something very grave is happening here. I don't want to put the blame on your shoulders, but you've never given your daughters any freedom. Martirio is lovesick. I don't care what you say. Why didn't you let her marry Enrique Humanas? Why, on the very day he was coming to her window did you send him a message not to come?

BERNARDA (*loudly*): I'd do it a thousand times over! My blood won't mingle with the Humanas' while I live! His father was a shepherd.

PONCIA: And you see now what's happening to you with these airs!

BERNARDA: I have them because I can afford to. And you don't have them because you know where you came from!

PONCIA (*with hate*): Don't remind me! I'm old now. I've always been grateful for your protection.

BERNARDA (*emboldened*): You don't seem so!

PONCIA (*with hate, behind softness*): Martirio will forget this.

BERNARDA: And if she doesn't — the worse for her. I don't believe this is that "very grave thing" that's happening here. Nothing's happening here. It's just that you wish it would! And if it should happen one day, you can be sure it won't go beyond these walls.

PONCIA: I'm not so sure of that! There are people in town who can also read hidden thoughts, from afar.

BERNARDA: How you'd like to see me and my daughters on our way to a whorehouse!

PONCIA: No one knows her own destiny!

BERNARDA: I know my destiny! And my daughters! The whorehouse was for a certain woman, already dead. . . .

PONCIA (*fiercely*): Bernarda, respect the memory of my mother!

BERNARDA: Then don't plague me with your evil thoughts!

(*Pause.*)

PONCIA: I'd better stay out of everything.

BERNARDA: That's what you ought to do. Work and keep your mouth shut. The duty of all who work for a living.

PONCIA: But we can't do that. Don't you think it'd be better for Pepe to marry Martirio or . . . yes! . . . Adela?

BERNARDA: No, I *don't* think so.

PONCIA (*with meaning*): Adela! She's Romano's real sweetheart!

BERNARDA: Things are never the way we want them!

PONCIA: But it's hard work to turn them from their destined course. For Pepe to be with Angustias seems wrong to me — and to other people — and even to the wind. Who knows if they'll get what they want?

BERNARDA: There you go again! Sneaking up on me — giving me bad dreams. But I won't listen to you, because if all you say should come to pass — I'd scratch your face.

PONCIA: Frighten someone else with that.

BERNARDA: Fortunately, my daughters respect me and have never gone against my will!

PONCIA: That's right! But, as soon as they break loose they'll fly to the rooftops!

BERNARDA: And I'll bring them down with stones!

PONCIA: Oh, yes! You were always the bravest one!

BERNARDA: I've always enjoyed a good fight!

PONCIA: But aren't people strange. You should see Angustias' enthusiasm for her lover, at her age! And he seems very smitten too. Yesterday my oldest son told me that when he passed by with the oxen at four-thirty in the morning they were still talking.

BERNARDA: At four-thirty?

ANGUSTIAS (*entering*): That's a lie!

PONCIA: That's what he told me.

BERNARDA (*to Angustias*): Speak up!

ANGUSTIAS: For more than a week Pepe has been leaving at one. May God strike me dead if I'm lying.

MARTIRIO (*entering*): I heard him leave at four too.

BERNARDA: But did you see him with your eyes?

MARTIRIO: I didn't want to look out. Don't you talk now through the side window?

ANGUSTIAS: We talk through my bedroom window.

(*Adela appears at the door.*)

MARTIRIO: Then . . .

BERNARDA: What's going on here?

PONCIA: If you're not careful, you'll find out! At least Pepe was at *one* of your windows — and at four in the morning too!

BERNARDA: Are you sure of that?

PONCIA: You can't be sure of anything in this life!

ADELA: Mother, don't listen to someone who wants us to lose everything we have.

BERNARDA: I know how to take care of myself! If the townspeople want to come bearing false witness against me, they'll run into a stone wall! Don't any of you talk about this! Sometimes other people try to stir up a wave of filth to drown us.

MARTIRIO: I don't like to lie.

PONCIA: So there must be something.

BERNARDA: There won't be anything. I was born to have my eyes always open. Now I'll watch without closing them 'til I die.

ANGUSTIAS: I have the right to know.

BERNARDA: You don't have any right except to obey. No one's going to fetch and carry for me. (*to La Poncia*) And don't meddle in our affairs. No one will take a step without my knowing it.

SERVANT (*entering*): There's a big crowd at the top of the street, and all the neighbors are at their doors!

BERNARDA (*to Poncia*): Run see what's happening!

(*The girls are about to run out.*)

Where are you going? I always knew you for window-watching women and breakers of your mourning. All of you, to the patio!

(*They go out. Bernarda leaves. Distant shouts are heard.*)
(*Martirio and Adela enter and listen, not daring to step farther than the front door.*)

MARTIRIO: You can be thankful I didn't happen to open my mouth.

ADELA: I would have spoken too.

MARTIRIO: And what were you going to say? Wanting isn't doing!

ADELA: I do what I can and what happens to suit me. You've wanted to, but haven't been able.

MARTIRIO: You won't go on very long.

ADELA: I'll have everything!

MARTIRIO: I'll tear you out of his arms!

ADELA (*pleadingly*): Martirio, let me be!

MARTIRIO: None of us will have him!

ADELA: He wants me for his house!

MARTIRIO: I saw how he embraced you!

ADELA: I didn't want him to. It's as if I were dragged by a rope.

MARTIRIO: I'll see you dead first!

(*Magdalena and Angustias look in. The tumult is increasing. A servant enters with Bernarda. Poncia also enters from another door.*)

PONCIA: Bernarda!

BERNARDA: What's happening?

PONCIA: Librada's daughter, the unmarried one, had a child and no one knows whose it is!

ADELA: A child?

PONCIA: And to hide her shame she killed it and hid it

under the rocks, but the dogs, with more heart than most Christians, dug it out and, as though directed by the hand of God, left it at her door. Now they want to kill her. They're dragging her through the streets — and down the paths and across the olive groves the men are coming, shouting so the fields shake.

BERNARDA: Yes, let them all come with olive whips and hoe handles — let them all come and kill her!

ADELA: No, not to kill her!

MARTIRIO: Yes — and let us go out too!

BERNARDA: And let whoever loses her decency pay for it!

(*Outside a woman's shriek and a great clamor is heard.*)

ADELA: Let her escape! Don't you go out!

MARTIRIO (*looking at Adela*): Let her pay what she owes!

BERNARDA (*at the archway*): Finish her before the guards come! Hot coals in the place where she sinned!

ADELA (*holding her belly*): No! No!

BERNARDA: Kill her! Kill her!

(*Curtain.*)

ACT 3

(*Four white walls, lightly washed in blue, of the interior patio of Bernarda Alba's house. The doorways, illumined by the lights inside the rooms, give a tenuous glow to the stage. At the center there is a table with a shaded oil lamp about which Bernarda and her daughters are eating. La Poncia serves them. Prudencia sits apart. When the curtain rises, there is a great silence interrupted only by the noise of plates and silverware.*)

PRUDENCIA: I'm going. I've made you a long visit.

(*She rises.*)

BERNARDA: But wait, Prudencia. We never see one another.

PRUDENCIA: Have they sounded the last call to rosary?

PONCIA: Not yet.

(*Prudencia sits down again.*)

BERNARDA: And your husband, how's he getting on?

PRUDENCIA: The same.

BERNARDA: We never see him either.

PRUDENCIA: You know how he is. Since he quarrelled with his brothers over the inheritance, he hasn't used the front door. He takes a ladder and climbs over the back wall.

BERNARDA: He's a real man! And your daughter?

PRUDENCIA: He's never forgiven her.

BERNARDA: He's right.

PRUDENCIA: I don't know what he told you. I suffer because of it.

BERNARDA: A daughter who's disobedient stops being a daughter and becomes an enemy.

PRUDENCIA: I let water run. The only consolation I've

left is to take refuge in the church, but, since I'm losing my sight, I'll have to stop coming so the children won't make fun of me.

(*A heavy blow is heard against the walls.*)

What's that?

BERNARDA: The stallion. He's locked in the stall and he kicks against the wall of the house.

(*Shouting.*)

Tether him and take him out in the yard!

(*In a lower voice.*)

He must be too hot.

PRUDENCIA: Are you going to put the new mares to him?

BERNARDA: At daybreak.

PRUDENCIA: You've known how to increase your stock.

BERNARDA: By dint of money and struggling.

PONCIA (*interrupting*): And she has the best herd in these parts. It's a shame that prices are low.

BERNARDA: Do you want a little cheese and honey?

PRUDENCIA: I have no appetite.

(*The blow is heard again.*)

PONCIA: My God!

PRUDENCIA: It quivered in my chest.

BERNARDA (*rising, furiously*): Do I have to say things twice? Let him out to roll on the straw.

(*Pause. Then, as though speaking to the stableman.*)

Well then, lock the mares in the corral, but let him run free or he may kick down the walls.

(*She returns to the table and sits again.*)

Ay, what a life!

PRUDENCIA: You have to fight like a man.

BERNARDA: That's it.

(*Adela gets up from the table.*)

Where are you going?

ADELA: For a drink of water.

BERNARDA (*raising her voice*): Bring a pitcher of cool water. (*to Adela*) You can sit down. (*Adela sits down.*)

PRUDENCIA: And Angustias, when will she get married?

BERNARDA: They're coming to ask for her within three days.

PRUDENCIA: You must be happy.

ANGUSTIAS: Naturally!

AMELIA (*to Magdalena*): You've spilled the salt!

MAGDALENA: You can't possibly have worse luck than you're having.

AMELIA: It always brings bad luck.

BERNARDA: That's enough!

PRUDENCIA (*to Angustias*): Has he given you the ring yet?

ANGUSTIAS: Look at it.

(*She holds it out.*)

PRUDENCIA: It's beautiful. Three pearls. In my day, pearls signified tears.

ANGUSTIAS: But things have changed now.

ADELA: I don't think so. Things go on meaning the same. Engagement rings should be diamonds.

PONCIA: The most appropriate.

BERNARDA: With pearls or without them, things are as one proposes.

MARTIRIO: Or as God disposes.

PRUDENCIA: I've been told your furniture is beautiful.

BERNARDA: It cost sixteen thousand *reales.*°

PONCIA (*interrupting*): The best is the wardrobe with the mirror.

PRUDENCIA: I never saw a piece like that.

BERNARDA: We had chests.

PRUDENCIA: The important thing is that everything be for the best.

ADELA: And that you never know.

BERNARDA: There's no reason why it shouldn't be.

(*Bells are heard very distantly.*)

PRUDENCIA: The last call. (*to Angustias*) I'll be coming back to have you show me your clothes.

ANGUSTIAS: Whenever you like.

PRUDENCIA: Good evening — God bless you!

BERNARDA: Good-bye, Prudencia.

ALL FIVE DAUGHTERS (*at the same time*): God go with you!

(*Pause. Prudencia goes out.*)

BERNARDA: Well, we've eaten.

(*They rise.*)

ADELA: I'm going to walk as far as the gate to stretch my legs and get a bit of fresh air.

(*Magdalena sits down in a low chair and leans against the wall.*)

AMELIA: I'll go with you.

MARTIRIO: I too.

ADELA (*with contained hate*): I'm not going to get lost!

AMELIA: One needs company at night.

(*They go out. Bernarda sits down. Angustias is clearing the table.*)

BERNARDA: I've told you once already! I want you to talk to your sister Martirio. What happened about the picture was a joke and you must forget it.

ANGUSTIAS: You know she doesn't like me.

BERNARDA: Each one knows what she thinks inside. I don't pry into anyone's heart, but I want to put up a good front and have family harmony. You understand?

ANGUSTIAS: Yes.

BERNARDA: Then that's settled.

MAGDALENA (*she is almost asleep*): Besides, you'll be gone in no time.

(*She falls asleep.*)

reales: Spanish silver coin. Sixteen thousand would have been a great sum.

ANGUSTIAS: Not soon enough for me.

BERNARDA: What time did you stop talking last night?

ANGUSTIAS: Twelve-thirty.

BERNARDA: What does Pepe talk about?

ANGUSTIAS: I find him absent-minded. He always talks to me as though he were thinking of something else. If I ask him what's the matter, he answers — "We men have our worries."

BERNARDA: You shouldn't ask him. And when you're married, even less. Speak if he speaks, and look at him when he looks at you. That way you'll get along.

ANGUSTIAS: But, Mother, I think he's hiding things from me.

BERNARDA: Don't try to find out. Don't ask him, and above all, never let him see you cry.

ANGUSTIAS: I should be happy, but I'm not.

BERNARDA: It's all the same.

ANGUSTIAS: Many nights I watch Pepe very closely through the window bars and he seems to fade away — as though he were hidden in a cloud of dust like those raised by the flocks.

BERNARDA: That's just because you're not strong.

ANGUSTIAS: I hope so!

BERNARDA: Is he coming tonight?

ANGUSTIAS: No, he went into town with his mother.

BERNARDA: Good, we'll get to bed early. Magdalena!

ANGUSTIAS: She's asleep.

(*Adela, Martirio and Amelia enter.*)

AMELIA: What a dark night!

ADELA: You can't see two steps in front of you.

MARTIRIO: A good night for robbers, for anyone who needs to hide.

ADELA: The stallion was in the middle of the corral. White. Twice as large. Filling all the darkness.

AMELIA: It's true. It was frightening. Like a ghost.

ADELA: The sky has stars as big as fists.

MARTIRIO: This one stared at them till she almost cracked her neck.

ADELA: Don't you like them up there?

MARTIRIO: What goes on over the roof doesn't mean a thing to me. I have my hands full with what happens under it.

ADELA: Well, that's the way it goes with you!

BERNARDA: And it goes the same for you as for her.

ANGUSTIAS: Good night.

ADELA: Are you going to bed now?

ANGUSTIAS: Yes, Pepe isn't coming tonight.

(*She goes out.*)

ADELA: Mother, why, when a stars falls or lightning flashes, does one say:
Holy Barbara, blessed on high
May your name be in the sky
With holy water written high?

BERNARDA: The old people know many things we've forgotten.

AMELIA: I close my eyes so I won't see them.

ADELA: Not I. I like to see what's quiet and been quiet for years on end, running with fire.

MARTIRIO: But all that has nothing to do with us.

BERNARDA: And it's better not to think about it.

ADELA: What a beautiful night! I'd like to stay up till very late and enjoy the breeze from the fields.

BERNARDA: But we have to go to bed. Magdalena!

AMELIA: She's just dropped off.

BERNARDA: Magdalena!

MAGDALENA (*annoyed*): Leave me alone!

BERNARDA: To bed!

MAGDALENA (*rising, in a bad humor*): You don't give anyone a moment's peace!

(*She goes off grumbling.*)

AMELIA: Good night!

(*She goes out.*)

BERNARDA: You two get along, too.

MARTIRIO: How is it Angustias' sweetheart isn't coming tonight?

BERNARDA: He went on a trip.

MARTIRIO (*looking at Adela*): Ah!

ADELA: I'll see you in the morning!

(*She goes out. Martirio drinks some water and goes out slowly, looking at the door to the yard. La Poncia enters.*)

PONCIA: Are you still here?

BERNARDA: Enjoying this quiet and not seeing anywhere the "very grave thing" that's happening here — according to you.

PONCIA: Bernarda, let's not go any further with this.

BERNARDA: In this house there's no question of a yes or a no. My watchfulness can take care of anything.

PONCIA: Nothing's happening outside. That's true, all right. Your daughters act and are as though stuck in a cupboard. But neither you nor anyone else can keep watch inside a person's heart.

BERNARDA: My daughters breathe calmly enough.

PONCIA: That's your business, since you're their mother. I have enough to do just with serving you.

BERNARDA: Yes, you've turned quiet now.

PONCIA: I keep my place — that's all.

BERNARDA: The trouble is you've nothing to talk about. If there were grass in this house, you'd make it your business to put the neighbors' sheep to pasture here.

PONCIA: I hide more than you think.

BERNARDA: Do your sons still see Pepe at four in the morning? Are they still repeating this house's evil litany?

PONCIA: They say nothing.

BERNARDA: Because they can't. Because there's nothing for them to sink their teeth in. And all because my eyes keep constant watch!

PONCIA: Bernarda, I don't want to talk about this because I'm afraid of what you'll do. But don't you feel so safe.

BERNARDA: Very safe!

PONCIA: Who knows, lightning might strike suddenly. Who knows but what all of a sudden, in a rush of blood, your heart might stop.

BERNARDA: Nothing will happen here. I'm on guard now against all your suspicions.

PONCIA: All the better for you.

BERNARDA: Certainly, all the better!

SERVANT (*entering*): I've just finished with the dishes. Is there anything else, Bernarda?

BERNARDA (*rising*): Nothing. I'm going to get some rest.

PONCIA: What time do you want me to call you?

BERNARDA: No time. Tonight I intend to sleep well.

(*She goes out.*)

PONCIA: When you're powerless against the sea, it's easier to turn your back on it and not look at it.

SERVANT: She's so proud! She herself pulls the blindfold over her eyes.

PONCIA: I can do nothing. I tried to head things off, but now they frighten me too much. You feel this silence? — in each room there's a thunderstorm and the day it breaks, it'll sweep all of us along with it. But I've said what I had to say.

SERVANT: Bernarda thinks nothing can stand against her, yet she doesn't know the strength a man has among women alone.

PONCIA: It's not all the fault of Pepe el Romano. It's true last year he was running after Adela; and she was crazy about him — but she ought to keep her place and not lead him on. A man's a man.

SERVANT: And some there are who believe he didn't have to talk many times with Adela.

PONCIA: That's true.

(*In a low voice.*)

And some other things.

SERVANT: I don't know what's going to happen here.

PONCIA: How I'd like to sail across the sea and leave this house, this battleground, behind!

SERVANT: Bernarda's hurrying the wedding and it's possible nothing will happen.

PONCIA: Things have gone much too far already. Adela is set no matter what comes, and the rest of them watch without rest.

SERVANT: Martirio too. . . ?

PONCIA: That one's the worst. She's a pool of poison. She sees El Romano is not for her, and she'd sink the world if it were in her hand to do so.

SERVANT: How bad they all are!

PONCIA: They're women without men, that's all. And in such matters even blood is forgotten. Sh-h-h-h!

(*She listens.*)

SERVANT: What's the matter?

PONCIA (*she rises*): The dogs are barking.

SERVANT: Someone must have passed by the back door.

(*Adela enters wearing a white petticoat and corselet.*)

PONCIA: Aren't you in bed yet?

ADELA: I want a drink of water.

(*She drinks from a glass on the table.*)

PONCIA: I imagined you were asleep.
ADELA: I got thirsty and woke up. Aren't you two going to get some rest?
SERVANT: Soon now.

(*Adela goes out.*)

PONCIA: Let's go.
SERVANT: We've certainly earned some sleep. Bernarda doesn't let me rest the whole day.
PONCIA: Take the light.
SERVANT: The dogs are going mad.
PONCIA: They're not going to let us sleep.

(*They go out. The stage is left almost dark. María Josefa enters with a lamb in her arms.*)

MARÍA JOSEFA (*singing*):
Little lamb, child of mine,
Let's go to the shore of the sea,
The tiny ant will be at his doorway,
I'll nurse you and give you your bread.
Bernarda, old leopard-face,
And Magdalena, hyena-face,
Little lamb . . .
Rock, rock-a-bye,
Let's go to the palms at Bethlehem's gate.

(*She laughs.*)

Neither you nor I would want to sleep
The door will open by itself
And on the beach we'll go and hide
In a little coral cabin.
Bernarda, old leopard-face,
And Magdalena, hyena-face,
Little lamb . . .
Rock, rock-a-bye,
Let's go to the palms at Bethlehem's gate.

(*She goes off singing.*)
(*Adela enters. She looks about cautiously and disappears out the door leading to the corral. Martirio enters by another door and stands in anguished watchfulness near the center of the stage. She also is in petticoats. She covers herself with a small black scarf. María Josefa crosses before her.*)

MARTIRIO: Grandmother, where are you going?
MARÍA JOSEFA: You are going to open the door for me? Who are you?
MARTIRIO: How did you get out here?
MARÍA JOSEFA: I escaped. You, who are you?
MARTIRIO: Go back to bed.
MARÍA JOSEFA: You're Martirio. Now I see you. Martirio, face of a martyr. And when are you going to have a baby? I've had this one.
MARTIRIO: Where did you get that lamb?
MARÍA JOSEFA: I know it's a lamb. But can't a lamb be a baby? It's better to have a lamb than not to have any-

thing. Old Bernarda, leopard-face, and Magdalena, hyena-face!
MARTIRIO: Don't shout.
MARÍA JOSEFA: It's true. Everything's very dark. Just because I have white hair you think I can't have babies, but I can — babies and babies and babies. This baby will have white hair, and I'd have *this* baby, and another, and this *one* other; and with all of us with snow white hair we'll be like the waves — one, then another, and another. Then we'll all sit down and all of us will have white heads, and we'll be seafoam. Why isn't there any seafoam here? Nothing but mourning shrouds here.
MARTIRIO: Hush, hush.
MARÍA JOSEFA: When my neighbor had a baby, I'd carry her some chocolate and later she'd bring me some, and so on — always and always and always. You'll have white hair, but your neighbors won't come. Now I have to go away, but I'm afraid the dogs will bite me. Won't you come with me as far as the fields? I don't like fields. I like houses, but open houses, and the neighbor women asleep in their beds with their little tiny tots, and the men outside sitting in their chairs. Pepe el Romano is a giant. All of you love him. But he's going to devour you because you're grains of wheat. No, not grains of wheat. Frogs with no tongues!
MARTIRIO (*angrily*): Come, off to bed with you.

(*She pushes her.*)

MARÍA JOSEFA: Yes, but then you'll open the door for me, won't you?
MARTIRIO: Of course.
MARÍA JOSEFA (*weeping*):
Little lamb, child of mine,
Let's go to the shore of the sea,
The tiny ant will be at his doorway,
I'll nurse you and give you your bread.

(*Martirio locks the door through which María Josefa came out and goes to the yard door. There she hesitates, but goes two steps farther.*)

MARTIRIO (*in a low voice*): Adela! (*Pause. She advances to the door. Then, calling.*) Adela!

(*Adela enters. Her hair is disarranged.*)

ADELA: And what are you looking for me for?
MARTIRIO: Keep away from him.
ADELA: Who are you to tell me that?
MARTIRIO: That's no place for a decent woman.
ADELA: How you wish *you'd* been there!
MARTIRIO (*shouting*): This is the moment for me to speak. This can't go on.
ADELA: This is just the beginning. I've had strength enough to push myself forward — the spirit and looks you lack. I've seen death under this roof, and gone out to look for what was mine, what belonged to me.
MARTIRIO: That soulless man came for another woman. You pushed yourself in front of him.

ADELA: He came for the money, but his eyes were always on me.

MARTIRIO: I won't allow you to snatch him away. He'll marry Angustias.

ADELA: You know better than I he doesn't love her.

MARTIRIO: I know.

ADELA: You know because you've seen — he loves me, me!

MARTIRIO (*desperately*): Yes.

ADELA (*close before her*): He loves me, *me!* He loves me, *me!*

MARTIRIO: Stick me with a knife if you like, but don't tell me that again.

ADELA: That's why you're trying to fix it so I won't go away with him. It makes no difference to you if he puts his arms around a woman he doesn't love. Nor does it to me. He could be a hundred years with Angustias, but for him to have his arms around me seems terrible to you — because you too love him! You love him!

MARTIRIO (*dramatically*): Yes! Let me say it without hiding my head. Yes! my breast's bitter, bursting like a pomegranate. I love him!

ADELA (*impulsively, hugging her*): Martirio, Martirio, I'm not to blame!

MARTIRIO: Don't put your arms around me! Don't try to smooth it over. My blood's no longer yours, and even though I try to think of you as a sister, I see you as just another woman.

(*She pushes her away.*)

ADELA: There's no way out here. Whoever has to drown — let her drown. Pepe is mine. He'll carry me to the rushes along the river bank. . . .

MARTIRIO: He won't!

ADELA: I can't stand this horrible house after the taste of his mouth. I'll be what he wants me to be. Everybody in the village against me, burning me with their fiery fingers; pursued by those who claim they're decent, and I'll wear, before them all, the crown of thorns that belongs to the mistress of a married man.

MARTIRIO: Hush!

ADELA: Yes, yes. (*In a low voice.*) Let's go to bed. Let's let him marry Angustias. I don't care any more, but I'll go off alone to a little house where he'll come to see me whenever he wants, whenever he feels like it.

MARTIRIO: That'll never happen! Not while I have a drop of blood left in my body.

ADELA: Not just weak you, but a wild horse I could force to his knees with just the strength of my little finger.

MARTIRIO: Don't raise that voice of yours to me. It irritates me. I have a heart full of a force so evil that, without my wanting to be, I'm drowned by it.

ADELA: You show us the way to love our sisters. God must have meant to leave me alone in the midst of darkness because I can see you as I've never seen you before.

(*A whistle is heard and Adela runs toward the door, but Martirio gets in front of her.*)

MARTIRIO: Where are you going?

ADELA: Get away from that door!

MARTIRIO: Get by me if you can!

ADELA: Get away!

(*They struggle.*)

MARTIRIO (*shouts*): Mother! Mother!

ADELA: Let me go!

(*Bernarda enters. She wears petticoats and a black shawl.*)

BERNARDA: Quiet! Quiet! How poor I am without even a man to help me!

MARTIRIO (*pointing to Adela*): She was with him. Look at those skirts covered with straw!

BERNARDA (*going furiously toward Adela*): That's the bed of a bad woman!

ADELA (*facing her*): There'll be an end to prison voices here! (*Adela snatches away her mother's cane and breaks it in two.*) This is what I do with the tyrant's cane. Not another step. No one but Pepe commands me!

(*Magdalena enters.*)

MAGDALENA: Adela!

(*La Poncia and Angustias enter.*)

ADELA: I'm his. (*to Angustias*) Know that — and go out in the yard and tell him. He'll be master in this house.

ANGUSTIAS: My God!

BERNARDA: The gun! Where's the gun?

(*She rushes out. La Poncia runs ahead of her. Amelia enters and looks on frightened, leaning her head against the wall. Behind her comes Martirio.*)

ADELA: No one can hold me back!

(*She tries to go out.*)

ANGUSTIAS (*holding her*): You're not getting out of here with your body's triumph! Thief! Disgrace of this house!

MAGDALENA: Let her go where we'll never see her again!

(*A shot is heard.*)

BERNARDA (*entering*): Just try looking for him now!

MARTIRIO (*entering*): That does away with Pepe el Romano.

ADELA: Pepe! My God! Pepe!

(*She runs out.*)

PONCIA: Did you kill him?

MARTIRIO: No. He raced away on his mare!

BERNARDA: It was my fault. A woman can't aim.

MAGDALENA: Then, why did you say . . . ?

MARTIRIO: For her! I'd like to pour a river of blood over her head!

PONCIA: Curse you!

MAGDALENA: Devil!

BERNARDA: Although it's better this way!

(*A thud is heard.*)

Adela! Adela!

PONCIA (*at her door*): Open this door!

BERNARDA: Open! Don't think the walls will hide your shame!

SERVANT (*entering*): All the neighbors are up!

BERNARDA (*in a low voice, but like a roar*): Open! Or I'll knock the door down!

(*Pause. Everything is silent.*)

Adela!

(*She walks away from the door.*)

A hammer!

(*La Poncia throws herself against the door. It opens and she goes in. As she enters, she screams and backs out.*)

What is it?

PONCIA (*she puts her hands to her throat*): May we never die like that!

(*The sisters fall back. The servant crosses herself. Bernarda screams and goes forward.*)

Don't go in!

BERNARDA: No, not I! Pepe, you're running now, alive in the darkness, under the trees, but another day you'll fall. Cut her down! My daughter died a virgin. Take her to another room and dress her as though she were a virgin. No one will say anything about this! She died a virgin. Tell them, so that at dawn, the bells will ring twice.

MARTIRIO: A thousand times happy she, who had him.

BERNARDA: And I want no weeping. Death must be looked at face to face. Silence!

(*To one daughter.*)

Be still, I said!

(*To another daughter.*)

Tears when you're alone! We'll drown ourselves in a sea of mourning. She, the youngest daughter of Bernarda Alba, died a virgin. Did you hear me? Silence, silence, I said. Silence!

COMMENTARY

John Gilmour (*b. 1939*)

RELIGION IN *THE HOUSE OF BERNARDA ALBA*   1992

In this commentary Gilmour examines the function of Christian faith in the play. He contrasts Christian charity with the repressive and ritualistic Christian regime that Bernarda imposes on her daughters. Gilmour also sees that the hypocrisy portrayed in the play is connected to Spain's intolerant social conditions at the time of Lorca's writing.

Bernarda may be very scrupulous about the way in which her family should show respect for the dead, and very familiar with Catholic ritual, but that is as far as her Christianity extends. Religion for her seems to mean blind, unquestioning adherence to an established set of rules which are there to be observed solely for the purpose of keeping up appearances. Her daughter Magdalena's sad comment, "nos pudrimos por el qué dirán" [we rot inside because of what people might say], is an indication of the destructive effect which this code of behavior has on her family's well-being. Nowhere is there room in this scheme of things for the more positive and fundamental aspects of the Christian faith, notably love and charity towards others. Ronaldo Cueto, in a recent article in which he investigates the religious significance of the character Bernarda Alba, makes the interesting point that Bernarda is the name commonly given in Spain to nuns of the Cistercian order whose main tenet of faith is "God is love." Yet it is surely hard to find a character as far removed from the true Bernardine spirit of love as Lorca's protagonist. A life of rigid conformity has corrupted her entire being, destroyed her soul and poisoned her home and social environment. Angustias describes the atmosphere inside their home as "un infierno" [a hell] — a damning indictment indeed of Bernarda's supposedly Christian regime. Bernarda shows no sign of being a loving mother. She is not prepared to trust her daughters with any kind of freedom (La Poncia tells her, "Tú no has dejado a tus hijas libres" [you never gave your daughters any freedom]). She keeps them prisoner in their own house (Magdelena complains of being "sentada días y días dentro de esta sala oscura" [sitting day after day in this dark room]). Like Yerma's sisters-in-law, she considers it her duty to stand guard over the family's honour; she blindly assures La Poncia, "Mi vigilancia lo puede todo . . . aquí no pasa nada" [My eyes kept constant watch . . . nothing gets by me]. She happily ruins the few chances which her daughters have to fall in love, either through snobbery ("Su padre fue gañán" [His father was a shepherd] is her explanation of why Martirio could not marry Enrique Humanas) or through social convention (Angustias's rich inheritance puts paid to Adela's relationship with Pepe el Romano). She thinks nothing of resorting to physical violence against her children. Angustias and Martirio are beaten to the ground amid a barrage of expletives which show the intensity of her fury. Not even the loss of Adela can release any emotion from her. Her "no quiero llantos" (I want no weeping) is the cold reaction of a mother whose only care appears to be that her daughter must be laid out "como una doncella" (like a virgin). Her stoicism in the face of tragedy is so remarkable as to be unnatural.

. . .

In their painful search for individual fulfillment, Lorca's tragic heroines in the rural plays reflect this bitter struggle to throw off the shackles of an ideologically dominant social institution which, in the eyes of the reformist Republicans of the 1930s, had for so long been synonymous with intolerance, immobilism, obscurantism and repression. Lorca may not have claimed allegiance to any particular left-wing political movement or party, but his depiction of a rural society, pious and ritualistic yet lacking the most basic Christian virtues, casts him as an outspoken opponent of conservative, bourgeois values. In short it is possibly his social conscience that makes him present religion in this negative manner.

Eugene O'Neill

Eugene O'Neill (1888–1953) is a major figure in American drama. His enormous output is in the tradition of realism established by Strindberg and Ibsen, and his early plays, such as *Anna Christie* (1921), introduced Americans to the techniques of the great European realists. Realism for Americans was a move away from the sentimental comedies, the pathetic dramas, and the melodrama that dominated the American stage from before the Civil War to World War I. Some of O'Neill's plays, such as *Strange Interlude* (1928) and *Dynamo* (1929), were expressionist in style, demonstrating a considerable range. O'Neill rejected the kind of theater in which his father had thrived. James O'Neill had long been a stage star, traveling across the country in his production of *The Count of Monte Cristo*, which had made him rich but had also made him a prisoner of a single role.

Eugene O'Neill won the Pulitzer Prize for drama three times in the 1920s and the Nobel Prize for literature in 1936. Although not popular successes in his own day, his plays — including those published posthumously — are now mainstays of the American theater. Some of America's finest actors have taken a strong interest in his work, both producing his plays and acting in them on the stage and on television. From the 1950s to the 1990s, the late Colleen Dewhurst and Jason Robards, Jr., in particular, gave some magnificent performances and interpretations of O'Neill's work.

The young O'Neill was a romantic in the popular sense of the word. After a year at Princeton University, he began to travel on the sea. His jaunts took him to South America, and he once wound up virtually broke and without resources in Buenos Aires. When he returned to America, he studied for a year with George Pierce Baker, the most famous drama teacher of his day. Eventually, he took up residence in Provincetown, Massachusetts, where a group of people dedicated to theater — including the playwright Susan Glaspell — began to put on plays in their living rooms. When their audiences spilled over, the group created the Provincetown Playhouse, the theater in which many of O'Neill's earliest pieces were first performed.

The subjects of many of O'Neill's plays were not especially appealing to general theater audiences. Those who hoped for light comedy and a good laugh or light melodrama and a good cry found the intensity of his dark vision of the world to be overwhelming. They came for mere entertainment, and he was providing them with frightening visions of the soul's interior. The glum and painful surroundings of *Anna Christie* (1921) and the brutality of the lower-class coal stoker in *The Hairy Ape* (1922) were foreign to the comfortable middle-class audiences who supported commercial theater in America. They found O'Neill's characters to be haunted by family agonies, affections never given, ambitions never realized, pains never assuaged. Despite his remarkable abilities and the power of his drama, audiences often did not know what to make of him. To a large extent, his acceptance came on waves of shock, as had the acceptance of the Scandinavian realists.

O'Neill's early work is marked by a variety of experiments with theatrical effects and moods. He tried to use the primary influences of Greek drama in such plays as *Desire under the Elms* (1924), which has been described by critics as Greek tragedy, and *Mourning Becomes Electra* (1931), based on the *Oresteia,* which took three days to perform. But many of his early plays now seem dated and strange. His most impressive plays are his later work, such as *Ah, Wilderness!* (1933), *The Iceman Cometh* (1939), *Long Day's Journey into Night* (1939–1941), *A Moon for the Misbegotten* (1943), and *A Touch of the Poet* (1935–1942), which was performed posthumously in 1957.

DESIRE UNDER THE ELMS

Desire under the Elms (1924) is Eugene O'Neill's first effort at writing in the style of Greek tragedy. He did not follow the Greek tradition and choose a great figure of noble birth about whom the fates would unravel their mystery. Rather, he was deliberately democratic, choosing a New England farmer and his family as the protagonists of his drama. Just as fate animates a Greek tragedy, the emotional forces of jealousy, resentment, lust, and incestuous love animate *Desire under the Elms*.

O'Neill set his play on a typically rocky New England soil, which in many ways bears a striking resemblance to the rocky soil of Athens and the Greek coastline. The unyielding toughness of life on that land contrasts with the easy life to be made from gold mining in California. Ephraim Cabot, the seventy-five-year-old father, has been made hard and physically powerful by his work. He has just taken a third wife, the young and scheming Abbie. His youngest son, Eben, has decided to stay on the farm while his two other sons plan to go to California and put New England behind them.

The sense of having been dispossessed of his farm by his new stepmother drives Eben to hate Abbie, who has married the elder Cabot merely to inherit his farm. At first the sparring between Abbie and Eben is based on calculating self-interest, but eventually their feelings overpower them. Lust turns to love, and the son they produce is passed off as old Cabot's, although the townspeople have no illusion about whose child it is.

The farm itself is a powerful presence in the play. Whenever old Cabot thinks he should give up and follow the promise of easy money in California, he feels God's presence urging him to stay. God operates for Ephraim as the oracle in *Oedipus Rex* does, giving him a message that is painful but must be obeyed. The rocks on the farm are unforgiving, and so is the fate that Abbie and Eben face. Theirs is an impossible love; everything they do to prove their love condemns them even more. The forces of fate center on the farm. When the play opens, Eben says of it, "God! Purty!" When the play ends, the sheriff praises the farm and says he surely would like to own it, striking a clear note of irony: the agony of the play is rooted in lust — lust for the farm that parallels the lust between Abbie and Eben.

The play is haunted by the ghost of Eben's mother, whom Ephraim married primarily for her farm. Her ghost is exorcised only after the cycle of retribution has begun. Old Cabot has committed a crime against her, and now he must become the victim.

The language of the dialogue is that of New England in the mid-nineteenth century. Living in New England, O'Neill understood the ways and the language of its people. He seems to have imagined the "down-east" flavor of Maine in the language, and he has been careful to build the proper pronunciation into the dialogue. This folksy way of speaking helps emphasize the peasantlike qualities in these New England farmers. O'Neill's careful use of language is reminiscent of Synge's masterful representation of the Irish-English speech in *Playboy of the Western World*.

The language of O'Neill's characters has a rocky toughness at times. Characters are laconic — they often answer in a single word: "Ay-eh." Faithful to his vision of the simple speech of country folk, O'Neill avoids giving them elaborate poetic soliloquies. Instead, he shows how, despite their limited language, rural people feel profound emotions and act on them.

O'Neill carefully links Abbie with Queen Phaedra, who in Euripides' play *Hippolytus* and in Racine's seventeenth-century play *Phaedra* finds herself uncontrollably desiring her husband's son as a lover. Racine and Racine's audience could easily imagine such intense emotions overwhelming a noblewoman because they thought that nobility felt more intensely and lived more intensely than ordinary people. But O'Neill is trying to make his audience see that even unlettered farm people can feel as deeply as tragic heroes of any age do. The Cabots are victims of passion. They share their fate with the great families of the Greek tragedies.

Desire under the Elms in Performance

Desire under the Elms was first performed in Greenwich Village in 1924 under the auspices of the Provincetown Players. A year later it appeared on Broadway for thirty-six weeks, a long run for a tragedy. Its first reviewers were courteous but puzzled. They compared the play with earlier O'Neill works, remarking on its "tragic gloom and irony" and praising its language. At the Los Angeles production in 1926, the cast was arrested for "giving an obscene play." The sexual themes offended theatergoers in California, and even those who defended the play admitted that the text would be offensive to some members of the audience.

Because the English censor banned the play until 1938, its first European production was in Prague's National Theatre in 1925. Its Czech title translated as "The Farm under the Elms." The director used a highly stylized set influenced by the Moscow Art Theatre and later described as "a sort of two-storied wooded edifice . . . rather like a log cabin multiplied by four."

Other earlier European productions followed in Moscow in 1932, in Stockholm in 1933, and finally in London in 1940. The 1952 New York revival was not successful. The 1963 revival at the Circle in the Square in New York starred George C. Scott and his wife, Colleen Dewhurst. Jose Quintero, a notable interpreter of O'Neill, directed. Critics complained about "awkward" echoes of Greek tragedy while admitting that the play had an uncanny power despite its flaws. It ran for 380 performances.

The play has often been revived: in Boston in 1967; at the Berkshire Theater Festival in 1974; at the Roundabout Theater in New York, directed by Terry Schrieber, in 1984; and by numerous local theater groups. In 1978 Edward Thomas staged it at Connecticut College in New London as an opera. A creditable production, it emphasized the play's American folk qualities.

Eugene O'Neill (1888–1953)

DESIRE UNDER THE ELMS

Characters

EPHRAIM CABOT
SIMEON
PETER } *his sons*
EBEN
ABBIE PUTNAM
YOUNG GIRL, TWO FARMERS, *the* FIDDLER, *a* SHERIFF, *and other folk from the neighboring farms.*

(Scene: *The action of the entire play takes place in, and immediately outside of, the Cabot farmhouse in New England, in the year 1850. The south end of the house faces front to a stone wall with a wooden gate at center opening on a country road. The house is in good condition but in need of paint. Its walls are a sickly grayish, the green of the shutters faded. Two enormous elms are on each side of the house. They bend their trailing branches down over the roof. They appear to protect and at the same time subdue. There is a sinister maternity in their aspect, a crushing, jealous absorption. They have developed from their intimate contact with the life of man in the house an appalling humaneness. They brood oppressively over the house. They are like exhausted women resting their sagging breasts and hands and hair on its roof, and when it rains their tears trickle down monotonously and rot on the shingles.*

There is a path running from the gate around the right corner of the house to the front door. A narrow porch is on this side. The end wall facing us has two windows in its upper story, two larger ones on the floor below. The two upper are those of the father's bedroom and that of the brothers. On the left, ground floor, is the kitchen — on the right, the parlor, the shades of which are always drawn down.)

PART I • Scene I

(*Exterior of the farmhouse. It is sunset of a day at the beginning of summer in the year 1850. There is no wind and everything is still. The sky above the roof is suffused with deep colors, the green of the elms glows, but the house is in shadow, seeming pale and washed out by contrast.*)

(*A door opens and Eben Cabot comes to the end of the porch and stands looking down the road to the right. He has a large bell in his hand and this he swings mechanically, awakening a deafening clangor. Then he puts his hands on his hips and stares up at the sky. He sighs with a puzzled awe and blurts out with halting appreciation.*)

EBEN: God! Purty! (*His eyes fall and he stares about him frowningly. He is twenty-five, tall and sinewy. His face is well formed, good-looking, but its expression is resentful and defensive. His defiant, dark eyes remind one of a wild animal's in captivity. Each day is a cage in which he finds himself trapped but inwardly unsubdued. There is a fierce repressed vitality about him. He has black hair, mustache, a thin curly trace of beard. He is dressed in rough farm clothes.*)

(*He spits on the ground with intense disgust, turns, and goes back into the house.*)

(*Simeon and Peter come in from their work in the fields. They are tall men, much older than their half-brother [Simeon is thirty-nine and Peter thirty-seven], built on a squarer, simpler model, fleshier in body, more bovine and homelier in face, shrewder and more practical. Their shoulders stoop a bit from years of farm work. They clump heavily along in their clumsy thick-soled boots caked with earth. Their clothes, their faces, hands, bare arms, and throats are earth-stained. They smell of earth. They stand together for a moment in front of the house and, as if with the one impulse, stare dumbly up at the sky, leaning on their hoes. Their faces have a compressed, unresigned expression. As they look upward, this softens.*)

SIMEON (*grudgingly*): Purty.
PETER: Ay-eh.
SIMEON (*suddenly*): Eighteen year ago.
PETER: What?
SIMEON: Jenn. My woman. She died.
PETER: I'd fergot.
SIMEON: I rec'lect — now an' agin. Makes it lonesome. She'd hair long's a hoss' tail — an' yeller like gold!
PETER: Waal — she's gone. (*This with indifferent finality — then after a pause.*) They's gold in the West, Sim.
SIMEON (*still under the influence of sunset — vaguely*): In the sky?
PETER: Waal — in a manner o' speakin' — that's the promise. (*Growing excited.*) Gold in the sky — in the West — Golden Gate — Californi-a! — Goldest West! — fields o' gold!
SIMEON (*excited in his turn*): Fortunes layin' just atop o' the ground waitin' t' be picked! Solomon's mines, they says! (*For a moment they continue looking up at the sky — then their eyes drop.*)
PETER (*with sardonic bitterness*): Here — it's stones atop o' the ground — stones atop o' stones — makin' stone walls — year atop o' year — him 'n' yew 'n' me 'n' then Eben — makin' stone walls fur him to fence us in!

SIMEON: We've wuked. Give our strength. Give our years. Plowed 'em under in the ground — (*He stamps rebelliously.*) — rottin' — makin' soil for his crops! (*A pause.*) Waal — the farm pays good for hereabouts.

PETER: If we plowed in Californi-a, they'd be lumps o' gold in the furrow!

SIMEON: Californi-a's t'other side o' earth, a'most. We got t' calc'late —

PETER (*after a pause*): 'Twould be hard fur me, too, to give up what we've 'arned here by our sweat. (*A pause. Eben sticks his head out of the dining room window, listening.*)

SIMEON: Ay-eh. (*A pause.*) Mebbe — he'll die soon.

PETER (*doubtfully*): Mebbe.

SIMEON: Mebbe — fur all we knows — he's dead now.

PETER: Ye'd need proof.

SIMEON: He's been gone two months — with no word.

PETER: Left us in the fields an evenin' like this. Hitched up an' druv off into the West. That's plum onnateral. He hadn't never been off this farm 'ceptin' t' the village in thirty year or more, not since he married Eben's maw. (*A pause. Shrewdly.*) I calc'late we might git him declared crazy by the court.

SIMEON: He skinned 'em too slick. He got the best o' all on 'em. They'd never b'lieve him crazy. (*A pause.*) We got t' wait — till he's underground.

EBEN (*with a sardonic chuckle*): Honor thy father! (*They turn startled, and stare at him. He grins, then scowls.*) I pray he's died. (*They stare at him. He continues matter-of-factly.*) Supper's ready.

SIMEON AND PETER (*together*): Ay-eh.

EBEN (*gazing up at the sky*): Sun's downin' purty.

SIMEON AND PETER (*together*): Ay-eh. They's gold in the West.

EBEN: Ay-eh. (*Pointing.*) Yonder atop o' the hill pasture, ye mean?

SIMEON AND PETER (*together*): In Californi-a!

EBEN: Hunh? (*Stares at them indifferently for a second, then drawls.*) Waal — supper's gittin' cold. (*He turns back into kitchen.*)

SIMEON (*startled — smacks his lips*): I air hungry!

PETER (*sniffing*): I smells bacon!

SIMEON (*with hungry appreciation*): Bacon's good!

PETER (*in same tone*): Bacon's bacon! (*They turn, shouldering each other, their bodies bumping and rubbing together as they hurry clumsily to their food, like two friendly oxen toward their evening meal. They disappear around the right corner of house and can be heard entering the door.*)

Scene II

(*The color fades from the sky. Twilight begins. The interior of the kitchen is now visible. A pine table is at center, a cook-stove in the right rear corner, four rough wooden chairs, a tallow candle on the table. In the middle of the rear wall is fastened a big advertising poster with a ship in full sail and the word "California"* in big letters. Kitchen utensils hang from nails. Everything is neat and in order but the atmosphere is of a men's camp kitchen rather than that of a home.)

(*Places for three are laid. Eben takes boiled potatoes and bacon from the stove and puts them on the table, also a loaf of bread and a crock of water. Simeon and Peter shoulder in, slump down in their chairs without a word. Eben joins them. The three eat in silence for a moment, the two elder as naturally unrestrained as beasts of the field, Eben picking at his food without appetite, glancing at them with a tolerant dislike.*)

SIMEON (*suddenly turns to Eben*): Looky here! Ye'd oughtn't t' said that, Eben.

PETER: 'Twa'n't righteous.

EBEN: What?

SIMEON: Ye prayed he'd died.

EBEN: Waal — don't yew pray it? (*A pause.*)

PETER: He's our Paw.

EBEN (*violently*): Not mine!

SIMEON (*dryly*): Ye'd not let no one else say that about yer Maw! Ha! (*He gives one abrupt sardonic guffaw. Peter grins.*)

EBEN (*very pale*): I meant — I hain't his'n — I hain't like him — he hain't me!

PETER (*dryly*): Wait till ye've growed his age!

EBEN (*intensely*): I'm Maw — every drop o' blood! (*A pause. They stare at him with indifferent curiosity.*)

PETER (*reminiscently*): She was good t' Sim 'n' me. A good Stepmaw's scurse.

SIMEON: She was good t' everyone.

EBEN (*greatly moved, gets to his feet and makes an awkward bow to each of them — stammering*): I be thankful t' ye. I'm her — her heir. (*He sits down in confusion.*)

PETER (*after a pause — judicially*): She was good even t' him.

EBEN (*fiercely*): An' fur thanks he killed her!

SIMEON (*after a pause*): No one never kills nobody. It's allus somethin'. That's the murderer.

EBEN: Didn't he slave Maw t' death?

PETER: He's slaved himself t' death. He's slaved Sim 'n' me 'n' yew t' death — on'y none o' us hain't died — yit.

SIMEON: It's somethin' — drivin' him — t' drive us!

EBEN (*vengefully*): Waal — I hold him t' jedgment! (*Then scornfully.*) Somethin'! What's somethin'?

SIMEON: Dunno.

EBEN (*sardonically*): What's drivin' yew to Californi-a, mebbe? (*They look at him in surprise.*) Oh, I've heerd ye! (*Then, after a pause.*) But ye'll never go t' the gold fields!

PETER (*assertively*): Mebbe!

EBEN: Whar'll ye git the money?

PETER: We kin walk. It's an a'mighty ways — Californi-a — but if yew was t' put all the steps we've walked on this farm end t' end we'd be in the moon!

EBEN: The Injuns'll skulp ye on the plains.

SIMEON (*with grim humor*): We'll mebbe make 'em pay a hair fur a hair!

EBEN (*decisively*): But t'aint that. Ye won't never go because ye'll wait here fur yer share o' the farm, thinkin' allus he'll die soon.

SIMEON (*after a pause*): We've a right.

PETER: Two-thirds belongs t'us.

EBEN (*jumping to his feet*): Ye've no right! She wa'n't yewr Maw! It was her farm! Didn't he steal it from her? She's dead. It's my farm.

SIMEON (*sardonically*): Tell that t' Paw — when he comes! I'll bet ye a dollar he'll laugh — fur once in his life. Ha! (*He laughs himself in one single mirthless bark.*)

PETER (*amused in turn, echoes his brother*): Ha!

SIMEON (*after a pause*): What've ye got held agin us, Eben? Year arter year it's skulked in yer eye — somethin'.

PETER: Ay-eh.

EBEN: Ay-eh. They's somethin'. (*Suddenly exploding.*) Why didn't ye never stand between him 'n' my Maw when he was slavin' her to her grave — t' pay her back fur the kindness she done t' yew? (*There is a long pause. They stare at him in surprise.*)

SIMEON: Waal — the stock'd got t' be watered.

PETER: 'R they was woodin' t' do.

SIMEON: 'R plowin'.

PETER: 'R hayin'.

SIMEON: 'R spreadin' manure.

PETER: 'R weedin'.

SIMEON: 'R prunin'.

PETER: 'R milkin'.

EBEN (*breaking in harshly*): An' makin' walls — stone atop o' stone — makin' walls till yer heart's a stone ye heft up out o' the way o' growth onto a stone wall t' wall in yer heart!

SIMEON (*matter-of-factly*): We never had no time t' meddle.

PETER (*to Eben*): Yew was fifteen afore yer Maw died — an' big fur yer age. Why didn't ye never do nothin'?

EBEN (*harshly*): They was chores t' do, wasn't they? (*A pause — then slowly.*) It was on'y arter she died I come to think o' it. Me cookin' — doin' her work — that made me know her, suffer her sufferin' — she'd come back t' help — come back t' bile potatoes — come back t' fry bacon — come back t' bake biscuits — come back all cramped up t' shake the fire, an' carry ashes, her eyes weepin' an' bloody with smoke an' cinders same's they used t' be. She still comes back — stands by the stove thar in the evenin' — she can't find it nateral sleepin' an' restin' in peace. She can't git used t' bein' free — even in her grave.

SIMEON: She never complained none.

EBEN: She'd got too tired. She'd got too used t' bein' too tired. That was what he done. (*With vengeful passion.*) An' sooner'r later, I'll meddle. I'll say the thin's I didn't say then t' him! I'll yell 'em at the top o' my lungs. I'll see t' it my Maw gits some rest an' sleep in her grave! (*He sits down again, relapsing into a brooding silence. They look at him with a queer indifferent curiosity.*)

PETER (*after a pause*): Whar in tarnation d'ye s'pose he went, Sim?

SIMEON: Dunno. He druv off in the buggy, all spick an' span, with the mare all breshed an' shiny, druv off clackin' his tongue an' wavin' his whip. I remember it right well. I was finishin' plowin', it was spring an' May an' sunset, an' gold in the West, an' he druv off into it. I yells "Whar ye goin', Paw?" an' he hauls up by the stone wall a jiffy. His old snake's eyes was glitterin' in the sun like he'd been drinkin' a jugful an' he says with a mule's grin: "Don't ye run away till I come back!"

PETER: Wonder if he knowed we was wantin' fur Californi-a?

SIMEON: Mebbe. I didn't say nothin' and he says, lookin' kinder queer an' sick: "I been hearin' the hens cluckin' an' the roosters crowin' all the durn day. I been listenin't the cows lowin' an' everythin' else kickin' up till I can't stand it no more. It's spring an' I'm feelin' damned," he says. "Damned like an old bare hickory tree fit on'y fur burnin'," he says. An' then I calc'late I must've looked a mite hopeful, fur he adds real spry and vicious: "But don't git no fool idee I'm dead. I've sworn t' live a hundred an' I'll do it, if on'y t' spite yer sinful greed! An' now I'm ridin' out t' learn God's message t' me in the spring, like the prophets done. An' yew git back t' yer plowin'," he says. An' he druv off singin' a hymn. I thought he was drunk — 'r I'd stopped him goin'.

EBEN (*scornfully*): No, ye wouldn't! Ye're scared o' him. He's stronger — inside — than both o' ye put together!

PETER (*sardonically*): An' yew — be yew Samson?°

EBEN: I'm gittin' stronger. I kin feel it growin' in me — growin' an' growin' — till it'll bust out — ! (*He gets up and puts on his coat and a hat. They watch him, gradually breaking into grins. Eben avoids their eyes sheepishly.*) I'm goin' out fur a spell — up the road.

PETER: T' the village.

SIMEON: T' see Minnie?

EBEN (*defiantly*): Ay-eh!

PETER (*jeeringly*): The Scarlet Woman!

SIMEON: Lust — that's what's growin' in ye!

EBEN: Waal — she's purty!

PETER: She's been purty fur twenty year.

SIMEON: A new coat o' paint'll make a heifer out of forty.

EBEN: She hain't forty!

PETER: If she hain't, she's teeterin' on the edge.

EBEN (*desperately*): What d'yew know —

PETER: All they is . . . Sim knew her — an' then me arter —

SIMEON: An' Paw kin tell yew somethin' too! He was fust!

EBEN: D'ye mean t' say he . . . ?

SIMEON (*with a grin*): Ay-eh! We air his heirs in everythin'!

Samson: A biblical hero known for his great physical strength.

EBEN (*intensely*): That's more to it! That grows on it! It'll bust soon! (*Then violently.*) I'll go smash my fist in her face! (*He pulls open the door in rear violently.*)

SIMEON (*with a wink at Peter — drawlingly*): Mebbe — but the night's wa'm — purty — by the time ye git thar mebbe ye'll kiss her instead!

PETER: Sart'n he will! (*They both roar with coarse laughter. Eben rushes out and slams the door — then the outside front door — comes around the corner of the house and stands still by the gate, staring up at the sky.*)

SIMEON (*looking after him*): Like his Paw.

PETER: Dead spit an' image!

SIMEON: Dog'll eat dog!

PETER: Ay-eh. (*Pause. With yearning.*) Mebbe a year from now we'll be in Californi-a.

SIMEON: Ay-eh. (*A pause. Both yawn.*) Let's git t'bed. (*He blows out the candle. They go out door in rear. Eben stretches his arms up to the sky — rebelliously.*)

EBEN: Waal — thar's a star, an' somewhar's they's him, an' here's me, an' thar's Min up the road — in the same night. What if I does kiss her? She's like t'night, she's soft 'n' wa'm, her eyes kin wink like a star, her mouth's wa'm, her arms're wa'm, she smells like a wa'm plowed field, she's purty . . . Ay-eh! By God A'mighty she's purty, an' I don't give a damn how many sins she's sinned afore mine or who she's sinned 'em with, my sin's as purty as any one on 'em! (*He strides off down the road to the left.*)

Scene III

(*It is the pitch darkness just before dawn. Eben comes in from the left and goes around to the porch, feeling his way, chuckling bitterly and cursing half-aloud to himself.*)

EBEN: The cussed old miser! (*He can be heard going in the front door. There is a pause as he goes upstairs, then a loud knock on the bedroom door of the brothers.*) Wake up!

SIMEON (*startledly*): Who's thar?

EBEN (*Pushing open the door and coming in, a lighted candle in his hand. The bedroom of the brothers is revealed. Its ceiling is the sloping roof. They can stand upright only close to the center dividing wall of the upstairs. Simeon and Peter are in a double bed, front. Eben's cot is to the rear. Eben has a mixture of silly grin and vicious scowl on his face.*): I be!

PETER (*angrily*): What in hell's-fire. . . ?

EBEN: I got news fur ye! Ha! (*He gives one abrupt sardonic guffaw.*)

SIMEON (*angrily*): Couldn't ye hold it 'til we'd got our sleep?

EBEN: It's nigh sunup. (*Then explosively.*) He's gone an' married agen!

SIMEON AND PETER (*explosively*): Paw?

EBEN: Got himself hitched to a female 'bout thirty-five — an' purty, they says . . .

SIMEON (*aghast*): It's a durn lie!

PETER: Who says?

SIMEON: They been stringin' ye!

EBEN: Think I'm a dunce, do ye? The hull village says. The preacher from New Dover, he brung the news — told it t'our preacher — New Dover, that's whar the old loon got himself hitched — that's whar the woman lived —

PETER (*no longer doubting — stunned*): Waal . . . !

SIMEON (*the same*): Waal . . . !

EBEN (*sitting down on a bed — with vicious hatred*): Ain't he a devil out o' hell? It's jest t' spite us — the damned old mule!

PETER (*after a pause*): Everythin'll go t'her now.

SIMEON: Ay-eh. (*A pause — dully.*) Waal — if it's done —

PETER: It's done us. (*Pause — then persuasively.*) They's gold in the fields o' Californi-a, Sim. No good a-stayin' here now.

SIMEON: Jest what I was a-thinkin'. (*Then with decision.*) S'well fust's last! Let's light out and git this mornin'.

PETER: Suits me.

EBEN: Ye must like walkin'.

SIMEON (*sardonically*): If ye'd grow wings on us we'd fly thar!

EBEN: Ye'd like ridin' better — on a boat, wouldn't ye? (*Fumbles in his pocket and takes out a crumpled sheet of foolscap.*) Waal, if ye sign this ye kin ride on a boat. I've had it writ out an' ready in case ye'd ever go. It says fur three hundred dollars t' each ye agree yewr shares o' the farm is sold t' me. (*They look suspiciously at the paper. A pause.*)

SIMEON (*wonderingly*): But if he's hitched agen —

PETER: An' whar'd yew git that sum o' money, anyways?

EBEN (*cunningly*): I know whar it's hid. I been waitin' — Maw told me. She knew whar it lay fur years, but she was waitin' . . . It's her'n — the money he hoarded from her farm an' hid from Maw. It's my money by rights now.

PETER: Whar's it hid?

EBEN (*cunningly*): Whar yew won't never find it without me. Maw spied on him —'r she'd never knowed. (*A pause. They look at him suspiciously, and he at them.*) Waal, is it fa'r trade?

SIMEON: Dunno.

PETER: Dunno.

SIMEON (*looking at window*): Sky's grayin'.

PETER: Ye better start the fire, Eben.

SIMEON: An' fix some vittles.

EBEN: Ay-eh. (*Then with a forced jocular heartiness.*) I'll git ye a good one. If ye're startin' t' hoof it t' Californi-a ye'll need somethin' that'll stick t' yer ribs. (*He turns to the door, adding meaningly.*) But ye kin ride on a boat if ye'll swap. (*He stops at the door and pauses. They stare at him.*)

SIMEON (*suspiciously*): Whar was ye all night?

EBEN (*defiantly*): Up t' Min's. (*Then slowly.*) Walkin' thar, fust I felt 's if I'd kiss her; then I got a-thinkin' o' what ye'd said o' him an' her an' I says, I'll bust her nose fur that! Then I got t' the village an' heerd the news an' I got madder'n hell an' run all the way t' Min's not knowin' what I'd do — (*He pauses — then sheepishly but more defiantly.*) Waal — when I seen her, I didn't hit her — nor I didn't kiss her nuther — I begun t' beller like a calf an' cuss at the same time, I was so durn mad — an' she got scared — an' I jest grabbed holt an' tuk her! (*Proudly.*) Yes, sirree! I tuk her. She may've been his'n — an' your'n, too — but she's mine now!

SIMEON (*dryly*): In love, air yew?

EBEN (*with lofty scorn*): Love! I don't take no stock in sech slop!

PETER (*winking at Simeon*): Mebbe Eben's aimin' t' marry, too.

SIMEON: Min'd make a true faithful he'pmeet! (*They snicker.*)

EBEN: What do I care fur her —'ceptin' she's round an' wa'm? The p'int is she was his'n — an' now she b'longs t' me! (*He goes to the door — then turns — rebelliously.*) An' Min hain't sech a bad un. They's worse'n Min in the world, I'll bet ye! Wait'll we see this cow the Old Man's hitched t'! She'll beat Min, I got a notion! (*He starts to go out.*)

SIMEON (*suddenly*): Mebbe ye'll try t' make her your'n, too?

PETER: Ha! (*He gives a sardonic laugh of relish at this idea.*)

EBEN (*spitting with disgust*): Her — here — sleepin' with him — stealin' my Maw's farm! I'd as soon pet a skunk 'r kiss a snake! (*He goes out. The two stare after him suspiciously. A pause. They listen to his steps receding.*)

PETER: He's startin' the fire.

SIMEON: I'd like t' ride t' Californi-a — but —

PETER: Min might o' put some scheme in his head.

SIMEON: Mebbe it's all a lie 'bout Paw marryin'. We'd best wait an' see the bride.

PETER: An' don't sign nothin' till we does!

SIMEON: Nor till we've tested it's good money! (*Then with a grin.*) But if Paw's hitched we'd be sellin' Eben somethin' we'd never git nohow!

PETER: We'll wait an' see. (*Then with sudden vindictive anger.*) An' till he comes, let's yew 'n' me not wuk a lick, let Eben tend to thin's if he's a mind t', let's us jest sleep an' eat an' drink likker, an' let the hull damned farm go t' blazes!

SIMEON (*excitedly*): By God, we've 'arned a rest! We'll play rich fur a change. I hain't a-going to stir outa bed till breakfast's ready.

PETER: An' on the table!

SIMEON (*after a pause — thoughtfully*): What d'ye cal-c'late she'll be like — our new Maw? Like Eben thinks?

PETER: More'n' likely.

SIMEON (*vindictively*): Waal — I hope she's a she-devil that'll make him wish he was dead an' livin' in the pit o' hell fur comfort!

PETER (*fervently*): Amen!

SIMEON (*imitating his father's voice*): "I'm ridin' out t' learn God's message t' me in the spring like the prophets done," he says. I'll bet right then an' thar he knew plumb well he was goin' whorin', the stinkin' old hypocrite!

Scene IV

(*Same as scene II — shows the interior of the kitchen with a lighted candle on table. It is gray dawn outside. Simeon and Peter are just finishing their breakfast. Eben sits before his plate of untouched food, brooding frown-ingly.*)

PETER (*glancing at him rather irritably*): Lookin' glum don't help none.

SIMEON (*sarcastically*): Sorrowin' over his lust o' the flesh!

PETER (*with a grin*): Was she yer fust?

EBEN (*angrily*): None o'yer business. (*A pause.*) I was thinkin' o' him. I got a notion he's gittin' near — I kin feel him comin' on like yew kin feel malaria chill afore it takes ye.

PETER: It's too early yet.

SIMEON: Dunno. He'd like t' catch us nappin' — jest t' have somethin' t' hoss us 'round over.

PETER (*Mechanically gets to his feet. Simeon does the same.*): Waal — let's git t'wuk. (*They both plod me-chanically toward the door before they realize. Then they stop short.*)

SIMEON (*grinning*): Ye're a cussed fool, Pete — and I be wuss! Let him see we hain't wukin'! We don't give a durn!

PETER (*as they go back to the table*): Not a damned durn! It'll serve t' show him we're done with him. (*They sit down again. Eben stares from one to the other with surprise.*)

SIMEON (*grins at him*): We're aimin' t' start bein' lilies o' the field.

PETER: Nary a toil 'r spin 'r lick o' wuk do we put in!

SIMEON: Ye're sole owner — till he comes — that's what ye wanted. Waal, ye got t' be sole hand, too.

PETER: The cows air bellerin'. Ye better hustle at the milkin'.

EBEN (*with excited joy*): Ye mean ye'll sign the paper?

SIMEON (*dryly*): Mebbe.

PETER: Mebbe.

SIMEON: We're considerin'. (*Peremptorily.*) Ye better git t' wuk.

EBEN (*with queer excitement*): It's Maw's farm agen! It's my farm! Them's my cows! I'll milk my durn fingers off fur cows o' mine! (*He goes out door in rear, they stare after him indifferently.*)

SIMEON: Like his Paw.

PETER: Dead spit 'n' image!

SIMEON: Waal — let dog eat dog! (*Eben comes out of front door and around the corner of the house. The sky is beginning to grow flushed with sunrise. Eben stops by the gate and stares around him with glowing, possessive eyes. He takes in the whole farm with his embracing glance of desire.*)

EBEN: It's purty! It's damned purty! It's mine! (*He suddenly throws his head back boldly and glares with hard, defiant eyes at the sky.*) Mine, d'ye hear? Mine! (*He turns and walks quickly off left, rear, toward the barn. The two brothers light their pipes.*)

SIMEON (*putting his muddy boots up on the table, tilting back his chair, and puffing defiantly*): Waal — this air solid comfort — fur once.

PETER: Ay-eh. (*He follows suit. A pause. Unconsciously they both sigh.*)

SIMEON (*suddenly*): He never was much o' a hand at milkin', Eben wa'n't.

PETER (*with a snort*): His hands air like hoofs! (*A pause.*)

SIMEON: Reach down the jug thar! Let's take a swaller. I'm feelin' kind o' low.

PETER: Good idee! (*He does so — gets two glasses — they pour out drinks of whisky.*) Here's t' the gold in Californi-a!

SIMEON: An' luck t' find it! (*They drink — puff resolutely — sigh — take their feet down from the table.*)

PETER: Likker don't pear t' sot right.

SIMEON: We hain't used t' it this early. (*A pause. They become very restless.*)

PETER: Gittin' close in this kitchen.

SIMEON (*with immense relief*): Let's git a breath o' air. (*They arise briskly and go out rear — appear around house and stop by the gate. They stare up at the sky with a numbed appreciation.*)

PETER: Purty!

SIMEON: Ay-eh. Gold's t' the East now.

PETER: Sun's startin' with us fur the Golden West.

SIMEON (*staring around the farm, his compressed face tightened, unable to conceal his emotion*): Waal — it's our last mornin' — mebbe.

PETER (*the same*): Ay-eh.

SIMEON (*stamps his foot on the earth and addresses it desperately*): Waal — ye've thirty year o' me buried in ye — spread out over ye — blood an' bone an' sweat — rotted away — fertilizin' ye — richin' yer soul — prime manure, by God, that's what I been t' ye!

PETER: Ay-eh! An' me.

SIMEON: An' yew, Peter. (*He sighs — then spits.*) Waal — no use'n cryin' over spilt milk.

PETER: They's gold in the West — an' freedom, mebbe. We been slaves t' stone walls here.

SIMEON (*defiantly*): We hain't nobody's slaves from this out — nor nothin's slaves nuther. (*A pause — restlessly.*) Speaking o' milk, wonder how Eben's managin'?

PETER: I s'pose he's managin'.

SIMEON: Mebbe we'd ought t' help — this once.

PETER: Mebbe. The cows knows us.

SIMEON: An' likes us. They don't know him much.

PETER: An' the hosses, an' pigs, an' chickens. They don't know him much.

SIMEON: They knows us like brothers — an' likes us! (*Proudly.*) Hain't we raised 'em t' be fust-rate, number one prize stock?

PETER: We hain't — not no more.

SIMEON (*dully*): I was fergittin'. (*Then resignedly.*) Waal, let's go help Eben a spell an' git waked up.

PETER: Suits me. (*They are starting off down left, rear, for the barn when Eben appears from there hurrying toward them, his face excited.*)

EBEN (*breathlessly*): Waal — har they be! The old mule an' the bride! I seen 'em from the barn down below at the turnin'.

PETER: How could ye tell that far?

EBEN: Hain't I as far-sight as he's near-sight? Don't I know the mare 'n' buggy, an' two people settin' in it? Who else . . . ? An' I tell ye I kin feel 'em a'comin', too! (*He squirms as if he had the itch.*)

PETER (*beginning to be angry*): Waal — let him do his own unhitchin'!

SIMEON (*angry in his turn*): Let's hustle in an' git our bundles an' be a-goin' as he's a-comin'. I don't want never t' step inside the door agen arter he's back. (*They both start back around the corner of the house. Eben follows them.*)

EBEN (*anxiously*): Will ye sign it afore ye go?

PETER: Let's see the color o' the old skinflint's money an' we'll sign. (*They disappear left. The two brothers clump upstairs to get their bundles. Eben appears in the kitchen, runs to window, peers out, comes back and pulls up a strip of flooring in under stove, takes out a canvas bag and puts it on table, then sets the floorboard back in place. The two brothers appear a moment after. They carry old carpetbags.*)

EBEN (*puts his hand on bag guardingly*): Have ye signed?

SIMEON (*shows paper in his hand*): Ay-eh. (*Greedily.*) Be that the money?

EBEN (*opens bag and pours out pile of twenty-dollar gold pieces*): Twenty-dollar pieces — thirty of 'em. Count 'em. (*Peter does so, arranging them in stacks of five, biting one or two to test them.*)

PETER: Six hundred. (*He puts them in bag and puts it inside his shirt carefully.*)

SIMEON (*handing paper to Eben*): Har ye be.

EBEN (*after a glance, folds it carefully and hides it under his shirt — gratefully*): Thank yew.

PETER: Thank yew fur the ride.

SIMEON: We'll send ye a lump o' gold fur Christmas. (*A pause. Eben stares at them and they at him.*)

PETER (*awkwardly*): Waal — we're a-goin'.

SIMEON: Comin' out t' the yard?

EBEN: No. I'm waitin' in here a spell. (*Another silence. The brothers edge awkwardly to door in rear — then turn and stand.*)

SIMEON: Waal — good-by.

PETER: Good-by.

EBEN: Good-by. (*They go out. He sits down at the table, faces the stove and pulls out the paper. He looks from it to the stove. His face, lighted up by the shaft of sunlight from the window, has an expression of trance. His lips move. The two brothers come out to the gate.*)

PETER (*looking off toward barn*): Thar he be — un-hitchin'.

SIMEON (*with a chuckle*): I'll bet ye he's riled!

PETER: An thar she be.

SIMEON: Let's wait 'n' see what our new Maw looks like.

PETER (*with a grin*): An' give him our partin' cuss!

SIMEON (*grinning*): I feel like raisin' fun. I feel light in my head an' feet.

PETER: Me, too. I feel like laffin' till I'd split up the middle.

SIMEON: Reckon it's the likker?

PETER: No. My feet feel itchin' t' walk an' walk — an' jump high over thin's — an'. . . .

SIMEON: Dance? (*A pause.*)

PETER (*puzzled*): It's plumb onnateral.

SIMEON (*a light coming over his face*): I calc'late it's 'cause school's out. It's holiday. Fur once we're free!

PETER (*dazedly*): Free?

SIMEON: The halter's broke — the harness is busted — the fence bars is down — the stone walls air crumblin' an' tumblin'! We'll be kickin' up an' tearin' away down the road!

PETER (*drawing a deep breath — oratorically*): Anybody that wants this stinkin' old rock-pile of a farm kin hev it. T'ain't our'n, no sirree!

SIMEON (*takes the gate off its hinges and puts it under his arm*): We harby 'bolishes shet gates, an' open gates, an' all gates, by thunder!

PETER: We'll take it with us fur luck an' let 'er sail free down some river.

SIMEON (*as a sound of voices comes from left, rear*): Har they comes! (*The two brothers congeal into two stiff, grim-visaged statues. Ephraim Cabot and Abbie Putnam come in. Cabot is seventy-five, tall and gaunt, with great, wiry, concentrated power, but stoop-shouldered from toil. His face is as hard as if it were hewn out of a boulder, yet there is a weakness in it, a petty pride in its own narrow strength. His eyes are small, close together, and extremely near-sighted, blinking continually in the effort to focus on objects, their stare having a straining, ingrowing quality. He is dressed in his dismal black Sunday suit. Abbie is thirty-five, buxom, full of vitality. Her round face is pretty but marred by its rather gross sensuality. There is strength and obstinacy in her jaw, a hard determination in her eyes, and about her whole personality the same unsettled, untamed, desperate quality which is so apparent in Eben.*)

CABOT (*as they enter — a queer strangled emotion in his dry cracking voice*): Har we be t' hum, Abbie.

ABBIE (*with lust for the word*): Hum! (*Her eyes gloating on the house without seeming to see the two stiff figures at the gate.*) It's purty — purty! I can't b'lieve it's r'ally mine.

CABOT (*sharply*): Yewr'n? Mine! (*He stares at her penetratingly. She stares back. He adds relentlessly.*) Our'n — mebbe! It was lonesome too long. I was growin' old in the spring. A hum's got t' hev a woman.

ABBIE (*her voice taking possession*): A woman's got t' hev a hum!

CABOT (*nodding uncertainly*): Ay-eh. (*Then irritably.*) Whar be they? Ain't thar nobody about —'r wukin' —'r nothin'?

ABBIE (*Sees the brothers. She returns their stare of cold appraising contempt with interest — slowly.*): Thar's two men loafin' at the gate an' starin' at me like a couple o' strayed hogs.

CABOT (*straining his eyes*): I kin see 'em — but I can't make out. . . .

SIMEON: It's Simeon.

PETER: It's Peter.

CABOT (*exploding*): Why hain't ye wukin'?

SIMEON (*dryly*): We're waitin' t' welcome ye hum — yew an' the bride!

CABOT (*confusedly*): Huh? Waal — this be yer new Maw, boys. (*She stares at them and they at her.*)

SIMEON (*turns away and spits contemptuously*): I see her!

PETER (*spits also*): An I see her!

ABBIE (*with the conqueror's conscious superiority*): I'll go in an' look at *my* house. (*She goes slowly around to porch.*)

SIMEON (*with a snort*): *Her* house!

PETER (*calls after her*): Ye'll find Eben inside. Ye better not tell him it's *yewr* house.

ABBIE (*mouthing the name*): Eben. (*Then quietly.*) I'll tell Eben.

CABOT (*with a contemptuous sneer*): Ye needn't heed Eben. Eben's a dumb fool — like his Maw — soft an' simple!

SIMEON (*with his sardonic burst of laughter*): Ha! Eben's a chip o' yew — spit 'n' image — hard 'n' bitter's a hickory tree! Dog'll eat dog. He'll eat ye yet, old man!

CABOT (*commandingly*): Ye git t' wuk.

SIMEON (*as Abbie disappears in house — winks at Peter and says tauntingly*): So that thar's our new Maw, be it? Whar in hell did ye dig her up? (*He and Peter laugh.*)

PETER: Ha! Ye'd better turn her in the pen with the other sows. (*They laugh uproariously, slapping their thighs.*)

CABOT (*so amazed at their effrontery that he stutters in confusion*): Simeon! Peter! What's come over ye? Air ye drunk?

SIMEON: We're free, old man — free o' yew an' the hull damned farm! (*They grow more and more hilarious and excited.*)

PETER: An' we're startin' out fur the gold fields o' Cali-forni-a!

SIMEON: Ye kin take this place an' burn it!

PETER: An' bury it — fur all we cares!

SIMEON: We're free, old man! (*He cuts a caper.*)

PETER: Free! (*He gives a kick in the air.*)

SIMEON (*in a frenzy*): Whoop!

PETER: Whoop! (*They do an absurd Indian war dance about the old man who is petrified between rage and the fear that they are insane.*)

SIMEON: We're free as Injuns! Lucky we don't skulp ye!

PETER: An' burn yer barn an' kill the stock!

SIMEON: An' rape yer new woman! Whoop! (*He and Peter stop their dance, holding their sides, rocking with wild laughter.*)

CABOT (*edging away*): Lust fur gold — fur the sinful, easy gold o' Californi-a! It's made ye mad!

SIMEON (*tauntingly*): Wouldn't ye like us to send ye back some sinful gold, ye old sinner?

PETER: They's gold besides what's in Californi-a! (*He retreats back beyond the vision of the old man and takes the bag of money and flaunts it in the air above his head, laughing.*)

SIMEON: And sinfuller, too!

PETER: We'll be voyagin' on the sea! Whoop! (*He leaps up and down.*)

SIMEON: Livin' free! Whoop! (*He leaps in turn.*)

CABOT (*suddenly roaring with rage*): My cuss on ye!

SIMEON: Take our'n in trade fur it! Whoop!

CABOT: I'll hev ye both chained up in the asylum!

PETER: Ye old skinflint! Good-by!

SIMEON: Ye old blood sucker! Good-by!

CABOT: Go afore I . . . !

PETER: Whoop! (*He picks a stone from the road. Simeon does the same.*)

SIMEON: Maw'll be in the parlor.

PETER: Ay-eh! One! Two!

CABOT (*frightened*): What air ye . . . ?

PETER: Three! (*They both throw, the stones hitting the parlor window with a crash of glass, tearing the shade.*)

SIMEON: Whoop!

PETER: Whoop!

CABOT (*in a fury now, rushing toward them*): If I kin lay hands on ye — I'll break yer bones fur ye! (*But they beat a capering retreat before him, Simeon with the gate still under his arm. Cabot comes back, panting with impotent rage. Their voices as they go off take up the song of the gold-seekers to the old tune of "Oh, Susannah!"*)

"I jumped aboard the Liza ship,
And traveled on the sea,
And every time I thought of home
I wished it wasn't me!
Oh! Californi-a,
That's the land fur me!
I'm off to Californi-a!
With my wash bowl on my knee."

(*In the meantime, the window of the upper bedroom on right is raised and Abbie sticks her head out. She looks down at Cabot — with a sigh of relief.*)

ABBIE: Waal — that's the last o' them two, hain't it? (*He doesn't answer. Then in possessive tones.*) This here's a nice bedroom, Ephraim. It's a r'al nice bed. Is it my room, Ephraim?

CABOT (*grimly — without looking up*): Our'n! (*She cannot control a grimace of aversion and pulls back her head slowly and shuts the window. A sudden horrible thought seems to enter Cabot's head.*) They been up to somethin'! Mebbe — mebbe they've pizened the stock —'r somethin'! (*He almost runs off down toward the barn. A moment later the kitchen door is slowly pushed open and Abbie enters. For a moment she stands looking at Eben. He does not notice her at first. Her eyes take him in penetratingly with a calculating appraisal of his strength as against hers. But under this her desire is dimly awakened by his youth and good looks. Suddenly he becomes conscious of her presence and looks up. Their eyes meet. He leaps to his feet, glowering at her speechlessly.*)

ABBIE (*in her most seductive tones which she uses all through this scene*): Be you — Eben? I'm Abbie — (*She laughs.*) I mean, I'm yer new Maw.

EBEN (*viciously*): No, damn ye!

ABBIE (*as if she hadn't heard — with a queer smile*): Yer Paw's spoke a lot o' yew. . . .

EBEN: Ha!

ABBIE: Ye mustn't mind him. He's an old man. (*A long pause. They stare at each other.*) I don't want t' pretend playin' Maw t' ye, Eben. (*Admiringly.*) Ye're too big an' too strong fur that. I want t' be frens with ye. Mebbe with me fur a fren ye'd find ye'd like livin' here better. I kin make it easy fur ye with him, mebbe. (*With a scornful sense of power.*) I calc'late I kin git him t' do most anythin' fur me.

EBEN (*with bitter scorn*): Ha! (*They stare again, Eben obscurely moved, physically attracted to her — in forced stilted tones.*) Yew kin go t' the devil!

ABBIE (*calmly*): If cussin' me does ye good, cuss all ye've a mind t'. I'm all prepared t' have ye agin me — at fust. I don't blame ye nuther. I'd feel the same at any stranger comin' t' take my Maw's place. (*He shudders. She is watching him carefully.*) Yew must've cared a lot fur yewr Maw, didn't ye? My Maw died afore I'd growed. I don't remember her none. (*A pause.*) But yew won't hate me long, Eben. I'm not the wust in the world — an' yew an' me've got a lot in common. I kin tell that by lookin' at ye. Waal — I've had a hard life, too — oceans o' trouble an' nuthin' but wuk fur reward. I was a orphan early an' had t' wuk fur others in other folks' hums. Then I married an' he turned out a drunken spreer an' so he had to wuk fur others an' me too agen in other folks' hums, an' the baby died, an' my husband got sick an' died too, an' I was glad sayin' now I'm free fur once, on'y I diskivered right away all I was free fur was t'wuk agen in other folks' hums, doin' other folks' wuk till I'd most give up hope o' ever doin' my own wuk in my own hum, an' then your Paw come . . . (*Cabot appears returning from the barn. He comes to the gate and looks down the road the brothers have gone. A faint strain of their retreating voices is heard: "Oh, Californi-a! That's the place for me." He stands glowering, his fist clenched, his face grim with rage.*)

EBEN (*fighting against his growing attraction and sympathy — harshly*): An' bought yew — like a harlot! (*She is stung and flushes angrily. She has been sincerely moved by the recital of her troubles. He adds furiously.*) An' the price he's payin' ye — this farm — was my Maw's, damn ye! — an' mine now!

ABBIE (*with a cool laugh of confidence*): Yewr'n? We'll see 'bout that! (*Then strongly.*) Waal — what if I did need a hum? What else'd I marry an old man like him fur?

EBEN (*maliciously*): I'll tell him ye said that!

ABBIE (*smiling*): I'll say ye're lyin' a-purpose — an' he'll drive ye off the place!

EBEN: Ye devil!

ABBIE (*defying him*): This be my farm — this be my hum — this be my kitchen — !

EBEN (*furiously, as if he were going to attack her*): Shut up, damn ye!

ABBIE (*walks up to him — a queer coarse expression of desire in her face and body — slowly*): An' upstairs — that be my bedroom — an' my bed! (*He stares into her eyes, terribly confused and torn. She adds softly.*) I hain't bad nor mean — 'ceptin' fur an enemy — but I got t' fight fur what's due me out o' life, if I ever 'spect t' git it. (*Then putting her hand on his arm — seductively.*) Let's yew 'n' me be frens, Eben.

EBEN (*stupidly — as if hypnotized*): Ay-eh. (*Then furiously flinging off her arm.*) No, ye durned old witch! I hate ye! (*He rushes out the door.*)

ABBIE (*looks after him smiling satisfiedly — then half to herself, mouthing the word*): Eben's nice. (*She looks at the table, proudly.*) I'll wash up *my* dishes now. (*Eben appears outside, slamming the door behind him. He comes around corner, stops on seeing his father, and stands staring at him with hate.*)

CABOT (*raising his arms to heaven in the fury he can no longer control*): Lord God o' Hosts, smite the undutiful sons with Thy wust cuss!

EBEN (*breaking in violently*): Yew 'n' yewr God! Allus cussin' folks — allus naggin' 'em!

CABOT (*oblivious to him — summoningly*): God o' the old! God o' the lonesome!

EBEN (*mockingly*): Naggin' His sheep t' sin! T' hell with yewr God! (*Cabot turns. He and Eben glower at each other.*)

CABOT (*harshly*): So it's yew. I might've knowed it. (*Shaking his finger threateningly at him.*) Blasphemin' fool! (*Then quickly.*) Why hain't ye t' wuk?

EBEN: Why hain't yew? They've went. I can't wuk it all alone.

CABOT (*contemptuously*): Nor noways! I'm wuth ten o' ye yit, old's I be! Ye'll never be more'n half a man! (*Then, matter-of-factly.*) Waal — let's git t' the barn. (*They go. A last faint note of the "Californi-a" song is heard from the distance. Abbie is washing her dishes.*)

PART II • *Scene I*

(*The exterior of the farmhouse, as in part I — a hot Sunday afternoon two months later. Abbie, dressed in her best, is discovered sitting in a rocker at the end of the porch. She rocks listlessly, enervated by the heat, staring in front of her with bored, half-closed eyes.*)

(*Eben sticks his head out of his bedroom window. He looks around furtively and tries to see — or hear — if anyone is on the porch, but although he has been careful to make no noise, Abbie has sensed his movement. She stops rocking, her face grows animated and eager, she waits attentively. Eben seems to feel her presence, he scowls back his thoughts of her and spits with exaggerated disdain — then withdraws back into the room. Abbie waits, holding her breath as she listens with passionate eagerness for every sound within the house.*)

(*Eben comes out. Their eyes meet; his falter. He is confused, he turns away and slams the door resentfully. At this gesture, Abbie laughs tantalizingly, amused but at the same time piqued and irritated. He scowls, strides off the porch to the path and starts to walk past her to the road with a grand swagger of ignoring her existence. He is dressed in his store suit, spruced up, his face shines from soap and water. Abbie leans forward on her chair, her eyes hard and angry now, and, as he passes her, gives a sneering, taunting chuckle.*)

EBEN (*stung — turns on her furiously*): What air yew cacklin' 'bout?

ABBIE (*triumphant*): Yew!

EBEN: What about me?

ABBIE: Ye look all slicked up like a prize bull.

EBEN (*with a sneer*): Waal — ye hain't so durned purty yerself, be ye? (*They stare into each other's eyes, his held by hers in spite of himself, hers glowingly possessive. Their physical attraction becomes a palpable force quivering in the hot air.*)

ABBIE (*softly*): Ye don't mean that, Eben. Ye may think ye mean it, mebbe, but ye don't. Ye can't. It's agin nature, Eben. Ye been fightin' yer nature ever since the day I come — tryin' t' tell yerself I hain't purty t'ye. (*She laughs a low humid laugh without taking her eyes from his. A pause — her body squirms desirously — she murmurs languorously.*) Hain't the sun strong an' hot? Ye kin feel it burnin' into the earth — Nature — makin' thin's grow — bigger 'n' bigger — burnin' inside ye — makin' ye want t' grow — into somethin' else — till ye're jined with it — an' it's your'n — but it owns ye, too — an' makes ye grow bigger — like a tree — like them elums — (*She laughs again softly, holding his eyes. He takes a step toward her, compelled against his will.*) Nature'll beat ye, Eben. Ye might's well own up t' it fust 's last.

EBEN (*trying to break from her spell — confusedly*): If Paw'd hear ye goin' on. . . . (*Resentfully.*) But ye've made such a damned idjit out o' the old devil . . . ! (*Abbie laughs.*)

ABBIE: Waal — hain't it easier fur yew with him changed softer?

EBEN (*defiantly*): No. I'm fightin' him — fightin' yew — fightin' fur Maw's rights t' her hum! (*This breaks her spell for him. He glowers at her.*) An' I'm onto ye. Ye hain't foolin' me a mite. Ye're aimin' t' swaller up everythin' an' make it your'n. Waal, you'll find I'm a heap sight bigger hunk nor yew kin chew! (*He turns from her with a sneer.*)

ABBIE (*trying to regain her ascendancy — seductively*): Eben!

EBEN: Leave me be! (*He starts to walk away.*)

ABBIE (*more commandingly*): Eben!

EBEN (*stops — resentfully*): What d'ye want?

ABBIE (*trying to conceal a growing excitement*): Whar air ye goin'?

EBEN (*with malicious nonchalance*): Oh — up the road a spell.

ABBIE: T' the village?

EBEN (*airily*): Mebbe.

ABBIE (*excitedly*): T' see that Min, I s'pose?

EBEN: Mebbe.

ABBIE (*weakly*): What d'ye want t' waste time on her fur?

EBEN (*revenging himself now — grinning at her*): Ye can't beat Nature, didn't ye say? (*He laughs and again starts to walk away.*)

ABBIE (*bursting out*): An ugly old hake!

EBEN (*with a tantalizing sneer*): She's purtier'n yew be!

ABBIE: That every wuthless drunk in the country has. . . .

EBEN (*tauntingly*): Mebbe — but she's better'n yew. She owns up fa'r 'n' squar' t' her doin's.

ABBIE (*furiously*): Don't ye dare compare. . . .

EBEN: She don't go sneakin' an' stealin' — what's mine.

ABBIE (*savagely seizing on his weak point*): Your'n? Yew mean — my farm?

EBEN: I mean the farm yew sold yerself fur like any other old whore — my farm!

ABBIE (*stung — fiercely*): Ye'll never live t' see the day when even a stinkin' weed on it'll belong t' ye! (*Then in a scream.*) Git out o' my sight! Go on t' yer slut — disgracin' yer Paw 'n' me! I'll git yer Paw t' horsewhip ye off the place if I want t'! Ye're only livin' here 'cause I tolerate ye! Git along! I hate the sight o' ye! (*She stops, panting and glaring at him.*)

EBEN (*returning her glance in kind*): An' I hate the sight o' yew! (*He turns and strides off up the road. She follows his retreating figure with concentrated hate. Old Cabot appears coming up from the barn. The hard, grim expression of his face has changed. He seems in some queer way softened, mellowed. His eyes have taken on a strange, incongruous dreamy quality. Yet there is no hint of physical weakness about him — rather he looks more robust and younger. Abbie sees him and turns away quickly with unconcealed aversion. He comes slowly up to her.*)

CABOT (*mildly*): War yew an' Eben quarrelin' agen?

ABBIE (*shortly*): No.

CABOT: Ye was talkin' a'mighty loud. (*He sits down on the edge of porch.*)

ABBIE (*snappishly*): If ye heerd us they hain't no need askin' questions.

CABOT: I didn't hear what ye said.

ABBIE (*relieved*): Waal — it wa'n't nothin' t' speak on.

CABOT (*after a pause*): Eben's queer.

ABBIE (*bitterly*): He's the dead spit 'n' image o' yew!

CABOT (*queerly interested*): D'ye think so, Abbie? (*After a pause, ruminatingly.*) Me 'n' Eben's allus fit 'n' fit. I never could b'ar him noways. He's so thunderin' soft — like his Maw.

ABBIE (*scornfully*): Ay-eh! 'Bout as soft as yew be!

CABOT (*as if he hadn't heard*): Mebbe I been too hard on him.

ABBIE (*jeeringly*): Waal — ye're gittin' soft now — soft as slop! That's what Eben was sayin'.

CABOT (*his face instantly grim and ominous*): Eben was sayin'? Waal, he'd best not do nothin' t' try me 'r he'll soon diskiver. . . . (*A pause. She keeps her face turned away. His gradually softens. He stares up at the sky.*) Purty, hain't it?

ABBIE (*crossly*): I don't see nothin' purty.

CABOT: The sky. Feels like a wa'm field up thar.

ABBIE (*sarcastically*): Air yew aimin' t' buy up over the farm too? (*She snickers contemptuously.*)

CABOT (*strangely*): I'd like t' own my place up thar. (*A pause.*) I'm gittin' old, Abbie. I'm gittin' ripe on the bough. (*A pause. She stares at him mystified. He goes on.*) It's allus lonesome cold in the house — even when it's bilin' hot outside. Hain't yew noticed?

ABBIE: No.

CABOT: It's wa'm down t' the barn — nice smellin' an' warm — with the cows. (*A pause.*) Cows is queer.

ABBIE: Like yew?

CABOT: Like Eben. (*A pause.*) I'm gittin' t' feel resigned t' Eben — jest as I got t' feel 'bout his Maw. I'm gittin' t' learn to b'ar his softness — jest like her'n. I calc'late I c'd a'most take t' him — if he wa'n't sech a dumb fool! (*A pause.*) I s'pose it's old age a-creepin' in my bones.

ABBIE (*indifferently*): Waal — ye hain't dead yet.

CABOT (*roused*): No, I hain't, yew bet — not by a hell of a sight — I'm sound 'n' tough as hickory! (*Then moodily.*) But arter three score and ten the Lord warns ye t' prepare. (*A pause.*) That's why Eben's come in my head. Now that his cussed sinful brothers is gone their path t' hell, they's no one left but Eben.

ABBIE (*resentfully*): They's me, hain't they? (*Agitatedly.*) What's all this sudden likin' ye've tuk to Eben? Why don't ye say nothin' 'bout me? Hain't I yer lawful wife?

CABOT (*simply*): Ay-eh. Ye be. (*A pause — he stares at her desirously — his eyes grow avid — then with a sudden movement he seizes her hands and squeezes them, declaiming in a queer camp meeting preacher's tempo.*) Yew air my Rose o' Sharon! Behold, yew air fair; yer eyes air doves; yer lips air like scarlet; yer two breasts air like two fawns; yer navel be like a round goblet; yer belly be like a heap o' wheat. . . . (*He covers her hand with kisses. She does not seem to notice. She stares before her with hard angry eyes.*)

ABBIE (*jerking her hands away — harshly*): So ye're plannin' t' leave the farm t' Eben, air ye?

CABOT (*dazedly*): Leave . . . ? (*Then with resentful obstinacy.*) I hain't a-givin' it t' no one!

ABBIE (*remorselessly*): Ye can't take it with ye.

CABOT (*thinks a moment — then reluctantly*): No, I calc'late not. (*After a pause — with a strange passion.*) But if I could, I would, by the Eternal! 'R if I could, in my dyin' hour, I'd set it afire an' watch it burn — this house an' every ear o' corn an' every tree down t' the last blade o' hay! I'd sit an' know it was all a-dying with me an' no one else'd ever own what was mine, what I'd made out o' nothin' with my own sweat 'n' blood! (*A pause — then he adds with a queer affection.*) 'Ceptin' the cows. Them I'd turn free.

ABBIE (*harshly*): An' me?

CABOT (*with a queer smile*): Ye'd be turned free, too.

ABBIE (*furiously*): So that's the thanks I git fur marryin' ye — t' have ye change kind to Eben who hates ye, an' talk o' turnin' me out in the road.

CABOT (*hastily*): Abbie! Ye know I wa'n't. . . .

ABBIE (*vengefully*): Just let me tell ye a thing or two 'bout Eben! Whar's he gone? T' see that harlot, Min! I tried fur t' stop him. Disgracin' yew an' me — on the Sabbath, too!

CABOT (*rather guiltily*): He's a sinner — nateral-born. It's lust eatin' his heart.

ABBIE (*enraged beyond endurance — wildly vindictive*): An' his lust fur me! Kin ye find excuses fur that?

CABOT (*stares at her — after a dead pause*): Lust — fur yew?

ABBIE (*defiantly*): He was tryin' t' make love t' me — when ye heerd us quarrelin'.

CABOT (*stares at her — then a terrible expression of rage comes over his face — he springs to his feet shaking all over*): By the A'mighty God — I'll end him!

ABBIE (*frightened now for Eben*): No! Don't ye!

CABOT (*violently*): I'll git the shotgun an' blow his soft brains t' the top o' them elums!

ABBIE (*throwing her arms around him*): No, Ephraim!

CABOT (*pushing her away violently*): I will, by God!

ABBIE (*in a quieting tone*): Listen, Ephraim. 'Twa'n't nothin' bad — on'y a boy's foolin' — 'twa'n't meant serious — jest jokin' an' teasin'. . . .

CABOT: Then why did ye say — lust?

ABBIE: It must hev sounded wusser'n I meant. An' I was mad at thinkin' — ye'd leave him the farm.

CABOT (*quieter but still grim and cruel*): Waal then, I'll horsewhip him off the place if that much'll content ye.

ABBIE (*reaching out and taking his hand*): No. Don't think o' me! Ye mustn't drive him off. 'Tain't sensible. Who'll ye get to help ye on the farm? They's no one hereabouts.

CABOT (*considers this — then nodding his appreciation*): Ye got a head on ye. (*Then irritably.*) Waal, let him stay. (*He sits down on the edge of the porch. She sits beside him. He murmurs contemptuously.*) I oughtn't t' git riled so — at that 'ere fool calf. (*A pause.*) But har's the p'int. What son o' mine'll keep on here t' the farm — when the Lord does call me? Simeon an' Peter air gone t' hell — an' Eben's follerin' 'em.

ABBIE: They's me.

CABOT: Ye're on'y a woman.

ABBIE: I'm yewr wife.

CABOT: That hain't me. A son is me — my blood — mine. Mine ought t' git mine. An' then it's still mine — even though I be six foot under. D'ye see?

ABBIE (*giving him a look of hatred*): Ay-eh. I see. (*She becomes very thoughtful, her face growing shrewd, her eyes studying Cabot craftily.*)

CABOT: I'm gittin' old — ripe on the bough. (*Then with a sudden forced reassurance.*) Not but what I hain't a hard nut t' crack even yet — an' fur many a year t' come! By the Eternal, I kin break most o' the young fellers' backs at any kind o' work any day o' the year!

ABBIE (*suddenly*): Mebbe the Lord'll give us a son.

CABOT (*turns and stares at her eagerly*): Ye mean — a son — t' me 'n' yew?

ABBIE (*with a cajoling smile*): Ye're a strong man yet, hain't ye? 'Tain't noways impossible, be it? We know that. Why d'ye stare so? Hain't ye never thought o' that afore? I been thinkin' o' it all along. Ay-eh — an' I been prayin' it'd happen, too.

CABOT (*his face growing full of joyous pride and a sort of religious ecstasy*): Ye been prayin', Abbie? — fur a son? — t' us?

ABBIE: Ay-eh. (*With a grim resolution.*) I want a son now.

CABOT (*excitedly clutching both of her hands in his*): It'd be the blessin' o' God, Abbie — the blessin' o' God A'mighty on me — in my old age — in my lonesomeness! They hain't nothin' I wouldn't do fur ye then, Abbie. Ye'd hev on'y t' ask it — anythin' ye'd a mind t'!

ABBIE (*interrupting*): Would ye will the farm t' me then — t' me an' it . . . ?

CABOT (*vehemently*): I'd do anythin' ye axed, I tell ye! I swar it! May I be everlastin' damned t' hell if I wouldn't! (*He sinks to his knees pulling her down with him. He trembles all over with the fervor of his hopes.*) Pray t' the Lord agen, Abbie. It's the Sabbath! I'll jine ye! Two prayers air better nor one. "An' God hearkened unto Rachel"! An' God hearkened unto Abbie! Pray, Abbie! Pray fur him to hearken! (*He bows his head, mumbling. She pretends to do likewise but gives him a side glance of scorn and triumph.*)

Scene II

(*About eight in the evening. The interior of the two bedrooms on the top floor is shown. Eben is sitting on the side of his bed in the room on the left. On account of the heat he has taken off everything but his undershirt and pants. His feet are bare. He faces front, brooding moodily, his chin propped on his hands, a desperate expression on his face.*)

(*In the other room Cabot and Abbie are sitting side by side on the edge of their bed, an old four-poster with feather mattress. He is in his nightshirt, she in her nightdress. He is still in the queer, excited mood into which the notion of a son has thrown him. Both rooms are lighted dimly and flickeringly by tallow candles.*)

CABOT: The farm needs a son.

ABBIE: I need a son.

CABOT: Ay-eh. Sometimes ye air the farm an' sometimes the farm be yew. That's why I clove t'ye in my lonesomeness. (*A pause. He pounds his knee with his fist.*) Me an' the farm has got t' beget a son!

ABBIE: Ye'd best go t' sleep. Ye're gittin' thin's all mixed.

CABOT (*with an impatient gesture*): No, I hain't. My mind's clear's a well. Ye don't know me, that's it. (*He stares hopelessly at the floor.*)

ABBIE (*indifferently*): Mebbe. (*In the next room Eben gets up and paces up and down distractedly. Abbie hears him. Her eyes fasten on the intervening wall with concentrated attention. Eben stops and stares. Their hot glances seem to meet through the wall. Unconsciously he stretches out his arms for her and she half rises. Then aware, he mutters a curse at himself and flings himself face downward on the bed, his clenched fists above his head, his face buried in the pillow. Abbie relaxes with a faint sigh but her eyes remain fixed on the wall; she listens with all her attention for some movement from Eben.*)

CABOT (*suddenly raises his head and looks at her — scornfully*): Will ye ever know me — 'r will any man 'r woman? (*Shaking his head.*) No. I calc'late wa'n't t' be. (*He turns away. Abbie looks at the wall. Then, evidently unable to keep silent about his thoughts, without looking at his wife, he puts out his hand and clutches her knee. She starts violently, looks at him, sees he is not watching her, concentrates again on the wall, and pays no attention to what he says.*) Listen, Abbie. When I come here fifty odd year ago — I was jest twenty an' the strongest an' hardest ye ever seen — ten times as strong an' fifty times as hard as Eben. Waal — this place was nothin' but fields o' stones. Folks laughed when I tuk it. They couldn't know what I knowed. When ye kin make corn sprout out o' stones, God's livin' in yew! They wa'n't strong enuf fur that! They reckoned God was easy. They laughed. They don't laugh no more. Some died hereabouts. Some went West an' died. They're all underground — fur follerin' arter an easy God. God hain't easy. (*He shakes his head slowly.*) An' I growed hard. Folks kept allus sayin' he's a hard man like 'twas sinful t' be hard, so's at last I said back at 'em: Waal then, by thunder, ye'll git me hard an' see how ye like it! (*Then suddenly.*) But I give in t' weakness once. 'Twas arter I'd been here two year. I got weak — despairful — they was so many stones. They was a party leavin', givin' up, goin' West. I jined 'em. We tracked on 'n on. We come t' broad medders, plains, whar the soil was black an' rich as gold. Nary a stone. Easy. Ye'd on'y to plow an' sow an' then set an' smoke yer pipe an' watch thin's grow. I could o' been a rich man — but somethin' in me fit me an' fit me — the voice o' God sayin': "This hain't wuth nothin' t' Me. Git ye back t' hum!" I got afeerd o' that voice an' I lit out back t' hum here, leavin' my claim an' crops t' whoever'd a mind t' take 'em. Ay-eh. I actoolly give up what was rightful mine! God's hard, not easy! God's in the stones! Build my church on a rock — out o' stones an' I'll be in them! That's what He meant t' Peter! (*He sighs heavily — a pause.*) Stones. I picked 'em up an' piled 'em into walls. Ye kin read the years o' my life in them walls, every day a hefted stone, climbin' over the hills up an' down, fencin' in the fields that was mine, whar I'd made thin's grow out o' nothin' — like the will o' God, like the servant o' His hand. It wa'n't easy. It was hard an' He made me hard fur it. (*He pauses.*) All the time I kept gittin' lonesomer. I tuk a wife. She bore Simeon an' Peter. She was a good woman. She wuked hard. We was married twenty year. She never knowed me. She helped but she never knowed what she was helpin'. I was allus lonesome. She died. After that it wa'n't so lonesome fur a spell. (*A pause.*) I lost count o' the years. I had no time t' fool away countin' 'em. Sim an' Peter helped. The farm growed. It was all mine! When I thought o' that I didn't feel lonesome. (*A pause.*) But ye can't hitch yer mind t' one thin' day an' night. I tuk another wife — Eben's Maw. Her folks was contestin' me at law over my deeds t' the farm — my farm! That's why Eben keeps a-talkin' his fool talk o' this bein' his Maw's farm. She bore Eben. She was purty — but soft. She tried t' be hard. She couldn't. She never knowed me nor nothin'. It was lonesomer 'n hell with her. After a matter o' sixteen odd years, she died. (*A pause.*) I lived with the boys. They hated me 'cause I was hard. I hated them 'cause they was soft. They coveted the farm without knowin' what it meant. It made me bitter 'n wormwood. It aged me — them coveting what I'd made fur mine. Then this spring the call come —

the voice o' God cryin' in my wilderness, in my lone-someness — t' go out an' seek an' find! (*Turning to her with strange passion.*) I sought ye an' I found ye! Yew air my Rose o' Sharon! Yer eyes air like.... (*She has turned a blank face, resentful eyes to his. He stares at her for a moment — then harshly.*) Air ye any the wiser fur all I've told ye?

ABBIE (*confusedly*): Mebbe.

CABOT (*pushing her away from him — angrily*): Ye don't know nothin' — nor never will. If ye don't hev a son t' redeem ye.... (*This in a tone of cold threat.*)

ABBIE (*resentfully*): I've prayed, hain't I?

CABOT (*bitterly*): Pray agen — fur understandin'!

ABBIE (*a veiled threat in her tone*): Ye'll have a son out o' me, I promise ye.

CABOT: How kin ye promise?

ABBIE: I got second-sight mebbe. I kin foretell. (*She gives a queer smile.*)

CABOT: I believe ye have. Ye give me the chills some-times. (*He shivers.*) It's cold in this house. It's oneasy. They's thin's pokin' about in the dark — in the cor-ners. (*He pulls on his trousers, tucking in his night-shirt, and pulls on his boots.*)

ABBIE (*surprised*): Whar air ye goin'?

CABOT (*queerly*): Down whar it's restful — whar it's warm — down t' the barn. (*Bitterly.*) I kin talk t' the cows. They know. They know the farm an' me. They'll give me peace. (*He turns to go out the door.*)

ABBIE (*a bit frightenedly*): Air ye ailin' tonight, Ephraim?

CABOT: Growin'. Growin' ripe on the bough. (*He turns and goes, his boots clumping down the stairs. Eben sits up with a start, listening. Abbie is conscious of his movement and stares at the wall. Cabot comes out of the house around the corner and stands by the gate, blinking at the sky. He stretches up his hands in a tortured gesture.*) God A'mighty, call from the dark! (*He listens as if expecting an answer. Then his arms drop, he shakes his head and plods off toward the barn. Eben and Abbie stare at each other through the wall. Eben sighs heavily and Abbie echoes it. Both become terribly nervous, uneasy. Finally Abbie gets up and listens, her ear to the wall. He acts as if he saw every move she was making, he becomes res-olutely still. She seems driven into a decision — goes out the door in rear determinedly. His eyes follow her. Then as the door of his room is opened softly, he turns away, waits in an attitude of strained fixity. Abbie stands for a second staring at him, her eyes burning with desire. Then with a little cry she runs over and throws her arms about his neck, she pulls his head back and covers his mouth with kisses. At first, he submits dumbly; then he puts his arms about her neck and returns her kisses, but finally, suddenly aware of his hatred, he hurls her away from him, springing to his feet. They stand speechless and breathless, panting like two animals.*)

ABBIE (*at last — painfully*): Ye shouldn't, Eben — ye shouldn't — I'd make ye happy!

EBEN (*harshly*): I don't want t' be happy — from yew!

ABBIE (*helplessly*): Ye do, Eben! Ye do! Why d'ye lie?

EBEN (*viciously*): I don't take t'ye, I tell ye! I hate the sight o' ye!

ABBIE (*with an uncertain troubled laugh*): Waal, I kissed ye anyways — an' ye kissed back — yer lips was burnin' — ye can't lie 'bout that! (*Intensely.*) If ye don't care, why did ye kiss me back — why was yer lips burnin'?

EBEN (*wiping his mouth*): It was like pizen on 'em. (*Then tauntingly.*) When I kissed ye back, mebbe I thought 'twas someone else.

ABBIE (*wildly*): Min?

EBEN: Mebbe.

ABBIE (*torturedly*): Did ye go t' see her? Did ye r'ally go? I thought ye mightn't. Is that why ye throwed me off jest now?

EBEN (*sneeringly*): What if it be?

ABBIE (*raging*): Then ye're a dog, Eben Cabot!

EBEN (*threateningly*): Ye can't talk that way t' me!

ABBIE (*with a shrill laugh*): Can't I? Did ye think I was in love with ye — a weak thin' like yew? Not much! I on'y wanted ye fur a purpose o' my own — an' I'll hev ye fur it yet 'cause I'm stronger'n yew be!

EBEN (*resentfully*): I knowed well it was on'y part o' yer plan t' swaller everythin'!

ABBIE (*tauntingly*): Mebbe!

EBEN (*furious*): Git out o' my room!

ABBIE: This air my room an' ye're on'y hired help!

EBEN (*threateningly*): Git out afore I murder ye!

ABBIE (*quite confident now*): I hain't a mite afeerd. Ye want me, don't ye? Yes, ye do! An' yer Paw's son'll never kill what he wants! Look at yer eyes! They's lust fur me in 'em, burnin' 'em up! Look at yer lips now! They're tremblin' an' longin' t' kiss me, an' yer teeth t' bite! (*He is watching her now with a horrible fascination. She laughs a crazy triumphant laugh.*) I'm a-goin' t' make all o' this hum my hum! They's one room hain't mine yet, but it's a-goin' t' be tonight. I'm a-goin' down now an' light up! (*She makes him a mocking bow.*) Won't ye come courtin' me in the best parlor, Mister Cabot?

EBEN (*staring at her — horribly confused — dully*): Don't ye dare! It hain't been opened since Maw died an' was laid out thar! Don't ye ...! (*But her eyes are fixed on his so burningly that his will seems to wither before hers. He stands swaying toward her help-lessly.*)

ABBIE (*holding his eyes and putting all her will into her words as she backs out the door*): I'll expect ye afore long, Eben.

EBEN (*Stares after her for a while, walking toward the door. A light appears in the parlor window. He murmurs.*): In the parlor? (*This seems to arouse con-notations, for he comes back and puts on his white shirt, collar, half ties the tie mechanically, puts on coat, takes his hat, stands barefooted looking about him in bewilderment, mutters wonderingly.*) Maw!

Abbie in the 1988 Pushkin Theatre (Moscow) production of *Desire under the Elms,* directed by Mark Lamos of the Hartford Stage Company.

Whar air yew? (*Then goes slowly toward the door in rear.*)

Scene III

(*A few minutes later. The interior of the parlor is shown. A grim, repressed room like a tomb in which the family has been interred alive. Abbie sits on the edge of the horsehair sofa. She has lighted all the candles and the room is revealed in all its preserved ugliness. A change has come over the woman. She looks awed and frightened now, ready to run away.*)

(*The door is opened and Eben appears. His face wears an expression of obsessed confusion. He stands staring at her, his arms hanging disjointedly from his shoulders, his feet bare, his hat in his hand.*)

ABBIE (*after a pause — with a nervous, formal politeness*): Won't ye set?

EBEN (*dully*): Ay-eh. (*Mechanically he places his hat carefully on the floor near the door and sits stiffly beside her on the edge of the sofa. A pause. They both remain rigid, looking straight ahead with eyes full of fear.*)

ABBIE: When I fust come in — in the dark — they seemed somethin' here.

EBEN (*simply*): Maw.

ABBIE: I kin still feel — somethin'. . . .

EBEN: It's Maw.

ABBIE: At fust I was feered o' it. I wanted t' yell an' run. Now — since yew come — seems like it's growin' soft an' kind t' me. (*Addressing the air — queerly.*) Thank yew.

EBEN: Maw allus loved me.

ABBIE: Mebbe it knows I love yew, too. Mebbe that makes it kind t' me.

EBEN (*dully*): I dunno. I should think she'd hate ye.

ABBIE (*with certainty*): No. I kin feel it don't — not no more.

EBEN: Hate ye fur stealin' her place — here in her hum — settin' in her parlor whar she was laid — (*He suddenly stops, staring stupidly before him.*)

ABBIE: What is it, Eben?

EBEN (*in a whisper*): Seems like Maw didn't want me t' remind ye.

ABBIE (*excitedly*): I knowed, Eben! It's kind t' me! It don't b'ar me no grudges fur what I never knowed an' couldn't help!

EBEN: Maw b'ars him a grudge.

ABBIE: Waal, so does all o' us.

EBEN: Ay-eh. (*With passion.*) I does, by God!

ABBIE (*taking one of his hands in hers and patting it*): Thar! Don't git riled thinkin' o' him. Think o' yer Maw who's kind t' us. Tell me about yer Maw, Eben.

EBEN: They hain't nothin' much. She was kind. She was good.

ABBIE (*Putting one arm over his shoulder. He does not seem to notice — passionately.*): I'll be kind an' good t' ye!

EBEN: Sometimes she used t' sing fur me.

ABBIE: I'll sing fur ye!

EBEN: This was her hum. This was her farm.

ABBIE: This is my hum! This is my farm!

EBEN: He married her t' steal 'em. She was soft an' easy. He couldn't 'preciate her.

ABBIE: He can't 'preciate me!

EBEN: He murdered her with his hardness.

ABBIE: He's murderin' me!

EBEN: She died. (*A pause.*) Sometimes she used to sing fur me. (*He bursts into a fit of sobbing.*)

ABBIE (*both her arms around him — with wild passion*): I'll sing fur ye! I'll die fur ye! (*In spite of her overwhelming desire for him, there is a sincere maternal love in her manner and voice — a horribly frank mixture of lust and mother love.*) Don't cry, Eben! I'll take yer Maw's place! I'll be everythin' she was t' ye! Let me kiss ye, Eben! (*She pulls his head around. He makes a bewildered pretense of resistance. She is tender.*) Don't be afeered! I'll kiss ye pure, Eben — same 's if I was a Maw t' ye — an' ye kin kiss me back 's if yew was my son — my boy — sayin' good-night t' me! Kiss me, Eben. (*They kiss in restrained fashion. Then suddenly wild passion overcomes her. She kisses him lustfully again and again and he flings his arms about her and returns her kisses. Suddenly, as in the bedroom, he frees himself from her violently and springs to his feet. He is trembling all over, in a strange state of terror. Abbie strains her arms toward him with fierce pleading.*) Don't ye leave me, Eben! Can't ye see it hain't enuf — lovin' ye like a Maw — can't ye see it's got t' be that an' more — much more — a hundred times more — fur me t' be happy — fur yew t' be happy?

EBEN (*to the presence he feels in the room*): Maw! Maw! What d'ye want? What air ye tellin' me?

ABBIE: She's tellin' ye t' love me. She knows I love ye an' I'll be good t' ye. Can't ye feel it? Don't ye know? She's tellin' ye t' love me, Eben!

EBEN: Ay-eh. I feel — mebbe she — but — I can't figger out — why — when ye've stole her place — here in her hum — in the parlor whar she was —

ABBIE (*fiercely*): She knows I love ye!

EBEN (*his face suddenly lighting up with a fierce, triumphant grin*): I see it! I sees why. It's her vengeance on him — so's she kin rest quiet in her grave!

ABBIE (*wildly*): Vengeance o' God on the hull o' us! What d'we give a durn? I love ye, Eben! God knows I love ye! (*She stretches out her arms for him.*)

EBEN (*throws himself on his knees beside the sofa and grabs her in his arms — releasing all his pent-up passion*): An' I love ye, Abbie! — now I kin say it! I been dyin' fur want o' ye — every hour since ye come! I love ye! (*Their lips meet in a fierce, bruising kiss.*)

Scene IV

(*Exterior of the farmhouse. It is just dawn. The front door at right is opened and Eben comes out and walks around to the gate. He is dressed in his working clothes. He seems changed. His face wears a bold and confident expression, he is grinning to himself with evident satisfaction. As he gets near the gate, the window of the parlor is heard opening and the shutters are flung back and Abbie sticks her head out. Her hair tumbles over her shoulders in disarray, her face is flushed, she looks at Eben with tender, languorous eyes and calls softly.*)

ABBIE: Eben. (*As he turns — playfully.*) Jest one more kiss afore ye go. I'm goin' to miss ye fearful all day.

EBEN: An' me yew, ye kin bet! (*He goes to her. They kiss several times. He draws away, laughingly.*) Thar. That's enuf, hain't it? Ye won't hev none left fur next time.

ABBIE: I got a million o' 'em left fur yew! (*Then a bit anxiously.*) D'ye r'ally love me, Eben?

EBEN (*emphatically*): I like ye better'n any gal I ever knowed! That's gospel!

ABBIE: Likin' hain't lovin'.

EBEN: Waal then — I love ye. Now air yew satisfied?

ABBIE: Ay-eh, I be. (*She smiles at him adoringly.*)

EBEN: I better git t' the barn. The old critter's liable t' suspicion an' come sneakin' up.

ABBIE (*with a confident laugh*): Let him! I kin allus pull the wool over his eyes. I'm goin' t' leave the shutters open and let in the sun 'n' air. This room's been dead long enuf. Now it's goin' t' be my room!

EBEN (*frowning*): Ay-eh.

ABBIE (*hastily*): I meant — our room.

EBEN: Ay-eh.

ABBIE: We made it our'n last night, didn't we? We give it life — our lovin' did. (*A pause.*)

EBEN (*with a strange look*): Maw's gone back t' her grave. She kin sleep now.

ABBIE: May she rest in peace! (*Then tenderly rebuking.*) Ye oughtn't t' talk o' sad thin's — this mornin'.

EBEN: It jest come up in my mind o' itself.

ABBIE: Don't let it. (*He doesn't answer. She yawns.*) Waal, I'm a-goin' t' steal a wink o' sleep. I'll tell the Old Man I hain't feelin' pert. Let him git his own vittles.

EBEN: I see him comin' from the barn. Ye better look smart an' git upstairs.

ABBIE: Ay-eh. Good-by. Don't ferget me. (*She throws him a kiss. He grins — then squares his shoulders and awaits his father confidently. Cabot walks slowly up from the left, staring up at the sky with a vague face.*)

EBEN (*jovially*): Mornin', Paw. Star-gazin' in daylight?

CABOT: Purty, hain't it?

EBEN (*looking around him possessively*): It's a durned purty farm.

CABOT: I mean the sky.

EBEN (*grinning*): How d'ye know? Them eyes o' your'n can't see that fur. (*This tickles his humor and he slaps his thigh and laughs.*) Ho-ho! That's a good un!

CABOT (*grimly sarcastic*): Ye're feelin' right chipper, hain't ye? Whar'd ye steal the likker?

EBEN (*good-naturedly*): 'Tain't likker. Jest life. (*Suddenly holding out his hand — soberly.*) Yew 'n' me is quits. Let's shake hands.

CABOT (*suspiciously*): What's come over ye?

EBEN: Then don't. Mebbe it's jest as well. (*A moment's pause.*) What's come over me? (*Queerly.*) Didn't ye feel her passin' — goin' back t' her grave?

CABOT (*dully*): Who?

EBEN: Maw. She kin rest now an' sleep content. She's quit with ye.

CABOT (*confusedly*): I rested. I slept good — down with the cows. They know how t' sleep. They're teachin' me.

EBEN (*suddenly jovial again*): Good fur the cows! Waal — ye better git t' work.

CABOT (*grimly amused*): Air yew bossin' me, ye calf?

EBEN (*beginning to laugh*): Ay-eh! I'm bossin' yew! Ha-ha-ha! See how ye like it! Ha-ha-ha! I'm the prize rooster o' this roost. Ha-ha-ha! (*He goes off toward the barn laughing.*)

CABOT (*looks after him with scornful pity*): Soft-headed. Like his Maw. Dead spit 'n' image. No hope in him! (*He spits with contemptuous disgust.*) A born fool! (*Then matter-of-factly.*) Waal — I'm gittin' peckish. (*He goes toward door.*)

PART III • *Scene 1*

(*A night in late spring the following year. The kitchen and the two bedrooms upstairs are shown. The two bedrooms are dimly lighted by a tallow candle in each. Eben is sitting on the side of the bed in his room, his chin propped on his fists, his face a study of the struggle he is making to understand his conflicting emotions. The noisy laughter and music from below where a kitchen dance is in progress annoy and distract him. He scowls at the floor.*)

(*In the next room a cradle stands beside the double bed.*)

(*In the kitchen all is festivity. The stove has been taken down to give more room to the dancers. The chairs, with wooden benches added, have been pushed back against the walls. On these are seated, squeezed in tight against one another, farmers and their wives and their young folks of both sexes from the neighboring farms. They are all chattering and laughing loudly. They evidently have some secret joke in common. There is no end of winking, of nudging, of meaning nods of the*

head toward Cabot who, in a state of extreme hilarious excitement increased by the amount he has drunk, is standing near the rear door where there is a small keg of whisky and serving drinks to all the men. In the left corner, front, dividing the attention with her husband, Abbie is sitting in a rocking chair, a shawl wrapped about her shoulders. She is very pale, her face is thin and drawn, her eyes are fixed anxiously on the open door in rear as if waiting for someone.*)

(*The musician is tuning up his fiddle, seated in the far right corner. He is a lanky young fellow with a long, weak face. His pale eyes blink incessantly and he grins about him slyly with a greedy malice.*)

ABBIE (*suddenly turning to a young girl on her right*): Whar's Eben?

YOUNG GIRL (*eyeing her scornfully*): I dunno, Mrs. Cabot. I hain't seen Eben in ages. (*Meaningly.*) Seems like he's spent most o' his time t' hum since yew come.

ABBIE (*vaguely*): I tuk his Maw's place.

YOUNG GIRL: Ay-eh. So I've heerd. (*She turns away to retail this bit of gossip to her mother sitting next to her. Abbie turns to her left to a big stoutish middle-aged man whose flushed face and starting eyes show the amount of "likker" he has consumed.*)

ABBIE: Ye hain't seen Eben, hev ye?

MAN: No, I hain't. (*Then he adds with a wink.*) If yew hain't, who would?

ABBIE: He's the best dancer in the county. He'd ought t' come an' dance.

MAN (*with a wink*): Mebbe he's doin' the dutiful an' walkin' the kid t' sleep. It's a boy, hain't it?

ABBIE (*nodding vaguely*): Ay-eh — born two weeks back — purty's a picter.

MAN: They all is — t' their Maws. (*Then in a whisper, with a nudge and a leer.*) Listen, Abbie — if ye ever git tired o' Eben, remember me! Don't fergit now! (*He looks at her uncomprehending face for a second — then grunts disgustedly.*) Waal — guess I'll likker agin. (*He goes over and joins Cabot who is arguing noisily with an old farmer over cows. They all drink.*)

ABBIE (*this time appealing to nobody in particular*): Wonder what Eben's a-doin'? (*Her remark is repeated down the line with many a guffaw and titter until it reaches the fiddler. He fastens his blinking eyes on Abbie.*)

FIDDLER (*raising his voice*): Bet I kin tell ye, Abbie, what Eben's doin'! He's down t' the church offerin' up prayers o' thanksgivin'. (*They all titter expectantly.*)

A MAN: What fur? (*Another titter.*)

FIDDLER: 'Cause unto him a — (*He hesitates just long enough.*) brother is born! (*A roar of laughter. They all look from Abbie to Cabot. She is oblivious, staring at the door. Cabot, although he hasn't heard the words, is irritated by the laughter and steps forward, glaring about him. There is an immediate silence.*)

CABOT: What're ye all bleatin' about — like a flock o' goats? Why don't ye dance, damn ye? I axed ye here t' dance — t' eat, drink an' be merry — an' thar ye set cacklin' like a lot o' wet hens with the pip! Ye've swilled my likker an' guzzled my vittles like hogs, hain't ye? Then dance fur me, can't ye? That's fa'r an' squar', hain't it? (*A grumble of resentment goes around but they are all evidently in too much awe of him to express it openly.*)

FIDDLER (*slyly*): We're waitin' fur Eben. (*A suppressed laugh.*)

CABOT (*with a fierce exultation*): T'hell with Eben! Eben's done fur now! I got a new son! (*His mood switching with drunken suddenness.*) But ye needn't t' laugh at Eben, none o' ye! He's my blood, if he be a dumb fool. He's better nor any o' yew! He kin do a day's work a'most up t' what I kin — an' that'd put any o' yew pore critters t' shame!

FIDDLER: An' he kin do a good night's work, too! (*A roar of laughter.*)

CABOT: Laugh, ye damn fools! Ye're right jist the same, Fiddler. He kin work day an' night too, like I kin, if need be!

OLD FARMER (*from behind the keg where he is weaving drunkenly back and forth — with great simplicity*): They hain't many t' touch ye, Ephraim — a son at seventy-six. That's a hard man fur ye! I be on'y sixty-eight an' I couldn't do it. (*A roar of laughter in which Cabot joins uproariously.*)

CABOT (*slapping him on the back*): I'm sorry fur ye, Hi. I'd never suspicion sech weakness from a boy like yew!

OLD FARMER: An' I never reckoned yew had it in ye nuther, Ephraim. (*There is another laugh.*)

CABOT (*suddenly grim*): I got a lot in me — a hell of a lot — folks don't know on. (*Turning to the fiddler.*) Fiddle 'er up, durn ye! Give 'em somethin' t' dance t'! What air ye, an ornament? Hain't this a celebration? Then grease yer elbow an' go it!

FIDDLER (*seizes a drink which the Old Farmer holds out to him and downs it*): Here goes! (*He starts to fiddle "Lady of the Lake." Four young fellows and four girls form in two lines and dance a square dance. The Fiddler shouts directions for the different movements, keeping his words in the rhythm of the music and interspersing them with jocular personal remarks to the dancers themselves. The people seated along the walls stamp their feet and clap their hands in unison. Cabot is especially active in this respect. Only Abbie remains apathetic, staring at the door as if she were alone in a silent room.*)

FIDDLER: Swing your partner t' the right! That's it, Jim! Give her a b'ar hug. Her Maw hain't lookin'. (*Laughter.*) Change partners! That suits ye, don't it, Essie, now ye got Reub afore ye? Look at her redden up, will ye? Waal, life is short an' so's love, as the feller says. (*Laughter.*)

CABOT (*excitedly, stamping his foot*): Go it, boys! Go it, gals!

FIDDLER (*with a wink at the others*): Ye're the spryest seventy-six ever I sees, Ephraim! Now if ye'd on'y

good eyesight . . . ! (*Suppressed laughter. He gives Cabot no chance to retort but roars.*) Promenade! Ye're walkin' like a bride down the aisle, Sarah! Waal, while they's life they's allus hope, I've heerd tell. Swing your partner to the left! Gosh A'mighty, look at Johnny Cook high-steppin'! They hain't goin' t' be much strength left fur howin' in the corn lot t'morrow. (*Laughter.*)

CABOT: Go it! Go it! (*Then suddenly, unable to restrain himself any longer, he prances into the midst of the dancers, scattering them, waving his arms about wildly.*) Ye're all hoofs! Git out o' my road! Give me room! I'll show ye dancin'. Ye're all too soft! (*He pushes them roughly away. They crowd back toward the walls, muttering, looking at him resentfully.*)

FIDDLER (*jeeringly*): Go it, Ephraim! Go it! (*He starts "Pop, Goes the Weasel," increasing the tempo with every verse until at the end he is fiddling crazily as fast as he can go.*)

CABOT (*Starts to dance, which he does very well and with tremendous vigor. Then he begins to improvise, cuts incredibly grotesque capers, leaping up and cracking his heels together, prancing around in a circle with body bent in an Indian war dance, then suddenly straightening up and kicking as high as he can with both legs. He is like a monkey on a string. And all the while he intersperses his antics with shouts and derisive comments.*): Whoop! Here's dancin' fur ye! Whoop! See that! Seventy-six, if I'm a day! Hard as iron yet! Beatin' the young 'uns like I allus done! Look at me! I'd invite ye t' dance on my hundredth birthday on'y ye'll all be dead by then. Ye're a sickly generation! Yer hearts air pink, not red! Yer veins is full o' mud an' water! I be the on'y man in the county! Whoop! See that! I'm a Injun! I've killed Injuns in the West afore ye was born — an' skulped 'em too! They's a arrer wound on my backside I c'd show ye! The hull tribe chased me. I outrun 'em all — with the arrer stuck in me! An' I tuk vengeance on 'em. Ten eyes fur an eye, that was my motter! Whoop! Look at me! I kin kick the ceilin' off the room! Whoop!

FIDDLER (*stops playing — exhaustedly*): God A'mighty, I got enuf. Ye got the devil's strength in ye.

CABOT (*delightedly*): Did I beat yew, too? Waal, ye played smart. Hev a swig. (*He pours whisky for himself and Fiddler. They drink. The others watch Cabot silently with cold, hostile eyes. There is a dead pause. The Fiddler rests. Cabot leans against the keg, panting, glaring around him confusedly. In the room above, Eben gets to his feet and tiptoes out the door in rear, appearing a moment later in the other bedroom. He moves silently, even frightenedly, toward the cradle and stands there looking down at the baby. His face is as vague as his reactions are confused, but there is a trace of tenderness, of interested discovery. At the same moment that he reaches the cradle, Abbie seems to sense something. She gets up weakly and goes to Cabot.*)

ABBIE: I'm goin' up t' the baby.

CABOT (*with real solicitation*): Air ye able fur the stairs? D'ye want me t' help ye, Abbie?

ABBIE: No. I'm able. I'll be down agen soon.

CABOT: Don't ye git wore out! He needs ye, remember — our son does! (*He grins affectionately, patting her on the back. She shrinks from his touch.*)

ABBIE (*dully*): Don't — tech me. I'm goin' — up. (*She goes. Cabot looks after her. A whisper goes around the room. Cabot turns. It ceases. He wipes his forehead streaming with sweat. He is breathing pantingly.*)

CABOT: I'm a-goin' out t' git fresh air. I'm feelin' a mite dizzy. Fiddle up thar! Dance, all o' ye! Here's likker fur them as wants it. Enjoy yerselves. I'll be back. (*He goes, closing the door behind him.*)

FIDDLER (*sarcastically*): Don't hurry none on our account! (*A suppressed laugh. He imitates Abbie.*) Whar's Eben? (*More laughter.*)

A WOMAN (*loudly*): What's happened in this house is plain as the nose on yer face! (*Abbie appears in the doorway upstairs and stands looking in surprise and adoration at Eben who does not see her.*)

A MAN: Ssshh! He's li'ble t' be listenin' at the door. That'd be like him. (*Their voices die to an intensive whispering. Their faces are concentrated on this gossip. A noise as of dead leaves in the wind comes from the room. Cabot has come out from the porch and stands by the gate, leaning on it, staring at the sky blinkingly. Abbie comes across the room silently. Eben does not notice her until quite near.*)

EBEN (*starting*): Abbie!

ABBIE: Ssshh! (*She throws her arms around him. They kiss — then bend over the cradle together.*) Ain't he purty? — dead spit 'n' image o' yew!

EBEN (*pleased*): Air he? I can't tell none.

ABBIE: E-zactly like!

EBEN (*frowningly*): I don't like this. I don't like lettin' on what's mine's his'n. I been doin' that all my life. I'm gittin' t' the end o' b'arin' it!

ABBIE (*putting her finger on his lips*): We're doin' the best we kin. We got t' wait. Somethin's bound t' happen. (*She puts her arms around him.*) I got t' go back.

EBEN: I'm goin' out. I can't b'ar it with the fiddle playin' an' the laughin'.

ABBIE: Don't git feelin' low. I love ye, Eben. Kiss me. (*He kisses her. They remain in each other's arms.*)

CABOT (*at the gate, confusedly*): Even the music can't drive it out — somethin'. Ye kin feel it droppin' off the elums, climbin' up the roof, sneakin' down the chimney, pokin' in the corners! They's no peace in houses, they's no rest livin' with folks. Somethin's always livin' with ye. (*With a deep sigh.*) I'll go t' the barn an' rest a spell. (*He goes wearily toward the barn.*)

FIDDLER (*tuning up*): Let's celebrate the old skunk gittin' fooled! We kin have some fun now he's went. (*He starts to fiddle "Turkey in the Straw." There is real merriment now. The young folks get up to dance.*)

Scene II

(*A half hour later — exterior — Eben is standing by the gate looking up at the sky, an expression of dumb pain bewildered by itself on his face. Cabot appears, returning from the barn, walking wearily, his eyes on the ground. He sees Eben and his whole mood immediately changes. He becomes excited, a cruel, triumphant grin comes to his lips, he strides up and slaps Eben on the back. From within comes the whining of the fiddle and the noise of stamping feet and laughing voices.*)

CABOT: So har ye be!

EBEN (*startled, stares at him with hatred for a moment — then dully*): Ay-eh.

CABOT (*surveying him jeeringly*): Why hain't ye been in t' dance? They was all axin' fur ye.

EBEN: Let 'em ax!

CABOT: They's a hull passel o' purty gals.

EBEN: T' hell with 'em!

CABOT: Ye'd ought t' be marryin' one o' 'em soon.

EBEN: I hain't marryin' no one.

CABOT: Ye might 'arn a share o' a farm that way.

EBEN (*with a sneer*): Like yew did, ye mean? I hain't that kind.

CABOT (*stung*): Ye lie! 'Twas yer Maw's folks aimed t' steal my farm from me.

EBEN: Other folks don't say so. (*After a pause — defiantly.*) An' I got a farm, anyways!

CABOT (*derisively*): Whar?

EBEN (*stamps a foot on the ground*): Har!

CABOT (*throws his head back and laughs coarsely*): Ho-ho! Ye hev, hev ye? Waal, that's a good un!

EBEN (*controlling himself — grimly*): Ye'll see!

CABOT (*stares at him suspiciously, trying to make him out — a pause — then with scornful confidence*): Ay-eh. I'll see. So'll ye. It's ye that's blind — blind as a mole underground. (*Eben suddenly laughs, one short sardonic bark: "Ha." A pause. Cabot peers at him with renewed suspicion.*) What air ye hawin' 'bout? (*Eben turns away without answering. Cabot grows angry.*) God A'mighty, yew air a dumb dunce! They's nothin' in that thick skull o' your'n but noise — like a empty keg it be! (*Eben doesn't seem to hear. Cabot's rage grows.*) Yewr farm! God A'mighty! If ye wa'n't a born donkey ye'd know ye'll never own stick nor stone on it, specially now arter him bein' born. It's his'n, I tell ye — his'n arter I die — but I'll live a hundred jest t' fool ye all — an' he'll be growed then — yewr age a'most! (*Eben laughs again his sardonic "Ha." This drives Cabot into a fury.*) Ha? Ye think ye kin git 'round that someways, do ye? Waal, it'll be her'n, too — Abbie's — ye won't git 'round her — she knows yer tricks — she'll be too much fur ye — she wants the farm her'n — she was afeerd o' ye — she told me ye was sneakin' 'round tryin' t' make love t' her t' git her on yer side . . . ye . . . ye mad fool, ye! (*He raises his clenched fists threateningly.*)

EBEN (*is confronting him, choking with rage*): Ye lie, ye old skunk! Abbie never said no sech thing!

CABOT (*suddenly triumphant when he sees how shaken Eben is*): She did. An' I says, I'll blow his brains t' the top o' them elums — an' she says no that hain't sense, who'll ye git t'help ye on the farm in his place — an' then she says yew'n me ought t' have a son — I know we kin, she says — an' I says, if we do, ye kin have anythin' I've got ye've a mind t'. An' she says, I wants Eben cut off so's this farm'll be mine when ye die! (*With terrible gloating.*) An' that's what's happened, hain't it? An' the farm's her'n! An' the dust o' the road — that's you'rn! Ha! Now who's hawin'?

EBEN (*has been listening, petrified with grief and rage — suddenly laughs wildly and brokenly*): Ha-ha-ha! So that's her sneakin' game — all along! — like I suspicioned at fust — t' swaller it all — an' me, too...! (*Madly.*) I'll murder her! (*He springs toward the porch but Cabot is quicker and gets in between.*)

CABOT: No, ye don't!

EBEN: Git out o' my road! (*He tries to throw Cabot aside. They grapple in what becomes immediately a murderous struggle. The old man's concentrated strength is too much for Eben. Cabot gets one hand on his throat and presses him back across the stone wall. At the same moment, Abbie comes out on the porch. With a stifled cry she runs toward them.*)

ABBIE: Eben! Ephraim! (*She tugs at the hand on Eben's throat.*) Let go, Ephraim! Ye're chokin' him!

CABOT (*Removes his hand and flings Eben sideways full length on the grass, gasping and choking. With a cry, Abbie kneels beside him, trying to take his head on her lap, but he pushes her away. Cabot stands looking down with fierce triumph.*): Ye needn't t've fret, Abbie, I wa'n't aimin' t' kill him. He hain't wuth hangin' fur — not by a hell of a sight! (*More and more triumphantly.*) Seventy-six an' him not thirty yit — an' look whar he be fur thinkin' his Paw was easy! No, by God, I hain't easy! An' him upstairs, I'll raise him t' be like me! (*He turns to leave them.*) I'm goin' in an' dance! — sing an' celebrate! (*He walks to the porch — then turns with a great grin.*) I don't calc'late it's left in him, but if he gits pesky, Abbie, ye jest sing out. I'll come a-runnin' an' by the Etarnal, I'll put him across my knee an' birch him! Ha-ha-ha! (*He goes into the house laughing. A moment later his loud "whoop" is heard.*)

ABBIE (*tenderly*): Eben. Air ye hurt? (*She tries to kiss him but he pushes her violently away and struggles to a sitting position.*)

EBEN (*gaspingly*): T'hell — with ye!

ABBIE (*not believing her ears*): It's me, Eben — Abbie — don't ye know me?

EBEN (*glowering at her with hatred*): Ay-eh — I know ye — now! (*He suddenly breaks down, sobbing weakly.*)

ABBIE (*fearfully*): Eben — what's happened t' ye — why did ye look at me 's if ye hated me?

EBEN (*violently, between sobs and gasps*): I do hate ye! Ye're a whore — a damn trickin' whore!

ABBIE (*shrinking back horrified*): Eben! Ye don't know what ye're sayin'!

EBEN (*scrambling to his feet and following her — accusingly*): Ye're nothin' but a stinkin' passel o' lies! Ye've been lyin' t' me every word ye spoke, day an' night, since we fust — done it. Ye've kept sayin' ye loved me....

ABBIE (*frantically*): I do love ye! (*She takes his hand but he flings hers away.*)

EBEN (*unheeding*): Ye've made a fool o' me — a sick, dumb fool — a-purpose! Ye've been on'y playin' yer sneakin', stealin' game all along — gittin' me t' lie with ye so's ye'd hev a son he'd think was his'n, an' makin' him promise he'd give ye the farm and let me eat dust, if ye did git him a son! (*Staring at her with anguished, bewildered eyes.*) They must be a devil livin' in ye! T'ain't human t' be as bad as that be!

ABBIE (*stunned — dully*): He told yew...?

EBEN: Hain't it true? It hain't no good in yew lyin'.

ABBIE (*pleadingly*): Eben, listen — ye must listen — it was long ago — afore we done nothin' — yew was scornin' me — goin' t' see Min — when I was lovin' ye — an' I said it t' him t' git vengeance on ye!

EBEN (*Unheedingly. With tortured passion.*): I wish ye was dead! I wish I was dead along with ye afore this come! (*Ragingly.*) But I'll git my vengeance too! I'll pray Maw t' come back t' help me — t' put her cuss on yew an' him!

ABBIE (*brokenly*): Don't ye, Eben! Don't ye! (*She throws herself on her knees before him, weeping.*) I didn't mean t' do bad t'ye! Fergive me, won't ye?

EBEN (*not seeming to hear her — fiercely*): I'll git squar' with the old skunk — an' yew! I'll tell him the truth 'bout the son he's so proud o'! Then I'll leave ye here t' pizen each other — with Maw comin' out o' her grave at nights — an' I'll go t' the gold fields o' Californi-a whar Sim an' Peter be!

ABBIE (*terrified*): Ye won't — leave me? Ye can't!

EBEN (*with fierce determination*): I'm a-goin', I tell ye! I'll git rich thar an' come back an' fight him fur the farm he stole — an' I'll kick ye both out in the road — t' beg an' sleep in the woods — an' yer son along with ye — t' starve an' die! (*He is hysterical at the end.*)

ABBIE (*with a shudder — humbly*): He's yewr son, too, Eben.

EBEN (*torturedly*): I wish he never was born! I wish he'd die this minit! I wish I'd never sot eyes on him! It's him — yew havin' him — a-purpose t' steal — that's changed everythin'!

ABBIE (*gently*): Did ye believe I loved ye — afore he come?

EBEN: Aye-eh — like a dumb ox!

ABBIE: An' ye don't believe no more?

EBEN: B'lieve a lyin' thief! Ha!

ABBIE (*shudders — then humbly*): An' did ye r'ally love me afore?

EBEN (*brokenly*): Ay-eh — an' ye was trickin' me!

ABBIE: An' ye don't love me now!

EBEN (*violently*): I hate ye, I tell ye!

ABBIE: An' ye're truly goin' West — goin' t' leave me — all account o' him being born?

EBEN: I'm a-goin' in the mornin' — or may God strike me t' hell!

ABBIE (*after a pause — with a dreadful cold intensity — slowly*): If that's what his comin's done t' me — killin' yewr love — takin' yew away — my on'y joy — the on'y joy I ever knowed — like heaven t' me — purtier'n heaven — then I hate him, too, even if I be his Maw!

EBEN (*bitterly*): Lies! Ye love him! He'll steal the farm fur ye! (*Brokenly.*) But t'ain't the farm so much — not no more — it's yew foolin' me — gittin' me t' love ye — lyin' yew loved me — jest t' git a son t' steal!

ABBIE (*distractedly*): He won't steal! I'd kill him fust! I do love ye! I'll prove t' ye . . . !

EBEN (*harshly*): T'ain't no use lyin' no more. I'm deaf t' ye! (*He turns away.*) I hain't seein' ye agen. Good-by!

ABBIE (*pale with anguish*): Hain't ye even goin' t' kiss me — not once — arter all we loved?

EBEN (*in a hard voice*): I hain't wantin' t' kiss ye never agen! I'm wantin' t' forgit I ever sot eyes on ye!

ABBIE: Eben! — ye mustn't — wait a spell — I want t' tell ye. . . .

EBEN: I'm a-goin' in t' git drunk. I'm a-goin' t' dance.

ABBIE (*clinging to his arm — with passionate earnestness*): If I could make it —'s if he'd never come up between us — if I could prove t' ye I wa'n't schemin' t' steal from ye — so's everythin' could be jest the same with us, lovin' each other jest the same, kissin' an' happy the same's we've been happy afore he come — if I could do it — ye'd love me agen, wouldn't ye? Ye'd kiss me agen? Ye wouldn't never leave me, would ye?

EBEN (*moved*): I calc'late not. (*Then shaking her hand off his arm — with a bitter smile.*) But ye hain't God, be ye?

ABBIE (*exultantly*): Remember ye've promised! (*Then with strange intensity.*) Mebbe I kin take back one thin' God does!

EBEN (*peering at her*): Ye're gittin' cracked, hain't ye? (*Then going toward door.*) I'm a-goin' t' dance.

ABBIE (*calls after him intensely*): I'll prove t' ye! I'll prove I love ye better'n. . . . (*He goes in the door, not seeming to hear. She remains standing where she is, looking after him — then she finishes desperately.*) Better'n everythin' else in the world!

Scene III

(*Just before dawn in the morning — shows the kitchen and Cabot's bedroom. In the kitchen, by the light of a tallow candle on the table, Eben is sitting, his chin propped on his hands, his drawn face blank and expressionless. His carpetbag is on the floor beside him. In the bedroom, dimly lighted by a small whale-oil lamp, Cabot lies asleep. Abbie is bending over the cradle, listening, her face full of terror yet with an undercurrent of desperate triumph. Suddenly, she breaks down and sobs, appears about to throw herself on her knees beside the cradle, but the old man turns restlessly, groaning in his sleep, and she controls herself, and, shrinking away from the cradle with a gesture of horror, backs swiftly toward the door in rear and goes out. A moment later she comes into the kitchen and, running to Eben, flings her arms about his neck and kisses him wildly. He hardens himself, he remains unmoved and cold, he keeps his eyes straight ahead.*)

ABBIE (*hysterically*): I done it, Eben! I told ye I'd do it! I've proved I love ye — better'n everythin' — so's ye can't never doubt me no more!

EBEN (*dully*): Whatever ye done, it hain't no good now.

ABBIE (*wildly*): Don't ye say that! Kiss me, Eben, won't ye? I need ye t' kiss me arter what I done! I need ye t' say ye love me!

EBEN (*kisses her without emotion — dully*): That's fur good-by. I'm a-goin' soon.

ABBIE: No! No! Ye won't go — not now!

EBEN (*going on with his own thoughts*): I been a-thinkin' — an' I hain't goin' t' tell Paw nothin'. I'll leave Maw t' take vengeance on ye. If I told him, the old skunk'd jest be stinkin' mean enuf to take it out on that baby. (*His voice showing emotion in spite of him.*) An' I don't want nothin' bad t' happen t' him. He hain't t' blame fur yew. (*He adds with a certain queer pride.*) An' he looks like me! An' by God, he's mine! An' some day I'll be a-comin' back an' . . . !

ABBIE (*too absorbed in her own thoughts to listen to him — pleadingly*): They's no cause fur ye t' go now — they's no sense — it's all the same's it was — they's nothin' come b'tween us now — arter what I done!

EBEN (*Something in her voice arouses him. He stares at her a bit frightenedly.*): Ye look mad, Abbie. What did ye do?

ABBIE: I — I killed him, Eben.

EBEN (*amazed*): Ye killed him?

ABBIE (*dully*): Ay-eh.

EBEN (*recovering from his astonishment — savagely*): An' serves him right! But we got t' do somethin' quick t' make it look s'if the old skunk'd killed himself when he was drunk. We kin prove by 'em all how drunk he got.

ABBIE (*wildly*): No! No! Not him! (*Laughing distractedly.*) But that's what I ought t' done, hain't it? I oughter killed him instead! Why didn't ye tell me?

EBEN (*appalled*): Instead? What d'ye mean?

ABBIE: Not him.

EBEN (*his face grown ghastly*): Not — not that baby!

ABBIE (*dully*): Ay-eh!

EBEN (*falls to his knees as if he'd been struck — his voice trembling with horror*): Oh, God A'mighty! A'mighty God! Maw, whar was ye, why didn't ye stop her?

ABBIE (*simply*): She went back t' her grave that night we fust done it, remember? I hain't felt her about since. (*A pause. Eben hides his head in his hands, trembling all over as if he had the ague. She goes on dully.*) I left the piller over his little face. Then he killed himself. He stopped breathin'. (*She begins to weep softly.*)

EBEN (*rage beginning to mingle with grief*): He looked like me. He was mine, damn ye!

ABBIE (*slowly and brokenly*): I didn't want t' do it. I hated myself fur doin' it. I loved him. He was so purty — dead spit 'n' image o' yew. But I loved yew more — an' yew was goin' away — far off whar I'd never see ye agen, never kiss ye, never feel ye pressed agin me agen — an' ye said ye hated me fur havin' him — ye said ye hated him an' wished he was dead — ye said if it hain't been fur him comin' it'd be the same's afore between us.

EBEN (*unable to endure this, springs to his feet in a fury, threatening her, his twitching fingers seeming to reach out for her throat*): Ye lie! I never said — I never dreamed ye'd — I'd cut off my head afore I'd hurt his finger!

ABBIE (*piteously, sinking on her knees*): Eben, don't ye look at me like that — hatin' me — not after what I done fur ye — fur us — so's we could be happy agen —

EBEN (*furiously now*): Shut up, or I'll kill ye! I see yer game now — the same old sneakin' trick — ye're aimin' t' blame me fur the murder ye done!

ABBIE (*moaning — putting her hands over her ears*): Don't ye, Eben! Don't ye! (*She grasps his legs.*)

EBEN (*his mood suddenly changing to horror, shrinks away from her*): Don't ye tech me! Ye're pizen! How could ye — t' murder a pore little critter — Ye must've swapped yer soul t' hell! (*Suddenly raging.*) Ha! I kin see why ye done it! Not the lies ye jest told — but 'cause ye wanted t' steal agen — steal the last thin' ye'd left me — my part o' him — no, the hull o' him — ye saw he looked like me — ye knowed he was all mine — an' ye couldn't b'ar it — I know ye! Ye killed him fur bein' mine! (*All this has driven him almost insane. He makes a rush past her for the door — then turns — shaking both fists at her, violently.*) But I'll take vengeance now! I'll git the Sheriff! I'll tell him everythin'! Then I'll sing "I'm off to Californi-a!" an' go — gold — Golden Gate — gold sun — fields o' gold in the West! (*This last he half shouts, half croons incoherently, suddenly breaking off passionately.*) I'm a-goin' fur the Sheriff t' come an' git ye! I want ye tuk away, locked up from me! I can't stand t' luk at ye! Murderer an' thief 'r not, ye still tempt me! I'll give ye up t' the Sheriff! (*He turns and runs out, around the corner of house,*

panting and sobbing, and breaks into a swerving sprint down the road.*)

ABBIE (*struggling to her feet, runs to the door, calling after him*): I love ye, Eben! I love ye! (*She stops at the door weakly, swaying, about to fall.*) I don't care what ye do — if ye'll on'y love me agen — (*She falls limply to the floor in a faint.*)

Scene IV

(*About an hour later. Same as scene III. Shows the kitchen and Cabot's bedroom. It is after dawn. The sky is brilliant with the sunrise. In the kitchen, Abbie sits at the table, her body limp and exhausted, her head bowed down over her arms, her face hidden. Upstairs, Cabot is still asleep but awakens with a start. He looks toward the window and gives a snort of surprise and irritation — throws back the covers and begins hurriedly pulling on his clothes. Without looking behind him, he begins talking to Abbie whom he supposes beside him.*)

CABOT: Thunder 'n' lightin', Abbie! I hain't slept this late in fifty year! Looks 's if the sun was full riz a'most. Must've been the dancin' an' likker. Must be gittin' old. I hope Eben's t' wuk. Ye might've tuk the trouble t' rouse me, Abbie. (*He turns — sees no one there — surprised.*) Waal — whar air she? Gittin' vittles, I calc'late. (*He tiptoes to the cradle and peers down — proudly.*) Mornin', sonny. Purty's a picter! Sleepin' sound. He don't beller all night like most o' 'em. (*He goes quietly out the door in rear — a few moments later enters kitchen — sees Abbie — with satisfaction.*) So thar ye be. Ye got any vittles cooked?

ABBIE (*without moving*): No.

CABOT (*coming to her, almost sympathetically*): Ye feelin' sick?

ABBIE: No.

CABOT (*Pats her on shoulder. She shudders.*): Ye'd best lie down a spell. (*Half jocularly.*) Yer son'll be needin' ye soon. He'd ought t' wake up with a gnashin' appetite, the sound way he's sleepin'.

ABBIE (*shudders — then in a dead voice*): He hain't never goin' t' wake up.

CABOT (*jokingly*): Takes after me this mornin'. I hain't slept so late in . . .

ABBIE: He's dead.

CABOT (*stares at her — bewilderedly*): What. . . .

ABBIE: I killed him.

CABOT (*stepping back from her — aghast*): Air ye drunk —'r crazy —'r . . . ?

ABBIE (*suddenly lifts her head and turns on him — wildly*): I killed him, I tell ye! I smothered him. Go up an' see if ye don't b'lieve me!

(*Cabot stares at her a second, then bolts out the rear door, can be heard bounding up the stairs, and rushes into the bedroom and over to the cradle. Abbie has sunk back lifelessly into her former position. Cabot puts his hand down on the body in the crib. An expression of fear and horror comes over his face.*)

CABOT (*shrinking away — tremblingly*): God A'mighty! God A'mighty. (*He stumbles out the door — in a short while returns to the kitchen — comes to Abbie, the stunned expression still on his face — hoarsely.*) Why did ye do it? Why? (*As she doesn't answer, he grabs her violently by the shoulder and shakes her.*) I ax ye why ye done it! Ye'd better tell me 'r . . . !

ABBIE (*gives him a furious push which sends him staggering back and springs to her feet — with wild rage and hatred*): Don't ye dare tech me! What right hev ye t' question me 'bout him? He wa'n't yewr son! Think I'd have a son by yew? I'd die fust! I hate the sight o' ye an' allus did! It's yew I should've murdered, if I'd had good sense! I hate ye! I love Eben. I did from the fust. An' he was Eben's son — mine an' Eben's — not your'n!

CABOT (*stands looking at her dazedly — a pause — finding his words with an effort — dully*): That was it — what I felt — pokin' round the corners — while ye lied — holdin' yerself from me — sayin' ye'd already conceived — (*He lapses into crushed silence — then with a strange emotion.*) He's dead, sart'n. I felt his heart. Pore little critter! (*He blinks back one tear, wiping his sleeve across his nose.*)

ABBIE (*hysterically*): Don't ye! Don't ye! (*She sobs unrestrainedly.*)

CABOT (*with a concentrated effort that stiffens his body into a rigid line and hardens his face into a stony mask — through his teeth to himself*): I got t' be — like a stone — a rock o' jedgment! (*A pause. He gets complete control over himself — harshly.*) If he was Eben's, I be glad he air gone! An' mebbe I suspicioned it all along. I felt they was somethin' onnateral — somewhars — the house got so lonesome — an' cold — drivin' me down t' the barn — t' the beasts o' the field. . . . Ay-eh. I must've suspicioned — somethin'. Ye didn't fool me — not altogether, leastways — I'm too old a bird — growin' ripe on the bough. . . . (*He becomes aware he is wandering, straightens again, looks at Abbie with a cruel grin.*) So ye'd liked t' hev murdered me 'steed o' him, would ye? Waal, I'll live to a hundred! I'll live t' see ye hung! I'll deliver ye up t' the jedgment o' God an' the law! I'll git the Sheriff now. (*Starts for the door.*)

ABBIE (*dully*): Ye needn't. Eben's gone fur him.

CABOT (*amazed*): Eben — gone fur the Sheriff?

ABBIE: Ay-eh.

CABOT: T' inform agen ye?

ABBIE: Ay-eh.

CABOT (*considers this — a pause — then in a hard voice*): Waal, I'm thankful fur him savin' me the trouble. I'll git t' wuk. (*He goes to the door — then turns — in a voice full of strange emotion.*) He'd ought t' been my son, Abbie. Ye'd ought t' loved me.

I'm a man. If ye'd loved me, I'd never told no Sheriff on ye no matter what ye did, if they was t' brile me alive!

ABBIE (*defensively*): They's more to it nor yew know, makes him tell.

CABOT (*dryly*): Fur yewr sake, I hope they be. (*He goes out — comes around to the gate — stares up at the sky. His control relaxes. For a moment he is old and weary. He murmurs despairingly.*) God A'mighty, I be lonesomer'n ever! (*He hears running footsteps from the left, immediately is himself again. Eben runs in, panting exhaustedly, wild-eyed and mad looking. He lurches through the gate. Cabot grabs him by the shoulder. Eben stares at him dumbly.*) Did ye tell the Sheriff?

EBEN (*nodding stupidly*): Ay-eh.

CABOT (*gives him a push away that sends him sprawling — laughing with withering contempt*): Good fur ye! A prime chip o' yer Maw ye be! (*He goes toward the barn, laughing harshly. Eben scrambles to his feet. Suddenly Cabot turns — grimly threatening.*) Git off this farm when the Sheriff takes her — or, by God, he'll have t' come back an' git me fur murder, too! (*He stalks off. Eben does not appear to have heard him. He runs to the door and comes into the kitchen. Abbie looks up with a cry of anguished joy. Eben stumbles over and throws himself on his knees beside her sobbing brokenly.*)

EBEN: Fergive me!

ABBIE (*happily*): Eben! (*She kisses him and pulls his head over against her breast.*)

EBEN: I love ye! Fergive me!

ABBIE (*ecstatically*): I'd fergive ye all the sins in hell fur sayin' that! (*She kisses his head, pressing it to her with a fierce passion of possession.*)

EBEN (*brokenly*): But I told the Sheriff. He's comin' fur ye!

ABBIE: I kin b'ar what happens t' me — now!

EBEN: I woke him up. I told him. He says, wait 'til I git dressed. I was waiting. I got to thinkin' o' yew. I got to thinkin' how I'd loved ye. It hurt like somethin' was bustin' in my chest an' head. I got t' cryin'. I knowed sudden I loved ye yet, an' allus would love ye!

ABBIE (*caressing his hair — tenderly*): My boy, hain't ye?

EBEN: I begun t' run back. I cut across the fields an' through the woods. I thought ye might have time t' run away — with me — an' . . .

ABBIE (*shaking her head*): I got t' take my punishment — t' pay fur my sin.

EBEN: Then I want t' share it with ye.

ABBIE: Ye didn't do nothin'.

EBEN: I put it in yer head. I wisht he was dead! I as much as urged ye t' do it!

ABBIE: No. It was me alone!

EBEN: I'm as guilty as yew be! He was the child o' our sin.

ABBIE (*lifting her head as if defying God*): I don't repent that sin! I hain't askin' God t' fergive that!

EBEN: Nor me — but it led up t' the other — an' the murder ye did, ye did 'count o' me — an' it's my murder, too, I'll tell the Sheriff — an' if ye deny it, I'll say we planned it t'gether — an' they'll all b'lieve me, fur they suspicion everythin' we've done, an' it'll seem likely an' true to 'em. An' it is true — way down. I did help ye — somehow.

ABBIE (*laying her head on his — sobbing*): No! I don't want yew t' suffer!

EBEN: I got t' pay fur my part o' the sin! An' I'd suffer wuss leavin' ye, goin' West, thinkin' o' ye day an' night, bein' out when yew was in — (*lowering his voice*) 'r bein' alive when yew was dead. (*A pause.*) I want t' share with ye, Abbie — prison 'r death 'r hell 'r anythin'! (*He looks into her eyes and forces a trembling smile.*) If I'm sharin' with ye, I won't feel lonesome, leastways.

ABBIE (*weakly*): Eben! I won't let ye! I can't let ye!

EBEN (*kissing her — tenderly*): Ye can't he'p yerself. I got ye beat fur once!

ABBIE (*forcing a smile — adoringly*): I hain't beat — s'long's I got ye!

EBEN (*hears the sound of feet outside*): Ssshh! Listen! They've come t' take us!

ABBIE: No, it's him. Don't give him no chance to fight ye, Eben. Don't say nothin' — no matter what he says. An' I won't neither. (*It is Cabot. He comes up from the barn in a great state of excitement and strides into the house and then into the kitchen. Eben is kneeling beside Abbie, his arm around her, hers around him. They stare straight ahead.*)

CABOT (*Stares at them, his face hard. A long pause — vindictively.*): Ye make a slick pair o' murderin' turtle doves! Ye'd ought t' be both hung on the same limb an' left thar t' swing in the breeze an' rot — a warnin' t' old fools like me t' b'ar their lonesomeness alone — an' fur young fools like ye t' hobble their lust. (*A pause. The excitement returns to his face, his eyes snap, he looks a bit crazy.*) I couldn't work today. I couldn't take no interest. T' hell with the farm! I'm leavin' it! I've turned the cows an' other stock loose! I've druv 'em into the woods whar they kin be free! By freein' 'em, I'm freein' myself! I'm quittin' here today! I'll set fire t' house an' barn an' watch 'em burn, an' I'll leave yer Maw t' haunt the ashes, an' I'll will the fields back t' God, so that nothin' human kin never touch 'em! I'll be a-goin' to Californi-a — t' jine Simeon an' Peter — true sons o' mine if they be dumb fools — an' the Cabots'll find Solomon's Mines t'gether! (*He suddenly cuts a mad caper.*) Whoop! What was the song they sung? "Oh, Californi-a! That's the land fur me." (*He sings this — then gets on his knees by the floorboard under which the money was hid.*) An' I'll sail thar on one o' the finest clippers I kin find! I've got the money! Pity ye didn't know whar this was hidden so's ye could steal. . . . (*He has pulled up the board. He stares —*

feels — stares again. A pause of dead silence. He slowly turns, slumping into a sitting position on the floor, his eyes like those of a dead fish, his face the sickly green of an attack of nausea. He swallows painfully several times — forces a weak smile at last.) So — ye did steal it!

EBEN (*emotionlessly*): I swapped it t' Sim an' Peter fur their share o' the farm — t' pay their passage t' Californi-a.

CABOT (*with one sardonic*): Ha! (*He begins to recover. Gets slowly to his feet — strangely.*) I calc'late God give it to 'em — not yew! God's hard, not easy! Mebbe they's easy gold in the West but it hain't God's gold. It hain't fur me. I kin hear His voice warnin' me agen t' be hard an' stay on my farm. I kin see his hand usin' Eben t' steal t' keep me from weakness. I kin feel I be in the palm o' His hand, His fingers guidin' me. (*A pause — then he mutters sadly.*) It's a-goin' t' be lonesomer now than ever it war afore — an' I'm gittin' old, Lord — ripe on the bough. . . . (*Then stiffening.*) Waal — what d'ye want? God's lonesome, hain't He? God's hard an' lonesome! (*A pause. The Sheriff with two men comes up the road from the left. They move cautiously to the door. The Sheriff knocks on it with the butt of his pistol.*)

SHERIFF: Open in the name o' the law! (*They start.*)

CABOT: They've come fur ye. (*He goes to the rear door.*) Come in, Jim! (*The three men enter. Cabot meets them in doorway.*) Jest a minit, Jim. I got 'em safe here. (*The Sheriff nods. He and his companions remain in the doorway.*)

EBEN (*suddenly calls*): I lied this mornin', Jim. I helped her to do it. Ye kin take me, too.

ABBIE (*brokenly*): No!

CABOT: Take 'em both. (*He comes forward — stares at Eben with a trace of grudging admiration.*) Purty good — fur yew! Waal, I got t' round up the stock. Good-by.

EBEN: Good-by.

ABBIE: Good-by. (*Cabot turns and strides past the men — comes out and around the corner of the house, his shoulders squared, his face stony, and stalks grimly toward the barn. In the meantime the Sheriff and men have come into the room.*)

SHERIFF (*embarrassedly*): Waal — we'd best start.

ABBIE: Wait. (*Turns to Eben.*) I love ye, Eben.

EBEN: I love ye, Abbie. (*They kiss. The three men grin and shuffle embarrassedly. Eben takes Abbie's hand. They go out the door in rear, the men following, and come from the house, walking hand in hand to the gate. Eben stops there and points to the sunrise sky.*) Sun's a-rizin'. Purty, hain't it?

ABBIE: Ay-eh. (*They both stand for a moment looking up raptly in attitudes strangely aloof and devout.*)

SHERIFF (*looking around at the farm enviously — to his companions*): It's a jim-dandy farm, no denyin'. Wished I owned it!

COMMENTARY

Stark Young (1881–1963)
REVIEW OF *DESIRE UNDER THE ELMS*   *1924*

Stark Young's sensitive review of this play contrasted with other reviewers. He saw the work as a significant advance for O'Neill and extensively discusses the drama in terms that reveal its importance. Young also gives particular praise to Walter Huston's performance and to the work's farmhouse setting. His final comments praise the writing in a specific scene "written with such poetry and terrible beauty as we rarely see in theatre."

Desire under the Elms, the first play by Eugene O'Neill to be produced since *Welded,* was presented last night at the Greenwich Village Theatre and proved to be as unlike that drama as it was unlike *The Hairy Ape* or *The Emperor Jones. Desire under the Elms* reverts in character to the earlier *Beyond the Horizon,* though it exhibits by comparison a fine progress in solidity and finish. It has less sentiment that this older piece and more passion; it is better written throughout; it has much tragic gloom and irony but a more mature conception and a more imaginative austerity.

Desire under the Elms is essentially a story of solitude, physical solitude, the solitude of the land, of men's dreams, of love, of life. The God behind the existence created on this New England farm is a harsh God, who is alone and is not understood. The minds of the people in this story are shaken and tinged with loneliness, with thwarted passion, with the trivial, the intense, the drab exaltation and denial of life. Underneath this solitude desire works, the redemption through love.

The children of old Cabot hate him. The youngest, the son of the second wife, remembers his dead mother, worked to death, and sees her about the place, risen from her grave. The father brings home a third wife. The two older sons go away to California; the younger stays and thinks to avenge his mother. In time he and the young wife come to love each other.

A son is born, which old Cabot thinks is to be heir to the farm, leaving the second wife's son adrift in the world. While a dance in honor of the newborn child goes on in the kitchen, the father and son quarrel outside; the son believes his father when he hears that the woman wanted a son only to cheat him out of the farm. He reviles her. To prove to him that it was the love of him and not the desire for the farm that had driven her to him, she kills the child. He runs off for the sheriff. The father turns the live stock loose in the woods and plans to go away, but when he finds the money gone from its hiding place, he believes that God another time has willed that he stand by the farm. The son returns from the sheriff's, he falls at the knees of the woman, takes part of the blame on himself, and they go away together to prison.

Robert Edmond Jones's setting for *Desire under the Elms* was profoundly dramatic. The end of a New England farmhouse with its overhanging elms was for all practical purposes built there on stage, with a wall of actual stone coming down to the footlights; a scene that was realistic but at the same time strangely and powerfully heightened in effect.

The general performance of the play was unusually adequate though not often on a level with the writing. Mary Morris, however, whose career as the fair Gertrude in *Fashion* last year was one of the flowers of the season's acting, played the wife in *Desire under the Elms* with a new and suppressed method that deepened at times into an admirable poignancy and a kind of grim, thin poetry that seemed the exact truth of her lines. Charles Ellis, though his work in earlier scenes was less successful or convincing, played with real poetry the passage where the boy is possessed with love for the woman and for his child. Walter Huston as the old man was everywhere trenchant, gaunt, fervid, harsh, as he should be in the part. In his ability to cover his gradations, to express the natural and convincing emotion, and to convey the harsh, inarticulate life embodied in this extraordinary portrait that Eugene O'Neill has drawn. Mr. Huston showed his talent and proved to be the best choice possible for the role.

The scene of *Desire under the Elms* that best illustrates the highest quality of the play is that in which we see the dance going on, the father outside the house, the young wife and her lover in the upstairs room in each other's arms beside the child's cradle, a scene written with such poetry and terrible beauty as we rarely see in the theatre, a scene that for these qualities of poetry, terror and at the same time unflinching realism rises above anything that Mr. O'Neill has written.

Bertolt Brecht

Among the most inventive and influential of modern playwrights, Bertolt Brecht (1898–1956) has left a legacy of important plays and theories about how those plays should be produced. Throughout most of his career he felt that drama should inform and awaken sensibilities, not just entertain or anesthetize an audience. Most of his plays concern philosophical and political issues, and some of them so threatened the Nazi regime that his works were burned publicly in Germany during the Third Reich.

At nineteen, Brecht worked as an orderly in a hospital during the last months of World War I. Seeing so much carnage and misery in the medical wards made him a lifelong pacifist. After the war he began writing plays while a student in Munich. His first successes in the Munich theater took the form of commentary on returned war veterans and on the questions of duty and heroism — which he treated negatively. His rejection of spiritual concepts was influenced by his readings of Hegel and the doctrines of Marx's dialectical materialism. Marx's theories predicted class struggles and based most social values in economic realities. Brecht eventually moved to Berlin, the theatrical center of Germany, and by 1926 was on his way to becoming a Communist.

Finding the political pressures in early Nazi Germany too frightening and dangerous for his writing, Brecht went into exile in 1933. He lived for a time in Scandinavia and later in the United States. After World War II Brecht and his wife returned to Berlin where, in 1949, he founded the Berliner Ensemble, which produced most of his later work. Brecht chose East Berlin as his home, in part because he felt his work could best be understood in a Communist setting. One irony is that his work has been even more widely appreciated and accepted in the West than in the former Communist eastern bloc.

Brecht wrote his most popular play in 1928, a musical in collaboration with the German composer Kurt Weill: *The Threepenny Opera*. The model for this play, the English writer John Gay's 1728 ballad opera *The Beggar's Opera*, provided Brecht with a perfect platform on which to comment satirically on the political and economic circumstances in Germany two hundred years after Gay wrote. The success of the Brecht-Weill collaboration — the work is still performed regularly — is due in part to Brecht's capacity to create appealing underworld characters such as Polly Peachum and Macheath, known as Mack the Knife. Brecht's wife, Helene Weigel, played Mrs. Peachum, the madam of the brothel in which the action takes place. Kurt Weill's second wife, Lotte Lenya, was an overnight sensation in the part of Jenny. She had a highly acclaimed reprise in New York almost twenty-five years later.

Brecht's most successful plays are *Galileo* (1938–1939), *Mother Courage* (1939), *The Good Woman of Setzuan* (1943), *The Private Lives of the Master Race* (1945), and *The Caucasian Chalk Circle* (1948). But these represent only a tiny fraction of a mass of work, including plays, poetry, criticism, and fiction.

His output is extraordinary in volume and quality. It includes plays borrowed not only from Gay but also from Sophocles, Molière, Gorky, Shakespeare, and John Webster, among others.

Brecht developed a number of theories regarding drama. He used the term *epic theater* to distinguish his own theater from traditional Aristotelian drama. Brecht expected his audience to observe critically, to draw conclusions, and to participate in an intellectual argument with the work at hand. The confrontational relationship he intended was designed to engage the audience in analyzing what they saw rather than in identifying with the main characters or in enjoying a wash of sentimentality or emotion.

One of the ways Brecht achieved his ends was by making the theatricality of the production's props, lights, sets, and equipment visible, thereby reminding the members of the audience that they were seeing a play. He used the term ALIENATION to define the effect he wanted his theater to have on an audience. He hoped that by alienating his audience from the drama he would keep them emotionally detached and intellectually alert. Brecht's theater was political. He saw a connection between an audience that could analyze theater critically and an audience that could analyze reality critically — and see that social, political, and economic conditions were not "natural" or fixed immutably but could (and should) be changed.

Brecht's theories produced interesting results and helped stimulate audiences that expected to be entertained by realistic or sentimental plays. His style spread rapidly throughout the world of theater, and it is still being used and developed by contemporary playwrights such as Heiner Müller and performers such as Pina Bausch.

MOTHER COURAGE

Since *Mother Courage* was first produced in 1941 in Zurich, it has become a classic of modern theater, performed successfully in the United States and most other Western countries. Brecht conceived of the drama as a powerful antiwar play. He set it in Germany during the Thirty Years' War, in which the German Protestants, supported by countries such as France, Denmark, and England, fought against the Hapsburg empire, which was allied with the Holy Roman Empire and the German Catholic princes. The war was actually a combination of many wars fought during the period of thirty years. It was bloody and seemingly interminable, devastating Germany's towns and citizenry as well as its agriculture and commerce. The armies fought to control territory, economic markets, and the religious differences between German Lutherans and Roman Catholics.

Brecht was not interested in the immediate causes underlying the Thirty Years' War. He was making a case against war entirely, regardless of its cause. To do this, he deliberately avoided making his play realistic. The stage setting is essentially barren; and the play is structured in scenes that are very intense but that avoid any sense of continuity of action. Audiences cannot become involved in unfolding action; they must always remain conscious of themselves as audience. Moreover, the lighting is high intensity, almost cruel at times, spotlighting the action in a way that is completely unnatural. In the early productions, Brecht included slide projections of the headings that accompany each of the twelve scenes so that the audience was always reminded of the presence of the playwright and the fact that they were seeing a play. These headings provided yet another break in the continuity of the action.

Although the printed text does not convey it, the play as Brecht produced it employed long silences, some of which were unsettling to the audience. When Swiss Cheese, Mother Courage's "honest" son, has a moment of rest in scene 3, he is in an intense ring of stage light as he comments on sitting in the sun in his shirtsleeves. As Swiss Cheese relaxes for the last time, the intense light becomes an ironic device: it seems to expose him as a thief, and he is dragged off to his death. While he is Mother Courage's "honest son," circumstances make it seem that he has been corrupted by the war, like everyone else.

Mother Courage herself lives off the war by selling goods to the soldiers. She and her children haul their wagon across the battlefields with no concern for who is winning, who is losing, or even where they are. Her only ambition is to stock her wagon, sell her goods, and make sure she does not get stuck with any useless inventory. When the chaplain tells her that peace has broken out, she laments their condition because without war the family has no livelihood.

As Mother Courage continues to pull her wagon across field after field, she learns how to survive. But she also loses her children, one by one, to the war. Eilif, seduced into joining the army by a recruitment officer, is led into battle thinking that war is a heroic adventure. Swiss Cheese thinks he found a good deal in a paymaster's uniform. Both are wrong: there is no security in war, and they eventually perish.

Kattrin, the daughter, is likewise a victim of the violence of war. Having been violated by a Swedish soldier, she becomes mute. Near the end of the play she is treated violently again, and the terrible scar on her face leaves her unmarriageable. At the end Kattrin dies while sounding an alarm to give the sleeping town warning of an imminent attack.

Finally, Mother Courage is left alone. She picks up her wagon and finds that she can maneuver it herself. The play ends as she circles the stage, with everything around her consumed by war.

Brecht's stated intentions were somewhat thwarted by the reactions of the play's first audiences. They were struck by the power of Brecht's characterization of Mother Courage and treated her with immense sympathy. They saw her as an indomitable woman whose strength in the face of adversity was so great that she could not be overwhelmed. But Brecht intended the audience to analyze Mother Courage further and to see in her a reflection of society's wrong values. She conducts business on the field of battle, paying no attention to the moral question of war itself. She makes her living from the war but cannot see that it is the war that causes her anguish.

In response to the audiences' sympathetic reactions, Brecht revised the play, adding new lines to help audiences see the venality of Mother Courage's motives. But subsequent audiences have continued to treat her as a survivor — almost a biblical figure. Brecht's German critics saw her as a model for one who

BRECHT • MOTHER COURAGE AND HER CHILDREN   **1001**

endures all the terrors of war and yet remains a testament for the resilience of humankind. No matter how one decides to interpret her, Mother Courage remains one of the most unusual and haunting characters in modern drama.

Mother Courage in Performance

Brecht wrote *Mother Courage* in three months, beginning in September 1939, while he and Helene Weigel were in Sweden in exile from Nazi Germany. Its first production was on April 19, 1941, in Zurich, Switzerland, while Brecht waited in Sweden for entry papers to the United States. Brecht and Weigel returned to Europe after the war. In 1948 they went to East Berlin to work with a new theater group explicitly to produce *Mother Courage* with Helene Weigel in the title role in January 1949. In October 1950 Brecht directed Thérèsa Giehse as Courage in Munich. Other productions were staged in provincial German towns and in other European cities, such as Rotterdam and Paris, both in 1951.

Brecht's productions are sometimes regarded as "canonical," although contemporary directors often modify his original plans. He usually began the performance with a half-curtain and a four-person orchestra playing an overture. Next, an unseen record player played a song associated with Courage; as Courage came on stage, she sang the second verse of her song herself. The stage had only a CYCLORAMA, a large curved curtain used as a backdrop, and a circle marked on the floor. This defined the space that was Mother Courage's world, and various sets were placed on the circle to accommodate successive scenes. The circle itself was a revolving turntable on which the wagon moved, going essentially nowhere. Brecht used placards to indicate changes in time and place as well as to indicate events in the life of Mother Courage and her children. The lighting was generally bright, and the effect was lively and colorful.

Brecht was not widely produced in the West during the cold war, but Leon Epp directed *Mother Courage* at the Volkstheater in Vienna in 1963. In the same year Jerome Robbins produced the play at the Martin Beck Theatre on Broadway, with sets by Ming Cho Lee. Anne Bancroft played Mother Courage, and Zohra Lampert was Kattrin. The reviews praised Bancroft for achieving a "lonely magnificence" at the end of the play and maintained that Brecht produced a considerable emotional intensity despite his theoretical distaste for such effects.

The next year Joseph Slowik produced the play in the Goodman Theater in Chicago with a partial student cast and the distinguished Eugenie Leontovich as Mother Courage. In England *Mother Courage* was produced twice in the 1950s in London. In 1961 and 1965 it was produced by the Old Vic. Numerous local theaters put on the play in the late 1960s and 1970s. In 1980 Ntozake Shange adapted it for its second New York production and reset it in the period after the American Civil War; Gloria Foster and Morgan Freeman had the major roles. Frank Rich praised the acting and the energy of the play but feared that Brecht's original vision was altered almost beyond recognition: Mother Courage becomes "an innocent victim of an entire system," which is exactly what Brecht argued against.

The Royal Shakespeare Company produced the play in London in 1984 with Judi Dench as Courage and Zoë Wanamaker as Kattrin. Both received fine reviews, as did the production itself. Diana Rigg was Mother Courage in the production at the Olivier Theatre in London (November 1995–January

1996), which featured a new colloquial translation by the playwright David Hare and which reset the play in the period of World War I. Like all these productions, it maintained the circular set that Brecht had originally used and experimented with Brecht's theories of alienation and distancing. The success of these productions indicates the play's appeal for our time.

Gwendolyn Mulamba played Mother Courage in the Classical Theater of Harlem's production in New York City in February 2004. Christopher McElroen directed. Clearly, Brecht's play speaks to all of us in the twenty-first century.

Bertolt Brecht (1898–1956)

MOTHER COURAGE AND HER CHILDREN   *1939*
A CHRONICLE OF THE THIRTY YEARS' WAR

TRANSLATED BY JOHN WILLETT

Characters

MOTHER COURAGE
KATTRIN, *her dumb daughter*
EILIF, *the elder son*
SWISS CHEESE, *the younger son*
THE RECRUITER
THE SERGEANT
THE COOK
THE GENERAL
THE CHAPLAIN
THE ARMOURER
YVETTE POTTIER
THE MAN WITH THE PATCH
ANOTHER SERGEANT
THE ANCIENT COLONEL
A CLERK
A YOUNG SOLDIER
AN OLDER SOLDIER
A PEASANT
THE PEASANT'S WIFE
THE YOUNG MAN
THE OLD WOMAN
ANOTHER PEASANT
HIS WIFE
THE YOUNG PEASANT
THE ENSIGN
SOLDIERS
A VOICE

SCENE 1

(*Spring 1624. The Swedish Commander-in-Chief Count Oxenstierna is raising troops in Dalecarlia for the Polish campaign. The canteen woman Anna Fierling, known under the name of Mother Courage, loses one son.*)
(*Country road near a town.*)
(*A sergeant and a recruiter stand shivering.*)

RECRUITER: How can you muster a unit in a place like this? I've been thinking about suicide, sergeant. Here am I, got to find our commander four companies before the twelfth of the month, and people round here are so nasty I can't sleep nights. S'pose I get hold of some bloke and shut my eye to his pigeon chest and varicose veins, I get him proper drunk, he signs on the line, I'm just settling up, he goes for a piss, I follow him to the door because I smell a rat; bob's your uncle, he's off like a flea with the itch. No notion of word of honour, loyalty, faith, sense of duty. This place has shattered my confidence in the human race, sergeant.

SERGEANT: It's too long since they had a war here; stands to reason. Where's their sense of morality to come from? Peace — that's just a mess; takes a war to restore order. Peacetime, the human race runs wild. People and cattle get buggered about, who cares? Everyone eats just as he feels inclined, a hunk of cheese on top of his nice white bread, and a slice of fat on top of the cheese. How many young blokes and good horses in that town there, nobody knows; they never thought of counting. I been in places ain't seen a war for nigh seventy years: folks hadn't got names to them, couldn't tell one another apart. Takes a war to get proper nominal rolls and inventories — shoes in bundles and corn in bags, and man and beast properly numbered and carted off, cause it stands to reason: no order, no war.

RECRUITER: Too true.

SERGEANT: Same with all good things, it's a job to get a war going. But once it's blossomed out there's no holding it; folk start fighting shy of peace like punters what can't stop for fear of having to tot up what they lost. Before that it's war they're fighting shy of. It's something new to them.

RECRUITER: Hey, here's a cart coming. Two tarts with two young fellows. Stop her, sergeant. If this one's a flop I'm not standing around in your spring winds any longer, I can tell you.

(*Sound of a jew's-harp. Drawn by two young fellows, a covered cart rolls in. On it sit Mother Courage and her dumb daughter Kattrin.*)

MOTHER COURAGE: Morning, sergeant.

SERGEANT (*blocking the way*): Morning, all. And who are you?

MOTHER COURAGE: Business folk. (*Sings.*)

> You captains, tell the drums to slacken
> And give your infanteers a break:
> It's Mother Courage with her waggon
> Full of the finest boots they make.
> With crawling lice and looted cattle
> With lumbering guns and straggling kit —
> How can you flog them into battle
> Unless you get them boots that fit?
>   The new year's come. The watchmen shout.
>   The thaw sets in. The dead remain.
>   Whatever life has not died out
>   It staggers to its feet again.
>
> Captains, how can you make them face it —
> Marching to death without a brew?
> Courage has rum with which to lace it
> And boil their souls and bodies through.
> Their musket primed, their stomach hollow —
> Captains, your men don't look so well.
> So feed them up and let them follow
> While you command them into hell.
>   The new year's come. The watchmen shout.
>   The thaw sets in. The dead remain.
>   Wherever life has not died out
>   It staggers to its feet again.

SERGEANT: Halt! Who are you with, you trash?

THE ELDER SON: Second Finnish Regiment.

SERGEANT: Where's your papers?

MOTHER COURAGE: Papers?

THE YOUNGER SON: What, mean to say you don't know Mother Courage?

SERGEANT: Never heard of her. What's she called Courage for?

MOTHER COURAGE: Courage is the name they gave me because I was scared of going broke, sergeant, so I drove me cart right through the bombardment of Riga with fifty loaves of bread aboard. They were going mouldy, it was high time, hadn't any choice really.

SERGEANT: Don't be funny with me. Your papers.

MOTHER COURAGE (*pulling a bundle of papers from a tin box and climbing down off the cart*): That's all my papers, sergeant. You'll find a whole big missal from Altötting in Bavaria for wrapping gherkins in, and a road map of Moravia, the Lord knows when I'll ever get there, might as well chuck it away, and here's a stamped certificate that my horse hasn't got foot-and-mouth, only he's dead worse luck, cost fifteen florins he did — not me luckily. That enough paper for you?

SERGEANT: You pulling my leg? I'll knock that sauce out of you. S'pose you know you got to have a licence.

MOTHER COURAGE: Talk proper to me, do you mind, and don't you dare say I'm pulling your leg in front of my unsullied children, 'tain't decent, I got no time for you. My honest face, that's me licence with the Second Regiment, and if it's too difficult for you to read there's nowt I can do about it. Nobody's putting a stamp on that.

RECRUITER: Sergeant, methinks I smell insubordination in this individual. What's needed in our camp is obedience.

MOTHER COURAGE: Sausage, if you ask me.

SERGEANT: Name.

MOTHER COURAGE: Anna Fierling.

SERGEANT: You all called Fierling then?

MOTHER COURAGE: What'd you mean? It's me's called Fierling, not them.

SERGEANT: Aren't all this lot your children?

MOTHER COURAGE: You bet they are, but why should they all have to be called the same, eh? (*Pointing to her elder son.*) For instance, that one's called Eilif Nojocki — Why? his father always claimed he was called Kojocki or Mojocki or something. The boy remembers him clearly, except that the one he remembers was someone else, a Frenchie with a little beard. Aside from that he's got his father's wits; that man knew how to snitch a peasant's pants off his bum without him noticing. This way each of us has his own name, see.

SERGEANT: What, each one different?

MOTHER COURAGE: Don't tell me you ain't never come across that.

SERGEANT: So I s'pose he's a Chinaman? (*Pointing to the younger son.*)

MOTHER COURAGE: Wrong. Swiss.

SERGEANT: After the Frenchman?

MOTHER COURAGE: What Frenchman? I never heard tell of no Frenchman. You keep muddling things up, we'll be hanging around here till dark. A Swiss, but called Fejos, and the name has nowt to do with his father. He was called something quite different and was a fortifications engineer, only drunk all the time.

(*Swiss Cheese beams and nods; dumb Kattrin too is amused.*)

SERGEANT: How in hell can he be called Fejos?

MOTHER COURAGE: I don't like to be rude, sergeant, but

you ain't got much imagination, have you? Course he's called Fejos, because when he arrived I was with a Hungarian, very decent fellow, had terrible kidney trouble though he never touched a drop. The boy takes after him.

SERGEANT: But he wasn't his father . . .

MOTHER COURAGE: Took after him just the same. I call him Swiss Cheese. (*Pointing to her daughter.*) And that's Kattrin Haupt, she's half German.

SERGEANT: Nice family, I must say.

MOTHER COURAGE: Aye, me cart and me have seen the world.

SERGEANT: I'm writing all this down. (*He writes.*) And you're from Bamberg in Bavaria; how d'you come to be here?

MOTHER COURAGE: Can't wait till war chooses to visit Bamberg, can I?

RECRUITER (*to Eilif*): You two should be called Jacob Ox and Esau Ox, pulling the cart like that. I s'pose you never get out of harness?

EILIF: Ma, can I clobber him one? I wouldn't half like to.

MOTHER COURAGE: And I says you can't; just you stop where you are. And now two fine officers like you, I bet you could use a good pistol, or a belt buckle, yours is on its last legs, sergeant.

SERGEANT: I could use something else. Those boys are healthy as young birch trees, I observe: chests like barrels, solid leg muscles. So why are they dodging their military service, may I ask?

MOTHER COURAGE (*quickly*): Nowt doing, sergeant. Yours is no trade for my kids.

RECRUITER: But why not? There's good money in it, glory too. Flogging boots is women's work. (*To Eilif.*) Come here, let's see if you've muscles in you or if you're a chicken.

MOTHER COURAGE: He's a chicken. Give him a fierce look, he'll fall over.

RECRUITER: Killing a young bull that happens to be in his way. (*Wants to lead him off.*)

MOTHER COURAGE: Let him alone, will you? He's nowt for you folk.

RECRUITER: He was crudely offensive and talked about clobbering me. The two of us are going to step into that field and settle it man to man.

EILIF: Don't you worry, mum, I'll fix him.

MOTHER COURAGE: Stop there! You varmint! I know you, nowt but fights. There's a knife down his boot. A slasher, that's what he is.

RECRUITER: I'll draw it out of him like a milk-tooth. Come along, sonny.

MOTHER COURAGE: Sergeant, I'll tell the colonel. He'll have you both in irons. The lieutenant's going out with my daughter.

SERGEANT: No rough stuff, chum. (*To Mother Courage.*) What you got against military service? Wasn't his own father a soldier? Died a soldier's death, too? Said it yourself.

MOTHER COURAGE: He's nowt but a child. You want to take him off to slaughterhouse, I know you lot. They'll give you five florins for him.

RECRUITER: First he's going to get a smart cap and boots, eh?

EILIF: Not from you.

MOTHER COURAGE: Let's both go fishing, said angler to worm. (*To Swiss Cheese.*) Run off, call out they're trying to kidnap your brother. (*She pulls a knife.*) Go on, you kidnap him, just try. I'll slit you open, trash. I'll teach you to make war with him. We're doing an honest trade in ham and linen, and we're peaceable folk.

SERGEANT: Peaceable I don't think; look at your knife. You should be ashamed of yourself; put that knife away, you old harridan. A minute back you were admitting you live off the war, how else should you live, what from? But how's anyone to have war without soldiers?

MOTHER COURAGE: No need for it to be my kids.

SERGEANT: Oh, you'd like war to eat the pips but spit out the apple? It's to fatten up your kids, but you won't invest in it. Got to look after itself, eh? And you called Courage, fancy that. Scared of the war that keeps you going? Your sons aren't scared of it, I can see that.

EILIF: Take more than a war to scare me.

SERGEANT: And why? Look at me: has army life done all that badly by me? Joined up at seventeen.

MOTHER COURAGE: Still got to reach seventy.

SERGEANT: I don't mind waiting.

MOTHER COURAGE: Under the sod, eh?

SERGEANT: You trying to insult me, saying I'll die?

MOTHER COURAGE: S'pose it's true? S'pose I can see the mark's on you? S'pose you look like a corpse on leave to me? Eh?

SWISS CHEESE: She's got second sight, Mother has.

RECRUITER: Go ahead, tell the sergeant's fortune, might amuse him.

MOTHER COURAGE: Gimme helmet. (*He gives it to her.*)

SERGEANT: It don't mean a bloody sausage. Anything for a laugh though.

MOTHER COURAGE (*taking out a sheet of parchment and tearing it up*): Eilif, Swiss Cheese and Kattrin, may all of us be torn apart like this if we lets ourselves get too mixed up in the war. (*To the sergeant.*) Just for you I'm doing it for free. Black's for death. I'm putting a big black cross on this slip of paper.

SWISS CHEESE: Leaving the other one blank, see?

MOTHER COURAGE: Then I fold them across and shake them. All of us is jumbled together like this from our mother's womb, and now draw a slip and you'll know. (*The sergeant hesitates.*)

RECRUITER (*to Eilif*): I don't take just anybody, they all know I'm choosey, but you got the kind of fire I like to see.

SERGEANT (*fishing in the helmet*): Too silly. Load of eyewash.

SWISS CHEESE: Drawn a black cross, he has. Write him off.

RECRUITER: They're having you on; not everybody's name's on a bullet.

SERGEANT (*hoarsely*): You've put me in the shit.

MOTHER COURAGE: Did that yourself the day you became a soldier. Come along, let's move on now. 'Tain't every day we have a war, I got to get stirring.

SERGEANT: God damn it, you can't kid me. We're taking that bastard of yours for a soldier.

EILIF: Swiss Cheese'd like to be a soldier too.

MOTHER COURAGE: First I've heard of that. You'll have to draw too, all three of you. (*She goes to the rear to mark crosses on further slips.*)

RECRUITER (*to Eilif*): One of the things they say against us is that it's all holy-holy in the Swedish camp; but that's a malicious rumour to do us down. There's no hymn-singing but Sundays, just a single verse, and then only for those got voices.

MOTHER COURAGE (*coming back with the slips, which she drops into the sergeant's helmet*): Trying to get away from their ma, the devils, off to war like calves to salt-lick. But I'm making you draw lots, and that'll show you the world is no vale of joys with "Come along, son, we need a few more generals." Sergeant, I'm so scared they won't get through the war. Such dreadful characters, all three of them. (*She hands the helmet to Eilif.*) Hey, come on, fish out your slip. (*He fishes one out, unfolds it. She snatches it from him.*) There you are, it's a cross. Oh, wretched mother that I am, o pain-racked giver of birth! Shall he die? Aye, in the springtime of life he is doomed. If he becomes a soldier he shall bite the dust, it's plain to see. He is too foolhardy, like his dad was. And if he ain't sensible he'll go the way of all flesh, his slip proves it. (*Shouts at him.*) You going to be sensible?

EILIF: Why not?

MOTHER COURAGE: Sensible thing is stay with your mother, never mind if they poke fun at you and call you chicken, just you laugh.

RECRUITER: If you're pissing in your pants I'll make do with your brother.

MOTHER COURAGE: I told you laugh. Go on, laugh. Now you draw, Swiss Cheese. I'm not so scared on account you're honest. (*He fishes in the helmet.*) Oh, why look at your slip in that strange way? It's got to be a blank. There can't be any cross on it. Surely I'm not going to lose *you*. (*She takes the slip.*) A cross? What, you too? Is that because you're so simple, perhaps? O Swiss Cheese, you too will be sunk if you don't stay utterly honest all the while, like I taught you from childhood when you brought the change back from the baker's. Else you can't save yourself. Look, sergeant, that's a black cross, ain't it?

SERGEANT: A cross, that's right. Can't think how I come to get one. I always stay in the rear. (*To the recruiter.*) There's no catch. Her own family get it too.

SWISS CHEESE: I get it too. But I listen to what I'm told.

MOTHER COURAGE (*to Kattrin*): And now you're the only one I know's all right, you're a cross yourself; got a kind heart you have. (*Holds the helmet up to*

her on the cart, but takes the slip out herself.) No, that's too much. That can't be right; must have made a mistake shuffling. Don't be too kind-hearted, Kattrin, you'll have to give it up, there's a cross above your path too. Lie doggo, girl, it can't be that hard once you're born dumb. Right, all of you know now. Look out for yourselves, you'll need to. And now up we get and on we go. (*She climbs on to the cart.*)

RECRUITER (*to the sergeant*): Do something.

SERGEANT: I don't feel very well.

RECRUITER: Must of caught a chill taking your helmet off in that wind. Involve her in a deal. (*Aloud.*) Might as well have a look at that belt-buckle, sergeant. After all, our friends here have to live by their business. Hey, you people, the sergeant wants to buy that belt-buckle.

MOTHER COURAGE: Half a florin. Two florins is what a belt like that's worth. (*Climbs down again.*)

SERGEANT: 'Tain't new. Let me get out of this damned wind and have a proper look at it. (*Goes behind the cart with the buckle.*)

MOTHER COURAGE: Ain't what I call windy.

SERGEANT: I s'pose it might be worth half a florin, it's silver.

MOTHER COURAGE (*joining him behind the cart*): It's six solid ounces.

RECRUITER (*to Eilif*): And then we men'll have one together. Got your bounty money here, come along. (*Eilif stands undecided.*)

MOTHER COURAGE: Half a florin it is.

SERGEANT: It beats me. I'm always at the rear. Sergeant's the safest job there is. You can send the others up front, cover themselves with glory. Me dinner hour's properly spoiled. Shan't be able to hold nowt down, I know.

MOTHER COURAGE: Mustn't let it prey on you so's you can't eat. Just stay at the rear. Here, take a swig of brandy, man. (*Gives him a drink.*)

RECRUITER (*has taken Eilif by the arm and is leading him away up stage*): Ten florins bounty money, then you're a gallant fellow fighting for the king and women'll be after you like flies. And you can clobber me for free for insulting you.

(*Exeunt both.°*)

(*Dumb Kattrin leans down from the cart and makes hoarse noises.*)

MOTHER COURAGE: All right, Kattrin, all right. Sergeant's just paying. (*Bites the half-florin.*) I got no faith in any kind of money. Burnt child, that's me, sergeant. This coin's good, though. And now let's get moving. Where's Eilif?

SWISS CHEESE: Went off with the recruiter.

MOTHER COURAGE (*stands quite still, then*): You simpleton. (*To Kattrin.*) 'Tain't your fault, you can't speak, I know.

SERGEANT: Could do with a swig yourself, ma. That's

Exeunt both: They both leave.

life. Plenty worse thing's than being a soldier. Want to live off war, but keep yourself and family out of it, eh?

MOTHER COURAGE: You'll have to help your brother pull now, Kattrin.

(*Brother and sister hitch themselves to the cart and start pulling. Mother Courage walks alongside. The cart rolls on.*)

SERGEANT (*looking after them*):
    Like the war to nourish you?
    Have to feed it something too.

SCENE 2

(*In the years 1625 and 1626 Mother Courage crosses Poland in the train of the Swedish armies. Before the fortress of Wallhof she meets her son again. Successful sale of a capon and heyday of her dashing son.*)
(*The general's tent.*)
(*Beside it, his kitchen. Thunder of cannon. The cook is arguing with Mother Courage, who wants to sell him a capon.*)

THE COOK: Sixty hellers for a miserable bird like that?

MOTHER COURAGE: Miserable bird? This fat brute? Mean to say some greedy old general — and watch your step if you got nowt for his dinner — can't afford sixty hellers for him?

THE COOK: I can get a dozen like that for ten hellers just down the road.

MOTHER COURAGE: What, a capon like this you can get just down the road? In time of siege, which means hunger that tears your guts. A rat you might get: "might" I say because they're all being gobbled up, five men spending best part of day chasing one hungry rat. Fifty hellers for a giant capon in time of siege!

THE COOK: But it ain't us having the siege, it's t'other side. We're conducting the siege, can't you get that in your head?

MOTHER COURAGE: But we got nowt to eat too, even worse than them in the town. Took it with them, didn't they? They're having a high old time, everyone says. And look at us! I been to the peasants, there's nowt there.

THE COOK: There's plenty. They're sitting on it.

MOTHER COURAGE (*triumphantly*): They ain't. They're bust, that's what they are. Just about starving. I saw some, were grubbing up roots from sheer hunger, licking their fingers after they boiled some old leather strap. That's way it is. And me got a capon here and supposed to take forty hellers for it.

THE COOK: Thirty, not forty. I said thirty.

MOTHER COURAGE: Here, this ain't just any old capon. It was such a gifted beast, I been told, it could only eat to music, had a military march of its own. It could count, it was that intelligent. And you say forty hellers is too much? General will make mincemeat of you if there's nowt on his table.

THE COOK: See what I'm doing? (*He takes a piece of beef and puts his knife to it.*) Here I got a bit of beef, I'm going to roast it. Make up your mind quick.

MOTHER COURAGE: Go on, roast it. It's last year's.

THE COOK: Last night's. That animal was still alive and kicking, I saw him myself.

MOTHER COURAGE: Alive and stinking, you mean.

THE COOK: I'll cook him five hours if need be. I'll just see if he's still tough. (*He cuts into it.*)

MOTHER COURAGE: Put plenty of pepper on it so his lordship the general don't smell the pong.

(*The general, a chaplain and Eilif enter the tent.*)

THE GENERAL (*slapping Eilif on the shoulder*): Now then, Eilif my son, into your general's tent with you and sit thou at my right hand. For you accomplished a deed of heroism, like a pious cavalier; and doing what you did for God, and in a war of religion at that, is something I commend in you most highly, you shall have a gold bracelet as soon as we've taken this town. Here we are, come to save their souls for them, and what do those insolent dung-encrusted yokels go and do? Drive their beef away from us. They stuff it into those priests of theirs all right, back and front, but you taught 'em manners, ha! So here's a pot of red wine for you, the two of us'll knock it back at one gulp. (*They do so.*) Piss all for the chaplain, the old bigot. And now, what would you like for dinner, my darling?

EILIF: A bit of meat, why not?

THE GENERAL: Cook! Meat!

THE COOK: And then he goes and brings guests when there's nowt there.

(*Mother Courage silences him so she can listen.*)

EILIF: Hungry job cutting down peasants.

MOTHER COURAGE: Jesus Christ, it's my Eilif.

THE COOK: Your what?

MOTHER COURAGE: My eldest boy. It's two years since I lost sight of him, they pinched him from me on the road, must think well of him if the general's asking him to dinner, and what kind of a dinner can you offer? Nowt. You heard what the visitor wishes to eat: meat. Take my tip, you settle for the capon, it'll be a florin.

THE GENERAL (*has sat down with Eilif, and bellows*): Food, Lamb, you foul cook, or I'll have your hide.

THE COOK: Give it over, dammit, this is blackmail.

MOTHER COURAGE: Didn't someone say it was a miserable bird?

THE COOK: Miserable; give it over, and a criminal price, fifty hellers.

MOTHER COURAGE: A florin, I said. For my eldest boy, the general's guest, no expense is too great for me.

THE COOK (*gives her the money*): You might at least pluck it while I see to the fire.

MOTHER COURAGE (*sits down to pluck the fowl*): He won't half be surprised to see me. He's my dashing clever son. Then I got a stupid one too, he's honest

Lotte Lenya as Mother Courage pulling her wagon in Brecht's 1979 Berliner Ensemble production of his play.

though. The girl's nowt. One good thing, she don't talk.

THE GENERAL: Drink up, my son, this is my best Falernian; only got a barrel or two left, but that's nothing to pay for a sign that there's still true faith to be found in my army. As for that shepherd of souls he can just look on, because all he does is preach, without the least idea how it's to be carried out. And now, my son Eilif, tell us more about the neat way you smashed those yokels and captured the twenty oxen. Let's hope they get here soon.

EILIF: A day or two at most.

MOTHER COURAGE: Thoughtful of our Eilif not to bring the oxen in till tomorrow, else you lot wouldn't have looked twice at my capon.

EILIF: Well, it was like this, see. I'd heard peasants had been driving the oxen they'd hidden, out of the forest into one particular wood, on the sly and mostly by night. That's where people from the town were

s'posed to come and pick them up. So I holds off and lets them drive their oxen together, reckoning they'd be better than me at finding 'em. I had my blokes slavering after the meat, cut their emergency rations even further for a couple of days till their mouths was watering at the least sound of any word beginning with "me-," like "measles" say.

THE GENERAL: Very clever of you.

EILIF: Possibly. The rest was a piece of cake. Except that the peasants had cudgels and outnumbered us three to one and made a murderous attack on us. Four of 'em shoved me into a thicket, knocked my sword from my hand and bawled out "Surrender!" What's the answer, I wondered; they're going to make mincemeat of me.

THE GENERAL: What did you do?

EILIF: I laughed.

THE GENERAL: You did what?

EILIF: Laughed. So we got talking. I put it on a business footing from the start, told them "Twenty florins a head's too much. I'll give you fifteen." As if I was meaning to pay. That threw them, and they began scratching their heads. In a flash I'd picked up my sword and was hacking 'em to pieces. Necessity's the mother of invention, eh, sir?

THE GENERAL: What is your view, pastor of souls?

THE CHAPLAIN: That phrase is not strictly speaking in the Bible, but when Our Lord turned the five loaves into five hundred there was no war on and he could tell people to love their neighbours as they'd had enough to eat. Today it's another story.

THE GENERAL (*laughs*): Quite another story. You can have a swig after all for that, you old Pharisee.° (*To Eilif.*) Hacked 'em to pieces, did you, so my gallant lads can get a proper bite to eat? What do the Scriptures say? "Whatsoever thou doest for the least of my brethren, thou doest for me." And what did you do for them? Got them a good square meal of beef, because they're not accustomed to mouldy bread, the old way was to fix a cold meal of rolls and wine in your helmet before you went out to fight for God.

EILIF: Aye, in a flash I'd picked up my sword and was hacking them to pieces.

THE GENERAL: You've the makings of a young Caesar. You ought to see the King.

EILIF: I have from a distance. He kind of glows. I'd like to model myself on him.

THE GENERAL: You've got something in common already. I appreciate soldiers like you, Eilif, men of courage. Somebody like that I treat as I would my own sort. (*He leads him over to the map.*) Have a look at the situation, Eilif; it's a long haul still.

MOTHER COURAGE (*who has been listening and now angrily plucks the fowl*): That must be a rotten general.

Pharisee: A member of a Jewish sect current in biblical days; the term is now commonly used to refer to a hypocritical, self-righteous person.

THE COOK: He's ravenous all right, but why rotten?

MOTHER COURAGE: Because he's got to have men of courage, that's why. If he knew how to plan a proper campaign what would he be needing men of courage for? Ordinary ones would do. It's always the same; whenever there's a load of special virtues around it means something stinks.

THE COOK: I thought it meant things is all right.

MOTHER COURAGE: No, that they stink. Look, s'pose some general or king is bone stupid and leads his men up shit creek, then those men've got to be fearless, there's another virtue for you. S'pose he's stingy and hires too few soldiers, then they got to be a crowd of Hercules's. And s'pose he's slapdash and don't give a bugger, then they got to be clever as monkeys else their number's up. Same way they got to show exceptional loyalty each time he gives them impossible jobs. Nowt but virtues no proper country and no decent king or general would ever need. In decent countries folk don't have to have virtues, the whole lot can be perfectly ordinary, average intelligence, and for all I know cowards.

THE GENERAL: I'll wager your father was a soldier.

EILIF: A great soldier, I been told. My mother warned me about it. There's a song I know.

THE GENERAL: Sing it to us. (Roars.) When's that dinner coming?

EILIF: It's called The Song of the Girl and the Soldier. (He sings it, dancing a war dance with his sabre.)

The guns blaze away, and the bay'nit'll slay
And the water can't hardly be colder.
What's the answer to ice? Keep off's my advice!
That's what the girl told the soldier.
Next thing the soldier, wiv' a round up the spout
Hears the band playing and gives a great shout:
Why, it's marching what makes you a soldier!
So it's down to the south and then northwards once
    more:
See him catching that bay'nit in his naked paw!
That's what his comrades done told her.

Oh, do not despise the advice of the wise
Learn wisdom from those that are older
And don't try for things that are out of your
    reach —
That's what the girl told the soldier.
Next thing the soldier, his bay'nit in place
Wades into the river and laughs in her face
Though the water comes up to his shoulder.
When the shingle roof glints in the light o' the
    moon
We'll be wiv' you again, not a moment too soon!
That's what his comrades done told her.

MOTHER COURAGE (takes up the song in the kitchen, beating on a pot with her spoon):

You'll go out like a light! And the sun'll take flight
For your courage just makes us feel colder.

Oh, that vanishing light! May God see that it's
    right! —
That's what the girl told the soldier.

EILIF: What's that?

MOTHER COURAGE (continues singing):

Next thing the soldier, his bay'nit in place
Was caught by the current and went down without
    trace
And the water couldn't hardly be colder.
Then the shingle roof froze in the light o' the
    moon
As both soldier and ice drifted down to their
    doom —
And d'you know what his comrades done told her?

He went out like a light. And the sunshine took
    flight
For his courage just made 'em feel colder.
Oh, do not despise the advice of the wise!
That's what the girl told the soldier.

THE GENERAL: The things they get up to in my kitchen these days.

EILIF (Has gone into the kitchen. He flings his arms round his mother.): Fancy seeing you again, ma! Where's the others?

MOTHER COURAGE (in his arms): Snug as a bug in a rug. They made Swiss Cheese paymaster of the Second Finnish; any road he'll stay out of fighting that way, I couldn't keep him out altogether.

EILIF: How's the old feet?

MOTHER COURAGE: Bit tricky getting me shoes on of a morning.

THE GENERAL (has joined them): So you're his mother, I hope you've got plenty more sons for me like this one.

EILIF: Ain't it my lucky day? You sitting out there in the kitchen, ma, hearing your son commended . . .

MOTHER COURAGE: You bet I heard. (Slaps his face.)

EILIF (holding his cheek): What's that for? Taking the oxen?

MOTHER COURAGE: No. Not surrendering when those four went for you and wanted to make mincemeat of you. Didn't I say you should look after yourself? You Finnish devil!

(The general and the chaplain stand in the doorway laughing.)

SCENE 3

(Three years later Mother Courage is taken prisoner along with elements of a Finnish regiment. She manages to save her daughter, likewise her covered cart, but her honest son is killed.)
(Military camp.)

(*Afternoon. A flagpole with the regimental pay. From her cart, festooned now with all kinds of goods, Mother Courage has stretched a washing line to a large cannon, across which she and Kattrin are folding the washing. She is bargaining at the same time with an armourer over a sack of shot. Swiss Cheese, now wearing a paymaster's uniform, is looking on. A comely person, Yvette Pottier, is sewing a gaily coloured hat, a glass of brandy before her. She is in her stockinged feet, having laid aside her red high-heeled boots.*)

THE ARMOURER: I'll let you have that shot for a couple of florins. It's cheap at the price, I got to have the money because the colonel's been boozing with his officers since two days back, and the drink's run out.

MOTHER COURAGE: That's troops' munitions. They catch me with that, I'm for court-martial. You crooks flog the shot, and troops got nowt to fire at enemy.

THE ARMOURER: Have a heart, can't you; you scratch my back and I'll scratch yours.

MOTHER COURAGE: I'm not taking army property. Not at that price.

THE ARMOURER: You can sell it on the q.t. tonight to the Fourth Regiment's armourer for five florins, eight even, if you let him have a receipt for twelve. He's right out of ammunition.

MOTHER COURAGE: Why not you do it?

THE ARMOURER: I don't trust him, he's a pal of mine.

MOTHER COURAGE (*takes the sack*): Gimme. (*To Kattrin.*) Take it away and pay him a florin and a half. (*The armourer protests.*) I said a florin and a half. (*Kattrin drags the sack upstage, the armourer following her. Mother Courage addresses Swiss Cheese.*) Here's your woollies, now look after them, it's October and autumn may set in any time. I ain't saying it's got to, cause I've learned nowt's got to come when you think it will, not even seasons of the year. But your regimental accounts got to add up right, come what may. Do they add up right?

SWISS CHEESE: Yes, mother.

MOTHER COURAGE: Don't you forget they made you paymaster cause you was honest, not dashing like your brother, and above all so stupid I bet you ain't even thought of clearing off with it, no not you. That's a big consolation to me. And don't lose those woollies.

SWISS CHEESE: No, mother, I'll put them under my mattress. (*Begins to go.*)

THE ARMOURER: I'll go along with you, paymaster.

MOTHER COURAGE: And don't you start learning him none of your tricks.

(*The armourer leaves with Swiss Cheese without any farewell gesture.*)

YVETTE (*waving to him*): No reason not to say goodbye, armourer.

MOTHER COURAGE (*to Yvette*): I don't like to see them together. He's wrong company for our Swiss Cheese. Oh well, war's off to a good start. Easily take four, five years before all countries are in. A bit of fore-sight, don't do nothing silly, and business'll flourish. Don't you know you ain't s'posed to drink before midday with your complaint?

YVETTE: Complaint, who says so, it's a libel.

MOTHER COURAGE: They all say so.

YVETTE: Because they're all telling lies, Mother Courage, and me at my wits' end cause they're all avoiding me like something the cat brought in thanks to those lies, what the hell am I remodelling my hat for? (*She throws it away.*) That's why I drink before midday. Never used to, gives you crows' feet, but now what the hell? All the Second Finnish know me. Ought to have stayed at home when my first fellow did me wrong. No good our sort being proud. Eat shit, that's what you got to do, or down you go.

MOTHER COURAGE: Now don't you start up again about that Pieter of yours and how it all happened, in front of my innocent daughter too.

YVETTE: She's the one should hear it, put her off love.

MOTHER COURAGE: Nobody can put 'em off that.

YVETTE: Then I'll go on, get it off my chest. It all starts with yours truly growing up in lovely Flanders, else I'd never of seen him and wouldn't be stuck here now in Poland, cause he was an army cook, fair-haired, a Dutchman but thin for once. Kattrin, watch out for the thin ones, only in those days I didn't know that, or that he'd got a girl already, or that they all called him Puffing Piet cause he never took his pipe out of his mouth when he was on the job, it meant that little to him. (*She sings the Song of Fraternisation.*)

When I was only sixteen
The foe came into our land.
He laid aside his sabre
And with a smile he took my hand.
After the May parade
The May light starts to fade.
The regiment dressed by the right
The drums were beaten, that's the drill.
The foe took us behind the hill
And fraternised all night.

There were so many foes then
But mine worked in the mess.
I loathed him in the daytime.
At night I loved him none the less.
After the May parade
The May light starts to fade.
The regiment dressed by the right
The drums were beaten, that's the drill.
The foe took us behind the hill
And fraternised all night.

The love which came upon me
Was wished on me by fate.
My friends could never grasp why
I found it hard to share their hate.
The fields were wet with dew
When sorrow first I knew.

The regiment dressed by the right
The drums were beaten, that's the drill.
And then the foe, my lover still
Went marching out of sight.

I followed him, fool that I was, but I never found him, and that was five years back. (*She walks unsteadily behind the cart.*)
MOTHER COURAGE: You left your hat here.
YVETTE: Anyone wants it can have it.
MOTHER COURAGE: Let that be a lesson, Kattrin. Don't you start anything with them soldiers. Love makes the world go round, I'm warning you. Even with fellows not in the army it's no bed of roses. He says he'd like to kiss the ground your feet walk on — reminds me, did you wash them yesterday? — and after that you're his skivvy. Be thankful you're dumb, then you can't contradict yourself and won't be wanting to bite your tongue off for speaking the truth; it's a godsend, being dumb is. And here comes the general's cook, now what's he after?

(*Enter the cook and the chaplain.*)

THE CHAPLAIN: I have a message for you from your son Eilif, and the cook has come along because you made such a profound impression on him.
THE COOK: I just came along to get a bit of air.
MOTHER COURAGE: That you can always do here if you behave yourself, and if you don't I can deal with you. What does he want? I got no spare cash.
THE CHAPLAIN: Actually I had a message for his brother the paymaster.
MOTHER COURAGE: He ain't here now nor anywhere else neither. He ain't his brother's paymaster. He's not to lead him into temptation nor be clever at his expense. (*Giving him money from the purse slung round her.*) Give him this, it's a sin, he's banking on mother's love and ought to be ashamed of himself.
THE COOK: Not for long, he'll have to be moving off with the regiment, might be to his death. Give him a bit extra, you'll be sorry later. You women are tough, then later on you're sorry. A little glass of brandy wouldn't have been a problem, but it wasn't offered and, who knows, a bloke may lie beneath the green sod and none of you people will ever be able to dig him up again.
THE CHAPLAIN: Don't give way to your feelings, cook. To fall in battle is a blessing, not an inconvenience, and why? It is a war of faith. None of your common wars but a special one, fought for the faith and therefore pleasing to God.
THE COOK: Very true. It's a war all right in one sense, what with requisitioning, murder and looting and the odd bit of rape thrown in, but different from all the other wars because it's a war of faith; stands to reason. But it's thirsty work at that, you must admit.
THE CHAPLAIN (*to Mother Courage, indicating the cook*): I tried to stop him, but he says he's taken a shine to you, you figure in his dreams.

THE COOK (*lighting a stumpy pipe*): Just want a glass of brandy from a fair hand, what harm in that? Only I'm groggy already cause the chaplain here's been telling such jokes all the way along you bet I'm still blushing.
MOTHER COURAGE: Him a clergyman too. I'd best give the pair of you a drink or you'll start making me immoral suggestions cause you've nowt else to do.
THE CHAPLAIN: Behold a temptation, said the court preacher, and fell. (*Turning back to look at Kattrin as he leaves.*) And who is this entrancing young person?
MOTHER COURAGE: That ain't an entrancing but a decent young person. (*The chaplain and the cook go behind the cart with Mother Courage. Kattrin looks after them, then walks away from her washing towards the hat. She picks it up and sits down, pulling the red boots towards her. Mother Courage can be heard in the background talking politics with the chaplain and the cook.*)
MOTHER COURAGE: Those Poles here in Poland had no business sticking their noses in. Right, our king moved in on them, horse and foot, but did they keep the peace? no, went and stuck their noses into their own affairs, they did, and fell on king just as he was quietly clearing off. They committed a breach of peace, that's what, so blood's on their own head.
THE CHAPLAIN: All our king minded about was freedom. The emperor had made slaves of them all, Poles and Germans alike, and the king had to liberate them.
THE COOK: Just what I say, your brandy's first rate, I weren't mistaken in your face, but talk of the king, it cost the king dear trying to give freedom to Germany, what with giving Sweden the salt tax, what cost the poor folk a bit, so I've heard, on top of which he had to have the Germans locked up and drawn and quartered cause they wanted to carry on slaving for the emperor. Course the king took a serious view when anybody didn't want to be free. He set out by just trying to protect Poland against bad people, particularly the emperor, then it started to become a habit till he ended up protecting the whole of Germany. They didn't half kick. So the poor old king's had nowt but trouble for all his kindness and expenses, and that's something he had to make up for by taxes of course, which caused bad blood, not that he'd let a little matter like that depress him. One thing he had on his side, God's word, that was a help. Because otherwise folk would of been saying he done it all for himself and to make a bit on the side. So he's always had a good conscience, which was the main point.
MOTHER COURAGE: Anyone can see you're no Swede or you wouldn't be talking that way about the Hero King.
THE CHAPLAIN: After all he provides the bread you eat.
THE COOK: I don't eat it, I bake it.
MOTHER COURAGE: They'll never beat him, and why, his men got faith in him. (*Seriously.*) To go by what the big shots say, they're waging war for almighty God and in the name of everything that's good and

lovely. But look closer, they ain't so silly, they're waging it for what they can get. Else little folk like me
wouldn't be in it at all.

THE COOK: That's the way it is.

THE CHAPLAIN: As a Dutchman you'd do better to
glance at the flag above your head before venting
your opinions here in Poland.

MOTHER COURAGE: All good Lutherans here. Prosit!°

(*Kattrin has put on Yvette's hat and begun strutting
around in imitation of her way of walking.*)

(*Suddenly there is a noise of cannon fire and shooting.
Drums. Mother Courage, the cook and the chaplain
rush out from behind the cart, the two last-named still
carrying their glasses. The armourer and another soldier
run up to the cannon and try to push it away.*)

MOTHER COURAGE: What's happening? Wait till I've
taken my washing down, you louts! (*She tries to rescue her washing.*)

THE ARMOURER: The Catholics! Broken through. Don't
know if we'll get out of here. (*To the soldier.*) Get
that gun shifted! (*Runs on.*)

THE COOK: God, I must find the general. Courage, I'll
drop by in a day or two for another talk.

MOTHER COURAGE: Wait, you forgot your pipe.

THE COOK (*in the distance*): Keep it for me. I'll be needing it.

MOTHER COURAGE: Would happen just as we're making
a bit of money.

THE CHAPLAIN: Ah well, I'll be going too. Indeed, if the
enemy is so close as that it might be dangerous.
Blessèd are the peacemakers is the motto in wartime.
If only I had a cloak to cover me.

MOTHER COURAGE: I ain't lending no cloaks, not on
your life. I been had too often.

THE CHAPLAIN: But my faith makes it particularly dangerous for me.

MOTHER COURAGE (*gets him a cloak*): Goes against my
conscience, this does. Now you run along.

THE CHAPLAIN: Thank you, dear lady, that's very generous of you, but I think it might be wiser for me to
remain seated here; it could arouse suspicion and
bring the enemy down on me if I were seen to run.

MOTHER COURAGE (*to the soldier*): Leave it, you fool,
who's going to pay you for that? I'll look after it for
you, you're risking your neck.

THE SOLDIER (*running away*): You can tell 'em I tried.

MOTHER COURAGE: Cross my heart. (*Sees her daughter
with the hat.*) What you doing with that strumpet's
hat? Take that lid off, you gone crazy? And the
enemy arriving any minute! (*Pulls the hat off Kattrin's head.*) Want 'em to pick you up and make a
prostitute of you? And she's gone and put those
boots on, whore of Babylon! Off with those boots!
(*Tries to tug them off her.*) Jesus Christ, chaplain,
gimme a hand, get those boots off her, I'll be right
back. (*Runs to the cart.*)

Prosit!: Cheers!

YVETTE (*arrives, powdering her face*): Fancy that, the
Catholics are coming. Where's my hat? Who's been
kicking it around? I can't go about looking like this if
the Catholics are coming. What'll they think of me?
No mirror either. (*To the chaplain.*) How do I look?
Too much powder?

THE CHAPLAIN: Exactly right.

YVETTE: And where are them red boots? (*Fails to find
them as Kattrin hides her feet under her skirt.*) I left
them here all right. Now I'll have to get to me tent
barefoot. It's an outrage.

(*Exit.*)

(*Swiss Cheese runs in carrying in a small box.*)

MOTHER COURAGE (*Arrives with her hands full of ashes.
To Kattrin.*): Here some ashes. (*To Swiss Cheese.*)
What's that you're carrying?

SWISS CHEESE: Regimental cash box.

MOTHER COURAGE: Chuck it away. No more paymas-
tering for you.

SWISS CHEESE: I'm responsible. (*He goes to the rear.*)

MOTHER COURAGE (*to the chaplain*): Take your clerical
togs off, padre, or they'll spot you under that cloak.
(*She rubs Kattrin's face with ash.*) Keep still, will you?
There you are, a bit of muck and you'll be safe. What
a disaster. Sentries were drunk. Hide your light under
a bushel, it says. Take a soldier, specially a Catholic
one, add a clean face, and there's your instant whore.
For weeks they get nowt to eat, then soon as they
manage to get it by looting they're falling on anything
in skirts. That ought to do. Let's have a look. Not
bad. Looks like you been grubbing in muckheap. Stop
trembling. Nothing'll happen to you like that. (*To
Swiss Cheese.*) Where d'you leave cash box?

SWISS CHEESE: Thought I'd put it in cart.

MOTHER COURAGE (*horrified*): What, my cart? Sheer
criminal idiocy. Only take me eyes off you one instant. Hang us all three, they will.

SWISS CHEESE: I'll put it somewhere else then, or clear
out with it.

MOTHER COURAGE: You sit on it, it's too late now.

THE CHAPLAIN (*who is changing his clothes downstage*):
For heaven's sake, the flag!

MOTHER COURAGE (*hauls down the regimental flag*):
Bozhe moi! I'd given up noticing it were there.
Twenty-five years I've had it.

(*The thunder of cannon intensifies.*)

(*A morning three days later. The cannon has gone.
Mother Courage, Kattrin, the chaplain and Swiss Cheese
are sitting gloomily over a meal.*)

SWISS CHEESE: That's three days I been sitting around
with nowt to do, and sergeant's always been kind to
me but any moment now he'll start asking where's
Swiss Cheese with the pay box?

MOTHER COURAGE: You thank your stars they ain't
after you.

THE CHAPLAIN: What can I say? I can't even hold a service here, it might make trouble for me. Whosoever

hath a full heart, his tongue runneth over, it says, but heaven help me if mine starts running over.

MOTHER COURAGE: That's how it goes. Here they sit, one with his faith and the other with his cash box. Dunno which is more dangerous.

THE CHAPLAIN: We are all of us in God's hands.

MOTHER COURAGE: Oh, I don't think it's as bad as that yet, though I must say I can't sleep nights. If it weren't for you, Swiss Cheese, things'd be easier. I think I got meself cleared. I told 'em I didn't hold with Antichrist, the Swedish one with horns on, and I'd observed left horn was a bit unserviceable. Half way through their interrogation I asked where I could get church candles not too dear. I knows the lingo cause Swiss Cheese's dad were Catholic, often used to make jokes about it, he did. They didn't believe me all that much, but they ain't got no regimental canteen lady. So they're winking an eye. Could turn out for the best, you know. We're prisoners, but same like fleas on dog.

THE CHAPLAIN: That's good milk. But we'll need to cut down our Swedish appetites a bit. After all, we've been defeated.

MOTHER COURAGE: Who's been defeated? Look, victory and defeat ain't bound to be same for the big shots up top as for them below, not by no means. Can be times the bottom lot find a defeat really pays them. Honour's lost, nowt else. I remember once up in Livonia our general took such a beating from enemy I got a horse off our baggage train in the confusion, pulled me cart seven months, he did, before we won and they checked up. As a rule you can say victory and defeat both come expensive to us ordinary folk. Best thing for us is when politics get bogged down solid. (To Swiss Cheese.) Eat up.

SWISS CHEESE: Got no appetite for it. What's sergeant to do when pay day comes round?

MOTHER COURAGE: They don't have pay days on a retreat.

SWISS CHEESE: It's their right, though. They needn't retreat if they don't get paid. Needn't stir a foot.

MOTHER COURAGE: Swiss Cheese, you're that conscientious it makes me quite nervous. I brought you up to be honest, you not being clever, but you got to know where to stop. Chaplain and me, we're off now to buy Catholic flag and some meat. Dunno anyone so good at sniffing meat, like sleepwalking it is, straight to target. I'd say he can pick out a good piece by the way his mouth starts watering. Well, thank goodness they're letting me go on trading. You don't ask tradespeople their faith but their prices. And Lutheran trousers keep cold out too.

THE CHAPLAIN: What did the mendicant say when he heard the Lutherans were going to turn everything in town and country topsy-turvy? "They'll always need beggars." (Mother Courage disappears into the cart.) So she's still worried about the cash box. So far they've taken us all for granted as part of the cart, but how long for?

SWISS CHEESE: I can get rid of it.

THE CHAPLAIN: That's almost more dangerous. Suppose you're seen. They have spies. Yesterday a fellow popped up out of the ditch in front of me just as I was relieving myself first thing. I was so scared I only just suppressed an ejaculatory prayer. That would have given me away all right. I think what they'd like best is to go sniffing people's excrement to see if they're Protestants. The spy was a little runt with a patch over one eye.

MOTHER COURAGE (clambering out of the cart with a basket): What have I found, you shameless creature? (She holds up the red boots in triumph.) Yvette's red high-heeled boots! Coolly went and pinched them, she did. Cause you put it in her head she was an enchanting young person. (She lays them in the basket.) I'm giving them back. Stealing Yvette's boots! She's wrecking herself for money. That's understandable. But you'd do it for nothing, for pleasure. What did I tell you: you're to wait till it's peace. No soldiers for you. You're not to start exhibiting yourself till it's peacetime.

THE CHAPLAIN: I don't find she exhibits herself.

MOTHER COURAGE: Too much for my liking. Let her be like a stone in Dalecarlia, where there's nowt else, so folk say "Can't see that cripple," that's how I'd lief have her. Then nowt'll happen to her. (To Swiss Cheese.) You leave that box where it is, d'you hear? And keep an eye on your sister, she needs it. The pair of you'll have me in grave yet. Sooner be minding a bagful of fleas.

(She leaves with the chaplain. Kattrin clears away the dishes.)

SWISS CHEESE: Won't be able to sit out in the sun in shirtsleeves much longer. (Kattrin points at a tree.) Aye, leaves turning yellow. (Kattrin asks by gestures if he wants a drink.) Don't want no drink. I'm thinking. (Pause.) Said she can't sleep. Best if I got rid of that box, found a good place for it. All right, let's have a glass. (Kattrin goes behind the cart.) I'll stuff it down the rat-hole by the river for the time being. Probably pick it up tonight before first light and take it to Regiment. How far can they have retreated in three days? Bet sergeant's surprised. I'm agreeably disappointed in you, Swiss Cheese, he'll say. I make you responsible for the cash, and you go and bring it back.

(As Kattrin emerges from behind the cart with a full glass in her hand, two men confront her. One is a sergeant, the other doffs his hat to her. He has a patch over one eye.)

THE MAN WITH THE PATCH: God be with you, mistress. Have you seen anyone round here from Second Finnish Regimental Headquarters?

(Kattrin, badly frightened, runs downstage, spilling the brandy. The two men look at one another, then withdraw on seeing Swiss Cheese sitting there.)

SWISS CHEESE (*interrupted in his thoughts*): You spilt half of it. What are those faces for? Jabbed yourself in eye? I don't get it. And I'll have to be off, I've thought it over, it's the only way. (*He gets up. She does everything possible to make him realise the danger. He only shrugs her off.*) Wish I knew what you're trying to say. Sure you mean well, poor creature, just can't get words out. What's it matter your spilling my brandy, I'll drink plenty more glasses yet, what's one more or less? (*He gets the box from the cart and takes it under his tunic.*) Be back in a moment. Don't hold me up now, or I'll be angry. I know you mean well. Too bad you can't speak.

(*As she tries to hold him back he kisses her and tears himself away. Exit. She is desperate, running hither and thither uttering little noises. The chaplain and Mother Courage return. Kattrin rushes to her mother.*)

MOTHER COURAGE: What's all this? Pull yourself together, love. They done something to you? Where's Swiss Cheese? Tell it me step by step, Kattrin. Mother understands you. What, so that bastard did take the box? I'll wrap it round his ears, the little hypocrite. Take your time and don't gabble, use your hands, I don't like it when you howl like a dog, what'll his reverence say? Makes him uncomfortable. What, a one-eyed man came along?

THE CHAPLAIN: That one-eyed man is a spy. Have they arrested Swiss Cheese? (*Kattrin shakes her head, shrugs her shoulders.*) We're done for.

MOTHER COURAGE (*fishes in her basket and brings out a Catholic flag, which the chaplain fixes to the mast*): Better hoist new flag.

THE CHAPLAIN (*bitterly*): All good Catholics here.

(*Voices are heard from the rear. The two men bring in Swiss Cheese.*)

SWISS CHEESE: Let me go, I got nowt. Don't twist my shoulder, I'm innocent.

SERGEANT: Here's where he came from. You know each other.

MOTHER COURAGE: Us? How?

SWISS CHEESE: I don't know them. Got no idea who she is, had nowt to do with them. I bought me dinner here, ten hellers it cost. You might have seen me sitting here, it was too salty.

SERGEANT: Who are you people, eh?

MOTHER COURAGE: We're law-abiding folk. That's right, he bought a dinner. Said it was too salty.

SERGEANT: Trying to pretend you don't know each other, that it?

MOTHER COURAGE: Why should I know him? Can't know everyone. I don't go asking 'em what they're called and are they a heretic; if he pays he ain't a heretic. You a heretic?

SWISS CHEESE: Go on.

THE CHAPLAIN: He sat there very properly, never opening his mouth except when eating. Then he had to.

SERGEANT: And who are you?

MOTHER COURAGE: He's just my potboy. Now I expect you gentlemen are thirsty, I'll get you a glass of brandy, you must be hot and tired with running.

SERGEANT: No brandy on duty. (*To Swiss Cheese.*) You were carrying something. Must have hidden it by the river. Was a bulge in your tunic when you left here.

MOTHER COURAGE: You sure it was him?

SWISS CHEESE: You must be thinking of someone else. I saw someone bounding off with a bulge in his tunic. I'm the wrong man.

MOTHER COURAGE: I'd say it was a misunderstanding too, such things happen. I'm a good judge of people, I'm Courage, you heard of me, everyone knows me, and I tell you that's an honest face he has.

SERGEANT: We're on the track of the Second Finnish Regiment's cash box. We got the description of the fellow responsible for it. Been trailing him two days. It's you.

SWISS CHEESE: It's not me.

SERGEANT: And you better cough it up, or you're a goner, you know. Where is it?

MOTHER COURAGE (*urgently*): Of course he'd give it over rather than be a goner. Right out he'd say: I got it, here it is, you're too strong. He ain't all that stupid. Speak up, stupid idiot, here's the sergeant giving you a chance.

SWISS CHEESE: S'pose I ain't got it.

SERGEANT: Then come along. We'll get it out of you. (*They lead him off.*)

MOTHER COURAGE (*calls after them*): He'd tell you. He's not that stupid. And don't you twist his shoulder! (*Runs after them.*)

(*Evening of the same day. The chaplain and dumb Kattrin are cleaning glasses and polishing knives.*)

THE CHAPLAIN: Cases like that, where somebody gets caught, are not unknown in religious history. It reminds me of the Passion of Our Lord and Saviour. There's an old song about that. (*He sings the Song of the Hours.°*)

In the first hour Jesus mild
Who had prayed since even
Was betrayed and led before
Pontius the heathen.

Pilate found him innocent
Free from fault and error
Therefore, having washed his hands
Sent him to King Herod.

In the third hour he was scourged
Stripped and clad in scarlet
And a plaited crown of thorns
Set upon his forehead.

Song of the Hours: Translated by Ralph Manheim.

On the Son of Man they spat
Mocked him and made merry.
Then the cross of death was brought
Given him to carry.

At the sixth hour with two thieves
To the cross they nailed him
And the people and the thieves
Mocked him and reviled him.

This is Jesus King of Jews
Cried they in derision
Till the sun withdrew its light
From that awful vision.

At the ninth hour Jesus wailed
Why hast thou me forsaken?
Soldiers brought him vinegar
Which he left untaken.

Then he yielded up the ghost
And the earth was shaken.
Rended was the temple's veil
And the saints were wakened.

Soldiers broke the two thieves' legs
As the night descended.
Thrust a spear in Jesus' side
When his life had ended.

Still they mocked, as from his wound
Flowed the blood and water
And blasphemed the Son of Man
With their cruel laughter.

MOTHER COURAGE (*entering excitedly*): It's touch and go. They say sergeant's open to reason though. Only we mustn't let on it's Swiss Cheese else they'll say we helped him. It's a matter of money, that's all. But where's money to come from? Hasn't Yvette been round? I ran into her, she's got her hooks on some colonel, maybe he'd buy her a canteen business.
THE CHAPLAIN: Do you really wish to sell?
MOTHER COURAGE: Where's money for sergeant to come from?
THE CHAPLAIN: What'll you live on, then?
MOTHER COURAGE: That's just it.

(*Yvette Pottier arrives with an extremely ancient colonel.*)

YVETTE (*embracing Mother Courage*): My dear Courage, fancy seeing you so soon. (*Whispers.*) He's not unwilling. (*Aloud.*) This is my good friend who advises me in business matters. I happened to hear you wanted to sell your cart on account of circumstances. I'll think it over.
MOTHER COURAGE: Pledge it, not sell, just not too much hurry, 'tain't every day you find a cart like this in wartime.

YVETTE (*disappointed*): Oh, pledge. I thought it was for sale. I'm not so sure I'm interested. (*To the colonel.*) How do you feel about it?
THE COLONEL: Just as you feel, pet.
MOTHER COURAGE: I'm only pledging it.
YVETTE: I thought you'd got to have the money.
MOTHER COURAGE (*firmly*): I got to have it, but sooner run myself ragged looking for a bidder than sell outright. And why? The cart's our livelihood. It's a chance for you, Yvette; who knows when you'll get another like it and have a special friend to advise you, am I right?
YVETTE: Yes, my friend thinks I should clinch it, but I'm not sure. If it's only a pledge . . . so you agree we ought to buy outright?
THE COLONEL: I agree, pet.
MOTHER COURAGE: Best look and see if you can find anything for sale then; maybe you will if you don't rush it, take your friend along with you, say a week or fortnight, might find something suits you.
YVETTE: Then let's go looking. I adore going around looking for things, I adore going around with you, Poldi, it's such fun, isn't it? No matter if it takes a fortnight. How soon would you pay the money back if you got it?
MOTHER COURAGE: I'd pay back in two weeks, maybe one.
YVETTE: I can't make up my mind, Poldi chéri, you advise me. (*Takes the colonel aside.*) She's got to sell, I know, no problem there. And there's that ensign, you know, the fair-haired one, he'd be glad to lend me the money. He's crazy about me, says there's someone I remind him of. What do you advise?
THE COLONEL: You steer clear of him. He's no good. He's only making use of you. I said I'd buy you something, didn't I, pussykins?
YVETTE: I oughtn't to let you. Of course if you think the ensign might try to take advantage . . . Poldi, I'll accept it from you.
THE COLONEL: That's how I feel too.
YVETTE: Is that your advice?
THE COLONEL: That is my advice.
YVETTE (*to Courage once more*): My friend's advice would be to accept. Make me out a receipt saying the cart's mine once two weeks are up, with all its contents, we'll check it now, I'll bring the two hundred florins later. (*To the colonel.*) You go back to the camp, I'll follow, I got to check it all and see there's nothing missing from my cart. (*She kisses him. He leaves. She climbs up on the cart.*) Not all that many boots, are there?
MOTHER COURAGE: Yvette, it's no time for checking your cart, s'posing it is yours. You promised you'd talk to sergeant about Swiss Cheese, there ain't a minute to lose, they say in an hour he'll be court-martialled.
YVETTE: Just let me count the shirts.
MOTHER COURAGE (*pulling her down by the skirt*): You bloody vampire. Swiss Cheese's life's at stake. And

not a word about who's making the offer, for God's sake, pretend it's your friend, else we're all done for cause we looked after him.

YVETTE: I fixed to meet that one-eyed fellow in the copse, he should be there by now.

THE CHAPLAIN: It doesn't have to be the whole two hundred either, I'd go up to a hundred and fifty, that may be enough.

MOTHER COURAGE: Since when has it been your money? You kindly keep out of this. You'll get your hotpot all right, don't worry. Hurry up and don't haggle, it's life or death. (*Pushes Yvette off.*)

THE CHAPLAIN: Far be it from me to interfere, but what are we going to live on? You're saddled with a daughter who can't earn her keep.

MOTHER COURAGE: I'm counting on regimental cash box, Mr. Clever. They'll allow it as his expenses.

THE CHAPLAIN: But will she get the message right?

MOTHER COURAGE: It's her interest I should spend her two hundred so she gets the cart. She's set on that, God knows how long that colonel of hers'll last. Kattrin, polish the knives, there's the pumice. And you, stop hanging round like Jesus on Mount of Olives,° get moving, wash them glasses, we'll have fifty or more of cavalry in tonight and I don't want to hear a lot of "I'm not accustomed to having to run about, oh my poor feet, we never ran in church." Thank the Lord they're corruptible. After all, they ain't wolves, just humans out for money. Corruption in humans is same as compassion in God. Corruption's our only hope. Long as we have it there'll be lenient sentences and even an innocent man'll have a chance of being let off.

YVETTE (*comes in panting*): They'll do it for two hundred. But it's got to be quick. Soon be out of their hands. Best thing is I go right away to my colonel with the one-eyed man. He's admitted he had the box, they put the thumbscrews on him. But he chucked it in the river soon as he saw they were on his track. The box is a write-off. I'll go and get the money from my colonel, shall I?

MOTHER COURAGE: Box is a write-off? How'm I to pay back two hundred then?

YVETTE: Oh, you thought you'd get it from the box, did you? And I was to be Joe Soap I suppose? Better not count on that. You'll have to pay up if you want Swiss Cheese back, or would you sooner I dropped the whole thing so's you can keep your cart?

MOTHER COURAGE: That's something I didn't allow for. Don't worry, you'll get your cart, I've said goodbye to it, had it seventeen years, I have. I just need a moment to think, it's bit sudden, what'm I to do, two hundred's too much for me, pity you didn't beat 'em down. Must keep a bit back, else any Tom, Dick and Harry'll be able to shove me in ditch. Go and tell

them I'll pay hundred and twenty florins, else it's all off, either way I'm losing me cart.

YVETTE: They won't do it. That one-eyed man's impatient already, keeps looking over his shoulder, he's so worked up. Hadn't I best pay them the whole two hundred?

MOTHER COURAGE (*in despair*): I can't pay that. Thirty years I been working. She's twenty-five already, and no husband. I got her to think of too. Don't push me, I know what I'm doing. Say a hundred and twenty, or it's off.

YVETTE: It's up to you. (*Rushes off.*)

(*Without looking at either the chaplain or her daughter, Mother Courage sits down to help Kattrin polish knives.*)

MOTHER COURAGE: Don't smash them glasses, they ain't ours now. Watch what you're doing, you'll cut yourself. Swiss Cheese'll be back, I'll pay two hundred if it comes to the pinch. You'll get your brother, love. For eighty florins we could fill a pack with goods and start again. Plenty of folk has to make do.

THE CHAPLAIN: The Lord will provide, it says.

MOTHER COURAGE: See they're properly dry. (*She cleans knives in silence. Kattrin suddenly runs behind the cart, sobbing.*)

YVETTE (*comes running in*): They won't do it. I told you so. The one-eyed man wanted to leave right away, said there was no point. He says he's just waiting for the drum-roll; that means sentence has been pronounced. I offered a hundred and fifty. He didn't even blink. I had to convince him to stay there so's I could have another word with you.

MOTHER COURAGE: Tell him I'll pay the two hundred. Hurry! (*Yvette runs off. They sit in silence. The chaplain has stopped polishing the glasses.*) I reckon I bargained too long.

(*In the distance drumming is heard. The chaplain gets up and goes to the rear. Mother Courage remains seated. It grows dark. The drumming stops. It grows light once more. Mother Courage is sitting exactly as before.*)

YVETTE (*arrives, very pale*): Well, you got what you asked for, with your haggling and trying to keep your cart. Eleven bullets they gave him, that's all. You don't deserve I should bother any more about you. But I did hear they don't believe the box really is in the river. They've an idea it's here and anyhow that you're connected with him. They're going to bring him here, see if you gives yourself away when you sees him. Thought I'd better warn you so's you don't recognise him, else you'll all be for it. They're right on my heels, best tell you quick. Shall I keep Kattrin away? (*Mother Courage shakes her head.*) Does she know? She mayn't have heard the drumming or know what it meant.

MOTHER COURAGE: She knows. Get her.

(*Yvette fetches Kattrin, who goes to her mother and stands beside her. Mother Courage takes her hand. Two*

Jesus on Mount of Olives: The Bible shows Jesus on the Mount of Olives when he preaches the Sermon on the Mount and when he prays in anguish before his betrayal by Peter.

lansequenets come carrying a stretcher with something lying on it covered by a sheet. The sergeant marches beside them. They set down the stretcher.)

SERGEANT: Here's somebody we dunno the name of. It's got to be listed, though, so everything's shipshape. He had a meal here. Have a look, see if you know him. (*He removes the sheet.*) Know him? (*Mother Courage shakes her head.*) What, never see him before he had that meal here? (*Mother Courage shakes her head.*) Pick him up. Chuck him in the pit. He's got nobody knows him. (*They carry him away.*)

SCENE 4

(*Mother Courage sings the Song of the Grand Capitulation.*)
(*Outside an officer's tent.*)
(*Mother Courage is waiting. A clerk looks out of the tent.*)

THE CLERK: I know you. You had a paymaster from the Lutherans with you, what was in hiding. I'd not complain if I were you.

MOTHER COURAGE: But I got a complaint to make. I'm innocent, would look as how I'd a bad conscience if I let this pass. Slashed everything in me cart to pieces with their sabres, they did, then wanted I should pay five taler fine for nowt, I tell you, nowt.

CLERK: Take my tip, better shut up. We're short of canteens, so we let you go on trading, specially if you got a bad conscience and pay a fine now and then.

MOTHER COURAGE: I got a complaint.

CLERK: Have it your own way. Then you must wait till the captain's free. (*Withdraws inside the tent.*)

YOUNG SOLDIER (*enters aggressively*): Bouque la Madonne! Where's that bleeding pig of a captain what's took my reward money to swig with his tarts? I'll do him.

OLDER SOLDIER (*running after him*): Shut up. They'll put you in irons.

YOUNG SOLDIER: Out of there, you thief! I'll slice you into pork chops, I will. Pocketing my prize money after I'd swum the river, only one in the whole squadron, and now I can't even buy meself a beer. I'm not standing for that. Come on out there so I can cut you up!

OLDER SOLDIER: Blessed Mother of God, he's asking for trouble.

MOTHER COURAGE: Is it some reward he weren't paid?

YOUNG SOLDIER: Lemme go, I'll slash you too while I'm at it.

OLDER SOLDIER: He rescued the colonel's horse and got no reward for it. He's young yet, still wet behind the ears.

MOTHER COURAGE: Let him go, he ain't a dog you got to chain up. Wanting your reward is good sound sense. Why be a hero otherwise?

YOUNG SOLDIER: So's he can sit in there and booze.

You're shit-scared, the lot of you. I done something special and I want my reward.

MOTHER COURAGE: Don't you shout at me, young fellow. Got me own worries, I have; any road you should spare your voice, be needing it when captain comes, else there he'll be and you too hoarse to make a sound, which'll make it hard for him to clap you in irons till you turn blue. People what shouts like that can't keep it up ever; half an hour, and they have to be rocked to sleep, they're so tired.

YOUNG SOLDIER: I ain't tired and to hell with sleep. I'm hungry. They make our bread from acorns and hemp-seed, and they even skimp on that. He's whoring away my reward and I'm hungry. I'll do him.

MOTHER COURAGE: Oh I see, you're hungry. Last year that general of yours ordered you all off roads and across fields so corn should be trampled flat; I could've got ten florins for a pair of boots s'pose I'd had boots and s'pose anyone'd been able to pay ten florins. Thought he'd be well away from that area this year, he did, but here he is, still there, and hunger is great. I see what you're angry about.

YOUNG SOLDIER: I won't have it, don't talk to me, it ain't fair and I'm not standing for that.

MOTHER COURAGE: And you're right; but how long? How long you not standing for unfairness? One hour, two hours? Didn't ask yourself that, did you, but it's the whole point, and why, once you're in irons it's too bad if you suddenly finds you can put up with unfairness after all.

YOUNG SOLDIER: What am I listening to you for, I'd like to know? Bouque la Madonne, where's that captain?

MOTHER COURAGE: You been listening to me because you knows it's like what I say, your anger has gone up in smoke already, it was just a short one and you needed a long one, but where you going to get it from?

YOUNG SOLDIER: Are you trying to tell me asking for my reward is wrong?

MOTHER COURAGE: Not a bit. I'm just telling you your anger ain't long enough, it's good for nowt, pity. If you'd a long one I'd be trying to prod you on. Cut him up, the swine, would be my advice to you in that case; but how about if you don't cut him up cause you feels your tail going between your legs? Then I'd look silly and captain'd take it out on me.

OLDER SOLDIER: You're perfectly right, he's just a bit crazy.

YOUNG SOLDIER: Very well, let's see if I don't cut him up. (*Draws his sword.*) When he arrives I'm going to cut him up.

CLERK (*looks out*): The captain'll be here in one minute. Sit down.

(*The young soldier sits down.*)

MOTHER COURAGE: He's sitting now. See, what did I say? You're sitting now. Ah, how well they know us, no one need tell 'em how to go about it. Sit down! and, bingo, we're sitting. And sitting and sedition don't mix. Don't try to stand up, you won't stand the way you was standing before. I shouldn't worry about what I think; I'm no better, not one moment. Bought up all our fighting spirit, they have. Eh? S'pose I kick back, might be bad for business. Let me tell you a thing or two about the Grand Capitulation. (*She sings the Song of the Grand Capitulation.*)

Back when I was young, I was brought to realise
What a very special person I must be
(Not just any old cottager's daughter, what with my
    looks and my talents and my urge towards
    Higher Things)
And insisted that my soup should have no hairs in it.
No one makes a sucker out of me!
(All or nothing, only the best is good enough, each
    man for himself, nobody's telling *me* what to do.)
Then I heard a tit
Chirp: Wait a bit!
    And you'll be marching with the band
    In step, responding to command
    And striking up your little dance:
    Now we advance.
    And now: parade, form square!
    Then men swear God's there —
    Not the faintest chance!

In no time at all anyone who looked could see
That I'd learned to take my medicine with good
    grace.
(Two kids on my hands and look at the price of
    bread, and things they expect of you!)
When they finally came to feel that they were
    through with me
They'd got me grovelling on my face.
(Takes all sorts to make a world, you scratch my
    back and I'll scratch yours, no good banging
    your head against a brick wall.)
Then I heard that tit
Chirp: Wait a bit!
    And you'll be marching with the band
    In step, responding to command
    And striking up your little dance:
    Now they advance.
    And now: parade, form square!
    Then men swear God's there —
    Not the faintest chance!

I've known people tried to storm the summits:
There's no star too bright or seems too far away.
(Dogged does it, where there's a will there's a way,
    by hook or by crook.)
As each peak disclosed fresh peaks to come, it's
Strange how much a plain straw hat could weigh.
(You have to cut your coat according to your cloth.)
Then I hear the tit
Chirp: Wait a bit!
    And they'll be marching with the band
    In step, responding to command

And striking up their little dance:
Now they advance.
And now: parade, form square!
Then men swear God's there —
Not the faintest chance!

MOTHER COURAGE (*to the young soldier*): That's why I reckon you should stay there with your sword drawn if you're truly set on it and your anger's big enough, because you got grounds, I agree, but if your anger's a short one best leave right away.

YOUNG SOLDIER: Oh stuff it. (*He staggers off with the older soldier following.*)

CLERK (*sticks his head out*): Captain's here now. You can make your complaint.

MOTHER COURAGE: I changed me mind. I ain't complaining.

(*Exit.*)

SCENE 5

(*Two years have gone by. The war is spreading to new areas. Ceaselessly on the move, Courage's little cart crosses Poland, Moravia, Bavaria, Italy then Bavaria again. 1631. Tilly's victory at Magdeburg costs Mother Courage four officers' shirts.*)
(*Mother Courage's cart has stopped in a badly shot-up village. Thin military music in the distance. Two soldiers at the bar being served by Kattrin and Mother Courage. One of them has a lady's fur coat over his shoulders.*)

MOTHER COURAGE: Can't pay, that it? No money, no schnapps. They give us victory parades, but catch them giving men their pay.

SOLDIER: I want my schnapps. I missed the looting. That double-crossing general only allowed an hour's looting in the town. He ain't an inhuman monster, he said. Town must of paid him.

THE CHAPLAIN (*stumbles in*): There are people still lying in that yard. The peasant's family. Somebody give me a hand. I need linen.

(*The second soldier goes off with him. Kattrin becomes very excited and tries to make her mother produce linen.*)

MOTHER COURAGE: I got none. All my bandages was sold to regiment. I ain't tearing up my officer's shirts for that lot.

CHAPLAIN (*calling back*): I need linen, I tell you.

MOTHER COURAGE (*blocking Kattrin's way into the cart by sitting on the step*): I'm giving nowt. They'll never pay, and why, nowt to pay with.

CHAPLAIN (*bending over a woman he has carried in*): Why d'you stay around during the gunfire?

PEASANT WOMAN (*feebly*): Farm.

MOTHER COURAGE: Catch them abandoning anything. But now I'm s'posed to foot the bill. I won't do it.

FIRST SOLDIER: Those are Protestants. What they have to be Protestants for?

MOTHER COURAGE: They ain't bothering about faith. They lost their farm.

SECOND SOLDIER: They're no Protestants. They're Catholics like us.

FIRST SOLDIER: No way of sorting 'em out in a bombardment.

A PEASANT (*brought in by the chaplain*): My arm's gone.

THE CHAPLAIN: Where's that linen?

MOTHER COURAGE: I can't give nowt. What with expenses, taxes, loan interest and bribes. (*Making guttural noises, Kattrin raises a plank and threatens her mother with it.*) You gone plain crazy? Put that plank away or I'll paste you one, you cow. I'm giving nowt, don't want to, got to think of meself. (*The chaplain lifts her off the steps and sets her on the ground, then starts pulling out shirts and tearing them into strips.*) My officers' shirts! Half a florin apiece! I'm ruined. (*From the house comes the cry of a child in pain.*)

THE PEASANT: The baby's in there still. (*Kattrin dashes in.*)

THE CHAPLAIN (*to the woman*): Don't move. They'll get it out.

MOTHER COURAGE: Stop her, roof may fall in.

THE CHAPLAIN: I'm not going back in there.

MOTHER COURAGE (*torn both ways*): Don't waste my precious linen.

(*Kattrin brings a baby out of the ruins.*)

MOTHER COURAGE: How nice, found another baby to cart around? Give it to its ma this instant, unless you'd have me fighting for hours to get it off you, like last time, d'you hear? (*To the second soldier.*) Don't stand there gawping, you go back and tell them cut out that music, we can see it's a victory with our own eyes. All your victories mean to me is losses.

THE CHAPLAIN (*tying a bandage*): Blood's coming through.

(*Kattrin is rocking the baby and making lullaby noises.*)

MOTHER COURAGE: Look at her, happy as a queen in all this misery; give it back at once, its mother's coming round. (*She catches the first soldier, who has been attacking the drinks and is trying to make off with one of the bottles.*) Psia krew! Thought you'd score another victory, you animal? Now pay.

FIRST SOLDIER: I got nowt.

MOTHER COURAGE (*pulling the fur coat off his back*): Then leave that coat, it's stolen any road.

THE CHAPLAIN: There's still someone under there.

SCENE 6

(*Outside the Bavarian town of Ingolstadt Courage participates in the funeral of the late Imperial commander Tilly. Discussions are held about war heroes and the war's duration. The chaplain complains that his talents are lying fallow, and dumb Kattrin gets the red boots. The year is 1632.*)

(*Inside a canteen tent.*)

(*It has a bar towards the rear. Rain. Sound of drums and Funeral music. The chaplain and the regimental clerk are playing a board game. Mother Courage and her daughter are stocktaking.*)

THE CHAPLAIN: Now the funeral procession will be moving off.

MOTHER COURAGE: Too bad about commander in chief — twenty-two pairs those socks — he fell by accident, they say. Mist over fields, that was the trouble. General had just been haranguing a regiment saying they must fight to last man and last round, he was riding back when mist made him lose direction so he was up front and a bullet got him in midst of battle — only four hurricane lamps left. (*A whistle from the rear. She goes to the bar.*) You scrim-shankers, dodging your commander in chief's funeral, scandal I call it. (*Pours drinks.*)

THE CLERK: They should never of paid troops out before the funeral. Instead of going now they're all getting pissed.

THE CHAPLAIN (*to the clerk*): Aren't you supposed to go to the funeral?

THE CLERK: Dodged it cause of the rain.

MOTHER COURAGE: It's different with you, your uniform might get wet. I heard they wanted to toll bells for funeral as usual, except it turned out all churches had been blown to smithereens by his orders, so poor old commander in chief won't be hearing no bells as they let the coffin down. They're going to let off three salvoes instead to cheer things up — seventeen belts.

SHOUTS (*from the bar*): Hey, Missis, a brandy!

MOTHER COURAGE: Let's see your money. No, I ain't having you in my tent with your disgusting boots. You can drink outside, rain or no rain. (*To the clerk.*) I'm only letting in sergeants and up. Commander in chief had been having his worries, they say. S'posed to have been trouble with Second Regiment cause he stopped their pay, said it was a war of faith and they should do it for free. (*Funeral march. All look to the rear.*)

THE CHAPLAIN: Now they'll be filing past the noble corpse.

MOTHER COURAGE: Can't help feeling sorry for those generals and emperors, there they are maybe thinking they're doing something extra special what folk'll talk about in years to come, and earning a public monument, like conquering the world for instance, that's a fine ambition for a general, how's he to know any better? I mean, he plagues hisself to death, then it all breaks down on account of ordinary folk what just wants their beer and bit of a chat, nowt higher. Finest plans get bolloxed up by the pettiness of them as should be carrying them out, because emperors can't do nowt themselves, they just counts on soldiers and people to back 'em up whatever happens, am I right?

THE CHAPLAIN (*laughs*): Courage, you're right, aside

from the soldiers. They do their best. Give me that lot outside there, for instance, drinking their brandy in the rain, and I'd guarantee to make you one war after another for a hundred years if need be, and I'm no trained general.

MOTHER COURAGE: You don't think war might end, then?

THE CHAPLAIN: What, because the commander in chief's gone? Don't be childish. They're two a penny, no shortage of heroes.

MOTHER COURAGE: Ee, I'm not asking for fun of it, but because I'm thinking whether to stock up, prices are low now, but if war's going to end it's money down the drain.

THE CHAPLAIN: I realise it's a serious question. There've always been people going round saying "the war can't go on for ever." I tell you there's nothing to stop it going on for ever. Of course there can be a bit of a breathing space. The war may need to get its second wind, it may even have an accident so to speak. There's no guarantee against that; nothing's perfect on this earth of ours. A perfect war, the sort you might say couldn't be improved on, that's something we shall probably never see. It can suddenly come to a standstill for some quite unforeseen reason, you can't allow for everything. A slight case of negligence, and it's bogged down up to the axles. And then it's a matter of hauling the war out of the mud again. But emperor and kings and popes will come to its rescue. So on the whole it has nothing serious to worry about, and will live to a ripe old age.

A SOLDIER (sings at the bar):

A schnapps, landlord, you're late!
A soldier cannot wait
To do his emperor's orders.

Make it a double, this is a holiday.

MOTHER COURAGE: S'pose I went by what you say . . .

THE CHAPLAIN: Think it out for yourself. What's to compete with the war?

THE SOLDIER (at the rear):

Your breast, my girl, you're late!
A soldier cannot wait
To ride across the borders.

THE CLERK (unexpectedly): And what about peace? I'm from Bohemia and I'd like to go home some day.

THE CHAPLAIN: Would you indeed? Ah, peace. Where is the hole once the cheese has been eaten?

THE SOLDIER (at the rear):

Lead trumps, my friend, you're late!
A soldier cannot wait.
His emperor needs him badly.

Your blessing, priest, you're late!
A soldier cannot wait.
Must lay his life down gladly.

THE CLERK: In the long run life's impossible if there's no peace.

THE CHAPLAIN: I'd say there's peace in war too; it has its peaceful moments. Because war satisfies all requirements, peaceable ones included, they're catered for, and it would simply fizzle out if they weren't. In war you can do a crap like in the depths of peacetime, then between one battle and the next you can have a beer, then even when you're moving up you can lay your head on your arms and have a bit of shuteye in the ditch, it's entirely possible. During a charge you can't play cards maybe, but nor can you in the depths of peacetime when you're ploughing, and after a victory there are various openings. You may get a leg blown off, then you start by making a lot of fuss as though it were serious, but afterwards you calm down or get given a schnapps, and you end up hopping around and the war's no worse off than before. And what's to stop you being fruitful and multiplying in the middle of all the butchery, behind a barn or something, in the long run you can't be held back from it, and then the war will have your progeny and can use them to carry on with. No, the war will always find an outlet, mark my words. Why should it ever stop?

(Kattrin has ceased working and is staring at the chaplain.)

MOTHER COURAGE: I'll buy fresh stock then. If you say so. (Kattrin suddenly flings a basket full of bottles to the ground and runs off.) Kattrin! (Laughs.) Damn me if she weren't waiting for peace. I promised her she'd get a husband soon as peace came. (Hurries after her.)

THE CLERK (standing up): I won. You been talking too much. Pay up.

MOTHER COURAGE (returning with Kattrin): Don't be silly, war'll go on a bit longer, and we'll make a bit more money, and peacetime'll be all the nicer for it. Now you go into town, that's ten minutes' walk at most, fetch things from Golden Lion, the expensive ones, we can fetch rest in cart later, it's all arranged, regimental clerk here will go with you. Nearly everybody's attending commander in chief's funeral, nowt can happen to you. Careful now, don't let them steal nowt, think of your dowry.

(Kattrin puts a cloth over her head and leaves with the clerk.)

THE CHAPLAIN: Is that all right to let her go with the clerk?

MOTHER COURAGE: She's not that pretty they'd want to ruin her.

THE CHAPLAIN: I admire the way you run your business and always win through. I see why they called you Courage.

MOTHER COURAGE: Poor folk got to have courage. Why, they're lost. Simply getting up in morning takes some doing in their situation. Or ploughing a field, and in a war at that. Mere fact they bring kids into world shows they got courage, cause there's no hope for them. They have to hang one another and slaughter one another, so just looking each other in face must call for courage. Being able to put up with emperor and pope shows supernatural courage, cause those two cost 'em their lives. (*She sits down, takes a little pipe from her purse and smokes.*) You might chop us a bit of kindling.

THE CHAPLAIN (*reluctantly removing his coat and preparing to chop up sticks*): I happen to be a pastor of souls, not a woodcutter.

MOTHER COURAGE: I got no soul, you see. Need firewood, though.

THE CHAPLAIN: Where's that stumpy pipe from?

MOTHER COURAGE: Just a pipe.

THE CHAPLAIN: What d'you mean, "just," it's a quite particular pipe, that.

MOTHER COURAGE: Aha?

THE CHAPLAIN: That stumpy pipe belongs to the Oxenstierna Regiment's cook.

MOTHER COURAGE: If you know that already why ask, Mr. Clever?

THE CHAPLAIN: Because I didn't know if you were aware what you're smoking. You might just have been rummaging around in your things, come across some old pipe or other, and used it out of sheer absence of mind.

MOTHER COURAGE: And why not?

THE CHAPLAIN: Because you didn't. You're smoking that deliberately.

MOTHER COURAGE: And why shouldn't I?

THE CHAPLAIN: Courage, I'm warning you. It's my duty. Probably you'll never clap eyes on the gentleman again, and that's no loss but your good fortune. He didn't make at all a reliable impression on me. Quite the opposite.

MOTHER COURAGE: Really? Nice fellow that.

THE CHAPLAIN: So he's what you would call a nice fellow? I wouldn't. Far be it from me to bear him the least ill-will, but nice is not what I would call him. More like one of those Don Juans, a slippery one. Have a look at that pipe if you don't believe me. You must admit it tells you a good deal about his character.

MOTHER COURAGE: Nowt that I can see. Worn out, I'd call it.

THE CHAPLAIN: Practically bitten through, you mean. A man of wrath. That is the pipe of an unscrupulous man of wrath; you must see that if you have any discrimination left.

MOTHER COURAGE: Don't chop my chopping block in two.

THE CHAPLAIN: I told you I'm not a woodcutter by trade. I studied to be a pastor of souls. My talent and abilities are being abused in this place, by manual labour. My God-given endowments are denied expression. It's a sin. You have never heard me preach. One sermon of mine can put a regiment in such a

frame of mind it'll treat the enemy like a flock of sheep. Life to them is a smelly old foot cloth which they fling away in a vision of final victory. God has given me the gift of speech. I can preach so you'll lose all sense of sight and hearing.

MOTHER COURAGE: I don't wish to lose my sense of sight and hearing. Where'd that leave me?

THE CHAPLAIN: Courage, I have often thought that your dry way of talking conceals more than just a warm heart. You too are human and need warmth.

MOTHER COURAGE: Best way for us to get this tent warm is have plenty of firewood.

THE CHAPLAIN: Don't change the subject. Seriously, Courage, I sometimes ask myself what it would be like if our relationship were to become somewhat closer. I mean, given that the whirlwind of war has so strangely whirled us together.

MOTHER COURAGE: I'd say it was close enough. I cook meals for you and you run around and chop firewood for instance.

THE CHAPLAIN (*coming closer*): You know what I mean by closer; it's not a relationship founded on meals and wood-chopping and other such base necessities. Let your head speak, harden thyself not.

MOTHER COURAGE: Don't you come at me with that axe. That'd be too close a relationship.

THE CHAPLAIN: You shouldn't make a joke of it. I'm a serious person and I've thought about what I'm saying.

MOTHER COURAGE: Be sensible, padre. I like you. I don't want to row you. All I'm after is get myself and children through all this with my cart. I don't see it as mine, and I ain't in the mood for private affairs. Right now I'm taking a gamble, buying stores just when commander in chief's fallen and all the talk's of peace. Where d'you reckon you'd turn if I'm ruined? Don't know, do you? You chop us some kindling wood, then we can keep warm at night, that's quite something these times. What's this? (*She gets up. Enter Kattrin, out of breath, with a wound above her eye. She is carrying a variety of stuff: parcels, leather goods, a drum and so on.*)

MOTHER COURAGE: What happened, someone assault you? On way back? She was assaulted on her way back. Bet it was that trooper was getting drunk here. I shouldn't have let you go, love. Drop that stuff. Not too bad, just a flesh wound you got. I'll bandage it and in a week it'll be all right. Worse than wild beasts, they are. (*She ties up the wound.*)

THE CHAPLAIN: It's not them I blame. They never went raping back home. The fault lies with those that start wars, it brings humanity's lowest instincts to the surface.

MOTHER COURAGE: Calm down. Didn't clerk come back with you? That's because you're respectable, they don't bother. Wound ain't a deep one, won't leave no mark. There you are, all bandaged up. You'll get something, love, keep calm. Something I put aside for you, wait till you see. (*She delves into a sack and brings out Yvette's red high-heeled boots.*) Made you open your eyes, eh? Something you always wanted. They're yours. Put 'em on quick, before I change me mind. Won't leave no mark, and what if it does? Ones I'm really sorry for's the ones they fancy. Drag them around till they're worn out, they do. Those they don't care for they leaves alive. I seen girls before now had pretty faces, then in no time looking fit to frighten a hyaena. Can't even go behind a bush without risking trouble, horrible life they lead. Same like with trees, straight well-shaped ones get chopped down to make beams for houses and crooked ones live happily ever after. So it's a stroke of luck for you really. Them boots'll be all right, I greased them before putting them away.

(*Kattrin leaves the boots where they are and crawls into the cart.*)

THE CHAPLAIN: Let's hope she's not disfigured.

MOTHER COURAGE: She'll have a scar. No use her waiting for peacetime now.

THE CHAPLAIN: She didn't let them steal the things.

MOTHER COURAGE: Maybe I shouldn't have dinned that into her so. Wish I knew what went on in that head of hers. Just once she stayed out all night, once in all those years. Afterwards she went around like before, except she worked harder. Couldn't get her to tell what had happened. Worried me quite a while, that did. (*She collects the articles brought by Kattrin, and sorts them angrily.*) That's war for you. Nice way to get a living!

(*Sound of cannon fire.*)

THE CHAPLAIN: Now they'll be burying the commander in chief. This is a historic moment.

MOTHER COURAGE: What I call a historic moment is them bashing my daughter over the eye. She's half wrecked already, won't get no husband now, and her so crazy about kids; anyway, she's only dumb from war, soldier stuffed something in her mouth when she was little. As for Swiss Cheese I'll never see him again, and where Eilif is God alone knows. War be damned.

SCENE 7

(*Mother Courage at the peak of her business career.*)
(*High road.*)
(*The chaplain, Mother Courage, and Kattrin are pulling the cart, which is hung with new wares. Mother Courage is wearing a necklace of silver coins.*)

MOTHER COURAGE: I won't have you folk spoiling my war for me. I'm told it kills off the weak, but they're write-off in peacetime too. And war gives its people a better deal. (*She sings.*)

And if you feel your forces fading
You won't be there to share the fruits.

But what is war but private trading
That deals in blood instead of boots?

And what's the use of settling down? Them as does are first to go. (*Sings.*)

Some people think to live by looting
The goods some others haven't got.
You think it's just a line they're shooting
Until you hear they have been shot.

And some I saw dig six feet under
In haste to lie down and pass out.
Now they're at rest perhaps they wonder
Just what was all their haste about.

(*They pull it further.*)

SCENE 8

(*The same year sees the death of the Swedish king Gustavus Adolphus at the battle of Lützen. Peace threatens to ruin Mother Courage's business. Courage's dashing son performs one heroic deed too many and comes to a sticky end.*)
(*Camp.*)
(*A summer morning. In front of the cart stand an old woman and her son. The son carries a large sack of bedding.*)

MOTHER COURAGE'S VOICE (*from inside the cart*): Does it need to be this ungodly hour?

THE YOUNG MAN: We walked twenty miles in the night and got to be back today.

MOTHER COURAGE'S VOICE: What am I to do with bedding? Folk've got no houses.

THE YOUNG MAN: Best have a look first.

THE OLD WOMAN: This place is no good either. Come on.

THE YOUNG MAN: What, and have them sell the roof over our head for taxes? She might pay three florins if you throw in the bracelet. (*Bells start ringing.*) Listen, mother.

VOICES (*from the rear*): Peace! Swedish king's been killed.

MOTHER COURAGE (*Sticks her head out of the cart. She has not yet done her hair.*): What's that bell-ringing about in mid-week?

THE CHAPLAIN (*crawling out from under the cart*): What are they shouting? Peace?

MOTHER COURAGE: Don't tell me peace has broken out just after I laid in new stock.

THE CHAPLAIN (*calling to the rear*): That true? Peace?

VOICES: Three weeks ago, they say, only no one told us.

THE CHAPLAIN (*to Courage*): What else would they be ringing the bells for?

VOICES: A whole lot of Lutherans have driven into town, they brought the news.

THE YOUNG MAN: Mother, it's peace. What's the matter?

(*The old woman has collapsed.*)

MOTHER COURAGE (*speaking into the cart*): Holy cow! Kattrin, peace! Put your black dress on, we're going to church. Least we can do for Swiss Cheese. Is it true, though?

THE YOUNG MAN: The people here say so. They've made peace. Can you get up? (*The old woman stands up dumbfounded.*) I'll get the saddlery going again. I promise. It'll all work out. Father will get his bedding back. Can you walk? (*To the chaplain.*) She came over queer. It's the news. She never thought there'd be peace again. Father always said so. We're going straight home. (*They go off.*)

MOTHER COURAGE'S VOICE: Give her a schnapps.

THE CHAPLAIN: They've already gone.

MOTHER COURAGE'S VOICE: What's up in camp?

THE CHAPLAIN: They're assembling. I'll go on over. Shouldn't I put on my clerical garb?

MOTHER COURAGE'S VOICE: Best check up before parading yourself as heretic. I'm glad about peace, never mind if I'm ruined. Any road I'll have got two of me children through the war. Be seeing Eilif again now.

THE CHAPLAIN: And who's that walking down the lines? Bless me, the army commander's cook.

THE COOK (*somewhat bedraggled and carrying a bundle*): What do I behold? The padre!

THE CHAPLAIN: Courage, we've got company.

(*Mother Courage clambers out.*)

THE COOK: I promised I'd drop over for a little talk soon as I had the time. I've not forgotten your brandy, Mrs. Fierling.

MOTHER COURAGE: Good grief, the general's cook! After all these years! Where's my eldest boy Eilif?

THE COOK: Hasn't he got here? He left before me, he was on his way to see you too.

THE CHAPLAIN: I shall don my clerical garb, just a moment.

(*Goes off behind the cart.*)

MOTHER COURAGE: Then he may be here any minute. (*Calls into the cart.*) Kattrin, Eilif's on his way. Get cook a glass of brandy, Kattrin! (*Kattrin does not appear.*) Drag your hair down over it, that's all right. Mr. Lamb's no stranger. (*Fetches the brandy herself.*) She don't like to come out, peace means nowt to her. Took too long coming, it did. They gave her a crack over one eye, you barely notice it now but she thinks folks are staring at her.

THE COOK: Ah yes. War. (*He and Mother Courage sit down.*)

MOTHER COURAGE: Cooky, you caught me at bad moment. I'm ruined.

THE COOK: What? That's hard.

MOTHER COURAGE: Peace'll wring my neck. I went and took chaplain's advice, laid in fresh stocks only t'other day. And now they're going to demobilise and I'll be left sitting on me wares.

THE COOK: What'd you want to go and listen to padre for? If I hadn't been in such a hurry that time, the Catholics arriving so quickly and all, I'd warned you against that man. All piss and wind, he is. So he's the authority around here, eh?

MOTHER COURAGE: He's been doing washing-up for me and helping pull.

THE COOK: Him pull! I bet he told you some of those jokes of his too, I know him, got a very unhealthy view of women, he has, all my good influence on him went for nowt. He ain't steady.

MOTHER COURAGE: You steady then?

THE COOK: Whatever else I ain't, I'm steady. Mud in your eye!

MOTHER COURAGE: Steady, that's nowt. I only had one steady fellow, thank God. Hardest I ever had to work in me life; he flogged the kids' blankets soon as autumn came, and he called me mouth-organ an unchristian instrument. Ask me, you ain't saying much for yourself admitting you're steady.

THE COOK: Still tough as nails, I see; but that's what I like about you.

MOTHER COURAGE: Now don't tell me you been dreaming of me nails.

THE COOK: Well, well, here we are, along with armistice bells and your brandy like what nobody else ever serves, it's famous, that is.

MOTHER COURAGE: I don't give two pins for your armistice bells just now. Can't see 'em handing out all the back pay what's owing, so where does that leave me with my famous brandy? Had your pay yet?

THE COOK (*hesitantly*): Not exactly. That's why we all shoved off. If that's how it is, I thought, I'll go and visit friends. So here I am sitting with you.

MOTHER COURAGE: Other words you got nowt.

THE COOK: High time they stopped that bloody clanging. Wouldn't mind getting into some sort of trade. I'm fed up being cook to that lot. I'm s'posed to rustle them up meals out of tree roots and old bootsoles, then they fling the hot soup in my face. Cook these days is a dog's life. Sooner do war service, only of course it's peacetime now. (*He sees the chaplain reappearing in his old garments.*) More about that later.

THE CHAPLAIN: It's still all right, only had a few moths in it.

THE COOK: Can't see why you bother. You won't get your old job back, who are you to inspire now to earn his pay honourably and lay down his life? What's more I got a bone to pick with you, cause you advised this lady to buy a lot of unnecessary goods saying war would go on for ever.

THE CHAPLAIN (*heatedly*): I'd like to know what concern that is of yours.

THE COOK: Because it's unscrupulous, that sort of thing is. How dare you meddle in other folks' business arrangements with your unwanted advice?

THE CHAPLAIN: Who's meddling? (*To Courage.*) I never knew this gentleman was such an intimate you had to account to him for everything.

MOTHER COURAGE: Keep your hair on, cook's only giving his personal opinion and you can't deny your war was a flop.

THE CHAPLAIN: You should not blaspheme against peace, Courage. You are a hyaena of the battlefield.

MOTHER COURAGE: I'm what?

THE COOK: If you're going to insult this lady you'll have to settle with me.

THE CHAPLAIN: It's not you I'm talking to. Your intentions are only too transparent. (*To Courage.*) But when I see you picking up peace betwixt your finger and your thumb like some dirty old snot-rag, then my humanity feels outraged; for then I see that you don't want peace but war, because you profit from it; in which case you shouldn't forget the ancient saying that whosoever sups with the devil needs a long spoon.

MOTHER COURAGE: I got no use for war, and war ain't got much use for me. But I'm not being called no hyaena, you and me's through.

THE CHAPLAIN: Then why grumble about peace when everybody's breathing sighs of relief? Because of some old junk in your cart?

MOTHER COURAGE: My goods ain't old junk but what I lives by, and you too up to now.

THE CHAPLAIN: Off war, in other words. Aha.

THE COOK (*to the chaplain*): You're old enough to know it's always a mistake offering advice. (*To Courage.*) Way things are, your best bet's to get rid of certain goods quick as you can before prices hit rock-bottom. Dress yourself and get moving, not a moment to lose.

MOTHER COURAGE: That ain't bad advice. I'll do that, I guess.

THE CHAPLAIN: Because cooky says it.

MOTHER COURAGE: Why couldn't you say it? He's right, I'd best go off to market. (*Goes inside the cart.*)

THE COOK: That's one to me, padre. You got no presence of mind. What you should of said was: what, me offer advice, all I done was discuss politics. Better not take me on. Cockfighting don't suit that get-up.

THE CHAPLAIN: If you don't stop your gob I'll murder you, get-up or no get-up.

THE COOK (*pulling off his boots and unwrapping his footcloths*): Pity the war made such a godless shit of you, else you'd easily get another parsonage now it's peacetime. Cooks won't be needed, there's nowt to cook, but faith goes on just the same, nowt changed in that direction.

THE CHAPLAIN: Mr. Lamb, I'm asking you not to elbow me out. Since I came down in the world I've become a better person. I couldn't preach to anyone now.

(*Enter Yvette Pottier in black, dressed up to the nines, carrying a cane. She is much older and fatter, and heavily powdered. She is followed by a manservant.*)

YVETTE: Hullo there, everybody. Is this Mother Courage's establishment?

THE CHAPLAIN: It is. And with whom have we the honour . . . ?

YVETTE: With the Countess Starhemberg, my good man. Where's Courage?

THE CHAPLAIN (*calls into the cart*): The Countess Starhemberg wishes to speak to you.

MOTHER COURAGE'S VOICE: Just coming.

YVETTE: It's Yvette.

MOTHER COURAGE'S VOICE: Oh, Yvette!

YVETTE: Come to see how you are. (*Sees the cook turn round aghast.*) Pieter!

THE COOK: Yvette!

YVETTE: Well I never! How d'you come to be here?

THE COOK: Got a lift.

THE CHAPLAIN: You know each other then? Intimately?

YVETTE: I should think so. (*She looks the cook over.*) Fat.

THE COOK: Not all that skinny yourself.

YVETTE: All the same I'm glad to see you, you shit. Gives me a chance to say what I think of you.

THE CHAPLAIN: You say it, in full; but don't start till Courage is out here.

MOTHER COURAGE (*coming out with all kinds of goods*): Yvette! (*They embrace.*) But what are you in mourning for?

YVETTE: Suits me, don't it? My husband the colonel died a few years back.

MOTHER COURAGE: That old fellow what nearly bought the cart?

YVETTE: His elder brother.

MOTHER COURAGE: Then you're sitting pretty. Nice to find somebody what's made it in this war.

YVETTE: Up and down and up again, that's the way it went.

MOTHER COURAGE: I'm not hearing a word against colonels, they make a mint of money.

THE CHAPLAIN: I would put my boots back on if I were you. (*To Yvette.*) You promised you would say what you think of the gentleman.

THE COOK: Don't kick up a stink here, Yvette.

MOTHER COURAGE: Yvette, this is a friend of mine.

YVETTE: That's old Puffing Piet.

THE COOK: Let's drop the nicknames. I'm called Lamb.

MOTHER COURAGE (*laughs*): Puffing Piet! Him as made all the women crazy! Here, I been looking after your pipe for you.

THE CHAPLAIN: Smoking it, too.

YVETTE: What luck I can warn you against him. Worst of the lot, he was, rampaging along the whole Flanders coastline. Got more girls in trouble than he has fingers.

THE COOK: That's all a long while ago. Tain't true anyhow.

YVETTE: Stand up when a lady brings you into the conversation! How I loved this man! All the time he had a little dark girl with bandy legs, got her in trouble too of course.

THE COOK: Got you into high society more like, far as I can see.

YVETTE: Shut your trap, you pathetic remnant! Better watch out for him, though; fellows like that are still dangerous even when on their last legs.

MOTHER COURAGE (*to Yvette*): Come along, got to get

rid of my stuff afore prices start dropping. You might be able to put a word in for me at regiment, with your connections. (*Calls into the cart.*) Kattrin, church is off, I'm going to market instead. When Eilif turns up, one of you give him a drink. (*Exit with Yvette.*)

YVETTE (*as she leaves*): Fancy a creature like that ever making me leave the straight and narrow path. Thank my lucky stars I managed to reach the top all the same. But I've cooked your goose, Puffing Piet, and that's something that'll be credited to me one day in the world to come.

THE CHAPLAIN: I would like to take as a text for our little talk "The mills of God grind slowly." Weren't you complaining about my jokes?

THE COOK: Dead out of luck, I am. It's like this, you see: I thought I might get a hot meal. Here am I starving, and now they'll be talking about me and she'll get quite a wrong picture. I think I'll clear out before she's back.

THE CHAPLAIN: I think so too.

THE COOK: Padre, I'm fed up already with this bloody peace. Human race has to go through fire and sword cause it's sinful from the cradle up. I wish I could be roasting a fat capon once again for the general, wherever he's got to, in mustard sauce with a carrot or two.

THE CHAPLAIN: Red cabbage. Red cabbage for a capon.

THE COOK: You're right, but carrots was what he had to have.

THE CHAPLAIN: No sense of what's fitting.

THE COOK: Not that it stopped you guzzling your share.

THE CHAPLAIN: With misgivings.

THE COOK: Anyway you must admit those were the days.

THE CHAPLAIN: I might admit it if pressed.

THE COOK: Now you've called her a hyaena your days here are finished. What you staring at?

THE CHAPLAIN: Eilif! (*Eilif arrives, followed by soldiers with pikes. His hands are fettered. His face is chalky-white.*) What's wrong?

EILIF: Where's mother?

THE CHAPLAIN: Gone into town.

EILIF: I heard she was around. They've allowed me to come and see her.

THE COOK (*to the soldiers*): What you doing with him?

A SOLDIER: Something not nice.

THE CHAPLAIN: What's he been up to?

THE SOLDIER: Broke into a peasant's place. The wife's dead.

THE CHAPLAIN: How could you do a thing like that?

EILIF: It's what I did last time, ain't it?

THE COOK: Aye, but it's peace now.

EILIF: Shut up. All right if I sit down till she comes?

THE SOLDIER: We've no time.

THE CHAPLAIN: In wartime they recommended him for that, sat him at the general's right hand. Dashing, it was, in those days. Any chance of a word with the provost-marshal?

THE SOLDIER: Wouldn't do no good. Taking some peasant's cattle, what's dashing about that?

THE COOK: Dumb, I call it.

EILIF: If I'd been dumb you'd of starved, clever bugger.

THE COOK: But as you were clever you're going to be shot.

THE CHAPLAIN: We'd better fetch Kattrin out anyhow.

EILIF: Sooner have a glass of schnapps, could do with that.

THE SOLDIER: No time, come along.

THE CHAPLAIN: And what shall we tell your mother?

EILIF: Tell her it wasn't any different, tell her it was the same thing. Or tell her nowt. (*The soldiers propel him away.*)

THE CHAPLAIN: I'll accompany you on your grievous journey.

EILIF: Don't need any bloody parsons.

THE CHAPLAIN: Wait and see. (*Follows him.*)

THE COOK (*calls after them*): I'll have to tell her, she'll want to see him.

THE CHAPLAIN: I wouldn't tell her anything. At most that he was here and will come again, maybe tomorrow. By then I'll be back and can break it to her. (*Hurries off.*)

(*The cook looks after him, shaking his head, then walks restlessly around. Finally he comes up to the cart.*)

THE COOK: Hoy! Don't you want to come out? I can understand you hiding away from peace. Like to do the same myself. Remember me, I'm general's cook? I was wondering if you'd a bit of something to eat while I wait for your mum. I don't half feel like a bit of pork, or bread even, just to fill the time. (*Peers inside.*) Head under blanket. (*Sound of gunfire off.*)

MOTHER COURAGE (*runs in, out of breath and with all her goods still*): Cooky, peacetime's over. War's been on again three days now. Heard news before selling me stuff, thank God. They're having a shooting match with Lutherans in town. We must get cart away at once. Kattrin, pack up! What you in the dumps for? What's wrong?

THE COOK: Nowt.

MOTHER COURAGE: Something is. I see it way you look.

THE COOK: Cause war's starting up again, I s'pose. Looks as if it'll be tomorrow night before I get next hot food inside me.

MOTHER COURAGE: You're lying, cooky.

THE COOK: Eilif was here. Had to leave almost at once, though.

MOTHER COURAGE: Was he now? Then we'll be seeing him on the march. I'm joining our side this time. How's he look?

THE COOK: Same as usual.

MOTHER COURAGE: Oh, he'll never change. Take more than war to steal him from me. Clever, he is. You going to help me get packed? (*Begins to pack up.*) What's his news? Still in general's good books? Say anything about his deeds of valour?

THE COOK (*glumly*): Repeated one of them, I'm told.

MOTHER COURAGE: Tell it me later, we got to move off. (*Kattrin appears.*) Kattrin, peacetime's finished now. We're moving on. (*To the cook.*) How about you?

THE COOK: Have to join up again.

MOTHER COURAGE: Why don't you . . . Where's padre?

THE COOK: Went into town with Eilif.

MOTHER COURAGE: Then you come along with us a way. Need somebody to help me.

THE COOK: That business with Yvette, you know . . .

MOTHER COURAGE: Done you no harm in my eyes. Opposite. Where there's smoke there's fire, they say. You coming along?

THE COOK: I won't say no.

MOTHER COURAGE: The Twelfth moved off already. Take the shaft. Here's a bit of bread. We must get round behind to Lutherans. Might even be seeing Eilif tonight. He's my favourite one. Short peace, wasn't it? Now we're off again. (*She sings as the cook and Kattrin harness themselves up.*)

> From Ulm to Metz, from Metz to Munich
> Courage will see the war gets fed.
> The war will show a well-filled tunic
> Given its daily shot of lead.
> But lead alone can hardly nourish
> It must have soldiers to subsist.
> It's you it needs to make it flourish.
> The war's still hungry. So enlist!

SCENE 9

(*It is the seventeenth year of the great war of faith. Germany has lost more than half her inhabitants. Those who survive the bloodbath are killed off by terrible epidemics. Once fertile areas are ravaged by famine, wolves roam the burnt-out towns. In autumn 1634 we find Courage in the Fichtelgebirge, off the main axis of the Swedish armies. The winter this year is early and harsh. Business is bad, so that there is nothing to do but beg. The cook gets a letter from Utrecht and is sent packing.*)
(*Outside a semi-dilapidated parsonage.*)
(*Grey morning in early winter. Gusts of wind. Mother Courage and the cook in shabby sheepskins, drawing the cart.*)

THE COOK: It's all dark, nobody up yet.

MOTHER COURAGE: Except it's parson's house. Have to crawl out of bed to ring bells. Then he'll have hot soup.

THE COOK: What from, when the whole village is burnt? We seen it.

MOTHER COURAGE: It's lived in, though, dog was barking.

THE COOK: S'pose parson's got, he'll give nowt.

MOTHER COURAGE: Maybe if we sing. . . .

THE COOK: I've had enough. (*Abruptly.*) Got a letter from Utrecht saying mother died of cholera and inn's mine. Here's letter if you don't believe me. No business of yours the way aunty goes on about my mode of existence, but have a look.

MOTHER COURAGE: (*Reads the letter.*) Lamb, I'm tired too of always being on the go. I feel like butcher's dog, dragging meat round customers and getting nowt off it. I got nowt left to sell, and folk got nowt left to buy nowt with. Saxony a fellow in rags tried landing me a stack of old books for two eggs, Württemberg they wanted to swap their plough for a titchy bag of salt. What's to plough for? Nowt growing no more, just brambles. In Pomerania villages are s'posed to have started in eating the younger kids, and nuns have been caught sticking folk up.

THE COOK: World's dying out.

MOTHER COURAGE: Sometimes I sees meself driving through hell with me cart selling brimstone, or across heaven with packed lunches for hungry souls. Give me my kids what's left, let's find some place they ain't shooting, and I'd like a few more years undisturbed.

THE COOK: You and me could get that inn going, Courage, think it over. Made up me mind in the night, I did: back to Utrecht with or without you, and starting today.

MOTHER COURAGE: Have to talk to Kattrin. That's a bit quick for me; I'm against making decisions all freezing cold and nowt inside you. Kattrin! (*Kattrin climbs out of the cart.*) Kattrin, got something to tell you. Cook and I want to go to Utrecht. He's been left an inn there. That'd be a settled place for you, let you meet a few people. Lots of 'em respect somebody mature, looks ain't everything. I'd like it too. I get on with cook. Say one thing for him, got a head for business. We'd have our meals for sure, not bad, eh? And your own bed too; like that, wouldn't you? Road's no life really. God knows how you might finish up. Lousy already, you are. Have to make up our minds, see, we could move with the Swedes, up north, they're somewhere up that way. (*She points to the left.*) Reckon that's fixed, Kattrin.

THE COOK: Anna, I got something private to say to you.

MOTHER COURAGE: Get back in cart, Kattrin.

(*Kattrin climbs back.*)

THE COOK: I had to interrupt, cause you don't understand, far as I can see. I didn't think there was need to say it, sticks out a mile. But if it don't, then let me tell you straight, no question of taking her along, not on your life. You get me, eh.

(*Kattrin sticks her head out of the cart behind them and listens.*)

MOTHER COURAGE: You mean I'm to leave Kattrin back here?

THE COOK: Use your imagination. Inn's got no room. It ain't one of the sort got three bar parlours. Put our backs in it we two'll get a living, but not three, no chance of that. She can keep cart.

MOTHER COURAGE: Thought she might find husband in Utrecht.

THE COOK: Go on, make me laugh. Find a husband, how? Dumb and that scar on top of it. And at her age?

MOTHER COURAGE: Don't talk so loud.

THE COOK: Loud or soft, no getting over facts. And that's another reason why I can't have her in the inn. Customers don't want to be looking at that all the time. Can't blame them.

MOTHER COURAGE: Shut your big mouth. I said not so loud.

THE COOK: Light's on in parson's house. We can try singing.

MOTHER COURAGE: Cooky, how's she to pull the cart on her own? War scares her. She'll never stand it. The dreams she must have . . . I hear her nights groaning. Mostly after a battle. What's she seeing in those dreams, I'd like to know. She's got a soft heart. Lately I found she'd got another hedgehog tucked away what we'd run over.

THE COOK: Inn's too small. (*Calls out.*) Ladies and gentlemen, domestic staff and other residents! We are now going to give you a song concerning Solomon, Julius Caesar and other famous personages what had bad luck. So's you can see we're respectable folk, which makes it difficult to carry on, particularly in winter. (*They sing.*)

> You saw sagacious Solomon
> You know what came of him.
> To him complexities seemed plain.
> He cursed the hour that gave birth to him
> And saw that everything was vain.
> How great and wise was Solomon!
> The world however didn't wait
> But soon observed what followed on.
> It's wisdom that had brought him to this state —
> How fortunate the man with none!

Yes, the virtues are dangerous stuff in this world, as this fine song proves, better not to have them and have a pleasant life and breakfast instead, hot soup for instance. Look at me: I haven't any but I'd like some. I'm a serving soldier but what good did my courage do me in all them battles, nowt, here I am starving and better have been shit-scared and stayed at home. For why?

> You saw courageous Caesar next
> You know what he became.
> They deified him in his life
> Then had him murdered just the same.
> And as they raised the fatal knife
> How loud he cried: You too, my son!
> The world however didn't wait
> But soon observed what followed on.
> It's courage that had brought him to that state.
> How fortunate the man with none!

(*Sotto voce.*) Don't even look out. (*Aloud.*) Ladies and gentlemen, domestic staff and other inmates! All right, you may say, gallantry never cooked a man's dinner, what about trying honesty? You can eat all you want then, or anyhow not stay sober. How about it?

> You heard of honest Socrates
> The man who never lied:
> They weren't so grateful as you'd think
> Instead the rulers fixed to have him tried
> And handed him the poisoned drink.
> How honest was the people's noble son!
> The world however didn't wait
> But soon observed what followed on.
> It's honesty that brought him to that state.
> How fortunate the man with none!

Ah yes, they say, be unselfish and share what you've got, but how about if you got nowt? It's all very well to say the do-gooders have a hard time, but you still got to have something. Aye, unselfishness is a rare virtue, cause it just don't pay.

> Saint Martin couldn't bear to see
> His fellows in distress.
> He met a poor man in the snow
> And shared his cloak with him, we know.
> Both of them therefore froze to death.
> His place in Heaven was surely won!
> The world however didn't wait
> But soon observed what followed on.
> Unselfishness had brought him to that state.
> How fortunate the man with none!

That's how it is with us. We're respectable folk, stick together, don't steal, don't murder, don't burn places down. And all the time you might say we're sinking lower and lower, and it's true what the song says, and soup is few and far between, and if we weren't like this but thieves and murderers I dare say we'd be eating our fill. For virtues aren't their own reward, only wickednesses are, that's how the world goes and it didn't ought to.

> Here you can see respectable folk
> Keeping to God's own laws.
> So far he hasn't taken heed.
> You who sit safe and warm indoors
> Help to relieve our bitter need!
> How virtuously we had begun!
> The world however didn't wait
> But soon observed what followed on.
> It's fear of God that brought us to that state.
> How fortunate the man with none!

VOICE (*from above*): Hey, you there! Come on up! There's hot soup if you want.

MOTHER COURAGE: Lamb, me stomach won't stand nowt. 'Tain't that it ain't sensible, what you say, but is that your last word? We got on all right.

THE COOK: Last word. Think it over.

MOTHER COURAGE: I've nowt to think. I'm not leaving her here.

THE COOK: That's proper senseless, nothing I can do about it though. I'm not a brute, just the inn's a small one. So now we better get on up, or there'll be nowt here either and wasted time singing in the cold.

MOTHER COURAGE: I'll get Kattrin.

THE COOK: Better bring a bit back for her. Scare them if they sees three of us coming. (*Exeunt both.*)

(*Kattrin climbs out of the cart with a bundle. She looks around to see if the other two have gone. Then she takes an old pair of trousers of the cook's and a skirt of her mother's, and lays them side by side on one of the wheels, so that they are easily seen. She has finished and is picking up her bundle to go, when Mother Courage comes back from the house.*)

MOTHER COURAGE (*with a plate of soup*): Kattrin! Will you stop there? Kattrin! Where you off to with that bundle? Has devil himself taken you over? (*She examines the bundle.*) She's packed her things. You been listening? I told him nowt doing, Utrecht, his rotten inn, what'd we be up to there? You and me, inn's no place for us. Still plenty to be got out of war. (*She sees the trousers and the skirt.*) You're plain stupid. S'pose I'd seen that, and you gone away? (*She holds Kattrin back as she tries to break away.*) Don't you start thinking it's on your account I given him the push. It was cart, that's it. Catch me leaving my cart I'm used to, it ain't you, it's for cart. We'll go off in t'other direction, and we'll throw cook's stuff out so he finds it, silly man. (*She climbs in and throws out a few other articles in the direction of the trousers.*) There, he's out of our business now, and I ain't having nobody else in, ever. You and me'll carry on now. This winter will pass, same as all the others. Get hitched up, it looks like snow.

(*They both harness themselves to the cart, then wheel it round and drag it off. When the cook arrives he looks blankly at his kit.*)

SCENE 10

(*During the whole of 1635 Mother Courage and her daughter Kattrin travel over the highroads of central Germany, in the wake of the increasingly bedraggled armies.*)

(*High road.*)

(*Mother Courage and Kattrin are pulling the cart. They pass a peasant's house inside which there is a voice singing.*)

THE VOICE:

> The roses in our arbour
> Delight us with their show:
> They have such lovely flowers
> Repaying all our labour
> After the summer showers.
> Happy are those with gardens now:
> They have such lovely flowers.

> When winter winds are freezing
> As through the woods they blow
> Our home is warm and pleasing.
> We fixed the thatch above it
> With straw and moss we wove it.
> Happy are those with shelter now
> When winter winds are freezing.

(*Mother Courage and Kattrin pause to listen, then continue pulling.*)

SCENE 11

(*January 1636. The emperor's troops are threatening the Protestant town of Halle. The stone begins to speak. Mother Courage loses her daughter and trudges on alone. The war is a long way from being over.*)

(*The cart is standing, much the worse for wear, alongside a peasant's house with a huge thatched roof, backing on a wall of rock. It is night.*)

(*An ensign and three soldiers in heavy armour step out of the wood.*)

THE ENSIGN: I want no noise now. Anyone shouts, shove your pike into him.

FIRST SOLDIER: Have to knock them up, though, if we're to find a guide.

THE ENSIGN: Knocking sounds natural. Could be a cow bumping the stable wall.

(*The soldiers knock on the door of the house. The peasant's wife opens it. They stop her mouth. Two soldiers go in.*)

MAN'S VOICE (*within*): What is it?

(*The soldiers bring out the peasant and his son.*)

THE ENSIGN (*pointing at the cart, where Kattrin's head has appeared*): There's another one. (*A Soldier drags her out.*) Anyone else live here beside you lot?

THE PEASANTS: This is our son. And she's dumb. Her mother's gone into town to buy stuff. For their business, cause so many people's getting out and selling things cheap. They're just passing through. Canteen folk.

THE ENSIGN: I'm warning you, keep quiet, or if there's the least noise you get a pike across your nut. Now I want someone to come with us and show us the path to the town. (*Points to the young peasant.*) Here, you.

THE YOUNG PEASANT: I don't know no path.

SECOND SOLDIER (*grinning*): He don't know no path.

THE YOUNG PEASANT: I ain't helping Catholics.

THE ENSIGN (*to the second soldier*): Stick your pike in his ribs.

THE YOUNG PEASANT (*forced to his knees, with the pike threatening him*): I won't do it, not to save my life.

FIRST SOLDIER: I know what'll change his mind. (*Goes towards the stable.*) Two cows and an ox. Listen, you: if you're not reasonable I'll chop up your cattle.

THE YOUNG PEASANT: No, not that!

THE PEASANT'S WIFE (*weeps*): Please spare our cattle, captain, it'd be starving us to death.

THE ENSIGN: They're dead if he goes on being obstinate.

FIRST SOLDIER: I'm taking the ox first.

THE YOUNG PEASANT (*to his father*): Have I got to? (*The wife nods.*) Right.

THE PEASANT'S WIFE: And thank you kindly, captain, for sparing us, for ever and ever, Amen.

(*The peasant stops his wife from further expressions of gratitude.*)

FIRST SOLDIER: I knew the ox was what they minded about most, was I right?

(*Guided by the young peasant, the ensign and his men continue on their way.*)

THE PEASANT: What are they up to, I'd like to know. Nowt good.

THE PEASANT'S WIFE: Perhaps they're just scouting. What you doing?

THE PEASANT (*putting a ladder against the roof and climbing up it*): Seeing if they're on their own. (*From the top.*) Something moving in the wood. Can see something down by the quarry. And there are men in armour in the clearing. And a gun. That's at least a regiment. God's mercy on the town and everyone in it!

THE PEASANT'S WIFE: Any lights in the town?

THE PEASANT: No. They'll all be asleep. (*Climbs down.*) If those people get in they'll butcher the lot.

THE PEASANT'S WIFE: Sentries're bound to spot them first.

THE PEASANT: Sentry in the tower up the hill must have been killed, or he'd have blown his bugle.

THE PEASANT'S WIFE: If only there were more of us.

THE PEASANT: Just you and me and that cripple.

THE PEASANT'S WIFE: Nowt we can do, you'd say. . . .

THE PEASANT: Nowt.

THE PEASANT'S WIFE: Can't possibly run down there in the blackness.

THE PEASANT: Whole hillside's crawling with 'em. We could give a signal.

THE PEASANT'S WIFE: What, and have them butcher us too?

THE PEASANT: You're right, nowt we can do.

THE PEASANT'S WIFE (*to Kattrin*): Pray, poor creature, pray! Nowt we can do to stop bloodshed. You can't talk, maybe, but at least you can pray. He'll hear you if no one else can. I'll help you. (*All kneel, Kattrin behind the two peasants.*) Our Father, which art in Heaven, hear Thou our prayer, let not the town be destroyed with all what's in it sound asleep and suspecting nowt. Arouse Thou them that they may get up and go to the walls and see how the enemy approacheth with picks and guns in the blackness across fields below the slope. (*Turning to Kattrin.*) Guard Thou our mother and ensure that the watch-

man sleepeth not but wakes up, or it will be too late. Succour our brother-in-law also, he is inside there with his four children, spare Thou them, they are innocent and know nowt. (*To Kattrin, who gives a groan.*) One of them's not two yet, the eldest's seven. (*Kattrin stands up distractedly.*) Our Father, hear us, for only Thou canst help; we look to be doomed, for why, we are weak and have no pike and nowt and can risk nowt and are in Thy hand along with our cattle and all the farm, and same with the town, it too is in Thy hand and the enemy is before the walls in great strength.

(*Unobserved, Kattrin has slipped away to the cart and taken from it something which she hides beneath her apron; then she climbs up the ladder on to the stable roof.*)

THE PEASANT'S WIFE: Forget not the children, what are in danger, the littlest ones especially, the old folk what can't move, and every living creature.

THE PEASANT: And forgive us our trespasses as we forgive them that trespass against us. Amen.

(*Sitting on the roof, Kattrin begins to beat the drum which she has pulled out from under her apron.*)

THE PEASANT'S WIFE: Jesus Christ, what's she doing?

THE PEASANT: She's out of her mind.

THE PEASANT'S WIFE: Quick, get her down.

(*The peasant hurries to the ladder, but Kattrin pulls it up on to the roof.*)

THE PEASANT'S WIFE: She'll do us in.

THE PEASANT: Stop drumming at once, you cripple!

THE PEASANT'S WIFE: Bringing the Catholics down on us!

THE PEASANT (*looking for stones to throw*): I'll stone you.

THE PEASANT'S WIFE: Where's your feelings? Where's your heart? We're done for if they come down on us. Slit our throats, they will.

(*Kattrin stares into the distance towards the town and carries on drumming.*)

THE PEASANT'S WIFE (*to her husband*): I told you we shouldn't have allowed those vagabonds on to farm. What do they care if our last cows are taken?

THE ENSIGN (*runs in with his soldiers and the young peasant*): I'll cut you to ribbons, all of you!

THE PEASANT'S WIFE: Please, sir, it's not our fault, we couldn't help it. It was her sneaked up there. A foreigner.

THE ENSIGN: Where's the ladder?

THE PEASANT: There.

THE ENSIGN (*calls up*): I order you, throw that drum down.

(*Kattrin goes on drumming.*)

THE ENSIGN: You're all in this together. It'll be the end of you.

THE PEASANT: They been cutting pine trees in that wood. How about if we got one of the trunks and poked her off. . . .

FIRST SOLDIER (*to the ensign*): Permission to make a suggestion, sir! (*He whispers something in the ensign's ear.*) Listen, we got a suggestion could help you. Get down off there and come into town with us right away. Show us which your mother is and we'll see she ain't harmed.

(*Kattrin goes on drumming.*)

THE ENSIGN (*pushes him roughly aside*): She doesn't trust you; with a mug like yours it's not surprising. (*Calls up.*) Suppose I gave you my word? I can give my word of honour as an officer.

(*Kattrin drums harder.*)

THE ENSIGN: Is nothing sacred to her?

THE YOUNG PEASANT: There's more than her mother involved, sir.

FIRST SOLDIER: This can't go on much longer. They're bound to hear in the town.

THE ENSIGN: We'll have somehow to make a noise that's louder than her drumming. What can we make a noise with?

FIRST SOLDIER: Thought we weren't s'posed to make no noise.

THE ENSIGN: A harmless one, you fool. A peaceful one.

THE PEASANT: I could chop wood with my axe.

THE ENSIGN: Good: you chop. (*The peasant fetches his axe and attacks a tree-trunk.*) Chop harder! Harder! You're chopping for your life.

(*Kattrin has been listening, drumming less loudly the while. She now looks wildly round, and goes on drumming.*)

THE ENSIGN: Not loud enough. (*To the first soldier.*) You chop too.

THE PEASANT: Only got the one axe. (*Stops chopping.*)

THE ENSIGN: We'll have to set the farm on fire. Smoke her out, that's it.

THE PEASANT: It wouldn't help, captain. If the townspeople see a fire here they'll know what's up.

(*Kattrin has again been listening as she drums. At this point she laughs.*)

THE ENSIGN: Look at her laughing at us. I'm not having that. I'll shoot her down, and damn the consequences. Fetch the harquebus.

(*Three soldiers hurry off. Kattrin goes on drumming.*)

THE PEASANT'S WIFE: I got it, captain. That's their cart. If we smash it up she'll stop. Cart's all they got.

THE ENSIGN (*to the young peasant*): Smash it up. (*Calls up.*) We're going to smash up your cart if you don't stop drumming. (*The young peasant gives the cart a few feeble blows.*)

THE PEASANT'S WIFE: Stop it, you animal!

(*Desperately looking towards the cart, Kattrin emits pitiful noises. But she goes on drumming.*)

THE ENSIGN: Where are those clodhoppers with the harquebus?

FIRST SOLDIER: Can't have heard nowt in town yet, else we'd be hearing their guns.

THE ENSIGN (*calls up*): They can't hear you at all. And now we're going to shoot you down. For the last time: throw down that drum!

THE YOUNG PEASANT (*suddenly flings away his plank*): Go on drumming! Or they'll all be killed! Go on, go on. . . .

(*The soldier knocks him down and beats him with his pike. Kattrin starts to cry, but she goes on drumming.*)

THE PEASANT'S WIFE: Don't strike his back! For God's sake, you're beating him to death!

(*The soldiers hurry in with the harquebus.*)

SECOND SOLDIER: Colonel's frothing at the mouth, sir. We're all for court-martial.

THE ENSIGN: Set it up! Set it up! (*Calls up while the gun is being erected.*) For the very last time: stop drumming! (*Kattrin, in tears, drums as loud as she can.*) Fire! (*The soldiers fire. Kattrin is hit, gives a few more drumbeats and then slowly crumples.*)

THE ENSIGN: That's the end of that.

(*But Kattrin's last drumbeats are taken up by the town's cannon. In the distance can be heard a confused noise of tocsins and gunfire.*)

FIRST SOLDIER: She's made it.

SCENE 12

(*Before first light. Sound of the fifes and drums of troops marching off into the distance.*)
(*In front of the cart Mother Courage is squatting by her daughter. The peasant family are standing near her.*)

THE PEASANTS (*with hostility*): You must go, missis. There's only one more regiment behind that one. You can't go on your own.

MOTHER COURAGE: I think she's going to sleep. (*She sings.*)

Lullaby baby
What's that in the hay?
Neighbours' kids grizzle
But my kids are gay.
Neighbours' are in tatters
And you're dressed in lawn
Cut down from the raiment an
Angel has worn.
Neighbours' kids go hungry
And you shall eat cake
Suppose it's too crumbly

You've only to speak.
Lullaby baby
What's that in the hay?
The one lies in Poland
The other — who can say?

Better if you'd not told her nowt about your brother-in-law's kids.

THE PEASANT: If you'd not gone into town to get your cut it might never of happened.

MOTHER COURAGE: Now she's asleep.

THE PEASANT'S WIFE: She ain't asleep. Can't you see she's passed over?

THE PEASANT: And it's high time you got away yourself. There are wolves around and, what's worse, marauders.

MOTHER COURAGE: Aye.

(*She goes and gets a tarpaulin to cover the dead girl with.*)

THE PEASANT'S WIFE: Ain't you got nobody else? What you could go to?

MOTHER COURAGE: Aye, one left. Eilif.

THE PEASANT (*as Mother Courage covers the dead girl*): Best look for him, then. We'll mind her, see she gets proper burial. Don't you worry about that.

MOTHER COURAGE: Here's money for expenses.

(*She counts out coins into the peasant's hands. The peasant and his son shake hands with her and carry Kattrin away.*)

THE PEASANT'S WIFE (*as she leaves*): I'd hurry.

MOTHER COURAGE (*harnessing herself to the cart*): Hope I can pull cart all right by meself. Be all right, nowt much inside it. Got to get back in business again.

(*Another regiment with its fifes and drums marches past in the background.*)

MOTHER COURAGE (*tugging the cart*): Take me along! (*Singing is heard from offstage.*)

With all its luck and all its danger
The war is dragging on a bit
Another hundred years or longer
The common man won't benefit.
Filthy his food, no soap to shave him
The regiment steals half his pay.
But still a miracle may save him:
Tomorrow is another day!
   The new year's come. The watchmen shout.
   The thaw sets in. The dead remain.
   Wherever life has not died out
   It staggers to its feet again.

COMMENTARIES

Bertolt Brecht (1898–1956)

THE ALIENATION EFFECT

1964

TRANSLATED BY JOHN WILLETT

In this short description, Brecht explains some of his theories of staging and acting. His alienation effect (A-effect) reminds the audience that the characters on stage are dramatic constructs, not real people suffering real emotions. As he explains, the A-effect is the opposite of traditional acting, which is designed to produce an empathy between actor and audience. The A-effect rejects that empathy.

What follows represents an attempt to describe a technique of acting which was applied in certain theaters with a view to taking the incidents portrayed and alienating them from the spectator. The aim of this technique, known as the alienation effect, was to make the spectator adopt an attitude of inquiry and criticism in his approach to the incident. The means were artistic.

The first condition for the A-effect's application to this end is that stage and auditorium must be purged of everything "magical" and that no "hypnotic tensions" should be set up. This ruled out any attempt to make the stage convey the flavor of a particular place (a room at evening, a road in the autumn), or to create atmosphere by relaxing the tempo of the conversation. The audience was not "worked up" by a display of temperament or "swept away" by acting with tautened muscles; in short, no attempt was made to put it in a trance and give it the illusion of watching an ordinary unrehearsed event. As will be seen presently, the audience's tendency to plunge into such illusions has to be checked by specific artistic means.

The first condition for the achievement of the A-effect is that the actor must invest what he has to show with a definite gest of showing. It is of course necessary to drop the assumption that there is a fourth wall cutting the audience off from the stage and the consequent illusion that the stage action is taking place in reality and without an audience. That being so, it is possible for the actor in principle to address the audience directly.

It is well known that contact between audience and stage is normally made on the basis of empathy. Conventional actors devote their efforts so exclusively to bringing about this psychological operation that they may be said to see it as the principal aim of their art. Our introductory remarks will already have made it clear that the technique which produces an A-effect is the exact opposite of that which aims at empathy. The actor applying it is bound not to try to bring about the empathy operation.

Yet in his efforts to reproduce particular characters and show their behavior he need not renounce the means of empathy entirely. He uses these means just as any normal person with no particular acting talent would use them if he wanted to portray someone else, i.e., show how he behaves. This showing of other people's behavior happens time and again in ordinary life (witnesses of an accident demonstrating to newcomers how the victim behaved, a facetious person imitating a friend's walk, etc.), without those involved making the least effort to subject their spectators to an illusion. At the same time they do feel their way into their characters' skins with a view to acquiring their characteristics.

As has already been said, the actor too will make use of this psychological operation. But whereas the usual practice in acting is to execute it during the actual performance, in the hope of stimulating the spectator into a similar operation, he will achieve it only at an earlier stage, at some time during rehearsals.

To safeguard against an unduly "impulsive," frictionless and uncritical creation of characters and incidents, more reading rehearsals can be held than usual. The actor should refrain from living himself into the part prematurely in any way, and should go on functioning as long as possible as a reader (which does not mean a reader-aloud). An important step is memorizing one's first impressions.

When reading his part the actor's attitude should be one of a man who is astounded and contradicts. Not only the occurrence of the incidents, as he reads about them, but the conduct of the man he is playing, as he experiences it, must be weighed up by him and their peculiarities understood; none can be taken as given, as something that "was bound to turn out that way," that was "only to be expected from a character like that." Before memorizing the words he must memorize what he felt astounded at and where he felt impelled to contradict. For these are dynamic forces that he must preserve in creating his performance.

When he appears on the stage, besides what he actually is doing he will at all essential points discover, specify, imply what he is not doing; that is to say he will act in such a way that the alternative emerges as clearly as possible, that his acting allows the other possibilities to be inferred and only represents one out of the possible variants. He will say for instance "You'll pay for that," and not say "I forgive you." He detests his children; it is not the case that he loves them. He moves down stage left and not up stage right. Whatever he doesn't do must be contained and conserved in what he does. In this way every sentence and every gesture signifies a decision; the character remains under observation and is tested. The technical term for this procedure is "fixing the 'not . . . but.'"

The actor does not allow himself to become completely transformed on the stage into the character he is portraying. He is not Lear, Harpagon, Schweik; he shows them. He reproduces their remarks as authentically as he can; he puts forward their way of behaving to the best of his abilities and knowledge of men; but he never tries to persuade himself (and thereby others) that this amounts to a complete transformation. Actors will know what it means if I say that a typical kind of acting without this complete transformation takes place when a producer or colleague shows one how to play a particular passage. It is not his own part, so he is not completely transformed; he underlines the technical aspect and retains the attitude of someone just making suggestions.

Once the idea of total transformation is abandoned the actor speaks his part not as if he were improvising it himself but like a quotation. At the same time he obviously has to render all the quotation's overtones, the remark's full human and concrete shape; similarly the gesture he makes must have the full substance of a human gesture even though it now represents a copy.

Given this absence of total transformation in the acting there are three aids which may help to alienate the actions and remarks of the characters being portrayed:

1. Transposition into the third person.
2. Transposition into the past.
3. Speaking the stage directions out loud.

Using the third person and the past tense allows the actor to adopt the right attitude of detachment. In addition he will look for stage directions and remarks that comment on his lines, and speak them aloud at rehearsal ("He stood up and exclaimed angrily, not having eaten: . . . ," or "He had never been told so before, and didn't know if it was true or not," or "He smiled, and said with forced nonchalance: . . . ."). Speaking the stage directions out loud in the third person results in a clash between two tones of voice, alienating the second of them, the text proper. This style of acting is further alienated by taking place on the stage after having already been outlined and announced in words. Transposing it into the past gives the speaker a standpoint from which he can look back at his sentence. The sentence too is thereby alienated without the speaker adopting an unreal point of view; unlike the spectator, he has read the play right through and is better placed to judge the sentence in accordance with the ending, with its consequences, than the former, who knows less and is more of a stranger to the sentence.

This composite process leads to an alienation of the text in the rehearsals which generally persists in the performance too. The directness of the relationship with the audience allows and indeed forces the actual speech delivery to be varied in accordance with the greater or smaller significance attaching to the sentences. Take the case of witnesses addressing a court. The underlinings, the characters' insistence on their remarks, must be developed as a piece of effective virtuosity. If the actor turns to the audience it must be a whole-hearted turn rather than the asides and soliloquizing technique of the old-fashioned theater. To get the full A-effect from the poetic medium the actor should start at rehearsal by paraphrasing the verse's content in vulgar prose, possibly accompanying this by the gestures designed for the verse. A daring and beautiful handling of verbal media will alienate the text. (Prose can be alienated by translation into the actor's native dialect.)

Gesture will be dealt with below, but it can at once be said that everything to do with the emotions has to be externalized; that is to say, it must be developed into a gesture. The actor has to find a sensibly perceptible outward expression for his character's emotions, preferably some action that gives away what is going on inside him. The emotion in question must be brought out, must lose all its restrictions so that it can be treated on a big scale. Special elegance, power and grace of gesture bring about the A-effect.

A masterly use of gesture can be seen in Chinese acting. The Chinese actor achieves the A-effect by being seen to observe his own movements.

Whatever the actor offers in the way of gesture, verse structure, etc., must be finished and bear the hallmarks of something rehearsed and rounded-off. The impression to be given is one of ease, which is at the same time one of difficulties overcome. The actor must make it possible for the audience to take his own art, his mastery of technique, lightly too. He puts an incident before the spectator with perfection and as he thinks it really happened or might have happened. He does not conceal the fact that he has rehearsed it, any more than an acrobat conceals his training, and he emphasizes that it is his own (actor's) account, view, version of the incident.

Because he doesn't identify himself with him he can pick a definite attitude to adopt towards the character whom he portrays, can show what he thinks of him and invite the spectator, who is likewise not asked to identify himself, to criticize the character portrayed.

The attitude which he adopts is a socially critical one. In his exposition of the incidents and in his characterization of the person he tries to bring out those features which come within society's sphere. In this way his performance becomes a discussion (about social conditions) with the audience he is addressing. He prompts the spectator to justify or abolish these conditions according to what class he belongs to.

The object of the A-effect is to alienate the social gest underlying every incident. By social gest is meant the mimetic and gestural expression of the social relationships prevailing between people of a given period.

It helps to formulate the incident for society, and to put it across in such a way that society is given the key, if titles are thought up for the scenes. These titles must have a historical quality.

This brings us to a crucial technical device: historicization.

The actor must play the incidents as historical ones. Historical incidents are unique, transitory incidents associated with particular periods. The conduct of the persons involved in them is not fixed and "universally human"; it includes elements that have been or may be overtaken by the course of history, and is subject to criticism from the immediately following period's point of view. The conduct of those born before us is alienated[1] from us by an incessant evolution.

It is up to the actor to treat present-day events and modes of behavior with the same detachment as the historian adopts with regard to those of the past. He must alienate these characters and incidents from us.

Characters and incidents from ordinary life, from our immediate surroundings, being familiar, strike us as more or less natural. Alienating them helps to make them seem remarkable to us. Science has carefully developed a technique of getting irritated with the everyday, "self-evident," universally accepted occurrence, and there is no reason why this infinitely useful attitude should not be taken over by art. It is an attitude which arose in science as a result of the growth in human productive powers. In art the same motive applies.

As for the emotions, the experimental use of the A-effect in the epic theater's German productions indicated that this way of acting too can stimulate them, though possibly a different class of emotion is involved from those of the orthodox theater. A critical attitude on the audience's part is a thoroughly artistic one. Nor does the actual practice of the A-effect seem anything like so unnatural as its description. Of course it is a way of acting that his nothing to do with stylization as commonly practiced. The main advantage of the epic theater with its A-effect, intended purely to show the world in such a way that it becomes manageable, is precisely its quality of being natural and earthly, its humor and its renunciation of all the mystical elements that have stuck to the orthodox theater from the old days.

[1]*Entfremdet.*

Bertolt Brecht (1898–1956)
NOTES FOR *MOTHER COURAGE,* SCENE 12   1949
TRANSLATED BY ERIC BENTLEY AND HUGO SCHMIDT

Brecht produced booklets for some of his work that supply a great deal of background information that does not appear in the text of the plays. Brecht's manner of producing his plays were important to him. While he did not expect every successive production to adhere strictly to the standards he established in commentaries such as this, he hoped his intentions would be substantially respected.

Twelfth Scene
Courage Moves On

The peasants have to convince Courage that Kattrin is dead. Kattrin's lullaby. Mother Courage pays for Kattrin's funeral and receives the expressions of sympathy of the peasants. Mother Courage harnesses herself to her empty covered wagon. Still hoping to get back into business, she follows the tattered army.

Basic Arrangement

The wagon stands on the empty stage. Mother Courage holds dead Kattrin's head in her lap. The peasants stand at the foot of the dead girl, huddled together and hostile. Courage talks as if her daughter were only sleeping, and deliberately overhears the reproach of the peasants that she was to blame for Kattrin's death.

Kattrin's lullaby. The mother's face is bent low over the face of the daughter. The song does not conciliate those who listen.

Mother Courage pays for Kattrin's funeral and receives expressions of sympathy from the peasants. After she has realized that her last child is dead, Courage gets up laboriously and hobbles around the corpse (right), along the footlights, behind the wagon. She returns with a tent cloth, and answers over her shoulder the peasant's question whether she had no one to turn to: "Oh yes, one. Eilif." And places the cloth over the body, with her back toward the footlights. At the head of the corpse, she pulls the cloth all the way over the face, then again takes her place behind the corpse. The peasant and his son shake hands with her and bow ceremoniously before carrying the body out (to the right). The peasant woman, too, shakes hands with Courage, walks to the right and stops once more, undecided. The two women exchange a few words, then the peasant woman exits.

Mother Courage harnesses herself to her empty covered wagon. Still hoping to get back into business, she follows the tattered army. Slowly, the old woman walks to the wagon, rolls up the rope which Dumb Kattrin had been pulling to this point, takes a stick, looks at it, slips it through the sling of the second rope, tucks the stick under her arm, and starts pulling. The turntable begins to move, and Courage circles the stage once. The curtain closes when she is upstage right for the second time.

The Peasants

The attitude of the peasants toward Courage is hostile. She got them into difficulties, and they will be saddled with her if she does not catch up with the regiments. Besides, she is to blame for the accident herself, in their opinion. And moreover the canteen woman is not part of the resident population, and now, in time of war, she belongs to the fleecers, cutthroats, and marauders in the wake of the armies. When they condole with her by shaking her hand, they merely follow custom.

The Bow

During this entire scene, Weigel, as Courage, showed an almost animal indifference. All the more beautiful was the deep bow that she made when the body was carried away.

The Lullaby

The lullaby must be sung without sentimentality and without the desire to arouse sentimentality. Otherwise, its significance does not get across. The thought that is the basis of this song is a murderous one: the child of this mother was supposed to be better off than other children of other mothers. Through a slight stress on the "you," Weigel revealed the treacherous hope of Courage to get her child, and perhaps only hers, through the war alive. The child to whom the most common things were denied was promised the uncommon.

Paying for the Funeral

Even when paying for the funeral, Weigel gave another hint at the character of Courage. She fished a few coins from her leather purse, put one back, and gave the rest to the peasant. The overpowering impression she gave of having been destroyed was not in the least diminished by this.

The Last Verse

While Courage slowly harnessed herself to her wagon, the last verse of her song was sung from the box in which the band had been placed. It expresses one more time her undestroyed hope to get something out of war anyway. It becomes more impressive in that it does not aim at the illusion that the song is actually sung by army units moving past in the distance.

Giehse in the Role of Courage

When covering up the body, Giehse put her head under the cloth, looking at her daughter one more time, before finally dropping it over her face.

Before she began pulling away her covered wagon — another beautiful variant — she looked into the distance, to figure out where to go, and before she started pulling, she blew her nose with her index finger.

Take Your Time

At the end of the play it is necessary that one see the wagon roll away. Naturally, the audience gets the idea when the wagon starts. If the movement is extended, a moment of irritation arises ("that's long enough, now"). If it is prolonged even further, deeper understanding sets in.

Pulling the Wagon in the Last Scene

For the 12th scene, farm house and stable with roof (of the 11th scene) were cleared away, and only the wagon and Dumb Kattrin's body were left. The act of dragging the wagon off — the large letters "Saxony" were pulled up (out of sight) when the music begins — took place on a completely empty stage: whereby one remembered the setting of the first scene. Courage and her wagon moved in a complete circle on the revolving stage. She passed the footlights once more. As usual, the stage was bathed in light.

Discoveries of the Realists

Wherein lies the effectiveness of Weigel's gesture when she mechanically puts one coin back into her purse, after having fished her money out, as she hands the peasant the funeral money for dead Kattrin? She shows that this tradeswoman, in all her grief, does not completely forget to count, since money is so hard to come by. And she shows this as a discovery about human nature that is shaped by certain conditions. This little feature has the power and the suddenness of a discovery. The art of the realists consists of digging out the truth from under the rubble of the evident, of connecting the particular with the general, of pinning down the unique within the larger process.

A Change of Text

After "I'll manage, there isn't much in it now," Courage added, in the Munich and then also in the Berlin production: "I must start up again in business."

Mother Courage Learns Nothing

In the last scene, Weigel's Courage appeared like an eighty-year-old woman. And she comprehends nothing. She reacts only to the statements that are connected with war, such as that one must not remain behind. She overhears the crude reproach of the peasants that Kattrin's death was her fault.

Courage's inability to learn from the unproductiveness of war was a prophecy in the year 1938 when the play was written. At the Berlin production in 1948 the desire was voiced that Courage should at least come to a realization in the play. To make it possible for the spectator to get something out of this realistic play, i.e., to make the spectator learn a lesson, theaters have to arrive at an acting style that does not seek an identification of the spectator with the protagonist.

Judging on the basis of reports of spectators and newspaper reviews, the Zurich world premiere — although artistically on a high level — presented only the image of war as a natural catastrophe and an inevitable fate, and thereby it underscored to the middle-class spectator in the orchestra his own indestructibility, his ability to survive. But even to the likewise middle-class Courage, the decision "Join in or don't join in" was always left open in the play. The production, it seems, must also have presented Courage's business dealings, profiteering, willingness to take risks, as quite natural, "eternally human" behavior, so that she had no other choice. Today, it is true, the man of the middle class can no longer stay out of war, as Courage could have. To him, a production of the play can probably teach nothing but a real hatred of war, and a certain insight into the fact that the big deals of which war consists are not made by the little people. In that sense, the play is more of a lesson than reality is, because here in the play the situation of war is more of an experimental situation, made for the sake of insights. I.e., the spectator attains the attitude of a student — as long as the acting style is correct. The part of the audience that belongs to the proletariat, i.e., the class that actually can struggle against and overcome war, should be given insight into the connection between business and war (again provided the acting style is correct): the proletariat as a class can do away with war by doing away with capitalism. Of course, as far as the proletarian part of the audience is concerned, one must also take into consideration the fact that this class is busy drawing its own conclusions — inside as well as outside the theater.

The Epic Element

The Epic element was certainly visible in the production at the Deutsches Theater — in the arrangement, in the presentation of the characters, in the minute execution of details, and in the pacing of the entire play. Also, contradictory elements were not eliminated but stressed, and the parts, visible as such, made a convincing whole. However, the goal of Epic Theater was not reached. Much became clear, but clarification was in the end absent. Only in a few recasting-rehearsals did it clearly emerge, for then the actors were only "pretending," i.e., they only showed to the newly added colleague the positions and intonations, and then the whole thing received that preciously loose, unlabored, non-urgent element that incites the spectator to have his own independent thoughts and feelings.

That the production did not have an Epic foundation was never remarked, however: which was probably the reason the actors did not dare provide one.

Concerning the Notes Themselves

We hope that the present notes, offering various explanations and inventions essential to the production of a play, will not have an air of spurious seriousness. It is admittedly hard to establish the lightness and casualness that are of the essence of theater. The arts, even when they are instructive, are forms of amusement.

Tennessee Williams

Tennessee Williams posing for a publicity photograph, circa 1949.

Tennessee Williams (1911–1983) was one of a handful of post–World War II American playwrights to achieve an international reputation. He was born Thomas Lanier Williams in Columbus, Mississippi, the first son of a traveling shoe salesman who eventually moved the family to a dark and dreary tenement in St. Louis. A precocious child, Williams was given a typewriter by his mother when he was eleven years old. The instrument helped him create fantasy worlds that seemed more real, more important to him than the dark and sometimes threatening world in which he lived. His parents, expecting a third child, their son Dakin, moved out of the tenement and bought a house whose gloominess depressed virtually everyone in it. His mother and father found themselves arguing, and his older sister, Rose, took refuge from the real world by closeting herself with a collection of glass animals.

Both Rose and Tennessee responded badly to their environment, and both had breakdowns. Tennessee was so ill that he suffered a partial paralysis of his legs, a disorder that made him a victim of bullies at school and a disappointment to his father at home. He could never participate in sports and was always somewhat frail; however, he was very advanced intellectually and published his first story when he was sixteen.

His education was sporadic. He attended the University of Missouri but, failing ROTC because of his physical limitations, soon dropped out to work in a shoe company. He then went to Washington University in St. Louis but dropped out again. Finally, he earned a bachelor's degree in playwriting at the State University of Iowa when he was twenty-four. During this time he was writing plays, some of which were produced at Washington University. Two years after he graduated, the Theatre Guild produced his first commercial play, *Battle of Angels* (1940), in Boston. It was such a distinct failure that he feared his fledgling career was stunted, but he kept writing and managed to live for a few years on foundation grants. It was not until the production of *The Glass Menagerie* (1944 in Chicago, 1945 in New York) that he achieved the kind of notice he knew he deserved. His first real success, the play was given the New York Drama Critics' Circle Award, the sign of his having achieved a measure of professional recognition and financial independence.

After trying several jobs, including an unsuccessful attempt at screenwriting, he had no more worries about work after *The Glass Menagerie* ran on Broadway for 561 performances. In 1947 his second success, *A Streetcar Named Desire,* starring the then-unknown Marlon Brando, was an even bigger box-office smash. It ran for 855 performances and won the Pulitzer Prize. By the time Tennessee Williams was thirty-six, he was regarded as one of the most important playwrights in America.

Williams followed these successes with a number of plays that were not all as well received as his first works. *Summer and Smoke* (1948), *The Rose Tattoo* (1951), and *Camino Real* (1953) were met with measured enthusiasm from the public, although the critics thought highly of Williams's work. These plays were followed by the saga of a southern family, *Cat on a Hot Tin Roof,* which won all the major drama prizes in 1955, including the Pulitzer.

Williams's energy was unfailing in the next several years. He authored a screenplay, *Baby Doll,* with the legendary director Elia Kazan, in 1956. In 1958 he wrote a one-act play, *Suddenly Last Summer,* and in 1959 *Sweet Bird of Youth.* Some of his later plays are *The Night of the Iguana* (1961), *The Milk Train Doesn't Stop Here Anymore* (1963), and *Small Craft Warnings* (1972). He also wrote a novel and several volumes of short stories, establishing himself as an important writer in many genres. His sudden death in 1983 was a blow to the theater world.

THE GLASS MENAGERIE

Tennessee Williams has often been accused of exorcising his family demons in his plays and of sometimes cloaking events in a personal symbolism that is impossible for an audience to penetrate totally. *The Glass Menagerie* (1944) certainly derives from his personal experience growing up in St. Louis in a tenement, the setting for the play. The characters are drawn from his own family, particularly the character Laura, who is based on his sister. But the symbolism in the play is not so obscure as to give an audience special difficulty.

In a way Williams thought of the play as a tribute to his sister, Rose. Rose's depressions were so severe that eventually she received a lobotomy, which rendered her more passive and more hopeless than before. The operation did not achieve anything positive, and Williams felt somewhat responsible because he had not urged the family to refuse the treatment.

In the play Amanda Wingfield is obsessed with finding gentlemen callers and a suitable career for her daughter, Laura, who walks with a slight limp and is exceedingly shy. Amanda lives in a world of imagination, endlessly retelling stories about a glorious past filled with suitors she could have had before she married. Amanda bullies Laura, whose only defense is to bury herself in her own fantasy world of spun-glass animals. Tom, the son and narrator of the play, is also a victim of Amanda's bullying, but he is more independent and better able to withstand her assaults.

Both children are great disappointments to Amanda. Tom is aloof, indolent, something like his father who is present only in his picture on the wall. Laura calls herself a cripple and has no self-esteem or hope for a future such as the one her mother conceives for her. Laura's shyness is almost uncontrollable. It has ruined any hope of a business career, to Amanda's intense distress. When Tom brings home Jim, and his sister recognizes him as a boy she admired from afar in high school, Laura is nearly too shy to come to the dinner table. And when it becomes clear that Jim is not the gentleman caller of Amanda's dreams, Amanda and Laura are left to face reality or to continue living in their fantasy worlds.

Amanda confronts Tom at the end of the play and asserts that he "live[s] in a dream" and "manufacture[s] illusions." She could be speaking about any character in the play, including Jim, who lives according to popular illusions about self-fulfillment. But the Wingfields in particular pay dearly for their illusions, perhaps Laura more than anyone because of her mother's inability to relinquish intense but unrealistic hopes for her daughter.

Williams's written presentation of the play provides more insights than usual for a reading audience. His stage directions are elaborate, poetic, and exceptionally evocative. Through Tom, as narrator, he says that the play is not realistic but rather is a memory play, an enactment of moments in Tom's memory.

Williams specifies a setting that is almost dreamlike, using Brechtian devices such as the visual images and screen legends flashed at appropriate moments. He uses music to establish a mood or stimulate an association. Because modern productions rarely follow Williams's directions, the dreamlike quality is sometimes lost. In fact, ironically, modern productions of this play are often realistic rather than symbolic, although they usually maintain the mood that Williams hoped to achieve.

The Glass Menagerie in Performance

The first production of *The Glass Menagerie* opened in Chicago on December 26, 1944, during World War II. Audiences were not drawn to it at first, but the critics' positive reviews began to attract people to the theater. In March 1945, when it was playing to full houses, the play transferred to New York and began a run of 561 performances. It won the Drama Critics' Circle Award as the best American play of the 1944–1945 season. Two road companies then toured the play around the country. The first London performance, in the large and distinguished Theatre Royal in Haymarket in July 1948, was directed by John Gielgud and starred Helen Hayes as Amanda Wingfield. A film version followed in 1950.

Revivals of the play have been both numerous and successful. Laurette Taylor, who played Amanda in the original New York production, set a standard with her interpretation of Williams's poetic language. Maureen Stapleton, whose more vigorous approach contrasted sharply with Taylor's, took the role in the 1965 production in the Brooks Atkinson Theater in New York. The critic Howard Taubman said, "Maureen Stapleton does not cause one to forget Miss Taylor. . . . Through the magic of her own sensitivity, she gives Amanda a strong, binding thread of sadness and tenderness." Katharine Hepburn's first television performance was as Amanda in 1973. "She gives a brilliant, multifaceted performance that is surely the acting tour de force of the year," said critic Percy Shain. Jessica Tandy performed the role in 1983 at the Eugene O'Neill Theater in New York, with Amanda Plummer as Laura. *New York Times* critic Frank Rich declared, "This Amanda is tough, and even her most comic badgerings leave a bitter aftertaste." The British director of that production, John Dexter, used some of the flash cards that Williams specified in the original published version but that had been omitted from previous productions. They flashed important speeches on the scrim during the performance.

Joanne Woodward played Amanda in the 1986 revival at the Long Wharf Theater in New Haven in a version that had been performed at the Williamstown Theatre Festival in 1982. Treat Williams was the son, James Naughton was the gentleman caller, and the Long Wharf production was impressively dreamlike and powerful. Woodward's husband, Paul Newman, directed the 1987 film version of the play.

Tennessee Williams (1911–1983)
THE GLASS MENAGERIE   *1944*

nobody, not even the rain, has such small hands — E. E. CUMMINGS

Production Notes by Tennessee Williams

Being a "memory play," *The Glass Menagerie* can be presented with unusual freedom of convention. Because of its considerably delicate or tenuous material, atmospheric touches and subtleties of direction play a particularly important part. Expressionism and all other unconventional techniques in drama have only one valid aim, and this is a closer approach to truth. When a play employs unconventional techniques, it is not, or certainly shouldn't be, trying to escape its responsibility of dealing with reality, or interpreting experience, but is actually or should be attempting to find a closer approach, or more penetrating and vivid expression of things as they are. The straight realistic play with its genuine frigidaire and authentic ice cubes, its characters that speak exactly as its audience speaks, corresponds to the academic landscape and has the same virtue of a photographic likeness. Everyone should know nowadays the unimportance of the photographic in art: that truth, life, or reality is an organic thing which the poetic imagination can represent or suggest, in essence, only through transformation, through changing into other forms than those which were merely present in appearance.

These remarks are not meant as a preface only to this particular play. They have to do with a conception of a new, plastic theatre which must take the place of the exhausted theatre of realistic conventions if the theatre is to resume vitality as a part of our culture.

The Screen Device. There is *only one important difference between the original and acting version of the play* and that is the *omission* in the latter of the device which I tentatively included in my *original* script. This device was the use of a screen on which were projected magic-lantern slides bearing images or titles. I do not regret the omission of this device from the present Broadway production. The extraordinary power of Miss Taylor's performance made it suitable to have the utmost simplicity in the physical production. But I think it may be interesting to some readers to see how this device was conceived. So I am putting it into the published manuscript. These images and legends, projected from behind, were cast on a section of wall between the front-room and dining-room areas, which should be indistinguishable from the rest when not in use.

The purpose of this will probably be apparent. It is to give accent to certain values in each scene. Each scene contains a particular point (or several) which is structurally the most important. In an episodic play, such as this, the basic structure or narrative line may be obscured from the audience; the effect may seem fragmentary rather than architectural. This may not be the fault of the play so much as a lack of attention in the audience. The legend or image upon the screen will strengthen the effect of what is merely allusion in the writing and allow the primary point to be made more simply and lightly than if the entire responsibility were on the spoken lines. Aside from this structural value, I think the screen will have a definite emotional appeal, less definable but just as important. An imaginative producer or director may invent many other uses for this device than those indicated in the present script. In fact the possibilities of the device seem much larger to me than the instance of this play can possibly utilize.

The Music. Another extra-literary accent in this play is provided by the use of music. A single recurring tune, "The Glass Menagerie," is used to give emotional emphasis to suitable passages. This tune is like circus music, not when you are on the grounds or in the immediate vicinity of the parade, but when you are at some distance and very likely thinking of something else. It seems under those circumstances to continue almost interminably and it weaves in and out of your preoccupied consciousness; then it is the lightest, most delicate music in the world and perhaps the saddest. It expresses the surface vivacity of life with the underlying strain of immutable and inexpressible sorrow. When you look at a piece of delicately spun glass you think of two things: how beautiful it is and how easily it can be broken. Both of those ideas should be woven into the recurring tune, which dips in and out of the play as if it were carried on a wind that changes. It serves as a thread of connection and allusion between the narrator with his separate point in time and space and the subject of his story. Between each episode it returns as reference to the emotion, nostalgia, which is the first condition of the play. It is primarily Laura's music and therefore comes out most clearly when the play focuses upon her and the lovely fragility of glass which is her image.

The Lighting. The lighting in the play is not realistic. In keeping with the atmosphere of memory, the stage is dim. Shafts of light are focused on selected areas or actors, sometimes in contradistinction to what is the apparent center. For instance, in the quarrel scene between Tom and Amanda, in which Laura has no active part, the clearest pool of light is on her figure. This is also true of the supper scene, when her silent figure on the sofa should remain the visual center. The light upon Laura should be distinct from the others, having a peculiar pristine clarity such as light used in early religious portraits of female saints or madonnas. A certain correspondence to light in religious paintings, such as El Greco's, where the figures are radiant in atmosphere that is relatively dusky, could be effectively used throughout the play. (It will also permit a more effective use of the screen.) A free, imaginative use of light can be of enormous value in giving a mobile, plastic quality to plays of a more or less static nature.

Characters

AMANDA WINGFIELD, *the mother. A little woman of great but confused vitality clinging frantically to another time and place. Her characterization must be carefully created, not copied from type. She is not paranoiac, but her life is paranoia. There is much to admire in Amanda, and as much to love and pity as there is to laugh at. Certainly she has endurance and a kind of heroism, and though her foolishness makes her unwittingly cruel at times, there is tenderness in her slight person.*

LAURA WINGFIELD, *her daughter. Amanda, having failed to establish contact with reality, continues to live vitally in her illusions, but Laura's situation is even graver. A childhood illness has left her crippled, one leg slightly shorter than the other, and held in a brace. This defect need not be more than suggested on the stage. Stemming from this, Laura's separation increases till she is like a piece of her own glass collection, too exquisitely fragile to move from the shelf.*

TOM WINGFIELD, *her son. And the narrator of the play. A poet with a job in a warehouse. His nature is not remorseless, but to escape from a trap he has to act without pity.*

JIM O'CONNOR, *the gentleman caller. A nice, ordinary, young man.*

Scene: *An alley in St. Louis.*
Part I: *Preparation for a Gentleman Caller.*
Part II: *The Gentleman Calls.*
Time: *Now and the Past.*

SCENE 1

(The Wingfield apartment is in the rear of the building, one of those vast hive-like conglomerations of cellular living-units that flower as warty growths in overcrowded urban centers of lower middle-class population and are symptomatic of the impulse of this largest and fundamentally enslaved section of American society to avoid fluidity and differentiation and to exist and function as one interfused mass of automatism.)

(The apartment faces an alley and is entered by a fire escape, a structure whose name is a touch of accidental poetic truth, for all of these huge buildings are always burning with the slow and implacable fires of human desperation. The fire escape is included in the set — that is, the landing of it and steps descending from it.)

(The scene is memory and is therefore nonrealistic. Memory takes a lot of poetic license. It omits some details; others are exaggerated, according to the emotional value of the articles it touches, for memory is seated predominantly in the heart. The interior is therefore rather dim and poetic.)

(At the rise of the curtain, the audience is faced with the dark, grim rear wall of the Wingfield tenement. This building, which runs parallel to the footlights, is flanked on both sides by dark, narrow alleys which run into murky canyons of tangled clotheslines, garbage cans, and the sinister latticework of neighboring fire escapes. It is up and down these side alleys that exterior entrances and exits are made, during the play. At the end of Tom's opening commentary, the dark tenement wall slowly reveals (by means of a transparency) the interior of the ground floor Wingfield apartment.)

(Downstage is the living room, which also serves as a sleeping room for Laura, the sofa unfolding to make her bed. Upstage, center, and divided by a wide arch or second proscenium with transparent faded portieres (or second curtain), is the dining room. In an old-fashioned what-not in the living room are seen scores of transparent glass animals. A blown-up photograph of the father hangs on the wall of the living room, facing the audience, to the left of the archway. It is the face of a very handsome young man in a doughboy's First World War cap. He is gallantly smiling, ineluctably smiling, as if to say, "I will be smiling forever.")

(The audience hears and sees the opening scene in the dining room through both the transparent fourth wall of the building and the transparent gauze portieres of the dining-room arch. It is during this revealing scene that the fourth wall slowly ascends, out of sight. This transparent exterior wall is not brought down again until the very end of the play, during Tom's final speech.)

(The narrator is an undisguised convention of the play. He takes whatever license with dramatic convention as is convenient to his purposes.)

(Tom enters dressed as a merchant sailor from alley, stage left, and strolls across the front of the stage to the fire escape. There he stops and lights a cigarette. He addresses the audience.)

TOM: Yes, I have tricks in my pocket, I have things up my sleeve. But I am the opposite of a stage magician. He gives you illusion that has the appearance of truth. I give you truth in the pleasant disguise of illusion. To begin with, I turn back time. I reverse it to that quaint period, the thirties, when the huge middle class of America was matriculating in a school for the blind. Their eyes had failed them, or they had failed their eyes, and so they were having their fingers pressed forcibly down on the fiery Braille alphabet of a dissolving economy. In Spain there was revolution. Here there was only shouting and confusion. In Spain there was Guernica. Here there were disturbances of labor, sometimes pretty violent, in otherwise peaceful cities such as Chicago, Cleveland, Saint Louis. . . . This is the social background of the play.

(Music.)

The play is memory. Being a memory play, it is dimly lighted, it is sentimental, it is not realistic. In memory everything seems to happen to music. That explains the fiddle in the wings. I am the narrator of the play, and also a character in it. The other characters are my mother, Amanda, my sister, Laura, and a gentleman caller who appears in the final scenes. He is the most realistic character in the play, being an emissary from a world of reality that we were somehow set apart from. But since I have a poet's weakness for symbols, I am using this character also as a symbol; he is the long delayed but always expected something that we live for. There is a fifth character in the play who doesn't appear except in this larger-than-life photograph over the mantel. This is our father who left us a long time ago. He was a telephone man who fell in love with long distances; he gave up his job with the telephone company and skipped the light fantastic out of town . . . The last we heard of him was a picture postcard from Mazatlan, on the Pacific coast of Mexico, containing a message of two words — "Hello — Good-bye!" and no address. I think the rest of the play will explain itself. . . .

(*Amanda's voice becomes audible through the portieres.*)
(*Legend on Screen: "Où Sont les Neiges."*)°
(*He divides the portieres and enters the upstage area.*)
(*Amanda and Laura are seated at a drop-leaf table. Eating is indicated by gestures without food or utensils. Amanda faces the audience. Tom and Laura are seated in profile.*)
(*The interior has lit up softly and through the scrim we see Amanda and Laura seated at the table in the upstage area.*)

AMANDA (*calling*): Tom?
TOM: Yes, Mother.
AMANDA: We can't say grace until you come to the table!
TOM: Coming, Mother. (*He bows slightly and withdraws, reappearing a few moments later in his place at the table.*)
AMANDA (*to her son*): Honey, don't *push* with your fingers. If you have to push with something, the thing to push with is a crust of bread. And chew — chew! Animals have sections in their stomachs which enable them to digest food without mastication, but human beings are supposed to chew their food before they swallow it down. Eat food leisurely, son, and really enjoy it. A well-cooked meal has lots of delicate flavors that have to be held in the mouth for appreciation. So chew your food and give your salivary glands a chance to function!

(*Tom deliberately lays his imaginary fork down and pushes his chair back from the table.*)

TOM: I haven't enjoyed one bite of this dinner because of your constant directions on how to eat it. It's you

Où Sont les Neiges: Where are the snows [of yesteryear].

that makes me rush through meals with your hawk-like attention to every bite I take. Sickening — spoils my appetite — all this discussion of animals' secretion — salivary glands — mastication!
AMANDA (*lightly*): Temperament like a Metropolitan° star! (*He rises and crosses downstage.*) You're not excused from the table.
TOM: I'm getting a cigarette.
AMANDA: You smoke too much.

(*Laura rises.*)

LAURA: I'll bring in the blancmange.

(*He remains standing with his cigarette by the portieres during the following.*)

AMANDA (*rising*): No, sister, no, sister — you be the lady this time and I'll be the darky.
LAURA: I'm already up.
AMANDA: Resume your seat, little sister — I want you to stay fresh and pretty — for gentlemen callers!
LAURA: I'm not expecting any gentlemen callers.
AMANDA (*crossing out to kitchenette. Airily*): Sometimes they come when they are least expected! Why, I remember one Sunday afternoon in Blue Mountain — (*Enters kitchenette.*)
TOM: I know what's coming!
LAURA: Yes. But let her tell it.
TOM: Again?
LAURA: She loves to tell it.

(*Amanda returns with bowl of dessert.*)

AMANDA: One Sunday afternoon in Blue Mountain — your mother received — *seventeen!* — gentlemen callers! Why, sometimes there weren't chairs enough to accommodate them all. We had to send the nigger over to bring in folding chairs from the parish house.
TOM (*remaining at portieres*): How did you entertain those gentlemen callers?
AMANDA: I understood the art of conversation!
TOM: I bet you could talk.
AMANDA: Girls in those days *knew* how to talk, I can tell you.
TOM: Yes?

(*Image: Amanda as a girl on a porch greeting callers.*)

AMANDA: They knew how to entertain their gentlemen callers. It wasn't enough for a girl to be possessed of a pretty face and a graceful figure — although I wasn't slighted in either respect. She also needed to have a nimble wit and a tongue to meet all occasions.
TOM: What did you talk about?
AMANDA: Things of importance going on in the world! Never anything coarse or common or vulgar. (*She addresses Tom as though he were seated in the vacant chair at the table though he remains by portieres. He plays this scene as though he held the book.*) My callers were gentlemen — all! Among my

Metropolitan: The Metropolitan Opera in New York City.

callers were some of the most prominent young planters of the Mississippi Delta — planters and sons of planters!

(*Tom motions for music and a spot of light on Amanda.*)
(*Her eyes lift, her face glows, her voice becomes rich and elegiac.*)
(*Screen legend: "Où Sont les Neiges."*)

There was young Champ Laughlin who later became vice-president of the Delta Planters Bank. Hadley Stevenson who was drowned in Moon Lake and left his widow one hundred and fifty thousand in Government bonds. There were the Cutrere brothers, Wesley and Bates. Bates was one of my bright particular beaux! He got in a quarrel with that wild Wainright boy. They shot it out on the floor of Moon Lake Casino. Bates was shot through the stomach. Died in the ambulance on his way to Memphis. His widow was also well-provided for, came into eight or ten thousand acres, that's all. She married him on the rebound — never loved her — carried my picture on him the night he died! And there was that boy that every girl in the Delta had set her cap for! That beautiful, brilliant young Fitzhugh boy from Greene County!

TOM: What did he leave his widow?

AMANDA: He never married! Gracious, you talk as though all of my old admirers had turned up their toes to the daisies!

TOM: Isn't this the first you mentioned that still survives?

AMANDA: That Fitzhugh boy went North and made a fortune — came to be known as the Wolf of Wall Street! He had the Midas touch, whatever he touched turned to gold! And I could have been Mrs. Duncan J. Fitzhugh, mind you! But — I picked your *father*!

LAURA (*rising*): Mother, let me clear the table.

AMANDA: No, dear, you go in front and study your typewriter chart. Or practice your shorthand a little. Stay fresh and pretty! — It's almost time for our gentlemen callers to start arriving. (*She flounces girlishly toward the kitchenette.*) How many do you suppose we're going to entertain this afternoon?

(*Tom throws down the paper and jumps up with a groan.*)

LAURA (*alone in the dining room*): I don't believe we're going to receive any, Mother.

AMANDA (*reappearing, airily*): What? No one — not one? You must be joking! (*Laura nervously echoes her laugh. She slips in a fugitive manner through the half-open portieres and draws them gently behind her. A shaft of very clear light is thrown on her face against the faded tapestry of the curtains. Music: "The Glass Menagerie" under faintly. Lightly.*) Not one gentleman caller? It can't be true! There must be a flood, there must have been a tornado!

LAURA: It isn't a flood, it's not a tornado, Mother. I'm just not popular like you were in Blue Mountain. . . .
(*Tom utters another groan. Laura glances at him*

with a faint, apologetic smile. Her voice catching a little.) Mother's afraid I'm going to be an old maid.

(*The scene dims out with "Glass Menagerie" music.*)

SCENE 2

(*"Laura, Haven't You Ever Liked Some Boy?"*)
(*On the dark stage the screen is lighted with the image of blue roses.*)
(*Gradually Laura's figure becomes apparent and the screen goes out.*)
(*The music subsides.*)
(*Laura is seated in the delicate ivory chair at the small clawfoot table.*)
(*She wears a dress of soft violet material for a kimono — her hair tied back from her forehead with a ribbon.*)
(*She is washing and polishing her collection of glass.*)
(*Amanda appears on the fire escape steps. At the sound of her ascent, Laura catches her breath, thrusts the bowl of ornaments away and seats herself stiffly before the diagram of the typewriter keyboard as though it held her spellbound. Something has happened to Amanda. It is written in her face as she climbs to the landing: a look that is grim and hopeless and a little absurd.*)
(*She has on one of those cheap or imitation velvety-looking cloth coats with imitation fur collar. Her hat is five or six years old, one of those dreadful cloche hats that were worn in the late twenties, and she is clasping an enormous black patent-leather pocketbook with nickel clasp and initials. This is her full-dress outfit, the one she usually wears to the D.A.R.°*)
(*Before entering she looks through the door.*)
(*She purses her lips, opens her eyes wide, rolls them upward and shakes her head.*)
(*Then she slowly lets herself in the door. Seeing her mother's expression Laura touches her lips with a nervous gesture.*)

LAURA: Hello, Mother, I was — (*She makes a nervous gesture toward the chart on the wall. Amanda leans against the shut door and stares at Laura with a martyred look.*)

AMANDA: Deception? Deception? (*She slowly removes her hat and gloves, continuing the swift suffering stare. She lets the hat and gloves fall on the floor — a bit of acting.*)

LAURA (*shakily*): How was the D.A.R. meeting? (*Amanda slowly opens her purse and removes a dainty white handkerchief which she shakes out delicately and delicately touches to her lips and nostrils.*) Didn't you go to the D.A.R. meeting, Mother?

D.A.R.: Daughters of the American Revolution, a patriotic organization for women whose ancestors were involved in the American Revolutionary War.

AMANDA (*faintly, almost inaudibly*): — No. — No. (*Then more forcibly*). I did not have the strength — to go to the D.A.R. In fact, I did not have the courage! I wanted to find a hole in the ground and hide myself in it forever! (*She crosses slowly to the wall and removes the diagram of the typewriter keyboard. She holds it in front of her for a second, staring at it sweetly and sorrowfully — then bites her lips and tears it in two pieces.*)

LAURA (*faintly*): Why did you do that, Mother? (*Amanda repeats the same procedure with the chart of the Gregg Alphabet.*) Why are you —

AMANDA: Why? Why? How old are you, Laura?

LAURA: Mother, you know my age.

AMANDA: I thought that you were an adult; it seems that I was mistaken. (*She crosses slowly to the sofa and sinks down and stares at Laura.*)

LAURA: Please don't stare at me, Mother.

(*Amanda closes her eyes and lowers her head. Count ten.*)

AMANDA: What are we going to do, what is going to become of us, what is the future?

(*Count ten.*)

LAURA: Has something happened, Mother? (*Amanda draws a long breath and takes out the handkerchief again. Dabbing process.*) Mother, has — something happened?

AMANDA: I'll be all right in a minute. I'm just bewildered — (*Count five.*) — by life. . . .

LAURA: Mother, I wish that you would tell me what's happened.

AMANDA: As you know, I was supposed to be inducted into my office at the D.A.R. this afternoon. (*Image: a swarm of typewriters.*) But I stopped off at Rubicam's Business College to speak to your teachers about your having a cold and ask them what progress they thought you were making down there.

LAURA: Oh. . . .

AMANDA: I went to the typing instructor and introduced myself as your mother. She didn't know who you were. Wingfield, she said. We don't have any such student enrolled at the school! I assured her she did, that you had been going to classes since early in January. "I wonder," she said, "if you could be talking about that terribly shy little girl who dropped out of school after only a few days' attendance?" "No," I said, "Laura, my daughter, has been going to school every day for the past six weeks!" "Excuse me," she said. She took the attendance book out and there was your name, unmistakably printed, and all the dates you were absent until they decided that you had dropped out of school. I still said, "No, there must have been some mistake! There must have been some mix-up in the records!" And she said, "No — I remember her perfectly now. Her hands shook so that she couldn't hit the right keys! The first time we gave a speed test, she broke down completely — was sick at the stomach and almost had to be carried into the wash-room! After that morning she never showed up any more. We phoned the house but never got any answer"— while I was working at Famous and Barr, I suppose, demonstrating those — Oh! I felt so weak I could barely keep on my feet. I had to sit down while they got me a glass of water! Fifty dollars' tuition, all of our plans — my hopes and ambitions for you — just gone up the spout, just gone up the spout like that. (*Laura draws a long breath and gets awkwardly to her feet. She crosses to the victrola and winds it up.*) What are you doing?

LAURA: Oh! (*She releases the handle and returns to her seat.*)

AMANDA: Laura, where have you been going when you've gone out pretending that you were going to business college?

LAURA: I've just been going out walking.

AMANDA: That's not true.

LAURA: It is. I just went walking.

AMANDA: Walking? Walking? In winter? Deliberately courting pneumonia in that light coat? Where did you walk to, Laura?

LAURA: All sorts of places — mostly in the park.

AMANDA: Even after you'd started catching that cold?

LAURA: It was the lesser of two evils, Mother. (*Image: winter scene in park.*) I couldn't go back up. I — threw up — on the floor!

AMANDA: From half past seven till after five every day you mean to tell me you walked around in the park, because you wanted to make me think that you were still going to Rubicam's Business College?

LAURA: It wasn't as bad as it sounds. I went inside places to get warmed up.

AMANDA: Inside where?

LAURA: I went in the art museum and the bird houses at the Zoo. I visited the penguins every day! Sometimes I did without lunch and went to the movies. Lately I've been spending most of my afternoons in the Jewel-box, that big glass house where they raise the tropical flowers.

AMANDA: You did all this to deceive me, just for the deception? (*Laura looks down.*) Why?

LAURA: Mother, when you're disappointed, you get that awful suffering look on your face, like the picture of Jesus' mother in the museum!

AMANDA: Hush!

LAURA: I couldn't face it.

(*Pause. A whisper of strings.*)
(*Legend: "The Crust of Humility."*)

AMANDA (*hopelessly fingering the huge pocketbook*): So what are we going to do the rest of our lives? Stay home and watch the parades go by? Amuse ourselves with the glass menagerie, darling? Eternally play those worn-out phonograph records your father left as a painful reminder of him? We won't have a business career — we've given that up because it gave us nervous indigestion! (*Laughs wearily.*) What is there left but dependency all our lives? I know so well what becomes of unmarried women who aren't prepared to occupy a position. I've seen such pitiful cases in the South — barely tolerated spinsters living upon the grudging patronage of sister's husband or brother's wife! — stuck away in some little mouse-trap of a room — encouraged by one in-law to visit another — little birdlike women without any nest — eating the crust of humility all their life! Is that the future that we've mapped out for ourselves? I swear it's the only alternative I can think of! It isn't a very pleasant alternative, is it? Of course — some girls do *marry*. (*Laura twists her hands nervously.*) Haven't you ever liked some boy?

LAURA: Yes. I liked one once. (*Rises.*) I came across his picture a while ago.

AMANDA (*with some interest*): He gave you his picture?

LAURA: No, it's in the yearbook.

AMANDA (*disappointed*): Oh — a high-school boy.

(*Screen image: Jim as high school hero bearing a silver cup.*)

LAURA: Yes. His name was Jim. (*Laura lifts the heavy annual from the clawfoot table.*) Here he is in *The Pirates of Penzance.*

AMANDA (*absently*): The what?

LAURA: The operetta the senior class put on. He had a wonderful voice and we sat across the aisle from each other Mondays, Wednesdays, and Fridays in the Aud. Here he is with the silver cup for debating! See his grin?

AMANDA (*absently*): He must have had a jolly disposition.

LAURA: He used to call me — Blue Roses.

(*Image: blue roses.*)

AMANDA: Why did he call you such a name as that?

LAURA: When I had that attack of pleurosis — he asked me what was the matter when I came back. I said pleurosis — he thought that I said Blue Roses! So that's what he always called me after that. Whenever he saw me, he'd holler, "Hello, Blue Roses!" I didn't care for the girl that he went out with. Emily Meisenbach. Emily was the best-dressed girl at Soldan. She never struck me, though, as being sincere . . . It says in the Personal Section — they're engaged. That's — six years ago! They must be married by now.

AMANDA: Girls that aren't cut out for business careers usually wind up married to some nice man. (*Gets up with a spark of revival.*) Sister, that's what you'll do!

(*Laura utters a startled, doubtful laugh. She reaches quickly for a piece of glass.*)

LAURA: But, Mother —

AMANDA: Yes? (*Crossing to photograph.*)

LAURA (*in a tone of frightened apology*): I'm — crippled!

(*Image: screen.*)

AMANDA: Nonsense! Laura, I've told you never, never to use that word. Why, you're not crippled, you just have a little defect — hardly noticeable, even! When people have some slight disadvantage like that, they cultivate other things to make up for it — develop charm — and vivacity — and — *charm!* That's all you have to do! (*She turns again to the photograph.*) One thing your father had *plenty of* — was *charm!*

(*Tom motions to the fiddle in the wings.*)
(*The scene fades out with music.*)

SCENE 3

(*Legend on screen: "After the Fiasco —"*)
(*Tom speaks from the fire escape landing.*)

TOM: After the fiasco at Rubicam's Business College, the idea of getting a gentleman caller for Laura began to play a more important part in Mother's calculations. It became an obsession. Like some archetype of the universal unconscious, the image of the gentleman caller haunted our small apartment. . . . (*Image: young man at door with flowers.*) An evening at home rarely passed without some allusion to this image, this specter, this hope. . . . Even when he wasn't mentioned, his presence hung in Mother's pre-occupied look and in my sister's frightened, apologetic manner — hung like a sentence passed upon the Wingfields! Mother was a woman of action as well as words. She began to take logical steps in the planned direction. Late that winter and in the early spring — realizing that extra money would be needed to properly feather the nest and plume the bird — she conducted a vigorous campaign on the telephone, roping in subscribers to one of those magazines for matrons called *The Home-maker's Companion,* the type of journal that features the serialized sublimations of ladies of letters who think in terms of delicate cuplike breasts, slim, tapering waists, rich, creamy thighs, eyes like wood smoke in autumn, fingers that soothe and caress like strains of music, bodies as powerful as Etruscan sculpture.

(*Screen image: glamor magazine cover.*)
(*Amanda enters with phone on long extension cord. She is spotted in the dim stage.*)

AMANDA: Ida Scott? This is Amanda Wingfield! We *missed* you at the D.A.R. last Monday! I said to myself: She's probably suffering with that sinus condition! How is that sinus condition? Horrors! Heaven have mercy! — You're a Christian martyr, yes, that's what you are, a Christian martyr! Well I just now happened to notice that your subscription to the *Companion*'s about to expire! Yes, it expires with the next issue, honey! — just when that wonderful new serial by Bessie Mae Hopper is getting off to such an exciting start. Oh, honey, it's something that you can't miss! You remember how *Gone with the Wind* took everybody by storm? You simply couldn't go out if you hadn't read it. All everybody *talked* was Scarlett O'Hara. Well, this is a book that critics already compare to *Gone with the Wind*. It's the *Gone with the Wind* of the post–World War generation! — What? — Burning? — Oh, honey, don't let them burn, go take a look in the oven and I'll hold the wire! Heavens — I think she's hung up!

(*Dim out.*)

(*Legend on screen: "You Think I'm in Love with Continental Shoemakers?"*)

(*Before the stage is lighted, the violent voices of Tom and Amanda are heard.*)

(*They are quarreling behind the portieres. In front of them stands Laura with clenched hands and panicky expression.*)

(*A clear pool of light on her figure throughout this scene.*)

TOM: What in Christ's name am I —
AMANDA (*shrilly*): Don't you use that —
TOM: Supposed to do!
AMANDA: Expression! Not in my —
TOM: Ohhh!
AMANDA: Presence! Have you gone out of your senses?
TOM: I have, that's true, *driven* out!
AMANDA: What is the matter with you, you — big — big — IDIOT!
TOM: Look — I've got *no thing,* no single thing —
AMANDA: Lower your voice!
TOM: In my life here that I can call my OWN! Everything is —
AMANDA: Stop that shouting!
TOM: Yesterday you confiscated my books! You had the nerve to —
AMANDA: I took that horrible novel back to the library — yes! That hideous book by that insane Mr. Lawrence. (*Tom laughs wildly.*) I cannot control the output of diseased minds or people who cater to them — (*Tom laughs still more wildly.*) BUT I WON'T ALLOW SUCH FILTH BROUGHT INTO MY HOUSE! No, no, no, no, no!
TOM: House, house! Who pays rent on it, who makes a slave of himself to —
AMANDA (*fairly screeching*): Don't you DARE to —
TOM: No, no, I mustn't say things! *I've* got to just —
AMANDA: Let me tell you —
TOM: I don't want to hear any more! (*He tears the portieres open. The upstage area is lit with a turgid smoky red glow.*)

(*Amanda's hair is in metal curlers and she wears a very old bathrobe, much too large for her slight figure, a relic of the faithless Mr. Wingfield.*)

(*An upright typewriter and a wild disarray of manuscripts are on the dropleaf table. The quarrel was probably precipitated by Amanda's interruption of his creative labor. A chair lying overthrown on the floor.*)

(*Their gesticulating shadows are cast on the ceiling by the fiery glow.*)

AMANDA: You *will* hear more, you —

TOM: No, I won't hear more, I'm going out!
AMANDA: You come right back in —
TOM: Out, out out! Because I'm —
AMANDA: Come back here, Tom Wingfield! I'm not through talking to you!
TOM: Oh, go —
LAURA (*desperately*): Tom!
AMANDA: You're going to listen, and no more insolence from you! I'm at the end of my patience! (*He comes back toward her.*)
TOM: What do you think I'm at? Aren't I supposed to have any patience to reach the end of, Mother? I know, I know. It seems unimportant to you, what I'm *doing* — what I *want* to do — having a little *difference* between them! You don't think that —
AMANDA: I think you've been doing things that you're ashamed of. That's why you act like this. I don't believe that you go every night to the movies. Nobody goes to the movies night after night. Nobody in their right minds goes to the movies as often as you pretend to. People don't go to the movies at nearly midnight, and movies don't let out at two A.M. Come in stumbling. Muttering to yourself like a maniac! You get three hours' sleep and then go to work. Oh, I can picture the way you're doing down there. Moping, doping, because you're in no condition.
TOM (*wildly*): No, I'm in no condition!
AMANDA: What right have you got to jeopardize your job? Jeopardize the security of us all? How do you think we'd manage if you were —
TOM: Listen! You think I'm crazy *about* the *warehouse?* (*He bends fiercely toward her slight figure.*) You think I'm in love with the Continental Shoemakers? You think I want to spend fifty-five *years* down there in that — *celotex interior!* with — *fluorescent* — *tubes!* Look! I'd rather somebody picked up a crowbar and battered out my brains — than go back mornings! I *go!* Every time you come in yelling that God damn "*Rise and Shine!*" "*Rise and Shine!*" I say to myself, "*How lucky dead* people are!" But I get up. I *go!* For sixty-five dollars a month I give up all that I dream of doing and being *ever!* And you say self — *self's* all I ever think of. Why, listen, if self is what I thought of, Mother, I'd be where he is — GONE! (*Pointing to father's picture.*) As far as the system of transportation reaches! (*He starts past her. She grabs his arm.*) Don't grab at me, Mother!
AMANDA: Where are you going?
TOM: I'm going to the *movies!*
AMANDA: I don't believe that lie!
TOM (*Crouching toward her, overtowering her tiny figure. She backs away, gasping.*): I'm going to opium dens! Yes, opium dens, dens of vice and criminals' hangouts, Mother. I've joined the Hogan gang, I'm a hired assassin, I carry a tommy-gun in a violin case! I run a string of cathouses in the Valley! They call me Killer, Killer Wingfield, I'm leading a double life, a simple, honest warehouse worker by day, by night, a

dynamic *czar* of the *underworld, Mother.* I go to gambling casinos, I spin away fortunes on the roulette table! I wear a patch over one eye and a false mustache, sometimes I put on green whiskers. On those occasions they call me — *El Diablo!* Oh, I could tell you things to make you sleepless! My enemies plan to dynamite this place. They're going to blow us all skyhigh some night! I'll be glad, very happy, and so will you! You'll go up, up on a broomstick, over Blue Mountain with seventeen gentlemen callers! You ugly — babbling old — *witch.* . . . (*He goes through a series of violent, clumsy movements, seizing his overcoat, lunging to the door, pulling it fiercely open. The women watch him, aghast. His arm catches in the sleeve of the coat as he struggles to pull it on. For a moment he is pinioned by the bulky garment. With an outraged groan he tears the coat off again, splitting the shoulders of it, and hurls it across the room. It strikes against the shelf of Laura's glass collection, there is a tinkle of shattering glass. Laura cries out as if wounded.*)

(*Music legend: "The Glass Menagerie."*)

LAURA (*shrilly*): My glass! — menagerie. . . . (*She covers her face and turns away.*)

(*But Amanda is still stunned and stupefied by the "ugly witch" so that she barely notices this occurrence. Now she recovers her speech.*)

AMANDA (*in an awful voice*): I won't speak to you — until you apologize! (*She crosses through portieres and draws them together behind her. Tom is left with Laura. Laura clings weakly to the mantel with her face averted. Tom stares at her stupidly for a moment. Then he crosses to shelf. Drops awkwardly to his knees to collect the fallen glass, glancing at Laura as if he would speak but couldn't.*)

(*"The Glass Menagerie" steals in as the scene dims out.*)

SCENE 4

(*The interior is dark. Faint light in the alley.*)

(*A deep-voiced bell in a church is tolling the hour of five as the scene commences.*)

(*Tom appears at the top of the alley. After each solemn boom of the bell in the tower, he shakes a little noisemaker or rattle as if to express the tiny spasm of man in contrast to the sustained power and dignity of the Almighty. This and the unsteadiness of his advance make it evident that he has been drinking.*)

(*As he climbs the few steps to the fire escape landing light steals up inside. Laura appears in nightdress, observing Tom's empty bed in the front room.*)

(*Tom fishes in his pockets for the door key, removing a motley assortment of articles in the search, including a perfect shower of movie ticket stubs and an empty bottle. At last he finds the key, but just as he is about to*

insert it, it slips from his fingers. He strikes a match and crouches below the door.*)

TOM (*bitterly*): One crack — and it falls through!

(*Laura opens the door.*)

LAURA: Tom! Tom, what are you doing?
TOM: Looking for a door key.
LAURA: Where have you been all this time?
TOM: I have been to the movies.
LAURA: All this time at the movies?
TOM: There was a very long program. There was a Garbo picture and a Mickey Mouse and a travelogue and a newsreel and a preview of coming attractions. And there was an organ solo and a collection for the milk fund — simultaneously — which ended up in a terrible fight between a fat lady and an usher!
LAURA (*innocently*): Did you have to stay through everything?
TOM: Of course! And, oh, I forgot! There was a big stage show! The headliner on this stage show was Malvolio the Magician. He performed wonderful tricks, many of them, such as pouring water back and forth between pitchers. First it turned to wine and then it turned to beer and then it turned to whiskey. I know it was whiskey it finally turned into because he needed somebody to come up out of the audience to help him, and I came up — both shows! It was Kentucky Straight Bourbon. A very generous fellow, he gave souvenirs. (*He pulls from his back pocket a shimmering rainbow-colored scarf.*) He gave me this. This is his magic scarf. You can have it, Laura. You wave it over a canary cage and you get a bowl of goldfish. You wave it over the goldfish bowl and they fly away canaries. . . . But the wonderfullest trick of all was the coffin trick. We nailed him into a coffin and he got out of the coffin without removing one nail. (*He has come inside.*) There is a trick that would come in handy for me — get me out of this 2 by 4 situation! (*Flops onto bed and starts removing shoes.*)
LAURA: Tom — Shhh!
TOM: What you shushing me for?
LAURA: You'll wake up Mother.
TOM: Goody, goody! Pay 'er back for all those "Rise an' Shines." (*Lies down, groaning.*) You know it don't take much intelligence to get yourself into a nailed-up coffin, Laura. But who in hell ever got himself out of one without removing one nail?

(*As if in answer, the father's grinning photograph lights up.*)

(*Scene dims out.*)

(*Immediately following: The church bell is heard striking six. At the sixth stroke the alarm clock goes off in Amanda's room, and after a few moments we hear her calling: "Rise and Shine! Rise and Shine! Laura, go tell your brother to rise and shine!"*)

TOM (*sitting up slowly*): I'll rise — but I won't shine.

(*The light increases.*)

AMANDA: Laura, tell your brother his coffee is ready.

(*Laura slips into front room.*)

LAURA: Tom! it's nearly seven. Don't make Mother nervous. (*He stares at her stupidly. Beseechingly.*) Tom, speak to Mother this morning. Make up with her, apologize, speak to her!

TOM: She won't to me. It's her that started not speaking.

LAURA: If you just say you're sorry she'll start speaking.

TOM: Her not speaking — is that such a tragedy?

LAURA: Please — please!

AMANDA (*calling from kitchenette*): Laura, are you going to do what I asked you to do, or do I have to get dressed and go out myself?

LAURA: Going, going — soon as I get on my coat! (*She pulls on a shapeless felt hat with nervous, jerky movement, pleadingly glancing at Tom. Rushes awkwardly for coat. The coat is one of Amanda's, inaccurately made over, the sleeves too short for Laura.*) Butter and what else?

AMANDA (*entering upstage*): Just butter. Tell them to charge it.

LAURA: Mother, they make such faces when I do that.

AMANDA: Sticks and stones may break my bones, but the expression on Mr. Garfinkel's face won't harm us! Tell your brother his coffee is getting cold.

LAURA (*at door*): Do what I asked you, will you, will you, Tom?

(*He looks sullenly away.*)

AMANDA: Laura, go now or just don't go at all!

LAURA (*rushing out*): Going — going! (*A second later she cries out. Tom springs up and crosses to the door. Amanda rushes anxiously in. Tom opens the door.*)

TOM: Laura?

LAURA: I'm all right. I slipped, but I'm all right.

AMANDA (*peering anxiously after her*): If anyone breaks a leg on those fire escape steps, the landlord ought to be sued for every cent he possesses! (*She shuts door. Remembers she isn't speaking and returns to other room.*)

(*As Tom enters listlessly for his coffee, she turns her back to him and stands rigidly facing the window on the gloomy gray vault of the areaway. Its light on her face with its aged but childish features is cruelly sharp, satirical as a Daumier print.*)

(*Music under: "Ave Maria."*)

(*Tom glances sheepishly but sullenly at her averted figure and slumps at the table. The coffee is scalding hot; he sips it and gasps and spits it back in the cup. At his gasp, Amanda catches her breath and half turns. Then catches herself and turns back to window.*)

(*Tom blows on his coffee, glancing sidewise at his mother. She clears her throat. Tom clears his. He starts to rise. Sinks back down again, scratches his head, clears his throat again. Amanda coughs. Tom raises his cup in both hands to blow on it, his eyes staring over the rim of it at his mother for several moments. Then he slowly sets the cup down and awkwardly and hesitantly rises from the chair.*)

TOM (*hoarsely*): Mother. I — I apologize. Mother. (*Amanda draws a quick, shuddering breath. Her face works grotesquely. She breaks into childlike tears.*) I'm sorry for what I said, for everything that I said, I didn't mean it.

AMANDA (*sobbingly*): My devotion has made me a witch and so I make myself hateful to my children!

TOM: No, you *don't.*

AMANDA: I worry so much, don't sleep, it makes me nervous!

TOM (*gently*): I understand that.

AMANDA: I've had to put up a solitary battle all these years. But you're my right-hand bower! Don't fall down, don't fail!

TOM (*gently*): I try, Mother.

AMANDA (*with great enthusiasm*): Try and you will SUCCEED! (*The notion makes her breathless.*) Why, you — you're just *full* of natural endowments! Both of my children — they're *unusual* children! Don't you think I know it? I'm so — *proud!* Happy and — feel I've — so much to be thankful for but — Promise me one thing, son!

TOM: What, Mother?

AMANDA: Promise, son, you'll — never be a drunkard!

LEFT: Laurette Taylor as Amanda in the original 1944 production of *The Glass Menagerie*. RIGHT: Julie Haydon as Laura. ABOVE: Jo Mielziner's drawing of the set for the original production of *The Glass Menagerie*.

Tom (*turns to her grinning*): I will never be a drunkard, Mother.

Amanda: That's what frightened me so, that you'd be drinking! Eat a bowl of Purina!

Tom: Just coffee, Mother.

Amanda: Shredded wheat biscuit?

Tom: No, no, Mother, just coffee.

Amanda: You can't put in a day's work on an empty stomach. You've got ten minutes — don't gulp! Drinking too-hot liquids makes cancer of the stomach. . . . Put cream in.

Tom: No, thank you.

Amanda: To cool it.

Tom: No! No, thank you, I want it black.

Amanda: I know, but it's not good for you. We have to do all that we can to build ourselves up. In these trying times we live in, all that we have to cling to is — each other. . . . That's why it's so important to — Tom, I — I sent out your sister so I could discuss something with you. If you hadn't spoken I would have spoken to you. (*Sits down.*)

Tom (*gently*): What is it, Mother, that you want to discuss?

Amanda: *Laura!*

(*Tom puts his cup down slowly.*)
(*Legend on screen: "Laura."*)
(*Music: "The Glass Menagerie."*)

Tom: — Oh. — Laura . . .

Amanda (*touching his sleeve*): You know how Laura is. So quiet but — still water runs deep! She notices things and I think she — broods about them. (*Tom looks up.*) A few days ago I came in and she was crying.

Tom: What about?

Amanda: You.

Tom: Me?

Amanda: She has an idea that you're not happy here.

Tom: What gave her that idea?

Amanda: What gives her any idea? However, you do act strangely. I — I'm not criticizing, understand *that!* I know your ambitions do not lie in the warehouse, that like everybody in the whole wide world — you've had to — make sacrifices, but — Tom — Tom — life's not easy, it calls for — Spartan endurance! There's so many things in my heart that I cannot describe to you! I've never told you but I — *loved your father.* . . .

Tom (*gently*): I know that, Mother.

Amanda: And you — when I see you taking after his ways! Staying out late — and — well, you *had* been drinking the night you were in that — terrifying condition! Laura says that you hate the apartment and that you go out nights to get away from it! Is that true, Tom?

Tom: No. You say there's so much in your heart that you can't describe to me. That's true of me, too. There's so much in my heart that I can't describe to *you!* So let's respect each other's —

Amanda: But, why — *why*, Tom — are you always so *restless?* Where do you go to, nights?

Tom: I — go to the movies.

Amanda: Why do you go to the movies so much, Tom?

Tom: I go to the movies because — I like adventure. Adventure is something I don't have much of at work, so I go to the movies.

Amanda: But, Tom, you go to the movies *entirely* too *much!*

Tom: I like a lot of adventure.

(*Amanda looks baffled, then hurt. As the familiar inquisition resumes he becomes hard and impatient again. Amanda slips back into her querulous attitude toward him.*)
(*Image on screen: sailing vessel with Jolly Roger.°*)

Amanda: Most young men find adventure in their careers.

Tom: Then most young men are not employed in a warehouse.

Amanda: The world is full of young men employed in warehouses and offices and factories.

Tom: Do all of them find adventure in their careers?

Amanda: They do or they do without it! Not everybody has a craze for adventure.

Tom: Man is by instinct a lover, a hunter, a fighter, and none of those instincts are given much play at the warehouse!

Amanda: Man is by instinct! Don't quote instinct to me! Instinct is something that people have got away from! It belongs to animals! Christian adults don't want it!

Tom: What do Christian adults want, then, Mother?

Amanda: Superior things! Things of the mind and the spirit! Only animals have to satisfy instincts! Surely your aims are somewhat higher than theirs! Than monkeys — pigs —

Tom: I reckon they're not.

Amanda: You're joking. However, that isn't what I wanted to discuss.

Tom (*rising*): I haven't much time.

Amanda (*pushing his shoulders*): Sit down.

Tom: You want me to punch in red at the warehouse, Mother?

Amanda: You have five minutes. I want to talk about Laura.

(*Legend: "Plans and Provisions."*)

Tom: All right! What about Laura?

Amanda: We have to be making plans and provisions for her. She's older than you, two years, and nothing has happened. She just drifts along doing nothing. It frightens me terribly how she just drifts along.

Tom: I guess she's the type that people call home girls.

Amanda: There's no such type, and if there is, it's a pity! That is unless the home is hers, with a husband!

Jolly Roger: The black flag with white skull and crossbones used by pirates.

Tom: What?

Amanda: Oh, I can see the handwriting on the wall as plain as I see the nose in front of my face! It's terrifying! More and more you remind me of your father! He was out all hours without explanation — Then *left! Good-bye!* And me with a bag to hold. I saw that letter you got from the Merchant Marine. I know what you're dreaming of. I'm not standing here blindfolded. Very well, then. Then *do* it! But not till there's somebody to take your place.

Tom: What do you mean?

Amanda: I mean that as soon as Laura has got somebody to take care of her, married, a home of her own, independent — why, then you'll be free to go wherever you please, on land, on sea, whichever way the wind blows you! But until that time you've got to look out for your sister. I don't say me because I'm old and don't matter! I say for your sister because she's young and dependent. I put her in business college — a dismal failure! Frightened her so it made her sick to her stomach. I took her over to the Young People's League at the church. Another fiasco. She spoke to nobody, nobody spoke to her. Now all she does is fool with those pieces of glass and play those worn-out records. What kind of a life is that for a girl to lead!

Tom: What can I do about it?

Amanda: Overcome selfishness! Self, self, self is all that you ever think of! (*Tom springs up and crosses to get his coat. It is ugly and bulky. He pulls on a cap with earmuffs.*) Where is your muffler? Put your wool muffler on! (*He snatches it angrily from the closet and tosses it around his neck and pulls both ends tight.*) Tom! I haven't said what I had in mind to ask you.

Tom: I'm too late to —

Amanda (*catching his arms — very importunately. Then shyly*): Down at the warehouse, aren't there some — nice young men?

Tom: No!

Amanda: There *must* be — *some* . . .

Tom: Mother —

(*Gesture.*)

Amanda: Find out one that's clean-living — doesn't drink and — ask him out for sister!

Tom: What?

Amanda: For *sister!* To *meet!* Get *acquainted!*

Tom (*stamping to door*): Oh, my *go-osh!*

Amanda: Will you? (*He opens door. Imploringly.*) Will you? (*He starts down.*) Will you? *Will* you, dear?

Tom (*calling back*): YES!

(*Amanda closes the door hesitantly and with a troubled but faintly hopeful expression.*)
    (*Screen image: glamor magazine cover.*)
    (*Spot° Amanda at phone.*)

Amanda: Ella Cartwright? This is Amanda Wingfield! How are you, honey? How is that kidney condition?

Spot: Spotlight.

(*Count five.*) Horrors! (*Count five.*) You're a Christian martyr, yes, honey, that's what you are, a Christian martyr! Well, I just happened to notice in my little red book that your subscription to the *Companion* has just run out! I knew that you wouldn't want to miss out on the wonderful serial starting in this new issue. It's by Bessie Mae Hopper, the first thing she's written since *Honeymoon for Three.* Wasn't that a strange and interesting story? Well, this one is even lovelier, I believe. It has a sophisticated society background. It's all about the horsey set on Long Island!

(*Fade out.*)

SCENE 5

(*Legend on screen "Annunciation." Fade with music.*)
    (*It is early dusk of a spring evening. Supper has just been finished in the Wingfield apartment. Amanda and Laura in light colored dresses are removing dishes from the table, in the upstage area, which is shadowy, their movements formalized almost as a dance or ritual, their moving forms as pale and silent as moths.*)
    (*Tom, in white shirt and trousers, rises from the table and crosses toward the fire escape.*)

Amanda (*as he passes her*): Son, will you do me a favor?

Tom: What?

Amanda: Comb your hair! You look so pretty when your hair is combed! (*Tom slouches on sofa with evening paper. Enormous caption "Franco Triumphs."*) There is only one respect in which I would like you to emulate your father.

Tom: What respect is that?

Amanda: The care he always took of his appearance. He never allowed himself to look untidy. (*He throws down the paper and crosses to fire escape.*) Where are you going?

Tom: I'm going out to smoke.

Amanda: You smoke too much. A pack a day at fifteen cents a pack. How much would that amount to in a month? Thirty times fifteen is how much, Tom? Figure it out and you will be astounded at what you could save. Enough to give you a night school course in accounting at Washington U! Just think what a wonderful thing that would be for you, son!

(*Tom is unmoved by the thought.*)

Tom: I'd rather smoke. (*He steps out on landing, letting the screen door slam.*)

Amanda (*sharply*): I know! That's the tragedy of it. . . . (*Alone, she turns to look at her husband's picture.*)

(*Dance music: "All the World is Waiting for the Sunrise!"*)

Tom (*to the audience*): Across the alley from us was the Paradise Dance Hall. On evenings in spring the windows and doors were open and the music came outdoors. Sometimes the lights were turned out except for a large glass sphere that hung from the ceiling. It would turn slowly about and filter the dusk with delicate rainbow colors. Then the orchestra played a waltz or a tango, something that had a slow and sensuous rhythm. Couples would come outside, to the relative privacy of the alley. You could see them kissing behind ash-pits and telephone poles. This was the compensation for lives that passed like mine, without any change or adventure. Adventure and change were imminent in this year. They were waiting around the corner for all these kids. Suspended in the mist over Berchtesgaden, caught in the folds of Chamberlain's umbrella — In Spain there was Guernica!° But here there was only hot swing music and liquor, dance halls, bars, and movies, and sex that hung in the gloom like a chandelier and flooded the world with brief, deceptive rainbows. . . . All the world was waiting for bombardments!

(*Amanda turns from the picture and comes outside.*)

AMANDA (*sighing*): A fire escape landing's a poor excuse for a porch. (*She spreads a newspaper on a step and sits down, gracefully and demurely as if she were settling into a swing on a Mississippi veranda.*) What are you looking at?

TOM: The moon.

AMANDA: Is there a moon this evening?

TOM: It's rising over Garfinkel's Delicatessen.

AMANDA: So it is! A little silver slipper of a moon. Have you made a wish on it yet?

TOM: Um-hum.

AMANDA: What did you wish for?

TOM: That's a secret.

AMANDA: A secret, huh? Well, I won't tell mine either. I will be just as mysterious as you.

TOM: I bet I can guess what yours is.

AMANDA: Is my head so transparent?

TOM: You're not a sphinx.

AMANDA: No, I don't have secrets. I'll tell you what I wished for on the moon. Success and happiness for my precious children! I wish for that whenever there's a moon, and when there isn't a moon, I wish for it, too.

TOM: I thought perhaps you wished for a gentleman caller.

AMANDA: Why do you say that?

TOM: Don't you remember asking me to fetch one?

AMANDA: I remember suggesting that it would be nice for your sister if you brought home some nice young man from the warehouse. I think I've made that suggestion more than once.

Berchtesgaden . . . Chamberlain . . . Guernica: All references to the approaches of World War II in Europe. Berchtesgaden was Hitler's summer home; Neville Chamberlain was the prime minister of England who signed the Munich Pact, which was regarded as a capitulation to Hitler; and the Spanish town Guernica was destroyed by German bombs during the Spanish Civil War in the late 1930s.

TOM: Yes, you have made it repeatedly.

AMANDA: Well?

TOM: We are going to have one.

AMANDA: *What?*

TOM: A gentleman caller!

(*The annunciation is celebrated with music.*)
    (*Amanda rises.*)
    (*Image on screen: caller with bouquet.*)

AMANDA: You mean you have asked some nice young man to come over?

TOM: Yep. I've asked him to dinner.

AMANDA: You really did?

TOM: I did!

AMANDA: You did, and did he — *accept?*

TOM: He did!

AMANDA: Well, well — well, well! That's — lovely!

TOM: I thought that you would be pleased.

AMANDA: It's definite, then?

TOM: Very definite.

AMANDA: Soon?

TOM: Very soon.

AMANDA: For heaven's sake, stop putting on and tell me some things, will you?

TOM: What things do you want me to tell you?

AMANDA: *Naturally* I would like to know when he's *coming!*

TOM: He's coming tomorrow.

AMANDA: *Tomorrow?*

TOM: Yep. Tomorrow.

AMANDA: But, Tom!

TOM: Yes, Mother?

AMANDA: Tomorrow gives me no time!

TOM: Time for what?

AMANDA: Preparations! Why didn't you phone me at once, as soon as you asked him, the minute that he accepted? Then, don't you see, I could have been getting ready!

TOM: You don't have to make any fuss.

AMANDA: Oh, Tom, Tom, Tom, of course I have to make a fuss! I want things nice, not sloppy! Not thrown together. I'll certainly have to do some fast thinking, won't I?

TOM: I don't see why you have to think at all.

AMANDA: You just don't know. We can't have a gentleman caller in a pigsty! All my wedding silver has to be polished, the monogrammed table linen ought to be laundered! The windows have to be washed and fresh curtains put up. And how about clothes? We have to *wear* something, don't we?

TOM: Mother, this boy is no one to make a fuss over!

AMANDA: Do you realize he's the first young man we've introduced to your sister? It's terrible, dreadful, disgraceful that poor little sister has never received a single gentleman caller! Tom, come inside! (*She opens the screen door.*)

TOM: What for?

AMANDA: I want to ask you some things.

TOM: If you're going to make such a fuss, I'll call it off, I'll tell him not to come.

AMANDA: You certainly won't do anything of the kind. Nothing offends people worse than broken engagements. It simply means I'll have to work like a Turk! We won't be brilliant, but we'll pass inspection. Come on inside. (*Tom follows, groaning.*) Sit down.

TOM: Any particular place you would like me to sit?

AMANDA: Thank heavens I've got that new sofa! I'm also making payments on a floor lamp I'll have sent out! And put the chintz covers on, they'll brighten things up! Of course I'd hoped to have these walls repapered. . . . What is the young man's name?

TOM: His name is O'Connor.

AMANDA: That, of course, means fish — tomorrow is Friday!° I'll have that salmon loaf — with Durkee's dressing! What does he do? He works at the warehouse?

TOM: Of course! How else would I —

AMANDA: Tom, he — doesn't drink?

TOM: Why do you ask me that?

AMANDA: Your father *did*!

TOM: Don't get started on that!

AMANDA: He *does* drink, then?

TOM: Not that I know of!

AMANDA: Make sure, be certain! The last thing I want for my daughter's a boy who drinks!

TOM: Aren't you being a little premature? Mr. O'Connor has not yet appeared on the scene!

AMANDA: But will tomorrow. To meet your sister, and what do I know about his character? Nothing! Old maids are better off than wives of drunkards!

TOM: Oh, my God!

AMANDA: Be still!

TOM (*leaning forward to whisper*): Lots of fellows meet girls whom they don't marry!

AMANDA: Oh, talk sensibly, Tom — and don't be sarcastic! (*She has gotten a hairbrush.*)

TOM: What are you doing?

AMANDA: I'm brushing that cowlick down! What is this young man's position at the warehouse?

TOM (*submitting grimly to the brush and the interrogation*): This young man's position is that of a shipping clerk, Mother.

AMANDA: Sounds to me like a fairly responsible job, the sort of a job *you* would be in if you just had more *get-up*. What is his salary? Have you got any idea.

TOM: I would judge it to be approximately eighty-five dollars a month.

AMANDA: Well — not princely, but —

TOM: Twenty more than I make.

AMANDA: Yes, how well I know! But for a family man, eighty-five dollars a month is not much more than you can just get by on. . . .

TOM: Yes, but Mr. O'Connor is not a family man.

---

fish . . . Friday: Until the 1960s Catholics were prohibited from eating meat on Fridays.

AMANDA: He might be, mightn't he? Some time in the future?

TOM: I see. Plans and provisions.

AMANDA: You are the only young man that I know of who ignores the fact that the future becomes the present, the present the past, and the past turns into everlasting regret if you don't plan for it!

TOM: I will think that over and see what I can make of it.

AMANDA: Don't be supercilious with your mother! Tell me some more about this — what do you call him?

TOM: James D. O'Connor. The D. is for Delaney.

AMANDA: Irish on *both* sides! *Gracious!* And doesn't drink?

TOM: Shall I call him up and ask him right this minute?

AMANDA: The only way to find out about those things is to make discreet inquiries at the proper moment. When I was a girl in Blue Mountain and it was suspected that a young man drank, the girl whose attentions he had been receiving, if any girl *was*, would sometimes speak to the minister of his church, or rather her father would if her father was living, and sort of feel him out on the young man's character. That is the way such things are discreetly handled to keep a young woman from making a tragic mistake!

TOM: Then how did you happen to make a tragic mistake?

AMANDA: That innocent look of your father's had everyone fooled! He *smiled* — the world was *enchanted*! No girl can do worse than put herself at the mercy of a handsome appearance! I hope that Mr. O'Connor is not too good-looking.

TOM: No, he's not too good-looking. He's covered with freckles and hasn't too much of a nose.

AMANDA: He's not right-down homely, though?

TOM: Not right-down homely. Just medium homely, I'd say.

AMANDA: Character's what to look for in a man.

TOM: That's what I've always said, Mother.

AMANDA: You've never said anything of the kind and I suspect you would never give it a thought.

TOM: Don't be suspicious of me.

AMANDA: At least I hope he's the type that's up and coming.

TOM: I think he really goes in for self-improvement.

AMANDA: What reason have you to think so?

TOM: He goes to night school.

AMANDA (*beaming*): Splendid! What does he do, I mean study?

TOM: Radio engineering and public speaking!

AMANDA: Then he has visions of being advanced in the world! Any young man who studies public speaking is aiming to have an executive job some day! And radio engineering? A thing for the future! Both of these facts are very illuminating. Those are the sort of things that a mother should know concerning any young man who comes to call on her daughter. Seriously or — not.

TOM: One little warning. He doesn't know about Laura.

I didn't let on that we had dark ulterior motives. I just said, why don't you come have dinner with us? He said okay and that was the whole conversation.

AMANDA: I bet it was! You're eloquent as an oyster. However, he'll know about Laura when he gets here. When he sees how lovely and sweet and pretty she is, he'll thank his lucky stars he was asked to dinner.

TOM: Mother, you mustn't expect too much of Laura.

AMANDA: What do you mean?

TOM: Laura seems all those things to you and me because she's ours and we love her. We don't even notice she's crippled anymore.

AMANDA: Don't say crippled! You know that I never allow that word to be used!

TOM: But face facts, Mother. She is and — that's not all —

AMANDA: What do you mean not all?

TOM: Laura is very different from other girls.

AMANDA: I think the difference is all to her advantage.

TOM: Not quite all — in the eyes of others — strangers — she's terribly shy and lives in a world of her own and those things make her seem a little peculiar to people outside the house.

AMANDA: Don't say peculiar.

TOM: Face the facts. She is.

(*The dance-hall music changes to a tango that has a minor and somewhat ominous tone.*)

AMANDA: In what way is she peculiar — may I ask?

TOM (*gently*): She lives in a world of her own — a world of — little glass ornaments, Mother. . . . (*Gets up. Amanda remains holding brush, looking at him, troubled.*) She plays old phonograph records and — that's about all — (*He glances at himself in the mirror and crosses to door.*)

AMANDA (*sharply*): Where are you going?

TOM: I'm going to the movies. (*Out screen door.*)

AMANDA: Not to the movies, every night to the movies! (*Follows quickly to screen door.*) I don't believe you always go to the movies! (*He is gone. Amanda looks worriedly after him for a moment. Then vitality and optimism return and she turns from the door. Crossing to portieres.*) Laura! Laura! (*Laura answers from kitchenette.*)

LAURA: Yes, Mother.

AMANDA: Let those dishes go and come in front! (*Laura appears with dish towel. Gaily.*) Laura, come here and make a wish on the moon!

LAURA (*entering*): Moon — moon?

AMANDA: A little silver slipper of a moon. Look over your left shoulder, Laura, and make a wish! (*Laura looks faintly puzzled as if called out of sleep. Amanda seizes her shoulders and turns her at an angle by the door.*) Now! Now, darling, *wish!*

LAURA: What shall I wish for, Mother?

AMANDA (*her voice trembling and her eyes suddenly filling with tears*): Happiness! Good Fortune!

(*The violin rises and the stage dims out.*)

SCENE 6

(*Image: high school hero.*)

TOM: And so the following evening I brought Jim home to dinner. I had known Jim slightly in high school. In high school Jim was a hero. He had tremendous Irish good nature and vitality with the scrubbed and polished look of white chinaware. He seemed to move in a continual spotlight. He was a star in basketball, captain of the debating club, president of the senior class and the glee club and he sang the male lead in the annual light operas. He was always running or bounding, never just walking. He seemed always at the point of defeating the law of gravity. He was shooting with such velocity through his adolescence that you would logically expect him to arrive at nothing short of the White House by the time he was thirty. But Jim apparently ran into more interference after his graduation from Soldan. His speed had definitely slowed. Six years after he left high school he was holding a job that wasn't much better than mine.

(*Image: clerk.*)

He was the only one at the warehouse with whom I was on friendly terms. I was valuable to him as someone who could remember his former glory, who had seen him win basketball games and the silver cup in debating. He knew of my secret practice of retiring to a cabinet of the washroom to work on poems when business was slack in the warehouse. He called me Shakespeare. And while the other boys in the warehouse regarded me with suspicious hostility, Jim took a humorous attitude toward me. Gradually his attitude affected the others, their hostility wore off and they also began to smile at me as people smile at an oddly fashioned dog who trots across their path at some distance.

I knew that Jim and Laura had known each other at Soldan, and I had heard Laura speak admiringly of his voice. I didn't know if Jim remembered her or not. In high school Laura had been as unobtrusive as Jim had been astonishing. If he did remember Laura, it was not as my sister, for when I asked him to dinner, he grinned and said, "You know, Shakespeare, I never thought of you as having folks!"

He was about to discover that I did. . . .

(*Light up stage.*)

(*Legend on screen: "The Accent of a Coming Foot."*)

(*Friday evening. It is about five o'clock of a late spring evening which comes "scattering poems in the sky."*)

(*A delicate lemony light is in the Wingfield apartment.*)

(*Amanda has worked like a Turk in preparation for the gentleman caller. The results are astonishing. The new floor lamp with its rose-silk shade is in place, a colored paper lantern conceals the broken light fixture in the ceiling, new billowing white curtains are at the windows, chintz covers are on chairs and sofa, a pair of new sofa pillows make their initial appearance.*)

(*Open boxes and tissue paper are scattered on the floor.*)

(*Laura stands in the middle with lifted arms while Amanda crouches before her, adjusting the hem of the new dress, devout and ritualistic. The dress is colored and designed by memory. The arrangement of Laura's hair is changed; it is softer and more becoming. A fragile, unearthly prettiness has come out in Laura: she is like a piece of translucent glass touched by light, given a momentary radiance, not actual, not lasting.*)

AMANDA (*impatiently*): Why are you trembling?
LAURA: Mother, you've made me so nervous!
AMANDA: How have I made you nervous?
LAURA: By all this fuss! You make it seem so important!
AMANDA: I don't understand you, Laura. You couldn't be satisfied with just sitting home, and yet whenever I try to arrange something for you, you seem to resist it. (*She gets up.*) Now take a look at yourself. No, wait! Wait just a moment — I have an idea!
LAURA: What is it now?

(*Amanda produces two powder puffs which she wraps in handkerchiefs and stuffs in Laura's bosom.*)

LAURA: Mother, what are you doing?
AMANDA: They call them "Gay Deceivers"!
LAURA: I won't wear them!
AMANDA: You will!
LAURA: Why should I?
AMANDA: Because, to be painfully honest, your chest is flat.
LAURA: You make it seem like we were setting a trap.
AMANDA: All pretty girls are a trap, a pretty trap, and men expect them to be. (*Legend: "A Pretty Trap."*) Now look at yourself, young lady. This is the prettiest you will ever be! I've got to fix myself now! You're going to be surprised by your mother's appearance! (*She crosses through portieres, humming gaily.*)

(*Laura moves slowly to the long mirror and stares solemnly at herself.*)

(*A wind blows the white curtains inward in a slow, graceful motion and with a faint, sorrowful sighing.*)

AMANDA (*offstage*): It isn't dark enough yet. (*She turns slowly before the mirror with a troubled look.*)

(*Legend on screen: "This Is My Sister: Celebrate Her with Strings!" Music.*)

AMANDA (*laughing, off*): I'm going to show you something. I'm going to make a spectacular appearance!
LAURA: What is it, Mother?
AMANDA: Possess your soul in patience — you will see! Something I've resurrected from that old trunk! Styles haven't changed so terribly much after all. . . . (*She parts the portieres.*) Now just look at your mother! (*She wears a girlish frock of yellowed voile with a blue silk sash. She carries a bunch of jonquils — the legend of her youth is nearly revived.*

Feverishly.) This is the dress in which I led the cotillion. Won the cakewalk twice at Sunset Hill, wore one spring to the Governor's ball in Jackson! See how I sashayed around the ballroom, Laura? (*She raises her skirt and does a mincing step around the room.*) I wore it on Sundays for my gentlemen callers! I had it on the day I met your father — I had malaria fever all that spring. The change of climate from East Tennessee to the Delta — weakened resistance — I had a little temperature all the time — not enough to be serious — just enough to make me restless and giddy! Invitations poured in — parties all over the Delta! — "Stay in bed," said Mother, "you have fever!"— but I just wouldn't. — I took quinine but kept on going, going! — Evenings, dances! — Afternoons, long, long rides! Picnics — lovely! — So lovely, that country in May. — All lacy with dogwood, literally flooded with jonquils! — That was the spring I had the craze for jonquils. Jonquils became an absolute obsession. Mother said, "Honey, there's no more room for jonquils." And still I kept on bringing in more jonquils. Whenever, wherever I saw them, I'd say, "Stop! Stop! I see jonquils!" I made the young men help me gather the jonquils! It was a joke, Amanda and her jonquils! Finally there were no more vases to hold them, every available space was filled with jonquils. No vases to hold them? All right, I'll hold them myself! And then I — (*She stops in front of the picture. Music.*) met your father! Malaria fever and jonquils and then — this — boy. . . . (*She switches on the rose-colored lamp.*) I hope they get here before it starts to rain. (*She crosses upstage and places the jonquils in bowl on table.*) I gave your brother a little extra change so he and Mr. O'Connor could take the service car home.
LAURA (*with altered look*): What did you say his name was?
AMANDA: O'Connor.
LAURA: What is his first name?
AMANDA: I don't remember. Oh, yes, I do. It was — Jim!

(*Laura sways slightly and catches hold of a chair.*)
(*Legend on screen: "Not Jim!"*)

LAURA (*faintly*): Not — Jim!
AMANDA: Yes, that was it, it was Jim! I've never known a Jim that wasn't nice!

(*Music: ominous.*)

LAURA: Are you sure his name is Jim O'Connor?
AMANDA: Yes. Why?
LAURA: Is he the one that Tom used to know in high school?
AMANDA: He didn't say so. I think he just got to know him at the warehouse.
LAURA: There was a Jim O'Connor we both knew in high school — (*Then, with effort.*) If that is the one that Tom is bringing to dinner — you'll have to excuse me, I won't come to the table.

AMANDA: What sort of nonsense is this?

LAURA: You asked me once if I'd ever liked a boy. Don't you remember I showed you this boy's picture?

AMANDA: You mean the boy you showed me in the yearbook?

LAURA: Yes, that boy.

AMANDA: Laura, Laura, were you in love with that boy?

LAURA: I don't know, Mother. All I know is I couldn't sit at the table if it was him!

AMANDA: It won't be him! It isn't the least bit likely. But whether it is or not, you will come to the table. You will not be excused.

LAURA: I'll have to be, Mother.

AMANDA: I don't intend to humor your silliness, Laura. I've had too much from you and your brother, both! So just sit down and compose yourself till they come. Tom has forgotten his key so you'll have to let them in, when they arrive.

LAURA (*panicky*): Oh, Mother — *you* answer the door!

AMANDA (*lightly*): I'll be in the kitchen — busy!

LAURA: Oh, Mother, please answer the door, don't make me do it!

AMANDA (*crossing into kitchenette*): I've got to fix the dressing for the salmon. Fuss, fuss — silliness! — over a gentleman caller!

(*Door swings shut. Laura is left alone.*)

(*Legend: "Terror!"*)

(*She utters a low moan and turns off the lamp — sits stiffly on the edge of the sofa, knotting her fingers together.*)

(*Legend on screen: "The Opening of a Door!"*)

(*Tom and Jim appear on the fire escape steps and climb to landing. Hearing their approach, Laura rises with a panicky gesture. She retreats to the portieres.*)

(*The doorbell. Laura catches her breath and touches her throat. Low drums.*)

AMANDA (*calling*): Laura, sweetheart! The door!

(*Laura stares at it without moving.*)

JIM: I think we just beat the rain.

TOM: Uh-huh. (*He rings again, nervously. Jim whistles and fishes for a cigarette.*)

AMANDA (*very, very gaily*): Laura, that is your brother and Mr. O'Connor! Will you let them in, darling?

(*Laura crosses toward kitchenette door.*)

LAURA (*breathlessly*): Mother — you go to the door!

(*Amanda steps out of kitchenette and stares furiously at Laura. She points imperiously at the door.*)

FAR LEFT: Amanda (Ruby Dee) and
Laura (Tonia Rowe) in the 1989 Arena
Stage production of *The Glass
Menagerie,* directed by Tazewell
Thompson. LEFT: Laura, Amanda, and
Tom (Jonathan Earl Peck). RIGHT:
Scene from *The Glass Menagerie.*

LAURA: Please, please!

AMANDA (*in a fierce whisper*): What is the matter with
  you, you silly thing?

LAURA (*desperately*): Please, you answer it, *please!*

AMANDA: I told you I wasn't going to humor you,
  Laura. Why have you chosen this moment to lose
  your mind?

LAURA: Please, please, please, you go!

AMANDA: You'll have to go to the door because I can't!

LAURA (*despairingly*): I can't either!

AMANDA: *Why?*

LAURA: I'm *sick!*

AMANDA: I'm sick, too — of your nonsense! Why can't
  you and your brother be normal people? Fantastic
  whims and behavior! (*Tom gives a long ring.*) Preposterous goings on! Can you give me one reason —
  (*Calls out lyrically.*) COMING! JUST ONE SECOND! —

why should you be afraid to open a door? Now you
  answer it, Laura!

LAURA: Oh, oh, oh . . . (*She returns through the portieres.
  Darts to the victrola and winds it frantically and turns
  it on.*)

AMANDA: Laura Wingfield, you march right to that door!

LAURA: Yes — yes, Mother!

(*A faraway, scratchy rendition of "Dardanella" softens
the air and gives her strength to move through it. She
slips to the door and draws it cautiously open.*)
(*Tom enters with the caller, Jim O'Connor.*)

TOM: Laura, this is Jim. Jim, this is my sister, Laura.

JIM (*stepping inside*): I didn't know that Shakespeare
  had a sister!

LAURA (*retreating stiff and trembling from the door*):
  How — how do you do?

JIM (*heartily extending his hand*): Okay!

(*Laura touches it hesitantly with hers.*)

JIM: Your hand's *cold*, Laura!

LAURA: Yes, well — I've been playing the victrola. . . .

JIM: Must have been playing classical music on it! You ought to play a little hot swing music to warm you up!

LAURA: Excuse me — I haven't finished playing the victrola. . . .

(*She turns awkwardly and hurries into the front room. She pauses a second by the victrola. Then catches her breath and darts through the portieres like a frightened deer.*)

JIM (*grinning*): What was the matter?

TOM: Oh — with Laura? Laura is — terribly shy.

JIM: Shy, huh? It's unusual to meet a shy girl nowadays. I don't believe you ever mentioned you had a sister.

TOM: Well, now you know. I have one. Here is the *Post Dispatch*. You want a piece of it?

JIM: Uh-huh.

TOM: What piece? The comics?

JIM: Sports! (*Glances at it.*) Ole Dizzy Dean is on his bad behavior.

TOM (*disinterest*): Yeah? (*Lights cigarette and crosses back to fire escape door.*)

JIM: Where are *you* going?

TOM: I'm going out on the terrace.

JIM (*goes after him*): You know, Shakespeare — I'm going to sell you a bill of goods!

TOM: What goods?

JIM: A course I'm taking.

TOM: Huh?

JIM: In public speaking! You and me, we're not the warehouse type.

TOM: Thanks — that's good news. But what has public speaking got to do with it?

JIM: It fits you for — executive positions!

TOM: Awww.

JIM: I tell you it's done a helluva lot for me.

(*Image: executive at desk.*)

TOM: In what respect?

JIM: In every! Ask yourself what is the difference between you an' me and men in the office down front? Brains? — No! — Ability? — No! Then what? Just one little thing —

TOM: What is that one little thing?

JIM: Primarily it amounts to — social poise! Being able to square up to people and hold your own on any social level!

AMANDA (*offstage*): Tom?

TOM: Yes, Mother?

AMANDA: Is that you and Mr. O'Connor?

TOM: Yes, Mother.

AMANDA: Well, you just make yourselves comfortable in there.

TOM: Yes, Mother.

AMANDA: Ask Mr. O'Connor if he would like to wash his hands.

JIM: Aw, — no — no — thank you — I took care of that at the warehouse. Tom —

TOM: Yes?

JIM: Mr. Mendoza was speaking to me about you.

TOM: Favorably?

JIM: What do you think?

TOM: Well —

JIM: You're going to be out of a job if you don't wake up.

TOM: I am waking up —

JIM: You show no signs.

TOM: The signs are interior.

(*Image on screen: the sailing vessel with Jolly Roger again.*)

TOM: I'm planning to change. (*He leans over the rail speaking with quiet exhilaration. The incandescent marquees and signs of the first-run movie houses light his face from across the alley. He looks like a voyager.*) I'm right at the point of committing myself to a future that doesn't include the warehouse and Mr. Mendoza or even a night school course in public speaking.

JIM: What are you gassing about?

TOM: I'm tired of the movies.

JIM: Movies!

TOM: Yes, movies! Look at them — (*A wave toward the marvels of Grand Avenue.*) All of those glamorous people — having adventures — hogging it all, gobbling the whole thing up! You know what happens? People go to the *movies* instead of *moving*! Hollywood characters are supposed to have all the adventures for everybody in America, while everybody in America sits in a dark room and watches them have them! Yes, until there's a war. That's when adventure becomes available to the masses! *Everyone's* dish, not only Gable's! Then the people in the dark room come out of the dark room to have some adventures themselves — Goody, goody! — It's our turn now, to go to the South Sea Island — to make a safari — to be exotic, far-off! — But I'm not patient. I don't want to wait till then. I'm tired of the *movies* and I am *about* to *move*!

JIM (*incredulously*): Move?

TOM: Yes.

JIM: When?

TOM: Soon!

JIM: Where? Where?

(*Theme three music seems to answer the question, while Tom thinks it over. He searches among his pockets.*)

TOM: I'm starting to boil inside. I know I seem dreamy, but inside — well, I'm boiling! Whenever I pick up a shoe, I shudder a little thinking how short life is and what I am doing! — Whatever that means. I know it doesn't mean shoes — except as something to wear on a traveler's feet! (*Finds paper.*) Look —

JIM: What?

TOM: I'm a member.

JIM (*reading*): The Union of Merchant Seamen.

TOM: I paid my dues this month, instead of the light bill.

JIM: You will regret it when they turn the lights off.

TOM: I won't be here.

JIM: How about your mother?

TOM: I'm like my father. The bastard son of a bastard! See how he grins? And he's been absent going on sixteen years!

JIM: You're just talking, you drip. How does your mother feel about it?

TOM: Shhh! — Here comes Mother! Mother is not acquainted with my plans!

AMANDA (*enters portieres*): Where are you all?

TOM: On the terrace, Mother.

(*They start inside. She advances to them. Tom is distinctly shocked at her appearance. Even Jim blinks a little. He is making his first contact with girlish Southern vivacity and in spite of the night school course in public speaking is somewhat thrown off the beam by the unexpected outlay of social charm.*)

(*Certain responses are attempted by Jim but are swept aside by Amanda's gay laughter and chatter. Tom is embarrassed but after the first shock Jim reacts very warmly. Grins and chuckles, is altogether won over.*)

(*Image: Amanda as a girl.*)

AMANDA (*coyly smiling, shaking her girlish ringlets*): Well, well, well, so this is Mr. O'Connor. Introductions entirely unnecessary. I've heard so much about you from my boy. I finally said to him, Tom — good gracious! — why don't you bring this paragon to supper? I'd like to meet this nice young man at the warehouse! — Instead of just hearing him sing your praises so much! I don't know why my son is so standoffish — that's not Southern behavior! Let's sit down and — I think we could stand a little more air in here! Tom, leave the door open. I felt a nice fresh breeze a moment ago. Where has it gone to? Mmm, so warm already! And not quite summer, even. We're going to burn up when summer really gets started. However, we're having — we're having a very light supper. I think light things are better fo' this time of year. The same as light clothes are. Light clothes an' light food are what warm weather calls fo'. You know our blood gets so thick during th' winter — it takes a while fo' us to *adjust* ou'selves! — when the season changes . . . It's come so quick this year. I wasn't prepared. All of a sudden — heavens! Already summer! — I ran to the trunk an' pulled out this light dress — Terribly old! Historical almost! But feels so good — so good an' co-ol, y'know. . . .

TOM: Mother —

AMANDA: Yes, honey?

TOM: How about — supper?

AMANDA: Honey, you go ask Sister if supper is ready! You know that Sister is in full charge of supper! Tell her you hungry boys are waiting for it. (*To Jim.*) Have you met Laura?

JIM: She —

AMANDA: Let you in? Oh, good, you've met already! It's rare for a girl as sweet an' pretty as Laura to be domestic! But Laura is, thank heavens, not only pretty but also very domestic. I'm not at all. I never was a bit. I never could make a thing but angel food cake. Well, in the South we had so many servants. Gone, gone, gone. All vestiges of gracious living! Gone completely! I wasn't prepared for what the future brought me. All of my gentlemen callers were sons of planters and so of course I assumed that I would be married to one and raise my family on a large piece of land with plenty of servants. But man proposes — and woman accepts the proposal! — To vary that old, old saying a little bit — I married no planter! I married a man who worked for the telephone company! — That gallantly smiling gentleman over there! (*Points to the picture.*) A telephone man who — fell in love with long distance! — Now he travels and I don't even know where! — But what am I going on for about my — tribulations! Tell me yours — I hope you don't have any! Tom?

TOM (*returning*): Yes, Mother?

AMANDA: Is supper nearly ready?

TOM: It looks to me like supper is on the table.

AMANDA: Let me look — (*She rises prettily and looks through portieres.*) Oh, lovely! — But where is Sister?

TOM: Laura is not feeling well and she says that she thinks she'd better not come to the table.

AMANDA: What? — Nonsense! — Laura? Oh, Laura!

LAURA (*offstage, faintly*): Yes, Mother.

AMANDA: You really must come to the table. We won't be seated until you come to the table! Come in, Mr. O'Connor. You sit over there, and I'll — Laura? Laura Wingfield! You're keeping us waiting, honey! We can't say grace until you come to the table!

(*The back door is pushed weakly open and Laura comes in. She is obviously quite faint, her lips trembling, her eyes wide and staring. She moves unsteadily toward the table.*)

(*Legend: "Terror!"*)

(*Outside a summer storm is coming abruptly. The white curtains billow inward at the windows and there is a sorrowful murmur and deep blue dusk.*)

(*Laura suddenly stumbles — she catches at a chair with a faint moan.*)

TOM: Laura!

AMANDA: Laura! (*There is a clap of thunder.*) (*Legend: "Ah!"*) (*Despairingly.*) Why, Laura, you *are* sick, darling! Tom, help your sister into the living room, dear! Sit in the living room, Laura — rest on the sofa. Well! (*To the gentleman caller.*) Standing over the hot stove made her ill! — I told her that it was just too warm this evening, but — (*Tom comes back in. Laura is on the sofa.*) Is Laura all right now?

TOM: Yes.

AMANDA: What *is* that? Rain? A nice cool rain has come up! (*She gives the gentleman caller a frightened look.*) I think we may — have grace — now . . . (*Tom looks at her stupidly.*) Tom, honey — you say grace!
TOM: Oh . . . "For these and all thy mercies —" (*They bow their heads, Amanda stealing a nervous glance at Jim. In the living room Laura, stretched on the sofa, clenches her hand to her lips, to hold back a shuddering sob.*) God's Holy Name be praised —

(*The scene dims out.*)

SCENE 7

(*A Souvenir*)
(*Half an hour later. Dinner is just being finished in the upstage area which is concealed by the drawn portieres.*)
(*As the curtain rises Laura is still huddled upon the sofa, her feet drawn under her, her head resting on a pale blue pillow, her eyes wide and mysteriously watchful. The new floor lamp with its shade of rose-colored silk gives a soft, becoming light to her face, bringing out the fragile, unearthly prettiness which usually escapes attention. There is a steady murmur of rain, but it is slackening and stops soon after the scene begins; the air outside becomes pale and luminous as the moon breaks out.*)
(*A moment after the curtain rises, the lights in both rooms flicker and go out.*)

JIM: Hey, there, Mr. Light Bulb!

(*Amanda laughs nervously.*)
(*Legend: "Suspension of a Public Service."*)

AMANDA: Where was Moses when the lights went out? Ha-ha. Do you know the answer to that one, Mr. O'Connor?
JIM: No, Ma'am, what's the answer?
AMANDA: In the dark! (*Jim laughs appreciably.*) Everybody sit still. I'll light the candles. Isn't it lucky we have them on the table? Where's a match? Which of you gentlemen can provide a match?
JIM: Here.
AMANDA: Thank you, sir.
JIM: Not at all, Ma'am!
AMANDA: I guess the fuse has burnt out. Mr. O'Connor, can you tell a burnt-out fuse? I know I can't and Tom is a total loss when it comes to mechanics. (*Sound: getting up: voices recede a little to kitchenette.*) Oh, be careful you don't bump into something. We don't want our gentleman caller to break his neck. Now wouldn't that be a fine howdy-do?
JIM: Ha-ha! Where is the fuse box?
AMANDA: Right here next to the stove. Can you see anything?
JIM: Just a minute.
AMANDA: Isn't electricity a mysterious thing? Wasn't it Benjamin Franklin who tied a key to a kite? We live in such a mysterious universe, don't we? Some people say

that science clears up all the mysteries for us. In my opinion it only creates more! Have you found it yet?
JIM: No, Ma'am. All these fuses look okay to me.
AMANDA: Tom!
TOM: Yes, Mother?
AMANDA: That light bill I gave you several days ago. The one I told you we got the notices about?
TOM: Oh. — Yeah.

(*Legend: "Ha!"*)

AMANDA: You didn't neglect to pay it by any chance?
TOM: Why, I —
AMANDA: Didn't! I might have known it!
JIM: Shakespeare probably wrote a poem on that light bill, Mrs. Wingfield.
AMANDA: I might have known better than to trust him with it! There's such a high price for negligence in this world!
JIM: Maybe the poem will win a ten-dollar prize.
AMANDA: We'll just have to spend the remainder of the evening in the nineteenth century, before Mr. Edison made the Mazda lamp!
JIM: Candlelight is my favorite kind of light.
AMANDA: That shows you're romantic! But that's no excuse for Tom. Well, we got through dinner. Very considerate of them to let us get through dinner before they plunged us into everlasting darkness, wasn't it, Mr. O'Connor?
JIM: Ha-ha!
AMANDA: Tom, as a penalty for your carelessness you can help me with the dishes.
JIM: Let me give you a hand.
AMANDA: Indeed you will not!
JIM: I ought to be good for something.
AMANDA: Good for something? (*Her tone is rhapsodic.*) You? Why, Mr. O'Connor, nobody, *nobody's* given me this much entertainment in years — as you have!
JIM: Aw, now, Mrs. Wingfield!
AMANDA: I'm not exaggerating, not one bit! But Sister is all by her lonesome. You go keep her company in the parlor! I'll give you this lovely old candelabrum that used to be on the altar at the church of the Heavenly Rest. It was melted a little out of shape when the church burnt down. Lightning struck it one spring. Gypsy Jones was holding a revival at the time and he intimated that the church was destroyed because the Episcopalians gave card parties.
JIM: Ha-ha.
AMANDA: And how about coaxing Sister to drink a little wine? I think it would be good for her! Can you carry both at once?
JIM: Sure. I'm Superman!
AMANDA: Now, Thomas, get into this apron!

(*The door of kitchenette swings closed on Amanda's gay laughter; the flickering light approaches the portieres.*)
(*Laura sits up nervously as he enters. Her speech at first is low and breathless from the almost intolerable strain of being alone with a stranger.*)

(*The legend: "I Don't Suppose You Remember Me at All!"*)

(*In her first speeches in this scene, before Jim's warmth overcomes her paralyzing shyness, Laura's voice is thin and breathless as though she has just run up a steep flight of stairs.*)

(*Jim's attitude is gently humorous. In playing this scene it should be stressed that while the incident is apparently unimportant, it is to Laura the climax of her secret life.*)

JIM: Hello, there, Laura.

LAURA (*faintly*): Hello. (*She clears her throat.*)

JIM: How are you feeling now? Better?

LAURA: Yes. Yes, thank you.

JIM: This is for you. A little dandelion wine. (*He extends it toward her with extravagant gallantry.*)

LAURA: Thank you.

JIM: Drink it — but don't get drunk! (*He laughs heartily. Laura takes the glass uncertainly; laughs shyly.*) Where shall I set the candles?

LAURA: Oh — oh, anywhere . . .

JIM: How about here on the floor? Any objections?

LAURA: No.

JIM: I'll spread a newspaper under to catch the drippings. I like to sit on the floor. Mind if I do?

LAURA: Oh, no.

JIM: Give me a pillow?

LAURA: What?

JIM: A pillow!

LAURA: Oh . . . (*Hands him one quickly.*)

JIM: How about you? Don't you like to sit on the floor?

LAURA: Oh — yes.

JIM: Why don't you, then?

LAURA: I — will.

JIM: Take a pillow! (*Laura does. Sits on the other side of the candelabrum. Jim crosses his legs and smiles engagingly at her.*) I can't hardly see you sitting way over there.

LAURA: I can — see you.

JIM: I know, but that's not fair, I'm in the limelight. (*Laura moves her pillow closer.*) Good! Now I can see you! Comfortable?

LAURA: Yes.

JIM: So am I. Comfortable as a cow. Will you have some gum?

LAURA: No, thank you.

JIM: I think that I will indulge, with your permission. (*Musingly unwraps it and holds it up.*) Think of the fortune made by the guy that invented the first piece of chewing gum. Amazing, huh? The Wrigley Building is one of the sights of Chicago. — I saw it summer before last when I went up to the Century of Progress. Did you take in the Century of Progress?

LAURA: No, I didn't.

JIM: Well, it was quite a wonderful exposition. What impressed me most was the Hall of Science. Gives you an idea of what the future will be in America, even more wonderful than the present time is!

(*Pause. Smiling at her.*) Your brother tells me you're shy. Is that right, Laura?

LAURA: I — don't know.

JIM: I judge you to be an old-fashioned type of girl. Well, I think that's a pretty good type to be. Hope you don't think I'm being too personal — do you?

LAURA (*hastily, out of embarrassment*): I believe I *will* take a piece of gum, if you — don't mind. (*Clearing her throat.*) Mr. O'Connor, have you — kept up with your singing?

JIM: Singing? Me?

LAURA: Yes. I remember what a beautiful voice you had.

JIM: When did you hear me sing?

(*Voice offstage in the pause.*)

VOICE: (*offstage*): O blow, ye winds, heigh-ho,
   A-roving I will go!
      I'm off to my love
      With a boxing glove —
   Ten thousand miles away!

JIM: You say you've heard me sing?

LAURA: Oh, yes! Yes, very often . . . I — don't suppose you remember me — at all?

JIM (*smiling doubtfully*): You know I have an idea I've seen you before. I had that idea soon as you opened the door. It seemed almost like I was about to remember your name. But the name that I started to call you — wasn't a name! And so I stopped myself before I said it.

LAURA: Wasn't it — Blue Roses?

JIM (*Springs up. Grinning.*): Blue Roses! My gosh, yes — Blue Roses! That's what I had on my tongue when you opened the door! Isn't it funny what tricks your memory plays? I didn't connect you with the high school somehow or other. But that's where it was; it was high school. I didn't even know you were Shakespeare's sister! Gosh, I'm sorry.

LAURA: I didn't expect you to. You — barely knew me!

JIM: But we did have a speaking acquaintance, huh?

LAURA: Yes, we — spoke to each other.

JIM: When did you recognize me?

LAURA: Oh, right away!

JIM: Soon as I came in the door?

LAURA: When I heard your name I thought it was probably you. I knew that Tom used to know you a little in high school. So when you came in the door — Well, then I was — sure.

JIM: Why didn't you *say* something, then?

LAURA (*breathlessly*): I didn't know what to say, I was — too surprised!

JIM: For goodness' sakes! You know, this sure is funny!

LAURA: Yes! Yes, isn't it, though . . .

JIM: Didn't we have a class in something together?

LAURA: Yes, we did.

JIM: What class was that?

LAURA: It was — singing — Chorus!

JIM: Aw!

LAURA: I sat across the aisle from you in the Aud.

JIM: Aw.

LAURA: Mondays, Wednesdays, and Fridays.

JIM: Now I remember — you always came in late.

LAURA: Yes, it was so hard for me, getting upstairs. I had that brace on my leg — it clumped so loud!

JIM: I never heard any clumping.

LAURA (*wincing at the recollection*): To me it sounded like — thunder!

JIM: Well, well, well, I never even noticed.

LAURA: And everybody was seated before I came in. I had to walk in front of all those people. My seat was in the back row. I had to go clumping all the way up the aisle with everyone watching!

JIM: You shouldn't have been self-conscious.

LAURA: I know, but I was. It was always such a relief when the singing started.

JIM: Aw, yes, I've placed you now! I used to call you Blue Roses. How was it that I got started calling you that?

LAURA: I was out of school a little while with pleurosis. When I came back you asked me what was the matter. I said I had pleurosis — you thought I said Blue Roses. That's what you always called me after that!

JIM: I hope you didn't mind.

LAURA: Oh, no — I liked it. You see, I wasn't acquainted with many — people. . . .

JIM: As I remember you sort of stuck by yourself.

LAURA: I — I — never had much luck at — making friends.

JIM: I don't see why you wouldn't.

LAURA: Well, I — started out badly.

JIM: You mean being —

LAURA: Yes, it sort of — stood between me —

JIM: You shouldn't have let it!

LAURA: I know, but it did, and —

JIM: You were shy with people!

LAURA: I tried not to be but never could —

JIM: Overcome it?

LAURA: No, I — I never could!

JIM: I guess being shy is something you have to work out of kind of gradually.

LAURA (*sorrowfully*): Yes — I guess it —

JIM: Takes time!

LAURA: Yes —

JIM: People are not so dreadful when you know them. That's what you have to remember! And everybody has problems, not just you, but practically everybody has got some problems. You think of yourself as having the only problems, as being the only one who is disappointed. But just look around you and you will see lots of people as disappointed as you are. For instance, I hoped when I was going to high school that I would be further along at this time, six years later, than I am now — You remember that wonderful write-up I had in *The Torch*?

LAURA: Yes! (*She rises and crosses to table.*)

JIM: It said I was bound to succeed in anything I went into! (*Laura returns with the annual.*) Holy Jeez! *The Torch*! (*He accepts it reverently. They smile across it with mutual wonder. Laura crouches beside him and*

they begin to turn through it. Laura's shyness is dissolving in his warmth.)

LAURA: Here you are in *Pirates of Penzance*!

JIM (*wistfully*): I sang the baritone lead in that operetta.

LAURA (*rapidly*): So — *beautifully*!

JIM (*protesting*): Aw —

LAURA: Yes, yes — beautifully — beautifully!

JIM: You heard me?

LAURA: All three times!

JIM: No!

LAURA: Yes!

JIM: All three performances?

LAURA (*looking down*): Yes.

JIM: Why?

LAURA: I — wanted to ask you to — autograph my program.

JIM: Why didn't you ask me to?

LAURA: You were always surrounded by your own friends so much that I never had a chance to.

JIM: You should have just —

LAURA: Well, I — thought you might think I was —

JIM: Thought I might think you was — what?

LAURA: Oh —

JIM (*with reflective relish*): I was beleaguered by females in those days.

LAURA: You were terribly popular!

JIM: Yeah —

LAURA: You had such a — friendly way —

JIM: I was spoiled in high school.

LAURA: Everybody — liked you!

JIM: Including you?

LAURA: I — yes, I — I did, too — (*She gently closes the book in her lap.*)

JIM: Well, well, well! — Give me that program, Laura. (*She hands it to him. He signs it with a flourish.*) There you are — better late than never!

LAURA: Oh, I — what a — surprise!

JIM: My signature isn't worth very much right now. But some day — maybe — it will increase in value! Being disappointed is one thing and being discouraged is something else. I am disappointed but I am not discouraged. I'm twenty-three years old. How old are you?

LAURA: I'll be twenty-four in June.

JIM: That's not old age!

LAURA: No, but —

JIM: You finished high school?

LAURA (*with difficulty*): I didn't go back.

JIM: You mean you dropped out?

LAURA: I made bad grades in my final examinations. (*She rises and replaces the book and the program. Her voice strained.*) How is — Emily Meisenbach getting along?

JIM: Oh, that kraut-head!

LAURA: Why do you call her that?

JIM: That's what she was.

LAURA: You're not still — going with her?

JIM: I never see her.

LAURA: It said in the Personal Section that you were — engaged!

JIM: I know, but I wasn't impressed by that — propaganda!

LAURA: It wasn't — the truth?

JIM: Only in Emily's optimistic opinion!

LAURA: Oh —

(*Legend: "What Have You Done since High School?"*)

(*Jim lights a cigarette and leans indolently back on his elbows smiling at Laura with a warmth and charm which lights her inwardly with altar candles. She remains by the table and turns in her hands a piece of glass to cover her tumult.*)

JIM (*after several reflective puffs on a cigarette*): What have you done since high school? (*She seems not to hear him.*) Huh? (*Laura looks up.*) I said what have you done since high school, Laura?

LAURA: Nothing much.

JIM: You must have been doing something these six long years.

LAURA: Yes.

JIM: Well, then, such as what?

LAURA: I took a business course at business college —

JIM: How did that work out?

LAURA: Well, not very — well — I had to drop out, it gave me — indigestion —

(*Jim laughs gently.*)

JIM: What are you doing now?

LAURA: I don't do anything — much. Oh, please don't think I sit around doing nothing! My glass collection takes up a good deal of my time. Glass is something you have to take good care of.

JIM: What did you say — about glass?

LAURA: Collection I said — I have one — (*She clears her throat and turns away again, acutely shy.*)

JIM (*abruptly*): You know what I judge to be the trouble with you? Inferiority complex! Know what that is? That's what they call it when someone low-rates himself! I understand it because I had it, too. Although my case was not so aggravated as yours seems to be. I had it until I took up public speaking, developed my voice, and learned that I had an aptitude for science. Before that time I never thought of myself as being outstanding in any way whatsoever! Now I've never made a regular study of it, but I have a friend who says I can analyze people better than doctors that make a profession of it. I don't claim that to be necessarily true, but I can sure guess a person's psychology, Laura! (*Takes out his gum.*) Excuse me, Laura. I always take it out when the flavor is gone. I'll use this scrap of paper to wrap it in. I know how it is to get it stuck on a shoe. Yep — that's what I judge to be your principal trouble. A lack of confidence in yourself as a person. You don't have the proper amount of faith in yourself. I'm basing that fact on a number of your remarks and also on certain observations I've made.

For instance that clumping you thought was so awful in high school. You say that you even dreaded to walk into class. You see what you did? You dropped out of school, you gave up an education because of a clump, which as far as I know was practically nonexistent! A little physical defect is what you have. Hardly noticeable even! Magnified thousands of times by imagination! You know what my strong advice to you is? Think of yourself as *superior* in some way!

LAURA: In what way would I think?

JIM: Why, man alive, Laura! Just look about you a little. What do you see? A world full of common people! All of 'em born and all of 'em going to die! Which of them has one-tenth of your good points! Or mine! Or anyone else's, as far as that goes — Gosh! Everybody excels in some one thing. Some in many! (*Unconsciously glances at himself in the mirror.*) All you've got to do is discover in what! Take me, for instance. (*He adjusts his tie at the mirror.*) My interest happens to lie in electro-dynamics. I'm taking a course in radio engineering at night school, Laura, on top of a fairly responsible job at the warehouse. I'm taking that course and studying public speaking.

LAURA: Ohhhh.

JIM: Because I believe in the future of television! (*Turning back to her.*) I wish to be ready to go up right along with it. Therefore I'm planning to get in on the ground floor. In fact, I've already made the right connections and all that remains is for the industry itself to get under way! Full steam — (*His eyes are starry.*) *Knowledge* — Zzzzzp! *Money* — Zzzzzzp! — *Power!* That's the cycle democracy is built on! (*His attitude is convincingly dynamic. Laura stares at him, even her shyness eclipsed in her absolute wonder. He suddenly grins.*) I guess you think I think a lot of myself!

LAURA: No — o-o-o, I —

JIM: Now how about you? Isn't there something you take more interest in than anything else?

LAURA: Well, I do — as I said — have my — glass collection —

(*A peal of girlish laughter from the kitchen.*)

JIM: I'm not right sure I know what you're talking about. What kind of glass is it?

LAURA: Little articles of it, they're ornaments mostly! Most of them are little animals made out of glass, the tiniest little animals in the world. Mother calls them a glass menagerie! Here's an example of one, if you'd like to see it! This one is one of the oldest. It's nearly thirteen. (*He stretches out his hand.*) (*Music: "The Glass Menagerie."*) Oh, be careful — if you breathe, it breaks!

JIM: I'd better not take it. I'm pretty clumsy with things.

LAURA: Go on, I trust you with him! (*Places it in his palm.*) There now — you're holding him gently! Hold him over the light, he loves the light! You see how the light shines through him?

JIM: It sure does shine!

LAURA: I shouldn't be partial, but he is my favorite one.

JIM: What kind of a thing is this one supposed to be?

LAURA: Haven't you noticed the single horn on his forehead?

JIM: A unicorn, huh?

LAURA: Mmm-hmmm!

JIM: Unicorns, aren't they extinct in the modern world?

LAURA: I know!

JIM: Poor little fellow, he must feel sort of lonesome.

LAURA (smiling): Well, if he does he doesn't complain about it. He stays on a shelf with some horses that don't have horns and all of them seem to get along nicely together.

JIM: How do you know?

LAURA (lightly): I haven't heard any arguments among them!

JIM (grinning): No arguments, huh? Well, that's a pretty good sign! Where shall I set him?

LAURA: Put him on the table. They all like a change of scenery once in a while!

JIM (stretching): Well, well, well, well — Look how big my shadow is when I stretch!

LAURA: Oh, oh, yes — it stretches across the ceiling!

JIM (crossing to door): I think it's stopped raining. (Opens fire escape door.) Where does the music come from?

LAURA: From the Paradise Dance Hall across the alley.

JIM: How about cutting the rug a little, Miss Wingfield?

LAURA: Oh, I —

JIM: Or is your program filled up? Let me have a look at it. (Grasps imaginary card.) Why, every dance is taken! I'll just have to scratch some out. (Waltz music: "La Golondrina.") Ahhh, a waltz! (He executes some sweeping turns by himself then holds his arms toward Laura.)

LAURA (breathlessly): I — can't dance!

JIM: There you go, that inferiority stuff!

LAURA: I've never danced in my life!

JIM: Come on, try!

LAURA: Oh, but I'd step on you!

JIM: I'm not made out of glass.

LAURA: How — how — how do we start?

JIM: Just leave it to me. You hold your arms out a little.

LAURA: Like this?

JIM: A little bit higher. Right. Now don't tighten up, that's the main thing about it — relax.

LAURA (laughing breathlessly): It's hard not to.

JIM: Okay.

LAURA: I'm afraid you can't budge me.

JIM: What do you bet I can't? (He swings her into motion.)

LAURA: Goodness, yes, you can!

JIM: Let yourself go, now, Laura, just let yourself go.

LAURA: I'm —

JIM: Come on!

LAURA: Trying!

JIM: Not so stiff — Easy does it!

LAURA: I know but I'm —

JIM: Loosen th' backbone! There now, that's a lot better.

LAURA: Am I?

JIM: Lots, lots better! (He moves her about the room in a clumsy waltz.)

LAURA: Oh, my!

JIM: Ha-ha!

LAURA: Oh, my goodness!

JIM: Ha-ha-ha! (They suddenly bump into the table. Jim stops.) What did we hit on?

LAURA: Table.

JIM: Did something fall off it? I think —

LAURA: Yes.

JIM: I hope that it wasn't the little glass horse with the horn!

LAURA: Yes.

JIM: Aw, aw, aw. Is it broken?

LAURA: Now it is just like all the other horses.

JIM: It's lost its —

LAURA: Horn! It doesn't matter. Maybe it's a blessing in disguise.

JIM: You'll never forgive me. I bet that that was your favorite piece of glass.

LAURA: I don't have favorites much. It's no tragedy, Freckles. Glass breaks so easily. No matter how careful you are. The traffic jars the shelves and things fall off them.

JIM: Still I'm awfully sorry that I was the cause.

LAURA (smiling): I'll just imagine he had an operation. The horn was removed to make him feel less — freakish! (They both laugh.) Now he will feel more at home with the other horses, the ones that don't have horns . . .

JIM: Ha-ha, that's very funny! (Suddenly serious.) I'm glad to see that you have a sense of humor. You know — you're — well — very different! Surprisingly different from anyone else I know! (His voice becomes soft and hesitant with a genuine feeling.) Do you mind me telling you that? (Laura is abashed beyond speech.) I mean it in a nice way . . . (Laura nods shyly, looking away.) You make me feel sort of — I don't know how to put it! I'm usually pretty good at expressing things, but — This is something that I don't know how to say! (Laura touches her throat and clears it — turns the broken unicorn in her hands.) (Even softer.) Has anyone ever told you that you were pretty? (Pause: Music.) (Laura looks up slowly, with wonder, and shakes her head.) Well, you are! In a very different way from anyone else. And all the nicer because of the difference, too. (His voice becomes low and husky. Laura turns away, nearly faint with the novelty of her emotions.) I wish that you were my sister. I'd teach you to have some confidence in yourself. The different people are not like other people, but being different is nothing to be ashamed of. Because other people are not such wonderful people. They're one hundred times one thousand. You're one times one! They walk all over the earth. You just stay here. They're common as — weeds, but — you — well, you're — Blue Roses!

(*Image on screen: blue roses.*)
(*Music changes.*)

LAURA: But blue is wrong for — roses . . .
JIM: It's right for you — You're — pretty!
LAURA: In what respect am I pretty?
JIM: In all respects — believe me! Your eyes — your hair — are pretty! Your hands are pretty! (*He catches hold of her hand.*) You think I'm making this up because I'm invited to dinner and have to be nice. Oh, I could do that! I could put on an act for you, Laura, and say lots of things without being very sincere. But this time I am. I'm talking to you sincerely. I happened to notice you had this inferiority complex that keeps you from feeling comfortable with people. Somebody needs to build your confidence up and make you proud instead of shy and turning away and — blushing — Somebody ought to — Ought to — *kiss* you, Laura! (*His hand slips slowly up her arm to her shoulder.*) (*Music swells tumultuously.*) (*He suddenly turns her about and kisses her on the lips. When he releases her Laura sinks on the sofa with a bright, dazed look. Jim backs away and fishes in his pocket for a cigarette.*) (*Legend on screen: "Souvenir."*) Stumble-john! (*He lights the cigarette, avoiding her look. There is a peal of girlish laughter from Amanda in the kitchen. Laura slowly raises and opens her hand. It still contains the little broken glass animal. She looks at it with a tender, bewildered expression.*) Stumble-john! I shouldn't have done that — That was way off the beam. You don't smoke, do you? (*She looks up, smiling, not hearing the question. He sits beside her a little gingerly. She looks at him speechlessly — waiting. He coughs decorously and moves a little farther aside as he considers the situation and senses her feelings, dimly, with perturbation. Gently.*) Would you — care for a — mint? (*She doesn't seem to hear him but her look grows brighter even.*) Peppermint — Life Saver? My pocket's a regular drugstore — wherever I go . . . (*He pops a mint in his mouth. Then gulps and decides to make a clean breast of it. He speaks slowly and gingerly.*) Laura, you know, if I had a sister like you, I'd do the same thing as Tom. I'd bring out fellows and — introduce her to them. The right type of boys of a type to — appreciate her. Only — well — he made a mistake about me. Maybe I've got no call to be saying this. That may not have been the idea in having me over. But what if it was? There's nothing wrong about that. The only trouble is that in my case — I'm not in a situation to — do the right thing. I can't take down your number and say I'll phone. I can't call up next week and — ask for a date. I thought I had better explain the situation in case you misunderstood it and — hurt your feelings. . . . (*Pause. Slowly, very slowly, Laura's look changes, her eyes returning slowly from his to the ornament in her palm.*)

(*Amanda utters another gay laugh in the kitchen.*)

LAURA (*faintly*): You — won't — call again?
JIM: No, Laura, I can't. (*He rises from the sofa.*) As I was just explaining, I've — got strings on me, Laura, I've — been going steady! I go out all the time with a girl named Betty. She's a home-girl like you, and Catholic, and Irish, and in a great many ways we — get along fine. I met her last summer on a moonlight boat trip up the river to Alton, on the *Majestic.* Well — right away from the start it was — love! (*Legend: Love!*) (*Laura sways slightly forward and grips the arm of the sofa. He fails to notice, now enrapt in his own comfortable being.*) Being in love has made a new man of me! (*Leaning stiffly forward, clutching the arm of the sofa, Laura struggles visibly with her storm. But Jim is oblivious, she is a long way off.*) The power of love is really pretty tremendous! Love is something that — changes the whole world, Laura! (*The storm abates a little and Laura leans back. He notices her again.*) It happened that Betty's aunt took sick, she got a wire and had to go to Centralia. So Tom — when he asked me to dinner — I naturally just accepted the invitation, not knowing that you — that he — that I — (*He stops awkwardly.*) Huh — I'm a stumble-john! (*He flops back on the sofa. The holy candles in the altar of Laura's face have been snuffed out! There is a look of almost infinite desolation. Jim glances at her uneasily.*) I wish that you would — say something. (*She bites her lip which was trembling and then bravely smiles. She opens her hand again on the broken glass ornament. Then she gently takes his hand and raises it level with her own. She carefully places the unicorn in the palm of his hand, then pushes his fingers closed upon it.*) What are you — doing that for? You want me to have him? — Laura? (*She nods.*) What for?
LAURA: A — souvenir . . .

(*She rises unsteadily and crouches beside the victrola to wind it up.*)

(*Legend on screen: "Things Have a Way of Turning out so Badly."*)

(*Or Image: "Gentleman Caller Waving Goodbye! — Gaily."*)

(*At this moment Amanda rushes brightly back in the front room. She bears a pitcher of fruit punch in an old-fashioned cut-glass pitcher and a plate of macaroons. The plate has a gold border and poppies painted on it.*)

AMANDA: Well, well, well! Isn't the air delightful after the shower? I've made you children a little liquid refreshment. (*Turns gaily to the gentleman caller.*) Jim, do you know that song about lemonade?
"Lemonade, lemonade
   Made in the shade and stirred with a spade —
Good enough for any old maid!"
JIM (*uneasily*): Ha-ha! No — I never heard it.
AMANDA: Why, Laura! You look so serious!
JIM: We were having a serious conversation.
AMANDA: Good! Now you're better acquainted!

JIM (*uncertainly*): Ha-ha! Yes.

AMANDA: You modern young people are much more serious-minded than my generation. I was so gay as a girl!

JIM: You haven't changed, Mrs. Wingfield.

AMANDA: Tonight I'm rejuvenated! The gaiety of the occasion, Mr. O'Connor! (*She tosses her head with a peal of laughter. Spills lemonade.*) Oooo! I'm baptizing myself!

JIM: Here — let me —

AMANDA (*setting the pitcher down*): There now. I discovered we had some maraschino cherries. I dumped them in, juice and all!

JIM: You shouldn't have gone to that trouble, Mrs. Wingfield.

AMANDA: Trouble, trouble? Why it was loads of fun! Didn't you hear me cutting up in the kitchen? I bet your ears were burning! I told Tom how out-done with him I was for keeping you to himself so long a time! He should have brought you over much, much sooner! Well, now that you've found your way, I want you to be a very frequent caller! Not just occasional but all the time. Oh, we're going to have a lot of gay times together! I see them coming! Mmm, just breathe that air! So fresh, and the moon's so pretty! I'll skip back out — I know where my place is when young folks are having a — serious conversation!

JIM: Oh, don't go out, Mrs. Wingfield. The fact of the matter is I've got to be going.

AMANDA: Going, now? You're joking! Why, it's only the shank of the evening, Mr. O'Connor!

JIM: Well, you know how it is.

AMANDA: You mean you're a young workingman and have to keep workingmen's hours. We'll let you off early tonight. But only on the condition that next time you stay later. What's the best night for you? Isn't Saturday night the best night for you workingmen?

JIM: I have a couple of time clocks to punch, Mrs. Wingfield. One at morning, another one at night!

AMANDA: My, but you *are* ambitious! You work at night, too?

JIM: No, Ma'am, not work but — Betty! (*He crosses deliberately to pick up his hat. The band at the Paradise Dance Hall goes into a tender waltz.*)

AMANDA: Betty? Betty? Who's — Betty! (*There is an ominous cracking sound in the sky.*)

JIM: Oh, just a girl. The girl I go steady with! (*He smiles charmingly. The sky falls.*)

(*Legend: "The Sky Falls."*)

AMANDA (*a long-drawn exhalation*): Ohhhh . . . Is it a serious romance, Mr. O'Connor?

JIM: We're going to be married the second Sunday in June.

AMANDA: Ohhhh — how nice! Tom didn't mention that you were engaged to be married.

JIM: The cat's not out of the bag at the warehouse yet. You know how they are. They call you Romeo and stuff like that. (*He stops at the oval mirror to put on his hat. He carefully shapes the brim and the crown to give a discreetly dashing effect.*) It's been a wonderful evening, Mrs. Wingfield. I guess this is what they mean by Southern hospitality.

AMANDA: It really wasn't anything at all.

JIM: I hope it don't seem like I'm rushing off. But I promised Betty I'd pick her up at the Wabash depot, an' by the time I get my jalopy down there her train'll be in. Some women are pretty upset if you keep 'em waiting.

AMANDA: Yes, I know — The tyranny of women! (*Extends her hand.*) Good-bye, Mr. O'Connor. I wish you luck — and happiness — and success! All three of them, and so does Laura! — Don't you, Laura?

LAURA: Yes!

JIM (*taking her hand*): Good-bye, Laura. I'm certainly going to treasure that souvenir. And don't you forget the good advice I gave you. (*Raises his voice to a cheery shout.*) So long, Shakespeare! Thanks again, ladies — Good night!

(*He grins and ducks jauntily out.*)

(*Still bravely grimacing, Amanda closes the door on the gentleman caller. Then she turns back to the room with a puzzled expression. She and Laura don't dare to face each other. Laura crouches beside the victrola to wind it.*)

AMANDA (*faintly*): Things have a way of turning out so badly. I don't believe that I would play the victrola. Well, well — well — Our gentleman caller was engaged to be married! Tom!

TOM (*from back*): Yes, Mother?

AMANDA: Come in here a minute. I want to tell you something awfully funny.

TOM (*enters with macaroon and a glass of the lemonade*): Has the gentleman caller gotten away already?

AMANDA: The gentleman caller has made an early departure. What a wonderful joke you played on us!

TOM: How do you mean?

AMANDA: You didn't mention that he was engaged to be married.

TOM: Jim? Engaged?

AMANDA: That's what he just informed us.

TOM: I'll be jiggered! I didn't know about that.

AMANDA: That seems very peculiar.

TOM: What's peculiar about it?

AMANDA: Didn't you call him your best friend down at the warehouse?

TOM: He is, but how did I know?

AMANDA: It seems extremely peculiar that you wouldn't know your best friend was going to be married!

TOM: The warehouse is where I work, not where I know things about people!

AMANDA: You don't know things anywhere! You live in a dream; you manufacture illusions! (*He crosses to door.*) Where are you going?

TOM: I'm going to the movies.

AMANDA: That's right, now that you've had us make such fools of ourselves. The effort, the preparations, all the expense! The new floor lamp, the rug, the clothes for Laura! All for what? To entertain some other girl's fiancé! Go to the movies, go! Don't think about us, a mother deserted, an unmarried sister who's crippled and has no job! Don't let anything interfere with your selfish pleasure! Just go, go, go — to the movies!

Tom: All right, I will! The more you shout about my selfishness to me the quicker I'll go, and I won't go to the movies!

Amanda: Go, then! Then go to the moon — you selfish dreamer!

(Tom smashes his glass on the floor. He plunges out on the fire escape, slamming the door. Laura screams — cut by door.)

(Dance hall music up. Tom goes to the rail and grips it desperately, lifting his face in the chill white moonlight penetrating the narrow abyss of the alley.)

(Legend on screen: "And so Good-bye . . .")

(Tom's closing speech is timed with the interior pantomime. The interior scene is played as though viewed through soundproof glass. Amanda appears to be making a comforting speech to Laura who is huddled upon the sofa. Now that we cannot hear the mother's speech, her silliness is gone and she has dignity and tragic beauty. Laura's dark hair hides her face until at the end of the speech she lifts it to smile at her mother. Amanda's gestures are slow and graceful, almost dancelike, as she comforts the daughter. At the end of her speech she glances a moment at the father's picture — then withdraws through the portieres. At close of Tom's speech, Laura blows out the candles, ending the play.)

Tom: I didn't go to the moon, I went much further — for time is the longest distance between two places — Not long after that I was fired for writing a poem on the lid of a shoebox. I left Saint Louis. I descended the steps of this fire escape for a last time and followed, from then on, in my father's footsteps, attempting to find in motion what was lost in space — I traveled around a great deal. The cities swept about me like dead leaves, leaves that were brightly colored but torn away from the branches. I would have stopped, but I was pursued by something. It always came upon me unawares, taking me altogether by surprise. Perhaps it was a familiar bit of music. Perhaps it was only a piece of transparent glass — Perhaps I am walking along a street at night, in some strange city, before I have found companions. I pass the lighted window of a shop where perfume is sold. The window is filled with pieces of colored glass, tiny transparent bottles in delicate colors, like bits of a shattered rainbow. Then all at once my sister touches my shoulder. I turn around and look into her eyes . . . Oh, Laura, Laura, I tried to leave you behind me, but I am more faithful than I intended to be! I reach for a cigarette, I cross the street, I run into the movies or a bar, I buy a drink, I speak to the nearest stranger — anything that can blow your candles out! *(Laura bends over the candles.)* — for nowadays the world is lit by lightning! Blow out your candles, Laura — and so good-bye. . . .

(She blows the candles out.)
(The scene dissolves.)

Commentaries

Tennessee Williams is a fascinating figure in American drama. He was a forceful personality who charmed his friends and the public alike, although his life was often filled with uncertainties and unresolved problems. Some of his best work derived from his private agonies. His work was taken seriously almost from the first, and a body of criticism has developed around it, including biographies, personal reminiscences of collaborators, critical commentaries, and scholarship.

In the *New York Times* review of *The Glass Menagerie* (included here), Lewis Nichols describes Laurette Taylor's performance as Amanda as "completely perfect." Donald Spoto, who wrote *The Kindness of Strangers: The Life of Tennessee Williams* (1985), says that Taylor, a powerful actress whose career had seemed finished when the part was offered to her, almost refused the role at first. But her interpretation established a point of reference to which later actresses had to pay homage. Spoto helps us understand the power of collaboration between actor and playwright that sometimes helps both expand their understanding of the work.

Benjamin Nelson explains that "*The Glass Menagerie* exhibits several of Williams's weaknesses as well as his strengths as a playwright." He discusses Williams's characterizations, especially of Laura and Amanda. He also points to "poetic passages" in the play that he feels are weaknesses. Ultimately, Nelson poses an interesting dramatic question: Is the play a tragedy? The search for an answer to this question involves a full consideration of the play's strengths and weaknesses, its success or failure.

Lewis Nichols (1903–1982)
REVIEW OF *THE GLASS MENAGERIE*   *1945*

Lewis Nichols's review of the New York premiere of The Glass Menagerie *focused on the stellar performance of Laurette Taylor, who played the Mother, Amanda. Nichols also points out the quality of Williams's writing and his ear for "faintly sardonic dialogue." He saw the play as a superb vehicle for sublime acting.*

The theatre opened its Easter basket the night before and found it a particularly rich one. Preceded by warm and tender reports from Chicago, *The Glass Menagerie* opened at the Playhouse on Saturday, and immediately it was clear that for once the advance notes were not in error. Tennessee Williams's simple play forms the framework for some of the finest acting to be seen in many a day. "Memorable" is an overworked word, but that is the only one to describe Laurette Taylor's performance. March left the theatre like a lioness.

Miss Taylor's picture of a blowsy, impoverished woman who is living on memories of a flower-scented Southern past is completely perfect. It combines qualities of humor and human understanding. The Mother of the play is an amusing figure and a pathetic one. Aged, with two children, living in an apartment off an alley in St. Louis, she recalls her past glories, her seventeen suitors, the old and better life. She is a bit of a scold, a bit of a snob; her finery has worn threadbare, but she has kept it for occasions of state. Miss Taylor makes her a person known by any other name to everyone in her audience. That is art.

In the story the Mother is trying to do the best she can for her children. The son works in a warehouse, although he wants to go to far places. The daughter, a cripple, never has been able to finish school. She is shy, she spends her time collecting glass animals — the title comes from this — and playing old phonograph records. The Mother thinks it is time she is getting married, but there has never been a Gentleman Caller at the house. Finally the son brings home another man from the warehouse and out comes the finery and the heavy if bent candlestick. Even the Gentleman Caller fails. He is engaged to another girl.

Mr. Williams's play is not all of the same caliber. A strict perfectionist could easily find a good many flaws. There are some unconnected odds and ends which have little to do with the story: Snatches of talk about the war, bits of psychology, occasional moments of rather flowery writing. But Mr. Williams has a real ear for faintly sardonic dialogue, unexpected phrases and an affection for his characters. Miss Taylor takes these many good passages and makes them sing. She plays softly and part of the time seems to be mumbling — a mumble that can be heard at the top of the gallery. Her accents, like the author's phrases, are unexpected, her gestures are vague and fluttery. There is no doubt she was a Southern belle; there is no doubt she is a great actress.

Eddie Dowling, who is coproducer, and, with Margo Jones, codirector, has the double job of narrator and the player of The Son. The narration is like that of *Our Town* and *I Remember Mama* and it probably is not essential to *The Glass Menagerie*. In the play itself Mr. Dowling gives his quiet, easy performance. Julie Haydon, very ethereal and slight, is good as the daughter, as is Anthony Ross as the Gentleman Caller. The Caller had been the hero in high school, but he, too, had been unsuccessful. Jo Mielziner's setting fits the play, as does Paul Bowles's music. In fact, everything fits. *The Glass Menagerie*, like spring, is a pleasure to have in the neighborhood.

Donald Spoto (b. 1941)
LAURETTE TAYLOR IN *THE GLASS MENAGERIE*   1985

Before the part of Amanda Wingfield was offered to her, Laurette Taylor had thought her career as an actress was over. Donald Spoto, Tennessee Williams's biographer, gives us a vision of how persistence and devotion to someone of genuine talent produced a legend in American acting.

That month [December 1944], the details moved together swiftly. [Actor-producer-director Eddie] Dowling, who had directed actress Julie Haydon in *The Time of Your Life,*° convinced her that (although she was thirty-four) she would be credible as the lame, fragile Laura, a character at least a decade younger. She, in turn, took the play to her friend and mentor (later her husband), the formidable critic George Jean Nathan, whose approval she felt obligatory. At the same time, the forty-nine-year-old Dowling announced — without a smile — that he would play young (twentyish) Tom, the shoe-warehouse clerk and aspiring poet; for the role of the gentleman caller, Anthony Ross was hired. The remaining role to be cast was Amanda Wingfield — the "little woman of great but confused vitality," as Williams described her in the play, "clinging frantically to another time and place." The role demanded not mere competence, but the nuances of dramatic greatness. Nathan suggested Laurette Taylor. Dowling and [Audrey] Wood [Williams's agent] and Williams saw his wisdom; they also panicked.

Laurette Taylor, then sixty, had been up to the 1930s one of the great ladies of the American stage. Those who had seen her in *Peg O'My Heart* (in 1912) or *The Furies* (in 1928) or *Outward Bound* (in 1938) knew her gifts. But for almost ten years she had herself become a woman of great but confused vitality, and a confirmed alcoholic.

At that time, Taylor was living in sad withdrawal from the theater, at a hotel on East 60th Street, where she was daily attended by a drama student named Eloise Sheldon. In return for acting lessons, the young woman cared for the practical details of Taylor's life and offered devoted companionship. The play reached Taylor

---

The Time of Your Life: A play (1939) by William Saroyan.

by the circuitous route of Wood to Dowling to Haydon to Nathan to Sheldon to Taylor. It also bore a new title — *The Glass Menagerie.*

"Of course her first reaction was to turn it down," Eloise Sheldon Armen recalled years later; "she thought her career was over. But we prevailed on her to see that no one could bring this character to life the way she could." At last, with the loving encouragement of Eloise —"a small flame," as Laurette Taylor's daughter appreciatively wrote of the young student, "guiding [Taylor] back to the paths of everyday life"— she accepted the part. She did not, however, stop drinking, nor did she seem to give much attention to memorizing lines before or during rehearsals.

In November, Dowling (with, Williams insisted, Margo Jones as codirector) began rehearsals in New York prior to a scheduled Chicago tryout at the end of December. Terrified that something like the history of *Battle of Angels* would be repeated — not because of the new play's content (which could not have been more different) but because he no longer believed the play was anything but "rather dull, too nice"— Williams fled New York for St. Louis. There he was interviewed on his life and work and hopes by the drama critic of the *Star-Times,* a man named William Inge. The resulting article was full of inaccuracies, half-truths, and Williams's typical alterations of personal history; the resulting friendship was much more intense and dramatic.

But Audrey and Dowling would not allow Williams to be an absentee author, and in December he was summoned to Chicago. The situation, he quickly realized, was as bleak as the fierce winter that had already descended.

First of all, Laurette Taylor — with only a week remaining before the December 26 premiere — attended the final rehearsals in what can only be called an alcoholic stupor, barely summarizing the dialogue and so broadly defining the woman's Southern accent and character that, as Williams wrote . . . , she made the play sound like the Aunt Jemima Pancake Hour. In addition, Jo Mielziner's stage designs were being followed with great difficulty, and the music Williams had commissioned from his old acquaintance Paul Bowles sounded harsh through the theater's crude sound system. Luggage had not arrived; a winter storm raged; the Civic Theatre was inconvenient to Chicago's main theater district; there was no budget for advertising or publicity; and everyone in the company (except Eddie Dowling and Julie Haydon) — cast, crew, author — submerged the fear of failure in strong drink. Margo Jones, Williams wrote . . . , was like a scoutmaster leading a wayward and desperate troop to their doom.

As late as Christmas Eve, the lines of the play had been neither "frozen" (fixed by the producer and playwright to be performed as written) nor completely memorized. Laurette Taylor managed only a martini mumble, Dowling was demanding rewrites, and the cast was stumbling into props and one another. "Mr. Dowling," Williams said quietly that night, "art is experience remembered in tranquillity. And I find no tranquillity in Chicago."

The night after Christmas, *The Glass Menagerie* was somehow performed for a small, diffident audience. By the afternoon of the twenty-seventh, the box office had taken in only four hundred dollars, and the producers prepared a closing notice. But then Audrey telephoned them to read two brief reviews: Critic Claudia Cassidy, writing in the *Chicago Daily Tribune,* said the play had "the stamina of success . . . [it] knows people and how they tick. . . . If it is your play, as it is mine, it reaches out . . . and you are caught in its spell." And Ashton Stevens, in the *Herald American,* said *The Glass Menagerie* "has the courage of true poetry couched in colloquial prose."

Before the end of that day, the mayor of Chicago, at the urging of the Civic The-atre's management, authorized a fifty-percent ticket subsidy for municipal employ-ees. On the third night, Laurette Taylor was not simply discharging a half-formed role, she was creating a legend, she had begun to draw a more wonderful portrait than anyone could have imagined — not Eddie Dowling (who resented the critics' subsequent raves about her), not Tennessee Williams nor Audrey Wood, not any-one connected with the play.

"Actually," according to the playwright, "she directed many of the scenes, par-ticularly the ones between mother and daughter, and she did a top-notch job. She was continually working on her part, putting in little things and taking them out — almost every night in Chicago there was something new, but she never disturbed the central characterization. Everything she did was absolutely in character."

The closing notice was removed — not, however, because box-office business dramatically improved, but because Claudia Cassidy and Ashton Stevens had been championing the play, returning almost nightly and telling and writing about it almost daily. "It gripped players and audiences alike," Cassidy wrote on January 7, 1945, "and created one of those rare evenings in the theater that make 'stagestruck' an honorable word." By the middle of the month, no tickets were available. In an unusual example of journalistic salvation, a play was for once not lost but kept alive because of critical support.

Benjamin Nelson
PROBLEMS IN *THE GLASS MENAGERIE*   *1961*

Benjamin Nelson's analysis of Williams's play recognizes the power of the cir-cumstances portrayed in the play. Nelson is concerned, however, that the charac-ters, especially Laura, are not as fully and carefully drawn as they need to be to make the play truly powerful. He also criticizes Williams for creating a universe that "does not allow tragedy."

The Glass Menagerie exhibits several of Williams's weaknesses as well as his strengths as a playwright. The great strength of the play is of course the delicate, sympathetic, yet objective creation of meaningful people in a meaningful situation. Williams has caught a decisive and desperate moment in the lives of four individu-als and given it illumination and a sense of deep meaning — no small feat for any writer.

His characterizations are not equally realized. He has been unable to create Laura on more than a single dimension, while Amanda is overwhelming in her multifaceted delineation. On a more technical level the play manifests a doubt on the part of its author toward the power of the written word. As a backdrop for *The Glass Menagerie*, Williams originally wished to use a screen to register emo-tions and present images from the past, present, and future. For example, when Jim O'Connor confesses to the family that he is going steady with another girl, the legend on the screen is to read, "The Sky Falls." Fortunately, [actor-director] Eddie Dowling deleted these touches of the poet from his production, but the play still abounds with a number of pretentious statements on the part of Tom as Narrator.

I assume that the final scene between Amanda and Laura is played in pantomime because Williams wished to portray Amanda's dignity through her gestures and her daughter's reaction rather than through the mother's speech, which during the course of the drama has been either shrill, simpering, or saucy. But in relegating this scene to background silence while Tom makes a self-conscious statement about drifting like a dead leaf "attempting to find in motion what was lost in space," he has substituted a painfully pretentious narration for what could have been an intense and luminous moment between the two women.

Again, on the credit side of the author, his play presents genuine situation, motivation, and, as Joseph Wood Krutch has noted, "a hard substantial core of shrewd observation and deft, economical characterization." But Mr. Krutch also noted that "this hard core is enveloped in a fuzzy haze of pretentious, sentimental, pseudopoetic verbiage."[1] In *The Glass Menagerie,* the strained lyricism runs parallel with dialogue that is fresh, alive, and highly characteristic, particularly in the speech of Amanda. This dialogue fortunately dominates the proceedings, but the excess of self-conscious "poetical" passages is quite apparent and is a fault of which Williams is to be guilty in much of his later work.

But the great weakness of *The Glass Menagerie* does not lie in its author's artistic or technical deficiencies. The weakness lies at the core of the play and evolves out of what is to become the playwright's hardening philosophical commitment. We can begin to comprehend this when we ask ourselves whether or not *The Glass Menagerie* is a tragedy. It presents a tragic situation and characters who, despite their moodiness and foolishness and self-deception, possess a sense of the tragic. With the possible exception of Laura, they are intensely genuine and the destruction of their dreams and aspirations bears the illusion of great importance. But the play is not a tragedy. The universe of *The Glass Menagerie* does not allow tragedy.

Everyone in the play is a failure and in the course of their drama they all perish a little. Amanda, the most heroic of the quartet, is pitiful but not tragic because from the outset she is doomed to failure despite her desperate struggle to right things. None of these people are given the opportunity to triumph against a fate which is as malignant as it is implacable. Their struggle is a rear-guard action against life, a continuous retreat. This retreat may be moving, pathetic, melodramatic, or boisterous, but it is always a withdrawal. After all, what is the world outside the glass menagerie?

> There was only hot swing music and liquor, dance halls, bars, and movies, and sex that hung in the gloom like a chandelier and flooded the world with brief, deceptive rainbows. . . . All the world was waiting for bombardments! (p. 1084)

The world outside the Wingfield apartment is a world of illusions, also, even more deceptive and destructive than those held by Amanda and Laura. It is the world of *Stairs to the Roof* and this time the escape is not to a new star but into the individual and personal illusions fostered by each of the characters as his private defense against destruction. Jim waits for the day when his "zzzzzp!" will at last disperse his fear and uncertainty; Laura creates her own sparkling, cold world which gives the illusion of warmth but is as eternal in its unreality as the glass from which it is composed; Amanda strikes out with all her power against her fate by clinging to the past as to a shield; and Tom, recognizing the plight of his family, can

[1]Joseph Wood Krutch, *The Nation* 14 April 1945:24.

do no more than drift away from them, rudderless, frightened, and never really as far from Amanda and Laura as he knows he should be.

Not one of these individuals can cope with his situation. They struggle and their hopes and the destruction of these hopes possess a sense of great importance because Williams has created genuine people in an intensely genuine situation, but they lack the completeness to truly cope with their dilemma. They are not responsible for what has happened to them and they are much too helpless to do more than delay the inevitable. And destruction is inevitable because it is implicit in the universe of Tennessee Williams.

> For the sins of the world are really only its partialities, and these are what sufferings must atone for. . . . The nature of man is full of such makeshift arrangements, devised by himself to cover his incompletion. He feels a part of himself to be like a missing wall or a room left unfurnished and he tries as well as he can to make up for it. The use of imagination, resorting to dreams or the loftier purpose of art, is a mask he devises to cover his incompletion. Or violence such as a war, between two men or among a number of nations, is also a blind and senseless compensation for that which is not yet formed in human nature. Then there is still another compensation. This one is found in the principle of atonement, the surrender of self to violent treatment by others with the idea of thereby cleansing one's self of his guilt.[2]

This statement emanates from the core of Williams's thought and is perhaps his most illuminating commentary about himself and his work. It represents a philosophy, or let us say an attitude toward man in his universe, which is to manifest itself in all his work. It is taken from his short story, "Desire and the Black Masseur," which deals with the final compensation cited in the above quotation: purification through violence. In this tale, a man atones for what the author feels is a cosmic fragmentation and guilt by allowing — and actually furthering — his destruction by a cannibal. In *Battle of Angels* and *The Purification*, we find this same kind of violent cleansing.

The Glass Menagerie is a far cry from any of these works; it is the most nonviolent drama written by Williams. Nevertheless it adheres to the belief set forth in the short story. The underlying belief in *The Glass Menagerie* is that there is very little, if any, reason for living. Man is by nature incomplete because his universe is fragmented. There is nothing to be done about this condition because nothing *can* be done about it. Human guilt becomes a corollary of universal guilt and man's life is an atonement for the human condition. In each character in *The Glass Menagerie* there is a part "like a missing wall or a room left unfurnished and he tries as well as he can to make up for it." The mask devised by Laura and Amanda and Tom and Jim is "the use of imagination, resorting to dreams." The Wingfields are broken, fragmented people because "the sins of the world are really only its partialities." They are really not at all responsible for their condition, and thus are in no way able to cope with it. They are trapped in a determined universe. Without some kind of responsibility on the part of the protagonist there is opportunity neither for tragic elevation nor tragic fall. The Wingfields were doomed the moment they were born. At best their struggles will allow them to survive . . . for a time. They will never be allowed to triumph. Thus their struggles, their hopes, and even their eventual destruction can never move far beyond pathos. The beauty and magic of *The Glass Menagerie* is that this pathos is genuine, objective, and deeply moving.

[2]Williams, "Desire and the Black Masseur," *One Arm and Other Stories* (New York, New Directions, 1948), 85.

CAT ON A HOT TIN ROOF

The title of the play comes from an offhand remark made by Tennessee Williams's father, Cornelius Williams, who told his wife that she sometimes made him "as nervous as a cat on a hot tin roof." In the play's first production Williams said that he saw his father in the character of Big Daddy. Reminiscence and family memory are as apparent in this play as in most of his work. The secret ingredient in the play, the secret that haunts Brick and torments Maggie, is homosexuality and Brick's relationship with his now-dead friend Skipper. Maggie seduced Skipper to find out what his relation with Brick was, and when he was unable to perform sexually with her, she felt she knew the truth. The theme of homosexuality extends to the previous inhabitants of Maggie and Brick's bedroom, the bachelors Jack Straw and Peter Ochello, the original owners of the plantation. Williams's note that the two "shared this room all their lives together" implies that their relationship was that of lovers. Williams had already become fully aware of his own homosexuality, although he revealed that personal element only obliquely in works such as *Cat on a Hot Tin Roof* until he "came out" during a television interview with David Frost in 1970.

Williams said in his *Memoirs* that this play was his favorite: "I believe that in *Cat* I reached beyond myself, in the second act, to a kind of crude eloquence of expression in Big Daddy that I have managed to give no other character of my creation." Critics have said that one reason Williams liked the play is that he was able to observe the unities of time, place, and action. Brick is confined to his room because he has broken his ankle in a drunken competition at the high school track. The central action of the play, the celebration of Big Daddy's sixty-fifth birthday, is thus brought to the bedroom, which is also at the center of one of the principal tensions in the play.

Big Daddy owns a cotton plantation and both his sons are a disappointment to him. Gooper, with his ambitious wife and his five "no-neck monsters," is weak and unappealing. Even though Gooper has become a lawyer and produced children in an effort to please his father, Big Daddy sees him as possessing none of the masculine qualities he expects in his heir. Brick, a former football player and Big Daddy's favorite, slipped into debilitating alcoholism after Skipper's death. At the time of the play he has no career and few prospects. Maggie sees that the only way she can secure Big Daddy's blessing in the form of Brick's inheritance is by having a child. And with Brick keeping a sexual distance from her, she has to find a way to help him over his grief.

Because Williams made Brick's homosexuality more or less ambiguous, some critics felt that the play's structure was inconclusive. For example, they reasoned that one sexual failure on the part of Skipper did not prove anything about his sexual preference. They also felt that Maggie and Brick's sexual efforts after the curtain falls on the last act may not be successful at all.

Williams's original version of the play — before it was performed — differed from his final version. Originally, Big Daddy did not appear after act 2, and Maggie and Brick did not vow to have a child or to get together at all. The play was changed because its first director, Elia Kazan, felt that Big Daddy was too brilliant a character to leave out of act 3. He argued with Williams until, against his will, Williams revised act 3 to imply a more positive ending, to bring back Big Daddy — who tells an elephant joke that caused the censor to complain in 1955 — and to make Maggie a softer, less acerbic, and much more appealing character. Williams later said that he agreed that the revision made the play stronger, although he preferred his original ending. He later published the play with two act 3s so that regional and other theaters could choose the ending they preferred.

Cat on a Hot Tin Roof in Performance

The play premiered at the Morosco Theater in New York in March 1955 with Burl Ives, then known best as a folk singer, as Big Daddy, Barbara Bel Geddes as Maggie, Ben Gazzara as Brick, and Mildred Dunnock as Big Mama. This powerful cast made the play a huge success. After 694 performances in New York, it toured for another 268 performances. It won Williams his second Pulitzer Prize and his third Drama Critics' Circle Award for best play of the season. Elia Kazan not only directed the play but also worked hard to help Williams alter his conception. Williams felt that the play should have a realistic production, since in his mind it was a realistic play. Kazan saw it otherwise and introduced soft lighting and a dreamy setting that established the play as moderately expressionistic.

London theaters were banned from performing the play as written, but a theater club produced it to mixed reviews in 1956. The 1958 film version originally was to have Grace Kelly as Maggie, but Elizabeth Taylor got the role, and Paul Newman played Brick. The film version removed all suggestions of homosexuality, focusing instead on Brick's immaturity and his need to grow up to the responsibilities of marriage. It was a highly successful film for its time.

Numerous revivals of the play have been performed in many countries, including a production in Tokyo in 1970. Williams revised the ending once more — putting back the elephant joke — for a restaging of the play in 1974 in Stratford, Connecticut, and then took it to New York for twenty weeks with Elizabeth Ashley as Maggie and Keir Dullea as Brick. That version (which we use in this book) was made into a television production in 1984 with Rip Torn as Big Daddy, Kim Stanley as Big Mama, Tommy Lee Jones as Brick, and Jessica Lange as Maggie. TV critic Richard Zoglin said, "The net effect is to retain the beefed-up dimensions of Maggie and Big Daddy from Broadway, but to leave Brick, at the end, a little more stuck in what Williams describes as a 'state of spiritual despair.'" *Newsweek* described the 1990 New York production, with Howard Davies directing Kathleen Turner as Maggie, as "one of the strongest Tennessee Williams revivals ever on Broadway." Charles Durning's Big Daddy was called "a powerhouse performance."

Another Big Daddy, Ned Beatty in the 2003 Broadway production, was hailed by Ben Brantley in his review in the *New York Times,* included in the commentaries following the play. Brantley says, "What Mr. Beatty does better than any other Big Daddy I've seen is to convey without caricature the monstrous, exhilarated egotism of a man who believes he has outrun death." Williams continues to be a force in American theater not only because he provides such great opportunities for actors, but because he provides much insight into American life.

Tennessee Williams *(1911–1983)*

CAT ON A HOT TIN ROOF

1955

Characters

MARGARET
BRICK
MAE, *sometimes called Sister Woman*
BIG MAMA
DIXIE, *a little girl*
BIG DADDY
REVEREND TOOKER
GOOPER, *sometimes called Brother Man*
DOCTOR BAUGH, *pronounced "Baw"*
LACEY, *a Negro servant*
SOOKEY, *another*
CHILDREN

Notes for the Designer

The set is the bed-sitting-room of a plantation home in the Mississippi Delta. It is along an up-stairs gallery which probably runs around the entire house; it has two pairs of very wide doors opening onto the gallery, showing white balus-trades against a fair summer sky that fades into dusk and night during the course of the play, which occupies precisely the time of its perfor-mance, excepting, of course, the fifteen minutes of intermission.

Perhaps the style of the room is not what you would expect in the home of the Delta's biggest cotton planter. It is Victorian with a touch of the Far East. It hasn't changed much since it was occu-pied by the original owners of the place, Jack Straw and Peter Ochello, a pair of old bachelors who shared this room all their lives together. In other words, the room must evoke some ghosts; it is gently and poetically haunted by a relationship that must have involved a tenderness which was uncommon. This may be irrelevant or unnecessary, but I once saw a reproduction of a faded photo-graph of the verandah of Robert Louis Stevenson's home on that Samoan Island where he spent his last years, and there was a quality of tender light on weathered wood, such as porch furniture made of bamboo and wicker, exposed to tropical suns and tropical rains, which came to mind when I

thought about the set for this play, bringing also to mind the grace and comfort of light, the reassur-ance it gives, on a late and fair afternoon in sum-mer, the way that no matter what, even dread of death, is gently touched and soothed by it. For the set is the background for a play that deals with human extremities of emotion, and it needs that softness behind it.

The bathroom door, showing only pale-blue tile and silver towel racks, is in one side wall; the hall door in the opposite wall. Two articles of furniture need mention: a big double bed which staging should make a functional part of the set as often as suitable, the surface of which should be slightly raked to make figures on it seen more easily; and against the wall space between the two huge double doors upstage: a monumental monstrosity peculiar to our times, a *huge* console combination of radio-phonograph (hi-fi with three speakers), TV set, *and* liquor cabinet, bearing and containing many glasses and bottles, all in one piece, which is a composition of muted silver tones, and the opalescent tones of reflecting glass, a chromatic link, this thing, between the sepia (tawny gold) tones of the interior and the cool (white and blue) tones of the gallery and sky. This piece of furniture (?!), this monument, is a very complete and com-pact little shrine to virtually all the comforts and illusions behind which we hide from such things as the characters in the play are faced with. . . .

The set should be far less realistic than I have so far implied in this description of it. I think the walls below the ceiling should dissolve mysteri-ously into air; the set should be roofed by the sky; stars and moon suggested by traces of milky pal-lor, as if they were observed through a telescope lens out of focus.

Anything else I can think of? Oh, yes, fanlights (transoms shaped like an open glass fan) above all the doors in the set, with panes of blue and amber, and above all, the designer should take as many pains to give the actors room to move about freely

1078

(to show their restlessness, their passion for breaking out) as if it were a set for a ballet.

An evening in summer. The action is continuous
with two intermissions.

ACT 1

(*At the rise of the curtain someone is taking a shower in
the bathroom, the door of which is half open. A pretty
young woman, with anxious lines in her face, enters the
bedroom and crosses to the bathroom door.*)

MARGARET (*shouting above roar of water*): One of those
no-neck monsters hit me with a hot buttered biscuit
so I have t' change!

(*Margaret's voice is both rapid and drawling. In her
long speeches she has the vocal tricks of a priest delivering a liturgical chant, the lines are almost sung, always
continuing a little beyond her breath so she has to gasp
for another. Sometimes she intersperses the lines with a
little wordless singing, such as "Da-da-daaaa!"*)

   (*Water turns off and Brick calls out to her, but is still
unseen. A tone of politely feigned interest, masking
indifference, or worse, is characteristic of his speech
with Margaret.*)

BRICK: Wha'd you say, Maggie? Water was on s' loud I
couldn't hearya. . . .

MARGARET: Well, I! — just remarked that! — one of th'
no-neck monsters messed up m' lovely lace dress so I
got t' — cha-a-ange. . . .

(*She opens and kicks shut drawers of the dresser.*)

BRICK: Why d'ya call Gooper's kiddies no-neck monsters?

MARGARET: Because they've got no necks! Isn't that a
good enough reason?

BRICK: Don't they have any necks?

MARGARET: None visible. Their fat little heads are set on
their fat little bodies without a bit of connection.

BRICK: That's too bad.

MARGARET: Yes, it's too bad because you can't wring
their necks if they've got no necks to wring! Isn't that
right, honey?

(*She steps out of her dress, stands in a slip of ivory satin
and lace.*)

Yep, they're no-neck monsters, all no-neck people
are monsters . . .

(*Children shriek downstairs.*)

Hear them? Hear them screaming? I don't know
where their voice boxes are located since they don't
have necks. I tell you I got so nervous at that table
tonight I thought I would throw back my head and
utter a scream you could hear across the Arkansas
border an' parts of Louisiana an' Tennessee. I said to

your charming sister-in-law, Mae, honey, couldn't
you feed those precious little things at a separate
table with an oilcloth cover? They make such a mess
an' the lace cloth looks *so* pretty! She made enormous eyes at me and said, "Ohhh, noooooo! On Big
Daddy's birthday? Why, he would never forgive me!"
Well, I want you to know, Big Daddy hadn't been at
the table two minutes with those five no-neck monsters slobbering and drooling over their food before
he threw down his fork an' shouted, "Fo' God's sake,
Gooper, why don't you put them pigs at a trough
in th' kitchen?" — Well, I swear, I simply could have
di-ieed!

Think of it, Brick, they've got five of them and
number six is coming. They've brought the whole
bunch down here like animals to display at a county
fair. Why, they have those children doin' tricks all the
time! "Junior, show Big Daddy how you do this,
show Big Daddy how you do that, say your little
piece fo' Big Daddy, Sister. Show your dimples,
Sugar. Brother, show Big Daddy how you stand on
your head!" — It goes on all the time, along with
constant little remarks and innuendos about the fact
that you and I have not produced any children, are
totally childless and therefore totally useless! — Of
course it's comical but it's also disgusting since it's so
obvious what they're up to!

BRICK (*without interest*): What are they up to, Maggie?

MARGARET: Why you know what they're up to!

BRICK (*appearing*): No, I don't know what they're up to.

(*He stands there in the bathroom doorway drying his
hair with a towel and hanging onto the towel rack
because one ankle is broken, plastered and bound. He is
still slim and firm as a boy. His liquor hasn't started tearing him down outside. He has the additional charm of
that cool air of detachment that people have who have
given up the struggle. But now and then, when disturbed, something flashes behind it, like lightning in a
fair sky, which shows that at some deeper level he is far
from peaceful. Perhaps in a stronger light he would
show some signs of deliquescence, but the fading, still
warm light from the gallery treats him gently.*)

MARGARET: I'll tell you what they're up to, boy of
mine! — They're up to cutting you out of your
father's estate, and —

(*She freezes momentarily before her next remark. Her
voice drops as if it were somehow a personally embarrassing admission.*)

   — Now we know that Big Daddy's dyin' of — cancer. . . .

(*There are voices on the lawn below: long-drawn calls
across distance. Margaret raises her lovely bare arms
and powders her armpits with a light sigh.*)

(*She adjusts the angle of a magnifying mirror to
straighten an eyelash, then rises fretfully saying:*)

There's so much light in the room it —
BRICK (*softly but sharply*): Do we?
MARGARET: Do we what?
BRICK: Know Big Daddy's dyin' of cancer?
MARGARET: Got the report today.
BRICK: Oh . . .
MARGARET (*letting down bamboo blinds which cast long, gold-fretted shadows over the room*): Yep, got th' report just now . . . it didn't surprise me, Baby. . . .

(*Her voice has range, and music; sometimes it drops low as a boy's and you have a sudden image of her playing boy's games as a child.*)

I recognized the symptoms soon's we got here last spring and I'm willin' to bet you that Brother Man and his wife were pretty sure of it, too. That more than likely explains why their usual summer migration to the coolness of the Great Smokies was passed up this summer in favor of — hustlin' down here ev'ry whipstitch with their whole screamin' tribe! And why so many allusions have been made to Rainbow Hill lately. You know what Rainbow Hill is? Place that's famous for treatin' alcoholics an' dope fiends in the movies!
BRICK: I'm not in the movies.
MARGARET: No, and you don't take dope. Otherwise you're a perfect candidate for Rainbow Hill, Baby, and that's where they aim to ship you — over my dead body! Yep, over my dead body they'll ship you there, but nothing would please them better. Then Brother Man could get a-hold of the purse strings and dole out remittances to us, maybe get power of attorney and sign checks for us and cut off our credit wherever, whenever he wanted! Son-of-a-bitch! — How'd you like that, Baby? — Well, you've been doin' just about ev'rything in your power to bring it about, you've just been doin' ev'rything you can think of to aid and abet them in this scheme of theirs! Quittin' work, devoting yourself to the occupation of drinkin'! — Breakin' your ankle last night on the high school athletic field: doin' what? Jumpin' hurdles? At two or three in the morning? Just fantastic! Got in the paper. *Clarksdale Register* carried a nice little item about it, human interest story about a well-known former athlete stagin' a one-man track meet on the Glorious Hill High School athletic field last night, but was slightly out of condition and didn't clear the first hurdle! Brother Man Gooper claims he exercised his influence t' keep it from goin' out over AP or UP or every goddamn "P."
     But, Brick? You still have one big advantage!

(*During the above swift flood of words, Brick has reclined with contrapuntal leisure on the snowy surface of the bed and has rolled over carefully on his side or belly.*)

BRICK (*wryly*): Did you *say* something, Maggie?
MARGARET: Big Daddy dotes on you, honey. And he can't stand Brother Man and Brother Man's wife, that monster of fertility, Mae. Know how I know? By little expressions that flicker over his face when that woman is holding fo'th on one of her choice topics such as — how she refused twilight sleep!° — when the twins were delivered! Because she feels motherhood's an experience that a woman ought to experience fully! — in order to fully appreciate the wonder and beauty of it! HAH! — and how she made Brother Man come in an' stand beside her in the delivery room so he would not miss out on the "wonder and beauty" of it either! — producin' those no-neck monsters. . . .

(*A speech of this kind would be antipathetic from almost anybody but Margaret; she makes it oddly funny, because her eyes constantly twinkle and her voice shakes with laughter which is basically indulgent.*)

     — Big Daddy shares my attitude toward those two! As for me, well — I give him a laugh now and then and he tolerates me. In fact! — I sometimes suspect that Big Daddy harbors a little unconscious "lech" fo' me. . . .
BRICK: What makes you think that Big Daddy has a lech for you, Maggie?
MARGARET: Way he always drops his eyes down my body when I'm talkin' to him, drops his eyes to my boobs an' licks his old chops! Ha ha!
BRICK: That kind of talk is disgusting.
MARGARET: Did anyone ever tell you that you're an ass-aching Puritan, Brick?
     I think it's mighty fine that that ole fellow, on the doorstep of death, still takes in my shape with what I think is deserved appreciation!
     And you wanta know something else? Big Daddy didn't know how many little Maes and Goopers had been produced! "How many kids have you got?" he asked at the table, just like Brother Man and his wife were new acquaintances to him! Big Mama said he was jokin', but that ole boy wasn't jokin', Lord, no!
     And when they infawmed him that they had five already and were turning out number six! — the news seemed to come as a sort of unpleasant surprise . . .

(*Children yell below.*)
     Scream, monsters!
(*Turns to Brick with a sudden, gay, charming smile which fades as she notices that he is not looking at her but into fading gold space with a troubled expression.*)
(*It is constant rejection that makes her humor "bitchy."*)

Yes, you should of been at that supper-table, Baby.

(*Whenever she calls him "baby" the word is a soft caress.*)

Y'know, Big Daddy, bless his ole sweet soul, he's the dearest ole thing in the world, but he does hunch over his food as if he preferred not to notice anything

twilight sleep: Anesthesia.

ABOVE LEFT: Maggie (Elizabeth
Ashley) in the 1974 American
Shakespeare Theater production
of *Cat on a Hot Tin Roof*. LEFT:
Brick (Keir Dullea) and Maggie.
ABOVE: Maggie and Big Daddy
(Fred Gwynne).

else. Well, Mae an' Gooper were side by side at the table, direckly across from Big Daddy, watchin' his face like hawks while they jawed an' jabbered about the cuteness an' brillance of th' no-neck monsters!

(*She giggles with a hand fluttering at her throat and her breast and her long throat arched.*)

(*She comes downstage and recreates the scene with voice and gesture.*)

And the no-neck monsters were ranged around the table, some in high chairs and some on th' *Books of Knowledge,* all in fancy little paper caps in honor of Big Daddy's birthday, and all through dinner, well, I want you to know that Brother Man an' his partner never once, for one moment, stopped exchanging pokes an' pinches an' kicks an' signs an' signals! — Why, they were like a couple of cardsharps fleecing a sucker. — Even Big Mama, bless her ole sweet soul, she isn't th' quickest an' brightest thing in the world, she finally noticed, at last, an' said to Gooper, "Gooper, what are you an' Mae makin' all these signs at each other about?" — I swear t' goodness, I nearly choked on my chicken!

(*Margaret, back at the dressing table, still doesn't see Brick. He is watching her with a look that is not quite definable — Amused? shocked? contemptuous? — part of those and part of something else.*)

Y'know — your brother Gooper still cherishes the illusion he took a giant step up on the social ladder when he married Miss Mae Flynn of the Memphis Flynns.

But I have a piece of Spanish news for Gooper. The Flynns never had a thing in this world but money and they lost that, they were nothing at all but fairly successful climbers. Of course, Mae Flynn came out in Memphis eight years before I made my debut in Nashville, but I had friends at Ward-Belmont who came from Memphis and they used to come to see me and I used to go to see them for Christmas and spring vacations, and so I know who rates an' who doesn't rate in Memphis society. Why, y'know ole Papa Flynn, he barely escaped doing time in the Federal pen for shady manipulations on th' stock market when his chain stores crashed, and as for Mae having been a cotton carnival queen, as they remind us so often, lest we forget, well, that's one honor that I don't envy her for! — Sit on a brass throne on a tacky float an' ride down Main Street, smilin', bowin', and blowin' kisses to all the trash on the street —

(*She picks out a pair of jeweled sandals and rushes to the dressing table.*)

Why, year before last, when Susan McPheeters was singled out fo' that honor, y' know what happened to her? Y'know what happened to poor little Susie McPheeters?

BRICK (*absently*): No. What happened to little Susie McPheeters?

MARGARET: Somebody spit tobacco juice in her face.

BRICK (*dreamily*): Somebody spit tobacco juice in her face?

MARGARET: That's right, some old drunk leaned out of a window in the Hotel Gayoso and yelled, "Hey, Queen, hey, hey, there, Queenie!" Poor Susie looked up and flashed him a radiant smile and he shot out a squirt of tobacco juice right in poor Susie's face.

BRICK: Well, what d'you know about that.

MARGARET (*gaily*): What do I know about it? I was there, I saw it!

BRICK (*absently*): Must have been kind of funny.

MARGARET: Susie didn't think so. Had hysterics. Screamed like a banshee. They had to stop th' parade an' remove her from her throne an' go on with —

(*She catches sight of him in the mirror, gasps slightly, wheels about to face him. Count ten.*)

— Why are you looking at me like that?

BRICK (*whistling softly, now*): Like what, Maggie?

MARGARET (*intensely, fearfully*): The way y' were lookin' at me just now, befo' I caught your eye in the mirror and you started t' whistle! I don't know how t' describe it but it froze my blood! — I've caught you lookin' at me like that so often lately. What are you thinkin' of when you look at me like that?

BRICK: I wasn't conscious of lookin' at you, Maggie.

MARGARET: Well, I was conscious of it! What were you thinkin'?

BRICK: I don't remember thinking of anything, Maggie.

MARGARET: Don't you think I know that — ? Don't you — ? — Think I know that — ?

BRICK (*cooly*): Know *what,* Maggie?

MARGARET (*struggling for expression*): That I've gone through this — *hideous!* — transformation, become — *hard!* Frantic!

(*Then she adds, almost tenderly:*)

— cruel!!
   That's what you've been observing in me lately. How could y' help but observe it? That's all right. I'm not — thin-skinned any more, can't afford t' be thin-skinned any more.

(*She is now recovering her power.*)

— But Brick? Brick?

BRICK: Did you say something?

MARGARET: I was goin t' say something: that I get — lonely. Very!

BRICK: Ev'rybody gets that . . .

MARGARET: Living with someone you love can be lonelier — than living entirely *alone!* — if the one that y' love doesn't love you. . . .

(*There is a pause. Brick hobbles downstage and asks, without looking at her:*)

BRICK: Would you like to live alone, Maggie?

(*Another pause: then — after she has caught a quick, hurt breath:*)

MARGARET: *No! — God! — I wouldn't!*

(*Another gasping breath. She forcibly controls what must have been an impulse to cry out. We see her deliberately, very forcibly, going all the way back to the world in which you can talk about ordinary matters.*)

Did you have a nice shower?
BRICK: Uh-huh.
MARGARET: Was the water cool?
BRICK: No.
MARGARET: But it made y' feel fresh, huh?
BRICK: Fresher. . . .
MARGARET: I know something would make y' feel *much* fresher!
BRICK: What?
MARGARET: An alcohol rub. Or cologne, a rub with cologne!
BRICK: That's good after a workout but I haven't been workin' out, Maggie.
MARGARET: You've kept in good shape, though.
BRICK (*indifferently*): You think so, Maggie?
MARGARET: I always thought drinkin' men lost their looks, but I was plainly mistaken.
BRICK (*wryly*): Why, thanks, Maggie.
MARGARET: You're the only drinkin' man I know that it never seems t' put fat on.
BRICK: I'm gettin' softer, Maggie.
MARGARET: Well, sooner or later it's bound to soften you up. It was just beginning to soften up Skipper when —

(*She stops short.*)

I'm sorry. I never could keep my fingers off a sore — I wish you *would* lose your looks. If you did it would make the martyrdom of Saint Maggie a little more bearable. But no such goddamn luck. I actually believe you've gotten better looking since you've gone on the bottle. Yeah, a person who didn't know you would think you'd never had a tense nerve in your body or a strained muscle.

(*There are sounds of croquet on the lawn below: the click of mallets, light voices, near and distant.*)

Of course, you always had that detached quality as if you were playing a game without much concern over whether you won or lost, and now that you've lost the game, not lost but just quit playing, you have that rare sort of charm that usually only happens in very old or hopelessly sick people, the charm of the defeated. — You look so cool, so cool, so enviably cool.
REVEREND TOOKER (*offstage right*): Now looka here, boy, lemme show you how to get outa that!
MARGARET: They're playing croquet. The moon has appeared and it's white, just beginning to turn a little bit yellow. . . .
 You were a wonderful lover. . . .
 Such a wonderful person to go to bed with, and I think mostly because you were really indifferent to it.

Isn't that right? Never had any anxiety about it, did it naturally, easily, slowly, with absolute confidence and perfect calm, more like opening a door for a lady or seating her at a table than giving expression to any longing for her. Your indifference made you wonderful at lovemaking — *strange?* — but true. . . .
REVEREND TOOKER: Oh! That's a beauty.
DOCTOR BAUGH: Yeah. I got you boxed.
MARGARET: You know, if I thought you would never, never, *never* make love to me again — I would go downstairs to the kitchen and pick out the longest and sharpest knife I could find and stick it straight into my heart, I swear that I would!
REVEREND TOOKER: Watch out, you're gonna miss it.
DOCTOR BAUGH: You just don't know me, boy!
MARGARET: But one thing I don't have is the charm of the defeated, my hat is still in the ring, and I am determined to win!

(*There is the sound of croquet mallets hitting croquet balls.*)

REVEREND TOOKER: Mmm — You're too slippery for me.
MARGARET: — What is the victory of a cat on a hot tin roof? — I wish I knew. . . .
 Just staying on it, I guess, as long as she can. . . .
DOCTOR BAUGH: Jus' like an eel, boy, jus' like an eel!

(*More croquet sounds.*)

MARGARET: Later tonight I'm going to tell you I love you an' maybe by that time you'll be drunk enough to believe me. Yes, they're playing croquet. . . .
 Big Daddy is dying of cancer. . . .
 What were you thinking of when I caught you looking at me like that? Were you thinking of Skipper?

(*Brick takes up his crutch, rises.*)

Oh, excuse me, forgive me, but laws of silence don't work! No, laws of silence don't work. . . .

(*Brick crosses to the bar, takes a quick drink, and rubs his head with a towel.*)

Laws of silence don't work. . . .
 When something is festering in your memory or your imagination, laws of silence don't work, it's just like shutting a door and locking it on a house on fire in hope of forgetting that the house is burning. But not facing a fire doesn't put it out. Silence about a thing just magnifies it. It grows and festers in silence, becomes malignant. . . .

(*He drops his crutch.*)

BRICK: Give me my crutch.

(*He has stopped rubbing his hair dry but still stands hanging onto the towel rack in a white towel-cloth robe.*)

MARGARET: Lean on me.
BRICK: No, just give me my crutch.

MARGARET: Lean on my shoulder.
BRICK: *I don't want to lean on your shoulder, I want my crutch!*

(*This is spoken like sudden lightning.*)

Are you going to give me my crutch or do I have to get down on my knees on the floor and —
MARGARET: *Here, here, take it, take it!*

(*She has thrust the crutch at him.*)

BRICK (*hobbling out*): Thanks . . .
MARGARET: We mustn't scream at each other, the walls in this house have ears. . . .

(*He hobbles directly to liquor cabinet to get a new drink.*)

— but that's the first time I've heard you raise your voice in a long time, Brick. A crack in the wall? — Of composure?
     — I think that's a good sign. . . .
          A sign of nerves in a player on the defensive!

(*Brick turns and smiles at her coolly over his fresh drink.*)

BRICK: It just hasn't happened yet, Maggie.
MARGARET: What?
BRICK: The click I get in my head when I've had enough of this stuff to make me peaceful. . . .
     Will you do me a favor?
MARGARET: Maybe I will. What favor?
BRICK: Just, just keep your voice down!
MARGARET (*in a hoarse whisper*): I'll do you that favor, I'll speak in a whisper, if not shut up completely, if *you* will do *me* a favor and make that drink your last one till after the party.
BRICK: What party?
MARGARET: Big Daddy's birthday party.
BRICK: Is this Big Daddy's birthday?
MARGARET: You know this is Big Daddy's birthday!
BRICK: No, I don't, I forgot it.
MARGARET: Well, I remembered it for you . . .

(*They are both speaking as breathlessly as a pair of kids after a fight, drawing deep exhausted breaths and looking at each other with faraway eyes, shaking and panting together as if they had broken apart from a violent struggle.*)

BRICK: Good for you, Maggie.
MARGARET: You just have to scribble a few lines on this card.
BRICK: You scribble something, Maggie.
MARGARET: It's got to be your handwriting; it's your present, I've given him my present; it's got to be your handwriting!

(*The tension between them is building again, the voices becoming shrill once more.*)

BRICK: I didn't get him a present.
MARGARET: I got one for you.

BRICK: All right. You write the card, then.
MARGARET: And have him know you didn't remember his birthday?
BRICK: I didn't remember his birthday.
MARGARET: You don't have to prove you didn't!
BRICK: I don't want to fool him about it.
MARGARET: Just write "Love, Brick!" for God's —
BRICK: No.
MARGARET: You've *got* to!
BRICK: I don't have to do anything I don't want to do. You keep forgetting the conditions on which I agreed to stay on living with you.
MARGARET (*out before she knows it*): I'm not living with you. We occupy the same cage.
BRICK: You've got to remember the conditions agreed on.
SONNY (*offstage*): Mommy, give it to me. I had it first.
MAE: Hush.
MARGARET: They're impossible conditions!
BRICK: Then why don't you — ?
SONNY: I want it, I want it!
MAE: Get away!
MARGARET: HUSH! Who is out there? Is somebody at the door?

(*There are footsteps in hall.*)

MAE (*outside*): May I enter a moment?
MARGARET: Oh, *you!* Sure. Come in, Mae.

(*Mae enters bearing aloft the bow of a young lady's archery set.*)

MAE: Brick, is this thing yours?
MARGARET: Why, Sister Woman — that's my Diana Trophy. Won it at the intercollegiate archery contest on the Ole Miss campus.
MAE: It's a mighty dangerous thing to leave exposed round a house full of nawmal rid-blooded children attracted t'weapons.
MARGARET: "Nawmal rid-blooded children attracted t'weapons" ought t'be taught to keep their hands off things that don't belong to them.
MAE: Maggie, honey, if you had children of your own you'd know how funny that is. Will you please lock this up and put the key out of reach?
MARGARET: Sister Woman, nobody is plotting the destruction of your kiddies. — Brick and I still have our special archers' license. We're goin' deer-huntin' on Moon Lake as soon as the season starts. I love to run with dogs through chilly woods, run, run leap over obstructions —

(*She goes into the closet carrying the bow.*)

MAE: How's the injured ankle, Brick?
BRICK: Doesn't hurt. Just itches.
MAE: Oh, my! Brick — Brick, you should've been downstairs after supper! Kiddies put on a show. Polly played the piano, Buster an' Sonny drums, an' then they turned out the lights an' Dixie an' Trixie puh-fawmed a toe dance in fairy costume with *spahkluhs!* Big Daddy just beamed! He just beamed!

MARGARET (*from the closet with a sharp laugh*): Oh, I bet. It breaks my heart that we missed it!

(*She reenters.*)

But Mae? Why did y'give dawgs' names to all your kiddies?
MAE: *Dogs'* names?
MARGARET (*sweetly*): Dixie, Trixie, Buster, Sonny, Polly! — Sounds like four dogs and a parrot . . .
MAE: Maggie?

(*Margaret turns with a smile.*)

Why are you so catty?
MARGARET: Cause I'm a cat! But why can't *you* take a joke, Sister Woman?
MAE: Nothin' pleases me more than a joke that's funny. You know the real names of our kiddies. Buster's real name is Robert. Sonny's real name is Saunders. Trixie's real name is Marlene and Dixie's —

(*Gooper downstairs calls for her. "Hey, Mae! Sister Woman, intermission is over!" — She rushes to door, saying:*)

Intermission is over! See ya later!
MARGARET: I wonder what Dixie's real name is?
BRICK: Maggie, being catty doesn't help things any . . .
MARGARET: I know! *WHY!* — Am I so catty? — Cause I'm consumed with envy an' eaten up with longing? — Brick, I'm going to lay out your beautiful Shantung silk suit from Rome and one of your monogrammed silk shirts. I'll put your cuff links in it, those lovely star sapphires I get you to wear so rarely. . . .
BRICK: I can't get trousers on over this plaster cast.
MARGARET: Yes, you can, I'll help you.
BRICK: I'm not going to get dressed, Maggie.
MARGARET: Will you just put on a pair of white silk pajamas?
BRICK: Yes, I'll do that, Maggie.
MARGARET: *Thank* you, thank you so *much!*
BRICK: Don't mention it.
MARGARET: *Oh, Brick!* How long does it have t' go on? This punishment? Haven't I done time enough, haven't I served my term, can't I apply for a — pardon?
BRICK: Maggie, you're spoiling my liquor. Lately your voice always sounds like you'd been running upstairs to warn somebody that the house was on fire!
MARGARET: Well, no wonder, no wonder. Y'know what I feel like, Brick?
    I feel all the time like a cat on a hot tin roof!
BRICK: Then jump off the roof, jump off it, cats can jump off roofs and land on their four feet uninjured!
MARGARET: Oh, yes!
BRICK: Do it! — fo' God's sake, do it . . .
MARGARET: Do what?
BRICK: Take a lover!
MARGARET: I can't see a man but you! Even with my eyes closed, I just see you! Why don't you get ugly, Brick, why don't you please get fat or ugly or something so I could stand it?

(*She rushes to hall door, opens it, listens.*)

The concert is still going on! Bravo, no-necks, bravo!

(*She slams and locks door fiercely.*)

BRICK: What did you lock the door for?
MARGARET: To give us a little privacy for a while.
BRICK: You know better, Maggie.
MARGARET: No, I don't know better. . . .

(*She rushes to gallery doors, draws the rose-silk drapes across them.*)

BRICK: Don't make a fool of yourself.
MARGARET: I don't mind makin' a fool of myself over you!
BRICK: I mind, Maggie. I feel embarrassed for you.
MARGARET: Feel embarrassed! But don't continue my torture. I can't live on and on under these circumstances.
BRICK: You agreed to —
MARGARET: I know but —
BRICK: — Accept that condition!
MARGARET: *I CAN'T! CAN'T! CAN'T!*

(*She seizes his shoulder.*)

BRICK: Let go!

(*He breaks away from her and seizes the small boudoir chair and raises it like a lion-tamer facing a big circus cat.*)
(*Count five. She stares at him with her fist pressed to her mouth, then bursts into shrill, almost hysterical laughter. He remains grave for a moment, then grins and puts the chair down.*)
(*Big Mama calls through closed door.*)

BIG MAMA: Son? Son? Son?
BRICK: What is it, Big Mama?
BIG MAMA (*outside*): Oh, son! We got the most wonderful news about Big Daddy. I just had t' run up an' tell you right this —

(*She rattles the knob.*)

— What's this door doin', locked, faw? You all think there's robbers in the house?
MARGARET: Big Mama, Brick is dressin, he's not dressed yet.
BIG MAMA: That's all right, it won't be the first time I've seen Brick not dressed. Come on, open this door!

(*Margaret, with a grimace, goes to unlock and open the hall door, as Brick hobbles rapidly to the bathroom and kicks the door shut. Big Mama has disappeared from the hall.*)

MARGARET: Big Mama?

(*Big Mama appears through the opposite gallery doors behind Margaret, huffing and puffing like an old bulldog. She is a short, stout woman; her sixty years and 170 pounds have left her somewhat breathless most of the time; she's always tensed like a boxer, or rather, a*)

Japanese wrestler. Her "family" was maybe a little superior to Big Daddy's, but not much. She wears a black or silver lace dress and at least half a million in flashy gems. She is very sincere.)

BIG MAMA (*loudly, startling Margaret*): Here — I come through Gooper's and Mae's gall'ry door. Where's Brick? *Brick* — Hurry on out of there son, I just have a second and want to give you the news about Big Daddy. — I hate locked doors in a house . . .

MARGARET (*with affected lightness*): I've noticed you do, Big Mama, but people have got to have *some* moments of privacy, don't they?

BIG MAMA: No, ma'am, not in *my* house. (*Without pause.*) Whacha took off you' dress faw? I thought that little lace dress was so sweet on yuh, honey.

MARGARET: I thought it looked sweet on me, too, but one of m' cute little table-partners used it for a napkin so — !

BIG MAMA (*picking up stockings on floor*): What?

MARGARET: You know, Big Mama, Mae and Gooper's so touchy about those children — thanks, Big Mama . . .

(*Big Mama has thrust the picked-up stockings in Margaret's hand with a grunt.*)

— that you just don't dare to suggest there's any room for improvement in their —

BIG MAMA: Brick, hurry out! — Shoot, Maggie, you just don't like children.

MARGARET: I do SO like children! Adore them! — well brought up!

BIG MAMA (*gentle — loving*): Well, why don't you have some and bring them up well, then, instead of all the time pickin' on Gooper's an' Mae's?

GOOPER (*shouting up the stairs*): Hey, hey, Big Mama, Betsy an' Hugh got to go, waitin' t' tell yuh g'by!

BIG MAMA: Tell 'em to hold their hawses, I'll be right down in a jiffy!

GOOPER: Yes ma'am!

(*She turns to the bathroom door and calls out.*)

BIG MAMA: Son? Can you hear me in there?

(*There is a muffled answer.*)

We just got the full report from the laboratory at the Ochsner Clinic, completely negative, son, ev'rything negative, right on down the line! Nothin' a-tall's wrong with him but some little functional thing called a spastic colon. Can you hear me, son?

MARGARET: He can hear you, Big Mama.

BIG MAMA: Then why don't he say something? God Almighty, a piece of news like that should make him shout. It made *me* shout, I can tell you. I shouted and sobbed and fell right down on my knees! — Look!

(*She pulls up her skirt.*)

See the bruises where I hit my kneecaps? Took both doctors to haul me back on my feet!

(*She laughs — she always laughs like hell at herself.*)

Big Daddy was furious with me! But ain't that wonderful news?

(*Facing bathroom again, she continues:*)

After all the anxiety we been through to git a report like that on Big Daddy's birthday? Big Daddy tried to hide how much of a load that news took off his mind, but didn't fool *me*. He was mighty close to crying about it *himself!*

(*Good-byes are shouted downstairs, and she rushes to door.*)

GOOPER: Big Mama!

BIG MAMA: *Hold those people down there, don't let them go!* — Now, git dressed we're all comin' up to this room fo' Big Daddy's birthday party because of your ankle. — How's his ankle, Maggie?

MARGARET: Well, he broke it, Big Mama.

BIG MAMA: I know he broke it.

(*A phone is ringing in hall. A Negro voice answers: "Mistuh Polly's res'dence."*)

I mean does it hurt him much still.

MARGARET: I'm afraid I can't give you that information, Big Mama. You'll have to ask Brick if it hurts much still or not.

SOOKEY (*in the hall*): It's Memphis, Mizz Polly, it's Miss Sally in Memphis.

BIG MAMA: Awright, Sookey.

(*Big Mama rushes into the hall and is heard shouting on the phone:*)

Hello, Miss Sally. How are you, Miss Sally? — Yes, well, I was just gonna call you about it. *Shoot!* —

MARGARET: Brick, don't!

(*Big Mama raises her voice to a bellow.*)

BIG MAMA: *Miss Sally? Don't ever call me from the Gayoso Lobby, too much talk goes on in that hotel lobby, no wonder you can't hear me!* Now listen, Miss Sally. They's nothin' serious wrong with Big Daddy. We got the report just now, they's nothin' wrong but a thing called a — spastic! SPASTIC! — colon . . .

(*She appears at the hall door and calls to Margaret.*)

— Maggie, come out here and talk to that fool on the phone. I'm shouted breathless!

MARGARET (*goes out and is heard sweetly at phone*): Miss Sally? This is Brick's wife, Maggie. So nice to hear your voice. Can you hear *mine*? Well, *good!* — Big Mama just wanted you to know that they've got the report from the Ochsner Clinic and what Big Daddy has is a spastic colon. Yes. Spastic colon, Miss Sally. That's right, spastic colon. *G'bye, Miss Sally, hope I'll see you real soon!*

(*Hangs up a little before Miss Sally was probably ready to terminate the talk. She returns through the hall door.*)

She heard me perfectly. I've discovered with deaf

people the thing to do is not shout at them but just enunciate clearly. My rich old Aunt Cornelia was deaf as the dead but I could make her hear me just by sayin' each word slowly, distinctly, close to her ear. I read her the *Commercial Appeal* ev'ry night, read her the classified ads in it, even, she never missed a word of it. But was she a mean ole thing! Know what I got when she died? Her unexpired subscriptions to five magazines and the Book-of-the-Month Club and a LIBRARY full of ev'ry dull book ever written! All else went to her hellcat of a sister . . . meaner than she was, even!

(*Big Mama has been straightening things up in the room during this speech.*)

BIG MAMA (*closing closet door on discarded clothes*): Miss Sally sure is a case! Big Daddy says she's always got her hand out fo' something. He's not mistaken. That poor ole thing always has her hand out fo' somethin'. I don't think Big Daddy gives her as much as he should.

GOOPER: Big Mama! Come on now! Betsy and Hugh can't wait no longer!

BIG MAMA (*shouting*): I'm comin'!

(*She starts out. At the hall door, turns and jerks a forefinger, first toward the bathroom door, then toward the liquor cabinet, meaning: "Has Brick been drinking?" Margaret pretends not to understand, cocks her head and raises her brows as if the pantomimic performance was completely mystifying to her.*)
(*Big Mama rushes back to Margaret:*)

Shoot! Stop playin' so dumb! — I mean has he been drinkin' that stuff much yet?

MARGARET (*with a little laugh*): Oh! I think he had a highball after supper.

BIG MAMA: Don't laugh about it! — Some single men stop drinkin' when they git married and others start! Brick never touched liquor before he — !

MARGARET (*crying out*): *THAT'S NOT FAIR!*

BIG MAMA: Fair or not fair I want to ask you a question, one question: D'you make Brick happy in bed?

MARGARET: Why don't you ask if he makes *me* happy in bed?

BIG MAMA: Because I know that —

MARGARET: *It works both ways!*

BIG MAMA: Something's not right! You're childless and my son drinks!

GOOPER: Come on, Big Mama!

(*Gooper has called her downstairs and she has rushed to the door on the line above. She turns at the door and points at the bed.*)

— When a marriage goes on the rocks, the rocks are *there*, right *there!*

MARGARET: That's —

(*Big Mama has swept out of the room and slammed the door.*)

— not — *fair* . . .

(*Margaret is alone, completely alone, and she feels it. She draws in, hunches her shoulders, raises her arms with fists clenched, shuts her eyes tight as a child about to be stabbed with a vaccination needle. When she opens her eyes again, what she sees is the long oval mirror and she rushes straight to it, stares into it with a grimace and says: "Who are you?" — Then she crouches a little and answers herself in a different voice which is high, thin, mocking: "I am Maggie the Cat!" — Straightens quickly as bathroom door opens a little and Brick calls out to her.*)

BRICK: Has Big Mama gone?
MARGARET: She's gone.

(*He opens the bathroom door and hobbles out, with his liquor glass now empty, straight to the liquor cabinet. He is whistling softly. Margaret's head pivots on her long, slender throat to watch him.*)
(*She raises a hand uncertainly to the base of her throat, as if it was difficult for her to swallow, before she speaks:*)

You know, our sex life didn't just peter out in the usual way, it was cut off short, long before the natural time for it to, and it's going to revive again, just as sudden as that. I'm confident of it. That's what I'm keeping myself attractive for. For the time when you'll see me again like other men see me. Yes, like other men see me. They still see me, Brick, and they like what they see. Uh-huh. Some of them would give their —
     Look, Brick!

(*She stands before the long oval mirror, touches her breast and then her hips with her two hands.*)

How high my body stays on me! — Nothing has fallen on me — not a fraction. . . .

(*Her voice is soft and trembling: a pleading child's. At this moment as he turns to glance at her — a look which is like a player passing a ball to another player, third down and goal to go — she has to capture the audience in a grip so tight that she can hold it till the first intermission without any lapse of attention.*)

Other men still want me. My face looks strained, sometimes, but I've kept my figure as well as you've kept yours, and men admire it. I still turn heads on the street. Why, last week in Memphis everywhere that I went men's eyes burned holes in my clothes, at the country club and in restaurants and department stores, there wasn't a man I met or walked by that didn't just eat me up with his eyes and turn around when I passed him and look back at me. Why, at Alice's party for her New York cousins, the best-lookin' man in the crowd — followed me upstairs and tried to force his way in the powder room with me, followed me to the door and tried to force his way in!

BRICK: Why didn't you let him, Maggie?
MARGARET: Because I'm not that common, for one

thing. Not that I wasn't almost tempted to. You like to know who it was? It was Sonny Boy Maxwell, that's who!

BRICK: Oh, yeah, Sonny Boy Maxwell, he was a good end-runner but had a little injury to his back and had to quit.

MARGARET: He has no injury now and has no wife and still has a lech for me!

BRICK: I see no reason to lock him out of a powder room in that case.

MARGARET: And have someone catch me at it? I'm not that stupid. Oh, I might sometime cheat on you with someone, since you're so insultingly eager to have me do it! — But if I do, you can be damned sure it will be in a place and a time where no one but me and the man could possibly know. Because I'm not going to give you any excuse to divorce me for being unfaithful or anything else. . . .

BRICK: Maggie, I wouldn't divorce you for being unfaithful or anything else. Don't you know that? Hell. I'd be relieved to know that you'd found yourself a lover.

MARGARET: Well, I'm taking no chances. No, I'd rather stay on this hot tin roof.

BRICK: A hot tin roof's 'n uncomfo'table place t' stay on. . . .

(He starts to whistle softly.)

MARGARET (through his whistle): Yeah, but I can stay on it just as long as I have to.

BRICK: You could leave me, Maggie.

(He resumes whistle. She wheels about to glare at him.)

MARGARET: *Don't want to and will not!* Besides if I did, you don't have a cent to pay for it but what you get from Big Daddy and he's dying of cancer!

(For the first time a realization of Big Daddy's doom seems to penetrate to Brick's consciousness, visibly, and he looks at Margaret.)

BRICK: Big Mama just said he *wasn't*, that the report was okay.

MARGARET: That's what she thinks because she got the same story that they gave Big Daddy. And was just as taken in by it as he was, poor ole things. . . .

But tonight they're going to tell her the truth about it. When Big Daddy goes to bed, they're going to tell her that he is dying of cancer.

(She slams the dresser drawer.)

— It's malignant and it's terminal.

BRICK: Does Big Daddy know it?

MARGARET: Hell, do they *ever* know it? Nobody says, "You're dying." You have to fool them. They have to fool *themselves*.

BRICK: Why?

MARGARET: *Why?* Because human beings dream of life everlasting, that's the reason! But most of them want it on earth and not in heaven.

(He gives a short, hard laugh at her touch of humor.)

Well. . . . (She touches up her mascara.) That's how it is, anyhow. . . . (She looks about.) Where did I put down my cigarette? Don't want to burn up the home-place, at least not with Mae and Gooper and their five monsters in it!

(She has found it and sucks at it greedily. Blows out smoke and continues:)

So this is Big Daddy's last birthday. And Mae and Gooper, they know it, oh, *they* know it, all right. They got the first information from the Ochsner Clinic. That's why they rushed down here with their no-neck monsters. Because. Do you know something? Big Daddy's made no will? Big Daddy's never made out any will in his life, and so this campaign's afoot to impress him, forcibly as possible, with the fact that you drink and I've borne no children!

(He continues to stare at her a moment, then mutters something sharp but not audible and hobbles rather rapidly out onto the long gallery in the fading, much faded, gold light.)

MARGARET (continuing her liturgical chant): Y'know, I'm *fond* of Big Daddy, I am genuinely fond of that old man, I really *am*, you know. . . .

BRICK (faintly, vaguely): Yes, I know you are. . . .

MARGARET: I've always sort of admired him in spite of his coarseness, his four-letter words and so forth. Because Big Daddy *is* what he *is*, and he makes no bones about it. He hasn't turned gentleman farmer, he's still a Mississippi redneck, as much of a redneck as he must have been when he was just overseer here on the old Jack Straw and Peter Ochello place. But he got hold of it an' built it into th' biggest an' finest plantation in the Delta. — I've always *liked* Big Daddy. . . .

(She crosses to the proscenium.)

Well, this is Big Daddy's last birthday. I'm sorry about it. But I'm facing the facts. It takes money to take care of a drinker and that's the office that I've been elected to lately.

BRICK: You don't have to take care of me.

MARGARET: Yes, I do. Two people in the same boat have got to take care of each other. At least you want money to buy more Echo Spring when this supply is exhausted, or will you be satisfied with a ten-cent beer?

Mae an' Gooper are plannin' to freeze us out of Big Daddy's estate because you drink and I'm child-less. But we can defeat that plan. We're *going* to defeat that plan!

Brick, y'know, I've been so God damn disgustingly poor all my life! — That's the *truth*, Brick!

BRICK: I'm not sayin' it isn't.

MARGARET: Always had to suck up to people I couldn't

stand because they had money and I was poor as Job's turkey. You don't know what that's like. Well, I'll tell you, it's like you would feel a thousand miles away from Echo Spring! — And had to get back to it on that broken ankle . . . without a crutch!

That's how it feels to be as poor as Job's turkey and have to suck up to relatives that you hated because they had money and all you had was a bunch of hand-me-down clothes and a few old moldy three-percent government bonds. My daddy loved his liquor, he fell in love with his liquor the way you've fallen in love with Echo Spring! — And my poor Mama, having to maintain some semblance of social position, to keep appearances up, on an income of one hundred and fifty dollars a month on those old government bonds!

When I came out, the year that I made my debut, I had just two evening dresses! One Mother made me from a pattern in *Vogue*, the other a hand-me-down from a snotty rich cousin I hated!

— The dress that I married you in was my grand-mother's weddin' gown. . . .

So that's why I'm like a cat on a hot tin roof!

(*Brick is still on the gallery. Someone below calls up to him in a warm Negro voice, "Hiya, Mistuh Brick, how yuh feelin'?" Brick raises his liquor glass as if that answered the question.*)

MARGARET: You can be young without money, but you can't be old without it. You've got to be old *with* money because to be old without it is just too awful, you've got to be one or the other, either *young* or *with money,* you can't be old and *without* it. — That's the *truth,* Brick. . . .

(*Brick whistles softly, vaguely.*)

Well, now I'm dressed, I'm all dressed, there's nothing else for me to do.

(*Forlornly, almost fearfully.*)

I'm dressed, all dressed, nothing else for me to do . . .

(*She moves about restlessly, aimlessly, and speaks, as if to herself.*)

What am I — ? Oh! — my bracelets. . . .

(*She starts working a collection of bracelets over her hands onto her wrists, about six on each, as she talks.*)

I've thought a whole lot about it and now I know when I made my mistake. Yes, I made my mistake when I told you the truth about that thing with Skipper. Never should have confessed it, a fatal error, tellin' you about that thing with Skipper.
BRICK: Maggie, shut up about Skipper. I mean it, Maggie; you got to shut up about Skipper.
MARGARET: You ought to understand that Skipper and I —
BRICK: You don't think I'm serious, Maggie? You're fooled by the fact that I am saying this quiet? Look,

Maggie. What you're doing is a dangerous thing to do. You're — you're — you're — foolin' with something that — nobody ought to fool with.
MARGARET: This time I'm going to finish what I have to say to you. Skipper and I made love, if love you could call it, because it made both of us feel a little bit closer to you. You see, you son of a bitch, you asked too much of people, of me, of him, of all the unlucky poor damned sons of bitches that happen to love you, and there was a whole pack of them, yes, there was a pack of them besides me and Skipper, you asked too goddamn much of people that loved you, you — superior creature! — you godlike being! — And so we made love to each other to dream it was you, both of us! Yes, yes, yes! Truth, truth! What's so awful about it? I like it, I think the truth is — yeah! I shouldn't have told you. . . .
BRICK (*holding his head unnaturally still and uptilted a bit*): It was Skipper that told me about it. Not you, Maggie.
MARGARET: I told you!
BRICK: After he told me!
MARGARET: What does it matter who — ?
DIXIE: I got your mallet, I got your mallet.
TRIXIE: Give it to me, give it to me. IT's mine.

(*Brick turns suddenly out upon the gallery and calls:*)

BRICK: Little girl! Hey, little girl!
LITTLE GIRL (*at a distance*): What, Uncle Brick?
BRICK: Tell the folks to come up! — Bring everybody upstairs!
TRIXIE: It's mine, it's mine.
MARGARET: I can't stop myself! I'd go on telling you this in front of them all, if I had to!
BRICK: Little girl! Go on, go on, will you? Do what I told you, call them!
DIXIE: Okay.
MARGARET: Because it's got to be told and you, you! — you never let me!

(*She sobs, then controls herself, and continues almost calmly.*)

It was one of those beautiful, ideal things they tell about in the Greek legends, it couldn't be anything else, you being you, and that's what made it so sad, that's what made it so awful, because it was love that never could be carried through to anything satisfying or even talked about plainly.
BRICK: Maggie, you gotta stop this.
MARGARET: Brick, I tell you, you got to believe me, Brick, I *do* understand all about it! I — I think it was — *noble!* Can't you tell I'm sincere when I say I respect it? My only point, the only point that I'm making, is life has got to be allowed to continue even after the *dream* of life is — all — over. . . .

(*Brick is without his crutch. Leaning on furniture, he crosses to pick it up as she continues as if possessed by a will outside herself:*)

ABOVE: Kathleen Turner as Maggie in the 1990 Eugene O'Neill Theatre production of *Cat on a Hot Tin Roof*, directed by Howard Davies. BELOW: Brick (Daniel Hugh Kelly) and Maggie. (Photos by Michael Tighe.)

Why I remember when we double-dated at college, Gladys Fitzgerald and I and you and Skipper, it was more like a date between you and Skipper. Gladys and I were just sort of tagging along as if it was necessary to chaperone you! — to make a good public impression —

BRICK (*turns to face her, half lifting his crutch*): Maggie, you want me to hit you with this crutch? Don't you know I could kill you with this crutch?

MARGARET: Good Lord, man, d' you think I'd care if you did?

BRICK: One man has one great good true thing in his life. One great good thing which is true! — I had friendship with Skipper. — You are naming it dirty!

MARGARET: I'm not naming it dirty! I am naming it clean.

BRICK: Not love with you, Maggie, but friendship with Skipper was that one great true thing, and you are naming it dirty!

MARGARET: Then you haven't been listenin', not understood what I'm saying! I'm naming it so damn clean that it killed poor Skipper! — You two had something that had to be kept on ice, yes, incorruptible, yes! — and death was the only icebox where you could keep it. . . .

BRICK: I married you, Maggie. Why would I marry you, Maggie, if I was — ?

MARGARET: Brick, let me finish! — I know, believe me I know, that it was only Skipper that harbored even any *unconscious* desire for anything not perfectly pure between you two! — Now let me skip a little. You married me early that summer we graduated out of Ole Miss, and we were happy, weren't we, we were blissful, yes, hit heaven together ev'ry time that we loved! But that fall you an' Skipper turned down wonderful offers of jobs in order to keep on bein' football heroes — pro-football heroes. You organized the Dixie Stars that fall, so you could keep on bein' teammates forever! But somethin' was not right with it! — *Me included!* — between you. Skipper began hittin' the bottle . . . you got a spinal injury — couldn't play the Thanksgivin' game in Chicago, watched it on TV from a traction bed in Toledo. I joined Skipper. The Dixie Stars lost because poor Skipper was drunk. We drank together that night all night in the bar of the Blackstone and when cold day was comin' up over the Lake an' we were comin' out drunk to take a dizzy look at it, I said, "SKIPPER! STOP LOVIN' MY HUSBAND OR TELL HIM HE'S GOT TO LET YOU ADMIT IT TO HIM!" — one way or another!

HE SLAPPED ME HARD ON THE MOUTH! — then turned and ran without stopping once, I am sure, all the way back into his room at the Blackstone. . . .

— When I came to his room that night, with a little scratch like a shy little mouse at his door, he made that pitiful, ineffectual little attempt to prove that what I had said wasn't true. . . .

(*Brick strikes at her with crutch, a blow that shatters the gemlike lamp on the table.*)

— In this way, I destroyed him, by telling him truth that he and his world which he was born and raised in, yours and his world, had told him could not be told?

— From then on Skipper was nothing at all but a receptacle for liquor and drugs. . . .

— Who shot cock robin? I with my —

(*She throws back her head with tight shut eyes.*)

— merciful arrow!

(*Brick strikes at her; misses.*)

Missed me! — Sorry, — I'm not tryin' to whitewash my behavior, Christ, no! Brick, I'm not good. I don't know why people have to pretend to be good, nobody's good. The rich or the well-to-do can afford to respect moral patterns, conventional moral patterns, but I could never afford to, yeah, but — I'm honest! Give me credit for just that, will you *please?* — Born poor, raised poor, expect to die poor unless I manage to get us something out of what Big Daddy leaves when he dies of cancer! But Brick?! — *Skipper is dead! I'm alive!* Maggie the cat is —

(*Brick hops awkwardly forward and strikes at her again with his crutch.*)

— alive! I am alive, alive! I am . . .

(*He hurls the crutch at her, across the bed she took refuge behind, and pitches forward on the floor as she completes her speech.*)

— alive!

(*A little girl, Dixie, bursts into the room, wearing an Indian war bonnet and firing a cap pistol at Margaret and shouting: "Bang, bang, bang!"*)

(*Laughter downstairs floats through the open hall door. Margaret had crouched gasping to bed at child's entrance. She now rises and says with cool fury:*)

Little girl, your mother or someone should teach you — (*gasping*) — to knock at a door before you come into a room. Otherwise people might think that you — lack — good breeding. . . .

DIXIE: Yanh, yanh, yanh, what is Uncle Brick doin' on th' floor?

BRICK: I tried to kill your Aunt Maggie, but I failed — and I fell. Little girl, give me my crutch so I can get up off th' floor.

MARGARET: Yes, give your uncle his crutch, he's a cripple, honey, he broke his ankle last night jumping hurdles on the high school athletic field!

DIXIE: What were you jumping hurdles for, Uncle Brick?

BRICK: Because I used to jump them, and people like to do what they used to do, even after they've stopped being able to do it. . . .

MARGARET: That's right, that's your answer, now go away, little girl.

(*Dixie fires cap pistol at Margaret three times.*)

    Stop, you stop that, monster! You little no-neck monster!

(*She seizes the cap pistol and hurls it through gallery doors.*)

DIXIE (*with a precocious instinct for the cruelest thing*): You're *jealous!* — You're just jealous because you can't have babies!

(*She sticks out her tongue at Margaret as she sashays past her with her stomach stuck out, to the gallery. Margaret slams the gallery doors and leans panting against them. There is a pause. Brick has replaced his spilt drink and sits, faraway, on the great four-poster bed.*)

MARGARET: You see? — they gloat over us being childless, even in front of their five little no-neck monsters!

(*Pauses. Voices approach on the stairs.*)

    Brick? — I've been to a doctor in Memphis, a — a gynecologist. . . .
    I've been completely examined, and there is no reason why we can't have a child whenever we want one. And this is my time by the calendar to conceive. Are you listening to me? Are you? Are you LISTENING TO ME!

BRICK: Yes. I hear you, Maggie.

(*His attention returns to her inflamed face.*)

    — But how in hell on earth do you imagine — that you're going to have a child by a man that can't stand you?

MARGARET: That's a problem that I will have to work out.

(*She wheels about to face the hall door.*)

MAE (*offstage left*): Come on, Big Daddy. We're all goin' up to Brick's room.

(*From offstage left, voices: Reverend Tooker, Doctor Baugh, Mae.*)

MARGARET: *Here they come!*

(*The lights dim.*)

ACT 2

(*There is no lapse of time. Margaret and Brick are in the same positions they held at the end of act 1.*)

MARGARET (*at door*): Here they come!

(*Big Daddy appears first, a tall man with a fierce, anxious look, moving carefully not to betray his weakness even, or especially, to himself.*)

GOOPER: I read in the *Register* that you're getting a new memorial window.

(*Some of the people are approaching through the hall, others along the gallery: voices from both directions. Gooper and Reverend Tooker become visible outside gallery doors, and their voices come in clearly.*)
(*They pause outside as Gooper lights a cigar.*)

REVEREND TOOKER (*vivaciously*): Oh, but St. Paul's in Grenada has three memorial windows, and the latest one is a Tiffany stained-glass window that cost twenty-five hundred dollars, a picture of Christ the Good Shepherd with a Lamb in His arms.

MARGARET: Big Daddy.

BIG DADDY: Well, Brick.

BRICK: Hello Big Daddy. — Congratulations!

BIG DADDY: — Crap. . . .

GOOPER: Who give that window, Preach?

REVEREND TOOKER: Clyde Fletcher's widow. Also presented St. Paul's with a baptismal font.

GOOPER: Y'know what somebody ought t' give your church is a *coolin'* system, Preach.

MAE (*almost religiously*): — Let's see now, they've had their *tyyy*-phoid shots, and their tetanus shots, their diphtheria shots and their hepatitis shots and their polio shots, they got *those* shots every month from May through September, and — Gooper? Hey! Gooper! — What all have the kiddies been shot faw?

REVEREND TOOKER: Yes, siree, Bob! And y'know what Gus Hamma's family gave in his memory to the church at Two Rivers? A complete new stone parish-house with a basketball court in the basement and a —

BIG DADDY (*uttering a loud barking laugh which is far from truly mirthful*): Hey, Preach! What's all this talk about memorials, Preach? Y' think somebody's about t' kick off around here? 'S that it?

(*Startled by this interjection, Reverend Tooker decides to laugh at the question almost as loud as he can.*)
(*How he would answer the question we'll never know, as he's spared that embarrassment by the voice of Gooper's wife, Mae, rising high and clear as she appears with "Doc" Baugh, the family doctor, through the hall door.*)

MARGARET (*overlapping a bit*): Turn on the hi-fi, Brick! Let's have some music t' start off th' party with!

BRICK: You turn it on, Maggie.

(*The talk becomes so general that the room sounds like a great aviary of chattering birds. Only Brick remains unengaged, leaning upon the liquor cabinet with his faraway smile, an ice cube in a paper napkin with which he now and then rubs his forehead. He doesn't respond to Margaret's command. She bounds forward and stoops over the instrument panel of the console.*)

GOOPER: We gave 'em that thing for a third anniversary present, got three speakers in it.

(*The room is suddenly blasted by the climax of a Wagnerian opera or a Beethoven symphony.*)

BIG DADDY: *Turn that damn thing off!*

(*Almost instant silence, almost instantly broken by the shouting charge of Big Mama, entering through hall door like a charging rhino.*)

BIG MAMA: *Wha's my Brick, wha's mah precious baby!!*
BIG DADDY: *Sorry! Turn it back on!*

(*Everyone laughs very loud. Big Daddy is famous for his jokes at Big Mama's expense, and nobody laughs louder at these jokes than Big Mama herself, though sometimes they're pretty cruel and Big Mama has to pick up or fuss with something to cover the hurt that the loud laugh doesn't quite cover.*)

   (*On this occasion, a happy occasion because the dread in her heart has also been lifted by the false report on Big Daddy's condition, she giggles, grotesquely, coyly, in Big Daddy's direction and bears down upon Brick, all very quick and alive.*)

BIG MAMA: Here he is, here's my precious baby! What's that you've got in your hand? You put that liquor down, son, your hand was made fo' holdin' some-thin' better than that!
GOOPER: Look at Brick put it down!

(*Brick has obeyed Big Mama by draining the glass and handing it to her. Again everyone laughs, some high, some low.*)

BIG MAMA: Oh, you bad boy, you, you're my bad little boy. Give Big Mama a kiss, you bad boy, you! — Look at him shy away, will you? Brick never liked bein' kissed or made a fuss over, I guess because he's always had too much of it!
   Son, you turn that thing off!

(*Brick has switched on the TV set.*)

   I can't stand TV, radio was bad enough but TV has gone it one better, I mean — (*plops wheezing in chair*) — one worse, ha ha! Now what'm I sittin' down here faw? I want t' sit next to my sweetheart on the sofa, hold hands with him and love him up a little!

(*Big Mama has on a black and white figured chiffon. The large irregular patterns, like the markings of some mas-sive animal, the luster of her great diamonds and many pearls, the brilliants set in the silver frames of her glasses, her riotous voice, booming laugh, have dominated the room since she entered. Big Daddy has been regarding her with a steady grimace of chronic annoyance.*)

BIG MAMA (*still louder*): Preacher, Preacher, hey, Preach!
   Give me you' hand an' help me up from this chair!
REVEREND TOOKER: None of your tricks, Big Mama!
BIG MAMA: What tricks? You give me you' hand so I can get up an' —

(*Reverend Tooker extends her his hand. She grabs it and pulls him into her lap with a shrill laugh that spans an octave in two notes.*)

Ever seen a preacher in a fat lady's lap? Hey, hey, folks! Ever seen a preacher in a fat lady's lap?

(*Big Mama is notorious throughout the Delta for this sort of inelegant horseplay. Margaret looks on with indulgent humor, sipping Dubonnet "on the rocks" and watching Brick, but Mae and Gooper exchange signs of humorless anxiety over these antics, the sort of behavior which Mae thinks may account for their failure to quite get in with the smartest young married set in Memphis, despite all. One of the Negroes, Lacey or Sookey, peeks in, cackling. They are waiting for a sign to bring in the cake and champagne. But Big Daddy's not amused. He doesn't understand why, in spite of the infinite mental relief he's received from the doctor's report, he still has these same old fox teeth in his guts. "This spastic condi-tion is something else," he says to himself, but aloud he roars at Big Mama:*)

BIG DADDY: *BIG MAMA, WILL YOU QUIT HORSIN'?* — You're too old an' too fat fo' that sort of crazy kid stuff an' besides a woman with your blood pressure — she had two hundred last spring! — is riskin' a stroke when you mess around like that. . . .

(*Mae blows on a pitch pipe.*)

BIG MAMA: *Here comes Big Daddy's birthday!*

(*Negroes in white jackets enter with an enormous birth-day cake ablaze with candles and carrying buckets of champagne with satin ribbons about the bottle necks.*)
   (*Mae and Gooper strike up song, and everybody, including the Negroes and Children, joins in. Only Brick remains aloof.*)

EVERYONE: Happy birthday to you.
   Happy birthday to you.
   Happy birthday, Big Daddy —

(*Some sing: "Dear, Big Daddy!"*)

   Happy birthday to you.

(*Some sing: "How old are you?"*)
   (*Mae has come down center and is organizing her children like a chorus. She gives them a barely audible: "One, two, three!" and they are off in the new tune.*)

CHILDREN: Skinamarinka — dinka — dink
   Skinamarinka — do
   We love you.
   Skinamarinka — dinka — dink
   Skinamarinka — do.

(*All together, they turn to Big Daddy.*)

   Big Daddy, you!

(*They turn back front, like a musical comedy chorus.*)

   We love you in the morning;
   We love you in the night.
   We love you when we're with you,
   And we love you out of sight.

Skinamarinka — dinka — dink
Skinamarinka — do.

(*Mae turns to Big Mama.*)

Big Mama, too!

(*Big Mama bursts into tears. The Negroes leave.*)

BIG DADDY: Now Ida, what the hell is the matter with you?

MAE: She's just so happy.

BIG MAMA: I'm just so happy, Big Daddy, I have to cry or something.

(*Sudden and loud in the hush:*)

Brick, do you know the wonderful news that Doc Baugh got from the clinic about Big Daddy? Big Daddy's one hundred percent!

MARGARET: Isn't that wonderful?

BIG MAMA: He's just one hundred percent. Passed the examination with flying colors. Now that we know there's nothing wrong with Big Daddy but a spastic colon, I can tell you something. I was worried sick half out of my mind, for fear that Big Daddy might have a thing like —

(*Margaret cuts through this speech, jumping up and exclaiming shrilly:*)

MARGARET: Brick, honey, aren't you going to give Big Daddy his birthday present?

(*Passing by him, she snatches his liquor glass from him.*)
(*She picks up a fancily wrapped package.*)

Here it is, Big Daddy, this is from Brick!

BIG MAMA: This is the biggest birthday Big Daddy's ever had, a hundred presents and bushels of telegrams from —

MAE (*at same time*): What is it, Brick?

GOOPER: I bet 500 to 50 that Brick don't *know* what it is.

BIG MAMA: The fun of presents is not knowing what they are till you open the package. Open your present, Big Daddy.

BIG DADDY: Open it you'self. I want to ask Brick somethin'! Come here, Brick.

MARGARET: Big Daddy's callin' you, Brick.

(*She is opening the package.*)

BRICK: Tell Big Daddy I'm crippled.

BIG DADDY: I see you're crippled. I want to know how you got crippled.

MARGARET (*making diversionary tactics*): Oh, look, oh, look, why, it's a cashmere robe!

(*She holds the robe up for all to see.*)

MAE: You sound surprised, Maggie.

MARGARET: I never saw one before.

MAE: That's funny. — *Hah!*

MARGARET (*turning on her fiercely, with a brilliant smile*): Why is it funny? All my family ever had was

family — and luxuries such as cashmere robes still surprise me!

BIG DADDY (*ominously*): Quiet!

MAE (*heedless in her fury*): I don't see how you could be so surprised when you bought it yourself at Loewenstein's in Memphis last Saturday. You know how I know?

BIG DADDY: I said, Quiet!

MAE: — I know because the salesgirl that sold it to you waited on me and said, Oh, Mrs. Pollitt, your sister-in-law just bought a cashmere robe for your husband's father!

MARGARET: Sister Woman! Your talents are wasted as a housewife and mother, you really ought to be with the FBI or —

BIG DADDY: QUIET!

(*Reverend Tooker's reflexes are slower than the others'. He finishes a sentence after the bellow.*)

REVEREND TOOKER (*to Doc Baugh*): — the Stork and the Reaper are running neck and neck!

(*He starts to laugh gaily when he notices the silence and Big Daddy's glare. His laugh dies falsely.*)

BIG DADDY: Preacher, I hope I'm not butting in on more talk about memorial stained-glass windows, am I, Preacher?

(*Reverend Tooker laughs feebly, then coughs dryly in the embarrassed silence.*)

Preacher?

BIG MAMA: Now, Big Daddy, don't you pick on Preacher!

BIG DADDY (*raising his voice*): You ever hear that expression all hawk and no spit? You bring that expression to mind with that little dry cough of yours, all hawk an' no spit. . . .

(*The pause is broken only by a short startled laugh from Margaret, the only one there who is conscious of and amused by the grotesque.*)

MAE (*raising her arms and jangling her bracelets*): I wonder if the mosquitoes are active tonight?

BIG DADDY: What's that, Little Mama? Did you make some remark?

MAE: Yes, I said I wondered if the mosquitoes would eat us alive if we went out on the gallery for a while.

BIG DADDY: Well, if they do, I'll have your bones pulverized for fertilizer!

BIG MAMA (*quickly*): Last week we had an airplane spraying the place and I think it done some good, at least I haven't had a —

BIG DADDY (*cutting her speech*): Brick, they tell me, if what they tell me is true, that you done some jumping last night on the high school athletic field?

BIG MAMA: Brick, Big Daddy is talking to you, son.

BRICK (*smiling vaguely over his drink*): What was that, Big Daddy?

BIG DADDY: They said you done some jumping on the high school track field last night.

BRICK: That's what they told me, too.

BIG DADDY: Was it jumping or humping that you were doing out there? What were you doing out there at three A.M., layin' a woman on that cinder track?

BIG MAMA: Big Daddy, you are off the sick-list, now, and I'm not going to excuse you for talkin' so —

BIG DADDY: Quiet!

BIG MAMA: — *nasty* in front of Preacher and —

BIG DADDY: *QUIET!* — I ast you, Brick, if you was cuttin' you'self a piece o' poon-tang last night on that cinder track? I thought maybe you were chasin' poon-tang on that track an' tripped over something in the heat of the chase — 'sthat it?

(*Gooper laughs, loud and false, others nervously following suit. Big Mama stamps her foot, and purses her lips, crossing to Mae and whispering something to her as Brick meets his father's hard, intent, grinning stare with a slow, vague smile that he offers all situations from behind the screen of his liquor.*)

BRICK: No, sir, I don't think so. . . .

MAE (*at the same time, sweetly*): Reverend Tooker, let's you and I take a stroll on the widow's walk.

(*She and the preacher go out on the gallery as Big Daddy says:*)

BIG DADDY: Then what the hell were you doing out there at three o'clock in the morning?

BRICK: Jumping the hurdles, Big Daddy, runnin' and jumpin' the hurdles, but those high hurdles have gotten too high for me, now.

BIG DADDY: Cause you was drunk?

BRICK (*his vague smile fading a little*): Sober I wouldn't have tried to jump the *low* ones. . . .

BIG MAMA (*quickly*): Big Daddy, blow out the candles on your birthday cake!

MARGARET (*at the same time*): I want to propose a toast to Big Daddy Pollitt on his sixty-fifth birthday, the biggest cotton planter in —

BIG DADDY (*bellowing with fury and disgust*): I told you to stop it, now stop it, quit this — !

BIG MAMA (*coming in front of Big Daddy with the cake*): Big Daddy, I will not allow you to talk that way, not even on your birthday, I —

BIG DADDY: I'll talk like I want to on my birthday, Ida, or any other goddamn day of the year and anybody here that don't like it knows what they can do!

BIG MAMA: You don't mean that!

BIG DADDY What makes you think I don't mean it?

(*Meanwhile various discreet signals have been exchanged and Gooper has also gone out on the gallery.*)

BIG MAMA: I just know you don't mean it.

BIG DADDY: You don't know a goddamn thing and you never did!

BIG MAMA: Big Daddy, you don't mean that.

BIG DADDY: Oh, yes, I do, oh, yes, I do, I mean it! I put up with a whole lot of crap around here because I thought I was dying. And you thought I was dying

and you started taking over, well, you can stop taking over now, Ida, because I'm not gonna die, you can just stop now this business of taking over because you're not taking over because I'm not dying, I went through the laboratory and the goddamn exploratory operation and there's nothing wrong with me but a spastic colon. And I'm not dying of cancer which you thought I was dying of. Ain't that so? Didn't you think that I was dying of cancer, Ida?

(*Almost everybody is out on the gallery but the two old people glaring at each other across the blazing cake.*)

(*Big Mama's chest heaves and she presses a fat fist to her mouth.*)

(*Big Daddy continues, hoarsely:*)

Ain't that so, Ida? Didn't you have an idea I was dying of cancer and now you could take control of this place and everything on it? I got that impression, I seemed to get that impression. Your loud voice everywhere, your fat old body butting in here and there!

BIG MAMA: Hush! The Preacher!

BIG DADDY: Fuck the goddamn preacher!

(*Big Mama gasps loudly and sits down on the sofa which is almost too small for her.*)

Did you hear what I said? I said fuck the goddamn preacher!

(*Somebody closes the gallery doors from outside just as there is a burst of fireworks and excited cries from the children.*)

BIG MAMA: I never seen you act like this before and I can't think what's got in you!

BIG DADDY: I went through all that laboratory and operation and all just so I would know if you or me was boss here! Well, now it turns out that I am and you ain't — and that's my birthday present — and my cake and champagne! — because for three years now you been gradually taking over. Bossing. Talking. Sashaying your fat old body around the place I made! I made this place! I was overseer on it! I was the overseer on the old Straw and Ochello plantation. I quit school at ten! I quit school at ten years old and went to work like a nigger in the fields. And I rose to be overseer of the Straw and Ochello plantation. And old Straw died and I was Ochello's partner and the place got bigger and bigger and bigger and bigger and bigger! I did all that myself with no goddamn help from you, and now you think you're just about to take over. Well, I am just about to tell you that you are not just about to take over, you are not just about to take over a God damn thing. Is that clear to you, Ida? Is that very plain to you, now? Is that understood completely? I been through the laboratory from A to Z. I've had the goddamn exploratory operation, and nothing is wrong with me but a spastic colon — made spastic, I guess, by *disgust!* By all the goddamn lies and liars that I have had to put up with and all the goddamn hypocrisy that I lived with all these forty years that we been livin' together!

Hey! Ida!! Blow out the candles on the birthday cake! Purse up your lips and draw a deep breath and blow out the goddamn candles on the cake!

BIG MAMA: Oh, Big Daddy, oh, oh, oh, Big Daddy!

BIG DADDY: What's the matter with you?

BIG MAMA: *In all these years you never believed that I loved you??*

BIG DADDY: Huh?

BIG MAMA: *And I did, I did so much, I did love you!* — I even loved your hate and your hardness, Big Daddy!

(*She sobs and rushes awkwardly out onto the gallery.*)

BIG DADDY (*to himself*): *Wouldn't it be funny if that was true. . . .*

(*A pause is followed by a burst of light in the sky from the fireworks.*)

BRICK! HEY, BRICK!

(*He stands over his blazing birthday cake.*)
(*After some moments, Brick hobbles in on his crutch, holding his glass.*)
(*Margaret follows him with a bright, anxious smile.*)

I didn't call you, Maggie. I called Brick.

MARGARET: I'm just delivering him to you.

(*She kisses Brick on the mouth which he immediately wipes with the back of his hand. She flies girlishly back out. Brick and his father are alone.*)

BIG DADDY: Why did you do that?

BRICK: Do what, Big Daddy?

BIG DADDY: Wipe her kiss off your mouth like she'd spit on you.

BRICK: I don't know. I wasn't conscious of it.

BIG DADDY: That woman of yours has a better shape on her than Gooper's but somehow or other they got the same look about them.

BRICK: What sort of look is that, Big Daddy?

BIG DADDY: I don't know how to describe it but it's the same look.

BRICK: They don't look peaceful, do they?

BIG DADDY: No, they sure in hell don't.

BRICK: They look nervous as cats?

BIG DADDY: That's right, they look nervous as cats.

BRICK: Nervous as a couple of cats on a hot tin roof?

BIG DADDY: That's right, boy, they look like a couple of cats on a hot tin roof. It's funny that you and Gooper being so different would pick out the same type of woman.

BRICK: Both of us married into society, Big Daddy.

BIG DADDY: Crap . . . I wonder what gives them both that look?

BRICK: Well. They're sittin' in the middle of a big piece of land, Big Daddy, twenty-eight thousand acres is a pretty big piece of land and so they're squaring off on it, each determined to knock off a bigger piece of it than the other whenever you let it go.

BIG DADDY: I got a surprise for those women. I'm not gonna let it go for a long time yet if that's what they're waiting for.

BRICK: That's right, Big Daddy. You just sit tight and let them scratch each other's eyes out. . . .

BIG DADDY: You bet your life I'm going to sit tight on it and let those sons of bitches scratch their eyes out, ha ha ha. . . .

But Gooper's wife's a good breeder, you got to admit she's fertile. Hell, at supper tonight she had them all at the table and they had to put a couple of extra leafs in the table to make room for them, she's got five head of them, now, and another one's comin'.

BRICK: Yep, number six is comin' . . .

BIG DADDY: Six hell, she'll probably drop a litter next time. Brick, you know, I swear to God, I don't know the way it happens.

BRICK: The way what happens, Big Daddy?

BIG DADDY: You git you a piece of land, by hook or crook, an' things start growin' on it, things accumulate on it, and the first thing you know it's completely out of hand, completely out of hand!

BRICK: Well, they say nature hates a vacuum, Big Daddy.

BIG DADDY: That's what they say, but sometimes I think that a vacuum is a hell of a lot better than some of the stuff that nature replaces it with.

Is someone out there by that door?

GOOPER: Hey Mae.

BRICK: Yep.

BIG DADDY: Who?

(*He has lowered his voice.*)

BRICK: Someone int'rested in what we say to each other.

BIG DADDY: Gooper? — GOOPER!

(*After a discreet pause, Mae appears in the gallery door.*)

MAE: Did you call Gooper, Big Daddy?

BIG DADDY: Aw, it was you.

MAE: Do you want Gooper, Big Daddy?

BIG DADDY: No, and I don't want you. I want some privacy here, while I'm having a confidential talk with my son Brick. Now it's too hot in here to close them doors, but if I have to close those fuckin' doors in order to have a private talk with my son Brick, just let me know and I'll close 'em. Because I hate eavesdroppers, I don't like any kind of sneakin' an' spyin'.

MAE: Why, Big Daddy —

BIG DADDY: You stood on the wrong side of the moon, it threw your shadow!

MAE: I was just —

BIG DADDY: You was just nothing but *spyin'* an you *know* it!

MAE (*begins to sniff and sob*): Oh, Big Daddy, you're so unkind for some reason to those that really love you!

BIG DADDY: Shut up, shut up, shut up! I'm going to move you and Gooper out of that room next to this! It's none of your goddamn business what goes on in here at night between Brick an' Maggie. You listen at night like a couple of rutten peekhole spies and go

and give a report on what you hear to Big Mama an'
she comes to me and says they say such and such and
so and so about what they heard goin' on between
Brick an' Maggie, and Jesus, it makes me sick. I'm
goin' to move you an' Gooper out of that room, I
can't stand sneakin' an' spyin', it makes me puke. . . .

(*Mae throws back her head and rolls her eyes heavenward and extends her arms as if invoking God's pity for
this unjust martyrdom; then she presses a handkerchief
to her nose and flies from the room with a loud swish of
skirts.*)

BRICK (*now at the liquor cabinet*): They listen, do they?
BIG DADDY: Yeah. They listen and give reports to Big
  Mama on what goes on in here between you and
  Maggie. They say that —

(*He stops as if embarrassed.*)

  — You won't sleep with her, that you sleep on the
  sofa. Is that true or not true? If you don't like Maggie,
  get rid of Maggie! — What are you doin' there now?
BRICK: Fresh'nin' up my drink.
BIG DADDY: Son, you know you got a real liquor prob-
  lem?
BRICK: Yes, sir, yes, I know.
BIG DADDY: Is that why you quit sports-announcing,
  because of this liquor problem?
BRICK: Yes, sir, yes, sir, I guess so.

(*He smiles vaguely and amiably at his father across his
replenished drink.*)

BIG DADDY: Son, don't guess about it, it's too important.
BRICK (*vaguely*): Yes, sir.
BIG DADDY: And listen to me, don't look at the damn
  chandelier. . . .

(*Pause. Big Daddy's voice is husky.*)

  — Somethin' else we picked up at th' big fire-sale in
  Europe.

(*Another pause.*)

  Life is important. There's nothing else to hold onto.
  A man that drinks is throwing his life away. Don't do
  it, hold onto your life. There's nothing else to hold
  onto. . . .
    Sit down over here so we don't have to raise our
  voices, the walls have ears in this place.
BRICK (*hobbling over to sit on the sofa beside him*): All
  right, Big Daddy.
BIG DADDY: Quit! — how'd that come about? Some
  disappointment?
BRICK: I don't know. Do you?
BIG DADDY: I'm askin' you, God damn it! How in hell
  would I know if you don't?
BRICK: I just got out there and found that I had a mouth
  full of cotton. I was always two or three beats behind
  what was goin' on on the field and so I —
BIG DADDY: Quit!

BRICK (*amiably*): Yes, quit.
BIG DADDY: Son?
BRICK: Huh?
BIG DADDY (*inhales loudly and deeply from his cigar;
then bends suddenly a little forward, exhaling loudly
and raising a hand to his forehead*): — Whew! — ha
  ha! — I took in too much smoke, it made me a little
  lightheaded. . . .

(*The mantel clock chimes.*)

  Why is it so damn hard for people to talk?
BRICK: Yeah. . . .

(*The clock goes on sweetly chiming till it has completed
the stroke of ten.*)

  — Nice peaceful-soundin' clock, I like to hear it all
  night. . . .

(*He slides low and comfortable on the sofa; Big Daddy
sits up straight and rigid with some unspoken anxiety.
All his gestures are tense and jerky as he talks. He
wheezes and pants and sniffs through his nervous speech,
glancing quickly, shyly, from time to time, at his son.*)

BIG DADDY: We got that clock the summer we wint to
  Europe, me an' Big Mama on that damn Cook's
  Tour, never had such an awful time in my life, I'm
  tellin' you, son, those gooks over there, they gouge
  your eyeballs out in their grand hotels. And Big
  Mama bought more stuff than you could haul in a
  couple of boxcars, that's no crap. Everywhere she
  wint on this whirlwind tour, she bought, bought,
  bought. Why, half that stuff she bought is still crated
  up in the cellar, under water last spring!

(*He laughs.*)

  That Europe is nothin' on earth but a great big auction, that's all it is, that bunch of old worn-out
  places, it's just a big fire-sale, the whole fuckin' thing,
  an' Big Mama wint wild in it, why, you couldn't hold
  that woman with a mule's harness! Bought, bought,
  bought! — lucky I'm a rich man, yes siree, Bob, an'
  half that stuff is mildewin' in th' basement. It's lucky
  I'm a rich man, it sure is lucky, well, I'm a rich man,
  Brick, yep, I'm a mighty rich man.

(*His eyes light up for a moment.*)

  Y'know how much I'm worth? Guess, Brick! Guess
  how much I'm worth!

(*Brick smiles vaguely over his drink.*)

  Close on ten million in cash an' blue-chip stocks, outside, mind you, of twenty-eight thousand acres of the
  richest land this side of the valley Nile!
    But a man can't buy his life with it, he can't buy
  back his life with it when his life has been spent,
  that's one thing not offered in the Europe fire-sale or
  in the American markets or any markets on earth, a
  man can't buy his life with it, he can't buy back his
  life when his life is finished. . . .

That's a sobering thought, a very sobering thought, and that's a thought that I was turning over in my head, over and over and over — until today. . . .

I'm wiser and sadder, Brick, for this experience which I just gone through. They's one thing else that I remember in Europe.

BRICK: What is that, Big Daddy?

BIG DADDY: The hills around Barcelona in the country of Spain and the children running over those bare hills in their bare skins beggin' like starvin' dogs with howls and screeches, and how fat the priests are on the streets of Barcelona, so many of them and so fat and so pleasant, ha ha! — Y'know I could feed that country? I got money enough to feed that goddamn country, but the human animal is a selfish beast and I don't reckon the money I passed out there to those howling children in the hills around Barcelona would more than upholster the chairs in this room, I mean pay to put a new cover on this chair!

Hell, I threw them money like you'd scatter feed corn for chickens, I threw money at them just to get rid of them long enough to climb back into th' car and — drive away. . . .

And then in Morocco, them Arabs, why, I remember one day in Marrakech, that old walled Arab city, I set on a broken-down wall to have a cigar, it was fearful hot there and this Arab woman stood in the road and looked at me till I was embarrassed, she stood stock still in the dusty hot road and looked at me till I was embarrassed. But listen to this. She had a naked child with her, a little naked girl with her, barely able to toddle, and after a while she set this child on the ground and give her a push and whispered something to her.

This child come toward me, barely able t' walk, come toddling up to me and —

Jesus, it makes you sick t' remember a thing like this! It stuck out its hand and tried to unbutton my trousers!

That child was not yet five! Can you believe me? Or do you think that I am making this up? I wint back to the hotel and said to Big Mama, Git packed! We're clearing out of this country. . . .

BRICK: Big Daddy, you're on a talkin' jag tonight.

BIG DADDY (*ignoring this remark*): Yes, sir, that's how it is, the human animal is a beast that dies but the fact that he's dying don't give him pity for others, no, sir, it —

— Did you say something?

BRICK: Yes.

BIG DADDY: What?

BRICK: Hand me over that crutch so I can get up.

BIG DADDY: Where you goin?

BRICK: I'm takin' a little short trip to Echo Spring.

BIG DADDY: To where?

BRICK: Liquor cabinet. . . .

BIG DADDY: Yes, sir, boy —

(*He hands Brick the crutch.*)

— the human animal is a beast that dies and if he's got money he buys and buys and buys and I think the reason he buys everything he can buy is that in the back of his mind he has the crazy hope that one of his purchases will be life everlasting! — Which it never can be. . . . The human animal is a beast that —

BRICK (*at the liquor cabinet*): Big Daddy, you sure are shootin' th' breeze here tonight.

(*There is a pause and voices are heard outside.*)

BIG DADDY: I been quiet here lately, spoke not a word, just sat and stared into space. I had something heavy weighing on my mind but tonight that load was took off me. That's why I'm talking. — The sky looks dif-f'rent to me. . . .

BRICK: You know what I like to hear most?

BIG DADDY: What?

BRICK: Solid quiet. Perfect unbroken quiet.

BIG DADDY: Why?

BRICK: Because it's more peaceful.

BIG DADDY: Man, you'll hear a lot of that in the grave.

(*He chuckles agreeably.*)

BRICK: Are you through talkin' to me?

BIG DADDY: Why are you so anxious to shut me up?

BRICK: Well, sir, ever so often you say to me, Brick, I want to have a talk with you, but when we talk, it never materializes. Nothing is said. You sit in a chair and gas about this and that and I look like I listen. I try to look like I listen, but I don't listen, not much. Communication is — awful hard between people an' — somehow between you and me, it just don't — happen.

BIG DADDY: Have you ever been scared? I mean have you ever felt downright terror of something?

(*He gets up.*)

Just one moment.

(*He looks off as if he were going to tell an important secret.*)

Brick?

BRICK: What?

BIG DADDY: Son, I thought I had it!

BRICK: Had what? Had what, Big Daddy?

BIG DADDY: Cancer!

BRICK: Oh . . .

BIG DADDY: I thought the old man made out of bones had laid his cold and heavy hand on my shoulder!

BRICK: Well, Big Daddy, you kept a tight mouth about it.

BIG DADDY: A pig squeals. A man keeps a tight mouth about it, in spite of a man not having a pig's advantage.

BRICK: What advantage is that?

BIG DADDY: Ignorance — of mortality — is a comfort. A man don't have that comfort, he's the only living thing that conceives of death, that knows what it is. The others go without knowing which is the way that anything living should go, go without knowing, without any knowledge of it, and yet a pig squeals, but a man sometimes, he can keep a tight mouth about it. Sometimes he —

(*There is a deep, smoldering ferocity in the old man.*)

— can keep a tight mouth about it. I wonder if —
BRICK: What, Big Daddy?
BIG DADDY: A whiskey highball would injure this spastic condition?
BRICK: No, sir, it might do it good.
BIG DADDY (*grins suddenly, wolfishly*): *Jesus, I can't tell you! The sky is open! Christ, it's open again! It's open, boy, it's open!*

(*Brick looks down at his drink.*)

BRICK: You feel better, Big Daddy?
BIG DADDY: Better? Hell! I can breathe! — All of my life I been like a doubled up fist. . . .

(*He pours a drink.*)

— Poundin', smashin', drivin'! — now I'm going to loosen these doubled-up hands and touch things *easy* with them. . . .

(*He spreads his hands as if caressing the air.*)

You know what I'm contemplating?
BRICK (*vaguely*): No, sir. What are you contemplating?
BIG DADDY: Ha ha! — *Pleasure!* — pleasure with *women!*

(*Brick's smile fades a little but lingers.*)

— Yes, boy. I'll tell you something that you might not guess. I still have desire for women and this is my sixty-fifth birthday.
BRICK: I think that's mighty remarkable, Big Daddy.
BIG DADDY: Remarkable?
BRICK: *Admirable*, Big Daddy.
BIG DADDY: You're damn right it is, remarkable and admirable both. I realize now that I never had me enough. I let many chances slip by because of scruples about it, scruples, convention — crap. . . . All that stuff is bull, bull, bull! — It took the shadow of death to make me see it. Now that shadow's lifted, I'm going to cut loose and have, what is it they call it, have me a — ball!
BRICK: A ball, huh?
BIG DADDY: That's right, a ball, a ball! Hell! — I slept with Big Mama till, let's see, five years ago, till I was sixty and she was fifty-eight, and never even liked her, never did!

(*The phone has been ringing down the hall. Big Mama enters, exclaiming:*)

BIG MAMA: Don't you men hear that phone ring? I heard it way out on the gall'ry.
BIG DADDY: There's five rooms off this front gall'ry that you could go through. Why do you go through this one?

(*Big Mama makes a playful face as she bustles out the hall door.*)

Hunh! — Why, when Big Mama goes out of a room, I can't remember what that woman looks like —
BIG MAMA: Hello.
BIG DADDY: — But when Big Mama comes back into the room, boy, then I see what she looks like, and I wish I didn't!

(*Bends over laughing at this joke till it hurts his guts and he straightens with a grimace. The laugh subsides to a chuckle as he puts the liquor glass a little distrustfully down the table.*)

BIG MAMA: Hello, Miss Sally.

(*Brick has risen and hobbled to the gallery doors.*)

BIG DADDY: Hey! Where you goin'?
BRICK: Out for a breather.
BIG DADDY: Not yet you ain't. Stay here till this talk is finished, young fellow.
BRICK: I thought it was finished, Big Daddy.
BIG DADDY: It ain't even begun.
BRICK: My mistake. Excuse me. I just wanted to feel that river breeze.
BIG DADDY: Set back down in that chair.

(*Big Mama's voice rises, carrying down the hall.*)

BIG MAMA: Miss Sally, you're a case! You're a caution, Miss Sally.
BIG DADDY: Jesus, she's talking to my old maid sister again.
BIG MAMA: Why didn't you give me a chance to explain it to you?
BIG DADDY: Brick, this stuff burns me.
BIG MAMA: Well, good-bye, now, Miss Sally. You come down real soon. Big Daddy's dying to see you.
BIG DADDY: Crap!
BIG MAMA: Yaiss, good-bye, Miss Sally. . . .

(*She hangs up and bellows with mirth. Big Daddy groans and covers his ears as she approaches.*)
(*Bursting in:*)

Big Daddy, that was Miss Sally callin' from Memphis again! You know what she done, Big Daddy? She called her doctor in Memphis to git him to tell her what that spastic thing is! Ha-*HAAAA!* — And called back to tell me how relieved she was that — Hey! Let me in!

(*Big Daddy has been holding the door half closed against her.*)

BIG DADDY: Naw I ain't. I told you not to come and go through this room. You just back out and go through those five other rooms.
BIG MAMA: Big Daddy? Big Daddy? Oh, Big Daddy! — You didn't mean those things you said to me, did you?

(*He shuts door firmly against her but she still calls.*)

Brick (Ben Gazzara) and Big Daddy (Burl Ives) in the original 1955 production of *Cat on a Hot Tin Roof*, directed by Elia Kazan.

Sweetheart? Sweetheart? Big Daddy? You didn't mean those awful things you said to me? — I know you didn't. I know you didn't mean those things in your heart. . . .

(*The childlike voice fades with a sob and her heavy foot-steps retreat down the hall. Brick has risen once more on his crutches and starts for the gallery again.*)

BIG DADDY: All I ask of that woman is that she leave me alone. But she can't admit to herself that she makes me sick. That comes of having slept with her too many years. Should of quit much sooner but that old woman she never got enough of it — and I was good in bed . . . I never should of wasted so much of it on her. . . . They say you got just so many and each one is numbered. Well, I got a few left in me, a few, and I'm going to pick me a good one to spend 'em on! I'm going to pick me a choice one, I don't care how much she costs, I'll smother her in — minks! Ha ha! I'll strip her naked and smother her in minks and choke her

with diamonds! Ha ha! I'll strip her naked and choke her with diamonds and smother her with minks and hump her from hell to breakfast. *Ha aha ha ha ha!*

MAE (*gaily at door*): Who's that laughin' in there?

GOOPER: Is Big Daddy laughin' in there?

BIG DADDY: Crap! — them two — *drips*. . . .

(*He goes over and touches Brick's shoulder.*)

Yes, son. Brick, boy. — I'm — *happy!* I'm happy, son, I'm happy!

(*He chokes a little and bites his under lip, pressing his head quickly, shyly against his son's head and then, coughing with embarrassment, goes uncertainly back to the table where he set down the glass. He drinks and makes a grimace as it burns his guts. Brick sighs and rises with effort.*)

What makes you so restless? Have you got ants in your britches?

BRICK: Yes, sir . . .

BIG DADDY: Why?

BRICK: — Something — hasn't — happened. . . .

BIG DADDY: Yeah? What is that!

BRICK (*sadly*): — the click. . . .

BIG DADDY: Did you say click?

BRICK: Yes, click.

BIG DADDY: What click?

BRICK: A click that I get in my head that makes me peaceful.

BIG DADDY: I sure in hell don't know what you're talking about, but it disturbs me.

BRICK: It's just a mechanical thing.

BIG DADDY: What is a mechanical thing?

BRICK: This click that I get in my head that makes me peaceful. I got to drink till I get it. It's just a mechanical thing, something like a — like a — like a —

BIG DADDY: Like a —

BRICK: Switch clicking off in my head, turning the hot light off and the cool night on and —

(*He looks up, smiling sadly.*)

— all of a sudden there's — peace!

BIG DADDY (*whistles long and soft with astonishment; he goes back to Brick and clasps his son's two shoulders*): Jesus! I didn't know it had gotten that bad with you. Why, boy, you're — *alcoholic!*

BRICK: That's the truth, Big Daddy. I'm alcoholic.

BIG DADDY: This shows how I — let things go!

BRICK: I have to hear that little click in my head that makes me peaceful. Usually I hear it sooner than this, sometimes as early as — noon, but —

— Today it's — dilatory. . . .

I just haven't got the right level of alcohol in my bloodstream yet!

(*This last statement is made with energy as he freshens his drink.*)

BIG DADDY: Uh — huh. Expecting death made me blind. I didn't have no idea that a son of mine was turning into a drunkard under my nose.

BRICK (*gently*): Well, now you do, Big Daddy, the news has penetrated.

BIG DADDY: UH-huh, yes, now I do, the news has — penetrated. . . .

BRICK: And so if you'll excuse me —

BIG DADDY: No, I won't excuse you.

BRICK: — I'd better sit by myself till I hear that click in my head, it's just a mechanical thing but it don't happen except when I'm alone or talking to no one. . . .

BIG DADDY: You got a long, long time to sit still, boy, and talk to no one, but now you're talkin' to me. At least I'm talking to you. And you set there and listen until I tell you the conversation is over!

BRICK: But this talk is like all the others we've ever had together in our lives! It's nowhere, nowhere! — it's — it's *painful*, Big Daddy. . . .

BIG DADDY: All right, then let it be painful, but don't you move from that chair! — I'm going to remove that crutch. . . .

(*He seizes the crutch and tosses it across room.*)

BRICK: I can hop on one foot, and if I fall, I can crawl!

BIG DADDY: If you ain't careful you're gonna crawl off this plantation and then, by Jesus, you'll have to hustle your drinks along Skid Row!

BRICK: That'll come, Big Daddy.

BIG DADDY: Naw, it won't. You're my son and I'm going to straighten you out; now that *I'm* straightened out, I'm going to straighten out you!

BRICK: Yeah?

BIG DADDY: Today the report come in from Ochsner Clinic. Y'know what they told me?

(*His face glows with triumph.*)

The only thing that they could detect with all the instruments of science in that great hospital is a little spastic condition of the colon! And nerves torn to pieces by all that worry about it.

(*A little girl bursts into room with a sparkler clutched in each fist, hops and shrieks like a monkey gone mad and rushes back out again as Big Daddy strikes at her.*)

(*Silence. The two men stare at each other. A woman laughs gaily outside.*)

I want you to know I breathed a sigh of relief almost as powerful as the Vicksburg tornado!

(*There is laughter outside, running footsteps, the soft, plushy sound and light of exploding rockets.*)

(*Brick stares at him soberly for a long moment; then makes a sort of startled sound in his nostrils and springs up on one foot and hops across the room to grab his crutch, swinging on the furniture for support. He gets the crutch and flees as if in horror for the gallery. His father seizes him by the sleeve of his white silk pajamas.*)

Stay here, you son of a bitch! — till I say go!

BRICK: I can't.

BIG DADDY: You sure in hell will, God damn it.

BRICK: No, I can't. We talk, you talk, in — circles! We get no where, no where! It's always the same, you say you want to talk to me and don't have a fuckin' thing to say to me!

BIG DADDY: Nothin' to say when I'm tellin' you I'm going to live when I thought I was dying?!

BRICK: Oh — *that!* — Is that what you have to say to me?

BIG DADDY: Why, you son of a bitch! Ain't that, ain't that — *important?!*

BRICK: Well, you said that, that's said, and now I —

BIG DADDY: Now you set back down.

BRICK: You're all balled up, you —

BIG DADDY: I ain't balled up!

BRICK: You are, you're all balled up!

BIG DADDY: Don't tell me what I am, you drunken whelp! I'm going to tear this coat sleeve off if you don't set down!

BRICK: Big Daddy —

BIG DADDY: Do what I tell you! I'm the boss here, now! I want you to know I'm back in the driver's seat now!

(*Big Mama rushes in, clutching her great heaving bosom.*)

BIG MAMA: Big Daddy!

BIG DADDY: What in hell do you want in here, Big Mama?

BIG MAMA: Oh, Big Daddy! Why are you shouting like that? I just cain't *stainnnnnnnd* — it. . . .

BIG DADDY (*raising the back of his hand above his head*): GIT! — outa here.

(*She rushes back out, sobbing.*)

BRICK (*softly, sadly*): Christ. . . .

BIG DADDY (*fiercely*): Yeah! Christ! — is right. . . .

(*Brick breaks loose and hobbles toward the gallery.*)
    (*Big Daddy jerks his crutch from under Brick so he steps with the injured ankle. He utters a hissing cry of anguish, clutches a chair and pulls it over on top of him on the floor.*)

    Son of a — tub of — hog fat. . . .

BRICK: Big Daddy! Give me my crutch.

(*Big Daddy throws the crutch out of reach.*)

    Give me that crutch, Big Daddy.

BIG DADDY: Why do you drink?

BRICK: Don't know, give me my crutch!

BIG DADDY: You better think why you drink or give up drinking!

BRICK: Will you please give me my crutch so I can get up off this floor?

BIG DADDY: First you answer my question. Why do you drink? Why are you throwing your life away, boy, like somethin' disgusting you picked up on the street?

BRICK (*getting onto his knees*): Big Daddy, I'm in pain, I stepped on that foot.

BIG DADDY: Good! I'm glad you're not too numb with the liquor in you to feel some pain!

BRICK: You — spilled my — drink . . .

BIG DADDY: I'll make a bargain with you. You tell me why you drink and I'll hand you one. I'll pour you the liquor myself and hand it to you.

BRICK: Why do I drink?

BIG DADDY: Yea! Why?

BRICK: Give me a drink and I'll tell you.

BIG DADDY: Tell me first!

BRICK: I'll tell you in one word.

BIG DADDY: What word?

BRICK: DISGUST!

(*The clock chimes softly, sweetly. Big Daddy gives it a short, outraged glance.*)

    Now how about that drink?

BIG DADDY: What are you disgusted with? You got to tell me that, first. Otherwise being disgusted don't make no sense!

BRICK: Give me my crutch.

BIG DADDY: You heard me, you got to tell me what I asked you first.

BRICK: I told you, I said to kill my disgust!

BIG DADDY: DISGUST WITH WHAT!

BRICK: You strike a hard bargain.

BIG DADDY: What are you disgusted with? — an' I'll pass you the liquor.

BRICK: I can hop on one foot, and if I fall, I can crawl.

BIG DADDY: You want liquor that bad?

BRICK (*dragging himself up, clinging to bedstead*): Yeah, I want it that bad.

BIG DADDY: If I give you a drink, will you tell me what it is you're disgusted with, Brick?

BRICK: Yes, sir, I will try to.

(*The old man pours him a drink and solemnly passes it to him.*)
    (*There is silence as Brick drinks.*)

    Have you ever heard the word "mendacity"?

BIG DADDY: Sure. Mendacity is one of them five dollar words that cheap politicians throw back and forth at each other.

BRICK: You know what it means?

BIG DADDY: Don't it mean lying and liars?

BRICK: Yes, sir, lying and liars.

BIG DADDY: Has someone been lying to you?

CHILDREN (*chanting in chorus offstage*):
    We want Big Dad-dee!
    We want Big Dad-dee!

(*Gooper appears in the gallery door.*)

GOOPER: Big Daddy, the kiddies are shouting for you out there.

BIG DADDY (*fiercely*): Keep out, Gooper!

GOOPER: 'Scuse *me*!

(*Big Daddy slams the doors after Gooper.*)

BIG DADDY: Who's been lying to you, has Margaret been lying to you, has your wife been lying to you about something, Brick?

BRICK: Not her. That wouldn't matter.

BIG DADDY: Then who's been lying to you, and what about?

BRICK: No one single person and no one lie. . . .

BIG DADDY: Then what, what then, for Christ's sake?

BRICK: — The whole, the whole — thing. . . .

BIG DADDY: Why are you rubbing your head? You got a headache?

BRICK: No, I'm tryin' to —

BIG DADDY: — Concentrate, but you can't because your brain's all soaked with liquor, is that the trouble? Wet brain!

(*He snatches the glass from Brick's hand.*)

What do you know about this mendacity thing? Hell! I could write a book on it! Don't you know that? I could write a book on it and still not cover the subject? Well, I could, I could write a goddamn book on it and still not cover the subject anywhere near enough!! — Think of all the lies I got to put up with! — Pretenses! Ain't that mendacity? Having to pretend stuff you don't think or feel or have any idea of? Having for instance to act like I care for Big Mama! — I haven't been able to stand the sight, sound, or smell of that woman for forty years now! — even when I *laid* her! — regular as a piston. . . .

Pretend to love that son of a bitch of a Gooper and his wife Mae and those five same screechers out there like parrots in a jungle? Jesus! Can't stand to look at 'em!

Church! — it bores the bejesus out of me but I go! — I go an' sit there and listen to the fool preacher!

Clubs! — Elks! Masons! Rotary! — *crap!*

(*A spasm of pain makes him clutch his belly. He sinks into a chair and his voice is softer and hoarser.*)

You I *do* like for some reason, did always have some kind of real feeling for — affection — respect — yes, always. . . .

You and being a success as a planter is all I ever had any devotion to in my whole life! — and that's the truth. . . .

I don't know why, but it is!

I've lived with mendacity! — Why can't *you* live with it? Hell, you *got* to live with it, there's nothing *else* to *live* with except mendacity, is there?

BRICK: Yes, sir. Yes, sir there is something else that you can live with!

BIG DADDY: What?

BRICK (*lifting his glass*): This! — Liquor. . . .

BIG DADDY: That's not living, that's dodging away from life.

BRICK: I want to dodge away from it.

BIG DADDY: Then why don't you kill yourself, man?

BRICK: I like to drink. . . .

BIG DADDY: Oh, God, I can't talk to you. . . .

BRICK: I'm sorry, Big Daddy.

BIG DADDY: Not as sorry as I am. I'll tell you something. A little while back when I thought my number was up —

(*This speech should have torrential pace and fury.*)

— before I found out it was just this — spastic — colon. I thought about you. Should I or should I not, if the jig was up, give you this place when I go — since I hate Gooper an' Mae an' know that they hate me, and since all five same monkeys are little Maes an' Goopers. — And I thought, No! — Then I thought, Yes! — I couldn't make up my mind. I hate Gooper and his five same monkeys and that bitch Mae! Why should I turn over twenty-eight thousand acres of the richest land this side of the valley Nile to not my kind? — But why in hell, on the other hand, Brick — should I subsidize a goddamn fool on the bottle? — Liked or not liked, well, maybe even — *loved!* — Why should I do that? — Subsidize worthless behavior? Rot? Corruption?

BRICK (*smiling*): I understand.

BIG DADDY: Well, if you do, you're smarter than I am, God damn it, because I don't understand. And this I will tell you frankly. I didn't make up my mind at all on that question and still to this day I ain't made out no will! — Well, now I don't *have* to. The pressure is gone. I can just wait and see if you pull yourself together or if you don't.

BRICK: That's right, Big Daddy.

BIG DADDY: You sound like you thought I was kidding.

BRICK (*rising*): No, sir, I know you're not kidding.

BIG DADDY: But you don't care — ?

BRICK (*hobbling toward the gallery door*): No, sir, I don't care. . . .

(*He stands in the gallery doorway as the night sky turns pink and green and gold with successive flashes of light.*)

BIG DADDY: *WAIT!* — Brick. . . .

(*His voice drops. Suddenly there is something shy, almost tender, in his restraining gesture.*)

Don't let's — leave it like this, like them other talks we've had, we've always — talked around things, we've — just talked around things for some fuckin' reason, I don't know what, it's always like something was left not spoken, something avoided because neither of us was honest enough with the — other. . . .

BRICK: I never lied to you, Big Daddy.

BIG DADDY: Did I ever to *you?*

BRICK: No, sir. . . .

BIG DADDY: Then there is at least two people that never lied to each other.

BRICK: But we've never *talked* to each other.

BIG DADDY: We can *now.*

BRICK: Big Daddy, there don't seem to be anything much to say.

BIG DADDY: You say that you drink to kill your disgust with lying.

BRICK: You said to give you a reason.

BIG DADDY: Is liquor the only thing that'll kill this disgust?

BRICK: Now. Yes.

BIG DADDY: But not once, huh?

BRICK: Not when I was still young an' believing. A drinking man's someone who wants to forget he isn't still young an' believing.

BIG DADDY: Believing what?

BRICK: Believing. . . .

BIG DADDY: Believing *what?*

BRICK (*stubbornly evasive*): Believing. . . .

BIG DADDY: I don't know what the hell you mean by believing and I don't think you know what you mean by believing, but if you still got sports in your blood, go back to sports announcing and —

BRICK: Sit in a glass box watching games I can't play? Describing what I can't do while players do it? Sweating out their disgust and confusion in contests I'm not fit for? Drinkin' a coke, half bourbon, so I can stand it? That's no goddamn good any more, no help — time just outran me, Big Daddy — got there first . . .

BIG DADDY: I think you're passing the buck.

BRICK: You know many drinkin' men?

BIG DADDY (*with a slight, charming smile*): I have known a fair number of that species.

BRICK: Could any of them tell you why he drank?

BIG DADDY: Yep, you're passin' the buck to things like time and disgust with "mendacity" and — crap! — if you got to use that kind of language about a thing, it's ninety-proof bull, and I'm not buying any.

BRICK: I had to give you a reason to get a drink!

BIG DADDY: You started drinkin' when your friend Skipper died.

(*Silence for five beats. Then Brick makes a startled movement, reaching for his crutch.*)

BRICK: What are you suggesting?

BIG DADDY: I'm suggesting nothing.

(*The shuffle and clop of Brick's rapid hobble away from his father's steady, grave attention.*)

— But Gooper an' Mae suggested that there was something not right exactly in your —

BRICK (*stopping short downstage as if backed to a wall*): "Not right"?

BIG DADDY: Not, well, exactly *normal* in your friendship with —

BRICK: They suggested that, too? I thought that was Maggie's suggestion.

(*Brick's detachment is at last broken through. His heart is accelerated; his forehead sweat-beaded; his breath becomes more rapid and his voice hoarse. The thing they're discussing, timidly and painfully on the side of Big Daddy, fiercely, violently on Brick's side, is the inadmissible thing that Skipper died to disavow between them. The fact that if it existed it had to be disavowed to "keep face" in the world they lived in, may be at the heart of the "mendacity" that Brick drinks to kill his disgust with. It may be the root of his collapse. Or maybe it is only a single manifestation of it, not even the most important. The bird that I hope to catch in the net of this play is not the solution of one man's psychological problem. I'm trying to catch the true quality of experience in a group of people, that cloudy, flickering, evanescent — fiercely charged! — interplay of live human beings in the thundercloud of a common crisis. Some mystery should be left in the revelation of character in a play, just as a great deal of mystery is always left in the revelation of character in life, even in one's own character to himself. This does not absolve the playwright of his duty to observe and probe as clearly and deeply as he legitimately can: But it should steer him away from "pat" conclusions, facile definitions which make a play just a play, not a snare for the truth of human experience.*)

(*The following scene should be played with great concentration, with most of the power leashed but palpable in what is left unspoken.*)

Who else's suggestion is it, is it *yours*? How many others thought that Skipper and I were —

BIG DADDY (*gently*): Now, hold on, hold on a minute, son. — I knocked around in my time.

BRICK: What's that got to do with —

BIG DADDY: I said "Hold on!" — I bummed, I bummed this country till I was —

BRICK: Whose suggestion, who else's suggestion is it?

BIG DADDY: Slept in hobo jungles and railroad Y's and flophouses in all cities before I —

BRICK: Oh, *you* think so, too, you call me your son and a queer. Oh! Maybe that's why you put Maggie and me in this room that was Jack Straw's and Peter Ochello's, in which that pair of old sisters slept in a double bed where both of 'em died!

BIG DADDY: *Now just don't go throwing rocks at* —

(*Suddenly Reverend Tooker appears in the gallery doors, his head slightly, playfully, fatuously cocked, with a practiced clergyman's smile, sincere as a birdcall blown on a hunter's whistle, the living embodiment of the pious, conventional lie.*)

(*Big Daddy gasps a little at this perfectly timed, but incongruous, apparition.*)

— What're you lookin' for, preacher?

REVEREND TOOKER: The gentleman's lavatory, ha ha! — heh, heh . . .

BIG DADDY (*with strained courtesy*): — Go back out and walk down to the other end of the gallery, Reverend Tooker, and use the bathroom connected with my bedroom, and if you can't find it, ask them where it is!

REVEREND TOOKER: Ah, thanks.

(*He goes out with a deprecatory chuckle.*)

BIG DADDY: It's hard to talk in this place . . .

BRICK: Son of a — !

BIG DADDY (*leaving a lot unspoken*): — I seen all things and understood a lot of them, till 1910. Christ, the year that — I had worn my shoes through, hocked my — I hopped off a yellow dog freight car half a mile down the road, slept in a wagon of cotton outside the gin — Jack Straw an' Peter Ochello took me in. Hired me to manage this place which grew into this one. — When Jack Straw died — why, old Peter Ochello quit eatin' like a dog does when its master's dead, and died, too!

BRICK: Christ!

BIG DADDY: I'm just saying I understand such —

BRICK (*violently*): Skipper is dead. I have not quit eating!

BIG DADDY: No, but you started drinking.

(*Brick wheels on his crutch and hurls his glass across the room shouting.*)

BRICK: YOU THINK SO, TOO?

(*Footsteps run on the gallery. There are women's calls.*)

(*Big Daddy goes toward the door.*)

(*Brick is transformed, as if a quiet mountain blew suddenly up in volcanic flame.*)

BRICK: You think so, too? You think so, too? You think me an' Skipper did, did, did! — *sodomy!* — together?

BIG DADDY: Hold — !

BRICK: That what you —

BIG DADDY: — *ON* — a minute!

BRICK: You think we did dirty things between us, Skipper an' —

BIG DADDY: Why are you shouting like that? Why are you —

BRICK: — Me, is that what you think of Skipper, is that —

BIG DADDY: — so excited? I don't think nothing. I don't know nothing. I'm simply telling you what —

BRICK: You think that Skipper and me were a pair of dirty old men?

BIG DADDY: Now that's —

BRICK: Straw? Ochello? A couple of —

BIG DADDY: Now just —

BRICK: — fucking sissies? Queers? Is that what you —

BIG DADDY: Shhh.

BRICK: — think?

(*He loses his balance and pitches to his knees without noticing the pain. He grabs the bed and drags himself up.*)

BIG DADDY: Jesus! — Whew. . . . Grab my hand!

BRICK: Naw, I don't want your hand. . . .

BIG DADDY: Well, I want yours. Git up!

(*He draws him up, keeps an arm about him with concern and affection.*)

You broken out in a sweat! You're panting like you'd run a race with —

BRICK (*freeing himself from his father's hold*): Big Daddy, you shock me, Big Daddy, you, you — *shock* me! Talkin' so —

(*He turns away from his father.*)

— casually! — about a — thing like that . . .

— Don't you know how people *feel* about things like that? How, how *disgusted* they are by things like that? Why, at Ole Miss when it was discovered a pledge to our fraternity, Skipper's and mine, did a, *attempted* to do a, unnatural thing with —

We not only dropped him like a hot rock! — We told him to git off the campus, and he did, he got! — All the way to —

(*He halts, breathless.*)

BIG DADDY: — Where?

BRICK: — North Africa, last I heard!

BIG DADDY: Well, I have come back from further away than that, I have just now returned from the other side of the moon, death's country, son, and I'm not easy to shock by anything here.

(*He comes downstage and faces out.*)

Always, anyhow, lived with too much space around me to be infected by ideas of other people. One thing you can grow on a big place more important than cotton! — is *tolerance!* — I grown it.

(*He returns toward Brick.*)

BRICK: Why can't exceptional friendship, *real, real, deep, deep friendship!* between two men be respected as something clean and decent without being thought of as —

BIG DADDY: It can, it is, for God's sake.

BRICK: — *Fairies.* . . .

(*In his utterance of this word, we gauge the wide and profound reach of the conventional mores he got from the world that crowned him with early laurel.*)

BIG DADDY: I told Mae an' Gooper —

BRICK: Frig Mae and Gooper, frig all dirty lies and liars! — Skipper and me had a clean, true thing between us! — had a clean friendship, practically all our lives, till Maggie got the idea you're talking about. Normal? No! — It was too rare to be normal, any true thing between two people is too rare to be normal. Oh, once in a while he put his hand on my shoulder or I'd put mine on his, oh, maybe even, when we were touring the country in profootball an' shared hotel rooms we'd reach across the space between the two beds and shake hands to say good-night, yeah, one or two times we —

BIG DADDY: Brick, nobody thinks that that's not normal!

BRICK: Well, they're mistaken, it was! It was a pure an' true thing an' that's not normal.

MAE (*offstage*): Big Daddy, they're startin' the fireworks.

(*They both stare straight at each other for a long moment. The tension breaks and both turn away as if tired.*)

BIG DADDY: Yeah, it's — hard t' — talk. . . .

BRICK: All right, then, let's — let it go. . . .

BIG DADDY: Why did Skipper crack up? Why have you?

(*Brick looks back at his father again. He has already decided, without knowing that he has made this decision, that he is going to tell his father that he is dying of cancer. Only this could even the score between them: one inadmissible thing in return for another.*)

BRICK (*ominously*): All right. You're asking for it, Big Daddy. We're finally going to have that real true talk you wanted. It's too late to stop it, now, we got to carry it through and cover every subject.

(*He hobbles back to the liquor cabinet.*)

Uh-huh.

(*He opens the ice bucket and picks up the silver tongs with slow admiration of their frosty brightness.*)

Maggie declares that Skipper and I went into pro-football after we left Ole Miss because we were scared to grow up . . .

(*He moves downstage with the shuffle and clop of a cripple on a crutch. As Margaret did when her speech became "recitative," he looks out into the house, commanding its attention by his direct, concentrated gaze — a broken, "tragically elegant" figure telling simply as much as he knows of "the Truth":*)

— Wanted to — keep on tossing — those long, long! — high, high! — passes that — couldn't be intercepted except by time, the aerial attack that made us famous! And so we did, we did, we kept it up for one season, that aerial attack, we held it high! — Yeah, but —

— that summer, Maggie, she laid the law down to me, said, Now or never, and so I married Maggie. . . .

BIG DADDY: How was Maggie in bed?

BRICK (*wryly*): Great! the greatest!

(*Big Daddy nods as if he thought so.*)

She went on the road that fall with the Dixie Stars. Oh, she made a great show of being the world's best sport. She wore a — wore a — tall bearskin cap! A shako, they call it, a dyed moleskin coat, a moleskin coat dyed red! — Cut up crazy! Rented hotel ballrooms for victory celebrations, wouldn't cancel them when it — turned out — defeat. . . .

MAGGIE THE CAT! Ha ha!

(*Big Daddy nods.*)

— But Skipper, he had some fever which came back on him which doctors couldn't explain and I got that injury — turned out to be just a shadow on the X-ray plate — and a touch of bursitis. . . .

I lay in a hospital bed, watched our games on TV, saw Maggie on the bench next to Skipper when he was hauled out of a game for stumbles, fumbles! — Burned me up the way she hung on his arm! — Y'know, I think that Maggie had always felt sort of left out because she and me never got any closer together than two people just get in bed, which is not much closer than two cats on a — fence humping. . . .

So! She took this time to work on poor dumb Skipper. He was a less than average student at Ole Miss, you know that, don't you?! — Poured in his mind the dirty, false idea that what we were, him and me, was a frustrated case of that ole pair of sisters that lived in this room, Jack Straw and Peter Ochello! — He, poor Skipper, went to bed with Maggie to prove it wasn't true, and when it didn't work out, he thought it *was* true! — Skipper broke in two like a rotten stick — nobody ever turned so fast to a lush — or died of it so quick. . . .

— Now are you satisfied?

(*Big Daddy has listened to this story, dividing the grain from the chaff. Now he looks at his son.*)

BIG DADDY: Are *you* satisfied?

BRICK: With what?

BIG DADDY: That half-ass story!

BRICK: What's half-ass about it?

BIG DADDY: Something's left out of that story. What did you leave out?

(*The phone has started ringing in the hall.*)

GOOPER (*offstage*): Hello.

(*As if it reminded him of something, Brick glances suddenly toward the sound and says:*)

BRICK: Yes! — I left out a long-distance call which I had from Skipper —

GOOPER: Speaking, go ahead.

BRICK: — In which he made a drunken confession to me and on which I hung up!

GOOPER: No.

BRICK: — Last time we spoke to each other in our lives . . .

GOOPER: No, sir.

BIG DADDY: You musta said something to him before you hung up.

BRICK: What could I say to him?

BIG DADDY: Anything. Something.

BRICK: Nothing.

BIG DADDY: Just hung up?

BRICK: Just hung up.

BIG DADDY: Uh-huh. Anyhow now! — we have tracked down the lie with which you're disgusted and which you are drinking to kill your disgust with, Brick. You been passing the buck. This disgust with mendacity is disgust with yourself.

You! — dug the grave of your friend and kicked him in it! — before you'd face truth with him!

BRICK: *His* truth, not *mine!*

BIG DADDY: His truth, okay! But you wouldn't face it with him!

BRICK: Who *can* face truth? Can *you?*

BIG DADDY: Now don't start passin' the rotten buck again, boy!

BRICK: How about these birthday congratulations, these many, many happy returns of the day, when ev'rybody knows there won't be any except you!

(*Gooper, who has answered the hall phone, lets out a high, shrill laugh; the voice becomes audible saying: "No, no, you got it all wrong! Upside down! Are you crazy?"*)

(*Brick suddenly catches his breath as he realizes that he has made a shocking disclosure. He hobbles a few paces, then freezes, and without looking at his father's shocked face says:*)

Let's, let's — go out, now, and — watch the fireworks. Come on, Big Daddy.

(*Big Daddy moves suddenly forward and grabs hold of the boy's crutch like it was a weapon for which they were fighting for possession.*)

BIG DADDY: Oh, no, no! No one's going out! What did you start to say?

BRICK: I don't remember.

BIG DADDY: "Many happy returns when they know there won't be any"?

BRICK: Aw, hell, Big Daddy, forget it. Come on out on the gallery and look at the fireworks they're shooting off for your birthday. . . .

BIG DADDY: First you finish that remark you were makin' before you cut off. "Many happy returns when they know there won't be any"? — Ain't that what you just said?

BRICK: Look, now. I can get around without that crutch if I have to but it would be a lot easier on the furniture an' glassware if I didn't have to go swinging along like Tarzan of th' —

BIG DADDY: FINISH! WHAT YOU WAS SAYIN'!

(*An eerie green glow shows in sky behind him.*)

BRICK (*sucking the ice in his glass, speech becoming thick*): Leave th' place to Gooper and Mae an' their five little same little monkeys. All I want is —

BIG DADDY: "LEAVE TH' PLACE," did you say?

BRICK (*vaguely*): All twenty-eight thousand acres of the richest land this side of the valley Nile.

BIG DADDY: Who said I was "leaving the place" to Gooper or anybody? This is my sixty-fifth birthday! I got fifteen years or twenty years left in me! I'll outlive *you*! I'll bury you an' have to pay for your coffin!

BRICK: Sure. Many happy returns. Now let's go watch the fireworks, come on, let's —

BIG DADDY: Lying, have they been lying? About the report from th' — clinic? Did they, did they — find something? — *Cancer.* Maybe?

BRICK: Mendacity is a system that we live in. Liquor is one way out an' death's the other. . . .

(*He takes the crutch from Big Daddy's loose grip and swings out on the gallery leaving the doors open.*)
(*A song, "Pick a Bale of Cotton," is heard.*)

MAE (*appearing in door*): Oh, Big Daddy, the field hands are singin' fo' you!

BRICK: I'm sorry, Big Daddy. My head don't work any more and it's hard for me to understand how anybody could care if he lived or died or was dying or cared about anything but whether or not there was liquor left in the bottle and so I said what I said without thinking. In some ways I'm no better than the others, in some ways worse because I'm less alive. Maybe it's being alive that makes them lie, and being almost *not* alive makes me sort of accidentally truthful — I don't know but — anyway — we've been friends . . .

— And being friends is telling each other the truth. . . .

(*There is a pause.*)

You told *me*! I told *you*!

BIG DADDY (*slowly and passionately*): CHRIST — DAMN —

GOOPER (*offstage*): Let her go!

(*Fireworks offstage right.*)

BIG DADDY: — ALL — LYING SONS OF — LYING BITCHES!

(*He straightens at last and crosses to the inside door. At the door he turns and looks back as if he had some des-*

perate question he couldn't put into words. Then he nods reflectively and says in a hoarse voice:)

Yes, all liars, all liars, all lying dying liars!

(*This is said slowly, slowly, with a fierce revulsion. He goes on out.*)

— Lying! Dying! Liars!

(*Brick remains motionless as the lights dim out and the curtain falls.*)

ACT 3

(*There is no lapse of time. Big Daddy is seen leaving as at the end of act 2.*)

BIG DADDY: ALL LYIN' — DYIN'! — LIARS! LIARS! — LIARS!

(*Margaret enters.*)

MARGARET: Brick, what in the name of God was goin' on in this room?

(*Dixie and Trixie enter through the doors and circle around Margaret shouting. Mae enters from the lower gallery window.*)

MAE: Dixie, Trixie, you quit that!

(*Gooper enters through the doors.*)

Gooper, will y' please get these kiddies to bed right now!

GOOPER: Mae, you seen Big Mama?

MAE: Not yet.

(*Gooper and kids exit through the doors. Reverend Tooker enters through the windows.*)

REVEREND TOOKER: Those kiddies are so full of vitality. I think I'll have to be starting back to town.

MAE: Not yet, Preacher. You know we regard you as a member of this family, one of our closest an' dearest, so you just got t' be with us when Doc Baugh gives Big Mama th' actual truth about th' report from the clinic.

MARGARET: Where do you think you're going?

BRICK: Out for some air.

MARGARET: Why'd Big Daddy shout "Liars"?

MAE: Has Big Daddy gone to bed, Brick?

GOOPER (*entering*): Now where is that old lady?

REVEREND TOOKER: I'll look for her.

(*He exits to the gallery.*)

MAE: Cain'tcha find her, Gooper?

GOOPER: She's avoidin' this talk.

MAE: I think she senses somethin'.

MARGARET (*going out on the gallery to Brick*): Brick, they're goin' to tell Big Mama the truth about Big Daddy and she's goin' to need you.

DOCTOR BAUGH: This is going to be painful.

MAE: Painful things caint always be avoided.

REVEREND TOOKER: I see Big Mama.

GOOPER: Hey, Big Mama, come here.

MAE: Hush, Gooper, don't holler.

BIG MAMA (*entering*): Too much smell of burnt fireworks makes me feel a little bit sick at my stomach. — Where is Big Daddy?

MAE: That's what I want to know, where has Big Daddy gone?

BIG MAMA: He must have turned in, I reckon he went to baid . . .

GOOPER: Well, then, now we can talk.

BIG MAMA: What *is* this talk, *what* talk?

(*Margaret appears on the gallery, talking to Doctor Baugh.*)

MARGARET (*musically*): My family freed their slaves ten years before abolition. My great-great-grandfather gave his slaves their freedom five years before the War between the States started!

MAE: Oh, for God's sake! Maggie's climbed back up in her family tree!

MARGARET (*sweetly*): What, Mae?

(*The pace must be very quick: great Southern animation.*)

BIG MAMA (*addressing them all*): I think Big Daddy was just worn out. He loves his family, he loves to have them around him, but it's a strain on his nerves. He wasn't himself tonight, Big Daddy wasn't himself, I could tell he was all worked up.

REVEREND TOOKER: I think he's remarkable.

BIG MAMA: Yaisss! Just remarkable. Did you all notice the food he ate at that table? Did you all notice the supper he put away? Why he ate like a hawss!

GOOPER: I hope he doesn't regret it.

BIG MAMA: What? Why that man — ate a huge piece of cawn bread with molasses on it! Helped himself twice to hoppin' John.

MARGARET: Big Daddy loves hoppin' John. — We had a real country dinner.

BIG MAMA (*overlapping Margaret*): Yaiss, he simply adores it! an' candied yams? Son? That man put away enough food at that table to stuff a *field* hand!

GOOPER (*with grim relish*): I hope he don't have to pay for it later on . . .

BIG MAMA (*fiercely*): What's *that*, Gooper?

MAE: Gooper says he hopes Big Daddy doesn't suffer tonight.

BIG MAMA: Oh, shoot, Gooper says, Gooper says! Why should Big Daddy suffer for satisfying a normal appetite? There's nothin' wrong with that man but nerves, he's sound as a dollar! And now he knows he is an' that's why he ate such a supper. He had a big load off his mind, knowin' he wasn't doomed t' — what he thought he was doomed to . . .

MARGARET (*sadly and sweetly*): Bless his old sweet soul . . .

BIG MAMA (*vaguely*): Yais, bless his heart, where's Brick?

MAE: Outside.

GOOPER: — Drinkin' . . .

BIG MAMA: I know he's drinkin'. Cain't I see he's drinkin' without you continually tellin' me that boy's drinkin'?

MARGARET: Good for you, Big Mama!

(*She applauds.*)

BIG MAMA: Other people *drink* and *have* drunk an' will *drink*, as long as they make that stuff an' put it in bottles.

MARGARET: That's the truth. I never trusted a man that didn't drink.

BIG MAMA: *Brick? Brick!*

MARGARET: He's still on the gall'ry. I'll go bring him in so we can talk.

BIG MAMA (*worriedly*): I don't know what this mysterious family conference is about.

(*Awkward silence. Big Mama looks from face to face, then belches slightly and mutters, "Excuse me . . . " She opens an ornamental fan suspended about her throat. A black lace fan to go with her black lace gown, and fans her wilting corsage, sniffing nervously and looking from face to face in the uncomfortable silence as Margaret calls "Brick?" and Brick sings to the moon on the gallery.*)

MARGARET: Brick, they're gonna tell Big Mama the truth an' she's gonna need you.

BIG MAMA: I don't know what's wrong here, you all have such long faces! Open that door on the hall and let some air circulate through here, will you please, Gooper?

MAE: I think we'd better leave that door closed, Big Mama, till after the talk.

MARGARET: Brick!

BIG MAMA: Reveren' Tooker, will *you* please open that door?

REVEREND TOOKER: I sure will, Big Mama.

MAE: I just didn't think we ought t' take any chance of Big Daddy hearin' a word of this discussion.

BIG MAMA: *I swan!* Nothing's going to be said in Big Daddy's house that he caint hear if he want to!

GOOPER: Well, Big Mama, it's —

(*Mae gives him a quick, hard poke to shut him up. He glares at her fiercely as she circles before him like a burlesque ballerina, raising her skinny bare arms over her head, jangling her bracelets, exclaiming:*)

MAE: A breeze! A breeze!

REVEREND TOOKER: I think this house is the coolest house in the Delta. — Did you all know that Halsey Banks's widow put air-conditioning units in the church and rectory at Friar's Point in memory of Halsey?

(*General conversation has resumed; everybody is chatting so that the stage sounds like a bird cage.*)

GOOPER: Too bad nobody cools your church off for you. I bet you sweat in that pulpit these hot Sundays, Reverend Tooker.

REVEREND TOOKER: Yes, my vestments are drenched. Last Sunday the gold in my chasuble faded into the purple.

GOOPER: Reveren', you musta been preachin' hell's fire last Sunday.

MAE (*at the same time to Doctor Baugh*): You reckon those vitamin B12 injections are what they're cracked up t' be, Doc Baugh?

DOCTOR BAUGH: Well, if you want to be stuck with something I guess they're as good to be stuck with as anything else.

BIG MAMA (*at the gallery door*): Maggie, Maggie, aren't you comin' with Brick?

MAE (*suddenly and loudly, creating a silence*): I have a strange feeling, I have a peculiar feeling!

BIG MAMA (*turning from the gallery*): What feeling?

MAE: That Brick said somethin' he shouldn't of said t' Big Daddy.

BIG MAMA: Now what on earth could Brick of said t' Big Daddy that he shouldn't say?

GOOPER: Big Mama, there's somethin' —

MAE: NOW, WAIT!

(*She rushes up to Big Mama and gives her a quick hug and kiss. Big Mama pushes her impatiently off.*)

DOCTOR BAUGH: In my day they had what they call the Keeley cure for heavy drinkers.

BIG MAMA: Shoot!

DOCTOR BAUGH: But now I understand they just take some kind of tablets.

GOOPER: They call them "Annie Bust" tablets.

BIG MAMA: *Brick* don't need to take *nothin'.*

(*Brick and Margaret appear in gallery doors, Big Mama unaware of his presence behind her.*)

That boy is just broken up over Skipper's death. You know how poor Skipper died. They gave him a big, big dose of that sodium amytal stuff at his home and then they called the ambulance and give him another big, big dose of it at the hospital and that and all of the alcohol in his system fo' months an' months just proved too much for his heart . . . I'm scared of needles! I'm more scared of a needle than the knife . . . I think more people have been needled out of this world than —

(*She stops short and wheels about.*)

Oh — here's Brick! My precious baby —

(*She turns upon Brick with short, fat arms extended, at the same time uttering a loud, short sob, which is both comic and touching. Brick smiles and bows slightly, making a burlesque gesture of gallantry for Margaret to pass before him into the room. Then he hobbles on his crutch directly to the liquor cabinet and there is absolute silence, with everybody looking at Brick as everybody*

has always looked at Brick when he spoke or moved or appeared. One by one he drops ice cubes in his glass, then suddenly, but not quickly, looks back over his shoulder with a wry, charming smile, and says:)

BRICK: I'm sorry! Anyone else?

BIG MAMA (*sadly*): No, son. I *wish* you wouldn't!

BRICK: I wish I didn't have to, Big Mama, but I'm still waiting for that click in my head which makes it all smooth out!

BIG MAMA: Ow, Brick, you — BREAK MY HEART!

MARGARET (*at same time*): Brick, go sit with Big Mama!

BIG MAMA: I just cain't staiiiiii-nnnnnnnd-it . . .

(*She sobs.*)

MAE: Now that we're all assembled —

GOOPER: We kin talk . . .

BIG MAMA: Breaks my heart . . .

MARGARET: Sit with Big Mama, Brick, and hold her hand.

(*Big Mama sniffs very loudly three times, almost like three drumbeats in the pocket of silence.*)

BRICK: You do that, Maggie. I'm a restless cripple. I got to stay on my crutch.

(*Brick hobbles to the gallery door; leans there as if waiting.*)
(*Mae sits beside Big Mama, while Gooper moves in front and sits on the end of the couch, facing her. Reverend Tooker moves nervously into the space between them; on the other side, Doctor Baugh stands looking at nothing in particular and lights a cigar. Margaret turns away.*)

BIG MAMA: Why're you all *surroundin'* me — like this? Why're you all starin' at me like this an' makin' signs at each other?

(*Reverend Tooker steps back startled.*)

MAE: Calm yourself, Big Mama.

BIG MAMA: Calm you'self, *you'self,* Sister Woman. How could I calm myself with everyone starin' at me as if big drops of blood had broken out on m'face? What's this all about, annh! What?

(*Gooper coughs and takes a center position.*)

GOOPER: Now, Doc Baugh.

MAE: Doc Baugh?

GOOPER: Big Mama wants to know the complete truth about the report we got from the Ochsner Clinic.

MAE (*eagerly*): — on Big Daddy's condition!

GOOPER: Yais, on Big Daddy's condition, we got to face it.

DOCTOR BAUGH: Well . . .

BIG MAMA (*terrified, rising*): Is there? Something? Something that I? Don't — know?

(*In these few words, this startled, very soft, question, Big Mama reviews the history of her forty-five years with Big Daddy, her great, almost embarrassingly true-hearted and simple-minded devotion to Big Daddy, who must have had something Brick has, who made himself loved so much by the "simple expedient" of not loving enough to disturb his charming detachment, also once coupled, like Brick, with virile beauty.)*

(Big Mama has a dignity at this moment; she almost stops being fat.)

DOCTOR BAUGH *(after a pause, uncomfortably)*: Yes? — Well —

BIG MAMA: I!!! — want to — *knowwwwwww . . .*

(Immediately she thrusts her fist to her mouth as if to deny that statement. Then for some curious reason, she snatches the withered corsage from her breast and hurls it on the floor and steps on it with her short, fat feet.)

    Somebody must be lyin'! — I want to know!

MAE: Sit down, Big Mama, sit down on this sofa.

MARGARET: Brick, go sit with Big Mama.

BIG MAMA: *What is it, what is it?*

DOCTOR BAUGH: I never have seen a more thorough examination than Big Daddy Pollitt was given in all my experience with the Ochsner Clinic.

GOOPER: It's one of the best in the country.

MAE: It's THE best in the country — bar *none!*

(For some reason she gives Gooper a violent poke as she goes past him. He slaps at her hand without removing his eyes from his mother's face.)

DOCTOR BAUGH: Of course they were ninety-nine and nine-tenths percent sure before they even started.

BIG MAMA: Sure of what, sure of what, sure of — what? — what?

(She catches her breath in a startled sob. Mae kisses her quickly. She thrusts Mae fiercely away from her, staring at the Doctor.)

MAE: Mommy, be a brave girl!

BRICK *(in the doorway, softly)*: "By the light, by the light, Of the sil-ve-ry mo-oo-n . . . "

GOOPER: Shut up! — Brick.

BRICK: Sorry . . .

(He wanders out on the gallery.)

DOCTOR BAUGH: But now, you see, Big Mama, they cut a piece of this growth, a specimen of the tissue and —

BIG MAMA: Growth? You told Big Daddy —

DOCTOR BAUGH: Now wait.

BIG MAMA *(fiercely)*: You told me and Big Daddy there wasn't a thing wrong with him but —

MAE: Big Mama, they always —

GOOPER: Let Doc Baugh talk, will yuh?

BIG MAMA: — little spastic condition of —

(Her breath gives out in a sob.)

DOCTOR BAUGH: Yes, that's what we told Big Daddy. But we had this bit of tissue run through the laboratory and I'm sorry to say the test was positive on it. It's — well — malignant . . .

(Pause.)

BIG MAMA: — Cancer?! Cancer?!

(Doctor Baugh nods gravely. Big Mama gives a long gasping cry.)

MAE AND GOOPER: Now, now, now, Big Mama, you had to know . . .

BIG MAMA: WHY DIDN'T THEY CUT IT OUT OF HIM? HANH? HANH?

DOCTOR BAUGH: Involved too much, Big Mama, too many organs affected.

MAE: Big Mama, the liver's affected and so's the kidneys, both! It's gone way past what they call a —

GOOPER: A surgical risk.

MAE: — Uh-huh . . .

(Big Mama draws a breath like a dying gasp.)

REVEREND TOOKER: Tch, tch, tch, tch, tch!

DOCTOR BAUGH: Yes it's gone past the knife.

MAE: *That's why he's turned yellow, Mommy!*

BIG MAMA: *Git away from me, git away from me, Mae!*

(She rises abruptly.)

    I want Brick! Where's Brick? Where is my only son?

MAE: Mama! Did she say "*only son*"?

GOOPER: What does that make *me*?

MAE: A sober responsible man with five precious children! — *Six!*

BIG MAMA: I want Brick to tell me! Brick! Brick!

MARGARET *(rising from her reflections in a corner)*: Brick was so upset he went back out.

BIG MAMA: *Brick!*

MARGARET: Mama, let *me* tell you!

BIG MAMA: No, no, leave me alone, you're not my blood!

GOOPER: *Mama, I'm your son!* Listen to *me!*

MAE: Gooper's your son, he's your first-born!

BIG MAMA: Gooper never liked Daddy.

MAE *(as if terribly shocked)*: *That's not TRUE!*

(There is a pause. The minister coughs and rises.)

REVEREND TOOKER *(to Mae)*: I think I'd better slip away at this point.

(Discreetly.)

    Good night, good night, everybody, and God bless you all . . . on this place . . .

(He slips out.)
(Mae coughs and points at Big Mama.)

GOOPER: Well, Big Mama . . .

(He sighs.)

BIG MAMA: It's all a mistake, I know it's just a bad dream.

DOCTOR BAUGH: We're gonna keep Big Daddy as comfortable as we can.

BIG MAMA: Yes, it's just a bad dream, that's all it is, it's just an awful dream.

GOOPER: In my opinion Big Daddy is having some pain but won't admit that he has it.

BIG MAMA: Just a dream, a bad dream.

DOCTOR BAUGH: That's what lots of them do, they think if they don't admit they're having the pain they can sort of escape the fact of it.

GOOPER (*with relish*): Yes, they get sly about it, they get real sly about it.

MAE: Gooper and I think —

GOOPER: Shut up, Mae! Big Mama, I think — Big Daddy ought to be started on morphine.

BIG MAMA: Nobody's going to give Big Daddy morphine.

DOCTOR BAUGH: Now, Big Mama, when that pain strikes it's going to strike mighty hard and Big Daddy's going to need the needle to bear it.

BIG MAMA: I tell you, nobody's going to give him morphine.

MAE: Big Mama, you don't want to see Big Daddy suffer, you know you —

(*Gooper, standing beside her, gives her a savage poke.*)

DOCTOR BAUGH (*placing a package on the table*): I'm leaving this stuff here, so if there's a sudden attack you all won't have to send out for it.

MAE: I know how to give a hypo.

BIG MAMA: Nobody's gonna give Big Daddy morphine.

GOOPER: Mae took a course in nursing during the war.

MARGARET: Somehow I don't think Big Daddy would want Mae to give him a hypo.

MAE: You think he'd want *you* to do it?

DOCTOR BAUGH: Well . . .

(*Doctor Baugh rises.*)

GOOPER: Doctor Baugh is goin'.

DOCTOR BAUGH: Yes, I got to be goin'. Well, keep your chin up, Big Mama.

GOOPER (*with jocularity*): She's gonna keep *both* chins up, aren't you, Big Mama?

(*Big Mama sobs.*)

Now stop that, Big Mama.

GOOPER (*at the door with Doctor Baugh*): Well, Doc, we sure do appreciate all you done. I'm telling you, we're surely obligated to you for —

(*Doctor Baugh has gone out without a glance at him.*)

— I guess that doctor has got a lot on his mind but it wouldn't hurt him to act a little more human . . .

(*Big Mama sobs.*)

Now be a brave girl, Mommy.

BIG MAMA: It's not true, I know that it's just not true!

GOOPER: Mama, those tests are infallible!

BIG MAMA: Why are you so determined to see your father daid?

MAE: Big Mama!

MARGARET (*gently*): I know what Big Mama means.

MAE (*fiercely*): Oh, do you?

MARGARET (*quietly and very sadly*): Yes, I think I do.

MAE: For a newcomer in the family you sure do show a lot of understanding.

MARGARET: Understanding is needed on this place.

MAE: I guess you must have needed a lot of it in your family, Maggie, with your father's liquor problem and now you've got Brick with his!

MARGARET: Brick does not have a liquor problem at all. Brick is devoted to Big Daddy. This thing is a terrible strain on him.

BIG MAMA: Brick is Big Daddy's boy, but he drinks too much and it worries me and Big Daddy, and, Margaret, you've got to cooperate with us, you've got to cooperate with Big Daddy and me in getting Brick straightened out. Because it will break Big Daddy's heart if Brick don't pull himself together and take hold of things.

MAE: Take hold of *what* things, Big Mama?

BIG MAMA: The place.

(*There is a quick violent look between Mae and Gooper.*)

GOOPER: Big Mama, you've had a shock.

MAE: Yais, we've all had a shock, but . . .

GOOPER: Let's be realistic —

MAE: — Big Daddy would never, would *never*, be foolish enough to —

GOOPER: — put this place in irresponsible hands!

BIG MAMA: Big Daddy ain't going to leave the place in anybody's hands; Big Daddy is *not* going to die. I want you to get that in your heads, all of you!

MAE: Mommy, Mommy, Big Mama, we're just as hopeful an' optimistic as you are about Big Daddy's prospects, we have faith in *prayer* — but nevertheless there are certain matters that have to be discussed an' dealt with, because otherwise —

GOOPER: Eventualities have to be considered and now's the time . . . Mae, will you please get my brief case out of our room?

MAE: Yes, honey.

(*She rises and goes out through the hall door.*)

GOOPER (*standing over Big Mama*): Now, Big Mom. What you said just now was not at all true and you know it. I've always loved Big Daddy in my own quiet way. I never made a show of it, and I know that Big Daddy has always been fond of me in a quiet way, too, and he never made a show of it neither.

(*Mae returns with Gooper's brief case.*)

MAE: Here's your brief case, Gooper, honey.

GOOPER (*handing the brief case back to her*): Thank you . . . Of cou'se, my relationship with Big Daddy is different from Brick's.

MAE: You're eight years older'n Brick an' always had t' carry a bigger load of th' responsibilities than Brick ever had t' carry. He never carried a thing in his life but a football or a highball.

GOOPER: Mae, will y' let me talk, please?

MAE: Yes, honey.

GOOPER: Now, a twenty-eight-thousand-acre plantation's a mighty big thing t' run.

MAE: Almost singlehanded.

(*Margaret has gone out onto the gallery and can be heard calling softly to Brick.*)

BIG MAMA: You never had to run this place! What are you talking about? As if Big Daddy was dead and in his grave, you had to run it? Why, you just helped him out with a few business details and had your law practice at the same time in Memphis!

MAE: Oh, Mommy, Mommy, Big Mommy! Let's be fair!

MARGARET: Brick!

MAE: Why, Gooper has given himself body and soul to keeping this place up for the past five years since Big Daddy's health started failing.

MARGARET: Brick!

MAE: Gooper won't say it, Gooper never thought of it as a duty, he just did it. And what did Brick do? Brick kept living in his past glory at college! Still a football player at twenty-seven!

MARGARET (*returning alone*): Who are you talking about now? Brick? A football player? He isn't a football player and you know it. Brick is a sports announcer on TV and one of the best-known ones in the country!

MAE: I'm talking about what he was.

MARGARET: Well, I wish you would just stop talking about my husband.

GOOPER: I've got a right to discuss my brother with other members of MY OWN family, which don't include *you*. Why don't you go out there and drink with Brick?

MARGARET: I've never seen such malice toward a brother.

GOOPER: How about his for me? Why, he can't stand to be in the same room with me!

MARGARET: This is a deliberate campaign of vilification for the most disgusting and sordid reason on earth, and I know what it is! It's *avarice, avarice, greed, greed!*

BIG MAMA: *Oh, I'll scream! I will scream in a moment unless this stops!*

(*Gooper has stalked up to Margaret with clenched fists at his sides as if he would strike her. Mae distorts her face again into a hideous grimace behind Margaret's back.*)

BIG MAMA (*sobs*): Margaret. Child. Come here. Sit next to Big Mama.

MARGARET: Precious Mommy. I'm sorry, I'm sorry, I — !

(*She bends her long graceful neck to press her forehead to Big Mama's bulging shoulder under its black chiffon.*)

MAE: How beautiful, how touching, this display of devotion! Do you know why she's childless? She's childless because that big beautiful athlete husband of hers won't go to bed with her!

GOOPER: You jest won't let me do this in a nice way, will yah? Aw right — I don't give a goddamn if Big Daddy likes me or don't like me or did or never did or will or will never! I'm just appealing to a sense of common decency and fair play. I'll tell you the truth. I've resented Big Daddy's partiality to Brick ever since Brick was born, and the way I've been treated like I was just barely good enough to spit on and sometimes not even good enough for that. Big Daddy is dying of cancer, and it's spread all through him and it's attacked all his vital organs including the kidneys and right now he is sinking into uremia, and you all know what uremia is, it's poisoning of the whole system due to the failure of the body to eliminate its poisons.

MARGARET (*to herself, downstage, hissingly*): *Poisons, poisons! Venomous thoughts and words! In hearts and minds! — That's poisons!*

GOOPER (*overlapping her*): I am asking for a square deal, and, by God, I expect to get one. But if I don't get one, if there's any peculiar shenanigans going on around here behind my back, well, I'm not a corporation lawyer for nothing, I know how to protect my own interests.

(*Brick enters from the gallery with a tranquil, blurred smile, carrying an empty glass with him.*)

BRICK: Storm coming up.

GOOPER: Oh! A late arrival!

MAE: Behold the conquering hero comes!

GOOPER: The fabulous Brick Pollitt! Remember him? — Who could forget him!

MAE: He looks like he's been injured in a game!

GOOPER: Yep, I'm afraid you'll have to warm the bench at the Sugar Bowl this year, Brick!

(*Mae laughs shrilly.*)

Or was it the Rose Bowl that he made that famous run in? —

(*Thunder.*)

MAE: The punch bowl, honey. It was in the punch bowl, the cut-glass punch bowl!

GOOPER: Oh, that's right, I'm getting the bowls mixed up!

MARGARET: Why don't you stop venting your malice and envy on a sick boy?

BIG MAMA: *Now you two hush, I mean it, hush, all of you, hush!*

DAISY, SOOKEY: Storm! Storm comin'! Storm! Storm!

LACEY: Brightie, close them shutters.

GOOPER: Lacey, put the top up on my Cadillac, will yuh?

LACEY: Yes, suh, Mistah Pollitt!

GOOPER (*at the same time*): Big Mama, you know it's necessary for me t' go back to Memphis in th' mornin' t' represent the Parker estate in a lawsuit.

(*Mae sits on the bed and arranges papers she has taken from the brief case.*)

BIG MAMA: Is it, Gooper?

MAE: Yaiss.

GOOPER: That's why I'm forced to — to bring up a problem that —

MAE: Somethin' that's too important t' be put off!

GOOPER: If Brick was sober, he ought to be in on this.

MARGARET: Brick is present; we're present.

GOOPER: Well, good. I will now give you this outline my partner, Tom Bullitt, an' me have drawn up — a sort of dummy — trusteeship.

MARGARET: Oh, that's it! You'll be in charge an dole out remittances, will you?

GOOPER: This we did as soon as we got the report on Big Daddy from th' Ochsner Laboratories. We did this thing, I mean we drew up this dummy outline with the advice and assistance of the Chairman of the Boa'd of Directors of th' Southern Plantahs Bank and Trust Company in Memphis, C. C. Bellowes, a man who handles estates for all th' prominent fam'lies in West Tennessee and th' Delta.

BIG MAMA: Gooper?

GOOPER (crouching in front of Big Mama): Now this is not — not final, or anything like it. This is just a preliminary outline. But it does provide a basis — a design — a — possible, feasible — *plan!*

MARGARET: Yes, I'll bet it's a plan.

(*Thunder.*)

MAE: It's a plan to protect the biggest estate in the Delta from irresponsibility an' —

BIG MAMA: Now you listen to me, all of you, you listen here! They's not goin' to be any more catty talk in my house! And Gooper, you put that away before I grab it out of your hand and tear it right up! I don't know what the hell's in it, and I don't want to know what the hell's in it. I'm talkin' in Big Daddy's language now; I'm his *wife*, not his *widow*, I'm still his *wife!* And I'm talkin' to you in his language an' —

GOOPER: Big Mama, what I have here is —

MAE (at the same time): Gooper explained that it's just a plan . . .

BIG MAMA: I don't care what you got there. Just put it back where it came from, an' don't let me see it again, not even the outside of the envelope of it! Is that understood? Basis! Plan! Preliminary! Design! I say — what is it Big Daddy always says when he's disgusted?

BRICK (from the bar): Big Daddy says "crap" when he's disgusted.

BIG MAMA (rising): That's right — CRAP! I say CRAP too, like Big Daddy!

(*Thunder.*)

MAE: Coarse language doesn't seem called for in this —

GOOPER: Somethin' in me is *deeply outraged* by hearin' you talk like this.

BIG MAMA: *Nobody's goin' to take nothin'!* — till Big Daddy lets go of it — maybe, just possibly, not — not even then! No, not even then!

(*Thunder.*)

MAE: Sookey, hurry up an' git that po'ch furniture cova-hed; want th' paint to come off?

GOOPER: Lacey, put mah car away!

LACEY: Caint, Mistah Pollitt, you got the keys!

GOOPER: Naw, you got 'em, man. Where th' keys to th' car, honey?

MAE: You got 'em in your pocket!

BRICK: "You can always hear me singin' this song, Show me the way to go home."

(*Thunder distantly.*)

BIG MAMA: Brick! Come here, Brick, I need you. Tonight Brick looks like he used to look when he was a little boy, just like he did when he played wild games and used to come home when I hollered myself hoarse for him, all sweaty and pink cheeked and sleepy, with his — red curls shining . . .

(*Brick draws aside as he does from all physical contact and continues the song in a whisper, opening the ice bucket and dropping in the ice cubes one by one as if he were mixing some important chemical formula.*)

(*Distant thunder.*)

Time goes by so fast. Nothin' can outrun it. Death commences too early — almost before you're half acquainted with life — you meet the other . . . Oh, you know we just got to love each other an' stay together, all of us, just as close as we can, especially now that such a *black* thing has come and moved into this place without invitation.

(*Awkwardly embracing Brick, she presses her head to his shoulder.*)

(*A dog howls offstage.*)

Oh, Brick, son of Big Daddy, Big Daddy does so love you. Y'know what would be his fondest dream come true? If before he passed on, if Big Daddy has to pass on . . .

(*A dog howls.*)

. . . you give him a child of yours, a grandson as much like his son as his son is like Big Daddy . . .

MARGARET: I know that's Big Daddy's dream.

BIG MAMA: That's his dream.

MAE: Such a pity that Maggie and Brick can't oblige.

BIG DADDY (off downstage right on the gallery): Looks like the wind was takin' liberties with this place.

SERVANT (offstage): Yes, sir, Mr. Pollitt.

MARGARET (crossing to the right door): Big Daddy's on the gall'ry.

(*Big Mama has turned toward the hall door at the sound of Big Daddy's voice on the gallery.*)

BIG MAMA: I can't stay here. He'll see somethin' in my eyes.

(*Big Daddy enters the room from upstage right.*)

BIG DADDY: Can I come in?

(*He puts his cigar in an ash tray.*)

MARGARET: Did the storm wake you up, Big Daddy?

BIG DADDY: Which stawm are you talkin' about — th' one outside or th' hullballoo in here?

(*Gooper squeezes past Big Daddy.*)

GOOPER: 'Scuse me.

(*Mae tries to squeeze past Big Daddy to join Gooper, but Big Daddy puts his arm firmly around her.*)

BIG DADDY: I heard some mighty loud talk. Sounded like somethin' important was bein' discussed. What was the powwow about?

MAE (*flustered*): Why — nothin', Big Daddy . . .

BIG DADDY (*crossing to extreme left center, taking Mae with him*): What is that pregnant-lookin' envelope you're puttin' back in your brief case, Gooper?

GOOPER (*at the foot of the bed, caught, as he stuffs papers into envelope*): That? Nothin', suh — nothin' much of anythin' at all . . .

BIG DADDY: Nothin'? It looks like a whole lot of nothin'!

(*He turns upstage to the group.*)

You all know th' story about th' young married couple —

GOOPER: Yes, sir!

BIG DADDY: Hello, Brick —

BRICK: Hello, Big Daddy.

(*The group is arranged in a semicircle above Big Daddy, Margaret at the extreme right, then Mae and Gooper, then Big Mama, with Brick at the left.*)

BIG DADDY: Young married couple took Junior out to th' zoo one Sunday, inspected all of God's creatures in their cages, with satisfaction.

GOOPER: Satisfaction.

BIG DADDY (*crossing to upstage center, facing front*): This afternoon was a warm afternoon in spring an' that ole elephant had somethin' else on his mind which was bigger'n peanuts. You know this story, Brick?

(*Gooper nods.*)

BRICK: No, sir, I don't know it.

BIG DADDY: Y'see, in th' cage adjoinin' they was a young female elephant in heat!

BIG MAMA (*at Big Daddy's shoulder*): Oh, Big Daddy!

BIG DADDY: What's the matter, preacher's gone, ain't he? All right. That female elephant in the next cage was permeatin' the atmosphere about her with a powerful and excitin' odor of female fertility! Huh! Ain't that a nice way to put it, Brick?

BRICK: Yes, sir, nothin' wrong with it.

BIG DADDY: Brick says th's nothin' wrong with it!

BIG MAMA: Oh, Big Daddy!

BIG DADDY (*crossing to downstage center*): So this ole bull elephant still had a couple of fornications left in him. He reared back his trunk an' got a whiff of that elephant lady next door! — began to paw at the dirt in his cage an' butt his head against the separatin' partition and, first thing y'know, there was a conspicuous change in his *profile* — very *conspicuous*! Ain't I tellin' this story in decent language, Brick?

BRICK: Yes, sir, too fuckin' decent!

BIG DADDY: So, the little boy pointed at it and said, "What's that?" His mama said, "Oh, that's — nothin'!" — His papa said, "She's spoiled!"

(*Big Daddy crosses to Brick at left.*)

You didn't laugh at that story, Brick.

(*Big Mama crosses to downstage right crying. Margaret goes to her. Mae and Gooper hold upstage right center.*)

BRICK: No, sir, I didn't laugh at that story.

BIG DADDY: What is the smell in this room? Don't you notice it, Brick? Don't you notice a powerful and obnoxious odor of mendacity in this room?

BRICK: Yes, sir, I think I do, sir.

GOOPER: Mae, Mae . . .

BIG DADDY: There is nothing more powerful. Is there, Brick?

BRICK: No, sir. No, sir, there isn't, an' nothin' more obnoxious.

BIG DADDY: Brick agrees with me. The odor of mendacity is a powerful and obnoxious odor an' the stawm hasn't blown it away from this room yet. You notice it, Gooper?

GOOPER: What, sir?

BIG DADDY: How about you, Sister Woman? You notice the unpleasant odor of mendacity in this room?

MAE: Why, Big Daddy, I don't even know what that is.

BIG DADDY: You can smell it. Hell it smells like death!

(*Big Mama sobs. Big Daddy looks toward her.*)

What's wrong with that fat woman over there, loaded with diamonds? Hey, what's-you-name, what's the matter with you?

MARGARET (*crossing toward Big Daddy*): She had a slight dizzy spell, Big Daddy.

BIG DADDY: You better watch that, Big Mama. A stroke is a bad way to go.

MARGARET (*crossing to Big Daddy at center*): Oh, Brick, Big Daddy has on your birthday present to him, Brick, he has on your cashmere robe, the softest material I have ever felt.

BIG DADDY: Yeah, this is my soft birthday, Maggie . . . Not my gold or my silver birthday, but my soft birthday, everything's got to be soft for Big Daddy on this soft birthday.

(*Maggie kneels before Big Daddy at center.*)

MARGARET: Big Daddy's got on his Chinese slippers that I gave him, Brick. Big Daddy, I haven't given you my big present yet, but now I will, now's the time for me to present it to you! I have an announcement to make!

MAE: What? What kind of announcement?

GOOPER: A sports announcement, Maggie?

MARGARET: Announcement of life beginning! A child is coming, sired by Brick, and out of Maggie the Cat! I have Brick's child in my body, an' that's my birthday present to Big Daddy on this birthday!

(*Big Daddy looks at Brick who crosses behind Big Daddy to downstage portal, left.*)

BIG DADDY: Get up, girl, get up off your knees, girl.

(*Big Daddy helps Margaret to rise. He crosses above her, to her right, bites off the end of a fresh cigar, taken from his bathrobe pocket, as he studies Margaret.*)

Uh-huh, this girl has life in her body, that's no lie!

BIG MAMA: BIG DADDY'S DREAM COME TRUE!

BRICK: JESUS!

BIG DADDY (*crossing right below wicker stand*): Gooper, I want my lawyer in the mornin'.

BRICK: Where are you goin', Big Daddy?

BIG DADDY: Son, I'm goin' up on the roof, to the belvedere on th' roof to look over my kingdom before I give up my kingdom — twenty-eight thousand acres of th' richest land this side of the valley Nile!

(*He exits through right doors, and down right on the gallery.*)

BIG MAMA (*following*): Sweetheart, sweetheart, sweetheart — can I come with you?

(*She exits downstage right.*)
    (*Margaret is downstage center in the mirror area. Mae has joined Gooper and she gives him a fierce poke, making a low hissing sound and a grimace of fury.*)

GOOPER (*pushing her aside*): Brick, could you possibly spare me one small shot of that liquor?

BRICK: Why, help yourself, Gooper boy.

GOOPER: I will.

MAE (*shrilly*): Of course we know that this is — a lie.

GOOPER: Be still, Mae.

MAE: I won't be still! I know she's made this up!

GOOPER: Goddamn it, I said shut up!

MARGARET: Gracious! I didn't know that my little announcement was going to provoke such a storm!

MAE: *That* woman isn't *pregnant*!

GOOPER: Who said she was?

MAE: *She* did.

GOOPER: The doctor didn't. Doc Baugh didn't.

MARGARET: I haven't gone to Doc Baugh.

GOOPER: Then who'd you go to, Maggie?

MARGARET: One of the best gynecologists in the South.

GOOPER: Uh huh, uh huh! — I see . . .

(*He takes out a pencil and notebook.*)

    — May we have his name, please?

MARGARET: No, you may not, Mister Prosecuting Attorney!

MAE: He doesn't have any name, he doesn't exist!

MARGARET: Oh, he exists all right, and so does my child, Brick's baby!

MAE: You can't conceive a child by a man that won't sleep with you unless you think you're —

(*Brick has turned on the phonograph. A scat song cuts Mae's speech.*)

GOOPER: *Turn that off!*

MAE: We know it's a lie because we hear you in here; he won't sleep with you, we hear you! So don't imagine you're going to put a trick over on us, to fool a dying man with a —

(*A long drawn cry of agony and rage fills the house. Margaret turns the phonograph down to a whisper. The cry is repeated.*)

MAE: Did you hear that, Gooper, did you hear that?

GOOPER: Sounds like the pain has struck.

MAE: Go see, Gooper!

GOOPER: Come along and leave these lovebirds together in their nest!

(*He goes out first. Mae follows but turns at the door, contorting her face and hissing at Margaret.*)

MAE: *Liar!*

(*She slams the door.*)
    (*Margaret exhales with relief and moves a little unsteadily to catch hold of Brick's arm.*)

MARGARET: Thank you for — keeping still . . .

BRICK: O.K., Maggie.

MARGARET: It was gallant of you to save my face!

(*He now pours down three shots in quick succession and stands waiting, silent. All at once he turns with a smile and says:*)

BRICK: *There!*

MARGARET: What?

BRICK: The *click* . . .

(*His gratitude seems almost infinite as he hobbles out on the gallery with a drink. We hear his crutch as he swings out of sight. Then, at some distance, he begins singing to himself a peaceful song. Margaret holds the big pillow forlornly as if it were her only companion, for a few moments, then throws it on the bed. She rushes to the liquor cabinet, gathers all the bottles in her arms, turns about undecidedly, then runs out of the room with them, leaving the door ajar on the dim yellow hall. Brick is heard hobbling back along the gallery, singing his peaceful song. He comes back in, sees the pillow on the bed, laughs lightly, sadly, picks it up. He has it under his arm as Margaret returns to the room. Margaret softly shuts the door and leans against it, smiling softly at Brick.*)

MARGARET: Brick, I used to think that you were stronger than me and I didn't want to be overpowered by you. But now, since you've taken to liquor — you know what? — I guess it's bad, but now I'm stronger than you and I can love you more truly! Don't move that pillow. I'll move it right back if you do! — Brick?

(*She turns out all the lamps but a single rose-silk-shaded one by the bed.*)

I really have been to a doctor and I know what to do and — Brick? — this is my time by the calendar to conceive?

BRICK: Yes, I understand, Maggie. But how are you going to conceive a child by a man in love with his liquor?

MARGARET: By locking his liquor up and making him satisfy my desire before I unlock it!

BRICK: Is that what you've done, Maggie?

MARGARET: Look and see. That cabinet's mighty empty compared to before!

BRICK: Well, I'll be a son of a —

(He reaches for his crutch but she beats him to it and rushes out on the gallery, hurls the crutch over the rail, and comes back in, panting.)

MARGARET: And so tonight we're going to make the lie true, and when that's done, I'll bring the liquor back here and we'll get drunk together, here, tonight, in this place that death has come into . . . — What do you say?

BRICK: I don't say anything. I guess there's nothing to say.

MARGARET: Oh, you weak people, you weak, beautiful people! — who give up with such grace. What you want is someone to —

(She turns out the rose-silk lamp.)

— take hold of you. — Gently, gently with love hand your life back to you, like somethin' gold you let go of. I *do* love you, Brick, I *do!*

BRICK *(smiling with charming sadness)*: Wouldn't it be funny if that was true?

COMMENTARIES

Tennessee Williams (1911–1983)
MEMOIRS   1972

Tennessee Williams published Memoirs *in 1972, after establishing himself as one of the most successful American playwrights. The excerpts included here concern his feelings about* Cat on a Hot Tin Roof *and his feelings about being a writer.*

Well, now, about plays, what about them? Plays are written and then, if they are lucky, they are performed, and if their luck still holds, which is not too frequently the case, their performance is so successful that both audience and critics at the first night are aware that they are being offered a dramatic work which is both honest and entertaining and also somehow capable of engaging their aesthetic appreciation.

I have never liked to talk about the professional side of my life. Am I afraid that it is a bird that will be startled away by discussion, as by a hawk's shadow? Something like that, I suppose.

People are always asking me, at those symposia to which I've been subjected in recent years, which is my favorite among the plays I have written, the number of which eludes my recollection, and I either say to them, "Always the latest" or I succumb to my instinct for the truth and say, "I suppose it must be the published version of *Cat on a Hot Tin Roof.*"

That play comes closest to being both a work of art and a work of craft. It is really very well put together, in my opinion, and all its characters are amusing and credible and touching. Also it adheres to the valuable edict of Aristotle that a tragedy must have unity of time and place and magnitude of theme.

The set in *Cat* never changes and its running time is exactly the time of its action, meaning that one act, timewise, follows directly upon the other, and I know of no other modern American play in which this is accomplished.

However my reasons for liking *Cat* best are deeper than that. I believe that in *Cat* I reached beyond myself, in the second act, to a kind of crude eloquence of expression in Big Daddy that I have managed to give no other character of my creation.

The story of *Cat*'s production in 1954 and the disaster that followed upon its enormous success must be told now.

[Director Elia] Kazan immediately shared Audrey's [Wood, Williams's agent] enthusiasm for *Cat* but he said that it was faulty in one act. I assumed that he meant the first act, but no, it was the third act. He wanted a more admirable heroine than the Maggie offered in the original script.

Inwardly I disagreed. I thought that in Maggie I had presented a very true and moving portrait of a young woman whose frustration in love and whose practicality drove her to the literal seduction of an unwilling young man. Seduction is too soft a word. Brick was literally forced back to bed by Maggie, when she confiscated his booze . . .

Then I also had to violate my own intuition by having Big Daddy re-enter the stage in Act Three. I saw nothing for him to do in that act when he re-entered and I did not think that it was dramatically proper that he should re-enter. Consequently I had him tell "the elephant story." This was assaulted by censors. I was told it must be removed. The material which I then had to put in its place was always offensive to me.

I would not tell you this except for the consequences to me as a writer after *Cat* had received its Critics' Award and its Pulitzer.

Even though I always go crazy on opening nights, the New York opening of *Cat* was particularly dreadful. I thought it was a failure, a distortion of what I had intended. After the show was over I thought I had heard coughs all during the performance. I suppose there weren't that many, probably the usual number. And it did become my biggest, my longest-running play. But after the show was over on opening night, Kazan said, "Let's go to my apartment until the reviews are out." He was totally confident that it would be a hit. I met Audrey Wood outside, and at the time I was totally dependent on her for any creative confidence; and so I said, "Audrey, we're all going up to the Kazans' to wait for the notices." She said, "Oh no, I have other plans." I was hurt, and said something mean. . . .

What is it like being a writer? I would say it is like being free.

I know that some writers aren't free, they are professionally employed, which is quite a different thing.

Professionally, they are probably better writers in the conventional sense of "better." They have an ear to the ground of best-seller demands: They please their publishers and presumably their public as well.

But they are not free and so they are not what I regard a true writer as being.

To be free is to have achieved your life.

It means any number of freedoms.

It means the freedom to stop when you please, to go where and when you please, it means to be voyager here and there, one who flees many hotels, sad or happy, without obstruction and without much regret.

It means the freedom of being. And someone has wisely observed, if you can't be yourself, what's the point of being anything at all?

I am not a frequent reader nor quoter of Scriptures and yet I love a piece of advice which occurs among them:

"Let thy light so shine among men that they see thy good works and glorify thy Father which is in heaven."

There is a New Journalism, there is a New Criticism, there is a new look and style of cinema and theater, of practically everything that we live with, but what I think we most need is a New Morality.

And I think we've arrived at a point where that is a necessity of continued and bearable existence.

Brenda Murphy (b. 1950)
TENNESSEE WILLIAMS AND ELIA KAZAN
COLLABORATE ON *CAT*   1991

Theater is a collaborative art, and numerous plays have been altered because of suggestions of director or actor. The collaboration of Tennessee Williams and director Elia Kazan was special because both were powerful personalities and each respected the other. The Cat on a Hot Tin Roof *that we know is much different from the one that Williams first wrote. He was willing to make many of the creative changes suggested by Kazan.*

[Director Elia Kazan's] imagination stimulated by Big Daddy's rhetorical power, Kazan developed the production around the impetus of direct communication between the characters and the audience. At the beginning of Act 2, for example, he made a note to himself to have Big Daddy come downstage facing the audience and talk straight out to them while the others remained way upstage, even out on the gallery. Williams agreed with Kazan about the power of Big Daddy's character and the centrality of words in the play. In *Memoirs* he wrote, "In *Cat* I reached beyond myself, in the second act, to a kind of crude eloquence of expression in Big Daddy that I have managed to give no other character of my creation."[1]

Although Williams had incorporated the idea of addressing the audience in the "recitative" speeches of Maggie and Brick in the early scripts, he had not counted on what was in 1955 the radical concept that Kazan devised for the production. As Kazan noted in a later interview, the conventions of representational realism were so entrenched in the Broadway theater of the fifties that foregrounding the production's theatricality to the extent of having the characters address the audience directly had been considered anathema for many years. The last time he could remember it being done was in the production of *Our Town*° in 1938.[2]

---

[1]Tennessee Williams, *Memoirs* (Garden City: Doubleday, 1975).
Our Town: In this play the Stage Manager speaks to the audience.
[2]Michel Ciment, *Kazan on Kazan* (New York: Viking, 1974) 47.

Kazan's pride in this rejection of realistic convention and his continuing interest in subjectifying theatrical experience were evident in an interview he gave in the early sixties:

> I was busting out of the goddamned proscenium theater uptown. In *Cat on a Hot Tin Roof* I had everybody address the audience continually. Every time they had one of those long speeches they'd turn and say it to the audience. Nobody thought anything of it once we opened. But there was a hell of a lot of bitching about it before. . . . The whole second act of *Cat* was a long address by Burl Ives to the audience. I had him address various members of the audience . . . "what would *you* do?" is implicit in this kind of staging. It sucks the audience into the experience and emotion of that moment.[3]

Kazan wrote in his autobiography that he had to convince Williams to accept his notion of how Burl Ives would play the part of Big Daddy. When Kazan said he was going to bring Ives right down to the edge of the forestage, have him "look the audience right in the eye, and speak it directly to them," Williams protested that *Cat* was a realistic play, and should be kept within the representational conventions. When pressed by Kazan to say whether old cotton planters actually talked that eloquently and that long without interruption, Williams replied that they did. After all, who would dare interrupt them?[4] Nonetheless Kazan pursued his concept for the production in the face of Williams's skepticism, if not his opposition.

The Design

When the central dynamic of the production had been established as direct communication between the characters and the audience, it had to imbue all the elements of the stage language. Here Kazan reports that he did run into opposition from Williams, who had a clear idea of what he thought the set should be like, an image that had evolved as he had revised the play. In the notes for the designer he prepared for the script preceding the November pre-rehearsal version, Williams described the basic plan of the set that was eventually used for the production: a bed–sitting room in a Mississippi Delta plantation, opening onto an upstairs gallery and showing white balustrades against a fair summer sky that fades into dusk and night during the course of the play. This is what is needed to support the action of the play which, as Williams was fond of pointing out, observed the unities of time and place, the action of the play being confined to the single set and occupying exactly the amount of time it took to enact on stage. The lighting was obviously crucial for this play, to show the passage of time that is a central thematic concern as well as a structural one.

Beyond this, however, Williams's original image of the set was strikingly different from the set Kazan and Jo Mielziner eventually devised between them. Williams described the room as Victorian, with a touch of the Far East, and poetically haunted by the tender relationship of Jack Straw and Peter Ochello. He noted that the room should not have changed much since Straw and Ochello's time. To suggest the style for the design, Williams referred the designer to the reproduction he had seen of a faded photograph of the verandah of Robert Louis Stevenson's home in Samoa: "There was a quality of tender light on weathered wood, such as porch-furniture made of bamboo and wicker, exposed to tropical suns and tropical rains,

[3] Quoted in Richard Schechner and Theodore Hoffman, "'Look, There's the American Theatre': An Interview with Elia Kazan," *Tulane Drama Review,* 9 (Winter 1964): 71.
[4] Elia Kazan, *Elia Kazan: A Life* (New York: Knopf, 1988) 541–42.

which came to mind when I thought about the set for this play" (RV xiii).° The photograph, he wrote, also brought to mind "the grace and comfort of light, the reassurance it gives, on a late and fair afternoon in summer, the way that no matter what, even dread of death, is gently touched and soothed by it. For the set is the background for a play that deals with human extremities of emotion and needs that softness behind it" (RV xiii).

Williams described in detail the big, slightly raked, double bed and the "entertainment center" that were the most significant objects in the set, and then he cautioned the designer, lest he feel that the previous description confined him to literal realism. As in the published "Note for the Designer," Williams envisioned that "the set should be far less realistic than I have so far implied in this description of it": The walls should dissolve mysteriously into the air below the ceiling; the set should be roofed by the sky; stars and moon suggested by traces of milky pallor, as if they were observed through a telescope lens out of focus (RV xiv). The original note, however, added the idea that a spiral nebula might be faintly suggested in order to suggest the "mystery of the cosmos," which Williams thought should be a visible presence in the play, almost as present as an actor in it. He also thought that the cloud effects and the sound effects for the windstorm in Act 3 should be as unrealistic as the set. As he revised the script, however, Williams began to reconceptualize the set as well. In November he sent off a rewrite of the scene description suggesting that the room should appear to have been remodeled since Straw and Ochello's time, and now had an open, Japanese effect. The canopied bed, he suggested, could appear to have been removed from an Italian renaissance palazzo when Big Daddy and Big Mama raided Europe a few years previously.

When Kazan and Mielziner began talking about the design, their concept of a production that foregrounded the characters' rhetorical appeals to the audience became the central element in their discussion. Kazan has written:

> Jo Mielziner and I had read the play in the same way; we saw its great merit was its brilliant rhetoric and its theatricality. Jo didn't see the play as realistic any more than I did. If it was to be done realistically, I would have to contrive stage business to keep the old man talking those great second-act speeches turned out front and pretend that it was just another day in the life of the Pollitt family. This would, it seemed to me, amount to an apology to the audience for the glory of the author's language. It didn't seem like just another day in the life of a cotton planter's family to Jo or to me; it seemed like the best kind of theater, the kind we were interested in encouraging, the theater theatrical, not pretending any longer that an audience wasn't out there to be addressed but having a performer as great as Burl Ives acknowledge their presence at all times and even make eye contact with individuals.[5]

Accordingly, Kazan wrote, "I caused Jo to design our setting as I wished, a large, triangular platform, tipped toward the audience and holding only one piece of furniture, an ornate bed. This brought the play down to its essentials and made it impossible for it to be played any way except as I preferred."[6]

The set was not quite so spare as Kazan remembered it, but the central point of his statement, that the presentational impulse was the dominant aesthetic factor in

---

RV: The reading version of the play (New York: New American Library, 1958), which has both versions of the third act.
[5]Kazan 542–43.
[6]Kazan 543.

creating the design, has been fully corroborated by Mielziner. In his memoir, Mielziner described their discussion about the design much as Kazan did. Asked how he thought the "elephant story" should be handled proxemically, Mielziner told Kazan that he thought it should receive as much emphasis as possible: "I suggested that we have an area of the stage on which Big Daddy could come down close to the audience and deliver the lines with dramatic force." Mielziner wrote that Kazan was delighted with his answer, and "from this discussion grew the idea of creating a stage within the stage. It would be steeply raked toward the audience with one corner actually jutting out over the footlights. In its final form it turned out to be a sort of thrust stage."[7]

Mielziner's design was a departure from the subjective realism he had employed in *Menagerie, Streetcar,* and *Summer and Smoke,* in that he did not try to suggest through the material elements of the stage language that the events unfolding on stage were filtered through the mind of one of the characters. Instead, the design of the set projected the action out toward the audience, forcing it to become involved as though it were one of the characters. Extremely spare, the set was composed of two platforms, a large diamond-shaped one, a corner of which projected beyond the proscenium, and a smaller rectangle a foot lower at stage right. There were no doors, such actions as opening doors and looking into the mirror being mimed in this production. The only items of furniture Mielziner drew in his sketches were the primary material signifiers: the large bed, which signified both Maggie and Brick's failing marriage and the lingering memory of Straw and Ochello; the entertainment center, which signified both Brick's immediate goal of escape from reality and the vacuous materialism that Williams saw in the fifties; and the daybed, which signified Brick's withdrawal from Maggie, their marriage, and life in general. The actual set, however, also held a wicker night table and a large wicker armchair which could accommodate either Burl Ives or two of the other actors. The overall effect was of a large playing space down front where the actors could address the audience as if from a bare platform.

The lines of the design contributed to this effect. The perspective was such that the corner of the ceiling came down to a point slightly to the left of upstage center, helping to focus the audience's attention on the point of the diamond where the characters addressed the audience. Mielziner took Williams's hints to give lighting a central function in the play, running a scrim from floor to ceiling along two sides of the set with strips of black velour indicating the lines of the columns outside the windows of the room when the light of the moon was projected through them. To signify sunlight, slide projections of blinds were thrown on the scrims, while the gallery and the lawn beyond the windows were blocked out. When characters on the gallery or the lawn were to be seen, the lights behind the scrim were brought up, making the actors visible to the audience, as had been done with *Streetcar.*

Two follow-spots were used in the production. One, on the audience's left, highlighted Maggie throughout Act 1 and picked up Big Mama, Maggie, and Brick in Act 2, as they were in turn nominally being addressed by Big Daddy, who was downstage talking to the audience. In Act 3 the light again shone on Maggie almost without interruption. The follow-spot on the audience's right highlighted the characters Maggie was addressing in Act 1, chiefly Brick, as she had her turn at "recitative." It shone on Big Daddy throughout Act 2 and picked up Brick, Big Mama,

[7]*Designing for Theatre: A Memoir and a Portfolio* (New York: Bram Hall House, 1965) 183.

Gooper, Mae, and Maggie at various times during Act 3, emphasizing a significant entrance or a significant reaction indexically as it occurred. Contributing to the generally "golden" look of the production's lighting, the follow-spots were amber except when a character went out onto the gallery, when they were changed to blue. The follow-spots not only helped to avoid confusion by focusing the audience's attention where Kazan wanted it to be, they also contributed to the fore-grounding of the theatricality in the production by "framing" specific characters and pieces of action. Kazan stylized the composition of his stage picture in *Cat*, and encoded a great deal of meaning through gesture, movement, and pose in the production. Using the follow-spots to highlight these formal compositions emphasized that what was happening onstage was not real life but theater.

In designing the furniture, both Kazan and Mielziner took their cue from Williams's earlier description of the set, emphasizing the qualities he had seen in the Robert Louis Stevenson photograph. Kazan had underlined elements of this description in his copy of the script. Listed together, they indicate quite well the direction Mielziner took with the design after their conferences:

Delta's biggest cotton planter
Far East
The room must evoke some ghosts
Gently . . . poetically haunted by a relationship . . . a tenderness which was uncommon
Samoan Island
tender light on weathered wood
Bamboo . . . wicker
[the entertainment center] monument . . . very complete . . . compact little shrine . . .
all the comforts . . . illusions . . . hide [written in the margin, "Brick hides"] such
things as the characters in the play are faced with (RV xii–xiv)

From these suggestions came the old wicker headboard with its huge and fantastically shaped design of two cornucopias, the matching wicker furniture, the carpet with its lushly fertile design of oversized flowers and vines, and the one object in the room that competed with the fertility symbol of the bed for the audience's attention, the oversized bar, hi-fi, radio, and television with its sleekly modern fifties lines. This object realized Williams's description of a compact modern shrine to all the comforts and illusions of contemporary life and signified Brick's retreat from human contact.

Kazan has said more than once that Williams did not like the set that Mielziner finally developed for *Cat* because he thought his play should be performed realistically. Kazan has also indicated that the set was a material signifier of his aesthetic vision in opposition to Williams's:

I had the setting I'd asked for; Jo had given me what I wanted. Tennessee had approved of it earlier, when he was ready to approve of damn near anything I asked for, because I was the director he wanted. Now the setting was up onstage, too late to change, and on that setting there was only one way for any human to conduct himself: "out front" it's called. Dear Tennessee was stuck with my vision, like it or not.[8]

[8]Kazan 543.

Ben Brantley (b. 1955)
BIG DADDY'S EGO DEFIES DEATH AND HIS FAMILY   2003

The drama critic for the New York Times *finds in a contemporary production of* Cat on a Hot Tin Roof *a new insight into the character of Big Daddy. The November 2003 production featuring Ned Beatty as Big Daddy breaks new ground and suggests a new light by which we can interpret his character in this play.*

There's nothing remotely feline about the critter who rules the new revival of "Cat on a Hot Tin Roof," which opened last night at the Music Box Theater. As the Southern patriarch Big Daddy in Tennessee Williams's Pulitzer Prize–winning drama of familial lies and loneliness, Ned Beatty brings to mind a rooster bred for cockfighting, just released from his cage and rarin' to ruffle feathers.

It may be rotten ole mendacity that Big Daddy insists he sniffs in his battle-ground of a homestead on his 65th birthday. But from the moment Mr. Beatty first shows up in the play's second act, he brings with him the invigorating breeze of passionate, scrupulously detailed acting. As long as he is allowed to dominate the stage, Anthony Page's production exhales the galvanizing honesty that is the elusive holy grail for Big Daddy, as it was for the playwright who invented him.

Before Mr. Beatty arrives, the predominant aroma is definitely more artificial, like a magnolia-scented air freshener. This mostly has to do with the undeniably luscious-looking movie star Ashley Judd as Maggie the Cat.

The first act largely belongs to Maggie, a blood-pumping life force of a woman, as she tries to win back the, er, affections of her terminally disgusted, alcoholically abstracted husband, Brick (Jason Patric, another luscious-looking film actor), Big Daddy's favorite son.

This should be the most purely entertaining part of "Cat." (It's all that a lot of people remember about it, thanks to the bowdlerized 1958 film version starring a lusty Elizabeth Taylor.) But in this production, it feels more like a teaser for the main event that is Mr. Beatty.

Ms. Judd, seen somewhat more advantageously on Broadway in a revival of "Picnic" in 1994, delivers her arialike monologues with clarity enough for the audience to savor their scorching wit and priceless Southern grotesqueries. But it's the performance of a self-conscious pupil in an elocution class.

As Ms. Judd gulps down a breath before taking on the next ornate hurdle of a sentence, you can imagine the penciled markings in her script. Although she is often funny (as well as beautiful) when Maggie gets really angry, this actress, so appealingly effortless in films like "Ruby in Paradise," shows little spontaneity in "Cat."

Fortunately, there is much more to "Cat" than Maggie. The play may have had the longest original run of any of Williams's works for reasons of notoriety. After all, "Cat" dared in 1955 not only to address the problems of a woman whose husband wouldn't sleep with her but also hinted at homosexual longings in a man as masculine as Ben Gazarra, who played Brick to Barbara Bel Geddes's Maggie.

But the core of "Cat" — and the reason it still resonates as one of the great American dramas — is both more primal and more complex. Williams's favorite among his plays, it is perhaps his most impassioned and articulate statement on human isolation, the wrenching problems of communication between people and the ways in which death defines life.

These sentiments are expressed most forcefully in Act II, when Big Daddy takes his shot at bringing Brick back to life. As Mr. Beatty plays the scene, which was inspired by one of Williams's last conversations with his terminally ill father, you understand why the playwright wrote that with Big Daddy he achieved "a kind of crude eloquence of expression . . . that I have managed to give no other character in my creation."

Big Daddy is dying of cancer but has been deceived into thinking he suffers from only a spastic colon. And Mr. Beatty, who wears his sand-colored suit as if sheathed in sunlight, projects the heady omnipotence of a man who believes he has "just now returned from the other side of the moon, death's country."

The form in which he has emerged from this journey has little in common with the mother of all Big Daddys: Burl Ives, who originated the part on stage and screen as a mythic, mountainous vulgarian. Mr. Beatty's patriarch is a strutting, jig-dancing bantam, a Napoleonic figure who has willed himself into wealth and power.

What Mr. Beatty does better than any other Big Daddy I've seen is to convey without caricature the monstrous, exhilarated egotism of a man who believes he has outrun death. This is especially evident in the giddy cruelty with which he dismisses Big Mama (the funny and affecting Margo Martindale), the wife he has only pretended to love for 40 years.

When he jokily threatens to hit her with his birthday cake, it's actually shocking. And he brings the casual contempt of a man waving away gnats to Big Daddy's dealings with the greedy Gooper (Michael Mastro), his older son, and Mae (Amy Hohn), Gooper's predatory wife, not to mention their hideous children, the immortally named "no-neck monsters."

Yet this is also a man who for the first time has applied his native shrewdness to cosmic questions. And Mr. Beatty makes it heart-stoppingly clear that it's Big Daddy's sudden awareness of life's brevity that leads him into confrontation with Brick, the one person he genuinely loves.

Mr. Beatty brings out the best in Mr. Patric. This chiseled-faced actor, who appears to have spent many hours watching Marlon Brando and James Dean movies, takes Brick's self-anesthetized state to sometimes exasperating extremes. If there's no discernible spark of life left in this former sports hero, who's in perpetual mourning for the death of his best friend, then there's no dramatic tension in the campaign to resurrect him. It's a losing game from the get-go.

But with Mr. Beatty's prodding, this Brick awakens reluctantly and desperately to long-suppressed emotions. The resulting indignation and agony sting like a salted wound.

Mr. Page — who directed a brilliant "Doll's House" in 1997 as well as "Cat" (also with Mr. Beatty) in London two years ago — does admirably in elucidating the play's patterns of evasion and power struggles. The late Maria Bjornson's airy rendering of Brick and Maggie's bedroom gracefully suggests an ephemeral world in which walls offer neither protection nor privacy.

The so-called fourth wall between stage and audience is used here as a bank of mirrors, in which people keep checking themselves and the reflections of others. And Mr. Page makes acutely pointed use of the injured Brick's crutch as a tool in family power plays.

You'll find in your program a note from Mr. Page about the play's third act. There are three versions of it, since Williams was asked by the director Elia Kazan to rewrite his original, bleaker ending. (The one used here is a variation on the adaptation Williams provided for the 1974 revival.)

No matter the version, it's the weakest of the acts, as the greedy Gooper and Mae — portrayed here with the usual gargoylish glee by Mr. Mastro and Ms. Hohn — get their comeuppance. Ms. Martindale, who finds depths of pathos as well as the sad silliness in Big Mama, and Mr. Beatty, in a fleeting reappearance, give the act what substance it has. But it's Ms. Judd who is required to make it sing, and she's simply not up to it.

That said, this "Cat" offers thought-plumbing pleasures too seldom found on Broadway these days. In an essay about "Cat," Williams spoke of his ability to open himself up to audiences in ways he felt he never could in social situations. "I want to go on talking to you as freely and intimately about what we live and die for as if I knew you better than anyone else whom you know," he wrote. Mr. Beatty guarantees that the conversation goes on.

Arthur Miller

Arthur Miller (b. 1915) has been the dean of American playwrights since the opening of *Death of a Salesman* in 1949. His steady output as a writer and a playwright began with his first publications after college in 1939, when he worked in the New York Federal Theatre Project, a branch of the Works Progress Administration (WPA), Franklin D. Roosevelt's huge Depression-era effort to put Americans back to work.

Miller, the son of a Jewish immigrant, was born and raised during his early years in the Harlem section of Manhattan and later in Brooklyn after his father's business failed. In high school Miller thought of himself more as an athlete than as a student, and he had trouble getting teachers' recommendations for college. After considerable struggle and waiting, he entered the University of Michigan, where his talent as a playwright emerged under the tutelage of Kenneth Rowe, his playwriting professor. His undergraduate plays won important university awards, and he became noticed by the Theatre Guild, a highly respected theater founded to present excellent plays (not necessarily commercial successes). His career was under way.

From 1939 to 1947 Miller wrote radio plays, screenplays, articles, stories, and a novel. His work covered a wide range of material, much of it growing out of his childhood memories of a tightly knit and somewhat eccentric family that provided him with a large gallery of characters. But he also dealt with political issues and problems of anti-Semitism, which was widespread in the 1930s and 1940s. Miller's political concerns have been a constant presence in his work since his earliest writings.

All My Sons (1947) was his first successful play. It ran on Broadway for three hundred performances, a remarkable record for a serious drama. The story centers on a man who knowingly produces defective parts for airplanes and then blames the subsequent crashes on his business partner, who is ruined and imprisoned. When the guilty man's son finds out the truth, he confronts his father and rebukes him. Ultimately, the man realizes not only that he has lost his son because of his deceit but that the dead pilots were also "all my sons." The play won the New York Drama Critics' Circle Award.

Miller's next play, *Death of a Salesman* (1949), was written in six weeks. Focusing on the American ideal of business success, its conclusions were a challenge to standard American business values. Willy Loman, first performed by Lee J. Cobb, was intended to be a warning for Americans in the postwar period of the cost of growing wealth and affluence.

His next play, *The Crucible* (1953), portrayed witch-hunts of seventeenth-century New England, but most people recognized the subtext: it was about contemporary anti-Communist witch-hunts. In the late 1940s and early 1950s the House Un-American Activities Committee (HUAC) held hearings to uncover suspected Communists in all areas of American life, particularly the arts. Many writers, artists, and performers came under close, often unfair, scrutiny by HUAC for their own political views and allegiances and were often asked to testify against their friends. Many were blacklisted (prevented from working in commercial theaters and movie companies), some were imprisoned for not testifying at others' trials, and some had their reputations and careers destroyed.

Arthur Miller was fearless in facing down HUAC, and he was convicted of contempt of court for not testifying against his friends. For a time he too was blacklisted, but his contempt citation was reversed, and he was not imprisoned. Given his personal political stance during this dangerous time, it is not a surprise to find that he usually chooses to write about matters of social concern.

In the 1990s Miller became the darling of the London stage while at the same time being somewhat neglected in the United States. One full-scale play, *Broken Glass* (1994), played in regional theater before going to a brief run on Broadway and then a longer run in London's West End. The play concerns a woman who becomes paralyzed in response to *Kristallnacht* (night of crystal), a night of violent rampages against Jews and Jewish property that resulted in 91 Jewish dead, hundreds injured, and 7,500 businesses and 177 synagogues gutted. After November 9, 1938, it was clear that Jews were no longer safe in Hitler's Germany. The subject of the play is intense, significant, and still timely.

The Ride Down Mount Morgan had its premiere in London in 1991; it then took seven years to open in New York in 1998. Its protagonist, Lyman Felt, played by Patrick Stewart in New York, was conceived as a Reaganite go-getter of the late 1980s: economically rapacious, sexually voracious, and amoral. When Felt's Porsche crashes on a ride down Mount Morgan, his two wives discover one another at the hospital. The play proceeds from there, examining the ethical values that permit Felt to live as he does. George Wolfe produced the play at the Joseph Papp Public Theatre. The Broadway production opened at the Ambassador Theater in April 2000, again with Patrick Stewart. The play was nominated for a Tony Award.

DEATH OF A SALESMAN

Death of a Salesman (1949) was a hit from its first performances and has remained at the center of modern American drama ever since. It has been successful in China, where there were no salesmen in 1983, and in Europe, where many salesmen dominate certain industries. Everywhere this play has touched the hearts and minds of its audiences. Its success is a phenomenon of American drama.

The play was first performed in an experimental environment. Miller had originally conceived of a model of a man's head as the stage setting. He has said: "The first image that occurred to me which was to result in *Death of a*

Salesman was of an enormous face the height of the proscenium arch which would appear and then open up, and we would see the inside of a man's head. In fact, *The Inside of His Head* was the first title." This technique was not used, but when Miller worked with the director and producer of the first production, he helped develop a setting that became a model for the "American style" in drama. The multilevel set permitted the play to shift from Willy Loman and his wife, Linda, having a conversation in their kitchen to their son's bedroom on the second level of the house. The set permitted portions of the stage to be reserved for Willy's visions of his brother, Ben, and for scenes outside the house such as Willy's interlude with the woman in Boston.

In a way, the setup of the stage respected Miller's original plan, but instead of portraying a cross-section of Willy's head, it presented a metaphor for a cross-section of his life. The audience was not looking in on just a living room, as in the nineteenth-century Ibsenist approach, but on an entire house and an entire life.

Using a cross-section of a house as a metaphor was an especially important device in this play because of the play's allusions to Greek tragedy. The great Greek tragedies usually portray the destruction of a house — such as the house of Atreus — in which "house" stands for a whole family, not a building. When Shakespeare's Hamlet dies, for example, his entire line dies with him. The death in *Death of a Salesman* implies the destruction of a family holding certain beliefs that have been wrong from the start.

The life of the salesman has given Willy a sense of dignity and worth, and he imagines that the modern world has corrupted that sense by robbing salesmen of the value of their personality. He thinks that the modern world has failed him, but he is wrong. His original belief — that what counts is not *what* you know but *whom* you know and how well you are liked — lies at the heart of his failure. When the play opens, he already has failed at the traveling salesman's job because he can no longer drive to his assigned territory. He cannot sell what he needs to sell.

Willy has inculcated his beliefs in his sons, Happy and Biff, and both are as ineffectual as their father. Willy doted on Biff and encouraged him to become a high school football star at the expense of his studies. But when Biff cannot pass an important course, and his plans to make up the work are subverted by his disillusionment in his father, his dreams of a college football career vanish. He cannot change and recover from this defeat. Happy, like his father, builds castles in the air and assumes somehow that he will be successful, though he has nothing to back himself up with. He wants the glory — and he spends time in fanciful imaginings, as Willy does — but he cannot do the basic work that makes it possible to achieve glory. Ironically, it is the "anemic" Bernard — who studies hard, stresses personal honesty and diligence, and never brags — who is successful.

Linda supports Willy's illusions, allowing him to be a fraud by sharing — or pretending to believe — in his dream. Willy has permitted himself to feel that integrity, honesty, and fidelity are not as important as being well liked.

The play ends with Willy still unable to face the deceptions he has perpetuated. He commits suicide, believing that his sons will be able to follow in his footsteps and succeed where he did not; he thinks that his insurance money will save the house and the family. What he does not realize is that his sons are no more capable than he is. They have been corrupted by his thinking, his values, his beliefs. And they cannot solve the problems that overwhelmed him.

Death of a Salesman has been given a privileged position in American drama because it is a modern tragedy. Aristotle felt that only characters of noble birth could be tragic heroes, but Miller confounds this theory, as Eugene O'Neill did, by showing the human integrity in even the most humble characters. Miller's Willy Loman is not a peasant, nor is he noble. In fact, Miller took a frightening risk in producing a figure that we find hard to like. Willy wants to be well liked, but as an audience we find it difficult to like a person who whines, complains, and accepts petty immorality as a normal way of life. Despite his character, we are awed by his fate.

One Chinese commentator said, after the Chinese production, that China is filled with such dreamers as Willy. Certainly America has been filled with them. Willy stands as an aspect of our culture, commercial and otherwise, that is at the center of our reflection of ourselves. Perhaps we react so strongly to Willy because we are afraid that we might easily become a Willy Loman if we are not vigilant about our moral views, our psychological well-being, and the limits of our commitment to success. Willy Loman has mesmerized audiences in America in many different economic circumstances: prosperity, recession, rapid growth, and cautious development. No matter what those circumstances, we have looked at the play as if looking in a mirror. What we have seen has always involved us, although it has not always made us pleased with ourselves.

Death of a Salesman in Performance

Death of a Salesman opened on Broadway on February 10, 1949, and won virtually every prize available for drama, including the Pulitzer Prize and the New York Drama Critics' Circle Award for best play. It ran on Broadway for an incredible 742 performances. Elia Kazan, director, was instrumental in establishing the play's innovative staging. Lee J. Cobb was cast as Willy, Mildred Dunnock as Linda, Arthur Kennedy as Biff, and Cameron Mitchell as Happy. The London production in July 1949, with Paul Muni as Willy and Kevin McCarthy as Biff, lasted 204 performances. Robert Coleman said of the New York production: "An explosion of emotional dynamite was set off last evening in the Morosco [Theater]. . . . In fashioning *Death of a Salesman* for them, author Arthur Miller and director Elia Kazan have collaborated on as exciting and devastating a theatrical blast as the nerves of modern playgoers can stand." Of Cobb, Howard Barnes said, "Cobb contributes a mammoth and magnificent portrayal of the central character. In his hands the salesman's frustration and final suicide are a matter of tremendous import."

An all-black production was directed by Lee Sankowich in Baltimore in 1972. Miller, in the audience on that production's opening night, commented that the play had been well received in "many countries and cultures" and that the Baltimore production further underscored the universality of the play. George C. Scott was praised for the power of his performance as Willy in New York's Circle in the Square production in 1975. A Chinese production directed by Arthur Miller was enormously successful in 1983. In the most celebrated revival of the play Dustin Hoffman portrayed Willy, John Malkovich played Biff, and Michael Rudman directed at the Broadhurst Theatre in New York in 1984. The critic Benedict Nightingale said of that production: "Somewhere at the core of him [Willy] an elaborate battle is being fought between dishonesty and honesty, glitter and substance, appearance and reality, between the promises or supposed promises of society and the claims of the self, between what Willy professes to value and what, perhaps without knowing it, he actually does value." In 1985 Dustin Hoffman brought his production of Miller's play to television, where it was viewed by an estimated twenty-five million people.

On February 10, 1999, exactly fifty years to the day from its original opening, the play's most recent production opened with Brian Dennehy as Willy Loman. The production was conceived in Chicago by the Goodman Theater Company, and in its revival Dennehy was praised by critics and theater-goers alike for presenting a powerful portrayal of Willy Loman for a new generation. Critics praised the timelessness of the drama — ultimately crowning it as an American classic.

Arthur Miller (b. 1915)

DEATH OF A SALESMAN   *1949*
CERTAIN PRIVATE CONVERSATIONS IN TWO ACTS AND A REQUIEM

Characters

WILLY LOMAN	UNCLE BEN
LINDA	HOWARD WAGNER
BIFF	JENNY
HAPPY	STANLEY
BERNARD	MISS FORSYTHE
THE WOMAN	LETTA
CHARLEY	

The action takes place in Willy Loman's house and yard and in various places he visits in the New York and Boston of today.

(Throughout the play, in the stage directions, left and right mean stage left and stage right.)

ACT I

(A melody is heard, played upon a flute. It is small and fine, telling of grass and trees and the horizon. The curtain rises.)

(Before us is the Salesman's house. We are aware of towering, angular shapes behind it, surrounding it on all sides. Only the blue light of the sky falls upon the house and forestage; the surrounding area shows an angry glow of orange. As more light appears, we see a solid vault of apartment houses around the small, fragile-

seeming home. An air of the dream clings to the place, a dream rising out of reality. The kitchen at center seems actual enough, for there is a kitchen table with three chairs, and a refrigerator. But no other fixtures are seen. At the back of the kitchen there is a draped entrance, which leads to the living room. To the right of the kitchen, on a level raised two feet, is a bedroom furnished only with a brass bedstead and a straight chair. On a shelf over the bed a silver athletic trophy stands. A window opens onto the apartment house at the side.)*

(Behind the kitchen, on a level raised six and a half feet, is the boys' bedroom, at present barely visible. Two beds are dimly seen, and at the back of the room a dormer window. [This bedroom is above the unseen living room.] At the left a stairway curves up to it from the kitchen.)

(The entire setting is wholly or, in some places, partially transparent. The roofline of the house is one-dimensional; under and over it we see the apartment buildings. Before the house lies an apron, curving beyond the forestage into the orchestra. This forward area serves as the back yard as well as the locale of all Willy's imaginings and of his city scenes. Whenever the action is in the present the actors observe the imaginary wall-lines, entering the house only through its door at the left. But in the scenes of the past these boundaries are broken, and characters enter or leave a room by stepping "through" a wall onto the forestage.)

[handwritten margin note: music playing (flute) whimsical music?]

(*From the right, Willy Loman, the Salesman, enters, carrying two large sample cases. The flute plays on. He hears but is not aware of it. He is past sixty years of age, dressed quietly. Even as he crosses the stage to the doorway of the house, his exhaustion is apparent. He unlocks the door, comes into the kitchen, and thankfully lets his burden down, feeling the soreness of his palms. A word-sigh escapes his lips — it might be "Oh, boy, oh, boy." He closes the door then carries his cases out into the living room, through the draped kitchen doorway.*)

(*Linda, his wife, has stirred in her bed at the right. She gets out and puts on a robe, listening. Most often jovial, she has developed an iron repression of her exceptions to Willy's behavior — she more than loves him, she admires him, as though his mercurial nature, his temper, his massive dreams and little cruelties, served her only as sharp reminders of the turbulent longings within him, longings which she shares but lacks the temperament to utter and follow to their end.*)

LINDA (*hearing Willy outside the bedroom, calls with some trepidation*): Willy!

WILLY: It's all right. I came back.

LINDA: Why? What happened? (*Slight pause.*) Did something happen, Willy?

WILLY: No, nothing happened.

LINDA: You didn't smash the car, did you?

WILLY (*with casual irritation*): I said nothing happened. Didn't you hear me?

LINDA: Don't you feel well?

WILLY: I'm tired to the death. (*The flute has faded away. He sits on the bed beside her, a little numb.*) I couldn't make it. I just couldn't make it, Linda.

LINDA (*very carefully, delicately*): Where were you all day? You look terrible.

WILLY: I got as far as a little above Yonkers. I stopped for a cup of coffee. Maybe it was the coffee.

LINDA: What?

WILLY (*after a pause*): I suddenly couldn't drive anymore. The car kept going off onto the shoulder, y'know?

LINDA (*helpfully*): Oh. Maybe it was the steering again. I don't think Angelo knows the Studebaker.

WILLY: No, it's me, it's me. Suddenly I realize I'm goin' sixty miles an hour and I don't remember the last five minutes. I'm — I can't seem to — keep my mind to it.

LINDA: Maybe it's your glasses. You never went for your new glasses.

WILLY: No, I see everything. I came back ten miles an hour. It took me nearly four hours from Yonkers.

LINDA (*resigned*): Well, you'll just have to take a rest, Willy, you can't continue this way.

WILLY: I just got back from Florida.

LINDA: But you didn't rest your mind. Your mind is overactive, and the mind is what counts, dear.

WILLY: I'll start out in the morning. Maybe I'll feel better in the morning. (*She is taking off his shoes.*) These goddam arch supports are killing me.

LINDA: Take an aspirin. Should I get you an aspirin? It'll soothe you.

WILLY (*with wonder*): I was driving along, you understand? And I was fine. I was even observing the scenery. You can imagine, me looking at scenery, on the road every week of my life. But it's so beautiful up there, Linda, the trees are so thick, and the sun is warm. I opened the windshield and just let the warm air bathe over me. And then all of a sudden I'm goin' off the road! I'm tellin' ya, I absolutely forgot I was driving. If I'd've gone the other way over the white line I might've killed somebody. So I went on again — and five minutes later I'm dreamin' again, and I nearly — (*He presses two fingers against his eyes.*) I have such thoughts, I have such strange thoughts.

LINDA: Willy, dear. Talk to them again. There's no reason why you can't work in New York.

WILLY: They don't need me in New York. I'm the New England man. I'm vital in New England.

LINDA: But you're sixty years old. They can't expect you to keep traveling every week.

WILLY: I'll have to send a wire to Portland. I'm supposed to see Brown and Morrison tomorrow morning at ten o'clock to show the line. Goddammit, I could sell them! (*He starts putting on his jacket.*)

LINDA (*taking the jacket from him*): Why don't you go down to the place tomorrow and tell Howard you've simply got to work in New York? You're too accommodating, dear.

WILLY: If old man Wagner was alive I'd a been in charge of New York now! That man was a prince, he was a masterful man. But that boy of his, that Howard, he don't appreciate. When I went north the first time, the Wagner Company didn't know where New England was!

LINDA: Why don't you tell those things to Howard, dear?

WILLY (*encouraged*): I will, I definitely will. Is there any cheese?

LINDA: I'll make you a sandwich.

WILLY: No, go to sleep. I'll take some milk. I'll be up right away. The boys in?

LINDA: They're sleeping. Happy took Biff on a date tonight.

WILLY (*interested*): That so?

LINDA: It was so nice to see them shaving together, one behind the other, in the bathroom. And going out together. You notice? The whole house smells of shaving lotion.

WILLY: Figure it out. Work a lifetime to pay off a house. You finally own it, and there's nobody to live in it.

LINDA: Well, dear, life is a casting off. It's always that way.

WILLY: No, no, some people — some people accomplish something. Did Biff say anything after I went this morning?

LINDA: You shouldn't have criticized him, Willy, especially after he just got off the train. You mustn't lose your temper with him.

WILLY: When the hell did I lose my temper? I simply asked him if he was making any money. Is that a criticism?

LINDA: But, dear, how could he make any money?

WILLY (*worried and angered*): There's such an undercurrent in him. He became a moody man. Did he apologize when I left this morning?

LINDA: He was crestfallen, Willy. You know how he admires you. I think if he finds himself, then you'll both be happier and not fight any more.

WILLY: How can he find himself on a farm? Is that a life? A farmhand? In the beginning, when he was young, I thought, well, a young man, it's good for him to tramp around, take a lot of different jobs. But it's more than ten years now and he has yet to make thirty-five dollars a week!

LINDA: He's finding himself, Willy.

WILLY: Not finding yourself at the age of thirty-four is a disgrace!

LINDA: Shh!

WILLY: The trouble is he's lazy, goddammit!

LINDA: Willy, please!

WILLY: Biff is a lazy bum!

LINDA: They're sleeping. Get something to eat. Go on down.

WILLY: Why did he come home? I would like to know what brought him home.

LINDA: I don't know. I think he's still lost, Willy. I think he's very lost.

WILLY: Biff Loman is lost. In the greatest country in the world a young man with such — personal attractiveness, gets lost. And such a hard worker. There's one thing about Biff — he's not lazy.

LINDA: Never.

WILLY (*with pity and resolve*): I'll see him in the morning; I'll have a nice talk with him. I'll get him a job selling. He could be big in no time. My God! Remember how they used to follow him around in high school? When he smiled at one of them their faces lit up. When he walked down the street . . . (*He loses himself in reminiscences.*)

LINDA (*trying to bring him out of it*): Willy, dear, I got a new kind of American-type cheese today. It's whipped.

WILLY: Why do you get American when I like Swiss?

LINDA: I just thought you'd like a change —

WILLY: I don't want a change! I want Swiss cheese. Why am I always being contradicted?

LINDA (*with a covering laugh*): I thought it would be a surprise.

WILLY: Why don't you open a window in here, for God's sake?

LINDA (*with infinite patience*): They're all open, dear.

WILLY: The way they boxed us in here. Bricks and windows, windows and bricks.

LINDA: We should've bought the land next door.

WILLY: The street is lined with cars. There's not a breath of fresh air in the neighborhood. The grass don't grow anymore, you can't raise a carrot in the back yard. They should've had a law against apartment houses. Remember those two beautiful elm trees out there? When I and Biff hung the swing between them?

LINDA: Yeah, like being a million miles from the city.

WILLY: They should've arrested the builder for cutting those down. They massacred the neighborhood. (*Lost.*) More and more I think of those days, Linda. This time of year it was lilac and wisteria. And then the peonies would come out, and the daffodils. What fragrance in this room!

LINDA: Well, after all, people had to move somewhere.

WILLY: No, there's more people now.

LINDA: I don't think there's more people. I think —

WILLY: There's more people! That's what's ruining this country! Population is getting out of control. The competition is maddening! Smell the stink from that apartment house! And another one on the other side . . . How can they whip cheese?

(*On Willy's last line, Biff and Happy raise themselves up in their beds, listening.*)

LINDA: Go down, try it. And be quiet.

WILLY (*turning to Linda, guiltily*): You're not worried about me, are you, sweetheart?

BIFF: What's the matter?

HAPPY: Listen!

LINDA: You've got too much on the ball to worry about.

WILLY: You're my foundation and my support, Linda.

LINDA: Just try to relax, dear. You make mountains out of molehills.

WILLY: I won't fight with him any more. If he wants to go back to Texas, let him go.

LINDA: He'll find his way.

WILLY: Sure. Certain men just don't get started till later in life. Like Thomas Edison, I think. Or B. F. Goodrich. One of them was deaf. (*He starts for the bedroom doorway.*) I'll put my money on Biff.

LINDA: And Willy — if it's warm Sunday we'll drive in the country. And we'll open the windshield, and take lunch.

WILLY: No, the windshields don't open on the new cars.

LINDA: But you opened it today.

WILLY: Me? I didn't. (*He stops.*) Now isn't that peculiar! Isn't that a remarkable — (*He breaks off in amazement and fright as the flute is heard distantly.*)

LINDA: What, darling?

WILLY: That is the most remarkable thing.

LINDA: What, dear?

WILLY: I was thinking of the Chevvy. (*Slight pause.*) Nineteen twenty-eight . . . when I had that red Chevvy — (*Breaks off.*) That funny? I coulda sworn I was driving that Chevvy today.

LINDA: Well, that's nothing. Something must've reminded you.

WILLY: Remarkable. Ts. Remember those days? The way Biff used to simonize that car? The dealer refused to believe there was eighty thousand miles on it. (*He shakes his head.*) Heh! (*To Linda.*) Close your eyes, I'll be right up. (*He walks out of the bedroom.*)

HAPPY (*to Biff*): Jesus, maybe he smashed up the car again!

LINDA (*calling after Willy*): Be careful on the stairs, dear! The cheese is on the middle shelf! (*She turns, goes over to the bed, takes his jacket, and goes out of the bedroom.*)

(*Light has risen on the boys' room. Unseen, Willy is heard talking to himself, "Eighty thousand miles," and a little laugh. Biff gets out of bed, comes downstage a bit, and stands attentively. Biff is two years older than his brother Happy, well built, but in these days bears a worn air and seems less self-assured. He has succeeded less, and his dreams are stronger and less acceptable than Happy's. Happy is tall, powerfully made. Sexuality is like a visible color on him, or a scent that many women have discovered. He, like his brother, is lost, but in a different way, for he has never allowed himself to turn his face toward defeat and is thus more confused and hard-skinned, although seemingly more content.*)

HAPPY (*getting out of bed*): He's going to get his license taken away if he keeps that up. I'm getting nervous about him, y'know, Biff?

BIFF: His eyes are going.

HAPPY: No, I've driven with him. He sees all right. He just doesn't keep his mind on it. I drove into the city with him last week. He stops at a green light and then it turns red and he goes. (*He laughs.*)

BIFF: Maybe he's color-blind.

HAPPY: Pop? Why he's got the finest eye for color in the business. You know that.

BIFF (*sitting down on his bed*): I'm going to sleep.

HAPPY: You're not still sour on Dad, are you, Biff?

BIFF: He's all right, I guess.

WILLY (*underneath them, in the living room*): Yes, sir, eighty thousand miles — eighty-two thousand!

BIFF: You smoking?

HAPPY (*holding out a pack of cigarettes*): Want one?

BIFF (*taking a cigarette*): I can never sleep when I smell it.

WILLY: What a simonizing job, heh!

HAPPY (*with deep sentiment*): Funny, Biff, y'know? Us sleeping in here again? The old beds. (*He pats his bed affectionately.*) All the talk that went across those two beds, huh? Our whole lives.

BIFF: Yeah. Lotta dreams and plans.

HAPPY (*with a deep and masculine laugh*): About five hundred women would like to know what was said in this room.

(*They share a soft laugh.*)

BIFF: Remember that big Betsy something — what the hell was her name — over on Bushwick Avenue?

HAPPY (*combing his hair*): With the collie dog!

BIFF: That's the one. I got you in there, remember?

HAPPY: Yeah, that was my first time — I think. Boy, there was a pig. (*They laugh, almost crudely.*) You taught me everything I know about women. Don't forget that.

BIFF: I bet you forgot how bashful you used to be. Especially with girls.

HAPPY: Oh, I still am, Biff.

BIFF: Oh, go on.

HAPPY: I just control it, that's all. I think I got less bashful and you got more so. What happened, Biff? Where's the old humor, the old confidence? (*He shakes Biff's knee. Biff gets up and moves restlessly about the room.*) What's the matter?

BIFF: Why does Dad mock me all the time?

HAPPY: He's not mocking you, he —

BIFF: Everything I say there's a twist of mockery on his face. I can't get near him.

HAPPY: He just wants you to make good, that's all. I wanted to talk to you about Dad for a long time, Biff. Something's — happening to him. He — talks to himself.

BIFF: I noticed that this morning. But he always mumbled.

HAPPY: But not so noticeable. It got so embarrassing I sent him to Florida. And you know something? Most of the time he's talking to you.

BIFF: What's he say about me?

HAPPY: I can't make it out.

BIFF: What's he say about me?

HAPPY: I think the fact that you're not settled, that you're still kind of up in the air . . .

BIFF: There's one or two other things depressing him, Happy.

HAPPY: What do you mean?

BIFF: Never mind. Just don't lay it all to me.

HAPPY: But I think if you just got started — I mean — is there any future for you out there?

BIFF: I tell ya, Hap, I don't know what the future is. I don't know — what I'm supposed to want.

HAPPY: What do you mean?

BIFF: Well, I spent six or seven years after high school trying to work myself up. Shipping clerk, salesman, business of one kind or another. And it's a measly manner of existence. To get on that subway on the hot mornings in summer. To devote your whole life to keeping stock, or making phone calls, or selling or buying. To suffer fifty weeks of the year for the sake of a two-week vacation, when all you really desire is to be outdoors, with your shirt off. And always to have to get ahead of the next fella. And still — that's how you build a future.

HAPPY: Well, you really enjoy it on a farm? Are you content out there?

BIFF (*with rising agitation*): Hap, I've had twenty or thirty different kinds of jobs since I left home before the war, and it always turns out the same. I just realized it lately. In Nebraska when I herded cattle, and the Dakotas, and Arizona, and now in Texas. It's why I came home now, I guess, because I realized it. This farm I work on, it's spring there now, see? And they've got about fifteen new colts. There's nothing more inspiring or — beautiful than the sight of a mare and a new colt. And it's cool there now, see?

Texas is cool now, and it's spring. And whenever spring comes to where I am, I suddenly get the feeling, my God, I'm not gettin' anywhere! What the hell am I doing, playing around with horses, twenty-eight dollars a week! I'm thirty-four years old, I oughta be makin' my future. That's when I come running home. And now, I get here, and I don't know what to do with myself. (*After a pause.*) I've always made a point of not wasting my life, and every time I come back here I know that all I've done is to waste my life.

HAPPY: You're a poet, you know that, Biff? You're a — you're an idealist!

BIFF: No, I'm mixed up very bad. Maybe I oughta get married. Maybe I oughta get stuck into something. Maybe that's my trouble. I'm like a boy. I'm not married, I'm not in business, I just — I'm like a boy. Are you content, Hap? You're a success, aren't you? Are you content?

HAPPY: Hell, no!

BIFF: Why? You're making money, aren't you?

HAPPY (*moving about with energy, expressiveness*): All I can do now is wait for the merchandise manager to die. And suppose I get to be merchandise manager? He's a good friend of mine, and he just built a terrific estate on Long Island. And he lived there about two months and sold it, and now he's building another one. He can't enjoy it once it's finished. And I know that's just what I would do. I don't know what the hell I'm workin' for. Sometimes I sit in my apartment — all alone. And I think of the rent I'm paying. And it's crazy. But then, it's what I always wanted. My own apartment, a car, and plenty of women. And still, goddammit, I'm lonely.

BIFF (*with enthusiasm*): Listen, why don't you come out West with me?

HAPPY: You and I, heh?

BIFF: Sure, maybe we could buy a ranch. Raise cattle, use our muscles. Men built like we are should be working out in the open.

HAPPY (*avidly*): The Loman Brothers, heh?

BIFF (*with vast affection*): Sure, we'd be known all over the counties!

HAPPY (*enthralled*): That's what I dream about, Biff. Sometimes I want to just rip my clothes off in the middle of the store and outbox that goddam merchandise manager. I mean I can outbox, outrun and outlift anybody in that store, and I have to take orders from those common, petty sons-of-bitches till I can't stand it anymore.

BIFF: I'm tellin' you, kid, if you were with me I'd be happy out there.

HAPPY (*enthused*): See, Biff, everybody around me is so false that I'm constantly lowering my ideals . . .

BIFF: Baby, together we'd stand up for one another, we'd have someone to trust.

HAPPY: If I were around you —

BIFF: Hap, the trouble is we weren't brought up to grub for money. I don't know how to do it.

HAPPY: Neither can I!

BIFF: Then let's go!

HAPPY: The only thing is — what can you make out there?

BIFF: But look at your friend. Builds an estate and then hasn't the peace of mind to live in it.

HAPPY: Yeah, but when he walks into the store the waves part in front of him. That's fifty-two thousand dollars a year coming through the revolving door, and I got more in my pinky finger than he's got in his head.

BIFF: Yeah, but you just said —

HAPPY: I gotta show some of those pompous, self-important executives over there that Hap Loman can make the grade. I want to walk into the store the way he walks in. Then I'll go with you, Biff. We'll be together yet, I swear. But take those two we had tonight. Now weren't they gorgeous creatures?

BIFF: Yeah, yeah, most gorgeous I've had in years.

HAPPY: I get that any time I want, Biff. Whenever I feel disgusted. The only trouble is, it gets like bowling or something. I just keep knockin' them over and it doesn't mean anything. You still run around a lot?

BIFF: Naa. I'd like to find a girl — steady, somebody with substance.

HAPPY: That's what I long for.

BIFF: Go on! You'd never come home.

HAPPY: I would! Somebody with character, with resistance! Like Mom, y'know? You're gonna call me a bastard when I tell you this. That girl Charlotte I was with tonight is engaged to be married in five weeks. (*He tries on his new hat.*)

BIFF: No kiddin'!

HAPPY: Sure, the guy's in line for the vice-presidency of the store. I don't know what gets into me, maybe I just have an overdeveloped sense of competition or something, but I went and ruined her, and furthermore I can't get rid of her. And he's the third executive I've done that to. Isn't that a crummy characteristic? And to top it all, I go to their weddings! (*Indignantly, but laughing.*) Like I'm not supposed to take bribes. Manufacturers offer me a hundred-dollar bill now and then to throw an order their way. You know how honest I am, but it's like this girl, see. I hate myself for it. Because I don't want the girl, and, still, I take it and — I love it!

BIFF: Let's go to sleep.

HAPPY: I guess we didn't settle anything, heh?

BIFF: I just got one idea that I think I'm going to try.

HAPPY: What's that?

BIFF: Remember Bill Oliver?

HAPPY: Sure, Oliver is very big now. You want to work for him again?

BIFF: No, but when I quit he said something to me. He put his arm on my shoulder, and he said, "Biff, if you ever need anything, come to me."

HAPPY: I remember that. That sounds good.

BIFF: I think I'll go to see him. If I could get ten thousand or even seven or eight thousand dollars I could buy a beautiful ranch.

HAPPY: I bet he'd back you. 'Cause he thought highly of you, Biff. I mean, they all do. You're well liked, Biff. That's why I say to come back here, and we both have the apartment. And I'm tellin' you, Biff, any babe you want . . .

BIFF: No, with a ranch I could do the work I like and still be something. I just wonder though. I wonder if Oliver still thinks I stole that carton of basketballs.

HAPPY: Oh, he probably forgot that long ago. It's almost ten years. You're too sensitive. Anyway, he didn't really fire you.

BIFF: Well, I think he was going to. I think that's why I quit. I was never sure whether he knew or not. I know he thought the world of me, though. I was the only one he'd let lock up the place.

WILLY (*below*): You gonna wash the engine, Biff?

HAPPY: Shh!

(*Biff looks at Happy, who is gazing down, listening. Willy is mumbling in the parlor.*)

HAPPY: You hear that?

(*They listen. Willy laughs warmly.*)

BIFF (*growing angry*): Doesn't he know Mom can hear that?

WILLY: Don't get your sweater dirty, Biff!

(*A look of pain crosses Biff's face.*)

HAPPY: Isn't that terrible? Don't leave again, will you? You'll find a job here. You gotta stick around. I don't know what to do about him, it's getting embarrassing.

WILLY: What a simonizing job!

BIFF: Mom's hearing that!

WILLY: No kiddin', Biff, you got a date? Wonderful!

HAPPY: Go on to sleep. But talk to him in the morning, will you?

BIFF (*reluctantly getting into bed*): With her in the house. Brother!

HAPPY (*getting into bed*): I wish you'd have a good talk with him.

(*The light on their room begins to fade.*)

BIFF (*to himself in bed*): That selfish, stupid . . .

HAPPY: Sh . . . Sleep, Biff.

(*Their light is out. Well before they have finished speaking, Willy's form is dimly seen below in the darkened kitchen. He opens the refrigerator, searches in there, and takes out a bottle of milk. The apartment houses are fading out, and the entire house and surroundings become covered with leaves. Music insinuates itself as the leaves appear.*)

WILLY: Just wanna be careful with those girls, Biff, that's all. Don't make any promises. No promises of any kind. Because a girl, y'know, they always believe what you tell 'em, and you're very young, Biff, you're too young to be talking seriously to girls.

(*Light rises on the kitchen. Willy, talking, shuts the refrigerator door and comes downstage to the kitchen table. He pours milk into a glass. He is totally immersed in himself, smiling faintly.*)

WILLY: Too young entirely, Biff. You want to watch your schooling first. Then when you're all set, there'll be plenty of girls for a boy like you. (*He smiles broadly at a kitchen chair.*) That so? The girls pay for you? (*He laughs.*) Boy, you must really be makin' a hit.

(*Willy is gradually addressing — physically — a point offstage, speaking through the wall of the kitchen, and his voice has been rising in volume to that of a normal conversation.*)

WILLY: I been wondering why you polish the car so careful. Ha! Don't leave the hubcaps, boys. Get the chamois to the hubcaps. Happy, use newspaper on the windows, it's the easiest thing. Show him how to do it, Biff! You see, Happy? Pad it up, use it like a pad. That's it, that's it, good work. You're doin' all right, Hap. (*He pauses, then nods in approbation for a few seconds, then looks upward.*) Biff, first thing we gotta do when we get time is clip that big branch over the house. Afraid it's gonna fall in a storm and hit the roof. Tell you what. We get a rope and sling her around, and then we climb up there with a couple of saws and take her down. Soon as you finish the car, boys, I wanna see ye. I got a surprise for you, boys.

BIFF (*offstage*): Whatta ya got, Dad?

WILLY: No, you finish first. Never leave a job till you're finished — remember that. (*Looking toward the "big trees."*) Biff, up in Albany I saw a beautiful hammock. I think I'll buy it next trip, and we'll hang it right between those two elms. Wouldn't that be something? Just swingin' there under those branches. Boy, that would be . . .

(*Young Biff and Young Happy appear from the direction Willy was addressing. Happy carries rags and a pail of water. Biff, wearing a sweater with a block "S," carries a football.*)

BIFF (*pointing in the direction of the car offstage*): How's that, Pop, professional?

WILLY: Terrific. Terrific job, boys. Good work, Biff.

HAPPY: Where's the surprise, Pop?

WILLY: In the back seat of the car.

HAPPY: Boy! (*He runs off.*)

BIFF: What is it, Dad? Tell me, what'd you buy?

WILLY (*laughing, cuffs him*): Never mind, something I want you to have.

BIFF (*turns and starts off*): What is it, Hap?

HAPPY (*offstage*): It's a punching bag!

BIFF: Oh, Pop!

WILLY: It's got Gene Tunney's signature on it!

(*Happy runs onstage with a punching bag.*)

BIFF: Gee, how'd you know we wanted a punching bag?

Biff (Kevin Anderson), Willy (Brian Dennehy), and Happy (Ted Koch) in a bright moment in
Robert Falls's 1999 Broadway revival of *Death of a Salesman*.

WILLY: Well, it's the finest thing for the timing.

HAPPY (*lies down on his back and pedals with his feet*):
I'm losing weight, you notice, Pop?

WILLY (*to Happy*): Jumping rope is good too.

BIFF: Did you see the new football I got?

WILLY (*examining the ball*): Where'd you get a new
ball?

BIFF: The coach told me to practice my passing.

WILLY: That so? And he gave you the ball, heh?

BIFF: Well, I borrowed it from the locker room. (*He
laughs confidentially.*)

WILLY (*laughing with him at the theft*): I want you to
return that.

HAPPY: I told you he wouldn't like it!

BIFF (*angrily*): Well, I'm bringing it back!

WILLY (*stopping the incipient argument, to Happy*):
Sure, he's gotta practice with a regulation ball,
doesn't he? (*To Biff.*) Coach'll probably congratulate
you on your initiative!

BIFF: Oh, he keeps congratulating my initiative all the
time, Pop.

WILLY: That's because he likes you. If somebody else

took that ball there'd be an uproar. So what's the
report, boys, what's the report?

BIFF: Where'd you go this time, Dad? Gee we were lonesome for you.

WILLY (*pleased, puts an arm around each boy and they
come down to the apron*): Lonesome, heh?

BIFF: Missed you every minute.

WILLY: Don't say? Tell you a secret, boys. Don't breathe
it to a soul. Someday I'll have my own business, and
I'll never have to leave home anymore.

HAPPY: Like Uncle Charley, heh?

WILLY: Bigger than Uncle Charley! Because Charley is
not — liked. He's liked, but he's not — well liked.

BIFF: Where'd you go this time, Dad?

WILLY: Well, I got on the road, and I went north to
Providence. Met the Mayor.

BIFF: The Mayor of Providence!

WILLY: He was sitting in the hotel lobby.

BIFF: What'd he say?

WILLY: He said, "Morning!" And I said, "You got a fine
city here, Mayor." And then he had coffee with me.
And then I went to Waterbury. Waterbury is a fine

city. Big clock city, the famous Waterbury clock. Sold a nice bill there. And then Boston — Boston is the cradle of the Revolution. A fine city. And a couple of other towns in Mass., and on to Portland and Bangor and straight home!

BIFF: Gee, I'd love to go with you sometime, Dad.

WILLY: Soon as summer comes.

HAPPY: Promise?

WILLY: You and Hap and I, and I'll show you all the towns. America is full of beautiful towns and fine, upstanding people. And they know me, boys, they know me up and down New England. The finest people. And when I bring you fellas up, there'll be open sesame for all of us, 'cause one thing, boys: I have friends. I can park my car in any street in New England, and the cops protect it like their own. This summer, heh?

BIFF AND HAPPY (*together*): Yeah! You bet!

WILLY: We'll take our bathing suits.

HAPPY: We'll carry your bags, Pop!

WILLY: Oh, won't that be something! Me comin' into the Boston stores with you boys carryin' my bags. What a sensation!

(*Biff is prancing around, practicing passing the ball.*)

WILLY: You nervous, Biff, about the game?

BIFF: Not if you're gonna be there.

WILLY: What do they say about you in school, now that they made you captain?

HAPPY: There's a crowd of girls behind him every time the classes change.

BIFF (*taking Willy's hand*): This Saturday, Pop, this Saturday — just for you, I'm going to break through for a touchdown.

HAPPY: You're supposed to pass.

BIFF: I'm takin' one play for Pop. You watch me, Pop, and when I take off my helmet, that means I'm breakin' out. Then you watch me crash through that line!

WILLY (*kisses Biff*): Oh, wait'll I tell this in Boston!

(*Bernard enters in knickers. He is younger than Biff, earnest and loyal, a worried boy.*)

BERNARD: Biff, where are you? You're supposed to study with me today.

WILLY: Hey, looka Bernard. What're you lookin' so anemic about, Bernard?

BERNARD: He's gotta study, Uncle Willy. He's got Regents next week.

HAPPY (*tauntingly, spinning Bernard around*): Let's box, Bernard!

BERNARD: Biff! (*He gets away from Happy.*) Listen, Biff, I heard Mr. Birnbaum say that if you don't start studyin' math he's gonna flunk you, and you won't graduate. I heard him!

WILLY: You better study with him, Biff. Go ahead now.

BERNARD: I heard him!

BIFF: Oh, Pop, you didn't see my sneakers! (*He holds up a foot for Willy to look at.*)

WILLY: Hey, that's a beautiful job of printing!

BERNARD (*wiping his glasses*): Just because he printed University of Virginia on his sneakers doesn't mean they've got to graduate him, Uncle Willy!

WILLY (*angrily*): What're you talking about? With scholarships to three universities they're gonna flunk him?

BERNARD: But I heard Mr. Birnbaum say —

WILLY: Don't be a pest, Bernard! (*To his boys.*) What an anemic!

BERNARD: Okay, I'm waiting for you in my house, Biff.

(*Bernard goes off. The Lomans laugh.*)

WILLY: Bernard is not well liked, is he?

BIFF: He's liked, but he's not well liked.

HAPPY: That's right, Pop.

WILLY: That's just what I mean. Bernard can get the best marks in school, y'understand, but when he gets out in the business world, y'understand, you are going to be five times ahead of him. That's why I thank Almighty God you're both built like Adonises. Because the man who makes an appearance in the business world, the man who creates personal interest, is the man who gets ahead. Be liked and you will never want. You take me, for instance. I never have to wait in line to see a buyer. "Willy Loman is here!" That's all they have to know, and I go right through.

BIFF: Did you knock them dead, Pop?

WILLY: Knocked 'em cold in Providence, slaughtered 'em in Boston.

HAPPY (*on his back, pedaling again*): I'm losing weight, you notice, Pop?

(*Linda enters as of old, a ribbon in her hair, carrying a basket of washing.*)

LINDA (*with youthful energy*): Hello, dear!

WILLY: Sweetheart!

LINDA: How'd the Chevvy run?

WILLY: Chevrolet, Linda, is the greatest car ever built. (*To the boys.*) Since when do you let your mother carry wash up the stairs?

BIFF: Grab hold there, boy!

HAPPY: Where to, Mom?

LINDA: Hang them up on the line. And you better go down to your friends, Biff. The cellar is full of boys. They don't know what to do with themselves.

BIFF: Ah, when Pop comes home they can wait!

WILLY (*laughs appreciatively*): You better go down and tell them what to do, Biff.

BIFF: I think I'll have them sweep out the furnace room.

WILLY: Good work, Biff.

BIFF (*goes through wall-line of kitchen to doorway at back and calls down*): Fellas! Everybody sweep out the furnace room! I'll be right down!

VOICES: All right! Okay, Biff.

BIFF: George and Sam and Frank, come out back! We're hangin' up the wash! Come on, Hap, on the double! (*He and Happy carry out the basket.*)

LINDA: The way they obey him!

WILLY: Well, that's training, the training. I'm tellin' you,

I was sellin' thousands and thousands, but I had to come home.

LINDA: Oh, the whole block'll be at that game. Did you sell anything?

WILLY: I did five hundred gross in Providence and seven hundred gross in Boston.

LINDA: No! Wait a minute, I've got a pencil. (*She pulls pencil and paper out of her apron pocket.*) That makes your commission . . . Two hundred — my God! Two hundred and twelve dollars!

WILLY: Well, I didn't figure it yet, but . . .

LINDA: How much did you do?

WILLY: Well, I — I did — about a hundred and eighty gross in Providence. Well, no — it came to — roughly two hundred gross on the whole trip.

LINDA (*without hesitation*): Two hundred gross. That's . . . (*She figures.*)

WILLY: The trouble was that three of the stores were half-closed for inventory in Boston. Otherwise I woulda broke records.

LINDA: Well, it makes seventy dollars and some pennies. That's very good.

WILLY: What do we owe?

LINDA: Well, on the first there's sixteen dollars on the refrigerator —

WILLY: Why sixteen?

LINDA: Well, the fan belt broke, so it was a dollar eighty.

WILLY: But it's brand new.

LINDA: Well, the man said that's the way it is. Till they work themselves in, y'know.

(*They move through the wall-line into the kitchen.*)

WILLY: I hope we didn't get stuck on that machine.

LINDA: They got the biggest ads of any of them!

WILLY: I know, it's a fine machine. What else?

LINDA: Well, there's nine-sixty for the washing machine. And for the vacuum cleaner there's three and a half due on the fifteenth. Then the roof, you got twenty-one dollars remaining.

WILLY: It don't leak, does it?

LINDA: No, they did a wonderful job. Then you owe Frank for the carburetor.

WILLY: I'm not going to pay that man! That goddam Chevrolet, they ought to prohibit the manufacture of that car!

LINDA: Well, you owe him three and a half. And odds and ends, comes to around a hundred and twenty dollars by the fifteenth.

WILLY: A hundred and twenty dollars! My God, if business don't pick up I don't know what I'm gonna do!

LINDA: Well, next week you'll do better.

WILLY: Oh, I'll knock 'em dead next week. I'll go to Hartford. I'm very well liked in Hartford. You know, the trouble is, Linda, people don't seem to take to me.

(*They move onto the forestage.*)

LINDA: Oh, don't be foolish.

WILLY: I know it when I walk in. They seem to laugh at me.

LINDA: Why? Why would they laugh at you? Don't talk that way, Willy.

(*Willy moves to the edge of the stage. Linda goes into the kitchen and starts to darn stockings.*)

WILLY: I don't know the reason for it, but they just pass me by. I'm not noticed.

LINDA: But you're doing wonderful, dear. You're making seventy to a hundred dollars a week.

WILLY: But I gotta be at it ten, twelve hours a day. Other men — I don't know — they do it easier. I don't know why — I can't stop myself — I talk too much. A man oughta come in with a few words. One thing about Charley. He's a man of few words, and they respect him.

LINDA: You don't talk too much, you're just lively.

WILLY (*smiling*): Well, I figure, what the hell, life is short, a couple of jokes. (*To himself.*) I joke too much! (*The smile goes.*)

LINDA: Why? You're —

WILLY: I'm fat. I'm very — foolish to look at, Linda. I didn't tell you, but Christmas time I happened to be calling on F. H. Stewarts, and a salesman I know, as I was going in to see the buyer I heard him say something about — walrus. And I — I cracked him right across the face. I won't take that. I simply will not take that. But they do laugh at me. I know that.

LINDA: Darling . . .

WILLY: I gotta overcome it. I know I gotta overcome it. I'm not dressing to advantage, maybe.

LINDA: Willy, darling, you're the handsomest man in the world —

WILLY: Oh, no, Linda.

LINDA: To me you are. (*Slight pause.*) The handsomest.

(*From the darkness is heard the laughter of a woman. Willy doesn't turn to it, but it continues through Linda's lines.*)

LINDA: And the boys, Willy. Few men are idolized by their children the way you are.

(*Music is heard as behind a scrim, to the left of the house, The Woman, dimly seen, is dressing.*)

WILLY (*with great feeling*): You're the best there is, Linda, you're a pal, you know that? On the road — on the road I want to grab you sometimes and just kiss the life outa you.

(*The laughter is loud now, and he moves into a brightening area at the left, where The Woman has come from behind the scrim and is standing, putting on her hat, looking into a "mirror" and laughing.*)

WILLY: 'Cause I get so lonely — especially when business is bad and there's nobody to talk to. I get the feeling that I'll never sell anything again, that I won't make a living for you, or a business, a business for the boys. (*He talks through The Woman's subsiding laughter; The Woman primps at the "mirror."*) There's so much I want to make for —

THE WOMAN: Me? You didn't make me, Willy. I picked you.

WILLY (*pleased*): You picked me?

THE WOMAN (*who is quite proper-looking, Willy's age*): I did. I've been sitting at that desk watching all the salesmen go by, day in, day out. But you've got such a sense of humor, and we do have such a good time together, don't we?

WILLY: Sure, sure. (*He takes her in his arms.*) Why do you have to go now?

THE WOMAN: It's two o'clock . . .

WILLY: No, come on in! (*He pulls her.*)

THE WOMAN: . . . my sisters'll be scandalized. When'll you be back?

WILLY: Oh, two weeks about. Will you come up again?

THE WOMAN: Sure thing. You do make me laugh. It's good for me. (*She squeezes his arm, kisses him.*) And I think you're a wonderful man.

WILLY: You picked me, heh?

THE WOMAN: Sure. Because you're so sweet. And such a kidder.

WILLY: Well, I'll see you next time I'm in Boston.

THE WOMAN: I'll put you right through to the buyers.

WILLY (*slapping her bottom*): Right. Well, bottoms up!

THE WOMAN (*slaps him gently and laughs*): You just kill me, Willy. (*He suddenly grabs her and kisses her roughly.*) You kill me. And thanks for the stockings. I love a lot of stockings. Well, good night.

WILLY: Good night. And keep your pores open!

THE WOMAN: Oh, Willy!

(*The Woman bursts out laughing, and Linda's laughter blends in. The Woman disappears into the dark. Now the area at the kitchen table brightens. Linda is sitting where she was at the kitchen table, but now is mending a pair of her silk stockings.*)

LINDA: You are, Willy. The handsomest man. You've got no reason to feel that —

WILLY (*coming out of The Woman's dimming area and going over to Linda*): I'll make it all up to you, Linda, I'll —

LINDA: There's nothing to make up, dear. You're doing fine, better than —

WILLY (*noticing her mending*): What's that?

LINDA: Just mending my stockings. They're so expensive —

WILLY (*angrily, taking them from her*): I won't have you mending stockings in this house! Now throw them out!

(*Linda puts the stockings in her pocket.*)

BERNARD (*entering on the run*): Where is he? If he doesn't study!

WILLY (*moving to the forestage, with great agitation*): You'll give him the answers!

BERNARD: I do, but I can't on a Regents! That's a state exam! They're liable to arrest me!

WILLY: Where is he? I'll whip him, I'll whip him!

LINDA: And he'd better give back that football, Willy, it's not nice.

WILLY: Biff! Where is he? Why is he taking everything?

LINDA: He's too rough with the girls, Willy. All the mothers are afraid of him!

WILLY: I'll whip him!

BERNARD: He's driving the car without a license!

(*The Woman's laugh is heard.*)

WILLY: Shut up!

LINDA: All the mothers —

WILLY: Shut up!

BERNARD (*backing quietly away and out*): Mr. Birnbaum says he's stuck up.

WILLY: Get outa here!

BERNARD: If he doesn't buckle down he'll flunk math! (*He goes off.*)

LINDA: He's right, Willy, you've gotta —

WILLY (*exploding at her*): There's nothing the matter with him! You want him to be a worm like Bernard? He's got spirit, personality . . .

(*As he speaks, Linda, almost in tears, exits into the living room. Willy is alone in the kitchen, wilting and staring. The leaves are gone. It is night again, and the apartment houses look down from behind.*)

WILLY: Loaded with it. Loaded! What is he stealing? He's giving it back, isn't he? Why is he stealing? What did I tell him? I never in my life told him anything but decent things.

(*Happy in pajamas has come down the stairs; Willy suddenly becomes aware of Happy's presence.*)

HAPPY: Let's go now, come on.

WILLY (*sitting down at the kitchen table*): Huh! Why did she have to wax the floors herself? Everytime she waxes the floors she keels over. She knows that!

HAPPY: Shh! Take it easy. What brought you back tonight?

WILLY: I got an awful scare. Nearly hit a kid in Yonkers. God! Why didn't I go to Alaska with my brother Ben that time! Ben! That man was a genius, that man was success incarnate! What a mistake! He begged me to go.

HAPPY: Well, there's no use in —

WILLY: You guys! There was a man started with the clothes on his back and ended up with diamond mines!

HAPPY: Boy, someday I'd like to know how he did it.

WILLY: What's the mystery? The man knew what he wanted and went out and got it! Walked into a jungle, and comes out, the age of twenty-one, and he's rich! The world is an oyster, but you don't crack it open on a mattress!

HAPPY: Pop, I told you I'm gonna retire you for life.

WILLY: You'll retire me for life on seventy goddam dollars a week? And your women and your car and your apartment, and you'll retire me for life! Christ's sake,

I couldn't get past Yonkers today! Where are you guys, where are you? The woods are burning! I can't drive a car!

(*Charley has appeared in the doorway. He is a large man, slow of speech, laconic, immovable. In all he says, despite what he says, there is pity, and, now, trepidation. He has a robe over pajamas, slippers on his feet. He enters the kitchen.*)

CHARLEY: Everything all right?

HAPPY: Yeah, Charley, everything's . . .

WILLY: What's the matter?

CHARLEY: I heard some noise. I thought something happened. Can't we do something about the walls? You sneeze in here, and in my house hats blow off.

HAPPY: Let's go to bed, Dad. Come on.

(*Charley signals to Happy to go.*)

WILLY: You go ahead, I'm not tired at the moment.

HAPPY (*to Willy*): Take it easy, huh? (*He exits.*)

WILLY: What're you doin' up?

CHARLEY (*sitting down at the kitchen table opposite Willy*): Couldn't sleep good. I had a heartburn.

WILLY: Well, you don't know how to eat.

CHARLEY: I eat with my mouth.

WILLY: No, you're ignorant. You gotta know about vitamins and things like that.

CHARLEY: Come on, let's shoot. Tire you out a little.

WILLY (*hesitantly*): All right. You got cards?

CHARLEY (*taking a deck from his pocket*): Yeah, I got them. Someplace. What is it with those vitamins?

WILLY (*dealing*): They build up your bones. Chemistry.

CHARLEY: Yeah, but there's no bones in a heartburn.

WILLY: What are you talkin' about? Do you know the first thing about it?

CHARLEY: Don't get insulted.

WILLY: Don't talk about something you don't know anything about.

(*They are playing. Pause.*)

CHARLEY: What're you doin' home?

WILLY: A little trouble with the car.

CHARLEY: Oh. (*Pause.*) I'd like to take a trip to California.

WILLY: Don't say.

CHARLEY: You want a job?

WILLY: I got a job, I told you that. (*After a slight pause.*) What the hell are you offering me a job for?

CHARLEY: Don't get insulted.

WILLY: Don't insult me.

CHARLEY: I don't see no sense in it. You don't have to go on this way.

WILLY: I got a good job. (*Slight pause.*) What do you keep comin' in here for?

CHARLEY: You want me to go?

WILLY (*after a pause, withering*): I can't understand it. He's going back to Texas again. What the hell is that?

CHARLEY: Let him go.

WILLY: I got nothin' to give him, Charley, I'm clean, I'm clean.

CHARLEY: He won't starve. None a them starve. Forget about him.

WILLY: Then what have I got to remember?

CHARLEY: You take it too hard. To hell with it. When a deposit bottle is broken you don't get your nickel back.

WILLY: That's easy enough for you to say.

CHARLEY: That ain't easy for me to say.

WILLY: Did you see the ceiling I put up in the living room?

CHARLEY: Yeah, that's a piece of work. To put up a ceiling is a mystery to me. How do you do it?

WILLY: What's the difference?

CHARLEY: Well, talk about it.

WILLY: You gonna put up a ceiling?

CHARLEY: How could I put up a ceiling?

WILLY: Then what the hell are you bothering me for?

CHARLEY: You're insulted again.

WILLY: A man who can't handle tools is not a man. You're disgusting.

CHARLEY: Don't call me disgusting, Willy.

(*Uncle Ben, carrying a valise and an umbrella, enters the forestage from around the right corner of the house. He is a stolid man, in his sixties, with a mustache and an authoritative air. He is utterly certain of his destiny, and there is an aura of far places about him. He enters exactly as Willy speaks.*)

WILLY: I'm getting awfully tired, Ben.

(*Ben's music is heard. Ben looks around at everything.*)

CHARLEY: Good, keep playing; you'll sleep better. Did you call me Ben?

(*Ben looks at his watch.*)

WILLY: That's funny. For a second there you reminded me of my brother Ben.

BEN: I only have a few minutes. (*He strolls, inspecting the place. Willy and Charley continue playing.*)

CHARLEY: You never heard from him again, heh? Since that time?

WILLY: Didn't Linda tell you? Couple of weeks ago we got a letter from his wife in Africa. He died.

CHARLEY: That so.

BEN (*chuckling*): So this is Brooklyn, eh?

CHARLEY: Maybe you're in for some of his money.

WILLY: Naa, he had seven sons. There's just one opportunity I had with that man . . .

BEN: I must make a train, William. There are several properties I'm looking at in Alaska.

WILLY: Sure, sure! If I'd gone with him to Alaska that time, everything would've been totally different.

CHARLIE: Go on, you'd froze to death up there.

WILLY: What're you talking about?

BEN: Opportunity is tremendous in Alaska, William. Surprised you're not up there.

WILLY: Sure, tremendous.

CHARLEY: Heh?

WILLY: There was the only man I ever met who knew the answers.

CHARLEY: Who?

BEN: How are you all?

WILLY (*taking a pot, smiling*): Fine, fine.

CHARLEY: Pretty sharp tonight.

BEN: Is Mother living with you?

WILLY: No, she died a long time ago.

CHARLEY: Who?

BEN: That's too bad. Fine specimen of a lady, Mother.

WILLY (*to Charley*): Heh?

BEN: I'd hoped to see the old girl.

CHARLEY: Who died?

BEN: Heard anything from Father, have you?

WILLY (*unnerved*): What do you mean, who died?

CHARLEY (*taking a pot*): What're you talkin' about?

BEN (*looking at his watch*): William, it's half-past eight!

WILLY (*as though to dispel his confusion he angrily stops Charley's hand*): That's my build!

CHARLEY: I put the ace —

WILLY: If you don't know how to play the game I'm not gonna throw my money away on you!

CHARLEY (*rising*): It was my ace, for God's sake!

WILLY: I'm through, I'm through!

BEN: When did Mother die?

WILLY: Long ago. Since the beginning you never knew how to play cards.

CHARLEY (*picks up the cards and goes to the door*): All right! Next time I'll bring a deck with five aces.

WILLY: I don't play that kind of game!

CHARLEY (*turning to him*): You ought to be ashamed of yourself!

WILLY: Yeah?

CHARLEY: Yeah! (*He goes out.*)

WILLY (*slamming the door after him*): Ignoramus!

BEN (*as Willy comes toward him through the wall-line of the kitchen*): So you're William.

WILLY (*shaking Ben's hand*): Ben! I've been waiting for you so long! What's the answer? How did you do it?

BEN: Oh, there's a story in that.

(*Linda enters the forestage, as of old, carrying the wash basket.*)

LINDA: Is this Ben?

BEN (*gallantly*): How do you do, my dear.

LINDA: Where've you been all these years? Willy's always wondered why you —

WILLY (*pulling Ben away from her impatiently*): Where is Dad? Didn't you follow him? How did you get started?

BEN: Well, I don't know how much you remember.

WILLY: Well, I was just a baby, of course, only three or four years old —

BEN: Three years and eleven months.

WILLY: What a memory, Ben!

BEN: I have many enterprises, William, and I have never kept books.

WILLY: I remember I was sitting under the wagon in — was it Nebraska?

BEN: It was South Dakota, and I gave you a bunch of wild flowers.

WILLY: I remember you walking away down some open road.

BEN (*laughing*): I was going to find Father in Alaska.

WILLY: Where is he?

BEN: At that age I had a very faulty view of geography, William. I discovered after a few days that I was heading due south, so instead of Alaska, I ended up in Africa.

LINDA: Africa!

WILLY: The Gold Coast!

BEN: Principally diamond mines.

LINDA: Diamond mines!

BEN: Yes, my dear. But I've only a few minutes —

WILLY: No! Boys! Boys! (*Young Biff and Happy appear.*) Listen to this. This is your Uncle Ben, a great man! Tell my boys, Ben!

BEN: Why, boys, when I was seventeen I walked into the jungle, and when I was twenty-one I walked out. (*He laughs.*) And by God I was rich.

WILLY (*to the boys*): You see what I been talking about? The greatest things can happen!

BEN (*glancing at his watch*): I have an appointment in Ketchikan Tuesday week.

WILLY: No, Ben! Please tell about Dad. I want my boys to hear. I want them to know the kind of stock they spring from. All I remember is a man with a big beard, and I was in Mamma's lap, sitting around a fire, and some kind of high music.

BEN: His flute. He played the flute.

WILLY: Sure, the flute, that's right!

(*New music is heard, a high, rollicking tune.*)

BEN: Father was a very great and a very wild-hearted man. We would start in Boston, and he'd toss the whole family into the wagon, and then he'd drive the team right across the country; through Ohio, and Indiana, Michigan, Illinois, and all the Western states. And we'd stop in the towns and sell the flutes that he'd made on the way. Great inventor Father. With one gadget he made more in a week than a man like you could make in a lifetime.

WILLY: That's just the way I'm bringing them up, Ben — rugged, well liked, all-around.

BEN: Yeah? (*To Biff.*) Hit that, boy — hard as you can. (*He pounds his stomach.*)

BIFF: Oh, no, sir!

BEN (*taking boxing stance*): Come on, get to me! (*He laughs.*)

WILLY: Go to it, Biff! Go ahead, show him!

BIFF: Okay! (*He cocks his fists and starts in.*)

LINDA (*to Willy*): Why must he fight, dear?

BEN (*sparring with Biff*): Good boy! Good boy!

WILLY: How's that, Ben, heh?

HAPPY: Give him the left, Biff!

LINDA: Why are you fighting?

BEN: Good boy! (*Suddenly comes in, trips Biff, and stands over him, the point of his umbrella poised over Biff's eye.*)

LINDA: Look out, Biff!

BIFF: Gee!

BEN (*patting Biff's knee*): Never fight fair with a stranger, boy. You'll never get out of the jungle that way. (*Taking Linda's hand and bowing.*) It was an honor and a pleasure to meet you, Linda.

LINDA (*withdrawing her hand coldly, frightened*): Have a nice — trip.

BEN (*to Willy*): And good luck with your — what do you do?

WILLY: Selling.

BEN: Yes. Well . . . (*He raises his hand in farewell to all.*)

WILLY: No, Ben, I don't want you to think . . . (*He takes Ben's arm to show him.*) It's Brooklyn, I know, but we hunt too.

BEN: Really, now.

WILLY: Oh, sure, there's snakes and rabbits and — that's why I moved out here. Why, Biff can fell any one of these trees in no time! Boys! Go right over to where they're building the apartment house and get some sand. We're gonna rebuild the entire front stoop right now! Watch this, Ben!

BIFF: Yes, sir! On the double, Hap!

HAPPY (*as he and Biff run off*): I lost weight, Pop, you notice?

(*Charley enters in knickers, even before the boys are gone.*)

CHARLEY: Listen, if they steal any more from that building the watchman'll put the cops on them!

LINDA (*to Willy*): Don't let Biff . . .

(*Ben laughs lustily.*)

WILLY: You shoulda seen the lumber they brought home last week. At least a dozen six-by-tens worth all kinds a money.

CHARLEY: Listen, if that watchman —

WILLY: I gave them hell, understand. But I got a couple of fearless characters there.

CHARLEY: Willy, the jails are full of fearless characters.

BEN (*clapping Willy on the back, with a laugh at Charley*): And the stock exchange, friend!

WILLY (*joining in Ben's laughter*): Where are the rest of your pants?

CHARLEY: My wife bought them.

WILLY: Now all you need is a golf club and you can go upstairs and go to sleep. (*To Ben.*) Great athlete! Between him and his son Bernard they can't hammer a nail!

BERNARD (*rushing in*): The watchman's chasing Biff!

WILLY (*angrily*): Shut up! He's not stealing anything!

LINDA (*alarmed, hurrying off left*): Where is he? Biff, dear! (*She exits.*)

WILLY (*moving toward the left, away from Ben*): There's nothing wrong. What's the matter with you?

BEN: Nervy boy. Good!

WILLY (*laughing*): Oh, nerves of iron, that Biff!

CHARLEY: Don't know what it is. My New England man comes back and he's bleedin', they murdered him up there.

WILLY: It's contacts, Charley, I got important contacts!

CHARLEY (*sarcastically*): Glad to hear it, Willy. Come in later, we'll shoot a little casino. I'll take some of your Portland money. (*He laughs at Willy and exits.*)

WILLY (*turning to Ben*): Business is bad, it's murderous. But not for me, of course.

BEN: I'll stop by on my way back to Africa.

WILLY (*longingly*): Can't you stay a few days? You're just what I need, Ben, because I — I have a fine position here, but I — well, Dad left when I was such a baby and I never had a chance to talk to him and I still feel — kind of temporary about myself.

BEN: I'll be late for my train.

(*They are at opposite ends of the stage.*)

WILLY: Ben, my boys — can't we talk? They'd go into the jaws of hell for me, see, but I —

BEN: William, you're being first-rate with your boys. Outstanding, manly chaps!

WILLY (*hanging on to his words*): Oh, Ben, that's good to hear! Because sometimes I'm afraid that I'm not teaching them the right kind of — Ben, how should I teach them?

BEN (*giving great weight to each word, and with a certain vicious audacity*): William, when I walked into the jungle, I was seventeen. When I walked out I was twenty-one. And, by God, I was rich! (*He goes off into darkness around the right corner of the house.*)

WILLY: . . . was rich! That's just the spirit I want to imbue them with! To walk into a jungle! I was right! I was right! I was right!

(*Ben is gone, but Willy is still speaking to him as Linda, in nightgown and robe, enters the kitchen, glances around for Willy, then goes to the door of the house, looks out and sees him. Comes down to his left. He looks at her.*)

LINDA: Willy, dear? Willy?

WILLY: I was right!

LINDA: Did you have some cheese? (*He can't answer.*) It's very late, darling. Come to bed, heh?

WILLY (*looking straight up*): Gotta break your neck to see a star in this yard.

LINDA: You coming in?

WILLY: Whatever happened to that diamond watch fob? Remember? When Ben came from Africa that time? Didn't he give me a watch fob with a diamond in it?

LINDA: You pawned it, dear. Twelve, thirteen years ago. For Biff's radio correspondence course.

WILLY: Gee, that was a beautiful thing. I'll take a walk.

LINDA: But you're in your slippers.

WILLY (*starting to go around the house at the left*): I was right! I was! (*Half to Linda, as he goes, shaking his head.*) What a man! There was a man worth talking to. I was right!

LINDA (*calling after Willy*): But in your slippers, Willy!

(*Willy is almost gone when Biff, in his pajamas, comes down the stairs and enters the kitchen.*)

BIFF: What is he doing out there?

LINDA: Sh!

BIFF: God Almighty, Mom, how long has he been doing this?

LINDA: Don't, he'll hear you.

BIFF: What the hell is the matter with him?

LINDA: It'll pass by morning.

BIFF: Shouldn't we do anything?

LINDA: Oh, my dear, you should do a lot of things, but there's nothing to do, so go to sleep.

(*Happy comes down the stair and sits on the steps.*)

HAPPY: I never heard him so loud, Mom.

LINDA: Well, come around more often, you'll hear him. (*She sits down at the table and mends the lining of Willy's jacket.*)

BIFF: Why didn't you ever write me about this, Mom?

LINDA: How would I write to you? For over three months you had no address.

BIFF: I was on the move. But you know I thought of you all the time. You know that, don't you, pal?

LINDA: I know, dear, I know. But he likes to have a letter. Just to know that there's still a possibility for better things.

BIFF: He's not like this all the time, is he?

LINDA: It's when you come home he's always the worst.

BIFF: When I come home?

LINDA: When you write you're coming, he's all smiles and talks about the future, and — he's just wonderful. And then the closer you seem to come, the more shaky he gets, and then, by the time you get here, he's arguing, and he seems angry at you. I think it's just that maybe he can't bring himself to — to open up to you. Why are you so hateful to each other? Why is that?

BIFF (*evasively*): I'm not hateful, Mom.

LINDA: But you no sooner come in the door than you're fighting!

BIFF: I don't know why. I mean to change. I'm tryin', Mom, you understand?

LINDA: Are you home to stay now?

BIFF: I don't know. I want to look around, see what's goin'.

LINDA: Biff, you can't look around all your life, can you?

BIFF: I just can't take hold, Mom. I can't take hold of some kind of a life.

LINDA: Biff, a man is not a bird, to come and go with the springtime.

BIFF: Your hair . . . (*He touches her hair.*) Your hair got so gray.

LINDA: Oh, it's been gray since you were in high school. I just stopped dyeing it, that's all.

BIFF: Dye it again, will ye? I don't want my pal looking old. (*He smiles.*)

LINDA: You're such a boy! You think you can go away

for a year and . . . You've got to get it into your head now that one day you'll knock on this door and there'll be strange people here —

BIFF: What are you talking about? You're not even sixty, Mom.

LINDA: But what about your father?

BIFF (*lamely*): Well, I meant him too.

HAPPY: He admires Pop.

LINDA: Biff, dear, if you don't have any feeling for him, then you can't have any feeling for me.

BIFF: Sure I can, Mom.

LINDA: No. You can't just come to see me, because I love him. (*With a threat, but only a threat, of tears.*) He's the dearest man in the world to me, and I won't have anyone making him feel unwanted and low and blue. You've got to make up your mind now, darling, there's no leeway any more. Either he's your father and you pay him that respect, or else you're not to come here. I know he's not easy to get along with — nobody knows that better than me — but . . .

WILLY (*from the left, with a laugh*): Hey, hey, Biffo!

BIFF (*starting to go out after Willy*): What the hell is the matter with him? (*Happy stops him.*)

LINDA: Don't — don't go near him!

BIFF: Stop making excuses for him! He always, always wiped the floor with you. Never had an ounce of respect for you.

HAPPY: He's always had respect for —

BIFF: What the hell do you know about it?

HAPPY (*surlily*): Just don't call him crazy!

BIFF: He's got no character — Charley wouldn't do this. Not in his own house — spewing out that vomit from his mind.

HAPPY: Charley never had to cope with what he's got to.

BIFF: People are worse off than Willy Loman. Believe me, I've seen them!

LINDA: Then make Charley your father, Biff. You can't do that, can you? I don't say he's a great man. Willy Loman never made a lot of money. His name was never in the paper. He's not the finest character that ever lived. But he's a human being, and a terrible thing is happening to him. So attention must be paid. He's not to be allowed to fall into his grave like an old dog. Attention, attention must be finally paid to such a person. You called him crazy —

BIFF: I didn't mean —

LINDA: No, a lot of people think he's lost his — balance. But you don't have to be very smart to know what his trouble is. The man is exhausted.

HAPPY: Sure!

LINDA: A small man can be just as exhausted as a great man. He works for a company thirty-six years this March, opens up unheard-of territories to their trademark, and now in his old age they take his salary away.

HAPPY (*indignantly*): I didn't know that, Mom.

LINDA: You never asked, my dear! Now that you get your spending money someplace else you don't trouble your mind with him.

HAPPY: But I gave you money last —

LINDA: Christmas time, fifty dollars! To fix the hot water it cost ninety-seven fifty! For five weeks he's been on straight commission, like a beginner, an unknown!

BIFF: Those ungrateful bastards!

LINDA: Are they any worse than his sons? When he brought them business, when he was young, they were glad to see him. But now his old friends, the old buyers that loved him so and always found some order to hand him in a pinch — they're all dead, retired. He used to be able to make six, seven calls a day in Boston. Now he takes his valises out of the car and puts them back and takes them out again and he's exhausted. Instead of walking he talks now. He drives seven hundred miles, and when he gets there no one knows him anymore, no one welcomes him. And what goes through a man's mind, driving seven hundred miles home without having earned a cent? Why shouldn't he talk to himself? Why? When he has to go to Charley and borrow fifty dollars a week and pretend to me that it's his pay? How long can that go on? How long? You see what I'm sitting here and waiting for? And you tell me he has no character? The man who never worked a day but for your benefit? When does he get the medal for that? Is this his reward — to turn around at the age of sixty-three and find his sons, who he loved better than his life, one a philandering bum —

HAPPY: Mom!

LINDA: That's all you are, my baby! (*To Biff.*) And you! What happened to the love you had for him? You were such pals! How you used to talk to him on the phone every night! How lonely he was till he could come home to you!

BIFF: All right, Mom. I'll live here in my room, and I'll get a job. I'll keep away from him, that's all.

LINDA: No, Biff. You can't stay here and fight all the time.

BIFF: He threw me out of this house, remember that.

LINDA: Why did he do that? I never knew why.

BIFF: Because I know he's a fake and he doesn't like anybody around who knows!

LINDA: Why a fake? In what way? What do you mean?

BIFF: Just don't lay it all at my feet. It's between me and him — that's all I have to say. I'll chip in from now on. He'll settle for half my pay check. He'll be all right. I'm going to bed. (*He starts for the stairs.*)

LINDA: He won't be all right.

BIFF (*turning on the stairs, furiously*): I hate this city and I'll stay here. Now what do you want?

LINDA: He's dying, Biff.

(*Happy turns quickly to her, shocked.*)

BIFF (*after a pause*): Why is he dying?

LINDA: He's been trying to kill himself.

BIFF (*with great horror*): How?

LINDA: I live from day to day.

BIFF: What're you talking about?

LINDA: Remember I wrote you that he smashed up the car again? In February?

BIFF: Well?

LINDA: The insurance inspector came. He said that they have evidence. That all these accidents in the last year — weren't — weren't — accidents.

HAPPY: How can they tell that? That's a lie.

LINDA: It seems there's a woman . . . (*She takes a breath as*)

BIFF (*sharply but contained*): ⎫ What woman?

LINDA (*simultaneously*): ⎭ . . . and this woman . . .

LINDA: What?

BIFF: Nothing. Go ahead.

LINDA: What did you say?

BIFF: Nothing. I just said what woman?

HAPPY: What about her?

LINDA: Well, it seems she was walking down the road and saw his car. She says that he wasn't driving fast at all, and that he didn't skid. She says he came to that little bridge, and then deliberately smashed into the railing, and it was only the shallowness of the water that saved him.

BIFF: Oh, no, he probably just fell asleep again.

LINDA: I don't think he fell asleep.

BIFF: Why not?

LINDA: Last month . . . (*With great difficulty.*) Oh, boys, it's so hard to say a thing like this! He's just a big stupid man to you, but I tell you there's more good in him than in many other people. (*She chokes, wipes her eyes.*) I was looking for a fuse. The lights blew out, and I went down the cellar. And behind the fuse box — it happened to fall out — was a length of rubber pipe — just short.

HAPPY: No kidding!

LINDA: There's a little attachment on the end of it. I knew right away. And sure enough, on the bottom of the water heater there's a new little nipple on the gas pipe.

HAPPY (*angrily*): That — jerk.

BIFF: Did you have it taken off?

LINDA: I'm — I'm ashamed to. How can I mention it to him? Every day I go down and take away that little rubber pipe. But, when he comes home, I put it back where it was. How can I insult him that way? I don't know what to do. I live from day to day, boys. I tell you, I know every thought in his mind. It sounds so old-fashioned and silly, but I tell you he put his whole life into you and you've turned your backs on him. (*She is bent over in the chair, weeping, her face in her hands.*) Biff, I swear to God! Biff, his life is in your hands!

HAPPY (*to Biff*): How do you like that damned fool!

BIFF (*kissing her*): All right, pal, all right. It's all settled now. I've been remiss. I know that, Mom. But now I'll stay, and I swear to you, I'll apply myself. (*Kneeling in front of her, in a fever of self-reproach.*) It's just — you see, Mom, I don't fit in business. Not that I won't try. I'll try, and I'll make good.

HAPPY: Sure you will. The trouble with you in business was you never tried to please people.

BIFF: I know, I —

HAPPY: Like when you worked for Harrison's. Bob Harrison said you were tops, and then you go and do some damn fool thing like whistling whole songs in the elevator like a comedian.

BIFF (*against Happy*): So what? I like to whistle sometimes.

HAPPY: You don't raise a guy to a responsible job who whistles in the elevator!

LINDA: Well, don't argue about it now.

HAPPY: Like when you'd go off and swim in the middle of the day instead of taking the line around.

BIFF (*his resentment rising*): Well, don't you run off? You take off sometimes, don't you? On a nice summer day?

HAPPY: Yeah, but I cover myself!

LINDA: Boys!

HAPPY: If I'm going to take a fade the boss can call any number where I'm supposed to be and they'll swear to him that I just left. I'll tell you something that I hate to say, Biff, but in the business world some of them think you're crazy.

BIFF (*angered*): Screw the business world!

HAPPY: All right, screw it! Great, but cover yourself!

LINDA: Hap, Hap!

BIFF: I don't care what they think! They've laughed at Dad for years, and you know why? Because we don't belong in this nuthouse of a city! We should be mixing cement on some open plain, or — or carpenters. A carpenter is allowed to whistle!

(*Willy walks in from the entrance of the house, at left.*)

WILLY: Even your grandfather was better than a carpenter. (*Pause. They watch him.*) You never grew up. Bernard does not whistle in the elevator, I assure you.

BIFF (*as though to laugh Willy out of it*): Yeah, but you do, Pop.

WILLY: I never in my life whistled in an elevator! And who in the business world thinks I'm crazy?

BIFF: I didn't mean it like that, Pop. Now don't make a whole thing out of it, will ye?

WILLY: Go back to the West! Be a carpenter, a cowboy, enjoy yourself!

LINDA: Willy, he was just saying —

WILLY: I heard what he said!

HAPPY (*trying to quiet Willy*): Hey, Pop, come on now . . .

WILLY (*continuing over Happy's line*): They laugh at me, heh? Go to Filene's, go to the Hub, go to Slattery's, Boston. Call out the name Willy Loman and see what happens! Big shot!

BIFF: All right, Pop.

WILLY: Big!

BIFF: All right!

WILLY: Why do you always insult me?

BIFF: I didn't say a word. (*To Linda.*) Did I say a word?

LINDA: He didn't say anything, Willy.

WILLY (*going to the doorway of the living room*): All right, good night, good night.

LINDA: Willy, dear, he just decided . . .

WILLY (*to Biff*): If you get tired hanging around tomorrow, paint the ceiling I put up in the living room.

BIFF: I'm leaving early tomorrow.

HAPPY: He's going to see Bill Oliver, Pop.

WILLY (*interestedly*): Oliver? For what?

BIFF (*with reserve, but trying, trying*): He always said he'd stake me. I'd like to go into business, so maybe I can take him up on it.

LINDA: Isn't that wonderful?

WILLY: Don't interrupt. What's wonderful about it? There's fifty men in the City of New York who'd stake him. (*To Biff.*) Sporting goods?

BIFF: I guess so. I know something about it and —

WILLY: He knows something about it! You know sporting goods better than Spalding, for God's sake! How much is he giving you?

BIFF: I don't know, I didn't even see him yet, but —

WILLY: Then what're you talkin' about?

BIFF (*getting angry*): Well, all I said was I'm gonna see him, that's all!

WILLY (*turning away*): Ah, you're counting your chickens again.

BIFF (*starting left for the stairs*): Oh, Jesus, I'm going to sleep!

WILLY (*calling after him*): Don't curse in this house!

BIFF (*turning*): Since when did you get so clean?

HAPPY (*trying to stop them*): Wait a . . .

WILLY: Don't use that language to me! I won't have it!

HAPPY (*grabbing Biff, shouts*): Wait a minute! I got an idea. I got a feasible idea. Come here, Biff, let's talk this over now, let's talk some sense here. When I was down in Florida last time, I thought of a great idea to sell sporting goods. It just came back to me. You and I, Biff — we have a line, the Loman Line. We train a couple of weeks, and put on a couple of exhibitions, see?

WILLY: That's an idea!

HAPPY: Wait! We form two basketball teams, see? Two water polo teams. We play each other. It's a million dollars' worth of publicity. Two brothers, see? The Loman Brothers. Displays in the Royal Palms — all the hotels. And banners over the ring and the basketball court: "Loman Brothers." Baby, we could sell sporting goods!

WILLY: That is a one-million-dollar idea!

LINDA: Marvelous!

BIFF: I'm in great shape as far as that's concerned.

HAPPY: And the beauty of it is, Biff, it wouldn't be like a business. We'd be out playin' ball again . . .

BIFF (*enthused*): Yeah, that's . . .

WILLY: Million-dollar . . .

HAPPY: And you wouldn't get fed up with it, Biff. It'd be the family again. There'd be the old honor, and comradeship, and if you wanted to go off for a swim or somethin' — well, you'd do it! Without some smart cooky gettin' up ahead of you!

WILLY: Lick the world! You guys together could absolutely lick the civilized world.

BIFF: I'll see Oliver tomorrow. Hap, if we could work that out . . .

LINDA: Maybe things are beginning to —

WILLY (*wildly enthused, to Linda*): Stop interrupting! (*To Biff.*) But don't wear sport jacket and slacks when you see Oliver.

BIFF: No, I'll —

WILLY: A business suit, and talk as little as possible, and don't crack any jokes.

BIFF: He did like me. Always liked me.

LINDA: He loved you!

WILLY (*to Linda*): Will you stop! (*To Biff.*) Walk in very serious. You are not applying for a boy's job. Money is to pass. Be quiet, fine, and serious. Everybody likes a kidder, but nobody lends him money.

HAPPY: I'll try to get some myself, Biff. I'm sure I can.

WILLY: I see great things for you kids, I think your troubles are over. But remember, start big and you'll end big. Ask for fifteen. How much you gonna ask for?

BIFF: Gee, I don't know —

WILLY: And don't say "Gee." "Gee" is a boy's word. A man walking in for fifteen thousand dollars does not say "Gee!"

BIFF: Ten, I think, would be top though.

WILLY: Don't be so modest. You always started too low. Walk in with a big laugh. Don't look worried. Start off with a couple of your good stories to lighten things up. It's not what you say, it's how you say it — because personality always wins the day.

LINDA: Oliver always thought the highest of him —

WILLY: Will you let me talk?

BIFF: Don't yell at her, Pop, will ye?

WILLY (*angrily*): I was talking, wasn't I?

BIFF: I don't like you yelling at her all the time, and I'm tellin' you, that's all.

WILLY: What're you, takin' over this house?

LINDA: Willy —

WILLY (*turning to her*): Don't take his side all the time, goddammit!

BIFF (*furiously*): Stop yelling at her!

WILLY (*suddenly pulling on his cheek, beaten down, guilt ridden*): Give my best to Bill Oliver — he may remember me. (*He exits through the living room doorway.*)

LINDA (*her voice subdued*): What'd you have to start that for? (*Biff turns away.*) You see how sweet he was as soon as you talked hopefully? (*She goes over to Biff.*) Come up and say good night to him. Don't let him go to bed that way.

HAPPY: Come on, Biff, let's buck him up.

LINDA: Please, dear. Just say good night. It takes so little to make him happy. Come. (*She goes through the living room doorway, calling upstairs from within the living room.*) Your pajamas are hanging in the bathroom, Willy!

HAPPY (*looking toward where Linda went out*): What a woman! They broke the mold when they made her. You know that, Biff?

BIFF: He's off salary. My God, working on commission!

HAPPY: Well, let's face it: he's no hot-shot selling man. Except that sometimes, you have to admit, he's a sweet personality.

BIFF (*deciding*): Lend me ten bucks, will ye? I want to buy some new ties.

HAPPY: I'll take you to a place I know. Beautiful stuff. Wear one of my striped shirts tomorrow.

BIFF: She got gray. Mom got awful old. Gee, I'm gonna go in to Oliver tomorrow and knock him for a —

HAPPY: Come on up. Tell that to Dad. Let's give him a whirl. Come on.

BIFF (*steamed up*): You know, with ten thousand bucks, boy!

HAPPY (*as they go into the living room*): That's the talk, Biff, that's the first time I've heard the old confidence out of you! (*From within the living room, fading off.*) You're gonna live with me, kid, and any babe you want just say the word . . . (*The last lines are hardly heard. They are mounting the stairs to their parents' bedroom.*)

LINDA (*entering her bedroom and addressing Willy, who is in the bathroom. She is straightening the bed for him.*): Can you do anything about the shower? It drips.

WILLY (*from the bathroom*): All of a sudden everything falls to pieces. Goddam plumbing, oughta be sued, those people. I hardly finished putting it in and the thing . . . (*His words rumble off.*)

LINDA: I'm just wondering if Oliver will remember him. You think he might?

WILLY (*coming out of the bathroom in his pajamas*): Remember him? What's the matter with you, you crazy? If he'd've stayed with Oliver he'd be on top by now! Wait'll Oliver gets a look at him. You don't know the average caliber any more. The average young man today — (*he is getting into bed*) — is got a caliber of zero. Greatest thing in the world for him was to bum around.

(*Biff and Happy enter the bedroom. Slight pause.*)

WILLY (*stops short, looking at Biff*): Glad to hear it, boy.

HAPPY: He wanted to say good night to you, sport.

WILLY (*to Biff*): Yeah. Knock him dead, boy. What'd you want to tell me?

BIFF: Just take it easy, Pop. Good night. (*He turns to go.*)

WILLY (*unable to resist*): And if anything falls off the desk while you're talking to him — like a package or something — don't you pick it up. They have office boys for that.

LINDA: I'll make a big breakfast —

WILLY: Will you let me finish? (*To Biff.*) Tell him you were in the business in the West. Not farm work.

BIFF: All right, Dad.

LINDA: I think everything —

WILLY (*going right through her speech*): And don't undersell yourself. No less than fifteen thousand dollars.

BIFF (*unable to bear him*): Okay. Good night, Mom. (*He starts moving.*)

WILLY: Because you got a greatness in you, Biff, remember that. You got all kinds of greatness . . . (*He lies back, exhausted. Biff walks out.*)

LINDA (*calling after Biff*): Sleep well, darling!

HAPPY: I'm gonna get married, Mom. I wanted to tell you.

LINDA: Go to sleep, dear.

HAPPY (*going*): I just wanted to tell you.

WILLY: Keep up the good work. (*Happy exits.*) God . . . remember that Ebbets Field game? The championship of the city?

LINDA: Just rest. Should I sing to you?

WILLY: Yeah. Sing to me. (*Linda hums a soft lullaby.*) When that team came out — he was the tallest, remember?

LINDA: Oh, yes. And in gold.

(*Biff enters the darkened kitchen, takes a cigarette, and leaves the house. He comes downstage into a golden pool of light. He smokes, staring at the night.*)

WILLY: Like a young god. Hercules — something like that. And the sun, the sun all around him. Remember how he waved to me? Right up from the field, with the representatives of three colleges standing by? And the buyers I brought, and the cheers when he came out — Loman, Loman, Loman! God Almighty, he'll be great yet. A star like that, magnificent, can never really fade away!

(*The light on Willy is fading. The gas heater begins to glow through the kitchen wall, near the stairs, a blue flame beneath red coils.*)

LINDA (*timidly*): Willy dear, what has he got against you?

WILLY: I'm so tired. Don't talk anymore.

(*Biff slowly returns to the kitchen. He stops, stares toward the heater.*)

LINDA: Will you ask Howard to let you work in New York?

WILLY: First thing in the morning. Everything'll be all right.

(*Biff reaches behind the heater and draws out a length of rubber tubing. He is horrified and turns his head toward Willy's room, still dimly lit, from which the strains of Linda's desperate but monotonous humming rise.*)

WILLY (*staring through the window into the moonlight*): Gee, look at the moon moving between the buildings!

(*Biff wraps the tubing around his hand and quickly goes up the stairs.*)

ACT II music playing

(*Music is heard, gay and bright. The curtain rises as the music fades away. Willy, in shirt sleeves, is sitting at the kitchen table, sipping coffee, his hat in his lap. Linda is filling his cup when she can.*)

WILLY: Wonderful coffee. Meal in itself.

LINDA: Can I make you some eggs?

WILLY: No. Take a breath.

LINDA: You look so rested, dear.

WILLY: I slept like a dead one. First time in months. Imagine, sleeping till ten on a Tuesday morning. Boys left nice and early, heh?

LINDA: They were out of here by eight o'clock.

WILLY: Good work!

LINDA: It was so thrilling to see them leaving together. I can't get over the shaving lotion in this house!

WILLY (*smiling*): Mmm —

LINDA: Biff was very changed this morning. His whole attitude seemed to be hopeful. He couldn't wait to get downtown to see Oliver.

WILLY: He's heading for a change. There's no question, there simply are certain men that take longer to get — solidified. How did he dress?

LINDA: His blue suit. He's so handsome in that suit. He could be a — anything in that suit!

(*Willy gets up from the table. Linda holds his jacket for him.*)

WILLY: There's no question, no question at all. Gee, on the way home tonight I'd like to buy some seeds.

LINDA (*laughing*): That'd be wonderful. But not enough sun gets back there. Nothing'll grow any more.

WILLY: You wait, kid, before it's all over we're gonna get a little place out in the country, and I'll raise some vegetables, a couple of chickens . . .

LINDA: You'll do it yet, dear.

(*Willy walks out of his jacket. Linda follows him.*)

WILLY: And they'll get married, and come for a weekend. I'd build a little guest house. 'Cause I got so many fine tools, all I'd need would be a little lumber and some peace of mind.

LINDA (*joyfully*): I sewed the lining . . .

WILLY: I could build two guest houses, so they'd both come. Did he decide how much he's going to ask Oliver for?

LINDA (*getting him into the jacket*): He didn't mention it, but I imagine ten or fifteen thousand. You going to talk to Howard today?

WILLY: Yeah. I'll put it to him straight and simple. He'll just have to take me off the road.

LINDA: And Willy, don't forget to ask for a little advance, because we've got the insurance premium. It's the grace period now.

WILLY: That's a hundred . . . ?

LINDA: A hundred and eight, sixty-eight. Because we're a little short again.

WILLY: Why are we short?

LINDA: Well, you had the motor job on the car . . .

WILLY: That goddam Studebaker!

LINDA: And you got one more payment on the refrigerator . . .

WILLY: But it just broke again!

LINDA: Well, it's old, dear.

WILLY: I told you we should've bought a well-advertised machine. Charley bought a General Electric and it's twenty years old and it's still good, that son-of-a-bitch.

LINDA: But, Willy —

WILLY: Whoever heard of a Hastings refrigerator? Once in my life I would like to own something outright before it's broken! I'm always in a race with the junkyard! I just finished paying for the car and it's on its last legs. The refrigerator consumes belts like a goddamn maniac. They time those things. They time them so when you finally paid for them, they're used up.

LINDA (*buttoning up his jacket as he unbuttons it*): All told, about two hundred dollars would carry us, dear. But that includes the last payment on the mortgage. After this payment, Willy, the house belongs to us.

WILLY: It's twenty-five years!

LINDA: Biff was nine years old when we bought it.

WILLY: Well, that's a great thing. To weather a twenty-five year mortgage is —

LINDA: It's an accomplishment.

WILLY: All the cement, the lumber, the reconstruction I put in this house! There ain't a crack to be found in it anymore.

LINDA: Well, it served its purpose.

WILLY: What purpose? Some stranger'll come along, move in, and that's that. If only Biff would take this house, and raise a family . . . (*He starts to go.*) Good-by, I'm late.

LINDA (*suddenly remembering*): Oh, I forgot! You're supposed to meet them for dinner.

WILLY: Me?

LINDA: At Frank's Chop House on Forty-eighth near Sixth Avenue.

WILLY: Is that so! How about you?

LINDA: No, just the three of you. They're gonna blow you to a big meal!

WILLY: Don't say! Who thought of that?

LINDA: Biff came to me this morning, Willy, and he said, "Tell Dad, we want to blow him to a big meal." Be there six o'clock. You and your two boys are going to have dinner.

WILLY: Gee whiz! That's really somethin'. I'm gonna knock Howard for a loop, kid. I'll get an advance, and I'll come home with a New York job. Goddammit, now I'm gonna do it!

LINDA: Oh, that's the spirit, Willy!

WILLY: I will never get behind a wheel the rest of my life!

LINDA: It's changing, Willy, I can feel it changing!

WILLY: Beyond a question. G'by, I'm late. (*He starts to go again.*)

LINDA (*calling after him as she runs to the kitchen table for a handkerchief*): You got your glasses?

WILLY (*feels for them, then comes back in*): Yeah, yeah, got my glasses.

LINDA (*giving him the handkerchief*): And a handkerchief.

WILLY: Yeah, handkerchief.

LINDA: And your saccharine?

WILLY: Yeah, my saccharine.

LINDA: Be careful on the subway stairs.

(*She kisses him, and a silk stocking is seen hanging from her hand. Willy notices it.*)

WILLY: Will you stop mending stockings? At least while I'm in the house. It gets me nervous. I can't tell you. Please.

(*Linda hides the stocking in her hand as she follows Willy across the forestage in front of the house.*)

LINDA: Remember, Frank's Chop House.

WILLY (*passing the apron*): Maybe beets would grow out there.

LINDA (*laughing*): But you tried so many times.

WILLY: Yeah. Well, don't work hard today. (*He disappears around the right corner of the house.*)

LINDA: Be careful!

(*As Willy vanishes, Linda waves to him. Suddenly the phone rings. She runs across the stage and into the kitchen and lifts it.*)

LINDA: Hello? Oh, Biff! I'm so glad you called, I just . . . Yes, sure, I just told him. Yes, he'll be there for dinner at six o'clock, I didn't forget. Listen, I was just dying to tell you. You know that little rubber pipe I told you about? That he connected to the gas heater? I finally decided to go down the cellar this morning and take it away and destroy it. But it's gone! Imagine? He took it away himself, it isn't there! (*She listens.*) When? Oh, then you took it. Oh — nothing, it's just that I'd hoped he'd taken it away himself. Oh, I'm not worried, darling, because this morning he left in such high spirits, it was like the old days! I'm not afraid any more. Did Mr. Oliver see you? . . . Well, you wait there then. And make a nice impression on him, darling. Just don't perspire too much before you see him. And have a nice time with Dad. He may have big news too! . . . That's right, a New York job. And be sweet to him tonight, dear. Be loving to him. Because he's only a little boat looking for a harbor. (*She is trembling with sorrow and joy.*) Oh, that's wonderful, Biff, you'll save his life. Thanks, darling. Just put your arm around him when he comes into the restaurant. Give him a smile. That's the boy . . . Good-by, dear. . . . You got your comb? . . . That's fine. Good-by, Biff dear.

(*In the middle of her speech, Howard Wagner, thirty-six, wheels in a small typewriter table on which is a wire-recording machine and proceeds to plug it in. This is on the left forestage. Light slowly fades on Linda as it rises on Howard. Howard is intent on threading the machine and only glances over his shoulder as Willy appears.*)

WILLY: Pst! Pst!

HOWARD: Hello, Willy, come in.

WILLY: Like to have a little talk with you, Howard.

HOWARD: Sorry to keep you waiting. I'll be with you in a minute.

WILLY: What's that, Howard?

HOWARD: Didn't you ever see one of these? Wire recorder.

WILLY: Oh. Can we talk a minute?

HOWARD: Records things. Just got delivery yesterday. Been driving me crazy, the most terrific machine I ever saw in my life. I was up all night with it.

WILLY: What do you do with it?

HOWARD: I bought it for dictation, but you can do anything with it. Listen to this. I had it home last night. Listen to what I picked up. The first one is my daughter. Get this. (*He flicks the switch and "Roll out the Barrel" is heard being whistled.*) Listen to that kid whistle.

WILLY: That is lifelike, isn't it?

HOWARD: Seven years old. Get that tone.

WILLY: Ts, ts. Like to ask a little favor if you . . .

(*The whistling breaks off, and the voice of Howard's daughter is heard.*)

HIS DAUGHTER: Now you, Daddy.

HOWARD: She's crazy for me! (*Again the same song is whistled.*) That's me! Ha! (*He winks.*)

WILLY: You're very good!

(*The whistling breaks off again. The machine runs silent for a moment.*)

HOWARD: Sh! Get this now, this is my son.

HIS SON: "The capital of Alabama is Montgomery; the capital of Arizona is Phoenix; the capital of Arkansas is Little Rock; the capital of California is Sacramento . . ." (*and on, and on.*)

HOWARD (*holding up five fingers*): Five years old, Willy!

WILLY: He'll make an announcer some day!

HIS SON (*continuing*): "The capital . . ."

HOWARD: Get that — alphabetical order! (*The machine breaks off suddenly.*) Wait a minute. The maid kicked the plug out.

WILLY: It certainly is a —

HOWARD: Sh, for God's sake!

HIS SON: "It's nine o'clock, Bulova watch time. So I have to go to sleep."

WILLY: That really is —

HOWARD: Wait a minute! The next is my wife.

(*They wait.*)

HOWARD'S VOICE: "Go on, say something." (*Pause.*) "Well, you gonna talk?"

HIS WIFE: "I can't think of anything."

HOWARD'S VOICE: "Well, talk — it's turning."

HIS WIFE (*shyly, beaten*): "Hello." (*Silence.*) "Oh, Howard, I can't talk into this . . ."

HOWARD (*snapping the machine off*): That was my wife.

WILLY: That is a wonderful machine. Can we —

HOWARD: I tell you, Willy, I'm gonna take my camera, and my bandsaw, and all my hobbies, and out they

go. This is the most fascinating relaxation I ever found.

WILLY: I think I'll get one myself.

HOWARD: Sure, they're only a hundred and a half. You can't do without it. Supposing you wanna hear Jack Benny, see? But you can't be at home at that hour. So you tell the maid to turn the radio on when Jack Benny comes on, and this automatically goes on with the radio . . .

WILLY: And when you come home you . . .

HOWARD: You can come home twelve o'clock, one o'clock, any time you like, and you get yourself a Coke and sit yourself down, throw the switch, and there's Jack Benny's program in the middle of the night!

WILLY: I'm definitely going to get one. Because lots of times I'm on the road, and I think to myself, what I must be missing on the radio!

HOWARD: Don't you have a radio in the car?

WILLY: Well, yeah, but who ever thinks of turning it on?

HOWARD: Say, aren't you supposed to be in Boston?

WILLY: That's what I want to talk to you about, Howard. You got a minute? (*He draws a chair in from the wing.*)

HOWARD: What happened? What're you doing here?

WILLY: Well . . .

HOWARD: You didn't crack up again, did you?

WILLY: Oh, no. No . . .

HOWARD: Geez, you had me worried there for a minute. What's the trouble?

WILLY: Well, tell you the truth, Howard. I've come to the decision that I'd rather not travel anymore.

HOWARD: Not travel! Well, what'll you do?

WILLY: Remember, Christmas time, when you had the party here? You said you'd try to think of some spot for me here in town.

HOWARD: With us?

WILLY: Well, sure.

HOWARD: Oh, yeah, yeah. I remember. Well, I couldn't think of anything for you, Willy.

WILLY: I tell ya, Howard. The kids are all grown up, y'know. I don't need much anymore. If I could take home — well, sixty-five dollars a week, I could swing it.

HOWARD: Yeah, but Willy, see I —

WILLY: I tell ya why, Howard. Speaking frankly and between the two of us, y'know — I'm just a little tired.

HOWARD: Oh, I could understand that, Willy. But you're a road man, Willy, and we do a road business. We've only got a half-dozen salesmen on the floor here.

WILLY: God knows, Howard, I never asked a favor of any man. But I was with the firm when your father used to carry you in here in his arms.

HOWARD: I know that, Willy, but —

WILLY: Your father came to me the day you were born and asked me what I thought of the name Howard, may he rest in peace.

HOWARD: I appreciate that, Willy, but there just is no

spot here for you. If I had a spot I'd slam you right in, but I just don't have a single solitary spot.

(*He looks for his lighter. Willy has picked it up and gives it to him. Pause.*)

WILLY (*with increasing anger*): Howard, all I need to set my table is fifty dollars a week.

HOWARD: But where am I going to put you, kid?

WILLY: Look, it isn't a question of whether I can sell merchandise, is it?

HOWARD: No, but it's business, kid, and everybody's gotta pull his own weight.

WILLY (*desperately*): Just let me tell you a story, Howard —

HOWARD: 'Cause you gotta admit, business is business.

WILLY (*angrily*): Business is definitely business, but just listen for a minute. You don't understand this. When I was a boy — eighteen, nineteen — I was already on the road. And there was a question in my mind as to whether selling had a future for me. Because in those days I had a yearning to go to Alaska. See, there were three gold strikes in one month in Alaska, and I felt like going out. Just for the ride, you might say.

HOWARD (*barely interested*): Don't say.

WILLY: Oh, yeah, my father lived many years in Alaska. He was an adventurous man. We've got quite a little streak of self-reliance in our family. I thought I'd go out with my older brother and try to locate him, and maybe settle in the North with the old man. And I was almost decided to go, when I met a salesman in the Parker House. His name was Dave Singleman. And he was eighty-four years old, and he'd drummed merchandise in thirty-one states. And old Dave, he'd go up to his room, y'understand, put on his green velvet slippers — I'll never forget — and pick up his phone and call the buyers, and without ever leaving his room, at the age of eighty-four, he made his living. And when I saw that, I realized that selling was the greatest career a man could want. 'Cause what could be more satisfying than to be able to go, at the age of eighty-four, into twenty or thirty different cities, and pick up a phone, and be remembered and loved and helped by so many different people? Do you know? When he died — and by the way he died the death of a salesman, in his green velvet slippers in the smoker of the New York, New Haven and Hartford, going into Boston — when he died, hundreds of salesmen and buyers were at his funeral. Things were sad on a lotta trains for months after that. (*He stands up. Howard has not looked at him.*) In those days there was personality in it, Howard. There was respect and comradeship, and gratitude in it. Today, it's all cut and dried, and there's no chance for bringing friendship to bear — or personality. You see what I mean? They don't know me any more.

HOWARD (*moving away, to the right*): That's just the thing, Willy.

WILLY: If I had forty dollars a week — that's all I'd need. Forty dollars, Howard.

HOWARD: Kid, I can't take blood from a stone, I —

WILLY (*desperation is on him now*): Howard, the year Al Smith was nominated, your father came to me and —

HOWARD (*starting to go off*): I've got to see some people, kid.

WILLY (*stopping him*): I'm talking about your father! There were promises made across this desk! You mustn't tell me you've got people to see — I put thirty-four years into this firm, Howard, and now I can't pay my insurance! You can't eat the orange and throw the peel away — a man is not a piece of fruit! (*After a pause.*) Now pay attention. Your father — in 1928 I had a big year. I averaged a hundred and seventy dollars a week in commissions.

HOWARD (*impatiently*): Now, Willy, you never averaged —

WILLY (*banging his hand on the desk*): I averaged a hundred and seventy dollars a week in the year of 1928! And your father came to me — or rather I was in the office here — it was right over this desk — and he put his hand on my shoulder —

HOWARD (*getting up*): You'll have to excuse me, Willy, I gotta see some people. Pull yourself together. (*Going out.*) I'll be back in a little while.

(*On Howard's exit, the light on his chair grows very bright and strange.*)

WILLY: Pull myself together! What the hell did I say to him? My God, I was yelling at him! How could I? (*Willy breaks off, staring at the light, which occupies the chair, animating it. He approaches this chair, standing across the desk from it.*) Frank, Frank, don't you remember what you told me that time? How you put your hand on my shoulder, and Frank . . . (*He leans on the desk and as he speaks the dead man's name he accidentally switches on the recorder, and instantly*)

HOWARD'S SON: ". . . of New York is Albany. The capital of Ohio is Cincinnati, the capital of Rhode Island is . . ." (*The recitation continues.*)

WILLY (*leaping away with fright, shouting*): Ha! Howard! Howard! Howard!

HOWARD (*rushing in*): What happened?

WILLY (*pointing at the machine, which continues nasally, childishly, with the capital cities*): Shut it off! Shut it off!

HOWARD (*pulling the plug out*): Look, Willy . . .

WILLY (*pressing his hands to his eyes*): I gotta get myself some coffee. I'll get some coffee . . .

(*Willy starts to walk out. Howard stops him.*)

HOWARD (*rolling up the cord*): Willy, look . . .

WILLY: I'll go to Boston.

HOWARD: Willy, you can't go to Boston for us.

WILLY: Why can't I go?

HOWARD: I don't want you to represent us. I've been meaning to tell you for a long time now.

WILLY: Howard, are you firing me?

HOWARD: I think you need a good long rest, Willy.

WILLY: Howard —

HOWARD: And when you feel better, come back, and we'll see if we can work something out.

WILLY: But I gotta earn money, Howard. I'm in no position to —

HOWARD: Where are your sons? Why don't your sons give you a hand?

WILLY: They're working on a very big deal.

HOWARD: This is no time for false pride, Willy. You go to your sons and you tell them that you're tired. You've got two great boys, haven't you?

WILLY: Oh, no question, no question, but in the meantime . . .

HOWARD: Then that's that, heh?

WILLY: All right, I'll go to Boston tomorrow.

HOWARD: No, no.

WILLY: I can't throw myself on my sons. I'm not a cripple!

HOWARD: Look, kid, I'm busy this morning.

WILLY (*grasping Howard's arm*): Howard, you've got to let me go to Boston!

HOWARD (*hard, keeping himself under control*): I've got a line of people to see this morning. Sit down, take five minutes, and pull yourself together, and then go home, will ya? I need the office, Willy. (*He starts to go, turns, remembering the recorder, starts to push off the table holding the recorder.*) Oh, yeah. Whenever you can this week, stop by and drop off the samples. You'll feel better, Willy, and then come back and we'll talk. Pull yourself together, kid, there's people outside.

(*Howard exits, pushing the table off left. Willy stares into space, exhausted. Now the music is heard — Ben's music — first distantly, then closer, closer. As Willy speaks, Ben enters from the right. He carries valise and umbrella.*)

WILLY: Oh, Ben, how did you do it? What is the answer? Did you wind up the Alaska deal already?

BEN: Doesn't take much time if you know what you're doing. Just a short business trip. Boarding ship in an hour. Wanted to say good-by.

WILLY: Ben, I've got to talk to you.

BEN (*glancing at his watch*): Haven't the time, William.

WILLY (*crossing the apron to Ben*): Ben, nothing's working out. I don't know what to do.

BEN: Now, look here, William. I've bought timberland in Alaska and I need a man to look after things for me.

WILLY: God, timberland! Me and my boys in those grand outdoors!

BEN: You've a new continent at your doorstep, William. Get out of these cities, they're full of talk and time payments and courts of law. Screw on your fists and you can fight for a fortune up there.

WILLY: Yes, yes! Linda, Linda!

(*Linda enters as of old, with the wash.*)

LINDA: Oh, you're back?

BEN: I haven't much time.

WILLY: No, wait! Linda, he's got a proposition for me in Alaska.

LINDA: But you've got — (*To Ben.*) He's got a beautiful job here.

WILLY: But in Alaska, kid, I could —

LINDA: You're doing well enough, Willy!

BEN (*to Linda*): Enough for what, my dear?

LINDA (*frightened of Ben and angry at him*): Don't say those things to him! Enough to be happy right here, right now. (*To Willy, while Ben laughs.*) Why must everybody conquer the world? You're well liked, and the boys love you, and someday — (*To Ben*) — why, old man Wagner told him just the other day that if he keeps it up he'll be a member of the firm, didn't he, Willy?

WILLY: Sure, sure. I am building something with this firm, Ben, and if a man is building something he must be on the right track, mustn't he?

BEN: What are you building? Lay your hand on it. Where is it?

WILLY (*hesitantly*): That's true, Linda, there's nothing.

LINDA: Why? (*To Ben.*) There's a man eighty-four years old —

WILLY: That's right, Ben, that's right. When I look at that man I say, what is there to worry about?

BEN: Bah!

WILLY: It's true, Ben. All he has to do is go into any city, pick up the phone, and he's making his living and you know why?

BEN (*picking up his valise*): I've got to go.

WILLY (*holding Ben back*): Look at this boy!

(*Biff, in his high school sweater, enters carrying suitcase. Happy carries Biff's shoulder guards, gold helmet, and football pants.*)

WILLY: Without a penny to his name, three great universities are begging for him, and from there the sky's the limit, because it's not what you do, Ben. It's who you know and the smile on your face! It's contacts, Ben, contacts! The whole wealth of Alaska passes over the lunch table at the Commodore Hotel, and that's the wonder, the wonder of this country, that a man can end with diamonds here on the basis of being liked! (*He turns to Biff.*) And that's why when you get out on that field today it's important. Because thousands of people will be rooting for you and loving you. (*To Ben, who has again begun to leave.*) And Ben! when he walks into a business office his name will sound out like a bell and all the doors will open to him! I've seen it, Ben, I've seen it a thousand times! You can't feel it with your hand like timber, but it's there!

BEN: Good-by, William.

WILLY: Ben, am I right? Don't you think I'm right? I value your advice.

BEN: There's a new continent at your doorstep, William. You could walk out rich. Rich! (*He is gone.*)

WILLY: We'll do it here, Ben! You hear me? We're gonna do it here!

music playing

(*Young Bernard rushes in. The gay music of the Boys is heard.*)

BERNARD: Oh, gee, I was afraid you left already!

WILLY: Why? What time is it?

BERNARD: It's half-past one!

WILLY: Well, come on, everybody! Ebbets Field next stop! Where's the pennants? (*He rushes through the wall-line of the kitchen and out into the living room.*)

LINDA (*to Biff*): Did you pack fresh underwear?

BIFF (*who has been limbering up*): I want to go!

BERNARD: Biff, I'm carrying your helmet, ain't I?

HAPPY: No, I'm carrying the helmet.

BERNARD: Oh, Biff, you promised me.

HAPPY: I'm carrying the helmet.

BERNARD: How am I going to get in the locker room?

LINDA: Let him carry the shoulder guards. (*She puts her coat and hat on in the kitchen.*)

BERNARD: Can I, Biff? 'Cause I told everybody I'm going to be in the locker room.

HAPPY: In Ebbets Field it's the clubhouse.

BERNARD: I meant the clubhouse. Biff!

HAPPY: Biff!

BIFF (*grandly, after a slight pause*): Let him carry the shoulder guards.

HAPPY (*as he gives Bernard the shoulder guards*): Stay close to us now.

(*Willy rushes in with the pennants.*)

WILLY (*handing them out*): Everybody wave when Biff comes out on the field. (*Happy and Bernard run off.*) You set now, boy?

(*The music has died away.*)

BIFF: Ready to go, Pop. Every muscle is ready.

WILLY (*at the edge of the apron*): You realize what this means?

BIFF: That's right, Pop.

WILLY (*feeling Biff's muscles*): You're comin' home this afternoon captain of the All-Scholastic Championship Team of the City of New York.

BIFF: I got it, Pop. And remember, pal, when I take off my helmet, that touchdown is for you.

WILLY: Let's go! (*He is starting out, with his arm around Biff, when Charley enters, as of old, in knickers.*) I got no room for you, Charley.

CHARLEY: Room? For what?

WILLY: In the car.

CHARLEY: You goin' for a ride? I wanted to shoot some casino.

WILLY (*furiously*): Casino! (*Incredulously.*) Don't you realize what today is?

LINDA: Oh, he knows, Willy. He's just kidding you.

WILLY: That's nothing to kid about!

CHARLEY: No, Linda, what's goin' on?

LINDA: He's playing in Ebbets Field.

CHARLEY: Baseball in this weather?

WILLY: Don't talk to him. Come on, come on! (*He is pushing them out.*)

CHARLEY: Wait a minute, didn't you hear the news?

WILLY: What?

CHARLEY: Don't you listen to the radio? Ebbets Field just blew up.

WILLY: You go to hell! (*Charley laughs. Pushing them out.*) Come on, come on! We're late.

CHARLEY (*as they go*): Knock a homer, Biff, knock a homer!

WILLY (*the last to leave, turning to Charley*): I don't think that was funny, Charley. This is the greatest day of his life.

CHARLEY: Willy, when are you going to grow up?

WILLY: Yeah, heh? When this game is over, Charley, you'll be laughing out of the other side of your face. They'll be calling him another Red Grange. Twenty-five thousand a year.

CHARLEY (*kidding*): Is that so?

WILLY: Yeah, that's so.

CHARLEY: Well, then, I'm sorry, Willy. But tell me something.

WILLY: What?

CHARLEY: Who is Red Grange?

WILLY: Put up your hands. Goddam you, put up your hands!   *music*

(*Charley, chuckling, shakes his head and walks away, around the left corner of the stage. Willy follows him. The music rises to a mocking frenzy.*)

WILLY: Who the hell do you think you are, better than everybody else? You don't know everything, you big, ignorant, stupid . . . Put up your hands!

(*Light rises, on the right side of the forestage, on a small table in the reception room of Charley's office. Traffic sounds are heard. Bernard, now mature, sits whistling to himself. A pair of tennis rackets and an overnight bag are on the floor beside him.*)

WILLY (*offstage*): What are you walking away for? Don't walk away! If you're going to say something say it to my face! I know you laugh at me behind my back. You'll laugh out of the other side of your goddam face after this game. Touchdown! Touchdown! Eighty thousand people! Touchdown! Right between the goal posts.

(*Bernard is a quiet, earnest, but self-assured young man. Willy's voice is coming from right upstage now. Bernard lowers his feet off the table and listens. Jenny, his father's secretary, enters.*)

JENNY (*distressed*): Say, Bernard, will you go out in the hall?

BERNARD: What is that noise? Who is it?

JENNY: Mr. Loman. He just got off the elevator.

BERNARD (*getting up*): Who's he arguing with?

JENNY: Nobody. There's nobody with him. I can't deal with him anymore, and your father gets all upset everytime he comes. I've got a lot of typing to do, and your father's waiting to sign it. Will you see him?

WILLY (*entering*): Touchdown! Touch — (*He sees Jenny.*)

Jenny, Jenny, good to see you. How're ya? Workin'? Or still honest?

JENNY: Fine. How've you been feeling?

WILLY: Not much any more, Jenny. Ha, ha! (*He is surprised to see the rackets.*)

BERNARD: Hello, Uncle Willy.

WILLY (*almost shocked*): Bernard! Well, look who's here! (*He comes quickly, guiltily, to Bernard and warmly shakes his hand.*)

BERNARD: How are you? Good to see you.

WILLY: What are you doing here?

BERNARD: Oh, just stopped by to see Pop. Get off my feet till my train leaves. I'm going to Washington in a few minutes.

WILLY: Is he in?

BERNARD: Yes, he's in his office with the accountant. Sit down.

WILLY (*sitting down*): What're you going to do in Washington?

BERNARD: Oh, just a case I've got there, Willy.

WILLY: That so? (*Indicating the rackets.*) You going to play tennis there?

BERNARD: I'm staying with a friend who's got a court.

WILLY: Don't say. His own tennis court. Must be fine people, I bet.

BERNARD: They are, very nice. Dad tells me Biff's in town.

WILLY (*with a big smile*): Yeah, Biff's in. Working on a very big deal, Bernard.

BERNARD: What's Biff doing?

WILLY: Well, he's been doing very big things in the West. But he decided to establish himself here. Very big. We're having dinner. Did I hear your wife had a boy?

BERNARD: That's right. Our second.

WILLY: Two boys! What do you know!

BERNARD: What kind of a deal has Biff got?

WILLY: Well, Bill Oliver — very big sporting-goods man — he wants Biff very badly. Called him in from the West. Long distance, carte blanche, special deliveries. Your friends have their own private tennis court?

BERNARD: You still with the old firm, Willy?

WILLY (*after a pause*): I'm — I'm overjoyed to see how you made the grade, Bernard, overjoyed. It's an encouraging thing to see a young man really — really — Looks very good for Biff — very — (*He breaks off, then.*) Bernard — (*He is so full of emotion, he breaks off again.*)

BERNARD: What is it, Willy?

WILLY (*small and alone*): What — what's the secret?

BERNARD: What secret?

WILLY: How — how did you? Why didn't he ever catch on?

BERNARD: I wouldn't know that, Willy.

WILLY (*confidentially, desperately*): You were his friend, his boyhood friend. There's something I don't understand about it. His life ended after that Ebbets Field game. From the age of seventeen nothing good ever happened to him.

BERNARD: He never trained himself for anything.

WILLY: But he did, he did. After high school he took so many correspondence courses. Radio mechanics; television; God knows what, and never made the slightest mark.

BERNARD (*taking off his glasses*): Willy, do you want to talk candidly?

WILLY (*rising, faces Bernard*): I regard you as a very brilliant man, Bernard. I value your advice.

BERNARD: Oh, the hell with the advice, Willy. I couldn't advise you. There's just one thing I've always wanted to ask you. When he was supposed to graduate, and the math teacher flunked him —

WILLY: Oh, that son-of-a-bitch ruined his life.

BERNARD: Yeah, but, Willy, all he had to do was go to summer school and make up that subject.

WILLY: That's right, that's right.

BERNARD: Did you tell him not to go to summer school?

WILLY: Me? I begged him to go. I ordered him to go!

BERNARD: Then why wouldn't he go?

WILLY: Why? Why! Bernard, that question has been trailing me like a ghost for the last fifteen years. He flunked the subject, and laid down and died like a hammer hit him!

BERNARD: Take it easy, kid.

WILLY: Let me talk to you — I got nobody to talk to. Bernard, Bernard, was it my fault? Y'see? It keeps going around in my mind, maybe I did something to him. I got nothing to give him.

BERNARD: Don't take it so hard.

WILLY: Why did he lay down? What is the story there? You were his friend!

BERNARD: Willy, I remember, it was June, and our grades came out. And he'd flunked math.

WILLY: That son-of-a-bitch!

BERNARD: No, it wasn't right then. Biff just got very angry, I remember, and he was ready to enroll in summer school.

WILLY (*surprised*): He was?

BERNARD: He wasn't beaten by it at all. But then, Willy, he disappeared from the block for almost a month. And I got the idea that he'd gone up to New England to see you. Did he have a talk with you then?

(*Willy stares in silence.*)

BERNARD: Willy?

WILLY (*with a strong edge of resentment in his voice*): Yeah, he came to Boston. What about it?

BERNARD: Well, just that when he came back — I'll never forget this, it always mystifies me. Because I'd thought so well of Biff, even though he'd always taken advantage of me. I loved him, Willy, y'know? And he came back after that month and took his sneakers — remember those sneakers with "University of Virginia" printed on them? He was so proud of those, wore them every day. And he took them down in the cellar, and burned them up in the furnace. We had a fist fight. It lasted at least half an hour. Just the two of us, punching each other down the cellar, and crying right through it. I've often thought of how strange it was that I knew he'd given up his life. What happened in Boston, Willy?

(*Willy looks at him as at an intruder.*)

BERNARD: I just bring it up because you asked me.

WILLY (*angrily*): Nothing. What do you mean, "What happened?" What's that got to do with anything?

BERNARD: Well, don't get sore.

WILLY: What are you trying to do, blame it on me? If a boy lays down is that my fault?

BERNARD: Now, Willy, don't get —

WILLY: Well, don't — don't talk to me that way! What does that mean, "What happened?"

(*Charley enters. He is in his vest, and he carries a bottle of bourbon.*)

CHARLEY: Hey, you're going to miss that train. (*He waves the bottle.*)

BERNARD: Yeah, I'm going. (*He takes the bottle.*) Thanks, Pop. (*He picks up his rackets and bag.*) Good-by, Willy, and don't worry about it. You know, "If at first you don't succeed . . ."

WILLY: Yes, I believe in that.

BERNARD: But sometimes, Willy, it's better for a man just to walk away.

WILLY: Walk away?

BERNARD: That's right.

WILLY: But if you can't walk away?

BERNARD (*after a slight pause*): I guess that's when it's tough. (*Extending his hand.*) Good-by, Willy.

WILLY (*shaking Bernard's hand*): Good-by, boy.

CHARLEY (*an arm on Bernard's shoulder*): How do you like this kid? Gonna argue a case in front of the Supreme Court.

BERNARD (*protesting*): Pop!

WILLY (*genuinely shocked, pained, and happy*): No! The Supreme Court!

BERNARD: I gotta run. 'By, Dad!

CHARLEY: Knock 'em dead, Bernard!

(*Bernard goes off.*)

WILLY (*as Charley takes out his wallet*): The Supreme Court! And he didn't even mention it!

CHARLEY (*counting out money on the desk*): He don't have to — he's gonna do it.

WILLY: And you never told him what to do, did you? You never took any interest in him.

CHARLEY: My salvation is that I never took any interest in anything. There's some money — fifty dollars. I got an accountant inside.

WILLY: Charley, look . . . (*With difficulty.*) I got my insurance to pay. If you can manage it — I need a hundred and ten dollars.

(*Charley doesn't reply for a moment; merely stops moving.*)

WILLY: I'd draw it from my bank but Linda would know, and I . . .

CHARLEY: Sit down, Willy.

WILLY (*moving toward the chair*): I'm keeping an account of everything, remember. I'll pay every penny back. (*He sits.*)

CHARLEY: Now listen to me, Willy.

WILLY: I want you to know I appreciate . . .

CHARLEY (*sitting down on the table*): Willy, what're you doin'? What the hell is goin' on in your head?

WILLY: Why? I'm simply . . .

CHARLEY: I offered you a job. You make fifty dollars a week. And I won't send you on the road.

WILLY: I've got a job.

CHARLEY: Without pay? What kind of a job is a job without pay? (*He rises.*) Now, look, kid, enough is enough. I'm no genius but I know when I'm being insulted.

WILLY: Insulted!

CHARLEY: Why don't you want to work for me?

WILLY: What's the matter with you? I've got a job.

CHARLEY: Then what're you walkin' in here every week for?

WILLY (*getting up*): Well, if you don't want me to walk in here —

CHARLEY: I'm offering you a job.

WILLY: I don't want your goddam job!

CHARLEY: When the hell are you going to grow up?

WILLY (*furiously*): You big ignoramus, if you say that to me again I'll rap you one! I don't care how big you are! (*He's ready to fight.*)

(*Pause.*)

CHARLEY (*kindly, going to him*): How much do you need, Willy?

WILLY: Charley, I'm strapped. I'm strapped. I don't know what to do. I was just fired.

CHARLEY: Howard fired you?

WILLY: That snotnose. Imagine that? I named him. I named him Howard.

CHARLEY: Willy, when're you gonna realize that them things don't mean anything? You named him Howard, but you can't sell that. The only thing you got in this world is what you can sell. And the funny thing is that you're a salesman, and you don't know that.

WILLY: I've always tried to think otherwise, I guess. I always felt that if a man was impressive, and well liked, that nothing —

CHARLEY: Why must everybody like you? Who liked J. P. Morgan?° Was he impressive? In a Turkish bath he'd look like a butcher. But with his pockets on he was very well liked. Now listen, Willy, I know you don't like me, and nobody can say I'm in love with you, but I'll give you a job because — just for the hell of it, put it that way. Now what do you say?

WILLY: I — I just can't work for you, Charley.

CHARLEY: What're you, jealous of me?

WILLY: I can't work for you, that's all, don't ask me why.

J. P. Morgan: (1837–1913), wealthy financier and art collector whose money was made chiefly in banking, railroads, and steel.

CHARLEY (*angered, takes out more bills*): You been jealous of me all your life, you dammed fool! Here, pay your insurance. (*He puts the money in Willy's hand.*)

WILLY: I'm keeping strict accounts.

CHARLEY: I've got some work to do. Take care of yourself. And pay your insurance.

WILLY (*moving to the right*): Funny, y'know? After all the highways, and the trains, and the appointments, and the years, you end up worth more dead than alive.

CHARLEY: Willy, nobody's worth nothin' dead. (*After a slight pause.*) Did you hear what I said?

(*Willy stands still, dreaming.*)

CHARLEY: Willy!

WILLY: Apologize to Bernard for me when you see him. I didn't mean to argue with him. He's a fine boy. They're all fine boys, and they'll end up big — all of them. Someday they'll all play tennis together. Wish me luck, Charley. He saw Bill Oliver today.

CHARLEY: Good luck.

WILLY (*on the verge of tears*): Charley, you're the only friend I got. Isn't that a remarkable thing? (*He goes out.*)

CHARLEY: Jesus! *music playing*

(*Charley stares after him a moment and follows. All light blacks out. Suddenly raucous music is heard, and a red glow rises behind the screen at right. Stanley, a young waiter, appears, carrying a table, followed by Happy, who is carrying two chairs.*)

STANLEY (*putting the table down*): That's all right, Mr. Loman, I can handle it myself. (*He turns and takes the chairs from Happy and places them at the table.*)

HAPPY (*glancing around*): Oh, this is better.

STANLEY: Sure, in the front there you're in the middle of all kinds of noise. Whenever you got a party, Mr. Loman, you just tell me and I'll put you back here. Y'know, there's a lotta people they don't like it private, because when they go out they like to see a lotta action around them because they're sick and tired to stay in the house by theirself. But I know you, you ain't from Hackensack. You know what I mean?

HAPPY (*sitting down*): So how's it coming, Stanley?

STANLEY: Ah, it's a dog life. I only wish during the war they'd a took me in the Army. I coulda been dead by now.

HAPPY: My brother's back, Stanley.

STANLEY: Oh, he come back, heh? From the Far West.

HAPPY: Yeah, big cattle man, my brother, so treat him right. And my father's coming too.

STANLEY: Oh, your father too!

HAPPY: You got a couple of nice lobsters?

STANLEY: Hundred percent, big.

HAPPY: I want them with the claws.

STANLEY: Don't worry, I don't give you no mice. (*Happy laughs.*) How about some wine? It'll put a head on the meal.

HAPPY: No. You remember, Stanley, that recipe I brought you from overseas? With the champagne in it?

STANLEY: Oh, yeah, sure. I still got it tacked up yet in the kitchen. But that'll have to cost a buck apiece anyways.

HAPPY: That's all right.

STANLEY: What'd you, hit a number or somethin'?

HAPPY: No, it's a little celebration. My brother is — I think he pulled off a big deal today. I think we're going into business together.

STANLEY: Great! That's the best for you. Because a family business, you know what I mean? — that's the best.

HAPPY: That's what I think.

STANLEY: 'Cause what's the difference? Somebody steals? It's in the family. Know what I mean? (*Sotto voce.°*) Like this bartender here. The boss is goin' crazy what kinda leak he's got in the cash register. You put it in but it don't come out.

HAPPY (*raising his head*): Sh!

STANLEY: What?

HAPPY: You notice I wasn't lookin' right or left, was I?

STANLEY: No.

HAPPY: And my eyes are closed.

STANLEY: So what's the — ?

HAPPY: Strudel's comin'.

STANLEY (*catching on, looks around*): Ah, no, there's no —

(*He breaks off as a furred, lavishly dressed girl enters and sits at the next table. Both follow her with their eyes.*)

STANLEY: Geez, how'd ya know?

HAPPY: I got radar or something. (*Staring directly at her profile.*) Oooooooo . . . Stanley.

STANLEY: I think that's for you, Mr. Loman.

HAPPY: Look at that mouth. Oh, God. And the binoculars.

STANLEY: Geez, you got a life, Mr. Loman.

HAPPY: Wait on her.

STANLEY (*going to the girl's table*): Would you like a menu, ma'am?

GIRL: I'm expecting someone, but I'd like a —

HAPPY: Why don't you bring her — excuse me, miss, do you mind? I sell champagne, and I'd like you to try my brand. Bring her a champagne, Stanley.

GIRL: That's awfully nice of you.

HAPPY: Don't mention it. It's all company money. (*He laughs.*)

GIRL: That's a charming product to be selling, isn't it?

HAPPY: Oh, gets to be like everything else. Selling is selling, y'know.

GIRL: I suppose.

HAPPY: You don't happen to sell, do you?

GIRL: No, I don't sell.

HAPPY: Would you object to a compliment from a stranger? You ought to be on a magazine cover.

GIRL (*looking at him a little archly*): I have been.

(*Stanley comes in with a glass of champagne.*)

Sotto voce: In a soft voice or stage whisper.

HAPPY: What'd I say before, Stanley? You see? She's a cover girl.

STANLEY: Oh, I could see, I could see.

HAPPY (*to the Girl*): What magazine?

GIRL: Oh, a lot of them. (*She takes the drink.*) Thank you.

HAPPY: You know what they say in France, don't you? "Champagne is the drink of the complexion" — Hya, Biff!

(*Biff has entered and sits with Happy.*)

BIFF: Hello, kid. Sorry I'm late.

HAPPY: I just got here. Uh, Miss — ?

GIRL: Forsythe.

HAPPY: Miss Forsythe, this is my brother.

BIFF: Is Dad here?

HAPPY: His name is Biff. You might've heard of him. Great football player.

GIRL: Really? What team?

HAPPY: Are you familiar with football?

GIRL: No, I'm afraid I'm not.

HAPPY: Biff is quarterback with the New York Giants.

GIRL: Well, that is nice, isn't it? (*She drinks.*)

HAPPY: Good health.

GIRL: I'm happy to meet you.

HAPPY: That's my name. Hap. It's really Harold, but at West Point they called me Happy.

GIRL (*now really impressed*): Oh, I see. How do you do? (*She turns her profile.*)

BIFF: Isn't Dad coming?

HAPPY: You want her?

BIFF: Oh, I could never make that.

HAPPY: I remember the time that idea would never come into your head. Where's the old confidence, Biff?

BIFF: I just saw Oliver —

HAPPY: Wait a minute. I've got to see that old confidence again. Do you want her? She's on call.

BIFF: Oh, no. (*He turns to look at the Girl.*)

HAPPY: I'm telling you. Watch this. (*Turning to the Girl*): Honey? (*She turns to him.*) Are you busy?

GIRL: Well, I am . . . but I could make a phone call.

HAPPY: Do that, will you, honey? And see if you can get a friend. We'll be here for a while. Biff is one of the greatest football players in the country.

GIRL (*standing up*): Well, I'm certainly happy to meet you.

HAPPY: Come back soon.

GIRL: I'll try.

HAPPY: Don't try, honey, try hard.

(*The Girl exits. Stanley follows, shaking his head in bewildered admiration.*)

HAPPY: Isn't that a shame now? A beautiful girl like that? That's why I can't get married. There's not a good woman in a thousand. New York is loaded with them, kid!

BIFF: Hap, look —

HAPPY: I told you she was on call!

BIFF (*strangely unnerved*): Cut it out, will ya? I want to say something to you.

HAPPY: Did you see Oliver?

BIFF: I saw him all right. Now look, I want to tell Dad a couple of things and I want you to help me.

HAPPY: What? Is he going to back you?

BIFF: Are you crazy? You're out of your goddam head, you know that?

HAPPY: Why? What happened?

BIFF (*breathlessly*): I did a terrible thing today, Hap. It's been the strangest day I ever went through. I'm all numb, I swear.

HAPPY: You mean he wouldn't see you?

BIFF: Well, I waited six hours for him, see? All day. Kept sending my name in. Even tried to date his secretary so she'd get me to him, but no soap.

HAPPY: Because you're not showin' the old confidence Biff. He remembered you, didn't he?

BIFF (*stopping Happy with a gesture*): Finally, about five o'clock, he comes out. Didn't remember who I was or anything. I felt like such an idiot, Hap.

HAPPY: Did you tell him my Florida idea?

BIFF: He walked away. I saw him for one minute. I got so mad I could've torn the walls down! How the hell did I ever get the idea I was a salesman there? I even believed myself that I'd been a salesman for him! And then he gave me one look and — I realized what a ridiculous lie my whole life has been! We've been talking in a dream for fifteen years. I was a shipping clerk.

HAPPY: What'd you do?

BIFF (*with great tension and wonder*): Well, he left, see. And the secretary went out. I was all alone in the waiting room. I don't know what came over me, Hap. The next thing I know I'm in his office — paneled walls, everything. I can't explain it. I — Hap, I took his fountain pen.

HAPPY: Geez, did he catch you?

BIFF: I ran out. I ran down all eleven flights. I ran and ran and ran.

HAPPY: That was an awful dumb — what'd you do that for?

BIFF (*agonized*): I don't know, I just — wanted to take something, I don't know. You gotta help me, Hap. I'm gonna tell Pop.

HAPPY: You crazy? What for?

BIFF: Hap, he's got to understand that I'm not the man somebody lends that kind of money to. He thinks I've been spiting him all these years and it's eating him up.

HAPPY: That's just it. You tell him something nice.

BIFF: I can't.

HAPPY: Say you got a lunch date with Oliver tomorrow.

BIFF: So what do I do tomorrow?

HAPPY: You leave the house tomorrow and come back at night and say Oliver is thinking it over. And he thinks it over for a couple of weeks, and gradually it fades away and nobody's the worse.

BIFF: But it'll go on forever!

HAPPY: Dad is never so happy as when he's looking forward to something!

(*Willy enters.*)

HAPPY: Hello, scout!

WILLY: Gee, I haven't been here in years!

(*Stanley has followed Willy in and sets a chair for him. Stanley starts off but Happy stops him.*)

HAPPY: Stanley!

(*Stanley stands by, waiting for an order.*)

BIFF (*going to Willy with guilt, as to an invalid*): Sit down, Pop. You want a drink?

WILLY: Sure, I don't mind.

BIFF: Let's get a load on.

WILLY: You look worried.

BIFF: N-no. (*To Stanley.*) Scotch all around. Make it doubles.

STANLEY: Doubles, right. (*He goes.*)

WILLY: You had a couple already, didn't you?

BIFF: Just a couple, yeah.

WILLY: Well, what happened, boy? (*Nodding affirmatively, with a smile.*) Everything go all right?

BIFF (*takes a breath, then reaches out and grasps Willy's hand*): Pal . . . (*He is smiling bravely, and Willy is smiling too.*) I had an experience today.

HAPPY: Terrific, Pop.

WILLY: That so? What happened?

BIFF (*high, slightly alcoholic, above the earth*): I'm going to tell you everything from first to last. It's been a strange day. (*Silence. He looks around, composes himself as best he can, but his breath keeps breaking the rhythm of his voice.*) I had to wait quite a while for him, and —

WILLY: Oliver?

BIFF: Yeah, Oliver. All day, as a matter of cold fact. And a lot of — instances — facts, Pop, facts about my life came back to me. Who was it, Pop? Who ever said I was a salesman with Oliver?

WILLY: Well, you were.

BIFF: No, Dad, I was a shipping clerk.

WILLY: But you were practically —

BIFF (*with determination*): Dad, I don't know who said it first, but I was never a salesman for Bill Oliver.

WILLY: What're you talking about?

BIFF: Let's hold on to the facts tonight, Pop. We're not going to get anywhere bullin' around. I was a shipping clerk.

WILLY (*angrily*): All right, now listen to me —

BIFF: Why don't you let me finish?

WILLY: I'm not interested in stories about the past or any crap of that kind because the woods are burning, boys, you understand? There's a big blaze going on all around. I was fired today.

BIFF (*shocked*): How could you be?

WILLY: I was fired, and I'm looking for a little good news to tell your mother, because the woman has waited and the woman has suffered. The gist of it is that I haven't got a story left in my head, Biff. So

don't give me a lecture about facts and aspects. I am not interested. Now what've you got to say to me?

(*Stanley enters with three drinks. They wait until he leaves.*)

WILLY: Did you see Oliver?

BIFF: Jesus, Dad!

WILLY: You mean you didn't go up there?

HAPPY: Sure he went up there.

BIFF: I did. I — saw him. How could they fire you?

WILLY (*on the edge of his chair*): What kind of a welcome did he give you?

BIFF: He won't even let you work on commission?

WILLY: I'm out! (*Driving.*) So tell me, he gave you a warm welcome?

HAPPY: Sure, Pop, sure!

BIFF (*driven*): Well, it was kind of —

WILLY: I was wondering if he'd remember you. (*To Happy.*) Imagine, man doesn't see him for ten, twelve years and gives him that kind of a welcome!

HAPPY: Damn right!

BIFF (*trying to return to the offensive*): Pop, look —

WILLY: You know why he remembered you, don't you? Because you impressed him in those days.

BIFF: Let's talk quietly and get this down to the facts, huh?

WILLY (*as though Biff had been interrupting*): Well, what happened? It's great news, Biff. Did he take you into his office or'd you talk in the waiting room?

BIFF: Well, he came in, see, and —

WILLY (*with a big smile*): What'd he say? Betcha he threw his arm around you.

BIFF: Well, he kinda —

WILLY: He's a fine man. (*To Happy.*) Very hard man to see, y'know.

HAPPY (*agreeing*): Oh, I know.

WILLY (*to Biff*): Is that where you had the drinks?

BIFF: Yeah, he gave me a couple of — no, no!

HAPPY (*cutting in*): He told him my Florida idea.

WILLY: Don't interrupt. (*To Biff.*) How'd he react to the Florida idea?

BIFF: Dad, will you give me a minute to explain?

WILLY: I've been waiting for you to explain since I sat down here! What happened? He took you into his office and what?

BIFF: Well — I talked. And — and he listened, see.

WILLY: Famous for the way he listens, y'know. What was his answer?

BIFF: His answer was — (*He breaks off, suddenly angry.*) Dad, you're not letting me tell you what I want to tell you!

WILLY (*accusing, angered*): You didn't see him, did you?

BIFF: I did see him!

WILLY: What'd you insult him or something? You insulted him, didn't you?

BIFF: Listen, will you let me out of it, will you just let me out of it!

HAPPY: What the hell!

WILLY: Tell me what happened!

Willy hearing things from the past which are upsetting him!

BIFF (*to Happy*): I can't talk to him!

(*A single trumpet note jars the ear. The light of green leaves stains the house, which holds the air of night and a dream. Young Bernard enters and knocks on the door of the house.*)

YOUNG BERNARD (*frantically*): Mrs. Loman, Mrs. Loman!

HAPPY: Tell him what happened!

BIFF (*to Happy*): Shut up and leave me alone!

WILLY: No, no! You had to go and flunk math!

BIFF: What math? What're you talking about?

YOUNG BERNARD: Mrs. Loman, Mrs. Loman!

(*Linda appears in the house, as of old.*)

WILLY (*wildly*): Math, math, math!

BIFF: Take it easy, Pop!

YOUNG BERNARD: Mrs. Loman!

WILLY (*furiously*): If you hadn't flunked you'd've been set by now!

BIFF: Now, look, I'm gonna tell you what happened, and you're going to listen to me.

YOUNG BERNARD: Mrs. Loman!

BIFF: I waited six hours —

HAPPY: What the hell are you saying?

BIFF: I kept sending in my name but he wouldn't see me. So finally he . . . (*He continues unheard as light fades low on the restaurant.*)

YOUNG BERNARD: Biff flunked math!

LINDA: No!

YOUNG BERNARD: Birnbaum flunked him! They won't graduate him!

LINDA: But they have to. He's gotta go to the university. Where is he? Biff! Biff!

YOUNG BERNARD: No, he left. He went to Grand Central.

LINDA: Grand — You mean he went to Boston!

YOUNG BERNARD: Is Uncle Willy in Boston?

LINDA: Oh, maybe Willy can talk to the teacher. Oh, the poor, poor boy!

(*Light on house area snaps out.*)

BIFF (*at the table, now audible, holding up a gold fountain pen*): . . . so I'm washed up with Oliver, you understand? Are you listening to me?

WILLY (*at a loss*): Yeah, sure. If you hadn't flunked —

BIFF: Flunked what? What're you talking about?

WILLY: Don't blame everything on me! I didn't flunk math — you did! What pen?

HAPPY: That was awful dumb, Biff, a pen like that is worth —

WILLY (*seeing the pen for the first time*): You took Oliver's pen?

BIFF (*weakening*): Dad, I just explained it to you.

WILLY: You stole Bill Oliver's fountain pen!

BIFF: I didn't exactly steal it! That's just what I've been explaining to you!

HAPPY: He had it in his hand and just then Oliver walked in, so he got nervous and stuck it in his pocket!

WILLY: My God, Biff!

BIFF: I never intended to do it, Dad!

OPERATOR'S VOICE: Standish Arms, good evening!

WILLY (*shouting*): I'm not in my room!

BIFF (*frightened*): Dad, what's the matter? (*He and Happy stand up.*)

OPERATOR: Ringing Mr. Loman for you!

WILLY: I'm not there, stop it!

BIFF (*horrified, gets down on one knee before Willy*): Dad, I'll make good, I'll make good. (*Willy tries to get to his feet. Biff holds him down.*) Sit down now.

WILLY: No, you're no good, you're no good for anything.

BIFF: I am, Dad, I'll find something else, you understand? Now don't worry about anything. (*He holds up Willy's face.*) Talk to me, Dad.

OPERATOR: Mr. Loman does not answer. Shall I page him?

WILLY (*attempting to stand, as though to rush and silence the Operator*): No, no, no!

HAPPY: He'll strike something, Pop.

WILLY: No, no . . .

BIFF (*desperately, standing over Willy*): Pop, listen! Listen to me! I'm telling you something good. Oliver talked to his partner about the Florida idea. You listening? He — he talked to his partner, and he came to me . . . I'm going to be all right, you hear? Dad, listen to me, he said it was just a question of the amount!

WILLY: Then you . . . got it?

HAPPY: He's gonna be terrific, Pop!

WILLY (*trying to stand*): Then you got it, haven't you? You got it! You got it!

BIFF (*agonized, holds Willy down*): No, no. Look, Pop. I'm supposed to have lunch with them tomorrow. I'm just telling you this so you'll know that I can still make an impression, Pop. And I'll make good somewhere, but I can't go tomorrow, see?

WILLY: Why not? You simply —

BIFF: But the pen, Pop!

WILLY: You give it to him and tell him it was an oversight!

HAPPY: Sure, have lunch tomorrow!

BIFF: I can't say that —

WILLY: You were doing a crossword puzzle and accidentally used his pen!

BIFF: Listen, kid, I took those balls years ago, now I walk in with his fountain pen? That clinches it, don't you see? I can't face him like that! I'll try elsewhere.

PAGE'S VOICE: Paging Mr. Loman!

WILLY: Don't you want to be anything?

BIFF: Pop, how can I go back?

WILLY: You don't want to be anything, is that what's behind it?

BIFF (*now angry at Willy for not crediting his sympathy*): Don't take it that way! You think it was easy walking into that office after what I'd done to him? A team of horses couldn't have dragged me back to Bill Oliver!

WILLY: Then why'd you go?

BIFF: Why did I go? Why did I go! Look at you! Look at what's become of you!

(*Off left, The Woman laughs.*)

WILLY: Biff, you're going to go to that lunch tomorrow, or —

BIFF: I can't go. I've got no appointment!

HAPPY: Biff, for . . . !

WILLY: Are you spiting me?

BIFF: Don't take it that way! Goddammit!

WILLY (*strikes Biff and falters away from the table*): You rotten little louse! Are you spiting me?

THE WOMAN: Someone's at the door, Willy!

BIFF: I'm no good, can't you see what I am?

HAPPY (*separating them*): Hey, you're in a restaurant! Now cut it out, both of you! (*The girls enter.*) Hello, girls, sit down.

(*The Woman laughs, off left.*)

MISS FORSYTHE: I guess we might as well. This is Letta.

THE WOMAN: Willy, are you going to wake up?

BIFF (*ignoring Willy*): How're ya, miss, sit down. What do you drink?

MISS FORSYTHE: Letta might not be able to stay long.

LETTA: I gotta get up very early tomorrow. I got jury duty. I'm so excited! Were you fellows ever on a jury?

BIFF: No, but I been in front of them! (*The girls laugh.*) This is my father.

LETTA: Isn't he cute? Sit down with us, Pop.

HAPPY: Sit him down, Biff!

BIFF (*going to him*): Come on, slugger, drink us under the table. To hell with it! Come on, sit down, pal.

(*On Biff's last insistence, Willy is about to sit.*)

THE WOMAN (*now urgently*): Willy, are you going to answer the door!

(*The Woman's call pulls Willy back. He starts right, befuddled.*)

BIFF: Hey, where are you going?

WILLY: Open the door.

BIFF: The door?

WILLY: The washroom . . . the door . . . where's the door?

BIFF (*leading Willy to the left*): Just go straight down.

(*Willy moves left.*)

THE WOMAN: Willy, Willy, are you going to get up, get up, get up, get up?

(*Willy exits left.*)

LETTA: I think it's sweet you bring your daddy along.

MISS FORSYTHE: Oh, he isn't really your father!

BIFF (*at left, turning to her resentfully*): Miss Forsythe, you've just seen a prince walk by. A fine, troubled prince. A hard-working, unappreciated prince. A pal, you understand? A good companion. Always for his boys.

LETTA: That's so sweet.

HAPPY: Well, girls, what's the program? We're wasting time. Come on, Biff. Gather round. Where would you like to go?

BIFF: Why don't you do something for him?

HAPPY: Me!

BIFF: Don't you give a damn for him, Hap?

HAPPY: What're you talking about? I'm the one who —

BIFF: I sense it, you don't give a good goddam about him. (*He takes the rolled-up hose from his pocket and puts it on the table in front of Happy.*) Look what I found in the cellar, for Christ's sake. How can you bear to let it go on?

HAPPY: Me? Who goes away? Who runs off and —

BIFF: Yeah, but he doesn't mean anything to you. You could help him — I can't! Don't you understand what I'm talking about? He's going to kill himself, don't you know that?

HAPPY: Don't I know it! Me!

BIFF: Hap, help him! Jesus . . . help him . . . Help me, help me, I can't bear to look at his face! (*Ready to weep, he hurries out, up right.*)

HAPPY (*starting after him*): Where are you going?

MISS FORSYTHE: What's he so mad about?

HAPPY: Come on, girls, we'll catch up with him.

MISS FORSYTHE (*as Happy pushes her out*): Say, I don't like that temper of his!

HAPPY: He's just a little overstrung, he'll be all right!

WILLY (*off left, as The Woman laughs*): Don't answer! Don't answer!

LETTA: Don't you want to tell your father —

HAPPY: No, that's not my father. He's just a guy. Come on, we'll catch Biff, and, honey, we're going to paint this town! Stanley, where's the check! Hey, Stanley!

(*They exit. Stanley looks toward left.*)

STANLEY (*calling to Happy indignantly*): Mr. Loman! Mr. Loman!

(*Stanley picks up a chair and follows them off. Knocking is heard off left. The Woman enters, laughing. Willy follows her. She is in a black slip; he is buttoning his shirt. Raw, sensuous music accompanies their speech.*)

WILLY: Will you stop laughing? Will you stop?

THE WOMAN: Aren't you going to answer the door? He'll wake the whole hotel.

WILLY: I'm not expecting anybody.

THE WOMAN: Whyn't you have another drink, honey, and stop being so damn self-centered?

WILLY: I'm so lonely.

THE WOMAN: You know you ruined me, Willy? From now on, whenever you come to the office, I'll see that you go right through to the buyers. No waiting at my desk anymore, Willy. You ruined me.

WILLY: That's nice of you to say that.

THE WOMAN: Gee, you are self-centered! Why so sad? You are the saddest, self-centeredest soul I ever did see-saw. (*She laughs. He kisses her.*) Come on inside, drummer boy. It's silly to be dressing in the middle of

[handwritten note: We see why Biff doesn't talk to Willy]

the night. (*As knocking is heard.*) Aren't you going to answer the door?

WILLY: They're knocking on the wrong door.

THE WOMAN: But I felt the knocking. And he heard us talking in here. Maybe the hotel's on fire!

WILLY (*his terror rising*): It's a mistake.

THE WOMAN: Then tell him to go away!

WILLY: There's nobody there.

THE WOMAN: It's getting on my nerves, Willy. There's somebody standing out there and it's getting on my nerves!

WILLY (*pushing her away from him*): All right, stay in the bathroom here, and don't come out. I think there's a law in Massachusetts about it, so don't come out. It may be that new room clerk. He looked very mean. So don't come out. It's a mistake, there's no fire.

(*The knocking is heard again. He takes a few steps away from her, and she vanishes into the wing. The light follows him, and now he is facing Young Biff, who carries a suitcase. Biff steps toward him. The music is gone.*)

BIFF: Why didn't you answer?

WILLY: Biff! What are you doing in Boston?

BIFF: Why didn't you answer? I've been knocking for five minutes, I called you on the phone —

WILLY: I just heard you. I was in the bathroom and had the door shut. Did anything happen home?

BIFF: Dad — I let you down.

WILLY: What do you mean?

BIFF: Dad . . .

WILLY: Biffo, what's this about? (*Putting his arm around Biff.*) Come on, let's go downstairs and get you a malted.

BIFF: Dad, I flunked math.

WILLY: Not for the term?

BIFF: The term. I haven't got enough credits to graduate.

WILLY: You mean to say Bernard wouldn't give you the answers?

BIFF: He did, he tried, but I only got a sixty-one.

WILLY: And they wouldn't give you four points?

BIFF: Birnbaum refused absolutely. I begged him, Pop, but he won't give me those points. You gotta talk to him before they close the school. Because if he saw the kind of man you are, and you just talked to him in your way, I'm sure he'd come through for me. The class came right before practice, see, and I didn't go enough. Would you talk to him? He'd like you, Pop. You know the way you could talk.

WILLY: You're on. We'll drive right back.

BIFF: Oh, Dad, good work! I'm sure he'll change it for you!

WILLY: Go downstairs and tell the clerk I'm checkin' out. Go right down.

BIFF: Yes, sir! See, the reason he hates me, Pop — one day he was late for class so I got up at the blackboard and imitated him. I crossed my eyes and talked with a lithp.

WILLY (*laughing*): You did? The kids like it?

BIFF: They nearly died laughing!

WILLY: Yeah? What'd you do?

BIFF: The thquare root of thixthy twee is . . . (*Willy bursts out laughing; Biff joins.*) And in the middle of it he walked in!

(*Willy laughs and The Woman joins in offstage.*)

WILLY (*without hesitation*): Hurry downstairs and —

BIFF: Somebody in there?

WILLY: No, that was next door.

(*The Woman laughs offstage.*)

BIFF: Somebody got in your bathroom!

WILLY: No, it's the next room, there's a party —

THE WOMAN (*enters, laughing. She lisps this.*): Can I come in? There's something in the bathtub, Willy, and it's moving!

(*Willy looks at Biff, who is staring open-mouthed and horrified at The Woman.*)

WILLY: Ah — you better go back to your room. They must be finished painting by now. They're painting her room so I let her take a shower here. Go back, go back . . . (*He pushes her.*)

THE WOMAN (*resisting*): But I've got to get dressed, Willy, I can't —

WILLY: Get out of here! Go back, go back . . . (*Suddenly striving for the ordinary.*) This is Miss Francis, Biff, she's a buyer. They're painting her room. Go back, Miss Francis, go back . . .

THE WOMAN: But my clothes, I can't go out naked in the hall!

WILLY (*pushing her offstage*): Get outa here! Go back, go back!

(*Biff slowly sits down on his suitcase as the argument continues offstage.*)

THE WOMAN: Where's my stockings? You promised me stockings, Willy!

WILLY: I have no stockings here!

THE WOMAN: You had two boxes of size nine sheers for me, and I want them!

WILLY: Here, for God's sake, will you get outa here!

THE WOMAN (*enters holding a box of stockings*): I just hope there's nobody in the hall. That's all I hope. (*To Biff.*) Are you football or baseball?

BIFF: Football.

THE WOMAN (*angry, humiliated*): That's me too. G'night. (*She snatches her clothes from Willy, and walks out.*)

WILLY (*after a pause*): Well, better get going. I want to get to the school first thing in the morning. Get my suits out of the closet. I'll get my valise. (*Biff doesn't move.*) What's the matter! (*Biff remains motionless, tears falling.*) She's a buyer. Buys for J. H. Simmons. She lives down the hall — they're painting. You don't imagine — (*He breaks off. After a pause.*) Now listen, pal, she's just a buyer. She sees merchandise in her room and they have to keep it looking just so . . . (*Pause. Assuming command.*) All right, get my suits. (*Biff doesn't move.*) Now stop crying and do as I say.

I gave you an order. Biff, I gave you an order! Is that what you do when I give you an order? How dare you cry! (*Putting his arm around Biff.*) Now look, Biff, when you grow up you'll understand about these things. You mustn't — you mustn't overemphasize a thing like this. I'll see Birnbaum first thing in the morning.

BIFF: Never mind.

WILLY (*getting down beside Biff*): Never mind! He's going to give you those points. I'll see to it.

BIFF: He wouldn't listen to you.

WILLY: He certainly will listen to me. You need those points for the U. of Virginia.

BIFF: I'm not going there.

WILLY: Heh? If I can't get him to change that mark you'll make it up in summer school. You've got all summer to —

BIFF (*his weeping breaking from him*): Dad . . .

WILLY (*infected by it*): Oh, my boy . . .

BIFF: Dad . . .

WILLY: She's nothing to me, Biff. I was lonely, I was terribly lonely.

BIFF: You — you gave her Mama's stockings! (*His tears break through and he rises to go.*)

WILLY (*grabbing for Biff*): I gave you an order!

BIFF: Don't touch me, you — liar!

WILLY: Apologize for that!

BIFF: You fake! You phony little fake! You fake! (*Overcome, he turns quickly and weeping fully goes out with his suitcase. Willy is left on the floor on his knees.*)

WILLY: I gave you an order! Biff, come back here or I'll beat you! Come back here! I'll whip you!

(*Stanley comes quickly in from the right and stands in front of Willy.*)

WILLY (*shouts at Stanley*): I gave you an order . . .

STANLEY: Hey, let's pick it up, pick it up, Mr. Loman. (*He helps Willy to his feet.*) Your boys left with the chippies. They said they'll see you home.

(*A second waiter watches some distance away.*)

WILLY: But we were supposed to have dinner together.

(*Music is heard, Willy's theme.*) music playing

STANLEY: Can you make it?

WILLY: I'll — sure, I can make it. (*Suddenly concerned about his clothes.*) Do I — I look all right?

STANLEY: Sure, you look all right. (*He flicks a speck off Willy's lapel.*)

WILLY: Here — here's a dollar.

STANLEY: Oh, your son paid me. It's all right.

WILLY (*putting it in Stanley's hand*): No, take it. You're a good boy.

STANLEY: Oh, no, you don't have to . . .

WILLY: Here — here's some more, I don't need it anymore. (*After a slight pause.*) Tell me — is there a seed store in the neighborhood?

STANLEY: Seeds? You mean like to plant?

(*As Willy turns, Stanley slips the money back into his jacket pocket.*)

WILLY: Yes. Carrots, peas . . .

STANLEY: Well, there's hardware stores on Sixth Avenue, but it may be too late now.

WILLY (*anxiously*): Oh, I'd better hurry. I've got to get some seeds. (*He starts off to the right.*) I've got to get some seeds, right away. Nothing's planted. I don't have a thing in the ground.

(*Willy hurries out as the light goes down. Stanley moves over to the right after him, watches him off. The other waiter has been staring at Willy.*)

STANLEY (*to the waiter*): Well, whatta you looking at?

(*The waiter picks up the chairs and moves off right. Stanley takes the table and follows him. The light fades on this area. There is a long pause, the sound of the flute coming over. The light gradually rises on the kitchen, which is empty. Happy appears at the door of the house, followed by Biff. Happy is carrying a large bunch of long-stemmed roses. He enters the kitchen, looks around for Linda. Not seeing her, he turns to Biff, who is just outside the house door, and makes a gesture with his hands, indicating "Not here, I guess." He looks into the living room and freezes. Inside, Linda, unseen, is seated, Willy's coat on her lap. She rises ominously and quietly and moves toward Happy, who backs up into the kitchen, afraid.*) Flute playing

HAPPY: Hey, what're you doing up? (*Linda says nothing but moves toward him implacably.*) Where's Pop? (*He keeps backing to the right, and now Linda is in full view in the doorway to the living room.*) Is he sleeping?

LINDA: Where were you?

HAPPY (*trying to laugh it off*): We met two girls, Mom, very fine types. Here, we brought you some flowers. (*Offering them to her.*) Put them in your room, Ma.

(*She knocks them to the floor at Biff's feet. He has now come inside and closed the door behind him. She stares at Biff, silent.*)

HAPPY: Now what'd you do that for? Mom, I want you to have some flowers —

LINDA (*cutting Happy off, violently to Biff*): Don't you care whether he lives or dies?

HAPPY (*going to the stairs*): Come upstairs, Biff.

BIFF (*with a flare of disgust, to Happy*): Go away from me! (*To Linda.*) What do you mean, lives or dies? Nobody's dying around here, pal.

LINDA: Get out of my sight! Get out of here!

BIFF: I wanna see the boss.

LINDA: You're not going near him!

BIFF: Where is he? (*He moves into the living room and Linda follows.*)

LINDA (*shouting after Biff*): You invite him for dinner. He looks forward to it all day — (*Biff appears in his parents' bedroom, looks around, and exits*) — and then you desert him there. There's no stranger you'd do that to!

HAPPY: Why? He had a swell time with us. Listen, when I — (*Linda comes back into the kitchen*) — desert him I hope I don't outlive the day!

LINDA: Get out of here!

HAPPY: Now look, Mom . . .

LINDA: Did you have to go to women tonight? You and your lousy rotten whores!

(*Biff reenters the kitchen.*)

HAPPY: Mom, all we did was follow Biff around trying to cheer him up! (*To Biff.*) Boy, what a night you gave me!

LINDA: Get out of here, both of you, and don't come back! I don't want you tormenting him any more. Go on now, get your things together! (*To Biff.*) You can sleep in his apartment. (*She starts to pick up the flowers and stops herself.*) Pick up this stuff, I'm not your maid anymore. Pick it up, you bum, you!

(*Happy turns his back to her in refusal. Biff slowly moves over and gets down on his knees, picking up the flowers.*)

LINDA: You're a pair of animals! Not one, not another living soul would have had the cruelty to walk out on that man in a restaurant!

BIFF (*not looking at her*): Is that what he said?

LINDA: He didn't have to say anything. He was so humiliated he nearly limped when he came in.

HAPPY: But, Mom, he had a great time with us —

BIFF (*cutting him off violently*): Shut up!

(*Without another word, Happy goes upstairs.*)

LINDA: You! You didn't even go in to see if he was all right!

BIFF (*still on the floor in front of Linda, the flowers in his hand; with self-loathing*): No. Didn't. Didn't do a damned thing. How do you like that, heh? Left him babbling in a toilet.

LINDA: You louse. You . . .

BIFF: Now you hit it on the nose! (*He gets up, throws the flowers in the wastebasket.*) The scum of the earth, and you're looking at him!

LINDA: Get out of here!

BIFF: I gotta talk to the boss, Mom. Where is he?

LINDA: You're not going near him. Get out of this house!

BIFF (*with absolute assurance, determination*): No. We're gonna have an abrupt conversation, him and me.

LINDA: You're not talking to him.

(*Hammering is heard from outside the house, off right. Biff turns toward the noise.*)

LINDA (*suddenly pleading*): Will you please leave him alone?

BIFF: What's he doing out there?

LINDA: He's planting the garden!

BIFF (*quietly*): Now? Oh, my God!

(*Biff moves outside, Linda following. The light dies down on them and comes up on the center of the apron as Willy walks into it. He is carrying a flashlight, a hoe, and a handful of seed packets. He raps the top of the hoe sharply to fix it firmly, and then moves to the left, measuring off the distance with his foot. He holds the flashlight to look at the seed packets, reading off the instructions. He is in the blue of night.*)

WILLY: Carrots . . . quarter-inch apart. Rows . . . one-foot rows. (*He measures it off.*) One foot. (*He puts down a package and measures off.*) Beets. (*He puts down another package and measures again.*) Lettuce. (*He reads the package, puts it down.*) One foot — (*He breaks off as Ben appears at the right and moves slowly down to him.*) What a proposition, ts, ts. Terrific, terrific. 'Cause she's suffered, Ben, the woman has suffered. You understand me? A man can't go out the way he came in, Ben, a man has got to add up to something. You can't, you can't — (*Ben moves toward him as though to interrupt.*) You gotta consider, now. Don't answer so quick. Remember, it's a guaranteed twenty-thousand-dollar proposition. Now look, Ben, I want you to go through the ins and outs of this thing with me. I've got nobody to talk to, Ben, and the woman has suffered, you hear me?

BEN (*standing still, considering*): What's the proposition?

WILLY: It's twenty thousand dollars on the barrelhead. Guaranteed, gilt-edged, you understand?

BEN: You don't want to make a fool of yourself. They might not honor the policy.

WILLY: How can they dare refuse? Didn't I work like a coolie to meet every premium on the nose? And now they don't pay off? Impossible!

BEN: It's called a cowardly thing, William.

WILLY: Why? Does it take more guts to stand here the rest of my life ringing up a zero?

BEN (*yielding*): That's a point, William. (*He moves, thinking, turns.*) And twenty thousand — that is something one can feel with the hand, it is there.

WILLY (*now assured, with rising power*): Oh, Ben, that's the whole beauty of it! I see it like a diamond, shining in the dark, hard and rough, that I can pick up and touch in my hand. Not like — like an appointment! This would not be another damned-fool appointment, Ben, and it changes all the aspects. Because he thinks I'm nothing, see, and so he spites me. But the funeral — (*Straightening up.*) Ben, that funeral will be massive! They'll come from Maine, Massachusetts, Vermont, New Hampshire! All the old-timers with the strange license plates — that boy will be thunderstruck, Ben, because he never realized — I am known! Rhode Island, New York, New Jersey — I am known, Ben and he'll see it with his eyes once and for all. He'll see what I am, Ben! He's in for a shock, that boy!

BEN (*coming down to the edge of the garden*): He'll call you a coward.

WILLY (*suddenly fearful*): No, that would be terrible.

BEN: Yes. And a damned fool.

WILLY: No, no, he mustn't, I won't have that! (*He is broken and desperate.*)

BEN: He'll hate you, William.

(*The gay music of the Boys is heard.*) music

WILLY: Oh, Ben, how do we get back to all the great times? Used to be so full of light, and comradeship, the sleigh-riding in winter, and the ruddiness on his cheeks. And always some kind of good news coming up, always something nice coming up ahead. And never even let me carry the valises in the house, and simonizing, simonizing that little red car! Why, why can't I give him something and not have him hate me?

BEN: Let me think about it. (*He glances at his watch.*) I still have a little time. Remarkable proposition, but you've got to be sure you're not making a fool of yourself.

(*Ben drifts off upstage and goes out of sight. Biff comes down from the left.*)

WILLY (*suddenly conscious of Biff, turns and looks up at him, then begins picking up the packages of seeds in confusion*): Where the hell is that seed? (*Indignantly.*) You can't see nothing out here! They boxed in the whole goddam neighborhood!

BIFF: There are people all around here. Don't you realize that?

WILLY: I'm busy. Don't bother me.

BIFF (*taking the hoe from Willy*): I'm saying good-by to you, Pop. (*Willy looks at him, silent, unable to move.*) I'm not coming back any more.

WILLY: You're not going to see Oliver tomorrow?

BIFF: I've got no appointment, Dad.

WILLY: He put his arm around you, and you've got no appointment?

BIFF: Pop, get this now, will you? Everytime I've left it's been a fight that sent me out of here. Today I realized something about myself and I tried to explain it to you and I — I think I'm just not smart enough to make any sense out of it for you. To hell with whose fault it is or anything like that. (*He takes Willy's arm.*) Let's just wrap it up, heh? Come on in, we'll tell Mom. (*He gently tries to pull Willy to left.*)

WILLY (*frozen, immobile, with guilt in his voice*): No, I don't want to see her.

BIFF: Come on! (*He pulls again, and Willy tries to pull away.*)

WILLY (*highly nervous*): No, no, I don't want to see her.

BIFF (*tries to look into Willy's face, as if to find the answer there*): Why don't you want to see her?

WILLY (*more harshly now*): Don't bother me, will you?

BIFF: What do you mean, you don't want to see her? You don't want them calling you yellow, do you? This isn't your fault; it's me, I'm a bum. Now come inside! (*Willy strains to get away.*) Did you hear what I said to you?

(*Willy pulls away and quickly goes by himself into the house. Biff follows.*)

LINDA (*to Willy*): Did you plant, dear?

BIFF (*at the door, to Linda*): All right, we had it out. I'm going and I'm not writing any more.

LINDA (*going to Willy in the kitchen*): I think that's the best way, dear. 'Cause there's no use drawing it out, you'll just never get along.

(*Willy doesn't respond.*)

BIFF: People ask where I am and what I'm doing, you don't know, and you don't care. That way it'll be off your mind, and you can start brightening up again. All right? That clears it, doesn't it? (*Willy is silent, and Biff goes to him.*) You gonna wish me luck, scout? (*He extends his hand.*) What do you say?

LINDA: Shake his hand, Willy.

WILLY (*turning to her, seething with hurt*): There's no necessity to mention the pen at all, y'know.

BIFF (*gently*): I've got no appointment, Dad.

WILLY (*erupting fiercely*): He put his arm around . . . ?

BIFF: Dad, you're never going to see what I am, so what's the use of arguing? If I strike oil I'll send you a check. Meantime forget I'm alive.

WILLY (*to Linda*): Spite, see?

BIFF: Shake hands, Dad.

WILLY: Not my hand.

BIFF: I was hoping not to go this way.

WILLY: Well, this is the way you're going. Good-by.

(*Biff looks at him a moment, then turns sharply and goes to the stairs.*)

WILLY (*stops him with*): May you rot in hell if you leave this house!

BIFF (*turning*): Exactly what is it that you want from me?

WILLY: I want you to know, on the train, in the mountains, in the valleys, wherever you go, that you cut down your life for spite!

BIFF: No, no.

WILLY: Spite, spite, is the word of your undoing! And when you're down and out, remember what did it. When you're rotting somewhere beside the railroad tracks, remember, and don't you dare blame it on me!

BIFF: I'm not blaming it on you!

WILLY: I won't take the rap for this, you hear?

(*Happy comes down the stairs and stands on the bottom step, watching.*)

BIFF: That's just what I'm telling you!

WILLY (*sinking into a chair at a table, with full accusation*): You're trying to put a knife in me — don't think I don't know what you're doing!

BIFF: All right, phony! Then let's lay it on the line. (*He whips the rubber tube out of his pocket and puts it on the table.*)

HAPPY: You crazy . . .

Dustin Hoffman as Willy Loman in the 1985 television version of *Death of a Salesman.*

LINDA: Biff! (*She moves to grab the hose, but Biff holds it down with his hand.*)

BIFF: Leave it there! Don't move it!

WILLY (*not looking at it*): What is that?

BIFF: You know goddam well what that is.

WILLY (*caged, wanting to escape*): I never saw that.

BIFF: You saw it. The mice didn't bring it into the cellar! What is this supposed to do, make a hero out of you? This supposed to make me sorry for you?

WILLY: Never heard of it.

BIFF: There'll be no pity for you, you hear it? No pity!

WILLY (*to Linda*): You hear the spite!

BIFF: No, you're going to hear the truth — what you are and what I am!

LINDA: Stop it!

WILLY: Spite!

HAPPY (*coming down toward Biff*): You cut it now!

BIFF (*to Happy*): The man don't know who we are! The man is gonna know! (*To Willy.*) We never told the truth for ten minutes in this house!

HAPPY: We always told the truth!

BIFF (*turning on him*): You big blow, are you the assistant buyer? You're one of the two assistants to the assistant, aren't you?

HAPPY: Well, I'm practically . . .

BIFF: You're practically full of it! We all are! and I'm through with it. (*To Willy.*) Now hear this, Willy, this is me.

WILLY: I know you!

BIFF: You know why I had no address for three months? I stole a suit in Kansas City and I was in jail. (*To Linda, who is sobbing.*) Stop crying. I'm through with it.

(*Linda turns away from them, her hands covering her face.*)

WILLY: I suppose that's my fault!

BIFF: I stole myself out of every good job since high school!

WILLY: And whose fault is that?

BIFF: And I never got anywhere because you blew me so full of hot air I could never stand taking orders from anybody! That's whose fault it is!

WILLY: I hear that!

LINDA: Don't, Biff!

BIFF: It's goddam time you heard that! I had to be boss big shot in two weeks, and I'm through with it!

WILLY: Then hang yourself! For spite, hang yourself!

BIFF: No! Nobody's hanging himself, Willy! I ran down eleven flights with a pen in my hand today. And suddenly I stopped, you hear me? And in the middle of that office building, do you hear this? I stopped in the middle of that building and I saw — the sky. I saw the things that I love in this world. The work and the food and time to sit and smoke. And I looked at the pen and said to myself, what the hell am I grabbing this for? Why am I trying to become what I don't want to be? What am I doing in an office, making a contemptuous begging fool of myself, when all I want is out there, waiting for me the minute I say I know who I am! Why can't I say that, Willy? (*He tries to make Willy face him, but Willy pulls away and moves to the left.*)

WILLY (*with hatred, threateningly*): The door of your life is wide open!

BIFF: Pop! I'm a dime a dozen, and so are you!

WILLY (*turning on him now in an uncontrolled outburst*): I am not a dime a dozen! I am Willy Loman, and you are Biff Loman!

(*Biff starts for Willy, but is blocked by Happy. In his fury, Biff seems on the verge of attacking his father.*)

BIFF: I am not a leader of men, Willy, and neither are you. You were never anything but a hard-working drummer who landed in the ash can like all the rest of them! I'm one dollar an hour, Willy! I tried seven states and couldn't raise it. A buck an hour! Do you gather my meaning? I'm not bringing home any prizes any more, and you're going to stop waiting for me to bring them home!

WILLY (*directly to Biff*): You vengeful, spiteful mutt!

(*Biff breaks from Happy. Willy, in fright, starts up the stairs. Biff grabs him.*)

BIFF (*at the peak of his fury*): Pop, I'm nothing! I'm nothing, Pop. Can't you understand that? There's no spite in it any more. I'm just what I am, that's all.

(*Biff's fury has spent itself and he breaks down, sobbing, holding on to Willy, who dumbly fumbles for Biff's face.*)

WILLY (*astonished*): What're you doing? What're you doing? (*To Linda.*) Why is he crying?

BIFF (*crying, broken*): Will you let me go, for Christ's sake? Will you take that phony dream and burn it before something happens? (*Struggling to contain himself he pulls away and moves to the stairs.*) I'll go in the morning. Put him — put him to bed. (*Exhausted, Biff moves up the stairs to his room.*)

WILLY (*after a long pause, astonished, elevated*): Isn't that — isn't that remarkable? Biff — he likes me!

LINDA: He loves you, Willy!

HAPPY (*deeply moved*): Always did, Pop.

WILLY: Oh, Biff! (*Staring wildly.*) He cried! Cried to me. (*He is choking with his love, and now cries out his promise.*) That boy — that boy is going to be magnificent!

(*Ben appears in the light just outside the kitchen.*)

BEN: Yes, outstanding, with twenty thousand behind him.

LINDA (*sensing the racing of his mind, fearfully, carefully*): Now come to bed, Willy. It's all settled now.

WILLY (*finding it difficult not to rush out of the house*): Yes, we'll sleep. Come on. Go to sleep, Hap.

BEN: And it does take a great kind of a man to crack the jungle.

(*In accents of dread, Ben's idyllic music starts up.*) music

HAPPY (*his arm around Linda*): I'm getting married, Pop, don't forget it. I'm changing everything. I'm gonna run that department before the year is up. You'll see, Mom. (*He kisses her.*)

BEN: The jungle is dark but full of diamonds, Willy.

(*Willy turns, moves, listening to Ben.*)

LINDA: Be good. You're both good boys, just act that way, that's all.

HAPPY: 'Night, Pop. (*He goes upstairs.*)

LINDA (*to Willy*): Come, dear.

BEN (*with greater force*): One must go in to fetch a diamond out.

WILLY (*to Linda, as he moves slowly along the edge of kitchen, toward the door*): I just want to get settled down, Linda. Let me sit alone for a little.

LINDA (*almost uttering her fear*): I want you upstairs.

WILLY (*taking her in his arms*): In a few minutes, Linda. I couldn't sleep right now. Go on, you look awful tired. (*He kisses her.*)

BEN: Not like an appointment at all. A diamond is rough and hard to the touch.

WILLY: Go on now. I'll be right up.

LINDA: I think this is the only way, Willy.

WILLY: Sure, it's the best thing.

BEN: Best thing!

WILLY: The only way. Everything is gonna be — go on, kid, get to bed. You look so tired.

LINDA: Come right up.

WILLY: Two minutes.

(*Linda goes into the living room, then reappears in her bedroom. Willy moves just outside the kitchen door.*)

Biff (Kevin Anderson) and
Willy (Brian Dennehy) try to
console one another in Robert
Falls's 1999 production of
Death of a Salesman.

WILLY: Loves me. (*Wonderingly.*) Always loved me. Isn't
that a remarkable thing? Ben, he'll worship me for it!
BEN (*with promise*): It's dark there, but full of diamonds.
WILLY: Can you imagine that magnificence with twenty
thousand dollars in his pocket?
LINDA (*calling from her room*): Willy! Come up!
WILLY (*calling into the kitchen*): Yes! yes. Coming! It's
very smart, you realize that, don't you, sweetheart?
Even Ben sees it. I gotta go, baby. 'By! 'By! (*Going
over to Ben, almost dancing.*) Imagine? When the
mail comes he'll be ahead of Bernard again!
BEN: A perfect proposition all around.
WILLY: Did you see how he cried to me? Oh, if I could
kiss him, Ben!
BEN: Time, William, time!
WILLY: Oh, Ben, I always knew one way or another we
were gonna make it, Biff and I!
BEN (*looking at his watch*): The boat. We'll be late. (*He
moves slowly off into the darkness.*)
WILLY (*elegiacally, turning to the house*): Now when
you kick off, boy, I want a seventy-yard boot, and get
right down the field under the ball, and when you hit,
hit low and hit hard, because it's important, boy. (*He
swings around and faces the audience.*) There's all
kinds of important people in the stands, and the first
thing you know . . . (*Suddenly realizing he is alone.*)
Ben! Ben, where do I . . . ? (*He makes a sudden
movement of search.*) Ben, how do I . . . ?
LINDA (*calling*): Willy, you coming up?
WILLY (*uttering a gasp of fear, whirling about as if to
quiet her*): Sh! (*He turns around as if to find his way;
sounds, faces, voices, seem to be swarming in upon*

him and he flicks at them, crying, Sh! Sh! Suddenly
music, faint and high, stops him. It rises in intensity,
almost to an unbearable scream. He goes up and
down on his toes, and rushes off around the house.)
Shhh!
LINDA: Willy?

(*There is no answer. Linda waits. Biff gets up off his
bed. He is still in his clothes. Happy sits up. Biff stands
listening.*)

LINDA (*with real fear*): Willy, answer me! Willy!

(*There is the sound of a car starting and moving away at
full speed.*)

LINDA: No!
BIFF (*rushing down the stairs*): Pop!

(*As the car speeds off, the music crashes down in a
frenzy of sound, which becomes the soft pulsation of a
single cello string. Biff slowly returns to his bedroom.
He and Happy gravely don their jackets. Linda slowly
walks out of her room. The music has developed into a
dead march. The leaves of day are appearing over everything. Charley and Bernard, somberly dressed, appear
and knock on the kitchen door. Biff and Happy slowly
descend the stairs to the kitchen as Charley and Bernard
enter. All stop a moment when Linda, in clothes of
mourning, bearing a little bunch of roses, comes
through the draped doorway into the kitchen. She goes
to Charley and takes his arm. Now all move toward the
audience, through the wall-line of the kitchen. At the
limit of the apron, Linda lays down the flowers, kneels,
and sits back on her heels. All stare down at the grave.*)

REQUIEM

CHARLEY: It's getting dark, Linda.

(*Linda doesn't react. She stares at the grave.*)

BIFF: How about it, Mom? Better get some rest, heh? They'll be closing the gate soon.

(*Linda makes no move. Pause.*)

HAPPY (*deeply angered*): He had no right to do that. There was no necessity for it. We would've helped him.

CHARLEY (*grunting*): Hmmm.

BIFF: Come along, Mom.

LINDA: Why didn't anybody come?

CHARLEY: It was a very nice funeral.

LINDA: But where are all the people he knew? Maybe they blame him.

CHARLEY: Naa. It's a rough world, Linda. They wouldn't blame him.

LINDA: I can't understand it. At this time especially. First time in thirty-five years we were just about free and clear. He only needed a little salary. He was even finished with the dentist.

CHARLEY: No man only needs a little salary.

LINDA: I can't understand it.

BIFF: There were a lot of nice days. When he'd come home from a trip; or on Sundays, making the stoop; finishing the cellar; putting on the new porch; when he built the extra bathroom; and put up the garage. You know something, Charley, there's more of him in that front stoop than in all the sales he ever made.

CHARLEY: Yeah. He was a happy man with a batch of cement.

LINDA: He was so wonderful with his hands.

BIFF: He had the wrong dreams. All, all, wrong.

HAPPY (*almost ready to fight Biff*): Don't say that!

BIFF: He never knew who he was.

CHARLEY (*stopping Happy's movement and reply. To Biff*): Nobody dast blame this man. You don't understand: Willy was a salesman. And for a salesman, there is no rock bottom to the life. He don't put a bolt to a nut, he don't tell you the law or give you medicine. He's a man way out there in the blue, riding on a smile and a shoeshine. And when they start not smiling back — that's an earthquake. And then you get yourself a couple of spots on your hat, and you're finished. Nobody dast blame this man. A salesman is got to dream, boy. It comes with the territory.

BIFF: Charley, the man didn't know who he was.

HAPPY (*infuriated*): Don't say that!

BIFF: Why don't you come with me, Happy?

HAPPY: I'm not licked that easily. I'm staying right in this city, and I'm gonna beat this racket! (*He looks at Biff, his chin set.*) The Loman Brothers!

BIFF: I know who I am, kid.

HAPPY: All right, boy. I'm gonna show you and everybody else that Willy Loman did not die in vain. He had a good dream. It's the only dream you can have — to come out number-one man. He fought it out here, and this is where I'm gonna win it for him.

BIFF (*with a hopeless glance at Happy, bends toward his mother*): Let's go, Mom.

LINDA: I'll be with you in a minute. Go on, Charley. (*He hesitates.*) I want to, just for a minute. I never had a chance to say good-by.

(*Charley moves away, followed by Happy. Biff remains a slight distance up and left of Linda. She sits there, summoning herself. The flute begins, not far away, playing behind her speech.*)

LINDA: Forgive me, dear. I can't cry. I don't know what it is, but I can't cry. I don't understand it. Why did you ever do that? Help me, Willy, I can't cry. It seems to me that you're just on another trip. I keep expecting you. Willy, dear, I can't cry. Why did you do it? I search and search and I search, and I can't understand it, Willy. I made the last payment on the house today. Today, dear. And there'll be nobody home. (*A sob rises in her throat.*) We're free and clear. (*Sobbing more fully, released.*) We're free. (*Biff comes slowly toward her.*) We're free . . . We're free . . .

(*Biff lifts her to her feet and moves out up right with her in his arms. Linda sobs quietly. Bernard and Charley come together and follow them, followed by Happy. Only the music of the flute is left on the darkening stage as over the house the hard towers of the apartment buildings rise into sharp focus, and the curtain falls.*)

COMMENTARIES

Arthur Miller (b. 1915)
IN MEMORIAM

1932

"In Memoriam," a short story about a salesman that Arthur Miller wrote in 1932 when he was seventeen, was published in 1995 after it was discovered in the Arthur Miller Archive at the University of Texas's Harry Ransom library. A note on the manuscript indicates that the real Schoenzeit threw himself in front of an elevated railway train the day after the incident the story records. While not providing the model for Death of a Salesman, *the story reminds us that Miller had experience with men like Willy Loman.*

Sitting here now, thinking of him, he seems to be a romantic figure, but really he wasn't. Yet I couldn't venture to call him "commonplace." I never knew him intimately, yet I feel as though I knew him more closely, more thoroughly, than I know myself. His was a salesman's profession, if one may describe such dignified slavery as a profession, and though he tried to interest himself in his work he never became entirely molded into the pot of that business. His emotions were displayed at the wrong times always, and he never quite knew when to laugh. Perhaps, if I may say so, he never was complete. He had lost something vital. There was an air of quiet solitude, of cryptic wondering about both him and his name.

Although he was ever simply and immaculately dressed, I always imagined he had been dressed by someone else.

When I first heard his name, I wondered if he hadn't forgotten some other and had merely been called this by men. His last name was Schoenzeit; the first I never learned, but it had to be Alfred. He always seemed to need that name. Especially when he sat at the small glass-topped table in my father's showroom, slowly perusing the columns of the *Times,* with tears of perspiration dotting the reddened ridge that his gray felt hat had made around his head. The shined, bulgy-toed shoes placed flatly and it seemed carefully on the carpet, his overcoat folded neatly on a chair, the bow of his tie stuck so perfectly into the crevice of a starched, rounded collar completed a setting where I am sure he never belonged.

Schoenzeit, as everyone called him, often was gay. I might add "happy," but of the last I shall never be sure. He laughed as superciliously as any of the others when someone was the object of a quip. But these occasions were rare and never lasted, as far as he was concerned. Always he returned to his fogged manner, and after the joke had faded from his mind the light which seemed to brighten his countenance, too, disappeared, and he was once more enigmatic and incomprehensible.

I had, on several occasions, been alone with him, and may truthfully say I deeply pitied such a dejected soul. At one time it was necessary for him to go to the Bronx to interview a large retail drygoods store, and I was instructed to carry his samples. It was late spring, the sky was cloudless and blue, a yellow sun was slowly warming the cool morning air, and the usual city hurriers were plying their trade.

1168

I had six coats in my arms, holding them against my chest, while he walked, leaning very slightly forward, by my side. His feet must have hurt him, for he pointed them outward, laying them flat on the ground at every step. When walking, he seemed to be striving against a stiff wind, his eyebrows peaked together, forming tiny creases at the bridge of his nose. His hat, placed straight on his head, shaded his eyes, which gazed seekingly ahead.

It was necessary to walk from Eighth to Third Avenue in order to reach the Elevated, and he offered many times to rest. I must have looked tired, because he turned to me once and laughed, saying in his cracked yet resonant baritone, "Hard work, eh, kid? Some business . . ." Of course, I didn't admit my weariness, and pitching my head to one side, raising my eyebrows and smiling, assured him that I was enjoying it as much as he was.

In due time, we approached the El, and about a block away he slowly and lightly touched my arm and, still looking ahead, he asked, "Arthur, do you get paid from the firm for carfare?" He said this in a low tone, as though he were trying to hide his point until it was absolutely necessary to take the plunge.

I thought for a moment and answered, "Well, whenever I have to go anywhere out of walking distance I am given money to ride, but I have no standing allowance for such purposes." He seemed to falter, and flushed a trifle before answering, and for a second I felt both rage and pity for this decrepit soul, who, it seemed, aged many years as he turned to me. I knew then that he felt as though his life were ended, that he was merely being pushed by outside forces. And though his body went on as before, the soul inside had crumpled and broken beyond repair.

He was asking me now for carfare. I knew he would rather have been pulled apart by a tiger, but he was asking me for carfare, a nickel to hold out to a corpulent, uninterested machine for his fare. My heart bled for him at that moment, and as we mounted the long stairway to the trains I realized that as low and shakingly embarrassed as I felt, his senses were that much more tormented and destroyed. And I marvelled at his poise under the circumstances. The coats were warm now against me, and I was thankful to God himself for this refuge for my gawky body which, with the expression of my eyes, must reveal to him my sensations.

I tried as best I could to make this situation seem as if it were common-place — I who had carried samples for so many salesmen. And when we reached the turnstile, I balanced my burden on one knee while I dipped my free hand into my pocket. Behind my throat, I cursed myself for not having the change. I turned from him in order to get the nickels required, and when I lifted my eyes to his figure I prayed, until my temples seemed to burst, for his salvation. At that moment, he looked so broken, so dejected and lost that I hastily lowered my gaze. He appeared to me then, as he stood there at the turnstile, like a small dog who has messed in the house, standing now, after his beating, waiting for his master to open the door to the back yard.

During the entire ride uptown, we two spoke but sparingly. The bright streets below changed constantly as we racketed past, and the windows of the houses facing the trains offered a haven for my confused and weary imagination.

He sold nothing that day and was profusely maltreated by the attending force at the buying office who, by virtue of their superior intelligence and ties to match, were vindicated even when they were consciously adding to the vicissitudes of a seller's life.

On the return trip, Alfred, as I subconsciously called him, became more voluble and questioned me as to my ambitions and my occupations in my leisure time.

Upon hearing that I owned an old car, he immediately became interested and spoke a little less haltingly than was his wont. From constant rebuff, he was loath to venture an opinion, and often embarrassed us both by ending a bountiful conversation unexpectedly.

He accompanied me to my father's place and, placing his hand on the small of my back, patted me lightly, and said with a faint smile, "Thanks, Arthur — and I'll . . . see you tomorrow."

With that farewell, he was off into the crowd, and his restless body faded slowly into the dark overcoats of unknowns as it willingly shrank from my sight.

I never saw him again and had forgotten him entirely when I heard of his death.

"Schoenzeit is dead," and my only recollection of that second when I heard those words is a slow exhaling of my breath and a cool, soft, glowing smile within my soul.

Arthur Miller (b. 1915)
TRAGEDY AND THE COMMON MAN   1949

One of the curious debates that arose around Death of a Salesman *was the question of whether it was a genuine tragedy. One of the requirements for traditional tragedy is that the hero be of noble birth. Miller countered that notion with a clear statement of modern purpose regarding tragedy.*

In this age few tragedies are written. It has often been held that the lack is due to a paucity of heroes among us, or else that modern man has had the blood drawn out of his organs of belief by the skepticism of science, and the heroic attack on life cannot feed on an attitude of reserve and circumspection. For one reason or another, we are often held to be below tragedy — or tragedy above us. The inevitable conclusion is, of course, that the tragic mode is archaic, fit only for the very highly placed, the kings or the kingly, and where this admission is not made in so many words it is most often implied.

I believe that the common man is as apt a subject for tragedy in its highest sense as kings were. On the face of it this ought to be obvious in the light of modern psychiatry, which bases its analysis upon classic formulations, such as the Oedipus and Orestes complexes, for instance, which were enacted by royal beings, but which apply to everyone in similar emotional situations.

More simply, when the question of tragedy in art is not at issue, we never hesitate to attribute to the well-placed and the exalted the very same mental processes as the lowly. And finally, if the exaltation of tragic action were truly a property of the high-bred character alone, it is inconceivable that the mass of mankind should cherish tragedy above all other forms, let alone be capable of understanding it.

As a general rule, to which there may be exceptions unknown to me, I think the tragic feeling is evoked in us when we are in the presence of a character who is ready to lay down his life, if need be, to secure one thing — his sense of personal dignity. From Orestes to Hamlet, Medea to Macbeth, the underlying struggle is that of the individual attempting to gain his "rightful" position in his society.

Sometimes he is one who has been displaced from it, sometimes one who seeks to attain it for the first time, but the fateful wound from which the inevitable events spiral is the wound of indignity, and its dominant force is indignation. Tragedy, then, is the consequence of a man's total compulsion to evaluate himself justly.

In the sense of having been initiated by the hero himself, the tale always reveals what has been called his "tragic flaw," a failing that is not peculiar to grand or elevated characters. Nor is it necessarily a weakness. The flaw, or crack in the character, is really nothing — and need be nothing — but his inherent unwillingness to remain passive in the face of what he conceives to be a challenge to his dignity, his image of his rightful status. Only the passive, only those who accept their lot without active retaliation, are "flawless." Most of us are in that category.

But there are among us today, as there always have been, those who act against the scheme of things that degrades them, and in the process of action everything we have accepted out of fear or insensitivity or ignorance is shaken before us and examined, and from this total onslaught by an individual against the seemingly stable cosmos surrounding us — from this total examination of the "unchangeable" environment — comes the terror and the fear that is classically associated with tragedy.

More important, from this total questioning of what has previously been unquestioned, we learn. And such a process is not beyond the common man. In revolutions around the world, these past thirty years, he has demonstrated again and again this inner dynamic of all tragedy.

Insistence upon the rank of the tragic hero, or the so-called nobility of his character, is really but a clinging to the outward forms of tragedy. If rank or nobility of character was indispensable, then it would follow that the problems of those with rank were the particular problems of tragedy. But surely the right of one monarch to capture the domain from another no longer raises our passions, nor are our concepts of justice what they were to the mind of an Elizabethan king.

The quality in such plays that does shake us, however, derives from the underlying fear of being displaced, the disaster inherent in being torn away from our chosen image of what and who we are in this world. Among us today this fear is as strong, and perhaps stronger, than it ever was. In fact, it is the common man who knows this fear best.

Now, if it is true that tragedy is the consequence of a man's total compulsion to evaluate himself justly, his destruction in the attempt posits a wrong or an evil in his environment. And this is precisely the morality of tragedy and its lesson. The discovery of the moral law, which is what the enlightenment of tragedy consists of, is not the discovery of some abstract or metaphysical quantity.

The tragic right is a condition of life, a condition in which the human personality is able to flower and realize itself. The wrong is the condition which suppresses man, perverts the flowing out of his love and creative instinct. Tragedy enlightens — and it must, in that it points the heroic finger at the enemy of man's freedom. The thrust for freedom is the quality in tragedy which exalts. The revolutionary questioning of the stable environment is what terrifies. In no way is the common man debarred from such thoughts or such actions.

Seen in this light, our lack of tragedy may be partially accounted for by the turn which modern literature has taken toward the purely psychiatric view of life, or the purely sociological. If all our miseries, our indignities, are born and bred within our minds, then all action, let alone the heroic action, is obviously impossible.

And if society alone is responsible for the cramping of our lives, then the protagonist must needs be so pure and faultless as to force us to deny his validity as a character. From neither of these views can tragedy derive, simply because neither represents a balanced concept of life. Above all else, tragedy requires the finest appreciation by the writer of cause and effect.

No tragedy can therefore come about when its author fears to question absolutely everything, when he regards any institution, habit, or custom as being either everlasting, immutable, or inevitable. In the tragic view the need of man to wholly realize himself is the only fixed star, and whatever it is that hedges his nature and lowers it is ripe for attack and examination. Which is not to say that tragedy must preach revolution.

The Greeks could probe the very heavenly origin of their ways and return to confirm the rightness of laws. And Job could face God in anger, demanding his right, and end in submission. But for a moment everything is in suspension, nothing is accepted, and in this stretching and tearing apart of the cosmos, in the very action of so doing, the character gains "size," the tragic stature which is spuriously attached to the royal or the highborn in our minds. The commonest of men may take on that stature to the extent of his willingness to throw all he has into the contest, the battle to secure his rightful place in his world.

There is a misconception of tragedy with which I have been struck in review after review, and in many conversations with writers and readers alike. It is the idea that tragedy is of necessity allied to pessimism. Even the dictionary says nothing more about the word than that it means a story with a sad or unhappy ending. This impression is so firmly fixed that I almost hesitate to claim that in truth tragedy implies more optimism in its author than does comedy, and that its final result ought to be the reinforcement of the onlooker's brightest opinions of the human animal.

For, if it is true to say that in essence the tragic hero is intent upon claiming his whole due as a personality, and if this struggle must be total and without reservation, then it automatically demonstrates the indestructible will of man to achieve his humanity.

The possibility of victory must be there in tragedy. Where pathos rules, where pathos is finally derived, a character has fought a battle he could not possibly have won. The pathetic is achieved when the protagonist is, by virtue of his witlessness, his insensitivity, or the very air he gives off, incapable of grappling with a much superior force.

Pathos truly is the mode for the pessimist. But tragedy requires a nicer balance between what is possible and what is impossible. And it is curious, although edifying, that the plays we revere, century after century, are the tragedies. In them, and in them alone, lies the belief — optimistic, if you will — in the perfectibility of man.

It is time, I think, that we who are without kings, took up this bright thread of our history and followed it to the only place it can possibly lead in our time — the heart and spirit of the average man.

Michiko Kakutani (b. 1955)
A SALESMAN WHO TRANSCENDS TIME   *1999*

> *Brian Dennehy revived* Death of a Salesman *fifty years after its premiere and discovered that the audiences were as deeply moved in 1999 as they were in 1949. Michiko Kakutani perceives the center of interest in the play shifting in this new production to emphasize the relationship of a father with his sons. Kakutani notes that, despite the play's flaws, its larger issues of love between father and son and longings for immortality have taken on even more significance.*

A half century after its premiere, *Death of a Salesman* has become an American classic — a perennial produced around the world, from Baltimore to Beijing, and routinely taught in high school English classes and mounted in community theaters. The play has become an institution, part of the accepted theater canon, and today even boasts its own Web site (www.deathofasalesman.com), where, in an ironic twist on its central theme, you will be able to purchase souvenirs.

With the opening on Wednesday of the Goodman Theater's new production of *Salesman* at the Eugene O'Neill Theatre on Broadway — fifty years to the day from the play's 1949 world premiere — it is clear that many of the debates that attended the original opening have long since become obsolete. We no longer question whether a play about a little man (a "low-man," as opposed to a king or powerful ruler) can be called a tragedy, just as we no longer question the ethnicity of the play's hero, the Jewishness or non-Jewishness of his locution.

At the same time, however, other debates persist. While *Salesman* opened to — and has continued to enjoy — enormous popular success, both the play and its author have maintained a less than stellar reputation among many highbrow critics. *Salesman* has been debunked as a didactic commentary on the bankruptcy of the American dream of success, while Mr. Miller has been dismissed as an epigone of Ibsenism, a preachy, pompous, and, yes, portentous writer who belongs, like Clifford Odets and Lillian Hellman, to a middlebrow, premodernist past. In retrospect, it is an overly simplistic judgment — especially when it comes to *Salesman,* Mr. Miller's most famous, most enduring, and in many ways most anomalous play.

Oddly enough, Mr. Miller's own ponderous pronouncements have tended to reinforce the perception of his work as an outmoded form of social realism. In one 1950 essay, he argued that *Death of a Salesman* — which chronicles the last day in the life of a salesman named Willy Loman, who has lost his job and, he fears, the love of his son Biff — is "the tragedy of a man who did believe that he alone was not meeting the qualifications laid down for mankind by those clean-shaven frontiersmen who inhabit the peaks of broadcasting and advertising offices."

Willy the failed salesman and willful suicide, Mr. Miller suggested in his own autobiography, represents the fate of a true believer in America's false dream of success: "This pseudo life that thought to touch the clouds by standing on top of a refrigerator, waving a paid-up mortgage at the moon, victorious at last." His singleminded pursuit of success has blinded him to the love of his own family, robbed him of his sense of self, and left him to subsist on a diet of illusions.

In contrast to Eugene O'Neill, who declared that he was "interested only in the relation of man and God," Mr. Miller has implied that the tragedy in his own work springs from the relation between man and the conditions that suppress him and pervert "the flowing out of his love and creative instinct." The playwright's own unhappy experiences during the Depression and the 1950s, when he was convicted of contempt of Congress for refusing to name names before the House Un-American Activities Committee, persuaded him, he has said, that politics "determines the exteriors of your personality," and he remained convinced, he once stated, that all serious plays ultimately address a single question: "How may a man make of the outside world a home?"

Truly great work, he declared in a 1958 interview, is "that work which will show at one and the same time the power and force of the human will working with and against the force of society upon it."

Yet in Robert Falls's darkly hued new staging from Chicago, *Death of a Salesman* seems less a social drama about what Harold Clurman called "the breakdown of the whole concept of salesmanship inherent in our society" than a fierce portrait of a father and son, caught in a fatal embrace of love and resentment and guilt. And Brian Dennehy's Willy Loman seems less a man, in Mr. Miller's words, who "embodies in himself some of the most terrible conflicts running through the streets of America today" than a perpetual adolescent caught in the dizzying gap between reality and his own expectations. This Willy Loman, like Dustin Hoffman's in 1984 on Broadway, may not be a tragic figure — to the last moment, self-awareness continues to elude him — but like Kierkegaard's "unhappiest man," he is a touching one, subsisting on past memory and future hope. His dilemmas are more psychological than sociological, more existential than environmental.

The play's structure, too, seems a far cry from the rough-hewn carpentry often associated with Mr. Miller's work. There is a dreamlike quality to *Salesman,* an expressionistic invocation of shifting moods and time frames that helps conceal the creaky stage machinery apparent in so many other Miller plays from *All My Sons* (1947) to *Broken Glass* (1994).

Certainly *Salesman,* too, has its problems: a paint-by-numbers Freudianism, a conveniently withheld secret that overshadows the second act, and supporting characters who are little more than cardboard cutouts. As written, Willy's long-suffering wife, Linda, is basically a doormat — a passive accomplice in her husband's denial, what we would today call an enabler. And Willy's successful brother, Ben — who walked into the jungle at seventeen, and walked out at twenty-one a rich man with diamonds in his pockets — remains a transparent symbol of rough and ready capitalism, a Horatio Alger joke.

These flaws, however, are subsumed by the play's visceral and deeply affecting portrait of father and son: Willy, intent for years on passing on to his son his own tarnished dreams; and Biff, finally shorn of those illusions, intent on making his father face the hard facts of his existence. The play limns Willy's fears of losing Biff's love and his own longings for immortality — his desire not just to be liked, but to be well liked — and it immerses the audience in Willy's conflicted, contradictory state of mind. In fact, Mr. Miller once noted that his original title for *Salesman* was "The Inside of His Head."

The play was constructed on the premise that Willy, in his growing panic and confusion, sees time not as a continuum but as a simultaneity of moments past and present. In the play's confessional structure, current anxieties fade into remembered guilts, and dreams and regrets blur and overlap — a structure not dissimilar to the narrative strategy adopted by Mr. Miller in his own 1987 autobiography, *Timebends.* The play, Mr. Miller wrote in that book, was meant to "cut through time like a knife through a layer cake or a road through a mountain revealing its geologic layers."

In later works like *After the Fall* (1964) and *The Price* (1968), Mr. Miller would again try to focus on his characters' inner lives, but never again with such urgency and skill as in *Salesman*. His other better-known plays would remain rooted in more topical concerns and feature characters who are more clearly symbols than flesh-and-blood human beings. *All My Sons* (1947) depicts a businessman — read greedy capitalist — covering up his role in the manufacture of defective parts that doomed twenty-one Air Force planes during World War II. *The Crucible* (1953) uses the Salem witch hunts of the late 1600s as a metaphor for the Communist witch hunts of the 1950s. *A View from the Bridge* (1955) examines the costs of McCarthy-era betrayal through its portrait of a longshoreman who rats on two illegal immigrants. *The American Clock* (1980), inspired by Studs Terkel's *Hard Times*, attempts to provide a panoramic portrait of the Depression. And *The Ride Down Mount Morgan* (1991) casts a cold eye on the rampant selfishness of the Reagan era. All too often in these works, Mr. Miller's efforts to "prove the theme" result in sanctimonious speechifying, message-driven melodramatics and two-dimensional characters who come across as illustrations of one or more social ills.

In recent years, the most successful productions of these works have played down the political, polemic aspects of the texts, to reveal their psychological subtext, the bedrock emotions of sexual passion and familial love, betrayal and guilt that lurk beneath the sociology. Last year, the Roundabout Theater Company's highly acclaimed production of *A View from the Bridge* shrugged off the play's McCarthy-era echoes to focus on the hero's secret obsession with his wife's teenage niece and the psychosexual drives that lead him to commit a shocking act of betrayal. Nicholas Hytner's dazzling 1996 movie version of *The Crucible* similarly stripped away that play's McCarthy-era moorings: by firmly grounding the story in the particulars of seventeenth-century Salem, the film uncovered the story's primal drama, its fascination with the consequences of lying and deception and sexual repression.

The success of such productions underscores the current renaissance that Mr. Miller has been enjoying — not just in England, where his work has found a ready audience among theatergoers reared, since the heyday of anti-Thatcherism, on politically committed playwriting, but also here in the States, where the Signature Theater Company recently completed a yearlong retrospective of his plays in New York.

What accounts for Mr. Miller's continuing appeal? Perhaps some of the very aspects of his work that seem so old-fashioned — his moral seriousness and fondness for mythic intonations (inspired by his favorite works, the Bible and Greek tragedies) — are refreshing anomalies in this age of relentless irony and cynicism.

In a day when the avant-garde has insistently purveyed a vision of a fractured, fragmented world, Mr. Miller's assumption that "life has meaning" appeals to our vestigial belief (or hope) that the dots *can* be connected, that a pattern *can* be found in the carpet. And in a day when the arts are increasingly becoming a form of entertainment, when the commercial theater has increasingly given us slice-of-life dramas, brittle satires, and glitzy theme-park musicals, his efforts, however ham-handed, to address the large questions of right and wrong suggest that the theater still matters, that it can still provide a venue for intellectual debate.

Indeed, his plays attest to his own belief that works of art can "change the consciousness of people and their estimate of who they are and what they stand for."

A PRODUCTION CASEBOOK

Death of a Salesman

The original staging of *Death of a Salesman* presented enormous challenges to everyone involved with the production. In many ways the play was radical in conception. Not only was the theory of tragedy challenged by the choice of a traveling salesman as the hero, but the approach to the drama itself, the sense that one needed to get inside Willy Loman's head, made the first production quite different from what theater-goers in 1949 would have expected. Arthur Miller's original title for the play, *The Inside of His Head,* was a rough guide to staging problems. The final production designs featured a novel transparency to the Lomans' house, so that the audience member was not just looking through a fourth wall, as in conventional stagings, but looking through a small world.

The designer for the stage, Jo Mielziner (1901–1976), was committed to innovation in stage design both before and after he was given the chance to work with director Elia Kazan on this project. In his notes, he discusses the ways in which the illusional realistic theater seemed to be limited in spite of extraordinary technical resources — the use of projections, film (or video), and multilevel staging — all of which could achieve effects that could only be suggested previously. He approached the problems of the play enthusiastically, as his journal excerpts and Brenda Murphy's essay on the design process for this set both reveal. While working on *Death of a Salesman* he was approached by Josh Logan to work on *South Pacific,* an upbeat and timeless American musical that must have provided an emotional relief of sorts while he dealt with the complexities of Miller's dark play.

It is perhaps unfair to refer to the play as dark, but when Miller sent the script to Elia Kazan, already a distinguished director, Kazan called him and said, "What a sad play." Miller thought that Kazan was rejecting the play. At that time Miller was famous as the author of *All My Sons,* but he was not at all confident that his new play would be acceptable for the stage. However, Kazan, whose voice sounded almost funereal, went on to talk about his own father; Miller later said Kazan was the first of many people who saw their own fathers in Willy Loman. The conversation with Kazan ended with a commitment to produce the play within the year. Kazan's "Directing *Death of a Salesman*" essay offers an overview of his experience as the play's director.

The problem of finding the right actor to play Willy Loman naturally challenged Kazan, who had Lee J. Cobb in mind right away even though Miller felt that the actor who played the part should be small in stature. Cobb was so large a man that Miller referred to him as "the walrus," and for a very long time Miller had no confidence in Cobb's ability to play the part. Deep into rehearsals, Cobb internalized the role and shocked Miller into seeing him as perfect. From the beginning, Cobb was convinced that this play was a masterpiece and that it would alter theater history.

As June Schlueter and James K. Flanagan point out, Willy Loman might well be the most memorable character in modern theater. Consequently, it is no surprise that a great variety of significant actors have played the role of Willy. In more recent years, Dustin Hoffman was notable as Willy and, because of his small size, closer to what Miller had originally intended. Interestingly, Hoffman played Bernard in 1965 with Lee J. Cobb as Willy when they produced a long-playing-record version of the play. Hume Cronyn and Brian Dennehy were each important in the part also, although Cronyn was almost too small in stature. Arthur Miller describes Ying Ruocheng, who translated the play into Chinese for Miller's 1983 production in Beijing, as a "brilliant" Willy.

Casting for the play involved a great deal of thought and agreement between the author and director. Arthur Miller, in his "Casting *Death of a Salesman*" essay, gives us some interesting insights into the complexities and the quirks that both actors and producers face. He gives us an engrossing description of the way in which Mildred Dunnock, a distinguished and well-known actress at that time, kept coming back for an audition even in the face of being told she was not right for the role of Linda. What this demonstrates is that minds can be changed even when firm decisions have been made, and that people can misjudge the ability of actors to do the work that needs doing. As it turned out, Mildred Dunnock was perfect for the part and breathed life into it as few actresses have done since.

Some of the interesting questions concerning the universality of the play were answered in the Asian productions, which have been enthusiastically received. One such production was the Taiwanese production reviewed by professor and director Catherine Diamond. The Beijing production was especially exciting because it came at a time when China was beginning to shift in its attitude toward capitalism. The all-black productions of the play, as well as versions in which some of the characters were played by black actors, presented their own issues. Brenda Murphy surveys some of the questions that those renditions raised in her essay, "Racial Consciousness in Casting *Death of a Salesman*." Any view that sees Willy Loman as restricted to a specific play and time seems to have been contradicted by the remarkable range of productions and producers, all of whom have faced considerable problems in staging and casting.

Perhaps the only generalization that can really be made is that the challenges the play presents seem to have been avenues into a boundless outgrowth of creativity.

Jo Mielziner (1901–1976)
DESIGNING A PLAY: *DEATH OF A SALESMAN* 1948–49

A seasoned and already respected set designer, Jo Mielziner reveals the detailed and demanding work that went into making the innovative designs for the first production of Death of a Salesman. *The late nights; the collaboration with electricians and carpenters, not to mention those with the director and producer; and all the worries and difficulties of conception — all these are revealed in the journal Mielziner kept as a record of his work on the play.*

Figure 16. Jo Mielziner's early sketch for the design of the original 1949 production of *Death of a Salesman*.

Figure 17. Jo Mielziner's painting of the original set, showing the backdrop of apartment buildings.

Figure 18. Mildred Dunnock (Linda), Lee J. Cobb (Willy), Arthur Kennedy (Biff), and Cameron Mitchell (Happy) on the original set of *Death of a Salesman* in 1949.

December 15, 1948

During my midweek check-up of unfinished *Salesman* chores, I realized that a large number of basic decisions still had to be made about the small scenes outside Willy Loman's house. Since rehearsals were due to start a couple of days after Christmas, I appealed to Kazan for a good long session.

During the previous weeks I had been receiving from Arthur Miller, scene by scene, the final version of the rehearsal script. Although he had done the basic rewriting, he had made no attempt to say how the transitions from one scene to another would be made. This was a problem for the director and the designer to work out together as we studied the model, the ground plan, and the cut-out cardboard symbols representing the props.

I pointed out to Kazan how difficult it would be in an office scene, for instance, to remove two desks, two chairs, and a hat rack (which the present script called for) and at the same time have an actor walk quickly across the stage and appear in "a hotel room in Boston where he meets a girl." I urged him to do even more cutting, not in the text but in the props called for in this latest version of the script. We finally got the office pared down to one desk and one chair. Then I suggested going so far as to use the same desk for both office scenes — first in Heiser's office and then, with a change of other props, in Charley's office. As usual, Kazan's imagination rose to the suggestion. He replied, "Sure, let's cut this down to the bone — we can play on practically anything." This is effective abstraction, giving the spectator the opportunity to "fill in."

I had felt from the outset that the cemetery scene at the end of the play would be done on the forestage, and I had actually drawn up a design for a trick trapdoor out of which would rise the small gravestone that we had thought necessary for this scene. I had shown Kazan the working drawing for the gravestone, explained how it would operate, and mentioned that because of union rules the man operating this mechanism would be doing this and nothing else, thereby adding a member to the crew for the sake of one effect. I had also mentioned that since the trap would be very close to the audience the sound of its opening might disturb the solemnity of the scene.

With some malice aforethought, I had also done a drawing showing the Salesman's widow sitting on the step leading to the forestage, with her two sons standing behind her, their heads bowed; on the floor at her feet was a small bouquet of flowers. The whole scene was bathed in a magic-lantern projection of autumn leaves. Here, again, leaves were symbolic. With this kind of lighting I thought I could completely obliterate the house in the background and evoke a sense of sadness and finality that might enable us to eliminate the gravestone itself.

My hints were not lost. "I get your point," Kazan said. "Let's do it without the gravestone. No matter how quietly you move it into place, everybody nearby is going to be so busy thinking, 'How is that done?' that they'll miss the mood of the scene."

I felt that this extreme simplicity would be the best theatre possible, and later, in dress rehearsal, it proved to be the right answer.

Kazan and I went over all the prop problems, especially the small hand props — who would bring them on, what actors would be handling them, were stagehands necessary on the set, how long could we black out the stage successfully for the changes?

A blackout is always difficult. As a rule, only a few seconds are permissible for a well-rehearsed stagehand to cross the stage in the darkness, pick up a prop, and exit without being seen by the audience. The eyes of those seated close to the stage soon become used to the sudden change of light, and figures onstage can be observed after six or eight seconds of the dark; gradually, everyone in the theatre can make them out. Stage blackouts are never complete anyway because there are masked and dimmed lights in the wings that must stay on for the control of the switchboard, the stage manager's desk with its telephones and master cue sheets, and the prop tables where the master property man gives hand props to actors waiting for entrance cues.

When we came to the scene in the Boston hotel room, Kazan said, "I don't need anything; just give me the feeling of a hotel room." I showed him a sketch of a panel of cheap wallpaper which I planned to project from the theatre balcony onto a background that was really a section of the trellis at one side of the Salesman's house. Projected images used in conjunction with scenery can be very valuable. In this case, the associations evoked by faded old wallpaper gave the audience a complete picture. Both the house and the exterior trellis faded away. The audience saw the Salesman in that cheap hotel room with that woman. I stress the phrase "in that room." Actors should never play against a scenic background but within the setting.

Kazan felt that the right actress cast in the role of the girl who visits Willy Loman in the hotel room, dressed in the right costume, plus the visual image of the wallpaper, would be enough to make this short scene come alive. There is no question that when a good actor is backed up by simple scenic treatment, his strong qualities are stressed. Of course, this can work in reverse, but Arthur Miller was lucky in the casting of *Salesman;* even the bit roles were played by vivid actors.

During these last weeks before rehearsals began, the producer's office was finishing the always difficult financing of the production, arranging details in preparation for the tryout and the New York run, organizing theatre parties, completing the casting. Arthur Miller was correcting and polishing the rehearsal version of the script. And Kazan was in constant communication with the author as well as the technical staff. I was busy enough myself. Although my wife and children were enjoying Christmas vacation in the country, I wasn't to join them until the day before Christmas.

January 19, 1949   This day was all mine. The stage was ready for me to set the lighting levels for the entire production. Backstage, property men were still unpacking and arranging hand props, and carpenters were finishing the masking of light leaks and cleaning up the paraphernalia; the acting company was still in New York for final run-throughs and costume fittings. The production stage manager had come down to Philadelphia to make notes from my lighting cues and to take over running the crew backstage; one of his assistants stayed in New York to be with Kazan and the company. The company manager was already in Philadelphia and had reported happily that advance sales were promising.

I had asked Del Hughes, the production stage manager, to enlist a couple of local drama students as volunteer stand-ins for my lighting rehearsal. For this process, without the company on hand, I always try to have someone on the set each time I set a light. It is easy to become so absorbed in lighting an empty stage that you wind up illuminating the scenery for its own sake; if I have stand-ins, not only can I see exactly what they themselves look like in the acting light, but I have figures in the foreground to give perspective when I am lighting the background.

I began by taking out every light in the theatre except those over the fire exits. We had to find out how much light the electricians needed on their boards, how much the fly men needed in the fly loft, and how much the property man needed in the wings; with these necessities as a base, I would know how much light there was to start with. Then, with my assistant sitting in back of me, the complete blueprint in my hands which showed the number of each pipe and area, and a speaker in front of me, I called out to Richard Raven, the chief electrician, "Light first pipe playing area right, blue circuit."

As the process went on, I could judge two things: what my predetermined color would look like on the set, and how well my assistant and the crew had angled the units. One by one, I looked at every group of lamps, every individual spot, every color, and every circuit. Then I looked at each projection individually.

The next phase was to create the mood of the background. For the opening of the play I had decided to start with lights behind the drop, which would illuminate the windows of the neighboring buildings painted on the face of the drop. I always start by telling my electrician, "When I call for something, don't bring it on full power, but start with it low on the dimmer." Dimmer controls have markings from one to ten, one being full power, nine and ten being lowest intensity. In this case, I said on the intercom, "Bring the tenth pipe amber up slowly from the bottom." When it reached about halfway, I said, "Hold it." Then I went to the lights on the face of the drop; for this we had two pipes of border lights. I had planned one to cover the top half of the drop; the other was to pick up and carry the bottom half. Each of these pipes contained three colors; one color at a time, I brought the lights up to a certain level, blending the three elements. In this way I gradually established the mood for the opening scene.

I next worked with a series of light pipes that gave a blue backlighting to the Loman house; this brought out the plastic element in that part of the set which was built three-dimensionally. When I had established these, I called backstage on the intercom to the chief electrician, "Mark it up carefully." It takes patience to sit in the dark of the auditorium and wait for what seems an endless time; but the boys on the switchboard, in this case three of them, have to look at each one of the many dimmer handles and mark meticulously at just what point I had called out to hold. This has to be checked and double-checked and then written down on each one of their cue sheets.

Because of the refusal of theatre owners to provide modern electronic lighting systems, almost all of the professional theatres in America are still forced to use the same manual switchboards that were in use fifty and more years ago. While university theatres and community playhouses throughout the country are decades ahead, the professional theatre still hauls in antiquated, heavy (even if serviceable) manual boards. All this, of course, means extra money for the management of a play. In this respect a theatrical producer is not unlike a person who might rent an expensive Fifth Avenue apartment and find a kitchen with an outlet plug for a stove and a refrigerator, but no stove or refrigerator. In most of the New York theatres even the outlets are inadequate in power for modern lighting. Many a time, not only in New York but in try out on the road, I have had every fuse in the place blow out because the electric service was being taxed beyond the limit.

I welcomed the chief electrician's voice on the intercom, saying, "O.K., Mr. M., we're all marked up; what next?" I was ready now for the playing areas, and the stage manager brought on the two young people who were going to stand in for the actors. I placed them first in the bedroom. The opening scene occurs late at night when the Salesman arrives home; I wanted just enough glow to bring out the forms in bed. I then traced through the entrance of Willy Loman and had the electricians mark down the "pre-set," the lights that can be set behind the curtain before it rises. When this was done, I planned the "follow-up"; this is the next cue, which the stage manager gives when he sees that the house curtain is all the way up and the lights in the auditorium can be brought up; these lights, of course, cannot be pre-set, since their beams would hit the house curtain when it was down, creating ugly patterns on its surface.

I had to be careful to judge the effect of light on the faces of people who were not in make-up and costume. For instance, the young lady stand-in had appeared in a white blouse, and I had borrowed a throw from the bed to put around her shoulders. The mere presence of that much white would have given me the illusion that I was getting much more light than was actually there. When I finished with a scene and was waiting for it to be noted on the electricians' cue sheets, I had the property man bring out the props that went with the scene at hand; this gave me a chance to see them not only in terms of distance but also in relationship to their surroundings. The color of the "oilcloth" on the kitchen table, for example, proved to be satisfactory on the surfaces facing the audience but too light on the top surface, where the bounce from the overhead spotlights brought it into competition with the actors' faces. This was swiftly remedied by spraying down the table top.

Knowing that we had about a hundred and fifty light cues to set, we decided to work straight through the night until we had at least a basic scheme and a basic cue for every part of the production. There was no time for polishing or for going back to rehearse the timing of cues, things I usually have been able to do on this day. As it was, we worked until midnight, sent out for coffee and sandwiches for all, and didn't finish the final scene until 4:30 in the morning. This added up to twenty and a half hours of pretty intense work, and the week had just begun.

During the afternoon Alex North and the musicians had arrived from New York, and I used what little time I had, while waiting for the electrical crew to do their mark-ups, to work out some details about the music. I checked to see that the dressing room which was to be the "sound studio" was properly equipped with microphones and a communication system. We had to put blankets on the floor and on the walls before North was satisfied with the quality of the sound as it came into the auditorium over the speaker system. At the same time the assistant electrician rigged a signal-and-sound system for the musicians so that the stage manager's voice announcing cue warnings and cues would be clear and unmistakable.

The process of lighting a musical is basically the same as for a play like *Death of a Salesman,* but there is less refinement in the musical because the picture is broader and the contrasts greater; less subtlety is needed, more vitality desired. Another difference is that in a legitimate play, with the acting areas more limited and the sets fewer, there is much greater need for extreme control of lighting equipment. During this day of setting the lighting for *Salesman* I occasionally had the two follow-spot men turn on their new and beautifully engineered lights, and the effect was fascinating. In the opening scene, for instance, when the Salesman makes his tiptoe entrance carrying his bags, we dimmed the follow-spot far down and played the beam just on the face of the stand-in. The effect was magical; there was so little light that there was no shadow behind him, and yet there was enough warmth in it so that the face stood out in the gray-blue night light. I was sure that this new experiment would come through very serviceably indeed.

How different this subtle and complex lighting was from earlier times! When I designed *Of Thee I Sing* in 1931 for Sam Harris, he was disturbed that I was not willing to use the 1900 type of stage lighting that had characterized his previous productions. This consisted of border lights, footlights, and old-fashioned floodlights for what were known as "entrances." There was no control of any segment of the stage, only a system of dimming and raising lights for the total acting area, with all people, all objects, and all scenery treated alike.

After Harris had finally agreed to let me try out "modern lighting," I was busy one day with the electrician, who had laid out several dozen new spotlights on the stage in preparation for hanging them. Harris walked on, gave a quizzical glance at the equipment, started to leave, and then turned and said, "You know, kid, my name is Sam Harris, not Uncle Sam." But the lighting stayed in and Harris' productions started to look like their contemporaries.

January 24, 1949   At last: Opening Night. Nerves take over backstage on this night of nights, and it is the rare actor or stage manager who isn't in a cold sweat until the performance moves into high gear. But from the very beginning of my career I have been favored. As I sit out front, I become fatalistic: I've done what I've done; good, bad, or indifferent, there it stands. I can no longer do anything about it. If something goes wrong, I may cringe, but I rarely get up to go backstage.

One of the fascinating aspects of theatre is the feeling I get when I am watching a familiar performance as a member of an audience for the first time. I do not mean an audience of fellow professionals or the people with whom I have been working for weeks on the production, but an audience of ordinary theatre-goers who are seeing the show for the first time. I become intensely aware of their response, and my own reactions, both intellectual and emotional, change completely from what they were the night before when only my fellow workers were around me. I become part of a community of 800 people, and my responses reflect the communal atmosphere.

The first public performance of *Death of a Salesman* gave us all the feeling that the play had it. There were scenes that didn't go well; others seemed a little long, and would later be cut or changed. But from the very beginning, long before any applause, there was a sense that the play really held the audience. There is nothing esoteric about being able to make a fairly reliable verdict on whether a show is going to be a hit after seeing an out-of-town performance. If there are serious doubts, the chances are that the play will not succeed. Of course, some plays received coolly out of town can become moderate successes on Broadway, but out of the more than 250 productions I have designed I cannot remember one really first-rate show that did not reveal its strength on first exposure.

Brenda Murphy (b. 1950)
DEATH OF A SALESMAN: THE DESIGN PROCESS   *1995*

Brenda Murphy examines the process by which the design for the set began to take shape. The distinguished set designer Jo Mielziner was presented with a highly novel concept in the action of the play, and his solution has spawned many imitations. His solution was to concentrate on the salesman's house, presenting it in a dramatic cross-section.

While the casting proceeded, the biggest unanswered question about the script, the design concept, was being addressed. On September 24, Jo Mielziner received a call from Kermit Bloomgarden asking whether he could come straight over and talk to him about "something very interesting." After learning that Kazan hoped to begin rehearsal of the play in two weeks, Mielziner left the meeting with the *Salesman* script to read. During that afternoon and evening, Mielziner began to understand the difficulty of the job he was faced with: "It was not only that there were so many different scenic locations but that the action demanded instantaneous time changes from the present to the past and back again. Actors playing a contemporaneous scene suddenly went back fifteen years in exactly the same setting — the Salesman's house."

As he looked for a design solution to the many changes in scene and time demanded by the script, Mielziner hit on the concept that was to become the key to the production:

The most important visual symbol in the play — the real background of the story — was the Salesman's house. Therefore, why should that house not be the main set, with all the other scenes — the corner of a graveyard, a hotel room in Boston, the corner of a business office, a lawyer's consultation room, and so on — played on a forestage? If I designed these little scenes in segments and fragments, with easily moved props and fluid lighting effects, I might be able, without ever lowering the curtain, to achieve the easy flow that the author dearly wanted.

The problem was that developing this design scheme would require more than the two weeks that remained before rehearsals were scheduled to begin. Miller would have to make substantial revisions in the script to change blackouts at the end of each scene to instantaneous scene changes, and Kazan would have to reconceive the whole production. What's more, if the play's opening was delayed, the pre-Broadway theatre bookings and the New York opening would have to be canceled and rescheduled. Mielziner asked for a meeting with Bloomgarden, Miller, and Kazan for that afternoon.

A long discussion followed Mielziner's presentation of his ideas on September 25. In the end, the aesthetic advantages of the single-set design scheme built around the material symbol of the house were determined to far outweigh the difficulties:

> To Arthur Miller, a design scheme allowing him as author to blend scenes at will without even the shortest break for physical changes was a significant decision. To Kazan, with his strong sense of movement, stimulated by his already proven genius as a film director, the scheme would permit use of some of the best cinematic techniques.

In the end, it was decided to postpone the start of rehearsals until the end of December and the New York opening until 10 February, allowing enough time for Miller's revisions and Kazan's rethinking of the direction as well as for the development of the design. Kazan was to consider Mielziner's "concept of a house standing like a specter behind all the scenes of the play, always present as it might be always present in Willy's mind, wherever his travels take him, even behind the office he visits, even behind the Boston hotel room and above his grave plot," the "single most critically important contribution and the key to the way [he] directed the play." Eloquently described by Miller on the opening pages of the published play, it has served the same purpose for millions of readers who have never seen a production of *Death of a Salesman.*

Mielziner set to work immediately to realize his ideas scenically. He made a number of rough sketches over the next few days, along with a ground plan of the stage, and worked on a breakdown of the script, which gave a page reference for each key scene and a notation of the needed lighting, scenery, props, and elevations. On September 28, he flew to Boston, where Kazan was rehearsing the pre-Broadway previews for *Love Life,* and went over his ideas at a breakfast meeting, leaving his director "after a brief hour with about ninety-percent approval." During the next week, Mielziner made about twenty black-and-white sketches representing the scenic design of the whole production and set his assistants to work on translating his sketches into an accurate floor plan and building a scale model of the set. When he met on October 4 with Bloomgarden, Kazan, and Miller, the designer had "a group of ground plans and sketches that . . . solved the major puzzles and were at least indications of the right style" for the production.

Mielziner's set was the culmination of a style of design he had been developing in his productions of Tennessee Williams's plays. In *The Glass Menagerie, A Streetcar Named Desire,* and *Summer and Smoke,* he had combined translucent scenery, expert lighting effects, and sets that went, as the eye traveled upward, from drab realistic interiors to light, delicate frameworks that were mere suggestions of buildings. The result was a style that was beginning to be recognized as his signature and that signaled to audiences a subjective realism in the play that juxtaposed ostensibly objective reality with a character's fantasy as easily as the scenery juxtaposed realism with symbolic abstraction.

Mielziner's *Salesman* set developed from his careful reading of the dialogue and the brief descriptive note that Miller had given him. Miller's note read: "[The house] had once been surrounded by open country, but it was now hemmed in with apartment houses. Trees that used to shade the house against the open sky and hot summer sun now were for the most part dead or dying." In the dialogue, Mielziner had underlined the lines "Boxed us in here"; "Bricks and windows, windows and bricks"; and "beautiful elm trees out there." From these visual suggestions, he conceived a tri-level set for the house, with Willy and Linda's bedroom on the lower floor, at stage right, one step up from the kitchen, which, at center stage, formed the largest playing space. On the far left of the kitchen were steps leading up to the boys' bedroom, above and behind the kitchen. All three rooms could be seen simultaneously. Although there was no wall between the parents' bedroom and the kitchen, the rear wall of each room was hung with translucent backdrops stenciled with "wallpaper" patterns. The lower floor also contained a bed, several chairs, a table, a telephone stand, and a refrigerator. Mielziner's original sketches also showed the hot water heater in the kitchen, but it was eventually hidden behind a curtain because it had become intrusive.

Rising above the lower floor there were only the skeletal rafters representing the gabled roof line and a platform holding the boys' beds and a chest. Behind the house was a translucent backdrop with two trees, the outline of the roof, and the boys' dormer window painted on the facing side. On the back were painted the outlines of bare, rectangular buildings with rectangular windows. When lit from the front with a soft golden light, the backdrop showed the Lomans' house as it used to be, a small but brave structure rising with hope and light to the sky. When lit from the back with a threatening reddish glow, it showed the house in the play's present, its fragile skeleton threatened by the huge, glowering apartment buildings.

On October 4, the main design problems that remained were lack of room for movement on the stage and transitions in time. The lack of room was solved only on December 8, when Kazan convinced Bloomgarden to take eleven seats out of the first row (at a cost of $323.40 per week in receipts) in order to extend the forestage. One of the biggest transition problems was getting Biff and Hap from the scene in their bedroom dressed in pajamas to the immediately following scene in which they appear to Willy in the kitchen as they were in the past, dressed in football uniforms. To manage this without closing the curtain or blacking the stage out, Mielziner had elevators built into the boys' beds so the actors could be moved unnoticed from one scene to the other. In order to give them time for a costume change, Miller expanded Willy's monologue about polishing the car by several minutes.

As the autumn progressed, Mielziner confronted the questions of lighting and props. Arthur Miller remembers that Mielziner and lighting expert Eddie Kook together "once worked an entire afternoon lighting a chair." The chair was the one that Willy addresses as if it were his old boss Frank Wagner in Howard's office, reminding him of the promises he had made. As Willy speaks to it, "the chair must become alive, quite as though his old boss were in it as he addresses him." Miller marveled that, "rather than being lit, the chair subtly seemed to begin emanating light" in the production. To achieve this effect, all of the surrounding lights on the stage had to be dimmed imperceptibly, rather than bringing up the spotlight on the chair, which would produce an effect too obvious to the audience.

This effect, and the attention that Mielziner and Kook gave to it, provide a good illustration of the designer's attitude toward the lighting of *Death of a Salesman*. Always a designer who made full artistic use of the scenic expression of lighting, Mielziner had decided that lighting was the key to *Salesman*'s time shifts. He decided to signify the passage of time on stage by creating two environments for the house through the lighting. When the set was first revealed, the audience saw the muslin backdrop lit from behind to show the oppressive apartment houses towering over the fragile house. When the scene shifted to the past, the lights behind the backdrop were dimmed out, and the buildings faded out as soft amber light and images of green leaves were projected onto the backdrop from a number of projection units that were carefully placed backstage, throughout the auditorium, and on the balcony. Mielziner felt that this visual symbol of the spring leaves, "liberating the house from the oppression of the surrounding structures and giving the stage a feeling of the free outdoors," was an "integral part of the Salesman's life story and had to be an easily recognized symbol of the springtime of that life." Combined with the music provided by Alex North, this lighting change would bring the audience effectively into the past along with Willy as each daydream began.

The painstaking work involved in the lighting of the original *Death of a Salesman* is almost inconceivable in these days of computerized stage lighting. Each of the 141 lighting units on the eight pipe battens above the stage had to be carefully hung and angled, and each light cue individually adjusted and marked up so that it could be re-created manually during each performance. It took three days for the hanging and angling, and another twenty-hour-day to set the approximately 150 light cues when the production was moved into the theater. In addition to the projection units, Mielziner had also persuaded Bloomgarden of the necessity of two special follow-spots, which could be manipulated to produce particular effects. Because their fine adjustments needed careful attention, each of these lights required a trained technician for its operation throughout the performance, a significant expense. Mielziner used the projection units to address spatial as well as temporal difficulties. He and Kazan had agreed early on that the most minimal of visual suggestions would suffice in creating the sets for the scenes to be played on the forestage — the Boston hotel room, the restaurant, and Howard's and Charley's offices. He created the hotel room by projecting a seedy wallpaper design from the theater balcony onto a section of the trellis at the side of the house. With the rest of the stage dimmed, this was enough to evoke the environment where Biff is disillusioned when he surprises Willy with The Woman.

This suggestiveness went along with the minimalism that Mielziner and Kazan had agreed on in the props. A few objects, such as the beds, the chairs, and the table, were required by the action on the stage. Most of the props, such as the refrigerator, the hot water heater, Willy's sample cases, the silk stockings, the rubber tubing, the hoe and seeds, and the gold fountain pen, served a necessary function but also took on a symbolic resonance. Kazan and Mielziner also agreed on several props which served primarily as material signifiers for the audience of some theme in the play, such as Biff's football trophy on a shelf over Willy's bed and a deflated football in the boys' room. The fact that props were kept to a minimum, with no attempt at realism, helped to foreground the few objects that did appear, encouraging the audience to perceive their symbolic significance.

Throughout the production process, the impulse was toward greater abstraction and symbolism, less realism. A good example is the Requiem scene, in which the original plan was to have a gravestone rise from a trick trapdoor in the forestage. Mielziner persuaded Kazan to use a simple bouquet of flowers to signify the grave instead, using a projection of autumn leaves to complete the symbolic statement of death in opposition to the life and hope suggested by the spring leaves in the day-dream scenes. What made the production's style unique, however, was the juxtaposition of the abstract and poetic with the real and prosaic. The props that were introduced into the abstract suggestiveness of the set were authentic, battered objects that the Lomans might very well have owned. The kitchen table was covered with a cloth painted with an "oilcloth" design. The refrigerator was a careful reproduction of a typical model from the 1929 Sears Roebuck catalogue. It was vital to the production's aesthetic that these objects signify a specific time, place, class, and way of life in juxtaposition with the insistent visions in Willy's mind, and that they resonate with symbolic significance in the context of the play as a total experience.

Brenda Murphy (b. 1950)
RACIAL CONSCIOUSNESS IN CASTING
DEATH OF A SALESMAN   *1995*

A number of interesting issues came to the surface when the 1972 Baltimore production of Death of a Salesman *cast all black actors. Race-blind casting had been common with other classic American plays and often with Shakespeare and other European plays. This play provided unexpected surprises, however, as Murphy explains.*

The Center Stage production in 1972 brought to the fore the issue of race and ethnicity in casting the play. Although it was the first professional production cast with African-Americans, it was not the first to raise the color issue. As early as 1960, Miller had turned down a request from Terry Carter to do a "Negro version" of *Salesman* Off-Broadway. Although Carter assured Miller that care would be taken to avoid interracial casting that might "distort" the play — the entire Loman family, as well as The Woman, Miss Forsythe, and Letta were to be played by black actors — the request was refused, presumably because of Miller's ban on professional productions in New York.[1] According to Miller, however, he approved a production in New York during the sixties that would have featured African-American Frederick O'Neal as Willy, although the production never materialized.[2] O'Neal had played Willy in a 1962 production directed by Esther Merle Jackson at Clark College in Atlanta with an all-black cast.

The Center Stage production featured Richard Ward, who had been a hit in *Ceremonies of Dark Old Men* at the theatre in the previous year. Miller attended the

[1]Unpublished letter from Terry Carter to Kay Brown, January 1960, HRHRC. [Harry Ransom Humanities Research Center]
[2]Unpublished letter from Arthur Miller to George [C. Scott], 28 April 1975, HRHRC.

opening night of the all-black production, and contributed a note to the program, saying:

> I have felt for many years that particularly with this play, which has been so well received in so many countries and cultures, the black actor would have an opportunity, if indeed that is needed anymore, to demonstrate to all his common humanity and his talent.[3]

The production was not particularly successful, chiefly because some inexperienced actors were cast in the minor roles. In several interviews, Ward made it clear that he had wanted to do the play with an integrated cast, particularly with Charley played by a white man, showing that "a white man and a black man can live next door to each other and care for each other . . . their children can grow up together and love each other."[4] Miller also was quoted as saying he would like to see the play done with an integrated cast, "just because it would allow a greater selection of players."[5] The producers reported that they had thought about an integrated cast, but decided that it "might be an attempt to make a statement that's not in the play." They had wanted to make Charley white, "but some black leaders in Baltimore pointed out that the neighbor ends up success[ful], and that a 'be white, be a success' message might come across."[6]

Not surprisingly, the production was analyzed almost exclusively in terms of the race issue. Mel Gussow asserted in the *New York Times* that "Black time has caught up to *Salesman*," and contended that "what makes this more than just an intriguing experiment, but an exciting concept, is not only what it tells us about *Death of a Salesman*, but what it tells us about the black experience."[7] In Gussow's view, "Willy Loman's values are white values — the elevation of personality, congeniality, conformity, salesmanship in the sense of selling oneself," so that in the context of an all-black production, "Willy becomes a black man embracing the white world as an example to be emulated."[8] Hollie West of the *Washington Post* found the concept less revealing. Putting black actors "in roles written for whites," she contended, required the actors to "shed the badge of their color. Without the nuances of black dialogue and a consciousness reflecting the unique customs and traditions of black life, such actors may ask the question: Am I playing a white black man?"[9] West did not think the production succeeded in transferring the circumstances of the lower-middle-class white family in New York during the 1930s and 1940s to "the black circumstances of the same period."[10] Although she found Ward's performance as Willy entirely convincing, she found historical and social reality impinging on the dramatic illusion of the other characters: "Have black women been willing to play secondary roles when their husbands were failing, as in the case of Mrs. Loman?" she asked. "Would Biff have been considered an outcast among thousands of similar black men a generation ago?"[11]

---

[3]Quoted in Mel Gussow, "Stage: Black *Salesman*," *New York Times,* 9 April 1972: 69.

[4]Quoted in Carl Schoettler, "Actor in *Death of a Salesman* Went on Stage at Age 13," Baltimore *Evening Sun,* 3 April 1972: C6. See also Larry Siddons, "A Black Willy Loman Talks of *Salesman*'s Soul," *New York Post,* 4 April 1972: 60.

[5]Quoted in Siddons, "A Black Willy Loman."

[6]*Ibid.*

[7]Gussow, "Black *Salesman*."

[8]*Ibid.*

[9]Hollie I. West, "*Death of a Salesman*," *Washington Post,* 14 April 1972: D1.

[10]*Ibid.,* D7.

[11]*Ibid.*

Despite his support for Richard Ward's desire for interracial casting in the Baltimore production, Miller made it clear three years later that he found the question of race in casting an extremely complex one. A year after taking over the direction of the Philadelphia Drama Guild production from Scott, Miller approved an Off-Broadway revival of *Salesman* at the Circle in the Square Theatre that Scott was to direct, with himself in the title role. When he learned that Scott was planning to cast a black actor as Charley, Miller wrote him a four-page single-spaced letter, warning him to consider carefully what the implications of this casting would be. So-called "color-blind casting, he believed, only worked when it was entirely color-blind, with Biff black and Happy white, for example. This, however, took the play out of the realm of realism, and made its relation to the social reality it depicted purely metaphorical, a conception which needed to be thoroughly thought through.[12]

In 1975, casting one "white" role with a black actor immediately foregrounded the issue of race. In the case of Charley, Miller did not think this would work. It would suggest that Willy, in daring to have a black man for his best friend during the thirties, would have it in him to rebel against accepted social values and prejudices, a quality antithetical to his character. It would also take away the sense that Charley is fundamentally the same as Willy, except for Willy's ruling passion, which destroys him. Miller felt that Charley should face the same conditions in life that Willy does, that he should be a representative of the American system when it functions as it should. He felt that adding the issue of race to this relationship would distort its dynamics as he had intended them to work.

[12]Unpublished letter from Arthur Miller to George [C. Scott], 28 April 1975, HRHRC.

Elia Kazan (1909–2003)
DIRECTING *DEATH OF A SALESMAN*   1988

Kazan speaks very personally about his involvement with Death of a Salesman, *beginning with his first reading of the script. He explains that the experience was like that of a brother speaking to him, someone who had shared his life experiences. And although he had directed the plays of Tennessee Williams and films such as* On the Waterfront, Death of a Salesman *was his favorite. The way in which he internalized the play may well parallel the responses of many readers and theatergoers, who might go home and wonder, as Kazan did, "Was I a good father? No? Why hadn't I done better?"*

Of all the plays I've directed, *Death of a Salesman* is my favorite. When I read it again recently, it hit me as hard as it had when I read it the first time, thirty-eight years ago — just as hard and in the same place, immediately, on page two! I am a man who has trained himself to let no pain show, but I felt tears coming as I turned that page. I suppose the play revives the memory, long at rest, of my father, a salesman of another product, of his hopes for his sons in this new country and the gently twisted Anatolian° smile on his face when he'd ask me, a muddle-headed kid of

Anatolian: Of the main portion of Turkey, in western Asia. Kazan was born Elia Kazanjoglous to a Greek family in Istanbul, then the capital of the multiethnic Turkish Ottoman Empire.

sixteen, "Who going support me my old age? Hey, you Elia, what you saying to that?" When I had nothing to say to that, but looked away, feeling threatened, he'd shrug and mutter — I'd hear it — "Hopeh-less case." That and more from those years of my life, as well as other memories, without words or faces, lying in wait with their burden of sadness, swarmed up when I read that damned disturbing play last week, just as they had when Art Miller, the day after he finished it in 1948, gave it to me.

After I'd read it that first time, I didn't wait for the next morning to see if I'd have a more "balanced" judgment, didn't delay as I generally did in those years to hear what Molly° might say about it, but called Art as I turned the back cover and told him his play had "killed" me. "I wrote it in eight weeks," he replied.

When I say this was my favorite play, I don't mean it was the best play. I am not a critic, and I do believe Williams wrote better. They were both Puritans, they were both concerned with morality — Tennessee more open about his "sins" and his problems, Miller more guarded. Still *Salesman* is the play that got to me most deeply. It's as if a brother was speaking of our common experience, a man who'd been through precisely the same life with his family that I had with mine. Art does an extraordinary thing there; he shows us a man who represents everything Art believes to be misguided about the system we live in, then goes on to make us feel affection and concern, pity and even love for this man. Then he goes deeper and we are aware of a tragic weight. Is it for the Salesman? Is it for ourselves? And along with arousing this sympathetic pain, his horrendous hero is able to make us laugh. He is ridiculous and he is tragic all at once. How is that accomplished? I don't know any other play in any other language that does all these things at the same time. But Arthur Miller did them all — that one time and never again.

I believe the reason he was able to do this was not that he was more understanding than anyone else about his fellow Americans and the system we live in, or knew better than the rest of us what was wrong with our civilization. It was because of his uncle. I remember — and I hope I remember correctly — that he derived Willy Loman from his uncle, "a very small man," the original stage direction reads, "who wears little shoes and little vests . . ." and "His emotions, in a word, are mercurial." Which is the way Art expected the part would be cast, not with Lee Cobb, certainly not great lumbering Leo Jacob Cobb. Art had this most ambivalent feeling about an actual person, thought him completely wrongheaded, believed he'd misguided his family and that everything he said that was meant to be serious was rubbish, but he still felt great affection for him and enjoyed his company and relished his passionate, nonsensical talk. The man made Art laugh, and Art likes to laugh. In short, he had the living model with that impossible combination of qualities in his own family, and he was smart enough, Art was, and talented enough to recognize that he had a character who could arouse affection and pity at the same time he evoked total condemnation and that both these reactions were significant separately, but together, in the same person, they were much more meaningful; together they could be tragic; together they were all of us.

Studying the play, as I was preparing to direct it, I began to see my father differently; I stopped being angry at him. I was ready at last to forget what I'd considered tyrannical and appreciate what he'd done for me. To gain an understanding of the play, one of the first things I did was sum up the similarities of my father to Willy Loman. George Kazan was a man full of violence that he dared release only at

Molly: His wife, Molly Day Thatcher (1932–1963).

home, where it was safe to be angry. But the possibility that he might blow up at any time kept us all in terrible fear.

He also had about him, my father along with Willy, the euphoria of a salesman. When it came time to seduce a customer, he was expressive to a theatrical degree. "Feel it!" I remember him shouting at a buyer, as he lifted the end of a large Kashan carpet and thrust it into the man's hand. "Go on, take it in your hand. Give yourself the pleasure. No charge. Like butter, right? Eh? What you say? Like sweet butter! Tell me where you find piece goods like this piece goods, tell me that much." And so on. People in the trade said he was a great salesman. But when I watched these mercantile revels, they embarrassed me.

"Baba" dressed as a salesman and had his shoes shined every day. Even when he went to my aunt's apple farm in the Catskills for a weekend's vacation, he'd bring along other rug merchants, to talk about prices and the market and the sources "on the other side," then to play poker or pinochle most of the night. Sundays, when he would supervise the shish-ke-bab, bending over the hot wood coals and carefully turning the spits thrust through the cubes of well-marinated lamb leg, he wore a hard collar and a bow tie. Sometimes he even wore the jacket of his business suit and a flat-brimmed straw hat. In the Catskills on a Sunday, he was a merchant waiting for Monday.

It's the essence of the salesman's philosophy that your success or failure depends on your impressing others not only with the goods you have for sale but with yourself. You must gain their approval of your personality, make them believe that anything you say is true, even when you know it's grossly exaggerated or even totally false. That is how my father lived, by saying with the passion of unqualified conviction what was useful in winning a customer. Come to think of it, it was not different from what actors do on stage; they must make an audience believe the poetry and the nonsense, even when they don't believe it themselves. They are rewarded not with a sale but with applause.

Like Willy, my father considered his eldest son a special failure and oh, God, this hurt him! And me! But how could I blame him for what he expected of me and didn't get? Obviously what his wife had produced for him, this silent, secretive, mysteriously sullen son, was not going to rally to his side and sell rugs, not any to anyone, ever. Father preferred his next two boys: one was bound to study medicine — Father already called him "the doctor" — and the other actually did show, for a time, an interest in the business that had been my father's life. But he was afraid to tell himself the truth about his eldest son, the truth being that I didn't give a damn about the Oriental rug trade and, despite his persisting hopes, would never go into it; and if I did, would soon defect; and if I stayed, be no damn good. But just as Willy did, George Kazan kept pumping up hope, and the burden of that hope was on my back.

Willy had Linda, ever-faithful, fiercely devoted Linda; my father had my mother, Athena. She'd stand behind him every night as he gulped the dinner she'd spent the day preparing, would sit to eat her own meal only after he'd moved to the sofa; typically Anatolian that, taking a quick nap after his *yehmek*.° Old lions sleep after eating what the lioness provides.

There is an unarticulated tragedy when a woman discovers that the man she married is not what she hoped he was when she married him. Both Linda and

yehmek: Meal.

Willy's best friend, Charley, saw through him but still loved him. Like Linda, my mother would not tolerate any criticism of my father from me; not while he was alive. If I indicated some disaffection, she'd turn on me and tell me he was a good man; "he never goes to other woman," she'd say, and someday I'd come to appreciate what he'd done for us all. He'd brought her to America, you see, not found her here, and she appreciated this. She protected him until the day he died; but when he was finally quiet in the grave, she surprised me one day by saying, "Your father was a stupid man." And soon afterward she said, "These years" — those following his death — "are best years of my life."

Art's play had such deep value for me because it forced me to understand my parents better. Even recently, when I read the play again, it made me wonder about the way I was treating my youngest son, ask myself if I was being as understanding of him as I should be. It disturbed me that I'd discovered my father's traits — even his facial expressions! — in myself. It disturbed me greatly when my youngest son told me that for years he'd lived in terror of my anger. I was repeating the pressure patterns of my father, and I was ashamed when I read Art's play and realized this. That damned play cut me where I was most vulnerable: Was I a good father? No? Why hadn't I done better?

I know it did this for many men; it was the only play I ever directed where men in the audience cried. I recall hearing sobs at the end of a performance, and they were mostly from men.

All the critics rushed to nail down the theme of the play, and Miller helped them with what's in the dialogue: "The man didn't know who he was," spoken over the grave, and a line even closer to the meaning, "He had the wrong dream," which is stated and restated. But it seemed to me that I, as the director, had to take another step and ask what that "wrong dream" was. I came to believe that the point was far more lethal than anything Art put into words. It's in the very fabric of the work, in the legend itself, which is where a theme should be. The Christian faith of this God-fearing civilization says we should love our brother as ourselves. Miller's story tells us that actually — as we have to live — we live by an opposite law, by which the purpose of life is to get the better of your brother, destroying him if necessary, yes, by in effect killing him. Even sex becomes a kind of aggression — to best your boss by taking his woman! That contrast between the ideal and the practice specific to our time is the sense in which the play is a "social drama," and this theme, so shameful and so final, permeates the work's fabric and is projected through the example of human behavior so there can be no avoiding it. Here is an antisystem play that is not "agitprop." We are out of the thirties at last — the audience does not have to suffer instruction or correction. The essence of our society, the capitalist system, is being destroyed not by rhetoric but by that unchallengeable vocabulary, action between people, which makes you believe that the terrible things that happen are true, are inevitable, and concern us all. Furthermore, the conflict we watch is between people who have every traditional reason to love each other. Miller makes us reach out for the lesson; it is not thrust down our throats. The question remains: Why do we live by that law when we know — and Art shows us this — that the result is so humanly destructive?

Art was trained first of all by Henrik Ibsen. The play has a strong structure. The viewer is immediately made aware, first by the title, then by Willy's revealing that he found himself driving off the road, that we are gathered together to watch the course of a suicide. That promise of terror and tragedy lies under every scene in the

A PRODUCTION CASEBOOK • DEATH OF A SALESMAN

action that follows and makes the tension continuous. You wait in anxiety as you watch this ridiculous, tragic, misguided, frantically obsessed man — whether Cobb plays him, or the actor is a smaller man like Miller's uncle, doesn't matter. What you watch is yourself, struggling against the fate you've made for yourself.

This production became the other half (with *Streetcar*)° of a theatre legend. The fascinating game of what is fact and what is public relations buildup began to be played. In the accounts of the production and in the remeasuring of the people involved, what had actually happened was replaced by what a hungry press needed — good copy! — and what the imaginations of the people who saw the production were prepared to believe. Furthermore, within each of the people involved there was a swell of confidence. We became convinced of our ability to do anything we chose to do. Success seemed the natural course for us all, the inevitable reward of our efforts. The great success of the play certified our worth. Truth was soon out of sight; we all puffed up. Our producers, Bloomgarden and Fried, Lee Cobb, Arthur Miller, and Elia Kazan were never the same again.

The play became, to the surprise of many theatre people, including its producers, a great success, selling out immediately. Kermit Bloomgarden, an excellent "line" producer, who had the ability to see to it that everything necessary for mounting a show arrived on time and in good working order, was now offered to the public as something more, the leading producer of "class" plays that no one else dared produce on Broadway. His pressman immediately set about creating an enlarged reputation. But how Kermit was able to acquire *Death of a Salesman* and what he thought of it is more interesting than this "puff." Daring is not a feature of the true story; luck is.

At the end of the triumphant opening night performance, Eddie Kook, who'd provided the equipment for lighting the show, was sitting behind Cheryl Crawford, listening to the applause storm. Eddie noticed tears in Cheryl's eyes and commented on the play's power. "That's not why I'm crying," she said. "I had this play and let it get away." This was true. When Art and I weren't sure which producer to entrust it to, I suggested we give it to Cheryl. To my surprise, the force it would have with an audience did not strike her. She hesitated; the time allowed for hesitation in the theatre is brief. Cheryl seemed especially dubious about the play's commercial potential. She'd given it to friends to read; they hadn't been sure either. Since a lively enthusiasm is a necessity for a successful ride through the obstacle course of a Broadway production, and Cheryl didn't show any, I told her to forget the play.

Now luck was loose. Art and I decided to pass the script on to another good friend, Kermit, and his associate, Walter Fried. They'd accepted the play for production, but, as had been the case with Cheryl, they were not sure of its box office strength. Kermit told me he'd consulted theatre owners and box office treasurers, and everyone had cautioned him that the word "Death" in a title invited death to the ticket window; this had been proven time and again, so they maintained.

One morning when I was in Kermit's side office, working on casting, he burst in and declared that he was convinced the title of the play had to be changed. He said there was an "upbeat" phrase in the play that would make a fine title, commercial

Streetcar: *A Streetcar Named Desire* by Tennessee Williams, which Kazan directed earlier in 1947. It was still running when *Death of a Salesman* opened.

as well as meaningful. Fried and he were determined that *Free and Clear* should be our title. When my reaction was negative, then obdurate, then — when they persisted — scornful, they asked if I'd mind if they talked to Miller without me there. I don't know why I was so damned gracious, because my emotions were violently hostile, but I did say, "Go ahead," and they summoned the author quickly for consultation. Art had to pass the small office where I was waiting with the door open. When he came by, I pulled him in, and without telling him what their proposal was, I said, "They want to talk to you about something I'm dead against. Don't you dare say yes." Art went in, they talked without me; our title was not changed.

But Kermit was a man who made it a matter of pride that he never changed his mind. Perhaps he thought that I, along with others who knew his original concerns about Miller's title, might think him weak if he altered his stand. Kermit had a horror of appearing weak. On opening night, he was cornered by Irving Hoffman, who wrote theatre reviews for the *Hollywood Reporter,* and although Irving didn't ask him what he thought of the title, Kermit volunteered, "I still don't like the title, but it's Arthur Miller's play and he wants the title we have and that's all right with me." Perhaps Kermit was throwing up a defense for himself in case Hoffman didn't like the title either. His anxiety about what Hoffman might think was not altogether unfounded. The "head" of the review in the *Hollywood Reporter* read: "Tragically We Roll Along."

The imaginative qualities of Art's play, the nonrealistic aspects, worked successfully on stage and added a great deal to the force of the theme. They were indeed innovative, and Art deserved all the praise he's been given. How they came to be in the production, however, is a story that brings credit to the theatre as an institution, as well as confirming a string of influences. As Tennessee Williams admired and was stirred by *All My Sons* ("It has the kind of eloquence we need now," he'd written me), so did Art benefit from *A Streetcar Named Desire*. I remember the night he came to see *Streetcar.* After the performance he appeared to be full of wonder at the theatre's expressive possibilities. He told me he was amazed at how simply and successfully the nonrealistic elements in the play — *"Flores! Flores para los muertos!"*° — blended with the realistic ones. These two men, completely different humans who never mixed socially, influenced each other's work and owed each other a debt.

After *Death of a Salesman* had made theatre history, it was published, and the sentence that follows "The Curtain rises" on the first printed pages is: "Before us is the Salesman's home . . . an air of a dream clings to the place, a dream rising out of reality." However, the stage direction in the original manuscript that Art gave me to read directly he'd finished it does not mention a home as a scenic element. It reads: "A pinpoint travelling spot lights a small area on stage left. The Salesman is revealed. He takes out his keys and opens an invisible door." It was a play waiting for a directorial solution.

The concept of a house standing like a specter behind all the scenes of the play, always present as it might be always present in Willy's mind, wherever his travels take him, even behind the office he visits, even behind the Boston hotel room and above his grave plot, is not even suggested in the original script. Although the spectral home is a directorial vision, it was not my idea any more than it was Art's. It

---

Flores! . . . muertos!: Flowers! Flowers for the dead!

was urged on us by the scenic designer, Jo Mielziner. I went for it — it solved many problems for me — and when we took it to Miller, he approved of it. In this production, it was the single most critically important contribution and the key to the way I directed the play. Both Miller and I were praised for what Jo had conceived; he never got the credit he deserved. Art rewrote his stage direction for the book based on Jo's design. A published play is often the record of a collaboration: The director's stage directions are incorporated, as are some of the contributions of others working on the show — actors' "business," designer's solutions, and so on. The theatre is not an exclusively literary form. Although the playscript is the essentially important element, after that is finished, actors, designers, directors, technicians "write" the play together.

Lee J. Cobb became the great star of that season; people marveled at his power and his brilliance. This adulation may have done him more harm than good. When I recommended that we cast Cobb as Willy, I knew him well from our days in the Group° and a road tour we'd played of *Golden Boy*. Our friendship had started close, but like many actors' friendships, it thinned out. I knew him for a mass of contradictions: loving and hateful, anxious yet still supremely pleased with himself, smug but full of doubt, guilty and arrogant, fiercely competitive but very withdrawn, publicly private, suspicious but always reaching for trust, boastful with a modest air, begging for total acceptance no matter what he did to others. In other words, the part was him; I knew that Willy was in Cobb, there to be pulled out.

When he received his fabulous notices, Lee awarded himself a status even higher than any the theatre world gave him. He was great as Willy Loman until he was told he was great and believed it — then he was less great. He was at his best during the last week of the tryout in Philadelphia, before his New York triumph. After we opened on Broadway, he began to share the audience's admiration for his performance and their pity for the character he played. Life on Broadway would not, because it could not, satisfy this man's hunger for unqualified recognition. He withdrew from our play before he should have, claiming that he was dangerously exhausted — which we might have appreciated except that we all saw he was dramatizing it beyond its measure. He said he was on the verge of a breakdown and demanded that I consult with his analyst. I did; we had a bad scene. I still don't know how serious Lee's trouble was; he was a very good actor and determined to prove that he had to leave the show.

Once he was "available" again, no more parts like Willy came his way. He began to masquerade as a martyr to an unappreciative theatre. Something pouting in his character waited for "justice," meaning that a role of great worth was his due and had to come soon. He'd certainly be the Lear of our time, he boasted. Friends agreed. But the theatre is no more just than life, and nothing came along that he found acceptable. Today, Cobb is remembered for Willy Loman and that is all; it became the story of his life.

Many actors are remembered because of a single great performance, but this comfort from history did not satisfy Cobb. When another season's crop of new plays came along with nothing for him, he decided to return west and to films. I brought him back east to my "location" in Hoboken, to play the corrupt labor

---

Group: The Group Theater was founded in New York in 1931.

boss in *Waterfront,* and he did well, even had an Academy Award nomination. But after that the roles offered him in films were beneath his talent. He felt aggrieved and insulted, and found that the people who dominated the film community were no less arrogant than I. To save his pride, he responded with arrogance. To release his tensions, he gambled more frequently and more seriously. I know only what I heard, the outside of the story. He disappeared from my view. Then suddenly he was dead, too young and — I agree — insufficiently rewarded. What a waste!

Thinkers who think about the theatre have said that success is a problem more difficult than failure — an astonishing thought to anyone who'd been hungry for recognition as long as I'd been. I didn't find success a problem; I was not uncomfortable sitting on a peak. I was credited with all kinds of magic and became the coy object of artistic temptation and commercial seduction. Every play of worth intended for Broadway was offered me first. I had to shrug them off. In films it was only a matter of what I wanted to do, name it. I could see no limit to what I might accomplish. I began to make notes on ambitious future projects, those I'd once only dreamed of. Now they were within reach; all I had to do was extend my hand. And work! That was easy; I had perfect health and boundless energy. I enjoyed the devotion and the intimate friendship of the two best playwrights of the day; one was writing a play, the other a film, both intended for me. I didn't have an enemy, not that I knew of; no, nothing but admiring followers. I was so successful there was no reason for anyone to be jealous of me: I was too far ahead of the pack. I was certain all this would endure — why would it not? — sure that my success would swell, my friendships deepen, my creative associations become richer. No longer suffering from self-doubt, I quit my analyst.

In time I had to confront some facts. I am a mediocre director except when a play or a film touches a part of my life's experience. Other times my cleverness and facility will not overcome my inadequacies. When I rely on mechanics, I do only what a good stage manager should be able to do. I am not catholic in my tastes. I dislike Beckett — his work. I am not an intellectual. I don't have great range. I am no good with music or with spectacles. The classics are beyond me. I enjoy humor and the great clowns, but I can't make up jokes or amusing bits of byplay and visual humor. What I need I steal. I have no ear for poetry. I have a pretty good eye but not a great eye. I do have courage, even some daring. I am able to talk to actors; I don't fear them and their questions. I've been able to arouse them to better work. I have strong, even violent, feelings, and they are assets. I am not shy about ripping the cover-guard off my own experiences; this encourages actors to overcome their inhibitions. I enjoy working with performers; they sense this and have been happy as well as successful with me. This is useful.

Molly used to say that I was too hard on myself. But I don't feel the above is inaccurate. I prefer this measure to the pumped-up state of fame I had after *Death of a Salesman* and *A Streetcar Named Desire.* It took me some years to face what I was as a director; in fact, it took a painful defeat at the Lincoln Center Repertory Theatre. At the time I'm writing about, I was mired in media mud; I'm afraid that for a time I believed what I read. When I see my photographs from that period, I don't like what I see. For three years I was on the very top, then life twisted, as it will; by surviving a great deal of pain and trouble, I became a different person. But that's looking too far ahead.

Arthur Miller (b. 1915)
CASTING *DEATH OF A SALESMAN*   1978

Reflecting on the process of casting both the main character, Willy, and Willy's wife, Linda, Miller considers some of the reasons for choosing one actor over another. He reminds us that the choices that producers and directors make are usually sound and sensible. Some actors have a great track record and recommend themselves in terms of their recent successes. Others have a quality that a director might remember and see as appropriate for the part. In addition, there are other actors who see themselves as the only viable choice for the part they want; their job, perhaps the most difficult, is to convince the decision makers that they are the right choice.

The basis upon which actors are hired or not hired is sometimes quite sound; for example, they may have been seen recently in a part which leads the director to believe they are right for the new role; but quite as often a horde of applicants is waiting beyond the door of the producer's private office and neither he nor the director nor the author has the slightest knowledge of any of them. It is at this point that things become painful, for the strange actor sits before them, so nervous and frightened that he either starts talking and can't stop, and sometimes *says* he can't stop, or is unable to say anything at all and says *that*. During the casting of one of my plays there entered a middle-aged woman who was so frightened she suddenly started to sing. The play being no musical, this was slightly beside the point, but the producer, the director, and myself, feeling so guilty ourselves, sat there and heard her through.

To further complicate matters there is each year the actor or actress who suddenly becomes what they call "hot." A hot performer is one not yet well-known, but who, for some mysterious reason, is generally conceded to be a coming star. It is possible, naturally, that a hot performer really has talent, but it is equally possible, and much more likely, that she or he is not a whit more attractive or more talented than a hundred others. Nevertheless, there comes a morning when every producer in these five blocks — some of them with parts the performer could never play — simply has to have him or her. Next season, of course, nobody hears about the new star and it starts all over again with somebody else.

All that is chancy in life, all that is fortuitous, is magnified to the bursting point at casting time; and that, I suspect, is one of the attractions of this whole affair, for it makes the ultimate winning of a part so much more zesty. It is also, to many actors, a most degrading process and more and more of them refuse to submit to these interviews until after the most delicate advances of friendship and hospitality are made to them. And their use of agents as intermediaries is often an attempt to soften the awkwardness of their applying for work.

The theatrical agents, in keeping with the unpredictable lunacy of the business, may be great corporations like the Music Corporation of America, which has an entire building on Madison Avenue, and will sell you anything from a tap dancer to a movie star, a symphony orchestra, saxophonists, crooners, scene designers, actors, and playwrights, to a movie script complete with cast; or they may be like Jane Broder, who works alone and can spread out her arms and touch both walls of her office. They may even be like Carl Cowl, who lives around the corner from me in Brooklyn. Carl is an ex-seaman who still ships out when he has no likely scripts on hand to sell, and when things get too nerveracking he stays up all night playing Mozart on his flute. MCA has antique desks, English eighteenth-century prints, old broken clocks and inoperative antique barometers hanging on its paneled walls, but Carl Cowl had a hole in his floor that the cat got into, and when he finally got the landlord to repair it he was happy and sat down to play his flute again; but he heard meowing, and they had to rip the floor open again to let out the cat. Still, Carl is not incapable of landing a hit play and neither more nor less likely than MCA to get it produced, and that is another handicraft aspect of this much publicized small business, a quality of opportunity which keeps people coming into it. The fact is that theatrical agents do not sell anyone or anything in the way one sells merchandise. Their existence is mainly due to the need theater people have for a home, some semblance of order in their lives, some sense of being wanted during the long periods when they have nothing to do. To have an agent is to have a kind of reassurance that you exist. The actor is hired, however, mainly because he is wanted for the role.

By intuition, then, by rumor, on the recommendation of an agent — usually heartfelt; out of sheer exhaustion, and upsurge of sudden hope or what not, several candidates for each role are selected in the office of the producer, and are called for readings on the stage of a theater.

It is here that the still unsolved mystery begins, the mystery of what makes a stage performer. There are persons who, in an office, seem exciting candidates for a role, but as soon as they step onto a stage the observers out front — if they are experienced — know that the blessing was not given them. For myself, I know it when, regardless of how well the actor is reading, my eyes begin to wander up to the brick wall back of the stage. Conversely, there are many who make little impression in an office, but once on the stage it is impossible to take one's attention from them. It is a question neither of technique nor of ability, I think, but some quality of surprise inherent in the person.

For instance, when we were searching for a woman to play Linda, the mother in *Death of a Salesman,* a lady came in whom we all knew but could never imagine in the part. We needed a woman who looked as though she had lived in a house dress all her life, even somewhat coarse and certainly less than brilliant. Mildred Dunnock insisted she was that woman, but she was frail, delicate, not long ago a teacher in a girl's college, and a cultivated citizen who probably would not be out of place in a cabinet post. We told her this, in effect, and she understood, and left.

And the next day the line of women formed again in the wings, and suddenly there was Milly again. Now she had padded herself from neck to hem line to look a bit bigger, and for a moment none of us recognized her, and she read again. As soon as she spoke we started to laugh at her ruse; but we saw, too, that she *was* a little more worn now, and seemed less well-maintained, and while she was not quite ordinary, she reminded you of women who were. But we all agreed, when she was finished reading, that she was not right, and she left.

Next day she was there again in another getup, and the next and the next, and each day she agreed with us that she was wrong; and to make a long story short when it came time to make the final selection it had to be Milly, and she turned out to be magnificent. But in this case we had known her work; there was no doubt that she was an excellent actress. The number of talented applicants who are turned down because they are unknown is very large. Such is the crap-shooting chanciness of the business, its chaos, and part of its charm. In a world where one's fate so often seems machined and standardized, and unlikely to suddenly change, these five blocks are like a stockade inside which are people who insist that the unexpected, the sudden chance, must survive. And to experience it they keep coming on all the trains.

But to understand its apparently deathless lure for so many it is necessary, finally, to have participated in the first production of a new play. When a director takes his place at the beaten-up wooden table placed at the edge of the stage, and the cast for the first time sit before him in a semicircle, and he gives the nod to the actor who has the opening lines, the world seems to be filling with a kind of hope, a kind of regeneration that, at the time, anyway, makes all the sacrifices worth while.

The production of a new play, I have often thought, is like another chance in life, a chance to emerge cleansed of one's imperfections. Here, as when one was very young, it seems possible again to attain even greatness, or happiness, or some otherwise unattainable joy. And when production never loses that air of hope through all its three-and-a-half-week rehearsal period, one feels alive as at no other imaginable occasion. At such a time, it seems to all concerned that the very heart of life's mystery is what must be penetrated. They watch the director and each other and they listen with the avid attention of deaf mutes who have suddenly learned to speak and hear. Above their heads there begins to form a tantalizing sort of cloud, a question, a challenge to penetrate the mystery of why men move and speak and act.

It is a kind of glamour that can never be reported in a newspaper column, and yet it is the center of all the lure theater has. It is a kind of soul-testing that ordinary people rarely experience except in the greatest emergencies. The actor who has always regarded himself as a strong spirit discovers now that his vaunted power somehow sounds querulous, and he must look within himself to find his strength. The actress who has made her way on her charm discovers that she appears not charming so much as shallow now, and must evaluate herself all over again, and create anew what she always took for granted. And the great performers are merely those who have been able to face themselves without remorse.

In the production of a good play with a good cast and a knowing director a kind of banding together occurs; there is formed a fraternity whose members share a mutual sense of destiny. In these five blocks, where the rapping of the tap-dancer's feet and the bawling of the phonographs in the record-shop doorways mix with the roar of the Broadway traffic; where the lonely, the perverted, and the lost wander like the souls in Dante's hell and the life of the spirit seems impossible, there are still little circles of actors in the dead silence of empty theaters, with a director in their center, and a new creation of life taking place.

There are always certain moments in such rehearsals, moments of such wonder that the memory of them serves to further entrap all who witness them into this most insecure of all professions. Remembering such moments the resolution to leave and get a "real" job vanishes, and they are hooked again.

I think of Lee Cobb, the greatest dramatic actor I ever saw, when he was creating the role of Willy Loman in *Death of a Salesman*. When I hear people scoffing at actors as mere exhibitionists, when I hear them ask why there must be a theater if it cannot support itself as any business must, when I myself grow sick and weary of the endless waste and the many travesties of this most abused of all arts, I think then of Lee Cobb making that role and I know that the theater can yet be one of the chief glories of mankind.

He sat for days on the stage like a great lump, a sick seal, a mourning walrus. When it came his time to speak lines, he whispered meaninglessly. Kazan, the director, pretended certainty, but from where I sat he looked like an ant trying to prod an elephant off his haunches. Ten days went by. The other actors were by now much further advanced: Milly Dunnock, playing Linda, was already creating a role; Arthur Kennedy as Biff had long since begun to reach for his high notes; Cameron Mitchell had many scenes already perfected; but Cobb stared at them, heavy-eyed, morose, even persecuted, it seemed.

And then, one afternoon, there on the stage of the New Amsterdam way up on top of a movie theater on Forty-second Street (this roof theater had once been Ziegfeld's private playhouse in the gilded times, and now was barely heated and misty with dust), Lee rose from his chair and looked at Milly Dunnock and there was a silence. And then he said, "I was driving along, you understand, and then all of a sudden I'm going off the road. . . ."

And the theater vanished. The stage vanished. The chill of an age-old recognition shuddered my spine; a voice was sounding in the dimly lit air up front, a created spirit, an incarnation, a Godlike creation was taking place; a new human being was being formed before all our eyes, born for the first time on this earth, made real by an act of will, by an artist's summoning up of all his memories and his intelligence; a birth was taking place above the meaningless traffic below; a man was here transcending the limits of his body and his own history. Through the complete concentration of his mind he had even altered the stance of his body, which now was strangely not the body of Lee Cobb (he was thirty-seven then) but of a sixty-year-old salesman; a mere glance of his eye created a window beside him, with the gentle touch of his hand on this empty stage a bed appeared, and when he glanced up at the emptiness above him a ceiling was there, and there was even a crack in it where his stare rested.

I knew then that something astounding was being made here. It would have been almost enough for me without even opening the play. The actors, like myself and Kazan and the producer, were happy, of course, that we might have a hit; but there was a good deal more. There was a new fact of life, there was an alteration of history for all of us that afternoon.

There is a certain immortality involved in theater, not created by monuments and books, but through the knowledge the actor keeps to his dying day that on a certain afternoon, in an empty and dusty theater, he cast a shadow of a being that was not himself but the distillation of all he had ever observed; all the unsingable heartsong the ordinary man may feel but never utter, he gave voice to. And by that he somehow joins the ages.

And that is the glamour that remains, but it will not be found in the gossip columns. And it is enough, once discovered, to make people stay with the theater, and others to come seeking it.

I think also that people keep coming into these five blocks because the theater is still so simple, so old-fashioned. And that is why, however often its obsequies are intoned, it somehow never really dies. Because underneath our shiny fronts of stone, our fascination with gadgets, and our new toys that can blow the earth into a million stars, we are still outside the doorway through which the great answers wait. Not all the cameras in Christendom nor all the tricky lights will move us one step closer to a better understanding of ourselves, but only, as it always was, the truly written word, the profoundly felt gesture, the naked and direct contemplation of man which is the enduring glamour of the stage.

June Schlueter (b. 1948) *and James K. Flanagan*
MEMORABLE WILLY   *1987*

The authors contend that there may be no more memorable character on the modern stage than Willy Loman. To an extent they base their statement on the effect that Willy has on the audience's imagination. The later audiences of the play seem to have been affected by Willy Loman even more than the original 1949 audience. The society had changed in twenty-five years, but in a direction that made Willy's values seem less connected with the Depression of the 1930s and more connected with the affluence of the 1970s.

When Walter Goodman reviewed the 1975 revival of *Death of a Salesman,* in which George C. Scott replaced Lee J. Cobb as the self-deluded drummer, he claimed that the play, though applauded in 1949 as the great American tragedy, might well mean more in 1975. Goodman argues that the sympathetic reception of so unmitigated a failure as Willy Loman could be expected from a people who had lived through the Great Depression and World War II, but identification with this loser of a salesman could not have lasted beyond the two-hour life of the play. For this audience was on its way to becoming the Affluent Society; in 1949, Willy Loman was "an anachronism, a relic of a Depression mentality." By 1975, however, America had again become a society ready to acknowledge that "attention must be paid," even to this unlikable, inept failure, whose condition rather than personality was moving. For the 1975 audience had lived through an unpopular, unnecessary war, which brought none of the enthusiasm or the nationalism of World War II; and it was disillusioned with two decades of an energetic prosperity that could not pause for failures nor accommodate a man who yearned to plant seeds or look at the moon.[1]

In 1984, Willy Loman appeared once again on the Broadway stage, this time a bit thinner and a bit smaller — more like the original "shrimp" Miller had created than the "walrus" into which Willy was metamorphosed when Lee J. Cobb was cast. Dustin Hoffman's portrayal of Willy was powerful and convincing, suggesting that the method actor had clearly found some coincidence between himself and the character that enabled him to create the role. But where America was in the mid-1980s did not seem to concern the critics. *Death of a Salesman* was no longer being viewed as time-bound commentary on capitalism and its victims, and audience response was not being judged in terms of economic or social circumstance. Miller's play had clearly earned its author's description of it as a play that raises "questions . . . whose answers define humanity,"[2] a description dramatically endorsed in 1983 when the play opened at the Beijing People's Art Theater in China.

That production, the first in China of an American play directed by an American, challenged the assumption that *Salesman* was culture-bound, meeting with enthusiastic responses in a country where peasants constitute 90 percent of the population and where there are no salesmen. Speaking of the opening in *"Salesman" in Beijing,* Miller noticed the odd laughs, the cruel laughs, beneath which he

[1]Walter Goodman, "Miller's *Salesman,* Created in 1949, May Mean More to 1975." *New York Times,* June 15, 1975, pp. 1, 5.

[2]Arthur Miller, introduction to *Arthur Miller's Collected Plays* (New York: Viking Press, 1957), p. 32.

sensed "a comprehension of Willy's character, a recognition. Which I suppose means they share these embarrassing weaknesses?"[3] Harry Moses, producer of the Bill Moyers show on PBS, which ran a special program on the production of *Death of a Salesman* in Beijing, told Miller the day after opening night that the last shot on the program would be of a young Chinese who spoke English, saying that "China was full of Willys, dreamers of the dream."[4]

But the problem with Willy — aside from his self-delusion, his ineptness, his self-pity, his misplaced pride, and his fraudulent morality — is that he has dreamed the wrong dream. About to be fired from his job, Willy cries out to the young upstart Howard, "You can't eat the orange and throw the peel away — a man is not a piece of fruit!" Though only the peel of Willy's dream remains, he refuses to discard it, deluding himself into believing that the dream of being a salesman with green velvet slippers, who was not only liked but well liked by the hundreds who mourned his death, was right for him.

There may well be no character in modern drama more memorable than Willy Loman. The image of the tired salesman, valise in hand, shoulders sloping, suit jacket hanging loosely about his weary frame, which appeared on the jacket of the Viking edition of the play for years, has sustained its power in the imagination of the theatergoing public. It has become a symbol of the pursuer of the American — and the universal — dream who met with the harsh consequences of not being able to keep up. Willy Loman is indeed a low man; no tragic hero of high degree, he is circumstantially and psychologically down. Surrounded by high-rise apartment buildings that deflect the sun from the backyard, Willy's little house in Brooklyn stands as a symbol of time past, when the world still had room for vegetable gardens and for salesmen who carried on their trade on the strength of a smile. There is a collective guilt in Willy's failure in which every theatergoer participates; it is a guilt occasioned by the knowledge that society cannot accommodate its failures in a system that relentlessly demands success.

[3]Arthur Miller, *"Salesman" in Beijing* (New York: Viking Press, 1984), p. 238.
[4]Miller, *"Salesman" in Beijing*, p. 245.

Catherine Diamond
DEATH OF A SALESMAN IN TAIPEI   *1993*

Diamond, who is a professor and director of the only English-language theater in Taiwan, felt that the Taiwanese production of Death of a Salesman *reflected Chinese values almost as much as it did American values. The political complexities of the production indicate the difficulties that the National Theater of Taipei overcame in order to produce the play. Diamond points to some of the interesting cultural differences that might be invisible to an American audience but that would be of considerable importance to the Chinese.*

DEATH OF A SALESMAN. By Arthur Miller. The Performance Workshop. The National Theater, Taipei, Taiwan, Republic of China. 18–26 April 1992.

In 1987, Yang Shipeng, director of the Hong Kong Repertory Theatre, was invited to direct a play at Taiwan's new National Theater. He requested permission from Arthur Miller to use a Taiwanese translation of *Death of a Salesman* because he could not use the Ying Ruocheng translation Miller used in Beijing. Miller initially gave his permission with the caveat that the translation be used only in Taiwan. The production was postponed and later, Yang heard from Miller's agent that only the Ying Ruocheng translation was acceptable. The reason for this change of mind has never been clearly determined, but the Taiwan press put the blame on Miller, insinuating his pro-communist sympathies. On the other hand, perhaps Miller, irritated that Taiwan's refusal of the mainland translation was based purely on political rather than artistic grounds, revoked his initial permission.

In 1991, Yang again wrote to Miller, asking whether he could use the Ying Ruocheng translation with some of his own emendations. Miller answered affirmatively. In both his alteration of the translation, in which he substituted Taipei idiom for the original Beijing idiom, and in his directing style, Yang strove for what he believed would appear most natural to the Taipei audience, neither emphasizing the play's Americanisms nor trying to adapt the story to a Taiwanese local.

The actors played the essence of relationships rather than their specifically American manifestations. However, there were some fundamental differences in social values that made it difficult for the audience to comprehend Willy's character and to sympathize with him. For example, virtually no Chinese father harbors aspirations for his son to become a professional sportsman, but desires instead for him to go to university — an American school preferably — and become a professor, doctor, manager, or lawyer. As an actor in Miller's *Salesman in Beijing* expressed it: "Every man wants his son to be a dragon." The audience clearly understood Willy's hopes for Biff and his ensuing disappointment, but since Taiwanese society so clearly admires the path taken by Willy's neighbor, the successful businessman Charley and his bookish son Bernard, people laughed at Willy's delusions, often failing to empathize with his particular dreams of success.

Despite some confusion caused by Willy's highly individualized character, other aspects of the play were almost written for modern day Taipei. The similarities between the United States in the wheeling-dealing 1920s and laissez faire capitalism in 1990s Taiwan are uncanny. Out-of-town extramarital affairs, children suffering from parental expectations, the high cost of housing, overcrowding, disappearance of green spaces, job obsolescence, increasing competition for jobs, and the struggle to maintain the esteem of others while facing failure are well-known phenomena in the postindustrial, newly-wealthy metropolis of Taipei. Yet the production did not challenge the audience to reflect upon these problems or the social values that cause them.

Director Yang had a clearcut goal of presenting an American play without any concessions to the Chinese actors or the Chinese audience, yet certain changes were inevitable. In the translation itself, the flavor of individual characters's speech gets attenuated, especially Happy's, which is slangy.

Another significant difference was in acting style. Modern Chinese stage acting tends to be broad, exaggerated and emphatic. This has roots in the traditional drama and is reinforced by television dramas which tend to be either contemporary soap operas or historical melodramas. Consequently the male actors in particular engaged in a great deal of demonstrative acting — pointing, waving their hands around, and touching each other to get attention. Seasoned stage actor Li Lichun played Willy's poignant scenes with admirable restraint, but Deng Chenghui, as the loyal wife Linda, evoked more sympathy. Her voice never broke until her last line

The 1992 Chinese production of *Death of a Salesman*, at the National Theater in Taipei, Taiwan, directed by Yang Shi-peng.

at Willy's grave: "We're free . . . we're free," and, because she held back her tears until the very end, the audience wept with her, moved more by her devotion than Willy's fall and final sacrifice.

In his Beijing production, Miller initially felt apprehensive that his play might be reduced to a political message — an indictment of American capitalism. This aspect was wholly absent from the Taipei production, where it might have been more justified. Instead, both director and actors stressed the pathos of the Loman family. Yang Shih-peng wanted to move the audience, but to what end, his production never made clear.

Samuel Beckett

Samuel Beckett (1906–1989) was born in Dublin to an upper-middle-class Protestant family. After a privileged education at the Portora Royal School, he went to Trinity College, Dublin, where he studied French and Italian. He was an exceptionally good student and, in 1928 after graduation, taught English at the École Normale Supérieure in Paris.

Beckett early on straddled two literary cultures: Irish and Anglo-Irish. Most of the literary energy in Ireland in the 1920s and 1930s was split between the essentially conservative Anglo-Irish Protestants, such as W. B. Yeats and Lady Gregory, and the more avant-garde Catholics, such as James Joyce, with whom Beckett formed an enduring personal and literary friendship in Paris. Although much younger than Joyce, Beckett developed a close artistic sympathy with him. Beckett's first published work (1929) was one of the earliest critical essays on Joyce's most radical literary composition, the not-yet-published *Finnegans Wake.*

When he was first in France, Beckett's reading of French philosophers, especially Descartes, exerted a strong influence on his work. Beckett's earliest writings appeared in Eugene Jolas's avant-garde literary journal *transition,* which put him in the center of Parisian literary activity in the late 1920s. After 1930, his series of short stories published under the title *More Pricks Than Kicks* (1934) established him as an important writer. After settling in Paris in 1937, Beckett wrote the novel *Murphy* (1938), on a recognizably Irish theme of economic impoverishment, alienation, and inward meditation and spiritual complexity.

When World War II began in 1939, Beckett took up the cause of the French Resistance. After his activity caught the eye of the Gestapo, for two years he lay low in unoccupied France by working as a farmhand and also writing another novel, *Watt* (written in 1944 but published in 1953). After the war he took up residence again in Paris and began writing most of his work in French. His greatest novels were written in the five years after the war, and they are often referred to as his trilogy: *Molloy, Malone Dies,* and *The Unnamable.* These three novels are about men who have become disaffected with society and who have strange and compelling urgencies to be alone and to follow exacting and repetitive patterns of behavior. In a sense, they are archetypes of the kinds of protagonists that Beckett created in most of his work.

Beckett's first published play, *Waiting for Godot* (1952), was produced in Paris (1953), in London (1955), and in Miami (1956). From the first, its repetitive, whimsical, and sometimes nonsensical style established the play as a major postwar statement. In a barren setting, Vladimir and Estragon, two tramps who echo the comic vision of Charlie Chaplin, wait for Godot to come. They amuse themselves by doing vaudeville routines, but their loneliness and isolation are painfully apparent to the audience. Godot has promised to come, and as they wait, Vladimir and Estragon speculate on whether or not he will.

The comic moments in the play, along with the enigma of Vladimir and Estragon's fruitless waiting, combined to capture the imagination of audiences and the press. They saw the play as a modern statement about the condition of humankind, although there was never any agreement on just what the statement was. Godot sends a boy to say that he will indeed come, but when the play ends, he has not arrived. The implication seems to be that he will never arrive. Most audiences saw Godot as a metaphor for God. Despite the critics' constant inquiries, Beckett never confirmed the view that Godot was God and kept Godot's identity open-ended.

The play itself was open-ended, as Beckett had hoped, and therefore could be interpreted in many ways. One interpretation was to see the play as a commentary on the futility of religion; another was to suggest that the play underscored the loneliness of humankind in an empty universe; yet a third implied that it was up to individuals, represented by the hapless Vladimir and Estragon, to shape the significance of their own lives, and their waiting represented that effort.

Many of the themes in *Waiting for Godot* are apparent in Beckett's later plays. The radio play *All That Fall* (1957) was followed by the very successful *Krapp's Last Tape* (1958). Also in 1957, *Endgame,* a play on the themes of the end of the world, was produced, followed in 1961 by *Happy Days*. Beckett experimented with minimalist approaches to drama, exemplified in *Act without Words I* and *Act without Words II*, both mime plays. Other plays experiment with minimalism in setting, props, and — in the mime plays — even words.

Beckett's plays reveal the deep influence of French postwar philosophers, such as Albert Camus and Jean-Paul Sartre, both existentialists. Their philosophy declares that people are not essentially good, bad, kind, or anything else but are what they make of themselves. Beckett's adaptation of existentialism sometimes borders on pessimism because his vision seems to negate many of the consolations of religious and secular philosophy. His style is antirealist, but the search for beliefs that are reasonable and plausible in a fundamentally absurd world, and the plight of individuals who must make their own meanings is central to most of his work.

Beckett's view of the world is not cheerful. But his vision is consistent, honest, and sympathetic to the persistence of his characters, who endure even in the face of apparent defeat. The significance of Beckett's achievements was recognized in 1969 when he was awarded the Nobel Prize for literature.

HAPPY DAYS

British writer and critic Nigel Dennis praised *Happy Days* (1961) for introducing a woman "spokesperson" into Beckett's cast of characters. Winnie, buried in a mound of earth first up to her waist, then up to her neck, is a nonstop talker who ruminates about every trivial thing around her. She looks at the contents of her bag and examines every item in detail to get some concrete information that she thinks is required for living sensibly. No matter what happens or does not happen, Winnie believes firmly that this day has been a happy day.

Winnie, a true believer, needs to know the truth, although her truths tend to be details that are essentially useless for a meaningful life. She does not seem to demand that her life be meaningful; she simply trusts that it is and lives a life that is essentially unexamined except for the trivial details.

Time and again she calls out to Willie, a portrait of an absent, newspaper-reading husband. His mere presence throughout the play provides one of the details that so please Winnie. At the end he himself appears in a full dress outfit and makes an effort to climb Winnie's mound apparently to reach her revolver. What his purposes are, we do not know. Winnie puts a good face on it and thinks his actions must be a sign of affection. The audience may think that he could simply be tired of her talking. He is, after all, as laconic as she is loquacious.

Winnie's situation is hopeless. She is rooted in the earth and cannot move. In this sense, she is a reflection of Oedipus — if Claude Lévi-Strauss is right about Oedipus' origins as a man plucked from the earth. Winnie is embedded in the earth. In act 2 she is drawn down even more deeply than in act 1, yet she never gives much notice of her confinement. She ignores this important detail of reality and insists on maintaining a number of broad illusions. One of them is her pious faith in religion, which opens the play. Another is her faith in Willie as a devoted husband and helpmate. Finally, she seems completely unaware that the earth that holds her so firmly is a metaphor for the grave.

Beckett may be graphically illustrating the fact that everyone alive is slowly slipping back into the earth from which we came. Beckett's philosophy of absurdism is especially bleak about facing the facts of life. Life is short; it is grim. It is — regardless of what we may do to endow it with meaning — meaningless. But these are facts that Winnie reveals no awareness of.

Beckett, like the Irish satirist Jonathan Swift, is rather savage in his treatment of those who willfully ignore the painful realities of life. The Miltonic allusion in the opening of act 2 ("Hail, holy light") reminds us that the characters in this play are their own Adam and Eve, but their paradise leaves much wanting. God walked in Eden with Adam and Eve, but Winnie's mound lacks the presence of God. In a way, it is paradise in reverse; although, if it is a Mephistophelean hell, Winnie is quite unaware of it.

Happy Days in Performance

The play premiered in September 1961 at the Cherry Lane Theatre in New York, directed by Alan Schneider, a close associate of Beckett. Ruth White played Winnie and John C. Becher played Willy. The Royal Court Theatre production in London by George Devine followed in November 1962 with Brenda Bruce and Peter Duguid. Roger Blin directed the 1963 French premiere with Madeleine Renaud as Winnie. Beckett directed a German version of the play in Berlin in 1971 and documented his experience for later directors. Peter Hall directed Peggy Ashcroft in the 1975 London production in the National Theatre. Billie Whitelaw played a memorable Winnie to Leonard Fenton's Willie in the 1979 Royal Court Theatre production, directed again by Samuel Beckett when he was seventy-two years old; his production notes have been published recently. At the same time, in the Public Theatre in New York, Andrei Serban directed a distinguished version with Irene Worth as Winnie. Beckett had set a standard with his productions in Berlin and London, and Serban essentially honored his wishes. In 2001, the Cherry Lane Theatre produced the play once again, this time directed by Joseph Chaiken, founder of the Open Theatre, with Joyce Aaron and Ron Faber. Sir Peter Hall directed the play again in London in November 2003 with the much-acclaimed comic actress Felicity Kendal. The play has attracted the talents of a number of great actresses and great directors and continues to be played in regional theaters in the United States and abroad.

Samuel Beckett (1906–1989)

HAPPY DAYS   *1961*

Characters

WINNIE, *a woman about fifty*
WILLIE, *a man about sixty*

ACT I

(*Expanse of scorched grass rising center to low mound. Gentle slopes down to front and either side of stage. Back an abrupter fall to stage level. Maximum of simplicity and symmetry.*)

(*Blazing light.*)

(*Very pompier trompe-l'oeil° backcloth to represent unbroken plain and sky receding to meet in far distance.*)

(*Imbedded up to above her waist in exact centre of mound, Winnie. About fifty, well preserved, blond for preference, plump, arms and shoulders bare, low bodice, big bosom, pearl necklet. She is discovered sleeping, her arms on the ground before her, her head on her arms. Beside her on ground to her left a capacious black bag, shopping variety, and to her right a collapsible collapsed parasol, beak of handle emerging from sheath.*)

(*To her right and rear, lying asleep on ground, hidden by mound, Willie.*)

(*Long pause. A bell rings piercingly, say ten seconds, stops. She does not move. Pause. Bell more piercingly, say five seconds. She wakes. Bell stops. She raises her head, gazes front. Long pause. She straightens up, lays her hands flat on ground, throws back her head and gazes at zenith. Long pause.*)

WINNIE (*gazing at zenith*): Another heavenly day. (*Pause. Head back level, eyes front, pause. She clasps hands to breast, closes eyes. Lips move in inaudible prayer,*

pompier trompe-l'oeil: Crudely illusionistic.

say ten seconds. Lips still. Hands remain clasped. Low.) For Jesus Christ sake Amen. (*Eyes open, hands unclasp, return to mound. Pause. She clasps hands to breast again, closes eyes, lips move again in inaudible addendum, say five seconds. Low.*) World without end Amen. (*Eyes open, hands unclasp, return to mound. Pause.*) Begin, Winnie. (*Pause.*) Begin your day, Winnie. (*Pause. She turns to bag, rummages in it without moving it from its place, brings out toothbrush, rummages again, brings out flat tube of toothpaste, turns back front, unscrews cap of tube, lays cap on ground, squeezes with difficulty small blob of paste on brush, holds tube in one hand and brushes teeth with other. She turns modestly aside and back to her right to spit out behind mound. In this position her eyes rest on Willie. She spits out. She cranes a little further back and down. Loud.*) Hoo-oo! (*Pause. Louder.*) Hoo-oo! (*Pause. Tender smile as she turns back front, lays down brush.*) Poor Willie — (*examines tube, smile off*) — running out — (*looks for cap*) — ah well — (*finds cap*) — can't be helped — (*screws on cap*) — just one of those old things — (*lays down tube*) — another of those old things — (*turns toward bag*) — just can't be cured — (*rummages in bag*) — cannot be cured — (*brings out small mirror, turns back front*) — ah yes — (*inspects teeth in mirror*) — poor dear Willie — (*testing upper front teeth with thumb, indistinctly*) — good Lord! — (*pulling back upper lip to inspect gums, do.*) — good God! — (*pulling back corner of mouth, mouth open, do.*) — ah well — (*other corner, do.*) — no worse — (*abandons inspection, normal speech*) — no better, no worse — (*lays down mirror*) — no change — (*wipes fingers on grass*) — no pain — (*looks for toothbrush*) — hardly any — (*takes up toothbrush*) — great thing that — (*examines handle of brush*) —

nothing like it — (*examines handle, reads*) — pure . . . what? — (*pause*) — what? — (*lays down brush*) — ah yes — (*turns toward bag*) — poor Willie — (*rummages in bag*) — no zest — (*rummages*) — for anything — (*brings out spectacles in case*) — no interest — (*turns back front*) — in life — (*takes spectacles from case*) — poor dear Willie — (*lays down case*) — sleep forever — (*opens spectacles*) — marvelous gift — (*puts on spectacles*) — nothing to touch it — (*looks for toothbrush*) — in my opinion — (*takes up toothbrush*) — always said so — (*examines handle of brush*) — wish I had it — (*examines handle, reads*) — genuine . . . pure . . . what? — (*lays down brush*) — blind next — (*takes off spectacles*) — ah well — (*lays down spectacles*) — seen enough — (*feels in bodice for handkerchief*) — I suppose — (*takes out folded handkerchief*) — by now — (*shakes out handkerchief*) — what are those wonderful lines — (*wipes one eye*) — woe woe is me — (*wipes the other*) — to see what I see — (*looks for spectacles*) — ah yes — (*takes up spectacles*) — wouldn't miss it — (*starts polishing spectacles, breathing on lenses*) — or would I? — (*polishes*) — holy light — (*polishes*) — bob up out of dark — (*polishes*) — blaze of hellish light. (*Stops polishing, raises face to sky, pause, head back level, resumes polishing, stops polishing, cranes back to her right and down.*) Ho-ooo! (*Pause. Tender smile as she turns back front and resumes polishing. Smile off.*) Marvelous gift — (*stops polishing, lays down spectacles*) — wish I had it — (*folds handkerchief*) — ah well — (*puts handkerchief back in bodice*) — can't complain — (*looks for spectacles*) — no no — (*takes up spectacles*) — mustn't complain — (*holds up spectacles, looks through lens*) — so much to be thankful for — (*looks through other lens*) — no pain — (*puts on spectacles*) — hardly any — (*looks for toothbrush*) — wonderful thing that — (*takes up toothbrush*) — nothing like it — (*examines handle of brush*) — slight headache sometimes — (*examines handle, reads*) — guaranteed . . . genuine . . . pure . . . what? — (*looks closer*) — genuine pure . . . — (*takes handkerchief from bodice*) — ah yes — (*shakes out handkerchief*) — occasional mild migraine — (*starts wiping handle of brush*) — it comes — (*wipes*) — then goes — (*wiping mechanically*) — ah yes — (*wiping*) — many mercies — (*wiping*) — great mercies — (*stops wiping, fixed lost gaze, brokenly*) — prayers perhaps not for naught — (*pause, do.*) — first thing — (*pause, do.*) — last thing — (*head down, resumes wiping, stops wiping, head up, calmed, wipes eyes, folds handkerchief, puts it back in bodice, examines handle of brush, reads*) — fully guaranteed . . . genuine pure . . . — (*looks closer*) — genuine pure . . . (*Takes off spectacles, lays them and brush down, gazes before her.*) Old things. (*Pause.*) Old eyes. (*Long pause.*) On, Winnie. (*She casts about her, sees parasol, considers it at length, takes it up, and develops from sheath a handle of surprising length. Hold-*

ing butt of parasol in right hand she cranes back and down to her right to hang over Willie.) Hoo-oo! (*Pause.*) Willie! (*Pause.*) Wonderful gift. (*She strikes down at him with beak of parasol.*) Wish I had it. (*She strikes again. The parasol slips from her grasp and falls behind mound. It is immediately restored to her by Willie's invisible hand.*) Thank you, dear. (*She transfers parasol to left hand, turns back front and examines right palm.*) Damp. (*Returns parasol to right hand, examines left palm.*) Ah well, no worse. (*Head up, cheerfully.*) No better, no worse, no change. (*Pause. Do.*) No pain. (*Cranes back to look down at Willie, holding parasol by butt as before.*) Don't go off on me again now dear will you please, I may need you. (*Pause.*) No hurry, no hurry, just don't curl up on me again. (*Turns back front, lays down parasol, examines palms together, wipes them on grass.*) Perhaps a shade off color just the same. (*Turns to bag, rummages in it, brings out revolver, holds it up, kisses it rapidly, puts it back, rummages, brings out almost empty bottle of red medicine, turns back front, looks for spectacles, puts them on, reads label.*) Loss of spirits . . . lack of keenness . . . want of appetite . . . infants . . . children . . . adults . . . six level . . . tablespoonfuls daily — (*head up, smile*) — the old style! — (*smile off, head down, reads*) — daily . . . before and after . . . meals . . . instantaneous . . . (*looks closer*) . . . improvement. (*Takes off spectacles, lays them down, holds up bottle at arm's length to see level, unscrews cap, swigs it off head well back, tosses cap and bottle away in Willie's direction. Sound of breaking glass.*) Ah that's better! (*Turns to bag, rummages in it, brings out lipstick, turns back front, examines lipstick.*) Running out. (*Looks for spectacles.*) Ah well. (*Puts on spectacles, looks for mirror.*) Musn't complain. (*Takes up mirror, starts doing lips.*) What is that wonderful line? (*Lips.*) Oh fleeting joys — (*lips*) — oh something lasting woe. (*Lips. She is interrupted by disturbance from Willie. He is sitting up. She lowers lipstick and mirror and cranes back and down to look at him. Pause. Top back of Willie's bald head, trickling blood, rises to view above slope, comes to rest. Winnie pushes up her spectacles. Pause. His hand appears with handkerchief, spreads it on skull, disappears. Pause. The hand appears with boater, club ribbon, settles it on head, rakish angle, disappears. Pause. Winnie cranes a little further back and down.*) Slip on your drawers, dear, before you get singed. (*Pause.*) No? (*Pause.*) Oh I see, you still have some of that stuff left. (*Pause.*) Work it well in, dear. (*Pause.*) Now the other. (*Pause. She turns back front, gazes before her. Happy expression.*) Oh this is going to be another happy day! (*Pause. Happy expression off. She pulls down spectacles and resumes lips. Willie opens newspaper, hands invisible. Tops of yellow sheets appear on either side of his head. Winnie finishes lips, inspects them in mirror held a little further*

Estelle Parsons as Winnie in
the 1998–99 Hartford Stage
Company production of *Happy
Days,* directed by Richard
Block.

Willie (Frank Raiter) reaches
out to Winnie (Estelle Parsons),
now buried up to her neck, in
Richard Block's 1998–99
production.

away.) Ensign crimson. (*Willie turns page. Winnie lays down lipstick and mirror, turns toward bag.*) Pale flag.

(*Willie turns page. Winnie rummages in bag, brings out small ornate brimless hat with crumpled feather, turns back front, straightens hat, smoothes feather, raises it toward head, arrests gesture as Willie reads.*)

WILLIE: His Grace and Most Reverend Father in God Dr. Carolus Hunter dead in tub.

(*Pause.*)

WINNIE (*gazing front, hat in hand, tone of fervent reminiscence*): Charlie Hunter! (*Pause.*) I close my eyes — (*she takes off spectacles and does so, hat in one hand, spectacles in other, Willie turns page*) — and am sitting on his knees again, in the back garden at Borough Green, under the horse-beech. (*Pause. She opens eyes, puts on spectacles, fiddles with hat.*) Oh the happy memories!

(*Pause. She raises hat toward head, arrests gesture as Willie reads.*)

WILLIE: Opening for smart youth.

(*Pause. She raises hat toward head, arrests gesture, takes off spectacles, gazes front, hat in one hand, spectacles in other.*)

WINNIE: My first ball! (*Long pause.*) My second ball! (*Long pause. Closes eyes.*) My first kiss! (*Pause. Willie turns page. Winnie opens eyes.*) A Mr. Johnson, or Johnston, or perhaps I should say John*stone.* Very bushy mustache, very tawny. (*Reverently.*) Almost ginger! (*Pause.*) Within a toolshed, though whose I cannot conceive. We had no toolshed and he most certainly had no toolshed. (*Closes eyes.*) I see the piles of pots. (*Pause.*) The tangles of bast. (*Pause.*) The shadows deepening among the rafters.

(*Pause. She opens eyes, puts on spectacles, raises hat toward head, arrests gesture as Willie reads.*)

WILLIE: Wanted bright boy.

(*Pause. Winnie puts on hat hurriedly, looks for mirror. Willie turns page. Winnie takes up mirror, inspects hat, lays down mirror, turns toward bag. Paper disappears. Winnie rummages in bag, brings out magnifying-glass, turns back front, looks for toothbrush. Paper reappears, folded, and begins to fan Willie's face, hand invisible. Winnie takes up toothbrush and examines handle through glass.*)

WINNIE: Fully guaranteed . . . (*Willie stops fanning*) . . . genuine pure . . . (*Pause. Willie resumes fanning. Winnie looks closer, reads.*) Fully guaranteed . . . (*Willie stops fanning*) . . . genuine pure . . . (*Pause. Willie resumes fanning. Winnie lays down glass and brush, takes handkerchief from bodice, takes off and polishes spectacles, puts on spectacles, looks for glass, takes up and polishes glass, lays down glass,*

looks for brush, takes up brush and wipes handle, lays down brush, puts handkerchief back in bodice, looks for glass, takes up glass, looks for brush, takes up brush and examines handle through glass.*) Fully guaranteed . . . (*Willie stops fanning*) . . . genuine pure . . . (*pause, Willie resumes fanning*) . . . hog's (*Willie stops fanning, pause*) . . . setae.° (*Pause. Winnie lays down glass and brush, paper disappears, Winnie takes off spectacles, lays them down, gazes front.*) Hog's setae. (*Pause.*) That is what I find so wonderful, that not a day goes by — (*smile*) — to speak in the old style — (*smile off*) — hardly a day, without some addition to one's knowledge however trifling, the addition I mean, provided one takes the pains. (*Willie's hand reappears with a postcard which he examines close to eyes.*) And if for some strange reason no further pains are possible, why then just close the eyes — (*she does so*) — and wait for the day to come — (*opens eyes*) — the happy day to come when flesh melts at so many degrees and the night of the moon has so many hundred hours. (*Pause.*) That is what I find so comforting when I lose heart and envy the brute beast. (*Turning toward Willie.*) I hope you are taking in — (*She sees postcard, bends lower.*) What is that you have there, Willie, may I see? (*She reaches down with hand and Willie hands her card. The hairy forearm appears above slope, raised in gesture of giving, the hand open to take back, and remains in this position till card is returned. Winnie turns back front and examines card.*) Heavens what are they up to! (*She looks for spectacles, puts them on and examines card.*) No but this is just genuine pure filth! (*Examines card.*) Make any nice-minded person want to vomit! (*Impatience of Willie's fingers. She looks for glass, takes it up and examines card through glass. Long pause.*) What does that creature in the background think he's doing? (*Looks closer.*) Oh no really! (*Impatience of fingers. Last long look. She lays down glass, takes edge of card between right forefinger and thumb, averts head, takes nose between left forefinger and thumb.*) Pah! (*Drops card.*) Take it away! (*Willie's arm disappears. His hand reappears immediately, holding card. Winnie takes off spectacles, lays them down, gazes before her. During what follows Willie continues to relish card, varying angles and distance from his eyes.*) Hog's setae. (*Puzzled expression.*) What exactly is a hog? (*Pause. Do.*) A sow of course I know, but a hog . . . (*Puzzled expression off.*) Oh well what does it matter, that is what I always say, it will come back, that is what I find so wonderful, all comes back. (*Pause.*) All? (*Pause.*) No, not all. (*Smile.*) No no. (*Smile off.*) Not quite. (*Pause.*) A part. (*Pause.*) Floats up, one fine day, out of the blue. (*Pause.*) That is what I find so wonderful. (*Pause. She turns toward bag. Hand and card disappear. She makes to rummage in bag, arrests gesture.*)

---

setae: Body organs.

No. (*She turns back front. Smile.*) No no. (*Smile off.*) Gently Winnie. (*She gazes front. Willie's hand reappears, takes off hat, disappears with hat.*) What then? (*Hand reappears, takes handkerchief from skull, disappears with handkerchief. Sharply, as to one not paying attention.*) Winnie! (*Willie bows head out of sight.*) What *is* the alternative? (*Pause.*) What *is* the al — (*Willie blows nose loud and long, head and hands invisible. She turns to look at him. Pause. Head reappears. Pause. Hand reappears with handkerchief, spreads it on skull, disappears. Pause. Hand reappears with boater, settles it on head, rakish angle, disappears. Pause.*) Would I had let you sleep on. (*She turns back front. Intermittent plucking at grass, head up and down, to animate following.*) Ah yes, if only I could bear to be alone, I mean prattle away with not a soul to hear. (*Pause.*) Not that I flatter myself you hear much, no Willie, God forbid. (*Pause.*) Days perhaps when you hear nothing. (*Pause.*) But days too when you answer. (*Pause.*) So that I may say at all times, even when you do not answer and perhaps hear nothing, something of this is being heard, I am not merely talking to myself, that is in the wilderness, a thing I could never bear to do — for any length of time. (*Pause.*) That is what enables me to go on, go on talking that is. (*Pause.*) Whereas if you were to die — (*smile*) — to speak in the old style — (*smile off*) — or go away and leave me, then what would I do, what *could* I do, all day long, I mean between the bell for waking and the bell for sleep? (*Pause.*) Simply gaze before me with compressed lips. (*Long pause while she does so. No more plucking.*) Not another word as long as I drew breath, nothing to break the silence of this place. (*Pause.*) Save possibly, now and then, every now and then, a sigh into my looking-glass. (*Pause.*) Or a brief . . . gale of laughter, should I happen to see the old joke again. (*Pause. Smile appears, broadens and seems about to culminate in laugh when suddenly replaced by expression of anxiety.*) My hair! (*Pause.*) Did I brush and comb my hair? (*Pause.*) I may have done. (*Pause.*) Normally I do. (*Pause.*) There is so little one *can* do. (*Pause.*) One does it all. (*Pause.*) All one can. (*Pause.*) Tis only human. (*Pause.*) Human nature. (*She begins to inspect mound, looks up.*) Human weakness. (*She resumes inspection of mound, looks up.*) Natural weakness. (*She resumes inspection of mound.*) I see no comb. (*Inspects.*) Nor any hairbrush. (*Looks up. Puzzled expression. She turns to bag, rummages in it.*) The comb is here. (*Back front. Puzzled expression. Back to bag. Rummages.*) The brush is here. (*Back front. Puzzled expression.*) Perhaps I put them back, after use. (*Pause. Do.*) But normally I do not put things back, after use, no, I leave them lying about and put them back all together, at the end of the day. (*Smile.*) To speak in the old style. (*Pause.*) The sweet old style. (*Smile off.*) And yet . . . I seem . . . to remember . . . (*Suddenly careless.*) Oh well, what does it matter,

that is what I always say, I shall simply brush and comb them later on, purely and simply, I have the whole — (*Pause. Puzzled.*) Them? (*Pause.*) Or it? (*Pause.*) Brush and comb it? (*Pause.*) Sounds improper somehow. (*Pause. Turning a little toward Willie.*) What would you say, Willie? (*Pause. Turning a little further.*) What would you say, Willie, speaking of your hair, them or it? (*Pause.*) The hair on your head, I mean. (*Pause. Turning a little further.*) The hair on your head, Willie, what would you say speaking of the hair on your head, them or it?

(*Long pause.*)

WILLIE: It.

WINNIE (*turning back front, joyful*): Oh you are going to talk to me today, this is going to be a happy day! (*Pause. Joy off.*) Another happy day. (*Pause.*) Ah well, where was I, my hair, yes, later on, I shall be thankful for it later on. (*Pause.*) I have my — (*raises hands to hat*) — yes, on, my hat on — (*lowers hands*) — I cannot take it off now. (*Pause.*) To think there are times one cannot take off one's hat, not if one's life were at stake. Times one cannot put it on, times one cannot take it off. (*Pause.*) How often I have said, Put on your hat now, Winnie, there is nothing else for it, take off your hat now, Winnie, like a good girl, it will do you good, and did not. (*Pause.*) Could not. (*Pause. She raises hand, frees a strand of hair from under hat, draws it toward eye, squints at it, lets it go, hand down.*) Golden you called it, that day, when the last guest was gone — (*hand up in gesture of raising a glass*) — to your golden . . . may it never (*voice breaks*) . . . may it never . . . (*Hand down. Head down. Pause. Low.*) That day. (*Pause. Do.*) What day? (*Pause. Head up. Normal voice.*) What now? (*Pause.*) Words fail, there are times when even they fail. (*Turning a little toward Willie.*) Is that not so, Willie? (*Pause. Turning a little further.*) Is not that so, Willie, that even words fail, at times? (*Pause. Back front.*) What is one to do then, until they come again? Brush and comb the hair, if it has not been done, or if there is some doubt, trim the nails if they are in need of trimming, these things tide one over. (*Pause.*) That is what I mean. (*Pause.*) That is all I mean. (*Pause.*) That is what I find so wonderful, that not a day goes by — (*smile*) — to speak in the old style — (*smile off*) — without some blessing — (*Willie collapses behind slope, his head disappears, Winnie turns toward event*) — in disguise. (*She cranes back and down.*) Go back into your hole now, Willie, you've exposed yourself enough. (*Pause.*) Do as I say, Willie, don't lie sprawling there in this hellish sun, go back into your hole. (*Pause.*) Go on now, Willie. (*Willie invisible starts crawling left toward hole.*) That's the man. (*She follows his progress with her eyes.*) Not head first, stupid, how are you going to turn? (*Pause.*) That's it . . . right round . . . now . . . back in. (*Pause.*) Oh I know it is not easy, dear, crawling backwards, but it is rewarding in the end. (*Pause.*) You have left your vaseline behind. (*She watches as he crawls back for vaseline.*) The lid! (*She watches as he crawls back toward hole. Irritated.*) Not head first, I tell you! (*Pause.*) More to the right. (*Pause.*) The right, I said. (*Pause. Irritated.*) Keep your tail down, can't you! (*Pause.*) Now. (*Pause.*) There! (*All these directions loud. Now in her normal voice, still turned toward him.*) Can you hear me? (*Pause.*) I beseech you, Willie, just yes or no, can you hear me, just yes or nothing.

(*Pause.*)

WILLIE: Yes.
WINNIE (*turning front, same voice*): And now?
WILLIE (*irritated*): Yes.
WINNIE (*less loud*): And now?
WILLIE (*more irritated*): Yes.
WINNIE (*still less loud*): And now? (*A little louder.*) And now?
WILLIE (*violently*): Yes!
WINNIE (*same voice*): Fear no more the heat o' the sun. (*Pause.*) Did you hear that?
WILLIE (*irritated*): Yes.
WINNIE (*same voice*): What? (*Pause.*) What?
WILLIE (*more irritated*): Fear no more.

(*Pause.*)

WINNIE (*same voice*): No more what? (*Pause.*) Fear no more what?
WILLIE (*violently*): Fear no more!
WINNIE (*normal voice, gabbled*): Bless you Willie I do appreciate your goodness I know what an effort it costs you, now you may relax I shall not trouble you again unless I am obliged to, by that I mean unless I come to the end of my own resources which is most unlikely, just to know that in theory you can hear me even though in fact you don't is all I need, just to feel you there within earshot and conceivably on the qui vive° is all I ask, not to say anything I would not wish you to hear or liable to cause you pain, not to be just babbling away on trust as it were not knowing and something gnawing at me. (*Pause for breath.*) Doubt. (*Places index and second finger on heart area, moves them about, brings them to rest.*) Here. (*Moves them slightly.*) Abouts. (*Hand away.*) Oh no doubt the time will come when before I can utter a word I must make sure you heard the one that went before and then no doubt another come another time when I must learn to talk to myself a thing I could never bear to do such wilderness. (*Pause.*) Or gaze before me with compressed lips. (*She does so.*) All day long. (*Gaze and lips again.*) No. (*Smile.*) No no. (*Smile off.*) There is of course the bag. (*Turns toward it.*) There will always be the bag. (*Back front.*) Yes, I suppose so. (*Pause.*) Even when you are gone, Willie.

on the qui vive: On the alert, on the lookout.

(*She turns a little toward him.*) You are going, Willie, aren't you? (*Pause. Louder.*) You *will* be going soon, Willie, won't you? (*Pause. Louder.*) Willie! (*Pause. She cranes back and down to look at him.*) So you have taken off your straw, that is wise. (*Pause.*) You do look snug, I must say, with your chin on your hands and the old blue eyes like saucers in the shadows. (*Pause.*) Can you see me from there I wonder, I still wonder. (*Pause.*) No? (*Back front.*) Oh I know it does not follow when two are gathered together — (*faltering*) — in this way — (*normal*) — that because one sees the other the other sees the one, life has taught me that . . . too. (*Pause.*) Yes, life I suppose, there is no other word. (*She turns a little toward him.*) Could you see me, Willie, do you think, from where you are, if you were to raise your eyes in my direction? (*Turns a little further.*) Lift up your eyes to me, Willie, and tell me can you see me, do that for me, I'll lean back as far as I can. (*Does so. Pause.*) No? (*Pause.*) Well never mind. (*Turns back painfully front.*) The earth is very tight today, can it be I have put on flesh, I trust not. (*Pause. Absently, eyes lowered.*) The great heat possibly. (*Starts to pat and stroke ground.*) All things expanding, some more than others. (*Pause. Patting and stroking.*) Some less. (*Pause. Do.*) Oh I can well imagine what is passing through your mind, it is not enough to have to listen to the woman, now I must look at her as well. (*Pause. Do.*) Well it is very understandable. (*Pause. Do.*) Most understandable. (*Pause. Do.*) One does not appear to be asking a great deal, indeed at times it would seem hardly possible — (*voice breaks, falls to a murmur*) — to ask less — of a fellow creature — to put it mildly — whereas actually — when you think about it — look into your heart — see the other — what he needs — peace — to be left in peace — then perhaps the moon — all this time — asking for the moon. (*Pause. Stroking hand suddenly still. Lively.*) Oh I say, what have we here? (*Bending head to ground, incredulous.*) Looks like life of some kind! (*Looks for spectacles, puts them on, bends closer. Pause.*) An emmet! (*Recoils. Shrill.*) Willie, an emmet, a live emmet! (*Seizes magnifying glass, bends to ground again, inspects through glass.*) Where's it gone? (*Inspects.*) Ah! (*Follows its progress through grass.*) Has like a little white ball in its arms. (*Follows progress. Hand still. Pause.*) It's gone in. (*Continues a moment to gaze at spot through glass, then slowly straightens up, lays down glass, takes off spectacles and gazes before her, spectacles in hand. Finally.*) Like a little white ball.

(*Long pause. Gesture to lay down spectacles.*)

WILLIE: Eggs.
WINNIE (*arresting gesture*): What?

(*Pause.*)

WILLIE: Eggs. (*Pause. Gesture to lay down glasses.*) Formication.

WINNIE (*arresting gesture*): What?

(*Pause.*)

WILLIE: Formication.

(*Pause. She lays down spectacles, gazes before her. Finally.*)

WINNIE (*murmur*): God. (*Pause. Willie laughs quietly. After a moment she joins in. They laugh quietly together. Willie stops. She laughs on a moment alone. Willie joins in. They laugh together. She stops. Willie laughs on a moment alone. He stops. Pause. Normal voice.*) Ah well what a joy in any case to hear you laugh again, Willie, I was convinced I never would, you never would. (*Pause.*) I suppose some people might think us a trifle irreverent, but I doubt it. (*Pause.*) How can one better magnify the Almighty than by sniggering with him at his little jokes, particularly the poorer ones? (*Pause.*) I think you would back me up there, Willie. (*Pause.*) Or were we perhaps diverted by two quite different things? (*Pause.*) Oh well, what does it matter, that is what I always say, so long as one . . . you know . . . what is that wonderful line . . . laughing wild . . . something something laughing wild amid severest woe (*Pause.*) And now? (*Long pause.*) Was I lovable once, Willie? (*Pause.*) Was I ever lovable? (*Pause.*) Do not misunderstand my question, I am not asking you if you loved me, we know all about that, I am asking you if you found me lovable — at one stage. (*Pause.*) No? (*Pause.*) You can't? (*Pause.*) Well I admit it is a teaser. And you have done more than your bit already, for the time being, just lie back now and relax, I shall not trouble you again unless I am compelled to, just to know you are there within hearing and conceivably on the semi-alert is . . . er . . . paradise enow. (*Pause.*) The day is now well advanced. (*Smile.*) To speak in the old style. (*Smile off.*) And yet it is perhaps a little soon for my song. (*Pause.*) To sing too soon is a great mistake, I find. (*Turning toward bag.*) There is of course the bag. (*Looking at bag.*) The bag. (*Back front.*) Could I enumerate its contents? (*Pause.*) No. (*Pause.*) Could I, if some kind person were to come along and ask, What all have you got in that big black bag, Winnie? give an exhaustive answer? (*Pause.*) No. (*Pause.*) The depths in particular, who knows what treasures. (*Pause.*) What comforts. (*Turns to look at bag.*) Yes, there is the bag. (*Back front.*) But something tells me. Do not overdo the bag, Winnie, make use of it of course, let it help you . . . along, when stuck, by all means, but cast your mind forward, something tells me, cast your mind forward, Winnie, to the time when words must fail — (*she closes eyes, pause, opens eyes*) — and do not overdo the bag. (*Pause. She turns to look at bag.*) Perhaps just one quick dip. (*She turns back front, closes eyes, throws out left arm, plunges hand in bag and brings out revolver. Disgusted.*) You again! (*She opens eyes, brings revolver front and contemplates it.*

Samuel Beckett himself directed this 1979 production of *Happy Days* for the Royal Court Theatre in London. Winnie is played by Billie Whitelaw.

She weighs it in her palm.) You'd think the weight of this thing would bring it down among the . . . last rounds. But no. It doesn't. Ever uppermost, like Browning. (*Pause.*) Brownie . . . (*Turning a little toward Willie.*) Remember Brownie, Willie? (*Pause.*) Remember how you used to keep on at me to take it away from you? Take it away, Winnie, take it away, before I put myself out of my misery. (*Back front. Derisive.*) *Your* misery! (*To revolver.*) Oh I suppose it's a comfort to know you're there, but I'm tired of you. (*Pause.*) I'll leave you out, that's what I'll do. (*She lays revolver on ground to her right.*) There, that's your home from this day out. (*Smile.*) The old style! (*Smile off.*) And now? (*Long pause.*) Is gravity what it was, Willie, I fancy not. (*Pause.*) Yes, the feeling more and more that if I were not held — (*gesture*) — in this way, I would simply float up into the blue. (*Pause.*) And that perhaps some day the earth will yield and let me go, the pull is so great, yes, crack all round me and let me out. (*Pause.*) Don't you ever have that feeling, Willie, of being sucked up? (*Pause.*)

Don't you have to cling on sometimes, Willie? (*Pause. She turns a little toward him.*) Willie.

(*Pause.*)

WILLIE: Sucked up?

WINNIE: Yes love, up into the blue, like gossamer. (*Pause.*) No? (*Pause.*) You don't? (*Pause.*) Ah well, natural laws, natural laws, I suppose it's like everything else, it all depends on the creature you happen to be. All I can say for my part is that for me they are not what they were when I was young and . . . foolish and . . . (*faltering, head down*) . . . beautiful . . . possibly . . . lovely . . . in a way . . . to look at. (*Pause. Head up.*) Forgive me, Willie, sorrow keeps breaking in. (*Normal voice.*) Ah well what a joy in any case to know you are there, as usual, and perhaps awake, and perhaps taking all this in, some of all this, what a happy day for me . . . it will have been. (*Pause.*) So far. (*Pause.*) What a blessing nothing grows, imagine if all this stuff were to start growing. (*Pause.*) Imagine. (*Pause.*) Ah yes, great mercies. (*Long pause.*) I can say no more. (*Pause.*) For the moment. (*Pause. Turns to look at bag. Back front. Smile.*) No no. (*Smile off. Looks at parasol.*) I suppose I might — (*takes up parasol*) — yes, I suppose I might . . . hoist this thing now. (*Begins to unfurl it. Following punctuated by mechanical difficulties overcome.*) One keeps putting off — putting up — for fear of putting up — too soon — and the day goes by — quite by — without one's having put up — at all. (*Parasol now fully open. Turned to her right she twirls it idly this way and that.*) Ah yes, so little to say, so little to do, and the fear so great, certain days, of finding oneself . . . left, with hours still to run, before the bell for sleep, and nothing more to say, nothing more to do, that the days go by, certain days go by, quite by, the bell goes, and little or nothing said, little or nothing done. (*Raising parasol.*) That is the danger. (*Turning front.*) To be guarded against. (*She gazes front, holding up parasol with right hand. Maximum pause.*) I used to perspire freely. (*Pause.*) Now hardly at all. (*Pause.*) The heat is much greater. (*Pause.*) The perspiration much less. (*Pause.*) That is what I find so wonderful. (*Pause.*) The way man adapts himself. (*Pause.*) To changing conditions. (*She transfers parasol to left hand. Long pause.*) Holding up wearies the arm. (*Pause.*) Not if one is going along. (*Pause.*) Only if one is at rest. (*Pause.*) That is a curious observation. (*Pause.*) I hope you heard that, Willie, I should be grieved to think you had not heard that. (*She takes parasol in both hands. Long pause.*) I am weary, holding it up, and I cannot put it down. (*Pause.*) I am worse off with it up than with it down, and I cannot put it down. (*Pause.*) Reason says, Put it down, Winnie, it is not helping you, put the thing down and get on with something else. (*Pause.*) I cannot. (*Pause.*) I cannot move. (*Pause.*) No, something must happen, in the world, take place, some change, I cannot, if I am to move again.

(*Pause.*) Willie. (*Mildly.*) Help. (*Pause.*) No? (*Pause.*) Bid me put this thing down, Willie, I would obey you instantly, as I have always done, honored and obeyed. (*Pause.*) Please, Willie. (*Mildly.*) For pity's sake. (*Pause.*) No? (*Pause.*) You can't? (*Pause.*) Well I don't blame you, no, it would ill become me, who cannot move, to blame my Willie because he cannot speak. (*Pause.*) Fortunately I am in tongue again. (*Pause.*) That is what I find so wonderful, my two lamps, when one goes out the other burns brighter. (*Pause.*) Oh yes, great mercies. (*Maximum pause. The parasol goes on fire. Smoke, flames if feasible. She sniffs, looks up, throws parasol to her right behind mound, cranes back to watch it burning. Pause.*) Ah earth you old extinguisher. (*Back front.*) I presume this has occurred before, though I cannot recall it. (*Pause.*) Can you, Willie? (*Turns a little toward him.*) Can you recall this having occurred before? (*Pause. Cranes back to look at him.*) Do you know what has occurred, Willie? (*Pause.*) Have you gone off on me again? (*Pause.*) I do not ask if you are alive to all that is going on, I merely ask if you have not gone off on me again. (*Pause.*) Your eyes appear to be closed, but that has no particular significance we know. (*Pause.*) Raise a finger, dear, will you please, if you are not quite senseless. (*Pause.*) Do that for me, Willie please, just the little finger, if you are still conscious. (*Pause. Joyful.*) Oh all five, you are a darling today, now I may continue with an easy mind. (*Back front.*) Yes, what ever occurred that did not occur before and yet . . . I wonder, yes, I confess I wonder. (*Pause.*) With the sun blazing so much fiercer down, and hourly fiercer, is it not natural things should go on fire never known to do so, in this way I mean, spontaneous like. (*Pause.*) Shall I myself not melt perhaps in the end, or burn, oh I do not mean necessarily burst into flames, no, just little by little be charred to a black cinder, all this — (*ample gesture of arms*) — visible flesh. (*Pause.*) On the other hand, did I ever know a temperate time? (*Pause.*) No. (*Pause.*) I speak of temperate times and torrid times, they are empty words. (*Pause.*) I speak of when I was not yet caught — in this way — and had my legs and had the use of my legs, and could seek out a shady place, like you, when I was tired of the sun, or a sunny place when I was tired of the shade, like you, and they are all empty words. (*Pause.*) It is no hotter today than yesterday, it will be no hotter tomorrow than today, how could it, and so on back into the far past, forward into the far future. (*Pause.*) And should one day the earth cover my breasts, then I shall never have seen my breasts, no one ever seen my breasts. (*Pause.*) I hope you caught something of that, Willie, I should be sorry to think you had caught nothing of all that, it is not every day I rise to such heights. (*Pause.*) Yes, something seems to have occurred, something has seemed to occur, and nothing has occurred, nothing at all, you are quite right, Willie. (*Pause.*) The sunshade will be

there again tomorrow, beside me on this mound, to
help me through the day. (*Pause. She takes up mirror.*) I take up this little glass, I shiver it on a stone —
(*does so*) — I throw it away — (*does so far behind
her*) — it will be in the bag again tomorrow, without
a scratch, to help me through the day. (*Pause.*) No,
one can do nothing. (*Pause.*) That is what I find so
wonderful, the way things . . . (*voice breaks, head
down*) . . . things . . . so wonderful. (*Long pause,
head down. Finally turns, still bowed, to bag, brings
out unidentifiable odds and ends, stuffs them back,
fumbles deeper, brings out finally musical-box, winds
it up, turns it on, listens for a moment holding it in
both hands, huddled over it, turns back front,
straightens up and listens to tune, holding box to
breast with both hands. It plays the Waltz Duet "I
love you so" from* The Merry Widow. *Gradually
happy expression. She sways to the rhythm. Music
stops. Pause. Brief burst of hoarse song without
words — musical-box tune — from Willie. Increase
of happy expression. She lays down box.*) Oh this
will have been a happy day! (*She claps hands.*) Again,
Willie, again! (*Claps.*) Encore, Willie, please! (*Pause.
Happy expression off.*) No? You won't do that for
me? (*Pause.*) Well it is very understandable, very
understandable. One cannot sing just to please someone, however much one loves them, no, song must
come from the heart, that is what I always say, pour
out from the inmost, like a thrush. (*Pause.*) How
often I have said, in evil hours, Sing now, Winnie,
sing your song, there is nothing else for it, and did
not. (*Pause.*) Could not. (*Pause.*) No, like the thrush,
or the bird of dawning, with no thought of benefit, to
oneself or anyone else. (*Pause.*) And now? (*Long
pause. Low.*) Strange feeling. (*Pause. Do.*) Strange
feeling that someone is looking at me. I am clear, then
dim, then gone, then dim again, then clear again, and
so on, back and forth, in and out of someone's eye.
(*Pause. Do.*) Strange? (*Pause. Do.*) No, here all is
strange. (*Pause. Normal voice.*) Something says, Stop
talking now, Winnie, for a minute, don't squander all
your words for the day, stop talking and do something for a change, will you? (*She raises hands and
holds them open before her eyes. Apostrophic.*) Do
something! (*She closes hands.*) What claws! (*She
turns to bag, rummages in it, brings out finally a nail-
file, turns back front and begins to file nails. Files for
a time in silence, then the following punctuated by
filing.*) There floats up — into my thoughts — a Mr.
Shower — a Mr. and perhaps a Mrs. Shower — no
— they are holding hands — his fiancée then more
likely — or just some — loved one. (*Looks closer at
nails.*) Very brittle today. (*Resumes filing.*) Shower —
Shower — does the name mean anything — to you,
Willie — evoke any reality, I mean — for you, Willie
— don't answer if you don't — feel up to it — you
have done more — than your bit — already —
Shower — Shower. (*Inspects filed nails.*) Bit more
like it. (*Raises head, gazes front.*) Keep yourself nice,

Winnie, that's what I always say, come what may,
keep yourself nice. (*Pause. Resumes filing.*) Yes —
Shower — Shower — (*stops filing, raises head, gazes
front, pause*) — or Cooker, perhaps I should say
Cooker. (*Turning a little toward Willie.*) Cooker,
Willie, does Cooker strike a chord? (*Pause. Turns a
little further. Louder.*) Cooker, Willie, does Cooker
ring a bell, the name Cooker? (*Pause. She cranes
back to look at him. Pause.*) Oh really! (*Pause.*) Have
you no handkerchief, darling? (*Pause.*) Have you no
delicacy? (*Pause.*) Oh, Willie, you're not eating it!
Spit it out, dear, spit it out! (*Pause. Back front.*) Ah
well, I suppose it's only natural. (*Break in voice.*)
Human. (*Pause. Do.*) What is one to do? (*Head
down. Do.*) All day long. (*Pause. Do.*) Day after
day. (*Pause. Head up. Smile. Calm.*) The old style!
(*Smile off. Resumes nails.*) No, done him. (*Passes on
to next.*) Should have put on my glasses. (*Pause.*)
Too late now. (*Finishes left hand, inspects it.*) Bit
more human. (*Starts right hand. Following punctuated as before.*) Well anyway — this man Shower —
or Cooker — no matter — and the woman — hand
in hand — in the other hands bags — kind of big
brown grips — standing there gaping at me — and at
last this man Shower — or Cooker — ends in er anyway — stake my life on that — What's she doing? he
says — What's the idea? he says — stuck up to her
diddies in the bleeding ground — coarse fellow —
What does it mean? he says — What's it meant to
mean? — and so on — lot more stuff like that —
usual drivel — Do you hear me? he says — I do, she
says, God help me — What do you mean, he says,
God help you? (*Stops filing, raises head, gazes front.*)
And you, she says, what's the idea of you, she says,
what are you meant to mean? It is because you're still
on your two flat feet, with your old ditty full of
tinned muck and changes of underwear, dragging me
up and down this fornicating wilderness, coarse creature, fit mate — (*with sudden violence*) — let go of
my hand and drop for God's sake, she says, drop!
(*Pause. Resumes filing.*) Why doesn't he dig her out?
he says — referring to you, my dear — What good is
she to him like that? — What good is he to her like
that? — and so on — usual tosh — Good! she says,
have a heart for God's sake — Dig her out, he says,
dig her out, no sense in her like that — Dig her out
with what? she says — I'd dig her out with my bare
hands, he says — must have been man and — wife.
(*Files in silence.*) Next thing they're away — hand in
hand — and the bags — dim — then gone — last
human kind — to stray this way. (*Finishes right
hand, inspects it, lays down file, gazes front.*) Strange
thing, time like this, drift up into the mind. (*Pause.*)
Strange? (*Pause.*) No, here all is strange. (*Pause.*)
Thankful for it in any case. (*Voice breaks.*) Most
thankful. (*Head down. Pause. Head up. Calm.*) Bow
and raise the head, bow and raise, always that.
(*Pause.*) And now? (*Long pause. Starts putting things
back in bag, toothbrush last. This operation, inter-

rupted by pauses as indicated, punctuates following.) It is perhaps a little soon — to make ready — for the night — (stops tidying, head up, smile) — the old style! — (smile off, resumes tidying) — and yet I do — make ready for the night — feeling it at hand — the bell for sleep — saying to myself — Winnie — it will not be long now, Winnie — until the bell for sleep. (Stops tidying, head up.) Sometimes I am wrong. (Smile.) But not often. (Smile off.) Sometimes all is over, for the day, all done, all said, all ready for the night, and the day not over, far from over, the night not ready, far, far from ready. (Smile.) But not often. (Smile off.) Yes, the bell for sleep when I feel it at hand, and so make ready for the night — (gesture) — in this way, sometimes I am wrong — (smile) — but not often. (Smile off. Resumes tidying.) I used to think — I say I used to think — that all these things — put back into the bag — if too soon — put back too soon — could be taken out again — if necessary — if needed — and so on — indefinitely — back into the bag — back out of the bag — until the bell — went. (Stops tidying, head up, smile.) But no. (Smile broader.) No no. (Smile off. Resumes tidying.) I suppose this — might seem strange — this — what shall I say — this what I have said — yes — (she takes up revolver) — strange — (she turns to put revolver in bag) — were it not — (about to put revolver in bag she arrests gesture and turns back front) — were it not — (she lays down revolver to her right, stops tidying, head up) — that all seems strange. (Pause.) Most strange. (Pause.) Never any change. (Pause.) And more and more strange. (Pause. She bends to mound again, takes up last object, i.e., toothbrush, and turns to put it in bag when her attention is drawn to disturbance from Willie. She cranes back and to her right to see. Pause.) Weary of your hole, dear? (Pause.) Well I can understand that. (Pause.) Don't forget your straw. (Pause.) Not the crawler you were, poor darling. (Pause.) No, not the crawler I gave my heart to. (Pause.) The hands and knees, love, try the hands and knees. (Pause.) The knees! The knees! (Pause.) What a curse, mobility! (She follows with eyes his progress toward her behind mound, i.e., toward place he occupied at beginning of act.) Another foot, Willie, and you're home. (Pause as she observes last foot.) Ah! (Turns back front laboriously, rubs neck.) Crick in my neck admiring you. (Rubs neck.) But it's (Long pause.) worth it, well worth it. (Turning slightly toward him.) Do you know what I dream sometimes? (Pause.) What I dream sometimes, Willie. (Pause.) That you'll come round and live this side where I could see you. (Pause. Back front.) I'd be a different woman. (Pause.) Unrecognizable. (Turning slightly toward him.) Or just now and then, come round this side just every now and then and let me feast on you. (Back front.) But you can't, I know. (Head down.) I know. (Pause. Head up.) Well anyway — (looks at toothbrush in her hand) — can't be long now —

(looks at brush) — until the bell. (Top back of Willie's head appears above slope. Winnie looks closer at brush.) Fully guaranteed . . . (head up) . . . what's this it was? (Willie's hand appears with handkerchief, spreads it on skull, disappears.) Genuine pure . . . fully guaranteed . . . (Willie's hand appears with boater, settles it on head, rakish angle, disappears) . . . genuine pure . . . ah! hog's setae. (Pause.) What is a hog exactly? (Pause. Turns slightly toward Willie.) What exactly is a hog, Willie, do you know, I can't remember. (Pause. Turning a little further, pleading.) What is a hog, Willie, please!

(Pause.)

WILLIE: Castrated male swine. (Happy expression appears on Winnie's face.) Reared for slaughter.

(Happy expression increases. Willie opens newspaper, hands invisible. Tops of yellow sheets appear on either side of his head. Winnie gazes before her with happy expression.)

WINNIE: Oh this is a happy day! This will have been another happy day! (Pause.) After all. (Pause.) So far.

(Pause. Happy expression off. Willie turns page. Pause. He turns another page. Pause.)

WILLIE: Opening for smart youth.

(Pause. Winnie takes off hat, turns to put it in bag, arrests gesture, turns back front. Smile.)

WINNIE: No. (Smile broader.) No no. (Smile off. Puts on hat again, gazes front, pause.) And now? (Pause.) Sing. (Pause.) Sing your song, Winnie. (Pause.) No? (Pause.) Then pray. (Pause.) Pray your prayer, Winnie.

(Pause. Willie turns page. Pause.)

WILLIE: Wanted bright boy.

(Pause. Winnie gazes before her. Willie turns page. Pause. Newspaper disappears. Long pause.)

WINNIE: Pray your old prayer, Winnie.

(Long pause.)

ACT II

(Scene as before.)

(Winnie imbedded up to neck, hat on head, eyes closed. Her head, which she can no longer turn, nor bow, nor raise, faces front motionless throughout act. Movements of eyes as indicated.)

(Bag and parasol as before. Revolver conspicuous to her right on mound.)

(Long pause.)

(Bell rings loudly. She opens eyes at once. Bell stops. She gazes front. Long pause.)

WINNIE: Hail, holy light. (Long pause. She closes her eyes. Bell rings loudly. She opens eyes at once. Bell

Legendary British director Peter Brook staged this 1997 production of *Happy Days* for Riverside Studios in London. Natasha Parry and Jean-Claude Perrin played Winnie and Willie.

stops. She gazes front. Long smile. Smile off. Long pause.) Someone is looking at me still. (*Pause.*) Caring for me still. (*Pause.*) That is what I find so wonderful. (*Pause.*) Eyes on my eyes. (*Pause.*) What is that unforgettable line? (*Pause. Eyes right.*) Willie. (*Pause. Louder.*) Willie. (*Pause. Eyes front.*) May one still speak of time? (*Pause.*) Say it is a long time now, Willie, since I saw you. (*Pause.*) Since I heard you. (*Pause.*) May one? (*Pause.*) One does. (*Smile.*) The old style! (*Smile off.*) There is so little one can speak of. (*Pause.*) One speaks of it all. (*Pause.*) All one can. (*Pause.*) I used to think . . . (*pause*) . . . I say I used to think that I would learn to talk alone. (*Pause.*) By that I mean to myself, the wilderness. (*Smile.*) But no. (*Smile broader.*) No no. (*Smile off.*) Ergo° you are there. (*Pause.*) Oh no doubt you are dead, like the others, no doubt you have died, or gone away and left me, like the others, it doesn't matter, you are there. (*Pause. Eyes left.*) The bag too is there, the same as ever, I can see it. (*Pause. Eyes right. Louder.*) The bag is there, Willie, as good as ever, the one you gave me that day . . . to go to market. (*Pause. Eyes front.*) That day. (*Pause.*) What day? (*Pause.*) I used to pray. (*Pause.*) I say I used to pray. (*Pause.*) Yes, I must confess I did. (*Smile.*) Not now. (*Smile broader.*) No no. (*Smile off. Pause.*) Then . . . now . . . what difficulties here, for the mind. (*Pause.*) To have been always what I am — and so changed from what I was. (*Pause.*) I am the one, I say the one, then the other. (*Pause.*) Now the one, then the other. (*Pause.*) There is so little one can say, one says it all. (*Pause.*) All one can. (*Pause.*) And no truth in it anywhere. (*Pause.*) My arms. (*Pause.*) My breasts. (*Pause.*)

Ergo: Latin for "therefore."

What arms? (*Pause.*) What breasts? (*Pause.*) Willie. (*Pause.*) What Willie? (*Sudden vehement affirmation.*) My Willie! (*Eyes right, calling.*) Willie! (*Pause. Louder.*) Willie! (*Pause. Eyes front.*) Ah well, not to know, not to know for sure, great mercy, all I ask. (*Pause.*) Ah yes . . . then . . . now . . . beechen green . . . this . . . Charlie . . . kisses . . . this . . . all that . . . deep trouble for the mind. (*Pause.*) But it does not trouble mine. (*Smile.*) Not now. (*Smile broader.*) No no. (*Smile off. Long pause. She closes eyes. Bell rings loudly. She opens eyes. Pause.*) Eyes float up that seem to close in peace . . . to see . . . in peace. (*Pause.*) Not mine. (*Smile.*) Not now. (*Smile broader.*) No no. (*Smile off. Long pause.*) Willie. (*Pause.*) Do you think the earth has lost its atmosphere, Willie? (*Pause.*) Do you, Willie? (*Pause.*) You have no opinion? (*Pause.*) Well that is like you, you never had any opinion about anything. (*Pause.*) It's understandable. (*Pause.*) Most. (*Pause.*) The earth-ball. (*Pause.*) I sometimes wonder. (*Pause.*) Perhaps not quite all. (*Pause.*) There always remains something. (*Pause.*) Of everything. (*Pause.*) Some remains. (*Pause.*) If the mind were to go. (*Pause.*) It won't of course. (*Pause.*) Not quite. (*Pause.*) Not mine. (*Smile.*) Not now. (*Smile broader.*) No no. (*Smile off. Long pause.*) It might be the eternal cold. (*Pause.*) Everlasting perishing cold. (*Pause.*) Just chance, I take it, happy chance. (*Pause.*) Oh yes, great mercies, great mercies. (*Pause.*) And now? (*Long pause.*) The face. (*Pause.*) The nose. (*She squints down.*) I can see it . . . (*squinting down*) . . . the tip . . . the nostrils . . . breath of life . . . that curve you so admired . . . (*pouts*) . . . a hint of lip . . . (*pouts again*) . . . if I pout them out . . . (*sticks out tongue*) . . . the tongue of course . . . you so admired . . . if I stick it out . . . (*sticks it out again*) . . . the tip . . . (*eyes up*) . . . suspicion of brow . . . eyebrow . . . imagination possibly . . . (*eyes left*) . . . cheek . . . no . . . (*eyes right*) . . . no . . . (*distends cheeks*) . . . even if I puff them out . . . (*eyes left, distends cheeks again*) . . . no . . . no damask. (*Eyes front.*) That is all. (*Pause.*) The bag of course . . . (*eyes left*) . . . a little blurred perhaps . . . but the bag. (*Eyes front. Offhand.*) The earth of course and sky. (*Eyes right.*) The sunshade you gave me . . . that day . . . (*pause*) . . . that day . . . the lake . . . the reeds. (*Eyes front. Pause.*) What day? (*Pause.*) What reeds? (*Long pause. Eyes close. Bell rings loudly. Eyes open. Pause. Eyes right.*) Brownie of course. (*Pause.*) You remember Brownie, Willie, I can see him. (*Pause.*) Brownie is there, Willie, beside me. (*Pause. Loud.*) Brownie is there, Willie. (*Pause. Eyes front.*) That is all. (*Pause.*) What would I do without them? (*Pause.*) What would I do without them, when words fail? (*Pause.*) Gaze before me, with compressed lips. (*Long pause while she does so.*) I cannot. (*Pause.*) Ah yes, great mercies, great mercies. (*Long pause. Low.*) Sometimes I hear sounds. (*Listening expression. Normal voice.*) But not often. (*Pause.*) They are a boon, sounds are a boon, they help me . . . through the day. (*Smile.*) The old style! (*Smile off.*) Yes, those are happy days, when there are sounds. (*Pause.*) When I hear sounds. (*Pause.*) I used to think . . . (*pause*) . . . I say I used to think they were in my head. (*Smile.*) But no. (*Smile broader.*) No no. (*Smile off.*) That was just logic. (*Pause.*) Reason. (*Pause.*) I have not lost my reason. (*Pause.*) Not yet. (*Pause.*) Not all. (*Pause.*) Some remains. (*Pause.*) Sounds. (*Pause.*) Like little . . . sunderings, little falls . . . apart. (*Pause. Low.*) It's things, Willie. (*Pause. Normal voice.*) In the bag, outside the bag. (*Pause.*) Ah yes, things have their life, that is what I always say, *things* have a life. (*Pause.*) Take my looking-glass, it doesn't need me. (*Pause.*) The bell. (*Pause.*) It hurts like a knife. (*Pause.*) A gouge. (*Pause.*) One cannot ignore it. (*Pause.*) How often . . . (*pause*) . . . I say how often I have said, Ignore it, Winnie, ignore the bell, pay no heed, just sleep and wake, sleep and wake, as you please, open and close the eyes, as you please, or in the way you find most helpful. (*Pause.*) Open and close the eyes, Winnie, open and close, always that. (*Pause.*) But no. (*Smile.*) Not now. (*Smile broader.*) No no. (*Smile off. Pause.*) What now? (*Pause.*) What now, Willie? (*Long pause.*) There is my story of course, when all else fails. (*Pause.*) A life. (*Smile.*) A long life. (*Smile off.*) Beginning in the womb, where life used to begin, Mildred has memories, she will have memories, of the womb, before she dies, the mother's womb. (*Pause.*) She is now four or five already and has recently been given a big waxen dolly. (*Pause.*) Fully clothed, complete outfit. (*Pause.*) Shoes, socks, undies, complete set, frilly frock, gloves. (*Pause.*) White mesh. (*Pause.*) A little white straw hat with a chin elastic. (*Pause.*) Pearly necklet. (*Pause.*) A little picture-book with

legends in real print to go under her arm when she takes her walk. (*Pause.*) China blue eyes that open and shut. (*Pause. Narrative.*) The sun was not well up when Milly rose, descended the steep . . . (*pause*) . . . slipped on her nightgown, descended all alone the steep wooden stairs, backwards on all fours, though she had been forbidden to do so, entered the . . . (*pause*) . . . tiptoed down the silent passage, entered the nursery and began to undress Dolly. (*Pause.*) Crept under the table and began to undress Dolly. (*Pause.*) Scolding her . . . the while. (*Pause.*) Suddenly a mouse — (*Long pause.*) Gently, Winnie. (*Long pause. Calling.*) Willie! (*Pause. Louder.*) Willie! (*Pause. Mild reproach.*) I sometimes find your attitude a little strange, Willie, all this time, it is not like you to be wantonly cruel. (*Pause.*) Strange? (*Pause.*) No. (*Smile.*) Not here. (*Smile broader.*) Not now. (*Smile off.*) And yet . . . (*Suddenly anxious.*) I do hope nothing is amiss. (*Eyes right, loud.*) Is all well, dear? (*Pause. Eyes front. To herself.*) God grant he did not go in head foremost! (*Eyes right, loud.*) You're not stuck, Willie? (*Pause. Do.*) You're not jammed, Willie? (*Eyes front, distressed.*) Perhaps he is crying out for help all this time and I do not hear him! (*Pause.*) I do of course hear cries. (*Pause.*) But they are in my head surely. (*Pause.*) Is it possible that . . . (*Pause. With finality.*) No no, my head was always full of cries. (*Pause.*) Faint confused cries. (*Pause.*) They come. (*Pause.*) Then go. (*Pause.*) As on a wind. (*Pause.*) That is what I find so wonderful. (*Pause.*) They cease. (*Pause.*) Ah yes, great mercies, great mercies. (*Pause.*) The day is now well advanced. (*Smile. Smile off.*) And yet it is perhaps a little soon for my song. (*Pause.*) To sing too soon is fatal, I always find. (*Pause.*) On the other hand it is possible to leave it too late. (*Pause.*) The bell goes for sleep and one has not sung. (*Pause.*) The whole day has flown — (*smile, smile off*) — flown by, quite by, and no song of any class, kind or description. (*Pause.*) There is a problem here. (*Pause.*) One cannot sing . . . just like that, no. (*Pause.*) It bubbles up, for some unknown reason, the time is ill chosen, one chokes it back. (*Pause.*) One says, Now is the time, it is now or never, and one cannot. (*Pause.*) Simply cannot sing. (*Pause.*) Not a note. (*Pause.*) Another thing, Willie, while we are on this subject. (*Pause.*) The sadness after song. (*Pause.*) Have you run across that, Willie? (*Pause.*) In the course of your experience. (*Pause.*) No? (*Pause.*) Sadness after intimate sexual intercourse one is familiar with of course. (*Pause.*) You would concur with Aristotle there, Willie, I fancy. (*Pause.*) Yes, that one knows and is prepared to face. (*Pause.*) But after song . . . (*Pause.*) It does not last of course. (*Pause.*) That is what I find so wonderful. (*Pause.*) It wears away. (*Pause.*) What are those exquisite lines? (*Pause.*) Go forget me why should something o'er that something shadow fling . . . go forget me . . . why should sorrow . . . brightly smile . . . go forget me . . . never hear me . . . sweetly smile . . . brightly sing . . . (*Pause. With a sigh.*) One loses one's classics. (*Pause.*) Oh not all. (*Pause.*) A part. (*Pause.*) A part remains. (*Pause.*) That is what I find so wonderful, a part remains, of one's classics, to help one through the day. (*Pause.*) Oh yes, many mercies, many mercies. (*Pause.*) And now? (*Pause.*) And now, Willie? (*Long pause.*) I call to the eye of the mind . . . Mr. Shower — or Cooker. (*She closes her eyes. Bell rings loudly. She opens her eyes. Pause.*) Hand in hand, in the other hands bags. (*Pause.*) Getting on . . . in life. (*Pause.*) No longer young, not yet old. (*Pause.*) Standing there gaping at me. (*Pause.*) Can't have been a bad bosom, he says, in its day. (*Pause.*) Seen worse shoulders, he says, in my time. (*Pause.*) Does she feel her legs? he says. (*Pause.*) Is there any life in her legs? he says. (*Pause.*) Has she anything on underneath? he says. (*Pause.*) Ask her, he says, I'm shy. (*Pause.*) Ask her what? she says. (*Pause.*) Is there any life in her legs? (*Pause.*) Has she anything on underneath. (*Pause.*) Ask her yourself, she says. (*Pause. With sudden violence.*) Let go of me for Christ sake and drop! (*Pause. Do.*) Drop dead! (*Smile.*) But no. (*Smile broader.*) No no. (*Smile off.*) I watch them recede. (*Pause.*) Hand in hand — and the bags. (*Pause.*) Dim. (*Pause.*) Then gone. (*Pause.*) Last human kind — to stray this way. (*Pause.*) Up to date. (*Pause.*) And now? (*Pause. Low.*) Help. (*Pause. Do.*) Help, Willie. (*Pause. Do.*) No? (*Long pause. Narrative.*) Suddenly a mouse . . . (*Pause.*) Suddenly a mouse ran up her little thigh and Mildred, dropping Dolly in her fright, began to scream — (*Winnie gives a sudden piercing scream*) — and screamed and screamed — (*Winnie screams twice*) — screamed and screamed and screamed and screamed till all came running, in their night attire, papa, mamma, Bibby and . . . old Annie, to see what was the matter . . . (*pause*) . . . what on earth could possibly be the matter. (*Pause.*) Too late. (*Pause.*) Too late. (*Long pause. Just audible.*) Willie. (*Pause. Normal voice.*) Ah well, not long now, Winnie, can't be long now, until the bell for sleep. (*Pause.*) Then you may close your eyes, then you *must* close your eyes — and keep them closed. (*Pause.*) Why say that again? (*Pause.*) I used to think . . . (*pause*) . . . I say I used to think there was no difference between one fraction of a second and the next. (*Pause.*) I used to say . . . (*pause*) . . . I say I used to say, Winnie, you are changeless, there is never any difference between one fraction of a second and the next. (*Pause.*) Why bring that up again? (*Pause.*) There is so little one can bring up, one brings up all. (*Pause.*) All one can. (*Pause.*) My neck is hurting me. (*Pause. With sudden violence.*) My neck is hurting me! (*Pause.*) Ah that's better. (*With mild irritation.*) Everything within reason. (*Long pause.*) I can do no more. (*Pause.*) Say no more. (*Pause.*) But I must say more. (*Pause.*) Problem here. (*Pause.*) No, something must move, in the world, I can't any more. (*Pause.*) A zephyr. (*Pause.*) A breath. (*Pause.*) What are those immortal lines? (*Pause.*) It might

be the eternal dark. (*Pause.*) Black night without end. (*Pause.*) Just chance, I take it, happy chance. (*Pause.*) Oh yes, abounding mercies. (*Long pause.*) And now? (*Pause.*) And now, Willie? (*Long pause.*) That day. (*Pause.*) The pink fizz. (*Pause.*) The flute glasses. (*Pause.*) The last guest gone. (*Pause.*) The last bumper with the bodies nearly touching. (*Pause.*) The look. (*Long pause.*) What day? (*Long pause.*) What look? (*Long pause.*) I hear cries. (*Pause.*) Sing. (*Pause.*) Sing your old song, Winnie.

(*Long pause. Suddenly alert expression. Eyes switch right. Willie's head appears to her right round corner of mound. He is on all fours, dressed to kill — top hat, morning coat, striped trousers, etc., white gloves in hand. Very long bushy white Battle of Britain mustache. He halts, gazes front, smoothes mustache. He emerges completely from behind mound, turns to his left, halts, looks up at Winnie. He advances on all fours toward center, halts, turns head front, gazes front, strokes mustache, straightens tie, adjusts hat, advances a little further, halts, takes off hat and looks up at Winnie. He is now not far from center and within her field of vision. Unable to sustain effort of looking up he sinks head to ground.*)

WINNIE (*mondaine*):° Well this is an unexpected pleasure! (*Pause.*) Reminds me of the day you came whining for my hand. (*Pause.*) I worship you, Winnie, be mine. (*He looks up.*) Life a mockery without Win. (*She goes off into a giggle.*) What a get up, you do look a sight! (*Giggles.*) Where are the flowers? (*Pause.*) That smile today. (*Willie sinks head.*) What's that on your neck, an anthrax? (*Pause.*) Want to watch that, Willie, before it gets a hold on you. (*Pause.*) Where were you all this time? (*Pause.*) What were you doing all this time? (*Pause.*) Changing? (*Pause.*) Did you not hear me screaming for you? (*Pause.*) Did you get stuck in your hole? (*Pause. He looks up.*) That's right, Willie, look at me. (*Pause.*) Feast your old eyes, Willie. (*Pause.*) Does anything remain? (*Pause.*) Any remains? (*Pause.*) No? (*Pause.*) I haven't been able to look after it, you know. (*He sinks his head.*) You are still recognizable, in a way. (*Pause.*) Are you thinking of coming to live this side now . . . for a bit maybe? (*Pause.*) No? (*Pause.*) Just a brief call? (*Pause.*) Have you gone deaf, Willie? (*Pause.*) Dumb? (*Pause.*) Oh I know you were never one to talk, I worship you Winnie be mine and then nothing from that day forth only titbits from Reynolds' News. (*Eyes front. Pause.*) Ah well, what matter, that's what I always say, it will have been a happy day, after all, another happy day. (*Pause.*) Not long now, Winnie. (*Pause.*) I hear cries. (*Pause.*) Do you ever hear cries, Willie? (*Pause.*) No? (*Eyes back on Willie.*) Willie. (*Pause.*) Look at me again, Willie. (*Pause.*) Once more, Willie. (*He looks up. Happily.*) Ah! (*Pause. Shocked.*) What ails you, Willie, I never

---

mondaine: Worldly.

saw such an expression! (*Pause.*) Put on your hat, dear, it's the sun, don't stand on ceremony, I won't mind. (*He drops hat and gloves and starts to crawl up mound toward her. Gleeful.*) Oh I say, this is terrific! (*He halts, clinging to mound with one hand, reaching up with the other.*) Come on, dear, put a bit of jizz into it, I'll cheer you on. (*Pause.*) Is it me you're after, Willie . . . or is it something else? (*Pause.*) Do you want to touch my face . . . again? (*Pause.*) Is it a kiss you're after, Willie . . . or is it something else? (*Pause.*) There was a time when I could have given you a hand. (*Pause.*) And then a time before that again when I did give you a hand. (*Pause.*) You were always in dire need of a hand, Willie. (*He slithers back to foot of mound and lies with face to ground.*) Brrum! (*Pause. He rises to hands and knees, raises his face toward her.*) Have another go, Willie, I'll cheer you on. (*Pause.*) Don't look at me like that! (*Pause. Vehement.*) Don't look at me like that! (*Pause. Low.*) Have you gone off your head, Willie? (*Pause. Do.*) Out of your poor old wits, Willie?

(*Pause.*)

WILLIE (*just audible*): Win.

(*Pause. Winnie's eyes front. Happy expression appears, grows.*)

WINNIE: Win! (*Pause.*) Oh this is a happy day, this will have been another happy day! (*Pause.*) After all. (*Pause.*) So far.

(*Pause. She hums tentatively beginning of song, then sings softly, musical-box tune.*)

> Though I say not
> What I may not
> Let you hear,
> Yet the swaying
> Dance is saying,
> Love me dear!
> Every touch of fingers
> Tells me what I know,
> Says for you,
> It's true, it's true,
> You love me so!

(*Pause. Happy expression off. She closes her eyes. Bell rings loudly. She opens her eyes. She smiles, gazing front. She turns her eyes, smiling, to Willie, still on his hands and knees looking up at her. Smile off. They look at each other. Long pause.*)

COMMENTARIES

Deirdre Bair (*b. 1935*)
THE FRENCH PRODUCTION OF *HAPPY DAYS*   1978

Beckett was enormously busy with writing, translating, and helping in the production of his work when Roger Blin scheduled his production of Oh les beaux jours (Happy Days). *Blin, who had acted in* Endgame, *another important Beckett play, recognized his role in the production and was careful not to conflict with Beckett's wishes. The problems of casting and staging were solved in slightly different ways than in the earlier U.S. and British productions.*

Because he stayed in Ulm-Donau longer than expected, there was no time for a holiday; he had promised Blin to be in Paris by the third week of June to start rehearsals of *Oh les beaux jours*. The previous winter, when Blin first read the script, he had told Beckett he was puzzled by Winnie and was unable to think of an actress who could portray her. He asked Beckett to describe Winnie as he envisioned her, so that he could look for an actress similar to Beckett's description.

Beckett described Winnie as "a little heavy, actually a little bit fat, about fifty, well-preserved. A virile woman, perhaps, with expressive eyes and a large bosom."[1]

This posed a problem for Blin, because the actresses who fit Beckett's description all verged on the comedic:

> I couldn't think of anyone who could have all the characteristics and not look merely ridiculous five minutes after the play started. That physique, in the situation where she was buried in the sand, constituted a kind of caricature. But the role necessitated an actress who had dramatic and comedic possibilities at the same time, someone who could suggest a whole range of possibilities.[2]

Blin thought of Madeleine Renaud, who was totally unlike Beckett's description:

> Although she didn't correspond to the physical character, she could project the total image of Winnie, and the role would be spoken by a voice which could bring the utmost to the text, which in this play was more important than the acting. There were two things of paramount importance in this play, Winnie's voice and the music — they constituted dramatic effect. If they were right, then the acting would be right, everything else would be right.[3]

Blin told Beckett that he wanted Renaud, and reluctantly Beckett agreed: "When you have the greatest voice in the French theatre, you do not insist on other, less important qualities."[4]

Beckett worked steadily with Renaud and Jean-Louis Barrault, who played Willie, from June until August. Because of Beckett's overpowering presence, Blin did not call himself the director, but instead billed it as a *"présentation de Roger Blin,"* which caused confusion among the critics, who thought he planned to make a speech before the play.[5] He did this on purpose, in an unsuccessful effort to give himself more authority, for he knew that Beckett would insist on a commanding role in the production and he wanted to protect his own part in it.

The first performances were given in the Odéon Petite Salle, a small theater inside the larger Odéon Théâtre de France, but almost immediately the play was moved into the larger theater. In order to keep a feeling of intimacy and confinement, Barrault limited the seating to the orchestra and the first balcony and moved the stage forward over the orchestra pit. Matias designed the setting, creating a bright orange sky for the background. In the New York production, the sky had been blue, but Matias wanted to stress heat more than pleasure. He wanted the audience to be discomfited by the intense glare brought on by a sky in gradations of a single color; the top was bright orange, and the very bottom was pale, which Blin remembers as so pale that it sometimes seemed to be gray. Renaud, as Winnie, was dressed in rose, and the strip of sky directly behind her also had a rosy glow. The platform which comprised her mound was all of orange shaded toward brown. Because the audience's eye was constantly disconcerted by all the orange, it was always drawn back to the actress, whose rosy glow was the only comforting area on the stage. As the play proceeded and Winnie's situation became more grim, the lights gradually faded until only one remained, casting a gray shadow on her, until

---

[1]Robert Blin (conversation). [Bair's note]
[2]Ibid.
[3]Ibid.
[4]Ibid.
[5]Ibid.

even that was extinguished. Beckett was delighted with this setting, and was ecstatic with the lighting, about which he had acquired a phenomenal expertise from the German production of *Play*.

No matter how much his cast urged him, Beckett would not go to Venice with them for the opening. He chose instead to steal away to Ussy, where he returned to the grind of translation, correspondence and proofs. While Blin was in Venice, where *Oh les beaux jours* was garnering impressive reviews, *Happy Days* opened in Dublin at the Eblana Theatre, with Marie Kean giving a performance as Winnie that won universal raves. To have a play so well received in Ireland was an astonishing piece of news, and it cheered Beckett for the coming opening in Paris.

As was his custom, he reserved a large block of seats for his Irish visitors, and was pleased to hear that H. O. White[6] planned to attend. White, retired from Trinity for several years, was in poor health and afraid to make the journey alone, so he invited R.B.D. French to go with him.[7] When they arrived at Orly on the morning of the first performance, they found Beckett waiting to drive them to Paris to take them to lunch. Beckett sat nervously throughout the meal, toying with a cigarette, then patiently assisted the fragile old man up the stairs to his hotel room before going off to take care of the last-minute details of the performance.

That night, White insisted on attending the play, even though he had to be led into the theater by someone on either side of him. Afterwards, Beckett hosted a party at the Falstaff, and against French's advice, White went. The party was festive because the play had gone well and everyone knew it. In fact, it was the biggest and happiest opening night celebration for any of Beckett's plays in Paris, and he was an unusually convivial host.[8] At 2 A.M., French returned to his hotel, leaving White, who insisted on staying until the very end. At 4 A.M., exhausted but exhilarated, White's long day ended when Beckett brought him back to his hotel. For the next few days, in spite of all the demands on his time now that the play had opened, Beckett entertained White.

White returned to Dublin in pouring rain, was led from the airplane directly into a wheelchair and then taken to his bed, from which he emerged only briefly until his death a short time later. His few days in Paris had been one of the happiest events of his life, and he told everyone who came to see him that Samuel Beckett was one of the truly good persons he had been privileged to know.[9]

[6]White was an English professor at Trinity College.
[7]R.B.D. French. [Bair's note]
[8]Madeleine Renaud, Roger Blin, Jean Martin, R.B.D. French and others. [Bair's note]
[9]R.B.D. French. [Bair's note]

Sidney Homan (b. 1938)
HAPPY DAYS: CREATION IN SPITE OF HABIT   1984

Sidney Homan's focus in his discussion of Happy Days *is on the question of sexuality, especially as it relates to Winnie. He sees the props and settings on stage as symbolic of sexual organs. He also sees interesting connections with the sexual imagination as expressed in other plays, such as* A Midsummer Night's Dream. *Homan is especially sensitive to the double-meanings implied in some of the play's language, and it is through a cautious but close interpretation of gestures and language that he builds his case for his approach to the play.*

Sexuality, in the broadest sense of the word, is inseparable from Winnie's creation. Even if they are immobile, or undesirable, Beckett's women all breathe a sexuality, wholesome or otherwise, that is either at one with their own sense of creativity or with that creativity they inspire in others. One thinks, first of all, of Mrs. Rooney in *All That Fall,* still eager, albeit somewhat incapacitated because of age and weight, to do the "trick," a creature lusting after something more than friendly taps on the shoulder. From her fertile mind spews a torrent of suggestive, symbolic, playful words. In *Embers,* Ada, however browbeaten by Henry, at length serves as stimulus for her husband, inspiring him with her description of his own Belacqua-like father. We might also think of the woman in the boat with Krapp, or the woman who berates Joe in Beckett's first television play, or the woman in the photograph examined by O in *Film,* even Sucky Moll in *Malone Dies,* serving the dying narrator, at the very least, as the subject for a fiction as he tries to escape his own death room.

As in Shakespeare's own *A Midsummer Night's Dream,* sex and the imagination are one: the poet is also a lover, giving birth to the creatures of his fictive venture. To love is to have empathy for that creation, for the ability to "go on." However inferior the shallow Athenians or the rustic Bottom are to the rationalist Theseus, the five lovers are still given the chance to experience Shakespeare's expansive, imaginative world, that forest expanding from finite Athens to the infinite dimensions of Oberon's kingdom. And this power, this chance is denied rationalists like Theseus. Similarly, in *The Taming of the Shrew* Petruchio's imaginative re-creation of Kate from shrew to model wife, or the imaginative capacity they both share in fashioning a world that denies the surface facts, is at one with their status as lovers. It is therefore no surprise that Winnie's sexuality, however faded, is stressed from the opening. We learn early that she is *"well preserved,"* with *"bare"* arms and shoulders, a *"low bodice, big bosom."* Though no shapely young girl, she is still miles beyond that dried virgin Miss Fitt.

If anything, the sexual problem in the play belongs to Willie, the husband, and this point is emphasized by the double entendres. Winnie's juxtaposition of commentary on the toothpaste and addresses to her husband suggests that, like the toothpaste, he is "running out," that the situation cannot be helped, and that both he and his sexual organ are "just one of those old things [which] . . . can't be cured." There is even a coda for this hymn joining fading toiletry and sexuality: "ah yes . . . poor dear Willie . . . good Lord."

Holding the butt of the parasol in her hand, a handle of *"surprising length,"* Winnie brings Willie into the comparison as she stretches back and to her right, hanging over him with "Willie" and then "wonderful gift." As she strikes her impotent husband with the handle, she cries, "Wish I had it," whereupon the parasol slips from her grasp and falls beneath the mound. After such sexual taunting she finds that her palm is "damp," perhaps as if from passion.

It is true that at times Winnie seems to be part of a large, symbolic travesty of sexuality: the various phallic instruments at her command (the parasol, the toothbrush, the revolver) arrayed against the vaginal hole into which Willie retreats, and the lubricant that she counsels him to "work it well in." The fact remains that it is Willie who seems to have lost his zest, his "jizz." Almost dead in his use of language, confined to a few monosyllabic utterances, some wordless play, and drawing comments not from his imagination but from the newspaper, he is, until the end of the play, almost extinct as a creative force. For Willie takes only a vicarious verbal pleasure from obscene postcards, from wordplay on "suck," or allusions to an old lover of Winnie. Winnie thus tries to lead him, to bring him out, both sexually and imaginatively. Again, sexuality and the imagination are inseparable: one feeds on the other. She reminds him that he once found her lovable, that in the past he had complimented her hair. Now the relationship is failing, despite Winnie's purposeful distortions of the situation: her attempts to dredge up a more romantic past and the fact that her standards for social intercourse have become so minimal that a mere grunt or monosyllable from Willie can move her to conclude that it will be a happy day.

Eugene Webb (*b. 1938*)
ON *HAPPY DAYS*

1972

Eugene Webb begins his discussion of the play with a description of what happens, emphasizing the setting and the visual circumstances of the action. He also focuses on the limitations that dominate the play: limitations of action, movement, and the design of the set. The symbolic value of Winnie's being buried in the earth suggests to Webb that her situation is one not only of necessity but of choice. He examines her uses of language and shows that "she talks so that she will not have to think." Talk has become a form of defense. The value of Willie as an audience for her talk becomes apparent by the end of the play.

The basic situation is . . . that of a person thrown into a condition with frustrating limitations and with the choice of either facing this directly and clearly or evading it. The central character in this case is Winnie, a rather full-blown, blond woman of about fifty, who is buried to above her waist in the center of a mound. Since Willie, her husband, rarely speaks or shows himself, he is largely peripheral to the play and is present primarily as an object of relationship for Winnie. All one sees of the earth is covered by scorched grass. On the backcloth an unbroken plain and sky recede to meet in the distance. The design of the set, with its *"maximum of simplicity and symmetry,"* carries our eyes to the center of attention, Winnie. The fact that she is buried in the earth is a symbol both of the way the absurd is closing in on her as death approaches, making it harder and harder for her to find distractions from herself, and also of the way she has given up her freedom to objects outside her by burying herself in that which is not herself. That the mound has not only been imposed on her by life but is also something she has chosen for herself is made clear by the reference to her feeling of having "to cling on" so as not to float up out of it.

The action begins when a piercing bell rings to awaken her. . . . It has to ring twice, first for ten seconds, then for five, before it finally gets through to her. Evidently she would prefer to remain asleep — in fact she says a little later that Willie's faculty for sleeping most of the time is a "marvelous gift" and that she wishes she had it — but nevertheless when she finally wakes, her first effort is to muster up her courage and look at life cheerfully: "Another heavenly day." Her next act is to pray in the traditional way — "For Jesus Christ sake Amen" — before commanding herself to "begin" her "day."

The fact that Winnie wants to make her experience a "day" is significant. Man cannot live without order, and in a world without a time scheme he will impose a pattern of his own making. There are no more days now, and when she is not busy making them up she knows this. "The old style," she says at one point when she sees the label on her medicine bottle telling her to take six level tablespoons "daily." "All day long" in the world she lives in now means only "between the bell for waking and the bell for sleep," but she likes the "old style" the way Hamm [in *Endgame*] liked the "old questions" and the "old answers" and does her best to retain what she can of it in her "daily" life.

In structuring her day she tries to give it, like an Aristotelian plot, a beginning, middle, and end. There has to be a time for brushing her teeth, which comes at the beginning, for rummaging among her things, for singing her song, which should come sometime near the end, and finally for going back to sleep when the bell rings. The trouble, of course, is that never knowing when the bell will ring to signal the end, she can never be certain the middle is being adequately arranged: "To sing too soon is fatal, I always find. . . . On the other hand it is possible to leave it too late. . . . The bell goes for sleep and one has not sung." Anxieties of this kind are something of a blessing for her, however; they distract her from the situation as it really is: a formless chaos on which patterns can be fitted only by self-deception.

Another important distraction, as well as a deep compulsion, is the need she has to know. The object of knowledge is not important; it need not be anything particularly significant. All that is required is that the search for it keep her mind occupied. There is her toothbrush, for example. When she finishes brushing her teeth, she looks at the handle of the brush and tries to make out the writing on it: ". . . genuine . . . pure . . . what?" She polishes her spectacles and tries again, then gets a magnifying glass out of her bag and finally manages to decipher it: "Fully guaranteed . . . genuine pure . . . hog's . . . setae." Every now and then, as in this instance, such a quest for knowledge brings her up against a reminder of the emptiness and sterility of this world in which "nothing grows." In this case, inquiring from Willie the difference between a hog and a swine, she finds that a hog is a "castrated male swine. . . . Reared for slaughter." She manages, however, to avoid thinking about the associations that go with this, the parallel to her own situation and to Willie's, by shifting her attention to her joy in the fact that Willie has finally spoken to her: "Oh this *is* a happy day!" Another object of curiosity, with similarly unpleasant associations for her, is a pornographic picture Willie shows her when she asks if she can see it. "No but this is just genuine pure filth," she exclaims as she examines it intently. "Make any nice-minded person want to vomit." Then she gets her magnifying glass to give it a better look: "What does that creature in the background think he's doing? (*Looks closer.*) Oh no really!" Finally she gives it a "last long look" before returning it with a "Pah! . . . Take it away!" No source of curiosity is too trivial or too repulsive to defeat her. She is always grateful for something — whether the hairs of the head are called "it" or "them," how the comb and brush got back into her bag if she did not put them there — that can keep her mind occupied and diverted from the real unpleasantness of her life.

And when these distractions fail her, when she loses heart and envies the brute beast, as she says, she turns to thoughts of death, either the death that will come, she hopes, with the end of the world — "the happy day to come when flesh melts at so many degrees and the night of the moon has so many hundred hours" — or suicide. Of course, as might be expected, her feelings about death are as equivocal as those of any of Beckett's other characters. This is made clear by her reaction to her revolver when she runs across it while rummaging in her bag: she brings it out, holds it up, "kisses it rapidly," then puts it back. She calls it by a pet name, "Brownie," and likes to know that it is there, but the sight of it makes her uncomfortable. Death is a pleasant fantasy as long as it remains at some remove, but when it comes too close it is as disturbing as reality itself.

The most important of her defenses is talk. Like Vladimir and Estragon [in *Waiting for Godot*], she talks so that she will not have to think, and what she is most afraid of is the possibility that there may come a time when she will no longer be able to talk, either because words will fail her — "Words fail, there are times when even they fail" — or because there will be nobody left to talk to. If it were simply words that failed she would still be able to occupy herself with her possessions, and consequently she is careful not to "overdo the bag" lest she exhaust its interest before the time when she will really need it. But if she were to lose Willie so that she were left entirely alone, she would have to face the emptiness that would be left in her by the absence of the other whose perception of her she had relied on to constitute her personality. The thought of no longer having an interlocutor to direct herself toward is especially abhorrent to her: "Oh no doubt the time will come when before I can utter a word I must make sure you heard the one that went before and then no doubt another come another time when I must learn to talk to myself a thing I could never bear to do such wilderness." Since what Winnie knows of her being is largely confined to that which is reflected in the eyes of others, to be deprived of those eyes, or ears, would be something more frightening to her than death itself. . . .

Does this steadfast refusal on Winnie's part to face reality mean . . . that her story is purely static, that she does not go through any kind of growth during the play? Not at all. Her life brings her closer to the vision she seeks to avoid even if it does so against her will. Reality presses upon her, both from the outside and from within. Even if it does not break through to her during the course of the play, we can see the direction in which things are moving. . . .

Act 2 carries this process of growth still further, even if not to completion. Whereas Winnie opened and closed the first act with conventional prayers and tried to persuade herself that they would be effective in bringing her relief from her misfortunes — "prayers perhaps not for naught," she says at one point on thinking of how sometimes her headaches go away — the second act opens without petitionary prayer, but only with "Hail, holy light" and an attempt to believe that "someone is looking at me still." Of course the "someone" is still the God of "the sweet old style," and the greeting to the "holy light" is a quotation from Milton's invocation to the uncreated light of God, but the fact that she is not explicitly praying for something to be given her would seem to indicate some growth in self-reliance. "I used to pray," she says, "I say I used to pray. . . . Yes, I must confess I did. (*Smile.*) Not now."

The reason she smiles as she says this is probably that she feels some degree of liberation in being able to get along without prayer. Her smile does not last, however; freedom may have its pleasant side, but it is also rather frightening. She stops to reflect that if this indicates a change in her, it is not clear what kind of change is involved and that perhaps it may be leading toward more change than she wants: "Then . . . now . . . what difficulties here, for the mind. (*Pause.*) To have been always what I am — and so changed from what I was." She goes on both to introduce and avoid the idea that something might be happening inside her that could eventually lead to a radical break with her past: "Eyes float up that seem to close in peace . . . to see . . . in peace. (*Pause.*) Not mine. (*Smile.*) Not now." The eyes she feels floating up inside her would seem to be the eyes of a new vision that would enable her to look on the reality of her world without anxiety over its lack of meaning. She does not want them yet, though: the "old style" is still too precious to her. She turns aside from these thoughts to return to the old question and answer game, to concern with her appearance, and to the last of her possessions, the gun. Even this flight from what is happening, however, leads her inescapably back to the heart of the problem. Thinking about her things she is forced to face for a moment the fact that like all the rest of reality they are not hers: they are only what they are. Possession is an artificial meaning imposed on an indifferent reality by man's imagination: "It's things, Willie. . . . In the bag, outside the bag. . . . Ah yes, things have their life, that is what I always say, *things* have a life. . . . Take my looking-glass, it doesn't need me." Things have a life of their own; they do not need her or any other person. Of course this is not what she "always" says — quite the contrary — but this thought, like so many others, feels more comfortable to her when she can take the edge off its newness by persuading herself that it is not unfamiliar.

These thoughts in turn lead to reflections on the role of the bell in her life, raising the question of the possibility of autonomy:

> The bell. . . . It hurts like a knife. . . . A gouge. . . . One cannot ignore it. . . . How often . . . I say how often I have said, Ignore it, Winnie, ignore the bell, pay no heed, just sleep and wake, sleep and wake, as you please, open and close the eyes as you please. . . . But no. (*Smile.*) Not now. (*Smile broader.*) No no.

Perhaps the new life that would emerge from the new vision that seems to be growing inside her would involve both freedom from the need to impose artificial patterns on a reality they do not fit and freedom to direct her own acts with her own will, no longer submitting to the authority of the bell any more than to that of the God she imagines or to that of the possessions which in fact possess her. This is not something she can accept, however. Freedom is no more endurable to her than meaninglessness.

She retreats into a story. Still, this turns out to be no more satisfactory an escape than any other. All roads lead to the same end: defeat. In this case the story is a thinly veiled projection of her own life into fiction. It is about a little girl named Mildred or Millie who has a doll with "china blue eyes that open and shut," like Winnie's, and a "pearly necklet," like that Winnie wears. Millie decides "to undress Dolly," rather the way the new self in Winnie represented by the eyes floating up from her depths is undressing Winnie by stripping from her all the conventional ideas that shield her from naked contact with the hard light of reality. Then suddenly a mouse appears in the story, disturbing Winnie sufficiently to make her discontinue it for a while. Evidently the mouse is a symbol to her of the destructive element she feels threatened by in the process of change she is undergoing. When she returns to the story later, she describes the mouse running up Millie's "little thigh." And as the little girl begins to scream in the story, Winnie gives a *"sudden piercing scream"* of her own, an indication of how closely she identifies with her protagonist. When the parents come, she says, it is "too late." Evidently Winnie feels the same of her own case: that the undressing that is taking place in her will lead to the destruction not only of her superficial identity, the self that lives in conventional ideas and in the eyes of others, but also of the deeper self within. She cannot believe that the loss of all her normal patterns of thought and behaviour would not destroy her very being as well.

At the end she retreats as usual to what she believes is the safer ground of her fortress of illusions, to the old dream of her "happy day." It does not seem likely, however, that this fortress will be able to stand indefinitely. The signs of change are too great. It is hard to tell just what it means when Willie appears, for the first time, dressed up in morning clothes, complete with top hat and white gloves, and tries without success to crawl up the mound to reach her. The attire suggests that the occasion is one of some solemnity, perhaps a death, though just what kind of death is not clear. Winnie makes of it what she must, a sign that this "will have been a happy day, after all, another happy day," and when Willie gasps her name, she rejoices and makes of it another occasion for flight into song. We already know of the sadness that comes after song, however, and we know how fragile the illusion of the "happy day" is. All we can be certain of about this ending is that Winnie will not find in it the meaning she expects. It would seem more likely that the process of change we have seen working itself out in her will lead her to an end she cannot imagine and into which we cannot follow her.

Lorraine Hansberry

Lorraine Hansberry (1930–1965), like John Millington Synge, died tragically young. Her loss to the American stage is incalculable; her successes were only beginning, and at her death she seemed on the verge of a remarkable career.

Hansberry grew up in a middle-class black family in Chicago. Her father, who was successful in real estate, founded one of the first banks for blacks in Chicago. However, he spent much of his life vainly trying to find a way to make a decent life for himself and his family in America. He eventually gave up on the United States, and, when he died in 1945, he was scouting for a place in Mexico where he could move his family to live comfortably.

Lorraine Hansberry went to college after her father died, and her first ambition was to become a visual artist. She attended the Art Institute of Chicago and numerous other schools before moving to New York. Once there, she became interested in some drama groups and soon married the playwright Howard Nemiroff. She began writing, sharing parts of her first play with friends in her own living room. They helped raise money to stage the play and, with black director Lloyd Richards and little-known Sidney Poitier as Walter Lee Younger, *A Raisin in the Sun* (1959) thrust her into the drama spotlight.

In 1959, only twenty-nine years old, Hansberry was the most promising woman writing for the American stage. She was also the first black American to win the New York Drama Critics' Circle Award for the best play of the year. She died of cancer the day her second produced play, *The Sign in Sidney Brustein's Window,* closed. She had finished a third play, *Les Blancs,* which was brought to Broadway by Nemiroff in 1970. Neither of her other plays was as popular as *Raisin,* but the two later plays demonstrate a deepening concern for and understanding of some of the key issues of racial and sexual politics that interested her throughout her career.

The hero in *The Sign in Sidney Brustein's Window* is a Jewish intellectual in the 1950s in Greenwich Village. Feeling that all the radical struggle of the 1930s has been lost, he agitates for personal involvement, for emotional and intellectual action. This idealistic play anticipates the political agitation in the United States during the mid-1960s and early 1970s. *Les Blancs* takes as its central character a black African intellectual, Tshembe, and explores his relationship to both Europe and Africa. In his uneasiness with both cultures he discovers that he cannot live outside his own history. *Les Blancs* reveals some of Hansberry's deep interest in Pan-Africanism and the search for a personal heritage.

A posthumous work was put together by Howard Nemiroff from Hansberry's notes, letters, and early writings. Titled *To Be Young, Gifted, and Black* (1971), it has helped solidify her achievements. Although we will never know just how Hansberry's career would have developed had she lived, her gifts were so remarkable that we can only lament that she is not writing for the stage today.

A RAISIN IN THE SUN

When produced on Broadway in 1959, *A Raisin in the Sun* was somewhat prophetic. Lorraine Hansberry's themes of blacks pressing forward with legitimate demands and expressing interest in their African heritage were to become primary themes of black culture in the 1960s, 1970s, and, indeed, to this day. The title of her play is from a poem by Langston Hughes, one of the poets of the Harlem Renaissance. It warns of the social explosions that might occur if society permits blacks to remain unequal and unfree.

The work appeared at the beginning of renewed political activity on the part of African Americans; it reveals its historical position in the use of the word *Negro,* which black activists rejected in the 1960s as an enslaving euphemism. This play illustrates the American dream as it is felt not just by African Americans but by all Americans: if you work hard, save your money, are honorable, and hope, then you can one day buy your own home and have the kind of space and privacy that permit people to live with dignity. Yet this very theme has plagued the play from the beginning: its apparent emphasis on middle-class, bourgeois values. On the surface, it seems to celebrate a mild form of consumerism — the desire for the house in the suburbs with the TV set inside to anesthetize its occupants. Hansberry was shocked when such criticisms, from black critics as well as white, were leveled against the play. She had written it very carefully to explore just those issues but in a context that demonstrated that black families' needs paralleled white families' while also having a different dimension that most white families could not understand.

Hansberry was quick to admit that Walter Lee Younger was affected by the same craziness influencing all Americans who lusted after possessions and the power they might confer. Walter wants to take his father's insurance money to buy a liquor store in partnership with a con man. Lena Younger argues against her son's plan as a profanation of her husband's memory as well as an abuse of the American dream: she believes that the product of a liquor store will further poison the community. What she wants is not a consumer product but the emblem of identity and security that she feels her family deserves.

Hansberry is painfully honest in this play. Walter Lee's weaknesses are recognizable. His male chauvinistic behavior undoes him. He is caught up in the old, failing pattern of male dominance over women. But none of the women in his life will tolerate his behavior. Hansberry also admits the social distinctions among African Americans. George Murchison is a young man from a wealthy black family, and when Beneatha tells Lena that she will not marry George, she says, "The only people in the world who are more snobbish than rich white people are rich colored people." Beneatha's desire to be a doctor is obviously not rooted in consumerism any more than in the middle-class need to be comfortable and rich.

The confusion brought to the family by a native African, Asagai, is realistically portrayed. In the early days of the Pan-African movement in the 1960s, blacks were often bemused by the way Africans presented themselves. Interest in Africa on the part of the American blacks was distorted by Tarzan movies and *National Geographic* articles, none of which presented black Africans as role models. Therefore, the adjustment to black African pride — while made swiftly — was not without difficulties. The Youngers are presented as no more sophisticated about black Africans than the rest of black society would be.

The dignity of the Younger family finally triumphs. When Walter Lee stands up for himself, he is asserting not macho domination but black manhood — a manhood that needs no domination over women. He is expressing not a desire for a big house — as he had done when he reflected on the possessions of his rich employer — but a desire to demonstrate to members of the Clybourne Park Improvement Association that the Youngers are their social equals and that they have a right to live wherever they choose.

A Raisin in the Sun in Performance

Lloyd Richards directed the first production at the Ethel Barrymore Theater in New York on March 11, 1959. The play won major prizes, and Sidney Poitier as a passionate Walter Lee Younger was a signal success. *New York Times* critic Brooks Atkinson said, "Since the performance is also honest and since Sidney Poitier is a candid actor, *A Raisin in the Sun* has vigor as well as veracity and is likely to destroy the complacency of any one who sees it." Critics were astonished that a first play could have the sophistication and depth they saw onstage.

The Theater Guild staged the play in 1960 in Boston with a different cast but the production received similar reviews. The film version, with most of the New York cast, was directed by Daniel Petrie in 1961. A revival in Chicago in 1983 at the Art Institute of Chicago — Hansberry's alma mater — was not altogether successful, but critics felt the text held up well. The Chicago revival, like the 1985 Merrimack Repertory Theater revival in Lowell, Massachusetts, demonstrated only that the play needs strong actors to have the desired impact. A twenty-fifth-anniversary production was directed by Lloyd Richards at the Yale Repertory Theatre in 1983. This production was taken to New York in 1986 and enjoyed a successful run. The setting was a realistic interior, emphasizing the play's realistic style. Critic Mel Gussow felt the revival demonstrated that the play is "an enduring work of contemporary theater." The production also revealed that Hansberry's language had not become dated, nor had the social issues of the play become any less critical and important for the lapse of twenty-five years. In fact, a production starring hip-hop artist and fashion mogul Sean "P. Diddy" Combs and Audra McDonald is scheduled for the 2004 season in New York City. Like the proletarian plays of Sean O'Casey, who inspired Lorraine Hansberry, this play continues to move us because its problems are serious and still remain.

Lorraine Hansberry *(1930–1965)*

A Raisin in the Sun

Harlem (A Dream Deferred)

What happens to a dream deferred?

Does it dry up
like a raisin in the sun?
Or fester like a sore —
And then run?
Does it stink like rotten meat?

Or crust and sugar over —
like a syrupy sweet?

Maybe it just sags
like a heavy load.

Or does it explode?   — LANGSTON HUGHES

Characters

RUTH YOUNGER
TRAVIS YOUNGER
WALTER LEE YOUNGER *(brother)*
BENEATHA YOUNGER
LENA YOUNGER *(Mama)*
JOSEPH ASAGAI
GEORGE MURCHISON
MRS. JOHNSON
KARL LINDNER
BOBO
MOVING MEN

The action of the play is set in Chicago's Southside, sometime between World War II and the present.

Act I
Scene I: *Friday morning.*
Scene II: *The following morning.*

Act II
Scene I: *Later, the same day.*
Scene II: *Friday night, a few weeks later.*
Scene III: *Moving day, one week later.*

Act III
An hour later.

ACT I • Scene I

(The Younger living room would be a comfortable and well-ordered room if it were not for a number of indestructible contradictions to this state of being. Its furnishings are typical and undistinguished and their primary feature now is that they have clearly had to accommodate the living of too many people for too many years — and they are tired. Still, we can see that at some time, a time probably no longer remembered by the family [except perhaps for Mama], the furnishings of this room were actually selected with care and love and even hope — and brought to this apartment and arranged with taste and pride.)

(That was a long time ago. Now the once loved pattern of the couch upholstery has to fight to show itself from under acres of crocheted doilies and couch covers which have themselves finally come to be more important than the upholstery. And here a table or a chair has been moved to disguise the worn places in the carpet; but the carpet has fought back by showing its weariness, with depressing uniformity, elsewhere on its surface.)

(Weariness has, in fact, won in this room. Everything has been polished, washed, sat on, used, scrubbed too often. All pretenses but living itself have long since vanished from the very atmosphere of this room.)

(Moreover, a section of this room, for it is not really a room unto itself, though the landlord's lease would make it seem so, slopes backward to provide a small kitchen area, where the family prepares the meals that are eaten in the living room proper, which must also serve as dining room. The single window that has been provided for these "two" rooms is located in this kitchen area. The sole natural light the family may enjoy in the course of a day is only that which fights its way through this little window.)

(At left, a door leads to a bedroom which is shared by Mama and her daughter, Beneatha. At right, opposite, is a second room [which in the beginning of the life of this apartment was probably a breakfast room] which serves as a bedroom for Walter and his wife, Ruth.)

(Time: Sometime between World War II and the present.)

(Place: Chicago's Southside.)

(At rise: It is morning dark in the living room. Travis is asleep on the make-down bed at center. An alarm clock sounds from within the bedroom at right, and presently Ruth enters from that room and closes the door behind her. She crosses sleepily toward the window. As she passes her sleeping son she reaches down and shakes him a little. At the window she raises the shade and a dusky Southside morning light comes in feebly. She fills a pot with water and puts it on to boil. She *calls to the boy, between yawns, in a slightly muffled voice.*)

(*Ruth is about thirty. We can see that she was a pretty girl, even exceptionally so, but now it is apparent that life has been little that she expected, and disappointment has already begun to hang in her face. In a few years, before thirty-five even, she will be known among her people as a "settled woman."*)

(*She crosses to her son and gives him a good, final, rousing shake.*)

RUTH: Come on now, boy, it's seven thirty! (*Her son sits up at last, in a stupor of sleepiness.*) I say hurry up, Travis! You ain't the only person in the world got to use a bathroom! (*The child, a sturdy, handsome little boy of ten or eleven, drags himself out of the bed and almost blindly takes his towels and "today's clothes" from drawers and a closet and goes out to the bathroom, which is in an outside hall and which is shared by another family or families on the same floor. Ruth crosses to the bedroom door at right and opens it and calls in to her husband.*) Walter Lee! . . . It's after seven thirty! Lemme see you do some waking up in there now! (*She waits.*) You better get up from there, man! It's after seven thirty I tell you. (*She waits again.*) All right, you just go ahead and lay there and next thing you know Travis be finished and Mr. Johnson'll be in there and you'll be fussing and cussing round here like a madman! And be late too! (*She waits, at the end of patience.*) Walter Lee — it's time for you to GET UP!

(*She waits another second and then starts to go into the bedroom, but is apparently satisfied that her husband has begun to get up. She stops, pulls the door to, and returns to the kitchen area. She wipes her face with a moist cloth and runs her fingers through her sleep-disheveled hair in a vain effort and ties an apron around her housecoat. The bedroom door at right opens and her husband stands in the doorway in his pajamas, which are rumpled and mismated. He is a lean, intense young man in his middle thirties, inclined to quick nervous movements and erratic speech habits — and always in his voice there is a quality of indictment.*)

WALTER: Is he out yet?

RUTH: What you mean *out*? He ain't hardly got in there good yet.

WALTER (*wandering in, still more oriented to sleep than to a new day*): Well, what was you doing all that yelling for if I can't even get in there yet? (*Stopping and thinking.*) Check coming today?

RUTH: They *said* Saturday and this is just Friday and I hopes to God you ain't going to get up here first thing this morning and start talking to me 'bout no money — 'cause I 'bout don't want to hear it.

WALTER: Something the matter with you this morning?

RUTH: No — I'm just sleepy as the devil. What kind of eggs you want?

WALTER: Not scrambled. (*Ruth starts to scramble eggs.*) Paper come? (*Ruth points impatiently to the rolled up Tribune on the table, and he gets it and spreads it out and vaguely reads the front page.*) Set off another bomb yesterday.

RUTH (*maximum indifference*): Did they?

WALTER (*looking up*): What's the matter with you?

RUTH: Ain't nothing the matter with me. And don't keep asking me that this morning.

WALTER: Ain't nobody bothering you. (*Reading the news of the day absently again.*) Say Colonel McCormick is sick.

RUTH (*affecting tea-party interest*): Is he now? Poor thing.

WALTER (*sighing and looking at his watch*): Oh, me. (*He waits.*) Now what is that boy doing in that bathroom all this time? He just going to have to start getting up earlier. I can't be being late to work on account of him fooling around in there.

RUTH (*turning on him*): Oh, no he ain't going to be getting up no earlier no such thing! It ain't his fault that he can't get to bed no earlier nights 'cause he got a bunch of crazy good-for-nothing clowns sitting up running their mouths in what is supposed to be his bedroom after ten o'clock at night . . .

WALTER: That's what you mad about, ain't it? The things I want to talk about with my friends just couldn't be important in your mind, could they?

(*He rises and finds a cigarette in her handbag on the table and crosses to the little window and looks out, smoking and deeply enjoying this first one.*)

RUTH (*almost matter of factly, a complaint too automatic to deserve emphasis*): Why you always got to smoke before you eat in the morning?

WALTER (*at the window*): Just look at 'em down there . . . Running and racing to work . . . (*He turns and faces his wife and watches her a moment at the stove, and then, suddenly.*) You look young this morning, baby.

RUTH (*indifferently*): Yeah?

WALTER: Just for a second — stirring them eggs. Just for a second it was — you looked real young again. (*He reaches for her; she crosses away. Then, drily.*) It's gone now — you look like yourself again!

RUTH: Man, if you don't shut up and leave me alone.

WALTER (*looking out to the street again*): First thing a man ought to learn in life is not to make love to no colored woman first thing in the morning. You all some eeevil people at eight o'clock in the morning.

(*Travis appears in the hall doorway, almost fully dressed and quite wide awake now, his towels and pajamas across his shoulders. He opens the door and signals for his father to make the bathroom in a hurry.*)

TRAVIS (*watching the bathroom*): Daddy, come on!

(*Walter gets his bathroom utensils and flies out to the bathroom.*)

RUTH: Sit down and have your breakfast, Travis.

TRAVIS: Mama, this is Friday. (*Gleefully.*) Check coming tomorrow, huh?

RUTH: You get your mind off money and eat your breakfast.

TRAVIS (*eating*): This is the morning we supposed to bring the fifty cents to school.

RUTH: Well, I ain't got no fifty cents this morning.

TRAVIS: Teacher say we have to.

RUTH: I don't care what teacher say. I ain't got it. Eat your breakfast, Travis.

TRAVIS: I *am* eating.

RUTH: Hush up now and just eat!

(*The boy gives her an exasperated look for her lack of understanding and eats grudgingly.*)

TRAVIS: You think Grandmama would have it?

RUTH: No! And I want you to stop asking your grandmother for money, you hear me?

TRAVIS (*outraged*): Gaaaleee! I don't ask her, she just gimme it sometimes!

RUTH: Travis Willard Younger — I got too much on me this morning to be —

TRAVIS: Maybe Daddy —

RUTH: *Travis!*

(*The boy hushes abruptly. They are both quiet and tense for several seconds.*)

TRAVIS (*presently*): Could I maybe go carry some groceries in front of the supermarket for a little while after school then?

RUTH: Just hush, I said. (*Travis jabs his spoon into his cereal bowl viciously and rests his head in anger upon his fists.*) If you through eating, you can get over there and make up your bed.

(*The boy obeys stiffly and crosses the room, almost mechanically, to the bed and more or less folds the bedding into a heap, then angrily gets his books and cap.*)

TRAVIS (*sulking and standing apart from her unnaturally*): I'm gone.

RUTH (*looking up from the stove to inspect him automatically*): Come here. (*He crosses to her and she studies his head.*) If you don't take this comb and fix this here head, you better! (*Travis puts down his books with a great sigh of oppression and crosses to the mirror. His mother mutters under her breath about his "slubbornness."*) 'Bout to march out of here with that head looking just like chickens slept in it! I just don't know where you get your slubborn ways . . . And get your jacket, too. Looks chilly out this morning.

TRAVIS (*with conspicuously brushed hair and jacket*): I'm gone.

RUTH: Get carfare and milk money — (*waving one finger*) — and not a single penny for no caps, you hear me?

TRAVIS (*with sullen politeness*): Yes'm.

(*He turns in outrage to leave. His mother watches after him as in his frustration he approaches the door almost comically. When she speaks to him, her voice has become a very gentle tease.*)

RUTH (*mocking; as she thinks he would say it*): Oh, Mama makes me so mad sometimes, I don't know what to do! (*She waits and continues to his back as he stands stock-still in front of the door.*) I wouldn't kiss that woman good-bye for nothing in this world this morning! (*The boy finally turns around and rolls his eyes at her, knowing the mood has changed and he is vindicated; he does not, however, move toward her yet.*) Not for nothing in this world! (*She finally laughs aloud at him and holds out her arms to him and we see that it is a way between them, very old and practiced. He crosses to her and allows her to embrace him warmly but keeps his face fixed with masculine rigidity. She holds him back from her presently and looks at him and runs her fingers over the features of his face. With utter gentleness —*) Now — whose little old angry man are you?

TRAVIS (*the masculinity and gruffness start to fade at last*): Aw gaalee — Mama . . .

RUTH (*mimicking*): Aw — gaaaaalleeeee, Mama! (*She pushes him, with rough playfulness and finality, toward the door.*) Get on out of here or you going to be late.

TRAVIS (*in the face of love, new aggressiveness*): Mama, could I *please* go carry groceries?

RUTH: Honey, it's starting to get so cold evenings.

WALTER (*coming in from the bathroom and drawing a make-believe gun from a make-believe holster and shooting at his son*): What is it he wants to do?

RUTH: Go carry groceries after school at the supermarket.

WALTER: Well, let him go . . .

TRAVIS (*quickly, to the ally*): I *have* to — she won't gimme the fifty cents . . .

WALTER (*to his wife only*): Why not?

RUTH (*simply, and with flavor*): 'Cause we don't have it.

WALTER (*to Ruth only*): What you tell the boy things like that for? (*Reaching down into his pants with a rather important gesture.*) Here, son —

(*He hands the boy the coin, but his eyes are directed to his wife's. Travis takes the money happily.*)

TRAVIS: Thanks, Daddy.

(*He starts out. Ruth watches both of them with murder in her eyes. Walter stands and stares back at her with defiance and suddenly reaches into his pocket again on an afterthought.*)

WALTER (*without even looking at his son, still staring hard at his wife*): In fact, here's another fifty cents . . . Buy yourself some fruit today — or take a taxicab to school or something!

TRAVIS: Whoopee —

(*He leaps up and clasps his father around the middle with his legs, and they face each other in mutual appreciation; slowly Walter Lee peeks around the boy to catch the violent rays from his wife's eyes and draws his head back as if shot.)*

WALTER: You better get down now — and get to school, man.

TRAVIS (*at the door*): O.K. Good-bye.

(*He exits.*)

WALTER (*after him, pointing with pride*): That's my boy. (*She looks at him in disgust and turns back to her work.*) You know what I was thinking 'bout in the bathroom this morning?

RUTH: No.

WALTER: How come you always try to be so pleasant!

RUTH: What is there to be pleasant 'bout!

WALTER: You want to know what I was thinking 'bout in the bathroom or not!

RUTH: I know what you thinking 'bout.

WALTER (*ignoring her*): 'Bout what me and Willy Harris was talking about last night.

RUTH (*immediately — a refrain*): Willy Harris is a good-for-nothing loudmouth.

WALTER: Anybody who talks to me has got to be a good-for-nothing loudmouth, ain't he? And what you know about who is just a good-for-nothing loudmouth? Charlie Atkins was just a "good-for-nothing loudmouth" too, wasn't he! When he wanted me to go in the dry-cleaning business with him. And now — he's grossing a hundred thousand a year. A hundred thousand dollars a year! You still call *him* a loudmouth!

RUTH (*bitterly*): Oh, Walter Lee . . .

(*She folds her head on her arms over the table.*)

WALTER (*rising and coming to her and standing over her*): You tired, ain't you? Tired of everything. Me, the boy, the way we live — this beat-up hole — everything. Ain't you? (*She doesn't look up, doesn't answer.*) So tired — moaning and groaning all the time, but you wouldn't do nothing to help, would you? You couldn't be on my side that long for nothing, could you?

RUTH: Walter, please leave me alone.

WALTER: A man needs for a woman to back him up . . .

RUTH: Walter —

WALTER: Mama would listen to you. You know she listen to you more than she do me and Bennie. She think more of you. All you have to do is just sit down with her when you drinking your coffee one morning and talking 'bout things like you do and — (*He sits down beside her and demonstrates graphically what he thinks her methods and tone should be.*) — you just sip your coffee, see, and say easy like that you been thinking 'bout that deal Walter Lee is so interested in, 'bout the store and all, and sip some more coffee, like what you saying ain't really that important to you — And the next thing you know, she be listening good and asking you questions and when I come home — I can tell her the details. This ain't no fly-by-night proposition, baby. I mean we figured it out, me and Willy and Bobo.

RUTH (*with a frown*): Bobo?

WALTER: Yeah. You see, this little liquor store we got in mind cost seventy-five thousand and we figured the initial investment on the place be 'bout thirty thousand, see. That be ten thousand each. Course, there's a couple of hundred you got to pay so's you don't spend your life just waiting for them clowns to let your license get approved —

RUTH: You mean graft?

WALTER (*frowning impatiently*): Don't call it that. See there, that just goes to show you what women understand about the world. Baby, don't *nothing* happen for you in this world 'less you pay *somebody* off!

RUTH: Walter, leave me alone! (*She raises her head and stares at him vigorously — then says, more quietly.*) Eat your eggs, they gonna be cold.

WALTER (*straightening up from her and looking off*): That's it. There you are. Man say to his woman: I got me a dream. His woman say: Eat your eggs. (*Sadly, but gaining in power.*) Man say: I got to take hold of this here world, baby! And a woman will say: Eat your eggs and go to work. (*Passionately now.*) Man say: I got to change my life, I'm choking to death, baby! And his woman say — (*in utter anguish as he brings his fists down on his thighs*) — Your eggs is getting cold!

RUTH (*softly*): Walter, that ain't none of our money.

WALTER (*not listening at all or even looking at her*): This morning, I was lookin' in the mirror and thinking about it . . . I'm thirty-five years old; I been married eleven years and I got a boy who sleeps in the living room — (*very, very quietly*) — and all I got to give him is stories about how rich white people live . . .

RUTH: Eat your eggs, Walter.

WALTER (*slams the table and jumps up*): — DAMN MY EGGS — DAMN ALL THE EGGS THAT EVER WAS!

RUTH: Then go to work.

WALTER (*looking up at her*): See — I'm trying to talk to you 'bout myself — (*shaking his head with the repetition*) — and all you can say is eat them eggs and go to work.

RUTH (*wearily*): Honey, you never say nothing new. I listen to you every day, every night and every morning, and you never say nothing new. (*Shrugging.*) So you would rather *be* Mr. Arnold than be his chauffeur. So — I would *rather* be living in Buckingham Palace.

WALTER: That is just what is wrong with the colored woman in this world . . . Don't understand about building their men up and making 'em feel like they somebody. Like they can do something.

RUTH (*drily, but to hurt*): There *are* colored men who do things.

WALTER: No thanks to the colored woman.

RUTH: Well, being a colored woman, I guess I can't help myself none.

(*She rises and gets the ironing board and sets it up and attacks a huge pile of rough-dried clothes, sprinkling them in preparation for the ironing and then rolling them into tight fat balls.*)

WALTER (*mumbling*): We one group of men tied to a race of women with small minds!

(*His sister Beneatha enters. She is about twenty, as slim and intense as her brother. She is not as pretty as her sister-in-law, but her lean, almost intellectual face has a handsomeness of its own. She wears a bright red flannel nightie, and her thick hair stands wildly about her head. Her speech is a mixture of many things; it is different from the rest of the family's insofar as education has permeated her sense of English — and perhaps the Mid-west rather than the South has finally — at last — won out in her inflection; but not altogether, because over all of it is a soft slurring and transformed use of vowels which is the decided influence of the Southside. She passes through the room without looking at either Ruth or Walter and goes to the outside door and looks, a little blindly, out to the bathroom. She sees that it has been lost to the Johnsons. She closes the door with a sleepy vengeance and crosses to the table and sits down a little defeated.*)

BENEATHA: I am going to start timing those people.

WALTER: You should get up earlier.

BENEATHA (*Her face in her hands. She is still fighting the urge to go back to bed.*): Really — would you suggest dawn? Where's the paper?

WALTER (*pushing the paper across the table to her as he studies her almost clinically, as though he has never seen her before*): You a horrible-looking chick at this hour.

BENEATHA (*drily*): Good morning, everybody.

WALTER (*senselessly*): How is school coming?

BENEATHA (*in the same spirit*): Lovely. Lovely. And you know, biology is the greatest. (*Looking up at him.*) I dissected something that looked just like you yesterday.

WALTER: I just wondered if you've made up your mind and everything.

BENEATHA (*gaining in sharpness and impatience*): And what did I answer yesterday morning — and the day before that?

RUTH (*from the ironing board, like someone disinterested and old*): Don't be so nasty, Bennie.

BENEATHA (*still to her brother*): And the day before that and the day before that!

WALTER (*defensively*): I'm interested in you. Something wrong with that? Ain't many girls who decide —

WALTER AND BENEATHA (*in unison*): — "to be a doctor."

(*Silence.*)

WALTER: Have we figured out yet just exactly how much medical school is going to cost?

RUTH: Walter Lee, why don't you leave that girl alone and get out of here to work?

BENEATHA (*exits to the bathroom and bangs on the door*): Come on out of there, please!

(*She comes back into the room.*)

WALTER (*looking at his sister intently*): You know the check is coming tomorrow.

BENEATHA (*turning on him with a sharpness all her own*): That money belongs to Mama, Walter, and it's for her to decide how she wants to use it. I don't care if she wants to buy a house or a rocketship or just nail it up somewhere and look at it. It's hers. Not ours — *hers.*

WALTER (*bitterly*): Now ain't that fine! You just got your mother's interest at heart, ain't you, girl? You such a nice girl — but if Mama got that money she can always take a few thousand and help you through school too — can't she?

BENEATHA: I have never asked anyone around here to do anything for me!

WALTER: No! And the line between asking and just accepting when the time comes is big and wide — ain't it!

BENEATHA (*with fury*): What do you want from me, Brother — that I quit school or just drop dead, which!

WALTER: I don't want nothing but for you to stop acting holy 'round here. Me and Ruth done made some sacrifices for you — why can't you do something for the family?

RUTH: Walter, don't be dragging me in it.

WALTER: You are in it — Don't you get up and go work in somebody's kitchen for the last three years to help put clothes on her back?

RUTH: Oh, Walter — that's not fair . . .

WALTER: It ain't that nobody expects you to get on your knees and say thank you, Brother; thank you, Ruth; thank you, Mama — and thank you, Travis, for wearing the same pair of shoes for two semesters —

BENEATHA (*dropping to her knees*): Well — I *do* — all right? — thank everybody! And forgive me for ever wanting to be anything at all! (*Pursuing him on her knees across the floor.*) FORGIVE ME, FORGIVE ME, FORGIVE ME!

RUTH: Please stop it! Your mama'll hear you.

WALTER: Who the hell told you you had to be a doctor? If you so crazy 'bout messing 'round with sick people — then go be a nurse like other women — or just get married and be quiet . . .

BENEATHA: Well — you finally got it said . . . It took you three years but you finally got it said. Walter, give up; leave me alone — it's Mama's money.

WALTER: *He was my father, too!*

BENEATHA: So what? He was mine, too — and Travis' grandfather — but the insurance money belongs to Mama. Picking on me is not going to make her give it to you to invest in any liquor stores — (*under breath, dropping into a chair*) — and I for one say, God bless Mama for that!

WALTER (*to Ruth*): See — did you hear? Did you hear!

RUTH: Honey, please go to work.

WALTER: Nobody in this house is ever going to understand me.

BENEATHA: Because you're a nut.

Ester Rolle as Lena Younger comforts her daughter-in-law Ruth in the Huntington Theatre Company's 1994 production of *A Raisin in the Sun*. Also in the scene are Marguerite Hannah as Ruth and B. W. Gonzalez as Beneatha.

WALTER: Who's a nut?

BENEATHA: You — you are a nut. Thee is mad, boy.

WALTER (*looking at his wife and his sister from the door, very sadly*): The world's most backward race of people, and that's a fact.

BENEATHA (*turning slowly in her chair*): And then there are all those prophets who would lead us out of the wilderness — (*Walter slams out of the house.*) — into the swamps!

RUTH: Bennie, why you always gotta be pickin' on your brother? Can't you be a little sweeter sometimes? (*Door opens. Walter walks in. He fumbles with his cap, starts to speak, clears throat, looks everywhere but at Ruth. Finally.*)

WALTER (*to Ruth*): I need some money for carfare.

RUTH (*looks at him, then warms; teasing, but tenderly*): Fifty cents? (*She goes to her bag and gets money.*) Here — take a taxi!

(*Walter exits. Mama enters. She is a woman in her early sixties, full-bodied and strong. She is one of those women of a certain grace and beauty who wear it so unobtrusively that it takes a while to notice. Her dark brown face is surrounded by the total whiteness of her hair, and, being a woman who has adjusted to many things in life and overcome many more, her face is full of strength. She has, we can see, wit and faith of a kind that keep her eyes lit and full of interest and expectancy. She is, in a word, a beautiful woman. Her bearing is perhaps most like the noble bearing of the women of the Hereros of Southwest Africa — rather as if she imagines that as she walks she still bears a basket or a vessel upon her head. Her speech, on the other hand, is as careless as her carriage is precise — she is inclined to slur everything — but her voice is perhaps not so much quiet as simply soft.)*

MAMA: Who that 'round here slamming doors at this hour?

(She crosses through the room, goes to the window, opens it, and brings in a feeble little plant growing doggedly in a small pot on the window sill. She feels the dirt and puts it back out.)

RUTH: That was Walter Lee. He and Bennie was at it again.

MAMA: My children and they tempers. Lord, if this little old plant don't get more sun than it's been getting it ain't never going to see spring again. *(She turns from the window.)* What's the matter with you this morning, Ruth? You looks right peaked. You aiming to iron all them things? Leave some for me. I'll get to 'em this afternoon. Bennie honey, it's too drafty for you to be sitting 'round half dressed. Where's your robe?

BENEATHA: In the cleaners.

MAMA: Well, go get mine and put it on.

BENEATHA: I'm not cold, Mama, honest.

MAMA: I know — but you so thin . . .

BENEATHA *(irritably)*: Mama, I'm not cold.

MAMA *(seeing the make-down bed as Travis has left it)*: Lord have mercy, look at that poor bed. Bless his heart — he tries, don't he?

(She moves to the bed Travis has sloppily made up.)

RUTH: No — he don't half try at all 'cause he knows you going to come along behind him and fix everything. That's just how come he don't know how to do nothing right now — you done spoiled that boy so.

MAMA *(folding bedding)*: Well — he's a little boy. Ain't supposed to know 'bout housekeeping. My baby, that's what he is. What you fix for his breakfast this morning?

RUTH *(angrily)*: I feed my son, Lena!

MAMA: I ain't meddling — *(Under breath; busybody-ish.)* I just noticed all last week he had cold cereal, and when it starts getting this chilly in the fall a child ought to have some hot grits or something when he goes out in the cold —

RUTH *(furious)*: I gave him hot oats — is that all right!

MAMA: I ain't meddling. *(Pause.)* Put a lot of nice butter on it? *(Ruth shoots her an angry look and does not reply.)* He likes lots of butter.

RUTH *(exasperated)*: Lena —

MAMA *(To Beneatha. Mama is inclined to wander conversationally sometimes.)*: What was you and your brother fussing 'bout this morning?

BENEATHA: It's not important, Mama.

(She gets up and goes to look out at the bathroom, which is apparently free, and she picks up her towels and rushes out.)

MAMA: What was they fighting about?

RUTH: Now you know as well as I do.

MAMA *(shaking her head)*: Brother still worrying hisself sick about that money?

RUTH: You know he is.

MAMA: You had breakfast?

RUTH: Some coffee.

MAMA: Girl, you better start eating and looking after yourself better. You almost thin as Travis.

RUTH: Lena —

MAMA: Un-hunh?

RUTH: What are you going to do with it?

MAMA: Now don't you start, child. It's too early in the morning to be talking about money. It ain't Christian.

RUTH: It's just that he got his heart set on that store —

MAMA: You mean that liquor store that Willy Harris want him to invest in?

RUTH: Yes —

MAMA: We ain't no business people, Ruth. We just plain working folks.

RUTH: Ain't nobody business people till they go into business. Walter Lee say colored people ain't never going to start getting ahead till they start gambling on some different kinds of things in the world — investments and things.

MAMA: What done got into you, girl? Walter Lee done finally sold you on investing.

RUTH: No. Mama, something is happening between Walter and me. I don't know what it is — but he needs something — something I can't give him anymore. He needs this chance, Lena.

MAMA *(frowning deeply)*: But liquor, honey —

RUTH: Well — like Walter say — I spec people going to always be drinking themselves some liquor.

MAMA: Well — whether they drinks it or not ain't none of my business. But whether I go into business selling it to 'em *is*, and I don't want that on my ledger this late in life. *(Stopping suddenly and studying her daughter-in-law.)* Ruth Younger, what's the matter with you today? You look like you could fall over right there.

RUTH: I'm tired.

MAMA: Then you better stay home from work today.

RUTH: I can't stay home. She'd be calling up the agency and screaming at them, "My girl didn't come in today — send me somebody! My girl didn't come in!" Oh, she just have a fit . . .

MAMA: Well, let her have it. I'll just call her up and say you got the flu —

RUTH *(laughing)*: Why the flu?

MAMA: 'Cause it sounds respectable to 'em. Something white people get, too. They know 'bout the flu. Otherwise they think you been cut up or something when you tell 'em you sick.

RUTH: I got to go in. We need the money.

MAMA: Somebody would of thought my children done all but starved to death the way they talk about money here late. Child, we got a great big old check coming tomorrow.

RUTH (*sincerely, but also self-righteously*): Now that's your money. It ain't got nothing to do with me. We all feel like that — Walter and Bennie and me — even Travis.

MAMA (*thoughtfully, and suddenly very far away*): Ten thousand dollars —

RUTH: Sure is wonderful.

MAMA: Ten thousand dollars.

RUTH: You know what you should do, Miss Lena? You should take yourself a trip somewhere. To Europe or South America or someplace —

MAMA (*throwing up her hands at the thought*): Oh, child!

RUTH: I'm serious. Just pack up and leave! Go on away and enjoy yourself some. Forget about the family and have yourself a ball for once in your life —

MAMA (*drily*): You sound like I'm just about ready to die. Who'd go with me? What I look like wandering 'round Europe by myself?

RUTH: Shoot — these here rich white women do it all the time. They don't think nothing of packing up they suitcases and piling on one of them big steamships and — swoosh! — they gone, child.

MAMA: Something always told me I wasn't no rich white woman.

RUTH: Well — what are you going to do with it then?

MAMA: I ain't rightly decided. (*Thinking. She speaks now with emphasis.*) Some of it got to be put away for Beneatha and her schoolin' — and ain't nothing going to touch that part of it. Nothing. (*She waits several seconds, trying to make up her mind about something, and looks at Ruth a little tentatively before going on.*) Been thinking that we maybe could meet the notes on a little old two-story somewhere, with a yard where Travis could play in the summertime, if we use part of the insurance for a down payment and everybody kind of pitch in. I could maybe take on a little day work again, few days a week —

RUTH (*studying her mother-in-law furtively and concentrating on her ironing, anxious to encourage without seeming to*): Well, Lord knows, we've put enough rent into this here rat trap to pay for four houses by now . . .

MAMA (*looking up at the words "rat trap" and then looking around and leaning back and sighing — in a suddenly reflective mood —*): "Rat trap" — yes, that's all it is. (*Smiling.*) I remember just as well the day me and Big Walter moved in here. Hadn't been married but two weeks and wasn't planning on living here no more than a year. (*She shakes her head at the dissolved dream.*) We was going to set away, little by little, don't you know, and buy a little place out in Morgan Park. We had even picked out the house. (*Chuckling a little.*) Looks right dumpy today. But Lord, child, you should know, all the dreams I had 'bout buying that house and fixing it up and making me a little garden in the back — (*She waits and stops smiling.*) And didn't none of it happen.

(*Dropping her hands in a futile gesture.*)

RUTH (*keeps her head down, ironing*): Yes, life can be a barrel of disappointments, sometimes.

MAMA: Honey, Big Walter would come in here some nights back then and slump down on that couch there and just look at the rug, and look at me and look at the rug and then back at me — and I'd know he was down then . . . really down. (*After a second very long and thoughtful pause; she is seeing back to times that only she can see.*) And then, Lord, when I lost that baby — little Claude — I almost thought I was going to lose Big Walter too. Oh, that man grieved hisself! He was one man to love his children.

RUTH: Ain't nothin' can tear at you like losin' your baby.

MAMA: I guess that's how come that man finally worked hisself to death like he done. Like he was fighting his own war with this here world that took his baby from him.

RUTH: He sure was a fine man, all right. I always liked Mr. Younger.

MAMA: Crazy 'bout his children! God knows there was plenty wrong with Walter Younger — hard-headed, mean, kind of wild with women — plenty wrong with him. But he sure loved his children. Always wanted them to have something — be something. That's where Brother gets all these notions, I reckon. Big Walter used to say, he'd get right wet in the eyes sometimes, lean his head back with the water standing in his eyes and say, "Seem like God didn't see fit to give the black man nothing but dreams — but He did give us children to make them dreams seem worthwhile." (*She smiles.*) He could talk like that, don't you know.

RUTH: Yes, he sure could. He was a good man, Mr. Younger.

MAMA: Yes, a fine man — just couldn't never catch up with his dreams, that's all.

(*Beneatha comes in, brushing her hair and looking up to the ceiling, where the sound of a vacuum cleaner has started up.*)

BENEATHA: What could be so dirty on that woman's rugs that she has to vacuum them every single day?

RUTH: I wish certain young women 'round here who I could name would take inspiration about certain rugs in a certain apartment I could also mention.

BENEATHA (*shrugging*): How much cleaning can a house need, for Christ's sakes.

MAMA (*not liking the Lord's name used thus*): Bennie!

RUTH: Just listen to her — just listen!

BENEATHA: Oh, God!

MAMA: If you use the Lord's name just one more time —

BENEATHA (*a bit of a whine*): Oh, Mama —

RUTH: Fresh — just fresh as salt, this girl!

BENEATHA (*drily*): Well — if the salt loses its savor —

MAMA: Now that will do. I just ain't going to have you 'round here reciting the scriptures in vain — you hear me?

BENEATHA: How did I manage to get on everybody's wrong side by just walking into a room?

RUTH: If you weren't so fresh —

BENEATHA: Ruth, I'm twenty years old.

MAMA: What time you be home from school today?

BENEATHA: Kind of late. (*With enthusiasm.*) Madeline is going to start my guitar lessons today.

(*Mama and Ruth look up with the same expression.*)

MAMA: Your *what* kind of lessons?

BENEATHA: Guitar.

RUTH: Oh, Father!

MAMA: How come you done taken it in your mind to learn to play the guitar?

BENEATHA: I just want to, that's all.

MAMA (*smiling*): Lord, child, don't you know what to do with yourself? How long it going to be before you get tired of this now — like you got tired of that little play-acting group you joined last year? (*Looking at Ruth.*) And what was it the year before that?

RUTH: The horseback-riding club for which she bought that fifty-five-dollar riding habit that's been hanging in the closet ever since!

MAMA (*to Beneatha*): Why you got to flit so from one thing to another, baby?

BENEATHA (*sharply*): I just want to learn to play the guitar. Is there anything wrong with that?

MAMA: Ain't nobody trying to stop you. I just wonders sometimes why you has to flit so from one thing to another all the time. You ain't never done nothing with all that camera equipment you brought home —

BENEATHA: I don't flit! I — I experiment with different forms of expression —

RUTH: Like riding a horse?

BENEATHA: — People have to express themselves one way or another.

MAMA: What is it you want to express?

BENEATHA (*angrily*): Me! (*Mama and Ruth look at each other and burst into raucous laughter.*) Don't worry — I don't expect you to understand.

MAMA (*to change the subject*): Who you going out with tomorrow night?

BENEATHA (*with displeasure*): George Murchison again.

MAMA (*pleased*): Oh — you getting a little sweet on him?

RUTH: You ask me, this child ain't sweet on nobody but herself — (*Under breath.*) Express herself!

(*They laugh.*)

BENEATHA: Oh — I like George all right, Mama. I mean I like him enough to go out with him and stuff, but —

RUTH (*for devilment*): What does *and stuff* mean?

BENEATHA: Mind your own business.

MAMA: Stop picking at her now, Ruth. (*She chuckles — then a suspicious sudden look at her daughter as she turns in her chair for emphasis.*) What DOES it mean?

BENEATHA (*wearily*): Oh, I just mean I couldn't ever really be serious about George. He's — he's so shallow.

RUTH: Shallow — what do you mean he's shallow? He's *Rich!*

MAMA: Hush, Ruth.

BENEATHA: I know he's rich. He knows he's rich, too.

RUTH: Well — what other qualities a man got to have to satisfy you, little girl?

BENEATHA: You wouldn't even begin to understand. Anybody who married Walter could not possibly understand.

MAMA (*outraged*): What kind of way is that to talk about your brother?

BENEATHA: Brother is a flip — let's face it.

MAMA (*to Ruth, helplessly*): What's a flip?

RUTH (*glad to add kindling*): She's saying he's crazy.

BENEATHA: Not crazy. Brother isn't really crazy yet — he — he's an elaborate neurotic.

MAMA: Hush your mouth!

BENEATHA: As for George. Well. George looks good — he's got a beautiful car and he takes me to nice places and, as my sister-in-law says, he is probably the richest boy I will ever get to know and I even like him sometimes — but if the Youngers are sitting around waiting to see if their little Bennie is going to tie up the family with the Murchisons, they are wasting their time.

RUTH: You mean you wouldn't marry George Murchison if he asked you someday? That pretty, rich thing? Honey, I knew you was odd —

BENEATHA: No I would not marry him if all I felt for him was what I feel now. Besides, George's family wouldn't really like it.

MAMA: Why not?

BENEATHA: Oh, Mama — The Murchisons are honest-to-God-real-*live*-rich colored people, and the only people in the world who are more snobbish than rich white people are rich colored people. I thought everybody knew that. I've met Mrs. Murchison. She's a scene!

MAMA: You must not dislike people 'cause they well off, honey.

BENEATHA: Why not? It makes just as much sense as disliking people 'cause they are poor, and lots of people do that.

RUTH (*A wisdom-of-the-ages manner. To Mama.*): Well, she'll get over some of this —

BENEATHA: Get over it? What are you talking about, Ruth? Listen, I'm going to be a doctor. I'm not worried about who I'm going to marry yet — if I ever get married.

MAMA AND RUTH: *If!*

MAMA: Now, Bennie —

BENEATHA: Oh, I probably will . . . but first I'm going to be a doctor, and George, for one, still thinks that's pretty funny. I couldn't be bothered with that. I am going to be a doctor and everybody around here better understand that!

MAMA (*kindly*): 'Course you going to be a doctor, honey, God willing.

BENEATHA (*drily*): God hasn't got a thing to do with it.

MAMA: Beneatha — that just wasn't necessary.

BENEATHA: Well — neither is God. I get sick of hearing about God.

MAMA: Beneatha!

BENEATHA: I mean it! I'm just tired of hearing about God all the time. What has He got to do with anything? Does he pay tuition?

MAMA: You 'bout to get your fresh little jaw slapped!

RUTH: That's just what she needs, all right!

BENEATHA: Why? Why can't I say what I want to around here, like everybody else?

MAMA: It don't sound nice for a young girl to say things like that — you wasn't brought up that way. Me and your father went to trouble to get you and Brother to church every Sunday.

BENEATHA: Mama, you don't understand. It's all a matter of ideas, and God is just one idea I don't accept. It's not important. I am not going out and be immoral or commit crimes because I don't believe in God. I don't even think about it. It's just that I get tired of Him getting credit for all the things the human race achieves through its own stubborn effort. There simply is no blasted God — there is only man and it is *he* who makes miracles!

(*Mama absorbs this speech, studies her daughter and rises slowly and crosses to Beneatha and slaps her powerfully across the face. After, there is only silence and the daughter drops her eyes from her mother's face, and Mama is very tall before her.*)

MAMA: Now — you say after me, in my mother's house there is still God. (*There is a long pause and Beneatha stares at the floor wordlessly. Mama repeats the phrase with precision and cool emotion.*) In my mother's house there is still God.

BENEATHA: In my mother's house there is still God.

(*A long pause.*)

MAMA (*Walking away from Beneatha, too disturbed for triumphant posture. Stopping and turning back to her daughter.*): There are some ideas we ain't going to have in this house. Not long as I am at the head of this family.

BENEATHA: Yes, ma'am.

(*Mama walks out of the room.*)

RUTH (*almost gently, with profound understanding*): You think you a woman, Bennie — but you still a little girl. What you did was childish — so you got treated like a child.

BENEATHA: I see. (*Quietly.*) I also see that everybody thinks it's all right for Mama to be a tyrant. But all the tyranny in the world will never put a God in the heavens!

(*She picks up her books and goes out. Pause.*)

RUTH (*goes to Mama's door*): She said she was sorry.

MAMA (*coming out, going to her plant*): They frightens me, Ruth. My children.

RUTH: You got good children, Lena. They just a little off sometimes — but they're good.

MAMA: No — there's something come down between me and them that don't let us understand each other and I don't know what it is. One done almost lost his mind thinking 'bout money all the time and the other done commence to talk about things I can't seem to understand in no form or fashion. What is it that's changing, Ruth.

RUTH (*soothingly, older than her years*): Now . . . you taking it all too seriously. You just got strong-willed children and it takes a strong woman like you to keep 'em in hand.

MAMA (*looking at her plant and sprinkling a little water on it*): They spirited all right, my children. Got to admit they got spirit — Bennie and Walter. Like this little old plant that ain't never had enough sunshine or nothing — and look at it . . .

(*She has her back to Ruth, who has had to stop ironing and lean against something and put the back of her hand to her forehead.*)

RUTH (*trying to keep Mama from noticing*): You . . . sure . . . loves that little old thing, don't you? . . .

MAMA: Well, I always wanted me a garden like I used to see sometimes at the back of the houses down home. This plant is close as I ever got to having one. (*She looks out of the window as she replaces the plant.*) Lord, ain't nothing as dreary as the view from this window on a dreary day, is there? Why ain't you singing this morning, Ruth? Sing that "No Ways Tired." That song always lifts me up so — (*She turns at last to see that Ruth has slipped quietly to the floor, in a state of semiconsciousness.*) Ruth! Ruth honey — what's the matter with you . . . Ruth!

Scene II

(*It is the following morning; a Saturday morning, and house cleaning is in progress at the Youngers'. Furniture has been shoved hither and yon and Mama is giving the kitchen-area walls a washing down. Beneatha, in dungarees, with a handkerchief tied around her face, is spraying insecticide into the cracks in the walls. As they work, the radio is on and a Southside disk jockey program is inappropriately filling the house with a rather exotic saxophone blues. Travis, the sole idle one, is leaning on his arms, looking out of the window.*)

TRAVIS: Grandmama, that stuff Bennie is using smells awful. Can I go downstairs, please?

MAMA: Did you get all them chores done already? I ain't seen you doing much.

TRAVIS: Yes'm — finished early. Where did Mama go this morning?

MAMA (*looking at Beneatha*): She had to go on a little errand.

(*The phone rings. Beneatha runs to answer it and reaches it before Walter, who has entered from bedroom.*)

TRAVIS: Where?

MAMA: To tend to her business.

BENEATHA: Haylo . . . (*Disappointed.*) Yes, he is. (*She tosses the phone to Walter, who barely catches it.*) It's Willie Harris again.

WALTER (*as privately as possible under Mama's gaze*): Hello, Willie. Did you get the papers from the lawyer? . . . No, not yet. I told you the mailman doesn't get here till ten-thirty . . . No, I'll come there . . . Yeah! Right away. (*He hangs up and goes for his coat.*)

BENEATHA: Brother, where did Ruth go?

WALTER (*as he exits*): How should I know!

TRAVIS: Aw come on, Grandma. Can I go outside?

MAMA: Oh, I guess so. You stay right in front of the house, though, and keep a good lookout for the post-man.

TRAVIS: Yes'm. (*He darts into bedroom for stickball and bat, reenters, and sees Beneatha on her knees spray-ing under sofa with behind upraised. He edges closer to the target, takes aim, and lets her have it. She screams.*) Leave them poor little cockroaches alone, they ain't bothering you none! (*He runs as she swings the spraygun at him viciously and playfully.*) Grandma! Grandma!

MAMA: Look out there, girl, before you be spilling some of that stuff on that child!

TRAVIS (*safely behind the bastion of Mama*): That's right — look out, now! (*He exits.*)

BENEATHA (*drily*): I can't imagine that it would hurt him — it has never hurt the roaches.

MAMA: Well, little boys' hides ain't as tough as South-side roaches. You better get over there behind the bureau. I seen one marching out of there like Napoleon yesterday.

BENEATHA: There's really only one way to get rid of them, Mama —

MAMA: How?

BENEATHA: Set fire to this building! Mama, where did Ruth go?

MAMA (*looking at her with meaning*): To the doctor, I think.

BENEATHA: The doctor? What's the matter? (*They exchange glances.*) You don't think —

MAMA (*with her sense of drama*): Now I ain't saying what I think. But I ain't never been wrong 'bout a woman neither.

(*The phone rings.*)

BENEATHA (*at the phone*): Hay-lo . . . (*Pause, and a moment of recognition.*) Well — when did you get back! . . . And how was it? . . . Of course I've missed you — in my way . . . This morning? No . . . house cleaning and all that and Mama hates it if I let people come over when the house is like this . . . You *have*? Well, that's different . . . What is it — Oh, what the hell, come on over . . . Right, see you then. *Arrivederci.*

(*She hangs up.*)

MAMA (*who has listened vigorously, as is her habit*): Who is that you inviting over here with this house looking like this? You ain't got the pride you was born with!

BENEATHA: Asagai doesn't care how houses look, Mama — he's an intellectual.

MAMA: *Who?*

BENEATHA: Asagai — Joseph Asagai. He's an African boy I met on campus. He's been studying in Canada all summer.

MAMA: What's his name?

BENEATHA: Asagai, Joseph. Ah-sah-guy . . . He's from Nigeria.

MAMA: Oh, that's the little country that was founded by slaves way back . . .

BENEATHA: No, Mama — that's Liberia.

MAMA: I don't think I never met no African before.

BENEATHA: Well, do me a favor and don't ask him a whole lot of ignorant questions about Africans. I mean, do they wear clothes and all that —

MAMA: Well, now, I guess if you think we so ignorant 'round here maybe you shouldn't bring your friends here —

BENEATHA: It's just that people ask such crazy things. All anyone seems to know about when it comes to Africa is Tarzan —

MAMA (*indignantly*): Why should I know anything about Africa?

BENEATHA: Why do you give money at church for the missionary work?

MAMA: Well, that's to help save people.

BENEATHA: You mean save them from *heathenism* —

MAMA (*innocently*): Yes.

BENEATHA: I'm afraid they need more salvation from the British and the French.

(*Ruth comes in forlornly and pulls off her coat with dejection. They both turn to look at her.*)

RUTH (*dispiritedly*): Well, I guess from all the happy faces — everybody knows.

BENEATHA: You pregnant?

MAMA: Lord have mercy, I sure hope it's a little old girl. Travis ought to have a sister.

(*Beneatha and Ruth give her a hopeless look for this grandmotherly enthusiasm.*)

BENEATHA: How far along are you?

RUTH: Two months.

BENEATHA: Did you mean to? I mean did you plan it or was it an accident?

MAMA: What do you know about planning or not plan-ning?

BENEATHA: Oh, Mama.

RUTH (*wearily*): She's twenty years old, Lena.

BENEATHA: Did you plan it, Ruth?

RUTH: Mind your own business.

BENEATHA: It is my business — where is he going to live, on the *roof*? (*There is silence following the remark as the three women react to the sense of it.*) Gee — I didn't mean that, Ruth, honest. Gee, I don't feel like that at all. I — I think it is wonderful.

RUTH (*dully*): Wonderful.

BENEATHA: Yes — really.

MAMA (*looking at Ruth, worried*): Doctor say everything going to be all right?

RUTH (*far away*): Yes — she says everything is going to be fine . . .

MAMA (*immediately suspicious*): "She" — What doctor you went to?

(*Ruth folds over, near hysteria.*)

MAMA (*worriedly hovering over Ruth*): Ruth honey — what's the matter with you — you sick?

(*Ruth has her fists clenched on her thighs and is fighting hard to suppress a scream that seems to be rising in her.*)

BENEATHA: What's the matter with her, Mama?

MAMA (*working her fingers in Ruth's shoulders to relax her*): She be all right. Women gets right depressed sometimes when they get her way. (*Speaking softly, expertly, rapidly.*) Now you just relax. That's right . . . just lean back, don't think 'bout nothing at all . . . nothing at all —

RUTH: I'm all right . . .

(*The glassy-eyed look melts and then she collapses into a fit of heavy sobbing. The bell rings.*)

BENEATHA: Oh, my God — that must be Asagai.

MAMA (*to Ruth*): Come on now, honey. You need to lie down and rest awhile . . . then have some nice hot food.

(*They exit, Ruth's weight on her mother-in-law. Beneatha, herself profoundly disturbed, opens the door to admit a rather dramatic-looking young man with a large package.*)

ASAGAI: Hello, Alaiyo —

BENEATHA (*holding the door open and regarding him with pleasure*): Hello . . . (*Long pause.*) Well — come in. And please excuse everything. My mother was very upset about my letting anyone come here with the place like this.

ASAGAI (*coming into the room*): You look disturbed too . . . Is something wrong?

BENEATHA (*still at the door, absently*): Yes . . . we've all got acute ghetto-itus. (*She smiles and comes toward him, finding a cigarette and sitting.*) So — sit down! No! Wait! (*She whips the spraygun off sofa where she had left it and puts the cushions back. At last perches on arm of sofa. He sits.*) So, how was Canada?

ASAGAI (*a sophisticate*): Canadian.

BENEATHA (*looking at him*): Asagai, I'm very glad you are back.

ASAGAI (*looking back at her in turn*): Are you really?

BENEATHA: Yes — very.

ASAGAI: Why? — you were quite glad when I went away. What happened?

BENEATHA: You went away.

ASAGAI: Ahhhhhhhh.

BENEATHA: Before — you wanted to be so serious before there was time.

ASAGAI: How much time must there be before one knows what one feels?

BENEATHA (*Stalling this particular conversation. Her hands pressed together, in a deliberately childish gesture.*): What did you bring me?

ASAGAI (*handing her the package*): Open it and see.

BENEATHA (*eagerly opening the package and drawing out some records and the colorful robes of a Nigerian woman*): Oh, Asagai! . . . You got them for me! . . . How beautiful . . . and the records too! (*She lifts out the robes and runs to the mirror with them and holds the drapery up in front of herself.*)

ASAGAI (*coming to her at the mirror*): I shall have to teach you how to drape it properly. (*He flings the material about her for the moment and stands back to look at her.*) Ah — Oh-pay-gay-day, oh-gbah-mu-shay. (*A Yoruba exclamation for admiration.*) You wear it well . . . very well . . . mutilated hair and all.

BENEATHA (*turning suddenly*): My hair — what's wrong with my hair?

ASAGAI (*shrugging*): Were you born with it like that?

BENEATHA (*reaching up to touch it*): No . . . of course not.

(*She looks back to the mirror, disturbed.*)

ASAGAI (*smiling*): How then?

BENEATHA: You know perfectly well how . . . as crinkly as yours . . . that's how.

ASAGAI: And it is ugly to you that way?

BENEATHA (*quickly*): Oh, no — not ugly . . . (*More slowly, apologetically.*) But it's so hard to manage when it's, well — raw.

ASAGAI: And so to accommodate that — you mutilate it every week?

BENEATHA: It's not mutilation!

ASAGAI (*laughing aloud at her seriousness*): Oh . . . please! I am only teasing you because you are so very serious about these things. (*He stands back from her and folds his arms across his chest as he watches her pulling at her hair and frowning in the mirror.*) Do you remember the first time you met me at school? . . . (*He laughs.*) You came up to me and you said — and I thought you were the most serious little thing I had ever seen — you said: (*He imitates her.*) "Mr. Asagai — I want very much to talk with you. About Africa. You see, Mr. Asagai, I am looking for my *identity!*"

(*He laughs.*)

BENEATHA (*turning to him, not laughing*): Yes —

(*Her face is quizzical, profoundly disturbed.*)

ASAGAI (*still teasing and reaching out and taking her face in his hands and turning her profile to him*): Well . . . it is true that this is not so much a profile of a Hollywood queen as perhaps a queen of the Nile — (*A mock dismissal of the importance of the question.*) But what does it matter? Assimilationism is so popular in your country.

BENEATHA (*wheeling, passionately, sharply*): I am not an assimilationist!

ASAGAI (*the protest hangs in the room for a moment and Asagai studies her, his laughter fading*): Such a serious one. (*There is a pause.*) So — you like the robes? You must take excellent care of them — they are from my sister's personal wardrobe.

BENEATHA (*with incredulity*): You — you sent all the way home — for me?

ASAGAI (*with charm*): For you — I would do much more . . . Well, that is what I came for. I must go.

BENEATHA: Will you call me Monday?

ASAGAI: Yes . . . We have a great deal to talk about. I mean about identity and time and all that.

BENEATHA: Time?

ASAGAI: Yes. About how much time one needs to know what one feels.

BENEATHA: You see! You never understood that there is more than one kind of feeling which can exist between a man and a woman — or, at least, there should be.

ASAGAI (*shaking his head negatively but gently*): No. Between a man and a woman there need be only one kind of feeling. I have that for you . . . Now even . . . right this moment . . .

BENEATHA: I know — and by itself — it won't do. I can find that anywhere.

ASAGAI: For a woman it should be enough.

BENEATHA: I know — because that's what it says in all the novels that men write. But it isn't. Go ahead and laugh — but I'm not interested in being someone's little episode in America or — (*with feminine vengeance*) — one of them! (*Asagai has burst into laughter again.*) That's funny as hell, huh!

ASAGAI: It's just that every American girl I have known has said that to me. White — black — in this you are all the same. And the same speech, too!

BENEATHA (*angrily*): Yuk, yuk, yuk!

ASAGAI: It's how you can be sure that the world's most liberated women are not liberated at all. You all talk about it too much!

(*Mama enters and is immediately all social charm because of the presence of a guest.*)

BENEATHA: Oh — Mama — this is Mr. Asagai.

MAMA: How do you do?

ASAGAI (*total politeness to an elder*): How do you do, Mrs. Younger. Please forgive me for coming at such an outrageous hour on a Saturday.

MAMA: Well, you are quite welcome. I just hope you understand that our house don't always look like this. (*Chatterish.*) You must come again. I would love to hear all about — (*not sure of the name*) — your country. I think it's so sad the way our American Negroes don't know nothing about Africa 'cept Tarzan and all that. And all that money they pour into these churches when they ought to be helping you people over there drive out them French and Englishmen done taken away your land.

(*The mother flashes a slightly superior look at her daughter upon completion of the recitation.*)

ASAGAI (*taken aback by this sudden and acutely unrelated expression of sympathy*): Yes . . . yes . . .

MAMA (*smiling at him suddenly and relaxing and looking him over*): How many miles is it from here to where you come from?

ASAGAI: Many thousands.

MAMA (*looking at him as she would Walter*): I bet you don't half look after yourself, being away from your mama either. I spec you better come 'round here from time to time to get yourself some decent home-cooked meals . . .

ASAGAI (*moved*): Thank you. Thank you very much. (*They are all quiet, then —*) Well . . . I must go. I will call you Monday, Alaiyo.

MAMA: What's that he call you?

ASAGAI: Oh — "Alaiyo." I hope you don't mind. It is what you would call a nickname, I think. It is a Yoruba word. I am a Yoruba.

MAMA (*looking at Beneatha*): I — I thought he was from — (*Uncertain.*)

ASAGAI (*understanding*): Nigeria is my country. Yoruba is my tribal origin —

BENEATHA: You didn't tell us what Alaiyo means . . . for all I know, you might be calling me Little Idiot or something . . .

ASAGAI: Well . . . let me see . . . I do not know how just to explain it . . . The sense of a thing can be so different when it changes languages.

BENEATHA: You're evading.

ASAGAI: No — really it is difficult . . . (*Thinking.*) It means . . . it means One for Whom Bread — Food — Is Not Enough. (*He looks at her.*) Is that all right?

BENEATHA (*understanding, softly*): Thank you.

MAMA (*looking from one to the other and not understanding any of it*): Well . . . that's nice . . . You must come see us again — Mr. ——

ASAGAI: Ah-sah-guy . . .

MAMA: Yes . . . Do come again.

ASAGAI: Good-bye.

(*He exits.*)

MAMA (*after him*): Lord, that's a pretty thing just went out here! (*Insinuatingly, to her daughter.*) Yes, I guess I see why we done commence to get so interested in Africa 'round here. Missionaries my aunt Jenny!

(*She exits.*)

BENEATHA: Oh, Mama! . . .

(*She picks up the Nigerian dress and holds it up to her in front of the mirror again. She sets the headdress on haphazardly and then notices her hair again and clutches at it and then replaces the headdress and frowns at herself. Then she starts to wriggle in front of the mirror as she thinks a Nigerian woman might. Travis enters and stands regarding her.)*

TRAVIS: What's the matter, girl, you cracking up?

BENEATHA: Shut up.

(She pulls the headdress off and looks at herself in the mirror and clutches at her hair again and squinches her eyes as if trying to imagine something. Then, suddenly, she gets her raincoat and kerchief and hurriedly prepares for going out.)

MAMA *(coming back into the room)*: She's resting now. Travis, baby, run next door and ask Miss Johnson to please let me have a little kitchen cleanser. This here can is empty as Jacob's kettle.

TRAVIS: I just came in.

MAMA: Do as you told. *(He exits and she looks at her daughter.)* Where you going?

BENEATHA *(halting at the door)*: To become a queen of the Nile!

(She exits in a breathless blaze of glory. Ruth appears in the bedroom doorway.)

MAMA: Who told you to get up?

RUTH: Ain't nothing wrong with me to be lying in no bed for. Where did Bennie go?

MAMA *(drumming her fingers)*: Far as I could make out — to Egypt. *(Ruth just looks at her.)* What time is it getting to?

RUTH: Ten twenty. And the mailman going to ring that bell this morning just like he done every morning for the last umpteen years.

(Travis comes in with the cleanser can.)

TRAVIS: She say to tell you that she don't have much.

MAMA *(angrily)*: Lord, some people I could name sure is tight-fisted! *(Directing her grandson.)* Mark two cans of cleanser down on the list there. If she that hard up for kitchen cleanser, I sure don't want to forget to get her none!

RUTH: Lena — maybe the woman is just short on cleanser —

MAMA *(not listening)*: — Much baking powder as she done borrowed from me all these years, she could of done gone into the baking business!

(The bell sounds suddenly and sharply and all three are stunned — serious and silent — mid-speech. In spite of all the other conversations and distractions of the morning, this is what they have been waiting for, even Travis, who looks helplessly from his mother to his grandmother. Ruth is the first to come to life again.)

RUTH *(to Travis)*: Get down them steps, boy!

(Travis snaps to life and flies out to get the mail.)

MAMA *(her eyes wide, her hand to her breast)*: You mean it done really come?

RUTH *(excited)*: Oh, Miss Lena!

MAMA *(collecting herself)*: Well . . . I don't know what

we all so excited about 'round here for. We known it was coming for months.

RUTH: That's a whole lot different from having it come and being able to hold it in your hands . . . a piece of paper worth ten thousand dollars . . . *(Travis bursts back into the room. He holds the envelope high above his head, like a little dancer, his face is radiant and he is breathless. He moves to his grandmother with sudden slow ceremony and puts the envelope into her hands. She accepts it, and then merely holds it and looks at it.)* Come on! Open it . . . Lord have mercy, I wish Walter Lee was here!

TRAVIS: Open it, Grandmama!

MAMA *(staring at it)*: Now you all be quiet. It's just a check.

RUTH: Open it . . .

MAMA *(still staring at it)*: Now don't act silly . . . We ain't never been no people to act silly 'bout no money —

RUTH *(swiftly)*: We ain't never had none before — OPEN IT!

(Mama finally makes a good strong tear and pulls out the thin blue slice of paper and inspects it closely. The boy and his mother study it raptly over Mama's shoulders.)

MAMA: *Travis!* *(She is counting off with doubt.)* Is that the right number of zeros.

TRAVIS: Yes'm . . . ten thousand dollars. Gaalee, Grandmama, you rich.

MAMA *(She holds the check away from her, still looking at it. Slowly her face sobers into a mask of unhappiness.)*: Ten thousand dollars. *(She hands it to Ruth.)* Put it away somewhere, Ruth. *(She does not look at Ruth; her eyes seem to be seeing something somewhere very far off.)* Ten thousand dollars they give you. Ten thousand dollars.

TRAVIS *(to his mother, sincerely)*: What's the matter with Grandmama — don't she want to be rich?

RUTH *(distractedly)*: You go on out and play now, baby. *(Travis exits. Mama starts wiping dishes absently, humming intently to herself. Ruth turns to her, with kind exasperation.)* You've gone and got yourself upset.

MAMA *(not looking at her)*: I spec if it wasn't for you all . . . I would just put that money away or give it to the church or something.

RUTH: Now what kind of talk is that. Mr. Younger would just be plain mad if he could hear you talking foolish like that.

MAMA *(stopping and staring off)*: Yes . . . he sure would. *(Sighing.)* We got enough to do with that money, all right. *(She halts then, and turns and looks at her daughter-in-law hard; Ruth avoids her eyes and Mama wipes her hands with finality and starts to speak firmly to Ruth.)* Where did you go today, girl?

RUTH: To the doctor.

MAMA *(impatiently)*: Now, Ruth . . . you know better than that. Old Doctor Jones is strange enough in his way but there ain't nothing 'bout him make some-body slip and call him "she" — like you done this morning.

RUTH: Well, that's what happened — my tongue slipped.

MAMA: You went to see that woman, didn't you?

RUTH (*defensively, giving herself away*): What woman you talking about?

MAMA (*angrily*): That woman who —

(*Walter enters in great excitement.*)

WALTER: Did it come?

MAMA (*quietly*): Can't you give people a Christian greeting before you start asking about money?

WALTER (*to Ruth*): Did it come? (*Ruth unfolds the check and lays it quietly before him, watching him intently with thoughts of her own. Walter sits down and grasps it close and counts off the zeros.*) Ten thousand dollars — (*He turns suddenly, frantically to his mother and draws some papers out of his breast pocket.*) Mama — look. Old Willy Harris put everything on paper —

MAMA: Son — I think you ought to talk to your wife . . . I'll go on out and leave you alone if you want —

WALTER: I can talk to her later — Mama, look —

MAMA: Son —

WALTER: WILL SOMEBODY PLEASE LISTEN TO ME TODAY!

MAMA (*quietly*): I don't 'low no yellin' in this house, Walter Lee, and you know it — (*Walter stares at them in frustration and starts to speak several times.*) And there ain't going to be no investing in no liquor stores.

WALTER: But, Mama, you ain't even looked at it.

MAMA: I don't aim to have to speak on that again.

(*A long pause.*)

WALTER: You ain't looked at it and you don't aim to have to speak on that again? You ain't even looked at it and *you* have decided — (*Crumpling his papers.*) Well, *you* tell that to my boy tonight when you put him to sleep on the living room couch . . . (*Turning to Mama and speaking directly to her.*) Yeah — and tell it to my wife, Mama, tomorrow when she has to go out of here to look after somebody else's kids. And tell it to *me*, Mama, every time we need a new pair of curtains and I have to watch *you* go out and work in somebody's kitchen. Yeah, you tell me then!

(*Walter starts out.*)

RUTH: Where you going?

WALTER: I'm going out!

RUTH: Where?

WALTER: Just out of this house somewhere —

RUTH (*getting her coat*): I'll come too.

WALTER: I don't want you to come!

RUTH: I got something to talk to you about, Walter.

WALTER: That's too bad.

MAMA (*still quietly*): Walter Lee — (*She waits and he finally turns and looks at her.*) Sit down.

WALTER: I'm a grown man, Mama.

MAMA: Ain't nobody said you wasn't grown. But you

still in my house and my presence. And as long as you are — you'll talk to your wife civil. Now sit down.

RUTH (*suddenly*): Oh, let him go on out and drink him-self to death! He makes me sick to my stomach! (*She flings her coat against him and exits to bedroom.*)

WALTER (*violently flinging the coat after her*): And you turn mine too, baby! (*The door slams behind her.*) That was my biggest mistake —

MAMA (*still quietly*): Walter, what is the matter with you?

WALTER: Matter with me? Ain't nothing the matter with *me!*

MAMA: Yes there is. Something eating you up like a crazy man. Something more than me not giving you this money. The past few years I been watching it happen to you. You get all nervous acting and kind of wild in the eyes — (*Walter jumps up impatiently at her words.*) I said sit there now, I'm talking to you!

WALTER: Mama — I don't need no nagging at me today.

MAMA: Seem like you getting to a place where you always tied up in some kind of knot about some-thing. But if anybody ask you 'bout it you just yell at 'em and bust out the house and go out and drink somewheres. Walter Lee, people can't live with that. Ruth's a good, patient girl in her way — but you get-ting to be too much. Boy, don't make the mistake of driving that girl away from you.

WALTER: Why — what she do for me?

MAMA: She loves you.

WALTER: Mama — I'm going out. I want to go off somewhere and be by myself for a while.

MAMA: I'm sorry 'bout your liquor store, son. It just wasn't the thing for us to do. That's what I want to tell you about —

WALTER: I got to go out, Mama —

(*He rises.*)

MAMA: It's dangerous, son.

WALTER: What's dangerous?

MAMA: When a man goes outside his home to look for peace.

WALTER (*beseechingly*): Then why can't there never be no peace in this house then?

MAMA: You done found it in some other house?

WALTER: No — there ain't no woman! Why do women always think there's a woman somewhere when a man gets restless. (*Picks up the check.*) Do you know what this money means to me? Do you know what this money can do for us? (*Puts it back.*) Mama — Mama — I want so many things . . .

MAMA: Yes, son —

WALTER: I want so many things that they are driving me kind of crazy . . . Mama — look at me.

MAMA: I'm looking at you. You a good-looking boy. You got a job, a nice wife, a fine boy and —

WALTER: A job. (*Looks at her.*) Mama, a job? I open and close car doors all day long. I drive a man around in his limousine and I say, "Yes, sir; no, sir; very good, sir; shall I take the Drive, sir?" Mama, that ain't no kind of job . . . that ain't nothing at all. (*Very quietly.*) Mama, I don't know if I can make you understand.

MAMA: Understand what, baby?

WALTER (*quietly*): Sometimes it's like I can see the future stretched out in front of me — just plain as day. The future, Mama. Hanging over there at the edge of my days. Just waiting for me — a big, looming blank space — full of *nothing*. Just waiting for *me*. But it don't have to be. (*Pause. Kneeling beside her chair.*) Mama — sometimes when I'm downtown and I pass them cool, quiet-looking restaurants where them white boys are sitting back and talking 'bout things . . . sitting there turning deals worth millions of dollars . . . sometimes I see guys don't look much older than me —

MAMA: Son — how come you talk so much 'bout money?

WALTER (*with immense passion*): Because it is life, Mama!

MAMA (*quietly*): Oh — (*Very quietly.*) So now it's life. Money is life. Once upon a time freedom used to be life — now it's money. I guess the world really do change . . .

WALTER: No — it was always money, Mama. We just didn't know about it.

MAMA: No . . . something has changed. (*She looks at him.*) You something new, boy. In my time we was worried about not being lynched and getting to the North if we could and how to stay alive and still have a pinch of dignity too . . . Now here come you and Beneatha — talking 'bout things we ain't never even thought about hardly, me and your daddy. You ain't satisfied or proud of nothing we done. I mean that you had a home, that we kept you out of trouble till you was grown, that you don't have to ride to work on the back of nobody's streetcar — You my children — but how different we done become.

WALTER (*A long beat. He pats her hand and gets up.*): You just don't understand, Mama, you just don't understand.

MAMA: Son — do you know your wife is expecting another baby? (*Walter stands, stunned, and absorbs what his mother has said.*) That's what she wanted to talk to you about. (*Walter sinks down into a chair.*) This ain't for me to be telling — but you ought to know. (*She waits.*) I think Ruth is thinking 'bout getting rid of that child.

WALTER (*slowly understanding*): — No — no — Ruth wouldn't do that.

MAMA: When the world gets ugly enough — a woman will do anything for her family. *The part that's already living.*

WALTER: You don't know Ruth, Mama, if you think she would do that.

(*Ruth opens the bedroom door and stands there a little limp.*)

RUTH (*beaten*): Yes I would too, Walter. (*Pause.*) I gave her a five-dollar down payment.

(*There is total silence as the man stares at his wife and the mother stares at her son.*)

MAMA (*presently*): Well — (*Tightly.*) Well — son, I'm waiting to hear you say something . . . (*She waits.*) I'm waiting to hear how you be your father's son. Be the man he was . . . (*Pause. The silence shouts.*) Your wife says she going to destroy your child. And I'm waiting to hear you talk like him and say we a people who give children life, not who destroys them — (*She rises.*) I'm waiting to see you stand up and look like your daddy and say we done give up one baby to poverty and that we ain't going to give up nary another one . . . I'm waiting.

WALTER: Ruth — (*He can say nothing.*)

MAMA: If you a son of mine, tell her! (*Walter picks up his keys and his coat and walks out. She continues, bitterly.*) You . . . you are a disgrace to your father's memory. Somebody get me my hat!

ACT II • *Scene 1*

(*Time: Later the same day.*)

(*At rise: Ruth is ironing again. She has the radio going. Presently Beneatha's bedroom door opens and Ruth's mouth falls and she puts down the iron in fascination.*)

RUTH: What have we got on tonight!

BENEATHA (*emerging grandly from the doorway so that we can see her thoroughly robed in the costume Asagai brought*): You are looking at what a well-dressed Nigerian woman wears — (*She parades for Ruth, her hair completely hidden by the headdress; she is coquettishly fanning herself with an ornate oriental fan, mistakenly more like Butterfly° than any Nigerian that ever was.*) Isn't it beautiful? (*She promenades to the radio and, with an arrogant flourish, turns off the good loud blues that is playing.*) Enough of this assimilationist junk! (*Ruth follows her with her eyes as she goes to the phonograph and puts on a record and turns and waits ceremoniously for the music to come up. Then, with a shout —*) OCOMOGOSIAY!

(*Ruth jumps. The music comes up, a lovely Nigerian melody. Beneatha listens, enraptured, her eyes far away — "back to the past." She begins to dance. Ruth is dumfounded.*)

RUTH: What kind of dance is that?

BENEATHA: A folk dance.

RUTH (*Pearl Bailey*): What kind of folks do that, honey?

BENEATHA: It's from Nigeria. It's a dance of welcome.

RUTH: Who you welcoming?

BENEATHA: The men back to the village.

RUTH: Where they been?

BENEATHA: How should I know — out hunting or something. Anyway, they are coming back now . . .

Butterfly: Madame Butterfly, the title character in the opera by Puccini, set in Japan.

RUTH: Well, that's good.

BENEATHA (*with the record*): *Alundi, alundi*
Alundi alunya
Jop pu a jeepua
Ang gu soooooooooo

Ai yai yue . . .
Ayehaye — alundi . . .

(*Walter comes in during this performance; he has obviously been drinking. He leans against the door heavily and watches his sister, at first with distaste. Then his eyes look off — "back to the past" — as he lifts both his fists to the roof, screaming.*)

WALTER: YEAH . . . AND ETHIOPIA STRETCH FORTH HER HANDS AGAIN! . . .

RUTH (*drily, looking at him*): Yes — and Africa sure is claiming her own tonight. (*She gives them both up and starts ironing again.*)

WALTER (*all in a drunken, dramatic shout*): Shut up! . . . I'm digging them drums . . . them drums move me! . . . (*He makes his weaving way to his wife's face and leans in close to her.*) In my *heart of hearts* — (*he thumps his chest*) — I am much warrior!

RUTH (*without even looking up*): In your heart of hearts you are much drunkard.

WALTER (*coming away from her and starting to wander around the room, shouting*): Me and Jomo . . . (*Intently, in his sister's face. She has stopped dancing to watch him in this unknown mood.*) That's my man, Kenyatta. (*Shouting and thumping his chest.*) FLAMING SPEAR! HOT DAMN! (*He is suddenly in possession of an imaginary spear and actively spearing enemies all over the room.*) OCOMOGOSIAY . . .

BENEATHA (*to encourage Walter, thoroughly caught up with this side of him*): OCOMOGOSIAY, FLAMING SPEAR!

WALTER: THE LION IS WAKING . . . OWIMOWEH! (*He pulls his shirt open and leaps up on the table and gestures with his spear.*)

BENEATHA: OWIMOWEH!

WALTER (*On the table, very far gone, his eyes pure glass sheets. He sees what we cannot, that he is a leader of his people, a great chief, a descendant of Chaka, and that the hour to march has come.*): Listen, my black brothers —

BENEATHA: OCOMOGOSIAY!

WALTER: — Do you hear the waters rushing against the shores of the coastlands —

BENEATHA: OCOMOGOSIAY!

WALTER: — Do you hear the screeching of the cocks in yonder hills beyond where the chiefs meet in council for the coming of the mighty war —

BENEATHA: OCOMOGOSIAY!

(*And now the lighting shifts subtly to suggest the world of Walter's imagination, and the mood shifts from pure comedy. It is the inner Walter speaking: the Southside chauffeur has assumed an unexpected majesty.*)

WALTER: — Do you hear the beating of the wings of the birds flying low over the mountains and the low places of our land —

BENEATHA: OCOMOGOSIAY!

WALTER: — Do you hear the singing of the women singing the war songs of our fathers to the babies in the great houses? Singing the sweet war songs! (*The doorbell rings.*) OH, DO YOU HEAR, MY *BLACK* BROTHERS —

BENEATHA (*completely gone*): We hear you, Flaming Spear —

(*Ruth shuts off the phonograph and opens the door. George Murchison enters.*)

WALTER: Telling us to prepare for the GREATNESS OF THE TIME! (*Lights back to normal. He turns and sees George.*) Black Brother!

(*He extends his hand for the fraternal clasp.*)

GEORGE: Black Brother, hell!

RUTH (*having had enough, and embarrassed for the family*): Beneatha, you got company — what's the matter with you? Walter Lee Younger, get down off that table and stop acting like a fool . . .

(*Walter comes down off the table suddenly and makes a quick exit to the bathroom.*)

RUTH: He's had a little to drink . . . I don't know what her excuse is.

GEORGE (*to Beneatha*): Look honey, we're going *to* the theater — we're not going to be *in* it . . . so go change, huh?

(*Beneatha looks at him and slowly, ceremoniously, lifts her hands and pulls off the headdress. Her hair is close-cropped and unstraightened. George freezes mid-sentence and Ruth's eyes all but fall out of her head.*)

GEORGE: What in the name of —

RUTH (*touching Beneatha's hair*): Girl, you done lost your natural mind? Look at your head!

GEORGE: What have you done to your head — I mean your hair!

BENEATHA: Nothing — except cut it off.

RUTH: Now that's the truth — it's what ain't been done to it! You expect this boy to go out with you with your head all nappy like that?

BENEATHA (*looking at George*): That's up to George. If he's ashamed of his heritage —

GEORGE: Oh, don't be so proud of yourself, Bennie — just because you look eccentric.

BENEATHA: How can something that's natural be eccentric?

GEORGE: That's what being eccentric means — being natural. Get dressed.

BENEATHA: I don't like that, George.

RUTH: Why must you and your brother make an argument out of everything people say?

BENEATHA: Because I hate assimilationist Negroes!

RUTH: Will somebody please tell me what assimila-whoever means!

GEORGE: Oh, it's just a college girl's way of calling people Uncle Toms — but that isn't what it means at all.

RUTH: Well, what does it mean?

BENEATHA (*cutting George off and staring at him as she replies to Ruth*): It means someone who is willing to give up his own culture and submerge himself completely in the dominant, and in this case *oppressive* culture!

GEORGE: Oh, dear, dear, dear! Here we go! A lecture on the African past! On our Great West African Heritage! In one second we will hear all about the great Ashanti empires; the great Songhay civilizations; and the great sculpture of Bénin — and then some poetry in the Bantu — and the whole monologue will end with the word *heritage!* (*Nastily.*) Let's face it, baby, your heritage is nothing but a bunch of raggedy-assed spirituals and some grass huts!

BENEATHA: GRASS HUTS! (*Ruth crosses to her and forcibly pushes her toward the bedroom.*) See there . . . you are standing there in your splendid ignorance talking about people who were the first to smelt iron on the face of the earth! (*Ruth is pushing her through the door.*) The Ashanti were performing surgical operations when the English — (*Ruth pulls the door to, with Beneatha on the other side, and smiles graciously at George. Beneatha opens the door and shouts the end of the sentence defiantly at George*) — were still tatooing themselves with blue dragons! (*She goes back inside.*)

RUTH: Have a seat, George. (*They both sit. Ruth folds her hands rather primly on her lap, determined to demonstrate the civilization of the family.*) Warm, ain't it? I mean for September. (*Pause.*) Just like they always say about Chicago weather: If it's too hot or cold for you, just wait a minute and it'll change. (*She smiles happily at this cliché of clichés.*) Everybody say it's got to do with them bombs and things they keep setting off. (*Pause.*) Would you like a nice cold beer?

GEORGE: No, thank you. I don't care for beer. (*He looks at his watch.*) I hope she hurries up.

RUTH: What time is the show?

GEORGE: It's an eight-thirty curtain. That's just Chicago, though. In New York standard curtain time is eight forty.

(*He is rather proud of this knowledge.*)

RUTH (*properly appreciating it*): You get to New York a lot?

GEORGE (*offhand*): Few times a year.

RUTH: Oh — that's nice. I've never been to New York.

(*Walter enters. We feel he has relieved himself, but the edge of unreality is still with him.*)

WALTER: New York ain't got nothing Chicago ain't. Just a bunch of hustling people all squeezed up together — being "Eastern."

(*He turns his face into a screw of displeasure.*)

GEORGE: Oh — you've been?

WALTER: *Plenty* of times.

RUTH (*shocked at the lie*): Walter Lee Younger!

WALTER (*staring her down*): Plenty! (*Pause.*) What we got to drink in this house? Why don't you offer this man some refreshment. (*To George.*) They don't know how to entertain people in this house, man.

GEORGE: Thank you — I don't really care for anything.

WALTER (*feeling his head; sobriety coming*): Where's Mama?

RUTH: She ain't come back yet.

WALTER (*looking Murchison over from head to toe, scrutinizing his carefully casual tweed sports jacket over cashmere V-neck sweater over soft eyelet shirt and tie, and soft slacks, finished off with white buckskin shoes*): Why all you college boys wear them faggoty-looking white shoes?

RUTH: Walter Lee!

(*George Murchison ignores the remark.*)

WALTER (*to Ruth*): Well, they look crazy as hell — white shoes, cold as it is.

RUTH (*crushed*): You have to excuse him —

WALTER: No he don't! Excuse me for what? What you always excusing me for! I'll excuse myself when I needs to be excused! (*A pause.*) They look as funny as them black knee socks Beneatha wears out of here all the time.

RUTH: It's the college *style*, Walter.

WALTER: Style, hell. She looks like she got burnt legs or something!

RUTH: Oh, Walter —

WALTER (*an irritable mimic*): Oh, Walter! Oh, Walter! (*To Murchison.*) How's your old man making out? I understand you all going to buy that big hotel on the Drive? (*He finds a beer in the refrigerator, wanders over to Murchison, sipping and wiping his lips with the back of his hand, and straddling a chair backward to talk to the other man.*) Shrewd move. Your old man is all right, man. (*Tapping his head and half winking for emphasis.*) I mean he knows how to operate. I mean he thinks *big*, you know what I mean, I mean for a *home*, you know? But I think he's kind of running out of ideas now. I'd like to talk to him. Listen, man, I got some plans that could turn this city upside down. I mean think like he does. *Big.* Invest big, gamble big, hell, lose *big* if you have to, you know what I mean. It's hard to find a man on this whole Southside who understands my kind of thinking — you dig? (*He scrutinizes Murchison again, drinks his beer, squints his eyes, and leans in close, confidential, man to man.*) Me and you ought to sit down and talk sometimes, man. Man, I got me some ideas . . .

MURCHISON (*with boredom*): Yeah — sometimes we'll have to do that, Walter.

WALTER (*understanding the indifference, and offended*): Yeah — well, when you get the time, man. I know you a busy little boy.

RUTH: Walter, please —

WALTER (*bitterly, hurt*): I know ain't nothing in this world as busy as you colored college boys with your fraternity pins and white shoes . . .

RUTH (*covering her face with humiliation*): Oh, Walter Lee —

WALTER: I see you all all the time — with the books tucked under your arms — going to your (*British A — a mimic*) "clahsses." And for what! What the hell you learning over there? Filling up your heads — (*counting off on his fingers*) — with the sociology and the psychology — but they teaching you how to be a man? How to take over and run the world? They teaching you how to run a rubber plantation or a steel mill? Naw — just to talk proper and read books and wear them faggoty-looking white shoes . . .

GEORGE (*looking at him with distaste, a little above it all*): You're all wacked up with bitterness, man.

WALTER (*intently, almost quietly, between the teeth, glaring at the boy*): And you — ain't you bitter, man? Ain't you just about had it yet? Don't you see no stars gleaming that you can't reach out and grab? You happy? — You contented son-of-a-bitch — you happy? You got it made? Bitter? Man, I'm a volcano. Bitter? Here I am a giant — surrounded by ants! Ants who can't even understand what it is the giant is talking about.

RUTH (*passionately and suddenly*): Oh, Walter — ain't you with nobody!

WALTER (*violently*): No! 'Cause ain't nobody with me! Not even my own mother!

RUTH: Walter, that's a terrible thing to say!

(*Beneatha enters, dressed for the evening in a cocktail dress and earrings, hair natural.*)

GEORGE: Well — hey — (*Crosses to Beneatha; thoughtful, with emphasis, since this is a reversal.*) You look great!

WALTER (*seeing his sister's hair for the first time*): What's the matter with your head?

BENEATHA (*tired of the jokes now*): I cut it off, Brother.

WALTER (*coming close to inspect it and walking around her*): Well, I'll be damned. So that's what they mean by the African bush . . .

BENEATHA: Ha ha. Let's go, George.

GEORGE (*looking at her*): You know something? I like it. It's sharp. I mean it really is. (*Helps her into her wrap.*)

RUTH: Yes — I think so, too. (*She goes to the mirror and starts to clutch at her hair.*)

WALTER: Oh no! You leave yours alone, baby. You might turn out to have a pin-shaped head or something!

BENEATHA: See you all later.

RUTH: Have a nice time.

GEORGE: Thanks. Good night. (*Half out the door, he reopens it. To Walter.*) Good night, Prometheus!°

Prometheus: Defiantly inventive Titan who stole fire from the gods and gave it to humans.

(*Beneatha and George exit.*)

WALTER (*to Ruth*): Who is Prometheus?

RUTH: I don't know. Don't worry about it.

WALTER (*in fury, pointing after George*): See there — they get to a point where they can't insult you man to man — they got to go talk about something ain't nobody never heard of!

RUTH: How do you know it was an insult? (*To humor him.*) Maybe Prometheus is a nice fellow.

WALTER: Prometheus! I bet there ain't even no such thing! I bet that simple-minded clown —

RUTH: Walter —

(*She stops what she is doing and looks at him.*)

WALTER (*yelling*): Don't start!

RUTH: Start what?

WALTER: Your nagging! Where was I? Who was I with? How much money did I spend?

RUTH (*plaintively*): Walter Lee — why don't we just try to talk about it . . .

WALTER (*not listening*): I been out talking with people who understand me. People who care about the things I got on my mind.

RUTH (*wearily*): I guess that means people like Willy Harris.

WALTER: Yes, people like Willy Harris.

RUTH (*with a sudden flash of impatience*): Why don't you all just hurry up and go into the banking business and stop talking about it!

WALTER: Why? You want to know why? 'Cause we all tied up in a race of people that don't know how to do nothing but moan, pray, and have babies!

(*The line is too bitter even for him and he looks at her and sits down.*)

RUTH: Oh, Walter . . . (*Softly.*) Honey, why can't you stop fighting me?

WALTER (*without thinking*): Who's fighting you? Who even cares about you?

(*This line begins the retardation of his mood.*)

RUTH: Well — (*She waits a long time, and then with resignation starts to put away her things.*) I guess I might as well go on to bed . . . (*More or less to herself.*) I don't know where we lost it . . . but we have . . . (*Then, to him.*) I — I'm sorry about this new baby, Walter. I guess maybe I better go on and do what I started . . . I guess I just didn't realize how bad things was with us . . . I guess I just didn't really realize — (*She starts out to the bedroom and stops.*) You want some hot milk?

WALTER: Hot milk?

RUTH: Yes — hot milk.

WALTER: Why hot milk?

RUTH: 'Cause after all that liquor you come home with you ought to have something hot in your stomach.

WALTER: I don't want no milk.

RUTH: You want some coffee then?

WALTER: No, I don't want no coffee. I don't want nothing hot to drink. (*Almost plaintively.*) Why you always trying to give me something to eat?

RUTH (*standing and looking at him helplessly*): What else can I give you, Walter Lee Younger?

(*She stands and looks at him and presently turns to go out again. He lifts his head and watches her going away from him in a new mood which began to emerge when he asked her "Who cares about you?"*)

WALTER: It's been rough, ain't it, baby? (*She hears and stops but does not turn around and he continues to her back.*) I guess between two people there ain't never as much understood as folks generally thinks there is. I mean like between me and you — (*She turns to face him.*) How we gets to the place where we scared to talk softness to each other. (*He waits, thinking hard himself.*) Why you think it got to be like that? (*He is thoughtful, almost as a child would be.*) Ruth, what is it gets into people ought to be close?

RUTH: I don't know, honey. I think about it a lot.

WALTER: On account of you and me, you mean? The way things are with us. The way something done come down between us.

RUTH: There ain't so much between us, Walter . . . Not when you come to me and try to talk to me. Try to be with me . . . a little even.

WALTER (*total honesty*): Sometimes . . . sometimes . . . I don't even know how to try.

RUTH: Walter —

WALTER: Yes?

RUTH (*coming to him, gently and with misgiving, but coming to him*): Honey . . . life don't have to be like this. I mean sometimes people can do things so that things are better . . . You remember how we used to talk when Travis was born . . . about the way we were going to live . . . the kind of house . . . (*She is stroking his head.*) Well, it's all starting to slip away from us . . .

(*He turns her to him and they look at each other and kiss, tenderly and hungrily. The door opens and Mama enters — Walter breaks away and jumps up. A beat.*)

WALTER: Mama, where have you been?

MAMA: My — them steps is longer than they used to be. Whew! (*She sits down and ignores him.*) How you feeling this evening, Ruth?

(*Ruth shrugs, disturbed at having been interrupted and watching her husband knowingly.*)

WALTER: Mama, where have you been all day?

MAMA (*still ignoring him and leaning on the table and changing to more comfortable shoes*): Where's Travis?

RUTH: I let him go out earlier and he ain't come back yet. Boy, is he going to get it!

WALTER: Mama!

MAMA (*as if she has heard him for the first time*): Yes, son?

WALTER: Where did you go this afternoon?

MAMA: I went downtown to tend to some business that I had to tend to.

WALTER: What kind of business?

MAMA: You know better than to question me like a child, Brother.

WALTER (*rising and bending over the table*): Where were you, Mama? (*Bringing his fists down and shouting.*) Mama, you didn't go do something with that insurance money, something crazy?

(*The front door opens slowly, interrupting him, and Travis peeks his head in, less than hopefully.*)

TRAVIS (*to his mother*): Mama, I —

RUTH: "Mama I" nothing! You're going to get it, boy! Get on in that bedroom and get yourself ready!

TRAVIS: But I —

MAMA: Why don't you all never let the child explain himself.

RUTH: Keep out of it now, Lena.

(*Mama clamps her lips together, and Ruth advances toward her son menacingly.*)

RUTH: A thousand times I have told you not to go off like that —

MAMA (*holding out her arms to her grandson*): Well — at least let me tell him something. I want him to be the first one to hear . . . Come here, Travis. (*The boy obeys, gladly.*) Travis — (*she takes him by the shoulder and looks into his face*) — you know that money we got in the mail this morning?

TRAVIS: Yes'm —

MAMA: Well — what you think your grandmama gone and done with that money?

TRAVIS: I don't know, Grandmama.

MAMA (*putting her finger on his nose for emphasis*): She went out and she bought you a house! (*The explosion comes from Walter at the end of the revelation and he jumps up and turns away from all of them in a fury. Mama continues, to Travis.*) You glad about the house? It's going to be yours when you get to be a man.

TRAVIS: Yeah — I always wanted to live in a house.

MAMA: All right, gimme some sugar then — (*Travis puts his arms around her neck as she watches her son over the boy's shoulder. Then, to Travis, after the embrace.*) Now when you say your prayers tonight, you thank God and your grandfather — 'cause it was him who give you the house — in his way.

RUTH (*taking the boy from Mama and pushing him toward the bedroom*): Now you get out of here and get ready for your beating.

TRAVIS: Aw, Mama —

RUTH: Get on in there — (*Closing the door behind him and turning radiantly to her mother-in-law.*) So you went and did it!

MAMA (*quietly, looking at her son with pain*): Yes, I did.

RUTH (*raising both arms classically*): PRAISE GOD! (*Looks at Walter a moment, who says nothing. She crosses rapidly to her husband.*) Please, honey — let me be glad . . . you be glad too. (*She has laid her hands on his shoulders, but he shakes himself free of her roughly, without turning to face her.*) Oh, Walter . . . a home . . . *a home.* (*She comes back to Mama.*) Well — where is it? How big is it? How much it going to cost?

MAMA: Well —

RUTH: When we moving?

MAMA (*smiling at her*): First of the month.

RUTH (*throwing back her head with jubilance*): *Praise God!*

MAMA (*tentatively, still looking at her son's back turned against her and Ruth*): It's — it's a nice house too . . . (*She cannot help speaking directly to him. An imploring quality in her voice, her manner, makes her almost like a girl now.*) Three bedrooms — nice big one for you and Ruth . . . Me and Beneatha still have to share our room, but Travis have one of his own and (*with difficulty*) I figure if the — new baby — is a boy, we could get one of them double-decker out- fits . . . And there's a yard with a little patch of dirt where I could maybe get to grow me a few flowers . . . And a nice big basement . . .

RUTH: Walter honey, be glad —

MAMA (*still to his back, fingering things on the table*): 'Course I don't want to make it sound fancier than it is . . . It's just a plain little old house — but it's made good and solid — and it will be *ours.* Walter Lee — it makes a difference in a man when he can walk on floors that belong to *him* . . .

RUTH: Where is it?

MAMA (*frightened at this telling*): Well — well — it's out there in Clybourne Park —

(*Ruth's radiance fades abruptly, and Walter finally turns slowly to face his mother with incredulity and hostility.*)

RUTH: Where?

MAMA (*matter-of-factly*): Four o six Clybourne Street, Clybourne Park.

RUTH: Clybourne Park? Mama, there ain't no colored people living in Clybourne Park.

MAMA (*almost idiotically*): Well, I guess there's going to be some now.

WALTER (*bitterly*): So that's the peace and comfort you went out and bought for us today!

MAMA (*raising her eyes to meet his finally*): Son — I just tried to find the nicest place for the least amount of money for my family.

RUTH (*trying to recover from the shock*): Well — well — 'course I ain't one never been 'fraid of no crackers,° mind you — but — well, wasn't there no other houses nowhere?

MAMA: Them houses they put up for colored in them areas way out all seem to cost twice as much as other houses. I did the best I could.

crackers: White people, often used to refer disparagingly to poor whites.

RUTH (*struck senseless with the news, in its various degrees of goodness and trouble, she sits a moment, her fists propping her chin in thought, and then she starts to rise, bringing her fists down with vigor, the radiance spreading from cheek to cheek again*): Well — well — All I can say is — if this is my time in life — MY TIME — to say good-bye — (*and she builds with momentum as she starts to circle the room with an exuberant, almost tearfully happy release*) — to these Goddamned cracking walls! — (*she pounds the walls*) — and these marching roaches! — (*she wipes at an imaginary army of marching roaches*) — and this cramped little closet which ain't now or never was no kitchen! . . . then I say it loud and good, HAL- LELUJAH! AND GOOD-BYE MISERY . . . I DON'T NEVER WANT TO SEE YOUR UGLY FACE AGAIN! (*She laughs joyously, having practically destroyed the apartment, and flings her arms up and lets them come down hap- pily, slowly, reflectively, over her abdomen, aware for the first time perhaps that the life therein pulses with happiness and not despair.*) Lena?

MAMA (*moved, watching her happiness*): Yes, honey?

RUTH (*looking off*): Is there — is there a whole lot of sunlight?

MAMA (*understanding*): Yes, child, there's a whole lot of sunlight.

(*Long pause.*)

RUTH (*collecting herself and going to the door of the room Travis is in*): Well — I guess I better see 'bout Travis. (*To Mama.*) Lord, I sure don't feel like whip- ping nobody today!

(*She exits.*)

MAMA (*the mother and son are left alone now and the mother waits a long time, considering deeply, before she speaks*): Son — you — you understand what I done, don't you? (*Walter is silent and sullen.*) I — I just seen my family falling apart today . . . just falling to pieces in front of my eyes . . . We couldn't of gone on like we was today. We was going backwards 'stead of forwards — talking 'bout killing babies and wish- ing each other was dead . . . When it gets like that in life — you just got to do something different, push on out and do something bigger . . . (*She waits.*) I wish you say something, son . . . I wish you'd say how deep inside you you think I done the right thing —

WALTER (*crossing slowly to his bedroom door and finally turning there and speaking measuredly*): What you need me to say you done right for? *You* the head of this family. You run our lives like you want to. It was your money and you did what you wanted with it. So what you need for me to say it was all right for? (*Bitterly, to hurt her as deeply as he knows is possible.*) So you butchered up a dream of mine — you — who always talking 'bout your children's dreams . . .

MAMA: Walter Lee —

(*He just closes the door behind him. Mama sits alone, thinking heavily.*)

Scene II

(*Time: Friday night. A few weeks later.*)

(*At rise: Packing crates mark the intention of the family to move. Beneatha and George come in, presumably from an evening out again.*)

GEORGE: O.K. . . . O.K., whatever you say . . . (*They both sit on the couch. He tries to kiss her. She moves away.*) Look, we've had a nice evening; let's not spoil it, huh? . . .

(*He again turns her head and tries to nuzzle in and she turns away from him, not with distaste but with momentary lack of interest; in a mood to pursue what they were talking about.*)

BENEATHA: I'm *trying* to talk to you.

GEORGE: We always talk.

BENEATHA: Yes — and I love to talk.

GEORGE (*exasperated; rising*): I know it and I don't mind it sometimes . . . I want you to cut it out, see — The moody stuff, I mean. I don't like it. You're a nice-looking girl . . . all over. That's all you need, honey, forget the atmosphere. Guys aren't going to go for the atmosphere — they're going to go for what they see. Be glad for that. Drop the Garbo routine. It doesn't go with you. As for myself, I want a nice — (*groping*) — simple (*thoughtfully*) — sophisticated girl . . . not a poet — O.K.?

(*He starts to kiss her, she rebuffs him again, and he jumps up.*)

BENEATHA: Why are you angry, George?

GEORGE: Because this is stupid! I don't go out with you to discuss the nature of "quiet desperation" or to hear all about your thoughts — because the world will go on thinking what it thinks regardless —

BENEATHA: Then why read books? Why go to school?

GEORGE (*with artificial patience, counting on his fingers*): It's simple. You read books — to learn facts — to get grades — to pass the course — to get a degree. That's all — it has nothing to do with thoughts.

(*A long pause.*)

BENEATHA: I see. (*He starts to sit.*) Good night, George.

(*George looks at her a little oddly and starts to exit. He meets Mama coming in.*)

GEORGE: Oh — hello, Mrs. Younger.

MAMA: Hello, George, how you feeling?

GEORGE: Fine — fine, how are you?

MAMA: Oh, a little tired. You know them steps can get you after a day's work. You all have a nice time tonight?

GEORGE: Yes — a fine time. A fine time.

MAMA: Well, good night.

GEORGE: Good night. (*He exits. Mama closes the door behind her.*)

MAMA: Hello, honey. What you sitting like that for?

BENEATHA: I'm just sitting.

MAMA: Didn't you have a nice time?

BENEATHA: No.

MAMA: No? What's the matter?

BENEATHA: Mama, George is a fool — honest. (*She rises.*)

MAMA (*Hustling around unloading the packages she has entered with. She stops.*): Is he, baby?

BENEATHA: Yes.

(*Beneatha makes up Travis's bed as she talks.*)

MAMA: You sure?

BENEATHA: Yes.

MAMA: Well — I guess you better not waste your time with no fools.

(*Beneatha looks up at her mother, watching her put groceries in the refrigerator. Finally she gathers up her things and starts into the bedroom. At the door she stops and looks back at her mother.*)

BENEATHA: Mama —

MAMA: Yes, baby —

BENEATHA: Thank you.

MAMA: For what?

BENEATHA: For understanding me this time.

(*She exits quickly and the mother stands, smiling a little, looking at the place where Beneatha just stood. Ruth enters.*)

RUTH: Now don't you fool with any of this stuff, Lena —

MAMA: Oh, I just thought I'd sort a few things out. Is Brother here?

RUTH: Yes.

MAMA (*with concern*): Is he —

RUTH (*reading her eyes*): Yes.

(*Mama is silent and someone knocks on the door. Mama and Ruth exchange weary and knowing glances and Ruth opens it to admit the neighbor, Mrs. Johnson,° who is a rather squeaky wide-eyed lady of no particular age, with a newspaper under her arm.*)

MAMA (*changing her expression to acute delight and a ringing cheerful greeting*): Oh — hello there, Johnson.

JOHNSON (*this is a woman who decided long ago to be enthusiastic about* EVERYTHING *in life and she is inclined to wave her wrist vigorously at the height of her exclamatory comments*): Hello there, yourself! H'you this evening, Ruth?

RUTH (*not much of a deceptive type*): Fine, Mis' Johnson, h'you?

JOHNSON: Fine. (*Reaching out quickly, playfully, and patting Ruth's stomach.*) Ain't you starting to poke out none yet! (*She mugs with delight at the overfamiliar remark and her eyes dart around looking at the crates and packing preparation; Mama's face is a cold sheet of endurance.*) Oh, ain't we getting ready round here, though! Yessir! Lookathere! I'm telling

Mrs. Johnson: This character and the scene of her visit were cut from the original production and early editions of the play.

you the Youngers is really getting ready to "move on up a little higher!" — Bless God!

MAMA (*a little drily, doubting the total sincerity of the Blesser*): Bless God.

JOHNSON: He's good, ain't He?

MAMA: Oh yes, He's good.

JOHNSON: I mean sometimes He works in mysterious ways . . . but He works, don't He!

MAMA (*the same*): Yes, he does.

JOHNSON: I'm just soooooo happy for y'all. And this here child — (*about Ruth*) looks like she could just pop open with happiness, don't she. Where's all the rest of the family?

MAMA: Bennie's gone to bed —

JOHNSON: Ain't no . . . (*the implication is pregnancy*) sickness done hit you — I hope . . . ?

MAMA: No — she just tired. She was out this evening.

JOHNSON (*all is a coo, an emphatic coo*): Aw — ain't that lovely. She still going out with the little Murchison boy?

MAMA (*drily*): Ummmm huh.

JOHNSON: That's lovely. You sure got lovely children, Younger. Me and Isaiah talks all the time 'bout what fine children you was blessed with. We sure do.

MAMA: Ruth, give Mis' Johnson a piece of sweet potato pie and some milk.

JOHNSON: Oh honey, I can't stay hardly a minute — I just dropped in to see if there was anything I could do. (*Accepting the food easily.*) I guess y'all seen the news what's all over the colored paper this week . . .

MAMA: No — didn't get mine yet this week.

JOHNSON (*lifting her head and blinking with the spirit of catastrophe*): You mean you ain't read 'bout them colored people that was bombed out their place out there?

(*Ruth straightens with concern and takes the paper and reads it. Johnson notices her and feeds commentary.*)

JOHNSON: Ain't it something how bad these here white folks is getting here in Chicago! Lord, getting so you think you right down in Mississippi! (*With a tremendous and rather insincere sense of melodrama.*) 'Course I thinks it's wonderful how our folks keeps on pushing out. You hear some of these Negroes round here talking 'bout how they don't go where they ain't wanted and all that — but not me, honey! (*This is a lie.*) Wilhemenia Othella Johnson goes anywhere, any time she feels like it! (*With head movement for emphasis.*) Yes I do! Why if we left it up to these here crackers the poor niggers wouldn't have nothing — (*She clasps her hand over her mouth.*) Oh, I always forgets you don't 'low that word in your house.

MAMA (*quietly, looking at her*): No — I don't 'low it.

JOHNSON (*vigorously again*): Me neither! I was just telling Isaiah yesterday when he come using it in front of me — I said, "Isaiah, it's just like Mis' Younger says all the time —"

MAMA: Don't you want some more pie?

JOHNSON: No — no thank you; this was lovely. I got to get on over home and have my midnight coffee. I hear some people say it don't let them sleep but I finds I can't close my eyes right lessen I done had that laaaast cup of coffee . . . (*She waits. A beat. Undaunted.*) My Good-night coffee, I calls it!

MAMA (*with much eye-rolling and communication between herself and Ruth*): Ruth, why don't you give Mis' Johnson some coffee.

(*Ruth gives Mama an unpleasant look for her kindness.*)

JOHNSON (*accepting the coffee*): Where's Brother tonight?

MAMA: He's lying down.

JOHNSON: Mmmmmmm, he sure gets his beauty rest, don't he? Good-looking man. Sure is a good-looking man! (*Reaching out to pat Ruth's stomach again.*) I guess that's how come we keep on having babies around here. (*She winks at Mama.*) One thing 'bout Brother, he always know how to have a *good* time. And soooooo ambitious! I bet it was his idea y'all moving out to Clybourne Park. Lord — I bet this time next month y'all's names will have been in the papers plenty — (*Holding up her hands to mark off each word of the headline she can see in front of her.*) "NEGROS INVADE CLYBOURNE PARK — BOMBED!"

MAMA (*she and Ruth look at the woman in amazement*): We ain't exactly moving out there to get bombed.

JOHNSON: Oh, honey — you know I'm praying to God every day that don't nothing like that happen! But you have to think of life like it is — and these here Chicago peckerwoods is some baaaad peckerwoods.

MAMA (*wearily*): We done thought about all that Mis' Johnson.

(*Beneatha comes out of the bedroom in her robe and passes through to the bathroom. Mrs. Johnson turns.*)

JOHNSON: Hello there, Bennie!

BENEATHA (*crisply*): Hello, Mrs. Johnson.

JOHNSON: How is school?

BENEATHA (*crisply*): Fine, thank you. (*She goes out.*)

JOHNSON (*insulted*): Getting so she don't have much to say to nobody.

MAMA: The child was on her way to the bathroom.

JOHNSON: I know — but sometimes she act like ain't got time to pass the time of day with nobody ain't been to college. Oh — I ain't criticizing her none. It's just — you know how some of our young people gets when they get a little education. (*Mama and Ruth say nothing, just look at her.*) Yes — well. Well, I guess I better get on home. (*Unmoving.*) 'Course I can understand how she must be proud and everything — being the only one in the family to make something of herself. I know just being a chauffeur ain't never satisfied Brother none. He shouldn't feel like that, though. Ain't nothing wrong with being a chauffeur.

MAMA: There's plenty wrong with it.

JOHNSON: What?

MAMA: Plenty. My husband always said being any kind of a servant wasn't a fit thing for a man to have to be. He always said a man's hands was made to make things, or to turn the earth with — not to drive nobody's car for 'em — or — (*she looks at her own hands*) carry they slop jars. And my boy is just like him — he wasn't meant to wait on nobody.

JOHNSON (*rising, somewhat offended*): Mmmmmmmmm. The Youngers is too much for me! (*She looks around.*) You sure one proud-acting bunch of colored folks. Well — I always thinks like Booker T. Washington said that time — "Education has spoiled many a good plow hand" —

MAMA: Is that what old Booker T. said?

JOHNSON: He sure did.

MAMA: Well, it sounds just like him. The fool.

JOHNSON (*indignantly*): Well — he was one of our great men.

MAMA: Who said so?

JOHNSON (*nonplussed*): You know, me and you ain't never agreed about some things, Lena Younger. I guess I better be going —

RUTH (*quickly*): Good night.

JOHNSON: Good night. Oh — (*Thrusting it at her.*) You can keep the paper! (*With a trill.*) 'Night.

MAMA: Good night, Mis' Johnson.

(*Mrs. Johnson exits.*)

RUTH: If ignorance was gold . . .

MAMA: Shush. Don't talk about folks behind their backs.

RUTH: You do.

MAMA: I'm old and corrupted. (*Beneatha enters.*) You was rude to Mis' Johnson, Beneatha, and I don't like it at all.

BENEATHA (*at her door*): Mama, if there are two things we, as a people, have got to overcome, one is the Klu Klux Klan — and the other is Mrs. Johnson. (*She exits.*)

MAMA: Smart aleck.

(*The phone rings.*)

RUTH: I'll get it.

MAMA: Lord, ain't this a popular place tonight.

RUTH (*at the phone*): Hello — Just a minute. (*Goes to door.*) Walter, it's Mrs. Arnold. (*Waits. Goes back to the phone. Tense.*) Hello. Yes, this is his wife speaking . . . He's lying down now. Yes . . . well, he'll be in tomorrow. He's been very sick. Yes — I know we should have called, but we were so sure he'd be able to come in today. Yes — yes, I'm very sorry. Yes . . . Thank you very much. (*She hangs up. Walter is standing in the doorway of the bedroom behind her.*) That was Mrs. Arnold.

WALTER (*indifferently*): Was it?

RUTH: She said if you don't come in tomorrow that they are getting a new man . . .

WALTER: Ain't that sad — ain't that crying sad.

RUTH: She said Mr. Arnold has had to take a cab for three days . . . Walter, you ain't been to work for three days! (*This is a revelation to her.*) Where you been, Walter Lee Younger? (*Walter looks at her and starts to laugh.*) You're going to lose your job.

WALTER: That's right . . . (*He turns on the radio.*)

RUTH: Oh, Walter, and with your mother working like a dog every day —

(*A steamy, deep blues pours into the room.*)

WALTER: That's sad too — Everything is sad.

MAMA: What you been doing for these three days, son?

WALTER: Mama — you don't know all the things a man what got leisure can find to do in this city . . . What's this — Friday night? Well — Wednesday I borrowed Willy Harris's car and I went for a drive . . . just me and myself and I drove and drove . . . Way out . . . way past South Chicago, and I parked the car and I sat and looked at the steel mills all day long. I just sat in the car and looked at them big black chimneys for hours. Then I drove back and I went to the Green Hat. (*Pause.*) And Thursday — Thursday I borrowed the car again and I got in it and I pointed it the other way and I drove the other way — for hours — way, way up to Wisconsin, and I looked at the farms. I just drove and looked at the farms. Then I drove back and I went to the Green Hat. (*Pause.*) And today — today I didn't get the car. Today I just walked. All over the Southside. And I looked at the Negroes and they looked at me and finally I just sat down on the curb at Thirty-ninth and South Parkway and I just sat there and watched the Negroes go by. And then I went to the Green Hat. You all sad? You all depressed? And you know where I am going right now —

(*Ruth goes out quietly.*)

MAMA: Oh, Big Walter, is this the harvest of our days?

WALTER: You know what I like about the Green Hat? I like this little cat they got there who blows a sax . . . He blows. He talks to me. He ain't but 'bout five feet tall and he's got a conked head and his eyes is always closed and he's all music —

MAMA (*rising and getting some papers out of her handbag*): Walter —

WALTER: And there's this other guy who plays the piano . . . and they got a sound. I mean they can work on some music . . . They got the best little combo in the world in the Green Hat . . . You can just sit there and drink and listen to them three men play and you realize that don't nothing matter worth a damn, but just being there —

MAMA: I've helped do it to you, haven't I, son? Walter I been wrong.

WALTER: Naw — you ain't never been wrong about nothing, Mama.

MAMA: Listen to me, now. I say I been wrong, son. That I been doing to you what the rest of the world been doing to you. (*She turns off the radio.*) Walter — (*She stops and he looks up slowly at her and she meets his eyes pleadingly.*) What you ain't never understood is that I ain't got nothing, don't own nothing, ain't never really wanted nothing that wasn't for you. There ain't nothing as precious to me . . . There ain't nothing worth holding on to, money, dreams, nothing else — if it means — if it means it's going to destroy my boy. (*She takes an envelope out of her handbag and puts it in front of him and he watches her without speaking or moving.*) I paid the man thirty-five hundred dollars down on the house. That leaves sixty-five hundred dollars. Monday morning I want you to take this money and take three thousand dollars and put it in a savings account for Beneatha's medical schooling. The rest you put in a checking account — with your name on it. And from now on any penny that come out of it or that go in it is for you to look after. For you to decide. (*She drops her hands a little helplessly.*) It ain't much, but it's all I got in the world and I'm putting it in your hands. I'm telling you to be the head of this family from now on like you supposed to be.

WALTER (*stares at the money*): You trust me like that, Mama?

MAMA: I ain't never stop trusting you. Like I ain't never stop loving you.

(*She goes out, and Walter sits looking at the money on the table. Finally, in a decisive gesture, he gets up and, in mingled joy and desperation, picks up the money. At the same moment, Travis enters for bed.*)

TRAVIS: What's the matter, Daddy? You drunk?

WALTER (*sweetly, more sweetly than we have ever known him*): No, Daddy ain't drunk. Daddy ain't going to never be drunk again . . .

TRAVIS: Well, good night, Daddy.

(*The father has come from behind the couch and leans over, embracing his son.*)

WALTER: Son, I feel like talking to you tonight.

TRAVIS: About what?

WALTER: Oh, about a lot of things. About you and what kind of man you going to be when you grow up. . . . Son — son, what do you want to be when you grow up?

TRAVIS: A bus driver.

WALTER (*laughing a little*): A what? Man, that ain't nothing to want to be!

TRAVIS: Why not?

WALTER: 'Cause, man — it ain't big enough — you know what I mean.

TRAVIS: I don't know then. I can't make up my mind. Sometimes Mama asks me that too. And sometimes when I tell her I just want to be like you — she says she don't want me to be like that and sometimes she says she does. . . .

WALTER (*gathering him up in his arms*): You know what, Travis? In seven years you going to be seventeen years old. And things is going to be very different with us in seven years Travis. . . . One day when

you are seventeen I'll come home — home from my office downtown somewhere —

TRAVIS: You don't work in no office, Daddy.

WALTER: No — but after tonight. After what your daddy gonna do tonight, there's going to be offices — a whole lot of offices. . . .

TRAVIS: What you gonna do tonight, Daddy?

WALTER: You wouldn't understand yet, son, but your daddy's gonna make a transaction . . . a business transaction that's going to change our lives. . . . That's how come one day when you 'bout seventeen years old I'll come home and I'll be pretty tired, you know what I mean, after a day of conferences and secretaries getting things wrong the way they do . . . 'cause an executive's life is hell man — (*The more he talks the farther away he gets.*) And I'll pull the car up on the driveway . . . just a plain black Chrysler, I think, with white walls — no — black tires. More elegant. Rich people don't have to be flashy . . . though I'll have to get something a little sportier for Ruth — maybe a Cadillac convertible to do her shopping in. . . . And I'll come up the steps to the house and the gardener will be clipping away at the hedges and he'll say, "Good evening, Mr. Younger." And I'll say, "Hello, Jefferson, how are you this evening?" And I'll go inside and Ruth will come downstairs and meet me at the door and we'll kiss each other and she'll take my arm and we'll go up to your room to see you sitting on the floor with the catalogues of all the great schools in America around you. . . . All the great schools in the world! And — and I'll say, all right son — it's your seventeenth birthday, what is it you've decided? . . . Just tell me where you want to go to school and you'll *go*. Just tell me, what it is you want to be — and you'll *be* it. . . . Whatever you want to be — Yessir! (*He holds his arms open for Travis.*) You just name it, son . . . (*Travis leaps into them*) and I hand you the world!

(*Walter's voice has risen in pitch and hysterical promise and on the last line he lifts Travis high.*)

Scene III

(*Time: Saturday, moving day, one week later.*)

(*Before the curtain rises, Ruth's voice, a strident, dramatic church alto, cuts through the silence.*)

(*It is, in the darkness, a triumphant surge, a penetrating statement of expectation: "Oh, Lord, I don't feel no ways tired! Children, oh, glory hallelujah!"*)

(*As the curtain rises we see that Ruth is alone in the living room, finishing up the family's packing. It is moving day. She is nailing crates and tying cartons. Beneatha enters, carrying a guitar case, and watches her exuberant sister-in-law.*)

RUTH: Hey!

BENEATHA (*putting away the case*): Hi.

RUTH (*pointing at a package*): Honey — look in that

package there and see what I found on sale this morning at the South Center. (*Ruth gets up and moves to the package and draws out some curtains.*) Lookahere — hand-turned hems!

BENEATHA: How do you know the window size out there?

RUTH (*who hadn't thought of that*): Oh — Well, they bound to fit something in the whole house. Anyhow, they was too good a bargain to pass up. (*Ruth slaps her head, suddenly remembering something.*) Oh, Bennie — I meant to put a special note on that carton over there. That's your mama's good china and she wants 'em to be very careful with it.

BENEATHA: I'll do it.

(*Beneatha finds a piece of paper and starts to draw large letters on it.*)

RUTH: You know what I'm going to do soon as I get in that new house?

BENEATHA: What?

RUTH: Honey — I'm going to run me a tub of water up to here . . . (*With her fingers practically up to her nostrils.*) And I'm going to get in it — and I am going to sit . . . and sit . . . and sit in that hot water and the first person who knocks to tell *me* to hurry up and come out —

BENEATHA: Gets shot at sunrise.

RUTH (*laughing happily*): You said it, sister! (*Noticing how large Beneatha is absent-mindedly making the note.*) Honey, they ain't going to read that from no airplane.

BENEATHA (*laughing herself*): I guess I always think things have more emphasis if they are big, somehow.

RUTH (*looking up at her and smiling*): You and your brother seem to have that as a philosophy of life. Lord, that man — done changed so 'round here. You know — you know what we did last night? Me and Walter Lee?

BENEATHA: What?

RUTH (*smiling to herself*): We went to the movies. (*Looking at Beneatha to see if she understands.*) We went to the movies. You know the last time me and Walter went to the movies together?

BENEATHA: No.

RUTH: Me neither. That's how long it been. (*Smiling again.*) But we went last night. The picture wasn't much good, but that didn't seem to matter. We went — and we held hands.

BENEATHA: Oh, Lord!

RUTH: We held hands — and you know what?

BENEATHA: What?

RUTH: When we come out of the show it was late and dark and all the stores and things was closed up . . . and it was kind of chilly and there wasn't many people on the streets . . . and we was still holding hands, me and Walter.

BENEATHA: You're killing me.

(*Walter enters with a large package. His happiness is deep in him; he cannot keep still with his newfound exu-*

berance. *He is singing and wiggling and snapping his fingers. He puts his package in a corner and puts a phonograph record which he has brought in with him, on the record player. As the music, soulful and sensuous, comes up he dances over to Ruth and tries to get her to dance with him. She gives in at last to his raunchiness and in a fit of giggling allows herself to be drawn into his mood. They dip and she melts into his arms in a classic, body-melding "slow drag."*)

BENEATHA (*regarding them a long time as they dance, then drawing in her breath for a deeply exaggerated comment which she does not particularly mean*): Talk about — olddddddddddd — fashionedddddddd — Negroes!

WALTER (*stopping momentarily*): What kind of Negroes?

(*He says this in fun. He is not angry with her today, nor with anyone. He starts to dance with his wife again.*)

BENEATHA: Old-fashioned.

WALTER (*as he dances with Ruth*): You know, when these *New Negroes* have their convention — (*pointing at his sister*) — that is going to be the chairman of the Committee on Unending Agitation. (*He goes on dancing, then stops.*) Race, race, race! . . . Girl, I do believe you are the first person in the history of the entire human race to successfully brainwash yourself. (*Beneatha breaks up and he goes on dancing. He stops again, enjoying his tease.*) Damn, even the N double A C P takes a holiday sometimes! (*Beneatha and Ruth laugh. He dances with Ruth some more and starts to laugh and stops and pantomimes someone over an operating table.*) I can just see that chick someday looking down at some poor cat on an operating table and before she starts to slice him, she says . . . (*pulling his sleeves back maliciously*) "By the way, what are your views on civil rights down there? . . ."

(*He laughs at her again and starts to dance happily. The bell sounds.*)

BENEATHA: Sticks and stones may break my bones but . . . words will never hurt me!

(*Beneatha goes to the door and opens it as Walter and Ruth go on with the clowning. Beneatha is somewhat surprised to see a quiet-looking middle-aged white man in a business suit holding his hat and a briefcase in his hand and consulting a small piece of paper.*)

MAN: Uh — how do you do, miss. I am looking for a Mrs. — (*he looks at the slip of paper*) Mrs. Lena Younger? (*He stops short, struck dumb at the sight of the oblivious Walter and Ruth.*)

BENEATHA (*smoothing her hair with slight embarrassment*): Oh — yes, that's my mother. Excuse me. (*She closes the door and turns to quiet the other two.*) Ruth! Brother! (*Enunciating precisely but soundlessly: "There's a white man at the door!"*) They stop dancing, Ruth cuts off the phonograph, Beneatha *opens the door. The man casts a curious quick glance at all of them.*) Uh — come in please.

MAN (*coming in*): Thank you.

BENEATHA: My mother isn't here just now. Is it business?

MAN: Yes . . . well, of a sort.

WALTER (*freely, the Man of the House*): Have a seat. I'm Mrs. Younger's son. I look after most of her business matters.

(*Ruth and Beneatha exchange amused glances.*)

MAN (*regarding Walter, and sitting*): Well — My name is Karl Lindner . . .

WALTER (*stretching out his hand*): Walter Younger. This is my wife — (*Ruth nods politely*) — and my sister.

LINDNER: How do you do.

WALTER (*amiably, as he sits himself easily on a chair, leaning forward on his knees with interest and looking expectantly into the newcomer's face*): What can we do for you, Mr. Lindner!

LINDNER (*some minor shuffling of the hat and briefcase on his knees*): Well — I am a representative of the Clybourne Park Improvement Association —

WALTER (*pointing*): Why don't you sit your things on the floor?

LINDNER: Oh — yes. Thank you. (*He slides the briefcase and hat under the chair.*) And as I was saying — I am from the Clybourne Park Improvement Association and we have had it brought to our attention at the last meeting that you people — or at least your mother — has bought a piece of residential property at — (*he digs for the slip of paper again*) — four o six Clybourne Street . . .

WALTER: That's right. Care for something to drink? Ruth, get Mr. Lindner a beer.

LINDNER (*upset for some reason*): Oh — no, really. I mean thank you very much, but no thank you.

RUTH: (*innocently*): Some coffee?

LINDNER: Thank you, nothing at all.

(*Beneatha is watching the man carefully.*)

LINDNER: Well, I don't know how much you folks know about our organization. (*He is a gentle man; thoughtful and somewhat labored in his manner.*) It is one of these community organizations set up to look after — oh, you know, things like block upkeep and special projects and we also have what we call our New Neighbors Orientation Committee . . .

BENEATHA (*drily*): Yes — and what do they do?

LINDNER (*turning a little to her and then returning the main force to Walter*): Well — it's what you might call a sort of welcoming committee, I guess. I mean they, we — I'm the chairman of the committee — go around and see the new people who move into the neighborhood and sort of give them the lowdown on the way we do things out in Clybourne Park.

BENEATHA (*with appreciation of the two meanings, which escape Ruth and Walter*): Un-huh.

LINDNER: And we also have the category of what the association calls — (*he looks elsewhere*) — uh — special community problems . . .

BENEATHA: Yes — and what are some of those?

WALTER: Girl, let the man talk.

LINDNER (*with understated relief*): Thank you. I would sort of like to explain this thing in my own way. I mean I want to explain to you in a certain way.

WALTER: Go ahead.

LINDNER: Yes. Well. I'm going to try to get right to the point. I'm sure we'll all appreciate that in the long run.

BENEATHA: Yes.

WALTER: Be still now!

LINDNER: Well —

RUTH (*still innocently*): Would you like another chair — you don't look comfortable.

LINDNER (*more frustrated than annoyed*): No, thank you very much. Please. Well — to get right to the point I — (*a great breath, and he is off at last*) I am sure you people must be aware of some of the incidents which have happened in various parts of the city when colored people have moved into certain areas — (*Beneatha exhales heavily and starts tossing a piece of fruit up and down in the air.*) Well — because we have what I think is going to be a unique type of organization in American community life — not only do we deplore that kind of thing — but we are trying to do something about it. (*Beneatha stops tossing and turns with a new and quizzical interest to the man.*) We feel — (*gaining confidence in his mission because of the interest in the faces of the people he is talking to*) — we feel that most of the trouble in this world, when you come right down to it — (*he hits his knee for emphasis*) — most of the trouble exists because people just don't sit down and talk to each other.

RUTH (*nodding as she might in church, pleased with the remark*): You can say that again, mister.

LINDNER (*more encouraged by such affirmation*): That we don't try hard enough in this world to understand the other fellow's problem. The other guy's point of view.

RUTH: Now that's right.

(*Beneatha and Walter merely watch and listen with genuine interest.*)

LINDNER: Yes — that's the way we feel out in Clybourne Park. And that's why I was elected to come here this afternoon and talk to you people. Friendly like, you know, the way people should talk to each other and see if we couldn't find some way to work this thing out. As I say, the whole business is a matter of *caring* about the other fellow. Anybody can see that you are a nice family of folks, hard-working and honest I'm sure. (*Beneatha frowns slightly, quizzically, her head tilted regarding him.*) Today everybody knows what it means to be on the outside of *something*. And of course, there is always somebody who is out to take advantage of people who don't always understand.

WALTER: What do you mean?

LINDNER: Well — you see our community is made up of people who've worked hard as the dickens for years to build up that little community. They're not rich and fancy people; just hard-working, honest people who don't really have much but those little homes and a dream of the kind of community they want to raise their children in. Now, I don't say we are perfect and there is a lot wrong in some of the things they want. But you've got to admit that a man, right or wrong, has the right to want to have the neighborhood he lives in a certain kind of way. And at the moment the overwhelming majority of our people out there feel that people get along better, take more of a common interest in the life of the community, when they share a common background. I want you to believe me when I tell you that race prejudice simply doesn't enter into it. It is a matter of the people of Clybourne Park believing, rightly or wrongly, as I say, that for the happiness of all concerned that our Negro families are happier when they live in their *own* communities.

BENEATHA (*with a grand and bitter gesture*): This, friends, is the Welcoming Committee!

WALTER (*dumfounded, looking at Lindner*): Is this what you came marching all the way over here to tell us?

LINDNER: Well, now we've been having a fine conversation. I hope you'll hear me all the way through.

WALTER (*tightly*): Go ahead, man.

LINDNER: You see — in the face of all the things I have said, we are prepared to make your family a very generous offer . . .

BENEATHA: Thirty pieces and not a coin less!

WALTER: Yeah!

LINDNER (*putting on his glasses and drawing a form out of the briefcase*): Our association is prepared, through the collective effort of our people, to buy the house from you at a financial gain to your family.

RUTH: Lord have mercy, ain't this the living gall!

WALTER: All right, you through?

LINDNER: Well, I want to give you the exact terms of the financial arrangement —

WALTER: We don't want to hear no exact terms of no arrangements. I want to know if you got any more to tell us 'bout getting together?

LINDNER (*taking off his glasses*): Well — I don't suppose that you feel . . .

WALTER: Never mind how I feel — you got any more to say 'bout how people ought to sit down and talk to each other? . . . Get out of my house, man.

(*He turns his back and walks to the door.*)

LINDNER (*looking around at the hostile faces and reaching and assembling his hat and briefcase*): Well — I don't understand why you people are reacting this way. What do you think you are going to gain by moving into a neighborhood where you just aren't wanted and where some elements — well — people

can get awful worked up when they feel that their whole way of life and everything they've ever worked for is threatened.

WALTER: Get out.

LINDNER (*at the door, holding a small card*): Well — I'm sorry it went like this.

WALTER: Get out.

LINDNER (*almost sadly regarding Walter*): You just can't force people to change their hearts, son.

(*He turns and puts his card on a table and exits. Walter pushes the door to with stinging hatred, and stands looking at it. Ruth just sits and Beneatha just stands. They say nothing. Mama and Travis enter.*)

MAMA: Well — this all the packing got done since I left out of here this morning. I testify before God that my children got all the energy of the *dead!* What time the moving men due?

BENEATHA: Four o'clock. You had a caller, Mama.

(*She is smiling, teasingly.*)

MAMA: Sure enough — who?

BENEATHA (*her arms folded saucily*): The Welcoming Committee.

(*Walter and Ruth giggle.*)

MAMA (*innocently*): Who?

BENEATHA: The Welcoming Committee. They said they're sure going to be glad to see you when you get there.

WALTER (*devilishly*): Yeah, they said they can't hardly wait to see your face.

(*Laughter.*)

MAMA (*sensing their facetiousness*): What's the matter with you all?

WALTER: Ain't nothing the matter with us. We just telling you 'bout the gentleman who came to see you this afternoon. From the Clybourne Park Improvement Association.

MAMA: What he want?

RUTH (*in the same mood as Beneatha and Walter*): To welcome you, honey.

WALTER: He said they can't hardly wait. He said the one thing they don't have, that they just *dying* to have out there is a fine family of fine colored people! (*To Ruth and Beneatha.*) Ain't that right!

RUTH (*mockingly*): Yeah! He left his card —

BENEATHA (*handing card to Mama*): In case.

(*Mama reads and throws it on the floor — understanding and looking off as she draws her chair up to the table on which she has put her plant and some sticks and some cord.*)

MAMA: Father, give us strength. (*Knowingly — and without fun.*) Did he threaten us?

BENEATHA: Oh — Mama — they don't do it like that anymore. He talked Brotherhood. He said everybody ought to learn how to sit down and hate each other with good Christian fellowship.

(*She and Walter shake hands to ridicule the remark.*)

MAMA (*sadly*): Lord, protect us . . .
RUTH: You should hear the money those folks raised to buy the house from us. All we paid and then some.
BENEATHA: What they think we going to do — eat 'em?
RUTH: No, honey, marry 'em.
MAMA (*shaking her head*): Lord, Lord, Lord . . .
RUTH: Well — that's the way the crackers crumble. (*A beat.*) Joke.
BENEATHA (*laughingly noticing what her mother is doing*): Mama, what are you doing?
MAMA: Fixing my plant so it won't get hurt none on the way . . .
BENEATHA: Mama, you going to take *that* to the new house?
MAMA: Un-huh —
BENEATHA: That raggedy-looking old thing?
MAMA (*stopping and looking at her*): It expresses ME!
RUTH (*with delight, to Beneatha*): So there, Miss Thing!

(*Walter comes to Mama suddenly and bends down behind her and squeezes her in his arms with all his strength. She is overwhelmed by the suddenness of it and, though delighted, her manner is like that of Ruth and Travis.*)

MAMA: Look out now, boy! You make me mess up my thing here!
WALTER (*his face lit, he slips down on his knees beside her, his arms still about her*): Mama . . . you know what it means to climb up in the chariot?
MAMA (*gruffly, very happy*): Get on away from me now . . .
RUTH (*near the gift-wrapped package, trying to catch Walter's eye*): Psst —
WALTER: What the old song say, Mama . . .
RUTH: Walter — Now?

(*She is pointing at the package.*)

WALTER (*speaking the lines, sweetly, playfully, in his mother's face*): I got wings . . . you got wings . . .
All God's Children got wings . . .
MAMA: Boy — get out of my face and do some work . . .
WALTER: When I get to heaven gonna put on my wings, Gonna fly all over God's heaven . . .
BENEATHA (*teasingly, from across the room*): Everybody talking 'bout heaven ain't going there!
WALTER (*to Ruth, who is carrying the box across to them*): I don't know, you think we ought to give her that . . . Seems to me she ain't been very appreciative around here.
MAMA (*eyeing the box, which is obviously a gift*): What is that?
WALTER (*taking it from Ruth and putting it on the table in front of Mama*): Well — what you all think? Should we give it to her?

RUTH: Oh — she was pretty good today.
MAMA: I'll good you —

(*She turns her eyes to the box again.*)

BENEATHA: Open it, Mama.

(*She stands up, looks at it, turns, and looks at all of them, and then presses her hands together and does not open the package.*)

WALTER (*sweetly*): Open it, Mama. It's for you. (*Mama looks in his eyes. It is the first present in her life without its being Christmas. Slowly she opens her package and lifts out, one by one, a brand-new sparkling set of gardening tools. Walter continues, prodding.*) Ruth made up the note — read it . . .
MAMA (*picking up the card and adjusting her glasses*): "To our own Mrs. Miniver — Love from Brother, Ruth and Beneatha." Ain't that lovely . . .
TRAVIS (*tugging at his father's sleeve*): Daddy, can I give her mine now?
WALTER: All right, son. (*Travis flies to get his gift.*)
MAMA: Now I don't have to use my knives and forks no more . . .
WALTER: Travis didn't want to go in with the rest of us, Mama. He got his own. (*Somewhat amused.*) We don't know what it is . . .
TRAVIS (*racing back in the room with a large hatbox and putting it in front of his grandmother*): Here!
MAMA: Lord have mercy, baby. You done gone and bought your grandmother a hat?
TRAVIS (*very proud*): Open it!

(*She does and lifts out an elaborate, but very elaborate, wide gardening hat, and all the adults break up at the sight of it.*)

RUTH: Travis, honey, what is that?
TRAVIS (*who thinks it is beautiful and appropriate*): It's a gardening hat! Like the ladies always have on in the magazines when they work in their gardens.
BENEATHA (*giggling fiercely*): Travis — we were trying to make Mama Mrs. Miniver — not Scarlett O'Hara!
MAMA (*indignantly*): What's the matter with you all! This here is a beautiful hat! (*Absurdly.*) I always wanted me one just like it!

(*She pops it on her head to prove it to her grandson, and the hat is ludicrous and considerably oversized.*)

RUTH: Hot dog! Go, Mama!
WALTER (*doubled over with laughter*): I'm sorry, Mama — but you look like you ready to go out and chop you some cotton sure enough!

(*They all laugh except Mama, out of deference to Travis's feelings.*)

MAMA (*gathering the boy up to her*): Bless your heart — this is the prettiest hat I ever owned — (*Walter, Ruth, and Beneatha chime in — noisily, festively, and insincerely congratulating Travis on his gift.*) What are we all standing around here for? We ain't finished packin' yet. Bennie, you ain't packed one book.

(*The bell rings.*)

BENEATHA: That couldn't be the movers . . . it's not hardly two good yet —

(*Beneatha goes into her room. Mama starts for door.*)

WALTER (*turning, stiffening*): Wait — wait — I'll get it.

(*He stands and looks at the door.*)

MAMA: You expecting company, son?

WALTER (*just looking at the door*): Yeah — yeah . . .

(*Mama looks at Ruth, and they exchange innocent and unfrightened glances.*)

MAMA (*not understanding*): Well, let them in, son.

BENEATHA (*from her room*): We need some more string.

MAMA: Travis — you run to the hardware and get me some string cord.

(*Mama goes out and Walter turns and looks at Ruth. Travis goes to a dish for money.*)

RUTH: Why don't you answer the door, man?

WALTER (*suddenly bounding across the floor to embrace her*): 'Cause sometimes it hard to let the future begin! (*Stooping down in her face.*)
I got wings! You got wings!
All God's children got wings!

(*He crosses to the door and throws it open. Standing there is a very slight little man in a not too prosperous business suit and with haunted frightened eyes and a hat pulled down tightly, brim up, around his forehead. Travis passes between the men and exits. Walter leans deep in the man's face, still in his jubilance.*) When I get to heaven gonna put on my wings, Gonna fly all over God's heaven . . . (*The little man just stares at him.*) Heaven — (*Suddenly he stops and looks past the little man into the empty hallway.*) Where's Willy, man?

BOBO: He ain't with me.

WALTER (*not disturbed*): Oh — come on in. You know my wife.

BOBO (*dumbly, taking off his hat*): Yes — h'you, Miss Ruth.

RUTH (*quietly, a mood apart from her husband already, seeing Bobo*): Hello, Bobo.

WALTER: You right on time today . . . Right on time. That's the way! (*He slaps Bobo on his back.*) Sit down . . . lemme hear.

(*Ruth stands stiffly and quietly in back of them, as though somehow she senses death, her eyes fixed on her husband.*)

BOBO (*his frightened eyes on the floor, his hat in his hands*): Could I please get a drink of water, before I tell you about it, Walter Lee?

(*Walter does not take his eyes off the man. Ruth goes blindly to the tap and gets a glass of water and brings it to Bobo.*)

WALTER: There ain't nothing wrong, is there?

BOBO: Lemme tell you —

WALTER: Man — didn't nothing go wrong?

BOBO: Lemme tell you — Walter Lee. (*Looking at Ruth and talking to her more than to Walter.*) You know how it was. I got to tell you how it was. I mean first I got to tell you how it was all the way . . . I mean about the money I put in, Walter Lee . . .

WALTER (*with taut agitation now*): What about the money you put in?

BOBO: Well — it wasn't much as we told you — me and Willy — (*He stops.*) I'm sorry, Walter. I got a bad feeling about it. I got a real bad feeling about it . . .

WALTER: Man, what you telling me about all this for? . . . Tell me what happened in Springfield . . .

BOBO: Springfield.

RUTH (*like a dead woman*): What was supposed to happen in Springfield?

BOBO (*to her*): This deal that me and Walter went into with Willy — Me and Willy was going to go down to Springfield and spread some money 'round so's we wouldn't have to wait so long for the liquor license . . . That's what we were going to do. Everybody said that was the way you had to do, you understand, Miss Ruth?

WALTER: Man — what happened down there?

BOBO (*a pitiful man, near tears*): I'm trying to tell you, Walter.

WALTER (*screaming at him suddenly*): THEN TELL ME, GODDAMMIT . . . WHAT'S THE MATTER WITH YOU?

BOBO: Man . . . I didn't go to no Springfield, yesterday.

WALTER (*halted, life hanging in the moment*): Why not?

BOBO (*the long way, the hard way to tell*): 'Cause I didn't have no reasons to . . .

WALTER: Man, what are you talking about!

BOBO: I'm talking about the fact that when I got to the train station yesterday morning — eight o'clock like we planned . . . Man — *Willy didn't never show up.*

WALTER: Why . . . where was he . . . where is he?

BOBO: That's what I'm trying to tell you . . . I don't know . . . I waited six hours . . . I called his house . . . and I waited . . . six hours . . . I waited in that train station six hours . . . (*Breaking into tears.*) That was all the extra money I had in the world . . . (*Looking up at Walter with the tears running down his face.*) Man, *Willy is gone.*

WALTER: Gone, what you mean Willy is gone? Gone where? You mean he went by himself. You mean he went off to Springfield by himself — to take care of getting the license — (*Turns and looks anxiously at Ruth.*) You mean maybe he didn't want too many people in on the business down there? (*Looks to Ruth again, as before.*) You know Willy got his own ways. (*Looks back to Bobo.*) Maybe you was late yesterday and he just went on down there without you. Maybe — maybe — he's been callin' you at home tryin' to tell you what happened or something. Maybe — maybe — he just got sick. He's somewhere — he's got to be somewhere. We just got to find him — me and you got to find him. (*Grabs Bobo senselessly by the collar and starts to shake him.*) We got to!

BOBO (*in sudden angry, frightened agony*): What's the matter with you, Walter! *When a cat take off with your money he don't leave you no road maps!*

WALTER (*turning madly, as though he is looking for Willy in the very room*): Willy! . . . Willy . . . don't do it . . . Please don't do it . . . Man, not with that money . . . Man, please, not with that money . . . Oh, God . . . Don't let it be true . . . (*He is wandering around, crying out for Willy and looking for him or perhaps for help from God.*) Man . . . I trusted you . . . Man, I put my life in your hands . . . (*He starts to crumple down on the floor as Ruth just covers her face in horror. Mama opens the door and comes into the room, with Beneatha behind her.*) Man . . . (*He starts to pound the floor with his fists, sobbing wildly.*) THAT MONEY IS MADE OUT MY FATHER'S FLESH ——

BOBO (*standing over him helplessly*): I'm sorry, Walter . . . (*Only Walter's sobs reply. Bobo puts on his hat.*) I had my life staked on this deal, too . . .

(*He exits.*)

MAMA (*to Walter*): Son — (*She goes to him, bends down to him, talks to his bent head.*) Son . . . Is it gone? Son, I gave you sixty-five hundred dollars. Is it gone? All of it? Beneatha's money too?

WALTER (*lifting his head slowly*): Mama . . . I never . . . went to the bank at all . . .

MAMA (*not wanting to believe him*): You mean . . . your sister's school money . . . you used that too . . . Walter? . . .

WALTER: Yessss! All of it . . . It's all gone . . .

(*There is total silence. Ruth stands with her face covered with her hands; Beneatha leans forlornly against a wall, fingering a piece of red ribbon from the mother's gift. Mama stops and looks at her son without recognition and then, quite without thinking about it, starts to beat him senselessly in the face. Beneatha goes to them and stops it.*)

BENEATHA: Mama!

(*Mama stops and looks at both of her children and rises slowly and wanders vaguely, aimlessly away from them.*)

MAMA: I seen . . . him . . . night after night . . . come in . . . and look at that rug . . . and then look at me . . . the red showing in his eyes . . . the veins moving in his head . . . I seen him grow thin and old before he was forty . . . working and working and working like somebody's old horse . . . killing him-

self . . . and you — you give it all away in a day — (*She raises her arms to strike him again.*)

BENEATHA: Mama —

MAMA: Oh, God . . . (*She looks up to Him.*) Look down here — and show me the strength.

BENEATHA: Mama —

MAMA (*folding over*): Strength . . .

BENEATHA (*plaintively*): Mama . . .

MAMA: Strength!

ACT III

(*An hour later.*)

(*At curtain, there is a sullen light of gloom in the living room, gray light not unlike that which began the first scene of act I. At left we can see Walter within his room, alone with himself. He is stretched out on the bed, his shirt out and open, his arms under his head. He does not smoke, he does not cry out, he merely lies there, looking up at the ceiling, much as if he were alone in the world.*)

(*In the living room Beneatha sits at the table, still surrounded by the now almost ominous packing crates. She sits looking off. We feel that this is a mood struck perhaps an hour before, and it lingers now, full of the empty sound of profound disappointment. We see on a line from her brother's bedroom the sameness of their attitudes. Presently the bell rings and Beneatha rises without ambition or interest in answering. It is Asagai, smiling broadly, striding into the room with energy and happy expectation and conversation.*)

ASAGAI: I came over . . . I had some free time. I thought I might help with the packing. Ah, I like the look of packing crates! A household in preparation for a journey! It depresses some people . . . but for me . . . it is another feeling. Something full of the flow of life, do you understand? Movement, progress . . . It makes me think of Africa.

BENEATHA: Africa!

ASAGAI: What kind of a mood is this? Have I told you how deeply you move me?

BENEATHA: He gave away the money, Asagai . . .

ASAGAI: Who gave away what money?

BENEATHA: The insurance money. My brother gave it away.

ASAGAI: Gave it away?

BENEATHA: He made an investment! With a man even Travis wouldn't have trusted with his most worn-out marbles.

ASAGAI: And it's gone?

BENEATHA: Gone!

ASAGAI: I'm very sorry . . . And you, now?

BENEATHA: Me? . . . Me? . . . Me, I'm nothing . . . Me. When I was very small . . . we used to take our sleds out in the wintertime and the only hills we had were the ice-covered stone steps of some houses down the street. And we used to fill them in with snow and make them smooth and slide down them all day . . . and it was very dangerous, you know . . . far too steep . . . and sure enough one day a kid named Rufus came down too fast and hit the sidewalk and we saw his face just split open right there in front of us . . . And I remember standing there looking at his bloody open face thinking that was the end of Rufus. But the ambulance came and they took him to the hospital and they fixed the broken bones and they sewed it all up . . . and the next time I saw Rufus he just had a little line down the middle of his face . . . I never got over that . . .

ASAGAI: What?

BENEATHA: That that was what one person could do for another, fix him up — sew up the problem, make him all right again. That was the most marvelous thing in the world . . . I wanted to do that. I always thought it was the one concrete thing in the world that a human being could do. Fix up the sick, you know — and make them whole again. This was truly being God . . .

ASAGAI: You wanted to be God?

BENEATHA: No — I wanted to cure. It used to be so important to me. I wanted to cure. It used to matter. I used to care. I mean about people and how their bodies hurt . . .

ASAGAI: And you've stopped caring?

BENEATHA: Yes — I think so.

ASAGAI: Why?

BENEATHA (*bitterly*): Because it doesn't seem deep enough, close enough to what ails mankind! It was a child's way of seeing things — or an idealist's.

ASAGAI: Children see things very well sometimes — and idealists even better.

BENEATHA: I know that's what you think. Because you are still where I left off. You with all your talk and dreams about Africa! You still think you can patch up the world. Cure the Great Sore of Colonialism — (*loftily, mocking it*) with the Penicillin of Independence —!

ASAGAI: Yes!

BENEATHA: Independence *and then what?* What about all the crooks and thieves and just plain idiots who will come into power and steal and plunder the same as before — only now they will be black and do it in the name of the new Independence — WHAT ABOUT THEM?!

ASAGAI: That will be the problem for another time. First we must get there.

BENEATHA: And where does it end?

ASAGAI: End? Who even spoke of an end? To life? To living?

BENEATHA: An end to misery! To stupidity! Don't you see there isn't any real progress, Asagai, there is only one large circle that we march in, around and around, each of us with our own little picture in front of us — our own little mirage that we think is the future.

ASAGAI: That is the mistake.

BENEATHA: What?

ASAGAI: What you just said — about the circle. It isn't a circle — it is simply a long line — as in geometry, you know, one that reaches into infinity. And because we cannot see the end — we also cannot see how it changes. And it is very odd but those who see the changes — who dream, who will not give up — are called idealists . . . and those who see only the circle — we call *them* the "realists"!

BENEATHA: Asagai, while I was sleeping in that bed in there, people went out and took the future right out of my hands! And nobody asked me, nobody consulted me — they just went out and changed my life!

ASAGAI: Was it your money?

BENEATHA: What?

ASAGAI: Was it your money he gave away?

BENEATHA: It belonged to all of us.

ASAGAI: But did you earn it? Would you have had it at all if your father had not died?

BENEATHA: No.

ASAGAI: Then isn't there something wrong in a house — in a world — where all dreams, good or bad, must depend on the death of a man? I never thought to see *you* like this, Alaiyo. You! Your brother made a mistake and you are grateful to him so that now you can give up the ailing human race on account of it! You talk about what good is struggle, what good is anything! Where are we all going and why are we bothering!

BENEATHA: AND YOU CANNOT ANSWER IT!

ASAGAI (*shouting over her*): I LIVE THE ANSWER! (*Pause.*) In my village at home it is the exceptional man who can even read a newspaper . . . or who ever sees a book at all. I will go home and much of what I will have to say will seem strange to the people of my village. But I will teach and work and things will happen, slowly and swiftly. At times it will seem that nothing changes at all . . . and then again the sudden dramatic events which make history leap into the future. And then quiet again. Retrogression even. Guns, murder, revolution. And I even will have moments when I wonder if the quiet was not better than all that death and hatred. But I will look about my village at the illiteracy and disease and ignorance and I will not wonder long. And perhaps . . . perhaps I will be a great man . . . I mean perhaps I will hold on to the substance of truth and find my way always with the right course . . . and perhaps for it I will be butchered in my bed some night by the servants of empire . . .

BENEATHA: *The martyr!*

ASAGAI (*he smiles*): . . . or perhaps I shall live to be a very old man, respected and esteemed in my new nation . . . And perhaps I shall hold office and this is what I'm trying to tell you, Alaiyo: Perhaps the things I believe now for my country will be wrong and outmoded, and I will not understand and do terrible things to have things my way or merely to keep my power. Don't you see that there will be young men and women — not British soldiers then, but my own black countrymen — to step out of the shadows some evening and slit my then useless throat? Don't you see they have always been there . . . that they always will be. And that such a thing as my own death will be an advance? They who might kill me even . . . actually replenish all that I was.

BENEATHA: Oh, Asagai, I know all that.

ASAGAI: Good! Then stop moaning and groaning and tell me what you plan to do.

BENEATHA: Do?

ASAGAI: I have a bit of a suggestion.

BENEATHA: What?

ASAGAI (*rather quietly for him*): That when it is all over — that you come home with me —

BENEATHA (*staring at him and crossing away with exasperation*): Oh — Asagai — at this moment you decide to be romantic!

ASAGAI (*quickly understanding the misunderstanding*): My dear, young creature of the New World — I do not mean across the city — I mean across the ocean: home — to Africa.

BENEATHA (*slowly understanding and turning to him with murmured amazement*): To Africa?

ASAGAI: Yes! . . . (*Smiling and lifting his arms playfully.*) Three hundred years later the African Prince rose up out of the seas and swept the maiden back across the middle passage over which her ancestors had come —

BENEATHA (*unable to play*): To — to Nigeria?

ASAGAI: Nigeria. Home. (*Coming to her with genuine romantic flippancy.*) I will show you our mountains and our stars; and give you cool drinks from gourds and teach you the old songs and the ways of our people — and, in time, we will pretend that — (*very softly*) — you have only been away for a day. Say that you'll come — (*He swings her around and takes her full in his arms in a kiss which proceeds to passion.*)

BENEATHA (*pulling away suddenly*): You're getting me all mixed up —

ASAGAI: Why?

BENEATHA: Too many things — too many things have happened today. I must sit down and think. I don't know what I feel about anything right this minute.

(*She promptly sits down and props her chin on her fist.*)

ASAGAI (*charmed*): All right, I shall leave you. No — don't get up. (*Touching her, gently, sweetly.*) Just sit awhile and think . . . Never be afraid to sit awhile and think. (*He goes to door and looks at her.*) How often I have looked at you and said, "Ah — so this is what the New World hath finally wrought . . ."

(*He exits. Beneatha sits on alone. Presently Walter enters from his room and starts to rummage through things, feverishly looking for something. She looks up and turns in her seat.*)

BENEATHA (*hissingly*): Yes — just look at what the New World hath wrought! . . . Just look! (*She gestures with bitter disgust.*) There he is! *Monsieur le petit bourgeois noir*° — himself! There he is — Symbol of a Rising Class! Entrepreneur! Titan° of the system! (*Walter ignores her completely and continues frantically and destructively looking for something and hurling things to floor and tearing things out of their place in his search. Beneatha ignores the eccentricity of his actions and goes on with the monologue of insult.*) Did you dream of yachts on Lake Michigan, Brother? Did you see yourself on that Great Day sitting down at the Conference Table, surrounded by all the mighty bald-headed men in America? All halted, waiting, breathless, waiting for your pronouncements on industry? Waiting for you — Chairman of the Board! (*Walter finds what he is looking for — a small piece of white paper — and pushes it in his pocket and puts on his coat and rushes out without ever having looked at her. She shouts after him.*) I look at you and I see the final triumph of stupidity in the world!

(*The door slams and she returns to just sitting again. Ruth comes quickly out of Mama's room.*)

RUTH: Who was that?

BENEATHA: Your husband.

RUTH: Where did he go?

BENEATHA: Who knows — maybe he has an appointment at U.S. Steel.

RUTH (*anxiously, with frightened eyes*): You didn't say nothing bad to him, did you?

BENEATHA: Bad? Say anything bad to him? No — I told him he was a sweet boy and full of dreams and everything is strictly peachy keen, as the ofay° kids say!

(*Mama enters from her bedroom. She is lost, vague, trying to catch hold, to make some sense of her former command of the world, but it still eludes her. A sense of waste overwhelms her gait; a measure of apology rides on her shoulders. She goes to her plant, which has remained on the table, looks at it, picks it up and takes it to the window sill and sits it outside, and she stands and looks at it a long moment. Then she closes the window, straightens her body with effort, and turns around to her children.*)

MAMA: Well — ain't it a mess in here, though? (*A false cheerfulness, a beginning of something.*) I guess we all better stop moping around and get some work done. All this unpacking and everything we got to do. (*Ruth raises her head slowly in response to the sense of the line; and Beneatha in similar manner turns very slowly to look at her mother.*) One of you all better call the moving people and tell 'em not to come.

RUTH: Tell 'em not to come?

MAMA: Of course, baby. Ain't no need in 'em coming all the way here and having to go back. They charges for that too. (*She sits down, fingers to her brow, think-*

Monsieur . . . noir: Mr. Black Lower Middle Class.
Titan: Person of great power; originally, a god.
ofay: White person, usually used disparagingly.

ing.) Lord, ever since I was a little girl, I always remembers people saying, "Lena — Lena Eggleston, you aims too high all the time. You needs to slow down and see life a little more like it is. Just slow down some." That's what they always used to say down home — "Lord, that Lena Eggleston is a high-minded thing. She'll get her due one day!"

RUTH: No, Lena . . .

MAMA: Me and Big Walter just didn't never learn right.

RUTH: Lena, no! We gotta go. Bennie — tell her . . . (*She rises and crosses to Beneatha with her arms outstretched. Beneatha doesn't respond.*) Tell her we can still move . . . the notes ain't but a hundred and twenty-five a month. We got four grown people in this house — we can work . . .

MAMA (*to herself*): Just aimed too high all the time —

RUTH (*turning and going to Mama fast — the words pouring out with urgency and desperation*): Lena — I'll work . . . I'll work twenty hours a day in all the kitchens in Chicago . . . I'll strap my baby on my back if I have to and scrub all the floors in America and wash all the sheets in America if I have to — but we got to MOVE! We got to get OUT OF HERE!!

(*Mama reaches out absently and pats Ruth's hand.*)

MAMA: No — I sees things differently now. Been thinking 'bout some of the things we could do to fix this place up some. I seen a second-hand bureau over on Maxwell Street just the other day that could fit right there. (*She points to where the new furniture might go. Ruth wanders away from her.*) Would need some new handles on it and then a little varnish and it look like something brand-new. And — we can put up them new curtains in the kitchen . . . Why this place be looking fine. Cheer us all up so that we forget trouble ever come . . . (*To Ruth.*) And you could get some nice screens to put up in your room round the baby's bassinet . . . (*She looks at both of them, pleadingly.*) Sometimes you just got to know when to give up some things . . . and hold on to what you got. . . .

(*Walter enters from the outside, looking spent and leaning against the door, his coat hanging from him.*)

MAMA: Where you been, son?

WALTER (*breathing hard*): Made a call.

MAMA: To who, son?

WALTER: To The Man. (*He heads for his room.*)

MAMA: What man, baby?

WALTER (*stops in the door*): The Man, Mama. Don't you know who The Man is?

RUTH: Walter Lee?

WALTER: *The Man.* Like the guys in the streets say — The Man. Captain Boss — Mistuh Charley . . . Old Cap'n Please Mr. Bossman . . .

BENEATHA (*suddenly*): Lindner!

WALTER: That's right! That's good. I told him to come right over.

BENEATHA (*fiercely, understanding*): For what? What do you want to see him for!

WALTER (*looking at his sister*): We going to do business with him.

MAMA: What you talking 'bout, son?

WALTER: Talking 'bout life, Mama. You all always telling me to see life like it is. Well — I laid in there on my back today . . . and I figured it out. Life just like it is. Who gets and who don't get. (*He sits down with his coat on and laughs.*) Mama, you know it's all divided up. Life is. Sure enough. Between the takers and the "tooken." (*He laughs.*) I've figured it out finally. (*He looks around at them.*) Yeah. Some of us always getting "tooken." (*He laughs.*) People like Willy Harris, they don't never get "tooken." And you know why the rest of us do? 'Cause we all mixed up. Mixed up bad. We get to looking 'round for the right and the wrong; and we worry about it and cry about it and stay up nights trying to figure out 'bout the wrong and the right of things all the time . . . And all the time, man, them takers is out there operating, just taking and taking. Willy Harris? Shoot — Willy Harris don't even count. He don't even count in the big scheme of things. But I'll say one thing for old Willy Harris . . . he's taught me something. He's taught me to keep my eye on what counts in this world. Yeah — (*Shouting out a little.*) Thanks, Willy!

RUTH: What did you call that man for, Walter Lee?

WALTER: Called him to tell him to come on over to the show. Gonna put on a show for the man. Just what he wants to see. You see, Mama, the man came here today and he told us that them people out there where you want us to move — well they so upset they willing to pay us *not* to move! (*He laughs again.*) And — and oh, Mama — you would of been proud of the way me and Ruth and Bennie acted. We told him to get out . . . Lord have mercy! We told the man to get out! Oh, we was some proud folks this afternoon, yeah. (*He lights a cigarette.*) We were still full of that old-time stuff . . .

RUTH (*coming toward him slowly*): You talking 'bout taking them people's money to keep us from moving in that house?

WALTER: I ain't just talking 'bout it, baby — I'm telling you that's what's going to happen!

BENEATHA: Oh, God! Where is the bottom! Where is the real honest-to-God bottom so he can't go any farther!

WALTER: See — that's the old stuff. You and that boy that was here today. You all want everybody to carry a flag and a spear and sing some marching songs, huh? You wanna spend your life looking into things and trying to find the right and the wrong part, huh? Yeah. You know what's going to happen to that boy someday — he'll find himself sitting in a dungeon, locked in forever — and the takers will have the key! Forget it, baby! There ain't no causes — there ain't nothing but taking in this world, and he who takes most is smartest — and it don't make a damn bit of difference *how.*

MAMA: You making something inside me cry, son. Some awful pain inside me.

WALTER: Don't cry, Mama. Understand. That white man is going to walk in that door able to write checks for more money than we ever had. It's important to him and I'm going to help him . . . I'm going to put on the show, Mama.

MAMA: Son — I come from five generations of people who was slaves and sharecroppers — but ain't nobody in my family never let nobody pay 'em no money that was a way of telling us we wasn't fit to walk the earth. We ain't never been that poor. (*Raising her eyes and looking at him.*) We ain't never been that — dead inside.

BENEATHA: Well — we are dead now. All the talk about dreams and sunlight that goes on in this house. It's all dead now.

WALTER: What's the matter with you all! I didn't make this world! It was give to me this way! Hell, yes, I want me some yachts someday! Yes, I want to hang some real pearls 'round my wife's neck. Ain't she supposed to wear no pearls? Somebody tell me — tell me, who decides which women is suppose to wear pearls in this world. I tell you I am a *man* — and I think my wife should wear some pearls in this world!

(*This last line hangs a good while and Walter begins to move about the room. The word "Man" has penetrated his consciousness; he mumbles it to himself repeatedly between strange agitated pauses as he moves about.*)

MAMA: Baby, how you going to feel on the inside?

WALTER: Fine! . . . Going to feel fine . . . a man . . .

MAMA: You won't have nothing left then, Walter Lee.

WALTER (*coming to her*): I'm going to feel fine, Mama. I'm going to look that son-of-a-bitch in the eyes and say — (*he falters*) — and say, "All right, Mr. Lindner — (*he falters even more*) — that's *your* neighborhood out there! You got the right to keep it like you want! You got the right to have it like you want! Just write the check and — the house is yours." And — and I am going to say — (*His voice almost breaks.*) "And you — you people just put the money in my hand and you won't have to live next to this bunch of stinking niggers! . . ." (*He straightens up and moves away from his mother, walking around the room.*) And maybe — maybe I'll just get down on my black knees . . . (*He does so; Ruth and Bennie and Mama watch him in frozen horror.*) "Captain, Mistuh, Bossman — (*Groveling and grinning and wringing his hands in profoundly anguished imitation of the slow-witted movie stereotype.*) A-hee-hee-hee! Oh, yassuh boss! Yasssssuh! Great white — (*voice breaking, he forces himself to go on*) — Father, just gi' ussen de money, fo' God's sake, and we's — we's ain't gwine come out deh and dirty up yo' white folks neighborhood . . ." (*He breaks down completely.*) And I'll feel fine! Fine! FINE! (*He gets up and goes into the bedroom.*)

BENEATHA: That is not a man. That is nothing but a toothless rat.

MAMA: Yes — death done come in this here house. (*She is nodding, slowly, reflectively.*) Done come walking in my house on the lips of my children. You what supposed to be my beginning again. You — what supposed to be my harvest. (*To Beneatha.*) You — you mourning your brother?

BENEATHA: He's no brother of mine.

MAMA: What you say?

BENEATHA: I said that that individual in that room is no brother of mine.

MAMA: That's what I thought you said. You feeling like you better than he is today? (*Beneatha does not answer.*) Yes? What you tell him a minute ago? That he wasn't a man? Yes? You give him up for me? You done wrote his epitaph too — like the rest of the world? Well, who give you the privilege?

BENEATHA: Be on my side for once! You saw what he just did, Mama! You saw him — down on his knees. Wasn't it you who taught me to despise any man who would do that? Do what he's going to do?

MAMA: Yes — I taught you that. Me and your daddy. But I thought I taught you something else too . . . I thought I taught you to love him.

BENEATHA: Love him? There is nothing left to love.

MAMA: There is *always* something left to love. And if you ain't learned that, you ain't learned nothing. (*Looking at her.*) Have you cried for that boy today? I don't mean for yourself and for the family 'cause we lost the money. I mean for him: what he been through and what it done to him. Child, when do you think is the time to love somebody the most? When they done good and made things easy for everybody? Well then, you ain't through learning — because that ain't the time at all. It's when he's at his lowest and can't believe in hisself 'cause the world done whipped him so! When you starts measuring somebody, measure him right, child, measure him right. Make sure you done taken into account what hills and valleys he come through before he got to wherever he is.

(*Travis bursts into the room at the end of the speech, leaving the door open.*)

TRAVIS: Grandmama — the moving men are downstairs! The truck just pulled up.

MAMA (*turning and looking at him*): Are they, baby? They downstairs?

(*She sighs and sits. Lindner appears in the doorway. He peers in and knocks lightly, to gain attention, and comes in. All turn to look at him.*)

LINDNER (*hat and briefcase in hand*): Uh — hello . . .

(*Ruth crosses mechanically to the bedroom door and opens it and lets it swing open freely and slowly as the lights come up on Walter within, still in his coat, sitting at the far corner of the room. He looks up and out through the room to Lindner.*)

RUTH: He's here.

(*A long minute passes and Walter slowly gets up.*)

LINDNER (*coming to the table with efficiency, putting his briefcase on the table and starting to unfold papers and unscrew fountain pens*): Well, I certainly was glad to hear from you people. (*Walter has begun the trek out of the room, slowly and awkwardly, rather like a small boy, passing the back of his sleeve across his mouth from time to time.*) Life can really be so much simpler than people let it be most of the time. Well — with whom do I negotiate? You, Mrs. Younger, or your son here? (*Mama sits with her hands folded on her lap and her eyes closed as Walter advances. Travis goes closer to Lindner and looks at the papers curiously.*) Just some official papers, sonny.

RUTH: Travis, you go downstairs —

MAMA (*opening her eyes and looking into Walter's*): No. Travis, you stay right here. And you make him understand what you doing, Walter Lee. You teach him good. Like Willy Harris taught you. You show where our five generations done come to. (*Walter looks from her to the boy, who grins at him innocently.*) Go ahead, son — (*She folds her hands and closes her eyes.*) Go ahead.

WALTER (*at last crosses to Lindner, who is reviewing the contract*): Well, Mr. Lindner. (*Beneatha turns away.*) We called you — (*there is a profound, simple groping quality in his speech*) — because, well, me and my family (*he looks around and shifts from one foot to the other*) Well — we are very plain people . . .

LINDNER: Yes —

WALTER: I mean — I have worked as a chauffeur most of my life — and my wife here, she does domestic work in people's kitchens. So does my mother. I mean — we are plain people . . .

LINDNER: Yes, Mr. Younger —

WALTER (*really like a small boy, looking down at his shoes and then up at the man*): And — uh — well, my father, well, he was a laborer most of his life. . . .

LINDNER (*absolutely confused*): Uh, yes — yes, I understand. (*He turns back to the contract.*)

WALTER (*a beat; staring at him*): And my father — (*With sudden intensity.*) My father almost *beat a man to death* once because this man called him a bad name or something, you know what I mean?

LINDNER (*looking up, frozen*): No, no, I'm afraid I don't —

WALTER (*A beat. The tension hangs; then Walter steps back from it.*): Yeah. Well — what I mean is that we come from people who had a lot of *pride.* I mean — we are very proud people. And that's my sister over there and she's going to be a doctor — and we are very proud —

LINDNER: Well — I am sure that is very nice, but —

WALTER: What I am telling you is that we called you over here to tell you that we are very proud and that this — (*Signaling to Travis.*) Travis, come here. (*Travis crosses and Walter draws him before him facing the man.*) This is my son, and he makes the sixth generation of our family in this country. And we have all thought about your offer —

LINDNER: Well, good . . . good —

WALTER: And we have decided to move into our house because my father — my father — he earned it for us brick by brick. (*Mama has her eyes closed and is rocking back and forth as though she were in church, with her head nodding the Amen yes.*) We don't want to make no trouble for nobody or fight no causes, and we will try to be good neighbors. And that's *all* we got to say about that. (*He looks the man absolutely in the eyes.*) We don't want your money. (*He turns and walks away.*)

LINDNER (*looking around at all of them*): I take it then — that you have decided to occupy . . .

BENEATHA: That's what the man said.

LINDNER (*to Mama in her reverie*): Then I would like to appeal to you, Mrs. Younger. You are older and wiser and understand things better I am sure . . .

MAMA: I am afraid you don't understand. My son said we was going to move and there ain't nothing left for me to say. (*Briskly.*) You know how these young folks is nowadays, mister. Can't do a thing with 'em! (*As he opens his mouth, she rises.*) Goodbye.

LINDNER (*folding up his materials*): Well — if you are that final about it . . . there is nothing left for me to say. (*He finishes, almost ignored by the family, who are concentrating on Walter Lee. At the door Lindner halts and looks around.*) I sure hope you people know what you're getting into.

(*He shakes his head and exits.*)

RUTH (*looking around and coming to life*): Well, for God's sake — if the moving men are here — LET'S GET THE HELL OUT OF HERE!

MAMA (*into action*): Ain't it the truth! Look at all this here mess. Ruth, put Travis's good jacket on him . . . Walter Lee, fix your tie and tuck your shirt in, you look like somebody's hoodlum! Lord have mercy, where is my plant? (*She flies to get it amid the general bustling of the family, who are deliberately trying to ignore the nobility of the past moment.*) You all start on down . . . Travis child, don't go empty-handed . . . Ruth, where did I put that box with my skillets in it? I want to be in charge of it myself . . . I'm going to make us the biggest dinner we ever ate tonight . . . Beneatha, what's the matter with them stockings? Pull them things up, girl . . .

(*The family starts to file out as two moving men appear and begin to carry out the heavier pieces of furniture, bumping into the family as they move about.*)

BENEATHA: Mama, Asagai asked me to marry him today and go to Africa —

MAMA (*in the middle of her getting-ready activity*): He did? You ain't old enough to marry nobody — (*Seeing the moving men lifting one of her chairs precariously.*) Darling, that ain't no bale of cotton, please handle it so we can sit in it again! I had that chair twenty-five years . . .

(*The movers sigh with exasperation and go on with their work.*)

BENEATHA (*girlishly and unreasonably trying to pursue the conversation*): To go to Africa, Mama — be a doctor in Africa . . .

MAMA (*distracted*): Yes, baby —

WALTER: *Africa!* What he want you to go to Africa for?

BENEATHA: To practice there . . .

WALTER: Girl, if you don't get all them silly ideas out your head! You better marry yourself a man with some loot . . .

BENEATHA (*angrily, precisely as in the first scene of the play*): What have you got to do with who I marry!

WALTER: Plenty. Now I think George Murchison —

BENEATHA: *George Murchison!* I wouldn't marry him if he was Adam and I was Eve!

(*Walter and Beneatha go out yelling at each other vigorously and the anger is loud and real till their voices diminish. Ruth stands at the door and turns to Mama and smiles knowingly.*)

MAMA (*fixing her hat at last*): Yeah — they something all right, my children . . .

RUTH: Yeah — they're something. Let's go, Lena.

MAMA (*stalling, starting to look around at the house*): Yes — I'm coming. Ruth —

RUTH: Yes?

MAMA (*quietly, woman to woman*): He finally come into his manhood today, didn't he? Kind of like a rainbow after the rain . . .

RUTH (*biting her lip lest her own pride explode in front of Mama*): Yes, Lena.

(*Walter's voice calls for them raucously.*)

WALTER (*offstage*): Y'all come on! These people charges by the hour you know!

MAMA (*waving Ruth out vaguely*): All right, honey — go on down. I be down directly.

(*Ruth hesitates, then exits. Mama stands, at last alone in the living room, her plant on the table before her as the lights start to come down. She looks around at all the walls and ceilings and suddenly, despite herself, while the children call below, a great heaving thing rises in her and she puts her fist to her mouth to stifle it, takes a final desperate look, pulls her coat about her, pats her hat, and goes out. The lights dim down. The door opens and she comes back in, grabs her plant, and goes out for the last time.*)

Wole Soyinka

Wole Soyinka (b. 1934) is one of Nigeria's several important writers to achieve international fame, winning the Nobel Prize for literature in 1986. His work includes novels, poems, and plays, but he admits that "there is no question at all that I think the Nobel Prize is for my drama."

Soyinka studied at University College, Ibadan, Nigeria, and began his literary career as an undergraduate, publishing poetry in the distinguished African literary magazine *Black Orpheus*. His work, especially his drama, has been an investigation of political, religious, and other forces in Nigerian culture. *The Swamp Dwellers* (1958) is a powerful play condemning African superstition. *The Lion and the Jewel* (1959) offers a comic view of Nigerian attitudes toward European values left over from the colonial period. Among his other plays are *The Trials of Brother Jero* (1960), about a corrupt evangelist, and *Kongi's Harvest* (1964). *A Dance of the Forests* (1960) was written to celebrate Nigerian independence, but it also alerted people to Nigeria's past violence and warned against its return.

Nigeria went through a bitter civil war in 1967, and Soyinka's political sympathies led to a term in prison, where he was placed in solitary confinement. He continued his writing, smuggling poems out of prison to give hope to his political allies. He even criticized his own tribe, the Yoruba, for murdering members of the Ibo during the war against Biafra.

Soyinka had studied at the University of Leeds after his schooling in Ibadan. Most of his writing is in English, but he still writes some of his poetry in his tribal language, Yoruba. He has recommended Swahili as the national language of Nigeria. Soyinka has spoken out against cultural parochialism, including its manifestation in the negritude movement, which rejects Western culture as a form of pollution. He expressed his philosophy to another great African writer, Leopold Senghor: "A tiger is not forever shouting about his tigritude"; a duiker antelope does not have to "prove his duikertude; you will know him by his elegant leap."

Soyinka has been chair of the drama department at Ife University as well as of his own University College, Ibadan. He has also lectured in Cambridge, England, and in universities in North America. One of his works, *A Play of Giants* (1984), is a scathing attack on abuse of power, indicting African tyrants such as Idi Amin, Jean-Bedel Bokassa, and others.

For all of his criticism of Nigerian politics, Soyinka has rooted his work in the religion and folklore of the Yoruba people. Ifa, the Yoruba religion, depends on a complex cosmology that sees experience as layered in interactive animal, mineral, and vegetable spheres. African critic Femi Osofisan has described Yoruba cosmology as holding "coeval the three historical, actual, and prospective planes of entity; . . . the animal and vegetable essences are correspondent; . . . the acknowledged deities are both anthropomorphic and symbiotic, each fusing in his personality a series of antinomies." Osofisan also notes "the comprehensive union of religious and secular intuition in the traditional Yoruba." Ifa plays a role in *The Strong Breed*, but the play is nonetheless understandable to those unfamiliar with the religion. Soyinka must be thought of as a traditional dramatist, writing in the tradition of his Yoruba people but reaching a worldwide audience.

THE STRONG BREED

The Strong Breed (1962), written at a time of political uncertainty in Nigeria, examines the interrelationship of ritual and community in African culture, describing one process by which a society renews itself. The "strong breed" are those men capable of the sacrifice needed annually to purify the community of its sins and to allow it to start over again. The community's sacrifice signals the beginning of a new year.

As the new year approaches, the elders of the community, Jaguna and Oroge, search for the appropriate "carrier" who can bear the burden of the community's guilt. The tradition in their community is to choose a stranger. Despite the elders' reluctance, Eman, one of the strong breed who has exiled himself from his own community, seems a logical choice until another outsider, the idiot Ifada, comes on the scene. Ifada seems heaven-sent to serve the community, but when he is chosen, he protests in terrified confusion. Eman explains to Jaguna and Oroge that no community should force a carrier to perform unwillingly. If he is unwilling, the guilt will not be carried away. Eman then offers himself as a willing sacrifice in Ifada's place.

The mythic pattern of sacrifice and renewal is basic to much Yoruba myth. Part of the tradition of Yoruba ritual drama is the reenactment of myths that resemble Eman's willing sacrifice. These are celebrated annually on the feast of Obatala, the god of creation. *The Strong Breed* has also been connected to ritual tragedies enacted in honor of Ogun, who suffers greatly for the good of the community.

The Strong Breed is informed by Soyinka's studies of Greek tragedy. Like Greek tragic figures, Soyinka's strong breed are genetically linked: they are fathers and sons who inherit their fathers' power. Soyinka's *The Bacchae of Euripides* (1973) deals with inspiration, intoxication, and mass hysteria. *Death and the King's Horseman* (1976), centering on death, also explores Greek themes of fate and inevitability. Soyinka demonstrates the universality of Greek themes in both European and African experience.

Certain patterns link Eman with Oedipus. Once Eman is identified by his father as one of the strong breed, he prepares himself for his mission by leaving his community. Like Oedipus, he unwittingly goes to another community where he ultimately must be sacrificed. Eman also resembles Christ: he is a teacher and healer; he refuses to exploit those around him; he lifts up the weak and has empathy for everyone, including the idiot Ifada. And, like Christ, those for whom he sacrifices himself do not hold him in high regard.

Despite its Greek and Christian overtones, the story is grounded in Yoruba tradition, with its initiation rites and concepts of heredity, community, and sacrifice. Soyinka's stagecraft includes traditional Yoruba music and dance as well as traditional Yoruba images, such as the effigy — the carrier doll — and the appearance of the human carrier in the form of Ifada. Soyinka demonstrates that everything in the past is part of the present by overlaying the ghosts of Omae, the woman Eman was to marry; his father (the Old Man); his tutor; and the priest. The past shapes the present just as his father's blood runs in his veins and shapes everything he does as a man.

The play leaves us wondering if Eman's sacrifice was wasteful or redeeming. Is the community led by Jaguna and Oroge worth dying for? Will Eman's death benefit Sunma, Ifada, and the Girl who betrayed him to his killers? Or does Eman die only because he is one of the strong breed, whose mission is to serve as the sacrifice for the community? Even the latter interpretation might imply a positive ending for the play, although it would be a different ending than suggesting that Eman has died *for* this village and thus has secured its renewal. Yoruba tradition implies that even if the community is unworthy, it shares in purification by the sacrifice of the willing. The subtlety of the issues in this play invites multiple interpretations.

The Strong Breed in Performance

In Ibadan in 1963, Soyinka created a twenty-five-minute version of *The Strong Breed* that omitted the flashbacks at the end of the play when Eman's past returns to him. This was done for Esso World Theatre and was included in the film *Culture in Transition*. The play was produced in its full-length version in 1964 at the Greenwich Mews Theatre in New York, and it has been performed by theater groups in several African nations. An African university theater group produced the play in its full-length version in Malawi in 1976 with Anthony Nazombe as Eman.

Wole Soyinka (b. 1934)

THE STRONG BREED

1962

Characters

EMAN, *a stranger*
SUNMA, *Jaguna's daughter*
IFADA, *an idiot*
A GIRL
JAGUNA
OROGE
ATTENDANT STALWARTS, *the villagers*

From Eman's past:
OLD MAN, *his father*
OMAE, *his betrothed*
TUTOR
PRIEST
ATTENDANTS, *the villagers*

The scenes are described briefly, but very often a darkened stage with lit areas will not only suffice but is necessary. Except for the one indicated place, there can be no break in the action. A distracting scene change would be ruinous.

(*A mud house, with space in front of it. Eman, in light buba and trousers stands at the window, looking out. Inside, Sunma is clearing the table of what looks like a modest clinic, putting the things away in a cupboard. Another rough table in the room is piled with exercise books, two or three worn textbooks, etc. Sunma appears agitated. Outside, just below the window crouches Ifada. He looks up with a shy smile from time to time, waiting for Eman to notice him.*)

SUNMA (*hesitant*): You will have to make up your mind soon, Eman. The lorry leaves very shortly.

(*As Eman does not answer, Sunma continues her work, more nervously. Two villagers, obvious travelers, pass hurriedly in front of the house, the man has a small raffia sack, the woman a cloth-covered basket, the man enters first, turns and urges the woman who is just emerging to hurry.*)

SUNMA (*seeing them, her tone is more intense*): Eman, are we going or aren't we? You will leave it till too late.

EMAN (*quietly*): There is still time — if you want to go.

SUNMA: If I want to go . . . and you?

(*Eman makes no reply.*)

SUNMA (*bitterly*): You don't really want to leave here. You never want to go away — even for a minute.

(*Ifada continues his antics. Eman eventually pats him on the head and the boy grins happily. Leaps up suddenly and returns with a basket of oranges which he offers to Eman.*)

EMAN: My gift for today's festival enh?

(*Ifada nods, grinning.*)

EMAN: They look ripe — that's a change.

SUNMA (*she has gone inside the room. Looks round the door*): Did you call me?

EMAN: No. (*She goes back.*) And what will you do tonight, Ifada? Will you take part in the dancing? Or perhaps you will mount your own masquerade?

(*Ifada shakes his head, regretfully.*)

EMAN: You won't? So you haven't any? But you would like to own one.

(*Ifada nods eagerly.*)

EMAN: Then why don't you make your own?

(*Ifada stares, puzzled by this idea.*)

EMAN: Sunma will let you have some cloth you know. And bits of wool . . .

SUNMA (*coming out*): Who are you talking to, Eman?

EMAN: Ifada. I am trying to persuade him to join the young maskers.

SUNMA (*losing control*): What does he want here? Why is he hanging round us?

EMAN (*amazed*): What . . . ? I said Ifada, Ifada.

SUNMA: Just tell him to go away. Let him go and play somewhere else!

EMAN: What is this? Hasn't he always played here?

SUNMA: I don't want him here. (*Rushes to the window.*) Get away, idiot. Don't bring your foolish face here anymore, do you hear? Go on, go away from here . . .

EMAN (*restraining her*): Control yourself, Sunma. What on earth has got into you?

(*Ifada, hurt and bewildered, backs slowly away.*)

SUNMA: He comes crawling round here like some horrible insect. I never want to lay my eyes on him again.

EMAN: I don't understand. It *is* Ifada you know. Ifada! The unfortunate one who runs errands for you and doesn't hurt a soul.

SUNMA: I cannot bear the sight of him.

EMAN: You can't do what? It can't be two days since he last fetched water for you.

SUNMA: What else can he do except that? He is useless. Just because we have been kind to him . . . Others would have put him in an asylum.

EMAN: You are not making sense. He is not a madman, he is just a little more unlucky than other children. (*Looks keenly at her.*) But what is the matter?

SUNMA: It's nothing. I only wish we had sent him off to one of those places for creatures like him.

EMAN: He is quite happy here. He doesn't bother anyone and he makes himself useful.

SUNMA: Useful! Is that one of any use to anybody? Boys of his age are already earning a living but all he can do is hang around and drool at the mouth.

EMAN: But he does work. You know he does a lot for you.

SUNMA: Does he? And what about the farm you started for him! Does he ever work on it? Or have you forgotten that it was really for Ifada you cleared that bush. Now you have to go and work it yourself. You spend all your time on it and you have no room for anything else.

EMAN: That wasn't his fault. I should first have asked him if he was fond of farming.

SUNMA: Oh, so he can choose? As if he shouldn't be thankful for being allowed to live.

EMAN: Sunma!

SUNMA: He does not like farming but he knows how to feast his dumb mouth on the fruits.

EMAN: But I want him to. I encourage him.

SUNMA: Well keep him. I don't want to see him anymore.

EMAN (*after some moments*): But why? You cannot be telling all the truth. What has he done?

SUNMA: The sight of him fills me with revulsion.

EMAN (*goes to her and holds her*): What really is it? (*Sunma avoids his eyes.*) It is almost as if you are forcing yourself to hate him. Why?

SUNMA: That is not true. Why should I?

EMAN: Then what is the secret? You've even played with him before.

SUNMA: I have always merely tolerated him. But I cannot anymore. Suddenly my disgust won't take him anymore. Perhaps . . . perhaps it is the new year. Yes, yes, it must be the new year.

EMAN: I don't believe that.

SUNMA: It must be. I am a woman, and these things matter. I don't want a misshape near me. Surely for one day in the year, I may demand some wholesomeness.

EMAN: I do not understand you. (*Sunma is silent.*) It was cruel of you. And to Ifada who is so helpless and alone. We are the only friends he has.

SUNMA: No, just you. I have told you, with me it has always been only an act of kindness. And now I haven't any pity left for him.

EMAN: No. He is not a wholesome being.

(*He turns back to looking through the window.*)

SUNMA (*half-pleading*): Ifada can rouse your pity. And yet if anything, I need more kindness from you. Every time my weakness betrays me, you close your mind against me . . . Eman . . . Eman . . .

(*A Girl comes in view, dragging an effigy° by a rope attached to one of its legs. She stands for a while gazing at Eman. Ifada, who has crept back shyly to his accustomed position, becomes somewhat excited when he sees the effigy. The Girl is unsmiling. She possesses in fact a kind of inscrutability which does not make her hard but is unsettling.*)

GIRL: Is the teacher in?

EMAN (*smiling*): No.

GIRL: Where is he gone?

EMAN: I don't really know. Shall I ask?

GIRL: Yes, do.

EMAN (*turning slightly*): Sunma, a girl outside wants to know . . .

(*Sunma turns away, goes into the inside room.*)

EMAN: Oh. (*Returns to the Girl, but his slight gaiety is lost.*) There is no one at home who can tell me.

GIRL: Why are you not in?

EMAN: I don't really know. Maybe I went somewhere.

GIRL: All right. I will wait until you get back.

(*She pulls the effigy to her, sits down.*)

EMAN (*slowly regaining his amusement*): So you are all ready for the new year.

GIRL (*without turning round*): I am not going to the festival.

EMAN: Then why have you got that?

GIRL: Do you mean my carrier? I am unwell you know. My mother says it will take away my sickness with the old year.

EMAN: Won't you share the carrier with your playmates?

GIRL: Oh, no. Don't you know I play alone? The other children won't come near me. Their mothers would beat them.

effigy: A figure or likeness in human shape.

EMAN: But I have never seen you here. Why don't you come to the clinic?

GIRL: My mother said No.

(*Gets up, begins to move off.*)

EMAN: You are not going away?

GIRL: I must not stay talking to you. If my mother caught me . . .

EMAN: All right, tell me what you want before you go.

GIRL (*stops. For some moments she remains silent*): I must have some clothes for my carrier.

EMAN: Is that all? You wait a moment.

(*Sunma comes out as he takes down a buba from the wall. She goes to the window and glares almost with hatred at the Girl. The Girl retreats hastily, still impassive.*)

By the way, Sunma, do you know who that girl is?

SUNMA: I hope you don't really mean to give her that.

EMAN: Why not? I hardly ever use it.

SUNMA: Just the same, don't give it to her. She is not a child. She is as evil as the rest of them.

EMAN: What has got into you today?

SUNMA: All right, all right. Do what you wish.

(*She withdraws. Baffled, Eman returns to the window.*)

EMAN: Here . . . will this do? Come and look at it.

GIRL: Throw it.

EMAN: What is the matter? I am not going to eat you.

GIRL: No one lets me come near them.

EMAN: But I am not afraid of catching your disease.

GIRL: Throw it.

(*Eman shrugs and tosses the buba. She takes it without a word and slips it on the effigy, completely absorbed in the task. Eman watches for a while, then joins Sunma in the inner room.*)

GIRL (*after a long, cool survey of Ifada*): You have a head like a spider's egg, and your mouth dribbles like a roof. But there is no one else. Would you like to play?

(*Ifada nods eagerly, quite excited.*)

GIRL: You will have to get a stick.

(*Ifada rushes around, finds a big stick, and whirls it aloft, bearing down on the carrier.*)

GIRL: Wait. I don't want you to spoil it. If it gets torn I shall drive you away. Now, let me see how you are going to beat it.

(*Ifada hits it gently.*)

GIRL: You may hit harder than that. As long as there is something left to hang at the end. (*She appraises him up and down.*) You are not very tall . . . will you be able to hang it from a tree?

(*Ifada nods, grinning happily.*)

GIRL: You will hang it up and I will set fire to it. (*Then, with surprising venom.*) But just because you are helping me, don't think it is going to cure you. I am the one who will get well at midnight, do you understand? It is my carrier and it is for me alone. (*She pulls at the rope to make sure that it is well attached to the leg.*) Well don't stand there drooling. Let's go.

(*She begins to walk off, dragging the effigy in the dust. Ifada remains where he is for some moments, seemingly puzzled. Then his face breaks into a large grin and he leaps after the procession, belaboring the effigy with all his strength. The stage remains empty for some moments. Then the horn of a lorry is sounded and Sunma rushes out. The hooting continues for some time with a rhythmic pattern. Eman comes out.*)

EMAN: I am going to the village . . . I shan't be back before nightfall.

SUNMA (*blankly*): Yes.

EMAN (*hesitates*): Well what do you want me to do?

SUNMA: The lorry was hooting just now.

EMAN: I didn't hear it.

SUNMA: It will leave in a few minutes. And you did promise we could go away.

EMAN: I promised nothing. Will you go home by yourself or shall I come back for you?

SUNMA: You don't even want me here?

EMAN: But you have to go home haven't you?

SUNMA: I had hoped we would watch the new year together — in some other place.

EMAN: Why do you continue to distress yourself?

SUNMA: Because you will not listen to me. Why do you continue to stay where nobody wants you?

EMAN: That is not true.

SUNMA: It is. You are wasting your life on people who really want you out of their way.

EMAN: You don't know what you are saying.

SUNMA: You think they love you? Do you think they care at all for what you — or I — do for them?

EMAN: *Them?* These are your own people. Sometimes you talk as if you were a stranger too.

SUNMA: I wonder if I really sprang from here. I know they are evil and I am not. From the oldest to the smallest child, they are nourished in evil and unwholesomeness in which I have no part.

EMAN: You knew this when you returned?

SUNMA: You reproach me then for trying at all?

EMAN: I reproach you with nothing. But you must leave me out of your plans. I can have no part in them.

SUNMA (*nearly pleading*): Once I could have run away. I would have gone and never looked back.

EMAN: I cannot listen when you talk like that.

SUNMA: I swear to you, I do not mind what happens afterwards. But you must help me tear myself away from here. I can no longer do it by myself . . . It is only a little thing. And we have worked so hard this past year . . . surely we can go away for a week . . . even a few days would be enough.

EMAN: I have told you, Sunma . . .

SUNMA (*desperately*): Two days, Eman. Only two days.

EMAN (*distressed*): But I tell you I have no wish to go.

SUNMA (*suddenly angry*): Are you so afraid then?

EMAN: Me? Afraid of what?

SUNMA: You think you will not want to come back.

EMAN (*pitying*): You cannot dare me that way.

SUNMA: Then why won't you leave here, even for an hour? If you are so sure that your life is settled here, why are you afraid to do this thing for me? What is so wrong that you will not go into the next town for a day or two?

EMAN: I don't want to. I do not have to persuade you or myself about anything. I simply have no desire to go away.

SUNMA (*his quiet confidence appears to incense her*): You are afraid. You accuse me of losing my sense of mission, but you are afraid to put yours to the test.

EMAN: You are wrong, Sunma. I have no sense of mission. But I have found peace here and I am content with that.

SUNMA: I haven't. For a while I thought that too, but I found there could be no peace in the midst of so much cruelty. Eman, tonight at least, the last night of the old year . . .

EMAN: No, Sunma. I find this too distressing; you should go home now.

SUNMA: It is the time for making changes in one's life, Eman. Let's breathe in the new year away from here.

EMAN: You are hurting yourself.

SUNMA: Tonight. Only tonight. We will come back tomorrow, as early as you like. But let us go away for this one night. Don't let another year break on me in this place . . . you don't know how important it is to me, but I will tell you, I will tell you on the way . . . but we must not be here today, Eman, do this one thing for me.

EMAN (*sadly*): I cannot.

SUNMA (*suddenly calm*): I was a fool to think it would be otherwise. The whole village may use you as they will but for me there is nothing. Sometimes I think you believe that doing anything for me makes you unfaithful to some part of your life. If it was a woman then I pity her for what she must have suffered.

(*Eman winces and hardens slowly. Sunma notices nothing.*)

Keeping faith with so much is slowly making you inhuman. (*Seeing the change in Eman.*) Eman. Eman. What is it?

(*As she goes toward him, Eman goes into the house.*)

SUNMA (*apprehensive, follows him*): What did I say? Eman, forgive me, forgive me please. (*Eman remains facing into the slow darkness of the room. Sunma, distressed, cannot decide what to do.*) I swear I didn't know . . . I would not have said it for all the world.

(*A lorry is heard taking off somewhere nearby. The sound comes up and slowly fades away into the distance. Sunma starts visibly, goes slowly to the window.*)

SUNMA (*as the sound dies off, to herself*): What happens now?

EMAN (*joining her at the window*): What did you say?

SUNMA: Nothing.

EMAN: Was that not the lorry going off?

SUNMA: It was.

EMAN: I am sorry I couldn't help you.

(*Sunma, about to speak, changes her mind.*)

EMAN: I think you ought to go home now.

SUNMA: No, don't send me away. It's the least you can do for me. Let me stay here until all the noise is over.

EMAN: But are you not needed at home? You have a part in the festival.

SUNMA: I have renounced it; I am Jaguna's eldest daughter only in name.

EMAN: Renouncing one's self is not so easy — surely you know that.

SUNMA: I don't want to talk about it. Will you at least let us be together tonight?

EMAN: But . . .

SUNMA: Unless you are afraid my father will accuse you of harboring me.

EMAN: All right, we will go out together.

SUNMA: Go out? I want us to stay here.

EMAN: When there is so much going on outside?

SUNMA: Someday you will wish that you went away when I tried to make you.

EMAN: Are we going back to that?

SUNMA: No. I promise you I will not recall it again. But you must know that it was also for your sake that I tried to get us away.

EMAN: For me? How?

SUNMA: By yourself you can do nothing here. Have you not noticed how tightly we shut out strangers? Even if you lived here for a lifetime, you would remain a stranger.

EMAN: Perhaps that is what I like. There is peace in being a stranger.

SUNMA: For a while perhaps. But they would reject you in the end. I tell you it is only I who stand between you and contempt. And because of this you have earned their hatred. I don't know why I say this now, except that somehow, I feel that it no longer matters. It is only I who have stood between you and much humiliation.

EMAN: Think carefully before you say any more. I am incapable of feeling indebted to you. This will make no difference at all.

SUNMA: I ask for nothing. But you must know it all the same. It is true I hadn't the strength to go by myself. And I must confess this now, if you had come with me, I would have done everything to keep you from returning.

EMAN: I know that.

SUNMA: You see, I bare myself to you. For days I had thought it over, this was to be a new beginning for us. And I placed my fate wholly in your hands. Now the thought will not leave me, I have a feeling which will not be shaken off, that in some way, you have tonight totally destroyed my life.

EMAN: You are depressed, you don't know what you are saying.

SUNMA: Don't think I am accusing you. I say all this only because I cannot help it.

EMAN: We must not remain shut up here. Let us go and be part of the living.

SUNMA: No. Leave them alone.

EMAN: Surely you don't want to stay indoors when the whole town is alive with rejoicing.

SUNMA: Rejoicing! Is that what it seems to you? No, let us remain here. Whatever happens I must not go out until all this is over.

(*There is silence. It has grown much darker.*)

EMAN: I shall light the lamp.

SUNMA (*eager to do something*): No, let me do it.

(*She goes into the inner room.*)

(*Eman paces the room, stops by a shelf and toys with the seeds in an "ayo" board, takes down the whole board and places it on a table, playing by himself.*)

(*The Girl is now seen coming back, still dragging her "carrier." Ifada brings up the rear as before. As he comes round the corner of the house two men emerge from the shadows. A sack is thrown over Ifada's head, the rope is pulled tight rendering him instantly helpless. The Girl has reached the front of the house before she turns round at the sound of scuffle. She is in time to see Ifada thrown over the shoulders and borne away. Her face betraying no emotion at all, the Girl backs slowly away, turns and flees, leaving the "carrier" behind. Sunma enters, carrying two kerosene lamps. She hangs one up from the wall.*)

EMAN: One is enough.

SUNMA: I want to leave one outside.

(*She goes out, hangs the lamp from a nail just above the door. As she turns she sees the effigy and gasps. Eman rushes out.*)

EMAN: What is it? Oh, is that what frightened you?

SUNMA: I thought . . . I didn't really see it properly.

(*Eman goes towards the object, stoops to pick it up.*)

EMAN: It must belong to that sick girl.

SUNMA: Don't touch it.

EMAN: Let's keep it for her.

SUNMA: Leave it alone. Don't touch it, Eman.

EMAN (*shrugs and goes back*): You are very nervous.

SUNMA: Let's go in.

EMAN: Wait. (*He detains her by the door, under the lamp.*) I know there is something more than you've told me. What are you afraid of tonight?

SUNMA: I was only scared by that thing. There is nothing else.

EMAN: I am not blind, Sunma. It is true I would not run away when you wanted me to, but that doesn't mean I do not feel things. What does tonight really mean that it makes you so helpless?

SUNMA: It is only a mood. And your indifference to me . . . let's go in.

(*Eman moves aside and she enters; he remains there for a moment and then follows.*)

(*She fiddles with the lamp, looks vaguely round the room, then goes and shuts the door, bolting it. When she turns, it is to meet Eman's eyes, questioning.*)

SUNMA: There is a cold wind coming in.

(*Eman keeps his gaze on her.*)

SUNMA: It *was* getting cold.

(*She moves guiltily to the table and stands by the "ayo" board, rearranging the seeds. Eman remains where he is a few moments, then brings a stool and sits opposite her. She sits down also and they begin to play in silence.*)

SUNMA: What brought you here at all, Eman? And what makes you stay?

(*There is another silence.*)

SUNMA: I am not trying to share your life. I know you too well by now. But at least we have worked together since you came. Is there nothing at all I deserve to know?

EMAN: Let me continue a stranger — especially to you. Those who have much to give fulfill themselves only in total loneliness.

SUNMA: Then there is no love in what you do.

EMAN: There is. Love comes to me more easily with strangers.

SUNMA: That is unnatural.

EMAN: Not for me. I know I find consummation only when I have spent myself for a total stranger.

SUNMA: It seems unnatural to me. But then I am a woman. I have a woman's longings and weaknesses. And the ties of blood are very strong in me.

EMAN (*smiling*): You think I have cut loose from all these — ties of blood.

SUNMA: Sometimes you are so inhuman.

EMAN: I don't know what that means. But I am very much my father's son.

(*They play in silence. Suddenly Eman pauses, listening.*)

EMAN: Did you hear that?

SUNMA (*quickly*): I heard nothing . . . it's your turn.

EMAN: Perhaps some of the mummers are coming this way.

(*Eman, about to play, leaps up suddenly.*)

SUNMA: What is it? Don't you want to play anymore?

(*Eman moves to the door.*)

SUNMA: No. Don't go out, Eman.

EMAN: If it's the dancers, I want to ask them to stay. At least we won't have to miss everything.

SUNMA: No, no. Don't open the door. Let us keep out everyone tonight.

(*A terrified and disordered figure bursts suddenly round the corner, past the window, and begins hammering at the door. It is Ifada. Desperate with terror, he pounds madly at the door, dumb-moaning all the while.*)

EMAN: Isn't that Ifada?

SUNMA: They are only fooling about. Don't pay any attention.

EMAN (*looks round the window*): That is Ifada. (*Begins to unbolt the door.*)

SUNMA (*pulling at his hands*): It is only a trick they are playing on you. Don't take any notice, Eman.

EMAN: What are you saying? The boy is out of his senses with fear.

SUNMA: No, no. Don't interfere, Eman. For God's sake, don't interfere.

EMAN: Do you know something of this then?

SUNMA: You are a stranger here, Eman. Just leave us alone and go your own way. There is nothing you can do.

EMAN (*he tries to push her out of the way but she clings fiercely to him*): Have you gone mad? I tell you the boy must come in.

SUNMA: Why won't you listen to me, Eman? I tell you it's none of your business. For your own sake, do as I say.

(*Eman pushes her off, unbolts the door. Ifada rushes in, clasps Eman round the knees, dumb-moaning against his legs.*)

EMAN (*manages to rebolt the door*): What is it, Ifada? What is the matter?

(*Shouts and voices are heard coming nearer the house.*)

SUNMA: Before it's too late, let him go. For once, Eman, believe what I tell you. Don't harbor him or you will regret it all your life.

(*Eman tries to calm Ifada who becomes more and more abject as the outside voices get nearer.*)

EMAN: What have they done to him? At least tell me that. What is going on, Sunma?

SUNMA (*with sudden venom*): Monster! Could you not take yourself somewhere else?

EMAN: Stop talking like that.

SUNMA: He could have run into the bush couldn't he? Toad! Why must he follow us with his own disasters!

VOICES OUTSIDE: It's here . . . Round the back . . . Spread, spread . . . this way . . . no, head him off . . . use the bush path and head him off . . . get some more lights . . .

(*Eman listens. Lifts Ifada bodily and carries him into the inner room. Returns at once, shutting the door behind him.*)

SUNMA (*slumps into a chair, resigned*): You always follow your own way.

JAGUNA (*comes round the corner followed by Oroge*

and three men, one bearing a torch): I knew he would come here.

OROGE: I hope our friend won't make trouble.

JAGUNA: He had better not. You, recall all the men and tell them to surround the house.

OROGE: But he may not be in the house after all.

JAGUNA: I know he is here . . . (*to the men*) . . . go on, do as I say. (*He bangs on the door.*) Teacher, open your door . . . you two, stay by the door. If I need you I will call you.

(*Eman opens the door.*)

JAGUNA (*speaks as he enters*): We know he is here.

EMAN: Who?

JAGUNA: Don't let us waste time. We are grown men, teacher. You understand me and I understand you. But we must take back the boy.

EMAN: This is my house.

JAGUNA: Daughter, you'd better tell your friend. I don't think he quite knows our ways. Tell him why he must give up the boy.

SUNMA: Father, I . . .

JAGUNA: Are you going to tell him or aren't you?

SUNMA: Father, I beg you, leave us alone tonight . . .

JAGUNA: I thought you might be a hindrance. Go home then if you will not use your sense.

SUNMA: But there are other ways . . .

JAGUNA (*turning to the men*): See that she gets home. I no longer trust her. If she gives trouble carry her. And see that the women stay with her until all this is over.

(*Sunma departs, accompanied by one of the men.*)

JAGUNA: Now, teacher . . .

OROGE (*restrains him*): You see, Mister Eman, it is like this. Right now, nobody knows that Ifada has taken refuge here. No one except us and our men — and they know how to keep their mouths shut. We don't want to have to burn down the house you see, but if the word gets around, we would have no choice.

JAGUNA: In fact, it may be too late already. A carrier should end up in the bush, not in a house. Anyone who doesn't guard his door when the carrier goes by has himself to blame. A contaminated house should be burnt down.

OROGE: But we are willing to let it pass. Only, you must bring him out quickly.

EMAN: All right. But at least you will let me ask you something.

JAGUNA: What is there to ask? Don't you understand what we have told you?

EMAN: Yes. But why did you pick on a helpless boy. Obviously he is not willing.

JAGUNA: What is the man talking about? Ifada is a godsend. Does he have to be willing?

EMAN: In my home, we believe that a man should be willing.

OROGE: Mister Eman, I don't think you quite understand. This is not a simple matter at all. I don't know what you do, but here, it is not a cheap task for any-

body. No one in his senses would do such a job. Why do you think we give refuge to idiots like him? We don't know where he came from. One morning, he is simply there, just like that. From nowhere at all. You see, there is a purpose in that.

JAGUNA: We only waste time.

OROGE: Jaguna, be patient. After all, the man has been with us for some time now and deserves to know. The evil of the old year is no light thing to load on any man's head.

EMAN: I know something about that.

OROGE: You do? (*Turns to Jaguna who snorts impatiently.*) You see I told you so didn't I? From the moment you came I saw you were one of the knowing ones.

JAGUNA: Then let him behave like a man and give back the boy.

EMAN: It is you who are not behaving like men.

JAGUNA (*advances aggressively*): That is a quick mouth you have . . .

OROGE: Patience, Jaguna . . . if you want the new year to cushion the land there must be no deeds of anger. What did you mean, my friend?

EMAN: It is a simple thing. A village which cannot produce its own carrier contains no men.

JAGUNA: Enough. Let there be no more talk or this business will be ruined by some rashness. You . . . come inside. Bring the boy out, he must be in the room there.

EMAN: Wait.

(*The men hesitate.*)

JAGUNA (*hitting the nearer one and propelling him forward*): Go on. Have you changed masters now that you listen to what he says?

OROGE (*sadly*): I am sorry you would not understand, Mister Eman. But you ought to know that no carrier may return to the village. If he does, the people will stone him to death. It has happened before. Surely it is too much to ask a man to give up his own soil.

EMAN: I know others who have done more.

(*Ifada is brought out, abjectly dumb-moaning.*)

EMAN: You can see him with your own eyes. Does it really have meaning to use one as unwilling as that.

OROGE (*smiling*): He shall be willing. Not only willing but actually joyous. I am the one who prepares them all, and I have seen worse. This one escaped before I began to prepare him for the event. But you will see him later tonight, the most joyous creature in the festival. Then perhaps you will understand.

EMAN: Then it is only a deceit. Do you believe the spirit of a new year is so easily fooled?

JAGUNA: Take him out. (*The men carry out Ifada.*) You see, it is so easy to talk. You say there are no men in this village because they cannot provide a willing carrier. And yet I heard Oroge tell you we only use strangers. There is only one other stranger in the village, but I have not heard him offer himself (*spits*). It is so easy to talk is it not? (*He turns his back on him.*)

(*They go off, taking Ifada with them, limp and silent. The only sign of life is that he strains his neck to keep his eyes on Eman till the very moment that he disappears from sight. Eman remains where they left him, staring after the group.*)

(*A blackout lasting no more than a minute. The lights come up slowly and Ifada is seen returning to the house. He stops at the window and looks in. Seeing no one, he bangs on the sill. Appears surprised that there is no response. He slithers down on his favorite spot, then sees the effigy still lying where the Girl had dropped it in her flight. After some hesitation, he goes towards it, begins to strip it of the clothing. Just then the Girl comes in.*)

GIRL: Hey, leave that alone. You know it's mine.

(*Ifada pauses, then speeds up his action.*)

GIRL: I said it is mine. Leave it where you found it.

(*She rushes at him and begins to struggle for possession of the carrier.*)

GIRL: Thief! Thief! Let it go, it is mine. Let it go. You animal, just because I let you play with it. Idiot! Idiot!

(*The struggle becomes quite violent. The Girl is hanging to the effigy and Ifada lifts her with it, flinging her all about. The Girl hangs on grimly.*)

GIRL: You are spoiling it . . . why don't you get your own? Thief! Let it go, you thief!

(*Sunma comes in walking very fast, throwing apprehensive glances over her shoulder. Seeing the two children, she becomes immediately angry. Advances on them.*)

SUNMA: So you've made this place your playground. Get away, you untrained pigs. Get out of here.

(*Ifada flees at once, the Girl retreats also, retaining possession of the "carrier."*)
    (*Sunma goes to the door. She has her hand on the door when the significance of Ifada's presence strikes her for the first time. She stands rooted to the spot, then turns slowly round.*)

SUNMA: Ifada! What are you doing here? (*Ifada is bewildered. Sunma turns suddenly and rushes into the house, flying into the inner room and out again.*) Eman! Eman! Eman! (*She rushes outside.*) Where did he go? Where did they take him? (*Ifada distressed, points. Sunma seizes him by the arm, drags him off.*) Take me there at once. God help you if we are too late. You loathsome thing, if you have let him suffer . . .

(*Her voice fades into other shouts, running footsteps, banged tins, bells, dogs, etc., rising in volume.*)

(*It is a narrow passageway between two mud houses. At the far end one man after another is seen running across the entry, the noise dying off gradually.*)

(*About halfway down the passage, Eman is crouching against the wall, tense with apprehension. As the noise dies off, he seems to relax, but the alert hunted look is still in his eyes, which are ringed in a reddish color. The rest of his body has been whitened with a floury substance. He is naked down to the waist, wears a baggy pair of trousers, calf-length, and around both feet are bangles.*)

EMAN: I will simply stay here till dawn. I have done enough.

(*A window is thrown open and a woman empties some slop from a pail. With a startled cry Eman leaps aside to avoid it and the woman puts out her head.*)

WOMAN: Oh, my head. What have I done! Forgive me, neighbor. . . . Eh, it's the carrier!

(*Very rapidly she clears her throat and spits on him, flings the pail at him, and runs off, shouting.*)

He's here. The carrier is hiding in the passage. Quickly, I have found the carrier!

(*The cry is taken up and Eman flees down the passage. Shortly afterwards his pursuers come pouring down the passage in full cry. After the last of them come Jaguna and Oroge.*)

OROGE: Wait, wait. I cannot go so fast.
JAGUNA: We will rest a little then. We can do nothing anyway.
OROGE: If only he had let me prepare him.
JAGUNA: They are the ones who break first, these fools who think they were born to carry suffering like a hat. What are we to do now?
OROGE: When they catch him I must prepare him.
JAGUNA: He? It will be impossible now. There can be no joy left in that one.
OROGE: Still, it took him by surprise. He was not expecting what he met.
JAGUNA: Why then did he refuse to listen? Did he think he was coming to sit down to a feast? He had not even gone through one compound before he bolted. Did he think he was taken round the people to be blessed? A woman, that is all he is.
OROGE: No, no. He took the beating well enough. I think he is the kind who would let himself be beaten from night till dawn and not utter a sound. He would let himself be stoned until he dropped dead.
JAGUNA: Then what made him run like a coward?
OROGE: I don't know. I don't really know. It is a night of curses, Jaguna. It is not many unprepared minds will remain unhinged under the load.
JAGUNA: We must find him. It is a poor beginning for a year when our own curses remain hovering over our homes because the carrier refused to take them.

(*They go. The scene changes. Eman is crouching beside some shrubs, torn and bleeding.*)

EMAN: They are even guarding my house . . . as if I would go there, but I need water . . . they could at least grant me that . . . I can be thirsty too . . . (*He pricks his ears.*) . . . there must be a stream nearby . . . (*As he looks round him, his eyes widen at a scene he encounters.*)

(*An Old Man, short and vigorous looking, is seated on a stool. He also is wearing calf-length baggy trousers, white. On his head, a white cap. An attendant is engaged in rubbing his body with oil. Round his eyes, two white rings have already been marked.*)

OLD MAN: Have they prepared the boat?
ATTENDANT: They are making the last sacrifice.
OLD MAN: Good. Did you send for my son?
ATTENDANT: He's on his way.
OLD MAN: I have never met the carrying of the boat with such a heavy heart. I hope nothing comes of it.
ATTENDANT: The gods will not desert us on that account.
OLD MAN: A man should be at his strongest when he takes the boat, my friend. To be weighed down inside and out is not a wise thing. I hope when the moment comes I shall have found my strength.

(*Enter Eman, a wrapper round his waist and a danski° over it.*)

OLD MAN: I meant to wait until after my journey to the river, but my mind is so burdened with my own grief and yours I could not delay it. You know I must have all my strength. But I sit here, feeling it all eaten slowly away by my unspoken grief. It helps to say it out. It even helps to cry sometimes.

(*He signals to the attendant to leave them.*)

Come nearer . . . we will never meet again, son. Not on this side of the flesh. What I do not know is whether you will return to take my place.
EMAN: I will never come back.
OLD MAN: Do you know what you are saying? Ours is a strong breed, my son. It is only a strong breed that can take this boat to the river year after year and wax stronger on it. I have taken down each year's evils for over twenty years. I hoped you would follow me.
EMAN: My life here died with Omae.
OLD MAN: Omae died giving birth to your child and you think the world is ended. Eman, my pain did not begin when Omae died. Since you sent her to stay with me, son, I lived with the burden of knowing that this child would die bearing your son.
EMAN: Father . . .
OLD MAN: Don't you know it was the same with you? And me? No woman survives the bearing of the strong ones. Son, it is not the mouth of the boaster that says he belongs to the strong breed. It is the tongue that is red with pain and black with sorrow. Twelve years you were away my son, and for those twelve years I knew the love of an old man for his daughter and the pain of a man helplessly awaiting his loss.

danski: A brief Yoruba garment.

EMAN: I wish I had stayed away. I wish I never came back to meet her.
OLD MAN: It had to be. But you know now what slowly ate away my strength. I awaited your return with love and fear. Forgive me then if I say that your grief is light. It will pass. This grief may drive you now from home. But you must return.
EMAN: You do not understand. It is not grief alone.
OLD MAN: What is it then? Tell me, I can still learn.
EMAN: I was away twelve years. I changed much in that time.
OLD MAN: I am listening.
EMAN: I am unfitted for your work, father. I wish to say no more. But I am totally unfitted for your call.
OLD MAN: It is only time you need, son. Stay longer and you will answer the urge of your blood.
EMAN: That I stayed at all was because of Omae. I did not expect to find her waiting. I would have taken her away, but hard as you claim to be, it would have killed you. And I was a tired man. I needed peace. Because Omae was peace, I stayed. Now nothing holds me here.
OLD MAN: Other men would rot and die doing this task year after year. It is strong medicine which only we can take. Our blood is strong like no other. Anything you do in life must be less than this, son.
EMAN: That is not true, father.
OLD MAN: I tell you it is true. Your own blood will betray you, son, because you cannot hold it back. If you make it do less than this, it will rush to your head and burst it open. I say what I know, my son.
EMAN: There are other tasks in life, father. This one is not for me. There are even greater things you know nothing of.
OLD MAN: I am very sad. You only go to give to others what rightly belongs to us. You will use your strength among thieves. They are thieves because they take what is ours, they have no claim of blood to it. They will even lack the knowledge to use it wisely. Truth is my companion at this moment, my son. I know everything I say will surely bring the sadness of truth.
EMAN: I am going, father.
OLD MAN: Call my attendant. And be with me in your strength for this last journey. A-ah, did you hear that? It came out without my knowing it; this is indeed my last journey. But I am not afraid.

(*Eman goes out. A few moments later, the attendant enters.*)

ATTENDANT: The boat is ready.
OLD MAN: So am I.

(*He sits perfectly still for several moments. Drumming begins somewhere in the distance, and the Old Man sways his head almost imperceptibly. Two men come in bearing a miniature boat, containing an indefinable mound. They rush it in and set it briskly down near the Old Man, and stand well back. The Old Man gets up slowly, the Attendant watching him keenly. He signs to the men, who lift the boat quickly onto the Old Man's head. As soon as it touches his head, he holds it down with both hands and runs off, the men give him a start, then follow at a trot.)*

(As the last man disappears Oroge limps in and comes face to face with Eman — as carrier — who is now seen still standing beside the shrubs, staring into the scene he has just witnessed. Oroge, struck by the look on Eman's face, looks anxiously behind him to see what has engaged Eman's attention. Eman notices him then, and the pair stare at each other. Jaguna enters, sees him and shouts, "Here he is," rushes at Eman who is whipped back to the immediate and flees, Jaguna in pursuit. Three or four others enter and follow them. Oroge remains where he is, thoughtful.)

JAGUNA (*reenters*): They have closed in on him now, we'll get him this time.

OROGE: It is nearly midnight.

JAGUNA: You were standing there looking at him as if he was some strange spirit. Why didn't you shout?

OROGE: You shouted didn't you? Did that catch him?

JAGUNA: Don't worry. We have him now. But things have taken a bad turn. It is no longer enough to drive him past every house. There is too much contamination about already.

OROGE (*not listening*): He saw something. Why may I not know what it was?

JAGUNA: What are you talking about?

OROGE: Hm. What is it?

JAGUNA: I said there is too much harm done already. The year will demand more from this carrier than we thought.

OROGE: What do you mean?

JAGUNA: Do we have to talk with the full mouth?

OROGE: S-sh . . . look!

(Jaguna turns just in time to see Sunma fly at him, clawing at his face like a crazed tigress.)

SUNMA: Murderer! What are you doing to him. Murderer! Murderer!

(Jaguna finds himself struggling really hard to keep off his daughter; he succeeds in pushing her off and striking her so hard on the face that she falls to her knees. He moves on her to hit her again.)

OROGE (*comes between*): Think what you are doing, Jaguna, she is your daughter.

JAGUNA: My daughter! Does this one look like my daughter? Let me cripple the harlot for life.

OROGE: That is a wicked thought, Jaguna.

JAGUNA: Don't come between me and her.

OROGE: Nothing in anger — do you forget what tonight is?

JAGUNA: Can you blame me for forgetting?

(Draws his hand across his cheek — it is covered with blood.)

OROGE: This is an unhappy night for us all. I fear what is to come of it.

JAGUNA: Let's go. I cannot restrain myself in this creature's presence. My own daughter . . . and for a stranger . . .

(They go off, Ifada, who came in with Sunma and had stood apart, horror-stricken, comes shyly forward. He helps Sunma up. They go off, he holding Sunma bent and sobbing.)

(Enter Eman — as carrier. He is physically present in the bounds of this next scene, a side of a round thatched hut. A young girl, about fourteen, runs in, stops beside the hut. She looks carefully to see that she is not observed, puts her mouth to a little hole in the wall.)

OMAE: Eman . . . Eman . . .

(Eman — as carrier — responds, as he does throughout the scene, but they are unaware of him.)

EMAN (*from inside*): Who is it?

OMAE: It is me, Omae.

EMAN: How dare you come here!

(Two hands appear at the hole and pushing outwards, create a much larger hole through which Eman puts out his head. It is Eman as a boy, the same age as the girl.)

Go away at once. Are you trying to get me into trouble!

OMAE: What is the matter?

EMAN: You. Go away.

OMAE: But I came to see you.

EMAN: Are you deaf? I say I don't want to see you. Now go before my tutor catches you.

OMAE: All right. Come out.

EMAN: Do what!

OMAE: Come out.

EMAN: You must be mad.

OMAE (*sits on the ground*): All right, if you don't come out I shall simply stay here until your tutor arrives.

EMAN (*about to explode, thinks better of it and the head disappears. A moment later he emerges from behind the hut*): What sort of a devil has got into you?

OMAE: None. I just wanted to see you.

EMAN (*his mimicry is nearly hysterical*): "None. I just wanted to see you." Do you think this place is the stream where you can go and molest innocent people?

OMAE (*coyly*): Aren't you glad to see me?

EMAN: I am not.

OMAE: Why?

EMAN: Why? Do you really ask me why? Because you are a woman and a most troublesome woman. Don't you know anything about this at all. We are not meant to see any woman. So go away before more harm's done.

OMAE (*flirtatious*): What is so secret about it anyway? What do they teach you?

EMAN: Nothing any woman can understand.

OMAE: Ha ha. You think we don't know eh? You've all come to be circumcised.

EMAN: Shut up. You don't know anything.

OMAE: Just think, all this time you haven't been circumcised, and you dared make eyes at us women.

EMAN: Thank you — woman. Now go.

OMAE: Do they give you enough to eat?

EMAN (*testily*): No. We are so hungry that when silly girls like you turn up, we eat them.

OMAE (*feigning tears*): Oh, oh, oh, he's abusing me. He's abusing me.

EMAN (*alarmed*): Don't try that here. Go quickly if you are going to cry.

OMAE: All right, I won't cry.

EMAN: Cry or no cry, go away and leave me alone. What do you think will happen if my tutor turns up now?

OMAE: He won't.

EMAN (*mimicking*): "He won't." I suppose you are his wife and he tells you where he goes. In fact this is just the time he comes round to our huts. He could be at the next hut this very moment.

OMAE: Ha-ha. You're lying. I left him by the stream, pinching the girls' bottoms. Is that the sort of thing he teaches you?

EMAN: Don't say anything against him or I shall beat you. Isn't it you loose girls who tease him, wiggling your bottoms under his nose?

OMAE (*going tearful again*): A-ah, so I am one of the loose girls eh?

EMAN: Now don't start accusing me of things I didn't say.

OMAE: But you said it. You said it.

EMAN: I didn't. Look, Omae, someone will hear you and I'll be in disgrace. Why don't you go before anything happens.

OMAE: It's all right. My friends have promised to hold your old rascal tutor till I get back.

EMAN: Then you go back right now. I have work to do. (*Going in.*)

OMAE (*runs after and tries to hold him. Eman leaps back, genuinely scared*): What is the matter? I was not going to bite you.

EMAN: Do you know what you nearly did? You almost touched me!

OMAE: Well?

EMAN: Well! Isn't it enough that you let me set my eyes on you? Must you now totally pollute me with your touch? Don't you understand anything?

OMAE: Oh, that.

EMAN (*nearly screaming*): It is not "oh that." Do you think this is only a joke or a little visit like spending the night with your grandmother? This is an important period of my life. Look, these huts, we built them with our own hands. Every boy builds his own. We learn things, do you understand? And we spend much time just thinking. At least, I do. It is the first time I have had nothing to do except think. Don't you see, I am becoming a man. For the first time, I understand that I have a life to fulfill. Has that thought ever worried you?

OMAE: You are frightening me.

EMAN: There. That is all you can say. And what use will

that be when a man finds himself alone — like that? (*Points to the hut.*) A man must go on his own, go where no one can help him, and test his strength. Because he may find himself one day sitting alone in a wall as round as that. In there, my mind could hold no other thought. I may never have such moments again to myself. Don't dare to come and steal any more of it.

OMAE (*this time, genuinely tearful*): Oh, I know you hate me. You only want to drive me away.

EMAN (*impatiently*): Yes, yes, I know I hate you — but go.

OMAE (*going, all tears. Wipes her eyes, suddenly all mischief*): Eman.

EMAN: What now?

OMAE: I only want to ask one thing . . . do you promise to tell me?

EMAN: Well, what is it?

OMAE (*gleefully*): Does it hurt?

(*She turns instantly and flees, landing straight into the arms of the returning tutor.*)

TUTOR: Te-he-he . . . what have we here? What little mouse leaps straight into the beak of the wise old owl eh?

(*Omae struggles to free herself, flies to the opposite side, grimacing with distaste.*)

TUTOR: I suppose you merely came to pick some fruits eh? You did not sneak here to see any of my children.

OMAE: Yes, I came to steal your fruits.

TUTOR: Te-he-he . . . I thought so. And that dutiful son of mine over there. He saw you and came to chase you off my fruit trees didn't he? Te-he-he . . . I'm sure he did, isn't that so, my young Eman?

EMAN: I was talking to her.

TUTOR: Indeed you were. Now be good enough to go into your hut until I decide your punishment. (*Eman withdraws.*) Te-he-he . . . now now, my little daughter, you need not be afraid of me.

OMAE (*spiritedly*): I am not.

TUTOR: Good. Very good. We ought to be friendly. (*His voice becomes leering.*) Now this is nothing to worry you, my daughter . . . a very small thing indeed. Although of course if I were to let it slip that your young Eman had broken a strong taboo, it might go hard on him you know. I am sure you would not like that to happen, would you?

OMAE: No.

TUTOR: Good. You are sensible, my girl. Can you wash clothes?

OMAE: Yes.

TUTOR: Good. If you will come with me now to my hut, I shall give you some clothes to wash, and then we will forget all about this matter eh? Well, come on.

OMAE: I shall wait here. You go and bring the clothes.

TUTOR: Eh? What is that? Now now, don't make me angry. You should know better than to talk back at your elders. Come now.

(*He takes her by the arm and tries to drag her off.*)

OMAE: No no, I won't come to your hut. Leave me. Leave me alone, you shameless old man.

TUTOR: If you don't come I shall disgrace the whole family of Eman, and yours too.

(*Eman reenters with a small bundle.*)

EMAN: Leave her alone. Let us go, Omae.

TUTOR: And where do you think you are going?

EMAN: Home.

TUTOR: Te-he-he . . . As easy as that eh? You think you can leave here any time you please? Get right back inside that hut!

(*Eman takes Omae by the arm and begins to walk off.*)

TUTOR: Come back at once.

(*He goes after him and raises his stick. Eman catches it, wrenches it from him, and throws it away.*)

OMAE (*hopping delightedly*): Kill him. Beat him to death.

TUTOR: Help! Help! He is killing me! Help!

(*Alarmed, Eman clamps his hand over his mouth.*)

EMAN: Old tutor, I don't mean you any harm, but you mustn't try to harm me either. (*He removes his hand.*)

TUTOR: You think you can get away with your crime. My report shall reach the elders before you ever get into town.

EMAN: You are afraid of what I will say about you? Don't worry. Only if you try to shame me, then I will speak. I am not going back to the village anyway. Just tell them I have gone, no more. If you say one word more than that I shall hear of it the same day and I shall come back.

TUTOR: You are telling me what to do? But don't think to come back next year because I will drive you away. Don't think to come back here even ten years from now. And don't send your children.

(*Goes off with threatening gestures.*)

EMAN: I won't come back.

OMAE: Smoked vulture! But Eman, he says you cannot return next year. What will you do?

EMAN: It is a small thing one can do in the big towns.

OMAE: I thought you were going to beat him that time. Why didn't you crack his dirty hide?

EMAN: Listen carefully, Omae . . . I am going on a journey.

OMAE: Come on. Tell me about it on the way.

EMAN: No, I go that way. I cannot return to the village.

OMAE: Because of that wretched man? Anyway you will first talk to your father.

EMAN: Go and see him for me. Tell him I have gone away for some time. I think he will know.

OMAE: But, Eman . . .

EMAN: I haven't finished. You will go and live with him till I get back. I have spoken to him about you. Look after him!

OMAE: But what is this journey? When will you come back?

EMAN: I don't know. But this is a good moment to go. Nothing ties me down.

OMAE: But, Eman, you want to leave me.

EMAN: Don't forget all I said. I don't know how long I will be. Stay in my father's house as long as you remember me. When you become tired of waiting, you must do as you please. You understand? You must do as you please.

OMAE: I cannot understand anything, Eman. I don't know where you are going or why. Suppose you never came back! Don't go, Eman. Don't leave me by myself.

EMAN: I must go. Now let me see you on your way.

OMAE: I shall come with you.

EMAN: Come with me! And who will look after you? Me? You will only be in my way, you know that! You will hold me back and I shall desert you in a strange place. Go home and do as I say. Take care of my father and let him take care of you.

(*He starts going but Omae clings to him.*)

OMAE: But, Eman, stay the night at least. You will only lose your way. Your father, Eman, what will he say? I won't remember what you said . . . come back to the village . . . I cannot return alone, Eman . . . come with me as far as the crossroads.

(*His face set, Eman strides off and Omae loses balance as he increases his pace. Falling, she quickly wraps her arms around his ankle, but Eman continues unchecked, dragging her along.*)

OMAE: Don't go, Eman . . . Eman, don't leave me, don't leave me . . . don't leave your Omae . . . don't go, Eman . . . don't leave your Omae . . .

(*Eman — as carrier — makes a nervous move as if he intends to go after the vanished pair. He stops but continues to stare at the point where he last saw them. There is stillness for a while. Then the Girl enters from the same place and remains looking at Eman. Startled, Eman looks apprehensively round him. The Girl goes nearer but keeps beyond arm's length.*)

GIRL: Are you the carrier?

EMAN: Yes. I am Eman.

GIRL: Why are you hiding?

EMAN: I really came for a drink of water . . . er . . . is there anyone in front of the house?

GIRL: No.

EMAN: But there might be people in the house. Did you hear voices?

GIRL: There is no one here.

EMAN: Good. Thank you. (*He is about to go, stops suddenly.*) Er . . . would you . . . you will find a cup on the table. Could you bring me the water out here? The water pot is in a corner.

(*The Girl goes. She enters the house, then, watching Eman carefully, slips out and runs off.*)

EMAN (*sitting*): Perhaps they have all gone home. It will be good to rest. (*He hears voices and listens hard.*) Too late. (*Moves cautiously nearer the house.*) Quickly, girl, I can hear people coming. Hurry up. (*Looks through the window.*) Where are you? Where is she? (*The truth dawns on him suddenly and he moves off, sadly.*)

(*Enter Jaguna and Oroge, led by the Girl.*)

GIRL (*pointing*): He was there.
JAGUNA: Ay, he's gone now. He is a sly one is your friend. But it won't save him forever.
OROGE: What was he doing when you saw him?
GIRL: He asked me for a drink of water.
JAGUNA: } Ah! (*They look at each other.*)
OROGE:
OROGE: We should have thought of that.
JAGUNA: He is surely finished now. If only we had thought of it earlier.
OROGE: It is not too late. There is still an hour before midnight.
JAGUNA: We must call back all the men. Now we need only wait for him — in the right place.
OROGE: Everyone must be told. We don't want anyone heading him off again.
JAGUNA: And it works so well. This is surely the help of the gods themselves, Oroge. Don't you know at once what is on the path to the stream?
OROGE: The sacred trees.
JAGUNA: I tell you it is the very hand of the gods. Let us go.

(*An overgrown part of the village. Eman wanders in, aimlessly, seemingly uncaring of discovery. Beyond him, an area lights up, revealing a group of people clustered round a spot, all the heads are bowed. One figure stands away and separate from them. Even as Eman looks, the group breaks up and the people disperse, coming down and past him. Only three people are left, a man [Eman] whose back is turned, the village priest, and the isolated one. They stand on opposite sides of the grave, the man on the mound of earth. The Priest walks round to the man's side and lays a hand on his shoulder.*)

PRIEST: Come.
EMAN: I will. Give me a few moments here alone.
PRIEST: Be comforted.

(*They fall silent.*)

EMAN: I was gone twelve years but she waited. She whom I thought had too much of the laughing child in her. Twelve years I was a pilgrim, seeking the vain shrine of secret strength. And all the time, strange knowledge, this silent strength of my child-woman.
PRIEST: We all saw it. It was a lesson to us; we did not know that such goodness could be found among us.
EMAN: Then why? Why the wasted years if she had to perish giving birth to my child? (*They are both silent.*) I do not really know for what great meaning I

searched. When I returned, I could not be certain I had found it. Until I reached my home and I found her a full-grown woman, still a child at heart. When I grew to believe it, I thought, this, after all, is what I sought. It was here all the time. And I threw away my new-gained knowledge. I buried the part of me that was formed in strange places. I made a home in my birthplace.
PRIEST: That was as it should be.
EMAN: Any truth of that was killed in the cruelty of her brief happiness.
PRIEST (*looks up and sees the figure standing away from them, the child in his arms. He is totally still*): Your father — he is over there.
EMAN: I knew he would come. Has he my son with him?
PRIEST: Yes.
EMAN: He will let no one take the child. Go and comfort him, priest. He loved Omae like a daughter, and you all know how well she looked after him. You see how strong we really are. In his heart of hearts the old man's love really awaited a daughter. Go and comfort him. His grief is more than mine.

(*The Priest goes. The Old Man has stood well away from the burial group. His face is hard and his gaze unswerving from the grave. The Priest goes to him, pauses, but sees that he can make no dent in the man's grief. Bowed, he goes on his way.*)
(*Eman, as carrier, walking towards the graveside, the other Eman having gone. His feet sink into the mound and he breaks slowly onto his knees, scooping up the sand in his hands and pouring it on his head. The scene blacks out slowly.*)

(*Enter Jaguna and Oroge.*)

OROGE: We have only a little time.
JAGUNA: He will come. All the wells are guarded. There is only the stream left him. The animal must come to drink.
OROGE: You are sure it will not fail — the trap, I mean.
JAGUNA: When Jaguna sets the trap, even elephants pay homage — their trunks downwards and one leg up in the sky. When the carrier steps on the fallen twigs, it is up in the sacred trees with him.
OROGE: I shall breathe again when this long night is over.

(*They go out.*)
(*Enter Eman — as carrier — from the same direction as the last two entered. In front of him is a still figure, the Old Man as he was, carrying the dwarf boat.*)

EMAN (*joyfully*): Father.

(*The figure does not turn round.*)

EMAN: It is your son, Eman. (*He moves nearer.*) Don't you want to look at me? It is I, Eman. (*He moves nearer still.*)
OLD MAN: You are coming too close. Don't you know what I carry on my head?

EMAN: But, Father, I am your son.

OLD MAN: Then go back. We cannot give the two of us.

EMAN: Tell me first where you are going.

OLD MAN: Do *you* ask that? Where else but to the river?

EMAN (*visibly relieved*): I only wanted to be sure. My throat is burning. I have been looking for the stream all night.

OLD MAN: It is the other way.

EMAN: But you said . . .

OLD MAN: I take the longer way, you know how I must do this. It is quicker if you take the other way. Go now.

EMAN: No, I will only get lost again. I shall go with you.

OLD MAN: Go back, my son. Go back.

EMAN: Why? Won't you even look at me?

OLD MAN: Listen to your father. Go back.

EMAN: But, father!

(*He makes to hold him. Instantly the old man breaks into a rapid trot. Eman hesitates, then follows, his strength nearly gone.*)

EMAN: Wait, father. I am coming with you . . . wait . . . wait for me, father . . .

(*There is a sound of twigs breaking, of a sudden trembling in the branches. Then silence.*)

(*The front of Eman's house. The effigy is hanging from the sheaves. Enter Sunma, still supported by Ifada, she stands transfixed as she sees the hanging figure. Ifada appears to go mad, rushes at the object, and tears it down. Sunma, her last bit of will gone, crumbles against the wall. Some distance away from them, partly hidden, stands the Girl, impassively watching. Ifada hugs the effigy to him, stands above Sunma. The Girl remains where she is, observing.*)

(*Almost at once, the villagers begin to return, subdued and guilty.*)

(*They walk across the front, skirting the house as widely as they can. No word is exchanged. Jaguna and Oroge eventually appear. Jaguna, who is leading, sees Sunma as soon as he comes in view. He stops at once, retreating slightly.*)

OROGE (*almost whispering*): What is it?

JAGUNA: The viper.

(*Oroge looks cautiously at the woman.*)

OROGE: I don't think she will even see you.

JAGUNA: Are you sure? I am in no frame of mind for another meeting with her.

OROGE: Let's go home.

JAGUNA: I am sick to the heart of the cowardice I have seen tonight.

OROGE: That is the nature of men.

JAGUNA: Then it is a sorry world to live in. We did it for them. It was all for their own common good. What did it benefit me whether the man lived or died. But did you see them? One and all they looked up at the man and words died in their throats.

OROGE: It was no common sight.

JAGUNA: Women could not have behaved so shamefully. One by one they crept off like sick dogs. Not one could raise a curse.

OROGE: It was not only him they fled. Do you see how unattended we are?

JAGUNA: There are those who will pay for this night's work!

OROGE: Ay, let us go home.

(*They go off. Sunma, Ifada, and the Girl remain as they are, the light fading slowly on them.*)

COMMENTARY

Lewis Nkosi (*b. 1935*)

INTERVIEW WITH WOLE SOYINKA   *1962*

> This early interview with Soyinka was taped in Lagos, Nigeria, in August 1962, while The Strong Breed *was very fresh in his mind. In fact, it had not yet had its first publication, which in Nigeria was in 1963. Nkosi in the interview highlights the impact of Bertolt Brecht's theater on Soyinka's writing.*

Nkosi: Well, Wole Soyinka, could you tell us what set you off on this road to writing?

Soyinka: I suppose that requires really going back a bit. I would say I began writing seriously, or rather taking myself seriously, taking my *writing* seriously about three, four years ago, but I can only presume that I have always been interested in writing. In school I wrote the usual little sketches for production, the occasional verse, you know, the short story, etc., and I think about 1951 I had the great excitement of having a short story of mine broadcast on the Nigerian Broadcasting Service and that was sort of my first public performance.

Nkosi: What schools did you attend?

Soyinka: I went to Government School, Ibadan; after that I spent a couple of years in the University College, Ibadan.

Nkosi: You have now published drama or rather you've had some plays produced?

Soyinka: Yes, "produced" is the correct word. I haven't had any plays published although some are in print right now and will come out shortly.

Nkosi: Could you tell us what those plays are?

Soyinka: There is *The Lion and the Jewel* which was the first play I wrote.

Nkosi: No, the second.

Soyinka: The first one I sent up, I suppose like most people do, is the *A Dance of Forests* which I wrote in 1960 and timed it for the Independence Celebrations; there is the *House of Banigeji* which has never been performed. And I have written about four one-acts including *The Trials of Brother Jero* which was done quite recently in Nigeria.

Nkosi: The *A Dance of the Forests* won you a prize, didn't it?

Soyinka: Yes, Nigerian Independence competition prize 1960.

Nkosi: Have you got any particular authors that have influenced you most?

Soyinka: This is a very difficult question for me because I am not aware of any conscious influence on my work, but I can say that if I wanted to aim at any particular kind of theater, I think, however subconsciously, I might aim at Brecht's kind of theater, which I admire tremendously, just his complete freedom with the medium of the theater.

Nkosi: In your last play, *A Dance of the Forests,* which caused a lot of people a tremendous amount of agony trying to figure out just exactly what it was trying to do — they felt that there were some hidden meanings contained in lots of symbolism which they couldn't gather. Now as you're the author, we are lucky to have you here, and we think that you probably might enlighten us about just what you were trying to say in that work of yours.

Soyinka: Well, let me say first of all that I think that my prime duty as a playwright is to provide excellent theater; in other words, I think that I have only one commitment to the public, and that is to my audience and that is to make sure they do not leave the theater bored. I don't believe that I have any obligation to enlighten, to instruct, to teach: I don't possess that sense of duty or didacticism — very much unlike Brecht for instance, for, you see, what I like in Brecht is his sort of theater, its liveliness and freedom, not so much his purpose or intentions. I believe my primary duty is just to see that I provide excellent theater for the audience. But inevitably, it is just common sense to say that one just cannot write about just nothing. In *A Dance of the Forests,* I was very much conscious of all the potentialities of existing theatrical idioms in Nigeria and I only know that there was one thing which motivated, maybe, guided the form and the shape of the play or the eventual fate of the characters. I use this word "motivated" quite cautiously because I do not think I consciously tried to preach or bring out, you know, a series of symbolisms at all, but the main thing was the realization that human beings are just destructive all over the world. I think this is it — I have thought about this again and again but during the production — I produced it myself — and in trying to see the play take shape on the stage, I find that the main thing is my own personal conviction or observation that human beings are simply cannibals all over the world so that their main preoccupation seems to be eating up one another. This I think is the main thing I would say was in the back of my mind when I wrote it.

Nkosi: Yes, that sounds very much like Tennessee Williams's idea of the world conscious of the evil.

Soyinka: Well, I don't sort of regard it so much as . . .

Nkosi: The ferocity of human beings.

Soyinka: Yes, the carnivorous nature of. . . .

Nkosi: Yes, I wonder whether now — have you pursued this theme in the other plays or are the other plays different?

Soyinka: . . . Fundamentally, I think they're different. I think that sort of semi-consciously the moment I realize I'm pursuing a theme again, it seems to ring a bell warning that I have preceded myself somewhere; I have such a feeling about this that I shirk from it but I would say there are traces of it in my other plays — in, for instance, my favorite one-act play which is *The Strong Breed*. I think this one is also very much mixed up with the whole element of sacrifice, so contrasting the idea of selfishness with willing self-sacrifice as opposed to the other general cannibalism of human beings.

Contemporary Drama

Experimentation

The experimentation in drama that flourished in the first half of the twentieth century has continued in contemporary drama. In fact, the achievements of Tennessee Williams, Arthur Miller, Samuel Beckett, and other midcentury playwrights encouraged later playwrights to experiment more daringly with mixing media such as film, video, opera, rock, and other music with live actors. Mixed-media approaches are still options for playwrights at the beginning of the twenty-first century, but most contemporary plays celebrated by critics and audiences have been relatively traditional. They build on the achievement of nineteenth-century realism and twentieth-century expressionism.

Harold Pinter's distinctive style, developed in the late 1950s and early 1960s, is connected with some of the absurdist experiments in drama. His dialogue is acerbic, repetitive, sometimes apparently aimless. However, he is able to produce intense emotional situations, such as that in *The Dumb Waiter* (1957), in which two "hit men" wait for instructions in a basement room. *The Caretaker* (1959) and *The Homecoming* (1965), his first commercial successes, established him as a major figure in modern theater. He has also been a screenwriter for such films as *The Quiller Memorandum* (1966), *The French Lieutenant's Woman* (1981), and *The Handmaid's Tale* (1990). His experiments with time and sequence in his full-length play *Betrayal* (1978), for which he also wrote the screenplay, have inspired other playwrights, such as Paula Vogel, to experiment with the backward movement of action.

Most of the interesting late twentieth-century experimental theater was done in groups such as Richard Schechner's Performance Group, which created what Schechner called ENVIRONMENTAL THEATER in New York City in the late 1960s, and Jerzy Grotowski's Polish Laboratory Theatre in Wroclaw, Poland, during the same period. Ensembles like the Bread and Puppet Theatre, San Francisco Mime Troupe, and Luis Valdez's El Teatro Campesino on the West Coast combined a radical political message with theatrical experimentation. The work of these groups is effective primarily at the level of performance; their texts are not representative of their impact on audiences.

Theater of Cruelty

The ensembles of the 1960s and 1970s were strongly influenced by the work of Antonin Artaud (1896–1948), French actor, director, and a theorist of theater. In creating what came to be known as the THEATER OF CRUELTY, he insisted on removing the comforting distance between actors and audience. Thus the audience was involved in a direct, virtually physical fashion with the dramatic action. Artaud designed theater to be a total experience — a sensational spectacle that did not depend on coherent plot or development. He concentrated on what he called a total theater that emphasized movement, gesture, music, sound, light, and other nonverbal elements to intensify the experience.

Artaud's manifestos collected in a work called *The Theater and Its Double* (1938) inspired some of the most important twentieth-century theater practitioners, including Peter Brook and Robert Wilson, among others. Artaud's notion of a "serious" theater is at the root of his influence:

> Our long habit of seeking diversion has made us forget the idea of a serious theater, which, overturning all our preconceptions, inspires us with the fiery magnetism of its images and acts upon us like a spiritual therapeutics whose touch can never be forgotten.
>
> Everything that acts is a cruelty. It is upon this idea of extreme action, pushed beyond all limits, that theater must be rebuilt.

Artaud compared the theater artist he envisioned to a victim "burnt at the stake, signaling through the flames."

Environmental Theater

Richard Schechner's most famous production, based on Euripides' *The Bacchae,* was *Dionysus in 69* (1968), in which Pentheus is torn to pieces in an impassioned frenzy. Part of the point of Schechner's production was to inspire the audience so much that they would take to the stage, becoming indistinguishable from the actors. *Dionysus in 69* was an effort to draw on the same spiritual energies tapped by Greek drama by connecting with the feasts of Dionysus, god of wine and ecstasy. The play was a spontaneous and partly improvised performance piece rather than a text meant to be read. At one point the audience and actors disrobed in a simulation of a Greek religious orgy, and Schechner's goal of involving audience and actors in a pagan ritual was realized night after night during the run.

In a similar way Julian Beck and Judith Malina's Living Theatre maintained a special relationship with the audience. Beck's plays were designed to break down the absolutes of dramatic space and audience space by having the actors roam through the audience and interact apparently at random with audience members. *Paradise Now* (1968) is his best-known play. Like Schechner's *Dionysus in 69,* it was essentially a performance piece. Certain segments were improvised; therefore, as a reading text, it has relatively little power.

"Poor Theater"

Jerzy Grotowski called his work "poor theater" because it was meant to contrast with the "rich theater" of the commercial stage, with its expensive lighting, decorated stages, rich costumes, numerous props, and elaborate settings. Grotowski's Laboratory Theatre, begun in 1959, relied on preexisting texts but interpreted them broadly through a total reconception of their meaning. For example, Grotowski's *Akropolis* (1962; revised frequently from 1963 to 1975) adapted an older Polish drama by Stanisław Wyspiański (1904) and reset it in modern times in Auschwitz with the actors, dressed in ragged sackcloth prison uniforms, looking wretched and starving. At the end of the play the prisoners follow a headless puppet-corpse, Christ, into an afterlife. They march in an eerie ritual procession offstage into the waiting prison camp ovens.

Grotowski's theater has been influential worldwide. When the Polish government clamped down on the Solidarity° movement in the late 1970s, Grotowski left Poland. After 1970 Grotowski shifted his focus from public performances to small, intense group workshops and to the ritual performances of cultures from all over the world. The first phase of his work with the Laboratory Theatre has remained the most influential. One of his actors, Richard Cieslak, traveled widely training people in Grotowski's methods.

Theater of Images

Robert Wilson experimented in the 1970s, 1980s, and 1990s with repetitive narratives that sometimes take eight hours to perform. His multimedia dramas involve huge casts and ordinarily cover an immense historic range (Figure 19). One of his most extraordinary successes was *Einstein on the Beach* (1976), an opera written in collaboration with composer Philip Glass. Eight hours long, it was originally produced in a conventional theater, but it uses dramatic techniques that involve extensive patterns of repetition, the creation of enigmatic and evocative images, and characters who are cartoonlike caricatures of historical people. The overall effect is hypnotic; one of the points of Wilson's work seems to be to induce a trancelike state in his audience. One of his multimedia productions, *CIVIL warS* (1983), continued to develop this concept of massive theater that transcends conventional dramatic boundaries. In 1994 Wilson produced a monologue version of *Hamlet* that received some acclaim.

Gay and Lesbian Theater and Other New Ensembles

Some of the most energetic theater of the late twentieth century came from groups that were excluded for long periods from representation in mainstream theater. Gay, lesbian, African American, Hispanic American, and Native American groups have been virtually ignored by commercial theater and as a result have formed their own collectives and groups.

One reason for the development of gay theater in the United States and Great Britain in the 1960s was the decriminalization of homosexuality beginning in 1967 in Boston. Depiction of homosexual love onstage waited even longer, until the Gay Workshop's plays in London beginning in 1976. The first openly gay play was Mart Crowley's *The Boys in the Band* (1968), a popular success produced just after the repeal of a New York law prohibiting homosexuality from being represented on stage.

The Ridiculous Theatrical Company, founded by Charles Ludlam (1940–1987) in 1969, produced a formidable body of work rooted in the experiences of the homosexual community of New York. Its influence spread to many parts of the world. One of Ludlam's catchphrases was "plays without the stink of art." His plays were often ridiculously funny. *Bluebeard* (1970), for example, focused on creating a third gender by inventing a third genital. *Camille* (1973), starring Ludlam himself in the title role, hilariously spoofed not only Dumas's play but most of the "Hallmark card" conventions about romantic love. A gifted female impersonator, Ludlam played Hedda Gabler at the American Ibsen Theatre in Pittsburgh. Under the direction of Ludlam's partner, Everett Quinton, the Ridiculous Theatrical Company continues to produce Ludlam's plays as well as new plays in his tradition.

Solidarity: A labor organizing movement in Communist Poland led by Lech Walesa.

Figure 19. Multimedia effects in Robert Wilson's *CIVIL warS*.

Many of the most-praised recent plays have addressed the issues of AIDS and its ravaging of the gay community. Harvey Fierstein's *Torch Song Trilogy* (1982) was named best play of the year and appeared several years later on television. *As Is* by William M. Hoffman (1985) has been described by Don Shewey as the "best gay play anyone has written on AIDS yet." Tony Kushner dazzled New York with *Angels in America Part One: Millennium Approaches* (1992) and *Part Two: Perestroika* (1992). This two-part drama approached the problems of gay life in America on both a personal and a public, political level. The plays are called a "fantasia" and use a free-form, nonrealistic style of presentation. HBO produced an award-winning version for television in late 2003 starring Al Pacino and Meryl Streep.

Lesbian theatrical groups have sprung up in the United States and Great Britain. They often merge with women's theater groups and address issues such as male violence, societal restrictions on women, and women's opportunities. A number of important collectives, such as the Rhode Island Women's Theater and At the Foot of the Mountain in Minneapolis, treated general women's issues in the 1970s. Groups such as Medusa's Revenge (founded 1976) and

Atlanta's Red Dyke Theater (1974) centered more on lesbian experience. These last two groups disbanded after a few years of successful productions. Megan Terry's Omaha Magic Theater, founded with Joanne Schmidman, has been a long-lasting theater focusing on women's issues. Other groups such as Spider-woman, consisting of three Native American sisters, and the highly successful Split Britches consider Cafe WOW in New York's East Village to be the home of lesbian theater. Gay and lesbian theater groups have often been concerned with erasing stereotypes while also celebrating gay and lesbian lifestyles. Plays that once played only to gay and lesbian audiences — such as Martin Sherman's (b. 1938) *Bent* (1977) and Larry Kramer's (b. 1936) *The Normal Heart* (1985) — are now shown in theaters worldwide.

Other important women playwrights have made their mark in contemporary theater, with plays such as María Irene Fornés's *Fefu and Her Friends* (1977), a sprawling play featuring women in roles traditionally reserved for men. It has become a cult classic, with many productions in regional theaters. Her *The Conduct of Life* (1985) is a cruel parody of macho values in a Latin American dictatorship. It won an Obie Award for best play of the year. Caryl Churchill has been a dominant figure in British drama since the first production of *Cloud Nine* (1979), a drama that critiques colonialism and gender stereotyping. *Top Girls* (1982) is one of her most successful plays. It centers on an employment agency for women but has as its premise the introduction of famous women from the past of several cultures. It is a powerful feminist statement. *Fen* (1983), *Serious Money* (1987), and *The Skriker* (1994) have solidified her reputation as an experimental, powerful dramatist. Marsha Norman's *Getting Out* (1977), *'night Mother* (1982), and *The Secret Garden* (1991) have been produced to considerable acclaim. Norman has become an important presence in American drama. Emily Mann's *Execution of Justice* (1983) centers on the trial of Dan White, who murdered Harvey Milk, an openly gay San Francisco city councilman. Anne Devlin's *Ourselves Alone* (1986); Lynn Siefert's *Coyote Ugly* (1986); Tina Howe's *Painting Churches* (1982); Anna Deavere Smith's *Fires in the Mirror: Crown Heights, Brooklyn and Other Identities* (1991) and *Twilight: Los Angeles 1992* (1992); Suzan-Lori Parks's *The Death of the Last Black Man in the Whole Entire World* (1990), *The America Play* (1993), *Venus* (1996), *In the Blood* (1999), and *Topdog/Underdog* (2001), which won the Pulitzer Prize for Drama, the first for a black woman; Dael Orlandersmith's *Yellowman* (2000); and Rebecca Gilman's *Spinning into Butter* (2000) have all added stature to the position of women in contemporary theater.

Through the 1970s, 1980s, and 1990s numerous black theatrical groups developed in many parts of the world. An important Afro-Caribbean theater group was formed in the Keskidee Center in North London, with Edgar White (b. 1947) as one of its directors. White's plays are often centered in Caribbean mystical experiences, including Rastafarianism. *The Nine Night* (1983), produced in London, focuses on a Jamaican funeral tradition designed to help the deceased enter the gates of heaven.

Experiments with Theater Space

Drama around the world has developed alternatives to the proscenium theater. Theater in the round, which seats audiences on all sides of the actors, has been exceptionally powerful for certain plays. Peter Weiss's *Persecution and Assassination of Jean-Paul Marat as Performed by the Inmates of the Asylum of Charenton under the Direction of the Marquis de Sade* (1964) was especially effective in this format. Other theatrical experiments explored the power of spaces one would not have thought appropriate for drama. For example, Wladimir Pereira Cardoso designed an elaborate welded-steel set for a production of Jean Genet's *The Balcony* in the Ruth Escobar Theater in São Paulo, Brazil. The set was a huge suspended cone in which people sat looking inward while the actors were suspended in the spherical space before them. The production was first staged in 1969 and was seen through 1971 and most of 1972 by many thousands of people. The set was constructed of eighty tons of iron assembled like a trellis and requiring 500,000 welds. The entire insides of the theater were torn out to accommodate the new set. The audience of 250 was seated on circular platforms and the actors moved through the space on ramps, on suspended cables, and on moving platforms. The same theater produced *The Voyage,* an adaptation of an epic poem, *The Lusiads,* about the origin of Portuguese people. That set used open welded platforms suggesting ships' decks. In Dubrovnik, Yugoslavia, a replica of Columbus's *Santa Maria* — built much larger than the original — was used to stage Miroslav Krleza's expressionist play *Christopher Columbus,* written in 1917. The ship was docked in Dubrovnik Harbor for the performances.

Richard Foreman's Ontological-Hysteric Theatre performs in a loft in New York City with all audience members facing in the same direction. This is not fundamentally different from the traditional proscenium theater, but the open loft space and the visible movements of actors offstage create a new relationship to the action. Foreman's work, such as *Sophia = (Wisdom)* (1970 and later), which has been performed in many parts, has none of the usually accepted narrative clues to its action. However, it aims to explore hitherto hidden aspects of experience, such as sexual taboos and unorthodox relationships. The relationship of the author to the performance is also experimental in his theater, since he directs his actors, often using a loud buzzer, as if they were extensions of his will. His work, begun in the 1960s, has continued to this day. He collaborated in the staging of Suzan-Lori Parks's *Venus* (1996).

Experimentation within the Tradition

Much of the powerful and lasting drama of the 1980s and 1990s through the early years of the twenty-first century has been achieved in a proscenium theater, using traditional methods of DRAMATURGY, the craft or techniques of dramatic composition. Contemporary dramatists are by no means shy of experimentation, but they are also sensitive to the continuing resources of the traditional stage as it was conceived by Chekhov and Ibsen and Miller. Marsha Norman, who wrote *'night, Mother,* has said that her plays are "wildly traditional. I'm a purist about structure. Plays are like plane rides. You [the audience] buy the ticket and you have to get where the ticket takes you. Or else you've been had."

Sam Shepard, one of the most prolific modern playwrights, experiments with his material, much of which premiered in small theaters in Greenwich Village, such as the La Mama Experimental Theater Club. But his most widely known plays, among them *Buried Child* (1978), are produced easily on conventional stages. Shepard's work is wide-ranging and challenging. His language is coarse, a representation of the way he has heard people speak, and the violence he portrays onstage is strong enough to alienate many in the audience. Shepard, important as he is, has not found a popular commercial audience for his plays. At root, his work is always experimental.

Brian Friel (b. 1929) began his career as an experimentalist in *Philadelphia, Here I Come!* (1964), in which Gar O'Donnell, the main character, appears both as his public self, represented by one actor, and as his private self, represented by another actor. This experimental drama ran for 326 performances on Broadway. Friel's political drama *Freedom of the City* (1974) addressed the "troubles" in Northern Ireland at a time of bombings and threats. *Translations* (1981) experiments with language — having Irish-speaking characters speak Irish to one another to baffle the British characters, while we "listen in" as if the Irish were being translated for us. *Faith Healer* (1980) presents characters onstage one at a time — with no interaction — telling us their stories in a powerful way. Throughout his career, Friel has been on the edge of experiment.

Athol Fugard, a South African, writes powerful plays that also work well on conventional proscenium stages. Like Shepard's, his subject matter is not the kind that permits an audience to sit back relaxed and appreciate the drama with a sense of detachment. Instead, the plays usually disturb audiences. His primary subject matter is the devastation — for blacks and whites — caused by apartheid in South Africa. Fugard's work with black actors in South Africa produced a vital experimental theater out of which his best early work grew.

Fugard's *The Blood Knot* (1961) and *Boesman and Lena* (1969), part of a trilogy on South Africa, are based on the theme of racial discrimination. But other plays, such as *A Lesson from Aloes* (1978) and *My Children! My Africa!* (1989), are involved with problems of individuals in relation to their political world. Fugard is in many ways a traditional playwright, except for his subject matter. His characters are thoroughly developed, but with great economy. In *"MASTER HAROLD" . . . and the boys,* for example, we are given a deep understanding of Hally and Sam, whose relationship, past, present, and future, is the center of the play. Fugard is not writing the well-made play, any more than the other contemporary playwrights in this collection are. There is nothing "mechanical" in Fugard's work but rather a sense of organic growth, of actions arising from perceptible conditions and historical circumstances. These contribute to the sense of integrity that his plays communicate.

Some of Caryl Churchill's plays, emphasizing themes of socialism, colonialism, and feminism, were developed in workshops and collaborations with actors and directors. When writing a play, she experiments early in the first stages by spending time in the environments her plays depict. When she worked on *Top Girls* (1982), she came up with the idea of setting the action in an employment agency after she had talked with many people whose lives are wrapped up in business. For *Serious Money* (1987), she and the group developing the play spent time at the London Stock Exchange, absorbing the atmosphere of frenetic buying and selling.

Although she claims to be a traditionalist, Marsha Norman has written experimental plays. Her first success, *Getting Out* (1977), portrays the same character at two periods in her life — as an adolescent and as an adult — on separate parts of the stage at the same time. Norman's *'night, Mother* is another traditionally structured play. It respects the Aristotelian unities of time, place, and action, and it is confrontational. Thelma and her daughter, Jessie, are in a power struggle over Jessie's right to commit suicide. The technique is naturalistic, and the play's subject matter, as in the plays of Strindberg and Ibsen, is discomforting to its contemporary audiences.

August Wilson has been working on a series of ten plays on the subject of black life in modern America. So far he has written nine of those plays, and each of the first four won the New York Drama Critics' Circle Award for best play of the year. All of Wilson's plays have explored the way the heritage of blacks enables them to live intelligently in the present, with understanding and dignity. People in his plays have lost touch with the past and, for that reason, risk a loss of self-understanding. Wilson's plays also show the pain endured by blacks in an America that is supposed to be the land of opportunity. Like Arthur Miller in *Death of a Salesman* and Lorraine Hansberry in *A Raisin in the Sun,* Wilson explores the nature and consequences of the American dream, especially for those effectively excluded from this dream. Blacks' frustration, exploitation, and suffering are presented in Wilson's powerful characters, such as Troy Maxson in *Fences* (1985). Troy is a garbage collector who was a star baseball player at a time when blacks could play only in their own leagues. (The major leagues were exclusively white until 1947, when Jackie Robinson joined the Brooklyn Dodgers and the game began to be integrated.) The play centers on Maxson's anger, his pride for his family, and his concerns for his son, who is growing up into a world in which he must empower himself to achieve what he most wants for himself. Cory, Troy's son, does not see the same kind of discrimination and has not felt the unfairness that was Troy's primary experience in growing up. Showing the world as Troy Maxson sees it is one of the functions of the play.

Wilson's plays have a naturalistic surface, but they also allude to the supernatural, as in *The Piano Lesson* (1990). Some of the roots of this tradition are in the black church and some in African religion, a source shared by Soyinka and Wilson, among others.

Among current playwrights, David Henry Hwang has been active in writing for both stage and film. His work has often centered on Chinese Americans and the problems they encounter in their experiences in the United States. Hwang has sensitized audiences to subjects about which playwrights had hitherto been silent. His first success, *FOB* (1980), focused on how new immigrants were viewed by Chinese Americans who had already assimilated. The play's title is an acronym for "fresh off the boat." Hwang's most successful play, *M. Butterfly* (1987), is about a romance between a French diplomat and a transvestite Chinese opera singer.

Since his short but intense *The Zoo Story* (1958), Edward Albee has been a powerful force in American theater. He has won three Pulitzer Prizes for drama: for *A Delicate Balance* (1966), *Seascape* (1974), and *Three Tall Women* (1991). He is better known for *Who's Afraid of Virginia Woolf?* (1961), however, a portrait of a violent, alcohol-filled academic marriage between George and Martha, portrayed memorably by Richard Burton and Elizabeth Taylor in Mike Nichols's 1966 film version. Not all his plays have been successful, but throughout his career he has maintained a reputation as an important experimentalist. His Tony Award–winning play, *The Goat, or Who Is Sylvia?* (2002) is a complex portrait of a prize-winning architect who falls in love with a goat. Albee thus pushes beyond the questions of hetero- or homosexuality into the taboo of bestiality. Beneath the surface, however, he presses the issues of tragedy as it is expressed in a modern situation.

David Mamet responds to a social situation in *Oleanna* (1992). The characters, a male college professor and a female student, at first adopt an ordinary teacher-student relationship; eventually, though, that relationship alters. Mamet explores questions of power and issues of sexual harassment. As the lines he draws shift back and forth, the audience never knows exactly how clear the lines are meant to be. The issues in the play are thus subject to a number of different interpretations. Widely considered Mamet's best play, *Glengarry Glen Ross* (1983) offers a savage portrait of the masculine world of salesmanship. Deception, competition, and outright theft dominate the play, demonstrating a failure of values of the main characters, all of whom feel justified in their willingness to push property on those who do not want or need it. Mamet's language carries the weight of a philosophy that scorns the get-ahead attitude of the salesman.

China's most distinguished modern playwright, Gao Xingjian, now lives and writes in Paris, after having lived through the Cultural Revolution of the 1960s, when all his plays and manuscripts were destroyed and he was forced to work as a laborer for several years. His work has been banned in China because it is seen as critical of the communist system in place in that country. Having lived in France since 1987, he has been influenced by playwrights such as Samuel Beckett and Bertolt Brecht. One of his plays, *Bus Stop* (1983), resembles Beckett's *Waiting for Godot* in that his characters wait patiently for the bus to come — a symbol of a positive change in their lives — but it never arrives. *The Other Shore* (1986) explores the religious aspirations of his characters from a perspective of Pure Land Buddhism, with the other shore being the land of the dead, a world with ambiguous virtues. Gao is also a novelist and wrote *Soul Mountain* (1989), a best-seller in its English translation (1999). Gao won the Nobel Prize in Literature in 2000.

Tony Kushner's two-part drama *Angels in America: Millennium Approaches* (1992) and *Perestroika* (1992) explores issues in modern American history, with an emphasis on religion, politics, and a variety of hysterias. The plays explore homophobia, red-baiting politics, and the impact of AIDS on contemporary society. The open, dynamic structure of the play is enormously powerful. The entire drama lasts six and a half hours and has been seen not only in San Francisco, where it opened, but also in New York, London, other European cities, and regional theaters throughout the United States. The Golden Globe award-winning 2003 HBO production made the play available to many millions of viewers and expanded some of Kushner's vision for the drama. His *Homebody/Kabul* (2001), which examines the political circumstances in Afghanistan in 1998 after American bombing raids, continues his interest in exploring contemporary historical events; his chamber opera *Caroline, or Change* (2003) considers racial issues in Louisiana in 1963.

In the late 1990s women and young men made important contributions to theater. José Rivera (b. 1955) presented two plays that drew on the tradition of magical realism that is prominent in Latin American fiction. *Marisol* (1992) and *Cloud Tectonics* (1995) are visually and emotionally impressive pieces that work counter to the Ibsenist tradition of realism. As especially theatrical pieces, they give the director a considerable degree of freedom in staging. Yasmina

Reza (b. 1959) had major success in France, England, the United States, and many other nations with her award-winning comedy *"Art,"* which raises unexpected questions about taste and friendship. Martin McDonagh (b. 1970) startled the London theater scene with his Leenane trilogy: *The Beauty Queen of Leenane* (1996), *A Skull in Connemara* (1997), and *The Lonesome West* (1997). The three plays and his *The Cripple of Inishmaan* (1996) were produced at the same time in London, a record for a twenty-seven-year-old playwright. Paula Vogel (b. 1951) created a portrait of an adolescent girl, Li'l Bit, involved with an incestuous Uncle Peck in *How I Learned to Drive* (1997). The play won the Pulitzer Prize that year and established her as one of the most important American playwrights. Her most recent play, *The Long Christmas Ride Home* (November 2003), continues her experimentation into the realm of puppet theater. The effect recalls techniques of Japanese Bunraku Theater.

Nilo Cruz (b. 1961) won the Pulitzer Prize in 2003 for *Anna in the Tropics.* He was the first Hispanic Pulitzer winner in drama. Among his many plays is *Lorca in a Green Dress* (2003), an experiment in literary allusion. The works of these playwrights demonstrate the vitality and energy that sustain drama in the twenty-first century.

Contemporary Drama Timeline

DATE	THEATER	POLITICAL	SOCIAL/CULTURAL
1950–present	**1951:** Anna Deavere Smith, African American playwright and actress, born. Among her works are *Fires in the Mirror* (1991) and *Twilight: Los Angeles, 1992* (1994). **1954:** Joseph Papp founds the New York Shakespeare festival. **1956:** John Osborne's *Look Back in Anger* is produced in London. **1956:** Tony Kushner, American playwright, born. He is best known for the plays *Angels in America, Parts 1 and 2* (1992). **1959:** Jerzy Grotowski establishes the Laboratory Theatre in Poland. In 1968 he publishes *Towards a Poor Theatre*. **1960s:** Off-Off-Broadway flourishes with the formation of such groups as Café Cino (1958), La Mama ETC (1962), the Open Theatre (1963), and the Performance Group (1967). **1962:** Peter Schumann founds the Bread and Puppet Theatre, an influential political ensemble, in New York City. **1963:** The National Theatre is established in London under the direction of Laurence Olivier. **1964:** Ariane Mnouchkine forms the Théâtre du Soleil in Paris. **1964:** Peter Brook's production of Peter Weiss's *Marat/Sade* opens at the Royal Shakespeare Company.	**1950:** U.S. Senator Joseph McCarthy begins his war on Communism by investigating the alleged "un-American activities" of hundreds of U.S. citizens. **1951:** The USSR explodes its first atomic bomb. **1953:** Joseph Stalin dies. **1954:** *Brown v. Board of Education* finds school segregation unconstitutional. **1954:** Senator Joseph McCarthy's witch hunt for Communist infiltration in the United States ends. **1955:** Communist Eastern European allies sign the Warsaw Pact. **1955:** Montgomery, Alabama, bus boycott **1958:** Fidel Castro begins total war against Batista in Cuba; in 1959 he becomes premier. **1958–1969:** Charles de Gaulle is president of France. **1960:** The Belgian Congo is granted independence. **1961:** The Berlin Wall blocks immigration to and from East and West Germany. **1962:** The cold war reaches one of its tensest moments when the United States confronts the USSR over Soviet nuclear missile bases in Cuba. **1962:** The first U.S. combat troops are sent to fight in South Vietnam. **1963:** President John F. Kennedy is assassinated in Dallas. **1965:** Malcolm X is assassinated in New York.	**1950:** Simone de Beauvoir (1908–1986), French author, publishes *The Second Sex*. **1952:** Ralph Ellison (1914–1994), African American novelist, publishes *Invisible Man*. **1954:** Elvis Presley (1935–1977) makes his first recording at Sun Studios. **1957:** Jack Kerouac (1922–1969) publishes *On the Road*. **1962:** James Watson and Francis Crick share the Nobel Prize for defining the 3-D molecular structure of DNA. **1962:** Cesar Chavez (1927–1993) organizes California migrant farm workers. **1962:** Alexander Solzhenitsyn's *One Day in the Life of Ivan Denisovich* describes life in the Soviet gulag. **1964:** The Beatles appear on the *Ed Sullivan Show*. **1965:** The National Endowment for the Arts is established by the U.S. government.

Contemporary Drama Timeline (continued)

DATE	THEATER	POLITICAL	SOCIAL/CULTURAL
1950–present (continued)	**1968:** The Negro Ensemble Company is established in the United States under the direction of Douglas Turner Ward.	**1967:** In the Six-Day War, Israel responds to Arab provocation by capturing territory from Egypt, Syria, and Jordan.	**1966:** The National Organization for Women (NOW) is established to end discrimination against women.
	1968: The Living Theatre produces its highly influential experimental work, *Paradise Now.*	**1967:** Thurgood Marshall (1908–1993) is the first African American appointed to the U.S. Supreme Court.	**1967:** Dr. Christiaan N. Barnard performs the world's first human heart transplant operation in South Africa.
	1968: Theatrical censorship, in place since the Licensing Act of 1737, is finally abolished in England.	**1968:** The American civil rights leader Martin Luther King Jr. is assassinated.	
	1968: *Hair!*, the first rock musical, hits Broadway; it is followed by *Jesus Christ Superstar* in 1971.	**1968:** Students demonstrate throughout France.	**1969:** U.S. astronaut Neil Armstrong walks on the moon.
	1968: The Performance Group produces *Dionysus in 69* under the direction of Richard Schechner.		**1969:** New York City police raid the Stonewall Inn, and the resulting three-day protest becomes a symbol for the emerging gay rights movement.
	1970: Peter Brook's acclaimed production of *A Midsummer Night's Dream* opens at the Royal Shakespeare Company.	**1970–1975:** Civil war is fought in Cambodia; Communist leader Pol Pot takes power in 1975 and begins genocidal campaign.	
		1972: U.S. President Richard Nixon and Soviet leader Leonid Brezhnev sign the Strategic Arms Limitation Treaty (SALT).	
		1972: Philippine President Ferdinand Marcos declares martial law and assumes dictatorial powers.	
		1973: In *Roe v. Wade*, the U.S. Supreme Court legalizes abortion.	
		1973: U.S. troops are withdrawn from Vietnam.	
		1974: President Nixon resigns from office as a result of the Watergate scandal.	
	1975: Michael Bennett's musical *A Chorus Line* opens on Broadway and runs until 1990.	**1975:** The Spanish dictator Francisco Franco dies.	
		1976: The Chinese Communist leader Mao Zedong dies. Deng Xiaoping emerges as the new Chinese leader in 1978.	**1976:** The Episcopal Church approves the ordination of women to be priests and bishops.
	1978: Harold Pinter's *Betrayal* premieres at the National Theatre in London.	**1976:** Waves of violence against apartheid in Cape Town, Soweto, and Johannesburg, South Africa	

1300

Contemporary Drama Timeline (continued)

DATE	THEATER	POLITICAL	SOCIAL/CULTURAL
1950–present (continued)	**1979:** Stephen Sondheim's *Sweeney Todd* opens on Broadway. Other musicals by the prolific composer include *Sunday in the Park with George* (1984), *Into the Woods* (1987), and *Passion* (1995).	**1979:** After the overthrow of Shah Mohammad Reza Pahlavi, the Ayatollah Khomeini establishes the Islamic Republic of Iran.	
	1980: Sam Shepard's *True West* premieres.	**1980:** The Iran-Iraq War begins when Iraq invades Iran; the war lasts for eight years.	
	1982: Athol Fugard's *"MASTER HAROLD" . . . and the boys* premieres at the Yale Repertory Theatre.	**1981:** General Idi Amin begins his eight-year reign of terror in Uganda.	**1981:** Sandra Day O'Connor becomes the first woman appointed to the U.S. Supreme Court.
	1982: Caryl Churchill's *Cloud Nine* premieres.	**1981:** Egyptian leader Anwar Sadat is assassinated by Muslim extremists.	**1981:** IBM markets its first personal computer.
	1983: Marsha Norman's *'night, Mother* opens at New York's Golden Theater and wins the Pulitzer Prize.		**1982:** Wisconsin becomes the first state to protect gays and lesbians under civil rights legislation.
	1985: August Wilson's *Fences* premieres at the Yale Repertory Theatre and wins the Pulitzer Prize in 1987.	**1985:** Mikhail Gorbachev becomes the leader of the Soviet Union and institutes a policy of *glasnost* (openness).	**1986:** In *Bowers v. Hardwick,* the U.S. Supreme Court upholds the constitutionality of the Georgia state law against sodomy.
	1987: The immensely popular Broadway adaptation of Victor Hugo's *Les Misérables* opens, then closes March 2003.	**1989:** A student demonstration in Beijing's Tiananmen Square results in bloodshed.	**1986:** The U.S. space shuttle *Challenger* explodes seconds after liftoff, killing all seven on board.
		1989: Communism crumbles in Eastern Europe, and the Berlin Wall is torn down.	
	1990s: In a proliferation of Shakespeare on film, new versions of *Hamlet, Henry V, Much Ado about Nothing, Othello,* and *Richard III* are released.	**1990:** Iraq invades Kuwait, which leads to the Gulf War in 1991.	**1990:** Octavio Paz, Mexican poet, receives the Nobel Prize for literature.
		1990: East and West Germany reunite after 45 years of separation.	**1990:** The National Endowment for the Arts is attacked when controversial awards are publicized.
		1990: The South African nationalist leader Nelson Mandela is released from prison.	
		1990–1991: South Africa repeals its apartheid laws.	
		1991: The Soviet Union collapses. U.S. President George H. W. Bush officially recognizes the twelve new countries created as a result.	

Contemporary Drama Timeline (continued)

DATE	THEATER	POLITICAL	SOCIAL/CULTURAL
1950–present (continued)	**1992:** David Mamet's *Oleanna* premiers off-Broadway and runs for over 250 performances.	**1991:** Yugoslavia dissolves. Croatia, Slovenia, Bosnia-Herzegovina, and Macedonia declare independence, and bitter fighting ensues for several years.	**1993:** Toni Morrison (b. 1931), African American novelist, is awarded the Nobel Prize for literature.
		1994: Nelson Mandela (b. 1918) is elected the first black president of South Africa after that nation's first multiracial elections.	**mid-1990s:** *Internet* and *World Wide Web* become household words.
		1994: Chechnya declares independence from Russia; Russian troops invade the republic in 1994 and again in 1999.	
	1996: Jonathan Larson's *Rent,* a musical based on Puccini's *La Bohème,* wins the Pulitzer Prize.	**1995:** The Israeli leader Yitzhak Rabin is assassinated.	**1995:** Shannon Faulkner is the first woman to be admitted to the Citadel military academy.
	1997: Martin McDonagh, at age 27, has four plays running simultaneously in London.	**1997:** Hong Kong is returned to China after 156 years as a British colony.	**1995:** The National Endowment for the Arts budget is slashed by the newly elected Republican Congress. The Public Broadcasting Corporation and the National Endowment for the Humanities also come under fire.
	1998: Paula Vogel's play *How I Learned to Drive* wins the Pulitzer Prize.	**1998:** Asian nations face dramatic recession after economic booms of the 1980s and early 1990s.	**1996:** In *Rome v. Evans,* the U.S. Supreme Court rules that the equal protection clause of the Constitution applies to lesbians and gay men.
	1998: Yasmina Reza's *"Art"* wins a Tony Award for best play.	**1999:** Congress impeaches President Clinton for his improper conduct in the White House, but the president remains in office.	**1997:** Scottish scientist Ian Wilmot clones a sheep.
		1999: U.N. troops keep a tentative peace between ethnic Albanians and Serbian Albanians in Kosovo.	
		1999: The United States transfers the Panama Canal to Panama.	
	2000: Lee Blessing's *Cobb* makes a political statement about baseball.	**2000:** Boris Yeltsin resigns as president of Russia.	
	2000: Gao Xingjian wins Nobel Prize for Literature.	**2001:** On September 11, Al Qaeda terrorists destroy the World Trade Center with two airliners. A third plane damages the Pentagon.	**2001:** The human genome is decoded.
	2002: Suzan-Lori Parks's *Topdog/Underdog* wins the Pulitzer Prize.	**2002:** U.S. attacks Taliban forces in Afghanistan.	
	2002: Edward Albee's *The Goat, or Who Is Sylvia?* wins Drama Desk Award for best play.	**2003:** U.S. attacks Saddam Hussein in Iraq, bringing down his government.	**2003:** A law barring partial-birth abortions comes under fire with legal challenges.
	2003: Nilo Cruz's *Anna in the Tropics* wins the Pulitzer Prize.		**2004:** Spirit and Rover explore the surface of Mars, sending back 3-D images.

Luis Valdez

Luis Valdez, one of ten children, was born in 1940 in Delano, California, to *campesinos*, or farm workers. When he was six years old, he watched a teacher use part of a paper bag to make papier-mâché masks for a theater production. This experience transformed his world view and eventually led him to the theater. His experiences in the fields, however, lasted until he was eighteen, when he went to San Jose State College. Although he began college as a math and physics major, in deference to his parents, after less than a year at San Jose State he joined the theater and declared a major in English. He wrote and acted in plays at San Jose State, where his first full-length play, *The Shrunken Head of Pancho Villa* (1964), was produced.

After college he joined the famous San Francisco Mime Troupe. In 1965, still a member of Cesar Chavez's United Farm Workers Union, he founded El Teatro Campesino, or the Farm Workers Theater, for which he became artistic director and playwright. The theater, which has won a number of awards and is now part of the Mexican American Centro Campesino Cultural in Fresno, began as a theater for striking farm workers and their union, earning money for the union and spreading news about its activities. Eventually, Valdez began writing plays on a number of related subjects, such as the Vietnam War in *Dark Root of a Scream* (1967). He wrote several plays in a form he called *mito*, or myth. One of them, *Bernabé* (1970), introduced a figure who was a zoot suiter and focused on historical issues concerning Chicanos. Another of his important plays, *Los Vendidos (The Sellouts)*, was written in 1967 and continues to be performed.

In 1978, Valdez produced *Zoot Suit*, his first major success; he went on to write *Bandido!* (1982), which he calls "an antimelodrama," about a Mexican bandit named Tiburcio Vásquez, who holds the unpleasant distinction of having been, in 1875, the last man publicly executed by the law in San Jose, California. *I Don't Have to Show You No Stinking Badges!* (1986), set in California during Ronald Reagan's presidency, concerns Buddy Villa and his wife Connie, who have spent their working lives as extras in TV and films. Videotaped inserts and music make this play a multimedia experience.

In addition to his activities as a playwright, Luis Valdez also directs films and plays. He directed the film *Zoot Suit* (1981) and the film *La Bamba* (1987), the biography of the Mexican American rock 'n' roll singer Richie Valens, who died in a plane crash with Buddy Holly in 1959. Valdez also wrote the script for that film. In 1987, he produced a television version of his 1983 play, *Corridos! Tales of Passion and Revolution*. Performances of *Corridos!* filled a relatively large house in San Francisco for six months before moving to Los Angeles. Its subject is Mexican history, something many in his audience knew little about. Valdez is currently working on a film on the life of Cesar Chavez.

ZOOT SUIT

In some sense *Zoot Suit* is a musical drama, although it can be read as a straight drama as well. A zoot suit had baggy pleated trousers with narrow, pegged ankles and a jacket with wide lapels and long tails (drape), usually to the back of the knees. With it, a zoot suiter usually wore a gold watch chain that came down almost to the ankles and a hat with a long feather. In 1942 it was the epitome of "cool" in jazz circles and was a style favored by some Chicano youths in Los Angeles. Wartime rationing effectively banned the production of the suit, although demand continued to flout the regulations. El Pachuco in this play is the "spirit" of the zoot suiter, and Henry Reyna is the leader of the zoot suiters, a loosely formed gang.

The language of the play is a dialect that mixes English, Spanish, and Los Angeles Spanish slang. It is called Caló (for California/Los Angeles) or *pachuco*. Valdez makes no effort to translate for English-only speakers, but the sense of the language is generally clear to most audiences.

The play is partially based on the zoot-suit riots in Los Angeles in 1942 in which military personnel stripped the suits from zoot suiters, whom they felt were unpatriotic, and during which a murder was committed. In the play, Henry Reyna is falsely accused and convicted of the murder and is imprisoned until an appeal can demonstrate that he was not involved in the crime. The play itself investigates the hopes and yearnings of Henry Reyna and his friends and family. The structure of the play takes us from a dance hall in Los Angeles to a court for the trial, and then to San Quentin prison where Henry becomes close friends with Alice, a member of the press who buoys his hopes for justice.

Justice, however, seems less and less likely to be accorded to Henry, partly because the "system" needs a scapegoat, and Henry is available. But Henry has to make choices for himself, and in the process he changes some of his thinking. Although Henry eventually wins his appeal, the play ends without an ending. Instead of one ending, Valdez provides several possibilities, depending on who you think Henry Reyna is: a leader, victim, warrior, friend, or someone else. The audience decides.

Zoot Suit in Performance

Zoot Suit opened on July 30, 1978, in Los Angeles and played to full houses for almost a year. It then moved to a Broadway production in New York, where it ran for a month. It remains the first and only Chicano play to be performed on Broadway. Luis Valdez directed the film version of the play in 1981 with Daniel Valdez, his brother, in the role of Henry Reyna. Daniel Valdez also composed the music for the film. Despite the obvious challenges in producing *Zoot Suit,* the play continues to be staged. El Teatro Campesino produced the play in San Juan Bautista, California, in late 2002. Illinois State University staged the play in November 2003 as part of its "new vision of multiculturalism."

Luis Valdez (b. 1940)
ZOOT SUIT

1978

Characters

EL PACHUCO°
HENRY REYNA

His Family:
ENRIQUE REYNA
DOLORES REYNA
LUPE REYNA
RUDY REYNA

His Friends:
GEORGE SHEARER
ALICE BLOOMFIELD

His Gang:
DELLA BARRIOS
SMILEY TORRES
JOEY CASTRO
TOMMY ROBERTS
ELENA TORRES
BERTHA VILLARREAL

The Downey Gang:
RAFAS
RAGMAN
HOBO
CHOLO
ZOOTER
GÜERA
HOBA
BLONDIE
LITTLE BLUE

Detectives:
LIEUTENANT EDWARDS
SERGEANT SMITH

The Press:
PRESS
CUB REPORTER
NEWSBOY

The Court:
JUDGE F. W. CHARLES
BAILIFF

The Prison:
GUARD

The Military:
BOSUN'S MATE
SAILORS
MARINE
SWABBIE
MANCHUKA
SHORE PATROLMAN

Others:
GIRLS
PIMP
CHOLO

Setting: *The giant facsimile of a newspaper front page serves as a drop curtain.*

The huge masthead reads: LOS ANGELES HERALD EXPRESS Thursday, June 3, 1943.

A headline cries out: ZOOT-SUITER HORDES INVADE LOS ANGELES. U.S. NAVY AND MARINES ARE CALLED IN.

Behind this are black drapes creating a place of haunting shadows larger than life. The somber shapes and outlines of pachuco images hang subtly, black on black, against a background of heavy fabric evoking memories and feelings like an old suit hanging forgotten in the depths of a closet somewhere, sometime. . . . Below this is a sweeping, curving place of levels and rounded corners with the hard, ingrained brilliance of countless spit shines, like the memory of a dance hall.

ACT 1 • *Prologue*

(A switchblade plunges through the newspaper. It slowly cuts a rip to the bottom of the drop. To the sounds of "Perdido" by Duke Ellington, El Pachuco

El Pachuco: For some people the word *pachuco* indicates someone from El Paso. However, it also refers to a specific form of Chicano subculture that was prevalent in the 1940s in the Southwest. Considered gangsters by some, pachucos were characterized by their distinctive clothing, appearance, and language. Though not the only youth group to wear the zoot suit (an oversized suit), this was one of their cultural practices. They also developed particular versions of Spanish dialect. Some scholars call it Caló and trace it back to the language of gypsies in Spain; others see this language practice as innovation based on the encounter between two cultures, Mexican and American. In this account it is seen as a form of code switching and language adaptation. Regardless of their particular mannerisms, pachucos shared a general distrust of assimilation and insisted on forming their own identity outside of the U.S. mainstream, something that made them suspicious to both the U.S. legal system and Mexicans and Mexican Americans who were trying to assimilate.

emerges from the slit. He adjusts his clothing, meticulously fussing with his collar, suspenders, cuffs. He tends to his hair, combing back every strand into a long luxurious ducktail, with infinite loving pains. Then he reaches into the slit and pulls out his coat and hat. He dons them. His fantastic costume is complete. It is a zoot suit. He is transformed into the very image of the pachuco myth, from his pork-pie hat to the tip of his four-foot watch chain. Now he turns to the audience. His three-soled shoes with metal taps click-clack as he proudly, slovenly, defiantly makes his way downstage. He stops and assumes a pachuco stance.)

PACHUCO: ¿Que le watcha a mis trapos, ese?
    ¿Sabe qué, carnal?
    Estas garras me las planté porque
    Vamos a dejarnos caer un play, ¿sabe?

(He crosses to center stage, models his clothes.)

5   Watcha mi tacuche, ese. Aliviánese con mis calcos, tando,
    lisa, tramos, y carlango, ese.

(Pause.)

    Nel, sabe qué, usted está muy verdolaga. Como se me hace
    que es puro square.°

(El Pachuco breaks character and addresses the audience in perfect English.)

10   Ladies and gentlemen
    the play you are about to see
    is a construct of fact and fantasy.
    The Pachuco Style was an act in Life
    and his language a new creation.
15   His will to be was an awesome force
    eluding all documentation . . .
    A mythical, quizzical, frightening being
    precursor of revolution
    Or a piteous, hideous heroic joke
    deserving of absolution?
20   I speak as an actor on the stage.
    The Pachuco was existential
    for he was an Actor in the streets
    both profane and reverential.
    It was the secret fantasy of every bato
25   in or out of the Chicanada°
    to put on a Zoot Suit and play the Myth
    más chucote que la chingada.°

(Puts hat back on and turns.)

    ¡Pos órale!°

(Music. The newspaper drop flies. El Pachuco begins his chuco stroll upstage, swinging his watch chain.)

Scene 1. Zoot Suit

(The scene is a barrio dance in the forties. Pachucos and Pachucas in zoot suits and pompadours.
    They are members of the 38th Street Gang, led by Henry Reyna, 21, dark, Indian-looking, older than his years, and Della Barrios, 20, his girlfriend in miniskirt and fingertip coat. A sailor called Swabbie dances with his girlfriend Manchuka among the Couples. Movement. Animation. El Pachuco sings.)

PACHUCO: PUT ON A ZOOT SUIT, MAKES YOU
        FEEL REAL ROOT
    LOOK LIKE A DIAMOND, SPARKLING,
        SHINING
    READY FOR DANCING
    READY FOR THE BOOGIE TONIGHT!

(The Couples, dancing, join the Pachuco in exclaiming the last term of each line in the next verse.)

    THE HEPCATS UP IN HARLEM WEAR THAT
        DRAPE SHAPE   5
    COMO LOS PACHUCONES° DOWN IN L.A.
    WHERE HUISAS° IN THEIR POMPADOURS
        LOOK REAL KEEN
    ON THE DANCE FLOOR OF THE BALLROOMS
    DONDE BAILAN° SWING.

    YOU BETTER GET HEP TONIGHT   10
    AND PUT ON THAT ZOOT SUIT!

(The Downey Gang, a rival group of pachucos enters upstage left. Their quick dance step becomes a challenge to 38th Street.)

DOWNEY GANG: Downey . . . ¡Rifa!°
HENRY *(gesturing back)*: ¡Toma!°

(The music is hot. El Pachuco slides across the floor and momentarily breaks the tension. Henry warns Rafas, the leader of the Downey Gang, when he sees him push his brother Rudy.)

    ¡Rafas!
PACHUCO *(sings)*: TRUCHA, ESE LOCO, VAMOS AL
        BORLO°   15
    WEAR THAT CARLANGO, TRAMOS Y TANDO

1, Prologue. 1–8. ¿Que le watcha . . . que es puro square: You're looking at my clothes, man? / You know what, brother (sense of soul brotherhood)? / I dressed up in these duds because / We are going to drop by a play, you know? Look at my suit, man. It goes well with my shoes, hat, / shirt, pants, and coat, dude. No, you know what, you are very inexperienced. It seems to me / that you're a pure square. **25. Chicanada:** Chicano world or community. **27. más chucote que la chingada:** More pachuco-like than hell.

28. ¡Pos órale!: Well listen! **1, 1. 6. COMO LOS PACHUCONES:** Like the pachucos. **7. HUISAS:** Girls. **9. DONDE BAILAN:** Where they dance. **12. ¡Rifa!:** The best. An equivalent expression might be "Rules!" **13. ¡Toma!:** Take that (referencing the gesture). **15. TRUCHA . . . AL BORLO:** Hey, crazy man, we are going to party (dance).

DANCE WITH YOUR HUISA
DANCE TO THE BOOGIE TONIGHT!

'CAUSE THE ZOOT SUIT IS THE STYLE IN
   CALIFORNIA
20 TAMBIÉN EN COLORADO Y ARIZONA°
THEY'RE WEARING THAT TACUCHE EN EL
   PASO
Y EN TODOS LOS SALONES DE CHICAGO°

YOU BETTER GET HEP TONIGHT
AND PUT ON THAT ZOOT SUIT!

Scene 2. The Mass Arrests

(*We hear a siren, then another, and another. It sounds like gangbusters. The dance is interrupted. Couples pause on the dance floor.*)

PACHUCO: Trucha, la jura. ¡Pélenle!°

(*Pachucos start to run out, but Detectives leap onstage with drawn guns. A Cub Reporter takes flash pictures.*)

SGT. SMITH: Hold it right there, kids!
LT. EDWARDS: Everybody get your hands up!
RUDY: Watcha! This way! (*Rudy escapes with some others.*)
5 LT. EDWARDS: Stop or I'll shoot!

(*Edwards fires his revolver into the air. A number of pachucos and their girlfriends freeze. The cops round them up. Swabbie, an American sailor, and Manchuka, a Japanese-American dancer, are among them.*)

SGT. SMITH: ¡Ándale!° (*Sees Swabbie.*) You! Get out of here.
SWABBIE: What about my girl?
SGT. SMITH: Take her with you.

(*Swabbie and Manchuka exit.*)

10 HENRY: What about my girl?
LT. EDWARDS: No dice, Henry. Not this time. Back in line.
SGT. SMITH: Close it up!
LT. EDWARDS: Spread!

(*The Pachucos turn upstage in a line with their hands up. The sirens fade and give way to the sound of a teletype. The Pachucos turn and form a lineup, and the Press starts shooting pictures as he speaks.*)

15 PRESS: The City of the Angels, Monday, August 2, 1942. The *Los Angeles Examiner* Headline:
THE LINEUP (*in chorus*): Death Awakens Sleepy Lagoon (*Breath.*) L.A. Shaken by Lurid "Kid" Murder.

PRESS: The City of the Angels, Monday, August 2, 1942. The *Los Angeles Times* Headline:
THE LINEUP: One Killed, Ten Hurt in Boy Wars: (*Breath.*) Mexican Boy Gangs Operating Within City.
PRESS: The City of the Angels, August 2, 1942. *Los Angeles Herald Express* Headline:
THE LINEUP: Police Arrest Mexican Youths. Black Widow Girls° in Boy Gangs.
PRESS: The City of the Angels . . .
PACHUCO (*sharply*): El Pueblo de Nuestra Señora la Reina de los Ángeles de Porciúncula, pendejo.°
PRESS (*eyeing the Pachuco cautiously*): The *Los Angeles Daily News* Headline:
BOYS IN THE LINEUP: Police Nab 300 in Roundup.
GIRLS IN THE LINEUP: Mexican Girls Picked Up in Arrests.
LT. EDWARDS: Press Release, Los Angeles Police Department: A huge showup of nearly 300 boys and girls rounded up by the police and sheriff's deputies will be held tonight at eight o'clock in Central Jail at First and Hill Street. Victims of assault, robbery, purse snatching, and similar crimes are asked to be present for the identification of suspects.
PRESS: Lieutenant . . . ?

(*Edwards poses as the Press snaps a picture.*)

LT. EDWARDS: Thank you.
PRESS: Thank you.

(*Smith gives a signal, and the lineup moves back, forming a straight line in the rear, leaving Henry up front by himself.*)

LT. EDWARDS: Move! Turn! Out!

(*As the rear line moves off to the left following Edwards, Smith takes Henry by the arm and pulls him downstage, shoving him to the floor.*)

Scene 3. Pachuco Yo

SGT. SMITH: Okay, kid you wait here till I get back. Think you can do that? Sure you can. You pachucos are regular tough guys.

(*Smith exits. Henry sits up on the floor. El Pachuco comes forward.*)

HENRY: Bastards. (*He gets up and paces nervously. Pause.*) ¿Ese? ¿Ese?°
PACHUCO (*behind him*): ¿Qué pues, nuez?°

---

20. TAMBIÉN . . . ARIZONA: Also in Colorado and Arizona. **21–22. TACUCHE . . . CHICAGO:** Zoot suit in El Paso and in all of the dance halls of Chicago. **1, 2. 1. Trucha . . . ¡Pélenle!:** Watch out, the police. Get out of here (beat it)! **6. ¡Ándale!:** Move it!

26–27. Black Widow Girls: Female gang whose members' distinctive dress included zoot jackets, short black skirts, and black fishnet stockings. **29–30. El Pueblo de . . . pendejo:** The city of Our Lady Queen of the Angels Portiuncula, idiot (the original Spanish name for Los Angeles). **1, 3. 5. ¿Ese? ¿Ese?: Man?** (Also dude or homeboy.) **6. ¿Qué pues, nuez?:** Well what, nut?

HENRY (*turning*): Where the hell you been, ese?

PACHUCO: Checking out the barrio. Qué desmadre, ¿no?°

HENRY: What's going on, ese? This thing is big.

10   PACHUCO: The city's cracking down on pachucos, carnal.° Don't you read the newspapers? They're screaming for blood.

HENRY: All I know is they got nothing on me. I didn't do anything.

15   PACHUCO: You're Henry Reyna, ese — Hank Reyna! The snarling juvenile delinquent. The zootsuiter. The bitter young pachuco gang leader of 38th Street. That's what they got on you.

HENRY: I don't like this, ese. (*Suddenly intense.*) I
20   DON'T LIKE BEING LOCKED UP!

PACHUCO: Calmantes montes, chicas patas.° Haven't I taught you to survive? Play it cool.

HENRY: They're going to do it again, ese! They're going to charge me with some phony rap and keep me until
25   they make something stick.

PACHUCO: So what's new?

HENRY (*pause*): I'm supposed to report for the Navy tomorrow. (*The Pachuco looks at him with silent disdain.*) You don't want me to go, do you?

30   PACHUCO: Stupid move, carnal.

HENRY (*hurt and angered by Pachuco's disapproval*): I've got to do something.

PACHUCO: Then hang tough. Nobody's forcing you to do shit.

HENRY: I'm forcing me, ese — ME, you understand?

35   PACHUCO: Muy patriotic, eh?

HENRY: Yeah.

PACHUCO: Off to fight for your country.

HENRY: Why not?

PACHUCO: Because this ain't your country. Look what's
40   happening all around you. The Japs have sewed up the Pacific. Rommel is kicking ass in Egypt but the Mayor of L.A. has declared all-out war on Chicanos. On you! ¿Te curas?°

HENRY: Órale.°

45   PACHUCO: Qué mamada, ¿no?° Is that what you want to go out and die for? Wise up. These bastard paddy cops have it in for you. You're a marked man. They think you're the enemy.

HENRY (*refusing to accept it*): Screw them bastard cops!

50   PACHUCO: And as soon as the Navy finds out you're in jail again, ya estuvo, carnal.° Unfit for military duty because of your record. Think about it.

HENRY (*pause*): You got a frajo?

PACHUCO: Simón. (*He pulls out a cigarette, hands it to Henry, lights it for him. Henry is pensive.*)

55   HENRY (*smokes, laughs ironically*): I was all set to come back a hero, see? Me la rayo.° For the first time in

my life I really thought Hank Reyna was going someplace.

PACHUCO: Forget the war overseas, carnal. Your war is on the homefront.   60

HENRY (*with new resolve*): What do you mean?

PACHUCO: The barrio needs you, carnal. Fight back! Stand up to them with some style. Show the world a Chicano has balls. Hang tough. You can take it. Remember, Pachuco Yo!   65

HENRY (*assuming the style*): Con safos, carnal.°

Scene 4. *The Interrogation*

(*The Press enters, followed by Edwards and Smith.*)

PRESS (*to the audience*): Final Edition, the *Los Angeles Daily News*. The police have arrested twenty-two members of the 38th Street Gang, pending further investigation of various charges.

LT. EDWARDS: Well, son, I was hoping I wouldn't see you   5
in here again.

HENRY: Then why did you arrest me?

LT. EDWARDS: Come on, Hank, you know why you're here.

HENRY: Yeah. I'm a Mexican.   10

LT. EDWARDS: Don't give me that. How long have I known you? Since '39?

HENRY: Yeah, when you got me for stealing a car, remember?

LT. EDWARDS: All right. That was a mistake. I didn't   15
know it was your father's car. I tried to make it up to you. Didn't I help you set up the youth club?

SGT. SMITH: They turned it into a gang, Lieutenant. Everything they touch turns to shit.

LT. EDWARDS: I remember a kid just a couple of years   20
back. Head boy at the Catholic Youth Center. His idea of fun was going to the movies. What happened to that nice kid, Henry?

PRESS: He's "Gone with the Wind," trying to look like Clark Gable.   25

SGT. SMITH: Now he thinks he's Humphrey Bogart.

PACHUCO: So who are you, puto? Pat O'Brien?

LT. EDWARDS: This is the wrong time to be antisocial, son. This country's at war, and we're under strict orders to crack down on all malcontents.   30

SGT. SMITH: Starting with all pachucos and draft dodgers.

HENRY: I ain't no draft dodger.

LT. EDWARDS: I know you're not. I heard you got accepted by the Navy. Congratulations. When do you   35
report?

HENRY: Tomorrow?

SGT. SMITH: Tough break!

LT. EDWARDS: It's still not too late, you know. I could still release you in time to get sworn in.   40

---

8. Qué desmadre, ¿no?: What a mess.   10–11. carnal: Brother.
21. Calmantes . . . patas: Take it easy, Chicano.   43. ¿Te curas?: Are you charged (excited)?   44. Órale: O.K.   45. Qué mamada, ¿no?: What stupidity, right?   51. ya estuvo, carnal: That's enough, brother.   56. Me la rayo: I would be in good circumstances.

---

66. Con safos, carnal: Be safe, brother.

HENRY: If I do what?

LT. EDWARDS: Tell me, Henry, what do you know about a big gang fight last Saturday night, out at Sleepy Lagoon?

45 PACHUCO: Don't tell 'em shit.

HENRY: Which Sleepy Lagoon?

LT. EDWARDS: You mean there's more than one? Come on, Hank, I know you were out there. I've got a statement from your friends that says you were beaten up.

50 Is that true? Were you and your girl attacked?

HENRY: I don't know anything about it. Nobody's ever beat me up.

SGT. SMITH: That's a lie and you know it. Thanks to your squealer friends, we've got enough dope on you

55 to indict for murder right now.

HENRY: Murder?

SGT. SMITH: Yeah, murder. Another greaser named José Williams.

HENRY: I never heard of the bato.

60 SGT. SMITH: Yeah, sure.

LT. EDWARDS: I've been looking at your record, Hank. Petty theft, assault, burglary, and now murder. Is that what you want? The gas chamber? Play square with me. Give me a statement as to what happened at the

65 Lagoon, and I'll go to bat for you with the Navy. I promise you.

PACHUCO: If that ain't a line of gabacho bullshit, I don't know what is.

LT. EDWARDS: Well?

70 PACHUCO: Spit in his pinche face.

SGT. SMITH: Forget it, Lieutenant. You can't treat these animals like people.

LT. EDWARDS: Shut up! I'm thinking of your family, Hank. Your old man would be proud to see you in

75 the Navy. One last chance, son. What do you say?

HENRY: I ain't your son, cop.

LT. EDWARDS: All right, Reyna, have it your way.

(Edwards and Press exit.)

PACHUCO: You don't deserve it, ese, but you're going to get it anyway.

80 SGT. SMITH: All right, muchacho, it's just me and you now. I hear tell you pachucos wear these monkey suits as a kind of armor. Is that right? How's it work? This is what you zooters need — a little old-fashioned discipline.

85 HENRY: Screw you, flatfoot.

SGT. SMITH: You greasy son of a bitch. What happened at the Sleepy Lagoon? Talk! Talk! Talk!

(Smith beats Henry with a rubber sap. Henry passes out and falls to the floor, with his hands still handcuffed behind his back. Dolores his mother appears in a spot upstage, as he falls.)

DOLORES: Henry!

(Lights change. Four Pachuco Couples enter, dancing a 40s pasodoble (two-step) around Henry on the floor, as they swing in a clothesline of newspaper sheets. Music.)

PACHUCO: Get up and escape, Henry . . .
  leave reality behind   90
  with your buenas garras
  muy chamberlain°
  escape through the barrio streets of your mind
  through a neighborhood of memories
  all chuckhole lined   95
  and the love
  and the pain
  as fine as wine . . .

(Henry sits up, seeing his mother Dolores folding newspaper sheets like clothes on a clothesline.)

DOLORES: Henry?

PACHUCO: It's a lifetime ago, last Saturday night . . . be-   100
  fore Sleepy Lagoon and the big bad fight.

DOLORES: Henry!

PACHUCO: Tu mamá, carnal.°

(He recedes into the background.)

DOLORES *(at the clothesline)*: Henry, ¿hijo? Ven a
  cenar.°   105

HENRY *(gets up off the floor)*: Sorry, jefita,° I'm not hungry. Besides, I got to pick up Della. We're late for the dance.

DOLORES: Dance? In this heat? Don't you muchachos ever think of anything else? God knows I suffer la   110
  pena negra° seeing you go out every night.

HENRY: This isn't just any night, jefa.° It's my last chance to use my tacuche.°

DOLORES: Tacuche? Pero tu padre . . .°

HENRY *(revealing a stubborn streak)*: I know what mi   115
  'apá° said, 'amá. I'm going to wear it anyway.

DOLORES *(sighs, resigns herself)*: Mira, hijo.° I know you work hard for your clothes. And I know how much they mean to you. Pero por diosito santo,° I just don't know what you see en esa cochinada de   120
  "soot zoot."°

HENRY *(smiling)*: Drapes, 'amá, we call them drapes.

DOLORES *(scolding playfully)*: Ay sí, drapes, muy funny, ¿verdad?° And what do the police call them, eh? They've put you in jail so many times. ¿Sabes qué?°   125
  I'm going to send them all your clothes!

HENRY: A qué mi 'amá.° Don't worry. By this time next week, I'll be wearing my Navy blues. Okay?

1, 4. 91–92. buenas . . . chamberlain: Good threads, very high class (literally, good rags). **103. Tu mamá, carnal:** Your mother, brother. **104–105. Henry . . . cenar:** Henry, son? Come to dinner. **106. jefita:** Mom (literally, little boss, an affectionate term for a parent). **110–111. la pena negra:** Through hell (literally, the black pain). **112. jefa:** Mom. **113. tacuche:** Zoot suit. **114. Pero tu padre:** But your father. **115–116. mi 'apá:** My dad. **117. Mira, hijo:** Look, son. **119. Pero . . . santo:** But for God's sake. **120–121. en esa "soot zoot":** In that filthy thing, that "soot zoot" (mispronunciation indicating her generational distance from pachuco culture). **124. ¿verdad?:** Truthfully. **125. ¿Sabes qué:** You know what? **127. A qué mi 'amá:** That's my mom.

DOLORES: Bendito sea Dios.° I still can't believe you're
130   going off to war. I almost wish you were going back
      to jail.
HENRY: ¡Órale!°

(*Lupe Reyna, 16, enters dressed in a short skirt and baggy coat. She is followed by Della Barrios, 17, dressed more modestly. Lupe hides behind a newspaper sheet on the line.*)

LUPE: Hank! Let's go, carnal. Della's here.
HENRY: Della . . . Órale, esa.° What are you doing here?
135   I told you I was going to pick you up at your house.
DELLA: You know how my father gets.
HENRY: What happened?
DELLA: I'll tell you later.
DOLORES: Della, hija, buenas noches.° How pretty you
140   look.
DELLA: Buenas noches.

(*Dolores hugs Della, then spots Lupe hiding behind the clothesline.*)

DOLORES (*to Lupe*): ¿Oye y tú?° What's wrong with
      you? What are you doing back there.
LUPE: Nothing, 'amá.
145   DOLORES: Well, come out then.
LUPE: We're late, 'amá.
DOLORES: Come out, te digo.°

(*Lupe comes out exposing her extremely short skirt. Dolores gasps.*)

      ¡Válgame Dios!° Guadalupe, are you crazy? Why
      bother to wear anything?
150   LUPE: Ay, 'amá, it's the style. Short skirt and fingertip
      coat. Huh, Hank?
HENRY: Uh, yeah, 'amá.
DOLORES: ¿Oh sí? And how come Della doesn't get to
      wear the same style?
155   HENRY: No . . . that's different. No, chale.°
ENRIQUE (*off*): ¡VIEJA!°
DOLORES: Ándale.° Go change before your father sees
      you.
ENRIQUE: I'm home. (*Coming into the scene.*) Buenas
160   noches, everybody. (*All respond. Enrique sees Lupe.*)
      ¡Ay, jijo!° Where's the skirt?!
LUPE: It's here.
ENRIQUE: Where's the rest of it?
DOLORES: She's going to the dance.
165   ENRIQUE: ¿Y a mí qué me importa?° Go and change
      those clothes. Ándale.
LUPE: Please, 'apá?

ENRIQUE: No, señorita.
LUPE: Chihuahua,° I don't want to look like a square.
ENRIQUE: ¡Te digo que no!° I will not have my daughter   170
      looking like a . . .
DOLORES: Like a puta° . . . I mean, a pachuca.
LUPE (*pleading for help*): Hank . . .
HENRY: Do what they say, sis.
LUPE: But you let Henry wear his drapes.   175
ENRIQUE: That's different. He's a man. Es hombre.
DOLORES: Sí, that's different. You men are all alike.
      From such a stick, such a splinter: De tal palo, tal
      astillota.
ENRIQUE: Natural, muy natural, and look how he came   180
      out. ¡Bien macho! Like his father. ¿Verdad, m'ijo?°
HENRY: If you say so, jefito.°
ENRIQUE (*to Della*): Buenas noches.
DELLA: Buenas noches.
HENRY: 'Apá, this is Della Barrios.   185
ENRIQUE: Mira, mira° . . . So this is your new girlfriend,
      eh? Muy bonita.° Quite a change from the last one.
DOLORES: Ay, señor.
ENRIQUE: It's true. What was her name?
DELLA: Bertha?   190
ENRIQUE: That's the one. The one with the tattoo.
DOLORES: Este hombre.° We have company.
ENRIQUE: That reminds me. I invited the compadres to
      the house mañana.°
DOLORES: ¿Que qué?°   195
ENRIQUE: I'm buying a big keg of cerveza° to go along
      with the menudo.°
DOLORES: Oye, ¿cuál menudo?°
ENRIQUE (*cutting her off*): ¡Qué caray, mujer!° It isn't
      every day a man's son goes off to fight for his   200
      country. I should know. Della, m'ija, when I was in
      the Mexican Revolution, I was not even as old as my
      son is.
DOLORES: N'ombre,° don't start with your revolution.
      We'll be here all night.   205
HENRY: Yeah, jefe, we've got to go.
LUPE (*comes forward. She has rolled down her skirt*):
      'Apá, is this better?
ENRIQUE: Bueno. And you leave it that way.
HENRY: Órale, pues.° It's getting late. Where's Rudy?
LUPE: He's still getting ready. Rudy!   210

(*Rudy Reyna, 19, comes downstage in an old suit made into a tacuche.*)°

RUDY: Let's go everybody. I'm ready.

---

129. **Bendito sea Dios:** Blessed be God.   132. **¡Órale!:** Come on!   134. **Órale, esa:** Hey, girl.   139. **hija, buenas noches:** Honey (literally, daughter), good evening.   142. **¿Oye y tú?:** Listen and you?   147. **te digo:** I told you.   148. **¡Válgame Dios!:** Goodness, gracious!   155. **No, chale:** No, no.   156. **¡VIEJA!:** Old woman (wife).   157. **Ándale:** That's it.   161. **¡Ay, jijo!:** My goodness!   165. **¿Y . . . importa?:** What difference does that make to me?

169. **Chihuahua:** Expression of frustration.   170. **¡Te digo que no!:** I told you no!   172. **puta:** Whore.   181. **¿Verdad, m'ijo?:** Right, son?   182. **jefito:** Dad.   186. **Mira, mira:** Look, look.   187. **Muy bonita:** Very pretty.   192. **Este hombre:** This man.   194. **mañana:** Tomorrow.   195. **¿Que qué?:** What's that?   196. **cerveza:** Beer.   197. **menudo:** Tripe soup, a dish eaten at special occasions.   198. **Oye, ¿cuál menudo?:** Hey, what menudo?   199. **¡Qué caray, mujer!:** Damn it, woman!   204. **N'ombre:** No, man.   209. **Órale, pues:** Come on, then.   210. **tacuche:** Zoot suit.

ENRIQUE: Oye, oye, ¿y tú?° What are you doing with my
    coat?

RUDY: It's my tacuche, 'apá.

215 ENRIQUE: ¡Me lleva la chingada!°

DOLORES: Enrique . . . ¡por el amor de Dios!°

ENRIQUE (*to Henry*): You see what you're doing? First
    that one and now this one. (*To Rudy.*) Hijo,° don't
    go out like that. Por favor. You look like an idiot,

220   pendejo.°

RUDY: Órale, Hank. Don't I look all right?

HENRY: Nel, ese,° you look fine. Watcha. Once I leave
    for the service, you can have my tacuche. Then you
    can really be in style. ¿Cómo la ves?°

225 RUDY: Chale.° Thanks, carnal, but if I don't join the ser-
    vice myself, I'm gonna get my own tacuche.

HENRY: You sure? I'm not going to need it where I'm
    going. ¿Tú sabes?°

RUDY: Are you serious?

230 HENRY: Simón.°

RUDY: I'll think about it.

HENRY: Pos, no hay pedo, ese.°

ENRIQUE: ¿Cómo que pedo? Nel, ¿Simón?° Since when
    did we stop speaking Spanish in this house? Have

235   you no respect?

DOLORES: Muchachos, muchachos, go to your dance.

(*Henry starts upstage.*)

HENRY: Buenas noches . . .

(*Enrique holds out his hand. Henry stops, looks, and
then returns to kiss his father's hand. Then he moves to
kiss his mother and Rudy in turn kisses Enrique's hand.
Enrique says "Buenas Noches" to each of his sons.*)

HENRY: Órale, we'd better get going . . .

(*General "goodbyes" from everybody.*)

ENRIQUE (*as Rudy goes past him*): Henry! Don't let your

240   brother drink beer.

RUDY: Ay, 'apá. I can take care of myself.

DOLORES: I'll believe that when I see it. (*She kisses him
    on the nose.*)

LUPE: Ahí te watcho, 'amá.°

ENRIQUE: ¿Que qué?°

245 LUPE: I mean, I'll see you later.

(*Henry, Della, Lupe, and Rudy turn upstage. Music
starts.*)

ENRIQUE: Mujer, why didn't you let me talk?

---

212. **Oye, oye, ¿y tú?:** Listen, listen, and you?   215. **¡Me lleva
la chingada!:** I'm (vulgar term)!   216. **¡por el amor de Dios!:**
For the love of God!   218. **Hijo:** Son.   220. **pendejo:** Idiot.
222. **Nel, ese:** No, man.   224. **¿Cómo la ves?:** How does that
seem to you?   225. **Chale:** No.   228. **¿Tú sabes?:** You know?
230. **Simón:** Yes.   232. **Pos . . . ese:** Well, that's no lie, man.
233. **¿Cómo . . . Simón?:** What's this nonsense? No, Yes? (He
is upset because his sons are speaking Chicano slang.)
243. **Ahí . . . 'amá:** See you later, mom.   244. **¿Que qué?:**
What's that?

DOLORES (*sighing*): Talk, señor, talk all you want. I'm
    listening.

(*Enrique and Dolores exit up right. Rudy and Lupe exit
up left. Lights change. We hear hot dance music. Henry
and Della dance at center stage. El Pachuco sings.*)

PACHUCO: CADA SÁBADO EN LA NOCHE
    YO ME VOY A BORLOTEAR   250
    CON MI LINDA PACHUCONA
    LAS CADERAS A MENEAR°

    ELLA LE HACE MUY DE AQUELLAS
    CUANDO EMPIEZA A GUARACHAR
    AL COMPÁS DE LOS TIMBALES   255
    YO ME SIENTO PETATEAR°

(*From upstage right, three pachucos now enter in a line,
moving to the beat. They are Joey Castro, 17; Smiley
Torres, 23; and Tommy Roberts, 19, Anglo. They all
come downstage left in a diagonal.*)

    LOS CHUCOS SUAVES BAILAN RUMBA
    BAILAN LA RUMBA Y LE ZUMBAN
    BAILAN GUARACHA SABROSÓN
    EL BOTECITO Y EL DANZÓN!°   260

(*Chorus repeats, the music fades. Henry laughs and happily embraces Della.*)

Scene 5. The Press

(*Lights change. El Pachuco escorts Della off right. The
Press appears at upstage center.*)

PRESS: *Los Angeles Times:* August 8, 1942.

(*A Newsboy enters, lugging in two more bundles of
newspapers, hawking them as he goes. People of various
walks of life enter at intervals and buy newspapers.
They arrange themselves in the background reading.*)

NEWSBOY: EXTRA! EXTRAAA! READ ALL ABOUT
    IT. SPECIAL SESSION OF L.A. COUNTY GRAND
    JURY CONVENES. D.A. CHARGES CONSPIRACY
    IN SLEEPY LAGOON MURDER. EXTRAAA!   5

(*A Cub Reporter emerges and goes to the Press, as Lieutenant Edwards enters.*)

CUB REPORTER: Hey, here comes Edwards!

(*Edwards is besieged by the Press, joined by Alice
Bloomfield, 26, a woman reporter.*)

249–252. **CADA . . . MENEAR:** Every Saturday night / I go to
party (dance) / With my beautiful pachuca / Shaking her hips.
253–256. **ELLA . . . PETATEAR:** She seems very fine / When
she begins to dance / To the rhythm of the drums / I feel like
I'm dying.   257–260. **LOS CHUCOS . . . DANZÓN!:** The
fine pachucos dance the rumba / Dance the rumba and they get
high / They dance the dance (similar to the flamenco) deliciously / The botecito (literally little jail or little boat; the name
of a dance) / And the danzón (a Cuban dance)!

PRESS: How about it, Lieutenant? What's the real scoop on the Sleepy Lagoon? Sex, violence . . .

CUB REPORTER: Marijuana?

10 NEWSBOY: Read all about it! Mexican Crime Wave Engulfs L.A.

LT. EDWARDS: Slums breed crime, fellas. That's your story.

ALICE: Lieutenant. What exactly is the Sleepy Lagoon?

15 CUB REPORTER: A great tune by Harry James, doll. Wanna dance?

(*Alice ignores the Cub.*)

LT. EDWARDS: It's a reservoir. An old abandoned gravel pit, really. It's on a ranch between here and Long Beach. Serves as a swimming hole for the younger
20 Mexican kids.

ALICE: Because they're not allowed to swim in the public plunges?

PRESS: What paper are you with, lady? The *Daily Worker*?

25 LT. EDWARDS: It also doubles as a sort of lovers' lane at night — which is why the gangs fight over it. Now they've finally murdered somebody.

NEWSBOY: EXTRA! EXTRA! ZOOT-SUITED GOONS OF SLEEPY LAGOON!

30 LT. EDWARDS: But we're not going to mollycoddle these youngsters any more. And you can quote me on that.

PRESS: One final question, Lieutenant. What about the 38th Street Gang — weren't you the first to arrest Henry Reyna?

35 LT. EDWARDS: I was. And I noticed right away the kid had great leadership potential. However . . .

PRESS: Yes?

LT. EDWARDS: You can't change the spots on a leopard.

PRESS: Thank you, sir.

(*People with newspapers crush them and throw them down as they exit. Edwards turns and exits. Alice turns toward Henry for a moment.*)

40 NEWSBOY: EXTRA, EXTRA. READ ALL ABOUT THE MEXICAN BABY GANGSTERS. EXTRA, EXTRA.

(*The Press and Cub Reporter rush out happily to file their stories. The Newsboy leaves, hawking his papers. Alice exits, with determination. Far upstage, Enrique enters with a rolling garbage can. He is a street sweeper. During the next scene he silently sweeps up the newspapers, pausing at the last to read one of the news stories.*)

Scene 6. *The People's Lawyer*

JOEY: ¡Chale, ese, chale! Qué pinche agüite.°

SMILEY: Mexican Baby Gangsters?!

TOMMY: Zoot-suited goons! I knew it was coming. Every time the D.A. farts, they throw us in the can.

1, 6. 1. **¡Chale . . . agüite:** No, man, no! What a damned nuisance.

SMILEY: Pos, qué chingados,° Hank. I can't believe this. 5
Are they really going to pin us with a murder rap?
I've got a wife and kid, man!

JOEY: Well, there's one good thing anyway. I bet you know that we've made the headlines. Everybody knows we got the toughest gang in town. 10

TOMMY: Listen to this pip-squeak. The biggest heist he ever pulled was a Tootsie Roll.

JOEY (*grabbing his privates*): Here's your Tootsie Roll, ese.

TOMMY: What, that? Get my microscope, Smiley. 15

JOEY: Why don't you come here and take a little bite, joto.

TOMMY: Joto? Who you calling a joto, maricón?°

JOEY: You, white boy. Did I ever tell you, you got the finest little duck ass in the world. 20

TOMMY: No, you didn't tell me that, culero.°

(*Joey and Tommy start sparring.*)

SMILEY (*furious*): Why don't you batos knock it off?

HENRY (*cool*): Cálmenla.°

SMILEY: ¡Pinches chavalos!° (*The batos stop.*)

JOEY: We're just cabuliando, ese. 25

TOMMY: Simón, ese. Horsing around. (*He gives Joey a final punch.*)

SMILEY (*with deep self-pity*): I'm getting too old for this pedo,° Hank. All this farting around con esos chavalillos.°

HENRY: Relax, carnal. No te agüites.° 30

SMILEY: You and me have been through a lot, Hank. Parties, chingazos,° jail. When you said let's join the pachucada,° I joined the pachucada. You and me started the 38th, bato. I followed you even after my kid was born, but what now, carnal? This pinche 35 pedo° is serious.

TOMMY: He's right, Hank. They indicted the whole gang.

JOEY: Yeah, you know the only one who ain't here is Rudy.

(*Henry turns sharply.*)

He was at the Sleepy Lagoon too, ese. Throwing 40 chingazos.°

HENRY: Yeah, but the cops don't know that, do they? Unless one of us turned stoolie.

JOEY: Hey, ese, don't look at me. They beat the shit out of me, but that's all they got. Shit. 45

TOMMY: That's all you got to give. (*Laughs.*)

HENRY: Okay! Let's keep it that way. I don't want my carnalillo° pulled into this. And if anybody asks

5. **Pos, qué chingados:** Anyhow, what (vulgar term). 18. **joto, maricón:** Homosexual (derogatory). 21. **culero:** (Vulgar term), son-of-a-bitch. 23. **Cálmenla:** Cool it. 24. **¡Pinches chavalos!:** Damned inexperienced boys. 28. **pedo:** Nonsense. 28–29. **con esos chavalillos:** With these little neophytes. 30. **No te agüites:** Don't let it get to you. 32. **chingazos:** Fights. 33. **pachucada:** World of the pachucos; pachuco population. 35–36. **pinche pedo:** Damned nonsense. 41. **chingazos:** Punches. 48. **carnalillo:** Little brother.

about him, you batos don't know nothing. You get
50   me?
      SMILEY: Simón.
      TOMMY: Crazy.
      JOEY (*throwing his palms out*): Say, Jackson, I'm cool.
          You know that.
55   HENRY: There's not a single paddy we can trust.
      TOMMY: Hey, ese, what about me?
      HENRY: You know what I mean.
      TOMMY: No, I don't know what you mean. I'm here
          with the rest of yous.
60   JOEY: Yeah, but you'll be the first one out, cabrón.°
      TOMMY: Gimme a break, maníaco. ¡Yo soy pachuco!°
      HENRY: Relax, ese. Nobody's getting personal with you.
          Don't I let you take out my carnala?° Well, don't I?
      TOMMY: Simón.
65   HENRY: That's because you respect my family. The rest
          of them paddies are after our ass.
      PACHUCO: Talk about paddies, ese, you got company.

      (*George Shearer enters upstage right and comes down.
      He is a middle-aged lawyer, strong and athletic, but with
      the slightly frazzled look of a people's lawyer.*)

      GEORGE: Hi, boys.
      HENRY: Trucha!°
70   GEORGE: My name is George Shearer. I've been retained
          by your parents to handle your case. Can we sit and
          talk for a little bit?

      (*Pause. The Boys eye George suspiciously. He slides a
      newspaper bundle a few feet upstage.*)

      PACHUCO: Better check him out, ese. He looks like a
          cop.
75   HENRY (*to the Guys, sotto voce*): Pónganse al alba. Este
          me huele a chota.°
      GEORGE: What was that? Did you say I could sit down?
          Thank you. (*He pulls a bundle upstage. He sits.*)
          Okay, let me get your names straight first. Who's José
80   Castro?
      JOEY: Right here, ese. What do you want to know?
      GEORGE: We'll get to that. Ismael Torres?
      SMILEY (*deadpan*): That's me. But they call me Smiley.
      GEORGE (*a wide grin*): Smiley? I see. You must be
85   Thomas Roberts.
      TOMMY: I ain't Zoot Suit Yokum.
      GEORGE: Which means you must be Henry Reyna.
      HENRY: What if I am. Who are you?
      GEORGE: I already told you, my name's George Shearer.
90   Your parents asked me to come.
      HENRY: Oh yeah? Where did they get the money for a
          lawyer?
      GEORGE: I'm a people's lawyer, Henry.
      SMILEY: People's lawyer?
95   JOEY: Simón, we're people.

      TOMMY: At least they didn't send no animal's lawyer.
      HENRY: So what does that mean? You doing this for free
          or what?
      GEORGE (*surprise turning to amusement*): I try not to
          work for free, if I can help it, but I do sometimes. In   100
          this case, I expect to be paid for my services.
      HENRY: So who's paying you? For what? And how
          much?
      GEORGE: Hey, hey, hold on there. I'm supposed to ask
          the questions. You're the one going on trial, not me.   105
      PACHUCO: Don't let him throw you, ese.
      GEORGE: I sat in on part of the Grand Jury. It was quite
          a farce, wasn't it? Murder one indictment and all.
      SMILEY: You think we stand a chance?
      GEORGE: There's always a chance, Smiley. That's what   110
          trials are for.
      PACHUCO: He didn't answer your question, ese.
      HENRY: You still didn't answer my question, mister.
          Who's paying you? And how much?
      GEORGE (*getting slightly peeved*): Well, Henry, it's really   115
          none of your damned business.

      (*The Boys react.*)

      But for whatever it's worth, I'll tell you a little story.
      The first murder case I ever tried, and won inciden-
      tally, was for a Filipino. I was paid exactly three dol-
      lars and fifty cents plus a pack of Lucky Strike   120
      cigarettes, and a note for a thousand dollars — never
      redeemed. Does that answer your question?
      HENRY: How do we know you're really a lawyer?
      GEORGE: How do I know you're Henry Reyna? What
          do you really mean, son? Do you think I'm a cop?   125
      HENRY: Maybe.
      GEORGE: What are you trying to hide from the cops?
          Murder?

      (*The Boys react.*)

      All right! Aside from your parents, I've been called
      into this case by a citizens' committee that's forming   130
      in your behalf, Henry. In spite of evidence to the con-
      trary, there are some people out there who don't
      want to see you get the shaft.
      HENRY: ¿Sabes qué, mister?° Don't do us any favors.
      GEORGE (*starting to leave*): All right, you want another   135
          lawyer? I'll talk to the Public Defender's office.
      JOEY (*grabbing his briefcase*): Hey, wait a minute, ese.
          Where are you going?
      TOMMY: De cinco se le va a volar la tapa.°
      JOEY: Nel, este bolillo no sabe nada.°   140
      GEORGE (*exploding*): All right, kids, cut the crap!
      SMILEY (*grabs his briefcase and crosses to Henry*): Let's
          give him a break, Hank. (*Smiley hands the briefcase
          to George.*)

      ---

      60. **cabrón:** Son-of-a-bitch. **61. maníaco . . . pachuco!:**
      Maniac. I'm a pachuco! **63. carnala:** Sister. **69. Trucha!:**
      Heads up! (Watch out!) **75–76. Pónganse . . . chota:** Put
      yourselves on alert. I will uncover this cop.

      134. **¿Sabes qué, mister?:** You know what, mister? **139. De
      cincho . . . tapa:** It's a cinch he's going to blow his top.
      140. Nel . . . nada: No, this Anglo (derogatory) doesn't know a
      thing.

GEORGE: Thank you. (*He starts to exit. Stops.*) You
145 know, you're making a big mistake. I wonder if you
know who your friends are? You boys are about to
get a mass trial. You know what that is? Well, it's a
new one on me too. The Grand Jury has indicted you
all on the same identical crime. Not just you four.
150 The whole so-called 38th Street Gang. And you
know who the main target is? You, Henry, because
they're saying you're the ringleader. (*Looks around
at the Guys.*) And I suppose you are. But you're leading your buddies here down a dead-end street. The
155 D.A.'s coming after you, son, and he's going to put
you and your whole gang right into the gas chamber.

(*George turns to leave. Smiley panics. Joey and Tommy
react with him.*)

SMILEY/JOEY/TOMMY (*all together*): Gas chamber! But
we didn't do nothing! We're innocent!
HENRY: ¡Cálmenla!°

(*The batos stop in their tracks.*)

160 Okay. Say we believe you're a lawyer, what does that
prove? The press has already tried and convicted us.
Think you can change that?
GEORGE: Probably not. But then, public opinion comes
and goes, Henry. What matters is our system of jus-
165 tice. I believe it works, however slowly the wheels
may grind. It could be a long uphill fight, fellas, but
we can make it. I know we can. I've promised your
parents the best defense I'm capable of. The question
is, Henry, will you trust me?
170 HENRY: Why should I? You're a gringo.
GEORGE (*calmly, deliberately*): ¿Cómo sabes?°
TOMMY (*shocked*): Hey, you speak Spanish?
GEORGE: Más o menos.°
JOEY: You mean you understood us a while ago?
175 GEORGE: More or less.
JOEY (*embarrassed*): ¡Híjole, qué gacho, ese!°
GEORGE: Don't worry. I'm not much on your pachuco
slang. The problem seems to be that I look like an
Anglo to you. What if I were to tell you that I had
180 Spanish blood in my veins? That my roots go back to
Spain, just like yours? What if I'm an Arab? What if
I'm a Jew? What difference does it make? The ques-
tion is, will you let me help you?

(*Pause. Henry glances at the Pachuco.*)

PACHUCO: ¡Chale!
185 HENRY (*pause*): Okay!
SMILEY: Me too!
JOEY: Same here!
TOMMY: ¡Órale!
GEORGE (*eagerly*): Okay! Let's go to work. I want to
190 know exactly what happened right from the begin-
ning. (*George sits down and opens his briefcase.*)

---

159. **¡Cálmenla!:** Cool it. 171. **¿Cómo sabes?:** How do you
know? 173. **Más o menos:** More or less. 176. **¡Híjole . . .
ese!:** Heavens, how bad is that!

HENRY: Well, I think the pedo° really started at the
dance last Saturday night . . .

(*El Pachuco snaps his fingers and we hear dance music.
Lights change. George exits.*)

Scene 7. *The Saturday Night Dance*

(*Swabbie and Manchuka come running onstage as the
barrio dance begins to take shape. Henry and the batos
move upstage to join other Pachucos and Pachucas
coming in. Henry joins Della Barrios; Joey teams up
with Bertha Villarreal, Tommy picks up Lupe Reyna;
and Smiley escorts his wife Elena Torres. They represent
the 38th Street neighborhood. Also entering the dance
comes the Downey Gang, looking mean. Rudy stands
upstage, in the background, drinking a bottle of beer. El
Pachuco sings.*)

PACHUCO: CUANDO SALGO YO A BAILAR
YO ME PONGO MUY CATRÍN
LAS HUISITAS TODAS GRITAN, DADDY
VAMOS A BAILAR EL SWING!°

(*The Couples dance. A lively swing number. The music
comes to a natural break and shifts into a slow number.
Bertha approaches Henry and Della downstage on the
dance floor.*)

BERTHA: Ese, ¡surote!° How about a dance for old time's   5
sake? No te hagas gacho.°
HENRY (*slow dancing with Della*): Sorry, Bertha.
BERTHA: Is this your new huisa? This little fly chick?
DELLA: Listen, Bertha . . .
HENRY (*stops her*): Chale. She's just jealous. Beat it,   10
Bertha.
BERTHA: Beat it yourself. Mira. You got no hold on me,
cabrón. Not any more. I'm as free as a bird.
SMILEY (*coming up*): Ese, Hank, that's the Downey Gang
in the corner. You think they're looking for trouble?   15
HENRY: There's only a couple of them.
BERTHA: That's all we need.
SMILEY: Want me to alert the batos?
HENRY: Nel, be cool.
BERTHA: Be cool? Huy, yu, yui. Forget it, Smiley. Since   20
he joined the Navy, this bato forgot the difference
between being cool and being cool-O.

(*She laughs and turns but Henry grabs her angrily by the
arm. Bertha pulls free and walks away cool and tough.
The music changes and the beat picks up. El Pachuco
sings as the Couples dance.*)

PACHUCO: CUANDO VOY AL VACILÓN
Y ME METO YO A UN SALÓN

---

192. **pedo:** Nonsense. **1, 7. 1–4. CUANDO . . . EL SWING!:**
When I go out dancing / I get dressed up very stylishly / The
girls all yell, Daddy / We're going to dance that swing! **5. Ese,
¡surote!:** Hey dude, two-timer! **6. No te hagas gacho:** Don't
become a bad man.

25 LAS CHAVALAS GRITAN, PAPI VENTE
    VAMOS A BAILAR DANSÓN!°

*(The dance turns Latin. The music comes to another
natural break and holds. Lupe approaches Henry on the
dance floor.)*

LUPE: Hank. Rudy's at it again. He's been drinking since
we got here.
HENRY *(glancing over at Rudy)*: He's okay, sis, let the
30   carnal enjoy himself.
RUDY *(staggering over)*: ¡Ese, carnal!
HENRY: What you say, brother?
RUDY: I'm flying high, Jackson. Feeling good.
LUPE: Rudy, if you go home drunk again, mi 'apá's
35   going to use you for a punching bag.

(Rudy kisses her on the cheek and moves on.)

DELLA: How are you feeling?
HENRY: Okay.
DELLA: Still thinking about Bertha?
HENRY: Chale, ¿qué traes?° Listen, you want to go out
40   to the Sleepy Lagoon? I've got something to tell you.
DELLA: What?
HENRY: Later, later.
LUPE: You better tell Rudy to stop drinking.
HENRY: Relax, sis. If he gets too drunk, I'll carry him
45   home. *(Music picks up again. El Pachuco sings a
    third verse.)*
PACHUCO: TOCAN MAMBO SABROSÓN
    SE ALBOROTA EL CORAZÓN
    Y CON UNA CHAVALONA VAMOS
    VAMOS A BAILAR EL MAMBO°

*(The Couples do the mambo. In the background, Rudy
gets into an argument with Rafas, the leader of the
Downey Gang. A fight breaks out as the music comes
to a natural break. Rafas pushes Rudy, half drunk, onto
the floor.)*

50 RAFAS: ¡Y a ti qué te importa, puto!°
    RUDY *(he falls)*: ¡Cabrón!
    HENRY *(reacting immediately)*: Hey!

*(The whole dance crowd tenses up immediately, split-
ting into separate camps. Batos from 38th clearly out-
number the Guys from Downey.)*

RAFAS: He started it, ese. El comenzó a chingar conmigo.°
RUDY: You chicken shit, ese! Tú me haces la puñeta,
55   ¡pirujo!°

RAFAS: Come over here and say that, puto!
HENRY *(pulling Rudy behind him)*: ¡Agüítala, carnal!°
    (Faces Rafas.) You're a little out of your territory,
    ¿que no Rafas?
RAFAS: It's a barrio dance, ese. We're from the barrio. 60
HENRY: You're from Downey.
RAFAS: Vale madre.° ¡Downey Rifa!
DOWNEY GANG: ¡SIMÓN!
RAFAS: What are you going to do about it?
HENRY: I'm going to kick your ass. 65

(The Two Sides start to attack each other.)

    ¡Cálmenla!

(All stop.)

RAFAS *(pulls out a switchblade)*: You and how many
    batos?
HENRY: Just me and you, cabrón. That's my carnalillo
    you started pushing around, see? And nobody chinga 70
    con mi familia° without answering to me, ese! Hank
    Reyna! *(He pulls out another switchblade.)*
BERTHA: ALL-RIGHT!
HENRY: Let's see if you can push me around like you did
    my little brother, ese. Come on . . . COME ON! 75

*(They knife fight. Henry moves in fast. Recoiling, Rafas
falls to the floor. Henry's blade is at his throat. El
Pachuco snaps his fingers. Everyone freezes.)*

PACHUCO: Qué mamada,° Hank. That's exactly what the
    play needs right now. Two more Mexicans killing
    each other. Watcha . . . Everybody's looking at you.
HENRY *(looks out at the audience)*: Don't give me that
    bullshit. Either I kill him or he kills me. 80
PACHUCO: That's exactly what they paid to see. Think
    about it.

(El Pachuco snaps again. Everybody unfreezes.)

HENRY *(kicks Rafas)*: Get out of here. ¡Píntate!°
BERTHA: What?
GÜERA *(Rafas's girlfriend runs forward)*: Rafas. ¡Vámo- 85
    nos!° *(She is stopped by other Downey batos.)*
RAFAS: Está suave.° I'll see you later.
HENRY: Whenever you want, cabrón.

*(The Downey Gang retreats, as the 38th razzes them all
the way out. Insults are exchanged. Bertha shouts
"¡Chinga tu madre!" and they are gone. The 38th
whoops in victory.)*

SMILEY: Órale, you did it, ese! ¡Se escamaron todos!°
TOMMY: We sure chased those jotos out of here. 90
BERTHA: I could have beat the shit out of those two
    rucas.°

23–26. CUANDO . . . DANSÓN!: When I go to the fiesta /
And I get to the dancehall / The girls yell, Daddy come / We
are going to dance the dansón! 39. Chale, ¿qué traes?: No,
what's bothering you? 46–49. TOCAN . . . MAMBO: They
play mambo deliciously / The heart falls in love (gets excited) /
With a sweetheart we go / We go to dance the mambo.
50. ¡Y . . . puto!: And what does it matter to you, male prostitute? 53. El comenzó . . . conmigo: He started to fight with
me. 54–55. Tú me . . . ¡pirujo!: I'm better than you are,
homosexual (derogatory)!

57. ¡Agüítala, carnal!: Calm down, brother! 62. Vale madre:
That doesn't mean anything. 70–71. chinga con mi familia: (Vulgar term) with my family. 76. Qué mamada: What
stupidity. 83. ¡Píntate!: Scram! 85–86. ¡Vámonos!: Let's
go! 87. Está suave: That's cool. 89. ¡Se escamaron todos!:
They all got scared! 92. rucas: Homegirls.

JOEY: That pinche° Rafas is yellow without his gang, ese.

95 LUPE: So why didn't you jump out there?

JOEY: Chale, Rudy ain't my baby brother.

RUDY (*drunk*): Who you calling a baby, pendejo? I'll show you who's a baby!

JOEY: Be cool, ese.

100 TOMMY: Man, you're lucky your brother was here.

BERTHA: Why? He didn't do nothing. The old Hank would have slit Rafas' belly like a fat pig.

HENRY: Shut your mouth, Bertha!

RUDY: ¿Por qué, carnal?° You backed down, ese. I could

105 have taken that sucker on by myself.

HENRY: That's enough, Rudy. You're drunk.

DELLA: Hank, what if Rafas comes back with all his gang?

HENRY (*reclaiming his leadership*): We'll kill the sons of

110 bitches.

JOEY: ¡Órale! ¡La 38th rifa!°

(*Music. Everybody gets back with furious energy. El Pachuco sings.*)

PACHUCO: DE LOS BAILES QUE MENTÉ
        Y EL BOLERO Y EL BEGUÍN
        DE TODOS LOS BAILES JUNTOS
115   ME GUSTA BAILAR EL SWING! HEY!°

(*The dance ends with a group exclamation: HEY!*)

Scene 8. *El Día de la Raza*

(*The Press enters upstage level, pushing a small hand truck piled high with newspaper bundles. The batos and rucas on the dance floor freeze in their final dance positions. El Pachuco is the only one who relaxes and moves.*)

PRESS: October 12, 1942: Columbus Day. Four Hundred and Fiftieth Anniversary of the Discovery of America. Headlines!

(*In their places, the Couples now stand straight and recite a headline before exiting. As they do so, the Press moves the bundles of newspapers on the floor to outline the four corners of a jail cell.*)

SMILEY/ELENA: President Roosevelt Salutes Good Neigh-
5   bors In Latin America.

(*Smiley and Elena exit.*)

TOMMY/LUPE: British Begin Drive to Oust Rommel From North Africa.

---

93. **pinche:** Damned.   104. **¿Por qué, carnal?:** Why, brother?
111. **¡Órale! ¡La 38th rifa!:** Right on! The 38th (street gang) rules!   112–15. **DE LOS . . . HEY!:** Of the dances that I mentioned / And the bolero and the beguine / Of all the dances joined together / I like to dance swing! Hey!

(*Tommy and Lupe exit.*)

RUDY/CHOLO: Japs In Death Grip On Pacific Isles.

(*Rudy and Cholo exit. Press tosses another bundle.*)

ZOOTER/LITTLE BLUE: Web Of Zoot Crime Spreads.

(*Zooter and Little Blue exit.*)

MANCHUKA/SWABBIE: U.S. Marines Land Bridgehead   10
On Guadalcanal.

(*Manchuka and Swabbie exit.*)

JOEY/BERTHA: First Mexican Braceros Arrive in U.S.A.

(*Joey and Bertha exit.*)

DELLA: Sleepy Lagoon Murder Trial Opens Tomorrow.

(*Della and the Press exit. As they exit, George and Alice enter upstage left. Henry is center, in a "cell" outlined by four newspaper bundles left by the Press.*)

GEORGE: Henry? How you doing, son? Listen, I've brought somebody with me that wants very much to   15
meet you. I thought you wouldn't mind.

(*Alice crosses to Henry.*)

ALICE: Hello! My name is Alice Bloomfield and I'm a reporter from the *Daily People's World*.

GEORGE: And . . . And I might add, a red hot member of the ad hoc committee that's fighting for you guys.   20

ALICE: Oh, George! I'd hardly call it fighting, for Pete's sake. This struggle has just barely begun. But we're sure going to win it, aren't we, Henry?

HENRY: I doubt it.

GEORGE: Oh come on, Henry. How about it, son? You   25
all set for tomorrow? Anything you need, anything I can get for you?

HENRY: Yeah. What about the clean clothes you promised me? I can't go to court looking like this.

GEORGE: You mean they didn't give them to you?   30

HENRY: What?

GEORGE: Your mother dropped them off two days ago. Clean pants, shirt, socks, underwear, the works. I cleared it with the Sheriff last week.

HENRY: They haven't given me nothing.   35

GEORGE: I'm beginning to smell something around here.

HENRY: Look, George, I don't like being like this. I ain't dirty. Go do something, man!

GEORGE: Calm down. Take it easy, son. I'll check on it right now. Oh! Uh, Alice?   40

ALICE: I'll be okay, George.

GEORGE: I'll be right back.   (*He exits.*)

ALICE (*pulling out a pad and pencil*): Now that I have you all to myself, mind if I ask you a couple of questions?   45

HENRY: I got nothing to say.

ALICE: How do you know? I haven't asked you anything yet. Relax. I'm from the progressive press. Okay?

(*Henry stares at her, not knowing quite how to react. Alice sits on a bundle and crosses her goodlooking legs. Henry concentrates on that.*)

50 Now. The regular press is saying the Pachuco Crime Wave is fascist inspired — any thoughts about that?
HENRY (*bluntly*): No.
ALICE: What about the American Japanese? Is it true they are directing the subversive activities of the pachucos from inside the relocation camps?

(*Henry turns to The Pachuco with a questioning look.*)

55 PACHUCO: This one's all yours, ese.
HENRY: Look, lady, I don't know what the hell you're talking about.
ALICE: I'm talking about you, Henry Reyna. And what the regular press has been saying. Are you aware
60 you're in here just because some bigshot up in San Simeon wants to sell more papers? It's true.
HENRY: So?
ALICE: So, he's the man who started this Mexican Crime Wave stuff. Then the police got into the act. Get the
65 picture? Somebody is using you as a patsy.
HENRY (*his machismo insulted*): Who you calling a patsy?
ALICE: I'm sorry, but it's true.
HENRY (*backing her up*): What makes you so goddamned smart?
ALICE (*starting to get scared and trying not to show it*):
70 I'm a reporter. It's my business to know.
PACHUCO: Puro pedo. She's just a dumb broad only good for you know what.
HENRY: Look, Miss Bloomfield, just leave me alone, all right?

(*Henry moves away. Alice takes a deep breath.*)

75 ALICE: Look, let's back up and start all over, okay? Hello. My name is Alice Bloomfield, and I'm not a reporter. I'm just somebody that wants very much to be your friend. (*Pause. With sincere feeling.*) Can you believe that?
80 HENRY: Why should I?
ALICE: Because I'm with you.
HENRY: Oh, yeah? Then how come you ain't in jail with me?
ALICE (*holding her head up*): We are all in jail, Henry.
85 Some of us just don't know it.
PACHUCO: Mmm, pues. No comment.

(*Pause. Henry stares at her, trying to figure her out. Alice tries a softer approach.*)

ALICE: Believe it or not, I was born in Los Angeles just like you. But for some strange reason I grew up here, not knowing very much about Mexicans at all. I'm
90 just trying to learn.
HENRY (*intrigued, but cynical*): What?
ALICE: Little details. Like that tattooed cross on your hand. Is that the sign of the pachuco?

(*Henry covers his right hand with an automatic reflex, then he realizes what he has done.*)

HENRY (*smiles to himself, embarrassed*): Órale.
95 ALICE: Did I embarrass you? I'm sorry. Your mother happened to mention it.
HENRY (*surprised*): My mother? You talked to my jefita?

ALICE (*with enthusiasm*): Yes! And your father and Lupe and Rudy. The whole family gave me a helluva interview. But your mother was sensational. I espe-
100 cially liked her story about the midnight raid. How the police rushed into your house with drawn guns, looking for you on some trumped up charge, and how your father told them you were already in jail . . . God, I would have paid to have seen the
105 cops' faces.
HENRY (*hiding his sentiment*): Don't believe anything my jefa tells you. (*Then quickly.*) There's a lot she doesn't know. I'm no angel.
ALICE: I'll just bet you're not. But you have been taken
110 in for suspicion a dozen times, kept in jail for a few days, then released for lack of evidence. And it's all stayed on your juvenile record.
HENRY: Yeah, well I ain't no punk, see.
ALICE: I know. You're an excellent mechanic. And you
115 fix all the guys' cars. Well, at least you're not one of the lumpen proletariat.
HENRY: The lumpen what?
ALICE: Skip it. Let's just say you're a classic social victim.
HENRY: Bullshit.
120 ALICE (*pause. A serious question*): Are you saying you're guilty?
HENRY: Of what?
ALICE: The Sleepy Lagoon Murder.
HENRY: What if I am?
125 ALICE: Are you?
HENRY (*pause, a serious answer*): Chale. I've pulled a lot of shit in my time, but I didn't do that.

(*George re-enters flushed and angry, trying to conceal his frustration.*)

GEORGE: Henry, I'm sorry, but dammit, something's coming off here, and the clothes have been withheld.
130 I'll have to bring it up in court.
HENRY: In court?
GEORGE: They've left me no choice.
ALICE: What's going on?
HENRY: It's a set up, George. Another lousy set up!
135 GEORGE: It's just the beginning, son. Nobody said this was going to be a fair fight. Well, if they're going to fight dirty, so am I. Legally, but dirty. Trust me.
ALICE (*passionately*): Henry, no matter what happens in the trial, I want you to know I believe you're inno-
140 cent. Remember that when you look out, and it looks like some sort of lynch mob. Some of us . . . a lot of us . . . are right there with you.
GEORGE: Okay, Alice, let's scram. I've got a million things to do. Henry, see you tomorrow under the big
145 top, son. Good luck, son.
ALICE: Thumbs up, Henry, we're going to beat this rap!

(*Alice and George exit. El Pachuco watches them go, then turns to Henry.*)

PACHUCO: "Thumbs up, Henry, we're going to beat this rap." You really think you're going to beat this one,
150 ese?

HENRY: I don't want to think about it.

PACHUCO: You've got to think about it, Hank. Everybody's playing you for a sucker. Wake up, carnal!

HENRY: Look, bato, what the hell do you expect me to do?

PACHUCO: Hang tough. (*Grabs his scrotum.*) Stop going soft.

HENRY: Who's going soft?

PACHUCO (*incisively*): You're hoping for something that isn't going to happen, ese. These paddies are leading you by the nose. Do you really believe you stand a chance?

HENRY (*stubborn all the more*): Yeah. I think I got a chance.

PACHUCO: Just because that white broad says so?

HENRY: Nel, ese, just because Hank Reyna says so.

PACHUCO: The classic social victim, eh?

HENRY (*furious but keeping his cool*): Mira, ese. Hank Reyna's no loser. I'm coming out of this on top. ¿Me entiendes,° Mendez? (*He walks away with a pachuco gait.*)

PACHUCO (*forcefully*): Don't try to out-pachuco ME, ese! We'll see who comes out on top. (*He picks up a bundle of newspapers and throws it upstage center. It lands with a thud.*) Let's go to court!

Scene 9. *Opening of the Trial*

(*Music. The Judge's bench, made up of more newspaper bundles piled squarely on a four-wheeled hand truck is pushed in by the batos. The Press rides it in, holding the State and Federal Flags. A Bailiff puts in place a hand cart: the Judge's throne. From the sides, spectators enter, including Henry's family and friends: Alice, Della, Bertha, Elena.*)

PRESS: The largest mass trial in the history of Los Angeles County opens this morning in the Superior Court at ten A.M. The infamous Sleepy Lagoon Murder case involves sixty-six charges against twenty-two defendants with seven lawyers pleading for the defense, two for the prosecution. The District Attorney estimates that over a hundred witnesses will be called and has sworn — I quote — "to put an end to Mexican baby gangsterism." End quote.

BAILIFF (*bangs a gavel on the bench*): The Superior Court of the State of California. In and For the County of Los Angeles. Department forty-three. The honorable F. W. Charles, presiding. All rise!

(*Judge Charles enters. All rise. El Pachuco squats. The Judge is played by the same actor that portrays Edwards.*)

JUDGE: Please be seated.

169–170. **¿Me entiendes:** You understand me?

(*All sit. Pachuco stands.*)

Call this case, Bailiff.

BAILIFF (*reading from a sheet*): The people of the State of California Versus Henry Reyna, Ismael Torres, Thomas Roberts, Jose Castro and eighteen other . . . (*slight hesitation*) . . . pa-coo-cos.

JUDGE: Is Counsel for the Defense present?

GEORGE (*rises*): Yes, Your Honor.

JUDGE: Please proceed. (*Signals the Press.*)

PRESS: Your Honor . . .

GEORGE (*moving in immediately*): If the Court please, it was reported to me on Friday that the District Attorney has absolutely forbidden the Sheriff's Office to permit these boys to have clean clothes or haircuts. Now, it's been three months since the boys were arrested . . .

PRESS (*jumping in*): Your Honor, there is testimony we expect to develop that the 38th Street Gang are characterized by their style of haircuts . . .

GEORGE: Three months, Your Honor.

PRESS: . . . the thick heavy heads of hair, the ducktail comb, the pachuco pants . . .

GEORGE: Your Honor, I can only infer that the Prosecution . . . is trying to make these boys look disreputable, like mobsters.

PRESS: Their appearance is distinctive, Your Honor. Essential to the case.

GEORGE: You are trying to exploit the fact that these boys look foreign in appearance! Yet clothes like these are being worn by kids all over America.

PRESS: Your Honor . . .

JUDGE (*bangs the gavel*): I don't believe we will have any difficulty if their clothing becomes dirty.

GEORGE: What about the haircuts, Your Honor?

JUDGE (*ruling*): The zoot haircuts will be retained throughout the trial for purposes of identification of defendants by witnesses.

PACHUCO: You hear that one, ese? Listen to it again.

(*Snaps. Judge repeats automatically.*)

JUDGE: The zoot haircuts will be retained throughout the trial for purposes of identification of defendants by witnesses.

PACHUCO: He wants to be sure we know who you are.

JUDGE: It has been brought to my attention the Jury is having trouble telling one boy from another, so I am going to rule the defendants stand each time their names are mentioned.

GEORGE: I object. If the Prosecution makes an accusation, it will mean self-incrimination.

JUDGE (*pause*): Not necessarily. (*To Press.*) Please proceed.

GEORGE (*still trying to set the stage*): Then if the Court please, might I request that my clients be allowed to sit with me during the trial so that I might consult with them?

JUDGE: Request denied.

GEORGE: May I inquire of Your Honor, if the defendant
70   Thomas Robert might rise from his seat and walk
        over to counsel table so as to consult with me during
        the trial?
JUDGE: I certainly will not permit it.
GEORGE: You will not?
75 JUDGE: No. This is a small courtroom, Mr. Shearer. We
        can't have twenty-two defendants all over the place.
GEORGE: Then I object. On the grounds that that is a
        denial of the rights guaranteed all defendants by both
        the federal and state constitutions.
80 JUDGE: Well, that is your opinion. (*Gavel.*) Call your
        first witness.
PRESS: The prosecution calls Lieutenant Sam Edwards
        of the Los Angeles Police Department.
PACHUCO (*snaps, does double take on Judge*): You know
85   what. We've already heard from that bato. Let's get
        on with the defense.

(*Snaps. Press sits. George stands.*)

GEORGE: The defense calls Adela Barrios.
BAILIFF (*calling out*): Adeela Barreeos to the stand.

(*Della Barrios comes forth out of the spectators. Bertha
leans forward.*)

BERTHA (*among the spectators*): Don't tell 'em nothing.

(*The Bailiff swears in Della silently.*)

90 PACHUCO: Look at your gang. They do look like mob-
        sters. Se watchan bien gachos.°

(*Henry looks at the batos, who are sprawled out in their
places.*)

HENRY (*under his breath*): Come on, Batos, sit up.
SMILEY: We're tired, Hank.
JOEY: My butt is sore.
95 TOMMY: Yeah, look at the soft chairs the jury's got.
HENRY: What did you expect? They're trying to make us
        look bad. Come on! Straighten up.
SMILEY: Simón, batos, Hank is right.
JOEY: ¡Más alba nalga!°
100 TOMMY: Put some class on your ass.
HENRY: Sit up! (*They all sit up.*)
GEORGE: State your name please.
DELLA: Adela Barrios. (*She sits.*)
GEORGE: Miss Barrios, were you with Henry Reyna on
105   the night of August 1, 1942?
DELLA: Yes.
JUDGE (*to Henry*): Please stand.

(*Henry stands.*)

GEORGE: Please tell the court what transpired that night.
DELLA (*pause, takes a breath*): Well, after the dance that
110   Saturday night, Henry and I drove out to the Sleepy
        Lagoon about eleven-thirty.

1, 9. 91. **Se watchan bien gachos:** They look like real bad guys.
99. **¡Más alba nalga!:** Sit up (literally, more alert rump)!

Scene 10. *Sleepy Lagoon*

(*Music: THE HARRY JAMES THEME. El Pachuco
creates the scene. The light changes. We see a shimmering pattern of light on the floor growing to the music. It
becomes the image of the Lagoon. As the music soars to
a trumpet solo, Henry reaches out to Della, and she
glides to her feet.*)

DELLA: There was a full moon that night, and as we
        drove up to the Lagoon we noticed right away the
        place was empty . . .

(*A pair of headlights silently pulls in from the black
background upstage center.*)

        Henry parked the car on the bank of the reservoir
        and we relaxed.   5

(*Headlights go off.*)

        It was such a warm, beautiful night, and the sky was
        so full of stars, we couldn't just sit in the car. So we
        got out, and Henry took my hand . . .

(*Henry stands and takes Della's hand.*)

        We went for a walk around the Lagoon. Neither of
        us said anything at first, so the only sounds we could   10
        hear were the crickets and the frogs . . .

(*Sounds of crickets and frogs, then music faintly in the
background.*)

        When we got to the other side of the reservoir, we
        began to hear music, so I asked Henry, what's that?
HENRY: Sounds like they're having a party.
DELLA: Where?   15
HENRY: Over at the Williams' Ranch. See the house
        lights.
DELLA: Who lives there?
HENRY: A couple of families. Mexicanos. I think they
        work on the ranch. You know, their name used to be   20
        Gonzales, but they changed it to Williams.
DELLA: Why?
HENRY: I don't know. Maybe they think it gives 'em
        more class.

(*We hear Mexican music.*)

        Ay, jijo.° They're probably celebrating a wedding or   25
        something.
DELLA: As soon as he said wedding, he stopped talking
        and we both knew why. He had something on his
        mind, something he was trying to tell me without
        sounding like a square.   30
HENRY: Della . . . what are you going to do if I don't
        come back from the war?
DELLA: That wasn't the question I was expecting, so I
        answered something dumb, like I don't know, what's
        going to keep you from coming back?   35

1, 10. 25. **Ay, jijo:** Heavens.

HENRY: Maybe wanting too much out of life, see? Ever since I was a kid, I've had this feeling like there's a big party going on someplace, and I'm invited, but I don't know how to get there. And I want to get there
40　so bad, I'll even risk my life to make it. Sounds crazy, huh?

(*Della and Henry kiss. They embrace and then Henry speaks haltingly.*)

　If I get back from the war . . . will you marry me?
DELLA: Yes! (*She embraces him and almost causes them to topple over.*)
HENRY: ¡Órale! You'll knock us into the Lagoon. Listen,
45　what about your old man? He ain't going to like you marrying me.
DELLA: I know. But I don't care. I'll go to hell with you if you want me to.
HENRY: ¿Sabes qué?° I'm going to give you the biggest
50　pachuco wedding L.A. has ever seen.

(*Another pair of headlights comes in from the left. Della goes back to her narration.*)

DELLA: Just then another car pulled up to the Lagoon. It was Rafas and some drunk guys in a gang from Downey. They got out and started to bust the windows on Henry's car. Henry yelled at them, and they
55　started cussing at us. I told Henry not to say anything, but he cussed them back!
HENRY: You stay here, Della.
DELLA: Henry, no! Don't go down there! Please don't go down there!
60　HENRY: Can't you hear what they're doing to my car?
DELLA: There's too many of them. They'll kill you!
HENRY: ¡Chale!

(*Henry turns and runs upstage, where he stops in a freeze.*)

DELLA: Henry! Henry ran down the back of the Lagoon and attacked the gang by himself. Rafas had about
65　ten guys with him and they jumped on Henry like a pack of dogs. He fought them off as long as he could, then they threw him on the ground hard and kicked him until he passed out . . .

(*Headlights pull off.*)

　After they left, I ran down to Henry and held him in
70　my arms until he came to. And I could tell he was hurt, but the first thing he said was . . .
PACHUCO: Let's go into town and get the guys.

(*Music: Glen Miller's "In the Mood." Henry turns to the batos and they stand. Smiley, Joey, and Tommy are joined by Rudy, Bertha, Lupe, and Elena, who enter from the side. They turn downstage in a body and freeze.*)

49. ¿Sabes qué?: You know what?

DELLA: It took us about an hour to go into town and come back. We got to the Lagoon with about eight cars, but the Downey gang wasn't there.　75
JOEY: Órale, ¿pos qué pasó?° Nobody here.
SMILEY: Then let's go to Downey.
THE BOYS (*ad lib*): Let's go!
HENRY: ¡Chale! ¡Chale!

(*Pause. They all stop.*)

　Ya estuvo.° Everybody go home.　80

(*A collective groan from The Boys.*)

　Go home!
DELLA: That's when we heard music coming from the Williams' Ranch again. We didn't know Rafas and his gang had been there too, causing trouble. So
85　when Joey said . . .
JOEY: Hey, there's a party! Bertha, let's crash it.
DELLA: We all went there yelling and laughing.

(*The group of batos turns upstage in a mimetic freeze.*)

　At the Williams' Ranch they saw us coming and thought we were the Downey Gang coming back again . . . They attacked us.　90

(*The group now mimes a series of tableaus showing the fight.*)

　An old man ran out of the house with a kitchen knife and Henry had to hit him. Then a girl grabbed me by the hair and in a second everybody was fighting! People were grabbing sticks from the fence, bottles, anything! It all happened so fast, we didn't know　95
what hit us, but Henry said let's go!
HENRY: ¡Vámonos!° Let's get out of here.
DELLA: And we started to back off . . . Before we got to the cars, I saw something out of the corner of my eye . . . It was a guy. He was hitting a man on the　100
ground with a big stick.

(*El Pachuco mimes this action.*)

　Henry called to him, but he wouldn't stop. He wouldn't stop . . . He wouldn't stop . . . He wouldn't stop . . .

(*Della in tears, holds Henry in her arms. The batos and rucas start moving back to their places, quietly.*)

　Driving back in the car, everybody was quiet, like　105
nothing had happened. We didn't know José Williams had died at the party that night and that the guys would be arrested the next day for murder.

(*Henry separates from her and goes back to stand in his place. Della resumes the witness stand.*)

76. Órale, ¿pos qué pasó?: Hey man, well what happened?
80. Ya estuvo: That's enough.　97. ¡Vámonos!: Let's go!

Scene 11. The Conclusion of the Trial

(*Lights change back to courtroom, as Judge Charles bangs his gavel. Everyone is seated back in place.*)

GEORGE: Your witness.

PRESS (*springing to the attack*): You say Henry Reyna hit the man with his fist. (*Indicates Henry standing.*) Is this the Henry Reyna?

5 DELLA: Yes. I mean, no. He's Henry, but he didn't . . .

PRESS: Please be seated.

(*Henry sits.*)

Now, after Henry Reyna hit the old man with his closed fist, is that when he pulled the knife?

DELLA: The old man had the knife.

10 PRESS: So Henry pulled one out, too?

GEORGE (*rises*): Your Honor, I object to counsel leading the witness.

PRESS: I am not leading the witness.

GEORGE: You are.

15 PRESS: I certainly am not.

GEORGE: Yes, you are.

JUDGE: I would suggest, Mr. Shearer, that you look up during the noon hour just what a leading question is.

GEORGE: If the Court please, I am going to assign that
20 remark of Your Honor as misconduct.

JUDGE (*to Press*): Proceed.

(*George crosses back to his chair.*)

PRESS: Where was Smiley Torres during all this? Is it not true that Smiley Torres grabbed a woman by the hair and kicked her to the ground? Will Smiley Torres
25 please stand? (*Smiley stands.*) Is this the man?

DELLA: Yes, it's Smiley, but he . . .

PRESS: Please be seated.

(*Smiley sits. Press picks up a two-by-four.*)

Wasn't José Castro carrying a club of some kind?

GEORGE (*on his feet again*): Your Honor, I object! No
30 such club was ever found. The Prosecution is implying that this two-by-four is associated with my client in some way.

PRESS: I'm not implying anything, Your Honor, I'm merely using this stick as an illustration.

35 JUDGE: Objection overruled.

PRESS: Will José Castro please stand?

(*Joey stands.*)

Is this the man who was carrying a club?

(*Della refuses to answer.*)

Answer the question please.

DELLA: I refuse.

40 PRESS: You are under oath. You can't refuse.

JUDGE: Answer the question, young lady.

DELLA: I refuse.

PRESS: Is this the man you saw hitting another man with a two-by-four? Your Honor . . .

JUDGE: I order you to answer the question. 45

GEORGE: Your Honor, I object. The witness is obviously afraid her testimony will be manipulated by the Prosecution.

PRESS: May I remind the court that we have a signed confession from one José Castro taken while in jail . . . 50

GEORGE: I object. Those were not confessions! Those are statements. They are false and untrue, Your Honor, obtained through beatings and coercion of the defendants by the police!

JUDGE: I believe the technical term is admissions, Mr. 55
Prosecutor. Objection sustained.

(*Applause from spectators.*)

At the next outburst, I will clear this courtroom. Go on, Mr. Prosecutor.

PRESS: Sit down please.

(*Joey sits. George goes back to his seat.*)

Is Henry Reyna the leader of the 38th Street Gang? 60

(*Henry stands.*)

DELLA: Not in the sense that you mean.

PRESS: Did Henry Reyna, pachuco ringleader of the 38th Street Gang, willfully murder José Williams?

DELLA: No. They attacked us first.

PRESS: I didn't ask for your comment. 65

DELLA: But they did, they thought we were the Downey gang.

PRESS: Just answer my questions.

DELLA: We were just defending ourselves so we could get out of there. 70

PRESS: Your Honor, will you instruct the witness to be cooperative.

JUDGE: I must caution you, young lady, answer the questions or I'll hold you in contempt.

PRESS: Was this the Henry Reyna who was carrying a 75
three-foot lead pipe?

GEORGE: I object!

JUDGE: Overruled.

DELLA: No.

PRESS: Was it a two-foot lead pipe? 80

GEORGE: Objection!

JUDGE: Overruled.

DELLA: No!

PRESS: Did he kick a woman to the ground?

DELLA: No, he was hurt from the beating. 85

PRESS: Sit down.

(*Henry sits.*)

Did Tommy Roberts rip stakes from a fence and hit a man on the ground?

GEORGE: Objection!

JUDGE: Overruled. 90

DELLA: I never saw him do anything.

PRESS: Did Joey Castro have a gun?

GEORGE: Objection!

JUDGE: Overruled.

(*Joey stands.*)

95 PRESS: Sit down.

(*Joey sits.*)

Did Henry Reyna have a blackjack in his hand?

(*Henry stands.*)

DELLA: No.
PRESS: A switchblade knife?
DELLA: No.
100 PRESS: A two-by-four?
DELLA: No.
PRESS: Did he run over to José Williams, hit him on the head, and kill him?
DELLA: He could barely walk, how could he run to any
105 place?
PRESS (*moving in for the kill*): Did Smiley Torres?

(*The batos stand and sit as their names are mentioned.*)

Did Joey Castro? Did Tommy Roberts? Did Henry Reyna? Did Smiley Torres? Did Henry Reyna? Did Henry Reyna? Did Henry Reyna kill José Williams?!
110 DELLA: No, no, no!
GEORGE (*on his feet again*): Your Honor, I object! The Prosecution is pulling out objects from all over the place, none of which were found at Sleepy Lagoon, and none of which have been proven to be associated
115 with my clients in any way.
JUDGE: Overruled.
GEORGE: If Your Honor please, I wish to make an assignment of misconduct!
JUDGE: We have only had one this morning. We might as
120 well have another now.
GEORGE: You have it, Your Honor.
JUDGE: One more remark like that and I'll hold you in contempt. Quite frankly, Mr. Shearer, I am getting rather tired of your repeated useless objections.
125 GEORGE: I have not made useless objections.
JUDGE: I am sorry. Somebody is using ventriloquism. We have a Charlie McCarthy using Mr. Shearer's voice.
GEORGE: I am going to assign that remark of Your Honor as misconduct.
130 JUDGE: Fine. I would feel rather bad if you did not make an assignment of misconduct at least three times every session. (*Gavel.*) Witness is excused.

(*Della stands.*)

However, I am going to remand her to the custody of the Ventura State School for Girls for a period of one
135 year . . .
HENRY: What?
JUDGE: . . . to be held there as a juvenile ward of the State. Bailiff?
GEORGE: If the court please . . . If the court please . . .

(*Bailiff crosses to Della and takes her off left.*)

140 JUDGE: Court is in recess until tomorrow morning.

(*Judge retires. Press exits. Henry meets George halfway across center stage. The rest of the batos stand and stretch in the background.*)

GEORGE: Now, Henry, I want you to listen to me, please. You've got to remember he's the judge, Hank. And this is his courtroom.
HENRY: But he's making jokes, George, and we're get-   145
ting screwed!
GEORGE: I know. I can't blame you for being bitter, but believe me, we'll get him.
HENRY: I thought you said we had a chance.
GEORGE (*passionately*): We do! This case is going to be   150
won on appeal.
HENRY: Appeal? You mean you already know we're going to lose?
PACHUCO: So what's new?
GEORGE: Don't you see, Henry, Judge Charles is hang-   155
ing himself as we go. I've cited over a hundred separate cases of misconduct by the bench, and it's all gone into the record. Prejudicial error, denial of due process, inadmissible evidence, hearsay . . .
HENRY: ¿Sabes qué, George? Don't tell me any more.

(*Henry turns. Alice and Enrique approach him.*)

ALICE: Henry . . . ?   160
HENRY (*turns furiously*): I don't want to hear it, Alice!

(*Henry sees Enrique, but neither father nor son can think of anything to say. Henry goes back upstage.*)

ALICE: George, is there anything we can do?
GEORGE: No. He's bitter, and he has a right to be.

(*Judge Charles pounds his gavel. All go back to their places and sit.*)

JUDGE: We'll now hear the Prosecution's concluding statement.   165
PRESS: Your Honor, ladies and gentlemen of the jury. What you have before you is a dilemma of our times. The City of Los Angeles is caught in the midst of the biggest, most terrifying crime wave in its history. A crime wave that threatens to engulf the very founda-   170
tions of our civic well-being. We are not only dealing with the violent death of one José Williams in a drunken barrio brawl. We are dealing with a threat and danger to our children, our families, our homes. Set these pachucos free, and you shall unleash the   175
forces of anarchy and destruction in our society. Set these pachucos free and you will turn them into heroes. Others just like them must be watching us at this very moment. What nefarious schemes can they be hatching in their twisted minds? Rape, drugs,   180
assault, more violence? Who shall be their next innocent victim in some dark alley way, on some lonely street? You? You? Your loved ones? No! Henry Reyna and his Latin juvenile cohorts are not heroes. They are criminals, and they must be stopped. The   185
specific details of this murder are irrelevant before the overwhelming danger of the pachuco in our

190 midst. I ask you to find these zoot-suited gangsters guilty of murder and to put them in the gas chamber where they belong.

(The Press sits down. George rises and takes center stage.)

GEORGE: Ladies and gentlemen of the jury, you have heard me object to the conduct of this trial. I have tried my best to defend what is most precious in our American society — a society now at war against the
195 forces of racial intolerance and totalitarian injustice. The prosecution has not provided one witness that actually saw, with his own eyes, who actually murdered José Williams. These boys are not the Downey gang, yet the evidence suggests that they were
200 attacked because the people at the ranch thought they were. Henry Reyna and Della Barrios were victims of the same bunch. Yes, they might have been spoiling for a revenge — who wouldn't under the circumstances — but not with the intent to conspire to
205 commit murder. So how did José Williams die? Was it an accident? Was it manslaughter? Was it murder? Perhaps we may never know. All the prosecution has been able to prove is that these boys wear long hair and zoot suits. And all the rest has been circumstan-
210 tial evidence, hearsay, and war hysteria. The prosecution has tried to lead you to believe that they are some kind of inhuman gangsters. Yet they are Americans. Find them guilty of anything more serious than a juvenile bout of fisticuffs, and you will condemn
215 all American youth. Find them guilty of murder, and you will murder the spirit of racial justice in America. *(George sits down.)*
JUDGE: The jury will retire to consider its verdict.

(The Press stands and starts to exit with the Bailiff. El Pachuco snaps. All freeze.)

PACHUCO: Chale. Let's have it.

(Snaps again. The Press turns and comes back again.)

220 JUDGE: Has the jury reached a verdict?
PRESS: We have, Your Honor.
JUDGE: How say you?
PRESS: We find the defendants guilty of murder in the first and second degrees.
225 JUDGE: The defendants will rise.

(The batos come to their feet.)

Henry Reyna, José Castro, Thomas Roberts, Ismael Torres, and so forth. You have been tried by a jury of your peers and found guilty of murder in the first and second degrees. The Law prescribes the capital pun-
230 ishment for this offense. However, in view of your youth and in consideration of your families, it is hereby the judgment of this court that you be sentenced to life imprisonment . . .
RUDY: No!
235 JUDGE: . . . and sent to the State Penitentiary at San Quentin. Court adjourned.

(Gavel. Judge exits. Dolores, Enrique, and family go to Henry. Bertha crosses to Joey; Lupe goes to Tommy. Elena crosses to Smiley. George and Alice talk.)

DOLORES: ¡Hijo mío! ¡Hijo de mi alma!°

(Bailiff comes down with a pair of handcuffs.)

BAILIFF: Okay, boys.

(He puts the cuffs on Henry. Rudy comes up.)

RUDY: ¿Carnal?

(Henry looks at the Bailiff, who gives him a nod of permission to spend a moment with Rudy. Henry embraces him with the cuffs on. George and Alice approach.)

240 GEORGE: Henry? I can't pretend to know how you feel, son. I just want you to know that our fight has just begun.
ALICE: We may have lost this decision, but we're going to appeal immediately. We're going to stand behind you until your name is absolutely clear. I swear it!   245
PACHUCO: What the hell are they going to do, ese? They just sent you to prison for life. Once a Mexican goes in, he never comes out.
BAILIFF: Boys?

(The Boys exit with the Bailiff. As they go Enrique calls after them.)

250 ENRIQUE *(holding back tears)*: Hijo. Be a man, hijo. *(Then to his family.)* Vámonos . . . ¡Vámonos!

(The family leaves and El Pachuco slowly walks to center stage.)

Pachuco: We're going to take a short break right now, so you can all go out and take a leak, smoke a frajo. Ahí los watcho.

(He exits up center and the newspaper backdrop comes down.)

ACT 2 • *Prologue*

(Lights up and El Pachuco emerges from the shadows. The newspaper drop is still down. Music.)

PACHUCO: Watchamos pachucos
los batos°
the dudes
street-corner warriors who fought and moved
like unknown soldiers in wars of their own   5
El Pueblo de Los was the battle zone
from Sleepy Lagoon to the Zoot Suit wars
when Marines and Sailors made their scores
stomping like Nazis on East L.A. . . .

---

237. ¡Hijo mío! ¡Hijo de mi alma!: My son! Son of my soul!
2, Prologue. 1–2. Watchamos . . . batos: We are watching pachucos, the dudes.

10   pero ¿saben qué?°
        That's later in the play. Let's pick it up in prison.
        We'll begin this scene
        inside the walls of San Quintín.

Scene 1. San Quentin

(*A bell rings as the drop rises. Henry, Joey, Smiley, and Tommy enter accompanied by a Guard.*)

GUARD: All right, people, lock up.

(*Boys move downstage in four directions. They step into "cells" simply marked by shadows of bars on the floor in their separate places. Newspaper handcarts rest on the floor as cots. Sound of cell doors closing. The Guard paces back and forth upstage level.*)

HENRY: San Quentin, California
        March 3, 1943
        Dear Family:
5   Coming in from the yard in the evening, we are
        quickly locked up in our cells. Then the clank and
        locking of the doors leaves one with a rather empty
        feeling. You are standing up to the iron door, waiting
        for the guard to come along and take the count, lis-
10   tening as his footsteps fade away in the distance. By
        this time there is a tense stillness that seems to crawl
        over the cellblock. You realize you are alone, so all
        alone.
PACHUCO: This all sounds rather tragic, doesn't it?
15 HENRY: But here comes the guard again, and he calls out
        your number in a loud voice . . .
    GUARD (*calls numbers; Boys call name*): 24-545
    HENRY: Reyna!
    GUARD: 24-546
20 JOEY: Castro!
    GUARD: 24-547
    TOMMY: Roberts!
    GUARD: 24-548
    SMILEY: Torres!

(*Guard passes through dropping letters and exits up left.*)

25 HENRY: You jump to your feet, stooping to pick up the
        letter . . .
    JOEY (*excited*): Or perhaps several letters . . .
    TOMMY: You are really excited as you take the letters
        from the envelope.
30 SMILEY: The censor has already broken the seal when he
        reads it.
    HENRY: You make a mental observation to see if you
        recognize the handwriting on the envelope.
    SMILEY (*anxious*): It's always nice to hear from home . . .
35 JOEY: Or a close comrade . . .
    TOMMY: Friends that you know on the outside . . .
    HENRY: Or perhaps it's from a stranger.

2, Prologue. 10. pero ¿saben qué?: But what did they know?

(*Pause. Spotlight at upstage center. Alice walks in with casual clothes on. Her hair is in pigtails, and she wears a pair of drapes. She is cheerful.*)

Scene 2. The Letters

Dear Boys,
Announcing the publication (mimeograph) of the Ap-
peal News, your very own newsletter, to be sent to you
twice a month for the purpose of keeping you reliably
informed of everything — the progress of the Sleeping   5
Lagoon Defense Committee (we have a name now) and,
of course, the matter of your appeal.
Signed,
Your editor
Alice Bloomfield.   10

(*Music. "Perdido" by Duke Ellington. Alice steps down and sits on the lip of the upstage level. The Boys start swinging the bat, dribbling the basketball, shadow-boxing, and exercising. Alice mimes typing movements and we hear the sounds of a typewriter. Music fades. Alice rises.*)

ALICE: The Appeal News Volume I, Number I, April
        7, 1943.
        Boys,
        You can, you must, and you will help us on the out-
        side by what you do on the inside. Don't forget, what   15
        you do affects others. You have no control over that.
        When the time comes, let us be proud to show the
        record.
        Signed,
        Your editor.   20

(*Music up again. The Boys go through their activities. Alice moves downstage center and the music fades.*)

SMILEY (*stepping toward her*): April 10, 1943
        Dear Miss Bloomfield,
        I have discovered from my wife that you are con-
        ducting door-to-door fund-raising campaigns in Los
        Angeles. She doesn't want to tell you, but she feels   25
        bad about doing such a thing. It's not our custom to
        go around the neighborhoods asking for money.
ALICE (*turning toward Smiley*): Dear Smiley,
        Of course, I understand your feelings . . .
SMILEY (*adamant*): I don't want my wife going around   30
        begging.
ALICE: It isn't begging — it's fund-raising.
SMILEY: I don't care what you call it. If that's what it's
        going to take, count me out.
ALICE: All right. I won't bother your wife if she really 35
        doesn't want me to. Okay?

(*Smiley looks at her and turns back to his upstage posi-tion. Music. The batos move again. Tommy crosses to Alice. Another fade.*)

TOMMY: April 18, 1943
        Dear Alice,

40 Trying to find the words and expression to thank you for your efforts in behalf of myself and the rest of the batos makes me realize what a meager vocabulary I possess . . .
ALICE: Dear Tommy,
Your vocabulary is just fine. Better than most.
45 TOMMY: Most what?
ALICE: People.
TOMMY (*glances at Henry*): Uh, listen, Alice. I don't want to be treated any different than the rest of the batos, see? And don't expect me to talk to you like
50 some square Anglo, some pinche gabacho.° You just better find out what it means to be Chicano, and it better be pretty damn quick.
ALICE: Look, Tommy, I didn't . . .
TOMMY: I know what you're trying to do for us and
55 that's reet, see? Shit. Most paddies would probably like to see us locked up for good. I been in jail a couple of times before, but never nothing this deep. Strange, ain't it, the trial in Los? I don't really know what happened or why. I don't give a shit what the
60 papers said. We didn't do half the things I read about. I also know that I'm in here just because I hung around with Mexicans . . . or pachucos. Well, just remember this, Alicia . . . I grew up right alongside most of these batos, and I'm pachuco too. Simón,
65 esa, you better believe it!

(*Music up. Movement. Tommy returns to his position. Henry stands. Alice turns toward him, but he walks over to The Pachuco, giving her his back.*)

JOEY (*stepping forward anxiously*): May 1, 1943
Dear Alice . . . Darling!
I can't help but spend my time thinking about you. How about sending us your retra — that is, your
70 photograph? Even though Tommy would like one of Rita Hayworth — he's always chasing Mexican skirts (Ha! Ha!) — I'd prefer to see your sweet face any day.
ALICE (*directly to him*): Dear Joey,
75 Thank you so much. I really appreciated receiving your letter.
JOEY: That's all reet, Grandma! You mind if I call you Grandma?
ALICE: Oh, no.
80 JOEY: Eres una ruca de aquellas.°
ALICE: I'm a what?
JOEY: Ruca. A fine chick.
ALICE (*pronounces the word*): Ruca?
JOEY: De aquellas. (*Makes a cool gesture, palms out at hip level.*)
85 ALICE (*imitating him*): De aquellas.
JOEY: All reet! You got it. (*Pause.*) P.S. Did you forget the photograph?
ALICE (*she hands it to him*): Dearest Joey,

Of course not. Here it is, attached to a copy of the Appeal News. I'm afraid it's not exactly a pin-up.
90 JOEY (*kissing the photo*): Alice, honey, you're a doll!

(*Joey shows the photo to Tommy, then Smiley, who is curious enough to come into the circle. Alice looks at Henry, but he continues to ignore her.*)

ALICE (*back at center*): The Appeal News, Volume I, Number 3, May 5, 1943.
Dear Boys,
95 Feeling that el Cinco de Mayo is a very appropriate day — the CIO radio program, "Our Daily Bread," is devoting the entire time this evening to a discussion of discrimination against Mexicans in general and against you guys in particular.

(*Music up. The repartee between Alice and the batos is now friendly and warm. Even Smiley is smiling with Alice. They check out her "drapes."*)

Scene 3. The Incorrigible Pachuco

(*Henry stands at downstage left, looks at the group, then decides to speak.*)

HENRY: May 17, 1943
Dear Miss Bloomfield,
I understand you're coming up to Q this weekend, and I would like to talk to you — in private. Can you arrange it?
5

(*The batos turn away, taking a hint.*)

ALICE (*eagerly*): Yes, yes, I can. What can I do for you, Henry?

(*Henry and Alice step forward toward each other. El Pachuco moves in.*)

HENRY: For me? ¡Ni madre!°
ALICE (*puzzled*): I don't understand.
HENRY: I wanted you to be the first to know, Alice. I'm 10 dropping out of the appeal.
ALICE (*unbelieving*): You're what?
HENRY: I'm bailing out, esa. Dropping out of the case, see?
ALICE: Henry, you can't! 15
HENRY: Why can't I?
ALICE: Because you'll destroy our whole case! If we don't present a united front, how can we ask the public to support us?
HENRY: That's your problem. I never asked for their 20 support. Just count me out.
ALICE (*getting nervous, anxious*): Henry, please, think about what you're saying. If you drop out, the rest of the boys will probably go with you. How can you even think of dropping out of the appeal? What about 25 George and all the people that have contributed their

2, 2. 50. **pinche gabacho:** Damned Anglo (derogatory).
80. Eres . . . aquellas: You are a fine chick.

2, 3. 8. **¡Ni madre!:** It doesn't matter, or, it's not worth a damn.

time and money in the past few months? You just can't quit on them!

HENRY: Oh no? Just watch me.

30 ALICE: If you felt this way, why didn't you tell me before?

HENRY: Why didn't you ask me? You think you can just move in and defend anybody you feel like? When did I ever ask you to start a defense committee for me? Or a newspaper? Or a fund-raising drive and all that

35 other shit? I don't need defending, esa. I can take care of myself.

ALICE: But what about the trial, the sentence. They gave you life imprisonment?

HENRY: It's my life!

40 ALICE: Henry, honestly — are you kidding me?

HENRY: You think so?

ALICE: But you've seen me coming and going. Writing to you, speaking for you, traveling up and down the state. You must have known I was doing it for you.

45 Nothing has come before my involvement, my attachment, my passion for this case. My boys have been everything to me.

HENRY: My boys? My boys! What the hell are we — your personal property? Well, let me set you straight,

50 lady, I ain't your boy.

ALICE: You know I never meant it that way.

HENRY: You think I haven't seen through your bullshit? Always so concerned. Come on, boys. Speak out, boys. Stand up for your people. Well, you leave my

55 people out of this! Can't you understand that?

ALICE: No, I can't understand that.

HENRY: You're just using Mexicans to play politics.

ALICE: Henry, that's the worst thing anyone has ever said to me.

60 HENRY: Who are you going to help next — the Colored People?

ALICE: No, as a matter of fact, I've already helped the Colored People. What are you going to do next — go to the gas chamber?

65 HENRY: What the hell do you care?

ALICE: I don't!

HENRY: Then get the hell out of here!

ALICE (*furiously*): You think you're the only one who doesn't want to be bothered? You ought to try work-

70 ing in the Sleepy Lagoon defense office for a few months. All the haggling, the petty arguments, the lack of cooperation. I've wanted to quit a thousand times. What the hell am I doing here? They're coming at me from all sides. You're too sentimental and emo-

75 tional about this, Alice. You're too cold hearted, Alice. You're collecting money and turning it over to the lawyers, while the families are going hungry. They're saying you can't be trusted because you're a Communist, because you're a Jew. Okay! If that's the

80 way they feel about me, then to hell with them! I hate them too. I hate their language, I hate their enchiladas, and I hate their goddamned mariachi music!

(*Pause. They look at each other. Henry smiles, then Alice — feeling foolish — and they both break out laughing.*)

HENRY: All right! Now you sound like you mean it.

ALICE: I do.

85 HENRY: Okay! Now we're talking straight.

ALICE: I guess I have been sounding like some square paddy chick. But, you haven't exactly been Mister Cool yourself . . . ese.

HENRY: So, let's say we're even Steven.

90 ALICE: Fair enough. What now?

HENRY: Why don't we bury the hatchet, you know what I mean?

ALICE: Can I tell George you'll go on with the appeal?

HENRY: Yeah. I know there's a lot of people out there

95 who are willing and trying to help us. People who feel that our conviction was an injustice. People like George . . . and you. Well, the next time you see them, tell them Hank Reyna sends his thanks.

ALICE: Why don't you tell them?

100 HENRY: You getting wise with me again?

ALICE: If you write an article — and I know you can — we'll publish it in the *People's World*. What do you say?

PACHUCO: Article! Pos who told you, you could write,

105 ese?

HENRY (*laughs*): Chale.

ALICE: I'm serious. Why don't you give it a try?

HENRY: I'll think about it. (*Pause.*) Listen, you think you and I could write each other . . . outside the news-

110 letter?

ALICE: Sure.

HENRY: Then it's a deal. (*They shake hands.*)

ALICE: I'm glad we're going to be communicating. I think we're going to be very good friends.

(*Alice lifts her hands to Henry's shoulder in a gesture of comradeship. Henry follows her hand, putting his on top of hers.*)

115 HENRY: You think so?

ALICE: I know so.

GUARD: Time, miss.

ALICE: I gotta go. Think about the article, okay? (*She turns to the Boys.*) I gotta go, boys.

120 JOEY: Goodbye, Grandma! Say hello to Bertha.

SMILEY: And to my wife!

TOMMY: Give my love to Lupe!

GUARD: Time!

ALICE: I've got to go. Goodbye, goodbye.

(*Alice exits, escorted by the Guard upstage left. As she goes, Joey calls after her.*)

125 JOEY: See you, Grandma.

TOMMY (*turning to Joey and Smiley*): She loves me.

PACHUCO: Have you forgotten what happened at the trial? You think the Appeals Court is any different? Some paddy judge sitting in the same fat-ass judg-

130 ment of your fate.

HENRY: Come on, ese, give me a break!

PACHUCO: One break, coming up!

(*He snaps his fingers. The Guard blows his whistle.*)

GUARD: Rec time!

Jorge Galvan as El Pachuco in *Zoot Suit* at the San Diego Repertory Theatre, 1997.

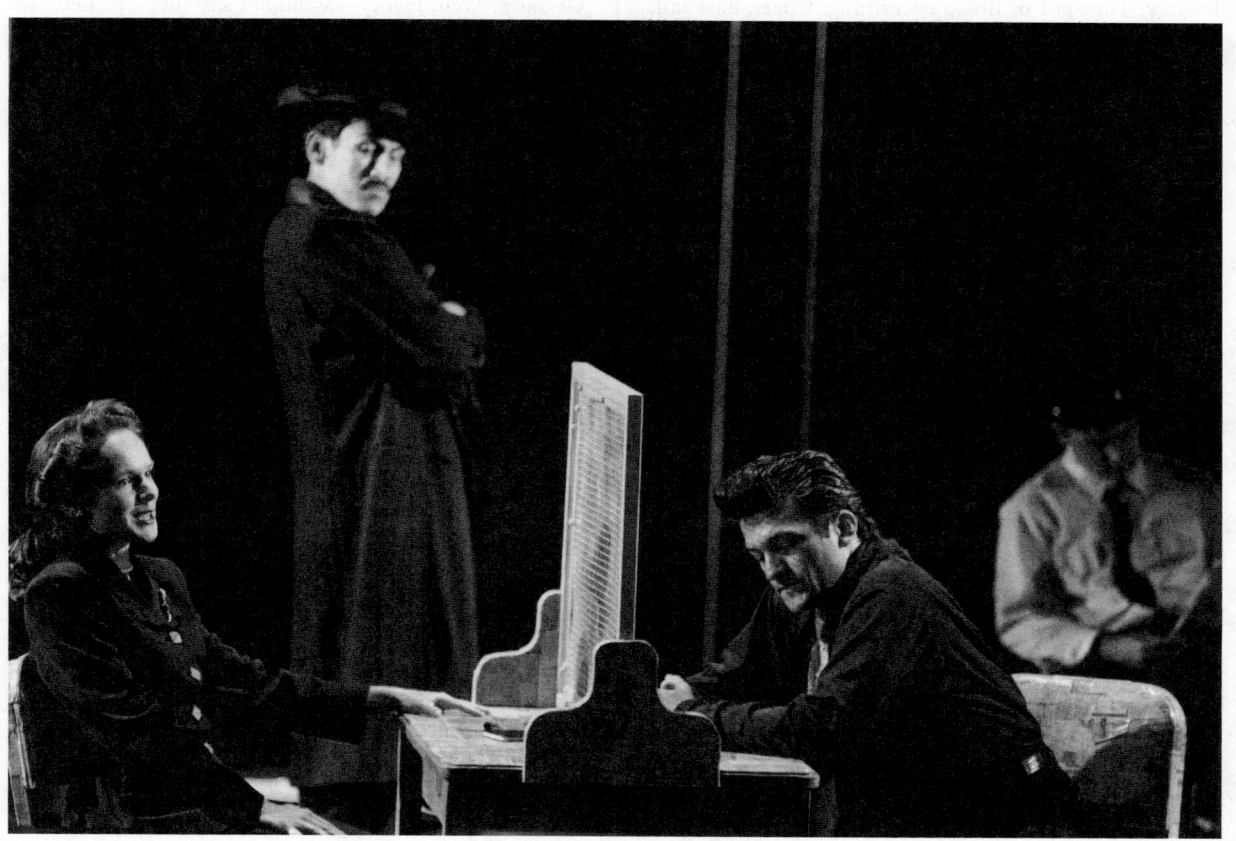

Alice Bloomfield (Carla Harting) and Henry Reyna (David Barrear) talking in prison in *Zoot Suit* at the San Diego Repertory Theatre, 1997. El Pachuco stands in the background.

(*The batos move upstage to the upper level. Music. The Boys mime a game of handball against the backdrop. During the game, George enters at stage right and comes downstage carrying his briefcase. The Guard blows a whistle and stops the game.*)

GUARD: Reyna, Castro, Roberts, Torres! — You got a
135   visitor.

Scene 4.   Major George

(*The Boys turn and see George. They come down enthusiastically.*)

JOEY: ¡Óra-leh! ¡Ese, Cheer!°
SMILEY: George!
GEORGE: Hi, guys!

(*The Boys shake his hand, pat him on the back. Henry comes to him last.*)

How are you all doing? You boys staying in shape?
5   JOEY: Ese, you're looking at the hero of the San Quentin athletic program. Right, batos? (*He shadowboxes a little.*)
TOMMY: Ten rounds with a busted ankle.
JOEY: ¡Simón! And I won the bout, too. I'm the terror of the flyweights, ese. The killer fly!
10   TOMMY: They got us doing everything, Cheer. Baseball, basketball.
SMILEY: Watch repairing.
GEORGE (*impressed*): Watch repairing?
SMILEY: I'm also learning to improve my English and
15   arithmetic.
GEORGE: Warden Duffy has quite a program. I hear he's a good man.
JOEY: Simón, he's a good man. We've learned our lesson . . . Well, anyway, I've learned my lesson, boy.
20   No more pachuquismo for me. Too many people depending on us to help out. The raza° here in Los. The whole Southwest. Mexico, South America! Like you and Grandma say, this is the people's world. If you get us out of here, I figure the only thing I could
25   do is become a union organizer. Or go into major league baseball.
GEORGE: Baseball?
JOEY: Simón, ese. You're looking at the first Mexican Babe Ruth. Or maybe, "Babe Root." Root! You get it?
30   TOMMY: How about "Baby Zoot"?
JOEY: Solid, Jackson.
GEORGE: Babe Zooter!
JOEY: Solid tudee, that's all reet, ese.
GEORGE: What about you, Henry? What have you been
35   doing?
HENRY: Time, George, I've been doing time.
TOMMY: Ain't it the truth?

2, 4. 1. ¡Ese, Cheer!: Hey it's Cheer! (nickname for George).
21. raza: The race, the people, Chicanos.

SMILEY: Yeah, George! When you going to spring us out of here, ese?
HENRY: How's the appeal coming?   40
GEORGE (*getting serious*): Not bad. There's been a development I have to talk to you about. But other than that . . .
HENRY: Other than what?
SMILEY (*pause*): Bad news?   45
GEORGE (*hedging*): It all depends on how you look at it, Smiley. It really doesn't change anything. Work on the brief is going on practically day and night. The thing is, even with several lawyers on the case now, it'll still be several months before we file. I want to be   50
honest about that.
HENRY (*suspiciously*): Is that the bad news?
GEORGE: Not exactly. Sit down, boys. (*Pause. He laughs to himself.*) I really don't mean to make such a big deal out of this thing. Fact is I'm still not quite used   55
to the idea myself. (*Pause.*) You see . . . I've been drafted.
JOEY: Drafted?
TOMMY: Into the Army?
SMILEY: You?   60
GEORGE: That's right. I'm off to war.
JOEY: But . . . you're old, Cheer.
HENRY (*a bitter edge*): Why you, George? Why did they pick on you?
GEORGE: Well, Henry, I wouldn't say they "picked" on   65
me. There's lots of men my age overseas. After all, it is war time and . . .
HENRY: And you're handling our appeal.
GEORGE (*pause*): We have other lawyers.
HENRY: But you're the one who knows the case!   70
GEORGE (*pause*): I knew you were going to take this hard. Believe me, Henry, my being drafted has nothing to do with your case. It's just a coincidence.
HENRY: Like our being in here for life is a coincidence?
GEORGE: No, that's another . . .   75
HENRY: Like our being hounded every goddam day of our life is a coincidence?
GEORGE: Henry . . .

(*Henry turns away furiously. There is a pause.*)

It's useless anger, son, believe me. Actually, I'm quite flattered by your concern, but I'm hardly indispens-   80
able.
HENRY (*deeply disturbed*): What the hell are you talking about, George?
GEORGE: I'm talking about all the people trying to get you out. Hundreds, perhaps thousands. Alice and I   85
aren't the only ones. We've got a heck of a fine team of lawyers working on the brief. With or without me, the appeal will be won. I promise you that.
HENRY: It's no use, George.
GEORGE: I realize all that sounds pretty unconvincing   90
under the circumstances, but it's true.
HENRY: Those bastard cops are never going to let us out of here. We're here for life and that's it.
GEORGE: You really believe that?

95 HENRY: What do you expect me to believe?
GEORGE: I wish I could answer that, son, but that's
    really for you to say.
GUARD: Time, Counselor.
GEORGE: Coming. (*Turns to the other Boys.*) Listen,
100 boys, I don't know where in the world I'll be the day
    your appeal is won — and it will be won — whether
    it's in the Pacific somewhere or in Europe or in a hole
    in the ground . . . Take care of yourselves.
TOMMY: See you around, George.
105 SMILEY: So long, George.
JOEY: 'Bye, Cheer.
GEORGE: Yeah. See you around. (*Pause.*) Goodbye,
    Henry. Good luck and God bless you.
HENRY: God bless you, too, George. Take care of your-
110 self.
TOMMY: Say, George, when you come back from the
    war, we're going to take you outa town and blast
    some weed.
JOEY: We'll get you a pair of buns you can hold in your
115 hands!
GEORGE: I may just take you up on that.

(*The Guard escorts George out, then turns back to the
Boys.*)

GUARD: All right, new work assignments. Everybody
    report to the jute mill. Let's go.

(*Smiley, Joey, and Tommy start to exit. Henry hangs
back.*)

    What's the matter with you, Reyna? You got lead in
120 your pants? I said let's go.
HENRY: We're supposed to work in the mess hall.
GUARD: You got a new assignment.
HENRY: Since when?
GUARD: Since right now. Get going!
125 HENRY (*hanging back*): The warden know about this?
GUARD: What the hell do you care? You think you're
    something special? Come on, greaseball. Move!
HENRY: Make me, you bastard!
GUARD: Oh yeah.

(*The Guard pushes Henry. Henry pushes back. The batos
react, as the Guard traps Henry with his club around the
chest. The Boys move to Henry's defense.*)

130 Back!
HENRY (*to the batos*): Back off! BACK OFF! Don't be
    stupid.
GUARD: Okay, Reyna, you got solitary! Bastard, huh?
    Into the hole!

(*He pushes Henry onto center stage. Lights down. A
single spot.*)

135 Line, greaseballs. Move out!

(*As they march.*)

    Quickly, quickly. You're too slow. Move, move, move.

(*The Boys exit with the Guard.*)

Scene 5. *Solitary*

(*A lone saxophone sets the mood.*)

PACHUCO: Too bad, ese. He set you up again.
HENRY (*long pause. He looks around*): Solitary, ese . . .
    they gave me solitary. (*He sits down on the floor, a
    forlorn figure.*)
PACHUCO: Better get used to it, carnal. That's what this
    stretch is going to be about, see? You're in here for   5
    life, bato.
HENRY: I can't accept it, ese.
PACHUCO: You've got to, Hank . . .
    only this reality is real now,
    only this place is real,   10
    sitting in the lonely cell of your will . . .
HENRY: I can't see my hands.
PACHUCO: Then tell your eyes to forget the light, ese
    Only the hard floor is there, carnal
    Only the cold hard edge of this reality   15
    and there is no time . . .
    Each second is a raw drop of blood from your brain
    that you must swallow
    drop by drop
    and don't even start counting   20
    or you'll lose your mind . . .
HENRY: I've got to know why I'm here, ese! I've got to
    have a reason for being here.
PACHUCO: You're here, Hank, because you chose to
    be — because you protected your brother and your   25
    family. And nobody knows the worth of that effort
    better than you, ese.
HENRY: I miss them, ese . . . my jefitos, my carnalillo, my
    sis . . . I miss Della.
PACHUCO (*a spot illuminates Henry's family standing up-
    stage; El Pachuco snaps it off*): Forget them!   30
    Forget them all.
    Forget your family and the barrio
    beyond the wall.
HENRY: There's still a chance I'll get out.
PACHUCO: Fat chance.   35
HENRY: I'm talking about the appeal!
PACHUCO: And I'm talking about what's real! ¿Qué traes,
    Hank?° Haven't you learned yet?
HENRY: Learned what?
PACHUCO: Not to expect justice when it isn't there.   40
    No court in the land's going to set you free.
    Learn to protect your loves by binding them
    in hate, ese! Stop hanging on to false hopes.
    The moment those hopes come crashing down,
    you'll find yourself on the ground foaming at   45
    the mouth. ¡Como loco!°
HENRY (*turning on him furiously*): ¿Sabes qué? Don't
    tell me any more. I don't need you to tell me what to
    do. Fuck off! FUCK OFF!

2, 5. 37–38. ¿Qué traes, Hank?: What's wrong, Hank?
46. ¡Como loco!: Like a lunatic!

(*Henry turns away from El Pachuco. Long pause. An anxious, intense moment. El Pachuco shifts gears and breaks the tension with a satirical twist. He throws his arms out and laughs.*)

50   PACHUCO: ¡Órale pues!°
        Don't take the pinche play so seriously, Jesús!
        Es puro vacilón!°
        Watcha.

(*He snaps his fingers. Lights change. We hear the sounds of the city.*)

        This is Los, carnal.
55   You want to see some justice for pachucos?
        Check out what's happening back home today.
        The Navy has landed, ese —
        on leave with full pay
        and war's breaking out in the streets of L.A.!

Scene 6. *Zoot Suit Riots*

(*We hear music: the bugle call from "Bugle Call Rag." Suddenly the stage is awash in colored lights. The city of Los Angeles appears in the background in a panoramic vista of lights tapering into the night horizon. Sailors and Girls jitterbug on the dance floor. It is the Avalon Ballroom. The music is hot, the dancing hotter. El Pachuco and Henry stand to the side.*

The scene is in dance and mostly pantomime. Occasionally words are heard over the music which is quite loud. On the floor are two Sailors [Swabbie is one] and a Marine dancing with the Girls. A Shore Patrolman speaks to the Cigarette Girl. A Pimp comes on and watches the action. Little Blue and Zooter are also on the floor. Rudy enters wearing Henry's zoot suit with Bertha and Lupe. Lupe takes their picture, then all three move up center to the rear of the ballroom. Cholo comes in down center, sees them and moves up stage. All four make an entrance onto the dance floor.

The Marine takes his girl aside after paying her. She passes the money to the Pimp. The Sailors try to pick up on Lupe and Bertha, and Cholo pushes one back. The Sailors complain to the Shore Patrol, who throws Cholo out the door down center. There is an argument that Rudy joins. The Sailors go back to Bertha and Lupe who resist. Cholo and Rudy go to their defense and a fight develops. Zooter and Little Blue split. Cholo takes the Girls out and Rudy pulls a knife. He is facing the three Sailors and the Marine, when The Pachuco freezes the action.)

PACHUCO (*forcefully*): Órale, that's enough!

(*El Pachuco takes Rudy's knife and with a tap sends him off-stage. Rudy exits with the Girls. El Pachuco is now*

facing the angry Servicemen. He snaps his fingers. The Press enters quickly to the beeping sound of a radio broadcast.*)

PRESS: Good evening, Mr. and Mrs. North and South America and all the ships at sea. Let's go to press. FLASH. Los Angeles, California, June 3, 1943. Seri- 5 ous rioting broke out here today as flying squadrons of Marines and soldiers joined the Navy in a new assault on zooter-infested districts. A fleet of twenty taxicabs carrying some two hundred servicemen pulled out of the Naval Armory in Chavez Ravine to- 10 night and assembled a task force that invaded the eastside barrio.

(*Unfreeze. The following speeches happen simultaneously.*)

MATE: You got any balls in them funny pants, boy?
SAILOR: He thinks he's tough . . .
SWABBIE: How about it, lardhead? You a tough guy or just a draft dodger? 15
PRESS: The Zoot Suiters, those gamin' dandies . . .
PACHUCO (*cutting them off*): Why don't you tell them what I really am, ese, or how you've been forbidden to use the very word . . .
PRESS: We are complying in the interest of the war. 20
PACHUCO: How have you complied?
PRESS: We're using other terms.
PACHUCO: Like *pachuco* and *zoot suiter*?
PRESS: What's wrong with that? The Zoot Suit Crime Wave is even beginning to push the war news off the 25 front page.
PACHUCO: The Press distorted the very meaning of the word "zoot suit."
        All it is for you guys is another way to say Mexican.
        But the ideal of the original chuco°
        was to look like a diamond 30
        to look sharp
        hip
        bonaroo°
        finding a style of urban survival
        in the rural skirts and outskirts 35
        of the brown metropolis of Los, cabrón.
PRESS: It's an afront to good taste.
PACHUCO: Like the Mexicans, Filipinos, and blacks who wear them.
PRESS: Yes! 40
PACHUCO: Even the white kids and the Wops and the Jews are putting on the drape shape.
PRESS: You are trying to outdo the white man in exaggerated white man's clothes!
PACHUCO: Because everybody knows 45
        that Mexicans, Filipinos, and blacks
        belong to the huarache°
        the straw hat and the dirty overall.

---

50. ¡Órale pues!: Listen then!   **52. Es puro vacilón!:** It's pure fantasy!

2, 6. 29. chuco: Pachuco.   **33. bonaroo:** Wonderful. **47. huarache:** Mexican sandal.

PRESS: You savages weren't even wearing clothes when
50   the white man pulled you out of the jungle.
MARINE: My parents are going without collars and cuffs
    so you can wear that shit.
PRESS: That's going too far, too goddamned far, and it's
    got to be stopped!
55 PACHUCO: Why?
PRESS: Don't you know there's a war on? Don't you
    fucking well know you can't get away with that shit?
    What are we fighting for if not to annihilate the ene-
    mies of the American way of life?
60 MATE: Let's tear it off his back!
SAILORS/MARINE: Let's strip him! Get him! (Etc.)
PRESS: KILL THE PACHUCO BASTARD!!

(*Music: "American Patrol" by Glenn Miller. The Press
gets a searchlight from upstage center while the Four
Servicemen stalk El Pachuco.*)

SAILOR: Heh, zooter. Come on, zooter!
SWABBIE: You think you're more important than the
65   war, zooter?
MATE: Let's see if you got any balls in them funny pants,
    boy.
SWABBIE: Watch out for the knife.
SAILOR: That's a real chango monkey suit he's got on.
70 MATE: I bet he's half monkey — just like the Filipinos
    and niggers that wear them.
SWABBIE: You trying to outdo the white man in them
    glad rags, Mex?

(*They fight now to the finish. El Pachuco is overpowered and stripped as Henry watches helplessly from his
position. The Press and Servicemen exit with pieces of
El Pachuco's zoot suit. El Pachuco stands. The only item
of clothing on his body is a small loincloth. He turns
and looks at Henry, with mystic intensity. He opens his
arms as an Aztec conch blows, and he slowly exits backward with powerful calm into the shadows. Silence.
Henry comes downstage. He absorbs the impact of what
he has seen and falls to his knees at center stage, spent
and exhausted. Lights down.*)

Scene 7. Alice

(*The Guard and Alice enter from opposite sides of the
stage. The Guard carries a handful of letters and is reading one of them.*)

GUARD: July 2, 1943.
ALICE: Dear Henry,
    I hope this letter finds you in good health and good
    spirits — but I have to assume you've heard about
5   the riots in Los Angeles. It was a nightmare, and it
    lasted for a week. The city is still in a state of shock.
GUARD (*folds letter back into envelope, then opens
    another*): August 5, 1943.
ALICE: Dear Henry,
    The riots here in L.A. have touched off race riots
10   all over the country — Chicago, Detroit, even little

Beaumont, Texas, for Christ's sake. But the one in
Harlem was the worst. Millions of dollars worth of
property damage. 500 people were hospitalized, and
five Negroes were killed.
GUARD: Things are rough all over.   15
ALICE: Please write to me and tell me how you feel.
GUARD (*the Guard folds up the second letter, stuffs it
    back into its envelope and opens a third*): August 20,
    1943.
ALICE: Dear Henry,
    Although I am disappointed not to have heard from   20
    you, I thought I would send you some good news for
    a change. Did you know we had a gala fund-raiser at
    the Mocambo?
GUARD: The Mocambo . . . Hotcha!°
ALICE: . . . and Rita Hayworth lent your sister Lupe a   25
    ball gown for the occasion. She got dressed at Cecil B.
    DeMille's house, and she looked terrific. Her escort
    was Anthony Quinn, and Orson Welles said . . .
GUARD: Orson Welles! Well! Sounds like Louella Par-
    sons. (*He folds up the letter.*) September 1, 1943.   30
ALICE: Henry, why aren't you answering my letters?
GUARD: He's busy. (*He continues to stuff the envelope.*)
ALICE: Henry, if there's something I've said or done . . . ?

(*The Guard shuffles the envelopes.*)

Henry . . .

(*Lights change. Guard crosses to center stage, where
Henry is still doubled up on the floor.*)

GUARD: Welcome back to the living, Reyna. It's been a   35
    long hot summer. Here's your mail.

(*The Guard tosses the letters to the floor directly in front
of Henry's head. Henry looks up slowly and grabs one
of the letters. He opens it, trying to focus. The Guard
exits.*)

ALICE: Henry, I just found out you did ninety days in
    solitary. I'm furious at the rest of the guys for keeping
    it from me. I talked to Warden Duffy, and he said you
    struck a guard. Did something happen I should know   40
    about? I wouldn't ask if it wasn't so important, but a
    clean record . . .

(*Henry rips up the letter he has been reading and scatters the others. Alarmed.*)

Henry?

(*Henry pauses, his instant fury spent and under control.
He sounds almost weary, but the anger is still there.*)

HENRY: You still don't understand, Alice.
ALICE (*softly, compassionate*): But I do! I'm not accus-   45
    ing you of anything. I don't care what happened or
    why they sent you there. I'm sure you had your rea-
    sons. But you know the public is watching you.
HENRY (*frustrated, a deep question*): Why do you do
    this, Alice?   50

2, 7. 24. **Hotcha!:** Expression used as a song lyric or title.

ALICE: What?

HENRY: The appeal, the case, all the shit you do. You think the public gives a goddamn?

55 ALICE (*with conviction*): Yes! We are going to get you out of here, Henry Reyna. We are going to win!

HENRY (*probing*): What if we lose?

ALICE (*surprised but moving on*): We're not going to lose.

HENRY (*forcefully, insistent, meaning more than he is saying*): What if we do? What if we get another
60 crooked judge, and he nixes the appeal?

ALICE: Then we'll appeal again. We'll take it to the Supreme Court. (*A forced laugh.*) Hell, we'll take it all the way to President Roosevelt!

HENRY (*backing her up — emotionally*): What if we still
65 lose?

ALICE (*bracing herself against his aggression*): We can't.

HENRY: Why can't we?

ALICE (*giving a political response in spite of herself*): Because we've got too much support. You should see the kinds of people responding to us. Unions, Mexi-
70 cans, Negroes, Oakies. It's fantastic.

HENRY (*driving harder*): Why can't we lose, Alice?

ALICE: I'm telling you.

HENRY: No, you're not.

ALICE (*starting to feel vulnerable*): I don't know what to
75 tell you.

HENRY: Yes, you do!

ALICE (*frightened*): Henry . . . ?

HENRY: Tell me why we can't lose, Alice!

ALICE (*forced to fight back, with characteristic passion*): Stop it, Henry! Please stop it! I won't have you treat
80 me this way. I never have been able to accept one person pushing another around . . . pushing me around! Can't you see that's why I'm here? Because I can't stand it happening to you. Because I'm a Jew, god-dammit! I have been there . . . I have been there! If
85 you lose, I lose.

(*Pause. The emotional tension is immense. Alice fights to hold back tears. She turns away.*)

HENRY: I'm sorry . . .

ALICE (*pause*): It's stupid for us to fight like this. I look forward to coming here for weeks. Just to talk to you, to be with you, to see your eyes.

90 HENRY (*pause*): I thought a lot about you when I was in the hole. Sometimes . . . sometimes I'd even see you walk in, in the dark, and talk to me. Just like you are right now. Same look, same smile, same perfume . . . (*He pauses.*) Only the other one never gave me so
95 much lip. She just listened. She did say one thing. She said . . .

ALICE (*trying to make light of it, then more gently*): I can't say that to you, Henry. Not the way you want it.

HENRY: Why not?

100 ALICE (*she means it*): Because I can't allow myself to be used to fill in for all the love you've always felt and always received from all your women.

HENRY (*with no self-pity*): Give it a chance, Alice.

ALICE (*beside herself*): Give it a chance? You crazy idiot. If I thought making love to you would solve all 105 your problems, I'd do it in a second. Don't you know that? But it won't. It'll only complicate things. I'm trying to help you, goddammit. And to do that, I have to be your friend, not your white woman.

HENRY (*getting angry*): What makes you think I want to 110 go to bed with you. Because you're white? I've had more white pieces of ass than you can count, ¿sabes? Who do you think you are? God's gift to us brown animals.

ALICE (*slaps him and stops, horrified, a whirlpool of emotions*): Oh, Hank. All the love and hate it's taken 115 to get us together in this lousy prison room. Do you realize only Hitler and the Second World War could have accomplished that? I don't know whether to laugh or cry.

(*Alice folds into her emotional spin, her body shaking. Suddenly she turns, whipping herself out of it with a cry, both laughing and weeping. They come to each other and embrace. Then they kiss — passionately. The Guard enters. He frowns.*)

GUARD: Time, Miss. 120

ALICE (*turning*): Already? Oh, my God, Henry, there's so many messages I was going to give you. Your mother and father send their love, of course. And Lupe and . . . Della. And . . . oh, yes. They want you to know Rudy's in the Marines. 125

HENRY: The Marines?

ALICE: I'll write you all about it. Will you write me?

HENRY (*a glance at the Guard*): Yes.

GUARD (*his tone getting harsher*): Let's go, lady. 130

HENRY: Goodbye, Licha.

ALICE: I'll see you on the outside . . . Hank.

(*Alice gives Henry a thumb up gesture, and the Guard escorts her out. Henry turns downstage, full of thoughts. He addresses El Pachuco, who is nowhere to be seen.*)

HENRY: You were wrong, ese . . . There is something to hope for. I know now we're going to win the appeal. Do you hear me, ese? Ese! (*Pause.*) Are you even there any more? 135

(*The Guard re-enters at a clip.*)

GUARD: Okay, Reyna, come on.

HENRY: Where to?

GUARD: We're letting you go . . .

(*Henry looks at him incredulously. The Guard smiles.*)

. . . to Folsom Prison with all the rest of the hardcore cons. You really didn't expect to walk out of here a 140 free man, did you? Listen, kid, your appeal stands about as much chance as the Japs and Krauts of win-ning the war. Personally, I don't see what that broad sees in you. I wouldn't give you the sweat off my balls. Come on! 145

(*Henry and the Guard turn upstage to leave. Lights change. El Pachuco appears halfway up the backdrop, fully dressed again and clearly visible. Henry stops with a jolt as he sees him. El Pachuco lifts his arms. Lights go down as we hear the high sound of a bomb falling to earth.*)

Scene 8. The Winning of the War

(*The aerial bomb explodes with a reverberating sound and a white flash that illuminates the form of pachuco images in the black backdrop. Other bombs fall and all hell breaks loose. Red flashes, artillery, gunfire, ack-ack. Henry and the Guard exit. The Four Servicemen enter as an honor guard. Music: Glen Miller's "Saint Louis Blues March." As the Servicemen march on we see Rudy down left in his marine uniform, belt undone. Enrique, Dolores, and Lupe join him. Dolores has his hat, Lupe her camera. Enrique fastens two buttons on the uniform as Rudy does up his belt. Dolores inspects his collar and gives him his hat. Rudy puts on his hat and all pose for Lupe. She snaps the picture and Rudy kisses them all and is off. He picks up the giant switchblade from behind a newspaper bundle and joins the Servicemen as they march down in drill formation. The family marches off, looking back sadly. The drill ends and Rudy and the Shore Patrol move to one side. As Rudy's interrogation goes on, People in the barrio come on with newspapers to mime daily tasks. The Press enters.*)

PRESS: The *Los Angeles Examiner,* July 1, 1943. Headline: WORLD WAR II REACHES TURNING POINT. If the late summer of 1942 was the low point, a year later the war for the Allies is pounding
5   its way to certain victory.

SHORE PATROL: July 10!

RUDY: U.S., British, and Canadian troops invade Sicily, Sir!

SHORE PATROL: August 6!

10 RUDY: U.S. troops occupy Solomon Island, Sir!

SHORE PATROL: September 5!

RUDY: MacArthur's forces land on New Guinea, Sir!

SHORE PATROL: October 1!

RUDY: U.S. Fifth Army enters Naples, Sir!

15 PRESS: On and on it goes. From Corsica to Kiev, from Tarawa to Anzio. The relentless advance of the Allied armies cannot be checked.

(*One by one, Henry's family and friends enter, carrying newspapers. They tear the papers into small pieces.*)

The *Los Angeles Times,* June 6, 1944. Headline: Allied forces under General Eisenhower land in Nor-
20 mandy.

SHORE PATROL: August 19!

RUDY: American First Army reaches Germany, Sir!

SHORE PATROL: October 17!

RUDY: MacArthur returns to the Philippines, Sir!

25 PRESS: On the homefront, Americans go on with their daily lives with growing confidence and relief, as the war pushes on toward inevitable triumph. (*Pause.*) The *Los Angeles Daily News,* Wednesday, November 8, 1944. Headline: District Court of Appeals decides in Sleepy Lagoon murder case . . . boys in pachuco   30 murder given . . .

PEOPLE: FREEDOM!!!

(*Music bursts forth as the joyous crowd tosses the shredded newspaper into the air like confetti. The Boys enter upstage center, and the crowd rushes to them, weeping and cheering. There are kisses and hugs and tears of joy. Henry is swept forward by the triumphal procession.*)

Scene 9. Return to the Barrio

(*The music builds and people start dancing. Others just embrace. The tune is "Soldado Razo" played to a lively corrido beat. It ends with joyous applause, laughter, and tears.*)

RUDY: ¡Ese carnal!

HENRY: Rudy!!

DOLORES: ¡Bendito sea Dios! Who would believe this day would ever come? Look at you — you're all home!   5

LUPE: I still can't believe it. We won! We won the appeal!

(*Cheers.*)

ENRIQUE: I haven't felt like this since Villa took Zacatecas. (*Laughter, cheers.*) ¡Pero mira!° Look who's here. Mis hijos. (*Puts his arm around Henry and*   10 *Rudy.*) It isn't every day a man has two grown sons come home from so far away — one from the war, the other from . . . bueno, who cares? The Sleepy Lagoon is history, hombre. For a change, los Mexicanos have won!   15

(*Cheers.*)

GEORGE: Well, Henry. I don't want to say I told you so, but we sure taught Judge Charles a lesson in misconduct, didn't we? (*More cheers.*) Do you realize this is the greatest victory the Mexican-American community has ever had in the history of this whole blasted   20 country?

DOLORES: Yes, but if it wasn't for the unselfish thoughtfulness of people like you and this beautiful lady — and all the people who helped out, Mexicanos, Negros, all Americanos — our boys would not be home   25 today.

GEORGE: I only hope you boys realize how important you are now.

JOEY: Pos, I realize it, ese.

(*Laughter.*)

2, 9. 9. ¡Pero mira!: But look!

30 RUDY: I came all the way from Hawaii just to get here, carnal. I only got a few days, but I'm going to get you drunk.

HENRY: Pos, we'll see who gets who drunk, ese.

(*Laughter and hoots. Henry spots El Pachuco entering from stage right.*)

DOLORES: Jorge, Licha, todos.° Let's go into the house,
35 eh? I've made a big pot of menudo, and it's for everybody.

ENRIQUE: There's ice-cold beer too. Vénganse, vamos todos.°

GEORGE (*to Alice*): Alice . . . Menudo, that's Mexican
40 chicken soup?

(*Everybody exits, leaving Henry behind with El Pachuco.*)

HENRY: It's good to see you again, ese. I thought I'd lost you.

PACHUCO: H'm pues, it'd take more than the U.S. Navy to wipe me out.

45 HENRY: Where you been?

PACHUCO: Pos, here in the barrio. Welcome back.

HENRY: It's good to be home.

PACHUCO: No hard feelings?

HENRY: Chale — we won, didn't we?

50 PACHUCO: Simón.

HENRY: Me and the batos have been in a lot of fights together, ese. But we won this one, because we learned to fight in a new way.

PACHUCO: And that's the perfect way to end this play —
55 happy ending y todo. (*Pachuco makes a sweeping gesture. Lights come down. He looks up at the lights, realizing something is wrong. He flicks his wrist, and the lights go back up again.*)

But life ain't that way, Hank.
The barrio's still out there, waiting and wanting.
The cops are still tracking us down like dogs.
The gangs are still killing each other,
60 Families are barely surviving,
And there in your own backyard . . . life goes on.

(*Soft music. Della enters.*)

DELLA: Hank?

(*Henry goes to her and they embrace.*)

HENRY: Where were you? Why didn't you come to the Hall of Justice to see us get out?

65 DELLA: I guess I was a little afraid things had changed. So much has happened to both of us.

PACHUCO: Simón. She's living in your house.

DELLA: After I got back from Ventura, my parents gave me a choice. Forget about you or get out.

70 HENRY: Why didn't you write to me?

34. **Jorge, Licha, todos:** George, Alice, everyone.   37–38. **Vénganse, vamos todos:** Come back, let's go everyone.

DELLA: You had your own problems. Your jefitos took care of me. Hey, you know what, Hank, I think they expect us to get married.

PACHUCO: How about it, ese? You still going to give her that big pachuco wedding you promised? 75

HENRY: I have to think about it.

ALICE (*off-stage*): Henry?

PACHUCO (*snaps fingers*): Wish you had the time. But here comes Licha.

ALICE (*entering*): Henry, I've just come to say good night. 80

(*Della freezes and Henry turns to Alice.*)

HENRY: Good night? Why are you leaving so soon?

ALICE: Soon? I've been here all afternoon. There'll be other times, Henry. You're home now, with your family, that's what matters.

HENRY: Don't patronize me, Alice. 85

ALICE (*surprised*): Patronize you?

HENRY: Yeah. I learned a few words in the joint.

ALICE: Yo también,° Hank. Te quiero.°

(*Pachuco snaps. Alice freezes, and Rudy enters.*)

RUDY: Ese, carnal, congratulations, the jefita just told me about you and Della. That's great, ese. But if you 90 want me to be best man, you better do it in the next three days.

HENRY: Wait a minute, Rudy, don't push me.

RUDY: Qué pues,° getting cold feet already?

(*Henry is beginning to be surrounded by separate conversations.*)

DELLA: If you don't want me here, I can move out. 95

RUDY: Watcha. I'll let you and Della have our room tonight, bato. I'll sleep on the couch.

ALICE: You aren't expecting me to sleep here, are you?

HENRY: I'm not asking you to.

PACHUCO/ALICE/RUDY/DELLA: Why not? 100

RUDY: The jefitos will never know, ese.

ALICE: Be honest, Henry.

DELLA: What do you want me to do?

HENRY: Give me a chance to think about it. Give me a second! 105

PACHUCO: One second!

(*Pachuco snaps. Enrique enters.*)

ENRIQUE: Bueno, bueno, pues,° what are you doing out here, hijo? Aren't you coming in for menudo?

HENRY: I'm just thinking, jefito.

ENRIQUE: ¿De qué, hombre?° Didn't you do enough of 110 that in prison? Andale, this is your house. Come in and live again.

HENRY: 'Apá, did you tell Della I was going to marry her?

ENRIQUE: Yes, but only after you did.

88. **Yo también:** Me too.   **Te quiero:** I love you.   94. **Qué pues:** Well what.   107. **Bueno, bueno, pues:** Good, good, certainly.   110. **¿De qué, hombre?:** About what, man?

115 RUDY: ¿Qué traes, carnal?° Don't you care about Della
     anymore?

     ALICE: If it was just me and you, Henry, it might be dif-
     ferent. But you have to think of your family.

     HENRY: I don't need you to tell me my responsibilities.

120 ALICE: I'm sorry.

     RUDY: Sorry, carnal.

     DELLA: I don't need anybody to feel sorry for me. I did
     what I did because I wanted to. All I want to know is
     what's going to happen now. If you still want me,

125 órale, suave. If you don't, that's okay, too. But I'm
     not going to hang around like a pendeja all my life.

     RUDY: Your huisa's looking finer than ever, carnal.

     ALICE: You're acting as if nothing has happened.

     ENRIQUE: You have your whole life ahead of you.

130 ALICE: You belong here, Henry. I'm the one that's out of
     place.

     RUDY: If you don't pick up on her, I'm going to have to
     step in.

     HENRY: That's bullshit. What about what we shared in

135 prison? I've never been that close to anybody.

     ALICE: That was in prison.

     HENRY: What the hell do you think the barrio is?

     RUDY: It's not bullshit!

     HENRY: Shut up, carnalillo!

140 RUDY: Carnalillo? How can you still call me that? I'm
     not your pinche little brother no more.

     GEORGE (entering): You guys have got to stop fighting,
     Henry, or the barrio will never change. Don't you
     realize you men represent the hope of your people?

145 ALICE: Della was in prison too. You know you had
     thousands of people clamoring for your release, but
     you were Della's only hope.

     HENRY: Look, esa, I know you did a year in Ventura. I
     know you stood up for me when it counted. I wish I

150 could make it up to you.

     DELLA: Don't give me your bullshit, Henry. Give it to
     Alice.

     ALICE: I think it's time for Alice Bloomfield to go home.

     HENRY: Don't be jealous, esa.

155 DELLA: Jealous? Mira, cabrón, I know I'm not the only
     one you ever took to the Sleepy Lagoon.

     RUDY: The Sleepy Lagoon ain't shit. I saw real lagoons
     in those islands, ese — killing Japs! I saw some pa-
     chucos go out there that are never coming back.

160 DELLA: But I was always there when you came back,
     wasn't I?

     DOLORES (entering): Henry? Come back inside, hijo.
     Everybody's waiting for you.

     RUDY: Why didn't you tell them I was there, carnal? I

165 was at the Sleepy Lagoon. Throwing chingazos with
     everybody!

     HENRY: Don't you understand, Rudy? I was trying to
     keep you from getting a record. Those bastard cops
     are never going to leave us alone.

GEORGE: You've got to forget what happened, Henry.   170

HENRY: What can I give you, Della? I'm an ex-con.

DELLA: So am I!

SMILEY (entering): Let's face it, Hank. There's no future
for us in this town. I'm taking my wife and kid and
moving to Arizona.   175

DOLORES (simultaneously):   ENRIQUE: If there's one
I know what you are   thing that will keep a
feeling, hijo, it's home   man off the streets it's
again. I know inside   his own familia.
you are afraid that   GEORGE: Don't let this   180
nothing has changed.   thing eat your heart out
That the police will   for the rest of your . . .
never leave you in   ALICE: Sometimes the best
peace. Pero no le hace.°   thing you can do for
Everything is going to   someone you love is   185
be fine now. Marry   walk away.
Della and fill this house   DELLA: What do you
with children. Just do   want, Hank?
one thing for me —   RUDY: It cost me more
forget the zoot suit   than it did you.   190
clothes.   SMILEY: We started the
                                  38th and I'll never for-
                                  get you, carnal. But I
                                  got to think about my
                                  family.   195

HENRY: Wait a minute! I don't know if I'll be back in
prison tomorrow or not! I have nothing to give you,
Della. Not even a piece of myself.

DELLA: I have my life to live, too, Hank. I love you. I
would even die for you. Pero me chingan la madre° if   200
I'm going to throw away my life for nothing.

HENRY: But I love you . . .

(Both Girls turn. Henry looks at Alice, then to the whole
group upstage of him. Still turning, he looks at Della
and goes to embrace her. The freeze ends and other
people enter.)

LUPE: ¡Órale, Hank! Watcha Joey. The crazy bato went
all the way to his house and put on his drapes.

JOEY: ¡Esos, batoooooosss! ¡Esas, huisaaaaaass!°   205

TOMMY: Look at this cat! He looks all reet.

LUPE: Yeah, like a parakeet!

HENRY: ¿Y tú, ese?° How come you put on your tacuche? Where's the party?

JOEY: Pos, ain't the party here?   210

RUDY: Yeah, ese, but this ain't the Avalon Ballroom. The
zoot suit died under fire here in Los. Don't you know
that, cabrón?

ENRIQUE: Rudolfo!

LUPE: And he was supposed to get Henry drunk.   215

RUDY: Shut up, esa!

ENRIQUE: ¡Ya pues!° Didn't you have any menudo?

---

184. Pero no le hace: But it doesn't happen.   **200. Pero me
chingan la madre:** But I'll be damned.   **205. ¡Esos . . .
huisaaaaaass!:** Hey dudes! Hey girls!   **208. ¿Y tú, ese?:** And
you man?   **217. ¡Ya pues!:** Enough already!

Vieja,° fix him a great big bowl of menudo and put plenty of chile in it. We're going to sweat it out of him.

220 RUDY: I don't need no pinche menudo.

HENRY: Watch your language, carnal.

RUDY: And I don't need you! I'm a man. I can take care of myself!

JOEY: Muy marine el bato° . . .

225 ENRIQUE: Rudy, hijo. Are you going to walk into the kitchen or do I have to drag you?

RUDY: Whatever you say, jefito.

GEORGE: Well, Alice. This looks like the place where we came in. I think it's about time we left.

230 ALICE: Say the word, George, just say the word.

DOLORES: No, no. You can't leave so soon.

JOEY: Chale, chale, chale. You can't take our Grandma. ¿Qué se trae, carnal? Póngase más abusado, ese. No se haga tan square.°

235 GEORGE: Okay, square I got. What was the rest of it?

JOEY: Pos, le estoy hablando en chicas patas, ese. Es puro chicano.°

RUDY: ¿Qué chicano? Ni que madre, cabrón.° Why don't you grow up?

240 JOEY: Grow up, ese?

RUDY: Try walking downtown looking like that. See if the sailors don't skin your ass alive.

JOEY: So what? It's no skin off your ass. Come on, Bertha.

245 RUDY: She's staying with me.

JOEY: She's mine.

RUDY: Prove it, punk.

(*Rudy attacks Joey and they fight. The Batos and Rucas take out Joey. Henry pacifies Rudy, who bursts out crying. Enrique, Della, Dolores, Alice, Lupe, and George are the only ones left. Rudy in a flush of emotion.*)

Cabrones, se amontonaron.° They ganged up on me, carnal. You left me and they ganged up on me. You
250 shouldn't have done it, carnal. Why didn't you take me with you. For the jefitos? The jefitos lost me anyway.

HENRY: Come on in the house, Rudy . . .

RUDY: No! I joined the Marines. I didn't have to join,
255 but I went. ¿Sabes por qué? Because they got me, carnal. Me chingaron, ese.° (*Sobs.*) I went to the pinche show with Bertha, all chingón in your tacuche, ese. I was wearing your zoot suit, and they got me. Twenty sailors, Marines. We were up in the balcony. They
260 came down from behind. They grabbed me by the

neck and dragged me down the stairs, kicking and punching and pulling my greña.° They dragged me out into the streets . . . and all the people watched while they stripped me. (*Sobs.*) They stripped me, carnal. Bertha saw them strip me. Hijos de la chin- 265 gada,° they stripped me.

(*Henry goes to Rudy and embraces him with fierce love and desperation. Pause. Tommy comes running in.*)

TOMMY: ¡Órale! There's cops outside. They're trying to arrest Joey.

(*George crosses to Tommy.*)

GEORGE (*bursting out*): Joey?

TOMMY: They got him up against your car. They're try- 270 ing to say he stole it!

GEORGE: Oh, God. I'll take care of this.

ALICE: I'll go with you.

(*George, Tommy, and Alice exit.*)

HENRY: Those fucking bastards! (*He starts to exit.*)

DELLA: Henry, no! 275

HENRY: What the hell do you mean no? Don't you see what's going on outside?

DELLA: They'll get you again! That's what they want.

HENRY: Get out of my way! (*He pushes her out of the way, toward Dolores.*)

ENRIQUE (*stands up before Henry*): ¡Hijo!

HENRY: Get out of my way, jefe!° 280

ENRIQUE: You will stay here!

HENRY: Get out of my way!

(*Enrique powerfully pushes him back and throws Henry to the floor and holds.*)

ENRIQUE: ¡TE DIGO QUE NO!

(*Silent moment. Henry stands up and offers to strike Enrique. But something stops him. The realization that if he strikes back or even if he walks out the door, the family bond is irreparably broken. Henry tenses for a moment, then relaxes and embraces his father. Della goes to them and joins the embrace. Then Dolores, then Lupe, then Rudy. All embrace in a tight little group. Press enters right and comes down.*)

PRESS: Henry Reyna went back to prison in 1947 for 285 robbery and assault with a deadly weapon. While incarcerated, he killed another inmate and he wasn't released until 1955, when he got into hard drugs. He died of the trauma of his life in 1972.

PACHUCO: That's the way you see it, ese. But there's 290 other ways to end this story.

RUDY: Henry Reyna went to Korea in 1950. He was

---

218. **Vieja:** Old woman (wife).   224. **Muy marine el bato:** The dude's acting like a marine.   233–234. **¿Qué . . . square:** What's wrong, brother? Smarten up, man. That doesn't seem very square.   236–237. **Pos . . . chicano:** Anyhow, I was speaking in Chicano, man. It's pure Chicano.   238. **¿Qué . . . cabrón:** What Chicano? Nothing that matters (vulgar term).   248. **Cabrones, se amontonaron:** (Vulgar term) they ganged up on me.   256. **Me chingaron, ese:** They (vulgar term) me up, man.

262. **greña:** Hair.   265–266. **Hijos de la chingada:** (Vulgar term).   281. **jefe:** Dad.

shipped across in a destroyer and defended the 38th
Parallel until he was killed at Inchon in 1952, being
295   posthumously awarded the Congressional Medal of
Honor.

ALICE: Henry Reyna married Della in 1948 and they
have five kids, three of them now going to the University, speaking calo and calling themselves Chi-
300   canos.

GEORGE: Henry Reyna, the born leader . . .

JUDGE: Henry Reyna, the social victim . . .

BERTHA: Henry Reyna, the street corner warrior . . .

SMILEY: Henry Reyna, el carnal de aquellas° . . .

JOEY: Henry Reyna, the zoot suiter . . .   305

TOMMY: Henry Reyna, my friend . . .

LUPE: Henry Reyna, my brother . . .

ENRIQUE: Henry Reyna . . .

DOLORES: Our son . . .

DELLA: Henry Reyna, my love . . .   310

PACHUCO: Henry Reyna . . . El Pachuco . . . The man . . .
the myth . . . still lives. (*Lights down and fade out.*)

304. el carnal de aquellas: The outstanding brother.

Harold Pinter

Harold Pinter (b. 1930) has written plays for the commercial stage, radio, and television as well as film scripts produced by some of the best directors of his time. Pinter was born into relatively humble circumstances in East London, but his early schooling distinguished him, and he eventually enrolled in London's prestigious Royal Academy of Dramatic Arts to study acting. When he finished his studies, he joined a company, toured for several years, and began to write for the stage. His previous writing efforts had been in prose: short stories and a long novel, *The Dwarfs* (1956), purportedly autobiographical, but never finished and not published until 1990. Produced as a radio play in 1960, it expresses some of the themes of his best work: the disintegration of a mind and the cruelty of people to their fellow beings.

In 1957 Pinter wrote three important plays, the one-act *The Room* and *The Dumb Waiter* and the full-length *The Birthday Party* (finished in 1958). All were well received. They established his method in dialogue and to a large extent the style that has dominated his work. The critic Martin Esslin, who coined the term "theater of the absurd," saw in Pinter's work an absurdist strain, especially in the nihilism — the belief in nothing — that sometimes shows up in his work. Pinter's characters usually reveal no spiritual awareness and no longing for spiritual values.

Pinter's dialogue sometimes has qualities of aimlessness, at least on the surface. But always the dialogue penetrates the unconsciousness of the audience and reveals the nature of the characters and their situation. Even the repetitious dialogue makes the audience more aware of the limitations and the pain of the circumstances in which Pinter's people find themselves.

Early reaction to the plays sometimes saw the aimless dialogue and the absurdist qualities as shortcomings rather than as indictments of the social order from which the plays arose. Yet the brutality of his characters to one another, their lack of sympathy for one another, and their demands for dominance have all become hallmarks of late-twentieth-century life.

The first of Pinter's plays to catch the attention of the general theater public was the commercially produced *The Caretaker* (1960), a play about two brothers, one of whom, Aston, invites a bewildered and all but mentally destroyed tramp, Davies, to become a caretaker in his room. Davies hardly knows who he is. His identity is essentially reduced to nothing by his soul-destroying life, and he speaks in broken language, especially when he is trying to explain that he left his identity papers in his beloved Sidcup — some fifteen years before — and that if they could find those papers, he would know where he was born and who he was. At the end of the play the younger brother, Mick, torments Davies, demanding that he leave, twisting his arm, verbally abusing him, but then relenting. The play ends with the shards of a life, as Davies says: "Listen . . . if I . . . go down . . . if I was to . . . get my papers . . . would you . . . would you let . . . would you . . . if I got down . . . and got my . . . (*Long silence.*)"

Pinter's *The Homecoming* (1965) has a brutal, shocking quality. A professor returns to England from America with his wife, and it becomes clear that he plans to return to America but that his wife will stay on as a mistress to his father and his brothers. The matter-of-factness with which the situation is treated and the way the relationships are portrayed provide part of the play's shock value.

In 1968 his play *Landscape* was censored for the use of obscenities, but eventually it and another short play, *Silence*, were produced in London in 1969 and in New York in 1970. *Old Times* was produced in London and in New York in 1971. Throughout the 1970s Pinter directed many plays by other playwrights and acted in films and on stage. *The Hothouse*, which was revived in 1995, was first produced in Hampstead in 1980. He later directed it himself in Providence, Rhode Island. He wrote the screenplay for *Betrayal* in 1982, when he also wrote the screenplay for *The French Lieutenant's Woman*, which received an Academy Award nomination for best film. In 1992 he adapted Kazuo Ishiguro's novel *Remains of the Day* for the screen and also wrote the screenplay for Franz Kafka's *The Trial*.

Recent plays include the full-length *Moonlight* (1993) and the short play *Ashes to Ashes* (1996). *Celebrations* (2000) is a short play and was paired at the Almeida Theatre in London with *The Room* (1957), his first play. Ordinarily, Pinter does not let his short plays be paired with other pieces. Even *Mountain Language* (1988), which lasted only twenty minutes, was produced alone by the Royal National Theatre in its Lyttelton Theatre. Pinter's most recent play, *War* (2003), includes a speech and eight poems on the theme of conflict. In addition to his playwriting, Pinter has also continued acting and appears in a major role as Sir Thomas Bertram in Patricia Rozema's film of Jane Austen's novel, *Mansfield Park* (1999).

BETRAYAL

Unlike many of Pinter's plays, in which people are specifically brutal toward one another, *Betrayal* shows people in an extraordinarily civil, although complex, relationship. The play concerns the betrayal of husbands and wives in adulterous relationships, but it also explores the power relations between the genders as well as the relationship between male friends. Jerry and Robert, best friends from college, are now business associates; Jerry, as literary agent, finds authors for Robert, who is a publisher. At first, the betrayal seems to have been committed by Jerry, the best man at Robert's marriage to Emma. As the play progresses, however, we see many levels of betrayal, including some appearing in the literature that Jerry promotes and Robert rejects, such as Spinks's novel, which Emma enjoys. Pinter examines the relationship of all three characters in great detail, revealing that Robert knew about Emma's affair with Jerry but never mentioned a word to his friend. Indeed, Robert and Jerry continued to have civilized lunches, drink together at bars, and generally enjoy each other's company as if nothing had happened. All the while and unknown to Emma and Jerry, Robert was himself having affairs. Part of the cruel fun of the play is watching the reactions of characters as they discover that such behavior had been going on without their knowledge.

The structure of the play is unusual. At first, it seems to progress normally, with the date 1977 displayed prominently at the top of the stage during the first two scenes, which follow chronologically. After those scenes, however, the play moves backward in time. During the first production in London this effect was powerful, if only because it was so unexpected. Pinter puts the audience into a special relationship with the characters and their circumstances because the audience understands the implied ironies in much of the dialogue, as for example in Robert's going off to read Yeats on the island of Torcello. Not only had Robert and Jerry discussed Yeats as undergraduates, but Yeats, the Irish poet, had also been "betrayed" by the one he loved, Maud Gonne, and had "betrayed" her in turn. It is especially ironic for Robert to tell Jerry that his early morning hours alone on Torcello were the high point of his trip to Venice, since it was the evening before that he had first discovered Emma and Jerry's affair.

The dialogue is pure Pinter. The speeches are very short at first, the words simple, often only one syllable, and often questions or observations are repeated in what seems an almost needless fashion. Yet the dialogue accretes and the significance of things that seem casual and almost irrelevant grows until we catch the innuendo and understand the deeper implications. One useful experience is going back to the opening scene after reading through the play. The emotional coolness of that scene is a powerful counterpoint to the intense closing scene of the play.

Betrayal in Performance

Betrayal was produced first at the National Theatre in London in 1978, then in New York in 1979. In London Michael Gambon was Jerry, Penelope Wilton was Emma, and Daniel Massey was Robert. In New York Raul Julia played Jerry, Blythe Danner was Emma, and Roy Scheider was Robert. Both productions were highly successful. The staging for both was similar, with realistic sets for the opening scene in the restaurant and the following scenes in the flat. The film version, which opened in February 1983, followed the structure of the play itself and stayed close to the original dialogue. Ben Kingsley was Robert, Jeremy Irons was Jerry, and a relative unknown, Patricia Hodge, played Emma. Of the film Vincent Canby wrote, "The writing is superb, and so quintessentially Pinter that it sometimes comes close to sounding like parody, though, in the screenplay, there's not one predictable line or gesture."

The play has been revived several times in London, first in 1983, then again at the Almeida Theatre in 1991. The Royal National Theatre produced the play at the Lyttelton Theatre in 1998. Sir Peter Hall directed the play in London's West End at The Duchess Theatre in October 2003. Janie Dee was Emma, Aden Gillett was Jerry, and Hugo Speer was Robert. It has also been produced regionally in the United States as a popular work in repertory.

Harold Pinter *(b. 1930)*

BETRAYAL

1978

Characters

EMMA
JERRY
ROBERT
A WAITER

In 1977 Emma is 38, Jerry and Robert are 40.

1977

Scene 1

Pub. 1977. Spring. *Noon.*
   Emma is sitting at a corner table. Jerry approaches with drinks, a pint of bitter for him, a glass of wine for her.
   He sits. They smile, toast each other silently, drink. He sits back and looks at her.

JERRY: Well . . .
EMMA: How are you?
JERRY: All right.
EMMA: You look well.
JERRY: Well, I'm not all that well, really.
EMMA: Why? What's the matter?
JERRY: Hangover.

(He raises his glass.)

   Cheers.

(He drinks.)

   How are you?
EMMA: I'm fine.

(She looks round the bar, back at him.)

   Just like old times.
JERRY: Mmn. It's been a long time.
EMMA: Yes.

(Pause.)

   I thought of you the other day.
JERRY: Good God. Why?

(She laughs.)

JERRY: Why?
EMMA: Well, it's nice, sometimes, to think back. Isn't it?
JERRY: Absolutely.

(Pause.)

   How's everything?

EMMA: Oh, not too bad.

(Pause.)

   Do you know how long it is since we met?
JERRY: Well I came to that private view, when was it — ?
EMMA: No, I don't mean that.
JERRY: Oh you mean alone?
EMMA: Yes.
JERRY: Uuh . . .
EMMA: Two years.
JERRY: Yes, I thought it must be. Mmnn.

(Pause.)

EMMA: Long time.
JERRY: Yes. It is.

(Pause.)

   How's it going? The Gallery?
EMMA: How do you think it's going?
JERRY: Well. Very well, I would say.
EMMA: I'm glad you think so. Well, it is, actually. I enjoy it.
JERRY: Funny lot, painters, aren't they?
EMMA: They're not at all funny.
JERRY: Aren't they? What a pity.

(Pause.)

   How's Robert?
EMMA: When did you last see him?
JERRY: I haven't seen him for months. Don't know why. Why?
EMMA: Why what?
JERRY: Why did you ask when I last saw him?
EMMA: I just wondered. How's Sam?
JERRY: You mean Judith.
EMMA: Do I?
JERRY: You remember the form. I ask about your husband, you ask about my wife.
EMMA: Yes, of course. How is your wife?
JERRY: All right.

(Pause.)

EMMA: Sam must be . . . tall.
JERRY: He is tall. Quite tall. Does a lot of running. He's a long distance runner. He wants to be a zoologist.
EMMA: No, really? Good. And Sarah?
JERRY: She's ten.
EMMA: God. I suppose she must be.
JERRY: Yes, she must be.

(Pause.)

   Ned's five, isn't he?

EMMA: You remember.
JERRY: Well, I would remember that.

(*Pause.*)

EMMA: Yes.

(*Pause.*)

You're all right, though?
JERRY: Oh . . . yes, sure.

(*Pause.*)

EMMA: Ever think of me?
JERRY: I don't need to think of you.
EMMA: Oh?
JERRY: I don't need to *think* of you.

(*Pause.*)

Anyway I'm all right. How are you?
EMMA: Fine, really. All right.
JERRY: You're looking very pretty.
EMMA: Really? Thank you. I'm glad to see you.
JERRY: So am I. I mean to see you.
EMMA: You think of me sometimes?
JERRY: I think of you sometimes.

(*Pause.*)

I saw Charlotte the other day.
EMMA: No? Where? She didn't mention it.
JERRY: She didn't see me. In the street.
EMMA: But you haven't seen her for years.
JERRY: I recognised her.
EMMA: How could you? How could you know?
JERRY: I did.
EMMA: What did she look like?
JERRY: You.
EMMA: No, what did you think of her, really?
JERRY: I thought she was lovely.
EMMA: Yes. She's very . . . She's smashing. She's thirteen.

(*Pause.*)

Do you remember that time . . . oh god it was . . . when you picked her up and threw her up and caught her?
JERRY: She was very light.
EMMA: She remembers that, you know.
JERRY: Really?
EMMA: Mmnn. Being thrown up.
JERRY: What a memory.

(*Pause.*)

She doesn't know . . . about us, does she?
EMMA: Of course not. She just remembers you, as an old friend.
JERRY: That's right.

(*Pause.*)

Yes, everyone was there that day, standing around, your husband, my wife, all the kids, I remember.
EMMA: What day?

JERRY: When I threw her up. It was in your kitchen.
EMMA: It was in your kitchen.

(*Silence.*)

JERRY: Darling.
EMMA: Don't say that.

(*Pause.*)

It all . . .
JERRY: Seems such a long time ago.
EMMA: Does it?
JERRY: Same again?

(*He takes the glasses, goes to the bar. She sits still. He returns, with the drinks, sits.*)

EMMA: I thought of you the other day.

(*Pause.*)

I was driving through Kilburn. Suddenly I saw where I was. I just stopped, and then I turned down Kinsale Drive and drove into Wessex Grove. I drove past the house and then stopped about fifty yards further on, like we used to do, do you remember?
JERRY: Yes.
EMMA: People were coming out of the house. They walked up the road.
JERRY: What sort of people?
EMMA: Oh . . . young people. Then I got out of the car and went up the steps. I looked at the bells, you know, the names on the bells. I looked for our name.

(*Pause.*)

JERRY: Green.

(*Pause.*)

Couldn't see it, eh?
EMMA: No.
JERRY: That's because we're not there any more. We haven't been there for years.
EMMA: No we haven't.

(*Pause.*)

JERRY: I hear you're seeing a bit of Casey.
EMMA: What?
JERRY: Casey. I just heard you were . . . seeing a bit of him.
EMMA: Where did you hear that?
JERRY: Oh . . . people . . . talking.
EMMA: Christ.
JERRY: The funny thing was that the only thing I really felt was irritation, I mean irritation that nobody gossiped about us like that, in the old days. I nearly said, now look, she may be having the occasional drink with Casey, who cares, but she and I had an affair for seven years and none of you bastards had the faintest idea it was happening.

(*Pause.*)

EMMA: I wonder. I wonder if everyone knew, all the time.

JERRY: Don't be silly. We were brilliant. Nobody knew. Who ever went to Kilburn in those days? Just you and me.

(*Pause.*)

Anyway, what's all this about you and Casey?

EMMA: What do you mean?

JERRY: What's going on?

EMMA: We have the occasional drink.

JERRY: I thought you didn't admire his work.

EMMA: I've changed. Or his work has changed. Are you jealous?

JERRY: Of what?

(*Pause.*)

I couldn't be jealous of Casey. I'm his agent. I advised him about his divorce. I read all his first drafts. I persuaded your husband to publish his first novel. I escort him to Oxford to speak at the Union. He's my . . . he's my boy. I discovered him when he was a poet, and that's a bloody long time ago now.

(*Pause.*)

He's even taken me down to Southampton to meet his Mum and Dad. I couldn't be jealous of Casey. Anyway it's not as if we're having an affair now, is it? We haven't seen each other for years. Really, I'm very happy if you're happy.

(*Pause.*)

What about Robert?

(*Pause.*)

EMMA: Well . . . I think we're going to separate.

JERRY: Oh?

EMMA: We had a long talk . . . last night.

JERRY: Last night?

EMMA: You know what I found out . . . last night? He's betrayed me for years. He's had . . . other women for years.

JERRY: No? Good Lord.

(*Pause.*)

But we betrayed him for years.

EMMA: And he betrayed me for years.

JERRY: Well I never knew that.

EMMA: Nor did I.

(*Pause.*)

JERRY: Does Casey know about this?

EMMA: I wish you wouldn't keep calling him Casey. His name is Roger.

JERRY: Yes. Roger.

EMMA: I phoned *you*. I don't know why.

JERRY: What a funny thing. We were such close friends, weren't we? Robert and me, even though I haven't seen him for a few months, but through all those years, all the drinks, all the lunches . . . we had together, I never even gleaned . . . I never suspected . . .

that there was anyone else . . . in his life but you. Never. For example, when you're with a fellow in a pub, or a restaurant, for example, from time to time he pops out for a piss, you see, who doesn't, but what I mean is, if he's making a crafty telephone call, you can sort of sense it, you see, you can sense the pip pip pips. Well, I never did that with Robert. He never made any pip pip telephone calls in any pub I was ever with him in. The funny thing is that it was me who made the pip pip calls — to you, when I left him boozing at the bar. That's the funny thing.

(*Pause.*)

When did he tell you all this?

EMMA: Last night. I think we were up all night.

(*Pause.*)

JERRY: You talked all night?

EMMA: Yes. Oh yes.

(*Pause.*)

JERRY: I didn't come into it, did I?

EMMA: What?

JERRY: I just —

EMMA: I just phoned you this morning, you know, that's all, because I . . . because we're old friends . . . I've been up all night . . . the whole thing's finished . . . I suddenly felt I wanted to see you.

JERRY: Well, look, I'm happy to see you. I am. I'm sorry . . . about . . .

EMMA: Do you remember? I mean, you do remember?

JERRY: I remember.

(*Pause.*)

EMMA: You couldn't really afford Wessex Grove when we took it, could you?

JERRY: Oh, love finds a way.

EMMA: I bought the curtains.

JERRY: You found a way.

EMMA: Listen, I didn't want to see you for nostalgia, I mean what's the point? I just wanted to see how you were. Truly. How are you?

JERRY: Oh what does it matter?

(*Pause.*)

You didn't tell Robert about me last night, did you?

EMMA: I had to.

(*Pause.*)

He told me everything. I told him everything. We were up . . . all night. At one point Ned came down. I had to take him up to bed, had to put him back to bed. Then I went down again. I think it was the voices woke him up. You know . . .

JERRY: You told him everything?

EMMA: I had to.

JERRY: You told him everything . . . about us?

EMMA: I had to.

(*Pause.*)

JERRY: But he's my oldest friend. I mean, I picked his own daughter up in my own arms and threw her up and caught her, in my kitchen. He watched me do it.

EMMA: It doesn't matter. It's all gone.

JERRY: Is it? What has?

EMMA: It's all all over.

(*She drinks.*)

1977
LATER

Scene 2

Jerry's House. Study. 1977. Spring. *Jerry sitting. Robert standing, with glass.*

JERRY: It's good of you to come.

ROBERT: Not at all.

JERRY: Yes, yes, I know it was difficult . . . I know . . . the kids . . .

ROBERT: It's all right. It sounded urgent.

JERRY: Well . . . You found someone, did you?

ROBERT: What?

JERRY: For the kids.

ROBERT: Yes, yes. Honestly. Everything's in order. Anyway, Charlotte's not a baby.

JERRY: No.

(*Pause.*)

Are you going to sit down?

ROBERT: Well, I might, yes, in a minute.

(*Pause.*)

JERRY: Judith's at the hospital . . . on night duty. The kids are . . . here . . . upstairs.

ROBERT: Uh-huh.

JERRY: I must speak to you. It's important.

ROBERT: Speak.

JERRY: Yes.

(*Pause.*)

ROBERT: You look quite rough.

(*Pause.*)

What's the trouble?

(*Pause.*)

It's not about you and Emma, is it?

(*Pause.*)

I know all about that.

JERRY: Yes. So I've . . . been told.

ROBERT: Ah.

(*Pause.*)

Well, it's not very important, is it? Been over for years, hasn't it?

JERRY: It is important.

ROBERT: Really? Why?

(*Jerry stands, walks about.*)

JERRY: I thought I was going to go mad.

ROBERT: When?

JERRY: This evening. Just now. Wondering whether to phone you. I had to phone you. It took me . . . two hours to phone you. And then you were with the kids . . . I thought I wasn't going to be able to see you . . . I thought I'd go mad. I'm very grateful to you . . . for coming.

ROBERT: Oh for God's sake! Look, what exactly do you want to say?

(*Pause.*)

(*Jerry sits.*)

JERRY: I don't know why she told you. I don't know how she could tell you. I just don't understand. Listen, I know you've got . . . look, I saw her today . . . we had a drink . . . I haven't seen her for . . . she told me, you know, that you're in trouble, both of you . . . and so on. I know that. I mean I'm sorry.

ROBERT: Don't be sorry.

JERRY: Why not?

(*Pause.*)

The fact is I can't understand . . . why she thought it necessary . . . after all these years . . . to tell you . . . so suddenly . . . last night . . .

ROBERT: Last night?

JERRY: Without consulting me. Without even warning me. After all, you and me . . .

ROBERT: She didn't tell me last night.

JERRY: What do you mean?

(*Pause.*)

I know about last night. She told me about it. You were up all night, weren't you?

ROBERT: That's correct.

JERRY: And she told you . . . last night . . . about her and me. Did she not?

ROBERT: No, she didn't. She didn't tell me about you and her last night. She told me about you and her four years ago.

(*Pause.*)

So she didn't have to tell me again last night. Because I knew. And she knew I knew because she told me herself four years ago.

(*Silence.*)

JERRY: What?

ROBERT: I think I will sit down.

(*He sits.*)

I thought you knew.

JERRY: Knew what?

ROBERT: That I knew. That I've known for years. I thought you knew that.

JERRY: You thought I knew?
ROBERT: She said you didn't. But I didn't believe that.

(*Pause.*)

Anyway I think I thought you knew. But you say you didn't?
JERRY: She told you . . . when?
ROBERT: Well, I found out. That's what happened. I told her I'd found out and then she . . . confirmed . . . the facts.
JERRY: When?
ROBERT: Oh, a long time ago, Jerry.

(*Pause.*)

JERRY: But we've seen each other . . . a great deal . . . over the last four years. We've had lunch.
ROBERT: Never played squash though.
JERRY: I was your best friend.
ROBERT: Well, yes, sure.

(*Jerry stares at him and then holds his head in his hands.*)

Oh, don't get upset. There's no point.

(*Silence.*)
(*Jerry sits up.*)

JERRY: Why didn't she tell me?
ROBERT: Well, I'm not her, old boy.
JERRY: Why didn't you tell me?

(*Pause.*)

ROBERT: I thought you might know.
JERRY: But you didn't know for *certain*, did you? You didn't *know*!
ROBERT: No.
JERRY: Then why didn't you tell me?

(*Pause.*)

ROBERT: Tell you what?
JERRY: That you knew. You bastard.
ROBERT: Oh, don't call me a bastard, Jerry.

(*Pause.*)

JERRY: What are we going to do?
ROBERT: You and I are not going to do anything. My marriage is finished. I've just got to make proper arrangements, that's all. About the children.

(*Pause.*)

JERRY: You hadn't thought of telling Judith?
ROBERT: Telling Judith what? Oh, about you and Emma. You mean she never knew? Are you quite sure?

(*Pause.*)

No, I hadn't thought of telling Judith, actually. You don't seem to understand. You don't seem to understand that I don't give a shit about any of this. It's true I've hit Emma once or twice. But that wasn't to defend a principle. I wasn't inspired to do it from any kind of moral standpoint. I just felt like giving her a good bashing. The old itch . . . you understand.

(*Pause.*)

JERRY: But you betrayed her for years, didn't you?
ROBERT: Oh yes.
JERRY: And she never knew about it. Did she?
ROBERT: Didn't she?

(*Pause.*)

JERRY: I didn't.
ROBERT: No, you didn't know very much about anything, really, did you?

(*Pause.*)

JERRY: No.
ROBERT: Yes you did.
JERRY: Yes I did. I lived with her.
ROBERT: Yes. In the afternoons.
JERRY: Sometimes very long ones. For seven years.
ROBERT: Yes, you certainly knew all there was to know about that. About the seven years of afternoons. I don't know anything about that.

(*Pause.*)

I hope she looked after you all right.

(*Silence.*)

JERRY: We used to like each other.
ROBERT: We still do.

(*Pause.*)

I bumped into old Casey the other day. I believe he's having an affair with my wife. We haven't played squash for years, Casey and me. We used to have a damn good game.
JERRY: He's put on weight.
ROBERT: Yes, I thought that.
JERRY: He's over the hill.
ROBERT: Is he?
JERRY: Don't you think so?
ROBERT: In what respect?
JERRY: His work. His books.
ROBERT: Oh his books. His art. Yes his art does seem to be falling away, doesn't it?
JERRY: Still sells.
ROBERT: Oh, sells very well. Sells very well indeed. Very good for us. For you and me.
JERRY: Yes.
ROBERT: Someone was telling me — who was it — must have been someone in the publicity department — the other day — that when Casey went up to York to sign his latest book, in a bookshop, you know, with Barbara Spring, you know, the populace queued for hours to get his signature on his book, while one old lady and a dog queued to get Barbara Spring's signature, on her book. I happen to think that Barbara Spring . . . is good, don't you?
JERRY: Yes.

(*Pause.*)

ROBERT: Still, we both do very well out of Casey, don't we?

JERRY: Very well.

(*Pause.*)

ROBERT: Have you read any good books lately?
JERRY: I've been reading Yeats.
ROBERT: Ah. Yeats. Yes.

(*Pause.*)

JERRY: You read Yeats on Torcello once.
ROBERT: On Torcello?
JERRY: Don't you remember? Years ago. You went over to Torcello in the dawn, alone. And read Yeats.
ROBERT: So I did. I told you that, yes.

(*Pause.*)

Yes.

(*Pause.*)

Where are you going this summer, you and the family?
JERRY: The Lake District.

1975

Scene 3

Flat. 1975. Winter. *Jerry and Emma. They are sitting.*

Silence.
JERRY: What do you want to do then?

(*Pause.*)

EMMA: I don't quite know what we're doing, any more, that's all.
JERRY: Mmnn.

(*Pause.*)

EMMA: I mean, this flat . . .
JERRY: Yes.
EMMA: Can you actually remember when we were last here?
JERRY: In the summer, was it?
EMMA: Well, was it?
JERRY: I know it seems —
EMMA: It was the beginning of September.
JERRY: Well, that's summer, isn't it?
EMMA: It was actually extremely cold. It was early autumn.
JERRY: It's pretty cold now.
EMMA: We were going to get another electric fire.
JERRY: Yes, I never got that.
EMMA: Not much point in getting it if we're never here.
JERRY: We're here now.
EMMA: Not really.

(*Silence.*)

JERRY: Well, things have changed. You've been so busy, your job, and everything.

EMMA: Well, I know. But I mean, I like it. I want to do it.
JERRY: No, it's great. It's marvellous for you. But you're not —
EMMA: If you're running a gallery you've got to run it, you've got to be there.
JERRY: But you're not free in the afternoons. Are you?
EMMA: No.
JERRY: So how can we meet?
EMMA: But look at the times you're out of the country. You're never here.
JERRY: But when I am here you're not free in the afternoons. So we can never meet.
EMMA: We can meet for lunch.
JERRY: We can meet for lunch but we can't come all the way out here for a quick lunch. I'm too old for that.
EMMA: I didn't suggest that.

(*Pause.*)

You see, in the past . . . we were inventive, we were determined, it was . . . it seemed impossible to meet . . . impossible . . . and yet we did. We met here, we took this flat and we met in this flat because we wanted to.
JERRY: It would not matter how much we wanted to if you're not free in the afternoons and I'm in America.

(*Silence.*)

Nights have always been out of the question and you know it. I have a family.
EMMA: I have a family too.
JERRY: I know that perfectly well. I might remind you that your husband is my oldest friend.
EMMA: What do you mean by that?
JERRY: I don't *mean* anything by it.
EMMA: But what are you trying to say by saying that?
JERRY: Jesus. I'm not *trying* to say anything. I've said precisely what I wanted to say.
EMMA: I see.

(*Pause.*)

The fact is that in the old days we used our imagination and we'd take a night and make an arrangement and go to an hotel.
JERRY: Yes. We did.

(*Pause.*)

But that was . . . in the main . . . before we got this flat.
EMMA: We haven't spent many nights . . . in this flat.
JERRY: No.

(*Pause.*)

Not many nights anywhere, really.

(*Silence.*)

EMMA: Can you afford . . . to keep it going, month after month?
JERRY: Oh . . .
EMMA: It's a waste. Nobody comes here. I just can't bear

to think about it, actually. Just . . . empty. All day and night. Day after day and night after night. I mean the crockery and the curtains and the bedspread and everything. And the tablecloth I brought from Venice. (*Laughs.*) It's ridiculous.

(*Pause.*)

It's just . . . an empty home.
JERRY: It's not a home.

(*Pause.*)

I know . . . I know what you wanted . . . but it could never . . . actually be a home. You have a home. I have a home. With curtains, etcetera. And children. Two children in two homes. There are no children here, so it's not the same kind of home.
EMMA: It was never intended to be the same kind of home. Was it?

(*Pause.*)

You didn't ever see it as a home, in any sense, did you?
JERRY: No, I saw it as a flat . . . you know.
EMMA: For fucking.
JERRY: No, for loving.
EMMA: Well, there's not much of that left, is there?

(*Silence.*)

JERRY: I don't think we don't love each other.

(*Pause.*)

EMMA: Ah well.

(*Pause.*)

What will you do about all the . . . furniture?
JERRY: What?
EMMA: The contents.

(*Silence.*)

JERRY: You know we can do something very simple, if we want to do it.
EMMA: You mean sell it to Mrs. Banks for a small sum and . . . and she can let it as a furnished flat?
JERRY: That's right. Wasn't the bed here?
EMMA: What?
JERRY: Wasn't it?
EMMA: We bought the bed. We bought everything. We bought the bed together.
JERRY: Ah. Yes.

(*Emma stands.*)

EMMA: You'll make all the arrangements, then? With Mrs. Banks?

(*Pause.*)

I don't want anything. Nowhere I can put it, you see. I have a home, with tablecloths and all the rest of it.
JERRY: I'll go into it, with Mrs. Banks. There'll be a few quid, you know, so . . .

EMMA: No, I don't want any *cash*, thank you very much.

(*Silence. She puts coat on.*)

I'm going now.

(*He turns, looks at her.*)

Oh here's my key.

(*Takes out keyring, tries to take key from ring.*)

Oh Christ.

(*Struggles to take key from ring.
Throws him the ring.*)

You take it off.

(*He catches it, looks at her.*)

Can you just do it please? I'm picking up Charlotte from school. I'm taking her shopping.

(*He takes key off.*)

Do you realise this is an afternoon? It's the Gallery's afternoon off. That's why I'm here. We close every Thursday afternoon. Can I have my keyring?

(*He gives it to her.*)

Thanks. Listen. I think we've made absolutely the right decision.

(*She goes.*)
(*He stands.*)

1974

Scene 4

Robert and Emma's House. Living room. 1974. Autumn.
Robert pouring a drink for Jerry. He goes to the door.

ROBERT: Emma! Jerry's here!
EMMA (*off*): Who?
ROBERT: Jerry.
EMMA: I'll be down.

(*Robert gives the drink to Jerry.*)

JERRY: Cheers.
ROBERT: Cheers. She's just putting Ned to bed. I should think he'll be off in a minute.
JERRY: Off where?
ROBERT: Dreamland.
JERRY: Ah. Yes, how is your sleep these days?
ROBERT: What?
JERRY: Do you still have bad nights? With Ned, I mean?
ROBERT: Oh, I see. Well, no. No, it's getting better. But you know what they say?
JERRY: What?
ROBERT: They say boys are worse than girls.
JERRY: Worse?
ROBERT: Babies. They say boy babies cry more than girl babies.

JERRY: Do they?

ROBERT: You didn't find that to be the case?

JERRY: Uh . . . yes, I think we did. Did you?

ROBERT: Yes. What do you make of it? Why do you think that is?

JERRY: Well, I suppose . . . boys are more anxious.

ROBERT: Boy babies?

JERRY: Yes.

ROBERT: What the hell are they anxious about . . . at their age? Do you think?

JERRY: Well . . . facing the world, I suppose, leaving the womb, all that.

ROBERT: But what about girl babies? They leave the womb too.

JERRY: That's true. It's also true that nobody talks much about girl babies leaving the womb. Do they?

ROBERT: I am prepared to do so.

JERRY: I see. Well, what have you got to say?

ROBERT: I was asking you a question.

JERRY: What was it?

ROBERT: Why do you assert that boy babies find leaving the womb more of a problem than girl babies?

JERRY: Have I made such an assertion?

ROBERT: You went on to make a further assertion, to the effect that boy babies are more anxious about facing the world than girl babies.

JERRY: Do you yourself believe that to be the case?

ROBERT: I do, yes.

(*Pause.*)

JERRY: Why do you think it is?

ROBERT: I have no answer.

(*Pause.*)

JERRY: Do you think it might have something to do with the difference between the sexes?

(*Pause.*)

ROBERT: Good God, you're right. That must be it.

(*Emma comes in.*)

EMMA: Hullo. Surprise.

JERRY: I was having tea with Casey.

EMMA: Where?

JERRY: Just around the corner.

EMMA: I thought he lived in . . . Hampstead or somewhere.

ROBERT: You're out of date.

EMMA: Am I?

JERRY: He's left Susannah. He's living alone round the corner.

EMMA: Oh.

ROBERT: Writing a novel about a man who leaves his wife and three children and goes to live alone on the other side of London to write a novel about a man who leaves his wife and three children —

EMMA: I hope it's better than the last one.

ROBERT: The last one? Ah, the last one. Wasn't that the one about the man who lived in a big house in Hampstead with his wife and three children and is writing a novel about — ?

JERRY (*to Emma*): Why didn't you like it?

EMMA: I've told you actually.

JERRY: I think it's the best thing he's written.

EMMA: It may be the best thing he's *written* but it's still bloody dishonest.

JERRY: Dishonest? In what way dishonest?

EMMA: I've told you, actually.

JERRY: Have you?

ROBERT: Yes, she has. Once when we were all having dinner, I remember, you, me, Emma and Judith, where was it, Emma gave a dissertation over the pudding about dishonesty in Casey with reference to his last novel. *Drying Out.* It was most stimulating. Judith had to leave unfortunately in the middle of it for her night shift at the hospital. How is Judith, by the way?

JERRY: Very well.

(*Pause.*)

ROBERT: When are we going to play squash?

JERRY: You're too good.

ROBERT: Not at all. I'm not good at all. I'm just fitter than you.

JERRY: But why? Why are you fitter than me?

ROBERT: Because I play squash.

JERRY: Oh, you're playing? Regularly?

ROBERT: Mmnn.

JERRY: With whom?

ROBERT: Casey, actually.

JERRY: Casey? Good Lord. What's he like?

ROBERT: He's a brutally honest squash player. No, really, we haven't played for years. We must play. You were rather good.

JERRY: Yes, I was quite good. All right. I'll give you a ring.

ROBERT: Why don't you?

JERRY: We'll make a date.

ROBERT: Right.

JERRY: Yes. We must do that.

ROBERT: And then I'll take you to lunch.

JERRY: No, no. I'll take you to lunch.

ROBERT: The man who wins buys the lunch.

EMMA: Can I watch?

(*Pause.*)

ROBERT: What?

EMMA: Why can't I watch and then take you both to lunch?

ROBERT: Well, to be brutally honest, we wouldn't actually want a woman around, would we, Jerry? I mean a game of squash isn't simply a game of squash, it's rather more than that. You see, first there's the game. And then there's the shower. And then there's the pint. And then there's lunch. After all, you've been at it. You've had your battle. What you want is your pint and your lunch. You really don't want a woman buying you lunch. You don't actually want a woman within a mile of the place, any of the places, really. You don't want her in the squash court, you don't want her in the shower, or the pub, or the restaurant. You see, at lunch you want to talk about squash, or cricket, or books, or even women, with your friend, and be able to warm to your theme without fear of improper interruption. That's what it's all about. What do you think, Jerry?

JERRY: I haven't played squash for years.

(*Pause.*)

ROBERT: Well, let's play next week.
JERRY: I can't next week. I'm in New York.
EMMA: Are you?
JERRY: I'm going over with one of my more celebrated writers, actually.
EMMA: Who?
JERRY: Casey. Someone wants to film that novel of his you didn't like. We're going over to discuss it. It was a question of them coming over here or us going over there. Casey thought he deserved the trip.
EMMA: What about you?
JERRY: What?
EMMA: Do you deserve the trip?
ROBERT: Judith going?
JERRY: No. He can't go alone. We'll have that game of squash when I get back. A week, or at the most ten days.
ROBERT: Lovely.
JERRY (*to Emma*): Bye. Thanks for the drink.
EMMA: Bye.

(*Robert and Jerry leave. She remains still.*)

(*Robert returns. He kisses her. She responds. She breaks away, puts her head on his shoulder, cries quietly. He holds her.*)

1973

Scene 5

Hotel Room. Venice. 1973. Summer. *Emma on bed reading. Robert at window looking out. She looks up at him, then back at the book.*

EMMA: It's Torcello tomorrow, isn't it?
ROBERT: What?
EMMA: We're going to Torcello tomorrow, aren't we?
ROBERT: Yes. That's right.
EMMA: That'll be lovely.
ROBERT: Mmn.
EMMA: I can't wait.

(*Pause.*)

ROBERT: Book good?
EMMA: Mmn. Yes.
ROBERT: What is it?

EMMA: This new book. This man Spinks.
ROBERT: Oh that. Jerry was telling me about it.
EMMA: Jerry? Was he?
ROBERT: He was telling me about it at lunch last week.
EMMA: Really? Does he like it?
ROBERT: Spinks is his boy. He discovered him.
EMMA: Oh. I didn't know that.
ROBERT: Unsolicited manuscript.

(*Pause.*)

You think it's good, do you?
EMMA: Yes, I do. I'm enjoying it.
ROBERT: Jerry thinks it's good too. You should have lunch with us one day and chat about it.
EMMA: Is that absolutely necessary?

(*Pause.*)

It's not as good as all that.
ROBERT: You mean it's not good enough for you to have lunch with Jerry and me and chat about it?
EMMA: What the hell are you talking about?
ROBERT: I must read it again myself, now it's in hard covers.
EMMA: Again?
ROBERT: Jerry wanted us to publish it.
EMMA: Oh, really?
ROBERT: Well, naturally. Anyway, I turned it down.
EMMA: Why?
ROBERT: Oh . . . not much more to say on that subject, really, is there?
EMMA: What do you consider the subject to be?
ROBERT: Betrayal.
EMMA: No, it isn't.
ROBERT: Isn't it? What is it then?
EMMA: I haven't finished it yet. I'll let you know.
ROBERT: Well, do let me know.

(*Pause.*)

Of course, I could be thinking of the wrong book.

(*Silence.*)

By the way, I went into American Express yesterday.

(*She looks up.*)

EMMA: Oh?
ROBERT: Yes. I went to cash some travellers cheques. You get a much better rate there, you see, than you do in an hotel.
EMMA: Oh, do you?
ROBERT: Oh yes. Anyway, there was a letter there for you. They asked me if you were any relation and I said yes. So they asked me if I wanted to take it. I mean, they gave it to me. But I said no, I would leave it. Did you get it?
EMMA: Yes.
ROBERT: I suppose you popped in when you were out shopping yesterday evening?
EMMA: That's right.
ROBERT: Oh well, I'm glad you got it.

(*Pause.*)

To be honest, I was amazed that they suggested I take it. It could never happen in England. But these Italians . . . so free and easy. I mean, just because my name is Downs and your name is Downs doesn't mean that we're the Mr. and Mrs. Downs that they, in their laughing Mediterranean way, assume we are. We could be, and in fact are vastly more likely to be, total strangers. So let's say I, whom they laughingly assume to be your husband, had taken the letter, having declared myself to be your husband but in truth being a total stranger, and opened it, and read it, out of nothing more than idle curiosity, and then thrown it in a canal, you would never have received it and would have been deprived of your legal right to open your own mail, and all this because of Venetian *je m'en foutisme.*° I've a good mind to write to the Doge of Venice about it.

(*Pause.*)

That's what stopped me taking it, by the way, and bringing it to you, the thought that I could very easily be a total stranger.

(*Pause.*)

What they of course did not know, and had no way of knowing, was that I am your husband.
EMMA: Pretty inefficient bunch.
ROBERT: Only in a laughing Mediterranean way.

(*Pause.*)

EMMA: It was from Jerry.
ROBERT: Yes, I recognised the handwriting.

(*Pause.*)

How is he?
EMMA: Okay.
ROBERT: Good. And Judith?
EMMA: Fine.

(*Pause.*)

ROBERT: What about the kids?
EMMA: I don't think he mentioned them.
ROBERT: They're probably all right, then. If they were ill or something he'd have probably mentioned it.

(*Pause.*)

Any other news?
EMMA: No.

(*Silence.*)

ROBERT: Are you looking forward to Torcello?

(*Pause.*)

How many times have we been to Torcello? Twice. I remember how you loved it, the first time I took you

there. You fell in love with it. That was about ten years ago, wasn't it? About . . . six months after we were married. Yes. Do you remember? I wonder if you'll like it as much tomorrow.

(*Pause.*)

What do you think of Jerry as a letter writer?

(*She laughs shortly.*)

You're trembling. Are you cold?
EMMA: No.
ROBERT: He used to write to me at one time. Long letters about Ford Madox Ford. I used to write to him too, come to think of it. Long letters about . . . oh, W. B. Yeats, I suppose. That was the time when we were both editors of poetry magazines. Him at Cambridge, me at Oxford. Did you know that? We were bright young men. And close friends. Well, we still are close friends. All that was long before I met you. Long before he met you. I've been trying to remember when I introduced him to you. I simply can't remember. I take it I *did* introduce him to you? Yes. But when? Can you remember?
EMMA: No.
ROBERT: You can't?
EMMA: No.
ROBERT: How odd.

(*Pause.*)

He wasn't best man at our wedding, was he?
EMMA: You know he was.
ROBERT: Ah yes. Well, that's probably when I introduced him to you.

(*Pause.*)

Was there any message for me, in his letter?

(*Pause.*)

I mean in the line of business, to do with the world of publishing. Has he discovered any new and original talent? He's quite talented at uncovering talent, old Jerry.
EMMA: No message.
ROBERT: No message. Not even his love?

(*Silence.*)

EMMA: We're lovers.
ROBERT: Ah. Yes. I thought it might be something like that, something along those lines.
EMMA: When?
ROBERT: What?
EMMA: When did you think?
ROBERT: Yesterday. Only yesterday. When I saw his handwriting on the letter. Before yesterday I was quite ignorant.
EMMA: Ah.

(*Pause.*)

I'm sorry.

je m'en foutisme: Vulgar phrase indicating a lax attitude.

ABOVE: Imogen Stubbs as
Emma and Anthony Calf as
Robert in the Royal National
Theatre's production of
Betrayal at the Lyttelton
Theatre, London, 1998.
RIGHT: Douglas Hodge as
Jerry and Imogen Stubbs as
Emma in *Betrayal* at the Royal
National Theatre's production
at the Lyttelton Theatre,
London, 1998.

ROBERT: *Sorry?*

(*Silence.*)

Where does it . . . take place? Must be a bit awkward. I mean we've got two kids, he's got two kids,
not to mention a wife . . .
EMMA: We have a flat.
ROBERT: Ah. I see.

(*Pause.*)

Nice?

(*Pause.*)

A flat. It's quite well established then, your . . .
uh . . . affair?
EMMA: Yes.
ROBERT: How long?
EMMA: Some time.
ROBERT: Yes, but how long exactly?
EMMA: Five years.
ROBERT: *Five years?*

(*Pause.*)

Ned is one year old.

(*Pause.*)

Did you hear what I said?
EMMA: Yes. He's your son. Jerry was in America. For
two months.

(*Silence.*)

ROBERT: Did he write to you from America?
EMMA: Of course. And I wrote to him.
ROBERT: Did you tell him that Ned had been conceived?
EMMA: Not by letter.
ROBERT: But when you did tell him, was he happy to
know I was to be a father?

(*Pause.*)

I've always liked Jerry. To be honest, I've always
liked him rather more than I've liked you. Maybe I
should have had an affair with him myself.

(*Silence.*)

Tell me, are you looking forward to our trip to Torcello?

1973
LATER

Scene 6

Flat. 1973. Summer. *Emma and Jerry standing, kissing.
She is holding a basket and a parcel.*

EMMA: Darling.
JERRY: Darling.

(*He continues to hold her. She laughs.*)

EMMA: I must put this down.

(*She puts basket on table.*)

JERRY: What's in it?
EMMA: Lunch.
JERRY: What?
EMMA: Things you like.

(*He pours wine.*)

How do I look?
JERRY: Beautiful.
EMMA: Do I look well?
JERRY: You do.

(*He gives her wine.*)

EMMA (*sipping*): Mmmnn.
JERRY: How was it?
EMMA: It was lovely.
JERRY: Did you go to Torcello?
EMMA: No.
JERRY: Why not?
EMMA: Oh, I don't know. The speedboats were on
strike, or something.
JERRY: On strike?
EMMA: Yes. On the day we were going.
JERRY: Ah. What about the gondolas?
EMMA: You can't take a gondola to Torcello.
JERRY: Well, they used to in the old days, didn't they?
Before they had speedboats. How do you think they
got over there?
EMMA: It would take hours.
JERRY: Yes, I suppose so.

(*Pause.*)

I got your letter.
EMMA: Good.
JERRY: Get mine?
EMMA: Of course. Miss me?
JERRY: Yes. Actually, I haven't been well.
EMMA: What?
JERRY: Oh nothing. A bug.

(*She kisses him.*)

EMMA: I missed you.

(*She turns away, looks about.*)

You haven't been here . . . at all?
JERRY: No.
EMMA: Needs Hoovering.°
JERRY: Later.

(*Pause.*)

I spoke to Robert this morning.
EMMA: Oh?

Hoovering: Vacuuming.

JERRY: I'm taking him to lunch on Thursday.

EMMA: Thursday? Why?

JERRY: Well, it's my turn.

EMMA: No, I meant why are you taking him to lunch?

JERRY: Because it's my turn. Last time he took me to lunch.

EMMA: You know what I mean.

JERRY: No. What?

EMMA: What is the subject or point of your lunch?

JERRY: No subject or point. We've just been doing it for years. His turn, followed by my turn.

EMMA: You've misunderstood me.

JERRY: Have I? How?

EMMA: Well, quite simply, you often do meet, or have lunch, to discuss a particular writer or a particular book, don't you? So to those meetings, or lunches, there is a point or a subject.

JERRY: Well, there isn't to this one.

(*Pause.*)

EMMA: You haven't discovered any new writers, while I've been away?

JERRY: No. Sam fell off his bike.

EMMA: No.

JERRY: He was knocked out. He was out for about a minute.

EMMA: Were you with him?

JERRY: No. Judith. He's all right. And then I got this bug.

EMMA: Oh dear.

JERRY: So I've had time for nothing.

EMMA: Everything will be better, now I'm back.

JERRY: Yes.

EMMA: Oh, I read that Spinks, the book you gave me.

JERRY: What do you think?

EMMA: Excellent.

JERRY: Robert hated it. He wouldn't publish it.

EMMA: What's he like?

JERRY: Who?

EMMA: Spinks.

JERRY: Spinks? He's a very thin bloke. About fifty. Wears dark glasses day and night. He lives alone, in a furnished room. Quite like this one, actually. He's . . . unfussed.

EMMA: Furnished rooms suit him?

JERRY: Yes.

EMMA: They suit me too. And you? Do you still like it? Our home?

JERRY: It's marvellous not to have a telephone.

EMMA: And marvellous to have me?

JERRY: You're all right.

EMMA: I cook and slave for you.

JERRY: You do.

EMMA: I bought something in Venice — for the house.

(*She opens the parcel, takes out a tablecloth. Puts it on the table.*)

Do you like it?

JERRY: It's lovely.

(*Pause.*)

EMMA: Do you think we'll ever go to Venice together?

(*Pause.*)

No. Probably not.

(*Pause.*)

JERRY: You don't think I should see Robert for lunch on Thursday, or on Friday, for that matter?

EMMA: Why do you say that?

JERRY: You don't think I should see him at all?

EMMA: I didn't say that. How can you not see him? Don't be silly.

(*Pause.*)

JERRY: I had a terrible panic when you were away. I was sorting out a contract, in my office, with some lawyers. I suddenly couldn't remember what I'd done with your letter. I couldn't remember putting it in the safe. I said I had to look for something in the safe. I opened the safe. It wasn't there. I had to go on with the damn contract . . . I kept seeing it lying somewhere in the house, being picked up . . .

EMMA: Did you find it?

JERRY: It was in the pocket of a jacket — in my wardrobe — at home.

EMMA: God.

JERRY: Something else happened a few months ago — I didn't tell you. We had a drink one evening. Well, we had our drink, and I got home about eight, walked in the door, Judith said, hello, you're a bit late. Sorry, I said, I was having a drink with Spinks. Spinks? she said, how odd, he's just phoned, five minutes ago, wanted to speak to you, he didn't mention he'd just seen you. You know old Spinks, I said, not exactly forthcoming, is he? He'd probably remembered something he'd meant to say but hadn't. I'll ring him later. I went up to see the kids and then we all had dinner.

(*Pause.*)

Listen. Do you remember, when was it, a few years ago, we were all in your kitchen, must have been Christmas or something, do you remember, all the kids were running about and suddenly I picked Charlotte up and lifted her high up, high up, and then down and up. Do you remember how she laughed?

EMMA: Everyone laughed.

JERRY: She was so light. And there was your husband and my wife and all the kids, all standing and laughing in your kitchen. I can't get rid of it.

EMMA: It was your kitchen, actually.

(*He takes her hand. They stand. They go to the bed and lie down.*)

Why shouldn't you throw her up?

(*She caresses him. They embrace.*)

1973
LATER

Scene 7

Restaurant. 1973. Summer. *Robert at table drinking white wine. The waiter brings Jerry to the table. Jerry sits.*

JERRY: Hullo, Robert.
ROBERT: Hullo.
JERRY (*to the waiter*): I'd like a Scotch on the rocks.
WAITER: With water?
JERRY: What?
WAITER: You want it with water?
JERRY: No. No water. Just on the rocks.
WAITER: Certainly signore.
ROBERT: Scotch? You don't usually drink Scotch at lunchtime.
JERRY: I've had a bug, actually.
ROBERT: Ah.
JERRY: And the only thing to get rid of this bug was Scotch — at lunchtime as well as at night. So I'm still drinking Scotch at lunchtime in case it comes back.
ROBERT: Like an apple a day.
JERRY: Precisely.

(*Waiter brings Scotch on rocks.*)

    Cheers.
ROBERT: Cheers.
WAITER: The menus, signori.

(*He passes the menus, goes.*)

ROBERT: How are you? Apart from the bug?
JERRY: Fine.
ROBERT: Ready for some squash?
JERRY: When I've got rid of the bug, yes.
ROBERT: I thought you had got rid of it.
JERRY: Why do you think I'm still drinking Scotch at lunchtime?
ROBERT: Oh yes. We really must play. We haven't played for years.
JERRY: How old are you now, then?
ROBERT: Thirty six.
JERRY: That means I'm thirty six as well.
ROBERT: If you're a day.
JERRY: Bit violent, squash.
ROBERT: Ring me. We'll have a game.
JERRY: How was Venice?
WAITER: Ready to order, signori?
ROBERT: What'll you have?

(*Jerry looks at him, briefly, then back to the menu.*)

JERRY: I'll have melone. And Piccata al limone with a green salad.
WAITER: Insalata verde. Prosciutto e melone?
JERRY: No. Just melone. On the rocks.
ROBERT: I'll have prosciutto and melone. Fried scampi. And spinach.
WAITER: E spinaci. Grazie, signore.

ROBERT: And a bottle of Corvo Bianco straight away.
WAITER: Si, signore. Molte grazie.

(*He goes.*)

JERRY: Is he the one who's always been here or is it his son?
ROBERT: You mean has his son always been here?
JERRY: No, is *he* his son? I mean, is he the son of the one who's always been here?
ROBERT: No, he's his father.
JERRY: Ah. Is he?
ROBERT: He's the one who speaks wonderful Italian.
JERRY: Yes. Your Italian's pretty good, isn't it?
ROBERT: No. Not at all.
JERRY: Yes it is.
ROBERT: No, it's Emma's Italian which is very good. Emma's Italian is very good.
JERRY: Is it? I didn't know that.

(*Waiter with bottle.*)

WAITER: Corvo Bianco, signore.
ROBERT: Thank you.
JERRY: How was it, anyway? Venice.
WAITER: Venice, signore? Beautiful. A most beautiful place of Italy. You see that painting on the wall? Is Venice.
ROBERT: So it is.
WAITER: You know what is none of in Venice?
JERRY: What?
WAITER: Traffico.

(*He goes, smiling.*)

ROBERT: Cheers.
JERRY: Cheers.
ROBERT: When were you last there?
JERRY: Oh, years.
ROBERT: How's Judith?
JERRY: What? Oh, you know, okay. Busy.
ROBERT: And the kids?
JERRY: All right. Sam fell off —
ROBERT: What?
JERRY: No, no, nothing. So how was it?
ROBERT: You used to go there with Judith, didn't you?
JERRY: Yes, but we haven't been there for years.

(*Pause.*)

    How about Charlotte? Did she enjoy it?
ROBERT: I think she did.

(*Pause.*)

    I did.
JERRY: Good.
ROBERT: I went for a trip to Torcello.
JERRY: Oh, really? Lovely place.
ROBERT: Incredible day. I got up very early and — whoomp — right across the lagoon — to Torcello. Not a soul stirring.
JERRY: What's the "whoomp"?
ROBERT: Speedboat.

JERRY: Ah. I thought —
ROBERT: What?
JERRY: It's so long ago, I'm obviously wrong. I thought one went to Torcello by gondola.
ROBERT: It would take hours. No, no, — whoomp — across the lagoon in the dawn.
JERRY: Sounds good.
ROBERT: I was quite alone.
JERRY: Where was Emma?
ROBERT: I think asleep.
JERRY: Ah.
ROBERT: I was alone for hours, as a matter of fact, on the island. Highpoint, actually, of the whole trip.
JERRY: Was it? Well, it sounds marvellous.
ROBERT: Yes. I sat on the grass and read Yeats.
JERRY: Yeats on Torcello?
ROBERT: They went well together.

(*Waiter with food.*)

WAITER: One melone. One prosciutto e melone.
ROBERT: Prosciutto for me.
WAITER: Buon appetito.
ROBERT: Emma read that novel of that chum of yours — what's his name?
JERRY: I don't know. What?
ROBERT: Spinks.
JERRY: Oh Spinks. Yes. The one you didn't like.
ROBERT: The one I wouldn't publish.
JERRY: I remember. Did Emma like it?
ROBERT: She seemed to be madly in love with it.
JERRY: Good.
ROBERT: You like it yourself, do you?
JERRY: I do.
ROBERT: And it's very successful?
JERRY: It is.
ROBERT: Tell me, do you think that makes me a publisher of unique critical judgement or a foolish publisher?
JERRY: A foolish publisher.
ROBERT: I agree with you. I am a very foolish publisher.
JERRY: No you're not. What are you talking about? You're a good publisher. What are you talking about?
ROBERT: I'm a bad publisher because I hate books. Or to be more precise, prose. Or to be even more precise, modern prose, I mean modern novels, first novels and second novels, all that promise and sensibility it falls upon me to judge, to put the firm's money on, and then to push for the third novel, see it done, see the dust jacket done, see the dinner for the national literary editors done, see the signing in Hatchards done, see the lucky author cook himself to death, all in the name of literature. You know what you and Emma have in common? You love literature. I mean you love modern prose literature, I mean you love the new novel by the new Casey or Spinks. It gives you both a thrill.
JERRY: You must be pissed.
ROBERT: Really? You mean you don't think it gives Emma a thrill?

JERRY: How do I know? She's your wife.

(*Pause.*)

ROBERT: Yes. Yes. You're quite right. I shouldn't have to consult you. I shouldn't have to consult anyone.
JERRY: I'd like some more wine.
ROBERT: Yes, yes. Waiter! Another bottle of Corvo Bianco. And where's our lunch? This place is going to pot. Mind you, it's worse in Venice. They really don't give a fuck there. I'm not drunk. You can't get drunk on Corvo Bianco. Mind you . . . last night . . . I was up late . . . I hate brandy . . . it stinks of modern literature. No, look, I'm sorry . . .

(*Waiter with bottle.*)

WAITER: Corvo Bianco.
ROBERT: Same glass. Where's our lunch?
WAITER: It comes.
ROBERT: I'll pour.

(*Waiter goes, with melon plates.*)

No, look, I'm sorry, have another drink. I'll tell you what it is, it's just that I can't bear being back in London. I was happy, such a rare thing, not in Venice, I don't mean that, I mean on Torcello, when I walked about Torcello in the early morning, alone, I was happy, I wanted to stay there forever.
JERRY: We all . . .
ROBERT: Yes, we all . . . feel that sometimes. Oh you do yourself, do you?

(*Pause.*)

I mean there's nothing really wrong, you see. I've got the family. Emma and I are very good together. I think the world of her. And I actually consider Casey to be a first rate writer.
JERRY: Do you really?
ROBERT: First rate. I'm proud to publish him and you discovered him and that was very clever of you.
JERRY: Thanks.
ROBERT: You've got a good nose and you care and I respect that in you. So does Emma. We often talk about it.
JERRY: How is Emma?
ROBERT: Very well. You must come and have a drink sometime. She'd love to see you.

1971

Scene 8

Flat. 1971. Summer. *Flat empty. Kitchen door open. Table set; crockery, glasses, bottle of wine. Jerry comes in through front door, with key.*

JERRY: Hullo.

(*Emma's voice from kitchen.*)

EMMA: Hullo.

(*Emma comes out of kitchen. She is wearing an apron.*)

I've only just got here. I meant to be here ages ago.
I'm making this stew. It'll be hours.

(*He kisses her.*)

Are you starving?

JERRY: Yes.

(*He kisses her.*)

EMMA: No really. I'll never do it. You sit down. I'll get it
on.

JERRY: What a lovely apron.

EMMA: Good.

(*She kisses him, goes into kitchen.*)
(*She calls. He pours wine.*)

EMMA: What have you been doing?

JERRY: Just walked through the park.

EMMA: What was it like?

JERRY: Beautiful. Empty. A slight mist.

(*Pause.*)

I sat down for a bit, under a tree. It was very quiet. I
just looked at the Serpentine.

(*Pause.*)

EMMA: And then?

JERRY: Then I got a taxi to Wessex Grove. Number 31.
And I climbed the steps and opened the front door
and then climbed the stairs and opened this door and
found you in a new apron cooking a stew.

(*Emma comes out of the kitchen.*)

EMMA: It's on.

JERRY: Which is now on.

(*Emma pours herself a vodka.*)

JERRY: Vodka? At lunchtime?

EMMA: Just feel like one.

(*She drinks.*)

I ran into Judith yesterday. Did she tell you?

JERRY: No, she didn't.

(*Pause.*)

Where?

EMMA: Lunch.

JERRY: Lunch?

EMMA: She didn't tell you?

JERRY: No.

EMMA: That's funny.

JERRY: What do you mean, lunch? Where?

EMMA: At Fortnum and Mason's.

JERRY: Fortnum and Mason's? What the hell was she
doing at Fortnum and Mason's?

EMMA: She was lunching with a lady.

JERRY: A lady?

EMMA: Yes.

(*Pause.*)

JERRY: Fortnum and Mason's is a long way from the
hospital.

EMMA: Of course it isn't.

JERRY: Well . . . I suppose not.

(*Pause.*)

And you?

EMMA: Me?

JERRY: What were you doing at Fortnum and Mason's?

EMMA: Lunching with my sister.

JERRY: Ah.

(*Pause.*)

EMMA: Judith . . . didn't tell you?

JERRY: I haven't really seen her. I was out late last night,
with Casey. And she was out early this morning.

(*Pause.*)

EMMA: Do you think she knows?

JERRY: Knows?

EMMA: Does she know? About us?

JERRY: No.

EMMA: Are you sure?

JERRY: She's too busy. At the hospital. And then the kids.
She doesn't go in for . . . speculation.

EMMA: But what about clues? Isn't she interested . . . to
follow clues?

JERRY: What clues?

EMMA: Well, there must be some . . . available to her . . .
to pick up.

JERRY: There are none . . . available to her.

EMMA: Oh. Well . . . good.

(*Pause.*)

JERRY: She has an admirer.

EMMA: Really?

JERRY: Another doctor. He takes her for drinks. It's . . .
irritating. I mean, she says that's all there is to it. He
likes her, she's fond of him, etcetera, etcetera . . . perhaps that's what I find irritating. I don't know exactly
what's going on.

EMMA: Oh, why shouldn't she have an admirer? I have
an admirer.

JERRY: Who?

EMMA: Uuh . . . you, I think.

JERRY: Ah. Yes.

(*He takes her hand.*)

I'm more than that.

(*Pause.*)

EMMA: Tell me . . . have you ever thought . . . of changing your life?

JERRY: Changing?

EMMA: Mmnn.

(*Pause.*)

JERRY: It's impossible.

(*Pause.*)

EMMA: Do you think she's being unfaithful to you?
JERRY: No. I don't know.
EMMA: When you were in America, just now, for instance?
JERRY: No.
EMMA: Have you ever been unfaithful?
JERRY: To whom?
EMMA: To me, of course.
JERRY: No.

(*Pause.*)

   Have you . . . to me?
EMMA: No.

(*Pause.*)

   If she was, what would you do?
JERRY: She isn't. She's busy. She's got lots to do. She's a very good doctor. She likes her life. She loves the kids.
EMMA: Ah.
JERRY: She loves me.

(*Pause.*)

EMMA: Ah.

(*Silence.*)

JERRY: All that means something.
EMMA: It certainly does.
JERRY: But I adore you.

(*Pause.*)

   I adore you.

(*Emma takes his hand.*)

EMMA: Yes.

(*Pause.*)

   Listen. There's something I have to tell you.
JERRY: What?
EMMA: I'm pregnant. It was when you were in America.

(*Pause.*)

   It wasn't anyone else. It was my husband.

(*Pause.*)

JERRY: Yes. Yes, of course.

(*Pause.*)

   I'm very happy for you.

1968

Scene 9

Robert and Emma's House. Bedroom. 1968. Winter.
The room is dimly lit. Jerry is sitting in the shadows. Faint music through the door.
   The door opens. Light. Music. Emma comes in, closes the door. She goes towards the mirror, sees Jerry.

EMMA: Good God.
JERRY: I've been waiting for you.
EMMA: What do you mean?
JERRY: I knew you'd come.

(*He drinks.*)

EMMA: I've just come in to comb my hair.

(*He stands.*)

JERRY: I knew you'd have to. I knew you'd have to comb your hair. I knew you'd have to get away from the party.

(*She goes to the mirror, combs her hair.
He watches her.*)

   You're a beautiful hostess.
EMMA: Aren't you enjoying the party?
JERRY: You're beautiful.

(*He goes to her.*)

   Listen. I've been watching you all night. I must tell you, I want to tell you, I have to tell you —
EMMA: Please —
JERRY: You're incredible.
EMMA: You're drunk.
JERRY: Nevertheless.

(*He holds her.*)

EMMA: Jerry.
JERRY: I was best man at your wedding. I saw you in white. I watched you glide by in white.
EMMA: I wasn't in white.
JERRY: You know what should have happened?
EMMA: What?
JERRY: I should have had you, in your white, before the wedding. I should have blackened you, in your white wedding dress, blackened you in your bridal dress, before ushering you into your wedding, as your best man.
EMMA: My husband's best man. Your best friend's best man.
JERRY: No. Your best man.
EMMA: I must get back.
JERRY: You're lovely. I'm crazy about you. All these words I'm using, don't you see, they've never been said before. Can't you see? I'm crazy about you. It's a whirlwind. Have you ever been to the Sahara Desert? Listen to me. It's true. Listen. You overwhelm me. You're so lovely.
EMMA: I'm not.
JERRY: You're so beautiful. Look at the way you look at me.
EMMA: I'm not . . . looking at you. Please.
JERRY: Look at the way you're looking at me. I can't wait for you, I'm bowled over, I'm totally knocked out, you dazzle me, you jewel, my jewel, I can't ever sleep again, no, listen, it's the truth, I won't walk, I'll be a cripple, I'll descend, I'll diminish, into total paralysis, my life is in your hands, that's what you're banishing

me to, a state of catatonia, do you know the state of catatonia? do you? do you? the state of . . . where the reigning prince is the prince of emptiness, the prince of absence, the prince of desolation. I love you.

EMMA: My husband is at the other side of that door.

JERRY: Everyone knows. The world knows. It knows. But they'll never know, they'll never know, they're in a different world. I adore you. I'm madly in love with you. I can't believe that what anyone is at this moment saying has ever happened has ever happened. Nothing has ever happened. Nothing. This is the only thing that has ever happened. Your eyes kill me. I'm lost. You're wonderful.

EMMA: No.

JERRY: Yes.

(He kisses her.
She breaks away.
He kisses her.)

(Laughter off.
She breaks away.
Door opens. Robert.)

EMMA: Your best friend is drunk.

JERRY: As you are my best and oldest friend and, in the present instance, my host, I decided to take this opportunity to tell your wife how beautiful she was.

ROBERT: Quite right.

JERRY: It is quite right, to . . . to face up to the facts . . . and to offer a token, without blush, a token of one's unalloyed appreciation, no holds barred.

ROBERT: Absolutely.

JERRY: And how wonderful for you that this is so, that this is the case, that her beauty is the case.

ROBERT: Quite right.

(Jerry moves to Robert and takes hold of his elbow.)

JERRY: I speak as your oldest friend. Your best man.

ROBERT: You are, actually.

(He clasps Jerry's shoulder, briefly, turns, leaves the room.)

(Emma moves towards the door. Jerry grasps her arm. She stops still.)

(They stand still, looking at each other.)

COMMENTARY

Katherine H. Burkman (b. 1934)

HAROLD PINTER'S *BETRAYAL:* LIFE BEFORE DEATH — AND AFTER   *1982*

> *Burkman's interest lies in the interplay of the characters and the dimensions of their betrayal of each other. She is concerned with Robert and Jerry's relationship and the role that Emma plays in their lives. The apparent simplicity of the play is belied by the complexities that lie beneath the surface, and Burkman's approach is to help reveal the play's depths.*

In scene five of Harold Pinter's *Betrayal,* just before Robert learns from his wife Emma that she has betrayed him for five years with his best friend Jerry, they discuss the book she is reading. It is a book that her publisher husband has, he tells her, refused to publish himself, despite the urging of Jerry (the author's agent, Robert's friend, and Emma's lover) because there isn't "much more to say on that subject."[1] He considers the subject to be betrayal. Emma does not think the book is

---

[1]Harold Pinter, *Betrayal* (New York: Grove Press, Inc., 1978), p. 78. All subsequent quotations from the play are from this edition as reprinted in *The Bedford Introduction to Drama,* Fifth Edition, and are hereafter given parenthetically in the body of the essay.

about betrayal, but she hasn't finished reading it yet; she promises to let Robert know what it is about when she is done.

In this nicely self-reflexive moment, Pinter invites us to look beneath the cross currents of this play's love affairs for what remains the primary subject in all of his dramas — renewal. In *A Slight Ache* and *The Homecoming* Pinter's depiction of women disposing of their husbands and taking on new partners had all of the ritual connotations attendant on Sir James Frazer's fertility goddesses in *The Golden Bough*. The prototype of these goddesses is Diana in the Grove of Nemi, who must unite with the new god-king-priest of her grove when he defeats the old, just as spring must follow winter — if spring is to follow winter.[2] One may look in vain in *Betrayal* for the lush summer setting of *A Slight Ache* (1959) in which Flora assumes a new mate who will understand and nourish the garden with which her old mate could no longer connect, just as one may look in vain for the environmental alternatives that attend Ruth, whose disposal of her husband and assumption of his family in *The Homecoming* (1965) is a desperate choice of life in the English jungle over death in the American desert. Still, the battle in *Betrayal* (1978) is a desperate one, its issue is renewal, and its strategies may be detected and charted as they operate beneath the seemingly casual game of betrayal in which the characters are ostensibly engaged.

Betrayal does not end, as do *A Slight Ache* and *The Homecoming*, with the breakup of a marriage; we learn at the very beginning that Emma and Robert's marriage is over. Emma returns in scene one to her now ex-lover Jerry, ostensibly to tell him the news. Lest Jerry have any doubts, Robert confirms that the marriage is over in scene two. The rest of the play, with the exception of scenes five, six, and seven, moves backward in time, exploring the life of the now dead triangle and ending at the triangle's inception or birth; the final tableau reveals Robert's intrusion on the scene of Jerry's first "pass" at Emma.

This backward narrative or exploration of the triangle's life before death may seem at times like an autopsy on characters who have never been very fully alive. "Instead of suffering hell-fire and damnation," writes one critic, "the characters simply fall apart from each other; their personal relationships disintegrate."[3] For others the characters fail to arouse our "concern or compassion."[4] It seems to me, however, that Pinter continues in his best tradition here to give us a vision of "life honed to the injured bone."[5] Combining his surgical precision and black humor with a haunting compassion, Pinter probes not only into the triangle's life before death, but for its life in death, and after. Without some form of death, after all, there can be no renewal.

There is little doubt in the opening scenes of the play that the relationships in the triangle are coming to an end, yet there is a kind of life that still bristles in what is now supposedly dead. Why, for example, has Emma sought out Jerry at this point in time? Not apparently to rekindle their affair; it has been over for two years and she is involved with somebody else, Casey, a writer whom Jerry has discovered and

[2]Sir James George Frazer, *The Golden Bough,* abr. ed. in 1 vol. (New York: The Macmillan Co., 1951), p. 823.

[3]*Wall Street Journal,* 11 January 1980, quoted in *New York Theatre Critics' Review,* 41 (1980) 392.

[4]John Beaufort, *The Christian Science Monitor,* 11 January 1980, p. 19.

[5]Walter Kerr, "Play: Pinter's 'Betrayal,' Story of an Affair," *New York Times,* 7 January 1980, quoted in *New York Theatre Critics' Review,* 41 (1980) 390.

Robert has published. What Emma seems to need to share with Jerry is not even any great sense of loss over the end of her marriage. Rather, it is her sense of being betrayed.

> EMMA: You know what I found out . . . last night? He's betrayed me for years. He's had . . . other women for years.
> JERRY: No? Good Lord.
>
> (*Pause.*)
>
> But we betrayed him for years.
> EMMA: And he betrayed me for years.
> JERRY: Well I never knew that.
> EMMA: Nor did I.
>
> (*Pause.*)
>
> JERRY: Does Casey know about this?   [p. 1373]

Emma, it seems, is still involved enough with both husband and lover to care that she has been betrayed by the one and to share that sense of betrayal with the other. Jerry, in turn, is involved enough with Emma to be jealous of her current affair with his protégé, Casey, a jealousy which exudes from his flagrant denials. "I couldn't be jealous of Casey. I'm his agent. I advised him about his divorce. I read all his first drafts. I persuaded your husband to publish his first novel. I escort him to Oxford to speak at the Union. He's my . . . he's my boy. . . ." (p. 1373).

Jerry also cares enough about Robert to be deeply concerned that Emma has told her husband about their affair in the previous night's conversation during which they decided to terminate their marriage. He is even more deeply dismayed in the following scene when he discovers that Emma has not, as she implied, told Robert about their affair the previous night but had told him four years ago. And even worse, in Jerry's eyes, is Robert's betrayal of him by continuing to pretend not to know.

> JERRY: Then why didn't you tell me?
>
> (*Pause.*)
>
> ROBERT: Tell you what?
> JERRY: That you knew. You bastard.
> ROBERT: Oh, don't call me a bastard, Jerry.   [p. 1375]

Robert too, it appears, despite his constant disclaimers about caring, cares. "You don't seem to understand that I don't give a shit about any of this," Robert points out in unconvincing tones to Jerry. "It's true I've hit Emma once or twice. But that wasn't to defend a principle. I wasn't inspired to do it from any kind of moral standpoint. I just felt like giving her a good bashing. The old itch . . . you understand." (p. 1375).

At the end of the first scene, when Emma tells Jerry, "It doesn't matter. It's all gone," and he replies, "Is it? What has?" (p. 1374), we share Jerry's confusion. The relationships in the triangle may be terminating, but the members of the triangle are still very much caught up in the anguish and complexities of their mutual betrayals; there is life in their dying. As Pinter moves us backward in time, however, the confusion clears up and we discover not only further betrayals and betrayals within betrayals but more of the rules of the game, the nature of the players, and the stakes of the battle that the game conceals and reveals. As in so many of Pinter's plays, much remains unstated; the characters are "subtly inarticulate, almost to the point of code."[6] However, if one can detect what is being said "underneath what is said," filling in the pauses and the silences as well, one can crack the code and come to know almost too much.[7]

Major clues to the life principle of the triangle lie in Robert's reaction to Emma's fifth scene confession of the affair with Jerry. He has become suspicious when asked at American Express to deliver a letter to his wife and has recognized the handwriting as Jerry's. Pretending to be incensed at the Italians who in their "laughing Mediterranean way" may have given the letter to a stranger with the same name, he has declined to deliver the letter. "That's what stopped me taking it, by the way," he explains to Emma, "and bringing it to you, the thought that I could very easily be a total stranger." (p. 1380). That husband and wife have become strangers is clear to both of them, and Robert expresses his bitterness when speaking of their planned trip from Venice to Torcello: "How many times have we been to Torcello? Twice. I remember how you loved it, the first time I took you there. You fell in love with it. That was about ten years ago, wasn't it? About . . . six months after we were married. Yes. Do you remember? I wonder if you'll like it as much tomorrow." (p. 1380).

Robert continues turning the ironical knife, reminding Emma that Jerry was best man at their wedding as he pushes her to confession. When confession comes, however, Robert is not so much shocked at the fact, which we later find out he has probably guessed much earlier, but at the arrangements that have attended the betrayal and its time span — five years of meeting in a flat. He wonders too if Ned, their four-year-old, is his. When reassured that Jerry was away at the time, Robert drives home to Emma the doubleness of her betrayal.

> ROBERT: Did you tell him that Ned had been conceived?
> EMMA: Not by letter.
> ROBERT: But when you did tell him, was he happy to know I was to be a father?
>
> (*Pause.*)
>
> I've always liked Jerry. To be honest, I've always liked him rather more than I've liked you. Maybe I should have had an affair with him myself.
>
> (*Silence.*)
>
> Tell me, are you looking forward to our trip to Torcello?   [p. 1382]

One wonders why Robert even needs to hit Emma when he is capable of such verbal thrusts.[8] Understandably bitter over what he considers Emma's double role as whore — betraying him with Jerry but also betraying Jerry with him by having their child — Robert's "honest" admission that he has always liked Jerry better than Emma provides a key for her behavior and for his.

---

[6]Clive Barnes, "Pinter's Back with 'Betrayal,'" *New York Post,* quoted in *New York Theatre Critics' Review,* 41 (1980) 392.

[7]Harold Pinter, quoted in Katherine H. Burkman, *The Dramatic World of Harold Pinter: Its Basis in Ritual* (Ohio: Ohio State University Press, 1971), p. 9.

[8]Robert certainly knows how to fight back better than Teddy did in *The Homecoming;* Teddy weakly protests to Ruth as she leans toward taking on his family by reminding her that he has taken her to Venice.

In an interview with Mel Gussow, Pinter noted that, "the play is about a nine-year relationship between two men who are best friends."[9] The nature of that friendship would seem to be a classical example of what René Girard calls triangular desire, a situation in which two men, through the mechanism of imitative desire, wish to possess the same woman. Imitative desire, as defined by Girard, is universal in human relationships and need not necessarily involve homosexuality or latent homosexuality, though it may: "The impulse toward the object is ultimately an impulse toward the mediator . . ."[10] What occurs is that one man (Jerry, in this case) desires another woman (Robert's) because the other man desires her. Robert, in turn, not only becomes the internal mediator of Jerry's desire (internal rather than external because of the nearness and involvement of the men in each other's sphere of action), but offers a case of what Girard calls double mediation as he founds his own desire on that of his disciple/rival. "The person who is mediator without realizing it may himself be incapable of spontaneous desire. Thus he will be tempted to copy the copy of his own desire. . . . We now have a subject-mediator and a mediator-subject, a model-disciple and a disciple-model."[11] Because of the nearness of the mediators to each other, the object of desire, Emma, becomes less real; she becomes more and more a mere object to the men.[12]

Evidence in the play, other than Robert's stated preference for Jerry, suggests that Emma, who seems to be doing the most betraying, is actually the triangle's major victim, a prize or object for which the men vie mostly because of their interest in each other.[13] In scene four, for example, when Jerry drops in to see Robert and Emma, having just had tea with Casey around the corner, Emma is pointedly excluded by Robert when she offers to come and watch them play squash and treat them to lunch. "Well, to be brutally honest," Robert informs his wife, "we wouldn't actually want a woman around, would we, Jerry?" (p. 1378). This is not only an exclusion of Emma from the battle they are engaged in, even though she may be the spoils of that battle, it is a triple put down of her. They have just discussed Casey's novel — which Emma has considered dishonest — hence the barb in Robert's, "Well, to be brutally honest." Robert has also just told Jerry that Emma has given her reaction to Casey's work when the two couples had dinner together, at which ". . . Emma gave a dissertation over the pudding about dishonesty in Casey with reference to his last novel" (p. 1378). Robert excludes Emma from lunch, mocks her daring to call another dishonest, and clearly objects to a woman interrupting male talk about books and giving her own opinions on them.

One could excuse Robert's behavior on the ground that he has learned in the next scene (going backwards in time) of the extent of Emma's affair with Jerry and is obviously very angry. But there is an implication in the speech that Emma has

[9]Mel Gussow, "An Interview with Harold Pinter," *Sunday New York Times*, 30 December 1979, quoted in The Goodman Theatre of the Art Institute of Chicago program for their production of *Betrayal*, January 16–February 22, 1981, p. 17.

[10]René Girard, *Deceit, Desire, and the Novel: Self and Other in Literary Structure*, trans. Yvonne Freccero (Maryland: The Johns Hopkins University Press, 1965), pp. 9–10.

[11]Girard, p. 99.

[12]"The closer the mediator comes, the greater his role becomes and the smaller that of the object." Girard, p. 45.

[13]One is reminded of Pinter's play, *The Collection*, in which Stella tells her husband James that she has had a one night affair with a dress designer, apparently in an effort to get her husband's fuller attention. Her effort backfires as the husband becomes vindictively interested in his wife's alleged lover, who is a homosexual.

really been an interruption in his relationship with Jerry with whom he still intends to "play." His subtextual sparring with Jerry over playing squash is fraught with his knowledge of the affair, though neither Jerry nor the audience knows at this point that Robert knows. Robert challenges Jerry to the game, assures Jerry that he is not better than he, as Jerry fears, only fitter from practice with Casey; he then reminds Jerry that he used to be good, almost suggesting to him that he is no longer a worthy opponent in their current war, as Casey is. Jerry counters by putting off "playing" with Robert since he must accompany Casey to New York to talk about film rights to the novel Emma has called dishonest, a neat put-down of Robert (Casey is *his*) and of Emma, whose judgment must be faulty if Casey has become so successful.

Actually, despite his invitations to Jerry to play squash, part of Robert's game involves not playing squash with him. When Jerry expresses his dismay in scene two at the way their friendship has continued over the years despite Robert's knowledge of the affair, Robert remarks, "Never played squash though" (p. 1375). Later in the scene he also mentions bumping into Casey recently. "I believe he's having an affair with my wife. We haven't played squash for years, Casey and me. We used to have a damn good game" (p. 1375). Invitations to the contrary, apparently Robert draws the line at playing squash with his wife's lovers, but he is nostalgic over the loss of this strictly masculine activity.

While Jerry's war with Robert, like Robert's war with Jerry, seems to be of more interest to him than his love for Emma, the quality of that love is suspect from the beginning-ending and at the ending-beginning — as well as in the middle. As Emma tries to get some support from Jerry in the opening scene (doubtless the affairs Robert has confessed to are symbolic to her of what she must always have sensed, his lack of involvement with her), Jerry is really only concerned with her betrayal of him by telling Robert of their affair. "But he's my oldest friend," Jerry protests. "I mean, I picked his own daughter up in my own arms and threw her up and caught her, in my kitchen. He watched me do it" (p. 1374). Later in the play, though earlier in time, when Jerry and Emma are breaking up their flat and their relationship, they speak of family obligations that have prevented them from meeting at night. "I might remind you," Jerry says testily to Emma, "that your husband is my oldest friend" (p. 1376), a remark that particularly offends her. Even when their affair is ostensibly at its height and Emma questions Jerry about his wife Judith's possible betrayal of him, Emma says to Jerry, "Oh, why shouldn't she have an admirer? I have an admirer" (p. 1386). When Jerry wants to know who that admirer is, Emma responds, "Uuh . . . you, I think" (p. 1386). Jerry's absentmindedness about Emma reveals her almost peripheral value for him in the drama of triangular desire and doubtless stems from the narcissistic quality of his initial attraction for her which we learn about when he first professes that love at the play's end. "You're so beautiful," Jerry says to her. "Look at the way you look at me" (p. 1387). Without her, he suggests, he will be "where the reigning prince is the prince of emptiness, the prince of absence, the prince of desolation" (p. 1388). With her, he is there too.

Betrayal is, in fact, a play in which the beginning is not only the ending, but the ending of the affair is suggested in its beginning at the play's end. Looking closely at the final conversation and movements among the three major characters at the end of the play, one gets a sense that at some level, despite the bitterness in his scene five discovery, Robert senses a good deal about the incipient affair before it really gets underway and that what the men are entering into is their own peculiar brand of squash, which they enjoy far more for sharing the sport than for Emma, the prize. In the concluding scene Emma assures Robert, as he enters and interrupts Jerry's lovemaking, that his "best friend is drunk," after which Jerry, admiring Emma's beauty, takes Robert by the elbow and assures him that he speaks "as your oldest friend. Your best man." When Robert replies, "You are, actually" (p. 1388), he leaves the room and leaves Emma to Jerry. The real passion here, restrained and understated, is between the two men, best friends become best enemies, both willing to sacrifice Emma for the fray — and in it. "Bit violent, squash," Jerry remarks of the game at one point in the play "Ring me. We'll have a game" (p. 1384) Robert replies.

If Jerry actually has any kind of passionate feelings for Emma, they are hostile feelings and relate back to Robert. Recalling how he was best man at her wedding at which he remembers her in white, a color which she denies having worn, he tells Emma of his fantasy: "I should have had you, in your white, before the wedding. I should have blackened you, in your white wedding dress, blackened you in your bridal dress, before ushering you into your wedding, as your best man" (p. 1387). Jerry's dream is not one of possessing Emma — he doesn't even recall the color of her dress properly. It is a dream of desecrating her virginity, blackening her whiteness, and then, rather than keeping her for himself, delivering her to Robert as damaged goods.

In terms of her relationship with the men, Emma seems to be very much like her daughter Charlotte who was thrown up in the air as a child and caught by Jerry in the midst of both Emma's and Jerry's families. The image is a central one. Emma first brings up the incident in scene one after Jerry tells her he has seen Charlotte on the street and recognized her because she looks like Emma. Jerry recalls throwing Charlotte up in the air in Emma's kitchen, which Emma corrects — it was in his kitchen. At the end of scene one, then, when he is dismayed that Emma has told Robert of their now dead affair, he again recalls throwing Charlotte up in front of Robert, this time in his own kitchen. He is suggesting, I think, that Robert trusted him with his daughter, or given the earlier connection Jerry made between Charlotte and Emma, with his wife. The memory is brought up again in scene six with Jerry reverting (not exactly reverting since it is earlier in time) to the idea that he threw Charlotte up in Robert's kitchen and Emma correcting him when she has returned from Venice and the affair is still going forward. They have been discussing the possibility that Judith could easily have found them out (Robert, Emma knows and we know from scene five, has found out) but the memory is a pleasant one here, emphasizing the friendship of both families and Emma's trust of Jerry. "Why shouldn't you throw her up?" (p. 1383) Emma asks as they embrace. [. . .]

Sam Shepard

Samuel Shepard Rogers VII was born in Illinois in 1943, but his father was a career man in the army, and, like most "army brats," Shepard found himself essentially uprooted, moving from base to base around the country. If he has roots as a writer, they are clearly in the American West, but not necessarily the West created by writers of westerns, comic books, and second-rate movies. Shepard's plays often have a surreal quality, as if they are set in a world of the imagination rather than in a real place like Paris, Texas.

Shepard has won numerous awards, including ten Obie Awards (given to off-Broadway plays) between 1966 and 1979, an Obie Award for sustained achievement in 1980, the New York Drama Critics' Circle Award for *A Lie of the Mind* in 1985, and a Pulitzer Prize for *Buried Child* in 1979. His work has been produced primarily in the experimental theater of downtown New York in places such as La Mama and in regional theaters throughout the United States known for artistic integrity but not for reaching a broad spectrum of theatergoers. In his way Shepard has been an underground playwright who has won the respect of most theater people, including the best playwrights.

Shepard's love for, and frustrations with, music have found their way into a major theme of his work. He plays drums and guitar and has never realized an early desire for a career in rock music. But the subversive qualities of rock and jazz — their implicit critique of middle-class life — appear in his plays in his analyses of the middle-class family. His primary themes center on the family and its complications, the nature of the person alone, and the myth of the Old West. In each theme Shepard expresses a deep sense of longing and of loss, emotions that his audiences have found significant.

Because his father began to drink and family life became intolerable, Shepard left home after a year at college and toured with the Bishops Company Repertory Players. At nineteen he wound up in New York working in one of the best jazz clubs of the day, the Village Gate. During this time in Greenwich Village he began to write one-act plays with extraordinary energy. Like Jack Kerouac, he almost never revised his work. He wrote it in a burst of energy and then had it performed to audiences whose admiration grew.

In the 1970s Shepard began acting in major motion pictures. One of the ironies of his life is that he became a matinee idol after appearing in movies such as *The Right Stuff, Fool for Love, Country,* and *Crimes of the Heart.* The critic Harry Haun said of him, "He is the Recluse as Superstar, the man who has arrived on his own terms, carefully sculpting a special myth for himself."

His output for the stage has been prodigious, with dozens of one-act plays, and he has a central body of work that has gained him an enviable reputation. *Operation Sidewinder* (1970) was performed at the Vivian Beaumont Theater — a public theater at Lincoln Center in New York City — to mixed reviews. The play, set in the West, involves a giant mechanical snake designed to make contact with outer space travelers; it includes Hopi snake dances and military scenes. *The Tooth of Crime* (1972) is about turf wars between an aging rock star and an up-and-coming young star. Its brutality and directness make it intense, exciting, and revealing of the California rock 'n' roll scene in the early 1970s.

Curse of the Starving Class (1977) and *Buried Child* (1978) both helped solidify Shepard's reputation. *Suicide in B-Flat* (1976) and *True West* (1980) only made it clearer that his work was developing in a consistent vein of black humor and dark criticism of the sanctity of family life. *A Lie of the Mind* (1985), like *Buried Child,* is about disturbed family life. It is filled with secrets: incest, murder, and sin. *New York Times* critic Mel Gussow said that it explores "the damage that one does to filial, fraternal, and marital bonds." Incest — or potential incest — is also a theme in *Fool for Love* (1983), in which Shepard starred on film. The play is set in the West and contains all the themes for which his work is known.

Shepard began his work with a sense of the West drawn from popular literature, reshaped it, and produced it in a new form. If the American West has a reality that survived its mythicization in the dime novel and John Wayne's movies, then Shepard is partly responsible for the way we now see it.

TRUE WEST

True West (1980) portrays a family, or part of a family, shattered by unknown circumstances into individuals isolated in their inability to understand and express their feelings for one another. The past is a strange, silent land that no one seems to be able to discover. The image of the desert that lingers throughout the play — in contrast with the cricket-drenched suburban setting — is an image of a pure, strange, and liberating environment. In some plays it might represent a nostalgia for a happy past. Instead, in *True West* it seems to imply a place where a person, like the religious hermits of the early Christian church, can be alone and somehow commune with an inner self.

The theme of loneliness is woven in complex ways into the play. The father is in a desert somewhere drinking himself into oblivion. Mom goes vacationing alone to Alaska, a cold glacial desert that leaves her with a sense of longing not for people but for her plants. When the play opens, Austin, the screenwriter, has taken Mom's house while she is away so he can be alone and write in peace and quiet. Lee, the older, outsider brother, breaks in on his peace and quiet in the same manner that he breaks into houses in the neighborhood and steals TVs. When he visits Mom's house and finds Austin, however, it is not a TV he ends up stealing: he steals Austin's livelihood and, in a fascinating way, his identity.

The struggle between Austin and Lee has a profound psychological quality that implies an almost unnatural terror. Lee and Austin are like two halves of the same person, but two halves that express totally antagonistic qualities. In their efforts to be one another, they are both trying to join the intellectual and violent sides of their nature. Early in the play Lee tells Austin, "I always wondered what'd be like to be you." Austin's surprised response is to tell Lee that he has always pictured him somewhere — which is to say that he has felt much the same way.

In their aloneness Austin and Lee acknowledge a sense of incompleteness. Such an awareness is not expressed by Mom, nor is it implied about the father. In this sense, Lee and Austin are very different from their parents. Whether that difference represents a hopeful sign is an unanswered question. The play ends with a power struggle between the brothers, but a struggle not so much for ultimate control as for a successful merger of their identities. The outcome of the action is in every sense in doubt as the play ends.

The title of the play carries special irony. Saul, the producer, tells Austin that Lee's outline for a story has the ring of truth to it. Austin knows the Hollywood scene, the dishonesty that produces three hundred thousand dollar deals. Sam Shepard knows it, too. His commentary is on the Hollywood shams that pretend to be true pictures of the American West. Lee and Austin represent a portrait of the true West; and to an extent the loneliness of the Mojave Desert represents the true West. But paying attention to the truth is painful. The true West is not a B movie; it is not a piece of escapist claptrap. It is an almost schizoid disunity, a play of opposites and painful discords.

True West in Performance

True West premiered in 1980, directed by Shepard's friend Robert Woodruff at San Francisco's Magic Theater, with Shepard as playwright in residence. That production garnered considerable praise from reviewers. The acting, lighting, set, and directing all impressed audiences enough that the famed Joseph Papp readied the play for the Public Theater in New York, where Papp had produced *Curse of the Starving Class* in 1978.

Unfortunately, Papp and Shepard had a falling out. Woodruff went to New York to assist in the production but was so horrified by the heavy-handed way Papp handled the acting and staging that he resigned from the project. The play opened in December 1980 to mixed reviews. Shepard disclaimed the production and swore he would never let Papp have another of his plays.

The revival of *True West* at the Cherry Lane Theater off-Broadway in October 1982 with John Malkovich as Lee and Gary Sinise as Austin (also as the director) marked the beginning of the play as we now think of it. Malkovich and Sinise, of Chicago's Steppenwolf Theatre Company, made their New York debut in *True West* and created a sensation. The reviews agreed that Malkovich and Sinise had perfectly embodied the characters and perfectly interpreted the play. The Public Broadcasting System produced a televised version of the play in the summer of 1998, also with Malkovich and Sinise as the brothers.

In the first Broadway production of *True West* (March 2000), in New York's Circle in the Square, John C. Reilly and Philip Seymour Hoffman alternated in the roles of Lee and Austin. Their version also received high acclaim from critics and theatergoers alike.

Sam Shepard (b. 1943)
TRUE WEST

Characters

AUSTIN, *early thirties, light blue sports shirt, light tan cardigan sweater, clean blue jeans, white tennis shoes*

LEE, *his older brother, early forties, filthy white t-shirt, tattered brown overcoat covered with dust, dark blue baggy pants from the Salvation Army, pink suede belt, pointed black forties dress shoes scuffed up, holes in the soles, no socks, no hat, long pronounced sideburns, "Gene Vincent" hairdo, two days' growth of beard, bad teeth*

SAUL KIMMER, *late forties, Hollywood producer, pink and white flower print sports shirt, white sports coat with matching polyester slacks, black and white loafers*

MOM, *early sixties, mother of the brothers, small woman, conservative white skirt and matching jacket, red shoulder bag, two pieces of matching red luggage*

Scene: *All nine scenes take place on the same set; a kitchen and adjoining alcove of an older home in a Southern California suburb, about 40 miles east of Los Angeles. The kitchen takes up most of the playing area to stage left. The kitchen consists of a sink, upstage center, surrounded by counter space, a wall telephone, cupboards, and a small window just above it bordered by neat yellow curtains. Stage left of sink is a stove. Stage right, a refrigerator. The alcove adjoins the kitchen to stage right. There is no wall division or door to the alcove. It is open and easily accessible from the kitchen and defined only by the objects in it: a small round glass breakfast table mounted on white iron legs, two matching white iron chairs set across from each other. The two exterior walls of the alcove which prescribe a corner in the upstage right are composed of many small windows, beginning from a solid wall about three feet high and extending to the ceiling. The windows look out to bushes and citrus trees. The alcove is filled with all sorts of house plants in various pots, mostly Boston ferns hanging in planters at different levels. The floor of the alcove is composed of green synthetic grass.*

All entrances and exits are made stage left from the kitchen. There is no door. The actors simply go off and come onto the playing area.

Note on Set and Costume: *The set should be constructed realistically with no attempt to distort its dimensions, shapes, objects, or colors. No objects should be introduced which might draw special attention to themselves other than the props demanded by the script. If a stylistic "concept" is grafted onto the set design it will only serve to confuse the evolution of the characters' situation, which is the most important focus of the play.*

Likewise, the costumes should be exactly representative of who the characters are and not added on to for the sake of making a point to the audience.

Note on Sound: *The coyote of Southern California has a distinct yapping, doglike bark, similar to a hyena. This yapping grows more intense and maniacal as the pack grows in numbers, which is usually the case when they lure and kill pets from suburban yards. The sense of growing frenzy in the pack should be felt in the background, particularly in Scenes VII and VIII. In any case, these coyotes never make the long, mournful, solitary howl of the Hollywood stereotype.*

The sound of crickets can speak for itself.

These sounds should also be treated realistically even though they sometimes grow in volume and numbers.

ACT I • *Scene I*

(*Night. Sound of crickets in dark. Candlelight appears in alcove, illuminating Austin, seated at glass table hunched over a writing notebook, pen in hand, cigarette burning in ashtray, cup of coffee, typewriter on table, stacks of paper, candle burning on table.*)

(*Soft moonlight fills kitchen illuminating Lee, beer in hand, six-pack on counter behind him. He's leaning against the sink, mildly drunk; takes a slug of beer.*)

LEE: So, Mom took off for Alaska, huh?

AUSTIN: Yeah.

LEE: Sorta' left you in charge.

AUSTIN: Well, she knew I was coming down here so she offered me the place.

LEE: You keepin' the plants watered?

AUSTIN: Yeah.

LEE: Keepin' the sink clean? She don't like even a single tea leaf in the sink ya' know.

AUSTIN (*trying to concentrate on writing*): Yeah, I know.

(*Pause.*)

LEE: She gonna' be up there a long time?

AUSTIN: I don't know.

LEE: Kinda' nice for you, huh? Whole place to yourself.

AUSTIN: Yeah, it's great.

LEE: Ya' got crickets anyway. Tons a' crickets out there. (*Looks around kitchen.*) Ya' got groceries? Coffee?

1368

[handwritten: Lee has improper speech in comparison to his brother Austin.]

AUSTIN (*looking up from writing*): What?

LEE: You got coffee?

AUSTIN: Yeah.

LEE: At's good. (*Short pause.*) Real coffee? From the bean?

AUSTIN: Yeah. You want some?

LEE: Naw. I brought some uh — (*Motions to beer.*)

AUSTIN: Help yourself to whatever's — (*Motions to refrigerator.*)

LEE: I will. Don't worry about me. I'm not the one to worry about. I mean I can uh — (*Pause.*) You always work by candlelight?

AUSTIN: No — uh — Not always.

LEE: Just sometimes?

AUSTIN (*puts pen down, rubs his eyes*): Yeah. Sometimes it's soothing.

LEE: Isn't that what the old guys did?

AUSTIN: What old guys?

LEE: The Forefathers. You know.

AUSTIN: Forefathers?

LEE: Isn't that what they did? Candlelight burning into the night? Cabins in the wilderness.

AUSTIN (*rubs hand through his hair*): I suppose.

LEE: I'm not botherin' you am I? I mean I don't wanna break into yer uh — concentration or nothin'.

AUSTIN: No, it's all right.

LEE: That's good. I mean I realize that yer line a' work demands a lota' concentration.

AUSTIN: It's okay.

LEE: You probably think that I'm not fully able to comprehend somethin' like that, huh?

AUSTIN: Like what?

LEE: That stuff yer doin'. That art. You know. Whatever you call it.

AUSTIN: It's just a little research.

LEE: You may not know it but I did a little art myself once.

AUSTIN: You did?

LEE: Yeah! I did some a' that. I fooled around with it. No future in it.

AUSTIN: What'd you do?

LEE: Never mind what I did! Just never mind about that. (*Pause.*) It was ahead of its time.

(*Pause.*)

AUSTIN: So, you went out to see the old man, huh?

LEE: Yeah, I seen him.

AUSTIN: How's he doing?

LEE: Same. He doin' just about the same.

AUSTIN: I was down there too, you know.

LEE: What d'ya' want, an award? You want some kinda' medal? You were down there. He told me all about you.

AUSTIN: What'd he say?

LEE: He told me. Don't worry.

(*Pause.*)

AUSTIN: Well —

LEE: You don't have to say nothin'.

AUSTIN: I wasn't.

LEE: Yeah, you were gonna' make somethin' up. Somethin' brilliant.

(*Pause.*)

AUSTIN: You going to be down here very long, Lee?

LEE: Might be. Depends on a few things.

AUSTIN: You got some friends down here?

LEE (*laughs*): I know a few people. Yeah.

AUSTIN: Well, you can stay here as long as I'm here.

LEE: I don't need your permission do I?

AUSTIN: No.

LEE: I mean she's my mother too, right?

AUSTIN: Right.

LEE: She might've just as easily asked me to take care of her place as you.

AUSTIN: That's right.

LEE: I mean I know how to water plants. *[handwritten: jealousy on Lee's side - fairly insulted]*

(*Long pause.*)

AUSTIN: So you don't know how long you'll be staying then?

LEE: Depends mostly on houses, ya' know.

AUSTIN: Houses?

LEE: Yeah. Houses. Electric devices. Stuff like that. I gotta' make a little tour first.

(*Short pause.*) *[handwritten: Learn of Lee's "occupation"]*

AUSTIN: Lee, why don't you just try another neighborhood, all right?

LEE (*laughs*): What'sa matter with this neighborhood? This is a great neighborhood. Lush. Good class a' people. Not many dogs.

AUSTIN: Well, our uh — Our mother just happens to live here. That's all.

LEE: Nobody's gonna' know. All they know is somethin's missing. That's all. She'll never even hear about it. Nobody's gonna' know.

AUSTIN: You're going to get picked up if you start walking around here at night.

LEE: Me? I'm gonna' git picked up? What about you? You stick out like a sore thumb. Look at you. You think yer regular lookin'?

AUSTIN: I've got too much to deal with here to be worrying about —

LEE: Yer not gonna' have to worry about me! I've been doin' all right without you. I haven't been anywhere near you for five years! Now isn't that true?

AUSTIN: Yeah.

LEE: So you don't have to worry about me. I'm a free agent.

AUSTIN: All right.

LEE: Now all I wanna' do is borrow yer car.

AUSTIN: No!

LEE: Just fer a day. One day.

AUSTIN: No!

LEE: I won't take it outside a twenty mile radius. I promise ya'. You can check the speedometer.

AUSTIN: You're not borrowing my car! That's all there is to it.

(*Pause.*)

LEE: Then I'll just take the damn thing.

AUSTIN: Lee, look — I don't want any trouble, all right?

LEE: That's a dumb line. That is a dumb fuckin' line. You git paid fer dreamin' up a line like that?

AUSTIN: Look, I can give you some money if you need money.

(*Lee suddenly lunges at Austin, grabs him violently by the shirt, and shakes him with tremendous power.*)

LEE: Don't you say that to me! Don't you ever say that to me! (*Just as suddenly he turns him loose, pushes him away, and backs off.*) You may be able to git away with that with the Old Man. Git him tanked up for a week! Buy him off with yer Hollywood blood money, but not me! I can git my own money my own way. Big money!

AUSTIN: I was just making an offer.

LEE: Yeah, well keep it to yourself!

(*Long pause.*)

Those are the most monotonous fuckin' crickets I ever heard in my life.

AUSTIN: I kinda' like the sound.

LEE: Yeah. Supposed to be able to tell the temperature by the number a' pulses. You believe that?

AUSTIN: The temperature?

LEE: Yeah. The air. How hot it is.

AUSTIN: How do you do that?

LEE: I don't know. Some woman told me that. She was a Botanist. So I believed her.

AUSTIN: Where'd you meet her?

LEE: What?

AUSTIN: The woman Botanist?

LEE: I met her on the desert. I been spendin' a lota' time on the desert.

AUSTIN: What were you doing out there?

LEE (*pause, stares in space*): I forgit. Had me a Pit Bull there for a while but I lost him.

AUSTIN: Pit Bull?

LEE: Fightin' dog. Damn I made some good money off that little dog. Real good money.

(*Pause.*)

AUSTIN: You could come up north with me, you know.

LEE: What's up there?

AUSTIN: My family.

LEE: Oh, that's right, you got the wife and kiddies now don't ya'. The house, the car, the whole slam. That's right.

AUSTIN: You could spend a couple of days. See how you like it. I've got an extra room.

LEE: Too cold up there.

(*Pause.*)

AUSTIN: You want to sleep for a while?

LEE (*pause, stares at Austin*): I don't sleep.

(*Lights to black.*)

Scene II

(*Morning. Austin is watering plants with a vaporizer, Lee sits at glass table in alcove drinking beer.*)

LEE: I never realized the old lady was so security-minded.

AUSTIN: How do you mean?

LEE: Made a little tour this morning. She's got locks on everything. Locks and double locks and chain locks and — What's she got that's so valuable?

AUSTIN: Antiques I guess. I don't know.

LEE: Antiques? Brought everything with her from the old place, huh. Just the same crap we always had around. Plates and spoons.

AUSTIN: I guess they have personal value to her.

LEE: Personal value. Yeah. Just a lota' junk. Most of it's phony anyway. Idaho decals. Now who in the hell wants to eat offa' plate with the State of Idaho starin' ya in the face. Every time ya' take a bite ya' get to see a little bit more.

AUSTIN: Well it must mean something to her or she wouldn't save it.

LEE: Yeah, well personally I don't wann' be invaded by Idaho when I'm eatin'. When I'm eatin' I'm home. Ya' know what I'm sayin'? I'm not driftin', I'm home. I don't need my thoughts swept off to Idaho. I don't need that!

(*Pause.*)

AUSTIN: Did you go out last night?

LEE: Why?

AUSTIN: I thought I heard you go out.

LEE: Yeah, I went out. What about it?

AUSTIN: Just wondered.

LEE: Damn coyotes kept me awake.

AUSTIN: Oh yeah, I heard them. They must've killed somebody's dog or something.

LEE: Yappin' their fool heads off. They don't yap like that on the desert. They howl. These are city coyotes here.

AUSTIN: Well, you don't sleep anyway do you?

(*Pause, Lee stares at him.*)

LEE: You're pretty smart aren't ya?

AUSTIN: How do you mean?

LEE: I mean you never had any more on the ball than I did. But here you are gettin' invited into prominent people's houses. Sittin' around talkin' like you know somethin'.

AUSTIN: They're not so prominent.

LEE: They're a helluva' lot more prominent than the houses I get invited into.

AUSTIN: Well you invite yourself.

LEE: That's right. I do. In fact I probably got a wider range a' choices than you do, come to think of it.

AUSTIN: I wouldn't doubt it.

LEE: In fact I been inside some pretty classy places in my time. And I never even went to an Ivy League school either.

Austin = responsible   Lee ≠
nas no guilty conscience either

John Malkovich as Lee in Steppenwolf Theatre Company's
Chicago production of *True West*. Gary Sinise, in the
background as Austin, directed the play in 1982.

AUSTIN: You want some breakfast or something?
LEE: Breakfast?
AUSTIN: Yeah. Don't you eat breakfast?
LEE: Look, don't worry about me pal. I can take care a'
    myself. You just go ahead as though I wasn't even
    here, all right?

(*Austin goes into kitchen, makes coffee.*)

AUSTIN: Where'd you walk to last night?

(*Pause.*)

LEE: I went up in the foothills there. Up in the San Ga-
    briels. Heat was drivin' me crazy.
AUSTIN: Well, wasn't it hot out on the desert?
LEE: Different kinda' heat. Out there it's clean. Cools off
    at night. There's a nice little breeze.
AUSTIN: Where were you, the Mojave?
LEE: Yeah. The Mojave. That's right.
AUSTIN: I haven't been out there in years.
LEE: Out past Needles there.
AUSTIN: Oh yeah.
LEE: Up here it's different. This country's real different.
AUSTIN: Well, it's been built up.
LEE: Built up? Wiped out is more like it. I don't even
    hardly recognize it.
AUSTIN: Yeah. Foothills are the same though, aren't they?
LEE: Pretty much. It's funny goin' up in there. The smells
    and everything. Used to catch snakes up there,
    remember?
AUSTIN: You caught snakes.
LEE: Yeah. And you'd pretend you were Geronimo or
    some damn thing. You used to go right out to lunch.
AUSTIN: I enjoyed my imagination.
LEE: That what you call it? Looks like yer still enjoyin' it.
AUSTIN: So you just wandered around up there, huh?
LEE: Yeah. With a purpose.
AUSTIN: See any houses?

(*Pause.*)

LEE: Couple. Couple a' real nice ones. One of 'em didn't
    even have a dog. Walked right up and stuck my head
    in the window. Not a peep. Just a sweet kinda' subur-
    ban silence.
AUSTIN: What kind of a place was it?
LEE: Like a paradise. Kinda' place that sorta' kills ya'
    inside. Warm yellow lights. Mexican tile all around.
    Copper pots hangin' over the stove. Ya' know like
    they got in the magazines. Blond people movin' in and
    outa' the rooms, talkin' to each other. (*Pause.*) Kinda'
    place you wish you sorta' grew up in, ya' know.
AUSTIN: That's the kind of place you wish you'd grown
    up in?
LEE: Yeah, why not?
AUSTIN: I thought you hated that kind of stuff.
LEE: Yeah, well you never knew too much about me did
    ya'?

(*Pause.*)

AUSTIN: Why'd you go out to the desert in the first place?
LEE: I was on my way to see the old man.
AUSTIN: You mean you just passed through there?
LEE: Yeah. That's right. Three months of passin' through.
AUSTIN: Three months?
LEE: Somethin' like that. Maybe more. Why?
AUSTIN: You lived on the Mojave for three months?
LEE: Yeah. What'sa matter with that?
AUSTIN: By yourself?
LEE: Mostly. Had a couple a' visitors. Had that dog for a
    while.

Philip Seymour Hoffman and
John C. Reilly in the 2000
revival of *True West* on
Broadway at Circle in the
Square. Hoffman and Reilly
alternated in the roles of
Austin and Lee.

AUSTIN: Didn't you miss people?

LEE (*laughs*): People?

AUSTIN: Yeah. I mean I go crazy if I have to spend three
nights in a motel by myself.

LEE: Yer not in a motel now.

AUSTIN: No, I know. But sometimes I have to stay in
motels.

LEE: Well, they got people in motels don't they?

AUSTIN: Strangers.

LEE: Yer friendly aren't ya'? Aren't you the friendly type?

(*Pause.*)

AUSTIN: I'm going to have somebody coming by here
later, Lee.

LEE: Ah! Lady friend?

AUSTIN: No, a producer.

LEE: Aha! What's he produce?

AUSTIN: Film. Movies. You know.

LEE: Oh, movies. Motion Pictures! A Big Wig Huh?

AUSTIN: Yeah.

LEE: What's he comin' by here for?

AUSTIN: We have to talk about a project.

LEE: Whadya' mean, "a project"? What's "a project"?

AUSTIN: A script.

LEE: Oh. That's what yer doin' with all these papers?

AUSTIN: Yeah.

LEE: Well, what's the project about?

AUSTIN: We're uh — it's a period piece.

LEE: What's "a period piece"?

AUSTIN: Look, it doesn't matter. The main thing is we
need to discuss this alone. I mean —

LEE: Oh, I get it. You want me outa' the picture.

AUSTIN: Not exactly. I just need to be alone with him for
a couple of hours. So we can talk.

LEE: Yer afraid I'll embarrass ya' huh?

AUSTIN: I'm not afraid you'll embarrass me!

LEE: Well, I tell ya' what — Why don't you just gimme
the keys to yer car and I'll be back here around six
o'clock or so. That give ya enough time?

AUSTIN: I'm not loaning you my car, Lee.

LEE: You want me to just git lost huh? Take a hike? Is
that it? Pound the pavement for a few hours while
you bullshit yer way into a million bucks.

AUSTIN: Look, it's going to be hard enough for me to
face this character on my own without —

LEE: You don't know this guy?

AUSTIN: No I don't know — He's a producer. I mean
I've been meeting with him for months but you never
get to know a producer.

LEE: Yer tryin' to hustle him? Is that it?

AUSTIN: I'm not trying to hustle him! I'm trying to work
out a deal! It's not easy.

LEE: What kinda' deal?

AUSTIN: Convince him it's a worthwhile story.

LEE: He's not convinced? How come he's comin' over
here if he's not convinced? I'll convince him for ya'.

AUSTIN: You don't understand the way things work
down here.

LEE: How do things work down here?

(*Pause.*)

AUSTIN: Look, if I loan you my car will you have it back
here by six?

LEE: On the button. With a full tank a' gas.

AUSTIN (*digging in his pocket for keys*): Forget about
the gas.

LEE: Hey, these days gas is gold, old buddy.

(*Austin hands the keys to Lee.*)

[handwritten marginal note:] (Pause)s are always after Lee's lines → Lee makes things quite awkward

Lee's speech pattern has changed significantly.

You remember that car I used to loan you?
AUSTIN: Yeah.
LEE: Forty Ford. Flathead.
AUSTIN: Yeah.
LEE: Sucker hauled ass didn't it?
AUSTIN: Lee, it's not that I don't want to loan you my car —
LEE: You are loanin' me yer car.

(*Lee gives Austin a pat on the shoulder, pause.*)

AUSTIN: I know. I just wish —
LEE: What? You wish what?
AUSTIN: I don't know. I wish I wasn't — I wish I didn't have to be doing business down here. I'd like to just spend some time with you.
LEE: I thought it was "Art" you were doin'.

(*Lee moves across the kitchen toward exit, tosses keys in his hand.*)

AUSTIN: Try to get back here by six, okay?
LEE: No sweat. Hey, ya' know, if that uh — story of yours doesn't go over with the guy — tell him I got a couple a' "projects" he might be interested in. Real commercial. Full a' suspense. True-to-life stuff.

(*Lee exits, Austin stares after Lee then turns, goes to papers at table, leafs through pages, lights fade to black.*)

Scene III

(*Afternoon. Alcove, Saul Kimmer and Austin seated across from each other at table.*)

SAUL: Well, to tell you the truth Austin, I have never felt so confident about a project in quite a long time.
AUSTIN: Well, that's good to hear, Saul.
SAUL: I am absolutely convinced we can get this thing off the ground. I mean we'll have to make a sale to television and that means getting a major star. Somebody bankable. But I think we can do it. I really do.
AUSTIN: Don't you think we need a first draft before we approach a star?
SAUL: No, no, not at all. I don't think it's necessary. Maybe a brief synopsis. I don't want you to touch the typewriter until we have some seed money.
AUSTIN: That's fine with me.
SAUL: I mean it's a great story. Just the story alone. You've really managed to capture something this time.
AUSTIN: I'm glad you like it, Saul.

(*Lee enters abruptly into kitchen carrying a stolen television set, short pause.*)

LEE: Aw shit, I'm sorry about that. I am really sorry Austin.
AUSTIN (*standing*): That's all right.
LEE (*moving toward them*): I mean I thought it was way past six already. You said to have it back here by six.
AUSTIN: We were just finishing up. (*To Saul.*) This is my, uh — brother, Lee.

SAUL (*standing*): Oh, I'm very happy to meet you.

(*Lee sets T.V. on sink counter, shakes hands with Saul.*)

LEE: I can't tell ya' how happy I am to meet you sir.
SAUL: Saul Kimmer.
LEE: Mr. Kipper.
SAUL: Kimmer.
AUSTIN: Lee's been living out on the desert and he just uh —
SAUL: Oh, that's terrific! (*To Lee.*) Palm Springs?
LEE: Yeah. Yeah, right. Right around in that area. Near uh — Bob Hope Drive there.
SAUL: Oh I love it out there. I just love it. The air is wonderful.
LEE: Yeah. Sure is. Healthy.
SAUL: And the golf. I don't know if you play golf, but the golf is just about the best.
LEE: I play a lota' golf.
SAUL: Is that right?
LEE: Yeah. In fact I was hoping I'd run into somebody out here who played a little golf. I've been lookin' for a partner.
SAUL: Well, I uh —
AUSTIN: Lee's just down for a visit while our mother's in Alaska.
SAUL: Oh, your mother's in Alaska?
AUSTIN: Yes. She went up there on a little vacation. This is her place.
SAUL: I see. Well isn't that something. Alaska.
LEE: What kinda' handicap do ya' have, Mr. Kimmer?
SAUL: Oh I'm just a Sunday duffer really. You know.
LEE: That's good 'cause I haven't swung a club in months.
SAUL: Well we ought to get together sometime and have a little game. Austin, do you play?

(*Saul mimes a Johnny Carson golf swing for Austin.*)

AUSTIN: No. I don't uh — I've watched it on T.V.
LEE (*to Saul*): How 'bout tomorrow morning? Bright and early. We could get out there and put in eighteen holes before breakfast.
SAUL: Well, I've got uh — I have several appointments —
LEE: No, I mean real early. Crack a' dawn. While the dew's still thick on the fairway.
SAUL: Sounds really great.
LEE: Austin could be our caddie.
SAUL: Now that's an idea. (*Laughs.*)
AUSTIN: I don't know the first thing about golf.
LEE: There's nothin' to it. Isn't that right, Saul? He'd pick it up in fifteen minutes.
SAUL: Sure. Doesn't take long. 'Course you have to play for years to find your true form. (*Chuckles.*)
LEE (*to Austin*): We'll give ya' a quick run-down on the club faces. The irons, the woods. Show ya' a couple pointers on the basic swing. Might even let ya' hit the ball a couple times. Whadya' think, Saul?
SAUL: Why not. I think it'd be great. I haven't had any exercise in weeks.
LEE: 'At's the spirit! We'll have a little orange juice right afterwards.

(*Pause.*)

SAUL: Orange juice?

LEE: Yea! Vitamin C! Nothin' like a shot a' orange juice after a round a' golf. Hot shower. Snappin' towels at each others' privates. Real sense a' fraternity.

SAUL (*smiles at Austin*): Well, you make it sound very inviting, I must say. It really does sound great.

LEE: Then it's a date.

SAUL: Well, I'll call the country club and see if I can arrange something.

LEE: Great! Boy, I sure am sorry that I busted in on ya' all in the middle of yer meeting.

SAUL: Oh that's quite all right. We were just about finished anyway.

LEE: I can wait out in the other room if you want.

SAUL: No really —

LEE: Just got Austin's color T.V. back from the shop. I can watch a little amateur boxing now.

(*Lee and Austin exchange looks.*)

SAUL: Oh — Yes.

LEE: You don't fool around in Television, do you Saul?

SAUL: Uh — I have in the past. Produced some T.V. Specials. Network stuff. But it's mainly features now.

LEE: That's where the big money is, huh?

SAUL: Yes. That's right.

AUSTIN: Why don't I call you tomorrow, Saul and we'll get together. We can have lunch or something.

SAUL: That'd be terrific.

LEE: Right after the golf.

(*Pause.*)

SAUL: What?

LEE: You can have lunch right after the golf.

SAUL: Oh, right.

LEE: Austin was tellin' me that yer interested in stories.

SAUL: Well, we develop certain projects that we feel have commercial potential.

LEE: What kinda' stuff do ya' go in for?

SAUL: Oh, the usual. You know. Good love interest. Lots of action. (*Chuckles at Austin.*)

LEE: Westerns?

SAUL: Sometimes.

AUSTIN: I'll give you a ring, Saul.

(*Austin tries to move Saul across the kitchen but Lee blocks their way.*)

LEE: I got a Western that'd knock yer lights out.

SAUL: Oh really?

LEE: Yeah. Contemporary Western. Based on a true story. 'Course I'm not a writer like my brother here. I'm not a man of the pen.

SAUL: Well —

LEE: I mean I can tell ya' a story off the tongue but I can't put it down on paper. That don't make any difference though does it?

SAUL: No, not really.

LEE: I mean plenty a' guys have stories don't they? True-

life stories. Musta' been a lota' movies made from real life.

SAUL: Yes, I suppose so.

LEE: I haven't seen a good Western since *Lonely Are the Brave*. You remember that movie?

SAUL: No, I'm afraid I —

LEE: Kirk Douglas. Helluva' movie. You remember that movie, Austin?

AUSTIN: Yes.

LEE (*to Saul*): The man dies for the love of a horse.

SAUL: Is that right.

LEE: Yeah. Ya' hear the horse screamin' at the end of it. Rain's comin' down. Horse is screamin'. Then there's a shot. BLAM! Just a single shot like that. Then nothin' but the sound of rain. And Kirk Douglas is ridin' in the ambulance. Ridin' away from the scene of the accident. And when he hears that shot he knows that his horse has died. He knows. And you see his eyes. And his eyes die. Right inside his face. And then his eyes close. And you know that he's died too. You know that Kirk Douglas has died from the death of his horse.

SAUL (*eyes Austin nervously*): Well, it sounds like a great movie. I'm sorry I missed it.

LEE: Yeah, you shouldn't a' missed that one.

SAUL: I'll have to try to catch it some time. Arrange a screening or something. Well, Austin, I'll have to hit the freeway before rush hour.

AUSTIN (*ushers him toward exit*): It's good seeing you, Saul.

(*Austin and Saul shake hands.*)

LEE: So ya' think there's room for a real Western these days? A true-to-life Western?

SAUL: Well, I don't see why not. Why don't you uh — tell the story to Austin and have him write a little outline.

LEE: You'd take a look at it then?

SAUL: Yes. Sure. I'll give it a read-through. Always eager for new material. (*Smiles at Austin.*)

LEE: That's great! You'd really read it then huh?

SAUL: It would just be my opinion of course.

LEE: That's all I want. Just an opinion. I happen to think it has a lota' possibilities.

SAUL: Well, it was great meeting you and I'll —

(*Saul and Lee shake.*)

LEE: I'll call you tomorrow about the golf.

SAUL: Oh. Yes, right.

LEE: Austin's got your number, right?

SAUL: Yes.

LEE: So long Saul. (*Gives Saul a pat on the back.*)

(*Saul exits, Austin turns to Lee, looks at T.V. then back to Lee.*)

AUSTIN: Give me the keys.

(*Austin extends his hand toward Lee, Lee doesn't move, just stares at Austin, smiles, lights to black.*)

Scene IV

(*Night. Coyotes in distance, fade, sound of typewriter in dark, crickets, candlelight in alcove, dim light in kitchen, lights reveal Austin at glass table typing, Lee sits across from him, foot on table, drinking beer and whiskey, the T.V. is still on sink counter, Austin types for a while, then stops.*)

LEE: All right, now read it back to me.

AUSTIN: I'm not reading it back to you, Lee. You can read it when we're finished. I can't spend all night on this.

LEE: You got better things to do?

AUSTIN: Let's just go ahead. Now what happens when he leaves Texas?

LEE: Is he ready to leave Texas yet? I didn't know we were that far along. He's not ready to leave Texas.

AUSTIN: He's right at the border.

LEE (*sitting up*): No, see this is one a' the crucial parts. Right here. (*Taps paper with beer can.*) We can't rush through this. He's not right at the border. He's a good fifty miles from the border. A lot can happen in fifty miles.

AUSTIN: It's only an outline. We're not writing an entire script now.

LEE: Well ya' can't leave things out even if it is an outline. It's one a' the most important parts. Ya' can't go leavin' it out.

AUSTIN: Okay, okay. Let's just — get it done.

LEE: All right. Now. He's in the truck and he's got his horse trailer and his horse.

AUSTIN: We've already established that.

LEE: And he sees this other guy comin' up behind him in another truck. And that truck is pullin' a gooseneck.

AUSTIN: What's a gooseneck?

LEE: Cattle trailer. You know the kind with a gooseneck, goes right down in the bed a' the pick-up.

AUSTIN: Oh. All right. (*Types.*)

LEE: It's important.

AUSTIN: Okay. I got it.

LEE: All these details are important.

(*Austin types as they talk.*)

AUSTIN: I've got it.

LEE: And this other guy's got his horse all saddled up in the back a' the gooseneck.

AUSTIN: Right.

LEE: So both these guys have got their horses right along with 'em, see.

AUSTIN: I understand.

LEE: Then this first guy suddenly realizes two things.

AUSTIN: The guy in front?

LEE: Right. The guy in front realizes two things almost at the same time. Simultaneous.

AUSTIN: What were the two things?

LEE: Number one, he realizes that the guy behind him is the husband of the woman he's been —

(*Lee makes gesture of screwing by pumping his arm.*)

AUSTIN (*sees Lee's gesture*): Oh. Yeah.

LEE: And number two, he realizes he's in the middle of Tornado Country.

AUSTIN: What's "Tornado Country"?

LEE: Panhandle.

AUSTIN: Panhandle?

LEE: Sweetwater. Around in that area. Nothin'. Nowhere, and number three —

AUSTIN: I thought there was only two.

LEE: There's three. There's a third unforeseen realization.

AUSTIN: And what's that?

LEE: That he's runnin' outa' gas.

AUSTIN (*stops typing*): Come on, Lee.

(*Austin gets up, moves to kitchen, gets a glass of water.*)

LEE: Whadya' mean, "come on"? That's what it is. Write it down! He's runnin' outa' gas.

AUSTIN: It's too —

LEE: What? It's too what? It's too real! That's what ya' mean isn't it? It's too much like real life!

AUSTIN: It's not like real life! It's not enough like real life. Things don't happen like that.

LEE: What! Men don't fuck other men's women?

AUSTIN: Yes. But they don't end up chasing each other across the Panhandle. Through "Tornado Country."

LEE: They do in this movie!

AUSTIN: And they don't have horses conveniently along with them when they run out of gas! And they don't run out of gas either!

LEE: These guys run outa' gas! This is my story and one a' these guys runs outa' gas!

AUSTIN: It's just a dumb excuse to get them into a chase scene. It's contrived.

LEE: It is a chase scene! It's already a chase scene. They been chasin' each other fer days.

AUSTIN: So now they're supposed to abandon their trucks, climb on their horses, and chase each other into the mountains?

LEE (*standing suddenly*): There aren't any mountains in the Panhandle! It's flat!

(*Lee turns violently toward windows in alcove and throws beer can at them.*)

LEE: Goddamn those crickets! (*Yells at crickets.*) Shut up out there! (*Pause, turns back toward table.*) This place is like a fuckin' rest home here. How're you supposed to think!

AUSTIN: You wanna' take a break?

LEE: No, I don't wanna' take a break! I wanna' get this done! This is my last chance to get this done.

AUSTIN (*moves back into alcove*): All right. Take it easy.

LEE: I'm gonna be leavin' this area. I don't have time to mess around here.

AUSTIN: Where are you going?

LEE: Never mind where I'm goin'! That's got nothin' to do with you. I just gotta' get this done. I'm not like you. Hangin' around bein' a parasite offa' other fools. I gotta' do this thing and get out.

(*Pause.*)

AUSTIN: A parasite? Me?

LEE: Yeah, you!

AUSTIN: After you break into people's houses and take their televisions!

LEE: They don't need their televisions! I'm doin' them a service.

AUSTIN: Give me back my keys, Lee.

LEE: Not until you write this thing! You're gonna' write this outline thing for me or that car's gonna wind up in Arizona with a different paint job.

AUSTIN: You think you can force me to write this? I was doing you a favor.

LEE: Git off yer high horse will ya'! Favor! Big favor. Handin' down favors from the mountain top.

AUSTIN: Let's just write it, okay? Let's sit down and not get upset and see if we can get through this.

(*Austin sits at typewriter.*)
(*Long pause.*)

LEE: Yer not gonna' even show it to him, are ya'?

AUSTIN: What?

LEE: This outline. You got no intention of showin' it to him. Yer just doin' this 'cause yer afraid a' me.

AUSTIN: You can show it to him yourself.

LEE: I will, boy! I'm gonna' read it to him on the golf course.

AUSTIN: And I'm not afraid of you either.

LEE: Then how come yer doin' it?

AUSTIN (*pause*): So I can get my keys back.

(*Pause as Lee takes keys out of his pocket slowly and throws them on table, long pause. Austin stares at keys.*)

LEE: There. Now you got yer keys back.

(*Austin looks up at Lee but doesn't take keys.*)

LEE: Go ahead. There's yer keys.

(*Austin slowly takes keys off table and puts them back in his own pocket.*)

Now what're you gonna' do? Kick me out?

AUSTIN: I'm not going to kick you out, Lee.

LEE: You couldn't kick me out, boy.

AUSTIN: I know.

LEE: So you can't even consider that one. (*Pause.*) You could call the police. That'd be the obvious thing.

AUSTIN: You're my brother.

LEE: That don't mean a thing. You go down to the L.A. Police Department there and ask them what kinda' people kill each other the most. What do you think they'd say?

AUSTIN: Who said anything about killing?

LEE: Family people. Brothers. Brothers-in-law. Cousins. Real American-type people. They kill each other in the heat mostly. In the Smog-Alerts. In the Brush Fire Season. Right about this time a' year.

AUSTIN: This isn't the same.

LEE: Oh no? What makes it different?

AUSTIN: We're not insane. We're not driven to acts of violence like that. Not over a dumb movie script. Now sit down.

(*Long pause, Lee considers which way to go with it.*)

LEE: Maybe not. (*He sits back down at the table across from Austin.*) Maybe you're right. Maybe we're too intelligent, huh? (*Pause.*) We got our heads on our shoulders. One of us has even got a Ivy League diploma. Now that means somethin' don't it? Doesn't that mean somethin'?

AUSTIN: Look, I'll write this thing for you, Lee. I don't mind writing it. I just don't want to get all worked up about it. It's not worth it. Now, come on. Let's just get through it, okay?

LEE: Nah. I think there's easier money. Maybe millions. I don't need this shit. I could go up to Sacramento Valley and steal me a diesel. Ten thousand a week dismantling one a' those suckers. Ten thousand a week!

(*Lee opens another beer, puts his foot back up on table.*)

AUSTIN: No, really, look, I'll write it out for you. I think it's a great idea.

LEE: Nah, you got yer own work to do. I don't wanna' interfere with yer life.

AUSTIN: I mean it'd be really fantastic if you could sell this. Turn it into a movie. I mean it.

(*Pause.*)

LEE: Ya' think so huh?

AUSTIN: Absolutely. You could really turn your life around, you know. Change things.

LEE: I could get a house maybe.

AUSTIN: Sure you could get a house. You could get a whole ranch if you wanted to.

LEE (*laughs*): A ranch? I could get a ranch?

AUSTIN: 'Course you could. You know what a screenplay sells for these days?

LEE: No. What's it sell for?

AUSTIN: A lot. A whole lot of money.

LEE: Thousands?

AUSTIN: Yeah. Thousands.

LEE: Millions?

AUSTIN: Well —

LEE: We could get the old man outa' hock then.

AUSTIN: Maybe.

LEE: Maybe? Whadya' mean, maybe?

AUSTIN: I mean it might take more than money.

LEE: You were just tellin' me it'd change my whole life around. Why wouldn't it change his?

AUSTIN: He's different.

LEE: Oh, he's of a different ilk huh?

AUSTIN: He's not gonna' change. Let's leave the old man out of it.

LEE: That's right. He's not gonna' change but I will. I'll just turn myself right inside out. I could be just like you then, huh? Sittin' around dreamin' stuff up. Gettin' paid to dream. Ridin' back and forth on the freeway just dreamin' my fool head off.

AUSTIN: It's not all that easy.

LEE: It's not, huh?

AUSTIN: No. There's a lot of work involved.

LEE: What's the toughest part? Deciding whether to jog or play tennis?

(*Long pause.*)

AUSTIN: Well, look. You can stay here — do whatever you want to. Borrow the car. Come in and out. Doesn't matter to me. It's not my house. I'll help you write this thing or — not. Just let me know what you want. You tell me.

LEE: Oh. So now suddenly you're at my service. Is that it?

AUSTIN: What do you want to do Lee?

(*Long pause, Lee stares at him then turns and dreams at windows.*)

LEE: I tell ya' what I'd do if I still had that dog. Ya' wanna' know what I'd do?

AUSTIN: What?

LEE: Head out to Ventura. Cook up a little match. God that little dog could bear down. Lota' money in dog fightin'. Big money.

(*Pause.*)

AUSTIN: Why don't we try to see this through, Lee. Just for the hell of it. Maybe you've really got something here. What do you think?

(*Pause, Lee considers.*)

LEE: Maybe so. No harm in tryin' I guess. You think it's such a hot idea. Besides, I always wondered what'd be like to be you.

AUSTIN: You did?

LEE: Yeah, sure. I used to picture you walkin' around some campus with yer arms fulla' books. Blondes chasin' after ya'.

AUSTIN: Blondes? That's funny.

LEE: What's funny about it?

AUSTIN: Because I always used to picture you somewhere.

LEE: Where'd you picture me?

AUSTIN: Oh, I don't know. Different places. Adventures. You were always on some adventure.

LEE: Yeah.

AUSTIN: And I used to say to myself, "Lee's got the right idea. He's out there in the world and here I am. What am I doing?"

LEE: Well you were settin' yourself up for somethin'.

AUSTIN: I guess.

LEE: We better get started on this thing then.

AUSTIN: Okay.

(*Austin sits up at typewriter, puts new paper in.*)

LEE: Oh. Can I get the keys back before I forget?

(*Austin hesitates.*)

You said I could borrow the car if I wanted, right? Isn't that what you said?

AUSTIN: Yeah. Right.

(*Austin takes keys out of his pocket, sets them on table, Lee takes keys slowly, plays with them in his hand.*)

LEE: I could get a ranch, huh?

AUSTIN: Yeah. We have to write it first though.

LEE: Okay. Let's write it.

(*Lights start dimming slowly to end of scene as Austin types, Lee speaks.*)

So they take off after each other straight into an endless black prairie. The sun is just comin' down and they can feel the night on their backs. What they don't know is that each one of 'em is afraid, see. Each one separately thinks that he's the only one that's afraid. And they keep ridin' like that straight into the night. Not knowing. And the one who's chasin' doesn't know where the other one is taking him. And the one who's being chased doesn't know where he's going.

(*Lights to black, typing stops in the dark, crickets fade.*)

ACT II • Scene V 2 night

(*Morning. Lee at the table in alcove with a set of golf clubs in a fancy leather bag, Austin at sink washing a few dishes.*)

AUSTIN: He really liked it, huh?

LEE: He wouldn't a' gave me these clubs if he didn't like it.

AUSTIN: He gave you the clubs?

LEE: Yeah. I told ya' he gave me the clubs. The bag too.

AUSTIN: I thought he just loaned them to you.

LEE: He said it was part a' the advance. A little gift like. Gesture of his good faith.

AUSTIN: He's giving you an advance?

LEE: Now what's so amazing about that? I told ya' it was a good story. You even said it was a good story.

AUSTIN: Well that is really incredible Lee. You know how many guys spend their whole lives down here trying to break into this business? Just trying to get in the door?

LEE (*pulling clubs out of bag, testing them*): I got no idea. How many?

(*Pause.*)

AUSTIN: How much of an advance is he giving you?

LEE: Plenty. We were talkin' big money out there. Ninth hole is where I sealed the deal.

AUSTIN: He made a firm commitment?

LEE: Absolutely.

AUSTIN: Well, I know Saul and he doesn't fool around when he says he likes something.

LEE: I thought you said you didn't know him.

AUSTIN: Well, I'm familiar with his tastes.

LEE: I let him get two up on me goin' into the back nine. He was sure he had me cold. You shoulda' seen his face when I pulled out the old pitching wedge and plopped it pin-high, two feet from the cup. He 'bout shit his pants. "Where'd a guy like you ever learn how to play golf like that?" he says.

(*Lee laughs, Austin stares at him.*)

AUSTIN: 'Course there's no contract yet. Nothing's final until it's on paper.

LEE: It's final, all right. There's no way he's gonna back out of it now. We gambled for it.

AUSTIN: Saul, gambled?

LEE: Yeah, sure. I mean he liked the outline already so he wasn't risking that much. I just guaranteed it with my short game.

(*Pause.*)

AUSTIN: Well, we should celebrate or something. I think Mom left a bottle of champagne in the refrigerator. We should have a little toast.

(*Austin gets glasses from cupboard, goes to refrigerator, pulls out bottle of champagne.*)

LEE: You shouldn't oughta' take her champagne, Austin. She's gonna' miss that.

AUSTIN: Oh, she's not going to mind. She'd be glad we put it to good use. I'll get her another bottle. Besides, it's perfect for the occasion.

(*Pause.*)

LEE: Yer gonna' get a nice fee for writin' the script a' course. Straight fee.

(*Austin stops, stares at Lee, puts glasses and bottle on table, pause.*)

AUSTIN: I'm writing the script?

LEE: That's what he said. Said we couldn't hire a better screenwriter in the whole town.

AUSTIN: But I'm already working on a script. I've got my own project. I don't have time to write two scripts.

LEE: No, he said he was gonna' drop that other one.

(*Pause.*)

AUSTIN: What? You mean mine? He's going to drop mine and do yours instead?

LEE (*smiles*): Now look, Austin, it's jest beginner's luck ya' know. I mean I sank a fifty foot putt for this deal. No hard feelings.

(*Austin goes to phone on wall, grabs it, starts dialing.*)

He's not gonna' be in, Austin. Told me he wouldn't be in 'til late this afternoon.

AUSTIN (*stays on phone, dialing, listens*): I can't believe this. I just can't believe it. Are you sure he said that? Why would he drop mine?

LEE: That's what he told me.

AUSTIN: He can't do that without telling me first. Without talking to me at least. He wouldn't just make a decision like that without talking to me!

LEE: Well I was kinda' surprised myself. But he was real enthusiastic about my story.

(*Austin hangs up phone violently, paces.*)

AUSTIN: What'd he say! Tell me everything he said!

LEE: I been tellin' ya! He said he liked the story a whole lot. It was the first authentic Western to come along in a decade.

AUSTIN: He liked that story! Your story?

LEE: Yeah! What's so surprisin' about that?

AUSTIN: It's stupid! It's the dumbest story I ever heard in my life.

LEE: Hey, hold on! That's my story yer talkin' about!

AUSTIN: It's a bullshit story! It's idiotic. Two lamebrains chasing each other across Texas! Are you kidding? Who do you think's going to go see a film like that?

LEE: It's not a film! It's a movie. There's a big difference. That's somethin' Saul told me.

AUSTIN: Oh he did, huh?

LEE: Yeah, he said, "In this business we make movies, American movies. Leave the films to the French."

AUSTIN: So you got real intimate with old Saul huh? He started pouring forth his vast knowledge of Cinema.

LEE: I think he liked me a lot, to tell ya' the truth. I think he felt I was somebody he could confide in.

AUSTIN: What'd you do, beat him up or something?

LEE (*stands fast*): Hey, I've about had it with the insults buddy! You think yer the only one in the brain department here? Yer the only one that can sit around and cook things up? There's other people got ideas too, ya' know!

AUSTIN: You must've done something. Threatened him or something. Now what'd you do Lee?

LEE: I convinced him!

(*Lee makes sudden menacing lunge toward Austin, wielding golf club above his head, stops himself, frozen moment, long pause, Lee lowers club.*)

AUSTIN: Oh, Jesus. You didn't hurt him did you?

(*Long silence, Lee sits back down at table.*)

Lee! Did you hurt him?

LEE: I didn't do nothin' to him! He liked my story. Pure and simple. He said it was the best story he'd come across in a long, long time.

AUSTIN: That's what he told me about my story! That's the same thing he said to me.

LEE: Well, he musta' been lyin'. He musta' been lyin' to one of us anyway.

AUSTIN: You can't come into this town and start pushing people around. They're gonna put you away!

LEE: I never pushed anybody around! I beat him fair and square. (*Pause.*) They can't touch me anyway. They can't put a finger on me. I'm gone. I can come in through the window and go out through the door.

They never knew what hit 'em. You, yer stuck. Yer the one that's stuck. Not me. So don't be warnin' me what to do in this town.

(*Pause, Austin crosses to table, sits at typewriter, rests.*)

AUSTIN: Lee, come on, level with me will you? It doesn't make any sense that suddenly he'd throw my idea out the window. I've been talking to him for months. I've got too much at stake. Everything's riding on this project.

LEE: What's yer idea?

AUSTIN: It's just a simple love story.

LEE: What kinda' love story?

AUSTIN (*stands, crosses into kitchen*): I'm not telling you!

LEE: Ha! 'Fraid I'll steal it huh? Competition's gettin' kinda' close to home isn't it?

AUSTIN: Where did Saul say he was going?

LEE: He was gonna' take my story to a couple studios.

AUSTIN: That's *my* outline you know! I wrote that outline! You've got no right to be peddling it around.

LEE: You weren't ready to take credit for it last night.

AUSTIN: Give me my keys!

LEE: What?

AUSTIN: The keys! I want my keys back!

LEE: Where you goin'?

AUSTIN: Just give me my keys! I gotta' take a drive. I gotta' get out of here for a while.

LEE: Where you gonna' go, Austin?

AUSTIN (*pause*): I might just drive out to the desert for a while. I gotta' think.

LEE: You can think here just as good. This is the perfect setup for thinkin'. We got some writin' to do here, boy. Now let's just have us a little toast. Relax. We're partners now.

(*Lee pops the cork of the champagne bottle, pours two drinks as the lights fade to black.*)

Scene VI

(*Afternoon. Lee and Saul in kitchen, Austin in alcove.*)

LEE: Now you tell him. You tell him, Mr. Kipper.

SAUL: Kimmer.

LEE: Kimmer. You tell him what you told me. He don't believe me.

AUSTIN: I don't want to hear it.

SAUL: It's really not a big issue, Austin. I was simply amazed by your brother's story and —

AUSTIN: Amazed? You lost a bet! You gambled with my material!

SAUL: That's really beside the point, Austin. I'm ready to go all the way with your brother's story. I think it has a great deal of merit.

AUSTIN: I don't want to hear about it, okay? Go tell it to the executives! Tell it to somebody who's going to turn it into a package deal or something. A T.V. series. Don't tell it to me.

SAUL: But I want to continue with your project too, Austin. It's not as though we can't do both. We're big enough for that aren't we?

AUSTIN: "We"? *I* can't do both! I don't know about "we."

LEE (*to Saul*): See, what'd I tell ya'. He's totally unsympathetic.

SAUL: Austin, there's no point in our going to another screenwriter for this. It just doesn't make sense. You're brothers. You know each other. There's a familiarity with the material that just wouldn't be possible otherwise.

AUSTIN: There's no familiarity with the material! None! I don't know what "Tornado Country" is. I don't know what a "gooseneck" is. And I don't want to know! (*Pointing to Lee.*) He's a hustler! He's a bigger hustler than you are! If you can't see that, then —

LEE (*to Austin*): Hey, now hold on. I didn't have to bring this bone back to you, boy. I persuaded Saul here that you were the right man for the job. You don't have to go throwin' up favors in my face.

AUSTIN: Favors! I'm the one who wrote the fuckin' outline! You can't even spell.

SAUL (*to Austin*): Your brother told me about the situation with your father.

(*Pause.*)

AUSTIN: What? (*Looks at Lee.*)

SAUL: That's right. Now we have a clear-cut deal here, Austin. We have big studio money standing behind this thing. Just on the basis of your outline.

AUSTIN (*to Saul*): What'd he tell you about my father?

SAUL: Well — that he's destitute. He needs money.

LEE: That's right. He does.

(*Austin shakes his head, stares at them both.*)

AUSTIN (*to Lee*): And this little assignment is supposed to go toward the old man? A charity project? Is that what this is? Did you cook this up on the ninth green too?

SAUL: It's a big slice, Austin.

AUSTIN (*to Lee*): I gave him money! I already gave him money. You know that. He drank it all up!

LEE: This is a different deal here.

SAUL: We can set up a trust for your father. A large sum of money. It can be doled out to him in parcels so he can't misuse it.

AUSTIN: Yeah, and who's doing the doling?

SAUL: Your brother volunteered.

(*Austin laughs.*)

LEE: That's right. I'll make sure he uses it for groceries.

AUSTIN (*to Saul*): I'm not doing this script! I'm not writing this crap for you or anybody else. You can't blackmail me into it. You can't threaten me into it. There's no way I'm doing it. So just give it up. Both of you.

(*Long pause.*)

SAUL: Well, that's it then. I mean this is an easy three hundred grand. Just for a first draft. It's incredible, Austin. We've got three different studios all trying to cut each other's throats to get this material. In one morning. That's how hot it is.

AUSTIN: Yeah, well you can afford to give me a percentage on the outline then. And you better get the genius here an agent before he gets burned.

LEE: Saul's gonna' be my agent. Isn't that right, Saul?

SAUL: That's right. (*To Austin.*) Your brother has really got something, Austin. I've been around too long not to recognize it. Raw talent.

AUSTIN: He's got a lota' balls is what he's got. He's taking you right down the river.

SAUL: Three hundred thousand, Austin. Just for a first draft. Now you've never been offered that kind of money before.

AUSTIN: I'm not writing it.

(*Pause.*)

SAUL: I see. Well —

LEE: We'll just go to another writer then. Right, Saul? Just hire us somebody with some enthusiasm. Somebody who can recognize the value of a good story.

SAUL: I'm sorry about this, Austin.

AUSTIN: Yeah.

SAUL: I mean I was hoping we could continue both things but now I don't see how it's possible.

AUSTIN: So you're dropping my idea altogether. Is that it? Just trade horses in midstream? After all these months of meetings.

SAUL: I wish there was another way.

AUSTIN: I've got everything riding on this, Saul. You know that. It's my only shot. If this falls through —

SAUL: I have to go with what my instincts tell me —

AUSTIN: Your instincts!

SAUL: My gut reaction.

AUSTIN: You lost! That's your gut reaction. You lost a gamble. Now you're trying to tell me you like his story? How could you possibly fall for that story? It's as phony as Hopalong Cassidy. What do you see in it? I'm curious.

SAUL: It has the ring of truth, Austin.

AUSTIN (*laughs*): Truth?

LEE: It is true.

SAUL: Something about the real West.

AUSTIN: Why? Because it's got horses? Because it's got grown men acting like little boys?

SAUL: Something about the land. Your brother is speaking from experience.

AUSTIN: So am I!

SAUL: But nobody's interested in love these days, Austin. Let's face it.

LEE: That's right.

AUSTIN (*to Saul*): He's been camped out on the desert for three months. Talking to cactus. What's he know about what people wanna' see on the screen! I drive on the freeway every day. I swallow the smog. I watch the news in color. I shop in the Safeway. I'm the one who's in touch! Not him!

SAUL: I have to go now, Austin.

(*Saul starts to leave.*)

AUSTIN: There's no such thing as the West anymore! It's a dead issue! It's dried up, Saul, and so are you.

(*Saul stops and turns to Austin.*)

SAUL: Maybe you're right. But I have to take the gamble, don't I?

AUSTIN: You're a fool to do this, Saul.

SAUL: I've always gone on my hunches. Always. And I've never been wrong. (*To Lee.*) I'll talk to you tomorrow, Lee.

LEE: All right, Mr. Kimmer.

SAUL: Maybe we could have some lunch.

LEE: Fine with me. (*Smiles at Austin.*)

SAUL: I'll give you a ring.

(*Saul exits, lights to black as brothers look at each other from a distance.*)

Scene VII ~3 night~

(*Night. Coyotes, crickets, sound of typewriter in dark, candlelight up on Lee at typewriter struggling to type with one finger system, Austin sits sprawled out on kitchen floor with whiskey bottle, drunk.*)

AUSTIN (*singing, from floor*): "Red sails in the sunset
Way out on the blue
Please carry my loved one
Home safely to me

Red sails in the sunset —"

LEE (*slams fist on table*): Hey! Knock it off will ya'! I'm tryin' to concentrate here.

AUSTIN (*laughs*): You're tryin' to concentrate?

LEE: Yeah. That's right.

AUSTIN: Now you're tryin' to concentrate.

LEE: Between you, the coyotes, and the crickets a thought don't have much of a chance.

AUSTIN: "Between me, the coyotes, and the crickets." What a great title.

LEE: I don't need a title! I need a thought.

AUSTIN (*laughs*): A thought! Here's a thought for ya'—

LEE: I'm not askin' fer yer thoughts! I got my own. I can do this thing on my own.

AUSTIN: You're going to write an entire script on your own?

LEE: That's right.

(*Pause.*) ~Change of position in characters~

AUSTIN: Here's a thought. Saul Kimmer —

LEE: Shut up will ya'!

AUSTIN: He thinks we're the same person.

LEE: Don't get cute.

AUSTIN: He does! He's lost his mind. Poor old Saul. (*Giggles.*) Thinks we're one and the same.

LEE: Why don't you ease up on that champagne.

AUSTIN (*holding up bottle*): This isn't champagne anymore. We went through the champagne a long time ago. This is serious stuff. The days of champagne are long gone.

LEE: Well, go outside and drink it.

AUSTIN: I'm enjoying your company, Lee. For the first time since your arrival I am finally enjoying your company. And now you want me to go outside and drink alone?

LEE: That's right.

(*Lee reads through paper in typewriter, makes an erasure.*)

AUSTIN: You think you'll make more progress if you're alone? You might drive yourself crazy.

LEE: I could have this thing done in a night if I had a little silence.

AUSTIN: Well you'd still have the crickets to contend with. The coyotes. The sounds of the Police Helicopters prowling above the neighborhood. Slashing their searchlights down through the streets. Hunting for the likes of you.

LEE: I'm a screenwriter now! I'm legitimate.

AUSTIN (*laughing*): A screenwriter!

LEE: That's right. I'm on salary. That's more'n I can say for you. I got an advance coming.

AUSTIN: This is true. This is very true. An advance. (*Pause.*) Well, maybe I oughta' go out and try my hand at your trade. Since you're doing so good at mine.

LEE: Ha!

(*Lee attempts to type some more but gets the ribbon tangled up, starts trying to rethread it as they continue talking.*)

AUSTIN: Well why not? You don't think I've got what it takes to sneak into people's houses and steal their T.V.s?

LEE: You couldn't steal a toaster without losin' yer lunch.

(*Austin stands with a struggle, supports himself by the sink.*)

AUSTIN: You don't think I could sneak into somebody's house and steal a toaster?

LEE: Go take a shower or somethin' will ya!

(*Lee gets more tangled up with the typewriter ribbon, pulling it out of the machine as though it was fishing line.*)

AUSTIN: You really don't think I could steal a crumby toaster? How much you wanna' bet I can't steal a toaster! How much? Go ahead! You're a gambler aren't you? Tell me how much yer willing to put on the line. Some part of your big advance? Oh, you haven't got that yet have you. I forgot.

LEE: All right. I'll bet you your car that you can't steal a toaster without gettin' busted.

AUSTIN: You already got my car!

LEE: Okay, your house then.

AUSTIN: What're you gonna' give me! I'm not talkin' about my house and my car, I'm talkin' about what are you gonna' give me. You don't have nothin' to give me.

LEE: I'll give you — shared screen credit. How 'bout that? I'll have it put in the contract that this was written by both of us.

AUSTIN: I don't want my name on that piece of shit! I want something of value. You got anything of value? You got any tidbits from the desert? Any Rattlesnake bones? I'm not a greedy man. Any little personal treasure will suffice.

LEE: I'm gonna' just kick yer ass out in a minute.

AUSTIN: Oh, so now you're gonna' kick me out! Now I'm the intruder. I'm the one who's invading your precious privacy.

LEE: I'm trying to do some screenwriting here!!

(*Lee stands, picks up typewriter, slams it down hard on table, pause, silence except for crickets.*)

AUSTIN: Well, you got everything you need. You got plenty a' coffee? Groceries. You got a car. A contract. (*Pause.*) Might need a new typewriter ribbon but other than that you're pretty well fixed. I'll just leave ya' alone for a while.

(*Austin tries to steady himself to leave, Lee makes a move toward him.*)

LEE: Where you goin'?

AUSTIN: Don't worry about me. I'm not the one to worry about.

(*Austin weaves toward exit, stops.*)

LEE: What're you gonna' do? Just go wander out into the night?

AUSTIN: I'm gonna' make a little tour.

LEE: Why don't ya' just go to bed for Christ's sake. Yer makin' me sick.

AUSTIN: I can take care a' myself. Don't worry about me.

(*Austin weaves badly in another attempt to exit, he crashes to the floor, Lee goes to him but remains standing.*)

LEE: You want me to call your wife for ya' or something?

AUSTIN (*from floor*): My wife?

LEE: Yeah. I mean maybe she can help ya' out. Talk to ya' or somethin'.

AUSTIN (*struggles to stand again*): She's five hundred miles away. North. North of here. Up in the North country where things are calm. I don't need any help. I'm gonna' go outside and I'm gonna' steal a toaster. I'm gonna' steal some other stuff too. I might even commit bigger crimes. Bigger than you ever dreamed of. Crimes beyond the imagination!

(*Austin manages to get himself vertical, tries to head for exit again.*)

LEE: Just hang on a minute, Austin.

AUSTIN: Why? What for? You don't need my help, right? You got a handle on the project. Besides, I'm lookin' forward to the smell of the night. The bushes. Orange blossoms. Dust in the driveways. Rain bird sprinklers. Lights in people's houses. You're right about the lights, Lee. Everybody else is livin' the life. Indoors. Safe. This is a Paradise down here. You know that? We're livin' in a Paradise. We've forgotten about that.

LEE: You sound just like the old man now.

AUSTIN: Yeah, well we all sound alike when we're sloshed. We just sorta' echo each other.

LEE: Maybe if we could work on this together we could bring him back out here. Get him settled down someplace.

(*Austin turns violently toward Lee, takes a swing at him, misses, and crashes to the floor again. Lee stays standing.*)

AUSTIN: I don't want him out here! I've had it with him! I went all the way out there! I went out of my way. I gave him money and all he did was play Al Jolson records and spit at me! I gave him money!

(*Pause.*)

LEE: Just help me a little with the characters, all right? You know how to do it, Austin.

AUSTIN (*on floor, laughs*): The characters!

LEE: Yeah. You know. The way they talk and stuff. I can hear it in my head but I can't get it down on paper.

AUSTIN: What characters?

LEE: The guys. The guys in the story.

AUSTIN: Those aren't characters.

LEE: Whatever you call 'em then. I need to write somethin' out.

AUSTIN: Those are illusions of characters.

LEE: I don't give a damn what ya call 'em! You know what I'm talkin' about!

AUSTIN: Those are fantasies of a long lost boyhood.

LEE: I gotta' write somethin' out on paper!!

(*Pause.*)

AUSTIN: What for? Saul's gonna' get you a fancy screenwriter isn't he?

LEE: I wanna' do it myself!

AUSTIN: Then do it! Yer on your own now, old buddy. You bulldogged yer way into contention. Now you gotta' carry it through.

LEE: I will but I need some advice. Just a couple a' things. Come on, Austin. Just help me get 'em talkin' right. It won't take much.

AUSTIN: Oh, now you're having a little doubt huh? What happened? The pressure's on, boy. This is it. You gotta' come up with it now. You don't come up with a winner on your first time out they just cut your head off. They don't give you a second chance ya' know.

LEE: I got a good story! I know it's a good story. I just need a little help is all.

AUSTIN: Not from me. Not from yer little old brother. I'm retired.

LEE: You could save this thing for me, Austin. I'd give ya' half the money. I would. I only need half anyway. With this kinda' money I could be a long time down the road. I'd never bother ya' again. I promise. You'd never even see me again.

AUSTIN (*still on floor*): You'd disappear?

LEE: I would for sure.

AUSTIN: Where would you disappear to?

LEE: That don't matter. I got plenty a' places.

AUSTIN: Nobody can disappear. The old man tried that. Look where it got him. He lost his teeth.

LEE: He never had any money.

AUSTIN: I don't mean that. I mean his teeth! His real teeth. First he lost his real teeth, then he lost his false teeth. You never knew that did ya? He never confided in you.

LEE: Nah, I never knew that.

AUSTIN: You wanna' drink?

(*Austin offers bottle to Lee, Lee takes it, sits down on kitchen floor with Austin, they share the bottle.*)

Yeah, he lost his real teeth one at a time. Woke up every morning with another tooth lying on the mattress. Finally, he decides he's gotta' get 'em all pulled out but he doesn't have any money. Middle of Arizona with no money and no insurance and every morning another tooth is lying on the mattress. (*Takes a drink.*) So what does he do?

LEE: I dunno'. I never knew about that.

AUSTIN: He begs the government. G.I. Bill or some damn thing. Some pension plan he remembers in the back of his head. And they send him out the money.

LEE: They did?

(*They keep trading the bottle between them, taking drinks.*)

AUSTIN: Yeah. They send him the money but it's not enough money. Costs a lot to have all yer teeth yanked. They charge by the individual tooth, ya' know. I mean one tooth isn't equal to another tooth. Some are very expensive. Like the big ones in the back —

LEE: So what happened?

AUSTIN: So he locates a Mexican dentist in Juarez who'll do the whole thing for a song. And he takes off hitchhiking to the border.

LEE: Hitchhiking?

AUSTIN: Yeah. So how long you think it takes him to get to the border? A man his age.

LEE: I dunno.

AUSTIN: Eight days it takes him. Eight days in the rain and the sun and every day he's droppin' teeth on the blacktop and nobody'll pick him up 'cause his mouth's full a' blood.

(*Pause, they drink.*)

So finally he stumbles into the dentist. Dentist takes all his money and all his teeth. And there he is, in Mexico, with his gums sewed up and his pockets empty.

(*Long silence, Austin drinks.*)

LEE: That's it?

AUSTIN: Then I go out to see him, see. I go out there and I take him out for a nice Chinese dinner. But he doesn't eat. All he wants to do is drink Martinis outa' plastic cups. And he takes his teeth out and lays 'em on the table 'cause he can't stand the feel of 'em. And we ask the waitress for one a' those doggie bags to take the Chop Suey home in. So he drops his teeth in the doggie bag along with the Chop Suey. And then we go out to hit all the bars up and down the highway. Says he wants to introduce me to all his buddies. And in one a' those bars, in one a' those bars up and down the highway, he left that doggie bag with his teeth laying in the Chop Suey.

LEE: You never found it?

AUSTIN: We went back but we never did find it. (*Pause.*) Now that's a true story. True to life.

(*They drink as lights fade to black.*)

Scene VIII

(*Very early morning, between night and day. No crickets, coyotes yapping feverishly in distance before light comes up, a small fire blazes up in the dark from alcove area, sound of Lee smashing typewriter with a golf club, lights coming up, Lee seen smashing typewriter methodically then dropping pages of his script into a burning bowl set on the floor of alcove, flames leap up, Austin has a whole bunch of stolen toasters lined up on the sink counter along with Lee's stolen T.V., the toasters are of a wide variety of models, mostly chrome, Austin goes up and down the line of toasters, breathing on them and polishing them with a dish towel, both men are drunk, empty whiskey bottles and beer cans litter floor of kitchen, they share a half empty bottle on one of the chairs in the alcove, Lee keeps periodically taking deliberate ax-chops at the typewriter using a nine-iron as Austin speaks, all of their mother's house plants are dead and drooping.*)

AUSTIN (*polishing toasters*): There's gonna' be a general lack of toast in the neighborhood this morning. Many, many unhappy, bewildered breakfast faces. I guess it's best not to even think of the victims. Not to even entertain it. Is that the right psychology?

LEE (*pauses*): What?

AUSTIN: Is that the correct criminal psychology? Not to think of the victims?

LEE: What victims?

(*Lee takes another swipe at typewriter with nine-iron, adds pages to the fire.*)

AUSTIN: The victims of crime. Of breaking and entering. I mean is it a prerequisite for a criminal not to have a conscience?

LEE: Ask a criminal.

(*Pause, Lee stares at Austin.*)

What're you gonna' do with all those toasters? That's the dumbest thing I ever saw in my life.

AUSTIN: I've got hundreds of dollars worth of household appliances here. You may not realize that.

LEE: Yeah, and how many hundreds of dollars did you walk right past?

AUSTIN: It was toasters you challenged me to. Only toasters. I ignored every other temptation.

LEE: I never challenged you! That's no challenge. Anybody can steal a toaster.

(*Lee smashes typewriter again.*)

AUSTIN: You don't have to take it out on my typewriter ya' know. It's not the machine's fault that you can't write. It's a sin to do that to a good machine.

LEE: A sin?

AUSTIN: When you consider all the writers who never even had a machine. Who would have given an eyeball for a good typewriter. Any typewriter.

(*Lee smashes typewriter again.*)

AUSTIN (*polishing toasters*): All the ones who wrote on matchbook covers. Paper bags. Toilet paper. Who had their writing destroyed by their jailers. Who persisted beyond all odds. Those writers would find it hard to understand your actions.

(*Lee comes down on typewriter with one final crushing blow of the nine-iron then collapses in one of the chairs, takes a drink from bottle, pause.*)

AUSTIN (*after pause*): Not to mention demolishing a perfectly good golf club. What about all the struggling golfers? What about Lee Trevino? What do you think he would've said when he was batting balls around with broomsticks at the age of nine. Impoverished.

(*Pause.*)

LEE: What time is it anyway?

AUSTIN: No idea. Time stands still when you're havin' fun.

LEE: Is it too late to call a woman? You know any women?

AUSTIN: I'm a married man.

LEE: I mean a local woman.

(*Austin looks out at light through window above sink.*)

AUSTIN: It's either too late or too early. You're the nature enthusiast. Can't you tell the time by the light in the sky? Orient yourself around the North Star or something?

LEE: I can't tell anything.

AUSTIN: Maybe you need a little breakfast. Some toast! How 'bout some toast?

(*Austin goes to cupboard, pulls out loaf of bread, and starts dropping slices into every toaster, Lee stays sitting, drinks, watches Austin.*)

LEE: I don't need toast. I need a woman.

AUSTIN: A woman isn't the answer. Never was.

LEE: I'm not talkin' about permanent. I'm talkin' about temporary.

AUSTIN (*putting toast in toasters*): We'll just test the merits of these little demons. See which brands have a tendency to burn. See which one can produce a perfectly golden piece of fluffy toast.

LEE: How much gas you got in yer car?

AUSTIN: I haven't driven my car for days now. So I haven't had an opportunity to look at the gas gauge.

LEE: Take a guess. You think there's enough to get me to Bakersfield?

AUSTIN: Bakersfield? What's in Bakersfield?

LEE: Just never mind what's in Bakersfield! You think there's enough goddamn gas in the car!

AUSTIN: Sure.

LEE: Sure. You could care less, right. Let me run outa' gas on the Grapevine. You could give a shit.

AUSTIN: I'd say there was enough gas to get you just about anywhere, Lee. With your determination and guts.

LEE: What the hell time is it anyway?

(*Lee pulls out his wallet, starts going through dozens of small pieces of paper with phone numbers written on them, drops some on the floor, drops others in the fire.*)

AUSTIN: Very early. This is the time of morning when the coyotes kill people's cocker spaniels. Did you hear them? That's what they were doing out there. Luring innocent pets away from their homes.

LEE (*searching through his papers*): What's the area code for Bakersfield? You know?

AUSTIN: You could always call the operator.

LEE: I can't stand that voice they give ya'.

AUSTIN: What voice?

LEE: That voice that warns you that if you'd only tried harder to find the number in the phone book you wouldn't have to be calling the operator to begin with.

(*Lee gets up, holding a slip of paper from his wallet, stumbles toward phone on wall, yanks receiver, starts dialing.*)

AUSTIN: Well I don't understand why you'd want to talk to anybody else anyway. I mean you can talk to me. I'm your brother.

LEE (*dialing*): I wanna' talk to a woman. I haven't heard a woman's voice in a long time.

AUSTIN: Not since the Botanist?

LEE: What?

AUSTIN: Nothing. (*Starts singing as he tends toast.*)
"Red sails in the sunset
Way out on the blue
Please carry my loved one.
Home safely to me."

LEE: Hey, knock it off will ya'! This is long distance here.

AUSTIN: Bakersfield?

LEE: Yeah, Bakersfield. It's Kern County.

AUSTIN: Well, what County are *we* in?

LEE: You better get yourself a 7-Up, boy.

AUSTIN: One County's as good as another.

(*Austin hums "Red Sails" softly as Lee talks on phone.*)

LEE (*to phone*): Yeah, operator look — first off I wanna' know the area code for Bakersfield. Right. Bakersfield! Okay. Good. Now I wanna' know if you can help me track somebody down. (*Pause.*) No, no I mean a phone number. Just a phone number. Okay. (*Holds a piece of paper up and reads it.*) Okay, the name is Melly Ferguson. Melly. (*Pause.*) I dunno'. Melly. Maybe. Yeah. Maybe Melanie. Yeah. Melanie Ferguson. Okay. (*Pause.*) What? I can't hear ya' so good. Sounds like yer under the ocean. (*Pause.*) You got ten Melanie Fergusons? How could that be? Ten Melanie Fergusons in Bakersfield? Well gimme all of 'em then. (*Pause.*) What d'ya mean? Gimme all ten Melanie Fergusons! That's right. Just a second. (*To Austin.*) Gimme a pen.

AUSTIN: I don't have a pen.

LEE: Gimme a pencil then!

AUSTIN: I don't have a pencil.

LEE (*to phone*): Just a second, operator. (*To Austin.*) Yer a writer and ya' don't have a pen or a pencil!

AUSTIN: I'm not a writer. You're a writer.

LEE: I'm on the phone here! Get me a pen or a pencil.

AUSTIN: I gotta' watch the toast.

LEE (*to phone*): Hang on a second, operator.

(*Lee lets the phone drop then starts pulling all the drawers in the kitchen out on the floor and dumping the contents, searching for a pencil, Austin watches him casually.*)

LEE (*crashing through drawers, throwing contents around kitchen*): This is the last time I try to live with people, boy! I can't believe it. Here I am! Here I am again in a desperate situation! This would never happen out on the desert. I would never be in this kinda' situation out on the desert. Isn't there a pen or a pencil in this house! Who lives in this house anyway!

AUSTIN: Our mother.

LEE: How come she don't have a pen or a pencil! She's a social person isn't she? Doesn't she have to make shopping lists? She's gotta' have a pencil. (*Finds a pencil.*) Aaha! (*He rushes back to phone, picks up receiver.*) All right operator. Operator? Hey! Operator! Goddamnit!

(*Lee rips the phone off the wall and throws it down, goes back to chair and falls into it, drinks, long pause.*)

AUSTIN: She hung up?

LEE: Yeah, she hung up. I knew she was gonna' hang up. I could hear it in her voice.

(*Lee starts going through his slips of paper again.*)

AUSTIN: Well, you're probably better off staying here with me anyway. I'll take care of you.

LEE: I don't need takin' care of! Not by you anyway.

AUSTIN: Toast is almost ready.

(*Austin starts buttering all the toast as it pops up.*)

LEE: I don't want any toast!

(*Long pause.*)

AUSTIN: You gotta' eat something. Can't just drink. How long have we been drinking anyway?

LEE (*looking through slips of paper*): Maybe it was Fresno. What's the area code for Fresno? How could I have lost that number! She was beautiful.

(*Pause.*)

AUSTIN: Why don't you just forget about that, Lee. Forget about the woman.

LEE: She had green eyes. You know what green eyes do to me?

AUSTIN: I know but you're not gonna' get it on with her now anyway. It's dawn already. She's in Bakersfield for Christ's sake.

(*Long pause, Lee considers the situation.*)

LEE: Yeah. (*Looks at windows.*) It's dawn?

AUSTIN: Let's just have some toast and —

LEE: What is this bullshit with the toast anyway! You make it sound like salvation or something. I don't want any goddamn toast! How many times I gotta' tell ya'! (*Lee gets up, crosses upstage to windows in alcove, looks out, Austin butters toast.*)

AUSTIN: Well it is like salvation sort of. I mean the smell. I love the smell of toast. And the sun's coming up. It makes me feel like anything's possible. Ya' know?

LEE (*back to Austin, facing windows upstage*): So go to church why don't ya'.

AUSTIN: Like a beginning. I love beginnings.

LEE: Oh yeah. I've always been kinda' partial to endings myself.

AUSTIN: What if I come with you, Lee?

LEE (*pause as Lee turns toward Austin*): What?

AUSTIN: What if I come with you out to the desert?

LEE: Are you kiddin'?

AUSTIN: No. I'd just like to see what it's like.

LEE: You wouldn't last a day out there pal.

AUSTIN: That's what you said about the toasters. You said I couldn't steal a toaster either.

LEE: A toaster's got nothin' to do with the desert.

AUSTIN: I could make it, Lee. I'm not that helpless. I can cook.

LEE: Cook?

AUSTIN: I can.

LEE: So what! You can cook. Toast.

AUSTIN: I can make fires. I know how to get fresh water from condensation.

(*Austin stacks buttered toast up in a tall stack on plate.*)
(*Lee slams table.*)

LEE: It's not somethin' you learn out of a Boy Scout handbook!

AUSTIN: Well how do you learn it then! How're you supposed to learn it!

(*Pause.*)

LEE: Ya' just learn it, that's all. Ya' learn it 'cause ya' have to learn it. You don't *have* to learn it.

AUSTIN: You could teach me.

LEE (*stands*): What're you, crazy or somethin'? You went to college. Here, you are down here, rollin' in bucks. Floatin' up and down in elevators. And you wanna' learn how to live on the desert!

AUSTIN: I do, Lee. I really do. There's nothin' down here for me. There never was. When we were kids here it was different. There was a life here then. But now — I keep comin' down here thinkin' it's the fifties or somethin'. I keep finding myself getting off the freeway at familiar landmarks that turn out to be unfamiliar. On the way to appointments. Wandering down streets I thought I recognized that turn out to be replicas of streets I remember. Streets I misremember. Streets I can't tell if I lived on or saw in a postcard. Fields that don't even exist anymore.

LEE: There's no point cryin' about that now.

AUSTIN: There's nothin' real down here, Lee! Least of all me!

LEE: Well I can't save you from that!

AUSTIN: You can let me come with you.

LEE: No dice, pal.

AUSTIN: You could let me come with you, Lee!

LEE: Hey, do you actually think I chose to live out in the middle a' nowhere? Do ya'? Ya' think it's some kinda' philosophical decision I took or somethin'? I'm livin' out there 'cause I can't make it here! And yer bitchin' to me about all yer success!

AUSTIN: I'd cash it all in in a second. That's the truth.

LEE (*pause, shakes his head*): I can't believe this.

AUSTIN: Let me go with you.

LEE: Stop sayin' that will ya'! Yer worse than a dog.

(*Austin offers out the plate of neatly stacked toast to Lee.*)

AUSTIN: You want some toast?

(*Lee suddenly explodes and knocks the plate out of Austin's hand, toast goes flying, long frozen moment where it appears Lee might go all the way this time when Austin breaks it by slowly lowering himself to his knees and begins gathering the scattered toast from the floor and stacking it back on the plate, Lee begins to circle Austin in a slow, predatory way, crushing pieces of toast in his wake, no words for a while, Austin keeps gathering toast, even the crushed pieces.*)

LEE: Tell ya' what I'll do, little brother. I might just consider makin' you a deal. Little trade. (*Austin continues gathering toast as Lee circles him through this.*) You write me up this screenplay thing just like I tell ya'. I mean you can use all yer usual tricks and stuff. Yer fancy language. Yer artistic hocus pocus. But ya' gotta' write everything like I say. Every move. Every time they run outa' gas, they run outa' gas. Every time they wanna' jump on a horse, they do just that. If they wanna' stay in Texas, by God they'll stay in Texas! (*Keeps circling.*) And you finish the whole thing up for me. Top to bottom. And you put my name on it. And I own all the rights. And every dime goes in my pocket. You do that and I'll sure enough take ya' with me to the desert. (*Lee stops, pause, looks down at Austin.*) How's that sound?

(*Pause as Austin stands slowly holding plate of demolished toast, their faces are very close, pause.*)

AUSTIN: It's a deal.

(*Lee stares straight into Austin's eyes, then he slowly takes a piece of toast off the plate, raises it to his mouth, and takes a huge crushing bite never taking his eyes off Austin's, as Lee crunches into the toast the lights black out.*)

Scene IX

(*Midday. No sound, blazing heat, the stage is ravaged; bottles, toasters, smashed typewriter, ripped out telephone, etc. All the debris from previous scene is now starkly visible in intense yellow light, the effect should be like a desert junkyard at high noon, the coolness of the preceding scenes is totally obliterated. Austin is seated at table in alcove, shirt open, pouring with sweat, hunched over a writing notebook, scribbling notes desperately with a ballpoint pen. Lee with no shirt, beer in hand, sweat pouring down his chest, is walking a slow circle around the table, picking his way through the objects, sometimes kicking them aside.*)

LEE (*as he walks*): All right, read it back to me. Read it back to me!

AUSTIN (*scribbling at top speed*): Just a second.

LEE: Come on, come on! Just read what ya' got.

AUSTIN: I can't keep up! It's not the same as if I had a typewriter.

LEE: Just read what we got so far. Forget about the rest.

AUSTIN: All right. Let's see — okay — (*wipes sweat from his face, reads as Lee circles*) Luke says uh —

LEE: Luke?

AUSTIN: Yeah.

LEE: His name's Luke? All right, all right — we can change the names later. What's he say? Come on, come on.

AUSTIN: He says uh — (*reading*) "I told ya' you were a fool to follow me in here. I know this prairie like the back a' my hand."

LEE: No, no no! That's not what I said. I never said that.

AUSTIN: That's what I wrote.

LEE: It's not what I said. I never said "like the back a' my hand." That's stupid. That's one a' those — whadya' call it? Whadya' call that?

AUSTIN: What?

LEE: Whadya' call it when somethin's been said a thousand times before. Whadya' call that?

AUSTIN: Um — a cliché?

LEE: Yeah. That's right. Cliché. That's what that is. A cliché. "The back a' my hand." That's stupid.

AUSTIN: That's what you said.

LEE: I never said that! And even if I did, that's where yer supposed to come in. That's where yer supposed to change it to somethin' better.

AUSTIN: Well how am I supposed to do that and write down what you say at the same time?

LEE: Ya' just do, that's all! You hear a stupid line you change it. That's yer job.

AUSTIN: All right. (*Makes more notes.*)

LEE: What're you changin' it to?

AUSTIN: I'm not changing it. I'm just trying to catch up.

LEE: Well change it! We gotta' change that, we can't leave that in there like that. "... the back a' my hand." That's dumb.

AUSTIN (*stops writing, sits back*): All right.

LEE (*pacing*): So what'll we change it to?

AUSTIN: Um — How 'bout — "I'm on intimate terms with this prairie."

LEE (*to himself considering line as he walks*): "I'm on intimate terms with this prairie." Intimate terms, intimate terms. Intimate — that means like uh — sexual right?

AUSTIN: Well — yeah — or —

LEE: He's on sexual terms with the prairie? How dya' figure that?

AUSTIN: Well it doesn't necessarily have to mean sexual.

LEE: What's it mean then?

AUSTIN: It means uh — close — personal —

LEE: All right. How's it sound? Put it into the uh — the line there. Read it back. Let's see how it sounds. (*To himself.*) "Intimate terms."

AUSTIN (*scribbles in notebook*): Okay. It'd go something like this: (*reads*) "I told ya' you were a fool to follow me in here. I'm on intimate terms with this prairie."

LEE: That's good. I like that. That's real good.

AUSTIN: You do?

LEE: Yeah. Don't you?

AUSTIN: Sure.

LEE: Sounds original now. "Intimate terms." That's good. Okay. Now we're cookin! That has a real ring to it.

(*Austin makes more notes, Lee walks around, pours beer on his arms and rubs it over his chest feeling good about the new progress, as he does this Mom enters unobtrusively down left with her luggage, she stops and stares at the scene still holding luggage as the two men continue, unaware of her presence, Austin absorbed in his writing, Lee cooling himself off with beer.*)

LEE (*continues*): "He's on intimate terms with this prairie." Sounds real mysterious and kinda threatening at the same time.

AUSTIN (*writing rapidly*): Good.

LEE: Now — (*Lee turns and suddenly sees Mom, he stares at her for a while, she stares back, Austin keeps writing feverishly, not noticing, Lee walks slowly over to Mom and takes a closer look, long pause.*)
LEE: Mom?

(*Austin looks up suddenly from his writing, sees Mom, stands quickly, long pause, Mom surveys the damage.*)

AUSTIN: Mom. What're you doing back?
MOM: I'm back.
LEE: Here, lemme take those for ya.

(*Lee sets beer on counter then takes both her bags but doesn't know where to set them down in the sea of junk so he just keeps holding them.*)

AUSTIN: I wasn't expecting you back so soon. I thought uh — How was Alaska?
MOM: Fine.
LEE: See any igloos?
MOM: No. Just glaciers.
AUSTIN: Cold huh?
MOM: What?
AUSTIN: It must've been cold up there?
MOM: Not really.
LEE: Musta' been colder than this here. I mean we're havin' a real scorcher here.
MOM: Oh? (*She looks at damage.*)
LEE: Yeah. Must be in the hundreds.
AUSTIN: You wanna' take your coat off, Mom?
MOM: No. (*Pause, she surveys space.*) What happened in here?
AUSTIN: Oh um — Me and Lee were just sort of celebrating and uh —
MOM: Celebrating?
AUSTIN: Yeah. Uh — Lee sold a screenplay. A story, I mean.
MOM: Lee did?
AUSTIN: Yeah.
MOM: Not you?
AUSTIN: No. Him.
MOM (*to Lee*): You sold a screenplay?
LEE: Yeah. That's right. We're sorta' finishing it up right now. That's what we're doing here.
AUSTIN: Me and Lee are going out to the desert to live.
MOM: You and Lee?
AUSTIN: Yeah. I'm taking off with Lee.
MOM (*she looks back and forth at each of them, pause*): You gonna go live with your father?
AUSTIN: No. We're going to a different desert Mom.
MOM: I see. Well, you'll probably wind up on the same desert sooner or later. What're all these toasters doing here?
AUSTIN: Well — we had kind of a contest.
MOM: Contest?
LEE: Yeah.
AUSTIN: Lee won.
MOM: Did you win a lot of money, Lee?
LEE: Well not yet. It's comin' in any day now.

MOM (*to Lee*): What happened to your shirt?
LEE: Oh. I was sweatin' like a pig and I took it off.

(*Austin grabs Lee's shirt off the table and tosses it to him, Lee sets down suitcases and puts his shirt on.*)

MOM: Well, it's one hell of a mess in here isn't it?
AUSTIN: Yeah, I'll clean it up for you, Mom. I just didn't know you were coming back so soon.
MOM: I didn't either.
AUSTIN: What happened?
MOM: Nothing. I just started missing all my plants.

(*She notices dead plants.*)

AUSTIN: Oh.
MOM: Oh, they're all dead aren't they. (*She crosses toward them, examines them closely.*) You didn't get a chance to water I guess.
AUSTIN: I was doing it and then Lee came and —
LEE: Yeah I just distracted him a whole lot here, Mom. It's not his fault.

(*Pause, as Mom stares at plants.*)

MOM: Oh well, one less thing to take care of I guess. (*Turns toward brothers.*) Oh, that reminds me — You boys will probably never guess who's in town. Try and guess.

(*Long pause, brothers stare at her.*)

AUSTIN: Whadya' mean, Mom?
MOM: Take a guess. Somebody very important has come to town. I read it, coming down on the Greyhound.
LEE: Somebody very important?
MOM: See if you can guess. You'll never guess.
AUSTIN: Mom — we're trying to uh — (*Points to writing pad.*)
MOM: Picasso. (*Pause.*) Picasso's in town. Isn't that incredible? Right now.   *Picasso visiting?*

(*Pause.*)

AUSTIN: Picasso's dead, Mom.
MOM: No, he's not dead. He's visiting the museum. I read it on the bus. We have to go down there and see him.
AUSTIN: Mom —
MOM: This is the chance of a lifetime. Can you imagine? We could all go down and meet him. All three of us.
LEE: Uh — I don't think I'm really up for meetin' anybody right now. I'm uh — What's his name?
MOM: Picasso! Picasso! You've never heard of Picasso? Austin, you've heard of Picasso.
AUSTIN: Mom, we're not going to have time.
MOM: It won't take long. We'll just hop in the car and go down there. An opportunity like this doesn't come along every day.
AUSTIN: We're gonna' be leavin' here, Mom!

(*Pause.*)

MOM: Oh.
LEE: Yeah.

(*Pause.*)

MOM: You're both leaving?
LEE (*looks at Austin*): Well we were thinkin' about that before but now I —
AUSTIN: No, we are! We're both leaving. We've got it all planned.
MOM (*to Austin*): Well you can't leave. You have a family.
AUSTIN: I'm leaving. I'm getting out of here.
LEE (*to Mom*): I don't really think Austin's cut out for the desert do you?
MOM: No. He's not.
AUSTIN: I'm going with you, Lee!
MOM: He's too thin.
LEE: Yeah, he'd just burn up out there.
AUSTIN (*to Lee*): We just gotta finish this screenplay and then we're gonna' take off. That's the plan. That's what you said. Come on, let's get back to work, Lee.
LEE: I can't work under these conditions here. It's too hot.
AUSTIN: Then we'll do it on the desert.
LEE: Don't be tellin' me what we're gonna do!
MOM: Don't shout in the house.
LEE: We're just gonna' have to postpone the whole deal.
AUSTIN: I can't postpone it! It's gone past postponing! I'm doing everything you said. I'm writing down exactly what you tell me.
LEE: Yeah, but you were right all along see. It is a dumb story. "Two lamebrains chasin' each other across Texas." That's what you said, right?
AUSTIN: I never said that.

(*Lee sneers in Austin's face then turns to Mom.*)

LEE: I'm gonna' just borrow some a' your antiques, Mom. You don't mind do ya'? Just a few plates and things. Silverware.

(*Lee starts going through all the cupboards in kitchen pulling out plates and stacking them on counter as Mom and Austin watch.*)

MOM: You don't have any utensils on the desert?
LEE: Nah, I'm fresh out.
AUSTIN (*to Lee*): What're you doing?
MOM: Well some of those are very old. Bone China.
LEE: I'm tired of eatin' outa' my bare hands, ya' know. It's not civilized.
AUSTIN (*to Lee*): What're you doing? We made a deal!
MOM: Couldn't you borrow the plastic ones instead? I have plenty of plastic ones.
LEE (*as he stacks plates*): It's not the same. Plastic's not the same at all. What I need is somethin' authentic. Somethin' to keep me in touch. It's easy to get outa' touch out there. Don't worry I'll get 'em back to ya'.

(*Austin rushes up to Lee, grabs him by shoulders.*)

AUSTIN: You can't just drop the whole thing, Lee!

(*Lee turns, pushes Austin in the chest knocking him backward into the alcove, Mom watches numbly, Lee returns to collecting the plates, silverware, etc.*)

MOM: You boys shouldn't fight in the house. Go outside and fight.
LEE: I'm not fightin'. I'm leavin'.
MOM: There's been enough damage done already.
LEE (*his back to Austin and Mom, stacking dishes on counter*): I'm clearin' outa' here once and for all. All this town does is drive a man insane. Look what it's done to Austin there. I'm not lettin' that happen to me. Sell myself down the river. No sir. I'd rather be a hundred miles from nowhere than let that happen to me.

(*During this Austin has picked up the ripped-out phone from the floor and wrapped the cord tightly around his hands, he lunges at Lee whose back is still to him, wraps the cord around Lee's neck, plants a foot in Lee's back and pulls back on the cord, tightening it, Lee chokes desperately, can't speak and can't reach Austin with his arms, Austin keeps applying pressure on Lee's back with his foot, bending him into the sink, Mom watches.*)

AUSTIN (*tightening cord*): You're not goin' anywhere! You're not takin' anything with you. You're not takin' my car! You're not takin' the dishes! You're not takin' anything! You're stayin' right here!
MOM: You'll have to stop fighting in the house. There's plenty of room outside to fight. You've got the whole outdoors to fight in.

(*Lee tries to tear himself away, he crashes across the stage like an enraged bull dragging Austin with him, he snorts and bellows but Austin hangs on and manages to keep clear of Lee's attempts to grab him, they crash into the table, to the floor, Lee is face down thrashing wildly and choking, Austin pulls cord tighter, stands with one foot planted on Lee's back and the cord stretched taut.*)

AUSTIN (*holding cord*): Gimme back my keys, Lee! Take the keys out! Take 'em out!

(*Lee desperately tries to dig in his pockets, searching for the car keys, Mom moves closer.*)

MOM (*calmly to Austin*): You're not killing him are you?
AUSTIN: I don't know. I don't know if I'm killing him. I'm stopping him. That's all. I'm just stopping him.

(*Lee thrashes but Austin is relentless.*)

MOM: You oughta' let him breathe a little bit.
AUSTIN: Throw the keys out, Lee!

(*Lee finally gets keys out and throws them on floor but out of Austin's reach, Austin keeps pressure on cord, pulling Lee's neck back, Lee gets one hand to the cord but can't relieve the pressure.*)

Reach me those keys would ya', Mom.

MOM (*not moving*): Why are you doing this to him?

AUSTIN: Reach me the keys!

MOM: Not until you stop choking him.

AUSTIN: I can't stop choking him! He'll kill me if I stop choking him!

MOM: He won't kill you. He's your brother.

AUSTIN: Just get me the keys would ya'!

(*Pause. Mom picks keys up off floor, hands them to Austin.*)

AUSTIN (*to Mom*): Thanks.

MOM: Will you let him go now?

AUSTIN: I don't know. He's not gonna' let me get outa' here.

MOM: Well you can't kill him.

AUSTIN: I can kill him! I can easily kill him. Right now. Right here. All I gotta' do is just tighten up. See? (*He tightens cord, Lee thrashes wildly, Austin releases pressure a little, maintaining control.*) Ya' see that?

MOM: That's a savage thing to do.

AUSTIN: Yeah well don't tell me I can't kill him because I can. I can just twist. I can just keep twisting. (*Austin twists the cord tighter, Lee weakens, his breathing changes to a short rasp.*)

MOM: Austin!

(*Austin relieves pressure, Lee breathes easier but Austin keeps him under control.*)

AUSTIN (*eyes on Lee, holding cord*): I'm goin' to the desert. There's nothing stopping me. I'm going by myself to the desert.

(*Mom moving toward her luggage.*)

MOM: Well, I'm going to go check into a motel. I can't stand this anymore.

AUSTIN: Don't go yet!

(*Mom pauses.*)

MOM: I can't stay here. This is worse than being homeless.

AUSTIN: I'll get everything fixed up for you, Mom. I promise. Just stay for a while.

MOM (*picking up luggage*): You're going to the desert.

AUSTIN: Just wait!

(*Lee thrashes, Austin subdues him, Mom watches holding luggage, pause.*)

MOM: It was the worst feeling being up there. In Alaska. Staring out a window. I never felt so desperate before. That's why when I saw that article on Picasso I thought —

AUSTIN: Stay here, Mom. This is where you live.

(*She looks around the stage.*)

MOM: I don't recognize it at all.

(*She exits with luggage, Austin makes a move toward her but Lee starts to struggle and Austin subdues him again with cord, pause.*)

AUSTIN (*holding cord*): Lee? I'll make ya' a deal. You let me get outa' here. Just let me get to my car. All right, Lee? Gimme a little headstart and I'll turn you loose. Just gimme a little headstart. All right?

(*Lee makes no response, Austin slowly releases tension cord, still nothing from Lee.*)

AUSTIN: Lee?

(*Lee is motionless, Austin very slowly begins to stand, still keeping a tenuous hold on the cord and his eyes riveted to Lee for any sign of movement, Austin slowly drops the cord and stands, he stares down at Lee who appears to be dead.*)

AUSTIN (*whispers*): Lee?

(*Pause, Austin considers, looks toward exit, back to Lee, then makes a small movement as if to leave. Instantly Lee is on his feet and moves toward exit, blocking Austin's escape. They square off to each other, keeping a distance between them. Pause, a single coyote heard in distance, lights fade softly into moonlight, the figures of the brothers now appear to be caught in a vast desertlike landscape, they are very still but watchful for the next move, lights go slowly to black as the after-image of the brothers pulses in the dark, coyote fades.*)

Brian Friel

Born in County Tyrone, Northern Ireland, in 1929, Brian Friel has become Ireland's major playwright. His distinction has grown in recent years with dramatic successes in Ireland, London, and New York. From 1950 to 1960 he was a schoolteacher, but since 1960 he has been a full-time writer. His first well-received play was *Philadelphia, Here I Come!* (1964), which tells the story of Gar O'Donnell, who is about to emigrate to the United States from his tiny hamlet of Ballybeg, County Donegal, the village Friel usually uses for his settings. Ballybeg is tiny, depressed, unable to offer work or dignity to its young men, and those with spirit find that their choices are circumscribed by the limitations of the economy. America offers the most hope, and that is where Gar decides to go. The play captured the imagination of many Irish Americans because of their response to the theme of emigration, but it transcends ethnic concerns. In many ways it has a universal theme — the story of all young men who grow up and realize they must break with their home and set out on their own.

The Loves of Cass McGuire (1966) was first broadcast as a radio play and then produced in New York, Belfast, and London. It tells the story of an old woman whose hopes in life have been dashed by circumstances, none of which improve during the play. Friel developed several strains in his work after demonstrating an interest in the pathos of individual lives such as those of Gar O'Donnell and Cass McGuire. He showed a satirical streak in the political play *The Mundy Scheme* (1969), which focuses on a crazy plan of Irish politicians to capitalize on the Irish specialty of holding wakes for the dead. Mundy's proposal is to convert Ireland into the graveyard of all Europe, thus turning much unarable land to good account. *Freedom of the City* was produced in Dublin, London, and Chicago in 1973 and in New York the following year. It tells the story of three very different people — Michael, twenty-two, and Skinner, twenty-one, both with differing social attitudes, and Lily, forty-three, mother of eleven — who occupy the mayor's office in the Guildhall (town hall) of Derry City during a student protest march. Eventually the three discover common political ground and through a series of unexpected incidents find themselves facing death at the hands of surrounding soldiers.

The Faith Healer (1979) ostensibly portrays a wandering man who heals people in a miraculous way. But the deep structure of the play is about art and the artist's responsibility for healing society. It played in New York and London to considerable acclaim. The most highly regarded of Friel's plays is *Translations* (1980). Produced in Derry, London, and New York to appreciative crowds, it is set in 1833 in Baile Beg (Ballybeg) and follows the efforts of English surveyors to rename Irish places while making survey maps. These maps translate Irish place names in high-handed, arbitrary fashion. For example, they choose Burnfoot for Bun na hAbhann, which in Irish means "mouth of the river," because Burnfoot is the closest they can get to the Irish word in English. Throughout the play Irish characters speak Irish — or at least we are to understand that they do — while the English speak English.

Much of Friel's work has concerned Irish political issues, but plays such as *Translations* are easy for non-Irish audiences to understand and appreciate. Despite its portrayal of the English as unconscious oppressors, audiences in London's National Theatre were wildly enthusiastic about it during its extensive 1981 run. *Making History* (1989), set in Elizabethan Ireland, also concerns English oppression and is part of a historical cycle of plays. Friel's *Dancing at Lughnasa* (1990) is a personal examination of a childhood in Ballybeg in the 1930s.

Brian Friel has never been an actor, but he brings to the stage a keen ear for language in the Irish tradition of William Congreve, Bernard Shaw, Oscar Wilde, Lady Gregory, John Millington Synge, Sean O'Casey, and Samuel Beckett. His characters' speeches are rich with the rhythms of everyday Irish country life and the color and metaphor of people whose joy in language is intense and satisfying. He is a member — along with critic Seamus Deane, poets Seamus Heaney and Tom Paulin, and actor Stephen Rea — of an Irish literary group called Field Day, which has its own press and publishes poetry, fiction, and drama and has produced an ambitious three-volume anthology of Irish literature. Friel has published *Selected Stories* (1979) and *The Diviner* (1983), a book of short stories. In addition to all this, he has also translated Chekhov's *Three Sisters* (1981) and adapted Turgenev's *Fathers and Sons* (1987) for the stage. He is a prodigious figure in contemporary literature.

TRANSLATIONS

When Brian Friel's play *Translations* was produced in 1980, he was already a famous international author with plays staged frequently in London, New York, and other major cities around the world. In Ireland at that time, unrest was evident in a steady campaign of bombings and guerrilla activities on the part of the outlawed Irish Republican Party. Consequently, the British army occupied Northern Ireland, a country separate from the Republic of Ireland but geographically part of the same island. On the streets of the country's capital, Belfast, at that time, one saw military vehicles, sentries on street corners, and chainlink fences some twenty feet high on both sides of the road to prevent rioters from tossing grenades into shops. The very building in which *Translations* was first presented had been bombed several times. The subject of politics was surely on everyone's mind in Belfast, Derry, and all other towns throughout Northern Ireland.

The circumstances of the play are essentially true to fact. In 1833, about a decade before the terrible Potato Famine (1845–1850), the English were surveying Ireland to create a reliable map of the terrain. They did not have enough trained surveyors to do the job, so they enlisted the help of the army. Like Yolland, the English officer in the play, these men were given a rough and ready introduction to the job and then set off. They, like Yolland and Captain Lancey, soon found the job very difficult and recruited local Irish to interpret for them and to identify the places whose Gaelic names they were to "normalize" into English. As Manus says in the middle of the play, referring to his brother Owen, who is helping the English, "But there are always the Rolands, aren't there?" The weight of this statement comes from the fact that Yolland continually calls Owen "Roland," in effect "translating" his Irish name into English. Manus is angry at his brother for collaborating with Yolland. Owen, however, feels he is liberating himself from a restricted culture bound by language and law. He also feels that Yolland is a decent man and that there is no reason to be prejudiced against him simply because he is English.

On the other hand, Owen watches and aids the alteration of Irish place names, filled with color and poetry, into common flat English prose. The fact that some places have several names does not bother the Irish, but it is intolerable to the surveyors, and they make arbitrary decisions about the final choices in the scenes in act 2 when the process is described. Much of this section of the play is based on fact. Since 1926, when the Irish Free State was established (today's Republic of Ireland wasn't proclaimed until 1949), some of the names have been changed back to Gaelic, such as Dun Laoghaire (pronounced Dun Leary), which the English had renamed Kingstown. Even today, in certain rural areas of Ireland, road signs in English have been blacked out so that only the Irish names are visible.

The implication is clear that, in Anglicizing the Irish names, more is lost than just a matter of naming. The entire culture is under threat, something Owen understands. He speaks both languages and has a foot in both cultures. The other people in Baile Beag primarily speak Irish and will be eventually forced to abandon their language and their culture in the name of progress and trade.

Simultaneously with the introduction of new place names, the English established a national school system in which the Irish were to have free schools taught in English. Prior to this, the system of hedge-schools had existed in Ireland for more than one hundred years. These schools were created because the English had denied Catholic school children in Ireland the right to go to school unless they converted to Protestantism. These laws forced the Irish to invent their own means of education. Friel's point in setting the play in such a hedge-school is that the system produced some exceptional scholars of Latin and Greek, all of whom studied in their vernacular Irish. They used barns, private homes, and any space they could find that would permit instruction. Hugh, the father of Owen and Manus, is an example of the beloved hedge-schoolmaster, urging on his students to become classically learned. The establishment of English schools meant the end of a long tradition. Friel, by contrasting the ignorance of the English officers — who know no Latin or Greek — with the knowledge of the Irish peasants, tells us something about the future of Irish education under the English system.

The romance between Yolland and Maire is exceptional for its ability to bridge the language gap, one of the main ideas in the play. One of the clever devices of *Translations* is its use of Irish-speaking characters whose language is "instantly" translated for us but is unintelligible to the English officers. Maire and Yolland do not understand each other, although they make an effort at the end of act 2. Yolland's Irish is essentially limited to place names, while Maire depends on Owen for translation from Irish to English. When Yolland and Maire are alone in scene 2 of act 2, they manage to communicate, but only in the roughest sense. Maire tries Latin, once the universal language of Europe, but Yolland did not have a grammar-school education and therefore does not understand. Ultimately, it is primarily each other's names that they can say and understand.

At the end of the play the place names are recited once more, but now they are translated back from English into Irish for Maire and others to understand. The purpose of the translation is to identify which places are to be destroyed by the English in reprisal for the supposed death of Lieutenant Yolland, who has disappeared.

Translations in Performance

The 1980 premiere was staged in Derry Guildhall in Northern Ireland to great acclaim. It was a major event in Ireland, and writers, artists, and politicians all came together peacefully to watch and admire what Friel had been able to do. The Field Day Company — established by Friel; poet Seamus Heaney; critic, poet, and novelist Seamus Deane; and other writers and artists to revitalize and politicize the Irish literary arts — produced the play. Actor Stephen Rea, also a member of the company, played Owen and went on to become an international film and stage actor. The reviews of the production were excellent both in Derry and at the Dublin Theatre Festival run the same year. Productions in New York and London quickly followed. In 1991, director Debra Freeberg saw the play in a small theater in Los Angeles and staged her own version at Calvin College, in Michigan, in 2000. The Abbey Theater in Dublin produced the play in 2000, again in 2001, and then brought it to the United States to play regionally. The Irish Classical Theatre in Buffalo, New York, produced the play in March 2004. _Translations_ has achieved the status of an Irish classic, performed frequently by professional and college theaters around the world.

Brian Friel (b. 1929)
TRANSLATIONS

1980

Persons in the Play

MANUS
SARAH
JIMMY JACK
MAIRE
DOALTY
BRIDGET
HUGH
OWEN
CAPTAIN LANCEY
LIEUTENANT YOLLAND

The action takes place in a hedge-school in the townland of Baile Beag/Ballybeg, an Irish-speaking community in County Donegal.

ACT ONE   An afternoon in late August 1833.

ACT TWO   A few days later.

ACT THREE The evening of the following day.

One-interval — between the two scenes in Act Two.

ACT ONE

The hedge-school is held in a disused barn or hay-shed or byre. Along the back wall are the remains of five or six stalls — wooden posts and chains — where cows were once milked and bedded. A double door left, large enough to allow a cart to enter. A window right. A wooden stairway without a banister leads to the upstairs living-quarters (off) of the schoolmaster and his son. Around the room are broken and forgotten implements: a cart-wheel, some lobster-pots, farming tools, a battle of hay, a churn, etc. There are also the stools and bench-seats which the pupils use and a table and chair for the master. At the door a pail of water and a soiled towel. The room is comfortless and dusty and functional — there is no trace of a woman's hand.

When the play opens, Manus is teaching Sarah to speak. He kneels beside her. She is sitting on a low stool her head down, very tense, clutching a slate on her knees. He is coaxing her gently and firmly and — as with everything he does — with a kind of zeal.

Manus is in his late twenties/early thirties; the master's older son. He is pale-faced, lightly built, intense, and works as an unpaid assistant — a monitor — to his father. His clothes are shabby; and when he moves we see that he is lame.

Sarah's speech is so bad that all her life she has been considered locally to be dumb and she has accepted this: when she wishes to communicate, she grunts and makes unintelligible nasal sounds. She has a waiflike appearance and could be any age from seventeen to thirty-five.

Jimmy Jack Cassie — known as the Infant Prodigy — sits by himself, contentedly reading Homer in Greek and smiling to himself. He is a bachelor in his sixties, lives alone, and comes to these evening classes partly for the company and partly for the intellectual stimulation. He is fluent in Latin and Greek but is in no way pedantic — to him it is perfectly normal to speak these tongues. He never washes. His clothes — heavy top coat, hat, mittens, which he wears now — are filthy and he lives in them summer and winter, day and night. He now reads in a quiet voice and smiles in profound satisfaction. For Jimmy the world of the gods and the ancient myths is as real and as immediate as everyday life in the townland of Baile Beag.

Manus holds Sarah's hands in his and he articulates slowly and distinctly into her face.

MANUS: We're doing very well. And we're going to try it once more — just once more. Now — relax and breathe in . . . deep . . . and out . . . in . . . and out . . .

[*Sarah shakes her head vigorously and stubbornly.*]

MANUS: Come on, Sarah. This is our secret.

[*Again vigorous and stubborn shaking of Sarah's head.*]

MANUS: Nobody's listening. Nobody hears you.
JIMMY: '*Ton d'emeibet epeita thea glaukopis Athene . . .*'°

Ton d'emeibet . . . Athene: The grey-eyed goddess Athene answered him (Homer, *Odyssey* 13.420).

MANUS: Get your tongue and your lips working. 'My name — ' Come on. One more try. 'My name is — ' Good girl.
SARAH: My . . .
MANUS: Great. 'My name — '
SARAH: My . . . my . . .
MANUS: Raise your head. Shout it out. Nobody's listening.
JIMMY: '. . . *alla hekelos estai en Atreidao domois . . .*'°
MANUS: Jimmy, please! Once more — just once more — 'My name — ' Good girl. Come on now. Head up. Mouth open.
SARAH: My . . .
MANUS: Good.
SARAH: My . . .
MANUS: Great.
SARAH: My name . . .
MANUS: Yes?
SARAH: My name is . . .
MANUS: Yes?

[*Sarah pauses. Then in a rush.*]

SARAH: My name is Sarah.
MANUS: Marvellous! Bloody marvellous!

[*Manus hugs Sarah. She smiles in shy, embarrassed pleasure.*]

Did you hear that, Jimmy? — 'My name is Sarah' — clear as a bell. [*To Sarah.*] The Infant Prodigy doesn't know what we're at.

[*Sarah laughs at this. Manus hugs her again and stands up.*]

Now we're really started! Nothing'll stop us now! Nothing in the wide world!

[*Jimmy, chuckling at his text, comes over to them.*]

JIMMY: Listen to this, Manus.
MANUS: Soon you'll be telling me all the secrets that have been in that head of yours all these years. Certainly, James — what is it? [*To Sarah.*] Maybe you'd set out the stools? [*Manus runs up the stairs.*]
JIMMY: Wait till you hear this, Manus.
MANUS: Go ahead. I'll be straight down.
JIMMY: '*Hos ara min phamene rabdo epemassat Athene—*' 'After Athene had said this, she touched Ulysses with her wand. She withered the fair skin of his supple limbs and destroyed the flaxen hair from off his head and about his limbs she put the skin of an old man . . .'! The divil! The divil!

[*Manus has emerged again with a bowl of milk and a piece of bread.*]

JIMMY: And wait till you hear! She's not finished with him yet!

[*As Manus descends the stairs he toasts Sarah with his bowl.*]

---

alla . . . domois: he [Telemachus] taking his ease in Menelaós' mansion . . . (Homer, *Odyssey* 13.423–4).

JIMMY: '*Knuzosen de oi osse*—'° 'She dimmed his two eyes that were so beautiful and clothed him in a vile ragged cloak begrimed with filthy smoke . . .'! D'you see! Smoke! Smoke! D'you see! Sure look at what the same turf-smoke has done to myself! [*He rapidly removes his hat to display his bald head.*] Would you call that flaxen hair?

MANUS: Of course I would.

JIMMY: 'And about him she cast the great skin of a filthy hind, stripped of the hair, and into his hand she thrust a staff and a wallet'! Ha-ha-ha! Athene did that to Ulysses! Made him into a tramp! Isn't she the tight one?

MANUS: You couldn't watch her, Jimmy.

JIMMY: You know what they call her?

MANUS: '*Glaukopis Athene.*'

JIMMY: That's it! The flashing-eyed Athene! By God, Manus, sir, if you had a woman like that about the house, it's not stripping a turf-bank you'd be thinking about—eh?

MANUS: She was a goddess, Jimmy.

JIMMY: Better still. Sure isn't our own Grania a class of a goddess and —

MANUS: Who?

JIMMY: Grania — Grania — Diarmuid's Grania.°

MANUS: Ah.

JIMMY: And sure she can't get her fill of men.

MANUS: Jimmy, you're impossible.

JIMMY: I was just thinking to myself last night: if you had the choosing between Athene and Artemis and Helen of Troy — all three of them Zeus's girls — imagine three powerful-looking daughters like that all in the one parish of Athens! — now, if you had the picking between them, which would you take?

MANUS [*to Sarah*]: Which should I take, Sarah?

JIMMY: No harm to Helen; and no harm to Artemis, and indeed no harm to our own Grania, Manus. But I think I've no choice but to go bull-straight for Athene. By God, sir, them flashing eyes would fair keep a man jigged up constant!

[*Suddenly and momentarily, as if in spasm, Jimmy stands to attention and salutes, his face raised in pained ecstasy. Manus laughs. So does Sarah. Jimmy goes back to his seat, and his reading.*]

MANUS: You're a dangerous bloody man, Jimmy Jack.

JIMMY: 'Flashing-eyed'! Hah! Sure Homer knows it all, boy. Homer knows it all.

[*Manus goes to the window and looks out.*]

MANUS: Where the hell has he got to?

[*Sarah goes to Manus and touches his elbow. She mimes rocking a baby.*]

MANUS: Yes, I know he's at the christening; but it doesn't take them all day to put a name on a baby, does it?

Knuzosen de oi osse: bleared his [Odysseus'] eyes.
Diarmuid's Grania: Diarmuid and Grania are lovers in Irish legend.

[*Sarah mimes pouring drinks and tossing them back quickly.*]

MANUS: You may be sure. Which pub?

[*Sarah indicates.*]

MANUS: Gracie's?

[*No. Further away.*]

MANUS: Con Connie Tim's?

[*No. To the right of there.*]

MANUS: Anna na mBreag's?

[*Yes. That's it.*]

MANUS: Great. She'll fill him up. I suppose I may take the class then.

[*Manus begins to distribute some books, slates and chalk, texts, etc., beside the seats. Sarah goes over to the straw and produces a bunch of flowers she has hidden there. During this:*]

JIMMY:. '*Autar o ek limenos prosebe —* ' 'But Ulysses went forth from the harbour and through the woodland to the place where Athene had shown him he could find the good swineherd who — *o oi biotoio malista kedeto'* — what's that, Manus?

MANUS: 'Who cared most for his substance.'

JIMMY: That's it! 'The good swineherd who cared most for his substance above all the slaves that Ulysses possessed . . .'

[*Sarah presents the flowers to Manus.*]

MANUS: Those are lovely, Sarah.

[*But Sarah has fled in embarrassment to her seat and has her head buried in a book. Manus goes to her.*]

MANUS: Flow-ers.

[*Pause. Sarah does not look up.*]

MANUS: Say the word: flow-ers. Come on — flow-ers.

SARAH: Flowers.

MANUS: You see? — you're off!

[*Manus leans down and kisses the top of Sarah's head.*]

MANUS: And they're beautiful flowers. Thank you.

[*Maire enters, a strong-minded, strong-bodied woman in her twenties with a head of curly hair. She is carrying a small can of milk.*]

MAIRE: Is this all's here? Is there no school this evening?

MANUS: If my father's not back, I'll take it. [*Manus stands awkwardly, having been caught kissing Sarah and with the flowers almost formally at his chest.*]

MAIRE: Well now, isn't that a pretty sight. There's your milk. How's Sarah?

[*Sarah grunts a reply.*]

MANUS: I saw you out at the hay.

[*Maire ignores this and goes to Jimmy.*]

MAIRE: And how's Jimmy Jack Cassie?
JIMMY: Sit down beside me, Maire.
MAIRE: Would I be safe?
JIMMY: No safer man in Donegal.

[*Maire flops on a stool beside Jimmy.*]

MAIRE: Ooooh. The best harvest in living memory, they say; but I don't want to see another like it. [*Showing Jimmy her hands.*] Look at the blisters.
JIMMY: *Esne fatigata?*
MAIRE: *Sum fatigatissima.*
JIMMY: *Bene! Optime!*°
MAIRE: That's the height of my Latin. Fit me better if I had even that much English.
JIMMY: English? I thought you had some English?
MAIRE: Three words. Wait — there was a spake I used to have off by heart. What's this it was? [*Her accent is strange because she is speaking a foreign language and because she does not understand what she is saying.*] 'In Norfolk we besport ourselves around the maypoll.' What about that!
MANUS: Maypole.

[*Again Maire ignores Manus.*]

MAIRE: God have mercy on my Aunt Mary — she taught me that when I was about four, whatever it means. Do you know what it means, Jimmy?
JIMMY: Sure you know I have only Irish like yourself.
MAIRE: And Latin. And Greek.
JIMMY: I'm telling you a lie: I know one English word.
MAIRE: What?
JIMMY: Bo-som.
MAIRE: What's a bo-som?
JIMMY: You know — [*he illustrates with his hands*] — bo-som — bo-som — you know — Diana, the huntress, she has two powerful bosom.
MAIRE: You may be sure that's the one English word you would know. [*Rises.*] Is there a drop of water about?

[*Manus gives Maire his bowl of milk.*]

MANUS: I'm sorry I couldn't get up last night.
MAIRE: Doesn't matter.
MANUS: Biddy Hanna sent for me to write a letter to her sister in Nova Scotia. All the gossip of the parish. 'I brought the cow to the bull three times last week but no good. There's nothing for it now but Big Ned Frank.'
MAIRE [*drinking*]: That's better.
MANUS: And she got so engrossed in that she forgot who she was dictating to: 'The aul drunken schoolmaster and that lame son of his are still footering about in the hedge-school, wasting people's good time and money.'

Esne fatigata . . . Optime!: Are you tired? / I am very tired / Good! Excellent!

[*Maire has to laugh at this.*]

MAIRE: She did not!
MANUS: And me taking it all down. 'Thank God one of them new national schools is being built above at Poll na gCaorach.' It was after midnight by the time I got back.
MAIRE: Great to be a busy man.

[*Maire moves away. Manus follows.*]

MANUS: I could hear music on my way past but I thought it was too late to call.
MAIRE [*to Sarah*]: Wasn't your father in great voice last night?

[*Sarah nods and smiles.*]

MAIRE: It must have been near three o'clock by the time you got home?

[*Sarah holds up four fingers.*]

MAIRE: Was it four? No wonder we're in pieces.
MANUS: I can give you a hand at the hay tomorrow.
MAIRE: That's the name of a hornpipe, isn't it? — 'The Scholar In The Hayfield' — or is it a reel?
MANUS: If the day's good.
MAIRE: Suit yourself. The English soldiers below in the tents, them sapper fellas, they're coming up to give us a hand. I don't know a word they're saying, nor they me; but sure that doesn't matter, does it?
MANUS: What the hell are you so crabbed about?!

[*Doalty and Bridget enter noisily. Both are in their twenties. Doalty is brandishing a surveyor's pole. He is an open-minded, open-hearted, generous and slightly thick young man. Bridget is a plump, fresh young girl, ready to laugh, vain, and with a countrywoman's instinctive cunning. Doalty enters doing his imitation of the master.*]

DOALTY: Vesperal salutations to you all.
BRIDGET: He's coming down past Carraig na Ri and he's as full as a pig!
DOALTY: *Ignari, stuli, rustici* — pot-boys and peasant whelps — semi-literates and illegitimates.
BRIDGET: He's been on the batter since this morning; he sent the wee ones home at eleven o'clock.
DOALTY: Three questions. Question A — Am I drunk? Question B — Am I sober? [*Into Maire's face.*] — *Responde — responde!*
BRIDGET: Question C, Master — When were you last sober?
MAIRE: What's the weapon, Doalty?
BRIDGET: I warned him. He'll be arrested one of these days.
DOALTY: Up in the bog with Bridget and her aul fella, and the Red Coats were just across at the foot of Croc na Mona, dragging them aul chains and peeping through that big machine they lug about everywhere with them — you know the name of it, Manus?
MAIRE: Theodolite.°

Theodolite: Surveyor's machine.

BRIDGET: How do you know?

MAIRE: They leave it in our byre at night sometimes if it's raining.

JIMMY: Theodolite — what's the etymology of that word, Manus?

MANUS: No idea.

BRIDGET: Get on with the story.

JIMMY: *Theo-theos* — something to do with a god. Maybe *thea* — a goddess! What shape's the yoke?°

DOALTY: 'Shape!' Will you shut up, you aul eejit you! Anyway, every time they'd stick one of these poles into the ground and move across the bog, I'd creep up and shift it twenty or thirty paces to the side.

BRIDGET: God!

DOALTY: Then they'd come back and stare at it and look at their calculations and stare at it again and scratch their heads. And cripes, d'you know what they ended up doing?

BRIDGET: Wait till you hear!

DOALTY: They took the bloody machine apart! [*And immediately he speaks in gibberish — an imitation of two very agitated and confused sappers in rapid conversation.*]

BRIDGET: That's the image of them!

MAIRE: You must be proud of yourself, Doalty.

DOALTY: What d'you mean?

MAIRE: That was a very clever piece of work.

MANUS: It was a gesture.

MAIRE: What sort of gesture?

MANUS: Just to indicate . . . a presence.

MAIRE: Hah!

BRIDGET: I'm telling you — you'll be arrested.

[*When Doalty is embarrassed — or pleased — he reacts physically. He now grabs Bridget around the waist.*]

DOALTY: What d'you make of that for an implement, Bridget? Wouldn't that make a great aul shaft for your churn?

BRIDGET: Let go of me, you dirty brute! I've a headline to do before Big Hughie comes.

MANUS: I don't think we'll wait for him. Let's get started.

[*Slowly, reluctantly they begin to move to their seats and specific tasks. Doalty goes to the bucket of water at the door and washes his hands. Bridget sets up a hand-mirror and combs her hair.*]

BRIDGET: Nellie Ruadh's baby was to be christened this morning. Did any of yous hear what she called it? Did you, Sarah?

[*Sarah grunts: No.*]

BRIDGET: Did you, Maire?

MAIRE: No.

BRIDGET: Our Seamus says she was threatening she was going to call it after its father.

DOALTY: Who's the father?

BRIDGET: That's the point, you donkey you!

yoke: slang for "thing."

DOALTY: Ah.

BRIDGET: So there's a lot of uneasy bucks about Baile Beag this day.

DOALTY: She told me last Sunday she was going to call it Jimmy.

BRIDGET: You're a liar, Doalty.

DOALTY: Would I tell you a lie? Hi, Jimmy, Nellie Ruadh's aul fella's looking for you.

JIMMY: For me?

MAIRE: Come on, Doalty.

DOALTY: Someone told him . . .

MAIRE: Doalty!

DOALTY: He heard you know the first book of the Satires of Horace off by heart . . .

JIMMY: That's true.

DOALTY: . . . and he wants you to recite it for him.

JIMMY: I'll do that for him certainly, certainly.

DOALTY: He's busting to hear it.

[*Jimmy fumbles in his pockets.*]

JIMMY: I came across this last night — this'll interest you — in Book Two of Virgil's *Georgics*.

DOALTY: Be God, that's my territory alright.

BRIDGET: You clown you. [*To Sarah.*] Hold this for me, would you? [*Her mirror.*]

JIMMY: Listen to this, Manus. '*Nigra fere et presso pinguis sub vomere terra . . .*'

DOALTY: Steady on now — easy, boys, easy — don't rush me, boys — [*He mimes great concentration.*]

JIMMY: Manus?

MANUS: 'Land that is black and rich beneath the pressure of the plough . . .'

DOALTY: Give *me* a chance!

JIMMY: 'And with *cui putre* — with crumbly soil — is in the main best for corn.' There you are!

DOALTY: There you are!

JIMMY: 'From no other land will you see more wagons wending homeward behind slow bullocks.' Virgil! There!

DOALTY: 'Slow bullocks'!

JIMMY: Isn't that what I'm always telling you? Black soil for corn. *That's* what you should have in that upper field of yours — corn, not spuds.

DOALTY: Would you listen to that fella! Too lazy be Jasus to wash himself and he's lecturing me on agriculture! Would you go and take a running race at yourself, Jimmy Jack Cassie! [*Grabs Sarah.*] Come away out of this with me, Sarah, and we'll plant some corn together.

MANUS: All right — all right. Let's settle down and get some work done. I know Sean Beag isn't coming — he's at the salmon. What about the Donnelly twins? [*To Doalty.*] Are the Donnelly twins not coming any more?

[*Doalty shrugs and turns away.*]

Did you ask them?

DOALTY: Haven't seen them. Not about these days.

[*Doalty begins whistling through his teeth. Suddenly the atmosphere is silent and alert.*]

MANUS: Aren't they at home?

DOALTY: No.

MANUS: Where are they then?

DOALTY: How would I know?

BRIDGET: Our Seamus says two of the soldiers' horses were found last night at the foot of the cliffs at Machaire Buidhe and . . . [*She stops suddenly and begins writing with chalk on her slate.*] D'you hear the whistles of this aul slate? Sure nobody could write on an aul slippery thing like that.

MANUS: What headline did my father set you?

BRIDGET: 'It's easier to stamp out learning than to re-call it.'

JIMMY: Book Three, the *Agricola* of Tacitus.

BRIDGET: God but you're a dose.

MANUS: Can you do it?

BRIDGET: There. Is it bad? Will he ate me?

MANUS: It's very good. Keep your elbow in closer to your side. Doalty?

DOALTY: I'm at the seven-times table. I'm perfect, skipper.

[*Manus moves to Sarah.*]

MANUS: Do you understand those sums?

[*Sarah nods: Yes. Manus leans down to her ear.*]

MANUS: My name is Sarah.

[*Manus goes to Maire. While he is talking to her the others swop books, talk quietly, etc.*]

MANUS: Can I help you? What are you at?

MAIRE: Map of America. [*Pause.*] The passage money came last Friday.

MANUS: You never told me that.

MAIRE: Because I haven't seen you since, have I?

MANUS: You don't want to go. You said that yourself.

MAIRE: There's ten below me to be raised and no man in the house. What do you suggest?

MANUS: Do you want to go?

MAIRE: Did you apply for that job in the new national school?

MANUS: No.

MAIRE: You said you would.

MANUS: I said I might.

MAIRE: When it opens, this is finished: nobody's going to pay to go to a hedge-school.

MANUS: I know that and I . . .

[*He breaks off because he sees Sarah, obviously listening at his shoulder. She moves away again.*]

I was thinking that maybe I could . . .

MAIRE: It's £56 a year you're throwing away.

MANUS: I can't apply for it.

MAIRE: You *promised* me you would.

MANUS: My father has applied for it.

MAIRE: He has not!

MANUS: Day before yesterday.

MAIRE: For God's sake, sure you know he'd never —

MANUS: I couldn't — I can't go in against him.

[*Maire looks at him for a second. Then:*]

MAIRE: Suit yourself. [*To Bridget.*] I saw your Seamus heading off to the Port fair early this morning.

BRIDGET: And wait till you hear this — I forgot to tell you this. He said that as soon as he crossed over the gap at Cnoc na Mona — just beyond where the soldiers are making the maps — the sweet smell was everywhere.

DOALTY: You never told me that.

BRIDGET: It went out of my head.

DOALTY: He saw the crops in Port?

BRIDGET: Some.

MANUS: How did the tops look?

BRIDGET: Fine — I think.

DOALTY: In flower?

BRIDGET: I don't know. I think so. He didn't say.

MANUS: Just the sweet smell — that's all?

BRIDGET: They say that's the way it snakes in, don't they? First the smell; and then one morning the stalks are all black and limp.

DOALTY: Are you stupid? It's the rotting stalks makes the sweet smell for God's sake. That's what the smell is — rotting stalks.

MAIRE: Sweet smell! Sweet smell! Every year at this time somebody comes back with stories of the sweet smell. Sweet God, did the potatoes ever fail in Baile Beag? Well, did they ever — ever? Never! There was never blight here. Never. Never. But we're always sniffing about for it, aren't we? — looking for disaster. The rents are going to go up again — the harvest's going to be lost — the herring have gone away for ever — there's going to be evictions. Honest to God, some of you people aren't happy unless you're miserable and you'll not be right content until you're dead!

DOALTY: Bloody right, Maire. And sure St Colmcille° prophesied there'd never be blight here. He said:

The spuds will bloom in Baile Beag
Till rabbits grow an extra lug.

And sure that'll never be. So we're all right. Seven threes are twenty-one, seven fours are twenty-eight; seven fives are forty-nine — Hi, Jimmy, do you fancy my chances as boss of the new national school?

JIMMY: What's that? — what's that?

DOALTY: Agh, g'way back home to Greece, son.

MAIRE: You ought to apply, Doalty.

DOALTY: D'you think so? Cripes, maybe I will. Hah!

BRIDGET: Did you know that you start at the age of six and you have to stick at it until you're twelve at least — no matter how smart you are or how much you know.

DOALTY: Who told you that yarn?

BRIDGET: And every child from every house has to go all day, every day, summer or winter. That's the law.

DOALTY: I'll tell you something — nobody's going to go near them — they're not going to take on — law or no law.

St Colmcille (521–97): Founded a monastery on the island of Iona and predicted the Viking invasions.

BRIDGET: And everything's free in them. You pay for nothing except the books you use, that's what our Seamus says.

DOALTY: 'Our Seamus.' Sure your Seamus wouldn't pay anyway. She's making this all up.

BRIDGET: Isn't that right, Manus?

MANUS: I think so.

BRIDGET: And from the very first day you go, you'll not hear one word of Irish spoken. You'll be taught to speak English and every subject will be taught through English and everyone'll end up as cute as the Buncrana people.

[*Sarah suddenly grunts and mimes a warning that the master is coming. The atmosphere changes. Sudden business. Heads down.*]

DOALTY: He's here, boys. Cripes, he'll make yella meal out of me for those bloody tables.

BRIDGET: Have you any extra chalk, Manus?

MAIRE: And the atlas for me.

[*Doalty goes to Maire who is sitting on a stool at the back.*]

DOALTY: Swop you seats.

MAIRE: Why?

DOALTY: There's an empty one beside the Infant Prodigy.

MAIRE: I'm fine here.

DOALTY: Please, Maire. I want to jouk in the back here.

[*Maire rises.*]

God love you. [*Aloud.*] Anyone got a bloody table-book? Cripes, I'm wrecked.

[*Sarah gives him one.*]

God, I'm dying about you.

[*In his haste to get to the back seat, Doalty bumps into Bridget who is kneeling on the floor and writing laboriously on a slate resting on top of a bench-seat.*]

BRIDGET: Watch where you're going, Doalty!

[*Doalty gooses Bridget. She squeals. Now the quiet hum of work: Jimmy reading Homer in a low voice; Bridget copying her headline; Maire studying the atlas; Doalty, his eyes shut tight, mouthing his tables; Sarah doing sums. After a few seconds: —*]

BRIDGET: Is this 'g' right, Manus? How do you put a tail on it?

DOALTY: Will you shut up! I can't concentrate!

[*A few more seconds of work. Then Doalty opens his eyes and looks around.*]

False alarm, boys. The bugger's not coming at all. Sure the bugger's hardly fit to walk.

[*And immediately Hugh enters. A large man, with residual dignity, shabbily dressed, carrying a stick. He has, as always, a large quantity of drink taken, but he is by no means drunk. He is in his early sixties.*]

HUGH: *Adsum*, Doalty, *adsum*. Perhaps not in *sobrietate perfecta°* but adequately *sobrius* to overhear your quip. Vesperal salutations to you all.

[*Various responses.*]

JIMMY: *Ave*, Hugh.

HUGH: James.

[*He removes his hat and coat and hands them and his stick to Manus, as if to a footman.*]

Apologies for my late arrival: we were celebrating the baptism of Nellie Ruadh's baby.

BRIDGET [*innocently*]: What name did she put on it, Master?

HUGH: Was it Eamon? Yes, it was Eamon.

BRIDGET: Eamon Donal from Tor! Cripes!

HUGH: And after the *caerimonia nominations* — Maire?

MAIRE: The ritual of naming.

HUGH: Indeed — we then had a few libations to mark the occasion. Altogether very pleasant. The derivation of the word 'baptize'? — where are my Greek scholars? Doalty?

DOALTY: Would it be — ah — ah —

HUGH: Too slow. James?

JIMMY: 'Baptizein' — to dip or immerse.

HUGH: Indeed — our friend Pliny Minor speaks of the 'baptisterium' — the cold bath.

DOALTY: Master.

HUGH: Doalty?

DOALTY: I suppose you could talk then about baptizing a sheep at sheep-dipping, could you?

[*Laughter. Comments.*]

HUGH: Indeed — the precedent is there — the day you were appropriately named Doalty — seven nines?

DOALTY: What's that, Master?

HUGH: Seven times nine?

DOALTY: Seven nines — seven nines — seven times nine — seven times nine are — cripes, it's on the tip of my tongue, Master — I knew it for sure this morning — funny that's the only one that foxes me —

BRIDGET [*prompt*]: Sixty-three.

DOALTY: What's wrong with me: sure seven nines are fifty-three, Master.

HUGH: Sophocles from Colonus would agree with Doalty Dan Doalty from Tulach Alainn: 'To know nothing is the sweetest life.' Where's Sean Beag?

MANUS: He's at the salmon.

HUGH: And Nora Dan?

MAIRE: She says she's not coming back any more.

HUGH: Ah. Nora Dan can now write her name — Nora Dan's education is complete. And the Donnelly twins?

[*Brief pause. Then: —*]

BRIDGET: They're probably at the turf. [*She goes to Hugh.*] There's the one-and-eight I owe you for last

adsum . . . sobrietate perfecta: I am here . . . not perfectly sober.

quarter's arithmetic and there's my one-and-six for this quarter's writing.

HUGH: *Gratias tibi ago.*° [*He sits at his table.*] Before we commence our *studia* I have three items of information to impart to you — [*to Manus*] a bowl of tea, strong tea, black —

[*Manus leaves.*]

Item A: on my perambulations today — Bridget? Too slow. Maire?

MAIRE: *Perambulare* — to walk about.

HUGH: Indeed — I encountered Captain Lancey of the Royal Engineers who is engaged in the ordnance survey of this area. He tells me that in the past few days two of his horses have strayed and some of his equipment seems to be mislaid. I expressed my regret and suggested he address you himself on these matters. He then explained that he does not speak Irish. Latin? I asked. None. Greek? Not a syllable. He speaks — on his own admission — only English; and to his credit he seemed suitably verecund — James?

JIMMY: *Verecundus* — humble.

HUGH: Indeed — he voiced some surprise that we did not speak his language. I explained that a few of us did, on occasion — outside the parish of course — and then usually for the purposes of commerce, a use to which his tongue seemed particularly suited — [*shouts*] and a slice of soda bread — and I went on to propose that our own culture and the classical tongues made a happier conjugation — Dolty?

DOALTY: *Conjugo* — I join together.

[*Doalty is so pleased with himself that he prods and winks at Bridget*]

HUGH: Indeed — English, I suggested, couldn't really express us. And again to his credit he acquiesced to my logic. Acquiesced — Maire?

[*Maire turns away impatiently. Hugh is unaware of the gesture.*]

Too slow. Bridget?

BRIDGET: *Acquiesco.*

HUGH: *Procede.*

BRIDGET: *Acquiesco, acquiescere, acquievi, acquietum.*

HUGH: Indeed — and Item B . . .

MAIRE: Master.

HUGH: Yes?

[*Maire gets to her feet uneasily but determinedly. Pause.*]

Well, girl?

MAIRE: We should all be learning to speak English. That's what my mother says. That's what I say. That's what Dan O'Connell° said last month in Ennis. He said the sooner we all learn to speak English the better.

Gratias . . . ago: I thank you.
Daniel O'Connell (1775–1847): Irish politician who achieved Catholic emancipation in 1829, permitting Catholics to hold office. O'Connell became a representative from Kerry.

[*Suddenly several speak together.*]

JIMMY: What's she saying? What? What?

DOALTY: It's Irish he uses when he's travelling around scrounging votes.

BRIDGET: And sleeping with married women. Sure no woman's safe from that fella.

JIMMY: Who-who-who? Who's this? Who's this?

HUGH: *Silentium!* [*Pause.*] Who is she talking about?

MAIRE: I'm talking about Daniel O'Connell.

HUGH: Does she mean that little Kerry politician?

MAIRE: I'm talking about the Liberator, Master, as you well know. And what he said was this: 'The old language is a barrier to modern progress.' He said that last month. And he's right. I don't want Greek. I don't want Latin. I want English.

[*Manus reappears on the platform above.*]

I want to be able to speak English because I'm going to America as soon as the harvest's all saved.

[*Maire remains standing. Hugh puts his hand into his pocket and produces a flask of whiskey. He removes the cap, pours a drink into it, tosses it back, replaces the cap, puts the flask back into his pocket. Then: —*]

HUGH: We have been diverted — *diverto* — *divertere* — Where were we?

DOALTY: Three items of information, Master. You're at Item B.

HUGH: Indeed — Item B — Item B — yes — On my way to the christening this morning I chanced to meet Mr George Alexander, Justice of the Peace. We discussed the new national school. Mr Alexander invited me to take charge of it when it opens. I thanked him and explained that I could do that only if I were free to run it as I have run this hedge-school for the past thirty-five years — filling what our friend Euripides calls the '*aplestos pithos*' — James?

JIMMY: 'The cask that cannot be filled.'

HUGH: Indeed — and Mr Alexander retorted courteously and emphatically that he hopes that is how it will be run.

[*Maire now sits.*]

Indeed. I have had a strenuous day and I am weary of you all. [*He rises.*] Manus will take care of you.

[*Hugh goes towards the steps. Owen enters. Owen is the younger son, a handsome, attractive young man in his twenties. He is dressed smartly — a city man. His manner is easy and charming: everything he does is invested with consideration and enthusiasm. He now stands framed in the doorway, a traveling bag across his shoulder.*]

OWEN: Could anybody tell me is this where Hugh Mor O'Donnell holds his hedge-school?

DOALTY: It's Owen — Owen Hugh! Look, boys — it's Owen Hugh!

[*Owen enters. As he crosses the room he touches and has a word for each person.*]

OWEN: Doalty! [*Playful punch.*] How are you, boy? *Jacobe, quid agis?°* Are you well?

JIMMY: Fine. Fine.

OWEN: And Bridget! Give us a kiss. Aaaaaah!

BRIDGET: You're welcome, Owen.

OWEN: It's not — Yes, it *is* Maire Chatach! God! A young woman!

MAIRE: How are you, Owen?

[*Owen is now in front of Hugh. He puts his two hands on his father's shoulders.*]

OWEN: And how's the old man himself?

HUGH: Fair — fair.

OWEN: Fair? For God's sake you never looked better! Come here to me. [*He embraces Hugh warmly and genuinely.*] Great to see you, Father. Great to be back.

[*Hugh's eyes are moist — partly joy, partly the drink.*]

HUGH: I — I'm — I'm — pay no attention to —

OWEN: Come on — come on — come on — [*He gives Hugh his handkerchief.*] Do you know what you and I are going to do tonight? We are going to go up to Anna na mBreag's . . .

DOALTY: Not there, Owen.

OWEN: Why not?

DOALTY: Her poteen's° worse than ever.

BRIDGET: They say she puts frogs in it!

OWEN: All the better. [*To Hugh.*] And you and I are going to get footless drunk. That's arranged.

[*Owen sees Manus coming down the steps with tea and soda bread. They meet at the bottom.*]

And Manus!

MANUS: You're welcome, Owen.

OWEN: I know I am. And it's great to be here. [*He turns round, arms outstretched.*] I can't believe it. I come back after six years and everything's just as it was! Nothing's changed! Not a thing! [*Sniffs.*] Even that smell — that's the same smell this place always had. What is it anyway? Is it the straw?

DOALTY: Jimmy Jack's feet.

[*General laughter. It opens little pockets of conversation round the room.*]

OWEN: And Doalty Dan Doalty hasn't changed either!

DOALTY: Bloody right, Owen.

OWEN: Jimmy, are you well?

JIMMY: Dodging about.

OWEN: Any word of the big day?

[*This is greeted with 'ohs' and 'ahs.'*]

Time enough, Jimmy. Homer's easier to live with, isn't he?

MAIRE: We heard stories that you own ten big shops in Dublin — is it true?

OWEN: Only nine.

Jacobe . . . agis?: James, how are you?
poteen: Homebrewed whiskey (pronounced: "pōcheen").

BRIDGET: And you've twelve horses and six servants.

OWEN: Yes — that's true. God Almighty, would you listen to them — taking a hand at me!

MANUS: When did you arrive?

OWEN: We left Dublin yesterday morning, spent last night in Omagh and got here half an hour ago.

MANUS: You're hungry then.

HUGH: Indeed — get him food — get him a drink.

OWEN: Not now, thanks; later. Listen — am I interrupting you all?

HUGH: By no means. We're finished for the day.

OWEN: Wonderful. I'll tell you why. Two friends of mine are waiting outside the door. They'd like to meet you and I'd like you to meet them. May I bring them in?

HUGH: Certainly. You'll all eat and have . . .

OWEN: Not just yet, Father. You've seen the sappers working in this area for the past fortnight, haven't you? Well, the older man is Captain Lancey . . .

HUGH: I've met Captain Lancey.

OWEN: Great. He's the cartographer in charge of this whole area. Cartographer — James? [*Owen begins to play this game — his father's game — partly to involve his classroom audience, partly to show he has not forgotten it, and indeed partly because he enjoys it.*]

JIMMY: A maker of maps.

OWEN: Indeed — and the younger man that I traveled with from Dublin, his name is Lieutenant Yolland and he is attached to the toponymic department — Father? — *responde — responde!*

HUGH: He gives names to places.

OWEN: Indeed — although he is in fact an orthographer — Doalty? — too slow — Manus?

MANUS: The correct spelling of those names.

OWEN: Indeed — indeed!

[*Owen laughs and claps his hands. Some of the others join in.*]

Beautiful! Beautiful! Honest to God, it's such a delight to be back here with you all again — 'civilized' people. Anyhow — may I bring them in?

HUGH: Your friends are our friends.

OWEN: I'll be straight back.

[*There is general talk as Owen goes towards the door. He stops beside Sarah.*]

OWEN: That's a new face. Who are you?

[*A very brief hesitation. Then: — *]

SARAH: My name is Sarah.

OWEN: Sarah who?

SARAH: Sarah Johnny Sally.

OWEN: Of course! From Bun na hAbhann! I'm Owen — Owen Hugh Mor. From Baile Beag. Good to see you.

[*During this Owen–Sarah exchange.*]

Come on now. Let's tidy this place up. [*He rubs the top of his table with his sleeve.*] Move, Doalty — lift those books off the floor.

The 1981 London production of *Translations*, directed by Donald McWhinnie, at the Hampstead Theatre with the following cast (from left to right): Anna Keaveney as Bridget, Ron Flanagan as Doalty, Maíre Ní Ghráinne as Sarah, Tony Doyle as Owen, Stephen Rea as Manus, and Ian Bannen as Hugh.

DOALTY: Right, Master; certainly, Master; I'm doing my best, Master.

[*Owen stops at the door.*]

OWEN: One small thing, Father.
HUGH: *Silentium!*
OWEN: I'm on their pay-roll.

[*Sarah, very elated at her success, is beside Manus.*]

SARAH: I said it, Manus!

[*Manus ignores Sarah. He is much more interested in Owen now.*]

MANUS: You haven't enlisted, have you?!

[*Sarah moves away.*]

OWEN: Me a soldier? I'm employed as a part-time, underpaid, civilian interpreter. My job is to translate the quaint, archaic tongue you people persist in speaking into the King's good English. [*He goes out.*]
HUGH: Move — move — move! Put some order on things! Come on, Sarah — hide that bucket. Whose are these slates? Somebody take these dishes away. *Festinate! Festinate!*°

[*Manus goes to Maire who is busy tidying.*]

MANUS: You didn't tell me you were definitely leaving.
MAIRE: Not now.
HUGH: Good girl, Bridget. That's the style.
MANUS: You might at least have told me.
HUGH: Are these your books, James?
JIMMY: Thank you.

Festinate!: Hurry!

MANUS: Fine! Fine! Go ahead! Go ahead!
MAIRE: You talk to me about getting married — with neither a roof over your head nor a sod of ground under your foot. I suggest you go for the new school; but no — 'My father's in for that.' Well now he's got it and now this is finished and now you've nothing.
MANUS: I can always . . .
MAIRE: What? Teach classics to the cows? Agh —

[*Maire moves away from Manus. Owen enters with Lancey and Yolland. Captain Lancey is middle-aged; a small, crisp officer expert in his field as cartographer but uneasy with people — especially civilians, especially these foreign civilians. His skill is with deeds, not words. Lieutenant Yolland is in his late twenties/early thirties. He is tall and thin and gangling, blond hair, a shy, awkward manner. A soldier by accident.*]

OWEN: Here we are. Captain Lancey — my father.
LANCEY: Good evening.

[*Hugh becomes expansive, almost courtly, with his visitors.*]

HUGH: You and I have already met, sir.
LANCEY: Yes.
OWEN: And Lieutenant Yolland — both Royal Engineers — my father.
HUGH: You're very welcome, gentlemen.
YOLLAND: How do you do.
HUGH: *Gaudeo vos hic adesse.*°
OWEN: And I'll make no other introductions except that these are some of the people of Baile Beag and — what? — well you're among the best people in Ire-

Gaudeo . . . adesse: You are welcome here.

land now. [*He pauses to allow Lancey to speak. Lancey does not.*] Would you like to say a few words, Captain.

HUGH: What about a drop, sir?

LANCEY: A what?

HUGH: Perhaps a modest refreshment? A little sampling of our *aqua vitae*?°

LANCEY: No, no.

HUGH: Later perhaps when —

LANCEY: I'll say what I have to say, if I may, and as briefly as possible. Do they speak *any* English, Roland?

OWEN: Don't worry. I'll translate.

LANCEY: I see. [*He clears his throat. He speaks as if he were addressing children — a shade too loudly and enunciating excessively.*] You may have seen me — seen me — working in this section — section? — working. We are here — here — in this place — you understand? — to make a map — a map — a map and —

JIMMY: *Nonne Latine loquitur?*°

[*Hugh holds up a restraining hand.*]

HUGH: James.

LANCEY [*to Jimmy*]: I do not speak Gaelic, sir. [*He looks at Owen.*]

OWEN: Carry on.

LANCEY: A map is a representation on paper — a picture — you understand picture? — a paper picture — showing, representing this country — yes? — showing your country in miniature — a scaled drawing on paper of — of — of —

[*Suddenly Doalty sniggers. Then Bridget. Then Sarah. Owen leaps in quickly.*]

OWEN: It might be better if you *assume* they understand you —

LANCEY: Yes?

OWEN: And I'll translate as you go along.

LANCEY: I see. Yes. Very well. Perhaps you're right. Well. What we are doing is this.

[*He looks at Owen. Owen nods reassuringly.*]

His Majesty's government has ordered the first ever comprehensive survey of this entire country — a general triangulation which will embrace detailed hydrographic and topographic information and which will be executed to a scale of six inches to the English mile.

HUGH [*pouring a drink*]: Excellent — excellent.

[*Lancey looks at Owen.*]

OWEN: A new map is being made of the whole country.

[*Lancey looks to Owen: Is that all? Owen smiles reassuringly and indicates to proceed.*]

LANCEY: This enormous task has been embarked on so that the military authorities will be equipped with up-to-date and accurate information on every corner of this part of the Empire.

OWEN: The job is being done by soldiers because they are skilled in this work.

LANCEY: And also so that the entire basis of land valuation can be reassessed for purposes of more equitable taxation.

OWEN: This new map will take the place of the estate agent's map so that from now on you will know exactly what is yours in law.

LANCEY: In conclusion I wish to quote two brief extracts from the white paper which is our governing charter: [*Reads*] 'All former surveys of Ireland originated in forfeiture and violent transfer of property; the present survey has for its object the relief which can be afforded to the proprietors and occupiers of land from unequal taxation.'

OWEN: The captain hopes that the public will cooperate with the sappers° and that the new map will mean that taxes are reduced.

HUGH: A worthy enterprise — *opus honestum!* And Extract B?

LANCEY: 'Ireland is privileged. No such survey is being undertaken in England. So this survey cannot but be received as proof of the disposition of this government to advance the interests of Ireland.' My sentiments, too.

OWEN: This survey demonstrates the government's interest in Ireland and the captain thanks you for listening so attentively to him.

HUGH: Our pleasure, Captain.

LANCEY: Lieutenant Yolland?

YOLLAND: I — I — I've nothing to say — really —

OWEN: The captain is the man who actually makes the new map. George's task is to see that the place-names on this map are . . . correct. [*To Yolland.*] Just a few words — they'd like to hear you. [*To class.*] Don't you want to hear George, too?

MAIRE: Has he anything to say?

YOLLAND [*to Maire*]: Sorry — sorry?

OWEN: She says she's dying to hear you.

YOLLAND [*to Maire*]: Very kind of you — thank you . . . [*To class.*] I can only say that I feel — I feel very foolish to — to — to be working here and not to speak your language. But I intend to rectify that — with Roland's help — indeed I do.

OWEN: He wants me to teach him Irish!

HUGH: You are doubly welcome, sir.

YOLLAND: I think your countryside is — is — is — is very beautiful. I've fallen in love with it already. I hope we're not too — too crude an intrusion on your lives. And I know that I'm going to be happy, very happy, here.

OWEN: He is already a committed Hibernophile —

---

aqua vitae: Lit. water of life, whiskey.
Nonne . . . loquitur?: He doesn't speak Latin?

sappers: Engineers.

JIMMY: He loves —

OWEN: All right, Jimmy — we know — he loves Baile Beag; and he loves you all.

HUGH: Please . . . May I . . . ? [*Hugh is now drunk. He holds on to the edge of the table.*]

OWEN: Go ahead, Father. [*Hands up for quiet.*] Please — please.

HUGH: And we, gentlemen, we in turn are happy to offer you our friendship, our hospitality, and every assistance that you may require. Gentlemen — welcome!

[*A few desultory claps. The formalities are over. General conversation. The soldiers meet the locals. Manus and Owen meet down stage.*]

OWEN: Lancey's a bloody ramrod but George's all right. How are you anyway?

MANUS: What sort of translation was that, Owen?

OWEN: Did I make a mess of it?

MANUS: You weren't saying what Lancey was saying!

OWEN: 'Uncertainty in meaning is incipient poetry' — who said that?

MANUS: There was nothing uncertain about what Lancey said: it's a bloody military operation, Owen! And what's Yolland's function? What's 'incorrect' about the place-names we have here?

OWEN: Nothing at all. They're just going to be standardized.

MANUS: You mean changed into English?

OWEN: Where there's ambiguity, they'll be Anglicized.

MANUS: And they call you Roland! They both call you Roland!

OWEN: Shhhhh. Isn't it ridiculous? They seemed to get it wrong from the very beginning — or else they can't pronounce Owen. I was afraid some of you bastards would laugh.

MANUS: Aren't you going to tell them?

OWEN: Yes — yes — soon — soon.

MANUS: But they . . .

OWEN: Easy, man, easy. Owen — Roland — what the hell. It's only a name. It's the same me, isn't it? Well, isn't it?

MANUS: Indeed it is. It's the same Owen.

OWEN: And the same Manus. And in a way we complement each other. [*He punches Manus lightly, playfully and turns to join the others. As he goes.*] All right — who has met whom? Isn't this a job for the go-between?

[*Manus watches Owen move confidently across the floor, taking Maire by the hand and introducing her to Yolland. Hugh is trying to negotiate the steps. Jimmy is lost in a text. Doalty and Bridget are reliving their giggling. Sarah is staring at Manus.*]

ACT TWO • Scene I

The sappers have already mapped most of the area. Yolland's official task, which Owen is now doing, is to take each of the Gaelic names — every hill, stream, rock, even every patch of ground which possessed its own distinctive Irish name and Anglicize it, either by changing it into its approximate English sound or by translating it into English words. For example, a Gaelic name like Cnoc Ban could become Knockban or — directly translated — Fair Hill. These new standardized names were entered into the Name-Book, and when the new maps appeared they contained all these new Anglicized names. Owen's official function as translator is to pronounce each name in Irish and then provide the English translation.

The hot weather continues. It is late afternoon some days later.

Stage right: an improvised clothes-line strung between the shafts of the cart and a nail in the wall; on it are some shirts and socks.

A large map — one of the new blank maps — is spread out on the floor. Owen is on his hands and knees, consulting it. He is totally engrossed in his task which he pursues with great energy and efficiency.

Yolland's hesitancy has vanished — he is at home here now. He is sitting on the floor, his long legs stretched out before him, his back resting against a creel, his eyes closed. His mind is elsewhere. One of the reference books — a church registry — lies open on his lap.

Around them are various reference books, the Name-Book, a bottle of poteen, some cups, etc.

Owen completes an entry in the Name-Book and returns to the map on the floor.

OWEN: Now. Where have we got to? Yes — the point where that stream enters the sea — that tiny little beach there. George!

YOLLAND: Yes. I'm listening. What do you call it? Say the Irish name again?

OWEN: Bun na hAbhann.

YOLLAND: Again.

OWEN: Bun na hAbhann.

YOLLAND: Bun na hAbhann.

OWEN: That's terrible, George.

YOLLAND: I know. I'm sorry. Say it again.

OWEN: Bun na hAbhann.

YOLLAND: Bun na hAbhann.

OWEN: That's better. Bun is the Irish word for bottom. And Abha means river. So it's literally the mouth of the river.

YOLLAND: Let's leave it alone. There's no English equivalent for a sound like that.

OWEN: What is it called in the church registry?

[*Only now does Yolland open his eyes.*]

YOLLAND: Let's see . . . Banowen.

OWEN: That's wrong. [*Consults text.*] The list of freeholders calls it Owenmore — that's completely wrong: Owenmore's the big river at the west end of the parish. [*Another text.*] And in the grand jury lists it's called — God! — Binhone! — wherever they got that. I suppose we could Anglicize it to Bunowen; but somehow that's neither fish nor flesh.

[*Yolland closes his eyes again.*]

YOLLAND: I give up.

OWEN [*at map*]: Back to first principles. What are we trying to do?

YOLLAND: Good question.

OWEN: We are trying to denominate and at the same time describe that tiny area of soggy, rocky, sandy ground where that little stream enters the sea, an area known locally as Bun na hAbhann . . . Burnfoot! What about Burnfoot?

YOLLAND [*indifferently*]: Good, Roland, Burnfoot's good.

OWEN: George, my name isn't . . .

YOLLAND: B-u-r-n-f-o-o-t?

OWEN: Are you happy with that?

YOLLAND: Yes.

OWEN: Burnfoot it is then. [*He makes the entry into the Name-Book.*] Bun na hAbhann — B-u-r-n-

YOLLAND: You're becoming very skilled at this.

OWEN: We're not moving fast enough.

YOLLAND [*opens eyes again*]: Lancey lectured me again last night.

OWEN: When does he finish here?

YOLLAND: The sappers are pulling out at the end of the week. The trouble is, the maps they've completed can't be printed without these names. So London screams at Lancey and Lancey screams at me. But I wasn't intimidated.

[*Manus emerges from upstairs and descends.*]

'I'm sorry, sir,' I said, 'But certain tasks demand their own tempo. You cannot rename a whole country overnight.' Your Irish air has made me bold. [*To Manus.*] Do you want us to leave?

MANUS: Time enough. Class won't begin for another half-hour.

YOLLAND: Sorry — sorry?

OWEN: Can't you speak English?

[*Manus gathers the things off the clothes-line. Owen returns to the map.*]

OWEN: We now come across that beach . . .

YOLLAND: Tra — that's the Irish for beach. [*To Manus*] I'm picking up the odd word, Manus.

MANUS: So.

OWEN: . . . on past Burnfoot; and there's nothing around here that has any name that I know of until we come down here to the south end, just about here . . . and there should be a ridge of rocks there . . . Have the sappers marked it? They have. Look, George.

YOLLAND: Where are we?

OWEN: There.

YOLLAND: I'm lost.

OWEN: Here. And the name of that ridge is Druim Dubh. Put English on that, Lieutenant.

YOLLAND: Say it again.

OWEN: Druim Dubh.

YOLLAND: Dubh means black.

OWEN: Yes.

YOLLAND: And Druim means . . . what? a fort?

OWEN: We met it yesterday in Druim Luachra.

YOLLAND: A ridge! The Black Ridge! [*To Manus.*] You see, Manus?

OWEN: We'll have you fluent at the Irish before the summer's over.

YOLLAND: Oh, I wish I were.

[*To Manus as he crosses to go back upstairs.*]

We got a crate of oranges from Dublin today. I'll send some up to you.

MANUS: Thanks. [*To Owen.*] Better hide that bottle. Father's just up and he'd be better without it.

OWEN: Can't you speak English before your man?

MANUS: Why?

OWEN: Out of courtesy.

MANUS: Doesn't he want to learn Irish? [*To Yolland.*] Don't you want to learn Irish?

YOLLAND: Sorry — sorry? I — I —

MANUS: I understand the Lanceys perfectly but people like you puzzle me.

OWEN: Manus, for God's sake!

MANUS [*still to Yolland*]: How's the work going?

YOLLAND: The work? — the work? Oh, it's — it's staggering along — I think — [*to Owen*] — isn't it? But we'd be lost without Roland.

MANUS [*leaving*]: I'm sure. But there are always the Rolands, aren't there? [*He goes upstairs and exits.*]

YOLLAND: What was that he said? — something about Lancey, was it?

OWEN: He said we should hide that bottle before Father gets his hands on it.

YOLLAND: Ah.

OWEN: He's always trying to protect him.

YOLLAND: Was he lame from birth?

OWEN: An accident when he was a baby: Father fell across his cradle. That's why Manus feels so responsible for him.

YOLLAND: Why doesn't he marry?

OWEN: Can't afford to, I suppose.

YOLLAND: Hasn't he a salary?

OWEN: What salary? All he gets is the odd shilling Father throws him — and that's seldom enough. I got out in time, didn't I?

[*Yolland is pouring a drink.*]

Easy with that stuff — it'll hit you suddenly.

YOLLAND: I like it.

OWEN: Let's get back to the job. Druim Dubh — what's it called in the jury lists? [*Consults texts.*]

YOLLAND: Some people here resent us.

OWEN: Dramduff — wrong as usual.

YOLLAND: I was passing a little girl yesterday and she spat at me.

OWEN: And it's Drimdoo here. What's it called in the registry?

YOLLAND: Do you know the Donnelly twins?

OWEN: Who?

YOLLAND: The Donnelly twins.

OWEN: Yes. Best fishermen about here. What about them?

YOLLAND: Lancey's looking for them.

OWEN: What for?

YOLLAND: He wants them for questioning.

OWEN: Probably stolen somebody's nets. Dramduffy! Nobody ever called it Dramduffy. Take your pick of those three.

YOLLAND: My head's addled. Let's take a rest. Do you want a drink?

OWEN: Thanks. Now, every Dubh we've come across we've changed to Duff. So if we're to be consistent, I suppose Druim Dubh has to become Dromduff.

[*Yolland is now looking out the window.*]

You can see the end of the ridge from where you're standing. But D-r-u-m- or D-r-o-m-? [*Name-Book.*] Do you remember — which did we agree on for Druim Luachra?

YOLLAND: That house immediately above where we're camped —

OWEN: Mm?

YOLLAND: The house where Maire lives.

OWEN: Maire? Oh, Maire Chatach.

YOLLAND: What does that mean?

OWEN: Curly-haired; the whole family are called the Catachs. What about it?

YOLLAND: I hear music coming from that house almost every night.

OWEN: Why don't you drop in?

YOLLAND: Could I?

OWEN: Why not? We used D-r-o-m then. So we've got to call it D-r-o-m-d-u-f-f — all right?

YOLLAND: Go back up to where the new school is being built and just say the names again for me, would you?

OWEN: That's a good idea. Poolkerry, Ballybeg —

YOLLAND: No, no; as they still are — in your own language.

OWEN: Poll na gCaorach,

[*Yolland repeats the names silently after him.*]

Baile Beag, Ceann Balor, Lis Maol, Machaire Buidhe, Baile na gGall, Carraig na Ri, Mullach Dearg —

YOLLAND: Do you think I could live here?

OWEN: What are you talking about?

YOLLAND: Settle down here — live here.

OWEN: Come on, George.

YOLLAND: I mean it.

OWEN: Live on what? Potatoes? Buttermilk?

YOLLAND: It's really heavenly.

OWEN: For God's sake! The first hot summer in fifty years and you think it's Eden. Don't be such a bloody romantic. You wouldn't survive a mild winter here.

YOLLAND: Do you think not? Maybe you're right.

[*Doalty enters in a rush.*]

DOALTY: Hi, boys, is Manus about?

OWEN: He's upstairs. Give him a shout.

DOALTY: Manus! The cattle's going mad in that heat — Cripes, running wild all over the place. [*To Yolland.*] How are you doing, skipper?

[*Manus appears.*]

YOLLAND: Thank you for — I — I'm very grateful to you for —

DOALTY: Wasting your time. I don't know a word you're saying. Hi, Manus, there's two bucks down the road there asking for you.

MANUS [*descending*]: Who are they?

DOALTY: Never clapped eyes on them. They want to talk to you.

MANUS: What about?

DOALTY: They wouldn't say. Come on. The bloody beasts'll end up in Loch an Iubhair if they're not capped. Good luck, boys!

[*Doalty rushes off. Manus follows him.*]

OWEN: Good luck! What were you thanking Doalty for?

YOLLAND: I was washing outside my tent this morning and he was passing with a scythe across his shoulder and he came up to me and pointed to the long grass and then cut a pathway round my tent and from the tent down to the road — so that my feet won't get wet with the dew. Wasn't that kind of him? And I have no words to thank him . . . I suppose you're right: I suppose I couldn't live here . . . Just before Doalty came up to me this morning, I was thinking that at that moment I might have been in Bombay instead of Ballybeg. You see, my father was at his wits end with me and finally he got me a job with the East India Company — some kind of clerkship. This was ten, eleven months ago. So I set off for London. Unfortunately I — I missed the boat. Literally. And since I couldn't face Father and hadn't enough money to hang about until the next sailing, I joined the army. And they stuck me into the Engineers and posted me to Dublin. And Dublin sent me here. And while I was washing this morning and looking across the Tra Bhan, I was thinking how very, very lucky I am to be here and not in Bombay.

OWEN: Do you believe in fate?

YOLLAND: Lancey's so like my father. I was watching him last night. He met every group of sappers as they reported in. He checked the field kitchens. He examined the horses. He inspected every single report — even examining the texture of the paper and commenting on the neatness of the handwriting. The perfect colonial servant: not only must the job be done — it must be done with excellence. Father has that drive, too; that dedication; that indefatigable energy. He builds roads — hopping from one end of the Empire to the other. Can't sit still for five minutes. He says himself the longest time he ever sat still was the night before Waterloo when they were waiting for Wellington° to make up his mind to attack.

Wellington: Irish-born Duke of Wellington defeated Napoleon at Waterloo (Belgium) in 1815.

OWEN: What age is he?

YOLLAND: Born in 1789 — the very day the Bastille° fell. I've often thought maybe that gave his whole life its character. Do you think it could? He inherited a new world the day he was born — The Year One. Ancient time was at an end. The world had cast off its old skin. There were no longer any frontiers to man's potential. Possibilities were endless and exciting. He still believes that. The Apocalypse is just about to happen . . . I'm afraid I'm a great disappointment to him. I've neither his energy, nor his coherence, nor his belief. Do I believe in fate? The day I arrived in Bally-beg — no, Baile Beag — the moment you brought me in here, I had a curious sensation. It's difficult to describe. It was a momentary sense of discovery; no — not quite a sense of discovery — a sense of recognition, of confirmation of something I half knew instinctively; as if I had stepped . . .

OWEN: Back into ancient time?

YOLLAND: No, no. It wasn't an awareness of *direction* being changed but of experience being of a totally different order. I had moved into a consciousness that wasn't striving nor agitated, but at its ease and with its own conviction and assurance. And when I heard Jimmy Jack and your father swapping stories about Apollo and Cuchulainn and Paris and Ferdia° — as if they lived down the road — it was then that I thought — I knew — perhaps I could live here . . . [*Now embarrassed.*] Where's the pot-een?

OWEN: Poteen.

YOLLAND: Poteen — poteen — poteen. Even if I did speak Irish I'd always be an outsider here, wouldn't I? I may learn the password but the language of the tribe will always elude me, won't it? The private core will always be . . . hermetic,° won't it?

OWEN: You can learn to decode us.

[*Hugh emerges from upstairs and descends. He is dressed for the road. Today he is physically and mentally jaunty and alert — almost self-consciously jaunty and alert. Indeed, as the scene progresses, one has the sense that he is deliberately parodying himself. The moment Hugh gets to the bottom of the steps Yolland leaps respectfully to his feet.*]

HUGH [*as he descends*]:

Quantumvis cursum longum fessumque moratur
Sol, sacro tandem carmine vesper adest.

I dabble in verse, Lieutenant, after the style of Ovid. [*To Owen.*] A drop of that to fortify me.

YOLLAND: You'll have to translate it for me.

HUGH: Let's see —
No matter how long the sun may linger on his long
    and weary journey
At length evening comes with its sacred song.

Bastille: Prison in Paris destroyed during the French Revolution; symbol of oppression.
Apollo . . . Ferdia: Greek and Celtic mythological figures.
hermetic: Secret, unrevealed.

YOLLAND: Very nice, sir.

HUGH: English succeeds in making it sound . . . plebeian.

OWEN: Where are you off to, Father?

HUGH: An *expeditio* with three purposes. Purpose A: to acquire a testimonial from our parish priest — [*to Yolland.*] a worthy man but barely literate; and since he'll ask me to write it myself, how in all modesty can I do myself justice? [*To Owen.*] Where did this [*drink*] come from?

OWEN: Anna na mBreag's.

HUGH [*to Yolland*]: In that case address yourself to it with circumspection. [*And Hugh instantly tosses the drink back in one gulp and grimaces.*] Aaaaaaagh! [*Holds out his glass for a refill.*] Anna na mBreag means Anna of the Lies. And Purpose B: to talk to the builders of the new school about the kind of living accommodation I will require there. I have lived too long like a journeyman tailor.

YOLLAND: Some years ago we lived fairly close to a poet — well, about three miles away.

HUGH: His name?

YOLLAND: Wordsworth — William Wordsworth.

HUGH: Did he speak of me to you?

YOLLAND: Actually I never talked to him. I just saw him out walking — in the distance.

HUGH: Wordsworth? . . . No. I'm afraid we're not familiar with your literature, Lieutenant. We feel closer to the warm Mediterranean. We tend to over-look your island.

YOLLAND: I'm learning to speak Irish, sir.

HUGH: Good.

YOLLAND: Roland's teaching me.

HUGH: Splendid.

YOLLAND: I mean — I feel so cut off from the people here. And I was trying to explain a few minutes ago how remarkable a community this is. To meet people like yourself and Jimmy Jack who actually converse in Greek, in Latin. And your place names — what was the one we came across this morning? — Ter-mon, from Terminus, the god of boundaries. It — it — it's really astonishing.

HUGH: We like to think we endure around truths immemorially posited.

YOLLAND: And your Gaelic literature — you're a poet yourself —

HUGH: Only in Latin, I'm afraid.

YOLLAND: I understand it's enormously rich and ornate.

HUGH: Indeed, Lieutenant. A rich language. A rich liter-ature. You'll find, sir, that certain cultures expend on their vocabularies and syntax acquisitive energies and ostentations entirely lacking in their material lives. I suppose you could call us a spiritual people.

OWEN [*not unkindly; more out of embarrassment before Yolland*]: Will you stop that nonsense, Father.

HUGH: Nonsense? What nonsense?

OWEN: Do you know where the priest lives?

HUGH: At Lis na Muc, over near . . .

OWEN: No, he doesn't. Lis na Muc, the Fort of the Pigs, has become Swinefort. [*Now turning the pages of the*

Name-Book — a page per name.] And to get to
Swinefort you pass through Greencastle and Fair
Head and Strandhill and Gort and Whiteplains. And
the new school isn't at Poll na gCaorach — it's at
Sheepsrock. Will you be able to find your way?

[*Hugh pours himself another drink. Then: —*]

HUGH: Yes, it is a rich language, Lieutenant, full of
the mythologies of fantasy and hope and self-
deception — a syntax opulent with tomorrows. It is
our response to mud cabins and a diet of potatoes;
our only method of replying to . . . inevitabilities.
[*To Owen.*] Can you give me the loan of half-a-
crown? I'll repay you out of the subscriptions I'm
collecting for the publication of my new book. [*To
Yolland.*] It is entitled: 'The Pentaglot° Preceptor or
Elementary Institute of the English, Greek, Hebrew,
Latin and Irish Languages; Particularly Calculated
for the Instruction of such Ladies and Gentlemen as
may Wish to Learn without the Help of a Master.'

YOLLAND [*laughs*]: That's a wonderful title!

HUGH: Between ourselves — the best part of the enterprise. Nor do I, in fact, speak Hebrew. And that last
phrase — 'without the Help of a Master' — that was
written before the new national school was thrust
upon me — do you think I ought to drop it now?
After all you don't dispose of the cow just because it
has produced a magnificent calf, do you?

YOLLAND: You certainly do not.

HUGH: The phrase goes. And I'm interrupting work of
moment. [*He goes to the door and stops there.*] To
return briefly to that other matter, Lieutenant. I
understand your sense of exclusion, of being cut off
from a life here; and I trust you will find access to us
with my son's help. But remember that words are signals, counters. They are not immortal. And it can
happen — to use an image you'll understand — it
can happen that a civilization can be imprisoned in a
linguistic contour which no longer matches the landscape of . . . fact. Gentlemen. [*He leaves.*]

OWEN: 'An *expeditio* with three purposes': the children
laugh at him: he always promises three points and he
never gets beyond A and B.

MANUS: He's an astute man.

OWEN: He's bloody pompous.

YOLLAND: But so astute.

OWEN: And he drinks too much. Is it astute not to be
able to adjust for survival? Enduring around truths
immemorially posited — hah!

YOLLAND: He knows what's happening.

OWEN: What is happening?

YOLLAND: I'm not sure. But I'm concerned about my
part in it. It's an eviction of sorts.

OWEN: We're making a six-inch map of the country. Is
there something sinister in that?

YOLLAND: Not in —

Pentaglot: Speaker of five languages.

OWEN: And we're taking place-names that are riddled
with confusion and —

YOLLAND: Who's confused? Are the people confused?

OWEN: — and we're standardizing those names as accurately and as sensitively as we can.

YOLLAND: Something is being eroded.

OWEN: Back to the romance again. All right! Fine! Fine!
Look where we've got to. [*He drops on his hands
and knees and stabs a finger at the map.*] We've come
to this crossroads. Come here and look at it, man!
Look at it! And we call that crossroads Tobair Vree.
And why do we call it Tobair Vree? I'll tell you why.
Tobair means a well. But what does Vree mean? It's a
corruption of Brian — Brian — an erosion of Tobair
Bhriain. Because a hundred-and-fifty years ago there
used to be a well there, not at the crossroads, mind
you — that would be too simple — but in a field
close to the crossroads. And an old man called Brian,
whose face was disfigured by an enormous growth,
got it into his head that the water in that well was
blessed; and every day for seven months he went
there and bathed his face in it. But the growth didn't
go away; and one morning Brian was found drowned
in that well. And ever since that crossroads is known
as Tobair Vree — even though that well has long
since dried up. I know the story because my grandfather told it to me. But ask Doalty — or Maire — or
Bridget — even my father — even Manus — why it's
called Tobair Vree; and do you think they'll know? I
know they don't know. So the question I put to you,
Lieutenant, is this: what do we do with a name like
that? Do we scrap Tobair Vree altogether and call
it — what? — The Cross? Crossroads? Or do we
keep piety with a man long dead, long forgotten, his
name 'eroded' beyond recognition, whose trivial
little story nobody in the parish remembers?

YOLLAND: Except you.

OWEN: I've left here.

YOLLAND: You remember it.

OWEN: I'm asking you: what do we write in the Name-
Book?

YOLLAND: Tobair Vree.

OWEN: Even though the well is a hundred yards from
the actual crossroads — and there's no well anyway — and what the hell does Vree mean?

YOLLAND: Tobair Vree.

OWEN: That's what you want?

YOLLAND: Yes.

OWEN: You're certain?

YOLLAND: Yes.

OWEN: Fine. Fine. That's what you'll get.

YOLLAND: That's what you want, too, Roland.

[*Pause.*]

OWEN [*explodes*]: George! For God's sake! *My name is
not Roland!*

YOLLAND: What?

OWEN [*softly*]: My name is Owen.

The 1993 Donmar Warehouse (London) production of *Translations,* directed by Sam Mendes with the following cast (front, from left to right): Tony Rohr as Jimmy Jack, Robert Patterson as Owen, Norman Rodway as Hugh, and Zara Turner as Maire.

James Larkin as Yolland in the 1993 Donmar Warehouse production.

[*Pause.*]

YOLLAND: Not Roland?
OWEN: Owen.
YOLLAND: You mean to say — ?
OWEN: Owen.
YOLLAND: But I've been —
OWEN: O-w-e-n.
YOLLAND: Where did Roland come from?
OWEN: I don't know.
YOLLAND: It was never Roland?

OWEN: Never.
YOLLAND: O my God!

[*Pause. They stare at one another. Then the absurdity of the situation strikes them suddenly. They explode with laughter. Owen pours drinks. As they roll about, their lines overlap.*]

YOLLAND: Why didn't you tell me?
OWEN: Do I look like a Roland?
YOLLAND: Spell Owen again.

OWEN: I was getting fond of Roland.
YOLLAND: O my God!
OWEN: O-w-e-n.
YOLLAND: What'll we write —
OWEN: — in the Name-Book?!
YOLLAND: R-o-w-e-n!
OWEN: Or what about Ol —
YOLLAND: Ol-what?
OWEN: Oland!

[*And again they explode. Manus enters. He is very elated.*]

MANUS: What's the celebration?
OWEN: A christening!
YOLLAND: A baptism!
OWEN: A hundred christenings!
YOLLAND: A thousand baptisms! Welcome to Eden!
OWEN: Eden's right! We name a thing and — bang! — it leaps into existence!
YOLLAND: Each name a perfect equation with its roots.
OWEN: A perfect congruence with its reality. [*To Manus.*] Take a drink.
YOLLAND: Poteen — beautiful.
OWEN: Lying Anna's poteen.
YOLLAND: Anna na mBreag's poteen.
OWEN: Excellent, George.
YOLLAND: I'll decode you yet.
OWEN [*offers drink*]: Manus?
MANUS: Not if that's what it does to you.
OWEN: You're right. Steady — steady — sober up — sober up.
YOLLAND: Sober as a judge, Owen.

[*Manus moves beside Owen.*]

MANUS: I've got good news! Where's Father?
OWEN: He's gone out. What's the good news?
MANUS: I've been offered a job.
OWEN: Where? [*Now aware of Yolland.*] Come on, man — speak in English.
MANUS: For the benefit of the colonist?
OWEN: He's a decent man.
MANUS: Aren't they all at some level?
OWEN: Please.

[*Manus shrugs.*]

He's been offered a job.
YOLLAND: Where?
OWEN: Well — tell us!
MANUS: I've just had a meeting with two men from Inis Meadhon. They want me to go there and start a hedge-school. They're giving me a free house, free turf, and free milk; a rood of standing corn; twelve drills of potatoes; and — [*He stops.*]
OWEN: And what?
MANUS: A salary of £42 a year!
OWEN: Manus, that's wonderful!
MANUS: You're talking to a man of substance.
OWEN: I'm delighted.
YOLLAND: Where's Inis Meadhon?

OWEN: An island south of here. And they came looking for you?
MANUS: Well, I mean to say . . .

[*Owen punches Manus.*]

OWEN: Aaaaagh! This calls for a real celebration.
YOLLAND: Congratulations.
MANUS: Thank you.
OWEN: Where are you, Anna?
YOLLAND: When do you start?
MANUS: Next Monday.
OWEN: We'll stay with you when we're there. [*To Yolland.*] How long will it be before we reach Inis Meadhon?
YOLLAND: How far south is it?
MANUS: About fifty miles.
YOLLAND: Could we make it by December?
OWEN: We'll have Christmas together. [*Sings.*] 'Christmas Day on Inis Meadhon . . .'
YOLLAND [*toast*]: I hope you're very content there, Manus.
MANUS: Thank you.

[*Yolland holds out his hand. Manus takes it. They shake warmly.*]

OWEN [*toast*]: Manus.
MANUS [*toast*]: To Inis Meadhon. [*He drinks quickly and turns to leave.*]
OWEN: Hold on — hold on — refills coming up.
MANUS: I've got to go.
OWEN: Come on, man; this is an occasion. Where are you rushing to?
MANUS: I've got to tell Maire.

[*Maire enters with her can of milk.*]

MAIRE: You've got to tell Maire what?
OWEN: He's got a job!
MAIRE: Manus?
OWEN: He's been invited to start a hedge-school in Inis Meadhon.
MAIRE: Where?
MANUS: Inis Meadhon — the island! They're giving me £42 a year and . . .
OWEN: A house, fuel, milk, potatoes, corn, pupils, what-not!
MANUS: I start on Monday.
OWEN: You'll take a drink. Isn't it great?
MANUS: I want to talk to you for —
MAIRE: There's your milk. I need the can back.

[*Manus takes the can and runs up the steps.*]

MANUS [*as he goes*]: How will you like living on an island?
OWEN: You know George, don't you?
MAIRE: We wave to each other across the fields.
YOLLAND: Sorry-sorry?
OWEN: She says you wave to each other across the fields.
YOLLAND: Yes, we do; oh, yes; indeed we do.
MAIRE: What's he saying?

OWEN: He says you wave to each other across the fields.
MAIRE: That's right. So we do.
YOLLAND: What's she saying?
OWEN: Nothing — nothing — nothing. [*To Maire.*] What's the news?

[*Maire moves away, touching the text books with her toe.*]

MAIRE: Not a thing. You're busy, the two of you.
OWEN: We think we are.
MAIRE: I hear the Fiddler O'Shea's about. There's some talk of a dance tomorrow night.
OWEN: Where will it be?
MAIRE: Maybe over the road. Maybe at Tobair Vree.
YOLLAND: Tobair Vree!
MAIRE: Yes.
YOLLAND: Tobair Vree! Tobair Vree!
MAIRE: Does he know what I'm saying?
OWEN: Not a word.
MAIRE: Tell him then.
OWEN: Tell him what?
MAIRE: About the dance.
OWEN: Maire says there may be a dance tomorrow night.
YOLLAND [*to Owen*]: Yes? May I come? [*To Maire.*] Would anybody object if I came?
MAIRE [*to Owen*]: What's he saying?
OWEN [*to Yolland*]: Who would object?
MAIRE [*to Owen*]: Did you tell him?
YOLLAND [*to Maire*]: Sorry-sorry?
OWEN [*to Maire*]: He says may he come?
MAIRE [*to Yolland*]: That's up to you.
YOLLAND [*to Owen*]: What does she say?
OWEN [*to Yolland*]: She says —
YOLLAND [*to Maire*]: What-what?
MAIRE [*to Owen*]: Well?
YOLLAND [*to Owen*]: Sorry-sorry?
OWEN [*to Yolland*]: Will you go?
YOLLAND [*to Maire*]: Yes, yes, if I may.
MAIRE [*to Owen*]: What does he say?
YOLLAND [*to Owen*]: What is she saying?
OWEN: Oh for God's sake! [*To Manus, who is descending with the empty can.*] You take on this job, Manus.
MANUS: I'll walk you up to the house. Is your mother at home? I want to talk to her.
MAIRE: What's the rush? [*To Owen.*] Didn't you offer me a drink?
OWEN: Will you risk Anna na mBreag?
MAIRE: Why not.

[*Yolland is suddenly intoxicated. He leaps up on a stool, raises his glass and shouts.*]

YOLLAND: Anna na mBreag! Baile Beag! Inis Meadhon! Bombay! Tobair Vree! Eden! And poteen — correct, Owen?
OWEN: Perfect.
YOLLAND: And bloody marvellous stuff it is, too. I love it! Bloody, bloody, bloody marvellous!

[*Simultaneously with his final 'bloody marvellous' bring up very loud the introductory music of the reel. Then immediately go to black. Retain the music throughout the very brief interval.*]

Scene II

The following night.
  This scene may be played in the schoolroom, but it would be preferable to lose — by lighting — as much of the schoolroom as possible, and to play the scene down front in a vaguely 'outside' area.
  The music rises to a crescendo. Then in the distance we hear Maire and Yolland approach — laughing and running. They run on, hand-in-hand. They have just left the dance. Fade the music to distant background. Then after a time it is lost and replaced by guitar music. Maire and Yolland are now down front, still holding hands and excited by their sudden and impetuous escape from the dance.

MAIRE: O my God, that leap across the ditch nearly killed me.
YOLLAND: I could scarcely keep up with you.
MAIRE: Wait till I get my breath back.
YOLLAND: We must have looked as if we were being chased.

[*They now realize they are alone and holding hands — the beginnings of embarrassment. The hands disengage. They begin to drift apart. Pause.*]

MAIRE: Manus'll wonder where I've got to.
YOLLAND: I wonder did anyone notice us leave.

[*Pause. Slightly further apart.*]

MAIRE: The grass must be wet. My feet are soaking.

[*Another pause. Another few paces apart. They are now a long distance from one another.*]

YOLLAND [*indicating himself*]: George.

[*Maire nods: Yes-yes. Then: —*]

MAIRE: Lieutenant George.
YOLLAND: Don't call me that. I never think of myself as Lieutenant.
MAIRE: What-what?
YOLLAND: Sorry-sorry. [*He points to himself again.*] George.

[*Maire nods: Yes-yes. Then points to herself.*]

MAIRE: Maire.
YOLLAND: Yes, I know you're Maire. Of course I know you're Maire. I mean I've been watching you night and day for the past —
MAIRE [*eagerly*]: What-what?
YOLLAND [*points*]: Maire. [*Points.*] George. [*Points both.*] Maire and George.

[*Maire nods: Yes-yes-yes.*]

I — I — I —

MAIRE: Say anything at all. I love the sound of your speech.

YOLLAND [*eagerly*]: Sorry-sorry? [*In acute frustration he looks around, hoping for some inspiration that will provide him with communicative means. Now he has a thought: he tries raising his voice and articulating in a staccato style and with equal and absurd emphasis on each word.*] Every-morning-I-see-you-feeding-brown-hens-and-giving-meal-to-black-calf — [*the futility of it.*] — O my God.

[*Maire smiles. She moves towards him. She will try to communicate in Latin.*]

MAIRE: *Tu es centurio in — in — in exercitu Britannico* — °

YOLLAND: Yes-yes? Go on — go on — say anything at all — I love the sound of your speech.

MAIRE: — *et es in castris quae — quae — quae sunt in agro* — ° [*the futility of it.*] — O my God.

[*Yolland smiles. He moves towards her. Now for her English words.*]

George — water.

YOLLAND: 'Water'? Water! Oh yes — water — water — very good — water — good — good.

MAIRE: Fire.

YOLLAND: Fire — indeed — wonderful — fire, fire, fire — splendid — splendid!

MAIRE: Ah . . . ah . . .

YOLLAND: Yes? Go on.

MAIRE: Earth.

YOLLAND: Earth?

MAIRE: Earth. Earth.

[*Yolland still does not understand. Maire stoops down and picks up a handful of clay. Holding it out.*]

Earth.

YOLLAND: Earth! Of course — earth! Earth. Earth. Good Lord, Maire, your English is perfect!

MAIRE [*eagerly*]: What-what?

YOLLAND: Perfect English. English perfect.

MAIRE: George —

YOLLAND: That's beautiful — oh, that's really beautiful.

MAIRE: George —

YOLLAND: Say it again — say it again —

MAIRE: Shhh. [*She holds her hand up for silence — she is trying to remember her one line of English. Now she remembers it and she delivers the line as if English were her language — easily, fluidly, conversationally.*] George, 'In Norfolk we besport ourselves around the maypoll.'

YOLLAND: Good God, do you? That's where my mother comes from — Norfolk. Norwich actually. Not exactly Norwich town but a small village called Little

Walsingham close beside it. But in our own village of Winfarthing we have a maypole too and every year on the first of May — [*He stops abruptly, only now realizing. He stares at her. She in turn misunderstands his excitement.*]

MAIRE [*to herself*]: Mother of God, my Aunt Mary wouldn't have taught me something dirty, would she?

[*Pause. Yolland extends his hand to Maire. She turns away from him and moves slowly across the stage.*]

YOLLAND: Maire.

[*She still moves away.*]

Maire Chatach.

[*She still moves away.*]

Bun na hAbhann? [*He says the name softly, almost privately, very tentatively, as if he were searching for a sound she might respond to. He tries again.*] Druim Dubh?

[*Maire stops. She is listening. Yolland is encouraged.*]

Poll na gCaorach. Lis Maol.

[*Maire turns towards him.*]

Lis na nGall.

MAIRE: Lis na nGradh.

[*They are now facing each other and begin moving — almost imperceptibly — towards one another.*]

MAIRE: Carraig an Phoill.

YOLLAND: Carraig na Ri. Loch na nEan.

MAIRE: Loch an Iubhair. Machaire Buidhe.

YOLLAND: Machaire Mor. Cnoc na Mona.

MAIRE: Cnoc na nGabhar.

YOLLAND: Mullach.

MAIRE: Port.

YOLLAND: Tor.

MAIRE : Lag.

[*She holds out her hands to Yolland. He takes them. Each now speaks almost to himself/herself.*]

YOLLAND: I wish to God you could understand me.

MAIRE: Soft hands; a gentleman's hands.

YOLLAND: Because if you could understand me I could tell you how I spend my days either thinking of you or gazing up at your house in the hope that you'll appear even for a second.

MAIRE: Every evening you walk by yourself along the Tra Bhan and every morning you wash yourself in front of your tent.

YOLLAND: I would tell you how beautiful you are, curly-headed Maire. I would so like to tell you how beautiful you are.

MAIRE: Your arms are long and thin and the skin on your shoulders is very white.

YOLLAND: I would tell you . . .

MAIRE: Don't stop — I know what you're saying.

Tu . . . Brittanico: You are a British soldier.
et . . . agro: And you camp in the field.

YOLLAND: I would tell you how I want to be here — to
   live here — always — with you — always, always.
MAIRE: 'Always'? What is that word — 'always'?
YOLLAND: Yes-yes; always.
MAIRE: You're trembling.
YOLLAND: Yes, I'm trembling because of you.
MAIRE: I'm trembling, too.

[*She holds his face in her hand.*]

YOLLAND: I've made up my mind . . .
MAIRE: Shhhh.
YOLLAND: I'm not going to leave here . . .
MAIRE: Shhh — listen to me. I want you, too, soldier.
YOLLAND: Don't stop — I know what you're saying.
MAIRE: I want to live with you — anywhere — any-
   where at all — always — always.
YOLLAND: 'Always'? What is that word — 'always'?
MAIRE: Take me away with you, George.

[*Pause. Suddenly they kiss. Sarah enters. She sees them.
She stands shocked, staring at them. Her mouth works.
Then almost to herself.*]

SARAH: Manus . . . Manus!

[*Sarah runs off. Music to crescendo.*]

ACT THREE

The following evening. It is raining.
   *Sarah and Owen alone in the schoolroom. Sarah,
more waiflike than ever, is sitting very still on a stool, an
open book across her knee. She is pretending to read but
her eyes keep going up to the room upstairs. Owen is
working on the floor as before, surrounded by his reference books, map, Name-Book, etc. But he has neither
concentration nor interest, and like Sarah he glances up
at the upstairs room.*
   *After a few seconds Manus emerges and descends,
carrying a large paper bag which already contains his
clothes. His movements are determined and urgent. He
moves around the classroom, picking up books, examining each title carefully, and choosing about six of them
which he puts into his bag. As he selects these books: —*

OWEN: You know that old limekiln beyond Con Connie
   Tim's pub, the place we call The Murren? — do you
   know why it's called The Murren?

[*Manus does not answer.*]

   I've only just discovered: it's a corruption of Saint
   Muranus. It seems Saint Muranus had a monastery
   somewhere about there at the beginning of the seventh
   century. And over the years the name became shortened to the Murren. Very unattractive name, isn't it? I
   think we should go back to the original — Saint
   Muranus. What do you think? The original's Saint
   Muranus. Don't you think we should go back to that?

[*No response. Owen begins writing the name into the
Name-Book. Manus is now rooting about among the*

*forgotten implements for a piece of rope. He finds a
piece. He begins to tie the mouth of the flimsy, overloaded bag — and it bursts, the contents spilling out on
the floor.*]

MANUS: Bloody, bloody, bloody hell!

[*His voice breaks in exasperation: he is about to cry.
Owen leaps to his feet.*]

OWEN: Hold on. I've a bag upstairs.
[*He runs upstairs. Sarah waits until Owen is off.
   Then: —*]
SARAH: Manus . . . Manus, I . . .

[*Manus hears Sarah but makes no acknowledgement.
He gathers up his belongings. Owen reappears with the
bag he had on his arrival.*]

OWEN: Take this one — I'm finished with it anyway.
   And it's supposed to keep out the rain.

[*Manus transfers his few belongings. Owen drifts back
to his task. The packing is now complete.*]

MANUS: You'll be here for a while? For a week or two
   anyhow?
OWEN: Yes.
MANUS: You're not leaving with the army?
OWEN: I haven't made up my mind. Why?
MANUS: Those Inis Meadhon men will be back to see
   why I haven't turned up. Tell them — tell them I'll
   write to them as soon as I can. Tell them I still want
   the job but that it might be three or four months
   before I'm free to go.
OWEN: You're being damned stupid, Manus.
MANUS: Will you do that for me?
OWEN: Clear out now and Lancey'll think you're involved somehow.
MANUS: Will you do that for me?
OWEN: Wait a couple of days even. You know George —
   he's a bloody romantic — maybe he's gone out to
   one of the islands and he'll suddenly reappear tomorrow morning. Or maybe the search party'll find him
   this evening lying drunk somewhere in the sandhills.
   You've seen him drinking that poteen — doesn't
   know how to handle it. Had he drink on him last
   night at the dance?
MANUS: I had a stone in my hand when I went out looking for him — I was going to fell him. The lame
   scholar turned violent.
OWEN: Did anybody see you?
MANUS [*again close to tears*]: But when I saw him standing there at the side of the road — smiling — and her
   face buried in his shoulder — I couldn't even go close
   to them. I just shouted something stupid — something like, 'You're a bastard, Yolland.' If I'd even said
   it in English . . . 'cos he kept saying 'Sorry-sorry?'
   The wrong gesture in the wrong language.
OWEN: And you didn't see him again?
MANUS: 'Sorry?'
OWEN: Before you leave tell Lancey that — just to clear
   yourself.

MANUS: What have I to say to Lancey? You'll give that message to the islandmen?

OWEN: I'm warning you: run away now and you're bound to be —

MANUS [to Sarah]: Will you give that message to the Inis Meadhon men?

SARAH: I will.

[Manus picks up an old sack and throws it across his shoulders.]

OWEN: Have you any idea where you're going?

MANUS: Mayo, maybe. I remember Mother saying she had cousins somewhere away out in the Erris Peninsula. [He picks up his bag.] Tell Father I took only the Virgil and the Caesar and the Aeschylus because they're mine anyway — I bought them with the money I got for that pet lamb I reared — do you remember that pet lamb? And tell him that Nora Dan never returned the dictionary and that she still owes him two-and-six for last quarter's reading — he always forgets those things.

OWEN: Yes.

MANUS: And his good shirt's ironed and hanging up in the press and his clean socks are in the butter-box under the bed.

OWEN: All right.

MANUS: And tell him I'll write.

OWEN: If Maire asks where you've gone . . . ?

MANUS: He'll need only half the amount of milk now, won't he? Even less than half — he usually takes his tea black. [Pause.] And when he comes in at night — you'll hear him; he makes a lot of noise — I usually come down and give him a hand up. Those stairs are dangerous without a banister. Maybe before you leave you'd get Big Ned Frank to put up some sort of a handrail. [Pause.] And if you can bake, he's very fond of soda bread.

OWEN: I can give you money. I'm wealthy. Do you know what they pay me? Two shillings a day for this — this — this —

[Manus rejects the offer by holding out his hand.]

Goodbye, Manus.

[Manus and Owen shake hands. Then Manus picks up his bag briskly and goes towards the door. He stops a few paces beyond Sarah, turns, comes back to her. He addresses her as he did in Act One but now without warmth or concern for her.]

MANUS: What is your name? [Pause.] Come on. What is your name?

SARAH: My name is Sarah.

MANUS: Just Sarah? Sarah what? [Pause.] Well?

SARAH: Sarah Johnny Sally.

MANUS: And where do you live? Come on.

SARAH: I live in Bun na hAbhann. [She is now crying quietly.]

MANUS: Very good, Sarah Johnny Sally. There's nothing to stop you now — nothing in the wide world.

[Pause. He looks down at her.] It's all right — it's all right — you did no harm — you did no harm at all. [He stoops over her and kisses the top of her head — as if in absolution. Then briskly to the door and off.]

OWEN: Good luck, Manus!

SARAH [quietly]: I'm sorry . . . I'm sorry . . . I'm so sorry, Manus . . .

[Owen tries to work but cannot concentrate. He begins folding up the map. As he does: —]

OWEN: Is there a class this evening?

[Sarah nods: yes.]

I suppose Father knows. Where is he anyhow?

[Sarah points.]

Where?

[Sarah mimes rocking a baby.]

I don't understand — where?

[Sarah repeats the mime and wipes away tears. Owen is still puzzled.]

It doesn't matter. He'll probably turn up.

[Bridget and Doalty enter, sacks over their heads against the rain. They are self-consciously noisier, more ebullient, more garrulous than ever — brimming over with excitement and gossip and brio.]

DOALTY: You're missing the crack,° boys! Cripes, you're missing the crack! Fifty more soldiers arrived an hour ago!

BRIDGET: And they're spread out in a big line from Sean Neal's over to Lag and they're moving straight across the fields towards Cnoc na nGabhar!

DOALTY: Prodding every inch of the ground in front of them with their bayonets and scattering animals and hens in all directions!

BRIDGET: And tumbling everything before them — fences, ditches, haystacks, turf-stacks!

DOALTY: They came to Barney Petey's field of corn — straight through it be God as if it was heather!

BRIDGET: Not a blade of it left standing!

DOALTY: And Barney Petey just out of his bed and running after them in his drawers: 'You hoors you! Get out of my corn, you hoors you!'

BRIDGET: First time he ever ran in his life.

DOALTY: Too lazy, the wee get, to cut it when the weather was good.

[Sarah begins putting out the seats.]

BRIDGET: Tell them about Big Hughie.

DOALTY: Cripes, if you'd seen your aul fella, Owen.

BRIDGET: They were all inside in Anna na mBreag's pub — all the crowd from the wake —

DOALTY: And they hear the commotion and they all come out to the street —

crack: Excitement, action.

BRIDGET: Your father in front; the Infant Prodigy foot-less behind him!

DOALTY: And your aul fella, he sees the army stretched across the countryside —

BRIDGET: O my God!

DOALTY: And Cripes he starts roaring at them!

BRIDGET: 'Visigoths! Huns! Vandals!'

DOALTY: *'Ignari! Stulti! Rustici!'*

BRIDGET: And wee Jimmy Jack jumping up and down and shouting, 'Thermopylae! Thermopylae!'°

DOALTY: You never saw crack like it in your life, boys. Come away on out with me, Sarah, and you'll see it all.

BRIDGET: Big Hughie's fit to take no class. Is Manus about?

OWEN: Manus is gone.

BRIDGET: Gone where?

OWEN: He's left — gone away.

DOALTY: Where to?

OWEN: He doesn't know. Mayo, maybe.

DOALTY: What's on in Mayo?

OWEN [*to Bridget*]: Did you see George and Maire Chat-ach leave the dance last night?

BRIDGET: We did. Didn't we, Doalty?

OWEN: Did you see Manus following them out?

BRIDGET: I didn't see him going out but I saw him com-ing in by himself later.

OWEN: Did George and Maire come back to the dance?

BRIDGET: No.

OWEN: Did you see them again?

BRIDGET: He left her home. We passed them going up the back road — didn't we, Doalty?

OWEN: And Manus stayed till the end of the dance?

DOALTY: We know nothing. What are you asking us for?

OWEN: Because Lancey'll question me when he hears Manus's gone. [*Back to Bridget.*] That's the way George went home? By the back road? That's where you saw him?

BRIDGET: Leave me alone, Owen. I know nothing about Yolland. If you want to know about Yolland, ask the Donnelly twins.

[*Silence. Doalty moves over to the window.*]

[*To Sarah.*] He's a powerful fiddler, O'Shea, isn't he? He told our Seamus he'll come back for a night at Hallowe'en.

[*Owen goes to Doalty who looks resolutely out the win-dow.*]

OWEN: What's this about the Donnellys? [*Pause.*] Were they about last night?

DOALTY: Didn't see them if they were. [*Begins whistling through his teeth.*]

OWEN: George is a friend of mine.

DOALTY: So.

OWEN: I want to know what's happened to him.

Thermopylae: Scene of a Greek victory over the Persians in 480 B.C.

DOALTY: Couldn't tell you.

OWEN: What have the Donnelly twins to do with it? [*Pause.*] Doalty!

DOALTY: I know nothing, Owen — nothing at all — I swear to God. All I know is this: on my way to the dance I saw their boat beached at Port. It wasn't there on my way home, after I left Bridget. And that's all I know. As God's my judge. The half-dozen times I met him I didn't know a word he said to me; but he seemed a right enough sort . . . [*With sudden exces-sive interest in the scene outside.*] Cripes, they're crawling all over the place! Cripes, there's millions of them! Cripes, they're levelling the whole land!

[*Owen moves away. Maire enters. She is bareheaded and wet from the rain; her hair in disarray. She attempts to appear normal but she is in acute distress, on the verge of being distraught. She is carrying the milk-can.*]

MAIRE: Honest to God, I must be going off my head. I'm halfway here and I think to myself, 'Isn't this can very light?' and I look into it and isn't it empty.

OWEN: It doesn't matter.

MAIRE: How will you manage for tonight?

OWEN: We have enough.

MAIRE: Are you sure?

OWEN: Plenty, thanks.

MAIRE: It'll take me no time at all to go back up for some.

OWEN: Honestly, Maire.

MAIRE: Sure it's better you have it than that black calf that's . . . that . . . [*She looks around.*] Have you heard anything?

OWEN: Nothing.

MAIRE: What does Lancey say?

OWEN: I haven't seen him since this morning.

MAIRE: What does he *think*?

OWEN: We really didn't talk. He was here for only a few seconds.

MAIRE: He left me home, Owen. And the last thing he said to me — he tried to speak in Irish — he said, 'I'll see you yesterday' — he meant to say 'I'll see you tomorrow.' And I laughed that much he pretended to get cross and he said 'Maypoll! Maypoll!' because I said that word wrong. And off he went, laughing — laughing, Owen! Do you think he's all right? What do *you* think?

OWEN: I'm sure he'll turn up. Maire.

MAIRE: He comes from a tiny wee place called Winfar-thing. [*She suddenly drops on her hands and knees on the floor — where Owen had his map a few min-utes ago — and with her finger traces out an outline map.*] Come here till you see. Look. There's Winfar-thing. And there's two other wee villages right beside it; one of them's called Barton Bendish — it's there; and the other's called Saxingham Nethergate — it's about there. And there's Little Walsingham — that's his mother's townland. Aren't they odd names? Sure they make no sense to me at all. And Winfarthing's near a big town called Norwich. And Norwich is in a county called Norfolk. And Norfolk is in the east of England. He drew a map for me on the wet strand and wrote the names on it. I have it all in my head now: Winfarthing — Barton Bendish — Saxingham Nethergate — Little Walsingham — Norwich — Norfolk. Strange sounds, aren't they? But nice sounds, like Jimmy Jack reciting his Homer. [*She gets to her feet and looks around; she is almost serene now. To Sarah.*] You were looking lovely last night, Sarah. Is that the dress you got from Boston? Green suits you. [*To Owen.*] Something very bad's happened to him, Owen. I know. He wouldn't go away without telling me. Where is he, Owen? You're his friend — where is he? [*Again she looks around the room; then sits on a stool.*] I didn't get a chance to do my geography last night. The master'll be angry with me. [*She rises again.*] I think I'll go home now. The wee ones have to be washed and put to bed and that black calf has to be fed . . . My hands are that rough; they're still blistered from the hay. I'm ashamed of them. I hope to God there's no hay to be saved in Brooklyn. [*She stops at the door.*] Did you hear? Nellie Ruadh's baby died in the middle of the night. I must go up to the wake. It didn't last long, did it?

[*Maire leaves. Silence. Then:*]

OWEN: I don't think there'll be any class. Maybe you should . . .

[*Owen begins picking up his texts. Doalty goes to him.*]

DOALTY: Is he long gone? — Manus.
OWEN: Half an hour.
DOALTY: Stupid bloody fool.
OWEN: I told him that.
DOALTY: Do they know he's gone?
OWEN: Who?
DOALTY: The army.
OWEN: Not yet.
DOALTY: They'll be after him like bloody beagles. Bloody, bloody fool, limping along the coast. They'll overtake him before night for Christ's sake.

[*Doalty returns to the window. Lancey enters — now the commanding officer.*]

OWEN: Any news? Any word?

[*Lancey moves into the centre of the room, looking around as he does.*]

LANCEY: I understood there was a class. Where are the others?
OWEN: There was to be a class but my father —
LANCEY: This will suffice. I will address them and it will be their responsibility to pass on what I have to say to every family in this section.

[*Lancey indicates to Owen to translate. Owen hesitates, trying to assess the change in Lancey's manner and attitude.*]

I'm in a hurry, O'Donnell.

OWEN: The captain has an announcement to make.
LANCEY: Lieutenant Yolland is missing. We are searching for him. If we don't find him, or if we receive no information as to where he is to be found, I will pursue the following course of action. [*He indicates to Owen to translate.*]
OWEN: They are searching for George. If they don't find him —
LANCEY: Commencing twenty-four hours from now we will shoot all livestock in Ballybeg.

[*Owen stares at Lancey.*]

At once.
OWEN: Beginning this time tomorrow they'll kill every animal in Baile Beag — unless they're told where George is.
LANCEY: If that doesn't bear results, commencing forty-eight hours from now we will embark on a series of evictions and levelling of every abode in the following selected areas —
OWEN: You're not —!
LANCEY: Do your job. Translate.
OWEN: If they still haven't found him in two days time they'll begin evicting and levelling every house starting with these townlands.

[*Lancey reads from his list.*]

LANCEY: Swinefort.
OWEN: Lis na Muc.
LANCEY: Burnfoot.
OWEN: Bun na hAbhann.
LANCEY: Dromduff.
OWEN: Druim Dubh.
LANCEY: Whiteplains.
OWEN: Machaire Ban.
LANCEY: Kings Head.
OWEN: Cnoc na Ri.
LANCEY: If by then the lieutenant hasn't been found, we will proceed until a complete clearance is made of this entire section.
OWEN: If Yolland hasn't been got by then, they will ravish the whole parish.
LANCEY: I trust they know exactly what they've got to do. [*Pointing to Bridget.*] I know you. I know where you live. [*Pointing to Sarah.*] Who are you? Name!

[*Sarah's mouth opens and shuts, opens and shuts. Her face becomes contorted.*]

What's your name?

[*Again Sarah tries frantically.*]

OWEN: Go on, Sarah. You can tell him.

[*But Sarah cannot. And she knows she cannot. She closes her mouth. Her head goes down.*]

OWEN: Her name is Sarah Johnny Sally.
LANCEY: Where does she live?
OWEN: Bun na hAbhann.
LANCEY: Where?

OWEN: Burnfoot.

LANCEY: I want to talk to your brother — is he here?

OWEN: Not at the moment.

LANCEY: Where is he?

OWEN: He's at a wake.

LANCEY: What wake?

[*Doalty, who has been looking out the window all through Lancey's announcements, now speaks — calmly, almost casually.*]

DOALTY: Tell him his whole camp's on fire.

LANCEY: What's your name? [*To Owen.*] Who's that lout?

OWEN: Doalty Dan Doalty.

LANCEY: Where does he live?

OWEN: Tulach Alainn.

LANCEY: What do we call it?

OWEN: Fair Hill. He says your whole camp is on fire.

[*Lancey rushes to the window and looks out. Then he wheels on Doalty.*]

LANCEY: I'll remember you, Mr Doalty. [*To Owen.*] You carry a big responsibility in all this. [*He goes off.*]

BRIDGET: Mother of God, does he mean it, Owen?

OWEN: Yes, he does.

BRIDGET: We'll have to hide the beasts somewhere — our Seamus'll know where. Maybe at the back of Lis na nGradh — or in the caves at the far end of the Tra Bhan. Come on, Doalty! Come on! Don't be standing about there!

[*Doalty does not move. Bridget runs to the door and stops suddenly. She sniffs the air. Panic.*]

The sweet smell! Smell it! It's the sweet smell! Jesus, it's the potato blight!

DOALTY: It's the army tents burning, Bridget.

BRIDGET: Is it? Are you sure? Is that what it is? God, I thought we were destroyed altogether. Come on! Come on!

[*She runs off. Owen goes to Sarah who is preparing to leave.*]

OWEN: How are you? Are you all right?

[*Sarah nods: Yes.*]

OWEN: Don't worry. It will come back to you again.

[*Sarah shakes her head.*]

OWEN: It will. You're upset now. He frightened you. That's all's wrong.

[*Again Sarah shakes her head, slowly, emphatically, and smiles at Owen. Then she leaves. Owen busies himself gathering his belongings. Doalty leaves the window and goes to him.*]

DOALTY: He'll do it, too.

OWEN: Unless Yolland's found.

DOALTY: Hah!

OWEN: Then he'll certainly do it.

DOALTY: When my grandfather was a boy they did the same thing. [*Simply, altogether without irony.*] And after all the trouble you went to, mapping the place and thinking up new names for it.

[*Owen busies himself. Pause. Doalty almost dreamily.*]

I've damned little to defend but he'll not put me out without a fight. And there'll be others who think the same as me.

OWEN: That's a matter for you.

DOALTY: If we'd all stick together. If we knew how to defend ourselves.

OWEN: Against a trained army.

DOALTY: The Donnelly twins know how.

OWEN: If they could be found.

DOALTY: If they could be found. [*He goes to the door.*] Give me a shout after you've finished with Lancey. I might know something then. [*He leaves.*]

[*Owen picks up the Name-Book. He looks at it momentarily, then puts it on top of the pile he is carrying. It falls to the floor. He stoops to pick it up — hesitates — leaves it. He goes upstairs. As Owen ascends, Hugh and Jimmy Jack enter. Both wet and drunk. Jimmy is very unsteady. He is trotting behind Hugh, trying to break in on Hugh's declamation. Hugh is equally drunk but more experienced in drunkenness: there is a portion of his mind which retains its clarity.*]

HUGH: There I was, appropriately dispositioned to proffer my condolences to the bereaved mother . . .

JIMMY: Hugh —

HUGH: . . . and about to enter the *domus lugubris* — Maire Chatach?

JIMMY: The wake house.

HUGH: Indeed — when I experience a plucking at my elbow: Mister George Alexander, Justice of the Peace. 'My tidings are infelicitous,' said he — Bridget? Too slow. Doalty?

JIMMY: *Infelix* — unhappy.

HUGH: Unhappy indeed. 'Master Bartley Timlin has been appointed to the new national school.' 'Timlin? Who is Timlin?' 'A schoolmaster from Cork. And he will be a major asset to the community: he is also a very skilled bacon-curer!'

JIMMY: Hugh —

HUGH: Ha-ha-ha-ha-ha! The Cork bacon-curer! *Barbarus hic ego sum quia non intelligor ulli* — James?

JIMMY: Ovid.

HUGH: *Procede.*

JIMMY: 'I am a barbarian in this place because I am not understood by anyone.'

HUGH: Indeed — [*Shouts.*] Manus! Tea! I will compose a satire on Master Bartley Timlin, schoolmaster and bacon-curer. But it will be too easy, won't it? [*Shouts.*] Strong tea! Black!

[*The only way Jimmy can get Hugh's attention is by standing in front of him and holding his arms.*]

JIMMY: Will you listen to me, Hugh!

HUGH: James. [*Shouts.*] And a slice of soda bread.

JIMMY: I'm going to get married.

HUGH: Well!

JIMMY: At Christmas.

HUGH: Splendid.

JIMMY: To Athene.

HUGH: Who?

JIMMY: Pallas Athene.

HUGH: *Glaukopis Athene?*

JIMMY: Flashing-eyed, Hugh, flashing-eyed! [*He attempts the gesture he has made before: standing to attention, the momentary spasm, the salute, the face raised in pained ecstasy — but the body does not respond efficiently this time. The gesture is grotesque.*]

HUGH: The lady has assented?

JIMMY: She asked *me* — I assented.

HUGH: Ah. When was this?

JIMMY: Last night.

HUGH: What does her mother say?

JIMMY: Metis from Hellespont? Decent people — good stock.

HUGH: And her father?

JIMMY: I'm meeting Zeus tomorrow. Hugh, will you be my best man?

HUGH: Honoured, James, profoundly honoured.

JIMMY: You know what I'm looking for, Hugh, don't you? I mean to say — you know — I — I — I joke like the rest of them — you know? — [*Again he attempts the pathetic routine but abandons it instantly.*] You know yourself, Hugh — don't you? — you know all that. But what I'm really looking for, Hugh — what I really want — companionship, Hugh — at my time of life, companionship, company, someone to talk to. Away up in Beann na Gaoithe — you've no idea how lonely it is. Companionship — correct, Hugh? Correct?

HUGH: Correct.

JIMMY: And I always liked her, Hugh. Correct?

HUGH: Correct, James.

JIMMY: Someone to talk to.

HUGH: Indeed.

JIMMY: That's all, Hugh. The whole story. You know it all now, Hugh. You know it all.

[*As Jimmy says those last lines he is crying, shaking his head, trying to keep his balance, and holding a finger up to his lips in absurd gestures of secrecy and intimacy. Now he staggers away, tries to sit on a stool, misses it, slides to the floor, his feet in front of him, his back against the broken cart. Almost at once he is asleep. Hugh watches all of this. Then he produces his flask and is about to pour a drink when he sees the Name-Book on the floor. He picks it up and leafs through it, pronouncing the strange names as he does. Just as he begins, Owen emerges and descends with two bowls of tea.*]

HUGH: Ballybeg. Burnfoot. King's Head. Whiteplains. Fair Hill. Dunboy. Green Bank.

[*Owen snatches the book from Hugh.*]

OWEN: I'll take that. [*In apology.*] It's only a catalogue of names.

HUGH: I know what it is.

OWEN: A mistake — my mistake — nothing to do with us. I hope that's strong enough [*tea*]. [*He throws the book on the table and crosses over to Jimmy.*] Jimmy. Wake up, Jimmy. Wake up, man.

JIMMY: What — what-what?

OWEN: Here. Drink this. Then go on away home. There may be trouble. Do you hear me, Jimmy? There may be trouble.

HUGH [*indicating Name-Book*]: We must learn those new names.

OWEN [*searching around*]: Did you see a sack lying about?

HUGH: We must learn where we live. We must learn to make them our own. We must make them our new home.

[*Owen finds a sack and throws it across his shoulders.*]

OWEN: I know where I live.

HUGH: James thinks he knows, too. I look at James and three thoughts occur to me: A — that it is not the literal past, the 'facts' of history, that shape us, but images of the past embodied in language. James has ceased to make that discrimination.

OWEN: Don't lecture me, Father.

HUGH: B — we must never cease renewing those images; because once we do, we fossilize. Is there no soda bread?

OWEN: And C, Father — one single, unalterable 'fact': if Yolland is not found, we are all going to be evicted. Lancey has issued the order.

HUGH: Ah. *Edictum imperatoris.*°

OWEN: You should change out of those wet clothes. I've got to go. I've got to see Doalty Dan Doalty.

HUGH: What about?

OWEN: I'll be back soon.

[*As Owen exits.*]

HUGH: Take care, Owen. To remember everything is a form of madness. [*He looks around the room, carefully, as if he were about to leave it forever. Then he looks at Jimmy, asleep again.*] The road to Sligo. A spring morning. 1798.° Going into battle. Do you remember, James? Two young gallants with pikes across their shoulders and the *Aeneid* in their pockets. Everything seemed to find definition that spring — a congruence, a miraculous matching of hope and past and present and possibility. Striding across the fresh, green land. The rhythms of perception heightened. The whole enterprise of consciousness accelerated. We were gods that morning, James; and I had recently married *my* goddess, Caitlin Dubh Nic Reactainn, may she rest in peace. And to leave

---

Edictum imperatoris: By imperial decree.
1798: Year of a rising against the British, resulting in defeat for the Irish.

her and my infant son in his cradle — that was heroic, too. By God, sir, we were magnificent. We marched as far as — where was it? — Glenties! All of twenty-three miles in one day. And it was there, in Phelan's pub, that we got homesick for Athens, just like Ulysses. The *desiderium nostrorum* — the need for our own. Our *pietas*, James, was for older, quieter things. And that was the longest twenty-three miles back I ever made. [*Toasts Jimmy.*] My friend, confusion is not an ignoble condition.

[*Maire enters.*]

MAIRE: I'm back again. I set out for somewhere but I couldn't remember where. So I came back here.

HUGH: Yes, I will teach you English, Maire Chatach.

MAIRE: Will you, Master? I must learn it. I need to learn it.

HUGH: Indeed you may well be my only pupil. [*He goes towards the steps and begins to ascend.*]

MAIRE: When can we start?

HUGH: Not today. Tomorrow, perhaps. After the funeral. We'll begin tomorrow. [*Ascending.*] But don't expect too much. I will provide you with the available words and the available grammar. But will that help you to interpret between privacies? I have no idea. But it's all we have. I have no idea at all. [*He is now at the top.*]

MAIRE: Master, what does the English word 'always' mean?

HUGH: *Semper — per omnia saecula.*° The Greeks called it 'aei'. It's not a word I'd start with. It's a silly word, girl.

[*He sits. Jimmy is awake. He gets to his feet. Maire sees the Name-Book, picks it up, and sits with it on her knee.*]

semper . . . saecula: Always, forever.

MAIRE: When he comes back, this is where he'll come to. He told me this is where he was happiest.

[*Jimmy sits beside Maire.*]

JIMMY: Do you know the Greek word *endogamein*? It means to marry within the tribe. And the word *exogamein* means to marry outside the tribe. And you don't cross those borders casually — both sides get very angry. Now, the problem is this: Is Athene sufficiently mortal or am I sufficiently godlike for the marriage to be acceptable to her people and to my people? You think about that.

HUGH: *Urbs antiqua fuit* — there was an ancient city which, 'tis said, Juno loved above all the lands. And it was the goddess's aim and cherished hope that here should be the capital of all nations — should the fates perchance allow that. Yet in truth she discovered that a race was springing from Trojan blood to overthrow some day these Tyrian towers — a people *late regem belloque superbum* — kings of broad realms and proud in war who would come forth for Lybia's downfall — such was — such was the course — such was the course ordained — ordained by fate . . . What the hell's wrong with me? Sure I know it backways. I'll begin again. *Urbs antiqua fuit* — there was an ancient city which, 'tis said, Juno loved above all the lands.

[*Begin to bring down the lights.*]

And it was the goddess's aim and cherished hope that here should be the capital of nations — should the fates perchance allow that. Yet in truth she discovered that a race was springing from Trojan blood to overthrow some day these Tyrian towers — a people kings of broad realms and proud in war who would come forth for Lybia's downfall . . .

Black

Caryl Churchill

Caryl Churchill (b. 1938) is in many ways a conventional middle-class woman. She was born in London to a comfortable family: her father was a political cartoonist and her mother a model. During World War II, her family emigrated to Canada, and much of her growing up was done in Montreal. She returned to England for college, receiving her degree in English literature at Oxford.

Churchill says that through all these years she did all the right things. She was a proper intellectual, a proper student, a proper person. She began writing plays in Oxford, where they were produced by students. After college, she married David Harter, also from Oxford, who became a lawyer in London. She raised three sons and at the same time tried to keep alive her dream of being a writer. Most of her early work was written for radio, and many of the plays were short. With so many children in the house, she says, it was difficult to sustain a long project.

Churchill's social conscience has been a significant part of her playwriting and her life. She found herself sometimes depressed by the dullness of the middle-class life demanded of the wife of a lawyer, and much of her early drama is satire directed at what many people thought was an enviable lifestyle.

In the early 1970s her husband left a very lucrative practice and has since devoted himself to helping the poor at a nearby legal aid center. She has become involved in theater groups, among them a group of women called Monstrous Regiment. She is closely aligned with the Royal Court Theatre in London, noted for producing satiric, biting, experimental drama with a punch.

Her first play staged at the Royal Court Theatre was a farcical but serious play called *Owners* (1972). It attacks the way that the concept of ownership destroys potential relationships. Churchill's basic socialist views are very apparent in the play, which is a critique of the values that most capitalists take for granted: being aggressive, getting ahead, doing well. Although this play is not explicitly feminist, Churchill combines socialism and feminism in most of her plays, thus producing an often unusual approach to her subject matter. *Owners* has been criticized for its Brechtian use of disconnected scenes and its loose plot, but when it was produced off Broadway in 1973 it marked Churchill as a serious playwright.

After a year as a playwright in residence at the Royal Court Theatre, Churchill produced *Objections to Sex and Violence* (1975). The play was not immensely successful, but it introduced themes of feminism into her work. Among other themes, the play examines in depth the domination of women by men and the relationship of violence to sex roles.

In 1976 Churchill produced *Vinegar Tom,* a play about witch hunts set in the seventeenth century. After researching witch trials, Churchill concluded that women were convenient scapegoats for men when times became difficult. A companion play also set in the seventeenth century is *Light Shining in*

Buckinghamshire, which studies revolutions. The play was developed by the Joint Stock Theatre Group and produced at the Royal Court Theatre to uniformly positive reviews.

Her first play to receive wide notice was *Cloud Nine* (1979). It treats several themes simultaneously, among them colonization. The first act is set in the Victorian era in a British colony of Africa. The play is broadly satirical, involving farcical moments in the relationships of colonialist and native, master and servant, and man and woman. Churchill cast certain parts of the play in a cross-gender fashion: a woman plays a sensitive schoolboy, a man plays an unfulfilled wife. The effect is both comic and instructive, since one of her most important purposes is to cast some light on gender distinctions. She said that she saw "parallels between the way colonizers treat the colonized and the way men tended to treat women in our own society." *Cloud Nine* was produced in the Lucille Lortel Theatre, where it ran for two years off Broadway and won an Obie award.

Top Girls (1982) played at the Royal Court Theatre in London and at the Public Theatre in New York, where the reviews were mixed. The play, essentially feminist in theme, was praised in England for being "the best British play ever from a woman dramatist." *Fen* (1983) was warmly praised by critics and audiences alike. A study of the effects of poverty on women, the play was developed with the Joint Stock Theatre Group and set in the area of England called the Fens, a flat country prone to flooding, where women work the fields and most of the people are poor.

Churchill's *Serious Money* (1987) is a verse play (like her first Oxford play) about the London stock market. It ran on Broadway to exceptional acclaim, partly because it played just after the stock market crash of October 1987. The play is a satiric study of those for whom only greed and getting ahead matter.

Churchill has written a number of plays for radio and television, such as *Lovesick, Abortive, Not Not Not Not Not Enough Oxygen, Schreber's Nervous Illness, The Hospital at the Time of the Revolution,* and *The Judge's Wife.* These are gathered in a volume called *Shorts* (1990). *The Skriker* (1994) is an experiment in fantasy, with a spirit world that parallels the real world. *Blue Heart* (1999) consists of two one-act plays: *Heart's Desire* and *Blue Kettle.* These are relatively realistic domestic dramas. *Heart's Desire* is a satire set in a sparkling kitchen where Alice and Brian wait, with Brian's sister Maisie, for the return of their daughter from Australia. Their peaceful setting is invaded by alcoholics and terrorists, among others, and yet the play has been described as "achingly, aggressively funny." *Blue Kettle* features a young man who searches for women who have given up children for adoption and then claims to be their lost son. It is a somber play and deals with the failure of language. Churchill has become one of the major dramatic voices of modern theater.

TOP GIRLS

Top Girls (1982), commissioned by the Royal Court Theatre in London, was first performed there under the direction of Max Stafford-Clark. Like many of the explosive Royal Court playwrights, Churchill had produced experimental, socially conscious plays that challenged the normal London and Broadway styles of production. She had established herself as a serious, significant writer.

The play has been produced in England and America by both important commercial theaters and smaller experimental and regional theaters. Although it is widely considered a feminist drama, Churchill is quick to point out that the play is often misunderstood; it is a critique not only of the dominance of males in the workplace but also of women who are satisfied to dominate the workplace in their turn and behave essentially like males. Churchill, an ardent socialist as well as a feminist, has said that *Top Girls* is an indictment of people, male or female, who get ahead at the cost of their humanity and their capacity to care for others.

The play opens with important legendary women gathering to share Marlene's celebration of her promotion with the Top Girls employment agency. The assembled group includes Pope Joan, a woman who posed as a man and became pope; Lady Nijo, a Japanese courtesan of the thirteenth century; Isabella Bird, a Victorian traveler who had many interesting adventures; Dull Gret, a figure from a Brueghel painting who led an attack on hell; and Patient Griselda, the obedient wife who inspired Chaucer.

Churchill creates characters who could be from a medieval allegory: Pope Joan succeeds by imitating a man physically; Lady Nijo succeeds by satisfying men; Isabella Bird attracts attention by displacing men (who were the legendary travelers); and Dull Gret and Patient Griselda, allegorical characters borrowed from other works of art, have their own ways of getting on in a "man's" world. Marlene is also allegorical: she stands for the woman who will succeed at all costs, including abandoning her own daughter.

Churchill alludes to medieval practice in another way. It was common in medieval poetic literature to tell stories about important historical and biblical women (as well as men). Such collections included incisive portraits of Eve, Cleopatra, the Witch of Endor, and Delilah. In the misogynist medieval period, such compilations of "top girls" focused on women who had caused scandal and harm to society. Such literature portrayed "bad girls."

One would think that the tables would be turned at the hands of a modern feminist, but Churchill's analysis is subtle. She demonstrates that Marlene and the other contemporary women have settled for demeaning themselves rather than demanding to re-create themselves. Most of the women in act II — Marlene, her coworkers, clients, and family — reveal their callousness, their indifference, and their basic incapacity to love. Marlene is unable to feel deeply even about those closest to her — her sister, her mother, and her daughter.

The ending of the play is a study of family relations. The failure of the two sisters is part of the message of the play. Marlene has paid an extraordinary price for her success. The play leaves us with the question of whether Marlene sees what she has done to herself and to her daughter and her sister. The play does not pull punches; it tries to illuminate the ways in which we make ourselves less human, less fulfilled, when we are driven to a success that is illusory and values that are false.

Top Girls in Performance

Max Stafford-Clark, the longtime director of London's Royal Court Theatre, helped Churchill develop the play and directed its first production in August 1982. With sixteen characters and seven actors, a good deal of multiple role-playing was required; for example, Deborah Finley played the roles of Isabella Bird, Joyce, and Mrs. Kidd, while Lindsay Duncan played Lady Nijo and Win. Gwen Taylor, who played Marlene, was the only actor not to play more than one role. This casting method is one of Churchill's frequent devices, as is the technique of having characters speak while other characters are talking.

Churchill originally wanted the play produced in three acts. However, consideration for the time taken by two intervals persuaded her to break the play into two acts, ending act one at what was originally act two, scene two. The production at the Royal Court Theatre was successful and drew good reviews. The play was then taken to Joseph Papp's Public Theatre in New York later in 1982, which led the *New York Time*'s Frank Rich to say, "*Top Girls* remains one of the few plays this season that allows its audience to watch a truly original theatrical mind at work." After its New York run, the play returned to the Royal Court Theatre in 1983. The Oxford Stage Company toured *Top Girls* in England in 2001 and brought it to London's Aldwych Theatre for a successful four-week run. James Forsythe directed the play at Brandon University in Canada in February 2002. *Top Girls* has been produced in regional theaters in the United States, England, and elsewhere to considerable acclaim.

Caryl Churchill (b. 1938)
TOP GIRLS

1982

Characters

MARLENE
WAITRESS/KIT/SHONA
ISABELLA BIRD/JOYCE/MRS. KIDD
LADY NIJO/WIN
DULL GRET/ANGIE
POPE JOAN/LOUISE
PATIENT GRISELDA/NELL/JEANINE

Act I
Scene I: *A Restaurant.*
Scene II: *Top Girls' Employment Agency, London.*
Scene III: *Joyce's backyard in Suffolk.*

Act II
Scene I: *Top Girls' Employment Agency.*
Scene II: *A Year Earlier. Joyce's kitchen.*

Production Note: *The seating order for Act I, Scene I in the original production at the Royal Court was (from right) Gret, Nijo, Marlene, Joan, Griselda, Isabella.*

The Characters

ISABELLA BIRD (1831–1904): Lived in Edinburgh, traveled extensively between the ages of forty and seventy.

LADY NIJO (b. 1258): Japanese, was an Emperor's courtesan and later a Buddhist nun who traveled on foot
through Japan.

DULL GRET: Is the subject of the Brueghel painting *Dulle
Griet,* in which a woman in an apron and armor
leads a crowd of women charging through hell and
fighting the devils.

POPE JOAN: Disguised as a man, is thought to have been
pope between 854 and 856.

PATIENT GRISELDA: Is the obedient wife whose story is
told by Chaucer in "The Clerk's Tale" of *The Canterbury Tales.*

The Layout: *A speech usually follows the one immediately before it but: (1) When one character starts speaking
before the other has finished, the point of interruption is
marked* /. *E.g.,*

ISABELLA: This is the Emperor of Japan? / I once met the
Emperor of Morocco.

NIJO: In fact he was the ex-Emperor.

*(2) A character sometimes continues speaking right
through another's speech. E.g.,*

ISABELLA: When I was forty I thought my life was over. /
Oh I was pitiful. I was

NIJO: I didn't say I felt it for twenty years. Not every
minute.

ISABELLA: sent on a cruise for my health and felt even
worse. Pains in my bones, pins and needles . . . etc.

*(3) Sometimes a speech follows on from a speech earlier
than the one immediately before it, and continuity is
marked*. E.g.,*

GRISELDA: I'd seen him riding by, we all had. And he'd
seen me in the fields with the sheep. *

ISABELLA: I would have been well suited to minding
sheep.

NIJO: And Mr. Nugent went riding by.

ISABELLA: Of course not, Nijo, I mean a healthy life in
the open air.

JOAN: *He just rode up while you were minding the
sheep and asked you to marry him?

*where "in the fields with the sheep" is the cue to both
"I would have been" and "He just rode up."*

ACT I • Scene I

*(Restaurant. Saturday night. There is a table with a
white cloth set for dinner with six places. The lights
come up on Marlene and the Waitress.)*

MARLENE: Excellent, yes, table for six. One of them's
going to be late but we won't wait. I'd like a bottle of
Frascati straight away if you've got one really cold.
(The Waitress goes. Isabella Bird arrives.) Here we
are. Isabella.

ISABELLA: Congratulations, my dear.

MARLENE: Well, it's a step. It makes for a party. I haven't
time for a holiday. I'd like to go somewhere exotic
like you but I can't get away. I don't know how you
could bear to leave Hawaii. / I'd like to lie

ISABELLA: I did think of settling.

MARLENE: in the sun forever, except of course I can't
bear sitting still.

ISABELLA: I sent for my sister Hennie to come and join
me. I said, Hennie we'll live here forever and help
the natives. You can buy two sirloins of beef for what
a pound of chops cost in Edinburgh. And Hennie
wrote back, the dear, that yes, she would come to
Hawaii if I wished, but I said she had far better stay
where she was. Hennie was suited to life in Tobermory.

MARLENE: Poor Hennie.

ISABELLA: Do you have a sister?

MARLENE: Yes in fact.

ISABELLA: Hennie was happy. She was good. I did miss
its face, my own pet. But I couldn't stay in Scotland. I
loathed the constant murk.

(Lady Nijo arrives.)

MARLENE *(seeing her)*: Ah! Nijo! *(The Waitress enters
with the wine.)*

NIJO: Marlene! *(To Isabella.)* So excited when Marlene
told me / you were coming.

ISABELLA: I'm delighted / to meet you.

MARLENE: I think a drink while we wait for the others. I
think a drink anyway. What a week. *(Marlene seats
Nijo. The Waitress pours the wine.)*

NIJO: It was always the men who used to get so drunk
I'd be one of the maidens, passing the sake.

ISABELLA: I've had sake.° Small hot drink. Quite fortify-
ing after a day in the wet.

NIJO: One night my father proposed three rounds of
three cups, which was normal, and then the Emperor
should have said three rounds of three cups, but he said
three rounds of nine cups, so you can imagine. Then the
Emperor passed his sake cup to my father and said, "Let
the wild goose come to me this spring."

MARLENE: Let the what?

NIJO: It's a literary allusion to a tenth-century epic, / His
Majesty was very cultured.

ISABELLA: This is the Emperor of Japan? / I once met the
Emperor of Morocco.

NIJO: In fact he was the ex-Emperor.

MARLENE: But he wasn't old? / Did you, Isabella?

NIJO: Twenty-nine.

ISABELLA: Oh it's a long story.

MARLENE: Twenty-nine's an excellent age.

NIJO: Well I was only fourteen and I knew he meant
something but I didn't know what. He sent me an
eight-layered gown and I sent it back. So when the
time came I did nothing but cry. My thin gowns were
badly ripped. But even that morning when he left /
he'd a green

sake: Japanese rice wine.

MARLENE: Are you saying he raped you?

NIJO: robe with a scarlet lining and very heavily embroidered trousers, I already felt different about him. It made me uneasy. No, of course not, Marlene, I belonged to him, it was what I was brought up for from a baby. I soon found I was sad if he stayed away. It was depressing day after day not knowing when he would come. I never enjoyed taking other women to him.

ISABELLA: I certainly never saw my father drunk. He was a clergyman. / And I didn't get married till I was fifty. (*The Waitress brings the menus.*)

NIJO: Oh, my father was a very religious man. Just before he died he said to me, "Serve His Majesty, be respectful, if you lose his favor enter holy orders."

MARLENE: But he meant stay in a convent, not go wandering round the country.

NIJO: Priests were often vagrants, so why not a nun? You think I shouldn't? / I still did what my father wanted.

MARLENE: No no, I think you should. / I think it was wonderful.

(*Dull Gret arrives.*)

ISABELLA: I tried to do what my father wanted.

MARLENE: Gret, good. Nijo. Gret / I know Griselda's going to be late, but should we wait for Joan? / Let's get you a drink.

ISABELLA: Hello, Gret! (*She continues to Nijo.*) I tried to be a clergyman's daughter. Needlework, music, charitable schemes. I had a tumor removed from my spine and spent a great deal of time on the sofa. I studied the metaphysical poets and hymnology. / I thought I enjoyed intellectual pursuits.

NIJO: Ah, you like poetry. I come of a line of eight generations of poets. Father had a poem / in the anthology.

ISABELLA: My father taught me Latin although I was a girl. / But really I was

MARLENE: They didn't have Latin at my school.

ISABELLA: more suited to manual work. Cooking, washing, mending, riding horses. / Better than reading

NIJO: Oh but I'm sure you're very clever.

ISABELLA: books, eh Gret? A rough life in the open air.

NIJO: I can't say I enjoyed my rough life. What I enjoyed most was being the Emperor's favorite / and wearing thin silk.

ISABELLA: Did you have any horses, Gret?

GRET: Pig.

(*Pope Joan arrives.*)

MARLENE: Oh Joan, thank God, we can order. Do you know everyone? We were just talking about learning Latin and being clever girls. Joan was by way of an infant prodigy. Of course you were. What excited you when you were ten?

JOAN: Because angels are without matter they are not individuals. Every angel is a species.

MARLENE: There you are. (*They laugh. They look at the menus.*)

ISABELLA: Yes, I forgot all my Latin. But my father was the mainspring of my life and when he died I was so grieved. I'll have the chicken, please, / and the soup.

NIJO: Of course you were grieved. My father was saying his prayers and he dozed off in the sun. So I touched his knee to rouse him. "I wonder what will happen," he said, and then he was dead before he finished the sentence. / If he'd

MARLENE: What a shock.

NIJO: died saying his prayers he would have gone straight to heaven. / Waldorf salad.

JOAN: Death is the return of all creatures to God.

NIJO: I shouldn't have woken him.

JOAN: Damnation only means ignorance of the truth. I was always attracted by the teachings of John the Scot, though he was inclined to confuse / God and the world.

ISABELLA: Grief always overwhelmed me at the time.

MARLENE: What I fancy is a rare steak. Gret?

ISABELLA: I am of course a member of the / Church of England.

MARLENE: Gret?

GRET: Potatoes.

MARLENE: I haven't been to church for years. / I like Christmas carols.

ISABELLA: Good works matter more than church attendance.

MARLENE: Make that two steaks and a lot of potatoes. Rare. But I don't do good works either.

JOAN: Canelloni, please, / and a salad.

ISABELLA: Well, I tried, but oh dear. Hennie did good works.

NIJO: The first half of my life was all sin and the second / all repentance.*

MARLENE: Oh what about starters?

GRET: Soup.

JOAN: *And which did you like best?

MARLENE: Were your travels just a penance? Avocado vinaigrette. Didn't you / enjoy yourself?

JOAN: Nothing to start with for me, thank you.

NIJO: Yes, but I was very unhappy. / It hurt to remember the past.

MARLENE: And the wine list.

NIJO: I think that was repentance.

MARLENE: Well I wonder.

NIJO: I might have just been homesick.

MARLENE: Or angry.

NIJO: Not angry, no, / why angry?

GRET: Can we have some more bread?

MARLENE: Don't you get angry? I get angry.

NIJO: But what about?

MARLENE: Yes let's have two more Frascati. And some more bread, please. (*The Waitress exits.*)

ISABELLA: I tried to understand Buddhism when I was in Japan but all this birth and death succeeding each other through eternities just filled me with the most profound melancholy. I do like something more active.

NIJO: You couldn't say I was inactive. I walked every day for twenty years.

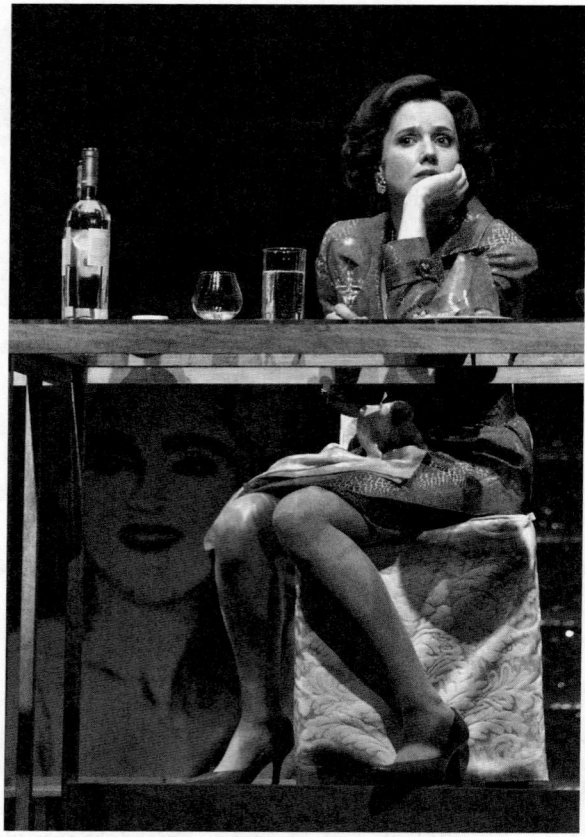

Bianca Amato as Marlene in the 2002–2003 Guthrie Lab production of *Top Girls* in Minneapolis, directed by Casey Stangl.

Eunice Wong as Win in *Top Girls* at the Guthrie Lab, 2002–2003.

ISABELLA: I don't mean walking. / I mean in the head.

NIJO: I vowed to copy five Mahayana sutras. / Do you know how long they are?

MARLENE: I don't think religious beliefs are something we have in common. Activity yes. (*Gret empties the bread basket into her apron.*)

NIJO: My head was active. / My head ached.

JOAN: It's no good being active in heresy.

ISABELLA: What heresy? She's calling the Church of England / a heresy.

JOAN: There are some very attractive / heresies.

NIJO: I had never heard of Christianity. Never / heard of it. Barbarians.

MARLENE: Well I'm not a Christian. / And I'm not a Buddhist.

ISABELLA: You have heard of it?

MARLENE: We don't all have to believe the same.

ISABELLA: I knew coming to dinner with a Pope we should keep off religion.

JOAN: I always enjoy a theological argument. But I won't try to convert you, I'm not a missionary. Anyway I'm a heresy myself.

ISABELLA: There are some barbaric practices in the east.

NIJO: Barbaric?

ISABELLA: Among the lower classes.

NIJO: I wouldn't know.

ISABELLA: Well theology always made my head ache.

MARLENE: Oh good, some food. (*The Waitress brings the first course, serves it during the following, then exits.*)

NIJO: How else could I have left the court if I wasn't a nun? When father died I had only His Majesty. So when I fell out of favor I had nothing. Religion is a kind of nothing / and I dedicated what was left of me to nothing.

ISABELLA: That's what I mean about Buddhism. It doesn't brace.

MARLENE: Come on, Nijo, have some wine.

NIJO: Haven't you ever felt like that? You've all felt / like that. Nothing will ever happen again. I am dead already.

ISABELLA: You thought your life was over but it wasn't.

JOAN: You wish it was over.

GRET: Sad.

MARLENE: Yes, when I first came to London I sometimes . . . and when I got back from America I did. But only for a few hours. Not twenty years.

ISABELLA: When I was forty I thought my life was over. / Oh I was pitiful. I was sent

NIJO: I didn't say I felt it for twenty years. Not every minute.

ISABELLA: on a cruise for my health and I felt even worse. Pains in my bones, pins and needles in my hands, swelling behind the ears, and — oh, stupidity. I shook all over, indefinable terror. And Australia seemed to me a hideous country, the acacias stank like drains. / I

NIJO: You were homesick. (*Gret steals a bottle of wine.*)

ISABELLA: had a photograph taken for Hennie but I told her I wouldn't send it, my hair had fallen out and my clothes were crooked, I looked completely insane and suicidal.

NIJO: So did I, exactly, dressed as a nun. / I was wearing walking shoes for the first time.

ISABELLA: I longed to go home, / but home to what? Houses are so perfectly dismal.*

NIJO: I longed to go back ten years.

MARLENE: *I thought traveling cheered you both up.

ISABELLA: Oh it did / of course. It was on

NIJO: I'm not a cheerful person, Marlene. I just laugh a lot.

ISABELLA: the trip from Australia to the Sandwich Isles, I fell in love with the sea. There were rats in the cabin and ants in the food but suddenly it was like a new world. I woke up every morning happy, knowing there would be nothing to annoy me. No nervousness. No dressing.

NIJO: Don't you like getting dressed? I adored my clothes. / When I was chosen

MARLENE: You had prettier colors than Isabella.

NIJO: to give sake to His Majesty's brother, the Emperor Kameyana, on his formal visit, I wore raw silk pleated trousers and a seven-layered gown in shades of red, and two outer garments, / yellow lined with green

MARLENE: Yes, all that silk must have been very — (*The Waitress enters, clears the first course and exits.*)

JOAN: I dressed as a boy when I left home.*

NIJO: and a light green jacket. Lady Betto had a five-layered gown in shades of green and purple.

ISABELLA: *You dressed as a boy?

MARLENE: Of course, / for safety.

JOAN: It was easy, I was only twelve. / Also women weren't allowed in the library. We wanted to study in Athens.

MARLENE: You ran away alone?

JOAN: No, not alone, I went with my friend. / He was

NIJO: Ah, an elopement.

JOAN: sixteen but I thought I knew more science than he did and almost as much philosophy.

ISABELLA: Well I always traveled as a lady and I repudi-

ated strongly any suggestion in the press that I was other than feminine.

MARLENE: I don't wear trousers in the office. / I could but I don't.

ISABELLA: There was no great danger to a woman of my age and appearance.

MARLENE: And you got away with it, Joan?

JOAN: I did then. (*The Waitress brings in the main course.*)

MARLENE: And nobody noticed anything?

JOAN: They noticed I was a very clever boy. / And

MARLENE: I couldn't have kept pretending for so long.

JOAN: when I shared a bed with my friend, that was ordinary — two poor students in a lodging house. I think I forgot I was pretending.

ISABELLA: Rocky Mountain Jim, Mr. Nugent, showed me no disrespect. He found it interesting, I think, that I could make scones and also lasso cattle. Indeed he declared his love for me, which was most distressing.

NIJO: What did he say? / We always sent poems first.

MARLENE: What did you say?

ISABELLA: I urged him to give up whiskey, / but he said it was too late.

MARLENE: Oh Isabella.

ISABELLA: He had lived alone in the mountains for many years.

MARLENE: But did you — ? (*The Waitress goes.*)

ISABELLA: Mr. Nugent was a man that any woman might love but none could marry. I came back to England.

NIJO: Did you write him a poem when you left? / Snow on the mountains. My sleeves

MARLENE: Did you never see him again?

ISABELLA: No, never.

NIJO: are wet with tears. In England no tears, no snow.

ISABELLA: Well, I say never. One morning very early in Switzerland, it was a year later, I had a vision of him as I last saw him / in his trapper's clothes with his

NIJO: A ghost!

ISABELLA: hair round his face, and that was the day, / I learned later, he died with a

NIJO: Ah!

ISABELLA: bullet in his brain. / He just bowed to me and vanished.

MARLENE: Oh Isabella.

NIJO: When your lover dies — One of my lovers died. / The priest Ariake.

JOAN: My friend died. Have we all got dead lovers?

MARLENE: Not me, sorry.

NIJO (*to Isabella*): I wasn't a nun, I was still at court, but he was a priest, and when he came to me he dedicated his whole life to hell. / He knew that when he died he would fall into one of the three lower realms. And he died, he did die.

JOAN (*to Marlene*): I'd quarreled with him over the teachings of John the Scot, who held that our ignorance of God is the same as his ignorance of himself. He only knows what he creates because he creates everything he knows but he himself is above being — do you follow?

MARLENE: No, but go on.

NIJO: I couldn't bear to think / in what shape would he be reborn.*

JOAN: St. Augustine maintained that the Neo-Platonic Ideas are indivisible

ISABELLA: *Buddhism is really most uncomfortable.

JOAN: from God, but I agreed with John that the created world is essences derived from Ideas which derived from God. As Denys the Areopagite said — the pseudo-Denys — first we give God a name, then deny it, / then reconcile the contradiction

NIJO: In what shape would he return?

JOAN: by looking beyond / those terms —

MARLENE: Sorry, what? Denys said what?

JOAN: Well we disagreed about it, we quarreled. And next day he was ill, / I was so annoyed with him

NIJO: Misery in this life and worse in the next, all because of me.

JOAN: all the time I was nursing him I kept going over the arguments in my mind. Matter is not a means of knowing the essence. The source of the species is the Idea. But then I realized he'd never understand my arguments again, and that night he died. John the Scot held that the individual disintegrates / and there is no personal immortality.

ISABELLA: I wouldn't have you think I was in love with Jim Nugent. It was yearning to save him that I felt.

MARLENE (to Joan): So what did you do?

JOAN: First I decided to stay a man. I was used to it. And I wanted to devote my life to learning. Do you know why I went to Rome? Italian men didn't have beards.

ISABELLA: The loves of my life were Hennie, my own pet, and my dear husband the doctor, who nursed Hennie in her last illness. I knew it would be terrible when Hennie died but I didn't know how terrible. I felt half of myself had gone. How could I go on my travels without that sweet soul waiting at home for my letters? It was Doctor Bishop's devotion to her in her last illness that made me decide to marry him. He and Hennie had the same sweet character. I had not.

NIJO: I thought His Majesty had sweet character because when he found out about Ariake he was so kind. But really it was because he no longer cared for me. One night he even sent me out to a man who had been pursuing me. / He lay awake on the other side of the screens and listened.

ISABELLA: I did wish marriage had seemed more of a step. I tried very hard to cope with the ordinary drudgery of life. I was ill again with carbuncles on the spine and nervous prostration. I ordered a tricycle, that was my idea of adventure then. And John himself fell ill, with erysipelas and anemia. I began to love him with my whole heart but it was too late. He was a skeleton with transparent white hands. I wheeled him on various seafronts in a bathchair. And he faded and left me. There was nothing in my life. The doctors said I had gout / and my heart was much affected.

NIJO: There was nothing in my life, nothing, without the Emperor's favor. The Empress had always been my enemy, Marlene, she said I had no right to wear three-layered gowns. / But I was the adopted daughter of my grandfather the Prime Minister. I had been publicly granted permission to wear thin silk.

JOAN: There was nothing in my life except my studies. I was obsessed with pursuit of the truth. I taught at the Greek School in Rome, which St. Augustine had made famous. I was poor, I worked hard, I spoke apparently brilliantly, I was still very young, I was a stranger, suddenly I was quite famous, I was everyone's favorite. Huge crowds came to hear me. The day after they made me cardinal I fell ill and lay two weeks without speaking, full of terror and regret. / But then I got up determined to

MARLENE: Yes, success is very . . .

JOAN: go on. I was seized again / with a desperate longing for the absolute.

ISABELLA: Yes, yes, to go on. I sat in Tobermory among Hennie's flowers and sewed a complete outfit in Jaeger flannel. / I was fifty-six years old.

NIJO: Out of favor but I didn't die. I left on foot, nobody saw me go. For the next twenty years I walked through Japan.

GRET: Walking is good. (*Meanwhile, the Waitress enters, pours lots of wine, then shows Marlene the empty bottle.*)

JOAN: Pope Leo died and I was chosen. All right then. I would be Pope. I would know God. I would know everything.

ISABELLA: I determined to leave my grief behind and set off for Tibet.

MARLENE: Magnificent all of you. We need some more wine, please, two bottles I think, Griselda isn't even here yet, and I want to drink a toast to you all. (*The Waitress exits.*)

ISABELLA: To yourself surely, / we're here to celebrate your success.

NIJO: Yes, Marlene.

JOAN: Yes, what is it exactly, Marlene?

MARLENE: Well it's not Pope but it is managing director.*

JOAN: And you find work for people.

MARLENE: Yes, an employment agency.

NIJO: *Over all the women you work with. And the men.

ISABELLA: And very well deserved too. I'm sure it's just the beginning of something extraordinary.

MARLENE: Well it's worth a party.

ISABELLA: To Marlene.*

MARLENE: And all of us.

JOAN: *Marlene.

NIJO: Marlene.

GRET: Marlene.

MARLENE: We've all come a long way. To our courage and the way we changed our lives and our extraordinary achievements. (*They laugh and drink a toast.*)

ISABELLA: Such adventures. We were crossing a mountain pass at seven thousand feet, the cook was all to pieces, the muleteers suffered fever and snow blindness. But even though my spine was agony I managed very well.*

MARLENE: Wonderful.

NIJO: *Once I was ill for four months lying alone at an inn. Nobody to offer a horse to Buddha. I had to live for myself, and I did live.

ISABELLA: Of course you did. It was far worse returning to Tobermory. I always felt dull when I was stationary. / That's why I could never stay anywhere.

NIJO: Yes, that's it exactly. New sights. The shrine by the beach, the moon shining on the sea. The goddess had vowed to save all living things. / She would even save the fishes. I was full of hope.

JOAN: I had thought the Pope would know everything. I thought God would speak to me directly. But of course he knew I was a woman.

MARLENE: But nobody else even suspected? (*The Waitress brings more wine and then exits.*)

JOAN: In the end I did take a lover again.*

ISABELLA: In the Vatican?

GRET: *Keep you warm.

NIJO: *Ah, lover.

MARLENE: *Good for you.

JOAN: He was one of my chamberlains. There are such a lot of servants when you're Pope. The food's very good. And I realized I did know the truth. Because whatever the Pope says, that's true.

NIJO: What was he like, the chamberlain?*

GRET: Big cock.

ISABELLA: Oh, Gret.

MARLENE: *Did he fancy you when he thought you were a fella?

NIJO: What was he like?

JOAN: He could keep a secret.

MARLENE: So you did know everything.

JOAN: Yes, I enjoyed being Pope. I consecrated bishops and let people kiss my feet. I received the King of England when he came to submit to the church. Unfortunately there were earthquakes, and some village reported it had rained blood, and in France there was a plague of giant grasshoppers, but I don't think that can have been my fault, do you?* (*Laughter.*) The grasshoppers fell on the English Channel / and were washed up on shore.

NIJO: I once went to sea. It was very lonely. I realized it made very little difference where I went.

JOAN: and their bodies rotted and poisoned the air and everyone in those parts died. (*Laughter.*)

ISABELLA: *Such superstition! I was nearly murdered in China by a howling mob. They thought the barbarians ate babies and put them under railway sleepers to make the tracks steady, and ground up their eyes to make the lenses of cameras. / So they were shouting,

MARLENE: And you had a camera!

ISABELLA: "Child-eater, child-eater." Some people tried to sell girl babies to Europeans for cameras or stew! (*Laughter.*)

MARLENE: So apart from the grasshoppers it was a great success.

JOAN: Yes, if it hadn't been for the baby I expect I'd have lived to an old age like Theodora of Alexandria, who lived as a monk. She was accused by a girl / who fell in love with her of being the father of her child and —

NIJO: But tell us what happened to your baby. I had some babies.

MARLENE: Didn't you think of getting rid of it?

JOAN: Wouldn't that be a worse sin than having it? / But a Pope with a child was about as bad as possible.

MARLENE: I don't know, you're the Pope.

JOAN: But I wouldn't have known how to get rid of it.

MARLENE: Other Popes had children, surely.

JOAN: They didn't give birth to them.

NIJO: Well you were a woman.

JOAN: Exactly and I shouldn't have been a woman. Women, children, and lunatics can't be Pope.

MARLENE: So the only thing to do / was to get rid of it somehow.

NIJO: You had to have it adopted secretly.

JOAN: But I didn't know what was happening. I thought I was getting fatter, but then I was eating more and sitting about, the life of a Pope is quite luxurious. I don't think I'd spoken to a woman since I was twelve. The chamberlain was the one who realized.

MARLENE: And by then it was too late.

JOAN: Oh I didn't want to pay attention. It was easier to do nothing.

NIJO: But you had to plan for having it. You had to say you were ill and go away.

JOAN: That's what I should have done I suppose.

MARLENE: Did you want them to find out?

NIJO: I too was often in embarrassing situations, there's no need for a scandal. My first child was His Majesty's, which unfortunately died, but my second was Akebono's. I was seventeen. He was in love with me when I was thirteen, he was very upset when I had to go the Emperor, it was very romantic, a lot of poems. Now His Majesty hadn't been near me for two months so he thought I was four months pregnant when I was really six, so when I reached the ninth month / I announced I was seriously ill,

JOAN: I never knew what month it was.

NIJO: and Akebono announced he had gone on a religious retreat. He held me round the waist and lifted me up as the baby was born. He cut the cord with a short sword, wrapped the baby in white and took it away. It was only a girl but I was sorry to lose it. Then I told the Emperor that the baby had miscarried because of my illness, and there you are. The danger was past.

JOAN: But, Nijo, I wasn't used to having a woman's body.

ISABELLA: So what happened?

JOAN: I didn't know of course that it was near the time. It was Rogation Day, there was always a procession. I was on the horse dressed in my robes and a cross was carried in front of me, and all the cardinals were following, and all the clergy of Rome, and a huge crowd of people. / We set off from St. Peter's to go

MARLENE: Total Pope. (*Gret pours the wine and steals the bottle.*)

The Oxford Stage Company production of *Top Girls* in 2002 at London's Aldwych Theatre with the following cast (from left to right): Helen Anderson as Lady Nijo, Joanna Scanlan as Pope Joan, Hattie Ladbury as Marlene, Sophie Shaw as Patient Griselda, and Elizabeth Berrington as Isabella Bird.

JOAN: to St. John's. I had felt a slight pain earlier, I thought it was something I'd eaten, and then it came back, and came back more often. I thought when this is over I'll go to bed. There were still long gaps when I felt perfectly all right and I didn't want to attract attention to myself and spoil the ceremony. Then I suddenly realized what it must be. I had to last out till I could get home and hide. Then something changed, my breath started to catch, I couldn't plan things properly anymore. We were in a little street that goes between St. Clement's and the Colosseum, and I just had to get off the horse and sit down for a minute. Great waves of pressure were going through my body, I heard sounds like a cow lowing, they came out of my mouth. Far away I heard people screaming, "The Pope is ill, the Pope is dying." And the baby just slid out onto the road.*

MARLENE: The cardinals / won't have known where to put themselves.

NIJO: Oh dear, Joan, what a thing to do! In the street!

ISABELLA: *How embarrassing.

GRET: In a field, yah. (*They are laughing.*)

JOAN: One of the cardinals said, "The Antichrist!" and fell over in a faint. (*They all laugh.*)

MARLENE: So what did they do? They weren't best pleased.

JOAN: They took me by the feet and dragged me out of town and stoned me to death. (*They stop laughing.*)

MARLENE: Joan, how horrible.

JOAN: I don't really remember.

NIJO: And the child died too?

JOAN: Oh yes, I think so, yes. (*The Waitress enters to clear the plates. Pause. They start talking very quietly.*)

ISABELLA (*to Joan*): I never had any children. I was very fond of horses.

NIJO (*to Marlene*): I saw my daughter once. She was three years old. She wore a plum-red / small sleeved gown. Akebono's wife

ISABELLA: Birdie was my favorite. A little Indian bay mare I rode in the Rocky Mountains.

NIJO: had taken the child because her own died. Everyone thought I was just a visitor. She was being brought up carefully so she could be sent to the palace like I was. (*Gret steals her empty plate.*)

ISABELLA: Legs of iron and always cheerful, and such a pretty face. If a stranger led her she reared up like a bronco.

NIJO: I never saw my third child after he was born, the son of Ariake the priest. Ariake held him on his lap the day he was born and talked to him as if he could understand, and cried. My fourth child was Ariake's too. Ariake died before he was born. I didn't want to see anyone, I stayed alone in the hills. It was a boy again, my third son. But oddly enough I felt nothing for him.

MARLENE: How many children did you have, Gret?

GRET: Ten.

ISABELLA: Whenever I came back to England I felt I had so much to atone for. Hennie and John were so good. I did no good in my life. I spent years in self-gratification. So I hurled myself into committees, I nursed the people of Tobermory in the epidemic of influenza, I lectured the Young Women's Christian Association on Thrift. I talked and talked explaining how the East was corrupt and vicious. My travels must do good to someone besides myself. I wore myself out with good causes.

MARLENE (*pause*): Oh God, why are we all so miserable?

JOAN (*pause*): The procession never went down that street again.

MARLENE: They rerouted it specially?

JOAN: Yes they had to go all round to avoid it. And they introduced a pierced chair.

MARLENE: A pierced chair?

JOAN: Yes, a chair made out of solid marble with a hole in the seat / and it was

MARLENE: You're not serious.

JOAN: in the Chapel of the Savior, and after he was elected the Pope had to sit in it.

MARLENE: And someone looked up his skirts? / Not really!

ISABELLA: What an extraordinary thing.

JOAN: Two of the clergy / made sure he was a man.

NIJO: On their hands and knees!

MARLENE: A pierced chair!

GRET: Balls!

(*Griselda arrives unnoticed.*)

NIJO: Why couldn't he just pull up his robe?

JOAN: He had to sit there and look dignified.

MARLENE: You could have made all your chamberlains sit in it.*

GRET: Big one. Small one.

NIJO: Very useful chair at court.

ISABELLA: *Or the Laird of Tobermory in his kilt.

(*They are quite drunk. They get the giggles. Marlene notices Griselda and gets up to welcome her. The others go on talking and laughing. Gret crosses to Joan and Isabella and pours them wine from her stolen bottles. The Waitress gives out the menus.*)

MARLENE: Griselda! / There you are. Do you want to eat?

GRISELDA: I'm sorry I'm so late. No, no, don't bother.

MARLENE: Of course it's no bother. / Have you eaten?

GRISELDA: No really, I'm not hungry.

MARLENE: Well have some pudding.

GRISELDA: I never eat pudding.

MARLENE: Griselda, I hope you're not anorexic. We're having pudding, I am, and getting nice and fat.

GRISELDA: Oh if everyone is. I don't mind.

MARLENE: Now who do you know? This is Joan who was Pope in the ninth century, and Isabella Bird, the Victorian traveler, and Lady Nijo from Japan, Emperor's concubine and Buddhist nun, thirteenth century, nearer your own time, and Gret who was painted by Brueghel. Griselda's in Boccaccio and Petrarch and Chaucer because of her extraordinary marriage. I'd like profiteroles because they're disgusting.

JOAN: Zabaglione, please.

ISABELLA: Apple pie / and cream.

NIJO: What's this?

MARLENE: Zabaglione, it's Italian, it's what Joan's having, / it's delicious.

NIJO: A Roman Catholic / dessert? Yes please.

MARLENE: Gret?

GRET: Cake.

GRISELDA: Just cheese and biscuits, thank you. (*The Waitress exits.*)

MARLENE: Yes, Griselda's life is like a fairy story, except it starts with marrying the prince.

GRISELDA: He's only a marquis, Marlene.

MARLENE: Well everyone for miles around is his liege and he'd absolute lord of life and death and you were the poor but beautiful peasant girl and he whisked you off. / Near enough a prince.

NIJO: How old were you?

GRISELDA: Fifteen.

NIJO: I was brought up in court circles and it was still a shock. Had you ever seen him before?

GRISELDA: I'd seen him riding by, we all had. And he'd seen me in the fields with the sheep.*

ISABELLA: I would have been well suited to minding sheep.

NIJO: And Mr. Nugent riding by.

ISABELLA: Of course not, Nijo, I mean a healthy life in the open air.

JOAN: *He just rode up while you were minding the sheep and asked you to marry him?

GRISELDA: No, no, it was on the wedding day. I was waiting outside the door to see the procession. Everyone wanted him to get married so there'd be an heir to look after us when he died, / and at last he

MARLENE: I don't think Walter wanted to get married. It is Walter? Yes.

GRISELDA: announced a day for the wedding but nobody knew who the bride was, we thought it must be a foreign princess, we were longing to see her. Then the carriage stopped outside our cottage and we couldn't see the bride anywhere. And he came and spoke to my father.

NIJO: And your father told you to serve the Prince.

GRISELDA: My father could hardly speak. The Marquis said it wasn't an order, I could say no, but if I said yes I must always obey him in everything.

MARLENE: That's when you should have suspected.

GRISELDA: But of course a wife must obey her husband. / And of course I must obey the Marquis.*

ISABELLA: I swore to obey dear John, of course, but it didn't seem to arise. Naturally I wouldn't have wanted to go abroad while I was married.

MARLENE: *Then why bother to mention it at all? He'd got a thing about it, that's why.

GRISELDA: I'd rather obey the Marquis than a boy from the village.

MARLENE: Yes, that's a point.

JOAN: I never obeyed anyone. They all obeyed me.

NIJO: And what did you wear? He didn't make you get married in your own clothes? That would be perverse.*

MARLENE: Oh, you wait.

GRISELDA: *He had ladies with him who undressed me and they had a white silk dress and jewels for my hair.

MARLENE: And at first he seemed perfectly normal?

GRISELDA: Marlene, you're always so critical of him. / Of course he was normal, he was very kind.

MARLENE: But, Griselda, come on, he took your baby.

GRISELDA: Walter found it hard to believe I loved him. He couldn't believe I would always obey him. He had to prove it.

MARLENE: I don't think Walter likes women.

GRISELDA: I'm sure he loved me, Marlene, all the time.

MARLENE: He just had a funny way / of showing it.

GRISELDA: It was hard for him too.

JOAN: How do you mean he took away your baby?

NIJO: Was it a boy?

GRISELDA: No, the first one was a girl.

NIJO: Even so it's hard when they take it away. Did you see it at all?

GRISELDA: Oh yes, she was six weeks old.

NIJO: Much better to do it straight away.

ISABELLA: But why did your husband take the child?

GRISELDA: He said all the people hated me because I was just one of them. And now I had a child they were restless. So he had to get rid of the child to keep them quiet. But he said he wouldn't snatch her, I had to agree and obey and give her up. So when I was feeding her a man came in and took her away. I thought he was going to kill her even before he was out of the room.

MARLENE: But you let him take her? You didn't struggle?

GRISELDA: I asked him to give her back so I could kiss her. And I asked him to bury her where no animals could dig her up. / It was Walter's child to do what he

ISABELLA: Oh, my dear.

GRISELDA: liked with.*

MARLENE: Walter was bonkers.

GRET: Bastard.

ISABELLA: *But surely, murder.

GRISELDA: I had promised.

MARLENE: I can't stand this. I'm going for a pee.

(Marlene goes out. The Waitress brings the dessert, serves it during the following, then exits.)

NIJO: No, I understand. Of course you had to, he was your life. And were you in favor after that?

GRISELDA: Oh yes, we were very happy together. We never spoke about what had happened.

ISABELLA: I can see you were doing what you thought was your duty. But didn't it make you ill?

GRISELDA: No, I was very well, thank you.

NIJO: And you had another child?

GRISELDA: Not for four years, but then I did, yes, a boy.

NIJO: Ah a boy. / So it all ended happily.

GRISELDA: Yes he was pleased. I kept my son till he was two years old. A peasant's grandson. It made the people angry. Walter explained.

ISABELLA: But surely he wouldn't kill his children / just because —

GRISELDA: Oh it wasn't true. Walter would never give in to the people. He wanted to see if I loved him enough.

JOAN: He killed his children / to see if you loved him enough?

NIJO: Was it easier the second time or harder?

GRISELDA: It was always easy because I always knew I would do what he said. (*Pause. They start to eat.*)

ISABELLA: I hope you didn't have any more children.

GRISELDA: Oh no, no more. It was twelve years till he tested me again.

ISABELLA: So whatever did he do this time? / My poor John, I never loved him enough, and he would never have dreamt . . .

GRISELDA: He sent me away. He said the people wanted him to marry someone else who'd give him an heir and he'd got special permission from the Pope. So I said I'd go home to my father. I came with nothing / so I went with nothing. I took

NIJO: Better to leave if your master doesn't want you.

GRISELDA: off my clothes. He let me keep a slip so he wouldn't be shamed. And I walked home barefoot. My father came out in tears. Everyone was crying except me.

NIJO: At least your father wasn't dead. / I had nobody.

ISABELLA: Well it can be a relief to come home. I loved to see Hennie's sweet face again.

GRISELDA: Oh yes, I was perfectly content. And quite soon he sent for me again.

JOAN: I don't think I would have gone.

GRISELDA: But he told me to come. I had to obey him. He wanted me to help prepare his wedding. He was getting married to a young girl from France / and nobody except me knew how to arrange things the way he liked them.

NIJO: It's always hard taking him another woman. (*Marlene comes back.*)

JOAN: I didn't live a woman's life. I don't understand it.

GRISELDA: The girl was sixteen and far more beautiful than me. I could see why he loved her. / She had her younger brother with her as a page. (*The Waitress enters.*)

MARLENE: Oh God, I can't bear it. I want some coffee. Six coffees. Six brandies. / Double brandies. Straightaway. (*The Waitress exits.*)

GRISELDA: They all went into the feast I'd prepared. And he stayed behind and put his arms round me and kissed me. / I felt half asleep with the shock.

NIJO: Oh, like a dream.

MARLENE: And he said, "This is your daughter and your son."

GRISELDA: Yes.

JOAN: What?

NIJO: Oh. Oh I see. You got them back.

ISABELLA: I did think it was remarkably barbaric to kill them but you learn not to say anything. / So he had them brought up secretly I suppose.

MARLENE: Walter's a monster. Weren't you angry? What did you do?

GRISELDA: Well I fainted. Then I cried and kissed the children. / Everyone was making a fuss of me.

NIJO: But did you feel anything for them?

GRISELDA: What?

NIJO: Did you feel anything for the children?

GRISELDA: Of course, I loved them.

JOAN: So you forgave him and lived with him?

GRISELDA: He suffered so much all those years.

ISABELLA: Hennie had the same sweet nature.

NIJO: So they dressed you again?

GRISELDA: Cloth of gold.

JOAN: I can't forgive anything.

MARLENE: You really are exceptional, Griselda.

NIJO: Nobody gave me back my children. (*She cries.*)

(*The Waitress brings the brandies and then exits. During the following, Joan goes to Nijo.*)

ISABELLA: I can never be like Hennie. I was always so busy in England, a kind of business I detested. The very presence of people exhausted my emotional reserves. I could not be like Hennie however I tried. I tried and was as ill as could be. The doctor suggested a steel net to support my head, the weight of my own head was too much for my diseased spine. It is dangerous to put oneself in depressing circumstances. Why should I do it?

JOAN (*to Nijo*): Don't cry.

NIJO: My father and the Emperor both died in the autumn. So much pain.

JOAN: Yes, but don't cry.

NIJO: They wouldn't let me into the palace when he was dying. I hid in the room with his coffin, then I couldn't find where I'd left my shoes, I ran after the funeral procession in bare feet, I couldn't keep up. When I got there it was over, a few wisps of smoke in the sky, that's all that was left of him. What I want to know is, if I'd still been at court, would I have been allowed to wear full mourning?

MARLENE: I'm sure you would.

NIJO: Why do you say that? You don't know anything about it. Would I have been allowed to wear full mourning?

ISABELLA: How can people live in this dim pale island and wear our hideous clothes? I cannot and will not live the life of a lady.

NIJO: I'll tell you something that made me angry. I was eighteen, at the Full Moon Ceremony. They make a special rice gruel and stir it with their sticks, and then they beat their women across the loins so they'll have sons and not daughters. So the Emperor beat us all / very hard as

MARLENE: What a sod. (*The Waitress enters with the coffees.*)

NIJO: usual — that's not it, Marlene, that's normal, what made us angry he told his attendants they could beat us too. Well they had a wonderful time. / So Lady Genki and I made a plan, and the ladies

MARLENE: I'd like another brandy, please. Better make it six. (*The Waitress exits.*)

NIJO: all hid in his rooms, and Lady Mashimizu stood guard with a stick at the door, and when His Majesty came in Genki seized him and I beat him till he cried out and promised he would never order anyone to hit us again. Afterward there was a terrible fuss. The nobles were horrified. "We wouldn't even dream of stepping on Your Majesty's shadow." And I had hit him with a stick. Yes, I hit him with a stick.

(*The Waitress brings the brandy bottle and tops up the glasses. Joan crosses in front of the table and back to her place while drunkenly reciting:*)

JOAN: Suave, mari magno turantibus aequora ventis,
e terra magnum alterius spectare laborem;
non quia vexari quemquamst iucunda voluptas,
sed quibus ipse malis careas quia cernere suave est.
Suave etiam belli certamina magna tueri
per campos instructa tua sine parse pericli.
Sed nil dulcius est, bene quam munita tenere
edita doctrine sapientum temple serena, /
despicere uncle queas alios passimque videre
errare atque viam palantis quaerere vitae,

GRISELDA: I do think — I do wonder — it would have been nicer if Walter hadn't had to.

ISABELLA: Why should I? Why should I?

MARLENE: Of course not.

NIJO: I hit him with a stick.

JOAN: certare ingenio, contendere nobilitate,
noctes atque dies niti praestante labore
ad summas emergere opes rerumque potiri.
O miseras hominum mentis, / o pectora caeca!*°

ISABELLA: O miseras!

NIJO: *Pectora caeca!

JOAN: qualibus in tenebris vitae quantisque periclis
degitur hoc aevi quodcumquest! / none videre
nil aliud sibi naturam latrare, nisi utqui
corpore seiunctus dolor absit, mente fruatur° . . .
    (*She subsides.*)

GRET: We come to hell through a big mouth. Hell's black and red. / It's

MARLENE (*to Joan*): Shut up, pet.

GRISELDA: Hush, please.

Suave, . . . o pectora caeca!: Joan's speech is from the Second Book of *On the Nature of Things* by Titus Lucretius Carus (97?–54 B.C.), the Latin poet and philosopher. The following translation of the passage is by Cyril Bailey: Sweet it is, when on the great sea the winds are buffeting the waters, to gaze from the land on another's great struggles; not because it is pleasure or joy that any one should be distressed, but because it is sweet to perceive from what misfortune you yourself are free. Sweet is it too, to behold great contests of war in full array over the plains, when you have no part in the danger. But nothing is more gladdening than to dwell in the calm high places, firmly embattled on the heights by the teaching of the wise, whence you can look down on others, and see them wandering hither and thither, going astray as they seek the way of life, in strife matching their wits or rival claims of birth, struggling night and day by surpassing effort to rise up to the height of power and gain possession of the world. Ah! miserable minds of men, blind hearts! **qualibus . . . fruatur:** In what darkness of life, in what great dangers ye spend this little span of years! to think that ye should not see that nature cries aloud for nothing else but that pain may be kept far sundered from the body, and that, withdrawn from care and fear, she may enjoy in mind the sense of pleasure!

ISABELLA: Listen, she's been to hell.

GRET: like the village where I come from. There's a river and a bridge and houses. There's places on fire like when the soldiers come. There's a big devil sat on a roof with a big hole in his arse and he's scooping stuff out of it with a big ladle and it's falling down on us, and it's money, so a lot of the women stop and get some. But most of us is fighting the devils. There's lots of little devils, our size, and we get them down all right and give them a beating. There's lots of funny creatures round your feet, you don't like to look, like rats and lizards, and nasty things, a bum with a face, and fish with legs, and faces on things that don't have faces on. But they don't hurt, you just keep going. Well we'd had worse, you see, we'd had the Spanish. We'd all had family killed. My big son die on a wheel. Birds eat him. My baby, a soldier run her through with a sword. I'd had enough, I was mad, I hate the bastards. I come out of my front door that morning and shout till my neighbors come out and I said, "Come on, we're going where the evil come from and pay the bastards out." And they all come out just as they was / from baking or

NIJO: All the ladies come.

GRET: washing in their aprons, and we push down the street and the ground opens up and we go through a big mouth into a street just like ours but in hell. I've got a sword in my hand from somewhere and I fill a basket with gold cups they drink out of down there. You just keep running on and fighting, / you didn't stop for nothing. Oh we give them devils such a beating.*

NIJO: Take that, take that.

JOAN: *Something something something mortisque timores

tum vacuum pectus° — damn.

Quod si ridicula —
something something on and on and on
and something splendorem purpureai.

ISABELLA: I thought I would have a last jaunt up the west river in China. Why not? But the doctors were so very grave I just went to Morocco. The sea was so wild I had to be landed by ship's crane in a coal bucket. / My horse was a terror to me, a powerful black charger.

GRET: Coal bucket good.

JOAN: nos in luce timemus
something
terrorem°

(Nijo is laughing and crying. Joan gets up and is sick. Griselda looks after her.)

GRISELDA: Can I have some water, please? (The Waitress exits.)

ISABELLA: So off I went to visit the Berber sheikhs in full blue trousers and great brass spurs. I was the only European woman ever to have seen the Emperor of Morocco. I was (the Waitress brings the water) seventy years old. What lengths to go to for a last chance of joy. I knew my return of vigor was only temporary, but how marvelous while it lasted.

Scene II

("Top Girls" Employment Agency. Monday morning. The lights come up on Marlene and Jeanine.)

MARLENE: Right, Jeanine, you are Jeanine aren't you? Let's have a look. O's and A's°. / No A's, all those

JEANINE: Six O's.

MARLENE: O's you probably could have got an A. / Speeds, not brilliant, not too bad.

JEANINE: I wanted to go to work.

MARLENE: Well, Jeanine, what's your present job like?

JEANINE: I'm a secretary.

MARLENE: Secretary or typist?

JEANINE: I did start as a typist but the last six months I've been a secretary.

MARLENE: To?

JEANINE: To three of them, really, they share me. There's Mr. Ashford, he's the office manager, and Mr. Philly / is sales, and —

MARLENE: Quite a small place?

JEANINE: A bit small.

MARLENE: Friendly?

JEANINE: Oh it's friendly enough.

MARLENE: Prospects?

JEANINE: I don't think so, that's the trouble. Miss Lewis is secretary to the managing director and she's been there forever, and Mrs. Bradford / is —

MARLENE: So you want a job with better prospects?

JEANINE: I want a change.

MARLENE: So you'll take anything comparable?

JEANINE: No, I do want prospects. I want more money.

MARLENE: You're getting — ?

JEANINE: Hundred.

MARLENE: It's not bad you know. You're what? Twenty?

Something . . . pectus: Fragments from Lucretius meaning "the dread of death leaves your heart empty . . ." Quod . . . pur-pureai. . . . nos in luce . . . terrorem: Fragments from the following passage by Lucretius: But if we see that these thoughts are mere mirth and mockery, and in very truth the fears of men and the cares that dog them fear not the clash of arms nor the weapons of war, but pass boldly among kings and lords of the world, nor dread the glitter that comes from gold nor the bright sheen of the purple robe, can you doubt that all such power belongs to reason alone, above all when the whole of life is but a struggle in darkness? For even as children tremble and fear everything in blinding darkness, so we sometimes dread in the light things that are no whit more to be feared than what children shudder at in the dark.   O's and A's: O-level and A-level examinations in the British education system. An O-level is a public examination for secondary-school students testing basic knowledge in various subjects; it is required before advancement to more specialized courses of study. A-level exams require advanced knowledge in a subject and are taken at the end of secondary school, usually two years after O-levels.

JEANINE: I'm saving to get married.

MARLENE: Does that mean you don't want a long-term job, Jeanine?

JEANINE: I might do.

MARLENE: Because where do the prospects come in? No kids for a bit?

JEANINE: Oh no, not kids, not yet.

MARLENE: So you won't tell them you're getting married?

JEANINE: Had I better not?

MARLENE: It would probably help.

JEANINE: I'm not wearing a ring. We thought we wouldn't spend on a ring.

MARLENE: Saves taking it off.

JEANINE: I wouldn't take it off.

MARLENE: There's no need to mention it when you go for an interview. / Now, Jeanine, do you have a feel

JEANINE: But what if they ask?

MARLENE: for any particular kind of company?

JEANINE: I thought advertising.

MARLENE: People often do think advertising. I have got a few vacancies but I think they're looking for something glossier.

JEANINE: You mean how I dress? / I can

MARLENE: I mean experience.

JEANINE: dress different. I dress like this on purpose for where I am now.

MARLENE: I have a marketing department here of a knitwear manufacturer. / Marketing is near enough

JEANINE: Knitwear?

MARLENE: advertising. Secretary to the marketing manager, he's thirty-five, married, I've sent him a girl before and she was happy, left to have a baby, you won't want to mention marriage there. He's very fair I think, good at his job, you won't have to nurse him along. Hundred and ten, so that's better than you're doing now.

JEANINE: I don't know.

MARLENE: I've a fairly small concern here, father and two sons, you'd have more say potentially, secretarial and reception duties, only a hundred but the job's going to grow with the concern and then you'll be in at the top with new girls coming in underneath you.

JEANINE: What is it they do?

MARLENE: Lampshades. / This would be my first choice for you.

JEANINE: Just lampshades?

MARLENE: There's plenty of different kinds of lampshade. So we'll send you there, shall we, and the knitwear second choice. Are you free to go for an interview any day they call you?

JEANINE: I'd like to travel.

MARLENE: We don't have any foreign clients. You'd have to go elsewhere.

JEANINE: Yes I know. I don't really . . . I just mean . . .

MARLENE: Does your fiancé want to travel?

JEANINE: I'd like a job where I was here in London and with him and everything but now and then — I expect it's silly. Are there jobs like that?

MARLENE: There's personal assistant to a top executive in a multinational. If that's the idea you need to be planning ahead. Is that where you want to be in ten years?

JEANINE: I might not be alive in ten years.

MARLENE: Yes but you will be. You'll have children.

JEANINE: I can't think about ten years.

MARLENE: You haven't got the speeds anyway. So I'll send you to these two shall I? You haven't been to any other agency? Just so we don't get crossed wires. Now, Jeanine, I want you to get one of these jobs, all right? If I send you that means I'm putting myself on the line for you. Your presentation's OK, you look fine, just be confident and go in there convinced that this is the best job for you and you're the best person for the job. If you don't believe it they won't believe it.

JEANINE: Do you believe it?

MARLENE: I think you could make me believe it if you put your mind to it.

JEANINE: Yes, all right.

Scene III

(*Joyce's back yard. Sunday afternoon. The house with a back door is upstage. Downstage is a shelter made of junk, made by children. The lights come up on two girls, Angie and Kit, who are squashed together in the shelter. Angie is sixteen, Kit is twelve. They cannot be seen from the house.*)

JOYCE (*off, calling from the house*): Angie. Angie, are you out there?

(*Silence. They keep still and wait. When nothing else happens they relax.*)

ANGIE: Wish she was dead.

KIT: Wanna watch *The Exterminator*?

ANGIE: You're sitting on my leg.

KIT: There's nothing on telly. We can have an ice cream. Angie?

ANGIE: Shall I tell you something?

KIT: Do you wanna watch *The Exterminator*?

ANGIE: It's X, innit?

KIT: I can get into Xs.

ANGIE: Shall I tell you something?

KIT: We'll go to something else. We'll go to Ipswich. What's on the Odeon?

ANGIE: She won't let me, will she.

KIT: Don't tell her.

ANGIE: I've no money.

KIT: I'll pay.

ANGIE: She'll moan though, won't she.

KIT: I'll ask her for you if you like.

ANGIE: I've no money, I don't want you to pay.

KIT: I'll ask her.

ANGIE: She don't like you.

KIT: I still got three pounds birthday money. Did she say she don't like me? I'll go by myself then.

ANGIE: Your mum don't let you. I got to take you.

KIT: She won't know.

ANGIE: You'd be scared who'd sit next to you.

KIT: No I wouldn't. She does like me anyway. Tell me then.

ANGIE: Tell you what?

KIT: It's you she doesn't like.

ANGIE: Well I don't like her so tough shit.

JOYCE (off): Angie. Angie. Angie. I know you're out there. I'm not coming out after you. You come in here. (Silence. Nothing happens.)

ANGIE: Last night when I was in bed. I been thinking yesterday could I make things move. You know, make things move by thinking about them without touching them. Last night I was in bed and suddenly a picture fell down off the wall.

KIT: What picture?

ANGIE: My gran, that picture. Not the poster. The photograph in the frame.

KIT: Had you done something to make it fall down?

ANGIE: I must have done.

KIT: But were you thinking about it?

ANGIE: Not about it, but about something.

KIT: I don't think that's very good.

ANGIE: You know the kitten?

KIT: Which one?

ANGIE:: There only is one. The dead one.

KIT: What about it?

ANGIE: I heard it last night.

KIT: Where?

ANGIE: Out here. In the dark. What if I left you here in the dark all night?

KIT: You couldn't. I'd go home.

ANGIE: You couldn't.

KIT: I'd / go home.

ANGIE: No you couldn't, not if I said.

KIT: I could.

ANGIE: Then you wouldn't see anything. You'd just be ignorant.

KIT: I can see in the daytime.

ANGIE: No you can't. You can't hear it in the daytime.

KIT: I don't want to hear it.

ANGIE: You're scared that's all.

KIT: I'm not scared of anything.

ANGIE: You're scared of blood.

KIT: It's not the same kitten anyway. You just heard an old cat, / you just heard some old cat.

ANGIE: You don't know what I heard. Or what I saw. You don't know nothing because you're a baby.

KIT: You're sitting on me.

ANGIE: Mind my hair / you silly cunt.

KIT: Stupid fucking cow, I hate you.

ANGIE: I don't care if you do.

KIT: You're horrible.

ANGIE: I'm going to kill my mother and you're going to watch.

KIT: I'm not playing.

ANGIE: You're scared of blood. (Kit puts her hand under dress, brings it out with blood on her finger.)

KIT: There, see, I got my own blood, so. (Angie takes Kit's hand and licks her finger.)

ANGIE: Now I'm a cannibal. I might turn into a vampire now.

KIT: That picture wasn't nailed up right.

ANGIE: You'll have to do that when I get mine.

KIT: I don't have to.

ANGIE: You're scared.

KIT: I'll do it, I might do it. I don't have to just because you say. I'll be sick on you.

ANGIE: I don't care if you are sick on me, I don't mind sick. I don't mind blood. If I don't get away from here I'm going to die.

KIT: I'm going home.

ANGIE. You can't go through the house. She'll see you.

KIT: I won't tell her.

ANGIE: Oh great, fine.

KIT: I'll say I was by myself. I'll tell her you're at my house and I'm going there to get you.

ANGIE: She knows I'm here, stupid.

KIT: Then why can't I go through the house?

ANGIE: Because I said not.

KIT: My mum don't like you anyway.

ANGIE: I don't want her to like me. She's a slag.

KIT: She is not.

ANGIE: She does it with everyone.

KIT: She does not.

ANGIE: You don't even know what it is.

KIT: Yes I do.

ANGIE: Tell me then.

KIT: We get it all at school, cleverclogs. It's on television. You haven't done it.

ANGIE: How do you know?

KIT: Because I know you haven't.

ANGIE: You know wrong then because I have.

KIT: Who with?

ANGIE: I'm not telling you / who with.

KIT: You haven't anyway.

ANGIE: How do you know?

KIT: Who with?

ANGIE: I'm not telling you.

KIT: You said you told me everything.

ANGIE: I was lying wasn't I.

KIT: Who with? You can't tell me who with because / you never —

ANGIE: Sh.

(Joyce has come out of the house. She stops halfway across the yard and listens. They listen.)

JOYCE: You there Angie? Kit? You there Kitty? Want a cup of tea? I've got some chocolate biscuits. Come on now I'll put the kettle on. Want a choccy biccy, Angie? (They all listen and wait.) Fucking rotten little cunt. You can stay there and die. I'll lock the door.

(They all wait. Joyce goes back to the house. Angie and Kit sit in silence for a while.)

KIT: When there's a war, where's the safest place?

ANGIE: Nowhere.

KIT: New Zealand is, my mum said. Your skin's burned right off. Shall we go to New Zealand?

ANGIE: I'm not staying here.

KIT: Shall we go to New Zealand?

ANGIE: You're not old enough.

KIT: You're not old enough.

ANGIE: I'm old enough to get married.

KIT: You don't want to get married.

ANGIE: No but I'm old enough.

KIT: I'd find out where they were going to drop it and stand right in the place.

ANGIE: You couldn't find out.

KIT: Better than walking round with your skin dragging on the ground. Eugh. / Would you like walking round with your skin dragging on the ground?

ANGIE: You couldn't find out, stupid, it's a secret.

KIT: Where are you going?

ANGIE: I'm not telling you.

KIT: Why?

ANGIE: It's a secret.

KIT: But you tell me all your secrets.

ANGIE: Not the true secrets.

KIT: Yes you do.

ANGIE: No I don't.

KIT: I want to go somewhere away from the war.

ANGIE: Just forget the war.

KIT: I can't.

ANGIE: You have to. It's so boring.

KIT: I'll remember it at night.

ANGIE: I'm going to do something else anyway.

KIT: What? Angie, come on. Angie.

ANGIE: It's a true secret.

KIT: It can't be worse than the kitten. And killing your mother. And the war.

ANGIE: Well I'm not telling you so you can die for all I care.

KIT: My mother says there's something wrong with you playing with someone my age. She says why haven't you got friends your own age. People your own age know there's something funny about you. She says you're a bad influence. She says she's going to speak to your mother. (*Angie twists Kit's arm till she cries out.*)

ANGIE: Say you're a liar.

KIT: She said it not me.

ANGIE: Say you eat shit.

KIT: You can't make me. (*Angie lets go.*)

ANGIE: I don't care anyway. I'm leaving.

KIT: Go on then.

ANGIE: You'll all wake up one morning and find I've gone.

KIT: Go on then.

ANGIE: You'll wake up one morning and find I've gone.

KIT: Good.

ANGIE: I'm not telling you when.

KIT: Go on then.

ANGIE: I'm sorry I hurt you.

KIT: I'm tired.

ANGIE: Do you like me?

KIT: I don't know.

ANGIE: You do like me.

KIT: I'm going home. (*She gets up.*)

ANGIE: No you're not.

KIT: I'm tired.

ANGIE: She'll see you.

KIT: She'll give me a chocolate biscuit.

ANGIE: Kitty.

KIT: Tell me where you're going.

ANGIE: Sit down.

KIT (*sitting down again*): Go on then.

ANGIE: Swear?

KIT: Swear.

ANGIE: I'm going to London. To see my aunt.

KIT: And what?

ANGIE: That's it.

KIT: I see my aunt all the time.

ANGIE: I don't see my aunt.

KIT: What's so special?

ANGIE: It is special. She's special.

KIT: Why?

ANGIE: She is.

KIT: Why?

ANGIE: She is.

KIT: Why?

ANGIE: My mother hates her.

KIT: Why?

ANGIE: Because she does.

KIT: Perhaps she's not very nice.

ANGIE: She is nice.

KIT: How do you know?

ANGIE: Because I know her.

KIT: You said you never see her.

ANGIE: I saw her last year. You saw her.

KIT: Did I?

ANGIE: Never mind.

KIT: I remember her. That aunt. What's so special?

ANGIE: She gets people jobs.

KIT: What's so special?

ANGIE: I think I'm my aunt's child. I think my mother's really my aunt.

KIT: Why?

ANGIE: Because she goes to America, now shut up.

KIT: I've been to London.

ANGIE: Now give us a cuddle and shut up because I'm sick.

KIT: You're sitting on my arm.

(*They curl up in each other's arms. Silence. Joyce comes out of the house and comes up to them quietly.*)

JOYCE: Come on.

KIT: Oh hello.

JOYCE: Time you went home.

KIT: We want to go to the Odeon.

JOYCE: What time?

KIT: Don't know.

JOYCE: What's on?

KIT: Don't know.

JOYCE: Don't know much do you?

KIT: That all right then?

JOYCE: Angie's got to clean her room first.

ANGIE: No I don't.

JOYCE: Yes you do, it's a pigsty.

ANGIE: Well I'm not.

JOYCE: Then you're not going. I don't care.

ANGIE: Well I am going.

JOYCE: You've no money, have you?

ANGIE: Kit's paying anyway.

JOYCE: No she's not.

KIT: I'll help you with your room.

JOYCE: That's nice.

ANGIE: No you won't. You wait here.

KIT: Hurry then.

ANGIE: I'm not hurrying. You just wait. (*Angie goes slowly into the house. Silence.*)

JOYCE: I don't know. (*Silence.*) How's school then?

KIT: All right.

JOYCE: What are you now? Third year?

KIT: Second year.

JOYCE: Your mum says you're good at English. (*Silence.*) Maybe Angie should've stayed on.

KIT: She didn't like it.

JOYCE: I didn't like it. And look at me. If your face fits at school it's going to fit other places too. It wouldn't make no difference to Angie. She's not going to get a job when jobs are hard to get. I'd be sorry for anyone in charge of her. She'd better get married. I don't know who'd have her, mind. She's one of those girls might never leave home. What do you want to be when you grow up, Kit?

KIT: Physicist.

JOYCE: What?

KIT: Nuclear physicist.

JOYCE: Whatever for?

KIT: I could, I'm clever.

JOYCE: I know you're clever, pet. (*Silence.*) I'll make a cup of tea. (*Silence.*) Looks like it's going to rain. (*Silence.*) Don't you have friends your own age?

KIT: Yes.

JOYCE: Well then.

KIT: I'm old for my age.

JOYCE: And Angie's simple is she? She's not simple.

KIT: I love Angie.

JOYCE: She's clever in her own way.

KIT: You can't stop me.

JOYCE: I don't want to.

KIT: You can't, so.

JOYCE: Don't be cheeky, Kitty. She's always kind to little children.

KIT: She's coming so you better leave me alone.

(*Angie comes out. She has changed into an old best dress, slightly small for her.*)

JOYCE: What you put that on for? Have you done your room? You can't clean your room in that.

ANGIE: I looked in the cupboard and it was there.

JOYCE: Of course it was there, it's meant to be there. Is that why it was a surprise, finding something in the right place? I should think she's surprised, wouldn't you, Kit, to find something in her room in the right place.

ANGIE: I decided to wear it.

JOYCE: Not today, why? To clean your room? You're not going to the pictures till you've done your room. You can put your dress on after if you like. (*Angie picks up a brick.*) Have you done your room? You're not getting out of it, you know.

KIT: Angie, let's go.

JOYCE: She's not going till she's done her room.

KIT: It's starting to rain.

JOYCE: Come on, come on then. Hurry and do your room, Angie, and then you can go to the cinema with Kit. Oh it's wet, come on. We'll look up the time in the paper. Does your mother know, Kit, it's going to be a late night for you, isn't it? Hurry up, Angie. You'll spoil your dress. You make me sick. (*Joyce and Kit run into the house. Angie stays where she is. There is the sound of rain. Kit comes out of the house.*)

KIT (*shouting*): Angie. Angie, come on, you'll get wet. (*She comes back to Angie.*)

ANGIE: I put on this dress to kill my mother.

KIT: I suppose you thought you'd do it with a brick.

ANGIE: You can kill people with a brick. (*She puts the brick down.*)

KIT: Well you didn't, so.

ACT II • *Scene 1*

(*"Top Girls" Employment Agency. Monday morning. There are three desks in the main office and a separate small interviewing area. The lights come up in the main office on Win and Nell who have just arrived for work.*)

NELL: Coffee coffee coffee coffee / coffee.

WIN: The roses were smashing. / Mermaid.

NELL: Ohhh.

WIN: Iceberg. He taught me all their names. (*Nell has some coffee now.*)

NELL: Ah. Now then.

WIN: He has one of the finest rose gardens in West Sussex. He exhibits.

NELL: He what?

WIN: His wife was visiting her mother. It was like living together.

NELL: Crafty, you never said.

WIN: He rang on Saturday morning.

NELL: Lucky you were free.

WIN: That's what I told him.

NELL: Did you hell.

WIN: Have you ever seen a really beautiful rose garden?

NELL: I don't like flowers. / I like swimming pools.

WIN: Marilyn. Esther's Baby. They're all called after birds.

NELL: Our friend's late. Celebrating all weekend I bet you.

WIN: I'd call a rose Elvis. Or John Conteh.

NELL: Is Howard in yet?

WIN: If he is he'll be bleeping us with a problem.

NELL: Howard can just hang on to himself.

WIN: Howard's really cut up.

NELL: Howard thinks because he's a fella the job was his as of right. Our Marlene's got far more balls than Howard and that's that.

WIN: Poor little bugger.

NELL: He'll live.

WIN: He'll move on.

NELL: I wouldn't mind a change of air myself.

WIN: Serious?

NELL: I've never been a staying-put lady. Pastures new.

WIN: So who's the pirate?

NELL: There's nothing definite.

WIN: Inquiries?

NELL: There's always inquiries. I'd think I'd got bad breath if there stopped being inquiries. Most of them can't afford me. Or you.

WIN: I'm all right for the time being. Unless I go to Australia.

NELL: There's not a lot of room upward.

WIN: Marlene's filled it up.

NELL: Good luck to her. Unless there's some prospects moneywise.

WIN: You can but ask.

NELL: Can always but ask.

WIN: So what have we got? I've got a Mr. Holden I saw last week.

NELL: Any use?

WIN: Pushy. Bit of a cowboy.

NELL: Goodlooker?

WIN: Good dresser.

NELL: High flyer?

WIN: That's his general idea certainly but I'm not sure he's got it up there.

NELL: Prestel wants six flyers and I've only seen two and a half.

WIN: He's making a bomb on the road but he thinks it's time for an office. I sent him to IBM but he didn't get it.

NELL: Prestel's on the road.

WIN: He's not overbright.

NELL: Can he handle an office?

WIN: Provided his secretary can punctuate he should go far.

NELL: Bear Prestel in mind then, I might put my head round the door. I've got that poor little nerd I should never had said I could help. Tender heart me.

WIN: Tender like old boots. How old?

NELL: Yes well forty-five.

WIN: Say no more.

NELL: He knows his place, he's not after calling himself a manager, he's just a poor little bod wants a better commission and a bit of sunshine.

WIN: Don't we all.

NELL: He's just got to relocate. He's got a bungalow in Dymchurch.

WIN: And his wife says.

NELL: The lady wife wouldn't care to relocate. She's going through the change.

WIN: It's his funeral, don't waste your time.

NELL: I don't waste a lot.

WIN: Good weekend you?

NELL: You could say.

WIN: Which one?

NELL: One Friday, one Saturday.

WIN: Aye — aye.

NELL: Sunday night I watched telly.

WIN: Which of them do you like best really?

NELL: Sunday was best, I like the Ovaltine.

WIN: Holden, Barker, Gardner, Duke.

NELL: I've a lady here thinks she can sell.

WIN: Taking her on?

NELL: She's had some jobs.

WIN: Services?

NELL: No, quite heavy stuff, electric.

WIN: Tough bird like us.

NELL: We could do with a few more here.

WIN: There's nothing going here.

NELL: No but I always want the tough ones when I see them. Hang on to them.

WIN: I think we're plenty.

NELL: Derek asked me to marry him again.

WIN: He doesn't know when he's beaten.

NELL: I told him I'm not going to play house, not even in Ascot.

WIN: Mind you, you could play house.

NELL: If I chose to play house I would play house ace.

WIN: You could marry him and go on working.

NELL: I could go on working and not marry him.

(*Marlene arrives.*)

MARLENE: Morning ladies. (*Win and Nell cheer and whistle.*) Mind my head.

NELL: Coffee coffee coffee.

WIN: We're tactfully not mentioning you're late.

MARLENE: Fucking tube.

WIN: We've heard that one.

NELL: We've used that one.

WIN: It's the top executive doesn't come in as early as the poor working girl.

MARLENE: Pass the sugar and shut your face, pet.

WIN: Well I'm delighted.

NELL: Howard's looking sick.

WIN: Howard is sick. He's got ulcers and heart. He told me.

NELL: He'll have to stop then, won't he?

WIN: Stop what?

NELL: Smoking, drinking, shouting. Working.

WIN: Well, working.

NELL: We're just looking through the day.

MARLENE: I'm doing some of Pam's ladies. They've been piling up while she's away.

NELL: Half a dozen little girls and an arts graduate who can't type.

WIN: I spent the whole weekend at his place in Sussex.

NELL: She fancies his rose garden.

WIN: I had to lie down in the back of the car so the neighbors wouldn't see me go in.

NELL: You're kidding.

WIN: It was funny.

NELL: Fuck that for a joke.

WIN: It was funny.

MARLENE: Anyway they'd see you in the garden.

WIN: The garden has extremely high walls.

NELL: I think I'll tell the wife.

WIN: Like hell.

NELL: She might leave him and you could have the rose garden.

WIN: The minute it's not a secret I'm out on my ear.

NELL: Don't know why you bother.

WIN: Bit of fun.

NELL: I think it's time you went to Australia.

WIN: I think it's pushy Mr. Holden time.

NELL: If you've any really pretty bastards, Marlene, I want some for Prestel.

MARLENE: I might have one this afternoon. This morning it's all Pam's secretarial.

NELL: Not long now and you'll be upstairs watching over us all.

MARLENE: Do you feel bad about it?

NELL: I don't like coming second.

MARLENE: Who does?

WIN: We'd rather it was you than Howard. We're glad for you, aren't we, Nell?

NELL: Oh yes. Aces.

(*Louise enters the interviewing area. The lights cross-fade to Win and Louise in the interviewing area. Nell exits.*)

WIN: Now, Louise, hello, I have your details here. You've been very loyal to the one job I see.

LOUISE: Yes I have.

WIN: Twenty-one years is a long time in one place.

LOUISE: I feel it is. I feel it's time to move on.

WIN: And you are what age now?

LOUISE: I'm in my early forties.

WIN: Exactly?

LOUISE: Forty-six.

WIN: It's not necessarily a handicap, well it is of course we have to face that, but it's not necessarily a disabling handicap, experience does count for something.

LOUISE: I hope so.

WIN: Now between ourselves is there any trouble, any reason why you're leaving that wouldn't appear on the form?

LOUISE: Nothing like that.

WIN: Like what?

LOUISE: Nothing at all.

WIN: No long-term understandings come to a sudden end, making for an insupportable atmosphere?

LOUISE: I've always completely avoided anything like that at all.

WIN: No personality clashes with your immediate superiors or inferiors?

LOUISE: I've always taken care to get on very well with everyone.

WIN: I only ask because it can affect the reference and it also affects your motivation, I want to be quite clear why you're moving on. So I take it the job itself no longer satisfies you. Is it the money?

LOUISE: It's partly the money. It's not so much the money.

WIN: Nine thousand is very respectable. Have you dependents?

LOUISE: No, no dependents. My mother died.

WIN: So why are you making a change?

LOUISE: Other people make changes.

WIN: But why are you, now, after spending most of your life in the one place?

LOUISE: There you are, I've lived for that company, I've given my life really you could say because I haven't had a great deal of social life, I've worked in the evenings. I haven't had office entanglements for the very reason you just mentioned and if you are committed to your work you don't move in many other circles. I had management status from the age of twenty-seven and you'll appreciate what that means. I've built up a department. And there it is, it works extremely well, and I feel I'm stuck there. I've spent twenty years in middle management. I've seen young men who I trained go on, in my own company or elsewhere, to higher things. Nobody notices me, I don't expect it, I don't attract attention by making mistakes, everybody takes it for granted that my work is perfect. They will notice me when I go, they will be sorry I think to lose me, they will offer me more money of course, I will refuse. They will see when I've gone what I was doing for them.

WIN: If they offer you more money you won't stay?

LOUISE: No I won't.

WIN: Are you the only woman?

LOUISE: Apart from the girls of course, yes. There was one, she was my assistant, it was the only time I took on a young woman assistant, I always had my doubts. I don't care greatly for working with women, I think I pass as a man at work. But I did take on this young woman, her qualifications were excellent, and she did well, she got a department of her own, and left the company for a competitor where she's now on the board and good luck to her. She has a different style, she's a new kind of attractive well dressed — I don't mean I don't dress properly. But there is a kind of woman who is thirty now who grew up in a different climate. They are not so careful. They take themselves for granted. I have had to justify my existence every minute, and I have done so, I have proved — well.

WIN: Let's face it, vacancies are ones where you'll be in competition with younger men. And there are companies that will value your experience enough that you'll be in with a chance. There are also fields that are easier for a woman, there is a cosmetic company here where your experience might be relevant. It's eight and a half, I don't know if that appeals.

LOUISE: I've proved I can earn money. It's more important to get away. I feel it's now or never. I sometimes / think —

WIN: You shouldn't talk too much at an interview.

LOUISE: I don't. I don't normally talk about myself. I know very well how to handle myself in an office situation. I only talk to you because it seems to me this is different, it's your job to understand me, surely. You asked the questions.

WIN: I think I understand you sufficiently.

LOUISE: Well good, that's good.

WIN: Do you drink?

LOUISE: Certainly not. I'm not a teetotaler, I think that's very suspect, it's seen as being an alcoholic if you're teetotal. What do you mean? I don't drink. Why?

WIN: I drink.

LOUISE: I don't.

WIN: Good for you.

(*The lights crossfade to the main office with Marlene sitting at her desk. Win and Louise exit. Angie arrives in the main office.*)

ANGIE: Hello.

MARLENE: Have you an appointment?

ANGIE: It's me. I've come.

MARLENE: What? It's not Angie?

ANGIE: It was hard to find this place. I got lost.

MARLENE: How did you get past the receptionist? The girl on the desk, didn't she try to stop you?

ANGIE: What desk?

MARLENE: Never mind.

ANGIE: I just walked in. I was looking for you.

MARLENE: Well you found me.

ANGIE: Yes.

MARLENE: So where's your mum? Are you up in town for the day?

ANGIE: Not really.

MARLENE: Sit down. Do you feel all right?

ANGIE: Yes thank you.

MARLENE: So where's Joyce?

ANGIE: She's at home.

MARLENE: Did you come up on a school trip then?

ANGIE: I've left school.

MARLENE: Did you come up with a friend?

ANGIE: No. There's just me.

MARLENE: You came up by yourself, that's fun. What have you been doing? Shopping? Tower of London?

ANGIE: No, I just come here. I come to you.

MARLENE: That's very nice of you to think of paying your aunty a visit. There's not many nieces make that the first port of call. Would you like a cup of coffee?

ANGIE: No thank you.

MARLENE: Tea, orange?

ANGIE: No thank you.

MARLENE: Do you feel all right?

ANGIE: Yes thank you.

MARLENE: Are you tired from the journey?

ANGIE: Yes, I'm tired from the journey.

MARLENE: You sit there for a bit then. How's Joyce?

ANGIE: She's all right.

MARLENE: Same as ever.

ANGIE: Oh yes.

MARLENE: Unfortunately you've picked a day when I'm rather busy, if there's ever a day when I'm not, or I'd take you out to lunch and we'd go to Madame Tussaud's. We could go shopping. What time do you have to be back? Have you got a day return?

ANGIE: No.

MARLENE: So what train are you going back on?

ANGIE: I came on the bus.

MARLENE: So what bus are you going back on? Are you staying the night?

ANGIE: Yes.

MARLENE: Who are you staying with? Do you want me to put you up for the night, is that it?

ANGIE: Yes please.

MARLENE: I haven't got a spare bed.

ANGIE: I can sleep on the floor.

MARLENE: You can sleep on the sofa.

ANGIE: Yes please.

MARLENE: I do think Joyce might have phoned me. It's like her.

ANGIE: This is where you work is it?

MARLENE: It's where I have been working the last two years but I'm going to move into another office.

ANGIE: It's lovely.

MARLENE: My new office is nicer than this. There's just the one big desk in it for me.

ANGIE: Can I see it?

MARLENE: Not now, no, there's someone else in it now. But he's leaving at the end of next week and I'm going to do his job.

ANGIE: Is that good?

MARLENE: Yes, it's very good.

ANGIE: Are you going to be in charge?

MARLENE: Yes I am.

ANGIE: I knew you would be.

MARLENE: How did you know?

ANGIE: I knew you'd be in charge of everything.

MARLENE: Not quite everything.

ANGIE: You will be.

MARLENE: Well we'll see.

ANGIE: Can I see it next week then?

MARLENE: Will you still be here next week?

ANGIE: Yes.

MARLENE: Don't you have to go home?

ANGIE: No.

MARLENE: Why not?

ANGIE: It's all right.

MARLENE: Is it all right?

ANGIE: Yes, don't worry about it.

MARLENE: Does Joyce know where you are?

ANGIE: Yes of course she does.

MARLENE: Well does she?

ANGIE: Don't worry about it.

MARLENE: How long are you planning to stay with me then?

ANGIE: You know when you came to see us last year?

MARLENE: Yes, that was nice wasn't it.

ANGIE: That was the best day of my whole life.

MARLENE: So how long are you planning to stay?

ANGIE: Don't you want me?

MARLENE: Yes yes, I just wondered.

ANGIE: I won't stay if you don't want me.

MARLENE: No, of course you can stay.

ANGIE: I'll sleep on the floor. I won't be any bother.

MARLENE: Don't get upset.

ANGIE: I'm not, I'm not. Don't worry about it.

(*Mrs. Kidd comes in.*)

MRS. KIDD: Excuse me.

MARLENE: Yes.

MRS. KIDD: Excuse me.

MARLENE: Can I help you?

MRS. KIDD: Excuse me bursting in on you like this but I have to talk to you.

MARLENE: I am engaged at the moment. / If you could go to reception —

MRS. KIDD: I'm Rosemary Kidd, Howard's wife, you don't recognize me but we did meet, I remember you of course / but you wouldn't —

MARLENE: Yes of course, Mrs. Kidd, I'm sorry, we did meet. Howard's about somewhere I expect, have you looked in his office?

MRS. KIDD: Howard's not about, no. I'm afraid it's you I've come to see if I could have a minute or two.

MARLENE: I do have an appointment in five minutes.

MRS. KIDD: This won't take five minutes. I'm very sorry. It is a matter of some urgency.

MARLENE: Well of course. What can I do for you?

MRS. KIDD: I just wanted a chat, an informal chat. It's not something I can simply — I'm sorry if I'm interrupting your work. I know office work isn't like housework / which is all interruptions.

MARLENE: No no, this is my niece. Angie. Mrs. Kidd.

MRS. KIDD: Very pleased to meet you.

ANGIE: Very well thank you.

MRS. KIDD: Howard's not in today.

MARLENE: Isn't he?

MRS. KIDD: He's feeling poorly.

MARLENE: I didn't know. I'm sorry to hear that.

MRS. KIDD: The fact is he's in a state of shock. About what's happened.

MARLENE: What has happened?

MRS. KIDD: You should know if anyone. I'm referring to you being appointed managing director instead of Howard. He hasn't been at all well all weekend. He hasn't slept for three nights. I haven't slept.

MARLENE: I'm sorry to hear that, Mrs. Kidd. Has he thought of taking sleeping pills?

MRS. KIDD: It's very hard when someone has worked all these years.

MARLENE: Business life is full of little setbacks. I'm sure Howard knows that. He'll bounce back in a day or two. We all bounce back.

MRS. KIDD: If you could see him you'd know what I'm talking about. What's it going to do to him working for a woman? I think if it was a man he'd get over it as something normal.

MARLENE: I think he's going to have to get over it.

MRS. KIDD: It's me that bears the brunt. I'm not the one that's been promoted. I put him first every inch of the way. And now what do I get? You women this, you women that. It's not my fault. You're going to have to be very careful how you handle him. He's very hurt.

MARLENE: Naturally I'll be tactful and pleasant to him, you don't start pushing someone around. I'll consult him over any decisions affecting his department. But that's no different, Mrs. Kidd, from any of my other colleagues.

MRS. KIDD: I think it is different, because he's a man.

MARLENE: I'm not quite sure why you came to see me.

MRS. KIDD: I had to do something.

MARLENE: Well you've done it, you've seen me. I think that's probably all we've time for. I'm sorry he's been taking it out on you. He really is a shit, Howard.

MRS. KIDD: But he's got a family to support. He's got three children. It's only fair.

MARLENE: Are you suggesting I give up the job to him then?

MRS. KIDD: It had crossed my mind if you were unavailable after all for some reason, he would be the natural second choice I think, don't you? I'm not asking.

MARLENE: Good.

MRS. KIDD: You mustn't tell him I came. He's very proud.

MARLENE: If he doesn't like what's happening here he can go and work somewhere else.

MRS. KIDD: Is that a threat?

MARLENE: I'm sorry but I do have some work to do.

MRS. KIDD: It's not that easy, a man of Howard's age. You don't care. I thought he was going too far but he's right. You're one of these ballbreakers, / that's what you

MARLENE: I'm sorry but I do have some work to do.

MRS. KIDD: are. You'll end up miserable and lonely. You're not natural.

MARLENE: Could you please piss off?

MRS. KIDD: I thought if I saw you at least I'd be doing something. (*Mrs. Kidd goes.*)

MARLENE: I've got to go and do some work now. Will you come back later?

ANGIE: I think you were wonderful.

MARLENE: I've got to go and do some work now.

ANGIE: You told her to piss off.

MARLENE: Will you come back later?

ANGIE: Can't I stay here?

MARLENE: Don't you want to go sightseeing?

ANGIE: I'd rather stay here.

MARLENE: You can stay here I suppose, if it's not boring.

ANGIE: It's where I most want to be in the world.

MARLENE: I'll see you later then.

(*Marlene goes. Shona and Nell enter the interviewing area. Angie sits at Win's desk. The lights crossfade to Nell and Shona in the interviewing area.*)

NELL: Is this right? You are Shona?

SHONA: Yeh.

NELL: It says here you're twenty-nine.

SHONA: Yeh.

NELL: Too many late nights, me. So you've been where you are for four years, Shona, you're earning six basic and three commission. So what's the problem?

SHONA: No problem.

NELL: Why do you want a change?

SHONA: Just a change.

NELL: Change of product, change of area?

SHONA: Both.

NELL: But you're happy on the road?

SHONA: I like driving.

NELL: You're not after management status?

SHONA: I would like management status.

NELL: You'd be interested in titular management status but not come off the road?

SHONA: I want to be on the road, yeh.

NELL: So how many calls have you been making a day?

SHONA: Six.

NELL: And what proportion of those are successful?

SHONA: Six.

NELL: That's hard to believe.

SHONA: Four.

NELL: You find it easy to get the initial interest do you?

SHONA: Oh yeh, I get plenty of initial interest.

NELL: And what about closing?

SHONA: I close, don't I?

NELL: Because that's what an employer is going to have doubts about with a lady as I needn't tell you, whether she's got the guts to push through to a closing situation. They think we're too nice. They think we listen to the buyer's doubts. They think we consider his needs and his feelings.

SHONA: I never consider people's feelings.

NELL: I was selling for six years, I can sell anything, I've sold in three continents, and I'm jolly as they come but I'm not very nice.

SHONA: I'm not very nice.

NELL: What sort of time do you have on the road with the other reps? Get on all right? Handle the chat?

SHONA: I get on. Keep myself to myself.

NELL: Fairly much of a loner are you?

SHONA: Sometimes.

NELL: So what field are you interested in?

SHONA: Computers.

NELL: That's a top field as you know and you'll be up against some very slick fellas there, there's some very pretty boys in computers, it's an American-style field.

SHONA: That's why I want to do it.

NELL: Video systems appeal? That's a high-flying situation.

SHONA: Video systems appeal OK.

NELL: Because Prestel have half a dozen vacancies I'm looking to fill at the moment. We're talking in the area of ten to fifteen thousand here and upwards.

SHONA: Sounds OK.

NELL: I've half a mind to go for it myself. But it's good money here if you've got the top clients. Could you fancy it do you think?

SHONA: Work here?

NELL: I'm not in a position to offer, there's nothing officially going just now, but we're always on the lookout. There's not that many of us. We could keep in touch.

SHONA: I like driving.

NELL: So the Prestel appeals.

SHONA: Yeh.

NELL: What about ties?

SHONA: No ties.

NELL: So relocation wouldn't be a problem.

SHONA: No problem.

NELL: So just fill me in a bit more could you about what you've been doing.

SHONA: What I've been doing. It's all down there.

NELL: The bare facts are down here but I've got to present you to an employer.

SHONA: I'm twenty-nine years old.

NELL: So it says here.

SHONA: We look young. Youngness runs in the family in our family.

NELL: So just describe your present job for me.

SHONA: My present job at present. I have a car. I have a Porsche. I go up the M1 a lot. Burn up the M1 a lot. Straight up the M1 in the fast lane to where the clients are, Staffordshire, Yorkshire, I do a lot in Yorkshire. I'm selling electric things. Like dishwashers, washing machines, stainless steel tubs are a feature and the reliability of the program. After sales service, we offer a very good after sales service, spare parts, plenty of spare parts. And fridges, I sell a lot of fridges specially in the summer. People want to buy fridges in the summer because of the heat melting the butter and you get fed up standing the milk in a basin of cold water with a cloth over, stands to reason people don't want to do that in this day and age. So I sell a lot of them. Big ones with big freezers. Big freezers. And I stay in hotels at night when I'm away from home. On my expense account. I stay in various hotels. They know me, the ones I go to. I check in, have a bath, have a shower. Then I go down to the bar, have a gin and tonic, have a chat. Then I go into the dining room and have dinner. I usually have fillet steak and mushrooms, I like mushrooms. I like smoked salmon very much. I like having a salad on the side. Green salad. I don't like tomatoes.

NELL: Christ what a waste of time.

SHONA: Beg your pardon?

NELL: Not a word of this is true, is it?

SHONA: How do you mean?

NELL: You just filled in the form with a pack of lies.
SHONA: Not exactly.
NELL: How old are you?
SHONA: Twenty-nine.
NELL: Nineteen?
SHONA: Twenty-one.
NELL: And what jobs have you done? Have you done any?
SHONA: I could though, I bet you.

(*The lights crossfade to the main office with Angie sitting as before. Win comes in to the main office. Shona and Nell exit.*)

WIN: Who's sitting in my chair?
ANGIE: What? Sorry.
WIN: Who's been eating my porridge?
ANGIE: What?
WIN: It's all right, I saw Marlene. Angie, isn't it? I'm Win. And I'm not going out for lunch because I'm knackered. I'm going to set me down here and have a yogurt. Do you like yogurt?
ANGIE: No.
WIN: That's good because I've only got one. Are you hungry?
ANGIE: No.
WIN: There's a café on the corner.
ANGIE: No thank you. Do you work here?
WIN: How did you guess?
ANGIE: Because you look as if you might work here and you're sitting at the desk. Have you always worked here?
WIN: No I was headhunted. That means I was working for another outfit like this and this lot came and offered me more money. I broke my contract, there was a hell of a stink. There's not many top ladies about. Your aunty's a smashing bird.
ANGIE: Yes I know.
MARLENE: Fan are you? Fan of your aunty's?
ANGIE: Do you think I could work here?
WIN: Not at the moment.
ANGIE: How do I start?
WIN: What can you do?
ANGIE: I don't know. Nothing.
WIN: Type?
ANGIE: Not very well. The letters jump up when I do capitals. I was going to do a CSE° in commerce but I didn't.
WIN: What have you got?
ANGIE: What?
WIN: CSE's, O's.
ANGIE: Nothing, none of that. Did you do all that?
WIN: Oh yes, all that, and a science degree funnily enough. I started out doing medical research but there's no money in it. I thought I'd go abroad. Did you know they sell Coca-Cola in Russia and Pepsi-Cola in China? You don't have to be qualified as much as you might think. Men are awful bullshitters,

CSE: Certificate of Secondary Education.

they like to make out jobs are harder than they are. Any job I ever did I started doing it better than the rest of the crowd and they didn't like it. So I'd get unpopular and I'd have a drink to cheer myself up. I lived with a fella and supported him for four years, he couldn't get work. After that I went to California. I like the sunshine. Americans know how to live. This country's too slow. Then I went to Mexico, still in sales, but it's no country for a single lady. I came home, went bonkers for a bit, thought I was five different people, got over that all right, the psychiatrist said I was perfectly sane and highly intelligent. Got married in a moment of weakness and he's inside now, he's been inside four years, and I've not been to see him too much this last year. I like this better than sales, I'm not really that aggressive. I started thinking sales was a good job if you want to meet people, but you're meeting people that don't want to meet you. It's no good if you like being liked. Here your clients want to meet you because you're the one doing them some good. They hope. (*Angie has fallen asleep. Nell comes in.*)
NELL: You're talking to yourself, sunshine.
WIN: So what's new?
NELL: Who is this?
WIN: Marlene's little niece.
NELL: What's she got, brother, sister? She never talks about her family.
WIN: I was telling her my life story.
NELL: Violins?
WIN: No, success story.
NELL: You've heard Howard's had a heart attack?
WIN: No, when?
NELL: I heard just now. He hadn't come in, he was at home, he's gone to hospital. He's not dead. His wife was here, she rushed off in a cab.
WIN: Too much butter, too much smoke. We must send him some flowers. (*Marlene comes in.*) You've heard about Howard?
MARLENE: Poor sod.
NELL: Lucky he didn't get the job if that's what his health's like.
MARLENE: Is she asleep?
WIN: She wants to work here.
MARLENE: Packer in Tesco more like.
WIN: She's a nice kid. Isn't she?
MARLENE: She's a bit thick. She's a bit funny.
WIN: She thinks you're wonderful.
MARLENE: She's not going to make it.

Scene II

(*Joyce's kitchen. Sunday evening, a year earlier. The lights come up on Joyce, Angie, and Marlene. Marlene is taking presents out of a bright carrier bag. Angie has already opened a box of chocolates.*)

MARLENE: Just a few little things. / I've
JOYCE: There's no need.

MARLENE: no memory for birthdays have I, and Christmas seems to slip by. So I think I owe Angie a few presents.

JOYCE: What do you say?

ANGIE: Thank you very much. Thank you very much, Aunty Marlene. (*She opens a present. It is the dress from Act I, new.*) Oh look, Mum, isn't it lovely?

MARLENE: I don't know if it's the right size. She's grown up since I saw her. / I knew she was always

ANGIE: Isn't it lovely?

MARLENE: tall for her age.

JOYCE: She's a big lump.

MARLENE: Hold it up, Angie, let's see.

ANGIE: I'll put it on, shall I?

MARLENE: Yes, try it on.

JOYCE: Go on to your room then, we don't want / a strip show thank you.

ANGIE: Of course I'm going to my room, what do you think. Look, Mum, here's something for you. Open it, go on. What is it? Can I open it for you?

JOYCE: Yes, you open it, pet.

ANGIE: Don't you want to open it yourself? / Go on.

JOYCE: I don't mind, you can do it.

ANGIE: It's something hard. It's — what is it? A bottle. Drink is it? No, it's what? Perfume, look. What a lot. Open it, look, let's smell it. Oh it's strong. It's lovely. Put it on me. How do you do it? Put it on me.

JOYCE: You're too young.

ANGIE: I can play wearing it like dressing up.

JOYCE: And you're too old for that. Here, give it here, I'll do it, you'll tip the whole bottle over yourself / and we'll have you smelling all summer.

ANGIE: Put it on you. Do I smell? Put it on Aunty too. Put it on Aunty too. Let's all smell.

MARLENE: I didn't know what you'd like.

JOYCE: There's no danger I'd have it already, / that's one thing.

ANGIE: Now we all smell the same.

MARLENE: It's a bit of nonsense.

JOYCE: It's very kind of you Marlene, you shouldn't.

ANGIE: Now I'll put on the dress and then we'll see. (*Angie goes.*)

JOYCE: You've caught me on the hop with the place in the mess. / If you'd let me

MARLENE: That doesn't matter.

JOYCE: know you was coming I'd have got something in to eat. We had our dinner dinnertime. We're just going to have a cup of tea. You could have an egg.

MARLENE: No, I'm not hungry. Tea's fine.

JOYCE: I don't expect you take sugar.

MARLENE: Why not?

JOYCE: You take care of yourself.

MARLENE: How do you mean you didn't know I was coming?

JOYCE: You could have written. I know we're not on the phone but we're not completely in the dark ages, / we do have a postman.

MARLENE: But you asked me to come.

JOYCE: How did I ask you to come?

MARLENE: Angie said when she phoned up.

JOYCE: Angie phoned up, did she.

MARLENE: Was it just Angie's idea?

JOYCE: What did she say?

MARLENE: She said you wanted me to come and see you. / It was a couple of

JOYCE: Ha.

MARLENE: weeks ago. How was I to know that's a ridiculous idea? My diary's always full a couple of weeks ahead so we fixed it for this weekend. I was meant to get here earlier but I was held up. She gave me messages from you.

JOYCE: Didn't you wonder why I didn't phone you myself?

MARLENE: She said you didn't like using the phone. You're shy on the phone and can't use it. I don't know what you're like, do I?

JOYCE: Are there people who can't use the phone?

MARLENE: I expect so.

JOYCE: I haven't met any.

MARLENE: Why should I think she was lying?

JOYCE: Because she's like what she's like.

MARLENE: How do I know / what she's like?

JOYCE: It's not my fault you don't know what she's like. You never come and see her.

MARLENE: Well I have now / and you don't seem over the moon.*

JOYCE: Good. *Well I'd have got a cake if she'd told me. (*Pause.*)

MARLENE: I did wonder why you wanted to see me.

JOYCE: I didn't want to see you.

MARLENE: Yes, I know. Shall I go?

JOYCE: I don't mind seeing you.

MARLENE: Great, I feel really welcome.

JOYCE: You can come and see Angie any time you like, I'm not stopping you. / You

MARLENE: Ta ever so.

JOYCE: know where we are. You're the one went away, not me. I'm right here where I was. And will be a few years yet I shouldn't wonder.

MARLENE: All right. All right. (*Joyce gives Marlene a cup of tea.*)

JOYCE: Tea.

MARLENE: Sugar? (*Joyce passes Marlene the sugar.*) It's very quiet down here.

JOYCE: I expect you'd notice it.

MARLENE: The air smells different too.

JOYCE: That's the scent.

MARLENE: No, I mean walking down the lane.

JOYCE: What sort of air you get in London then?

(*Angie comes in, wearing the dress. It fits.*)

MARLENE: Oh, very pretty. / You do look pretty, Angie.

JOYCE: That fits all right.

MARLENE: Do you like the color?

ANGIE: Beautiful. Beautiful.

JOYCE: You better take it off, / you'll get it dirty.

ANGIE: I want to wear it. I want to wear it.

MARLENE: It is for wearing after all. You can't just hang it up and look at it.

Royal Court production of *Top Girls* in 1991 with Lesley Manville as Marlene (left) and Deborah Findlay as Joyce.

ANGIE: I love it.

JOYCE: Well if you must you must.

ANGIE: If someone asks me what's my favorite color I'll tell them it's this. Thank you very much Aunty Marlene.

MARLENE: You didn't tell your mum you asked me down.

ANGIE: I wanted it to be a surprise.

JOYCE: I'll give you a surprise / one of these days.

ANGIE: I thought you'd like to see her. She hasn't been here since I was nine. People do see their aunts.

MARLENE: Is it that long? Doesn't time fly.

ANGIE: I wanted to.

JOYCE: I'm not cross.

ANGIE: Are you glad?

JOYCE: I smell nicer anyhow, don't I?

(*Kit comes in without saying anything, as if she lived there.*)

MARLENE: I think it was a good idea, Angie, about time. We are sisters after all. It's a pity to let that go.

JOYCE: This is Kitty, / who lives up the road. This is Angie's Aunty Marlene.

KIT: What's that?

ANGIE: It's a present. Do you like it?

KIT: It's all right. / Are you coming out?*

MARLENE: Hello, Kitty.

ANGIE: *No.

KIT: What's that smell?

ANGIE: It's a present.

KIT: It's horrible. Come on.*

MARLENE: Have a chocolate.

ANGIE: *No, I'm busy.

KIT: Coming out later?

ANGIE: No.

KIT (*to Marlene*): Hello. (*Kit goes without a chocolate.*)

JOYCE: She's a little girl Angie sometimes plays with because she's the only child lives really close. She's like a little sister to her really. Angie's good with little children.

MARLENE: Do you want to work with children, Angie? / Be a teacher or a nursery nurse?

JOYCE: I don't think she's ever thought of it.

MARLENE: What do you want to do?

JOYCE: She hasn't an idea in her head what she wants to do. / Lucky to get anything.

MARLENE: Angie?

JOYCE: She's not clever like you. (*Pause.*)

MARLENE: I'm not clever, just pushy.

JOYCE: True enough. (*Marlene takes a bottle of whiskey out of the bag.*) I don't drink spirits.

ANGIE: You do at Christmas.

JOYCE: It's not Christmas, is it?

ANGIE: It's better than Christmas.

MARLENE: Glasses?

JOYCE: Just a small one then.

MARLENE: Do you want some, Angie?

ANGIE: I can't, can I?

JOYCE: Taste it if you want. You won't like it. (*Angie tastes it.*)

ANGIE: Mmm.

MARLENE: We got drunk together the night your grandfather died.

JOYCE: We did not get drunk.

MARLENE: I got drunk. You were just overcome with grief.

JOYCE: I still keep up the grave with flowers.

MARLENE: Do you really?

JOYCE: Why wouldn't I?

MARLENE: Have you seen Mother?

JOYCE: Of course I've seen Mother.

MARLENE: I mean lately.

JOYCE: Of course I've seen her lately, I go every Thursday.

MARLENE (to Angie): Do you remember your grandfather?

ANGIE: He got me out of the bath one night in a towel.

MARLENE: Did he? I don't think he ever gave me a bath. Did he give you a bath, Joyce? He probably got soft in his old age. Did you like him?

ANGIE: Yes of course.

MARLENE: Why?

ANGIE: What?

MARLENE: So what's the news? How's Mrs. Paisley? Still going crazily? / And Dorothy. What happened to Dorothy?*

ANGIE: Who's Mrs. Paisley?

JOYCE: *She went to Canada.

MARLENE: Did she? What to do?

JOYCE: I don't know. She just went to Canada.

MARLENE: Well / good for her.

ANGIE: Mr. Connolly killed his wife.

MARLENE: What, Connolly at Whitegates?

ANGIE: They found her body in the garden. / Under the cabbages.

MARLENE: He was always so proper.

JOYCE: Stuck up git, Connolly. Best lawyer money could buy but he couldn't get out of it. She was carrying on with Matthew.

MARLENE: How old's Matthew then?

JOYCE: Twenty-one. / He's got a motorbike.

MARLENE: I think he's about six.

ANGIE: How can he be six? He's six years older than me. / If he was six I'd be nothing, I'd be just born this minute.

JOYCE: Your aunty knows that, she's just being silly. She means it's so long since she's been here she's forgotten about Matthew.

ANGIE: You were here for my birthday when I was nine. I had a pink cake. Kit was only five then, she was four, she hadn't started school yet. She could read already when she went to school. You remember my birthday? / You remember me?

MARLENE: Yes, I remember the cake.

ANGIE: You remember me?

MARLENE: Yes, I remember you.

ANGIE: And Mum and Dad was there, and Kit was.

MARLENE: Yes, how is your dad? Where is he tonight? Up the pub?

JOYCE: No, he's not here.

MARLENE: I can see he's not here.

JOYCE: He moved out.

MARLENE: What? When did he? / Just recently?*

ANGIE: Didn't you know that? You don't know much.

JOYCE: *No, it must be three years ago. Don't be rude, Angie.

ANGIE: I'm not, am I, Aunty? What else don't you know?

JOYCE: You was in America or somewhere. You sent a postcard.

ANGIE: I've got that in my room. It's the Grand Canyon. Do you want to see it? Shall I get it? I can get it for you.

MARLENE: Yes, all right. (Angie goes.)

JOYCE: You could be married with twins for all I know. You must have affairs and break up and I don't need to know about any of that so I don't see what the fuss is about.

MARLENE: What fuss? (Angie comes back with the postcard.)

ANGIE: "Driving across the states for a new job in L.A. It's a long way but the car goes very fast. It's very hot. Wish you were here. Love from Aunty Marlene."

JOYCE: Did you make a lot of money?

MARLENE: I spent a lot.

ANGIE: I want to go to America. Will you take me?

JOYCE: She's not going to America, she's been to America, stupid.

ANGIE: She might go again, stupid. It's not something you do once. People who go keep going all the time, back and forth on jets. They go on Concorde and Laker and get jet lag. Will you take me?

MARLENE: I'm not planning a trip.

ANGIE: Will you let me know?

JOYCE: Angie, / you're getting silly.

ANGIE: I want to be American.

JOYCE: It's time you were in bed.

ANGIE: No it's not. / I don't have to go to bed at all tonight.

JOYCE: School in the morning.

ANGIE: I'll wake up.

JOYCE: Come on now, you know how you get.

ANGIE: How do I get? / I don't get anyhow.*

JOYCE: Angie. *Are you staying the night?

MARLENE: Yes, if that's all right. / I'll see you in the morning.

ANGIE: You can have my bed. I'll sleep on the sofa.

JOYCE: You will not, you'll sleep in your bed. / Think

ANGIE: Mum.

JOYCE: I can't see through that? I can just see you going to sleep / with us talking.

ANGIE: I would, I would go to sleep, I'd love that.

JOYCE: I'm going to get cross, Angie.

ANGIE: I want to show her something.

JOYCE: Then bed.

ANGIE: It's a secret.

JOYCE: Then I expect it's in your room so off you go. Give us a shout when you're ready for bed and your aunty'll be up and see you.

ANGIE: Will you?

MARLENE: Yes of course. (Angie goes. Silence.) It's cold tonight.

JOYCE: Will you be all right on the sofa? You can / have my bed.

MARLENE: The sofa's fine.

JOYCE: Yes the forecast said rain tonight but it's held off.

MARLENE: I was going to walk down to the estuary but I've left it a bit late. Is it just the same?

JOYCE: They cut down the hedges a few years back. Is that since you were here?

MARLENE: But it's not changed down the end, all the mud. And the reeds? We used to pick them up when they were bigger than us. Are there still lapwings?

JOYCE: You get strangers walking there on a Sunday. I expect they're looking at the mud and the lapwings, yes.

MARLENE: You could have left.

JOYCE: Who says I wanted to leave?

MARLENE: Stop getting at me then, you're really boring.

JOYCE: How could I have left?

MARLENE: Did you want to?

JOYCE: I said how, / how could I?

MARLENE: If you'd wanted to you'd have done it.

JOYCE: Christ.

MARLENE: Are we getting drunk?

JOYCE: Do you want something to eat?

MARLENE: No, I'm getting drunk.

JOYCE: Funny time to visit, Sunday evening.

MARLENE: I came this morning. I spent the day —

ANGIE (*off*): Aunty! Aunty Marlene!

MARLENE: I'd better go.

JOYCE: Go on then.

MARLENE: All right.

ANGIE (*off*): Aunty! Can you hear me? I'm ready.

(*Marlene goes. Joyce goes on sitting, clears up, sits again. Marlene comes back.*)

JOYCE: So what's the secret?

MARLENE: It's a secret.

JOYCE: I know what it is anyway.

MARLENE: I bet you don't. You always said that.

JOYCE: It's her exercise book.

MARLENE: Yes, but you don't know what's in it.

JOYCE: It's some game, some secret society she has with Kit.

MARLENE: You don't know the password. You don't know the code.

JOYCE: You're really in it, aren't you. Can you do the handshake?

MARLENE: She didn't mention a handshake.

JOYCE: I thought they'd have a special handshake. She spends hours writing that but she's useless at school. She copies things out of books about black magic, and politicians out of the paper. It's a bit childish.

MARLENE: I think it's a plot to take over the world.

JOYCE: She's been in the remedial class the last two years.

MARLENE: I came up this morning and spent the day in Ipswich. I went to see Mother.

JOYCE: Did she recognize you?

MARLENE: Are you trying to be funny?

JOYCE: No, she does wander.

MARLENE: She wasn't wandering at all, she was very lucid thank you.

JOYCE: You were very lucky then.

MARLENE: Fucking awful life she's had.

JOYCE: Don't tell me.

MARLENE: Fucking waste.

JOYCE: Don't talk to me.

MARLENE: Why shouldn't I talk? Why shouldn't I talk to you? / Isn't she my mother too?

JOYCE: Look, you've left, you've gone away, / we can do without you.

MARLENE: I left home, so what, I left home. People do leave home / it is normal.

JOYCE: We understand that, we can do without you.

MARLENE: We weren't happy. Were you happy?

JOYCE: Don't come back.

MARLENE: So it's just your mother is it, your child, you never wanted me round, / you were jealous

JOYCE: Here we go.

MARLENE: of me because I was the little one and I was clever.

JOYCE: I'm not clever enough for all this psychology / if that's what it is.

MARLENE: Why can't I visit my own family / without

JOYCE: Aah.

MARLENE: all this?

JOYCE: Just don't go on about Mum's life when you haven't been to see her for how many years. / I go

MARLENE: It's up to me.

JOYCE: and see her every week.

MARLENE: Then don't go and see her every week.

JOYCE: Somebody has to.

MARLENE: No they don't. / Why do they?

JOYCE: How would I feel if I didn't go?

MARLENE: A lot better.

JOYCE: I hope you feel better.

MARLENE: It's up to me.

JOYCE: You couldn't get out of here fast enough. (*Pause.*)

MARLENE: Of course I couldn't get out of here fast enough. What was I going to do? Marry a dairyman who'd come home pissed? / Don't you fucking this

JOYCE: Christ.

MARLENE: fucking that fucking bitch fucking tell me what to fucking do fucking.

JOYCE: I don't know how you could leave your own child.

MARLENE: You were quick enough to take her.

JOYCE: What does that mean?

MARLENE: You were quick enough to take her.

JOYCE: Or what? Have her put in a home? Have some stranger / take her would you rather?

MARLENE: You couldn't have one so you took mine.

JOYCE: I didn't know that then.

MARLENE: Like hell, / married three years.

JOYCE: I didn't know that. Plenty of people / take that long.

MARLENE: Well it turned out lucky for you, didn't it?

JOYCE: Turned out all right for you by the look of you. You'd be getting a few less thousand a year.

MARLENE: Not necessarily.

JOYCE: You'd be stuck here / like you said.

MARLENE: I could have taken her with me.

JOYCE: You didn't want to take her with you. It's no good coming back now, Marlene, / and saying —

MARLENE: I know a managing director who's got two children, she breastfeeds in the board room, she pays a hundred pounds a week on domestic help alone and she can afford that because she's an extremely high-powered lady earning a great deal of money.

JOYCE: So what's that got to do with you at the age of seventeen?

MARLENE: Just because you were married and had somewhere to live —

JOYCE: You could have lived at home. / Or live

MARLENE: Don't be stupid.

JOYCE: with me and Frank. / You

MARLENE: You never suggested.

JOYCE: said you weren't keeping it. You shouldn't have had it / if you wasn't

MARLENE: Here we go.

JOYCE: going to keep it. You was the most stupid, / for someone so clever you was the most stupid, get yourself pregnant, not go to the doctor, not tell.

MARLENE: You wanted it, you said you were glad, I remember the day, you said I'm glad you never got rid of it, I'll look after it, you said that down by the river. So what are you saying, sunshine, you don't want her?

JOYCE: Course I'm not saying that.

MARLENE: Because I'll take her, / wake her up and pack now.

JOYCE: You wouldn't know how to begin to look after her.

MARLENE: Don't you want her?

JOYCE: Course I do, she's my child.

MARLENE: Then what are you going on about / why did I have her?

JOYCE: You said I got her off you / when you didn't —

MARLENE: I said you were lucky / the way it —

JOYCE: Have a child now if you want one. You're not old.

MARLENE: I might do.

JOYCE: Good. (*Pause.*)

MARLENE: I've been on the pill so long / I'm probably sterile.

JOYCE: Listen when Angie was six months I did get pregnant and I lost it because I was so tired looking after your fucking baby / because she cried so

MARLENE: You never told me.

JOYCE: much — yes I did tell you — / and the doctor

MARLENE: Well I forgot.

JOYCE: said if I'd sat down all day with my feet up I'd've kept it / and that's the only chance I ever had because after that —

MARLENE: I've had two abortions, are you interested? Shall I tell you about them? Well I won't, it's boring, it wasn't a problem. I don't like messy talk about blood / and what a bad time we all had. I

JOYCE: If I hadn't had your baby. The doctor said.

MARLENE: don't want a baby. I don't want to talk about gynecology.

JOYCE: Then stop trying to get Angie off of me.

MARLENE: I come down here after six years. All night you've been saying I don't come often enough. If I don't come for another six years she'll be twenty-one, will that be OK?

JOYCE: That'll be fine, yes, six years would suit me fine. (*Pause.*)

MARLENE: I was afraid of this. I only came because I thought you wanted . . . I just want . . . (*She cries.*)

JOYCE: Don't grizzle, Marlene, for God's sake. Marly? Come on, pet. Love you really. Fucking stop it, will you? (*She goes to Marlene.*)

MARLENE: No, let me cry. I like it. (*They laugh, Marlene begins to stop crying.*) I knew I'd cry if I wasn't careful.

JOYCE: Everyone's always crying in this house. Nobody takes any notice.

MARLENE: You've been wonderful looking after Angie.

JOYCE: Don't get carried away.

MARLENE: I can't write letters but I do think of you.

JOYCE: You're getting drunk. I'm going to make some tea.

MARLENE: Love you. (*Joyce goes to make tea.*)

JOYCE: I can see why you'd want to leave. It's a dump here.

MARLENE: So what's this about you and Frank?

JOYCE: He was always carrying on, wasn't he. And if I wanted to go out in the evening he'd go mad, even if it was nothing, a class, I was going to go to an evening class. So he had this girlfriend, only twenty-two poor cow, and I said go on, off you go, hoppit. I don't think he even likes her.

MARLENE: So what about money?

JOYCE: I've always said I don't want your money.

MARLENE: No, does he send you money?

JOYCE: I've got four different cleaning jobs. Adds up. There's not a lot round here.

MARLENE: Does Angie miss him?

JOYCE: She doesn't say.

MARLENE: Does she see him?

JOYCE: He was never that fond of her to be honest.

MARLENE: He tried to kiss me once. When you were engaged.

JOYCE: Did you fancy him?

MARLENE: No, he looked like a fish.

JOYCE: He was lovely then.

MARLENE: Ugh.

JOYCE: Well I fancied him. For about three years.

MARLENE: Have you got someone else?

JOYCE: There's not a lot round here. Mind you, the minute you're on your own, you'd be amazed how

your friends' husbands drop by. I'd sooner do without.

MARLENE: I don't see why you couldn't take my money.

JOYCE: I do, so don't bother about it.

MARLENE: Only got to ask.

JOYCE: So what about you? Good job?

MARLENE: Good for a laugh. / Got back

JOYCE: Good for more than a laugh I should think.

MARLENE: from the US of A a bit wiped out and slotted
into this speedy employment agency and still there.

JOYCE: You can always find yourself work then?

MARLENE: That's right.

JOYCE: And men?

MARLENE: Oh there's always men.

JOYCE: No one special?

MARLENE: There's fellas who like to be seen with a high-
flying lady. Shows they've got something really good
in their pants. But they can't take the day to day.
They're waiting for me to turn into the little woman.
Or maybe I'm just horrible of course.

JOYCE: Who needs them.

MARLENE: Who needs them. Well I do. But I need
adventures more. So on on into the sunset. I think the
eighties are going to be stupendous.

JOYCE: Who for?

MARLENE: For me. / I think I'm going up up up.

JOYCE: Oh for you. Yes, I'm sure they will.

MARLENE: And for the country, come to that. Get the
economy back on its feet and whoosh. She's a tough
lady, Maggie. I'd give her a job. / She just needs to
hang

JOYCE: You voted for them, did you?

MARLENE: in there. This country needs to stop whining. / Monetarism is not

JOYCE: Drink your tea and shut up, pet.

MARLENE: stupid. It takes time, determination. No more
slop. / And

JOYCE: Well I think they're filthy bastards.

MARLENE: who's got to drive it on? First woman prime
minister. Terrifico. Aces. Right on. / You must admit.
Certainly gets my vote.

JOYCE: What good's first woman if it's her? I suppose
you'd have liked Hitler if he was a woman. Ms.
Hitler. Got a lot done, Hitlerina. / Great adventures.

MARLENE: Bosses still walking on the worker's faces?
Still dadda's little parrot? Haven't you learned to
think for yourself? I believe in the individual. Look at
me.

JOYCE: I am looking at you.

MARLENE: Come on, Joyce, we're not going to quarrel
over politics.

JOYCE: We are though.

MARLENE: Forget I mentioned it. Not a word about the
slimy unions will cross my lips. (*Pause.*)

JOYCE: You say Mother had a wasted life.

MARLENE: Yes I do. Married to that bastard.

JOYCE: What sort of life did he have? /

MARLENE: Violent life?

JOYCE: Working in the fields like an animal. / Why

MARLENE: Come off it.

JOYCE: wouldn't he want a drink? You want a drink. He
couldn't afford whiskey.

MARLENE: I don't want to talk about him.

JOYCE: You started, I was talking about her. She had a rotten life because she had nothing. She went hungry.

MARLENE: She was hungry because he drank the
money. / He used to hit her.

JOYCE: It's not all down to him / Their

MARLENE: She didn't hit him.

JOYCE: lives were rubbish. They were treated like rubbish. He's dead and she'll die soon and what sort of
life / did they have?

MARLENE: I saw him one night. I came down.

JOYCE: Do you think I didn't? / They

MARLENE: I still have dreams.

JOYCE: didn't get to America and drive across it in a fast
car. / Bad nights, they had bad days.

MARLENE: America, America, you're jealous. / I had to
get out, I knew when I

JOYCE: Jealous?

MARLENE: was thirteen, out of their house, out of them,
never let that happen to me, / never let him, make my
own way, out.

JOYCE: Jealous of what you've done, you'd be ashamed
of me if I came to your office, your smart friends,
wouldn't you, I'm ashamed of you, think of nothing
but yourself, you've got on, nothing's changed for
most people, / has it?

MARLENE: I hate the working class / which is what

JOYCE: Yes you do.

MARLENE: you're going to go on about now, it doesn't
exist any more, it means lazy and stupid. / I don't

JOYCE: Come on, now we're getting it.

MARLENE: like the way they talk. I don't like beer guts
and football vomit and saucy tits / and brothers and
sisters —

JOYCE: I spit when I see a Rolls Royce, scratch it with my
ring / Mercedes it was.

MARLENE: Oh very mature —

JOYCE: I hate the cows I work for / and their dirty dishes
with blanquette of fucking veau.

MARLENE: and I will not be pulled down to their level by
a flying picket and I won't be sent to Siberia / or a
loony bin just because I'm original. And I support

JOYCE: No, you'll be on a yacht, you'll be head of Coca-
Cola and you wait, the eighties is going to be stupendous all right because we'll get you lot off our
backs —

MARLENE: Reagan even if he is a lousy movie star
because the reds are swarming up his map and I want
to be free in a free world —

JOYCE: What? / What?

MARLENE: I know what I mean / by that — not shut up
here.

JOYCE: So don't be round here when it happens because
if someone's kicking you I'll just laugh. (*Silence.*)

MARLENE: I don't mean anything personal. I don't believe in class. Anyone can do anything if they've got what it takes.

JOYCE: And if they haven't?

MARLENE: If they're stupid or lazy or frightened, I'm not going to help them get a job, why should I?

JOYCE: What about Angie?

MARLENE: What about Angie?

JOYCE: She's stupid, lazy, and frightened, so what about her?

MARLENE: You run her down too much. She'll be all right.

JOYCE: I don't expect so, no. I expect her children will say what a wasted life she had. If she has children. Because nothing's changed and it won't with them in.

MARLENE: Them, them. / Us and them?

JOYCE: And you're one of them.

MARLENE: And you're us, wonderful us, and Angie's us / and Mum and Dad's us.

JOYCE: Yes, that's right, and you're them.

MARLENE: Come on, Joyce, what a night. You've got what it takes.

JOYCE: I know I have.

MARLENE: I didn't really mean all that.

JOYCE: I did.

MARLENE: But we're friends anyway.

JOYCE: I don't think so, no.

MARLENE: Well it's lovely to be out in the country. I really must make the effort to come more often. I want to go to sleep. I want to go to sleep. (*Joyce gets blankets for the sofa.*)

JOYCE: Goodnight then. I hope you'll be warm enough.

MARLENE: Goodnight. Joyce —

JOYCE: No, pet. Sorry. (*Joyce goes. Marlene sits wrapped in a blanket and has another drink. Angie comes in.*)

ANGIE: Mum?

MARLENE: Angie? What's the matter?

ANGIE: Mum?

MARLENE: No, she's gone to bed. It's Aunty Marlene.

ANGIE: Frightening.

MARLENE: Did you have a bad dream? What happened in it? Well you're awake now, aren't you, pet?

ANGIE: Frightening.

COMMENTARY

Kathleen Betsko, Rachel Koenig, and Emily Mann
AN INTERVIEW WITH CARYL CHURCHILL   1984

Kathleen Betsko and Rachel Koenig interviewed Caryl Churchill in New York on February 25, 1984, but found their tape was incomplete. Fortunately, Emily Mann, a playwright, was able to complete the interview with Churchill at London's Riverside Studio on November 23, 1984. The excerpts presented here combine the two sessions, emphasizing Top Girls *and some of the interesting responses to Churchill's drama.*

Interviewer: Is there a female aesthetic? And we'd like you to wrap this question up once and for all. [Laughter]

Churchill: I don't see how you can tell until there are so many plays by women that you can begin to see what they have in common that's different from the way men have written, and there are still relatively so few. And we have things in common with male playwrights who are worried about similar things in their particular country and who have worked in the same theaters with the same directors. So it's hard to separate out and think of "women playwrights" rather than just "playwrights." Though I do remember before I wrote *Top Girls* thinking about women barristers — how they were in a minority and had to imitate men to succeed — and I was thinking of them as different from me. And then I thought, "Wait a minute, my whole concept of what plays might be is from plays written by men. I don't have to put on a wig, speak in a special voice, but how far do I assume things that have been defined by men?" There isn't a simple answer to that. And I remember long before that thinking of the "maleness" of the traditional structure of plays, with conflict and building in a certain way to a climax. But it's not something I think about very often. Playwriting will change not just because more women are doing it but because more women are doing other things as well. And of course men will be influenced by that too. So maybe you'll still be no nearer to defining a female aesthetic.

Interviewer: Some of the playwrights we've interviewed suggest there are no "lost masterpieces" and that "the cream will rise to the top" in terms of women's writing for the stage.

Churchill: Most theaters are still controlled by men and people do tend to be able to see promise in people who are like themselves. Women directors have pointed out to me how established men tend to take a young male director under their wing, and seem to feel more uncomfortable with a woman director because they can't quite see where she is, because they weren't like that at her age. I think the same thing can happen with writers: If you're at the stage where you are promising but not doing it all that well yet, it's perhaps easier for a man choosing plays to see the potential in a man writer. I don't know about "lost masterpieces" but people don't usually start out writing masterpieces and women may have less chance of getting started. Having productions does seem to make people write better.

Interviewer: Has the political climate for women dramatists changed drastically since you began writing plays?

Churchill: I began writing plays in 1958, and I don't think I knew of any other women playwrights then. Luckily, I didn't think about it. Do you know Tillie Olsen's book *Silences*? She says that at different times, whole categories of people are enabled to write. You tend to think of your own development only having to do with yourself and it's exciting to discover it in a historical context. When I began it was quite hard for any playwrights to get started in London. The English Stage Company had just started a policy of doing new writing at the Royal Court, but that was almost the only place. I had student productions at first, and then wrote for radio. In the late sixties and early seventies there was a surge of fringe theaters and interest in new writing, starting with the Theatre Upstairs and the Royal Court, and that was the first place to do a professional stage production of one of my plays, *Owners*, in 1972. For a while, a lot of writers were getting produced for the first time, though far fewer women than men. Gradually during the seventies the number of women increased, coming partly through fringe theaters and partly through women's theater groups. In the last five years there seem to be far more women playwrights and some theaters are more open to them, though others still aren't. At the moment, because of the financial cuts, it's again become quite hard for all playwrights. Theaters are having to do co-productions with other theaters because they haven't enough money to do a whole year's work on their grants, so it means one new play gets done instead of two. The Royal Court, for instance, can now only afford to do four new plays in the main house instead of eight. But I get the impression life is even harder for playwrights in the United States than in England because of there not being a subsidized theater.

Interviewer: In Laurie Stone's *Village Voice* interview [March 1, 1983], you talked about women becoming Coca-Cola executives and you said, "Well, that's not what I mean by feminism." What exactly do you mean by feminism?

Churchill: When I was in the States in '79 I talked to some women who were saying how well things were going for women in America now with far more top executives being women, and I was struck by the difference between that and the feminism I was used to in England, which is far more closely connected with socialism. And that was one of the ideas behind writing *Top Girls,* that achieving things isn't necessarily good, it matters *what* you achieve.

Thatcher° had just become prime minister; there was talk about whether it was an advance to have a woman prime minister if it was someone with policies like hers: She may be a woman but she isn't a sister, she may be a sister but she isn't a comrade. And, in fact, things have got much worse for women under Thatcher. So that's the context of that remark. I do find it hard to conceive of a right-wing feminism. Of course, socialism and feminism aren't synonymous, but I feel strongly about both and wouldn't be interested in a form of one that didn't include the other.

Interviewer: Do you think it's odd, given the fact that there is at best indifference, at worst hostility, to political plays in America, that your works are so popular here?

Churchill: Is it true that on the whole plays here tend to be more family-centered, personal, individual-centered?

Interviewer: Yes, more psychological.

Churchill: Whereas I've been quite heavily exposed to a tradition of looking at the larger context of groups of people. It doesn't mean you don't look at families or individuals within that, but you are also looking at bigger things. Like with the kind of work Joint Stock Theatre Group has done, where you go and research a subject and where you have a lot of characters, even if played by only a few people. It tends to open things out.

Interviewer: The critics do ask, "Where are the American plays with the larger social issues?" Unfortunately, when one comes along our own critics usually turn thumbs down if the politics are overt. An overt political position is considered poor craft or preaching. . . .

Interviewer: Does the playwright have an obligation to take a moral and political stance?

Churchill: It's almost impossible not to take one, whether you intend to or not. Most plays can be looked at from a political perspective and have said something, even if it isn't what you set out to say. If you wrote a West End comedy relying on conventional sexist jokes, that's taking a moral and political stance, though the person who wrote it might say, "I was just writing an entertaining show." Whatever you do your point of view is going to show somewhere. It usually only gets noticed and called "political" if it's against the status quo. There are times when I feel I want to deal with immediate issues and times when I don't. I do like the stuff of theater, in the same way people who are painting like paint; and of course when you say "moral and political" that doesn't have to imply reaching people logically or overtly, because theater can reach people on all kinds of other levels too. Sometimes one side or the other is going to have more weight. Sometimes it's going to be about images, more like a dream to people, and sometimes it's going to be more like reading an article. And there's room for all that. But either way, the issues you feel strongly about are going to come through, and they're going to be a moral and political stance in some form. Sometimes more explicitly, sometimes less. . . .

Thatcher: Margaret (Hilda) Thatcher (b. 1925), British Prime Minister, 1979–1990, and a strong political conservative.

Mann: Let's talk about your play *Top Girls*.

Churchill: When I wrote *Top Girls* I was writing it by myself and not for a company. I wanted to write about women doing different kinds of work and didn't feel I knew enough about it. Then I thought, this is ridiculous, if you were with a company you'd go out and talk to people, so I did. Which is how I came up with the employment agency in the second act.

Mann: Are there specific characters in *Top Girls* that have their real life counterparts?

Churchill: Quite a few of the things Win tells Angie about her life are things different people said to me. And of course the dead women at the dinner are all based on someone [from art, literature or history]. But apart from that, it's imaginary.

Mann: Tell me about the ways in which *Top Girls* has been misunderstood.

Churchill: What I was intending to do was make it first look as though it was celebrating the achievements of women and then — by showing the main character, Marlene, being successful in a very competitive, destructive, capitalist way — ask, what kind of achievement is that? The idea was that it would start out looking like a feminist play and turn into a socialist one, as well. And I think on the whole it's mostly been understood like that. A lot of people have latched on to Marlene leaving her child, which interestingly was something that came very late. Originally the idea was just that Marlene was "writing off" her niece, Angie, because she'd never make it; I didn't yet have the plot idea that Angie was actually Marlene's own child. Of course women are pressured to make choices between working and having children in a way that men aren't, so it *is* relevant, but it isn't the main point of it.

There's another thing that I've recently discovered with other productions of *Top Girls*. In Greece, for example, where fewer women go out to work, the attitude from some men seeing it was, apparently, that the women in the play who'd gone out to work weren't very nice, weren't happy, and they abandoned their children. They felt the play was obviously saying women *shouldn't* go out to work — they took it to mean what they were wanting to say about women themselves, which is depressing. Highly depressing. [laughter] Another example of its being open to misunderstanding was a production in Cologne, Germany, where the women characters were played as miserable and quarrelsome and competitive at the dinner, and the women in the office were neurotic and incapable. The waitress slunk about in a catsuit like a bunnygirl and Win changed her clothes on stage in the office. It just turned into a complete travesty of what it was supposed to be. So that's the sort of moment when you think you'd rather write novels, because the productions can't be changed.

Mann: I don't know whether we're safer in the theater or not. . . .

Churchill: With a play you do leave more room for other things and that's one of the attractions, that people can keep coming to it fresh and doing it differently.

Athol Fugard

Athol Fugard (b. 1932) was an actor before becoming a playwright. Fugard's wife, the actress Sheila Meiring, stimulated his interest in theater, and in 1956 he began working with a theater group called the Serpent Company in Cape Town, South Africa. The group included both black and white actors at a time when racial mixing was illegal and went on to make a notable contribution to world drama.

Fugard, who is white, met Zakes Mokae, a black musician and actor, in the early days of the Serpent players, and the two collaborated on several works. Mokae has said that the tradition in Africa was not so much for a solitary playwright to compose a work that others would act out as it was for people to develop a communal approach to drama, crafting a dramatic piece through their interaction. To some extent, Fugard in his early efforts did just that. He worked with actors, watched the developments among them, and then shaped the drama accordingly.

In 1960 he began to write a two-person play called *The Blood Knot* while he was in England trying to establish a theater group there. This play was part of a trilogy called *The Family,* with *Hello and Goodbye* (1965) and *Boesman and Lena* (1969). *The Blood Knot* was given its first performance in Dorkay House in Johannesburg, South Africa, late in 1961. As Fugard has said, the entire production, which starred Fugard and Mokae, was put together so quickly that the government never had time to stop it. The play is about two brothers, one black, the other light-skinned enough to pass for white. It is exceptionally powerful, and in the play's first performances in Johannesburg, it was a sensation. It toured South Africa and had a revival in New Haven and in New York in 1984 and 1985.

While they toured South Africa, Fugard and Mokae were victims of the country's apartheid policies. They could not travel in the same train car: Fugard went first class, and Mokae had to go in special cars for blacks. After *The Blood Knot*'s success the government passed laws making it all but impossible for black and white actors to work together on the stage, but that policy has now changed.

Fugard has had a considerable number of plays produced in New York and London over the years. *Sizwe Banzi Is Dead* (1972), written with black actors John Kani and Winston Ntshona, is about a man who exchanges identity with a corpse as a way of avoiding the racial laws of South Africa; it was well received. *The Island* (1975), also written with Kani and Ntshona, starred the latter two, who have become associated with Fugard and his work. They portray prisoners who, while putting on *Antigone,* become immersed in the political themes of the play, seeing it as an example of the political repression they experience in their own lives. A revival in New York in April 2003, with Kani and Ntshona in a mildly revised version, received excellent reviews.

Fugard's plays *A Lesson from Aloes* (1978) and *The Road to Mecca* (1984) were successful in their first American productions at the Yale Repertory Theatre and on Broadway. Fugard's works are not always concerned with racial problems, but they usually center on political issues and the stress that individuals feel in trying to be themselves in an intolerant society.

The situation in South Africa has improved since *"MASTER HAROLD"...and the boys* was first produced in 1982. Apartheid has been abolished, and the government is in the hands of the African National Congress. The shift has been more successful than white South Africans expected, although political tensions still exist. Fugard's attachment and commitment to South Africa remain deep and lifelong. He has been criticized by black writers for dealing with themes they feel belong to them, while also being criticized by whites for his sympathies toward blacks. In the new South Africa some of these problems have begun to sort themselves out. *Valley Song* (1996), produced at London's Royal Court Theatre, explores the problems and the promise of the new South Africa. Fugard's most recent plays have premiered at the McCarter Theatre in Princeton, New Jersey. In May 1998 *The Captain's Tiger* was directed by Fugard, who also acted in the role of Tiger, a character on board a ship. Fugard himself had left university to work on ships around Africa. In May 2001, Fugard directed *Sorrows and Rejoicing,* a play about a man who dies and whose white wife and colored mistress meet at his funeral. Another play, *The Abbess,* is under development. It is based on the life of Saint Hildegard of Bingen (1098–1179) — a Benedictine abbess known for her correspondence; her work in medicine; and her music, poems, writing, and drama.

"MASTER HAROLD"...
AND THE BOYS

Athol Fugard has said that *"MASTER HAROLD"...and the boys* (1982) is a very personal play in which he exorcises personal guilt (Fugard's entire name is Harold Athol Lannigan Fugard). As a white South African he has written numerous plays that represent the racial circumstances of life in that troubled nation. This play has won international distinction and has made a reputation for its stars, especially Zakes Mokae, with whom Fugard has worked for more than thirty years.

Hally, the teenage son of the restaurant's owners, reveals throughout the play (which is set in 1950) that he is more attached emotionally to Sam, the black waiter who has befriended him, than he is even to his own parents, owners of the restaurant where Sam works. His attitude toward his father is complicated by his father's alcoholism and confinement. At that time in South Africa even such an alcoholic was considered automatically superior to a black man such as Sam, who is intelligent, quick, thoughtful, and generous. When Hally reveals his anxiety about his father, Sam warns him that it is dishonorable to treat one's father the way he does, but Sam's presumption in admonishing Hally triggers Hally's meanspirited outburst toward him.

Zakes Mokae, who created the role of Sam in the first performance of the play at the Yale Repertory Theatre, has commented extensively about his role and the character of Sam. He has observed that some black audience members called out during a performance that he should beat up Hally the minute Hally demands that Sam call him Master Harold. But other black audience members spoke with him after the performance and agreed that, because Sam had never taken that kind of stand against Harold or his father, he was getting what he deserved. Mokae himself has pointed out that Sam is probably not living in Port Elizabeth legally and that to have taken action, even if he wanted to, would have ended with his removal from the town into exile.

Zakes Mokae understands the character from his perspective as a black South African, and he realizes Sam's limits. But he has said that in his version of the play Sam would give Hally a beating and "suffer the consequences." He points out, however, that he is an urban South African, unlike Sam, and his attitude is quite different from anything that Sam would have understood. As an urban black, Mokae could not have been sent into exile, although he could certainly have been punished, for beating a white boy.

On the question of whether the play made a positive contribution to white-black relations in South Africa, Mokae feels that a play cannot change people's minds. Audiences were not likely to seek to change the government of South Africa simply because they had seen a play. At the same time, however, he feels that it was productive to talk about the apartheid and racial distrust in South Africa.

Unfortunately, the government of South Africa decided that the play was too inflammatory for performance in its country, and it was banned briefly from performance in Johannesburg and other theatrical centers in South Africa. This suggests that, while Zakes Mokae did not feel that one play would have much impact on injustices in South Africa, it is likely that the government feared otherwise.

In an important way, *"MASTER HAROLD" . . . and the boys* is a personal statement by Fugard that establishes the extent to which apartheid damages even a person sympathetic to black rights. It is astonishing in retrospect to think, as his interviewer, Heinrich von Staden, once said, that Hally could grow up to be Athol himself. If this is true, then it is also true that the play is hopeful.

One sign of hope is that the violence in the play is restrained. Sam does not beat Hally for humiliating him, although he probably would like to. And no one in the play makes a move to be physically threatening to Sam. However faint, these are signs of hope. And as Zakes Mokae has said about the situation in his homeland, "One is always optimistic. It can't go on forever." He was right. On June 5, 1991, Parliament abandoned apartheid, and South Africa had a new beginning.

"MASTER HAROLD" . . . and the boys in Performance

The world premiere of *"MASTER HAROLD" . . . and the boys* was at the Yale Repertory Theatre in March 1982. Fugard himself directed the play, with Zakes Mokae as Sam, Danny Glover as Willie, and Željko Ivanek as Hally. It was the first of his plays to premiere outside South Africa. Fugard chose New

Haven, Connecticut, in part because the play's setting was so personal that he feared it might disturb his brother and sister if it were produced first in South Africa. The setting was a bright tea room — a restaurant that serves light meals — interpreted to look like the tea room Fugard's mother actually ran in Port Elizabeth when he was a child. The space was open, the walls a whitish hue, everything simple and plain in decoration.

New York Times critic Frank Rich reviewed the premiere, saying, "*'MASTER HAROLD' . . . and the boys* is only an anecdote, really, and it's often as warm and musical as the men's dance. But somewhere along the way it rises up and breaks over the audience like a storm." Alan Stern of the *Boston Phoenix* linked the play with Greek tragedy:

> One reason for the play's potency is that, as in Greek tragedy, the events seem preordained — they're the by-product of social forces and human nature. Even as he spits in Sam's face, Hally realizes the magnitude of his action, that he is the one who will be harmed by it. And yet he can't help himself. Power corrupts, and in a society that sanctions the domination of one man — or set of men — over another, all relationships, even the promising ones, are poisoned.

Zakes Mokae and Danny Glover starred in the Broadway production in May 1982. After a brief period in which it was banned, the play was produced in Johannesburg, South Africa, in March 1983 with a South African cast. Joseph Lelyveld, in the *New York Times,* said of that production: "Athol Fugard's confessional drama about a white adolescent's initiation in the uses of racial power has come home to South Africa, and it left its multiracial audience . . . visibly shaken and stunned. . . . Many, blacks and whites, were crying."

The play was televised in 1984 with Matthew Broderick as Hally. It has had revivals in 1985 by the Trinity Repertory Company in Providence, in 1986 by the Boston Shakespeare Company in Boston, and in 1987 at the American Stage Festival in Milford, New Hampshire. These productions, although without Fugard's direction and without a "star" cast, had the same effect on their audiences as the major productions in New York and Johannesburg. Clifford Gallo in the *Boston Globe* called the American Stage Festival production "a devastating look at the loss of racial innocence in a nation where political and social inequality are the norm." Danny Glover revived the play in June 2003 in New York's Royale Theatre. This time he played Sam, whereas twenty years before he had played Willie.

Athol Fugard (b. 1932)

"MASTER HAROLD" . . . AND THE BOYS
1982

Characters

WILLIE
SAM
HALLY

(*The St. George's Park Tea Room on a wet and windy Port Elizabeth afternoon.*)

(*Tables and chairs have been cleared and are stacked on one side except for one which stands apart with a single chair. On this table a knife, fork, spoon and side plate in anticipation of a simple meal, together with a pile of comic books.*)

(*Other elements: a serving counter with a few stale cakes under glass and a not very impressive display of sweets, cigarettes and cool drinks, etc.; a few cardboard advertising handouts — Cadbury's Chocolate, Coca-Cola — and a blackboard on which an untrained hand has chalked up the prices of Tea, Coffee, Scones, Milk-shakes — all flavors — and Cool Drinks; a few sad ferns in pots; a telephone; an old-style jukebox.*)

(*There is an entrance on one side and an exit into a kitchen on the other.*)

(*Leaning on the solitary table, his head cupped in one hand as he pages through one of the comic books, is Sam. A black man in his mid-forties. He wears the white coat of a waiter. Behind him on his knees, mopping down the floor with a bucket of water and a rag, is Willie. Also black and about the same age as Sam. He has his sleeves and trousers rolled up.*)

(*The year: 1950.*)

WILLIE (*singing as he works*): "She was scandalizin'
　　my name,
She took my money
She called me honey
But she was scandalizin' my name.
Called it love but was playin' a game. . . ."

(*He gets up and moves the bucket. Stands thinking for a moment, then, raising his arms to hold an imaginary partner, he launches into an intricate ballroom dance step. Although a mildly comic figure, he reveals a reasonable degree of accomplishment.*)

Hey, Sam.

(*Sam, absorbed in the comic book, does not respond.*)

Hey, Boet° Sam!

(*Sam looks up.*)

Boet: Brother.

I'm getting it. The quickstep. Look now and tell me. (*He repeats the step.*) Well?

SAM (*encouragingly*): Show me again.

WILLIE: Okay, count for me.

SAM: Ready?

WILLIE: Ready.

SAM: Five, six, seven, eight. . . . (*Willie starts to dance.*) A-n-d one two three four . . . and one two three four. . . . (*Ad libbing as Willie dances.*) Your shoulders, Willie . . . your shoulders! Don't look down! Look happy, Willie! Relax, Willie!

WILLIE (*desperate but still dancing*): I am relax.

SAM: No, you're not.

WILLIE (*he falters*): Ag no man, Sam! Mustn't talk. You make me make mistakes.

SAM: But you're stiff.

WILLIE: Yesterday I'm not straight . . . today I'm too stiff!

SAM: Well, you are. You asked me and I'm telling you.

WILLIE: Where?

SAM: Everywhere. Try to glide through it.

WILLIE: Glide?

SAM: Ja, make it smooth. And give it more style. It must look like you're enjoying yourself.

WILLIE (*emphatically*): I wasn't.

SAM: Exactly.

WILLIE: How can I enjoy myself? Not straight, too stiff and now it's also glide, give it more style, make it smooth. . . . Haai! Is hard to remember all those things, Boet Sam.

SAM: That's your trouble. You're trying too hard.

WILLIE: I try hard because it *is* hard.

SAM: But don't let me see it. The secret is to make it look easy. Ballroom must look happy, Willie, not like hard work. It must. . . . Ja! . . . it must look like romance.

WILLIE: Now another one! What's romance?

SAM: Love story with happy ending. A handsome man in tails, and in his arms, smiling at him, a beautiful lady in evening dress!

WILLIE: Fred Astaire, Ginger Rogers.

SAM: You got it. Tapdance or ballroom, it's the same. Romance. In two weeks' time when the judges look at you and Hilda, they must see a man and a woman who are dancing their way to a happy ending. What I saw was you holding her like you were frightened she was going to run away.

WILLIE: Ja! Because that is what she wants to do! I got no romance left for Hilda anymore, Boet Sam.

SAM: Then pretend. When you put your arms around Hilda, imagine she is Ginger Rogers.

WILLIE: With no teeth? You try.

SAM: Well, just remember, there's only two weeks left.

WILLIE: I know, I know! (*To the jukebox.*) I do it better with music. You got sixpence for Sarah Vaughan?

SAM: That's a slow foxtrot. You're practicing the quickstep.

WILLIE: I'll practice slow foxtrot.

SAM (*shaking his head*): It's your turn to put money in the jukebox.

WILLIE: I only got bus fare to go home. (*He returns disconsolately to his work.*) Love story and happy ending! She's doing it all right, Boet Sam, but is not me she's giving happy endings. Fuckin' whore! Three nights now she doesn't come practice. I wind up gramophone, I get record ready and I sit and wait. What happens? Nothing. Ten o'clock I start dancing with my pillow. You try and practice romance by yourself, Boet Sam. Struesgod, she doesn't come tonight I take back my dress and ballroom shoes and I find me new partner. Size twenty-six. Shoes size seven. And now she's also making trouble for me with the baby again. Reports me to Child Wellfed, that I'm not giving her money. She lies! Every week I am giving her money for milk. And how do I know is my baby? Only his hair looks like me. She's fucking around all the time I turn my back. Hilda Samuels is a bitch! (*Pause.*) Hey, Sam!

SAM: Ja.

WILLIE: You listening?

SAM: Ja.

WILLIE: So what you say?

SAM: About Hilda?

WILLIE: Ja.

SAM: When did you last give her a hiding?

WILLIE (*reluctantly*): Sunday night.

SAM: And today is Thursday.

WILLIE (*he knows what's coming*): Okay.

SAM: Hiding on Sunday night, then Monday, Tuesday, and Wednesday she doesn't come to practice . . . and you are asking me why?

WILLIE: I said okay, Boet Sam!

SAM: You hit her too much. One day she's going to leave you for good.

WILLIE: So? She makes me the hell-in too much.

SAM (*emphasizing his point*): *Too* much and *too* hard. You had the same trouble with Eunice.

WILLIE: Because she also make the hell-in, Boet Sam. She never got the steps right. Even the waltz.

SAM: Beating her up every time she makes a mistake in the waltz? (*Shaking his head.*) No, Willie! That takes the pleasure out of ballroom dancing.

WILLIE: Hilda is not too bad with the waltz, Boet Sam. Is the quickstep where the trouble starts.

SAM (*teasing him gently*): How's your pillow with the quickstep?

WILLIE (*ignoring the tease*): Good! And why? Because it got no legs. That's her trouble. She can't move them quick enough, Boet Sam. I start the record and before halfway Count Basie is already winning. Only time we catch up with him is when gramophone runs down. (*Sam laughs.*) Haaikona, Boet Sam, is not funny.

SAM (*snapping his fingers*): I got it! Give her a handicap.

WILLIE: What's that?

SAM: Give her a ten-second start and then let Count Basie go. Then I put my money on her. Hot favorite in the Ballroom Stakes: Hilda Samuels ridden by Willie Malopo.

WILLIE (*turning away*): I'm not talking to you no more.

SAM (*relenting*): Sorry, Willie. . . .

WILLIE: It's finish between us.

SAM: Okay, okay . . . I'll stop.

WILLIE: You can also fuck off.

SAM: Willie, listen! I want to help you!

WILLIE: No more jokes?

SAM: I promise.

WILLIE: Okay. Help me.

SAM (*his turn to hold an imaginary partner*): Look and learn. Feet together. Back straight. Body relaxed. Right hand placed gently in the small of her back and wait for the music. Don't start worrying about making mistakes or the judges or the other competitors. It's just you, Hilda and the music, and you're going to have a good time. What Count Basie do you play?

WILLIE: "You the cream in my coffee, you the salt in my stew."

SAM: Right. Give it to me in strict tempo.

WILLIE: Ready?

SAM: Ready.

WILLIE: A-n-d . . . (*Singing.*)
"You the cream in my coffee.
You the salt in my stew.
You will always be my necessity.
I'd be lost without you. . . ." (*etc.*)

(*Sam launches into the quickstep. He is obviously a much more accomplished dancer than Willie. Hally enters. A seventeen-year-old white boy. Wet raincoat and school case. He stops and watches Sam. The demonstration comes to an end with a flourish. Applause from Hally and Willie.*)

HALLY: Bravo! No question about it. First place goes to Mr. Sam Semela.

WILLIE (*in total agreement*): You was gliding with style, Boet Sam.

HALLY (*cheerfully*): How's it, chaps?

SAM: Okay, Hally.

WILLIE (*springing to attention like a soldier and saluting*): At your service, Master Harold!

HALLY: Not long to the big event, hey!

SAM: Two weeks.

HALLY: You nervous?

SAM: No.

HALLY: Think you stand a chance?

SAM: Let's just say I'm ready to go out there and dance.

HALLY: It looked like it. What about you, Willie?

(*Willie groans.*)

What's the matter?

SAM: He's got leg trouble.

HALLY (*innocently*): Oh, sorry to hear that, Willie.

WILLIE: Boet Sam! You promised. (*Willie returns to his work.*)

(*Hally deposits his school case and takes off his raincoat. His clothes are a little neglected and untidy: black blazer with school badge, gray flannel trousers in need of an ironing, khaki shirt and tie, black shoes. Sam has fetched a towel for Hally to dry his hair.*)

HALLY: God, what a lousy bloody day. It's coming down cats and dogs out there. Bad for business, chaps. . . . (*Conspiratorial whisper.*) . . . but it also means we're in for a nice quiet afternoon.

SAM: You can speak loud. Your Mom's not here.

HALLY: Out shopping?

SAM: No. The hospital.

HALLY: But it's Thursday. There's no visiting on Thursday afternoons. Is my Dad okay?

SAM: Sounds like it. In fact, I think he's going home.

HALLY (*stopped short by Sam's remark*): What do you mean?

SAM: The hospital phoned.

HALLY: To say what?

SAM: I don't know. I just heard your Mom talking.

HALLY: So what makes you say he's going home?

SAM: It sounded as if they were telling her to come and fetch him.

(*Hally thinks about what Sam has said for a few seconds.*)

HALLY: When did she leave?

SAM: About an hour ago. She said she would phone you. Want to eat?

(*Hally doesn't respond.*)

Hally, want your lunch?

HALLY: I suppose so. (*His mood has changed.*) What's on the menu? . . . as if I don't know.

SAM: Soup, followed by meat pie and gravy.

HALLY: Today's?

SAM: No.

HALLY: And the soup?

SAM: Nourishing pea soup.

HALLY: Just the soup. (*The pile of comic books on the table.*) And these?

National Theatre of London's 1983 production of *"MASTER HAROLD"* . . . *and the boys* with (from left to right) Ramolao Makene as Willie, Duart Sylwain as Hally, and John Kani as Sam.

SAM: For your Dad. Mr. Kempston brought them.

HALLY: You haven't been reading them, have you?

SAM: Just looking.

HALLY (*examining the comics*): *Jungle Jim . . . Batman and Robin . . . Tarzan . . .* God, what rubbish! Mental pollution. Take them away.

(*Sam exits waltzing into the kitchen. Hally turns to Willie.*)

HALLY: Did you hear my Mom talking on the telephone, Willie?

WILLIE: No, Master Hally. I was at the back.

HALLY: And she didn't say anything to you before she left?

WILLIE: She said I must clean the floors.

HALLY: I mean about my Dad.

WILLIE: She didn't say nothing to me about him, Master Hally.

HALLY (*with conviction*): No! It can't be. They said he needed at least another three weeks of treatment. Sam's definitely made a mistake. (*Rummages through his school case, finds a book and settles down at the table to read.*) So, Willie!

WILLIE: Yes, Master Hally! Schooling okay today?

HALLY: Yes, okay. . . . (*He thinks about it.*) . . . No, not really. Ag, what's the difference? I don't care. And Sam says you've got problems.

WILLIE: Big problems.

HALLY: Which leg is sore?

(*Willie groans.*)

Both legs.

WILLIE: There is nothing wrong with my legs. Sam is just making jokes.

HALLY: So then you *will* be in the competition.

WILLIE: Only if I can find a partner.

HALLY: But what about Hilda?

SAM (*returning with a bowl of soup*): She's the one who's got trouble with her legs.

HALLY: What sort of trouble, Willie?

SAM: From the way he describes it, I think the lady has gone a bit lame.

HALLY: Good God! Have you taken her to see a doctor?

SAM: I think a vet would be better.

HALLY: What do you mean?

SAM: What do you call it again when a racehorse goes very fast?

HALLY: Gallop?

SAM: That's it!

WILLIE: Boet Sam!

HALLY: "A gallop down the homestretch to the winning post." But what's that got to do with Hilda?

SAM: Count Basie always gets there first.

(*Willie lets fly with his slop rag. It misses Sam and hits Hally.*)

HALLY (*furious*): For Christ's sake, Willie! What the hell do you think you're doing?

WILLIE: Sorry, Master Hally, but it's him. . . .

HALLY: Act your bloody age! (*Hurls the rag back at Willie.*) Cut out the nonsense now and get on with your work. And you too, Sam. Stop fooling around.

(*Sam moves away.*)

No. Hang on. I haven't finished! Tell me exactly what my Mom said.

SAM: I have. "When Hally comes, tell him I've gone to the hospital and I'll phone him."

HALLY: She didn't say anything about taking my Dad home?

SAM: No. It's just that when she was talking on the phone. . . .

HALLY (*interrupting him*): No, Sam. They can't be discharging him. She would have said so if they were. In any case, we saw him last night and he wasn't in good shape at all. Staff nurse even said there was talk about taking more X-rays. And now suddenly today he's better? If anything, it sounds more like a bad turn to me . . . which I sincerely hope it isn't. Hang on . . . how long ago did you say she left?

SAM: Just before two . . . (*His wrist watch.*) . . . hour and a half.

HALLY: I know how to settle it. (*Behind the counter to the telephone. Talking as he dials.*) Let's give her ten minutes to get to the hospital, ten minutes to load him up, another ten, at the most, to get home, and another ten to get him inside. Forty minutes. They should have been home for at least half an hour already. (*Pause — he waits with the receiver to his ear.*) No reply, chaps. And you know why? Because she's at his bedside in hospital helping him pull through a bad turn. You definitely heard wrong.

SAM: Okay.

(*As far as Hally is concerned, the matter is settled. He returns to his table, sits down, and divides his attention between the book and his soup. Sam is at his school case and picks up a textbook.*)

Modern Graded Mathematics for Standards Nine and Ten. (*Opens it at random and laughs at something he sees.*) Who is this supposed to be?

HALLY: Old fart-face Prentice.

SAM: Teacher?

HALLY: Thinks he is. And believe me, that is not a bad likeness.

SAM: Has he seen it?

HALLY: Yes.

SAM: What did he say?

HALLY: Tried to be clever, as usual. Said I was no Leonardo da Vinci and that bad art had to be punished. So, six of the best, and his are bloody good.

SAM: On your bum?

HALLY: Where else? The days when I got them on my hands are gone forever, Sam.

SAM: With your trousers down!

HALLY: No. He's not quite that barbaric.

SAM: That's the way they do it in jail.

HALLY (*flicker of morbid interest*): Really?

SAM: Ja. When the magistrate sentences you to "strokes with a light cane."

HALLY: Go on.

SAM: They make you lie down on a bench. One policeman pulls down your trousers and holds your ankles, another one pulls your shirt over your head and holds your arms. . . .

HALLY: Thank you! That's enough.

SAM: . . . and the one that gives you the strokes talks to you gently and for a long time between each one. (*He laughs.*)

HALLY: I've heard enough, Sam! Jesus! It's a bloody awful world when you come to think of it. People can be real bastards.

SAM: That's the way it is, Hally.

HALLY: It doesn't *have* to be that way. There is something called progress, you know. We don't exactly burn people at the stake anymore.

SAM: Like Joan of Arc.

HALLY: Correct. If she was captured today, she'd be given a fair trial.

SAM: And then the death sentence.

HALLY (*a world-weary sigh*): I know, I know! I oscillate between hope and despair for this world as well, Sam. But things will change, you wait and see. One day somebody is going to get up and give history a kick up the backside and get it going again.

SAM: Like who?

HALLY (*after thought*): They're called social reformers. Every age, Sam, has got its social reformer. My history book is full of them.

SAM: So where's ours?

HALLY: Good question. And I hate to say it, but the answer is: I don't know. Maybe he hasn't even been born yet. Or is still only a babe in arms at his mother's breast. God, what a thought.

SAM: So we just go on waiting.

HALLY: Ja, looks like it. (*Back to his soup and the book.*)

SAM (*reading from the textbook*): "Introduction: In some mathematical problems only the magnitude. . . ." (*He mispronounces the word "magnitude."*)

HALLY (*correcting him without looking up*): Magnitude.

SAM: What's it mean?

HALLY: How big it is. The size of the thing.

SAM (*reading*): ". . . magnitude of the quantities is of importance. In other problems we need to know whether these quantities are negative or positive. For example, whether there is a debit or credit bank balance . . ."

HALLY: Whether you're broke or not.

SAM: ". . . whether the temperature is above or below Zero. . . ."

HALLY: Naught degrees. Cheerful state of affairs! No cash and you're freezing to death. Mathematics won't get you out of that one.

SAM: "All these quantities are called . . ." (*spelling the word*) . . . s-c-a-l- . . .

HALLY: Scalars.

SAM: Scalars! (*Shaking his head with a laugh.*) You understand all that?

HALLY (*turning a page*): No. And I don't intend to try.

SAM: So what happens when the exams come?

HALLY: Failing a maths exam isn't the end of the world, Sam. How many times have I told you that examination results don't measure intelligence?

SAM: I would say about as many times as you've failed one of them.

HALLY (*mirthlessly*): Ha, ha, ha.

SAM (*simultaneously*): Ha, ha, ha.

HALLY: Just remember Winston Churchill didn't do particularly well at school.

SAM: You've also told me that one many times.

HALLY: Well, it just so happens to be the truth.

SAM (*enjoying the word*): Magnitude! Magnitude! Show me how to use it.

HALLY (*after thought*): An intrepid social reformer will not be daunted by the magnitude of the task he has undertaken.

SAM (*impressed*): Couple of jaw-breakers in there!

HALLY: I gave you three for the price of one. Intrepid, daunted, and magnitude. I did that once in an exam. Put five of the words I had to explain in one sentence. It was half a page long.

SAM: Well, I'll put my money on you in the English exam.

HALLY: Piece of cake. Eighty percent without even trying.

SAM (*another textbook from Hally's case*): And history?

HALLY: So-so. I'll scrape through. In the fifties if I'm lucky.

SAM: You didn't do too badly last year.

HALLY: Because we had World War One. That at least has some action. You try to find that in the South African Parliamentary system.

SAM (*reading from the history textbook*): "Napoleon and the principle of equality." Hey! This sounds interesting. "After concluding peace with Britain in 1802, Napoleon used a brief period of calm to insti-tute . . ."

HALLY: Introduce.

SAM: ". . . many reforms. Napoleon regarded all people as equal before the law and wanted them to have equal opportunities for advancement. All ves-ti-ges of the feu-dal sys-tem with its oppression of the poor were abol-ished." Vestiges, feudal system, and abolished. I'm all right on oppression.

HALLY: I'm thinking. He swept away . . . abol-ished . . . the last remains . . . vestiges . . . of the bad old days . . . feudal system.

SAM: Ha! There's the social reformer we're waiting for. He sounds like a man of some magnitude.

HALLY: I'm not so sure about that. It's a damn good title for a book, though. A man of magnitude!

SAM: He sounds pretty big to me, Hally.

HALLY: Don't confuse historical significance with greatness. But maybe I'm being a bit prejudiced. Have a look in there and you'll see he's two chapters long. And hell! . . . has he only got dates, Sam, all of which you've got to remember! This campaign and that campaign, and then, because of all the fighting, the next thing is we get Peace Treaties all over the place. And what's the end of the story? Battle of Waterloo, which he loses. Wasn't worth it. No, I don't know about him as a man of magnitude.

SAM: Then who would you say was?

HALLY: To answer that, we need a definition of greatness, and I suppose that would be somebody who . . . somebody who benefited all mankind.

SAM: Right. But like who?

HALLY (*he speaks with total conviction*): Charles Darwin. Remember him? That big book from the library. *The Origin of the Species.*

SAM: Him?

HALLY: Yes. For his Theory of Evolution.

SAM: You didn't finish it.

HALLY: I ran out of time. I didn't finish it because my two weeks were up. But I'm going to take it out again after I've digested what I read. It's safe. I've hidden it away in the Theology section. Nobody ever goes in there. And anyway who are you to talk? You hardly even looked at it.

SAM: I tried. I looked at the chapters in the beginning and I saw one called "The Struggle for an Existence." Ah ha, I thought. At last! But what did I get? Something called the mistiltoe which needs the apple tree and there's too many seeds and all are going to die except one . . . ! No, Hally.

HALLY (*intellectually outraged*): What do you mean, No! The poor man had to start somewhere. For God's sake, Sam, he revolutionized science. Now we know.

SAM: What?

HALLY: Where we come from and what it all means.

SAM: And that's a benefit to mankind? Anyway, I still don't believe it.

HALLY: God, you're impossible. I showed it to you in black and white.

SAM: Doesn't mean I got to believe it.

HALLY: It's the likes of you that kept the Inquisition in business. It's called bigotry. Anyway, that's my man of magnitude. Charles Darwin! Who's yours?

SAM (*without hesitation*): Abraham Lincoln.

HALLY: I might have guessed as much. Don't get sentimental, Sam. You've never been a slave, you know. And anyway we freed your ancestors here in South Africa long before the Americans. But if you want to thank somebody on their behalf, do it to Mr. William Wilberforce.° Come on. Try again. I want a real genius.

(*Now enjoying himself, and so is Sam. Hally goes behind the counter and helps himself to a chocolate.*)

SAM: William Shakespeare.

HALLY (*no enthusiasm*): Oh. So you're also one of them,

Mr. William Wilberforce: (1759–1833), British statesman who supported a bill outlawing the slave trade and suppressing slavery in the British Empire.

are you? You're basing that opinion on only one play, you know. You've only read my *Julius Caesar* and even I don't understand half of what they're talking about. They should do what they did with the old Bible: bring the language up to date.

SAM: That's all you've got. It's also the only one *you've* read.

HALLY: I know. I admit it. That's why I suggest we reserve our judgment until we've checked up on a few others. I've got a feeling, though, that by the end of this year one is going to be enough for me, and I can give you the names of twenty-nine other chaps in the Standard Nine class of the Port Elizabeth Technical College who feel the same. But if you want him, you can have him. My turn now. (*Pacing.*) This is a damned good exercise, you know! It started off looking like a simple question and here it's got us really probing into the intellectual heritage of our civilization.

SAM: So who is it going to be?

HALLY: My next man . . . and he gets the title on two scores: social reform and literary genius . . . is Leo Nikolaevich Tolstoy.

SAM: That Russian.

HALLY: Correct. Remember the picture of him I showed you?

SAM: With the long beard.

HALLY (*trying to look like Tolstoy*): And those burning, visionary eyes. My God, the face of a social prophet if ever I saw one! And remember my words when I showed it to you? Here's a *man*, Sam!

SAM: Those were words, Hally.

HALLY: Not many intellectuals are prepared to shovel manure with the peasants and then go home and write a "little book" called *War and Peace.* Incidentally, Sam, he was somebody else who, to quote, ". . . did not distinguish himself scholastically."

SAM: Meaning?

HALLY: He was also no good at school.

SAM: Like you and Winston Churchill.

HALLY (*mirthlessly*): Ha, ha, ha.

SAM (*simultaneously*): Ha, ha, ha.

HALLY: Don't get clever, Sam. That man freed his serfs of his own free will.

SAM: No argument. He was a somebody, all right. I accept him.

HALLY: I'm sure Count Tolstoy will be very pleased to hear that. Your turn. Shoot. (*Another chocolate from behind the counter.*) I'm waiting, Sam.

SAM: I've got him.

HALLY: Good. Submit your candidate for examination.

SAM: Jesus.

HALLY (*stopped dead in his tracks*): Who?

SAM: Jesus Christ.

HALLY: Oh, come on, Sam!

SAM: The Messiah.

HALLY: Ja, but still . . . No, Sam. Don't let's get started on religion. We'll just spend the whole afternoon arguing again. Suppose I turn around and say Mohammed?

SAM: All right.

HALLY: You can't have them both on the same list!

SAM: Why not? You like Mohammed, I like Jesus.

HALLY: I *don't* like Mohammed. I never have. I was merely being hypothetical. As far as I'm concerned, the Koran is as bad as the Bible. No. Religion is out! I'm not going to waste my time again arguing with you about the existence of God. You know perfectly well I'm an atheist . . . and I've got homework to do.

SAM: Okay, I take him back.

HALLY: You've got time for one more name.

SAM (*after thought*): I've got one I know we'll agree on. A simple straightforward great Man of Magnitude . . . and no arguments. And *he* really *did* benefit all mankind.

HALLY: I wonder. After your last contribution I'm beginning to doubt whether anything in the way of an intellectual agreement is possible between the two of us. Who is he?

SAM: Guess.

HALLY: Socrates? Alexandre Dumas? Karl Marx? Dostoevsky? Nietzsche?

(*Sam shakes his head after each name.*)

Give me a clue.

SAM: The letter *P* is important. . . .

HALLY: Plato!

SAM: . . . and his name begins with an *F*.

HALLY: I've got it. Freud and Psychology.

SAM: No. I didn't understand him.

HALLY: That makes two of us.

SAM: Think of moldy apricot jam.

HALLY (*after a delighted laugh*): Penicillin and Sir Alexander Fleming! And the title of the book: *The Microbe Hunters.* (*Delighted.*) Splendid, Sam! Splendid. For once we are in total agreement. The major breakthrough in medical science in the Twentieth Century. If it wasn't for him, we might have lost the Second World War. It's deeply gratifying, Sam, to know that I haven't been wasting my time in talking to you. (*Strutting around proudly.*) Tolstoy may have educated his peasants, but I've educated you.

SAM: Standard Four to Standard Nine.

HALLY: Have we been at it as long as that?

SAM: Yep. And my first lesson was geography.

HALLY (*intrigued*): Really? I don't remember.

SAM: My room there at the back of the old Jubilee Boarding House. I had just started working for your Mom. Little boy in short trousers walks in one afternoon and asks me seriously: "Sam, do you want to see South Africa?" Hey man! Sure I wanted to see South Africa!

HALLY: Was that me?

SAM: . . . So the next thing I'm looking at a map you had just done for homework. It was your first one and you were very proud of yourself.

HALLY: Go on.

SAM: Then came my first lesson. "Repeat after me, Sam: Gold in the Transvaal, mealies in the Free State, sugar in Natal, and grapes in the Cape." I still know it!

HALLY: Well, I'll be buggered. So that's how it all started.

SAM: And your next map was one with all the rivers and the mountains they came from. The Orange, the Vaal, the Limpopo, the Zambezi. . . .

HALLY: You've got a phenomenal memory!

SAM: You should be grateful. That is why you started passing your exams. You tried to be better than me.

(*They laugh together. Willie is attracted by the laughter and joins them.*)

HALLY: The old Jubilee Boarding House. Sixteen rooms with board and lodging, rent in advance and one week's notice. I haven't thought about it for donkey's years . . . and I don't think that's an accident. God, was I glad when we sold it and moved out. Those years are not remembered as the happiest ones of an unhappy childhood.

WILLIE (*knocking on the table and trying to imitate a woman's voice*): "Hally, are you there?"

HALLY: Who's that supposed to be?

WILLIE: "What you doing in there, Hally? Come out at once!"

HALLY (*to Sam*): What's he talking about?

SAM: Don't you remember?

WILLIE: "Sam, Willie . . . is he in there with you boys?"

SAM: Hiding away in our room when your mother was looking for you.

HALLY (*another good laugh*): Of course! I used to crawl and hide under your bed! But finish the story, Willie. Then what used to happen? You chaps would give the game away by telling her I was in there with you. So much for friendship.

SAM: We couldn't lie to her. She knew.

HALLY: Which meant I got another rowing for hanging around the "servants' quarters." I think I spent more time in there with you chaps than anywhere else in that dump. And do you blame me? Nothing but bloody misery wherever you went. Somebody was always complaining about the food, or my mother was having a fight with Micky Nash because she'd caught her with a petty officer in her room. Maud Meiring was another one. Remember those two? They were prostitutes, you know. Soldiers and sailors from the troopships. Bottom fell out of the business when the war ended. God, the flotsam and jetsam that life washed up on our shores! No joking, if it wasn't for your room, I would have been the first certified ten-year-old in medical history. Ja, the memories are coming back now. Walking home from school and thinking: "What can I do this afternoon?" Try out a few ideas, but sooner or later I'd end up in there with you fellows. I bet you I could still find my way to your room with my eyes closed. (*He does exactly that.*) Down the corridor . . . telephone on the right, which my Mom keeps locked because somebody is using it on the sly and not paying . . . past the kitchen and unappetizing cooking smells . . . around the corner into the backyard, hold my breath again because there are more smells coming when I pass your lavatory, then into that little passageway, first door on the right and into your room. How's that?

SAM: Good. But, as usual, you forgot to knock.

HALLY: Like that time I barged in and caught you and Cynthia . . . at it. Remember? God, was I embarrassed! I didn't know what was going on at first.

SAM: Ja, that taught you a lesson.

HALLY: And about a lot more than knocking on doors, I'll have you know, and I don't mean geography either. Hell, Sam, couldn't you have waited until it was dark?

SAM: No.

HALLY: Was it that urgent?

SAM: Yes, and if you don't believe me, wait until your time comes.

HALLY: No, thank you. I am not interested in girls. (*Back to his memories. . . . Using a few chairs he recreates the room as he lists the items.*) A gray little room with a cold cement floor. Your bed against that wall . . . and I now know why the mattress sags so much! . . . Willie's bed . . . it's propped up on bricks because one leg is broken . . . that wobbly little table with the washbasin and jug of water . . . Yes! . . . stuck to the wall above it are some pin-up pictures from magazines. Joe Louis. . . .

WILLIE: Brown Bomber. World Title. (*Boxing pose.*) Three rounds and knockout.

HALLY: Against who?

SAM: Max Schmeling.

HALLY: Correct. I can also remember Fred Astaire and Ginger Rogers, and Rita Hayworth in a bathing costume which always made me hot and bothered when I looked at it. Under Willie's bed is an old suitcase with all his clothes in a mess, which is why I never hide there. Your things are neat and tidy in a trunk next to your bed, and on it there is a picture of you and Cynthia in your ballroom clothes, your first silver cup for third place in a competition and an old radio which doesn't work anymore. Have I left out anything?

SAM: No.

HALLY: Right, so much for the stage directions. Now the characters. (*Sam and Willie move to their appropriate positions in the bedroom.*) Willie is in bed, under his blankets with his clothes on, complaining nonstop about something, but we can't make out a word of what he's saying because he's got his head under the blankets as well. You're on your bed trimming your toenails with a knife — not a very edifying sight — and as for me. . . . What am I doing?

SAM: You're sitting on the floor giving Willie a lecture about being a good loser while you get the checkerboard and pieces ready for a game. Then you go to Willie's bed, pull off the blankets and make him play

with you first because you know you're going to win, and that gives you the second game with me.

HALLY: And you certainly were a bad loser, Willie!

WILLIE: Haai!

HALLY: Wasn't he, Sam? And so slow! A game with you almost took the whole afternoon. Thank God I gave up trying to teach you how to play chess.

WILLIE: You and Sam cheated.

HALLY: I never saw Sam cheat, and mine were mostly the mistakes of youth.

WILLIE: Then how is it you two was always winning?

HALLY: Have you ever considered the possibility, Willie, that it was because we were better than you?

WILLIE: Every time better?

HALLY: Not every time. There were occasions when we deliberately let you win a game so that you would stop sulking and go on playing with us. Sam used to wink at me when you weren't looking to show me it was time to let you win.

WILLIE: So then you two didn't play fair.

HALLY: It was for your benefit, Mr. Malopo, which is more than being fair. It was an act of self-sacrifice. (*To Sam.*) But you know what my best memory is, don't you?

SAM: No.

HALLY: Come on, guess. If your memory is so good, you must remember it as well.

SAM: We got up to a lot of tricks in there, Hally.

HALLY: This one was special, Sam.

SAM: I'm listening.

HALLY: It started off looking like another of those useless nothing-to-do afternoons. I'd already been down to Main Street looking for adventure, but nothing had happened. I didn't feel like climbing trees in the Donkin Park or pretending I was a private eye and following a stranger . . . so as usual: See what's cooking in Sam's room. This time it was you on the floor. You had two thin pieces of wood and you were smoothing them down with a knife. It didn't look particularly interesting, but when I asked you what you were doing, you just said, "Wait and see, Hally. Wait . . . and see". . . in that secret sort of way of yours, so I knew there was a surprise coming. You teased me, you bugger, by being deliberately slow and not answering my questions!

(*Sam laughs.*)

And whistling while you worked away! God, it was infuriating! I could have brained you! It was only when you tied them together in a cross and put that down on the brown paper that I realized what you were doing. "Sam is making a kite?" And when I asked you and you said, "Yes". . . ! (*Shaking his head with disbelief.*) The sheer audacity of it took my breath away. I mean, seriously, what the hell does a black man know about flying a kite? I'll be honest with you, Sam, I had no hopes for it. If you think I was excited and happy, you got another guess coming. In fact, I was shit-scared that we were going to make fools of ourselves. When we left the boarding house to go up onto the hill, I was praying quietly that there wouldn't be any other kids around to laugh at us.

SAM (*enjoying the memory as much as Hally*): Ja, I could see that.

HALLY: I made it obvious, did I?

SAM: Ja. You refused to carry it.

HALLY: Do you blame me? Can you remember what the poor thing looked like? Tomato-box wood and brown paper! Flour and water for glue! Two of my mother's old stockings for a tail, and then all those bits and pieces of string you made me tie together so that we could fly it! Hell, no, that was now only asking for a miracle to happen.

SAM: Then the big argument when I told you to hold the string and run with it when I let go.

HALLY: I was prepared to run, all right, but straight back to the boarding house.

SAM (*knowing what's coming*): So what happened?

HALLY: Come on, Sam, you remember as well as I do.

SAM: I want to hear it from you.

(*Hally pauses. He wants to be as accurate as possible.*)

HALLY: You went a little distance from me down the hill, you held it up ready to let it go. . . . "This is it," I thought. "Like everything else in my life, here comes another fiasco." Then you shouted, "Go, Hally!" and I started to run. (*Another pause.*) I don't know how to describe it, Sam. Ja! The miracle happened! I was running, waiting for it to crash to the ground, but instead suddenly there was something alive behind me at the end of the string, tugging at it as if it wanted to be free. I looked back . . . (*Shakes his head.*) . . . I still can't believe my eyes. It was flying! Looping around and trying to climb even higher into the sky. You shouted to me to let it have more string. I did, until there was none left and I was just holding that piece of wood we had tied it to. You came up and joined me. You were laughing.

SAM: So were you. And shouting, "It works, Sam! We've done it!"

HALLY: And we had! I was so proud of us! It was the most splendid thing I had ever seen. I wished there were hundreds of kids around to watch us. The part that scared me, though, was when you showed me how to make it dive down to the ground and then just when it was on the point of crashing, swoop up again!

SAM: You didn't want to try yourself.

HALLY: Of course not! I would have been suicidal if anything had happened to it. Watching you do it made me nervous enough. I was quite happy just to see it up there with its tail fluttering behind it. You left me after that, didn't you? You explained how to get it down, we tied it to the bench so that I could sit and watch it, and you went away. I wanted you to stay,

you know. I was a little scared of having to look after it by myself.

SAM (*quietly*): I had work to do, Hally.

HALLY: It was sort of sad bringing it down, Sam. And it looked sad again when it was lying there on the ground. Like something that had lost its soul. Just tomato-box wood, brown paper and two of my mother's old stockings! But, hell, I'll never forget that first moment when I saw it up there. I had a stiff neck the next day from looking up so much.

(*Sam laughs. Hally turns to him with a question he never thought of asking before.*)

Why did you make that kite, Sam?

SAM (*evenly*): I can't remember.

HALLY: Truly?

SAM: Too long ago, Hally.

HALLY: Ja, I suppose it was. It's time for another one, you know.

SAM: Why do you say that?

HALLY: Because it feels like that. Wouldn't be a good day to fly it, though.

SAM: No. You can't fly kites on rainy days.

HALLY (*He studies Sam. Their memories have made him conscious of the man's presence in his life.*): How old are you, Sam?

SAM: Two score and five.

HALLY: Strange, isn't it?

SAM: What?

HALLY: Me and you.

SAM: What's strange about it?

HALLY: Little white boy in short trousers and a black man old enough to be his father flying a kite. It's not every day you see that.

SAM: But why strange? Because the one is white and the other black?

HALLY: I don't know. Would have been just as strange, I suppose, if it had been me and my Dad . . . cripple man and a little boy! Nope! There's no chance of me flying a kite without it being strange. (*Simple statement of fact — no self-pity.*) There's a nice little short story there. "The Kite-Flyers." But we'd have to find a twist in the ending.

SAM: Twist?

HALLY: Yes. Something unexpected. The way it ended with us was too straightforward . . . me on the bench and you going back to work. There's no drama in that.

WILLIE: And me?

HALLY: You?

WILLIE: Yes me.

HALLY: You want to get into the story as well, do you? I got it! Change the title: "Afternoons in Sam's Room". . . expand it and tell all the stories. It's on its way to being a novel. Our days in the old Jubilee. Sad in a way that they're over. I almost wish we were still in that little room.

SAM: We're still together.

HALLY: That's true. It's just that life felt the right size in there . . . not too big and not too small. Wasn't so hard to work up a bit of courage. It's got so bloody complicated since then.

(*The telephone rings. Sam answers it.*)

SAM: St. George's Park Tea Room . . . Hello, Madam . . . Yes, Madam, he's here. . . . Hally, it's your mother.

HALLY: Where is she phoning from?

SAM: Sounds like the hospital. It's a public telephone.

HALLY (*relieved*): You see! I told you. (*The telephone.*) Hello, Mom . . . Yes . . . Yes no fine. Everything's under control here. How's things with poor old Dad? . . . Has he had a bad turn? . . . What? . . . Oh, God! . . . Yes, Sam told me, but I was sure he'd made a mistake. But what's this all about, Mom? He didn't look at all good last night. How can he get better so quickly? . . . Then very obviously you must say no. Be firm with him. You're the boss. . . . You know what it's going to be like if he comes home. . . . Well then, don't blame me when I fail my exams at the end of the year. . . . Yes! How am I expected to be fresh for school when I spend half the night massaging his gammy leg? . . . So am I! . . . So tell him a white lie. Say Dr. Colley wants more X-rays of his stump. Or bribe him. We'll sneak in double tots of brandy in future. . . . What? . . . Order him to get back into bed at once! If he's going to behave like a child, treat him like one. . . . All right, Mom! I was just trying to . . . I'm sorry. . . . I said I'm sorry. . . . Quick, give me your number. I'll phone you back. (*He hangs up and waits a few seconds.*) Here we go again! (*He dials.*) I'm sorry, Mom. . . . Okay. . . . But now listen to me carefully. All it needs is for you to put your foot down. Don't take no for an answer. . . . Did you hear me? And whatever you do, don't discuss it with him. . . . Because I'm frightened you'll give in to him. . . . Yes, Sam gave me lunch. . . . I ate all of it! . . . No, Mom not a soul. It's still raining here. . . . Right, I'll tell them. I'll just do some homework and then lock up. . . . But remember now, Mom. Don't listen to anything he says. And phone me back and let me know what happens. . . . Okay. Bye, Mom. (*He hangs up. The men are staring at him.*) My Mom says that when you're finished with the floors you must do the windows. (*Pause.*) Don't misunderstand me, chaps. All I want is for him to get better. And if he was, I'd be the first person to say: "Bring him home." But he's not, and we can't give him the medical care and attention he needs at home. That's what hospitals are there for. (*Brusquely.*) So don't just stand there! Get on with it!

(*Sam clears Hally's table.*)

You heard right. My Dad wants to go home.

SAM: Is he better?

HALLY (*sharply*): No! How the hell can he be better when last night he was groaning with pain? This is not an age of miracles!

SAM: Then he should stay in hospital.

HALLY (*seething with irritation and frustration*): Tell me something I don't know, Sam. What the hell do you think I was saying to my Mom? All I can say is fuck-it-all.

SAM: I'm sure he'll listen to your Mom.

HALLY: You don't know what she's up against. He's already packed his shaving kit and pajamas and is sitting on his bed with his crutches, dressed and ready to go. I know him when he gets in that mood. If she tries to reason with him, we've had it. She's no match for him when it comes to a battle of words. He'll tie her up in knots. (*Trying to hide his true feelings.*)

SAM: I suppose it gets lonely for him in there.

HALLY: With all the patients and nurses around? Regular visits from the Salvation Army? Balls! It's ten times worse for him at home. I'm at school and my mother is here in the business all day.

SAM: He's at least got you at night.

HALLY (*before he can stop himself*): And we've got him! Please! I don't want to talk about it anymore. (*Unpacks his school case, slamming down books on the table.*) Life is just a plain bloody mess, that's all. And people are fools.

SAM: Come on, Hally.

HALLY: Yes, they are! They bloody well deserve what they get.

SAM: Then don't complain.

HALLY: Don't try to be clever, Sam. It doesn't suit you. Anybody who thinks there's nothing wrong with this world needs to have his head examined. Just when things are going along all right, without fail someone or something will come along and spoil everything. Somebody should write that down as a fundamental law of the Universe. The principle of perpetual disappointment. If there is a God who created this world, he should scrap it and try again.

SAM: All right, Hally, all right. What you got for homework?

HALLY: Bullshit, as usual. (*Opens an exercise book and reads.*) "Write five hundred words describing an annual event of cultural or historical significance."

SAM: That should be easy enough for you.

HALLY: And also plain bloody boring. You know what he wants, don't you? One of their useless old ceremonies. The commemoration of the landing of the 1820 Settlers, or if it's going to be culture, Carols by Candlelight every Christmas.

SAM: It's an impressive sight. Make a good description, Hally. All those candles glowing in the dark and the people singing hymns.

HALLY: And it's called religious hysteria. (*Intense irritation.*) Please, Sam! Just leave me alone and let me get on with it. I'm not in the mood for games this afternoon. And remember my Mom's orders . . . you're to help Willie with the windows. Come on now, I don't want any more nonsense in here.

SAM: Okay, Hally, okay.

(*Hally settles down to his homework; determined preparations . . . pen, ruler, exercise book, dictionary, another cake . . . all of which will lead to nothing.*)

(*Sam waltzes over to Willie and starts to replace tables and chairs. He practices a ballroom step while doing so. Willie watches. When Sam is finished, Willie tries.*)

Good! But just a little bit quicker on the turn and only move in to her after she's crossed over. What about this one?

(*Another step. When Sam is finished, Willie again has a go.*)

Much better. See what happens when you just relax and enjoy yourself? Remember that in two weeks' time and you'll be all right.

WILLIE: But I haven't got partner, Boet Sam.

SAM: Maybe Hilda will turn up tonight.

WILLIE: No, Boet Sam. (*Reluctantly.*) I gave her a good hiding.

SAM: You mean a bad one.

WILLIE: Good bad one.

SAM: Then you mustn't complain either. Now you pay the price for losing your temper.

WILLIE: I also pay two pounds ten shilling entrance fee.

SAM: They'll refund you if you withdraw now.

WILLIE (*appalled*): You mean, don't dance?

SAM: Yes.

WILLIE: No! I wait too long and I practice too hard. If I find me new partner, you think I can be ready in two weeks? I ask Madam for my leave now and we practice every day.

SAM: Quickstep nonstop for two weeks. World record, Willie, but you'll be mad at the end.

WILLIE: No jokes, Boet Sam.

SAM: I'm not joking.

WILLIE: So then what?

SAM: Find Hilda. Say you're sorry and promise you won't beat her again.

WILLIE: No.

SAM: Then withdraw. Try again next year.

WILLIE: No.

SAM: Then I give up.

WILLIE: Haaikona, Boet Sam, you can't.

SAM: What do you mean, I can't? I'm telling you: I give up.

WILLIE (*adamant*): No! (*Accusingly.*) It was you who start me ballroom dancing.

SAM: So?

WILLIE: Before that I use to be happy. And is you and Miriam who bring me to Hilda and say here's partner for you.

SAM: What are you saying, Willie?

WILLIE: You!

SAM: But me what? To blame?

WILLIE: Yes.

SAM: Willie . . . ? (*Bursts into laughter.*)

WILLIE: And now all you do is make jokes at me. You wait. When Miriam leaves you is my turn to laugh. Ha! Ha! Ha!

SAM (*he can't tak*
leave me tonig
an imaginary
dances and si
"Just a fellov
Dancin' like
In an autum

WILLIE: There

(*Sam goes on*

Boet Sam!

SAM: There's the a
nouncement in two weeks' tim
men, the winner in the open section . . . Mr.
Malopo and his pillow!"

(*This is too much for a now really angry Willie. He goes for Sam, but the latter is too quick for him and puts Hally's table between the two of them.*)

HALLY (*exploding*): For Christ's sake, you two!

WILLIE (*still trying to get at Sam*): I donner you, Sam! Struesgod!

SAM (*still laughing*): Sorry, Willie . . . Sorry. . . .

HALLY: Sam! Willie! (*Grabs his ruler and gives Willie a vicious whack on the bum.*) How the hell am I supposed to concentrate with the two of you behaving like bloody children!

WILLIE: Hit him too!

HALLY: Shut up, Willie.

WILLIE: He started jokes again.

HALLY: Get back to your work. You too, Sam. (*His ruler.*) Do you want another one, Willie?

(*Sam and Willie return to their work. Hally uses the opportunity to escape from his unsuccessful attempt at homework. He struts around like a little despot, ruler in hand, giving vent to his anger and frustration.*)

Suppose a customer had walked in then? Or the Park Superintendent. And seen the two of you behaving like a pair of hooligans. That would have been the end of my mother's license, you know. And your jobs? Well, this is the end of it. From now on there will be no more of your ballroom nonsense in here. This is a business establishment, not a bloody New Brighton dancing school. I've been far too lenient with the two of you. (*Behind the counter for a green cool drink and a dollop of ice cream. He keeps up his tirade as he prepares it.*) But what really makes me bitter is that I allow you chaps a little freedom in here when business is bad and what do you do with it? The foxtrot! Specially you, Sam. There's more to life than trotting around a dance floor and I thought at least you knew it.

SAM: It's a harmless pleasure, Hally. It doesn't hurt anybody.

HALLY: It's also a rather simple one, you know.

SAM: You reckon so? Have you ever tried?

HALLY: Of course not.

SAM: Why don't you? Now.

HALLY: . . . you mean? Me dance?

SAM: . . . show you a simple step — the waltz — . . . try it.

HALLY: . . . at will that prove?

SAM: . . . t it might not be as easy as you think.

HALLY: . . . I didn't say it was easy. I said it was simple — . . . ke in simple-minded, meaning mentally retarded. . . . You can't exactly say it challenges the intellect.

SAM: It does other things.

HALLY: Such as?

SAM: Make people happy.

HALLY (the glass in his hand): So do American cream sodas with ice cream. For God's sake, Sam, you're not asking me to take ballroom dancing serious, are you?

SAM: Yes.

HALLY (sigh of defeat): Oh, well, so much for trying to give you a decent education. I've obviously achieved nothing.

SAM: You still haven't told me what's wrong with admiring something that's beautiful and then trying to do it yourself.

HALLY: Nothing. But we happen to be talking about a foxtrot, not a thing of beauty.

SAM: But that is just what I'm saying. If you were to see two champions doing, two masters of the art . . . !

HALLY: Oh God, I give up. So now it's also art!

SAM: Ja.

HALLY: There's a limit, Sam. Don't confuse art and entertainment.

SAM: So then what is art?

HALLY: You want a definition?

SAM: Ja.

HALLY (He realizes he has got to be careful. He gives the matter a lot of thought before answering.): Philosophers have been trying to do that for centuries. What is Art? What is Life? But basically I suppose it's . . . the giving of meaning to matter.

SAM: Nothing to do with beautiful?

HALLY: It goes beyond that. It's the giving of form to the formless.

SAM: Ja, well, maybe it's not art, then. But I still say it's beautiful.

HALLY: I'm sure the word you mean to use is entertaining.

SAM (adamant): No. Beautiful. And if you want proof come along to the Centenary Hall in New Brighton in two weeks' time.

(The mention of the Centenary Hall draws Willie over to them.)

HALLY: What for? I've seen the two of you prancing around in here often enough.

SAM (he laughs): This isn't the real thing, Hally. We're just playing around in here.

HALLY: So? I can use my imagination.

SAM: And what do you get?

HALLY: A lot of people dancing around and having a so-called good time.

SAM: That all?

HALLY: Well, basically it is that, surely.

SAM: No, it isn't. Your imagination hasn't helped you at all. There's a lot more to it than that. We're getting ready for the championships, Hally, not just another dance. There's going to be a lot of people, all right, and they're going to have a good time, but they'll only be spectators, sitting around and watching. It's just the competitors out there on the dance floor. Party decorations and fancy lights all around the walls! The ladies in beautiful evening dresses!

HALLY: My mother's got one of those, Sam, and, quite frankly, it's an embarrassment every time she wears it.

SAM (undeterred): Your imagination left out the excitement.

(Hally scoffs.)

Oh, yes. The finalists are not going to be out there just to have a good time. One of those couples will be the 1950 Eastern Province Champions. And your imagination left out the music.

WILLIE: Mr. Elijah Gladman Guzana and his Orchestral Jazzonions.

SAM: The sound of the big band, Hally. Trombone, trumpet, tenor and alto sax. And then, finally, your imagination also left out the climax of the evening when the dancing is finished, the judges have stopped whispering among themselves and the Master of Ceremonies collects their scorecards and goes up onto the stage to announce the winners.

HALLY: All right. So you make it sound like a bit of a do. It's an occasion. Satisfied?

SAM (victory): So you admit that!

HALLY: Emotionally yes, intellectually no.

SAM: Well, I don't know what you mean by that, all I'm telling you is that it is going to be the event of the year in New Brighton. It's been sold out for two weeks already. There's only standing room left. We've got competitors coming from Kingwilliamstown, East London, Port Alfred.

(Hally starts pacing thoughtfully.)

HALLY: Tell me a bit more.

SAM: I thought you weren't interested . . . intellectually.

HALLY (mysteriously): I've got my reasons.

SAM: What do you want to know?

HALLY: It takes place every year?

SAM: Yes. But only every third year in New Brighton. It's East London's turn to have the championships next year.

HALLY: Which, I suppose, makes it an even more significant event.

SAM: Ah ha! We're getting somewhere. Our "occasion" is now a "significant event."

HALLY: I wonder.

SAM: What?

HALLY: I wonder if I would get away with it.

SAM: But what?

HALLY (to the table and his exercise book): "Write five hundred words describing an annual event of cultural or historical significance." Would I be stretching poetic license a little too far if I called your ballroom championships a cultural event?

SAM: You mean . . . ?

HALLY: You think we could get five hundred words out of it, Sam?

SAM: Victor Sylvester has written a whole book on ballroom dancing.

WILLIE: You going to write about it, Master Hally?

HALLY: Yes, gentlemen, that is precisely what I am considering doing. Old Doc Bromely — he's my English teacher — is going to argue with me, of course. He doesn't like natives. But I'll point out to him that in strict anthropological terms the culture of a primitive black society includes its dancing and singing. To put my thesis in a nutshell: The war-dance has been replaced by the waltz. But it still amounts to the same thing: the release of primitive emotions through movement. Shall we give it a go?

SAM: I'm ready.

WILLIE: Me also.

HALLY: Ha! This will teach the old bugger a lesson. (*Decision taken.*) Right. Let's get ourselves organized. (*This means another cake on the table. He sits.*) I think you've given me enough general atmosphere, Sam, but to build the tension and suspense I need facts. (*Pencil poised.*)

WILLIE: Give him facts, Boet Sam.

HALLY: What you called the climax . . . how many finalists?

SAM: Six couples.

HALLY (*making notes*): Go on. Give me the picture.

SAM: Spectators seated right around the hall. (*Willie becomes a spectator.*)

HALLY: . . . and it's a full house.

SAM: At one end, on the stage, Gladman and his Orchestral Jazzonions. At the other end is a long table with the three judges. The six finalists go onto the dance floor and take up their positions. When they are ready and the spectators have settled down, the Master of Ceremonies goes to the microphone. To start with, he makes some jokes to get people laughing. . . .

HALLY: Good touch. (*As he writes.*) " . . . creating a relaxed atmosphere which will change to one of tension and drama as the climax is approached."

SAM (*onto a chair to act out the M.C.*): "Ladies and gentlemen, we come now to the great moment you have all been waiting for this evening. . . . The finals of the 1950 Eastern Province Open Ballroom Dancing Championships. But first let me introduce the finalists! Mr. and Mrs. Welcome Tchabalala from Kingwilliamstown . . ."

WILLIE (*he applauds after every name*): Is when the people clap their hands and whistle and make a lot of noise, Master Hally.

SAM: "Mr. Mulligan Njikelane and Miss Nomhle Nkonyeni of Grahamstown; Mr. and Mrs. Norman Nchinga from Port Alfred; Mr. Fats Bokolane and

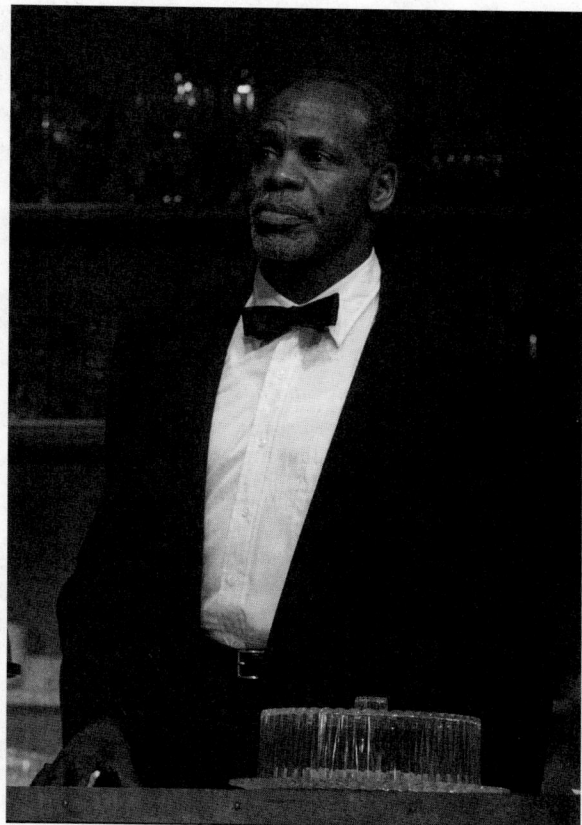

Danny Glover, who played Willie in the 1982 Broadway production, played the older waiter, Sam, in the 2003 New York revival of *"MASTER HAROLD" . . . and the boys,* directed by Lonny Price.

Miss Dina Plaatjies from East London; Mr. Sipho Dugu and Mrs. Mable Magada from Peddie; and from New Brighton our very own Mr. Willie Malopo and Miss Hilda Samuels."

(*Willie can't believe his ears. He abandons his role as spectator and scrambles into position as a finalist.*)

WILLIE: Relaxed and ready to romance!

SAM: The applause dies down. When everybody is silent, Gladman lifts up his sax, nods at the Orchestral Jazzonions. . . .

WILLIE: Play the jukebox please, Boet Sam!

SAM: I also only got bus fare, Willie.

HALLY: Hold it, everybody. (*Heads for the cash register behind the counter.*) How much is in the till, Sam?

SAM: Three shillings. Hally . . . Your Mom counted it before she left.

(*Hally hesitates.*)

HALLY: Sorry, Willie. You know how she carried on the last time I did it. We'll just have to pool our combined imaginations and hope for the best. (*Returns to the table.*) Back to work. How are the points scored, Sam?

SAM: Maximum of ten points each for individual style, deportment, rhythm, and general appearance.

WILLIE: Must I start?

HALLY: Hold it for a second, Willie. And penalties?

SAM: For what?

HALLY: For doing something wrong. Say you stumble or bump into somebody . . . do they take off any points?

SAM (*aghast*): Hally . . . !

HALLY: When you're dancing. If you and your partner collide into another couple.

(*Hally can get no further. Sam has collapsed with laughter. He explains to Willie.*)

SAM: If me and Miriam bump into you and Hilda. . . .

(*Willie joins him in another good laugh.*)

Hally, Hally . . . !

HALLY (*perplexed*): Why? What did I say?

SAM: There's no collisions out there, Hally. Nobody trips or stumbles or bumps into anybody else. That's what that moment is all about. To be one of those finalists on that dance floor is like . . . like being in a dream about a world in which accidents don't happen.

HALLY (*genuinely moved by Sam's image*): Jesus, Sam! That's beautiful!

WILLIE (*can endure waiting no longer*): I'm starting!

(*Willie dances while Sam talks.*)

SAM: Of course it is. That's what I've been trying to say to you all afternoon. And it's beautiful because that is what we want life to be like. But instead, like you said, Hally, we're bumping into each other all the time. Look at the three of us this afternoon: I've bumped into Willie, the two of us have bumped into you, you've bumped into your mother, she bumping into your Dad. . . . None of us knows the steps and there's no music playing. And it doesn't stop with us. The whole world is doing it all the time. Open a newspaper and what do you read? America has bumped into Russia, England is bumping into India, rich man bumps into poor man. Those are big collisions, Hally. They make for a lot of bruises. People get hurt in all that bumping, and we're sick and tired of it now. It's been going on for too long. Are we never going to get it right? . . . Learn to dance life like champions instead of always being just a bunch of beginners at it?

HALLY (*deep and sincere admiration of the man*): You've got a vision, Sam!

SAM: Not just me. What I'm saying to you is that everybody's got it. That's why there's only standing room left for the Centenary Hall in two weeks' time. For as long as the music lasts, we are going to see six couples get it right, the way we want life to be.

HALLY: But is that the best we can do, Sam . . . watch six finalists dreaming about the way it should be?

SAM: I don't know. But it starts with that. Without the dream we won't know what we're going for. And anyway I reckon there are a few people who have got past just dreaming about it and are trying for something real. Remember that thing we read once in the paper about the Mahatma Gandhi? Going without food to stop those riots in India?

HALLY: You're right. He certainly was trying to teach people to get the steps right.

SAM: And the Pope.

HALLY: Yes, he's another one. Our old General Smuts° as well, you know. He's also out there dancing. You know, Sam, when you come to think of it, that's what the United Nations boils down to . . . a dancing school for politicians!

SAM: And let's hope they learn.

HALLY (*a little surge of hope*): You're right. We mustn't despair. Maybe there's some hope for mankind after all. Keep it up, Willie. (*Back to his table with determination.*) This is a lot bigger than I thought. So what have we got? Yes, our title: "A World Without Collisions."

SAM: That sounds good! "A World Without Collisions."

HALLY: Subtitle: "Global Politics on the Dance Floor." No. A bit too heavy, hey? What about "Ballroom Dancing as a Political Vision"?

(*The telephone rings. Sam answers it.*)

SAM: St. George's Park Tea Room . . . Yes, Madam . . . Hally, it's your Mom.

HALLY (*back to reality*): Oh, God, yes! I'd forgotten all about that. Shit! Remember my words, Sam? Just when you're enjoying yourself, someone or something will come along and wreck everything.

SAM: You haven't heard what she's got to say yet.

HALLY: Public telephone?

SAM: No.

HALLY: Does she sound happy or unhappy?

SAM: I couldn't tell. (*Pause.*) She's waiting, Hally.

HALLY (*to the telephone*): Hello, Mom . . . No, everything is okay here. Just doing my homework. . . . What's your news? . . . You've what? . . . (*Pause. He takes the receiver away from his ear for a few seconds. In the course of Hally's telephone conversation, Sam and Willie discreetly position the stacked tables and chairs. Hally places the receiver back to his ear.*) Yes, I'm still here. Oh, well, I give up now. Why did you do it, Mom? . . . Well, I just hope you know what you've let us in for. . . . (*Loudly.*) I said I hope you know what you've let us in for! It's the end of the peace and quiet we've been having. (*Softly.*) Where is he? (*Normal voice.*) He can't hear us from

General Smuts: (1870–1950), South African statesman who fought the British in the Boer War in 1899, was instrumental in forming the Union of South Africa in 1910, and was active in the creation of the United Nations.

in there. But for God's sake, Mom, what happened? I told you to be firm with him. . . . Then you and the nurses should have held him down, taken his crutches away. . . . I know only too well he's my father! . . . I'm not being disrespectful, but I'm sick and tired of emptying stinking chamber pots full of phlegm and piss. . . . Yes, I do! When you're not there, he asks *me* to do it. . . . If you really want to know the truth, that's why I've got no appetite for my food. . . . Yes! There's a lot of things you don't know about. For your information, I still haven't got that science textbook I need. And you know why? He borrowed the money you gave me for it. . . . Because I didn't want to start another fight between you two. . . . He says that every time. . . . All right, Mom! (*Viciously.*) Then just remember to start hiding your bag away again, because he'll be at your purse before long for money for booze. And when he's well enough to come down here, you better keep an eye on the till as well, because that is also going to develop a leak. . . . Then don't complain to me when he starts his old tricks. . . . Yes, you do. I get it from you on one side and from him on the other, and it makes life hell for me. I'm not going to be the peacemaker anymore. I'm warning you now: when the two of you start fighting again, I'm leaving home. . . . Mom, if you start crying, I'm going to put down the receiver. . . . Okay. . . . (*Lowering his voice to a vicious whisper.*) Okay, Mom. I heard you. (*Desperate.*) No. . . . Because I don't want to. I'll see him when I get home! Mom! . . . (*Pause. When he speaks again, his tone changes completely. It is not simply pretense. We sense a genuine emotional conflict.*) Welcome home, chum! . . . What's that? . . . Don't be silly, Dad. You being home is just about the best news in the world. . . . I bet you are. Bloody depressing there with everybody going on about their ailments, hey! . . . How you feeling? . . . Good. . . . Here as well, pal. Coming down cats and dogs. . . . That's right. Just the day for a kip° and a toss in your old Uncle Ned. . . . Everything's just hunky-dory on my side, Dad. . . . Well, to start with, there's a nice pile of comics for you on the counter. . . . Yes, old Kemple brought them in. *Batman and Robin, Submariner* . . . just your cup of tea. . . . I will. . . . Yes, we'll spin a few yarns tonight. . . . Okay, chum, see you in a little while. . . . No, I promise. I'll come straight home. . . . (*Pause — his mother comes back on the phone.*) Mom? Okay. I'll lock up now. . . . What? . . . Oh, the brandy . . . Yes, I'll remember! . . . I'll put it in my suitcase now, for God's sake. I know well enough what will happen if he doesn't get it. . . . (*Places a bottle of brandy on the counter.*) I *was* kind to him, Mom. I didn't say anything nasty! . . . All right. Bye. (*End of telephone conversation. A desolate Hally doesn't move. A strained silence.*)

kip: Nap.

SAM (*quietly*): That sounded like a bad bump, Hally.
HALLY (*Having a hard time controlling his emotions. He speaks carefully.*): Mind your own business, Sam.
SAM: Sorry. I wasn't trying to interfere. Shall we carry on? Hally? (*He indicates the exercise book. No response from Hally.*)
WILLIE (*also trying*): Tell him about when they give out the cups, Boet Sam.
SAM: Ja! That's another big moment. The presentation of the cups after the winners have been announced. You've got to put that in.

(*Still no response from Hally.*)

WILLIE: A big silver one, Master Hally, called floating trophy for the champions.
SAM: We always invite some big-shot personality to hand them over. Guest of honor this year is going to be His Holiness Bishop Jabulani of the All African Free Zionist Church.

(*Hally gets up abruptly, goes to his table, and tears up the page he was writing on.*)

HALLY: So much for a bloody world without collisions.
SAM: Too bad. It was on its way to being a good composition.
HALLY: Let's stop bullshitting ourselves, Sam.
SAM: Have we been doing that?
HALLY: Yes! That's what all our talk about a decent world has been . . . just so much bullshit.
SAM: We did say it was still only a dream.
HALLY: And a bloody useless one at that. Life's a fuckup and it's never going to change.
SAM: Ja, maybe that's true.
HALLY: There's no maybe about it. It's a blunt and brutal fact. All we've done this afternoon is waste our time.
SAM: Not if we'd got your homework done.
HALLY: I don't give a shit about my homework, so, for Christ's sake, just shut up about it. (*Slamming books viciously into his school case.*) Hurry up now and finish your work. I want to lock up and get out of here. (*Pause.*) And then go where? Home-sweet-fucking-home. Jesus, I hate that word.

(*Hally goes to the counter to put the brandy bottle and comics in his school case. After a moment's hesitation, he smashes the bottle of brandy. He abandons all further attempts to hide his feelings. Sam and Willie work away as unobtrusively as possible.*)

Do you want to know what is really wrong with your lovely little dream, Sam? It's not just that we are all bad dancers. That does happen to be perfectly true, but there's more to it than just that. You left out the cripples.
SAM: Hally!
HALLY (*now totally reckless*): Ja! Can't leave them out, Sam. That's why we always end up on our backsides on the dance floor. They're also out there dancing . . . like a bunch of broken spiders trying to do the quickstep! (*An ugly attempt at laughter.*) When you come

to think of it, it's a bloody comical sight. I mean, it's bad enough on two legs . . . but one and a pair of crutches! Hell, no, Sam. That's guaranteed to turn that dance floor into a shambles. Why you shaking your head? Picture it, man. For once this afternoon let's use our imaginations sensibly.

SAM: Be careful, Hally.

HALLY: Of what? The truth? I seem to be the only one around here who is prepared to face it. We've had the pretty dream, it's time now to wake up and have a good long look at the way things really are. Nobody knows the steps, there's no music, the cripples are also out there tripping up everybody and trying to get into the act, and it's all called the All-Comers-How-to-Make-a-Fuckup-of-Life Championships. (*Another ugly laugh.*) Hang on, Sam! The best bit is still coming. Do you know what the winner's trophy is? A beautiful big chamber pot with roses on the side, and it's full to the brim with piss. And guess who I think is going to be this year's winner.

SAM (*almost shouting*): Stop now!

HALLY (*suddenly appalled by how far he has gone*): Why?

SAM: Hally? It's your father you're talking about.

HALLY: So?

SAM: Do you know what you've been saying?

(*Hally can't answer. He is rigid with shame. Sam speaks to him sternly.*)

No, Hally, you mustn't do it. Take back those words and ask for forgiveness! It's a terrible sin for a son to mock his father with jokes like that. You'll be punished if you carry on. Your father is your father, even if he is a . . . cripple man.

WILLIE: Yes, Master Hally. Is true what Sam say.

SAM: I understand how you are feeling, Hally, but even so. . . .

HALLY: No, you don't!

SAM: I think I do.

HALLY: And I'm telling you you don't. Nobody does. (*Speaking carefully as his shame turns to rage at Sam.*) It's your turn to be careful, Sam. Very careful! You're treading on dangerous ground. Leave me and my father alone.

SAM: I'm not the one who's been saying things about him.

HALLY: What goes on between me and my Dad is none of your business!

SAM: Then don't tell me about it. If that's all you've got to say about him, I don't want to hear.

(*For a moment Hally is at loss for a response.*)

HALLY: Just get on with your bloody work and shut up.

SAM: Swearing at me won't help you.

HALLY: Yes, it does! Mind your own fucking business and shut up!

SAM: Okay. If that's the way you want it, I'll stop trying.

(*He turns away. This infuriates Hally even more.*)

HALLY: Good. Because what you've been trying to do is meddle in something you know nothing about. All that concerns you in here, Sam, is to try and do what you get paid for — keep the place clean and serve the customers. In plain words, just get on with your job. My mother is right. She's always warning me about allowing you to get too familiar. Well, this time you've gone too far. It's going to stop right now.

(*No response from Sam.*)

You're only a servant in here, and don't forget it.

(*Still no response. Hally is trying hard to get one.*)

And as far as my father is concerned, all you need to remember is that he is your boss.

SAM (*needled at last*): No, he isn't. I get paid by your mother.

HALLY: Don't argue with me, Sam!

SAM: Then don't say he's my boss.

HALLY: He's a white man and that's good enough for you.

SAM: I'll try to forget you said that.

HALLY: Don't! Because you won't be doing me a favor if you do. I'm telling you to remember it.

(*A pause. Sam pulls himself together and makes one last effort.*)

SAM: Hally, Hally . . . ! Come on now. Let's stop before it's too late. You're right. We *are* on dangerous ground. If we're not careful, somebody is going to get hurt.

HALLY: It won't be me.

SAM: Don't be so sure.

HALLY: I don't know what you're talking about, Sam.

SAM: Yes, you do.

HALLY (*furious*): Jesus, I wish you would stop trying to tell me what I do and what I don't know.

(*Sam gives up. He turns to Willie.*)

SAM: Let's finish up.

HALLY: Don't turn your back on me! I haven't finished talking.

(*He grabs Sam by the arm and tries to make him turn around. Sam reacts with a flash of anger.*)

SAM: Don't do that, Hally! (*Facing the boy.*) All right, I'm listening. Well? What do you want to say to me?

HALLY (*pause as Hally looks for something to say*): To begin with, why don't you also start calling me Master Harold, like Willie.

SAM: Do you mean that?

HALLY: Why the hell do you think I said it?

SAM: And if I don't?

HALLY: You might just lose your job.

SAM (*quietly and very carefully*): If you make me say it once, I'll never call you anything else again.

HALLY: So? (*The boy confronts the man.*) Is that meant to be a threat?

SAM: Just telling you what will happen if you make me do that. You must decide what it means to you.

HALLY: Well, I have. It's good news. Because that is exactly what Master Harold wants from now on.

Think of it as a little lesson in respect, Sam, that's long overdue, and I hope you remember it as well as you do your geography. I can tell you now that somebody who will be glad to hear I've finally given it to you will be my Dad. Yes! He agrees with my Mom. He's always going on about it as well. "You must teach the boys to show you more respect, my son."

SAM: So now you can stop complaining about going home. Everybody is going to be happy tonight.

HALLY: That's perfectly correct. You see, you mustn't get the wrong idea about me and my Dad, Sam. We also have our good times together. Some bloody good laughs. He's got a marvelous sense of humor. Want to know what our favorite joke is? He gives out a big groan, you see, and says: "It's not fair, is it, Hally?" Then I have to ask: "What, chum?" And then he says: "A nigger's arse" . . . and we both have a good laugh.

(*The men stare at him with disbelief.*)

What's the matter, Willie? Don't you catch the joke? You always were a bit slow on the uptake. It's what is called a pun. You see, fair means both light in color and to be just and decent. (*He turns to Sam.*) I thought *you* would catch it, Sam.

SAM: Oh ja, I catch it all right.

HALLY: But it doesn't appeal to your sense of humor.

SAM: Do you really laugh?

HALLY: Of course.

SAM: To please him? Make him feel good?

HALLY: No, for heavens sake! I laugh because I think it's a bloody good joke.

SAM: You're really trying hard to be ugly, aren't you? And why drag poor old Willie into it? He's done nothing to you except show you the respect you want so badly. That's also not being fair, you know . . . and *I* mean just or decent.

WILLIE: It's all right, Sam. Leave it now.

SAM: It's me you're after. You should just have said "Sam's arse" . . . because that's the one you're trying to kick. Anyway, how do you know it's not fair? You've never seen it. Do you want to? (*He drops his trousers and underpants and presents his backside for Hally's inspection.*) Have a good look. A real Basuto arse . . . which is about as nigger as they can come. Satisfied? (*Trousers up.*) Now you can make your Dad even happier when you go home tonight. Tell him I showed you my arse and he is quite right. It's not fair. And if it will give him an even better laugh next time, I'll also let *him* have a look. Come, Willie, let's finish up and go.

(*Sam and Willie start to tidy up the tea room. Hally doesn't move. He waits for a moment when Sam passes him.*)

HALLY (*quietly*): Sam . . .

(*Sam stops and looks expectantly at the boy. Hally spits in his face. A long and heartfelt groan from Willie. For a few seconds Sam doesn't move.*)

SAM (*taking out a handkerchief and wiping his face*): It's all right, Willie.

(*To Hally.*)

Ja, well, you've done it . . . Master Harold. Yes, I'll start calling you that from now on. It won't be difficult anymore. You've hurt yourself, Master Harold. I saw it coming. I warned you, but you wouldn't listen. You've just hurt yourself *bad*. And you're a coward, Master Harold. The face you should be spitting in is your father's . . . but you used mine, because you think you're safe inside your fair skin . . . and this time I don't mean just or decent. (*Pause, then moving violently toward Hally.*) Should I hit him, Willie?

WILLIE (*stopping Sam*): No, Boet Sam.

SAM (*violently*): Why not?

WILLIE: It won't help, Boet Sam.

SAM: I don't want to help! I want to hurt him.

WILLIE: You also hurt yourself.

SAM: And if he had done it to you, Willie?

WILLIE: Me? Spit at me like I was a dog? (*A thought that had not occurred to him before. He looks at Hally.*) Ja. Then I want to hit him. I want to hit him hard!

(*A dangerous few seconds as the men stand staring at the boy. Willie turns away, shaking his head.*)

But maybe all I do is go cry at the back. He's little boy, Boet Sam. Little *white* boy. Long trousers now, but he's still little boy.

SAM (*his violence ebbing away into defeat as quickly as it flooded*): You're right. So go on, then: groan again, Willie. You do it better than me. (*To Hally.*) You don't know all of what you've just done . . . Master Harold. It's not just that you've made me feel dirtier than I've ever been in my life . . . I mean, how do I wash off yours and your father's filth? . . . I've also failed. A long time ago I promised myself I was going to try and do something, but you've just shown me . . . Master Harold . . . that I've failed. (*Pause.*) I've also got a memory of a little white boy when he was still wearing short trousers and a black man, but they're not flying a kite. It was the old Jubilee days, after dinner one night. I was in my room. You came in and just stood against the wall, looking down at the ground, and only after I'd asked you what you wanted, what was wrong, I don't know how many times, did you speak and even then so softly I almost didn't hear you. "Sam, please help me to go and fetch my Dad." Remember? He was dead drunk on the floor of the Central Hotel Bar. They'd phoned for your Mom, but you were the only one at home. And do you remember how we did it? You went in first by yourself to ask permission for me to go into the bar. Then I loaded him onto my back like a baby and carried him back to the boarding house with you following behind carrying his crutches. (*Shaking his head as he remembers.*) A crowded Main Street with all the people watching a little white boy following his drunk father on a nigger's back! I felt for that little boy . . . Master Harold. I felt for him. After that we still had to clean him up, remember? He'd messed in his trousers, so we had to clean him up and get him into bed.

HALLY (*great pain*): I love him, Sam.

SAM: I know you do. That's why I tried to stop you from saying these things about him. It would have been so simple if you could have just despised him for being a weak man. But he's your father. You love him and you're ashamed of him. You're ashamed of so much! . . . And now that's going to include yourself. That was the promise I made to myself: to try and stop that happening. (*Pause.*) After we got him to bed you came back with me to my room and sat in a corner and carried on just looking down at the ground. And for days after that! You hadn't done anything wrong, but you went around as if you owed the world an apology for being alive. I didn't like seeing that! That's not the way a boy grows up to be a man! . . . But the one person who should have been teaching you what that means was the cause of your shame. If you really want to know, that's why I made you that kite. I wanted you to look up, be proud of something, of yourself . . . (*bitter smile at the memory*) . . . and you certainly were that when I left you with it up there on the hill. Oh, ja . . . something else! . . . If you ever do write it as a short story, there *was* a twist in our ending. I couldn't sit down there and stay with you. It was a "Whites Only" bench. You were too young, too excited to notice then. But not anymore. If you're not careful . . . Master Harold . . . you're going to be sitting up there by yourself for a long time to come, and there won't be a kite in the sky. (*Sam has got nothing more to say. He exits into the kitchen, taking off his waiter's jacket.*)

WILLIE: Is bad. Is all bad in here now.

HALLY (*books into his school case, raincoat on*): Willie . . . (*It is difficult to speak.*) Will you lock up for me and look after the keys?

WILLIE: Okay.

(*Sam returns. Hally goes behind the counter and collects the few coins in the cash register. As he starts to leave. . . .*)

SAM: Don't forget the comic books.

(*Hally returns to the counter and puts them in his case. He starts to leave again.*)

SAM (*to the retreating back of the boy*): Stop . . . Hally. . . .

(*Hally stops, but doesn't turn to face him.*)

Hally . . . I've got no right to tell you what being a man means if I don't behave like one myself, and I'm

not doing so well at that this afternoon. Should we try again, Hally?

HALLY: Try what?

SAM: Fly another kite, I suppose. It worked once, and this time I need it as much as you do.

HALLY: It's still raining, Sam. You can't fly kites on rainy days, remember.

SAM: So what do we do? Hope for better weather tomorrow?

HALLY (*helpless gesture*): I don't know. I don't know anything anymore.

SAM: You sure of that, Hally? Because it would be pretty hopeless if that was true. It would mean nothing has been learnt in here this afternoon, and there was a hell of a lot of teaching going on . . . one way or the other. But anyway, I don't believe you. I reckon there's one thing you know. You don't *have* to sit up there by yourself. You know what that bench means now, and you can leave it any time you choose. All you've got to do is stand up and walk away from it.

(*Hally leaves. Willie goes up quietly to Sam.*)

WILLIE: Is okay, Boet Sam. You see. Is . . . (*he can't find any better words*) . . . is going to be okay tomorrow. (*Changing his tone.*) Hey, Boet Sam! (*He is trying hard.*) You right. I think about it and you right. Tonight I find Hilda and say sorry. And make promise I won't beat her no more. You hear me, Boet Sam?

SAM: I hear you, Willie.

WILLIE: And when we practice I relax and romance with her from beginning to end. Nonstop! You watch! Two weeks' time: "First prize for promising newcomers: Mr. Willie Malopo and Miss Hilda Samuels." (*Sudden impulse.*) To hell with it! I walk home. (*He goes to the jukebox, puts in a coin and selects a record. The machine comes to life in the gray twilight, blushing its way through a spectrum of soft, romantic colors.*) How did you say it, Boet Sam? Let's dream. (*Willie sways with the music and gestures for Sam to dance.*)

(*Sarah Vaughan sings.*)

"Little man you're crying,
I know why you're blue,
Someone took your kiddy car away;
Better go to sleep now,
Little man you've had a busy day." (*etc., etc.*)
You lead. I follow.

(*The men dance together.*)

"Johnny won your marbles,
Tell you what we'll do;
Dad will get you new ones right away;
Better go to sleep now,
Little man you've had a busy day."

COMMENTARIES

Heinrich von Staden (*b. 1939*)
INTERVIEW WITH ATHOL FUGARD   *1982*

When "MASTER HAROLD" . . . and the boys was first produced at the Yale Repertory Theatre, Athol Fugard had the chance to respond to some questions about its significance to him. He revealed that the play was deeply personal and that through it he had been able to exorcise a demon that had haunted him for some time. In this interview Fugard details his involvement with South African drama and black actors in South Africa. He also comments on the extent to which censorship and other political pressures in South Africa made it difficult for his work to be produced in his own country.

von Staden: The bombs of fiction — Athol, aren't they more explosive than TNT?

Fugard: I'd like to believe that. You understand I've got to be careful about that one. I've got to be careful about flattering myself about the potency of the one area of activity which I've got, which is theater and being a writer.

von Staden: How often have there been productions of your plays for nonsegregated audiences in South Africa?

Fugard: I've had to change my tactics in terms of that over the years. At a period when the policy on segregated audiences in South Africa was rigid and very strictly enforced, I had to make a decision whether to take on an act of silence, just be silent because I couldn't go into a theater that was decent in my terms, or whether to take on the compromising circumstances of segregated audiences simply because I felt that if a play has got something to say, at least say it. And there were years when I decided to do the latter. I did perform before segregated audiences. In a sense I regret that decision now. I think I might possibly have looked after myself — and maybe the situation — better by not accepting that compromise. But I did.

von Staden: But do you think you had a genuine choice at that time?

Fugard: I had a choice between silence or being heard.

von Staden: Let me ask you along similar lines, when you are writing a play or a novel like *Tsotsi,* do you sense constraints on the way you are writing in view of the fact that certain things are anathema to the government, also in fiction?

Fugard: I would like to believe that I have operated at the table at which I sit and write, that I have operated totally without self-censorship. Maybe some awareness of what is possible and is not possible has operated subconsciously and is deciding choices I make in terms of what I favor. I think it may be pertinent to the conversation we are having, that *"MASTER HAROLD" . . . and the boys* is the first play of mine in twenty-four years of writing that will have its premiere outside of South Africa. And one of the reasons why I'm doing that this time is that there are elements in *"MASTER HAROLD" . . . and the boys* that might have run into censorship problems. [. . .]

von Staden: Here you are, a person who, critics say, has achieved exceptional insight into human nature, and you never obtained a university degree. What institutions, what processes do you think contributed most to the insights you have?

Fugard: Well, I think to be a South African is in a way to be at a university that teaches you about that. The South African experience is certainly one in which, if you're prepared to keep your eyes open and look, you're going to see a lot of suffering. But then, in terms of personal specifics, I suppose for me there was a very, very important relationship, a friendship, with a black man in what I suppose is any person's most formative and definitive years, the age between eleven, ten up until the age of twenty-one. It was a black man in Port Elizabeth, and my play *"MASTER HAROLD"... and the boys* reflects something of that friendship, tries to talk about it, look at it. I left South Africa, hitchhiked through the African continent, ended up as a sailor on a ship which, apart from the officers and engineers, had a totally nonwhite, had a totally black crew, and I was a sailor in a totally black crew. There was that, I think I can't nail down any one specific traumatic incident as being totally decisive. But I could be certain that *"MASTER HAROLD"... and the boys* deals with one specific moment which I'm trying to exorcise out of my soul.

von Staden: In all of your plays and in the novel you always have a South African setting. Yet your plays and your novels, though so rooted in the specifics of the South African situation, seem to have a tremendous appeal to audiences that are largely ignorant of the situation there. To what do you ascribe that?

Fugard: You take a chance. As a storyteller one year ago, I took a chance [. . .] I realized that it was finally time to deal with the story of a seventeen-year-old boy and his friendship with two black men. And it's a gamble. There's no formula. There is no way that you can make or decide or guarantee before the event that that story is going to resonate outside of its specific context. You just take a bloody chance.

Athol Fugard (*b. 1932*)
From *Notebooks 1960–1977*   *1983*

Like most playwrights, Athol Fugard is a journal writer. In his notebooks he has written scraps of memory that have special meaning to him. In one entry for March 1961, long before he began to write "MASTER HAROLD"... and the boys (1982), he describes one of his childhood memories. It concerns the real-life Sam, and it reveals — very painfully — exactly what the personal crime was that Fugard's play deals with. His gesture of contempt for the man who was like a grandfather to him became a demon that had to be exorcised.

Sam Semela — Basuto — with the family fifteen years. Meeting him again when he visited Mom set off string of memories.

The kite which he produced for me one day during those early years when Mom ran the Jubilee Hotel and he was a waiter there. He had made it himself: brown paper, its ribs fashioned from thin strips of tomato-box plank which he had smoothed down, a paste of flour and water for glue. I was surprised and bewildered that he had made it for me.

I vaguely recall shyly "haunting" the servants' quarters in the well of the hotel — cold, cement-gray world — the pungent mystery of the dark little rooms — a world I didn't understand. Frightened to enter any of the rooms. Sam, broad-faced, broader based — he smelled of woodsmoke. The "kaffir smell" of South Africa is the smell of poverty — woodsmoke and sweat.

Later, when he worked for her at the Park café, Mom gave him the sack: ". . . he became careless. He came late for work. His work went to hell. He didn't seem to care no more." I was about thirteen and served behind the counter while he waited on table.

Realize now he was the most significant — the only — friend of my boyhood years. On terrible windy days when no one came to swim or walk in the park, we would sit together and talk. Or I was reading — Introductions to Eastern Philosophy or Plato and Socrates — and when I had finished he would take the book back to New Brighton.

Can't remember now what precipitated it, but one day there was a rare quarrel between Sam and myself. In a truculent silence we closed the café, Sam set off home to New Brighton on foot and I followed a few minutes later on my bike. I saw him walking ahead of me and, coming out of a spasm of acute loneliness, as I rode up behind him I called his name, he turned in mid-stride to look back and, as I cycled past, I spat in his face. Don't suppose I will ever deal with the shame that overwhelmed me the second after I had done that.

Now he is thin. We had a long talk. He told about the old woman ("Ma") whom he and his wife have taken in to look after their house while he goes to work — he teaches ballroom dancing. "Ma" insists on behaving like a domestic — making Sam feel guilty and embarrassed. She brings him an early morning cup of coffee. Sam: "No, Ma, you mustn't, man." Ma: "I must." Sam: "Look, Ma, if I want it, I can make it." Ma: "No, I must."

Occasionally, when she is doing something, Sam feels like a cup of tea but is too embarrassed to ask her, and daren't make one for himself. Similarly, with his washing. After three days or a week away in other towns, giving dancing lessons, he comes back with underclothes that are very dirty. He is too shy to give them out to be washed so washes them himself. When Ma sees this she goes and complains to Sam's wife that he doesn't trust her, that it's all wrong for him to do the washing.

Of tsotsis,° he said: "They grab a old man, stick him with a knife, and ransack him. And so he must go to hospital and his kids is starving with hungry." Of others: "He's got some little moneys. So he is facing starvation for the weekend."

Of township snobs, he says there are the educational ones: "If you haven't been to the big school, like Fort Hare, what you say isn't true." And the money ones: "If you aren't selling shops or got a business or a big car, man, you're nothing."

Sam's incredible theory about the likeness of those "with the true seed of love." Starts with Plato and Socrates — they were round. "Man is being shrinking all the time. An Abe Lincoln, him too, taller, but that's because man is shrinking." Basically, those with the true seed of love look the same —"It's in the eyes."

He spoke admiringly of one man, a black lawyer in East London, an educated man — university background — who was utterly without snobbery, looking down on no one — any man, educated or ignorant, rich or poor, was another *man* to him, another human being, to be respected, taken seriously, to be talked to, listened to.

"They" won't allow Sam any longer to earn a living as a dancing teacher. "You must get a job!" One of his fellow teachers was forced to work at Fraser's Quarries.

tsotsis: Gang members.

David Mamet

The title of one of David Mamet's plays, *A Life in the Theatre* (1977), may have been autobiographically inspired. Mamet has spent his life — from high school onward — in the theater, as actor, director, playwright, and screenwriter. Born in Chicago in 1947, he graduated with an English major from Goddard College in Vermont, where he wrote several plays, including his undergraduate thesis, *Camel* (1968). *Sexual Perversity in Chicago* (1975), Mamet's first resounding commercial success, was first drafted when he was at Goddard. In the same year, *American Buffalo* premiered in the Goodman Theatre in Chicago, beginning a series of productions around the country. The Broadway production was not especially well received, but it was the first American play produced at London's new National Theatre in 1978. After a 1980 revival in New Haven's Long Wharf Theater with Al Pacino as Teach, it moved to Circle in the Square in New York in 1981 and then to Broadway in 1983. A study of petty thieves living a darkly comic underground life, *American Buffalo* has become one of Mamet's most highly regarded plays.

His much-acclaimed *Glengarry Glen Ross* (1983) premiered in London at the National Theatre, then moved to Broadway the following year, where it won the Pulitzer Prize and many other awards. This tale of scheming real estate salesmen derives in part from Mamet's experience working in a real estate office as a young man. The portrait of avarice and deceit is an indictment of one aspect of American business. *Glengarry Glen Ross* was eventually revised for film.

In the 1980s and 1990s Mamet wrote many stage plays, radio plays, and film scripts. He adapted Chekhov's *The Cherry Orchard* (1985), wrote *Goldberg Street* for radio performance, and wrote the screenplays for *The Untouchables* (1987), *House of Games* (1987, nominated for a Golden Globe Award), *Things Change* (1988), and *Homicide* (1991). *Speed the Plow* (1988) opened on Broadway with Madonna playing a secretary from a temp agency. It draws on Mamet's experience in the film industry and explores the insecurities and double-dealing of those who make decisions about producing movies. *The Cryptogram* (1994) was produced first in London in June 1994, then in February 1995 at the American Repertory Theatre in Boston; the New York production was at the Westside Arts Theater in March 1995. *Boston Marriage* (1999) examines a lesbian relationship between Victorian blue-bloods, a novel subject for Mamet, who is sometimes criticized as being misogynistic.

In the early 1970s Mamet was involved in Chicago's St. Nicholas Theatre Company, a group that gathered to produce a variety of plays, including some of his own. William H. Macy, Steven Schacter, and Patricia Cox were the principal actors, and others joined with them. Soon, however, Mamet's responsibilities as a writer and his occasional stints as a university professor at Goddard and elsewhere led him to leave Chicago and center himself in New York.

GLENGARRY GLEN ROSS

Mamet's examination of the world of sleazy real estate salesmen is at once both comic and savage. The level of deceit that pervades the play is so deep that one almost begins to accept the views of Shelly "the Machine" Levene, who, as he ages, loses his credibility as a sales "closer" but continues to deceive himself and anyone who will listen into thinking he can still "do the job" and sell the way he once did. Of course, with Shelly it is difficult to know what to believe. Perhaps he once was a top-notch salesman, but, then again, his ability to fabricate stories about himself is so advanced that it is possible he was never "on top" and that he has always been a tissue of excuses. In the opening scene in the Chinese restaurant, he reveals himself to Williamson, the office manager who seems to be the "nephew of somebody," as a man willing to exaggerate his achievements and explain away his defeats as things beyond his control.

The question of whether or not Shelly Levene is a sympathetic character may depend on the point of view of the individual reader or audience member. Although he does not project the image of a man who was once useful and is now being cast aside because of age, he may be seen as a remote likeness of Willy Loman in *Death of a Salesman*. On the other hand, like Willy, he seems to have consistently chosen values that would ultimately doom him as a man. The language of the play constantly reminds us that these salesmen are men. MEN in capital letters, men who seem to be comparable to yesterday's warriors. In act 2, Roma tells us that only men can do this job because it takes a man, by which he suggests that there is something noble, something daring about going out and selling property to people who may not even want it. Roma, almost aware of Mamet's judgment, says, "it's not a world of men, Machine . . . it's a world of clock watchers, bureaucrats, officeholders . . . what it is, it's a fucked-up world . . . there's no adventure *to* it." Mamet's imagery constantly defaults back to a revelation of male homosocial behavior, implying a brutal world built of conflict and survival, a world of predatory behavior resembling that of primitive hunters. Yet in actuality, these men are more like con men than like hunter-gatherers.

In act 2, Roma sets up a con when Mr. Lingk comes into the office to ask for his money back. Lingk knows that he has three days in which to make up his mind to get a refund, and Roma tries to con him into thinking that he can wait four days. One important detail is that the "deal" they make occurs casually between Roma and Lingk in a restaurant in scene 3 of act 1. They begin their casual conversation when they are sitting in different booths from one another. They are just guys having a conversation. However, because one of the guys, Roma, is a skilled salesman, he is able to take the relatively untutored Lingk into his confidence and sell him property. In a marvelous twist, Lingk comes back in act 2 in the middle of a robbery investigation at the insistence of his wife. He reveals that it is not his decision to ask for his money back, but his wife's. She demands that he get their check back or she will go to the attorney general. She is the force behind his request and it is she who undoes all the macho posturing of Roma, who tries everything he can think of, including having Levene masquerade as a very important customer who has "purchased" a great deal of property. In a sense, Roma is trying to "rob" Lingk of both his money and his will to resist. Simultaneously, the actual robbery of the real estate office is under investigation, further bewildering Lingk. Shelly Levene has let himself be drawn into a ridiculous scheme to steal leads — the names and addresses of people with enough resources to be potential buyers — and sell them to a competing firm. The entire scheme is self-defeating in the long run, but it produces immediate cash. Levene is so unsuccessful as a salesman that he has no money and sees this scheme as a temporary way out. In the process, as if displaying his lack of awareness, Levene seems to have skimmed off one of the leads and then had a "sit" with Bruce and Harriett Nyborg and "sold" them $82,000 worth of property. Near the end of the play, Williamson is astonished at Levene's naïveté: "They're nuts . . . they used to call in every week." The Nyborgs just like to talk to people — they are not legitimate customers, and Levene allows himself to be conned by them.

Levene is delusional when he tells Williamson that, although he's committed a crime, it has taught him something: "What it taught me, that you've got to get *out* there. Big deal. So I wasn't cut out to be a thief. I was cut out to be a salesman." In Mamet's play, there is not much of a distinction.

Glengarry Glen Ross in Performance

The play premiered at the Cottesloe Theatre, London, part of the South Bank group of National Theatres, on September 21, 1983. Derek Newark played Levene and Jack Shepherd played Roma. The American premiere followed on February 6, 1984, in Chicago at the Goodman Theatre, with Robert Prosky as Levene, Joe Mantegna as Roma, and Mike Nussbaum as Aaronow. J. T. Walsh played Williamson. Both productions were well received by reviewers and audiences alike, and the play won the Pulitzer Prize for 1984. Numerous productions have followed both regionally and abroad. The film version (1992), with Jack Lemmon as Levene and Al Pacino as Roma, was not a box-office success, but has since become a cult classic. The first major theatrical revival was at the McCarter Theatre in Princeton, New Jersey, on February 18, 2000, with Scott Zigler directing. Charles Durning played Levene, Daniel Benzali played Moss, and Ruben Santiago-Hudson played Roma. Daniel L. Lewis in *Variety* said, "David Mamet's scorching 1984 drama *Glengarry Glen Ross* has lost none of its bite or blistering dramatic thrust in director Scott Zigler's McCarter Theatre production." Amy Morton directed the play at Steppenwolf Theatre in Chicago in November 2001–January 2002. In her production Mike Nussbaum, who had played Aaronow in 1984, now played Shelly Levene. The reviews noted that, even without any recognizable "stars" in the performance, the play still had power and verve.

David Mamet *(b. 1947)*

GLENGARRY GLEN ROSS

1983

Always be closing. — PRACTICAL SALES MAXIM

The Characters

WILLIAMSON
BAYLEN
ROMA
LINGK
} Men in their early forties.

LEVENE
MOSS
AARONOW
} Men in their fifties.

THE SCENE

The three scenes of ACT ONE *take place in a Chinese restaurant.*

ACT TWO *takes place in a real estate office.*

ACT ONE • Scene One

A booth at a Chinese restaurant, Williamson and Levene are seated at the booth.

LEVENE: John . . . John . . . John. Okay. John. John. Look (*Pause.*) The Glengarry Highland's leads, you're sending Roma out. Fine. He's a good man. We know what he is. He's fine. All I'm saying, you look at the *board*, he's throwing . . . wait, wait, wait, he's throwing them *away*, he's throwing the leads away. All that I'm saying, that you're wasting leads. I don't want to tell you your *job*. All that I'm saying, things get *set*, I know they do, you get a certain *mindset*. . . . guy gets a reputation. We know how this . . . all I'm saying, put a *closer* on the job. There's more than one man for the . . . Put a . . . wait a second, put a *proven man out* . . . and you watch, now *wait* a second — and you watch your *dollar* volumes. . . . You start closing them for *fifty* 'stead of *twenty-five* . . . you put a *closer* on the . . .

WILLIAMSON: Shelly, you blew the last . . .

LEVENE: No. John. No. Let's wait, let's back up here, I did . . . will you please? Wait a second. Please. I didn't "blow" them. No. I didn't "blow" them. No. One kicked *out*, one I closed . . .

WILLIAMSON: . . . you didn't close . . .

LEVENE: . . . I, if you'd *listen* to me. Please. I *closed* the cocksucker. His *ex*, John, his *ex*, I didn't know he was married . . . he, the *judge* invalidated the . . .

WILLIAMSON: Shelly . . .

LEVENE: . . . and what is that, John? What? Bad *luck*. That's all it is. I pray in your *life* you will never find it runs in streaks. That's what it does, that's all it's doing. Streaks. I pray it misses you. That's all I want to say.

WILLIAMSON (*Pause*): What about the other two?

LEVENE: What two?

WILLIAMSON: Four. You had four leads. One kicked out, one the *judge*, you say . . .

LEVENE: . . . you want to see the court records? John? Eh? You want to go down . . .

WILLIAMSON: . . . no . . .

LEVENE: . . . do you want to go down*town* . . . ?

WILLIAMSON: . . . no . . .

LEVENE: . . . then . . .

WILLIAMSON: . . . I only . . .

LEVENE: . . . then what is this "you *say*" shit, what is that? (*Pause.*) What is that . . . ?

WILLIAMSON: All that I'm saying . . .

LEVENE: What is this "you *say*"? A deal kicks out . . . I got to *eat*. *Shit*, Williamson, *shit*. You . . . Moss . . . Roma . . . look at the *sheets* . . . look at the *sheets*. Nineteen *eighty*, eighty-one . . . eighty-*two* . . . six months of eighty-two . . . who's there? Who's up there?

WILLIAMSON: Roma.

LEVENE: Under him?

WILLIAMSON: Moss.

LEVENE: Bullshit. John. Bull*shit*. April, September 1981. It's *me*. It isn't *fucking* Moss. Due respect, he's an *order* taker, John. He *talks*, he talks a good game, look at the *board*, and it's *me*, John, it's me . . .

WILLIAMSON: Not lately it isn't.

LEVENE: Lately kiss my ass lately. That isn't how you build an org . . . talk, talk to Murray. Talk to Mitch. When we were on Peterson, who paid for his fucking *car*? You talk to him. The *Seville*. . . ? He came in, "You bought that for me Shelly." Out of *what*? Cold *calling*. *Nothing*. Sixty-*five*, when we were there, with Glen *Ross* Farms? You call 'em downtown. What was that? *Luck*? That was "luck"? *Bull*shit, John. You're burning my ass, I can't get a fucking *lead* . . . you think that was luck. My stats for those years? Bull*shit* . . . over that period of time. . . ? Bull*shit*. It wasn't luck. It was *skill*. You want to throw that away, John. . . ? You want to throw that away?

WILLIAMSON: It isn't me . . .

LEVENE: . . . it isn't you. . . ? Who *is* it? Who is this I'm talking to? I need the *leads* . . .

1483

WILLIAMSON: . . . after the thirtieth . . .

LEVENE: Bull*shit* the thirtieth, I don't get on the board the thirtieth, they're going to can my ass. I need the leads. I need them now. Or I'm gone, and you're going to miss me, John, I swear to you.

WILLIAMSON: Murray . . .

LEVENE: . . . you *talk* to Murray . . .

WILLIAMSON: I have. And my job is to marshal those leads . . .

LEVENE: Marshal the leads . . . marshal the leads? What the fuck, what bus did *you* get off of, we're here to fucking *sell*. *Fuck* marshaling the leads. What the fuck talk is that? What the fuck talk is that? Where did you learn that? In school? (*Pause.*) That's "talk," my friend, that's "talk." Our job is to *sell*. I'm the *man* to sell. I'm getting garbage. (*Pause.*) You're giving it to me, and what I'm saying is it's *fucked*.

WILLIAMSON: You're saying that I'm fucked.

LEVENE: Yes. (*Pause.*) I am. I'm sorry to antagonize you.

WILLIAMSON: Let me . . .

LEVENE: . . . and I'm going to get bounced and you're . . .

WILLIAMSON: . . . let me . . . are you listening to me . . . ?

LEVENE: Yes.

WILLIAMSON: Let me tell you something, Shelly. I do what I'm hired to do. I'm . . . wait a second. I'm *hired* to watch the leads. I'm given . . . hold on, I'm given a *policy*. *My* job is to *do* that. What I'm *told*. That's it. You, wait a second, *anybody* falls below a certain mark I'm not *permitted* to give them the premium leads.

LEVENE: Then how do they come up above that mark? With *dreck*. . . ? That's *nonsense*. Explain this to me. 'Cause it's a waste, and it's a stupid waste. I want to tell you something . . .

WILLIAMSON: You know what those leads cost?

LEVENE: The premium leads. Yes. I know what they cost. John. Because *I*, *I* generated the dollar revenue sufficient to *buy* them. Nineteen senny-*nine*, you know what I made? Senny-*nine*? Ninety-six thousand dollars. John? For *Murray* . . . For *Mitch* . . . look at the sheets . . .

WILLIAMSON: Murray said . . .

LEVENE: *Fuck* him. *Fuck* Murray. John? You know? You tell him I said so. What does *he* fucking know? He's going to have a "sales" contest . . . you know what our sales contest used to be? *Money*. A *fortune*. Money lying on the ground. Murray? When was the last time *he* went out on a sit? Sales contest? It's *laughable*. It's cold out there now, John. It's tight. Money is *tight*. This ain't sixty-five. It ain't. It just ain't. See? See? Now, I'm a good *man* — but I need a . . .

WILLIAMSON: Murray said . . .

LEVENE: John. John . . .

WILLIAMSON: Will you please wait a second. Shelly. Please. Murray told me: the hot leads . . .

LEVENE: . . . ah, *fuck* this . . .

WILLIAMSON: The . . . Shelly? (*Pause.*) The hot leads are assigned according to the board. During the contest. *Period*. Anyone who beats fifty per . . .

LEVENE: That's fucked. That's fucked. You don't look at the fucking *percentage*. You look at the *gross*.

WILLIAMSON: Either way. You're out.

LEVENE: I'm out.

WILLIAMSON: Yes.

LEVENE: I'll tell you why I'm out. I'm *out*, you're giving me toilet paper. John. I've *seen* those leads. I saw them when I was at Homestead, we pitched those cocksuckers Rio Rancho nineteen sixty-*nine* they wouldn't buy. They couldn't buy a fucking *toaster*. They're *broke*, John. They're cold. They're deadbeats, you can't judge on that. Even so. Even so. Alright. Fine. Fine. Even so. I go in, FOUR FUCKING LEADS they got their money in a *sock*. They're fucking *Polacks*, John. Four leads. I close two. *Two*. Fifty per . . .

WILLIAMSON: . . . they kicked out.

LEVENE: They *all* kick out. You run in *streaks*, pal. *Streaks*. I'm . . . I'm . . . *don't* look at the *board*, look at *me*. Shelly Levene. *Anyone*. Ask them on Western. Ask Getz at Homestead. Go ask Jerry Graff. You know who I am . . . I NEED A SHOT. I got to get on the fucking board. Ask them. *Ask* them. Ask them who ever picked up a check I was flush. Moss, Jerry Graff, Mitch himself . . . Those guys *lived* on the business I brought in. They *lived* on it . . . and so did Murray, John. You were here you'd of benefited from it too. And now I'm saying this. Do I want charity? Do I want *pity*? I want *sits*. I want leads don't come right out of a *phone book*. Give me a lead hotter than that, I'll go in and close it. Give me a chance. That's all I want. I'm going to *get* up on that fucking board and all I want is a chance. It's a *streak* and I'm going to turn it around. (*Pause.*) I need your help. (*Pause.*)

WILLIAMSON: I can't do it, Shelly. (*Pause.*)

LEVENE: Why?

WILLIAMSON: The leads are assigned randomly . . .

LEVENE: *Bullshit, bullshit*, you assign them. . . . What are you *telling* me?

WILLIAMSON: . . . apart from the top men on the contest board.

LEVENE: Then put me on the board.

WILLIAMSON: You start closing again, you'll *be* on the board.

LEVENE: I can't close these leads, John. No one can. It's a joke. John, look, just give me a hot lead. Just give me two of the premium leads. As a "test," alright? As a "test" and I promise you . . .

WILLIAMSON: I can't do it, Shel. (*Pause.*)

LEVENE: I'll give you ten percent. (*Pause.*)

WILLIAMSON: Of what?

LEVENE: Of my end what I close.

WILLIAMSON: And what if you don't close.

LEVENE: I *will* close.

WILLIAMSON: What if you *don't* close. . . ?

LEVENE: I *will* close.

WILLIAMSON: What if you *don't*? Then I'm *fucked*. You see. . . ? Then it's *my* job. That's what I'm *telling* you.

LEVENE: I *will* close. John, John, ten percent. I can get hot. You *know* that . . .

WILLIAMSON: Not lately you can't . . .

LEVENE: Fuck that. That's defeatist. Fuck that. Fuck it. . . . Get on my side. *Go* with me. Let's *do* something. You want to run this office, *run* it.

WILLIAMSON: Twenty percent. (*Pause.*)

LEVENE: Alright.

WILLIAMSON: And fifty bucks a lead.

LEVENE: John. (*Pause.*) Listen. I want to talk to you. Permit me to do this a second. I'm older than you. A man acquires a reputation. On the street. What he does when he's *up*, what he does otherwise. . . . I said "ten," you said "no." You said "twenty." I said "fine," I'm not going to fuck with you, how can I beat that, you tell me? . . . Okay. Okay. We'll . . . Okay. Fine. We'll . . . Alright, twenty percent, and fifty bucks a lead. That's fine. For now. That's fine. A month or two we'll talk. A month from now. Next month. After the thirtieth. (*Pause.*) We'll talk.

WILLIAMSON: What are we going to say?

LEVENE: No. You're right. That's for later. We'll talk in a month. What have you got? I want two sits. Tonight.

WILLIAMSON: I'm not sure I have two.

LEVENE: I saw the board. You've got *four* . . .

WILLIAMSON (*Snaps*): I've got *Roma*. Then I've got Moss . . .

LEVENE: *Bullshit.* They ain't been in the office yet. Give 'em some stiff. We have a deal or not? Eh? Two sits. The Des Plaines. Both of 'em, six and ten, you can do it . . . six and ten . . . eight and eleven, I don't give a shit, you set 'em up? Alright? The two sits in Des Plaines.

WILLIAMSON: Alright.

LEVENE: Good. Now we're talking. (*Pause.*)

WILLIAMSON: A hundred bucks. (*Pause.*)

LEVENE: Now? (*Pause.*) *Now?*

WILLIAMSON: Now. (*Pause.*) Yes . . . When?

LEVENE: Ah, *shit*, John. (*Pause.*)

WILLIAMSON: I wish I could.

LEVENE: You fucking asshole. (*Pause.*) I haven't got it. (*Pause.*) I haven't got it, John. (*Pause.*) I'll pay you tomorrow. (*Pause.*) I'm coming in here with the sales, I'll pay you *tomorrow.* (*Pause.*) I haven't *got* it, when I pay, the *gas* . . . I get back the hotel, I'll bring it in tomorrow.

WILLIAMSON: Can't do it.

LEVENE: I'll give you thirty on them now, I'll bring the rest tomorrow. I've got it at the hotel. (*Pause.*) John? (*Pause.*) We do that, for chrissake?

WILLIAMSON: No.

LEVENE: I'm asking you. As a favor to me? (*Pause.*) John. (*Long pause.*) John: my *daughter* . . .

WILLIAMSON: I can't do it, Shelly.

LEVENE: Well, I want to tell you something, fella, wasn't long I could pick up the phone, call *Murray* and I'd have your job. You know that? Not too *long* ago. For what? For *nothing.* "Mur, this new kid burns my ass." "Shelly, he's out." You're gone before I'm back from lunch. I bought him a trip to Bermuda once . . .

WILLIAMSON: I have to go . . . (*Gets up.*)

LEVENE: Wait. Alright. Fine. (*Starts going in pocket for money.*) The one. Give me the lead. Give me the one lead. The best one you have.

WILLIAMSON: I can't split them. (*Pause.*)

LEVENE: Why?

WILLIAMSON: Because I say so.

LEVENE (*Pause*): Is that it? Is that *it*? You want to do business that way. . . ?

Williamson gets up, leaves money on the table.

LEVENE: You want to do business that way. . . ? Alright. Alright. Alright. Alright. What is there on the other list. . . ?

WILLIAMSON: You want something off the B list?

LEVENE: *Yeah.* Yeah.

WILLIAMSON: Is that what you're saying?

LEVENE: That's what I'm saying. Yeah. (*Pause.*) I'd like something off the other list. Which, very least, that I'm entitled to. If I'm still *working* here, which for the moment I guess that I am. (*Pause.*) What? I'm sorry I spoke harshly to you.

WILLIAMSON: That's alright.

LEVENE: The deal still stands, our other thing.

Williamson shrugs. Starts out of the booth.

LEVENE: Good. Mmm. I, you know, I left my wallet back at the hotel.

Scene Two

A booth at the restaurant. Moss and Aaronow seated. After the meal.

MOSS: Polacks and deadbeats.

AARONOW: . . . Polacks . . .

MOSS: Deadbeats *all.*

AARONOW: . . . they hold on to their money . . .

MOSS: All of 'em. They, *hey*: it happens to us all.

AARONOW: Where am I going to work?

MOSS: You have to cheer up, George, you aren't out yet.

AARONOW: I'm not?

MOSS: You missed a fucking sale. Big deal. A deadbeat Polack. Big deal. How you going to sell 'em in the *first* place. . . ? Your mistake, you shoun'a took the lead.

AARONOW: I had to.

MOSS: You had to, yeah. Why?

AARONOW: To get on the . . .

MOSS: To get on the board. Yeah. How you goan'a get on the board sell'n a Polack? And I'll tell you, I'll tell you what *else.* You listening? I'll tell you what else: don't ever try to sell an Indian.

AARONOW: I'd never try to sell an Indian.

MOSS: You get those names come up, you ever get 'em, "Patel"?

AARONOW: Mmm . . .

MOSS: You ever get 'em?

AARONOW: Well, I think I had one once.

MOSS: You did?

AARONOW: I . . . I don't know.

MOSS: You had one you'd know it. *Patel.* They keep coming up. I don't know. They like to talk to salesmen. (*Pause.*) They're *lonely,* something. (*Pause.*) They like to feel *superior,* I don't know. Never bought a fucking thing. You're sitting down "The Rio Rancho *this,* the blah blah blah," "The Mountain View — " "Oh yes. My brother told me that. . . ." They got a grapevine. Fuckin' Indians, George. Not my cup of tea. Speaking of which I want to tell you something: (*Pause*) I never got a cup of tea with them. You see them in the restaurants. A supercilious race. What is this *look* on their face all the time? I don't know. (*Pause.*) I don't know. Their broads all look like they just got fucked with a dead *cat, I* don't know. (*Pause.*) I don't know. I don't like it. Christ . . .

AARONOW: What?

MOSS: The whole fuckin' thing . . . The pressure's just too great. You're ab . . . you're absolu . . . they're too important. All of them. You go in the door. I . . . "I got to *close* this fucker, or I don't eat lunch," "or I don't win the *Cadillac.* . . ." We fuckin' work too hard. You work too hard. We all, I remember when we were at Platt . . . huh? Glen Ross Farms . . . *didn't* we sell a bunch of that. . . ?

AARONOW: They came in and they, you know . . .

MOSS: Well, they fucked it up.

AARONOW: They did.

MOSS: They killed the goose.

AARONOW: They did.

MOSS: And now . . .

AARONOW: We're stuck with *this* . . .

MOSS: We're stuck with *this* fucking shit . . .

AARONOW: . . . *this* shit . . .

MOSS: It's too . . .

AARONOW: It is.

MOSS: Eh?

AARONOW: It's too . . .

MOSS: You get a bad month, all of a . . .

AARONOW: You're on this . . .

MOSS: All of, they got you on this "board . . ."

AARONOW: I, I . . . I . . .

MOSS: Some *contest* board . . .

AARONOW: I . . .

MOSS: It's not right.

AARONOW: It's not.

MOSS: No. (*Pause.*)

AARONOW: And it's not right to the *customers.*

MOSS: I know it's not. I'll tell you, you got, you know, you got . . . what did I learn as a kid on Western? Don't sell a guy one car. Sell him *five* cars over fifteen years.

AARONOW: That's right?

MOSS: Eh. . . ?

AARONOW: That's right?

MOSS: Goddamn right, that's right. Guys come on: "Oh, the blah blah blah, *I* know what I'll do: I'll go in and rob everyone blind and go to Argentina cause nobody ever *thought* of this before."

AARONOW: . . . that's right . . .

MOSS: Eh?

AARONOW: No. That's absolutely right.

MOSS: And so they kill the goose. I, I, I'll . . . and a fuckin' *man,* worked all his *life* has got to . . .

AARONOW: . . . that's right . . .

MOSS: . . . cower in his boots . . .

AARONOW (*simultaneously with "boots"*): Shoes, boots, yes . . .

MOSS: For some fuckin' "Sell ten thousand and you win the steak knives . . ."

AARONOW: For some *sales* pro . . .

MOSS: . . . sales promotion, "You *lose,* then we fire your . . ." No. It's *medieval* . . . it's wrong. "Or we're going to fire your ass." It's wrong.

AARONOW: Yes.

MOSS: Yes, it is. And you know who's responsible?

AARONOW: Who?

MOSS: You know who it is. It's Mitch. And Murray. 'Cause it doesn't have to be this way.

AARONOW: No.

MOSS: Look at Jerry Graff. He's *clean,* he's doing business for *himself,* he's got his, that *list* of his with the *nurses* . . . see? You see? That's *thinking.* Why take ten percent? A ten percent comm . . . why are we giving the rest away? What are we giving ninety per . . . for *nothing.* For some jerk sit in the office tell you "Get out there and close." "Go win the Cadillac." Graff. He goes out and *buys.* He pays top dollar for the . . . you see?

AARONOW: Yes.

MOSS: That's *thinking.* Now, he's got the leads, he goes in business for *himself.* He's . . . that's what I . . . that's *thinking*! "Who? Who's got a steady *job,* a couple bucks nobody's touched, who?"

AARONOW: Nurses.

MOSS: So Graff buys a fucking list of nurses, one grand — if he paid two I'll eat my hat — four, five thousand nurses, and he's going *wild* . . .

AARONOW: He is?

MOSS: He's doing *very* well.

AARONOW: I heard that they were running cold.

MOSS: The nurses?

AARONOW: Yes.

MOSS: You hear a *lot* of things. . . . He's doing very well. He's doing *very* well.

AARONOW: With River Oaks?

MOSS: River Oaks, Brook Farms. *All* of that shit. Somebody told me, you know what he's clearing *himself*? Fourteen, fifteen grand a *week.*

AARONOW: Himself?

MOSS: That's what I'm *saying.* Why? The *leads.* He's got the good leads . . . what are we, we're sitting in the shit here. Why? We have to go to *them* to *get* them. Huh. Ninety percent our sale, we're *paying* to the *office* for the *leads.*

AARONOW: The leads, the overhead, the telephones, there's *lots* of things.

MOSS: What do you need? A *telephone,* some broad to say "Good morning," nothing . . . nothing . . .

AARONOW: No, it's not that simple, Dave . . .

MOSS: *Yes.* It *is*. It *is* simple, and you know what the hard part is?

AARONOW: What?

MOSS: Starting up.

AARONOW: What hard part?

MOSS: Of doing the thing. The dif . . . the difference. Between me and Jerry Graff. Going to business for yourself. The hard part is . . . you know what it is?

AARONOW: What?

MOSS: Just the *act*.

AARONOW: What act?

MOSS: To say "I'm going on my own." 'Cause what you do, George, let me tell you what you do: you find yourself in *thrall* to someone else. And we *enslave* ourselves. To *please*. To win some fucking *toaster* . . . to . . . to . . . and the guy who got there first made *up* those . . .

AARONOW: That's right . . .

MOSS: He made *up* those rules, and we're working for *him*.

AARONOW: That's the truth . . .

MOSS: That's the *God's* truth. And it gets me depressed. I *swear* that it does. At MY AGE. To see a goddamn: "Somebody wins the Cadillac this month. P.S. Two guys get fucked."

AARONOW: *Huh*.

MOSS: You don't *ax* your sales force.

AARONOW: No.

MOSS: You . . .

AARONOW: You . . .

MOSS: You *build* it!

AARONOW: That's what I . . .

MOSS: You fucking *build* it! Men come . . .

AARONOW: Men come *work* for you . . .

MOSS: . . . you're absolutely right.

AARONOW: They . . .

MOSS: They have . . .

AARONOW: When they . . .

MOSS: Look look look look, when they *build* your business, then you can't fucking turn around, *enslave* them, treat them like *children*, fuck them up the ass, leave them to fend for themselves . . . no. (*Pause.*) No. (*Pause.*) You're absolutely right, and I want to tell you something.

AARONOW: What?

MOSS: I want to tell you what somebody should do.

AARONOW: What?

MOSS: Someone should stand up and strike *back*.

AARONOW: What do you mean?

MOSS: *Somebody* . . .

AARONOW: Yes. . . ?

MOSS: Should do something to *them*.

AARONOW: What?

MOSS: Something. To pay them back. (*Pause.*) Someone, someone should hurt them. Murray and Mitch.

AARONOW: Someone should hurt them.

MOSS: Yes.

AARONOW (*Pause.*): How?

MOSS: How? Do something to hurt them. Where they live.

AARONOW: What? (*Pause.*)

MOSS: Someone should rob the office.

AARONOW: Huh.

MOSS: That's what I'm *saying*. We were, if we were that kind of guys, to knock it off, and *trash* the joint, it looks like robbery, and *take* the fuckin' leads out of the files . . . go to Jerry Graff. (*Long pause.*)

AARONOW: What could somebody get for them?

MOSS: What could we *get* for them? I don't know. Buck a *throw* . . . buck-a-half a throw . . . I don't know. . . . Hey, who knows what they're worth, what do they *pay* for them? All told . . . must be, I'd . . . three bucks a throw . . . *I* don't know.

AARONOW: How many leads have we got?

MOSS: The *Glengarry* . . . the premium leads. . . ? I'd say we got five thousand. Five. Five thousand leads.

AARONOW: And you're saying a fella could take and sell these leads to Jerry Graff.

MOSS: Yes.

AARONOW: How do you know he'd buy them?

MOSS: Graff? Because I worked for him.

AARONOW: You haven't talked to him.

MOSS: No. What do you mean? Have I talked to him about *this*? (*Pause.*)

AARONOW: Yes. I mean are you actually *talking* about this, or are we just . . .

MOSS: No, we're just . . .

AARONOW: We're just *"talking"* about it.

MOSS: We're just *speaking* about it. (*Pause.*) As an *idea*.

AARONOW: As an idea.

MOSS: Yes.

AARONOW: We're not actually *talking* about it.

MOSS: No.

AARONOW: Talking about it as a . . .

MOSS: *No*.

AARONOW: As a *robbery*.

MOSS: As a "robbery"?! No.

AARONOW: *Well*. Well . . .

MOSS: Hey. (*Pause.*)

AARONOW: So all this, um, you didn't, actually, you didn't actually go talk to Graff.

MOSS: Not actually, no. (*Pause.*)

AARONOW: You didn't?

MOSS: No. Not actually.

AARONOW: Did you?

MOSS: What did I say?

AARONOW: What did you say?

MOSS: Yes. (*Pause.*) I said, "Not actually." The fuck *you* care, George? We're just *talking* . . .

AARONOW: We are?

MOSS: Yes. (*Pause.*)

AARONOW: Because, because, you know, it's a *crime*.

MOSS: That's right. It's a crime. It is a crime. It's also very safe.

AARONOW: You're actually *talking* about this?

MOSS: That's right. (*Pause.*)

AARONOW: You're going to steal the leads?

MOSS: Have I said that? (*Pause.*)

AARONOW: Are you? (*Pause.*)

MOSS: Did I say that?

AARONOW: Did you talk to Graff?

MOSS: Is that what I said?

AARONOW: What did he say?

MOSS: What did he say? He'd *buy* them. (*Pause.*)

AARONOW: You're going to steal the leads and sell the leads to him? (*Pause.*)

MOSS: Yes.

AARONOW: What will he pay?

MOSS: A buck a shot.

AARONOW: For five thousand?

MOSS: However they are, that's the deal. A buck a throw. Five thousand dollars. Split it half and half.

AARONOW: You're saying "me."

MOSS: Yes. (*Pause.*) Twenty-five hundred apiece. One night's work, and the job with Graff. Working the premium leads. (*Pause.*)

AARONOW: A job with Graff.

MOSS: Is that what I said?

AARONOW: He'd give me a job.

MOSS: He would take you on. Yes. (*Pause.*)

AARONOW: Is that the truth?

MOSS: Yes. It is, George. (*Pause.*) Yes. It's a big decision. (*Pause.*) And it's a big reward. (*Pause.*) It's a big reward. For one night's work. (*Pause.*) But it's got to be tonight.

AARONOW: What?

MOSS: What? What? The *leads*.

AARONOW: You have to steal the leads tonight?

MOSS: That's *right,* the guys are moving them downtown. After the thirtieth. Murray and Mitch. After the contest.

AARONOW: You're, you're saying so you have to go in there tonight and . . .

MOSS: *You* . . .

AARONOW: I'm sorry?

MOSS: *You.* (*Pause.*)

AARONOW: Me?

MOSS: *You* have to go in. (*Pause.*) *You* have to get the leads. (*Pause.*)

AARONOW: I do?

MOSS: Yes.

AARONOW: I . . .

MOSS: It's not something for nothing, George, I took you in on this, you have to go. That's your thing. I've made the deal with Graff. I can't go. I can't go in, I've spoken on this too much. I've got a big mouth. (*Pause.*) "The fucking leads" et cetera, blah blah blah ". . . the fucking tight ass company . . ."

AARONOW: They'll know when you go over to Graff . . .

MOSS: What will they know? That I stole the leads? I *didn't* steal the leads, I'm going to the *movies* tonight with a friend, and then I'm going to the Como Inn. Why did I go to Graff? I got a better deal. *Period.* Let 'em prove something. They can't prove anything that's not the case. (*Pause.*)

AARONOW: *Dave.*

MOSS: Yes.

AARONOW: You want me to break into the office tonight and steal the leads?

MOSS: Yes. (*Pause.*)

AARONOW: No.

MOSS: Oh, yes, George.

AARONOW: What does that mean?

MOSS: Listen to this. I have an alibi, I'm going to the Como Inn, why? Why? The place gets robbed, they're going to come looking for *me.* Why? Because I probably did it. Are you going to turn me in? (*Pause.*) George? Are you going to turn me in?

AARONOW: What if you don't get caught?

MOSS: They come to you, you going to turn me in?

AARONOW: Why would they come to me?

MOSS: They're going to come to *everyone.*

AARONOW: Why would I *do* it?

MOSS: You wouldn't, George, that's why I'm talking to you. Answer me. They come to you. You going to turn me in?

AARONOW: No.

MOSS: Are you sure?

AARONOW: Yes. I'm sure.

MOSS: Then listen to this: I have to get those leads tonight. That's something I have to do. If I'm not at the *movies* . . . if I'm not eating over at the inn . . . If you don't do this, then *I* have to come in here . . .

AARONOW: . . . you don't have to come in . . .

MOSS: . . . and *rob* the place . . .

AARONOW: . . . I thought that we were only talking . . .

MOSS: . . . they *take* me, then. They're going to ask me who were my accomplices.

AARONOW: *Me?*

MOSS: Absolutely.

AARONOW: That's ridiculous.

MOSS: Well, to the law, you're an accessory. Before the fact.

AARONOW: I didn't ask to be.

MOSS: Then tough luck, George, because you are.

AARONOW: Why? *Why,* because you only *told* me about it?

MOSS: That's right.

AARONOW: Why are you doing this to me, Dave. Why are you talking this way to me? I don't understand. Why are you doing this at *all.* . . ?

MOSS: That's none of your fucking business . . .

AARONOW: Well, well, well, *talk* to me, we sat down to eat *dinner,* and here I'm a *criminal* . . .

MOSS: You *went* for it.

AARONOW: In the abstract . . .

MOSS: So I'm making it concrete.

AARONOW: Why?

MOSS: Why? Why *you* going to give me five grand?

AARONOW: Do you need five grand?

MOSS: Is that what I just said?

AARONOW: You need money? Is that the . . .

MOSS: Hey, hey, let's just keep it simple, what I need is not the . . . what do *you* need. . . ?

AARONOW: What is the five grand? (*Pause.*) What is the, you said that we were going to *split* five . . .

MOSS: I lied. (*Pause.*) Alright? My end is *my* business. Your end's twenty-five. In or out. You tell me, you're out you take the consequences.

AARONOW: I do?

MOSS: Yes. (*Pause.*)

AARONOW: And why is that?

MOSS: Because you listened.

Scene Three

The restaurant. Roma is seated alone at the booth. Lingk is at the booth next to him. Roma is talking to him.

ROMA: . . . all train compartments smell vaguely of shit. It gets so you don't mind it. That's the worst thing that I can confess. You know how long it took me to get there? A long time. When you *die* you're going to regret the things you don't do. You think you're *queer*. . . ? I'm going to tell you something: we're *all* queer. You think that you're a *thief*? So *what*? You get befuddled by a middle-class morality. . . ? Get *shut* of it. Shut it out. You cheated on your wife. . . ? You *did* it, *live* with it. (*Pause.*) You fuck little girls, so *be* it. There's an absolute morality? May *be*. And *then* what? If you *think* there is, then *be* that thing. Bad people go to hell? I don't *think* so. If you think that, act that way. A hell exists on earth? Yes. I won't live in it. That's *me*. You ever take a dump made you feel you'd just slept for twelve hours. . . ?

LINGK: Did I. . . ?

ROMA: Yes.

LINGK: I don't know.

ROMA: Or a *piss*. . . ? A great meal fades in reflection. Everything else gains. You know why? 'Cause it's only food. This shit we eat, it keeps us going. But it's only food. The great fucks that you may have had. What do you remember about them?

LINGK: What do I. . . ?

ROMA: Yes.

LINGK: Mmmm . . .

ROMA: I don't know. For *me*, I'm saying, what it is, it's probably not the orgasm. Some broads, forearms on your neck, something her *eyes* did. There was a *sound* she made . . . or, me, lying, in the, I'll tell you: me lying in bed; the next day she brought me café au lait. She gives me a cigarette, my balls feel like concrete. Eh? What I'm saying, what is our life? (*Pause.*) It's looking forward or it's looking back. And that's our life. That's *it*. Where is the *moment*? (*Pause.*) And what is it that we're afraid of? Loss. What else? (*Pause.*) The *bank* closes. We get *sick*, my wife died on a plane, the stock market collapsed . . . the house burnt down . . . what of these happen. . . ? None of 'em. We worry anyway. What does this mean? I'm not *secure*. How can I be secure? (*Pause.*) Through amassing wealth beyond all measure? No. And what's beyond all measure? That's a sickness. That's a trap. There is no measure. Only greed. How can we act? The right way, we would say, to deal with this: "There is a one-in-a-million chance that so and so will happen. . . . *Fuck* it, it won't happen to *me*. . . ." No. We know that's not the right way I think. (*Pause.*) We say the *correct* way to deal with this is "There is a one-in-so-and-so chance this will happen . . . God *protect* me. I am powerless, let it not happen to me. . . ." But no to *that*. I say. There's something else. What is it? "If it happens, AS IT MAY for that is not within our powers, I will *deal* with it, just as I do *today* with what draws my concern today." I say *this* is how we must act. I do those things which seem correct to me *today*. I trust myself. And if security concerns me, I do that which *today* I think will make me secure. And every day I *do* that, when that day *arrives* that I need a reserve, (a) odds are that I have it, and (b) the *true* reserve that I have is the strength that I have of *acting each day* without fear. (*Pause.*) According to the dictates of my mind. (*Pause.*) Stocks, bonds, objects of art, real estate. Now: what are they? (*Pause.*) An opportunity. To what? To make money? Perhaps. To *lose* money? Perhaps. To "indulge" and to "learn" about ourselves? Perhaps. *So fucking what?* What *isn't*? They're an *opportunity*. That's all. They're an *event*. A guy comes up to you, you make a call, you send in a brochure, it doesn't matter, "There're these *properties* I'd like for you to see." What does it mean? What you *want* it to mean. (*Pause.*) Money? (*Pause.*) If that's what it signifies to you. Security? (*Pause.*) Comfort? (*Pause.*) All it is is THINGS THAT HAPPEN TO YOU. (*Pause.*) That's all it is. How are they different? (*Pause.*) Some poor newly married guy gets run down by a cab. Some *busboy* wins the lottery. (*Pause.*) All it is, it's a carnival. What's special . . . what *draws* us? (*Pause.*) We're all different. (*Pause.*) We're not the same. (*Pause.*) We are not the same. (*Pause.*) Hmmm. (*Pause. Sighs.*) It's been a long day. (*Pause.*) What are you drinking?

LINGK: Gimlet.

ROMA: Well, let's have a couple more. My name is Richard Roma, what's yours?

LINGK: Lingk. James Lingk.

ROMA: James. I'm glad to meet you. (*They shake hands.*) I'm glad to meet you, James. (*Pause.*) I want to show you something. (*Pause.*) It might mean *nothing* to you . . . and it might not. I don't know. I don't know anymore. (*Pause. He takes out a small map and spreads it on a table.*) What is that? Florida. Glengarry Highlands. Florida. "Florida. *Bullshit.*" And maybe that's true; and that's what *I* said: but look *here*: what is this? This is a piece of land. Listen to what I'm going to tell you now:

ACT TWO

The real estate office. Ransacked. A broken plate-glass window boarded up, glass all over the floor. Aaronow and Williamson standing around, smoking.

Pause.

AARONOW: People used to say that there are numbers of such magnitude that multiplying them by two made no difference. (*Pause.*)

WILLIAMSON: Who used to say that?

AARONOW: In school. (*Pause.*)

Baylen, a detective, comes out of the inner office.

BAYLEN: Alright. . . ?

Roma enters from the street.

ROMA: *Williamson . . . Williamson,* they stole the con-tracts. . . ?

BAYLEN: Excuse me, sir . . .

ROMA: Did they get my contracts?

WILLIAMSON: They got . . .

BAYLEN: Excuse me, fella.

ROMA: . . . did they . . .

BAYLEN: Would you excuse us, please. . . ?

ROMA: Don't *fuck* with me, fella. I'm talking about a fuckin' Cadillac car that you owe me . . .

WILLIAMSON: They didn't get your contract. I filed it before I left.

ROMA: They didn't get my contracts?

WILLIAMSON: They — excuse me . . . (*He goes back into inner room with the Detective.*)

ROMA: Oh, *fuck. Fuck.* (*He starts kicking the desk.*) FUCK FUCK FUCK! WILLIAMSON!!! WILLIAM-ON!!! (*Goes to the door Williamson went into, tries the door; it's locked.*) OPEN THE FUCKING . . . WILLIAMSON . . .

BAYLEN (*coming out*): Who are you?

Williamson comes out.

WILLIAMSON: They didn't get the contracts.

ROMA: Did they . . .

WILLIAMSON: They got, listen to me . . .

ROMA: Th . . .

WILLIAMSON: Listen to me: They got *some* of them.

ROMA: Some of them . . .

BAYLEN: Who told you. . . ?

ROMA: Who told me wh. . . ? You've got a fuckin', you've . . . a . . . who is this. . . ? You've got a board-up on the window. . . . *Moss* told me.

BAYLEN (*Looking back toward the inner office.*): Moss . . . Who told him?

ROMA: How the fuck do *I* know? (*To Williamson:*) *What . . . talk* to me.

WILLIAMSON: They took *some* of the con . . .

ROMA: . . . some of the contracts . . . Lingk. James Lingk. I closed . . .

WILLIAMSON: You closed him yesterday.

ROMA: *Yes.*

WILLIAMSON: It went down. I filed it.

ROMA: You did?

WILLIAMSON: Yes.

ROMA: Then I'm over the fucking top and you owe me a Cadillac.

WILLIAMSON: I . . .

ROMA: And I don't want any fucking shit and I don't give a shit, Lingk puts me over the top, you filed it, that's fine, any other shit kicks out *you* go back. You . . . *you* reclose it, 'cause I *closed* it and you . . . you owe me the car.

BAYLEN: Would you excuse us, please.

AARONOW: I, um, and may . . . maybe they're in . . . they're in . . . you should, John, if we're ins . . .

WILLIAMSON: I'm sure that we're insured, George . . . (*Going back inside.*)

ROMA: Fuck insured. You owe me a car.

BAYLEN (*Stepping back into the inner room*): Please don't leave. I'm going to talk to you. What's your name?

ROMA: Are you talking to me? (*Pause.*)

BAYLEN: Yes. (*Pause.*)

ROMA: My name is Richard Roma.

Baylen goes back into the inner room.

AARONOW: I, you know, they should be insured.

ROMA: What do *you* care. . . ?

AARONOW: Then, you know, they wouldn't be so ups . . .

ROMA: Yeah. That's swell. Yes. You're right. (*Pause.*) How are you?

AARONOW: I'm fine. You mean the *board*? You mean the *board. . . ?*

ROMA: I don't . . . yes. Okay, the board.

AARONOW: I'm, I'm, I'm, I'm fucked on the board. *You.* You see how . . . I . . . (*Pause.*) I can't . . . my mind must be in other places. 'Cause I can't do any . . .

ROMA: *What?* You can't do any *what?* (*Pause.*)

AARONOW: I can't close 'em.

ROMA: Well, they're old. I saw the shit that they were giving you.

AARONOW: Yes.

ROMA: Huh?

AARONOW: Yes. They are old.

ROMA: They're ancient.

AARONOW: Clear . . .

ROMA: Clear Meadows. That shit's dead. (*Pause.*)

AARONOW: It *is* dead.

ROMA: It's a waste of time.

AARONOW: Yes. (*Long pause.*) I'm no fucking good.

ROMA: That's . . .

AARONOW: Everything I . . . *you* know . . .

ROMA: That's not . . . Fuck that shit, George. You're a, *hey,* you had a bad month. You're a good man, George.

AARONOW: I am?

ROMA: You hit a bad streak. We've all . . . look at this: fifteen units Mountain View, the fucking things get stole.

AARONOW: He said he filed . . .

ROMA: He filed half of them, he filed the *big* one. All the little ones, I have, I have to go back and . . . ah, *fuck,* I got to go out like a fucking schmuck hat in my hand and reclose the . . . (*Pause.*) I mean, talk about a bad streak. That would sap *anyone's* self confi . . . I got to go out and reclose all my . . . Where's the phones?

AARONOW: They stole . . .

ROMA: They stole the . . .

AARONOW: What. What kind of outfit are we running where . . . where anyone . . .

ROMA (*To himself*): They stole the phones.

AARONOW: Where criminals can come in here . . . they take the . . .

ROMA: They stole the phones. They stole the leads. They're . . . *Christ.* (*Pause.*) What am I going to do this month? Oh, *shit* . . . (*Starts for the door.*)

AARONOW: You think they're going to catch . . . where are you going?

ROMA: Down the street.

WILLIAMSON (*Sticking his head out of the door*): Where are you going?

ROMA: To the restaura . . . what do you fucking. . . ?

WILLIAMSON: Aren't you going out today?

ROMA: With what? (*Pause.*) With what, John, they took the leads . . .

WILLIAMSON: I have the stuff from last year's . . .

ROMA: Oh. Oh. Oh, your "nostalgia" file, that's fine. No. Swell. 'Cause I don't have to . . .

WILLIAMSON: . . . you want to go out today. . . ?

ROMA: 'Cause I don't have to *eat* this month. No. Okay. *Give* 'em to me . . . (*To himself:*) Fucking Mitch and Murray going to shit a br . . . what am I going to *do* all . . .

Williamson starts back into the office. He is accosted by Aaronow.

AARONOW: Were the leads . . .

ROMA: . . . what am I going to *do* all month. . . ?

AARONOW: Were the leads insured?

WILLIAMSON: I don't know, George, why?

AARONOW: 'Cause, you know, 'cause they weren't, I know that Mitch and Murray uh . . . (*Pause.*)

WILLIAMSON: What?

AARONOW: That they're going to be upset.

WILLIAMSON: That's right. (*Going back into his office. Pause. To Roma:*) You want to go out today. . . ?

Pause. Williamson returns to his office.

AARONOW: He said we're all going to have to go talk to the guy.

ROMA: What?

AARONOW: He said we . . .

ROMA: To the cop?

AARONOW: Yeah.

ROMA: Yeah. That's swell. *Another* waste of time.

AARONOW: A waste of time? Why?

ROMA: *Why?* 'Cause they aren't going to find the guy.

AARONOW: The cops?

ROMA: Yes. The cops. No.

AARONOW: They aren't?

ROMA: No.

AARONOW: Why don't you think so?

ROMA: Why? Because they're *stupid.* "Where were you last night . . ."

AARONOW: Where were you?

ROMA: Where was *I?*

AARONOW: Yes.

ROMA: I was at home, where were *you?*

AARONOW: At home.

ROMA: *See.* . . ? Were you the guy who broke in?

AARONOW: Was I?

ROMA: Yes.

AARONOW: No.

ROMA: Then don't sweat it, George, you know why?

AARONOW: No.

ROMA: You have nothing to hide.

AARONOW (*Pause*): When I talk to the police, I get nervous.

ROMA: Yeah. You know who doesn't?

AARONOW: No, who?

ROMA: Thieves.

AARONOW: Why?

ROMA: They're inured to it.

AARONOW: You think so?

ROMA: Yes. (*Pause.*)

AARONOW: But what should I *tell* them?

ROMA: The truth, George. Always tell the truth. It's the easiest thing to remember.

Williamson comes out of the office with leads. Roma takes one, reads it.

ROMA: *Patel?* Ravidam *Patel?* How am I going to make a living on these deadbeat *wogs?* Where did you get this, from the *morgue?*

WILLIAMSON: If you don't want it, give it back.

ROMA: I don't "want" it, if you catch my drift.

WILLIAMSON: I'm giving you *three* leads. You . . .

ROMA: What's the fucking point in *any* case. . . ? What's the *point.* I got to argue with *you,* I got to knock heads with the *cops,* I'm busting my *balls,* sell you *dirt* to fucking *deadbeats* money in the *mattress,* I come back you can't even manage to keep the contracts safe, I have to go back and close them *again.* . . . What the fuck am I wasting my time, fuck this shit. I'm going out and reclose last week's . . .

WILLIAMSON: The word from Murray is: leave them alone. If we need a new signature he'll go out himself, he'll be the *president,* just come *in,* from out of *town* . . .

ROMA: Okay, okay, okay, gimme this shit. Fine. (*Takes the leads.*)

WILLIAMSON: Now, I'm giving you three . . .

ROMA: Three? I count *two.*

WILLIAMSON: Three.

ROMA: Patel? Fuck *you.* Fuckin' *Shiva* handed him a million dollars, told him "sign the deal," he wouldn't sign. And Vishnu, too. Into the bargain. Fuck *that,* John. You know your business, I know mine. Your business is being an *asshole,* and I find out whose fucking *cousin* you are, I'm going to go to him and figure out a way to have your *ass* . . . fuck you — I'll wait for the new leads.

Shelly Levene enters.

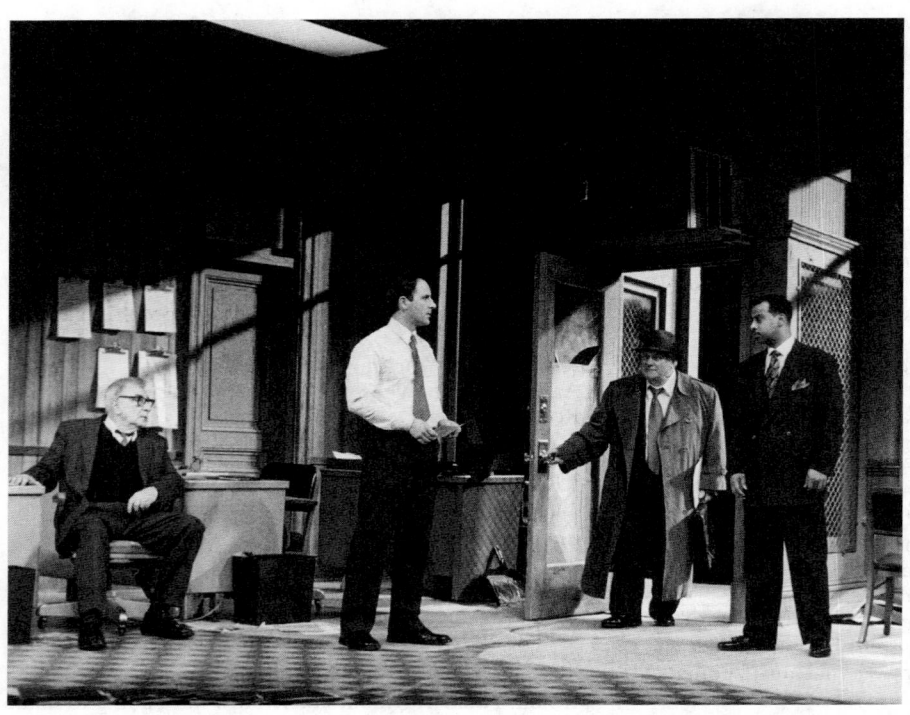

Above: The 2000 McCarter Theatre production of *Glengarry Glen Ross* with the following cast (left to right): Sam Coppola as Aaronow, Jordan Lage as Williamson, Charles Durning as Shelly Levene, and Ruben Santiago-Hudson as Roma. Right: Charles Durning as Shelly Levene in director Scott Zigler's 2000 production of *Glengarry Glen Ross* at the McCarter Theatre in Princeton, New Jersey.

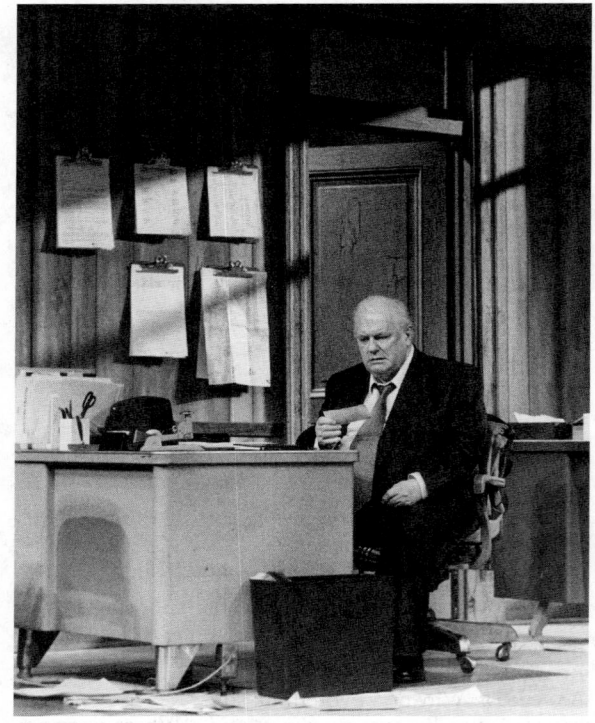

LEVENE: Get the *chalk*. Get the *chalk* . . . get the *chalk*! I closed 'em! I *closed* the cocksucker. Get the chalk and put me on the *board*. I'm going to Hawaii! Put me on the Cadillac board, Williamson! Pick up the fuckin' chalk. Eight units. Mountain View.

ROMA: You sold eight Mountain View?

LEVENE: You bet your ass. Who wants to go to lunch? Who wants to go to lunch? I'm buying. (*Slaps contract down on Williamson's desk.*) Eighty-two fucking grand. And twelve grand in commission. John. (*Pause.*) On fucking deadbeat magazine subscription leads.

WILLIAMSON: Who?

LEVENE (*Pointing to contract*): *Read* it. Bruce and Harriett Nyborg. (*Looking around.*) What happened here?

AARONOW: Fuck. I had them on River Glen.

Levene looks around.

LEVENE: What happened?

WILLIAMSON: Somebody broke in.

ROMA: Eight units?

LEVENE: That's right.

ROMA: *Shelly*. . . !

LEVENE: Hey, big fucking deal. Broke a bad streak . . .

AARONOW: Shelly, the Machine, Levene.

LEVENE: You . . .

AARONOW: That's great.

LEVENE: Thank you, George.

Baylen sticks his head out of the room; calls in, "Aaronow." Aaronow goes into the side room.

LEVENE: Williamson, get on the phone, call Mitch . . .

ROMA: They took the phones . . .

LEVENE: They . . .

BAYLEN: *Aaronow* . . .

ROMA: They took the typewriters, they took the leads, they took the cash, they took the *contracts* . . .

LEVENE: Wh . . . wh . . . Wha. . . ?

AARONOW: We had a robbery. (*Goes into the inner room.*)

LEVENE (*Pause.*): When?

ROMA: Last night, this morning. (*Pause.*)

LEVENE: They took the leads?

ROMA: Mmm.

Moss comes out of the interrogation.

MOSS: Fuckin' asshole.

ROMA: What, they beat you with a rubber bat?

MOSS: Cop couldn't find his dick two hands and a map. Anyone talks to this guy's an *asshole* . . .

ROMA: You going to turn State's?

MOSS: Fuck you, Ricky. I ain't going out today. I'm going home. I'm going home because nothing's *accomplished* here. . . . Anyone *talks* to this guy is . . .

ROMA: Guess what the Machine did?

MOSS: Fuck the Machine.

ROMA: Mountain View. Eight units.

MOSS: Fuckin' cop's got no right talk to me that way. I didn't rob the place . . .

ROMA: You hear what I said?

MOSS: Yeah. He closed a deal.

ROMA: Eight units. Mountain View.

MOSS (*To Levene*): You did that?

LEVENE: Yeah. (*Pause.*)

MOSS: Fuck you.

ROMA: Guess who?

MOSS: When . . .

LEVENE: Just now.

ROMA: Guess who?

MOSS: You just this morning . . .

ROMA: Harriett and blah blah Nyborg.

MOSS: You did that?

LEVENE: Eighty-two thousand dollars. (*Pause.*)

MOSS: Those fuckin' *deadbeats* . . .

LEVENE: My ass. I told 'em. (*To Roma:*) Listen to this: I said . . .

MOSS: Hey, I don't want to hear your fucking war stories . . .

ROMA: Fuck *you*, Dave . . .

LEVENE: "You have to believe in your*self* . . . you" — look — "alright. . . ?"

MOSS (*To Williamson*): Give me some leads. I'm going out . . . I'm getting out of . . .

LEVENE: ". . . you have to believe in your*self* . . ."

MOSS: Na, fuck the leads, I'm going home.

LEVENE: "Bruce, Harriett . . . Fuck *me*, believe in your*self* . . ."

ROMA: We haven't got a lead . . .

MOSS: Why not?

ROMA: They took 'em . . .

MOSS: Hey, they're fuckin' garbage any case. . . . This whole goddamn . . .

LEVENE: ". . . You look around, you say, 'This one has so-and-so, and I have nothing . . .'"

MOSS: *Shit.*

LEVENE: "'*Why*? Why don't I get the opportunities. . . ?'"

MOSS: And did they steal the contracts. . . ?

ROMA: Fuck *you* care. . . ?

LEVENE: "I want to tell you something, Harriett . . ."

MOSS: . . . the fuck is *that* supposed to mean. . . ?

LEVENE: Will you shut up, I'm telling you this . . .

Aaronow sticks his head out.

AARONOW: Can we get some coffee. . . ?

MOSS: How ya doing? (*Pause.*)

AARONOW: Fine.

MOSS: Uh-huh.

AARONOW: If anyone's going, I could use some coffee.

LEVENE: "You *do* get the . . ." (*To Roma:*) Huh? Huh?

MOSS: *Fuck* is that supposed to mean?

LEVENE: "You *do* get the opportunity. . . . You *get* them. As *I* do, as *anyone* does . . ."

MOSS: Ricky? . . . That I don't care they stole the contracts. . . ? (*Pause.*)

LEVENE: I got 'em in the kitchen. I'm eating her crumb cake.

MOSS: What does that mean?

ROMA: It *means*, Dave, you haven't closed a good one in a month, none of my business, you want to push me to answer you. (*Pause.*) And so you haven't got a contract to get stolen or so forth.

MOSS: You have a mean streak in you, Ricky, you know that. . . ?

LEVENE: Rick. Let me tell you. Wait, we're in the . . .

MOSS: Shut the fuck up. (*Pause.*) Ricky. You have a mean streak in you. . . . (*To Levene:*) And what the fuck are *you* babbling about. . . ? (*To Roma:*) Bring that shit up. Of my volume. You were on a bad one and I brought it up to *you* you'd harbor it. (*Pause.*) You'd harbor it a long long while. And you'd be right.

ROMA: Who said "Fuck the Machine"?

MOSS: *"Fuck the Machine"? "Fuck the Machine"?* What is this. *Courtesy* class. . . ? You're *fucked,* Rick — are you fucking *nuts?* You're hot, so you think you're the *ruler* of this place. . . ?! You want to . . .

LEVENE: Dave . . .

MOSS: . . . Shut up. Decide who should be dealt with how? Is that the thing? I come into the fuckin' office today, I get humiliated by some jagoff cop. I get accused of . . . I get this *shit* thrown in my face by you, you genuine shit, because you're top name on the board . . .

ROMA: Is that what I did? Dave? I humiliated you? My *God* . . . I'm *sorry* . . .

MOSS: Sittin' on top of the *world,* sittin' on top of the *world,* everything's fucking *peachfuzz* . . .

ROMA: Oh, and I don't get a moment to spare for a bust-out *humanitarian* down on his luck lately. Fuck *you,* Dave, you know you got a big *mouth,* and *you* make a close the whole *place* stinks with your *farts* for a week. "How much you just ingested," what a big *man* you are, "Hey, let me buy you a pack of gum. I'll show you how to *chew* it." Your *pal* closes, all that comes out of your mouth is *bile,* how fucked *up* you are . . .

MOSS: *Who's* my pal. . . ? And what are you, Ricky, huh, what are you, Bishop *Sheean?* Who the fuck are *you,* Mr. Slick. . . ? What are you, friend to the *workingman?* Big deal. Fuck *you,* you got the memory a fuckin' *fly.* I never liked you.

ROMA: What is this, your farewell speech?

MOSS: I'm going home.

ROMA: Your farewell to the troops?

MOSS: I'm not going home. I'm going to Wis*con*sin.

ROMA: Have a good trip.

MOSS (*Simultaneously with "trip"*): And fuck *you.* Fuck the *lot* of you. Fuck you *all.*

Moss exits. Pause.

ROMA (*To Levene*): You were saying? (*Pause.*) Come on. Come on, you got them in the kitchen, you got the stats spread out, you're in your shirt-sleeves, you can *smell* it. Huh? Snap out of it, you're eating her *crumb* cake. (*Pause.*)

LEVENE: I'm eating her *crumb* cake . . .

ROMA: How was it. . . ?

LEVENE: From the store.

ROMA: Fuck *her* . . .

LEVENE: "What we have to do is *admit* to ourself that we see that opportunity . . . and *take* it. (*Pause.*) And that's it." And we *sit* there. (*Pause.*) I got the pen out . . .

ROMA: "Always be closing . . ."

LEVENE: That's what I'm *saying.* The *old* ways. The *old* ways . . . convert the motherfucker . . . *sell* him . . . *sell* him . . . *make him sign the check.* (*Pause.*) The . . . Bruce, Harriett . . . the kitchen, blah: they got their money in *government* bonds. . . . I say *fuck* it, we're going to go the whole route. I plat it out eight units. Eighty-two grand. I tell them. "This is now. This is that *thing* that you've been dreaming of, you're going to find that suitcase on the train, the guy comes in the door, the bag that's full of money. This is it, *Harri-ett* . . ."

ROMA (*Reflectively*): Harriett . . .

LEVENE: *Bruce* . . . "I don't want to fuck *around* with you. I don't want to go *round* this, and *pussyfoot* around the thing, you have to look back on this. I do, too. I came here to do good for you and me. For *both* of us. Why take an interim position? *The only arrangement I'll accept* is full investment. Period. The whole eight units. I know that you're saying 'be safe,' I know what you're saying. I know if I left you to yourselves, you'd say 'come back tomorrow,' and when I walked out that door, you'd make a cup of *coffee* . . . you'd sit *down* . . . and you'd think 'let's be safe . . .' and not to disappoint me you'd go *one* unit or maybe two, because you'd become scared because you'd met possi*bi*lity. But this won't do, and that's not the subject. . . ." Listen to this, I actually said this. "That's not the subject of our *evening* together." Now I handed them the pen. I held it in my hand. I turned the contract, eight units eighty-two grand. "Now I want you to sign." (*Pause.*) I sat there. Five minutes. Then, I sat there, Ricky, *twenty-two minutes* by the kitchen clock. (*Pause.*) Twenty-two minutes by the kitchen clock. Not a *word,* not a *motion.* What am I thinking? "My arm's getting tired?" *No.* I *did* it. I *did* it. Like in the *old* days, Ricky. Like I was taught . . . Like, like, like I *used* to do . . . I did it.

ROMA: Like you taught me . . .

LEVENE: Bullshit, you're . . . No. That's raw . . . well, if I *did,* then I'm *glad* I did. I, *well.* I locked on them. All on them, nothing on me. All my thoughts are on them. I'm holding the last thought that I spoke: "Now is the time." (*Pause.*) They signed, Ricky. It was *great.* It was fucking great. It was like they wilted all at once. No *gesture* . . . nothing. Like together. They, I swear to God, they both kind of *imperceptibly slumped.* And he reaches and takes the pen and signs, he passes it to her, she signs. It was so fucking solemn. I just let it sit. I nod like this. I nod again. I grasp his hands. I shake his hands. I grasp *her* hands. I nod at her like this. "Bruce . . . Harriett . . ." I'm beaming at them. I'm nodding like this. I point back in the living room, back to the sideboard. (*Pause.*) *I didn't fucking know there was a sideboard there!!* He goes back, he brings us a drink. Little shot glasses. A pattern in 'em. And we toast. In silence. (*Pause.*)

ROMA: That was a great sale, Shelly. (*Pause.*)

LEVENE: Ah, fuck. Leads! Leads! Williamson! (*Williamson sticks his head out of the office.*) Send me *out*! Send me *out*!

WILLIAMSON: The leads are coming.

LEVENE: *Get* 'em to me!

WILLIAMSON: I talked to Murray and Mitch an hour ago. They're coming in, you understand they're a bit *upset* over this morning's . . .

LEVENE: Did you tell 'em my sale?

WILLIAMSON: How could I tell 'em your sale? Eh? I don't have a tel . . . I'll tell 'em your sale when they bring in the leads. Alright? Shelly. Alright? We had a little . . . You closed a deal. You made a good sale. Fine.

LEVENE: It's better than a good sale. It's a . . .

WILLIAMSON: Look: I have a lot of things on my mind, they're coming in, alright, they're very upset, I'm trying to make some *sense* . . .

LEVENE: All that I'm *telling* you: that one thing you can tell them it's a remarkable sale.

WILLIAMSON: The only thing remarkable is who you made it to.

LEVENE: What does *that* fucking mean?

WILLIAMSON: That if the sale sticks, it will be a miracle.

LEVENE: Why should the sale not stick? Hey, *fuck* you. That's what I'm saying. You have no idea of your job. A man's his job and you're *fucked* at yours. You hear what I'm saying to you? Your "end of month board . . ." You can't run an office. I don't care. You don't know what it *is*, you don't have the *sense*, you don't have the *balls*. You ever been on a sit? *Ever*? Has this cocksucker ever been . . . you ever sit down with a cust . . .

WILLIAMSON: I were you, I'd calm down, Shelly.

LEVENE: *Would* you? *Would* you. . . ? Or you're gonna *what*, fire me?

WILLIAMSON: It's not impossible.

LEVENE: On an eighty-thousand dollar *day*? And it ain't even *noon*.

ROMA: You closed 'em today?

LEVENE: Yes. I did. This *morning*. (*To Williamson:*) What I'm *saying* to you: things can *change*. You *see*? This is where you fuck *up*, because this is something you don't *know*. You can't look down the *road*. And see what's *coming*. Might be someone *else*, John. It might be someone *new*, eh? Someone *new*. And you can't look *back*. 'Cause you don't know *history*. You ask them. When we were at Rio Rancho, who was top man? A month. . . ? Two months. . . ? Eight months in twelve for three years in a row. You know what that means? You know what that means? Is that *luck*? Is that some, some, some purloined leads? That's *skill*. That's *talent*, that's, that's . . .

ROMA: . . . *yes* . . .

LEVENE: . . . and you don't *remember*. 'Cause you weren't *around*. That's cold *calling*. Walk up to the door. I don't even know their *name*. I'm selling something they don't even *want*. You talk about soft sell . . . before we had a name for it . . . before we called it anything, we did it.

ROMA: That's right, Shel.

LEVENE: And, and, and, I *did* it. And I put a kid through *school*. She . . . and . . . Cold *calling*, fella. Door to door. But you don't know. You don't know. You never heard of a *streak*. You never heard of "marshaling your sales force. . . ." What are you, you're a *secretary*, John. Fuck *you*. That's my message to you. Fuck you and kiss my ass. You don't like it, I'll go talk to Jerry Graff. Period. Fuck you. Put me on the board. And I want three worthwhile leads today and I don't want any bullshit about them and I want 'em close together 'cause I'm going to hit them all today. That's all I have to say to you.

ROMA: He's right, Williamson.

Williamson goes into a side office. Pause.

LEVENE: It's not right. I'm sorry, and I'll tell you who's to blame is Mitch and Murray.

Roma sees something outside the window.

ROMA (*Sotto*): Oh, Christ.

LEVENE: The hell with him. We'll go to lunch, the leads won't be up for . . .

ROMA: You're a client. I just sold you five waterfront Glengarry Farms. I rub my head, throw me the cue "Kenilworth."

LEVENE: What is it?

ROMA: Kenilw . . .

Lingk enters the office.

ROMA (*To Levene*): I own the property, my *mother* owns the property, I put her *into* it. I'm going to show you on the plats. You look when you get home A–3 through A–14 and 26 through 30. You take your time and if you still feel.

LEVENE: No, Mr. Roma. I don't need the time, I've made a lot of *investments* in the last . . .

LINGK: I've got to talk to you.

ROMA (*Looking up*): Jim! What are you doing here? Jim Lingk, D. Ray Morton . . .

LEVENE: Glad to meet you.

ROMA: I just put Jim into Black Creek . . . are you acquainted with . . .

LEVENE: No . . . Black *Creek*. Yes. In *Florida*?

ROMA: Yes.

LEVENE: I wanted to *speak* with you about . . .

ROMA: Well, we'll do that this weekend.

LEVENE: My *wife* told me to look into . . .

ROMA: *Beautiful*. Beautiful rolling land. I was telling Jim and Jinny, Ray, I want to tell you something. (*To Levene:*) You, Ray, you eat in a lot of restaurants. I know you do. . . . (*To Lingk:*) Mr. Morton's with American

Express . . . he's . . . (*To Levene:*) I can tell Jim what you do. . . ?

LEVENE: Sure.

ROMA: Ray is director of all European sales and services for American Ex . . . (*To Levene:*) But I'm saying you haven't had a *meal* until you've tasted . . . I was at the Lingks' last . . . as a matter of fact, what was that service feature you were talking about. . . ?

LEVENE: Which . . .

ROMA: "Home Cooking" . . . what did you call it, you said it . . . it was a tag phrase that you had . . .

LEVENE: Uh . . .

ROMA: Home . . .

LEVENE: Home cooking . . .

ROMA: The monthly interview. . . ?

LEVENE: Oh! For the *magazine* . . .

ROMA: Yes. Is this something that I can talk ab . . .

LEVENE: Well, it isn't coming *out* until the February iss . . . *sure.* Sure, go ahead, Ricky.

ROMA: You're sure?

LEVENE (*nods*): Go ahead.

ROMA: Well, Ray was eating at one of his company's men's home in France . . . the man's French, isn't he?

LEVENE: No, his *wife* is.

ROMA: Ah. Ah, his wife is. Ray: what *time* do you have. . . ?

LEVENE: Twelve-fifteen.

ROMA: Oh! My God . . . I've got to get you on the *plane*!

LEVENE: Didn't I say I was taking the two o' . . .

ROMA: No. You said the one. That's why you said we couldn't talk till Kenilworth.

LEVENE: Oh, my God, you're right! I'm on the one. . . . (*Getting up.*) Well, let's *scoot* . . .

LINGK: I've got to talk to you . . .

ROMA: I've got to get Ray to O'Hare . . . (*To Levene:*) Come on, let's hustle. . . . (*Over his shoulder:*) John! Call American Express in *Pittsburgh* for Mr. Morton, will you, tell them he's on the one o'clock. (*To Lingk:*) I'll see you. . . . Christ, I'm sorry you came all the way in. . . . I'm running Ray over to O'Hare. . . . You wait here, I'll . . . no. (*To Levene:*) I'm meeting your man at the bank. . . . (*To Lingk:*) I wish you'd phoned. . . . I'll tell you, wait: are you and Jinny going to be home tonight? (*Rubs forehead.*)

LINGK: I . . .

LEVENE: Rick.

ROMA: What?

LEVENE: *Kenilworth*. . . ?

ROMA: I'm sorry. . . ?

LEVENE: *Kenilworth.*

ROMA: Oh, God . . . Oh, God . . . (*Roma takes Lingk aside, sotto*) Jim, excuse me. . . . Ray, I told you, who he is is *the* senior vice-president American Express. His family owns 32 per. . . . Over the past years I've sold him . . . I can't tell you the dollar amount, but *quite* a lot of land. I promised five *weeks* ago that I'd go to the wife's birthday party in Kenilworth tonight. (*Sighs.*) I *have* to go. You understand. They treat me

like a member of the family, so I have to go. It's funny, you know, you get a picture of the Corporation-Type Company Man, all business . . . this man, *no.* We'll go out to his home sometime. Let's see. (*He checks his datebook.*) Tomorrow. No. Tomorrow, I'm in L.A. . . . *Monday* . . . I'll take you to lunch, where would you like to go?

LINGK: My wife . . . (*Roma rubs his head.*)

LEVENE (*Standing in the door*): Rick. . . ?

ROMA: I'm sorry, Jim. I can't talk now. I'll call you tonight . . . I'm sorry. I'm coming, Ray. (*Starts for the door.*)

LINGK: My wife said I have to cancel the deal.

ROMA: It's a common reaction, Jim. I'll tell you what it is, and I know that that's why you married her. One of the reasons is *prudence.* It's a sizable investment. One thinks *twice* . . . it's also something *women* have. It's just a reaction to the size of the investment. *Monday,* if you'd invite me for dinner again . . . (*To Levene:*) This woman can *cook* . . .

LEVENE (*Simultaneously*): I'm sure she can . . .

ROMA (*To Lingk*): We're going to talk. I'm going to *tell* you something. Because (*Sotto:*) there's something about your acreage I want you to know. I can't talk about it now. I really shouldn't. And, in fact, by *law,* I . . . (*Shrugs, resigned.*) The man next to you, he bought his lot at forty-*two,* he phoned to say that he'd *already* had an offer . . . (*Roma rubs his head.*)

LEVENE: Rick. . . ?

ROMA: I'm coming, Ray . . . what a day! I'll call you this evening, Jim. I'm sorry you had to come in . . . Monday, lunch.

LINGK: My wife . . .

LEVENE: Rick, we really have to go.

LINGK: My wife . . .

ROMA: Monday.

LINGK: She called the consumer . . . the attorney, I don't know. The attorney gen . . . they said we have three days . . .

ROMA: *Who* did she call?

LINGK: I don't know, the attorney gen . . . the . . . some consumer office, umm . . .

ROMA: Why did she do *that,* Jim?

LINGK: I don't know. (*Pause.*) They said we have three days. (*Pause.*) They said we have three days.

ROMA: Three days.

LINGK: To . . . you know. (*Pause.*)

ROMA: No, I don't know. *Tell* me.

LINGK: To change our minds.

ROMA: Of *course* you have three days. (*Pause.*)

LINGK: So we can't talk *Monday.* (*Pause.*)

ROMA: Jim, Jim, you saw my book . . . I *can't,* you saw my book . . .

LINGK: But we have to *before* Monday. To get our money ba . . .

ROMA: Three *business* days. They mean three *business* days.

LINGK: Wednesday, Thursday, Friday.

ROMA: I don't understand.

Kevin Spacey as Williamson (left) and Jack Lemmon as Levene (right) in the 1992 film version of *Glengarry Glen Ross* (New Line Cinema), directed by James Foley.

The premiere production of *Glengarry Glen Ross* in 1983 at the Cottesloe Theatre in London, directed by Bill Bryden, with Jack Shepherd as Roma (left) and Tony Haygarth as Lingk (right).

LINGK: That's what they are. Three business . . . if I wait till Monday, my time limit runs out.

ROMA: You don't count Saturday.

LINGK: I'm not.

ROMA: No, I'm saying you don't include Saturday . . . in your three days. It's not a *business* day.

LINGK: But I'm not *counting* it. (*Pause.*) Wednesday. Thursday. Friday. So it would have elapsed.

ROMA: What would have elapsed?

LINGK: If we wait till Mon . . .

ROMA: When did you write the check?

LINGK: Yest . . .

ROMA: What was yesterday?

LINGK: Tuesday.

ROMA: And when was that check cashed?

LINGK: I don't know.

ROMA: What was the *earliest* it could have been cashed? (*Pause.*)

LINGK: I don't know.

ROMA: *Today.* (*Pause.*) *Today.* Which, in any case, it was not, as there were a couple of points on the agreement I wanted to go over with you in any case.

LINGK: The check wasn't cashed?

ROMA: I just called downtown, and it's on their desk.

LEVENE: Rick . . .

ROMA: One moment, I'll be right with you. (*To Lingk:*) In fact, a . . . *one* point, which I spoke to you of which (*Looks around.*) I can't talk to you about here.

Detective puts his head out of the doorway.

BAYLEN: Levene!!!

LINGK: I, I . . .

ROMA: Listen to me, the *statute*, it's for your protection. I have no complaints with that, in fact, I was a member of the board when we *drafted* it, so quite the *opposite*. It *says* that you can change your mind three working days from the time the deal is closed.

BAYLEN: Levene!

ROMA: Which, wait a second, which is not until the check is cashed.

BAYLEN: Levene!!

Aaronow comes out of the Detective's office.

AARONOW: I'm *through*, with *this* fucking meshugaas. No one should talk to a man that way. How are you *talking* to me that. . . ?

BAYLEN: Levene! (*Williamson puts his head out of the office.*)

AARONOW: . . . how can you *talk* to me that . . . that . . .

LEVENE (*To Roma*): Rick, I'm going to flag a cab.

AARONOW: *I didn't rob* . . .

Williamson sees Levene.

WILLIAMSON: Shelly: get in the office.

AARONOW: *I didn't* . . . why should *I* . . . "Where were you last . . ." Is anybody listening to me . . . ? Where's Moss . . . ? Where. . . ?

BAYLEN: Levene? (*To Williamson:*) Is this Lev . . . (*Baylen accosts Lingk.*)

LEVENE (*Taking Baylen into the office*): Ah. Ah. Perhaps I can advise you on that. . . . (*To Roma and Lingk, as he exits:*) *Excuse* us, will you. . . ?

AARONOW (*Simultaneous with Levene's speech above*): . . . Come in here . . . I *work* here, I don't come in here to be *mistreated* . . .

WILLIAMSON: Go to *lunch,* will you . . .

AARONOW: I want to *work* today, that's why I came . . .

WILLIAMSON: The leads come in, I'll let . . .

AARONOW: . . . that's why I came in. I thought I . . .

WILLIAMSON: Just go to lunch.

AARONOW: I don't *want* to go to lunch.

WILLIAMSON: Go to lunch, George.

AARONOW: Where does he get off to talk that way to a working man? It's not . . .

WILLIAMSON (*Buttonholes him*): Will you take it outside, we have people trying to do *business* here . . .

AARONOW: That's what, that's what, that's what *I* was trying to do. (*Pause.*) That's why I came *in* . . . I meet *gestapo* tac . . .

WILLIAMSON (*Going back into his office*): Excuse me . . .

AARONOW: I meet *gestapo* tactics . . . I meet *gestapo* tactics. . . . That's not right. . . . No man has the right to . . . "Call an attorney," that means you're guilt . . . you're under sus . . . "Co. . . ," he says, "cooperate" or we'll go downtown. *That's* not . . . as long as I've . . .

WILLIAMSON (*Bursting out of his office*): Will you get out of here. Will you get *out* of here. Will you. I'm trying to run an *office* here. Will you go to lunch? Go to lunch. Will you go to lunch? (*Retreats into office.*)

ROMA (*To Aaronow*): Will you excuse . . .

AARONOW: Where did Moss. . . ? I . . .

ROMA: Will you excuse us please?

AARONOW: Uh, uh, did he go to the restaurant? (*Pause.*) I . . . I . . . (*Exits.*)

ROMA: I'm *very* sorry, Jimmy. I apologize to you.

LINGK: It's not me, it's my wife.

ROMA (*Pause.*): What is?

LINGK: I told you.

ROMA: Tell me again.

LINGK: What's going on here?

ROMA: Tell me again. Your wife.

LINGK: I told you.

ROMA: You tell me again.

LINGK: She wants her money back.

ROMA: We're going to speak to her.

LINGK: No. She told me "right now."

ROMA: We'll speak to her, Jim . . .

LINGK: She won't listen.

Detective sticks his head out.

BAYLEN: *Roma.*

LINGK: She told me if not, I have to call the State's attorney.

ROMA: No, no. That's just something she "said." We don't have to do that.

LINGK: She told me I *have* to.

ROMA: No, Jim.

LINGK: I *do.* If I don't get my *money* back . . .

Williamson points out Roma to Baylen.

BAYLEN: Roma! (*To Roma:*) I'm talking to you . . .

ROMA: I've . . . look. (*Generally:*) Will someone get this guy off my back.

BAYLEN: You have a problem?

ROMA: Yes, I have a problem. Yes, I *do,* my fr . . . It's not me that ripped the joint off, I'm doing *business.* I'll be with you in a *while.* You got it. . . ? (*Looks back. Lingk is heading for the door.*) Where are you going?

LINGK: I'm . . .

ROMA: Where are you going. . . ? This is *me.* . . . This is Ricky, Jim. Jim, anything you *want,* you *want* it, you *have* it. You understand? This is *me.* Something *upset* you. Sit down, now sit down. You tell me what it is. (*Pause.*) Am I going to help you fix it? You're goddamned right I am. Sit down. Tell you something. . . ? *Sometimes* we need someone from *outside.* It's . . . no, sit down. . . . Now *talk* to me.

LINGK: I can't negotiate.

ROMA: What does that mean?

LINGK: That . . .

ROMA: . . . what, what, *say* it. Say it to me . . .

LINGK: I . . .

ROMA: What. . . ?

LINGK: I . . .

ROMA: What. . . ? Say the words.

LINGK: I don't have the *power.* (*Pause.*) I said it.

ROMA: What power?

LINGK: The power to negotiate.

ROMA: To negotiate what? (*Pause.*) To negotiate what?

LINGK: *This.*

ROMA: What, "this"? (*Pause.*)

LINGK: The deal.

ROMA: The "deal," *forget* the deal. *Forget* the deal, you've got something on your mind, Jim, what is it?

LINGK (*rising*): I can't talk to you, *you* met my wife, I . . . (*Pause.*)

ROMA: What? (*Pause.*) What? (*Pause.*) What, Jim: I tell you what, let's get out of here . . . let's go get a drink.

LINGK: She told me not to talk to you.

ROMA: Let's . . . no one's going to know, let's go around the *corner* and we'll get a drink.

LINGK: She told me I had to get back the check or call the State's att . . .

ROMA: *Forget* the deal, Jimmy. (*Pause.*) *Forget* the deal . . . you know me. The deal's *dead.* Am I talking about the *deal?* That's *over.* Please. Let's talk about *you.* Come on. (*Pause. Roma rises and starts walking toward the front door.*) Come on. (*Pause.*) Come on, Jim. (*Pause.*) I want to tell you something. Your life is your own. You have a contract with your wife. You have certain things you do *jointly,* you have a *bond* there . . . and there are *other* things. Those things are yours. You needn't feel *ashamed,* you needn't feel that you're being *untrue* . . . or that she would abandon you if she knew. This is your life. (*Pause.*) Yes.

Now I want to *talk* to you because you're obviously upset and that *concerns* me. Now let's go. Right now.

Lingk gets up and they start for the door.

BAYLEN (*Sticks his head out of the door*): Roma . . .

LINGK: . . . and . . . and . . . (*Pause.*)

ROMA: What?

LINGK: And the check is . . .

ROMA: What did I *tell* you? (*Pause.*) What did I say about the three days. . . ?

BAYLEN: Roma, would you, I'd like to get some lunch . . .

ROMA: I'm talking with Mr. Lingk. If you please, I'll be back in. (*Checks watch.*) I'll be back in a while. . . . I told you, check with Mr. Williamson.

BAYLEN: The people downtown said . . .

ROMA: You call them again. Mr. Williamson . . . !

WILLIAMSON: Yes.

ROMA: Mr. Lingk and I are going to . . .

WILLIAMSON: Yes. Please. Please. (*To Lingk:*) The police (*Shrugs.*) can be . . .

LINGK: What are the police doing?

ROMA: It's nothing.

LINGK: What are the *police* doing here . . . ?

WILLIAMSON: We had a slight burglary last night.

ROMA: It was nothing . . . I was assuring Mr. Lingk . . .

WILLIAMSON: Mr. Lingk. James Lingk. Your contract went out. Nothing to . . .

ROMA: John . . .

WILLIAMSON: Your contract went out to the bank.

LINGK: You cashed the check?

WILLIAMSON: We . . .

ROMA: . . . Mr. Williamson . . .

WILLIAMSON: Your check was cashed yesterday afternoon. And we're completely insured, as you know, in *any* case. (*Pause.*)

LINGK (*To Roma*): You cashed the check?

ROMA: Not to my knowledge, no . . .

WILLIAMSON: I'm sure we can . . .

LINGK: Oh, Christ . . . (*Starts out the door.*) Don't follow me. . . . Oh, Christ. (*Pause. To Roma:*) I know I've let you down. I'm sorry. For . . . Forgive . . . for . . . I don't know anymore. (*Pause.*) Forgive me. (*Lingk exits. Pause.*)

ROMA (*To Williamson*): You stupid fucking cunt. *You,* Williamson . . . I'm talking to *you,* shithead. . . . You just cost me *six thousand dollars.* (*Pause.*) Six thousand dollars. And one Cadillac. That's right. What are you going to do about it? What are you going to do about it, asshole. You fucking *shit.* Where did you learn your *trade.* You stupid fucking *cunt.* You *idiot.* Whoever told you you could work with *men?*

BAYLEN: Could I . . .

ROMA: I'm going to have your *job,* shithead. I'm going *downtown* and talk to Mitch and Murray, and I'm going to Lemkin. I don't care *whose* nephew you are, who you know, whose dick you're sucking on. You're going *out,* I swear to you, you're going . . .

BAYLEN: Hey, fella, let's get this done . . .

ROMA: Anyone in this office lives on their *wits*. . . . (*To Baylen:*) I'm going to be with you in a second. (*To Williamson:*) What you're hired for is to *help* us — does that seem clear to you? To *help* us. *Not* to fuck us up . . . to help *men* who are going *out* there to try to earn a *living*. You *fairy*. You company man . . . I'll tell you something else. I hope you knocked the joint off, I can tell our friend here something might help him catch you. (*Starts into the room.*) You want to learn the first rule you'd know if you ever spent a day in your life . . . you never open your mouth till you know what the shot is. (*Pause.*) You fucking *child* . . . (*Roma goes to the inner room.*)

LEVENE: You *are* a shithead, Williamson . . . (*Pause.*)

WILLIAMSON: Mmm.

LEVENE: You can't think on your feet you should keep your mouth closed. (*Pause.*) You hear me? I'm *talking* to you. Do you hear me. . . ?

WILLIAMSON: Yes. (*Pause.*) I hear you.

LEVENE: You can't learn that in an office. Eh? He's right. You have to learn it on the streets. You can't *buy* that. You have to *live* it.

WILLIAMSON: Mmm.

LEVENE: *Yes.* Mmm. *Yes. Precisely. Precisely.* 'Cause your partner *depends* on it. (*Pause.*) I'm *talking* to you, I'm trying to tell you something.

WILLIAMSON: You are?

LEVENE: Yes, I am.

WILLIAMSON: What are you trying to tell me?

LEVENE: What Roma's trying to tell you. What I told you yesterday. Why you don't belong in this business.

WILLIAMSON: Why I don't . . .

LEVENE: You listen to me, someday you might say, "Hey . . ." No, fuck that, you just listen what I'm going to say: your partner *depends* on you. Your partner . . . a man who's your "partner" *depends* on you . . . you have to go *with* him and *for* him . . . or you're shit, you're *shit*, you can't exist alone . . .

WILLIAMSON (*Brushing past him*): Excuse me . . .

LEVENE: . . . excuse you, *nothing*, you be as cold as you want, but you just fucked a good man out of six thousand dollars and his goddamn bonus 'cause you didn't know the *shot*, if you can do that and you aren't man enough that it gets you, then I don't know what, if you can't take *some* thing from that . . . (*Blocking his way.*) you're *scum*, you're fucking white-bread. You be as cold as you want. A *child* would know it, he's right. (*Pause.*) You're going to make something up, be sure it will *help* or keep your mouth closed. (*Pause.*)

WILLIAMSON: Mmm. (*Levene lifts up his arm.*)

LEVENE: Now I'm done with you. (*Pause.*)

WILLIAMSON: How do you know I made it up?

LEVENE (*Pause*): What?

WILLIAMSON: How do you know I made it up?

LEVENE: What are you talking about?

WILLIAMSON: You said, "You don't make something up unless it's sure to help." (*Pause.*) How did you know that I made it up?

LEVENE: What are you talking about?

WILLIAMSON: I told the customer that his contracts had gone to the bank.

LEVENE: Well, hadn't it?

WILLIAMSON: No. (*Pause.*) It hadn't.

LEVENE: Don't *fuck* with me, John, don't *fuck* with me . . . what are you saying?

WILLIAMSON: Well, I'm saying this, Shel: usually I take the contracts to the bank. Last night I didn't. How did you know that? One night in a year I left a contract on my desk. Nobody knew that but *you*. Now how did you know that? (*Pause.*) You want to talk to me, you want to talk to someone *else* . . . because this is *my* job. This is my job on the line, and you are going to *talk* to me. Now how did you know that contract was on my desk?

LEVENE: You're so full of shit.

WILLIAMSON: You robbed the office.

LEVENE (*Laughs*): Sure! I robbed the office. Sure.

WILLIAMSON: What'd you do with the leads? (*Pause. Points to the Detective's room.*) You want to go in there? I tell him what I know, he's going to dig up *something*. . . . You got an alibi last night? You better have one. What did you do with the leads? If you tell me what you did with the leads, we can talk.

LEVENE: I don't know what you are saying.

WILLIAMSON: If you tell me where the leads are, I won't turn you in. If you *don't*, I am going to tell the cop you stole them, Mitch and Murray will see that you go to jail. Believe me they will. Now, what did you do with the leads? I'm walking in that door — you have five seconds to tell me: or you are going to jail.

LEVENE: I . . .

WILLIAMSON: I don't care. You understand? *Where are the leads?* (*Pause.*) Alright. (*Williamson goes to open the office door.*)

LEVENE: I sold them to Jerry Graff.

WILLIAMSON: How much did you get for them? (*Pause.*) How much did you get for them?

LEVENE: Five thousand. I kept half.

WILLIAMSON: Who kept the other half? (*Pause.*)

LEVENE: Do I have to tell you? (*Pause. Williamson starts to open the door.*) Moss.

WILLIAMSON: *That* was easy, *wasn't* it? (*Pause.*)

LEVENE: It was his idea.

WILLIAMSON: *Was* it?

LEVENE: I . . . I'm sure he got more than the five, actually.

WILLIAMSON: Uh-huh?

LEVENE: He told me my share was twenty-five.

WILLIAMSON: Mmm.

LEVENE: Okay: I . . . look: I'm going to make it worth your while. I am. I turned this thing around. I closed the *old* stuff, I can do it again. *I'm* the one's going to close 'em. *I* am! I am! 'Cause I turned this thing a . . . I can do *that*, I can do *anyth* . . . last night. I'm going to tell you, I was ready to Do the Dutch. Moss gets me, "Do this, we'll get well. . . ." Why not. Big fuckin' deal. I'm halfway hoping to get caught. To put me out of my . . . (*Pause.*) But it *taught* me some-

[handwritten marginalia: "Levene slipped up"]

[handwritten marginalia: "Levene confesses and sells Moss out!"]

thing. What it taught me, that you've got to get *out* there. Big deal. So I wasn't cut out to be a thief. I was cut out to be a salesman. And now I'm back, and I got my *balls* back . . . and, you know, John, you have the *advantage* on me now. Whatever it takes to make it right, we'll make it right. We're going to make it right.

WILLIAMSON: I want to tell you something, Shelly. You have a big mouth. (*Pause.*)

LEVENE: What?

WILLIAMSON: You've got a big mouth, and now I'm going to show you an even bigger one. (*Starts toward the Detective's door.*)

LEVENE: Where are you going, John? . . . you can't do that, you don't want to do that . . . hold, hold on . . . hold on . . . wait . . . wait . . . wait . . . (*Pulls money out of his pockets.*) Wait . . . uh, look . . . (*Starts splitting money.*) Look, twelve, twenty, two, twen . . . twenty-five hundred, it's . . . take it. (*Pause.*) Take it all. . . . (*Pause.*) Take it!

WILLIAMSON: No, I don't think so, Shel.

LEVENE: I . . .

WILLIAMSON: No, I think I don't want your money. I think you fucked up my office. And I think you're going away.

LEVENE: I . . . what? Are you, are you, that's why . . . ? Are you nuts? I'm . . . I'm going to *close* for you, I'm going to . . . (*Thrusting money at him.*) Here, here, I'm going to *make* this office . . . I'm going to be back there Number One. . . . Hey, hey, hey! This is only the beginning. . . . List . . . list . . . listen. Listen. Just one moment. List . . . here's what . . . here's what we're going to do. Twenty percent. I'm going to give you twenty percent of my sales. . . . (*Pause.*) Twenty percent. (*Pause.*) For as long as I am with the firm. (*Pause.*) Fifty percent. (*Pause.*) You're going to be my partner. (*Pause.*) Fifty percent. Of all my sales.

WILLIAMSON: What sales?

LEVENE: What sales. . . ? I just *closed* eighty-two grand. . . . Are you fuckin' . . . I'm *back* . . . I'm *back*, this is only the beginning.

WILLIAMSON: Only the beginning . . .

LEVENE: Abso . . .

WILLIAMSON: Where have you been, Shelly? Bruce and Harriett Nyborg. Do you want to see the *memos* . . . ? They're nuts . . . they used to call in every week. When I was with Webb. And we were selling Arizona . . . they're nuts . . . did you see how they were *living*? How can you delude yours . . .

LEVENE: I've got the check . . .

WILLIAMSON: Forget it. Frame it. It's worthless. (*Pause.*)

LEVENE: The check's no good?

WILLIAMSON: You stick around I'll pull the memo for you. (*Starts for the door.*) I'm busy now . . .

LEVENE: Their check's no good? They're nuts . . . ?

WILLIAMSON: Call up the bank. *I* called them.

LEVENE: You did?

WILLIAMSON: I called them when we had the lead . . . four months ago. (*Pause.*) The people are insane. They just like talking to salesmen. (*Williamson starts for door.*)

LEVENE: Don't.

WILLIAMSON: I'm sorry.

LEVENE: *Why?*

WILLIAMSON: Because I don't like you.

LEVENE: John: John: . . . my *daughter* . . .

WILLIAMSON: Fuck you. (*Roma comes out of the Detective's door. Williamson goes in.*)

ROMA (*To Baylen*): Asshole . . . (*To Levene:*) Guy couldn't find his fuckin' couch the *living room* . . . Ah, Christ . . . what a day, what a day . . . I haven't even had a cup of *coffee*. . . . Jagoff John opens his mouth he blows my Cadillac. . . . (*Sighs.*) I swear . . . it's not a world of men, Machine . . . it's a world of clock watchers, bureaucrats, officeholders . . . what it is, it's a fucked-up world . . . there's no adventure *to* it. (*Pause.*) Dying breed. Yes it is. (*Pause.*) We are the members of a dying breed. That's . . . that's . . . that's why we have to stick together. Shel: I want to talk to you. I've wanted to talk to you for some time. For a long time, actually. I said, "The Machine, there's a man I would work with. There's a man. . . ." You know? I never said a thing. I should have, don't know why I didn't. And that shit you were slinging on my guy today was *so* good . . . it . . . it was, and, excuse me, 'cause it isn't even my place to say it. It was admirable . . . it was the old stuff. Hey, I've been on a hot streak, so *what?* There's things that I could learn from you. You eat today?

LEVENE: Me.

ROMA: Yeah.

LEVENE: Mm.

ROMA: Well, you want to swing by the Chinks, watch me eat, we'll talk?

LEVENE: I think I'd better stay here for a while.

Baylen sticks his head out of the room:

BAYLEN: Mr. *Levene*. . . ?

ROMA: You're done, come down and let's . . .

BAYLEN: Would you come in here, please?

ROMA: And let's put this together. Okay? Shel? Say okay. (*Pause.*)

LEVENE (*Softly, to himself*): Huh.

BAYLEN: Mr. Levene, I think we have to talk.

ROMA: I'm going to the Chinks. You're done, come down, we're going to smoke a cigarette.

LEVENE: I . . .

BAYLEN (*Comes over*): . . . Get in the room.

ROMA: Hey, hey, hey, *easy* friend, that's the "Machine." That is Shelly "The Machine" Lev

BAYLEN: Get in the goddamn room. (*Baylen starts manhandling Shelly into the room.*)

LEVENE: Ricky, I . . .

ROMA: Okay, okay, I'll be at the resta . . .

LEVENE: Ricky . . .

BAYLEN: "Ricky" can't help you, pal.

LEVENE: . . . I only want to . . .

BAYLEN: Yeah. What do you want? You want to *what?* (*He pushes Levene into the room, closes the door behind him. Pause.*)

ROMA: Williamson: listen to me: when the *leads* come in . . . listen to me: when the *leads* come in I want my top two off the list. For *me*. My usual two. Anything you give *Levene* . . .

WILLIAMSON: . . . I wouldn't worry about it.

ROMA: Well I'm *going* to worry about it, and so are you, so shut up and *listen*. (*Pause.*) I GET HIS ACTION. My stuff is *mine*, whatever *he* gets for himself, I'm talking half. You put me in with him.

Aaronow enters.

AARONOW: Did they. . . ?

ROMA: You understand?

AARONOW: Did they catch. . . ?

ROMA: Do you understand? My stuff is mine, his stuff is ours. I'm taking half of his commissions — now, *you* work it out.

WILLIAMSON: Mmm.

AARONOW: Did they find the guy who broke into the office yet?

ROMA: No. *I* don't know. (*Pause.*)

AARONOW: Did the leads come in yet?

ROMA: No.

AARONOW (*Settling into a desk chair*): Oh, God, I hate this job.

ROMA (*Simultaneous with "job," exiting the office*): I'll be at the restaurant.

COMMENTARIES

Anne Dean

GLENGARRY GLEN ROSS

1990

In her discussion, Anne Dean focuses on the economic issues in Mamet's play — the central question of capitalism and the competition that makes it such an efficient economic system. In the play, the salesmen compete for the prize, a Cadillac, the symbol of success in America. Those who fail, however, face the possibility of being let go entirely. Dean compares the salesmen in Glengarry Glen Ross *with Willy Loman in Arthur Miller's* Death of a Salesman. *Underlying both is the quest for success.*

At the end of Arthur Miller's *Death of Salesman*, Charley offers a valediction on Willy Loman:

> for a salesman, there is no rock bottom to the life. . . . He's a man way out there in the blue, riding on a smile and a shoe shine. . . . A salesman is got to dream, boy. It comes with the territory.[1]

Like Willy, the salesmen in Mamet's *Glengarry Glen Ross* all have their dreams. They dream of the rich customer who will enable them to stop working for those who exploit them and they dream, continually, of success. For several generations of writers who have criticized the American Dream, the salesman has symbolized its shortcomings. It is true that such a profession can be the route to great wealth, the means for an ordinary man to make good by sheer hard work, but this is not the aspect that such writers choose to emphasize. To them, a society that advocates this kind of "self-improvement" is a consumer society based on materialism and has, at its heart, an emptiness that cannot be assuaged by yet more

[1]Arthur Miller, "Requiem," *Death of a Salesman* (London: Penguin, 1980), p. 111.

money in the bank. Just as the salesmen's lives are fueled by the promise of happiness and contentment in return for material success, so too are the lives of their clients; the clients are as much a part of the capitalist hegemony as the men from whom they purchase their symbols of material success. Their purchases are invested by the salesmen with amazing, life-enhancing properties that somehow hold the promise of a better future. The truth is, however, usually rather different. In the same way as the salesmen's endless quest for spurious success is essentially a chimera, so the goods they sell are probably quite worthless. The salesmen are, therefore, exploiting those who, like them, need to dream and to believe in a brighter future. It is a vicious circle.

Probably the most famous literary salesman is Miller's Willy Loman, whose frustrated dreams eventually split his family and destroy him. His relentless quest for success, together with an unrealistic view of the world, results, as Eleanor Clark puts it, in his being "done . . . in" largely due to "the capitalist system."[2] Similarly, G. F. Babbitt in Sinclair Lewis's satirical novel, *Babbitt,* neglects his emotional life in the belief that "the one purpose of the real-estate business was to make money for George F. Babbitt,"[3] although he finds that success does not bring him the happiness he seeks. Hickey, that hypocritical shatterer of illusions in Eugene O'Neill's *The Iceman Cometh,* is undone not directly through capitalism — although there is certainly a suggestion that the need for professional kudos is at least partly to blame for his tragedy — but through his need to hang onto the "pipe dreams" he exhorts his friends to eschew. Hickey is the archetypal salesman in literature, a peculiar mixture of both victim and oppressor whose downfall is brought about by self-delusion and societal pressure.

Mamet has commented on the theme of capitalism that runs through both *Glengarry Glen Ross* and *American Buffalo* (which was written about nine years earlier). Both plays are, he says, "set deeply in the milieu of capitalism [which is] obviously an idea whose time has come and gone."[4]

He goes on to explain how

in America we're still suffering from loving a frontier ethic — that is to say, take the land from the Indians and give it to the railroad. Take the money from the blacks and give it to the rich. The ethic was always something for nothing. It never really existed when the American frontier was open . . . it never was anything more transcendent than something for nothing . . . The idea of go West and make your fortune, there's gold lying in the ground, was an idea promulgated by the storekeepers in the gold rush and the railroads in the westward expansion as a way of enslaving the common man and woman . . . playing on their greed. As W. C. Fields said, you can't cheat an honest man. So, because we've been rather dishonest about our basic desire to get something for nothing in this country we've always been enslaved by the myth of the happy capitalist. Familiar American pieties are always linked to criminality. That's why they're familiar American pieties.[5]

Elsewhere he notes that "American capitalism comes down to one thing. . . . The operative axiom is 'Hurrah for me and fuck you.' Anything else is a lie."[6] Thus, Mamet lays the blame for modern-day greed and corruption on the ethics that have

[2]Eleanor Clark cited in Dennis Welland, *Miller the Playwright* (London and New York: Eyre Methuen, 1983), p. 39.
[3]Sinclair Lewis, *Babbitt* (New York: Harcourt, Brace & Co., 1922), p. 49.
[4]Christopher Bigsby, *Contemporary Writers: David Mamet* (London: Methuen, 1985), p. 111.
[5]Ibid.
[6]Program notes for *Glengarry Glen Ross.*

existed since the early days of the American Republic. From the outset, people have been urged to live falsely, to seek financial success by any means open to them, including cheating and stealing. Mamet believes that this has led to the diminishment of important emotional bonds whose value is then viewed only as a means of achieving pecuniary gain. His plays are frequently concerned with the fact that ordinary human relationships have been corrupted and subverted by social fiats, and *Glengarry Glen Ross* is perhaps the most frightening example of this tendency. The archaic — although still powerful — New World ethos of seizing rapaciously what is denied by right is exposed as both immoral and callous and, in these plays, Mamet draws attention to the deforming effect upon individual morality. His characters are, therefore, essentially very unhappy; on the surface they may be tough and smiling, but underneath this brittle veneer, they are aware of a terrible void in their lives. Mamet has noted how

> the American ethic of business, of boosterism, never made anybody happy. It has made a lot of people rich, but it never made anybody happy. So we live in a very, very unhappy country here. I have always considered it to be part of my job to talk about the things that I see, and certainly the most pervasive aspect of America is that we are so damned unhappy over here, but we are smiling all the time.[7]

Glengarry Glen Ross is, he says, an attempt to write about "those guys you see on planes. They all sit together, and you can never understand what they're talking about, and they all have these papers filled with columns and figures. They're all named Bob. And when they laugh, it's 'Ha-*ha*!' — this imitation laugh."[8] During an interview with Mel Gussow, Mamet recalled a conversation he had had with his wife's stepfather about the cruelty and ruthlessness of the world of salesmanship. He had been told how "as an effect of the recession, how 'vicious the competition was for jobs and sales, especially among older men.' He described one incident in which an older salesman was so terrified about making a presentation that he had a heart attack on the spot, 'and the new president of the company stepped over his body to leave the room.'"[9]

Mamet's characters must convince themselves that material gain is the ultimate achievement — there is simply nothing else. In this world, business has become an end in itself; people frantically pursue their individual goals for success and happiness and find it to be an endless pursuit. Once they reach one pinnacle, they must move on to another. Mamet demonstrates how inextricably people can become enmeshed in their jobs, almost losing their identity behind a job title. Certainly his salesmen seem to have little life outside the office. One of them actually says, "A man's his job" (act 2), which suggests that he has become a mere extension of his livelihood. There are very few moments in the play when the characters use any language that is not expressly concerned with business and even when they do it quickly becomes apparent that it is a ploy designed to coerce a colleague or cheat a client. When Roma talks to a customer about his wife, he uses the vocabulary of the boardroom to make his point:

> *Roma:* . . . You have a contract with your wife. You have certain things you do *jointly*, you have a *bond* there . . . (act 2)

[7]*Kaleidoscope,* Radio 4 (B.B.C. Radio) 19 April 1985.
[8]Jennifer Allen, "David Mamet's Hard Sell," *New York,* 9 April 1984, p. 40.
[9]Mel Gussow, "Real Estate World a Model for Mamet," *New York Times,* 28, March 1984, p. C19.

It is as if the world has ceased to exist outside of the office; Roma and his cronies have distorted speech so much through cunning and artifice — and downright professional obsession — that it seems they no longer have a need for language that does not immediately relate to their business interests. Mamet is not, however, out to condemn such characters, but merely to expose a system that has created them. He insists that it was not his intention to offer an indictment or a commentary: "My job is to create a closed moral universe,"[10] he says, and to leave evaluation to the audience. To Mamet, the "play is about a society based on business . . . a society with only one bottom line: How much money you make."[11]

The premise upon which *Glengarry Glen Ross* is based is, in a way, a paradigm of capitalism. The company's bosses have organized a sales competition in which the salesman with the highest "grosses" — financial profit — wins a Cadillac and is automatically guaranteed the best "leads" (addresses of prospective land buyers), the runners-up win a set of steak knives, and the losers are sacked. That the successful salesman is given the best leads while the runners-up are forced to accept inferior leads from the "B" list or are even dismissed, underlines the unfairness of a system that penalizes those who are weak and needy but rewards those who least need such support. With no other choice but to capitulate to the demands of their employers, it is not surprising that the salesmen should rail against the iniquities of an unfair system. Their jobs may be their lives, but they should be *better* jobs; despite their refusal to look beneath the shallowness of their lives, there remains a level at which they are conscious of a serious deficiency.

Corrupted by the constant need to beat their colleagues at any cost, these men have become expert manipulators. Their ability to cajole and confuse with superbly calculated verbal onslaughts is quite mesmerizing. Jack Shepherd, who played Richard Roma in the National Theatre production remarks that they are "vicious existentialists, experts in deception, superb liars. . . . persuasive, ruthless, competitive, disloyal."[12] These men think nothing of trampling over anyone who stands in their way. Theirs is a world in which loyalty and trust have almost no place and where language can no longer be trusted as a means of straightforward communication. Merely listening to the wrong words can mean dire consequences, as Aaronow finds to his cost. A major theme in this play is the corruption of the function of language, and Robert Cushman has observed how Mamet drives home his point about the unreliability of language through his characters' "intoxicating mixture of evasions, pleadings, browbeatings, stonewalling and spiel."[13] The language in *Glengarry Glen Ross* is quite stunning in its versatility, and Mamet's command over dialogue reaches its most dazzling pitch. What is perhaps most striking is the almost operatic quality of some of the verbal set pieces. The terse, sometimes stichomythic quality of his earlier dialogue still exists here, but Mamet now seems to be experimenting with new and more lengthy forms of linguistic control. There are in this work a number of bravura monologues and brilliantly sustained "duets" that the salesmen utilize to bewilder and impress their audience. In *Sexual Perversity in Chicago,* some of Bernie Litko's absurdly inflated fantasies take a similar form, but even they are a pale prelude to the heights achieved here. Mamet demonstrates with consummate skill his ability to condense and expand salient aspects of

[10]Ibid.
[11]Ibid.
[12]Jack Shepherd, National Theatre Study Notes for *Glengarry Glen Ross,* p. 7.
[13]Robert Cushman, *The Observer,* 11 September 1983, p. 31.

the American language into what truly become the "tainted arias"[14] of which Christopher Bigsby has spoken. Roma's mesmerizing monologue in the company of the inarticulate Lingk, Levene's poetic and almost orgasmic evocation of a great sale, and the brilliant entrapment of Aaronow into criminal culpability by his colleague, Moss, surpass even Mamet's own dizzying standards of linguistic invention.

The world of sales and salesmanship offers myriad opportunities for those who enjoy spinning a yarn and acting a part. In the brutally competitive world in which he moves, the salesman must become expert in linguistic technique; so long as he can keep his narrative flowing and uninterrupted he is able to feel, at least momentarily, safe. Through the pattern of his words, he can manipulate and persuade and thus his fantasies of success and those of his client can become a temporary reality. As Barbara Hardy observes, storytellers of any kind must be "fluent and vivid . . . artists who keep an eye on the subject, on the listeners, and on the occasion. They are sincerely involved and engrossed in their stories but are self-consciously practised in that manipulation of effect which belongs to all oratory and is essential to the art of narrative improvisation."[15] In *Glengarry Glen Ross*, Mamet's salesmen spill out their endless, brilliant chatter to anyone who is prepared to listen but at the heart of their manipulation lies aridity and emptiness. Behind the foulmouthed, incessantly "macho" bravado lies a desperate bluster, a braggadocio show of power by men who are only too aware of their own powerlessness. They may live by victimizing their colleagues and clients, but the most abject victims of their trade are themselves.

This play is Mamet's most successful to date. It was premiered at the National Theatre in London in 1983, winning two British drama awards before opening on Broadway where it won the Pulitzer Prize in 1984. Despite the fact that it is by far the most abrasive and scatological that Mamet has yet written, it has been much praised for its poetic qualities. Benedict Nightingale comments upon the "gaudy, swaggering poetry [Mamet] has fashioned out of the street-wise idiom of Chicago [which] sucks us in, carries us along, bouncing us over minor implausibilities like a stream over rusty cans."[16] Connie Booth describes the work as one of "poetic brilliance . . . It is caustic, sharp, and tragic. The language isn't easy or melodic but it is certainly true poetry in every sense of the word."[17] Mamet was worried about the play when he read it through for the first time. The mixture of an episodic first act with a conventionally structured second act prompted him to send a copy to Harold Pinter for his comments. Pinter told him that, in his opinion, the only thing wrong with the play was that it was not currently in production. Mamet now believes that its structure gives the work an extra dimension, and adds to its appeal. He has noted, "people love my new play . . . Because I finally had the will to write a second act. I wrote a million episodic plays. I can write them with my left hand. So what? Who cares? Fortunately, I got sick of it before [the audience] did."[18]

[14]Bigsby, *Contemporary Writers,* p. 126.

[15]Barbara Hardy, *Tellers and Listeners: The Narrative Imagination* (London: The Athlone Press, 1975), p. 135.

[16]Bernard Nightingale, "Bard of Modern Immorality," p. 5.

[17]Connie Booth, interview with author, 2 December 1986, Hampstead, London.

[18]Allen, "Mamet's Hard Sell," p. 41.

Hersh Zeifman

PHALLUS IN WONDERLAND

1992

Hersh Zeifman, a professor at York University in Ontario, Canada, compares Mamet's American Buffalo *(1975) and* Glengarry Glen Ross, *with an eye toward the question of masculinity and macho behavior. Zeifman shows to what extent the language reveals the underpinnings of the characters' attitude toward their own masculinity and the lack of it in others.*

The most sustained torrent of abuse in *Glengarry*, however, is reserved for Williamson, the despised office manager who sits behind a desk and so, unlike the salesmen, never tests his manhood in the arena of "battle." Predictably, the terms of that abuse are misogynistic and homophobic. Levene's scorn for him is withering: "You don't know what it *is*, you don't have the *sense*, you don't have the *balls*. You ever been on a sit? *Ever? Has this cocksucker ever been . . .*" (1525). (In the rehearsal typescript of the play, Levene further accused "You don't have the *blood*, John. You don't have the *blood*. . . ,"[1] thus emphasizing the sheer animal savagery of the business world; as one of the characters in Mamet's *Reunion* [1976] comments: "It's a fucking jungle out there.")[2] But the strongest abuse of Williamson is unleashed by Roma, livid with rage that Williamson has blown one of his deals:

> You stupid fucking *cunt*. You *idiot*. Whoever told you you could work with *men*? . . . I don't care . . . whose dick you're sucking on. You're going *out*. . . . What you're hired for is to *help* us — does that seem clear to you? To *help* us. Not to fuck us up . . . to help *men* who are going *out* there to try to earn a *living*. You *fairy*. . . . You fucking *child*. . . . [pp. 1529–30]

For Roma, as for Moss and indeed *all* the characters of this exclusively male world in which machismo rules, "cunt," "fairy," and "child" are synonymous terms of abuse; each is equivalent to "non-man," and thus to nothing, to worse than nothing.

The arena of "battle" entered into by the salesmen of *Glengarry* reminds us that, once again, Mamet is linking business with other traditional male homosocial institutions. When Moss turns viciously on Roma, for example, the invective spewing out of him in great bursts of bile, Roma retorts: "What is this, your farewell speech? . . . Your farewell to the troops?" (1524). Similarly, Levene's boasting of his incredible sale is interrupted by Moss's "Hey, I don't want to hear your fucking war stories . . ." (1523). Levene's description of closing that sale is, indeed, very like that of a military engagement; the language he uses suggests both an epic battle and, in its compulsively orgasmic rhythm, a sexual conquest, casting his customers in the role of the enemy who must at all costs not simply be defeated but *annihilated*. "They signed, Ricky," he exults to Roma. "It was *great*. It was fucking great. It was like they *wilted* all at once. . . . They, I swear to God, they both kind of *imperceptibly slumped*" (1524). A businessman, Levene implies, is constantly putting his life on the line — like a soldier, like a cop. "You can't learn [what it takes] in an

[1]C. W. E. Bigsby, *David Mamet* (London and New York: Methuen, 1987), p. 121.
[2]David Mamet, "Reunion" in *Reunion and Dark Pony* (New York: Grove, 1979), p. 23.

1507

office . . . ," Levene instructs the deskbound Williamson. "You have to learn it on the streets. . . . 'Cause your partner *depends* on it. . . . Your partner . . . a man who's your 'partner' *depends* on you . . . you have to go *with* him and *for* him . . ." (1530).

Levene's mock-heroic rhetoric, however, is belied by the play's action. There are, finally, no "partners" in *Glengarry Glen Ross,* nor — given the "values" of this world — could there be; each salesman is out strictly for himself. Don's definition of business in *Buffalo* — "People taking *care* of themselves" (7) — is dramatized with a vengeance in *Glengarry,* where the Practical Sales Maxim "ALWAYS BE CLOSING" (1513), used by Mamet as the play's epigraph, applies to *all* relationships. Everyone in *Glengarry* exists potentially to be "sold": the customers, the salesmen, even the audience. Thus both acts end with a magisterial "selling" job by Ricky Roma, in which the audience too is "buffaloed": in act one when we ultimately realize that Roma's conversation with James Lingk is not simply a philosophical chat with a stranger over a drink but the cunning seduction of a sales pitch, and more lethally in act two, when "tricky Ricky" suddenly and viciously betrays his self-proclaimed "friend" and "partner" Levene.

"ALWAYS BE CLOSING" might also stand as *Mamet's* credo in *Glengarry.* For Mamet has once again "closed" this play about American business to women, excluding the "feminine" and its reputed values from the sphere of dramatic action; once again there is no place for such values in a world ruled by machismo. As in *Buffalo,* women haunt the margins of the text but never break through to the stage. Their presence is evoked only metonymically, as terms of abuse, or else in the form of "spirits" whose essence threatens male values. The most prominent of these off-stage women is the wife of James Lingk, who has ordered her husband to cancel the business deal into which Roma has "suckered" him. Roma tries desperately to change Lingk's mind, predictably lapsing into the language of commerce in characterizing Lingk's relationship with his wife — predictably, because Ricky can conceive of human intercourse only in commercial terms: "Come on, Jim. (*Pause.*) I want to tell you something. Your life is your own. You have a contract with your wife. You have certain things you do *jointly,* you have a *bond* there . . . and there are *other* things. Those things are yours" (1529). Although Roma ridicules and attempts to dismiss her "prudence" as "something *women* have" (1526) — akin to menstrual cramps, perhaps — Mrs. Lingk in fact implicitly challenges his macho code of behavior; she has a different agenda from his, a far less cutthroat one. Excluded from the stage, she is the "missing Lingk" whose values could destroy Roma's very existence.

Mamet once declared in an interview that he views his plays as "iconoclastic," "in the sense of tearing down the icons of American business, and some of the myths about this country."[3] In *American Buffalo* and *Glengarry Glen Ross,* one of the most powerful ways in which this iconoclasm is dramatized is through the exclusion from the stage of women and of the values traditionally associated with them. There are, of course, a number of potential problems here. First, to characterize women *as a gender* as compassionate, tender, empathetic, etc., is a remarkably sentimental notion; Mamet certainly doesn't sustain this view in his critical writings, say, or more significantly in those plays of his in which women actually

---

[3]Henry I. Schvey, "Celebrating the Capacity for Self-Knowledge" [an interview with Mamet], (*New Theatre Quarterly,* 4, No. 13 (February 1988), p. 96.

appear.[4] Second, and far more serious, to use women metaphorically in this way, to inscribe them with certain values (however "positive" those values might be), may itself be a form of misogyny. Thus Michelene Wandor has noted that, even in plays by male dramatists in which women become "the conscience of humanity, . . . the perspective still remains male-determined . . .":

> What is interesting is that these plays simply represent variants on the "feminine." . . . Using woman as a metaphor may look like a compliment, but it is an unconscious way of denying her a real part of the stage action.[5]

Mamet has himself partially acknowledged this danger: "Men *generally* expect more of women than we do of ourselves," he has written. "We feel, based on constant evidence, that women are better, stronger, more truthful, than men. You can call this sexism, or reverse sexism, or whatever you wish, but it is my experience."[6] If there's a sense in which Mamet might be accused of misogyny in *Buffalo* and *Glengarry,* it's in this latter sense only — not that he shares the crudely misogynist views of those plays' male characters (which both plays clearly and explicitly condemn), but in this far more subtle essentialist reduction of women to a gender stereotype. Yet whether suspect in these ways or not, Mamet's insistence on all-male casts in *American Buffalo* and *Glengarry Glen Ross* makes his thematic point crystal clear. Both plays could thus have been titled *Sexual Perversity in Chicago,* for the perverse denial of an entire gender and its metaphorical import brilliantly exposes the moral wilderness of a business "ethic" ruled solely by the vile and violent values of a debased machismo.

---

[4]See, for example, such plays as *Sexual Perversity in Chicago* (1974), *The Woods* (1977), and *Speed the Plow* (1988). See also Mamet's description of women in the business world he knows best, that of theater and films: "The coldest, cruelest, most arrogant behavior I have ever seen in my professional life has been — and *consistently* has been — on the part of women producers in the movies and the theater. I have seen women do things that the worst man would never entertain the thought of — I do not imply that he would be stopped by conscience, but that he *would* be stopped by the fear of censure, which takes us back to [women's] inability to compromise." Mamet, "Women," in *Some Freaks* (New York: Viking, 1989), p. 28.

[5]Michelene Wandor, *Carry On, Understudies: Theatre and Sexual Politics* (London and New York: Routledge & Kegan Paul, 1986), p. 157.

[6]Mamet, "Women," in *Some Freaks,* p. 24.

Gao Xingjian

Gao Xingjian was born in eastern China in 1940. He received a degree in French from the Beijing Foreign Languages Institute in 1962, the same year he joined the Communist Party. In 1989, however, following the massacre in Tiananmen Square, he renounced his party membership. He became a noted writer during the Cultural Revolution (1966–1976), a period of extraordinary upheaval in China. The government tried to suppress China's professionals, purge intellectuals, and destroy works of art. Gao wrote fiction, poetry, and drama early in this period and was denounced to the authorities by his own wife on the grounds that he was writing "literature" at a time when such activity was both suspect and prohibited. Not only was he forced to labor in the fields, but he was made to destroy all his manuscripts, among them fifteen plays.

He was sent to a remote camp for reeducation, along with thousands of others who had become suspect citizens at that time. He was eventually reintegrated into society, and after 1976 he was able to begin writing and publishing again.

Gao also produced a number of books on writing. *A Preliminary Discussion of the Art of Modern Fiction* (1981) and *In Search of a Modern Form of Dramatic Representation* (1987) demonstrate his interest in theoretical issues relative to literature. He published *Collected Plays* in 1985.

In 1982 he was misdiagnosed with lung cancer; after thinking he was dying, he was given a reprieve. This prompted him to begin a spiritual journey in 1983 through remote regions of China, spending some six months wandering and meeting people as he traced the Yangtze River's path. He is said to have walked almost ten thousand miles. From that experience he wrote a highly respected and popular novel, *Soul Mountain* (1989; tr. 1999). In 2000 he was awarded the Nobel Prize for Literature, the first Chinese writer so honored.

In China, however, he has been accused of "spiritual pollution" because his works do not follow the Communist Party line. His first notable play was *Bus Stop* (1983), which bore a resemblance to Samuel Beckett's *Waiting for Godot*. The people at the bus stop wait years and never see the bus they need. This play stirred a great deal of public controversy and debate in newspapers. Condemned by the authorities as "intellectual pollution," it has been described as the "most pernicious work" since the founding of the People's Republic. It goes almost without saying that this play has been banned in China.

In 1986 *The Other Shore* was also banned in China and was eventually produced in Hong Kong and Taiwan. At this point, Gao realized he could not remain in China and continue to be a productive voice in theater or literature. Because he was also a distinguished painter, he was given permission as a painter to travel to France. In 1987 he requested political asylum in France and settled in Paris. He had studied French in China as a young man and found

France hospitable to his ideas. Today he is a French citizen. He has continued to write in both Chinese and French and, while he remains concerned about events in China, he persists in describing himself as professing "nothingism," rather than communism or capitalism. He wishes to remain aloof from both ideologies as well as any others that might come along.

In his Nobel Prize acceptance speech he said,

> From my experience in writing, I can say that literature is inherently man's affirmation of the value of his own self and that this is validated during the writing; literature is born primarily of the writer's need for self-fulfillment. Whether it has any impact on society comes after the completion of a work and that impact certainly is not determined by the wishes of the writer.

Gao admits to having been influenced in his dramatic writing by some of the modernist French writers as well as Samuel Beckett, who wrote some of his work in French. He is an admirer of Eugene Ionesco (1909–1994), author of *The Bald Soprano* and *The Lesson,* as well as Antonin Artaud (1896–1948), a playwright and author of manifestos on the Theatre of Cruelty. These are all experimental writers searching for new ways to create dramatic tension and to explore the effects of theater. Gao's dramatic work, too, follows some of their ideas and attempts to break new ground.

One of Gao's approaches is an attempt to refine our conception of the actor. The "Tripartite actor" is his approach to training actors to work in his plays. He asks the actors to consider themselves first as they actually are, then as actors in the abstract, then as actors playing specific characters. Gao tries to help those who work in his plays to understand themselves in relation to the drama in a complex system of relationships to the text and their roles. As his translator, Gilbert C. F. Fong, says, "Gao Xingjian maintains that the actor has to be self-conscious of his craft, being aware not only of the character he is playing but also of the fact that he is putting on a performance as a performer. This awareness is in contrast to Stanislavsky's total immersion method, and to an extent it is also distinguished from Brecht's 'alienation,' which breaks the illusion of realism and underlines the distance between performance and audience."[1]

[1]Gilbert Fong, *The Other Shore* (Hong Kong: The Chinese University Press, 1999), p. xix.

THE OTHER SHORE

The Other Shore refers to a Buddhist concept, the land of enlightenment. The metaphor of crossing a river to a new world is based on the belief that the world of the senses, our material world, is essentially an illusion and that once one has achieved — or rather, *if* one achieves — enlightenment, one will move to that other shore on which illusion will be stripped away and reality perceived.

In the play, however, once the characters cross over, they do not automatically achieve the peace they crave. Instead, they bring their earthly attitudes with them and these worldly beliefs trap them once again. The opening of the play, which centers on exercises and games with ropes that connect individuals and lead them to a collectivism, establishes the social basis of the play. Critics sometimes connect this collectivism with that of Communism. The failure of the idealism implied by the communication naturally casts suspicion on the programs of collectivism worldwide.

The violence in the play derives from the failure of individuals to communicate. Even in the section in which language is absent, there is no peace, and the resumption of language brings with it the potential for deceit and manipulation. The large abstractions of Mother, Master, and Man are philosophical counters in the play, implying a basic attitude toward experience that the actors are unable to let go.

The structure of the play may seem arbitrary on the surface, but Gao moves from human relationships through a number of human experiences. The card player introduces the concept of chance and risk in life, while the Zen Master introduces religious virtues through Buddhism. The dog-plaster seller is the healer, and the mad woman a whore who insists on life's pleasures as a significant value. The Shadow is described as "your heart," meaning Man's heart, and implies a constant emotional presence in the life of the characters. The Man is described as a "weirdo" because he does not know what he wants, while the others are obsessed with what they want. The female mannequin near the end of the play introduces the idea of Asian puppet theater, which then raises another question about the humanity of characters in the play.

Gao has said that he wrote the play as a vehicle to help develop his three-part view of the actor. He views each segment of the play — segments that are, in Brechtian fashion, not absolutely coherent with each other — as a step in helping the actors explore themselves first as they really are, then as actors, then as actors portraying particular characters. This self-awareness is part of Gao's view of how the actor must approach this play, and the play is designed to help the actor keep an intense awareness present throughout the play.

The Other Shore in Performance

The 1986 Beijing production was banned immediately, but the play was produced that same year in Taiwan. In 1995 Gao Xingjian himself directed *The Other Shore* in Hong Kong at the Hong Kong Academy of Performing Arts in what has been described as its premiere. The New York premiere of the play was performed outdoors in Washington Square Park by the Trilogy Theatre in August 2001, directed by Cara Blouin. Dondrie Burnham played both the Mother and the Madwoman. The West Coast premiere took place in November 2003, directed by Jeffrey Wienckowski with the Sons of Beckett Theatre Company as part of the Edge of the World Theater Festival at Theatre/Theater in Hollywood, California. Boston University Theater produced a version in February 2004. Since 1995, the effective premiere of the play, *The Other Shore* has found a niche in experimental theater in the United States and elsewhere.

Gao Xingjian (b. 1940)

THE OTHER SHORE

1986

TRANSLATED BY GILBERT FONG

Time: The time cannot be defined or stated precisely.

Location: From the real world to the nonexistent other shore.

Characters

AN ACTOR PLAYING WITH ROPES	SHADOW
	HEART
CARD PLAYER	MOTHER
"DOGSKIN" PLASTER SELLER	FATHER
WOMAN	ZEN MASTER
YOUNG GIRL	OLD LADY
MAD WOMAN	STABLE KEEPER
MODEL	ACTORS
MAN	CROWD
YOUNG MAN	

(*The play can be performed in a theatre, a living room, a rehearsal room, an empty warehouse, a gymnasium, the hall of a temple, a circus tent, or any empty space as long as the necessary lighting and sound equipment can be properly installed. Lighting can be dispensed with if the play is performed during the day. The actors may be among the audience, or the audience among the actors. The two situations are the same and will not make any difference to the play.*)

ACTOR PLAYING WITH ROPES: Here's a rope. Let's play a game, but we've got to be serious, as if we're children playing their game. Our play starts with a game.

Okay, I want you to take hold of this end of the rope. You see, this way a relationship is established between us. Before that you were you and I was I, but with this rope between us we're tied to each other and it becomes you and I.

Let's try running in opposite directions. See, now you're pulling me, but then again I'm also holding you back, like two locusts tied to the same string, neither of us can get away from each other. Of course, we're also like husband and wife. (*Pauses.*) But that's not a good metaphor. If I were to pull the rope real hard towards me, then we'd have to see who's stronger. The stronger one pulls and the weaker is being pulled. It becomes a tug-of-war, a competition of strength, and there'll be a winner and a loser, victory and defeat.

Now if I carry this rope on my back like this and pull even harder, you'll be like a dead dog; likewise if you manage to gain control of this rope, I'll be like a horse or a cow, and you'll be able to drive me around like cattle. In other words, you'll be running the show. So you see, our relationship is not at all constant, it's not at all unchanging.

Or we can establish an even more complex relationship. For instance if you revolve around me, I'll be the centre of your orbit, and you'll become my satellite. But if you don't wish to revolve around me, I can rotate on my own, thinking that all of you are revolving around me. Are you revolving or am I the one who's revolving? I could be revolving around you or you could be revolving around me. Who knows? Perhaps we're both turning at the same time, or maybe we're both revolving around other people, or maybe those other people are revolving around us both or maybe all of us are revolving around God — maybe there isn't a God after all, maybe there's only a universe rotating by itself like a millstone — now we're touching on philosophy. Never mind, we'll leave philosophy to the philosophers, let's just continue to play our game.

Everyone of you can pick up a rope and play different kinds of games, the possibilities are endless. Playing with ropes is such a game, that it can be a manifestation of all kinds of interpersonal relationships.

(*The actors each choose a partner to play the game, using a piece of rope. They can switch partners or briefly make contact with other pairs of players, but the contacts are soon broken. The game becomes increasingly lively, tense, and exciting, accompanied by all kinds of salutations and screams.*)

ACTOR PLAYING WITH ROPES: Okay everybody, let's knock it off for a moment. Let's make this game bigger and more complex. Now I want all of you to hold on to one end of your rope and give me the other end. This way you'll be able to establish all kinds of relationships with me, some tense, some lax, some distant, and some close, and soon your individual attitudes will have a strong impact on me. Society is complex and ever-changing, we're constantly pulling and being pulled. (*Pauses.*) Just like a fly that's fallen into a spider's web. (*Pauses.*) Or just like a spider. (*Pauses.*) The rope is like our hands. (*He lets go one rope and his partner also lets go. The rope falls on the ground.*) Or like an extended antenna. (*He lets go another and his partner follows.*) Or like the language we use, for instance when we say "Good Morning" or "How are you!" (*Another rope falls to the ground.*) Or perhaps it's like looking at each other, (*Replaces another rope.*) or like the thoughts in our minds. (*His back is against his current partner, but the two sides are still communicating.*) Either you're thinking of her, or she's thinking of someone

else. (*He brushes past her shoulders. She and someone else are gazing into each other's eyes.*) In this way
the rope is pulling all of us, binding us together.
We look —

(*The actors are communicating with one another
through pieces of imaginary ropes.*)

We observe —
We stare —
Then there's temptation and attraction —
Orders and obedience —

(*In the following, the performance is accompanied by all
kinds of sighs and screams but without resorting to the
use of language.*)

Conflicts —
Intimacy —
Exclusion —
Entanglement —
Abandonment —
Emulation —
Evasion —
Repulsion —
Pursuit —
Encirclement —
Congregation —
Fragmentation —
Dismiss!
At ease!
Now there is a river in front of us, not a piece of rope.
Let's cross the river and try to reach the other shore.

ACTORS: (*One after another.*) Yes, to the other shore! To
the other shore!
The other shore! To the other shore! To the other
shore!
The other shore!
Oh — Oh — Oh
The water in the river is so clear!
So cool!
Watch out, the stones are killing my feet!
How nice!
(*Gradually there comes the sound of running water.*)
My skirt's soaking wet!
Is the river deep?
Let's swim across to the other shore!
Don't go by yourself!
Look at the water spray, how it sparkles in the sun-
shine!
What fun, just like a waterfall.
A dam, a river flowing gently down the dam.
Form a line in the middle of the river.
Further down the water's dark blue, it's got to be
really deep there.
I've got some fish wriggling between my legs . . .
So exciting!
I'm going to fall.
Don't worry, hold on to me.
There's an eddy over there —
Look after one another, hold hands.

To the rapid waters.
To the other shore!
No one can see the other shore.
Cut the poetry crap! I'm falling.
Hold tight, one after another now.
Over there the water is deep blue . . .
Aahh! The water's over my waist all of a sudden!
I'm getting dizzy.
Close your eyes for a while.
Look in front of you, look ahead, keep your eyes
open!
All looking at the other shore.
How come I can't see it?
We'll drown, all of us.
We'll all be fish food.
If we're going to die, let's die together.
Girls, stop blabbing, try to concentrate.
The current is very strong, tread in the shallows, try,
going up stream!
I can't make it across, I'm sure I can't make it.
Where's the other shore?
Sometimes it's dark, sometimes it's bright.
Are there lights on the other shore?
There are flowers, lots of flowers on the other shore,
it's a world of flowers.
I'm afraid I can't make it, please don't leave me
behind.
(*Sobs.*)
Can you feel it? We're drifting in the river.
Like corks on a string.
And like water weed.
Why are we going to the other shore? I really don't
understand.
Right, why do we want to go to the other shore?
The other shore is the other shore, you'll never
reach it.
But you still want to go, to see what it's like over
there.
I can't see anything.
No oasis, and no light.
In total darkness.
It's like this . . .
No, I can't make it.
We haven't been there before.
We must get there.
But why?
To make a long-time wish come true, the other shore,
the other shore.
No, I can't make it, I want to go home!
None of us can.
Can't go back at all.
O — !
Who is it? Don't know.
(*Silence, only the sound of water gurgling.*)
Was somebody screaming? Did you hear it?
You must have heard it, but nobody answered.
(*Silence. Sound of sobbing.*)
This is a ditch of dead water.
There's only oblivion.

Actors playing with ropes in the 2001 New York premiere of *The Other Shore,* which was directed by Cara Blouin and performed outdoors by the Trilogy Theatre in Washington Square Park.

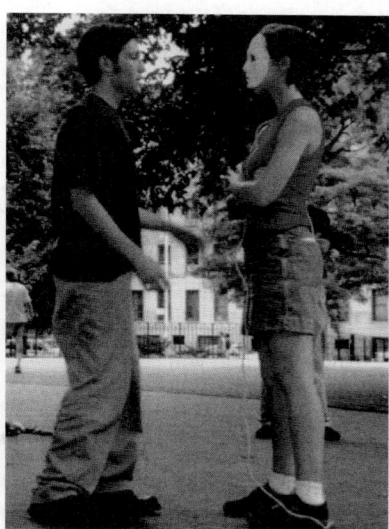

Jared McGuire as Man/Young Man and Suzie Syta as Young Girl/Stable Keeper in the Trilogy Theatre production of *The Other Shore.*

(*Bewildered, the Crowd slowly walk out of the dead water. Music is faintly heard. The Crowd gradually reach the shore and lie down totally exhausted on the ground. Woman appears in darkness. Like a strand of light mist, she walks around to inspect the people who have lost their memories. She drifts among them, touching and waking them up one by one. They lazily open their eyes and look up, turning their bodies and staring at her. They try to speak but in vain.*)

WOMAN: (*Raises her hand.*) Look here, this is a hand.

(*The Crowd utter muddled sounds from their throat.*)

WOMAN: This is a hand.
CROWD: (*Still mumbling.*) Th . . . The . . . This . . . ee . . . ha . . . han . . . hand.
WOMAN: Hand —
CROWD: Hand — band — sand — hand —
WOMAN: This is a foot.
CROWD: Th . . . Th . . . This . . . ee . . . fo . . . foo . . . foot.
WOMAN: (*Pointing to her eye.*) Eye.
CROWD: Ee . . . ee . . . eye . . . eye . . .
WOMAN: (*Gesturing.*) Your eyes are looking at your foot!
CROWD: (*Totally confused.*) Eyes . . . cook . . . cook your . . . own . . . coot . . .

(*Woman laughs, and the Crowd join in the laughter with her, giggling.*)

WOMAN: (*Stops laughing, somewhat sad.*) This is a hand —

CROWD: This is a hand, this is a band, this is a sand, this is a hand . . .
WOMAN: This is a foot —
CROWD: This is a boot, this is a hoot, this is a root, this is a foot . . .
WOMAN: This is a body — your body —
CROWD: This is a body, this is a body, this is a body your body, this is your body is a body is a body is your body your . . .
WOMAN: (*Shakes her head, gesturing more slowly and still being patient.*) My hand — my body — my foot — this is me.
CROWD: My band, my hand, my body, my coot, my hand's body's foot's my coot's hand's foot's body this is my hand's foot's body is meat!
WOMAN: Say, me —
CROWD: Say me say me say me say me say me!
WOMAN: (*Shakes her head and points to herself, from her eyes to her mouth, and from her body to her feet.*) Me.
CROWD: (*Together at last.*) Me.
WOMAN: Good!
CROWD: Food! Hood! Good! Wood!
WOMAN: (*At once she waves her hand in disagreement. After thinking for a moment, she points at one person among the crowd.*) You.
CROWD: (*All pointing at the person.*) You!
THE PERSON: (*He looks around him and then points at himself.*) You!
WOMAN: (*Shakes her head and helps him to point his finger at someone else.*) You.

CROWD: You.

WOMAN: (*Gesturing.*) Me and you.

CROWD: Me and you.

WOMAN: (*Laughs.*) Good!

CROWD: (*Also laugh.*) Good!

(*Music. Gradually the tempo of the music becomes faster.*)

WOMAN: Me and him!

CROWD: Me and him!

WOMAN: Them and me.

CROWD: Them and me.

WOMAN: Me and you.

CROWD: Me and you.

WOMAN: You and us.

CROWD: You and us.

WOMAN: Now follow me when you're seeing with your eyes —

CROWD: See —

WOMAN: Tell me, who do you see?

CROWD: (*One after another.*) See him, see you, see me, see them, they see you, you see us, we see them . . .

WOMAN: Now say touch, give, like, and love, and you won't feel lonely any more.

CROWD: (*Becoming active.*) I touch you, you give me, I like him, he loves you, you touch me, I give him, he likes you, you love me . . .

(*Man comes out from among the Crowd.*)

MAN: Who are you?

WOMAN: I'm one of you.

MAN: Where are we now?

WOMAN: The other shore, which we wanted to reach but couldn't.

MAN: Are you the same person who drowned while we were crossing the river? (*Woman shakes her head.*) Are you her soul? (*Woman still shakes her head.*) Have you been hiding in our thoughts, do you appear only when we think of you? Or are you something like a kind of consciousness? Did you guide us to the other shore so that we wouldn't get lost?

CROWD: (*At the same time.*) I detest you.

You touched me!

I'll beat you up!

You hate me?

I'll torture her.

He cheats on me.

You're swearing at him!

I'll tell on you.

You punish him!

He plots against me!

I hate you!

You curse him!

I'll kill you . . .

MAN: (*To Woman.*) You're so kind.

CROWD: (*Turn to face Woman one after another, playing with words.*)

You're so generous.

You're so lovely.

You're so despicable.

He's a bastard.

You don't say what you mean, you're a crook.

You're a double-dealing no-good tramp!

She butters you up, but she's actually jealous of you.

You're snaky, you teach us words so that you can talk to our men and seduce them!

You may look so kind and gentle, but who knows if you're a whore or not?

She's trying to seduce our husbands!

Stirring up trouble among our brothers.

A buttered bun, look, just look at her —

Keep the girls away from her, she'll turn them into whores.

She may look prim and proper, but she's really more corrupt than a common whore.

She's the one, she makes people panic, there'll be no more peace in this world.

(*Woman draws back as the Crowd surrounds her from all sides. They are excited by their own increasingly venomous language. She cannot escape from the stares of the Crowd, so she turns to Man for help and hangs on to him.*)

CROWD: (*Getting more angry.*)

Whore!

Venomous snake!

Witch!

Shameless slut!

(*Woman holds on to Man and pleads for his protection. The Crowd go wild.*)

CROWD: Look, go and take a look!

Pooh!

Dump her!

Drag her away!

Get a hold of her!

Strip her!

Wring her neck! The shameless whore!

(*The Crowd drag her away from Man and jump on her. In the confusion they strangle her to death. When Man pushes his way into the Crowd and shakes her body, there is no response.*) (*Witnessing this, the Crowd is stunned.*)

CROWD: Dead.

Dead?

Dead?

She's dead!

(*The Crowd disperse in a hurry.*)

Was she strangled to death?

It's you —

No, he started it.

You shouted first!

I was only following you, you were all shouting.

Who shouted first? Who?

Who shouted first to grab her, strip her and strangle her?

Who?
We all shouted.
I shouted because you did.
I shouted because all of you were shouting.
But she's dead! Strangled alive!
I didn't kill her.
I didn't kill her.
I didn't kill her.
I didn't kill her.
I didn't kill her.
I didn't.
I didn't.
Didn't.
Didn't.
Didn't.
But she's dead for sure, so lovely even when she's dead.
So beautiful, nobody could help loving her.
Her skin is like jade, it's got no blemishes, it's so pure.
Look at her pretty little hands, they've got her endless tenderness in them.
My, she's like a statue of the Bodhisattva!°
So pure, so prim and proper.
She gave us language, she brought us wisdom, but she was murdered!
This is the greatest sin of all, you despicable lot!
Who are you talking about?
Murderers! You, all of you!
How dare you smear me? You bastard!
You're a thug!
You're a rascal!

(*The Crowd fight among themselves.*)

MAN: Are you finished? We killed her, there's no question about it. It's you, it's him, it's me, and it's all of us. We're all in it together! On this desolate other shore, she gave us language, but we didn't know how to cherish it; she gave us wisdom, but we didn't know how to use it! We ought to be shocked by what we did, but we're cowards, we're too spineless to feel any shame.

CROWD: What do you think we should do?
We need a leader, a flock of sheep also needs a leader. We'll follow you.

MAN: I detest you, I detest myself. It's better for us to go our separate ways.

CROWD: No, don't abandon us.
We've made up our mind to follow you, and you want to leave us?

MAN: Follow me where? Where can I lead you? (*He leaves by himself. The Crowd follow behind.*) Don't follow me! (*Troubled.*) I don't even know where I want to go myself. (*Stops and tries to figure out where to go. The Crowd still follow him at a distance.*)

(*Mother appears in front of him.*)

Bodhisattva: One who has achieved enlightenment and become a Buddha.

MOTHER: Do you still remember me?
MAN: Yes, mother.
MOTHER: You've almost forgotten me, haven't you?
MAN: (*On his knees.*) Yes, mother.
MOTHER: (*Stroking his head.*) Find yourself a girl, you really should start a family.
MAN: But I want to make something of myself.
MOTHER: You're too ambitious.
MAN: (*Looks down.*) I'm still your son.
MOTHER: Are they all following you? Where are you going to take them?
MAN: I don't know. I only know we should go forward, is that right, mother?
MOTHER: My good son. (*Embraces his head.*)
MAN: Your hands are cold! (*Shocked by his discovery.*) Mother, is this the world of the dead? Am I in another dimension?
MOTHER: There's nothing to be scared of, son. It's just a bit dark, a bit cold and damp, that's all.
MAN: (*Leaves her.*) How do I get out of here? Mother, I haven't lived long enough!

(*Mother turns and disappears. He hesitates for a moment and then follows in a hurry. A young girl blocks his way.*)

MAN: Who are you? I've seen you somewhere, but I can't recall your name. It seems like we used to live on the same street or something, many years ago. Every day on my way to school I always hoped that I could catch a glimpse of you, even if it's only your back. My heart would keep on pounding whenever I saw your long ponytail and your crimson red dress, you seemed to be wearing that crimson dress all that time. . . . I used to follow you, follow you right to your doorsteps, hoping that when you turned around to close the door, you'd at least say one word to me before you went inside, or smile at me just once. But every time you'd only look at me, saying nothing. Oh, I can see those eyes of yours again . . . (*He rubs his eyes and looks more closely, but she has disappeared into the dark shadows of the Crowd.*)

(*To the Crowd.*) We've got to get out of this ghastly place. Once we're away from this darkness we'll find light ahead of us. With the light there'll be houses, and we'll be able to dry our clothes around the stove and drink some hot tea. (*Incitingly.*) We'd be able to return to our homes, see our families, our wives and husbands, our children and parents, and all our loved ones and those who love us!

(*Young Girl appears again from behind the Crowd.*) Who are you?

(*Blocking her way.*) Wait, your name is on the tip of my tongue! It seems like I used to write poetry for you, that we used to go to the movies together and I held your hand in the dark, those tiny frail hands of yours . . . (*She turns and gets away from his grasp. She is now behind him, becoming more illusory. He turns around but cannot see her, no matter how hard he tries.*)

She always appeared in my dreams to torment me whenever I was worried and couldn't set my mind free. I couldn't recall her name, I couldn't see her face clearly, I couldn't even get hold of her presence in any way, but she still kept on tormenting me.

(*Speaking to the shadowy Crowd.*) Why do you keep following me? I need some peace and quiet, I need to be alone! I don't need to be stared at by a crowd, I don't need you, just as you don't need me. What you need is someone who can guide you, to show you the way, even though once you've found a way out, or think you have, you'd put on a spurt, darting away faster than rabbits. And you'd abandon your guide without even taking a second look, just like throwing away a worn-out shoe. I understand, I understand it only too well. You've all experienced loving and being loved, possessing and being possessed. I, too, have a right to be in love, to love a woman and to possess a woman, and to be loved and possessed by her. I'm human just like you are, so full of desires and ambitions, I'm what you may call a career-minded man, a man who is competitive yet extremely weak sometimes, and a man who is righteous, compassionate, willing to sacrifice himself and . . . (*He rolls on the ground and wails loudly like a fretting and self-indulgent child.*)

(*The Crowd is stunned. When Man has had enough wailing and is totally exhausted, he settles down and gets up from the floor. He continues his way forward and the Crowd follow silently behind him. A faint light in the dark becomes brighter. A man is seen drinking and playing cards alone under an oil lamp. Man mimes knocking on the door. The Crowd clap their hands three times.*)

MAN: Sorry to bother you.

CARD PLAYER: (*Without lifting his head.*) Come in. Take a seat.

MAN: May I ask —

CARD PLAYER: (*Tosses a card from his hand. Looks up.*) You play cards?

MAN: I've played before.

(*The Crowd try to squeeze in through the door.*)

CARD PLAYER: Come in, come in. Do you all want to play cards? Close the door for me. I hate draughts, they make the light flicker, which is bad for a card player's eyes. Alright, let's form a circle, I'll be the banker here. All of you will each take a card, and I'll take one myself, only one, just like you. That's only fair. The card in my hand will be the trump, there's got to be a trump, right? And it's better if I choose the trump card instead of you, it's more convenient that way. (*Turns over his card.*) My card is the two of spades. I'm not trying to fly low, luck is all you need when you're playing cards. Now if you pick a spade, any spade, you'd have a higher number than mine and I'd be the loser and you'd be the winner. But if you didn't pick a

spade, you'd lose no matter what, it doesn't matter which card you've picked. You got me?

MAN: What happens if one wins or loses?

CARD PLAYER: The winner gets to drink the wine in this pot.

MAN: And the loser?

CARD PLAYER: There'll be a penalty.

MAN: I have no money, no land, no property, and no wife.

CARD PLAYER: But you do have a face, haven't you?

MAN: I don't get it.

CARD PLAYER: You'll find out soon enough. All of you, anyone who loses will stick a piece of paper on his face for me.

CROWD: That's easy enough.
How big is the paper?
Any paper?
The thing is, have you really got wine in your pot?

CARD PLAYER: Have a taste first.

CROWD: It's good.
What aroma!
Of course, it's the real thing.
Let me have a sip.
It's worth playing for.

CARD PLAYER: In a moment you'll pick your cards. I've shown you my card, all of you have seen it, right? Now you can only look at your own card, no ganging up, that's a no-no.

CROWD: (*Eager to pick their cards.*)
That's nothing, it's fine with me.
We should play our own games.
Don't worry, I won't look even if you let me.
Me, I'm honesty personified.
Integrity comes first, winning and losing second.
Hear! Hear!

(*Those who have picked their cards are silent.*)

CARD PLAYER: (*To the person who picks first.*) Show me your card. You lose.

THIS PERSON: (*Nods.*) What's the penalty?

(*Card Player takes a piece of paper and spits on it. He sticks the paper onto the cheek of This Person, who mutters something. The Crowd watch and laugh. This Person is relieved and laughs with them.*)

CARD PLAYER: (*Turns to another person.*) My friend, how about you? (*That Person shows his card.*) You lose too.

THAT PERSON: Well, give it to me.

CARD PLAYER: Stick it under your chin.

(*That Person takes a piece of paper, spits on it, and sticks it under his chin. He is somewhat embarrassed, but when he sees the Crowd laughing, he is himself again.*)

THIRD PERSON (FEMALE): It's fun.

CARD PLAYER: (*Turns towards her.*) And you? (*She shows her card and hurriedly takes it back.*)

CROWD: Did you win?
You won!

Did you really win?

(*She frets demurely and shakes her head.*)

Why aren't you sticking the paper on your face?

Stick the paper on, stick it on!

Come on, it's the rule, no exceptions allowed.

If you don't stick it on, we won't either.

THIRD PERSON (FEMALE): It's too embarrassing.

CROWD: You think we're not?

That won't do. Stick it on the ear.

Right, on the ear.

Stick it on the nose!

It must be different with everybody, okay? No repetitions.

Everybody gets one.

(*When the Card Player looks at someone, the person will show his card and then obediently stick a piece of paper on his face.*)

CROWD: (*Sticking paper to their own faces.*)

Fair and square.

No doubt about that.

Nobody tells you to lose, but when you do, you've got to take what comes.

Everyone gets a penalty, everyone sticks a paper on their face.

If you haven't got a paper on your face, you'll look odd and out of place, and people will be afraid of you.

(*The strange-looking, papered faces all turn towards Man.*)

CARD PLAYER: My friend, it's your turn now.

MAN: I don't play.

CARD PLAYER: Everybody plays, why don't you?

MAN: I find the whole thing very silly. What's more, I've got to go.

CROWD: Yes, that's right. We should all be going.

Don't go by yourself.

Where are we going?

Right, where exactly are we going?

MAN: In any case I've got to go.

CARD PLAYER: I've got the whole place lit up and I've prepared wine. I went through all these troubles just to play cards with you people. I've never heard of anyone who comes here and leaves without playing. You shouldn't have come in the first place!

CROWD: (*Stopping Man.*) Play!

Come on, be a good sport. Don't be such a party pooper. Just play one game. Just one.

Play once and then we'll go.

MAN: Don't you understand? You're not really playing cards, he's playing a trick on you. You can't win. Your card, yours, and yours are all no trumps, including all the cards still in the deck. The only spade in the deck is in his hand! (*Card Player giggles.*) Let's go! Why waste our time on this guy.

CARD PLAYER: There is no such thing as time here. (*He blows on the oil lamp and the light flickers, and it gradually turns brighter again.*) There is only eternal light.

(*He takes the lamp and shines on everyone from below the chin. The papered faces look like gargoyles.*) I'm a sucker for big crowds. You're scared, aren't you?

MAN: You're a devil.

CARD PLAYER: Why don't you try feeling their arses? They've all got a bristly tail down there! (*He points to the Crowd's bottoms and laughs out loud. Then he pushes a deck of cards in front of Man.*) Take a card! Let everyone see if it's a spade or no trumps? (*Turns over a no trump card and flashes it in front of the Crowd.*) What is it, is it a spade or not?

PERSON A: I can't really tell.

CARD PLAYER: What'd you say?

PERSON B: It looked like —

CARD PLAYER: You must have seen it clearly.

PERSON C: I think I saw a — spade.

CARD PLAYER: That's right! Young lady, what do you think?

OBEDIENT GIRL: Spades.

CARD PLAYER: That a girl. You've made my day. Old Sir, how about you?

PERSON D: Spades, how can it not be spades?

CARD PLAYER: Bless you. (*Suddenly explodes.*) How can we let him bullshit us like this and tell us that they're all no trumps? Huh?

CROWD: It's spades.

Of course it's spades. It can't be anything else.

No mistake about it.

We all saw it.

We're all witnesses!

CARD PLAYER: You heard what they said, didn't you? Why did you lie, why did you insist that a spade is no trump? You're scared, aren't you? Have you ever tried eating rat meat? A bouncing baby rat, its hair not fully grown and its eyes unopened, the little creature still squeaking when you dip it in the sauce and put it in your mouth, ready for a bite? If you had, then you'd be brave enough to tell the truth. My friend, I'm gonna give you one more chance to tell the truth. Tell me, was it spades or a no trump?

MAN: I think . . . that's still a no trump.

CARD PLAYER: You're no fun, you make people miserable. Tell me, people, is this guy bad or what?

CROWD: (*Passing the wine pot and taking sips one after another.*) Bad, bad, bad, bad, bad, bad, bad, bad . . .

CARD PLAYER: (*Takes the wine from them.*) What shall we do with this bad guy?

CROWD: (*Surround Man.*) Throw him out!

Tell him to get out of here!

Trouble-maker.

A real pest.

When he's here, we've got no wine to drink.

Teach him a lesson!

Spank him!

Strip him!

Take off his pants!

(*The Crowd try to take off Man's pants.*)

CARD PLAYER: I'm gonna give you a second chance. Think clearly. Think again!

MAN: (*Holding up his pants.*) But I remember . . . it looked like a . . . no trump.

(*Card Player tucks the wine pot under his arm and turns away. The Crowd pull at Man as if they were teasing a bird.*)

CROWD: Tell him to fly!
  What? What did you say?
  Fly like a bird!
  Men are not birds, why should they learn to fly like birds?
  Wow, it's so fun!
  Fly!
  Lower your head, let your arms fly!

CARD PLAYER: My friend, I refuse to believe that you're a stubborn man.

OBEDIENT GIRL: (*Takes pity on Man.*) You can't turn a spade into a no trump. What's with you? Please, try to take hold of yourself.

MAN: Maybe it was really a spade . . .

OBEDIENT GIRL: Then why did you say it was a no trump?

MAN: I think it should be . . .

OBEDIENT GIRL: But what should be is not necessarily the truth.

CARD PLAYER: You're a loser because you're a pighead. What do you mean by "should be"? It either is or isn't. To hell with "should be."

MAN: But why can't we have "should be"?

CARD PLAYER: (*Irritated.*) Should be my foot! What do you say, should be or not should be?

CROWD: (*Immediately tear at Man.*) We don't want any "should be"!
  We want "yes" or "no"!
  We want spades, not no trumps!
  Down with no trumps!
  Spades are the best!

MAN: It . . . seemed . . . like a . . . sp . . .

CROWD: (*Beating their chests and stamping their feet.*)
  Speak up!
  Louder!
  Can't hear you!
  You've got to clear this up!

MAN: Sp . . . Spa . . . It's spades . . . (*On his knees and collapses.*)

(*The Crowd surround Card Player and perform a strange and awkward dance. They exit.*)

A woman dressed in a white cotton skirt appears. She covers Man with her skirt, bends down and wraps herself in it as well. The two form a white object which disappears with the gradually approaching drumbeat. The drumbeat builds up into a heart-thumping bang. A scrawny monk comes out jumping and beating a gigantic drum with his fingers, palms, elbows, and knees as if he were bewitched. Zen Master enters, dressed in a Buddhist robe of kasaya, his hands clasped together and his

right shoulder bare. Other monks and nuns, all cloaked in grey kasaya, follow Zen Master onto the stage. The Crowd enter in a single file, chanting "Amitabha"° as they come. Their chanting is not in any particular order, each singing their own tune and at their own pitch. The chanting comes and goes, combining with the drumbeat into a cacophony of intersecting sounds. Man is following the Crowd; he also chants and looks around him at times. The Crowd all put down a futon, on which they sit with their legs crossed. Man does the same. The drum stops, followed by the sound of a wooden fish° and an inverted bell.)

ZEN MASTER: (*Recites the Vajraccedika prajna paramita sutra,° his palms clasped together and his right knee on the ground.*) ". . . How much the Bodhisattvas, the great beings, have been helped with the greatest help by the Tathagata, the Fully Enlightened One. It is wonderful, O Lord, how much the Bodhisattvas, the great beings, have been favoured with the highest favour by the Tathagata, the Fully Enlightened One. How then, O Lord, should good men and women stand, who seek the supreme wisdom, how progress, how control their thoughts?"

  After these words the Lord said to the Venerable Subhuti°: "Well said, well said, Subhuti! So it is, Subhuti, so it is as you say! The Tathagata has helped the Bodhisattvas, the great beings with the greatest help, and he has favoured them with the highest favour. Therefore, Subhuti, listen well, and attentively! . . ."

(*Incense smoke permeates the whole place during the chanting. The Crowd close their eyes in meditation, and Man gradually does so as well. Young Girl appears, her eyes slightly closed. She is squatting in a corner and doing her mental exercise, like a baby who is sleeping not too tightly in a transparent egg shell, its hands and feet pressed against the four walls of the shell. Young Man, who has been hiding behind her, gets up slowly and walks towards Young Girl in gingerly steps. The chanting gradually fades. The Crowd disappear.*)

ZEN MASTER: (*The sound of chanting can still be heard faintly.*) "Monks of the Buddha, nuns of the Buddha, I will teach you how they should stand, who seek the supreme wisdom, how progress, how control their thoughts."

  "So be it, O Lord. With a joyful heart we long to hear," the Venerable Subhuti replied to the Lord.

  The Lord said: "Here, Subhuti, someone who seeks supreme wisdom should produce a thought in this manner . . ."

Amitabha: Chant of Pure Land Buddhism, one of three schools of Mahayana ("great vehicle") Buddhism. **wooden fish:** A percussion instrument made of a hollow wooden block, used by Buddhist priests to make rhythm while chanting scriptures. [Fong's note]. **sutra:** A Buddhist religious text that teaches that all appearances are illusions. Also called the Diamond Sutra. **Subhuti:** A disciple of Buddha.

(*Young Man stretches his hand to touch Young Girl's fingers. Surprised, she wakes and withdraws her hand immediately.*)

YOUNG GIRL: Stop it!

YOUNG MAN: Are you doing your mental exercise?

YOUNG GIRL: Yes.

YOUNG MAN: May I ask what kind of exercise are you doing?

YOUNG GIRL: They say it's called Small Circular Heaven.

YOUNG MAN: Is there a Big Circular Heaven as well?

YOUNG GIRL: I don't know.

YOUNG MAN: You're doing something you don't know anything about?

YOUNG GIRL: (*Nervously.*) Stop interrogating me! Just stop it!

YOUNG MAN: (*Mischievously.*) Then perhaps you don't know what's the use of this exercise? (*Grabs her hand.*)

YOUNG GIRL: No, don't, you can't do that —

YOUNG MAN: Why not?

YOUNG GIRL: I'm scared . . .

YOUNG MAN: What's there to be scared of?

YOUNG GIRL: Don't touch me!

YOUNG MAN: What if I do?

YOUNG GIRL: Then I'd feel the pain.

YOUNG MAN: So you don't feel any pain right now?

YOUNG GIRL: (*Painfully.*) I can't say for sure . . .

YOUNG MAN: (*Grabs her hand by force.*) Then for once I'll let you feel the pain!

YOUNG GIRL: (*Begging him and trying to struggle free.*) Oh no, don't . . .

(*Father enters carrying an umbrella. The chanting Zen Master and the meditating Crowd have all disappeared. Only Man is left sitting on the futon with his eyes closed.*)

YOUNG MAN: Father!

FATHER: Don't get into trouble. Come home with me, now!

(*Father drags Young Man along.*)

(*Young Girl disappears.*)

YOUNG MAN: (*Turns back to look. Nonchalantly.*) Why? It's not raining.

FATHER: I tell you it will.

YOUNG MAN: But it's not raining now.

FATHER: It'll be too late if it does.

YOUNG MAN: What if it doesn't.

FATHER: It's going to rain sooner or later! Look, what do you think I've brought my umbrella for?

YOUNG MAN: You've brought it because you have nothing else to do.

FATHER: I've been carrying an umbrella all my life!

YOUNG MAN: You've brought it upon yourself.

FATHER: How dare you talk to your father like that?

YOUNG MAN: Fine, I won't say anything then.

FATHER: Get away from me! Go as far as you possibly can! Don't even bother coming back to see me. I don't have a son like you! (*Exits angrily.*)

(*Young Man is bewildered. Man is still sitting on the futon meditating. The sound of chanting approaches, but there is no sign of Zen Master.*)

CHANTING SOUND: The Buddha said: Here, Subhuti, someone who seeks supreme wisdom should produce a thought in this manner: "As many beings as there are in the universe of beings, comprehended under the term 'beings' — egg-born, born from a womb, moisture-born, or miraculously born; with or without form; with perception, without perception, — as far as any conceivable form of beings is conceived: all these I must lead to Nirvana, into that Realm of Nirvana which leaves nothing behind. . . ."

(*Young Man turns and finds a wall of people behind him. He tries unsuccessfully to find a way to get over it. Old Lady comes out from a crack in the "wall."*)

OLD LADY: Young man, do you want to go over there?

YOUNG MAN: I just want to take a look.

OLD LADY: Look, look. Everybody wants to take a look. Do you have any money?

YOUNG MAN: (*He searches all his pockets and finally takes out a coin.*) Here.

OLD LADY: (*Laughs out loud.*) You want to take care of me with this? Don't you have anything valuable on you at all? Something your mother gave you, for example?

YOUNG MAN: (*Suddenly understands.*) I've got this fountain pen, it has a gold nib, my mother gave it to me for my birthday. (*Takes the pen out and hands it over to her.*)

OLD LADY: (*Takes the pen and inspects it carefully.*) Hmm, this is quite nice. (*Stuffs the pen into her waist bag and steps aside to reveal a crack in the "wall."*) Now you can go ahead.

YOUNG MAN: (*Hesitating.*) I'm afraid my mother might find out . . .

OLD LADY: Will she beat you?

YOUNG MAN: I . . . I can't say . . .

OLD LADY: You'll just have to lie to her, tell her that you've lost it. Don't you know how to lie?

YOUNG MAN: Mother wouldn't allow it.

OLD LADY: That's why you're still such a kid. I'm telling you, there's no adult who doesn't lie, and you know, without lying there'd be no more happy days. All right, just go right through.

(*Crawling, Young Man goes through the crack of the wall of people. When he looks up he sees Young Girl sobbing quietly on the other side, her hands covering her face. He tries to get up, but two thugs approach and take turns beating him up. Young Girl and the sound of chanting disappear at the same time. Only Man is left sitting on the futon and meditating with his eyes closed.*)

PLASTER SELLER: Dogskin Plasters! Dogskin Plasters! Thirteen generations in the family. Give me internal wounds, external wounds, fractures, strains and contusions, give me rabies, heart-attacks, infant convulsions, geriatric strokes, lovesick young men and women, unspeakable depravity and the possessed, stick one on and you'll be as good as new. The first don't work, the second will. . . . Dogskin Plasters! Dogskin Plasters! Taken junky home remedy? Swallowed the wrong drug? No problem! Infertile women, impotent men, sinners and delinquents? Sure thing! Oh yes, and the stutterers, the crooked mouthed, jealous women, avenging men, fathers who love not the mothers, sons who listen not to their old men, pock-marked faces, tinea feet, one plaster cures all. The first don't work, the second will. Satisfaction guaranteed or your money gladly refunded. . . . Dogskin Plasters! Come and get the miracle Dogskin Plasters! Don't miss this golden opportunity! Your chance in a life time!

(*Young man, on the outside of the Crowd's circle, finally manages to get up from his feet. Mad Woman enters.*)

MAD WOMAN: (*Approaching Young Man.*) They say I'm a whore, but they didn't say anything when they sneaked into my bed to sleep with me. They say I'm bad as if they haven't been bad before, as if they haven't had fun with a woman's body before!

(*Young Man retreats and hides himself from her. The Crowd turn to face them.*)

CROWD: Here comes the mad woman.
  The mad woman's here!
  The mad woman's here!
MAD WOMAN: You're mad!
CROWD: Look, look at her.
  She's talking crazy again.
MAD WOMAN: You're talking crazy.

(*The Crowd happily break out in laughter.*)

PLASTER SELLER: (*At the same time.*) If you've got money, give me money, if you don't, stay and watch the show! Dogskin Plasters for sale! (*Throws a bundle of plasters on the ground.*) Big sacrifice! Everything must go! Pay what you will. Cheap! Cheap! Cheap! . . . Pooh! You stinking whore! (*Puts away plasters and exits.*)
MAD WOMAN: You're cheap! (*The Crowd laugh at her again.*) What are you laughing at? Go laugh at yourselves! What things you wouldn't do to get into a woman's pants! You all look like you're human, but actually you're all dogs, dogs, dirty dogs.
MEN IN CROWD: (*To women in the Crowd.*) Stop her wagging tongue. Take her away.
MAD WOMAN: Why? You're scared because I'll tell on you, right? You're hiding something, aren't you? Right, keep away from me, as far away as you can. I know exactly what's going on in those shitty little heads of yours. (*Snickers.*)
MEN IN CROWD: Take her away! Take her away!

(*Women in the Crowd come forward to drag Mad Woman away.*)

MAD WOMAN: You're afraid too, aren't you? You're afraid I'll say that all of your husbands, every single one of them, have slept with me? Afraid because you'll become like me, dumped by your men after they've gotten their rocks off? Afraid your husbands will know you've screwed other men? Afraid people will find out you'd lost your cherry before you got married?
CROWD: Gag her!
  With horse shit!
  With bull shit!
  Shut her big mouth!
MAD WOMAN: (*Grappling with Women in the Crowd.*) Haven't you got off with a man before? You're like me, you can't take your hands off your men after they've screwed you . . .

(*The Crowd move forward to tie up Mad Woman with ropes and gag her mouth. Crying and wailing, she becomes hysterical, but is finally dragged away by the Crowd. Young Man watches in astonishment and leaves with the Crowd. Man, who has been sitting and meditating on the futon, also disappears at the same time. Immediately afterwards, he returns from the other side with his Shadow. Shadow is dressed in black and has on black headgear which covers his face. Man and Shadow do not look at each other. They talk only to themselves, but their steps and movements are synchronized.*)

MAN: A seed falls on to the soil —
SHADOW: A child is born onto the world —
MAN: A gust of wind blows through the forest —
SHADOW: A horse gallops on the plateau —
MAN: A grain of sand falls into the eye —
SHADOW: An eye is crying tears —
MAN: The tears fall on the parched desert —
SHADOW: Like entering a bustling marketplace —
MAN: People squashing people, but their eyes can't be seen —
SHADOW: Seeing dead fish one by one —
MAN: That's a lonely city —
SHADOW: Pop singers are yelling and screaming to exhaustion —
MAN: Only the stars can hear the wind chimes ringing —
SHADOW: It is not our hearts that are ringing —
MAN: It's the electric guitars picking your nerves —
SHADOW: You jump three times, nine times, eight times, seven times and you're out of breath —
MAN: Just because you're no hero —
SHADOW: More like a popular and low-minded farce —
MAN: An out-of-tune trumpet blows, blows, blows, blows and blows —
SHADOW: The conductor has to be right —
MAN: Everyone says he's 180% painful —
SHADOW: Only one minute's happiness —
MAN: It's not the time for drinking beer —
SHADOW: Chicago Nuremberg —
MAN: Once there was a war —
SHADOW: Only sparrows were killed —

MAN: Soldiers didn't fight, they only stood on guard —

SHADOW: And those standing on guard got to wear medals —

MAN: Who is the person speaking to me?

SHADOW: It is your shadow, your thoughts spoken out loud —

MAN: You're always following me —

SHADOW: When you have lost your self —

MAN: You'll come and remind me and double my trouble?

SHADOW: What are you looking for so desperately?

MAN: Now that you've reminded me! I've definitely lost something, can you tell me where to look for it?

SHADOW: (*Sarcastically.*) You probably do not know what you are looking for?

MAN: It appears to be . . . isn't everyone looking for it?

(*The Crowd enter. They form a circle and bend down to look for something in the circle, like children at play.*)

SHADOW: It would not hurt to ask them what you are looking for. (*Takes the chance to leave and disappear.*)

MAN: Excuse me, are you looking for —

PERSON A: A needle, they say you can lead a camel through the eye of this needle.

MAN: (*To another person.*) Excuse me, can you tell me what you're looking for?

PERSON B: Looking for a place where I can sit comfortably and securely. Once I'm there, I won't leave the seat ever again. (*Whispering.*) I have haemorrhoids, I can't sit on any wooden bench.

MAN: And, what are you looking for?

PERSON C: (*Stuttering.*) I . . . I . . . I am . . . looking for a . . . a . . . mouth . . . which can . . . s . . . s . . . peak . . . for me. I . . . I . . . have to s . . . s . . . speak a lot . . . of . . . of . . . words ev . . . every . . . every day.

MAN: And you, young man?

PERSON D: I'm looking for a rice bowl! You have everything, but I don't even have a rice bowl!

MAN: Of course, I know, I know it's very important to have a rice bowl. Go for it. Keep looking. (*To another person.*) Excuse me, I didn't do it on purpose. (*Removes his foot.*) What are you looking for?

PERSON E: I'm looking for a pair of shoes that fits. I don't know why my shoes pinch. I want to know —

MAN: I'm also looking for —

PERSON E: Do your shoes pinch too?

MAN: My shoes don't pinch, but I don't know where my feet should be going.

PERSON E: You just have to follow other people's footsteps.

MAN: Are you also looking for other people's footsteps?

PERSON F: (*Laughing playfully.*) I'm looking for a hole I can sneak through without anyone noticing me. And then I'll come out on the other side swaggering.

MAN: How about you, my friend? You don't look like the sneaky type.

PERSON G: You're right.

MAN: Can you tell me what are you looking for?

PERSON G: Looking for my childhood dream.

MAN: It must be a very beautiful dream. (*To another*) And you? Are you looking for a dream too?

PERSON H: No, I'm looking for a sentence.

MAN: Are you writing a poem?

PERSON H: Everybody can write poetry, just like everybody knows how to make love.

MAN: Then you're —

PERSON H: Thinking! Everyone's got a mind, but not everyone can think.

MAN: You're right. What you're looking for must be an epigram.

PERSON H: I'm not sure if it's an epigram. The problem is, if I didn't find this sentence my thoughts would be cut off, and thoughts which have been cut off are like a cut-off kite, you'll never be able to retrieve it again. Without a sentence you just can't think, because thinking is like a chain, each ring is linked to the next one. You understand?

MAN: Young lady, how about you? What are you looking for?

YOUNG LADY: Take a guess.

MAN: It must be something to do with love.

YOUNG LADY: You're so right! I'm waiting for a pair of eyes, tender, profound, and burning with passion —

(*He avoids the young lady, but he bumps into another person.*)

PERSON I: Don't step on my toes!

MAN: Oh, I beg your pardon.

PERSON I: Never seen anyone who walks like you.

MAN: Neither have I. I'm going that way.

PERSON I: Everyone's looking here, what are you going to do over there?

MAN: There is nothing I want here.

PERSON I: What are you looking for?

MAN: (*Troubled.*) I don't know what I'm looking for.

PERSON I: Everybody, look! The man is a weirdo, he doesn't know what he's looking for!

PERSON J: He must have found it already.

(*The Crowd surround Man.*)

MAN: No, I haven't. Really I haven't. (*Walks away.*)

STABLE KEEPER: (*Coming out from the Crowd.*) Where are you going?

MAN: Over there.

STABLE KEEPER: You haven't found anything yet, right? How come you're going over there?

MAN: I'm not going to look for anything any more. I just want to go over there.

STABLE KEEPER: We're all looking here, but you insist on going there.

EVERYBODY: Shall we let him?

CROWD: No!
  Absolutely not!
  He can't go.
  Just wait until we've all found it, then you can go.

MAN: Let me explain.

CROWD: There's no need, we already know.

We've been looking, you've been looking, everybody's been looking, but no one's found anything. Why do you want to go there now?

It won't do.

When we say no, we mean no.

If you quit looking and we quit looking, then you can go there. But everybody's still looking right now and you insist on going, of course we won't let you. How can you?

If we're going to quit, we should all quit. So if we're going to look, we should all be looking, right?

MAN: I don't have anything to do with you.

STABLE KEEPER: My friend, we're treating you like a friend, don't you see? (*To the Crowd.*) Try again to make him understand. Okay, let's start from the beginning.

CROWD: (*One after the other.*) That's to say, yes, no, everybody looks or nobody looks, even if nobody looks or everybody looks, not looking is not the same as not wanting to look, the question is whether we can look and find it —

MAN: What if I don't want to look?

CROWD: You don't want to look, sure, okay, we can't force you to if you don't want to, if you don't want to look, it doesn't mean nobody should look, and if everybody looks then you can't be not looking, nobody looks you don't look no more, everybody wants to look and you don't look, everybody looks for everybody, you don't look for everybody, you don't look and everybody looks, you look or not you don't look everybody looks you look or not nobody looks you look everybody looks —

MAN: (*Can't control himself.*) I'm going my way! I'm not bothering anybody, and nobody's going to bother me, okay?

STABLE KEEPER: I'll give it to you straight: No way! You've found it but we haven't, it just won't wash!

MAN: But I haven't found anything!

STABLE KEEPER: Then keep looking.

MAN: I'm not looking here any more. I — want — to — go — there.

STABLE KEEPER: Don't you know the rules here? We've told you over and over again, why can't you admit that you're wrong and change your ways?

CROWD: What's happening?

What's happening?

Son of a bitch, he's looking for trouble!

STABLE KEEPER: Wait, this is no good, it's so uncivilized. If he doesn't want to repent, let him. We won't make it difficult for him. Just tell him to crawl through here. (*Pointing to his crotch.*) What do you say?

CROWD: (*Bursting into laughter.*) Wonderful!

(*Silence. Surprisingly, Man crawls through Stable Keeper's crotch. The Crowd is shocked and disappears. Man picks up a key while he is crawling. Shadow enters immediately.*)

SHADOW: A key? That is correct. You must have been looking for a key like this one. Yes, yes, the key is what you have been looking for!

(*Man is on his knees, inspecting the key in his hand. He then stands up and walks to centre stage and uses the key to open an imaginary door. He pulls hard on the big and heavy door and manages to open it. He walks inside. Shadow exits. Silence everywhere.*)

MAN: (*Inquiring.*) Hello — (*Echo: Hello — hello — hello — hello . . . hello . . .*) Ah — (*Ah — Ah — Ah — Ah . . . Ah . . . Ah . . . The echoes seem to make the room more hollow and deserted.*) Anybody home? (*Echo: Anybody home? Anybody home? Anybody home? Anybody home? Anybody home? . . .*) Nobody has ever set foot in here before for sure . . . (*Echolike murmuring: so lonely, so lonely, so lonely, so lonely.*)

(*Man looks around and finds that some objects are hidden under the cover of a piece of black cloth. He carefully pulls out a bare woman's arm from under the black cloth.*)

MAN: (*Shocked.*) O —

(*Simulated female voice sighs, echoing: O . . . O . . . O . . . O . . . O . . . The voice seems to make him more enthusiastic. He begins to clear out what lies beneath the black cloth more diligently, and he pulls out a woman's leg.*)

MAN: (*Excited.*) Ah!

(*There is another series of simulated female voices calling urgently: Ah! Ah! Ah! Ah! Ah! Ah! . . . Finally Man discovers a female mannequin hidden under the black cloth. He lifts the mannequin out and lays it down carefully. He admires it and then starts to move its hands and feet. And with increasing passion and energy, he fiddles with its shoulders, arms and the whole body, bringing it to a rather awkward forward leaning position. He turns the head around, and groping and touching, he manages to create various facial expressions. Every change he makes on the mannequin is accompanied by a simulated female voice akin to mechanical sound. The different expressions on the mannequin's face, including joy, pain, bewilderment, and peaceful staring, are also accompanied by music expressing the same sentiments in a simulated female voice. He puts the head straight so that it is staring at a not-so-distant place in front. . . . Then he stops and tries to figure out what to do next.*

He becomes more excited now. One by one he pulls out more male and female mannequins and arranges them into a kind of pattern. After thinking for a while, he decides to put a piece of headgear on the first model. He keeps rearranging the pattern, his feet dancing to the beat of the increasingly loud music. The pattern changes according to one or more rules of his own making and at a speed which can only be observed in an instant. Gradually he finds himself hemmed in by the pattern and becomes one of its composite parts, and he crawls busily back and forth in between the mannequins. The process is a sustained and intense consumption of will power and strength.

Now the mannequins form a gigantic collective pattern using the first mannequin as its centre. As they move about, the pattern keeps changing slowly yet unstoppably. Man runs around in a hurry, jumping, moving, and rolling among his own creations. Highly excited, he calls out and responds to the mannequins in all kinds of non-language shouts and screams. This is a process of constant discovery, renewal, rediscovery, and further renewal. But gradually the objects no longer obey his commands and the sounds they make begin to overwhelm his shouts. As he is totally drawn in among them, he gradually becomes weaker, and it becomes difficult for him to get out. After a long while he finally manages to crawl out like a worm, utterly exhausted. His creations roaringly gyrate past him and slowly disappear.)

(Shadow appears again, keeping a certain distance from him.)

SHADOW: (*Narrates in a serene voice.*) Then winter came along. It was snowing hard that day, and you walked barefoot on the ice to experience the bone-chilling cold. You seemed to feel that you were Jesus Christ, that you were the loneliest person, the only person who was suffering in this world. You felt that you were pervaded by the spirit of self-sacrifice, even though you were not sure for whom you would be sacrificing yourself. Yes, you did leave your footprints in the snow, and in the distance was a hazy, misty forest.

(Totally worn out, Man walks into a simulated forest made of human bodies.)

SHADOW: (*Following him.*) You walked into the dark and shady forest. The trees, every one of them, had already shed their leaves, stretching out their shaven branches like naked women. Somberly they stood in the snow, lonely and speechless. You could not help wanting to tell them about your sorrows and torments. You recalled the time of your youth, when you waited for her on the roadside for a long long time. That day it was also snowing, and you were determined to tell her that you loved her. You want to say that at the time you were still young and innocent, but now you have sinned deeply, and you will never be able to go back to those early days any more. You have long lost your faith in people, your heart has grown old and it will not love again. Your only wish is to go walking among the trees in the forest until you are totally exhausted. Then you will collapse somewhere, hoping never to be found.

(Finally Man leans against a tree to take a breath. Shadow comes closer and closer, observing him.)

SHADOW: In fact it is nothing more than a kind of self-pity. You are unwilling to end like this, you are so vain. (*Exits.*)

(The tree Man has been leaning against bends down its trunk and speaks in a human-like voice: "Oh, here you are." Then all the trees in the forest move slowly towards him like monsters. They reveal their human forms and become the Crowd, all dressed in mourning clothes.)

CROWD: (*They speak and move, but they are unfeeling and expressionless.*)
We've been looking all over for you.
Come on, take us to the pub to have a drink.
You're our host, how come you're here in the snow?
You're a giant, and we have to look up to see you.
You're famous, so famous that we're scared of you.
We admire you, but we don't want to idolize you.
You're no more than a crook, only we don't have your tricks.
Get up and come with us.
You should donate money to our charities for children, you must know that children need money the most.
You went through the forest alone, a forest even the devil fears to tread, you're number one.
You're a pathfinder, you've walked out a road nobody wants to walk on, you've led people astray.
You're lucky, not everyone is as lucky as you are.
It's not that you're more talented than the others, it's only that they don't get the chance to show what they've got.
You're the tops, let's us give him a pat on the behind!

(The Crowd laugh coldly and sinisterly. Some start to pull at him and grapple with him.)

CROWD: (*Suddenly.*) Here he comes!
Talk of the devil.
Make way.

(Shadow backs in as the Crowd step aside to make way for him.)

MAN: (*Weakly.*) Who are you?
SHADOW: Your heart.

(As the Crowd watch the drooping, blind, and deaf heart slouching past them, Shadow quietly drags Man away. The Crowd slowly follow behind the heart which is extremely old and actually invisible. All exit.)

(One by one the Actors enter from the other side.)

ACTORS: We set off before dawn. The morning dew was thick, and in the dark we heard the cows breathing while they were chewing grass on a small hill nearby. In the distance, the river bend was enveloped in a shade of deep blue light brighter than the sky.
He told us a fable.
I dreamed that there's a piece of ivory in my stomach, it scared me to death!
Have you thought of becoming a bird?

Why a bird? I'm happy with the way I am, and he says he loves me.
Faulkner.
I like "Roses for Emily."°
I called you up many times.
Do you know how to read palms?
No need for any explanations, you don't have to explain any more!
This kitten is so cute.
I think I've seen you somewhere.
I have a sweet tooth, and I'm also a sucker for sour milk.

"Roses . . . Emily": Reference to William Faulkner's (1897–1962) short story "A Rose for Emily."

Your hair looks so nice, is it real?

(*The sound of a baby crying.*)

Sweetie, oh, sorry, I forgot to change your diapers!

(*The sound of a car engine starting.*)

How are you going to get back?
It's so bad, what kind of stupid play is this anyway?
Are you doing anything tomorrow? Shall we have dinner together?

(*Sounds of a baby crying, a car engine starting and running, bicycle bells and the trickle of running water from a tap, and in the distance, the siren of an ambulance.*)

The End

August Wilson

August Wilson was born in Pittsburgh in 1945, the son of a white father who never lived with his family and a black mother who had come from North Carolina to a Pittsburgh slum, where she worked to keep her family together. Wilson's early childhood was spent in an environment very similar to that of his play *Fences,* and Troy Maxson seems to be patterned somewhat on Wilson's stepfather.

Wilson's writing is rooted to a large extent in music, specifically the blues. As a poet, writing over several years, Wilson found himself interested in the speech patterns and rhythms that were familiar to him from black neighborhoods, but the value of those patterns became clearer to him when he grew older and moved from Pittsburgh to Minneapolis. From a distance, he was able to see more clearly what had attracted him to the language and to begin to use the language more fully in his work.

In the 1960s and 1970s Wilson became involved in the civil rights movement and began to describe himself as a black nationalist, a term he has said he feels comfortable with. He began writing plays in the 1960s in Pittsburgh and then took a job in St. Paul writing dramatic skits for the Science Museum of Minnesota. He founded the Playwrights Center in Minneapolis and wrote a play, *Jitney,* about a gypsy cab station, which was first produced in 1982 and which was staged in New York in April 2000 in a revised version at the Second Stage Theater. *Fullerton Street,* about Pittsburgh, was another play written in this early period. Wilson's first commercial success, *Ma Rainey's Black Bottom,* eventually premiered at the Yale Repertory Theatre in 1984 and then went to Broadway, where it enjoyed 275 performances and won the New York Drama Critics' Circle Award.

Ma Rainey's Black Bottom was the first of a planned sequence of ten plays based on the black American experience. As Wilson said, "I think the black Americans have the most dramatic story of all mankind to tell." The concept of such a vast project echoes Eugene O'Neill's projected group of eleven plays based on the Irish-American experience. (Unfortunately, O'Neill destroyed all but *A Touch of the Poet, More Stately Mansions,* and part of *Calms of Capricorn* in his series.) Wilson's project, however, is ongoing and intense and so far has produced some of the most successful plays in the recent American theater.

Ma Rainey is about the legendary black blues singer who preceded Bessie Smith and Billie Holiday. The play is about the ways in which she was exploited by white managers and recording executives and the way in which she knowingly dealt with her exploitation. In the cast of the play are several black musicians in the backup band. Levee, the trumpet player, has a dream of leading his own band and establishing himself as an important jazz musician. But he is haunted by memories of seeing his mother raped by a gang of white men when he was a boy. He wants to "improve" the session he's playing by making the old jazz tune "Black Bottom" swing in the new jazz style, but Ma Rainey keeps him in tow and demands that they play the tune in the old way. Levee finally cracks under the pressure, and the play ends painfully. In a February 2003 revival at the Royale Theatre in New York, Whoopi Goldberg played Ma Rainey.

Fences opened at the Yale Repertory Theatre in 1985 and in New York in early 1987, where it won the Pulitzer Prize as well as the New York Drama Critics' Circle Award. This long-running success established Wilson firmly as an important writer. *Joe Turner's Come and Gone* opened at the Yale Repertory Theatre in late 1986 and moved to New York in early 1988, where it too has been hailed as an important play, winning its author another New York Drama Critics' Circle Award. Set in a rooming house in Pittsburgh in 1911, *Joe Turner* is a study of the children of former slaves. They have come north to find work, and some of them have been found by the legendary bounty hunter Joe Turner. As a study of a people in transition, the play is a quiet masterpiece. It incorporates a number of important African traditions, especially religious rituals of healing as performed by Bynum, the "bone man," a seer and a medicine man. In this play and others, Wilson makes a special effort to highlight the elements of African heritage that white society strips away from blacks.

The next play in Wilson's projected series, *The Piano Lesson,* which premiered at the Yale Repertory Theatre in 1987, also portrays the complexity of black attitudes toward the past and black heritage. The piano represents two kinds of culture: the white culture that produced the musical instrument and the black culture, in the form of Papa Boy Willie, who carved into it images from black Africa. The central question in the play is whether Boy Willie should sell the piano and use the money for a down payment on land and therefore on the future. Or should he follow his sister Berniece's advice and keep it because it is too precious to sell? The conflict is deep and the play ultimately focuses on a profound moment of spiritual exorcism. How one exorcises the past — how one lives with it or without it — is a central theme in Wilson's work.

His next play, *Two Trains Running,* is set in 1969, in the decade that saw the Vietnam War, racial and political riots, and the assassinations of John and Robert Kennedy, Malcolm X, and Martin Luther King Jr. The play premiered at the Yale Repertory Theatre in 1990 and opened on Broadway at the Walter Kerr Theater in April 1992, directed by Lloyd Richards. The characters remain in Memphis Lee's diner — scheduled for demolition — throughout the play. The two trains in the title are heading to Africa and to the old South, but the characters are immobile and seem indifferent to both of them. Wilson moved away from the careful structure of the well-made play in this work and produced an open-ended conclusion, leaving the racial and philosophical tensions unresolved.

Seven Guitars (1996) takes place in a backyard in Pittsburgh in 1948 on the eve of the landmark boxing match between Joe Louis and "Jersey" Joe Walcott. The play focuses on a blues musician, Floyd Barton, who hopes to regain his lost love, put his band back together, and move to Chicago to make his second recording. *Seven Guitars* emphasizes the blues, especially in its long first act, with Barton's friends gathered in his backyard to mourn his death and the loss of his talent. People did much the same when Joe Louis, the "Brown Bomber," lost his fight, a loss that punctuated the end of an era. The second act focuses on Hedley, a West Indian boarder, whom critic Margo Jefferson describes as "half madman and half prophet." Hedley recites a litany of racial injustices and gives voice to a torrent of wrongs. Hedley's voice is a counterpoint to the blues; he gives us a powerful range of responses to the condition of being black in Pittsburgh in the late 1940s.

Wilson's most recent play in the series is set in 1985. *King Hedley II* (1999) picks up some of the characters of *Seven Guitars,* including the character Hedley, and develops further the experience of living in the Hill District of Pittsburgh. Wilson describes *King Hedley II* as focusing on "the breakdown of the black community's extended-family structure." The sequence of the plays detailing the African American experience for each decade of the twentieth century needs only the first and last decades' coverage. In development now are the two final plays in the series: *Gem of the Ocean,* scheduled for Broadway in the fall of 2004, and *Radio Golf,* premiering at the Yale Repertory Theatre in 2005. Wilson now lives primarily in Seattle, but he returned to his hometown for the December 1999 premiere of *King Hedley II,* the first play produced in the new O'Reilly Theater by the Pittsburgh Public Theater. It moved in March 2000 to the Seattle Repertory Theater.

FENCES

Fences (1985), like most of August Wilson's recent plays, was directed by Lloyd Richards, who also directed the first production of Lorraine Hansberry's *A Raisin in the Sun.* Richards was, until 1991, the dean of the School of Drama at Yale University and ran the Yale Repertory Theatre, where he directed the first several of the plays Wilson has written in his projected ten-play cycle about black American life.

Fences presents a slice of life in a black tenement in Pittsburgh in the 1950s. Its main character, Troy Maxson, is a garbage collector who has taken great pride in keeping his family together and providing for them. When the play opens, he and his friend Bono are talking about Troy's challenge to the company and the union about blacks' ability to do the same "easy" work that whites do. Troy's rebellion and frustration set the tone of the entire play: he is looking for his rights, and, at age fifty-three, he has missed many opportunities to get what he deserves.

Troy's struggle for fairness becomes virtually mythic as he describes his wrestling with death during a bout with pneumonia in 1941. He describes a three-day struggle in which he eventually overcame his foe. Troy — a good baseball player who was relegated to the Negro leagues — sees death as nothing but a fastball, and he could always deal with a fastball. Both Bono and Troy's wife, Rose, show an intense admiration for him as he describes his ordeal.

The father-son relationship that begins to take a central role in the drama is complicated by strong feelings of pride and independence on both sides. Troy's son Cory wants to play football, and Troy wants him to work on the fence he's mending. Cory's youthful enthusiasm probably echoes Troy's own youthful innocence, but Troy resents it in Cory, seeing it as partly responsible for his own predicament. Cory cannot see his father's point of view and feels that he is exempt from the kind of prejudice his father suffered.

The agony of the father-son relationship, their misperceptions of each other, persist through the play. Rose's capacity to cope with the deepest of Troy's anxieties — his fear of death — is one of her most important achievements in the play. At the end of the play Rose demands that Cory give Troy the respect he deserves, although Cory's anger and inexperience make it all but impossible for him to see his father as anything other than an oppressor. Cory feels that he must say no to his father once, but Rose will not let him deny his father. When the play ends with Gabriel's fantastic ritualistic dance, the audience feels a sense of closure, of spiritual finish.

Fences in Performance

Like many of America's best plays, *Fences* began in a workshop production. Its first version was performed in a reading without full production — no sets, no full lighting, actors working "on book" instead of fully memorizing the play — in the summer of 1983 at the Eugene O'Neill Center in Waterford, Connecticut. This early version was four hours long.

Once Wilson found the focus of his play, it premiered in 1985 at the Yale Repertory Theatre in New Haven. Lloyd Richards, then dean of Yale Drama School, directed this as well as the New York production. The New York opening on March 27, 1987, starred Mary Alice, James Earl Jones, and Ray Aranha, the cast from New Haven. Frank Rich in the *New York Times* praised James Earl Jones, congratulating him on finding "what may be the best role of his career." Rich also said, "*Fences* leaves no doubt that Mr. Wilson is a major writer, combining a poet's ear for vernacular with a robust sense of humor (political and sexual), a sure instinct for crackling dramatic incident and a passionate commitment to a great subject."

From the first, *Fences* was recognized as an important play. It won four Tony Awards: best play, best actor, best supporting actress, and best director. It also won the New York Drama Critics' Circle Award for best play. Before the New York production, it had traveled to Chicago, San Francisco, and Seattle. It has been performed numerous times since. Wilson is working on the script for a film version of the play.

August Wilson (b. 1945)

FENCES

Characters

TROY MAXSON
JIM BONO, *Troy's friend*
ROSE, *Troy's wife*
LYONS, *Troy's oldest son by previous marriage*
GABRIEL, *Troy's brother*
CORY, *Troy and Rose's son*
RAYNELL, *Troy's daughter*

Setting: *The setting is the yard which fronts the only entrance to the Maxson household, an ancient two-story brick house set back off a small alley in a big-city neighborhood. The entrance to the house is gained by two or three steps leading to a wooden porch badly in need of paint.*

A relatively recent addition to the house and running its full width, the porch lacks congruence. It is a sturdy porch with a flat roof. One or two chairs of dubious value sit at one end where the kitchen window opens onto the porch. An old-fashioned icebox stands silent guard at the opposite end.

The yard is a small dirt yard, partially fenced, except for the last scene, with a wooden sawhorse, a pile of lumber, and other fence-building equipment set off to the side. Opposite is a tree from which hangs a ball made of rags. A baseball bat leans against the tree. Two oil drums serve as garbage receptacles and sit near the house at right to complete the setting.

The Play: *Near the turn of the century, the destitute of Europe sprang on the city with tenacious claws and an honest and solid dream. The city devoured them. They swelled its belly until it burst into a thousand furnaces and sewing machines, a thousand butcher shops and bakers' ovens, a thousand churches and hospitals and funeral parlors and money-lenders. The city grew. It nourished itself and offered each man a partnership limited only by his talent, his guile, and his willingness and capacity for hard work. For the immigrants of Europe, a dream dared and won true.*

The descendants of African slaves were offered no such welcome or participation. They came from places called the Carolinas and the Virginias, Georgia, Alabama, Mississippi, and Tennessee. They came strong, eager, searching. The city rejected them and they fled and settled along the riverbanks and under bridges in shallow, ramshackle houses made of sticks and tarpaper. They collected rags and wood. They sold the use of their muscles and their bodies. They cleaned houses and washed clothes, they shined shoes, and in quiet desperation and vengeful pride, they stole, and lived in pursuit of their own dream. That they could breathe free, finally, and stand to meet life with the force of dignity and whatever eloquence the heart could call upon.

By 1957, the hard-won victories of the European immigrants had solidified the industrial might of America. War had been confronted and won with new energies that used loyalty and patriotism as its fuel. Life was rich, full, and flourishing. The Milwaukee Braves won the World Series, and the hot winds of change that would make the sixties a turbulent, racing, dangerous, and provocative decade had not yet begun to blow full.

ACT I • Scene I

(It is 1957. Troy and Bono enter the yard, engaged in conversation. Troy is fifty-three years old, a large man with thick, heavy hands; it is this largeness that he strives to fill out and make an accommodation with. Together with his blackness, his largeness informs his sensibilities and the choices he has made in his life.)

(Of the two men, Bono is obviously the follower. His commitment to their friendship of thirty-odd years is rooted in his admiration of Troy's honesty, capacity for hard work, and his strength, which Bono seeks to emulate.)

(It is Friday night, payday, and the one night of the week the two men engage in a ritual of talk and drink. Troy is usually the most talkative and at times he can be crude and almost vulgar, though he is capable of rising to profound heights of expression. The men carry lunch buckets and wear or carry burlap aprons and are dressed in clothes suitable to their jobs as garbage collectors.)

BONO: Troy, you ought to stop that lying!

TROY: I ain't lying! The nigger had a watermelon this big.

(He indicates with his hands.)

Talking about . . . "What watermelon, Mr. Rand?" I liked to fell out! "What watermelon, Mr. Rand?" . . . And it sitting there big as life.

BONO: What did Mr. Rand say?

TROY: Ain't said nothing. Figure if the nigger too dumb to know he carrying a watermelon, he wasn't gonna get much sense out of him. Trying to hide that great big old watermelon under his coat. Afraid to let the white man see him carry it home.

BONO: I'm like you . . . I ain't got no time for them kind of people.

TROY: Now what he look like getting mad cause he see the man from the union talking to Mr. Rand?

BONO: He come to me talking about . . . "Maxson gonna get us fired." I told him to get away from me with that. He walked away from me calling you a troublemaker. What Mr. Rand say?

TROY: Ain't said nothing. He told me to go down the Commissioner's office next Friday. They called me down there to see them.

BONO: Well, as long as you got your complaint filed, they can't fire you. That's what one of them white fellows tell me.

TROY: I ain't worried about them firing me. They gonna fire me cause I asked a question? That's all I did. I went to Mr. Rand and asked him, "Why? Why you got the white mens driving and the colored lifting?" Told him "what's the matter, don't I count? You think only white fellows got sense enough to drive a truck. That ain't no paper job! Hell, anybody can drive a truck. How come you got all whites driving and the colored lifting?" He told me "take it to the union." Well, hell, that's what I done! Now they wanna come up with this pack of lies.

BONO: I told Brownie if the man come and ask him any questions . . . just tell the truth! It ain't nothing but something they done trumped up on you cause you filed a complaint on them.

TROY: Brownie don't understand nothing. All I want them to do is change the job description. Give everybody a chance to drive the truck. Brownie can't see that. He ain't got that much sense.

BONO: How you figure he be making out with that gal be up at Taylors' all the time . . . that Alberta gal?

TROY: Same as you and me. Getting just as much as we is. Which is to say nothing.

BONO: It is, huh? I figure you doing a little better than me . . . and I ain't saying what I'm doing.

TROY: Aw, nigger, look here . . . I know you. If you had got anywhere near that gal, twenty minutes later you be looking to tell somebody. And the first one you gonna tell . . . that you gonna want to brag to . . . is gonna be me.

BONO: I ain't saying that. I see where you be eyeing her.

TROY: I eye all the women. I don't miss nothing. Don't never let nobody tell you Troy Maxson don't eye the women.

BONO: You been doing more than eyeing her. You done bought her a drink or two.

TROY: Hell yeah, I bought her a drink! What that mean? I bought you one, too. What that mean cause I buy her a drink? I'm just being polite.

BONO: It's all right to buy her one drink. That's what you call being polite. But when you wanna be buying two or three . . . that's what you call eyeing her.

TROY: Look here, as long as you known me . . . you ever known me to chase after women?

BONO: Hell yeah! Long as I done known you. You forgetting I knew you when.

TROY: Naw, I'm talking about since I been married to Rose?

BONO: Oh, not since you been married to Rose. Now, that's the truth, there. I can say that.

TROY: All right then! Case closed.

BONO: I see you be walking up around Alberta's house. You supposed to be at Taylors' and you be walking up around there.

TROY: What you watching where I'm walking for? I ain't watching after you.

BONO: I seen you walking around there more than once.

TROY: Hell, you liable to see me walking anywhere! That don't mean nothing cause you see me walking around there.

BONO: Where she come from anyway? She just kinda showed up one day.

TROY: Tallahassee. You can look at her and tell she one of them Florida gals. They got some big healthy women down there. Grow them right up out the ground. Got a little bit of Indian in her. Most of them niggers down in Florida got some Indian in them.

BONO: I don't know about that Indian part. But she damn sure big and healthy. Woman wear some big stockings. Got them great big old legs and hips as wide as the Mississippi River.

TROY: Legs don't mean nothing. You don't do nothing but push them out of the way. But them hips cushion the ride!

BONO: Troy, you ain't got no sense.

TROY: It's the truth! Like you riding on Goodyears!

(*Rose enters from the house. She is ten years younger than Troy, her devotion to him stems from her recognition of the possibilities of her life without him: a succession of abusive men and their babies, a life of partying and running the streets, the Church, or aloneness with its attendant pain and frustration. She recognizes Troy's spirit as a fine and illuminating one and she either ignores or forgives his faults, only some of which she recognizes. Though she doesn't drink, her presence is an integral part of the Friday night rituals. She alternates between the porch and the kitchen, where supper preparations are under way.*)

ROSE: What you all out here getting into?

TROY: What you worried about what we getting into for? This is men talk, woman.

ROSE: What I care what you all talking about? Bono, you gonna stay for supper?

BONO: No, I thank you, Rose. But Lucille say she cooking up a pot of pigfeet.

TROY: Pigfeet! Hell, I'm going home with you! Might even stay the night if you got some pigfeet. You got something in there to top them pigfeet, Rose?

ROSE: I'm cooking up some chicken. I got some chicken and collard greens.

TROY: Well, go on back in the house and let me and

Bono finish what we was talking about. This is men talk. I got some talk for you later. You know what kind of talk I mean. You go on and powder it up.

ROSE: Troy Maxson, don't you start that now!

TROY (*puts his arm around her*): Aw, woman . . . come here. Look here, Bono . . . when I met this woman . . . I got out that place, say, "Hitch up my pony, saddle up my mare . . . there's a woman out there for me somewhere. I looked here. Looked there. Saw Rose and latched on to her." I latched on to her and told her — I'm gonna tell you the truth — I told her, "Baby, I don't wanna marry, I just wanna be your man." Rose told me . . . tell him what you told me, Rose.

ROSE: I told him if he wasn't the marrying kind, then move out the way so the marrying kind could find me.

TROY: That's what she told me. "Nigger, you in my way. You blocking the view! Move out the way so I can find me a husband." I thought it over two or three days. Come back —

ROSE: Ain't no two or three days nothing. You was back the same night.

TROY: Come back, told her . . . "Okay, baby . . . but I'm gonna buy me a banty rooster and put him out there in the backyard . . . and when he see a stranger come, he'll flap his wings and crow . . ." Look here, Bono, I could watch the front door by myself . . . it was that back door I was worried about.

ROSE: Troy, you ought not talk like that. Troy ain't doing nothing but telling a lie.

TROY: Only thing is . . . when we first got married . . . forget the rooster . . . we ain't had no yard!

BONO: I hear you tell it. Me and Lucille was staying down there on Logan Street. Had two rooms with the outhouse in the back. I ain't mind the outhouse none. But when that goddamn wind blow through there in the winter . . . that's what I'm talking about! To this day I wonder why in the hell I ever stayed down there for six long years. But see, I didn't know I could do no better. I thought only white folks had inside toilets and things.

ROSE: There's a lot of people don't know they can do no better than they doing now. That's just something you got to learn. A lot of folks still shop at Bella's.

TROY: Ain't nothing wrong with shopping at Bella's. She got fresh food.

ROSE: I ain't said nothing about if she got fresh food. I'm talking about what she charge. She charge ten cents more than the A&P.

TROY: The A&P ain't never done nothing for me. I spends my money where I'm treated right. I go down to Bella, say, "I need a loaf of bread, I'll pay you Friday." She give it to me. What sense that make when I got money to go and spend it somewhere else and ignore the person who done right by me? That ain't in the Bible.

ROSE: We ain't talking about what's in the Bible. What sense it make to shop there when she overcharge?

TROY: You shop where you want to. I'll do my shopping where the people been good to me.

ROSE: Well, I don't think it's right for her to overcharge. That's all I was saying.

BONO: Look here . . . I got to get on. Lucille going be raising all kind of hell.

TROY: Where you going, nigger? We ain't finished this pint. Come here, finish this pint.

BONO: Well, hell, I am . . . if you ever turn the bottle loose.

TROY (*hands him the bottle*): The only thing I say about the A&P is I'm glad Cory got that job down there. Help him take care of his school clothes and things. Gabe done moved out and things getting tight around here. He got that job. . . . He can start to look out for himself.

ROSE: Cory done went and got recruited by a college football team.

TROY: I told that boy about that football stuff. The white man ain't gonna let him get nowhere with that football. I told him when he first come to me with it. Now you come telling me he done went and got more tied up in it. He ought to go and get recruited in how to fix cars or something where he can make a living.

ROSE: He ain't talking about making no living playing football. It's just something the boys in school do. They gonna send a recruiter by to talk to you. He'll tell you he ain't talking about making no living playing football. It's a honor to be recruited.

TROY: It ain't gonna get him nowhere. Bono'll tell you that.

BONO: If he be like you in the sports . . . he's gonna be all right. Ain't but two men ever played baseball as good as you. That's Babe Ruth and Josh Gibson.° Them's the only two men ever hit more home runs than you.

TROY: What it ever get me? Ain't got a pot to piss in or a window to throw it out of.

ROSE: Times have changed since you was playing baseball, Troy. That was before the war. Times have changed a lot since then.

TROY: How in hell they done changed?

ROSE: They got lots of colored boys playing ball now. Baseball and football.

BONO: You right about that, Rose. Times have changed, Troy. You just come along too early.

TROY: There ought not never have been no time called too early! Now you take that fellow . . . what's that fellow they had playing right field for the Yankees back then? You know who I'm talking about, Bono. Used to play right field for the Yankees.

ROSE: Selkirk?

TROY: Selkirk! That's it! Man batting .269, understand? .269. What kind of sense that make? I was hitting .432 with thirty-seven home runs! Man batting .269 and playing right field for the Yankees! I saw Josh Gibson's daughter yesterday. She walking around

Josh Gibson: (1911–1947), powerful black baseball player known in the 1930s as the Babe Ruth of the Negro leagues.

with raggedy shoes on her feet. Now I bet you Selkirk's daughter ain't walking around with raggedy shoes on her feet! I bet you that!

ROSE: They got a lot of colored baseball players now. Jackie Robinson was the first. Folks had to wait for Jackie Robinson.

TROY: I done seen a hundred niggers play baseball better than Jackie Robinson. Hell, I know some teams Jackie Robinson couldn't even make! What you talking about Jackie Robinson. Jackie Robinson wasn't nobody. I'm talking about if you could play ball then they ought to have let you play. Don't care what color you were. Come telling me I come along too early. If you could play . . . then they ought to have let you play.

(*Troy takes a long drink from the bottle.*)

ROSE: You gonna drink yourself to death. You don't need to be drinking like that.

TROY: Death ain't nothing. I done seen him. Done wrassled with him. You can't tell me nothing about death. Death ain't nothing but a fastball on the outside corner. And you know what I'll do to that! Lookee here, Bono . . . am I lying? You get one of them fastballs, about waist high, over the outside corner of the plate where you can get the meat of the bat on it . . . and good god! You can kiss it goodbye. Now, am I lying?

BONO: Naw, you telling the truth there. I seen you do it.

TROY: If I'm lying . . . that 450 feet worth of lying!

(*Pause.*)

That's all death is to me. A fastball on the outside corner.

ROSE: I don't know why you want to get on talking about death.

TROY: Ain't nothing wrong with talking about death. That's part of life. Everybody gonna die. You gonna die, I'm gonna die. Bono's gonna die. Hell, we all gonna die.

ROSE: But you ain't got to talk about it. I don't like to talk about it.

TROY: You the one brought it up. Me and Bono was talking about baseball . . . you tell me I'm gonna drink myself to death. Ain't that right, Bono? You know I don't drink this but one night out of the week. That's Friday night. I'm gonna drink just enough to where I can handle it. Then I cuts it loose. I leave it alone. So don't you worry about me drinking myself to death. 'Cause I ain't worried about Death. I done seen him. I done wrestled with him.

Look here, Bono . . . I looked up one day and Death was marching straight at me. Like Soldiers on Parade! The Army of Death was marching straight at me. The middle of July, 1941. It got real cold just like it be winter. It seem like Death himself reached out and touched me on the shoulder. He touch me just like I touch you. I got cold as ice and Death standing there grinning at me.

ROSE: Troy, why don't you hush that talk.

TROY: I say . . . What you want, Mr. Death? You be wanting me? You done brought your army to be getting me? I looked him dead in the eye. I wasn't fearing nothing. I was ready to tangle. Just like I'm ready to tangle now. The Bible say be ever vigilant. That's why I don't get but so drunk. I got to keep watch.

ROSE: Troy was right down there in Mercy Hospital. You remember he had pneumonia? Laying there with a fever talking plumb out of his head.

TROY: Death standing there staring at me . . . carrying that sickle in his hand. Finally he say, "You want bound over for another year?" See, just like that . . . "You want bound over for another year?" I told him, "Bound over hell! Let's settle this now!"

It seem like he kinda fell back when I said that, and all the cold went out of me. I reached down and grabbed that sickle and threw it just as far as I could throw it . . . and me and him commenced to wrestling.

We wrestled for three days and three nights. I can't say where I found the strength from. Every time it seemed like he was gonna get the best of me, I'd reach way down deep inside myself and find the strength to do him one better.

ROSE: Every time Troy tell that story he find different ways to tell it. Different things to make up about it.

TROY: I ain't making up nothing. I'm telling you the facts of what happened. I wrestled with Death for three days and three nights and I'm standing here to tell you about it.

(*Pause.*)

All right. At the end of the third night we done weakened each other to where we can't hardly move. Death stood up, throwed on his robe . . . had him a white robe with a hood on it. He throwed on that robe and went off to look for his sickle. Say, "I'll be back." Just like that. "I'll be back." I told him, say, "Yeah, but . . . you gonna have to find me!" I wasn't no fool. I wan't going looking for him. Death ain't nothing to play with. And I know he's gonna get me. I know I got to join his army . . . his camp followers. But as long as I keep my strength and see him coming . . . as long as I keep up my vigilance . . . he's gonna have to fight to get me. I ain't going easy.

BONO: Well, look here, since you got to keep up your vigilance . . . let me have the bottle.

TROY: Aw hell, I shouldn't have told you that part. I should have left out that part.

ROSE: Troy be talking that stuff and half the time don't even know what he be talking about.

TROY: Bono know me better than that.

BONO: That's right. I know you. I know you got some Uncle Remus° in your blood. You got more stories than the devil got sinners.

Uncle Remus: Black storyteller who recounts traditional African American tales in the book by Joel Chandler Harris.

TROY: Aw hell, I done seen him too! Done talked with the devil.

ROSE: Troy, don't nobody wanna be hearing all that stuff.

(*Lyons enters the yard from the street. Thirty-four years old, Troy's son by a previous marriage, he sports a neatly trimmed goatee, sport coat, white shirt, tieless and buttoned at the collar. Though he fancies himself a musician, he is more caught up in the rituals and "idea" of being a musician than in the actual practice of the music. He has come to borrow money from Troy, and while he knows he will be successful, he is uncertain as to what extent his lifestyle will be held up to scrutiny and ridicule.*)

LYONS: Hey, Pop.

TROY: What you come "Hey, Popping" me for?

LYONS: How you doing, Rose?

(*He kisses her.*)

Mr. Bono. How you doing?

BONO: Hey, Lyons . . . how you been?

TROY: He must have been doing all right. I ain't seen him around here last week.

ROSE: Troy, leave your boy alone. He come by to see you and you wanna start all that nonsense.

TROY: I ain't bothering Lyons.

(*Offers him the bottle.*)

Here . . . get you a drink. We got an understanding. I know why he come by to see me and he know I know.

LYONS: Come on, Pop . . . I just stopped by to say hi . . . see how you was doing.

TROY: You ain't stopped by yesterday.

ROSE: You gonna stay for supper, Lyons? I got some chicken cooking in the oven.

LYONS: No, Rose . . . thanks. I was just in the neighborhood and thought I'd stop by for a minute.

TROY: You was in the neighborhood all right, nigger. You telling the truth there. You was in the neighborhood cause it's my payday.

LYONS: Well, hell, since you mentioned it . . . let me have ten dollars.

TROY: I'll be damned! I'll die and go to hell and play blackjack with the devil before I give you ten dollars.

BONO: That's what I wanna know about . . . that devil you done seen.

LYONS: What . . . Pop done seen the devil? You too much, Pops.

TROY: Yeah, I done seen him. Talked to him too!

ROSE: You ain't seen no devil. I done told you that man ain't had nothing to do with the devil. Anything you can't understand, you want to call it the devil.

TROY: Look here, Bono . . . I went down to see Hertzberger about some furniture. Got three rooms for two-ninety-eight. That what it say on the radio. "Three rooms . . . two-ninety-eight." Even made up a little song about it. Go down there . . . man tell me

I can't get no credit. I'm working every day and can't get no credit. What to do? I got an empty house with some raggedy furniture in it. Cory ain't got no bed. He's sleeping on a pile of rags on the floor. Working every day and can't get no credit. Come back here — Rose'll tell you — madder than hell. Sit down . . . try to figure what I'm gonna do. Come a knock on the door. Ain't been living here but three days. Who know I'm here? Open the door . . . devil standing there bigger than life. White fellow . . . got on good clothes and everything. Standing there with a clipboard in his hand. I ain't had to say nothing. First words come out of his mouth was . . . "I understand you need some furniture and can't get no credit." I liked to fell over. He say, "I'll give you all the credit you want, but you got to pay the interest on it." I told him, "Give me three rooms worth and charge whatever you want." Next day a truck pulled up here and two men unloaded them three rooms. Man what drove the truck give me a book. Say send ten dollars, first of every month to the address in the book and everything will be all right. Say if I miss a payment the devil was coming back and it'll be hell to pay. That was fifteen years ago. To this day . . . the first of the month I send my ten dollars, Rose'll tell you.

ROSE: Troy lying.

TROY: I ain't never seen that man since. Now you tell me who else that could have been but the devil? I ain't sold my soul or nothing like that, you understand. Naw, I wouldn't have truck with the devil about nothing like that. I got my furniture and pays my ten dollars the first of the month just like clockwork.

BONO: How long you say you been paying this ten dollars a month?

TROY: Fifteen years!

BONO: Hell, ain't you finished paying for it yet? How much the man done charged you.

TROY: Ah hell, I done paid for it. I done paid for it ten times over! The fact is I'm scared to stop paying it.

ROSE: Troy lying. We got that furniture from Mr. Glickman. He ain't paying no ten dollars a month to nobody.

TROY: Aw hell, woman. Bono know I ain't that big a fool.

LYONS: I was just getting ready to say . . . I know where there's a bridge for sale.

TROY: Look here, I'll tell you this . . . it don't matter to me if he was the devil. It don't matter if the devil give credit. Somebody has got to give it.

ROSE: It ought to matter. You going around talking about having truck with the devil . . . God's the one you gonna have to answer to. He's the one gonna be at the Judgment.

LYONS: Yeah, well, look here, Pop . . . let me have that ten dollars. I'll give it back to you. Bonnie got a job working at the hospital.

TROY: What I tell you, Bono? The only time I see this nigger is when he wants something. That's the only time I see him.

LYONS: Come on, Pop, Mr. Bono don't want to hear all that. Let me have the ten dollars. I told you Bonnie working.

TROY: What that mean to me? "Bonnie working." I don't care if she working. Go ask her for the ten dollars if she working. Talking about "Bonnie working." Why ain't you working?

LYONS: Aw, Pop, you know I can't find no decent job. Where am I gonna get a job at? You know I can't get no job.

TROY: I told you I know some people down there. I can get you on the rubbish if you want to work. I told you that the last time you came by here asking me for something.

LYONS: Naw, Pop . . . thanks. That ain't for me. I don't wanna be carrying nobody's rubbish. I don't wanna be punching nobody's time clock.

TROY: What's the matter, you too good to carry people's rubbish? Where you think that ten dollars you talking about come from? I'm just supposed to haul people's rubbish and give my money to you cause you too lazy to work. You too lazy to work and wanna know why you ain't got what I got.

ROSE: What hospital Bonnie working at? Mercy?

LYONS: She's down at Passavant working in the laundry.

TROY: I ain't got nothing as it is. I give you that ten dollars and I got to eat beans the rest of the week. Naw . . . you ain't getting no ten dollars here.

LYONS: You ain't got to be eating no beans. I don't know why you wanna say that.

TROY: I ain't got no extra money. Gabe done moved over to Miss Pearl's paying her the rent and things done got tight around here. I can't afford to be giving you every payday.

LYONS: I ain't asked you to give me nothing. I asked you to loan me ten dollars. I know you got ten dollars.

TROY: Yeah, I got it. You know why I got it? Cause I don't throw my money away out there in the streets. You living the fast life . . . wanna be a musician . . . running around in them clubs and things . . . then, you learn to take care of yourself. You ain't gonna find me going and asking nobody for nothing. I done spent too many years without.

LYONS: You and me is two different people, Pop.

TROY: I done learned my mistake and learned to do what's right by it. You still trying to get something for nothing. Life don't owe you nothing. You owe it to yourself. Ask Bono. He'll tell you I'm right.

LYONS: You got your way of dealing with the world . . . I got mine. The only thing that matters to me is the music.

TROY: Yeah, I can see that! It don't matter how you gonna eat . . . where your next dollar is coming from. You telling the truth there.

LYONS: I know I got to eat. But I got to live too. I need something that gonna help me to get out of the bed in the morning. Make me feel like I belong in the world. I don't bother nobody. I just stay with my music cause that's the only way I can find to live in the world. Otherwise there ain't no telling what I might do. Now I don't come criticizing you and how you live. I just come by to ask you for ten dollars. I don't wanna hear all that about how I live.

TROY: Boy, your mamma did a hell of a job raising you.

LYONS: You can't change me, Pop. I'm thirty-four years old. If you wanted to change me, you should have been there when I was growing up. I come by to see you . . . ask for ten dollars and you want to talk about how I was raised. You don't know nothing about how I was raised.

ROSE: Let the boy have ten dollars, Troy.

TROY (to Lyons): What the hell you looking at me for? I ain't got no ten dollars. You know what I do with my money.

(To Rose.)

Give him ten dollars if you want him to have it.

ROSE: I will. Just as soon as you turn it loose.

TROY (handing Rose the money): There it is. Seventy-six dollars and forty-two cents. You see this, Bono? Now, I ain't gonna get but six of that back.

ROSE: You ought to stop telling that lie. Here, Lyons. (She hands him the money.)

LYONS: Thanks, Rose. Look . . . I got to run . . . I'll see you later.

TROY: Wait a minute. You gonna say, "thanks, Rose" and ain't gonna look to see where she got that ten dollars from? See how they do me, Bono?

LYONS: I know she got it from you, Pop. Thanks. I'll give it back to you.

TROY: There he go telling another lie. Time I see that ten dollars . . . he'll be owing me thirty more.

LYONS: See you, Mr. Bono.

BONO: Take care, Lyons!

LYONS: Thanks, Pop. I'll see you again.

(Lyons exits the yard.)

TROY: I don't know why he don't go and get him a decent job and take care of that woman he got.

BONO: He'll be all right, Troy. The boy is still young.

TROY: The *boy* is thirty-four years old.

ROSE: Let's not get off into all that.

BONO: Look here . . . I got to be going. I got to be getting on. Lucille gonna be waiting.

TROY (puts his arm around Rose): See this woman, Bono? I love this woman. I love this woman so much it hurts. I love her so much . . . I done run out of ways of loving her. So I got to go back to basics. Don't you come by my house Monday morning talking about time to go to work . . . 'cause I'm still gonna be stroking!

ROSE: Troy! Stop it now!

BONO: I ain't paying him no mind, Rose. That ain't nothing but gin-talk. Go on, Troy. I'll see you Monday.

TROY: Don't you come by my house, nigger! I done told you what I'm gonna be doing.

(The lights go down to black.)

Scene II

(*The lights come up on Rose hanging up clothes. She hums and sings softly to herself. It is the following morning.*)

ROSE (*sings*): Jesus, be a fence all around me every day
  Jesus, I want you to protect me as I travel on my way.
  Jesus, be a fence all around me every day.

(*Troy enters from the house.*)

  Jesus, I want you to protect me
  As I travel on my way.
  (*To Troy.*) 'Morning. You ready for breakfast? I can fix it soon as I finish hanging up these clothes.

TROY: I got the coffee on. That'll be all right. I'll just drink some of that this morning.

ROSE: That 651 hit yesterday. That's the second time this month. Miss Pearl hit for a dollar . . . seem like those that need the least always get lucky. Poor folks can't get nothing.

TROY: Them numbers don't know nobody. I don't know why you fool with them. You and Lyons both.

ROSE: It's something to do.

TROY: You ain't doing nothing but throwing your money away.

ROSE: Troy, you know I don't play foolishly. I just play a nickel here and a nickel there.

TROY: That's two nickels you done thrown away.

ROSE: Now I hit sometimes . . . that makes up for it. It always comes in handy when I do hit. I don't hear you complaining then.

TROY: I ain't complaining now. I just say it's foolish. Trying to guess out of six hundred ways which way the number gonna come. If I had all the money niggers, these Negroes, throw away on numbers for one week — just one week — I'd be a rich man.

ROSE: Well, you wishing and calling it foolish ain't gonna stop folks from playing numbers. That's one thing for sure. Besides . . . some good things come from playing numbers. Look where Pope done bought him that restaurant off of numbers.

TROY: I can't stand niggers like that. Man ain't had two dimes to rub together. He walking around with his shoes all run over bumming money for cigarettes. All right. Got lucky there and hit the numbers . . .

ROSE: Troy, I know all about it.

TROY: Had good sense, I'll say that for him. He ain't throwed his money away. I seen niggers hit the numbers and go through two thousand dollars in four days. Man bought him that restaurant down there . . . fixed it up real nice . . . and then didn't want nobody to come in it! A Negro go in there and can't get no kind of service. I seen a white fellow come in there and order a bowl of stew. Pope picked all the meat out the pot for him. Man ain't had nothing but a bowl of meat! Negro come behind him and ain't got nothing but the potatoes and carrots. Talk-

ing about what numbers do for people, you picked a wrong example. Ain't done nothing but make a worser fool out of him than he was before.

ROSE: Troy, you ought to stop worrying about what happened at work yesterday.

TROY: I ain't worried. Just told me to be down there at the Commissioner's office on Friday. Everybody think they gonna fire me. I ain't worried about them firing me. You ain't got to worry about that.

(*Pause.*)

  Where's Cory? Cory in the house? (*Calls.*) Cory?

ROSE: He gone out.

TROY: Out, huh? He gone out 'cause he know I want him to help me with this fence. I know how he is. That boy scared of work.

(*Gabriel enters. He comes halfway down the alley and, hearing Troy's voice, stops.*)

TROY (*continues*): He ain't done a lick of work in his life.

ROSE: He had to go to football practice. Coach wanted them to get in a little extra practice before the season start.

TROY: I got his practice . . . running out of here before he get his chores done.

ROSE: Troy, what is wrong with you this morning? Don't nothing set right with you. Go on back in there and go to bed . . . get up on the other side.

TROY: Why something got to be wrong with me? I ain't said nothing wrong with me.

ROSE: You got something to say about everything. First it's the numbers . . . then it's the way the man runs his restaurant . . . then you done got on Cory. What's it gonna be next? Take a look up there and see if the weather suits you . . . or is it gonna be how you gonna put up the fence with the clothes hanging in the yard.

TROY: You hit the nail on the head then.

ROSE: I know you like I know the back of my hand. Go on in there and get you some coffee . . . see if that straighten you up. 'Cause you ain't right this morning.

(*Troy starts into the house and sees Gabriel. Gabriel starts singing. Troy's brother, he is seven years younger than Troy. Injured in World War II, he has a metal plate in his head. He carries an old trumpet tied around his waist and believes with every fiber of his being that he is the Archangel Gabriel. He carries a chipped basket with an assortment of discarded fruits and vegetables he has picked up in the strip district and which he attempts to sell.*)

GABRIEL (*singing*): Yes, ma'am, I got plums
  You ask me how I sell them
  Oh ten cents apiece
  Three for a quarter
  Come and buy now
  'Cause I'm here today
  And tomorrow I'll be gone

(*Gabriel enters.*)

Hey, Rose!

ROSE: How you doing, Gabe?

GABRIEL: There's Troy . . . Hey, Troy!

TROY: Hey, Gabe.

(*Exit into kitchen.*)

ROSE (*to Gabriel*): What you got there?

GABRIEL: You know what I got, Rose. I got fruits and vegetables.

ROSE (*looking in basket*): Where's all these plums you talking about?

GABRIEL: I ain't got no plums today, Rose. I was just singing that. Have some tomorrow. Put me in a big order for plums. Have enough plums tomorrow for St. Peter and everybody.

(*Troy reenters from kitchen, crosses to steps.*)
(*To Rose.*)

Troy's mad at me.

TROY: I ain't mad at you. What I got to be mad at you about? You ain't done nothing to me.

GABRIEL: I just moved over to Miss Pearl's to keep out from in your way. I ain't mean no harm by it.

TROY: Who said anything about that? I ain't said anything about that.

GABRIEL: You ain't mad at me, is you?

TROY: Naw . . . I ain't mad at you, Gabe. If I was mad at you I'd tell you about it.

GABRIEL: Got me two rooms. In the basement. Got my own door too. Wanna see my key?

(*He holds up a key.*)

That's my own key! Ain't nobody else got a key like that. That's my key! My two rooms!

TROY: Well, that's good, Gabe. You got your own key . . . that's good.

ROSE: You hungry, Gabe? I was just fixing to cook Troy his breakfast.

GABRIEL: I'll take some biscuits. You got some biscuits? Did you know when I was in heaven . . . every morning me and St. Peter would sit down by the gate and eat some big fat biscuits? Oh, yeah! We had us a good time. We'd sit there and eat us them biscuits and then St. Peter would go off to sleep and tell me to wake him up when it's time to open the gates for the judgment.

ROSE: Well, come on . . . I'll make up a batch of biscuits.

(*Rose exits into the house.*)

GABRIEL: Troy . . . St. Peter got your name in the book. I seen it. It say . . . Troy Maxson. I say . . . I know him! He got the same name like what I got. That's my brother!

TROY: How many times you gonna tell me that, Gabe?

GABRIEL: Ain't got my name in the book. Don't have to have my name. I done died and went to heaven. He got your name though. One morning St. Peter was looking at his book . . . marking it up for the judgment . . . and he let me see your name. Got it in there under M. Got Rose's name . . . I ain't seen it like I seen yours . . . but I know it's in there. He got a great big book. Got everybody's name what was ever been born. That's what he told me. But I seen your name. Seen it with my own eyes.

TROY: Go on in the house there. Rose going to fix you something to eat.

GABRIEL: Oh, I ain't hungry. I done had breakfast with Aunt Jemimah. She come by and cooked me up a whole mess of flapjacks. Remember how we used to eat them flapjacks?

TROY: Go on in the house and get you something to eat now.

GABRIEL: I got to go sell my plums. I done sold some tomatoes. Got me two quarters. Wanna see?

(*He shows Troy his quarters.*)

I'm gonna save them and buy me a new horn so St. Peter can hear me when it's time to open the gates.

(*Gabriel stops suddenly. Listens.*)

Hear that? That's the hellhounds. I got to chase them out of here. Go on get out of here! Get out!

(*Gabriel exits singing.*)

Better get ready for the judgment
Better get ready for the judgment
My Lord is coming down

(*Rose enters from the house.*)

TROY: He gone off somewhere.

GABRIEL (*offstage*): Better get ready for the judgment
Better get ready for the judgment morning
Better get ready for the judgment
My God is coming down

ROSE: He ain't eating right. Miss Pearl say she can't get him to eat nothing.

TROY: What you want me to do about it, Rose? I done did everything I can for the man. I can't make him get well. Man got half his head blown away . . . what you expect?

ROSE: Seem like something ought to be done to help him.

TROY: Man don't bother nobody. He just mixed up from that metal plate he got in his head. Ain't no sense for him to go back in the hospital.

ROSE: Least he be eating right. They can help him take care of himself.

TROY: Don't nobody wanna be locked up, Rose. What you wanna lock him up for? Man go over there and fight the war . . . messin' around with them Japs, get half his head blown off . . . and they give him a lousy three thousand dollars. And I had to swoop down on that.

ROSE: Is you fixing to go into that again?

TROY: That's the only way I got a roof over my head . . . cause of that metal plate.

ROSE: Ain't no sense you blaming yourself for nothing. Gabe wasn't in no condition to manage that money. You done what was right by him. Can't nobody say you ain't done what was right by him. Look how long you took care of him . . . till he wanted to have his own place and moved over there with Miss Pearl.

TROY: That ain't what I'm saying, woman! I'm just stating the facts. If my brother didn't have that metal plate in his head . . . I wouldn't have a pot to piss in or a window to throw it out of. And I'm fifty-three years old. Now see if you can understand that!

(*Troy gets up from the porch and starts to exit the yard.*)

ROSE: Where you going off to? You been running out of here every Saturday for weeks. I thought you was gonna work on this fence.

TROY: I'm gonna walk down to Taylors'. Listen to the ball game. I'll be back in a bit. I'll work on it when I get back.

(*He exits the yard. The lights go to black.*)

Scene III

(*The lights come up on the yard. It is four hours later. Rose is taking down the clothes from the line. Cory enters carrying his football equipment.*)

ROSE: Your daddy like to had a fit with you running out of here this morning without doing your chores.

CORY: I told you I had to go to practice.

ROSE: He say you were supposed to help him with this fence.

CORY: He been saying that the last four or five Saturdays, and then he don't never do nothing but go down to Taylors'. Did you tell him about the recruiter?

ROSE: Yeah, I told him.

CORY: What he say?

ROSE: He ain't said nothing too much. You get in there and get started on your chores before he gets back. Go on and scrub down them steps before he gets back here hollering and carrying on.

CORY: I'm hungry. What you got to eat, Mama?

ROSE: Go on and get started on your chores. I got some meat loaf in there. Go on and make you a sandwich . . . and don't leave no mess in there.

(*Cory exits into the house. Rose continues to take down the clothes. Troy enters the yard and sneaks up and grabs her from behind.*)

Troy! Go on, now. You liked to scared me to death. What was the score of the game? Lucille had me on the phone and I couldn't keep up with it.

TROY: What I care about the game? Come here, woman. (*He tries to kiss her.*)

ROSE: I thought you went down Taylors' to listen to the game. Go on, Troy! You supposed to be putting up this fence.

TROY (*attempting to kiss her again*): I'll put it up when I finish with what is at hand.

ROSE: Go on, Troy. I ain't studying you.

TROY (*chasing after her*): I'm studying you . . . fixing to do my homework!

ROSE: Troy, you better leave me alone.

TROY: Where's Cory? That boy brought his butt home yet?

ROSE: He's in the house doing his chores.

TROY (*calling*): Cory! Get your butt out here, boy!

(*Rose exits into the house with the laundry. Troy goes over to the pile of wood, picks up a board, and starts sawing. Cory enters from the house.*)

TROY: You just now coming in here from leaving this morning?

CORY: Yeah, I had to go to football practice.

TROY: Yeah, what?

CORY: Yessir.

TROY: I ain't but two seconds off you noway. The garbage sitting in there overflowing . . . you ain't done none of your chores . . . and you come in here talking about "Yeah."

CORY: I was just getting ready to do my chores now, Pop . . .

TROY: Your first chore is to help me with this fence on Saturday. Everything else come after that. Now get that saw and cut them boards.

(*Cory takes the saw and begins cutting the boards. Troy continues working. There is a long pause.*)

CORY: Hey, Pop . . . why don't you buy a TV?

TROY: What I want with a TV? What I want one of them for?

CORY: Everybody got one. Earl, Ba Bra . . . Jesse!

TROY: I ain't asked you who had one. I say what I want with one?

CORY: So you can watch it. They got lots of things on TV. Baseball games and everything. We could watch the World Series.

TROY: Yeah . . . and how much this TV cost?

CORY: I don't know. They got them on sale for around two hundred dollars.

TROY: Two hundred dollars, huh?

CORY: That ain't that much, Pop.

TROY: Naw, it's just two hundred dollars. See that roof you got over your head at night? Let me tell you something about that roof. It's been over ten years since that roof was last tarred. See now . . . the snow come this winter and sit up there on that roof like it is . . . and it's gonna seep inside. It's just gonna be a little bit . . . ain't gonna hardly notice it. Then the next thing you know, it's gonna be leaking all over the house. Then the wood rot from all that water and you gonna need a whole new roof. Now, how much you think it cost to get that roof tarred?

CORY: I don't know.

TROY: Two hundred and sixty-four dollars . . . cash money. While you thinking about a TV, I got to be thinking about the roof . . . and whatever else go wrong around here. Now if you had two hundred dollars, what would you do . . . fix the roof or buy a TV?

CORY: I'd buy a TV. Then when the roof started to leak . . . when it needed fixing . . . I'd fix it.

TROY: Where you gonna get the money from? You done spent it for a TV. You gonna sit up and watch the water run all over your brand new TV.

CORY: Aw, Pop. You got money. I know you do.

TROY: Where I got it at, huh?

CORY: You got it in the bank.

TROY: You wanna see my bankbook? You wanna see that seventy-three dollars and twenty-two cents I got sitting up in there.

CORY: You ain't got to pay for it all at one time. You can put a down payment on it and carry it on home with you.

TROY: Not me. I ain't gonna owe nobody nothing if I can help it. Miss a payment and they come and snatch it right out your house. Then what you got? Now, soon as I get two hundred dollars clear, then I'll buy a TV. Right now, as soon as I get two hundred and sixty-four dollars, I'm gonna have this roof tarred.

CORY: Aw . . . Pop!

TROY: You go on and get you two hundred dollars and buy one if ya want it. I got better things to do with my money.

CORY: I can't get no two hundred dollars. I ain't never seen two hundred dollars.

TROY: I'll tell you what . . . you get you a hundred dollars and I'll put the other hundred with it.

CORY: All right, I'm gonna show you.

TROY: You gonna show me how you can cut them boards right now.

(*Cory begins to cut the boards. There is a long pause.*)

CORY: The Pirates won today. That makes five in a row.

TROY: I ain't thinking about the Pirates. Got an all-white team. Got that boy . . . that Puerto Rican boy . . . Clemente. Don't even half-play him. That boy could be something if they give him a chance. Play him one day and sit him on the bench the next.

CORY: He gets a lot of chances to play.

TROY: I'm talking about playing regular. Playing every day so you can get your timing. That's what I'm talking about.

CORY: They got some white guys on the team that don't play every day. You can't play everybody at the same time.

TROY: If they got a white fellow sitting on the bench . . . you can bet your last dollar he can't play! The colored guy got to be twice as good before he get on the team. That's why I don't want you to get all tied up in them sports. Man on the team and what it get him? They got colored on the team and don't use them. Same as not having them. All them teams the same.

CORY: The Braves got Hank Aaron and Wes Covington. Hank Aaron hit two home runs today. That makes forty-three.

TROY: Hank Aaron ain't nobody. That's what you supposed to do. That's how you supposed to play the game. Ain't nothing to it. It's just a matter of timing . . . getting the right follow-through. Hell, I can hit forty-three home runs right now!

CORY: Not off no major-league pitching, you couldn't.

TROY: We had better pitching in the Negro leagues. I hit seven home runs off of Satchel Paige.° You can't get no better than that!

CORY: Sandy Koufax. He's leading the league in strike-outs.

TROY: I ain't thinking of no Sandy Koufax.

CORY: You got Warren Spahn and Lew Burdette. I bet you couldn't hit no home runs off of Warren Spahn.

TROY: I'm through with it now. You go on and cut them boards.

(*Pause.*)

Your mama tell me you done got recruited by a college football team? Is that right?

CORY: Yeah. Coach Zellman say the recruiter gonna be coming by to talk to you. Get you to sign the permission papers.

Satchel Paige: (1906–1982), legendary black pitcher in the Negro leagues.

TROY: I thought you supposed to be working down there at the A&P. Ain't you suppose to be working down there after school?

CORY: Mr. Stawicki say he gonna hold my job for me until after the football season. Say starting next week I can work weekends.

TROY: I thought we had an understanding about this football stuff? You suppose to keep up with your chores and hold that job down at the A&P. Ain't been around here all day on a Saturday. Ain't none of your chores done . . . and now you telling me you done quit your job.

CORY: I'm gonna be working weekends.

TROY: You damn right you are! And ain't no need for nobody coming around here to talk to me about signing nothing.

CORY: Hey, Pop . . . you can't do that. He's coming all the way from North Carolina.

TROY: I don't care where he coming from. The white man ain't gonna let you get nowhere with that football noway. You go on and get your book-learning so you can work yourself up in that A&P or learn how to fix cars or build houses or something, get you a trade. That way you have something can't nobody take away from you. You go on and learn how to put your hands to some good use. Besides hauling people's garbage.

CORY: I get good grades, Pop. That's why the recruiter wants to talk with you. You got to keep up your grades to get recruited. This way I'll be going to college. I'll get a chance . . .

ABOVE LEFT: Lynn Thigpen and James Earl Jones in the 1987 production of *Fences*. ABOVE: James Earl Jones as Troy Maxson in *Fences*. RIGHT: Jones and Courtney Vance as his son Cory.

TROY: First you gonna get your butt down there to the A&P and get your job back.

CORY: Mr. Stawicki done already hired somebody else 'cause I told him I was playing football.

TROY: You a bigger fool than I thought . . . to let somebody take away your job so you can play some football. Where you gonna get your money to take out your girlfriend and whatnot? What kind of foolishness is that to let somebody take away your job?

CORY: I'm still gonna be working weekends.

TROY: Naw . . . naw. You getting your butt out of here and finding you another job.

CORY: Come on, Pop! I got to practice. I can't work after school and play football too. The team needs me. That's what Coach Zellman say . . .

TROY: I don't care what nobody else say. I'm the boss . . . you understand? I'm the boss around here. I do the only saying what counts.

CORY: Come on, Pop!

TROY: I asked you . . . did you understand?

CORY: Yeah . . .

TROY: What?!

CORY: Yessir.

TROY: You go on down there to that A&P and see if you can get your job back. If you can't do both . . . then you quit the football team. You've got to take the crookeds with the straights.

CORY: Yessir.

(*Pause.*)

Can I ask you a question?

TROY: What the hell you wanna ask me? Mr. Stawicki the one you got the questions for.

CORY: How come you ain't never liked me?

TROY: Liked you? Who the hell say I got to like you? What law is there say I got to like you? Wanna stand up in my face and ask a damn fool-ass question like that. Talking about liking somebody. Come here, boy, when I talk to you.

(*Cory comes over to where Troy is working. He stands slouched over and Troy shoves him on his shoulder.*)

Straighten up, goddammit! I asked you a question . . . what law is there say I got to like you?

CORY: None.

TROY: Well, all right then! Don't you eat every day?

(*Pause.*)

Answer me when I talk to you! Don't you eat every day?

CORY: Yeah.

TROY: Nigger, as long as you in my house, you put that sir on the end of it when you talk to me!

CORY: Yes . . . sir.

TROY: You eat every day.

CORY: Yessir!

TROY: Got a roof over your head.

CORY: Yessir!

TROY: Got clothes on your back.

CORY: Yessir.

TROY: Why you think that is?

CORY: Cause of you.

TROY: Ah, hell I know it's 'cause of me . . . but why do you think that is?

CORY (*hesitant*): Cause you like me.

TROY: Like you? I go out of here every morning . . . bust my butt . . . putting up with them crackers° every day . . . cause I like you? You about the biggest fool I ever saw.

(*Pause.*)

It's my job. It's my responsibility! You understand that? A man got to take care of his family. You live in my house . . . sleep you behind on my bedclothes . . . fill you belly up with my food . . . cause you my son. You my flesh and blood. Not 'cause I like you! Cause it's my duty to take care of you. I owe a responsibility to you! Let's get this straight right here . . . before it go along any further . . . I ain't got to like you. Mr. Rand don't give me my money come payday cause he likes me. He gives me cause he owe me. I done give you everything I had to give you. I gave you your life! Me and your mama worked that out between us. And liking your black ass wasn't part of the bargain. Don't you try and go through life worrying about if somebody like you or not. You best be making sure they doing right by you. You understand what I'm saying, boy?

CORY: Yessir.

TROY: Then get the hell out of my face, and get on down to that A&P.

(*Rose has been standing behind the screen door for much of the scene. She enters as Cory exits.*)

ROSE: Why don't you let the boy go ahead and play football, Troy? Ain't no harm in that. He's just trying to be like you with the sports.

TROY: I don't want him to be like me! I want him to move as far away from my life as he can get. You the only decent thing that ever happened to me. I wish him that. But I don't wish him a thing else from my life. I decided seventeen years ago that boy wasn't getting involved in no sports. Not after what they did to me in the sports.

ROSE: Troy, why don't you admit you was too old to play in the major leagues? For once . . . why don't you admit that?

TROY: What do you mean too old? Don't come telling me I was too old. I just wasn't the right color. Hell, I'm fifty-three years old and can do better than Selkirk's .269 right now!

ROSE: How's was you gonna play ball when you were over forty? Sometimes I can't get no sense out of you.

TROY: I got good sense, woman. I got sense enough not to let my boy get hurt over playing no sports. You

crackers: White people (derogatory).

been mothering that boy too much. Worried about if people like him.

ROSE: Everything that boy do . . . he do for you. He wants you to say "Good job, son." That's all.

TROY: Rose, I ain't got time for that. He's alive. He's healthy. He's got to make his own way. I made mine. Ain't nobody gonna hold his hand when he get out there in that world.

ROSE: Times have changed from when you was young, Troy. People change. The world's changing around you and you can't even see it.

TROY (*slow, methodical*): Woman . . . I do the best I can do. I come in here every Friday. I carry a sack of potatoes and a bucket of lard. You all line up at the door with your hands out. I give you the lint from my pockets. I give you my sweat and my blood. I ain't got no tears. I done spent them. We go upstairs in that room at night . . . and I fall down on you and try to blast a hole into forever. I get up Monday morning . . . find my lunch on the table. I go out. Make my way. Find my strength to carry me through to the next Friday.

(*Pause.*)

That's all I got, Rose. That's all I got to give. I can't give nothing else.

(*Troy exits into the house. The lights go down to black.*)

Scene IV

(*It is Friday. Two weeks later. Cory starts out of the house with his football equipment. The phone rings.*)

CORY (*calling*): I got it!

(*He answers the phone and stands in the screen door talking.*)

Hello? Hey, Jesse. Naw . . . I was just getting ready to leave now.

ROSE (*calling*): Cory!

CORY: I told you, man, them spikes is all tore up. You can use them if you want, but they ain't no good. Earl got some spikes.

ROSE (*calling*): Cory!

CORY (*calling to Rose*): Mam? I'm talking to Jesse.

(*Into phone.*)

When she say that? (*Pause.*) Aw, you lying, man. I'm gonna tell her you said that.

ROSE (*calling*): Cory, don't you go nowhere!

CORY: I got to go to the game, Ma!

(*Into the phone.*)

Yeah, hey, look, I'll talk to you later. Yeah, I'll meet you over Earl's house. Later. Bye, Ma.

(*Cory exits the house and starts out the yard.*)

ROSE: Cory, where you going off to? You got that stuff all pulled out and thrown all over your room.

CORY (*in the yard*): I was looking for my spikes. Jesse wanted to borrow my spikes.

ROSE: Get up there and get that cleaned up before your daddy get back in here.

CORY: I got to go to the game! I'll clean it up *when I get back*.

(*Cory exits.*)

ROSE: That's all he need to do is see that room all messed up.

(*Rose exits into the house. Troy and Bono enter the yard. Troy is dressed in clothes other than his work clothes.*)

BONO: He told him the same thing he told you. Take it to the union.

TROY: Brownie ain't got that much sense. Man wasn't thinking about nothing. He wait until I confront them on it . . . then he wanna come crying seniority.

(*Calls.*)

Hey, Rose!

BONO: I wish I could have seen Mr. Rand's face when he told you.

TROY: He couldn't get it out of his mouth! Liked to bit his tongue! When they called me down there to the Commissioner's office . . . he thought they was gonna fire me. Like everybody else.

BONO: I didn't think they was gonna fire you. I thought they was gonna put you on the warning paper.

TROY: Hey, Rose!

(*To Bono.*)

Yeah, Mr. Rand like to bit his tongue.

(*Troy breaks the seal on the bottle, takes a drink, and hands it to Bono.*)

BONO: I see you run right down to Taylors' and told that Alberta gal.

TROY (*calling*): Hey, Rose! (*To Bono.*) I told everybody. Hey, Rose! I went down there to cash my check.

ROSE (*entering from the house*): Hush all that hollering, man! I know you out here. What they say down there at the Commissioner's office?

TROY: You supposed to come when I call you, woman. Bono'll tell you that.

(*To Bono.*)

Don't Lucille come when you call her?

ROSE: Man, hush your mouth. I ain't no dog . . . talk about "come when you call me."

TROY (*puts his arm around Rose*): You hear this Bono? I had me an old dog used to get uppity like that. You say, "C'mere, Blue!" . . . and he just lay there and look at you. End up getting a stick and chasing him away trying to make him come.

ROSE: I ain't studying you and your dog. I remember you used to sing that old song.

TROY (*he sings*): Hear it ring! Hear it ring! I had a dog his name was Blue.

ROSE: Don't nobody wanna hear you sing that old song.

TROY (*sings*): You know Blue was mighty true.

ROSE: Used to have Cory running around here singing that song.

BONO: Hell, I remember that song myself.

TROY (*sings*): You know Blue was a good old dog.
    Blue treed a possum in a hollow log.
    That was my daddy's song. My daddy made up that song.

ROSE: I don't care who made it up. Don't nobody wanna hear you sing it.

TROY (*makes a song like calling a dog*): Come here, woman.

ROSE: You come in here carrying on, I reckon they ain't fired you. What they say down there at the Commissioner's office?

TROY: Look here, Rose . . . Mr. Rand called me into his office today when I got back from talking to them people down there . . . it come from up top . . . he called me in and told me they was making me a driver.

ROSE: Troy, you kidding!

TROY: No I ain't. Ask Bono.

ROSE: Well, that's great, Troy. Now you don't have to hassle them people no more.

(*Lyons enters from the street.*)

TROY: Aw hell, I wasn't looking to see you today. I thought you was in jail. Got it all over the front page of the *Courier* about them raiding Sefus' place . . . where you be hanging out with all them thugs.

LYONS: Hey, Pop . . . that ain't got nothing to do with me. I don't go down there gambling. I go down there to sit in with the band. I ain't got nothing to do with the gambling part. They got some good music down there.

TROY: They got some rogues . . . is what they got.

LYONS: How you been, Mr. Bono? Hi, Rose.

BONO: I see where you playing down at the Crawford Grill tonight.

ROSE: How come you ain't brought Bonnie like I told you. You should have brought Bonnie with you, she ain't been over in a month of Sundays.

LYONS: I was just in the neighborhood . . . thought I'd stop by.

TROY: Here he come . . .

BONO: Your daddy got a promotion on the rubbish. He's gonna be the first colored driver. Ain't got to do nothing but sit up there and read the paper like them white fellows.

LYONS: Hey, Pop . . . if you knew how to read you'd be all right.

BONO: Naw . . . naw . . . you mean if the nigger knew how to *drive* he'd be all right. Been fighting with them people about driving and ain't even got a license. Mr. Rand know you ain't got no driver's license?

TROY: Driving ain't nothing. All you do is point the truck where you want it to go. Driving ain't nothing.

BONO: Do Mr. Rand know you ain't got no driver's license? That's what I'm talking about. I ain't asked if driving was easy. I asked if Mr. Rand know you ain't got no driver's license.

TROY: He ain't got to know. The man ain't got to know my business. Time he find out, I have two or three driver's licenses.

LYONS (*going into his pocket*): Say, look here, Pop . . .

TROY: I knew it was coming. Didn't I tell you, Bono? I know what kind of "Look here, Pop" that was. The nigger fixing to ask me for some money. It's Friday night. It's my payday. All them rogues down there on the avenue . . . the ones that ain't in jail . . . and Lyons is hopping in his shoes to get down there with them.

LYONS: See, Pop . . . if you give somebody else a chance to talk sometime, you'd see that I was fixing to pay you back your ten dollars like I told you. Here . . . I told you I'd pay you when Bonnie got paid.

TROY: Naw . . . you go ahead and keep that ten dollars. Put it in the bank. The next time you feel like you wanna come by here and ask me for something . . . you go on down there and get that.

LYONS: Here's your ten dollars, Pop. I told you I don't want you to give me nothing. I just wanted to borrow ten dollars.

TROY: Naw . . . you go on and keep that for the next time you want to ask me.

LYONS: Come on, Pop . . . here go your ten dollars.

ROSE: Why don't you go on and let the boy pay you back, Troy?

LYONS: Here you go, Rose. If you don't take it I'm gonna have to hear about it for the next six months.

(*He hands her the money.*)

ROSE: You can hand yours over here too, Troy.

TROY: You see this, Bono. You see how they do me.

BONO: Yeah, Lucille do me the same way.

(*Gabriel is heard singing offstage. He enters.*)

GABRIEL: Better get ready for the Judgment! Better get ready for . . . Hey! . . . Hey! . . . There's Troy's boy!

LYONS: How are you doing, Uncle Gabe?

GABRIEL: Lyons . . . The King of the Jungle! Rose . . . hey, Rose. Got a flower for you.

(*He takes a rose from his pocket.*)

Picked it myself. That's the same rose like you is!

ROSE: That's right nice of you, Gabe.

LYONS: What you been doing, Uncle Gabe?

GABRIEL: Oh, I been chasing hellhounds and waiting on the time to tell St. Peter to open the gates.

LYONS: You been chasing hellhounds, huh? Well . . . you doing the right thing, Uncle Gabe. Somebody got to chase them.

GABRIEL: Oh, yeah . . . I know it. The devil's strong. The devil ain't no pushover. Hellhounds snipping at everybody's heels. But I got my trumpet waiting on the judgment time.

LYONS: Waiting on the Battle of Armageddon, huh?

GABRIEL: Ain't gonna be too much of a battle when God get to waving that Judgment sword. But the people's gonna have a hell of a time trying to get into heaven if them gates ain't open.

LYONS (*putting his arm around Gabriel*): You hear this, Pop. Uncle Gabe, you all right!

GABRIEL (*laughing with Lyons*): Lyons! King of the Jungle!

ROSE: You gonna stay for supper, Gabe. Want me to fix you a plate?

GABRIEL: I'll take a sandwich, Rose. Don't want no plate. Just wanna eat with my hands. I'll take a sandwich.

ROSE: How about you, Lyons? You staying? Got some short ribs cooking.

LYONS: Naw, I won't eat nothing till after we finished playing.

(*Pause.*)

You ought to come down and listen to me play, Pop.

TROY: I don't like that Chinese music. All that noise.

ROSE: Go on in the house and wash up, Gabe . . . I'll fix you a sandwich.

GABRIEL (*to Lyons, as he exits*): Troy's mad at me.

LYONS: What you mad at Uncle Gabe for, Pop.

ROSE: He thinks Troy's mad at him cause he moved over to Miss Pearl's.

TROY: I ain't mad at the man. He can live where he want to live at.

LYONS: What he move over there for? Miss Pearl don't like nobody.

ROSE: She don't mind him none. She treats him real nice. She just don't allow all that singing.

TROY: She don't mind that rent he be paying . . . that's what she don't mind.

ROSE: Troy, I ain't going through that with you no more. He's over there cause he want to have his own place. He can come and go as he please.

TROY: Hell, he could come and go as he please here. I wasn't stopping him. I ain't put no rules on him.

ROSE: It ain't the same thing, Troy. And you know it.

(*Gabriel comes to the door.*)

Now, that's the last I wanna hear about that. I don't wanna hear nothing else about Gabe and Miss Pearl. And next week . . .

GABRIEL: I'm ready for my sandwich, Rose.

ROSE: And next week . . . when that recruiter come from that school . . . I want you to sign that paper and go on and let Cory play football. Then that'll be the last I have to hear about that.

TROY (*to Rose as she exits into the house*): I ain't thinking about Cory nothing.

LYONS: What . . . Cory got recruited? What school he going to?

TROY: That boy walking around here smelling his piss . . . thinking he's grown. Thinking he's gonna do what he want, irrespective of what I say. Look here, Bono . . . I left the Commissioner's office and went down to the A&P . . . that boy ain't working down there. He lying to me. Telling me he got his job back . . . telling me he working weekends . . . telling me he working after school . . . Mr. Stawicki tell me he ain't working down there at all!

LYONS: Cory just growing up. He's just busting at the seams trying to fill out your shoes.

TROY: I don't care what he's doing. When he get to the point where he wanna disobey me . . . then it's time for him to move on. Bono'll tell you that. I bet he ain't never disobeyed his daddy without paying the consequences.

BONO: I ain't never had a chance. My daddy came on through . . . but I ain't never knew him to see him . . . or what he had on his mind or where he went. Just moving on through. Searching out the New Land. That's what the old folks used to call it. See a fellow moving around from place to place . . . woman to woman . . . called it searching out the New Land. I can't say if he ever found it. I come along, didn't want no kids. Didn't know if I was gonna be in one place long enough to fix on them right as their daddy. I figured I was going searching too. As it turned out I been hooked up with Lucille near about as long as your daddy been with Rose. Going on sixteen years.

TROY: Sometimes I wish I hadn't known my daddy. He ain't cared nothing about no kids. A kid to him wasn't nothing. All he wanted was for you to learn how to walk so he could start you to working. When it come time for eating . . . he ate first. If there was anything left over, that's what you got. Man would sit down and eat two chickens and give you the wing.

LYONS: You ought to stop that, Pop. Everybody feed their kids. No matter how hard times is . . . everybody care about their kids. Make sure they have something to eat.

TROY: The only thing my daddy cared about was getting them bales of cotton in to Mr. Lubin. That's the only thing that mattered to him. Sometimes I used to wonder why he was living. Wonder why the devil hadn't come and got him. "Get them bales of cotton in to Mr. Lubin" and find out he owe him money . . .

LYONS: He should have just went on and left when he saw he couldn't get nowhere. That's what I would have done.

TROY: How he gonna leave with eleven kids? And where he gonna go? He ain't knew how to do nothing but farm. No, he was trapped and I think he knew it. But I'll say this for him . . . he felt a responsibility toward us. Maybe he ain't treated us the way I felt he should have . . . but without that responsibility he could have walked off and left us . . . made his own way.

BONO: A lot of them did. Back in those days what you talking about . . . they walk out their front door and just take on down one road or another and keep on walking.

LYONS: There you go! That's what I'm talking about.

BONO: Just keep on walking till you come to something else. Ain't you never heard of nobody having the walking blues? Well, that's what you call it when you just take off like that.

TROY: My daddy ain't had them walking blues! What you talking about? He stayed right there with his family. But he was just as evil as he could be. My mama couldn't stand him. Couldn't stand that evilness. She run off when I was about eight. She sneaked off one night after he had gone to sleep. Told me she was coming back for me. I ain't never seen her no more. All his women run off and left him. He wasn't good for nobody.

When my turn come to head out, I was fourteen and got to sniffing around Joe Canewell's daughter. Had us an old mule we called Greyboy. My daddy sent me out to do some plowing and I tied up Greyboy and went to fooling around with Joe Canewell's daughter. We done found us a nice little spot, got real cozy with each other. She about thirteen and we done figured we was grown anyway . . . so we down there enjoying ourselves . . . ain't thinking about nothing. We didn't know Greyboy had got loose and wandered back to the house and my daddy was looking for me. We down there by the creek enjoying ourselves when my daddy come up on us. Surprised us. He had them leather straps off the mule and commenced to whupping me like there was no tomorrow. I jumped up, mad and embarrassed. I was scared of my daddy. When he commenced to whupping on me . . . quite naturally I run to get out of the way.

(*Pause.*)

Now I thought he was mad cause I ain't done my work. But I see where he was chasing me off so he could have the gal for himself. When I see what the matter of it was, I lost all fear of my daddy. Right there is where I become a man . . . at fourteen years of age.

(*Pause.*)

Now it was my turn to run him off. I picked up them same reins that he had used on me. I picked up them reins and commenced to whupping on him. The gal jumped up and run off . . . and when my daddy turned to face me, I could see why the devil had never come to get him . . . cause he was the devil himself. I don't know what happened. When I woke up, I was laying right there by the creek, and Blue . . . this old dog we had . . . was licking my face. I thought I was blind. I couldn't see nothing. Both my eyes were swollen shut. I layed there and cried. I didn't know what I was gonna do. The only thing I knew was the time had come for me to leave my daddy's house. And right there the world suddenly got big. And it was a long time before I could cut it down to where I could handle it.

Part of that cutting down was when I got to the place where I could feel him kicking in my blood and knew that the only thing that separated us was the matter of a few years.

(*Gabriel enters from the house with a sandwich.*)

LYONS: What you got there, Uncle Gabe?

GABRIEL: Got me a ham sandwich. Rose gave me a ham sandwich.

TROY: I don't know what happened to him. I done lost touch with everybody except Gabriel. But I hope he's dead. I hope he found some peace.

LYONS: That's a heavy story, Pop. I didn't know you left home when you was fourteen.

TROY: And didn't know nothing. The only part of the world I knew was the forty-two acres of Mr. Lubin's land. That's all I knew about life.

LYONS: Fourteen's kinda young to be out on your own. (*Phone rings.*) I don't even think I was ready to be out on my own at fourteen. I don't know what I would have done.

TROY: I got up from the creek and walked on down to Mobile. I was through with farming. Figured I could do better in the city. So I walked the two hundred miles to Mobile.

LYONS: Wait a minute . . . you ain't walked no two hundred miles, Pop. Ain't nobody gonna walk no two hundred miles. You talking about some walking there.

BONO: That's the only way you got anywhere back in them days.

LYONS: Shhh. Damn if I wouldn't have hitched a ride with somebody!

TROY: Who you gonna hitch it with? They ain't had no cars and things like they got now. We talking about 1918.

ROSE (*entering*): What you all out here getting into?

TROY (*to Rose*): I'm telling Lyons how good he got it. He don't know nothing about this I'm talking.

ROSE: Lyons, that was Bonnie on the phone. She say you supposed to pick her up.

LYONS: Yeah, okay, Rose.

TROY: I walked on down to Mobile and hitched up with some of them fellows that was heading this way. Got up here and found out . . . not only couldn't you get a job . . . you couldn't find no place to live. I thought I was in freedom. Shhh. Colored folks living down there on the riverbanks in whatever kind of shelter they could find for themselves. Right down there under the Brady Street Bridge. Living in shacks made of sticks and tarpaper. Messed around there and went from bad to worse. Started stealing. First it was food. Then I figured, hell, if I steal money I can buy me some food. Buy me some shoes too! One thing led to another. Met your mama. I was young and anxious to be a man. Met your mama and had you. What I do that for? Now I got to worry about feeding you and her. Got to steal three times as much. Went out one day looking for somebody to rob . . . that's what I was, a robber. I'll tell you the truth. I'm ashamed of it today. But it's the truth. Went to rob this fellow . . . pulled out my knife . . . and he pulled out a gun. Shot me in the chest. It felt just like somebody had taken a hot branding iron and laid it on me. When he shot me I jumped at him with my knife. They told me I killed him and they put me in the penitentiary and locked me up for fifteen years. That's where I met Bono. That's where I learned how to play baseball. Got out that place and your mama had taken you and went on to make life without me. Fifteen years was a long time for her to wait. But that fifteen years cured me of that robbing stuff. Rose'll tell you. She asked me when I met her if I had gotten all that foolishness out of my system. And I told her, "Baby, it's you and baseball all what count with me." You hear me, Bono? I meant it too. She say "Which one comes first?" I told her, "Baby, ain't no doubt it's baseball . . . but you stick and get old with me and we'll both outlive this baseball." Am I right, Rose? And it's true.

ROSE: Man, hush your mouth. You ain't said no such thing. Talking about, "Baby, you know you'll always be number one with me." That's what you was talking.

TROY: You hear that, Bono. That's why I love her.

BONO: Rose'll keep you straight. You get off the track, she'll straighten you up.

ROSE: Lyons, you better get on up and get Bonnie. She waiting on you.

LYONS (*gets up to go*): Hey, Pop, why don't you come on down to the Grill and hear me play?

TROY: I ain't going down there. I'm too old to be sitting around in them clubs.

BONO: You got to be good to play down at the Grill.

LYONS: Come on, Pop . . .

TROY: I got to get up in the morning.

LYONS: You ain't got to stay long.

TROY: Naw, I'm gonna get my supper and go on to bed.

LYONS: Well, I got to go. I'll see you again.

TROY: Don't you come around my house on my payday.

ROSE: Pick up the phone and let somebody know you coming. And bring Bonnie with you. You know I'm always glad to see her.

LYONS: Yeah, I'll do that, Rose. You take care now. See you, Pop. See you, Mr. Bono. See you, Uncle Gabe.

GABRIEL: Lyons! King of the Jungle!

(*Lyons exits.*)

TROY: Is supper ready, woman? Me and you got some business to take care of. I'm gonna tear it up too.

ROSE: Troy, I done told you now!

TROY (*puts his arm around Bono*): Aw hell, woman . . . this is Bono. Bono like family. I done known this nigger since . . . how long I done know you?

BONO: It's been a long time.

TROY: I done known this nigger since Skippy was a pup. Me and him done been through some times.

BONO: You sure right about that.

TROY: Hell, I done know him longer than I known you. And we still standing shoulder to shoulder. Hey, look here, Bono . . . a man can't ask for no more than that.

(*Drinks to him.*)

I love you, nigger.

BONO: Hell, I love you too . . . but I got to get home see my woman. You got yours in hand. I got to go get mine.

(*Bono starts to exit as Cory enters the yard, dressed in his football uniform. He gives Troy a hard, uncompromising look.*)

CORY: What you do that for, Pop?

(*He throws his helmet down in the direction of Troy.*)

ROSE: What's the matter? Cory . . . what's the matter?

CORY: Papa done went up to the school and told Coach Zellman I can't play football no more. Wouldn't even let me play the game. Told him to tell the recruiter not to come.

ROSE: Troy . . .

TROY: What you Troying me for. Yeah, I did it. And the boy know why I did it.

CORY: Why you wanna do that to me? That was the one chance I had.

ROSE: Ain't nothing wrong with Cory playing football, Troy.

TROY: The boy lied to me. I told the nigger if he wanna play football . . . to keep up his chores and hold down that job at the A&P. That was the conditions. Stopped down there to see Mr. Stawicki . . .

CORY: I can't work after school during the football season, Pop! I tried to tell you that Mr. Stawicki's holding my job for me. You don't never want to listen to nobody. And then you wanna go and do this to me!

TROY: I ain't done nothing to you. You done it to yourself.

CORY: Just cause you didn't have a chance! You just scared I'm gonna be better than you, that's all.

TROY: Come here.

ROSE: Troy . . .

(*Cory reluctantly crosses over to Troy.*)

TROY: All right! See. You done made a mistake.

CORY: I didn't even do nothing!

TROY: I'm gonna tell you what your mistake was. See . . . you swung at the ball and didn't hit it. That's strike one. See, you in the batter's box now. You swung and you missed. That's strike one. Don't you strike out!

(*Lights fade to black.*)

ACT II • Scene I

(*The following morning. Cory is at the tree hitting the ball with the bat. He tries to mimic Troy, but his swing is awkward, less sure. Rose enters from the house.*)

ROSE: Cory, I want you to help me with this cupboard.

CORY: I ain't quitting the team. I don't care what Poppa say.

ROSE: I'll talk to him when he gets back. He had to go see about your Uncle Gabe. The police done arrested him. Say he was disturbing the peace. He'll be back directly. Come on in here and help me clean out the top of this cupboard.

(*Cory exits into the house. Rose sees Troy and Bono coming down the alley.*)

Troy . . . what they say down there?

TROY: Ain't said nothing. I give them fifty dollars and they let him go. I'll talk to you about it. Where's Cory?

ROSE: He's in there helping me clean out these cupboards.

TROY: Tell him to get his butt out here.

(*Troy and Bono go over to the pile of wood. Bono picks up the saw and begins sawing.*)

TROY (*to Bono*): All they want is the money. That makes six or seven times I done went down there and got him. See me coming they stick out their *hands.*

BONO: Yeah. I know what you mean. That's all they care about . . . that money. They don't care about what's right.

(*Pause.*)

Nigger, why you got to go and get some hard wood? You ain't doing nothing but building a little old fence. Get you some soft pine wood. That's all you need.

TROY: I know what I'm doing. This is outside wood. You put pine wood inside the house. Pine wood is inside wood. This here is outside wood. Now you tell me where the fence is gonna be?

BONO: You don't need this wood. You can put it up with pine wood and it'll stand as long as you gonna be here looking at it.

TROY: How you know how long I'm gonna be here, nigger? Hell, I might just live forever. Live longer than old man Horsely.

BONO: That's what Magee used to say.

TROY: Magee's a damn fool. Now you tell me who you ever heard of gonna pull their own teeth with a pair of rusty pliers.

BONO: The old folks . . . my granddaddy used to pull his teeth with pliers. They ain't had no dentists for the colored folks back then.

TROY: Get clean pliers! You understand? Clean pliers! Sterilize them! Besides we ain't living back then. All Magee had to do was walk over to Doc Goldblum's.

BONO: I see where you and that Tallahassee gal . . . that Alberta . . . I see where you all done got tight.

TROY: What you mean "got tight"?

BONO: I see where you be laughing and joking with her all the time.

TROY: I laughs and jokes with all of them, Bono. You know me.

BONO: That ain't the kind of laughing and joking I'm talking about.

(*Cory enters from the house.*)

CORY: How you doing, Mr. Bono?

TROY: Cory? Get that saw from Bono and cut some wood. He talking about the wood's too hard to cut. Stand back there, Jim, and let that young boy show you how it's done.

BONO: He's sure welcome to it.

(*Cory takes the saw and begins to cut the wood.*)

Whew-e-e! Look at that. Big old strong boy. Look like Joe Louis. Hell, must be getting old the way I'm watching that boy whip through that wood.

CORY: I don't see why Mama want a fence around the yard noways.

TROY: Damn if I know either. What the hell she keeping out with it? She ain't got nothing nobody want.

BONO: Some people build fences to keep people out . . . and other people build fences to keep people in. Rose wants to hold on to you all. She loves you.

TROY: Hell, nigger, I don't need nobody to tell me my wife loves me, Cory . . . go on in the house and see if you can find that other saw.

CORY: Where's it at?

TROY: I said find it! Look for it till you find it!

(*Cory exits into the house.*)

What's that supposed to mean? Wanna keep us in?

BONO: Troy . . . I done known you seem like damn near my whole life. You and Rose both. I done know both of you all for a long time. I remember when you met Rose. When you was hitting them baseball out the park. A lot of them old gals was after you then. You had the pick of the litter. When you picked Rose, I was happy for you. That was the first time I knew you had any sense. I said . . . My man Troy knows what he's doing . . . I'm gonna follow this nigger . . . he might take me somewhere. I been following you too. I done learned a whole heap of things about life watching you. I done learned how to tell where the shit lies. How to tell it from the alfalfa. You done learned me a lot of things. You showed me how to not make the same mistakes . . . to take life as it comes along and keep putting one foot in front of the other.

(*Pause.*)

Rose a good woman, Troy.

TROY: Hell, nigger, I know she a good woman. I been married to her for eighteen years. What you got on your mind, Bono?

BONO: I just say she a good woman. Just like I say anything. I ain't got to have nothing on my mind.

TROY: You just gonna say she a good woman and leave it hanging out there like that? Why you telling me she a good woman?

BONO: She loves you, Troy. Rose loves you.

TROY: You saying I don't measure up. That's what you trying to say. I don't measure up cause I'm seeing this other gal. I know what you trying to say.

BONO: I know what Rose means to you, Troy. I'm just trying to say I don't want to see you mess up.

TROY: Yeah, I appreciate that, Bono. If you was messing around on Lucille I'd be telling you the same thing.

BONO: Well, that's all I got to say. I just say that because I love you both.

TROY: Hell, you know me . . . I wasn't out there looking for nothing. You can't find a better woman than Rose. I know that. But seems like this woman just stuck onto me where I can't shake her loose. I done wrestled with it, tried to throw her off me . . . but she just stuck on tighter. Now she's stuck on for good.

BONO: You's in control . . . that's what you tell me all the time. You responsible for what you do.

TROY: I ain't ducking the responsibility of it. As long as it sets right in my heart . . . then I'm okay. Cause that's all I listen to. It'll tell me right from wrong every time. And I ain't talking about doing Rose no bad turn. I love Rose. She done carried me a long ways and I love and respect her for that.

BONO: I know you do. That's why I don't want to see you hurt her. But what you gonna do when she find out? What you got then? If you try and juggle both of them . . . sooner or later you gonna drop one of them. That's common sense.

TROY: Yeah, I hear what you saying, Bono. I been trying to figure a way to work it out.

BONO: Work it out right, Troy. I don't want to be getting all up between you and Rose's business . . . but work it so it come out right.

TROY: Ah hell, I get all up between you and Lucille's business. When you gonna get that woman that refrigerator she been wanting? Don't tell me you ain't got no money now. I know who your banker is. Mellon don't need that money bad as Lucille want that refrigerator. I'll tell you that.

BONO: Tell you what I'll do . . . when you finish building this fence for Rose . . . I'll buy Lucille that refrigerator.

TROY: You done stuck your foot in your mouth now!

(*Troy grabs up a board and begins to saw. Bono starts to walk out the yard.*)

Hey, nigger . . . where you going?

BONO: I'm going home. I know you don't expect me to help you now. I'm protecting my money. I wanna see you put that fence up by yourself. That's what I want to see. You'll be here another six months without me.

TROY: Nigger, you ain't right.

BONO: When it comes to my money . . . I'm right as fireworks on the Fourth of July.

TROY: All right, we gonna see now. You better get out your bankbook.

(*Bono exits, and Troy continues to work. Rose enters from the house.*)

ROSE: What they say down there? What's happening with Gabe?

TROY: I went down there and got him out. Cost me fifty dollars. Say he was disturbing the peace. Judge set up a hearing for him in three weeks. Say to show cause why he shouldn't be recommitted.

ROSE: What was he doing that cause them to arrest him?

TROY: Some kids was teasing him and he run them off home. Say he was howling and carrying on. Some folks seen him and called the police. That's all it was.

ROSE: Well, what's you say? What'd you tell the judge?

TROY: Told him I'd look after him. It didn't make no sense to recommit the man. He stuck out his big greasy palm and told me to give him fifty dollars and take him on home.

ROSE: Where's he at now? Where'd he go off to?

TROY: He's gone on about his business. He don't need nobody to hold his hand.

ROSE: Well, I don't know. Seem like that would be the best place for him if they did put him into the hospital. I know what you're gonna say. But that's what I think would be best.

TROY: The man done had his life ruined fighting for what? And they wanna take and lock him up. Let him be free. He don't bother nobody.

ROSE: Well, everybody got their own way of looking at it I guess. Come on and get your lunch. I got a bowl of lima beans and some cornbread in the oven. Come on get something to eat. Ain't no sense you fretting over Gabe.

(*Rose turns to go into the house.*)

TROY: Rose . . . got something to tell you.

ROSE: Well, come on . . . wait till I get this food on the table.

TROY: Rose!

(*She stops and turns around.*)

I don't know how to say this.

(*Pause.*)

I can't explain it none. It just sort of grows on you till it gets out of hand. It starts out like a little bush . . . and the next thing you know it's a whole forest.

ROSE: Troy . . . what is you talking about?

TROY: I'm talking, woman, let me talk. I'm trying to find a way to tell you . . . I'm gonna be a daddy. I'm gonna be somebody's daddy.

ROSE: Troy . . . you're not telling me this? You're gonna be . . . what?

TROY: Rose . . . now . . . see . . .

ROSE: You telling me you gonna be somebody's daddy? You telling your *wife* this?

(*Gabriel enters from the street. He carries a rose in his hand.*)

GABRIEL: Hey, Troy! Hey, Rose!

ROSE: I have to wait eighteen years to hear something like this.

GABRIEL: Hey, Rose . . . I got a flower for you.

(*He hands it to her.*)

That's a rose. Same rose like you is.

ROSE: Thanks, Gabe.

GABRIEL: Troy, you ain't mad at me is you? Them bad mens come and put me away. You ain't mad at me is you?

TROY: Naw, Gabe, I ain't mad at you.

ROSE: Eighteen years and you wanna come with this.

GABRIEL (*takes a quarter out of his pocket*): See what I got? Got a brand new quarter.

TROY: Rose . . . it's just . . .

ROSE: Ain't nothing you can say, Troy. Ain't no way of explaining that.

GABRIEL: Fellow that give me this quarter had a whole mess of them. I'm gonna keep this quarter till it stop shining.

ROSE: Gabe, go on in the house there. I got some watermelon in the frigidaire. Go on and get you a piece.

GABRIEL: Say, Rose . . . you know I was chasing hellhounds and them bad mens come and get me and take me away. Troy helped me. He come down there and told them they better let me go before he beat them up. Yeah, he did!

ROSE: You go on and get you a piece of watermelon, Gabe. Them bad mens is gone now.

GABRIEL: Okay, Rose . . . gonna get me some watermelon. The kind with the stripes on it.

(*Gabriel exits into the house.*)

ROSE: Why, Troy? Why? After all these years to come dragging this in to me now. It don't make no sense at your age. I could have expected this ten or fifteen years ago, but not now.

TROY: Age ain't got nothing to do with it, Rose.

ROSE: I done tried to be everything a wife should be. Everything a wife could be. Been married eighteen years and I got to live to see the day you tell me you been seeing another woman and done fathered a child by her. And you know I ain't never wanted no half nothing in my family. My whole family is half. Everybody got different fathers and mothers . . . my two sisters and my brother. Can't hardly tell who's who. Can't never sit down and talk about Papa and Mama. It's your papa and your mama and my papa and my mama . . .

TROY: Rose . . . stop it now.

ROSE: I ain't never wanted that for none of my children. And now you wanna drag your behind in here and tell me something like this.

TROY: You ought to know. It's time for you to know.

ROSE: Well, I don't want to know, goddamn it!

TROY: I can't just make it go away. It's done now. I can't wish the circumstance of the thing away.

ROSE: And you don't want to either. Maybe you want to wish me and my boy away. Maybe that's what you want? Well, you can't wish us away. I've got eighteen years of my life invested in you. You ought to have stayed upstairs in my bed where you belong.

TROY: Rose . . . now listen to me . . . we can get a handle on this thing. We can talk this out . . . come to an understanding.

ROSE: All of a sudden it's "we." Where was "we" at when you was down there rolling around with some godforsaken woman? "We" should have come to an understanding before you started making a damn fool of yourself. You're a day late and a dollar short when it comes to an understanding with me.

TROY: It's just . . . She gives me a different idea . . . a different understanding about myself. I can step out of this house and get away from the pressures and problems . . . be a different man. I ain't got to wonder how I'm gonna pay the bills or get the roof fixed. I can just be a part of myself that I ain't never been.

ROSE: What I want to know . . . is do you plan to continue seeing her. That's all you can say to me.

TROY: I can sit up in her house and laugh. Do you understand what I'm saying. I can laugh out loud . . . and it feels good. It reaches all the way down to the bottom of my shoes.

(*Pause.*)

Rose, I can't give that up.

ROSE: Maybe you ought to go on and stay down there with her . . . if she's a better woman than me.

TROY: It ain't about nobody being a better woman or nothing. Rose, you ain't the blame. A man couldn't ask for no woman to be a better wife than you've been. I'm responsible for it. I done locked myself into a pattern trying to take care of you all that I forgot about myself.

ROSE: What the hell was I there for? That was my job, not somebody else's.

TROY: Rose, I done tried all my life to live decent . . . to live a clean . . . hard . . . useful life. I tried to be a good husband to you. In every way I knew how. Maybe I come into the world backwards, I don't know. But . . . you born with two strikes on you before you come to the plate. You got to guard it closely . . . always looking for the curve ball on the inside corner. You can't afford to let none get past you. You can't afford a call strike. If you going down . . . you going down swinging. Everything lined up against you. What you gonna do. I fooled them, Rose. I bunted. When I found you and Cory and a halfway decent job . . . I was safe. Couldn't nothing touch me. I wasn't gonna strike out no more. I wasn't going back to the penitentiary. I wasn't gonna lay in the streets with a bottle of wine. I was safe. I had me a family. A job. I wasn't gonna get that last strike. I was on first looking for one of them boys to knock me in. To get me home.

ROSE: You should have stayed in my bed, Troy.

TROY: Then when I saw that gal . . . she firmed up my backbone. And I got to thinking that if I tried . . . I just might be able to steal second. Do you understand after eighteen years I wanted to steal second.

ROSE: You should have held me tight. You should have grabbed me and held on.

TROY: I stood on first base for eighteen years and I thought . . . well, goddamn it . . . go on for it!

ROSE: We're not talking about baseball! We're talking about you going off to lay in bed with another woman . . . and then bring it home to me. That's what we're talking about. We ain't talking about no baseball.

TROY: Rose, you're not listening to me. I'm trying the best I can to explain it to you. It's not easy for me to admit that I been standing in the same place for eighteen years.

ROSE: I been standing with you! I been right here with you, Troy. I got a life too. I gave eighteen years of my life to stand in the same spot with you. Don't you think I ever wanted other things? Don't you think I had dreams and hopes? What about my life? What about me. Don't you think it ever crossed my mind to want to know other men? That I wanted to lay up somewhere and forget about my responsibilities? That I wanted someone to make me laugh so I could feel good? You not the only one who's got wants and needs. But I held on to you, Troy. I took all my feelings, my wants and needs, my dreams . . . and I buried them inside you. I planted a seed and watched and prayed over it. I planted myself inside you and waited to bloom. And it didn't take me no eighteen years to find out the soil was hard and rocky and it wasn't never gonna bloom.

But I held on to you, Troy. I held you tighter. You was my husband. I owed you everything I had. Every part of me I could find to give you. And upstairs in that room . . . with the darkness falling in on me . . . I gave everything I had to try and erase the doubt that you wasn't the finest man in the world. And wherever you was going . . . I wanted to be there with you. Cause you was my husband. Cause that's the only way I was gonna survive as your wife. You always talking about what you give . . . and what you don't have to give. But you take too. You take . . . and don't even know nobody's giving!

(*Rose turns to exit into the house; Troy grabs her arm.*)

TROY: You say I take and don't give!

ROSE: Troy! You're hurting me!

TROY: You say I take and don't give.

ROSE: Troy . . . you're hurting my arm! Let go!

TROY: I done give you everything I got. Don't you tell that lie on me.

ROSE: Troy!

TROY: Don't you tell that lie on me!

(*Cory enters from the house.*)

CORY: Mama!

ROSE: Troy. You're hurting me.

TROY: Don't you tell me about no taking and giving.

(*Cory comes up behind Troy and grabs him. Troy, surprised, is thrown off balance just as Cory throws a glancing blow that catches him on the chest and knocks him down. Troy is stunned, as is Cory.*)

ROSE: Troy. Troy. No!

(*Troy gets to his feet and starts at Cory.*)

Troy . . . no. Please! Troy!

(*Rose pulls on Troy to hold him back. Troy stops himself.*)

TROY (*to Cory*): All right. That's strike two. You stay away from around me, boy. Don't you strike out. You living with a full count. Don't you strike out.

(*Troy exits out the yard as the lights go down.*)

Scene II

(*It is six months later, early afternoon. Troy enters from the house and starts to exit the yard. Rose enters from the house.*)

ROSE: Troy, I want to talk to you.

TROY: All of a sudden, after all this time, you want to talk to me, huh? You ain't wanted to talk to me for months. You ain't wanted to talk to me last night. You ain't wanted no part of me then. What you wanna talk to me about now?

ROSE: Tomorrow's Friday.

TROY: I know what day tomorrow is. You think I don't know tomorrow's Friday? My whole life I ain't done nothing but look to see Friday coming and you got to tell me it's Friday.

ROSE: I want to know if you're coming home.

TROY: I always come home, Rose. You know that. There ain't never been a night I ain't come home.

ROSE: That ain't what I mean . . . and you know it. I want to know if you're coming straight home after work.

TROY: I figure I'd cash my check . . . hang out at Taylors' with the boys . . . maybe play a game of checkers . . .

ROSE: Troy, I can't live like this. I won't live like this. You livin' on borrowed time with me. It's been going on six months now you ain't been coming home.

TROY: I be here every night. Every night of the year. That's 365 days.

ROSE: I want you to come home tomorrow after work.

TROY: Rose . . . I don't mess up my pay. You know that now. I take my pay and I give it to you. I don't have no money but what you give me back. I just want to have a little time to myself . . . a little time to enjoy life.

ROSE: What about me? When's my time to enjoy life?

TROY: I don't know what to tell you, Rose. I'm doing the best I can.

ROSE: You ain't been home from work but time enough to change your clothes and run out . . . and you wanna call that the best you can do?

TROY: I'm going over to the hospital to see Alberta. She went into the hospital this afternoon. Look like she might have the baby early. I won't be gone long.

ROSE: Well, you ought to know. They went over to Miss Pearl's and got Gabe today. She said you told them to go ahead and lock him up.

TROY: I ain't said no such thing. Whoever told you that is telling a lie. Pearl ain't doing nothing but telling a big fat lie.

ROSE: She ain't had to tell me. I read it on the papers.

TROY: I ain't told them nothing of the kind.

ROSE: I saw it right there on the papers.

TROY: What it say, huh?

ROSE: It said you told them to take him.

TROY: Then they screwed that up, just the way they screw up everything. I ain't worried about what they got on the paper.

ROSE: Say the government send part of his check to the hospital and the other part to you.

TROY: I ain't got nothing to do with that if that's the way it works. I ain't made up the rules about how it work.

ROSE: You did Gabe just like you did Cory. You wouldn't sign the paper for Cory . . . but you signed for Gabe. You signed that paper.

(The telephone is heard ringing inside the house.)

TROY: I told you I ain't signed nothing, woman! The only thing I signed was the release form. Hell, I can't read, I don't know what they had on that paper! I ain't signed nothing about sending Gabe away.

ROSE: I said send him to the hospital . . . you said let him be free . . . now you done went down there and signed him to the hospital for half his money. You went back on yourself, Troy. You gonna have to answer for that.

TROY: See now . . . you been over there talking to Miss Pearl. She done got mad cause she ain't getting Gabe's rent money. That's all it is. She's liable to say anything.

ROSE: Troy, I seen where you signed the paper.

TROY: You ain't seen nothing I signed. What she doing got papers on my brother anyway? Miss Pearl telling a big fat lie. And I'm gonna tell her about it too! You ain't seen nothing I signed. Say . . . you ain't seen nothing I signed.

(Rose exits into the house to answer the telephone. Presently she returns.)

ROSE: Troy . . . that was the hospital. Alberta had the baby.

TROY: What she have? What is it?

ROSE: It's a girl.

TROY: I better get on down to the hospital to see her.

ROSE: Troy . . .

TROY: Rose . . . I got to go see her now. That's only right . . . what's the matter . . . the baby's all right, ain't it?

ROSE: Alberta died having the baby.

TROY: Died . . . you say she's dead? Alberta's dead?

ROSE: They said they done all they could. They couldn't do nothing for her.

TROY: The baby? How's the baby?

ROSE: They say it's healthy. I wonder who's gonna bury her.

TROY: She had family, Rose. She wasn't living in the world by herself.

ROSE: I know she wasn't living in the world by herself.

TROY: Next thing you gonna want to know if she had any insurance.

ROSE: Troy, you ain't got to talk like that.

TROY: That's the first thing that jumped out your mouth. "Who's gonna bury her?" Like I'm fixing to take on that task for myself.

ROSE: I am your wife. Don't push me away.

TROY: I ain't pushing nobody away. Just give me some space. That's all. Just give me some room to breathe.

(Rose exits into the house. Troy walks about the yard.)

TROY (with a quiet rage that threatens to consume him): All right . . . Mr. Death. See now . . . I'm gonna tell you what I'm gonna do. I'm gonna take and build me a fence around this yard. See? I'm gonna build me a fence around what belongs to me. And then I want you to stay on the other side. See? You stay over there until you're ready for me. Then you come on. Bring your army. Bring your sickle. Bring your wrestling clothes. I ain't gonna fall down on my vigilance this time. You ain't gonna sneak up on me no more. When you ready for me . . . when the top of your list say Troy Maxson . . . that's when you come around here. You come up and knock on the front door. Ain't nobody else got nothing to do with this. This is between you and me. Man to man. You stay on the other side of that fence until you ready for me. Then you come up and knock on the front door. Anytime you want. I'll be ready for you.

(The lights go down to black.)

Scene III

(The lights come up on the porch. It is late evening three days later. Rose sits listening to the ball game waiting for Troy. The final out of the game is made and Rose switches off the radio. Troy enters the yard carrying an infant wrapped in blankets. He stands back from the house and calls.)

(Rose enters and stands on the porch. There is a long, awkward silence, the weight of which grows heavier with each passing second.)

TROY: Rose . . . I'm standing here with my daughter in my arms. She ain't but a wee bittie little old thing. She don't know nothing about grownups' business. She innocent . . . and she ain't got no mama.

ROSE: What you telling me for, Troy?

(*She turns and exits into the house.*)

TROY: Well . . . I guess we'll just sit out here on the porch.

(*He sits down on the porch. There is an awkward indelicateness about the way he handles the baby. His largeness engulfs and seems to swallow it. He speaks loud enough for Rose to hear.*)

A man's got to do what's right for him. I ain't sorry for nothing I done. It felt right in my heart.

(*To the baby.*)

What you smiling at? Your daddy's a big man. Got these great big old hands. But sometimes he's scared. And right now your daddy's scared cause we sitting out here and ain't got no home. Oh, I been homeless before. I ain't had no little baby with me. But I been homeless. You just be out on the road by your lonesome and you see one of them trains coming and you just kinda go like this . . .

(*He sings as a lullaby.*)

Please, Mr. Engineer let a man ride the line
Please, Mr. Engineer let a man ride the line
I ain't got no ticket please let me ride the blinds

(*Rose enters from the house. Troy hearing her steps behind him, stands and faces her.*)

She's my daughter, Rose. My own flesh and blood. I can't deny her no more than I can deny them boys.

(*Pause.*)

You and them boys is my family. You and them and this child is all I got in the world. So I guess what I'm saying is . . . I'd appreciate it if you'd help me take care of her.

ROSE: Okay, Troy . . . you're right. I'll take care of your baby for you . . . cause . . . like you say . . . she's innocent . . . and you can't visit the sins of the father upon the child. A motherless child has got a hard time.

(*She takes the baby from him.*)

From right now . . . this child got a mother. But you a womanless man.

(*Rose turns and exits into the house with the baby. Lights go down to black.*)

Scene IV

(*It is two months later. Lyons enters from the street. He knocks on the door and calls.*)

LYONS: Hey, Rose! (*Pause.*) Rose!

ROSE (*from inside the house*): Stop that yelling. You gonna wake up Raynell. I just got her to sleep.

LYONS: I just stopped by to pay Papa this twenty dollars I owe him. Where's Papa at?

ROSE: He should be here in a minute. I'm getting ready to go down to the church. Sit down and wait on him.

LYONS: I got to go pick up Bonnie over her mother's house.

ROSE: Well, sit it down there on the table. He'll get it.

LYONS (*enters the house and sets the money on the table*): Tell Papa I said thanks. I'll see you again.

ROSE: All right, Lyons. We'll see you.

(*Lyons starts to exit as Cory enters.*)

CORY: Hey, Lyons.

LYONS: What's happening, Cory. Say man, I'm sorry I missed your graduation. You know I had a gig and couldn't get away. Otherwise, I would have been there, man. So what you doing?

CORY: I'm trying to find a job.

LYONS: Yeah I know how that go, man. It's rough out here. Jobs are scarce.

CORY: Yeah, I know.

LYONS: Look here, I got to run. Talk to Papa . . . he know some people. He'll be able to help get you a job. Talk to him . . . see what he say.

CORY: Yeah . . . all right, Lyons.

LYONS: You take care. I'll talk to you soon. We'll find some time to talk.

(*Lyons exits the yard. Cory wanders over to the tree, picks up the bat, and assumes a batting stance. He studies an imaginary pitcher and swings. Dissatisfied with the result, he tries again. Troy enters. They eye each other for a beat. Cory puts the bat down and exits the yard. Troy starts into the house as Rose exits with Raynell. She is carrying a cake.*)

TROY: I'm coming in and everybody's going out.

ROSE: I'm taking this cake down to the church for the bake sale. Lyons was by to see you. He stopped by to pay you your twenty dollars. It's laying in there on the table.

TROY (*going into his pocket*): Well . . . here go this money.

ROSE: Put it in there on the table, Troy. I'll get it.

TROY: What time you coming back?

ROSE: Ain't no use in you studying me. It don't matter what time I come back.

TROY: I just asked you a question, woman. What's the matter . . . can't I ask you a question?

ROSE: Troy, I don't want to go into it. Your dinner's in there on the stove. All you got to do is heat it up. And don't you be eating the rest of them cakes in there. I'm coming back for them. We having a bake sale at the church tomorrow.

(*Rose exits the yard. Troy sits down on the steps, takes a pint bottle from his pocket, opens it, and drinks. He begins to sing.*)

TROY: Hear it ring! Hear it ring!
Had an old dog his name was Blue
You know Blue was mighty true
You know Blue as a good old dog
Blue trees a possum in a hollow log
You know from that he was a good old dog

(*Bono enters the yard.*)

BONO: Hey, Troy.

TROY: Hey, what's happening, Bono?

BONO: I just thought I'd stop by to see you.

TROY: What you stop by and see me for? You ain't stopped by in a month of Sundays. Hell, I must owe you money or something.

BONO: Since you got your promotion I can't keep up with you. Used to see you every day. Now I don't even know what route you working.

TROY: They keep switching me around. Got me out in Greentree now . . . hauling white folks' garbage.

BONO: Greentree, huh? You lucky, at least you ain't got to be lifting them barrels. Damn if they ain't getting heavier. I'm gonna put in my two years and call it quits.

TROY: I'm thinking about retiring myself.

BONO: You got it easy. You can *drive* for another five years.

TROY: It ain't the same, Bono. It ain't like working the back of the truck. Ain't got nobody to talk to . . . feel like you working by yourself. Naw, I'm thinking about retiring. How's Lucille?

BONO: She all right. Her arthritis get to acting up on her sometime. Saw Rose on my way in. She going down to the church, huh?

TROY: Yeah, she took up going down there. All them preachers looking for somebody to fatten their pockets.

(*Pause.*)

Got some gin here.

BONO: Naw, thanks. I just stopped by to say hello.

TROY: Hell, nigger . . . you can take a drink. I ain't never known you to say no to a drink. You ain't got to work tomorrow.

BONO: I just stopped by. I'm fixing to go over to Skinner's. We got us a domino game going over his house every Friday.

TROY: Nigger, you can't play no dominoes. I used to whup you four games out of five.

BONO: Well, that learned me. I'm getting better.

TROY: Yeah? Well, that's all right.

BONO: Look here . . . I got to be getting on. Stop by sometime, huh?

TROY: Yeah, I'll do that, Bono. Lucille told Rose you bought her a new refrigerator.

BONO: Yeah, Rose told Lucille you had finally built your fence . . . so I figured we'd call it even.

TROY: I knew you would.

BONO: Yeah . . . okay. I'll be talking to you.

TROY: Yeah, take care, Bono. Good to see you. I'm gonna stop over.

BONO: Yeah. Okay, Troy.

(*Bono exits. Troy drinks from the bottle.*)

TROY: Old Blue died and I dig his grave
Let him down with a golden chain

Every night when I hear old Blue bark
I know Blue treed a possum in Noah's Ark.
Hear it ring! Hear it ring!

(*Cory enters the yard. They eye each other for a beat. Troy is sitting in the middle of the steps. Cory walks over.*)

CORY: I got to get by.

TROY: Say what? What's you say?

CORY: You in my way. I got to get by.

TROY: You got to get by where? This is my house. Bought and paid for. In full. Took me fifteen years. And if you wanna go in my house and I'm sitting on the steps . . . you say excuse me. Like your mama taught you.

CORY: Come on, Pop . . . I got to get by.

(*Cory starts to maneuver his way past Troy. Troy grabs his leg and shoves him back.*)

TROY: You just gonna walk over top of me?

CORY: I live here too!

TROY (*advancing toward him*): You just gonna walk over top of me in my own house?

CORY: I ain't scared of you.

TROY: I ain't asked if you was scared of me. I asked if you was fixing to walk over top of me in my own house? That's the question. You ain't gonna say excuse me? You just gonna walk over top of me?

CORY: If you wanna put it like that.

TROY: How else am I gonna put it?

CORY: I was walking by you to go into the house cause you sitting on the steps drunk, singing to yourself. You can put it like that.

TROY: Without saying excuse me???

(*Cory doesn't respond.*)

I asked you a question. Without saying excuse me???

CORY: I ain't got to say excuse me to you. You don't count around here no more.

TROY: Oh, I see . . . I don't count around here no more. You ain't got to say excuse me to your daddy. All of a sudden you done got so grown that your daddy don't count around here no more . . . Around here in his own house and yard that he done paid for with the sweat of his brow. You done got so grown to where you gonna take over. You gonna take over my house. Is that right? You gonna wear my pants. You gonna go in there and stretch out on my bed. You ain't got to say excuse me cause I don't count around here no more. Is that right?

CORY: That's right. You always talking this dumb stuff. Now, why don't you just get out my way.

TROY: I guess you got someplace to sleep and something to put in your belly. You got that, huh? You got that? That's what you need. You got that, huh?

CORY: You don't know what I got. You ain't got to worry about what I got.

TROY: You right! You one hundred percent right! I done spent the last seventeen years worrying about what you got. Now it's your turn, see? I'll tell you what to do. You grown . . . we done established that. You a man. Now, let's see you act like one. Turn your behind around and walk out this yard. And when you get out there in the alley . . . you can forget about this house. See? 'Cause this is my house. You go on and be a man and get your own house. You can forget about this. 'Cause this is mine. You go on and get yours 'cause I'm through with doing for you.

CORY: You talking about what you did for me . . . what'd you ever give me?

TROY: Them feet and bones! That pumping heart, nigger! I give you more than anybody else is ever gonna give you.

CORY: You ain't never gave me nothing! You ain't never done nothing but hold me back. Afraid I was gonna be better than you. All you ever did was try and make me scared of you. I used to tremble every time you called my name. Every time I heard your footsteps in the house. Wondering all the time . . . what's Papa gonna say if I do this? . . . What's he gonna say if I do that? . . . What's Papa gonna say if I turn on the radio? And Mama, too . . . she tries . . . but she's scared of you.

TROY: You leave your mama out of this. She ain't got nothing to do with this.

CORY: I don't know how she stand you . . . after what you did to her.

TROY: I told you to leave your mama out of this!

(*He advances toward Cory.*)

CORY: What you gonna do . . . give me a whupping? You can't whup me no more. You're too old. You just an old man.

TROY (*shoves him on his shoulder*): Nigger! That's what you are. You just another nigger on the street to me!

CORY: You crazy! You know that?

TROY: Go on now! You got the devil in you. Get on away from me!

CORY: You just a crazy old man . . . talking about I got the devil in me.

TROY: Yeah, I'm crazy! If you don't get on the other side of that yard . . . I'm gonna show you how crazy I am! Go on . . . get the hell out of my yard.

CORY: It ain't your yard. You took Uncle Gabe's money he got from the army to buy this house and then you put him out.

TROY (*Troy advances on Cory*): Get your black ass out of my yard!

(*Troy's advance backs Cory up against the tree. Cory grabs up the bat.*)

CORY: I ain't going nowhere! Come on . . . put me out! I ain't scared of you.

TROY: That's my bat!

CORY: Come on!

TROY: Put my bat down!

CORY: Come on, put me out.

(*Cory swings at Troy, who backs across the yard.*)

What's the matter? You so bad . . . put me out!

(*Troy advances toward Cory.*)

CORY (*backing up*): Come on! Come on!

TROY: You're gonna have to use it! You wanna draw that bat back on me . . . you're gonna have to use it.

CORY: Come on! . . . Come on!

(*Cory swings the bat at Troy a second time. He misses. Troy continues to advance toward him.*)

TROY: You're gonna have to kill me! You wanna draw that bat back on me. You're gonna have to kill me.

(*Cory, backed up against the tree, can go no farther. Troy taunts him. He sticks out his head and offers him a target.*)

Come on! Come on!

(*Cory is unable to swing the bat. Troy grabs it.*)

TROY: Then I'll show you.

(*Cory and Troy struggle over the bat. The struggle is fierce and fully engaged. Troy ultimately is the stronger and takes the bat from Cory and stands over him ready to swing. He stops himself.*)

Go on and get away from around my house.

(*Cory, stung by his defeat, picks himself up, walks slowly out of the yard and up the alley.*)

CORY: Tell Mama I'll be back for my things.

TROY: They'll be on the other side of that fence.

(*Cory exits.*)

TROY: I can't taste nothing. Helluljah! I can't taste nothing no more. (*Troy assumes a batting posture and begins to taunt Death, the fastball on the outside corner.*) Come on! It's between you and me now! Come on! Anytime you want! Come on! I be ready for you . . . but I ain't gonna be easy.

(*The lights go down on the scene.*)

Scene V

(*The time is 1965. The lights come up in the yard. It is the morning of Troy's funeral. A funeral plaque with a light hangs beside the door. There is a small garden plot off to the side. There is noise and activity in the house as Rose, Gabriel, and Bono have gathered. The door opens and Raynell, seven years old, enters dressed in a flannel nightgown. She crosses to the garden and pokes around with a stick. Rose calls from the house.*)

ROSE: Raynell!

RAYNELL: Mam?

ROSE: What you doing out there?

RAYNELL: Nothing.

(*Rose comes to the door.*)

ROSE: Girl, get in here and get dressed. What you doing?
RAYNELL: Seeing if my garden growed.
ROSE: I told you it ain't gonna grow overnight. You got to wait.
RAYNELL: It don't look like it never gonna grow. Dag!
ROSE: I told you a watched pot never boils. Get in here and get dressed.
RAYNELL: This ain't even no pot, Mama.
ROSE: You just have to give it a chance. It'll grow. Now you come on and do what I told you. We got to be getting ready. This ain't no morning to be playing around. You hear me?
RAYNELL: Yes, mam.

(*Rose exits into the house. Raynell continues to poke at her garden with a stick. Cory enters. He is dressed in a Marine corporal's uniform, and carries a duffel bag. His posture is that of a military man, and his speech has a clipped sternness.*)

CORY (*to Raynell*): Hi.

(*Pause.*)

I bet your name is Raynell.
RAYNELL: Uh huh.
CORY: Is your mama home?

(*Raynell runs up on the porch and calls through the screen door.*)

RAYNELL: Mama . . . there's some man out here. Mama?

(*Rose comes to the door.*)

ROSE: Cory? Lord have mercy! Look here, you all!

(*Rose and Cory embrace in a tearful reunion as Bono and Lyons enter from the house dressed in funeral clothes.*)

BONO: Aw, looka here . . .
ROSE: Done got all grown up!
CORY: Don't cry, Mama. What you crying about?
ROSE: I'm just so glad you made it.
CORY: Hey Lyons. How you doing, Mr. Bono.

(*Lyons goes to embrace Cory.*)

LYONS: Look at you, man. Look at you. Don't he look good, Rose. Got them Corporal stripes.
ROSE: What took you so long.
CORY: You know how the Marines are, Mama. They got to get all their paperwork straight before they let you do anything.
ROSE: Well, I'm sure glad you made it. They let Lyons come. Your Uncle Gabe's still in the hospital. They don't know if they gonna let him out or not. I just talked to them a little while ago.
LYONS: A Corporal in the United States Marines.
BONO: Your daddy knew you had it in you. He used to tell me all the time.

LYONS: Don't he look good, Mr. Bono?
BONO: Yeah, he remind me of Troy when I first met him.

(*Pause.*)

Say, Rose, Lucille's down at the church with the choir. I'm gonna go down and get the pallbearers lined up. I'll be back to get you all.
ROSE: Thanks, Jim.
CORY: See you, Mr. Bono.
LYONS (*with his arm around Raynell*): Cory . . . look at Raynell. Ain't she precious? She gonna break a whole lot of hearts.
ROSE: Raynell, come and say hello to your brother. This is your brother, Cory. You remember Cory.
RAYNELL: No, Mam.
CORY: She don't remember me, Mama.
ROSE: Well, we talk about you. She heard us talk about you. (*To Raynell.*) This is your brother, Cory. Come on and say hello.
RAYNELL: Hi.
CORY: Hi. So you're Raynell. Mama told me a lot about you.
ROSE: You all come on into the house and let me fix you some breakfast. Keep up your strength.
CORY: I ain't hungry, Mama.
LYONS: You can fix me something, Rose. I'll be in there in a minute.
ROSE: Cory, you sure you don't want nothing. I know they ain't feeding you right.
CORY: No, Mama . . . thanks. I don't feel like eating. I'll get something later.
ROSE: Raynell . . . get on upstairs and get that dress on like I told you.

(*Rose and Raynell exit into the house.*)

LYONS: So . . . I hear you thinking about getting married.
CORY: Yeah, I done found the right one, Lyons. It's about time.
LYONS: Me and Bonnie been split up about four years now. About the time Papa retired. I guess she just got tired of all them changes I was putting her through.

(*Pause.*)

I always knew you was gonna make something out yourself. Your head was always in the right direction. So . . . you gonna stay in . . . make it a career . . . put in your twenty years?
CORY: I don't know. I got six already, I think that's enough.
LYONS: Stick with Uncle Sam and retire early. Ain't nothing out here. I guess Rose told you what happened with me. They got me down the workhouse. I thought I was being slick cashing other people's checks.
CORY: How much time you doing?
LYONS: They give me three years. I got that beat now. I ain't got but nine more months. It ain't so bad. You learn to deal with it like anything else. You got to

take the crookeds with the straights. That's what Papa used to say. He used to say that when he struck out. I seen him strike out three times in a row . . . and the next time up he hit the ball over the grandstand. Right out there in Homestead Field. He wasn't satisfied hitting in the seats . . . he want to hit it over everything! After the game he had two hundred people standing around waiting to shake his hand. You got to take the crookeds with the straights. Yeah, Papa was something else.

CORY: You still playing?

LYONS: Cory . . . you know I'm gonna do that. There's some fellows down there we got us a band . . . we gonna try and stay together when we get out . . . but yeah, I'm still playing. It still helps me to get out of bed in the morning. As long as it do that I'm gonna be right there playing and trying to make some sense out of it.

ROSE (*calling*): Lyons, I got these eggs in the pan.

LYONS: Let me go on and get these eggs, man. Get ready to go bury Papa.

(*Pause.*)

How you doing? You doing all right?

(*Cory nods. Lyons touches him on the shoulder and they share a moment of silent grief. Lyons exits into the house. Cory wanders about the yard. Raynell enters.*)

RAYNELL: Hi.

CORY: Hi.

RAYNELL: Did you used to sleep in my room?

CORY: Yeah . . . that used to be my room.

RAYNELL: That's what Papa call it. "Cory's room." It got your football in the closet.

(*Rose comes to the door.*)

ROSE: Raynell, get in there and get them good shoes on.

RAYNELL: Mama, can't I wear these. Them other one hurt my feet.

ROSE: Well, they just gonna have to hurt your feet for a while. You ain't said they hurt your feet when you went down to the store and got them.

RAYNELL: They didn't hurt then. My feet done got bigger.

ROSE: Don't you give me no backtalk now. You get in there and get them shoes on.

(*Raynell exits into the house.*)

Ain't too much changed. He still got that piece of rag tied to that tree. He was out here swinging that bat. I was just ready to go back in the house. He swung that bat and then he just fell over. Seem like he swung it and stood there with this grin on his face . . . and then he just fell over. They carried him on down to the hospital, but I knew there wasn't no need . . . why don't you come on in the house?

CORY: Mama . . . I got something to tell you. I don't know how to tell you this . . . but I've got to tell you . . . I'm not going to Papa's funeral.

ROSE: Boy, hush your mouth. That's your daddy you talking about. I don't want hear that kind of talk this morning. I done raised you to come to this? You standing there all healthy and grown talking about you ain't going to your daddy's funeral?

CORY: Mama . . . listen . . .

ROSE: I don't want to hear it, Cory. You just get that thought out of your head.

CORY: I can't drag Papa with me everywhere I go. I've got to say no to him. One time in my life I've got to say no.

ROSE: Don't nobody have to listen to nothing like that. I know you and your daddy ain't seen eye to eye, but I ain't got to listen to that kind of talk this morning. Whatever was between you and your daddy . . . the time has come to put it aside. Just take it and set it over there on the shelf and forget about it. Disrespecting your daddy ain't gonna make you a man, Cory. You got to find a way to come to that on your own. Not going to your daddy's funeral ain't gonna make you a man.

CORY: The whole time I was growing up . . . living in his house . . . Papa was like a shadow that followed you everywhere. It weighed on you and sunk into your flesh. It would wrap around you and lay there until you couldn't tell which one was you anymore. That shadow digging in your flesh. Trying to crawl in. Trying to live through you. Everywhere I looked, Troy Maxson was staring back at me . . . hiding under the bed . . . in the closet. I'm just saying I've got to find a way to get rid of that shadow, Mama.

ROSE: You just like him. You got him in you good.

CORY: Don't tell me that, Mama.

ROSE: You Troy Maxson all over again.

CORY: I don't want to be Troy Maxson. I want to be me.

ROSE: You can't be nobody but who you are, Cory. That shadow wasn't nothing but you growing into yourself. You either got to grow into it or cut it down to fit you. But that's all you got to make life with. That's all you got to measure yourself against that world out there. Your daddy wanted you to be everything he wasn't . . . and at the same time he tried to make you into everything he was. I don't know if he was right or wrong . . . but I do know he meant to do more good than he meant to do harm. He wasn't always right. Sometimes when he touched he bruised. And sometimes when he took me in his arms he cut.

When I first met your daddy I thought . . . Here is a man I can lay down with and make a baby. That's the first thing I thought when I seen him. I was thirty years old and had done seen my share of men. But when he walked up to me and said "I can dance a waltz that'll make you dizzy," I thought, Rose Lee, here is a man that you can open yourself up to and be filled to bursting. Here is a man that can fill all them empty spaces you been tipping around the edges of. One of them empty spaces was being somebody's mother.

I married your daddy and settled down to cooking his supper and keeping clean sheets on the bed. When your daddy walked through the house he was so big he filled it up. That was my first mistake. Not to make him leave some room for me. For my part in the matter. But at that time I wanted that. I wanted a house that I could sing in. And that's what your daddy gave me. I didn't know to keep up his strength I had to give up little pieces of mine. I did that. I took on his life as mine and mixed up the pieces so that you couldn't hardly tell which was which anymore. It was my choice. It was my life and I didn't have to live it like that. But that's what life offered me in the way of being a woman and I took it. I grabbed hold of it with both hands.

By the time Raynell came into the house, me and your daddy had done lost touch with one another. I didn't want to make my blessing off of nobody's misfortune . . . but I took on to Raynell like she was all them babies I had wanted and never had.

(*The phone rings.*)

Like I'd been blessed to relive a part of my life. And if the Lord see fit to keep up my strength . . . I'm gonna do her just like your daddy did you . . . I'm gonna give her the best of what's in me.

RAYNELL (*entering, still with her old shoes*): Mama . . . Reverend Tollivier on the phone.

(*Rose exits into the house.*)

RAYNELL: Hi.
CORY: Hi.
RAYNELL: You in the Army or the Marines?
CORY: Marines.
RAYNELL: Papa said it was the Army. Did you know Blue?
CORY: Blue? Who's Blue?
RAYNELL: Papa's dog what he sing about all the time.
CORY (*singing*): Hear it ring! Hear it ring!
  I had a dog his name was Blue
  You know Blue was mighty true
  You know Blue was a good old dog
  Blue treed a possum in a hollow log
  You know from that he was a good old dog.
  Hear it ring! Hear it ring!

(*Raynell joins in singing.*)

CORY AND RAYNELL: Blue treed a possum out on a limb
  Blue looked at me and I looked at him
  Grabbed that possum and put him in a sack
  Blue stayed there till I came back
  Old Blue's feets was big and round
  Never allowed a possum to touch the ground.

  Old Blue died and I dug his grave
  I dug his grave with a silver spade
  Let him down with a golden chain

  And every night I call his name
  Go on Blue, you good dog you
  Go on Blue, you good dog you

RAYNELL: Blue laid down and died like a man
  Blue laid down and died . . .
BOTH: Blue laid down and died like a man
  Now he's treeing possums in the Promised Land
  I'm gonna tell you this to let you know
  Blue's gone where the good dogs go
  When I hear old Blue bark
  When I hear old Blue bark
  Blue treed a possum in Noah's Ark
  Blue treed a possum in Noah's Ark.

(*Rose comes to the screen door.*)

ROSE: Cory, we gonna be ready to go in a minute.
CORY (*to Raynell*): You go on in the house and change them shoes like Mama told you so we can go to Papa's funeral.
RAYNELL: Okay, I'll be back.

(*Raynell exits into the house. Cory gets up and crosses over to the tree. Rose stands in the screen door watching him. Gabriel enters from the alley.*)

GABRIEL (*calling*): Hey, Rose!
ROSE: Gabe?
GABRIEL: I'm here, Rose. Hey Rose, I'm here!

(*Rose enters from the house.*)

ROSE: Lord . . . Look here, Lyons!
LYONS: See, I told you, Rose . . . I told you they'd let him come.
CORY: How you doing, Uncle Gabe?
LYONS: How you doing, Uncle Gabe?
GABRIEL: Hey, Rose. It's time. It's time to tell St. Peter to open the gates. Troy, you ready? You ready, Troy. I'm gonna tell St. Peter to open the gates. You get ready now.

(*Gabriel, with great fanfare, braces himself to blow. The trumpet is without a mouthpiece. He puts the end of it into his mouth and blows with great force, like a man who has been waiting some twenty-odd years for this single moment. No sound comes out of the trumpet. He braces himself and blows again with the same result. A third time he blows. There is a weight of impossible description that falls away and leaves him bare and exposed to a frightful realization. It is a trauma that a sane and normal mind would be unable to withstand. He begins to dance. A slow, strange dance, eerie and life-giving. A dance of atavistic signature and ritual. Lyons attempts to embrace him. Gabriel pushes Lyons away. He begins to howl in what is an attempt at song, or perhaps a song turning back into itself in an attempt at speech. He finishes his dance and the gates of heaven stand open as wide as God's closet.*)

That's the way that go!

COMMENTARIES

David Savran (b. 1950)
INTERVIEW WITH AUGUST WILSON   *1987*

August Wilson is interested not only in the characters in his plays but also in their political circumstances. One of his primary efforts has been to help strip away the black male stereotypes so that his audiences can see his people as he sees them. In this interview he discusses the social conditions of African Americans and the relationship between Troy Maxson and his son Cory. Wilson's views about their relationship may be surprising, since he interprets it in a way that differs from many of the critics' interpretations.

Savran: In reading *Fences,* I came to view Troy more and more critically as the play progressed, sharing Rose's point of view. We see that Troy has been crippled by his father. That's being replayed in Troy's relationship with Cory. Do you think there's a way out of that cycle?

Wilson: Surely. First of all, we're all like our parents. The things we are taught early in life, how to respond to the world, our sense of morality — everything, we get from them. Now you can take that legacy and do with it anything you want to do. It's in your hands. Cory is Troy's son. How can he be Troy's son without sharing Troy's values? I was trying to get at why Troy made the choices he made, how they have influenced his values and how he attempts to pass those along to his son. Each generation gives the succeeding generation what they think they need. One question in the play is "Are the tools we are given sufficient to compete in a world that is different from the one our parents knew?" I think they are — it's just that we have to do different things with the tools. That's all Troy has to give. Troy's flaw is that he does not recognize that the world was changing. That's because he spent fifteen years in a penitentiary.

As African-Americans, we should demand to participate in society as Africans. That's the way out of the vicious cycle of poverty and neglect that exists in 1987 in America, where you have a huge percentage of blacks living in the equivalent of South African townships, in housing projects. No one is inviting these people to participate in society. Look at the poverty levels — $8,500 for a family of four, if you have $8,501 you're not counted. Those statistics would go up enormously if we had an honest assessment of the cost of living in America. I don't know how anybody can support a family of four on $8,500. What I'm saying is that 85 or 90 percent of blacks in America are living in abject poverty and, for the most part, are crowded into what amount to concentration camps. The situation for blacks in America is worse than it was forty years ago. Some sociologists will tell you about the tremendous progress we've made. They didn't put me out when I walked in the door. And you can always point to someone who works on Wall Street, or is a doctor. But they don't count in the larger scheme of things.

Savran: Do you have any idea how these political changes could take place?

Wilson: I'm not sure. I know that blacks must be allowed their cultural differences. I think the process of assimilation to white American society was a big mistake. We don't want to be like you. Blacks living in housing projects are isolated from the society, for the most part — living as they choose, as Africans. Only they don't realize the value in what they're doing because they have accepted their victimization. They've marked themselves as victims. Once they recognize that, they can begin to move through society in a different manner, from a stronger position, and claim what is theirs.

Savran: A project of yours is to point up what happens when oppression is internalized.

Wilson: Yes, transfer of aggression to the wrong target. I think it's interesting that the two roads open to blacks for "full participation" are entertainment and sports. *Ma Rainey* and *Fences,* and I didn't plan it that way. I don't think that they're the correct roads. I think Troy's right. Now with the benefit of historical perspective, I can say that the athletic scholarship was actually a way of exploiting. Now you've got two million kids who think they're going to play in the NBA. In the sixties the universities made a lot of money off of athletics. You had kids playing for free who, by and large, were not getting educated, were taking courses in basketweaving. Some of them could barely read.

Savran: Troy may be right about that issue, but it seems that he has passed on certain destructive traits in spite of himself. Take the hostility between father and son.

Wilson: I think every generation says to the previous generation: you're in my way, I've got to get by. The father-son conflict is actually a normal generational conflict that happens all the time.

Savran: So it's a healthy and a good thing?

Wilson: Oh, sure. Troy is seeing this boy walk around, smelling his piss. Two men cannot live in the same household. Troy would have been tremendously disappointed if Cory had not challenged him. Troy knows that this boy has to go out and do battle with that world: "So I had best prepare him because I know that's a harsh, cruel place out there. But that's going to be easy compared to what he's getting here. Ain't nobody gonna whip your ass like I'm gonna whip it." He has a tremendous love for the kid. But he's not going to say, "I love you," he's going to demonstrate it. He's carrying garbage for seventeen years just for the kid. The only world Troy knows is the one that he made. Cory's going to go on to find another one, he's going to arrive at the same place as Troy. I think one of the most important lines in the play is when Troy is talking about his father: "I got to the place where I could feel him kicking in my blood and knew that the only thing that separated us was the matter of a few years."

Hopefully, Cory will do things a bit differently with his son. For Troy, sports was not the way to go, the white man wouldn't let him get away with that. "Get you a job, with your hands, something that nobody can take away from you." The idea of school — he doesn't know what that is. That's for white folks. Very few blacks had paperwork jobs. But if you knew how to fix cars, you could always make some money. That's what Troy wants for Cory. There aren't many people who ever jumped up in Troy's face. So he's proud of the kid at the same time that he expresses a hurt that all men feel. You got to cut your kid loose at some point. There's that sense of loss and separation. You find out how Troy left his father's house and you see how Cory leaves his house. I suspect with Cory it will repeat with some differences and maybe, after five or six generations, they'll find a different way to do it.

Savran: Where Cory ends up is very ambiguous, as a marine in 1965.

Wilson: Yes. For the average black kid on the street, that was an alternative. You went into the army because you could learn how to do something. I can remember my parents talking about the son of some friends: "He's in the navy. He *did* something"— as opposed to standing on the street corner, shooting drugs, drinking wine, and robbing stores. Lyons says to Cory, "I always knew you were going to make something out of yourself." It really wounds me. He's a corporal in the marines. For blacks, that is a sense of accomplishment. Therein lies one of the tragedies of blacks in America. Cory says, "I don't know. I put in six years. That's enough." Anyone who goes into the army and makes a career out of it is a loser. They sit there and are nurtured by the army and they don't have to confront life. Then they get out of the army and find there's nothing to do. They didn't learn any skills. And if they did, they can't find a job. Four months later, they're shooting dope. In the sixties a whole bunch of blacks went over, fought and died in the Vietnam War. The survivors came back to the same street corners and found out nothing had changed. They still couldn't get a job.

At the end of *Fences* every person, with the exception of Raynell, is institutionalized. Rose is in a church. Lyons is in a penitentiary. Gabriel's in a mental hospital and Cory's in the marines. The only free person is the girl, Troy's daughter, the hope for the future. That was conscious on my part because in '57 that's what I saw. Blacks have relied on institutions which are really foreign — except for the black church, which has been our saving grace. I have some problems with it but I recognize it as a central social organization and sometimes an economic organization for the black community. I would like to see blacks develop their own institutions that respond to their needs.

Frank Rich (b. 1949)
REVIEW OF *FENCES*   *1987*

Frank Rich, the New York Times *drama critic, reviews* Fences *in context with August Wilson's other plays. Rich criticizes the old-fashioned structure of the plot, which he characterizes as "clunky," but he also admits that the play is "gripping," especially in the second act. Rich focuses on the struggle between father and son, which he sees as meaningful to "theatergoers from all kinds of families."*

To hear his wife tell it, Troy Maxson, the middle-aged Pittsburgh sanitation worker at the center of *Fences,* is "so big" that he fills up his tenement house just by walking through it. Needless to say, that description could also apply to James Earl Jones, the actor who has found what may be the best role of his career in August Wilson's new play, at the 46th Street Theater. But the remarkable stature of the character — and of the performance — is not a matter of sheer size. If Mr. Jones's Troy is a mountainous man prone to tyrannical eruptions of rage, he is also a dignified, delicate figure capable of cradling a tiny baby, of pleading gravely to his wife for understanding, of standing still to stare death unflinchingly in the eye. A black man, a free man, a descendant of slaves, a menial laborer, a father, a husband, a lover — Mr. Jones's Troy embraces all the contradictions of being black and male and American in his time.

That time is 1957 — three decades after the period of Mr. Wilson's previous and extraordinary *Ma Rainey's Black Bottom*. For blacks like Troy in the industrial North of *Fences*, social and economic equality is more a legal principle than a reality: the Maxson's slum neighborhood, a panorama of grimy brick and smokestack-blighted sky in James D. Sandefur's eloquent design, is a cauldron of busted promises, waiting to boil over. The conflagration is still a decade away — the streetlights burn like the first sparks of distant insurrection — so Mr. Wilson writes about the pain of an extended family lost in the wilderness of de facto segregation and barren hope.

It speaks of the power of the play — and of the cast assembled by the director, Lloyd Richards — that Mr. Jones's patriarch doesn't devour the rest of *Fences* so much as become the life force that at once nurtures and stunts the characters who share his blood. The strongest countervailing player is his wife, Rose, luminously acted by Mary Alice. Rose is a quiet woman who, as she says, "planted herself" in the "hard and rocky" soil of her husband. But she never bloomed: marriage brought frustration and betrayal in equal measure with affection.

Even so, Ms. Alice's performance emphasizes strength over self-pity, open anger over festering bitterness. The actress finds the spiritual quotient in the acceptance that accompanies Rose's love for a scarred, profoundly complicated man. It's rare to find a marriage of any sort presented on stage with such balance — let alone one in which the husband has fathered children by three different women. Mr. Wilson grants both partners the right to want to escape the responsibilities of their domestic drudgery while affirming their respective claims to forgiveness.

The other primary relationship of *Fences* is that of Troy to his son Cory (Courtney B. Vance) — a promising 17-year-old football player being courted by a college recruiter. Troy himself was once a baseball player in the Negro Leagues — early enough to hit homers off Satchel Paige, too early to benefit from Jackie Robinson's breakthrough — and his bitter, long-ago disappointment leads him to decree a different future for his son. But while Troy wants Cory to settle for a workhorse trade guaranteeing a weekly paycheck, the boy resists. The younger Maxson is somehow convinced that the dreams of his black generation need not end in the city's mean alleys with the carting of white men's garbage.

The struggle between father and son over conflicting visions of black identity, aspirations and values is the play's narrative fulcrum, and a paradigm of violent divisions that would later tear apart a society. As written, the conflict is also a didactic one, reminiscent of old-fashioned plays, black and white, about disputes between first-generation American parents and their rebellious children.

In *Ma Rainey* — set at a blues recording session — Mr. Wilson's characters were firecrackers exploding in a bottle, pursuing jagged theatrical riffs reflective of their music and of their intimacy with the Afro-American experience that gave birth to that music. The relative tameness of *Fences* — with its laboriously worked-out titular metaphor, its slow-fused Act I exposition — is as much an expression of its period as its predecessor was of the hotter 20s. Intentionally or not — and perhaps to the satisfaction of those who found the more esthetically daring *Ma Rainey* too "plotless"— Mr. Wilson invokes the clunkier dramaturgy of Odets, Miller and Hansberry on this occasion.

Such formulaic theatrical tidiness, while exasperating at times, proves a minor price for the gripping second act (strengthened since the play's Yale debut in 1985) and for the scattered virtuoso passages throughout. Like *Ma Rainey* and the latest Wilson work seen at Yale (*Joe Turner's Come and Gone,* also promised for New York), *Fences* leaves no doubt that Mr. Wilson is a major writer, combining a poet's ear for vernacular with a robust sense of humor (political and sexual), a sure instinct for crackling dramatic incident and a passionate commitment to a great subject.

Mr. Wilson continues to see history as fully as he sees his characters. In one scene, Troy and his oldest friend (played with brimming warmth by Ray Aranha) weave an autobiographical "talking blues"— a front-porch storytelling jaunt from the antebellum plantation through the pre-industrial urban South, jail and northward migration. *Fences* is pointedly bracketed by two disparate wars that swallowed up black manhood, and, as always with Mr. Wilson, is as keenly cognizant of its characters' bonds to Africa, however muted here, as their bondage to white America. One hears the cadences of a centuries-old heritage in Mr. Jones's efforts to shout down the devil. It is a frayed scrap of timeless blues singing, unpretty but unquenchable, that proves the over-powering cathartic link among the disparate branches of the Maxson family tree.

Under the exemplary guidance of Mr. Richards — whose staging falters only in the awkward scene transitions — the entire cast is impressive, including Frankie R. Faison in the problematic (but finally devastating) role of a brain-damaged, horn-playing uncle named Gabriel, and Charles Brown, as a Maxson son who falls into the sociological crack separating the play's two principal generations. As Cory, Courtney B. Vance is not only formidable in challenging Mr. Jones to a psychological (and sometimes physical) kill-or-be-killed battle for supremacy but also seems to grow into Troy's vocal timbre and visage by the final scene. Like most sons, Mr. Vance just can't elude "the shadow" of his father, no matter how hard he tries. Such is the long shadow Mr. Jones's father casts in *Fences* that theatergoers from all kinds of families may find him impossible to escape.

David Henry Hwang

Born in 1957, David Henry Hwang was raised in California's San Gabriel Valley by Asian-born parents. His father, a native of Shanghai, China, is a successful banker; his mother, born in the Philippines, is a professor of piano. As a child, Hwang was a proficient violinist, and today his sister makes a living as a cellist. Hwang plays jazz violin occasionally and has appeared on friends' albums. While art and music were influential as he grew, so too was his awareness of his ethnic roots; his interest in Asian American experience developed out of personal observation. Much of his early focus in drama has been on assimilation and on the power of Chinese culture, but he is also aware that he has other issues to explore in his writing.

Hwang's first play, *FOB* (1980), was written while an undergraduate at Stanford. The title of the play is an acronym standing for "Fresh Off the Boat," and the play examines the problems of immigrant assimilation. It is set in a restaurant in Chinatown with college-age characters who all reveal difficulties in fitting into the American way of life. Assimilated immigrants make fun of a young man who has just arrived from China. Hwang strips off the social pretensions of those who feel that getting ahead calls for abandoning their roots and humiliating others. The play, developed at the O'Neill Playwright's Conference, was then brought to the Public Theater in New York by Joseph Papp. It won a 1981 Obie Award for best play.

The Dance and the Railroad (1981) was developed in New York with the assurance that Joseph Papp would produce it. Hwang worked with actor John Lone, who had trained in Chinese opera in Hong Kong and who starred in the play. Hwang says that he tried to learn from Lone everything he could about the history and tradition of Chinese opera. This play demonstrates the need to understand and participate in the traditions of one's culture. The dance and operatic forms that Lone practices and values are at first rejected by Ma, the other central character in the play, but eventually win him over.

Hwang's other plays are *Family Devotions* (1981), *The House of Sleeping Beauties* (1983), *The Sound of a Voice* (1983), *Rich Relations* (1986), and *M. Butterfly* (1988), for which he is best known. *M. Butterfly* has been an international success, winning a Tony Award for best play in 1988. The story of a French diplomat's affair with a Chinese actress in the Peking Opera, it culminates in the astonishing discovery that the actress is a man. Further, their relationship, based on a true story of a more than two-decade affair, includes espionage and intrigue.

Hwang's activity since *M. Butterfly* has included more plays, films, and an opera libretto. He collaborated with Philip Glass on *1000 Airplanes on the Roof* (1988), a science fiction musical; and on *The Voyage* (1992), Glass's full-length opera. Hwang's *Bondage* (1992), a one-act play that premiered at the Humana Theatre Festival, explores the psychology of sadomasochism. Hwang's parody of the musical *Miss Saigon,* called *Face Value* (1993), desentimentalizes the popular treatment of Vietnam. His film *Golden Gate* (1994) was based on a story he heard about Chinese immigrants arrested for sending money back to China. Hwang received an Obie Award for *Golden Child* (1997), a play loosely based on his own great-grandfather's break with Confucian tradition by converting to Christianity and unbinding his daughter's feet. In 2002, Hwang co-wrote the screenplay for the movie *Possession,* based on the novel by A. S. Byatt.

M. BUTTERFLY

In his afterword to *M. Butterfly,* David Henry Hwang explains how he found the original material from which he built his play. A French diplomat had a twenty-year affair with an actor in the Peking Opera, during which time the Chinese actor was also a spy for Communist China. Eventually, the diplomat learned that the actor was not a woman, as he thought, but a man. To some extent, the drama is designed to begin answering the question of how the diplomat could have spent twenty years not knowing his lover was a man.

Hwang explains that he saw a connection between the story he read in the newspaper and the Puccini opera *Madame Butterfly* (1904), in which Pinkerton, an American naval officer, appears to marry a Japanese girl, Cio-Cio-San, but leaves for America without her. He eventually returns with his American wife, expecting to retrieve his child, and Cio-Cio-San, realizing that she has waited in vain to be reunited with her "husband," kills herself.

Hwang began the project without knowing details of the narrative of Puccini's opera and with a decision to do no research into the details of the original news article. This strategy left him free to explore his feelings about the opera and about the relationship of West to East.

At root, *M. Butterfly* examines both racist and sexist attitudes common to the Western male. As Song Liling, the actor who masquerades as a woman, tells us late in the play, "being an Oriental, I could never be completely a man." In explaining the role of stereotypes in the deception he also tells the judge: "The West thinks of itself as masculine — big guns, big industry, big money — so the East is feminine — weak, delicate, poor . . . but good at art, and full of inscrutable wisdom — the feminine mystique."

Hwang saw that all these qualities were prominent in Puccini's opera. The powerful American naval officer did exactly as he wished with his Madame Butterfly, with no understanding of her deepest feelings. The opening of *M. Butterfly* provides enough background on the opera for the audience to see the parallels to the story Gallimard tells us. But in Hwang's version, the Westerner is beguiled and imprisoned, and the "Oriental woman" is free. It is not by accident that this story is narrated primarily from Gallimard's dank prison cell and that the outcome of Hwang's narrative is exactly the reverse of Puccini's. The cell and reversal help explain what Hwang meant by his intention to deconstruct the story of *Madame Butterfly.*

The ingenious development of the dramatic line keeps us always aware that Gallimard behaves in a manner rooted in Puccini's opera. Like Pinkerton, he considers himself honorable in respecting Song Liling's "modesty" when "she" refuses to disrobe in light of what he thinks are normal Chinese customs. Gallimard is admittedly backward and reserved in relation to women. He expects women to be weaker, but he also expects that his passivity will be rewarded with ardor. Hwang places the explanation for the deception's success deep in the psychology of Gallimard. However, he explains a portion of that psychology in terms of what Song Liling describes as a "rape mentality."

Ironically, we learn at the end of the play that Gallimard's role in French intelligence is so hopeless that all his predictions — based on his superior "knowledge" of the Chinese — are completely false. In other words, French intelligence, or Western intelligence as represented by Gallimard, is false intelligence. The vaunted diplomat is essentially unintelligent when it comes to understanding the Chinese, just as he is unintelligent in understanding Song Liling. Hwang may have chosen the name Gallimard because it is also the name of a prominent French publisher whose books on the Orient attempt to explain the East.

M. Butterfly in Performance

The play premiered in Washington, D.C., in 1988 to generally good reviews. John Dexter was the director. In New York the play was received with enthusiasm and became a major success, winning a Tony Award for best play. John Lithgow played Gallimard and B. D. Wong played Song Liling. The staging featured a rounded ascending ramp, designed by Eiko Ishioka, on which Song Liling dominates the space, while below, in a space resembling a prison cell, Gallimard can only look up as at a performance of an opera. The opening scenes of the production used Chinese red as a primary color both in the staging and the lighting, producing a rich sensuousness to contrast with the darkness of Gallimard's cell.

After its New York run, M. Butterfly toured across the United States and has enjoyed revivals in major cities in the United States and around the world. It has proven to be a durable drama with a major appeal to a wide variety of audiences.

David Henry Hwang (b. 1957)
M. BUTTERFLY   1988

The Characters

RENÉ GALLIMARD
SONG LILING
MARC/MAN NO. 2/CONSUL SHARPLESS
RENÉE/WOMAN AT PARTY/PINUP GIRL
COMRADE CHIN/SUZUKI/SHU-FANG
HELGA
TOULON/MAN NO. 1/JUDGE
DANCERS

Time and Place: *The action of the play takes place in a Paris prison in the present, and, in recall, during the decade 1960–1970 in Beijing, and from 1966 to the present in Paris.*

Playwright's Notes: *A former French diplomat and a Chinese opera singer have been sentenced to six years in jail for spying for China after a two-day trial that traced a story of clandestine love and mistaken sexual identity. . . .*

Mr. Boursicot was accused of passing information to China after he fell in love with Mr. Shi, whom he believed for twenty years to be a woman.
— THE NEW YORK TIMES, *May 11, 1986*

This play was suggested by international newspaper accounts of a recent espionage trial. For purposes of dramatization, names have been changed, characters created, and incidents devised or altered, and this play does not purport to be a factual record of real events or real people.

I could escape this feeling
With my China girl . . .   — DAVID BOWIE & IGGY POP

ACT I • Scene I

(*M. Gallimard's prison cell. Paris. 1988.*

Lights fade up to reveal René Gallimard, sixty-five, in a prison cell. He wears a comfortable bathrobe and looks old and tired. The sparsely furnished cell contains a wooden crate, upon which sits a hot plate with a kettle and a portable tape recorder. Gallimard sits on the crate staring at the recorder, a sad smile on his face.

Upstage Song, who appears as a beautiful woman in traditional Chinese garb, dances a traditional piece from the Peking Opera, surrounded by the percussive clatter of Chinese music.

Then, slowly, lights and sound cross-fade; the Chinese opera music dissolves into a Western opera, the "Love Duet" from Puccini's Madame Butterfly. *Song continues dancing, now to the Western accompaniment. Though her movements are the same, the difference in music now gives them a balletic quality.*

Gallimard rises, and turns upstage towards the figure of Song, who dances without acknowledging him.)

GALLIMARD: Butterfly, Butterfly . . .

(*He forces himself to turn away, as the image of Song fades out, and talks to us.*)

The limits of my cell are as such: four-and-a-half meters by five. There's one window against the far wall; a door, very strong, to protect me from autograph hounds. I'm responsible for the tape recorder, the hot plate, and this charming coffee table.

When I want to eat, I'm marched off to the dining room — hot, steaming slop appears on my plate. When I want to sleep, the light bulb turns itself off — the work of fairies. It's an enchanted space I occupy. The French — we know how to run a prison.

But, to be honest, I'm not treated like an ordinary prisoner. Why? Because I'm a celebrity. You see, I make people laugh.

I never dreamed this day would arrive. I've never been considered witty or clever. In fact, as a young boy, in an informal poll among my grammar school classmates, I was voted "least likely to be invited to a party." It's a title I managed to hold on to for many years. Despite some stiff competition.

But now, how the tables turn! Look at me: the life of every social function in Paris. Paris? Why be modest: My fame has spread to Amsterdam, London, New York. Listen to them! In the world's smartest parlors. I'm the one who lifts their spirits!

(*With a flourish, Gallimard directs our attention to another part of the stage.*)

Scene II

(*A party. 1988.*

Lights go up on a chic-looking parlor, where a well-dressed trio, two men and one woman, make conversation. Gallimard also remains lit; he observes them from his cell.)

WOMAN: And what of Gallimard?
MAN 1: Gallimard?
MAN 2: Gallimard!
GALLIMARD (*to us*): You see? They're all determined to say my name, as if it were some new dance.
WOMAN: He still claims not to believe the truth.
MAN 1: What? Still? Even since the trial?
WOMAN: Yes. Isn't it mad?
MAN 2 (*laughing*): He says . . . it was dark . . . and she was very modest!

(*The trio break into laughter.*)

MAN 1: So — what? He never touched her with his hands?
MAN 2: Perhaps he did, and simply misidentified the equipment. A compelling case for sex education in the schools.
WOMAN: To protect the National Security — the Church can't argue with that.
MAN 1: That's impossible! How could he not know?
MAN 2: Simple ignorance.
MAN 1: For twenty years?
MAN 2: Time flies when you're being stupid.
WOMAN: Well, I thought the French were ladies' men.
MAN 2: It seems Monsieur Gallimard was overly anxious to live up to his national reputation.
WOMAN: Well, he's not very good-looking.
MAN 1: No, he's not.
MAN 2: Certainly not.
WOMAN: Actually, I feel sorry for him.
MAN 2: A toast! To Monsieur Gallimard!
WOMAN: Yes! To Gallimard!
MAN 1: To Gallimard!
MAN 2: *Vive la différence!*

(*They toast, laughing. Lights down on them.*)

Scene III

(*M. Gallimard's cell.*)

GALLIMARD (*smiling*): You see? They toast me. I've become a patron saint of the socially inept. Can they really be so foolish? Men like that — they should be scratching at my door, begging to learn my secrets! For I, René Gallimard, you see, I have known, and been loved by . . . the Perfect Woman.

Alone in this cell, I sit night after night, watching our story play through my head, always searching for a new ending, one which redeems my honor, where she returns at last to my arms. And I imagine you — my ideal audience — who come to understand and even, perhaps just a little, to envy me.

(*He turns on his tape recorder. Over the house speakers, we hear the opening phrases of* Madame Butterfly.)

GALLIMARD: In order for you to understand what I did and why, I must introduce you to my favorite opera: *Madame Butterfly*. By Giacomo Puccini. First produced at La Scala, Milan, in 1904, it is now beloved throughout the Western world.

(*As Gallimard describes the opera, the tape segues in and out to sections he may be describing.*)

GALLIMARD: And why not? Its heroine, Cio-Cio-San, also known as Butterfly, is a feminine ideal, beautiful and brave. And its hero, the man for whom she gives up everything, is — (*He pulls out a naval officer's cap from under his crate, pops it on his head, and struts about.*) — not very good-looking, not too bright, and pretty much a wimp: Benjamin Franklin Pinkerton of the U.S. Navy. As the curtain rises, he's just closed on two great bargains: one on a house, the other on a woman — call it a package deal.

Pinkerton purchased the rights to Butterfly for one hundred yen — in modern currency, equivalent to about . . . sixty-six cents. So, he's feeling pretty pleased with himself as Sharpless, the American consul, arrives to witness the marriage.

(*Marc, wearing an official cap to designate Sharpless, enters and plays the character.*)

SHARPLESS/MARC: Pinkerton!

PINKERTON/GALLIMARD: Sharpless! How's it hangin'? It's a great day, just great. Between my house, my wife, and the rickshaw ride in from town, I've saved nineteen cents just this morning.

SHARPLESS: Wonderful. I can see the inscription on your tombstone already: "I saved a dollar, here I lie." (*He looks around.*) Nice house.

PINKERTON: It's artistic. Artistic, don't you think? Like the way the shoji screens slide open to reveal the wet bar and disco mirror ball? Classy, huh? Great for impressing the chicks.

SHARPLESS: "Chicks"? Pinkerton, you're going to be a married man!

PINKERTON: Well, sort of.

SHARPLESS: What do you mean?

PINKERTON: This country — Sharpless, it is okay. You got all these geisha girls running around —

SHARPLESS: I know! I live here!

PINKERTON: Then, you know the marriage laws, right? I split for one month, it's annulled!

SHARPLESS: Leave it to you to read the fine print. Who's the lucky girl?

PINKERTON: Cio-Cio-San. Her friends call her Butterfly. Sharpless, she eats out of my hand!

SHARPLESS: She's probably very hungry.

PINKERTON: Not like American girls. It's true what they say about Oriental girls. They want to be treated bad!

SHARPLESS: Oh, please!

PINKERTON: It's true!

SHARPLESS: Are you serious about this girl?

PINKERTON: I'm marrying her, aren't I?

SHARPLESS: Yes — with generous trade-in terms.

PINKERTON: When I leave, she'll know what it's like to have loved a real man. And I'll even buy her a few nylons.

SHARPLESS: You aren't planning to take her with you?

PINKERTON: Huh? Where?

SHARPLESS: Home!

PINKERTON: You mean, America? Are you crazy? Can you see her trying to buy rice in St. Louis?

SHARPLESS: So, you're not serious.

(*Pause.*)

PINKERTON/GALLIMARD (*as Pinkerton*): Consul, I am a sailor in port. (*As Gallimard.*) They then proceed to sing the famous duet, "The Whole World Over."

(*The duet plays on the speakers. Gallimard, as Pinkerton, lip-syncs his lines from the opera.*)

GALLIMARD: To give a rough translation: "The whole world over, the Yankee travels, casting his anchor wherever he wants. Life's not worth living unless he can win the hearts of the fairest maidens, then hotfoot it off the premises ASAP." (*He turns towards Marc.*) In the preceding scene, I played Pinkerton, the womanizing cad, and my friend Marc from school . . . (*Marc bows grandly for our benefit.*) played Sharpless, the sensitive soul of reason. In life, however, our positions were usually — no, always — reversed.

Scene IV

(*École Nationale.° Aix-en-Provence. 1947.*)

GALLIMARD: No, Marc, I think I'd rather stay home.

MARC: Are you crazy?! We are going to Dad's condo in Marseilles! You know what happened last time?

GALLIMARD: Of course I do.

École Nationale: National School.

MARC: Of course you don't! You never know. . . . They stripped, René!

GALLIMARD: Who stripped?

MARC: The girls!

GALLIMARD: Girls? Who said anything about girls?

MARC: René, we're a buncha university guys goin' up to the woods. What are we gonna do — talk philosophy?

GALLIMARD: What girls? Where do you get them?

MARC: Who cares? The point is, they come. On trucks. Packed in like sardines. The back flips open, babes hop out, we're ready to roll.

GALLIMARD: You mean, they just — ?

MARC: Before you know it, every last one of them — they're stripped and splashing around my pool. There's no moon out, they can't see what's going on, their boobs are flapping, right? You close your eyes, reach out — it's grab bag, get it? Doesn't matter whose ass is between whose legs, whose teeth are sinking into who. You're just in there, going at it, eyes closed, on and on for as long as you can stand. (*Pause.*) Some fun, huh?

GALLIMARD: What happens in the morning?

MARC: In the morning, you're ready to talk some philosophy. (*Beat.*) So how 'bout it?

GALLIMARD: Marc, I can't . . . I'm afraid they'll say no — the girls. So I never ask.

MARC: You don't have to ask! That's the beauty — don't you see? They don't have to say yes. It's perfect for a guy like you, really.

GALLIMARD: You go ahead . . . I may come later.

MARC: Hey, René — it doesn't matter that you're clumsy and got zits — they're not looking!

GALLIMARD: Thank you very much.

MARC: Wimp.

(*Marc walks over to the other side of the stage, and starts waving and smiling at women in the audience.*)

GALLIMARD (*to us*): We now return to my version of *Madame Butterfly* and the events leading to my recent conviction for treason.

(*Gallimard notices Marc making lewd gestures.*)

GALLIMARD: Marc, what are you doing?

MARC: Huh? (*Sotto voce.*) René, there're a lotta great babes out there. They're probably lookin' at me and thinking, "What a dangerous guy."

GALLIMARD: Yes — how could they help but be impressed by your cool sophistication?

(*Gallimard pops the Sharpless cap on Marc's head, and points him offstage. Marc exits, leering.*)

Scene V

(*M. Gallimard's cell.*)

GALLIMARD: Next, Butterfly makes her entrance. We learn her age — fifteen . . . but very mature for her years.

(*Lights come up on the area where we saw Song dancing at the top of the play. She appears there again, now dressed as Madame Butterfly, moving to the "Love Duet." Gallimard turns upstage slightly to watch, transfixed.*)

GALLIMARD: But as she glides past him, beautiful, laughing softly behind her fan, don't we who are men sigh with hope? We, who are not handsome, nor brave, nor powerful, yet somehow believe, like Pinkerton, that we deserve a Butterfly. She arrives with all her possessions in the folds of her sleeves, lays them all out, for her man to do with as he pleases. Even her life itself — she bows her head as she whispers that she's not even worth the hundred yen he paid for her. He's already given too much, when we know he's really had to give nothing at all.

(*Music and lights on Song out. Gallimard sits at his crate.*)

GALLIMARD: In real life, women who put their total worth at less than sixty-six cents are quite hard to find. The closest we come is in the pages of these magazines. (*He reaches into his crate, pulls out a stack of girlie magazines, and begins flipping through them.*) Quite a necessity in prison. For three or four dollars, you get seven or eight women.

I first discovered these magazines at my uncle's house. One day, as a boy of twelve. The first time I saw them in his closet . . . all lined up — my body shook. Not with lust — no, with power. Here were women — a shelfful — who would do exactly as I wanted.

(*The "Love Duet" creeps in over the speakers. Special comes up, revealing, not Song this time, but a pinup girl in a sexy negligee, her back to us. Gallimard turns upstage and looks at her.*)

GIRL: I know you're watching me.

GALLIMARD: My throat . . . it's dry.

GIRL: I leave my blinds open every night before I go to bed.

GALLIMARD: I can't move.

GIRL: I leave my blinds open and the lights on.

GALLIMARD: I'm shaking. My skin is hot, but my penis is soft. Why?

GIRL: I stand in front of the window.

GALLIMARD: What is she going to do?

GIRL: I toss my hair, and I let my lips part . . . barely.

GALLIMARD: I shouldn't be seeing this. It's so dirty. I'm so bad.

GIRL: Then, slowly, I lift off my nightdress.

GALLIMARD: Oh, god. I can't believe it. I can't —

GIRL: I toss it to the ground.

GALLIMARD: Now, she's going to walk away. She's going to —

GIRL: I stand there, in the light, displaying myself.

GALLIMARD: No. She's — why is she naked?

GIRL: To you.

GALLIMARD: In front of a window? This is wrong. No —

GIRL: Without shame.

GALLIMARD: No, she must . . . like it.

GIRL: I like it.

GALLIMARD: She . . . she wants me to see.

GIRL: I want you to see.

GALLIMARD: I can't believe it! She's getting excited!

GIRL: I can't see you. You can do whatever you want.

GALLIMARD: I can't do a thing. Why?

GIRL: What would you like me to do . . . next?

(*Lights go down on her. Music off. Silence, as Gallimard puts away his magazines. Then he resumes talking to us.*)

GALLIMARD: Act Two begins with Butterfly staring at the ocean. Pinkerton's been called back to the U.S., and he's given his wife a detailed schedule of his plans. In the column marked "return date," he's written "when the robins nest." This failed to ignite her suspicions. Now, three years have passed without a peep from him. Which brings a response from her faithful servant, Suzuki.

(*Comrade Chin enters, playing Suzuki.*)

SUZUKI: Girl, he's a loser. What'd he ever give you? Nineteen cents and those ugly Day-Glo stockings? Look, it's finished! Kaput! Done! And you should be glad! I mean, the guy was a woofer! He tried before, you know — before he met you, he went down to geisha central and plunked down his spare change in front of the usual candidates — everyone else gagged! These are hungry prostitutes, and they were not interested, get the picture? Now, stop slathering when an American ship sails in, and let's make some bucks — I mean, yen! We are broke!

Now, what about Yamadori? Hey, hey — don't look away — the man is a prince — figuratively, and, what's even better, literally. He's rich, he's handsome, he says he'll die if you don't marry him — and he's even willing to overlook the little fact that you've been deflowered all over the place by a foreign devil. What do you mean, "But he's Japanese"? What do you think you are? You think you've been touched by the whitey god? He was a sailor with dirty hands!

(*Suzuki stalks offstage.*)

GALLIMARD: She's also visited by Consul Sharpless, sent by Pinkerton on a minor errand.

(*Marc enters, as Sharpless.*)

SHARPLESS: I hate this job.

GALLIMARD: This Pinkerton — he doesn't show up personally to tell his wife he's abandoning her. No, he sends a government diplomat . . . at taxpayers' expense.

SHARPLESS: Butterfly? Butterfly? I have some bad — I'm going to be ill. Butterfly, I came to tell you —

GALLIMARD: Butterfly says she knows he'll return and if he doesn't she'll kill herself rather than go back to her own people. (*Beat.*) This causes a lull in the conversation.

SHARPLESS: Let's put it this way . . .

GALLIMARD: Butterfly runs into the next room, and returns holding —

(*Sound cue: a baby crying. Sharpless, "seeing" this, backs away.*)

SHARPLESS: Well, good. Happy to see things going so well. I suppose I'll be going now. Ta ta. Ciao. (*He turns away. Sound cue out.*) I hate this job. (*He exits.*)

GALLIMARD: At that moment, Butterfly spots in the harbor an American ship — the *Abramo Lincoln!*

(*Music cue: "The Flower Duet." Song, still dressed as Butterfly, changes into a wedding kimono, moving to the music.*)

GALLIMARD: This is the moment that redeems her years of waiting. With Suzuki's help, they cover the room with flowers —

(*Chin, as Suzuki, trudges onstage and drops a lone flower without much enthusiasm.*)

GALLIMARD: — and she changes into her wedding dress to prepare for Pinkerton's arrival.

(*Suzuki helps Butterfly change. Helga enters, and helps Gallimard change into a tuxedo.*)

GALLIMARD: I married a woman older than myself — Helga.

HELGA: My father was ambassador to Australia. I grew up among criminals and kangaroos.

GALLIMARD: Hearing that brought me to the altar —

(*Helga exits.*)

GALLIMARD: — where I took a vow renouncing love. No fantasy woman would ever want me, so, yes, I would settle for a quick leap up the career ladder. Passion, I banish, and in its place — practicality!

But my vows had long since lost their charm by the time we arrived in China. The sad truth is that all men want a beautiful woman, and the uglier the man, the greater the want.

(*Suzuki makes final adjustments of Butterfly's costume, as does Gallimard of his tuxedo.*)

GALLIMARD: I married late, at age thirty-one. I was faithful to my marriage for eight years. Until the day when, as a junior-level diplomat in puritanical Peking, in a parlor at the German ambassador's house, during the "Reign of a Hundred Flowers,"° I first saw her . . . singing the death scene from *Madame Butterfly.*

(*Suzuki runs offstage.*)

Reign of a Hundred Flowers: A brief period in 1957 when freedom of expression was allowed in China.

Scene VI

(*German ambassador's house. Beijing. 1960.*

The upstage special area now becomes a stage. Several chairs face upstage, representing seating for some twenty guests in the parlor. A few "diplomats"— Renée, Marc, Toulon — in formal dress enter and take seats.

Gallimard also sits down, but turns towards us and continues to talk. Orchestral accompaniment on the tape is now replaced by a simple piano. Song picks up the death scene from the point where Butterfly uncovers the hara-kiri knife.)

GALLIMARD: The ending is pitiful. Pinkerton, in an act of great courage, stays home and sends his American wife to pick up Butterfly's child. The truth, long deferred, has come up to her door.

(*Song, playing Butterfly, sings the lines from the opera in her own voice — which, though not classical, should be decent.*)

SONG: "Con onor muore / chi non puo serbar / vita con onore."

GALLIMARD (*simultaneously*): "Death with honor / Is better than life / Life with dishonor."

(*The stage is illuminated; we are now completely within an elegant diplomat's residence. Song proceeds to play out an abbreviated death scene. Everyone in the room applauds. Song, shyly, takes her bows. Others in the room rush to congratulate her. Gallimard remains with us.*)

GALLIMARD: They say in opera the voice is everything. That's probably why I'd never before enjoyed opera. Here . . . here was a Butterfly with little or no voice — but she had the grace, the delicacy . . . I believed this girl. I believed her suffering. I wanted to take her in my arms — so delicate, even I could protect her, take her home, pamper her until she smiled.

(*Over the course of the preceding speech, Song has broken from the upstage crowd and moved directly upstage of Gallimard.*)

SONG: Excuse me. Monsieur . . . ?

(*Gallimard turns upstage, shocked.*)

GALLIMARD: Oh! Gallimard. Mademoiselle . . . ? A beautiful . . .
SONG: Song Liling.
GALLIMARD: A beautiful performance.
SONG: Oh, please.
GALLIMARD: I usually —
SONG: You make me blush. I'm no opera singer at all.
GALLIMARD: I usually don't like *Butterfly*.
SONG: I can't blame you in the least.
GALLIMARD: I mean, the story —
SONG: Ridiculous.
GALLIMARD: I like the story, but . . . what?
SONG: Oh, you like it?

GALLIMARD: I . . . what I mean is, I've always seen it played by huge women in so much bad makeup.
SONG: Bad makeup is not unique to the West.
GALLIMARD: But, who can believe them?
SONG: And you believe me?
GALLIMARD: Absolutely. You were utterly convincing. It's the first time —
SONG: Convincing? As a Japanese woman? The Japanese used hundreds of our people for medical experiments during the war, you know. But I gather such an irony is lost on you.
GALLIMARD: No! I was about to say, it's the first time I've seen the beauty of the story.
SONG: Really?
GALLIMARD: Of her death. It's a . . . a pure sacrifice. He's unworthy, but what can she do? She loves him . . . so much. It's a very beautiful story.
SONG: Well, yes, to a Westerner.
GALLIMARD: Excuse me?
SONG: It's one of your favorite fantasies, isn't it? The submissive Oriental woman and the cruel white man.
GALLIMARD: Well, I didn't quite mean . . .
SONG: Consider it this way: what would you say if a blonde homecoming queen fell in love with a short Japanese businessman? He treats her cruelly, then goes home for three years, during which time she prays to his picture and turns down marriage from a young Kennedy. Then, when she learns he has remarried, she kills herself. Now, I believe you would consider this girl to be a deranged idiot, correct? But because it's an Oriental who kills herself for a Westerner — ah! — you find it beautiful.

(*Silence.*)

GALLIMARD: Yes . . . well . . . I see your point . . .
SONG: I will never do Butterfly again, Monsieur Gallimard. If you wish to see some real theater, come to the Peking Opera sometime. Expand your mind.

(*Song walks offstage. Other guests exit with her.*)

GALLIMARD (*to us*): So much for protecting her in my big Western arms.

Scene VII

(*M. Gallimard's apartment. Beijing. 1960.*

Gallimard changes from his tux into a casual suit. Helga enters.)

GALLIMARD: The Chinese are an incredibly arrogant people.
HELGA: They warned us about that in Paris, remember?
GALLIMARD: Even Parisians consider them arrogant. That's a switch.
HELGA: What is it that Madame Su says? "We are a very old civilization." I never know if she's talking about her country or herself.
GALLIMARD: I walk around here, all I hear every day,

everywhere is how *old* this culture is. The fact that "old" may be synonymous with "senile" doesn't occur to them.

HELGA: You're not going to change them. "East is east, west is west, and . . ." whatever that guy said.

GALLIMARD: It's just that — silly. I met . . . at Ambassador Koening's tonight — you should've been there.

HELGA: Koening? Oh god, no. Did he enchant you all again with the history of Bavaria?

GALLIMARD: No. I met, I suppose, the Chinese equivalent of a diva. She's a singer in the Chinese opera.

HELGA: They have an opera, too? Do they sing in Chinese? Or maybe — in Italian?

GALLIMARD: Tonight, she did sing in Italian.

HELGA: How'd she manage that?

GALLIMARD: She must've been educated in the West before the Revolution. Her French is very good also. Anyway, she sang the death scene from *Madame Butterfly*.

HELGA: *Madame Butterfly!* Then I should have come. (*She begins humming, floating around the room as if dragging long kimono sleeves.*) Did she have a nice costume? I think it's a classic piece of music.

GALLIMARD: That's what *I* thought, too. Don't let her hear you say that.

HELGA: What's wrong?

GALLIMARD: Evidently the Chinese hate it.

HELGA: She hated it, but she performed it anyway? Is she perverse?

GALLIMARD: They hate it because the white man gets the girl. Sour grapes if you ask me.

HELGA: Politics again? Why can't they just hear it as a piece of beautiful music? So, what's in their opera?

GALLIMARD: I don't know. But, whatever it is, I'm sure it must be *old*.

(*Helga exits.*)

Scene VIII

(*Chinese opera house and the streets of Beijing. 1960. The sound of gongs clanging fills the stage.*)

GALLIMARD: My wife's innocent question kept ringing in my ears. I asked around, but no one knew anything about the Chinese opera. It took four weeks, but my curiosity overcame my cowardice. This Chinese diva — this unwilling Butterfly — what did she do to make her so proud?

The room was hot, and full of smoke. Wrinkled faces, old women, teeth missing — a man with a growth on his neck, like a human toad. All smiling, pipes falling from their mouths, cracking nuts between their teeth, a live chicken pecking at my foot — all looking, screaming, gawking . . . at her.

(*The upstage area is suddenly hit with a harsh white light. It has become the stage for the Chinese opera performance. Two dancers enter, along with Song. Gallimard stands apart, watching. Song glides gracefully*

amidst the two dancers. Drums suddenly slam to a halt. Song strikes a pose, looking straight at Gallimard. Dancers exit. Light change. Pause, then Song walks right off the stage and straight up to Gallimard.)

SONG: Yes. You. White man. I'm looking straight at you.

GALLIMARD: Me?

SONG: You see any other white men? It was too easy to spot you. How often does a man in my audience come in a tie?

(*Song starts to remove her costume. Underneath, she wears simple baggy clothes. They are now backstage. The show is over.*)

SONG: So, you are an adventurous imperialist?

GALLIMARD: I . . . thought it would further my education.

SONG: It took you four weeks. Why?

GALLIMARD: I've been busy.

SONG: Well, education has always been undervalued in the West, hasn't it?

GALLIMARD (*laughing*): I don't think that's true.

SONG: No, you wouldn't. You're a Westerner. How can you objectively judge your own values?

GALLIMARD: I think it's possible to achieve some distance.

SONG: Do you? (*Pause.*) It stinks in here. Let's go.

GALLIMARD: These are the smells of your loyal fans.

SONG: I love them for being my fans, I hate the smell they leave behind. I too can distance myself from my people. (*She looks around, then whispers in his ear.*) "Art for the masses" is a shitty excuse to keep artists poor. (*She pops a cigarette in her mouth.*) Be a gentleman, will you? And light my cigarette.

(*Gallimard fumbles for a match.*)

GALLIMARD: I don't . . . smoke.

SONG (*lighting her own*): Your loss. Had you lit my cigarette, I might have blown a puff of smoke right between your eyes. Come.

(*They start to walk about the stage. It is a summer night on the Beijing streets. Sounds of the city play on the house speakers.*)

SONG: How I wish there were even a tiny café to sit in. With cappuccinos, and men in tuxedos, and bad expatriate jazz.

GALLIMARD: If my history serves me correctly, you weren't even allowed into the clubs in Shanghai before the Revolution.

SONG: Your history serves you poorly, Monsieur Gallimard. True, there were signs reading "No dogs and Chinamen." But a woman, especially a delicate Oriental woman — we always go where we please. Could you imagine it otherwise? Clubs in China filled with pasty, big-thighed white women, while thousands of slender lotus blossoms wait just outside the door? Never. The clubs would be empty. (*Beat.*) We have always held a certain fascination for you Caucasian men, have we not?

GALLIMARD: But . . . that fascination is imperialist, or so you tell me.

SONG: Do you believe everything I tell you? Yes. It is always imperialist. But sometimes . . . sometimes, it is also mutual. Oh — this is my flat.

GALLIMARD: I didn't even —

SONG: Thank you. Come another time and we will further expand your mind.

(*Song exits. Gallimard continues roaming the streets as he speaks to us.*)

GALLIMARD: What was that? What did she mean, "Sometimes . . . it is mutual"? Women do not flirt with me. And I normally can't talk to them. But tonight, I held up my end of the conversation.

Scene IX

(*Gallimard's bedroom. Beijing. 1960.
Helga enters.*)

HELGA: You didn't tell me you'd be home late.

GALLIMARD: I didn't intend to. Something came up.

HELGA: Oh? Like what?

GALLIMARD: I went to the . . . to the Dutch ambassador's home.

HELGA: Again?

GALLIMARD: There was a reception for a visiting scholar. He's writing a six-volume treatise on the Chinese revolution. We all gathered that meant he'd have to live here long enough to actually write six volumes, and we all expressed our deepest sympathies.

HELGA: Well, I had a good night too. I went with the ladies to a martial arts demonstration. Some of those men — when they break those thick boards — (*she mimes fanning herself*) whoo-whoo!

(*Helga exits. Lights dim.*)

GALLIMARD: I lied to my wife. Why? I've never had any reason to lie before. But what reason did I have tonight? I didn't do anything wrong. That night, I had a dream. Other people, I've been told, have dreams when angels appear. Or dragons, or Sophia Loren in a towel. In my dream, Marc from school appeared.

(*Marc enters, in a nightshirt and cap.*)

MARC: René! You met a girl!

(*Gallimard and Marc stumble down the Beijing streets. Night sounds over the speakers.*)

GALLIMARD: It's not that amazing, thank you.

MARC: No! It's so monumental, I heard about it halfway around the world in my sleep!

GALLIMARD: I've met girls before, you know.

MARC: Name one. I've come across time and space to congratulate you. (*He hands Gallimard a bottle of wine.*)

GALLIMARD: Marc, this is expensive.

MARC: On those rare occasions when you become a formless spirit, why not steal the best?

(*Marc pops open the bottle, begins to share it with Gallimard.*)

GALLIMARD: You embarrass me. She . . . there's no reason to think she likes me.

MARC: "Sometimes, it is mutual"?

GALLIMARD: Oh.

MARC: "Mutual"? "Mutual"? What does that mean?

GALLIMARD: You heard?

MARC: It means the money is in the bank, you only have to write the check!

GALLIMARD: I am a married man!

MARC: And an excellent one too. I cheated after . . . six months. Then again and again, until now — three hundred girls in twelve years.

GALLIMARD: I don't think we should hold that up as a model.

MARC: Of course not! My life — it is disgusting! Phooey! Phooey! But, you — you are the model husband.

GALLIMARD: Anyway, it's impossible. I'm a foreigner.

MARC: Ah, yes. She cannot love you, it is taboo, but something deep inside her heart . . . she cannot help herself . . . she must surrender to you. It is her destiny.

GALLIMARD: How do you imagine all this?

MARC: The same way you do. It's an old story. It's in our blood. They fear us, René. Their women fear us. And their men — their men hate us. And, you know something? They are all correct.

(*They spot a light in a window.*)

MARC: There! There, René!

GALLIMARD: It's her window.

MARC: Late at night — it burns. The light — it burns for you.

GALLIMARD: I won't look. It's not respectful.

MARC: We don't have to be respectful. We're foreign devils.

(*Enter Song, in a sheer robe, her face completely swathed in black cloth. The "One Fine Day" aria creeps in over the speakers. With her back to us, Song mimes attending to her toilette. Her robe comes loose, revealing her white shoulders.*)

MARC: All your life you've waited for a beautiful girl who would lay down for you. All your life you've smiled like a saint when it's happened to every other man you know. And you see them in magazines and you see them in movies. And you wonder, what's wrong with me? Will anyone beautiful ever want me? As the years pass, your hair thins and you struggle to hold on to even your hopes. Stop struggling, René. The wait is over. (*He exits.*)

GALLIMARD: Marc? Marc?

(*At that moment, Song, her back still towards us, drops her robe. A second of her naked back, then a sound cue: a phone ringing, very loud. Blackout, followed in the next beat by a special up on the bedroom area, where a*) *phone now sits. Gallimard stumbles across the stage and picks up the phone. Sound cue out. Over the course of his conversation, area lights fill in the vicinity of his bed. It is the following morning.*)

GALLIMARD: Yes? Hello?
SONG (*offstage*): Is it very early?
GALLIMARD: Why, yes.
SONG (*offstage*): How early?
GALLIMARD: It's . . . it's 5:30. Why are you — ?
SONG (*offstage*): But it's light outside. Already.
GALLIMARD: It is. The sun must be in confusion today.

(*Over the course of Song's next speech, her upstage special comes up again. She sits in a chair, legs crossed, in a robe, telephone to her ear.*)

SONG: I waited until I saw the sun. That was as much discipline as I could manage for one night. Do you forgive me?
GALLIMARD: Of course . . . for what?
SONG: Then I'll ask you quickly. Are you really interested in the opera?
GALLIMARD: Why, yes. Yes I am.
SONG: Then come again next Thursday. I am playing *The Drunken Beauty.* May I count on you?
GALLIMARD: Yes. You may.
SONG: Perfect. Well, I must be getting to bed. I'm exhausted. It's been a very long night for me.

(*Song hangs up; special on her goes off. Gallimard begins to dress for work.*)

Scene X

(*Song Liling's apartment. Beijing. 1960.*)

GALLIMARD: I returned to the opera that next week, and the week after that . . . she keeps our meetings so short — perhaps fifteen, twenty minutes at most. So I am left each week with a thirst which is intensified. In this way, fifteen weeks have gone by. I am starting to doubt the words of my friend Marc. But no, not really. In my heart, I know she has . . . an interest in me. I suspect this is her way. She is outwardly bold and outspoken, yet her heart is shy and afraid. It is the Oriental in her at war with her Western education.
SONG (*offstage*): I will be out in an instant. Ask the servant for anything you want.
GALLIMARD: Tonight, I have finally been invited to enter her apartment. Though the idea is almost beyond belief, I believe she is afraid of me.

(*Gallimard looks around the room. He picks up a picture in a frame, studies it. Without his noticing, Song enters, dressed elegantly in a black gown from the twenties. She stands in the doorway looking like Anna May Wong.°*)

Anna May Wong: (1905–1961), Chinese American actor known for her exotic beauty and most often cast as a villain.

SONG: That is my father.
GALLIMARD (*surprised*): Mademoiselle Song . . .

(*She glides up to him, snatches away the picture.*)

SONG: It is very good that he did not live to see the Revolution. They would, no doubt, have made him kneel on broken glass. Not that he didn't deserve such a punishment. But he is my father. I would've hated to see it happen.
GALLIMARD: I'm very honored that you've allowed me to visit your home.

(*Song curtseys.*)

SONG: Thank you. Oh! Haven't you been poured any tea?
GALLIMARD: I'm really not —
SONG (*to her offstage servant*): Shu-Fang! Cha! Kwai-lah! (*To Gallimard.*) I'm sorry. You want everything to be perfect —
GALLIMARD: Please.
SONG: — and before the evening even begins —
GALLIMARD: I'm really not thirsty.
SONG: — it's ruined.
GALLIMARD (*sharply*): Mademoiselle Song!

(*Song sits down.*)

SONG: I'm sorry.
GALLIMARD: What are you apologizing for now?

(*Pause; Song starts to giggle.*)

SONG: I don't know!

(*Gallimard laughs.*)

GALLIMARD: Exactly my point.
SONG: Oh, I am silly. Light-headed. I promise not to apologize for anything else tonight, do you hear me?
GALLIMARD: That's a good girl.

(*Shu-Fang, a servant girl, comes out with a tea tray and starts to pour.*)

SONG (*to Shu-Fang*): No! I'll pour myself for the gentleman!

(*Shu-Fang, staring at Gallimard, exits.*)

GALLIMARD: You have a beautiful home.
SONG: No, I . . . I don't even know why I invited you up.
GALLIMARD: Well, I'm glad you did.

(*Song looks around the room.*)

SONG: There is an element of danger to your presence.
GALLIMARD: Oh?
SONG: You must know.
GALLIMARD: It doesn't concern me. We both know why I'm here.
SONG: It doesn't concern me either. No . . . well perhaps . . .
GALLIMARD: What?
SONG: Perhaps I am slightly afraid of scandal.
GALLIMARD: What are we doing?
SONG: I'm entertaining you. In my parlor.
GALLIMARD: In France, that would hardly —
SONG: France. France is a country living in the modern era.

Perhaps even ahead of it. China is a nation whose soul is firmly rooted two thousand years in the past. What I do, even pouring the tea for you now . . . it has . . . implications. The walls and windows say so. Even my own heart, strapped inside this Western dress . . . even it says things — things I don't care to hear.

(*Song hands Gallimard a cup of tea. Gallimard puts his hand over both the teacup and Song's hand.*)

GALLIMARD: This is a beautiful dress.
SONG: Don't.
GALLIMARD: What?
SONG: I don't even know if it looks right on me.
GALLIMARD: Believe me —
SONG: You are from France. You see so many beautiful women.
GALLIMARD: France? Since when are the European women — ?
SONG: Oh! What am I trying to do, anyway?!

(*Song runs to the door, composes herself, then turns towards Gallimard.*)

SONG: Monsieur Gallimard, perhaps you should go.
GALLIMARD: But . . . why?
SONG: There's something wrong about this.
GALLIMARD: I don't see what.
SONG: I feel . . . I am not myself.
GALLIMARD: No. You're nervous.
SONG: Please. Hard as I try to be modern, to speak like a man, to hold a Western woman's strong face up to my own . . . in the end, I fail. A small, frightened heart beats too quickly and gives me away. Monsieur Gallimard, I'm a Chinese girl. I've never . . . never invited a man up to my flat before. The forwardness of my actions makes my skin burn.
GALLIMARD: What are you afraid of? Certainly not me, I hope.
SONG: I'm a modest girl.
GALLIMARD: I know. And very beautiful. (*He touches her hair.*)
SONG: Please — go now. The next time you see me, I shall again be myself.
GALLIMARD: I like you the way you are right now.
SONG: You are a cad.
GALLIMARD: What do you expect? I'm a foreign devil.

(*Gallimard walks downstage. Song exits.*)

GALLIMARD (*to us*): Did you hear the way she talked about Western women? Much differently than the first night. She does — she feels inferior to them — and to me.

Scene XI

(*The French embassy. Beijing. 1960.
Gallimard moves towards a desk.*)

GALLIMARD: I determined to try an experiment. In *Madame Butterfly*, Cio-Cio-San fears that the West-

ern man who catches a butterfly will pierce its heart with a needle, then leave it to perish. I began to wonder: had I, too, caught a butterfly who would writhe on a needle?

(*Marc enters, dressed as a bureaucrat, holding a stack of papers. As Gallimard speaks, Marc hands papers to him. He peruses, then signs, stamps, or rejects them.*)

GALLIMARD: Over the next five weeks, I worked like a dynamo. I stopped going to the opera, I didn't phone or write her. I knew this little flower was waiting for me to call, and, as I wickedly refused to do so, I felt for the first time that rush of power — the absolute power of a man.

(*Marc continues acting as the bureaucrat, but he now speaks as himself.*)

MARC: René! It's me.
GALLIMARD: Marc — I hear your voice everywhere now. Even in the midst of work.
MARC: That's because I'm watching you — all the time.
GALLIMARD: You were always the most popular guy in school.
MARC: Well, there's no guarantee of failure in life like happiness in high school. Somehow I knew I'd end up in the suburbs working for Renault and you'd be in the Orient picking exotic women off the trees. And they say there's no justice.
GALLIMARD: That's why you were my friend?
MARC: I gave you a little of my life, so that now you can give me some of yours. (*Pause.*) Remember Isabelle?
GALLIMARD: Of course I remember! She was my first experience.
MARC: We all wanted to ball her. But she only wanted me.
GALLIMARD: I had her.
MARC: Right. You balled her.
GALLIMARD: You were the only one who ever believed me.
MARC: Well, there's a good reason for that. (*Beat.*) C'mon. You must've guessed.
GALLIMARD: You told me to wait in the bushes by the cafeteria that night. The next thing I knew, she was on me. Dress up in the air.
MARC: She never wore underwear.
GALLIMARD: My arms were pinned to the dirt.
MARC: She loved the superior position. A girl ahead of her time.
GALLIMARD: I looked up, and there was this woman . . . bouncing up and down on my loins.
MARC: Screaming, right?
GALLIMARD: Screaming, and breaking off the branches all around me, and pounding my butt up and down into the dirt.
MARC: Huffing and puffing like a locomotive.
GALLIMARD: And in the middle of all this, the leaves were getting into my mouth, my legs were losing circulation, I thought, "God. So this is *it*?"
MARC: You thought that?

GALLIMARD: Well, I was worried about my legs falling off.

MARC: You didn't have a good time?

GALLIMARD: No, that's not what I — I had a great time!

MARC: You're sure?

GALLIMARD: Yeah. Really.

MARC: 'Cuz I wanted you to have a good time.

GALLIMARD: I did.

(*Pause.*)

MARC: Shit. (*Pause.*) When all is said and done, she was kind of a lousy lay, wasn't she? I mean, there was a lot of energy there, but you never knew what she was doing with it. Like when she yelled "I'm coming!"— hell, it was so loud, you wanted to go, "Look, it's not that big a deal."

GALLIMARD: I got scared. I thought she meant someone was actually coming. (*Pause.*) But, Marc?

MARC: What?

GALLIMARD: Thanks.

MARC: Oh, don't mention it.

GALLIMARD: It was my first experience.

MARC: Yeah. You got her.

GALLIMARD: I got her.

MARC: Wait! Look at that letter again!

(*Gallimard picks up one of the papers he's been stamping, and rereads it.*)

GALLIMARD (*to us*): After six weeks, they began to arrive. The letters.

(*Upstage special on Song, as Madame Butterfly. The scene is underscored by the "Love Duet."*)

SONG: Did we fight? I do not know. Is the opera no longer of interest to you? Please come — my audiences miss the white devil in their midst.

(*Gallimard looks up from the letter, towards us.*)

GALLIMARD (*to us*): A concession, but much too dignified. (*Beat; he discards the letter.*) I skipped the opera again that week to complete a position paper on trade.

(*The bureaucrat hands him another letter.*)

SONG: Six weeks have passed since last we met. Is this your practice — to leave friends in the lurch? Sometimes I hate you, sometimes I hate myself, but always I miss you.

GALLIMARD (*to us*): Better, but I don't like the way she calls me "friend." When a woman calls a man her "friend," she's calling him a eunuch or a homosexual. (*Beat; he discards the letter.*) I was absent from the opera for the seventh week, feeling a sudden urge to clean out my files.

(*Bureaucrat hands him another letter.*)

SONG: Your rudeness is beyond belief. I don't deserve this cruelty. Don't bother to call. I'll have you turned away at the door.

GALLIMARD (*to us*): I didn't. (*He discards the letter; bureaucrat hands him another.*) And then finally, the letter that concluded my experiment.

SONG: I am out of words. I can hide behind dignity no longer. What do you want? I have already given you my shame.

(*Gallimard gives the letter back to Marc, slowly. Special on Song fades out.*)

GALLIMARD (*to us*): Reading it, I became suddenly ashamed. Yes, my experiment had been a success. She was turning on my needle. But the victory seemed hollow.

MARC: Hollow?! Are you crazy?

GALLIMARD: Nothing, Marc. Please go away.

MARC (*exiting, with papers*): Haven't I taught you anything?

GALLIMARD: "I have already given you my shame." I had to attend a reception that evening. On the way, I felt sick. If there is a God, surely he would punish me now. I had finally gained power over a beautiful woman, only to abuse it cruelly. There must be justice in the world. I had the strange feeling that the ax would fall this very evening.

Scene XII

(*Ambassador Toulon's residence. Beijing. 1960.*
Sound cue: party noises. Light change. We are now in a spacious residence. Toulon, the French ambassador, enters and taps Gallimard on the shoulder.)

TOULON: Gallimard? Can I have a word? Over here.

GALLIMARD (*to us*): Manuel Toulon. French ambassador to China. He likes to think of us all as his children. Rather like God.

TOULON: Look, Gallimard, there's not much to say. I've liked you. From the day you walked in. You were no leader, but you were tidy and efficient.

GALLIMARD: Thank you, sir.

TOULON: Don't jump the gun. Okay, our needs in China are changing. It's embarrassing that we lost Indochina. Someone just wasn't on the ball there. I don't mean you personally, of course.

GALLIMARD: Thank you, sir.

TOULON: We're going to be doing a lot more information-gathering in the future. The nature of our work here is changing. Some people are just going to have to go. It's nothing personal.

GALLIMARD: Oh.

TOULON: Want to know a secret? Vice-Consul LeBon is being transferred.

GALLIMARD (*to us*): My immediate superior!

TOULON: And most of his department.

GALLIMARD (*to us*): Just as I feared! God has seen my evil heart —

TOULON: But not you.

GALLIMARD (*to us*): — and he's taking her away just as . . . (*To Toulon.*) Excuse me, sir?

TOULON: Scare you? I think I did. Cheer up, Gallimard. I want you to replace LeBon as vice-consul.

GALLIMARD: You — ? Yes, well, thank you, sir.

TOULON: Anytime.

GALLIMARD: I . . . accept with great humility.

TOULON: Humility won't be part of the job. You're going to coordinate the revamped intelligence division. Want to know a secret? A year ago, you would've been out. But the past few months, I don't know how it happened, you've become this new aggressive confident . . . thing. And they also tell me you get along with the Chinese. So I think you're a lucky man, Gallimard. Congratulations.

(*They shake hands. Toulon exits. Party noises out. Gallimard stumbles across a darkened stage.*)

GALLIMARD: Vice-consul? Impossible! As I stumbled out of the party, I saw it written across the sky: There is no God. Or, no — say that there is a God. But that God . . . understands. Of course! God who creates Eve to serve Adam, who blesses Solomon with his harem but ties Jezebel to a burning bed° — that God is a man. And he understands! At age thirty-nine, I was suddenly initiated into the way of the world.

Scene XIII

(*Song Liling's apartment. Beijing. 1960.*
Song enters, in a sheer dressing gown.)

SONG: Are you crazy?

GALLIMARD: Mademoiselle Song —

SONG: To come here — at this hour? After . . . after eight weeks?

GALLIMARD: It's the most amazing —

SONG: You bang on my door? Scare my servants, scandalize the neighbors?

GALLIMARD: I've been promoted. To vice-consul.

(*Pause.*)

SONG: And what is that supposed to mean to me?

GALLIMARD: Are you my Butterfly?

SONG: What are you saying?

GALLIMARD: I've come tonight for an answer: are you my Butterfly?

SONG: Don't you know already?

GALLIMARD: I want you to say it.

SONG: I don't want to say it.

GALLIMARD: So, that is your answer?

SONG: You know how I feel about —

GALLIMARD: I do remember one thing.

God who creates Eve . . . burning bed: Eve, Adam, Solomon, and Jezebel are biblical characters. See Gen. 2:18–25; I Kings 11:1–8; and II Kings 9:11–37.

SONG: What?

GALLIMARD: In the letter I received today.

SONG: Don't.

GALLIMARD: "I have already given you my shame."

SONG: It's enough that I even wrote it.

GALLIMARD: Well, then —

SONG: I shouldn't have it splashed across my face.

GALLIMARD: — if that's all true —

SONG: Stop!

GALLIMARD: Then what is one more short answer?

SONG: I don't want to!

GALLIMARD: Are you my Butterfly? (*Silence; he crosses the room and begins to touch her hair.*) I want from you honesty. There should be nothing false between us. No false pride.

(*Pause.*)

SONG: Yes, I am. I am your Butterfly.

GALLIMARD: Then let me be honest with you. It is because of you that I was promoted tonight. You have changed my life forever. My little Butterfly, there should be no more secrets: I love you.

(*He starts to kiss her roughly. She resists slightly.*)

SONG: No . . . no . . . gently . . . please, I've never . . .

GALLIMARD: No?

SONG: I've tried to appear experienced, but . . . the truth is . . . no.

GALLIMARD: Are you cold?

SONG: Yes. Cold.

GALLIMARD: Then we will go very, very slowly.

(*He starts to caress her; her gown begins to open.*)

SONG: No . . . let me . . . keep my clothes . . .

GALLIMARD: But . . .

SONG: Please . . . it all frightens me. I'm a modest Chinese girl.

GALLIMARD: My poor little treasure.

SONG: I am your treasure. Though inexperienced, I am not . . . ignorant. They teach us things, our mothers, about pleasing a man.

GALLIMARD: Yes?

SONG: I'll do my best to make you happy. Turn off the lights.

(*Gallimard gets up and heads for a lamp. Song, propped up on one elbow, tosses her hair back and smiles.*)

SONG: Monsieur Gallimard?

GALLIMARD: Yes, Butterfly?

SONG: "*Vieni, vieni!*"

GALLIMARD: "Come, darling."

SONG: "*Ah! Dolce notte!*"

GALLIMARD: "Beautiful night."

SONG: "*Tutto estatico d'amor ride il ciel!*"

GALLIMARD: "All ecstatic with love, the heavens are filled with laughter."

(*He turns off the lamp. Blackout.*)

ACT II • *Scene I*

(M. Gallimard's cell. Paris. 1988.
Lights up on Gallimard. He sits in his cell, reading from a leaflet.)

GALLIMARD: This, from a contemporary critic's commentary on *Madame Butterfly:* "Pinkerton suffers from . . . being an obnoxious bounder whom every man in the audience itches to kick." Bully for us men in the audience! Then, in the same note: "Butterfly is the most irresistibly appealing of Puccini's 'Little Women.' Watching the succession of her humiliations is like watching a child under torture." *(He tosses the pamphlet over his shoulder.)* I suggest that, while we men may all want to kick Pinkerton, very few of us would pass up the opportunity to *be* Pinkerton.

(Gallimard moves out of his cell.)

Scene II

(Gallimard and Butterfly's flat. Beijing. 1960.
We are in a simple but well-decorated parlor. Gallimard moves to sit on a sofa, while Song, dressed in a cheongsam,° enters and curls up at his feet.)

GALLIMARD *(to us)*: We secured a flat on the outskirts of Peking. Butterfly, as I was calling her now, decorated our "home" with Western furniture and Chinese antiques. And there, on a few stolen afternoons or evenings each week, Butterfly commenced her education.
SONG: The Chinese men — they keep us down.
GALLIMARD: Even in the "New Society"?
SONG: In the "New Society," we are all kept ignorant equally. That's one of the exciting things about loving a Western man. I know you are not threatened by a woman's education.
GALLIMARD: I'm no saint, Butterfly.
SONG: But you come from a progressive society.
GALLIMARD: We're not always reminding each other how "old" we are, if that's what you mean.
SONG: Exactly. We Chinese — once, I suppose, it is true, we ruled the world. But so what? How much more exciting to be part of the society ruling the world today. Tell me — what's happening in Vietnam?
GALLIMARD: Oh, Butterfly — you want me to bring my work home?
SONG: I want to know what you know. To be impressed by my man. It's not the particulars so much as the fact that you're making decisions which change the shape of the world.
GALLIMARD: Not the world. At best, a small corner.

(Toulon enters, and sits at a desk upstage.)

John Lithgow as René Gallimard and B. D. Wong as Song Liling in *M. Butterfly* at Broadway's Eugene O'Neill Theatre in 1988.

---

cheongsam: A fitted dress with a mandarin collar and side slits in the skirt.

Scene III

(*French embassy. Beijing. 1961.*
   Gallimard moves downstage, to Toulon's desk. Song remains upstage, watching.)

TOULON: And a more troublesome corner is hard to imagine.

GALLIMARD: So, the Americans plan to begin bombing?

TOULON: This is very secret, Gallimard: yes. The Americans don't have an embassy here. They're asking us to be their eyes and ears. Say Jack Kennedy signed an order to bomb North Vietnam, Laos. How would the Chinese react?

GALLIMARD: I think the Chinese will squawk —

TOULON: Uh-huh.

GALLIMARD: — but, in their hearts, they don't even like Ho Chi Minh.°

(*Pause.*)

TOULON: What a bunch of jerks. Vietnam was *our* colony. Not only didn't the Americans help us fight to keep them, but now, seven years later, they've come back to grab the territory for themselves. It's very irritating.

GALLIMARD: With all due respect, sir, why should the Americans have won our war for us back in fifty-four if we didn't have the will to win it ourselves?

TOULON: You're kidding, aren't you?

(*Pause.*)

GALLIMARD: The Orientals simply want to be associated with whoever shows the most strength and power. You live with the Chinese, sir. Do you think they like Communism?

TOULON: I live in China. Not with the Chinese.

GALLIMARD: Well, I —

TOULON: *You* live with the Chinese.

GALLIMARD: Excuse me?

TOULON: I can't keep a secret.

GALLIMARD: What are you saying?

TOULON: Only that I'm not immune to gossip. So, you're keeping a native mistress? Don't answer. It's none of my business. (*Pause.*) I'm sure she must be gorgeous.

GALLIMARD: Well . . .

TOULON: I'm impressed. You had the stamina to go out into the streets and hunt one down. Some of us have to be content with the wives of the expatriate community.

GALLIMARD: I do feel . . . fortunate.

TOULON: So, Gallimard, you've got the inside knowledge — what *do* the Chinese think?

GALLIMARD: Deep down, they miss the old days. You know, cappuccinos, men in tuxedos —

TOULON: So what do we tell the Americans about Vietnam?

Ho Chi Minh: (1890–1969), first president of North Vietnam (1945–1969).

GALLIMARD: Tell them there's a natural affinity between the West and the Orient.

TOULON: And that you speak from experience?

GALLIMARD: The Orientals are people too. They want the good things we can give them. If the Americans demonstrate the will to win, the Vietnamese will welcome them into a mutually beneficial union.

TOULON: I don't see how the Vietnamese can stand up to American firepower.

GALLIMARD: Orientals will always submit to a greater force.

TOULON: I'll note your opinions in my report. The Americans always love to hear how "welcome" they'll be. (*He starts to exit.*)

GALLIMARD: Sir?

TOULON: Mmmm?

GALLIMARD: This . . . rumor you've heard.

TOULON: Uh-huh?

GALLIMARD: How . . . widespread do you think it is?

TOULON: It's only widespread within this embassy. Where nobody talks because everybody is guilty. We were worried about you, Gallimard. We thought you were the only one here without a secret. Now you go and find a lotus blossom . . . and top us all. (*He exits.*)

GALLIMARD (*to us*): Toulon knows! And he approves! I was learning the benefits of being a man. We form our own clubs, sit behind thick doors, smoke — and celebrate the fact that we're still boys. (*He starts to move downstage, towards Song.*) So, over the —

(*Suddenly Comrade Chin enters. Gallimard backs away.*)

GALLIMARD (*to Song*): No! Why does she have to come in?

SONG: René, be sensible. How can they understand the story without her? Now, don't embarrass yourself.

(*Gallimard moves down center.*)

GALLIMARD (*to us*): Now, you will see why my story is so amusing to so many people. Why they snicker at parties in disbelief. Please — try to understand it from my point of view. We are all prisoners of our time and place. (*He exits.*)

Scene IV

(*Gallimard and Butterfly's flat. Beijing. 1961.*)

SONG (*to us*): 1961. The flat Monsieur Gallimard rented for us. An evening after he has gone.

CHIN: Okay, see if you can find out when the Americans plan to start bombing Vietnam. If you can find out what cities, even better.

SONG: I'll do my best, but I don't want to arouse his suspicions.

CHIN: Yeah, sure, of course. So, what else?

SONG: The Americans will increase troops in Vietnam to 170,000 soldiers with 120,000 militia and 11,000 American advisors.

CHIN (*writing*): Wait, wait, 120,000 militia and —
SONG: — 11,000 American —
CHIN: — American advisors. (*Beat.*) How do you re-member so much?
SONG: I'm an actor.
CHIN: Yeah. (*Beat.*) Is that how come you dress like that?
SONG: Like what, Miss Chin?
CHIN: Like that dress! You're wearing a dress. And every time I come here, you're wearing a dress. Is that because you're an actor? Or what?
SONG: It's a . . . disguise, Miss Chin.
CHIN: Actors, I think they're all weirdos. My mother tells me actors are like gamblers or prostitutes or —
SONG: It helps me in my assignment.

(*Pause.*)

CHIN: You're not gathering information in any way that violates Communist Party principles, are you?
SONG: Why would I do that?
CHIN: Just checking. Remember: when working for the Great Proletarian State, you represent our Chairman Mao in every position you take.
SONG: I'll try to imagine the Chairman taking my posi-tions.
CHIN: We all think of him this way. Good-bye, comrade. (*She starts to exit.*) Comrade?
SONG: Yes?
CHIN: Don't forget: there is no homosexuality in China!
SONG: Yes, I've heard.
CHIN: Just checking. (*She exits.*)
SONG (*to us*): What passes for a woman in modern China.

(*Gallimard sticks his head out from the wings.*)

GALLIMARD: Is she gone?
SONG: Yes, René. Please continue in your own fashion.

Scene V

(*Beijing. 1961–1963.*
Gallimard moves to the couch where Song still sits. He lies down in her lap, and she strokes his forehead.)

GALLIMARD (*to us*): And so, over the years 1961, '62, '63, we settled into our routine, Butterfly and I. She would always have prepared a light snack and then, ever so delicately, and only if I agreed, she would start to pleasure me. With her hands, her mouth . . . too many ways to explain, and too sad, given my present situation. But mostly we would talk. About my life. Perhaps there is nothing more rare than to find a woman who passionately listens.

(*Song remains upstage, listening, as Helga enters and plays a scene downstage with Gallimard.*)

HELGA: René, I visited Dr. Bolleart this morning.
GALLIMARD: Why? Are you ill?
HELGA: No, no. You see, I wanted to ask him . . . that question we've been discussing.

GALLIMARD: And I told you, it's only a matter of time. Why did you bring a doctor into this? We just have to keep trying — like a crapshoot, actually.
HELGA: I went, I'm sorry. But listen: he says there's noth-ing wrong with me.
GALLIMARD: You see? Now, will you stop — ?
HELGA: René, he says he'd like you to go in and take some tests.
GALLIMARD: Why? So he can find there's nothing wrong with both of us?
HELGA: René, I don't ask for much. One trip! One visit! And then, whatever you want to do about it — you decide.
GALLIMARD: You're assuming he'll find something defective!
HELGA: No! Of course not! Whatever he finds — if he finds nothing, we decide what to do about nothing! But go!
GALLIMARD: If he finds nothing, we keep trying. Just like we do now.
HELGA: But at least we'll know! (*Pause.*) I'm sorry. (*She starts to exit.*)
GALLIMARD: Do you really want me to see Dr. Bolleart?
HELGA: Only if you want a child, René. We have to face the fact that time is running out. Only if you want a child. (*She exits.*)
GALLIMARD (*to Song*): I'm a modern man, Butterfly. And yet, I don't want to go. It's the same old voodoo. I feel like God himself is laughing at me if I can't pro-duce a child.
SONG: You men of the West — you're obsessed by your odd desire for equality. Your wife can't give you a child, and *you're* going to the doctor?
GALLIMARD: Well, you see, she's already gone.
SONG: And because this incompetent can't find the defect, you now have to subject yourself to him? It's unnatural.
GALLIMARD: Well, what is the "natural" solution?
SONG: In Imperial China, when a man found that one wife was inadequate, he turned to another — to give him his son.
GALLIMARD: What do you — ? I can't . . . marry you, yet.
SONG: Please. I'm not asking you to be my husband. But I am already your wife.
GALLIMARD: Do you want to . . . have my child?
SONG: I thought you'd never ask.
GALLIMARD: But, your career . . . your —
SONG: Phooey on my career! That's your Western mind, twisting itself into strange shapes again. Of course I love my career. But what would I love most of all? To feel something inside me — day and night — something I know is yours. (*Pause.*) Promise me . . . you won't go to this doctor. Who is this West-ern quack to set himself as judge over the man I love? I know who is a man, and who is not. (*She exits.*)
GALLIMARD (*to us*): Dr. Bolleart? Of course I didn't go. What man would?

Scene VI

(*Beijing. 1963.*

Party noises over the house speakers. Renée enters, wearing a revealing gown.)

GALLIMARD: 1963. A party at the Austrian embassy. None of us could remember the Austrian ambassador's name, which seemed somehow appropriate. (*To Renée.*) So, I tell the Americans, Diem° must go. The U.S. wants to be respected by the Vietnamese, and yet they're propping up this nobody seminarian as her president. A man whose claim to fame is his sister-in-law imposing fanatic "moral order" campaigns? Oriental women — when they're good, they're very good, but when they're bad, they're Christians.

RENÉE: Yeah.

GALLIMARD: And what do you do?

RENÉE: I'm a student. My father exports a lot of useless stuff to the Third World.

GALLIMARD: How useless?

RENÉE: You know. Squirt guns, confectioner's sugar, Hula Hoops . . .

GALLIMARD: I'm sure they appreciate the sugar.

RENÉE: I'm here for two years to study Chinese.

GALLIMARD: Two years!

RENÉE: That's what everybody says.

GALLIMARD: When did you arrive?

RENÉE: Three weeks ago.

GALLIMARD: And?

RENÉE: I like it. It's primitive, but . . . well, this is the place to learn Chinese, so here I am.

GALLIMARD: Why Chinese?

RENÉE: I think it'll be important someday.

GALLIMARD: You do?

RENÉE: Don't ask me when, but . . . that's what I think.

GALLIMARD: Well, I agree with you. One hundred percent. That's very farsighted.

RENÉE: Yeah. Well of course, my father thinks I'm a complete weirdo.

GALLIMARD: He'll thank you someday.

RENÉE: Like when the Chinese start buying Hula Hoops?

GALLIMARD: There're a billion bellies out there.

RENÉE: And if they end up taking over the world — well, then I'll be lucky to know Chinese too, right?

(*Pause.*)

GALLIMARD: At this point, I don't see how the Chinese can possibly take —

RENÉE: You know what I *don't* like about China?

GALLIMARD: Excuse me? No — what?

RENÉE: Nothing to do at night.

GALLIMARD: You come to parties at embassies like everyone else.

Diem: Ngo Dinh Diem (1901–1963), president of South Vietnam (1955–1963), assassinated in a coup d'état supported by the United States.

RENÉE: Yeah, but they get out at ten. And then what?

GALLIMARD: I'm afraid the Chinese idea of a dance hall is a dirt floor and a man with a flute.

RENÉE: Are you married?

GALLIMARD: Yes. Why?

RENÉE: You wanna . . . fool around?

(*Pause.*)

GALLIMARD: Sure.

RENÉE: I'll wait for you outside. What's your name?

GALLIMARD: Gallimard. René.

RENÉE: Weird. I'm Renée too. (*She exits.*)

GALLIMARD (*to us*): And so, I embarked on my first extra-extramarital affair. Renée was picture perfect. With a body like those girls in the magazines. If I put a tissue paper over my eyes, I wouldn't have been able to tell the difference. And it was exciting to be with someone who wasn't afraid to be seen completely naked. But is it possible for a woman to be *too* uninhibited, *too* willing, so as to seem almost too . . . masculine?

(*Chuck Berry° blares from the house speakers, then comes down in volume as Renée enters, toweling her hair.*)

RENÉE: You have a nice weenie.

GALLIMARD: What?

RENÉE: Penis. You have a nice penis.

GALLIMARD: Oh. Well, thank you. That's very . . .

RENÉE: What — can't take a compliment?

GALLIMARD: No, it's very . . . reassuring.

RENÉE: But most girls don't come out and say it, huh?

GALLIMARD: And also . . . what did you call it?

RENÉE: Oh. Most girls don't call it a "weenie," huh?

GALLIMARD: It sounds very —

RENÉE: Small, I know.

GALLIMARD: I was going to say, "young."

RENÉE: Yeah. Young, small, same thing. Most guys are pretty, uh, sensitive about that. Like, you know, I had a boyfriend back home in Denmark. I got mad at him once and called him a little weeniehead. He got so mad! He said at least I should call him a great big weeniehead.

GALLIMARD: I suppose I just say "penis."

RENÉE: Yeah. That's pretty clinical. There's "cock," but that sounds like a chicken. And "prick" is painful, and "dick" is like you're talking about someone who's not in the room.

GALLIMARD: Yes. It's a . . . bigger problem than I imagined.

RENÉE: I — I think maybe it's because I really don't know what to do with them — that's why I call them "weenies."

GALLIMARD: Well, you did quite well with . . . mine.

RENÉE: Thanks, but I mean, really *do* with them. Like, okay, have you ever looked at one? I mean, really?

Chuck Berry: American musician (b. 1926) often called the father of rock 'n' roll music.

GALLIMARD: No, I suppose when it's part of you, you sort of take it for granted.

RENÉE: I guess. But, like, it just hangs there. This little . . . flap of flesh. And there's so much fuss that we make about it. Like, I think the reason we fight wars is because we wear clothes. Because no one knows — between the men, I mean — who has the biggest . . . weenie. So, if I'm a guy with a small one, I'm going to build a really big building or take over a really big piece of land or write a really long book so the other men don't know, right? But, see, it never really works, that's the problem. I mean, you conquer the country, or whatever, but you're still wearing clothes, so there's no way to prove absolutely whose is bigger or smaller. And that's what we call a civilized society. The whole world run by a bunch of men with pricks the size of pins. (*She exits.*)

GALLIMARD (*to us*): This was simply not acceptable.

(*A high-pitched chime rings through the air. Song, dressed as Butterfly, appears in the upstage special. She is obviously distressed. Her body swoons as she attempts to clip the stems of flowers she's arranging in a vase.*)

GALLIMARD: But I kept up our affair, wildly, for several months. Why? I believe because of Butterfly. She knew the secret I was trying to hide. But, unlike a Western woman, she didn't confront me, threaten, even pout. I remembered the words of Puccini's *Butterfly*:

SONG: "*Noi siamo gente avvezza / alle piccole cose / umili e silenziose.*"

GALLIMARD: "I come from a people / Who are accustomed to little / Humble and silent." I saw Pinkerton and Butterfly, and what she would say if he were unfaithful . . . nothing. She would cry, alone, into those wildly soft sleeves, once full of possessions, now empty to collect her tears. It was her tears and her silence that excited me, every time I visited Renée.

TOULON (*offstage*): Gallimard!

(*Toulon enters. Gallimard turns towards him. During the next section, Song, up center, begins to dance with the flowers. It is a drunken, reckless dance, where she breaks small pieces off the stems.*)

TOULON: They're killing him.

GALLIMARD: Who? I'm sorry? What?

TOULON: Bother you to come over at this late hour?

GALLIMARD: No . . . of course not.

TOULON: Not after you hear my secret. Champagne?

GALLIMARD: Um . . . thank you.

TOULON: You're surprised. There's something that you've wanted, Gallimard. No, not a promotion. Next time. Something in the world. You're not aware of this, but there's an informal gossip circle among intelligence agents. And some of ours heard from some of the Americans —

GALLIMARD: Yes?

TOULON: That the U.S. will allow the Vietnamese generals to stage a coup . . . and assassinate President Diem.

(*The chime rings again. Toulon freezes. Gallimard turns upstage and looks at Butterfly, who slowly and deliberately clips a flower off its stem. Gallimard turns back towards Toulon.*)

GALLIMARD: I think . . . that's a very wise move!

(*Toulon unfreezes.*)

TOULON: It's what you've been advocating. A toast?

GALLIMARD: Sure. I consider this a vindication.

TOULON: Not exactly. "To the test. Let's hope you pass."

(*They drink. The chime rings again. Toulon freezes. Gallimard turns upstage, and Song clips another flower.*)

GALLIMARD (*to Toulon*): The test?

TOULON (*unfreezing*): It's a test of everything you've been saying. I personally think the generals probably will stop the Communists. And you'll be a hero. But if anything goes wrong, then your opinions won't be worth a pig's ear. I'm sure that won't happen. But sometimes it's easier when they don't listen to you.

GALLIMARD: They're your opinions too, aren't they?

TOULON: Personally, yes.

GALLIMARD: So we agree.

TOULON: But my opinions aren't on that report. Yours are. Cheers.

(*Toulon turns away from Gallimard and raises his glass. At that instant Song picks up the vase and hurls it to the ground. It shatters. Song sinks down amidst the shards of the vase, in a calm, childlike trance. She sings softly, as if reciting a child's nursery rhyme.*)

SONG (*repeat as necessary*): "The whole world over, the white man travels, setting anchor, wherever he likes. Life's not worth living, unless he finds, the finest maidens, of every land . . ."

(*Gallimard turns downstage towards us. Song continues singing.*)

GALLIMARD: I shook as I left his house. That coward! That worm! To put the burden for his decisions on my shoulders!

I started for Renée's. But no, that was all I needed. A schoolgirl who would question the role of the penis in modern society. What I wanted was revenge. A vessel to contain my humiliation. Though I hadn't seen her in several weeks, I headed for Butterfly's.

(*Gallimard enters Song's apartment.*)

SONG: Oh! René . . . I was dreaming!

GALLIMARD: You've been drinking?

SONG: If I can't sleep, then yes, I drink. But then, it gives me these dreams which — René, it's been almost three weeks since you visited me last.

GALLIMARD: I know. There's been a lot going on in the world.

SONG: Fortunately I am drunk. So I can speak freely. It's not the world, it's you and me. And an old problem. Even the softest skin becomes like leather to a man who's touched it too often. I confess I don't know how to stop it. I don't know how to become another woman.

GALLIMARD: I have a request.

SONG: Is this a solution? Or are you ready to give up the flat?

GALLIMARD: It may be a solution. But I'm sure you won't like it.

SONG: Oh well, that's very important. "Like it?" Do you think I "like" lying here alone, waiting, always waiting for your return? Please — don't worry about what I may not "like."

GALLIMARD: I want to see you . . . naked.

(*Silence.*)

SONG: I thought you understood my modesty. So you want me to — what — strip? Like a big cowboy girl? Shiny pasties on my breasts? Shall I fling my kimono over my head and yell "ya-hoo" in the process? I thought you respected my shame!

GALLIMARD: I believe you gave me your shame many years ago.

SONG: Yes — and it is just like a white devil to use it against me. I can't believe it. I thought myself so repulsed by the passive Oriental and the cruel white man. Now I see — we are always most revolted by the things hidden within us.

GALLIMARD: I just mean —

SONG: Yes?

GALLIMARD: — that it will remove the only barrier left between us.

SONG: No, René. Don't couch your request in sweet words. Be yourself — a cad — and know that my love is enough, that I submit — submit to the worst you can give me. (*Pause.*) Well, come. Strip me. Whatever happens, know that you have willed it. Our love, in your hands. I'm helpless before my man.

(*Gallimard starts to cross the room.*)

GALLIMARD: Did I not undress her because I knew, somewhere deep down, what I would find? Perhaps. Happiness is so rare that our mind can turn somersaults to protect it.

At the time, I only knew that I was seeing Pinkerton stalking towards his Butterfly, ready to reward her love with his lecherous hands. The image sickened me, pulled me to my knees, so I was crawling towards her like a worm. By the time I reached her, Pinkerton . . . had vanished from my heart. To be replaced by something new, something unnatural, that flew in the face of all I'd learned in the world — something very close to love.

(*He grabs her around the waist; she strokes his hair.*)

GALLIMARD: Butterfly, forgive me.

SONG: René . . .

GALLIMARD: For everything. From the start.

SONG: I'm . . .

GALLIMARD: I want to —

SONG: I'm pregnant. (*Beat.*) I'm pregnant. (*Beat.*) I'm pregnant.

(*Beat.*)

GALLIMARD: I want to marry you!

Scene VII

(*Gallimard and Butterfly's flat. Beijing. 1963.*
    Downstage, Song paces as Comrade Chin reads from her notepad. Upstage, Gallimard is still kneeling. He remains on his knees throughout the scene, watching it.)

SONG: I need a baby.

CHIN (*from pad*): He's been spotted going to a dorm.

SONG: I need a baby.

CHIN: At the Foreign Language Institute.

SONG: I need a baby.

CHIN: The room of a Danish girl. . . . What do you mean, you need a baby?!

SONG: Tell Comrade Kang — last night, the entire mission, it could've ended.

CHIN: What do you mean?

SONG: Tell Kang — he told me to strip.

CHIN: Strip?!

SONG: Write!

CHIN: I tell you, I don't understand nothing about this case anymore. Nothing.

SONG: He told me to strip, and I took a chance. Oh, we Chinese, we know how to gamble.

CHIN (*writing*): ". . . told him to strip."

SONG: My palms were wet, I had to make a split-second decision.

CHIN: Hey! Can you slow down?!

(*Pause.*)

SONG: You write faster, I'm the artist here. Suddenly, it hit me —"All he wants is for her to submit. Once a woman submits, a man is always ready to become 'generous.'"

CHIN: You're just gonna end up with rough notes.

SONG: And it worked! He gave in! Now, if I can just present him with a baby. A Chinese baby with blond hair — he'll be mine for life!

CHIN: Kang will never agree! The trading of babies has to be a counterrevolutionary act!

SONG: Sometimes, a counterrevolutionary act is necessary to counter a counterrevolutionary act.

(*Pause.*)

CHIN: Wait.

SONG: I need one . . . in seven months. Make sure it's a boy.

CHIN: This doesn't sound like something the Chairman would do. Maybe you'd better talk to Comrade Kang yourself.

SONG: Good. I will.

(*Chin gets up to leave.*)

SONG: Miss Chin? Why, in the Peking Opera, are women's roles played by men?

CHIN: I don't know. Maybe, a reactionary remnant of male —

SONG: No. (*Beat.*) Because only a man knows how a woman is supposed to act.

(*Chin exits. Song turns upstage, towards Gallimard.*)

GALLIMARD (*calling after Chin*): Good riddance! (*To Song.*) I could forget all that betrayal in an instant, you know. If you'd just come back and become Butterfly again.

SONG: Fat chance. You're here in prison, rotting in a cell. And I'm on a plane, winging my way back to China. Your President pardoned me of our treason, you know.

GALLIMARD: Yes, I read about that.

SONG: Must make you feel . . . lower than shit.

GALLIMARD: But don't you, even a little bit, wish you were here with me?

SONG: I'm an artist, René. You were my greatest . . . acting challenge. (*She laughs.*) It doesn't matter how rotten I answer, does it? You still adore me. That's why I love you, René. (*She points to us.*) So — you were telling your audience about the night I announced I was pregnant.

(*Gallimard puts his arms around Song's waist. He and Song are in the positions they were in at the end of Scene VI.*)

Scene VIII

(*Same.*)

GALLIMARD: I'll divorce my wife. We'll live together here, and then later in France.

SONG: I feel so . . . ashamed.

GALLIMARD: Why?

SONG: I had begun to lose faith. And now, you shame me with your generosity.

GALLIMARD: Generosity? No, I'm proposing for very selfish reasons.

SONG: Your apologies only make me feel more ashamed. My outburst a moment ago!

GALLIMARD: Your outburst? What about my request?!

SONG: You've been very patient dealing with my . . . eccentricities. A Western man, used to women freer with their bodies —

GALLIMARD: It was sick! Don't make excuses for me.

SONG: I have to. You don't seem willing to make them for yourself.

(*Pause.*)

GALLIMARD: You're crazy.

SONG: I'm happy. Which often looks like crazy.

GALLIMARD: Then make me crazy. Marry me.

(*Pause.*)

SONG: No.

GALLIMARD: What?

SONG: Do I sound silly, a slave, if I say I'm not worthy?

GALLIMARD: Yes. In fact you do. No one has loved me like you.

SONG: Thank you. And no one ever will. I'll see to that.

GALLIMARD: So what is the problem?

SONG: René, we Chinese are realists. We understand rice, gold, and guns. You are a diplomat. Your career is sky-rocketing. Now, what would happen if you divorced your wife to marry a Communist Chinese actress?

GALLIMARD: That's not being realistic. That's defeating yourself before you begin.

SONG: We conserve our strength for the battles we can win.

GALLIMARD: That sounds like a fortune cookie!

SONG: Where do you think fortune cookies come from!

GALLIMARD: I don't care.

SONG: You do. So do I. And we should. That is why I say I'm not worthy. I'm worthy to love and even to be loved by you. But I am not worthy to end the career of one of the West's most promising diplomats.

GALLIMARD: It's not that great a career! I made it sound like more than it is!

SONG: Modesty will get you nowhere. Flatter yourself, and you flatter me. I'm flattered to decline your offer. (*She exits.*)

GALLIMARD (*to us*): Butterfly and I argued all night. And, in the end, I left, knowing I would never be her husband. She went away for several months — to the countryside, like a small animal. Until the night I received her call.

(*A baby's cry from offstage. Song enters, carrying a child.*)

SONG: He looks like you.

GALLIMARD: Oh! (*Beat; he approaches the baby.*) Well, babies are never very attractive at birth.

SONG: Stop!

GALLIMARD: I'm sure he'll grow more beautiful with age. More like his mother.

SONG: "*Chi vide mai / a bimbo del Giappon . . .*"

GALLIMARD: "What baby, I wonder, was ever born in Japan"— or China, for that matter —

SONG: "*. . . occhi azzurrini?*"

GALLIMARD: "With azure eyes"— they're actually sort of brown, wouldn't you say?

SONG: "*E il labbro.*"

GALLIMARD: "And such lips!" (*He kisses Song.*) And such lips.

SONG: "*E i ricciolini d'oro schietto?*"

GALLIMARD: "And such a head of golden"— if slightly patchy —"curls?"

SONG: I'm going to call him "Peepee."

GALLIMARD: Darling, could you repeat that because I'm sure a rickshaw just flew by overhead.

SONG: You heard me.

GALLIMARD: "Song Peepee"? May I suggest Michael, or Stephan, or Adolph?

SONG: You may, but I won't listen.

GALLIMARD: You can't be serious. Can you imagine the time this child will have in school?

SONG: In the West, yes.

GALLIMARD: It's worse than naming him Ping Pong or Long Dong or —

SONG: But he's never going to live in the West, is he?

(*Pause.*)

GALLIMARD: That wasn't my choice.

SONG: It is mine. And this is my promise to you: I will raise him, he will be our child, but he will never burden you outside of China.

GALLIMARD: Why do you make these promises? I want to be burdened! I want a scandal to cover the papers!

SONG (*to us*): Prophetic.

GALLIMARD: I'm serious.

SONG: So am I. His name is as I registered it. And he will never live in the West.

(*Song exits with the child.*)

GALLIMARD (*to us*): Is it possible that her stubbornness only made me want her more? That drawing back at the moment of my capitulation was the most brilliant strategy she could have chosen? It is possible. But it is also possible that by this point she could have said, could have done . . . anything, and I would have adored her still.

Scene IX

(*Beijing. 1966.*
A driving rhythm of Chinese percussion fills the stage.)

GALLIMARD: And then, China began to change. Mao became very old, and his cult became very strong. And, like many old men, he entered his second childhood. So he handed over the reins of state to those with minds like his own. And children ruled the Middle Kingdom° with complete caprice. The doctrine of the Cultural Revolution° implied continuous anarchy. Contact between Chinese and foreigners became impossible. Our flat was confiscated. Her fame and my money now counted against us.

(*Two dancers in Mao suits and red-starred caps enter, and begin crudely mimicking revolutionary violence, in an agitprop fashion.*)

GALLIMARD: And somehow the American war went wrong too. Four hundred thousand dollars were being spent for every Viet Cong° killed; so General

---

Middle Kingdom: The royal domain of China during its feudal period.
Cultural Revolution: Reform campaign of 1965–1967 to purge counterrevolutionary thought in China that challenged Mao Zedong.
Viet Cong: Member of the National Liberation Front of South Vietnam, against which U.S. forces were fighting.

Westmoreland's° remark that the Oriental does not value life the way Americans do was oddly accurate. Why weren't the Vietnamese people giving in? Why were they content instead to die and die and die again?

(*Toulon enters. Percussion and dancers continue upstage.*)

TOULON: Congratulations, Gallimard.

GALLIMARD: Excuse me, sir?

TOULON: Not a promotion. That was last time. You're going home.

GALLIMARD: What?

TOULON: Don't say I didn't warn you.

GALLIMARD: I'm being transferred . . . because I was wrong about the American war?

TOULON: Of course not. We don't care about the Americans. We care about your mind. The quality of your analysis. In general, everything you've predicted here in the Orient . . . just hasn't happened.

GALLIMARD: I think that's premature.

TOULON: Don't force me to be blunt. Okay, you said China was ready to open to Western trade. The only thing they're trading out there are Western heads. And, yes, you said the Americans would succeed in Indochina. You were kidding, right?

GALLIMARD: I think the end is in sight.

TOULON: Don't be pathetic. And don't take this personally. You were wrong. It's not your fault.

GALLIMARD: But I'm going home.

TOULON: Right. Could I have the number of your mistress? (*Beat.*) Joke! Joke! Eat a croissant for me.

(*Toulon exits. Song, wearing a Mao suit, is dragged in from the wings as part of the upstage dance. They "beat" her, then lampoon the acrobatics of the Chinese opera, as she is made to kneel onstage.*)

GALLIMARD (*simultaneously*): I don't care to recall how Butterfly and I said our hurried farewell. Perhaps it was better to end our affair before it killed her.

(*Gallimard exits. Percussion rises in volume. The lampooning becomes faster, more frenetic. At its height, Comrade Chin walks across the stage with a banner reading: "The Actor Renounces His Decadent Profession!" She reaches the kneeling Song. At the moment Chin touches Song's chin, percussion stops with a thud. Dancers strike poses.*)

CHIN: Actor-oppressor, for years you have lived above the common people and looked down on their labor. While the farmer ate millet —

SONG: I ate pastries from France and sweetmeats from silver trays.

CHIN: And how did you come to live in such an exalted position?

General Westmoreland: William Westmoreland (b. 1914), commander of American troops in Vietnam from 1964 to 1968.

SONG: I was a plaything for the imperialists!

CHIN: What did you do?

SONG: I shamed China by allowing myself to be corrupted by a foreigner . . .

CHIN: What does this mean? The People demand a full confession!

SONG: I engaged in the lowest perversions with China's enemies!

CHIN: What perversions? Be more clear!

SONG: I let him put it up my ass!

(*Dancers look over, disgusted.*)

CHIN: Aaaa-ya! How can you use such sickening language?!

SONG: My language . . . is only as foul as the crimes I committed . . .

CHIN: Yeah. That's better. So — what do you want to do . . . now?

SONG: I want to serve the people!

(*Percussion starts up, with Chinese strings.*)

CHIN: What?

SONG: I want to serve the people!

(*Dancers regain their revolutionary smiles, and begin a dance of victory.*)

CHIN: What?!

SONG: I want to serve the people!!

(*Dancers unveil a banner: "The Actor Is Re-Habilitated!" Song remains kneeling before Chin, as the dancers bounce around them, then exit. Music out.*)

Scene X

(*A commune. Hunan Province. 1970.*)

CHIN: How you planning to do that?

SONG: I've already worked four years in the fields of Hunan, Comrade Chin.

CHIN: So? Farmers work all their lives. Let me see your hands.

(*Song holds them out for her inspection.*)

CHIN: Goddamn! Still so smooth! How long does it take to turn you actors into good anythings? Hunh. You've just spent too many years in luxury to be any good to the Revolution.

SONG: I served the Revolution.

CHIN: Serve the Revolution? Bullshit! You wore dresses! Don't tell me — I was there. I saw you! You and your white vice-consul! Stuck up there in your flat, living off the People's Treasury! Yeah, I knew what was going on! You two . . . homos! Homos! Homos! (*Pause; she composes herself.*) Ah! Well . . . you will serve the people, all right. But not with the Revolution's money. This time, you use your own money.

SONG: I have no money.

CHIN: Shut up! And you won't stink up China anymore with your pervert stuff. You'll pollute the place where pollution begins — the West.

SONG: What do you mean?

CHIN: Shut up! You're going to France. Without a cent in your pocket. You find your consul's house, you make him pay your expenses —

SONG: No.

CHIN: And you give us weekly reports! Useful information!

SONG: That's crazy. It's been four years.

CHIN: Either that, or back to rehabilitation center!

SONG: Comrade Chin, he's not going to support me! Not in France! He's a white man! I was just his plaything —

CHIN: Oh yuck! Again with the sickening language? Where's my stick?

SONG: You don't understand the mind of a man.

(*Pause.*)

CHIN: Oh no? No I don't? Then how come I'm married, huh? How come I got a man? Five, six years ago, you always tell me those kind of things, I felt very bad. But not now! Because what does the Chairman say? He tells us *I'm* now the smart one, you're now the nincompoop! *You're* the blockhead, the harebrain, the nitwit! You think you're so smart? You understand "The Mind of a Man"? Good! Then *you* go to France and be a pervert for Chairman Mao!

(*Chin and Song exit in opposite directions.*)

Scene XI

(*Paris. 1968–1970.*
Gallimard enters.)

GALLIMARD: And what was waiting for me back in Paris? Well, better Chinese food than I'd eaten in China. Friends and relatives. A little accounting, regular schedule, keeping track of traffic violations in the suburbs. . . . And the indignity of students shouting the slogans of Chairman Mao at me — in French.

HELGA: René? René? (*She enters, soaking wet.*) I've had a . . . problem.

(*She sneezes.*)

GALLIMARD: You're wet.

HELGA: Yes, I . . . coming back from the grocer's. A group of students, waving red flags, they —

(*Gallimard fetches a towel.*)

HELGA: — they ran by, I was caught up along with them. Before I knew what was happening —

(*Gallimard gives her the towel.*)

HELGA: Thank you. The police started firing water cannons at us. I tried to shout, to tell them I was the wife of a diplomat, but — you know how it is . . .

(*Pause.*) Needless to say, I lost the groceries. René, what's happening to France?

GALLIMARD: What's — ? Well, nothing, really.

HELGA: Nothing?! The storefronts are in flames, there's glass in the streets, buildings are toppling — and I'm wet!

GALLIMARD: Nothing! . . . that I care to think about.

HELGA: And is that why you stay in this room?

GALLIMARD: Yes, in fact.

HELGA: With the incense burning? You know something? I hate incense. It smells so sickly sweet.

GALLIMARD: Well, I hate the French. Who just smell — period!

HELGA: And the Chinese were better?

GALLIMARD: Please — don't start.

HELGA: When we left, this exact same thing, the riots —

GALLIMARD: No, no . . .

HELGA: Students screaming slogans, smashing down doors —

GALLIMARD: Helga —

HELGA: It was all going on in China, too. Don't you remember?!

GALLIMARD: Helga! Please! (*Pause.*) You have never understood China, have you? You walk in here with these ridiculous ideas, that the West is falling apart, that China was spitting in our faces. You come in, dripping of the streets, and you leave water all over my floor. (*He grabs Helga's towel, begins mopping up the floor.*)

HELGA: But it's the truth!

GALLIMARD: Helga, I want a divorce.

(*Pause; Gallimard continues mopping the floor.*)

HELGA: I take it back. China is . . . beautiful. Incense, I like incense.

GALLIMARD: I've had a mistress.

HELGA: So?

GALLIMARD: For eight years.

HELGA: I knew you would. I knew you would the day I married you. And now what? You want to marry her?

GALLIMARD: I can't. She's in China.

HELGA: I see. You know that no one else is ever going to marry me, right?

GALLIMARD: I'm sorry.

HELGA: And you want to leave. For someone who's not here, is that right?

GALLIMARD: That's right.

HELGA: You can't live with her, but still you don't want to live with me.

GALLIMARD: That's right.

(*Pause.*)

HELGA: Shit. How terrible that I can figure that out. (*Pause.*) I never thought I'd say it. But, in China, I was happy. I knew, in my own way, I knew that you were not everything you pretended to be. But the pretense — going on your arm to the embassy ball, visiting your office and the guards saying, "Good morning, good morning, Madame Gallimard"— the

pretense . . . was very good indeed. (*Pause.*) I hope everyone is mean to you for the rest of your life. (*She exits.*)

GALLIMARD (*to us*): Prophetic.

(*Marc enters with two drinks.*)

GALLIMARD (*to Marc*): In China, I was different from all other men.

MARC: Sure. You were white. Here's your drink.

GALLIMARD: I felt . . . touched.

MARC: In the head? René, I don't want to hear about the Oriental love goddess. Okay? One night — can we just drink and throw up without a lot of conversation?

GALLIMARD: You still don't believe me, do you?

MARC: Sure I do. She was the most beautiful, et cetera, et cetera, blasé, blasé.

(*Pause.*)

GALLIMARD: My life in the West has been such a disappointment.

MARC: Life in the West is like that. You'll get used to it. Look, you're driving me away. I'm leaving. Happy, now? (*He exits, then returns.*) Look, I have a date tomorrow night. You wanna come? I can fix you up with —

GALLIMARD: Of course. I would love to come.

(*Pause.*)

MARC: Uh — on second thought, no. You'd better get ahold of yourself first.

(*He exits; Gallimard nurses his drink.*)

GALLIMARD (*to us*): This is the ultimate cruelty, isn't it? That I can talk and talk and to anyone listening, it's only air — too rich a diet to be swallowed by a mundane world. Why can't anyone understand? That in China, I once loved, and was loved by, very simply, the Perfect Woman.

(*Song enters, dressed as Butterfly in wedding dress.*)

GALLIMARD (*to Song*): Not again. My imagination is hell. Am I asleep this time? Or did I drink too much?

SONG: René!

GALLIMARD: God, it's too painful! That you speak?

SONG: What are you talking about? René — touch me.

GALLIMARD: Why?

SONG: I'm real. Take my hand.

GALLIMARD: Why? So you can disappear again and leave me clutching at the air? For the entertainment of my neighbors who — ?

(*Song touches Gallimard.*)

SONG: René?

(*Gallimard takes Song's hand. Silence.*)

GALLIMARD: Butterfly? I never doubted you'd return.

SONG: You hadn't . . . forgotten — ?

GALLIMARD: Yes, actually, I've forgotten everything. My mind, you see — there wasn't enough room in this hard head — not for the world *and* for you. No, there was only room for one. (*Beat.*) Come, look. See? Your bed has been waiting, with the Klimt° poster you like, and — see? The *xiang lu*° you gave me?

SONG: I . . . I don't know what to say.

GALLIMARD: There's nothing to say. Not at the end of a long trip. Can I make you some tea?

SONG: But where's your wife?

GALLIMARD: She's by my side. She's by my side at last.

(*Gallimard reaches to embrace Song. Song sidesteps, dodging him.*)

GALLIMARD: Why?!

SONG (*to us*): So I did return to René in Paris. Where I found —

GALLIMARD: Why do you run away? Can't we show them how we embraced that evening?

SONG: Please. I'm talking.

GALLIMARD: You have to do what I say! I'm conjuring you up in *my* mind!

SONG: René, I've never done what you've said. Why should it be any different in your mind? Now split — the story moves on, and I must change.

GALLIMARD: I welcomed you into my home! I didn't have to, you know! I could've left you penniless on the streets of Paris! But I took you in!

SONG: Thank you.

GALLIMARD: So . . . please . . . don't change.

SONG: You know I have to. You know I will. And anyway, what difference does it make? No matter what your eyes tell you, you can't ignore the truth. You already know too much.

(*Gallimard exits. Song turns to us.*)

SONG: The change I'm going to make requires about five minutes. So I thought you might want to take this opportunity to stretch your legs, enjoy a drink, or listen to the musicians. I'll be here, when you return, right where you left me.

(*Song goes to a mirror in front of which is a wash basin of water. She starts to remove her makeup as stagelights go to half and houselights come up.*)

ACT III • *Scene I*

(*A courthouse in Paris. 1986.*

As he promised, Song has completed the bulk of his transformation onstage by the time the houselights go down and the stagelights come up full. As he speaks to us, he removes his wig and kimono, leaving them on the floor. Underneath, he wears a well-cut suit.)

SONG: So I'd done my job better than I had a right to expect. Well, give him some credit, too. He's right — I was in a fix when I arrived in Paris. I walked from

---

Klimt: Gustav Klimt (1863–1918), Austrian painter in the art nouveau style, whose most famous painting is *The Kiss.* ***xiang lu:*** Incense burner.

the airport into town, then I located, by blind groping, the Chinatown district. Let me make one thing clear: whatever else may be said about the Chinese, they are stingy! I slept in doorways three days until I could find a tailor who would make me this kimono on credit. As it turns out, maybe I didn't even need it. Maybe he would've been happy to see me in a simple shift and mascara. But . . . better safe than sorry.

That was 1970, when I arrived in Paris. For the next fifteen years, yes, I lived a very comfy life. Some relief, believe me, after four years on a fucking commune in Nowheresville, China. René supported the boy and me, and I did some demonstrations around the country as part of my "cultural exchange" cover. And then there was the spying.

(*Song moves upstage, to a chair. Toulon enters as a judge, wearing the appropriate wig and robes. He sits near Song. It's 1986, and Song is testifying in a courtroom.*)

SONG: Not much at first. René had lost all his high-level contacts. Comrade Chin wasn't very interested in parking-ticket statistics. But finally, at my urging, René got a job as a courier, handling sensitive documents. He'd photograph them for me, and I'd pass them on to the Chinese embassy.

JUDGE: Did he understand the extent of his activity?

SONG: He didn't ask. He knew that I needed those documents, and that was enough.

JUDGE: But he must've known he was passing classified information.

SONG: I can't say.

JUDGE: He never asked what you were going to do with them?

SONG: Nope.

(*Pause.*)

JUDGE: There is one thing that the court — indeed, that all of France — would like to know.

SONG: Fire away.

JUDGE: Did Monsieur Gallimard know you were a man?

SONG: Well, he never saw me completely naked. Ever.

JUDGE: But surely, he must've . . . how can I put this?

SONG: Put it however you like. I'm not shy. He must've felt around?

JUDGE: Mmmmm.

SONG: Not really. I did all the work. He just laid back. Of course we did enjoy more . . . complete union, and I suppose he *might* have wondered why I was always on my stomach, but. . . . But what you're thinking is, "Of course a wrist must've brushed . . . a hand hit . . . over twenty years!" Yeah. Well, Your Honor, it was my job to make him think I was a woman. And chew on this: it wasn't all that hard. See, my mother was a prostitute along the Bundt before the Revolution. And, uh, I think it's fair to say she learned a few things about Western men. So I borrowed her knowledge. In service to my country.

JUDGE: Would you care to enlighten the court with this secret knowledge? I'm sure we're all very curious.

SONG: I'm sure you are. (*Pause.*) Okay, Rule One is: Men always believe what they want to hear. So a girl can tell the most obnoxious lies and the guys will believe them every time —"This is my first time"— "That's the biggest I've ever seen"— or *both,* which, if you really think about it, is not possible in a single lifetime. You've maybe heard those phrases a few times in your own life, yes, Your Honor?

JUDGE: It's not my life, Monsieur Song, which is on trial today.

SONG: Okay, okay, just trying to lighten up the proceedings. Tough room.

JUDGE: Go on.

SONG: Rule Two: As soon as a Western man comes into contact with the East — he's already confused. The West has sort of an international rape mentality towards the East. Do you know rape mentality?

JUDGE: Give us your definition, please.

SONG: Basically, "Her mouth says no, but her eyes say yes."

The West thinks of itself as masculine — big guns, big industry, big money — so the East is feminine — weak, delicate, poor . . . but good at art, and full of inscrutable wisdom — the feminine mystique.

Her mouth says no, but her eyes say yes. The West believes the East, deep down, *wants* to be dominated — because a woman can't think for herself.

JUDGE: What does this have to do with my question?

SONG: You expect Oriental countries to submit to your guns, and you expect Oriental women to be submissive to your men. That's why you say they make the best wives.

JUDGE: But why would that make it possible for you to fool Monsieur Gallimard? Please — get to the point.

SONG: One, because when he finally met his fantasy woman, he wanted more than anything to believe that she was, in fact, a woman. And second, I am an Oriental. And being an Oriental, I could never be completely a man.

(*Pause.*)

JUDGE: Your armchair political theory is tenuous, Monsieur Song.

SONG: You think so? That's why you'll lose in all your dealings with the East.

JUDGE: Just answer my question: did he know you were a man?

(*Pause.*)

SONG: You know, Your Honor, I never asked.

Scene II

(*Same.*

Music from the "Death Scene" from Butterfly blares over the house speakers. It is the loudest thing we've heard in this play.

Gallimard enters, crawling towards Song's wig and kimono.)

GALLIMARD: Butterfly? Butterfly?

(*Song remains a man, in the witness box, delivering a testimony we do not hear.*)

GALLIMARD (*to us*): In my moment of greatest shame, here, in this courtroom — with that . . . person up there, telling the world. . . . What strikes me especially is how shallow he is, how glib and obsequious . . . completely . . . without substance! The type that prowls around discos with a gold medallion stinking of garlic. So little like my Butterfly.

Yet even in this moment my mind remains agile, flip-flopping like a man on a trampoline. Even now, my picture dissolves, and I see that . . . witness . . . talking to me.

(*Song suddenly stands straight up in his witness box, and looks at Gallimard.*)

SONG: Yes. You. White man.

(*Song steps out of the witness box, and moves downstage towards Gallimard. Light change.*)

GALLIMARD (*to Song*): Who? Me?

SONG: Do you see any other white men?

GALLIMARD: Yes. There're white men all around. This is a French courtroom.

SONG: So you are an adventurous imperialist. Tell me, why did it take you so long? To come back to this place?

GALLIMARD: What place?

SONG: This theater in China. Where we met many years ago.

GALLIMARD (*to us*): And once again, against my will, I am transported.

(*Chinese opera music comes up on the speakers. Song begins to do opera moves, as he did the night they met.*)

SONG: Do you remember? The night you gave your heart?

GALLIMARD: It was a long time ago.

SONG: Not long enough. A night that turned your world upside down.

GALLIMARD: Perhaps.

SONG: Oh, be honest with me. What's another bit of flattery when you've already given me twenty years' worth? It's a wonder my head hasn't swollen to the size of China.

GALLIMARD: Who's to say it hasn't?

SONG: Who's to say? And what's the shame? In pride? You think I could've pulled this off if I wasn't already full of pride when we met? No, not just pride. Arrogance. It takes arrogance, really — to believe you can will, with your eyes and your lips, the destiny of another. (*He dances.*) C'mon. Admit it. You still want me. Even in slacks and a button-down collar.

GALLIMARD: I don't see what the point of —

SONG: You don't? Well maybe, René, just maybe — I want you.

GALLIMARD: You do?

SONG: Then again, maybe I'm just playing with you. How can you tell? (*Reprising his feminine character, he sidles up to Gallimard.*) "How I wish there were even a small café to sit in. With men in tuxedos, and cappuccinos, and bad expatriate jazz." Now you want to kiss me, don't you?

GALLIMARD (*pulling away*): What makes you — ?

SONG: — so sure? See? I take the words from your mouth. Then I wait for you to come and retrieve them. (*He reclines on the floor.*)

GALLIMARD: Why?! Why do you treat me so cruelly?

SONG: Perhaps I *was* treating you cruelly. But now — I'm being nice. Come here, my little one.

GALLIMARD: I'm not your little one!

SONG: My mistake. It's I who am *your* little one, right?

GALLIMARD: Yes, I —

SONG: So come get your little one. If you like, I may even let you strip me.

GALLIMARD: I mean, you were! Before . . . but not like this!

SONG: I was? Then perhaps I still am. If you look hard enough. (*He starts to remove his clothes.*)

GALLIMARD: What — what are you doing?

SONG: Helping you to see through my act.

GALLIMARD: Stop that! I don't want to! I don't —

SONG: Oh, but you asked me to strip, remember?

GALLIMARD: What? That was years ago! And I took it back!

SONG: No. You postponed it. Postponed the inevitable. Today, the inevitable has come calling.

(*From the speakers, cacophony: Butterfly mixed in with Chinese gongs.*)

GALLIMARD: No! Stop! I don't want to see!

SONG: Then look away.

GALLIMARD: You're only in my mind! All this is in my mind! I order you! To stop!

SONG: To what? To strip? That's just what I'm —

GALLIMARD: No! Stop! I want you — !

SONG: You want me?

GALLIMARD: To stop!

SONG: You know something, René? Your mouth says no, but your eyes say yes. Turn them away. I dare you.

GALLIMARD: I don't have to! Every night, you say you're going to strip, but then I beg you and you stop!

SONG: I guess tonight is different.

GALLIMARD: Why? Why should that be?

SONG: Maybe I've become frustrated. Maybe I'm saying "Look at me, you fool!" Or maybe I'm just feeling . . . sexy. (*He is down to his briefs.*)

GALLIMARD: Please. This is unnecessary. I know what you are.

SONG: You do? What am I?

GALLIMARD: A — a man.

SONG: You don't really believe that.

GALLIMARD: Yes I do! I knew all the time somewhere that my happiness was temporary, my love a deception. But my mind kept the knowledge at bay. To make the wait bearable.

SONG: Monsieur Gallimard — the wait is over.

(*Song drops his briefs. He is naked. Sound cue out. Slowly, we and Song come to the realization that what*

we had thought to be Gallimard's sobbing is actually his laughter.)

GALLIMARD: Oh god! What an idiot! Of course!

SONG: René — what?

GALLIMARD: Look at you! You're a man! (*He bursts into laughter again.*)

SONG: I fail to see what's so funny!

GALLIMARD: "You fail to see — !" I mean, you never did have much of a sense of humor, did you? I just think it's ridiculously funny that I've wasted so much time on just a man!

SONG: Wait. I'm not "just a man."

GALLIMARD: No? Isn't that what you've been trying to convince me of?

SONG: Yes, but what I mean —

GALLIMARD: And now, I finally believe you, and you tell me it's not true? I think you must have some kind of identity problem.

SONG: Will you listen to me?

GALLIMARD: Why?! I've been listening to you for twenty years. Don't I deserve a vacation?

SONG: I'm not just any man!

GALLIMARD: Then, what exactly are you?

SONG: René, how can you ask — ? Okay, what about this?

(*He picks up Butterfly's robes, starts to dance around. No music.*)

GALLIMARD: Yes, that's very nice. I have to admit.

(*Song holds out his arm to Gallimard.*)

SONG: It's the same skin you've worshipped for years. Touch it.

GALLIMARD: Yes, it does feel the same.

SONG: Now — close your eyes.

(*Song covers Gallimard's eyes with one hand. With the other, Song draws Gallimard's hand up to his face. Gallimard, like a blind man, lets his hands run over Song's face.*)

GALLIMARD: This skin, I remember. The curve of her face, the softness of her cheek, her hair against the back of my hand . . .

SONG: I'm your Butterfly. Under the robes, beneath everything, it was always me. Now, open your eyes and admit it — you adore me. (*He removes his hand from Gallimard's eyes.*)

GALLIMARD: You, who knew every inch of my desires — how could you, of all people, have made such a mistake?

SONG: What?

GALLIMARD: You showed me your true self. When all I loved was the lie. A perfect lie, which you let fall to the ground — and now, it's old and soiled.

SONG: So — you never really loved me? Only when I was playing a part?

GALLIMARD: I'm a man who loved a woman created by a man. Everything else — simply falls short.

(*Pause.*)

Song: What am I supposed to do now?

Gallimard: You were a fine spy, Monsieur Song, with an even finer accomplice. But now I believe you should go. Get out of my life!

Song: Go where? René, you can't live without me. Not after twenty years.

Gallimard: I certainly can't live with you — not after twenty years of betrayal.

Song: Don't be stubborn! Where will you go?

Gallimard: I have a date . . . with my Butterfly.

Song: So, throw away your pride. And come . . .

Gallimard: Get away from me! Tonight, I've finally learned to tell fantasy from reality. And, knowing the difference, I choose fantasy.

Song: *I'm* your fantasy!

Gallimard: You? You're as real as hamburger. Now get out! I have a date with my Butterfly and I don't want your body polluting the room! (*He tosses Song's suit at him.*) Look at these — you dress like a pimp.

Song: Hey! These are Armani slacks and — ! (*He puts on his briefs and slacks.*) Let's just say . . . I'm disappointed in you, René. In the crush of your adoration, I thought you'd become something more. More like . . . a woman.

But no. Men. You're like the rest of them. It's all in the way we dress, and make up our faces, and bat our eyelashes. You really have so little imagination!

Gallimard: You, Monsieur Song? Accuse me of too little imagination? You, if anyone, should know — I am pure imagination. And in imagination I will remain. Now get out!

(*Gallimard bodily removes Song from the stage, taking his kimono.*)

Song: René! I'll never put on those robes again! You'll be sorry!

Gallimard (*to Song*): I'm already sorry! (*Looking at the kimono in his hands.*) Exactly as sorry . . . as a Butterfly.

Scene III

(*M. Gallimard's prison cell. Paris. 1988.*)

Gallimard: I've played out the events of my life night after night, always searching for a new ending to my story, one where I leave this cell and return forever to my Butterfly's arms.

Tonight I realize my search is over. That I've looked all along in the wrong place. And now, to you, I will prove that my love was not in vain — by returning to the world of fantasy where I first met her.

(*He picks up the kimono; dancers enter.*)

Gallimard: There is a vision of the Orient that I have. Of slender women in cheongsams and kimonos who die for the love of unworthy foreign devils. Who are born and raised to be the perfect women. Who take whatever punishment we give them, and bounce back, strengthened by love, unconditionally. It is a vision that has become my life.

(*Dancers bring the washbasin to him and help him make up his face.*)

Gallimard: In public, I have continued to deny that Song Liling is a man. This brings me headlines, and is a source of great embarrassment to my French colleagues, who can now be sent into a coughing fit by the mere mention of Chinese food. But alone, in my cell, I have long since faced the truth.

And the truth demands a sacrifice. For mistakes made over the course of a lifetime. My mistakes were simple and absolute — the man I loved was a cad, a bounder. He deserved nothing but a kick in the behind, and instead I gave him . . . all my love.

Yes — love. Why not admit it all? That was my undoing, wasn't it? Love warped my judgment, blinded my eyes, rearranged the very lines on my face . . . until I could look in the mirror and see nothing but . . . a woman.

(*Dancers help him put on the Butterfly wig.*)

Gallimard: I have a vision. Of the Orient. That, deep within its almond eyes, there are still women. Women willing to sacrifice themselves for the love of a man. Even a man whose love is completely without worth.

(*Dancers assist Gallimard in donning the kimono. They hand him a knife.*)

Gallimard: Death with honor is better than life . . . life with dishonor. (*He sets himself center stage, in a seppuku position.*) The love of a Butterfly can withstand many things — unfaithfulness, loss, even abandonment. But how can it face the one sin that implies all others? The devastating knowledge that, underneath it all, the object of her love was nothing more, nothing less than . . . a man. (*He sets the tip of the knife against his body.*) It is 1988. And I have found her at last. In a prison on the outskirts of Paris. My name is René Gallimard — also known as Madame Butterfly.

(*Gallimard turns upstage and plunges the knife into his body, as music from the "Love Duet" blares over the speakers. He collapses into the arms of the dancers, who lay him reverently on the floor. The image holds for several beats. Then a tight special up on Song, who stands as a man, staring at the dead Gallimard. He smokes a cigarette; the smoke filters up through the lights. Two words leave his lips.*)

Song: Butterfly? Butterfly?

(*Smoke rises as lights fade slowly to black.*)

COMMENTARIES

John Louis DiGaetani (b. 1943)
M. BUTTERFLY: AN INTERVIEW
WITH DAVID HENRY HWANG   *1989*

> *John Louis DiGaetani and David Henry Hwang discuss some of the more inter-*
> *esting aspects of the playwright's approach to writing* M. Butterfly. *He explores the*
> *ideas that lay behind "orientalism" as Hwang worked with it in the play, and he*
> *comments on connections with Puccini's* Madame Butterfly.

David Henry Hwang's *M. Butterfly* went into rehearsal during the first week of January 1988 and into preview on February 6 at the National Theater in Washington, D.C. On February 10 the play opened and played to excellent reviews until the first week in March. On March 20, 1988, the play opened on Broadway at the Eugene O'Neill Theatre, where it has been successfully running ever since.

M. Butterfly takes place today in a Paris prison, and, in recall, the years 1960 to 1985 in Beijing and Paris. The events of the play were suggested by recent newspaper accounts of an actual international spy scandal. A French diplomat by the name of Boursicot (Gallimard in the play) was stationed in Beijing, China, during the period of the American war in Vietnam. During Boursicot's stay, he started a long-term affair with someone he thought was a female star of the Beijing Opera. When the lovers tried to enter France, they were both charged with espionage. Only then did the diplomat discover that his mistress was a spy for the Chinese government — and also a man. M. Boursicot was tried, found guilty of espionage, and sentenced to prison. He was released from prison in 1988.

I spoke with Mr. Hwang in New York City in September 1988.

Hwang: I wrote *M. Butterfly* as an attempt to deal with some aspects of orientalism. I assumed that many in the audience would be coming to the theater because they hoped to see something exotic and mysterious, but what exactly is behind the desire to see the "exotic East"?

DiGaetani: One of the things I found interesting is that your play suggested the Western naivete about the East. Many Westerners tend to think of the East as a pretty little Madame Butterfly rather than seeing what is actually there in the orient. It's a kind of racism combined with sexism.

Hwang: Yes, that's true. The play has been taken as a commentary or a criticism of Western attitudes toward the East, and I think that's accurate. But I would like to think that the play is fairly even-handed in saying that the East also misperceives the West. The East is guilty or complicit in this dual form of cultural stereotyping. The West, having had the advantage of being the colonial power and of being the more powerful of the two over the past couple of hundred years, has an attitude of condescension toward the East. But the East has played up to that to its short-term

1592

advantage without thinking of the long-term ill effects that reinforcing those racial stereotypes causes. I think both parties are equally guilty.

In terms of Western misperceptions, there is Edward Said's term, "orientalism." I read Said's book after I wrote the play. John Dexter, the play's director, recommended it. It was one of the reasons he was interested in doing the play. This notion that the East is mysterious, inscrutable, and therefore ultimately inferior, is something that definitely is consistent with themes in Puccini's *Madame Butterfly*.

DiGaetani: Well, an aspect of the Puccini opera that I think is often overlooked is its attack on that Western view. Pinkerton is one of the great heels in all opera. Puccini presents the West as oafish and insensitive.

Hwang: Puccini presents that view at the same time that he presents a view of the East as helpless to resist. I think that the East has played into that stereotype by saying, "Oh, yes, we are helpless" and therefore trying to manipulate the situation to its own advantage.

DiGaetani: Naivete can be used as a ploy. One of the interesting things about the Puccini opera is that it presents the East as a place in the early stages of its victimization by an imperialist power. In other words, in the beginning people think that the changes are all wonderful and mean progress and the modern way. They don't realize that they are being used. Of course Madame Butterfly does eventually realize the horrible consequences of being colonized. Are you an opera fan?

Hwang: I was trained as a musician, so I'm a music fan in general. Opera is actually something that I've only become interested in during the past couple of years, and to some degree because of *M. Butterfly*. Ironically, when I decided I wanted to incorporate the plot of Puccini's *Madame Butterfly* into the play, I actually didn't know much about opera. So I started listening to a lot more of it, and particularly during the rehearsals for the play I started listening to the Puccini opera and I really learned to appreciate it. My play, which sets out to lampoon opera, has made me an opera buff.

DiGaetani: Your play brings up lots of interesting questions, one of which is: Can we love a person as a person if we are unsure of that person's gender?

Hwang: The play is to some degree about the nature of seduction — in the sense that we seduce ourselves. Sometimes when you have the desire to fall in love or you desire to have someone to be some kind of ideal, you can make that person ideal in your own mind whether or not the actual facts correspond to the reality. I think that it's often true in a smaller, less extreme sense that we get involved with people and decide to blind ourselves to their faults so that they can be the perfect love that we've always wanted. And on some level we're aware that that is not the case. But we prefer the fantasy over the reality. The play presents an obviously more extreme and less common situation, where the reality is so radically different from fantasy that at the core, even the simple, fundamental fact that it's a man instead of a woman is something that the person in love chooses to block out. But it's not actually that different qualitatively from everyday types of deceptions that people make in order to convince themselves they're in love.

DiGaetani: I remember when I first read the story in the newspaper. I thought, how could this have happened? What was your reaction?

Hwang: Of course, I had the same reactions as everybody else — how could it have happened? But then on some level it seemed natural to me that it should have happened, that given the degree of misperception generally between East and West and between men and women, it seemed inevitable that a mistake of this magnitude would one day take place. As a metaphor, the story made perfect sense in the context of the general misunderstanding that I have always perceived takes place between these different groups. In retrospect, it seems to me that that was what really piqued my imagination. I felt the impossibility of the situation and the inevitability of it, both at the same time.

DiGaetani: Men playing women is of course very much a part of Western theater. But one of the ways I interpret your play, and I'd like your comments about this, is that Gallimard was really a homosexual from day one. He was living in a much more homophobic period than today, and the thing about his affair with Song Liling, the thing about the mirage that he and Song Liling created, was that he never had to face his own homosexuality. In other words, he had an affair with a man and never told anyone, not even himself.

Hwang: The lines between gay and straight become very blurred in this play, but I think he knows he's having an affair with a man. Therefore, on some level he is gay. Our director John Dexter told me that he never found the situation to be that unbelievable because of an experience he once had. Dexter once shot a movie for Columbia called *Virgin Soldiers.* He hired macho Englishmen and brought them to Singapore where they went to Boogie Street, the transvestite street. A few of these men picked up these guys, I mean these women who were really men, and the next day Dexter overheard them talking and they said, "No, it was a girl. I know men and I know women, and that was a woman." If you want to believe it's a woman, that's fine. I mean, the fact is you're sleeping with a man, but if you choose to believe you're heterosexual, then that's your prerogative, to live in that fantasy. I think this would apply today to people in Chinese, Italian, Spanish, and some of the other Latin cultures. People in these cultures believe that if you have sex with a man and you do the screwing, you are not gay, but if you're screwed, you're gay. I mean, that sort of distinction has existed since time immemorial.

DiGaetani: Oh, the Chinese believe this is true?

Hwang: So what does gay mean at that point? I don't know.

DiGaetani: In what you're saying, gay means being a passive homosexual. If you're not passive, you're not gay.

Hwang: Correct. So, the situation in *M. Butterfly* is not so far-fetched. Gallimard chooses to believe he is heterosexual.

DiGaetani: Is Gallimard still in jail?

Hwang: The name of the real Gallimard is Boursicot and he just got out of jail.

DiGaetani: Have you tried to contact him?

Hwang: No. I think we may want to have some kind of legal arrangement with him, but we'll see what happens.

DiGaetani: He might want a cut of the royalties.

Hwang: Probably.

DiGaetani: And he deserves it?

Hwang: I wouldn't mind giving him a little.

DiGaetani: Not a lot?

Hwang: No, since the play is not literally based on him. I don't know that it's his story. But on the other hand, I think the guy's been in jail, he's suffered a lot of indignity, so since it's him, why not?

DiGaetani: Have you tried to incorporate many elements of Oriental opera or theater into this play? Or was it primarily Dexter who wanted to do this?

Hwang: The main reason we ended up using Chinese opera was because it was relevant. In reality, Song Liling was a practitioner of Chinese opera. But I also wanted to explore why it is that in Asian theater and also in Shakespearean theater men play women's roles. It's just touched on briefly. Song Liling says, "Why are women's roles played by men?" And the answer is: "Because only a man knows how a woman should act." Let's look at that in kabuki terms because in kabuki it's expressed much more clearly. In kabuki they say that a woman can only be a woman whereas a man can be the idealization of a woman. This is obscene, and it's inherently sexist. What it's saying is that only a man can be a man's idealization of a woman.

DiGaetani: Not a woman's.

Hwang: Right. Song Liling is able to be such an effective fantasy for Gallimard because, as a man, she knows how a man wants to see women, and therefore can become a man's woman — which is why Gallimard says toward the end of the play: "I was a man in love with a woman created by a man, and now everything else simply falls short." I thought the play was a very interesting way to deal with the concept of the onnagata° in the context of a Western play.

DiGaetani: Another interesting conflict I saw in the play was between Japanese and Chinese cultures. They're really different.

Hwang: One of the things I wanted to do was to indicate both the differences between cultures as perceived by Asians and the similarities as perceived by Westerners. In other words, the West looks at the "East" as sort of a monolith. Whether we've been at war against Japan or Korea or Vietnam or in a cold war with China, it's all "Oriental." But of course the Asians see themselves as very different. I also have to say, again, that the reverse is true, that Asians tend to see the West as very monolithic. Perhaps from each point of view, it's a legitimate position to take because there are probably more similarities between the Asian cultures as opposed to the West than differences, and vice versa. But from the point of view of the West, America does not consider itself to be the same as France. And Japan does not consider itself to be China.

I think one of the more simple things the play's trying to say is that eventually one must look past all the cultural stereotyping we do of each other, West to East and East to West, and deal with each other just as humans if we're really to reach any point of true understanding.

onnagata: A male actor who plays a female role. In Chinese opera and Japanese kabuki drama, male actors study and perfect the art of female impersonation over the course of their careers.

John Gross (*b. 1935*)
REVIEW OF *M. BUTTERFLY*   *1988*

John Gross reviewed David Henry Hwang's play in the New York Times *in April 1988 and took issue with a number of the details in the text. His review is not an attack, but it does examine some of the ideas that Hwang centers in the play and calls them into question in an interesting fashion.*

If you want to be taken seriously as a playwright, the quickest way is to set up as a thinker. Nothing is more calculated to make audiences assume a respectful expression than the suggestion that they are about to have some ideas dished out to them, and in a theater world that generally offers little in the way of intellectual nourishment, it is easy enough to see why.

But some ideas are better than others. It isn't enough, when a play raises large and far-reaching questions, to be grateful for the mere show of thinking; a certain amount of attention also needs to be paid to the quality of thought.

In *M. Butterfly*, which has recently opened at the Eugene O'Neill Theatre, David Henry Hwang has seized on a story that fairly bristles with opportunities for exploring social, cultural, and sexual themes. A true story that, as they say, nobody could have invented.

In 1966 a former French diplomat, Bernard Boursicot, and his Chinese lover, a former diva in the Beijing Opera called Shi Peipu, were both sentenced by a French court to six years in jail for spying for China. (Shi was subsequently deported.) They had begun their affair more than 20 years earlier, when Mr. Boursicot was stationed in Beijing; later Shi had followed him back to Paris with the child he was said to have fathered. It was only during the course of the trial that it was revealed, to Boursicot's consternation, that the singer was in fact a man.

There are a number of ways in which such a story could be tackled by a playwright — as a comedy of duplicity and gullibility, for instance, or as a chapter (a serious chapter, for all its outlandishness) in the annals of espionage. To Mr. Hwang, he tells us, it represents a chance to air some of his concerns about racism, sexism, and imperialism, all of them underlined by the analogies he draws with *Madama Butterfly*.

Puccini's opera (adapted from a turn-of-the-century play by an American, David Belasco) is a fable of submission, both female and Oriental, of a kind that no enlightened audience could comfortably endorse today. In Mr. Hwang's fictionalized version of the Boursicot story, the diplomat (for some reason he has been given the name of a celebrated French publisher, Gallimard) assumes that the singer (now known as Song Liling) is a modest, fluttering Butterfly, a delusion that Song skillfully abets. And although Gallimard himself is clumsy and inexperienced, he is soon preening himself on his supposed conquest. If he had a mustache, he'd be twirling it.

His new he-man confidence quickly spills over into his politics. With the conflict in Vietnam growing more intense (ominous roll of drums), he advises the French ambassador to Beijing to advise the Americans to hit the North Vietnamese hard; and when Ngo Dinh Diem's leadership in the South starts proving a liability, he recommends his assassination.

As an explanation of the Vietnam War, the play leaves something to be desired; but for the audience, the more immediate problem is that Gallimard's hawkishness seems utterly out of keeping with everything else about him. It isn't only that he is a dupe — he could, after all, have been a sinister or a belligerent dupe — but that he is generally so comic and pathetic and inept. (It may be just a chance physical resemblance, but watching John Lithgow in the part, I more than once found myself thinking of Basil Fawlty.°)

Then what of the lesser and presumably more representative Western characters in the play, such as Gallimard's wife and his old friend Marc? They are almost all

Basil Fawlty: Comic hotel proprietor of the British sitcom *Fawlty Towers* played by John Cleese.

clumsy caricatures of the attitudes they are meant to represent — and, one might add, disconcertingly American-style caricatures. Marc, for example, may be a prime example of what French feminists call a phallocrate, a male chauvinist, but the particular brand of chauvinism he spouts was unmistakably born in the U.S.A.

Perhaps this doesn't matter very much in itself; perhaps it doesn't matter that Song is Chinese and that Madama Butterfly was Japanese (although at one point Westerners are upbraided for not understanding the difference, and for being unaware of Japanese atrocities in China in the 1930s and 40s). Both blurrings of the boundaries contribute, however, to a more pervasive sense of middle.

So do such episodes as the one featuring a sexy blonde, who makes a speech explaining the urge to make war in terms of masculine fears about sexual inadequacy. The sentiments seem to chime with Mr. Hwang's own, and with his presentation of Gallimard; but the blonde is another caricature of a Westerner, and the speech itself is a dreadful affair, with its leering talk. Where does it all leave us?

The most glaring discrepancy in the play is between its generalized view of the East as feminine victim and its rather more complex view of the actual regime in Beijing that Song serves. *Complexity* here is a strictly relative term: we don't learn all that much about the regime, either. But we are shown the Cultural Revolution working its ravages, with Song sentenced to hard labor in Hunan while a guard bawls at him through a loudspeaker and taunts him with cries of "homo!"

The only reasonable conclusion is that Song is far more victimized by the regime than he is by Gallimard (who is at least as much Song's victim, anyway). Toward the end of the play the original message is hammered home, rather desperately: the West is masculine, the East is feminine, and the West has a "rape mentality." But after everything that we have been shown, it doesn't really add up.

Yet if *M. Butterfly* is a mess, intellectually speaking, that doesn't mean that it isn't very well worth seeing. It can boast one truly outstanding performance in B. D. Wong's Song, and one very good one in John Lithgow's Gallimard; it has moments of undoubted theatrical power, especially the big transformation scenes and role reversals; and at its best it sweeps one up in a tense emotional drama.

That drama is almost wholly the story of two individuals, however. A strange story, certainly: whatever the truth of the relationship may have been in real life, it is hard to believe that, as presented on stage, it doesn't have strong homosexual undercurrents. But watching Gallimard and Song, one isn't inclined to fuss over such matters, or to dabble in amateur psychoanalysis. What we are left with is a tragedy of love, betrayal, and loss, and one that holds together on its own terms.

It would have been better, in fact, if Mr. Hwang hadn't been tempted to pile on the ideas; if he had kept them, at best, in second place, as implications and overtones. As it is, they clutter up the foreground of the play and seriously coarsen its texture. But luckily, despite these handicaps, the central action survives: bitter, affecting, and finally driven on by an anguish that even approaches — just a little — the passion of *Madama Butterfly*.

Tony Kushner

Tony Kushner was born in 1956 in New York City, but his family soon moved to Louisiana, where his father ran the family lumberyard. His parents were classical musicians, and their home was filled with art. Kushner dates his interest in theater to early memories of seeing his mother onstage. He also recollects from childhood "fairly clear memories of being gay since I was six." He did not, however, "come out" until after he had tried psychotherapy to change his sexual orientation.

After finishing his undergraduate education at Columbia University, Kushner studied directing in graduate school at New York University, partly because he was not confident of his chances to become a playwright. Among his early plays are *Yes, Yes, No, No* (1985), a children's play produced in St. Louis; *Stella* (1987), an adaptation from Goethe produced in New York; *A Bright Room Called Day* (1987), produced in San Francisco; and *The Illusion* (1988), adapted from Corneille, produced in New York, then in Hartford in 1990. He worked with Argentinian playwright Ariel Dorfman to adapt Dorfman's *Widows,* produced in Los Angeles in 1991. *A Bright Room Called Day,* about left-wing politics in Nazi Germany, was not well reviewed after its New York production in 1991. Frank Rich, for example, said that it was "an early front-runner for the most infuriating play of 1991." But some people saw in it the power that was to show up later in his work. The Eureka Theater in San Francisco commissioned him to write a play that ultimately turned out to be *Angels in America: A Gay Fantasia on National Themes* (1992), the play that catapulted him to international prominence.

Among Kushner's current projects is a series of three plays that he describes as having money as its subject — meaning, in part, the effects of economics, in the forms of both poverty and wealth, on individuals. The first of these plays, titled *Henry Box Brown,* centers on the true story of a black American who escaped slavery by being smuggled out of the South in a crate. Brown eventually made his way to England where he joined with a number of other former slaves in producing dramatic "panoramas" intended to discourage the English from buying slave-picked cotton, on which their textile industry largely relied. Kushner has said, "I've always been drawn to writing historical characters. . . . The best stories are the ones you find in history."

Kushner's play, *Homebody/Kabul* (2001), seems connected with history, too. It is set in London and Afghanistan in 1998, after a U.S. bombing raid. Some of the dialog is in Pashto. It was described by Paul Taylor, a London critic, as "a deeply felt expansively ruminative drama."

Among his many projects is a chamber opera about a black maid working for a Jewish family in Louisiana, *Caroline, or Change* (2003) at the Joseph Papp Public Theatre in New York, written in collaboration with Jeanine Tesori.

ANGELS IN AMERICA: MILLENNIUM APPROACHES

Kushner began work on this play shortly after Oskar Eustis of the Eureka Theater commissioned a two-and-a-half hour play with songs. Once Kushner got a presentable version, he showed it to Eustis and realized that, even incomplete, it was already longer than a one-evening play. Eventually, *Millennium Approaches* and *Perestroika,* the second part of *Angels* (not included here), grew to be more than seven hours long. Although the two parts are thematically linked and contain many of the same characters, both parts of *Angels* stand on their own as complete plays. Kushner said that he never expected to see his play produced anywhere but in a small theater in San Francisco; certainly he never expected it to be a smash hit on Broadway. It won the 1993 Pulitzer Prize for drama, another surprise.

Angels in America has epic, Brechtian proportions. Kushner has said that he set out to write a play on "AIDS, Mormons, and Roy Cohn." He chose AIDS because it is a scourge that has destroyed large numbers of the gay community. He chose Mormons because he saw in them a group that valued goodness and godliness but that could not tolerate gays. He chose Roy Cohn because, when Cohn was an aid to Senator Joseph McCarthy during the anti-Communist hysteria of the 1950s, he persecuted gays although he was himself a closet homosexual. His homosexuality did not become public until he contracted AIDS and died in 1986. In Cohn, Kushner had found a villain whose rapacious individualism and unquenchable thirst for power helped symbolize the selfishness of the 1980s. In its New York production Ron Liebman was an overbearingly powerful Cohn, shouting orders, raising hypocrisy to an art form, with depths of contempt matching a profound love of power.

Kushner indicated that his play was a "fantasia on national themes," and it certainly lives up to its title. Kushner set his play in 1985, during the second presidential term of Ronald Reagan. He critiques the values of the Reagan years and politics in general. Jews, WASPs, and Mormons all suffer under his scrutiny. Moreover, he goes beyond national themes and introduces cosmological themes, notably with the introduction of an angel descending through the ceiling at the end of *Millennium Approaches*.

The play focuses as well on problems of individuals. Cohn's friend and protégé Joe Pitt works for the Reagan administration and struggles with his growing awareness that he is gay. A conservative Mormon, Joe faces honestly and painfully these complex, threatening feelings. Harper, Joe's wife, relies on pills, listens all day to talk shows, and has no job but thinks of herself as part of a traditional marriage and fights to hold on to it. Louis Ironson, a liberal but not profoundly political homosexual, is partnered with Prior Walter, dying from AIDS. Louis has hidden his sexuality from his family and finds it impossible to stay with Prior as his lover's illness worsens. Kushner makes sure that we see all these sets of people interrelated throughout the play, despite their distinctness and the unlikeliness of their ever knowing one another.

Though the scope of the play is enormous, its focus is essentially on politics. Kushner's own views contrast sharply with Cohn's conservative politics, and he is surprised that both conservatives and liberals found the play rewarding, since Kushner felt it to be a pointed attack on conservative values.

Angels in America: Millennium Approaches in Performance

The 1991 premiere of the play was in a workshop version in the Eureka Theater in San Francisco. Its first full-scale production came in July 1992 at London's Royal National Theatre, where it was a sensation. Some reviewers speculated that in London the political theater of Caryl Churchill and other playwrights such as David Hare and David Edgar prepared the way for this play. The audiences were enormously enthusiastic, and the positive reviews the play received attracted attention in the United States. Despite Kushner's relatively unknown status, the two parts of the drama (over seven hours long) were staged in the Mark Taper Forum in Los Angeles in 1992, directed by Oskar Eustis and Tony Taccone. *Millennium Approaches* appeared on Broadway in April 1993 at the Walter Kerr Theater, directed by George C. Wolfe. Frank Rich gave it a strong, positive review in the *New York Times* and said, "When first seen a year or so ago, the play seemed defined by its anger at the reigning political establishment, which tended to reward the Roy Cohns and ignore the Prior Walters. Mr. Kushner has not revised the text since — a crony of Cohn's still boasts of a Republican lock on the White House until the year 2000 — but the shift in Washington has had the subliminal effect of making *Angels in America* seem more focused on what happens next than on the past."

The second part of the work, *Perestroika*, arrived on Broadway in November 1993. Frank Rich in the *New York Times* said it was "also a true millennial work of art, uplifting, hugely comic and pantheistically religious in a very American style." After its Broadway run, the play moved to regional theaters, touring throughout the United States. The staging of the drama includes moments that may be described as magical realism featuring ghosts, hallucinations, and other illusions. But Kushner has said, "The play benefits from a pared-down style of presentation, with minimal scenery and scene shifts done rapidly (no blackouts!), employing the cast as well as stagehands — which makes for an actor-driven event, as this must be." He said that it was not a problem if "wires showed," "but the magic should at the same time be thoroughly amazing."

One of Kushner's signal successes in 2003 was seeing *Angels in America* air in a six-part production over two evenings on Home Box Office (HBO) cable television, with Al Pacino in the role of Roy Cohn, Meryl Streep as both Hannah Pitt and Eleanor Rosenberg, and Emma Thompson as the Angel. The production was well done and won a Golden Globe award. Kushner expects more inroads in television with the 2004 HBO production of *Homebody/Kabul* (2001).

Tony Kushner (b. 1956)

ANGELS IN AMERICA: MILLENNIUM APPROACHES

A GAY FANTASIA ON NATIONAL THEMES

1992

Characters

ROY M. COHN, *a successful New York lawyer and unofficial power broker*

JOSEPH PORTER PITT, *chief clerk for Justice Theodore Wilson of the Federal Court of Appeals, Second Circuit*

HARPER AMATY PITT, *Joe's wife, an agoraphobic with a mild Valium addiction*

LOUIS IRONSON, *a word processor working for the Second Circuit Court of Appeals*

PRIOR WALTER, *Louis's boyfriend. Occasionally works as a club designer or caterer, otherwise lives very modestly but with great style off a small trust fund.*

HANNAH PORTER PITT, *Joe's mother, currently residing in Salt Lake City, living off her deceased husband's army pension*

BELIZE, *a former drag queen and former lover of Prior's. A registered nurse. Belize's name was originally Norman Arriaga; Belize is a drag name that stuck.*

THE ANGEL, *four divine emanations, Fluor, Phosphor, Lumen and Candle; manifest in One: the Continental Principality of America. She has magnificent steel-gray wings.*

Other Characters in Part One

RABBI ISISOR CHEMELWITZ, *an orthodox Jewish rabbi, played by the actor playing Hannah*

MR. LIES, *Harper's imaginary friend, a travel agent, who in style of dress and speech suggests a jazz musician; he always wears a large lapel badge emblazoned "IOTA" (The International Order of Travel Agents). He is played by the actor playing Belize.*

THE MAN IN THE PARK, *played by the actor playing Prior*

THE VOICE, *the voice of The Angel*

HENRY, *Roy's doctor, played by the actor playing Hannah*

EMILY, *a nurse, played by the actor playing The Angel*

MARTIN HELLER, *a Reagan Administration Justice Department flackman, played by the actor playing Harper*

SISTER ELLA CHAPTER, *a Salt Lake City real-estate saleswoman, played by the actor playing the Angel*

PRIOR 1, *the ghost of a dead Prior Walter from the 13th century, played by the actor playing Joe. He is a blunt, gloomy medieval farmer with a guttural Yorkshire accent.*

PRIOR 2, *the ghost of a dead Prior Walter from the 17th century, played by the actor playing Roy. He is a Londoner, sophisticated, with a High British accent.*

THE ESKIMO, *played by the actor playing Joe*

THE WOMAN IN THE SOUTH BRONX, *played by the actor playing the Angel*

ETHEL ROSENBERG, *played by the actor playing Hannah*

Playwright's Notes

A Disclaimer: Roy M. Cohn, the character, is based on the late Roy M. Cohn (1927–1986), who was all too real; for the most part the acts attributed to the character Roy, such as his illegal conferences with Judge Kaufmann during the trial of Ethel Rosenberg, are to be found in the historical record. But this Roy is a work of dramatic fiction; his words are my invention, and liberties have been taken.

A Note about the Staging: The play benefits from a pared-down style of presentation, with minimal scenery and scene shifts done rapidly (no blackouts!), employing the cast as well as stagehands — which makes for an actor-driven event, as this must be. The moments of magic — the appearance and disappearance of Mr. Lies and the ghosts, the Book hallucination, and the ending — are to be fully realized, as bits of wonderful theatrical illusion — which means it's OK if the wires show, and maybe it's good that they do, but the magic should at the same time be thoroughly amazing.

In a murderous time
the heart breaks and breaks
and lives by breaking.
— STANLEY KUNITZ
"THE TESTING-TREE"

ACT 1
BAD NEWS • *October–November 1985*

Scene 1

(The last days of October. Rabbi Isidor Chemelwitz alone onstage with a small coffin. It is a rough pine box with two wooden pegs, one at the foot and one at the head, holding the lid in place. A prayer shawl embroidered with a Star of David is draped over the lid, and by the head a yarzheit candle is burning.)

RABBI ISIDOR CHEMELWITZ (*he speaks sonorously, with a heavy Eastern European accent, unapologetically consulting a sheet of notes for the family names*): Hello and good morning. I am Rabbi Isidor

Chemelwitz of the Bronx Home for Aged Hebrews. We are here this morning to pay respects at the passing of Sarah Ironson, devoted wife of Benjamin Ironson, also deceased, loving and caring mother of her sons Morris, Abraham, and Samuel, and her daughters Esther and Rachel; beloved grandmother of Max, Mark, Louis, Lisa, Maria . . . uh . . . Lesley, Angela, Doris, Luke and Eric. (*Looks more closely at paper.*) Eric? This is a Jewish name? (*Shrugs.*) Eric. A large and loving family. We assemble that we may mourn collectively this good and righteous woman.

(*He looks at the coffin.*)

This woman. I did not know this woman. I cannot accurately describe her attributes, nor do justice to her dimensions. She was. . . . Well, in the Bronx Home of Aged Hebrews are many like this, the old, and to many I speak but not to be frank with this one. She preferred silence. So I do not know her and yet I know her. She was . . .

(*he touches the coffin*)

. . . not a person but a whole kind of person, the ones who crossed the ocean, who brought with us to America the villages of Russia and Lithuania — and how we struggled, and how we fought, for the family, for the Jewish home, so that you would not grow up *here*, in this strange place, in the melting pot where nothing melted. Descendants of this immigrant woman, you do not grow up in America, you and your children and their children with the goyische names. You do not live in America. No such place exists. Your clay is the clay of some Litvak shtetl, your air the air of the steppes — because she carried the old world on her back across the ocean, in a boat, and she put it down on Grand Concourse Avenue, or in Flatbush, and she worked that earth into your bones, and you pass it to your children, this ancient, ancient culture and home.

(*Little pause.*)

You can never make that crossing that she made, for such Great Voyages in this world do not any more exist. But every day of your lives the miles that voyage between that place and this one you cross. Every day. You understand me? In you that journey is.

So . . .

She was the last of the Mohicans, this one was. Pretty soon . . . all the old will be dead.

Scene 2

(*Same day. Roy and Joe in Roy's office. Roy at an impressive desk, bare except for a very elaborate phone system, rows and rows of flashing buttons which bleep and beep and whistle incessantly, making chaotic music underneath Roy's conversations. Joe is sitting, waiting. Roy conducts business with great energy, impatience and sensual abandon: gesticulating, shouting, cajoling, crooning, playing the phone, receiver and hold button with virtuosity and love.*)

ROY (*hitting a button*): Hold. (*To Joe.*) I wish I was an octopus, a fucking octopus. Eight loving arms and all those suckers. Know what I mean?

JOE: No, I . . .

ROY (*gesturing to a deli platter of little sandwiches on his desk*): You want lunch?

JOE: No, that's OK really I just . . .

ROY (*hitting a button*): Ailene? Roy Cohn. Now what kind of a greeting is. . . . I thought we were friends, Ai. . . . Look Mrs. Soffer you don't have to get. . . . You're upset. You're yelling. You'll aggravate your condition, you shouldn't yell, you'll pop little blood vessels in your face if you yell. . . . No that was a joke, Mrs. Soffer, I was joking. . . . I already apologized sixteen times for that, Mrs. Soffer, you . . . (*While she's fulminating, Roy covers the mouthpiece with his hand and talks to Joe.*) This'll take a minute, eat already, what is this tasty sandwich here it's — (*He takes a bite of a sandwich.*) Mmmmm, liver or some. . . . Here.

(*He pitches the sandwich to Joe, who catches it and returns it to the platter.*)

ROY (*back to Mrs. Soffer*): Uh huh, uh huh. . . . No, I already told you, it wasn't a vacation, it was business, Mrs. Soffer, I have clients in Haiti, Mrs. Soffer, I. . . . Listen, Ailene, YOU THINK I'M THE ONLY GODDAM LAWYER IN HISTORY EVER MISSED A COURT DATE? Don't make such a big fucking. . . . Hold. (*He hits the hold button.*) You HAG!

JOE: If this is a bad time . . .

ROY: *Bad* time? This is a *good* time! (*Button.*) Baby doll, get me. . . . Oh fuck, wait . . . (*Button, button.*) Hello? Yah. Sorry to keep you holding, Judge Hollins, I. . . . Oh *Mrs.* Hollins, sorry dear deep voice you got. Enjoying your visit? (*Hand over mouthpiece again, to Joe.*) She sounds like a truckdriver and he sounds like Kate Smith, very confusing. Nixon appointed him, all the geeks are Nixon appointees . . . (*To Mrs. Hollins.*) Yeah yeah right good so how many tickets dear? Seven. For what, *Cats, 42nd Street,* what? No you wouldn't like *La Cage,* trust me, I know. Oh for godsake. . . . Hold. (*Button, button.*) Baby doll, seven for *Cats* or something, anything hard to get, I don't give a fuck what and neither will they. (*Button; to Joe.*) You see *La Cage?*

JOE: No, I . . .

ROY: Fabulous. Best thing on Broadway. Maybe ever. (*Button.*) Who? Aw, Jesus H. Christ, Harry, *no,* Harry, Judge John Francis Grimes, Manhattan Family Court. Do I have to do every goddam thing myself? *Touch* the bastard, Harry, and don't call me on this line again, I told you not to . . .

JOE (*starting to get up*): Roy, uh, should I wait outside or . . .

ROY (*to Joe*): Oh sit. (*To Harry.*) You hold. I pay you to hold fuck you Harry you jerk. (*Button.*) Half-wit dick-brain. (*Instantly philosophical.*) I see the universe, Joe, as a kind of sandstorm in outer space with winds of mega-hurricane velocity, but instead of grains of sand it's shards and splinters of glass. You ever feel that way? Ever have one of those days?

JOE: I'm not sure I . . .

ROY: So how's life in Appeals? How's the Judge?

JOE: He sends his best.

ROY: He's a good man. Loyal. Not the brightest man on the bench, but he has manners. And a nice head of silver hair.

JOE: He gives me a lot of responsibility.

ROY: Yeah, like writing his decisions and signing his name.

JOE: Well . . .

ROY: He's a nice guy. And you cover admirably.

JOE: Well, thanks, Roy, I . . .

ROY (*button*): Yah? Who is *this*? Well who the fuck are *you*? Hold — (*button*) Harry? Eighty-seven grand, something like that. Fuck him. Eat me. New Jersey, chain of porno film stores in, uh, Weehawken. That's — Harry, that's the beauty of the law. (*Button.*) So, baby doll, what? Cats? Bleah. (*Button.*) *Cats!* It's about cats. Singing cats, you'll love it. Eight o'clock, the theatre's always at eight. (*Button.*) Fucking tourists. (*Button, then to Joe.*) Oh live a little, Joe, *eat* something for Christ sake —

JOE: Um, Roy, could you . . .

ROY: What? (*To Harry.*) Hold a minute. (*Button.*) Mrs. Soffer? Mrs. . . . (*Button.*) God-fucking-dammit to hell, where is . . .

JOE (*overlapping*): Roy, I'd really appreciate it if . . .

ROY (*overlapping*): Well she was here a minute ago, baby doll, see if . . .

(*The phone starts making three different beeping sounds, all at once.*)

ROY (*smashing buttons*): Jesus fuck this goddam thing . . .

JOE (*overlapping*): I really wish you wouldn't . . .

ROY (*overlapping*): Baby doll? Ring the *Post* get me Suzy see if . . .

(*The phone starts whistling loudly.*)

ROY: CHRIST!

JOE: *Roy.*

ROY (*into receiver*): Hold. (*Button; to Joe.*) *What?*

JOE: Could you please not take the Lord's name in vain (*Pause.*)
I'm sorry. But please. At least while I'm . . .

ROY (*laughs, then*): Right. Sorry. Fuck. Only in America. (*Punches a button.*) Baby doll, tell 'em all to fuck off. Tell 'em I died. You handle Mrs. Soffer. Tell her it's on the way. Tell her I'm schtupping the judge. I'll call her back. I *will* call her. I *know* how much I borrowed. She's got four hundred times that stuffed up her. . . . Yeah, tell her I said that. (*Button. The phone is silent.*) So, Joe.

JOE: I'm sorry Roy, I just . . .

ROY: No no no no, principles count, I respect principles, I'm not religious but I like God and God likes me. Baptist, Catholic?

JOE: Mormon.

ROY: Mormon. Delectable. Absolutely. Only in America. So, Joe. Whattya think?

JOE: It's . . . well . . .

ROY: Crazy life.

JOE: Chaotic.

ROY: Well but God bless chaos. Right?

JOE: Ummm . . .

ROY: Huh. Mormons. I knew Mormons, in, um, Nevada.

JOE: Utah, mostly.

ROY: No, these Mormons were in Vegas.
So. So, how'd you like to go to Washington and work for the Justice Department?

JOE: Sorry?

ROY: How'd you like to go to Washington and work for the Justice Department? All I gotta do is pick up the phone, talk to Ed, and you're in.

JOE: In . . . what, exactly?

ROY: Associate Assistant Something Big. Internal Affairs, heart of the woods, something nice with clout.

JOE: Ed . . . ?

ROY: Meese. The Attorney General.

JOE: Oh.

ROY: I just have to pick up the phone . . .

JOE: I have to think.

ROY: Of course.
(*Pause.*)
It's a great time to be in Washington, Joe.

JOE: Roy, it's incredibly exciting . . .

ROY: And it would mean something to me. You understand?

(*Little pause.*)

JOE: I . . . can't say how much I appreciate this Roy, I'm sort of . . . well, stunned, I mean. . . . Thanks, Roy. But I have to give it some thought. I have to ask my wife.

ROY: Your wife. Of course.

JOE: But I really appreciate . . .

ROY: Of course. Talk to your wife.

Scene 3

(*Later that day. Harper at home, alone. She is listening to the radio and talking to herself, as she often does. She speaks to the audience.*)

HARPER: People who are lonely, people left alone, sit talking nonsense to the air, imagining . . . beautiful systems dying, old fixed orders spiraling apart . . .
When you look at the ozone layer, from outside, from a spaceship, it looks like a pale blue halo, a gentle, shimmering aureole encircling the atmosphere encircling the earth. Thirty miles above our heads, a thin layer of three-atom oxygen molecules, product of photosynthesis, which explains the fussy vegetable preference for visible light, its rejection of darker rays

and emanations. Danger from without. It's a kind of gift, from God, the crowning touch to the creation of the world: guardian angels, hands linked, make a spherical net, a blue-green nesting orb, a shell of safety for life itself. But everywhere, things are collapsing, lies surfacing, systems of defense giving way. . . . This is why, Joe, this is why I shouldn't be left alone.

> (*Little pause.*)

I'd like to go traveling. Leave you behind to worry. I'll send postcards with strange stamps and tantalizing messages on the back. "Later maybe." "Nevermore . . ."

(*Mr. Lies, a travel agent, appears.*)

HARPER Oh! You startled me!

MR. LIES: Cash, check or credit card?

HARPER: I remember you. You're from Salt Lake. You sold us the plane tickets when we flew here. What are you doing in Brooklyn?

MR. LIES: You said you wanted to travel . . .

HARPER: And here you are. How thoughtful.

MR. LIES: Mr. Lies. Of the International Order of Travel Agents. We mobilize the globe, we set people adrift, we stir the populace and send nomads eddying across the planet. We are adepts of motion, acolytes of the flux. Cash, check or credit card. Name your destination.

HARPER: Antarctica, maybe. I want to see the hole in the ozone. I heard on the radio . . .

MR. LIES (*he has a computer terminal in his briefcase*): I can arrange a guided tour. Now?

HARPER: Soon. Maybe soon. I'm not safe here you see. Things aren't right with me. Weird stuff happens . . .

MR. LIES: Like?

HARPER: Well, like you, for instance. Just appearing. Or last week . . . well never mind.

> People are like planets, you need a thick skin. Things get to me, Joe stays away and now. . . . Well look. My dreams are talking back to me.

MR. LIES: It's the price of rootlessness. Motion sickness. The only cure: keep moving.

HARPER: I'm undecided. I feel . . . that something's going to give. It's 1985. Fifteen years till the third millennium. Maybe Christ will come again. Maybe seeds will be planted, maybe there'll be harvests then, maybe early figs to eat, maybe new life, maybe fresh blood, maybe companionship and love and protection, safety from what's outside, maybe the door will hold, or maybe . . . maybe the troubles will come, and the end will come, and the sky will collapse and there will be terrible rains and showers of poison light, or maybe my life is really fine, maybe Joe loves me and I'm only crazy thinking otherwise, or maybe not, maybe it's even worse than I know, maybe . . . I want to know, maybe I don't. The suspense, Mr. Lies, it's killing me.

MR. LIES: I suggest a vacation.

HARPER (*hearing something*): That was the elevator. Oh God, I should fix myself up, I. . . . You have to go, you shouldn't be here . . . you aren't even real.

MR. LIES: Call me when you decide . . .

HARPER: Go!

(*The Travel Agent vanishes as Joe enters.*)

JOE: Buddy?

> Buddy? Sorry I'm late. I was just . . . out. Walking. Are you mad?

HARPER: I got a little anxious.

JOE: Buddy kiss.

(*They kiss.*)

JOE: Nothing to get anxious about.

> So. So how'd you like to move to Washington?

Scene 4

(*Same day. Louis and Prior outside the funeral home, sitting on a bench, both dressed in funereal finery, talking. The funeral service for Sarah Ironson has just concluded and Louis is about to leave for the cemetery.*)

LOUIS: My grandmother actually saw Emma Goldman speak. In Yiddish. But all Grandma could remember was that she spoke well and wore a hat.

> What a weird service. That rabbi . . .

PRIOR: A definite find. Get his number when you go to the graveyard. I want him to bury me.

LOUIS: Better head out there. Everyone gets to put dirt on the coffin once it's lowered in.

PRIOR: Oooh. Cemetery fun. Don't want to miss that.

LOUIS: It's an old Jewish custom to express love. Here, Grandma, have a shovelful. Latecomers run the risk of finding the grave completely filled.

> She was pretty crazy. She was up there in that home for ten years, talking to herself. I never visited. She looked too much like my mother.

PRIOR (*hugs him*): Poor Louis. I'm sorry your grandma is dead.

LOUIS: Tiny little coffin, huh?

> Sorry I didn't introduce you to. . . . I always get so closety at these family things.

PRIOR: Butch. You get butch. (*Imitating.*) "Hi Cousin Doris, you don't remember me I'm Lou, Rachel's boy." Lou, not Louis, because if you say Louis they'll hear the sibilant S.

LOUIS: I don't have a . . .

PRIOR: I don't blame you, hiding. Bloodlines. Jewish curses are the worst. I personally would dissolve if anyone ever looked me in the eye and said "Feh." Fortunately WASPs don't say "Feh." Oh and by the way, darling, cousin Doris is a dyke.

LOUIS: No.

> Really?

PRIOR: You don't notice anything. If I hadn't spent the last four years fellating you I'd swear you were straight.

LOUIS: You're in a pissy mood. Cat still missing?

(*Little pause.*)

PRIOR: Not a furball in sight. It's your fault.

LOUIS: It is?

PRIOR: I warned you, Louis. Names are important. Call an animal "Little Sheba" and you can't expect it to stick around. Besides, it's a dog's name.

LOUIS: I wanted a dog in the first place, not a cat. He sprayed my books.

PRIOR: He was a female cat.

LOUIS: Cats are stupid, high-strung predators. Babylonians sealed them up in bricks. Dogs have brains.

PRIOR: Cats have intuition.

LOUIS: A sharp dog is as smart as a really dull two-year-old child.

PRIOR: Cats know when something's wrong.

LOUIS: Only if you stop feeding them.

PRIOR: They know. That's why Sheba left, because she knew.

LOUIS: Knew what?

(*Pause.*)

PRIOR: I did my best Shirley Booth this morning, floppy slippers, housecoat, curlers, can of Little Friskies; "Come back, Little Sheba, come back. . . ." To no avail. Le chat, elle ne reviendra jamais, jamais . . .°

(*He removes his jacket, rolls up his sleeve, shows Louis a dark-purple spot on the underside of his arm near the shoulder.*)

See.

LOUIS: That's just a burst blood vessel.

PRIOR: Not according to the best medical authorities.

LOUIS: What?

(*Pause.*)

Tell me.

PRIOR: K.S., baby. Lesion number one. Lookit. The wine-dark kiss of the angel of death.

LOUIS (*very softly, holding Prior's arm*): Oh please . . .

PRIOR: I'm a lesionnaire. The Foreign Lesion. The American Lesion. Lesionnaire's disease.

LOUIS: Stop.

PRIOR: My troubles are lesion.

LOUIS: Will you *stop.*

PRIOR: Don't you think I'm handling this well?
I'm going to die.

LOUIS: Bullshit.

PRIOR: Let go of my arm.

LOUIS: No.

PRIOR: Let go.

LOUIS (*grabbing Prior, embracing him ferociously*): No.

PRIOR: I can't find a way to spare you baby. No wall like the wall of hard scientific fact. K.S. Wham. Bang your head on that.

LOUIS: Fuck you. (*Letting go.*) Fuck you fuck you fuck you.

PRIOR: Now that's what I like to hear. A mature reaction.

Le chat . . . jamais: The cat will never ever return.

Let's go see if the cat's come home.
Louis?

LOUIS: When did you find this?

PRIOR: I couldn't tell you.

LOUIS: Why?

PRIOR: I was scared, Lou.

LOUIS: Of what?

PRIOR: That you'll leave me.

LOUIS: Oh.

(*Little pause.*)

PRIOR: Bad timing, funeral and all, but I figured as long as we're on the subject of death . . .

LOUIS: I have to go bury my grandma.

PRIOR: Lou?
(*Pause.*)
Then you'll come home?

LOUIS: Then I'll come home.

Scene 5

(*Same day, later on. Split scene: Joe and Harper at home; Louis at the cemetery with Rabbi Isidor Chemelwitz and the little coffin.*)

HARPER: Washington?

JOE: It's an incredible honor, buddy, and . . .

HARPER: I have to think.

JOE: Of course.

HARPER: Say no.

JOE: You said you were going to think about it.

HARPER: I don't want to move to Washington.

JOE: Well I do.

HARPER: It's a giant cemetery, huge white graves and mausoleums everywhere.

JOE: We could live in Maryland. Or Georgetown.

HARPER: We're happy here.

JOE: That's not really true, buddy, we . . .

HARPER: Well happy enough! Pretend-happy. That's better than nothing.

JOE: It's time to make some changes, Harper.

HARPER: No changes. Why?

JOE: I've been chief clerk for four years. I make twenty-nine thousand dollars a year. That's ridiculous. I graduated fourth in my class and I make less than anyone I know. And I'm . . . I'm tired of being a clerk, I want to go where something good is happening.

HARPER: Nothing good happens in Washington. We'll forget church teachings and buy furniture at . . . at *Conran's* and become yuppies. I have too much to do here.

JOE: Like what?

HARPER: I *do* have things . . .

JOE: What things?

HARPER: I have to finish painting the bedroom.

JOE: You've been painting in there for over a year.

HARPER: I know, I. . . . It just isn't done because I never get time to finish it.

JOE: Oh that's . . . that doesn't make sense. You have all the time in the world. You could finish it when I'm at work.

HARPER: I'm afraid to go in there alone.

JOE: Afraid of what?

HARPER: I heard someone in there. Metal scraping on the wall. A man with a knife, maybe.

JOE: There's no one in the bedroom, Harper.

HARPER: Not now.

JOE: Not this morning either.

HARPER: How do you know? You were at work this morning. There's something creepy about this place. Remember *Rosemary's Baby*?

JOE: *Rosemary's Baby*?

HARPER: Our apartment looks like that one. Wasn't that apartment in Brooklyn?

JOE: No, it was . . .

HARPER: Well, it looked like this. It did.

JOE: Then let's move.

HARPER: Georgetown's worse. *The Exorcist* was in Georgetown.

JOE: The devil, everywhere you turn, huh, buddy.

HARPER: Yeah. Everywhere.

JOE: How many pills today, buddy?

HARPER: None. One. Three. Only three.

LOUIS (*pointing at the coffin*): Why are there just two little wooden pegs holding the lid down?

RABBI ISIDOR CHEMELWITZ: So she can get out easier if she wants to.

LOUIS: I hope she stays put.
  I pretended for years that she was already dead. When they called to say she had died it was a surprise. I abandoned her.

RABBI ISIDOR CHEMELWITZ: "Sharfer vi di tson fun a shlang iz an umdankbar kind!"

LOUIS: I don't speak Yiddish.

RABBI ISIDOR CHEMELWITZ: Sharper than the serpent's tooth is the ingratitude of children. Shakespeare. *King Lear*.

LOUIS: Rabbi, what does the Holy Writ say about someone who abandons someone he loves at a time of great need?

RABBI ISIDOR CHEMELWITZ: Why would a person do such a thing?

LOUIS: Because he has to. Maybe because this person's sense of the world, that it will change for the better with struggle, maybe a person who has this neo-Hegelian positivist sense of constant historical progress towards happiness or perfection or something, who feels very powerful because he feels connected to these forces, moving uphill all the time . . . maybe that person can't, um, incorporate sickness into his sense of how things are supposed to go. Maybe vomit . . . and sores and disease . . . really frighten him, maybe . . . he isn't so good with death.

RABBI ISIDOR CHEMELWITZ: The Holy Scriptures have nothing to say about such a person.

LOUIS: Rabbi, I'm afraid of the crimes I may commit.

RABBI ISIDOR CHEMELWITZ: Please, mister. I'm a sick old rabbi facing a long drive home to the Bronx. You want to confess, better you should find a priest.

LOUIS: But I'm not a Catholic, I'm a Jew.

RABBI ISIDOR CHEMELWITZ: Worse luck for you, bubbulah. Catholics believe in forgiveness. Jews believe in Guilt. (*He pats the coffin tenderly.*)

LOUIS: You just make sure those pegs are in good and tight.

RABBI ISIDOR CHEMELWITZ: Don't worry, mister. The life she had, she'll stay put. She's better off.

JOE: Look, I know this is scary for you. But try to understand what it means to me. Will you try?

HARPER: Yes.

JOE: Good. Really try.
  I think things are starting to change in the world.

HARPER: But I don't want . . .

JOE: Wait. For the good. Change for the good. America has rediscovered itself. Its sacred position among nations. And people aren't ashamed of that like they used to be. This is a great thing. The truth restored. Law restored. That's what President Reagan's done, Harper. He says "Truth exists and can be spoken proudly." And the country responds to him. We become better. More good. I need to be a part of that, I need something big to lift me up. I mean, six years ago the world seemed in decline, horrible, hopeless, full of unsolvable problems and crime and confusion and hunger and . . .

HARPER: But it still seems that way. More now than before. They say the ozone layer is . . .

JOE: Harper . . .

HARPER: And today out the window on Atlantic Avenue there was a schizophrenic traffic cop who was making these . . .

JOE: Stop it! I'm trying to make a point.

HARPER: So am I.

JOE: You aren't even making sense, you . . .

HARPER: My point is the world seems just as . . .

JOE: It only seems that way to you because you never go out in the world, Harper, and you have emotional problems.

HARPER: I do so get out in the world.

JOE: You don't. You stay in all day, fretting about imaginary . . .

HARPER: I get out. I do. You don't know what I do.

JOE: You don't stay in all day.

HARPER: No.

JOE: Well. . . . Yes you do.

HARPER: That's what you think.

JOE: Where do you go?

HARPER: Where do *you* go? When you walk.
  (*Pause, then angrily.*) And I DO NOT have emotional problems.

JOE: I'm sorry.

HARPER: And if I do have emotional problems it's from living with you. Or . . .

JOE: I'm sorry buddy, I didn't mean to . . .

HARPER: Or if you do think I do then you should never have married me. You have all these secrets and lies.

JOE: I want to be married to you, Harper.

HARPER: You shouldn't. You never should.
(*Pause.*)
Hey buddy. Hey buddy.

JOE: Buddy kiss . . .

(*They kiss.*)

HARPER: I heard on the radio how to give a blowjob.

JOE: What?

HARPER: You want to try?

JOE: You really shouldn't listen to stuff like that.

HARPER: Mormons can give blowjobs.

JOE: *Harper.*

HARPER (*imitating his tone*): *Joe.*
It was a little Jewish lady with a German accent. This is a good time. For me to make a baby.

(*Little pause. Joe turns away.*)

HARPER: Then they went on to a program about holes in the ozone layer. Over Antarctica. Skin burns, birds go blind, icebergs melt. The world's coming to an end.

Scene 6

(*First week of November. In the men's room of the offices of the Brooklyn Federal Court of Appeals; Louis is crying over the sink; Joe enters.*)

JOE: Oh, um. . . . Morning.

LOUIS: Good morning, counselor.

JOE (*he watches Louis cry*): Sorry, I . . . I don't know your name.

LOUIS: Don't bother. Word processor. The lowest of the low.

JOE (*holding out hand*): Joe Pitt. I'm with Justice Wilson . . .

LOUIS: Oh, I know that. Counselor Pitt. Chief Clerk.

JOE: Were you . . . are you OK?

LOUIS: Oh, yeah. Thanks. What a nice man.

JOE: Not so nice.

LOUIS: What?

JOE: Not so nice. Nothing. You sure you're . . .

LOUIS: Life sucks shit. Life . . . just sucks shit.

JOE: What's wrong?

LOUIS: Run in my nylons.

JOE: Sorry . . . ?

LOUIS: Forget it. Look, thanks for asking.

JOE: Well . . .

LOUIS: I mean it really is nice of you.
(*He starts crying again.*)
Sorry, sorry, sick friend . . .

JOE: Oh, I'm sorry.

LOUIS: Yeah, yeah, well, that's sweet.
Three of your colleagues have preceded you to this baleful sight and you're the first one to ask. The

others just opened the door, saw me, and fled. I hope they had to pee real bad.

JOE (*handing him a wad of toilet paper*): They just didn't want to intrude.

LOUIS: Hah. Reaganite heartless macho asshole lawyers.

JOE: Oh, that's unfair.

LOUIS: What is? Heartless? Macho? Reaganite? Lawyer?

JOE: I voted for Reagan.

LOUIS: You did?

JOE: Twice.

LOUIS: Twice? Well, oh boy. A Gay Republican.

JOE: Excuse me?

LOUIS: Nothing.

JOE: I'm not . . .
Forget it.

LOUIS: Republican? Not Republican? Or . . .

JOE: What?

LOUIS: What?

JOE: Not gay. I'm not gay.

LOUIS: Oh. Sorry.
(*Blows his nose loudly.*) It's just . . .

JOE: Yes?

LOUIS: Well, sometimes you can tell from the way a person sounds that . . . I mean you *sound* like a . . .

JOE: No I don't. Like what?

LOUIS: Like a Republican.

(*Little pause. Joe knows he's being teased; Louis knows he knows. Joe decides to be a little brave.*)

JOE (*making sure no one else is around*): Do I? Sound like a . . . ?

LOUIS: What? Like a . . . ? Republican, or . . . ? Do I?

JOE: Do you what?

LOUIS: Sound like a . . . ?

JOE: Like a . . . ?
I'm . . . confused.

LOUIS: Yes.
My name is Louis. But all my friends call me Louise. I work in Word Processing. Thanks for the toilet paper.

(*Louis offers Joe his hand, Joe reaches, Louis feints and pecks Joe on the cheek, then exits.*)

Scene 7

(*A week later. Mutual dream scene. Prior is at a fantastic makeup table, having a dream, applying the face. Harper is having a pill-induced hallucination. She has these from time to time. For some reason, Prior has appeared in this one. Or Harper has appeared in Prior's dream. It is bewildering.*)

PRIOR (*alone, putting on makeup, then examining the results in the mirror; to the audience*): "I'm ready for my closeup, Mr. DeMille."
One wants to move through life with elegance and grace, blossoming infrequently but with exquisite taste, and perfect timing, like a rare bloom, a zebra

orchid. . . . One wants. . . . But one so seldom gets what one wants, does one? No. One does not. One gets fucked. Over. One . . . dies at thirty, robbed of . . . decades of majesty.

Fuck this shit. Fuck this shit.

(*He almost crumbles; he pulls himself together; he studies his handiwork in the mirror.*)

I look like a corpse. A corpsette. Oh my queen; you know you've hit rock-bottom when even drag is a drag.

(*Harper appears.*)

HARPER: Are you. . . . Who are you?

PRIOR: Who are you?

HARPER: What are you doing in my hallucination?

PRIOR: I'm not in your hallucination. You're in my dream.

HARPER: You're wearing makeup.

PRIOR: So are you.

HARPER: But you're a man.

PRIOR (*feigning dismay, shock, he mimes slashing his throat with his lipstick and dies, fabulously tragic. Then*): The hands and feet give it away.

HARPER: There must be some mistake here. I don't recognize you. You're not. . . . Are you my . . . some sort of imaginary friend?

PRIOR: No. Aren't you too old to have imaginary friends?

HARPER: I have emotional problems. I took too many pills. Why are you wearing makeup?

PRIOR: I was in the process of applying the face, trying to make myself feel better — I swiped the new fall colors at the Clinique counter at Macy's. (*Showing her.*)

HARPER: You stole these?

PRIOR: I was out of cash; it was an emotional emergency!

HARPER: Joe will be so angry. I promised him. No more pills.

PRIOR: These pills you keep alluding to?

HARPER: Valium. I take Valium. Lots of Valium.

PRIOR: And you're dancing as fast as you can.

HARPER: I'm not *addicted*. I don't believe in addiction, and I never . . . well, I *never* drink. And I *never* take drugs.

PRIOR: Well, smell *you*, Nancy Drew.

HARPER: Except Valium.

PRIOR: Except Valium; in wee fistfuls.

HARPER: It's terrible. Mormons are not supposed to be addicted to anything. I'm a Mormon.

PRIOR: I'm a homosexual.

HARPER: Oh! In my church we don't believe in homosexuals.

PRIOR: In my church we don't believe in Mormons.

HARPER: What church do . . . oh! (*She laughs.*) I get it.

I don't understand this. If I didn't ever see you before and I don't think I did then I don't think you should be here, in this hallucination, because in my experience the mind, which is where hallucinations come from, shouldn't be able to make up anything that wasn't there to start with, that didn't enter it from experience, from the real world. Imagination can't create anything new, can it? It only recycles bits and pieces from the world and reassembles them into visions. . . . Am I making sense right now?

PRIOR: Given the circumstances, yes.

HARPER: So when we think we've escaped the unbearable ordinariness and, well, untruthfulness of our lives, it's really only the same old ordinariness and falseness rearranged into the appearance of novelty and truth. Nothing unknown is knowable. Don't you think it's depressing?

PRIOR: The limitations of the imagination?

HARPER: Yes.

PRIOR: It's something you learn after your second theme party: It's All Been Done Before.

HARPER: The world. Finite. Terribly, terribly. . . . Well . . .

This is the most depressing hallucination I've ever had.

PRIOR: Apologies. I do try to be amusing.

HARPER: Oh, well, don't apologize, you. . . . I can't expect someone who's really sick to entertain me.

PRIOR: How on earth did you know . . .

HARPER: Oh that happens. This is the very threshhold of revelation sometimes. You can see things . . . how sick you are. Do you see anything about me?

PRIOR: Yes.

HARPER: What?

PRIOR: You are amazingly unhappy.

HARPER: Oh big deal. You meet a Valium addict and you figure out she's unhappy. That doesn't count. Of course I. . . . Something else. Something surprising.

PRIOR: Something surprising.

HARPER: Yes.

PRIOR: Your husband's a homo.

(*Pause.*)

HARPER: Oh, ridiculous.

(*Pause, then very quietly.*)

Really?

PRIOR (*shrugs*): Threshhold of revelation.

HARPER: Well I don't like your revelations. I don't think you intuit well at all. Joe's a very normal man, he . . .

Oh God. Oh God. He. . . . Do homos take, like, lots of long walks?

PRIOR: Yes. We do. In stretch pants with lavender coifs. I just looked at you, and there was . . .

HARPER: A sort of blue streak of recognition.

PRIOR: Yes.

HARPER: Like you knew me incredibly well.

PRIOR: Yes.

HARPER: Yes.

I have to go now, get back, something just . . . fell apart.

Oh God, I feel so sad . . .

PRIOR: I . . . I'm sorry. I usually say, "Fuck the truth," but mostly, the truth fucks you.

HARPER: I see something else about you . . .

PRIOR: Oh?

HARPER: Deep inside you, there's a part of you, the most inner part, entirely free of disease. I can see that.

PRIOR: Is that. . . . That isn't true.

HARPER: Threshold of revelation.

Home . . .

(*She vanishes.*)

PRIOR: People come and go so quickly here . . .

(*To himself in the mirror.*) I don't think there's any uninfected part of me. My heart is pumping polluted blood. I feel dirty.

(*He begins to wipe makeup off with his hands, smearing it around. A large gray feather falls from up above. Prior stops smearing the makeup and looks at the feather. He goes to it and picks it up.*)

A VOICE (*it is an incredibly beautiful voice*): Look up!

PRIOR (*looking up, not seeing anyone*): Hello?

A VOICE: Look up!

PRIOR: Who is that?

A VOICE: Prepare the way!

PRIOR: I don't see any . . .

(*There is a dramatic change in lighting, from above.*)

A VOICE: Look up, look up,
    prepare the way
    the infinite descent
    A breath in air
    floating down
    Glory to . . .

(*Silence.*)

PRIOR: Hello? Is that it? Helloooo!
    What the fuck . . . ? (*He holds himself.*)
    Poor me. Poor poor me. Why me? Why poor poor me? Oh I don't feel good right now. I really don't.

Scene 8

(*That night. Split scene: Harper and Joe at home; Prior and Louis in bed.*)

HARPER: Where were you?

JOE: Out.

HARPER: Where?

JOE: Just out. Thinking.

HARPER: It's late.

JOE: I had a lot to think about.

HARPER: I burned dinner.

JOE: Sorry.

HARPER: Not my dinner. My dinner was fine. Your dinner. I put it back in the oven and turned everything up as high as it could go and I watched till it burned black. It's still hot. Very hot. Want it?

JOE: You didn't have to do that.

HARPER: I know. It just seemed like the kind of thing a mentally deranged sex-starved pill-popping house-wife would do.

JOE: Uh huh.

HARPER: So I did it. Who knows anymore what I have to do?

JOE: How many pills?

HARPER: A bunch. Don't change the subject.

JOE: I won't talk to you when you . . .

HARPER: No. No. Don't do that! I'm . . . I'm fine, pills are not the problem, not our problem, I WANT TO KNOW WHERE YOU'VE BEEN! I WANT TO KNOW WHAT'S GOING ON!

JOE: Going on with what? The job?

HARPER: Not the job.

JOE: I said I need more time.

HARPER: Not the job!

JOE: Mr. Cohn, I talked to him on the phone, he said I had to hurry . . .

HARPER: Not the . . .

JOE: But I can't get you to talk sensibly about anything so . . .

HARPER: SHUT UP!

JOE: Then what?

HARPER: Stick to the subject.

JOE: I don't know what that is. You have something you want to ask me? Ask me. Go.

HARPER: I . . . can't. I'm scared of you.

JOE: I'm tired, I'm going to bed.

HARPER: Tell me without making me ask. Please.

JOE: This is crazy, I'm not . . .

HARPER: When you come through the door at night your face is never exactly the way I remembered it. I get sur-prised by something . . . mean and hard about the way you look. Even the weight of you in the bed at night, the way you breathe in your sleep seems unfamiliar.

You terrify me.

JOE (*cold*): I know who you are.

HARPER: Yes. I'm the enemy. That's easy. That doesn't change.

You think you're the only one who hates sex; I do; I hate it with you; I do. I dream that you batter away at me till all my joints come apart, like wax, and I fall into pieces. It's like a punishment. It was wrong of me to marry you. I knew you . . . (*She stops herself.*) It's a sin, and it's killing us both.

JOE: I can always tell when you've taken pills because it makes you red-faced and sweaty and frankly that's very often why I don't want to . . .

HARPER: Because . . .

JOE: Well, you aren't pretty. Not like this.

HARPER: I have something to ask you.

JOE: Then ASK! ASK! What in hell are you . . .

HARPER: Are you a homo?

(*Pause.*)

Are you? If you try to walk out right now I'll put your dinner back in the oven and turn it up so high the whole building will fill with smoke and everyone in it will asphyxiate. So help me God I will.

Now answer the question.

JOE: What if I . . .

(*Small pause.*)

HARPER: Then tell me, please. And we'll see.
JOE: No. I'm not.
   I don't see what difference it makes.

LOUIS: Jews don't have any clear textual guide to the afterlife; even that it exists. I don't think much about it. I see it as a perpetual rainy Thursday afternoon in March. Dead leaves.
PRIOR: Eeeugh. Very Greco-Roman.
LOUIS: Well for us it's not the verdict that counts, it's the act of judgment. That's why I could never be a lawyer. In court all that matters is the verdict.
PRIOR: You could never be a lawyer because you are oversexed. You're too distracted.
LOUIS: Not distracted; *ab*stracted. I'm trying to make a point:
PRIOR: Namely:
LOUIS: It's the judge in his or her chambers, weighing, books open, pondering the evidence, ranging freely over categories: good, evil, innocent, guilty; the judge in the chamber of circumspection, not the judge on the bench with the gavel. The shaping of the law, not its execution.
PRIOR: The point, dear, the point . . .
LOUIS: That it should be the questions and shape of a life, its total complexity gathered, arranged and considered, which matters in the end, not some stamp of salvation or damnation which disperses all the complexity in some unsatisfying little decision — the balancing of the scales . . .
PRIOR: I like this; very zen; it's . . . reassuringly incomprehensible and useless. We who are about to die thank you.
LOUIS: You are not about to die.
PRIOR: It's not going well, really . . . two new lesions. My leg hurts. There's protein in my urine, the doctor says, but who knows what the fuck that portends. Anyway it shouldn't be there, the protein. My butt is chapped from diarrhea and yesterday I shat blood.
LOUIS: I really hate this. You don't tell me . . .
PRIOR: You get too upset, I wind up comforting you. It's easier . . .
LOUIS: Oh thanks.
PRIOR: If it's bad I'll tell you.
LOUIS: Shitting blood sounds bad to me.
PRIOR: And I'm telling you.
LOUIS: And I'm handling it.
PRIOR: Tell me some more about justice.
LOUIS: I *am* handling it.
PRIOR: Well Louis you win Trooper of the Month.

(*Louis starts to cry.*)

PRIOR: I take it back. You aren't Trooper of the Month.
   This isn't working . . .
   Tell me some more about justice.
LOUIS: You are not about to die.
PRIOR: Justice . . .
LOUIS: . . . is an immensity, a confusing vastness. Justice is God.
   Prior?

PRIOR: Hmmm?
LOUIS: You love me.
PRIOR: Yes.
LOUIS: What if I walked out on this?
   Would you hate me forever?

(*Prior kisses Louis on the forehead.*)

PRIOR: Yes.

JOE: I think we ought to pray. Ask God for help. Ask him together . . .
HARPER: God won't talk to me. I have to make up people to talk to me.
JOE: You have to keep asking.
HARPER: I forgot the question.
   Oh yeah. God, is my husband a . . .
JOE (*scary*): Stop it. Stop it. I'm warning you.
   Does it make any difference? That I might be one thing deep within, no matter how wrong or ugly that thing is, so long as I have fought, with everything I have, to kill it. What do you want from me? What do you want from me, Harper? More than that? For God's sake, there's nothing left, I'm a shell. There's nothing left to kill.
   As long as my behavior is what I know it has to be. Decent. Correct. That alone in the eyes of God.
HARPER: No, no, not that, that's Utah talk, Mormon talk, I hate it, Joe, tell me, say it . . .
JOE: All I will say is that I am a very good man who has worked very hard to become good and you want to destroy that. You want to destroy me, but I am not going to let you do that.

(*Pause.*)

HARPER: I'm going to have a baby.
JOE: Liar.
HARPER: You liar.
   A baby born addicted to pills. A baby who does not dream but who hallucinates, who stares up at us with big mirror eyes and who does not know who we are.

(*Pause.*)

JOE: Are you really . . .
HARPER: No. Yes. No. Yes. Get away from me.
   Now we both have a secret.
PRIOR: One of my ancestors was a ship's captain who made money bringing whale oil to Europe and returning with immigrants — Irish mostly, packed in tight, so many dollars per head. The last ship he captained foundered off the coast of Nova Scotia in a winter tempest and sank to the bottom. He went down with the ship — la Grande Geste — but his crew took seventy women and kids in the ship's only longboat, this big, open rowboat, and when the weather got too rough, and they thought the boat was overcrowded, the crew started lifting people up and hurling them into the sea. Until they got the ballast right. They walked up and down the longboat, eyes to the water-

line, and when the boat rode low in the water they'd grab the nearest passenger and throw them into the sea. The boat was leaky, see; seventy people; they arrived in Halifax with nine people on board.

LOUIS: Jesus.

PRIOR: I think about that story a lot now. People in a boat, waiting, terrified, while implacable, unsmiling men, irresistibly strong, seize . . . maybe the person next to you, maybe you, and with no warning at all, with time only for a quick intake of air you are pitched into freezing, turbulent water and salt and darkness to drown.

I like your cosmology, baby. While time is running out I find myself drawn to anything that's suspended, that lacks an ending — but it seems to me that it lets you off scot-free.

LOUIS: What do you mean?

PRIOR: No judgment, no guilt or responsibility.

LOUIS: For me.

PRIOR: For anyone. It was an editorial "you."

LOUIS: Please get better. Please.

Please don't get any sicker.

Scene 9

(*Third week in November. Roy and Henry, his doctor, in Henry's office.*)

HENRY: Nobody knows what causes it. And nobody knows how to cure it. The best theory is that we blame a retrovirus, the Human Immunodeficiency Virus. Its presence is made known to us by the useless antibodies which appear in reaction to its entrance into the bloodstream through a cut, or an orifice. The antibodies are powerless to protect the body against it. Why, we don't know. The body's immune system ceases to function. Sometimes the body even attacks itself. At any rate it's left open to a whole horror house of infections from microbes which it usually defends against.

Like Kaposi's sarcomas. These lesions. Or your throat problem. Or the glands.

We think it may also be able to slip past the blood-brain barrier into the brain. Which is of course very bad news.

And it's fatal in we don't know what percent of people with suppressed immune responses.

(*Pause.*)

ROY: This is very interesting, Mr. Wizard, but why the fuck are you telling me this?

(*Pause.*)

HENRY: Well, I have just removed one of three lesions which biopsy results will probably tell us is a Kaposi's sarcoma lesion. And you have a pronounced swelling of glands in your neck, groin, and armpits — lymphadenopathy is another sign. And you

have oral candidiasis and maybe a little more fungus under the fingernails of two digits on your right hand. So that's why . . .

ROY: This disease . . .

HENRY: Syndrome.

ROY: Whatever. It afflicts mostly homosexuals and drug addicts.

HENRY: Mostly. Hemophiliacs are also at risk.

ROY: Homosexuals and drug addicts. So why are you implying that I . . .

(*Pause.*)

What are you implying, Henry?

HENRY: I don't . . .

ROY: I'm not a drug addict.

HENRY: Oh come on Roy.

ROY: What, what, come on Roy what? Do you think I'm a junkie, Henry, do you see tracks?

HENRY: This is absurd.

ROY: Say it.

HENRY: Say what?

ROY: Say, "Roy Cohn, you are a . . ."

HENRY: Roy.

ROY: "You are a. . . ." Go on. Not "Roy Cohn you are a drug fiend." "Roy Marcus Cohn, you are a . . ."

Go on, Henry, it starts with an "H."

HENRY: Oh I'm not going to . . .

ROY: *With an "H,"* Henry, and it isn't "Hemophiliac." Come on . . .

HENRY: What are you doing, Roy?

ROY: No, say it. I mean it. Say: "Roy Cohn, you are a homosexual."

(*Pause.*)

And I will proceed, systematically, to destroy your reputation and your practice and your career in New York State, Henry. Which you know I can do.

(*Pause.*)

HENRY: Roy, you have been seeing me since 1958. Apart from the facelifts I have treated you for everything from syphilis . . .

ROY: From a whore in Dallas.

HENRY: From syphilis to venereal warts. In your rectum. Which you may have gotten from a whore in Dallas, but it wasn't a female whore.

(*Pause.*)

ROY: So say it.

HENRY: Roy Cohn, you are . . .

You have had sex with men, many many times, Roy, and one of them, or any number of them, has made you very sick. You have AIDS.

ROY: AIDS.

Your problem, Henry, is that you are hung up on words, on labels, that you believe they mean what they seem to mean. AIDS. Homosexual. Gay. Lesbian. You think these are names that tell you who someone sleeps with, but they don't tell you that.

HENRY: No?

ROY: No. Like all labels they tell you one thing and one

thing only: where does an individual so identified fit in the food chain, in the pecking order? Not ideology, or sexual taste, but something much simpler: clout. Not who I fuck or who fucks me, but who will pick up the phone when I call, who owes me favors. This is what a label refers to. Now to someone who does not understand this, homosexual is what I am because I have sex with men. But really this is wrong. Homosexuals are not men who sleep with other men. Homosexuals are men who in fifteen years of trying cannot get a pissant antidiscrimination bill through City Council. Homosexuals are men who know nobody and who nobody knows. Who have zero clout. Does this sound like me, Henry?

HENRY: No.

ROY: No. I have clout. A lot. I can pick up this phone, punch fifteen numbers, and you know who will be on the other end in under five minutes, Henry?

HENRY: The President.

ROY: Even better, Henry. His wife.

HENRY: I'm impressed.

ROY: I don't want you to be impressed. I want you to understand. This is not sophistry. And this is not hypocrisy. This is reality. I have sex with men. But unlike nearly every other man of whom this is true, I bring the guy I'm screwing to the White House and President Reagan smiles at us and shakes his hand. Because *what* I am is defined entirely by *who* I am. Roy Cohn is not a homosexual. Roy Cohn is a heterosexual man, Henry, who fucks around with guys.

HENRY: OK, Roy.

ROY: And what is my diagnosis, Henry?

HENRY: You have AIDS, Roy.

ROY: No, Henry, no. AIDS is what homosexuals have. I have liver cancer.

(*Pause.*)

HENRY: Well, whatever the fuck you have, Roy, it's very serious, and I haven't got a damn thing for you. The NIH in Bethesda has a new drug called AZT with a two-year waiting list that not even I can get you onto. So get on the phone, Roy, and dial the fifteen numbers, and tell the First Lady you need in on an experimental treatment for liver cancer, because you can call it any damn thing you want, Roy, but what it boils down to is very bad news.

ACT 2
IN VITRO • *December 1985–January 1986*

Scene 1

(*Night, the third week in December. Prior alone on the floor of his bedroom; he is much worse.*)

PRIOR: Louis, Louis, please wake up, oh God.

(*Louis runs in.*)

PRIOR: I think something horrible is wrong with me I can't breathe . . .

LOUIS (*starting to exit*): I'm calling the ambulance.

PRIOR: No, wait, I . . .

LOUIS: *Wait?* Are you fucking crazy? Oh God you're on fire, your head is on fire.

PRIOR: It hurts, it hurts . . .

LOUIS: I'm calling the ambulance.

PRIOR: I don't want to go to the hospital, I don't want to go to the hospital please let me lie here, just . . .

LOUIS: No, no, God, Prior, stand up . . .

PRIOR: DON'T TOUCH MY LEG!

LOUIS: We have to . . . oh God this is so crazy.

PRIOR: I'll be OK if I just lie here Lou, really, if I can only sleep a little . . .

(*Louis exits.*)

PRIOR: Louis?
    NO! NO! Don't call, you'll send me there and I won't come back, please, please Louis I'm begging, baby, please . . .
    (*Screams.*) LOUIS!!

LOUIS (*from off; hysterical*): WILL YOU SHUT THE FUCK UP!

PRIOR (*trying to stand*): Aaaah. I have . . . to go to the bathroom. Wait. Wait, just . . . oh. Oh God. (*He shits himself.*)

LOUIS (*entering*): Prior? They'll be here in . . .
    Oh my God.

PRIOR: I'm sorry, I'm sorry.

LOUIS: What did . . . ? What?

PRIOR: I had an accident.

(*Louis goes to him.*)

LOUIS: This is blood.

PRIOR: Maybe you shouldn't touch it . . . me. . . . I . . . (*He faints.*)

LOUIS (*quietly*): Oh help. Oh help. Oh God oh God oh God help me I can't I can't I can't.

Scene 2

(*Same night. Harper is sitting at home, all alone, with no lights on. We can barely see her. Joe enters, but he doesn't turn on the lights.*)

JOE: Why are you sitting in the dark? Turn on the light.

HARPER: *No.* I heard the sounds in the bedroom again. I know someone was in there.

JOE: No one was.

HARPER: Maybe actually in the bed, under the covers with a knife.
    Oh, boy. Joe. I, um, I'm thinking of going away. By which I mean: I think I'm going off again. You . . . you know what I mean?

JOE: Please don't. Stay. We can fix it. I pray for that. This is my fault, but I can correct it. You have to try too . . .

(*He turns on the light. She turns it off again.*)

HARPER: When you pray, what do you pray for?

JOE: I pray for God to crush me, break me up into little pieces and start all over again.

HARPER: Oh. Please. Don't pray for that.

JOE: I had a book of Bible stories when I was a kid. There was a picture I'd look at twenty times every day: Jacob wrestles with the angel. I don't really remember the story, or why the wrestling — just the picture. Jacob is young and very strong. The angel is . . . a beautiful man, with golden hair and wings, of course. I still dream about it. Many nights. I'm. . . . It's me. In that struggle. Fierce, and unfair. The angel is not human, and it holds nothing back, so how could anyone human win, what kind of a fight is that? It's not just. Losing means your soul thrown down in the dust, your heart torn out from God's. But you can't not lose.

HARPER: In the whole entire world, you are the only person, the only person I love or have ever loved. And I love you terribly. Terribly. That's what's so awfully, irreducibly real. I can make up anything but I can't dream that away.

JOE: Are you . . . are you really going to have a baby?

HARPER: It's my time, and there's no blood. I don't really know. I suppose it wouldn't be a great thing. Maybe I'm just not bleeding because I take too many pills. Maybe I'll give birth to a pill. That would give a new meaning to pill-popping, huh?

  I think you should go to Washington. Alone. Change, like you said.

JOE: I'm not going to leave you, Harper.

HARPER: Well maybe not. But I'm going to leave you.

Scene 3

(*One AM, the next morning. Louis and a nurse, Emily, are sitting in Prior's room in the hospital.*)

EMILY: He'll be all right now.

LOUIS: No he won't.

EMILY: No. I guess not. I gave him something that makes him sleep.

LOUIS: Deep asleep?

EMILY: Orbiting the moons of Jupiter.

LOUIS: A good place to be.

EMILY: Anyplace better than here. You his . . . uh?

LOUIS: Yes. I'm his uh.

EMILY: This must be hell for you.

LOUIS: It is. Hell. The After Life. Which is not at all like a rainy afternoon in March, by the way, Prior. A lot more vivid than I'd expected. Dead leaves, but the crunchy kind. Sharp, dry air. The kind of long, luxurious dying feeling that breaks your heart.

EMILY: Yeah, well we all get to break our hearts on this one.

  He seems like a nice guy. Cute.

LOUIS: Not like this.

  Yes, he is. Was. Whatever.

EMILY: Weird name. Prior Walter. Like, "The Walter before this one."

LOUIS: Lots of Walters before this one. Prior is an old old family name in an old old family. The Walters go back to the Mayflower and beyond. Back to the Norman Conquest. He says there's a Prior Walter stitched into the Bayeux tapestry.

EMILY: Is that impressive?

LOUIS: Well, it's old. Very old. Which in some circles equals impressive.

EMILY: Not in my circle. What's the name of the tapestry?

LOUIS: The Bayeux tapestry. Embroidered by La Reine Mathilde.

EMILY: I'll tell my mother. She embroiders. Drives me nuts.

LOUIS: Manual therapy for anxious hands.

EMILY: Maybe you should try it.

LOUIS: Mathilde stitched while William the Conqueror was off to war. She was capable of . . . more than loyalty. Devotion.

  She waited for him, she stitched for years. And if he had come back broken and defeated from war, she would have loved him even more. And if he had returned mutilated, ugly, full of infection and horror, she would still have loved him; fed by pity, by a sharing of pain, she would love him even more, and even more, and she would never, never have prayed to God, please let him die if he can't return to me whole and healthy and able to live a normal life. . . . If he had died, she would have buried her heart with him.

  So what the fuck is the matter with me?

(*Little pause.*)

Will he sleep through the night?

EMILY: At least.

LOUIS: I'm going.

EMILY: Its one A.M. Where do you have to go at . . .

LOUIS: I know what time it is. A walk. Night air, good for the. . . . The park.

EMILY: Be careful.

LOUIS: Yeah. Danger.

  Tell him, if he wakes up and you're still on, tell him goodbye, tell him I had to go.

Scene 4

(*An hour later. Split scene. Joe and Roy in a fancy [straight] bar; Louis and a Man in the Rambles in Central Park. Joe and Roy are sitting at the bar; the place is brightly lit. Joe has a plate of food in front of him but he isn't eating. Roy occasionally reaches over the table and forks small bites off Joe's plate. Roy is drinking heavily, Joe not at all. Louis and the Man are eyeing each other, each alternating interest and indifference.*)

JOE: The pills were something she started when she miscarried or . . . no, she took some before that. She had a really bad time at home, when she was a kid, her home was really bad. I think a lot of drinking and physical stuff. She doesn't talk about that, instead she talks about . . . the sky falling down, people with knives hiding under sofas. Monsters. Mormons. Everyone thinks Mormons don't come from homes like that, we aren't supposed to behave that way, but we do. It's not lying, or being two-faced. Everyone tries very hard to live up to God's strictures, which are very . . . um . . .

ROY: Strict.

JOE: I shouldn't be bothering you with this.

ROY: No, please. Heart to heart. Want another. . . . What is that, seltzer?

JOE: The failure to measure up hits people very hard. From such a strong desire to be good they feel very far from goodness when they fail.

What scares me is that maybe what I really love in her is the part of her that's farthest from the light, from God's love; maybe I was drawn to that in the first place. And I'm keeping it alive because I need it.

ROY: Why would you need it?

JOE: There are things. . . . I don't know how well we know ourselves. I mean, what if? I know I married her because she . . . because I loved it that she was always wrong, always doing something wrong, like one step out of step. In Salt Lake City that stands out. I never stood out, on the outside, but inside, it was hard for me. To pass.

ROY: Pass?

JOE: Yeah.

ROY: Pass as what?

JOE: Oh. Well. . . . As someone cheerful and strong. Those who love God with an open heart unclouded by secrets and struggles are cheerful; God's easy simple love for them shows in how strong and happy they are. The saints.

ROY: But you had secrets? Secret struggles . . .

JOE: I wanted to be one of the elect, one of the Blessed. You feel you ought to be, that the blemishes are yours by choice, which of course they aren't. Harper's sorrow, that really deep sorrow, she didn't choose that. But it's there.

ROY: You didn't put it there.

JOE: No.

ROY: You sound like you think you did.

JOE: I am responsible for her.

ROY: Because she's your wife.

JOE: That. And I do love her.

ROY: Whatever. She's your wife. And so there are obligations. To her. But also to yourself.

JOE: She'd fall apart in Washington.

ROY: Then let her stay here.

JOE: She'll fall apart if I leave her.

ROY: Then bring her to Washington.

JOE: I just can't, Roy. She needs me.

ROY: Listen, Joe. I'm the best divorce lawyer in the business.

(*Little pause.*)

JOE: Can't Washington wait?

ROY: You do what you need to do, Joe. What *you* need. *You.* Let her life go where it wants to go. You'll both be better for that. *Somebody* should get what they want.

MAN: What do you want?

LOUIS: I want you to fuck me, hurt me, make me bleed.

MAN: I want to.

LOUIS: Yeah?

MAN: I want to hurt you.

LOUIS: Fuck me.

MAN: Yeah?

LOUIS: Hard.

MAN: Yeah? You been a bad boy?

(*Pause. Louis laughs, softly.*)

LOUIS: Very bad. Very bad.

MAN: You need to be punished, boy?

LOUIS: Yes. I do.

MAN: Yes what?

(*Little pause.*)

LOUIS: Um, I . . .

MAN: Yes *what*, boy?

LOUIS: Oh. Yes sir.

MAN: I want you to take me to your place, boy.

LOUIS: No, I can't do that.

MAN: No *what*?

LOUIS: No sir, I can't, I . . . I don't live alone, sir.

MAN: Your lover know you're out with a man tonight, boy?

LOUIS: No sir, he . . . My lover doesn't know.

MAN: Your lover know you . . .

LOUIS: Let's change the subject, OK? Can we go to your place?

MAN: I live with my parents.

LOUIS: Oh.

ROY: Everyone who makes it in this world makes it because somebody older and more powerful takes an interest. The most precious asset in life, I think, is the ability to be a good son. You have that, Joe. Somebody who can be a good son to a father who pushes them farther than they would otherwise go. I've had many fathers, I owe my life to them, powerful, powerful men. Walter Winchell, Edgar Hoover. Joe McCarthy most of all. He valued me because I am a good lawyer, but he loved me because I was and am a good son. He was a very difficult man, very guarded and cagey; I brought out something tender in him. He would have died for me. And me for him. Does this embarrass you?

JOE: I had a hard time with my father.

ROY: Well sometimes that's the way. Then you have to find other fathers, substitutes, I don't know. The father-son relationship is central to life. Women are for birth, beginning, but the father is continuance.

The son offers the father his life as a vessel for carrying forth his father's dream. Your father's living?

JOE: Um, dead.

ROY: He was . . . what? A difficult man?

JOE: He was in the military. He could be very unfair. And cold.

ROY: But he loved you.

JOE: I don't know.

ROY: No, no, Joe, he did, I know this. Sometimes a father's love has to be very, very hard, unfair even, cold to make his son grow strong in a world like this. This isn't a good world.

MAN: Here, then.

LOUIS: I. . . . Do you have a rubber?

MAN: I don't use rubbers.

LOUIS: You should. (*He takes one from his coat pocket.*) Here.

MAN: I don't use them.

LOUIS: Forget it, then. (*He starts to leave.*)

MAN: No, wait.
    Put it on me. Boy.

LOUIS: Forget it, I have to get back. Home. I must be going crazy.

MAN: Oh come on please he won't find out.

LOUIS: It's cold. Too cold.

MAN: It's never too cold, let me warm you up. Please?

(*They begin to fuck.*)

MAN: Relax.

LOUIS (*a small laugh*): Not a chance.

MAN: It . . .

LOUIS: What?

MAN: I think it broke. The rubber. You want me to keep going? (*Little pause.*) Pull out? Should I . . .

LOUIS: Keep going.
    Infect me.
    I don't care. I don't care.

(*Pause. The Man pulls out.*)

MAN: I . . . um, look, I'm sorry, but I think I want to go.

LOUIS: Yeah.
    Give my best to mom and dad.

(*The Man slaps him.*)

LOUIS: Ow!

(*They stare at each other.*)

LOUIS: It was a joke.

(*The Man leaves.*)

ROY: How long have we known each other?

JOE: Since 1980.

ROY: Right. A long time. I feel close to you, Joe. Do I advise you well?

JOE: You've been an incredible friend, Roy, I . . .

ROY: I want to be family. Familia, as my Italian friends call it. La Familia. A lovely word. It's important for me to help you, like I was helped.

JOE: I owe practically everything to you, Roy.

ROY: I'm dying, Joe. Cancer.

JOE: Oh my God.

ROY: Please. Let me finish.
    Few people know this and I'm telling you this only because. . . . I'm not afraid of death. What can death bring that I haven't faced? I've lived; life is the worst. (*Gently mocking himself.*) Listen to me, I'm a philosopher.
    Joe. You must do this. You must must must. Love; that's a trap. Responsibility; that's a trap too. Like a father to a son I tell you this: Life is full of horror; nobody escapes, nobody; save yourself. Whatever pulls on you, whatever needs from you, threatens you. Don't be afraid; people are so afraid; don't be afraid to live in the raw wind, naked, alone. . . . Learn at least this: What you are capable of. Let nothing stand in your way.

Scene 5

(*Three days later. Prior and Belize in Prior's hospital room. Prior is very sick but improving. Belize has just arrived.*)

PRIOR: Miss Thing.

BELIZE: Ma cherie bichette.

PRIOR: Stella.

BELIZE: Stella for star. Let me see. (*Scrutinizing Prior.*) You look like shit, why yes indeed you do, comme la merde!°

PRIOR: Merci.

BELIZE (*taking little plastic bottles from his bag, handing them to Prior*): Not to despair, Belle Reeve. Lookie! Magic goop!

PRIOR (*opening a bottle, sniffing*): Pooh! What kinda crap is that?

BELIZE: Beats me. Let's rub it on your poor blistered body and see what it does.

PRIOR: This is not Western medicine, these bottles . . .

BELIZE: Voodoo cream. From the botanica° 'round the block.

PRIOR: And you a registered nurse.

BELIZE (*sniffing it*): Beeswax and cheap perfume. Cut with Jergen's Lotion. Full of good vibes and love from some little black Cubana witch in Miami.

PRIOR: Get that trash away from me, I am immune-suppressed.

BELIZE: I *am* a health professional. I *know* what I'm doing.

PRIOR: It stinks. Any word from Louis?

(*Pause. Belize starts giving Prior a gentle massage.*)

PRIOR: Gone.

---

comme la merde: Like shit.
botanica: Shop that sells magic charms and herbs.

BELIZE: He'll be back. I know the type. Likes to keep a girl on edge.

PRIOR: It's been . . .

(*Pause.*)

BELIZE (*trying to jog his memory*): How long?

PRIOR: I don't remember.

BELIZE: How long have you been here?

PRIOR (*getting suddenly upset*): I don't remember, I don't give a fuck. I want Louis. I want my fucking boyfriend, where the fuck is he? I'm dying, I'm dying, where's Louis?

BELIZE: Shhhh, shhh . . .

PRIOR: This is a very strange drug, this drug. Emotional lability, for starters.

BELIZE: Save a tab or two for me.

PRIOR: Oh no, not this drug, ce n'est pas pour la joyeux noël et la bonne année, this drug she is serious poisonous chemistry, ma pauvre bichette.°
And not just disorienting. I hear things. Voices.

BELIZE: Voices.

PRIOR: A voice.

BELIZE: Saying what?

(*Pause.*)

PRIOR: I'm not supposed to tell.

BELIZE: You better tell the doctor. Or I will.

PRIOR: No no don't. Please. I want the voice; it's wonderful. It's all that's keeping me alive. I don't want to talk to some intern about it.
You know what happens? When I hear it, I get hard.

BELIZE: Oh my.

PRIOR: Comme ça. (*He uses his arm to demonstrate.*) And you know I am slow to rise.

BELIZE: My jaw aches at the memory.

PRIOR: And would you deny me this little solace — betray my concupiscence to Florence Nightingale's storm troopers?

BELIZE: Perish the thought, ma bébé.°

PRIOR: They'd change the drug just to spoil the fun.

BELIZE: You and your boner can depend on me.

PRIOR: Je t'adore, ma belle nègre.°

BELIZE: All this girl-talk shit is politically incorrect, you know. We should have dropped it back when we gave up drag.

PRIOR: I'm sick, I get to be politically incorrect if it makes me feel better. You sound like Lou.
(*Little pause.*)
Well, at least I have the satisfaction of knowing he's in anguish somewhere. I loved his anguish. Watching him stick his head up his asshole and eat his guts out over some relatively minor moral conundrum — it was the best show in town. But Mother warned me: if they get overwhelmed by the little things . . .

BELIZE: They'll be belly-up bustville when something big comes along.

PRIOR: Mother warned me.

BELIZE: And they do come along.

PRIOR: But I didn't listen.

BELIZE: No. (*Doing Hepburn.*) Men are beasts.

PRIOR (*also Hepburn*): The absolute lowest.

BELIZE: I have to go. If I want to spend my whole lonely life looking after white people I can get underpaid to do it.

PRIOR: You're just a Christian martyr.

BELIZE: Whatever happens, baby, I will be here for you.

PRIOR: Je t'aime.°

BELIZE: Je t'aime. Don't go crazy on me, girlfriend, I already got enough crazy queens for one lifetime. For two. I can't be bothering with dementia.

PRIOR: I promise.

BELIZE (*touching him; softly*): Ouch.

PRIOR: Ouch. Indeed.

BELIZE: Why'd they have to pick on you?
And eat more, girlfriend, you really do look like shit.

(*Belize leaves.*)

PRIOR (*after waiting a beat*): He's gone.
Are you still . . .

VOICE: I can't stay. I will return.

PRIOR: Are you one of those "Follow me to the other side" voices?

VOICE: No. I am no nightbird. I am a messenger . . .

PRIOR: You have a beautiful voice, it sounds . . . like a viola, like a perfectly tuned, tight string, balanced, the truth. . . . Stay with me.

VOICE: Not now. Soon I will return, I will reveal myself to you; I am glorious, glorious; my heart, my countenance and my message. You must prepare.

PRIOR: For what? I don't want to . . .

VOICE: No death, no:
A marvelous work and a wonder we undertake, an edifice awry we sink plumb and straighten, a great Lie we abolish, a great error correct, with the rule, sword and broom of Truth!

PRIOR: What are you talking about, I . . .

VOICE: I am on my way; when I am manifest, our Work begins:
Prepare for the parting of the air,
The breath, the ascent,
Glory to . . .

Scene 6

(*The second week of January. Martin, Roy and Joe in a fancy Manhattan restaurant.*)

MARTIN: It's a revolution in Washington, Joe. We have a new agenda and finally a real leader. They got back

---

ce n'est pas . . . bichette: This drug isn't for a merry Christmas or a happy new year . . . my poor little bitch.
ma bébé: My baby.
Je t'adore . . . nègre: I adore you, my beautiful negro.

Je t'aime: I love you.

the Senate but we have the courts. By the nineties the Supreme Court will be block-solid Republican appointees, and the Federal bench — Republican judges like land mines, everywhere, everywhere they turn. Affirmative action? Take it to court. Boom! Land mine. And we'll get our way on just about everything: abortion, defense, Central America, family values, a live investment climate. We have the White House locked till the year 2000. And beyond. A permanent fix on the Oval Office? It's possible. By '92 we'll get the Senate back, and in ten years the South is going to give us the House. It's really the end of Liberalism. The end of New Deal Socialism. The end of ipso facto secular humanism. The dawning of a genuinely American political personality. Modeled on Ronald Wilson Reagan.

JOE: It sounds great, Mr. Heller.

MARTIN: Martin. And Justice is the hub. Especially since Ed Meese took over. He doesn't specialize in Fine Points of the Law. He's a flatfoot, a cop. He reminds me of Teddy Roosevelt.

JOE: I can't wait to meet him.

MARTIN: Too bad, Joe, he's been dead for sixty years!

(*There is a little awkwardness. Joe doesn't respond.*)

MARTIN: Teddy Roosevelt. You said you wanted to. . . . Little joke. It reminds me of the story about the . . .

ROY (*smiling, but nasty*): Aw shut the fuck up Martin.
   (*To Joe.*) You see that? Mr. Heller here is one of the mighty, Joseph, in D.C. he sitteth on the right hand of the man who sitteth on the right hand of The Man. And yet I can say "shut the fuck up" and he will take no offense. Loyalty. He . . .
   Martin?

MARTIN: Yes, Roy?

ROY: Rub my back.

MARTIN: Roy . . .

ROY: No no really, a sore spot, I get them all the time now, these. . . . Rub it for me darling, would you do that for me?

(*Martin rubs Roy's back. They both look at Joe.*)

ROY (*to Joe*): How do you think a handful of Bolsheviks turned St. Petersburg into Leningrad in one afternoon? *Comrades.* Who do for each other. Marx and Engels. Lenin and Trotsky. Josef Stalin and Franklin Delano Roosevelt.

(*Martin laughs.*)

ROY: *Comrades*, right Martin?

MARTIN: This man, Joe, is a Saint of the Right.

JOE: I know, Mr. Heller, I . . .

ROY: And you see what I mean, Martin? He's special, right?

MARTIN: Don't embarrass him, Roy.

ROY: Gravity, decency, smarts! His strength is as the strength of ten because his heart is pure! *And* he's a Royboy, one hundred percent.

MARTIN: We're on the move, Joe. On the move.

JOE: Mr. Heller, I . . .

MARTIN (*ending backrub*): We can't wait any longer for an answer.

(*Little pause.*)

JOE: Oh. Um, I . . .

ROY: Joe's a married man, Martin.

MARTIN: Aha.

ROY: With a wife. She doesn't care to go to D.C., and so Joe cannot go. And keeps us dangling. We've seen that kind of thing before, haven't we? These men and their wives.

MARTIN: Oh yes. Beware.

JOE: I really can't discuss this under . . .

MARTIN: Then *don't* discuss. Say yes, Joe.

ROY: Now.

MARTIN: Say yes I will.

ROY: Now.
   Now. I'll hold my breath till you do, I'm turning blue waiting. . . . *Now*, goddammit!

MARTIN: Roy, calm down, it's not . . .

ROY: Aw, fuck it. (*He takes a letter from his jacket pocket, hands it to Joe.*)
   Read. Came today.

(*Joe reads the first paragraph, then looks up.*)

JOE: Roy. This is . . . Roy, this is terrible.

ROY: You're telling me.
   A letter from the New York State Bar Association, Martin.
   They're gonna try and disbar me.

MARTIN: Oh my.

JOE: Why?

ROY: Why, Martin?

MARTIN: Revenge.

ROY: The whole Establishment. Their little rules. Because I know no rules. Because I don't see the Law as a dead and arbitrary collection of antiquated dictums, thou shall, thou shalt not, because, because I know the Law's a pliable, breathing, sweating . . . *organ*, because, because . . .

MARTIN: Because he borrowed half a million from one of his clients.

ROY: Yeah, well, there's that.

MARTIN: *And* he forgot to *return* it.

JOE: Roy, that's. . . . You borrowed money from a client?

ROY: I'm deeply ashamed.

(*Little pause.*)

JOE (*very sympathetic*): Roy, you know how much I admire you. Well I mean I know you have unorthodox ways, but I'm sure you only did what you thought at the time you needed to do. And I have faith that . . .

ROY: Not so damp, please. I'll deny it was a loan. She's got no paperwork. Can't prove a fucking thing.

(*Little pause. Martin studies the menu.*)

JOE (*handing back the letter, more official in tone*): Roy I really appreciate your telling me this, and I'll do whatever I can to help.

ROY (*holding up a hand, then, carefully*): I'll tell you what you can do.

I'm about to be tried, Joe, by a jury that is not a jury of my peers. The disbarment committee: genteel gentleman Brahmin lawyers, country-club men. I offend them, to these men . . . I'm what, Martin, some sort of filthy little Jewish troll?

MARTIN: Oh well, I wouldn't go so far as . . .

ROY: Oh well I would.

Very fancy lawyers, these disbarment committee lawyers, fancy lawyers with fancy corporate clients and complicated cases. Antitrust suits. Deregulation. Environmental control. Complex cases like these need Justice Department cooperation like flowers need the sun. Wouldn't you say that's an accurate assessment, Martin?

MARTIN: I'm not here, Roy. I'm not hearing any of this.

ROY: No. Of course not.

Without the light of the sun, Joe, these cases, and the fancy lawyers who represent them, will wither and die.

A well-placed friend, someone in the Justice Department, say, can turn off the sun. Cast a deep shadow on my behalf. Make them shiver in the cold. If they overstep. They would fear that.

(*Pause.*)

JOE: Roy. I don't understand.

ROY: You do.

(*Pause.*)

JOE: You're not asking me to . . .

ROY: Sssshhhh. Careful.

JOE (*a beat, then*): Even if I said yes to the job, it would be illegal to interfere. With the hearings. It's unethical. No. I can't.

ROY: Un-ethical.

Would you excuse us, Martin?

MARTIN: Excuse you?

ROY: Take a walk, Martin. For real.

(*Martin leaves.*)

ROY: Un-ethical. Are you trying to embarrass me in front of my friend?

JOE: Well it is unethical, I can't . . .

ROY: Boy, you are really something. What the fuck do you think this is, Sunday School?

JOE: No, but Roy this is . . .

ROY: This is . . . this is gastric juices churning, this is enzymes and acids, this is intestinal is what this is, bowel movement and blood-red meat — this stinks, this is *politics*, Joe, the game of being alive. And you think you're. . . . What? Above that? Above alive is what? Dead! In the clouds! You're on earth, goddammit! Plant a foot, stay a while.

I'm sick. They smell I'm weak. They want blood

this time. I must have eyes in Justice. In Justice you will protect me.

JOE: Why can't Mr. Heller . . .

ROY: Grow up, Joe. The administration can't get involved.

JOE: But I'd be part of the administration. The same as him.

ROY: Not the same. Martin's Ed's man. And Ed's Reagan's man. So Martin's Reagan's man.

And you're mine.

(*Little pause. He holds up the letter.*)

This will never be. Understand me?

(*He tears the letter up.*)

I'm gonna be a lawyer, Joe, I'm gonna be a lawyer, Joe, I'm gonna be a goddam motherfucking legally licensed member of the bar lawyer, just like my daddy was, till my last bitter day on earth, Joseph, until the day I die.

(*Martin returns.*)

ROY: Ah, Martin's back.

MARTIN: So are we agreed?

ROY: Joe?

(*Little pause.*)

JOE: I will think about it.

(*To Roy.*) I will.

ROY: Huh.

MARTIN: It's the fear of what comes after the doing that makes the doing hard to do.

ROY: Amen.

MARTIN: But you can almost always live with the consequences.

Scene 7

(*That afternoon. On the granite steps outside the Hall of Justice, Brooklyn. It is cold and sunny. A Sabrett wagon is selling hot dogs. Louis, in a shabby overcoat, is sitting on the steps contemplatively eating one. Joe enters with three hot dogs and a can of Coke.*)

JOE: Can I . . . ?

LOUIS: Oh sure. Sure. Crazy cold sun.

JOE (*sitting*): Have to make the best of it.

How's your friend?

LOUIS: My . . . ? Oh. He's worse. My friend is worse.

JOE: I'm sorry.

LOUIS: Yeah, well. Thanks for asking. It's nice. You're nice. I can't believe you voted for Reagan.

JOE: I hope he gets better.

LOUIS: Reagan?

JOE: Your friend.

LOUIS: He won't. Neither will Reagan.

JOE: Let's not talk politics, OK?

LOUIS (*pointing to Joe's lunch*): You're eating *three* of those?

JOE: Well . . . I'm . . . hungry.

LOUIS: They're really terrible for you. Full of rat-poo and beetle legs and wood shavings 'n' shit.

JOE: Huh.

LOUIS: And . . . um . . . irridium, I think. Something toxic.

JOE: You're eating one.

LOUIS: Yeah, well, the shape, I can't help myself, plus I'm *trying* to commit suicide, what's your excuse?

JOE: I don't have an excuse. I just have Pepto-Bismol.

(*Joe takes a bottle of Pepto-Bismol and chugs it. Louis shudders audibly.*)

JOE: Yeah I know but then I wash it down with Coke.

(*He does this. Louis mimes barfing in Joe's lap. Joe pushes Louis's head away.*)

JOE: Are you *always* like this?

LOUIS: I've been worrying a lot about his kids.

JOE: Whose?

LOUIS: Reagan's. Maureen and Mike and little orphan Patti and Miss Ron Reagan Jr., the you-should-pardon-the-expression heterosexual.

JOE: Ron Reagan Jr. is *not*. . . . You shouldn't just make these assumptions about people. How do you know? About him? What he is? You don't know.

LOUIS (*doing Tallulah*): Well darling he never sucked *my* cock but . . .

JOE: Look, if you're going to get vulgar . . .

LOUIS: No no really I mean. . . . What's it like to be the child of the Zeitgeist? To have the American Animus as your dad? It's not really a *family*, the Reagans, I read *People*, there aren't any connections there, no love, they don't ever even speak to each other except through their agents. So what's it like to be Reagan's kid? Enquiring minds want to know.

JOE: You can't believe everything you . . .

LOUIS (*looking away*): But . . . I think we all know what that's like. Nowadays. No connections. No responsibilities. All of us . . . falling through the cracks that separate what we owe to our selves and . . . and what we owe to love.

JOE: You just. . . . Whatever you feel like saying or doing, you don't care, you just . . . do it.

LOUIS: Do what?

JOE: It. Whatever. Whatever it is you want to do.

LOUIS: Are you trying to tell me something?

(*Little pause, sexual. They stare at each other. Joe looks away.*)

JOE: No, I'm just observing that you . . .

LOUIS: Impulsive.

JOE: Yes, I mean it must be scary, you . . .

LOUIS (*shrugs*): Land of the free. Home of the brave. Call me irresponsible.

JOE: It's kind of terrifying.

LOUIS: Yeah, well, freedom is. Heartless, too.

JOE: Oh you're not heartless.

LOUIS: You don't know.
        Finish your weenie.

(*He pats Joe on the knee, starts to leave.*)

JOE: Um . . .

(*Louis turns, looks at him. Joe searches for something to say.*)

JOE: Yesterday was Sunday but I've been a little unfocused recently and I thought it was Monday. So I came here like I was going to work. And the whole place was empty. And at first I couldn't figure out why, and I had this moment of incredible . . . fear and also. . . . It just flashed through my mind: The whole Hall of Justice, it's empty, it's deserted, it's gone out of business. Forever. The people that make it run have up and abandoned it.

LOUIS (*looking at the building*): Creepy.

JOE: Well yes but. I felt that I was going to scream. Not because it was creepy, but because the emptiness felt so *fast*.
        And . . . well, good. A . . . happy scream.
        I just wondered what a thing it would be . . . if overnight everything you owe anything to, justice, or love, had really gone away. Free.
        It would be . . . heartless terror. Yes. Terrible, and . . .
        Very great. To shed your skin, every old skin, one by one and then walk away, unencumbered, into the morning.
        (*Little pause. He looks at the building.*)
        I can't go in there today.

LOUIS: Then don't.

JOE (*not really hearing Louis*): I can't go in, I need . . .
        (*He looks for what he needs. He takes a swig of Pepto-Bismol.*)
        I can't *be* this anymore. I need . . . a change, I should just . . .

LOUIS (*not a come-on, necessarily; he doesn't want to be alone*): Want some company? For whatever?

(*Pause. Joe looks at Louis and looks away, afraid. Louis shrugs.*)

LOUIS: Sometimes, even if it scares you to death, you have to be willing to break the law. Know what I mean?

(*Another little pause.*)

JOE: Yes.

(*Another little pause.*)

LOUIS: I moved out. I moved out on my . . .
        I haven't been sleeping well.

JOE: Me neither.

(*Louis goes up to Joe, licks his napkin and dabs at Joes mouth.*)

LOUIS: Antacid moustache.
        (*Points to the building.*) Maybe the court won't convene. Ever again. Maybe we are free. To do whatever.

Children of the new morning, criminal minds. Selfish and greedy and loveless and blind. Reagan's children.

You're scared. So am I. Everybody is in the land of the free. God help us all.

Scene 8

(*Late that night. Joe at a payphone phoning Hannah at home in Salt Lake City.*)

JOE: Mom?

HANNAH: Joe?

JOE: Hi.

HANNAH: You're calling from the street. It's . . . it must be four in the morning. What's happened?

JOE: Nothing, nothing, I . . .

HANNAH: It's Harper. Is Harper. . . . Joe? Joe?

JOE: Yeah, hi. No, Harper's fine. Well, no, she's . . . not fine. How are you, Mom?

HANNAH: What's happened?

JOE: I just wanted to talk to you. I, uh, wanted to try something out on you.

HANNAH: Joe, you haven't . . . have you been drinking, Joe?

JOE: Yes ma'am. I'm drunk.

HANNAH: That isn't like you.

JOE: No. I mean, who's to say?

HANNAH: Why are you out on the street at four A.M.? In that crazy city. It's dangerous.

JOE: Actually, Mom, I'm not on the street. I'm near the boathouse in the park.

HANNAH: What park?

JOE: Central Park.

HANNAH: CENTRAL PARK! Oh my Lord. What on earth are you doing in Central Park at this time of night? Are you . . .

Joe, I think you ought to go home right now. Call me from home.

(*Little pause.*)

Joe?

JOE: I come here to watch, Mom. Sometimes. Just to watch.

HANNAH: Watch what? What's there to watch at four in the . . .

JOE: Mom, did Dad love me?

HANNAH: What?

JOE: Did he?

HANNAH: You ought to go home and call from there.

JOE: Answer.

HANNAH: Oh now really. This is maudlin. I don't like this conversation.

JOE: Yeah, well, it gets worse from here on.

(*Pause.*)

HANNAH: Joe?

JOE: Mom. Momma. I'm a homosexual, Momma.

Boy, did that come out awkward.

(*Pause.*)

Hello? Hello?

I'm a homosexual.

(*Pause.*)

Please, Momma. Say something.

HANNAH: You're old enough to understand that your father didn't love you without being ridiculous about it.

JOE: What?

HANNAH: You're ridiculous. You're being ridiculous.

JOE: I'm . . .

What?

HANNAH: You really ought to go home now to your wife. I need to go to bed. This phone call. . . . We will just forget this phone call.

JOE: Mom.

HANNAH: No more talk. Tonight. This . . .

(*Suddenly very angry.*) Drinking is a sin! A sin! I raised you better than that. (*She hangs up.*)

Scene 9

(*The following morning, early. Split scene: Harper and Joe at home; Louis and Prior in Prior's hospital room. Joe and Louis have just entered. This should be fast and obviously furious; overlapping is fine; the proceedings may be a little confusing but not the final results.*)

HARPER: Oh God. Home. The moment of truth has arrived.

JOE: Harper.

LOUIS: I'm going to move out.

PRIOR: The fuck you are.

JOE: Harper. Please listen. I still love you very much. You're still my best buddy; I'm not going to leave you.

HARPER: No, I don't like the sound of this. I'm leaving.

LOUIS: I'm leaving.

I already have.

JOE: Please listen. Stay. This is really hard. We have to talk.

HARPER: We are talking. Aren't we. Now please shut up. OK?

PRIOR: Bastard. Sneaking off while I'm flat out here, that's low. If I could get up now I'd beat the holy shit out of you.

JOE: Did you take pills? How many?

HARPER: No pills. Bad for the . . . (*Pats stomach.*)

JOE: You aren't pregnant. I called your gynecologist.

HARPER: I'm seeing a new gynecologist.

PRIOR: You have no right to do this.

LOUIS: Oh, that's ridiculous.

PRIOR: No right. It's criminal.

JOE: Forget about that. Just listen. You want the truth. This is the truth.

I knew this when I married you. I've known this I guess for as long as I've known anything, but . . . I don't know, I thought maybe that with enough effort and will I could change myself . . . but I can't . . .

PRIOR: Criminal.

LOUIS: There oughta be a law.

PRIOR: There is a law. You'll see.

JOE: I'm losing ground here, I go walking, you want to know where I walk, I . . . go to the park, or up and down 53rd Street, or places where. . . . And I keep swearing I won't go walking again, but I just can't.

LOUIS: I need some privacy.

PRIOR: That's new.

LOUIS: Everything's new, Prior.

JOE: I try to tighten my heart into a knot, a snarl, I try to learn to live dead, just numb, but then I see someone I want, and it's like a nail, like a hot spike right through my chest, and I know I'm losing.

PRIOR: Apartment too small for three? Louis and Prior comfy but not Louis and Prior and Prior's disease?

LOUIS: Something like that.

I won't be judged by you. This isn't a crime, just — the inevitable consequence of people who run out of — whose limitations. . . .

PRIOR: Bang bang bang. The court will come to order.

LOUIS: I mean let's talk practicalities, schedules; I'll come over if you want, spend nights with you when I can, I can . . .

PRIOR: Has the jury reached a verdict?

LOUIS: I'm doing the best I can.

PRIOR: Pathetic. Who cares?

JOE: My whole life has conspired to bring me to this place, and I can't despise my whole life. I think I believed when I met you I could save you, you at least if not myself, but . . .

I don't have any sexual feelings for you, Harper. And I don't think I ever did.

(*Little pause.*)

HARPER: I think you should go.

JOE: Where?

HARPER: Washington. Doesn't matter.

JOE: What are you talking about?

HARPER: Without me.

Without me, Joe. Isn't that what you want to hear?

(*Little pause.*)

JOE: Yes.

LOUIS: You can love someone and fail them. You can love someone and not be able to . . .

PRIOR: You *can*, theoretically, yes. A person can, maybe an editorial "you" can love, Louis, but not *you*, specifically you, I don't know, I think you are excluded from that general category.

HARPER: You were going to save me, but the whole time you were spinning a lie. I just don't understand that.

PRIOR: A person could theoretically love and maybe many do but we both know now you can't.

LOUIS: I do.

PRIOR: You can't even say it.

LOUIS: I love you, Prior.

PRIOR: I repeat. Who cares?

HARPER: This is so scary, I want this to stop, to go back . . .

PRIOR: We have reached a verdict, your honor. This man's heart is deficient. He loves, but his love is worth nothing.

JOE: Harper . . .

HARPER: Mr. Lies, I want to get away from here. Far away. Right now. Before he starts talking again. Please, please . . .

JOE: As long as I've known you Harper you've been afraid of . . . Of men hiding under the bed, men hiding under the sofa, men with knives.

PRIOR (*shattered; almost pleading; trying to reach him*): I'm dying! You stupid fuck! Do you know what that is! Love! Do you know what love means? We lived together four-and-a-half years, you animal, you idiot.

LOUIS: I have to find some way to save myself.

JOE: Who are these men? I never understood it. Now I know.

HARPER: What?

JOE: It's me.

HARPER: It is?

PRIOR: GET OUT OF MY ROOM!

JOE: I'm the man with the knives.

HARPER: You are?

PRIOR: If I could get up now I'd kill you. I would. Go away. Go away or I'll scream.

HARPER: Oh God . . .

JOE: I'm sorry . . .

HARPER: It is you.

LOUIS: Please don't scream.

PRIOR: Go.

HARPER: I recognize you now.

LOUIS: Please . . .

JOE: Oh. Wait, I. . . . Oh!

(*He covers his mouth with his hand, gags, and removes his hand, red with blood.*)

I'm bleeding.

(*Prior screams.*)

HARPER: Mr. Lies.

MR. LIES (*appearing, dressed in antarctic explorer's apparel*): Right here.

HARPER: I want to go away. I can't see him anymore.

MR. LIES: Where?

HARPER: Anywhere. Far away.

MR. LIES: Absolutamento.

(*Harper and Mr. Lies vanish. Joe looks up, sees that she's gone.*)

PRIOR (*closing his eyes*): When I open my eyes you'll be gone.

(*Louis leaves.*)

JOE: Harper?

PRIOR (*opening his eyes*): Huh. It worked.

JOE (*calling*): Harper?

PRIOR: I hurt all over. I wish I was dead.

Scene 10

(*The same day, sunset. Hannah and Sister Ella Chapter, a real-estate saleswoman, Hannah Pitt's closest friend, in front of Hannah's house in Salt Lake City.*)

SISTER ELLA CHAPTER: Look at that view! A view of heaven. Like the living city of heaven, isn't it, it just fairly glimmers in the sun.
HANNAH: Glimmers.
SISTER ELLA CHAPTER: Even the stone and brick it just glimmers and glitters like heaven in the sunshine. Such a nice view you get, perched up on a canyon rim. Some kind of beautiful place.
HANNAH: It's just Salt Lake, and you're selling the house *for* me, not *to* me.
SISTER ELLA CHAPTER: I like to work up an enthusiasm for my properties.
HANNAH: Just get me a good price.
SISTER ELLA CHAPTER: Well, the market's off.
HANNAH: At least fifty.
SISTER ELLA CHAPTER: Forty'd be more like it.
HANNAH: Fifty.
SISTER ELLA CHAPTER: Wish you'd wait a bit.
HANNAH: Well I can't.
SISTER ELLA CHAPTER: Wish you would. You're about the only friend I got.
HANNAH: Oh well now.
SISTER ELLA CHAPTER: Know why I decided to like you? I decided to like you 'cause you're the only unfriendly Mormon I ever met.
HANNAH: Your wig is crooked.
SISTER ELLA CHAPTER: Fix it.

(*Hannah straightens Sister Ella's wig.*)

SISTER ELLA CHAPTER: New York City. All they got there is tiny rooms.
    I always thought: People ought to stay put. That's why I got my license to sell real estate. It's a way of saying: Have a house! Stay put! It's a way of saying traveling's no good. Plus I needed the cash. (*She takes a pack of cigarettes out of her purse, lights one, offers pack to Hannah.*)
HANNAH: Not out here, anyone could come by.
    There's been days I've stood at this ledge and thought about stepping over.
    It's a hard place, Salt Lake: baked dry. Abundant energy; not much intelligence. That's a combination that can wear a body out. No harm looking someplace else. I don't need much room.
    My sister-in-law Libby thinks there's radon gas in the basement.
SISTER ELLA CHAPTER: Is there gas in the . . .
HANNAH: Of course not. Libby's a fool.
SISTER ELLA CHAPTER: 'Cause I'd have to include that in the description.
HANNAH: There's no gas, Ella. (*Little pause.*) Give a puff. (*She takes a furtive drag of Ella's cigarette.*) Put it away now.

SISTER ELLA CHAPTER: So I guess it's goodbye.
HANNAH: You'll be all right, Ella, I wasn't ever much of a friend.
SISTER ELLA CHAPTER: I'll say something but don't laugh, OK?
    This is the home of saints, the godliest place on earth, they say, and I think they're right. That mean there's no evil here? No. Evil's everywhere. Sin's everywhere. But this . . . is the spring of sweet water in the desert, the desert flower. Every step a Believer takes away from here is a step fraught with peril. I fear for you, Hannah Pitt, because you are my friend. Stay put. This is the right home of saints.
HANNAH: Latter-day saints.
SISTER ELLA CHAPTER: Only kind left.
HANNAH: But still. Late in the day . . . for saints and everyone. That's all. That's all.
    Fifty thousand dollars for the house, Sister Ella Chapter; don't undersell. It's an impressive view.

ACT 3
NOT-YET-CONSCIOUS, FORWARD DAWNING • *January 1986*

Scene 1

(*Late night, three days after the end of act 2. The stage is completely dark. Prior is in bed in his apartment, having a nightmare. He wakes up, sits up and switches on a nightlight. He looks at his clock. Seated by the table near the bed is a man dressed in the clothing of a 13th-century British squire.*)

PRIOR (*terrified*): Who are you?
PRIOR 1: My name is Prior Walter.

(*Pause.*)

PRIOR: My name is Prior Walter.
PRIOR 1: I know that.
PRIOR: Explain.
PRIOR 1: You're alive. I'm not. We have the same name. What do you want me to explain?
PRIOR: A ghost?
PRIOR 1: An ancestor.
PRIOR: Not *the* Prior Walter? The Bayeux tapestry Prior Walter?
PRIOR 1: His great-great grandson. The fifth of the name.
PRIOR: I'm the thirty-fourth, I think.
PRIOR 1: Actually the thirty-second.
PRIOR: Not according to Mother.
PRIOR 1: She's including the two bastards, then; I say leave them out. I say no room for bastards. The little things you swallow . . .
PRIOR: Pills.
PRIOR 1: Pills. For the pestilence. I too . . .
PRIOR: Pestilence. . . . You too what?

PRIOR 1: The pestilence in my time was much worse than now. Whole villages of empty houses. You could look outdoors and see Death walking in the morning, dew dampening the ragged hem of his black robe. Plain as I see you now.

PRIOR: You died of the plague.

PRIOR 1: The spotty monster. Like you, alone.

PRIOR: I'm not alone.

PRIOR 1: You have no wife, no children.

PRIOR: I'm gay.

PRIOR 1: So? Be gay, dance in your altogether for all I care, what's that to do with not having children?

PRIOR: Gay homosexual, not bonny, blithe and . . . never mind.

PRIOR 1: I had twelve. When I died.

(*The second ghost appears, this one dressed in the clothing of an elegant 17th-century Londoner.*)

PRIOR 1 (*pointing to Prior 2*): And I was three years younger than him.

(*Prior sees the new ghost, screams.*)

PRIOR: Oh God another one.

PRIOR 2: Prior Walter. Prior to you by some seventeen others.

PRIOR 1: He's counting the bastards.

PRIOR: Are we having a convention?

PRIOR 2: We've been sent to declare her fabulous incipience. They love a well-paved entrance with lots of heralds, and . . .

PRIOR 1: The messenger come. Prepare the way. The infinite descent, a breath in air . . .

PRIOR 2: They chose us, I suspect, because of the mortal affinities. In a family as long-descended as the Walters there are bound to be a few carried off by plague.

PRIOR 1: The spotty monster.

PRIOR 2: Black Jack. Came from a water pump, half the city of London, can you imagine? His came from fleas. Yours, I understand, is the lamentable consequence of venery . . .

PRIOR 1: Fleas on rats, but who knew that?

PRIOR: Am I going to die?

PRIOR 2: We aren't allowed to discuss . . .

PRIOR 1: When you do, you don't get ancestors to help you through it. You may be surrounded by children but you die alone.

PRIOR: I'm afraid.

PRIOR 1: You should be. There aren't even torches, and the path's rocky, dark and steep.

PRIOR 2: Don't alarm him. There's good news before there's bad.

We two come to strew rose petal and palm leaf before the triumphal procession. Prophet. Seer. Revelator. It's a great honor for the family.

PRIOR 1: He hasn't got a family.

PRIOR 2: I meant for the Walters, for the family in the larger sense.

PRIOR (*singing*): All I want is a room somewhere, Far away from the cold night air . . .

PRIOR 2 (*putting a hand on Prior's forehead*): Calm, calm, this is no brain fever . . .

(*Prior calms down, but keeps his eyes closed. The lights begin to change. Distant Glorious Music.*)

PRIOR 1 (*low chant*): Adonai, Adonai,
Olam ha-yichud,
Zefirot, Zazahot,
Ha-adam, ha-gadol
Daughter of Light,
Daughter of Splendors,
Fluor! Phosphor!
Lumen! Candle!

PRIOR 2 (*simultaneously*): Even now,
From the mirror-bright halls of heaven,
Across the cold and lifeless infinity of space,
The Messenger comes
Trailing orbs of light,
Fabulous, incipient,
Oh Prophet,
To you . . .

PRIOR 1 AND PRIOR 2: Prepare, prepare,
The Infinite Descent,
A breath, a feather,
Glory to . . .

(*They vanish.*)

Scene 2

(*The next day. Split scene. Louis and Belize in a coffee shop. Prior is at the outpatient clinic at the hospital with Emily, the nurse; she has him on a pentamidine IV drip.*)

LOUIS: Why has democracy succeeded in America? Of course by succeeded I mean comparatively, not literally, not in the present, but what makes for the prospect of some sort of radical democracy spreading outward and growing up? Why does the power that was once so carefully preserved at the top of the pyramid by the original framers of the Constitution seem drawn inexorably downward and outward in spite of the best effort of the Right to stop this? I mean it's the really hard thing about being Left in this country, the American Left can't help but trip over all these petrified little fetishes: freedom, that's the worst; you know, *Jeane Kirkpatrick*° for God's sake will go on and on about freedom and so what does that mean, the word freedom, when she talks about it, or human rights; you have Bush talking about human rights, and so what are these people talking about, they might as well be talking about the mating habits of Venusians, these people don't begin to know what, ontologically, freedom is or human

Jeane Kirkpatrick: Former U.S. ambassador to the United Nations. Kirkpatrick (b. 1920) remains a Senior Fellow of the American Enterprise Institute for Public Policy and Research, a conservative think tank.

rights, like they see these bourgeois property-based Rights-of-Man-type rights but that's not enfranchisement, not democracy, not what's implicit, what's potential within the idea, not the idea with blood in it. That's just liberalism, the worst kind of liberalism, really, bourgeois tolerance, and what I think is that what AIDS shows us is the limits of tolerance, that it's not enough to be tolerated, because when the shit hits the fan you find out how much tolerance is worth. Nothing. And underneath all the tolerance is intense, passionate hatred.

BELIZE: Uh huh.

LOUIS: Well don't you think that's true?

BELIZE: Uh huh. It is.

LOUIS: *Power* is the object, not being tolerated. Fuck assimilation. But I mean in spite of all this the thing about America, I think, is that ultimately we're different from every other nation on earth, in that, with people here of every race, we can't. . . . Ultimately what defines us isn't race, but politics. Not like any European country where there's an insurmountable fact of a kind of racial, or ethnic, monopoly, or monolith, like all Dutchmen, I mean Dutch people, are well, Dutch, and the Jews of Europe were never Europeans, just a small problem. Facing the monolith. But here there are so many small problems, it's really just a collection of small problems, the monolith is missing. Oh, I mean, of course I suppose there's the monolith of White America. White Straight Male America.

BELIZE: Which is not unimpressive, even among monoliths.

LOUIS: Well, no, but when the race thing gets taken care of, and I don't mean to minimalize how major it is, I mean I know it is, this is a really, really incredibly racist country but it's like, well, the British. I mean, all these blue-eyed pink people. And it's just weird, you know, I mean I'm not all that Jewish-looking, or . . . well, maybe I am but, you know, in New York, everyone is . . . well, not everyone, but so many are but so but in England, in London I walk into bars and I feel like Sid the Yid, you know I mean like Woody Allen in *Annie Hall,* with the payess and the gabardine coat, like never, never anywhere so much — I mean, not actively despised, not like they're Germans, who I think are still terribly anti-Semitic, and racist too, I mean black-racist, they pretend otherwise but, anyway, in London, there's just . . . and at one point I met this black gay guy from Jamaica who talked with a lilt but he said his family'd been living in London since before the Civil War — the American one — and how the English never let him forget for a minute that he wasn't blue-eyed and pink and I said yeah, me too, these people are anti-Semites and he said yeah but the British Jews have the clothing business all sewed up and blacks there can't get a foothold. And it was an incredibly awkward moment of just. . . . I mean there we were, in this bar that was gay but it was a *pub,* you know,

the beams and the plaster and those horrible little, like, two-day-old fish and egg sandwiches — and just so British, so *old,* and I felt, well, there's no way out of this because both of us are, right now, too much immersed in this history, hope is dissolved in the sheer age of this place, where race is what counts and there's no real hope of change — it's the racial destiny of the Brits that matters to them, not their political destiny, whereas in America . . .

BELIZE: Here in America race doesn't count.

LOUIS: No, no, that's not. . . . I mean you *can't* be hearing that . . .

BELIZE: I . . .

LOUIS: It's — look, race, yes, but ultimately race here is a political question, right? Racists just try to use race here as a tool in a political struggle. It's not really about race. Like the spiritualists try to use that stuff, are you enlightened, are you centered, channeled, whatever, this reaching out for a spiritual past in a country where no indigenous spirits exist — only the Indians, I mean Native American spirits and we killed them off so now, there are no gods here, no ghosts and spirits in America, there are no angels in America, no spiritual past, no racial past, there's only the political, and the decoys and the ploys to maneuver around the inescapable battle of politics, the shifting downwards and outwards of political power to the people . . .

BELIZE: POWER to the People! AMEN! (*Looking at his watch.*) *OH MY GOODNESS!* Will you look at the time, I gotta . . .

LOUIS: Do you. . . . You think this is, what, racist or naive or something?

BELIZE: Well it's certainly *something.* Look, I just remembered I have an appointment . . .

LOUIS: What? I mean I really don't want to, like, speak from some position of privilege and . . .

BELIZE: I'm sitting here, thinking, eventually he's *got* to run out of steam, so I let you rattle on and on saying about maybe seven or eight things I find really offensive.

LOUIS: What?

BELIZE: But I know you, Louis, and I know the guilt fueling this peculiar tirade is obviously already swollen bigger than your hemorrhoids.

LOUIS: I don't have hemorrhoids.

BELIZE: I hear different. May I finish?

LOUIS: Yes, but I don't have hemorrhoids.

BELIZE: So finally, when I . . .

LOUIS: Prior told you, he's an asshole, he shouldn't have . . .

BELIZE: You promised, Louis. Prior is not a subject.

LOUIS: You brought him up.

BELIZE: I brought up hemorrhoids.

LOUIS: So it's indirect. Passive-aggressive.

BELIZE: Unlike, I suppose, banging me over the head with your theory that America doesn't have a race problem.

LOUIS: Oh be fair I never said that.

BELIZE: Not exactly, but . . .

LOUIS: I said . . .

BELIZE: . . . but it was close enough, because if it'd been that blunt I'd've just walked out and . . .

LOUIS: You deliberately misinterpreted! I . . .

BELIZE: Stop interrupting! I haven't been able to . . .

LOUIS: Just let me . . .

BELIZE: NO! What, *talk*? You've been running your mouth nonstop since I got here, yaddadda yaddadda blah blah blah, up the hill, down the hill, playing with your MONOLITH . . .

LOUIS (*overlapping*): Well, you could have joined in at any time instead of . . .

BELIZE (*continuing over Louis*): . . . and girlfriend it is truly an *awesome* spectacle but I got better things to do with my time than sit here listening to this racist bullshit just because I feel sorry for you that . . .

LOUIS: I am not a racist!

BELIZE: Oh come on . . .

LOUIS: So maybe I am a racist but . . .

BELIZE: Oh I really hate that! It's no fun picking on you Louis; you're so guilty, it's like throwing darts at a glob of jello, there's no satisfying hits, just quivering, the darts just blop in and vanish.

LOUIS: I just think when you are discussing lines of oppression it gets very complicated and . . .

BELIZE: Oh is that a fact? You know, we black drag queens have a rather intimate knowledge of the complexity of the lines of . . .

LOUIS: *Ex*-black drag queen.

BELIZE: Actually ex-ex.

LOUIS: You're doing drag again?

BELIZE: I don't. . . . Maybe. I don't have to tell you. Maybe.

LOUIS: I think it's sexist.

BELIZE: I didn't ask you.

LOUIS: Well it is. The gay community, I think, has to adopt the same attitude towards drag as black women have to take towards black women blues singers.

BELIZE: Oh my we *are* walking dangerous tonight.

LOUIS: Well, it's all internalized oppression, right, I mean the masochism, the stereotypes, the . . .

BELIZE: Louis, are you deliberately trying to make me hate you?

LOUIS: No, I . . .

BELIZE: I mean, are you deliberately transforming yourself into an arrogant, sexual-political Stalinist-slash-racist flag-waving thug for my benefit?

(*Pause.*)

LOUIS: You know what I think?

BELIZE: What?

LOUIS: You hate me because I'm a Jew.

BELIZE: I'm leaving.

LOUIS: It's true.

BELIZE: You have no basis except your . . .

　Louis, it's good to know you haven't changed; you are still an honorary citizen of the Twilight Zone, and after your pale, pale white polemics on behalf of racial insensitivity you have a flaming *fuck* of a lot of nerve calling me an anti-Semite. Now I really gotta go.

LOUIS: You called me Lou the Jew.

BELIZE: That was a joke.

LOUIS: I didn't think it was funny. It was hostile.

BELIZE: It was three years ago.

LOUIS: So?

BELIZE: You just called yourself Sid the Yid.

LOUIS: That's not the same thing.

BELIZE: Sid the Yid is different from Lou the Jew.

LOUIS: Yes.

BELIZE: Someday you'll have to explain that to me, but right now . . .

　You hate me because you hate black people.

LOUIS: I do not. But I do think most black people are anti-Semitic.

BELIZE: "Most black people." *That's* racist, Louis, and I think most Jews . . .

LOUIS: Louis Farrakhan.

BELIZE: Ed Koch.

LOUIS: Jesse Jackson.

BELIZE: Jackson. Oh really, Louis, this is . . .

LOUIS: Hymietown! Hymietown!

BELIZE: Louis, you voted for Jesse Jackson. You send checks to the Rainbow Coalition.

LOUIS: I'm ambivalent. The checks bounced.

BELIZE: All your checks bounce, Louis; you're ambivalent about everything.

LOUIS: What's that supposed to mean?

BELIZE: You may be dumber than shit but I refuse to believe you can't figure it out. Try.

LOUIS: I was never ambivalent about Prior. I love him. I do. I really do.

BELIZE: Nobody said different.

LOUIS: Love and ambivalence are. . . . Real love isn't ambivalent.

BELIZE: "Real love isn't ambivalent." I'd swear that's a line from my favorite bestselling paperback novel, *In Love with the Night Mysterious*, except I don't think you ever read it.

(*Pause.*)

LOUIS: I never read it, no.

BELIZE: You ought to. Instead of spending the rest of your life trying to get through *Democracy in America*. It's about this white woman whose Daddy owns a plantation in the Deep South in the years before the Civil War — the American one — and her name is Margaret, and she's in love with her Daddy's number-one slave, and his name is Thaddeus, and she's married but her white slave-owner husband has AIDS: Antebellum Insufficiently Developed Sex-organs. And there's a lot of hot stuff going down when Margaret and Thaddeus can catch a spare torrid ten under the cotton-picking moon, and then of course the Yankees come, and they set the slaves free, and the slaves string up old Daddy, and so on.

Historical fiction. Somewhere in there I recall Margaret and Thaddeus find the time to discuss the nature of love; her face is reflecting the flames of the burning plantation — you know, the way white people do — and his black face is dark in the night and she says to him, "Thaddeus, real love isn't ever ambivalent.'"

(*Little pause. Emily enters and turns off IV drip.*)

BELIZE: Thaddeus looks at her; he's contemplating her thesis; and he isn't sure he agrees.
EMILY (*removing IV drip from Prior's arm*): Treatment number . . . (*consulting chart*) four.
PRIOR: Pharmaceutical miracle. Lazarus breathes again.
LOUIS: Is he. . . . How bad is he?
BELIZE: You want the laundry list?
EMILY: Shirt off, let's check the . . .

(*Prior takes his shirt off. She examines his lesions.*)

BELIZE: There's the weight problem and the shit problem and the morale problem.
EMILY: Only six. That's good. Pants.

(*He drops his pants. He's naked. She examines.*)

BELIZE: And. He thinks he's going crazy.
EMILY: Looking good. What else?
PRIOR: Ankles sore and swollen, but the leg's better. The nausea's mostly gone with the little orange pills. BM's pure liquid but not bloody anymore, for now, my eye doctor says everything's OK, for now, my dentist says "Yuck!" when he sees my fuzzy tongue, and now he wears little condoms on his thumb and forefinger. And a mask. So what? My dermatologist is in Hawaii and my mother . . . well leave my mother out of it. Which is usually where my mother is, out of it. My glands are like walnuts, my weight's holding steady for week two, and a friend died two days ago of bird tuberculosis; bird tuberculosis; that scared me and I didn't go to the funeral today because he was an Irish Catholic and it's probably open casket and I'm afraid of . . . something, the bird TB or seeing him or. . . . So I guess I'm doing OK. Except for of course I'm going nuts.
EMILY: We ran the toxoplasmosis series and there's no indication . . .
PRIOR: I know, I know, but I feel like something terrifying is on its way, you know, like a missile from outer space, and it's plummeting down towards the earth, and I'm ground zero, and . . . I am generally known where I am known as one cool, collected queen. And I am ruffled.
EMILY: There's really nothing to worry about. I think that shochen bamromim hamtzeh menucho nechono al kanfey haschino.
PRIOR: What?
EMILY: Everything's fine. Bemaalos k'doshim ut'horim kezohar horokeea mazhirim . . .
PRIOR: Oh I don't understand what you're . . .
EMILY: Es nishmas Prior sheholoch leolomoh, baavur shenodvoo z'dokoh b'ad hazkoras nishmosoh.

PRIOR: Why are you doing that?! Stop it! Stop it!
EMILY: Stop what?
PRIOR: You were just . . . weren't you just speaking in Hebrew or something.
EMILY: *Hebrew?* (*Laughs.*) I'm basically Italian-American. No. I didn't speak in Hebrew.
PRIOR: Oh no, oh God please I really think I . . .
EMILY: Look, I'm sorry, I have a waiting room full of. . . . I think you're one of the lucky ones, you'll live for years, probably — you're pretty healthy for someone with no immune system. Are you seeing someone? Loneliness is a danger. A therapist?
PRIOR: No, I don't need to see anyone, I just . . .
EMILY: Well think about it. You aren't going crazy. You're just under a lot of stress. No wonder . . . (*She starts to write in his chart.*)

(*Suddenly there is an astonishing blaze of light, a huge chord sounded by a gigantic choir, and a great book with steel pages mounted atop a molten-red pillar pops up from the stage floor. The book opens; there is a large Aleph inscribed on its pages, which bursts into flames. Immediately the book slams shut and disappears instantly under the floor as the lights become normal again. Emily notices none of this, writing. Prior is agog.*)

EMILY (*laughing, exiting*): Hebrew . . .

(*Prior flees.*)

LOUIS: Help me.
BELIZE: I beg your pardon?
LOUIS: You're a nurse, give me something, I . . . don't know what's to do anymore, I. . . . Last week at work I screwed up the Xerox machine like permanently and so I . . . then I tripped on the subway steps and my glasses broke and I cut my forehead, here, see, and now I can't see much and my forehead . . . it's like the Mark of Cain,° stupid, right, but it won't heal and every morning I see it and I think, Biblical things, Mark of Cain, Judas Iscariot° and his silver and his noose, people who . . . in betraying what they love betray what's truest in themselves, I feel . . . nothing but cold for myself, just cold, and every night I miss him, I miss him so much but then . . . those sores, and the smell and . . . where I thought it was going. . . . I could be . . . I could be . . . sick too, maybe I'm sick too. I don't know.
  Belize. Tell him I love him. Can you do that?
BELIZE: I've thought about it for a very long time, and I still don't understand what love is. Justice is simple. Democracy is simple. Those things are unambivalent. But love is very hard. And it goes bad for you if you violate the hard law of love.
LOUIS: I'm dying.
BELIZE: He's dying. You just wish you were.

Mark of Cain: In Genesis Cain murdered his brother Abel and subsequently was marked on his forehead by God.
Judas Iscariot: An apostle who betrayed Jesus for thirty pieces of silver.

Oh cheer up, Louis. Look at that heavy sky out there.

LOUIS: Purple.

BELIZE: *Purple?* Boy, what kind of a homosexual are you, anyway? That's not purple, Mary, that color up there is (*very grand*) mauve.

All day today it's felt like Thanksgiving. Soon, this . . . ruination will be blanketed white. You can smell it — can you smell it?

LOUIS: Smell what?

BELIZE: Softness, compliance, forgiveness, grace.

LOUIS: No . . .

BELIZE: I can't help you learn that. I can't help you, Louis. You're not my business. (*He exits.*)

(*Louis puts his head in his hands, inadvertently touching his cut forehead.*)

LOUIS: Ow FUCK! (*He stands slowly, looks towards where Belize exited.*) Smell what?

(*He looks both ways to be sure no one is watching, then inhales deeply, and is surprised.*) Huh. Snow.

Scene 3

(*Same day. Harper in a very white, cold place, with a brilliant blue sky above; a delicate snowfall. She is dressed in a beautiful snowsuit. The sound of the sea, faint.*)

HARPER: Snow! Ice! Mountains of ice! Where am I? I . . .

I feel better, I do, I . . . feel better. There are ice crystals in my lungs, wonderful and sharp. And the snow smells like cold, crushed peaches. And there's something . . . some current of blood in the wind, how strange, it has that iron taste.

MR. LIES: Ozone.

HARPER: Ozone! Wow! Where am I?

MR. LIES: The Kingdom of Ice, the bottommost part of the world.

HARPER (*looking around, then realizing*): Antarctica. This is Antarctica!

MR. LIES: Cold shelter for the shattered. No sorrow here, tears freeze.

HARPER: Antarctica, Antarctica, oh boy oh boy, LOOK at this, I. . . . Wow, I must've really snapped the tether, huh?

MR. LIES: Apparently

HARPER: That's great. I want to stay here forever. Set up camp. Build things. Build a city, an enormous city made up of frontier forts, dark wood and green roofs and high gates made of pointed logs and bonfires burning on every street corner. I should build by a river. Where are the forests?

MR. LIES: No timber here. Too cold. Ice, no trees.

HARPER: Oh details! I'm sick of details! I'll plant them and grow them. I'll live off caribou fat, I'll melt it over the bonfires and drink it from long, curved goat-horn cups. It'll be great. I want to make a new world here. So that I never have to go home again.

MR. LIES: As long as it lasts. Ice has a way of melting . . .

HARPER: No. Forever. I can have anything I want here — maybe even companionship, someone who has . . . desire for me. You, maybe.

MR. LIES: It's against the by-laws of the International Order of Travel Agents to get involved with clients. Rules are rules. Anyway, I'm not the one you really want.

HARPER: There isn't anyone . . . maybe an Eskimo. Who could ice-fish for food. And help me build a nest for when the baby comes.

MR. LIES: There are no Eskimo in Antarctica. And you're not really pregnant. You made that up.

HARPER: Well all of this is made up. So if the snow feels cold I'm pregnant. Right? Here, I can be pregnant. And I can have any kind of a baby I want.

MR. LIES: This is a retreat, a vacuum, its virtue is that it lacks everything; deep-freeze for feelings. You can be numb and safe here, that's what you came for. Respect the delicate ecology of your delusions.

HARPER: You mean like no Eskimo in Antarctica.

MR. LIES: Correcto. Ice and snow, no Eskimo. Even hallucinations have laws.

HARPER: Well then who's that?

(*The Eskimo appears.*)

MR. LIES: An Eskimo.

HARPER: An antarctic Eskimo. A fisher of the polar deep.

MR. LIES: There's something wrong with this picture.

(*The Eskimo beckons.*)

HARPER: I'm going to like this place. It's my own National Geographic Special! Oh! Oh! (*She holds her stomach.*) I think . . . I think I felt her kicking. Maybe I'll give birth to a baby covered with thick white fur, and that way she won't be cold. My breasts will be full of hot cocoa so she doesn't get chilly. And if it gets really cold, she'll have a pouch I can crawl into. Like a marsupial. We'll mend together. That's what we'll do; we'll mend.

Scene 4

(*Same day. An abandoned lot in the South Bronx. A homeless Woman is standing near an oil drum in which a fire is burning. Snowfall. Trash around. Hannah enters dragging two heavy suitcases.*)

HANNAH: Excuse me? I said excuse me? Can you tell me where I am? Is this Brooklyn? Do you know a Pineapple Street? Is there some sort of bus or train or . . . ?

I'm lost, I just arrived from Salt Lake. City. Utah? I took the bus that I was told to take and I got off — well it was the very last stop, so I had to get off, and I *asked* the driver was this Brooklyn, and he nodded yes but he was from one of those foreign countries where they think it's good manners to nod at everything even if you have no idea what it is you're nodding at, and in truth I think he spoke no English at all, which I think would make him ineligible for employment on public transportation. The public being English-speaking, mostly. Do you speak English?

(*The Woman nods.*)

HANNAH: I was supposed to be met at the airport by my son. He didn't show and I don't wait more than three and three-quarters hours for *anyone*. I should have been patient, I guess, I. . . . Is this . . .
WOMAN: Bronx.
HANNAH: Is that. . . . The *Bronx*? Well how in the name of Heaven did I get to the Bronx when the bus driver said . . .
WOMAN (*talking to herself*): Slurp slurp slurp will you STOP that disgusting slurping! YOU DISGUSTING SLURPING FEEDING ANIMAL! Feeding yourself, just feeding yourself, what would it matter, to you or to ANYONE, if you just stopped. Feeding. And DIED?

(*Pause.*)

HANNAH: Can you just tell me where I . . .
WOMAN: Why was the Kosciusko Bridge named after a Polack?
HANNAH: I don't know what you're . . .
WOMAN: That was a joke.
HANNAH: Well what's the punchline?
WOMAN: I don't know.
HANNAH (*looking around desperately*): Oh for pete's sake, is there anyone else who . . .
WOMAN (*again, to herself*): Stand further off you fat loathsome whore, you can't have any more of this soup, slurp slurp slurp you animal, and the — I know you'll just go pee it all away and where will you do that? Behind what bush? It's FUCKING COLD out here and I . . .
Oh that's right, because it was supposed to have been a tunnel!
That's not very funny.
Have you read the prophecies of Nostradamus?
HANNAH: Who?
WOMAN: Some guy I went out with once somewhere, Nostradamus. Prophet, outcast, eyes like. . . . Scary shit, he . . .
HANNAH: Shut up. Please. Now I want you to stop jabbering for a minute and pull your wits together and tell me how to get to Brooklyn. Because you know! And you are going to tell me! Because there is no one else around to tell me and I am wet and cold and I am very angry! So I am sorry you're psychotic but just make the effort — take a deep breath — DO IT!

(*Hannah and the Woman breathe together.*)

HANNAH: That's good. Now exhale.

(*They do.*)

HANNAH: Good. Now how do I get to Brooklyn?
WOMAN: Don't know. Never been. Sorry. Want some soup?
HANNAH: Manhattan? Maybe you know . . . I don't suppose you know the location of the Mormon Visitor's . . .
WOMAN: 65th and Broadway.
HANNAH: How do you . . .
WOMAN: Go there all the time. Free movies. Boring, but you can stay all day.
HANNAH: Well. . . . So how do I.
WOMAN: Take the D Train. Next block make a right.
HANNAH: Thank you.
WOMAN: Oh yeah. In the new century I think we will all be insane.

Scene 5

(*Same day. Joe and Roy in the study of Roy's brownstone. Roy is wearing an elegant bathrobe. He has made a considerable effort to look well. He isn't well, and he hasn't succeeded much in looking it.*)

JOE: I can't. The answer's no. I'm sorry.
ROY: Oh, well, apologies . . .
I can't see that there's anyone asking for apologies.

(*Pause.*)

JOE: I'm sorry, Roy.
ROY: Oh, well, apologies.
JOE: My wife is missing, Roy. My mother's coming from Salt Lake to . . . to help look, I guess. I'm supposed to be at the airport now, picking her up but. . . . I just spent two days in a hospital, Roy, with a bleeding ulcer, I was spitting up blood.
ROY: Blood, huh? Look, I'm very busy here and . . .
JOE: It's just a job.
ROY: A job? A *job*? *Washington*! Dumb Utah Mormon hick shit!
JOE: Roy . . .
ROY: *WASHINGTON!* When Washington called me I was younger than you, you think I said "Aw fuck no I can't go I got two fingers up my asshole and a little moral nosebleed to boot!" When Washington calls you my pretty young punk friend you go or you can go fuck yourself sideways 'cause the train has pulled out of the station, and you are *out,* nowhere, out in the cold. Fuck you, Mary Jane, get outta here.
JOE: Just let me . . .
ROY: Explain? Ephemera. You broke my heart. Explain that. Explain that.
JOE: I love you. Roy.
There's so much that I want, to be . . . what you see in me, I want to be a participant in the world, in your world, Roy, I want to be capable of that, I've

tried, really I have but . . . I can't do this. Not because I don't believe in you, but because I believe in you so much, in what you stand for, at heart, the order, the decency. I would give anything to protect you, but. . . . There are laws I can't break. It's too ingrained. It's not me. There's enough damage I've already done.
   Maybe you were right, maybe I'm dead.
ROY: You're not dead, boy, you're a sissy.
   You love me; that's moving, I'm moved. It's nice to be loved. I warned you about her, didn't I, Joe? But you don't listen to me, why, because you say Roy is smart and Roy's a friend but Roy . . . well, he isn't nice, and you wanna be nice. Right? A nice, nice man!
      (*Little pause.*)
   You know what my greatest accomplishment was, Joe, in my life, what I am able to look back on and be proudest of? And I have helped make Presidents and unmake them and mayors and more goddam judges than anyone in NYC ever — AND several million dollars, tax-free — and what do you think means the most to me?
   You ever hear of Ethel Rosenberg? Huh, Joe, huh?
JOE: Well, yeah, I guess I. . . . Yes.
ROY: Yes. Yes. You have heard of Ethel Rosenberg. Yes. Maybe you even read about her in the history books.
   If it wasn't for me, Joe, Ethel Rosenberg would be alive today, writing some personal-advice column for *Ms.* magazine. She isn't. Because during the trial, Joe, I was on the phone every day, talking with the judge . . .
JOE: Roy . . .
ROY: Every day, doing what I do best, talking on the telephone, making sure that timid Yid nebbish on the bench did his duty to America, to history. That sweet unprepossessing woman, two kids, boo-hoo-hoo, reminded us all of our little Jewish mamas — she came this close to getting life; I pleaded till I wept to put her in the chair. Me. I did that. I would have fucking pulled the switch if they'd have let me. Why? Because I fucking hate traitors. Because I fucking hate communists. Was it legal? Fuck legal. Am I a nice man? Fuck nice. They say terrible things about me in the *Nation.* Fuck the *Nation.* You want to be Nice, or you want to be Effective? Make the law, or subject to it. Choose. Your wife chose. A week from today, she'll be back. SHE knows how to get what SHE wants. Maybe I ought to send *her* to Washington.
JOE: I don't believe you.
ROY: Gospel.
JOE: You can't possibly mean what you're saying.
   Roy, you were the Assistant United States Attorney on the Rosenberg case, ex-parte communication with the judge during the trial would be . . . censurable, at least, probably conspiracy and . . . in a case that resulted in execution, it's . . .
ROY: What? Murder?
JOE: You're not well is all.
ROY: What do you mean, not well? Who's not well?

(*Pause.*)

JOE: You said . . .
ROY: No I didn't. I said what?
JOE: Roy, you have cancer.
ROY: No I don't.

(*Pause.*)

JOE: You told me you were dying.
ROY: What the fuck are you talking about, Joe? I never said that. I'm in perfect health. There's not a goddam thing wrong with me.
      (*He smiles.*)
   Shake?

(*Joe hesitates. He holds out his hand to Roy. Roy pulls Joe into a close, strong clinch.*)

ROY (*more to himself than to Joe*): It's OK that you hurt me because I love you, baby Joe. That's why I'm so rough on you.

(*Roy releases Joe. Joe backs away a step or two.*)

ROY: Prodigal son. The world will wipe its dirty hands all over you.
JOE: It already has, Roy.
ROY: Now go.

(*Roy shoves Joe, hard. Joe turns to leave. Roy stops him, turns him around.*)

ROY (*smoothing Joe's lapels, tenderly*): I'll always be here, waiting for you . . .
      (*Then again, with sudden violence, he pulls Joe close, violently.*)
   What did you want from me, what was all this, what do you want, treacherous ungrateful little . . .

(*Joe, very close to belting Roy, grabs him by the front of his robe, and propels him across the length of the room. He holds Roy at arm's length, the other arm ready to hit.*)

ROY (*laughing softly, almost pleading to be hit*): Transgress a little, Joseph.

(*Joe releases Roy.*)

ROY: There are so many laws; find one you can break.

(*Joe hesitates, then leaves, backing out. When Joe has gone, Roy doubles over in great pain, which he's been hiding throughout the scene with Joe.*)

ROY: Ah, Christ . . .
   Andy! Andy! Get in here! Andy!

(*The door opens, but it isn't Andy. A small Jewish Woman dressed modestly in a fifties hat and coat stands in the doorway. The room darkens.*)

ROY: Who the fuck are you? The new nurse?

(*The figure in the doorway says nothing. She stares at Roy. A pause. Roy looks at her carefully, gets up, crosses to her. He crosses back to the chair, sits heavily.*)

ROY: Aw, fuck. Ethel.

ETHEL ROSENBERG (*her manner is friendly, her voice is ice-cold*): You don't look good, Roy.

ROY: Well, Ethel. I don't feel good.

ETHEL ROSENBERG: But you lost a lot of weight. That suits you. You were heavy back then. Zaftig, mit hips.

ROY: I haven't been that heavy since 1960. We were all heavier back then, before the body thing started. Now I look like a skeleton. They stare.

ETHEL ROSENBERG: The shit's really hit the fan, huh, Roy?

(*Little pause. Roy nods.*)

ETHEL ROSENBERG: Well the fun's just started.

ROY: What is this, Ethel, Halloween? You trying to scare me?

(*Ethel says nothing.*)

ROY: Well you're wasting your time! I'm scarier than you any day of the week! So beat it, Ethel! BOOO! BETTER DEAD THAN RED! Somebody trying to shake me up? HAH HAH! From the throne of God in heaven to the belly of hell, you can all fuck yourselves and then go jump in the lake because I'M NOT AFRAID OF YOU OR DEATH OR HELL OR ANYTHING!

ETHEL ROSENBERG: Be seeing you soon, Roy. Julius sends his regards.

ROY: Yeah, well send this to Julius!

(*He flips the bird in her direction, stands and moves towards her. Halfway across the room he slumps to the floor, breathing laboriously, in pain.*)

ETHEL ROSENBERG: You're a very sick man, Roy.

ROY: Oh God . . . ANDY!

ETHEL ROSENBERG: Hmmm. He doesn't hear you, I guess. We should call the ambulance.
    (*She goes to the phone.*)
    Hah! Buttons! Such things they got now.
    What do I dial, Roy?

(*Pause. Roy looks at her, then:*)

ROY: 911.

ETHEL ROSENBERG (*dials the phone*): It sings!
    (*Imitating dial tones.*) La la la . . .
    Huh.
    Yes, you should please send an ambulance to the home of Mister Roy Cohn, the famous lawyer.
    What's the address, Roy?

ROY (*a beat, then*): 244 East 87th.

ETHEL ROSENBERG: 244 East 87th Street. No apartment number, he's got the whole building.
    My name? (*A beat.*) Ethel Greenglass Rosenberg.
    (*Small smile.*) Me? No I'm not related to Mr. Cohn. An old friend.
    (*She hangs up.*)
    They said a minute.

ROY: I have all the time in the world.

ETHEL ROSENBERG: You're immortal.

ROY: I'm immortal. Ethel. (*He forces himself to stand.*)
    I have *forced* my way into history. I ain't never gonna die.

ETHEL ROSENBERG (*a little laugh, then*): History is about to crack wide open. Millennium approaches.

Scene 6

(*Late that night. Prior's bedroom. Prior 1 watching Prior in bed, who is staring back at him, terrified. Tonight Prior 1 is dressed in weird alchemical robes and hat over his historical clothing and he carries a long palm-leaf bundle.*)

PRIOR 1: Tonight's the night! Aren't you excited? Tonight she arrives! Right through the roof! Ha-adam, Ha-gadol . . .

FAR LEFT: Ron Liebman as Roy Cohn in the Broadway production of *Angels in America: Millennium Approaches*. LEFT: Scene from the end of *Angels in America: Millennium Approaches*.

PRIOR 2 (*appearing, similarly attired*): Lumen! Phosphor! Fluor! Candle! An unending billowing of scarlet and . . .

PRIOR: Look. Garlic. A mirror. Holy water. A crucifix. FUCK OFF! Get the fuck out of my room! GO!

PRIOR 1 (*to Prior 2*): Hard as a hickory knob, I'll bet.

PRIOR 2: We all tumesce when they approach. We wax full, like moons.

PRIOR 1: Dance.

PRIOR: Dance?

PRIOR 1: Stand up, dammit, give us your hands, dance!

PRIOR 2: Listen . . .

(*A lone oboe begins to play a little dance tune.*)

PRIOR 2: Delightful sound. Care to dance?

PRIOR: Please leave me alone, please just let me sleep . . .

PRIOR 2: Ah, he wants someone familiar. A partner who knows his steps. (*To Prior.*) Close your eyes. Imagine . . .

PRIOR: I don't . . .

PRIOR 2: Hush. Close your eyes.

(*Prior does.*)

PRIOR 2: Now open them.

(*Prior does. Louis appears. He looks gorgeous. The music builds gradually into a full-blooded, romantic dance tune.*)

PRIOR: Lou.

LOUIS: Dance with me.

PRIOR: I can't, my leg, it hurts at night . . .
    Are you . . . a ghost, Lou?

LOUIS: No. Just spectral. Lost to myself. Sitting all day on cold park benches. Wishing I could be with you. Dance with me, babe . . .

(*Prior stands up. The leg stops hurting. They begin to dance. The music is beautiful.*)

PRIOR 1 (*to Prior 2*): Hah. Now I see why he's got no children. He's a sodomite.

PRIOR 2: Oh be quiet, you medieval gnome, and let them dance.

PRIOR 1: I'm not interfering, I've done my bit. Hooray, hooray, the messenger's come, now I'm blowing off. I don't like it here.

(*Prior 1 vanishes.*)

PRIOR 2: The twentieth century. Oh dear, the world has gotten so terribly, terribly old.

(*Prior 2 vanishes. Louis and Prior waltz happily. Lights fade back to normal. Louis vanishes.*
Prior dances alone.
Then suddenly, the sound of wings fills the room.)

Scene 7

(*Split scene. Prior alone in his apartment; Louis alone in the park.*
Again, a sound of beating wings.)

PRIOR: Oh don't come in here don't come in . . . LOUIS!! No. My name is Prior Walter, I am . . . the scion of an ancient line, I am . . . abandoned I . . . no, my name is . . . is . . . Prior and I live . . . *here and now,* and . . . in the dark, in the dark, the Recording Angel opens its hundred eyes and snaps the spine of the Book of Life and . . . hush! Hush!
    I'm talking nonsense, I . . .
    No more mad scene, hush, hush.

(*Louis in the park on a bench. Joe approaches, stands at a distance. They stare at each other, then Louis turns away.*)

LOUIS: Do you know the story of Lazarus?

JOE: Lazarus?

LOUIS: Lazarus. I can't remember what happens, exactly.

JOE: I don't. . . . Well, he was dead, Lazarus, and Jesus breathed life into him. He brought him back from death.

LOUIS: Come here often?

JOE: No. Yes. Yes.

LOUIS: Back from the dead. You believe that really happened?

JOE: I don't know anymore what I believe.

LOUIS: This is quite a coincidence. Us meeting.

JOE: I followed you.
    From work. I . . . followed you here.

(*Pause.*)

LOUIS: You followed me.
    You probably saw me that day in the washroom and thought: there's a sweet guy, sensitive, cries for friends in trouble.

JOE: Yes.

LOUIS: You thought maybe I'll cry for you.

JOE: Yes.

LOUIS: Well I fooled you. Crocodile tears. Nothing . . . (*He touches his heart, shrugs.*)

(*Joe reaches tentatively to touch Louis's face.*)

LOUIS (*pulling back*): What are you doing? Don't do that.

JOE (*withdrawing his hand*): Sorry. I'm sorry.

LOUIS: I'm . . . just not . . . I think, if you touch me, your hand might fall off or something. Worse things have happened to people who have touched me.

JOE: Please.
    Oh, boy . . .
    Can I . . .
    I . . . want . . . to touch you. Can I please just touch you . . . um, here?
    (*He puts his hand on one side of Louis's face. He holds it there.*)
    I'm going to hell for doing this.

LOUIS: Big deal. You think it could be any worse than New York City?
    (*He puts his hand on Joe's hand. He takes Joe's hand away from his face, holds it for a moment, then:*) Come on.

JOE: Where?

LOUIS: Home. With me.

JOE: This makes no sense. I mean I don't know you.

LOUIS: Likewise.

JOE: And what you do know about me you don't like.

LOUIS: The Republican stuff?

JOE: Yeah, well for starters.

LOUIS: I don't not like that. I *hate* that.

JOE: So why on earth should we . . .

(*Louis goes to Joe and kisses him.*)

LOUIS: Strange bedfellows. I don't know. I never made it with one of the damned before.
    I would really rather not have to spend tonight alone.

JOE: I'm a pretty terrible person, Louis.

LOUIS: Lou.

JOE: No, I really really am. I don't think I deserve being loved.

LOUIS: There? See? We already have a lot in common.

(*Louis stands, begins to walk away. He turns, looks back at Joe. Joe follows. They exit.*)

(*Prior listens. At first no sound, then once again, the sound of beating wings, frighteningly near.*)

PRIOR: That sound, that sound, it. . . . What is that, like birds or something, like a *really* big bird, I'm frightened, I . . . no, no fear, find the anger, find the . . .

anger, my blood is clean, my brain is fine, I can handle pressure, I am a gay man and I am used to pressure, to trouble, I am tough and strong and. . . . Oh. Oh my goodness. I . . . (*He is washed over by an intense sexual feeling.*) Ooohhhh. . . . I'm hot, I'm . . . so . . . aw Jeez what is going on here I . . . must have a fever I . . .

(*The bedside lamp flickers wildly as the bed begins to roll forward and back. There is a deep bass creaking and groaning from the bedroom ceiling, like the timbers of a ship under immense stress, and from above a fine rain of plaster dust.*)

PRIOR: OH!
    PLEASE, OH PLEASE! Something's coming in here, I'm scared, I don't like this at all, something's approaching and I. . . . OH!

(*There is a great blaze of triumphal music, heralding. The light turns an extraordinary harsh, cold, pale blue, then a rich, brilliant warm golden color, then a hot, bil-ious green, and then finally a spectacular royal purple. Then silence.*)

PRIOR (*an awestruck whisper*): God almighty . . .
    Very Steven Spielberg.

(*A sound, like a plummeting meteor, tears down from very, very far above the earth, hurtling at an incredible velocity towards the bedroom; the light seems to be sucked out of the room as the projectile approaches; as the room reaches darkness, we hear a terrifying CRASH as something immense strikes earth; the whole building shudders and a part of the bedroom ceiling, lots of plaster and lathe and wiring, crashes to the floor. And then in a shower of unearthly white light, spreading great opalescent gray-silver wings, the Angel descends into the room and floats above the bed.*)

ANGEL: Greetings, Prophet;
    The Great Work begins:
    The Messenger has arrived.

(*Blackout.*)

COMMENTARY

Andrea Bernstein
INTERVIEW WITH TONY KUSHNER   *1995*

> *Andrea Bernstein, a freelance cultural critic, engaged Tony Kushner in a discussion of the politics in his plays. Kushner's responses to her questions establish his credentials as a left-thinking critic of contemporary political life. His discussion of his work is centered much more in political reality than it is in dramatic technique or concern for theater. Yet Kushner is able to zero in on the dramatic moment and present contemporary politics as a dialectical struggle.*

Tony Kushner, a gay Jewish socialist who was raised in Louisiana, won a Pulitzer Prize and two Tony Awards for his two-part, seven-hour Broadway production of *Angels in America: A Gay Fantasia on National Themes*. Other plays, *A Bright Room Called Day* (1985) and *Slavs!* (1994), are also concerned with the moral responsibilities of people in politically repressive times. Such concerns may be especially relevant in America today, where, as he observes: "What used to be called liberal is now called radical, what used to be called radical is now called insane, what used to be called reactionary is now called moderate, and what used to be called insane is now called solid conservative thinking."

Q: Angels in America opened on Broadway just months after the Clinton inauguration. It ends with a very hopeful speech about healing. Do you still feel that hope?

A: You have to have hope. It's irresponsible to give *false* hope, which I think a lot of playwrights are guilty of. But I also think it's irresponsible to simply be a nihilist, which quite a lot of playwrights, especially playwrights younger than me, have become guilty of. I don't believe you would bother to write a play if you really had no hope. That passage was one of the very first things I ever wrote when I was working on *Angels.* I read it to the woman who I was originally writing the part of the angel for, who died of breast cancer before the play was finished. In one of my last conversations with her, she told me that she thought about that image a lot and that she hoped I would include it in the play. I think I wouldn't have included it otherwise, but I'm glad I did now.

Q: Angels in America was a political play — and that's something Americans and critics frequently resist. How did you overcome that resistance?

A: What I found in the audience response is a huge hunger for political issues and political discussion. So I always wonder: Is it that Americans don't like politics, or is it that so much theater that is political isn't well-done? One of the things I learned in *Slavs!* is that it's much easier to talk about being gay than it is to talk about being a socialist. People are afraid of socialism, and plays that deal with economics are scarier to them. I'll learn more about that — my next three plays are all about money.

Also, *Angels* is very entertaining. It does things formally that are new, and people were excited by the size and the scope. It's a good play and that makes all the difference.

Thelma and Louise, for instance, is a really terrific movie, and genuinely left in its political sensibilities. It's well-made, so the fact that it is unquestionably coming from a feminist perspective didn't make it absolutely marginal the way you would expect such a film to be. It had guns — that probably helped.

Q: People loved *Forrest Gump,* too.

A: People shouldn't trust artists and they shouldn't trust art. Part of the fun of art is that it invites you to interpret it.

There's a very complicated relationship between form and content and between aesthetics and politics. Good politics will produce good aesthetics, really good politics will produce really good aesthetics, and really good aesthetics, if somebody's really asking the hard questions and answering them honestly, they'll probably produce truth, which is to say progressive politics.

Q: Is it hard to write characters that are not caricatures and to overcome the barrier that people have about listening to politics from a character on stage?

A: I think that a character's politics have to live in the same sort of relationship to the character's psyche that people's politics live in relationship to their own psyches. People are never consistent. People will always do surprising things, both good and bad, and the way that people surprise themselves and their audience are the most interesting moments of human behavior. The space between what we'd like to be and what we actually are is where you find out the most interesting things.

Q: Do you see your plays as part of a political movement?

A: I do. I would hate to write anything that wasn't. I would like my plays to be of use to progressive people. I think preaching to the converted is exactly what art ought to do.

I am happiest when people who are politically engaged in the world say, "Your play meant a lot to me; it helped me think about something, or made me feel like I wasn't the only person who felt this way."

It's the way you feel when you go to a demo, which is the only way to keep sane a lot of the time. You need to remind yourself there are many bodies who are as angry about something as you are.

When I teach writing, I always tell my students you should assume that the audience you're writing for is smarter than you. You can't write if you don't think they're on your side, because then you start to yell at them or preach down to them.

Q: The character Prelapsarianov — the "world's oldest living Bolshevik"— gives the same speech in both *Angels* and *Slavs!:* "How are we to proceed without theory? Is it enough to reject the past, is it wise to move forward in this blind fashion, without the cold brilliant light of theory to guide the way? . . . You who live in this sour little age cannot imagine the sheer grandeur of the prospect we gazed upon."

A: In both *Perestroika* [part two of *Angels*] and *Slavs!,* the whole play proceeds from the question: If you don't know where you're going, can you move? And do you even have a choice, or do you just dive in and work it out as you're going?

That speech came out of a fight I had with my friend Oskar Eustis about Gorbachev. Oskar's point, which became the basis of Prelapsarianov's speech, is that if you don't have a theory to start with — Gorbachev pretended to be about democratic socialism but actually sort of was and sort of wasn't; he was also sort of about preserving the Communist Party power elite — what do you do? It's one of those big conundrums.

Q: So what *do* you do?

A: You can't stay back. The fundamental question is: Are we made by history or do we make history — and the answer is yes. I was rereading Marx's *Eighteenth Brumaire of Louis Bonaparte* recently. The whole tradition in socialist struggle is looking to the past for an antecedent form upon which the present revolutionary response is to be modeled. We may need to stop doing that.

Q: Why does the play *Slavs!* end with the question: "What is to be done?"

A: I wanted someone to ask the question: What if this really is the end of history? What if there really is literally nothing to be done, and we're simply stuck with capitalism — although I don't really think it is a possibility.

I still believe in a dialectical ordering of the universe. There is a dynamic principle at work — it isn't always mechanically moving things toward the good, but there's always either some sort of progress or decay. And there's too much misery in the world. That is not something that can hold.

Q: What do you think is to be done?

A: I'm 38 now. One of the painful rites of passage that everyone on the left goes through is to realize it's a lifelong struggle. What we're dealing with from Nixon on as a counter-reaction to the '60s is a very widespread, long-term historical trend. It's going to take many years and probably a few decades to reverse. People need to be willing to take an issue that they feel passionately about, address themselves to it as extensively as they are capable of and build common cause between issue groups.

Everybody on the left needs to start talking about how to create, first on local levels and eventually on a national level, a third party or at least a party that could establish some kind of position in Congress. That's the eternal dream of the left.

Q: You think there's no hope for revitalizing the Democratic Party?

A: It's a waste of time at this point. There's a famous story about Paul Wellstone refusing to shake Jesse Helms' hand and being chastised by everyone in the Senate because he wouldn't do it — he was told this is a gentlemen's club where we're all colleagues. That's what's wrong.

Q: One of the characters in *A Bright Room Called Day* keeps saying — as Nazism progressively snatches power and the Weimar Republic falls — that each turn for the worse would be the essential spur for people to rise up and oppose fascism. That didn't happen. Do you see parallels today?

A: You don't want to be opportunistic about it and say, "Oh, goody, millions of people are going to be thrown out of their homes — now we'll really get things cooking." It's like people saying the AIDS epidemic helped organize the gay and lesbian community.

Q: Speaking of which, there's a lot of discussion now about the second wave of the AIDS epidemic, and about gay men not practicing safer sex. Where do you weigh in?

A: It's very difficult to ask people to abstain from pleasure indefinitely, especially sexual erotic pleasure, which is so incredibly important to human beings and the enjoyment of which among homosexuals is so much of a political battlefield. There is absolutely no question that safer sex is not as gratifying and that given all the despair and the unbelievably imponderable weight of loss that the community has had to deal with, self-destructive behaviors are going to be engaged in.

Q: Do you think the gay community should be discussing this publicly?

A: Of course it's going to be discussed publicly. But you have to be smart. When you make a public utterance you are responsible for being responsible. We're still an embattled community, and if you're stupid about it you'll give aid to the enemy.

Q: Do you have that conundrum as a playwright?

A: You have to say: What am I feeding into? I think you should ask yourself that question and then make the decision based on the answers you come up with. I regret having made the only black person in *Angels* a nurse; that was an inept thing to do.

I was very scared about writing a play where there's a couple, one has AIDS and the other walks out. I thought, this is transgressive and scary and am I going to become public enemy number one in the gay community for having written a character like Louis?

On the other hand, you have to be willing to scare the horses. You have to be interesting and you have to be daring and you have to be willing to write things that shock. Shock is part of art. Art that's polite is not much fun.

Anna Deavere Smith

Anna Deavere Smith was born in 1950. Besides teaching at Stanford University where she was the Ann O'Day Maples Professor of the Arts, and at New York University, she is a poet, director, playwright, and a notable actor, appearing in the films *Philadelphia* (1993) and *The American President* (1995). She has also taught at Carnegie-Mellon University, Yale University, New York University, in the Drama Division of the University of Southern California, and at American Conservatory Theatre, her alma mater.

She is well known for her work on a series of theatrical pieces that she calls *On the Road: A Search for American Character,* the first of which was produced in Berkeley, California, in 1983, followed by *Aye, Aye, Aye, I'm Integrated,* a 1984 off-Broadway production. She has also done a one-woman show called *A Birthday Card and Aunt Julia's Shoes.* Her sensational *Fires in the Mirror: Crown Heights, Brooklyn and Other Identities* (1991), the thirteenth work in the *On the Road* series, was a one-woman show in which she played all the roles. It won the Obie award, was a runner-up for the Pulitzer Prize in drama in 1992, and was shown on the Public Broadcasting System in 1993.

Smith became nationally known for *Fires in the Mirror* and for developing what the *New York Times* called "documentary theater, which has the immediacy of live drama and the fluidity of film." Smith's technique is to interview many people connected with a traumatic social event; she then refines their dialogue and enacts it herself, using a minimum of makeup, wigs, costumes, and props. She relies heavily on her body language, on gesture and speech pattern, and on facial expression to create character. Smith is a performance artist as well as a playwright. Her dynamic approach to the roles convinces her audience that she has "become" the parts she plays, from gang members to city officials, from prostitutes to housewives. She portrays African American men, Asian merchants, white suburbanites — and all convincingly.

In 1993, Smith presented *Twilight: Los Angeles 1992,* a performance piece developed in a fashion similar to *Fires in the Mirror.* This play is based on reactions to the Rodney King beating and the subsequent riots in Los Angeles after the police, who were videotaped beating King, were declared not guilty. This was one of the worst riots in the United States since 1960 and was widely televised by news helicopters. *Twilight: Los Angeles 1992* was produced at the Joseph Papp Public Theater in New York, directed by George C. Wolfe, one of the characters in *Fires in the Mirror.* In 1996, Smith was awarded a MacArthur Fellowship, which gave her financial support for five years to work on her creative projects.

Currently, Smith is professor at the Tisch School at New York University. Her most recent plays are *House Arrest* (1997) and *Piano* (2000). She appears periodically in the television series *The West Wing,* playing a military advisor to the president. Her film career continues as well, with such recent credits as Mrs. Silk in *The Human Stain* (2003), the film made of Philip Roth's novel, and the headmistress in *Living the Lie* (2004).

FIRES IN THE MIRROR: CROWN HEIGHTS, BROOKLYN AND OTHER IDENTITIES

Because this is a performance piece performed by a single actress, Anna Deavere Smith, it depends on the skills of impersonation and representation that are unique to her. As a project, it resembles a number of documentary efforts that have developed since she began her work. *The Laramie Project* (2002), produced first as a play and then as a cable-television film, records in a similar fashion the reactions of the town of Laramie, Wyoming, to the murder of Matthew Shepard, a young man killed because he was gay. In the film adaptation, however, the characters are interviewed directly and no effort is made to reproduce Smith's style of playing all the parts herself. A gifted actress, Smith is able to adopt convincing personas for all the characters she represents, even those who, like Al Sharpton, presidential candidate in 2004, are well-known television personalities. Smith has inspired a number of other younger actors; one such actor is John Leguizamo (b. 1964), who produced the one-man *Mambo Mouth* and *Spic-o-Rama,* both performance pieces in the style of Anna Deavere Smith.

Fires in the Mirror portrays reactions to terrible events in Crown Heights, Brooklyn, in August 1991. The Grand Rebbe, Menachem M. Schneerson — the leader of the orthodox Jewish Lubavitch Hasids — was riding in a cavalcade following a visit to a cemetery when one of the three cars in the cavalcade lost its way and raced through a red light. The result was a crash that killed a black boy named Gavin Cato, age 7, and injured his cousin, Angela Cato. The details of the event are narrated in the play, but the most important points are that Gavin Cato was killed and that the gathering crowd of African Americans realized a Jewish driver had run the children down. Two ambulances, the first from a private Hasidic service and the second from the city, arrived on the scene within minutes. The accounts of what followed are conflicting. Police claim they ordered the Hasidic ambulance to tend to the Jewish men injured in the crash and leave the scene immediately to defuse the situation, because the other ambulance had already arrived and an angry, distraught crowd was growing. The city ambulance did treat the children, but word quickly spread among the crowd that the Hasidic ambulance had intentionally ignored the two black children in favor of treating the white Jewish men. In reaction, a riot occurred in which a great deal of anti-Jewish sentiment was voiced and an innocent Jewish student coming to the scene, Yankel Rosenbaum, was stabbed to death by an African American, Lemrick Nelson. The tensions between the orthodox Hasidic and the African American communities, who share the Crown Heights neighborhood, had been significant up to that point, but they did not turn violent until that evening in August.

In her retelling of these events, Smith portrays people who are well known in the larger New York community as well as people who are essentially residents or bystanders. She treats them with equal authority and gives them equal weight in the development of the play. They speak frankly, much more honestly than one would expect if they thought they were on a television news program. They voice anti-Jewish and anti-black sentiments just as they generalize broadly on what they perceive to be the characteristic behavior of the various ethnic groups in the community. They discuss the police, rap music, religion, violence, and all the issues that are central to their concerns in Crown Heights.

In presenting the views and thoughts of each character, Smith begins by describing them physically. She adopts their clothing and their style, and she "becomes" the character as she speaks. However, in the headnotes to the characters, she also explains who they are and what they were doing and wearing when the interview took place. She begins with a statement that seems to be one-half of a telephone conversation with playwright Ntozake Shange (Paulette Williams, b. 1948), author of *For Colored Girls Who Have Considered Suicide When the Rainbow is Enuf* (1975). Her focus is on the issue of identity, which is central to the entire play. The characters generally feel that the ethnic groups are identifiable in specific ways and that their identities are recognizable, defined, and permanently established.

The presentations of other characters focus on general political reactions, such as those of Al Sharpton, and on an effort to simply get the facts down, as in Rabbi Spielman's conversation. Letty Cottin Pogrebin provides background on the Nazi Holocaust in Europe in which Jews were gassed and murdered wholesale, while Professor Jeffries discusses the problems associated with the making of the film *Roots,* which attempts to portray the heritage of African Americans and the legacy of slavery. Each group has paid a terrible price for simple survival, but instead of seeing themselves as sharing a similar cultural tragedy, they see themselves as very different.

On the one hand, this play is sociological in nature — and perhaps would even be a sociological document if each role were played by the original speaker. In the hands of Smith, however, sociology is transcended. Her sense of drama, the shaping of the material, and the brilliance of her portrayals are mesmerizing and elevate the newslike material into a universal human experience pertinent to any physical locale in which different ethnic groups find themselves in uneasy peace or occasional conflict.

Fires in the Mirror: Crown Heights, Brooklyn and Other Identities in Performance

Anna Deavere Smith performed all thirty roles herself in the PBS television production in 1993. She went on to perform selections in Cambridge, Massachusetts, that same year. Then in 1996 she produced *Fires in the Mirror* with the Trinity Repertory Theatre in Providence, Rhode Island, using two actresses, one white and one black, to perform the roles. Brian Kulick directed and Barbara Meek and Becky London acted. The play has been performed frequently by both professional and amateur groups, although, when such groups perform, they use a number of actors taking on several roles each. The Lab! student theater company at the University of North Carolina produced the play in 1999; Mark Franceschini directed the production by the Silver Spring Stage in Maryland in June 2003. The play has a wide appeal and offers powerful dramatic portrayals.

Anna Deavere Smith (b. 1950)

FIRES IN THE MIRROR: CROWN HEIGHTS, BROOKLYN AND OTHER IDENTITIES

1991

This book is dedicated to the residents of Crown Heights, Brooklyn, and in the memory of Gavin Cato and Yankel Rosenbaum

The Characters

NTOZAKE SHANGE, *Playwright, poet, novelist.*

ANONYMOUS LUBAVITCHER WOMAN, *Preschool teacher.*

GEORGE C. WOLFE, *Playwright, director, producing director of the New York Shakespeare Festival.*

AARON M. BERNSTEIN, *Physicist at Massachusetts Institute of Technology.*

ANONYMOUS GIRL, *Junior high school black girl of Haitian descent. Lives in Brooklyn near Crown Heights.*

REVEREND AL SHARPTON, *Well-known New York activist, minister.*

RIVKAH SIEGAL, *Lubavitcher woman, graphic designer.*

ANGELA DAVIS, *Author, orator, activist, scholar. Professor in the History of Consciousness Department at the University of California, Santa Cruz.*

MONIQUE "BIG MO" MATTHEWS, *Los Angeles rapper.*

LEONARD JEFFRIES, *Professor of African American Studies at City University of New York, former head of the department.*

LETTY COTTIN POGREBIN, *Author* Deborah, Golda, and Me. *One of the founding editors of* Ms. *magazine.*

CONRAD MOHAMMED, *New York minister for the Honorable Louis Farrakhan.*

ROBERT SHERMAN, *Director, Mayor of the City of New York's Increase the Peace Corps.*

RABBI JOSEPH SPIELMAN, *Spokesperson in the Lubavitcher community.*

THE REVEREND CANON DOCTOR HERON SAM, *Pastor, St. Mark's, Crown Heights Church.*

ANONYMOUS YOUNG MAN #1, *Crown Heights resident.*

MICHAEL S. MILLER, *Executive Director at the Jewish Community Relations Council.*

HENRY RICE, *Crown Heights resident.*

NORMAN ROSENBAUM, *Brother of Yankel Rosenbaum. A barrister from Australia.*

ANONYMOUS YOUNG MAN #2, *African American young man, late teens, early twenties. Resident of Crown Heights.*

SONNY CARSON, *Activist.*

RABBI SHEA HECHT, *Lubavitcher rabbi, spokesperson.*

RICHARD GREEN, *Director, Crown Heights Youth Collective. Codirector Project CURE, a Black-Hasidic basketball team that developed after the riots.*

ROSLYN MALAMUD, *Lubavitcher resident of Crown Heights.*

REUVEN OSTROV, *Lubavitcher male; at the time of the riot, was seventeen years old. Worked as assistant chaplain at Kings County Hospital.*

CARMEL CATO, *Father of Gavin Cato. Crown Heights resident, originally from Guyana.*

IDENTITY • *Ntozake Shange*
The Desert

(This interview was done on the phone at about 4:00 P.M. Philadelphia time. The only cue Ntozake gave about her physical appearance was that she took one earring off to talk on the phone. On stage we placed her upstage center in an arm chair, smoking. Then we placed her standing, downstage.)

Hummmm.

Identity —

it, is, uh . . . in a way it's, um . . . it's sort of, it's uh . . .

it's a psychic sense of place

it's a way of knowing I'm not a rock or that tree?

I'm this other living creature over here?

And it's a way of knowing that no matter where I put myself

that I am not necessarily

what's around me.

I am part of my surroundings

and I become separate from them

and it's being able to make those differentiations clearly

that lets us have an identity

and what's inside our identity

is everything that's ever happened to us.

Everything that's ever happened

to us as well as our responses to it

'cause we might be alone in a trance state,

someplace like the desert

and we begin to feel as though

we are part of the desert —

which we are right at that minute —

but we are not the desert,

uh . . .

we are part of the desert,

and when we go home

we take with us that part of the desert that the desert gave us,

but we're still not the desert.

It's an important differentiation to make because you
      don't know
what you're giving if you don't know what you have
      and you don't
know what you're taking if you don't know what's
      yours and what's
somebody else's.

Anonymous Lubavitcher° Woman
Static

(*This interview was actually done on the phone. Based
on what she told me she was doing, and on the three visits I had made to her home for other interviews, I
devised this physical scene. A Lubavitcher woman, in a
wig, and loose-fitting clothes. She is in her mid-thirties.
She is folding clothes. There are several children around.
Three boys of different ages are lying together on the
couch. The oldest is reading to the younger two. A teenage girl with long hair, a button-down-collar shirt, and
skirt is sweeping the floor.*)

Well,
it was um,
getting toward the end of Shabbas,°
like around five in the afternoon,
and it was summertime
and sunset isn't until about eight, nine o'clock,
so there were still quite a few hours left to go
and my baby had been playing with the knobs on the
      stereo system
then all of a sudden he pushed the button —
the *on* button —
and all of a sudden came blaring out,
at full volume,
sort of like a half station
of polka music.
But just like with the static,
it was blaring, blaring
and we can't turn off,
we can't turn off electrical,
you know electricity, on Shabbas.
So um,
uh . . .
there was —
we just were trying to ignore it,
but a young boy that was visiting us,
he was going nuts already, he said
it was giving him such a headache could we do some-
      thing about it,
couldn't we get a baby
to turn it off;
we can't make the baby turn it off but if the baby,
but if a child under three

Lubavitcher: Member of a Hasidic sect of Orthodox Judaism.
Shabbas: The Sabbath.

turns something on or turns something off it's not con-
      sidered against the Torah,
so we put the baby by it and tried to get the baby to turn
      it off,
he just probably made it worse,
so the guest was so uncomfortable that I said I would go
      outside
and see if I can find someone who's not Jewish and see if
      they would
like to —
see if they could turn it off,
so you can have somebody who's not Jewish do a simple
      act like
turning on the light or turning off the light,
and I hope I have the law correct,
but you can ask them to do it directly.
If they wanna do it of their own free will —
and hopefully they would get some benefit from it too,
so I went outside
and I saw
a little
boy in the neighborhood
who I didn't know and didn't know me —
not Jewish, he was black and he wasn't wearing a yar-
      mulke because you can't —
so I went up to him and I said to him
that my radio is on really loud and I can't turn it off,
could he help me,
so he looked at me a little crazy like,
Well?
And I said I don't know what to do,
so he said okay,
so he followed me into the house
and he hears this music on so loud
and so unpleasant
and so
he goes over to the
stereo
and he says, "You see this little button here
that says on and off?
Push that in
and that turns it off."
And I just sort of stood there looking kind of dumb
and then he went and pushed it,
and we laughed that he probably thought:
And people say Jewish people are really smart and they
      don't know
how to turn off their radios.

George C. Wolfe
101 Dalmatians

(*The Mondrian Hotel in Los Angeles. Morning, Sunny.
A very nice room. George is wearing denim jeans, a light
blue denim shirt, and white leather tennis shoes. His
hair is in a ponytail. He wears tortoise/wire spectacles.
He is drinking tea with milk. The tea is served on a tray,*

the cups and teapot are delicate porcelain. George is sit-
ting on a sofa, with his feet up on the coffee table.)

I mean I grew up on a black —
a one-block street —
that was black.
My grandmother lived on that street
my cousins lived around the corner.
I went to this
Black — Black —
private Black grade school
where
I was extraordinary.
Everybody there was extraordinary.
You were told you were extraordinary.
It was very clear
that I could not go to see *101 Dalmatians* at the Capital
    Theatre
because it was segregated.
And at the same time
I was treated like I was the most extraordinary creature
    that had
been born.
So I'm on my street in my house,
at my school —
and I was very spoiled too —
so I was treated like I was this special special creature.
And then I would go beyond a certain point
I was treated like I was insignificant.
Nobody was
hosing me down or calling me nigger.
It was just that I was insignificant.

(Slight pause)

You know what I mean so it was very clear of

(Teacup on saucer strike twice on "very clear")

where my extraordinariness lived.
You know what I mean.
That I was extraordinary as long as I was Black.
But I am — not — going — to place myself

(Pause)

in relationship to your whiteness.
I will talk about your whiteness if we want to talk about
    that.
But I,
but what,
that which,
what I —
what am I saying?
My blackness does not resis — ex — re —
exist in relationship to your whiteness.

(Pause)

You know

(Not really a question, more like a hum)

(Slight pause)

it does not exist in relationship to —

it *exists*
it exists.
I come —
you know what I mean —
like I said, I, I, I,
I come from —
it's a very *complex,*
confused,
neu-rotic,
at times destructive
reality, but it is completely
and totally a reality
contained and, and,
and full unto itself.
It's complex.
It's demonic.
It's ridiculous.
It's absurd.
It's evolved.
It's all the stuff.
That's the way I grew up.

(Slight pause)

So that *therefore* —
and then you're White —

(Quick beat)

And then there's a point when,
and then these two things come into contact.

MIRRORS • *Aaron M. Bernstein*
Mirrors and Distortions

(Evening, Cambridge, Massachusetts. Fall. He is a man
in his fifties, wearing a sweater and a shirt with a pen
guard. He is seated at a round wooden table with a low-
hanging lamp.)

Okay, so a mirror is something that reflects light.
It's the simplest instrument to understand,
okay?
So a simple mirror is just a flat
reflecting
substance, like,
for example,
it's a piece of glass which is silvered on the back,
okay?
Now the notion of distortion also goes back into litera-
    ture,
okay?
I'm trying to remember from art —
You probably know better than I.
You know you have a pretty young woman and she
    looks in a mirror
and she's a witch

(He laughs)

because she's evil on the inside.
That's not a real mirror,

as everyone knows —
you see the inner thing.
Now that really goes back in literature.
So everyone understood that mirrors don't distort,
so that was a play
not on words
but a concept.
But physicists do
talk about distortion.
It's a big
subject, distortions.
I'll give you an example —
if you wanna see the
stars
you make a big
reflecting mirror —
that's one of the ways —
you make a big telescope
so you can gather in a lot of light
and then it focuses at a point
and then there's always something called the circle of
    confusion.
So if ya don't make the thing perfectly spherical or per-
    fectly
parabolic
then,
then, uh, if there are errors in the construction
which you can see, it's easy, if it's huge,
then you're gonna have a circle of confusion,
you see?
So that's the reason for making the
telescope as large as you can,
because you want that circle
to seem smaller,
and you want to easily see errors in the construction.
So, you see, in physics it's very practical —
you wanna look up in the heavens
and see the stars as well as you can
without distortion.
If you're counting stars, for example,
and two look like one,
you've blown it.

HAIR • *Anonymous Girl*
        Look in the Mirror

(*Morning. Spring. A teen-age Black girl of Haitian descent. She has hair which is straightened, and is wearing
a navy blue jumper and a white shirt. She is seated in a
stairwell at her junior high school in Brooklyn.*)

When I look in the mirror . . .
I don't know.
How did I find out I was Black . . .

(*Tongue sound*)

When I grew up and I look in the mirror and saw I was
    Black.

When I look at my parents,
That's how I knew I was Black.
Look at my skin.
You Black?
Black is beautiful.
I don't know.
That's what I always say.
I think White is beautiful too.
But I think Black is beautiful too.
In my class nobody is White, everybody's Black,
and some of them is Hispanic.
In my class
you can't call any of them Puerto Ricans.
They despise Puerto Ricans, I don't know why.
They think that Puerto Ricans are stuck up and every-
    thing.
They say, Oh my Gosh my nail broke, look at that cute
    guy and everything.
But they act like that themselves.
They act just like White girls.
Black girls is not like that.
Please, you should be in my class.
Like they say that Puerto Ricans act like that
and they don't see that they act like that themselves.
Black girls, they do bite off the Spanish girls,
they bite off of your clothes.
You don't know what that means? biting off?
Like biting off somebody's clothes
Like cop, following,
and last year they used to have a lot of girls like that.
They come to school with a style, right?
And if they see another girl with that style?
Oh my gosh look at her.
What she think she is,
she tryin' to bite off of me in some way
no don't be bitin' off of my sneakers
or like that.
Or doin' a hairstyle
I mean Black people are into hairstyles.
So they come to school, see somebody with a certain
    style,
they say uh-huh I'm gonna get me one just like that uh-
    huh,
that's the way Black people are
Yea-ah!
They don't like people doing that to them
and they do that to other people,
so the Black girls they won't follow the Spanish girls.
The Spanish girls don't bite off of us.
Some of the Black girls follow them.
But they don't mind
They don't care.
They follow each other.
Like there's three girls in my class,
they from the Dominican Republic.
They all stick together like glue.
They all three best friends.
They don't follow nobody,
like there's none of them lead or anything.

They don't hang around us either.
They're
by themselves.

The Reverend Al Sharpton
Me and James's Thing

(Early afternoon. Fall. A small room that is a part of a suite of offices in a building on West Fifty-seventh Street and Seventh Avenue in New York. A very large Black man with straightened hair. Reverend Sharpton's hair is in the style of James Brown's hair. He is wearing a suit, colorful tie, and a gold medallion that was given to him by Martin Luther King, Jr. Reverend Sharpton has a pinky ring, a very resonant voice even in this small room. There is a very built, very tall man who sits behind me during the interview. Reverend Sharpton's face is much younger, and more innocent than it appears to be in the media. His humor is in his face. He is very direct. The interview only lasts fifteen minutes because he had been called out of a meeting in progress to do the interview.)

James Brown° raised me.
Uh . . .
I never had a father.
My father left when I was ten.
James Brown took me to the beauty parlor one day
and made my hair like his.
And made me promise
to wear it like that
'til I die.
It's a personal family thing
between me and James Brown.
I always wanted a father
and he filled that void.
And the strength that he's demonstrated —
I don't know anybody that reached his heights,
and then had to go as low as he did and come back.
And I think that if anybody I met in life deserved that
    type of
tribute from
somebody
that he wanted a kid
to look like him
and be like his son . . .
I just came home from spending a weekend with him
    now,
uh, uh,
I think James deserved that.
And just like
he was the father I never had,
his kids never even visited him when he went to jail.
So I was like the kid he never had.
And if I had to choose between arguing with people
    about my

James Brown: Singer (b. 1933) who helped create the funk musical style out of soul and gospel music. He champions black pride.

hairstyle
or giving him that one tribute
he axed,
I'd rather give him that tribute
because he filled a void for me.
And I really don't give a damn
who doesn't understand it.
The press and everybody do
their thing on that.
It's a personal thing between me and James Brown.
And just like
in other communities
people do their cultural thing
with who they like,
uh,
there's nothing wrong with me doing
that with James.
It's, it's, *us.*
I mean in the fifties it was a slick.
It was acting like White folks.
But today
people don't wear their hair like that.
James and I the only ones out there doing that.
So it's certainlih not
a reaction to Whites.
It's me and James's thing.

Rivkah Siegal
Wigs

(Early afternoon. Spring. The kitchen of an apartment in Crown Heights. A very pretty Lubavitcher woman, with clear eyes and a direct gaze, wearing a wig and a knit sweater, that looks as though it might be hand knit. A round wooden table. Coffee mug. Sounds of children playing in the street are outside. A neighbor, a Lubavitcher woman with light blond hair who no longer wears the wig, observes the interview at the table.)

Your hair —
It only has to be —
there's different,
uhm,
customs in different
Hasidic groups.
Lubavitch
the system is
it should be two inches
long.
It's —
some groups
have
the custom
to shave their
heads.
There's —
the reason is,

when you go to the mikvah°
you may, maybe,
it's better if it's short
because of what you —
the preparation
that's involved
and that
you have to go under the water.
The hair has a tendency to float
and you have to be completely submerged
including your hair.
So . . .
And I got married
when I was a little older,
and I really wanted to be married
and I really wanted to, um . . .
In some ways I was eager to cover my head.
Now if I had grown up in a Lubavitch household
and then had to cut it,
I don't know what that would be like.
I really don't.
But now that I'm wearing the wig,
you see,
with my hair I can keep it very simple
and I can change it all the time.
So with a wig you have to have like five wigs if you want
    to do that.
But I, uh,
I feel somehow like it's fake,
I feel like it's not me.
I try to be as much myself as I can,
and it just
bothers me
that I'm kind of fooling the world.
I used to go to work.
People . . .
and I would wear a different wig,
and they'd say I like your new haircut
and I'd say it's not mine!
You know,
and it was very hard for me to say it
and
it became very difficult.
I mean, I've gone through a lot with wearing wigs and
    not wearing
wigs.
It's been a big issue for me.

Angela Davis
Ropes

(*Morning. Spring. Oakland, California. In reality this
interview was done on the phone, with myself and Thulani Davis. Thulani and I were calling from an office at
the Public Theatre. We do not know exactly what Angela*

mikvah: A spiritual cleansing.

*was doing or wearing. I believe, from things she said,
that she was sitting on her deck in her home in Oakland,
which overlooks a beautiful panorama of trees.*)

Race, um —
of course
for many years in the history
of African Americans in this country —
was synonymous with community.
As a matter of fact
we were race women and race men.
Billie Holiday for example
called herself a race woman
because she supported the community
and as a child growing up in the South
my assumptions were
that if anybody in the race
came under attack
then I had to be there
to support that person,
to support the race.
I was saying to my students just the other day,
I said,
if in 1970,
when I was
in jail,
someone had told me
that in 1991,
a black man
who
said that his, um . . .
hero —

(*Increased volume, speed, and energy*)

one of his heroes
was Malcolm X —
would be nominated to the Supreme Court
I would have celebrated
and I don't think it would have been possible at that
    time
to convince me
that I would
be absolutely opposed,
a black candidate —
I mean like absolutely —

(*A new attack, more energy*)

or that if anyone would have told me that
a *woman* . . .
finally be elected to the Supreme Court,
it would have been very difficult,
as critical as I am with respect to feminism,
as critical as I have always been with what I used to call,
you know, narrow nationalism?
I don't think
it would have been possible to convince me that things
    would have so absolutely
shifted that
someone could have evoked

Anna Deavere Smith in two of her roles in the 1993 premiere production of *Fires in the Mirror,* performed at the Joseph Papp Public Theater.

the specter of lynching
on national television
and that specter of lynching would be used to violate
     our history.
And I still feel that we have to point out the racism
     involved
in the razing of a Black man
and a Black woman
in that way.
I mean Kennedy° was sitting right there
and it had never occurred to anyone to bring him up
before
the world,
which is not to say that I don't think it should happen.
And it is actually a sign of how we,
in our various oppressed
marginalized communities,
have been able to turn
terrible acts of racism directed against us
into victory . . .
And therefore I think
Anita Hill did that,
and so it's very complicated,
but I have no problems aligning myself politically
against Clarence Thomas° in a real passionate way,
but at the same time I can talk about the racism that led
     to the possibility
of constructing those kinds of hearings
and the same thing with Mike Tyson.°
So I guess that would be,
um . . .
the way in which I would begin to look at community,
and would therefore think
that race has become, uh,
an increasingly obsolete way
of constructing community
because it is based on unchangeable
immutable biological
facts
in a very pseudo-scientific way,
alright?
Now
racism is entirely different
because see *racism,*
uh,
actually I think
is
at the origins of this concept of race.
It's not —

it's not the other way around,
that there were racists,
and then the racists —
one race came to dominate
the others.
As a matter of fact
in order for a European colonialist
to attempt
to conquer the world,
to colonize the world,
they had to construct this notion
of,
uh,
the populations of the earth being divided into certain,
uh,
firm biological, uh,
communities,
and that's what I think we have to go back and look at.
So when I use the word race now I put it in quotations.
Because if we don't transform
this . . . this intransigent
rigid
notion of race,
we will be caught up in this cycle
of genocidal
violence
that, um,
is at the origins of our history.
So I think —
and I'm
I'm convinced — and this is what I'm working on in my
     political practice right now —
is that we have to find ways of coming together in a dif-
     ferent way,
not the old notion of coalition in which we anchor our-
     selves very solidly
in our,
um,
communities,
and simply voice
our
solidarity with other people.
I'm not suggesting that we do not anchor ourselves in
     our communities;
I feel very anchored in,
um,
my various communities,
but I think that,
you know,
to use a metaphor, the rope
attached to that anchor should be long enough to allow
     us to move
into other communities
to understand and learn.
I've been thinking a lot about the need to make more
     intimate
these connections and associations and to really take on
     the responsibility

Kennedy: Reference to Senator Ted Kennedy's 1969 automobile accident in Chappaquidick, Massachusetts, in which a campaign worker, Mary Jo Kopechne, was killed and he did not report the accident for ten hours. **Clarence Thomas:** Anita Hill accused Clarence Thomas of committing sexual harassment before he was appointed to the Supreme Court. Thomas is a conservative; Davis is a political radical. **Mike Tyson:** (b. 1966) Former heavyweight champion — also from Brooklyn.

of learning.
So I think that we need to —
in order to find ways of working with
and understanding
the vastness
of our many cultural heritages
and ways of coming together without
rendering invisible all of that heterogeneity —
I don't have the answer,
you know
I don't know.
What I'm interested in is communities
that are not static,
that
can change, that can respond to new historical needs.
So I think it's a very exciting moment.

RHYTHM • *Monique "Big Mo" Matthews*
Rhythm and Poetry

(In reality this interview was done on an afternoon in the spring of 1989, while I was in residence at the University of California, Los Angeles, as a fellow at the Center for Afro-American Studies. Mo was a student of mine. We were sitting in my office, which was a narrow office, with sunlight. I performed Mo in many shows, and in the course of performing her, I changed the setting to a performance setting, with microphone. I was inspired by a performance that I saw of Queen Latifah° in San Francisco, and by Mo's behavior in my class, which was performance behavior, to change the setting to one that was more theatrical, since Mo's everyday speech was as theatrical as Latifah's performance speech. Speaking directly to the audience, pacing the stage.)

And she say, "This is for the fellas,"
and she took off all her clothes and she had on a leotard
that had all cuts and stuff in it,
and she started doin' it on the floor.
They were like
"Go, girl!"
People like, "That look really stink."
But that's what a lot of female rappers do —
like to try to get off,
they sell they body or pimp they body
to, um, get play.
And you have people like Latifah who doesn't, you
    know,
she talks intelligent.
You have Lyte who's just hard and people are scared by
    her hardness,
her strength of her words.
She encompasses that whole, New York–street sound.
It's like, you know, she'll like . . .
what's a line?

Queen Latifah: (b. 1970) Rap music and film star.

What's a line
like "Paper Thin,"
"IN ONE EAR AND RIGHT OUT THE OTHUH."
It's like,
"I don't care what you have to say,
I'm gittin' done what's gotta be done.
Man can't come across me.
A female she can't stand against me.
I'm just the toughest, I'm just the hardest/You just can't
    come up
against me/if you do you get waxed!"
It's like a lot of my songs,
I don't know if I'm gonna get blacklisted for it.
The image that I want is a strong strong African strong
    Black woman
and I'm not down with what's going on, like Big Daddy
    Kane° had a song
out called "Pimpin Ain't Easy," and he sat there and he
    talk for the
whole song, and I sit there I wanna slap him, I wanna
    slap him so
hard, and he talks about, it's one point he goes, yeah
um,
"Puerto Rican girls Puerto Rican girls call me Papi and
White girls say
even White girls say I'm a hunk!"
I'm like,
"What you mean 'even'?
Oh! Black girls ain't good enough for you huh?"
And one of my songs has a line that's like
"PIMPIN' AIN'T EASY BUT WHORIN' AIN'T
    PROPER. RESPECT AND
CHERISH THE ORIGINAL MOTHER."
And a couple of my friends were like,
"Aww, Mo, you good but I can't listen to you 'cause you
    be Men bashin'."
I say,
"It ain't men bashin', it's female assertin'."
Shit.
I'm tired of it.
I'm tired of my friends just acceptin'
that they just considered to be a ho.
You got a song,
"Everybody's a Hotty."
A "hotty" means you a freak, you a ho,
and it's like Too Short
gets up there and he goes,
"B I AYYYYYYYYYYYYE."
Like he stretches "bitch" out for as long as possible,
like you just a ho and you can't be saved,
and 2 Live Crew. . . . "we want some pussy," and the
    girls!
"La le la le la le la,"
it's like my friends say,
"Mo, if you so bad how come you don't never say
    nothin' about Two

Kane: Rap singer Antonio Hardy (b. 1968), known for his "Brooklyn style" rapping.

Live Crew?"
When I talk about rap,
and I talk about people demeaning rap,
I don't even mention them
because they don't understand the fundamentals of rap.
Rap, rap
is basically
broken down
Rhythm
and Poetry.
And poetry is expression.
It's just like poetry; you release so much through poetry
    you get
angry, you get it?
Poetry is like
intelligence.
You just release it all and if you don't have a complex
    rhyme
it's like,
"I'm goin' to the store."
What rhymes with store?
More store for more bore
"I'm going to the store I hope I don't get bored,"
it's like,
"WHAT YOU SAYIN', MAN? WHO CARES?"
You have something that flows.
You have to be def,
D-E-F.
I guess I have to think of something for you that ain't
    slang.
Def is dope, def is live
when you say somethin's dope
it means it is the epitome of the experience
and you have to be def by your very presence
because you have to make people happy.
And we are living in a society where people are not
    happy with their everyday lives.

SEVEN VERSES • *Leonard Jeffries*
Roots

(3:00 P.M. Wednesday, November 20, 1991. A very large conference room in the African American Studies Department at CUNY. Drawn venetian blinds, fluorescent lighting. Dr. Jeffries wears a light, multicolored African top, and a multicolored African hat. His shoes are black functional shoes, like the shoes to a uniform. He sits facing the table, and often sits back with the chair back from the table, often touches the table, and often sits back with the chair on its back legs only. Sometimes he scratches his head by throwing his hat forward on his head with great ease and authority. There is a bodyguard, a large heavy-set African American man, present.)

People are asking who is this guy Jeffries?
When they find out my background they're gonna be
    surprised.

They are gonna find out that I was even related to Alex
    Haley.°
In fact I was a major consultant for *Roots*.
In fact there might not have been a *Roots* without me.
Now when I say that,
that's my own personal in-group joke wit' Alex.
He was in Philadelphia
getting his ticket to go down to Jamaica
and
Roots was lost.
He had it in a duffel bag,
a big duffel bag like this,
the whole manuscript.
It was lost in the airport of Philadelphia.
I got on my horse and ran around the airport of Phila-
    delphia
and found *Roots*.
So that's my joke.
He had this manuscript,
Alex didn't have anything else but this manuscript.
Now if he had lost that, that would have been it.
He didn't have any photocopies.
Alex did everything on a shoestring.
uhm
so for him to deny me now . . .
He never even acknowledged
Pat
Alexander
his girlfriend/secretary who he had paid with affection
    and not with
resources.
So I didn't expect him to acknowledge me.
He called me to come down.
I called my wife who was working on her Ph.D. at Yale.
I said, "Rosalind, Alex wants us to come down to
    Brunswick, Georgia,
they're filming *Roots*."
She said yes she'd come down and we'd go, then she
    called me back.
She said, "I got too much work," so I went down to
    Brunswick, Georgia.
He introduced me to Margulies,°
who was the, um, director
of *Roots*,
as the leading expert in America on Africa, and I said,
    "Wow," to
myself, "that's kind of high."
When Margulies said,
"That makes me number two," then I realized what
    Alex was doing to keep *Roots* honest.
So for two weeks I tried to change *Roots*.
Alex would say, "Wait a
minute, let's consult the experts."
After two weeks they got tired of me, sat me down
and said, "Dr. Jeffries," at lunch,

Haley: Alex Haley (1921–1992), author of *Roots*.   **Margulies:** Stan Margulies was the producer of *Roots*, along with David Wolper.

"we are very happy to have you here
but we just bought the rights to the book *Roots*
and we are under no obligation to maintain the integrity
    of the book
and we certainly don't have to deal with the truth of
    Black history."
Now,
this was a wipeout for me
I
I, there's been very few trau*matic*
moments

(*Longest pause in his text*)

uh, just to think.
Now I wasn't even prepared for this
but Pat had called me before and said,
"Len, I'm looking at this document and I don't know
    what to make of it."
I said, "What is it, Pat, what is it?"
and I knew she was nervous, she said,
"I'm reading a contract that says
"*Roots* has been sold to David Wolper and their heirs
    for ever and
ever

(*He is thumping his hand on table*)

and their heirs for ever and ever."
Alex had signed the contract for fifty thousand dollars.

(*He is thumping his hand on table*)

Fifty thousand dollars for paperback *Roots*.
Something that made how much?
Three hundred million dollars?
He was suing them for years.
The millions he made out to TV *Roots* he spent a lot of
    it to sue
Doubleday to get a better deal — I don't know if he ever
    got it.
Roots was a devastation.
The tens of millions and hundreds of millions made on
    Roots
went to produce,
not to make more Black series,
like *Roots*,
but they went to produce a *series*
maybe a dozen mini-series on *Jewish* history
as opposed to Black history.
You can document what was produced in terms of Black
    history
compared to what was produced of Jewish history.
It's a devastation.
But the *one* thing that came out of this for me,
was that when these people told me, you know,
"We bought your research
We bought your history
You really have no . . ."
I was thrown off
I had to get out of there.
I stayed for another couple of days.

I told Alex I had to make a pilgrimage to my grandfa-
    ther's grave.
Never saw my grandfather.
Then I watched one more scene in the Alex Haley thing
and that finished it for me.
A cutaway of a slave ship
that was so real that they had to bring in these high
    school kids,
and once these high school kids played the enslaved Af-
    ricans greased
down in simulated vomit
and feces
they couldn't come back,
so they had to continue to get,
go take these youngsters,
and some little White woman
who was there sleeping with one of those guys,
they told her, "You cannot take these kids without au-
    thorization."
But she would drive a bus
up to the schoolyard,
put the kids in it, and bring them to the set.
And it almost produced a riot
there.
But anyway this slave scene
was so realistic
the trainer's up on a lower deck
and Kunta Kinte's on a bottom deck
and they call down to each other,
and the trainer says,
"Kunta Kinte,
Be strong! Be strong!
We may have to fight.
Kill the White man and return to Mother Africa."
This was high drama.
All of us grown men over hiding in the shadows in *tears*.
Then
Green rushes out and said, "Break! Break!"
He said he didn't want the scene.
We said, "What?"
Even Lou Gossett° and them were ready to *fight*!
You know 'cause they had —
a movie script is just
a skeleton,
you have to put your soul in a movie script,
and they put their heart and soul into what would have
    been . . .
And with the African —
because the "earth is mother" all over Africa.
So to say to go back to Mother Africa is a very meaning-
    ful phrase.
But this
Englishman refused
to accept it,
and they almost had a physical fight on the set.

Gossett: Lou Gossett, Jr. (b. 1936) acted in *Roots*. He was born
in Brooklyn.

They compromised and said,
"We — are — all — from — one — village,"

(*Hitting his hand rhythmically on the desk*)

which is not the same thing.
After that I said, "I have to go."
I said I have to go,
and I rented a —
I flew out with Lorne Greene° of all people.
He saw me and we had known each other for a couple of weeks from
the set,
and he's sitting there drinking his little drinks
talking about "Isn't *Roots* wonderful.
It's everybody's history,"
and I'm dying.

(*Pause*)

Get to Atlanta.
Rent a car. Cut across the Georgia countryside.
came to a fork in the road,
made the right turn,
and there on a bluff
was a clapboard church
made by my grandfather
and
four
other trustees.
Then when
I went across the cemetery
to see, uh,
the gravesite where he was —
the tallest tombstone in the graveyard was his.
Uhm,
It was an obelisk.
On it was a Masonic symbol.
He was the master of the lodge.
On it was his vital statistics:
"Born August the tenth 1868."
At the birth of the Fourteenth Amendment.
I later learned that his brother Sam was born
1865 at the birth of the Thirteenth Amendment!
And this is why people say,
"Who is he?
What is he?
Why is he?"
If they only know
I've had one of the best educations on the planet.
Yeah.
So . . .
When I went to Albany
in July,
I went knowing that you might not have
much time,
just like my wife said on the radio today:
"When we speak

we speak as though it is the last speech we're gonna make."
But I knew what was at stake
ever since they branded me a conspiracy theorist,
February 12, 1990,
two-column editorial in the *New York Times*.
That was,
in the concept of Jewish thinking,
the kiss of death.
I knew I had been targeted.
Arthur Schlesinger° went and wrote a book
called *The Disuniting of America*.
He has everybody in the margin
except a half-page photo of myself
which said to us,
"This is the one they got to kill."
We knew that Schlesinger
and his people had sent out a thousand letters
to CEOs around the country
and foundation heads
not to have anything to do with
all of us involved in these studies
for multicultural curriculum
so, uh . . .
Knowing that I had taken this beating for two and a half years
it was my chance to strike out,
but people don't understand
that that was my way of saying,
"You bastids! . . .
for starting this process
of destroying *me*."
That was my striking out.
But people don't know the context.
They don't know that for two and a half years
I bore this burden
by myself
and I bore it well.
And now they've got a problem.
'Cause after they destroyed me,
here he is resurrected!!!!!
I spoke at Columbia, I spoke at Queens College. . . .

Letty Cottin Pogrebin
Near Enough to Reach

(*Evening. The day before Thanksgiving, 1991. On the phone. Direct, passionate, confident, lots of volume. She is in a study with a rolltop desk and a lot of books.*)

I think it's about rank frustration and the old story
that you pick a scapegoat
that's much more, I mean Jews and Blacks,
that's manageable,
because we're near,

Greene: Lorne Greene (1915–1987) was a star in the TV series *Bonanza*.

Schlesinger: Arthur Schlesinger (b. 1917), historian and author.

we're still near enough to each other to reach!
I mean, what can you do about the people who voted for
    David Duke°?
Are Blacks going to go there and deal with that?
No, it's much easier to deal with Jews who are also pan-
    icky.
We're the only ones that pay any attention

(*Her voice makes an upward inflection*)

Do you hear?
Well, Jeffries did speak about the Mafia being, um,
Mafia,
and the Jews in Hollywood.
I didn't see
this tremendous outpouring of Italian
reaction.
Only *Jews* listen,
only *Jews* take Blacks seriously,
only *Jews* view Blacks as full human beings that you
should *address*
in their rage
and, um,
people don't seem to notice that.
But Blacks, it's like a little child kicking up against Arnold
Schwarzenegger°
when they,
when they have anything to say about the dominant cul-
    ture
nobody listens! Nobody reacts!
To get a headline,
to get on the evening news,
you have to attack a Jew.
Otherwise you're ignored.
And it's a shame.
We all play into it.

Minister Conrad Mohammed
Seven Verses

(*April 1992, morning. A café/restaurant. Roosevelt Island,
New York. We are sitting in the back, in an area that
is surrounded by glass floor-to-ceiling windows. Mr. Mohammed is impeccably dressed in a suit of an elegant
fabric. He wears a blue shirt and a bow tie. He has on fine
shoes, designer socks, and a large fancy watch and wedding ring. His hair is closely cropped. He drinks black
coffee, and uses a few packs of sugar. He is traveling with
another man, also a Muslim, in the clothing of a Muslim,
impeccable, who sits at another table and watches us.*)

The condition of the Black man in America today is part
    and parcel,
through the devlishment
that permitted Caucasian people

Duke: David Duke, white extremist candidate for president in
1992. **Schwarzenegger:** Arnold Schwarzenegger (b. 1947),
action movie star elected as governor of California in 2003.

to rob us of our humanity,
and put us in the throes of slavery . . .
The fact that our — our Black
parents
were actually taken
as cattle
and as, as
animals
and packed into
slave ships
like sardines
amid feces
and urine —
and the suffering of our people,
for months,
in the middle passage —
Our women,
raped
before our own eyes,
so that today
some look like you,
some look like me,
some look like a brother . . .
(indicating his companion)
This is a crime of tremendous proportion.
In fact,
no crime in the history of humanity
has before or since
equaled that crime.
The Holocaust did not equal it
Oh, absolutely not.
First of all,
that was a horrible crime
and that is something that is a disgrace in the eyes of
    civilized
people.
That, uh, crime also stinks
in the nostrils of God.
But it in no way compares with the slavery of our people
because we lost over a hundred
and some say two hundred and fifty,
million
in the middle passage
coming from Africa
to America.
We were so thoroughly robbed.
We didn't just lose six million.
We didn't just
endure this
for, for
five or six years
or from '38 to '45 or '39 to —
We endured this for over three hundred years —
the total subjugation of the Black man.
You can go into Bangladesh today,
Calcutta,

(*He strikes the table with a sugar packet three or four
times*)

New Delhi,
Nigeria,
some really
so-called underdeveloped nation,
and I don't care how low that person's humanity is

(*He opens the sugar packet*)

whether they never
had running water,
if they'd never seen a television or anything.
They are in better condition than the Black man and
  woman
in America today
right now.
Even at Harvard.
They have a contextual understanding of what their destiny is.

(*He strikes the table with another sugar packet three or
four times and opens it*)

But the Black man has no knowledge of that;
he's an amnesia victim

(*Starts stirring his coffee*)

He has lost knowledge of himself

(*Stirring his coffee*)

and he's living a beast life.

(*Stirring his coffee*)

So this proves that it was the greatest
crime.
Because we were cut off from our past.
Not only were we killed and murdered,
not only were our women raped
in front of their own children.
Not only did the slave master stick

(*The spoon drops onto saucer*)

at times,
daggers into a pregnant woman's stomach,
slice the stomach open
push the baby out on the ground and crush the head of
  the baby
to instill fear in the Massas of the plantation.

(*Stirring again*)

Not only were these things done,
not only were our thumbs

(*Spoon drops*)

put in, in devices
that would just slowly torture the slave
and tear the thumb off from the root.
Not only were we sold on the auction block
like cattle,
not permitted to marry.
See these are the crimes
of slavery that nobody wants to talk about.

But the most significant crime —
because we could have recovered from all of that —
but the fact that they cut off all knowledge from us,
told us that we were animals,
told us that we were subhuman,
took from us our names,
gave us names like
Smith
and Jones
and today we wear those names
with dignity
and pride,
yet these were the names given to us in one of the greatest crimes
ever committed on the face of the earth.
So this kind of thing,
Sister,
is what qualifies slavery
as the greatest
crime
ever committed.
They have stolen
our garment.
Stolen our identity.
The Honorable Louis Farrakhan°
teaches us
that *we* are the chosen of God.
We are those people
that almighty God Allah
has selected as his chosen,
and they are masquerading in our garment —
the Jews.
We don't have an identity today.
Because we are the people . . .
There are seven verses
in the Bible
seven verses,
I believe it is in Deuteronomy,
that the Jews base
their chosen people, uh, uh,
claim the theology,
the whole theological exegesis
with respect
of being the chosen
is based upon seven verses
in the Scripture that talk
about a covenant
with Abraham.

Letty Cottin Pogrebin
Isaac

(*Morning. Spring. On the phone. She is in her office in
her home on West 67th Street and Central Park West in
Manhattan. Her office has an old-fashioned wooden*

Farrakhan: Louis Farrakhan (b. 1933), born Louis Eugene
Walcott, head of the Nation of Islam.

rolltop desk and bookcases filled with books. She says
she was wearing leggings and a loose shirt.)

Well,
it's hard for me to do that
because
I think there's a tendency to make hay
with the Holocaust,
to push
all the buttons.
And I mean this story about my uncle Isaac — makes
   me cry
and it's going to make your audience cry
and I'm beginning to worry
that
we're trotting out our Holocaust stories
too regularly and that we're going to inure each other to
   the truth of
them.
But
I think
maybe if you let me read it,
I would prefer to read it:

(*Reading from* Deborah, Golda, and Me)°

"I remember my mother's cousin
Isaac who came to New York
immediately after the war and lived with us for several
   months.
Isaac is my connection to dozens of other family members who
were murdered in the concentration camps.
Because he was blond and blue-eyed he had been
chosen as the designated survivor of his town.
That is the Jewish councils had instructed him to do
   anything
to stay alive and tell the story.
For Isaac
anything turned out to mean this.
The Germans accepted his forged Aryan papers and
   decided that he
would have to prove by his actions that he was not a Jew.
They put him on a transport train with the Jews of his
   town
and then gave him the task of herding into the gas chambers
everyone in his train load.
After he had fulfilled that assignment
with patriotic
German efficiency,
the Nazis accepted the authenticity of his identity papers
and let him go.
Among those whom Isaac packed into the gas chambers
   that day
dispassionately as if shoving a few more items into an
   overstuffed

Deborah . . . Me: A Jewish feminist book (1992) by Letty Cottin Pogrebin (b. 1939).

closet
were his wife
and
two children.
The designated survivor
arrived in America
at about age forty

(*Breathes in*)

with prematurely white hair and a dead gaze within the
   sky blue
eyes that's helped save his life.
As promised he told his story to dozens of Jewish agencies
and community leaders and to groups of families and
   friends which
is how I heard the account
translated from his Yiddish
by my mother.
For months he talked,
speaking the unspeakable.
Describing a horror
that American Jews had suspected but could not conceive.
A monstrous tale
that dwarfed the demonology of legend
and gave me the nightmare I still dream to this day.
And as he talked
Isaac seemed to grow older and older
until one night a few months later
when he finished telling everything he knew
he died."

Robert Sherman
Lousy Language

(*11:00 A.M. Wednesday, November 13, 1991. A very*
sunny and large, elegant living room in a large apart-
ment near the Brooklyn Museum. Mr. Sherman is sitting
in an armchair near an enormous bouquet of flowers
for the birth of his first child. He wears sweats, and a
bright orange long-sleeved tee shirt. Smiles frequently,
upbeat, impassioned. Fingers his wedding ring. Each
phrase builds on the next, pauses are all sustained inten-
sity, never lets up. Full. Lots of volume, clear enunci-
ation, teeth, and tongue very involved in his speech.
Good-humored, seems to like the act of speech.)

Do you have demographic information on Crown
   Heights?
The important thing to remember is that —
and I will check these numbers when I get back to the
   office —
I think the
Hasidim°
comprise only ten percent

Hasidim: A sect of Orthodox Jews.

of the population
of the neighborhood.
The Crown Heights conflict has been brewing on and
    off for twenty years
since the Hasidic community
developed some serious numbers
and some strength in Crown Heights and as African
    Americans and
Caribbean Americans came to make up the dominant
    culture in
Crown Heights.
Very important to remember that
those things that are expressed really as
bias,
those things
that we at the Human Rights Commission
would consider to be bias,
have the same trappings of bias,
which is complaints based on a characteristic, not on a
    knowledge of a
specific person.
There sort of is a soup
of bias — prejudice, racism, and discrimination.
I think bias really does relate to
feelings with a valence,
feelings with a, uhm,

(*Breathing in*)

feelings that can go in a direction positive or negative
although we usually use bias to mean a negative.
What it means usually
is negative attitudes
that can lead to negative behaviors:
biased
acts, biased incidents,
or biased crimes.
Racism is hatred based on race.
Discrimination refers to
acts against somebody . . .
so that the words
actually tangle up.
I think in part
because vocabulary
follows general awareness. . . .
I think you know
the Eskimos have seventy words for snow?
We probably have seventy different kinds of bias, preju-
    dice, racism, and
discrimination,
but it's not in our mind-set to be clear about it,
so I think that we have
sort of lousy language
on the subject
and that
is a reflection
of our unwillingness
to deal with it honestly
and to sort it out.
I think we have very, very bad language.

CROWN HEIGHTS, BROOKLYN
AUGUST 1991 • *Rabbi Joseph Spielman*
No Blood in His Feet

(*9:30 A.M. Tuesday, November 12, 1991. A large home on President Street in Crown Heights. Only natural light, not very much light. Dark wood. A darkish dining room with an enormous table, could seat twenty. The rabbi sits at the head of the table. Lots of stuff on the table. He wears Hasidic clothing, a black fedora, black jacket, and reading glasses. As he talks, he slightly slides around the tape-recorder microphone, which is in front of him at the table. The furniture in the dining room including his chair is, for the most part, very old, solid wood. There are children playing quietly in another room, and people come in and out frequently, but always whispering and walking carefully not to make noise, unless they speak to him directly. The children at one point came over and stared at me.*)

Many people were on the sidewalk,
talking, playing,
drinking
beer or whatever —
being that type of neighborhood.
A car
driven by an individual —
a Hasidic individual —
went through the intersection,
was hit by another car,
thereby causing it to go onto the sidewalk.
The driver on seeing
himself in such a position that he felt he was going to
    definitely hit
someone,
because of the amount of people on the sidewalk,
he steered at the building,
so as to get out of the way of the people.
Obviously, for the most part,
he was successful.
But regrettably,
one child was killed
and another child
was wounded.
Um,
seeing what happened,
he jumped out of the car
and, realizing
there may be a child under the car,
he tried to physically lift
the car
from the child.
Well, as he was doing this
the Afro-Americans were beating him already.
He was beaten so much he needed stitches in the scalp
    and the face,
fifteen or sixteen stitches
and also

there were three other passengers in the car
that were being beaten too.
One of the passengers was calling 911
on the cellular phone.
A Black person
pulled the phone out of his hand and ran.
Just stole the — stole the telephone.
The Jewish community
has a volunteer
ambulance corps
which is funded totally from the nations —
there is not one penny of government funds —
and manned by volunteers —
who many times at their expense —
supplied the equipment that they carry in order to save
    lives.
As one of the EMS ambulances were coming,
one of the Hasidic ambulances or the Jewish ambu-
    lances came
on the scene.
The EMS responded with three ambulances on the
    scene.
They were there before
the Jewish ambulance came.
Two or three police cars were already on the scene.
The police saw the potential for violence
and saw that the occupants of the car
were being beaten and were afraid for their safety.
At the same time the EMS asked
the Hasidic ambulances for certain pieces of equipment
    that they
were out of,
that they needed to take care of the Cato kid,
and,
um,
in fact, I was . . .
The Hasidic ambulance left, leaving behind one of the
    passengers.
That passenger had a walkie-talkie and he requested
    that I
come down to pick him up.
And at that time there was a lot of screaming and shout-
    ing
and it was a mixed crowd, Hasidic and Afro-American.
The police said, "Rabbi get your people out of here."
I told them to leave and I left.
Now,
a few hours later,
two and a half hours later,
in a different part of Crown Heights,
a scholar
from Australia,
Yankel Rosenbaum,
who, urr,
I think he had a doctorate or he was working on his doc-
    torate,
was walking on the street
on his own —
I mean he was totally oblivious —

and he was accosted by a group of young Blacks
about twenty of them strong
which was being egged on by a Black
male approximately
forty years old and balding,
telling them,
"Kill all Jews —
look what they did to the kid,
kill all Jews,"
and all the epithets that go along with it,
"Heil Hitler" and all of it.
They stabbed him,
which later on the stab wounds were fatal
and he passed away in the hospital.
The Mayor,
hearing about the Cato kid,
came to the Kings County Hospital
to give condolences to the family of the child who had
    regrettably been killed.
At the meantime they had already wheeled in
Mr. Rosenbaum.
He was in the emergency room
and I was at the hospital at the same time,
and the Mayor, seeing me there,
expressed his concern
that a child,
uh, innocent child, had been killed.
Where I explained to him
the fact
that,
whereas the child was killed from an unfortunate acci-
    dent
where there was no malicious intent,
here
there was an individual lying in the emergency room
who had been stabbed with malicious intent
and for the sole reason —
not that he did anything to anyone —
just from the fact that he happened to be Jewish.
And the Mayor went with me to the emergency room
to visit Mr. Rosenbaum.
This was approximately one and a half hours before he
    passed away.
I noticed at the time that his feet
were
completely white.
And I complained to the doctor
on the scene,
"He's having a problem with blood circulation
because there's no blood in his feet."
And she gave me some asinine answer.
And the Mayor asked her what his condition is:
"Serious but stable."
In the meantime he was screaming and in pain
and they weren't doing anything.
Subsequently they, um,
they started giving him anaesthesia in a time that
    they weren't allowed to give him anaesthesia
and while he was under anaesthesia,

he passed away.
So there was totally mismanagement in his case.
So whereas the Mayor,
had been fed . . .
his people got
whatever information he got out of the Black commu-
    nity was
that
the driver had run a red light
and also,
and that the ambulance,
the Hasidic ambulance,
refused to take care of the Black child that was dying
    and
rather took care of their own.
Nenh?
And this is what was fed amongst the Black community.
And it was false,
it was totally false
and it was done maliciously
only with the intent to get the riots,
to start up the resulting riots.

The Reverend Canon Doctor Heron Sam
Mexican Standoff

(*November 12, 1991, 4:00 P.M. The rectory office at St.
Mark's Church in Crown Heights. A small, short office.
Lived in but impeccably ordered. Some light from lamps,
some from overhead. Plaques and awards everywhere.
The reverend is wearing a yellow shirt, priest's collar,
tan summer jacket. He wears spectacles. There are
clocks that make noise and sound the hour in his office
and outside church bells sound during the interview,
loud. Throughout the talk he is trying to get the corner
of a calendar to stay down, but it continues to stick up.
Finally he uses a paperweight to keep it down.*)

You can't have that kind of accident
if people are observing the speed limits.
People knew it was the Grand Rebbe.°
People have seen the Grand Rebbe
charging through the community.
He is worried
about a threat on his life
from the Satmars.°
These Lubavitcher people
are really very,
uh, enigmatic people.
They move so easily between
simplicity and sophistication.
Because
they fear for his life,

Rebbe: Menachem M. Schneerson (1902–1994), leader of
Lubavitcher Hasidic Jews. **Satmars:** Satmar Hasidic Jews,
rival to the Lubavitchers.

---

because the Satmars
who are their sworn enemies

(*He laughs/chuckles*)

have threatened to *kill*
the Rebbe.
So whenever he comes out
he's gotta be *whisked*!
You know like a President
or even better than a President.
He says he's an intuhnational figuh
like a Pope!
I say
then, "Why don't you get the Swiss guards
to escort you
rather than using the police
and taxpayers' money?"
He's gotta be
whisked!
Quickly through the neighborhood.
Can't walk around.
He used to walk.
When I first came here.
Now he doesn't walk at all.
They drive him.
And when he walked
you could tell he was in front
because there was,
he was protected all around
and they spilled out onto the streets
and buses had to stop
because this BIG BAND
had to escort
the Rebbe from his house over there
to the synagogue.
So the Rebbe goes to the cemetery.
Every time the Rebbe goes to the cemetery,
which is once a week
to visit his dead wife
and father-in-law,
the police
lead him in escort
charging down the street
at seventy miles an hour in a metropolis —
what do you want?

(*Swift increase in volume and suddenly businesslike*)

It happened that on this occasion that as they were com-
    ing back,
uh,
the police car
with its siren,
had gone over a main
intersection with the light
in favor
of the police car.
The Rebbe's Cadillac had passed
when the lights had become amber
and nobody expected the bodyguard van,

uh,
station wagon
to deliberately go through the red light.
So the traffic
that had the right of way kept coming and
BANG!
came the collision and the careening
onto the sidewalk
had to damage whoever was there
and then, um, they were more concerned about licking
    their own
wounds.
Rather than pick
the car off the boy
who died as a result.
And then the ambulance that came —
the Jewish ambulance —
was concerned about the people in the van
while some boy lay dead,
a black boy lay dead on the street.
The people showed their —

(*Increase in volume*)

they burned and whatever else,
upturned
police cars
and looted,
and as a result,
I think in retaliation, murdered one of the Hasidics.
But that was just the match that lit the powder keg.
It's gonna happen again and again.
There's a Mexican standoff right now
But it's gonna happen again.

Anonymous Young Man #1
Wa Wa Wa

(*7:00 or 8:00 P.M. Spring. A recreation room at Ebbets Field apartments. A very handsome young Caribbean American man with dreadlocks, in his late teens or early twenties, wearing a bright, loose-fitting shirt. The room is ill equipped. There are a few pieces of broken furniture. It is poorly lit. A woman, Kym, with dreadlocks and shells in her hair, is at the interview. It was originally scheduled to be her interview. The Anonymous Young Man #1 and the other Anonymous Young Man, #2, started by watching the interview from the side of the room but soon approached me and began to join in. Anonymous Young Man #1 was the most vocal. Anonymous Young Man #2 stood lurking in the shadows. A third young man, younger than both of them, wearing wire spectacles and a blue Windbreaker, who looks quite like a young Spike Lee, sat silent with his hands and head on the table the entire time. There is a very bad radio or tape recorder playing music in the background.*)

What I saw was
she was pushin'

her brother on the bike like
this,
right?
She was pushin'
him
and he kept dippin' around
like he didn't know how
to ride the bike.
So she kept runnin'
and pushin' him to the side.
So she was already runnin'
when the car was comin'.
So I don't know if she was runnin' toward him
because we was watchin' the car
weavin',
and we was goin'
"Oh, yo
it's a Jew, man.
He broke the stop light, they never get arrested."
At first we was laughin', man, we was like
you see they do anything
and get away with it,
and then
we saw that he was out of control,
and den
we started regrettin' laughin',
because then
we saw where he was goin'.
First he hit a car, right,
then tore a whole front fender off a car,
and then we was like
Oh
my god,
man, look at the kids,
you know,
so we was already runnin' over there
by the time the accident happened.
That's how we know he was drinkin'
cause he was like
Wa Wa Wa Wa
and I was like
"Yo, man, he's drunk.
Grab him,
grab him.
Don't let him go anywhere."
I said,
"Grab him."
I didn't want him to limp off
in some apartment somewhere
and come back in a different black jacket.
So I was like,
"Grab him,"
and then I was like, "Is the ambulance comin' for the
    kids?"
'Cause I been in a lot of confrontations with Jews before
and I know that when they said an ambulance
is comin'
it most likely meant for them.
And they was like,

"oh, oh."
Jews right?
"Ambulance comin', ambulance comin',
calm down, calm down,
God will help them,
God will help them if you believe."
And he was actin' like he was dyin'.
"Wa Aww,
me too,
I'm hurt, I'm hurt, I'm hurt too."
Wan nothin' wrong with him,
wan nothin' wrong with him.
They say that we beat up on that man
that he had to have stitches because of us.
You don't come out of an accident like that unmarked,
without a scratch.
The most he got from us was slapped
by a little kid.
And here come the ambulance
and I was like, "That's not a city ambulance,"
not like this I was upset right
and I was like,
"YO,
the man is drunk!
He ran a red light!
You all ain't gonna do nothin'."
Everybody started comin' around, right,
'cause I was talkin' about
these kids is dyin' man!
I'm talkin' about the skull of the baby is on the ground
    man!
and he's walkin'!
I was like, "Don't let him get into that ambulance!"
And the Jews,
the Jews
was like private, private ambulance
I was like, "Grab him,"
but my buddies was like,
"We can't touch them."
Nobody wanted to grab him,
nobody wanted to touch him,
An' I was breakin' fool, man,
I was goin' mad,
I couldn't believe it.
Everybody just stood
there,
and that made me cry.
I was cryin'
so I left, I went home and watched the rest of it on TV,
it was too lackadazee
so it was like me, man, instigatin' the whole thing.
I got arrested for it
long after
in Queens.
Can't tell you no more about that,
you know.
Hey, wait a minute,
they got eyes and ears everywhere.
What color is the Israeli flag?

And what color are the police cars?
The man was *drunk,*
I open up his car door,
I was like, when —
I was like, he'd been drinkin'
I know our words don't have no meanin',
as Black people in Crown Heights.
You realize, man,
ain't no justice,
ain't never been no justice,
ain't never gonna be no justice.

Michael S. Miller
"Heil Hitler"

(*A large airy office in Manhattan on Lexington in the fifties. Mr. Miller sits behind a big desk in a high-backed swivel chair drinking coffee. He's wearing a yarmulke. Plays with the swizzle stick throughout. There is an intercom in the office, so that when the receptionist calls him, you can hear it, and when she calls others in other offices, you can hear it, like a page in a public place, faintly.*)

I was at Gavin Cato's° funeral,
at nearly every public event
that was conducted by the Lubavitcher community and
    the Jewish
community as a whole.
Words of comfort
were offered to the family of Gavin Cato.
I can show you a letter that we sent
to the Cato family expressing, uh,
our sorrow over the loss,
unnecessary loss, of their son.
I am not aware of a word
that was spoken at that funeral.
I am not aware of a —
and I was taking notes —
of a word that was uttered
of comfort to the family of Yankel Rosenbaum.°
Frankly this was a political rally rather than a funeral.
The individuals you mentioned —
and again,
I am not going to participate in verbal acrimony,
not only
were there cries of, "Kill the Jews"
or,
"Kill the Jew,"
there were cries of, "Heil Hitler."
There were cries of, "Hitler didn't finish the job."
There were cries of,
"Throw them back into the ovens again."
To hear in *Crown Heights* —

Gavin Cato: (1984–1991) died in the runaway car accident.
Yankel Rosenbaum: (1962–1991) Jewish student stabbed in the riot by Lemrick Nelson.

and Hitler was no lover of Blacks —
"Heil Hitler"?
"Hitler didn't finish the job"?
"We should heat up the ovens"?
From *Blacks*?
Is more inexplicable
or unexplainable
or any other word that I cannot fathom.
The hatred is so
deep seated
and the hatred
knows no boundaries.
There is no boundary
to anti-Judaism.
The anti-*Judaism* —
if people don't want me
to use,
hear me use the word anti-Semitism.
And I'll be damned if,
if preferential treatment is gonna
be the excuse
for every bottle,
rock,
or pellet that's, uh, directed
toward a Jew
or the window of a Jewish home
or a Jewish store.
And, frankly,
I think the response of the Lubavitcher community was
    relatively
passive.

Henry Rice
Knew How to Use Certain Words

(*Thursday, November 21, 1991. The Jackson Hole res-*
taurant on Lexington Avenue in the thirties in Manhat-
tan. Lunchtime, dimly lit, a reddish haze on everything,
perhaps from a neon light. Mr. Rice, very neatly dressed,
is eating a large, messy hamburger and horizontally
chopped pickles. Drinking a Miller Lite. Beer is in a bottle
next to a red plastic glass. He's wearing a baseball cap over
very closely cut hair and a bright, multicolored, expen-
sive-looking colored nylon jacket. Heavy new Timber-
land boots. Struggling to eat without making a mess of
the food. At some point sits up from food and has his
right hand or fist on his hip — a very unaffected but truly
authoritative stance. Good-natured, handsome, healthy.
Patsy Cline's "Crazy" is very loud on the jukebox.)

I went back home and got my bike
because I knew I would have to be
illusive.
I was there in body and in spirit
but I didn't participate in any of the violence
because basically I have a lot to lose.
But I was there
and I would have defended myself if it was necessary,

most definitely.
I weaved around trouble.
When something broke out, I moved back,
when it calmed down, I would move back in on the
    front line.
I was always there.
And Richard Green heard me saying something to a
    bunch of kids
about *voting*
about the power of *vote*
the power of *numbers*
and he said,
uh,
I said, "Get away from me, you're an Uncle Tom,
get away from me.
Get back in your Mercedes-Benz!"
No! I said that to Clarence Norman
and to Richard Green,
both of them.
I was tearing them apart.
Richard Green was very persistent.
He said,
"Look, Mr. Rice,
I like the way you speak.
I need you.
Please help me.
I'm a community activist. . . .
ba, ba, ba, ba, ba."

(*He drops some food on his clothes, or so it seems, he*
looks and grins)

It didn't get on me.
"I'm a community activist.
I need your help,
please help me,"
and so forth.
Again,
I didn't pay him no mind
but we spoke
some
the next day after that,
after the incidents that took place on that corner
of Albany Avenue.
A brother was beat up —
cops rushing into the Black crowd
didn't rush into the Jewish crowd,
cops rushed into the Black crowd
started beatin' up
Black people.
But the next day Richard came by in a yellow van,
a New York City Department of Transportation van,
with a megaphone,
yellow light flashing,

(*Music segues from Patsy Cline's "Crazy" to Public*
Enemy's "Can't Truss It," or Naughty by Nature's
"O.P.P.")

the whole works
and, um,

he said,
"Henry, I need you in this van.
Drive around with me.
Let's keep some of these kids off the street tonight."
I said, "Okay."
He said,
"The blood
of Black men are on your hands tonight!"
I said, "Okay."
We drive around in the van,
"Young people stay in the house!
Mothers keep your children in the house,
please."
So I began fillin'
I began feeling like
I had to do it
after he told me that,
"the blood of the Black man"
were on my hands,
you know.
Richard Green sure know how to use certain words.

(*He giggles*)

I remember reaching Albany Avenue —
kids were being chased by the police.
I jump out with a portable megaphone,
I tell them, "Stop running!
The cops won't chase you!
and they won't hit you!"
The next thing I know,
cop grabs my megaphone hits me in the head with a
     stick,
handcuffs me,
and takes the megaphone out of my hand.
So I'm like
"Wait a minute
I'm doing a community service for the mayor's office."
They don't want to hear it.
Matter of fact,
they still have the megaphone 'til this day.
I'm like,
"Richard Green get me
out of this police car, please!"
So a Black captain came by,
thank God,
and he says, "What's goin' on?"
Richard Green explained it to him.
He said, "Let him go."
Get back in the van,
there's another Brother in van,
starts saying,
"Non violence!"
to the young Brothers.
They begin throwing bottles at the, uh,
at the van.
One guy got so upset
he had a nine-millimeter
fully loaded.
He said, "Get the hell out of this neighborhood!"

The next day
more violence:
fires,
cars being burnt,
stores being broken into,
a perception that Black youth
are going crazy in Crown Heights
like we were angry over
nothing,
understand?

Norman Rosenbaum
My Brother's Blood

(*A Sunday afternoon. Spring. Crisp, clear, and windy. Across from City Hall in New York City. Crowds of people, predominantly Lubavitcher, with placards. A rally that was organized by Lubavitcher women. All of the speakers were men, but the women stand close to the stage. Mr. Rosenbaum, an Australian, with a beard, hat, and wearing a pinstripe suit, speaks passionately and loudly from the microphone on a stage with a podium. Behind him is a man in an Australian bush hat with a very large Australian flag which blows dramatically in the wind. It is so windy that Mr. Rosenbaum has to hold his hat to keep it on his head.*)

Al do lay achee so achee aylay alo.dalmo
My brother's blood cries out from the ground.
Let me make it clear
why I'm here.
In August of 1991,
as you all have heard before today,
my brother was killed in the streets of Crown Heights
for no other reason
than that he was a Jew!
The only miracle was
that my brother was the only victim
who paid for being a Jew with his life.
When my brother was surrounded,
each and every American was surrounded.
When my brother was stabbed four times,
each and every American was stabbed four times
and as my brother bled to death in this city,
while the medicos stood by
and let him bleed
to death, it was the gravest of indictments against this
     country.
One person out of twenty gutless individuals
who attacked my brother has been arrested.
I for one am not convinced that it is beyond the ability
     of the New York police
to arrest others.
Let me tell you, Mayor Dinkins,
let me tell you, Commissioner Brown:
I'm here,
I'm not going home,
until there is justice.

Norman Rosenbaum
Sixteen Hours Difference

(7:00 A.M. *Spring. Newark Airport, Departure Gate, Continental Airlines. Mr. Rosenbaum is moments before his flight to LA and then back to Australia. Wearing a pinstripe suit with an Australian fit. Hat. Suitcase. He has sparkling blue eyes with a twinkle, rosy cheeks, and a large smile throughout the interview.*)

There's sixteen hours difference between New York and
    Melbourne
and I had just gotten back to my office
and I had a phone call from my wife,
and she said she wanted me to come home straight away
and I sensed the urgency in her voice.
I said, "are you all right?" She said, "Yeah."
I said, "are the children all right, you know the kids?"
    She says, "yeah."
So I'm driving home and I'm thinking, I wonder what's
    the problem now, you know?
We had some carpenters doing some work, I wonder if
    there has been a disaster,
some sort of domestic problem,
and I thought, oh my God, you know, my parents,
I didn't even ask after them,
how insensitive not to even ask after my parents,
and I've got a grandmother eighty-five years old, same
    sort of thing.
So I get home,
I walk in the door, and a friend of mine was standing
    there,
close friend,
does the same sort of work as me, he's a barrister and an
    academic,
and he sees me and he says,
"There's got a pro —
uh,
we've got a problem. There's a problem."
I thought he was talking about a case we were working
    on together,
he says, "'Z come,
come and sit down."
He goes to me,
"There's been a riot in New York,
been a riot in Crown Heights,
Yankel's been stabbed and he's dead."
And
my brother was the last in the world,
I hadn't even given him a thought.
I mean the fact that my brother
could be attacked
or die,
it just hadn't even entered my mind.
At first I appeared all cool, calm and collected.
I then
started asking questions
like who told you,
how do you know,

are you sure?
I just asked the question,
you know,
are you sure?

Anonymous Young Man #2
Bad Boy

(*Evening. Spring. The same recreation room as interview with Anonymous Young Man #1. Young Man #2 is wearing a black jacket over his clothes. He has a gold tooth. He has some dreadlocks, and a very odd-shaped multicolored hat. He is soft-spoken, and has a direct gaze. He seems to be very patient with his explanation.*)

That youth,
that sixteen-year-old
didn't murder that Jew.

(*Pause*)

For one thing,
he played baseball, right?
He was a atha-lete,
right?
A bad boy
does
bad things.
Only a bad boy coulda stabbed the man.
Somebody who
does those type a things,
or who sees
those types a things.
A atha-lete
sees people,
is interested in athletics,
stretchin',
exercisin',
goin' to his football games,
or his baseball games.
He's not interested
in stabbin'
people.
so
it's not in his mind
to stab,
to just jump into somethin',
that he has no idea about
and
sta —
and kill a man.
A bad boy,
somebody who's groomed in badness,
or did badness
before,
stabbed the man.
Because I used to be a atha-lete
and I used to be a bad boy,
and when I was a atha-lete,

I was a atha-lete.
All I thought about was atha-lete.
I'm not gonna jeopardize my athleticism
or my career to do anything
that bad people do.
And when I became a bad boy
I'm not a athalete no more.
I'm a bad boy,
and I'm groomin' myself in things that is bad.
You understand, so
he's a athalete,
he's not a bad boy.
It's a big difference.
Like,
mostly the Black youth in Crown Heights have two
    things to do —
either DJ or be a bad boy, right?
You either
DJ, be a MC, a rapper
or Jamaican rapper,
ragamuffin,
or you be a bad boy,
you sell drugs or you rob people.
What do you do?
I sell drugs.
What do you do?
I rap.
That's how it is in Crown Heights.
I been livin' in Crown Heights mosta my life.
I know for a fact that that youth, that sixteen-year-old,
didn't kill that Jew.
That's between me and my Creator.

Sonny Carson
Chords

(*Lunchtime. Spring. A fancy restaurant in Brooklyn.
Sonny tells me it's where all the judges come for lunch.
White linen tablecloths. Light wood walls, lamplight
next to the table. Tile floor. He is eating crab cakes. He
is dressed in a black turtleneck and a gray jacket. He has
on a mud cloth hat. He has an authority stick with him,
and it lays on the table. His bodyguard, wearing a black
leather jacket, enters in the middle of the interview.
Sonny chides him for being late.*)

It's going to be a long hot summer.
I'm connected up with the young people all over the
    country
and there's a thread
leading to an eruption
and Crown Heights began the whole thing.
And the Jews come second to the police
when it comes to feelings of dislike among Black folks.
The police,
the police,
believe me, the police —
I know the police and the police know me

and they turn that whole place into an occupied camp
with the Seventy-first Precinct as the overseers.
And don't think that everything is OK within that
    precinct among those officers
either.
Don't think that,
don't think that.
You know the media has always painted me as the bad
    guy —
that's OK!
I'm a good guy to pick on.
Their viewers don't like me either,
they really don't like me because I *am* the bad guy,
I am the ultimate bad guy
because of my relationship to the young people in the
    city.
I understand their language.
I respect them as the future.
I speak their language. They don't even engage in long
    dialogue
anymore
just short
"words."
It always amazes me
how the city fathers,
the power brokers,
just continue to deny what's happening.
And it is just getting intolerable for me to continue to
    watch
this small
arrogant
group of people continue to get this kind of preferential
    treatment.
They sit on the school board.
A board of nine
and they have
four members, and their kids don't even go to public
    school.
So that's the kind of arrogance I'm talking about.
I have no reason to be eagerly awaiting the coming
    together of our
people.
They owe me first.
I'm not givin' in just like that,
I don't want it.
You can have it.
Like my grandmother said,
"Help the bear!
If you see me and the bear in a fight,
help the bear —
don't help me,
help the bear."
I don't need any of it from them!
And I'm not gonna advocate any coming together and
    healing of
America
and all that shit.
You kiddin'?
You kiddin'?

Just 'cause I can have the fortune of walking in here
and sitting and talking
and having a drink,
it appear that I have all the same kinds of abilities
of other folks in here.
No, it's not that way.
'Cause tonight
by nighttime it could all change for me.
So I'm always aware of that, and that's what keeps me
    goin'
today
and each day!

(*He eats*)

I have
this idea
about a film.
See,
these kids, they got
another kinda rhythm now,
there's a whole new kinda
step that they do.
When I first heard rap
I was sittin' in a huge open kinda stadium,
boys and girls high school field,
and I heard these kids come out and start rappin',
and I'm listening
but it's not really clickin',
but I was mesmerized though.
But it was simontaneouis
all around the country
and I said, "Oh shit,"
and everybody I knew who was young was listenin' to it
and I said, "Wow."
Because I have always been involved with young people
and all of a sudden I got it,
I really heard the rhythm,
the chords
the discord.
There's a whole new sound
that the crackers are tryin' to get, but they can't get it.
I heard it on a television commercial.
One of the most beautiful pieces of art
that I ever witnessed
was a play
called
um,
um,
um,
'bout, 'bout the Puerto Rican gang —
no, no, no, no, no —
the Puerto Rican gang,
the musical
that was on Broad —
yeah,
West Side Story —
the answer should be
a musical.

Rabbi Shea Hecht
Ovens

(*Morning. Spring. A building on Eastern Parkway. A large room with a very long conference table. There are pictures of Lubavitcher men on the walls. Rabbi Hecht is wearing a shirt, open at the neck. He has several crisp one-dollar bills in his shirt pocket. These are, apparently, dollar bills that the Rebbe has given him. It is the custom that the Rebbe gives out one-dollar bills on Sunday. Rabbi Hecht has a beard. He wears glasses, traditional Hasidic garb, including tsitses (ceremonial fringes that hang over his belt) and a red yarmulke with gold trim which is ripped. His daughter comes in frequently to get money from him. He keeps telling her to wait until he is finished. She becomes more and more agitated. His brother also enters frequently to ask him questions, and to tell him he's late.*)

What is my goal?
My goal is not
to give anybody a message
that we plan on working things out
by integrating
our two
things.
By a person understanding more of their own religion
they will automatically respect another person.
The respect that my religion teaches me has nothing to do
with understanding you.
See, there's a problem.
If
the only way I'm going to respect you
is based on how much I understand you,
no matter what it is
in certain circles you're gonna run into problems.
Number one,
we are different,
and we think we should and can be different.
When the Rebbe said to the Mayor
that we were all
one people,
I think
what the Rebbe is talking about is that,
that common denominator that we're all children of
    God, and the
respect we all have to give each other under that banner.
But that does not mean that I have to invite you to my
    house for
dinner,
because I cannot go back to your home for dinner,
because you're not gonna give me kosher food.
And I said,
so, like one Black said,
I'll bring in kosher food.
I said eh-eh.
We can't use your ovens,
we can't use your dishes,

it's, it —
it's not just a question of buying certain food,
it's buying the food,
preparing it a certain way.
We can't use your dishes, we can't use your oven.
The — the higher you go
the more common denominator.
And what the Rebbe was saying,
you as the Mayor
don't get caught up in the differences,
you're —
from your position is —
you have to look at it as one city
and one
human race.
We are all New Yorkers
and therefore I will protect all New Yorkers.
You see
preferential treatment
suggests
that you're giving the person
the police car
not because they need the police car
but because
they are who they are.
You're not gonna
give them the housing
because they
need the housing —
you're giving it because of who they are.
But
just because I'm a Jew
therefore I
shouldn't get the police car.
The question is
a synagogue
that has five thousand Jews
leave
the synagogue
at the same time,
do they have a police car to stop the traffic?
The answer is every — single — synagogue,
temple,
mosque,
in
the
world
stops traffic
when five thousand people have to walk out
at the same time.

Reverend Al Sharpton
Rain

The D.A.
came back with no indictment.
Uh, so then our only course

was to ask for a special prosecutor
which is appointed by the Governor,
who's been hostile,
and to sue civilly.
When we went into civil court
we went to get an order to show cause.
The judge signed it and gave me a deadline of three days.
The driver left the country. . . .
No one even said, "Why would he run?
If he did no wrong."
If you and I were in an accident we'd have to go to civil
    court.
Why is this man
above the law?
So they said, "He's in Israel."
So I said,
"Well, I'll go to Israel to show best effits."
And the deadline
was,
I had to serve him by Tuesday,
which was Yom Kippur —
that was the judge's decision not mine.
So we went.
Alton Maddox° and I
got on a plane,
left Monday night,
landed Tuesday morning,
went and served the American embassy, uh,
so that
if this man had any decency at all
he could come to the American embassy and receive ser-
    vice,
which he has not done to this day.
Come back,
went to court
and showed the judge the receipts,
and the judge said, "You made best effits,
therefore you are now permitted,
by default,
to go ahead
and sue the rabbi or whomever
because you cannot do the driver."
So it wasn't just a media grandstand.
We wanted to show the world
one, this man *ran*
and was *allowed* to run, and, two, we wanted to be able
    to legally go
around him,
to sue the people he was working for so that we can
    bring them into
court and establish *why* and what happened.
And it came out in the paper the other day
that the driver in the other car didn't even have a driver's
    license.
So we're dealing with a *complete* outrage here,
we're dealing with a double standard,

Alton Maddox: Activist lawyer.

we're dealing with uh, uh, a, a
situation where
Blacks do not have equal protection under the law
and the media is used to castigate us
that merely asked for justice
rather than castigate those that would hit a kid
and walk away like he just stepped on a roach!
Uh,
there also is the media
contention of the young Jewish scholar
that was stabbed that night
and they've even distorted
saying *my words at the funeral.*
I *preached* the funeral.
Uh, [the newspaper said I]
helped to, to, uh, uh,
spark or, or, or, or, or *inspire* or *incite* people to kill him
    [Yankel Rosenbaum]
when he was dead the day before
I came out there.
He was killed the night
that the young man
was killed with the car accident.
I didn't even get a call
from the family
'til eighteen hours later.
So there's a whole media distortion
to protect them [the Lubavitchers].
Nobody is talking about,
"Why
is this guy
in flight?"
If I was a rabbi
(I am a ministuh)
and my driver hit a kid,
I would not let the driver *leave*
and I certainlih would give my condolences,
or anything else I could,
to the family,
I don't care what race they are.
To this minute the Rebbe has never even uttered a word of
sympathy
to the family,
not even sent 'em a *card*
a *flower* or *nothing*!
So it's treating us with absolute contempt
and I don't care how controversial it makes us.
I *won't* tolerate being insulted.
If you piss in my face I'm gonna call it *piss.*
I'm not gonna call it rain.

Richard Green
Rage

(2:00 P.M. *in a big red van. Green is in the front. He has
a driver. I am in the back. Green wears a large knit hat
with reggae colors over long dreadlocks. Driving from*

Crown Heights to Brooklyn College. *He turns sideways
to face me in the back, and bends down, talking with his
elbow on his knee.*)

Sharpton, Carson, and Reverend Herbert Daughtry
didn't have any power out there really.
The media gave them power.
But they weren't turning those youfs on and off.
Nobody knew who controlled the switch out there.
Those young people had rage like an oil-well fire
that has to burn out.
All they were doin' was sort of orchestratin' it.
Uh, they were not really the ones that were saying, "Well
stop, go, don't go, stop, turn around, go up."
It wasn't like that.
Those young people had rage out there,
that didn't matter who was in control of that —
that rage had to get out
and that rage
has been building up.
When all those guys have come and gone,
that rage is still out here.
I can show you that rage every day
right up and down this avenue.
We see, sometimes in one month, we see three bodies
in one month. That's rage,
and that's something that nobody has control of.
And I don't know who told you that it was preferential
    treatment for
Blacks that the Mayor kept the cops back. . . .
If the Mayor had turned those cops on?
We would still be in a middle of a battle.
And
I pray on both sides of the fence,
and I tell the people in the Jewish community the same
    thing,
"This is not something that force will hold."
Those youfs were running on cops without nothing in
    their hands,
seven- and eight- and nine- and ten-year-old boys were
    running at
those cops
with nothing,
just running at 'em.
That's rage.
Those young people out there are angry
and that anger has to be vented,
it has to be negotiated.
And they're not angry at the Lubavitcher community
they're just as angry at you and me,
if it comes to that.
They have no
role models,
no guidance
so they're just out there growin' up on their own,
their peers are their role models,
their peers is who teach them how to move
so when they see the Lubavitch
they don't know the difference between "Heil Hitler"

and, uh, and uh, whatever else.
They don't know the difference.
When you ask 'em to say who Hitler was they wouldn't even be able
to tell you.

(*Phone rings, Richard picks it up, it's a mobile phone*)

"Richard Green, can I help?
Aw, man I tol' you I want some color
up on that wall. Give me some colors.
Look, I'm in the middle of somethin'."

(*He returns to the conversation*)

Half them don't even know three quarters of 'em.
Just as much as they don't know who Frederick Douglass° was.
They know Malcolm°
because Malcolm has been played up to such an extent now
that they know Malcolm.
But ask who Nat Turner was or Mary McCleod Bethune or Booker T.°
Because the system has given 'em
Malcolm is convenient and
Spike is goin' to give 'em Malcolm even more.
It's convenient.

Roslyn Malamud
The Coup

(*Spring. Midafternoon. The sunny kitchen of a huge, beautiful house on Eastern Parkway in Crown Heights. It's a large, very well-equipped kitchen. We are sitting at a table in a breakfast nook area, which is separated by shelves from the cooking area. There is a window to the side. There are newspapers on the chair at the far side of the table. Mrs. Malamud offers me food at the beginning of the interview. We are drinking coffee. She is wearing a sweatshirt with a large sequined cat. Her tennis shoes have matching sequined cats. She has on a black skirt and is wearing a wig. Her nails are manicured. She has beautiful eyes that sparkle, are very warm, and a very resonant voice. There is a lot of humor in her face.*)

Do you know what happened in August here?
You see when you read the newspapers.
I mean my son filmed what was going on,
but when you read the newspapers . . .
Of course I was here
I couldn't leave my house.
I only would go out early during the day.
The police were barricading here.

Douglass: Frederick Douglass (1818–1895), leading Black abolitionist.   **Malcolm:** Malcolm X (Little) (1925–1965), Black Muslim leader and spokesman.   **Nat . . . Booker T.:** Nat Turner (1800–1831), leader of a slave revolt; Mary McLeod Bethune (1875–1955), prominent African American teacher; Booker T. Washington (1856–1915), American educator.

You see,
I wish
I could just like
go on television.
I wanna scream to the whole world.
They said
that the Blacks were rioting against the Jews in Crown Heights
and that the Jews were fighting back.
Do you know that the Blacks who came here to riot were not my
neighbors?
I don't love my neighbors.
I don't know my Black neighbors.
There's one lady on President Street —
Claire —
I adore her.
She's my girl friend's next-door neighbor.
I've had a manicure
done in her house and we sit and kibbitz
and stuff
but I don't know them.
I told you we don't mingle socially
because of the difference
of food
and religion
and what have you here.
But
the people in this community
want exactly
what I want out of life.
They want to live
in nice homes.
They all go to work.
They couldn't possibly
have houses here
if they didn't
generally — They have
two,
um,
incomes
that come in.
They want to send their kids to college.
They wanna live a nice quiet life.
They wanna shop for their groceries and cook their meals and go to
their Sunday picnics!
They just want to have decent homes and decent lives!
The people who came to riot here
were brought here
by this famous
Reverend Al Sharpton,
which I'd like to know who ordained him?
And he brought in a bunch of kids.
I wish you could see the *New York Times*,
unfortunately it was on page twenty,
but,
he brought in a bunch of kids who didn't have jobs in the summertime

when you don't have a job
and you're hanging out all day.
I mean, they interviewed
one of the Black girls on Utica Avenue.
She said,
"The guys will make you pregnant
at night
and in the morning not know who you are."

(*Almost whispering*)

And if you're sitting on a front stoop and its very, very hot
and you have no money
and you have nothing to do with your time
and someone says, "Come on, you wanna riot?"
You know how kids are.
The fault lies with the police department.
The police department did nothing to stop them.
I was sitting here in the front of the house
when bottles were being thrown
and the sergeant tells five hundred policemen
with clubs and helmets and guns
to duck.
And I said to him,
"You're telling them to duck?
What should I do?
I don't have a club and a gun."
Had they put it —
stopped it on the first night
this kid who came from Australia . . .

(*She sucks her teeth*)

You know,
his parents were Holocaust survivors, he didn't have to
    die.
He worked,
did a lot of research in Holocaust studies.
He didn't have to die.
What happened on Utica Avenue
was an accident.
JEWISH PEOPLE
DO NOT DRIVE VANS INTO SEVEN-YEAR-OLD
    BOYS.
YOU WANT TO KNOW SOMETHING? BLACK
    PEOPLE DO NOT DRIVE
VANS INTO SEVEN-YEAR-OLD BOYS.
HISPANIC PEOPLE DON'T DRIVE VANS INTO
    SEVEN-YEAR-OLD BOYS.
IT'S JUST NOT DONE.
PEOPLE LIKE JEFFREY DAHMER° MAYBE THEY
    DO IT.
BUT AVERAGE CITIZENS DO NOT GO OUT AND
    TRY TO KILL

(*Sounds like a laugh but it's just a sound*)

SEVEN-YEAR-OLD BOYS.

Jeffrey Dahmer: (1960–1994), mass murderer and cannibal.

It was an accident!
But it was allowed to fester and to steam and all that.
When you come here do you see anything that's going
    on, riots?
No.
But Al Sharpton and the likes of him like *Dowerty*,
who by the way has been in prison
and all of a sudden he became Reverend *Dowerty* —
they once did an exposé on him —
but
these guys live off of this,
you understand?
People are not gonna give them money,
contribute to their causes
unless they're out there rabble-rousing
My Black neighbors?
I mean I spoke to them.
They were hiding in their houses just like I was.
We were scared.
I was scared!
I was really frightened.
I had five hundred policemen standing in front of my
    house
every day
I had mounted police,
but I couldn't leave my block,
because when it got dark I couldn't come back in.
I couldn't meet anyone for dinner.
Thank God, I told you my children were all out of town.
My son was in Russia.
The coup
was exactly the same day as the riot
and I was very upset about it.
He was in Russia running a camp
and I was very concerned when I had heard about that.
I hadn't heard from him
that night the riot started.
When I did hear from him I told him to stay in Russia,
    he'd be safer
there than here.
And he was.

Reuven Ostrov
Pogroms°

(*9:00 P.M. November 1991. In a basement of a Crown
Heights house. Mr. Ostrov wears a yarmulke. Eating
popcorn and sliced apples. Very low, gentle-sounding
nigunim° music plays in the background, it almost
sounds like New Age music, perhaps because traditional
music is played on a modern electronic keyboard instrument. In the show, I wore a basketball jacket with the
team's insignia, and used a basketball — which Mr.*

Pogrom: Systematic persecution of Jews.   **nigunim:** Popular
Jewish music.

*Ostrov did not do at this interview, but previously had
at a basketball game. He has no beard, which is unusual
for a man his age who does have a beard if grown. He
has a very rich, deep voice.)*

I was working in a hospital.
I work as an assistant chaplain at
Down State Kings County Hospital.
I heard that Yankel Rosenbaum was stabbed and, um,
    they
were gonna give him an *aurtopsy*
and they asked if he had an
aurtopsy
or not because in the Jewish religion a person is not
    allowed to have
an aurtopsy
and I found out later that he did have one
a few days later.
I found a Jewish man in a room,
a Russian man.
His mother committed suicide
because she was, uhm, she was terrified.
She jumped out of the third floor of her apartment
    building,
committed suicide.
The mother originally came from Russia.
I was speaking to her son
in one of the rooms near the morgue
trying to get his mother not to have an aurtopsy
and he was telling me that the mother
came from Russia eleven years ago
and the mother left Russia eleven years ago
because of the hardships that they had over there,
and when they came to America
and when this thing started to happen in Crown
    Heights.
It became painful
and it felt like, like there was no place to go.
It's like you're trapped,
everywhere you go there's Jew haters.
And then he told me she commit suicide,
told me the next morning he woke up
he heard the doorbell ring.
He wasn't,
she wasn't there.
He noticed that the window was open,
which is never open
because she was afraid of the cold
even in the summertime.
And he saw his mother
with blood all over her
landed head first
on the concrete side of the apartment building.
After that we already knew this was getting serious,
because we had,
we had Sonny Carson come down
and we had, um,
Reverend Al Sharpton come down
start making pogroms.

Carmel Cato
Lingering

(7:00 P.M. *The corner where the accident occurred in
Crown Heights. An altar to Gavin is against the wall
where the car crashed. Many pieces of cloth are draped.
Some writing in color is on the wall. Candle wax is
everywhere. There is a rope around the area. Cato is
wearing a trench coat, pulled around him. He stands
very close to me. Dark outside. Reggae music is in the
background. Lights come from stores on each corner.
Busy intersection. Sounds from outside. Traffic. Stores
open. People in and out of shops. Sounds from inside
apartments, televisions, voices, cooking, etc. He speaks
in a pronounced West Indian accent.)*

In the meanwhile
it was two.
Angela was on the ground
but she was trying to move. Gavin was still.
They was trying to pound him.
I was the father.
I was 'it, chucked, and pushed,
and a lot of
sarcastic words were passed towards me
from the police
while I was trying to explain: It was my kid!
These are my children.
The child was hit you know.
I saw everything, everything,
the guy radiator burst
all the hoses,
the steam,
all the garbage buckets along the building.
And it was very loud,
everything burst.
It's like an atomic bomb,
and that's why all these people comin' round
wanna know what's happening.
Oh it was very outrageous.
Numerous numbers.
All the time the police sayin'
you can't get in,
you can't pass,
and the children laying on the ground.
He was hit at exactly eight-thirty.
Why?
I was standing over there.
There was a little child —
a friend of mine
came up with a little child —
and I lift the child up
and she look at her watch at the same time
and she say it was eight-thirty.
I gave the child back to her.
And then it happen.
Um, Um . . .
My child, these are the things I never dream about.
I take care of my children.

You know it's a funny thing,
if a child get sick and he dies
it won't hurt me so bad,
or if a child run out into the street
it wouldn't hurt me.
That's what's hurtin' me.
And the whole week
that Gavin died
my body was changing,
I was having different feelings.
I stop eating,
I didn't et
nothin',
only drink water,
for two weeks;
and I was very touchy —
any least thing that drop
or any song I hear
it would effect me.
Every time I try to do something
I would have to stop.
I was
lingering, lingering, lingering, lingering,
all the time.
But I can do things,
I can see things,
I know that for a fact.
I was telling myself,
"Something is wrong somewhere,"
but I didn't want to see,
I didn't want to accept,
and it was inside of me,
and even when I go home I tell my friends,
"Something coming I could feel it
but I didn't want to see,"
and all the time I just deny deny deny,
and I never thought it was Gavin,
but I didn't have a clue.
I thought it was one of the other children —

the bigger boys
or the girl,
because she worry me,
she won't et —
but Gavin 'ee was 'ealtee,
and he don't cause no trouble.
That's what's devastating me now.
Sometime it make me feel like it's no justice,
like, uh,
the Jewish people,
they are very high up,
it's a very big thing,
they runnin' the whole show
from the judge right down.
And something I don't understand:
The Jewish people, they told me
there are certain people I can not be seen with
and certain things I can not say
and certain people I can not talk to.
They made that very clear to me — the Jewish people —
they can throw the case out
unless
I go to them with pity.
I don't know what they talkin' about.
So I don't know what kind of crap is that.
And make me say things I don't wanna say
and make me do things I don't wanna do.
I am a special person.
I was born different.
I'm a man born by my foot.
I born by my foot.
Anytime a baby comin' by the foot
they either cut the mother
or the baby dies.
But I was born with my foot.
I'm one of the special.
There's no way they can overpower me.
No there's nothing to hide,
you can repeat every word I say.

Paula Vogel

Paula Vogel (b. 1951) came from a Washington, DC, working-class family and knew she would have to make it on her own if she made it at all. For her, that knowledge was essentially the best inheritance she could have had. Her early years were marred by her parents' divorce and the loss of a father whom she came to know only in later years when her closest sibling, Carl, was dying of AIDS. Her earliest efforts in playwriting also met with rejection. After losing her scholarship to Bryn Mawr College, she devoted herself to dramatic literature and graduated from Catholic University in Washington, then was turned down by the Yale School of Drama. Her earliest plays were also turned down by the Eugene O'Neill National Playwright's Conference. In retrospect, she feels that these were good things because they made her learn her craft in a difficult — and original — way, which led eventually to her winning the Pulitzer Prize for *How I Learned to Drive*.

Vogel's earliest exposure to theater was in Washington, D.C. She talks about having "stumbled into drama class" when she was a sophomore in high school and beginning to find her way in theater. Her high school drama teacher was gay, and she feels he must have realized that she was herself a lesbian. She resisted taking acting roles — although she coached other students — and spent her years in high school as a stage manager. As a young playwright she found other friends who were trying to write, and they gathered together to read each other's work. They occasionally did exercises, some of which became useful teaching tools for Vogel at Brown University. For example, they wrote complete plays in forty-eight hours as a way of getting the essentials down as quickly as possible. Some of her earliest work had its origin in these experiments, including a version of *How I Learned to Drive*.

Some of her plays have startling images, such as a bizarre Groucho Marx–like doctor treating a dying AIDS patient in *The Baltimore Waltz* (which won an Obie Award for best play in 1992), a play about the death of her beloved brother Carl, who had begun a professional career as an English professor but switched to being a librarian. He was gay, and homophobia, according to Vogel, hurt him more than the disease that killed him. Her plays are famous for scatological humor, jokes about the body, and extremely plain talk.

Among her early plays is one about lesbians who parent several little boys: *And Baby Makes Seven* (1984) — a daring excursion into territory that few playwrights have explored. Another early play, *The Oldest Profession* (1988), treats older prostitutes. *Hot 'n' Throbbing* (1994) examines the effect of theater on its characters. *The Mineola Twins* (1996) was written before *How I Learned to Drive* but was produced later, in 1999. Vogel thinks of this play as a comedy and something of a contrast to *How I Learned to Drive*, which is, if not a tragedy, certainly serious in nature. Yet it too has moments of genuine comedy.

Paula Vogel's most recent play is *The Long Chrismas Ride Home*, which opened in June 2003 in Providence's Trinity Repertory Company. It moved into the Vineyard Theatre in New York in December 2003 to good reviews. *New York Times* critic Ben Brantley said of the June production that: "*The Long Christmas Ride Home* is partly a latter-day answer to the works of Thornton Wilder, including *Our Town,* and the short pieces *The Long Christmas Dinner* and *The Happy Journey to Trenton and Camden.*"[1] The play employs half-size puppets, borrowing from the Japanese Bunraku-style theater. Using puppets to help portray a dysfunctional family has been widely praised for producing appropriate and subtle emotional nuances. The 2004 production at Long Wharf Theatre was enormously effective and powerful theater.

HOW I LEARNED TO DRIVE

How I Learned to Drive was first produced in New York off-Broadway in 1997. It won not only the Pulitzer Prize but also the New York Drama Critics' Circle, Drama Desk, and Obie awards for best play of the year. It is published in a volume with *The Mineola Twins* called *The Mammary Plays*. Vogel explains that large-busted women remained an emblem for her in the construction of both plays. As a feminist, Vogel is interested in our fetishization of women's bodies, and both these plays move toward revealing the way the culture, both men and women, regard women's bodies, even while praising their minds.

All the characters in Li'l Bit's family are named in an unusual way. Li'l Bit explains, "In my family, if we call someone 'Big Papa,' it's not because he's tall. In my family, folks tend to get nicknamed for their genitalia. Uncle Peck, for example. My mamma's adage was 'the titless wonder.' Even Li'l Bit was named after she was physically examined at birth. Uncle Peck, married to Li'l Bit's mother's sister Mary, is not a blood relation — a fact he constantly stresses to Li'l Bit — and he tells her he has loved her since she was small enough to hold in his hand. Even Big Papa chases Grandma around the house: it's an unusual and curious family.

The play is about sexual molestation — but about many other things, too. It is about families, about growing up, about becoming independent, and most of all about being a survivor. In an interview with Arthur Holmberg, literary director of American Repertory Theatre, Vogel has said, "My play dramatizes the gifts we receive from people who hurt us." When asked what gift Li'l Bit received, Vogel responded, "She received the gift of how to survive." Vogel uses learning to drive as a complex metaphor for sexual initiation. At the same time, the metaphor examines what a man expects from a close relationship with a woman and what a woman expects from a close relationship with a man. Uncle Peck is careful never to hurt Li'l Bit and always reminds her that he doesn't want her to do anything she doesn't wish to do. But at the same time,

Uncle Peck "has a way" with adolescent girls, as his wife tells us. He listens to Li'l Bit and becomes her confidante, patiently waiting for her to accept him on his own terms.

Although he is a predator, Uncle Peck is not necessarily a villain in the play. He takes advantage of Li'l Bit starting at age eleven and continues until she is eighteen and in college. For Vogel, part of the learning process for Li'l Bit is, as Vogel has said, becoming "an adult looking at and understanding her complicity." Then the next step is self-forgiveness. This step is essential to moving forward in her life.

How I Learned to Drive in Performance

The Vineyard Theatre in New York produced the play in February 1997 and moved it to the large Century Theater in April. It was reviewed warmly and received positively by audiences, eventually winning Vogel the Pulitzer Prize for drama for 1997. The play relies on an interesting device, the Greek Chorus, a character who speaks in the voice of characters alluded to but not present, such as Li'l Bit's mother, grandmother, grandfather, and aunt. Vogel also wanted to have slides shown at critical moments, such as the scene in which Uncle Peck is taking photographs of Li'l Bit and in the scene in which Uncle Peck rhapsodizes over 1950s automobiles. Not all directors use the slides. For example, they were not used in the original New York production. Vogel's method of writing, like that of many playwrights, is to respond to the actors' interpretation of lines during rehearsal and rewriting. *How I Learned to Drive* benefited from that method.

In 1998 *How I Learned to Drive* had twenty-six regional productions and was the most produced play in the United States. Many more regional and international productions have followed, with numerous university productions in 2002, 2003, and 2004.

Paula Vogel (b. 1951)
HOW I LEARNED TO DRIVE

1997

Characters

LI'L BIT, *A woman who ages forty-something to eleven years old.*

PECK, *Attractive man in his forties. Despite a few problems, he should be played by an actor one might cast in the role of Atticus in* To Kill A Mockingbird.

THE GREEK CHORUS, *If possible, these three members should be able to sing three-part harmony.*

> MALE GREEK CHORUS, *Plays Grandfather, Waiter, High School Boys. Thirties–forties.*

FEMALE GREEK CHORUS, *Plays Mother, Aunt Mary, High School Girls. Thirty–fifty.*
TEENAGE GREEK CHORUS, *Plays Grandmother, High School Girls, and the voice of eleven-year-old Li'l Bit. Note on the casting of this actor: I would strongly recommend casting a young woman who is "of legal age," that is, twenty-one to twenty-five years old, who can look as close to eleven as possible. The contrast with the other cast members will help. If the actor is too young, the audience may feel uncomfortable.*

(As the house lights dim, a Voice announces:)

Safety First — You and Driver Education.

(*Then the sound of a key turning the ignition of a car. Li'l Bit steps into a spotlight on the stage; "well-endowed," she is a softer-looking woman in the present time than she was at seventeen.*)

Lɪ'ʟ Bɪᴛ: Sometimes to tell a secret, you first have to teach a lesson. We're going to start our lesson tonight on an early, warm summer evening.

In a parking lot overlooking the Beltsville Agricultural Farms in suburban Maryland.

Less than a mile away, the crumbling concrete of U.S. One wends its way past one-room revival churches, the porno drive-in, and boarded up motels with For Sale signs tumbling down.

Like I said, it's a warm summer evening.

Here on the land the Department of Agriculture owns, the smell of sleeping farm animals is thick on the air. The smells of clover and hay mix in with the smells of the leather dashboard. You can still imagine how Maryland used to be, before the malls took over. This countryside was once dotted with farmhouses — from their porches you could have witnessed the Civil War raging in the front fields.

Oh yes. There's a moon over Maryland tonight, that spills into the car where I sit beside a man old enough to be — did I mention how still the night is? Damp soil and tranquil air. It's the kind of night that makes a middle-aged man with a mortgage feel like a country boy again.

It's 1969. And I am very old, very cynical of the world, and I know it all. In short, I am seventeen years old, parking off a dark lane with a married man on an early summer night.

(*Lights up on two chairs facing front — or a Buick Riviera, if you will. Waiting patiently, with a smile on his face, Peck sits sniffing the night air. Li'l Bit climbs in beside him, seventeen years old and tense. Throughout the following, the two sit facing directly front. They do not touch. Their bodies remain passive. Only their facial expressions emote.*)

Pᴇᴄᴋ: Ummm. I love the smell of your hair.
Lɪ'ʟ Bɪᴛ: Uh-huh.
Pᴇᴄᴋ: Oh, Lord. Ummmm. (*Beat.*) A man could die happy like this.
Lɪ'ʟ Bɪᴛ: Well, *don't.*
Pᴇᴄᴋ: What shampoo is this?
Lɪ'ʟ Bɪᴛ: Herbal Essence.
Pᴇᴄᴋ: Herbal Essence. I'm gonna buy me some. Herbal Essence. And when I'm all alone in the house, I'm going to get into the bathtub, and uncap the bottle and —
Lɪ'ʟ Bɪᴛ: — Be good.
Pᴇᴄᴋ: What?
Lɪ'ʟ Bɪᴛ: Stop being . . . bad.
Pᴇᴄᴋ: What did you think I was going to say? What do you think I'm going to do with the shampoo?

Lɪ'ʟ Bɪᴛ: I don't want to know. I don't want to hear it.
Pᴇᴄᴋ: I'm going to wash my hair. That's all.
Lɪ'ʟ Bɪᴛ: Oh.
Pᴇᴄᴋ: What did you think I was going to do?
Lɪ'ʟ Bɪᴛ: Nothing . . . I don't know. Something . . . nasty.
Pᴇᴄᴋ: With shampoo? Lord, gal — your mind!
Lɪ'ʟ Bɪᴛ: And whose fault is it?
Pᴇᴄᴋ: Not mine. I've got the mind of a boy scout.
Lɪ'ʟ Bɪᴛ: Right. A horny boy scout.
Pᴇᴄᴋ: Boy scouts are always horny. What do you think the first Merit Badge is for?
Lɪ'ʟ Bɪᴛ: There. You're going to be nasty again.
Pᴇᴄᴋ: Oh, no. I'm good. Very good.
Lɪ'ʟ Bɪᴛ: It's getting late.
Pᴇᴄᴋ: Don't change the subject. I was talking about how good I am. (*Beat.*) Are you ever gonna let me show you how good I am?
Lɪ'ʟ Bɪᴛ: Don't go over the line now.
Pᴇᴄᴋ: I won't. I'm not gonna do anything you don't want me to do.
Lɪ'ʟ Bɪᴛ: That's right.
Pᴇᴄᴋ: And I've been good all week.
Lɪ'ʟ Bɪᴛ: You have?
Pᴇᴄᴋ: Yes. All week. Not a single drink.
Lɪ'ʟ Bɪᴛ: Good boy.
Pᴇᴄᴋ: Do I get a reward? For not drinking?
Lɪ'ʟ Bɪᴛ: A small one. It's getting late.
Pᴇᴄᴋ: Just let me undo you. I'll do you back up.
Lɪ'ʟ Bɪᴛ: All right. But be quick about it.

(*Peck pantomimes undoing Li'l Bit's brassiere with one hand.*)

You know, that's amazing. The way you can undo the hooks through my blouse with one hand.
Pᴇᴄᴋ: Years of practice.
Lɪ'ʟ Bɪᴛ: You would make an incredible brain surgeon with that dexterity.
Pᴇᴄᴋ: I'll bet Clyde — what's the name of the boy taking you to the prom?
Lɪ'ʟ Bɪᴛ: Claude Souders.
Pᴇᴄᴋ: Claude Souders. I'll bet it takes him two hands, lights on, and you helping him on to get to first base.
Lɪ'ʟ Bɪᴛ: Maybe.

(*Beat.*)

Pᴇᴄᴋ: Can I . . . kiss them? Please?
Lɪ'ʟ Bɪᴛ: I don't know.
Pᴇᴄᴋ: Don't make a grown man beg.
Lɪ'ʟ Bɪᴛ: Just one kiss.
Pᴇᴄᴋ: I'm going to lift your blouse.
Lɪ'ʟ Bɪᴛ: It's a little cold.

(*Peck laughs gently.*)

Pᴇᴄᴋ: That's not why you're shivering.

(*They sit, perfectly still, for a long moment of silence. Peck makes gentle, concentric circles with his thumbs in the air in front of him.*)

How does that feel?

(*Li'l Bit closes her eyes, carefully keeps her voice calm:*)

LI'L BIT: It's . . . okay.

(*Sacred music, organ music or a boy's choir swells beneath the following.*)

PECK: I tell you, you can keep all the cathedrals of Europe. Just give me a second with these — these celestial orbs —

(*Peck bows his head as if praying. But he is kissing her nipple. Li'l Bit, eyes still closed, rears back her head on the leather Buick car seat.*)

LI'L BIT: Uncle Peck — we've got to go. I've got graduation rehearsal at school tomorrow morning. And you should get on home to Aunt Mary —

PECK: — All right, Li'l Bit.

LI'L BIT: — *Don't call me that no more.* (*Calmer.*) Any more. I'm a big girl now, Uncle Peck. As you know.

(*Li'l Bit pantomimes refastening her bra behind her back.*)

PECK: That you are. Going on eighteen. Kittens will turn into cats. (*Sighs.*) I live all week long for these few minutes with you — you know that?

LI'L BIT: I'll drive.

(*A Voice cuts in with:*)

Idling in the Neutral Gear.

(*Sound of car revving cuts off the sacred music; Li'l Bit, now an adult, rises out of the car and comes to us.*)

LI'L BIT: In most families, relatives get names like "Junior," or "Brother," or "Bubba." In my family, if we call someone "Big Papa," it's not because he's tall. In my family, folks tend to get nicknamed for their genitalia. Uncle Peck, for example. My mama's adage was "the titless wonder," and my cousin Bobby got branded for life as "B.B."

(*In unison with Greek Chorus:*)

LI'L BIT: For blue balls.   GREEK CHORUS: For blue balls.

FEMALE GREEK CHORUS (*as Mother*): And of course, we were so excited to have a baby girl that when the nurse brought you in and said, "It's a girl! It's a baby girl!" I just had to see for myself. So we whipped your diapers down and parted your chubby little legs — and right between your legs there was —

(*Peck has come over during the above and chimes along:*)

PECK: Just a little bit.   GREEK CHORUS: Just a little bit.

FEMALE GREEK CHORUS (*as Mother*): And when you were born, you were so tiny that you fit in Uncle Peck's outstretched hand.

(*Peck stretches his hand out.*)

PECK: Now that's a fact. I held you, one day old, right in this hand.

(*A traffic signal is projected of a bicycle in a circle with a diagonal red slash.*)

LI'L BIT: Even with my family background, I was sixteen or so before I realized that pedophilia did not mean people who loved to bicycle . . . .

(*A Voice intrudes:*)

Driving in First Gear.

LI'L BIT: 1969. A typical family dinner.

FEMALE GREEK CHORUS (*as Mother*): Look, Grandma. Li'l Bit's getting to be as big in the bust as you are.

LI'L BIT: Mother! Could we please change the subject?

TEENAGE GREEK CHORUS (*as Grandmother*): Well, I hope you are buying her some decent bras. I never had a decent bra, growing up in the Depression, and now my shoulders are just crippled — crippled from the weight hanging on my shoulders — the dents from my bra straps are big enough to put your finger in. — Here, let me show you —

(*As Grandmother starts to open her blouse:*)

LI'L BIT: Grandma! Please don't undress at the dinner table.

PECK: I thought the entertainment came *after* the dinner.

LI'L BIT (*to the audience*): This is how it always starts. My grandfather, Big Papa, will chime in next with —

MALE GREEK CHORUS (*as Grandfather*): Yup. If Li'l Bit gets any bigger, we're gonna haveta buy her a wheelbarrow to carry in front of her —

LI'L BIT: — Damn it —

PECK: — How about those Redskins on Sunday, Big Papa?

LI'L BIT (*to the audience*): The only sport Big Papa followed was chasing Grandma around the house —

MALE GREEK CHORUS (*as Grandfather*): — Or we could write to Kate Smith. Ask her for somma her used brassieres she don't want anymore — she could maybe give to Li'l Bit here —

LI'L BIT: — I can't stand it. I can't.

PECK: Now, honey, that's just their way —

FEMALE GREEK CHORUS (*as Mother*): I tell you, Grandma, Li'l Bit's at that age. She's so sensitive, you can't say boo —

LI'L BIT: I'd like some privacy, that's all. Okay? Some goddamn privacy —

PECK: — Well, at least she didn't use the savior's name —

LI'L BIT (*to the audience*): And Big Papa wouldn't let a dead dog lie. No sirree.

MALE GREEK CHORUS (*as Grandfather*): Well, she'd better stop being so sensitive. 'Cause five minutes before Li'l Bit turns the corner, her tits turn first —

LI'L BIT (*starting to rise from the table*): — That's it. That's it.

PECK: Li'l Bit, you can't let him get to you. Then he wins.

LI'L BIT: I hate him. *Hate* him.

PECK: That's fine. But hate him and eat a good dinner at the same time.

(*Li'l Bit calms down and sits with perfect dignity.*)

LI'L BIT: The gumbo is really good, Grandma.

MALE GREEK CHORUS (*as Grandfather*): A'course, Li'l Bit's got a big surprise coming for her when she goes to that fancy college this fall —

PECK: Big Papa — let it go.

MALE GREEK CHORUS (*as Grandfather*): What does she need a college degree for? She's got all the credentials she'll need on her chest —

LI'L BIT: — Maybe I want to learn things. Read. Rise above my cracker° background —

PECK: — Whoa, now, Li'l Bit —

MALE GREEK CHORUS (*as Grandfather*): What kind of things do you want to read?

LI'L BIT: There's a whole semester course, for example, on Shakespeare —

(*Greek Chorus, as Grandfather, laughs until he weeps.*)

MALE GREEK CHORUS (*as Grandfather*): Shakespeare. That's a good one. Shakespeare is really going to help you in life.

PECK: I think it's wonderful. And on scholarship!

MALE GREEK CHORUS (*as Grandfather*): How is Shakespeare going to help her lie on her back in the dark?

(*Li'l Bit is on her feet.*)

LI'L BIT: You're getting old, Big Papa. You are going to die — very very soon. Maybe even *tonight*. And when you get to heaven, God's going to be a beautiful black woman in a long white robe. She's gonna look at your chart and say: Uh-oh. Fornication. Dog-ugly mean with blood relatives. Oh. Uh-oh. Voted for George Wallace. Well, one last chance: If you can name the play, all will be forgiven. And then she'll quote: "The quality of mercy is not strained." Your answer? Oh, too bad — *Merchant of Venice:* Act IV, Scene iii. And then she'll send your ass to fry in hell with all the other crackers. Excuse me, please.

(*To the audience.*) And as I left the house, I would always hear Big Papa say:

MALE GREEK CHORUS (*as Grandfather*): Lucy, your daughter's got a mouth on her. Well, no sense in wasting good gumbo. Pass me her plate, Mama.

LI'L BIT: And Aunt Mary would come up to Uncle Peck:

FEMALE GREEK CHORUS (*as Aunt Mary*): Peck, go after her, will you? You're the only one she'll listen to when she gets like this.

PECK: She just needs to cool off.

FEMALE GREEK CHORUS (*as Aunt Mary*): Please, honey — Grandma's been on her feet cooking all day.

cracker: A derogatory term for a poor, Southern, white person.

PECK: All right.

LI'L BIT: And as he left the room, Aunt Mary would say:

FEMALE GREEK CHORUS (*as Aunt Mary*): Peck's so good with them when they get to be this age.

(*Li'l Bit has stormed to another part of the stage, her back turned, weeping with a teenage fury. Peck, cautiously, as if stalking a deer, comes to her. She turns away even more. He waits a bit.*)

PECK: I don't suppose you're talking to family. (*No response.*) Does it help that I'm in-law?

LI'L BIT: Don't you dare make fun of this.

PECK: I'm not. There's nothing funny about this. (*Beat.*) Although I'll bet when Big Papa is about to meet his maker, he'll remember *The Merchant of Venice*.

LI'L BIT: I've got to get away from here.

PECK: You're going away. Soon. Here, take this.

(*Peck hands her his folded handkerchief. Li'l Bit uses it, noisily. Hands it back. Without her seeing, he reverently puts it back.*)

LI'L BIT: I hate this family.

PECK: Your grandfather's ignorant. And you're right — he's going to die soon. But he's family. Family is . . . family.

LI'L BIT: Grown-ups are always saying that. Family.

PECK: Well, when you get a little older, you'll see what we're saying.

LI'L BIT: Uh-huh. So family is another acquired taste, like French kissing?

PECK: Come again?

LI'L BIT: You know, at first it really grosses you out, but in time you grow to like it?

PECK: Girl, you are . . . a handful.

LI'L BIT: Uncle Peck — you have the keys to your car?

PECK: Where do you want to go?

LI'L BIT: Just up the road.

PECK: I'll come with you.

LI'L BIT: No — please? I just need to . . . to drive for a little bit. Alone.

(*Peck tosses her the keys.*)

PECK: When can I see you alone again?

LI'L BIT: Tonight.

(*Li'l Bit crosses to center stage while the lights dim around her. A Voice directs:*)

Shifting Forward from First to Second Gear.

LI'L BIT: There were a lot of rumors about why I got kicked out of that fancy school in 1970. Some say I got caught with a man in my room. Some say as a kid on scholarship I fooled around with a rich man's daughter.

(*Li'l Bit smiles innocently at the audience.*) I'm not talking.

But the real truth was I had a constant companion

in my dorm room — who was less than discreet. Canadian V.O. A fifth a day.

1970. A Nixon recession. I slept on the floors of friends who were out of work themselves. Took factory work when I could find it. A string of dead-end jobs that didn't last very long.

What I did, most nights, was cruise the Beltway and the back roads of Maryland, where there was still country, past the battlefields and farm houses. Racing in a 1965 Mustang — and as long as I had gasoline for my car and whiskey for me, the nights would pass. Full tanked, I would speed past the churches and the trees on the bend, thinking just one notch of the steering wheel would be all it would take, and yet some . . . reflex took over. My hands on the wheel in the nine and three o'clock position — I never so much as got a ticket. He taught me well.

(*A Voice announces:*)

You and the Reverse Gear.

LI'L BIT: Back up. 1968. On the Eastern Shore. A celebration dinner.

(*Li'l Bit joins Peck at a table in a restaurant.*)

PECK: Feeling better, missy?

LI'L BIT: The bathroom's really amazing here, Uncle Peck! They have these little soaps — instead of borax or something — and they're in the shape of shells.

PECK: I'll have to take a trip to the gentleman's room just to see.

LI'L BIT: How did you know about this place?

PECK: This inn is famous on the Eastern Shore — it's been open since the seventeenth century. And I know how you like history. . . .

(*Li'l Bit is shy and pleased.*)

LI'L BIT: It's great.

PECK: And you've just done your first, legal, long-distance drive. You must be hungry.

LI'L BIT: I'm starved.

PECK: I would suggest a dozen oysters to start, and the crab imperial. . . . (*Li'l Bit is genuinely agog.*) You might be interested to know the town history. When the British sailed up this very river in the dead of night — see outside where I'm pointing? — they were going to bombard the heck out of this town. But the town fathers were ready for them. They crept up all the trees with lanterns so that the British would think they saw the town lights and they aimed their cannons too high. And that's why the inn is still here for business today.

LI'L BIT: That's a great story.

PECK (*casually*): Would you like to start with a cocktail?

LI'L BIT: You're not . . . you're not going to start drinking, are you, Uncle Peck?

PECK: Not me. I told you, as long as you're with me, I'll never drink. I asked you if *you'd* like a cocktail before dinner. It's nice to have a little something with the oysters.

LI'L BIT: But . . . I'm not . . . legal. We could get arrested. Uncle Peck, they'll never believe I'm twenty-one!

PECK: So? Today we celebrate your driver's license — on the first try. This establishment reminds me a lot of places back home.

LI'L BIT: What does that mean?

PECK: In South Carolina, like here on the Eastern Shore, they're . . . (*Searches for the right euphemism.*) . . . "European." Not so puritanical. And very understanding if gentlemen wish to escort very attractive young ladies who might want a before-dinner cocktail. If you want one, I'll order one.

LI'L BIT: Well — sure. Just . . . one.

(*The Female Greek Chorus appears in a spot.*)

FEMALE GREEK CHORUS (*as Mother*): A Mother's Guide to Social Drinking:

A lady never gets sloppy — she may, however, get tipsy and a little gay.

Never drink on an empty stomach. Avail yourself of the bread basket and generous portions of butter. *Slather* the butter on your bread.

Sip your drink, slowly, let the beverage linger in your mouth — interspersed with interesting, fascinating conversation. Sip, never . . . slurp or gulp. Your glass should always be three-quarters full when his glass is empty.

Stay away from *ladies'* drinks: drinks like pink ladies, slow gin fizzes, piña coladas, mai tais, planter's punch, white Russians, black Russians, red Russians, melon balls, blue balls, hummingbirds, hemorrhages, and hurricanes. In short, avoid anything with sugar, or anything with an umbrella. Get your vitamin C from *fruit*. Don't order anything with Voodoo or Vixen in the title or sexual positions in the name like Dead Man Screw or the Missionary. (*She sort of titters.*)

Believe me, they are lethal. . . . I think you were conceived after one of those.

Drink, instead, like a man: straight up or on the rocks, with plenty of water in between.

Oh, yes. And never mix your drinks. Stay with one all night long, like the man you came in with: bourbon, gin, or tequila till dawn, damn the torpedoes, full speed ahead!

(*As the Female Greek Chorus retreats, the Male Greek Chorus approaches the table as a Waiter.*)

MALE GREEK CHORUS (*as Waiter*): I hope you all are having a pleasant evening. Is there something I can bring you, sir, before you order?

(*Li'l Bit waits in anxious fear. Carefully, Uncle Peck says with command:*)

PECK: I'll have a plain iced tea. The lady would like a drink, I believe.

(*The Male Greek Chorus does a double take; there is a moment when Uncle Peck and he are in silent communication.*)

MALE GREEK CHORUS (*as Waiter*): Very good. What would the . . . lady like?
LI'L BIT (*a bit flushed*): Is there . . . is there any sugar in a martini?
PECK: None that I know of.
LI'L BIT: That's what I'd like then — a dry martini. And could we maybe have some bread?
PECK: A drink fit for a woman of the world. — Please bring the lady a dry martini, be generous with the olives, straight up.

(*The Male Greek Chorus anticipates a* large *tip.*)

MALE GREEK CHORUS (*as Waiter*): Right away. Very good, sir.

(*The Male Greek Chorus returns with an empty martini glass which he puts in front of Li'l Bit.*)

PECK: Your glass is empty. Another martini, madam?
LI'L BIT: Yes, thank you.

(*Peck signals the Male Greek Chorus, who nods.*)

So why did you leave South Carolina, Uncle Peck?
PECK: I was stationed in D.C. after the war, and decided to stay. Go North, Young Man, someone might have said.
LI'L BIT: What did you do in the service anyway?
PECK (*suddenly taciturn*): I . . . I did just this and that. Nothing heroic or spectacular.
LI'L BIT: But did you see fighting? Or go to Europe?
PECK: I served in the Pacific Theater. It's really nothing interesting to talk about.
LI'L BIT: It is to me. (*The Waiter has brought another empty glass.*) Oh, goody. I love the color of the swizzle sticks. What were we talking about?
PECK: Swizzle sticks.
LI'L BIT: Do you ever think of going back?
PECK: To the Marines?
LI'L BIT: No — to South Carolina.
PECK: Well, we do go back. To visit.
LI'L BIT: No, I mean to live.
PECK: Not very likely. I think it's better if my mother doesn't have a daily reminder of her disappointment.
LI'L BIT: Are these floorboards slanted?
PECK: Yes, the floor is very slanted. I think this is the original floor.
LI'L BIT: Oh, good.

(*The Female Greek Chorus as Mother enters swaying a little, a little past tipsy.*)

FEMALE GREEK CHORUS (*as Mother*): Don't leave your drink unattended when you visit the ladies' room. There is such a thing as white slavery; the modus operandi is to spike an unsuspecting young girl's drink with a "mickey" when she's left the room to powder her nose.

But if you feel you have had more than your sufficiency in liquor, do go to the ladies' room — often. Pop your head out of doors for a refreshing breath of the night air. If you must, wet your face and head with tap water. Don't be afraid to dunk your head if necessary. A wet woman is still less conspicuous than a drunk woman.

(*The Female Greek Chorus stumbles a little; conspiratorially.*) When in the course of human events it becomes necessary, go to a corner stall and insert the index and middle finger down the throat almost to the epiglottis. Divulge your stomach contents by such persuasion, and then wait a few moments before rejoining your beau waiting for you at your table.

Oh, no. Don't be shy or embarrassed. In the very best of establishments, there's always one or two debutantes crouched in the corner stalls, their beaded purses tossed willy-nilly, sounding like cats in heat, heaving up the contents of their stomachs.

(*The Female Greek Chorus begins to wander off.*)
I wonder what is it they do in the men's rooms. . . .
LI'L BIT: So why is your mother disappointed in you, Uncle Peck?
LI'L BIT: Every mother in Horry County has Great Expectations.
LI'L BIT: — Could I have another mar-ti-ni, please?
PECK: I think this is your last one.

(*Peck signals the Waiter. The Waiter looks at Li'l Bit and shakes his head no. Peck raises his eyebrow, raises his finger to indicate one more, and then rubs his fingers together. It looks like a secret code. The Waiter sighs, shakes his head sadly, and brings over another empty martini glass. He glares at Peck.*)

LI'L BIT: The name of the county where you grew up is "Horry"? (*Li'l Bit, plastered, begins to laugh. Then she stops.*) I think your mother should be proud of you.

(*Peck signals for the check.*)

PECK: Well, missy, she wanted me to do — to *be* everything my father was not. She wanted me to amount to something.
LI'L BIT: But you have! You've amounted a lot. . . .
PECK: I'm just a very ordinary man.

(*The Waiter has brought the check and waits. Peck draws out a large bill and hands it to the Waiter. Li'l Bit is in the soppy stage.*)

LI'L BIT: I'll bet your mother loves you, Uncle Peck.

(*Peck freezes a bit. To Male Greek Chorus as Waiter:*)

PECK: Thank you. The service was exceptional. Please keep the change.
MALE GREEK CHORUS (*as Waiter, in a tone that could freeze*): Thank you, sir. Will you be needing any help?

PECK: I think we can manage, thank you.

(*Just then, the Female Greek Chorus as Mother lurches on stage; the Male Greek Chorus as Waiter escorts her off as she delivers:*)

FEMALE GREEK CHORUS (*as Mother*): Thanks to judicious planning and several trips to the ladies' loo, your mother once out-drank an entire regiment of British officers on a good-will visit to Washington! Every last man of them! Milquetoasts! How'd they ever kick Hitler's cahones, huh? No match for an American lady — I could drink every man in here under the table.

  (*She delivers one last crucial hint before she is gently "bounced."*)

  As a last resort, when going out for an evening on the town, be sure to wear a skin-tight girdle — so tight that only a surgical knife or acetylene torch can get it off you — so that if you do pass out in the arms of your escort, he'll end up with rubber burns on his fingers before he can steal your virtue —

(*A Voice punctures the interlude with:*)

Vehicle Failure.
Even with careful maintenance and preventive operation of your automobile, it is all too common for us to experience an unexpected breakdown. If you are driving at any speed when a breakdown occurs, you must slow down and guide the automobile to the side of the road.

(*Peck is slowly propping up Li'l Bit as they work their way to his car in the parking lot of the inn.*)

PECK: How are you doing, missy?

LI'L BIT: It's so far to the car, Uncle Peck. Like the lanterns in the trees the British fired on. . . .

(*Li'l Bit stumbles. Peck swoops her up in his arms.*)

PECK: Okay, I think we're going to take a more direct route.

(*Li'l Bit closes her eyes.*)

  Dizzy?

(*She nods her head.*)

  Don't look at the ground. Almost there — do you feel sick to your stomach?

(*Li'l Bit nods. They reach the "car." Peck gently deposits her on the front seat.*)

  Just settle here a little while until things stop spinning.

(*Li'l Bit opens her eyes.*)

LI'L BIT: What are we doing?

PECK: We're just going to sit here until your tummy settles down.

LI'L BIT: It's such nice upholst'ry —

PECK: Think you can go for a ride, now?

LI'L BIT: Where are you taking me?

PECK: Home.

LI'L BIT: You're not taking me — upstairs? There's no room at the inn? (*Li'l Bit giggles.*)

PECK: Do you want to go upstairs?

(*Li'l Bit doesn't answer.*)

  Or home?

LI'L BIT: — This isn't right, Uncle Peck.

PECK: What isn't right?

LI'L BIT: What we're doing. It's wrong. It's very wrong.

PECK: What are we doing?

(*Li'l Bit does not answer.*)

  We're just going out to dinner.

LI'L BIT: You know. It's not nice to Aunt Mary.

PECK: You let me be the judge of what's nice and not nice to my wife.

(*Beat.*)

LI'L BIT: Now you're mad.

PECK: I'm not mad. It's just that I thought you . . . understood me, Li'l Bit. I think you're the only one who does.

LI'L BIT: Someone will get hurt.

PECK: Have I forced you to do anything?

(*There is a long pause as Li'l Bit tries to get sober enough to think this through.*)

LI'L BIT: . . . I guess not.

PECK: We are just enjoying each other's company. I've told you, nothing is going to happen between us until you want it to. Do you know that?

LI'L BIT: Yes.

PECK: Nothing is going to happen until you want it. (*A second more, with Peck staring ahead at the river while seated at the wheel of his car. Then, softly:*) Do you want something to happen?

(*Peck reaches over and strokes her face, very gently. Li'l Bit softens, reaches for him, and buries her head in his neck. Then she kisses him. Then she moves away, dizzy again.*)

LI'L BIT: . . . I don't know.

(*Peck smiles; this has been good news for him — it hasn't been a "no."*)

PECK: Then I'll wait. I'm a very patient man. I've been waiting for a long time. I don't mind waiting.

LI'L BIT: Someone is going to get hurt.

PECK: No one is going to get hurt. (*Li'l Bit closes her eyes.*) Are you feeling sick?

LI'L BIT: Sleepy.

(*Carefully, Peck props Li'l Bit up on the seat.*)

PECK: Stay here a second.

LI'L BIT: Where're you going?

PECK: I'm getting something from the back seat.

LI'L BIT (*scared; too loud*): What? What are you going to do?

(*Peck reappears in the front seat with a lap rug.*)

PECK: Shhh. (*Peck covers Li'l Bit. She calms down.*) There. Think you can sleep?

(*Li'l Bit nods. She slides over to rest on his shoulder. With a look of happiness, Peck turns the ignition key. Beat. Peck leaves Li'l Bit sleeping in the car and strolls down to the audience.* Wagner's Flying Dutchman *comes up faintly.*) (*A Voice interjects:*)

Idling in the Neutral Gear.

TEENAGE GREEK CHORUS: Uncle Peck Teaches Cousin Bobby How to Fish.

PECK: I get back once or twice a year — supposedly to visit Mama and the family, but the real truth is to fish. I miss this the most of all. There's a smell in the Low Country — where the swamp and fresh inlet join the saltwater — a scent of sand and cypress, that I haven't found anywhere yet.

I don't say this very often up North because it will just play into the stereotype everyone has, but I will tell you: I didn't wear shoes in the summertime until I was sixteen. It's unnatural down here to pen up your feet in leather. Go ahead — take 'em off. Let yourself breathe — it really will make you feel better.

We're going to aim for some pompano today — and I have to tell you, they're a very shy, mercurial fish. Takes patience, and psychology. You have to believe it doesn't matter if you catch one or not.

Sky's pretty spectacular — there's some beer in the cooler next to the crab salad I packed, so help yourself if you get hungry. Are you hungry? Thirsty? Holler if you are.

Okay. You don't want to lean over the bridge like that — pompano feed in shallow water, and you don't want to get too close — they're frisky and shy little things — wait, check your line. Yep, something's been munching while we were talking.

Okay, look: We take the sand flea and you take the hook like this — right through his little sand flea rump. Sand fleas should always keep their backs to the wall. Okay. Cast it in, like I showed you. That's great! I can taste that pompano now, sautéed with some pecans and butter, a little bourbon — now — let it lie on the bottom — now, reel, jerk, reel, jerk —

Look — look at your line. There's something calling, all right. Okay, tip the rod up — not too sharp — hook it — all right, now easy, reel and then rest — let it play. And reel — play it out, that's right — really good! I can't believe it! It's a pompano. — Good work! Way to go! You are an official fisherman now. Pompano are hard to catch. We are going to have a delicious little —

What? Well, I don't know how much pain a fish feels — you can't think of that. Oh, no, don't cry, come on now, it's just a fish — the other guys are going to see you. — No, no, you're just real sensitive, and I think that's wonderful at your age — look, do you want me to cut it free? You do?

Okay, hand me those pliers — look — I'm cutting the hook — okay? And we're just going to drop it in — no I'm not mad. It's just for fun, okay? There — it's going to swim back to its lady friend and tell her what a terrible day it had and she's going to stroke him with her fins until he feels better, and then they'll do something alone together that will make them both feel good and sleepy. . . .

(*Peck bends down, very earnest.*) I don't want you to feel ashamed about crying. I'm not going to tell anyone, okay? I can keep secrets. You know, men cry all the time. They just don't tell anybody, and they don't let anybody catch them. There's nothing you could do that would make me feel ashamed of you. Do you know that? Okay. (*Peck straightens up, smiles.*)

Do you want to pack up and call it a day? I tell you what — I think I can still remember — there's a really neat tree house where I used to stay for days. I think it's still here — it was the last time I looked. But it's a secret place — you can't tell anybody we've gone there — least of all your mom or your sisters. — This is something special just between you and me. Sound good? We'll climb up there and have a beer and some crab salad — okay, B.B.? Bobby? Robert. . . .

(*Li'l Bit sits at a kitchen table with the two Female Greek Chorus members.*)

LI'L BIT (*to the audience*): Three women, three generations, sit at the kitchen table.

On Men, Sex, and Women: Part I:

FEMALE GREEK CHORUS (*as Mother*): Men only want one thing.

LI'L BIT (*wide-eyed*): But what? What is it they want?

FEMALE GREEK CHORUS (*as Mother*): And once they have it, they lose all interest. So Don't Give It to Them.

TEENAGE GREEK CHORUS (*as Grandmother*): I never had the luxury of the rhythm method. Your grandfather is just a big bull. A big bull. Every morning, every evening.

FEMALE GREEK CHORUS (*as Mother, whispers to Li'l Bit*): And he used to come home for lunch every day.

LI'L BIT: My god, Grandma!

TEENAGE GREEK CHORUS (*as Grandmother*): Your grandfather only cares that I do two things: have the table set and the bed turned down.

FEMALE GREEK CHORUS (*as Mother*): And in all that time, Mother, you never have experienced — ?

LI'L BIT (*to the audience*): — Now my grandmother believed in all the sacraments of the church, to the day she died. She believed in Santa Claus and the Easter Bunny until she was fifteen. But she didn't believe in —

TEENAGE GREEK CHORUS (*as Grandmother*): — Orgasm! That's just something you and Mary have made up! I don't believe you.

FEMALE GREEK CHORUS (*as Mother*): Mother, it happens to women all the time —

TEENAGE GREEK CHORUS (*as Grandmother*): — Oh, now you're going to tell me about the G force!

LI'L BIT: No, Grandma, I think that's astronauts —

FEMALE GREEK CHORUS (*as Mother*): Well, Mama, after all, you were a child bride when Big Papa came and got you — you were a married woman and you still believed in Santa Claus.

TEENAGE GREEK CHORUS (*as Grandmother*): It was legal, what Daddy and I did! I was fourteen and in those days, fourteen was a grown-up woman —

(*Big Papa shuffles in the kitchen for a cookie.*)

MALE GREEK CHORUS (*as Grandfather*): — Oh, now we're off on Grandma and the Rape of the Sa-bean Women!

TEENAGE GREEK CHORUS (*as Grandmother*): Well, you were the one in such a big hurry —

MALE GREEK CHORUS (*as Grandfather to Li'l Bit*): — I picked your grandmother out of that herd of sisters just like a lion chooses the gazelle — the plump, slow, flaky gazelle dawdling at the edge of the herd — your sisters were too smart and too fast and too scrawny —

LI'L BIT (*to the audience*): — The family story is that when Big Papa came for Grandma, my Aunt Lily was waiting for him with a broom — and she beat him over the head all the way down the stairs as he was carrying out Grandma's hope chest —

MALE GREEK CHORUS (*as Grandfather*): — And they were *mean*. 'Specially Lily.

FEMALE GREEK CHORUS (*as Mother*): Well, you were robbing the baby of the family!

TEENAGE GREEK CHORUS (*as Grandmother*): I still keep a broom handy in the kitchen! And I know how to use it! So get your hand out of the cookie jar and don't you spoil your appetite for dinner — out of the kitchen!

(*Male Greek Chorus as Grandfather leaves chuckling with a cookie.*)

FEMALE GREEK CHORUS (*as Mother*): Just one thing a married woman needs to know how to use — the rolling pin or the broom. I prefer a heavy, cast-iron fry pan — they're great on a man's head, no matter how thick the skull is.

TEENAGE GREEK CHORUS (*as Grandmother*): Yes, sir, your father is ruled by only two bosses! Mr. Gut and Mr. Peter! And sometimes, first thing in the morning, Mr. Sphincter Muscle!

FEMALE GREEK CHORUS (*as Mother*): It's true. Men are like children. Just like little boys.

TEENAGE GREEK CHORUS (*as Grandmother*): Men are bulls! Big bulls!

(*The Greek Chorus is getting aroused.*)

FEMALE GREEK CHORUS (*as Mother*): They'd still be crouched on their haunches over a fire in a cave if we hadn't cleaned them up!

TEENAGE GREEK CHORUS (*as Grandmother, flushed*): Coming in smelling of sweat —

FEMALE GREEK CHORUS (*as Mother*): — Looking at those naughty pictures like boys in a dime store with a dollar in their pockets!

TEENAGE GREEK CHORUS (*as Grandmother; raucous*): No matter to them what they smell like! They've got to have it, right then, on the spot, right there! Nasty! —

FEMALE GREEK CHORUS (*as Mother*): — Vulgar!

TEENAGE GREEK CHORUS (*as Grandmother*): Primitive! —

FEMALE GREEK CHORUS (*as Mother*): — Hot! —

LI'L BIT: And just about then, Big Papa would shuffle in with —

MALE GREEK CHORUS (*as Grandfather*): — What are you all cackling about in here?

TEENAGE GREEK CHORUS (*as Grandmother*): Stay out of the kitchen! This is just for girls!

(*As Grandfather leaves:*)

MALE GREEK CHORUS (*as Grandfather*): Lucy, you'd better not be filling Mama's head with sex! Every time you and Mary come over and start in about sex, when I ask a simple question like, "What time is dinner going to be ready?," Mama snaps my head off!

TEENAGE GREEK CHORUS (*as Grandmother*): Dinner will be ready when I'm good and ready! Stay out of this kitchen!

(*Li'l Bit steps out.*)

(*A Voice directs:*)

When Making a Left Turn, You Must Downshift While Going Forward.

LI'L BIT: 1979. A long bus trip to Upstate New York. I settled in to read, when a young man sat beside me.

MALE GREEK CHORUS (*as Young Man; voice cracking*): "What are you reading?"

LI'L BIT: He asked. His voice broke into that miserable equivalent of vocal acne, not quite falsetto and not tenor, either. I glanced a side view. He was appealing in an odd way, huge ears at a defiant angle springing forward at ninety degrees. He must have been shaving, because his face, with a peach sheen, was speckled with nicks and styptic. "I have a class tomorrow," I told him.

MALE GREEK CHORUS (*as Young Man*): "You're taking a class?"

LI'L BIT: "I'm teaching a class." He concentrated on lowering his voice.

MALE GREEK CHORUS (*as Young Man*): "I'm a senior. Walt Whitman High."

LI'L BIT: The light was fading outside, so perhaps he was — with a very high voice.

I felt his "interest" quicken. Five steps ahead of the hopes in his head, I slowed down, waited, pretended surprise, acted at listening, all the while knowing we would get off the bus, he would just then seem to think to ask me to dinner, he would chivalrously insist on walking me home, he would continue to converse in the street until I would casually invite him up to my room — and — I was only into the second moment of conversation and I could see the whole evening before me.

And dramaturgically speaking, after the faltering and slightly comical "first act," there was the very briefest of intermissions, and an extremely capable and forceful and *sustained* second act. And after the second act climax and a gentle denouement — before the post-play discussion — I lay on my back in the dark and I thought about you, Uncle Peck. Oh. Oh — this is the allure. Being older. Being the first. Being the translator, the teacher, the epicure, the already jaded. This is how the giver gets taken.

(*Li'l Bit changes her tone.*) On Men, Sex, and Women: Part II:

(*Li'l Bit steps back into the scene as a fifteen-year-old, gawky and quiet, as the gazelle at the edge of the herd.*)

TEENAGE GREEK CHORUS (*as Grandmother, to Li'l Bit*): You're being mighty quiet, missy. Cat Got Your Tongue?

LI'L BIT: I'm just listening. Just thinking.

TEENAGE GREEK CHORUS (*as Grandmother*): Oh, yes, Little Miss Radar Ears? Soaking it all in? Little Miss Sponge? Penny for your thoughts?

(*Li'l Bit hesitates to ask but she really wants to know.*)

LI'L BIT: Does it — when you do it — you know, theoretically when I do it and I haven't done it before — I mean — does it hurt?

FEMALE GREEK CHORUS (*as Mother*): Does what hurt, honey?

LI'L BIT: When a . . . when a girl does it for the first time — with a man — does it hurt?

TEENAGE GREEK CHORUS (*as Grandmother; horrified*): *That's* what you're thinking about?

FEMALE GREEK CHORUS (*as Mother, calm*): Well, just a little bit. Like a pinch. And there's a little blood.

TEENAGE GREEK CHORUS (*as Grandmother*): Don't tell her that! She's too young to be thinking those things!

FEMALE GREEK CHORUS (*as Mother*): Well, if she doesn't find out from me, where is she going to find out? In the street?

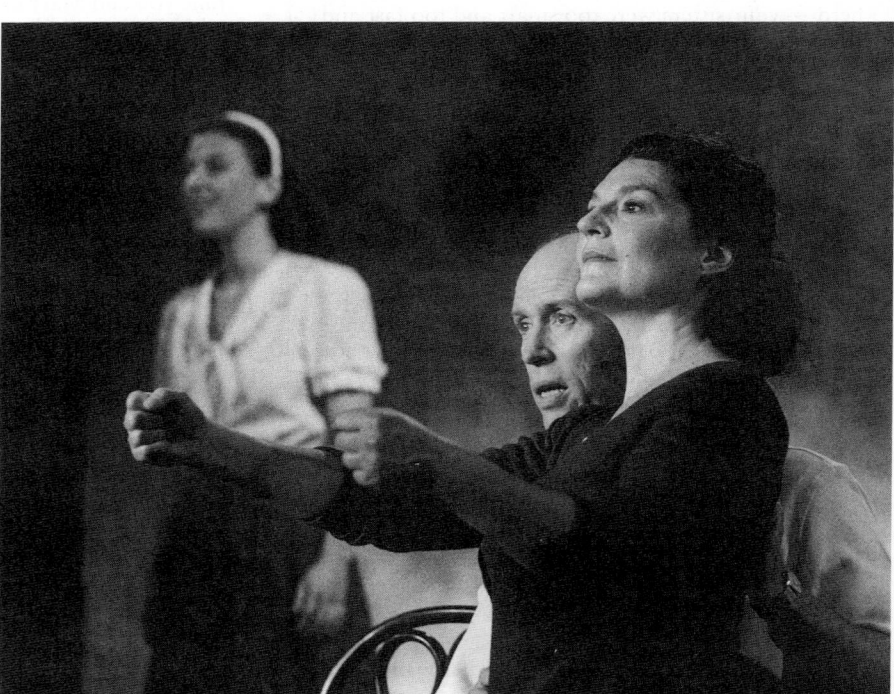

Tim Crowe as Uncle Peck and Annie Sullivan as Li'l Bit in the Trinity Repertory Theater's production of *How I Learned to Drive.*

TEENAGE GREEK CHORUS (*as Grandmother*): Tell her it hurts! It's agony! You think you're going to die! Especially if you do it before marriage!

FEMALE GREEK CHORUS (*as Mother*): Mama! I'm going to tell her the truth! Unlike you, you left me and Mary completely in the dark with fairy tales and told us to go to the priest! What does an eighty-year-old priest know about lovemaking with girls!

LI'L BIT (*getting upset*): It's not fair!

FEMALE GREEK CHORUS (*as Mother*): Now, see, she's getting upset — you're scaring her.

TEENAGE GREEK CHORUS (*as Grandmother*): Good! Let her be good and scared! It hurts! You bleed like a stuck pig! And you lay there and say, "Why, O Lord, have you forsaken me?!"

LI'L BIT: It's not fair! Why does everything have to hurt for girls? Why is there always blood?

FEMALE GREEK CHORUS (*as Mother*): It's not a lot of blood — and it feels wonderful after the pain subsides. . . .

TEENAGE GREEK CHORUS (*as Grandmother*): You're encouraging her to just go out and find out with the first drugstore joe who buys her a milkshake!

FEMALE GREEK CHORUS (*as Mother*): Don't be scared. It won't hurt you — if the man you go to bed with really loves you. It's important that he loves you.

TEENAGE GREEK CHORUS (*as Grandmother*): — Why don't you just go out and rent a motel room for her, Lucy?

FEMALE GREEK CHORUS (*as Mother*): I believe in telling my daughter the truth! We have a very close relationship! I want her to be able to ask me anything — I'm not scaring her with stories about Eve's sin and snakes crawling on their bellies for eternity and women bearing children in mortal pain —

TEENAGE GREEK CHORUS (*as Grandmother*): — If she stops and thinks before she takes her knickers off, maybe someone in this family will finish high school!

(*Li'l Bit knows what is about to happen and starts to retreat from the scene at this point.*)

FEMALE GREEK CHORUS (*as Mother*): Mother! If you and Daddy had helped me — I wouldn't have had to marry that — that no-good-son-of-a —

TEENAGE GREEK CHORUS (*as Grandmother*): — He was good enough for you on a full moon! I hold you responsible!

FEMALE GREEK CHORUS (*as Mother*): — You could have helped me! You could have told me something about the facts of life!

TEENAGE GREEK CHORUS (*as Grandmother*): — I told you what my mother told me! A girl with her skirt up can outrun a man with his pants down!

(*The Male Greek Chorus enters the fray; Li'l Bit edges farther downstage.*)

FEMALE GREEK CHORUS (*as Mother*): And when I turned to you for a little help, all I got afterwards was —

MALE GREEK CHORUS (*as Grandfather*): You Made Your Bed; Now Lie On It!

(*The Greek Chorus freezes, mouths open, argumentatively.*)

LI'L BIT (*to the audience*): Oh, please! I still can't bear to listen to it, after all these years —

(*The Male Greek Chorus "unfreezes," but out of his open mouth, as if to his surprise, comes a bass refrain from a Motown song.*)

MALE GREEK CHORUS: "Do-Bee-Do-Wah!"

(*The Female Greek Chorus member is also surprised; but she, too, unfreezes.*)

FEMALE GREEK CHORUS: "Shoo-doo-be-doo-be-doo; shoo-doo-be-doo-be-doo."

(*The Male and Female Greek Chorus members continue with their harmony, until the Teenage member of the Chorus starts in with Motown lyrics such as "Dedicated to the One I Love," or "In the Still of the Night," or "Hold Me" — any Sam Cooke will do. The three modulate down into three-part harmony, softly, until they are submerged by the actual recording playing over the radio in the car in which Uncle Peck sits in the driver's seat, waiting. Li'l Bit sits in the passenger's seat.*)

LI'L BIT: Ahh. That's better.

(*Uncle Peck reaches over and turns the volume down; to Li'l Bit:*)

PECK: How can you hear yourself think?

(*Li'l Bit does not answer.*)

(*A Voice insinuates itself in the pause:*)

Before You Drive.
Always check under your car for obstructions — broken bottles, fallen tree branches, and the bodies of small children. Each year hundreds of children are crushed beneath the wheels of unwary drivers in their own driveways. Children depend on you *to watch them.*

(*Pause.*)

(*The Voice continues:*)

You and the Reverse Gear.

(*In the following section, it would be nice to have slides of erotic photographs of women and cars: women posed over the hood; women draped along the sideboards; women with water hoses spraying the car; and the actress playing Li'l Bit with a Bel Air or any 1950s car one can find for the finale.*)

LI'L BIT: 1967. In a parking lot of the Beltsville Agricultural Farms. The Initiation into a Boy's First Love.

PECK (*with a soft look on his face*): Of course, my favorite car will always be the '56 Bel Air Sports Coupe. Chevy sold more '55s, but the '56! — a V-8 with Corvette option, 225 horsepower; went from zero to sixty miles per hour in 8.9 seconds.

LI'L BIT (*to the audience*): Long after a mother's tits, but before a woman's breasts:

PECK: Super-Turbo-Fire! What a Power Pack — mechanical lifters, twin four-barrel carbs, lightweight valves, dual exhausts —

LI'L BIT (*to the audience*): After the milk but before the beer:

PECK: A specific intake manifold, higher-lift camshaft, and the tightest squeeze Chevy had ever made —

LI'L BIT (*to the audience*): Long after he's squeezed down the birth canal but before he's pushed his way back in: The boy falls in love with the thing that bears his weight with speed.

PECK: I want you to know your automobile inside and out. — Are you there? Li'l Bit?

(*Slides end here.*)

LI'L BIT: — What?

PECK: You're drifting. I need you to concentrate.

LI'L BIT: Sorry.

PECK: Okay. Get into the driver's seat. (*Li'l Bit does.*) Okay. Now. Show me what you're going to do before you start the car.

(*Li'l Bit sits, with her hands in her lap. She starts to giggle.*)

LI'L BIT: I don't know, Uncle Peck.

PECK: Now, come on. What's the first thing you're going to adjust?

LI'L BIT: My bra strap? —

PECK: — Li'l Bit. What's the most important thing to have control of on the inside of the car?

LI'L BIT: That's easy. The radio. I tune the radio from Mama's old fart tunes to —

(*Li'l Bit turns the radio up so we can hear a 1960s tune. With surprising firmness, Peck commands:*)

PECK: — Radio off. Right now. (*Li'l Bit turns the radio off.*) When you are driving your car, with your license, you can fiddle with the stations all you want. But when you are driving with a learner's permit in my car, I want all your attention to be on the road.

LI'L BIT: Yes, sir.

PECK: Okay. Now the seat — forward and up. (*Li'l Bit pushes it forward.*) Do you want a cushion?

LI'L BIT: No — I'm good.

PECK: You should be able to reach all the switches and controls. Your feet should be able to push the accelerator, brake and clutch all the way down. Can you do that?

LI'L BIT: Yes.

PECK: Okay, the side mirrors. You want to be able to see just a bit of the right side of the car in the right mirror — can you?

LI'L BIT: Turn it out more.

PECK: Okay. How's that?

LI'L BIT: A little more. . . . Okay, that's good.

PECK: Now the left — again, you want to be able to see behind you — but the left lane — adjust it until you feel comfortable. (*Li'l Bit does so.*) Next. I want you to check the rearview mirror. Angle it so you have a clear vision of the back. (*Li'l Bit does so.*) Okay. Lock your door. Make sure all the doors are locked.

LI'L BIT (*making a joke of it*): But then I'm locked in with you.

PECK: Don't fool.

LI'L BIT: All right. We're locked in.

PECK: We'll deal with the air vents and defroster later. I'm teaching you on a manual — once you learn manual, you can drive anything. I want you to be able to drive any car, any machine. Manual gives you *control*. In ice, if your brakes fail, if you need more power — okay? It's a little harder at first, but then it becomes like breathing. Now. Put your hands on the wheel. I never want to see you driving with one hand. Always two hands. (*Li'l Bit hesitates.*) What? What is it now?

LI'L BIT: If I put my hands on the wheel — how do I defend myself?

PECK (*softly*): Now listen. Listen up close. We're not going to fool around with this. This is serious business. I will never touch you when you are driving a car. Understand?

LI'L BIT: Okay.

PECK: Hands on the nine o'clock and three o'clock position gives you maximum control and turn.

(*Peck goes silent for a while. Li'l Bit waits for more instruction.*)

Okay. Just relax and listen to me, Li'l Bit, okay? I want you to lift your hands for a second and look at them.

(*Li'l Bit feels a bit silly, but does it.*)

Those are your two hands. When you are driving, your life is in your own two hands. Understand?

(*Li'l Bit nods.*)

I don't have any sons. You're the nearest to a son I'll ever have — and I want to give you something. Something that really matters to me.

There's something about driving — when you're in control of the car, just you and the machine and the road — that nobody can take from you. A power. I feel more myself in my car than anywhere else. And that's what I want to give to you.

There's a lot of assholes out there. Crazy men, arrogant idiots, drunks, angry kids, geezers who are blind — and you have to be ready for them. I want to teach you to drive like a man.

LI'L BIT: What does that mean?

PECK: Men are taught to drive with confidence — with aggression. The road belongs to them. They drive defensively — always looking out for the other guy. Women tend to be polite — to hesitate. And that can be fatal.

You're going to learn to think what the other guy is going to do before he does it. If there's an accident, and ten cars pile up, and people get killed, you're the one who's gonna steer through it, put your foot on the gas if you have to, and be the only one to walk away. I don't know how long you or I are going to live, but we're for damned sure not going to die in a car.

So if you're going to drive with me, I want you to take this very seriously.

LI'L BIT: I will, Uncle Peck. I want you to teach me to drive.

PECK: Good. You're going to pass your test on the first try. Perfect score. Before the next four weeks are over, you're going to know this baby inside and out. Treat her with respect.

LI'L BIT: Why is it a "she"?

PECK: Good question. It doesn't have to be a "she" — but when you close your eyes and think of someone who responds to your touch — someone who performs just for you and gives you what you ask for — I guess I always see a "she." You can call her what you like.

LI'L BIT (*to the audience*): I closed my eyes — and decided not to change the gender.

(*A Voice:*)

Defensive driving involves defending yourself from hazardous and sudden changes in your automotive environment. By thinking ahead, the defensive driver can adjust to weather, road conditions, and road kill. Good defensive driving involves mental and physical preparation. Are you prepared?

(*Another Voice chimes in:*)

You and the Reverse Gear.

LI'L BIT: 1966. The Anthropology of the Female Body in Ninth Grade — Or A Walk Down Mammary Lane.

(*Throughout the following, there is occasional rhythmic beeping, like a transmitter signaling. Li'l Bit is aware of it, but can't figure out where it is coming from. No one else seems to hear it.*)

MALE GREEK CHORUS: In the hallway of Francis Scott Key Middle School.

(*A bell rings; the Greek Chorus is changing classes and meets in the hall, conspiratorially.*)

TEENAGE GREEK CHORUS: She's coming!

(*Li'l Bit enters the scene; the Male Greek Chorus member has a sudden, violent sneezing and lethal allergy attack.*)

FEMALE GREEK CHORUS: Jerome? Jerome? Are you all right?

MALE GREEK CHORUS: I — don't — know. I can't breathe — get Li'l Bit —

TEENAGE GREEK CHORUS: — He needs oxygen! —

FEMALE GREEK CHORUS: — Can you help us here?

LI'L BIT: What's wrong? Do you want me to get the school nurse —

(*The Male Greek Chorus member wheezes, grabs his throat and sniffs at Li'l Bit's chest, which is beeping away.*)

MALE GREEK CHORUS: No — it's okay — I only get this way when I'm around an allergy trigger —

LI'L BIT: Golly. What are you allergic to?

MALE GREEK CHORUS (*with a sudden grab of her breast*): Foam rubber.

(*The Greek Chorus members break up with hilarity; Jerome leaps away from Li'l Bit's kicking rage with agility; as he retreats:*)

LI'L BIT: Jerome! Creep! Cretin! Cro-Magnon!

TEENAGE GREEK CHORUS: Rage is not attractive in a girl.

FEMALE GREEK CHORUS: Really. Get a Sense of Humor.

(*A Voice echoes:*)

Good defensive driving involves mental and physical preparation. Were You Prepared?

FEMALE GREEK CHORUS: Gym Class: In the showers.

(*The sudden sound of water; the Female Greek Chorus members and Li'l Bit, while fully clothed, drape towels across their fronts, miming nudity. They stand, hesitate, at an imaginary shower's edge.*)

LI'L BIT: Water looks hot.

FEMALE GREEK CHORUS: Yesss. . . .

(*Female Greek Chorus members are not going to make the first move. One dips a tentative toe under the water, clutching the towel around her.*)

LI'L BIT: Well, I guess we'd better shower and get out of here.

FEMALE GREEK CHORUS: Yep. You go ahead. I'm still cooling off.

LI'L BIT: Okay. — Sally? Are you gonna shower?

TEENAGE GREEK CHORUS: After you —

(*Li'l Bit takes a deep breath for courage, drops the towel and plunges in: The two Female Greek Chorus members look at Li'l Bit in the all together, laugh, gasp and high-five each other.*)

TEENAGE GREEK CHORUS: Oh my god! Can you believe —

FEMALE GREEK CHORUS: Told you! It's not foam rubber! I win! Jerome owes me fifty cents!

(*A Voice editorializes:*)

Were You Prepared?

(*Li'l Bit tries to cover up; she is exposed, as suddenly 1960s Motown fills the room and we segue into:*)

FEMALE GREEK CHORUS: The Sock Hop.

(*Li'l Bit stands up against the wall with her female classmates. Teenage Greek Chorus is mesmerized by the music and just sways alone, lip-synching the lyrics.*)

LI'L BIT: I don't know. Maybe it's just me — but — do you ever feel like you're just a walking Mary Jane joke?
FEMALE GREEK CHORUS: I don't know what you mean.
LI'L BIT: You haven't heard the Mary Jane jokes? (*Female Greek Chorus member shakes her head no.*) Okay. "Little Mary Jane is walking through the woods, when all of a sudden this man who was hiding behind a tree *jumps* out, *rips* open Mary Jane's blouse, and *plunges* his hands on her breasts. And Little Mary Jane just laughed and laughed because she knew her money was in her shoes."

(*Li'l Bit laughs; the Female Greek Chorus does not.*)

FEMALE GREEK CHORUS: You're weird.

(*In another space, in a strange light, Uncle Peck stands and stares at Li'l Bit's body. He is setting up a tripod, but he just stands, appreciative, watching her.*)

LI'L BIT: Well, don't you ever feel . . . self-conscious? Like you're being looked at all the time?
FEMALE GREEK CHORUS: That's not a problem for me. — Oh — look — Greg's coming over to ask you to dance.

(*Teenage Creek Chorus becomes attentive, flustered. Male Greek Chorus member, as Greg, bends slightly as a very short young man, whose head is at Li'l Bit's chest level. Ardent, sincere, and socially inept, Greg will become a successful gynecologist.*)

TEENAGE GREEK CHORUS (*softly*): Hi, Greg.

(*Greg does not hear. He is intent on only one thing.*)

MALE GREEK CHORUS (*as Greg, to Li'l Bit*): Good evening. Would you care to dance?
LI'L BIT (*gently*): Thank you very much, Greg — but I'm going to sit this one out.
MALE GREEK CHORUS (*as Greg*): Oh. Okay. I'll try my luck later.

(*He disappears.*)

TEENAGE GREEK CHORUS: Oohhh.

(*Li'l Bit relaxes. Then she tenses, aware of Peck's gaze.*)

FEMALE GREEK CHORUS: Take pity on him. Someone should.
LI'L BIT: But he's so short.
TEENAGE GREEK CHORUS: He can't help it.
LI'L BIT: But his head comes up to (*Li'l Bit gestures*) here. And I think he asks me on the fast dances so he can watch me — you know — jiggle.
FEMALE GREEK CHORUS: I wish I had your problems.

(*The tune changes; Greg is across the room in a flash.*)

MALE GREEK CHORUS (*as Greg*): Evening again. May I ask you for the honor of a spin on the floor?
LI'L BIT: I'm . . . very complimented, Greg. But I . . . I just don't do fast dances.
MALE GREEK CHORUS (*as Greg*): Oh. No problem. That's okay.

(*He disappears. Teenage Greek Chorus watches him go.*)

TEENAGE GREEK CHORUS: That is just so — sad.

(*Li'l Bit becomes aware of Peck waiting.*)

FEMALE GREEK CHORUS: You know, you should take it as a compliment that the guys want to watch you jiggle. They're guys. That's what they're supposed to do.
LI'L BIT: I guess you're right. But sometimes I feel like these alien life forces, these two mounds of flesh have grafted themselves onto my chest, and they're using me until they can "propagate" and take over the world and they'll just keep growing, with a mind of their own until I collapse under their weight and they suck all the nourishment out of my body and I finally just waste away while they get bigger and bigger and — (*Li'l Bit's classmates are just staring at her in disbelief.*)
FEMALE GREEK CHORUS: — You are the strangest girl I have ever met.

(*Li'l Bit's trying to joke but feels on the verge of tears.*)

LI'L BIT: Or maybe someone's implanted radio transmitters in my chest at a frequency I can't hear, that girls can't detect, but they're sending out these signals to men who get mesmerized, like sirens, calling them to dash themselves on these "rocks" —

(*Just then, the music segues into a slow dance, perhaps a Beach Boys tune like "Little Surfer," but over the music there's a rhythmic, hypnotic beeping transmitted, which both Greg and Peck hear. Li'l Bit hears it too, and in horror she stares at her chest. She, too, is almost hypnotized. In a trance, Greg responds to the signals and is called to her side — actually, her front. Like a zombie, he stands in front of her, his eyes planted on her two orbs.*)

MALE GREEK CHORUS (*as Greg*): This one's a slow dance. I hope your dance card isn't . . . filled?

(*Li'l Bit is aware of Peck; but the signals are calling her to him. The signals are no longer transmitters, but an electromagnetic force, pulling Li'l Bit to his side, where he again waits for her to join him. She must get away from the dance floor.)*

LI'L BIT: Greg — you really are a nice boy. But I don't like to dance.

MALE GREEK CHORUS (*as Greg*): That's okay. We don't have to move or anything. I could just hold you and we could just *sway* a little —

LI'L BIT: — No! I'm sorry — but I think I have to leave; I hear someone calling me —

(Li'l Bit starts across the dance floor, leaving Greg behind. The beeping stops. The lights change, although the music does not. As Li'l Bit talks to the audience, she continues to change and prepare for the coming session. She should be wearing a tight tank top or a sheer blouse and very tight pants. To the audience:)

> In every man's home some small room, some zone in his house, is set aside. It might be the attic, or the study, or a den. And there's an invisible sign as if from the old treehouse: Girls Keep Out. Here, away from female eyes, lace doilies and crochet, he keeps his manly toys: the Vargas pinups, the tackle. A scent of tobacco and WD-40. *(She inhales deeply.)* A dash of his Bay Rum. Ahhh . . . *(Li'l Bit savors it for just a moment more.)* Here he keeps his secrets: a violin or saxophone, drum set or darkroom, and the stacks of *Playboy.* *(In a whisper.)* Here, in my aunt's home, it was the basement. Uncle Peck's turf.

(A Voice commands:)

You and the Reverse Gear.

LI'L BIT: 1965. The Photo Shoot.

(Li'l Bit steps into the scene as a nervous but curious thirteen-year-old. Music, from the previous scene, continues to play, changing into something like Roy Orbison later — something seductive with a beat. Peck fiddles, all business, with his camera. As in the driving lesson, he is all competency and concentration. Li'l Bit stands awkwardly. He looks through the Leica camera on the tripod, adjusts the back lighting, etc.)

PECK: Are you cold? The lights should heat up some in a few minutes —

LI'L BIT: — Aunt Mary is?

PECK: At the National Theatre matinee. With your mother. We have time.

LI'L BIT: But — what if —

PECK: — And so what if they return? I told them you and I were going to be working with my camera. They won't come down.

(Li'l Bit is quiet, apprehensive.)

> Look, are you sure you want to do this?

LI'L BIT: I said I'd do it. But —

PECK: — I know. You've drawn the line.

LI'L BIT (*reassured*): That's right. No frontal nudity.

PECK: Good heavens, girl, where did you pick that up?

LI'L BIT (*defensive*): I read.

(Peck tries not to laugh.)

PECK: And I read *Playboy* for the interviews. Okay. Let's try some different music.

(Peck goes to an expensive reel-to-reel and forwards. Something like "Sweet Dreams" begins to play.)

LI'L BIT: I didn't know you listened to this.

PECK: I'm not dead, you know, I try to keep up. Do you like this song?

(Li'l Bit nods with pleasure.)

> Good. Now listen — at professional photo shoots, they always play music for the models. Okay? I want you to just enjoy the music. Listen to it with your body, and just — respond.

LI'L BIT: Respond to the music with my . . . body?

PECK: Right. Almost like dancing. Here — let's get you on the stool, first. *(Peck comes over and helps her up.)*

LI'L BIT: But nothing showing —

(Peck firmly, with his large capable hands, brushes back her hair, angles her face. Li'l Bit turns to him like a plant to the sun.)

PECK: Nothing showing. Just a peek.

(He holds her by the shoulders, looking at her critically. Then he unbuttons her blouse to the midpoint, and runs his hands over the flesh of her exposed sternum, arranging the fabric, just touching her. Deliberately, calmly. Asexually. Li'l Bit quiets, sits perfectly still, and closes her eyes.)

> Okay?

LI'L BIT: Yes.

(Peck goes back to his camera.)

PECK: I'm going to keep talking to you. Listen without responding to what I'm saying; you want to *listen* to the music. Sway, move just your torso or your head — I've got to check the light meter.

LI'L BIT: But — you'll be watching.

PECK: No — I'm not here — just my voice. Pretend you're in your room all alone on a Friday night with your mirror — and the music feels good — just move for me, Li'l Bit —

(Li'l Bit closes her eyes. At first self-conscious; then she gets more into the music and begins to sway. We hear the camera start to whir. Throughout the shoot, there can be a slide montage of actual shots of the actor playing Li'l Bit — interspersed with other models à la Playboy, *Calvin Klein, and Victoriana/Lewis Carroll's Alice Liddell.)*

> That's it. That looks great. Okay. Just keep doing that. Lift your head up a bit more, good, good, just keep moving, that a girl — you're a very beautiful young woman. Do you know that?

(*Li'l Bit looks up, blushes. Peck shoots the camera. The audience should see this shot on the screen.*)

Li'l Bit: No. I don't know that.

Peck: Listen to the music.

(*Li'l Bit closes her eyes again.*)

Well you are. For a thirteen-year-old, you have a body a twenty-year-old woman would die for.

Li'l Bit: The boys in school don't think so.

Peck: The boys in school are little Neanderthals in short pants. You're ten years ahead of them in maturity; it's gonna take a while for them to catch up.

(*Peck clicks another shot; we see a faint smile on Li'l Bit on the screen.*)

Girls turn into women long before boys turn into men.

Li'l Bit: Why is that?

Peck: I don't know, Li'l Bit. But it's a blessing for men.

(*Li'l Bit turns silent.*)

Keep moving. Try arching your back on the stool, hands behind you, and throw your head back.

(*The slide shows a* Playboy *model in this pose.*)

Oohh, great. That one was great. Turn your head away, same position. (*Whir.*) Beautiful.

(*Li'l Bit looks at him a bit defiantly.*)

Li'l Bit: I think Aunt Mary is beautiful.

(*Peck stands still.*)

Peck: My wife is a very beautiful woman. Her beauty doesn't cancel yours out. (*More casually; he returns to the camera.*) All the women in your family are beautiful. In fact, I think all women are. You're not listening to the music. (*Peck shoots some more film in silence.*) All right, turn your head to the left. Good. Now take the back of your right hand and put it on your right cheek — your elbow angled up — now slowly, slowly, stroke your cheek, draw back your hair with the back of your hand. (*Another classic* Playboy *or* Vargas.) Good. One hand above and behind your head; stretch your body; smile. (*Another pose.*) Li'l Bit. I want you to think of something that makes you laugh —

Li'l Bit: I can't think of anything.

Peck: Okay. Think of Big Papa chasing Grandma around the living room.

(*Li'l Bit lifts her head and laughs. Click. We should see this shot.*)

Good. Both hands behind your head. Great! Hold that. (*From behind his camera.*) You're doing great work. If we keep this up, in five years we'll have a really professional portfolio.

(*Li'l Bit stops.*)

Li'l Bit: What do you mean in five years?

Peck: You can't submit work to *Playboy* until you're eighteen. —

(*Peck continues to shoot; he knows he's made a mistake.*)

Li'l Bit: — Wait a minute. You're joking, aren't you, Uncle Peck?

Peck: Heck, no. You can't get into *Playboy* unless you're the very best. And you are the very best.

Li'l Bit: I would never do that!

(*Peck stops shooting. He turns off the music.*)

Peck: Why? There's nothing wrong with *Playboy* — it's a very classy maga —

Li'l Bit (*more upset*): But I thought you said I should go to college!

Peck: Wait — Li'l Bit — it's nothing like that. Very respectable women model for *Playboy* — actresses with major careers — women in college — there's an Ivy League issue every —

Li'l Bit: — I'm never doing anything like that! You'd show other people these — other *men* — what I'm doing. — Why would you do that?! Any *boy* around here could just pick up, just go into The Stop & Go and *buy* — Why would you ever want to — to share —

Peck: — Whoa, whoa. Just stop a second and listen to me. Li'l Bit. Listen. There's nothing wrong in what we're doing. I'm very proud of you. I think you have a wonderful body and an even more wonderful mind. And of course I want other people to *appreciate* it. It's not anything shameful.

Li'l Bit (*hurt*): But this is something — that I'm only doing for you. This is something — that you said was just between us.

Peck: It is. And if that's how you feel, five years from now, it will remain that way. Okay? I know you're not going to do anything you don't feel like doing. (*He walks back to the camera.*) Do you want to stop now? I've got just a few more shots on this roll —

Li'l Bit: I don't want anyone seeing this.

Peck: I swear to you. No one will. I'll treasure this — that you're doing this only for me.

(*Li'l Bit, still shaken, sits on the stool. She closes her eyes.*)

Li'l Bit? Open your eyes and look at me.

(*Li'l Bit shakes her head no.*)

Come on. Just open your eyes, honey.

Li'l Bit: If I look at you — if I look at the camera: You're gonna know what I'm thinking. You'll see right through me —

Peck: — No, I won't. I want you to look at me. All right, then. I just want you to listen. Li'l Bit.

(*She waits.*)

I love you.

(Li'l Bit opens her eyes; she is startled. Peck captures the shot. On the screen we see right through her. Peck says softly.)

Do you know that?

(Li'l Bit nods her head yes.)

I have loved you every day since the day you were born.

Li'l Bit: Yes.

(Li'l Bit and Peck just look at each other. Beat. Beneath the shot of herself on the screen, Li'l Bit, still looking at her uncle, begins to unbutton her blouse.

A neutral Voice cuts off the above scene with:)

Implied Consent.
As an individual operating a motor vehicle in the state of Maryland, you must abide by "Implied Consent." If you do not consent to take the blood alcohol content test, there may be severe penalties: a suspension of license, a fine, community service, and a possible jail sentence.

(The Voice shifts tone:)

Idling in the Neutral Gear.

Male Greek Chorus *(announcing)*: Aunt Mary on behalf of her husband.

(Female Greek Chorus checks her appearance, and with dignity comes to the front of the stage and sits down to talk to the audience.)

Female Greek Chorus *(as Aunt Mary)*: My husband was such a good man — is. Is such a good man. Every night, he does the dishes. The second he comes home, he's taking out the garbage, or doing yard work, lifting the heavy things I can't. Everyone in the neighborhood borrows Peck — it's true — women with husbands of their own, men who just don't have Peck's abilities — there's always a knock on our door for a jump start on cold mornings, when anyone needs a ride, or help shoveling the sidewalk — I look out, and there Peck is, without a coat, pitching in.

I know I'm lucky. The man works from dawn to dusk. And the overtime he does every year — my poor sister. She sits every Christmas when I come to dinner with a new stole, or diamonds, or with the tickets to Bermuda.

I know he has troubles. And we don't talk about them. I wonder, sometimes, what happened to him during the war. The men who fought World War II didn't have "rap sessions" to talk about their feelings. Men in his generation were expected to be quiet about it and get on with their lives. And sometimes I can feel him just fighting the trouble — whatever has

burrowed deeper than the scar tissue — and we don't talk about it. I know he's having a bad spell because he comes looking for me in the house, and just hangs around me until it passes. And I keep my banter light — I discuss a new recipe, or sales, or gossip — because I think domesticity can be a balm for men when they're lost. We sit in the house and listen to the peace of the clock ticking in his well-ordered living room, until it passes.

(Sharply.) I'm not a fool. I know what's going on. I wish you could feel how hard Peck fights against it — he's swimming against the tide, and what he needs is to see me on the shore, believing in him, knowing he won't go under, he won't give up —

And I want to say this about my niece. She's a sly one, that one is. She knows exactly what she's doing; she's twisted Peck around her little finger and thinks it's all a big secret. Yet another one who's borrowing my husband until it doesn't suit her anymore.

Well. I'm counting the days until she goes away to school. And she manipulates someone else. And then he'll come back again, and sit in the kitchen while I bake, or beside me on the sofa when I sew in the evenings. I'm a very patient woman. But I'd like my husband back.

I am counting the days.

(A Voice repeats:)

You and the Reverse Gear.

Male Greek Chorus: Li'l Bit's Thirteenth Christmas. Uncle Peck Does the Dishes. Christmas 1964.

(Peck stands in a dress shirt and tie, nice pants, with an apron. He is washing dishes. He's in a mood we haven't seen. Quiet, brooding. Li'l Bit watches him a moment before seeking him out.)

Li'l Bit: Uncle Peck?

(He does not answer. He continues to work on the pots.)

I didn't know where you'd gone to.

(He nods. She takes this as a sign to come in.)

Don't you want to sit with us for a while?

Peck: No. I'd rather do the dishes.

(Pause. Li'l Bit watches him.)

Li'l Bit: You're the only man I know who does dishes.

(Peck says nothing.)

I think it's really nice.

Peck: My wife has been on her feet all day. So's your grandmother and your mother.

Li'l Bit: I know. *(Beat.)* Do you want some help?

Peck: No. *(He softens a bit towards her.)* You can help by just talking to me.

Li'l Bit: Big Papa never does the dishes. I think it's nice.

PECK: I think men should be nice to women. Women are always working for us. There's nothing particularly manly in wolfing down food and then sitting around in a stupor while the women clean up.

LI'L BIT: That looks like a really neat camera that Aunt Mary got you.

PECK: It is. It's a very nice one.

(*Pause, as Peck works on the dishes and some demon that Li'l Bit intuits.*)

LI'L BIT: Did Big Papa hurt your feelings?

PECK (*tired*): What? Oh, no — it doesn't hurt me. Family is family. I'd rather have him picking on me than — I don't pay him any mind, Li'l Bit.

LI'L BIT: Are you angry with us?

PECK: No, Li'l Bit. I'm not angry.

(*Another pause.*)

LI'L BIT: We missed you at Thanksgiving. . . . I did. I missed you.

PECK: Well, there were . . . "things" going on. I didn't want to spoil anyone's Thanksgiving.

LI'L BIT: Uncle Peck? (*Very carefully.*) Please don't drink anymore tonight.

PECK: I'm not . . . overdoing it.

LI'L BIT: I know. (*Beat.*) Why do you drink so much?

(*Peck stops and thinks, carefully.*)

PECK: Well, Li'l Bit — let me explain it this way. There are some people who have a . . . a "fire" in the belly. I think they go to work on Wall Street or they run for office. And then there are people who have a "fire" in their heads — and they become writers or scientists or historians. (*He smiles a little at her.*) You. You've got a "fire" in the head. And then there are people like me.

LI'L BIT: Where do you have . . . a fire?

PECK: I have a fire in my heart. And sometimes the drinking helps.

LI'L BIT: There's got to be other things that can help.

PECK: I suppose there are.

LI'L BIT: Does it help — to talk to me?

PECK: Yes. It does. (*Quiet.*) I don't get to see you very much.

LI'L BIT: I know. (*Li'l Bit thinks.*) You could talk to me more.

PECK: Oh?

LI'L BIT: I could make a deal with you, Uncle Peck.

PECK: I'm listening.

LI'L BIT: We could meet and talk — once a week. You could just store up whatever's bothering you during the week — and then we could talk.

PECK: Would you like that?

LI'L BIT: As long as you don't drink. I'd meet you somewhere for lunch or for a walk — on the weekends — as long as you stop drinking. And we could talk about whatever you want.

PECK: You would do that for me?

LI'L BIT: I don't think I'd want Mom to know. Or Aunt Mary. I wouldn't want them to think —

PECK: — No. It would just be us talking.

LI'L BIT: I'll tell Mom I'm going to a girlfriend's. To study. Mom doesn't get home until six, so you can call me after school and tell me where to meet you.

PECK: You get home at four?

LI'L BIT: We can meet once a week. But only in public. You've got to let me — draw the line. And once it's drawn, you mustn't cross it.

PECK: Understood.

LI'L BIT: Would that help?

(*Peck is very moved.*)

PECK: Yes. Very much.

LI'L BIT: I'm going to join the others in the living room now. (*Li'l Bit turns to go.*)

PECK: Merry Christmas, Li'l Bit.

(*Li'l Bit bestows a very warm smile on him.*)

LI'L BIT: Merry Christmas, Uncle Peck.

(*A Voice dictates:*)

Shifting Forward from Second to Third Gear.

(*The Male and Female Greek Chorus members come forward.*)

MALE GREEK CHORUS: 1969. Days and Gifts: A Countdown:

FEMALE GREEK CHORUS: A note. "September 3, 1969. Li'l Bit: You've only been away two days and it feels like months. Hope your dorm room is cozy. I'm sending you this tape cassette — it's a new model — so you'll have some music in your room. Also that music you're reading about for class — *Carmina Burana*. Hope you enjoy. Only ninety days to go! — Peck."

MALE GREEK CHORUS: September 22. A bouquet of roses. A note: "Miss you like crazy. Sixty-nine days . . ."

TEENAGE GREEK CHORUS: September 25. A box of chocolates. A card: "Don't worry about the weight gain. You still look great. Got a post office box — write to me there. Sixty-six days. — Love, your candy man."

MALE GREEK CHORUS: October 16. A note: "Am trying to get through the Jane Austen you're reading — *Emma* — here's a book in return: *Liaisons Dangereuses*. Hope you're saving time for me." Scrawled in the margin the number: "47."

FEMALE GREEK CHORUS: November 16. "Sixteen days to go! — Hope you like the perfume. — Having a hard time reaching you on the dorm phone. You must be in the library a lot. Won't you think about me getting you your own phone so we can talk?"

TEENAGE GREEK CHORUS: November 18. "Li'l Bit — got a package returned to the P.O. Box. Have you changed dorms? Call me at work or write to the P.O. Am still on the wagon. Waiting to see you. Only two weeks more!"

MALE GREEK CHORUS: November 23. A letter. "Li'l Bit. So disappointed you couldn't come home for the turkey. Sending you some money for a nice dinner out — nine days and counting!"

GREEK CHORUS (*in unison*): November 25th. A letter:

LI'L BIT: "Dear Uncle Peck: I am sending this to you at work. Don't come up next weekend for my birthday. I will not be here —"

(*A Voice directs:*)

Shifting Forward from Third to Fourth Gear.

MALE GREEK CHORUS: December 10, 1969. A hotel room. Philadelphia. There is no moon tonight.

(*Peck sits on the side of the bed while Li'l Bit paces. He can't believe she's in his room, but there's a desperate edge to his happiness. Li'l Bit is furious, edgy. There is a bottle of champagne in an ice bucket in a very nice hotel room.*)

PECK: Why don't you sit?

LI'L BIT: I don't want to. — What's the champagne for?

PECK: I thought we might toast your birthday —

LI'L BIT: — I am so pissed off at you, Uncle Peck.

PECK: Why?

LI'L BIT: I mean, are you crazy?

PECK: What did I do?

LI'L BIT: You scared the holy crap out of me — sending me that stuff in the mail —

PECK: — They were gifts! I just wanted to give you some little perks your first semester —

LI'L BIT: — Well, what the hell were those numbers all about! Forty-four days to go — only two more weeks. — And then just numbers — 69 — 68 — 67 — like some serial killer!

PECK: Li'l Bit! Whoa! This is me you're talking to — I was just trying to pick up your spirits, trying to celebrate your birthday.

LI'L BIT: My *eighteenth* birthday. I'm not a child, Uncle Peck. You were counting down to my eighteenth birthday.

PECK: So?

LI'L BIT: So? So statutory rape is not in effect when a young woman turns eighteen. And you and I both know it.

(*Peck is walking on ice.*)

PECK: I think you misunderstand.

LI'L BIT: I think I understand all too well. I know what you want to do five steps ahead of you doing it. Defensive Driving 101.

PECK: Then why did you suggest we meet here instead of the restaurant?

LI'L BIT: I don't want to have this conversation in public.

PECK: Fine. Fine. We have a lot to talk about.

LI'L BIT: Yeah. We do.

(*Li'l Bit doesn't want to do what she has to do.*)
Could I . . . have some of that champagne?

PECK: Of course, madam! (*Peck makes a big show of it.*) Let me do the honors. I wasn't sure which you might prefer — Taittingers or Veuve Clicquot — so I thought we'd start out with an old standard — Perrier Jouet. (*The bottle is popped.*)

Quick — Li'l Bit — your glass! (*Uncle Peck fills Li'l Bit's glass. He puts the bottle back in the ice and goes for a can of ginger ale.*) Let me get some of this ginger ale — my bubbly — and toast you.

(*He turns and sees that Li'l Bit has not waited for him.*)

LI'L BIT: Oh — sorry, Uncle Peck. Let me have another.

(*Peck fills her glass and reaches for his ginger ale; she stops him.*)

Uncle Peck — maybe you should join me in the champagne.

PECK: You want me — to drink?

LI'L BIT: It's not polite to let a lady drink alone.

PECK: Well, missy, if you insist. . . . (*Peck hesitates.*) — Just one. It's been a while. (*Peck fills another flute for himself.*) There. I'd like to propose a toast to you and your birthday! (*Peck sips it tentatively.*) I'm not used to this anymore.

LI'L BIT: You don't have anywhere to go tonight, do you?

(*Peck hopes this is a good sign.*)

PECK: I'm all yours. — God, it's good to see you! I've gotten so used to . . . to . . . talking to you in my head. I'm used to seeing you every week — there's so much — I don't quite know where to begin. How's school, Li'l Bit?

LI'L BIT: I — it's hard. Uncle Peck. Harder than I thought it would be. I'm in the middle of exams and papers and — I don't know.

PECK: You'll pull through. You always do.

LI'L BIT: Maybe. I . . . might be flunking out.

PECK: You always think the worst, Li'l Bit, but when the going gets tough —

(*Li'l Bit shrugs and pours herself another glass.*)

— Hey, honey, go easy on that stuff, okay?

LI'L BIT: Is it very expensive?

PECK: Only the best for you. But the cost doesn't matter — champagne should be "sipped."

(*Li'l Bit is quiet.*)

Look — if you're in trouble in school — you can always come back home for a while.

LI'L BIT: *No* — (*Li'l Bit tries not to be so harsh.*) — Thanks, Uncle Peck, but I'll figure some way out of this.

PECK: You're supposed to get in scrapes, your first year away from home.

LI'L BIT: Right. How's Aunt Mary?

PECK: She's fine. (*Pause.*) Well — how about the new car?

LI'L BIT: It's real nice. What is it, again?

PECK: It's a Cadillac El Dorado.

LI'L BIT: Oh. Well, I'm real happy for you, Uncle Peck.

PECK: I got it for you.

LI'L BIT: What?

PECK: I always wanted to get a Cadillac — but I thought, Peck, wait until Li'l Bit's old enough — and thought maybe you'd like to drive it, too.

LI'L BIT (*confused*): Why would I want to drive your car?

PECK: Just because it's the best — I want you to have the best.

(*They are running out of "gas"; small talk.*)

LI'L BIT: Listen, Uncle Peck, I don't know how to begin this, but —	PECK: I have been thinking of how to say this in my head, over and over —

PECK: Sorry.

LI'L BIT: You first.

PECK: Well, your going away — has just made me realize how much I miss you. Talking to you and being alone with you. I've really come to depend on you, Li'l Bit. And it's been so hard to get in touch with you lately — the distance and — and you're never in when I call — I guess you've been living in the library —

LI'L BIT: — No — the problem is, I haven't been in the library —

PECK: — Well, it doesn't matter — I hope you've been missing me as much.

LI'L BIT: Uncle Peck — I've been thinking a lot about this — and I came here tonight to tell you that — I'm not doing very well. I'm getting very confused — I can't concentrate on my work — and now that I'm away — I've been going over and over it in my mind — and I don't want us to "see" each other anymore. Other than with the rest of the family.

PECK (*quiet*): Are you seeing other men?

LI'L BIT (*getting agitated*): I — no, that's not the reason — I — well, yes, I am seeing other — listen, it's not really anybody's business!

PECK: Are you in love with anyone else?

LI'L BIT: That's not what this is about.

PECK: Li'l Bit — you're scared. Your mother and your grandparents have filled your head with all kinds of nonsense about men — I hear them working on you all the time — and you're scared. It won't hurt you — if the man you go to bed with really loves you. (*Li'l Bit is scared. She starts to tremble.*) And I have loved you since the day I held you in my hand. And I think everyone's just gotten you frightened to death about something that is just like breathing —

LI'L BIT: Oh, my god — (*She takes a breath.*) I can't see you anymore, Uncle Peck.

(*Peck downs the rest of his champagne.*)

PECK: Li'l Bit. Listen. Listen. Open your eyes and look at me. Come on. Just open your eyes, honey. (*Li'l Bit, eyes squeezed shut, refuses.*) All right then. I just want you to listen. Li'l Bit — I'm going to ask you just this once. Of your own free will. Just lie down on the bed with me — our clothes on — just lie down with me, a man and a woman . . . and let's . . . hold one another. Nothing else. Before you say anything else. I want the chance to . . . hold you. Because sometimes the body knows things that the mind isn't listening to . . . and after I've held you, then I want you to tell me what you feel.

LI'L BIT: You'll just . . . hold me?

PECK: Yes. And then you can tell me what you're feeling.

(*Li'l Bit — half wanting to run, half wanting to get it over with, half wanting to be held by him:*)

LI'L BIT: Yes. All right. Just hold. Nothing else.

(*Peck lies down on the bed and holds his arms out to her. Li'l Bit lies beside him, putting her head on his chest. He looks as if he's trying to soak her into his pores by osmosis. He strokes her hair, and she lies very still. The Male Greek Chorus member and the Female Greek Chorus member as Aunt Mary come into the room.*)

MALE GREEK CHORUS: Recipe for a Southern Boy:

FEMALE GREEK CHORUS (*as Aunt Mary*): A drawl of molasses in the way he speaks.

MALE GREEK CHORUS: A gumbo of red and brown mixed in the cream of his skin.

(*While Peck lies, his eyes closed, Li'l Bit rises in the bed and responds to her aunt.*)

LI'L BIT: Warm brown eyes —

FEMALE GREEK CHORUS (*as Aunt Mary*): Bedroom eyes —

MALE GREEK CHORUS: A dash of Southern Baptist Fire and Brimstone —

LI'L BIT: A curl of Elvis on his forehead —

FEMALE GREEK CHORUS (*as Aunt Mary*): A splash of Bay Rum —

MALE GREEK CHORUS: A closely shaven beard that he razors just for you —

FEMALE GREEK CHORUS (*as Aunt Mary*): Large hands — rough hands —

LI'L BIT: Warm hands —

MALE GREEK CHORUS: The steel of the military in his walk —

LI'L BIT: The slouch of the fishing skiff in his walk —

MALE GREEK CHORUS: Neatly pressed khakis —

FEMALE GREEK CHORUS (*as Aunt Mary*): And under the wide leather of the belt —

LI'L BIT: Sweat of cypress and sand —

MALE GREEK CHORUS: Neatly pressed khakis —

LI'L BIT: His heart beating Dixie —

FEMALE GREEK CHORUS (*as Aunt Mary*): The whisper of the zipper — you could reach out with your hand and —

LI'L BIT: His mouth —

Mary Louise Parker as Li'l Bit and David Morse as Uncle Peck in *How I Learned to Drive* in 1997 at the Vineyard Theatre, New York City.

FEMALE GREEK CHORUS (*as Aunt Mary*): You could just reach out and —
LI'L BIT: Hold him in your hand —
FEMALE GREEK CHORUS (*as Aunt Mary*): And his mouth —

(*Li'l Bit rises above her uncle and looks at his mouth; she starts to lower herself to kiss him — and wrenches herself free. She gets up from the bed.*)

LI'L BIT: — I've got to get back.
PECK: Wait — Li'l Bit. Did you . . . feel nothing?
LI'L BIT (*lying*): No. Nothing.
PECK: Do you — do you think of me?

(*The Greek Chorus whispers:*)

FEMALE GREEK CHORUS: Khakis —
MALE GREEK CHORUS: Bay Rum —
FEMALE GREEK CHORUS: The whisper of the —
LI'L BIT: — No.

(*Peck, in a rush, trembling, gets something out of his pocket.*)

PECK: I'm forty-five. That's not old for a man. And I haven't been able to do anything else but think of you. I can't concentrate on my work — Li'l Bit. You've got to — I want you to think about what I am about to ask you.
LI'L BIT: I'm listening.

(*Peck opens a small ring box.*)

PECK: I want you to be my wife.
LI'L BIT: This isn't happening.
PECK: I'll tell Mary I want a divorce. We're not blood-related. It would be legal —
LI'L BIT: — What have you been thinking! You are married to my aunt, Uncle Peck. She's my family. You have — you have gone way over the line. Family is family.
   (*Quickly, Li'l Bit flies through the room, gets her coat.*) I'm leaving. Now. I am not seeing you. Again.

(*Peck lies down on the bed for a moment, trying to absorb the terrible news. For a moment, he almost curls into a fetal position.*)

   I'm not coming home for Christmas. You should go home to Aunt Mary. Go home now, Uncle Peck.

(*Peck gets control, and sits, rigid.*)

   Uncle Peck? — I'm sorry but I have to go.

(*Pause.*)

   Are you all right?

(*With a discipline that comes from being told that boys don't cry, Peck stands upright.*)

PECK: I'm fine. I just think — I need a real drink.

(*The Male Greek Chorus has become a bartender. At a small counter, he is lining up shots for Peck. As Li'l Bit*)

*narrates, we see Peck sitting, carefully and calmly down-
ing shot glasses.)*

LI'L BIT (*to the audience*): I never saw him again. I
stayed away from Christmas and Thanksgiving for
years after.

　　It took my uncle seven years to drink himself to
death. First he lost his job, then his wife, and finally
his driver's license. He retreated to his house, and
had his bottles delivered.

*(Peck stands, and puts his hands in front of him —
almost like Superman flying.)*

　　One night he tried to go downstairs to the basement — and he flew down the steep basement stairs.
My aunt came by weekly to put food on the porch,
and she noticed the mail and the papers stacked up,
uncollected.

　　They found him at the bottom of the stairs. Just
steps away from his dark room.

　　Now that I'm old enough, there are some questions I would have liked to have asked him. Who did
it to you, Uncle Peck? How old were you? Were you
eleven?

(Peck moves to the driver's seat of the car and waits.)

　　Sometimes I think of my uncle as a kind of Flying
Dutchman. In the opera, the Dutchman is doomed to
wander the sea; but every seven years he can come
ashore, and if he finds a maiden who will love him of
her own free will — he will be released.

　　And I see Uncle Peck in my mind, in his Chevy
'56, a spirit driving up and down the back roads of
Carolina — looking for a young girl who, of her own
free will, will love him. Release him.

(A Voice states:)

You and the Reverse Gear.

LI'L BIT: The summer of 1962. On Men, Sex, and
Women: Part III:

(Li'l Bit steps, as an eleven-year-old, into:)

FEMALE GREEK CHORUS (*as Mother*): It is out of the
question. End of Discussion.

LI'L BIT: But why?

FEMALE GREEK CHORUS (*as Mother*): Li'l Bit — we are
not discussing this. I said no.

LI'L BIT: But I could spend an extra week at the beach!
You're not telling me why!

FEMALE GREEK CHORUS (*as Mother*): Your uncle pays
entirely too much attention to you.

LI'L BIT: He listens to me when I talk. And — and he
talks to me. He teaches me about things. Mama —
he knows an awful lot.

FEMALE GREEK CHORUS (*as Mother*): He's a small town
hick who's learned how to mix drinks from Hugh
Hefner.

LI'L BIT: Who's Hugh Hefner?

(Beat.)

FEMALE GREEK CHORUS (*as Mother*): I am not letting an
eleven-year-old girl spend seven hours alone in the
car with a man. . . . I don't like the way your uncle
looks at you.

LI'L BIT: For god's sake, mother! Just because you've
gone through a bad time with my father — you think
every man is evil!

FEMALE GREEK CHORUS (*as Mother*): Oh no, Li'l Bit —
not all men. . . . We . . . we just haven't been very
lucky with the men in our family.

LI'L BIT: Just because you lost your husband — I still
deserve a chance at having a father! Someone! A man
who will look out for me! Don't I get a chance?

FEMALE GREEK CHORUS (*as Mother*): I will feel terrible
if something happens.

LI'L BIT: Mother! It's in your head! Nothing will happen! I can take care of myself. And I can certainly
handle Uncle Peck.

FEMALE GREEK CHORUS (*as Mother*): All right. But I'm
warning you — if anything happens, I hold you
responsible.

(Li'l Bit moves out of this scene and toward the car.)

LI'L BIT: 1962. On the Back Roads of Carolina: The
First Driving Lesson.

*(The Teenage Greek Chorus member stands apart on
stage. She will speak all of Li'l Bit's lines. Li'l Bit sits
beside Peck in the front seat. She looks at him closely,
remembering.)*

PECK: Li'l Bit? Are you getting tired?

TEENAGE GREEK CHORUS: A little.

PECK: It's a long drive. But we're making really good time.
We can take the back road from here and see . . . a
little scenery. Say — I've got an idea — (*Peck checks
his rearview mirror.*)

TEENAGE GREEK CHORUS: Are we stopping, Uncle Peck?

PECK: There's no traffic here. Do you want to drive?

TEENAGE GREEK CHORUS: I can't drive.

PECK: It's easy. I'll show you how. I started driving when
I was your age. Don't you want to? —

TEENAGE GREEK CHORUS: — But it's against the law at
my age!

PECK: And that's why you can't tell anyone I'm letting
you do this —

TEENAGE GREEK CHORUS: — But — I can't reach the
pedals.

PECK: You can sit in my lap and steer. I'll push the pedals
for you. Did your father ever let you drive his car?

TEENAGE GREEK CHORUS: No way.

PECK: Want to try?

TEENAGE GREEK CHORUS: Okay. (*Li'l Bit moves into
Peck's lap. She leans against him, closing her eyes.*)

PECK: You're just a little thing, aren't you? Okay — now
think of the wheel as a big clock — I want you to put
your right hand on the clock where three o'clock

would be; and your left hand on the nine —

(*Li'l Bit puts one hand to Peck's face, to stroke him. Then, she takes the wheel.*)

TEENAGE GREEK CHORUS: Am I doing it right?
PECK: That's right. Now, whatever you do, don't let go of the wheel. You tell me whether to go faster or slower —
TEENAGE GREEK CHORUS: Not so fast, Uncle Peck!
PECK: Li'l Bit — I need you to watch the road —

(*Peck puts his hands on Li'l Bit's breasts. She relaxes against him, silent, accepting his touch.*)

TEENAGE GREEK CHORUS: Uncle Peck — what are you doing?
PECK: Keep driving. (*He slips his hands under her blouse.*)
TEENAGE GREEK CHORUS: Uncle Peck — please don't do this —
PECK: — Just a moment longer . . . (*Peck tenses against Li'l Bit.*)
TEENAGE GREEK CHORUS (*trying not to cry*): This isn't happening.

(*Peck tenses more, sharply. He buries his face in Li'l Bit's neck, and moans softly. The Teenage Greek Chorus exits, and Li'l Bit steps out of the car. Peck, too, disappears.*)
(*A Voice reflects:*)

Driving in Today's World.

LI'L BIT: That day was the last day I lived in my body. I retreated above the neck, and I've lived inside the "fire" in my head ever since.
   And now that seems like a long, long time ago. When we were both very young.
   And before you know it, I'll be thirty-five. That's getting up there for a woman. And I find myself believing in things that a younger self vowed never to believe in. Things like family and forgiveness.
   I know I'm lucky. Although I still have never known what it feels like to jog or dance. Any thing

that . . . "jiggles." I do like to watch people on the dance floor, or out on the running paths, just jiggling away. And I say — good for them. (*Li'l Bit moves to the car with pleasure.*)
   The nearest sensation I feel — of flight in the body — I guess I feel when I'm driving. On a day like today. It's five A.M. The radio says it's going to be clear and crisp. I've got five hundred miles of highway ahead of me — and some back roads too. I filled the tank last night, and had the oil checked. Checked the tires, too. You've got to treat her . . . with respect.
   First thing I do is: Check under the car. To see if any two year olds or household cats have crawled beneath, and strategically placed their skulls behind my back tires. (*Li'l Bit crouches.*)
   Nope. Then I get in the car. (*Li'l Bit does so.*)
   I lock the doors. And turn the key. Then I adjust the most important control on the dashboard — the radio — (*Li'l Bit turns the radio on: We hear all of the Greek Chorus overlapping, and static:*)
FEMALE GREEK CHORUS (*overlapping*): — "You were so tiny you fit in his hand —"
MALE GREEK CHORUS (*overlapping*): — "How is Shakespeare gonna help her lie on her back in the —"
TEENAGE GREEK CHORUS (*overlapping*): — "Am I doing it right?"

(*Li'l Bit fine-tunes the radio station. A song like "Dedicated to the One I Love" or Orbison's "Sweet Dreams" comes on, and cuts off the Greek Chorus.*)

LI'L BIT: Ahh . . . (*Beat.*) I adjust my seat. Fasten my seat belt. Then I check the right side mirror — check the left side. (*She does.*) Finally, I adjust the rearview mirror.

(*As Li'l Bit adjusts the rearview mirror, a faint light strikes the spirit of Uncle Peck, who is sitting in the back seat of the car. She sees him in the mirror. She smiles at him, and he nods at her. They are happy to be going for a long ride together. Li'l Bit slips the car into first gear; to the audience:*)

And then — I floor it.

(*Sound of a car taking off. Blackout.*)

COMMENTARIES

Christopher Bigsby
PAULA VOGEL   *1999*

In this excerpt from his discussion of Paula Vogel, English theater scholar Christopher Bigsby examines some of the complexities of How I Learned to Drive. *He comments on the attractive qualities of Peck and the seductive qualities of Li'l Bit, while also examining the subtleties of the metaphors of driving embedded in the play. He also reminds us that for Vogel the attraction for pedophiles is not the gender of the prey, but the age. Bigsby sees the play as a complex structure that avoids psychological cliché.*

[. . .] Peck is an attractive man in his forties. He should, Vogel instructs, and despite what she calls "a few problems," be played by an actor one might cast in the role of Atticus in *To Kill a Mockingbird,* hence his name (Gregory Peck playing that role in the movie). Li'l Bit is by turns a woman in her thirties or forties and a prematurely developed young girl seen at various moments from the age of eleven through her twenties. The action takes place in suburban Maryland, described by the older Li'l Bit as near the crumbling concrete of U.S. One, which "winds its way past one-room revival churches, the porno drive-in, and boarded up motels with For Sale signs tumbling down." Once there had been another Maryland, "before the Malls took over," but even then innocence had been tainted: "This country-side was once dotted with farmhouses — from their porches you could have witnessed the Civil War raging in the front fields." This is a moralized landscape, invested with the qualities of a country whose own insistent innocence had itself never been entirely plausible, never quite realized. *How I Learned to Drive,* indeed, is surely in part about an America which struggles to sustain notions of innocence, spiritual concern, and family values while flooding its consciousness with sexual titillation: a cheerleader culture of prepubescent beauty pageants, eroticized movies and advertisements, as though sex were a language in which it is necessary to become fluent as soon as possible. In such a context, moral affront at Lolita-like affairs becomes more difficult to sustain or at least more profoundly ambiguous. [. . .]

The audience's attitude to Peck, and to his relationship with Li'l Bit, is in part shaped by the fact of the play's broken chronology. The first scene finds the young girl at seventeen, "going on eighteen," allowing what Blanche DuBois (who herself conducts affairs with teenage boys) would have called "little familiarities" at the hands of a man who is, admittedly, more than twice her age. Despite the disproportion between their ages, however, this seems a relationship which if disturbing is relaxed and not overtly exploitative. Though hardly an innocent encounter it is presented as little more than a parodic teenage tryst. If the genders were reversed we would have *Tea and Sympathy.* Peck partly undresses and fondles Li'l Bit but Vogel instructs that this is to be performed in mime while the mock solemnity with which it is enacted — "Sacred music, organ music or a boys' choir" swells as she permits the intimacies — defuses its potential for affront. If anything, power seems to reside with the young woman and not the man whose behavior makes him seem younger than he is, and more dependent.

In *How I Learned to Drive* we see the effect before we understand the cause, detect the trauma before being told its root. We learn early that at eighteen Li'l Bit leaves college for a string of dead-end jobs because of her fondness for alcohol, spending the nights driving through the countryside "thinking just one notch of the steering wheel would be all it would take" to end it all. However, it takes much of the play to understand what lies behind this suicidal impulse.

Meanwhile, though Peck damages Li'l Bit, she is his lifeline, all that stops him free-falling towards death, and despite his calculated seduction of a vulnerable girl he still offers her an understanding that no one else in her family cares to do, and, ultimately, warns her against himself, thus surrendering the one thing that holds him back from despair, an action that has led Vogel to call him "heroic." As Vogel observed, "I see him as teaching her ego formation, as giving her the tools to grow up and reject him and destroy him."

Peck never forces himself on Li'l Bit, though he plots his campaign with the skill of a practiced seducer and there are suggestions that she has not been his only victim. When she storms out of the family home in a teenage fury Peck's wife, Aunt Mary, observes that "Peck's so good with them when they get to be this age," while his approach to the weeping girl is described in a stage note to be "like stalking a deer."

His method is obliquely exposed in what is one of the most disturbing scenes in the play, when he describes a fishing trip back in South Carolina with a young male cousin. His strategy with fish mirrors that which he adopts with the young woman he desires: "they're very shy, mercurial, fish. Takes patience and psychology. You have to believe it doesn't matter if you catch one or not . . . you don't want to get close — they're frisky and shy little things . . . easy, reel and then net — let it play." And when the fish is landed his comments to his young cousin are a displaced version of his relationship with the young Li'l Bit: "I don't want you to feel ashamed about crying. I'm not going to tell anyone, okay? I can keep secrets . . . There's nothing you could do that would make me feel ashamed of you . . . you can't tell anybody . . . least of all your mom or your sisters. This is something special between you and me." It is Peck's apparently genuine gentleness combined with his patient cunning that is the source of his seductive power. He is driven by his sexual need but that very need gives him an insight into the vulnerabilities of others.

For Vogel, it is clear that Peck does molest his young cousin. Indeed she saw his equal attraction to young girls and boys as a necessary counterbalance to assumptions that pedophiles are gay: "it is the age that is the attraction, not the gender." When she was invited to delete the scene she insisted on retaining it, not least because she felt she owed a debt to her gay brother to clarify what she saw as a slur on gay men. At the same time the scene had not featured in her own outline for the play. It was a product of the process of writing, but it gave her and the audience what she came to feel was a crucial sense of distance, and became a vital element in the drama.

Vogel reminds her audience of the arbitrariness of the lines drawn by society. What is legitimate at eighteen is statutory rape at the age of seventeen. As Li'l Bit's grandmother reminds her daughter, "It was legal, what Daddy and I did! I was fourteen and in those days, fourteen was a grown-up woman." As a gay writer Vogel knows all too well the capricious nature of sexual prohibitions. But, as the play progresses so she raises the stakes and the audience is forced to revise its reaction to the early scene, forced to question its liberal or sentimental response as Li'l Bit becomes first seventeen, then sixteen, then fifteen and, finally, eleven. If the line was not crossed in the opening scene then it is later and we are led, little by little, into the heart of that darkness, a darkness which Li'l Bit herself, however, eventually begins to understand or at least to find echoed in her own experience.

At the age of twenty-seven she experiences the same thrill that she imagines, in retrospect, Peck must have felt as she meets a teenage boy on a bus and seduces him, staging a drama in which she is author, director and principal actor: "dramatically speaking," she explains,

> after the faltering and slightly comical "first act," there was the very briefest of intermissions, and an extremely capable and forceful and *sustained* [. . .] discussion — I lay on my back in the dark and I thought about you, Uncle Peck. Oh. Oh — this is the allure. Being older. Being the first. Being the translator, the teacher, the epicure, the already jaded. This is how the giver gets taken.

In one sense this could be seen as an account of how abused becomes abuser but it is equally an attempt to understand the seductiveness of seduction, the allure of innocence, the compelling nature of power, the fascination that lies in devising a plot that will enfold another's life. And the fact that Vogel chooses a theatrical metaphor is, perhaps, not without its significance in that the playwright, too, deals in the manipulation of emotions, the seduction of others. She, too, takes her audience to places they have not been, exposes them to experiences which threaten their composure, moral assurance and, ultimately, therefore, innocence. She, too, works by stealth. The description of Peck's fishing technique could, indeed, be seen as an account of her own dramatic strategy in *How I Learned to Drive*: "reel and then rest — let it play."

As the play's title suggests, the principal metaphor is that of the driving lesson. On a literal level it is this that enables Peck to secure time alone with Li'l Bit. But beyond this it charts their developing relationship and Li'l Bit's increasing autonomy. When Peck insists that "when you are driving, your life is in your own two hands," he is offering her a lesson in responsibility for her own life. When he speaks of the power it conveys, he is explaining the necessity for her to realize her own strength. Most significantly, when he instructs her in the need to "think what the other guy is going to do before he does it," this is something more than a piece of roadcraft advice. It is, we later realize, a genuine warning against his own planned action, a moment of honesty, a proffered grace. To think ahead, he insists, is to be the only one to survive an impending disaster. Indeed it is tempting to think that perhaps Peck has summoned Li'l Bit into being, or at least forged her into a weapon against himself, precisely to be his nemesis, to punish himself for past, present and future sins. Certainly he trains her to survive without him while simultaneously struggling to hold on to her.

Throughout the play, a Voice, of "the type . . . that driver education films employ" [. . .], offers a commentary on driver skills which likewise comments, often ironically, on Li'l Bit's unfolding relationship with Peck. Thus, at this moment, it remarks that "Good defensive driving involves mental and physical preparation" and asks *Are you prepared?* Another Voice immediately adds: "You and the

Reverse Gear." Li'l Bit does not go into reverse any more than does Peck and the drive (automotive and sexual) continues, as does the journey on which they are, apparently mutually, engaged. The question *"Are you prepared?"* however, echoes throughout the text.

The references to driving thus apply as much to Li'l Bit's relationship with Peck as to road safety awareness, and that fact is underlined by phrases which implicitly comment on the unfolding action: Idling in Neutral Gear, Shifting Forward from First Gear to Second Gear, You and the Reverse Gear (the last displayed as the action moves back into the past), *Vehicle failure* (displayed as Li'l Bit is incapacitated by drink), *Implied consent, Children depend on you to watch them.* These comments, in turn, are accompanied by projected signs with equally evident ambiguities: Slow Children, Dangerous Curves, One Way. Indeed, this parallel even infiltrates the stage directions, Vogel referring to Li'l Bit and Peck as "running out of gas," a phrase glossed as meaning "running out of small talk."

Where does responsibility lie in this relationship? Clearly with Peck, but there is a level at which Li'l Bit colludes. There is, in the words of the Voice, an "Implied consent," and this is where the play treads dangerous ground. Plainly in *Lolita* the young girl is a knowing collaborator in her own seduction. In Vogel's play she is led to such implied consent by Peck's seductive skills, but also by their shared sense of exclusion. She responds to his evident need as he in turn offers her understanding. He exploits her youth and innocence, damages her, but also, in his own terms, seeks her consent and will not transgress the terms of that consent. He indulges his own needs, subordinating hers to his, rationalizing his behavior, and yet, finally, hands her back her life at ultimate cost to himself. Nothing he does justifies his actions but his own vulnerabilities are real. There is a kind of innocence even at the center of his corrupting power, for there is no reason to doubt that at the heart of his obsession there is love, as at the heart of his love there is obsession. [. . .]

Meanwhile, beneath his practical competency, his air of quiet assurance, Peck is plainly lonely and disturbed, driven by demons he can neither name nor defeat. His wife can do nothing to address his needs. Aware of his relationship with their niece, she sees it as a temporary infatuation inspired by a manipulative girl. Yet whatever pain lies at the heart of Peck's life all she can offer is domesticity, routine and what she imagines to be a restorative banality, as if this man could settle for something as prosaic as that. She lives with a stranger and seems to understand nothing beyond the fact of his suffering. The plight of her niece, meanwhile, matters not at all. She offers less love than a baffled and frustrated attempt at understanding.

Li'l Bit, by contrast, does care for Peck. On their last encounter in a hotel we are told that she is "half wanting to run, half wanting to get it over with, half wanting to be held by him." She comes close to kissing him but tears herself away. He is destroyed. The lifeline cut, he is, finally, lost. As Li'l Bit explains: "It took my uncle seven years to drink himself to death. First he lost his job, then his wife, and finally his driver's license. He retreated to his house, and had his bottles delivered." The loss of his driver's license is simultaneously a fact and a symbol as he loses that power over his direction, that command of his life, which he had once tried to teach the young girl he both abused and loved as they sat side by side and he taught her the ambiguous lessons of life.

Nor is Li'l Bit shown as ultimately damaged. This is not an accusatory play. Indeed, it ends on a note of reconciliation. As Li'l Bit drives off in her car, in the final scene, she looks in her rearview mirror and smiles at the spirit of Peck who sits behind her. She is now in charge of the car. She did, in the end, accept his advice and anticipated the problems coming towards her. She is, as he had urged her to be, the only one to survive the accident. [. . .]

Vogel has talked of her alarm at the growth of a victim culture in the United States — the desire to shuffle off responsibility for one's life by locating some external cause for failure. "I hate the word victim," she has said. "It's a buzz word people use these days. We're all victims just by virtue of being alive."[1] Li'l Bit's education is thus not only in the occasional cruelties and disabling selfishness of others, but the knowledge and acceptance of her ultimate responsibility for her own life. She comes to recognize in herself a desire for power as well as that unfocused need which had characterized Peck, until he chose to focus it on a girl whose very innocence made her a *tabula rasa,* a place to inscribe his own desperation. [. . .] And if Li'l Bit learns from Peck how cruelly exploitative some people are she also learns their potential for something which perhaps could only be called love.

She learns that her own life consists of everything that has happened to her and that a life of blame or regret is no life at all. Ironically, she never accuses him of the crime which in truth he committed. Indeed, in some ways she devises the rules of the deeply suspect games they play. Even as a woman in her thirties (who, after all, narrates this play much as did Tom in *The Glass Menagerie*) revisiting her own past, she does so not to lay blame or make accusations but to understand her life so that she may live it without regret. As a result, the audience does not reject Peck but grants him his own pain, his own bruised dignity, his own curious courage in the face of feelings he struggles to contain. But they do so not because of the man himself — manipulative, exploitative, dangerous but also compassionate, understanding, self-sacrificing — but because Li'l Bit accepts him in all his confusions and moral equivocations. The man we see is the man she reconstitutes in her memory. She declines the opportunity retrospectively to invent him as pure villain and herself as simple victim, and as a result can take her life in her hands and not, finally, cede it to another, not entomb herself in a myth that can only leave her the helpless product of circumstance, the residue of process and the result of abuse. As Vogel has said, "I had no interest in a movie-of-the-week drama about child-molesting." She wished, rather, "to see if audiences will *allow* themselves to find this erotic; otherwise, they only see victimization without empowerment."[2] To her, the essence of the play lay not simply in the fact of the relationship but its consequence. As she explained, "it seems to me that one thing that gets left out when we're talking about trauma is the victim's responsibility to look the experience squarely in the eye and then to move on. That's the journey I wanted to craft here" (*Playbill,* Century Theatre).

How I Learned to Drive plays against our expectations. It seeks to go beyond the labels, the categories which do little to explain ourselves to ourselves. It is about a love affair which, if not mutual, nevertheless, and not entirely paradoxically, does have love on each side. It is about a man whose loneliness is too deep to be filled, who looks for consolation in the wrong place but loves enough eventually to release the object of that love, a man who inhabits a society that is itself deeply confused as to the role of sexuality. The music to which Vogel wrote the play and which she suggests should accompany the action, is, as she has said, "rife with pedophilia," a word she seldom uses in interviews: "Dream Baby," "You're Sixteen," "Little Surfer Girl,"

[1]Steven Druckman, "A Playwright on the Edge," *New York Times* (March 16, 1997), H6.
[2]Ibid.

"This Girl Is a Woman Now," "Come Back When You Grow Up." Peck, in other words, is not some aberration, someone to be labeled and filed away. He inhabits an ambiguity that reaches out beyond the parameters of his own special need.

David Savran (b. 1950)
PAULA VOGEL   *1999*

David Savran, Paula Vogel's colleague in the English Department at Brown University, is well known for his series of interviews with contemporary playwrights. His interview with Paula Vogel appears in his book The Playwright's Voice *(1999), but this excerpt is his review of Vogel's career and precedes the interview itself. His observations describe in an economical fashion the special features of her work.*

In her playwriting classes, Paula Vogel always asks her students to write the impossible: a play with a dog as protagonist, a play that cannot be staged, a play that dramatizes the end of the world in five pages. And while these provocative exercises stretch students' imaginations in remarkable ways, they also inadvertently reveal much about Vogel's own playwriting. For all her plays endeavor to stage the impossible. They defy traditional theater logic, subtly calling conventions into question or, in some cases, pushing them well past their limits. What other playwright would dare memorialize her brother in a play filled with fart jokes and riotous sex, whose medical authority, a cross between Dr. Strangelove and Groucho Marx, ends up drinking his own piss? What other feminist would dare write so many jokes about tits?

For a Vogel play is never simply a politely dramatized fiction, it is always a meditation on the theater itself — on role-playing, on the socially sanctioned scripts from which characters diverge at their peril, and on a theatrical tradition that has punished women who don't remain quiet, passive and demure. Take, for example, *The Mineola Twins* (1996), which plays deliriously and chillingly with the age-old farcical convention of using one virtuosic actor (and a battery of wigs) to play two startlingly dissimilar identical twins. Or *Hot 'n' Throbbing* (1994), which transforms a theater into a living room and a living room into a theater in order to dramatize the fatal consequences of stage directions gone out of control. Or her Pulitzer Prize–winning *How I Learned to Drive* (1997), which does far more than explain the effects of sexual predation on a young girl; it literally splits her into two — a body and a voice — in order to represent the radical alienation from Self that results from having been molested.

In *How I Learned to Drive,* Vogel turns the theater itself into a vehicle for memory, using first gear to move forward in time and reverse to move backwards. By reenacting the driving lessons given her by her Uncle Peck, Li'l Bit remembers her strangely — and literally — intoxicating sexual initiation. For there is no question but that her uncle's seduction has caused her to retreat "above the neck." At the same time, Peck, that most charming of pedophiles and himself a victim of abuse, is the only member of her family who makes a real effort to understand, nurture, and help her grow up. For *How I Learned to Drive* is the story not only of Li'l Bit's molestation. It is also a slyly subversive dramatization of how a girl — perhaps any girl — becomes an adult.

At the beginning of the play, Li'l Bit remembers the suburban Maryland of her youth, completely absorbed in the touch, smell, and taste of a "warm summer evening." These sensory perceptions connect her to the past, to the land and to her own body as she renders herself miraculously whole again through the power of memory. But as Li'l Bit knows all too well — and any adult will tell you — this primordial wholeness cannot last, and the remainder of the play shows her being taken for a drive that will lead her into another realm, one dominated by the senses of sight and hearing. For if touch, smell, and taste are the tokens of intimacy and wholeness, then sight and hearing are undeniably the most objectifying of the senses; they introduce a radical separation between subject and object. This is perhaps why the very center of the play is a photo shoot, for it is in this scene that Li'l Bit most graphically becomes an object for Uncle Peck and, more ominously, for herself as well. Yet this sequence is so effective theatrically because it tacitly recognizes that sight and hearing are also the senses, by no mere coincidence, upon which theater depends. It demonstrates that the theater, like the photo shoot, will always produce figures who are subjected to the scrutiny of voyeuristic spectators (or lascivious uncles). Li'l Bit, in other words, suddenly discovers that she has become an actor in a drama that has been scripted for her by an exploitative, if well-meaning spectator who is, in turn, the product of a society that values women for their allure. Yet *How I Learned to Drive* is no more an indictment of theater than it is of eroticism. For it is precisely the theater that gives Li'l Bit the time and the place to remember, that is, to reconstruct herself, to put herself back together. In learning to drive, the play shows us, Li'l Bit learns how to desire, how to use the theater, and the act of self-presentation, to put herself quite literally in the driver's seat.

In *How I Learned to Drive*, Li'l Bit is literally haunted by the unquiet spirit of her Uncle Peck in the same way that Anna in *The Baltimore Waltz* (1992) — and Vogel herself — is haunted by the spirit of her dead brother, Carl. For in attempting to remember, Vogel's theater calls up ghosts, figures lighter than air yet heavy with the past. It is obsessed with commemorating what has been lost, while understanding that loss always pays a kind of dividend that is experienced both on a personal and cultural level. For Vogel's ghosts always materialize at the place where memory turns into history, the particular into the universal. Thus, *Baltimore Waltz* becomes an exhilarating tribute and love letter not only to Carl, but to everyone who has died of AIDS, in the same way that *Drive*, by staging Li'l Bit's singular journey, dramatizes the relentless process by which we are each being produced as the subjects and objects of our own dramas.

For all their precision in documenting the act of remembering, Vogel's plays are perhaps unique in the way that they locate memory in the body. For it is far more than her punning sensibility that inspires her to title her most recent collection *The Mammary Plays* (TCG, 1998). Summoning up the "full-figured gal" of TV-commercial fame, both *Drive* and *The Mineola Twins* simultaneously exploit and critique the cliché of this "stacked" femme fatale. Both tacitly acknowledge that female bodies are steeped in history, that "sometimes the body," as Uncle Peck puts it, "knows things that the mind isn't listening to." And like her other plays, they are intent on listening to and reclaiming that lost, forgotten history. For as a feminist writer, Vogel not only attends to the deeply contradictory representations of women in our culture, but also delineates female characters who are prepared to use their physical charms (if need be) to wrest control of their lives. From the sprightly geriatric prostitutes of *The Oldest Profession* (1988) who have seized the means of production; to Myra, Mineola's answer to Patricia Hearst and Patricia Ireland; to the lesbian parents of three imaginary little boys in *And Baby Makes Seven* (1984); Vogel's women are themselves playwrights who attempt to write their way out of difficult situations and script more creative, bountiful lives. Like Vogel herself, they are committed to redressing a history of oppression by rewriting the scenes they have been handed. By so turning her female characters (and her students!) into playwrights of no mean accomplishments, she suggests that although a triumphal feminist theater seems an impossibility in our time, one may nonetheless endeavor to stage that impossibility, along with the glittering promises it holds.

Jill Dolan (b. 1957)
REVIEW OF *HOW I LEARNED TO DRIVE*   *1997*

Jill Dolan reviewed the Vineyard Theatre production of How I Learned to Drive *and examines the ways in which Paula Vogel establishes sympathy for Uncle Peck despite revealing him as a pedophile. Dolan sees sexuality as unstable and a matter of exploration in the drama, especially on Li'l Bit's part. In the process of commenting on the play Dolan gives us useful insights into the staging of the drama.*

Playwright Paula Vogel tends to select sensitive, difficult, fraught issues to theatricalize, and to spin them with a dramaturgy that's at once creative, highly imaginative, and brutally honest. In *How I Learned to Drive* — which won the 1997 Drama Desk Award for Best Play and several Obie Awards — Vogel's conceits remain personal, political, and highly theatrical. In a nonlinear narrative, Li'l Bit (Mary Louise Parker) tries to understand her relationship with her Uncle Peck (David Morse), whose driving lessons taught her as much about gender relations and her own sexuality as they did about the proper use of rearview mirrors, gearshifts, and turn signals.

Driving becomes the action that evokes Li'l Bit's memories; driving metaphors chart Li'l Bit's growth into automotive mastery and sexual mystery, punctuating the play's movement back and forth in time. Sitting in straight-backed chairs on a nearly bare set, Morse and Parker evoke the car rides that shape and intertwine their lives. Mark Brokaw's crisp, unsparing direction allows them to craft the scene with gesture and light, leaving the production unencumbered by more than minimal props and set pieces. The sparse set is framed by a map of Baltimore in the 1950s and 1960s, when the play's first memories occur. The geographical snippets, covered with interstates, route numbers, town names, and zip codes that move in and out of sight, remind spectators how difficult it is to truly map the territory of relationships, sexuality, and desire.

Vogel's choice to remember Li'l Bit and Peck's relationship nonchronologically illustrates its complexity, and allows the playwright to build sympathy for a man who might otherwise be despised and dismissed as a child molester. As played with affable gentility and gentleness by Morse, Peck is charming, kind, and sympathetic, a man driven toward children by his own demons but attentive to Li'l Bit's adolescent needs in ways that are never violent, paternalistic, or condescending. Peck takes the young woman seriously, and she takes great pleasure from believing that she helps him emotionally. Vogel paints their relationship as flirtatious and sexual, but also as a careful balance of power between Peck's adult desires and Li'l Bit's inchoate, exploratory impulses. Parker's lithe, erotic performance captures in subtle gestures and in postures weighted with ambivalence and desire the pleasure Li'l Bit takes in the power of saying no while her body urges her to say yes. The attraction between them becomes more urgent and mutual as the play progresses, along with Li'l Bit's knowledge that the relationship is not right. Li'l Bit's isolation in the face of strong emotions she can not understand is palpable; Parker's virtuosic performance illustrates the nuances of Li'l Bit's desire and loathing for a man who taught her so much and could finally give her so little.

Vogel builds the relationship in scenes sculpted with spare efficiency by Brokaw that crystallize moments of trust, disappointment, longing, and desire. When Peck's loneliness grips him, a very young Li'l Bit offers solace with weekly outings that are as much about companionship as they come to be about sex or driving lessons. Later, Peck photographs Li'l Bit in his basement studio, and although it's clear his motives are not pure, the experience instills in Li'l Bit a sense of her own allure, a glimpse of a budding sexuality that's powerful to her in a family life in which she is otherwise naive and powerless. Peck takes her to dinner at a sophisticated restaurant out of town when she passes her driving test. Under the disapproving eye of a sanctimonious waiter, Li'l Bit drinks martinis while one of the female chorus relates how to stay safe sexually while leaving the shores of sobriety in masculine company.

These interventions are delivered with wry and empathetic clarity directly to the audience by a three-actor chorus that shifts agilely through roles as family members and other commentators. The actors transform precisely and pointedly, with help from iconic costume pieces like glasses or scarves, into those who either deny or judge the relationship. Brokaw directs them on a nearly empty set, using chairs and the occasional table to evoke the car, the restaurant, the basement photo studio. The physical performances his actors achieve imaginatively flesh out the edges of this searing portrait.

How I Learned to Drive is only "about" incest after the scene of Li'l Bit's first molestation scene, when Li'l Bit asks the audience rhetorically, "How old were you when someone did this to you?" The moment is startling, because although the audience has witnessed Peck in an early scene prepare to molest a little boy (the boy is imagined and Morse elegantly, chillingly mimes the actions), the play has been about more than incest. Through Parker's and Morse's multilayered performances, power and danger are always present, but so are moments of understanding and mutuality.

Parker and Morse are empathetic and moving, and Johanna Day, Kerry O'Malley, and Michael Showalter, as the chorus, present tight economical sketches of Li'l Bit's family and the social characters with whom Li'l Bit and Peck interact. Vogel's wry, insightful humor captures the pain and awkward pleasure of growing into social awareness and understanding. Vogel's play is about forgiveness and family, about the instability of sexuality, about the unpredictable ways in which we learn who we are, how we desire, and how our growth is built on loss.

Suzan-Lori Parks

Suzan-Lori Parks (b. 1964) was named by Mel Gussow in the *New York Times* as the "year's most promising playwright" in 1989. She lives in Venice, California, with her husband, Paul Oscher, a blues musician who has played with Muddy Waters. Currently, Parks teaches drama and playwriting at the California Institute of the Arts in Valencia and is head of the A. S. K. (Audrey Skirball-Kenis) Theatre project, searching for new plays in the Los Angeles area. Parks's work has been supported by grants from numerous agencies, including the Rockefeller and Ford Foundations and the National Endowment for the Arts, from which she has twice received a playwriting fellowship. She also received a MacArthur Award in 1986. Her work has been seen primarily in off-Broadway theaters in New York as well as in important regional theaters.

Parks was the child of an army officer and grew up in several different locations. She says, "I've heard horrible stories about twelve-step groups for army people. But I had a great childhood. My parents were really into experiencing the places we lived." She lived, for example, in a small town in Germany and attended German schools, studying in German. She went to Hampshire College, where she studied writing with James Baldwin. After that experience she went to London for a year to study acting. "It really made a difference in my writing. It dawned on me that a lot of people write with ideas in mind. . . . But I never really have ideas, per se. I have these movements, these gestures. Then I figure out how to put those gestures into words."

She is aware of being influenced by a number of important literary figures, among them Gertrude Stein, James Joyce, William Faulkner, and Samuel Beckett, but echoes of other writers such as Shakespeare and Richard Wright can be heard in *The Death of the Last Black Man in the Whole Entire World* (1990). Parks's approach to language is partly vernacular as she attempts to reproduce speech both as it is spoken and as her audience assumes it may be spoken. But she is interested in the hypnotic and musical value of words, which accounts for much of the patterning of repetition that marks her work.

Her plays have been performed in the BACA (Brooklyn Arts Council Association) Downtown Theater, Manhattan Theater Club, and the Joseph Papp Public Theater in Manhattan. Her early short plays are *Betting on the Dust Commander, Fishes, The Sinners' Place,* and *The America Play.* Her full-length play *Imperceptible Mutabilities in the Third Kingdom,* directed by her long-time collaborator Liz Diamond, won the Obie Award for the best off-Broadway play of 1990. One section of *Mutabilities* takes place on Emancipation Day in 1865 and is played in whiteface by African American actors. Another section, "Greeks," makes reference to her own family, with a character called Mr. Sergeant Smith. Parts of the play have been described as "like a choral poem."

Parks has produced a film, *Anemone Me* (1990), that has been shown in New York. Her *Devotees in the Garden of Love* (1992) premiered at the

Actors Theatre of Louisville, Kentucky. Her next play, *Venus* (1996), was a coproduction of the Joseph Papp Public Theater and Yale Repertory Theatre. It was directed by Richard Foreman, the founder of the Ontological-Hysteric Theater. The play focuses on the life of a black woman brought to England as the Venus Hottentot, a sideshow freak displaying "an intensely ugly figure, distorted beyond all European notions of beauty." The authorities put an end to the sideshow, and Parks explores this mysterious woman's life. Parks has also written *Girl 6* (1996), a film directed by Spike Lee.

Parks's *In the Blood* (1999) focuses on Hester, a welfare mother of five. She faces poverty, the welfare system's workfare, and sterilization. The play examines our attitudes toward poverty and responsibility.

Topdog/Underdog (2001) won the Pulitzer Prize for drama, the first awarded to a black woman playwright. She followed this with *Fucking A* (2003), with the A standing for abortion rather than adultery, as it does in Nathaniel Hawthorne's novel *The Scarlet Letter*. Parks's protagonist, like Hawthorne's, is also Hester, a carryover from *In the Blood*. Parks has said that characters stay with her, as in the case also of the black Lincoln impersonator who is central to *The America Play*, and she feels free to follow up with new plays on old themes. In 2003 Parks published her first novel, *Getting Mother's Body*, inspired by a novel by William Faulkner. Parks is an energetic, carefully focused, and clearly directed playwright with a special interest in the language of speech and the language of gesture — in almost equal measure.

TOPDOG/UNDERDOG

Although Lincoln is listed as the topdog, and Booth the underdog, Parks has said they shift from moment to moment in this drama. John Wilkes Booth shot and killed Abraham Lincoln in 1865, but Booth was hunted down twelve days later and either shot or burned to death by federal troops. Lincoln is history's topdog, but the real Booth thought Lincoln was a tyrant who needed to be put to death not only because the South lost the war but because Lincoln planned to give blacks citizenship and voting rights in addition to their freedom. Modern historians have pointed out that Lincoln's personal views on matters of race were complex and sometimes contradictory. He believed, for example, that only very bright blacks should have voting rights. He also believed that blacks and whites would probably not be able to live together as social equals, and, as a result, he hoped that the white race would essentially be top dog in the future.

Naturally, it is a striking irony to have Lincoln, the elder brother in the play, play the part of Abraham Lincoln in an entertainment arcade where he sits staring into a shiny metal electrical box while customers pay for the privilege of shooting him with a pistol loaded with blanks. He plays the part in whiteface and gets less pay than the previous "Lincoln," a white man. Nevertheless, he feels the job is an opportunity. He likes the work and hopes to continue and build something for himself. The fact that he is let go because of belt-tightening on the part of the arcade owners is emblematic of patterns of black hiring: "last hired, first fired." For Lincoln, this job represents a way out of the pattern of hustling and petty crime that has been his heritage.

Lincoln's younger brother, Booth, has a real gun. He carries it with him and it remains a threatening presence throughout the play. He spends much of his time "boosting" goods from stores. He also practices the street con card game, Three-Card Monte, in which the dealer throws down three cards and then permits a "mark" to gamble on finding the ace of spades among the cards. It's a dishonest game, using sleight of hand and a number of sidekicks who act as shills or make-believe players. Lincoln is the very best at the game, but he has left the street and wants to make a go of the "straight" life with a job that has potential and benefits. He has abandoned his game and refuses in act 1 to touch the cards. Booth, on the other hand, has no plans of going straight and pleads with Lincoln to teach him how the game works. He expects to be the best that ever was at Three-Card Monte. Booth is even willing to change his name to Three-Card and he envisions getting Lincoln's "old gang" together again to work with him.

In the process, the brothers examine their backgrounds, beginning with the fact that their parents separated and individually left them to fend for themselves when Lincoln was sixteen and Booth was thirteen. Booth points out that he got an inheritance from each of his parents of $500. The money that his mother gave him, we learn in act 2, is safe in a stocking that he has never opened. The final struggle in the last act seems focused on that "bequest," although it also has its roots in jealousy and brotherly competition of the kind found in the Bible's story of Cain and Abel.

The fact that they were abandoned as children weighs on both brothers, as does the fact that they were named Lincoln and Booth by their father as a joke. In other words, they were burdened by a violent history, unaware that, as the Chinese have said, "One's name is one's fate." In addition to reliving the personal history of Lincoln and Booth (both in the arcade and beyond it), however, they also live through the history of slavery and its aftermath. Their heritage is one of hustling and insecurity, and when Lincoln tries to emulate the virtues of his namesake — "Honest Abe" — he finds that, indeed, he likes the feeling of being honest and making an honest living. He does not want to go back to the street hustle, whereas Booth sees that there is no hope of finding himself a role in the working world. He does not even try. In the end, however, Lincoln, having tried and temporarily succeeded, finds himself replaced because of cutbacks not by another actor, but by a wax dummy — essentially a wax machine that sits there and is shot, combined with a recording apparatus that can cry out appropriately at the proper moment.

In his review of the second New York performance, critic Ben Brantley said, "Brotherly love and hatred is translated into the terms of men who have known betrayal since their youth, when their parents walked out on them, and who will never be able entirely to trust anyone, including (and especially) each other. Implicit in their relationship is the idea that to live is to con."[1]

[1]*New York Times,* April 8, 2002, p. E1.

Topdog/Underdog
in Performance

The first production was July 22, 2001, at the Joseph Papp Public Theater/ New York Shakespeare Festival. George C. Wolfe was the producer and director. Don Cheadle played Booth and Jeffrey Wright played Lincoln. With the success of this production, the play moved to the larger Ambassador Theatre on Broadway in April 2002 with Jeffrey Wright as Lincoln and the hip-hop artist Mos Def as Booth. The reviews of the production cited the intensity and brilliance of this performance. The energy displayed by Mos Def was extraordinary, and the interplay with Jeffrey Wright was so powerful that at times one wondered how they could contain themselves to get to the end of the play. The setting, by Riccardo Hernández, suggested the gloominess of a mid-nineteenth-century rooming house, adding to the tension and darkness of the drama.

Suzan-Lori Parks (*b.* 1964)

TOPDOG/UNDERDOG

2001

I am God in nature;
I am a weed by the wall.   — RALPH WALDO EMERSON
                                       From "Circles"
                                       Essays: First Series (1841)

The Players

LINCOLN, *the topdog*
BOOTH (*aka 3-Card*), *the underdog*

Author's Notes: From the "Elements of Style"

I'm continuing the use of my slightly unconventional theatrical elements. Here's a road map.

- (*Rest*)
  Take a little time, a pause, a breather; make a transition.

- A Spell
  An elongated and heightened (*Rest*). Denoted by repetition of figures' names with no dialogue. Has sort of an architectural look:

  LINCOLN
  BOOTH
  LINCOLN
  BOOTH

  This is a place where the figures experience their pure true simple state. While no action or stage business is necessary, directors should fill this moment as they best see fit.

- [Brackets in the text indicate optional cuts for production.]

- (Parentheses around dialogue indicate softly spoken passages (asides; sotto voce)).

SCENE ONE

Thursday evening. A seedily furnished rooming house room. A bed, a reclining chair, a small wooden chair, some other stuff but not much else. Booth, a black man in his early 30s, practices his 3-card monte scam on the classic setup: 3 playing cards and the cardboard playing board atop 2 mismatched milk crates. His moves and accompanying patter are, for the most part, studied and awkward.

BOOTH: Watch me close watch me close now: who-see-thuh-red-card-who-see-thuh-red-card? I-see-thuh-red-card. Thuh-red-card-is-thuh-winner. Pick-thuh-red-card-you-pick-uh-winner. Pick-uh-black-card-you-pick-uh-loser. Theres-thuh-loser, yeah, theres-thuh-black-card, theres-thuh-other-loser-and-theres-thuh-red-card, thuh-winner.

(*Rest*)

Watch me close watch me close now: 3-Card-throws-thuh-cards-lightning-fast. 3-Card-thats-me-and-Ima-last. Watch-me-throw-cause-here-I-go. One-good-pickll-get-you-in, 2-good-picks-and-you-gone-win. See-thuh-red-card-see-thuh-red-card-who-see-thuh-red-card?

(*Rest*)

Dont touch my cards, man, just point to thuh one you want. You-pick-that-card-you-pick-a-loser, yeah, that-cards-a-loser. You-pick-that-card-thats-thuh-other-loser. You-pick-that-card-you-pick-a-winner. Follow that card. You gotta chase that card. You-pick-thuh-dark-deuce-thats-a-loser-other-dark-deuces-thuh-other-loser, red-deuce, thuh-deuce-of-heartsll-win-it-all. Follow thuh red card.

(*Rest*)

Ima show you thuh cards: 2 black cards but only one heart. Now watch me now. Who-sees-thuh-red-card-who-knows-where-its-at? Go on, man, point to thuh card. Put yr money down cause you aint no clown. No? Ah you had thuh card, but you didnt have thuh heart.

(*Rest*)

You wanna bet? 500 dollars? Shoot. You musta been watching 3-Card real close. Ok. Lay the cash in my hand cause 3-Cards thuh man. Thank you, mister. This card you say?

(*Rest*)

Wrong! Sucker! Fool! Asshole! Bastard! I bet yr daddy heard how stupid you was and drank himself to death just cause he didnt wanna have nothing to do witchu! I bet yr mama seen you when you comed out and she walked away from you with thuh after-birth still hanging from out twixt her legs, sucker! Ha Ha Ha! And 3-Card, once again, wins all thuh money!!

(*Rest*)

What? Cops looking my way? Fold up thuh game, and walk away. Sneak outa sight. Set up on another corner.

(*Rest*)

Yeah.

(*Rest*)

Having won the imaginary loot and dodged the imaginary cops, Booth sets up his equipment and starts practicing his scam all over again. Lincoln comes in quietly. He is a black man in his later 30s. He is dressed in an antique frock coat and wears a top hat and fake beard, that is, he is dressed to look like Abraham Lincoln. He surreptitiously walks into the room to stand right behind Booth, who, engrossed in his cards, does not notice Lincoln right away.

BOOTH: Watch me close watch me close now: who-see-thuh-red-card-who-see-thuh-red-card? I-see-thuh-red-card. Thuh-red-card-is-thuh-winner. Pick-thuh-red-card-you-pick-uh-winner. Pick-uh-black-card-you-pick-uh-loser. Theres-thuh-loser-yeah-theres-thuh-black-card, theres-thuh-other-loser-and-theres-thuh-red-card, thuh-winner. Dont touch my cards, man, dont —

(*Rest*)

Dont do that shit. Dont do that shit. Dont do that shit!

Booth, sensing someone behind him, whirls around, pulling a gun from his pants. While the presence of Lincoln doesnt surprise him, the Lincoln costume does.

BOOTH: And woah, man dont *ever* be doing that shit! Who thuh fuck you think you is coming in my shit all spooked out and shit. You pull that one more time I'll shoot you!
LINCOLN: I only had a minute to make the bus.
BOOTH: Bullshit.
LINCOLN: Not completely. I mean, its either bull or shit, but not a complete lie so it aint bullshit, right?

(*Rest*)

Put yr gun away.
BOOTH: Take off the damn hat at least.

Lincoln takes off the stovepipe hat. Booth puts his gun away.

LINCOLN: Its cold out there. This thing kept my head warm.
BOOTH: I dont like you wearing that bullshit, that shit that bull that disguise that getup that motherdisfuckinguise anywhere in the vicinity of my humble abode.

Lincoln takes off the beard.

LINCOLN: Better?
BOOTH: Take off the damn coat too. Damn, man. Bad enough you got to wear that shit all day you come up in here wearing it. What my women gonna say?
LINCOLN: What women?
BOOTH: I got a date with Grace tomorrow. Shes in love with me again but she dont know it yet. Aint no man can love her the way I can. She sees you in that getup its gonna reflect bad on me. She coulda seen you coming down the street. Shit. Could be standing outside right now taking her ring off and throwing it on the sidewalk.

Booth takes a peek out the window.

BOOTH: I got her this ring today. Diamond. Well, diamond-esque, but it looks just as good as the real thing. Asked her what size she wore. She say 7 so I go boost a size 6 and a half, right? Show it to her and she loves it and I shove it on her finger and its a tight fit right, so she cant just take it off on a whim, like she did the last one I gave her. Smooth, right?

Booth takes another peek out the window.

LINCOLN: She out there?
BOOTH: Nope. Coast is clear.
LINCOLN: You boosted a ring?
BOOTH: Yeah. I thought about spending my inheritance on it but — take off that damn coat, man, you make me nervous standing there looking like a spook, and that damn face paint, take it off You should take all of it off at work and leave it there.

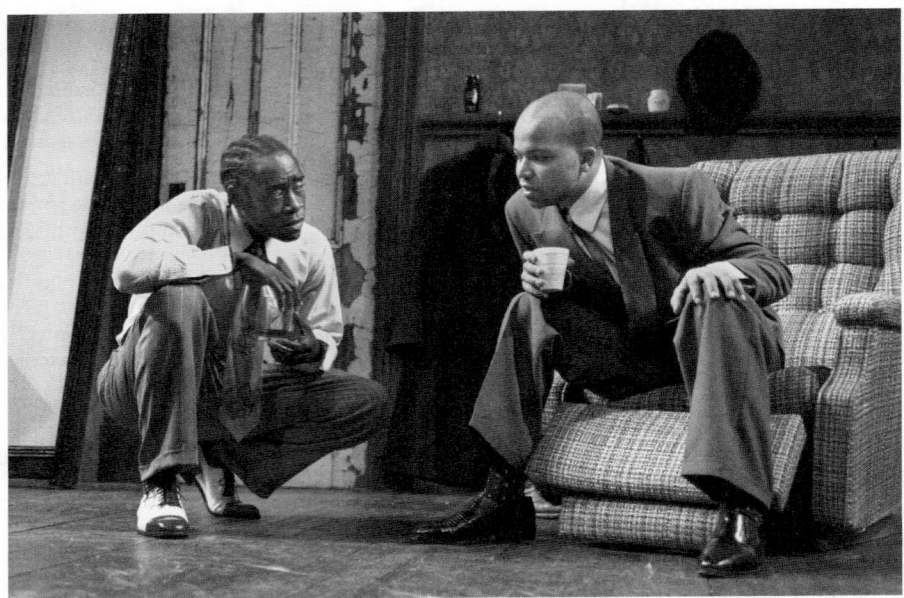

ABOVE: Don Cheadle as Booth and Jeffrey Wright as Lincoln in the original 2001 production of *Topdog/Underdog* at the Joseph Papp Public Theater in New York, directed and produced by George C. Wolfe. RIGHT: Mos Def as Booth, playing three-card monte in the 2002 New York production at the Ambassador Theater on Broadway.

LINCOLN: I dont bring it home someone might steal it.
BOOTH: At least take it *off* there, then.
LINCOLN: Yeah.

(*Rest*)

Lincoln takes off the frock coat and applies cold cream,
removing the whiteface.

LINCOLN: I was riding the bus. Really I only had a minute
to make my bus and I was sitting in the arcade thinking, should I change into my street clothes or should I
make the bus? Nobody was in there today anyway.
Middle of week middle of winter. Not like on weekends. Weekends the place is packed. So Im riding the
bus home. And this kid asked me for my autograph. I
pretended I didnt hear him at first. I'd had a long day.
But he kept asking. Theyd just done Lincoln in history class and he knew all about him, he'd been to
the arcade but, I dunno, for some reason he was tripping cause there was Honest Abe right beside him
on the bus. I wanted to tell him to go fuck hisself.
But then I got a look at him. A little rich kid. Born
on easy street, you know the type. So I waited until I
could tell he really wanted it, the autograph, and I
told him he could have it for 10 bucks. I was gonna
say 5, cause of the Lincoln connection but something
in me made me ask for 10.
BOOTH: But he didnt have a 10. All he had was a penny.
So you took the penny.
LINCOLN: All he had was a *20.* So I took the 20 and told
him to meet me on the bus tomorrow and Honest
Abe would give him the change.
BOOTH: Shit.
LINCOLN: Shit is right.

(*Rest*)

BOOTH: Whatd you do with thuh 20?
LINCOLN: Bought drinks at Luckys. A round for every-
body. They got a kick out of the getup.
BOOTH: You shoulda called me down.
LINCOLN: Next time, bro.

(*Rest*)

You making bookshelves? With the milk crates, you
making bookshelves?
BOOTH: Yeah, big bro, Im making bookshelves.
LINCOLN: Whats the cardboard part for?
BOOTH: Versatility.
LINCOLN: Oh.
BOOTH: I was thinking we dont got no bookshelves we
dont got no dining room table so Im making a sorta
modular unit you put the books in the bottom and
the table top on top. We can eat and store our books.
We could put the photo album in there.

Booth gets the raggedy family photo album and puts it
in the milk crate.

BOOTH: Youd sit there, I'd sit on the edge of the bed.
Gathered around the dinner table. Like old times.

LINCOLN: We just gotta get some books but thats great,
Booth, thats real great.
BOOTH: Dont be calling me Booth no more, K?
LINCOLN: You changing yr name?
BOOTH: Maybe.
LINCOLN
BOOTH
LINCOLN: What to?
BOOTH: Im not ready to reveal it yet.
LINCOLN: You already decided on something?
BOOTH: Maybe.
LINCOLN: You gonna call yrself something african? That
be cool. Only pick something thats easy to spell and
pronounce, man, cause you know, some of them
african names, I mean, ok, Im down with the power
to the people thing, but, no ones gonna hire you if
they cant say yr name. And some of them fellas who
got they african names, no one can say they names
and they cant say they names neither. I mean, you
dont want yr new handle to obstruct yr employment
possibilities.
BOOTH
LINCOLN
BOOTH: You bring dinner?
LINCOLN: "Shango" would be a good name. The name
of the thunder god. If you aint decided already Im
just throwing it in the pot. I brought chinese.
BOOTH: Lets try the table out.
LINCOLN: Cool.

They both sit at the new table. The food is far away near
the door.

LINCOLN
BOOTH
LINCOLN: I buy it you set it up. Thats the deal. Thats the
deal, right?
BOOTH: You like this place?
LINCOLN: Ssallright.
BOOTH: But a little cramped sometimes, right?
LINCOLN: You dont hear me complain. Although that
recliner sometimes Booth, man — no Booth, right —
man, Im too old to be sleeping in that chair.
BOOTH: Its my place. You dont got a place. Cookie, she
threw you out. And you cant seem to get another
woman. Yr lucky I let you stay.
LINCOLN: Every Friday you say *mi casa es su casa.*°
BOOTH: Every Friday you come home with yr paycheck.
Today is Thursday and I tell you brother, its a long
way from Friday to Friday. All kinds of things can
happen. All kinds of bad feelings can surface and
erupt while yr little brother waits for you to bring in
yr share.

(*Rest*)

I got my Thursday head on, Link. Go get the food.

Lincoln doesnt budge.

---

mi . . . casa: My house is your house.

LINCOLN: You dont got no running water in here, man.

BOOTH: So?

LINCOLN: You dont got no toilet you dont got no sink.

BOOTH: Bathrooms down the hall.

LINCOLN: You living in thuh Third World, fool! Hey, I'll get thuh food.

Lincoln goes to get the food. He sees a stray card on the floor and examines it without touching it. He brings the food over, putting it nicely on the table.

LINCOLN: You been playing cards?

BOOTH: Yeah.

LINCOLN: Solitaire?

BOOTH: Thats right. Im getting pretty good at it.

LINCOLN: Thats soup and thats sauce. I got you the meat and I got me the skrimps.

BOOTH: I wanted the skrimps.

LINCOLN: You said you wanted the meat. This morning when I left you said you wanted the meat.

(*Rest*)

Here man, take the skrimps. No sweat.

They eat. Chinese food from styrofoam containers, cans of soda, fortune cookies. Lincoln eats slowly and carefully, Booth eats ravenously.

LINCOLN: Yr getting good at solitaire?

BOOTH: Yeah. How about we play a hand after eating?

LINCOLN: Solitaire?

BOOTH: Poker or rummy or something.

LINCOLN: You know I dont touch thuh cards, man.

BOOTH: Just for fun.

LINCOLN: I dont touch thuh cards.

BOOTH: How about for money?

LINCOLN: You dont got no money. All the money you got I bring in here.

BOOTH: I got my inheritance.

LINCOLN: Thats like saying you dont got no money cause you aint never gonna do nothing with it so its like you dont got it.

BOOTH: At least I still got mines. You blew yrs.

LINCOLN

BOOTH

LINCOLN: You like the skrimps?

BOOTH: Ssallright.

LINCOLN: Whats yr fortune?

BOOTH: "Waste not want not." Whats yrs?

LINCOLN: "Your luck will change!"

Booth finishes eating. He turns his back to Lincoln and fiddles around with the cards, keeping them on the bed, just out of Lincolns sight. He mutters the 3-card patter under his breath. His moves are still clumsy. Every once and a while he darts a look over at Lincoln who does his best to ignore Booth.

((((Watch me close watch me close now: who-see-thuh-red-card who-see-thuh-red-card? I-see-thuh-red-card. Thuh-red-card-is-thuh-winner. Pick-thuh-red-card-you-pick-uh-winner. Pick-uh-black-card-and-you-pick-uh-loser. Theres-thuh-loser, yeah, theres-thuh-black-card, theres-thuh-other-loser-and-theres-thuh-red-card, thuh-winner! Cop C, Stick, Cop C! Go on —))))

LINCOLN: ((Shit.))

BOOTH: (((((((One-good-pickll-get-you-in, 2-good-picks-and-you-gone-win. Dont touch my cards, man, just point to thuh one you want. You-pick-that-card-you-pick-uh-loser, yeah, that-cards-uh-loser. You-pick-that-card-thats-thuh-other-loser. You-pick-that-card-you-pick-uh-winner. Follow-that-card. You-gotta-chase-that-card!)))))))

LINCOLN: You wanna hustle 3-card monte, you gotta do it right, you gotta break it down. Practice it in smaller bits. Yr trying to do the whole thing at once thats why you keep fucking it up.

BOOTH: Show me.

LINCOLN: No. Im just saying you wanna do it you gotta do it right and if you gonna do it right you gotta work on it in smaller bits, thatsall.

BOOTH: You and me could team up and do it together. We'd clean up, Link.

LINCOLN: I'll clean up — bro.

Lincoln cleans up. As he clears the food, Booth goes back to using the "table" for its original purpose.

BOOTH: My new names 3-Card. 3-Card, got it? You wanted to know it so now you know it. 3-card monte by 3-Card. Call me 3-Card from here on out.

LINCOLN: 3-Card. Shit.

BOOTH: Im getting everybody to call me 3-Card. Grace likes 3-Card better than Booth. She says 3-Cards got something to it. Anybody not calling me 3-Card gets a bullet.

LINCOLN: Yr too much, man.

BOOTH: Im making a point.

LINCOLN: Point made, 3-Card. Point made.

Lincoln picks up his guitar. Plays at it.

BOOTH: Oh, come on, man, we could make money you and me. Throwing down the cards. 3-Card and Link: look out! We could clean up you and me. You would throw the cards and I'd be yr Stickman. The one in the crowd who looks like just an innocent passerby, who looks like just another player, like just another customer, but who gots intimate connections with you, the Dealer, the one throwing the cards, the main man. I'd be the one who brings in the crowd, I'd be the one who makes them want to put they money down, you do yr moves and I do mines. You turn yr head and I turn the card —

LINCOLN: It aint as easy as all that. Theres —

BOOTH: We could be a team, man. Rake in the money! Sure thered be some cats out there with fast eyes, some brothers and sisters who would watch real close and pick the right card, and so thered be some days when we would lose money, but most of the days we would come out on top! Pockets bulging, plenty of cash! And the ladies would be thrilling! You could afford to get laid! Grace would be all over me again.

LINCOLN: I thought you said she was all over you.

BOOTH: She is she is. Im seeing her tomorrow but today we gotta solidify the shit twixt you and me. Big brother Link and little brother Booth —

LINCOLN: 3-Card.

BOOTH: Yeah. Scheming and dreaming. No one throws the cards like you, Link. And with yr moves and my magic, and we get Grace and a girl for you to round out the posse. We'd be golden, bro! Am I right?

LINCOLN

BOOTH

BOOTH: Am I right?

LINCOLN: I dont touch thuh cards, 3-Card. I dont touch thuh cards no more.

LINCOLN

BOOTH

LINCOLN

BOOTH

BOOTH: You know what Mom told me when she was packing to leave? You was at school motherfucker you was at school. You got up that morning and sat down in yr regular place and read the cereal box while Dad read the sports section and Mom brought you yr dick toast and then you got on the damn school bus cause you didnt have the sense to do nothing else you was so into yr own shit that you didnt have the sense to feel nothing else going on. I had the sense to go back cause I was feeling something going on man, I was feeling something changing. So I —

LINCOLN: Cut school that day like you did almost every day —

BOOTH: She was putting her stuff in bags. She had all them nice suitcases but she was putting her stuff in bags.

(Rest)

Packing up her shit. She told me to look out for you. I told her I was the little brother and the big brother should look out after the little brother. She just said it again. That I should look out for you. Yeah. So who gonna look out for me. Not like you care. Here I am interested in an economic opportunity, willing to work hard, willing to take risks and all you can say you shiteating motherfucking pathetic limpdick uncle tom, all you can tell me is how you dont do no more what I be wanting to do. Here I am trying to earn a living and you standing in my way. YOU STANDING IN MY WAY, LINK!

LINCOLN: Im sorry.

BOOTH: Yeah, you sorry all right.

LINCOLN: I cant be hustling no more, bro.

BOOTH: What you do all day aint no hustle?

LINCOLN: Its honest work.

BOOTH: Dressing up like some crackerass white man, some dead president and letting people shoot at you sounds like a hustle to me.

LINCOLN: People know the real deal. When people know the real deal it aint a hustle.

BOOTH: We do the card game people will know the real deal. Sometimes we will win sometimes they will win. They fast they win, we faster we win.

LINCOLN: I aint going back to that, bro. I aint going back.

BOOTH: You play Honest Abe. You aint going back but you going all the way back. Back to way back then when folks was slaves and shit.

LINCOLN: Dont push me.

BOOTH

LINCOLN

BOOTH: You gonna have to leave.

LINCOLN: I'll be gone tomorrow.

BOOTH: Good. Cause this was only supposed to be a temporary arrangement.

LINCOLN: I will be gone tomorrow.

BOOTH: Good.

Booth sits on his bed. Lincoln, sitting in his easy chair with his guitar, plays and sings.

LINCOLN:
My dear mother left me, my fathers gone away
My dear mother left me and my fathers gone away
I dont got no money, I dont got no place to stay.

My best girl, she threw me out into the street
My favorite horse, they ground him into meat
Im feeling cold from my head down to my feet.

My luck was bad but now it turned to worse
My luck was bad but now it turned to worse
Dont call me up a doctor, just call me up a hearse.

BOOTH: You just made that up?

LINCOLN: I had it in my head for a few days.

BOOTH: Sounds good.

LINCOLN: Thanks.

(Rest)

Daddy told me once why we got the names we do.

BOOTH: Yeah?

LINCOLN: Yeah.

(Rest)

He was drunk when he told me, or maybe I was drunk when he told me. Anyway he told me, may not be true, but he told me. Why he named us both. Lincoln and Booth.

BOOTH: How come. How come, man?

LINCOLN: It was his idea of a joke.

Both men relax back as the lights fade.

SCENE TWO

Friday evening. The very next day. Booth comes in looking like he is bundled up against the cold. He makes sure his brother isnt home, then stands in the middle of the room. From his big coat sleeves he pulls out one new shoe then another, from another sleeve come two more shoes. He then slithers out a belt from each sleeve. He removes his coat. Underneath he wears a very nice new suit. He removes the jacket and pants revealing another new suit underneath. The suits still have the price tags on them. He takes two neckties from his pockets and two folded shirts from the back of his pants. He pulls a magazine from the front of his pants. Hes clearly had a busy day of shoplifting. He lays one suit out on Lincolns easy chair. The other he lays out on his own bed. He goes out into the hall returning with a folding screen which he sets up between the bed and the recliner creating 2 separate spaces. He takes out a bottle of whiskey and two glasses, setting them on the two stacked milk crates. He hears footsteps and sits down in the small wooden chair reading the magazine. Lincoln, dressed in street clothes, comes in.

LINCOLN: Taaaaadaaaaaaaa!
BOOTH: Lordamighty, Pa, I smells money!
LINCOLN: Sho nuff, Ma. Poppas brung home thuh bacon.
BOOTH: Bringitherebringitherebringithere.

With a series of very elaborate moves Lincoln brings the money over to Booth.

BOOTH: Put it in my hands, Pa!
LINCOLN: I want ya tuh smells it first, Ma!
BOOTH: Put it neath my nose then, Pa!
LINCOLN: Take yrself a good long whiff of them green-backs.
BOOTH: Oh lordamighty Ima faint, Pa! Get me muh med-sin!

Lincoln quickly pours two large glasses of whiskey.

LINCOLN: Dont die on me, Ma!
BOOTH: Im fading fast, Pa!
LINCOLN: Thinka thuh children, Ma! Thinka thuh farm!
BOOTH: 1-2-3.

Both men gulp down their drinks simultaneously.

LINCOLN AND BOOTH: AAAAAAAAAAAAAAAAAAAAAH!

Lots of laughing and slapping on the backs.

LINCOLN: Budget it out man budget it out.
BOOTH: You in a hurry?
LINCOLN: Yeah. I wanna see how much we got for the week.
BOOTH: You rush in here and dont even look around. Could be a fucking A-bomb in the middle of the floor you wouldnt notice. Yr wife, Cookie —
LINCOLN: X-wife —
BOOTH: — could be in my bed you wouldnt notice —
LINCOLN: She was once —
BOOTH: Look the fuck around please.

Lincoln looks around and sees the new suit on his chair.

LINCOLN: Wow.
BOOTH: Its yrs.
LINCOLN: Shit.
BOOTH: Got myself one too.

LINCOLN: Boosted?
BOOTH: Yeah, I boosted em. Theys stole from a big-ass department store. That store takes in more money in one day than we will in our whole life. I stole and I stole generously. I got one for me and I got one for you. Shoes belts shirts ties socks in the shoes and everything. Got that screen too.
LINCOLN: You all right, man.
BOOTH: Just cause I aint good as you at cards dont mean I cant do nothing.
LINCOLN: Lets try em on.

They stand in their separate sleeping spaces, Booth near his bed, Lincoln near his recliner, and try on their new clothes.

BOOTH: Ima wear mine tonight. Gracell see me in this and *she* gonna ask me tuh marry *her*.

(Rest)

I got you the blue and I got me the brown. I walked in there and walked out and they didnt as much as bat an eye. Thats how smooth lil bro be, Link.
LINCOLN: You did good. You did real good, 3-Card.
BOOTH: All in a days work.
LINCOLN: They say the clothes make the man. All day long I wear that getup. But that dont make me who I am. Old black coat not even real old just fake old. Its got worn spots on the elbows, little raggedy places thatll break through into holes before the winters out. Shiny strips around the cuffs and the collar. Dust from the cap guns on the left shoulder where they shoot him, where they shoot me I should say but I never feel like they shooting me. The fella who had the gig before I had it wore the same coat. When I got the job they had the getup hanging there waiting for me. Said thuh fella before me just took it off one day and never came back.

(Rest)

Remember how Dads clothes used to hang in the closet?
BOOTH: Until you took em outside and burned em.

(Rest)

He had some nice stuff. What he didnt spend on booze he spent on women. What he didnt spend on them two he spent on clothes. He had some nice stuff I would look at his stuff and calculate thuh how long it would take till I was big enough to fit it. Then you went and burned it all up.
LINCOLN: I got tired of looking at em without him in em.

(Rest)

They said thuh fella before me — he took off the getup one day, hung it up real nice, and never came back. And as they offered me thuh job, saying of course I would have to wear a little makeup and accept less than what they would offer a — another guy —

BOOTH: Go on, say it. "White." Theyd pay you less than theyd pay a white guy.

LINCOLN: I said to myself thats exactly what I would do: wear it out and then leave it hanging there and not come back. But until then, I would make a living at it. But it dont make me. Worn suit coat, not even worn by the fool that Im supposed to be playing, but making fools out of all those folks who come crowding in for they chance to play at something great. Fake beard. Top hat. Dont make me into no Lincoln. I was Lincoln on my own before any of that.

The men finish dressing. They style and profile.

BOOTH: Sharp, huh?

LINCOLN: Very sharp.

BOOTH: You look sharp too, man. You look like the real you. Most of the time you walking around all bedraggled and shit. You look good. Like you used to look back in thuh day when you had Cookie in love with you and all the women in the world was eating out of yr hand.

LINCOLN: This is real nice, man. I dont know where Im gonna wear it but its real nice.

BOOTH: Just wear it around. Itll make you feel good and when you feel good yll meet someone nice. Me I aint interested in meeting no one nice, I mean, I only got eyes for Grace. You think she'll go for me in this?

LINCOLN: I think thuh tie you gave me'll go better with what you got on.

BOOTH: Yeah?

LINCOLN: Grace likes bright colors dont she? My ties bright, yrs is too subdued.

BOOTH: Yeah. Gimmie yr tie.

LINCOLN: You gonna take back a gift?

BOOTH: I stole the damn thing didnt I? Gimmie yrs! I'll give you mines.

They switch neckties. Booth is pleased. Lincoln is more pleased.

LINCOLN: Do thuh budget.

BOOTH: Right. Ok lets see: we got 314 dollars. We put 100 aside for the rent. 100 a week times 4 weeks makes the rent and —

LINCOLN AND BOOTH: — we dont want thuh rent spent.

BOOTH: That leaves 214. We put aside 30 for the electric leaving 184. We put aside 50 for thuh phone leaving 134.

LINCOLN: We dont got a phone.

BOOTH: We pay our bill theyll turn it back on.

LINCOLN: We dont need no phone.

BOOTH: How you gonna get a woman if you dont got a phone? Women these days are more cautious, more whaddacallit, more circumspect. You go into a club looking like a fast daddy, you get a filly to give you her numerophono and gone is the days when she just gives you her number and dont ask for yrs.

LINCOLN: Like a woman is gonna call me.

BOOTH: She dont wanna call you she just doing a preliminary survey of the property. Shit, Link, you dont know nothin no more.

(Rest)

She gives you her number and she asks for yrs. You give her yr number. The phone number of yr home. Thereby telling her 3 things: 1) you got a home, that is, you aint no smooth talking smooth dressing *homeless* joe; 2) that you is in possession of a telephone and a working telephone number which is to say that you got thuh cash and thuh wherewithal to acquire for yr self the worlds most revolutionary communication apparatus and you together enough to pay yr bills!

LINCOLN: Whats 3?

BOOTH: You give her yr number you telling her that its cool to call if she should so please, that is, that you aint got no wife or wife approximation on the premises.

(Rest)

50 for the phone leaving 134. We put aside 40 for "med-sin."

LINCOLN: The price went up. 2 bucks more a bottle.

BOOTH: We'll put aside 50, then. That covers the bills. We got 84 left. 40 for meals together during the week leaving 44. 30 for me 14 for you. I got a woman I gotta impress tonight.

LINCOLN: You didnt take out for the phone last week.

BOOTH: Last week I was depressed. This week things is looking up. For both of us.

LINCOLN: Theyre talking about cutbacks at the arcade. I only been there 8 months, so —

BOOTH: Dont sweat it man, we'll find something else.

LINCOLN: Not nothing like this. I like the job. This is sit down, you know, easy work. I just gotta sit there all day. Folks come in kill phony Honest Abe with the phony pistol. I can sit there and let my mind travel.

BOOTH: Think of women.

LINCOLN: Sometimes.

(Rest)

All around the whole arcade is buzzing and popping. Thuh whirring of thuh duckshoot, baseballs smacking the back wall when someone misses the stack of cans, some woman getting happy cause her fella just won the ring toss. The Boss playing the barker talking up the fake freaks. The smell of the ocean and cotton candy and rat shit. And in thuh middle of all that, I can just sit and let my head go quiet. Make up songs, make plans. Forget.

(Rest)

You should come down again.

BOOTH: Once was plenty, but thanks.

(Rest)

Yr Best Customer, he come in today?

LINCOLN: Oh, yeah, he was there.

BOOTH: He shoot you?

LINCOLN: He shot Honest Abe, yeah.

BOOTH: He talk to you?

LINCOLN: In a whisper. Shoots on the left whispers on the right.

BOOTH: Whatd he say this time?

LINCOLN: "Does thuh show stop when no ones watching or does thuh show go on?"

BOOTH: Hes getting deep.

LINCOLN: Yeah.

BOOTH: Whatd he say, that one time? "Yr only yrself — "

LINCOLN: " — when no ones watching," yeah.

BOOTH: Thats deep shit.

(*Rest*)

Hes a brother, right?

LINCOLN: I think so.

BOOTH: He know yr a brother?

LINCOLN: I dunno. Yesterday he had a good one. He shoots me, Im playing dead, and he leans in close then goes: "God aint nothing but a parasite."

BOOTH: Hes one *deep* black brother.

LINCOLN: Yeah. He makes the day interesting.

BOOTH (*Rest*): Thats a fucked-up job you got.

LINCOLN: Its a living.

BOOTH: But you aint living.

LINCOLN: Im alive aint I?

(*Rest*)

One day I was throwing the cards. Next day Lonny died. Somebody shot him. I knew I was next, so I quit. I saved my life.

(*Rest*)

The arcade gig is the first lucky break Ive ever had. And Ive actually grown to like the work. And now theyre talking about cutting me.

BOOTH: You was lucky with thuh cards.

LINCOLN: Lucky? Aint nothing lucky about cards. Cards aint luck. Cards is work. Cards is skill. Aint never nothing lucky about cards.

(*Rest*)

I dont wanna lose my job.

BOOTH: Then you gotta jazz up yr act. Elaborate yr moves, you know. You was always too stiff with it. You cant just sit there! Maybe, when they shoot you, you know, leap up flail yr arms then fall down and wiggle around and shit so they gotta shoot you more than once. Blam Blam Blam! Blam!

LINCOLN: Help me practice. I'll sit here like I do at work and you be like one of the tourists.

BOOTH: No thanks.

LINCOLN: My paychecks on the line, man.

BOOTH: I got a date. Practice on yr own.

(*Rest*)

I got a rendezvous with Grace. Shit she so sweet she makes my teeth hurt.

(*Rest*)

Link, uh, howbout slipping me an extra 5 spot. Its the biggest night of my life.

LINCOLN

BOOTH

Lincoln gives Booth a 5er.

BOOTH: Thanks.

LINCOLN: No sweat.

BOOTH: Howabout I run through it with you when I get back. Put on yr getup and practice till then.

LINCOLN: Sure.

Booth leaves. Lincoln stands there alone. He takes off his shoes, giving them a shine. He takes off his socks and his fancy suit, hanging it neatly over the little wooden chair. He takes his getup out of his shopping bag. He puts it on, slowly, like an actor preparing for a great role: frock coat, pants, beard, top hat, necktie. He leaves his feet bare. The top hat has an elastic band which he positions securely underneath his chin. He picks up the white pancake makeup but decides against it. He sits. He pretends to get shot, flings himself on the floor and thrashes around. He gets up, considers giving the new moves another try, but instead pours himself a big glass of whiskey and sits there drinking.

SCENE THREE

Much later that same Friday evening. The recliner is reclined to its maximum horizontal position and Lincoln lies there asleep. He wakes with a start. He is horrific, bleary eyed and hungover, in his full Lincoln regalia. He takes a deep breath, realizes where he is and reclines again, going back to sleep. Booth comes in full of swagger. He slams the door trying to wake his brother who is dead to the world. He opens the door and slams it again. This time Lincoln wakes up, as hungover and horrid as before. Booth swaggers about, his moves are exaggerated, rooster-like. He walks round and round Lincoln making sure his brother sees him.

LINCOLN: You hurt yrself?

BOOTH: I had me "an evening to remember."

LINCOLN: You look like you hurt yrself.

BOOTH: Grace Grace Grace. *Grace.* She wants me back. She wants me back so bad she wiped her hand over the past where we wasnt together just so she could say we aint never been apart. She wiped her hand over our breakup. She wiped her hand over her childhood, her teenage years, her first boyfriend, just so she could say that she been mine since the dawn of time.

LINCOLN: Thats great, man.

BOOTH: And all the shit I put her through: she wiped it clean. And the women I saw while I was seeing her —

LINCOLN: Wiped clean too?

BOOTH: Mister Clean, Mister, Mister Clean!

LINCOLN: Whered you take her?

BOOTH: We was over at her place. I brought thuh food. Stopped at the best place I could find and stuffed my coat with only the best. We had candlelight, we had music we had —

LINCOLN: She let you do it?

BOOTH: Course she let me do it.

LINCOLN: She let you do it without a rubber?

BOOTH: — Yeah.

LINCOLN: Bullshit.

BOOTH: I put my foot down — and she *melted*. And she was — huh — she was something else. I dont wanna get you jealous, though.

LINCOLN: Go head, I dont mind.

BOOTH (*Rest*): Well, you know what she looks like.

LINCOLN: She walks on by and the emergency room fills up cause all the guys get whiplash from lookin at her.

BOOTH: Thats right thats right. Well — she comes to the door wearing nothing but her little nightie, eats up the food I'd brought like there was no tomorrow and then goes and eats on me.

(*Rest*)

LINCOLN: Go on.

BOOTH: I dont wanna make you feel bad, man.

LINCOLN: Ssallright. Go on.

BOOTH (*Rest*): Well, uh, you know what shes like. Wild. Goodlooking. So sweet my teeth hurt.

LINCOLN: Sexmachine.

BOOTH: Yeah.

LINCOLN: Hotsy-Totsy.

BOOTH: Yeah.

LINCOLN: Amazing Grace.

BOOTH: Amazing Grace! Yeah. Thats right. She let me do her how I wanted. And no rubber.

(*Rest*)

LINCOLN: Go on.

BOOTH: You dont wanna hear the mushy shit.

LINCOLN: Sure I do.

BOOTH: You hate mushy shit. You always hated thuh mushy shit.

LINCOLN: Ive changed. Go head. You had "an evening to remember," remember? I was just here alone sitting here. Drinking. Go head. Tell Link thuh stink.

(*Rest*)

Howd ya do her?

BOOTH: Dogstyle.

LINCOLN: Amazing Grace.

BOOTH: In front of a mirror.

LINCOLN: So you could see her. Her face her breasts her back her ass. Graces got a great ass.

BOOTH: Its all right.

LINCOLN: Amazing Grace!

Booth goes into his bed area and takes off his suit, tossing the clothes on the floor.

BOOTH: She said next time Ima have to use a rubber. She let me have my way this time but she said that next time I'd have to put my boots on.

LINCOLN: Im sure you can talk her out of it.

BOOTH: Yeah.

(*Rest*)

What kind of rubbers you use, I mean, when you was with Cookie.

LINCOLN: We didnt use rubbers. We was married, man.

BOOTH: Right. But you had other women on the side. What kind you use when you was with them?

LINCOLN: Magnums.

BOOTH: Thats thuh kind I picked up. For next time. Grace was real strict about it.

While Booth sits on his bed fiddling with his box of condoms, Lincoln sits in his chair and resumes drinking.

LINCOLN: Im sure you can talk her out of it. You put yr foot down and she'll melt.

BOOTH: She was real strict. Sides I wouldnt wanna be taking advantage of her or nothing. Putting my foot down and her melting all over thuh place.

LINCOLN: Magnums then.

(*Rest*)

Theyre for "the larger man."

BOOTH: Right. Right.

Lincoln keeps drinking as Booth, sitting in the privacy of his bedroom, fiddles with the condoms, perhaps trying to put one on.

LINCOLN: Thats right.

BOOTH: Graces real different from them fly-by-night gals I was making do with. Shes in school. Making something of herself. Studying cosmetology. You should see what she can do with a womans hair and nails.

LINCOLN: Too bad you aint a woman.

BOOTH: What?

LINCOLN: You could get yrs done for free, I mean.

BOOTH: Yeah. She got this way of sitting. Of talking. Everything she does is. Shes just so hot.

(*Rest*)

We was together 2 years. Then we broke up. I had my little employment difficulty and she needed time to think.

LINCOLN: And shes through thinking now.

BOOTH: Thats right.

LINCOLN

BOOTH

LINCOLN: Whatcha doing back there?

BOOTH: Resting. That girl wore me out.

LINCOLN: You want some med-sin?

BOOTH: No thanks.

LINCOLN: Come practice my moves with me, then.

BOOTH: Lets hit it tomorrow, K?

LINCOLN: I been waiting. I got all dressed up and you said if I waited up — come on, man, they gonna replace me with a wax dummy.

BOOTH: No shit.

LINCOLN: Thats what theyre talking about. Probably just talk, but — come on, man, I even lent you 5 bucks.

BOOTH: Im tired.

LINCOLN: You didnt get shit tonight.

BOOTH: You jealous, man. You just jail-us.

LINCOLN: You laying over there yr balls blue as my boosted suit. Laying over there waiting for me to go back to sleep or black out so I wont hear you rustling thuh pages of yr fuck book.

BOOTH: Fuck you, man.

LINCOLN: I was over there looking for something the other week and theres like 100 fuck books under yr bed and theyre matted together like a bad fro, bro, cause you spunked in the pages and didnt wipe them off.

BOOTH: Im hot. I need constant sexual release. If I wasnt taking care of myself by myself I would be out there running around on thuh town which costs cash that I dont have so I would be doing worse: I'd be out there doing who knows what, shooting people and shit. Out of a need for unresolved sexual release. I'm a hot man. I aint apologizing for it. When I dont got a woman, I gotta make do. Not like you, Link. When you dont got a woman you just sit there. Letting yr shit fester. Yr dick, if it aint falled off yet, is hanging there between yr legs, little whiteface shriveled-up blank-shooting grub worm. As goes thuh man so goes thuh mans dick. Thats what I say. Least my shits intact.

(Rest)

You a limp dick jealous whiteface motherfucker whose wife dumped him cause he couldnt get it up and she told me so. Came crawling to me cause she needed a man.

(Rest)

I gave it to Grace good tonight. So goodnight.

LINCOLN (Rest): Goodnight.

LINCOLN
BOOTH
LINCOLN
BOOTH
LINCOLN
BOOTH

Lincoln sitting in his chair. Booth lying in bed. Time passes. Booth peeks out to see if Lincoln is asleep. Lincoln is watching for him.

LINCOLN: You can hustle 3-card monte without me you know.

BOOTH: Im planning to.

LINCOLN: I could contact my old crew. You could work with them. Lonny aint around no more but theres the rest of them. Theyre good.

BOOTH: I can get my own crew. I dont need yr crew. Buncha has-beens. I can get my own crew.

LINCOLN: My crews experienced. We usedta pull down a thousand a day. Thats 7 G a week. That was years ago. They probably do twice, 3 times that now.

BOOTH: I got my own connections, thank you.

LINCOLN: Theyd take you on in a heartbeat. With my say. My say still counts with them. They know you from before, when you tried to hang with us but — wernt ready yet. They know you from then, but I'd talk you up. I'd say yr my bro, which they know, and I'd say youd been working the west coast. Little towns. Mexican border. Taking tourists. I'd tell them you got moves like I dreamed of having. Meanwhile youd be working out yr shit right here, right in this room, getting good and getting better every day so when I did do the reintroductions youd have some marketable skills. Youd be passable.

BOOTH: I'd be more than passable, I'd be the be all end all.

LINCOLN: Youd be the be all end all. And youd have my say. If yr interested.

BOOTH: Could do.

LINCOLN: Youd have to get a piece. They all pack pistols, bro.

BOOTH: I *got* a piece.

LINCOLN: Youd have to be packing something more substantial than that pop gun, 3-Card. These hustlers is upper echelon hustlers they pack upper echelon heat, not no Saturday night shit, now.

BOOTH: Whata you know of heat? You aint hung with those guys for 6, 7 years. You swore off em. Threw yr heat in thuh river and you "Dont touch thuh cards." I know more about heat than you know about heat.

LINCOLN: Im around guns every day. At the arcade. Theyve all been reworked so they only fire caps but I see guns every day. Lots of guns.

BOOTH: What kinds?

LINCOLN: You been there, you seen them. Shiny deadly metal each with their own deadly personality.

BOOTH: Maybe I *could* visit you over there. I'd boost one of them guns and rework it to make it shoot for real again. What kind you think would best suit my personality?

LINCOLN: You aint stealing nothing from the arcade.

BOOTH: I go in there and steal if I want to go in there and steal I go in there and steal.

LINCOLN: It aint worth it. They dont shoot nothing but blanks.

BOOTH: Yeah, like you. Shooting blanks.

(Rest)

(Rest)

You ever wonder if someones gonna come in there with a real gun? A real gun with real slugs? Someone with uh axe tuh grind or something?

LINCOLN: No.

BOOTH: Someone who hates you come in there and guns you down and gets gone before anybody finds out.

LINCOLN: I dont got no enemies.

BOOTH: Yr X.

LINCOLN: Cookie dont hate me.

BOOTH: Yr Best Customer? Some miscellaneous stranger?

LINCOLN: I cant be worrying about the actions of miscellaneous strangers.

BOOTH: But there they come day in day out for a chance to shoot Honest Abe.

(*Rest*)

Who are they mostly?

LINCOLN: I dont really look.

BOOTH: You must see something.

LINCOLN: Im supposed to be staring straight ahead. Watching a play, like Abe was.

BOOTH: All day goes by and you never ever take a sneak peek at who be pulling the trigger.

Pulled in by his own curiosity, Booth has come out of his bed area to stand on the dividing line between the two spaces.

LINCOLN: Its pretty dark. To keep thuh illusion of thuh whole thing.

(*Rest*)

But on thuh wall opposite where I sit theres a little electrical box, like a fuse box. Silver metal. Its got uh dent in it like somebody hit it with they fist. Big old dent so everything reflected in it gets reflected upside down. Like yr looking in uh spoon. And thats where I can see em. The assassins.

(*Rest*)

Not behind me yet but I can hear him coming. Coming in with his gun in hand, thuh gun he already picked out up front when he paid his fare. Coming on in. But not behind me yet. His dress shoes making too much noise on the carpet, the carpets too thin, Boss should get a new one but hes cheap. Not behind me yet. Not behind me yet. Cheap lightbulb just above my head.

(*Rest*)

And there he is. Standing behind me. Standing in position. Standing upside down. Theres some feet shapes on the floor so he knows just where he oughta stand. So he wont miss. Thuh gun is always cold. Winter or summer thuh gun is always cold. And when the gun touches me he can feel that Im warm and he knows Im alive. And if Im alive then he can shoot me dead. And for a minute, with him hanging back there behind me, its real. Me looking at him upside down and him looking at me looking like Lincoln. Then he shoots.

(*Rest*)

I slump down and close my eyes. And he goes out thuh other way. More come in. Uh whole day full. Bunches of kids, little good for nothings, in they

school uniforms. Businessmen smelling like two for one martinis. Tourists in they theme park t-shirts trying to catch it on film. Housewives with they mouths closed tight, shooting more than once.

(*Rest*)

They all get so into it. I do my best for them. And now they talking bout replacing me with uh wax dummy. Itll cut costs.

BOOTH: You just gotta show yr boss that you can do things a wax dummy cant do. You too dry with it. You gotta add spicy shit.

LINCOLN: Like what.

BOOTH: Like when they shoot you, I dunno, scream or something.

LINCOLN: Scream?

Booth plays the killer without using his gun.

BOOTH: Try it. I'll be the killer. Bang!

LINCOLN: Aaaah!

BOOTH: Thats good.

LINCOLN: A wax dummy can scream. They can put a voicebox in it and make it like its screaming.

BOOTH: You can curse. Try it. Bang!

LINCOLN: Motherfucking cocksucker!

BOOTH: Thats good, man.

LINCOLN: They aint going for that, though.

BOOTH: You practice rolling and wiggling on the floor?

LINCOLN: A little.

BOOTH: Lemmie see. Bang!

Lincoln slumps down, falls on the floor and silently wiggles around.

BOOTH: You look more like a worm on the sidewalk. Move yr arms. Good. Now scream or something.

LINCOLN: Aaaah! Aaaaah! Aaaah!

BOOTH: A little tougher than that, you sound like yr fucking.

LINCOLN: Aaaaaah!

BOOTH: Hold yr head or something, where I shotcha. Good. And look at me! I am the assassin! *I am Booth!!* Come on man this is life and death! Go all out!

Lincoln goes all out.

BOOTH: Cool, man thats cool. Thats enough.

LINCOLN: Whatdoyathink?

BOOTH: I dunno, man. Something about it. I dunno. It was looking too real or something.

LINCOLN: They dont want it looking too real. I'd scare the customers. Then I'd be out for sure. Yr trying to get me fired.

BOOTH: Im trying to help. Cross my heart.

LINCOLN: People are funny about they Lincoln shit. Its historical. People like they historical shit in a certain way. They like it to unfold the way they folded it up. Neatly like a book. Not raggedy and bloody and screaming. You trying to get me fired.

(Rest)

I am uh brother playing Lincoln. Its uh stretch for anyones imagination. And it aint easy for me neither. Every day I put on that shit, I leave my own shit at the door and I put on that shit and I go out there and I make it work. I make it look easy but its hard. That shit is hard. But it works. Cause I work it. And you trying to get me fired.

(Rest)

I swore off them cards. Took nowhere jobs. Drank. Then Cookie threw me out. What thuh fuck was I gonna do? I seen that "Help Wanted" sign and I went up in there and I looked good in the getup and agreed to the whiteface and they really dug it that me and Honest Abe got the same name.

(Rest)

Its a sit down job. With benefits. I dont wanna get fired. They wont give me a good reference if I get fired.

BOOTH: Iffen you was tuh get fired, then, well — then you and me could — hustle the cards together. We'd have to support ourselves somehow.

(Rest)

Just show me how to do the hook part of the card hustle, man. The part where the Dealer looks away but somehow he sees —

LINCOLN: I couldnt remember if I wanted to.

BOOTH: Sure you could.

LINCOLN: No.

(Rest)

Night, man.

BOOTH: Yeah.

Lincoln stretches out in his recliner. Booth stands over him waiting for him to get up, to change his mind. But Lincoln is fast asleep. Booth covers him with a blanket then goes to his bed, turning off the lights as he goes. He quietly rummages underneath his bed for a girlie magazine which, as the lights fade, he reads with great interest.

SCENE FOUR

Saturday. Just before dawn. Lincoln gets up. Looks around. Booth is fast asleep, dead to the world.

LINCOLN: No fucking running water.

He stumbles around the room looking for something which he finally finds: a plastic cup, which he uses as a urinal. He finishes peeing and finds an out of the way place to stow the cup. He claws at his Lincoln getup, removing it and tearing it in the process. He strips down to his t-shirt and shorts.

LINCOLN: Hate falling asleep in this damn shit. Shit. Ripped the beard. I can just hear em tomorrow.

Busiest day of the week. They looking me over to make sure Im presentable. They got a slew of guys working but Im the only one they look over every day. "Yr beards ripped, pal. Sure, we'll getcha new one but its gonna be coming outa yr pay." Shit. I should quit right then and there. I'd yank off the beard, throw it on the ground and stomp it, then go strangle the fucking boss. Thatd be good. My hands around his neck and his bug eyes bugging out. You been ripping me off since I took this job and now Im gonna have to take it outa *yr* pay, motherfucker. Shit.

(Rest)

Sit down job. With benefits.

(Rest)

Hustling. Shit, I was good. I was great. Hell I was the be all end all. I was throwing cards like throwing cards was made for me. Made for me and me alone. I was the best anyone ever seen. Coast to coast. Everybody said so. And I never lost. Not once. Not one time. Not never. Thats how much them cards was mines. I was the be all end all. I was that good.

(Rest)

Then you woke up one day and you didnt have the taste for it no more. Like something in you knew — . Like something in you knew it was time to quit. Quit while you was still ahead. Something in you was telling you — . But hells no. Not Link thuh stink. So I went out there and threw one more time. What thuh fuck. And Lonny died.

(Rest)

Got yrself a good job. And when the arcade lets you go yll get another good job. I dont gotta spend my whole life hustling. Theres more to Link than that. More to me than some cheap hustle. More to life than cheating some idiot out of his paycheck or his life savings.

(Rest)

Like that joker and his wife from out of town. Always wanted to see the big city. I said you could see the bigger end of the big city with a little more cash. And if they was fast enough, faster than me, and here I slowed down my moves I slowed em way down and my Lonny, my right hand, my Stickman, spanish guy who looked white and could draw a customer in like nothing else, Lonny could draw a fly from fresh shit, he could draw Adam outa Eve just with that look he had, Lonny always got folks playing.

(Rest)

Somebody shot him. They dont know who. Nobody knows nobody cares.

(Rest)

We took that man and his wife for hundreds. No, thousands. We took them for everything they had and everything they ever wanted to have. We took a father for the money he was gonna get his kids new bike with and he cried in the street while we vanished. We took a mothers welfare check, she pulled a knife on us and we ran. She threw it but her aim werent shit. People shopping. Greedy. Thinking they could take me and they got took instead.

(*Rest*)

Swore off thuh cards. Something inside me telling me — . But I was good.
LINCOLN
LINCOLN

He sees a packet of cards. He studies them like an alcoholic would study a drink. Then he reaches for them, delicately picking them up and choosing 3 cards.

LINCOLN: Still got my moves. Still got my touch. Still got my chops. Thuh feel of it. And I aint hurting no one, God. Link is just here hustling hisself.

(*Rest*)

Lets see whatcha got.

He stands over the monte setup. Then he bends over it placing the cards down and moving them around. Slowly at first, aimlessly, as if hes just making little ripples in water. But then the game draws him in. Unlike Booth, Lincolns patter and moves are deft, dangerous, electric.

LINCOLN: (((Lean in close and watch me now: who see thuh black card who see thuh black card I see thuh black card black cards thuh winner pick thuh black card thats thuh winner pick thuh red card thats thuh loser pick thuh other red card thats thuh other loser pick thuh black card you pick thuh winner. Watch me as I throw thuh cards. Here we go.)))

(*Rest*)

(((Who see thuh black card who see thuh black card? You pick thuh red card you pick a loser you pick that red card you pick a loser you pick thuh black card thuh deuce of spades you pick a winner who sees thuh deuce of spades thuh one who sees it never fades watch me now as I throw thuh cards. Red losers black winner follow thuh deuce of spades chase thuh black deuce. Dark deuce will get you thuh win.)))

Even though Lincoln speaks softly, Booth wakes and, unbeknownst to Lincoln, listens intently.

(*Rest*)

LINCOLN: ((10 will get you 20, 20 will get you 40.))

(*Rest*)

((Ima show you thuh cards: 2 red cards but only one spade. Dark winner in thuh center and thuh red losers on thuh sides. Pick uh red card you got a loser

pick thuh other red card you got a loser pick thuh black card you got a winner. One good pickll get you in, 2 good picks and you gone win. Watch me come on watch me now.))

(*Rest*)

((Who sees thuh winner who knows where its at? You do? You sure? Go on then, put yr money where yr mouth is. Put yr money down you aint no clown. No? Ah, you had thuh card but you didnt have thuh heart.))

(*Rest*)

((Watch me now as I throw thuh cards watch me real close. Ok, man, you know which card is the deuce of spades? Was you watching Links lightning fast express? Was you watching Link cause he the best? So you sure, huh? Point it out first, then place yr bet and Linkll show you yr winner.))

(*Rest*)

((500 dollars? You thuh man of thuh hour you thuh man with thuh power. You musta been watching Link real close. You must be thuh man who know thuh most. Ok. Lay the cash in my hand cause Link the man. Thank you, mister. This card you say?))

(*Rest*)

((Wrong! Ha!))

(*Rest*)

((Thats thuh show. We gotta go.))

Lincoln puts the cards down. He moves away from the monte setup. He sits on the edge of his easy chair, but he can't take his eyes off the cards.

Intermission

SCENE FIVE

Several days have passed. Its now Wednesday night. Booth is sitting in his brand-new suit. The monte setup is nowhere in sight. In its place is a table with two nice chairs. The table is covered with a lovely tablecloth and there are nice plates, silverware, champagne glasses and candles. All the makings of a very romantic dinner for two. The whole apartment in fact takes its cue from the table. Its been cleaned up considerably. New curtains on the windows, a doily-like object on the recliner. Booth sits at the table darting his eyes around, making sure everything is looking good.

BOOTH: Shit.

He notices some of his girlie magazines visible from underneath his bed. He goes over and nudges them out of sight. He sits back down. He notices that theyre still visible. He goes over and nudges them some more, kicking at them finally. Then he takes the spread from his bed and pulls it down, hiding them. He sits back down. He gets up. Checks the champagne on much melted ice. Checks the food.

BOOTH: Foods getting cold, Grace!! Dont worry man, she'll get here, she'll get here.

He sits back down. He goes over to the bed. Checks it for springiness. Smoothes down the bedspread. Double-checks 2 matching silk dressing gowns, very expensive, marked "His" and "Hers." Lays the dressing gowns across the bed again. He sits back down. He cant help but notice the visibility of the girlie magazines again. He goes to the bed, kicks them fiercely, then on his hands and knees shoves them. Then he begins to get under the bed to push them, but he remembers his nice clothing and takes off his jacket. After a beat he removes his pants and, in this half-dressed way, he crawls under the bed to give those telltale magazines a good and final shove. Lincoln comes in. At first Booth, still stripped down to his underwear, thinks its his date. When he realizes its his brother, he does his best to keep Lincoln from entering the apartment. Lincoln wears his frock coat and carries the rest of his getup in a plastic bag.

LINCOLN: You in the middle of it?
BOOTH: What the hell you doing here?
LINCOLN: If yr in thuh middle of it I can go. Or I can just be real quiet and just — sing a song in my head or something.
BOOTH: The casas off limits to you tonight.
LINCOLN: You know when we lived in that 2-room place with the cement backyard and the frontyard with nothing but trash in it, Mom and Pops would do it in the middle of the night and I would always hear them but I would sing in my head, cause, I dunno, I couldnt bear to listen.
BOOTH: You gotta get out of here.
LINCOLN: I would make up all kinds of songs. Oh, sorry, yr all up in it. No sweat, bro. No sweat. Hey, Grace, howyadoing?!
BOOTH: She aint here yet, man. Shes running late. And its a good thing too cause I aint all dressed yet. Yr gonna spend thuh night with friends?
LINCOLN: Yeah.

Booth waits for Lincoln to leave. Lincoln stands his ground.

LINCOLN: I lost my job.
BOOTH: Hunh.
LINCOLN: I come in there right on time like I do every day and that motherfucker gives me some song and dance about cutbacks and too many folks complaining.
BOOTH: Hunh.
LINCOLN: Showd me thuh wax dummy — hes buying it right out of a catalog.

(Rest)

I walked out still wearing my getup.

(Rest)

I could go back in tomorrow. I could tell him I'll take another pay cut. Thatll get him to take me back.
BOOTH: Link. Yr free. Dont go crawling back. Yr free at last! Now you can do anything you want. Yr not tied down by that job. You can — you can do something else. Something that pays better maybe.
LINCOLN: You mean Hustle.
BOOTH: Maybe. Hey, Graces on her way. You gotta go.

Lincoln flops into his chair. Booth is waiting for him to move. Lincoln doesnt budge.

LINCOLN: I'll stay until she gets here. I'll act nice. I wont embarrass you.
BOOTH: You gotta go.
LINCOLN: What time she coming?
BOOTH: Shes late. She could be here any second.
LINCOLN: I'll meet her. I met her years ago. I'll meet her again.

(Rest)

How late is she?
BOOTH: She was supposed to be here at 8.
LINCOLN: Its after 2 a.m. Shes — shes late.

(Rest)

Maybe when she comes you could put the blanket over me and I'll just pretend like Im not here.

(Rest)

I'll wait. And when she comes I'll go. I need to sit down. I been walking around all day.
BOOTH
LINCOLN

Booth goes to his bed and dresses hurriedly.

BOOTH: Pretty nice, right? The china thuh silver thuh crystal.
LINCOLN: Its great.

(Rest)

Boosted?
BOOTH: Yeah.
LINCOLN: Thought you went and spent yr inheritance for a minute, you had me going I was thinking shit, Booth — 3-Card — that 3-Cards gone and spent his inheritance and the gal is — late.
BOOTH: Its boosted. Every bit of it.

(Rest)

Fuck this waiting bullshit.
LINCOLN: She'll be here in a minute. Dont sweat it.
BOOTH: Right.

Booth comes to the table. Sits. Relaxes as best he can.

BOOTH: How come I got a hand for boosting and I dont got a hand for throwing cards? Its sorta the same thing — you gotta be quick — and slick. Maybe yll show me yr moves sometime.

LINCOLN
BOOTH
LINCOLN
BOOTH
LINCOLN: Look out the window. When you see Grace coming, I'll go.
BOOTH: Cool. Cause youd jinx it, youd really jinx it. Maybe you being here has jinxed it already. Naw. Shes just a little late. You aint jinxed nothing.

Booth sits by the window, glancing out, watching for his date. Lincoln sits in his recliner. He finds the whiskey bottle, sips from it. He then rummages around, finding the raggedy photo album. He looks through it.

LINCOLN: There we are at that house. Remember when we moved in?
BOOTH: No.
LINCOLN: You were 2 or 3.
BOOTH: I was 5.
LINCOLN: I was 8. We all thought it was the best fucking house in the world.
BOOTH: Cement backyard and a frontyard full of trash, yeah, dont be going down memory lane man, yll jinx thuh vibe I got going in here. Gracell be walking in here and wrinkling up her nose cause you done jinxed up thuh joint with yr raggedy recollections.
LINCOLN: We had some great times in that house, bro. Selling lemonade on thuh corner, thuh treehouse out back, summers spent lying in thuh grass and looking at thuh stars.
BOOTH: We never did none of that shit.
LINCOLN: But we had us some good times. That row of nails I got you to line up behind Dads car so when he backed out the driveway to work —
BOOTH: He came back that night, only time I ever seen his face go red, 4 flat tires and yelling bout how thuh white man done sabotaged him again.
LINCOLN: And neither of us flinched. Neither of us let on that itd been us.
BOOTH: It was at dinner, right? What were we eating?
LINCOLN: Food.
BOOTH: We was eating pork chops, mashed potatoes and peas. I remember cause I had to look at them peas real hard to keep from letting on. And I would glance over at you, not really glancing not actually turning my head, but I was looking at you out thuh corner of my eye. I was sure he was gonna find us out and then he woulda whipped us good. But I kept glancing at you and you was cool, man. Like nothing was going on. You was cooooool.

(Rest)

What time is it?
LINCOLN: After 3.

(Rest)

You should call her. Something mighta happened.
BOOTH: No man, Im cool. She'll be here in a minute. Patience is a virtue. She'll be here.

LINCOLN: You look sad.
BOOTH: Nope. Im just, you know, Im just —
LINCOLN: Cool.
BOOTH: Yeah. Cool.

Booth comes over, takes the bottle of whiskey and pours himself a big glassful. He returns to the window looking out and drinking.

BOOTH: They give you a severance package, at thuh job?
LINCOLN: A weeks pay.
BOOTH: Great.
LINCOLN: I blew it. Spent it all.
BOOTH: On what?
LINCOLN: — . Just spent it.

(Rest)

It felt good, spending it. Felt really good. Like back in thuh day when I was really making money. Throwing thuh cards all day and strutting and rutting all night. Didnt have to take no shit from no fool, didnt have to worry about getting fired in favor of some damn wax dummy. I was thuh shit and they was my fools.

(Rest)

Back in thuh day.

(Rest)

(Rest)

Why you think they left us, man?
BOOTH: Mom and Pops? I dont think about it too much.
LINCOLN: I dont think they liked us.
BOOTH: Naw. That aint it.
LINCOLN: I think there was something out there that they liked more than they liked us and for years they was struggling against moving towards that more liked something. Each of them had a special something that they was struggling against. Moms had hers. Pops had his. And they was struggling. We moved out of that nasty apartment into a house. A whole house. It wernt perfect but it was a house and theyd bought it and they brought us there and everything we owned, figuring we could be a family in that house and them things, them two separate things each of them was struggling against, would just leave them be. Them things would see thuh house and be impressed and just leave them be. Would see thuh job Pops had and how he shined his shoes every night before he went to bed, shining them shoes whether they needed it or not, and thuh thing he was struggling against would see all that and just let him be, and thuh thing Moms was struggling against, it would see the food on the table every night and listen to her voice when she'd read to us sometimes, the clean clothes, the buttons sewed on all right and it would just let her be. Just let us all be, just regular people living in a house. That wernt too much to ask.
BOOTH: Least we was grown when they split.
LINCOLN: 16 and 13 aint grown.

BOOTH: 16s grown. Almost. And I was ok cause you were there.

(*Rest*)

Shit man, it aint like they both one day both, together packed all they shit up and left us so they could have fun in thuh sun on some tropical island and you and me would have to grub in thuh dirt forever. They didnt leave together. That makes it different. She left. 2 years go by. Then he left. Like neither of them couldnt handle it no more. She split then he split. Like thuh whole family mortgage bills going to work thing was just too much. And I dont blame them. You dont see me holding down a steady job. Cause its bullshit and I know it. I seen how it cracked them up and I aint going there.

(*Rest*)

It aint right me trying to make myself into a one woman man just because she wants me like that. One woman rubber-wearing motherfucker. Shit. Not me. She gonna walk in here looking all hot and shit trying to see how much she can get me to sweat, how much she can get me to give her before she gives me mines. Shit.

LINCOLN

BOOTH

LINCOLN: Moms told me I shouldnt never get married.

BOOTH: She told me thuh same thing.

LINCOLN: They gave us each 500 bucks then they cut out.

BOOTH: Thats what Im gonna do. Give my kids 500 bucks then cut out. Thats thuh way to do it.

LINCOLN: You dont got no kids.

BOOTH: Im gonna have kids then Im gonna cut out.

LINCOLN: Leaving each of yr offspring 500 bucks as yr splitting.

BOOTH: Yeah.

(*Rest*)

Just goes to show Mom and Pops had some agreement between them.

LINCOLN: How so.

BOOTH: Theyd stopped talking to eachother. Theyd stopped *screwing* eachother. But they had an agreement. Somewhere in there when it looked like all they had was hate they sat down and did thuh "split" budget.

(*Rest*)

When Moms splits she gives me 5 hundred-dollar bills rolled up and tied up tight in one of her nylon stockings. She tells me to put it in a safe place, to spend it only in case of an emergency, and not to tell nobody I got it, not even you. 2 years later Pops splits and before he goes —

LINCOLN: He slips me 10 fifties in a clean handkerchief: "Hide this somewheres good, dont go blowing it, dont tell no one you got it, especially that Booth."

BOOTH: Theyd been scheming together all along. They left separately but they was in agreement. Maybe they arrived at the same place at the same time, maybe they renewed they wedding vows, maybe they got another family.

LINCOLN: Maybe they got 2 new kids. 2 boys. Different than us, though. Better.

BOOTH: Maybe.

Their glasses are empty. The whiskey bottle is empty too. Booth takes the champagne bottle from the ice tub. He pops the cork and pours drinks for his brother and himself.

BOOTH: I didnt mind them leaving cause you was there. Thats why Im hooked on us working together. If we could work together it would be like old times. They split and we got that room downtown. You was done with school and I stopped going. And we had to run around doing odd jobs just to keep the lights on and the heat going and thuh child protection bitch off our backs. It was you and me against thuh world, Link. It could be like that again.

LINCOLN

BOOTH

LINCOLN

BOOTH

LINCOLN: Throwing thuh cards aint as easy as it looks.

BOOTH: I aint stupid.

LINCOLN: When you hung with us back then, you was just on thuh sidelines. Thuh perspective from thuh sidelines is thuh perspective of a customer. There was all kinds of things you didnt know nothing about.

BOOTH: Lonny would entice folks into thuh game as they walked by. Thuh 2 folks on either side of ya looked like they was playing but they was only pretending tuh play. Just tuh generate excitement. You was moving thuh cards as fast as you could hoping that yr hands would be faster than yr customers eyes. Sometimes you won sometimes you lost what else is there to know?

LINCOLN: Thuh customer is actually called the "Mark." You know why?

BOOTH: Cause hes thuh one you got yr eye on. You mark him with yr eye.

LINCOLN

LINCOLN

BOOTH: Im right, right?

LINCOLN: Lemmie show you a few moves. If you pick up these yll have a chance.

BOOTH: Yr playing.

LINCOLN: Get thuh cards and set it up.

BOOTH: No shit.

LINCOLN: Set it up set it up.

In a flash, Booth clears away the romantic table setting by gathering it all up in the tablecloth and tossing it aside. As he does so he reveals the "table" underneath: the 2 stacked monte milk crates and the cardboard playing surface. Lincoln lays out the cards. The brothers are ready. Lincoln begins to teach Booth in earnest.

LINCOLN: Thuh deuce of spades is thuh card tuh watch.

BOOTH: I work with thuh deuce of hearts. But spades is cool.

LINCOLN: Theres thuh Dealer, thuh Stickman, thuh Sides, thuh Lookout and thuh Mark. I'll be thuh Dealer.

BOOTH: I'll be thuh Lookout. Lemmie be thuh Lookout, right? I'll keep an eye for thuh cops. I got my piece on me.

LINCOLN: You got it on you right now?

BOOTH: I always carry it.

LINCOLN: Even on a date? In yr own home?

BOOTH: You never know, man.

(*Rest*)

So Im thuh Lookout.

LINCOLN: Gimmie yr piece.

Booth gives Lincoln his gun. Lincoln moves the little wooden chair to face right in front of the setup. He then puts the gun on the chair.

LINCOLN: We dont need nobody standing on the corner watching for cops cause there aint none.

BOOTH: I'll be thuh Stickman, then.

LINCOLN: Stickman knows the game inside out. You aint there yet. But you will be. You wanna learn good, be my Sideman. Playing along with the Dealer, moving the Mark to lay his money down. You wanna learn, right?

BOOTH: I'll be thuh Side.

LINCOLN: Good.

(*Rest*)

First thing you learn is what is. Next thing you learn is what aint. You dont know what is you dont know what aint, you dont know shit.

BOOTH: Right.

LINCOLN

BOOTH

BOOTH: Whatchu looking at?

LINCOLN: Im sizing you up.

BOOTH: Oh yeah?!

LINCOLN: Dealer always sizes up thuh crowd.

BOOTH: Im yr Side, Link, Im on yr team, you dont go sizing up yr own team. You save looks like that for yr Mark.

LINCOLN: Dealer always sizes up thuh crowd. Everybody out there is part of the crowd. His crew is part of the crowd, he himself is part of the crowd. Dealer always sizes up thuh crowd.

Lincoln looks Booth over some more then looks around at an imaginary crowd.

BOOTH: Then what then what?

LINCOLN: Dealer dont wanna play.

BOOTH: Bullshit man! Come on you promised!

LINCOLN: Thats thuh Dealers attitude. He *acts* like he dont wanna play. He holds back and thuh crowd, with their eagerness to see his skill and their willing-

ness to take a chance, and their greediness to win his cash, the larceny in their hearts, all goad him on and push him to throw his cards, although of course the Dealer has been wanting to throw his cards all along. Only he dont never show it.

BOOTH: Thats some sneaky shit, Link.

LINCOLN: It sets thuh mood. You wanna have them in yr hand before you deal a hand, K?

BOOTH: Cool. — K.

LINCOLN: Right.

LINCOLN

BOOTH

BOOTH: You sizing me up again?

LINCOLN: Theres 2 parts to throwing thuh cards. Both parts are fairly complicated. Thuh moves and thuh grooves, thuh talk and thuh walk, thuh patter and thuh pitter pat, thuh flap and thuh rap: what yr doing with yr mouth and what yr doing with yr hands.

BOOTH: I got thuh words down pretty good.

LINCOLN: You need to work on both.

BOOTH: K.

LINCOLN: A goodlooking walk and a dynamite talk captivates their entire attention. The Mark focuses with 2 organs primarily: his eyes and his ears. Leave one out you lose yr shirt. Captivate both, yr golden.

BOOTH: So them times I seen you lose, them times I seen thuh Mark best you, that was a time when yr hands werent fast enough or yr patter werent right.

LINCOLN: You could say that.

BOOTH: So, there was plenty of times —

Lincoln moves the cards around.

LINCOLN: You see what Im doing? Dont look at my hands, man, look at my eyes. Know what is and know what aint.

BOOTH: What is?

LINCOLN: My eyes.

BOOTH: What aint?

LINCOLN: My hands. Look at my eyes not my hands. And you standing there thinking how thuh fuck I gonna learn how tuh throw thuh cards if I be looking in his eyes? Look into my eyes and get yr focus. Dont think about learning how tuh throw thuh cards. Dont think about nothing. Just look into my eyes. Focus.

BOOTH: Theyre red.

LINCOLN: Look into my eyes.

BOOTH: You been crying?

LINCOLN: Just look into my eyes, fool. Now. Look down at thuh cards. I been moving and moving and moving them around. Ready?

BOOTH: Yeah.

LINCOLN: Ok, Sideman, thuh Marks got his eye on you. Yr gonna show him its easy.

BOOTH: K.

LINCOLN: Pick out thuh deuce of spades. Dont pick it up just point to it.

BOOTH: This one, right?

LINCOLN: Dont ask thuh Dealer if yr right, man, point to yr card with confidence.

Booth points.

BOOTH: That one.

(*Rest*)

Flip it over, man.

Lincoln flips over the card. It is in fact the deuce of spades. Booth struts around gloating like a rooster. Lincoln is mildly crestfallen.

BOOTH: Am I right or am I right?! Make room for 3-Card! Here comes thuh champ!

LINCOLN: Cool. Stay focused. Now we gonna add the second element. Listen.

Lincoln moves the cards and speaks in a low hypnotic voice.

LINCOLN: Lean in close and watch me now: who see thuh black card who see thuh black card I see thuh black card black cards thuh winner pick thuh black card thats thuh winner pick thuh red card thats thuh loser pick thuh other red card thats thuh other loser pick thuh black card you pick thuh winner. Watch me as I throw thuh cards. Here we go.

(*Rest*)

Who see thuh black card who see thuh black card? You pick thuh red card you pick a loser you pick that red card you pick a loser you pick thuh black card thuh deuce of spades you pick a winner who sees thuh deuce of spades thuh one who sees it never fades watch me now as I throw thuh cards. Red losers black winner follow thuh deuce of spades chase thuh black deuce. Dark deuce will get you thuh win. One good pickll get you in 2 good picks you gone win. 10 will get you 20, 20 will get you 40.

(*Rest*)

Ima show you thuh cards: 2 red cards but only one spade. Dark winner in thuh center and thuh red losers on thuh sides. Pick uh red card you got a loser pick thuh other red card you got a loser pick thuh black card you got a winner. Watch me watch me watch me now.

(*Rest*)

Ok, 3-Card, you know which cards thuh deuce of spades?

BOOTH: Yeah.

LINCOLN: You sure? Yeah? You sure you sure or you just think you sure? Oh you sure you sure huh? Was you watching Links lightning fast express? Was you watching Link cause he the best? So you sure, huh? Point it out. Now, place yr bet and Linkll turn over yr card.

BOOTH: What should I bet?

LINCOLN: Dont bet nothing man, we just playing. Slap me 5 and point out thuh deuce.

Booth slaps Lincoln 5, then points out a card which Lincoln flips over. It is in fact again the deuce of spades.

BOOTH: Yeah, baby! 3-Card got thuh moves! You didnt know lil bro had thuh stuff, huh? Think again, Link, think again.

LINCOLN: You wanna learn or you wanna run yr mouth?

BOOTH: Thought you had fast hands. Wassup? What happened tuh "Links Lightning Fast Express"? Turned into uh local train looks like tuh me.

LINCOLN: Thats yr whole motherfucking problem. Yr so busy running yr mouth you aint never gonna learn nothing! You think you something but you aint shit.

BOOTH: I aint shit, I am *The* Shit. Shit. Wheres thuh dark deuce? Right there! *Yes*, baby!

LINCOLN: Ok, 3-Card. Cool. Lets switch. Take thuh cards and show me whatcha got. Go on. Dont touch thuh cards too heavy just — its a light touch. Like yr touching Graces skin. Or, whatever, man, just a light touch. Like uh whisper.

BOOTH: Like uh whisper.

Booth moves the cards around, in an awkward imitation of his brother.

LINCOLN: Good.

BOOTH: Yeah. All right. Look into my eyes.

Booths speech is loud and his movements are jerky. He is doing worse than when he threw the cards at the top of the play.

BOOTH: Watch-me-close-watch-me-close-now: who-see-thuh-dark-card-who-see-thuh-dark-card? I-see-thuh-dark-card. Here-it-is. Thuh-dark-card-is-thuh-winner. Pick-thuh-dark-card-and-you-pick-uh-winner. Pick-uh-red-card-and-you-pick-uh-loser. Theres-thuh-loser-yeah-theres-thuh-red-card, theres-thuh-other-loser-and-theres-thuh-black-card, thuh-winner. Watch-me-close-watch-me-close-now: 3-Card-throws-thuh-cards-lightning-fast. 3-Card-thats-me-and-Ima-last. Watch-me-throw-cause-here-I-go. See thuh black card? Yeah? Who see I see you see thuh black card?

LINCOLN: Hahahahhahahahahahahah!

Lincoln doubles over laughing. Booth puts on his coat and pockets his gun.

BOOTH: What?

LINCOLN: Nothing, man, nothing.

BOOTH: *What?!*

LINCOLN: Yr just, yr just a little wild with it. You talk like that on thuh street cards or no cards and theyll lock you up, man. Shit. Reminds me of that time when you hung with us and we let you try being thuh Stick cause you wanted to so bad. Thuh hustle was so simple. Remember? I told you that when I put my hand in my left pocket you was to get thuh Mark tuh pick thuh card on that side. You got to thinking something like Links left means my left some dyslexic shit and turned thuh wrong card. There was 800 bucks on the line and you fucked it up.

(*Rest*)

But it was cool, little bro, cause we made the money back. It worked out cool.

(*Rest*)

So, yeah, I said a light touch, little bro. Throw thuh cards light. Like uh whisper.

BOOTH: Like Graces skin.

LINCOLN: Like Graces skin.

BOOTH: What time is it?

Lincoln holds up his watch. Booth takes a look.

BOOTH: Bitch. *Bitch!* She said she was gonna show up around 8. 8-a-fucking-clock.

LINCOLN: Maybe she meant 8 *a.m.*

BOOTH: Yeah. She gonna come all up in my place talking bout how she *love* me. How she cant stop *thinking* bout me. Nother mans shit up in her nother mans thing in her nother mans dick on her breath.

LINCOLN: Maybe something happened to her.

BOOTH: Something happened to her all right. She trying to make a chump outa me. I aint her chump. I aint nobodys chump.

LINCOLN: Sit. I'll go to the payphone on the corner. I'll —

BOOTH: Thuh world puts its foot in yr face and you dont move. You tell thuh world tuh keep on stepping. But Im my own man, Link. I aint you.

Booth goes out, slamming the door behind him.

LINCOLN: You got that right.

After a moment Lincoln picks up the cards. He moves them around fast, faster, faster.

SCENE SIX

Thursday night. The room looks empty, as if neither brother is home. Lincoln comes in. Hes fairly drunk. He strides in, leaving the door slightly ajar.

LINCOLN: Taaadaaaa!

(*Rest*)

(*Rest*

Taadaa. motherfucker. Taadaa!

(*Rest*)

Booth — uh, 3-Card — you here? Nope. Good. Just as well. HaHa *Ha Ha Ha*!

He pulls an enormous wad of money from his pocket. He counts it, slowly and luxuriously, arranging and smoothing the bills and sounding the amounts under his breath. He neatly rolls up the money, secures it with a rubber band and puts it back in his pocket. He relaxes in his chair. Then he takes the money out again, counting it all over again, but this time quickly, with the touch of an expert hustler.

LINCOLN: You didnt go back, Link, you got back, you got it back you got yr shit back in thuh saddle, man, you got back in business. Walking in Luckys and you seen how they was looking at you? Lucky starts pouring for you when you walk in. And the women. You see how they was looking at you? Bought drinks for everybody. Bought drinks for Lucky. Bought drinks for Luckys damn dog. Shit. And thuh women be hanging on me and purring. And I be feeling that old call of thuh wild calling. I got more phone numbers in my pockets between thuh time I walked out that door and thuh time I walked back in than I got in my whole life. Cause my shit is *back*. And back better than it was when it left too. Shoot. Who thuh man? Link. Thats right. Purrrrring all up on me and letting me touch them and promise them shit. 3 of them sweethearts in thuh restroom on my dick all at once and I was *there* my shit was there. And Cookie just went out of my mind which is cool which is very cool. 3 of them. Fighting over it. Shit. Cause they knew I'd been throwing thuh cards. Theyd seen me on thuh corner with thuh old crew or if they aint seed me with they own eyes theyd heard word. Links thuh stink! Theyd heard word and they seed uh sad face on some poor sucker or a tear in thuh eye of some stupid fucking tourist and they figured it was me whod just took thuh suckers last dime, it was me who had all thuh suckers loot. They knew. They knew.

Booth appears in the room. He was standing behind the screen, unseen all this time. He goes to the door, soundlessly, just stands there.

LINCOLN: And they was all in Luckys. Shit. And they was waiting for me to come in from my last throw. Cant take too many fools in one day, its bad luck, Link, so they was all waiting in there for me to come in thuh door and let thuh liquor start flowing and thuh music start going and let thuh boys who dont have thuh balls to get nothing but a regular job and uh weekly paycheck, let them crowd around and get in somehow on thuh excitement, and make way for thuh ladies, so they can run they hands on my clothes and feel thuh magic and imagine thuh man, with plenty to go around, living and breathing underneath.

(*Rest*)

They all thought I was down and out! They all thought I was some NoCount HasBeen LostCause motherfucker. But I got my shit back. Thats right. They stepped on me and kept right on stepping. Not no more. Who thuh man?! Goddamnit, who thuh —

Booth closes the door.

LINCOLN
BOOTH

(*Rest*)

LINCOLN: Another evening to remember, huh?

BOOTH (*Rest*): Uh — yeah, man, yeah. Thats right, thats right.
LINCOLN: Had me a memorable evening myself.
BOOTH: I got news.

(*Rest*)

What you been up to?
LINCOLN: Yr news first.
BOOTH: Its good.
LINCOLN: Yeah?
BOOTH: Yeah.
LINCOLN: Go head then.
BOOTH (*Rest*): Grace got down on her knees. Down on her knees, man. Asked *me* tuh marry *her*.
LINCOLN: Shit.
BOOTH: Amazing Grace!
LINCOLN: Lucky you, man.
BOOTH: And guess where she was, I mean, while I was here waiting for her. She was over at her house watching tv. I'd told her come over Thursday and I got it all wrong and was thinking I said Wednesday and here I was sitting waiting my ass off and all she was doing was over at her house just watching tv.
LINCOLN: Howboutthat.
BOOTH: She wants to get married right away. Shes tired of waiting. Feels her clock ticking and shit. Wants to have my baby. But dont look so glum man, we gonna have a boy and we gonna name it after you.
LINCOLN: Thats great, man. Thats really great.
BOOTH
LINCOLN
BOOTH: Whats yr news?
LINCOLN (*Rest*) Nothing.
BOOTH: Mines good news, huh?
LINCOLN: Yeah. Real good news, bro.
BOOTH: Bad news is — well, shes real set on us living together. And she always did like this place.

(*Rest*)

Yr gonna have to leave. Sorry.
LINCOLN: No sweat.
BOOTH: This was only a temporary situation anyhow.
LINCOLN: No sweat man. You got a new life opening up for you, no sweat. Graces moving in today? I can leave right now.
BOOTH: I dont mean to put you out.
LINCOLN: No sweat. I'll just pack up.

Lincoln rummages around finding a suitcase and begins to pack his things.

BOOTH: Just like that, huh? "No sweat"?! Yesterday you lost yr damn job. You dont got no cash. You dont got no friends, no nothing, but you clearing out just like that and its "no sweat"?!
LINCOLN: Youve been real generous and you and Grace need me gone and its time I found my own place.
BOOTH: No sweat.
LINCOLN: No sweat.

(*Rest*)

K. I'll spill it. I got another job, so getting my own place aint gonna be so bad.
BOOTH: You got a new job! Doing what?
LINCOLN: Security guard.
BOOTH (*Rest*): Security guard. Howaboutthat.

Lincoln continues packing the few things he has. He picks up a whiskey bottle.

BOOTH: Go head, take thuh med-sin, bro. You gonna need it more than me. I got, you know, I got my love to keep me warm and shit.
LINCOLN: You gonna have to get some kind of work, or are you gonna let Grace support you?
BOOTH: I got plans.
LINCOLN: She might want you now but she wont want you for long if you dont get some kind of job. Shes a smart chick. And she cares about you. But she aint gonna let you treat her like some pack mule while shes out working her ass off and yr laying up in here scheming and dreaming to cover up thuh fact that you dont got no skills.
BOOTH: Grace is very cool with who I am and where Im at, thank you.
LINCOLN: It was just some advice. But, hey, yr doing great just like yr doing.
LINCOLN
BOOTH
LINCOLN
BOOTH
BOOTH: When Pops left he didnt take nothing with him. I always thought that was fucked-up.
LINCOLN: He was a drunk. Everything he did was always half regular and half fucked-up.
BOOTH: Whyd he leave his clothes though? Even drunks gotta wear clothes.
LINCOLN: Whyd he leave his clothes whyd he leave us? He was uh drunk, bro. He — whatever, right? I mean, you aint gonna figure it out by thinking about it. Just call it one of thuh great unsolved mysteries of existence.
BOOTH: Moms had a man on thuh side.
LINCOLN: Yeah? Pops had side shit going on too. More than one. He would take me with him when he went to visit them. Yeah.

(*Rest*)

Sometimes he'd let me meet the ladies. They was all very nice. Very polite. Most of them real pretty. Sometimes he'd let me watch. Most of thuh time I was just outside on thuh porch or in thuh lobby or in thuh car waiting for him but sometimes he'd let me watch.
BOOTH: What was it like?
LINCOLN: Nothing. It wasnt like nothing. He made it seem like it was this big deal this great thing he was letting me witness but it wasnt like nothing.

(*Rest*)

One of his ladies liked me, so I would do her after he'd done her. On thuh sly though. He'd be laying

there, spent and sleeping and snoring and her and me
would be sneaking it.
BOOTH: Shit.
LINCOLN: It was alright.
BOOTH
LINCOLN

*Lincoln takes his crumpled Abe Lincoln getup from the
closet. Isnt sure what to do with it.*

BOOTH: Im gonna miss you coming home in that getup. I
dont even got a picture of you in it for the album.
LINCOLN (*Rest*): Hell, I'll put it on. Get thuh camera get
thuh camera.
BOOTH: Yeah?
LINCOLN: What thuh fuck, right?
BOOTH: Yeah, what thuh fuck.

*Booth scrambles around the apartment and finds the
camera. Lincoln quickly puts on the getup, including 2
thin smears of white pancake makeup, more like war
paint than whiteface.*

LINCOLN: They didnt fire me cause I wasnt no good. They
fired me cause they was cutting back. Me getting dis-
missed didnt have no reflection on my performance.
And I was a damn good Honest Abe considering.
BOOTH: Yeah. You look great man, really great. Fix yr
hat. Get in thuh light. Smile.
LINCOLN: Lincoln didnt never smile.
BOOTH: Sure he smiled.
LINCOLN: No he didnt, man, you seen thuh pictures of
him. In all his pictures he was real serious.
BOOTH: You got a new job, yr having a good day, right?
LINCOLN: Yeah.
BOOTH: So smile.
LINCOLN: Snapshots gonna look pretty stupid with me —

Booth takes a picture.

BOOTH: Thisll look great in thuh album.
LINCOLN: Lets take one together, you and me.
BOOTH: No thanks. Save the film for the wedding.
LINCOLN: This wasnt a bad job. I just outgrew it. I could
put in a word for you down there, maybe when busi-
ness picks up again theyd hire you.
BOOTH: No thanks. That shit aint for me. I aint into pre-
tending Im someone else all day.
LINCOLN: I was just sitting there in thuh getup. I wasnt
pretending nothing.
BOOTH: What was going on in yr head?
LINCOLN: I would make up songs and shit.
BOOTH: And think about women.
LINCOLN: Sometimes.
BOOTH: Cookie.
LINCOLN: Sometimes.
BOOTH: And how she came over here one night looking
for you.
LINCOLN: I was at Luckys.
BOOTH: She didnt know that.
LINCOLN: I was drinking.

BOOTH: All she knew was you couldnt get it up. You
couldnt get it up with her so in her head you was
tired of her and had gone out to screw somebody
new and this time maybe werent never coming back.

(*Rest*)

She had me pour her a drink or 2. I didnt want to. She
wanted to get back at you by having some fun of her
own and when I told her to go out and have it, she
said she wanted to have her fun right here. With me.

(*Rest*)

[And then, just like that, she changed her mind.

(*Rest*)

But she'd hooked me. That bad part of me that I fight
down everyday. You beat yrs down and it stays there
dead but mine keeps coming up for another round.
And she hooked the bad part of me. And the bad part
of me opened my mouth and started promising her
things. Promising her things I knew she wanted and
you couldnt give her. And the bad part of me took
her clothing off and carried her into thuh bed and
had her, Link, yr Cookie. It wasnt just thuh bad part
of me it was all of me, man,] I had her. Yr damn wife.
Right in that bed.
LINCOLN: I used to think about her all thuh time but I
dont think about her no more.
BOOTH: I told her if she dumped you I'd marry her but I
changed my mind.
LINCOLN: I dont think about her no more.
BOOTH: You dont go back.
LINCOLN: Nope.
BOOTH: Cause you cant. No matter what you do you
cant get back to being who you was. Best you can do
is just pretend to be yr old self.
LINCOLN: Yr outa yr mind.
BOOTH: Least Im still me!
LINCOLN: Least I work. You never did like to work. You
better come up with some kinda way to bring home
the bacon or Gracell drop you like a hot rock.
BOOTH: I got plans!
LINCOLN: Yeah, you gonna throw thuh cards, right?
BOOTH: Thats right!
LINCOLN: You a double left-handed motherfucker who
dont stand a chance in all get out there throwing
no cards.
BOOTH: You scared.
LINCOLN: Im gone.

Lincoln goes to leave.

BOOTH: Fuck that!
LINCOLN: Yr standing in my way.
BOOTH: You scared I got yr shit.
LINCOLN: The only part of my shit you got is the part of
my shit you think you got and that aint shit.
BOOTH: Did I pick right them last times? Yes. Oh, I got
yr shit.
LINCOLN: Set up the cards.

BOOTH: Thought you was gone.

LINCOLN: Set it up.

BOOTH: I got yr shit and Ima go out there and be thuh man and you aint gonna be nothin.

LINCOLN: Set it up!

Booth hurriedly sets up the milk crates and cardboard top. Lincoln throws the cards.

LINCOLN: Lean in close and watch me now: who see thuh black card who see thuh black card I see thuh black card black cards thuh winner pick thuh black card thats thuh winner pick thuh red card thats thuh loser pick thuh other red card thats thuh other loser pick thuh black card you pick thuh winner. Who see thuh black card who see thuh black card? You pick thuh red card you pick a loser you pick that red card you pick a loser you pick thuh black card thuh deuce of spades you pick a winner who sees thuh deuce of spades thuh one who sees it never fades watch me now as I throw thuh cards. Red losers black winner follow thuh deuce of spades chase thuh black deuce. Dark deuce will get you thuh win. 10 will get you 20, 20 will get you 40. One good pickll get you in 2 good picks and you gone win.

(Rest)

Ok, man, wheres thuh black deuce?

Booth points to a card. Lincoln flips it over. It is the deuce of spades.

BOOTH: Who thuh man?!

Lincoln turns over the other 2 cards, looking at them confusedly.

LINCOLN: Hhhhh.

BOOTH: Who thuh man, Link?! Huh? Who thuh man, Link?!?!

LINCOLN: You thuh man, man.

BOOTH: I got yr shit down.

LINCOLN: Right.

BOOTH: "Right"? All you saying is "right"?

(Rest)

You was out on the street throwing. Just today. Werent you? You wasnt gonna tell me.

LINCOLN: Tell you what?

BOOTH: That you was out throwing.

LINCOLN: I was gonna tell you, sure. Cant go and leave my little bro out thuh loop, can I? Didnt say nothing cause I thought you heard. Did all right today but Im still rusty, I guess. But hey — yr getting good.

BOOTH: But I'll get out there on thuh street and still fuck up, wont I?

LINCOLN: You seem pretty good, bro.

BOOTH: You gotta do it for real, man.

LINCOLN: I am doing it for real. And yr getting good.

BOOTH: I dunno. It didnt feel real. Kinda felt — well it didnt feel real.

LINCOLN: We're missing the essential elements. The crowd, the street, thuh traffic sounds, all that.

BOOTH: We missing something else too, thuh thing thatll really make it real.

LINCOLN: Whassat, bro?

BOOTH: Thuh cash. Its just bullshit without thuh money. Put some money down on thuh table then itd be real, then youd do it for real, then I'd win it for real.

(Rest)

And dont be looking all glum like that. I know you got money. A whole pocketful. Put it down.

LINCOLN

BOOTH

BOOTH: You scared of losing it to thuh man, chump? Put it down, less you think thuh kid who got two left hands is gonna give you uh left hook. Put it down, bro, put it down.

Lincoln takes the roll of bills from his pocket and places it on the table.

BOOTH: How much you got there?

LINCOLN: 500 bucks.

BOOTH: Cool.

(Rest)

Ready?

LINCOLN: Does it feel real?

BOOTH: Yeah. Clean slate. Take it from the top. "One good pickll get you in 2 good picks and you gone win."

(Rest)

Go head.

LINCOLN: Watch me now:

BOOTH: Woah, man, woah.

(Rest)

You think Ima chump.

LINCOLN: No I dont.

BOOTH: You aint going full out.

LINCOLN: I was just getting started.

BOOTH: But when you got good and started you wasnt gonna go full out. Ye wasnt gonna go all out. You was gonna do thuh pussy shit, not thuh real shit.

LINCOLN: I put my money down. Money makes it real.

BOOTH: But not if I dont put no money down tuh match it.

LINCOLN: You dont got no money.

BOOTH: I got money!

LINCOLN: You aint worked in years. You dont got shit.

BOOTH: I got money.

LINCOLN: Whatcha been doing, skimming off my weekly paycheck and squirreling it away?

BOOTH: I got money.

(Rest)

They stand there sizing eachother up. Booth breaks away, going over to his hiding place from which he gets an old nylon stocking with money in the toe, a knot holding the money secure.

LINCOLN
BOOTH
BOOTH: You know she was putting her stuff in plastic bags? She was just putting her stuff in plastic bags not putting but shoving. She was shoving her stuff in plastic bags and I was standing in thuh doorway watching her and she was so busy shoving thuh shit she didnt see me. "I aint made of money," thats what he always saying. The guy she had on the side. I would catch them together sometimes. Thuh first time I cut school I got tired of hanging out so I goes home — figured I could tell Mom I was sick and cover my ass. Come in thuh house real slow cause Im sick and moving slow and quiet. He had her bent over. They both had all they clothes on like they was about to do something like go out dancing cause they was dressed to thuh 9s but at thuh last minute his pants had fallen down and her dress had flown up and theyd ended up doing something else.

(*Rest*)

They didnt see me come in, they didnt see me watching them, they didnt see me going out. That was uh Thursday. Something told me tuh cut school thuh next Thursday and sure enough — . He was her Thursday man. Every Thursday. Yeah. And Thursday nights she was always all cleaned up and fresh and smelling nice. Serving up dinner. And Pops would grab her cause she was all bright and she would look at me, like she didnt know that I knew but she was asking me not to tell nohow. She was asking me to — oh who knows.

(*Rest*)

She was talking with him one day, her sideman, her Thursday dude, her backdoor man, she needed some money for something, thered been some kind of problem some kind of mistake had been made some kind of mistake that needed cleaning up and she was asking Mr. Thursday for some money to take care of it. "I aint made of money," he says. He was putting his foot down. And then there she was 2 months later not showing yet, maybe she'd got rid of it maybe she hadnt maybe she'd stuffed it along with all her other things in them plastic bags while he waited outside in thuh car with thuh motor running. She musta known I was gonna walk in on her this time cause she had my payoff — my *inheritance* — she had it all ready for me. 500 dollars in a nylon stocking. Huh.

He places the stuffed nylon stocking on the table across from Lincolns money roll.

BOOTH: Now its real.
LINCOLN: Dont put that down.
BOOTH: Throw thuh cards.
LINCOLN: I dont want to play.

BOOTH: Throw thuh fucking cards, man!!
LINCOLN (*Rest*): 2 red cards but only one black. Pick thuh black you pick thuh winner. All thuh cards are face down you point out thuh cards and then you move them around. Now watch me now, now watch me real close. Put thuh winning deuce down in the center put thuh loser reds on either side then you just move thuh cards around. Move them slow or move them fast, Links thuh king he gonna last.

(*Rest*)

Wheres thuh deuce of spades?

Booth chooses a card and chooses correctly.

BOOTH: HA!
LINCOLN: One good pickll get you in 2 good picks and you gone win.
BOOTH: I know man I know.
LINCOLN: Im just doing thuh talk.
BOOTH: Throw thuh fucking cards!

Lincoln throws the cards.

LINCOLN: Lean in close and watch me now: who see thuh black card who see thuh black card I see thuh black card black cards thuh winner pick thuh black card thats thuh winner pick thuh red card thats thuh loser pick thuh other red card thats thuh other loser pick thuh black card you pick thuh winner. Watch me as I throw thuh cards. Here we go.

(*Rest*)

Ima show you thuh cards: 2 red cards but only one spade. Dark winner in thuh center and thuh red losers on thuh sides. Pick uh red card you got a loser pick thuh other red card you got a loser pick thuh black card you got a winner. Watch me watch me watch me now.

(*Rest*)

Who see thuh black card who see thuh black card? You pick thuh red card you pick a loser you pick that red card you pick a loser you pick thuh black card thuh deuce of spades you pick a winner who sees thuh deuce of spades thuh one who sees it never fades watch me now as I throw thuh cards. Red losers black winner follow thuh deuce of spades chase thuh black deuce. Dark deuce will get you thuh win.

(*Rest*)

Ok, 3-Card, you know which cards thuh deuce of spades? This is for real now, man. You pick wrong Im in yr wad and I keep mines. You pick wrong Im in yr wad and I keep mines.
BOOTH: I pick right I got yr shit.
LINCOLN: Yeah.
BOOTH: Plus I beat you for real.
LINCOLN: Yeah.

(*Rest*)

You think we're really brothers?

BOOTH: Huh?

LINCOLN: I know we *brothers,* but is we really brothers, you know, blood brothers or not, you and me, what-duhyathink?

BOOTH: I think we're brothers.

BOOTH

LINCOLN

BOOTH

LINCOLN

BOOTH

LINCOLN

LINCOLN: Go head man, wheres thuh deuce?

In a flash Booth points out a card.

LINCOLN: You sure?

BOOTH: Im sure!

LINCOLN: Yeah? Dont touch thuh cards, now.

BOOTH: Im sure.

The 2 brothers lock eyes. Lincoln turns over the card that Booth selected and Booth, in a desperate break of concentration, glances down to see that he has chosen the wrong card.

LINCOLN: Deuce of hearts, bro. Im sorry. Thuh deuce of spades was this one.

(Rest)

I guess all this is mines.

He slides the money toward himself.

LINCOLN: You were almost right. Better luck next time.

(Rest)

Aint yr fault if yr eyes aint fast. And you cant help it if you got 2 left hands, right? Throwing cards aint thuh whole world. You got other shit going for you. You got Grace.

BOOTH: Right.

LINCOLN: Whassamatter?

BOOTH: Mm.

LINCOLN: Whatsup?

BOOTH: Nothing.

LINCOLN:

(Rest)

It takes a certain kind of understanding to be able to play this game.

(Rest)

I still got thuh moves, dont I?

BOOTH: Yeah you still got thuh moves.

Lincoln cant help himself. He chuckles.

LINCOLN: I aint laughing at you, bro, Im just laughing. Shit there is so much to this game. This game is — there is just so much to it.

Lincoln, still chuckling, flops down in the easy chair. He takes up the nylon stocking and fiddles with the knot.

LINCOLN: Woah, she sure did tie this up tight, didnt she?

BOOTH: Yeah. I aint opened it since she gived it to me.

LINCOLN: Yr kidding. 500 and you aint never opened it? Shit. Sure is tied tight. She said heres 500 bucks and you didnt undo thuh knot to get a look at the cash? You aint needed to take a peek in all these years? Shit. I woulda opened it right away. Just a little peek.

BOOTH: I been saving it.

(Rest)

Oh, dont open it, man.

LINCOLN: How come?

BOOTH: You won it man, you dont gotta go opening it.

LINCOLN: We gotta see whats in it.

BOOTH: We *know* whats in it. Dont open it.

LINCOLN: You are a chump, bro. There could be millions in here! There could be nothing! I'll open it.

BOOTH: Dont.

LINCOLN

BOOTH

(Rest)

LINCOLN: Shit this knot aint coming out. I could cut it, but that would spoil the whole effect, wouldnt it? Shit. Sorry. I aint laughing at you Im just laughing. Theres so much about those cards. You think you can learn them just by watching and just by playing but there is more to them cards than that. And — . Tell me something, Mr. 3-Card, she handed you this stocking and she said there was money in it and then she split and you say you didnt open it. Howd you know she was for real?

BOOTH: She was for real.

LINCOLN: How you know? She coulda been jiving you, bro. Jiving you that there really *was* money in this thing. Jiving you big time. Its like thuh cards. And ooooh you certainly was persistent. But you was in such a hurry to learn thuh last move that you didnt bother learning thuh first one. That was yr mistake. Cause its thuh first move that separates thuh Player from thuh Played. And thuh first move is to know that there aint no winning. It may look like you got a chance but the only time you pick right is when thuh man lets you. And when its thuh real deal, when its thuh real fucking deal, bro, and thuh moneys on thuh line, thats when thuh man wont want you picking right. He will want you picking wrong so he will make you pick wrong. Wrong wrong wrong. Ooooh, you thought you was finally happening, didnt you? You thought yr ship had come in or some shit, huh? Thought you was uh Player. But I played you, bro.

BOOTH: Fuck you. Fuck you FUCK YOU *FUCK YOU*!!

LINCOLN: Whatever, man. Damn this knot is tough. Ima cut it.

Lincoln reaches in his boot, pulling out a knife. He chuckles all the while.

LINCOLN: Im not laughing at you, bro, Im just laughing.

Booth chuckles with him. Lincoln holds the knife high, ready to cut the stocking.

LINCOLN: Turn yr head. You may not wanna look.

Booth turns away slightly. They both continue laughing. Lincoln brings the knife down to cut the stocking.

BOOTH: I popped her.
LINCOLN: Huh?
BOOTH: Grace. I popped her. Grace.

(Rest)

> Who thuh fuck she think she is doing me like she done? Telling me I dont got nothing going on. I showed her what I got going on. Popped her good. Twice. 3 times. Whatever.

(Rest)

> She aint dead.

(Rest)

> She werent wearing my ring I gived her. Said it was too small. Fuck that. Said it hurt her. Fuck that. Said she was into bigger things. *Fuck* that. Shes alive not to worry, she aint going out that easy, shes alive shes shes — .

LINCOLN: Dead. Shes —
BOOTH: Dead.
LINCOLN: Ima give you back yr stocking, man. Here, bro —
BOOTH: Only so long I can stand that little brother shit. Can only take it so long. Im telling you —
LINCOLN: Take it back, man —
BOOTH: That little bro shit had to go —
LINCOLN: Cool —
BOOTH: Like Booth went —
LINCOLN: Here, 3-Card —
BOOTH: That Booth shit is over. 3-Cards thuh man now —
LINCOLN: Ima give you yr stocking back, 3-Card —
BOOTH: Who thuh man now, huh? Who thuh man now?! Think you can fuck with me, motherfucker think again motherfucker think again! Think you can take me like Im just some chump some two left-handed pussy dickbreath chump who you can take and then go laugh at. Aint laughing at me you was just laughing bunch uh bullshit and you know it.
LINCOLN: Here. Take it.
BOOTH: I aint gonna be needing it. Go on. You won it you open it.
LINCOLN: No thanks.
BOOTH: Open it open it open it open it. OPEN IT!!!

(Rest)

> Open it up, bro.

LINCOLN
BOOTH

Lincoln brings the knife down to cut the stocking. In a flash, Booth grabs Lincoln from behind. He pulls his gun and thrusts it into the left side of Lincolns neck. They stop there poised.

LINCOLN: Dont.

Booth shoots Lincoln. Lincoln slumps forward, falling out of his chair and onto the floor. He lies there dead. Booth paces back and forth, like a panther in a cage, holding his gun.

BOOTH: Think you can take my shit? My shit. That shit was mines. I kept it. Saved it. All this while. Through thick and through thin. Through fucking thick and through fucking thin, motherfucker. And you just gonna come up in here and mock my shit and call me two lefthanded talking bout how she coulda been jiving me then go steal from me? My *inheritance.* You stole my *inheritance,* man. That aint right. That aint right and you know it. You had yr own. And you blew it. You *blew* it, motherfucker! I saved mines and you blew yrs. Thinking you all that and blew yr shit. And I *saved* mines.

(Rest)

> You aint gonna be needing yr fucking money-roll no more, dead motherfucker, so I will pocket it thank you.

(Rest)

> Watch me close watch me close now: Ima go out there and make a name for myself that dont have nothing to do with you. And 3-Cards gonna be in everybodys head and in everybodys mouth like Link was.

(Rest)

> Ima take back my inheritance too. It was mines anyhow. Even when you stole it from me it was still mines cause she gave it to me. She didnt give it to you. And I been saving it all this while.

He bends to pick up the money-filled stocking. Then he just crumples. As he sits beside Lincolns body, the money-stocking falls away. Booth holds Lincolns body, hugging him close. He sobs.

BOOTH: *AAAAAAAAAAAAAAAAAAAAH!*

COMMENTARY

Joshua Wolf Shenk
BEYOND A BLACK-AND-WHITE LINCOLN   *2002*

Shenk, who is working on a book on Abraham Lincoln, provides some useful background to Lincoln as he is perceived by contemporary historians and how that history informs the viewer of Topdog/Underdog. *Shenk emphasizes the paradox of Lincoln's ambivalence toward blacks while also emphasizing his repugnance for slavery.*

Abraham Lincoln thought slavery was a "moral, social and political evil," devoted himself to preventing its spread and, as president, issued the Emancipation Proclamation. In the last speech of his life, he supported public schooling for black people and limited suffrage.

At the same time, Lincoln believed there was a "physical difference between the white and black races" that would "forever forbid the two races living together on terms of social and political equality." And, he continued in this 1858 speech, "I, as much as any other man, am in favor of having the superior position assigned to the white race." As president, he ordered emancipation only as a war measure, and even then limited it to slaves living in rebel territory. In the last speech of his life, he said he thought only former Union soldiers and "very intelligent" black people should be able to vote.

Generations who followed Lincoln — heirs to the country he remade — have struggled to resolve these apparent contradictions into a complex whole. What is his legacy for the descendants of slaves? Two plays by Suzan-Lori Parks — one of which, "Topdog/Underdog," is opening tonight on Broadway — offer a fresh and compelling answer.

It has never been easy to talk about Lincoln for what he was, a paradox. In 1922, for instance, W. E. B. Du Bois wrote in the N.A.A.C.P. magazine *The Crisis* that Lincoln was "big enough to be inconsistent — cruel, merciful; peace-loving, a fighter; despising Negroes and letting them fight and vote; protecting slavery and freeing slaves."

Du Bois's readers were so outraged that he had to recant in a subsequent issue. Most blacks then considered Lincoln the "Great Emancipator" of history and a spiritual ally in their struggle. A folk tale had Lincoln rising from the dead to right the wrongs of the Jim Crow South. With Marian Anderson's concert there in 1939 and the Rev. Dr. Martin Luther King Jr.'s "I Have a Dream" speech, the Lincoln Memorial became a kind of civil rights mecca.

Even by 1963, though, when Dr. King invoked Lincoln as a "great American, in whose symbolic shadow we stand today," many blacks objected to this romantic portrait. Today, popular accounts of Lincoln often portray him as an enemy, not a friend. In "The Debt: What America Owes to Blacks," Randall Robinson says blacks can find little succor in the memory of a man who supported shipping them back to Africa. Lerone Bennett Jr.'s "Forced Into Glory: Abraham Lincoln's White Dream" portrays Lincoln as a white supremacist whose policies aimed at "racial cleansing." "Everything he did," writes Mr. Bennett, the executive editor of *Ebony* magazine, "was based on this racist idea."

Noting the popularity of Mr. Bennett's book — a best seller in black-interest bookstores — the Lincoln scholar Allen Guelzo calls it "an important marker of a longterm shift, and that is the withdrawal of blacks from the ranks of Lincoln admirers."

At first glance, the two plays by Suzan-Lori Parks might seem another illustration of this trend. A 38-year-old playwright with a MacArthur Foundation grant and two Obie Awards, Ms. Parks has written, among a number of plays, two that involve black men who dress up as Lincoln and get shot.

The main character of the 1994 "America Play" is constantly told he looks just like Lincoln. In the midst of a spiritual crisis, he begins to speak some of Lincoln's words, then invites people to throw old food at him. "And when someone remarked that he played Lincoln so well he ought to be shot, it was as if the Great Man's footsteps had been suddenly revealed." From then on, his entire act is to sit in a box and invite the public to "Shoot Mr. Lincoln."

This character seems diminished, even humiliated by Lincoln. He doesn't even have a name of his own. The text calls him "The Foundling Father, as Abraham Lincoln," and he refers to himself as "the Lesser Known" in comparison to "the Great Man."

The second play, "Topdog/Underdog," is at the Ambassador Theater. Directed by George C. Wolfe, it had a run earlier this season Off Broadway at the Joseph Papp Public Theater and is the story of two black brothers named Lincoln and Booth. Lincoln (played by Jeffrey Wright) works at a boardwalk arcade, dressing up as the other Lincoln — the usual stovepipe hat, frock coat, fake beard, plus whiteface — so that tourists can shoot him with cap guns. He got the job because his boss liked the idea that he and Honest Abe had the same name, though he gets paid less than the white man who had the job before him.

Like the Foundling Father, this heir to Lincoln seems simultaneously abandoned by a history that could nourish him and bound to repeat much of its violence. Both characters get shot, over and over again. In "Topdog/Underdog," this happens offstage. But then Lincoln comes home to a brother named Booth (Mos Def), who asks, "You ever wonder if someone's gonna come in there with a real gun?"

But Ms. Parks does not intend to judge Lincoln in these plays. She is interested in the way he shows up in the lives of her characters. And when he does, it is with all the ambiguity that he and his legacy demand.

"To me," Ms. Parks said in an interview, "Lincoln is the closest thing we have to a mythic figure. In days of great Greek drama, they had Apollo and Medea and Oedipus — these larger-than-life figures that walked the earth and spoke — and they turned them into plays. Shakespeare had kings and queens that he fashioned into his stories. Lincoln, to me, is one of those."

"This is a subterranean thing I keep dipping into," she continued, "that I don't go into to solve. It just keeps pulling me into it."

The image of Lincoln's assassination also has a strong pull on Ms. Parks. "It's like Lincoln created an opening with that hole in his head," she said. "We've all passed through it into now, you know, like the eye of a needle. Everything that happens, from 1865 to today, has to pass through that wound."

While one individual might see in this image anger about Lincoln's racism, another might see the opposite: that Lincoln was in a sense a martyr for racial progress. (John Wilkes Booth, who had long considered a scheme to kidnap Lincoln, apparently decided to kill him when he came to believe that Lincoln would push for citizenship for blacks.)

Ms. Parks, who emphasized that she had not given much thought to the controversy over Lincoln's legacy, said: "Can Lincoln be the Great Emancipator and a white supremacist? Hmmm. Yes. Both, both. I think both."

Her plays render this paradox. The characters in "The America Play" and "Topdog/Underdog" are in a struggle to know who they are — and so they dig at, sift through and "play" the old stories that shape their lives. Abraham Lincoln is a burden to them but also a source of life. And this is true for all the layers of history that they are wrapped in. The brothers Lincoln and Booth were abandoned by their parents, and they both resent and long for them. Similarly, they need each other to survive (perhaps even to exist) but are also locked in a battle, the origins of which they can never fully know.

"There's a relationship with the past, an important one," Ms. Parks said. "But I think to focus on that relationship and de-emphasize the relationship of the person right in the room with you is the great mistake of American culture and the mistake of history. We have to deal with what's happening right now."

Like others of Ms. Parks's plays ("In the Blood," for instance, and "The Death of the Last Black Man in the Whole Entire World") "The America Play" and "Topdog/Underdog" may provoke old questions about race and power. But Ms. Parks is never content with old answers. The program for "Topdog/Underdog" notes that Booth is the "underdog" and Lincoln the "topdog." But, Ms. Parks said, "It shifts back and forth."

Is the same true with whites and blacks? "Yes," she said. "I think it shifts back and forth more than we're willing to admit. I think it's constantly in flux, case by case, any given moment."

But if Lincoln is a god and was in fact a white man, does Ms. Parks, as an African-American woman, feel excluded from this American mythology? "No," she said, "I've gotten two plays out of it."

Edward Albee

Like Eugene O'Neill, Edward Albee (b. 1928) has won three Pulitzer Prizes for drama: *A Delicate Balance* (1966), *Seascape* (1974), and *Three Tall Women* (1991). However, some of his earlier plays are much better known and are considered much more powerful, such as his first, a one-act play called *The Zoo Story* (1958); *The Death of Bessie Smith* (1959); *The American Dream* (1960); and *Who's Afraid of Virginia Woolf?* (1961), which was made into a memorable film. Albee is known as an experimental writer, concerned with style and ideas in equal measure, but also concerned with jolting the audience into awareness.

Critics have dissected some of Albee's plays based on their homoerotic themes; Albee certainly does not limit himself to such issues, although certain plays, such as *Tiny Alice* (1964), sometimes rely on sexual slang for their effect. His portrait of the savage marital battle between George and Martha (echoing the names of our country's founding "father" and "mother") in *Who's Afraid of Virginia Woolf?* has sometimes been used as an example of Albee's distaste for conventional heterosexual marriage. In *Three Tall Women,* the main character is in bed, dying. She has turned her back on her gay son, and while her mind wanders she is visited by two women who help clarify the nature of her life. *The Goat, or Who Is Sylvia?* (2002) stimulated considerable controversy because of its perceived bestiality in Martin's confession that he had fallen in love with a goat. Clearly, the sexual quotient in Albee's plays takes on a special importance.

Albee is unusual in that his first plays made him a major figure in American drama. He was born in Washington, D.C., and adopted by Reed and Frances Albee. His father was part owner of a vaudeville circuit, so in one sense it may be said that Albee was born into a theatrical family. He grew up in Larchmont, New York, although his parents wintered in warm climates; eventually Edward had to go to boarding school. The one he liked most was Choate, in Connecticut, where he was encouraged to write. He attended Trinity College in Hartford for only two years. When he left school he knew he wanted to write, and to give himself the space to do that he took a number of jobs that did not make serious intellectual demands on him. He also had a trust fund to supplement his income and, thus, had few financial worries. His first play was written in three weeks when he was thirty, but no New York producer would take it. *The Zoo Story,* in which a conservative gentleman and a young man from the counterculture have an emotional encounter, was first produced in 1959 in Berlin, Germany. Later that year it was produced at the Provincetown Playhouse in Greenwich Village on the same bill with Samuel Beckett's *Krapp's Last Tape.*

After his early successes, Albee had a number of plays produced that brought him no acclaim. Some were panned outright, and all tended to lessen his impact as a major playwright. The period from the late 1970s through the 1980s was especially problematic, with a string of failures: *The Lady from Dubuque* (1977), *Another Part of the Zoo* (1981), *The Man Who Had Three*

Arms (1981), *Finding the Sun* (1982), and *The Marriage Play* (1987). Albee came roaring back with *Three Tall Women* in 1991, despite the fact that it opened off-Broadway. Today Albee is regarded as one of America's most important living playwrights. His plays are produced regularly in the United States and abroad, and theaters such as the Goodman in Chicago have staged Albee festivals to honor his lifelong achievement.

THE GOAT, OR WHO IS SYLVIA?

The subtitle of the play, "Who Is Sylvia?" alludes to Shakespeare's song in *Two Gentlemen of Verona*. "Who is Silvia? What is she? / That all our swains commend her? / Holy, fair, and wise is she; / The heaven such grace did lend her / That she might admired be." In Shakespeare, the allusion is to a sylvan (or rural) sweet love, innocent and pure, and Albee plays on several levels of irony by introducing his barnyard beloved into the lives of Martin, Stevie, Billy, and Ross.

The controversy stimulated by this play centered naturally on the question of bestiality, sexual intercourse with an animal. It seemed to those who studied Albee that he had found a way to deal with sexuality in a fashion that would shock an otherwise unshockable audience, and it was the shock value that drove the play. In the process of developing that idea, reviewers did not emphasize the details that pointed in a somewhat different direction.

The surface of the narrative is plain enough. Martin Gray, celebrating his fiftieth birthday with a TV interview conducted by his oldest friend, reveals to his wife of more than twenty years that he is in love with a goat named Sylvia. This news is at first thought to be a bit of light comedy. Eventually, however, Martin's wife, Stevie, begins to take it seriously and regards it as an affront that cannot be undone. She explains at the end of scene 2 that what Martin has done is unforgivable, that it has shattered the glass of their lives. Martin cannot explain what he has done or even what he feels, other than to explain a love for a fellow animal. He constantly reminds Stevie and his friend Ross that he cannot explain it and they cannot understand his feelings.

That Martin's bestiality may strike him as deviant behavior is plain from his attending an AA-style group in which a man describes his affair with a pig and a woman talks about her relations with her German shepherd. Stevie and Martin even have a mutual friend in the group who has an affair with her dog. Martin tries to understand his feelings in relation to the members of the group, some of whom feel they have been "cured," but he cannot imagine what a cure might be. Despite his visit to this group, he feels that he is doing what is natural, and when he tells Stevie he makes no excuses for his behavior.

Albee's portrayals of sexuality also include the heterosexual relationship between Martin and Stevie and the homosexual orientation of Billy, who is still in school — an all-boys' school, for which he thanks his father. What Albee tries to remind us of is the polymorphous nature of sexuality and the erotic, even to the point of explaining how a baby can cause a man, Martin in this case, to feel a sexual urge. Even the intense kiss of father and son in the last scene of the play figures in Albee's equation of varieties of sexual "normality."

The play has another level as well, however. If we approach the play from another direction we can see that Albee is working with a concept of tragedy that is peculiarly modern. The printed text offers a subtitle in parentheses: "(Notes toward a definition of tragedy)." For one thing, the Greek word for tragedy derives from a term that can be defined as "goat-song." The goat is a symbol of sacrifice, and tragedies are stories of things that people do that cannot be undone. What Martin has done cannot be undone, as he is told at the end of the play. His career is threatened by his behavior. His reputation will be shattered. His friend Ross tells him "this isn't going to whores and coming down with the clap, or whatever, you know. This isn't the stuff that stops a career in its tracks for a little while — humiliation, public remorse, and then back up again. This is *beyond* that — *way* beyond it!" Ross tells him "there are prison terms for this" . . . "Some states they kill you for it."

When we think back to the start of the play we realize that Martin takes on the familiar role of the tragic hero, who begins the play at the top of his world. Martin is a famous architect who has won the most prestigious prize any architect could win — the Pritzker — at the age of fifty (an incredibly young age for such an achievement in this field). He has also received a commission for a $200 billion project to design The World City, the "dream city of the future." Martin can rise no higher than this and, like most tragic heroes, can only go downward. Even Stevie reminds him how perfect their relationship is, how perfect his life is. But Martin woos his goat the way Oedipus wooed his own tragedy — and the results are similar. In some ways Albee has found an ingenious analysis of the tragic in everyone's life, not only by revealing the goat of the tragic goat-song, but also by implying a relationship with the goat-god Pan, whose sexuality drives the entire world of biological life. As the Irish writer James Stephens has said, "civilization is built on a volcano," and that volcano is sex. In *The Goat,* the volcano erupts.

The Goat, or Who Is Sylvia? in Performance

The play premiered in March 2002 in New York City at the Golden Theatre on Broadway. Martin was played by Bill Pullman, Stevie was played by Mercedes Ruehl, Ross by Stephen Rowe, and Billy by Jeffrey Carlson. The production was praised on a number of levels, especially for the acting of Ruehl and Pullman; the latter, a popular movie star, surprised reviewers with the subtlety of his performance. Sally Field and Bill Irwin took over the parts in September 2002 and also garnered good reviews. *The Goat, or Who Is Sylvia?* won The Critics Circle award as the best play of 2002, as well as the Tony for best play and the Drama Desk Award for best play. The Fairfax Theatre in Melbourne, Australia, produced the play in February 2003; the Goodman Theatre in Chicago followed in November 2003; and the distinguished Almeida Theatre's 2004 production in London moved in April to the Apollo Theatre, also in London. All of this tells us that this is a play with considerable international appeal that will become a central component of Albee's achievement as a playwright.

Edward Albee (b. 1928)

The Goat, or Who Is Sylvia?

The Goat *had its world premiere in New York City on March 10, 2002, at the Golden Theatre, produced by Elizabeth Ireland McCann, Daryl Roth, Carole Shorenstein Hays, Terry Allen Kramer, Scott Rudin, Bob Boyett, Scott Nederlander, and Sine/ZPI. It was directed by David Esbjornson, with the following cast:*

STEVIE, *Mercedes Ruehl*
MARTIN, *Bill Pullman*
ROSS, *Stephen Rowe*
BILLY, *Jeffrey Carlson*

The scenic design was by John Arnone, costume design by Elizabeth Hope Clancy, lighting design by Kenneth Posner, and sound design by Mark Bennett. The production stage manager was Erica Schwartz. The general manager was Joey Parnes. The company manager was Elizabeth Blitzer. The casting was done by Bernard Telsey Casting. The press representative was Sam Rudy of Shirley Herz Associates.

On September 13, 2002, the roles of Stevie and Martin were taken over by Sally Field and Bill Irwin, respectively.

SCENE ONE

(The living room)

(Stevie onstage, arranging flowers)

STEVIE (*Calling offstage*): What time are they coming? (*No response*) Martin? What time are they coming?
MARTIN (*Offstage*): What?
STEVIE (*A little smile; a slowish statement*): What . . . time . . . are . . . they . . . coming.
MARTIN: Who? (*Recalling*) Oh! Oh. (*Looks at watch*) Soon; very soon. Why can't I remember anything?
STEVIE (*Finishing flowers*): Why can't you remember?
MARTIN: Anything; nothing; can't remember a thing. This morning — so far! — I couldn't remember where I'd put the new head for the razor; I couldn't recall Ross's son's name — still can't; two cards in my jacket make no sense to me whatever, and I'm not sure I know why I came in here.
STEVIE: Todd.
MARTIN: What?
STEVIE: Ross's son is called Todd.
MARTIN (*Slaps his forehead*): Right! Why the flowers?
STEVIE: To brighten up the corner . . .
MARTIN: . . . where you *are*? Where *I* am?

STEVIE: . . . where you'll probably be sitting, to make the cameras happy.
MARTIN (*Smelling the flowers*): What are they?
STEVIE: Cameras?
MARTIN: No; these.
STEVIE: Ranunculus. I (*Then*) I: ranunculi.
MARTIN: Pretty. Why don't they smell?
STEVIE: They're secretive; probably too subtle for your forgetful nose.
MARTIN (*Shakes his head, mock concern*): Every sense going! Taste next! Touch; hearing. Hah! Hearing!
STEVIE: What?
MARTIN: What?
STEVIE: And to think you're only fifty. Did you find it?
MARTIN: What?
STEVIE: The new head for the razor.
MARTIN: Right! A new head! I'll need that next — the whole thing.
STEVIE: Why did you want to remember Todd's name?
MARTIN: Well, to begin with, I shouldn't be forgetting it, and when Ross shows up and he asks about Billy I can't say "He's fine; how's . . . you know . . . *your* son . . ."
STEVIE: Todd.
MARTIN: Todd. "How's old Todd?"
STEVIE: Young Todd.
MARTIN: Yes. It's the little slips.
STEVIE: I wouldn't worry about it. Are you going to offer them stuff? Coffee? Beer?
MARTIN (*Preoccupied*): Probably. Do you think it means anything?
STEVIE: I don't know what "it" is.
MARTIN: That I can't remember anything.
STEVIE: Probably not: you have too much to remember, that's all. You could go in for a checkup . . . if you can remember our doctor's name.
MARTIN (*Nailing it*): Percy!
STEVIE: Right!
MARTIN (*To himself*): Who could forget that? Nobody has a doctor named Percy. (*To Stevie*) What's the matter with me?
STEVIE: You're fifty.
MARTIN: No; more than that.
STEVIE: The old foreboding? The sense that everything going right is a sure sign that everything's going wrong, of all the awful to come? All that?
MARTIN (*Rueful*): Probably. Why did I come in here?
STEVIE: I heard you in the hall; I called you.
MARTIN: Aha.
STEVIE: What's my *name*?

MARTIN: Pardon?

STEVIE: Who *am* I? Who am *I*?

MARTIN (*Acted*): You're the love of my life, the mother of my handsome and worrisome son, my playmate, my cook, my bottlewasher. Do you?

STEVIE: What?

MARTIN: Wash my bottles?

STEVIE (*Puzzles it*): Not as a habit. I may have — washed one of your bottles. Do you have bottles?

MARTIN: Everyone has bottles.

STEVIE: Right. But what's my *name*?

MARTIN (*Pretending confusion*): Uh . . . Stevie?

STEVIE: Good. Will this be a long one?

MARTIN: A long what?

STEVIE: Interview.

MARTIN: The usual, I guess. Ross said it wasn't going to be a feature — sort of a catch-up.

STEVIE: On your fiftieth.

MARTIN (*Nods*): On my fiftieth. I wonder if I should tell him that my mind's going? If I can remember.

STEVIE (*Laughs; hugs him from behind*): Your mind's not going.

MARTIN: My what?

STEVIE: Your mind, darling; it's not going . . . anywhere.

MARTIN (*Serious*): Am I too young for Alzheimer's?

STEVIE: Probably. Isn't it nice to be too young for something?

MARTIN (*Mind elsewhere*): Um-hum.

STEVIE: The joke is, if you can remember what it's called you don't have it.

MARTIN: Have what?

STEVIE: Alz . . . (*they both laugh; he kisses her forehead*) Oh, you know how to turn a girl on! Forehead kisses! (*Sniffs him*) Where have you been?

MARTIN (*Releases her; preoccupied*): What time are they coming?

STEVIE: Soon, you said; very soon.

MARTIN: I did? Good.

STEVIE: Did you find it?

MARTIN: What?

STEVIE: The head for your razor.

MARTIN: No; it's around somewhere. (*Fishes in a pocket, brings out cards*) But these! Now these! What the hell are these!? "Basic Services, Limited." Basic Services, Limited?? Limited to what!? (*The other card*) "Clarissa Atherton." (*Shrugs*) Clarissa Atherton? No number, no . . . internet thing? Clarissa Atherton?

STEVIE: Basic services? Clarissa Atherton, basic services?

MARTIN: Hm? Every time someone gives me one of these, I know I'm supposed to give them one back, and I don't have them. It's embarrassing.

STEVIE: I've told you to have them made . . . cards.

MARTIN: I don't want to.

STEVIE: Then don't. Who is she?

MARTIN: Who?

STEVIE: Clarissa Atherton, basic services. Does she smell funny?

MARTIN: I don't know. (*Afterthought*) I don't know who she is, as far as I know. Where were we this week?

STEVIE (*Overly casual; stretches*): Oh, it doesn't matter sweetie. If you're seeing this Atherton woman, this . . . dominatrix . . . who smells funny . . .

MARTIN: How could I be seeing her — whoever she is? There's nothing on the card. Dominatrix!?

STEVIE: Why not?

MARTIN: Maybe you know things I don't.

STEVIE: Maybe.

MARTIN: And I probably know one or two things you *don't*.

STEVIE: It evens out.

MARTIN: Yes. Do I look OK?

STEVIE: For the TV? Yes.

MARTIN: Yes. (*Turning*) Really?

STEVIE: I said: yes; fine. (*Indicates*) The old prep school tie?

MARTIN (*Genuine, as he looks*): Is it? Oh, yeah; so it is.

STEVIE (*Not letting him have it*): *No* one puts on their prep school tie by accident. *No* one.

MARTIN (*Considers*): What if you can't remember that's what it is?

STEVIE: *No* one!! If you do get Alzheimer's, and you get to the stage you don't know who I am, who *Billy* is, who *you* are, for that matter . . .

MARTIN: Billy?

STEVIE (*Laughs*): Stop it! When you get to the point you can't remember anything, someone will hand you that (*indicates his tie*) and you'll look at it and you'll say (*terrible imitation of aged man*) "Ahhhhh! My prep school tie! My prep school tie!"

(*They chuckle; the doorbell rings/chimes*)

MARTIN: Ah! Doom time!

STEVIE (*Quite matter of fact*): If you *are* seeing that woman, I think we'd better talk about it.

MARTIN (*Stops. Long pause; matter of fact*): If I *were* . . . we *would*.

STEVIE (*As offhand as possible*): If not the dominatrix, then some blonde half your age, some . . . chippie, as they used to call them . . .

MARTIN: . . . or, worst of all, someone just like you? As bright; as resourceful; as intrepid; . . . merely . . . new?

STEVIE (*Warm smile; shake of head*): You win 'em all, don't you.

MARTIN (*Same smile*): Enough.

(*Door again. The next several speeches are done in a greatly exaggerated Noel Coward manner: English accents, flamboyant gestures*)

STEVIE: Something's going on, isn't it!?

MARTIN: Yes! I've fallen in love!

STEVIE: I knew it!

MARTIN: Hopelessly!

STEVIE: I knew it!

MARTIN: I fought against it!

STEVIE: Oh, you poor darling!

MARTIN: Fought hard!

STEVIE: I suppose you'd better tell me!

MARTIN: I can't! I can't!

STEVIE: Tell me! Tell me!

MARTIN: Her name is Sylvia!

STEVIE: Sylvia? Who is Sylvia?

MARTIN: She's a goat; Sylvia is a goat! (*Acting manner dropped; normal tone now; serious, flat*) She's a goat.

STEVIE (*Long pause; she stares, finally smiles. She giggles, chortles, moves toward the hall; normal tone*): You're too much! (*Exits*)

MARTIN: I am? (*Shrugs; to himself*) You try to *tell* them; you try to be *honest*. What do they do? They laugh at you. (*Imitation*) "You're too much!" (*Thinks about it*) I suppose I am.

ROSS: Hey honey.

STEVIE: Hi Ross. (*Ross enters with Stevie*)

ROSS: Hello there, old man!

MARTIN: I'm fifty!

ROSS: It's a term of endearment. Nice flowers.

MARTIN: It is?

ROSS: What? What is?

MARTIN: "Hello there, old man." Ranunculi.

ROSS: Pardon?

STEVIE: The proper plural of ranunculus — the flowers, according to old Martin here.

MARTIN: Some say ranunculuses, but that sounds wrong, even though it's probably perfectly acceptable.

ROSS (*Not interested*): Aha! Let's move that chair over to the . . . whatever they are . . . the flowers. (*To Martin*) Are you happy in that chair?

MARTIN: Am I happy in it? I don't even know if I've ever sat in it. (*To Stevie*) Have I? Have I ever sat in it?

STEVIE: You just did, and you sat in it the last time Ross did the program with you.

ROSS: That's *right*!

MARTIN: Yes . . . but was I happy? Did I sit there and did contentment bathe me in its warm light?

ROSS: You got me, fella.

STEVIE: Yes; contentment fell; you sat there and I watched it bathe you in its warm light. I've got to go.

MARTIN: Where are you going?

STEVIE (*No information*): Out.

MARTIN: Are we in tonight?

STEVIE: Yes. I think Billy's going out.

MARTIN: Naturally!

STEVIE: We're in. (*Glee*) TV time! I'm getting my hair done, and then I thought I'd stop by the feed store. (*Exits, giggling*)

ROSS: By *what*? She's going to stop by *what*?

MARTIN (*Staring after her*): Nothing; nowhere. (*To Ross*) No crew?

ROSS: Just me this time — the old hand-held. (*Indicates camera*) You ready for the chair?

MARTIN (*Sing-song*): Ha, ha. (*Suddenly remembering*) How's old *Todd*!?

ROSS: "Old Todd?"

MARTIN: You know: old *Todd*!

ROSS: You mean my baby son who just last week it seems I dandled on my knee? *That* old Todd?

MARTIN: Lovely word — dandled. Yes: *that* old Todd.

ROSS: Who I cannot accept having become eighteen?

MARTIN: Whom.

ROSS: Maybe.

MARTIN: Yes; that one. Can any of us? Ever?

ROSS: Pushing me further into middle age?

MARTIN: Yes; that one.

ROSS (*Offhand*): He's OK. (*Laughs*) He asked me last week — first time since he was four, or something — why he didn't have a brother, or a sister, or whatever — why April and I never had another kid.

MARTIN: April, May, June — the pastel months. You name girl babies after them.

ROSS (*Doesn't care*): Right. (*Does care*) I told him if you do it right the first time, why take a chance on another.

MARTIN: Did he like that one?

ROSS: Seemed to. Of course, I could have told him the whole graduating class got together and vowed that we would all have only one kid each — keep the population down. Speaking of which, how's Billy? How's *yours* — *your* one and only?

MARTIN (*Attempted throw-away tone*): Ohhhh, seventeen last week — didn't Todd come to the party? No, I guess he didn't. Real cute kid, Billy, bright as you'd ever want, gay as the nineties.

ROSS: Passing phase. Have you had the old serious talk?

MARTIN: The "You'll get over it once you meet the right girl" lecture? Nah, I'm too smart for that, so's he, so's Billy. I told him to be sure. Says he's sure; loves it, he says.

ROSS: Well, of course he loves it; he's getting laid, for God's sake! Don't worry about him.

MARTIN: Who?

ROSS: Billy! Seventeen; it's a phase.

MARTIN: Like the moon, eh?

ROSS: He'll straighten out — to make a pun. (*To quash the subject*) Billy'll come out of it; he'll be OK.

MARTIN (*Reassuring if a bit patronizing*): Sure.

ROSS: Voice test? Phone off?

MARTIN: I assume Stevie did it.

ROSS: I hear a kind of . . . rushing sound, like a . . . woooooosh!, or . . . wings, or something.

MARTIN: It's probably the Eumenides.

ROSS: More like the dishwasher. There; it stopped.

MARTIN: Then it probably wasn't the Eumenides: they don't stop.

ROSS (*Agreeing*): They go right on.

MARTIN: Right.

ROSS: Why is Stevie going to the feed store?

MARTIN: She isn't.

ROSS: Then why did she . . .

MARTIN: It's a joke.

ROSS: A standing joke?

MARTIN: No, a new one; a brand-new one.

ROSS: OK? Ready? Ready Martin; here we go; just . . . be yourself.

MARTIN: Really?

ROSS (*A tiny bit testy*): Well, no; maybe not. Put on your public face.

MARTIN (*Overly cheerful*): OK!!

ROSS: And don't switch in the middle.
MARTIN (*More*): OK!!
ROSS (*Under his breath*): Jesus! (*Announcer voice*) Good evening. This is Ross Tuttle. Welcome to People Who Matter. Some people have birthdays and no one pays them any mind. Well . . . family, of course, friends. And others . . . well, some people are . . . I was going to say special, but that's a . . . dumb word, for everyone matters, everyone's special. But some people matter in extraordinary ways, in ways which affect the lives of the rest of us — enrich them, inform them. Some people, I guess, are, well . . . more extraordinary than others. Martin Gray — whom you've met on this program before — is such a man, such a person. Good evening, Martin.
MARTIN: Good . . . uh, evening, Ross. (*sotto voce*) It's mid-afternoon.
ROSS (*Quiet snarl*): I know. Shut up! (*Announcer voice*) Three things happened to you this week, Martin. You became the youngest person ever to win the Pritzker Prize, architecture's version of the Nobel. Also this week you were chosen to design The World City, the two hundred billion dollar dream city of the future, financed by U.S. electronics technology and set to rise in the wheatfields of our Middle West. Also, this week, you celebrated your fiftieth birthday. Happy birthday, Martin, and congratulations!
MARTIN (*Brief pause; casual*): Thanks, Ross.
ROSS: Quite a week, Martin!
MARTIN (*A little puzzled*): Yes; yes it was. Quite a week.
ROSS (*Big*): How does it feel, Martin?
MARTIN: Becoming fifty?
ROSS (*Pushing*): No. *All* of it. Yes.
MARTIN: Well . . .
ROSS (*Sensing no answer is coming*): It must be amazing! No, thrilling!
MARTIN: Turning fifty? No: not really.
ROSS (*Not amused*): No! The other! The World City! The Pritzker! All that!
MARTIN (*Genuine surprise*): Oh, that! Well, yes . . . amazing, thrilling.
ROSS (*Prompting*): For one so young.
MARTIN (*Innocent*): Fifty is young?
ROSS (*Controlling himself*): For the Pritzker Prize! Where were you when they told you?
MARTIN: I was at the gym; I'd taken all my clothes off, and Stevie called me there.
ROSS: Stevie is your wife.
MARTIN: I know that.
ROSS: How did it make you feel?
MARTIN: Stevie being my wife?
ROSS: No: the Prize.
MARTIN: Well, it was . . . gratifying — not being naked, but . . . hearing about it — the Prize.
ROSS (*Exuberant*): Weren't you . . . thunderstruck!?
MARTIN: Well, no; they'd hinted at it — the Prize, I mean, and . . .
ROSS (*Heavily prompting*): But it was pretty wonderful, wasn't it?

MARTIN (*Understanding what to say*): Yes; yes it was pretty wonderful — *is* pretty wonderful.
ROSS: Tell us about The World City.
MARTIN: Well, you just *did*: two hundred billion dollars, and all, the wheatfields of Kansas, or whatever . . .
ROSS: What an honor! What a duo of honors! You're at the . . . pinnacle of your success, Martin . . .
MARTIN (*Considers that*): You mean it's all downhill from here?
ROSS: CUT! CUT! (*Camera down. To Martin*) What's the matter with you!?
MARTIN: Sorry?
ROSS: I can't shoot that! You were a million miles away!!
MARTIN (*Considering*): That far.
ROSS: You want to try again?
MARTIN: Try what?
ROSS: The taping! The program!
MARTIN (*As if seeing the camera for the first time*): Oooooh.
ROSS: We're taping!
MARTIN (*Unhappy*): Yes; I know.
ROSS (*Nicely concerned*): Something the matter?
MARTIN: I think so. Yes; probably.
ROSS: Do you want to talk about it, as they say?
MARTIN: About what?
ROSS: About what's the matter.
MARTIN (*Concerned*): Why? What's the matter?
ROSS: You said something was the matter, that you think something's the matter.
MARTIN (*Far away*): Oh.
ROSS: Forty years, Martin; we've known each other forty years — since we were ten.
MARTIN (*Trying to understand*): Yes. That gives you something? Rights, or something?
ROSS: I'm your oldest friend.
MARTIN: No; my aesthetics professor at college; I still see him; he's a lot older than you; he's over ninety.
ROSS (*So patient*): Your longest friend: the person you've known the longest.
MARTIN: No; my Aunt Sarah; she's known me . . .
ROSS (*Trying to stay patient*): She's not a friend!
MARTIN (*Deep, quiet surprise*): Oh?
ROSS (*Close to giving up*): No; she's a relative; relatives are not friends!
MARTIN: Oh, now . . .
ROSS: Are not the same as friends. Jesus!
MARTIN: Aha! Yes; well, you're right. I've known you longer as a friend than anyone. (*Tiny pause*) Why is that relevant?
ROSS: Because you're troubled, and I thought that as your oldest friend I might be able to . . .
MARTIN: I am? Is that true?
ROSS: You said that something was the matter!
MARTIN (*Not remembering*): I did, hunh?
ROSS: Why are you so . . . ? (*Can't find the word*)
MARTIN: Are you still shooting? Are you still on?
ROSS (*Heavy sigh*): No. We'll try to do it at the studio later. Sorry.
MARTIN: Can I get up now?

Ross: If you want to; if you're not happy.
Martin: Why are you talking to me like I was a child?
Ross: Because you're acting like one.
Martin (*Innocent*): I am?
Ross: Probably the most important week of your life . . .
Martin (*Impressed, if uninvolved*): Really!
Ross: . . . and you act like you don't know whether you're coming or going, like you don't know where you are.
Martin (*Self-absorbed, almost to himself*): Maybe it's . . . love or something.
Ross: Maybe what is?
Martin: Like a child.
Ross (*Bingo!*): You're having an affair!
Martin: SHHHHHHHH! I mean, Jesus!
Ross (*Shrugs*): It's OK; he's not having an affair.
Martin: Jesus! Too bad you didn't bring the crew; they'd love this.
Ross (*Cool*): They know their business.
Martin: And . . . ?
Ross: And . . . ?
Martin: Aren't you guys friendly anymore?
Ross: They know their business. What do you want me to do — have them over for *dinner*? Have every crew over for dinner?
Martin (*Puzzled*): No, I guess not. (*Afterthought*) Why *not*?
Ross: Hm?
Martin: Why *not* have them over for dinner?
Ross: Oh, for God's sake, Martin!
Martin (*Hands up, defensively*) Ok! OK! Jesus!
Ross: It's just that . . . it's just that I don't . . . mix with . . .
Martin (*Joyful*): The *help*?! You don't mix with the *help*!?
Ross: What *is* wrong with you today!? That's not what I meant, and you *know* it.
Martin (*Half-serious, half-joking*): You're a snob! I guess I've always known that. For all your left-wing, proletarian background, you're a *snob*: worst kind.
Ross (*A plea; a warning*): We're best friends, remember?
Martin: Meaning . . . ?
Ross: We like each other.
Martin ("*So, that's it!*"): Ohhhhhhh!
Ross: More than anyone.
Martin (*Ibid*): Ohhhhh! (*Considers it*) Right; yes. Who else can I be cranky with?
Ross: Stevie??
Martin: Ya know, Stevie doesn't take too well to cranky anymore. If she's developed a flaw, it's that. "Don't be so cranky, Martin."
Ross: Pity.

(*They've gentled down now*)

Martin (*Shrugs*): Well . . . *you* know.
Ross (*Pause*): So you're in love.
Martin: With Stevie? Sure! Twenty-two years now.
Ross: No, I mean . . . "in love." Ficky-fack! Humpty-doodle!
Martin: What on earth are you talking about!? "Humpty-doodle!?"

Ross: You said you were in love — outside of Stevie, as I read it.
Martin (*Genuine*): Really? I don't remember.
Ross (*Impatient sigh; abrupt*): O . . . K! That does it!
Martin (*As Ross gathers up stuff; true innocence*): Where are you going?
Ross (*Staring him down*): I'm gathering my things and I'm taking my left-wing . . . what was it?
Martin: Uh . . . proletarian.
Ross: . . . proletarian self outa here.
Martin: "But, why!" as the . . .
Ross: Look, I came here to fucking interview you.
Martin: Fine.
Ross: To boost your ego even more than . . .
Martin: I have no ego.
Ross: Bullshit! Even more than where it is already and you fuck that up.
Martin: Fine. You say fuck a lot.
Ross: You say fine a lot. (*He laughs; so does Martin*)
Martin: Words beginning with F.
Ross (*Smiles*): Yeah. (*Pause*) So; tell me about it.
Martin (*Shy*): About . . . ?
Ross (*Gently urging*): Your new love.
Martin: Oh; that.
Ross: Yes.
Martin: I don't know that I want to.
Ross: Yes; you do.
Martin: . . . that I can.
Ross: Try.
Martin (*Small smile*): You're persistent.
Ross: Best friend. (*Martin tries to talk; can't*) Best friend.
Martin (*Frustrated explosion*): OK!! OK!! (*Heavy, slow sigh; long pause*) I don't know if I ever thought that . . . well, that Stevie and I would be . . . well, no; we're not. (*Pause*)
Ross: Are you telling me about it?
Martin: I'm starting to . . . or maybe I'm beginning to start.
Ross: Oh; OK.
Martin: As I said, it never occurred to me that anything like this would come up. 'Cause we've always been good together — good in bed, good out; always honest, always . . . considerate. I've not been unfaithful our whole marriage; I want you to know this; never physically untrue, as they say.
Ross: That's amazing. It's wonderful, but . . . wow!
Martin: Yes: wow. Oh, I've been groped in the kitchen by a cutie or two, late, a party, once or twice, and I've had my hand a couple of places a couple of times, but I've never . . . *done* anything. You follow.
Ross: Yes; I follow.
Martin: It never seemed . . . well, necessary, either to be able to do a comparison, or . . . even for its own sake. I never needed it, I guess. Do you remember that time, that college reunion weekend you and I decided to call that service they'd told us about . . . the gang had told us about?
Ross (*Rueful laugh*): The Ladies Aid Society?
Martin: Yeah, and you called them, and . . .

ROSS: . . . and we had a couple of bimbos over . . .

MARTIN: Bimbi.

ROSS: Yes? (*Broad*) Ohhhhh, I remember.

MARTIN: . . . and you were married already, and Stevie and I were dating . . . or going together . . .

ROSS: . . . or whatever.

MARTIN: Yes.

ROSS (*Trying to recall*): What were their names?

MARTIN: Mine was Alice.

ROSS: Big girl.

MARTIN: Large Alice.

ROSS: Right! Mine was Trudy, or Trixie, or . . .

MARTIN: April.

ROSS: Yes? April?

MARTIN: Yes; April.

ROSS (*Interior*): Oh, shit; April's called April.

MARTIN (*Registering it*): Yes; she is.

ROSS: Shit. (*Pause; recovers*) And we had them up to our room — two beds, two hookers.

MARTIN: Just like when we roomed together.

ROSS: A kind of reunion for the reunion.

MARTIN: Yes, I guess so. And do you remember what happened?

ROSS: I don't know. What happened?

MARTIN: I couldn't do it? Couldn't perform?

ROSS (*Recalls*): Oh, yeah. You'd never had that problem when we were undergrads! I'd be pumping away, you pumping away in the next bed.

MARTIN: I hadn't met Stevie.

ROSS (*Soberer*): Right.

MARTIN: That night at the reunion with large Alice . . .

ROSS: You were going with Stevie . . .

MARTIN: Right.

ROSS: I remember.

MARTIN: I don't know why I ever thought I wanted to . . . *you* know.

ROSS: No. Right.

MARTIN: I was already in love with Stevie and I didn't know how much.

ROSS (*A little deriding*): Amazing theory: the heart rules the dick. I always thought that the dick was driven by . . .

MARTIN: Don't be cynical.

ROSS: Oh, a new part of my left-wing . . . what?

MARTIN: Proletarian.

ROSS: Yes. My left-wing, proletarian, snobbish, *cynical* self.

MARTIN: Right, and not new. (*They both smile*) You *do* see, don't you? In love with Stevie, she owns every part of me. Look, when I'm traveling, and Stevie's *here*, and I get itchy . . .

ROSS: You give yourself a handjob and you think about Stevie — about you and Stevie.

MARTIN (*Shy*): Yes.

ROSS (*Shakes his head; noncommittal*): Wonderful.

MARTIN: I didn't catch your tone.

ROSS: There wasn't any. Go on; how did you fuck it up?

MARTIN (*Truly confused*): What? Fuck *what* up?

ROSS: Are you playing games?

MARTIN: No. Fuck *what* up?

ROSS (*Serious*): Your life, apparently — you and Stevie. How'd you fuck it up?

MARTIN (*Pause*): Oh. (*Pause*) That.

ROSS (*Impatient*): Getting an answer out of you . . .

MARTIN: OK! OK! As I told you, I've never been unfaithful, never needed it . . . never . . .

ROSS: Yeah, yeah; right. You told me.

MARTIN: And then . . . one day . . . (*Stops*)

ROSS (*After a silence*): Yeah!?

MARTIN: And then one day. (*Says nothing more*)

ROSS (*Long pause*): That's it!?

MARTIN (*Goes ahead*): And then one day . . . one day . . . well, I was house-hunting — barn hunting, actually. Stevie and I had decided it was time to have a real country place — a farm, maybe — we deserved it. So, I was in the car about sixty miles out from the city. Stevie couldn't come with me.

ROSS: Beyond the suburbs.

MARTIN: Yes; beyond the suburbs. Farms around it, small farms. And I found a wonderful place, a wonderful old farmhouse, and a lot of land.

ROSS: The old back twenty, or whatever it is.

MARTIN: Right! Whatever. And I called Stevie, and told her she had to see it, and I'd put a hold on it 'til she could see it. And Stevie was . . . well, "A farm?" she said, but I said "Wait!" And the real estate guy was OK with that for a while. And I was driving out of the town back to the highway, and I stopped at the top of a hill.

ROSS: Crest.

MARTIN: Right. And I stopped, and the view was . . . well, not spectacular, but . . . wonderful. Fall, you know?, with leaves turning and the town below me and great scudding clouds and those country smells.

ROSS: Cow shit, and all that.

MARTIN (*Broad country parody*): New-mown hay, fella! The smell a country; the smell a apples! (*Normal tone again*) The roadside stands, with corn and other stuff piled high, and baskets full of other things — beans and tomatoes and those great white peaches you only get late summer . . .

ROSS (*Broad*): The whole thing; right.

MARTIN (*Shakes his head*): Oh, you city boys! And from up there I could trace the roads out toward the farm, and it gave me a kind of shiver.

ROSS: The ludicrous often does.

MARTIN: Anyway . . .

ROSS: Anyway.

MARTIN: Anyway, it was pretty wonderful. And I was getting back in the car, about to get back in the car, all my loot — vegetables and stuff . . . (*change of tone to quiet wonder*) and it was then that I saw her. (*Sees it*) Just . . . just looking at me.

ROSS: Daisy Mae! Blonde hair to her shoulders, big tits in the calico blouse, bare midriff, blonde down at the navel, piece a straw in her teeth . . .

MARTIN (*Gentle, admonishing smile*): You don't understand.

ROSS: No? No blonde hair? No tits?

MARTIN: No. And there she was, looking at me with those eyes.

ROSS: And it was love.

MARTIN: You don't understand.

ROSS: No? It *wasn't* love?

MARTIN: No. Yes; yes, it was love, but I didn't know it right then. (*To himself*) How could I?

ROSS: Right then it was good old lust, eh? Dick starting to get big in your pants . . .

MARTIN (*Sad*): You *don't* understand. (*Pause*) I didn't know *what* it was — what I was feeling. It was . . . it wasn't like anything I'd felt before; it was . . . so . . . amazing, so . . . extraordinary! There she was, just looking at me, with those *eyes* of hers, and . . .

ROSS (*Impatient*): Well, did you *talk* to her?

MARTIN (*Incredulous laugh*): Did I *what*!?

ROSS: Did you *talk* to her!?

MARTIN (*Considers it*): Hunh! Yes; yes, I did. I went up to her, to where she was, and I spoke to her, and she came toward me and . . . and those eyes, and I touched her face, and . . . (*Abrupt*) I don't want to talk about it; I can't *talk* about it.

ROSS: All right; let me help you. You're *seeing* her.

MARTIN (*Sad laugh*): Yes; oh, yes; I'm *seeing* her.

ROSS: You're having an affair with her.

MARTIN (*Confused*): A what? Having a *what*!?

ROSS (*Hard*): You're *screwing* her.

MARTIN (*Sudden vision of it*): Yes; yes; I'm *screwing* her. Oh, Jesus!

ROSS (*Softer*): And you're in love.

MARTIN: That's it, you see.

ROSS: What is? What do I see?

MARTIN: I *am* seeing her; I *am* having . . . an affair, I guess. No! That's not the right word. I am . . . (*winces*) screwing her, as you put it — all of which is . . . beyond even . . . yes, I'm doing all that.

ROSS (*Prompting*): . . . and you're in love with her.

MARTIN (*Begins to cry*): Yes! Yes! I am! I'm in love with her. Oh, Jesus! Oh, Sylvia! Oh, Sylvia!

ROSS (*After a respectful pause*): I almost dare not ask this, but . . . who is Sylvia?

MARTIN: I can't tell you!

ROSS: Who else *but* me? You can't tell Stevie, it would . . .

MARTIN: NO!!

ROSS: Then, who is she? Who is Sylvia?

(*Martin pauses; goes to wallet, brings out photo, looks at it, hesitates, then hands it to Ross, not looking as he does so. Ross takes photo, looks at it, double-takes, begins a huge guffaw, which becomes a coughing*)

MARTIN (*Shy*): Don't laugh. Please; don't laugh.

ROSS (*Staring at photo; straightforward*): This is Sylvia.

MARTIN (*Nods*): Yes.

ROSS (*Pinning it down*): This is Sylvia . . . who you're fucking.

MARTIN (*Winces*): Don't say that. (*It just comes out*) Whom.

ROSS: . . . with whom you're having an affair.

MARTIN (*Soft; nodding*): Yes. (*Pause*) Yes.

ROSS: How long now?

MARTIN (*Soft*): Six months.

ROSS: Jesus. You *have* to tell Stevie.

MARTIN: I can't! I couldn't do that!

ROSS: You *have* to . . . and if you don't, I will.

MARTIN (*Begging*): No! Ross! Please!

ROSS (*Genuine*): You're in very serious trouble.

MARTIN (*Pause; little boy*): I am?

ROSS (*Quiet; shaking his head as he looks at the photo*): You sure are, buddy; you sure are.

MARTIN: But, Ross, you don't under . . .

ROSS (*Huge*): THIS IS A GOAT! YOU'RE HAVING AN AFFAIR WITH A GOAT! YOU'RE FUCKING A GOAT!

MARTIN (*Long pause; factual*): Yes.

End of Scene One

SCENE TWO

(*Same living room; a day later. Martin, Stevie, and Billy; Stevie holding a letter*)

BILLY (*To Martin*): You're doing *what*?! You're fucking a *goat*?!

MARTIN (*Indicating Stevie, who is at window, facing out*): Billy! Please!

BILLY: Jesus Christ!

MARTIN: Don't swear.

BILLY (*Scoffing laugh*): Don't *what*?!

MARTIN: Don't swear; you're too young.

BILLY (*Considers a moment, then*): FUCK THAT!!

MARTIN: Billy! Your mother!

BILLY (*Scoffing laugh*): You're fucking a fucking goat and you tell me not to *swear*?!

MARTIN: You know, your *own* sex life leaves a little to . . .

STEVIE (*Still at window; ice*): All right, you two!

BILLY (*To Martin*): At least what I do is with . . . per-sons!

STEVIE (*Turning into the room*): I said, all right, you two!

BILLY: Goat fucker!

MARTIN: Fucking faggot!

STEVIE: I said, all right!

(*A silence*)

BILLY (*To Martin; soft, hurt*): Fucking faggot? You called me a fucking *faggot*?!

MARTIN (*Gentle; to Billy*): I'm . . . I'm sorry.

STEVIE (*Even*): Your father's sorry, Billy.

MARTIN: I'm sorry. (*To get rid of the whole subject*) You're gay, and that's fine, and I don't give a shit what you put where. (*Thinks about it*) I don't care one way or the other is what I mean.

BILLY: Yeah! Sure!

STEVIE (*Cool*): I said your father's sorry for calling you a fucking faggot because he's not that kind of man. He's a decent, liberal, right-thinking, talented, famous, gentle man (*hard*) who right now would appear to be fucking a goat; and *I* would like to talk about *that*, if you don't mind. *Or* . . . even if you *do*.

BILLY (*Nice*): Sure, Mom; I'm sorry; you go right ahead.

MARTIN (*Sighs*): Oh, dear.

STEVIE (*Objective*): Let's review Ross's letter, shall we? (*waves it*)

MARTIN (*Hurt and enraged*): How *could* he!! How could he do such a thing?!

STEVIE (*Ice*): How could he — best friend to both of us, a man you would trust with your wife — no? . . .

MARTIN: . . . sure; sure . . .

STEVIE: How could Ross write me this letter? (*waves it again*)

MARTIN: YES!!

STEVIE (*Composed; cool; quoting*): ". . . because I love you, Stevie, as much as I love Martin, because I love you both — respect you, love you — I can't stay silent at a time of crisis for you both, for Martin's public image, and your own deeply devoted . . ."

MARTIN: BULLSHIT!

STEVIE: Yes?

MARTIN: Yes!

STEVIE: So; anyhow; let's not pretend he never wrote the letter; let's not pretend I didn't get it in the mail today — nice that: no electronic nonsense — and let us not pretend that I did not read it.

MARTIN: No; no, of course not.

STEVIE: And let us not pretend that Ross does not tell me that you are having an affair with . . . (*looks*) how does he put it? . . . "an affair with a certain Sylvia who, I am mortified to tell you . . ." He does get flowery, doesn't he!

MARTIN: Yes; yes, he does.

STEVIE: "I am mortified to tell you is a goat."

BILLY: Jesus!

STEVIE & MARTIN: Will you be still!!?

BILLY (*Dramatically cowering*): Hey! Sure! Jesus!

STEVIE (*Back to business; quoting again*): "You will, of course, be shocked and greatly distressed . . ." No kidding! Uh . . . "shocked and greatly distressed to know of this, but I felt it my obligation to be the one to bear these tidings . . ."

MARTIN (*Some disbelief*): Tidings?

STEVIE: Yes; "tidings."

MARTIN: Jesus! Of comfort and joy?

STEVIE: ". . . as I'm sure you'd rather hear it all from a dear friend . . ." As opposed to *what*! The ASPCA?!

MARTIN (*Woe*): Oh, God; oh, God.

STEVIE: "Doubtless, Martin . . ." Doubtless?

MARTIN: Probably.

STEVIE: ". . . doubtless Martin will tell you all I have not, all I cannot." (*To Martin*) What are friends for, eh?

BILLY (*Really sad*): Oh, Dad!

MARTIN: Poor Dad?

BILLY: What?

MARTIN: Nothing.

STEVIE (*Level*): So, now you will tell me all that Ross has not, cannot. After you tell me what friends are for, of course.

MARTIN: Oh . . . Stevie . . . (*Starts to move to her*)

STEVIE (*Abrupt; cold*): Stay away from me; stay there. You smell of goat, you smell of shit, you smell of all I cannot imagine being able to smell. Stay *away* from me!

MARTIN (*Arms wide; hopeless*): I *love* you!

BILLY (*Softly*): Jesus.

STEVIE: You *love* me. Let's see if I understand the phrase. You *love* me.

MARTIN: Yes!

STEVIE: But I'm a human being; I have only two breasts; I walk upright; I give milk only on special occasions; I use the toilet. (*Begins to cry*) You love me? I don't understand.

MARTIN (*More hopeless*): Oh, God!

STEVIE: How can you love me when you love so much less?

MARTIN (*Even more hopeless*): Oh, God.

BILLY: Fucking a goat?!

MARTIN (*To Billy; sharp*): That does it! Out!

BILLY (*To Stevie; arms wide*): What did I *say*? I said he was . . .

MARTIN: Enough!

BILLY: For Christ's sake, I . . .

MARTIN: Go to your room!

STEVIE (*Almost laughing*): Oh, really, Martin!

BILLY (*Incredulous*): Go to my room?!

MARTIN: Go to your *room*!

BILLY: What am I — eight, or something? Go to my *room*?

STEVIE: You'd better go, Billy. If you stay you might learn something.

MARTIN (*To Stevie*): Nicely put.

STEVIE (*Coldly*): Thanks.

BILLY (*To Stevie*): You want me to leave you here with this . . . this . . . *pervert*?!

STEVIE (*To help*): Just go to your room, Billy, or go outside, or . . .

MARTIN: . . . or go to one of your public urinals, or one of those death clubs, or . . .

BILLY: KNOCK IT OFF!!

MARTIN (*Impressed*): Wow!

BILLY (*Sneering*): You seem to know a lot about all that.

MARTIN (*Not defensive*): I *read*.

BILLY: Sure. (*To Stevie*) I'll go if you think it's OK, Ma; I'll go. (*To Martin*) But not to your . . . "places." I will probably go to my room, and I'll probably close my door, and I'll probably lie down on my bed, and I'll probably start crying and it'll probably get louder and worse, but you probably won't hear it — either of you — because you'll be too busy killing each other. But I'll be there, and my little eight-year-old heart will for certain be breaking — in twain, as they say.

MARTIN (*Some awe; no contempt*): Very good; very good.

STEVIE (*Preoccupied*): Yes; very good, Billy.

BILLY (*Fleeing; near tears*): Jesus Christ!

STEVIE (*As he exits*): Billy . . .

MARTIN (*Quietly*): Let him go. (*Silence; quietly*) Well, now; just you and me.

Stevie and Martin (played by Mercedes Ruehl and Bill Pullman, respectively) fighting in the 2002 Broadway premiere of *The Goat, or Who Is Sylvia?* at the Golden Theatre, directed by David Esbjornson.

STEVIE (*Pause*): Yes.

MARTIN (*Pause*): I take it you want to talk about it?

STEVIE (*Awful chuckle*): Oh, God! (*Afterthought*) You *take* it?

MARTIN: Is that a "yes"?

STEVIE (*Cold; precise*): I was out shopping today — dress gloves, if you want to know. I still wear them — for weddings and things . . .

MARTIN (*Puzzled*): Who's getting married?

STEVIE (*Huge*): SHUT UP!

MARTIN (*Winces*): Sorry.

STEVIE (*Normal tone again*): . . . dress gloves, and then to the fish people for shad roe — it's just come in — and then back home, and you were gone and I heard Billy's music up in his room and there was the mail. You'd gone out before it came — not that it would have mattered: we don't read each other's.

MARTIN: Would that we did.

STEVIE: Oh? I would have found out sooner or later. And there was Ross's letter. "Ross? Writing to me? Whatever for!"

MARTIN (*Softly*): Oh, God.

STEVIE: . . . and I was standing in the pantry. I'd put the roe away and had left the kitchen and was moving to the dining room on my way to the stairs when I began to read it.

MARTIN: Ross shouldn't have done this. He *knows* he shouldn't have done . . .

STEVIE (*Reading; steady, almost amused*): "Dearest Stevie . . ."

MARTIN: Oh, God.

STEVIE: "This is the hardest letter I've ever had to write."

MARTIN: Sure!

STEVIE: You doubt it? ". . . the hardest letter I've ever had to write, and to my dearest friends. But because I love you, Stevie, as much as I love Martin, because I love you both — respect you, love you — I can't stay silent at a time of crisis for you both, for Martin's public image and your own deeply devoted . . ."

MARTIN: As I said, bullshit.

STEVIE: . . . "self. I must put it baldly, for hinting would only put off the inevitable. Martin — as he told me this himself" . . . (*aside*) I would have liked to have been listening to *that* conversation!

MARTIN: No you wouldn't.

STEVIE (*Reading again*): "Martin is having an affair with a certain Sylvia . . ." (*To Martin*) Oh, God, I thought; at least it's someone I don't know; at least it's not Ross's first wife, the one I thought you might if you were going to . . .

MARTIN (*Surprise*): Rebecca?

STEVIE: Yes, or maybe your new assistant . . .

MARTIN (*Bewildered*): Who? Ted Ryan?

STEVIE: No; the *other* one — the one with the hooters.

MARTIN: Oh; Lucy something.

STEVIE: Yes: Lucy "something." You men are the end. Where was I? (*reads again*) . . . "an affair with a certain Sylvia who, I am mortified to tell you . . . is a goat. You will, of course, be shocked and greatly disturbed to know of this, but I felt it my obligation to be the one to bear these tidings, as I'm sure you'd rather hear it from a dear friend. Doubtless, Martin . . ." Doubtless?

MARTIN (*Shrugs*): Sounds right.

STEVIE: "Doubtless, Martin will tell you all I have not . . . all I cannot. With profound affection for you both, Ross." (*Pause*) Well.

MARTIN: Yes. "Well."

STEVIE (*Not eager; dogged*): We will now discuss it.

MARTIN (*Heavy sigh*): Of course, though you won't understand.

STEVIE: Oh? Do you know what I thought — what I thought after I'd read the letter, right to the end?

MARTIN: No, I don't want to know . . . or guess.

STEVIE: Well, I laughed, of course: a grim joke but an awfully funny one. "That Ross, I tell you, that Ross! You go too far, Ross. It's funny . . . in its . . . awful way, but it's way overboard, Ross!" So, I shook my head and laughed — at the awfulness of it, the absurdity, the awfulness; some things are so awful you have to laugh — and then I listened to myself laughing, and I began to wonder why I *was* — *laughing*. "It's not funny when you come right down to it, Ross." Why *was* I laughing? And just like that (*snaps her fingers*) I stopped; I stopped laughing. I realized — probably in the way if you suddenly fell off a building — oh, shit! I've fallen off a building and I'm going to die; I'm going to go splat on the sidewalk; like *that* — that it wasn't a joke at all; it was awful and absurd, but it wasn't a joke. And everything tied in — Ross coming here to interview you yesterday, the funny smell, the Noel Coward bit we did about you having an affair, and with a goat. You said it right out and I laughed. You told me! You came right out and fucking *told* me, and I laughed, and I made jokes about going to the feed store, and I *laughed*. I fucking laughed! Until it stopped; until the laughter stopped. Until it all came together — Ross's letter and all the rest: that odd smell . . . the mistress's perfume on you. And so I knew.

MARTIN: Stevie, I'm so . . .

STEVIE: Shut up. And so I knew. And next, of course, came believing it. Knowing it — knowing it's true is one thing, but *believing* what you *know* . . . well, there's the tough part. We all prepare for jolts along the way, disturbances of the peace, the lies, the evasions, the infidelities — *if* they happen. (*Very offhand*) I've never had an affair, by the way, all our years together; not even with a cat, or . . . *anything*.

MARTIN: Oh, Stevie . . .

STEVIE: We prepare for . . . things, for lessenings, even; inevitable . . . lessenings, and we think we can handle everything, whatever comes along, but we don't know, do we! (*Right at Martin*) Do we!

MARTIN (*Bereaved*): No; no, we don't.

STEVIE: Fucking *right* we don't! (*Didactic*) Something can happen that's outside the rules, that doesn't relate to The Way the Game Is Played. Death before you're ready to even think about it — that's part of

the game. A stroke that leaves you sitting looking at an eggplant the week before had been your husband — that's another. Emotional disengagement, gradual, so gradual you don't know it's happening, or sudden — not very often, but occasionally — that's another. You've read about spouses — God! I hate that word! — "spouses" who all of a sudden start wearing dresses — yours, or their own collection — wives gone dyke . . . but if there's one thing you *don't* put on your plate, no matter how exotic your tastes may be is . . . bestiality.

MARTIN: Don't! You don't understand.

STEVIE: The fucking of animals! No, that's one thing you haven't thought about, one thing you've overlooked as a byway on the road of life, as the old soap has it. "Well, I wonder when he'll start cruising livestock. I must ask Mother whether Dad did it and how *she* handled it." No, that's the one thing you haven't thought about — nor could you conceive of. (*Pause; grimly cheerful*) So! How was *your* day?

MARTIN (*Pause; attempting the casual*): Well . . . I had a good day at the office. Made the design for The World City even larger than . . .

STEVIE (*Fixed smile*): Oh, good!

MARTIN: . . . and then I stopped by the haberdasher . . .

STEVIE (*Pretending to puzzle*): Ha-ber-dash-er. That's someone who makes haberdash?

MARTIN: Haber, I think. Dash is part of doing it.

STEVIE: Ah! *Then* what?

MARTIN: Hm? Well, then I drove back home, and . . .

STEVIE: What! You didn't stop by to see your ladyfriend? Get a lick in?

MARTIN: She's in the country. Please, Stevie . . . *don't*!

STEVIE (*Feigned wonder*): She's in the *country*!

MARTIN: I keep her there.

STEVIE: Where!?

MARTIN: Please! Don't!

STEVIE: Martin, did you ever think you'd come back from your splendid life, walk into your living room and find you had no life left?

MARTIN: Not specifically; no. (*Looks down*)

STEVIE: I think we'd better talk about this. If I'm going to kill you I need to know exactly why — all the details.

MARTIN (*Shy*): You really want to?

STEVIE: What? Kill you?

MARTIN: No; learn about it.

STEVIE (*Big*): No! I *don't* really want to! (*Normal tone again*) I want the whole day to rewind — start over. I want the reel to reverse: to see the mail on the hall table where Billy's left it, then *not* see it because I haven't opened the door yet — not having gotten the fish yet because I haven't bought the gloves yet because I haven't left the house yet because I haven't gotten out of our bed because I haven't *waked* UP YET!! (*Quieter*) But . . . since I can't reverse time . . . yes, I *do* want to know. I'm reeling with it. (*Pleading*) Make me not *believe* it! Please, make me *not believe* it.

MARTIN (*Pause*): Why aren't you crying?

STEVIE: Because this is too serious. Do goats cry, by the way?

MARTIN: I . . . I don't know. I haven't . . .

STEVIE: . . . made her cry yet!? What's the *matter* with you?!

MARTIN (*Begging*): Stevie . . .

STEVIE (*As if to someone else*): He can't even make a *goat* cry. What *good* is he? His son's probably weeping as we speak. That was pretty awful what you said to him, Martin, pretty awful. His son's probably lying on his bed, tears flowing; his wife *would* be crying (*harder*) except she can't be that weak right now. And you can't even make a goat cry?! Jeez!

MARTIN (*Dogmatic*): I didn't say I *couldn't;* I said I *haven't.*

STEVIE: Well, the goats of this world must be very happy. Oh, you kid!

MARTIN (*Starting to leave*): I can't *have* this conversation. I can't listen to you when you're . . .

STEVIE (*Blocking him*): You *stay* where you *are*! You will *have* this conversation, and with *me* and right *now*!

MARTIN (*Retreating; sighing*): Where shall I start?

STEVIE (*A threat*): Right at the beginning! (*Afterthought*) Why do you call her Sylvia, by the way? Did she have a tag, or something? Or, was it more:
Who is Sylvia,
Fair is she
That all our goats commend her . . .

MARTIN (*Trying to be rational*): No, it just seemed right. Very good, by the way.

STEVIE: Thank you. You saw this . . . *thing* . . . this goat, and you said to yourself "This is Sylvia." Or did you talk to it: "Hello, Sylvia." How the hell did you know it was a she — was a female? Bag of nipples dragging in the dung? Or, isn't this your first?!

MARTIN (*Very quiet*): She is my first; she is my only. But you don't understand. You . . .

STEVIE (*Contemptuous*): Awww; I'm trying not to throw up.

MARTIN: Well, if that's the way you . . .

STEVIE: *No!!* Tell me.

MARTIN (*Sighs*): All right. As I said to Ross . . .

STEVIE (*Broad parody*): "As I said to Ross . . ." NO! Not "As I said to Ross." To *me*! As you say to *me*!

MARTIN (*Annoyed*): In any event . . .

STEVIE: Not "in any event!" No! *This* event!

MARTIN (*Won't let it go*): As I said to Ross . . .

STEVIE (*Impatient acquiescence*): *Very* well; as you said to Ross.

MARTIN: Thank you. As I said to Ross, I'd gone to the country . . . to find the place we wanted, our . . . country *place.*

STEVIE (*Fact*): You went out a lot.

MARTIN: Well, if you're after Utopia . . . (*Shrugs*)

STEVIE: Sure.

MARTIN: . . . unless you're one of those people finds it right off: "That's it; that's the place." Unless you're one of those, you've got to search; look around.

Close enough in to make it practical for our country needs. No more than an hour or so from . . .

STEVIE (*Scoffing*): Our "country needs"?

MARTIN: *You're* the one who said it. Verdancy: flowers and green leaves against steel and stone. OK?

STEVIE (*Shrugs*): OK. (*Angry*) And it's lovely. Now get to the *goat*!

MARTIN: I'm *getting* there. I'm *getting* to her.

STEVIE: Stop calling it *her*!

MARTIN (*Defending*): *That* is what she *is*! It is a *she*! She is a *she*!

STEVIE (*Pathetic sneer*): I suppose I should be grateful it wasn't a *male, isn't* a male goat.

MARTIN: Funny you should ask — as they say. There was a place I went to . . .

STEVIE: Oh?

MARTIN: Well, when I realized something was wrong. I mean, when I realized people would *think* something was wrong, that what I was doing wasn't . . .

STEVIE (*Dispassionate*): I *am* going to kill you.

MARTIN (*Preoccupied*): Yes; probably. It was a therapy place, a place people went to . . . to talk about it, about what they were doing . . . and with whom.

STEVIE: *What!* Not *whom! What!* With *what*!

MARTIN (*Sharp*): Whatever! A place! Please! Let me finish this! (*Stevie is silent*) A place to talk about it; like AA, like Alcoholics Anonymous.

STEVIE (*Sneers*): Goat-fuckers Anonymous?

MARTIN (*Oddly shocked*): Please! (*Stevie hoots. Quieter*) Please?

STEVIE: Sorry. Destroy me.

MARTIN: It had no cute name; no AA; no . . . no nothing. Just . . . a place.

STEVIE: How did you find it?

MARTIN: Online.

STEVIE (*Toneless*): Of course.

MARTIN: I went there . . . and there were — what? — ten of us . . . a group leader, of course.

STEVIE: What was *he* fucking? *Who;* sorry.

MARTIN: He was cured, he said — odd phrase. Was off it.

STEVIE (*Very calm*): Very well. What *had* he been fucking?

MARTIN (*Matter of fact*): A pig. A young pig.

(*Stevie rises, finds a big ceramic table plate, smashes it, resits, or whatever*)

STEVIE (*Without emotion*): Go on.

MARTIN (*Indicates*): Is there going to be a lot of that?

STEVIE: Probably.

MARTIN: You don't want Billy down here; some things . . .

STEVIE (*Steaming*): Some things are . . . *what*?! Private? Sacred? Husband telling wifey about a very peculiar therapy session? A *pig*?!

MARTIN (*A little embarrassed*): A small one, he said.

STEVIE: Jesus!

(*Billy rushes in from the hall*)

BILLY: You two OK?

MARTIN: Yes-we're-fine-go-away-Billy.

BILLY: Who's throwing things?

STEVIE: I am; your mother is throwing things.

BILLY: Is there going to be more?

STEVIE: I imagine so.

BILLY (*Retrieving a small vase*): I gave you this one; I think I'll take it upstairs.

STEVIE (*As Billy turns to go*): I would have noticed, Billy.

BILLY (*Shaking his head*): Sure. You guys hold it down. (*Exits*)

STEVIE (*After him*): I *would* have. (*Uncertain*) I *think* I would have.

MARTIN (*Pause*): So, anyway; it was this place.

STEVIE (*Reconcentrating*): A pig? Really?

MARTIN: Well, everyone had . . . *you* know . . .

STEVIE: . . . some*one*, or some*thing*.

MARTIN: Yes.

STEVIE (*Lightbulb*): And was Clarissa Atherton there?

MARTIN: Who? Yes! That's where I got the card, and . . .

STEVIE: And what is *she* fucking? *Who?*

MARTIN (*Matter of fact*): A dog, I think.

(*Stevie finds a vase, crashes it to the floor*)

STEVIE: A dog you *think*.

MARTIN: Why would she lie? Why would anyone there lie?

STEVIE: Damned if *I* know.

MARTIN (*Sighs*): And so I went there, and . . .

STEVIE (*There is chaos behind the civility, of course*): Did you all take your . . . friends with you — your pigs, your dogs, your goats, your . . .

MARTIN: No. We weren't there to talk about *them;* we were there about ourselves, our . . . our problems, as they called them.

STEVIE: The livestock was all happy, you mean.

MARTIN: Well, no; there was this one . . . goose, I think it was . . . (*Stevie finds a vase, crashes it to the floor*) Shall we go outside?

STEVIE (*Hands on hips*): Get *on* with it.

MARTIN (*So calm*): All right; there was this one goose . . .

STEVIE: *Not* geese! *Not* pigs! *Not* dogs! *Goats!* The subject is *goats!*

MARTIN: The subject is *a* goat; the subject is Sylvia. (*He sees Stevie looking for something to throw*) No! Don't; please! Just listen! Sit and listen!

STEVIE (*Has a small bowl in her hands; sits*): All right. I'm listening.

MARTIN: I said, most of the people there were having problems, were . . . ashamed, or — what is the word? — conflicted . . . were . . . needed to talk about it while . . . while I went there, I guess, to find out why they were all there.

STEVIE (*As if the language were unfamiliar*): Pardon?

MARTIN: I didn't understand why they were there — why they were all so . . . unhappy; what was wrong with . . . with . . . being in love . . . like that. (*Stevie gently separates hands, letting bowl fall between her legs, break*) There's so much I have to explain.

STEVIE (*Deep, quiet irony*): Oh?

MARTIN (*Rises, moves a little away*): You must promise to be still. Sit there and please listen, and then maybe when I've finished you . . . just listen; please.

STEVIE (*Sad smile*): How could I not?

MARTIN: I went there . . . because I couldn't come to *you* with it.

STEVIE: Oh?

MARTIN: Well . . . *think* about it.

STEVIE (*Does*): I suppose you're right.

MARTIN: And most of them had a problem, had a long history. The man with the pig was a farmboy, and he and his brothers, when they were kids, just . . . *did* it . . . *naturally;* it was what they did . . . with the pigs. (*Knits brow*) Or piglets, perhaps; that wasn't clear.

STEVIE: Naturally; of course.

MARTIN: Are you agreeing?

STEVIE: No. Just get on with it.

MARTIN: It was what they did. Maybe it was better than . . .

STEVIE: . . . than with each other, or their sisters, or their grandmothers? You've got to be kidding!

MARTIN: No one got hurt.

STEVIE: HUNH!!

MARTIN: We'll talk about that.

STEVIE: You *bet* we will!

MARTIN (*Sighs*): Most of them had a reason, the man with the pig more a matter of . . . habit than anything else, I guess . . . comfort, familiarity.

STEVIE (*Eyes heavenward*): Jesus!

MARTIN: Though he was off it . . . "cured," as he put it, which I found odd.

STEVIE: Of course.

MARTIN: I mean . . . if he was happy . . .

(*Stevie knocks over the small side table where she is sitting, never taking her eyes off Martin*)

STEVIE (*Ironic*): Ooops!

MARTIN: When he was doing it, I mean. Must you? Though I suppose he wasn't . . . no longer was happy.

STEVIE (*Feigned surprise*): You mean you didn't *ask* him?

MARTIN: No; no, I didn't. The lady with the German Shepherd . . .

STEVIE: Clarissa?

MARTIN: No; another one. The lady with the Shepherd, it turned out she had been raped by her father *and* her brother when she was twelve, or so . . . continually raped, one watching the other, she told us . . .

STEVIE: . . . and so she took up with a *dog*?!

MARTIN (*No opinion*): Yes; it would seem. The man with the goose was . . . hideously ugly — I could barely look at him — and I suppose he thought he could never . . . *you* know.

STEVIE (*Cool*): Do I?

MARTIN: Try and imagine.

STEVIE (*Calm; sad*): I doubt I can.

MARTIN: *Try:* so ugly, no woman — no *man* — would even *think* of . . . "doing it" with you — *ever.*

STEVIE: One in the hand, et cetera. But . . . a goose!?

MARTIN (*Sad smile*): Not everyone is satisfied that way . . . one in the hand. No matter. And *I* was unhappy there, for *they* were all unhappy.

STEVIE: My goodness.

MARTIN: And I didn't know why.

STEVIE (*Considers it*): Really? I think we've hit upon why I'm going to kill you.

MARTIN (*Onward*): There's something else I want you to understand.

STEVIE (*Sarcasm*): Oh? Something else?

MARTIN: It's something I told Ross.

STEVIE: Not him again.

MARTIN: He *is* my best friend.

STEVIE (*Actress-y*): Oh? And I thought *I* was!

MARTIN (*Undeterred; calm*): I told him that in all our time together — yours and mine — all our marriage — I've never been unfaithful.

STEVIE (*A beat; fake astonishment*): Hunh!!

MARTIN (*Onward*): Never in all our years. Oh, early on, one of your friends would grope me in the kitchen at a party, or . . .

STEVIE: I love my friends; they have taste.

MARTIN: Never unfaithful; never once. I've never even wanted to. We're so good together, you and I.

STEVIE: A perfect fit, eh?

MARTIN (*Sincere*): Yes!

STEVIE: You'd never imagine that a marriage could be so perfect.

MARTIN: Yes! I mean *no; I hadn't.*

STEVIE (*Advertisement*): Great sex, good cook, even does windows.

MARTIN: Be serious!

STEVIE: No! It's too serious for that. (*Afterthought*) Fuck you, by the way.

MARTIN: Never once! People looked at me, said "What's the matter with you?!" "Don't you have any . . . you know, lust?" And "Sure," I said, "I've got plenty. All for Stevie."

STEVIE (*Shakes her head; sing-song*): La-di-da; la-di-fuckin'-da!

MARTIN (*Rage*): Listen to me!

STEVIE (*Army drill*): Yes, Sir! (*Softer*) Yes, Sir.

MARTIN: All the men I knew were "having affairs" . . . *see*ing other women, and laughing about it — at the club, on the train. I felt . . . well, I almost felt like a misfit. "What's the matter with you, Martin!? You mean you're only doing it with your wife!? What kind of man *are* you?!"

STEVIE: You men *must* be fun together.

MARTIN: Odd man out. I only wanted *you.*

STEVIE (*Pause; quietly*): And *I* have something to tell *you.*

MARTIN (*Anticipating, with dread*): Oh, no! Don't tell me that you've been with . . .

STEVIE (*Hands up; shakes her head*): Hush. In all our marriage I've never even wanted anyone but you.

MARTIN (*Deeply sad*): Oh, Stevie.

STEVIE: My mother told me — we really *were* good friends; I'm sorry you never knew her.

MARTIN: I am, too.

STEVIE: We talked together like sisters, by God; we talked the night away, two "girls" talking; we were that good friends, but she sure knew how to be a "parent" when she needed to, when she wanted to keep me very . . . level. And she said to me — I never told you this — "Be sure you marry someone you're in love with — deeply and wholly in love with — but be careful who you fall in love with, because you might marry him." (*Martin chuckles, quietly, ruefully*) "Your father and I have the best marriage anyone could possibly have," she said to me, over and over. "Be sure you do, too."

MARTIN: Stevie, I . . .

STEVIE: "Be careful who you marry," she said to me. And I *was.* I *fell* in love with you? No . . . I rose into love with you and have — what — *cherished*? you, all these years, been proud of all you've done, been happy with our . . . funny son, been . . . well, happy. I guess that's the word. No, I don't guess; I *know.* (*Begins to cry*) I've been happy. (*More*) Look at me, Mother; I've married the man I loved (*more*) and I've been . . . so . . . happy.

MARTIN (*Moves to her; touches her*): Oh, Stevie . . .

STEVIE (*Huge; swipes objects off the coffee table*): GET YOUR GOAT-FUCKING HANDS OFF ME!!! (*Retreats to wall, arms wide, sobbing greatly*)

MARTIN (*Reacts as if he's touched a hot stove*): All right! No more!

STEVIE: Yes! *More!* Finish it! Vomit it all up! Puke it out all over me. I'll never be less ready. So . . . *do* it! *DO IT!!* I've laid it all out for you; I'm naked on the table; take all your knives! Cut me! Scar me forever!

MARTIN (*Thinks a moment*): Before or *after* I vomit on you? (*Gently; hands up to appease*) Sorry; sorry.

STEVIE (*A shaking voice*): Women in deep woe often mix their metaphors.

MARTIN (*Pacifying*): Yes; yes.

STEVIE: Get *on* with it! (*Afterthought*) Very good, by the way.

MARTIN (*Rue*): Thanks.

STEVIE: . . . and hopelessly inappropriate.

MARTIN: Yes; sorry.

STEVIE (*Casually overturns a chair*): Get on with it, I said.

MARTIN: Are you going to do that with *all* the furniture?

STEVIE (*Looks around*): I think so. You may have to help me with some of it.

MARTIN: Truce! Truce!

STEVIE (*Takes a painting, breaks it over something*): NO! NO TRUCE! *All* of it! Now!

MARTIN: That was my mother's painting.

STEVIE: It still is! (*Prompting*) You found us our lovely country place.

MARTIN (*Girds*): And the day I found it — I called you. You remember: I told you I'd put a hold on it.

STEVIE: I'll never forget.

MARTIN: And I was driving out of the town, back to the highway, and I stopped at the top of a hill . . .

STEVIE: Crest.

MARTIN: What!? Who *are* you!?

STEVIE: You stopped at the crest of a hill — on it, actually.

MARTIN: Yes. And I stopped, and the view was . . . wonderful. Not spectacular, but wonderful — fall, the leaves turning . . .

STEVIE (*Staring at him*): A regular bucolic.

MARTIN: Yes; a regular bucolic. I stopped and got us things — vegetables and things. *You* remember.

STEVIE (*Denial*): No; I don't.

MARTIN (*Realizing, going on*): No matter. And it was then that I saw her.

STEVIE (*Grotesque incomprehension*): Who!?

MARTIN (*Deeply sad*): Oh, Stevie . . .

STEVIE (*Heavy irony*): Who!? Who could you have seen!?

MARTIN (*Dogged*): I'm going on with this. You asked. I'm going to get it all out.

STEVIE (*Eyes hard on him*): Serves *me* right, I guess.

MARTIN: And I closed the trunk of the car, with all that I'd gotten — (*pause*) . . . and it was then that I saw her. And she was looking at me with . . . with those eyes.

STEVIE (*Staring at him*): Oh, those eyes! (*Afterthought*) *THEM* eyes!

MARTIN (*Slow; deliberate*): And what I felt was . . . it was unlike anything I'd ever felt before. It was so . . . amazing. There she was.

STEVIE (*Grotesque enthusiasm*): Who!? Who!?

MARTIN: Don't. She was looking at me with those eyes of hers and . . . I melted, I think. I think that's what I did: I melted.

STEVIE (*Hideous enthusiasm*): You melted!!

MARTIN (*Waves her off*): I'd never seen such an expression. It was pure . . . and trusting and . . . and innocent; so . . . so guileless.

STEVIE (*Sardonic echo*): Guileless; innocent; pure. You've never seen children, or anything? You never saw Billy when he was a kid?

MARTIN (*Pleading*): Of course I did. Don't *mock* me.

STEVIE (*Shooting harsh chuckle*): Don't mock *me.*

MARTIN: I . . . I went over to where she was — to the fence where she was, and I knelt there, eye level . . .

STEVIE (*Quiet loathing*): *Goat* level.

MARTIN (*Angry; didactic*): I will *finish* this! You *asked* for it, and you're going to *get* it! So . . . shut your tragic mouth! (*Stevie does a sharp intake of breath, puts her fingers over her mouth*) All right. Listen to me. It was as if an alien came out of whatever it was, and it . . . took me with it, and it was . . . an ecstasy and a purity, and a . . . love of a . . . (*dogmatic*) un-i-mag-in-able kind, and it relates to nothing *whatever*, to nothing that can be *related* to! Don't you see!? Don't you see the . . . don't you see the "thing" that happened to me? What nobody understands? Why I can't feel what I'm supposed to? Because it relates to nothing? It can't have happened! It did, but it *can't* have! (*Stevie shakes her head*) What are you doing?

STEVIE (*Removes fingers*): Being tragic. I bet a psychiatrist would love all this.

MARTIN: I knelt there, eye level, and there was a . . . a what!? . . . an understanding so intense, so natural . . .

STEVIE: There are some things you *can* remember, eh?

MARTIN (*Closes his eyes, reopens them*): . . . an understanding so . . .

STEVIE (*Awful, high-pitched little voice*): I can't remember why I come into rooms, where I put the thing for the razor . . .

MARTIN (*Refusing to be drawn in*): . . . an understanding so natural, so intense that I will *never* forget it, as intense as the night you and I finally came at the same time. What was it . . . a month after we began? (*Where is she, emotionally?*) Stevie? It wasn't happening . . . but it *was!*

STEVIE (*Shaking her head; oddly objective*): How *much* do you hate me?

MARTIN (*Hopeless*): I *love* you. (*Pause*) And I love *her.* (*Pause*) And there it is.

(*Stevie howls three times, slowly, deliberately; a combination of rage and hurt*)

STEVIE (*Then; calmly*): Go on.

MARTIN (*Apologetic*): I have to do it.

STEVIE: Yes? (*Martin nods*) Right.

MARTIN (*Starting again*) And there was a connection there — a communication — that, well . . . an epiphany, I guess comes closest, and I knew what was going to happen.

STEVIE (*Mildly interested in the fact*): I think I'm going to be sick.

MARTIN: *Please* don't. (*Back to it*) Epiphany! And when it happens there's no retreating, no holding back. I put my hands through the wires of the fence and she came toward me, slipped her face between my hands, brought her nose to mine at the wires and . . . and nuzzled.

STEVIE: I am a grown woman; a grown married woman. (*As if she's never heard the word before*) Nuzzled; nuzzled.

MARTIN: Her breath . . . her breath was . . . so sweet, warm and . . . (*Hears something; stops*)

STEVIE: Go on. Tell the grown-up married woman . . .

MARTIN (*Warning hand up*): I hear Billy.

(*Billy enters*)

BILLY: Are you hitting her!? (*Sees the carnage*) What the fuck!?

STEVIE: We're redecorating, honey. No, he's not, by the way — hitting me. I'm hitting myself.

BILLY (*Near tears*): I hear you two! I'm up there and I *hear* you! STOP IT! JESUS GOD, STOP IT!!

MARTIN (*Gentle*): We will, Billy; we're not quite done.

STEVIE: Go away, Billy. Go out and play.

BILLY: Go out and . . . ?

STEVIE (*Harder*): Leave the house! Leave us alone!

BILLY: But . . .

MARTIN (*Calm*): Do what your Mother says. "Go out and play." Make mudpies; climb a tree . . .

BILLY (*A finger in Martin's face*): If I come back and find you've hurt her, I'll . . . I'll . . . (*Billy lunges at Martin, shoves him, recoils. Martin steps forward, stops. Billy sobs, runs from the room. We hear the front door slam*)

STEVIE (*After*): Mudpies?

MARTIN: Well . . . whatever.

STEVIE (*Calm*): What *will* you do if he comes back and finds you've hurt me? . . . *when* he comes back and finds you've hurt me?

MARTIN (*Absorbed in something*): What?

STEVIE (*Smiles*): Down from the trees, hands all muddy? (*Sad*) Nothing. (*Cold*) You were in the middle of your Epiphany.

MARTIN (*Sighs*): Yes.

STEVIE (*Sad*): God, I wish you were stupid.

MARTIN (*He, too*): Yes; I wish *you* were stupid, too.

STEVIE (*Pause; businesslike*): Epiphany!

MARTIN: Yes. It was at that moment that I realized . . .

STEVIE: . . . that you and the fucking goat were destined for one another!

MARTIN: . . . that she and I were . . . (*Softly; embarrassed*) that she and I were going to go to bed together.

STEVIE: To stall together! To hay! *Not* to bed!

MARTIN (*Sits*): Whatever. That what could not happen was *going* to. That we wanted each other very much, that I had to have her, that I . . . (*Stevie screams — a deep-throated rage — and lunges at Martin. He rises, grabs her wrists and shoves her into a chair. She attempts to get up, but he shoves her back again*) Now stop it! Let me finish!

STEVIE: You'll be fucking Billy next.

MARTIN (*Ice*): He's not my type.

STEVIE (*Rising again. Rage*): He's not your type!? He's not your fucking type!?

MARTIN: No; he's not. (*She is about to strike him*) You're my type. (*The shock of this stays her gesture; we see her confusion*) You're my type.

STEVIE (*Stands where she is; hard*): Thank you!

MARTIN: You're welcome. (*A gesture*) Oh, Stevie, I . . .

STEVIE: I'm your type and so is she; so is the goat. (*Harder*) So long as it's female, eh? So long as it's got a cunt it's all right with you!

MARTIN (*Huge*): A SOUL!! Don't you know the difference!? Not a cunt, a soul!

STEVIE (*After a little; tears again*): You can't fuck a soul.

MARTIN: No; and it isn't about fucking.

STEVIE: YES!!

MARTIN (*As gentle as possible*): No; no, Stevie, it isn't.

STEVIE (*Pause; then, even more sure*): Yes! It is about fucking! It is about you being an animal!

MARTIN (*Thinks a moment; quietly*): I thought I was.

STEVIE (*Contempt*): Hunh!

MARTIN: I thought I was; I thought we *all* were . . . animals.

STEVIE (*Cold rage*): We stay with our own kind!

MARTIN (*Gentle; rational*): Oh, we fall in love with *many* other creatures . . . dogs and cats, and . . .

STEVIE: We don't *fuck* them! You're a monster!

MARTIN (*Pinning it down*): I am a deeply troubled, greatly divided . . .

STEVIE (*No quarter*): *Animal* fucker!

MARTIN: Sylvia and I . . .

STEVIE (*Hideous*): You're going to tell me she *wants* you.

MARTIN (*Simply put*): Yes.

STEVIE: What does she do — back into you making awful little bleating sounds?

MARTIN: That's sheep.

STEVIE: *Whatever!! Presented* herself? Down on her forelegs, her head turned, her eyes on you, her . . .

MARTIN: Stop it! I won't go into the specifics of our sex with you!

STEVIE (*Contempt*): *Thank* you! You take advantage of this . . . creature!? You . . . *rape* this . . . animal and convince yourself that it has to do with *love*!?

MARTIN (*Helpless*): I love her . . . and she loves me, and . . .

STEVIE (*A huge animal sound: rage; sweeps the bookcase of whatever is on it, or overturns a piece of furniture. Silence; then starting quietly, building*): Now, you listen to me. I have listened to you. I have heard you tell me how much you love me, how you've never even wanted another woman, how we have been a more perfect marriage than chance would even *allow*. We're both too bright for *most* of the shit. We see the deep and awful humor of things go over the heads of most people; we see what's hideously wrong in what most people accept as normal; we have both the joys and the sorrows of all that. We have a straight line through life, right all the way to dying, but that's OK because it's a good line . . . so long as we don't screw up.

MARTIN: I know; I know.

STEVIE (*Don't interrupt me!*): Shut up; so long as we don't screw up. (*Points at him*) And *you've* screwed *up*!

MARTIN: Stevie, I . . .

STEVIE: I said, shut up. Do you know *how* you've done it? How you've screwed up?

MARTIN (*Mumbled*): Because I was at the vegetable stand one day, and I looked over to my right and I saw . . .

STEVIE (*Hard and slow*): Because you've broken something and it can't be fixed!

MARTIN: Stevie . . .

STEVIE: Fall out of love with me? Fine! No, not fine, but that can be fixed . . . time . . . whatever! But tell me you love me and an animal — both of us! — equally? The same way? That you go from my bed — *our* bed . . . (*aside-ish*) it's amazing, you know, how good we are, still, how we please each other *and* ourselves so . . . fully, so . . . fresh each time . . . (*aside over*) . . . you go from our bed, wash your dick, get in your car and go to her, and do with her what I cannot imagine myself imagining? Or — worse! . . . that you've come *from* her, to *my* bed!? To *our* bed!? . . . and you do with me what I *can* imagine . . . love . . . *want* you for!?

MARTIN (*Deep sadness*): Oh, Stevie . . .

STEVIE (*Not listening*): That you can do these two things . . . and not understand how it . . . SHAT-TERS THE GLASS!!?? How it cannot be dealt with — how stop and forgiveness have nothing to do with it? and how I am destroyed? How *you* are? How I cannot admit it though I *know* it!? How I cannot deny it because I cannot *admit* it!? Cannot admit it, because it is outside of denying!?

MARTIN: Stevie, I . . . I promise you, I'll stop; I'll . . .

STEVIE: How stopping has nothing to do with having started?! How nothing has anything to do with anything!? (*Tears — if there — stop*) You have brought me down, you goat-fucker; you love of my life! You have brought me down to *nothing*! (*Accusatory finger right at him*) You have brought me down, and, Christ!, I'll bring you down with me!

(*Brief pause; she turns on her heel, exits. We hear the front door slam.*)

MARTIN (*After she leaves; after he hears the door; little boy*): Stevie? (*Pause*) Stevie?

End of Scene Two

SCENE THREE

(*An hour or so later. Martin is sitting in the ruins. Maybe he is examining a broken piece of something. The room is as it was at the end of Scene Two. The front door slams; Billy enters; Martin rises and stands in the middle of the room.*)

BILLY (*Looking around*): Wow!

MARTIN (*Realizing Billy is there*): Yes; wow.

BILLY (*Seemingly casual*): You guys really had it out, hunh.

MARTIN (*Subdued; almost laughing*): Oh, yes.

BILLY: Where is she?

MARTIN: Hm? Who?

BILLY (*Not friendly; overly articulated*): My mother. Where is my mother?

MARTIN (*Mocking*): Where is "my mother"? Not "Mother — where's Mother?" Not that, but . . . "Where is my mother?"

BILLY (*Anger rising*): Whatever! Where *is* she? Where is *my mother*?

MARTIN (*Arms out; helplessly*): I . . . I . . .

BILLY (*Angrier*): Where *is* she?! What did you do . . . kill her?

MARTIN (*Softly*): Yes; I think so.

BILLY (*Dropping something he has picked up*): What!!?

MARTIN (*Quietly, with a restraining hand*): Stop. No. No, I did not kill her — of *course* not — but I think I might as well have. I think we've killed each other.

BILLY (*Driving*): Where *is* she!?

MARTIN (*Simply*): I don't know.

BILLY: What do you mean you don't . . .

MARTIN (*Loud*): She left!

BILLY: What do you mean she left? Where . . .

MARTIN (*Snappish*): Stop asking me what I mean! (*Quieter*) She said what she wanted to say; she finished . . . and she left. She slammed the front door and left. I assume she drove somewhere.

BILLY: Yeah, the wagon's gone. (*Harder*) Where *is* she!?

MARTIN (*Loud*): She *left*! I don't know where she *is*! It's English! "She left." It's English. No, I did not kill her, yes, I think I did, I think we killed each other. That's English, too: one of your courses!

BILLY (*Is his rage close to tears? Probably*): I know who you *are*. I know you're my father. I know who you are, and I know who you're supposed to be, but . . .

MARTIN: You, too?

BILLY: Hunh?

MARTIN: You don't know who I *am* anymore.

BILLY (*Flat*): No.

MARTIN: Well . . . neither does your mother.

BILLY (*Trying to explain, but, still, rage underneath*): Parents fight; I know that; all kids know that. There are good times and rotten ones, and sometimes the blanket is pulled out from under you, and . . .

MARTIN (*Can't help saying it*): You're mixing your metaphors.

BILLY (*Furious*): What!?

MARTIN: Never mind; probably not the best time to bring it up. You were saying . . . "There are good times and rotten ones"?

BILLY: Yes. (*Quick sarcasm*) Thanks.

MARTIN (*Noncommittal*): Welcome.

BILLY: But sometimes the whatever is pulled out from under you.

MARTIN: Rug. I think.

BILLY: Right! Now shut the fuck up! (*Martin opens his mouth, closes it. Spits out*) Semanticist!

MARTIN: Very good! Where did you learn that?

BILLY: I go to a good school. Remember?

MARTIN: Yes, but still . . .

BILLY: I said, shut the fuck up!

MARTIN (*Subsiding*): Right.

BILLY: There are good times, and there are rotten ones. There are times we are so . . . deep in content, in happiness, that we think we'll probably drown in it but we won't mind. There are *some* of those — not too many. There are times we don't know what the fuck's going on — *to* us, *with* us, *about* us — and that's most of the time. I'm talking about us so-called adolescents.

MARTIN: I know.

BILLY: And then there are the times we wish we were old enough to . . . just walk out the door and start all over again, somewhere else — blank it all out.

MARTIN (*Quietly*): And this?

BILLY (*Hard*): One guess, you *fuck*!! (*Huge*) What have you done with my *mother*!!??

MARTIN (*Calm*): We finished our conversation (*gestures at ruined room*) — you see how we talk? — we finished our conversation, and she said a final . . . *thing*, and she left. She walked out, out the front door, slam.

BILLY: How long ago?

MARTIN (*Shrugs*): An hour; maybe more; maybe two. I'm not very good at time and stuff right now.

BILLY: Two hours? And you haven't . . .

MARTIN (*A little angry himself*): What!? called the police? (*Awful imitation of distress*) "Oh, Officer, help me! My wife just found out I've been doing it with livestock, and she's run off, and can you help me find her?" What!? Take off after her!? She's a grown woman; she could be having her hair done, for all I know.

BILLY (*Dogged*): What did she *say* to you?

MARTIN (*Rueful chuckle*): Oh . . . quite a few things.

BILLY (*Bigger*): When she left! What did she say when she left!?

MARTIN: Something about . . . bringing me down — or whatever.

BILLY: Be specific.

MARTIN: Well, it's hard to be specific. We *were* busy after all, and . . .

BILLY (*Big*): Exactly what she said, and *now*!

MARTIN (*Clears his throat*): "You have brought me down, and . . . I will bring you down with me."

BILLY (*Puzzled; trying to get it*): What does that *mean*?

MARTIN (*Almost sweet*): No one's ever brought you down? No, I suppose not — not yet. It means . . . (*fails*) it means what it says: that you have done to me what cannot be undone and . . . and you won't get away with it.

(*Billy stands for a moment and then spontaneously cries for a little, stops*)

BILLY (*Wiping his eyes*): I see.

MARTIN (*Further explanation*): You destroy me — I destroy you.

BILLY: Yes; I see. (*Indicates wreckage*) Then there's no point in setting all this right.

MARTIN (*Sad chuckle*): It does look pretty awful, *doesn't* it.

BILLY: Let's do it anyway.

MARTIN: Set the stage for the next round? (*Some self-pity and irony*) Hunh! *what* next round!? It's all behind me, isn't it? — everything? All hope . . . all . . . "salvation"? (*Fast litany*) Dead-end-rock-bottom-out-with-the-garbage-flushed-down-the-toilet-ground-up-spit-out-over-the-edge with heavy weights, down-down-sunk . . . whatever? All hope, everything? Gone? Right?

BILLY (*Shrugs*): Whatever. (*Billy begins to right a few things, not much; then quits*) What is it going to be then? Divorce?

MARTIN (*Simply*): I don't know, Billy; I don't know that there are any rules for where we are.

BILLY: Beyond all the rules, eh?

MARTIN (*Some rue*): I think so.

BILLY: I wouldn't know. I guess I've never been in love. *Yet,* I mean. Oh, lots of crushes, and all.

MARTIN: Only twice for me — your mother and . . . Sylvia.

BILLY: You're really holding onto this, *aren't* you.

MARTIN: To . . . ?

BILLY (*Sneering*): This goat! This big love affair!

MARTIN (*Shrugs*): It's true.

BILLY: Grow up!

MARTIN: Ah! Is *that* it! (*Billy laughs, in spite of himself. Martin tries to right a chair*) Help me with this. (*Billy helps him*) Thanks!

BILLY (*Shrugs*): Any time. (*Pause*) They asked us at school — when? Last week, last month? — they asked each of us in this class to talk about how normal our lives were, how . . . how conventional it all was and how did we feel about it.

MARTIN: What kind of school *is* this!?

BILLY (*Shrugs*): You chose it; you two chose it. And a lot of the guys got up and talked about — you know — our home lives, how our parents get on, and all; and it wasn't very special except the guys whose parents are divorced or one has died or gone crazy, or whatever.

MARTIN: Really? Crazy?

BILLY: Sure. Good private school. All guys, too; thanks. I mean, it was all about what you'd expect. Maybe everybody left all the juicy stuff out, or they didn't know it. (*Picks up a shard*) Where does this go?

MARTIN: Trash, I suspect.

BILLY (*Looks at it*): Too bad. (*Drops it*) So, it was all pretty dull, pretty much what you'd expect.

MARTIN: I take it you haven't gotten up and spoken yet.

BILLY (*Noncommittal*): Nope. Haven't. (*Waits a little*) You know what I'm going to tell them — when I get up there on my hind legs?

MARTIN (*Winces*): Do I *want* to know?

BILLY: Sure; you're a big guy.

MARTIN: I am diminished.

BILLY: Yeah? Well . . . whatever. I think what I'll tell them is this: that I've been living with two people about as splendid as you can get; that if I'd been born to other people, it couldn't have been any better. (*Martin sighs heavily, puts a protesting hand up*) No; really; I mean it. You two guys are about as good as they come. You're smart, and fair, and you have a sense of humor — both of you — and . . . and you're Democrats. You *are* Democrats, aren't you?

MARTIN: More than *they* are, sometimes.

BILLY: That's what I thought, and you've figured out that raising a kid does *not* include making him into a carbon copy of *you,* that you're letting me think you're putting up with me being gay far better than you probably really are.

MARTIN: Oh, now . . .

BILLY: Thank you, by the way.

MARTIN: It's the least.

BILLY (*Nodding*): Right.

MARTIN (*Feigned surprise*): You're *gay*!?

BILLY (*Smiles*): Shut up. Anyway, you've let me have it better than a lot of kids, better than a lot of "Moms and Dads" have, a lot closer to what being grown up will look like — as far as I can tell. Good guidance; it's great to see how two people can love each other . . .

MARTIN: Don't!

BILLY: At least that's what I thought — until yesterday, until the shit hit the fan!

MARTIN: Billy, please don't.

BILLY (*Big crying underneath*): . . . until the shit hit the fan, and the talk I was going to do at school became history. (*Exaggerated*) What will I say *now*!? Goodness me! The Good Ship Lollipop has gone and sunk. (*More normal tone*) What will I say!? Well, let's see: I came home yesterday and everything had been great — absolutely normal, therefore great. Great parents, great house, great trees, great cars — you know: the old "great." (*Bigger now, more exaggerated*) But then today I come home, and what do I *find*? I find my great Mom and my great Dad talking about a letter from great good friend Ross . . .

MARTIN (*Deep anger*): Fuck Ross!!

BILLY: Yes? A letter from great good friend Ross written to great good Mom about how great good Dad has been out in the barnyard fucking *animals*!!

MARTIN: Don't . . . *do* this.

BILLY: Animals! Well, one in particular. A goat! A fucking goat! You see, guys, your stories are swell or whatever, but I've got one'll knock your socks off, as they used to say, wipe the tattoos right off your butts. Ya see, while great old Mom and great old Dad have been doing the great old parent thing, one of them has been underneath the house, down in the cellar, digging a pit so deep!, so wide!, so . . . HUGE! . . . we'll all fall in and (*crying now*) and never . . . be . . . able . . . to . . . climb . . . out . . . again — no matter how much we want to, how hard we try. And you see, kids, fellow students, you see, I love these people. I love the man who's been down there digging — when he's not giving it to a goat! I love this man! I love him! (*Drops whatever he's holding, moves to Martin, arms out*) I love him! (*Wraps his arms around Martin, who doesn't know what to do. Starts kissing Martin on the hands, then on the neck, crying the while. Then it turns — or does it? — and he kisses Martin full on the mouth — a deep, sobbing, sexual kiss. Ross has entered, stands watching. Martin tries to disengage from Billy, but Billy moans, holds on. Finally Martin shoves him away. Billy stands there, still sobbing, arms around nothing. They have not seen Ross.*)

MARTIN: Don't *do* that!!

BILLY: I *love* you!

MARTIN: Sure you do, you . . . you . . .

BILLY: Faggot? You faggot?

MARTIN (*Enraged*): That's not what I was going to say!!

BILLY (*So sad; so sincere*): Dad! I *love* you! Hold me! Please!

MARTIN (*Holds him; strokes him*): Shhhhhh; shhhh; shhhhh now.

BILLY (*Disengaging finally*): I'm sorry; I didn't mean to . . .

MARTIN: No; it's all right. (*Arms out*) Here; let me hold you.

(*Billy moves to him again; a momentary silent embrace*)

ROSS: Excuse me. (*They are startled, split. Maybe Billy stumbles over something.*) I'm sorry; I didn't mean to interrupt your little . . .

MARTIN (*Cold fury*): What!? See a man and his son kissing? That would go nicely in one of your fucking letters. Judas! Get out of here!

BILLY (*To Ross*): It wasn't what you think!

MARTIN (*At Billy*): Yes! Yes, it was! Don't apologize. (*To Ross*) Too bad you couldn't have brought your fucking TV crew over! Don't you and *your* son ever kiss? Don't you and — what's his name? — *Todd* love one another?

ROSS (*Hard; contemptuous*): Not *that* way!

MARTIN (*Angry and reckless*): *That* way!? *What* way!? (*Points vigorously at Billy*) This boy is hurt! I've hurt him, and he still loves me! You fucker! He loves his father, and if it . . . clicks over and becomes — what? — sexual for . . . just a moment . . . so what!? So fucking what!? He's hurt and he's lonely and mind your own fucking business!

ROSS (*A sneer*): You're sicker than I thought.

MARTIN: No! I'm hysterical!

BILLY (*Rueful wonder*): It *did*. It clicked over, and you were just another . . .

MARTIN: It's all right.

BILLY: . . . another man. I get confused . . . sex and love; loving and . . . (*To Ross*) I probably *do* want to sleep with him. (*Rueful laugh*) I want to sleep with everyone.

MARTIN (*To quiet him*): It's all right.

BILLY (*Still to Ross*): Except you, probably.

ROSS: Jesus! Sick! What is it . . . contagious?

BILLY (*Confused*): What? Is what?

MARTIN (*Moves over to comfort Billy*): There was a man told me once — a friend; we went to the same gym — he told me he had his kid on his lap one day — not even old enough to be a boy or a girl: a baby — and he had . . . *it* on his lap, and it was gurgling at him and making giggling sounds, and he had it with his arms around it, (*demonstrates*) in his lap, shifting it a little from side to side to make it happier, to make it giggle more . . . and all at once he realized he was getting hard.

ROSS: Jesus!

BILLY: Oh my God . . .

MARTIN: . . . that the baby in his lap was making him hard — not arousing him; it wasn't sexual, but it was happening.

ROSS: Jesus!

MARTIN: . . . his dick was rising to the baby in his lap — his baby; his lap. And when he realized what was happening, he thought he would die; his pulse was going a mile a minute; his ears were ringing — loud! Very *loud*! And he was going to faint; he *knew* it, and then the moment passed, and he knew it had all been an accident, that it meant . . . nothing — that nothing was connected to anything else. His wife came in;

she smiled; he smiled and handed her the baby. And that was it; it was over. (*Shrugs*) Things happen. Besides — I'm hysterical. Remember?

ROSS: What are you doing? *Defending* yourself?! Jesus. You're sick.

MARTIN (*Contempt*): Do you have any other words? Sick and Jesus? Is that all you have?

BILLY (*Shy*): Was it me? Was it me, Dad? Was the baby me?

MARTIN (*To Billy; after a pause; gently*): Hush.

BILLY (*Almost frightened*): Was it?

MARTIN (*Turning to Ross*): So, what do you want here now, motherfucker!? Judas!?

ROSS: Stevie called — what? An hour ago? More? She said you needed me; she said to come over.

MARTIN: I don't! Get out! (*Surprise*) She *called* you?

ROSS: Yes. (*Shakes his head*) Getting hard with a baby! Is there anything you people don't get off on!?

BILLY (*Once more*): Was it, Dad?

MARTIN (*So clearly a lie; gently*): Of course not, Billy. (*To Ross; hard, eyes narrowing*) Is there anything "we people" don't get off on? Is there anything anyone doesn't get off on, whether we admit it or not — whether we *know* it or not? Remember Saint Sebastian with all the arrows shot into him? He probably came! God knows the faithful did! Shall I go on!? You want to hear about the cross!?

BILLY (*Quietly; smiling*): No, of course it wasn't . . . wasn't me.

ROSS (*Shaking his head; sad, but with a lip curled*): Sick; sick; sick.

MARTIN (*At Ross; growing rage*): I'll tell you what's sick! Writing that fucking letter to Stevie — why doesn't it matter!! — that's what's sick! I *tell* you about it; I share it with you, the . . . the . . . whole . . . awful . . . thing, because I think I've lost it, maybe; I *tell* you; I *share* it with you because you're . . . what!? . . . you're my best friend in the whole world? Because I need to tell *somebody*, somebody with his head on straight enough to hear it? I *tell* you, and you fucking turn around and . . .

ROSS: I *had* to!

MARTIN: *No!* You *didn't!* You didn't *have* to!

ROSS (*Dogmatic*): I couldn't let you *continue!*

MARTIN (*Near tears*): I could have worked it out. I could have stopped, and no one would have known. Except you, motherfucker. Mister one strike and you're out. I could have . . .

ROSS: No! You couldn't!

MARTIN: I could have worked it out! And now nothing can *ever* be put back together! *Ever!*

BILLY (*Trying to help*): Dad . . .

MARTIN (*Savage*): You shut up! (*Billy winces. Martin reacts*) Oh, God! I'm sorry. (*To Ross*) Yes; all right, it *was* sick, and yes, it *was* compulsive, and . . .

ROSS: IS! Not *was!* IS!

MARTIN (*Stopped in his tracks*): I . . . I . . .

ROSS: IS!

MARTIN (*Gathering himself*): Is. All right. Is. Is sick; *is* compulsive.

ROSS (*Pushing*): And it was *wrong!*

MARTIN: It was . . . it was . . . what?

ROSS: Wrong! Deeply, destructively *wrong!*

MARTIN: Whatever you want. (*Rage growing*) But I could have handled it! You didn't have to bring it all down! You didn't have to destroy both of us; you didn't have to destroy Stevie, too!

ROSS: Me!? *Me* bring you down!? This isn't . . . embezzlement, honey; this isn't stealing from helpless widows; this isn't going to whores and coming down with the clap, or whatever, you know. This isn't the stuff that stops a career in its tracks for a little while — humiliation, public remorse, and then back up again. This is *beyond* that — *way* beyond it! You go on and you'll slip up one day. Somebody'll see you. Somebody'll surprise you one day, in whatever barn you put her in, no matter where you put her. Somebody'll see you, on your knees behind the damn animal; your pants around your ankles. Somebody will *catch* you at it.

BILLY: Let him alone. For God's sake, Ross . . .

ROSS (*Waving Billy off; to Martin*): Do you know there are prison terms for this? Some states they kill you for it? Do you know what they'd *do* to you. The press? Everybody? Down it all comes — your career; your life . . . everything. (*So cold; so rational*) For fucking a goat. (*Shakes his head sadly; Billy is weeping quietly*)

MARTIN (*Long pause*): Is *that* what it is, then? That people will *know*!? That people will find *out*!? That I can do whatever I want, and that's what matters!? That people will find *out*!? Fuck the . . . thing *itself*!? Fuck what it *means*!? That people will find *out*!?

ROSS: Your soul is your own business. The rest I can *help* you with.

MARTIN: Of course it's my business, and clearly you don't have one.

ROSS (*Mild interest*): Oh?

MARTIN: So that's what it comes down to, eh? . . . what we can get away with?

ROSS: Sure.

MARTIN (*Heavy irony*): Oh, thank God! It's so simple! I thought it was . . . I thought it had to do with love and loss, and it's only about . . . getting *by*. Well, Stevie and I have been wrestling with the wrong angel! When she comes back — *if* she comes back — I'll have to set her straight about what matters. (*Intense; not looking at Ross or Billy; pounding his hands on his knees perhaps*) Does anybody understand what happened!?

ROSS: Oh, for Christ's sake, Martin!

BILLY: Dad . . .

MARTIN (*Crying a little*): Why can't anyone understand this . . . that I am *alone* . . . all . . . *alone!*

(*A silence. Then we hear a sound at the door.*)

BILLY: Mom? (*Billy going into the hall. Gone.*)
MARTIN (*Pause; to Ross, begging*): You *do* understand; *don't* you.
ROSS (*Long pause; shakes his head*): No.

(*Stevie is dragging a dead goat. The goat's throat is cut; the blood is down Stevie's dress, on her arms. She stops*)

ROSS: Oh, my God.
MARTIN: What have you done!?
STEVIE: Here.
BILLY (*Generally; to no one; helpless; a quiet plea*): Help. Help.
ROSS: Oh, my God.

(*Martin moves toward Stevie*)

MARTIN: What have you done!? Oh, my God, what have you *done*!?

(*Billy is crying. Stevie regards Martin for a moment; Ross is immobile.*)

STEVIE (*Turns to face him; evenly, without emotion*): I went where Ross told me I would find . . . your friend. I found her. I killed her. I brought her here to you. (*Odd little question*) No?
MARTIN (*A profound cry*): ANNNNNNH!
STEVIE: Why are you surprised? What did you expect me to do?
MARTIN (*Crying*): What did she *do*!? What did she ever *do*!? (*To Stevie*) I ask you: what did she ever *do*!?
STEVIE (*Pause; quietly*): She loved you . . . you say. As much as *I* do.
MARTIN (*To Stevie; empty*): I'm sorry. (*To Billy; empty*) I'm sorry. (*Then . . .*) I'm sorry.
BILLY (*To one, then the other; no reaction from them*): Dad? Mom?

(*Tableau*)

End

Nilo Cruz

Nilo Cruz, born in 1961, was brought out of Cuba in 1970 by his parents in a freedom flight to Miami. (After his first, failed attempt to get his family out of Cuba, Nilo's father, a shoemaker, was imprisoned for two years. During that time his mother worked as a seamstress to support the family.) Nilo was only nine years old when he left, but he keeps the memory of Cuba in his plays and feels a commitment to writing about the Latino experience. He has said, "What I want to document is what we as Cubans and Latinos are trying to provide, our cultural gift of art to the Anglo world. We have beautiful, powerful traditions. As a writer and a human being, I want to share them."[1]

Cruz began in the theater as an actor but soon switched to writing when one of his teachers at Miami-Dade Community College convinced him he could write. Eventually, Cruz had several plays produced in South Florida and came to the attention of playwright Paula Vogel, who heads the Graduate Playwriting Program at Brown University in Rhode Island. She was so impressed by his work that she admitted him to the program as a graduate student even though he did not have an undergraduate degree. Earlier, Cruz had worked with another distinguished playwright, María Irene Fornes, who was also born in Cuba. She was both influential and reassuring, and showed her confidence in Cruz by having him work with her and her group in Florida.

Many of Cruz's plays have premiered at the South Coast Repertory Theatre in Costa Mesa, California, as well as the Magic Theatre in San Francisco and the McCarter Theatre in Princeton, New Jersey. *Two Sisters and a Piano* (1999) began at South Coast and then moved to the Public Theater in New York. It tells the story of two sisters under house arrest in modern Cuba. His earlier work, *Night Train to Bolina* (1993), is a daring play that features two children, a boy and a girl, who dream of freedom on their own terms. *Dancing on Her Knees* also went to the Public Theater in New York. *Ay Carmella!* (2001) was produced at the Warehouse, Croydon, London. *Hortensia and the Museum of Dreams* (2000–2001) was produced at the New Theatre in Coral Gables and at South Coast Repertory in 2003. Among Cruz's other plays are *A Park in Our House* (1995), an exploration of political values in 1970 Cuba; *A Bicycle Country* (1999), about life and love in Cuba in the midst of dreams of escaping from an ocean "jail"; and *Beauty of the Father* (2002).

Cruz has been inspired by the Spanish playwright Federico García Lorca (1898–1936), whose own remarkable career as a playwright and poet was cut short by political assassins at the beginning of the Nationalists' war against the Republicans in Spain. Lorca was an opponent of the fascist General Franco, whose forces succeeded in destroying what were perceived as Communist republicans during the Spanish Civil War. Lorca was branded as a Communist;

[1]Anders, Gigi. "Nilo Cruz's Play Wins Pulitzer Despite Great Odds." *Hispanic Magazine.Com.* June 2003. 10 Jan. 2003 <www.hispaniconline.com/magazine/2003/june/Features/nilo.html>.

because he was also known to be a homosexual, he was considered undesirable by the Catholic Church. His death increased his stature as a writer, however, and today he is considered the greatest modern Spanish playwright and one of the greatest modern poets. Cruz has written an homage to Lorca called *Lorca in a Green Dress,* produced at the Oregon Shakespeare Festival in July 2003. It is an ambitious play that moves in a relatively unlinear fashion, with Lorca observing his life in certain key moments, including one dramatic scene in which he wears a green dress — worn with great effect in the Oregon production by Cristofer Jean.

Nilo Cruz has taught playwriting at the University of Iowa, Brown University, and Yale University. He has won numerous awards in addition to the Pulitzer Prize. He received a Rockefeller Foundation grant; an NEA/TCG (National Endowment for the Arts/Theatre Communications Group) National Theatre Artist Residency Grant, which funded both him and the New Theatre while he developed *Anna in the Tropics;* a Kennedy Center Funds for New American Plays award; and others. His work has been produced in many theaters in cities around the United States.

ANNA IN THE TROPICS

The original working title of this play was *Ybor City,* the location near Tampa of the cigar factory in which the play takes place. Cruz developed the play from an idea centering on the use of lectors — readers — who in the early years of the twentieth century came into the factories to read to the workers, predominantly women, who rolled cigars. The work was both demanding and boring at the same time, and the lector relieved the boredom by reading newspapers, magazine articles, and occasionally books, often to people who could not themselves read. The lectors were also sometimes rather dashing men whose good looks and smart clothes — in addition to their education and sophistication — excited romantic interest on the part of some of the workers. It was not uncommon for the lectors to be looked upon as something of a threat to the virtue of the women involved in the work.

In developing the premise of the play, Cruz discovered that, because the working conditions in the factories were less than ideal, a general leftist sympathy existed among the workers, especially in the aftermath of the Russian Revolution (1917), when the promise of Communism and its benefits to the ordinary worker was widely promulgated among factory hands. Cruz found that Leo Tolstoy's (1828–1910) great Russian novel *Anna Karenina* (1877), which portrays a profoundly romantic adulterous affair, would have been an appropriate book for the time.

Following a long literary tradition, stretching from Dante's recounting in *Inferno* of the affair of Abelard and Heloise, who seduced each other by reading romances to one another, Cruz demonstrates the seductive power of literature, ultimately re-creating a situation in Ybor City that parallels the situation in the Russian novel.

In the process, Cruz reveals the intimate details of life in Ybor City and in the cigar factories of the time. He also reveals the inner lives of people living in a circumscribed world of work. Most of all, he demonstrates the power of literature to inspire romance and, perhaps most critically, independence of mind in the women in the play. Palomo is clearly involved with another woman, and his wife Conchita tells him it's all right as long as she has the right to take a lover of her own. In a strange and complex way, Conchita's affair with Juan Julian, the lector, stimulates her own marriage so that at the end of the play things are hopeful for her and Palomo. For Cheché, however, things are different. He has lost his wife to another man and now begins to find Conchita's younger sister Marela desirable. Both he and Marela are stimulated by *Anna Karenina*, but it is clear that Marela finds Juan Julian more attractive than Cheché, whom she rejects. The play ends with Cheché's act of desperation.

Anna in the Tropics won the 2003 $15,000 American Theatre Critics/ Steinberg New Play Award at the Humana Festival of New American Plays in Louisville, an award given to plays produced outside New York. One of Arthur Miller's plays was a runner up to Cruz. When the play won the Pulitzer Prize, Edward Albee's *The Goat, or Who Is Sylvia?* was his primary competition. The most surprising detail concerning the awarding of this prize is that none of the judges saw the original production in Miami. They gave the award on the basis of reading the script alone, something that has happened only once before — with Robert Schenkkan's *The Kentucky Cycle* in 1992.

Anna in the Tropics in Performance

The first performance took place in 2002 at the New Theatre, a 100-seat theater in Coral Gables, Florida, near Miami University. The power of that production was brought to the attention of the theater world by *Miami Herald* theater critic Christine Dolen, who felt that American theater is too "New York–centric" and that more attention should be paid to the work being done in Miami. Happily, her wish became reality. *Anna in the Tropics* was quickly produced in California at the South Coast Repertory Theater. Almost as quickly, the distinguished playwright and producer Emily Mann brought the play to the McCarter Theater in Princeton, New Jersey, in September 2003, with Jimmy Smits as the lector. That production moved in December 2003 to the Royale Theatre in New York City for its Broadway production, which closed on February 22, 2004. The cast was entirely Latino: Jimmy Smits, David Zayas, Priscilla López, Victor Argo, Vanessa Aspillaga, John Ortiz, and Daphne Rubin-Vega. This was the first all-Latino cast for any Broadway play.

Nilo Cruz *(b. 1961)*

ANNA IN THE TROPICS

Characters

SANTIAGO, *Owner of a cigar factory, late fifties*
CHECHÉ, *His half-brother; half-Cuban, half-American, early forties*
OFELIA, *Santiago's wife, fifties*
MARELA, *Ofelia and Santiago's daughter, twenty-two*
CONCHITA, *Her sister, thirty-two*
PALOMO, *Her husband, forty-one*
JUAN JULIAN, *The lector, thirty-eight*
ELIADES, *Local gamester, runs cockfights, forties*

Time and Place

1929. Tampa, Florida. A small town called Ybor City.

Set

An old warehouse.

Costumes

These workers are always well dressed. They use a lot of white and beige linen and their clothes are always well pressed and starched.

Playwright's Note

After 1931, the lectors were removed from the factories, and what remained of the cigar rollers consisted of low-paid American workers who operated machines. The end of a tradition.

Quotations from Anna Karenina *by Leo Tolstoy:*

"Looking at him" (PAGE 1799)
Part 2, Chapter 11

"If there are as many minds" (PAGE 1801)
Part 2, Chapter 7

"At first Anna sincerely thought" (PAGE 1804)
Part 2, Chapter 4

"Anna Karenina had stepped into a new life" (PAGE 1804)
Part 2, Chapter 11

"Anna Karenina's husband did not see anything peculiar" (PAGE 1808)
Part 2, Chapter 8

"Anna Karenina prepared herself for the journey" (PAGE 1812)
Part 1, Chapter 29

"In his youth, Anna Karenina's husband had been intrigued" (PAGE 1813)
Part 3, Chapter 13

"By the time he arrived in Petersburg" (PAGE 1814)
Part 3, Chapter 14

ACT ONE • Scene 1

Sounds of a crowd at a cockfight. Santiago and Cheché are betting their money on cockfights. They've been drinking, but are not drunk. They wear typical, long-sleeve, white linen shirts (guayabera), white pants and two-tone shoes. Eliades collects the money and oversees all the operations of this place.

ELIADES: Cockfights! See the winged beauties fighting in midair! Cockfights! I'll take five, ten, fifteen, twenty dollars on Picarubio. Five, ten, twenty on Espuela de Oro. Picarubio against Espuela de Oro. Espuela de Oro against Picarubio.
SANTIAGO: I'll bet a hundred on Picarubio.
ELIADES: A hundred on Picarubio.
CHECHÉ: Eighty on Espuela de Oro.
ELIADES: Eighty on Espuela de Oro.
SANTIAGO: Ten more on Picarubio.
ELIADES: Ten more on Picarubio. Ten more on Espuela de Oro?
CHECHÉ: No, that's enough.
ELIADES: I'll take five, ten, twenty dollars. Picarubio against Espuela de Oro. Espuela de Oro against Picarubio.

(Sound of a ship approaching the harbor. Marela, Conchita and their mother Ofelia are standing by the seaport. They are holding white handkerchiefs and are waiting for a ship to arrive.)

MARELA: Is that the ship approaching in the distance?
CONCHITA: I think it is.
OFELIA: It's the only ship that's supposed to arrive around this time.
MARELA: Then that must be it. Oh, I'm so excited! Let me look at the picture again, Mamá.
OFELIA: How many times are you going to look at it?
MARELA: Many times. We have to make sure we know what he looks like.
CONCHITA: You just like looking at his face.
MARELA: I think he is elegant and good looking.

(Ofelia opens a letter and takes out a photograph.)

OFELIA: That he is. But what's essential is that he has good vocal chords, deep lungs and a strong voice.
CONCHITA: What's more important is that he has good diction when he reads.
MARELA: As long as he reads with feeling and gusto, I'm content. *(Looks at the photo)* Look at his face and the way he signs his name.

(*Sounds of a crowd at a cockfight.*)

ELIADES: We have a winner! We have a winner! Espuela de Oro is the winner! Espuela de Oro!

CHECHÉ: Winner here.

ELIADES (*Counting money*): Ten, twenty, thirty, forty, fifty, sixty.

SANTIAGO: You're a lucky man.

ELIADES: Next fight! I'll take five, ten, fifteen, twenty dollars . . . Cuello de Jaca against Uñaroja. Uñaroja against Cuello de Jaca.

SANTIAGO: Eighty on Cuello de Jaca.

ELIADES: Eighty on Cuello de Jaca.

CHECHÉ: Eighty on Uñaroja.

ELIADES: Eighty on Uñaroja. (*To the audience*) Uñaroja against Cuello de Jaca! Cuello de Jaca against Uñaroja!

(*Sound of a ship approaching the harbor*)

OFELIA: Don't tell your father, but I took some money from the safe to pay for the lector's trip.

CONCHITA: You did well, Mamá.

OFELIA: Oh, I don't feel a bit guilty. Doesn't your father spend his money gambling? Then I'll do as I wish with my money. I'll spend my money on the best lector we can get. The gentleman who recommended him says that he is the best lector west of Havana.

MARELA: Well, I'm glad, because poor old Teodoro used to spit a little too much when he read to us. Sometimes it felt like sprinkles of rain were coming out of his mouth.

OFELIA: Marela! The poor man was eighty years old.

MARELA: That he was!

OFELIA: Have more respect — he died three months ago.

MARELA: Oh, I respect him, but let the truth be told.

OFELIA: The poor fellow, for ten years he read to us.

MARELA (*With satire*): Oh, I loved him . . . I loved him, like an uncle, like a grandfather. May he rest in peace! But he should've given up being a lector a long time ago. His heart couldn't take the love stories. He couldn't take the poetry and tragedy in the novels. Sometimes he had to sit down after reading a profound and romantic passage.

CONCHITA: Oh, that's why I liked him, because I knew that he read to us with his heart.

MARELA: But it was too much. It took him three months to read the last novel to us.

OFELIA: Ah! But it was *Wuthering Heights*, and none of us wanted it to end, including you.

CONCHITA: Well, I hope this new lector turns out to be as good as Teodoro, because the one who replaced him didn't last . . .

MARELA: Look, the ship is getting closer. Oh, I'm so excited, I just want him to disembark and have him here once and for all.

CONCHITA (*Looking into the distance*): He's probably going to bring a lot of new books from Argentina and Spain and France, because so many ships make stops in Cuba.

(*Sounds of a crowd at a cockfight.*)

ELIADES: We have a winner! We have a winner! Uñaroja! Uñaroja is the winner!

CHECHÉ: Winner here. Uñaroja.

(*Eliades pays Cheché, then continues announcing the next fight.*)

ELIADES: Twenty, forty, sixty, eighty, one hundred . . . Twenty, forty sixty . . . Ready for the next fight! We have Colabrava against Falcón de Acero. I'll take five, ten, fifteen, twenty dollars . . . Colabrava against Falcón de Acero . . . (*Continuing his announcement*)

SANTIAGO: Lend me some money, Cheché.

CHECHÉ: How much?

SANTIAGO: Two hundred.

CHECHÉ: I don't lend any money when I'm gambling, and I don't lend any money when I'm drinking.

SANTIAGO: Are you going to make me walk home to get more money?

CHECHÉ: Ah, just give it up!

SANTIAGO: Are you going to make me walk back to my house?

CHECHÉ: It's not a good night for you! You've lost all your money.

SANTIAGO: Lend me some money, Cheché. I'll pay you back.

CHECHÉ: You're drunk, Santiago.

SANTIAGO: Give me some money and I'll show you my luck. Come on, you've got the lucky money! With your lucky money I'll show you what I can do.

CHECHÉ: And when are you going to pay me back?

SANTIAGO: I guarantee you that I'll pay you back.

CHECHÉ: You got to give me your word.

SANTIAGO: I'll give you my word. Give me a paper. I'll sign a paper. You got paper?

CHECHÉ: No, I don't have any paper.

SANTIAGO: Then lift up your foot.

CHECHÉ: What do you mean lift up my foot?

SANTIAGO (*Grabbing Cheché's leg*): Lift up your foot, hombre!

CHECHÉ: What the hell? . . .

SANTIAGO: Let me have the sole of your shoe.

(*Santiago takes out a knife.*)

CHECHÉ: What are you going to do? (*Lifting up his foot*)

SANTIAGO: I'm signing my name on the sole of your shoe.

(*Santiago carves his name on Cheché's shoe.*)

CHECHÉ: What for?

SANTIAGO: Proof. Testament that I'll pay you back. See here: "S" for Santiago. How much are you going to lend me?

CHECHÉ: Twenty.

SANTIAGO: Twenty? Cheapskate. I'm writing a hundred.

CHECHÉ: A hundred?

SANTIAGO: A hundred. There you go.

CHECHÉ: A hundred?

SANTIAGO: A hundred. That's what I wrote.

CHECHÉ: Are you . . ?

SANTIAGO: I'll pay you back. I'm your brother, for God's sake!

(*Sound of a ship approaching the harbor*)

OFELIA: There is the ship. Wave your handkerchief.

MARELA: Do you see him?

CONCHITA: All the men look the same with their hats.

OFELIA: Oh, why do I get so emotional every time I see a ship?

MARELA: Don't get mad at me, Mamá, but I wrote the lector's name on a piece of paper and placed it in a glass of water with brown sugar and cinnamon.

OFELIA: What for?

MARELA: Carmela, the palm reader, told me that if I sweeten his name, the reader would come our way.

OFELIA: That's like casting a spell on him.

MARELA: It's only sugar and cinnamon. And it worked.

OFELIA: I told you about playing with spells. It's not right, Marela. One should never alter other people's destiny.

MARELA: I didn't alter his destiny. With a little sugar I sweetened his fate.

CONCHITA: That's how witches get started — with brown sugar. Then they begin to play with fire. Look at what happened to Rosario, she put a spell on her lover and the man died. And not only did she lose her man; she's gone to hell herself.

OFELIA (*To Marela*): Did you hear that?

CONCHITA: They say she couldn't stop crying after her lover's death. That her whole face became an ocean of tears, and the father had to take her back to Cuba, to see if she would get better. But a fever would possess the girl at night. They say she'd run to the sea naked. She'd run there to meet the dead lover.

MARELA: Now you're making me feel awful.

(*Sounds of a crowd at a cockfight.*)

ELIADES: Kikiriki . . . Ready for the next fight! We have Diamante Negro against Crestafuerte . . . I'll take five, ten, fifteen, twenty dollars . . . Diamante Negro against Crestafuerte. Crestafuerte against Diamante Negro.

SANTIAGO: Lift up your foot again.

CHECHÉ: What for?

SANTIAGO: Lift up your foot and let me see the sole of your shoe.

CHECHÉ: What for?

(*Santiago carves something on the sole of Cheché's shoe.*)

SANTIAGO: I'm borrowing two hundred more.

CHECHÉ: No. You can't. You're jinxed tonight.

SANTIAGO: I'll pay you back. It's written on your shoe already.

CHECHÉ: Then cross it out.

SANTIAGO: I can't cross it out. I've got my totals there. If I don't pay you, part of the factory is yours.

(*Immediately Cheché takes off his shoe.*)

CHECHÉ: Then write it down. Write it down. I want it in writing.

SANTIAGO: I'll write it down. (*Takes the knife and carves out his promise*) There you go.

(*Cheché looks at the sole of his shoe. He gives Santiago more money.*)

CHECHÉ: Here. Let's go.

SANTIAGO: Well, put on your shoe, hombre!

CHECHÉ: No, I'm not putting it on.

SANTIAGO: Why not?

CHECHÉ: Because this here is our contract, and I don't want it erased.

SANTIAGO: And you're going to walk with just one shoe.

CHECHÉ: Yes!

SANTIAGO: You bastard!

(*Sound of a ship approaching.*)

OFELIA: Well, there's no sign of him. Let's see if you spoiled it for us.

MARELA: Ah, don't say that! I'm so nervous I think I'm going to pee-pee on myself.

CONCHITA: Is he that man waving his hat?

OFELIA: Is it? I can't see very well from here.

CONCHITA: No. He's got to be younger.

MARELA: How is he going to recognize us?

OFELIA: I told him that I was going to wear a white hat.

MARELA: Oh Lord! There are more than fifty women with white hats.

OFELIA: But I told him that my hat would have a gardenia.

CONCHITA: Is it the man with the blue suit?

MARELA: No, too fat.

OFELIA: When you get home take his name out of that sweet water.

MARELA: Oh Lord, I feel awful. He's nowhere to be found. I'm going home. I'm going home. I've ruined it. (*Starts to exit*)

OFELIA: Marela!

MARELA: No. I've ruined it.

OFELIA: Come back here. A little bit of sugar can't do any harm.

(*The lector, Juan Julian, enters. He is wearing a Panama hat and a white linen suit.*)

MARELA: I don't want to spoil it.

OFELIA: Marela, don't be foolish.

JUAN JULIAN: Señora Ofelia?

OFELIA (*Turning to look*): Yes . . .

JUAN JULIAN: The gardenia on your hat, am I correct? Señora Ofelia.

(*Juan Julian takes off his hat.*)

OFELIA (*Dumbstruck*): Oh!

CONCHITA: Say yes, Mamá!

OFELIA: Ah, yes! I'm Ofelia.

JUAN JULIAN: Juan Julian Rios, at your service!

OFELIA: Ah! Ofelia . . . Ofelia Alcalar. What an honor!

(*We hear Marela pee on herself from nervousness. There is an awkward pause. All of them notice.*)

(*Dissimulating*) Oh! Do you have everything, Señor Juan Julian? Do you have your luggage?

JUAN JULIAN: I'll have to tell the steward that I found you.

OFELIA: Go find him . . . We'll wait here.

(*Juan Julian runs off.*)

(*Turning to Marela*) Marela, what happened?

MARELA (*Dumbstruck*): I don't know.

OFELIA: Oh dear! But you've wet yourself, like a child.

MARELA: I couldn't hold it in, Mamá.

(*Music plays. Lights change.*)

Scene 2

The cigar factory. Juan Julian is holding a few books strapped with a belt. Cheché enters. He wears one shoe and holds the other in his hand.

CHECHÉ: Are you here to see someone?

JUAN JULIAN: I'm here to see Ofelia.

CHECHÉ: Ofelia hasn't come yet. Can I help you?

JUAN JULIAN: She told me she'd be here around this time.

CHECHÉ: She should be getting here soon. Can I be of any service?

JUAN JULIAN: No, thank you. I'll wait.

CHECHÉ: What are you, a lector?

JUAN JULIAN: Yes, I am. I just arrived from the island. Today is my first day . . .

CHECHÉ: If you're looking for a job, we're not hiring . . .

JUAN JULIAN: No, I'm . . . I'm the new lector. Doña Ofelia —

CHECHÉ: I heard. You just arrived and I'm telling you we're not hiring . . .

JUAN JULIAN: Well, I imagine you are not hiring because Señora Ofelia . . .

(*Ofelia and her daughters enter.*)

CHECHÉ: Ofelia, the señor . . . this gentleman is here to see you. I told him we're not hiring . . .

OFELIA (*With conviction*): He's been hired by me, Chester.

CHECHÉ: Oh, I see. I see. (*Pause*) Oh, well.

(*Cheché exits.*)

OFELIA: Welcome, Juan Julian. Some of the cigar rollers who work in front told me they already met you. They're very excited that you're here.

JUAN JULIAN: Ah yes. I was talking to the gentleman wearing the fedora who sits all the way to the right.

OFELIA: Peppino Mellini. He's the best buncher we have. He is from Napoli. He has a soft spot for the love stories. He is the one that sings Neapolitan songs at the end of the day.

JUAN JULIAN: And I also met Palomo, the gentleman with the Panama hat.

CONCHITA: My husband. He is a roller like us.

OFELIA: And did you meet Manola?

JUAN JULIAN: Is she the lady with the picture of Valentino° on top of her table?

OFELIA: Yes, she does the stuffing. Oh, she's delighted that you are here. Sometimes she's a sea of tears when she listens to the stories.

JUAN JULIAN: And the gentleman with the handkerchief around his neck?

OFELIA: Ah, that's Pascual Torino from Spain. He does the wrapping. A nostalgic at heart, wants to go back to his country and die in Granada.

JUAN JULIAN: And the gentleman that was just here?

MARELA: Chester is a clown.

(*Conchita and Marela laugh.*)

OFELIA: Marela! We call him Cheché. He is my husband's half-brother. We didn't know he was part of the family, but one day he showed up at the factory with a birth certificate and said he was my father-in-law's son. So we took him in, and ever since, he's been part of the family. But he is really from a town up north. (*Laughs*) My father-in-law got around.

JUAN JULIAN: I think that my presence offends him.

MARELA: Oh, that can't be. Don't pay him any mind.

JUAN JULIAN: When I entered the factory this morning he turned his back on me and then he . . .

MARELA: Cheché thinks he owns the factory. (*Breaks into laughter*)

OFELIA: My husband has given him a little too much power. But it's my husband who really runs the factory.

CONCHITA: Don't mind him. Cheché has a knack for turning the smallest incident into a loud and tragic event.

JUAN JULIAN: But I didn't do anything to the man.

MARELA: He doesn't like lectors.

OFELIA: He doesn't understand the purpose of having someone like you read stories to the workers.

JUAN JULIAN: But that has always been the tradition.

CONCHITA: He's from another culture.

MARELA: He thinks that lectors are the ones who cause trouble.

JUAN JULIAN: Why? Because we read novels to the workers, because we educate them and inform them?

MARELA: No. It's more complicated than that. His wife ran away from home with a lector.

OFELIA: Marela! He doesn't need to know these things!

MARELA: But it's true. She disappeared one day with the lector that was working here. She was a southern belle from Atlanta and he was from Guanabacoa. Her skin was pale like a lily and he was the color of saffron. And of course, now Cheché is against all lectors and the love stories they read.

Valentino: Rudolph Valentino (1895–1926), one of silent films' greatest romantic stars.

JUAN JULIAN: But he can't put the blame . . .

MARELA: Cheché thinks the love stories got under her skin. That's why she left him.

OFELIA: That's enough, Marela! When all this happened the poor man was desperate, angry and sad. He couldn't accept reality, so he blamed the lectors and the love stories for his misfortune.

CONCHITA: If he's ever disrespectful you should talk to our father.

OFELIA: Don't you worry. I'll take care of him.

MARELA: What are you planning to read to us?

JUAN JULIAN: First, Tolstoy, *Anna Karenina*.

MARELA: *Anna Karenina*. I already like the title. Is it romantic?

JUAN JULIAN: Yes. Quite romantic.

MARELA: Ah, *Anna Karenina* will go right to Cheché's heart. The poor man. He won't be able to take it.

JUAN JULIAN: I could pick another book. I've brought many.

CONCHITA: No, read *Anna Karenina* if that's the book that you chose.

MARELA: He needs to listen to another love story and let the words make nests in his hair, so he can find another woman.

OFELIA: And how do you like Tampa so far, Juan Julian?

JUAN JULIAN: Well, I . . . I . . . It's very . . . It seems like it's a city in the making.

OFELIA: That it is. We are still trying to create a little city that resembles the ones we left back in the island.

JUAN JULIAN: It's curious, there are no mountains or hills here. Lots of sky I have noticed . . . And clouds . . . The largest clouds I've ever seen, as if they had soaked up the whole sea. It's all so flat all around. That's why the sky seems so much bigger here and infinite. Bigger than the sky I know back home. And there's so much light. There doesn't seem to be a place where one could hide.

MARELA: One can always find shade in the park. There's always a hiding place to be found, and if not, one can always hide behind light.

JUAN JULIAN: Really. And how does one hide behind light?

(*The women laugh nervously.*)

MARELA: Depends what you are hiding from.

JUAN JULIAN: Perhaps light itself.

MARELA: Well, there are many kinds of light. The light of fires. The light of stars. The light that reflects off rivers. Light that penetrates through cracks. Then there's the type of light that reflects off the skin. Which one?

JUAN JULIAN: Perhaps the type that reflects off the skin.

MARELA: That's the most difficult one to escape.

(*The women laugh. Cheché enters. He is still holding the shoe in his hand.*)

CHECHÉ: Ofelia, why didn't Santiago come to work today?

OFELIA: He went to Camacho's house. Is there a problem, Cheché?

CHECHÉ: No, I'd just like to talk about . . . Will he come by later?

OFELIA: I don't know. What's wrong with your foot?

CHECHÉ: Oh, it's a long story. You see . . . I . . .

OFELIA: Did you fall? Did you hurt yourself?

CHECHÉ: No. I . . . It's nothing.

OFELIA: I know my feet are worse each day. If it isn't a bunion hurting, it's an ingrown nail.

CHECHÉ: No, Ofelia. Nothing of the sort.

OFELIA: Then why are you walking . . . ?

CHECHÉ: Well, you see . . . My shoes for work . . . I . . . I took them to the shoemaker yesterday and they weren't ready today.

OFELIA: So, these are new shoes and they hurt your feet.

CHECHÉ: No, you see . . . I mean . . . Last night Santiago and I . . . We . . . You see, we went to the cockfights.

OFELIA: Ha! That explains it. You lost all your money and your shoes.

CHECHÉ: No, I didn't lose my money. Your husband lost all his money and some of mine.

(*Ofelia laughs.*)

OFELIA: So are you giving me this shoe so I can throw it at him and break his head?

(*The women laugh.*)

CHECHÉ: No, Ofelia . . . I . . .

OFELIA: So what's with the shoe? Are you collecting alms? Instead of passing the bucket or the hat are you passing the shoe?

CHECHÉ: Well, I'm sort of passing it to you.

OFELIA: I don't have any money, Cheché.

CHECHÉ: I'm not asking you for money.

(*Juan Julian and the sisters exit.*)

OFELIA: Then why are you pointing this thing at me?

CHECHÉ: You see here. Right here, on the sole of my shoe, Santiago wrote how much he owes me.

OFELIA: And how much does he owe you?

CHECHÉ: The total is here.

(*Ofelia looks at the shoe.*)

OFELIA: That's a lot of money.

CHECHÉ: That's how much he owes me.

OFELIA: Where did you get so much money?

CHECHÉ: I was winning.

OFELIA: And you drank and gave it all away.

CHECHÉ: No. I . . . Well, he wanted to continue playing. He didn't want to walk home to get more money, so I lent him what I had. And he told me he'd sign my shoe and write the totals. And I trust that he'll pay me back.

OFELIA: So what do you want me to do?

CHECHÉ: Well, this here is a bill. A document.

OFELIA: You're not serious!

CHECHÉ: No. This here is an agreement. If he doesn't pay me . . . You see here. You see his initials . . . He signed this! He signed it! He told me that if he didn't pay me, another share of the factory would be mine.

Jimmy Smits as the lector and Daphne Rubin-Vega as Conchita in the 2003 production of *Anna in the Tropics* at the McCarter Theatre in Princeton, New Jersey, directed by Emily Mann.

The 2003 McCarter Theatre production of *Anna in the Tropics*, with (from left to right) Vanessa Aspillaga as Marela, Daphne Rubin-Vega as Conchita, and Priscilla López as Ofelia.

OFELIA: Get this thing out of my sight.
CHECHÉ: But Ofelia . . .
OFELIA: Get it out my sight, I said.
CHECHÉ: But Ofelia . . .
OFELIA: I don't know what went on between you and your brother, but I don't have anything to do with it. And you better go to a shoemaker and get your shoes mended.

(*Music plays. Lights change.*)

Scene 3

Juan Julian strides around the cigar workers reading from Tolstoy's Anna Karenina. *He reads with passion and fervor. The cigar workers roll, but are completely immersed in the story.*

JUAN JULIAN (*Reading*):

> Looking at him, Anna Karenina felt a physical humiliation and could not say another word. Her beloved felt what a killer must feel when he looks at the body he has deprived of life. The body he had deprived of life was their love, the beginning of their love. There was something dreadful and revolting in the recollection of what had been paid for by this awful price of shame. The shame Anna sensed from their spiritual nakedness destroyed her and affected him. But in spite of the killer's horror when he faces the body of his victim, the killer must cut the body to pieces and conceal it, and he must make use of what he has gained by his crime. And with the same fury and passion as the killer throws himself upon the body and drags it and cuts it, he covered her face and shoulders with kisses. "Yes, these kisses — these kisses are what have been bought by my shame."

(*Juan Julian closes the book.*)

That's all for today from *Anna Karenina*.

(*The workers applaud.*)

MARELA (*Still enraptured by the story*): Why does he always end when he gets to the good part?
OFELIA: To keep us in suspense.
CONCHITA: To keep us wanting more.
MARELA: He's really a fine lector.
OFELIA: That's why he's called the Persian Canary, because it's like hearing a bird sing when he reads.
MARELA: Me, too.
CHECHÉ: I would've preferred a detective story.
MARELA: They're not very literary, Chester.
CONCHITA: Well. I don't know about you, but ever since he started reading *Anna Karenina* my mind wanders to Russia.
MARELA: Me, too. I have dreams and they are full of white snow, and Anna Karenina is dancing waltzes with Vronsky. Then I see them in a little room, and all the snow melts from the heat of their bodies and their skin. And I just want to borrow a fur coat from my friend Cookie Salazar and go to Russia.
OFELIA: He chose the right book. There is nothing like reading a winter book in the middle of summer. It's like having a fan or an icebox by your side to relieve the heat and the caloric nights.
CHECHÉ (*To Palomo*): Help me with the boxes.

(*The men exit.*)

MARELA: What was that last line? "And, as with fury and passion the killer throws himself upon . . ."
CONCHITA: "Upon the body," he said, "And drags it and cuts it, he covered her face and shoulders with kisses."
MARELA: Does it mean that when you're in love your body is stolen from life?
CONCHITA: No. The body robbed of life was their love. The love of Anna and her beloved.
OFELIA: It must be terrible living that way.
MARELA: Why?
OFELIA: How the three of them live! Anna, the husband and the lover. It must be a nightmare.
MARELA: Of course not!

(*Conchita refers to the story, but also to her own life.*)

CONCHITA: Yes. Anna said it herself. It's like a curse, she said. She was talking about it at the end, when she said that his kisses have been bought by her shame. She's got to be miserable.
MARELA: Miserable? Enraptured maybe.
OFELIA: You don't listen to the story, Marela.
MARELA: Of course I listen to the story.
CONCHITA: Then you ought to know that it is misery for her. It's pure agony for Anna's husband and for the lover, too. They probably couldn't endure it any longer, if it weren't for some kind of hope.
MARELA: Then why would she take on a lover?
OFELIA: She has no choice. It's something she can't escape. That's why the writer describes love as a thief. The thief is the mysterious fever that poets have been studying for years. Remember Anna Karenina's last words.
CONCHITA: She never remembers anything.
MARELA: I do. I just don't cling to every word the way you do. I don't try to understand everything they say. I let myself be taken. When Juan Julian starts reading, the story enters my body and I become the second skin of the characters.
OFELIA: Don't be silly.
MARELA: We can always dream.
OFELIA: Ah yes. But we have to take a yardstick and measure our dreams.
MARELA: Then I will need a very long yardstick. The kind that could measure the sky.
CONCHITA: How foolish you are, Marela!
MARELA (*To Conchita*): No, everything in life dreams. A bicycle dreams of becoming a boy, an umbrella dreams of becoming the rain, a pearl dreams of becoming a woman, and a chair dreams of becoming a gazelle and running back to the forest.
OFELIA: But, my child, people like us . . . We have to remember to keep our feet on the ground and stay living inside our shoes and not have lofty illusions.

(*A bell rings. Palomo enters.*)

Ah, workday has come to an end. Good. I rolled more than two hundred cigars today.

MARELA: And I've wedded more than a thousand. That's what I like about putting the bands around the cigars. It's like marrying all these men without actually seeing them.

OFELIA: Men marry their cigars, my dear, and the white smoke becomes the veil of their brides. My mother used to say, "When a man marries, he marries two women, his bride and his cigar." Are you coming, Conchita?

CONCHITA: No. Palomo and I are working till late.

OFELIA: We'll see you for dinner. Adios.

CONCHITA: Adios.

OFELIA: Till later, Palomo.

PALOMO: Adios.

MARELA: Adios.

PALOMO: Is your father in trouble again and that's why . . . ?

CONCHITA: He is.

PALOMO: How much did he lose this time?

CONCHITA: Plenty.

PALOMO: Plenty can be a lot of money.

CONCHITA: Yes, you're right. And I don't know what good he gets from losing all that money.

PALOMO: Oh, that's something we'll never know. (*Beginning to roll*)

CONCHITA: And how do you like the novel that Juan Julian is reading to us?

PALOMO: I like it very much.

CONCHITA: Doesn't it make you uncomfortable?

PALOMO: Why would it make me uncomfortable?

CONCHITA: The part about the lover.

PALOMO: It seems like in every novel there's always a love affair.

CONCHITA: And do you ever think about everything that's happening between Anna Karenina and her husband?

PALOMO: I do . . . But I . . .

CONCHITA: So what goes through your mind when you listen to the story?

PALOMO: I think of the money all those people have.

CONCHITA: You would say something like that.

PALOMO: Why? Because I like money?

CONCHITA: I'm talking about literature and you talk about money.

PALOMO: And what do you want me to say?

CONCHITA: I want you to talk about the story, the characters . . .

PALOMO: Wouldn't you like to have all the money they have? So you don't have to spend the whole day rolling cigars and working after hours so we can save money and have our own business.

CONCHITA: I don't mind rolling cigars.

PALOMO: And what's so good about rolling cigars?

CONCHITA: My mind wanders to other places.

PALOMO: What places?

CONCHITA: Places and things money can't buy.

PALOMO: Money can buy everything.

CONCHITA: Not the places I go to in my mind.

PALOMO: And what kind of places are you talking about?

CONCHITA: Places made of dreams.

PALOMO (*Laughs; becoming playful*): You're a strange creature, Conchita. I don't know why I married you.

CONCHITA: You married me because the day you met me, I gave you a cigar I had rolled especially for you and when you smoked it, you told me I had slipped into your mouth like a pearl diver.

PALOMO: I told you that?

CONCHITA: Yes, you did. After blowing a blue ring of smoke out of your mouth. And the words lingered in the air like a zeppelin and I thought to myself, I could fall in love with that mouth.

PALOMO: As far as I can remember, I married you because I couldn't untie your father's hands from around my neck.

CONCHITA: Ah, the truth comes out. That explains everything. You never really cared for me.

PALOMO: Are you trying to start a fight?

CONCHITA: No. I asked you a simple question about a love story and you're being foolish.

PALOMO: Never mind.

CONCHITA: You don't care about anything, do you? Juan Julian could be reading a book by José Martí° or Shakespeare and everything goes in one ear and out the other.

PALOMO: I pay attention to what he reads. I just don't take everything to heart the way you do.

CONCHITA: Well, you should. Do you remember that part of the book in which Anna Karenina's husband is suspicious of her having an affair with Vronsky? Remember when he paces the room, like a lost animal.

PALOMO: I know what you're getting at.

CONCHITA: I just want to have a civilized conversation. The same way the characters speak to each other in the novel. I've learned many things from this book.

PALOMO: Such as?

CONCHITA: Jealousy. For Anna's husband jealousy is base and almost animalistic. And he's right. He would never want Anna to think that he's capable of such vile and shameful emotions.

PALOMO: But you can't help being jealous. It's part of your nature.

CONCHITA: Not anymore.

PALOMO: Well, that's a change.

CONCHITA: Oh, I could see the husband so clear in the novel. How the thoughts would take shape in his mind, as they have in my own mind. I mean, not the same . . . No, no . . . Not the same, because he's an educated man, surrounded by culture and wealth, and I'm just a cigar roller in a factory. He is well bred and sophisticated. I barely get by in life.

José Martí: Martí (1853–1895) was a writer and fighter for Cuba's independence from Spain. He died fighting in Cuba.

But with this book I'm seeing everything through new eyes. What is happening in the novel has been happening to us.

No. Don't look at me that way. You might not want to admit it, but Anna and her husband remind me of us. Except I'm more like the husband.

PALOMO: So what does that make me then, Anna Karenina?

CONCHITA: You are the one who has the secret love, not me.

PALOMO: Oh, come on. It's late. Let's go home. I can't work like this.

CONCHITA: That's exactly what Anna said when the husband confronted her about the lover: "It's late. Let's go to sleep."

PALOMO: I think you're taking this a little too far.

CONCHITA: Am I? Have you ever heard the voice of someone who's deaf? The voice is crude and ancient, because it has no sense of direction or place, because it doesn't hear itself and it doesn't know if anybody else in the world hears it. Sometimes I want to have a long conversation with you, like this. Like a deaf person. As if I couldn't hear you or myself. But I would just talk and talk, and say everything that comes to my mind, like a shell that shouts with the voice of the sea and it doesn't care if anybody ever hears it. That's how I want to speak to you, and ask you things.

PALOMO: And what's the use of talking like this? What sort of things do you want to ask me?

CONCHITA: Things that you wouldn't tell me, afraid that I might not understand.

PALOMO: Like what?

CONCHITA: I'd like to know what she's like. And what does she do to make you happy?

PALOMO: Ah, let's go home.

CONCHITA: Why?

PALOMO (*Abruptly*): Because I don't want to talk about these things!

(*A pause.*)

CONCHITA: So what's going to happen to us, Palomo?

PALOMO: I don't know. Do you want a divorce? We could travel to Reno and be divorced in six weeks. But your family will be opposed to it, and the same with mine. So divorce is out of the question.

CONCHITA: And if I tell you that I want to cut my hair, change the way I dress and take on a lover.

PALOMO: Say that again?

CONCHITA: What I just said.

PALOMO: You want to have a lover?

CONCHITA: Yes, like you do.

PALOMO: Ave Maria purissima!

CONCHITA: I have the same right as you do.

PALOMO: This book will be the end of us.

CONCHITA: Don't you think we've already come to the end?

PALOMO: No . . . I . . .

CONCHITA: You don't make love to me like you used to.

PALOMO: Well, we . . . You and I . . . We . . .

CONCHITA: It's all right, Palomo. It's all right. (*She touches his arm*) There's something that Anna Karenina said and I keep repeating it to myself: "If there are as many minds as there are heads, then there are as many kinds of love as there are hearts." I can try to love you in a different way. I can do that. And you should try to do the same.

(*Music plays. Lights change.*)

Scene 4

A square of light on the floor suggests the interior of the family's house. Ofelia and Santiago are not on speaking terms. She sits on one side of the room, he sits on the other; Marela stands by Santiago. The dialogue moves fast. Marela runs back and forth as a communicator.

SANTIAGO: Ask your mother for some money to buy me a pack of cigarettes. She's not talking to me.

MARELA: Papá wants money for a pack of cigarettes.

OFELIA: Ask him when is he going back to work.

MARELA: She wants to know when you're going back to work.

SANTIAGO: Tell her as soon as I get money from Camacho to pay Cheché.

MARELA: He says as soon as he gets money from Camacho to pay Cheché.

OFELIA: Tell him to give up smoking till then, that I'm not giving him any money.

SANTIAGO: What did she say?

MARELA: She says —

SANTIAGO: I heard her. (*In loud voice, to Ofelia*) Tell her that she's insane!

MARELA: He says you're insane.

OFELIA: And tell him he's a drunk, a thief and a-good-for-nothing gambler.

MARELA: She says —

SANTIAGO: I heard.

MARELA: He heard you, Mamá.

OFELIA: Good!

MARELA: Good, she says.

SANTIAGO: You're a crazy woman! Crazy woman!

OFELIA: Tell him I didn't hear that. I told him I don't want him to talk to me.

SANTIAGO: Ah, she heard me!

OFELIA: Tell him I don't want to hear his barbarism.

MARELA: Did you hear that, Papá? She doesn't want to hear your barbarism.

SANTIAGO: Tell her . . .

(*Marela starts to walk toward her father.*)

OFELIA (*Infuriated*): Come here, Marela . . .

(*Marela walks toward her mother.*)

SANTIAGO: Marela, come here . . .

MARELA: Wait! It's not your turn, Mamá.

OFELIA: Marela . . .

MARELA: Stop! I can't be here and there at the same time!

(*Silence. Ofelia and Santiago shake their heads as if giving up on the whole thing.*)

OFELIA AND SANTIAGO: This is insane!

MARELA: Well, you both heard that.

(*Marela tries to put in a word, but they don't give her a chance.*)

SANTIAGO: Tell her I'm going to a pawnshop to sell my wedding ring.

OFELIA: Tell him he should've done that a long time ago.

SANTIAGO: She's right, I should've done it a long time ago.

OFELIA: Yes, before his finger got numb.

SANTIAGO: She's right, my finger got numb.

OFELIA: You see, I was right. Numb, like everything else.

SANTIAGO: She's wrong. Not like everything else.

OFELIA: Nothing works on his body. Just his rotten teeth to chew away money.

MARELA: I'm leaving.

OFELIA: Marela!

SANTIAGO: Marela!

MARELA: You can fight without me!

(*Marela walks out of the room. Silence.*
   Then, Ofelia and Santiago begin to speak to each other without looking at each other.)

SANTIAGO: I've been listening to the new lector from up here.

OFELIA: You have?

SANTIAGO: He's good. He has a solid voice and I like the novel that he's reading.

OFELIA: Yes, a solid voice he has and I like the novel, too.

SANTIAGO: I 'specially like the character that lives in the countryside.

OFELIA (*With delight*): Yes.

SANTIAGO: Yes, him.

OFELIA: The one that has the farm?

SANTIAGO: Yes. The one that has the farm. What is his name?

OFELIA: His name is Levin.

SANTIAGO: That's right, Levin.

OFELIA: The one that lives in the forest surrounded by trees.

SANTIAGO: That Levin reminds me of when I was young and my father left me to run the factory. It seems as if Levin has dedicated his whole life to his farm.

OFELIA: Yes, he's a dedicated man.

SANTIAGO: I used to be like him.

OFELIA: Yes, you used to be like him.

SANTIAGO: I like the part of the book when Anna's brother is going to sell the estate next to Levin's property and Levin counsels him not to sell it.

OFELIA: Yes, that's a good part. And I can't believe that you almost gave another share of the factory to Cheché.

SANTIAGO: You're right, I lost my mind. I shouldn't drink.

OFELIA: That's right, drink you shouldn't. That's an idiotic thing to do, give away another share of the business. Cheché doesn't know what he's doing. He's like a scarecrow. He's been talking about bringing machines and replacing some of the workers. You need to go back to the factory.

SANTIAGO: Yes, you're right. To the factory I need to go back.

(*Ofelia looks at him.*)

OFELIA: Santiago, what's eating you? You haven't gone to work. You don't eat. You don't sleep well.

SANTIAGO: I've acted like a fool, Ofelia. I'm ashamed of myself and I'm angry and bitter. And I can't shake off this damn agony!

OFELIA: Do you want me to call a doctor?

SANTIAGO: No. I don't need a doctor.

OFELIA: But you can't go on like this. Sooner or later you have to go back and face the workers.

SANTIAGO: I will. When I get the money and I can face Cheché.

OFELIA: And are you going to stay here until then?

SANTIAGO: Yes.

OFELIA: That's silly.

SANTIAGO: That's the way I am.

OFELIA: Well, I'm going to bed.

(*Ofelia starts to exit.*)

SANTIAGO: Ofelia.

OFELIA: Yes.

SANTIAGO: Stay up a while longer.

OFELIA: I'm tired. You didn't work like I did today.

SANTIAGO: Talk to me about the novel. I can't always hear very well from up here. This fellow, Levin . . . This character that I admire . . . He's the one who is in love with the young girl in the story, isn't he?

OFELIA (*A burst of energy*): Ah yes! He's in love with Kitty. Levin is in love with Kitty, and Kitty is in love with Vronsky. And Vronsky is in love with Anna Karenina. And Anna Karenina is married, but she's in love with Vronsky. Ay, everybody is in love in this book!

SANTIAGO: But for Levin . . . For Levin there's only one woman.

OFELIA: Yes, for him there's only one woman.

SANTIAGO (*Full of love, he looks at her*): Ofelia.

OFELIA: Yes .

(*Santiago swallows the gulp of love.*)

SANTIAGO: No. Nothing.

OFELIA (*Fanning herself*): Ah, the night breeze is making its way to us again. There's nothing like this Tampa breeze, always a punctual visitor around this time.

SANTIAGO: You know, Ofelia, when I gamble I try to repeat the same motions . . . I try to repeat everything I did the day I won. And when I lose I try to take inventory of what I did wrong. I think to myself, Did I get up from bed with my left foot first? Did I forget to polish my shoes? Did I leave the house in a state of disorder? Was I unkind to someone and that's why luck didn't come my way? Lately, I've been in a fog and I don't know what to do.

Every time I lose, I feel that something has been taken from me. Something bigger than money. And I see a line of little ants carrying breadcrumbs on their backs. But the crumbs they are taking away are my pride and my self-respect. My dignity. (*Looks at her again*) Have I lost you too, Ofelia? Have I lost you?

OFELIA: If you had lost me, I wouldn't be here. If you had lost me, I wouldn't be by your side. How can you say that you've lost me! (*She hugs him*)

(*Music plays. Lights change.*)

Scene 5

Juan Julian, Marela and Conchita at the factory.

JUAN JULIAN: I don't really like cities. In the country one has freedom. When I'm in a city I feel asphyxiated. I feel constriction in my lungs. The air feels thick and dense, as if the buildings breathe and steal away the oxygen. As my father used to say, living in a city is like living inside the mouth of a crocodile, buildings all around you like teeth. The teeth of culture, the mouth and tongue of civilization. It's a silly comparison, but it makes sense to me.

Every time I go to a park, I'm reminded of how we always go back to nature. We build streets and buildings. We work five to six days a week, building and cementing our paths and down come tumbling trees and nests, a whole paradise of insects. And all for what? On Sundays we return to a park where we could still find greenery. The verdure of nature.

CONCHITA: You're right. I don't know what I would do without my walks to the park. Why did you choose to read Tolstoy?

JUAN JULIAN: Because Tolstoy understands humanity like no other writer does.

CONCHITA: That's a good enough reason to read him.

JUAN JULIAN: Someone told me that at the end of his life, when he knew he was going to die, he abandoned his house and he was found dead at a train station. The same as . . .
Oh, perhaps I shouldn't tell you this.

CONCHITA: He was probably on his way to visit God.

JUAN JULIAN: That has always been my suspicion.

MARELA: Pardon me, but I must go. (*She exits*)

(*There is an awkward pause as Juan Julian and Conchita watch Marela leave.*)

CONCHITA: How did you become a lector?

JUAN JULIAN: I discovered books one summer. My father owed a lot of money to a creditor and we had to close ourselves up in our house and hide for a while. For my family, keeping up appearances was important. We had to pretend that we had gone away on a trip. We told neighbors that my mother was ill and she had to recuperate somewhere else. We stayed in that closed-up house for more than two months, while my father worked abroad. I remember it was hot and all the windows were kept closed. The heat was unbearable. The maid was the only one who went out to buy groceries. And while being closed up in our own home my mother read books to the family. And that's when I became a listener and I learned to appreciate stories and the sound of words. (*Smiles*) Have you ever been to New England?

CONCHITA: No.

JUAN JULIAN: I always wanted to go there. I wonder what New Englanders are like. Here I have met workers from other parts of the world, but I haven't met anybody from up North.

CONCHITA: Cheché is from up North.

JUAN JULIAN: Cheché is from a world of his own.

CONCHITA: I knew a fellow from New London. He was modest and reserved. So shy was this boy, that when he expressed any sort of feeling, he would excuse himself. (*Laughs*) One day I gave him a braid that I'd cut from my hair and told him to bury it under a tree. I explained to him that back in the island most women cut their hair once a year on the 2nd of February, when plants and trees are pruned, for the feast of Saint Candelaria. I told him how women offer their hair to the earth and the trees, for all the greenery and fruits to come. And I gave him my little braid in a box and told him to choose a tree in the park.

And the boy looked at me with a strange face and said that he would feel embarrassed digging a hole in the middle of the park, in front of everybody. And that's when I took my braid back from him, took a shovel, dug a hole and put him to shame. From then on he never talked to me again. So he's the only person from New England that I've met.

(*Palomo enters. He watches from a distance.*)

JUAN JULIAN (*Laughs*): And do you still cut your hair every 2nd of February?

CONCHITA: Yes. My father always does me the honor of burying it.

JUAN JULIAN: Your father! And why not your husband? It should be an honor for any man . . . If I were your husband I would find an old, wise, banyan tree and I would bury your hair by its roots, and I'm sure it would accept the offering like rainwater.

CONCHITA: Well, I'm cutting my hair short like Clara Bow° and that will be the end of the ritual.

JUAN JULIAN: I would offer to find a strong-looking tree. But the ritual won't count if it's not done on February 2nd.

CONCHITA: I believe everything counts if you have faith.

JUAN JULIAN: So are you telling me that I should pick a strong-looking tree?

CONCHITA: Yes, if you wish.

Clara Bow: (1905–1965), one of the most popular silent film stars of the 1920s. She was called the "It" Girl.

JUAN JULIAN: And why me?

CONCHITA: Because you offer to. And you are the reader of the love stories, and anybody who dedicates his life to reading books believes in rescuing things from oblivion.

JUAN JULIAN: So is there a story in your hair?

CONCHITA: There will be the day I cut it, and that story will come to an end.

JUAN JULIAN: And how does one read the story of your hair?

CONCHITA: The same way one reads a face or a book.

JUAN JULIAN: Then we shouldn't bury your hair under a tree. We should place it inside a manuscript. The same way Victorian women used to press flowers or a lock of hair between the pages of a book.

CONCHITA: Then I would leave it to you to choose the book.

JUAN JULIAN: How about this one?

CONCHITA: My hair will be in good company with *Anna Karenina*.

JUAN JULIAN: Then close your eyes and choose a page.

(*Conchita closes her eyes. She opens the book and chooses a page. Juan Julian reads:*)

> At first Anna sincerely thought that she was annoyed because he insisted on pursuing her; but very soon after her return from Moscow, when she went to an evening party where she expected to see him, but which he did not attend, she came to the realization by the sadness that overwhelmed her, that she was deceiving herself.

CONCHITA: Then here, cut my hair.

(*Conchita hands him the scissors. She loosens her hair and turns her back to him. He combs her hair with his fingers. He kisses her shoulder. She then turns around to return his kiss.*)

ACT TWO • Scene 1

Darkness. Music.

As the lights start to come up, we hear the recorded voice of the lector narrating a passage from Anna Karenina.

JUAN JULIAN (*Recorded voice*):

> Anna Karenina had stepped into a new life and she could not convey through words her sense of shame, rapture and horror, and she did not want to talk about it and profane this feeling through simple words. And as time passed by, the next day and the next, she still could not find the proper words to express the complexity of her feelings, and could not even find thoughts with which to reflect on all that was in her soul.

(*Juan Julian and Conchita are at the factory making love. She is lying on top of a table, half naked, her skirt tucked up. He is there between her legs, shirtless and full of sweat. They have transgressed the limits of their bodies, and he now kisses her gently.*)

I'd like to stop seeing you here.

CONCHITA: And where do you want to meet?

JUAN JULIAN: In my room where we could be —

CONCHITA: That would be impossible.

(*They start dressing.*)

JUAN JULIAN: Then we should meet in a hotel.

CONCHITA: Hotels are cold and impersonal like hospitals.

JUAN JULIAN: Like hospitals?

CONCHITA: Yes. Every guest is looking for a remedy, whether it's a temporary relief from the world or a temporary rest from life.

JUAN JULIAN (*Touching her face playfully*): Then we should meet in a hospital, because sometimes I detect sad trees in your eyes after we make love.

CONCHITA: Then I must have a terrible malady.

JUAN JULIAN: Yes, and I recommend that you buy a canary and hear it sing five minutes a day . . . (*He starts kissing her neck*)

CONCHITA: And what if I can't find a canary?

JUAN JULIAN: Then you must come hear me sing when I take a shower.

(*We hear people outside.*)

CONCHITA: Go . . . Go . . . Someone's coming . . . Go . . .

(*We hear Cheché in an argument. Juan Julian takes his shirt and rushes out. Conchita fixes her dress and her hair, then runs to sit at her table.*)

CHECHÉ: Wait . . . wait . . . You don't let me finish!!! You don't let me finish!!! That's one of the problems that we have, I own shares in this factory and now that your husband . . .

(*The cigar workers enter and gather around Cheché. Next to him is a large machine wrapped in paper.*
There is a heated controversy over the machine. We hear the workers complaining.)

OFELIA: I'm the owner of the factory and I have the last word . . .

CHECHÉ: But Ofelia . . .

OFELIA: Someone go upstairs and call Santiago!

CHECHÉ: Ofelia . . . All I'm trying to say is that all these other companies are succeeding . . .

PALOMO: But, Cheché, that has nothing to do with machines. . . .

OFELIA: I don't want to listen to this. He's not the owner of this factory. Will someone call my husband!

(*Cheché stands up on a chair and addresses the crowd:*)

CHECHÉ: Just let me talk!!! Let's back up here! I'm trying to make a point, and you don't let me speak . . .

MARELA: Let the man talk, Mamá!

CHECHÉ: Ofelia . . . Ofelia . . . All these other cigar companies have the leads. I can name them all: Caprichos, Entreactos, Petit Bouquet, Regalia de Salón, Coquetas, Conchas Finas . . . They all have the leads . . .

OFELIA: Bah! They don't roll cigars like we do.

CHECHÉ: It doesn't matter how they roll their cigars. That's what I'm trying to tell you.

OFELIA: It matters to us.

CHECHÉ: Then we're never going to get anywhere.

OFELIA: And who's in a hurry to get anywhere? Are you going somewhere, Conchita?

CONCHITA: No.

OFELIA: Are you going somewhere, Palomo?

PALOMO: I wouldn't mind going to the Canary Islands to see my grandma . . .

(*Laughter from the crowd.*)

OFELIA: In that case I want to go to Spain . . .

MARELA: And I'd like to go to Russia . . .

(*Laughter from the crowd. Juan Julian enters.*)

CHECHÉ: I'm not joking, fellow workers. I'm talking about the modern world. Modernity. Progress. Advancement.

OFELIA: If working with machines means being modern then we're not interested in the modern world.

(*Applause from the workers.*)

CONCHITA: Bravo!

CHECHÉ: Do you want to see our sales records? Do you want to see our records?

OFELIA: I don't have to see the sales records. I know how much we sell and we're not doing that badly.

CHECHÉ: How can we be doing well when we had to let go of two employees?

MARELA: One employee, Cheché. The other one was your wife and she left on her own accord.

(*Laughter from the workers.*)

CHECHÉ: My point is that machines . . .

PALOMO: Machines are stealing our jobs.

MARELA: That's right.

(*The crowd is getting anxious.*)

CHECHÉ: I've been given more shares in this factory. I'm — (*He is interrupted*) Wait a second. And from now on I'm going to set things straight. (*Another interruption*) Hold on! Do you want to know the problems we have with our factory? Do you want to know? We are stuck in time. And why are we stuck in time? We are operating in the same manner that we were twenty, thirty, fifty years ago . . . (*Another interruption*) Hold on . . . Hold on . . . And why are we stuck? We are stuck because we are not part of the new century. Because we are still rolling cigars the same way that Indians rolled them hundreds of years ago. I mean, we might as well wear feathers and walk half naked with bones in our noses. There are machines that do tobacco stuffing at the speed of light: bunching machines, stripping machines . . .

OFELIA: And with all those machines, do they have any workers left?

CHECHÉ: Are you kidding me! The workers operate the machines. The workers run the machines.

PALOMO: Leonardo over at the Aurora factory says . . .

CHECHÉ: Ah, Leonardo is a lector! What does he know about machines?

PALOMO: He doesn't talk about machines like you do. But I can tell you what he says. He's always talking about maintaining our ways. Our methods. The old process we use. What we brought with us from the island. (*Raises his hands*) We brought these to roll our cigars, so we don't need an apparatus or whatever you want to call it . . .

(*Assertive comments from the crowd.*)

CHECHÉ: Leonardo is a lector. That's why he doesn't value machines. The lectors are being fired from all the factories, because nobody can hear them read over the sound of the machines. And that's another thing I wanted to talk about. I don't know about the rest of you, but I'm not interested in giving any more money from my pocket, from my wages to listen to a lector read me romantic novels.

CONCHITA: It's literature, Cheché.

(*Palomo looks at his wife, then turns to look at Juan Julian.*)

CHECHÉ: Literature, romance novels . . . It's all the same to me . . .

MARELA: No. It's not the same. We learn things. And the words he reads are like a breeze that breaks the monotony of this factory.

CHECHÉ: Well, some of these companies have done away . . .

JUAN JULIAN: Señor Chester, allow me to say something. My father used to say that the tradition of having readers in the factories goes back to the Taino Indians. He used to say that tobacco leaves whisper the language of the sky. And that's because through the language of cigar smoke the Indians used to communicate to the gods. Obviously I'm not an Indian, but as a lector I am a distant relative of the Cacique, the Chief Indian, who used to translate the sacred words of the deities. The workers are the oidores. The ones who listen quietly, the same way Taino Indians used to listen. And this is the tradition that you're trying to destroy with your machine. Instead of promoting and popularizing machines, why don't you advertise our cigars? Or are you working for the machine industry?

OFELIA: He's right. We need more advertising, so we can sell more cigars.

JUAN JULIAN: Let's face it, Chester, workers, cigars aren't popular anymore. Moving pictures now feature their stars smoking cigarettes: Valentino, Douglas Fairbanks° . . . They are all smoking little fags and not cigars. You can go to Hollywood and offer our cigars to producers.

Douglas Fairbanks: (1883–1939), a major action/adventure film star of the 1920s.

CHECHÉ: You're being cynical . . .

JUAN JULIAN: No, I'm warning you. This fast mode of living with machines and moving cars affects cigar consumption. And do you want to know why, Señor Chester? Because people prefer a quick smoke, the kind you get from a cigarette. The truth is that machines, cars, are keeping us from taking walks and sitting on park benches, smoking a cigar slowly and calmly. The way they should be smoked. So you see, Chester, you want modernity, and modernity is actually destroying our very own industry. The very act of smoking a cigar.

(All the workers applaud except for Cheché and Palomo.)

OFELIA: Bravo!

JUAN JULIAN: I can certainly step out of the room if you want to take a vote.

(Juan Julian puts his hat on and starts to exit.)

OFELIA: You don't have to go out of the room. It's obvious that we want you to stay.

JUAN JULIAN: No, let's do it the democratic way. We are in America. I'll step out of the room and you vote. Go ahead, Chester.

(Santiago enters.)

SANTIAGO: What's going on here?

OFELIA: Ah, good! I'm glad you're here. We are about to take a vote.

SANTIAGO: What are you voting for?

OFELIA: Machines. Cheché brought a stuffing machine.

SANTIAGO: And do the workers want machines?

WORKERS *(In unison)*: No.

SANTIAGO: So what are you voting for?

OFELIA: To do it the American way.

SANTIAGO: And what's the American way if everybody said no?

OFELIA: You talk to Cheché. Everything has gone up to his head. He also wants to get rid of the lector.

CHECHÉ: Wait a minute . . .

SANTIAGO: Is that true, Cheché?

CHECHÉ: I asked the workers if they wanted to continue to pay for the lector. That's all I did.

JUAN JULIAN: And I was about to go out, so the workers could vote.

SANTIAGO: You don't have to go anywhere. You stay here. I am glad to meet you. I am Santiago.

JUAN JULIAN: Juan Julian Ríos, at your service

SANTIAGO *(To the workers)*: I've heard that many factories are getting rid of their lectors. But is this what we want, workers? Let's raise our hands if this is what we want.

(Cheché and Palomo are the only ones who raise their hands. Conchita is shocked to see Palomo's decision.)

Two votes. Then that's the answer. We are not getting rid of Juan Julian. And I have good news, workers. We are coming up with a new cigar brand and it will be called Anna Karenina.

OFELIA: Bravo!

SANTIAGO: And Marela, if you will do us the honor, I would like you to pose as Anna Karenina for the label.

MARELA: Me?

SANTIAGO: If you like.

MARELA: Of course!

SANTIAGO: Here are some clothes for you to wear.

(Santiago gives her a box. She opens the box, which contains an elegant winter coat with fur trimming and a fancy fur hat.)

MARELA: I'll go try them on. *(She exits)*

(Santiago addresses the workers:)

SANTIAGO: Tomorrow we will start making plans for production. We have much work ahead of us, workers. But I promise that we will all benefit from the fruit of our work. I'm glad to be back.

(Applause from the workers. They exit. Cheché pulls Santiago aside. Santiago hands him an envelope.)

This is for you, Cheché. Here's your money.

CHECHÉ: Santiago, what is this new cigar brand that you're talking about? We don't have the money . . .

SANTIAGO: And what is this apparatus that you've brought to our factory?

CHECHÉ: Santiago, the sales are down. You haven't been here . . . The price of tobacco coming from Cuba is sky high . . .

SANTIAGO: Should we spend our money buying machines then?

CHECHÉ: We can benefit . . .

SANTIAGO: It's out of the question. Return that apparatus to the factory where you got it from. And get me a calendar.

CHECHÉ: But Santiago . . .

SANTIAGO: I got a loan, Cheché. This time I'm betting my money on the factory. Get me a calendar, I said.

(Cheché runs to get a calendar. He hands it to Santiago.)

What's today's date?

CHECHÉ: The twenty-first.

SANTIAGO: How can it be the twenty-first when you've already crossed out the twenty-first on the calendar?

CHECHÉ: That's how I do it.

SANTIAGO: You've already crossed out today's date!

CHECHÉ: I know.

SANTIAGO: You might have a problem, Cheché.

CHECHÉ: And what kind of problem do you think I might have?

SANTIAGO: You are crossing out the new day before you start taking part in it.

CHECHÉ: What's the use anyway when nothing changes in this place?

SANTIAGO: That's not a good attitude.

CHECHÉ: Then what do you want me to do?

SANTIAGO: For one thing, get rid of this crap. Why don't you get the kind of calendar I have? The kind that you tear off the pages.

CHECHÉ: And do you think the page of a calendar can make a difference in one's life?

SANTIAGO: Of course. Something as simple as crossing out your days before you live them can have an effect on the mind. It can cause apprehension, anxiety and even despair.

CHECHÉ: Then I'm going straight to hell, 'cause everything here feels the same. Today feels like yesterday and the day before that.

SANTIAGO: What in the world is wrong with you, Cheché?

CHECHÉ: This factory. I can't stand it. Working here is like hitting my head against a wall . . . I try to make changes, modernize this place. But it's like facing a wall of concrete every time I try to do something.

SANTIAGO: Is that what it is, Chester?

CHECHÉ: Well, then there's Mildred. Ever since she left me I'm not the same. Something is missing. Have you ever seen the tail of a lizard when it's been cut off? The tail twists and moves from side to side like a worm that's been removed from the soil. The thing moves on its own, like a nerve that still has life and it's looking for the rest of the body that's been slashed away. That's how I feel sometimes. I turn from side to side on my bed at night.

I wake up in the morning looking for her in the kitchen, thinking that she's there making coffee. I look for her in the garden. And then when I come here there's this moron reading the same story every day to remind me of her.

And I hate it! I hate him! It's like there's no end to it and I just want to . . .

(*Marela enters wearing the elegant coat and fur hat. She does a turn, feeling the smooth material of the coat, enjoying the warmth it provides.*)

MARELA: How do I look, Papá?

SANTIAGO: You'll make a great Anna. But you have to wear a flower in your hair and make her look like one of our women. I'll get you a flower, my dear. We'll talk later, Chester. We need to talk.

(*Santiago exits. Cheché turns to Marela. He contemplates her beauty. Marela looks at her clothes and then she does a turn, as if she were dancing a waltz.*)

MARELA: Well, do you think I can pose for the label?

CHECHÉ: You look beautiful.

(*Juan Julian enters.*)

JUAN JULIAN: Ah, who is this Russian lady?

MARELA: Do I pass the test?

JUAN JULIAN: You look wonderful. Your father is right in choosing you. It's going to be a great picture. I'm looking for my book. I think I left it here.

MARELA: I didn't see it.

JUAN JULIAN (*Looking around*): No. It's not here. I must've left it outside. (*He exits*)

MARELA (*To herself*): I wish you would take a picture of me with your eyes.

(*Marela takes off the coat and hat. Then she takes out a box and starts pasting magazine cutouts on her work table.*)

CHECHÉ: Are you staying until late tonight?

MARELA: I am.

CHECHÉ: I'm going over the books. And you?

MARELA: I'm decorating my table with pictures I like. Photographs of movie stars, and this of a street in Moscow, so I can picture the people in the novel walking through it.

CHECHÉ: You're really obsessed with this book.

MARELA: I am.

CHECHÉ: Just the book or the lector?

MARELA: That's none of your business.

CHECHÉ: But it is. I've been watching you while you work.

MARELA: And what are you doing looking at me when I work?

CHECHÉ: You have to pay less attention to the reader and more attention to what you're doing.

MARELA: Oh, you're just trying to find any excuse to get rid of the lector. Next thing, you'll tell my father that he's distracting all the workers.

CHECHÉ: As a matter of fact he is. He is distracting you. Some of the cigars you rolled today were faulty, and you're going to get the same dickens that everyone gets.

MARELA: Yes. The new lector is getting to you with *Anna Karenina.*

CHECHÉ: I don't let any book or lector get to me.

MARELA: Sure. You probably remember your wife every time he reads a page.

CHECHÉ: My wife's dead to me.

MARELA: Dead behind your eyes, so everywhere you look you see her.

CHECHÉ: Do you want to see all the cigars you've ruined?

MARELA: Show me. I pride myself in my work. I'm one of the fastest rollers in this whole place.

(*Cheché pulls out a bag of cigars.*)

CHECHÉ: But fast isn't always good, Marela.

MARELA: Nothing's wrong with it.

CHECHÉ: Here. Feel it. Hollow. A soft spot.

MARELA: Thank you, Chester. Is there anything else? Can I start pasting . . . ?

CHECHÉ: As a matter of fact there's something else . . .

MARELA: What, Chester?

CHECHÉ: Sometimes you get so distracted by the Russian story that I've seen you take shortcuts when you're rolling.

MARELA: What kind of shortcuts?

CHECHÉ: Sometimes you bring a cigar to your mouth and you bite the end of it, instead of reaching for the knife.

MARELA: You've seen me do that?

CHECHÉ: Yes, I've seen you do that and a lot more.

MARELA: Really?

CHECHÉ: Yes. When your mind wanders away from your work and you go far to your own little Russia.

You forget the paste jar and you lick the last tobacco leaf, as if you were sealing a letter to a lover or playing with the mustache of a Russian man. Is that what it is, little Marela, you're playing with some man in your mind and you forget that you're bringing a cigar to your mouth and licking it, instead of pasting it?

MARELA (*Laughs*): Oh, Chester . . .

CHECHÉ: Do you actually forget that you are working in a little factory where it gets real hot in the summer, and we have to wet the tobacco leaves, because they get dry from the heat and they need moisture, like the wet lick of your tongue.

MARELA: Don't look at me that way, Chester.

CHECHÉ (*Touching her hair*): And how do you want me to look at you?

MARELA: Don't touch me.

(*She moves away. He follows her.*)

CHECHÉ: Why not?

MARELA: Because I don't like it.

CHECHÉ: But I do. Every time I listen to that story I do see my wife . . .

(*He moves closer to her.*)

MARELA: Get away from me!

(*He tries to kiss her. She struggles to get away from him.*)

CHECHÉ: Marela, please. Come close . . . You don't know . . .

MARELA: Get away from me! Get away from me!

(*She pushes him away. He falls to the floor.*)

Don't you ever touch me again!

(*Marela exits. Cheché remains on the floor. Music plays. Lights change.*)

Scene 2

Spotlight on Juan Julian sitting on a chair. He begins to recite a passage from Anna Karenina. *He remains isolated from the action of the scene.*

JUAN JULIAN:

Anna Karenina's husband did not see anything peculiar or improper in his wife's sitting together with Vronsky at a separate table and having a lively conversation with him; but he noticed that the others sitting in the drawing room considered it peculiar and improper, and so it seemed improper to him, too. He decided that he must have a conversation with his wife about it.

(*Conchita enters. She goes to her table and begins to roll cigars. Palomo enters. He is like a lost animal. Juan Julian continues to read in silence.*)

PALOMO: At what time do you meet your lover?
CONCHITA: At the agreed time.
PALOMO: And what time is that?
CONCHITA: It changes like the moon.

PALOMO: Where do you meet besides this place?
CONCHITA: I can't tell you these things.
PALOMO: Why not?
CONCHITA: Because that's the way it is.
PALOMO: Does he read to you?
CONCHITA: Sometimes when he says that I look sad.
PALOMO: You get sad.
CONCHITA: It's not sadness. Sometimes I feel frightened.
PALOMO: Frightened of what?
CONCHITA: Frightened of something I have never felt or done before.
PALOMO: But isn't this what you wanted?
CONCHITA: Yes. But sometimes I can't help the guilt.
PALOMO: And how does he respond when you tell him this?
CONCHITA: He tells me that we have to make love all over again. That I have to get used to it. To him. To his body.
PALOMO: And what else does he say to you?
CONCHITA: He says things a woman likes to hear.
PALOMO: Like what?
CONCHITA: That I taste sweet and mysterious like the water hidden inside fruits and that our love will be white and pure like tobacco flowers. And it will grow at night, the same way that tobacco plants grow at night.
PALOMO: And what else does he tell you?
CONCHITA: Private things.
PALOMO: Like what?
CONCHITA: Obscenities.
PALOMO: And you like that?
CONCHITA: He knows when and how to say them.
PALOMO: And when does he talk to you this way?
CONCHITA: When we're both deep inside each other and we could almost surrender to death. When he pounds so hard inside me as if to kill me. As if to revive me from that drowning place, from that deep place where he takes me.
PALOMO: I see.
CONCHITA: Why so curious, Palomo?
PALOMO: Because I don't know . . . Because . . . You seem different. You've changed.
CONCHITA: It happens when lovers do what they are supposed to do.
PALOMO: Do you ever talk to him about me?
CONCHITA: Yes. He wanted to know why you stopped loving me.
PALOMO: And what did you tell him?
CONCHITA: I told him that it just happened one day, like everything else in life.
PALOMO: And what was his response?
CONCHITA: He wanted to know what I felt and I told him the truth. I told him that I desire and love you just the same.
PALOMO: And was he fine with that?
CONCHITA: He told me to show him how I love you. To show him on his body.
PALOMO: And what did you do?
CONCHITA: It was terrifying.

PALOMO: What was terrifying?

CONCHITA: I thought it would be impossible. That nobody could occupy that space in me. But he did. He did. And everything seemed so recognizable, as if he had known me all along. His room became a theatre and his bed a stage, and we became like actors in a play. Then I asked him to play my role, to pretend to be me and I dressed him in my clothes. And he was compliant. It was as if I was making love to myself, because he knew what to do, where to go and where to take me.

PALOMO: Show me.

CONCHITA: Show you what?

PALOMO: Show me . . . Show me what he did to you and how he did it.

CONCHITA: You would have to do as actors do.

PALOMO: And what is that?

CONCHITA: Actors surrender. They stop playing themselves and they give in. You would have to let go of yourself and enter the life of another human being, and in this case it would be me.

PALOMO: Teach me then.

CONCHITA: Here, in the factory?

PALOMO: Yes, back there, where you meet him.

(*Soft music plays. Conchita traces Palomo's neck and shoulders with her hand. He leads her out of the room. Lights change. Juan Julian closes the book. The soft music fades.*)

Scene 3

A danzón plays. It's the inauguration of the new cigar brand. There's a party. The workers start filing in, dressed in their best clothes. Santiago and Ofelia enter with two bottles of rum and glasses.

OFELIA: Did you get enough rum, Santiago?

SANTIAGO: Did I get enough rum? Tell her how much rum I got, Juan Julian.

JUAN JULIAN: He's got enough rum to get an elephant drunk.

OFELIA: Then give me some before anybody gets here, so I can calm my nerves.

SANTIAGO: What are you nervous about?

OFELIA: Oh, I have the heart of a seal and when I get excited it wants to swim out of my chest.

(*Santiago gives her a drink.*)

SANTIAGO: Let's have a drink, the three of us. We ought to have a private toast before anybody gets here.

(*Santiago serves drinks.*)

We really haven't done that badly this year. Sales were down last month but we're still staying above water.

OFELIA: We'll do well, Santiago. People need to blow out smoke and vent themselves.

SANTIAGO (*Toasting*): That's right, salud!

OFELIA: Salud.

JUAN JULIAN: Salud.

OFELIA: Let's bring out the lanterns.

(*The three of them exit. Cheché and Palomo, both elegantly dressed, enter with palm leaves to decorate the factory. They are engaged in conversation.*)

PALOMO: Sometimes I think . . . I keep wondering if they're still together, if they see each other. I can feel it. Or it's just me. My mind. At night I can't sleep. I lie there awake thinking, imagining the two of them together. I can still smell him on her skin, her clothes and her handkerchief. I can see him on her face and her eyes, and I don't know what to do . . .

CHECHÉ: You should move up North to Trenton and start a new life. Take her away from here. That's what I wanted to do with Mildred. I'd figure we could live up North. The two of us could work in a cigar factory. There are plenty of them in Trenton. And there are no lectors and no good-for-nothing love stories, which put ideas into women's heads and ants inside their pants . . .

(*Juan Julian enters with a garland of Chinese lanterns.*)

JUAN JULIAN: Would you give me a hand with the lanterns?

PALOMO: Ah, we were just talking about the love stories.

JUAN JULIAN: It's obvious that you don't care much for them. You almost made me lose my job the other day.

PALOMO: Oh, I'm curious as to how the story ends.

CHECHÉ: Yeah! Does the husband ever think of killing the lover? (*Laughs*) I would've killed the bastard a long time ago.

JUAN JULIAN: The husband would probably choose a duel, instead of killing the lover in cold blood.

CHECHÉ: I would've shot the son of a bitch a long time ago.

JUAN JULIAN: But that's not the way things were done in those days.

CHECHÉ: Then the husband is a coward and a stinker.

PALOMO: Oh, I don't see the husband as a coward. He might be more clever than the three of us. Wouldn't you say so, Juan Julian?

JUAN JULIAN: Well, the husband is acting according to his status. He is a man of power. He has one of the most important positions in the ministry. And we're talking about Saint Petersburg society — everyone knows each other and he doesn't want Anna's affair to turn into a big scandal.

CHECHÉ: The husband is a pansy if you ask me.

PALOMO: So what character do you identify with in the novel?

JUAN JULIAN: I like them all. I learn things from all of them.

PALOMO: And what have you learned from Anna's lover?

JUAN JULIAN: Oh, I don't know . . . I . . .

PALOMO: I'm intrigued as to how he became interested in her.

(*Juan Julian knows where Palomo is trying to go with this.*)

JUAN JULIAN: Well, it's very obvious in the novel.

PALOMO: And what's your personal opinion?

JUAN JULIAN: She came to him because she thought that he could help her.

PALOMO: Help her how?

JUAN JULIAN: Help her to love again. Help her to recognize herself as a woman all over again. She had probably known only one man and that was the husband. With the lover she learns a new way of loving. And it's this new way of loving that makes her go back to the lover over and over again. But that's my interpretation.

(*Santiago and Ofelia enter*)

SANTIAGO: Good! You are all here. We are celebrating the whole day today. Let's have another drink.

OFELIA: Remember you have a speech to make.

SANTIAGO (*Lifting the bottle*): This will inspire me.

OFELIA: At the rate we're going we'll be drunk before the party gets started.

SANTIAGO (*Laughs*): Enjoy yourself. Today I'm the happiest man on earth.

(*Conchita enters. She's dressed in a chiffon paisley dress.*)

CONCHITA: Are you drinking without me?

SANTIAGO: Of course not. Come have a drink with us. Where's your sister? You look beautiful in that dress, my child. I've never seen you wear it.

CONCHITA: Papá, just a month ago I wore it. We were invited to a party. I remember as if it were yesterday. (*She looks at her mother*) Mamá hates paisleys.

OFELIA: No, I don't, my child.

CONCHITA: You said I looked like an old lady the last time I wore it.

OFELIA: Frankly, I just didn't think much of it when you had it made. But now that you cut your hair and you look so different, it's actually very becoming.

PALOMO: You do look beautiful, my love.

OFELIA: I like paisleys.

CONCHITA: They remind me of gypsies and bohemians.

PALOMO: You actually look very bohemian.

JUAN JULIAN: It's true. Paisleys look dreamy, as if they come from a floating world.

(*Palomo looks at Juan Julian. Juan Julian lifts his glass. Palomo brings Conchita close to him and wraps his arm around her.*)

Señores, one question. As an outsider, as a foreigner in this country, I have something to ask. Why do Americans prohibit something as divine as whiskey and rum?°

SANTIAGO: Because Americans are not socialists when they drink.

(*Laughter from the crowd*)

---

prohibit . . . rum: The 18th amendment to the U.S. Constitution prohibited the sale of alcoholic beverages from 1920 to 1933, when the amendment was repealed.

PALOMO: I have another answer to your question. Alcohol is prohibited in this country because alcohol is like literature. Literature brings out the best and the worst part of ourselves. If you're angry it brings out your anger. If you are sad, it brings out your sadness. And some of us are . . . Let's just say, not very happy.

(*Ofelia, who is a little tipsy, taps her glass to make a speech.*)

OFELIA (*Doing a dance step*): Ah, but rum brings out your best steps if you are a good dancer. If you have two left feet, it's better if you don't dance at all. So let's face it, señores, Americans are good at making movies, radios and cars, but when it comes to dancing, it's better if . . . With the exception of the colored folks, of course. They've got what it takes to dance up a storm. That's why I think alcohol is prohibited, because most Americans don't know how to dance.
   (*Grabbing Santiago by the hand*) Let's go, I feel like dancing.

SANTIAGO: No. We can't dance yet, because I have an announcement to make. Where's Marela?

OFELIA: She must be putting on her costume.

SANTIAGO: Well, señoras y señores, today we've taken time from work to drink and dance, and to celebrate the new cigar brand we are launching into the market. (*He takes out a cigar from his shirt pocket*) This well-crafted cigar is wrapped in the finest leaves from Vuelta Abajo in Pinar del Río, the tip of the island of Cuba. The length of this new cigar is six and one-eighth inches. The ring gauge is fifty-two. I truly believe this is our finest toro.
   Where's Marela? She should be here.

(*Marela enters dressed in an elegant black gown. She is like Anna on the night of the ball.*)

MARELA: I'm here, Papá.

SANTIAGO: Let me look at you, my little blue sky.

OFELIA: But my child, you look beautiful.

SANTIAGO: You came just in time . . . I was just about to say that since most cigars are named after women and romantic love stories, today we are baptizing our new cigar with the name Anna Karenina! This cigar will sell for ten cents and we are hoping this new brand will bring us fortune and prosperity. So now that we are all gathered here, I would like to ask my beloved Ofelia to do us the honor of officially lighting the first Anna Karenina.

(*Applause from the crowd. The cigar is passed to Ofelia. Santiago lights it with a match. Ofelia takes a puff and blows out a ring of smoke.*)

   Well?

OFELIA: It's . . . It's . . . Aaaah! It burns like a blue dream.

(*The crowd applauds.*)

PALOMO: Bravo! Bravo!

(*Ofelia passes the cigar to Santiago and he gives it to Marela.*)

SANTIAGO: And to the youngest one in the family, our very own Anna.

(*Marela takes a puff coughs a little. She laughs. She passes the cigar to another. This person presents it to Santiago.*)

MARELA: Mhm! Lovely!

(*Santiago takes a puff*)

SANTIAGO: Ah! It's glorious. Perfecto.

(*Applause from the crowd.*)

    Chester.

(*Santiago hands the cigar to someone, who passes it to Cheché. He takes a puff.*)

CHECHÉ: Burns well. Pleasant aroma. I detect a little bit of cherry. I think it's our finest horse.

(*Applause. The cigar is passed to Palomo. Palomo passes it to Conchita. She takes a puff.*)

CONCHITA: Ah! It speaks of forests and orchids.

(*Applause. Conchita hands the cigar to Marela. Marela gives it Palomo. He takes a puff.*)

PALOMO: Mhm! Magnifico! Definitely like aged rum. Sweet like mangoes.

(*Palomo passes it to Santiago.*)

SANTIAGO: You forgot Juan Julian.
PALOMO: Ah, yes we can't forget our lector, who brought us the world of *Anna Karenina.*

(*Santiago passes the cigar back to Palomo. Palomo takes off his hat and gives Juan Julian the cigar. This is an offense since the cigar should never be handed directly to the person that is supposed to smoke. There has to be a mediator to facilitate communication with the gods.*

Juan Julian smiles. He smells the cigar, looks up and makes a gesture to the gods.)

JUAN JULIAN: Sweet aroma. (*Taking a puff*) It sighs like a sunset and it has a little bit of cocoa beans and cedar. I believe we have a cigar, señores!
SANTIAGO: We do have a cigar, señores! We have a champion!
OFELIA (*A little tipsy*): Indeed we have a champion!
MARELA: Papá, let's go out into the streets and tell the world about our cigar. Let's give our new cigars to the people.
SANTIAGO: And go bankrupt, my child! No, I propose a gunshot!
OFELIA: A gunshot! Santiago, you're drunk. Stop drinking.
SANTIAGO: No inauguration is complete without the breaking of a bottle or a gunshot.
MARELA: I propose two gunshots then!

SANTIAGO: Can't have two gunshots. It's got to be three.
MARELA: Then I'll shoot the third one.

(*Laughter.*)

SANTIAGO: Let's go. Let's shoot!
OFELIA: Just make sure you aim up high, but don't shoot the moon!

(*They all laugh. The workers bring the party outside. As Conchita starts to leave, Palomo grabs her by the arm.*)

PALOMO: Where are you going?
CONCHITA: Outside.
PALOMO: You've been looking at him the whole night. You're falling in love with this man.
CONCHITA: Maybe just as much as you are.
PALOMO: I don't like men.

(*Sound of a celebratory gunshot. Laughter.*)

CONCHITA: Then why do you always want me to tell you what I do with him?
PALOMO: Because it's part of the old habit we have of listening. We are listeners.
CONCHITA: No, there's something else.
PALOMO: You're right there's something else. And it's terrible sometimes.
CONCHITA: Then nothing makes sense to me anymore.

(*Another gunshot. More laughter.*)

PALOMO (*Grabbing her arm*): I want you to go back to him and tell him you want to make love like a knife.
CONCHITA: Why a knife?
PALOMO: Because everything has to be killed.

(*Another gunshot. More laughter. Ofelia, Santiago, Marela and Juan Julian reenter.*)

OFELIA: Señores, I have a confession to make. When I was seventeen, and that was yesterday, I was chosen to pose for a cigar brand that was called Aida, like the opera. And, of course, just the thought of my face being on a cigar ring and in so many men's hands and lips, my mother was scandalized. You see, we weren't cigar people, we were in the guava jelly business. So when my mother forbid me to pose for the label, I told her that I wanted a picture of my face on a can of guava marmalade. And it was only fair. So, they dressed me up in a red dress and I had a red carnation behind my ear. They had me looking lovely sitting in a hammock and a parrot by my side . . .

(*Everyone laughs.*)

SANTIAGO: Let's go, my dear. We have smoked, we have fired a gun and you've had too much to drink.
OFELIA: Bah, you just want to take advantage of me because I'm drunk.
MARELA (*Embarrassed*): Mamá!

(*Santiago laughs. He takes Ofelia by the hand. They start to exit.*)

SANTIAGO: Good night!

MARELA: Good night!
OFELIA: Marela, are you coming with us?
MARELA: I'll be there in a minute.
OFELIA: Don't be too long. (*They exit*)
PALOMO (*Grabbing Conchita's hand*): Let's go home. (*To the others*) We'll see you tomorrow.
JUAN JULIAN: Adios!
CONCHITA: Adios!

(*Conchita and Palomo exit, leaving Marela and Juan Julian alone.*)

MARELA: Oh, I don't want this night to end. I could stay up all night. I don't want to sleep. We sleep too much. We spend more than a third of our lives sleeping, sleeping. Darkness descends and everything is a mystery to us. We don't know if trees really walk at night, as I've heard in legends. We don't really know if statues and spirits dance in the squares unbeknown to us. And how would we ever know if we sleep? We sleep and sleep . . .
JUAN JULIAN: Oh, I want to have what you drank. What did you drink?
MARELA: Oh, I didn't drink. I just feel gladness. Papá was so happy. I like to see him that way. And Mamá was so full of joy. (*Laughs*) She's the one who drinks a little too much.
JUAN JULIAN: It's good to drink a little once in a while.

(*Cheché reenters. He stays at a distance, watching.*)

MARELA: Yes, we deserve a little drink. We work hard enough. We deserve all that life offers us, and life is made of little moments. Little moments as small as violet petals. Little moments I could save in a jar and keep forever, like now talking to you.
JUAN JULIAN (*Playfully*): Ah! So you are a collector. And what sort of things do you like to collect besides a night like this one?
MARELA: The first time you read and the day you walked me to the pharmacy.
JUAN JULIAN: So I'm in one of your jars.
MARELA: In many.
JUAN JULIAN (*Smiles*): Many. (*Beat. Looks at her tenderly*) You are clear and fresh as water. Did anybody ever tell you this?
MARELA: No, never.
JUAN JULIAN: Then people are blind.
MARELA: Blind? Do you think so? And how can one teach the blind to see?
JUAN JULIAN: I wouldn't know. I'm not blind.
MARELA: But we are all blind in the eyes of those who can't see.
JUAN JULIAN: You're right.
MARELA: We just have to learn to use our eyes in the dark. We have to learn to see through words and sound, through our hands. (*Touches his hand*)
JUAN JULIAN: I'm sure those who are blind will see your beauty once they touch your face. (*Touches her face tenderly*)
    I must go now. Sleep well.

MARELA: Adios.
JUAN JULIAN: Adios.

(*Just as Juan Julian is about to exit:*)

MARELA: Juan Julian . . .
JUAN JULIAN: Yes.
MARELA: Lend me the book.
JUAN JULIAN (*Not realizing that he is holding it*): What book?
MARELA: The book in your hand.
JUAN JULIAN: Oh!
MARELA: I promise not to get ahead of the story.
JUAN JULIAN: Bring it tomorrow morning or I won't have a book to read.
MARELA: May you dream of angels!
JUAN JULIAN (*Kissing her face*): You, too.

(*As Juan Julian exits, Marela stays looking at him in the distance. She brings the book to her chest, then she opens it and reads, as if to find consolation, the sort one seeks in the lonely hours of the night.*)

MARELA:

Anna Karenina prepared herself for the journey with joy and willfulness. With small, skillful hands she opened a red bag and took out a little cushion, which she placed on her knees before closing the bag.

(*Cheché emerges from the shadows. He takes a handkerchief from his pocket and dries his face. He looks at Marela. His glance is full of desire. Marela sees him. She closes the book. Cheché grabs her arm.*

    Blackout.)

Scene 4

Palomo enters the factory carrying a couple of heavy boxes. Conchita is clearing up the mess from the night before.

PALOMO: Where's Cheché?
CONCHITA: He hasn't come in yet.
PALOMO: I hope someone gets here with the keys to the safe. The boy who delivered these boxes is out there and he wants to get paid.
CONCHITA: I'll go to the house and ask Mamá for the keys.
PALOMO: No. You got to help me take inventory of all these boxes. (*Hands her some papers*)
CONCHITA: As soon as I finish with this. I wonder why Papá isn't here.
PALOMO: He's probably still in bed. He did drink . . .
CONCHITA: Yes you're right. Mamá must be putting cold compresses on his forehead. It always happens.

(*Santiago and Ofelia enter. Santiago is trying to get rid of his hangover by rubbing his forehead.*)

OFELIA: Morning!
CONCHITA: Morning!

PALOMO: Santiago, I need the key to the safe. I have to pay for this delivery.

SANTIAGO: Ofelia has them.

OFELIA: I just left them at the office on top of the desk.

(*Palomo exits. Ofelia sits down and starts rolling cigars.*)

SANTIAGO: Where's Cheché?

CONCHITA: He hasn't arrived yet.

SANTIAGO: I don't blame him. I would've stayed in bed myself. But your mother is like a rooster. When she gets up from bed nobody . . .

OFELIA: I didn't wake you up.

SANTIAGO: I didn't say you did. It's those slippers you use to walk around the house. They are louder than a running train. (*Makes noise*) Shoo . . . Shoo . . . Everywhere . . . One day I'm going to throw them out the window.

OFELIA: You do that and I'll give your Sunday shoes to the chimney cleaner.

SANTIAGO: See, now the pain got worse! This woman, how she likes to bother me! Ay!

CONCHITA: Do you want my bottle of spirits, Papá?

SANTIAGO: Give me anything you have, my child. Your mother doesn't take care of me.

(*Conchita gives him the bottle of spirits. He sniffs. Marela enters wearing the long coat. She goes to her table and starts to roll cigars.*)

MARELA: Morning!

CONCHITA: Marela, why are you wearing that coat? Aren't you warm? . . .

MARELA: No. Some coats keep winter inside them. You wear them and you find pockets full of December, January and February. All those months that cover the earth with snow and make everything still. That's how I want to be, layered and still.

OFELIA: My child, are you all right?

MARELA: I'm fine, Mamá. Don't worry about me.

(*Juan Julian enters.*)

JUAN JULIAN: Good morning!

ALL: Good morning!

MARELA: Here's your book. (*Hands him the book*)

(*Juan Julian notices Marela's coat, and that she seems to be in a state of dismay.*)

JUAN JULIAN: Thank you.

(*Palomo reenters.*)

PALOMO: Has Cheché come in yet?

CONCHITA: No. He's just late. Sit down. Juan Julian is going to read to us.

JUAN JULIAN: Today I'll begin by reading Part 3, Chapter 13, of *Anna Karenina*:

In his youth Anna Karenina's husband had been intrigued by the idea of dueling because he was physically a coward and was well aware of this fact. In his youth this terror had often forced him to think about dueling and imagining

himself in a situation in which it was necessary to endanger his life.

(*Cheché enters unnoticed. His head is heavy with dark thoughts.*)

This old ingrained feeling now reasserted itself. Let's suppose I challenge him. Let's suppose someone teaches me how to do it, he went on thinking.

(*Cheché pulls out a gun.*)

They put us in position, I squeeze the trigger, he said to himself, and it turns out I've killed him. He shook his head to drive away such silly thoughts. What would be the sense of killing a man in order to define one's own relations with a woman . . .

(*Cheché shoots Juan Julian. Then shoots again. The sound of the gun echoes and echoes as Juan Julian falls to the floor.*
The workers are shocked. Some of them look up to see where the shot came from. The shot still echoes throughout the room as Marela reaches out to touch the dying lector.
The lights fade to black.)

Scene 5

Three days have passed. The factory workers are rolling cigars and organizing the tobacco leaves by their proper size and shape. Marela is still wearing her coat.

OFELIA: What silence! I never knew that silence could have so much weight. Can someone say something? Can someone read? We are listeners! We are oidores! I can't get used to this silence all around us. It's as if a metal blanket has fallen on us.

PALOMO: The same silence we had when our last reader died.

OFELIA: No, this silence is louder. Much louder. Much louder.

SANTIAGO: That's because Juan Julian died before his time, and the shadows of the young are heavier and they linger over the earth like a cloud.

MARELA: I should write his name on a piece of paper and place it in a glass of water with brown sugar, so his spirit knows that he is welcomed in this factory, and he can come here and drink sweet water. And nobody better tell me that it's wrong for me to do this! You hear me, Mamá! (*For the first time tears come to her eyes*)

SANTIAGO: Your mother hasn't said anything, my child.

MARELA: I know she hasn't. But we must look after the dead, so they can feel part of the world. So they don't forget us and we could count on them when we cross to the other side.

CONCHITA: We should continue reading, Papá!

MARELA: Yes, we should continue reading the story in his honor, so he doesn't feel that he left his job undone. He should know that we're still his faithful listeners.

CONCHITA: If I could, I would read, but I know that if I open that book I'll be weak.

MARELA: We shouldn't cry. Tears are for the weak that mourn the knife and the killer, and the trickle of blood that streams from this factory all the way to the house where he was born.

OFELIA: Could someone read?

(*Pause.*)

PALOMO: I will read.

OFELIA: That's it, read, so we can get rid of this silence and this heat. And we can pause over a few lines and sigh and be glad that we are alive.

SANTIAGO: But read something else. Read something cheerful.

MARELA: Stories should be finished, Papá. Let him finish the book.

CONCHITA: She's right. Stories should be finished or they suffer the same fate as those who die before their time.

(*Palomo opens the book. He looks at Conchita.*)

PALOMO: *Anna Karenina.* Part 3, Chapter 14:

> By the time he arrived in Petersburg, Anna Karenina's husband was not only completely determined to carry out his decision, but he had composed in his head a letter he would write to his wife.

(*He looks up from the book and stares at Conchita.*)

> In his letter he was going to write everything he'd been meaning to tell her.

(*The lights begin to fade.*)

END OF PLAY

COMMENTARY

Christine Dolen
ANNA IN THE TROPICS SHINES ON BROADWAY   *2003*

Christine Dolen, theater reviewer for the Miami Herald, *saw the earliest version of Cruz's play and spread the word that it was exceptional and that the theater world should pay attention to what Cruz had achieved. Dolen is also a shrewd critic, however, and in the New York production she sees areas where she feels the play has been "tweaked," as she says, a little too much in an effort to make it appeal to a broad audience. Nonetheless, she sees this play as an important contribution to contemporary theater.*

Anna in the Tropics, the Pulitzer Prize–winning play born in New Theater's tiny space in Coral Gables, has made it to the biggest stage in all of American theater.

Broadway's Royale Theatre, where Nilo Cruz's heady mixture of poetic language, vanished tradition and aching passion opened on Sunday evening, is now home to a work that, whatever its fate with New York critics and audiences, will forever have the distinction of being the first play to win drama's highest honor for a Latino playwright — the Cuban-American Cruz, who spent his formative years and discovered his passion for writing in Miami.

This high-profile production of Cruz's play about Cuban-American cigar-makers in Ybor City on the eve of the Great Depression was put together in September at the McCarter Theatre Center in nearby Princeton, N.J. The entire cast of that production, including marquee name Jimmy Smits, has come with it to Broadway. Yet it's obvious, the strong reviews *Anna* got in Princeton notwithstanding, that the actors and director Emily Mann have continued their work on the play.

On Broadway, *Anna in the Tropics* is warmer, more vibrant, more detailed than it was in Princeton. The actors have added more flourishes to their performances, taking them up a notch or three to match the scale of the larger, more traditional Royale.

At times, though, they edge a little too close stylistically to *telenovela*° territory. *Anna in the Tropics* has always had its share of organic, character-drive humor to counterbalance the emotional turbulence and loss that flow through the play.

But if you stood outside the Royale on Friday evening during one of the show's official press performances, you'd think Cruz had written a Pulitzer Prize–winning *comedy*. It's appropriate to laugh when younger daughter Marela (Vanessa Aspillaga) is gushing over the factory's handsome new *lector* Juan Julian (Smits); it's excruciating to hear laughter when the second act begins with Juan Julian and Marela's married sister Conchita (Daphne Rubin-Vega) making adulterous love on the factory floor. That moment is supposed to be thrilling and passionate, not something that elicits hoots and guffaws, and it's a sign that *Anna* has been tweaked too much.

Even so, the power of Cruz's beautiful, image-filled language sings in the words of actors who obviously connect with it, adore it and understand its musical nuances.

As the lector who reads to the cigar-makers and alters their lives, Smits is sweetly seductive, matinee-idol handsome in a tropical white suit, a man who rides the passion of Leo Tolstoy's *Anna Karenina* to a different tragic ending.

The other men — John Ortiz as Conchita's cheating husband Palomo, Victor Argo as the depressed factory owner Santiago, David Zayas as his volatile half-brother Cheché — rant and charm and cajole, holding their own against the play's strong women.

And those women — Aspillaga as the fleshy, dreamily girlish Marela; Rubin-Vega as the wounded, risk-taking Conchita; Priscilla Lopez as their mother Ofelia, a steely but womanly Cuban matriarch — all deserve Tony Award consideration.

The production's design, from Robert Brill's spare but exquisite set to Peter Kaczorowski's lighting (with its suggestions of tropical heat and shuttered windows) to the powerful scene-connecting thrum of a solo guitar, serves as a powerful but unobtrusive frame surrounding the artistry of Cruz's vivid, inspired linguistic pictures.

telenovela: Soap opera.

Writing about Drama

Why Write about Drama?

The act of writing involves making a commitment to ideas, and that commitment helps clarify your thinking. Your writing forces you to examine the details, the elements of a play that might otherwise pass unnoticed, and it helps you develop creative interpretations that enrich your appreciation of the plays you read. Besides deepening your own understanding, your writing can contribute to that of your peers and readers, as the commentaries in this book are meant to do.

Because every reader of plays has a unique experience and background, every reader can contribute something to the experience and awareness of others. You will see things that others do not. You will interpret things in a way that others will not. Naturally, every reader's aim is to respect the text, but it is not reasonable to think that there is only one way to interpret a text. Nor is it reasonable to think that only a few people can give "correct" interpretations. One of the most interesting aspects of writing about drama is that it is usually preceded by discussion, through which a range of possible interpretations begins to appear. When you start to write, you commit yourself to working with certain ideas, and you begin to deepen your thinking about those ideas as you write.

Conventions in Writing Criticism about Drama

Ordinarily, when you are asked to write about a play, you are expected to produce a critical and analytical study. A critical essay will go beyond any subjective experience and include a discussion of what the play achieves and how it does so. If you have a choice, you should choose a play that you admire and enjoy. If you have special background material on that play, such as a playbill or newspaper article, or if you have seen a production, these aids will be especially useful to you in writing.

For a critical study you will need to go far beyond retelling the events of the play. You may have to describe what you feel happens in a given scene or moment in a play, but simply rewriting the plot of the play in your own words does not constitute an interpretation. A critical reading of the play demands that you isolate evidence and comment on it. For example, you may want to quote passages of dialogue or stage direction to point out an idea that plays a key role in the drama. When you do so, quote in moderation. A critical essay that is merely a string of quotations linked together with a small amount of your commentary will not suffice. Further, make sure that the quotations you use are illustrations of your point; explain clearly their importance to your discussion.

1786

Approaches to Criticism

Many critical approaches are available to the reader of drama. One approach might emphasize the response of audience members or readers, recognizing that the audience brings a great deal to the play even before the action begins. The audience's or reader's previous experience with drama influences expectations about what will happen on stage and about how the central characters will behave. Personal and cultural biases also influence how an audience member reacts to the unfolding drama. Reader response criticism pays close attention to these responses and to what causes them.

Another critical approach might treat the play as the coherent work of a playwright who intends the audience to perceive certain meanings in the play. This approach assumes that a careful analysis, or close reading, of the play will reveal the author's meanings.

Either approach can lead to engaging essays on drama. In the pages that follow, you will find directions on how to pay attention to your responses as an audience member or reader and advice about how to read a play with close attention to dialogue, images, and patterns of action.

Reader Response Criticism

Response criticism depends on a full experience of the text — a good understanding of its meaning as well as of its conventions of staging and performance.

Your responses to various elements of the drama, whether to the characters, the setting, the theme, or the dialogue, may change and grow as you see a play or read it through. You might have a very different reaction to a play during a second reading or viewing of it. Keeping a careful record of your responses as you read is a first step in response criticism.

There is, however, a big difference between recording your responses and examining them. Douglas Atkins of the University of Kansas speaks not only of reader response in criticism but of reader responsibility, by which he means that readers have the responsibility to respond on more than a superficial level when they read drama. This book helps you reach deeper critical levels because you can read each play in light of the history of drama. This book also gives you important background material and commentary from the playwrights and from professional critics. Reading such criticism helps you understand what the critic's role is and what a critic can say about drama.

Reading drama in a historical perspective is important because it can highlight similarities between plays of different eras. Anyone who has read *Oedipus Rex* and *Antigone* will be better prepared to respond to *Hamlet*. In addition to the history and criticism of drama presented in this book, the variety of style, subject matter, and scope of the plays gives you the opportunity to read and respond to a broad range of drama. The more plays you read carefully, the better you will become at responding to drama and writing about it.

When you write response criticism, keep these guidelines in mind:

1. As you read, make note of the important effects the text has on you. Annotate in the margins moments that are especially effective. Do you find yourself alarmed, disturbed, sympathetic, or unsympathetic to a character? Do you sense suspense, or are you confused about what is happening? Do you feel personally involved with the action, or is it very distant? Do you find the situation funny? What overall response do you find yourself giving the play?

1788 WRITING ABOUT DRAMA

2. By analyzing the following two elements of your response, establish why the play had the effects you observe. Do you think it would have those effects on others? Have you observed that it does?

First, determine what it is about the play that causes you to have the response you do. Is it the structure of the play, the way the characters behave, their talk? Is it an unusual use of language, allusions to literature you know (or don't know)? Is the society portrayed especially familiar (or especially unfamiliar) to you? What does the author seem to expect the audience to know before the play begins?

Second, determine what it is about you, the reader, that causes you to respond as you do. Were you prepared for the dramatic conventions of the play, in terms of its genre as tragedy, comedy, or tragicomedy, or in terms of its place in the history of drama? How does your preparation affect your response? Did you have difficulty interpreting the language of the play because of unfamiliarity? Are you especially responsive to certain kinds of plays because of familiarity?

3. What do your responses to the play tell you about your own limitations, your own expertise, your own values, and your own attitudes toward social behavior, uses of language, and your sense of what is "normal"? Be sure to be willing to face your limitations as well as your strengths.[1]

Reader response criticism is flexible and useful in the way it allows you to explore possible interpretations of a text. Everyone is capable of responding to drama, and everyone's response will differ depending on his or her preparation and background.

Close Reading

Analyzing a play by close reading means examining the text in detail, looking for patterns that might not be evident with a less attentive approach to the text. Annotation is the key to close reading, since the critic's job is to keep track of elements in the play that, innocent though they may seem alone, imply a greater significance when seen together.

Close reading implies rereading, because you do not know the first time through a text just what will be meaningful as the play unfolds, and you will want to read it again to confirm and deepen your impressions. You will usually make only a few discoveries the first time through. However, it is important to annotate the text even the first time you read it.

In annotating a play try following these guidelines:

1. Underline all the speeches and images you think are important. Look for dialogue that you think reveals the play's themes, the true nature of the characters, and the position of the playwright.

2. Watch for repetition of imagery (such as the garden and weed imagery in *Hamlet*) and keep track of it through annotation. Do the same for repeated ideas in the dialogue and for repeated comments on government or religion or psychology. Such repetitions will reveal their importance to the playwright.

3. Color-code or number-code various patterns in the text; then gather them either in photocopies or in lists for examination before you begin to plan your essay.

[1] Adapted from Kathleen McCormick, "Theory in the Reader: Bleich, Holland, and Beyond," *College English* 47 (1985): 838.

Criticism that uses the techniques of close reading pays very careful attention to the elements of drama — plot, characterization, setting, dialogue (use of language), movement, and theme — which were discussed earlier in relation to Lady Gregory's *The Rising of the Moon*. As you read a play, keep track of its chief elements because often they will give you useful ideas for your paper. You may find it helpful to refer to the earlier discussion of the elements in *The Rising of the Moon* since a short critical essay about that play is presented here (pp. 1822–24).

Annotating the special use of any of the primary elements will help you decide how important they are and whether a close study of them can contribute to an interesting interpretation of the play. You may not want to discuss all the elements in an essay, or if you do, only one may be truly dominant, but you should be aware of them in any play you write about.

From Prewriting to Final Draft: A Sample Essay on *The Rising of the Moon*

Most good writing results from good planning. When you write criticism about drama, consider these important stages:

1. When possible, choose a play that you enjoy.
2. Annotate the play very carefully.
3. Spend time prewriting.
4. Write a good first draft, then revise for content, organization, style, and mechanics.

The essay on Lady Gregory's *The Rising of the Moon* at the end of this section involved several stages of writing. First, the writer read and annotated the play. In the process of doing so, she noticed the unusual stage direction beginning the play, *Moonlight,* and noticed also that when the two policemen leave the Sergeant, they take the lantern, but the Sergeant reminds them that it is very lonely waiting there "with nothing but the moon." Second, she used the stage directions regarding moonlight to guide her in several important techniques of prewriting, including brainstorming, clustering, freewriting, drafting a trial thesis, and outlining.

The first stage, brainstorming, involved listing ideas, words, or phrases suggested by reading the play. The idea of moonlight and the moon recurred often. Then the writer practiced clustering: beginning with *moon,* a key term developed from brainstorming, then radiating from it all the associations that naturally suggested themselves. (See the cluster diagram on p. 1790.)

Next the student chose the term *romance* because it had generated a number of responses, and she performed a freewriting exercise around that term. Freewriting is a technique in which a writer takes four or five minutes to write whatever comes to mind. The technique is designed to be done quickly, so the conscious censor has to be turned off. Anything you write in freewriting may be useful because you may produce ideas you did not know you had.

The following passage is part of the freewriting exercise the student wrote using *romance* as a key term. The passage is also an example of invisible writing because the writing was done on a computer and the writer turned off the monitor so that she could not censor or erase what she was writing. The writer could only go forward, as fast as possible.

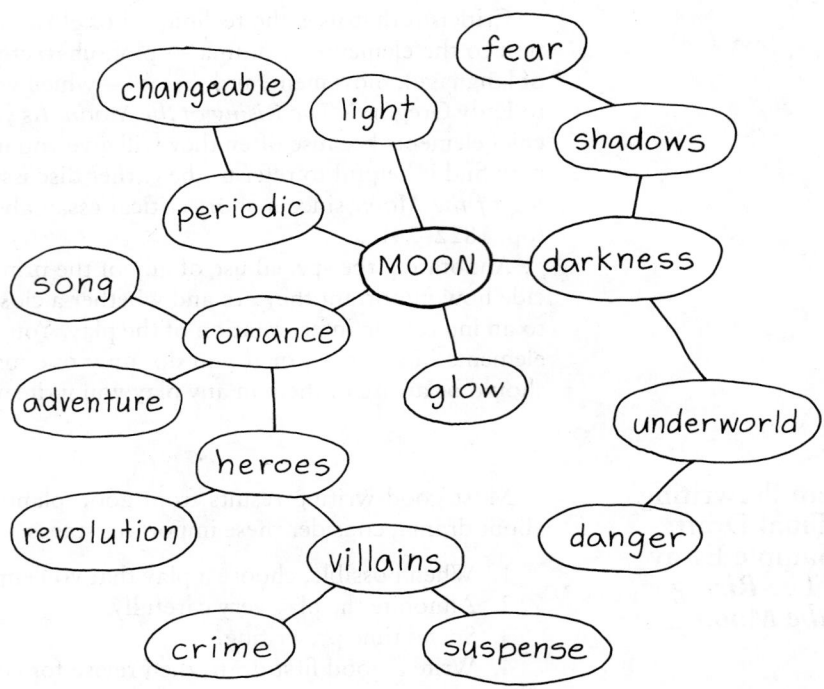

The setting of the play is completely romantic. In a lot of ways
the play wouldn't work in a different setting. When you think
about it the moon in the title is what makes all the action
possible. Moon associated with darkness, underworld, world of
fairies, so the moon is what makes all the action possible. Moon
makes Sergeant look at things differently. The moon is the rebel
moon--that's what title means. Rebel moon is rising, always
rising. So the world the policeman lives in--sun lights up
everything in practical and nonromantic way--is like lantern that
second policeman brings to dockside. It shows things in a harsh
light. Moon shows things in soft light. Without the moon there
would be a different play.

The freewriting gave the writer a new direction — discussing the setting of
the play, especially the role of light. The clustering began with the moon,
veered off to the concept of the romantic elements in the play, and then came
back to the way the moon and the lantern function in the play. The writer was
now ready to work up a trial thesis:

Lady Gregory uses light to create a romantic setting that helps us
understand the relationship between the rebel and the Sergeant and
the values that they each stand for.

Because the thesis is drafted before the essay is written, the thesis is like a trial balloon. It may work or it may not. At this point it gives the writer direction.

Next the student outlined the essay. Because the writer did not know the outcome of the essay yet, her outline was necessarily sketchy:

I. Moonlight is associated with romance and rebellion; harsh light of lantern is associated with repressiveness of police.

   A. Rebel is associated with romance.

   B. Sergeant is associated with practicality and the law.

II. Without the lantern the Sergeant is under the influence of the romantic moon and the rebel.

   A. Sergeant feels resentment about his job.

   B. Rebel sings forbidden song and Sergeant reveals his former sympathies.

   C. Sergeant admits he was romantic when young.

III. Sergeant must choose between moon and lantern.

   A. Sergeant seems ready to arrest rebel.

   B. When police return with lantern the Sergeant sends them away.

   C. Rebel escapes and Sergeant remains in moonlight.

The prewriting strategies of brainstorming, clustering, freewriting, drafting a thesis, and outlining helped the student generate ideas and material for her first draft. After writing this draft, she revised it carefully for organization, clarity, expression, punctuation, and format. What follows is her final draft.

Andrea James

Professor Jacobus

English 233

19 October

The Use of Light in The Rising of the Moon

Lady Gregory uses light imagery in The Rising of the Moon to contrast rebellion and repressiveness. Her initial stage direction is basic: Moonlight. She suggests some of the values associated with moonlight, such as rebellion and romance, caution and secrecy, daring exploits, and even the underworld. All these are set against the policemen, who are governed not by the moon, which casts shadows and makes the world look magical, but by the lantern, which casts a harsh light that even the Sergeant eventually rejects.

The ballad singer, the rebel, is associated with romance from the start: "Dark hair--dark eyes, smooth face. . . . There isn't another man in Ireland would have broken jail the way he did" (27-28). He is dark, handsome, and recklessly brave. The Sergeant, by contrast, is a practical man, no romantic. He sees that he might have a chance to arrest the rebel and gain the reward for his capture if he stays right on the quay, a likely place for the rebel to escape from. But he unknowingly spoils his chances by refusing to keep the lantern the policemen offer. He tells the policemen, "You can take the lantern. Don't be too long now. It's very lonesome here with nothing but the moon" (28). What he does not realize is that with the lantern as his guiding light, he will behave like a proper Sergeant. But with the moon to guide him, he will side with the rebel.

It takes only a few minutes for the rebel to show up on the scene. At first, the Sergeant is very tough and abrupt with the rebel, who is disguised as "Jimmy Walsh, a ballad singer." The rebel tells the Sergeant that he is a traveler, that he is from Ennis, and that he has been to Cork. Unlike the Sergeant, who has stayed in one place and is a family man, the ballad singer appears to be a romantic figure, in the sense that he follows his mind to go where he wants to, sings what he wants to, and does what he wants to.

When the ballad singer begins singing, the Sergeant reacts badly, telling the singer, "Stop that noise" (28). Maybe he is envious of the ballad singer's freedom. When the Sergeant tries to make the rebel leave, the rebel instead begins telling stories about the man the Sergeant is looking for. He reminds the Sergeant of deeds done that would frighten anyone. "It was after the time of the attack on the police barrack at Kilmallock. . . . Moonlight . . . just like this" (29). The moonlight of the tale and the moonlight of the setting combine to add mystery and suspense to the situation.

The effect of the rebel's talk--and of the moonlight--is to make the Sergeant feel sorry for himself in a thankless job. "It's little we get but abuse from the people, and no choice but to obey our orders," he says bitterly while sitting on the barrel sharing a pipe with the singer (29). When the rebel sings an illegal song, the Sergeant corrects a few words, revealing his former sympathies with the people. The rebel realizes this, telling the Sergeant,

"It was with the people you were, and not with the law you were, when you were a young man" (30). The Sergeant admits that when he was young he too was a romantic, but now that he is older he is practical and law-abiding: "Well, if I was foolish then, that time's gone. . . . I have my duties and I know them" (30).

Pulled by his past and his present, the Sergeant is suddenly forced to choose when the ballad singer's signal to his friend reveals the singer's identity to the Sergeant. He must decide whether his heart is with the world of moonlight or the world of the lantern. He seizes the rebel's hat and wig and seems about to arrest him when the policemen, with their lantern, come back. The Sergeant orders the policemen back to the station, and they offer to leave the lantern with him. But the Sergeant refuses. We know that he will not turn the rebel in. He has chosen the world of moonlight, of the rebel.

Before they leave the policemen try to make the world of the lantern seem the right choice. Policeman B says:

> Well, I thought it might be a comfort to you. I often think when I have it in my hand and can be flashing it about into every dark corner (doing so) that it's the same as being beside the fire at home, and the bits of bogwood blazing up now and again. (Flashes it about, now on the barrel, now on Sergeant.) (31)

The Sergeant reacts furiously and tells them to get out--"your-selves and your lantern!"

The play ends with the Sergeant giving the hat and wig back to the rebel, obviously having chosen the side of the people. When the rebel leaves, the Sergeant wonders if he himself was crazy for losing his chance at the reward. But as the curtain goes down, the Sergeant is still in the moonlight.

How to Write a Review

What Is the Purpose of a Review?

A review is more than a critical essay because it covers the actual performance of a play. As a reviewer you write after digesting an evening's entertainment and observing how actors and a director present a production for your enjoyment. Your responsibility is to respond both to the production and to the text of the play; thus, you will discuss the quality of the acting, the effectiveness of the setting, the interpretation of the text, and the power of the direction.

Reviews of plays ordinarily appear in daily newspapers or in weekly or semiweekly publications timely enough to help a prospective playgoer decide on whether to see the play. Considering the cost of tickets in contemporary theater, the best reviewers can perform a valuable service by letting readers know what they feel is most worth seeing. Regular reviewers, such as Ben Brantley and Vincent Canby in the *New York Times,* John Simon in *Newsweek,* and John Lahr in *The New Yorker,* develop their own following because playgoers know from experience whether they can rely on these reviewers' judgments.

Another purpose of theater reviews is to set a standard to which producers aspire. Criticism can promote excellence because experienced and demanding critics force producers of drama to maintain high standards. The power of theater critics in major cities is legendary: more than a few plays have closed prematurely after savage reviews in London, New York, Chicago, and elsewhere. Knowing that they risk close examination by knowledgeable reviewers convinces writers, directors, actors, and producers to do their best.

What You Need to Write a Good Review

The best reviewers ordinarily bring three qualities to their work: experience in the theater, a knowledge of theatrical history, and a sensitivity to dramatic production. Some reviewers have had experience onstage as actors or as production assistants. They are familiar with the process of preparing a play for the stage and in some cases may actually have written for the stage. Other reviewers who have not had such experience have, instead, spent hours in the theater watching plays; their rich experience of seeing a variety of plays enables them to make useful comparisons.

Knowledge of the basics of theater history is fundamental equipment for a good reviewer. New plays that borrow from the traditions of the Greek chorus, or plays that emulate medieval pageants or nineteenth-century melodrama, need reviewers who understand their sources. Suzan-Lori Parks, for example, admits responding to the influence of Bertolt Brecht and Samuel Beckett. While expecting her audience to recognize some of that influence, she knows that her reviewers will spot most or all of it. This book is structured around the history of drama so that readers will better understand drama's roots and evolution. In that sense this book is an aid in helping a theater enthusiast to become a competent reviewer.

Besides knowing the history of drama, the reviewer needs also to be extremely well read. Some reviewers, for example, have not had the opportunity to see all of Shakespeare's plays, but a good reviewer will have read most of them and can refer to them as necessary. The same will be true of the plays of Bernard Shaw, as many have not been produced in the last dozen years or so. In the case of contemporary playwrights, it is common for a reviewer to refer to the playwright's earlier work to put the current production in a useful context. A knowledgeable reviewer knows not only the history of theater but also the work of other playwrights that may be relevant to the play under review.

Most students of theater have enough sensitivity to dramatic productions to write adequate reviews. The most sensitive reviewers will pay close attention to the suitability of the acting almost as a matter of first importance, especially if the play is well known. Most contemporary reviews single out actors and comment on their performance in some detail. Reviewers usually know the work of the most busy actors, and in some cases they will make comparisons with earlier roles. They will also indicate whether the actor has developed further as an artist or has perhaps walked mechanically through the part. The reviewer's sensitivity to individual actors is developed in part from past experience and therefore from having a benchmark against which to match a performance. Curiosity about an actor's performance sometimes drives a review, as in Ben Brantley's examination of Fiona Shaw's acting in *Medea* (p. 161), which was the main focus of his essay on the play.

Obviously, neither Ben Brantley nor any other reviewer is going to review *Medea* with an eye toward telling us that it is a good or bad play; the history of criticism has already done that. The reviewer of *Medea,* like the reviewer of any of Euripides' great plays, will aim to tell us about the quality of the acting or the effectiveness of the setting, as in John Corbin's review of Chekhov's *The Cherry Orchard* (p. 824). Being sensitive to the effective use of lighting, props, costumes, and stage design is essential for any reviewer, but it is probably even more essential for a reviewer of classic theater.

Preparing to Review a Classic Play

If you have the opportunity to review a play that is well established — like most of the plays in this collection — you need special preparation. Besides having read the text before seeing the play, you need to imagine how the play should be staged. Once you understand what the play is about and what its implications may be, you then need to consult reviews or descriptions of early productions. You may do so by referring to the index of any major newspaper or to *New York Theatre Critics' Reviews,* which includes multiple reviews of important productions over the years. The point is simply to come to the experience of the drama as a fully informed viewer. Knowing how the play has been staged in the past will help you see the innovations and special interpretation of the current production.

Preparing to Review a New Play

Sometime you may have the opportunity to review a new play — one that playgoers, including the reviewers, have not had the chance to read in advance. In that case you need to pay special attention to the text, taking notes when necessary, to follow the development of the drama's ideas and issues. You are still responsible for commenting on the acting and the production, but in the case of a new play, your responsibility shifts to preparing the prospective audience to understand and respond to the play. They will need to know what the play is about, how it presents the primary issues in the drama, and what is at stake. You may need to tell something of the plot, but always with an eye toward not giving too much away, especially if the play involves suspense. Ask yourself how much the reader needs to know to decide whether to see the play.

Reviewers of new plays usually include a special commentary on a new or relatively unknown playwright. The most important information here would be any previous work of the playwright. The best reviewers will have seen that work and are prepared to relate it to the new play at hand. Reviewers of August Wilson, for example, spent time in the late 1980s establishing his credentials as a playwright. Now, when a new play of his is produced, reviewers usually attempt to describe how the new play fits into the growing body of his work. Since Wilson is in the process of writing a series of plays on African American life centering on specific decades of the twentieth century, the reviewer does the reader a service by explaining how a new play fits into his overall scheme.

Guidelines for
Writing Reviews

Good reviewers approach the job of writing reviews from many different angles. Some of the reviews in this book begin with a generalization on the theme. Some begin with a personal observation about the play at hand or a personal experience in the theater. Others begin with a note on the background of the playwright, the actors, or the director. There is no one way to write a review, but the following suggestions can help you to structure your reaction.

1. If you are reviewing a professionally produced play, request a press kit from the theater. These kits usually include a great deal of information that could interest readers.

2. In your review provide any necessary background on a playwright who is contemporary or relatively unknown. The press kit should contain some information; if not, the program may do so. Check with the press representative or with the box office manager to see if the playwright is in the house and, before the play begins, ask to arrange an interview.

Sample Review

Because August Wilson's *Fences* (1987) was completely unknown to his readers, Frank Rich takes special care to discuss the details of the play's narrative and to comment on Wilson's other work, much of which may not be familiar to his audience. Rich carefully establishes the time period of the play, 1957, and the neighborhood in which it is set. He then goes on to examine the "mountainous" stature of Troy Maxson, played by James Earl Jones in what Rich feels may be one of his best roles. The struggle between Troy, the one-time player in the Negro baseball leagues, and his son, who is being courted by college football coaches, is central to the drama, and Rich helps us understand its import and its relevance to life in general, not just the play.

Rich reviews each of the main actors: James Earl Jones, Courtney Vance, Mary Alice, and Ray Aranha, clarifying the strength of their work. However, Rich also qualifies his praise of the play by suggesting that Wilson's earlier play, *Ma Rainey's Black Bottom*, is "more aesthetically daring." Yet that does not stop him from approving the power of Wilson's use of the "talking blues," and "Mr. Jones's efforts to shout down the devil." Rich ends with a useful comment on Lloyd Richards's direction and the dominant struggle, both psychological and physical, between father and son that ends the play. Rich leaves the reader with no question about the importance of going to see *Fences*.

Analysis of any of the other reviews in this book will show variations on Rich's structure. When you write your own review, be sure to set up a checklist based on the one that follows here:

Author and title of play	Description of the action
What the play is about	Direction
The play's main issues	Theater and dates of performance
Actors	Your recommendation
Setting	

Take the list to the theater with you and keep your notes on it. When you begin writing your review look at some of the tips in this discussion and some of the reviews elsewhere in this book. Your review should provide your readers a valuable service.

Glossary of Dramatic Terms

Act. A major division in the action of a play. Most plays from the Elizabethan era until the nineteenth century were divided into five acts by the playwrights or by later editors. In the nineteenth century many writers began to write four-act plays. Today one-, two-, and three-act plays are most common.

Action. What happens in a play; the events that make up the **plot**.

Agon. The Greek word for "contest." In Greek tragedy the *agon* was often a formal debate in which the **chorus** divided and took the sides of the disputants.

Alienation effect. In his **epic theater**, Bertolt Brecht (1898–1956) tried to make the familiar unfamiliar (or to alienate it) to show the audience that familiar, seemingly "natural," and therefore unalterable social conditions could be changed. Different devices achieved the alienation effect by calling attention to the theater as theater — stage lights brought in front of the curtain, musicians put onstage instead of hidden in an orchestra pit, placards indicating scene changes and interrupting the linear flow of the action, actors distancing themselves from their characters to invite the audience to analyze and criticize the characters instead of empathizing with them. These alienating devices prevented the audience from losing itself in the illusion of reality. (See **epic theater**.)

Allegory. A literary work that is coherent on at least two levels simultaneously: a literal level consisting of recognizable characters and events and an allegorical level in which the literal characters and events represent moral, political, religious, or other ideas and meanings.

Anagnorisis. Greek term for a character's discovery or recognition of someone or something previously unknown. *Anagnorisis* often paves the way for a reversal of fortune (see *peripeteia*). An example in *Oedipus Rex* is Oedipus's discovery of his true identity.

Antagonist. A character or force in conflict with the **protagonist**. The antagonist is often another character but may also be an intangible force such as nature or society. The dramatic conflict can also take the form of a struggle with the protagonist's own character.

Anticlimax. See **plot**.

Antimasque. See **masque**.

Antistrophe. The second of the three parts of the verse ode sung by the **chorus** in Greek drama. While singing the **strophe** the chorus moves in a dance rhythm from right to left; during the antistrophe it moves from left to right back to its original position. The third part, the **epode,** was sung standing still.

Apron stage. The apron is the part of the stage extending in front of the **proscenium arch.** A stage is an apron stage if all or most of it is in front of any framing structures. The Elizabethan stage, which the audience surrounded on three sides, is an example of an apron stage.

Arena stage. A stage surrounded on all sides by the audience, actors make exits and entrances through the aisles. Usually used in **theater in the round.**

Arras. A curtain hung at the back of the Elizabethan playhouse to partition off an alcove or booth. The curtain could be pulled back to reveal a room or a cave.

Aside. A short speech made by a character to the audience which, by **convention**, the other characters onstage cannot hear.

Atellan farce. Broad and sometimes coarse popular humor indigenous to the town of Atella in Italy. By the third century B.C., the Romans had imported the Atellan farce, which they continued to modify and develop.

Blank verse. An unrhymed verse form often used in writing drama. Blank verse is composed of ten-syllable lines accented on the second, fourth, sixth eighth, and tenth syllables (**iambic pentameter**).

Bombast. A loud, pompous speech whose inflated diction is disproportionate to the subject matter it expresses.

Bourgeois drama. Drama that treats middle-class subject matter or characters rather than the lives of the rich and powerful.

Braggart soldier. A **stock character** in comedy who is usually cowardly, parasitical, pompous, and easily victimized by practical jokers. Sir John Falstaff in Shakespeare's *Henry IV* (parts 1, 2) is an example of this type.

Burla (plural, *burle*). Jests or practical jokes that were part of the comic **stage business** in the **commedia dell'arte.**

Buskin. A thick-soled boot possibly worn by Greek tragedians to increase their stature. Later called a *cothurnus.*

Catastrophe. See **plot.**

Catharsis. The feeling of emotional purgation or release that, according to Aristotle, an audience should feel after watching a tragedy.

Ceremonial drama. Egyptian passion play about the god Osiris.

Character. Any person appearing in a drama or narrative.

> **Stock character.** A stereotypical character type whose behavior, qualities, or beliefs conform to familiar dramatic **conventions,** such as the clever servant or the **braggart soldier.** (Also called *type character.*)

Chiton. Greek tunic worn by Roman actors.

Choregos. An influential citizen chosen to pay for the training and costuming of the **chorus** in Greek drama competitions. He probably also paid for the musicians and met other financial production demands not paid for by the state.

Chorus. A masked group that sang and danced in Greek tragedy. The chorus usually chanted in unison, offering advice and commentary on the action but rarely participating. See also **strophe, antistrophe,** and **epode.**

City Dionysia. See **Dionysus.**

Climax. See **plot.**

Closet drama. A drama, usually in verse, meant for reading rather than for performance. Hrosvitha's *Dulcitius,* Percy Bysshe Shelley's *Prometheus Unbound,* and John Milton's *Samson Agonistes* are examples.

Comedy. A type of drama intended to interest and amuse rather than to concern the audience deeply. Although characters experience various discomfitures, the audience feels confident that they will overcome their ill fortune and find happiness at the end.

Comedy of humors. Form of comedy developed by Ben Jonson in the seventeenth century in which characters' actions are determined by the preponderance in their systems of one of the four bodily fluids or humors — blood, phlegm, choler (yellow bile), and melancholy (black bile). Characters' dispositions are exaggerated and stereotyped; common types are the melancholic and the belligerent bully.

Comedy of manners. Realistic, often satiric comedy concerned with the manners and conventions of high society. Usually refers to the Restoration comedies of late seventeenth-century England, which feature witty dialogue or **repartee.** An example is William Congreve's *The Way of the World.*

Drawing room comedy. A type of comedy of manners concerned with life in polite society. The action generally takes place in a drawing room.

Farce. A short dramatic work that depends on exaggerated, improbable situations, incongruities, coarse wit, and horseplay for its comic effect.

High comedy. Comedy that appeals to the intellect, often focusing on the pretensions, foolishness, and incongruity of human behavior. **Comedy of manners** with its witty dialogue is a type of high comedy.

Low comedy. Comedy that lacks the intellectual appeal of **high comedy,** depending instead on boisterous buffoonery, "gags," and jokes for its comic effect.

Middle Comedy. This transitional Greek style of comedy extended from 375 to about 330 B.C. It marks a change, especially in language, which grew less formal and closer to the way people spoke. Little evidence of Middle Comedy exists, but from surviving statuettes we can surmise that costumes on stage resembled what Athenians actually wore on the street.

New Comedy. Emerging between the fourth and third centuries B.C. in ancient Greece, New Comedy replaced the farcical **Old Comedy.** New Comedy, usually associated with Menander, is witty and intellectually engaging; it is often thought of as the first **high comedy.**

Old Comedy. Greek comedy of the fifth century B.C. that uses bawdy farce to attack satirically social, religious, and political institutions. Old Comedy is usually associated with Aristophanes.

Sentimental comedy. Comedy populated by stereotypical virtuous **protagonists** and villainous **antagonists** that resolves the domestic trials of middle-class people in a pat, happy ending.

Slapstick. Low comedy that involves little plot or character development but consists of physical horseplay or practical jokes.

Comic relief. The use of humorous characters, speeches, or scenes in an otherwise serious or tragic drama.

Commedia dell'arte. Italian **low comedy** dating from around the mid-sixteenth century in which professional actors playing **stock characters** improvised dialogue to fit a given **scenario.**

Complication. See **plot.**

Conflict. See **plot.**

Convention. Any feature of a literary work that has become standardized over time, such as the **aside** or the **stock character.** Often refers to an unrealistic device (such as Danish characters speaking English in *Hamlet*) that the audience tacitly agrees to accept.

Coryphaeus. See *koryphaios.*

Cosmic irony. See **irony.**

Cothurnus. See **buskin.**

Craft play. Medieval sacred drama based on Old and New Testament stories. Craft plays were performed outside the church by members of a particular trade guild, and their subject matter often reflected the guild's trade. The fisherman's guild, for example, might present the story of Noah and the flood.

Crisis. Same as **climax.** See **plot.**

Cycle. A group of medieval **mystery plays** written in the vernacular (the language in common use rather than Latin) for performance outside the church. Cycles, each of which treated biblical stories from creation through the last judgment, are named after the town in which they were produced. Most extant mystery plays are from the York, Chester, Wakefield (Towneley), and N-Town cycles.

Decorum. A quality that exists when the style of a work is appropriate to the speaker, the occasion, and the subject matter. Kings should speak in a "high style" and clowns in a "low style," according to many Renaissance authors. Decorum was a guiding critical principle in **neoclassicism.**

Defamiliarization effect (*Verfremdungseffekt*). See **alienation effect.**

Denouement. See **plot.**

Deus ex machina. Latin for "a god out of a machine." In Greek drama, a mechanical device called a *mechane* could lower "gods" onto the stage to solve the seemingly unsolvable problems of mortal characters. Also used to describe a playwright's use of a forced or improbable solution to plot complications — for example, the discovery of a lost will or inheritance that will pay off the evil landlord.

Dialogue. Spoken interchange or conversation between two or more characters. Also see **soliloquy.**

Diction. A playwright's choice of words or the match between language and subject matter. Also refers collectively to an actor's phrasing, enunciation, and manner of speaking.

Dionysus. Greek nature god of wine, mystic revelry, and irrational impulse. Greek tragedy probably sprang from dramatized ritual choral celebrations in his honor.

City Dionysia. (Also called Great or Greater Dionysia.) The most important of the four Athenian festivals in honor of Dionysus. This spring festival sponsored the first tragedy competitions; comedy was associated with the winter festival, the Lenaea.

Director. The person responsible for a play's interpretation and staging and for the guidance of the actors.

Disguising. Medieval entertainment featuring a masked procession of actors performing short plays in pantomime; probably the origin of the court **masque.**

Dithyramb. Ancient Greek choral hymn sung and danced to honor **Dionysus;** originally divided into an improvised story sung by a choral leader and a traditional refrain sung by the **chorus.** Believed by some to be the origin of Greek tragedy.

Domestic tragedy. A serious play usually focusing on the family and depicting the fall of a middle-class **protagonist** rather than of a powerful or noble hero. Also called *bourgeois tragedy.* An example is Arthur Miller's *Death of a Salesman,* which traces the emotional collapse and eventual suicide of Willy Loman, a traveling salesman.

Double plot. See **plot.**

Drama. A play written in prose or verse that tells a story through **dialogue** and actions performed by actors impersonating the characters of the story.

Dramatic illusion. The illusion of reality created by drama and accepted by the audience for the duration of the play.

Dramatic irony. See **irony.**

Dramatist. The author of a play; playwright.

Dramaturge. One who represents the playwright and guides the production. In some cases, the dramaturge researches different aspects of the production or earlier productions of the play.

Dramaturgy. The art of writing plays.

Drawing room comedy. See **comedy.**

Empathy. The sense of feeling *with* a character. (Distinct from sympathy, which is feeling *for* a character.)

Ensemble acting. Performance by a group of actors, usually members of a **repertory** company, in which the integrated acting of all members is emphasized over individual star performances. The famous nineteenth-century director Konstantin Stanislavsky promoted this type of acting in the Moscow Art Theatre.

Environmental theater. A term used by Richard Schechner, director of the Performance Group in the late 1960s and early 1970s, to describe his work and the work of other theater companies, including the Bread and Puppet Theatre, Open Theatre, and Living Theatre. He also used the term to describe the indigenous theater of Africa and Asia. Environmental theater occupies the whole of a performance space; it is not confined to a stage separated from the audience. Action can take place in and around the audience, and audience members are often encouraged to participate in the theater event.

Epic theater. A type of theater first associated with German director Erwin Piscator (1893–1966). Bertolt Brecht (1898–1956) used the term to distinguish his own theater from the "dramatic" theater that created the illusion of reality and invited the audience to identify and empathize with the characters. Brecht criticized the dramatic theater for encouraging the audience to believe that social conditions were "natural" and therefore unalterable. According to Brecht, the theater should show human beings as dependent on certain political and economic factors and at the same time as capable of altering them. "The spectator is given the chance to criticize human behavior from a social point of view, and the scene is played as a piece of history," he wrote. Epic theater calls attention to itself as theater, bringing the stage lights in front of the curtain and interrupting the linear flow of the action to help the audience analyze the action and characters onstage. (See **alienation effect.**)

Epilogue. A final speech added to the end of a play. An example is Puck's "If we shadows have offended . . ." speech that ends Shakespeare's *A Midsummer Night's Dream.*

Epitasis. Ancient term for the **rising action** of a **plot.** (See also **plot.**)

Epode. The third of three parts of the verse ode sung by the **chorus** in a Greek drama. The epode follows the **strophe** and **antistrophe.**

Exodos. The concluding scene, which includes the exit of all characters and the **chorus,** of a Greek drama.

Exposition. See **plot.**

Expressionism. Early twentieth-century literary movement in Germany that posited that art should represent powerful emotional states and moods. Expressionists abandon **realism** and **verisimilitude,** producing distorted, nightmarish images of the individual unconscious.

Falling action. See **plot.**

Farce. See **comedy.**

First Folio. The first collected edition of thirty-six of Shakespeare's plays, collected by two of his fellow actors and published posthumously in 1623.

Foil. A character who, through difference or similarity, brings out a particular aspect of another character. Laertes, reacting to the death of his father, acts as a foil for Hamlet.

Foreshadowing. Ominous hints of events to come that help to create an air of suspense in a drama.

Frons scaena. The elaborately decorated facade of the *scaena* or stage house used in presenting Roman drama. (Also called *scaena frons.*)

Hamartia. An error or wrong act through which the fortunes of the **protagonist** are reversed in a tragedy.

High comedy. See **comedy.**

History play. A drama set in a time other than that in which it was written. The term usually refers to Elizabethan drama, such as Shakespeare's Henry plays, that draws its plots from English historical materials such as Holinshed's *Chronicles.*

Hubris (or *hybris*). Excessive pride or ambition. In ancient Greek tragedy hubris often causes the **protagonist's** fall.

Humor character. A stereotyped character in the **comedy of humors** (see **comedy**). Clever plots often play on the character's personality distortions (caused by an imbalance of humors), revealing his or her absurdity.

Iambic pentameter. A poetic meter that divides a line into five parts (or feet), each part containing an unaccented syllable followed by an accented syllable. The line "When I consider everything that grows" is an example of iambic pentameter verse.

Imitation. See *mimesis.*

Impressionism. A highly personal style of writing in which the author presents characters, scenes, or moods as they appear to him or her at a particular moment rather than striving for an objectively realistic description.

Interlude. A short play, usually either farcical or moralistic, performed between the courses of a feast or between the acts of a longer play. The interlude thrived during the late fifteenth and early sixteenth centuries in England.

Irony. The use of words to suggest a meaning that is the opposite of the literal meaning, as in "I can't wait to take the exam." Irony is present in a literary work that gives expression to contradictory attitudes or impulses to entertain ambiguity or to maintain detachment.

Cosmic irony. Irony present when destiny or the gods seem to be in favor of the **protagonist** but are actually engineering his or her downfall. (Same as *irony of fate.*)

Dramatic irony. Irony present when the outcome of an event or situation is the opposite of what a character expects.

Tragic irony. Irony that exists when a character's lack of complete knowledge or understanding (which the audience possesses) results in his or her fall or has tragic consequences for loved ones. An example from *Oedipus Rex* is Oedipus's declaration that he will stop at nothing to banish King Laios's murderer, whom the audience knows to be Oedipus himself.

Jongleur. Early medieval French musical entertainer who recited lyrics, ballads, and stories. Forerunner of the minstrel.

Koryphaios. The leader of the **chorus** in Greek drama.

Kothornos. See **buskin.**

Lazzo (plural, *lazzi*). Comic routines or **stage business** associated with the stock situations and characters of the Italian **commedia dell'arte**. A scenario might, for example, call for the *lazzo* of fear.

Liturgical drama. Short dramatized sections of the medieval church service. Some scholars believe that these playlets evolved into the vernacular **mystery plays,** which were performed outside the church by lay people.

Low comedy. See **comedy.**

Mansion. Scenic structures used in medieval drama to indicate the locale or scene of the action. Mansions were areas inside the church used for performing liturgical drama; later more elaborate structures were built on pageant wagons to present **mystery plays** outside the church.

Mask. A covering used to disguise or ornament the face; used by actors in Greek drama and revived in the later **commedia dell'arte** and court **masque** to heighten dramatic effect.

Masque (also *mask*). A short but elaborately staged court drama, often mythological and allegorical, principally acted and danced by masked courtiers. (Professional actors often performed the major speaking and singing roles.) Popular in England during the late sixteenth and early seventeenth centuries, masques were often commissioned to honor a particular person or occasion. Ben Jonson was the most important masque writer; the genre's most elaborate sets and costumes were designed by Jonson's occasional partner Inigo Jones.

Antimasque. A parody of the court **masque** developed by Ben Jonson featuring broad humor, grotesque characters, and ludicrous actions.

Melodrama. A suspenseful play filled with situations that appeal to the audience's emotions. Justice triumphs in a happy ending: the good characters (completely virtuous) are rewarded and the bad characters (thoroughly villainous) are punished.

Method acting. A naturalistic technique of acting developed by the Russian director Konstantin Stanislavsky and adapted for American actors by Lee Strasberg, among others. The Method actor identifies with the **character** he or she portrays and experiences the emotions called for by the play in an effort to render the character with emotional **verisimilitude.**

Middle Comedy. See **comedy.**

Mimesis. The Greek word for "imitation." Aristotle used the term to define the role of art as an imitation of an action.

Miracle play. A type of medieval sacred drama that depicts the lives of saints, focusing especially on the miracles performed by saints.

Mise-en-scène. The stage setting of a play, including the use of scenery, props, and stage movement.

Moira. Greek word for "fate."

Morality play. Didactic late medieval drama (flourishing in England c. 1400–1550) that uses **allegory** to dramatize some aspects of the Christian moral life. Abstract qualities or entities such as Virtue, Vice, Good Deeds, Knowledge, and Death are cast as characters who discuss with the **protagonist** issues related to salvation and the afterlife. *Everyman* is an example.

Motivation. The reasons for a character's actions in a drama. For drama to be effective, the audience must believe that a character's actions are justified and plausible given what they know about him or her.

Mouth of hell. A stage prop in medieval drama suggesting the entrance to hell. Often in the shape of an open-mouthed monster's head, the mouth of hell was positioned over a smoke-and-fire-belching pit in the stage that appeared to swallow up sinners.

Mystery play. A sacred medieval play dramatizing biblical events such as the creation, the fall of Adam and Eve, and Christ's birth and resurrection. The genre probably evolved from **liturgical drama;** mystery plays were often incorporated into larger **cycles** of plays.

Naturalism. Literary philosophy popularized during the nineteenth century that casts art's role as the scientifically accurate reflection of a "slice of life." Naturalism is aligned with the belief that each person is a product of heredity and environment driven by internal and external forces beyond his or her control. August Strindberg's *Miss Julie,* with its focus on reality's sordidness and humankind's powerlessness, draws on naturalism.

Neoclassicism. A movement in sixteenth-century Italy and seventeenth-century France to revive and emulate classical attitudes toward art based on principles of order, harmony, unity, restrained wit, and **decorum.** The neoclassical movement in France gave rise to a corresponding movement in England during the late seventeenth and eighteenth centuries.

New Comedy. See **comedy.**

Ode. A dignified Greek three-part song sung by the **chorus** in Greek drama. The parts are the **strophe,** the **antistrophe,** and the **epode.**

Old Comedy. See **comedy.**

Orchestra. Literally the "dancing place"; the circular stage where the Greek **chorus** performed.

Pageant. A movable stage or wagon (often called a pageant wagon) on which a set was built for the performance of medieval drama. The term can also refer to the spectacle itself.

Pallium. Long white cloak or mantle worn by Greek actors or Romans in Greek-based plays.

Pantomime. Silent acting using facial expression, body movement, and gesture to convey the plot and the characters' feelings.

Parodos. The often stately entrance song of the **chorus** in Greek drama. The term also refers to the aisles (plural, *paradoi*) on either side of the orchestra by which the chorus entered the Greek theater.

Pastoral drama. A dramatic form glorifying shepherds and rural life in an idealized natural setting; usually implies a negative comparison to urban life.

Pathos. The quality of evoking pity.

Performance art. A mid-twentieth-century form that often mixes media: music, video, film, opera, dance, and spoken text. It was originally defined in terms of artists using a live production for dramatic effect, such as Anna Deavere Smith. However, it has widened to include performances that cross defined dramatic "boundaries." Dancers Martha Clarke and Pina Bausch, musicians such as Laurie Anderson, and experimental directors such as Richard Foreman have been identified as performance artists.

Peripeteia. A reversal of fortune, for better or worse, for the **protagonist.** Used especially to describe the main character's fall in Greek tragedy.

Phallus. An appendage meant to suggest the penis added to the front of blatantly comic male characters' costumes in some Greek comedy; associated chiefly with the Greek **satyr play.**

Play. A literary genre whose plot is usually presented dramatically by actors portraying characters before an audience.

Play-within-the-play. A brief secondary drama presented to or by the characters of a play that reflects or comments on the larger work. An example is the Pyramus and Thisbe episode in Shakespeare's *A Midsummer Night's Dream.*

Plot. The events of a play or narrative. The sequence and relative importance a **dramatist** assigns to these events.

Anticlimax. An unexpectedly trivial or significant conclusion to a series of significant events; an unsatisfying resolution that often occurs in place of a conventional **climax.**

Catastrophe. The outcome or conclusion of a play; usually applied specifically to tragedy. (**Denouement** is a parallel term applied to both comedy and tragedy.)

Climax. The turning point in a drama's action, preceded by the **rising action** and followed by the **falling action.** Same as **crisis.**

Complication. The part of the plot preceding the **climax** that establishes the entanglements to be untangled in the **denouement.** Part of the **rising action.**

Conflict. The struggle between the **protagonist** and the **antagonist** that propels the **rising action** of the plot and is resolved in the **denouement.**

Denouement. The "unknotting" of the plot's **complication;** the resolution of a drama's action. See **catastrophe.**

Double plot. A dramatic structure in which two related plots function simultaneously.

Exposition. The presentation of essential information, especially about events that have occurred prior to the first scene of a play. The exposition appears early in the play and initiates the **rising action.**

Falling action. The events of the plot following the **climax** and ending in the **catastrophe** or resolution.

Rising action. The events of the plot leading up to the **climax.**

Subplot. A secondary plot intertwined with the main plot, often reflecting or commenting on the main plot.

Underplot. Same as **subplot.**

Problem play. A drama that argues a point or presents a problem (usually a social problem). Ibsen is a notable writer of problem plays.

Prologos. In Greek drama, an introductory scene for actor or actors that precedes the entrance of the **chorus.** This **convention** has evolved into the modern dramatic introductory monologue or **prologue.**

Prologue. A preface or introduction preceding the play proper.

Proscaena. The space in front of the *scaena* in a Roman theater.

Proscenium arch. An arched structure over the front of the stage from which a curtain often hangs. The arch frames the action onstage and separates the audience from the action.

Proskenion. The playing space in front of the *skene* or scene house in Greek drama.

Protagonist. The main character in a drama. This character is usually the most interesting and sympathetic and is the person involved in the **conflict** driving the **plot.**

Protasis. Classical term for the introductory act or **exposition** of a drama.

Psychomachia. Psychological struggle; a war of souls.

Quem Quaeritis **trope.** A brief dramatized section of the medieval church's Easter liturgy. The oldest extant **trope** and the probable origin of liturgical drama, it enacts the visit of the three Marys to Christ's empty tomb (*quem quaeritis* means "whom do you seek?" in Latin).

Realism. The literary philosophy holding that art should accurately reproduce an image of life. Avoiding the use of dramatic **conventions** such as asides and soliloquies, it depicts ordinary people in ordinary situations. Ibsen's *A Doll House* is an example of realism in drama.

Recognition. See *anagnorisis.*

Repartee. Witty and pointed verbal exchanges usually found in the **comedy of manners.**

Repertory. A theater company or group of actors that presents a set of plays alternately throughout a season. The term also refers to the set of plays itself.

Restoration comedy. A type of **comedy of manners** that developed in England in the late seventeenth century. Often features **repartee** in the service of complex romantic plots. Oliver Goldsmith's *She Stoops to Conquer* is an example.

Revenge tragedy. Sensational tragedy popularized during the Elizabethan age that is notable for bloody plots involving such elements as murder, ghosts, insanity, and crimes of lust.

Reversal. See *peripeteia.*

Riposte. A quick or sharp reply; similar to **repartee.**

Rising action. See **plot.**

Ritual. Repeated formalized or ceremonial practices, many of which have their roots in primitive cultures. Certain theorists hold that primitive ritual evolved into drama.

Satire. A work that makes fun of a social institution or human foible, often in an intellectually sophisticated way, to persuade the audience to share the author's views. Molière's *The Misanthrope* contains social satire.

Satyr play. A comic play performed after the tragic trilogy in Greek tragedy competitions. The satyr play provided **comic relief** and was usually a farcical, boisterous treatment of mythological material.

Scaena. The stage house in Roman drama; the facade of the *scaena* (called the *frons scaena*) was often elaborately ornamented.

Scenario. The plot outline around which professional actors of the **commedia dell'arte** improvised their plays. Most scenarios specified the action's sequence and the entrances of the main characters.

Scene. Division of an **act** in a drama. By traditional definition a scene has no major shift in place or time frame, and it is performed by a static group of actors onstage (in French drama, if an actor enters or exits, the group is altered and the scene, technically, should change). The term also refers to the physical surroundings or locale in which a play's action is set.

Scenery. The backdrop and set (furniture and so on) onstage that suggest to the audience the surroundings in which a play's **action** takes place.

Scenography. Painting of backdrops and hangings.

Senecan tragedy. Tragic drama modeled on plays written by Seneca. The genre usually has five acts and features a **chorus;** it is notable for its thematic concern with bloodshed, revenge, and unnatural crimes. (See also **revenge tragedy.**)

Sentimental. Refers to tender emotions in excess of what the situation calls for.

Setting. All details of time, location, and environment relating to a play.

Skene. The building or scene house in the Greek theater that probably began as a dressing room and eventually was incorporated into the action as part of the scenery.

Slapstick. See **comedy.**

Slice of life. See **naturalism.**

Social problem play. Same as **problem play.**

Sock. Derived from the Latin *soccus,* the term refers to a light slipper or sock worn by Roman comic actors.

Soliloquy. A speech in which an actor, usually alone onstage, utters his or her thoughts aloud, revealing personal feelings. Hamlet's "To be, or not to be" speech is an example.

Spectacle. In Aristotle's terms, the costumes and scenery in a drama — the elements that appeal to the eye.

Stage business. Minor physical action, including an actor's posture and facial expression, and the use of props, all of which make up a particular interpretation of a character.

Stichomythia. Dialogue in which two speakers engage in a verbal duel in alternating lines.

Stock character. See **character.**

Strophe. The first of three parts of the verse **ode** sung by the Greek **chorus.** While singing the strophe the chorus moves in a dancelike pattern from right to left. See also **antistrophe** and **epode.**

Subplot. See **plot.**

Subtext. A level of meaning implicit in or underlying the surface meaning of a text.

Surrealism. A literary movement flourishing in France during the early twentieth century that valued the unwilled expression of the unconscious (usually as revealed in dreams) over a rendering of "reality" structured by the conscious mind.

Suspense. The sense of tension aroused by an audience's uncertainty about the resolution of dramatic conflicts.

Suspension of disbelief. An audience's willingness to accept the world of the drama as reality during the course of a play.

Symbolism. A literary device in which an object, event, or action is used to suggest a meaning beyond its literal meaning. The lantern in *The Rising of the Moon* has a symbolic function.

Theater. The building in which a play is performed. Also used to refer to drama as an art form.

Theater in the round. The presentation of a play on an **arena stage** surrounded by the audience.

Theater of the absurd. A type of twentieth-century drama presenting the human condition as meaningless, absurd, and illogical. An example of the genre is Samuel Beckett's *Happy Days*.

Theater of cruelty. A type of drama created by Antonin Artaud in the 1930s that uses shock techniques to expose the audience's primitive obsessions with cruelty and sexuality. The purpose was to overwhelm spectators' rational minds, leading them to understand and even participate in the cycle of cruelty and ritual purgation dramatized in the performance.

Three unities. Aristotle noted that a play's action usually occurs in one day or a little more and that the plot should reveal clearly ordered actions and incidents moving toward the plot's resolution. Later scholars and critics, especially those in the neoclassical tradition, interpreted Aristotle's ideas as rules (unity of time and unity of action) and added a third, unity of place (a play's action should occur in a single locale).

Thrust stage. A stage extending beyond the **proscenium arch,** usually surrounded on three sides by the audience.

Tiring house. From "attiring house," the backstage space in Elizabethan public theaters used for storage and as a dressing room. The term also refers to the changing space beneath the medieval pageant wagon.

Total theater. A concept of the theater as an experience synthesizing all the expressive arts including music, dance, lighting, and so on.

Tragedy. Serious drama in which a **protagonist,** traditionally of noble position, suffers a series of unhappy events culminating in a **catastrophe** such as death or spiritual breakdown. Shakespeare's *Hamlet*, which ends with the prince's death, is an example of Elizabethan tragedy.

Tragicomedy. A play that combines elements of tragedy and comedy. Chekhov's *The Cherry Orchard* is an example. Tragicomedies often include a serious plot in which the expected tragic **catastrophe** is replaced by a happy ending.

Trope. Interpolation into or expansion of an existing medieval liturgical text. These expansions, such as the *Quem Quaeritis* **trope,** gave rise to **liturgical drama.**

Type character. See **character.**

Underplot. See **plot.**

Unity. The sense that the events of a play and the actions of the characters follow one another naturally to form one complete action. Unity is present when characters' behavior seems **motivated** and the work is perceived to be a connected artistic whole. See also **three unities.**

Verfremdungseffekt. German term coined by Bertolt Brecht to mean "alienation." See also **alienation effect.**

Verisimilitude. The degree to which a dramatic representation approximates an appearance of reality.

Well-made play. Drama that relies for effect on the suspense generated by its logical, cleverly constructed plot rather than on characterization. Plots often involve a withheld secret, a battle of wits between hero and villain, and a resolution in which the secret is revealed and the **protagonist** saved. The plays of Eugène Scribe (1791–1861) have defined the type.

Selected Bibliography

Selected References for Periods of Drama

GREEK DRAMA

Aylen, Leo. *The Greek Theater*. Rutherford: Fairleigh Dickinson UP, 1985.

Bieber, Margaret. *The History of the Greek and Roman Theater*. 2nd ed. Princeton: Princeton UP, 1961.

Easterling, P. E., ed. *The Cambridge Companion to Greek Tragedy*. Cambridge: Cambridge UP, 1997.

Green, John R. *Theatre in Ancient Greek Society*. New York: Routledge, 1994.

Hamilton, Edith. *The Greek Way*. New York: Norton, 1983.

Hartigan, Karelisa V. *Greek Tragedy on the American Stage: Ancient Drama in the Commercial Theater 1882–1994*. Westport: Greenwood, 1995.

Havelock, Eric. "The Double Vision of Greek Tragedy." Hudson Review 37 (1984): 244–70.

Kitto, H. D. F. *Form and Meaning in Drama: A Study of Six Greek Plays and of Hamlet*. 2nd ed. New York: Barnes, 1968.

———. *Greek Tragedy: A Literary Study*. 3rd ed. London: Methuen, 1966.

Knox, Bernard M. *Word and Action: Essays on the Ancient Theater*. Baltimore: Johns Hopkins UP, 1979.

Mills, Sophie. *Theseus, Tragedy, and the Athenian Empire*. Oxford: Oxford UP, 1997.

Pickard-Cambridge, Arthur W. *Dramatic Festivals of Athens*. 2nd ed. Revised by John Gould and D. M. Lewis. Oxford: Clarendon, 1962.

Silk, M. S., ed. *Tragedy and the Tragic: Greek Theatre and Beyond*. Oxford: Clarendon, 1996.

Steiner, George. *The Death of Tragedy*. New York: Knopf, 1961.

Taplin, Oliver. *Greek Tragedy in Action*. Berkeley: U of California P, 1978.

Taylor, David. *The Greek and Roman Stage*. Bristol: Bristol Classical, 1999.

Trendall, A. D., and T. B. L. Webster. *Illustrations of Greek Drama*. London: Phaidon, 1971.

Vickers, Brian. *Towards Greek Tragedy: Drama, Myth, Society*. London: Longman, 1973.

Walcot, Peter. *Greek Drama in Its Theatrical and Social Context*. Cardiff: U of Wales P, 1976.

Walton, Michael J. *Living Greek Theater: A Handbook of Classical Performance and Modern Production*. New York: Greenwood, 1987.

Webster, T. B. L. *Greek Theater Production*. 2nd ed. London: Methuen, 1970.

Winkler, John J., and Froma I. Zeitlin. *Nothing to Do with Dionysus? Athenian Drama in Its Social Context*. Princeton: Princeton UP, 1990.

Wise, Jennifer. *Dionysus Writes: The Invention of Theatre in Ancient Greece*. Ithaca: Cornell UP, 1998.

Zinman, Toby. "Still Dangerous after All These Years: Now's Your Chance to Get Reacquainted with Greek Tragedy's High-and-Mighty Heroines." *American Theatre* 16.3 (1999): 18–21, 62–63.

ROMAN DRAMA

Beare, William. *The Roman Stage*. 3rd ed. London: Methuen, 1969.

Bieber, Margaret. *The History of the Greek and Roman Theater*. 2nd ed. Princeton: Princeton UP, 1961.

Dodwell, Charles R. *Anglo-Saxon Gestures and the Roman Stage*. New York: Cambridge UP, 1999.

Duckworth, George E. *The Nature of Roman Comedy: A Study in Popular Entertainment*. Princeton: Princeton UP, 1952.

Grant, M. D. "Plautus and Seneca: Acting in Nero's Rome." *Greece and Rome* 46.1 (1999): 27–33.

Hunter, R. L. *The New Comedy of Greece and Rome*. New York: Cambridge UP, 1985.

Kenney, E. J., ed. *The Cambridge History of Classical Literature*. 2 vols. New York: Cambridge UP, 1982.

Konstan, David. *Roman Comedy*. Ithaca: Cornell UP, 1983.

Reinheimer, David A. "The Roman Actor, Censorship, and Dramatic Autonomy." *Studies in English Literature 1500–1900* 38.2 (1998): 317–32.

Segal, Erich. *Roman Laughter*. Cambridge: Harvard UP, 1968.

Wiles, David. *The Masks of Menander: Sign and Meaning in Greek and Roman Performances*. New York: Cambridge UP, 1991.

Wiseman, Timothy P. *Roman Drama and Roman History*. Exeter: University of Exeter Press, 1998.

MEDIEVAL DRAMA

Bevington, David, ed. *Medieval Drama*. Boston: Houghton, 1975.

Briscoe, Marianne G., and John C. Coldewey. *Contexts for Early English Drama*. Bloomington: Indiana UP, 1989.

Chambers, Edmund K. *English Literature at the Close of the Middle Ages*. Oxford: Clarendon, 1945.

———. *The Medieval Stage*. 2 vols. London: Oxford UP, 1967.

Cox, John D., and David S. Kastan, eds. *A New History of Early English Drama*. New York: Columbia UP, 1997.

Craig, Hardin. *English Religious Drama of the Middle Ages*. 2nd ed. Westport: Greenwood, 1978.

Davidson, Clifford, et al., eds. *Drama in the Middle Ages*. New York: AMS, 1982.

———. *Material Culture and Medieval Drama*. Kalamazoo: Medieval Institute, 1999.

Dillon, Janette. *Language and Stage in Medieval and Renaissance England*. Cambridge: Cambridge UP, 1998.

Elliott, John R. *Playing God: Medieval Mysteries on the Modern Stage*. Toronto: U Toronto P, 1989.

Enders, Jody. *The Medieval Theater of Cruelty: Rhetoric, Memory, Violence*. Ithaca: Cornell UP, 1999.

Ernst, Earle. *Three Japanese Plays from the Traditional Theatre*. London: Oxford UP, 1959.

Fenollosa, Ernest, and Ezra Pound. *The Classic Noh Theatre of Japan*. New York: New Directions, 1959.

Gassner, John, ed. *Medieval and Tudor Drama*. New York: Bantam, 1971.

Hardison, O. B., Jr. *Christian Rite and Christian Drama in the Middle Ages: Essays in the Origin and Early History of Modern Drama*. Baltimore: Johns Hopkins UP, 1965.

Keene, Donald. *Nō: The Classic Theatre of Japan*. Tokyo and Palo Alto: Kodansha International, 1966.

Keene, Donald. *No and Bunraku*. New York: Columbia UP, 1990.

Ortolani, Benito. *The Japanese Theatre*. rev. ed. Princeton: Princeton UP, 1995.

Spinrad, Phoebe. *The Summons of Death on the Medieval and Renaissance English Stage*. Columbus: Ohio State UP, 1987.

Tyler, Royall. *Japanese No Dramas*. New York: Penguin, 1993.

Vince, Ronald W. *Ancient and Medieval Theatre: A Historiographical Handbook*. Westport: Greenwood, 1984.

Wickham, Glynne. *The Medieval Theatre*. 3rd ed. New York: Cambridge UP, 1987.

Woolf, Rosemary. *The English Mystery Plays*. Berkeley: U of California P, 1972.

Wright, Stephen K. "The Betrayer's Art: Translating Medieval Drama for Modern Readers." *Research Opportunities in Renaissance Drama* 35 (1996): 85–96.

RENAISSANCE DRAMA

Adams, John C. *The Globe Playhouse*. 2nd ed. New York: Barnes, 1961.

Altman, Joel B. *The Tudor Play of Mind: Rhetorical Inquiry and the Development of Elizabethan Drama*. Berkeley: U of California P, 1978.

Axton, Richard. *European Drama of the Early Middle Ages*. London: Hutchinson, 1974.

Bevington, David. *From Mankind to Marlowe: Growth of Structure in the Popular Drama of Tudor England*. Cambridge: Harvard UP, 1962.

Bradbrook, Muriel C. *The Growth and Structure of Elizabethan Comedy*. London: Chatto, 1955.

Braunmuller, A. R., and Michael Hathaway. *The Cambridge Companion to Renaissance Drama*. New York: Cambridge UP, 1990.

Bush, Douglas. *The Renaissance and English Humanism*. Toronto: U of Toronto P, 1939.

Bushnell, Rebecca W. *Tragedies of Tyrants: Political Thought and Theater in the English Renaissance*. Ithaca: Cornell UP, 1990.

Cairns, Christopher, ed. *The Renaissance Theatre: Texts, Performance, Design*. Aldershot: Ashgate, 1999.

Cartwright, Kent. *Theatre and Humanism: English Drama in the Sixteenth Century*. Cambridge: Cambridge UP, 1999.

Cerasano, S. P., and Marion Wynne-Davies, eds. *Readings in Renaissance Women's Drama: Criticism, History, and Performance, 1594–1998*. London: Routledge, 1998.

Chambers, E. K. *The Elizabethan Stage*. 4 vols. Oxford: Clarendon, 1923.

Coyle, Martin. "*Hamlet*, Gertrude and the Ghost: The Punishment of Women in Renaissance Drama." *Q/W/E/R/T/Y* 6 (1996): 29–38.

Farnham, W. *The Medieval Heritage of Elizabethan Tragedy*. Berkeley: U of California P, 1936.

Findaly, Alison. *A Feminist Perspective on Renaissance Drama*. Oxford: Blackwell Publishers, 1999.

Fumerton, Patricia, and Simon Hunt, eds. *Renaissance Culture and the Everyday*. Philadelphia: U of Philadelphia P, 1999.

Happe, Peter. *English Drama Before Shakespeare*. London: Longman, 1999.

Hussey, Maurice. *The World of Shakespeare and His Contemporaries: A Visual Approach*. New York: Viking, 1972.

Kernodle, George. *From Art to Theatre: Form and Convention in the Renaissance*. Chicago: U of Chicago P, 1944.

Lea, Kathleen M. *Italian Popular Comedy: A Study of the Commedia dell'Arte, 1560–1620*. 2 vols. Oxford: Clarendon, 1934.

Leggatt, Alexander. *Introduction to English Renaissance Comedy*. Manchester: Manchester UP, 1999.

Leinwand, Theodore B. *Theatre, Finance, and Society in Early Modern England*. Cambridge: Cambridge UP, 1999.

Loomba, Ania. *Gender, Race, and Renaissance Drama.* New York: Manchester UP, 1989.

Marcus, Leah S. *Unediting the Renaissance: Shakespeare, Marlowe, Milton.* London: Routledge, 1996.

Masten, Jeffrey, and Wendy Wall. *Renaissance Drama.* Evanston: Northwestern UP, 1999.

McLuskie, Kathleen. *Renaissance Dramatists.* Atlantic Highlands: Humanities International, 1989.

Nicoll, Allardyce. *The World of Harlequin.* Cambridge: Cambridge UP, 1963.

Rose, Mary Beth. *The Expense of Spirit: Love and Sexuality in English Renaissance Drama.* Ithaca: Cornell UP, 1988.

Rose, Mary Beth, ed. *Renaissance Dramatic Culture.* Evanston: Northwestern UP, 1998.

Tetzell, Kurt von Rosador. "The Power of Magic: From Endimion to *The Tempest.*" *Shakespeare Survey* 43 (1991): 1–13.

Waith, Eugene M. *Patterns and Perspectives in English Renaissance Drama.* Newark: U of Delaware P, 1988.

Welsford, Enid. *The Court Masque.* Cambridge: Cambridge UP, 1927.

White, Martin. *Renaissance Drama in Action: An Introduction to Aspects of Theatre Practice and Performance.* London: Routledge, 1998.

Wind, Edgar. *Pagan Mysteries in the Renaissance.* New Haven: Yale UP, 1958.

Woodbridge, Linda. *Woman and the English Renaissance: Literature and the Nature of Womankind, 1540–1620.* Urbana: U of Illinois P, 1984.

Yates, Frances A. *Theatre of the World.* Chicago: U of Chicago P, 1969.

LATE SEVENTEENTH- AND EIGHTEENTH-CENTURY DRAMA

Barber, Charles L. *The Idea of Honour in the English Drama, 1591–1700.* Stockholm: Göteborg, 1957.

Brandon, James R. ed. *Chūshingura: Studies in Kabuki and the Puppet Theater.* Honolulu: U of Hawaii P, 1982.

Brandon, James R., and Samuel L. Leiter, eds. *Kabuki Plays on Stage: Darkness and Desire, 1804–1864.* Honolulu: U of Hawaii P, 2002.

Cox, Jeffrey N. *In the Shadows of Romance.* Athens: Ohio UP, 1987.

Ernst, Earle. *The Kabuki Theatre.* rev. ed. Honolulu: U of Hawaii P, 1974.

Grene, Nicholas. *Shakespeare, Jonson, Molière: The Comic Contract.* Totowa: Barnes, 1980.

Holland, Norman N. *The First Modern Comedies: The Significance of Etherege, Wycherley, and Congreve.* Cambridge: Harvard UP, 1959.

Hume, Robert. *The Rakish Stage: Studies in English Drama, 1660–1800.* Carbondale: Southern Illinois UP, 1983.

Kaplan, Deborah. "Representing the Nation: Restoration Comedies on the Early Twentieth-Century London Stage." *Theatre Survey* 36.2 (1995): 37–61.

Keene, Donald. *Bunraku, the Art of the Japanese Puppet Theatre.* Tokyo and Palo Alto: Kodansha International, 1965.

Leiter, Samuel L. *A Kabuki Reader: History and Performance (Japan in the Modern World).* Armonk: M.E. Sharpe, 2001.

Loftis, John, ed. *Restoration Drama.* New York: Oxford UP, 1966.

Lynch, Kathleen M. *The Social Mode of Restoration Comedy.* New York: Farrar, 1975.

Marshall, Geoffrey. *Restoration Serious Drama.* Norman: U of Oklahoma P, 1975.

McMillin, Scott, ed. *Restoration and Eighteenth-Century Comedy.* 2nd ed. New York: Norton, 1997.

Nicoll, Allardyce. *A History of Restoration Drama, 1600–1700.* New York: Cambridge UP, 1923.

Owen, Susan J. *Restoration Theatre and Crisis.* Oxford: Clarendon P, 1996.

Peters, Julie Stone. "'Things Govern'd by Words': Late Seventeenth-Century Comedy and the Reformers." *English Studies* 68 (1987): 142–53.

Powell, Jocelyn. *Restoration Theatre Production.* Boston: Routledge, 1984.

Price, Cecil. *Theatre in the Age of Garrick.* Oxford: Oxford UP, 1973.

Richards, K. R., ed. *Essays on the Eighteenth Century English Stage.* London: Methuen, 1972.

Rothstein, Eric. *The Designs of Carolean Comedy.* Carbondale: Southern Illinois UP, 1988.

Scott, A. C. *The Kabuki Theatre of Japan.* Mineola: Dover Publications, 1999.

Stynan, J. L. *Restoration Comedy in Performance.* New York: Cambridge UP, 1986.

Turnell, Martin. *The Classical Movement: Studies in Corneille, Molière, and Racine.* New York: New Directions, 1948.

NINETEENTH-CENTURY DRAMA THROUGH THE TURN OF THE TWENTIETH CENTURY

Bank, Rosemarie K. *Theatre Culture in America, 1825–1860.* Cambridge Studies in American Theatre and Drama. Cambridge: Cambridge UP, 1997.

Bentley, Eric. *The Playwright as Thinker: A Study of Drama in Modern Times.* New York: Harcourt, 1967.

Bogard, Travis, ed. *Modern Drama: Essays in Criticism.* New York: Oxford UP, 1965.

Booth, Michael. *English Melodrama.* London: Jenkins, 1965.

Brustein, Robert. *The Theatre of Revolt.* Boston: Little, 1964.

Cole, Toby, ed. *Playwrights on Playwriting: The Meaning and Making of Modern Drama from Ibsen to Ionesco.* New York: Hill, 1960.

Detsi-Diamanti, Zoe. *Early American Women Dramatists, 1775–1860.* Garland Studies in American Popular History and Culture. New York: Garland, 1998.

Driver, Tom Faw. *Romantic Quest and Modern Query: A History of the Modern Theatre.* New York: Delacorte, 1970.

Finney, Gail. *Women in Modern Drama: Freud, Feminism, and European Theater at the Turn of the Century.* Ithaca: Cornell UP, 1989.

Fisher, Judith L., and Stephen Watt, eds. *When They Weren't Doing Shakespeare: Essays on Nineteenth-Century British and American Theatre.* Athens: U of Georgia P, 1989.

Gilman, Richard. *The Making of Modern Drama: A Study of Buchner, Ibsen, Strindberg, Chekhov, Pirandello, Brecht, Beckett, Handke.* New York: Farrar, 1974.

Jewett, William. *Fatal Autonomy: Romantic Drama and the Rhetoric of Agency.* Ithaca: Cornell UP, 1997.

Krasner, David. *Resistance, Parody, and Double Consciousness in African American Theatre, 1895–1910.* Basingstoke: Macmillan, 1997.

Marker, Fredrick J., and Christopher Innes, eds. *Modernism in European Drama: Ibsen, Strindberg, Pirandello, Beckett.* Toronto: U of Toronto P, 1998.

Newey, Katharine. "Melodrama and Metatheatre: Theatricality in the Nineteenth Century Theatre." *Journal of Dramatic Theory and Criticism* 11.2 (1997): 85–100.

Quinsey, Katherine M., ed. *Broken Boundaries: Women and Feminism in Restoration Drama.* Lexington: U of Kentucky P, 1996.

Riis, Thomas. "Opera and the Operatic, Drama and the Melodramatic: What Was the State of Things in Nineteenth-Century America?" *Nineteenth Century Theatre* 23.1–2 (1995): 76–89.

Stynan, J. L. *Modern Drama in Theory and Practice.* 3 vols. New York: Cambridge UP, 1980.

Valency, Maurice Jacques. *The Flower and the Castle: An Introduction to Modern Drama.* New York: Schocken, 1982.

Whitaker, Thomas R. *Fields of Play in Modern Drama.* Princeton: Princeton UP, 1977.

Williams, Raymond. *Drama from Ibsen to Eliot.* New York: Oxford UP, 1953.

DRAMA IN THE EARLY AND MID-TWENTIETH CENTURY

Artaud, Antonin. *The Theatre and Its Double.* Trans. Mary C. Richards. New York: Grove, 1958.

Bentley, Eric. *The Theatre of Commitment and Other Essays on Drama in Our Society.* New York: Atheneum, 1967.

Blau, Herbert, *The Impossible Theatre: A Manifesto.* New York: Macmillan, 1964.

Bogard, Travis, and William I. Oliver, eds. *Modern Drama: Essays in Criticism.* New York: Oxford UP, 1965.

Booth, Michael R., and Joel H. Kaplan, eds. *The Edwardian Theatre: Essays on Performance and the Stage.* Cambridge: Cambridge UP, 1996.

Bordman, Gerald Martin. *American Theatre: A Chronicle of Comedy and Drama, 1930–1969.* New York: Oxford UP, 1996.

Brater, Enoch, and Ruby Cohn, eds. *Around the Absurd: Essays on Modern and Postmodern Drama.* Ann Arbor: U of Michigan P, 1990.

Brockett, Oscar G. *History of the Theatre.* 5th ed. Boston: Allyn, 1987.

Brook, Peter. *The Empty Space.* New York: Avon, 1968.

Cohn, Ruby. *From Desire to Godot: Pocket Theater of Postwar Paris.* Berkeley: U of California P, 1987.

Davidson, Clifford, C. J. Gianakaris, and John H. Stroupe, eds. *Drama in the Twentieth Century: Comparative and Critical Essays.* New York: AMS, 1984.

Demastes, William W., and Katherine E. Kelly. *British Playwrights, 1880–1956: A Research and Production Sourcebook.* Westport: Greenwood, 1996.

Esslin, Martin. *The Theatre of the Absurd.* Woodstock, NY: Overlook, 1973.

Fearnow, Mark. *The American Stage and the Great Depression: A Cultural History of the Grotesque.* Cambridge Studies in American Theatre and Drama. Cambridge: Cambridge UP, 1997.

Gassner, John. *Theatre at the Crossroads.* New York: Holt, 1960.

Goldberg, RosaLee. *Performance: Live Art 1909 to the Present.* New York: Abrams, 1979.

Hebel, Udo J. "Early American Women Playwrights (1916–1930) and the Remapping of Twentieth-Century American Drama." *Arbeiten aus Anglistik und Amerikanistik* 21.2 (1996): 267–86.

Kernan, Alvin B., ed. *The Modern American Theater: A Collection of Critical Essays.* Englewood Cliffs: Prentice, 1967.

Kirby, Michael. *A Formalist Theatre.* Philadelphia: U of Pennsylvania P, 1987.

Mason, Jeffrey D., and Ellen Gainer, eds. *Performing America: Cultural Nationalism in American Theater.* Ann Arbor: U of Michigan P, 1999.

Miller, Jordan Yale. *American Drama between the Wars: A Critical History.* Twayne's Critical History of American Drama. Boston: Twayne, 1997.

Murray, Christopher. "Modern Drama from Ibsen to Fugard." *Moderna Sprak* 88.1 (1994): 98–100.

Orr, John. *Tragic Drama and Modern Society: Studies in Social and Literary Theory of Drama from 1870 to the Present.* New York: Macmillan, 1981.

Piscator, Erwin. *The Political Theatre: A History, 1914–1929.* Trans. Hugh Rorrison. London: Eyre Methuen, 1980.

Roose-Evans, James. *Experimental Theatre: From Stanislavsky to Today.* 2nd ed. London: Studio Vista, 1973.

Smith, Wendy. *Real Life Drama: The Group Theatre and America, 1931–1940.* New York: Knopf, 1990.

Szilassy, Zolt N. *American Theater of the 1960s.* Carbondale: U of Illinois P, 1986.

CONTEMPORARY DRAMA

Andreach, Robert J. *Creating Self in the Contemporary American Theatre.* Carbondale: Southern Illinois UP, 1998.

Betsko, Kathleen, and Rachel Koenig. *Interviews with Contemporary Women Playwrights.* New York: Beech Tree, 1987.

Bigsby, Christopher W. E. *Contemporary American Playwrights.* Cambridge: Cambridge UP, 1999.

Blau, Herbert. *Eye of Prey: Subversions of the Postmodern.* Bloomington: Indiana UP, 1987.

Blumenthal, Eileen. *Joseph Chaikin: Exploring at the Boundaries of Theatre.* New York: Cambridge UP, 1984.

Brecht, Stefan. *The Theatre of Visions: Robert Wilson.* Frankfurt am Main: Suhrkamp, 1978.

Carpenter, Charles A. *Modern Drama: Scholarship and Criticism, 1981–1990: An International Bibliography.* Toronto: U of Toronto P, 1997.

Cheney, Sheldon. *New Movement in the Theatre.* Westport: Greenwood, 1971.

Coen, Stephanie. "No Comparisons." *American Theatre* 11.6 (1994): 26.

DiGaetani, John L. "David Ives." *Interviews with Contemporary Playwrights.* Ed. John L. DiGaetani. Westport: Greenwood, 1991. 183–90.

Dobrez, Livio A. C. *The Existential and Its Exits: Literary and Philosophical Perspectives on the Works of Beckett, Ionesco, Genet, and Pinter.* New York: St. Martin's, 1986.

Grotowski, Jerzy. *Towards a Poor Theatre.* New York: Simon, 1968.

Hart, Lynda, ed. *Making a Spectacle: Feminist Essays on Contemporary Women's Theatre.* Ann Arbor: U of Michigan P, 1989.

Hayman, Ronald. *Theatre and Anti-Theatre: New Movements since Beckett.* New York: Oxford UP, 1979.

Heilpern, John. *How Good Is David Mamet Anyway? Writings on Theatre and Why It Matters.* New York: Routledge, 1999.

Hill, Errol, ed. *The Theatre of Black Americans.* 2 vols. Englewood Cliffs: Prentice, 1980.

Inverso, MaryBeth. *The Gothic Impulse in Contemporary Drama.* Ann Arbor: U of Michigan P, 1990.

Marranca, Bonnie, ed. *The Theatre of Images.* New York: Drama Book Specialists, 1977.

McDonough, Carla J. *Staging Masculinity: Male Identity in Contemporary American Drama.* Jefferson: McFarland, 1997.

Orr, John. *Tragicomedy and Contemporary Culture: Play and Performance from Beckett to Shepard.* Ann Arbor: U of Michigan P, 1990.

Parker, Dorothy. *Essays on Modern American Drama: Williams, Miller, Albee, and Shepard.* Toronto: U of Toronto P, 1987.

Peacock, D. Keith. *Thatcher's Theatre: British Theatre and Drama in the Eighties.* Contributions in Drama and Theatre Studies 88. Westport: Greenwood, 1999.

Roudané, Matthew Charles. *American Drama since 1960: A Critical History.* New York: Twayne, 1997.

Savran, David. *In Their Own Words: Contemporary American Playwrights.* New York: Theatre Communications Group, 1988.

Schechner, Richard. *Environmental Theater.* New York: Hawthorn, 1973.

Sinfield, Alan. *Out on Stage: Lesbian and Gay Theatre in the Twentieth Century.* New Haven: Yale UP, 1999.

Smith, Iris. "Authors in America: Tony Kushner, Arthur Miller, and Anna Deveare Smith." *Centennial Review* 40.1 (1996): 125–42.

Watt, Stephen. *Postmodern Drama: Reading the Contemporary Stage.* Ann Arbor: U of Michigan P, 1998.

Wellworth, George E. *The Theater of Protest and Paradox.* New York: New York UP, 1971.

Selected References for Playwrights and Plays

AESCHYLUS

Brooks, Otis. *Cosmos and Tragedy: An Essay on the Meaning of Aeschylus.* Chapel Hill: U of North Carolina P, 1981.

Conacher, D. J. *Aeschylus' Oresteia: A Literary Commentary.* Toronto: U of Toronto P, 1987.

Gannon, J. F. "Aeschylus's *Agamemnon.*" *Classical Quarterly* 39.1 (1989): 254–57.

Goldhill, Simon. *Language, Sexuality, Narrative, the Oresteia.* Cambridge (Cambridgeshire); New York: Cambridge UP, 1984.

Harrington, J. C. *Aeschylus.* New Haven: Yale UP, 1986.

Ireland, S. *Aeschylus, Greece and Rome.* 1947. Classical Association 18. Oxford: Clarendon, 1986.

Konishi, H. "Agamemnon's Reason for Yielding." *American Journal of Philology* 110 (1989): 210–22.

Podlecki, Anthony J. *The Political Background of Aeschylean Tragedy.* Ann Arbor: U of Michigan P, 1966.

Rosenmeyer, Thomas G. *The Art of Aeschylus.* Berkeley: U of California P, 1982.

Spatz, Lois. *Aeschylus.* Twayne's World Authors Series 675. Boston: Twayne, 1982.

Thalmann, W. G. "Aeschylus's Physiology of the Emotions." *American Journal of Philology* 107 (1986): 489–511.

Thomson, George Derwent. *Aeschylus and Athens: A Study in the Social Origins of Drama.* 2nd ed. London: Lawrence & Wishart, 1967.

Valentini, Valentina. "The 'Orestei' of the Soìetas Raffaelo Sanzio." *Performance Research* 2.3 (1997): 58–64.

Winnington-Ingram, R. P. [Reginald Pepys]. *Studies in Aeschylus.* New York: Cambridge UP, 1983.

EDWARD ALBEE

Bigsby, C. W. E. *Albee.* Edinburgh, Oliver & Boyd, 1969.

Bloom, Harold, ed. *Edward Albee (Modern Critical Views)*. New York: Chelsea House, 2000.

Gussow, Mel. *Edward Albee: A Singular Journey*: A Biography. New York: Simon & Schuster, 1999.

Hayman, Ronald. *Edward Albee*. London, Heinemann, 1971.

Horn, Barbara Lee. *Edward Albee: A Research and Production Sourcebook*. Westport: Praeger, 2003.

Mann, Bruce J., ed. *Edward Albee: A Casebook*. New York: Routledge, 2003.

McCarthy, Gerry. *Edward Albee*. New York: St. Martin's Press, 1987.

Paolucci, Anne. *From Tension to Tonic: The Plays of Edward Albee*. Wilmington, DE: Griffon House Press, 2000.

Roudané, Matthew Charles. *Understanding Edward Albee*. Columbia, S.C.: U of South Carolina P, 1987.

ARISTOPHANES

Bowie, A. M. *Aristophanes: Myth, Ritual, and Comedy*. Cambridge UP, 1996.

Colvin, Stephen. *Dialect in Aristophanes and the Politics of Language in Ancient Greek Literature*. Oxford: Clarendon, 1999.

Dane, Joseph A. *Parody: Critical Concepts versus Literary Practices, Aristophanes to Sterne*. Norman: U of Oklahoma P, 1988.

Deardon, C. W. *The Stage of Aristophanes*. London: Athlone, 1976.

Dover, K. J. *Aristophanic Comedy*. Berkeley: U of California P, 1972.

Forrest, W. G. "Aristophanes' *Lysistrata*." *Classical Quarterly* 45.1 (1995): 240–41.

Harriott, Rosemary. *Aristophanes: Poet and Dramatist*. Baltimore: Johns Hopkins UP, 1986.

Henderson, Jeffrey. *Aristophanes' Lysistrata*. New York: Oxford UP, 1987.

Matz, D. "Ensuring That the Flea Wears Wax Slippers When Teaching Aristophanes and a One-Person Reenactment of a Choral Entry from *Lysistrata* in the Classroom." *Classical Journal* 87.1 (1991): 55–58.

McLeish, Kenneth. *The Theatre of Aristophanes*. New York: Taplinger, 1980.

Murray, Gilbert. *Aristophanes*. Oxford: Clarendon, 1933.

Reckford, Kenneth. *Aristophanes' Old-and-New Comedy*. Chapel Hill: U of North Carolina P, 1987.

Russo, Carlo Ferdinando. *Aristophanes: An Author for the Stage*. London: Routledge, 1997.

Segal, Erich, ed. *Oxford Readings in Aristophanes*. Oxford: Oxford UP, 1996.

Ussher, Robert Glenn. *Aristophanes*. New York: Oxford UP, 1979.

SAMUEL BECKETT

Andonian, Cathleen Culotta, ed. *The Critical Response to Samuel Beckett*. Westport, CT: Greenwood, 1998.

Astro, Alan. *Understanding Beckett*. Columbia: U of South Carolina P, 1990.

Athanason, Arthur N. Endgame: *The Ashbin Play*. New York: Twayne, 1993.

Begam, Richard. *Samuel Beckett and the End of Modernity*. Stanford: Stanford UP, 1996.

Beja, Morris, S. E. Gontarski, and Pierre Astier, eds. *Samuel Beckett: Humanistic Perspectives*. Columbus: Ohio State UP, 1983.

Ben-Zvi, Linda, ed. *Women in Beckett: Performance and Critical Perspectives*. Urbana: U of Illinois P, 1990.

Brater, Enoch, ed. *Beckett at 80: Beckett in Context*. New York: Oxford UP, 1986.

———. *Why Beckett: With 122 Illustrations*. New York: Thames, 1989.

Buning, Marius, and Lois Oppenheim, eds. *Beckett in the 1990s*. Amsterdam: Rodopi, 1993.

Burkman, Katherine. *Myth and Ritual in the Plays of Samuel Beckett*. Rutherford: Fairleigh Dickinson UP, 1987.

Butler, Lance S., and Robin J. Davis, eds. *Rethinking Beckett: A Collection of Critical Essays*. New York: St. Martin's, 1990.

Cohn, Ruby. *Just Play: Beckett's Theater*. Princeton: Princeton UP, 1980.

———, ed. *Samuel Beckett: A Collection of Criticism*. New York: McGraw, 1975.

Connor, Steven, ed. *Gender in Transition*: Waiting for Godot and Endgame. New York: St. Martin's, 1992.

Cronin, Anthony. *Samuel Beckett: The Last Modernist*. New York. Harper, 1997.

Dearlove, J. E. *Accommodating the Chaos: Samuel Beckett's Nonrelational Art*. Durham: Duke UP, 1982.

Doll, Mary Aswell. *Beckett and Myth: An Archetypal Approach*. Syracuse: Syracuse UP, 1988.

Esslin, Martin, ed. *Samuel Beckett: A Collection of Critical Essays*. Englewood Cliffs: Prentice, 1965.

Fletcher, Beryl S., et al. *A Student's Guide to the Plays of Samuel Beckett*. 2nd ed. Boston: Faber, 1985.

Fletcher, John. *Beckett: The Playwright*. New York: Hill, 1985.

Gidal, Peter. *Understanding Beckett*. New York: St. Martin's, 1986.

Gontarski, S. E. *Beckett's* Happy Days: *A Manuscript Study*. Columbus: Ohio State UP, 1977.

———. *On Beckett: Essays and Criticism*. New York: Grove, 1986.

Gordon, Lois G. *The World of Samuel Beckett*. New Haven: Yale UP, 1996.

Kenner, Hugh. *A Reader's Guide to Samuel Beckett*. New York: Farrar, 1973.

Knowlson, James. *Damned to Fame: The Life of Samuel Beckett*. London: Bloomsbury, 1997.

Lyons, Charles R. *Samuel Beckett*. New York: Grove, 1983.

Rosen, Steven J. *Samuel Beckett and the Pessimistic Tradition*. New Brunswick: Rutgers UP, 1976.

Smith, Joseph H., ed. *The World of Samuel Beckett*. Baltimore: Johns Hopkins UP, 1991.

Tassi, Marguerite. "Shakespeare and Beckett Revisited: A Phenomenology of Theatre." *Comparative Drama* 31 (1997): 248–76.

Uhlmann, Anthony. *Beckett and Poststructuralism.* Cambridge: Cambridge UP, 1999.

Worth, Katharine. *Samuel Beckett's Theatre: Life-Journeys.* Oxford: Clarendon, 1999.

———. Waiting for Godot *and* Happy Days. Basingstoke: Macmillan, 1990.

Aphra Behn

Armistid, J. M. *Four Restoration Playwrights: A Reference Guide to Thomas Shadwell, Aphra Behn, Nathaniel Lee, and Thomas Otway.* Boston: Hall, 1984.

Copeland, Nancy. "'Once a Whore and Ever'? Whore and Virgin in *The Rover* and Its Antecedents." *Early Women Writers: 1600–1720.* Ed. Anita Pacheco. London: Longman, 1998. 149–59.

DeRitter, Jones. "The Gypsy, The Rover, and the Wanderer: Aphra Behn's Revision of Thomas Killigrew." *Restoration: Studies in English Literary Culture, 1660–1700* 10.2 (1986): 82–92.

Diamond, Elin. "Gestus and Signature in Aphra Behn's *The Rover.*" *Early Women Writers: 1600–1720.* Ed. Anita Pacheco. London: Longman, 1998. 160–82.

Gallagher, Catherine. "Who Was That Masked Woman? The Prostitute and the Playwright in the Comedies of Aphra Behn." *Last Laughs.* Ed. Gina Barreca. New York: Gordon, 1989. 23–42.

Jones, Jane. "New Light on the Background and Early Life of Aphra Behn." *Notes and Queries* 37 (1990): 288–93.

Link, Frederick M. *Aphra Behn.* Boston: Twayne, 1969.

Lussier, Mark. "'The Vile Mercandize of Fortune': Women, Economy, and Desire in Aphra Behn." *Women's Studies* 18.4 (1991): 379–93.

Mendelson, Sara Heller. *The Mental World of Stuart Women: Three Studies.* Amherst: U of Massachusetts P, 1987.

Munns, Jessica. "'I by a Double Right Thy Bounties Claim': Aphra Behn and Sexual Space." *Curtain Calls: British and American Women and the Theater, 1660–1820.* Ed. Mary Anne Schofield and Cecilia Macheski. Athens: Ohio UP, 1991.

Szilagyi, Stephen. "The Sexual Politics of Behn's *Rover* — After Patriarchy." *Studies in Philology* 95 (1998): 435–55.

Todd, Janet. *Aphra Behn.* New Casebooks. Basingstoke: Macmillan, 1999.

———. *Aphra Behn Studies.* Cambridge: Cambridge UP, 1996.

———. *The Critical Fortunes of Aphra Behn.* Columbia: Camden House, 1998.

———. *The Secret Life of Aphra Behn.* London: Pandora, 1999.

Wiseman, S. J. *Aphra Behn.* Plymouth: Northcote House, 1996.

Bertolt Brecht

Bai, Ronnie. "Dances with Mei Lanfang: Brecht and the Alienation Effect." *Comparative Drama* 32 (1998): 389–433.

Bail, Henry, and Carol Martin, eds. *Bertolt Brecht: A Critical Anthology.* London: Routledge, 1999.

Beckley, Richard. "Brecht: The Reality and the Ideal." *Gestus* 2.1 (1986): 37–46.

Bodek, Richard. *Proletarian Performance in Weimar Berlin: Agitprop, Chorus, and Brecht.* Columbia: Camden House, 1997.

Brecht, Bertolt. *Brecht on Theatre: The Development of an Aesthetic.* Ed. and trans. John Willett. New York: Hill, 1964.

Brown, Russell E. *Intimacy and Intimidation: Three Essays on Bertolt Brecht.* Stuttgart: Steiner, 1990.

Bryant-Bertail, Sarah. "Women, Space, Ideology: Mutter Courage und Ihre Kinder." *The Brecht Yearbook* 12 (1983): 43–61.

Cima, Gay Gibson, Maarten Van Dijk, Liz Diamond, et al. "Brecht/'Brecht': A Symposium." *Theater* 25.2 (1994): 24–41.

Demetz, Peter, ed. *Brecht: A Collection of Critical Essays.* Englewood Cliffs: Prentice, 1962.

Docherty, Brian, ed. *Twentieth-Century European Drama.* New York: St. Martin's, 1994.

Eddershaw, Margaret. *Performing Brecht.* New York: Routledge, 1996.

Esslin, Martin. *Brecht: The Man and His Works.* Garden City: Doubleday, 1971.

Ewen, Frederick. *Bertolt Brecht: His Life, His Art and His Times.* New York: Citadel, 1967.

Fuegi, John. *Bertolt Brecht: Chaos, According to Plan.* New York: Cambridge UP, 1987.

———. *Brecht and Company: Sex, Politics, and the Making of Modern Drama.* New York: Grove, 1994.

Giles, Steve, and Rodney Livingstone, eds. *Bertolt Brecht: Centenary Essays.* Amsterdam: Rodopi, 1998.

Gleitman, Claire. "All in the Family: *Mother Courage* and the Ideology in the Gestus." *Comparative Drama* 25.2 (1991): 147–67.

Gray, Ronald. *Bertolt Brecht.* New York: Grove, 1967.

Harrington, R. "*Mother Courage and Her Children.*" *Appalachian Journal* 24.2 (1997): 141–43.

Hill, Claude. *Bertolt Brecht.* New York: Twayne, 1975.

Jameson, Fredric. *Brecht and Method.* London: Verso, 1998.

Kleber, Pia, and Colin Visser, eds. *Re-Interpreting Brecht: His Influence on Contemporary Drama and Film.* Cambridge: Cambridge UP, 1990.

Mews, Siegfried, ed. *A Bertolt Brecht Reference Companion.* Westport: Greenwood, 1997.

———, comp. *Critical Essays on Bertolt Brecht.* Boston: Hall, 1989.

Munk, Erika, ed. "On Brecht." *Theater* 25.2 (1994): 9–55.

Potter, Robert. "Writing *Mother Courage.*" *The Brecht Yearbook* 24 (1999): 14–23.

Rouse, John. "Brecht and the Contradictory Actor." *Theatre Journal* 36.1 (1984): 25–41.

Schoeps, Karl Heinz. *Bertolt Brecht: Life, Work, and Criticism.* Fredericton: York, 1989.

Silberman, Marc. "A Postmodernized Brecht?" *Theatre Journal* 45.1 (1993): 1–19.

Spalter, Max. *Brecht's Tradition.* Baltimore: Johns Hopkins UP, 1967.

Speirs, Ronald. *Bertolt Brecht.* New York: St. Martin's, 1987.

Stern, Guy. "Enriching *Mother Courage.*" *Communications from the International Brecht Society* 25.1 (1996): 60–68.

Thomson, Peter, and Glendyr Sachs, eds. *The Cambridge Companion to Brecht.* Cambridge: Cambridge UP, 1994.

Tian, Min. "Alienation-Effect for Whom? Brecht's (Mis)interpretation of the Classical Chinese Theatre." *Asian Theatre Journal* 14.2 (1997): 200–22.

Willet, John. *Brecht in Context: Comparative Approaches.* 2nd ed. London: Methuen, 1998.

———. *The Theatre of Bertolt Brecht.* New York, 1959.

Willits, Ross D. "The Through-line of Meaning in *Mother Courage* and Brecht." *Text and Presentation.* Ed. Karelisa Hartigan. Lanham: UP of America, 1989.

PEDRO CALDERÓN DE LA BARCA

Cascardi, Anthony J. *The Limits of Illusion: A Critical Study of Calderón.* Cambridge, Cambridge UP, 1984.

De Armas, Frederick Alfred, David M. Gitlitz, and José A. Madrigal, eds. *Critical Perspectives on Calderón de la Barca.* Lincoln: Society of Spanish and Spanish-American Studies, 1986.

Delgado, Manuel. *The Calderónian Stage: Body and Soul.* Lewisburg: Bucknell UP, 1997.

Greer, Margaret Rich. *The Play of Power: Mythological Court Dramas of Calderón de la Barca.* Princeton: Princeton UP, 1991.

Hesse, Everett W. *Calderón de la Barca.* New York: Twayne, 1967.

Honig, Edwin. *Calderón and the Seizures of Honor.* Cambridge: Harvard UP, 1972.

Levin, Leslie. *Metaphors of Conversion in Seventeenth Century Spanish Drama.* Colección Tamesis. Serie A, Monografías 174. Woodbridge: Tamesis, 1999.

Lund, Henry. *Pedro Calderón de la Barca: A Biography.* Edingburg: Andres Noriega P, 1963.

McGaha, Michael D., ed. *Approaches to the Theatre of Calderón.* Washington: UP of America, 1982.

O'Conner, Thomas Austin. *Myth and Mythology in the Theatre of Pedro Calderón de la Barca.* San Antonio: Trinity UP, 1988.

Parker, Alexander Augustine. *The Allegorical Drama of Calderón: An Introduction to the Autos Sacramentales.* Oxford: Dolphin, 1991.

———. *The Mind and Art of Calderón: Essays on the Comedias.* Cambridge: Cambridge UP, 1988.

Sloman, Albert E. *The Dramatic Craftsmanship of Calderón.* Oxford: Oxford UP, 1958.

Suscavage, Charlene E. *Calderón: The Imagery of Tragedy.* New York: P. Lang, 1991.

Wardropper, Bruce W., ed. *Critical Essays in the Theatre of Calderón.* New York: New York UP, 1965.

ANTON CHEKHOV

Baldwin, James. "Chekhov, the Rediscovery of Realism: Michel Saint-Denis' Productions of *Three Sisters* and *The Cherry Orchard.*" *Theatre Notebook* 53.2 (1999): 96–115.

Barricelli, Jean-Pierre, ed. *Chekhov's Great Plays: A Critical Anthology.* New York: New York UP, 1981.

Clayton, J. Douglas, ed. *Chekhov Then and Now: The Reception of Chekhov in World Culture.* New York: Peter Lang, 1997.

Eekman, Thomas A. *Critical Essays on Anton Chekhov.* Boston: Hall, 1989.

Emeljanow, Victor. *Chekhov: The Critical Heritage.* Boston: Routledge, 1981.

Hingley, Ronald. *Chekhov: A Biographical and Critical Study.* New York: Barnes, 1966.

Jackson, Robert Louis. *Chekhov: A Collection of Critical Essays.* Englewood Cliffs: Prentice, 1967.

Karlinsky, Simon, and Michael Heim, eds. *Anton Chekhov's Life and Thought: Selected Letters and Commentary.* Berkeley: U of California P, 1975.

Magarshak, David. *Chekhov the Dramatist.* New York: Hill, 1960.

Meister, Charles. *Chekhov Criticism 1880 through 1986.* New York: McFarland, 1988.

Peace, Richard. *Chekhov: A Study of the Four Major Plays.* New Haven: Yale UP, 1983.

Rayfield, Donald. *Anton Chekhov: A Life.* London: Harper, 1997.

———. *Understanding Chekhov: A Critical Study of Chekhov's Prose and Drama.* Bristol: Bristol Classical, 1999.

Russell, Robert, and Andrew Barratt, eds. *Russian Theatre in the Age of Modernism.* New York: St. Martin's, 1990.

Senderovich, Savely. "*The Cherry Orchard:* Chekhov's Last Testament." *Russian Literature* 35 (1994): 223–42.

Senelick, Laurence. *The Chekhov Theatre: A Century of Plays in Performance.* Cambridge: Cambridge UP, 1999.

Stanislavsky, Konstantin. *My Life in Art.* New York: Routledge Chapman and Hall, 1924.

Stynan, J. L. *Chekhov in Performance.* Cambridge: Cambridge UP, 1971.

Toumanova, Princess Nina Andronikova. *Anton Chekhov: The Voice of Twilight Russia.* New York: Columbia UP, 1960.

Tulloch, John, Tom Burvill, and Andrew Hood. "Reinhabiting *The Cherry Orchard:* Class and History in

Performing Chekhov." *New Theatre Quarterly* 13 (1997): 318–28.

Valency, Maurice. *The Breaking String: The Plays of Anton Chekhov.* New York: Oxford UP, 1966.

Welleck, Rene, and Nonna D. Welleck, eds. *Chekhov: New Perspectives.* Englewood Cliffs: Prentice, 1984.

Williams, Lee J. *Anton Chekhov, the Iconoclast.* Scranton: U of Scranton P, 1989.

CHIKAMATSU MONZAEMON

Gerstle, C. Andrew. *Circles of Fantasy: Convention in the Plays of Chikamatsu.* Cambridge: Harvard UP, 1986.

———. "Heroic Honor: Chikamatsu and the Samurai Ideal." *Harvard Journal of Asiatic Studies* 57.2 (1997): 307–81.

Lee, William. "Chikamatsu and Dramatic Literature in the Meiji Period." *Inventing the Classics: Modernity, National Identity, and Japanese Literature.* Ed. Haruo Shirane and Tomi Suzuki. Stanford: Stanford UP, 2000. 179–98.

Matisoff, Susan K. "No as Transformed by Chikamatsu." *Journal of the Association of Teachers of Japanese* 11.2–3 (1976): 201–16.

Sasayama, Takashi. "Tragedy and Emotion: Shakespeare and Chikamatsu." *Shakespeare and the Japanese Stage.* Ed. Takashi Sasayama, J. R. Mulyrne, and Margaret Shwring. Cambridge: Cambridge UP, 1998. 145–58.

CARYL CHURCHILL

Aston, Elaine. *Caryl Churchill. Writers and Their Work.* Plymouth: Northcote House, 1997.

Brater, Enoch, and Ruby Cohn, eds. *Feminine Focus: The New Women Playwrights.* Oxford: Oxford UP, 1989.

Fitzsimmons, Linda. "'I Won't Turn Back for You or Anyone': Caryl Churchill's Socialist-Feminist Theatre." *Essays in Theatre* 6.1 (1987): 19–29.

Gardner, Janet E. "Caryl Churchill's *Top Girls:* Defining and Reclaiming Feminism in Thatcher's Britain." *New England Theatre Journal* 10 (1999): 89–110.

Marohl, Joseph. "De-Realised Women: Performance and Identity in Churchill's *Top Girls:* Essays from Modern Drama." *Contemporary British Drama 1970–1990.* Ed. Hersh Zeifman and Cynthia Zimmerman. Toronto: U of Toronto P, 1993. 307–22.

Nischik, Reingard M. "Betrayal Psychohistorically: The Representation of Emotions in the British Drama of Manners." *Anglistentag 1991 Dusseldorf.* Ed. Wilhelm B. Busse. Tubingen: Niemeyer, 1992. 189–204.

Rabillard, Sheila Mary, ed. *Essays on Caryl Churchill: Contemporary Representations.* Winnipeg: Blizzard, 1998.

Randall, Phyllis R., ed. *Caryl Churchill: A Casebook.* New York: Garland, 1988.

Tonnies, Merle. "(Post)modernist Play with New Purposes: The Functioning of Language in Contemporary British Drama." *Zeitschrift für Anglistick und Amerikanistik* 46 (1998): 325–37.

Vanden-Heuvel, Michael. "Performing Gender(s)." *Contemporary Literature* 35.4 (1994): 804–13.

EURIPIDES

Barlow, Shirley Anne. "Stereotype and Reversal in Euripides' *Medea.*" *Greece and Rome* 36 (1989): 158–71.

Burian, Peter, ed. *Directions in Euripidean Criticism.* Durham: Duke UP, 1985.

Collard, Christopher. *Euripides.* New York: Oxford UP, 1981.

Conacher, D. J. *Euripides and the Sophists: Some Dramatic Treatments of Philosophical Ideas.* London: Duckworth, 1998.

Foley, Helene P. "Medea's Divided Self." *Classical Antiquity* 8 (1989): 61–85.

———. *Ritual Irony: Poetry and Sacrifice in Euripides.* Ithaca: Cornell UP, 1985.

Halleran, Michael P. *Stagecraft in Euripides.* Totowa: Barnes, 1985.

Marks, Peter. "Theater Review: Anguish, Freeze-Dried and Served with Precision." *New York Times* 25 Sept. 1998: B1+.

Meagher, Robert E. *Mortal Vision: The Wisdom of Euripides.* New York: St. Martin's, 1989.

Michelini, Ann N. *Euripides and the Tragic Tradition.* Madison: U of Wisconsin P, 1987.

O'Connor, E. A. M. E. *Aspects of Human Sacrifice in the Tragedies of Euripides.* Amsterdam: Grüner, 1987.

Pucci, Pietro. *The Violence of Pity in Euripides'* Medea. Ithaca: Cornell UP, 1980.

Segal, Erich, ed. *Euripides: A Collection of Critical Essays.* Englewood Cliffs: Prentice, 1968.

Whitman, Cedric Hubbell. *Euripides and the Full Circle of Myth.* Cambridge: Harvard UP, 1974.

EVERYMAN

Bevington, David M. *From Mankind to Marlowe: Growth of Structure in the Popular Drama of Tudor England.* Cambridge: Harvard UP, 1962.

Cawley, A. C. *Everyman.* Manchester: Manchester UP, 1977.

———, ed. Everyman *and Medieval Miracle Plays.* New York: Dutton, 1977.

Cunningham, John. "Comedic and Liturgical Restoration in *Everyman.*" *Drama in the Middle Ages: Comparative and Critical Essays.* Second Series. Ed. Clifford Davidson and John H. Stroupe. New York: AMS, 1990.

Garner, Stanton B., Jr. "Theatricality in Mankind and *Everyman.*" *Studies in Philology* 84.3 (1987): 272–85.

Gilman, Donald, ed. Everyman *and Company: Essays on the Theme and Structure of the European Moral Play.* New York: AMS, 1989.

Pietropoli, Cecilia. "Towards a New *Everyman*: Medieval Drama as a Link between Classical and Renaissance Comedy." *International Conference on Aspects of European Medieval Drama*. 2 vols. Camerino: University degli Studi di Camerino, 1996.

Spinrad, Phoebe S. "The Last Temptation of *Everyman*." *Philological Quarterly* 64.2 (1985): 185–94.

Staub, August W., and Michael J. Hussey. "Saints and Cyborgs: Mystical Performance Spaces (Re)visioned." *Journal of Dramatic Theory and Criticism* 13.1 (1998): 177–82.

Tanner, Ron. "Humor in *Everyman* and the Middle English Morality Play." *Philological Quarterly* 70 (1991): 149–61.

White, D. Jerry. *Early English Drama*: Everyman *to 1580, A Reference Guide*. Boston: Hall, 1986.

BRIAN FRIEL

Baker, Charles. "'It's the Same Me, Isn't It?' The Language Question and Brian Friel's *Translations*." *Midwest Quarterly: A Journal of Contemporary Thought* 41.3 (2000): 264–75.

Delaney, Paul, ed. *Brian Friel in Conversation*. Ann Arbor: U Michigan P, 2000.

Friel, Brian. *Brian Friel: Essays, Diaries, Interviews 1964–1998*. Ed. Christopher Murray. London; New York: Faber, 2000.

Harp, Richard, ed. *A Companion to Brian Friel*. West Cornwall: Locust Hill, 2002.

Kerwin, William, ed. *Brian Friel: A Casebook*. New York: Garland, 1997.

Krause, David. "The Failed Words of Brian Friel." *Modern Drama* 40.3 (1997): 359–73.

McGrath, Francis Charles. *Brian Friel's (Post) Colonial Drama: Language, Illusion, and Politics*. Syracuse: Syracuse UP, 1999.

O'Brien, George. *Brian Friel: A Reference Guide, 1962–1992*. New York: Hall, 1995.

———. *The Diviner: The Art of Brian Friel*. Dublin: U College Dublin P, 1999.

———. "Meet Brian Friel." *Irish University Review* 29.1 (1999): 30–41.

Pine, Richard. *Brian Friel and Ireland's Drama*. London: Routledge, 1990.

ATHOL FUGARD

Barbera, Jack. "Athol Fugard Issue." *Twentieth-Century Literature* 39.4 (1993).

Benson, Mary. *Athol Fugard and Barney Simon: Bare Stage, A Few Props, Great Theatre*. Randburg: Ravan, 1997.

———. "Keeping an Appointment with the Future: The Theatre of Athol Fugard." *Theatre Quarterly* 7 (1977–78): 77–83.

Daymond, M. J., J. A. Jacobs, and Margaret Lenta, eds. *Momentum: On Recent South African Writing*. Pietermaritzburg: U of Natal P, 1984.

Durbach, Errol. " 'MASTER HAROLD'. . . *and the boys*: Athol Fugard and the Psychopathology of Apartheid." *Modern Drama* 30.4 (1987): 505–13.

Fugard, Athol. "Fugard on Actors, Actors on Fugard." *Theatre Quarterly* 7 (1977–78): 83–7.

———. "Fugard on Fugard." *Yale Theatre* 1 (Winter 1973): 41–54.

———. "Letter from Athol Fugard." *Classic* 1 (1966): 78–80.

———. *Notebooks 1960–1977*. New York: Knopf, 1983.

Gray, Stephen, ed. *Athol Fugard*. Southern Africa Literature Series 1. Johannesburg: McGraw, 1982.

Heywood, Christopher. *Aspects of South African Literature*. London: Heinemann, 1976.

Hoegberg, David. E. "'*Master Harold*' and the Bard: Education and Succession in Fugard and Shakespeare." *Comparative Drama* 29.4 (1996): 415–35.

Jordan, John O. "Life in the Theatre: Politics and Romance in 'MASTER HAROLD'. . . *and the boys*." *Twentieth-Century Literature* 39.4 (1993): 461–72.

Kavanagh, Robert Mshengu. *Theatre and Cultural Struggle in South Africa*. London: Zed, 1985.

Post, Robert M. "Racism in Athol Fugard's 'MASTER HAROLD'. . . *and the boys*." *World Literature Written in English* 30.1 (1990): 97–102.

Seidenspinner, Margarete. *Exploring the Labyrinth: Athol Fugard's Approach to South African Drama*. Essen: Verlag Die Blaue Eule, 1986.

Sutton, Brian. "Fugard's 'Master Harold'. . . and the Boys." *Explicator* 59.2 (2001): 109–11.

Vandenbroucke, Russell. *Truths the Hand Can Touch: The Theatre of Athol Fugard*. New York: Theatre Communications Group, 1985.

Walder, Dennis. *Athol Fugard*. New York: Grove, 1985.

Weales, Gerald. "Fugard Masters the Code." *Twentieth-Century Literature* 39.4 (1993): 503–16.

Wertheim, Albert. "Ballroom Dancing, Kites and Politics: Athol Fugard's 'MASTER HAROLD'. . . *and the boys*." *SPAN* 30 (1990): 141–55.

———. "Triangles of Race: Athol Fugard's *Master Harold . . . and the Boys* and Paul Slabolepszy's *Saturday Night at the Palace*." *Commonwealth Essays and Studies* 20.1 (1997): 86–95.

GAO XINGJIAN

Tam, Kwok-Kan, ed. *The Soul of Chaos: Critical Perspectives on Gao Xingjian*. Hong Kong: The Chinese University Press, 2001.

SUSAN GLASPELL

Ben-Zvi, Linda. "'Murder, She Wrote': The Genesis of Susan Glaspell's *Trifles*." *Theatre Journal* 44.2 (1992): 141–62.

———, ed. *Susan Glaspell: Essays on Her Theater and Fiction*. Ann Arbor: U of Michigan P, 1995.

———. "Susan Glaspell's Contributions to Contemporary Women Playwrights." *Feminine Focus: The*

New Women Playwrights. Ed. Enoch Brater and Ruby Cohn. Oxford: Oxford UP, 1989.

Dymkowski, Christine. "On the Edge: The Plays of Susan Glaspell." *Modern Drama* 31.1 (1988): 91–105.

Kattwinkel, Susan. "Absence as a Site for Debate: Modern Feminism and Victorianism in the Plays of Susan Glaspell." *New England Theatre Journal* 7 (1996): 37–55.

Larabee, Ann E. " 'Meeting the Outside Face to Face': Susan Glaspell, Djuna Barnes, and O'Neill's *The Emperor Jones.*" *Modern American Drama: The Female Canon.* Ed. June Schlueter. Rutherford: Fairleigh Dickinson UP, 1990. 77–85.

Mael, Phyllis. "*Trifles*: The Path to Sisterhood." *Literature-Film Quarterly* 17.4 (1989): 281–84.

Makowsky, Veronica. *Susan Glaspell's Century of American Women: A Critical Interpretation of Her Work.* New York: Oxford UP, 1993.

Mustazza, Leonard. "Generic Translation and Thematic Shift in Susan Glaspell's *Trifles* and 'A Jury of Her Peers.' " *Studies in Short Fiction* 26.4 (1989): 489–96.

Noe, Marcia. "Region as Metaphor in the Plays of Susan Glaspell." *Western Illinois Regional Studies* 4.1 (1981): 77–85.

———. "Reconfiguring the Subject/Recuperating Realism: Susan Glaspell's Unseen Woman." *American Drama* 4.2 (1995): 36–54.

Ozieblo, Barbara. "Rebellion and Rejection: The Plays of Susan Glaspell.*" Modern American Drama: The Female Canon.* Ed. June Schlueter. Rutherford: Fairleigh Dickinson UP, 1990.

———. "Susan Glaspell." *American Drama.* Ed. Clive Bloom. New York: St. Martin's, 1995. 6–20.

Papke, Mary E. *Susan Glaspell: A Research and Production Sourcebook.* Westport: Greenwood, 1993.

Russell, Judith K. "Glaspell's *Trifles.*" *Explicator* 55.2 (1997): 88–90.

OLIVER GOLDSMITH

Bloom, Harold, ed. *Oliver Goldsmith (Modern Critical View, Series).* New York: Chelsea House, 1987.

Irving, Washington. *Oliver Goldsmith: A Biography.* New York: Haskell House, 1973.

Jackson, Robert W. *Oliver Goldsmith: Essays Towards an Interpretation.* Dublin: Ayer, 1951.

Rousseau, G. S., ed. *Goldsmith: The Critical Heritage.* London: Routledge, 1974.

Shafer, Yvonne. "*She Stoops to Conquer.*" *Theatre Journal* 54, no. 4 (2002): Baltimore: Johns Hopkins UP, 648–50.

Thompson, James. "Recent Studies in the Restoration and Eighteenth Century." *Studies in English Literature, 1500–1900,* 36 (1996): 693–746.

LADY GREGORY (ISABELLA AUGUSTA GREGORY)

Adams, Hazard. *Lady Gregory.* Lewisburg: Bucknell UP, 1973.

Conlon, John J. "Shaw, Lady Gregory and the Abbey: A Correspondence and A Record." *English Literature in Transition 1880–1920.* 40.3 (1997): 345–47.

Coxhead, Elizabeth. *Lady Gregory: A Literary Portrait.* New York: Harcourt, 1961.

Gregory, Lady. *Lady Gregory's Diaries, 1892–1902.* New York: Oxford UP, 1996.

———. *Lady Gregory's Journals, 1910–1930.* New York: Oxford UP, 1978.

———. *Our Irish Theatre.* Gerrards Cross: Smythe, 1972.

Kiberg, Declan. *Inventing Ireland: The Literature of the Modern Nation.* London: Vintage, 1996.

Kohfeldt, Mary Lou. *Lady Gregory: The Woman Behind the Irish Renaissance.* New York: Atheneum, 1985.

Kopper, E. A., Jr. "Lady Gregory's *The Rising of the Moon.*" *Explicator* 47 (1989): 29–31.

Lenox-Conyngham, Melosina. *Diaries of Ireland: An Anthology, 1590–1987.* Dublin: Lilliput, 1998.

Maxwell, D. E. S. *A Critical History of Modern Irish Drama: 1891–1980.* New York: Cambridge UP, 1984.

O'Connor, Ulick. *All the Olympians.* New York: Atheneum, 1984.

Owens, C'il'n D., and Joan N. Radner. *Irish Drama: 1900–1980.* Washington: Catholic U of America P, 1990.

Saddlemyer, Ann. *In Defense of Lady Gregory, Playwright.* Dublin: Dolmen, 1966.

———. *Lady Gregory, Fifty Years After.* Totowa: Barnes, 1987.

LORRAINE HANSBERRY

Ashley, Leonard R. "Lorraine Hansberry and the Great Black Way." *Modern American Drama: The Female Canon.* Ed. June Schlueter. Rutherford: Fairleigh Dickinson UP, 1990. 151–60.

Carter, Steven R. *Hansberry's Drama: Commitment and Complexity.* Urbana: U of Illinois P, 1991.

Cheney, Anne. *Lorraine Hansberry.* Boston: Twayne, 1984.

Freedman, Morris. *American Drama in Social Context.* Carbondale: Southern Illinois UP, 1971.

Keyssar, Helene. "Rites and Responsibilities: The Drama of Black American Women." *The New Women Playwrights.* Ed. Enoch Brater and Ruby Cohn. Oxford: Oxford UP, 1989. 226–40.

Kodat, Catherine Gunther. "Confusion in a Dream Deferred: Context and Culture in Teaching *A Raisin in the Sun.*" *Studies in the Literary Imagination* 31.1 (1998): 149–64.

Leeson, Richard M. *Lorraine Hansberry: A Research and Production Sourcebook.* Westport: Greenwood, 1997.

McKelly, James C. "Hymns of Sedition: Portraits of the Artist in Contemporary African-American Drama." *Arizona Quarterly* 48.1 (1992): 87–107.

Scheader, Catherine. *Lorraine Hansberry: Playwright and Voice of Justice.* Springfield, NJ: Enslow, 1998.

————. *They Found a Way: Lorraine Hansberry.* Chicago: Children's, 1978.

Schlueter, June, ed. *Modern American Drama: The Female Canon.* Rutherford: Fairleigh Dickinson UP, 1990.

Seaton, Sandra. "*A Raisin in the Sun*: A Study in Afro-American Culture." *Midwestern Miscellany* 20 (1992): 40–49.

Sinnott, Susan. *Lorraine Hansberry: Award-Winning Playwright and Civil Rights Activist.* Berkeley: Conari P, 1999.

Washington, J. Charles. "*A Raisin in the Sun* Revisited." *Black American Literature Forum* 22.1 (1988): 109–24.

Weales, Gerald. "Lorraine Hansberry." *Contemporary Dramatists.* Ed. D. L. Kirkpatrick. 4th ed. Chicago: St. James, 1988. 653–54.

Wilkerson, Margaret B. "Excavating Our History: The Importance of Biographies of Women of Color." *Black American Forum* 24.1 (1990): 73–84.

Williams, Mance. *Black Theatre in the 1960s and 1970s.* Westport: Greenwood, 1985.

HROSVITHA

Carlson, Marvin. "Impassive Bodies: Hrotsvit Stages Martyrdom." *Theatre Journal* 50.4 (1998): 473–87.

Schmitt, Miriam. "Hrotsvit: Medieval Playwright." *Medieval Women Monastics: Wisdom's Wellsprings.* Ed. Miriam Schmitt and Linda Kulzer. Collegeville: Liturgical Press, 1996.

Wilson, Katharine M. *Hrotsvit of Gandersheim: The Ethics of Authorial Stance.* New York: Brill, 1988.

————. *Hrotsvit of Gandersheim: Rara Avis in Saxonia? A Collection of Essays.* Ann Arbor: MARC, 1987.

Zeydel, Edwin H. "Hrotsvit von Gandersheim and the Eternal Womanly." *Studies in the German Drama: A Festschrift in Honor of Walter Silz.* Chapel Hill: U of North Carolina P, 1974. 1–14.

DAVID HENRY HWANG

Cooperman, Robert. "Across the Boundaries of Cultural Identity: An Interview with David Henry Hwang." *Staging Difference: Cultural Pluralism in American Theatre and Drama.* Ed. Marc Maufort. New York: Peter Lang, 1995.

DiGaetani, John Louis. "*M. Butterfly*: An Interview with David Henry Hwang." *The Drama Review* 33.3 (Fall 1989): 141–53.

Frockt, Deborah. "David Henry Hwang." *The Playwright's Art: Conversations with Contemporary American Dramatists.* Ed. Jackson Bryer. New Brunswick: Rutgers UP, 1995. 123–46.

Hwang, David Henry. "Evolving a Multicultural Tradition." *MELUS* 16.3 (1989–90): 16–19.

Lye, Colleen. "M. Butterfly and the Rhetoric of Antiessentialism: Minority Discourse in an International Frame." *The Ethic Canon: Histories, Institu-tions, and Interventions.* Ed. David Palumbo-Liu. Minneapolis: U of Minnesota P, 1995. 260–89.

Lyons, Bonnie. "'Making His Muscles Work for Himself': An Interview with David Henry Hwang." *The Literary Review* 42.2 (1999): 230–44.

Pao, Angela. "M. Butterfly by David Henry Hwang." *A Resource Guide to Asian American Literature.* Ed. Sau-ling Cynthia Wong and Stephen H. Sumida. New York: MLA, 2001. 200–08.

Saal, Ilka. "Performance and Perception: Gender, Sexuality, and Culture in David Henry Hwang's *M. Butterfly.*" *American Studies* 43.4 (1998): 629–44.

Shin, Andrew. "Projected Bodies in David Henry Hwang's M. Butterfly and Golden Gate." *MELUS: The Journal of the Society for the Study of Multi-Ethnic Literature of the United States* 27.1 (2002): 177–97.

Skloot, Robert. "Breaking the Butterfly: The Politics of David Henry Hwang." *Modern Drama* 33.1 (1990): 59–66.

Street, Douglas. *David Henry Hwang.* Western Writers Series no. 90. Boise: Boise State U, 1989.

Trudeau, Lawrence. *Asian American Literature: Reviews and Criticism of Works by American Writers of Asian Descent.* Detroit: Gale Research, 1999.

HENRIK IBSEN

Ackerman, Gretchen P. *Ibsen and the English Stage, 1889–1903.* New York: Garland, 1987.

Chamberlain, John S. *Ibsen: The Open Vision.* London: Athlone, 1982.

Egan, Michael, ed. *Ibsen: The Critical Heritage.* London: Routledge, 1972.

Ferguson, Robert. *Henrik Ibsen: A New Biography.* London, R. Cohen, 1996.

Fjelde, Rolf, ed. *Ibsen: A Collection of Critical Essays.* Englewood Cliffs: Prentice, 1965.

Gaskell, Ronald. *Drama and Reality: The European Theatre since Ibsen.* London: Routledge, 1972.

Goldman, Michael. *Ibsen: The Dramaturgy of Fear.* New York: Columbia UP, 1999.

Lebowitz, Naomi. *Ibsen and the Great World.* Baton Rouge: Louisiana UP, 1990.

Marker, Frederick J. *Ibsen's Lively Art: A Performance Study of the Major Plays.* New York: Cambridge UP, 1989.

McFarlane, James, ed. *Discussions of Henrik Ibsen.* Boston: Heath, 1962.

Meyer, Michael, *Henrik Ibsen: A Biography.* 3 vols. Garden City: Doubleday, 1971.

Noreng, Harald, et al., eds. *Contemporary Approaches to Ibsen.* Oslo: Universitetsforlaget, 1977.

Northam, John. *Ibsen: A Critical Study.* Cambridge: Cambridge UP, 1973.

Shaw, Bernard. *The Quintessence of Ibsenism.* New York: Hill, 1957.

Shepherd-Barr, Kirsten. *Ibsen and Early Modernist Theatre, 1890–1900.* Westport: Greenwood, 1997.

Theoharis, Theoharis Constantine. *Ibsen's Drama: Right Action and Tragic Joy.* New York: St. Martin's, 1996.

Thomas, David. *Henrik Ibsen.* New York: Grove, 1984.

A Doll House

Andreas-Salomé, Lou. *Ibsen's Heroines.* Ed. and trans. Siegfried Mandel. Austrian/German Culture Series. Redding Ridge: Black Swan, 1985.

Bradbrook, M. C. "*A Doll's House* and the Unweaving of the Web." *Women and Literature, 1779–1982.* Vol. 2. Totowa: Barnes, 1982. 81–92. 2 vols.

Drake, David B. "Ibsen's *A Doll House.*" *Explicator* 53.1 (1994): 32–34.

Durbach, Errol. *A Doll's House: Ibsen's Myth of Transformation.* Boston: Twayne, 1991.

Ibsen, Henrik. "*Doll's House*" [Ibsen's notes on *A Doll House*]. *Playwrights on Playwriting.* Ed. Toby Cole. New York: Hill, 1960. 151–54.

Mitchell, Hayley R. *Readings on* A Doll's House. San Diego: Greenhaven, 1999.

Sprinchorn, E. M. "Ibsen and the Actors." *Ibsen and the Theatre.* Ed. Errol Durbach. New York: New York UP, 1980. 118–30.

Tornqvist, Egil. "Comparative Performance Semiotics: The End of Ibsen's *A Doll House.*" Theatre Research International 19.2 (1994): 156–164.

BEN JONSON

Butler, Martin, ed. *Re-presenting Ben Jonson: Text, History, Performance.* New York: St. Martin's, 1999.

Floyd-Wilson, Mary. "Temperature, Temperance, and Racial Difference in Ben Jonson's *The Masque of Blackness.*" *English Literary Renaissance* 28.2 (1998): 183–209.

Hirsh, James, ed. *New Perspectives on Ben Jonson.* Madison: Fairleigh Dickinson UP, 1997.

Orgel, Stephen. *Marginal Jonson.* Cambridge: Cambridge UP, 1998.

Sanders, Julie. *Ben Jonson's Theatrical Republics.* Basingstoke: Macmillan, 1998.

——, ed., with Kate Chedgzoy and Susan Wiseman. *Refashioning Ben Jonson: Gender, Politics, and the Jonsonian Canon.* New York: St. Martin's, 1998.

Summers, Claude J. *Ben Jonson Revised.* New York: Twayne, 1999.

Watson, Robert N. *Critical Essays on Ben Jonson.* New York: Hall, 1997.

TONY KUSHNER

Arons, Wendy. " 'Preaching to the Converted?' 'You Couldn't Possibly Do Any Better!': An Interview with Tony Kushner." *Communications from the International Brecht Society* 23.2 (1994): 51–59.

Blask, Per K. *Essays on Kushner's Angels.* Winnipeg: Blizzard, 1996.

Fisher, James. *The Theater of Tony Kushner: Living Past Hope.* New York: Routledge, 2001.

Geis, Deborah R., and Steven F. Kuger, eds. *Approaching the Millennium: Essays on Angels in America.* Ann Arbor: U of Michigan P, 1997.

Kiefer, Daniel. "*Angels in America* and the Failure of Revelation." *American Drama* 4.1 (1994): 21–38.

Lowenthal, Michael. "On Art, Angels, and 'Postmodern Fascism.' " *Harvard Gay and Lesbian Review* 2.2 (1995): 10–12.

Montgomery, Benilde. "Angels in America as Medieval Mystery." *Modern Drama* 41.4 (1998): 596–606.

Posnock, Ross. "Roy Cohn in America." *Raritan* 13.3 (1994): 64–77.

Quinn, John R. "Corpus Juris Terium: Redemptive Jurisprudence in *Angels in America.*" *Theatre Journal* 48.1 (1996): 79–90.

Rogoff, Gordon. "*Angels in America*, Devils in the Wings." *Theater* 24.2 (1993): 21–29.

Savran, David. "Tony Kushner." *Speaking on Stage: Interviews with Contemporary American Playwrights.* Ed. Philip C. Kolin and Colby H. Kullman. Tuscaloosa: U of Alabama P, 1996. 291–313.

——. "Tony Kushner Considers the Longstanding Problems of Virtue and Happiness." *American Theatre* 11.8 (1994): 20–27+.

Steyn, Mark. "Communism Is Dead: Long Live the King." *New Criterion*: 13.6 (1995): 49–53.

Vorlicky, Robert, and Tony Kushner, eds. *Tony Kushner in Conversation.* Ann Arbor: U of Michigan P, 1998.

FEDERICO GARCÍA LORCA

Anderson, Andrew. "On Broadway, Off Broadway: García Lorca and the New York Theatre, 1929–1930." *Gestos* 8.16 (1993): 135–48.

Colecchia, Francesca. "A Selected Bibliography of Studies on García Lorca's *La casa de Bernarda Alba.*" *Estreno-Cuadernos del Teatro Espa–ol Contemporaneo* 21.2 (1995): 39–41.

Dempsey, Andrew, ed. *A Life of Lorca: Drawings, Photographs, Words.* Norwich: U of East Anglia, 1997.

Duran, Manuel, and Francesca Colecchia, eds. *Lorca's Legacy: Essays on Lorca's Life, Poetry, and Theatre.* New York: Lang, 1991.

Fitzpatrick, Tim, and Sean Batten. "Watching the Watchers Watch: Some Implications of Audience Attention Patterns." *Gestos* 6.12 (1991): 11–31.

Gabriele, John P. "Of Mothers and Freedom: Adela's Struggle for Freedom in *La Casa de Bernardo Alba.*" *Symposium* 47.3 (1993): 188–99.

Handley, Sharon. "Garcia-Lorca: Poet of the Inmensa-Minora? Or Voice of the Andalusian Pueblo?" *Critica Hispanica* 18.2 (1996): 298–312.

Harvard, Robert, ed. *Lorca: Poet and Playwright.* Cardiff: U of Wales, 1992.

Hoeg, Jerry. "Steps to an Ecology of *La casa de Bernarda Alba.*" *Revista de Estudios Hispanicos* 30.1 (1996): 81–101.

Klein, Dennis A. *Blood Wedding, Yerma, and The House of Bernarda Alba: García Lorca's Tragic Trilogy.* Boston: Twayne, 1991.

Lanters, Jose. "The Theatre of Thomas Murphy and Federico García Lorca." *Modern Drama* 36.4 (1993): 481–89.

Parilla, Catherine Arturi. *A Theory for Reading Dramatic Texts: Selected Texts by Pirandello and García Lorca.* New York: P. Lang, 1995.

Podol, Peter L. "*La Casa de Bernarda Alba* in Performance: Three Productions in Three Media." *Estreno-Cuadernos del Teatro Español Contemporaneo* 21.2 (1995): 42–44.

Rees, Margaret A., ed. *Leeds Papers on Hispanic Drama.* Leeds: Trinity and All Saints College, 1991.

Soufas, C. Christopher. *Audience and Authority in the Modernist Theater of Federico García Lorca.* Tuscaloosa: U of Alabama P, 1996.

———. "Dialectics of Vision: Pictorial vs. Photographic Representation in Lorca's *La Casa de Bernarda Alba.*" *Ojancano* 5 (1991): 52–66.

Wellington, Beth. *Reflections on Lorca's Private Mythology: Once Five Years Pass and the Rural Plays.* New York: P. Lang, 1993.

DAVID MAMET

Almansi, Guido. "David Mamet: A Virtuoso of Invective." *Critical Angles: European Views of Contemporary American Literature.* Ed. Marc Chenetier. Carbondale: Southern Illinois UP, 1986.

Bigsby, Christopher, ed. *The Cambridge Companion to David Mamet.* Cambridge, UK; New York: Cambridge UP, 2004.

Blumberg, Marcia. "Eloquent Stammering in the Fog: O'Neill's Heritage in Mamet." *Perspectives on O'Neill: New Essays.* Ed. Shyamal Bagchee. Victoria: U of Victoria P, 1988. 97–111.

Boon, Kevin Alexander. "Dialogue, Discourse and Dialectics: The Rhetoric of Capitalism in *Glengarry Glen Ross.*" *Creative Screenwriting* 5.3 (1998): 50–57.

Dean, Anne. *David Mamet: Language as Dramatic Action.* Rutherford: Fairleigh Dickinson UP, 1990.

Esche, Edward J. "David Mamet." *American Drama.* Ed. Clive Bloom. New York: St. Martin's, 1995. 165–77.

Hubert, Liebler Pascale. "Dominance and Anguish: The Teacher-Student Relationship in the Plays of David Mamet." *Modern Drama* 31.4 (1988): 557–70.

Jacobs, Dorothy H. "Working Worlds in David Mamet's Dramas." *Midwestern Miscellany* 14 (1986): 47–57.

Kane, Leslie, ed. *David Mamet's* Glengarry Glen Ross: *Text and Performance.* New York: Garland, 1996.

———. *Weasels and Wisemen: Ethics and Ethnicity in the Work of David Mamet.* Basingstoke: Macmillan, 1999.

Kolin, Philip C. "Mitch and Murray in David Mamet's *Glengarry Glen Ross.*" *Notes on Contemporary Literature,* 18.2 (1988): 3–5.

Lubin, Robert I. "Differing Dramatic Dynamics in the Stage and Screen Versions of *Glengarry Glen Ross.*" *American Drama* 10.1 (2002): 38–55.

Lundon, Edward. "Mamet and Mystery." *Publications of the Mississippi Philological Association* (1988): 106–14.

Maufort, Marc. "Narrative Patterns in the Plays of David Mamet." *BELL* (1991): 112–19.

McDonough, Carla J. "Every Fear Hides a Wish: Unstable Masculinity in Mamet's Drama." *Theatre Journal* 44.2 (1992): 195–205.

———. *Staging Masculinity: Male Identity in Contemporary American Drama.* Jefferson, NC: McFarland, 1997.

Mufson, Daniel. "The Critical Eye: Sexual Perversity in *Viragos.*" *Theater* 24.1 (1993): 111–13.

Price, Steven. "AT&T: Anxiety, Telecommunications and the Theatre of David Mamet." *Cynos* 12.1 (1995): 59–67.

Roudané, Matthew. "David Mamet." *Speaking on Stage: Interviews with Contemporary American Playwrights.* Ed. Philip C. Kolin and Colby H. Kullman. Tuscaloosa: U of Alabama P, 1996.

———. "An Interview with David Mamet." *Studies in American Drama 1945–Present* 1 (1986): 73–81.

Sauer, David K., and Janice A. Sauer. *David Mamet: A Research and Production Sourcebook.* Westport: Praeger, 2003.

Zinman, Toby Silverman. "Jewish Aporia: The Rhythm of Talking in Mamet." *Theatre Journal* 44.2 (1992): 207–15.

CHRISTOPHER MARLOWE

Bartels, Emily C. "Authorizing Subversion: Strategies of Power in Marlowe's *Doctor Faustus.*" *Renaissance Papers* (1989): 65–74.

———, ed. *Critical Essays on Christopher Marlowe.* New York: Prentice, 1997.

Birrenger, Johannes. "Between Body and Language: 'Writing' *The Damnation of Faust.*" *Theatre Journal* 36.3 (1984): 301–20.

Bloom, Harold, ed. *Christopher Marlowe.* New York: Chelsea, 1986.

———. *Christopher Marlowe's* Doctor Faustus. New York: Chelsea, 1988.

Cole, Douglas. *Suffering and Evil in the Plays of Christopher Marlowe.* Princeton: Princeton UP, 1962.

Cox, John D. "Devils and Power in Marlowe and Shakespeare." *Yearbook of English Studies* 23 (1993): 46–64.

Cutts, John P. *The Left Hand of God.* Haddonfield: Haddonfield, 1973.

Ellis-Fermor, Una Mary. *Christopher Marlowe.* Hamden: Anchor, 1967.

Farnham, Willard, comp. *Twentieth-Century Interpretation of Doctor Faustus: A Collection of Critical Essays.* Englewood Cliffs: Prentice, 1969.

Friedenreich, Kenneth, Roma Gill, and Constance Kuriyama, eds. *New Essays on Christopher Marlowe.* New York: AMS, 1988.

Godshalk, W. L. *The Marlovian World Picture.* The Hague: Mouton, 1974.

Golden, Kenneth. "Myth, Psychology and Marlowe's *Doctor Faustus.*" *College Literature* 12.3 (1985): 202–10.

Honigmann, Ernst. "Ten Problems in *Doctor Faustus.*" *The Arts of Performance in Elizabethan and Early Stuart Drama.* Ed. Murray Biggs et al. Edinburgh: Edinburgh UP, 1991. 173–191.

Jones, John Henry, ed. *The English Faust Book: A Critical Edition Based on the Text of 1592.* Cambridge: Cambridge UP, 1994.

Jones, Louise Conley. "A Textual Analysis of Marlowe's *Doctor Faustus* with Director's Book: Stage Action as Metaphor." *Studies in Renaissance Literature* 12. Lewiston: Mellen, 1996.

Keefer, Michael H. "History and the Canon: The Case of *Doctor Faustus.*" *University of Toronto Quarterly* 56.4 (1987): 498–522.

Leech, Clifford, ed. *Marlowe: A Collection of Critical Essays.* Englewood Cliffs: Prentice, 1964.

Levin, Harry. *The Overreacher, A Study of Christopher Marlowe.* Boston: Beacon, 1964.

Marlowe, Christopher. *Complete Plays.* Ed., intro, and notes, Irving Ribner. New York: Odyssey, 1963.

McAlindon, T. Doctor Faustus: *Divine in Show.* New York: Twayne, 1994.

Muir, Kenneth. "Three Marlowe Texts (*Doctor Faustus, The Jew of Malta* and *The Massacre at Paris*)." *Notes and Queries* 43.2 (1996): 142–44.

Ricks, Christopher. "*Doctor Faustus* and Hell on Earth." *Essays in Criticism* 35.2 (1985): 101–20.

Roberts, Peter, and Darryll Grantley, eds. *Christopher Marlowe and English Renaissance Culture.* Aldershot: Ashgate, 1999.

Steane, J. B. *Marlowe: A Critical Study.* Cambridge: Cambridge UP, 1964.

Stover, David F. "The Individualism of *Doctor Faustus.*" *North Dakota Quarterly* 57.4 (1989): 146–61.

Wilson, Richard, ed. *Christopher Marlowe.* Longman Critical Readers. London: Longman, 1999.

ARTHUR MILLER

Anderson, M. C. "*Death of a Salesman*: A Consideration of Willy Loman's Role in Twentieth-Century Tragedy." *CRUX* 20.2 (1986): 25–29.

Babcock, Granger. "'What's the Secret?': Willy Loman as Desiring Machine." *American Drama* 2.1 (1992): 59–83.

Balakian, Jan. "Arthur Miller." *Speaking on Stage: Interviews with Contemporary American Playwrights.* Ed. Philip C. Kolin and Colby H. Kullman. Tuscaloosa: U of Alabama P, 1996. 40–57.

Bigsby, Christopher W. E. *Arthur Miller.* Cambridge Companions to Literature. Cambridge: Cambridge UP, 1997.

Bloom, Harold. *Arthur Miller.* Philadelphia: Chelsea, 1999.

———, ed. *Arthur Miller's* Death of a Salesman. New York: Chelsea, 1988.

———. *Willy Loman.* New York: Chelsea, 1990.

Brucher, Richard T. "Willy Loman and the Soul of a New Machine: Technology and the Common Man." *Journal of American Studies* 17.3 (1983): 325–36.

Carson, Neil. *Arthur Miller.* London: Macmillan; 1982.

Centola, Steven R. "Family Values in *Death of a Salesman.*" *College Language Association Journal* 37.1 (1993): 29–41.

Corrigan, Robert W., ed. *Arthur Miller: A Collection of Critical Essays.* Englewood Cliffs: Prentice, 1969.

Goldstein, Laurence, ed. "Aurthur Miller." *Michigan Quarterly Review* 37.4 [Special Issue] (1998).

Griffin, Alice. *Understanding Arthur Miller.* Columbia: U of South Carolina P, 1996.

Hadomi, Leah. "Fantasy and Reality: Dramatic Rhythm in *Death of a Salesman.*" *Modern Drama* 31.2 (1988): 157–74.

Harder, Harry. "*Death of a Salesman*: An American Classic." *Censored Books: Critical Viewpoints.* Ed. Nicholas J. Karolides, Lee Burress, and John M. Kean. Metuchen: Scarecrow, 1993.

Hayman, Ronald. *Arthur Miller.* New York: Ungar, 1972.

Huftel, Sheila. *Arthur Miller: The Burning Glass.* New York: Citadel, 1965.

Jenckes, Norma, ed. "Arthur Miller." *American Drama* 6.1 [Special Issue] (1996).

Koon, Helene Wickham. Twentieth Century Interpretations of *Death of a Salesman.* Englewood Cliffs: Prentice, 1983.

Martin, Robert A., ed. *Arthur Miller: New Perspectives.* Englewood Cliffs: Prentice, 1982.

———. "The Nature of Tragedy in Arthur Miller's *Death of a Salesman.*" *South Atlantic Review* 61.4 (1996): 97–106.

Miller, Arthur. *Collected Plays.* New York: Viking, 1957.

———. *The Theater Essays of Arthur Miller.* Ed. and intro., Robert A. Martin. New York: Viking, 1978.

———. *Timebends: A Life.* New York: Grove, 1987.

Murphy, Brenda. "Arthur Miller: Revisioning Realism." *Realism and the American Dramatic Tradition.* Ed. William W. Demastes. Tuscaloosa: U of Alabama P, 1996. 189–202.

Roudane, Matthew C., ed. *Conversations with Arthur Miller.* Jackson: UP of Mississippi, 1987.

Schlueter, June, and James K. Flanagan. *Arthur Miller.* New York: Ungar, 1987.

Schockley, John S. "*Death of a Salesman* and American Leadership: Life Imitates Art." *Journal of American Culture* 17.2 (1994): 49–56.

Siebold, Thomas, ed. *Readings on Arthur Miller.* San Diego: Greenhaven, 1997.

———, ed. *Readings on Death of a Salesman.* San Diego: Greenhaven, 1999.

Stanton, Kay. "Women and the American Dream of *Death of a Salesman.*" *Feminist Rereadings of Modern American Drama.* Ed. June Schlueter. Rutherford: Fairleigh Dickinson UP, 1989.

MOLIÈRE (JEAN BAPTISTE POQUELIN)

Bermel, Albert. *Molière's Theatrical Bounty: A New View of the Plays.* Carbondale: Southern Illinois UP, 1990.

Edney, David. "Molière in North America: Problems of Translation and Adaptation." *Modern Drama* 41.1 (1998): 60–76.

Gaines, James F., and Michael S. Koppisch eds. *Approaches to Teaching Molière's Tartuffe and Other Plays.* New York: Modern Language Association of America, 1995.

———. *Molière's Theater.* Columbus: Ohio State UP, 1984.

Gross, Nathan. *From Gesture to Idea: Esthetics and Ethics in Molière's Comedy.* New York: Columbia UP, 1982.

Guicharnaud, Jacques. *Molière: A Collection of Critical Essays.* Englewood Cliffs: Prentice, 1964.

Hall, H. Gaston. *Comedy in Context: Essays on Molière.* Jackson: UP of Mississippi, 1984.

———. "Molière's Roles Written for Himself." *Australian Journal of French Studies* 33 (1996): 414–27.

Jagendorf, Zvi. *The Happy End of Comedy: Jonson, Molière, and Shakespeare.* Newark: U of Delaware P, 1984.

Knutson, Harold C. *The Triumph of Wit: Molière and Restoration Comedy.* Columbus: Ohio State UP, 1988.

Lalande, Roxanne Decker. *Intruders in the Play World: The Dynamics of Gender in Molière's Comedies.* Madison: Fairleigh Dickinson UP, 1996.

Molière. *Tartuffe: Comedy in Five Acts.* Trans. Richard Wilbur. New York: Harcourt, 1963.

Spingler, Michael, ed. *Molière Today.* Amsterdam: Harwood, 1997.

Walker, Hallam. *Molière.* Rev. ed. Boston: Twayne, 1990.

EUGENE O'NEILL

Ahuja, Chaman. *Tragedy, Modern Temper, and O'Neill.* Atlantic Highlands: Humanities, 1984.

Berlin, Normand. *Eugene O'Neill.* New York: Grove, 1987.

Black, Stephen A. *Eugene O'Neill: Beyond Mourning and Tragedy.* New Haven: Yale UP, 1999.

Bogard, Travis. *Contour in Time: The Plays of Eugene O'Neill.* New York: Oxford UP, 1988.

Cargill, Oscar, N. Bryllion Fagan, and William J. Fisher, eds. *O'Neill and His Plays: Four Decades of Criticism.* New York: New York UP, 1961.

Cunningham, Frank R. "Eugene O'Neill and Reality in America." *Realism and the American Dramatic Tra-*

dition. Ed. William W. Demastes. Tuscaloosa: U of Alabama P, 1996.

Fleche, Anne. *Mimetic Disillusion: Eugene O'Neill, Tennessee Williams, and U.S. Dramatic Realism.* Tuscaloosa: U of Alabama P, 1997.

Floyd, Virginia. *The Plays of Eugene O'Neill: A New Assessment.* New York: Ungar, 1985.

Frenz, Horst, and Susan Tuck, eds. *Eugene O'Neill's Critics: Voices from Abroad.* Boulder: netLibrary, 1999.

Gallup, Donald. *Eugene O'Neill and His Eleven-Play Cycle: "A Tale of Possessors Self-Possessed."* New Haven: Yale UP, 1998.

Gassner, John, ed. *O'Neill: A Collection of Critical Essays.* Englewood Cliffs: Prentice, 1964.

Leech, Clifford. *Eugene O'Neill.* New York: Grove, 1963.

Manheim, Michael, ed. *Eugene O'Neill.* Cambridge Companions to Literature. Cambridge: Cambridge UP, 1998.

Maufort, Marc, ed. *Eugene O'Neill and the Emergence of American Drama.* Atlanta: Rodopi, 1989.

Miller, Jordan Yale. *Eugene O'Neill and American Criticism: A Bibliographical Checklist.* 2nd ed. Hamden: Anchor, 1973.

Moorton, Richard F., Jr. *Eugene O'Neill's Century: Centennial Views on America's Foremost Critic.* Westport: Greenwood, 1991.

Mottram, Eric. "Eugene O'Neill." *American Drama.* Ed. Clive Bloom. New York: St. Martin's, 1995. 21–45.

O'Neill, Eugene. *Long Day's Journey into Night.* New Haven: Yale UP, 1956.

———. *The Plays of Eugene O'Neill.* 3 vols. New York: Modern Library, 1982.

Pfister, Joel. *Staging Depth: Eugene O'Neill and the Politics of Psychological Discourse.* Boulder: netLibrary, 1999.

Porter, Laurin. *The Banished Prince: Time, Memory, and Ritual in the Late Plays of Eugene O'Neill.* Ann Arbor: UMI Research, 1988.

Ranald, Margaret Loftus. *The Eugene O'Neill Companion.* Westport: Greenwood, 1984.

Siebold, Thomas. *Readings on Eugene O'Neill.* San Diego: Greenhaven, 1998.

Wainscott, Ronald Harold. *Staging O'Neill: The Experimental Years, 1920–1934.* New Haven: Yale UP, 1988.

SUZAN-LORI PARKS

Carr, C. "Review of Imperceptible Mutabilities in the Third Kingdom." *Artforum* November 1989: 154.

Gussow, Mel. Review of *The Death of the Last Black Man in the Whole Entire World. New York Times* 25 Sept. 1990: C15.

———. Review of Imperceptible Mutabilities in the Third Kingdom. *New York Times* 20 Sept. 1989: C24.

Holden, Stephen. Review of Betting on the Dust Commander. *New York Times* 26 June 1991: C12.

Jiggetts, Shelby. "Interviews with Suzan-Lori Parks." *Callaloo.* 19.2 (1996): 309–17.

HAROLD PINTER

Aragay, Mireia. "Writing, Politics, and Ashes to Ashes: An Interview with Harold Pinter." *Pinter Review: Annual Essays* (1996).

Barnett, Claudia. "The Metadramatic Prison of *Betrayal.*" *The Pinter Review: Annual Essays* (1992–93):69–72.

Behera, Charan. *Reality and Illusion in the Plays of Harold Pinter.* New Delhi: Atlantic, 1998.

Billington, Michael. *The Life and Work of Harold Pinter.* London: Faber, 1996.

Bloom, Harold, ed. *Harold Pinter.* New York: Chelsea, 1987.

Bold, Alan, ed. *Harold Pinter: You Never Heard Such Silence.* Critical Studies Series. Totowa: Barnes, 1985.

Burkman, Katherine H. *The Dramatic World of Harold Pinter.* Columbia: Ohio State UP, 1971.

Chevallier, Genevieve, ed. "Harold Pinter." *Cycnos* 14.1 [Special Issue] (1997).

Conklin, Robert. "*Old Times* and *Betrayal* as Rorschach Test." *Pinter Review* (1992–93): 69–72.

Deer, Harriet. "Melodramatic Problematics in Pinter's Film of *Betrayal.*" *Pinter Review* (1990): 61–70.

Diamond, Elin. *Pinter's Comic Play.* Lewisburg: Bucknell UP, 1985.

Dukore, Bernard F. *Harold Pinter.* 2nd ed. New York: Macmillan, 1988.

Esslin, Martin. *Pinter: The Playwright.* New York: Methuen, 1984.

Gaggi, Silvio. "Pinter's Betrayal: Problems of Language or Grand Metatheatre?" *Theatre Journal* 22.4 (1981): 504–16.

Gale, Steven H., ed. *Critical Essays on Harold Pinter.* Boston: Hall, 1990.

———. "Harold Pinter." *British Playwrights, 1956–1995: A Research and Production Sourcebook.* Ed. William W. Demastes. Westport: Greenwood, 1996. 301–25.

———. *Harold Pinter: Critical Approaches.* Rutherford: Fairleigh Dickinson UP, 1986.

Ganz, Arthur F., ed. *Pinter: A Collection of Critical Essays.* Englewood Cliffs: Prentice, 1979.

Gordon, Lois, ed. *Pinter at 70: A Casebook.* New York: Routledge, 2001.

Hayman, Ronald. *Harold Pinter.* New York: Ungar, 1973.

Hinchliffe, Arnold P. *Harold Pinter.* Boston: Twayne, 1981.

Jalote, S. R. *The Plays of Harold Pinter: A Study in Neurotic Anxiety.* New Delhi: Harman House, 1996.

Kerr, Walter. *Harold Pinter.* New York: Columbia UP, 1967.

Knowles, Ronald. *Understanding Harold Pinter.* Columbia: U of South Carolina P, 1995.

Mayberry, Bob. *Theatre of Discord: Dissonance in Beckett, Albee, and Pinter.* Rutherford: Fairleigh Dickinson UP, 1989.

Peacock, D. Keith. *Harold Pinter and the New British Theatre.* Westport: Greenwood, 1997.

Pearce, Howard. "The Doll House in Harold Pinter's *Betrayal.*" *Text and Presentation* 17 (1996): 46–52.

Pinter, Harold. *Complete Works.* 3 vols. New York: Grove, 1977–78.

Quigley, Austin E. *The Pinter Problem.* Princeton: Princeton UP, 1975.

Strunk, Volker. *Harold Pinter: Towards a Poetics of His Plays.* New York: Lang, 1989.

Sykes, Arlene. *Harold Pinter.* New York: Humanities, 1970.

Woodroffe, Graham. "From Kinsale Drive to Wessex Grove: A Psychoanalytical Study of Harold Pinter's *Betrayal.*" *Literature and Psychology* 35.3 (1989): 43–63.

Zeifman, Hersh, and Cynthia Zimmerman, eds. *Contemporary British Drama 1970–90.* Toronto: U of Toronto P, 1993.

LUIGI PIRANDELLO

Bassabesem, Fiora A. *Understanding Luigi Pirandello.* Columbia: U of South Carolina P, 1997.

Bassnett, Susan. *File on Pirandello.* London: Methuen, 1989.

Bassnett-McGuire, Susan. *Luigi Pirandello.* New York: Grove, 1983.

Bentley, Eric. *The Pirandello Commentaries.* Evanston: Northwestern UP, 1986.

Biasin, Gian-Paolo, and Manuela Gieri, eds. *Luigi Pirandello: Contemporary Perspectives.* Toronto: U of Toronto P, 1999.

Bloom, Harold. *Luigi Pirandello.* New York: Chelsea, 1989.

Büdel, Oscar. *Pirandello.* New York: Hillary, 1969.

Caesar, Ann. *Characters and Authors in Luigi Pirandello.* Oxford: Clarendon, 1998.

Cambon, Glauco, ed. *Pirandello: A Collection of Critical Essays.* Englewood Cliffs: Prentice, 1967.

Caputi, Anthony. *Pirandello and the Crisis of Modern Consciousness.* Urbana: U of Illinois P, 1988.

Dashwood, Julie R. *Luigi Pirandello: The Theatre of Paradox.* Lewiston: Mellen, 1996.

Guidice, Gaspare. *Pirandello: A Biography.* Trans. Alastair Hamilton. New York: Oxford UP, 1975.

Hornby, Richard. "Three Modern Playwrights (Pirandello, Strindberg, Chekhov)." *Seewanee Review* 105 (1997): 595–99.

Mariani, Umberto. "The 'Pirandellian' Character." *Canadian Journal of Italian Studies* 12.38–39 (1989): 1–9.

Mazzaro, Jerome. "Pirandello's *Sei Personaggi* and Expressive Form." *Comparative Drama* 30 (1996–97): 503–24.

Oliver, Roger W. *Dreams of Passion: The Theater of Luigi Pirandello.* New York: New York UP, 1979.

Paolucci, Anne. *Pirandello's Theater.* Carbondale: Southern Illinois UP, 1974.

Pirandello, Luigi. *Naked Masks, Five Plays.* Ed. Eric Bentley. New York: Dutton, 1952.

———. *Short Stories.* Ed. and trans. Frederick May. New York: Oxford UP, 1965.

Ragusa, Olga. "Comparative Perspectives on Pirandello." *Atenea* 8.1 (1988): 19–36.

Starkie, Walter. *Luigi Pirandello, 1867–1936.* 3rd ed. Berkeley: U of California P, 1965.

Stone, Jennifer. *Pirandello's Naked Prompt: The Structure of Repetition in Modernism.* Ravenna: Longo Editore, 1989.

PLAUTUS

Anderson, William Scovil. *Barbarian Play: Plautus' Roman Comedy.* Toronto: U of Toronto P, 1996.

Moore, Timothy J. *The Theater of Plautus: Playing to the Audience.* Austin: U of Texas P, 1999.

Segal, Erich. *Roman Laughter: The Comedy of Plautus.* New York: Oxford UP, 1987.

———, ed. *Oxford Readings in Menander, Plautus, and Terence.* Oxford: Oxford UP, 2001.

Slater, Niall W. *Plautus in Performance: The Theater of the Mind.* Princeton: Princeton UP, 1985.

SECOND SHEPHERDS' PAGEANT

Harris, John Wesley. *Medieval Theatre in Context: An Introduction.* London: Routledge, 1992.

Nelson, Alan H. *The Medieval English Stage: Corpus Christi Pageants and Plays.* Chicago: U of Chicago P, 1974.

SENECA

Fairweather, Janet. *Seneca the Elder.* New York: Cambridge UP, 1981.

Stewart, J. "Challenging Prescriptions for Discourse: Seneca's Use of Paradox and Psymoron." *Mosaic* 30.1 (1997): 1–17.

Tarrant, R. J. *Seneca's Thyestes.* Atlanta: Scholars, 1985.

WILLIAM SHAKESPEARE

Bamber, Linda. *Comic Women, Tragic Men: A Study of Gender and Genre in Shakespeare.* Stanford: Stanford UP, 1982.

Barber, C. L. *Shakespeare's Festive Comedy.* Princeton: Princeton UP, 1968.

Bloom, Harold. *Shakespeare: The Invention of the Human.* London: Fourth Estate, 1999.

Bradley, A. C. *Shakespearean Tragedy.* New York: Meridian, 1955.

Bullough, Geoffrey, ed. *Narrative and Dramatic Sources of Shakespeare.* 8 vols. New York: Columbia UP, 1957–75.

Chute, Marchette. *Shakespeare of London.* New York: Dutton, 1949.

Doran, Madeleine. *Shakespeare's Dramatic Language.* Madison: U of Wisconsin P, 1976.

Drakakis, John, ed. *Alternative Shakespeares.* New York: Methuen, 1985.

Dusinberre, Juliet. *Shakespeare and the Nature of Women.* 2nd. ed. New York: St. Martin's, 1996.

Dutton, Richard. *Shakespeare: A Literary Life.* New York: St. Martin's, 1989.

Eagleton, Terry. *William Shakespeare.* New York: Blackwell, 1986.

Erikson, Peter. *Rewriting Shakespeare, Rewriting Ourselves.* Berkeley: U of California P, 1991.

Frye, Northrop. *On Shakespeare.* New Haven: Yale UP, 1986.

Goddard, Harold C. *The Meaning of Shakespeare.* Chicago: U of Chicago P, 1951.

Grady, Hugh. *The Modernist Shakespeare: Critical Texts in a Material World.* New York: Oxford UP, 1991.

Granville-Barker, H. *Prefaces to Shakespeare.* Princeton: Princeton UP, 1946.

Greene, G., et al., eds. *The Women's Part: Feminist Criticism of Shakespeare.* Urbana: U of Illinois P, 1980.

Honan, Park. *Shakespeare: A Life.* Oxford: Oxford UP, 2000.

Hyland, Peter. *An Introduction to Shakespeare: The Dramatist in His Context.* Houndmills: Macmillan, 1996.

Ioppolo, Grace. *Revising Shakespeare.* Cambridge: Harvard UP, 1991.

Jacobus, Lee. *Shakespeare and the Dialectic of Certainty.* New York: St. Martin's, 1992.

Jardine, Lisa. *Still Harping on Daughters: Women and Drama in the Age of Shakespeare.* Totowa: Barnes, 1983.

Kermode, Frank, ed. *Four Centuries of Shakespearean Criticism.* New York: Avon, 1974.

Kiernan, Pauline. *Shakespeare's Theory of Drama.* Cambridge: Cambridge UP, 1998.

Kiernan, Ryan, ed. *Shakespeare: Texts and Contexts.* New York: St. Martin's, 1999.

Kott, Jan. *Shakespeare Our Contemporary.* New York: Norton, 1974.

McDonald, Russ. *The Bedford Companion to Shakespeare: An Introduction with Documents.* Boston: Bedford, 1996.

Meagher, John C. *Shakespeare's Shakespeare: How the Plays Were Made.* New York: Continuum, 1997.

Orgel, Stephen and Sean Keilen. *Shakespeare in the Theatre.* Shakespeare: The Critical Complex 8. New York: Garland, 1999.

Righter, Anne. *Shakespeare and the Idea of the Play.* London: Chatto, 1962.

Schoenbaum, Samuel. *William Shakespeare: A Documentary Life.* New York: Oxford UP, 1975.

Schwartz, Murray M., and Coppelia Kahn, eds. *Representing Shakespeare: New Psychoanalytic Essays.* Baltimore: Johns Hopkins UP, 1981.

Scott, Michael. *Shakespeare and the Modern Dramatist.* New York: St. Martin's, 1989.

Shakespeare Quarterly. Annual Bibliography.

Shakespeare Survey 9.

Shellard, Dominic. *William Shakespeare.* The British Library Writers' Lives. New York: Oxford UP, 1998.

Wells, Stanley W., ed. *Shakespeare and Language.* Cambridge: Cambridge UP, 1997.

———, ed. *Shakespeare in the Theatre: An Anthology of Criticism.* Oxford: Clarendon, 1997.

———. *Shakespeare: The Poet and His Plays.* London: Methuen, 1997.

Hamlet

Berkoff, Steven. *I Am Hamlet.* New York: Grove, 1990.

Bloom, Harold, ed. *William Shakespeare's* Hamlet. New York: Chelsea, 1986.

Calderwood, James. *To Be and Not to Be: Negation and Metadrama in* Hamlet. New York: Columbia UP, 1983.

Cantor, Paul A. *Shakespeare,* Hamlet. New York: Cambridge UP, 1989.

Charney, Maurice. Hamlet's *Fictions.* New York: Routledge, 1988.

Cohen, Michael. Hamlet *in My Mind's Eye.* Athens: U of Georgia P, 1989.

Duffy, Kevin Thomas. *The Elsinor Appeal: People vs.* Hamlet. New York: St. Martin's, 1996.

Farley-Hills, David, ed. "Critical Responses to *Hamlet,* 1600–1900." *The Hamlet Collection 3.* New York: AMS, 1999.

Frye, Northrop. *Fools of Time: Studies in Shakespearean Tragedy.* Buffalo: U of Toronto P, 1973.

Gay, Jean de. "Playing (with) Shakespeare." *New Theatre Quarterly* 14 (1998): 125–38.

Jones, Ernest. *Hamlet and Oedipus.* New York: Norton, 1976.

Lacan, Jacques. "Desire and the Interpretation of Desire in *Hamlet.*" *Literature and Psychoanalysis: The Question of Reading Otherwise.* Ed. Shoshana Felman. Baltimore: Johns Hopkins UP, 1982.

Levin, Harry. *The Question of Hamlet.* New York: Oxford UP, 1959.

Mills, John A. Hamlet *on Stage: The Great Tradition.* Westport: Greenwood, 1985.

Prosser, Eleanor. Hamlet *and Revenge.* Stanford: Stanford UP, 1967.

Ribner, Irving. *Patterns in Shakespearean Tragedy.* New York: Barnes, 1960.

Showalter, Elaine. "Representing Ophelia: Women, Madness, and the Responsibilities of Feminist Criticism." *Shakespeare and the Question of Theory.* Ed. Patricia Parker and Geoffrey Hartman. New York: Methuen, 1985.

Trewin, J. C. *Five and Eighty Hamlets.* New York: New Amsterdam, 1987.

Wilson, John Dover. *What Happens in* Hamlet. Cambridge: Cambridge UP, 1967.

A Midsummer Night's Dream

Bloom, Harold, ed. *William Shakespeare's* A Midsummer Night's Dream. New York: Chelsea, 1987.

Brown, John Russell. *Shakespeare and His Comedies.* London: Methuen, 1968.

Fleissner, Robert F. "Shakespeare's *A Midsummer Night's Dream.*" *Explicator* 55.2 (1997): 72–73.

Garber, Marjorie. *Dream in Shakespeare: From Metaphor to Metamorphosis.* New Haven: Yale UP, 1974.

Girard, Rene. "Myth and Ritual in Shakespeare: *A Midsummer Night's Dream.*" *Textual Strategies: Perspectives in Post-Structuralist Criticism.* Ithaca: Cornell UP, 1979.

Griffiths, Trevor R., ed. *A Midsummer Night's Dream.* Shakespeare in Production. Cambridge: Cambridge UP, 1996.

Hawkes, Terrence. *A Midsummer Night's Dream.* New Casebooks. New York: St. Martin's, 1996.

Hendricks, Margo. "Obscured by Dreams, Race, Empire, and Shakespeare's *A Midsummer Night's Dream.*" *Shakespeare Quarterly* 47.1 (1996): 37–60.

Kehler, Dorothea, ed. A Midsummer Night's Dream: *Critical Essays.* New York: Garland, 1998.

Latham, Minor White. *The Elizabethan Fairies: The Fairies of Folklore and the Fairies of Shakespeare.* New York: Columbia UP, 1930.

Legatt, Alexander. A Midsummer Night's Dream: *Shakespeare's Comedy of Love.* London: Methuen, 1974.

Montrose, Louis Adrian. "'Shaping Fantasies': Figurations of Gender and Power in Elizabethan Culture." *Representations* 1.2 (1983): 61–94.

Paster, Gail Kern and Skiles Howard, eds. A Midsummer Night's Dream: *Texts and Contexts.* Boston: Bedford, 1999.

Shelbourne, David. *The Making of* A Midsummer Night's Dream. London: Methuen, 1982.

Wiles, David. "The Carnivalesque in *A Midsummer Night's Dream.*" *Shakespeare and Carnival: After Bakhtin.* Ed. Ronald Knowles. New York: St. Martin's, 1998. 61–82.

Young. David P. *Something of Great Constancy: The Art of* A Midsummmer Night's Dream. New Haven: Yale UP, 1966.

Othello

Bernard, J. "Theatricality and Textuality: The Example of *Othello.*" *New Literary History* 26 (1995): 931–49.

Ghazoul, Ferial J. The Arabization of *Othello.*" *Comparative Literature* 50.1 (1998): 1–31.

Hadfield, Andrew. "Race in *Othello*: The 'History and Description of Africa' and the Black Legend." *Notes and Queries* 45 (1998): 336–38.

Hogan, Patrick C. "*Othello,* Racism, and Despair." *College Language Association Journal* 41 (1998): 431–51.

Honigmann, E. A. J. *The Texts of* Othello *and Shakespearean Revision.* London: Routledge, 1996.

Pechter, Edward. Othello *and Interpretive Traditions.* Iowa City: U of Iowa P, 1999.

Widmayer, M. "Brabantio and Othello." *English Studies* 77.2 (1996): 113–26.

Xiaojing, Zhou. "Othello's Color in Shakespeare's Tragedy." *College Language Association Journal* 41 (1998): 335–48.

BERNARD SHAW

Bentley, Eric. *Bernard Shaw*. 2nd ed. London: Methuen, 1967.

Berst, Charles A. *Bernard Shaw and the Art of Drama*. Urbana: U of Illinois P, 1973.

Bloom, Harold, ed. *George Bernard Shaw*. New York: Chelsea, 1987.

Bloomfield, Zachary. "America's Response to George Bernard Shaw: A Study of Professional Productions." *Theatre Studies* 36 (1991): 5–17.

Bosha, Francis J. "William James's Unpublished Correspondence with Bernard Shaw." *Notes and Queries* 37 (1990): 432–33.

Brown, John Ivor. *Shaw in His Time*. London: Nelson, 1965.

Evans, T. F. *Shaw: The Critical Heritage*. Boston: Routledge, 1976.

Fisher, James. "Edy Craig and the Pioneer Players' Production of *Mrs. Warren's Profession*." *Shaw: The Annual of Bernard Shaw Studies* 15 (1995): 37–56.

Gainor, J. Ellen. "G. B. S. and the New Woman." *New England Theatre Journal* 1.1 (1990): 1–17.

———. *Shaw's Daughters: Dramatic and Narrative Constructions of Gender*. Ann Arbor: U of Michigan P, 1991.

Ganz, Arthur F. *George Bernard Shaw*. New York: Grove, 1983.

Gibbs, A. M. *The Art and Mind of Shaw: Essays in Criticism*. New York: St. Martin's, 1983.

———, ed. *Shaw: Interviews and Recollections*. Iowa City: U of Iowa P, 1990.

Gordon, David J. *Bernard Shaw and the Comic Sublime*. New York: St. Martin's, 1990.

Grecco, Stephen. "Vivie Warren's Profession: A New Look at *Mrs. Warren's Profession*." *Shaw: The Annual of Bernard Shaw Studies* 10 (1967): 93–99.

Greene, Nicholas. *Bernard Shaw: A Critical View*. New York: St. Martin's, 1984.

Hugo, Leon. *Edwardian Shaw: The Writer and His Age*. Basingstoke: Macmillan, 1999.

Innes, Christopher D., ed. *George Bernard Shaw*. Cambridge Companions to Literature. Cambridge: Cambridge UP, 1998.

Kauffmann, Stanley. "The Late Beginner: Bernard Shaw Becoming a Dramatist." *South Atlantic Quarterly* 91.2 (1992): 289–301.

Kaufman, R. J., ed. *G. B. Shaw: A Collection of Critical Essays*. Englewood Cliffs: Prentice, 1965.

Larson, Gale K. *Shaw and History*. University Park: Pennsylvania State UP, 1999.

May, Keith M. *Ibsen and Shaw*. New York: St. Martin's, 1985.

Mudford, Peter. "*Mrs. Warren's Profession*." *The Shavian: The Journal of Bernard Shaw* 6.5 (1987): 4–10.

Peters, Sally. *Bernard Shaw: The Ascent of the Superman*. New Haven: Yale UP, 1996.

Shaw, Bernard. *An Autobiography*. Ed. Stanley Weintraub. 2 vols. New York: Weybright, 1969.

———. *Collected Letters*. Ed. Dan H. Laurence. New York: Dodd, 1972.

———. *Complete Plays with Prefaces*. New York: Dodd, 1962.

———. *Plays and Players: Essays on the Theatre*. Ed. A. C. Ward. New York: Oxford UP, 1963.

———. *Shaw on Shakespeare: An Anthology of Bernard Shaw's Writings on the Plays and Production of Shakespeare*. Ed. Edwin Wilson. New York: Dutton, 1961.

Silver, Arnold. *Bernard Shaw: The Darker Side*. Stanford: Stanford UP, 1982.

Skidelsky, R. "Doing Good and Being Good: The Conflicting Ideals of Bernard Shaw and John Maynard Keynes." *Times Literary Supplement* 26 March 1999: 12–14.

Sterner, Mark H. "The Changing Status of Women in Late Victorian Drama." *Within the Dramatic Spectrum*. Ed. Karelisa Hartigan. Lanham: UP of America, 1986. 199–212.

Turner, Tramble T. *George Bernard Shaw*. Westport: Greenwood, 1997.

Valency, Maurice. *The Cart and the Trumpet: The Plays of George Bernard Shaw*. New York: Schocken, 1983.

Weintraub, Stanley. *The Unexpected Shaw: Biographical Approaches to G.B.S. and His Work*. New York: Ungar, 1982.

Wiley, Catherine. "The Matter with Manners: The New Woman and the Problem Play." *Women in Theatre*. Ed. James Redmond. Cambridge: Cambridge UP, 1989. 109–27.

Wisenthal, J.L. "Wilde, Shaw and the Play of Conversation." *Modern Drama* 37.1 (1994): 206–19.

Yae, Young-soo. "Individual Will and Social Environment in G. B. Shaw's *Mrs. Warren's Profession*." *Journal of English Language and Literature* 37.1 (1991): 213–32.

Yorks, Samuel A. *The Evolution of Bernard Shaw*. Lanham: UP of America, 1981.

SAM SHEPARD

Auerbach, Doris. *Sam Shepard, Arthur Kopit, and the Off-Broadway Theatre*. Twayne's United States Author Series 432. Boston: Twayne, 1982.

Bottoms, Stephen J. *The Theatre of Sam Shepard: States of Crisis*. Cambridge: Cambridge UP, 1998.

Callens, Johan, ed. *Sam Shepard: Between the Margin and the Center*. 2 vols. Contemporary Theatre Review 8, 3–4. Chur, Switz.: Harwood, 1998.

Cohn, Ruby. *New American Dramatists: 1960–1980*. New York: Grove, 1982.

Cott, Jonathan. "The Rolling Stone Interview: Sam Shepard." *Rolling Stone* 18 Dec. 1986–1 Jan. 1987: 166–72+.

Falk, Florence. "The Role of Performance in Sam Shepard's Plays." *Theatre Journal* May 1981: 182–98.

Gilman, Richard. Introduction. *Sam Shepard: Seven Plays.* New York: Bantam, 1981. ix–xiv.

Hart, Lynda. *Sam Shepard's Metaphorical Stages.* Westport: Greenwood, 1987.

King, Kimball, ed. *Sam Shepard: A Casebook.* New York: Garland, 1988.

Lanier, Gregory W. "*True West?* Sam Shepard's Mythic Misdirection." *Text and Presentation* 12 (1992): 49–54.

March, Christie. "The Real and Illusory in Sam Shepard's *True West.*" *The Image of the American West in Literature, the Media, and Society.* Ed. Will Wright and Stephen Kaplan. Pueblo: U of Southern Colorado, 1996. 251–54.

Mottram, Ron. *Inner Landscapes: The Theater of Sam Shepard.* Columbia: U of Missouri P, 1984.

Orbison, Tucker. "Mythic Levels in Sam Shepard's *True West.*" *Modern Drama* 27 (Dec. 1984): 506–19.

Oumano, Ellen. *Sam Shepard: The Life and Work of an American Dreamer.* New York: St. Martin's, 1986.

Sessums, Kevin. "Geography of a Horse Dreamer: Playwright, Actor, and Movie Director Sam Shepard." *Interview* Sept. 1988: 70–78.

Shewey, Don. *Sam Shepard.* 2nd ed. New York: Da Capo, 1997.

St. Pierre, Ronald. "'True-to-Life-Stuff': Versions of the West in Shepard's *True West.*" *Shoin Literary Review* 29 (1996): 37–50.

Wade, Leslie A. *Sam Shepard and the American Theatre.* Westport, CT: Praeger, 1997.

Williams, Megan. "Nowhere Man and the Twentieth-Century Cowboy: Images of Identity and American History in Sam Shepard's *True West.*" *Modern Drama* 40 (1997): 57–73.

Wilson, Ann. "Fool of Desire: The Spectator to the Plays of Sam Shepard." *Modern Drama* 30.1 (1987): 46–57.

———, ed. *Rereading Shepard: Contemporary Critical Essays on the Plays of Sam Shepard.* New York: St. Martin's, 1993.

ANNA DEAVERE SMITH

Lyons, Charles R. "Anna Deavere Smith: Perspectives on Her Performance within the Context of Critical Theory." *Journal of Dramatic Theory and Criticism* 9.1 (1994): 43–66.

Reinelt, Janelle. "Performing Race: Anna Deavere Smith's Fires in the Mirror." *Modern Drama* 39.4 (1996): 609–17.

Thompson, Debby. "'Is Race a Trope': Anna Deavere Smith and the Question of Racial Performativity." *African American Review* 37.1 (2003): 127–38.

SOPHOCLES

Bloom, Harold, ed. *Sophocles.* New York: Chelsea, 1990.

———, ed. *Sophocles' Oedipus Plays:* Oedipus the King, Oedipus at Colonus, *and* Antigone. Bloom's Notes. Broomhall: Chelsea, 1999.

Bowra, Sir Maurice. *Sophoclean Tragedy.* Oxford: Clarendon, 1944.

Burton, Reginald William Boteler. *The Chorus in Sophocles' Tragedies.* New York: Oxford UP, 1980.

Bushnell, Rebecca. *Prophesying Tragedy: Sign and Voice in Sophocles' Theban Plays.* Ithaca: Cornell UP, 1988.

Buxton, R. G. A. *Sophocles.* New York: Clarendon, 1984.

Gardiner, Cynthia P. *The Sophoclean Chorus: A Study of Character and Function.* Iowa City: U of Iowa P, 1987.

Hogan, James C. *A Commentary on the Plays of Sophocles.* Boulder: netLibrary, 1999.

Kitto, H. D. F. *Sophocles: Dramatist and Philosopher.* London: Oxford UP, 1958.

Knox, Bernard M. *Sophocles at Thebes: Sophocles' Tragic Hero and His Time.* New York: Norton, 1971.

Reinhardt, Karl. *Sophokles.* Trans. D. Harvey and H. Harvey. New York: Barnes, 1978.

Scodel, Ruth. *Sophocles.* Boston: Twayne, 1984.

Segal, Charles. *Tragedy and Civilization: An Interpretation of Sophocles.* Cambridge: Harvard UP, 1981.

Waldock, A. J. A. *Sophocles the Dramatist.* Cambridge: Cambridge UP, 1951.

Wiles, David. *The Masks of Menander: Sign and Meaning in Greek and Roman Performances.* Cambridge: Cambridge UP, 1991.

Winnington-Ingram, R. P. *Sophocles: An Interpretation.* New York: Cambridge UP, 1980.

Woodard, T. M, ed. *Sophocles: A Collection of Critical Essays.* Englewood Cliffs: Prentice, 1966.

Antigone

Brown, Andrew. *A New Companion to Greek Tragedy.* Totowa: Barnes, 1983.

Chanter, Tina. "Tragic Discolations: Antigone's Modern Theatrics." *Differences: A Journal of Feminist Cultural Studies* 10.1 (1998): 75–97.

Goheen, R. F. *The Imagery of Sophocles'* Antigone: *A Study of Poetic Language and Structure.* Princeton: Princeton UP, 1951.

Linforth, I. M. *Antigone and Creon.* Berkeley: U of California P, 1961.

"Review: *Antigone.*" *Theatre Record* 18.6 (1998): 320–21.

Steiner, George. *Antigones.* New York: Clarendon, 1984.

Oedipus Rex

Bloom, Harold. *Sophocles'* Oedipus Rex. New York: Chelsea, 1988.

Cameron, Alister. *The Identity of Oedipus the King: Five Essays on the "Oedipus Tyrannus."* New York: New York UP, 1968.

Edmonds, Lowell. *Oedipus: The Ancient Legend and Its Later Analogues*. Baltimore: Johns Hopkins UP, 1985.

Fergusson, Francis. *The Idea of a Theater*. Princeton: Princeton UP, 1949.

———. "*Oedipus Rex*: The Tragic Rhythm of Action." *Ritual and Myth: Robertson Smith, Farzer, Hooke, and Harrison*. Ed. Robert A. Segal. New York: Garland, 1996. 67–95.

O'Brien, M. J., ed. *Twentieth Century Interpretations of Oedipus Rex*. Englewood Cliffs: Prentice, 1968.

Rudnytsky, Peter L. *Freud and Oedipus*. New York: Columbia UP, 1987.

Tonelli, Franco. "Sophocles' *Oedipus* and the Tale of the Theatre." *Speculum Artium Series* 12. Ravenna: Longo Editore, 1983.

Verhoeff, Han, and Harly Sonne. "Does Oedipus Have His Complex?" *Style* 18.3 (1984): 261–83.

WOLE SOYINKA

Adah, Anthony, ed., "Soyinka and Postcolonialism." *Modern Drama* 45.3 (2002): 335–493.

Byam, Dale. "Art, Exile and Resistance." *American Theatre* 14.1 (1997): 26–29.

Euba, Femi. "Wole Soyinka (1934)." *Postcolonial African Writers: A Bio-Bibliographical Critical Source Book*. Ed. Naidu Parekh et al. Westport: Greenwood, 1998. 438–54.

Gibbs, James. "The BBC Became a Glutton for Punishment: Wole Soyinka's Dealings with the BBC (1953–1959)." *Crisis and Creativity in the New Literatures in English: Cross/Cultures*. Ed. Geoffrey Davis and Hena Maes-Jelinek. Amsterdam: Rodopi, 1990. 205–17.

———. *Critical Perspectives on Wole Soyinka*. Washington: Three Continents, 1980.

———. "'Marrying Earth to Heaven': A Nobel Laureate at the End of the Eighties." *International Literature in English: Essays on the Major Writers*. Ed. Robert L. Ross. New York: Garland, 1991.

———. *Wole Soyinka*. New York: Grove, 1986.

Hepburn, Joan. "Mediators of Ritual Closure." *Black American Literature Forum* 22.3 (1988): 576–614.

Jeyifo, Biodun, ed. *Perspectives on Wole Soyinka: Freedom and Complexity*. Jackson: UP of Mississippi, 2001.

Jones, Eldred D. *The Writing of Wole Soyinka*. Portsmouth: Heinemann, 1988.

Katrak, Ketu H. *Wole Soyinka and Modern Tragedy: A Study of Dramatic Theory and Practice*. Westport: Greenwood, 1986.

King, Bruce, ed. *Post-Colonial English Drama: Commonwealth Drama since 1960*. New York: St. Martin's, 1992.

Larsen, Stephan. *A Writer and His Gods: A Study of the Importance of Yoruba Myths and Religious Ideas to the Writing of Wole Soyinka*. Stockholm: U of Stockholm P, 1983.

Lindfors, Bernth. "Beating the White Man at His Own Game: Nigerian Reactions to the Nobel Prize in Literature." *Literary Criterion* 25.1 (1990): 43–59.

Maduakor, Obi. *Wole Soyinka: An Introduction to His Writings*. New York: Garland, 1987.

Maja-Pearce, Adewale. *Who's Afraid of Wole Soyinka? Essays on Censorship*. London: Heinemann, 1991.

———, ed. *Wole Soyinka: An Appraisal*. Oxford: Heinemann, 1994.

McMahon, Christina S. "Interview with Wole Soyinka." *Theatron* (Spring 2003): 89–95.

Moody, David. "The Prodigal Father: Discursive Rupture in the Plays of Wole Soyinka." *ARIEL* 23.1 (1992): 25–38.

Ndiava, Marieme. "Female Stereotypes in Wole Soyinka's *The Strong Breed* and *The Lion and the Jewel*." *Bridges* 5 (1993): 19–24.

Ogbaa, Kalu, ed. *The Gong and the Flute: African Literary Development and Celebration*. Westport: Greenwood, 1994.

Ojewuyi, Olesegun. "Wole Soyinka: The Hunter, the Hunt." *Theater* 28.1 (1998): 58–59.

———, and Shawn-Marie Garrett. "A World of Amusement and Pity." *Theater* 28.1 (1998): 61–68.

Okome, Onookome. *Ogun's Children: The Literature and Politics of Wole Soyinka Since the Nobel Prize*. Trenton: Africa World P, 1999.

Soyinka, Wole. *Ake: The Years of Childhood*. New York: Random, 1981.

———. *Isara: A Voyage Round Essay*. New York: Random, 1989.

———. *The Man Died: The Prison Notes of Wole Soyinka*. London: Collings, 1972.

———. "Twice Bitten: The Fate of Africa's Culture Producers." *PMLA* 105.1 (1990): 110–120.

Wright, Derek. "Ritual and Revolution: Soyinka's Dramatic Theory." *ARIEL* 23.1 (1992): 39–53.

———. "Wole Soyinka as Yoruba Theatre Historian." *Post-Colonial Stages: Critical and Creative Views on Drama, Theatre and Performance*. Ed. Helen Gilbert. London: Dangaroo, 1999. 161–73.

———. *Wole Soyinka: Life, Work and Criticism*. Fredericton: York, 1996.

———. *Wole Soyinka Revisited*. New York: Twayne, 1993.

AUGUST STRINDBERG

Carlson, Harry Gilbert. *Out of Inferno: Strindberg's Reawakening as an Artist*. Seattle: U of Washington P, 1996.

———. *Strindberg and the Poetry of Myth*. Berkeley: U of California P, 1982.

Chaudhuri, U. "Private Part: Sex, Class, and Stage Space in *Miss Julie*." *Theatre Journal* 45.3 (1993): 317–32.

Franchuk, E. S. "Symbolism in *Miss Julie*." *Theatre Research International* 18 (1993): 11–15.

Lally, M. L. K. "Strindberg's *Miss Julie*." *Explicator* 48.3 (1990): 196–98.

Lucas, F. L. *The Drama of Ibsen and Strindberg*. London: Cassell, 1962.

Meidal, Bjorn. "A Strindberg Forgery: Carl Ohman's August Strindberg and the Origin of Scenic Expressionism." *Scandinavica* 34.1 (1995): 61–69.

Parker, Brian. "Strindberg's *Miss Julie* and the Legend of Salome." *Modern Drama* 32 (1989): 469–84.

Reinert, Otto, ed. *Strindberg: A Collection of Critical Essays*. Englewood Cliffs: Prentice, 1971.

Robinson, Michael. "August Strindberg: His True Life?" *Scandinavica* 28.2 (1989): 185–91.

———. *Studies in Strindberg*. Norwich: Norvik, 1998.

Shideler, Ross. "The Absent Authority: From Darwin to Nora and Julie." *Space and Boundaries in Literature*. Proceedings of the Twelfth Congress of the International Comparative Literature Association. Ed. Roger Bauer and Donwe Fokkema. Munich: Iudicium, 1990.

Sprinchorn, Evert. *Strindberg as Dramatist*. New Haven: Yale UP, 1982.

Steene, Birgitta. *The Greatest Fire: A Study of August Strindberg*. Carbondale: Southern Illinois UP, 1973.

Stockenstrom, Goran, ed. *Strindberg's Dramaturgy*. Minneapolis: U of Minnesota P, 1988.

Tornqvist, Egil. *Strindberg's "Miss Julie": A Play and Its Transpositions*. Norwich: Norvik, 1988.

JOHN MILLINGTON SYNGE

Benson, Eugene. *J. M. Synge*. New York: Grove, 1983.

Casey, Daniel J., ed. *Critical Essays on John Millington Synge*. New York: Hall, 1994.

Corkery, Daniel. *Synge and Anglo-Irish Literature*. Cork: Cork UP, 1955.

Gerstenberger, Donna Lorine. *John Millington Synge*. 2nd ed. Boston: Twayne, 1990.

Gonzales, Alexander G. *Assessing the Achievement of J. M. Synge*. Westport: Greenwood, 1996.

Greene, David H., and Edward M. Stephens. *John Millington Synge, 1871–1909*. 2nd ed. New York: New York UP, 1989.

Grene, N. *Synge: A Critical Study Interpretation of the Plays*. London: Macmillan, 1975.

Kiberd, Declan. *Synge and the Irish Language*. London: Macmillan, 1979.

King, Mary C. *The Drama of J. M. Synge*. Syracuse: Syracuse UP, 1985.

Kopper, Edward A. *A John Millington Synge Literary Companion*. Westport: Greenwood, 1988.

Price, Alan. *Synge and Anglo-Irish Drama*. London: Methuen, 1961.

Roche, A. "Friel and Synge: Towards a Theatrical Language." *Irish University Review* 29.1 (1999): 145–61.

Skelton, Robin. *J. M. Synge and His World*. New York: Viking, 1971.

———. *The Writings of J. M. Synge*. London: Thames, 1971.

TERENCE

Forehand, Walter. *Terence*. Boston: Twayne, 1985.

Goldberg, Sander M. *Understanding Terence*. Princeton: Princeton UP, 1986.

Segal, Erich, ed. *Oxford Readings in Menander, Plautus, and Terence*. Oxford: Oxford UP, 2001.

LUIS VALDEZ

Elam, Harry Justin. *Taking it to the Streets: The Social Protest Theatre of Luis Valdez and Amiri Baraka*. Ann Arbor: U of Michigan P, 1997.

Morton, Carlos. *Critical Response to Zoot Suit and Corridos*. El Paso: U of Texas at El Paso, 1984.

Pizzato, M. "Brechtian and Aztec Violence in Valdez' Zoot Suit." *Journal of Popular Film and Television* 26.2 (1998): 52–61.

Valdez, Luis. *Luis Valdez—Early Works: Actors, Bernabé, and Pensamiento serpentino*. Houston: Arte Publico, 1990.

PAULA VOGEL

Kimbrough, Andrew. "The Pedophile in Me: The Ethics of How I Learned to Drive." *Journal of Dramatic Theory and Criticism* 16.2 (2002): 47–67.

Parker, Mary-Louise. "Paula Vogel." *Bomb* 61 (1997): 44–49.

Savran, David. "Driving Ms. Vogel." *American Theatre* 15.8 (1998): 16–19, 96–106.

Sova, Kathy. "Time to Laugh." *American Theatre* 14.2 (1997): 24.

OSCAR WILDE

Beckson, Karl E. *The Oscar Wilde Encyclopedia*. New York: AMS, 1998.

Bloom, Harold. *Oscar Wilde's* The Importance of Being Earnest. New York: Chelsea, 1988.

Byrne, Patrick. *The Wildes of Merrion Square: The Family of Oscar Wilde*. New York: Staples, 1953.

Calloway, Stephen. *Oscar Wilde: An Exquisite Life*. London: Orion Media, 1999.

Cohen, Ed. "Writing Gone Wild: Homoerotic Desire in the Closet of Representation." *PMLA* 102 (1987): 801–13.

Cohen, Philip K. *The Moral Vision of Oscar Wilde*. Rutherford: Fairleigh Dickinson UP, 1978.

Danson, Lawrence. *Wilde's Intentions. The Artist in His Criticism*. Oxford: Clarendon, 1997.

Ellmann, Richard. *Oscar Wilde*. New York: Knopf, 1988.

———. *Oscar Wilde: A Collection of Critical Essays*. Englewood Cliffs: Prentice, 1969.

Eltis, Sos. *Revisiting Wilde: Society and Subversion in the Plays of Oscar Wilde*. Oxford: Clarendon, 1996.

Erikson, Donald. *Oscar Wilde*. Boston: Twayne, 1977.

Gagnier, Regenia. *Idylls of the Marketplace: Oscar Wilde and the Victorian Public*. Stanford: Stanford UP, 1986.

Haley, Bruce. "Wilde's 'Decadence' and the Positivist Tradition." *Victorian Studies* 28 (1985): 215–29.

Hart-Davis, Rupert, ed. *Letters of Oscar Wilde*. New York: Harcourt, 1962.

———. *More Letters of Oscar Wilde*. New York: Vanguard, 1985.

Hodge, James H. *Famous Trials*. Baltimore: Penguin, 1963.

Mackie, W. Craven. "Bunburry Pure and Simple." *Modern Drama* 41.2 (1998): 327–30.

McCormack, Jerusha Hull, ed. *Wilde the Irishman*. New Haven: Yale UP, 1998.

Mikhail, E. H. *Oscar Wilde: Interviews and Recollections*. New York: Barnes, 1979.

Miller, Robert Keith. *Oscar Wilde*. New York: Ungar, 1982.

Poznar, Walter. "Life and Play in Wilde's *The Importance of Being Earnest*." *Midwest Quarterly* 30.4 (1989): 515–28.

Raby, Peter, ed. *The Cambridge Companion to Oscar Wilde*. Cambridge: Cambridge UP, 1997.

———. "The Origins of *The Importance of Being Earnest*." *Modern Drama* 37.1 (1994): 139–47.

San Juan, Epifanio. *The Art of Oscar Wilde*. Princeton: Princeton UP, 1963.

Smith, Philip E., and Michael S. Heffland, eds. *Oscar Wilde's Oxford Notebooks*. New York: Oxford UP, 1989.

Sullivan, Kevin. *Oscar Wilde*. Columbia Essays on Modern Writers 64. New York: Columbia UP, 1972.

Varty, Anne. *A Preface to Oscar Wilde*. Preface Books. London: Longman, 1998.

Weintraub, Stanley. *The Literary Criticism of Oscar Wilde*. Lincoln: U of Nebraska P, 1968.

Wilde, Oscar. *The Complete Works*. New York: Doubleday, 1923.

———. *The Plays of Oscar Wilde*. New York: Random, 1980.

TENNESSEE WILLIAMS

Aisbong, Emmanuel B. *Tennessee Williams: The Tragic Tension*. Elms Court: Stockwell, 1978.

Boxill, Roger. *Tennessee Williams*. New York: St. Martin's, 1987.

Bruhm, Steven. "Blackmailed by Sex: Tennessee Williams and the Economics of Desire." *Modern Drama* 34.4 (1991): 528–37.

Cranell, George W., ed. *The Critical Response to Tennessee Williams*. Westport: Greenwood, 1996.

Devlin, Albert J., ed. *Conversations with Tennessee Williams*. Jackson: UP of Mississippi, 1986.

Donahue, Francis. *The Dramatic World of Tennessee Williams*. New York: Ungar, 1964.

Falk, Signi Lenea. *Tennessee Williams*. 2nd ed. Boston: Twayne, 1978.

Griffin, Alice. *Understanding Tennessee Williams*. Columbia: U of South Carolina P, 1995.

Hayman, Ronald. *Tennessee Williams: Everyone Else Is an Audience*. New Haven: Yale UP, 1993.

Koprince, Susan. "Tennessee Williams's Unseen Characters." *Southern Quarterly* 33.1 (1994): 87–95.

Leavitt, Richard Freeman, ed. *The World of Tennessee Williams*. New York: Putnam's, 1978.

Leverich, Lyle. *Tom: The Unknown Tennessee Williams*. London: Scepter, 1996.

Martin, Robert A., ed. *Critical Essays on Tennessee Williams*. New York: Hall, 1997.

Parker, R. B., ed. The Glass Menagerie: *A Collection of Critical Essays*. Englewood Cliffs: Prentice, 1983.

Roudané, Matthew Charles, ed. *The Cambridge Companion to Tennessee Williams*. Cambridge: Cambridge UP, 1997.

Sarotte, Georges-Michel. "Fluidity and Differentiation in Three Plays by Tennessee Williams: *The Glass Menagerie, A Streetcar Named Desire*, and *Cat on a Hot Tin Roof*." *Staging Difference: Cultural Pluralism in American Theatre and Drama*. Ed. Marc Maufort. New York: Peter Lang, 1995. 141–56.

Savran, David. " 'By coming suddenly into a room that I thought was empty': Mapping the Closet with Tennessee Williams." *Studies in the Literary Imagination* 24.2 (1991): 57–74.

———. *Communists, Cowboys and Queers: The Politics of Masculinity in the Work of Arthur Miller and Tennessee Williams*. Minneapolis: U of Minnesota P, 1992.

Spoto, Donald. *The Kindness of Strangers: The Life of Tennessee Williams*. Boston: Little, 1985.

Stanton, Stephen, ed. *Tennessee Williams: A Collection of Critical Essays*. Englewood Cliffs: Prentice, 1977.

Thompson, Judith. *Tennessee Williams' Plays: Memory, Myth, and Symbol*. New York: Lang, 1987.

Wilhelmi, Nancy O. "The Language of Power and Powerlessness: Verbal Combat in the Plays of Tennessee Williams." *The Text and Beyond: Essays in Literary Linguistics*. Ed. Cynthia Goldin-Bernstein. Tuscaloosa: U of Alabama P, 1994.

Williams, Dakin, with Shepherd Mead. *Tennessee Williams: An Intimate Biography*. New York: Arbor, 1983.

Williams, Tennessee. *Memoirs*. Garden City: Doubleday, 1975

Cat on a Hot Tin Roof

Atkinson, Brooks. "Williams' 'Tin Roof.' " *New York Times* 3 Apr. 1955: B1.

Huzzard, Jere. "Williams' *Cat on a Hot Tin Roof*." *Explicator* 43.2 (1985):46–47.

Inge, Thomas M. "The South, Tragedy and Comedy in Tennessee Williams's *Cat on a Hot Tin Roof*." *The United States South: Regionalism and Identity*. Ed. Tjebbe Westendorp. Rome: Bulzone, 1991.

Kalem, T. E. "Fate Strikes the Delta." *Time* 6 Dec. 1976: 97–98.

"London Sees Cat; Opinion Is Divided." *New York Times* 31 Jan. 1958: 24.

Mayberry, Susan Nela. "A Study of Illusion and the Grotesque in Tennessee Williams' *Cat on a Hot Tin Roof.*" *Southern Studies* 22.4 (1983): 359–65.

Rev. of *Cat on a Hot Tin Roof. New York Theatre Critics' Reviews* 20 Mar. 1955: 342–43.

Rev. of *Cat on a Hot Tin Roof. New York Theatre Critics' Reviews* 25 Sept. 1974: 242–46.

The Glass Menagerie

Bloom, Harold. *Tennessee Williams's* The Glass Menagerie. New York: Chelsea, 1988.

Cardullo, Bert. "The Blue Rose of St. Louis: Laura, Romanticism, and *The Glass Menagerie.*" *Tennessee Williams Annual Review* (1998).

Greiff, Louis K. "Fathers, Daughters, and Spiritual Sisters: Marsha Norman's *'night, Mother* and Tennessee Williams's *The Glass Menagerie.*" *Text and Performance Quarterly* 9.3 (1989): 224–28.

Jones, John H. "The Missing Link: The Father in *The Glass Menagerie.*" *Notes on Mississippi Writers* 20.1 (1988): 29–38.

Kolin, Philip C. "The Black and Multi-Racial Productions of Tennessee Williams's *The Glass Menagerie.*" *Journal of Dramatic Theory and Criticism* 9.2 (1995): 96–128.

Levy, Eric P. "Through Soundproof Glass: The Prison of Self-Consciousness in *The Glass Menagerie.*" *Modern Drama* 36.4 (1993): 529–37.

Parker, R. B. "The Circle Closed: A Psychological Reading of *The Glass Menagerie* and the Two Character Play." *Modern Drama* 28 (1985): 517–34.

Presley, Delma Eugene. The Glass Menagerie: *An American Memory.* Boston: Twayne, 1990.

Reynolds, James. "The Failure of Technology in *The Glass Menagerie.*" *Modern Drama* 34.4 (1991): 522–27.

Siebold, Thomas., ed. *Readings on* The Glass Menagerie. San Diego: Greenhaven, 1998.

Smith, William Jay. "Tom: The Making of *The Glass Menagerie.*" *The New Criterion* 14 (1996): 72–77.

Thierfelder, William R. "Williams's *The Glass Menagerie.*" *Explicator* 48.4 (1990): 284–85.

Usui, Masami. "'A World of Her Own' in Tennessee Williams's *The Glass Menagerie.*" *Studies in Culture and the Humanities* 1 (1992): 21–37.

AUGUST WILSON

Arthur, Thomas H. "Looking for My Relatives: The Political Implications of 'Family' in Selected Works of Athol Fugard and August Wilson." *South African Theatre Journal* 6.2 (1992): 5–16.

Bogumil, Mary L. *Understanding August Wilson.* Columbia: U of South Carolina P, 1999.

DiGaetani, John L. *A Search for a Postmodern Theater: Interviews with Contemporary Playwrights.* Westport: Greenwood, 1991.

Elkins, Marilyn, ed. *August Wilson: A Casebook.* New York: Garland, 1994.

Freedman, Samuel G. "A Voice from the Streets." *New York Times Magazine* 15 Mar. 1987: 33+.

———. "Wilson's New *Fences* Nurtures a Partnership." *New York Times* 5 May 1985, sec. I: 80.

Gerard, Jeremy. "Waterford to Broadway: Well-Traveled *Fences.*" *New York Times* 9 April 1987, sec. 3: 21.

Henderson, Heather. "Building Fences: An Interview with Mary Alice and James Earl Jones." *Yale Theater* 12 (Summer/Fall 1985): 67–70.

Herrington, Joan. *I Ain't Sorry for Nothin' I Done: August Wilson's Process of Playwrighting.* New York: Limelight, 1998.

Kelley, Kevin. "August Wilson an Heir to O'Neill." *Boston Globe* 24 Jan. 1988: A1+.

Lyons, B. "An Interview with August Wilson." *Contemporary Literature* 40.1 (1999): 1–21.

Nadel, Alan, ed. *May All Your Fences Have Gates: Essays on the Drama of August Wilson.* Iowa City: U of Iowa P, 1994.

Pereira, Kim. *August Wilson and the African American Odyssey.* Urbana: U of Illinois P, 1995.

Plum, Jay. "Blues, History and the Dramaturgy of August Wilson." *African American Review* 27.4 (1993): 561–67.

Rich, Frank. "Theater: Family Ties in Wilson's *Fences.*" *New York Times* 27 Mar. 1987, sec. II: 1.

Shannon, Sandra, "Blues, History, and Dramaturgy: An Interview with August Wilson." *African American Review* 27.4 (1993): 539–59.

———. "Conversing with the Past: *Joe Turner's Come and Gone* and *The Piano Lesson.*" *CEA Magazine* 4.1 (1991): 33–42.

Sterling, E. "Protecting Home: Patriarchal Authority in August Wilson's *Fences.*" *Essays in Theatre-Etudes Theatrales* 17.1 (1996): 53–62.

Wang, Qun. *An In-Depth Study of the Major Plays of African American Playwright August Wilson: Vernacularizing the Blues on Stage.* Lewiston: Mellen, 1999.

Wessling, J. H. "Wilson's *Fences.*" *Explicator* 57.2 (1999): 123–27.

ZEAMI MOTOKIYO

Hare, Thomas Blenman. *Zeami's Style: The Noh Plays of Zeami Motokiyo.* Stanford: Stanford UP, 1996.

Rimer, J. Thomas, and Yamazaki Masakazu, *On the Art of the No Drama: The Major Treatises of Zeami.* Princeton: Princeton UP, 1984.

Selected List of Film, Video, and Audiocassette Resources

The following list of audiovisual resources supplements the teaching of plays in *The Bedford Introduction to Drama*. The resources are listed alphabetically by playwright.

The films and videos marked with an asterisk (*) are available for rental from member institutions of the Consortium of College and University Media Centers. For further information, consult Media Sources: Consortium of College and University Media Centers, 1st ed. on CD-ROM.

Many of the videos are available for rental from local video outlets. Others are available through a distributor. Check the Directory of Distributors following this list for information.

AESCHYLUS

Aeschylus, *The Oresteia*. 230 minutes, 1985. VHS, Beta, 3/4″ U-matic cassette. Directed by Peter Hall. The National Theatre of Great Britain performs Aeschylus's classic dramas, each available separately. Distributed by Films for the Humanities and Sciences.

Aeschylus and the Death of Tragedy. 80 minutes, 1963. Audiocassette. Walter Kaufmann. Kaufmann argues that although Aeschylus is generally considered the creator of tragedy, his world-view contains central elements that are usually associated with the death of tragedy in our time. The *Oresteia* trilogy is examined. Distributed by Audio-Forum.

EDWARD ALBEE

Edward Albee. 52 minutes, color. VHS, DVD. This program looks at Edward Albee's work from 1962's *Who's Afraid of Virginia Woolf?* to his 1994 Pulitzer Prize–winning drama *Three Tall Women*. Distributed by Films for the Humanities and Sciences.

ANONYMOUS

Anonymous, *Everyman*. 25 minutes, color, 1971. 16 mm film. Abridged by H. Frances Clark. Distributed by Coronet/MTI Film & Video.

Anonymous, *Everyman*. 53 minutes, color, 1991. VHS. Produced in conjunction with medieval literature scholar Holward Schless of Columbia University. Authentically staged in period costume. Distributed by Insight Media.

ANONYMOUS

Anonymous (or the Wakefield Master), *The Second Shepherds' Play*. Titled *Medieval Drama: From Sanctuary to Stage*. 48 minutes. VHS. Excerpts from *The Second Shepherd's Play*, *Everyman*, *Ordo Virtutum* and the York Mystery Cycle. Distributed by Films for the Humanities and Sciences.

ARISTOPHANES

Aristophanes, *Lysistrata*. 97 minutes, color, 1987. VHS, Beta. A contemporary adaptation, shot on location at the Acropolis. In Greek with English subtitles. Distributed by New York Film Annex.

SAMUEL BECKETT

Beckett on Film. 2002. DVD. This 4-DVD set presents acclaimed productions of Beckett's 19 plays. Disc 3 includes *Happy Days*. Distributed by Insight Media.

Samuel Beckett. 80 minutes, color, 1989. Beta, VHS, 3/4″ U-matic cassette. An autobiographical portrait of Beckett's artistic life through his work. Distributed by Films for the Humanities and Sciences.

Samuel Beckett, *Happy Days*. Color, 2003. VHS, DVD. Starring Irene Worth and George Voskovec. Directed by David Heeley. Distributed by Kultur.

APHRA BEHN

Approaching Literature: Aphra Behn's **The Rover.** 181 minutes, color, 1997. VHS, DVD. This program presents a complete performance of Behn's *The Rover.* Distributed by Insight Media.

BERTOLT BRECHT

Bertolt Brecht. 55 minutes, color, 1989. VHS, 3/4″ U-matic cassette. A biographical portrait of Brecht through his works. Distributed by Films for the Humanities and Sciences.

Gisela May: Reflections on the Theater of Brecht. 30 minutes, color, 1979. Beta, VHS, 1/2″ open reel (EIAJ), 3/4″ U-matic cassette, 2″ quadraplex open reel. Gisela May of the Berliner Ensemble performs excerpts from Brecht's plays. Distributed by Camera Three Productions Inc. and Creative Arts Television Archive.

PEDRO CALDERÓN DE LA BARCA

Pedro Calderón de la Barca, **Life Is a Dream.** 100 minutes, color, in French, with English subtitles, 1988. Film. Directed by Raul Ruiz.

ANTON CHEKHOV

Anton Chekhov. 30 minutes, color and b/w, 1996. VHS. A documentary filmed where Chekhov lived and worked. Part of the Great Authors series. Distributed by Kultur.

Anton Chekhov, **The Cherry Orchard.** 3 audiocassettes. Translated by Leonid Kipnis and performed by Jessica Tandy and Hume Cronyn. Distributed by Caedmon/Harper Audio.

Anton Chekhov, **The Cherry Orchard, Part I: Chekhov, Innovator of Modern Drama.** 21 minutes, color and b/w, 1968. Beta, VHS, 3/4″ U-matic cassette, 16-mm film. Important scenes with discussion led by Norris Houghton. Distributed by Encyclopaedia Britannica Educational Corp.

Anton Chekhov, **The Cherry Orchard, Part II: Comedy or Tragedy?** 21 minutes, color and b/w, 1967. Beta, VHS, 3/4″ U-matic cassette, 16-mm film. Important scenes with discussion led by Norris Houghton. Covers Chekhov's technique of dramatization of interior actions and examines the notion of subtext. Distributed by Encyclopaedia Britannica Educational Corp.

Anton Chekhov: A Writer's Life. 37 minutes, b/w, 1974. VHS, 3/4″ U-matic cassette. A biographical portrait of the playwright. Distributed by Films for the Humanities and Sciences.

Chekhov. 1080 minutes, 1989. 12 audiocassettes. By Henri Troyat, read by Wolfram Kandinsky. A biography of the writer. Distributed by Books on Tape, Inc.

Chekhov: Humanity's Advocate. 46 minutes, 1968. Audiocassette. By Ernest J. Simmons. Explores various facets of Chekhov's works and his artistic principals. Classics of Russian Literature Series. Distributed by Audio-Forum.

CHIKAMATSU MONZAEMON

Chikamatsu Monogatari. 179 minutes, b&w, in Japanese, with English subtitles, 1954. VHS. Based on a story by Chikamatsu and derived from a Bunraku play. Starring Kazuo Hasegawa, Kyoko Kagawa, Eitaro Shindo, and Sakae Ozawa. Directed by Kenji Mizoguchi. Distributed by Facets Multimedia, Inc.

Double Suicide (*Shinjo ten no amijima*). 104 minutes, b&w, in Japanese, with English subtitles, 1969. VHS. A Bunraku-style production based on the play by Chikamatsu. Starring Kamatari Fujiwara, Tokie Hidari, Shima Iwashita, and Yoshi Kato. Directed by Masahiro Shinoda. Distributed by Criterion.

Gonza the Spearman (*Yari no gonza*). 126 minutes, color, in Japanese, with English subtitles, 1986. VHS. Adaptation of a Chikamatsu play set during the Tokugawa shogunate in the early 1700s. Directed by Masahiro Shinoda. Distributed by Kino Video.

General

Kabuki. 36 minutes, color, 1988. VHS, DVD. Distributed by Films for the Humanities and Sciences.

Kabuki Acting Techniques, Part 1 and 2. Color, 1980. VHS. Distributed by Insight Media.

Theater in Japan: Yesterday and Today. 53 minutes, color, 1989. VHS, DVD. Distributed by Films for the Humanities and Sciences.

CARYL CHURCHILL

Approaching Literature: Caryl Churchill's **Top Girls.** 179 minutes, color, 1997. VHS, DVD. This 1991 televised performance of Churchill's play *Top Girls* also features interviews with the playwright. Distributed by Insight Media.

EURIPIDES

Euripides, **Medea.** 107 minutes, b/w, 1959. VHS. With Judith Anderson and Colleen Dewhurst. Directed by Jose Quintero. Distributed by Ivy Video.

Euripides, **Medea.** 118 minutes, color, 1970. Beta, VHS. With Maria Callas, Guiseppe Gentile, and Laurent Tarzieff. Directed by Pier Paolo Passolini. In Italian with English subtitles. Distributed by Video Artists International.

Euripides, **Medea.** 70 minutes, color, 1979. VHS. With Marina Goderdzishvili and Vladimir Julukhadze. A free adaptation for ballet. Distributed by Kultur.

Euripides, **Medea.** 90 minutes, color, 1982. VHS, 3/4″ U-matic cassette. With Zoe Caldwell and Judith Anderson. A Kennedy Center production based on the poet Robinson Jeffers's version. Distributed by Films for the Humanities and Sciences.

Euripides, *Medea.* 2 audiocassettes. Translated by Rex Warner. Performed by Judith Anderson and Anthony Quayle. Distributed by Caedmon/Harper Audio.

BRIAN FRIEL

Brian Friel, *Dancing at Lughnasa.* 94 minutes, color, 1998. VHS, DVD. Starring Meryl Streep and Michael Gambon. Directed by Pat O'Connor. Distributed by Columbia Tristar.

ATHOL FUGARD

Athol Fugard, *"MASTER HAROLD" . . . and the boys.* 90 minutes, color, 1984. Beta, VHS. With Matthew Broderick. Directed by Michael Lindsay-Hogg. A made-for-cable production. Distributed by Warner Home Video, Inc.

GAO XINGJIANG

Gao Xingjiang, *Nobel Lecture.* 37 minutes, color, in Chinese, with English subtitles, 2000. Available online via the Nobel Prize Web site at <nobel.se/literature/laureates/2000/gao-lecture.html>.

OLIVER GOLDSMITH

Oliver Goldsmith, *She Stoops to Conquer.* Color, 2003. VHS, DVD. The 2002 Out of Joint/National Theatre coproduction of Goldsmith's play. Directed by Max Stafford-Clark.

LORRAINE HANSBERRY

Lorraine Hansberry: The Black Experience in the Creation of Drama. 35 minutes, color, 1975. Beta, VHS, 3/4" U-matic cassette. With Sidney Poitier, Ruby Dee, and Al Freeman, Jr. Narrated by Claudia McNeil. A profile of the playwright's life and work. Distributed by Films for the Humanities and Sciences.
Lorraine Hansberry Speaks Out: Art and the Black Revolution. Audiocassette. By Lorraine Hansberry, edited by Robert Nemiroff. Distributed by Caedmon/HarperAudio.
Lorraine Hansberry, A Raisin in the Sun. 128 minutes, b/w, 1961. Beta, VHS, DVD. With Sidney Poitier, Claudia McNeil and Ruby Dee. Directed by Daniel Petrie. Distributed by Columbia Tristar.
Lorraine Hansberry, A Raisin in the Sun. 171 minutes, color, 1989. Beta, VHS, DVD. With Danny Glover, Esther Rolle, and Starletta DuPois. Directed by Bill Duke. An American Playhouse made-for-television production. Distributed by Chuck Fries Productions.
Lorraine Hansberry, A Raisin in the Sun. 141 minutes. 2 audiocassettes. Dramatization performed by Ossie Davis and Ruby Dee. Distributed by Caedmon/Harper Audio.

To Be Young, Gifted, and Black. 90 minutes, color, 1981. Beta, VHS, 1/2" open reel (EIAJ), 3/4" U-matic cassette, 16-mm film. With Ruby Dee, Al Freeman, Jr., Claudia McNeil, Barbara Barrie, Lauren Jones, Roy Scheider, and Blythe Danner. A play about the life of Lorraine Hansberry. Distributed by Monterey Home Video.

DAVID HENRY HWANG

David Henry Hwang, *M. Butterfly.* 101 minutes, color, 1994. VHS. With Jeremy Irons, Ian Richardson, and Barbara Sukowa. Distributed by Warner Home Video.
David Henry Hwang, *M. Butterfly.* 2 audiocassettes. Directed by Steve Albrezzi. With John Lithgow, Margaret Cho, and B.D. Wong. Distributed by the L.A. Theater Works.

HENRIK IBSEN

A Doll's House. 180 minutes, 1993. 3 audiocassettes. Read by Flo Gibson. Distributed by Audio Book Contractors.
A Doll's House, Part I: The Distinction of Illusion. 34 minutes, color, 1968. Beta, VHS, 3/4" U-matic cassette, 16-mm film. Norris Houghton discusses the subsurface tensions in the play. Distributed by Encyclopaedia Britannica Educational Corp.
A Doll's House, Part II: Ibsen's Themes. 29 minutes, color, 1968. Beta, VHS, 3/4" U-matic cassette, 16-mm film. Norris Houghton examines the case of characters and the themes in the play. Distributed by Encyclopaedia Britannica Educational Corp.
Henrik Ibsen, *A Doll's House.* 89 minutes, b/w, 1959. Beta, VHS, 3/4" U-matic cassette. With Julie Harris, Christopher Plummer, Jason Robards, Hume Cronyn, Eileen Heckart, and Richard Thomas. An original television production. Distributed by MGM/UA Entertainment.
Henrik Ibsen, *A Doll's House.* 98 minutes, color, 1973. VHS, 16-mm film. With Jane Fonda, Edward Fox, and Trevor Howard. Screenplay by Christopher Hampton. Distributed by Prism Entertainment.
Henrik Ibsen, *A Doll's House.* 39 minutes, color, 1973. VHS, DVD. With Claire Bloom, Anthony Hopkins, and Ralph Richardson. Distributed by AIMS Media.
Ibsen's Life and Times, Part I: Youth and Self-Imposed Exile. 28 minutes, color. VHS. The conflict between individual and society is illustrated in scenes from *Ghosts,* featuring Beatrice Straight as Mrs. Alving. Includes a biographical segment on the playwright. Distributed by Insight Media.
Ibsen's Life and Times, Part II: The Later Years. 24 minutes, color. VHS. Includes scenes from *The Master Builder* and *Lady from the Sea,* emphasizing the realism in Ibsen's plays. A biographical segment includes on-location footage. Distributed by Insight Media.

TONY KUSHNER

Tony Kushner, *Angels in America*. 352 minutes (premiere version), color, 2003. DVD. Starring Al Pacino, Meryl Streep, Emma Thompson, Mary-Louise Parker, and Jeffrey Wright. Directed by Mike Nichols. HBO adaptation of Tony Kushner's play, aired as a mini-series after its premiere.

FEDERICO GARCÍA LORCA

Federico García Lorca: El Balcon Abierto. 90 minutes, color. VHS, 3/4″ U-matic cassette. In Spanish. An examination of García Lorca's work, life, and violent death. Distributed by Films for the Humanities and Sciences.

Lorca: A Murder in Granada. 55 minutes, 1983. VHS, 3/4″ U-matic cassette. In Spanish and English. The authoritative film biography of García Lorca. Distributed by Films for the Humanities and Sciences.

DAVID MAMET

David Mamet, *Glengarry Glen Ross*. 100 minutes, 1992. VHS, DVD. With Jack Lemmon, Al Pacino, and Kevin Spacey. Directed by James Foley. Distributed by Artisan Entertainment.

CHRISTOPHER MARLOWE

Christopher Marlowe, *Doctor Faustus*. 93 minutes, 1968. VHS, Beta, DVD. Adaptation of Marlowe's classic. With Richard Burton and Elizabeth Taylor. Directed by Richard Burton and Neville Coghill. Distributed by Columbia Tristar Home Video.

ARTHUR MILLER

Death of a Salesman. 135 minutes, color, 1985. Beta, VHS, DVD. With Dustin Hoffman, John Malkovich, Charles Durning, and Stephen Lang. Directed by Volker Schlondorff. A made-for-television adaptation of the play. Distributed by Facets Multimedia and Warner Home Video.

Arthur Miller, *Death of a Salesman*. 2 audiocassettes. Performed by Lee J. Cobb and Mildred Dunnock. Distributed by Caedmon/Harper Audio.

Arthur Miller, *Death of a Salesman*. 44 minutes, 1986. Audiocassette. Dramatization performed by Paul Douglas. Distributed by Sounddeluxe Audio Publishing.

Private Conversations on the Set of Death of a Salesman. 82 minutes, color, 1985. Beta, VHS. With Arthur Miller, Dustin Hoffman, Volker Schlondorff, and John Malkovich. This PBS documentary presents heated discussion between actor, director, and playwright. Various interpretations of the play emerge and viewers gain insight into how each part contributed to the final production. Distributed by Video Learning Library.

MOLIÈRE

Molière, *Le Misanthrope*. 52 minutes, color, 1975. VHS. With Cyril Ritchard, Edward Petherbridge, and Neil Stacy. Distributed by Films for the Humanities and Sciences.

Molière, *Le Misanthrope*. 140 minutes, color, 1986. VHS, 3/4″ U-matic cassette. In French with English subtitles. Distributed by Films for the Humanities and Sciences.

Molière, *Le Misanthrope*. 89 minutes. 2 audiocassettes. With Richard Easton. Distributed by Caedmon.

Molière, *Le Misanthrope*. 104 minutes. 2 audiocassettes. Recorded live as part of L.A. Theater Works' The Play's the Thing series of performance productions. Distributed by L.A. Theater Works.

EUGENE O'NEILL

Eugene O'Neill. 30 minutes, b/w and color, 1996. VHS. A commentary on the author's life. Part of the Famous Authors series. Distributed by Kultur.

Eugene O'Neill, *Desire under the Elms*. 111 minutes, b/w, 1958. Beta, VHS, LaserDisc. Starring Anthony Perkins, Burl Ives, and Sophia Loren. Directed by Delbert Mann. Distributed by Paramount Home Video.

HAROLD PINTER

Harold Pinter, *Betrayal*. 95 minutes, color, 1983. VHS. With Ben Kingsley, Patricia Hodge, and Jeremy Irons. Directed by David Jones. Distributed by CBS/Fox Video.

Harold Pinter with Benedict Nightingale. 55 minutes, 1989. VHS. Interview with Pinter. Distributed by Insight Media.

LUIGI PIRANDELLO

Luigi Pirandello, *Six Characters in Search of an Author*. 52 minutes, color, 1976. VHS, 3/4″ U-matic cassette. Joseph Heller discusses the boundaries between reality and fiction. Distributed by Films for the Humanities and Sciences.

Luigi Pirandello, *Six Characters in Search of an Author*. 60 minutes, color, 1978. VHS, 3/4″ U-matic cassette. Hosted by Jose Ferrer. As an accompaniment to the play, Ossie Davis discusses Pirandello's work in the theater. Distributed by RMI Media Production, Inc.

Luigi Pirandello, *Six Characters in Search of an Author*. 96 minutes, b/w, 1992. VHS, DVD. A BBC Production featuring John Hurt, Brian Cox, and Tara Fitzgerald. Distributed by Films for the Humanities and Sciences.

PLAUTUS

Plautus, *A Funny Thing Happened on the Way to the Forum*. 100 minutes, color, 1966. VHS. Starring Zero

Mostel, Phil Silvers, and Buster Keaton. Directed by Richard Lester. Distributed by Facets Multimedia.

WILLIAM SHAKESPEARE

Hamlet

Hamlet: The Age of Elizabeth, I. 30 minutes, color, 1979. Beta, VHS, 3/4″ U-matic cassette, 16-mm film. An introduction to Elizabethan theater. Distributed by Encyclopaedia Britannica Educational Corp.

Hamlet: The Poisoned Kingdom, III. 30 minutes, color, 1959. Beta, VHS, 3/4″ U-matic cassette, 16-mm film. Observes that poisoning in the play is both literal and figurative and affects all the characters. Distributed by Encyclopaedia Britannica Educational Corp.

Hamlet: The Readiness Is All, IV. 30 minutes, color, 1959. Beta, VHS, 3/4″ U-matic cassette, 16-mm film. *Hamlet* is presented as a coming-of-age story. Distributed by Encyclopaedia Britannica Educational Corp.

Hamlet: The Trouble with Hamlet. 23 minutes, color, 1969. 16-mm film. Emphasizes Hamlet's existentialist dilemma. Distributed by the National Broadcasting Company.

Hamlet: What Happens in Hamlet, II. 30 minutes, color and b/w, 1959. Beta, VHS, 3/4″ U-matic cassette, 16-mm film. Analyzes the play as a ghost story, a detective story, and a revenge story. Uses scenes from Acts I, III, and V to introduce the principal characters and present the structure of each substory. Distributed by Encyclopaedia Britannica Educational Films.

Shakespeare and His Stage: Approaches to Hamlet. 45 minutes, color, 1979. VHS. Includes footage of the four greatest Hamlets of this century: John Barrymore, Laurence Olivier, John Gielgud, and Nicol Williamson. Shows a young actor learning the role. Narrated by Gielgud. Distributed by Films for the Humanities and Sciences.

William Shakespeare, *Hamlet*. 153 minutes, b/w, 1948. VHS, beta, laser disc, DVD. With Laurence Olivier, Basil Sydney, Felix Aylmer, Jean Simmons, Stanley Holloway, Peter Cushing, and Christopher Lee. Voice of John Gielgud. Directed by Olivier. Photographed in Denmark. Cut scenes include all of Rosencrantz and Guildenstern. Emphasizes Oedipal implications in the play. Distributed by Paramount Home Video.

William Shakespeare, *Hamlet*. 115 minutes, color, 1969. With Nicol Williamson and Anthony Hopkins. Directed by Tony Richardson. Distributed by Filmic Archives.

William Shakespeare, *Hamlet*. 222 minutes, color, 1979. VHS, other formats by arrangement. Directed by Derek Jacobi. Distributed by Filmic Archives.

William Shakespeare, *Hamlet*. 135 minutes, color, 1990. VHS, DVD. With Mel Gibson, Glenn Close, Alan Bates, Paul Scofield, Ian Holm, and Helena Bonham-Carter. Directed by Franco Zeffirelli. Distributed by Critics' Choice.

William Shakespeare, *Hamlet*. 242 minutes, color, 1996. Laser, DDS, VHS. With Kenneth Branagh, Kate Winslet, Julie Christie, and Charlton Heston. Directed by Kenneth Branagh. Distributed by Columbia Tristar Home Video.

William Shakespeare, *Hamlet*. 112 minutes, b/w color, 2000. VHS, DVD. Starring Ethan Hawke, Kyle MacLachlan, Sam Shepard, Bill Murray, Diane Verona, Liev Schreiber, and Julia Stiles. Directed by Michael Almereyda. Distributed by Miramax Home Entertainment.

William Shakespeare, *Hamlet*. 3 audiocassettes. Performed by Paul Scofield and Diana Wynyard. Distributed by Caedmon/Harper Audio.

The Tragedie of Hamlet: Prince of Denmark. 22 minutes, color, 1988. VHS. Actors depict Shakespeare and his contemporary, Richard Burbage, rehearsing the play. "Shakespeare" gives a line-by-line analysis of scenes from the play along with insight into plot and character. Part of the Shakespeare in Rehearsal Series. Distributed by Coronet/MTI Film & Video.

A Midsummer Night's Dream

A Midsummer Night's Dream. 120 minutes. 2 audiocassettes. Performed by Robert Helpmann and Moira Shearer. An Old Vic production. Distributed by Durkin Hayes Publishing.

William Shakespeare, *A Midsummer Night's Dream*. 118 minutes, b/w, 1935. VHS. With James Cagney, Mickey Rooney, Olivia DeHaviland, and Dick Powell. Distributed by Critics' Choice.

William Shakespeare, *A Midsummer Night's Dream*. 111 minutes, b/w, 1963. Beta, VHS, 3/4″ U-matic cassette. With Patrick Allen, Eira Heath, Cyril Luckham, Tony Bateman, and Jill Bennett. A live BBC-TV performance, with Mendelssohn's incidental music. Distributed by Video Yesteryear.

William Shakespeare, *A Midsummer Night's Dream*. 120 minutes, 1968. VHS. With Diana Rigg and David Warner. Directed by Peter Hall. A Royal Shakespeare Company performance. Distributed by Critics' Choice.

William Shakespeare, *A Midsummer Night's Dream*. 120 minutes, color, 1982. Beta, VHS. With Helen Mirren, Peter McEnery, and Brian Glover. Distributed by Filmic Archives.

William Shakespeare, *A Midsummer Night's Dream*. 165 minutes, color, 1983. Beta, VHS, 3/4″ U-matic cassette. With William Hurt and Michelle Shay. A lively interpretation by Joseph Papp. Distributed by Films for the Humanities and Sciences.

William Shakespeare, *A Midsummer Night's Dream*. 194 minutes, color, 1987. VHS. With Ileana Cotrubas, James Bowman, and Curt Appelgren. Directed by Peter Hall. A performance of the Benjamin Britten opera, taped at the Glyndebourne Festival Opera. Distributed by Critics' Choice.

William Shakespeare, *A Midsummer Night's Dream.* 115 minutes, color, 1999. VHS, DVD. Starring Kevin Kline, Michelle Pfeiffer, Calista Flockhart, and Stanley Tucci. Distributed by Twentieth Century Fox.

William Shakespeare, *A Midsummer Night's Dream.* 2 audio compact discs. Dramatization performed by Paul Scofield and Joy Parker. With an introductory essay by scholar Harold Bloom. Distributed by Caedmon/Harper Audio.

Othello

Otello. 146 minutes, color, 1997. VHS. With Placido Domingo, Kiri Te Kanawa, and Sergei Leiferkus. Opera by Giuseppe Verdi. Conducted by Georg Solti. Production at the Royal Opera House, Covent Garden, London. Distributed by Public Media/Home Vision.

William Shakespeare, *Othello.* 92 minutes, b/w, 1952. VHS, laser disc, DVD. Directed by Orson Welles. The original version as it appeared in the 1952 Cannes Film Festival. Distributed by Voyager.

William Shakespeare, *Othello.* 208 minutes, color, 1982. VHS. With Bob Hoskins and Anthony Hopkins. Distributed by Ambrose Video Publishing, Inc.

William Shakespeare, *Othello.* 90 minutes, color, 1993. Various actors perform key scenes as scholars provide commentary. Distributed by the Video Catalog.

William Shakespeare, *Othello.* 124 minutes, color, 1995, VHS, DVD. With Laurence Fishburne, Kenneth Branagh, and Irene Jacob. Distributed by Castle Rock Entertainment.

William Shakespeare, *Othello.* 2 audiocassettes. Performed by Cyril Cusack and Alan Bates. Distributed by Caedmon/Harper Audio.

General

The Life and Times of William Shakespeare 1: The Historical Setting. 25 minutes, color, 1978. VHS. An overview of Elizabethan England. Distributed by the University of Wyoming Audio-Visual Services.

The Life and Times of William Shakespeare 2: English Drama. 20 minutes, color, 1978. VHS. History of drama from the Greeks to that of Shakespeare's time. Distributed by the University of Wyoming Audio-Visual Services.

The Life and Times of William Shakespeare 3: Stratford Years. 18 minutes, color, 1978. VHS. Deals with Shakespeare's early life. Distributed by the University of Wyoming Audio-Visual Services.

The Life and Times of William Shakespeare 4: London Years. 33 minutes, color, 1978. VHS. A history of the center of the English-speaking world. Distributed by the University of Wyoming Audio-Visual Services.

Shakespeare and the Globe. 31 minutes, color, 1985. VHS, 3/4" U-matic cassette. A survey of Shakespeare's life, work, and cultural milieu. Distributed by Films for the Humanities and Sciences.

Shakespeare and His Stage. 47 minutes, color, 1975. VHS, 16-mm film. Provides a montage of Shakespearean background, including scenes from Hamlet and the preparation of various actors for the role. Distributed by Films for the Humanities and Sciences.

Shakespeare's Heritage. 29 minutes, color, 1988. 16-mm film. Narrated by Anthony Quayle. Explores Stratford and the life of the playwright. Distributed by Encyclopaedia Britannica Educational Corp.

Shakespeare's Theater. 13 minutes, color, 1946. 16-mm film. Re-creates the experience of going to a play at the Globe Theatre in Shakespeare's time. Distributed by the Indiana University Instructional Support Services.

Shakespeare's Theater: The Globe Playhouse. 18 minutes, b/w, 1953. VHS. Provides a model of the Globe Theater and a discussion of the original staging of some of Shakespeare's plays. Distributed by the University of California Extension Media Center.

The Two Traditions. 50 minutes, color, 1983. VHS. Deals with the problem of overcoming barriers of time and culture to make Shakespeare relevant today. Examples from *Hamlet, Coriolanus, The Merchant of Venice,* and *Othello.* Part of the Playing Shakespeare Series. Distributed by Films for the Humanities and Sciences.

Understanding Shakespeare: His Sources. 20 minutes, color, 1972. Beta, VHS, 3/4" U-matic cassette, 16-mm film, other formats by special arrangement. Examines how Shakespeare's plays grew out of sources available to him, and how he enhanced the material with his own imagination. Distributed by Coronet/MTI Film & Video.

GEORGE BERNARD SHAW

George Bernard Shaw. 30 minutes, b/w and color, 1996. VHS. An examination of the social and political forces relevant to Shaw's work. Part of the Famous Authors series. Distributed by Kultur.

George Bernard Shaw, *Mrs. Warren's Profession.* 115 minutes, color, 1976. VHS. Directed by Herbert Wise. With Coral Browne, Penelope Wilton, and James Grout. Distributed by Time-Life Multimedia.

George Bernard Shaw, *Mrs. Warren's Profession.* 1 audiocassette. Directed by Nicholas Rudall. With Paul Gutrecht, Kaitlin Hopkins, and Shirley Knight. Recorded live as part of L.A. Theater Works' The Play's the Thing, a series of recorded performances. Distributed by L.A. Theater Works.

SAM SHEPARD

Sam Shepard, *True West.* 110 minutes, color, 1983. Directed by Gary Sinise. With John Malkovich and Gary Sinise. Distributed by Academy Home Entertainments.

ANNA DEAVERE SMITH

Anna Deavere Smith, *Fires in the Mirror.* 87 minutes, color, 1993. VHS. Directed by George C. Wolfe. Starring Anna Deavere Smith. Distributed by Monterey Media.

SOPHOCLES

Antigone

Antigone: Rites of Passion. 85 minutes, color, 1992. VHS. With Amy Greenfield, Bertram Ross, and Janet Eilber. Directed by Amy Greenfield. A retelling of Sophocles' tragedy through action, dance, and rock music. Distributed by Mystic Fire Video.

Antigone. 2 audiocassettes. Dramatization of the Fitts and Fitzgerald translation. Performed by Dorothy Tutin and Max Adrian. Distributed by Caedmon/Harper Audio.

Sophocles, *Antigone.* 88 minutes, b/w, 1962. VHS. With Irene Papas. Directed by George Tzavellas. In Greek with English subtitles. Distributed by Ivy Video.

Sophocles, *Antigone.* 120 minutes, 1987. VHS, 3/4″ U-matic cassette, DVD. With Juliet Stevenson, John Shrapnel, and John Gielgud. Staged version. Distributed by Films for the Humanities and Sciences.

Sophocles, *Antigone.* 58 minutes, color, 1994. VHS. With Seymour Simon. Distributed by RMI Media Productions.

Oedipus

Oedipus Rex: Age of Sophocles, I. 31 minutes, color and b/w, 1959. Beta, VHS, 3/4″ U-matic cassette, 16-mm film. Discusses Greek civilization, the classic Greek theater, and the theme of man's fundamental nature. Distributed by Encyclopaedia Britannica Educational Corp.

Oedipus Rex: The Character of Oedipus, II. 31 minutes, color and b/w, 1959. Beta, VHS, 3/4″ U-matic cassette, 16-mm film. Debates whether Oedipus's trouble is a result of character flaws or of fate. Distributed by Encyclopaedia Britannica Educational Corp.

Oedipus Rex: Man and God, III. 30 minutes, color and b/w, 1959. Beta, VHS, 3/4″ U-matic cassette, 16-mm film. Deals with the idea that Oedipus, although a worldly ruler, cannot overcome the gods and his destiny. Distributed by Encyclopaedia Britannica Educational Corp.

Oedipus Rex: Recovery of Oedipus, IV. 30 minutes, color and b/w, 1959. Beta, VHS, 3/4″ U-matic cassette, 16-mm film. Deals with man's existence in between God and beast. Distributed by Encyclopaedia Britannica Educational Corp.

Sophocles, *Oedipus Rex.* 20 minutes, color, 1957. Beta, VHS, 3/4″ U-matic cassette. Sophocles' play, presented in a signed version for the deaf. Distributed by Gallaudet University Library.

Sophocles, *Oedipus Rex.* 87 minutes, color, 1957. VHS, 16-mm film, DVD. With Douglas Campbell, Douglas Rain, Eric House, and Eleanor Stuart. Based on William Yeats's translation. Directed by Tyrone Guthrie. Contained and highly structured rendering by the Stratford (Ontario) Festival Players. Distributed by Water Bearer Films.

Sophocles, *Oedipus the King.* 97 minutes, color, 1967. VHS. With Donald Sutherland, Christopher Plummer, Lilli Palmer, Orson Welles, Cyril Cusack, Richard Johnson, and Roger Livesey. Directed by Philip Saville. Simplified film version of the play, filmed in Greece using an old amphitheater to serve as the background for much of the action. Distributed by Crossroads Video.

Sophocles, *Oedipus the King.* 45 minutes, color, 1975. Beta, VHS, 3/4″ U-matic cassette, 16-mm film. With Anthony Quayle, James Mason, Claire Bloom, and Ian Richardson. A production by the Athens Classical Theatre Company, with an English soundtrack. Distributed by Films for the Humanities and Sciences.

Sophocles, *Oedipus the King.* 120 minutes, color, 1987. VHS, DVD. With John Gielgud, Michael Pennington, and Claire Bloom. Distributed by Films for the Humanities and Sciences.

Sophocles, *Oedipus Rex.* 2 audiocassettes. Translated by William Butler Yeats. Performed by Douglas Campbell and Eric House. Dramatization. Distributed by Caedmon/Harper Audio.

Sophocles, *Oedipus at Colonus.* 120 minutes, color, 1987. Beta, VHS, DVD, 3/4″ U-matic cassette. With Anthony Quayle, Juliet Stevenson, and Kenneth Haigh. Staged version. Distributed by Films for the Humanities and Sciences.

Sophocles: The Theban Plays. 360 minutes, color, 1986. 3 videocassettes, VHS, 3/4″ U-matic cassette. Distributed by Films for the Humanities and Sciences.

WOLE SOYINKA

Wole Soyinka. 50 minutes, color, 1985. VHS, 3/4″ U-matic cassette. An interview with the playwright, who discusses political and cultural life in Africa and the United States and what it means to be an artist. Distributed by The Roland Collection.

Wole Soyinka. 50 minutes, 1989. VHS. From the Writers in Conversation Series. Soyinka lectures on creative traditions and the "climate of terror" in which they are born. Also discusses the growth of contemporary African self-awareness. Distributed by the Roland Collection.

AUGUST STRINDBERG

August Strindberg, *Miss Julie.* 90 minutes, b/w, 1950. VHS. Starring Anita Bjork and Ulf Palme. Directed by Alf Sjoberg. Distributed by Public Media/Home Vision.

August Strindberg, *Miss Julie.* 105 minutes, color, 1972. VHS. With Helen Mirren. A production of the Royal Shakespeare Company. Distributed by MasterVision.

August Strindberg, *Miss Julie.* 60 minutes, color, 1978. Beta, VHS, 3/4″ U-matic cassette. Ancillary materials available. With Patrick Stewart and Lisa Harrow. Hosted by Jose Ferrer. Opens with the rehearsal of a crucial scene and closes with a full-dress production of the play. In between, the actors show different ways of interpreting a scene. Distributed by Films, Inc.

August Strindberg, *Miss Julie.* 100 minutes, color, 1997. VHS. Directed by Michael Simpson. Distributed by Films for the Humanities and Sciences.

August Strindberg, *Miss Julie.* 103 minutes, color, 1999. VHS, DVD. Starring Saffron Burrows and Peter Mullan. Directed by Mike Figgis. Distributed by MGM/UA.

JOHN MILLINGTON SYNGE

John Millington Synge, *Riders to the Sea.* 60 minutes, color, 1989. VHS, DVD. Starring Geraldine Page and Amanda Plummer. Directed by Ronan O'Leary. Distributed by Diamond Entertainment.

John Millington Synge, *Riders to the Sea* and *In the Shadow of the Glen.* 1986. Audiocassettes. Distributed by Spoken Arts.

LUIS VALDEZ

Luis Valdez, *Zoot Suit.* 92 minutes, color, 1981. VHS, DVD. The film adaptation of Valdez's play. Distributed by Universal Pictures.

OSCAR WILDE

Oscar Wilde, *The Importance of Being Earnest.* 95 minutes, color, 1952. Beta, VHS, DVD. With Michael Redgrave, Edith Evans, Margaret Rutherford, Michael Dennison, and Joan Greenwood. Directed by Anthony Asquith. Staged version. Distributed by Paramount Home Video.

Oscar Wilde, *The Importance of Being Earnest.* 2 audiocassettes. Performed by Lynn Redgrave and Gladys Cooper. Distributed by Caedmon/Harper Audio.

Oscar Wilde: Spendthrift of Genius. 60 minutes, color, 1989. VHS. A portrait of this multitalented author. Distributed by Films for the Humanities and Sciences.

Oscar Wilde, *The Importance of Being Earnest.* 97 minutes, color, 2002. VHS, DVD. With Rupert Everett, Colin Firth, Reese Witherspoon, Judi Dench, and Tom Wilkinson. Directed by Oliver Parker. Distributed by Buena Vista Home Video.

TENNESSEE WILLIAMS

Cat on a Hot Tin Roof

Tennessee Williams, *Cat on a Hot Tin Roof.* 108 minutes, color, 1958. VHS, DVD. With Paul Newman, Burl Ives, Elizabeth Taylor, and Jack Carson. Directed by Richard Brooks. Distributed by MGM/UA Home Video.

Tennessee Williams, *Cat on a Hot Tin Roof.* 148 minutes, color, 1984. VHS, DVD. With Jessica Lange, Tommy Lee Jones, and Rip Torn. Directed by Jack Hofsiss. Distributed by MGM/UA Home Video.

The Glass Menagerie

The Glass Menagerie. 134 minutes, color, 1987. Beta, VHS. With Joanne Woodward, Karen Allen, John Malkovich, and James Naughton. Directed by Paul Newman. See local retailer.

Tennessee Williams, *The Glass Menagerie.* 2 audiocassettes. Performed by Montgomery Clift and Julie Harris. Distributed by Caedmon/Harper Audio.

Tennessee Williams, *Tennessee Williams Reads "The Glass Menagerie" and Others.* Audiocassette. Read by Tennessee Williams. Includes *The Glass Menagerie* (opening monologue and closing scene); "Cried the Fox"; "The Eyes"; "The Summer Belvedere"; "Some Poems Meant for Music"; "Little Horse"; "Which Is My Little Boy"; "Little One"; "Gold-Tooth Blues"; "Kitchen-Door Blues"; "Heavenly Grass"; and "The Yellow Bird." Distributed by Caedmon/Harper Audio.

The Glass Menagerie. Audiocassette. Read by Tennessee Williams. Includes "The Yellow Bird" (short story) and poems. Distributed by the American Audio Prose Library.

General

In the Country of Tennessee Williams. 30 minutes, color, 1977. Beta, VHS, 1/2″ reel, 3/4″ U-matic cassette, 2″ Quad. A one-act play about how Williams developed as a writer. Distributed by the New York State Education Department.

Tennessee Williams: Orpheus of the American Stage. 97 minutes, color, 1994. VHS, DVD. The only film study of Tennessee Williams's life and work as a whole. Distributed by Films for the Humanities and Sciences.

AUGUST WILSON

August Wilson: The American Dream in Black and White. 52 minutes, color, 1990. Interview with Wilson offering a review of his life and career. Also includes excerpts from a number of his plays. Distributed by Films for the Humanities and Sciences.

ZEAMI MOTOKIYO

Noh: Classical Theatre of Japan. 28 minutes, color, 1980. VHS. Includes excerpts of performances by Akira Matsui of the Kita Noh School of *Benkei on the Bridge* and *The Lady Han.* Distributed by Insight Media.

General

This is Noh. 40 minutes, color, 2000. VHS. Scripted by the actors of the Noh Association, Kyoto Branch, this video features excerpts from numerous plays, rehearsals, and dances.

Bunraku: Masters of Japanese Puppet Theater. 53 minutes, color, 2001. VHS, DVD. Features two of Japan's greatest puppeteer masters, Tamao Yoshida and chanter Sumitayu Takemoto. Distributed by Films for the Humanities and Sciences.

General Resources

Black Theatre: The Making of a Movement. 113 minutes, color, VHS, 1978. A look at black theater born from the Civil Rights movement of the 1950s, 1960s, and 1970s. Recollections from Ossie Davis, James Earl Jones, Amiri Baraka, and Ntozake Shange. Distributed by California Newsreel.

A Day at the Globe. 30 minutes, color. VHS. Starts with a brief overview of early drama and of seventeenth-century England, then discusses the Globe Theater, using still images. Explains how actors, artisans, and other company members prepared for performances and presents dramatic readings, period costumes, music, and sound effects in order to help students envision how Shakespearean drama actually looked. Distributed by Insight Media.

Drama Comes of Age. 30 minutes, b/w, 1957. 16-mm film. Discusses the Shakespearean theater and neoclassic drama. Demonstrates early realism with a scene from *Hedda Gabler.* Distributed by the Indiana University Instructional Support Services.

Drama: How It Began. 30 minutes, b/w, 1957. 16-mm film. Discusses the early beginnings of the theater. Explains the techniques of the Greek theater and how playwriting developed. Illustrates the chorus technique with a scene from *Oedipus the King.* Distributed by the Indiana University Instructional Support Services.

The Elizabethan Age. 30 minutes, color. VHS. A discussion of the resurgence of enthusiasm for the arts and letters that swept seventeenth-century England. Uses original sources. Distributed by Insight Media.

Greek Tragedy. Audiocassette. Works of Euripides and Sophocles, Performed by Katina Paxinou and Alexis Minotis. Distributed by Caedmon/Harper Audio.

The Theatre in Ancient Greece. 26 minutes, color, 1989. Beta, VHS, 3/4" U-matic cassette. Program explores ancient theatre design, the origins or tragedy, the audience, the comparative roles of the writer/director and actors, and the use of landscape in many plays. Examines the theaters of Herodus, Atticus, Epidauros, Corinth, and numerous others. Distributed by Films for the Humanities and Sciences.

Directory of Distributors

AIMS Multimedia, 9710 DeSoto Avenue, Chatsworth, CA 91311-4409, (818) 773-4300, (800) 367-2467

Ambrose Video Publishing Inc., 145 West 45th Street, Suite 1115, New York, NY 10036, (212) 768-7373, (800) 526-4663

American Audio Prose Library, PO Box 842, 600 Crestland Avenue, Columbia, MO 65203, (573) 443-0361

Annenberg/CPB, P.O. Box 2345, South Burlington, VT 05407-2345, (800) LEARNER

Applause Learning Resources, 85-A Fernwood Lane, Roslyn, NY 11576, (800) 277-5287

Artisan Entertainment Inc., 2700 Colorado Ave., 2nd Fl., Santa Monica, CA 90404, (310) 449-9200

Audio Book Contractors, PO Box 40115, Washington, DC 20016, (202) 363-3429.

Audio-Forum, Jeffrey Norton Publishers, One Orchard Park Road, Madison, CT 06443, (800) 243-1234

BFS Entertainment & Multimedia Limited, 360 Newkirk Road, Richmond Hill, Ontario, Canada L4C 3G7, (905) 884–2323

Books on Tape, Inc., P.O. Box 25122, Santa Ana, CA 92799-5122

Buena Vista Home Entertainment, a division of Walt Disney Company. See local retailers.

Caedmon/Harper Audio, HarperCollins Publishers, 10 East 53rd Street, New York, NY 10022, (212) 207-7000

California Newsreel, 500 Third Street, Suite 505, San Francisco, CA 94107, (415) 284-7800

Camera Three Productions and Creative Arts Television Archive, Box 739, Kent, CT 06757, (860) 868-1771

Castle Rock Entertainment. See local retailers.

CBS/FOX Video. See local retailers.

Chuck Fries Productions, 6922 Hollywood Boulevard, Los Angeles, CA 90028, (323) 466-2266

Columbia Tristar Home Video. See local retailers.

Coronet/MTI Film & Video, 2349 Chaffee Drive, St. Louis, MO 63146, (314) 569-0211, (800) 221-1274

Criterion. See local retailers.

Crossroads Video, 15 Buckminster Lane, Manhasset, NY 11030, (516) 365-3715, (800) 548-5757

Diamond Entertainment, 800 Tucker Lane, Walnut, CA 91789, (909) 839–1989

Durkin Hayes Publishing, 2221 Niagara Falls Boulevard, Niagara Falls, NY 14304, (716) 731-9177, (800) 962-5200

Encyclopaedia Britannica Educational Corporation, 310 South Michigan Avenue, Chicago, IL 60604, (312) 347-7900, (800) 621-3900

Facets Multimedia Inc., 1517 West Fullerton Avenue, Chicago, IL 60614, (773) 281-9075 (800) 331-6197

Filmic Archives, The Cinema Center, Botsford, CT 06404, (800) 366-1920, (203) 261-1920

Films for the Humanities and Sciences, PO Box 2053, Princeton, NJ 08543-2053, (609) 275-1400, (800) 257-5126

Gallaudet University Library, Gallaudet Media Distribution, 800 Florida Avenue NE, Washington, DC 20002, (202) 651-5579, (202) 651-5440

Hallmark Home Entertainment. See local retailers.

Home Vision Entertainment, 4411 North Ravenswood Avenue, Chicago, IL 60640, (773) 878-2600, (800) 826-3456

Image Entertainment, 9333 Oso Avenue, Chatsworth, CA 91311

Indiana University Instructional Support Services, Franklin Hall, Room 0001, Bloomington, IN 47405-5901, (812) 855-2853

Insight Media, 2162 Broadway, New York, NY 10024, (212) 721-6316

Ivy Video, PO Box 18376, Asheville, NC 28814, (828) 285-9995, (800) 669-4057

Kino International Corp., 333 W. 39th Street, Suite 503, New York, NY 10018, (800) 562-3330

Kultur, 195 Highway #36, West Long Branch, NJ 07764, (732) 229-0066, (800) 4-KULTUR

Library Video Company, PO Box 580, Wynnewood, PA 19096, (800) 843–3620

Madacy Entertainment, 3333 Graham Boulevard, Suite 102, Montreal, Quebec, Canada H3R 3L5, (514) 341–5600

MasterVision, 969 Park Avenue, New York, NY 10028, (212) 879-0448

MGM/UA. See local retailers.

Miramax. See local retailers.

Monterey Home Video, 566 St. Charles Drive, Thousand Oaks, CA 91360, (805) 494-7199, (800) 424-2593

Mystic Fire Video, PO Box 422, Prince Street Station, New York, NY 10012, (212) 941-0999

National Broadcasting Company, 30 Rockefeller Plaza, New York, NY 10112, (212) 664-4444

National Public Radio, Audience Services, 635 Massachusetts Avenue NW, Washington, DC 20001, (202) 414-3232

New York Film Annex, 1618 West 4th Street, Brooklyn, NY 11223, (718) 382-8868

New York State Education Department, Media Distribution Network, Room 7-C-CEC, Empire State Plaza, Albany, NY 12230, (518) 474-3168

Paramount Home Video. See local retailers.

PBS Video, 1320 Braddock Place, Alexandria, VA 22314, (800) 344-3337

Prism Entertainment, 1888 Century Park East, Suite 350, Los Angeles, CA 90067, (310) 277-3270

RMI Media Productions, Inc., 1365 Winchester, Olathe, KS, 66061, (913) 768-1696, (800) 745-5480

The Roland Collection, 22D Hollywood Avenue, Ho-Ho-Kus, NJ 07423, (201) 251-8200, (800) 59-ROLAND

Smithsonian Institution Press, 470 L'Enfante Plaza, Suite 7100, Washington, DC 20650, (202) 287-3738

Sounddeluxe, Box H, Novato City, CA 94949, (800) 227-2020

Spoken Arts, 195 South White Rock Road, Holmes, NY 12531, (800) 326–4090

The Teaching Company, 4151 Lafayette Center Drive, Suite 100, Chantilly, VA 20151, (800) TEACH-12

Time-Life Video and Television, 1450 East Parham Road, Richmond, VA 23280, (800) 621-7026

Twentieth Century Fox Film Corporation. See local retailers.

Universal Studios Home Video. See local retailers.

University of California Extension Media Center, 2000 Center Street, Suite 400, Berkeley, CA 94704, (510) 642-0460

University of Wyoming Audio-Visual Services, Box 3273, Laramie, WY 82071, (307) 766-3184

Video Artists International, 109 Wheeler Avenue, Pleasantville, NY 10570, (914) 769-3691, (800) 477-7146

The Video Catalog Company, Inc., 561 Broadway, New York, NY 10012, (212) 334-0340

Video Learning Library, 15838 North 62 Street, Suite 101, Scottsdale, AZ 85254, (602) 596-9970, (800) 383-8811

Video Yesteryear, Box C, Sandy Hook, CT 06482, (800) 243-0987

Voyager, 424 35 Avenue, Seattle, WA 98122, (206) 323-1112

Warner Home Video. See local retailers.

Water Bearer Films, 20 West 20th St., 2nd floor, New York, NY 10011, (212) 242-8686

Acknowledgments

Greek Drama

Figure 1. The Theater of Epidauros, Greece. CORBIS/Michael Nicholson.

Figure 2. Theater at Epidauros from *The Theatre of Dionysus in Athens* by Arthur Wallace Pickard-Cambridge. Reprinted by permission of Oxford University Press.

Agamemnon from *The Oresteia by Aeschylus: A New Translation for the State,* by David Greene and Wendy Doniger O'Flaherty. Copyright © 1989 by The University of Chicago. Reprinted by permission of The University of Chicago Press. Photo: © Richard Feldman.

"Orestes and the Gods" by Albrecht Dihle, excerpt from *A History of Greek Literature,* translated by Clare Krojzl. Reprinted with the permission of International Thomson Publishing Services.

"*Oresteia:* Trilogy Preserved" from *Aeschylus* by Lois S. Spatz. Copyright © 1982, Twayne Publishers. Reprinted by permission of The Gale Group.

Photo: A sculptural bust of Sophocles in marble. Museo Capitolino, Rome, Italy. Photo: CORBIS/Gianni Dagli Orti.

Oedipus Rex from *Sophocles: The Oedipus Cycle, An English Version* by Dudley Fitts and Robert Fitzgerald, copyright © 1949 by Harcourt, Inc. and renewed 1977 by Cornelia Fitts and Robert Fitzgerald. Reprinted by permission of the publisher. Photos: Henry S. Kranzler, all rights reserved; Museum for Gestaltung Zurich; © Dr. Jaromir Svoboda; Act One, Ltd./Michael Paul.

"Poetics: Comedy and Epic and Tragedy" by Aristotle, from *Poetics,* translated by Gerald F. Else. Copyright © 1967. Reprinted with the permission of The University of Michigan Press.

Excerpt from "The Structural Study of Myth" by Claude Lévi-Strauss. Reprinted from *The Bibliographical and Special Series* of the American Folklore Society, Vol. 5 (1955). Copyright © 1955 by Indiana University Press.

Antigone from *Sophocles: The Oedipus Cycle, An English Version* by Dudley Fitts and Robert Fitzgerald, copyright © 1939 by Harcourt, Inc. and renewed 1967 by Dudley Fitts and Robert Fitzgerald. Reprinted with the permission of the publisher. CAUTION: All rights, including professional, amateur, motion picture, recitation, lecturing, performance, public reading, radio broadcasting, and television, are strictly reserved. Inquiries on all rights should be addressed to Harcourt, Inc., Permissions Department, Orlando, FL 32887-6777. Photos: © Martha Swope (5).

"Emotion and Meaning in Greek Tragedy," excerpt from *Greek Tragedy in Action* by Oliver Taplin. Reprinted with the permission of International Thomson Publishing Services.

Excerpt from *Antigone* by Jean Anouilh, translated by Lewis Galantière. Copyright © 1946 by Random House, Inc. and renewed 1974 by Lewis Galantière. Used by permission of Random House, Inc.

Medea is reprinted from *Three Plays of Euripides: Alcestis, Medea, The Bacchae,* translated by Paul Roche, with the permission of W. W. Norton & Company, Inc. Copyright © 1974 by Paul Roche. Photos: © 2003 Stephanie Berger. All Rights Reserved; © Joan Marcus.

"Murder, She Wrought" by John Simon. Review of *Medea* from *New York Magazine* (1994). Copyright © 1994 by K-III Magazine Corporation. All rights reserved. Reprinted with the permission of *New York Magazine.*

"A 'Medea' for the World Today." Review of *Medea* by Ben Brantley. From *The New York Times,* October 4, 2002. Copyright © 2002 by The New York Times Company. Reprinted with permission.

Lysistrata: An English Version from *Aristophanes: Four Comedies* by Dudley Fitts, copyright © 1954 by Harcourt, Inc. and renewed 1982 by Cornelia Fitts, Daniel H. Fitts, and Deborah W. Fitts. Reprinted with the permission of the publisher. CAUTION: Professional and amateurs are hereby warned that all titles included in this volume, being fully protected under the copyright laws of the United States of America, Canada, the British Empire, and all other countries which are signatories to the Universal Copyright Convention and the International Copyright Union, are subject to royalty. All rights, including professional, amateur, motion picture, recitation, lecturing, performance, public reading, radio broadcasting and television, are strictly reserved. Inquiries on professional rights should be addressed to Lucy Kroll Agency, 390 West End Avenue, New York, NY 10024. Inquiries on all other rights should be addressed to Harcourt, Inc., Permissions Department, Orlando, FL 32887-6777. Photo: © Donald Cooper/PHOTOSTAGE.

Roman Drama

Figure 3. The ancient Theater of Sabratha, in Sabratha, Libya. CORBIS/Roger Wood.

Figure 4. Theater of Marcellus from *The History of Greek and Roman Theater* by Margarete Bieber. Copyright 1939, 1961 by Princeton University Press. Fig. 641 after Peruzzi; redrawn by Mrs. Wadhams. Reprinted by permission of Princeton University Press.

Excerpt from *The Twin Menaechmi* from *Six Plays of Plautus* by Plautus, translated by Lionel Casson. Copyright © 1963 by Lionel Casson. Used by permission of Doubleday, a division of Random House, Inc.

Excerpt from *The Brothers* from *The Mother-in-Law* by Terence from *Comedies of Terence,* translated by Robert Graves. Reprinted with the permission of A. P. Watt Ltd. on behalf of Carcanet Press Limited and The Trustees of the Robert Grave Copyright Trust.

Excerpt from *Thyestes* by Seneca from *The Complete Roman Drama* by George E. Duckworth. Translated by Ella Isabel Harris. Copyright © 1942 and renewed 1970 by Random House, Inc. Used by permission of Random House, Inc.

Medieval Drama

Figure 5. Pageant wagon from *Early English Stages 1300 to 1660* by Glynne William Gladstone Wickham. Reprinted by permission of Columbia University Press and Routledge & Kegan Paul Ltd.

Figure 6. Plan of the No stage.

Dulcitius by Hrotsvitha. From "Dulcitius: The Martyrdom of the Holy Virgins Agape, Chionia, and Hirena." In *The Plays of Hrosvit of Gandersheim,* Volume 51, Series B, translated by Kathrina M. Wilson. Copyright © 1989. Reprinted with the permission of the translator.

"Reading Hrosvit's Tormented Bodies" excerpted from "Impassive Bodies: Hrotsvit Stages Martyrdom" by Marla Carlson. From *Theatre Journal,* 50, December 1998. Copyright © by The Johns Hopkins University Press. Reprinted with permission of The Johns Hopkins University Press.

"Re-viewing Hrotsvit" excerpted from "Reviewing Hrotsvit" by Sue Ellen Case. From *Theatre Journal* 35, December 1983. © by The Johns Hopkins University Press. Reprinted with permission of The Johns Hopkins University Press.

Lady Han by Zeami Motokiyo from *Japanese No Dramas,* edited and translated with an introduction and notes by Royall Tyler. Copyright © 1992 by Royall Tyler. Reprinted with the permission of Penguin Books Ltd.

The Second Shepherds' Play from *Everyman and Medieval Miracle Plays,* edited by A. C. Cawley. Copyright © 1962 by A. C. Cawley. Reprinted with permission. Photos: Joe Cocks Studio. Courtesy of The Shakespearean Birthplace Trust.

Everyman from the *Everyman's Library* edition, edited and with footnotes by A. C. Cawley, 1974. Reprinted with the permission of David Campbell Publishers Ltd. Photo: Act One, Ltd./Michael Paul.

Renaissance Drama

Figure 7. Teatro Olimpico in Vicenza, Italy, Alinari/Art Resource New York.

Figure 8. Perspective setting designed by Baldassare Peruzzi, Scala/Art Resource New York.

Figure 9. C. Walter Hodges, diagram of the Globe Theatre from *The Globe Restored,* published by Oxford University Press. © 1968 by C. Walter Hodges. Reprinted by permission of Oxford University Press.

Doctor Faustus by Christopher Marlowe. "The Tragical History of the Life and Death of Doctor Faustus" from *Doctor Faustus: Text and Major Criticism,* edited with notes by Irving Ribner. Copyright © 1985. Reprinted with the permission of Pearson Education, Inc., Upper Saddle River, NJ. Photos: Donald Cooper/PHOTOSTAGE. Orson Wells as Doctor Faustus/Photofest.

Excerpt from "Ten Problems in Dr. Faustus" by Ernst Honigmann. From *The Arts of Performance in Elizabethan and Early Stuart Drama,* edited by Murray Biggs et al. (Edinburgh, 1991), reprinted by permission of Edinburgh University Press.

Photo: Image of William Shakespeare included on the First Folio. Reprinted by permission of The Folger Shakespeare Library.

A Midsummer Night's Dream and *Hamlet* by William Shakespeare from *The Complete Works of Shakespeare,* 4th edition edited by David Bevington. Copyright © 1997 by Addison-Wesley Educational Publishers, Inc. Reprinted with permission of Pearson Education, Inc. Photos: Richard M. Feldman; Mario Tursi © 1999 Twentieth Century Fox Film Corporation; Monarchy Enterprises B.V. and Regency Entertainment (USA), Inc.; © Martha Swope; Österreichisches Theatermuseum; © Donald Cooper/PHOTOSTAGE; Rolf Konow © Castle Rock Entertainment; Hamlet dueling Laertes from Kenneth Branagh film of *Hamlet*/Photofest; Bill Murray as Polonius in 2000 film adaptation of *Hamlet*/Photofest.

"Masque Elements in *A Midsummer Night's Dream*" by Enid Welsford from *The Court Masque.* Reprinted with the permission of Cambridge University Press.

"On *A Midsummer Night's Dream*" by Linda Bamber. Reprinted from *Comic Women, Tragic Men: A Study of Gender and Genre in Shakespeare.* Copyright © 1982 by The Board of Trustees of Leland Stanford Junior University. Reprinted with the permission of Stanford University Press.

"The Play Is the Message . . ." by Peter Brook from *The Shifting Point: Theatre, Film, Opera* by Peter Brook. Copyright © 1987 by Peter Brook. Reprinted with the permission of HarperCollins Publishers, Inc.

Review of *A Midsummer Night's Dream* by Clive Barnes. "A Magical 'Midsummer Night's Dream'" from *The New York Times,* January 21, 1991. Copyright © 1991 by The New York Times Company. Reprinted with permission.

"Hamlet and His Problems" from "Hamlet" in *Selected Essays* by T. S. Eliot, copyright © 1950 by Harcourt, Inc. Renewed © 1978 by Esme Valerie Eliot. Reprinted with the permission of Harcourt, Inc. and Faber and Faber Ltd.

Othello by William Shakespeare, text and notes by Gerald Eades Bentley. Copyright © 1958, 1970 by Penguin Books. © 2000 by Penguin Putnam Inc. Used by permission of Penguin, a division of Penguin Group (USA) Inc. Photos: Harvard Theatre Collection; T. Charles Erickson Photography; Rolf Konow © Castle Rock Entertainment; Special Collections and University Archives, Rutgers University Libraries.

Casebook Photos: Portrait of Abdul El-Ouahed Ben Messasud. Oil on panel. Artist unknown. University of Birmingham Collections. The Shakespeare Theatre's 1997–98 production of *Othello.* Photo: Carol Rosegg.

"Going It Alone: A Review of Olivier's *Othello*" by John Holstrom from "Plays and Players" in *Theatre Magazine* (June 1964). Reprinted with the permission of Duke University Press.

"Macready's *Othello*" by Virginia Mason Vaughan from *Othello: A Contextual History.* Copyright © 1994. Reprinted with the permission of Cambridge University Press.

Excerpt from *Mandeville's Travels* by Sir John Mandeville, 1357. Edited by M. C. Seymour. Copyright © 1968. Reprinted with the permission of Oxford University Press.

Excerpt from "*Othello* and Colour Prejudice" by G. K. Hunter from *Dramatic Identities and Cultural Tradition: Studies in Shakespeare and His Contemporaries* by G. K. Hunter, © 1978. Reprinted with the permission of Liverpool University Press.

Excerpt from *Shakespeare without Tears* by Margaret Webster. Copyright © 1942 by Margaret Webster. Reprinted by permission of McGraw-Hill, Inc.

The Masque of Blackness by Ben Jonson from *Ben Jonson: The Complete Masques,* edited by Stephen Orgel. Copyright © 1969 by Yale University. Reprinted by permission of Yale University Press. Photo: Devonshire Collection, Chatsworth.

"Africa in English Masque and Pageantry" by Eldred Jones from *Othello's Countrymen* by Eldred Jones. Copyright © 1965. Reprinted with the permission of the author.

Life Is a Dream by Pedro Calderón de la Barca from *Life Is a Dream and Other Spanish Classics,* translated by Roy Campbell and edited by

Eric Bentley. Copyright © 1959, 1958 by Eric Bentley. Reprinted with the permission of Applause Theater Book Publishers. Photos: T. Charles Erickson Photography; Douglas Robertson.

Review of the 1998 Edinburgh Festival Production of *Life Is a Dream,* by Michael Billington from the *Guardian,* August 20, 1998. Copyright © 1998 by the *Guardian.* Reprinted with permission of Guardian Newspapers Limited.

"Review of José Rivera's Production of *Sueño*" by Ed Morales from *American Theatre* 15:5 (May/June 1998). Reprinted by permission of Theatre Communications Group.

"The *Hamlet* of Spain, in a Fevered Setting" by Matt Wolf. From *The New York Times,* October 10, 1999. Copyright © 1999 by The New York Times Company. Reprinted with permission.

Late Seventeenth- and Eighteenth-Century Drama

Figure 10. Early Restoration Theater, illustration by Peter Kahn. From *The Frohlicks; or, The Lawyer Cheated* by Elizabeth Polwhele, edited by Judith Milhous and Robert D. Hume, Cornell University Press, 1977. Used by permission of the publisher, Cornell University Press.

The Misanthrope by Molière, translated by Richard Wilbur, copyright © 1955 and renewed 1983 by Richard Wilbur, reprinted with the permission of Harcourt, Inc. CAUTION: Professionals and amateurs are hereby warned that this translation, being fully protected under the copyright laws of the United States of America, the Dominion of Canada, the British Empire, and all other countries which are signatories to the Universal Copyright Convention, is subject to royalty. All rights, including professional, amateur, motion picture, recitation, lecturing, public reading, radio broadcasting, and television, are strictly reserved. Particular emphasis is laid on the question of readings, permission for which must be secured from the author's agent in writing. Inquiries on professional rights should be addressed to Mr. Gilbert Parker, William Morris Agency, 1350 Avenue of the Americas, New York, NY 10019. Inquiries on all other rights should be addressed to Harcourt, Inc., Permissions Department, Orlando, FL 32887-6777. The amateur acting rights of *The Misanthrope* are controlled exclusively by the Dramatists Play Service, Inc., 440 Park Avenue South, New York, NY 10016. No amateur performance of the play may be given without obtaining in advance written permission of the Dramatists Play Service, Inc. and paying the requisite fee. Photo: Courtesy of the Williamstown Theatre Festival. Photo by Michael C. Durling.

"Alceste's Love for Célimène," excerpt from *Men and Masks: A Study of Molière* by Lionel Grossman. Copyright © 1963. Reprinted with the permission of Johns Hopkins University Press.

The Rover; or, The Banished Cavaliers. Photo: Courtesy of the Williamstown Theatre Festival. Photo by Nina Krieger.

"On Aphra Behn," excerpt from *A Room of One's Own* by Virginia Woolf. Copyright © 1929 by Harcourt, Inc. and renewed © 1957 by Leonard Woolf. Reprinted with the permission of the publisher.

"Courtship and Marriage in *The Rover*," excerpt from *Virtue of Necessity: English Women's Writing* by Elaine Hobby. Copyright © 1988 by Elaine Hobby. Reprinted with the permission of the author.

The Love Suicides at Sonezaki by Chikamatsu Monzaemon. From *Major Plays of Chikamatsu,* translated by Donald Keene. Copyright © 1961, 1990 by Donald Keene. Reprinted with the permission of Columbia University Press.

Japanese Theater casebook photos: © Michael W. Yamashita/CORBIS; Werner Forman/Art Resource NY (2); Burstein Collection/CORBIS; Réunion des Musées Nationaux/Art Resource NY; Library of Congress.

"The Genroku Period—The Golden Age," excerpt from *Audience and Actors: A Story of Their Interaction in the Japanese Traditional Theater* by Jacob Raz. Copyright © 1983 by Jacob Raz. Reprinted with the permission of E. J. Brill.

"Return to the Puppets," excerpt from *Japanese Theatre* by Faubion Bowers. Copyright © 1952 by Faubion Bowers. Reprinted with the permission of Hermitage House.

"The Playwright Chikamatsu," excerpt from *Bunraku: The Puppet Theater* by Tsuruo Ando. Copyright © 1970 by Tsuruo Ando. Reprinted with the permission of Walker and Company.

"The Development of Theater Buildings," excerpt from "The Social Environment of Tokugawa Kabuki" in *Studies in Kabuki: Its Acting,*

Music, and Historical Context by James R. Berandon, William P. Malm, and Donald H. Shively. Copyright © 1978. Reprinted with the permission of the University of Hawaii Press.

"The Evolution of the Kabuki Stage" from *The Kabuki Theatre* by Earle Ernst. Copyright © 1956, 1974 by Earle Ernst. Reprinted with the permission of the University of Hawaii Press.

"Background of Kabuki and Joruri" from *The Japanese Theatre, Revised Edition.* Copyright 1990, 1995 by Benito Ortolani. Reprinted with the permission of E. J. Brill.

She Stoops to Conquer photos: 2002 Out of Joint production and Queen's Theatre's 1993 production. © Donald Cooper/PHOTOSTAGE.

Nineteenth-Century Drama through the Turn of the Twentieth Century

Figure 11. Auditorium, Chicago, 1889. Photo: Henrich Blessing. Courtesy of the Auditorium Theatre Council.

Figure 12. Realistic setting in Anton Chekhov's *The Cherry Orchard,* Harvard Theatre Collection.

Photos: Henrik Ibsen (c. 1896), CORBIS/Bettmann; Realistic stage setting of Ibsen's *The Wild Duck,* Bibliothèque de l'Arsenal, Paris; Edvard Munch's stage design for Ibsen's *Ghosts,* Munch Museum, Oslo Photo: Munch Museum.

A Doll House from *The Complete Major Prose Plays of Henrik Ibsen,* translated by Rolf Fjelde. Translation copyright © 1965, 1970, 1978 by Rolf Fjelde. Reprinted with the permission of Dutton Signet, a division of Penguin Group (USA) Inc. Photos: © 1992 Martha Swope; Donald Cooper/PHOTOSTAGE; Sara Krulwich/NYT Pictures.

"*A Doll's House:* Ibsen the Moralist" by Muriel C. Bradbrook from *Ibsen the Norwegian* by Muriel C. Bradbrook. Reprinted with the permission of Random House, Inc. and Chatto & Windus/The Random House Group, Ltd.

Miss Julie by August Strindberg, and excerpt from the Preface to *Miss Julie* from *Five Plays,* edited and translated by Harry G. Carlson. Copyright © 1983 by The Regents of the University of California. Reprinted with permission of the University of California Press. Photo: Donald Cooper/PHOTOSTAGE.

The Importance of Being Earnest. Photos: © Richard Feldman; Carol Rosegg.

"An Unpublished Letter from Oscar Wilde on *The Importance of Being Earnest*" from "The Making of *The Importance of Being Earnest*" by Peter Raby. *Times Literary Supplement* No. 4629, December 1991. Reprinted by permission of Peter Raby. Oscar Wilde's "Letter to Sir George Alexander on *The Importance of Being Earnest* (1894)." Copyright © by Merlin Holland. Reprinted with the permission of Mr. Merlin Holland and the Clark Library.

The Cherry Orchard by Anton Chekhov from *The Major Plays of Anton Chekhov,* translated by Ann Dunnigan. Translation copyright © 1964 by Ann Dunnigan. Reprinted with the permission of New American Library, a division of Penguin Group (USA) Inc. Photos: © Richard Feldman.

"Two Letters." From *Letters of Anton Chekhov,* translated by Michael Henry Heim and Simon Karlinsky. Copyright © 1973 by Harper & Row Publishers, Inc. Reprinted with the permission of HarperCollins Publishers, Inc.

Excerpt from "Recollections" by Maxim Gorky from *Reminiscences of Tolstoy, Chekhov, and Andreyev,* translated by Katherine Mansfield. Reprinted with the permission of Random Century.

Review of *The Cherry Orchard* by John Corbin. From *The New York Times,* January 23, 1923. Copyright © 1923 by The New York Times Company. Reprinted with permission.

"The Play is the Message . . ." and "On Chekhov" from *The Shifting Point: Theatre, Film, Opera* by Peter Brook. Copyright © 1987 by Peter Brook. Reprinted by permission of HarperCollins Publishers, Inc.

Mrs. Warren's Profession. Photos: T. Charles Erickson Photography.

Casebook Photos: Scene from a brothel from *National Police Gazette,* July 26, 1879, © Collection of the New York Historical Society; directory of brothels from *The Gentleman's Directory, Temples of Love, Address Listings,* 1870, © Collection of the New York Historical Society.

"The Woman Question: Women's Rights" from the Preface to *Getting Married,* Part I, by August Strindberg. Translated from the Swedish by Mary Sandbach. Copyright © 1972 by Sandbach Cheetham. Reprinted with the permission of Victor Gollancz Ltd.

"A Nineteenth-Century Husband's Letter to His Wife, 1844," translated by Hans Panofsky. Original German text in the Archive of the Leo Baeck Institute, New York (Mosse Family Collection, AR99). Reprinted by permission of the Leo Baeck Institute and Margaret A. Panofsky.

Drama in the Early and Mid-Twentieth Century

Figure 13. Expressionistic setting in Arthur Miller's *Death of a Salesman,* the Billy Rose Theatre Collection of New York Public Library for the Performing Arts/Astor, Lenox, and Tilden Foundations.

Riders to the Sea. Photos: © Donald Cooper/PHOTOSTAGE.

Trifles. Photo by Ellen Lacy. Courtesy of the Echo Theatre, Dallas, TX.

"On the Edge: The Plays of Susan Glaspell" by Christine Dymkowski from *Modern Drama 31* (March 1988). Reprinted by permission of *Modern Drama,* University of Toronto Press.

Six Characters in Search of an Author. Photo: © Richard Feldman.

The House of Bernarda Alba by Federico García Lorca, translated by James Graham-Lujan and Richard L. O'Connell from *Three Tragedies.* Copyright © 1947 by New Directions Publishing Corporation. Reprinted with the permission of New Directions Publishing Corporation. Photo: © Carol Rosegg.

"Religion in *The House of Bernarda Alba*" by John Gilmour in "The Cross of Pain and Death: Religion in the Rural Tragedies" from *Lorca: Poet and Playwright,* edited by Robert Harvard. Copyright © 1992 by Robert Harvard. Reprinted by permission of Palgrave Macmillan.

Desire under the Elms by Eugene O'Neill. Copyright 1924 and renewed 1952 by Eugene O'Neill. Reprinted from *The Plays of Eugene O'Neill* by Eugene O'Neill by permission of Random House, Inc. Photo: T. Charles Erickson Photography (p. 1006).

Review of *Desire under the Elms* by Stark Young. Copyright © 1924 by The New York Times Company. Reprinted by permission.

Mother Courage and Her Children by Bertolt Brecht, translated by John Willett. Copyright 1940 by Arvid Englind Teaterforlag, a.b., renewed 1967 by Stefan S. Brecht. Photo: Photofest.

"The Alienation Effect" by Bertolt Brecht. From *Brecht on Theatre,* edited and translated by John Willett. Translation copyright © 1964, renewed 1992 by John Willett. Reprinted with the permission of Hill and Wang, a division of Farrar, Straus & Giroux, LLC.

"Notes for *Mother Courage,* Scene 12," translated by John Willett. Translated by Eric Bentley and Hugo Schmidt, from *Directors on Directing,* edited by Toby Cole and Helen Krich Chinoy. Copyright © 1963. Reprinted with the permission of Prentice-Hall, Inc.

Photo: Tennessee Williams on set of *Glass Menagerie* smoking a cigarette.

The Glass Menagerie by Tennessee Williams. Copyright 1945 by Tennessee Williams and Edwina D. Williams. Renewed 1973 by Tennessee Williams. Used by permission of Random House, Inc. Photos: The Billy Rose Theatre Collection of the New York Public Library for the Performing Arts/Astor, Lenox, and Tilden Foundations; by permission of the Estate of Jo Mielziner; Joan Marcus/Arena Stage.

Review of *The Glass Menagerie* by Lewis Nichols. From *The New York Times,* April 8, 1945. Copyright © 1945 by The New York Times Company. Reprinted by permission.

"Laurette Taylor in *The Glass Menagerie,*" excerpt from *The Kindness of Strangers: The Life of Tennessee Williams* by Donald Spoto. Copyright © 1985 by Donald Spoto. Reprinted with the permission of Little, Brown and Company.

"Problems in *The Glass Menagerie*" by Benjamin Nelson. From *Tennessee Williams: The Man and His Work* by Benjamin Nelson. Copyright © 1961 by Benjamin Nelson. Reprinted with the permission of the author.

Cat on a Hot Tin Roof by Tennessee Williams. Copyright © 1954, 1955, 1971, 1975 by Tennessee Williams. Reprinted with the permission of New Directions Publishing Corporation. Photos: 1992 Martha Swope; Michael Tighe/Visages 1992; Fred Fehl/the Billy Rose Theatre Collection of the New York Public Library for the Performing Arts/Astor, Lenox, and Tilden Foundations.

Excerpt from *Tennessee Williams: Memoirs* by Tennessee Williams. Copyright © 1972, 1975 by Tennessee Williams. Reprinted with the permission of Doubleday, a division of Random House, Inc.

"Tennessee Williams and Elia Kazan Collaborate on *Cat*," excerpt from *Tennessee Williams and Elia Kazan: A Collaboration in the Theatre* by Brenda Murphy. Copyright © 1991 by Cambridge University Press. Reprinted with the permission of Cambridge University Press.

Review of *Cat on a Hot Tin Roof* by Ben Brantley, "Big Daddy's Ego Defies Death and His Family." From *The New York Times*, November 3, 2003. Copyright © 2003 by The New York Times. Reprinted with permission.

Death of a Salesman by Arthur Miller. Copyright © 1949, renewed © 1977 by Arthur Miller. All rights reserved. Reprinted with the permission of Viking Penguin, a division of Penguin Group (USA) Inc. Photos: Goodman Theatre production of *Death of a Salesman* by Eric Y. Exit; Photofest.

"In Memoriam" by Arthur Miller. From *The New Yorker* (1932). Copyright © 1995 by Arthur Miller. Reprinted with the permission of the author and International Creative Management, Inc.

"Tragedy and the Common Man," excerpt from *The Theatre Essays of Arthur Miller* edited by Robert A. Martin. Copyright © 1949, renewed 1977 by Arthur Miller. Used by the permission of Viking Penguin, a division of Penguin Group (USA), Inc.

"A Salesman Who Transcends Time" (excerpt) by Michiko Kakutani. From *The New York Times*, February 7, 1999. Copyright © 1999 by The New York Times Company. Reprinted by permission.

"Designing of a Play: *Death of a Salesman*." Excerpts from *Designing for the Theatre: A Memoir and a Portfolio* by Jo Mielziner. Copyright © 1965 by Jo Mielziner. Reprinted with the permission of Scribner, an imprint of Simon and Schuster Adult Publishing Group. Photos: Jo Mielziner's design sketch and painting of backdrop apartment buildings for *Death of a Salesman*. Actors on original set of *Death of a Salesman*. Courtesy of Jo Mielziner.

Excerpts from *Death of a Salesman: The Design Process*. "The Design Process" and "Racial Consciousness in Casting *Death of a Salesman*" by Brenda Murphy. Copyright © 1995. Reprinted with the permission of Cambridge University Press.

"Casting *Death of a Salesman*" by Arthur Miller. From *The Theater Essays of Arthur Miller*, by Arthur Miller, edited by Robert A. Martin. Copyright © 1978 by Robert A. Martin. Used by permission of Viking Penguin, a division of Penguin Group (USA), Inc.

"Directing *Death of a Salesman*." Excerpt from *Elia Kazan: A Life* by Elia Kazan. Copyright © 1988 by Elia Kazan. Reprinted with the permission of Alfred A. Knopf, a division of Random House, Inc.

"Racial Consciousness in Casting *Death of a Salesman*." Copyright © 1995. Reprinted with the permission of Cambridge University Press.

"Memorable Willy" from *Arthur Miller* by June Schlueter and James K. Flanagan. Copyright © 1987 by June Schlueter and James K. Flanagan. Reprinted by permission.

"*Death of a Salesman* in Taipei" from *Theatre Review* 45 (1993). Copyright © 1993 by Catherine Diamond. Photo: *Death of a Salesman* at the National Theatre, Taipei, Taiwan, 1992. Reprinted with the permission of Catherine Diamond.

Happy Days by Samuel Beckett. Copyright © 1961 by Grove Press, Inc. Copyright renewed © 1989 by Samuel Beckett. Used by permission of Grove/Atlantic, Inc. Photos: © T. Charles Erickson; © Donald Cooper/PHOTOSTAGE.

"The French Production." Excerpt from *Samuel Beckett: A Biography* by Deirdre Bair. Copyright © 1978 by Deirdre Bair. Reprinted with the permission of the Elaine Markson Literary Agency.

"*Happy Days*: Creation in Spite of Habit" by Sidney Holman. From *Beckett's Theaters: Interpretations for Performance*. Reprinted with the permission of Associated University Presses.

"On *Happy Days*" from *The Plays of Samuel Beckett* by Eugene Webb. Copyright © 1972 by the University of Washington Press. Reprinted with the permission of the publishers.

A Raisin in the Sun by Lorraine Hansberry. Copyright © 1958 by Robert Nemiroff, as an unpublished work. Copyright © 1959, 1966, 1984 by Robert Nemiroff. Used by permission of Random House, Inc.

"Harlem (A Dream Deferred)" by Langston Hughes from *The Panther and the Lash* by Langston Hughes. Copyright © 1951 by Langston Hughes. Used by permission of Alfred A. Knopf, a division of Random House, Inc.

The Strong Breed by Wole Soyinka. From *Wole Soyinka: Collected Plays 1*. Copyright © 1964 by Oxford University Press. Reprinted with the permission of Oxford University Press.

"Interview with Wole Soyinka" by Lewis Nkosi. From *African Writers Talking: A Collection of Radio Interviews*, edited by Cosmo Pieterse and Dennis Duerden. Copyright © 1972 by Cosmo Pieterse and Dennis Duerden. Reprinted with the permission of the publisher.

Contemporary Drama

Figure 14. Multimedia effects in Robert Wilson's *CIVIL warS*, Richard M. Feldman.

Zoot Suit by Luis Valdez from *Zoot Suit and Other Plays*. Copyright © 1992 by Luis Valdez. Reprinted with the permission of Arte Publico Press—University of Houston. Photos: Ken Jacques.

Betrayal by Harold Pinter copyright © 1978 by Harold Pinter Ltd. Used by permission of Grove/Atlantic, Inc.

"Harold Pinter's *Betrayal*: Life before Death—and After" by Katherine H. Burkman. From *Theatre Journal*, December 1982. Copyright © by The Johns Hopkins University Press. Reprinted with the permission of The Johns Hopkins University Press.

True West by Sam Shepard from *Seven Plays*. Copyright © 1981 by Sam Shepard. Used by permission of Bantam Books, a division of Random House, Inc. Photo: Michael Brosilow; © Joan Marcus.

Translations by Brian Friel from *Selected Plays of Brian Friel*. Copyright © 1984 by Catholic University of America Press. Reprinted with the permission of Faber & Faber, Ltd.

Top Girls by Caryl Churchill. Copyright © 1982 by Caryl Churchill. Reprinted with the permission of Methuen Publishing Ltd. Photos: © Michal Daniel, 2003 (2); Donald Cooper (2).

"Interview with Caryl Churchill" from *Interviews with Contemporary Women Playwrights* by Kathleen Betsko and Rachel Koenig. Copyright © 1987 by Kathleen Betsko and Rachel Koenig. Reprinted by permission of HarperCollins Publishers, Inc.

"*Master Harold* . . . and the Boys" by Athol Fugard. Copyright © 1982 by Athol Fugard. Used by permission of Alfred A. Knopf, a division of Random House, Inc. Photos: © Donald Cooper/PHOTOSTAGE; © Joan Marcus.

"Interview with Athol Fugard" by Heinrich von Staden from *Theater* (Winter 1982). Reprinted with the permission of the author.

Excerpt from *Notebooks 1960-1977* by Athol Fugard. Copyright © 1983 by Athol Fugard. Used by permission of Alfred A. Knopf, a division of Random House, Inc.

Glengarry Glen Ross by David Mamet. Copyright © 1982, 1983 by David Mamet. Used by permission of Grove/Atlantic, Inc. Photos: © T. Charles Erickson (2); © Photofest; © Donald Cooper/PHOTOSTAGE.

"Glengarry Glen Ross," excerpt from *David Mamet: Language as Dramatic Action*. Copyright © 1990 by Anna Dean. Reprinted with the permission of Fairleigh Dickinson University Press/Associated University Presses.

"Phallus in Wonderland" from *David Mamet: A Casebook* by Leslie Kane. Copyright © 1992 by Leslie Kane. Reprinted with the permission of Routledge/Taylor & Francis Books, Inc.

The Other Shore by Gao Xingjian. Translated by Gilbert C. Fong. Copyright © 1999 by Gilbert C. Fong. Reprinted with permission of The Chinese University Press. Photos: by Cara Blouin, courtesy of Stone Soup Theatre Arts, New York, NY (2).

Fences by August Wilson. Copyright © 1986 by August Wilson. Reprinted with permission of Dutton Signet, a division of Penguin Group (USA) Inc. Photos: Photofest.

"Interview with August Wilson" by David Savran from *In Their Own Voices*. Copyright © 1999 by David Savran. Reprinted with the permission of Theatre Communications Group.

"Family Ties in Wilson's *Fences*" by Frank Rich from *The New York Times*, March 27, 1987. Copyright © 1987 by The New York Times Company. Reprinted with permission.

M. Butterfly by David Henry Hwang. Copyright © 1986, 1987, 1988 by David Henry Hwang. Reprinted with the permission of Dutton Signet, a division of Penguin Group (USA) Inc. Photo: Joan Marcus.

"*M. Butterfly*: An Interview with David Henry Hwang" by John Louis DiGaetani. From *The Drama Review 33* (Fall 1989). Copyright © 1989 by New York University and the Massachusetts Institute of Technology. Reprinted by permission.